Encyclopedia of Music in Canada

Encyclopedia of Music in Canada

Edited by
Helmut Kallmann, Gilles Potvin, Kenneth Winters

University of Toronto Press
TORONTO BUFFALO LONDON

Toronto Buffalo London
Printed in Canada

ISBN 0-8020-5509-5

Canadian Cataloguing in Publication Data

Main entry under title:
Encyclopedia of music in Canada

Includes bibliographies and index.
ISBN 0-8020-5509-5

1. Music – Canada – Dictionaries. I. Kallmann, Helmut, 1922– II. Potvin, Gilles, 1923– III. Winters, Kenneth, 1929–

ML106.C36E52 780'.971 C81-094855-9

This book has been published with the help of a grant from the Canadian Federation for the Humanities, using funds provided by the Social Sciences and Humanities Research Council of Canada; grants from the Canada Council and the Ontario Arts Council under their block grant programs; and a grant from the Publications Fund of the University of Toronto Press.

The enterprise,
enthusiasm, and generosity of spirit of

FLOYD S. CHALMERS

were fundamental to the initiation
and the completion of the
Encyclopedia of Music in Canada.
In recognition of this and his other
contributions to cultural life in Canada
this encyclopedia is dedicated to him.

Encyclopedia of Music in Canada

BOARD OF DIRECTORS

Contents

Foreword

It would surprise no one who knows Floyd S. Chalmers that in 1969 he was reading *Musicanada*, or that he was moved to action by something he found there. The prompting came from an article by John Beckwith regretting the lack of printed information about Canada's musical culture. A few lines in *Grove's* and other reference works were not sufficient for Chalmers, a distinguished retired Toronto publisher. Under his leadership a group of musicians, scholars, and businessmen was brought together to launch the *Encyclopedia of Music in Canada* and fill the gap. With typical generosity, Chalmers was the first to donate funds towards its preparation, and his own and the Floyd S. Chalmers Foundation's several donations were the project's only private funding.

The arduous project of preparing the manuscript is described by the editors in the introduction which follows, and the help they received is discussed in their acknowledgments. In this preamble I should like to thank the directors of the encyclopedia for their nine years of service; the three editors, who perhaps would not have undertaken the task had they compiled an encyclopedia previously; and the government bodies which demonstrated their faith in this major Canadian project. The national scope of the project was recognized at all levels of government. Generous subsidies were received from the Canada Council, the Social Sciences and Humanities Research Council of Canada, and the Canadian Federation for the Humanities; provincial support came in a major way from the Ontario Arts Council and Wintario, and substantial grants were received also from the British Columbia Cultural Fund and the Western Canada Lottery Foundation, Alberta Culture, the Alberta Foundation for the Performing Arts and the Western Canada Lottery Foundation (Alberta Division), and the Ministère des Affaires culturelles du Québec. Valued support was received from Metropolitan Toronto and the City of Toronto. A particular word of thanks is owed to the National Library of Canada for making available its resources, and to the University of Toronto for space and support services.

Members of the executive committee of the board – of necessity located in Toronto where the project's administrative offices were situated – participated in many long meetings and gave freely of their time and experience: Keith MacMillan and John Beckwith from the world of music; Floyd Chalmers and his daughter Joan from the world of philanthropy; and Rodney Anderson, CA, from the world of accountancy. With Anderson I reworked the ever increasing budget for the project with alarming frequency. To all these individuals the creation of the encyclopedia owes a major debt.

MICHAEL M. KOERNER

Introduction

The concept

The *Encyclopedia of Music in Canada* is about music in Canada and Canada's musical relations with the rest of the world; it is not a Canadian version of a general reference work on music. It relates the activities and contributions of Canadian individuals and organizations in their great diversity and discusses general topics in their Canadian aspects. For these topics brief definitions and explanations of technical terms are given and where necessary the world context is sketched, but *EMC* does not attempt to provide, for instance, an introduction to electronic composition in the world at large or to explain the mechanisms of different types of reed organs. There are many excellent music dictionaries which may be consulted for such purposes.

The idea of devoting a dictionary to the music of one country has been realized before, but the editors are not aware of any previous attempt to describe a nation's musical culture in all its breadth and depth: the historical and the current aspects of popular, folk, religious, concert, and other forms of music, and the educational, critical, administrative, and commercial manifestations. The editors believe that some of *EMC*'s approaches to musical information break new ground: entries on the relationships with other countries and with sister arts; on the memorials that a nation provides for its musicians; on the musical involvements of 'Sovereigns, statesmen, and other public figures'; or on the reflection in music of 'Wars, rebellions, and uprisings,' 'Lakes,' 'Mountains,' 'Rivers,' 'Sports,' 'Transportation,' and that annually recurring Canadian condition 'Winter.' It is believed, also, that *EMC* provides new emphases in including in city entries lists of the names of some of the cities' sons and daughters who contributed to musical life and also in including lists of outstanding pupils of a teacher (most reference works name a musician's teachers but rarely his pupils) and indications of the location of deceased musicians' surviving papers.

Since by definition encyclopedias and dictionaries break down their main subjects into alphabetical sequences of constituent or component subjects, it was not regarded as *EMC*'s task to provide a single 'historical outline' or a single 'survey of composition.' For many such large subjects, however, *EMC* has provided 'reader's guides' (eg, Education, Religions and music, Universities) which list entries on specific aspects of those subjects.

The reader who wishes to gain an impression of the course of musical development in Canada will find certain basic themes recurring in many of *EMC*'s broad survey articles: the coincidence of the three-and-a-half centuries of Canada's colonization with the period of the creation of the vast majority of the works which appear in the standard western concert repertoire of the 20th century; the expansion of co-existing (and sometimes cross-fertilizing) musical cultures, beginning with the Indians, Inuit, and French and expanding into the 'musical United Nations' that Canada has become; the diversification of genres, beginning with native, folk, and church music, growing into an ever more complex web of specialized repertoires with specialized audiences; the urbanization and industrialization of musical life, reflected in the formation of large organizations for the teaching and performance of music, supported by a diversified system of patronage; the establishment of a professional stratum of musicians, in addition to the amateur; the continuing and overwhelming foreign influence on musical composition, teaching, and audience tastes, giving way only gradually to homegrown traditions.

Several decisions regarding presentation and coverage of information were made at the outset. It was agreed that *EMC* should address itself to a wide range of readers – laymen as well as experts, students as well as advanced scholars – and that statements should be unambiguous and supported by facts. To these ends the editors have striven for clear and nontechnical language, compromising only in some technological and ethnomusicological entries and in some descriptions of the works of advanced composers. It was agreed to supplement articles with bibliographies, discographies, and other lists. It was agreed also that musicians from all regions should be given due attention (of paramount importance in a country of Canada's size and diversity), and that the temptation to give disproportionate prominence to major figures in the larger cities should be kept in check.

It was understood further that *EMC* should be published in English and French versions containing the same information. About two-thirds of the entries were written in English and one-third in French, and all have been translated into the other language. The French edition is entitled *Encyclopédie de la musique au Canada*.

The need

Between the late 19th century and the mid-20th little information on Canadian music and musicians appeared in European and US journals and reference works. The *Musical Times* of London, the *Guide musical* of Brussels, the *Musical Courier* of Philadelphia, and *Musical America* of New York rarely featured reports from Canadian cities, and Pazdírek's *Universal-Handbuch der Musikliteratur*, a turn-of-the-century list of 'all' published music, ignored Canada (forgivably perhaps, since few Canadian publishers issued catalogues). Even in the late 1960s, by which time a vigorous generation of Canadian composers had reached maturity, dictionaries and surveys of the world's music gave Canada only spotty coverage. This was not entirely the fault of the compilers or authors of these works; in many cases accurate, up-to-date information representative of all parts of

Canada was all but impossible to obtain.

The few useful Canadian reference works – eg, the *Dictionnaire biographique des musiciens canadiens* (1935) and *Catalogue of Canadian Composers* (1952) – were limited in scope and were aging. *Contemporary Canadian Composers* was still unpublished; when it did appear, in 1975 in English and in 1977 in French, it represented a vast advance over its forerunners, but it too had the limitations indicated by its title: it treated only composers, and only the composers of the 20th century. Even so, its 144 entries (160 in the French-language edition) were one indication of the staggering rate at which music had developed since the end of World War II, and of the keenly felt need for a survey and record – indeed, a general stock-taking – of music and musical life in Canada. *Music in Canada* (1955) and *Aspects of Music in Canada* (1969, 1970) had been attempts to fill the need, and may be said to have succeeded to the degree that essay-volumes could, but they also indicated that the growing mass of information in future could no longer be treated in essay form. The step from narrative survey under broad headings to encyclopedic coverage under specific headings seemed preordained; the very absence of such a work had become palpable; the need for it lay in the air. John Beckwith's article 'About Canadian music: the P.R. failure' (*Musicanada*, 21, Jul–Aug 1969), though it was concerned specifically with the coverage of Canadian composition in the major and purportedly international reference works (coverage which, he demonstrated with wit and example, ranged from non-existent to condescending to complacently mistaken), gave one focus to the need. To Floyd S. Chalmers, who read the Beckwith article with the eye of a publisher, it pointed up what it did not actually articulate: the necessity for a nation to provide systematic published discussion of its own music before it could expect other nations to enter that discussion. He saw the clear need for an encyclopedia that would be Canada's own statement about its music and decided to do something about it. In the early fall of 1970 he approached Keith MacMillan, the editor of *Musicanada*, and with his help set up a committee to study the feasibility of producing such a work. It was a measure of Chalmers' conviction and determination and of the committee's enthusiasm that by the end of 1971 the three editors had been enlisted, by 15 Dec 1972 the board of directors had been incorporated, and by 30 Dec 1972 the first $65,000 of a promised grant of $100,000 from the Floyd S. Chalmers Foundation had been received, all *before* the arrival (5 Feb 1973) of a $5000 feasibility grant from the Canada Council. (Once the project was established, however, the council was to prove a staunch ally and major contributor.) The first articles were written in the summer of 1973.

The realization

Most old-world or US music encyclopedias have been harvesters of existing, completed research and have been able to call upon the resources of solid ranks of recognized experts. By contrast *EMC* to an unusual extent has been a sower of seeds, a mobilizer and developer of writers and experts, and a stimulator of research by national organizations into their own pasts. Of course it has harvested as well – for example in the area of folk music, in which scholarship has been established for a long time – and it would be an exaggeration to suggest either that Canada is deficient in musical authorities or that all of its authorities were too busy or too little interested to contribute. *EMC* was fortunate in finding experts on many specific subjects: certain contemporary composers, the musical life among some individual ethnic minorities, the musical histories of some organizations, or the activities in certain genres of popular music, to give only a few examples. But these pockets of expertise were outweighed by a general scarcity of reliable and ready writers on other aspects of Canadian musical life, eg, the musical histories of some cities, traditional dance music, or piano building.

Thus, for many contributors and certainly for the editors *EMC* has been a journey of discovery, arduous but rewarded by the revelation of a rich fabric of activity and achievement. Pioneering achievements in recorded sound and electronic instruments, an international operatic career which began with an irrepressible youngster singing persistently in a prairie town, an astonishing survival of Moravian hymns in an Inuit settlement, a great piano-building firm which grew out of a workshop in the house of an immigrant European craftsman, a middle-aged woman with a lot of children to feed singing out of her poverty and leaving a legacy of songs which became the prototype for a new genre in Quebec – the stories of these* and of many hundreds of other people, institutions, and accomplishments reveal something of the energy that has flowed ceaselessly through Canadian musical endeavours over the years.

*See Recorded sound, Hugh Le Caine, and Morse Robb; Jon Vickers; Moravian missions; Heintzman Ltd; La Bolduc.

Preparations

Five main activities occupied the editors and their assistants and advisers during the preparatory stage: the establishment of criteria of inclusion and treatment; the compilation of standards of style (spellings, abbreviations, etc); the preparation of lists of entry headings with tentative estimations of word length; the search for potential contributors; and the exploration of bibliographical and other sources of information. These activities overlapped and in fact continued long after assigning, writing, and editing had begun, since many questions of inclusion, style, and word length could be settled only through trial and error.

The original list of entries compiled by the editors had about 3000 headings. After circulation among the directors of *EMC* and among some 60 consultants selected according to field of specialization and geographical region the list had swollen to 4300. Some suggestions were discarded; some subjects were amalgamated into larger units and others were broken up into smaller ones; if a subject was not familiar to the editors, an assignment might be made and a decision regarding inclusion reached only after it was written. The final result, embodied in this encyclopedia, is 3162 entries and 164 reference entries.

The discovery of contributors who had the willingness, ability, and time to write, and the matching of contributor and subject – no easy task – were carried out by the assignments officer in close collaboration with the editors. Visits to the major Canadian cities by the English-language editor and the assignments officer resulted in the enlistment of a large number of interested writers. Not all the writers were able to be productive; many were unable to fulfil their assignments because they could not obtain the necessary information, even by direct interview. The disappointments inherent in this situation and the concurrent development of research techniques and materials by *EMC*'s staff led eventually to the assignment to the staff of all remaining entries and all those on newly prominent subjects. It was decided also, regretfully, to postpone entries on some subjects to a later edition (eg, those on barbershop quartet societies, on certain economic aspects of musical life, and on the sociology of the post-1960 Anglo-Canadian folksong revival).

The sources of information for *EMC*'s content may be listed in the following order, roughly according to importance:

1 the personal knowledge, sometimes embodied in previous publications, of *EMC* contributors, editors, editorial assistants, and non-contributing specialists;
2 the resources of the National Library of Canada with its vast collections of Canadian sheet music and scores, recordings, and music periodicals, its information and picture files, its city directories and other historical Canadiana, and its many bibliographical and discographical tools;
3 the Canadian Music Centre's thorough documentation of

contemporary Canadian composition, particularly at its Montreal and Toronto offices;
4 the resources of certain other libraries with large holdings of Canadian music, eg, the Metropolitan Toronto and Montreal City libraries, and the Canadian Centre for Folk Culture Studies of the National Museum of Man;
5 the files and information services of many organizations, such as PRO Canada, CAPAC, the CBC's Toronto and Montreal reference libraries, and the RCMT registrar's office;
6 data collected by means of questionnaires or interviews, or through subscription to mailing lists;
7 the current daily press, periodicals, and newscasts;
8 information and literature (clippings, leaflets, programs, etc) supplied by dedicated contributors and informants in addition to the material contained in their own assignments.

One might mention the books most frequently cited – the *Jesuit Relations* in the modern edition by R.G. Thwaites and *Roll Back the Years* by Edward B. Moogk probably would take the lead. As of 1980 the 17th century still was better documented than the early 18th, and the relatively few newspapers, travel accounts, and personal diaries of the 1790s had been indexed and scanned more diligently than the innumerable newspapers of the early 20th century; moreover, no library held certain volumes of English-language Canadian music journals. Knowledge of many Ontario musicians and musical societies of that time comes from vague recollections and hastily compiled surveys, not enough to provide cohesive and accurate entries. For certain Quebec musicians it has been necessary to continue to depend on the reminiscences written by Nazaire LeVasseur ca 1920. The existence of the *Dictionnaire biographique des musiciens canadiens* of 1935 at least makes possible the inclusion of entries on the Quebec equivalents of those Ontario musicians, but much of the information in the *Dictionnaire* could be neither enlarged upon nor confirmed and verified. And while often the apprenticeship of a musician has been possible to document, just as often his final years have remained shrouded in darkness; see, eg, W. Waugh Lauder, Djane Lavoie-Hertz, Adele Lount-Tyson, Eva Rose York, and even some musicians of the present era.

Criteria

The decisions to include or exclude entries on certain musicians have been among the most difficult to make. There is no sure way to translate merit into a point system, and no two judges would select the same names from a suggested list. How many times did the editors of *EMC* hear the comment: 'If you want to include an entry on so-and-so, I can name you five others just as important or more so!' And how many times was a suggestion taken up only to be found unjustifiable when the entry was completed. But dividing lines had to be drawn, according to merit and also to a reasonable duration of residence or substantial activity in Canada, and no undue apologies are made for occasional misjudgment and unavoidable injustice. It is believed that on the whole musical merit, historical significance, and readers' interest have been brought into balanced consideration. Thus are included some pioneers of bygone days whose accomplishments, by modern standards, may have been quite modest, and some pop musicians of recent years whose successes have made them objects of legitimate interest whatever their degree of musical accomplishment. The editors have been aware that clever promotion, premature praise of a young prize-winning artist, or treatment in earlier publications can prejudice selection and have attempted to counterbalance the temptation to include such vivid but perhaps ephemeral presences by reaching out to neglected or forgotten musicians whose considerable contributions have not been recorded in other histories or dictionaries. In 'borderline cases' preference has been given to combinations of talent: among the hundreds of excellent piano teachers, church organists, university teachers, or orchestral players – other factors being equal – to those who have made 'extra' contributions as, for instance, writers of instruction books, founders of choirs, presidents of professional organizations, or performers of chamber music.

Canadian-born and Canadian-trained musicians whose adult careers have been pursued in other countries are discussed briefly under the entries for those countries (this treatment has applied in particular to those established in the USA), unless they have maintained close and active contacts with Canada. But no rigid formula for inclusion could be applied. (See Emigration.)

Foreign-born musicians have received individual entries if they have made noteworthy contributions to Canada. It has made no difference whether they remained in Canada or moved on to other countries, but few are included who have not lived in Canada at least five years. However, certain orchestra conductors who are sufficiently prominent to deserve entries have been treated under the entries for the orchestras which have been the only focus of their work in Canada. Many Canadian-born musicians also have been given only capsule biographies in the entries on the societies, institutions, or topics (eg, Country music, Fiddling, Jazz) most closely related to their spheres of activity. Discussion of their activities may be traced through the index.

Next to the basic decisions of inclusion and exclusion few aspects of a work of this kind cause more criticism than that of the relative space alotted to subjects. It is a pitfall, however, to equate length with significance. To a large extent length is determined by the complexity of the externals of a story: the career of a composer who held many academic positions in succession and had a great facility in his craft requires more space to describe and document than that of an equally worthy colleague who occupied one position throughout his career, did not sit on executive boards, and created a relatively limited quantity of music in a slow and self-critical process. Likewise the length of an entry on a choir is influenced by the number of its conductors and name changes over a given period of time. It is far more reasonable to expect a consistent relationship between significance and scale of detail than between significance and length of an article. This consistency has been striven for, and the editors are open to criticism on the extent to which they have succeeded. Two prejudices should be admitted in this connection: that towards performers and ensembles who make a specialty of introducing new Canadian works, and that towards composers of concert music; both have been treated generously.

The balancing act that is part of the editors' job has come further into play in the juxtaposition of factual data and evaluative opinion. Solid facts, in particular accurate forms and spellings of names and titles, and precise dates, are the very foundation of authoritativeness. To a certain extent, also, facts imply significance, and it should be necessary only in the rarest of cases to point out that a certain musician made an 'important contribution.' But factual data alone do not suffice to complete satisfactorily even a brief biographical article. A long list of diplomas and degrees earned, appointments held, prizes won, or operatic roles sung will not add up in itself to the recognition of human qualities and historical significance. Behind the record of a teacher-pupil relationship there may be a fruitful passing-on of skill and wisdom or an unhappy mismatching. The teacher who moves from university to university may be an ambitious or restless seeker of the perfect environment or an incompetent lecturer. It is important to ask: 'What are the strengths and weaknesses of a performer's style, and what are the stylistic characteristics and aesthetic convictions of a composer?' A 'Who's Who' may ignore such questions; an encyclopedia may not. The editors have gone to great pains to solicit evaluations, and in the case of composers have been fairly successful. In the case of performers, however, it often was necessary to go back to the contributor and ask: 'What characterizes this pianist's playing?' 'How would you describe this voice?' or 'Did this group play rock or country music?' Often, when the reply was unsatisfactory, a concert review which expressed an opinion could be found and a quotation from it added to the entry; but regrettably a number of biographical entries had to remain unilluminated by analytical and critical insights.

Editorial processes

The wide variations in coverage and format in the contributors' responses to their assignments left no doubt that the editorial tasks of *EMC* would be pioneering, creative, and re-creative. Moreover, the musical life of Canada was transforming itself in innumerable ways even as the latest transformations were being noted. Thus, no entry, even a well organized and tightly written one, could remain as it was when it arrived. The result at *EMC*'s editorial offices was a complex system of work-flow, work-scheduling, and work-distribution. Upon receipt each article was read for information, coverage, balance, relationship to articles on hand, and style. In the majority of cases the initial reading was followed by a thorough effort to verify facts, fill gaps, and resolve discrepancies between different sources.

Name changes and founding dates of musical societies were among the most frequent and most difficult quests, since available sources often provided no more than 'was in its ninth season in 1928' (leaving the reader to guess whether reference is to the 1927–8 or 1928–9 season and whether the years were counted from the time of foundation, possibly in October, or the date of the first concert, perhaps the following February). Some birth dates presented particular challenges. Rosario Bourdon was born in 1865 according to the *Musiciens canadiens*, 1889 according to the *ASCAP Dictionary*, and 1895 according to *Grove's*. *EMC* found 1885 to be his actual birth year. *EMC* has been able to correct other such long-perpetuated errors, eg, those committed in connection with the death date of Adam Schott (1840 according to the *New Grove Dictionary*, but actually 1864) and the founding dates of two of Canada's most important music businesses, Heintzman and Nordheimer; and *EMC* research may not have solved but at least it has brought closer to solution the puzzles surrounding the creation and first performance of 'O Canada.' In all cases, in seeking accurate data, the editors and staff consulted the sources listed above, and many others as well. All that was possible in some cases was to identify doubtful information or provide alternative data. No doubt inaccuracies, over-simplifications, oversights, and downright errors will persist. The editors will be grateful for corrections and additions from readers who have noted errors or possess well-documented information that the editors may have overlooked.

A main emphasis during the first years of the preparation of *EMC* was on the production of articles on historical subjects, leaving those on currently active musicians to a later stage in order to minimize the necessity for updating. Ironically, the years after 1973 produced not only the foreseen career expansions, new talents, new compositions, and new organizations, but also much new historical research and much long-lost archival and printed material. In 1978 contributors were given the opportunity to update their articles, and many did. In the end, updating became an encyclopedia-wide necessity. In general, entries may be considered current to the end of 1979, but an attempt has been made to include later available news of major significance in the areas of appointments, premiere performances, deaths, dissolutions or name changes of ensembles and organizations, and other such information. In some instances it was possible to update only through the means of an additional bibliographic item.

An invaluable aid in the work of revision was the index that was prepared as articles assumed final shape. This provided the means for avoiding inconsistent name spellings and birthplaces, and for tracing pupil-teacher connections, and also yielded information helpful when many of the large survey articles (eg, those on cities, relations with other countries, the playing and teaching of instruments, and publications) were prepared.

Not all the individual contributions to the editorial process can be enumerated here, but one fact needs stressing: the preparation of *EMC* has been a team effort. It had been assumed at the outset that the three editors would have equal rank but distinct responsibilities – Helmut Kallmann for content, Gilles Potvin for the French text, and Kenneth Winters for the English text – but in practice these functions have overlapped throughout the project; each editor has felt free to revise content and to criticize style. By extension it is true to say that there has not been one member of the supporting staff who has not supplied some special knowledge and who has not exercised at one time or another the function of a critical reader. On virtually every entry there has been spirited discussion, involving contributor, editors, editorial assistants, and sometimes outside consultants; in most cases the information content was increased. All those who participated in this exploration of Canada's music and musical life will remember the experience with gratitude and pleasure.

EMC is a beginning, in more senses than one. As a first edition it is inevitably the beginning of a long process of correcting, updating, filling of gaps, and reinterpretation. And like anything that is written about music, it is the beginning of a process of understanding that has only one justifiable end: a deeper participation in music itself, as listener, interpreter, or creator. *EMC* is also the beginning of an orderly all-encompassing record of Canadian musical life (there having been several notable achievements in documenting specific aspects). This documentation, the editors fervently hope, not only will contribute to a new level of efficiency and accuracy in the day-to-day dissemination of information on music in Canada, but also will create a new consciousness of, and a new pride in, Canada's multifaceted record of musical achievement.

HELMUT KALLMANN, GILLES POTVIN, KENNETH WINTERS

Acknowledgments

The editors wish to express their gratitude to *EMC*'s board of directors, staff, and several hundred contributors, to the University of Toronto Press editors, and to the many individuals and institutions who provided information, advice, and other services. *EMC* is their work as much as the editors'.

The board of directors has assumed many burdens. Besides bearing the responsibility for administrative planning and financing, all the directors have shown keen interest in matters of editorial policy and content and have lent their knowledge, wisdom, and experience without interfering in the editors' areas of decision making. Special admiration is due the board's chairman, Michael Koerner, who was always approachable and was willing to give of his time despite a busy schedule of his own, who showed a great interest in the work of *EMC* yet was never obtrusive, and who brought to his tasks a diplomat's skill for solving problems and reconciling divergent views. A director whose help on many fronts has been of paramount importance is Floyd S. Chalmers, truly the father of *EMC*. Without his vision, his initiative, his continuing counsel (based on vast editorial, financial, and administrative experience), and his generous financial assistance the project would have been neither begun nor completed.

Some directors have played significant roles in suggesting topics and persons to be included in the book, in enlisting the services of expert writers, and in locating missing information. Others have contributed editorial, translator's, and business skills and several have contributed articles. Particular thanks are owed Rodney Anderson, a chartered accountant and music lover, for his help in budget and systems planning; Helen Creighton for her unswerving interest in matters dealing with folk music and with the Maritimes; John Beckwith, whose wide knowledge of Canadian music and whose critical intelligence and editorial experience were channelled into countless hours of voluntary work; Jean Papineau-Couture, whose critical reading of many articles and of translations (into English as well as French) has been of great help; and Keith MacMillan, who in the early stages of *EMC* helped Floyd Chalmers to transform an idea into an organization willing to undertake the project, who made available his practical knowledge of the Canadian musical scene, and who continued to help throughout the years of preparation.

The editors have been rewarded also by their staff's grasp of the objectives of *EMC* and of the techniques used to fulfil these. Several members of that staff came to regard *EMC* as a service to an ideal rather than mere employment, and all who served for any length of time could be observed to grow as researchers, writers, and experts in the areas of their work. Skills varied and musical tastes and opinions differed, but all were exercised in a spirit of compromise and teamwork and a determination to get on with the job. Each person contributed not only to the specific task assigned but eventually also to the totality of the editorial process according to his or her special knowledge and critical sense.

The editors wish to pay particular tribute to those *EMC* staff members who have assumed senior or special responsibilities.

Mabel Laine's efficiency, orderliness, and resourcefulness have been fundamental to the administrative control of the project from near its beginning to its end. Mrs Laine served first as accountant, secretary, assignments officer, and manager of the Toronto office, and later as administrator for the project as a whole. Throughout the long journey she monitored deadlines, supervised the intricate paper flow, and lent her strength to the practical solution of innumerable problems.

In Claire Versailles the Montreal office was fortunate to have, during the last half of the project, an equally protean, well-organized, and dedicated supervisor. Mme Versailles's duties were as various as the needs that arose, and she served as compiler, researcher, writer, proofreader, liaison between the English-language and French-language offices, and office manager.

Mark Miller's conscientious assumption of responsibility for the coverage of jazz and popular music made him the project's only subject editor; besides reading and revising all articles in these fields for the editors' approval he researched and wrote much of the original copy. He also assisted with the revision of copy in other fields and showed acumen in discussions on format and proportion.

Patricia Wardrop brought a librarian's skills to her daunting main duties as indexer and bibliographer. She went far beyond the call of those duties, however, to assist in many aspects of the editorial process, contributing fresh research, preparing special lists, monitoring spellings and dates, helping to eradicate innumerable discrepancies in information, and working to co-ordinate related detail in separate entries.

During the eight-year preparation of *EMC* the total staff at work in *EMC*'s three offices (Montreal, Ottawa, and Toronto) never numbered more than 23 at any one time, and usually it was much smaller. Some members were employed for nearly the entire project, others worked part-time, and still others worked intensively for periods as short as three months. All except the editors themselves and the four senior staff members singled out above are included in the following list, and the editors thank them for their devoted service.

RESEARCH AND WRITING

Toronto: John Berke, Clifford Ford (also lists of compositions), Jane Glassco, Marjorie Hale, Nancy McGregor (also bibliographies, discographies, lists of compositions, and rewriting), Joseph Petric (also cataloguing), Philip M. Wults (also rewriting)

Ottawa: Florence Hayes (also illustrations), Denise Ménard

Montreal: Chantal Gauthier, Brigitte Hébert, Hélène Panneton, Hélène Plouffe (also proofreading), Annick Poussart (also translations and revising translations), Micheline Tessier, Suzanne Thomas (also cross-referencing and indexing French edition)

SPECIAL ASSISTANTS

Toronto: Mary Maude (revising translations, French to English); William B. Barker, Elizabeth Church, Margaret Matheson, Nancy Viglietti (proofreading)

Ottawa: Lisa Whyte (research)

Montreal: Suzanne Huot (cross-referencing; revising translations, English to French)

TRANSLATION

Toronto: Marc Destrubé, Edward Farrant, Richard Howard, Danièle Pascal, Harvey Starkman, Leslie Starkman

Montreal: Willie Chevalier, Jacques Dupire, Véronique Robert

TYPING OF MANUSCRIPTS

Toronto: Catherine Adamson, Nancy Beck (also bookkeeping, indexing, and proofreading), Penny Nettlefold

Montreal: Monique Clerk, Françoise Cloutier, Hélène Langlois-Labrèche, Denise de Passillé, Marie-José Roy

CLERICAL ASSISTANCE

Toronto: Felicity Coulter, Nancy Gregoire (also bookkeeping), Stephen Knott (also bookkeeping)

Ottawa: Ruth Kallmann

Montreal: Paule Daunais, Bernard Dion, Lise Dion, Françoise Marchand, Louise Ostiguy (also proofreading)

The editors would like also to pay tribute to the publisher's editorial staff, in particular the three – Joan Bulger, Margaret Parker, and John Parry – who were assigned to the detailed preparation of the completed manuscript for the printer, but whose actual assistance, reflected in shrewd questions, wide knowledge, and balanced advice, far exceeded the merely technical, to the betterment of the whole text.

It is more difficult to express the editors' gratitude to the many individual contributors (see list on p xvi) whose articles have made *EMC* a reality. The difficulties and the expense of time entailed in compiling data on subjects never researched previously are well understood, as are the frustrations encountered in attempts to treat briefly subjects which cry out for twice the length assigned. In many cases the editors were able to outline the desired scope of an assignment and to provide bibliographical references, but often no such guidance could be given. Many an article which went beyond the assigned word length and scale of detail persuaded the editors of the justice of extending its planned length.

The editors are indebted to a great many people in all parts of Canada who served as consultants. Of those living in provinces other than Ontario and Quebec, however, a few helped not only occasionally but repeatedly, devoting many hours to collecting information, finding addresses, corroborating data, and in general providing vital liaison between their regions of the country or areas of knowledge and *EMC*. The editors owe them particular thanks. They are:

William L. Brandhagen, Regina
Casimir Carter, Winnipeg
Gladys Deutsch, St John's, Nfld
Bryan N.S. Gooch, Vancouver
Helen Lawson, Charlottetown
Nancy Vogan, Sackville, NB

Of the many others consulted or asked for advice during the preparation of *EMC* the following were particularly helpful in individual subject areas: Joan Baillie (opera), Hunter Bishop (Toronto Arts and Letters Club), †François Brassard (Franco-Canadian folk music), Marcelle Corneille (education), Peter Dala (church music and Hungarian names), Ruth Parent Du Montet (discography), Corinne Dupuis-Maillet (Casavant Society), Richard Flohil (pop music), Edith Fowke (Anglo-Canadian folk music), Réal Gagnier (early Montreal), Geneviève Gauthier (education), Clyde Gilmour (recordings), Alice Giroux (education), Peter Goddard (pop music), Walt Grealis (pop music), J. Paul Green (bands, education, universities), Christopher Jackson (Louis Mitchell), John Kraglund (Toronto concerts), Gabriel Labbé (Quebec folk music), Claire Laplante (education), Gérald Locas (St-Hyacinthe, Que), Thelma Reid Lower (Vancouver choirs), Frank McGuire (bands), James B. McPherson (opera), Maurice Meerte (dance bands), †Edward Moogk (pop music, recordings), Clément Morin (Roman Catholic church music), William Munson (rock), Marie-Thérèse Paquin (general), Kenneth Peacock (native and ethnic music), Benoît Plamondon (Plamondon family), Bill Smith (jazz), Alfred Strombergs (art song), Richard Warren (Toronto Symphony).

Institutions and their individual staff members have been extremely co-operative, supplying information, advice and, in some cases, illustrations. Not all those institutions can be listed here, but the editors would like to single out the following: Alberta Culture, Edmonton; archives, notably the Public Archives of Canada and the various provincial archives, in particular the Archives d'état civil du Québec, in Montreal; Association of Canadian Orchestras, Toronto; Canadian Music Centre, Montreal and Toronto offices; Canadian Music Council, Ottawa; CAPAC, Toronto and Montreal offices; CBC Montreal, Toronto, Winnipeg, and Vancouver offices and libraries; Fraser-Hickson Institute, Montreal; Glenbow-Alberta Institute, Calgary; libraries of every major city in Canada, especially the Bibliothèque nationale du Québec in Montreal, the National Library of Canada in Ottawa, and the libraries of Canadian universities; Montreal Symphony Orchestra; National Gallery of Canada; National Museum of Man, Ottawa; Ontario Arts Council, Toronto; Ontario Choral Federation, Toronto; P.R.O. Canada, Toronto and Montreal offices; Royal Canadian College of Organists, Toronto; Royal Conservatory of Music, Toronto; Société St-Jean-Baptiste, Montreal.

†Deceased

Contributors

The authorship of an *EMC* entry may be identified after the entry's concluding line by the initials of one or more of the contributors listed below.

Contributors' initials are given without parentheses when the information and the phrasing substantially represent the contributor's work in its original form. Initials have been placed in parentheses when the contribution was revised considerably or was a supplementary or partial one.

Unsigned entries are usually of a brief and factual nature, written in the *EMC* offices from questionnaires or publicity material. Larger unsigned entries represent collective efforts of members of the editorial staff.

AB	Antoine Bouchard, Quebec City
AC	Arthur Crighton, Edmonton
ACN	Agnes C. Nyland, Ottawa
AD	Andrée Desautels, Montreal
ADV	Alix de Vaulchier, Montreal
AEB	A. Elizabeth Baird, Ottawa
AF	Alfred Fisher, Edmonton
AG	Alfred Garson, Montreal
AGra	Alan Graham, Alberton, PEI
AHC	Alan H. Cowle, Toronto
AKT	A. Kerr Twaddle, Winnipeg
AL	Alan Lessem, Toronto
AM	Alex Murray, Milliken, Ont
AMG	Alan M. Gillmor, Ottawa
A-MG	Anne-Marie Grégoire, Ste-Martine, Que
AP	Annick Poussart, Montreal
APW	Adam P. Woog, Vancouver
AR	Anna Valerie Rand, Montreal
AS	Ann Speedie, Niagara Falls, Ont
ASDJ	Audrey St Denys Johnson, Victoria, BC
AW	Anthony Whittingham, Kingston, Ont
BAC	Beverley A. Cavanagh, Kingston, Ont
BC	Brian Cherney, Montreal
BCl	Beth Cooil, Winnipeg
BCn	Bernice Cunnington, Winnipeg
BD	Bernard Deaville, Winnipeg
BE	Brian Ellard, Sherbrooke, Que
BH	Brian Harris, Edmonton
BHe	Brigitte Hébert, Lachute, Que
BHr	Benjamin Horch, Winnipeg
BJE	Barry J. Edwards, Toronto
BL	Bibiane Lapointe, Montreal
BLH	Benoît L'Herbier, Longueuil, Que
BM	Benoît Marineau, Quebec City
BN	Boyd Neel, Toronto
BNSG	Bryan N.S. Gooch, Vancouver
BR	Bruno Roy, Roxboro, Que
BSm	Bob Smith, Vancouver
B-SS	Bang-song Song, Seoul, Korea
BSt	Ben Steinberg, Toronto
CA	Carolyn Allworth, Yarmouth, NS
CAl	Catherine Allison, Ottawa
CAP	C. Alex Pincombe, Moncton, NB
CB	Carole Boudreault, Montreal
CC	Casimir Carter, Winnipeg
CCr	Claire Caron, Montreal
CDG	Céline De Guise, Montreal
CEB	†Charles E. Borden, Vancouver
CEG	C. Edward Gartshore, Sault Ste Marie, Ont
CEH	Carol E. Harris, St John's, Nfld
CF	Clifford Ford, Montreal
CG	Charles Girard, Montreal
CGa	Chantal Gauthier, Montreal
CGl	Christopher Gledhill, Charlottetown
CGr	Conrad Grimes, Winnipeg
CH	Cécile Huot, Montreal
CL	Conrad Laforte, Quebec City
CLE	Claire L'Écuyer, Repentigny, Que
CM	Carl Morey, Toronto
CMl	Calum Macleod, Antigonish, NS
CMr	Clément Morin, Montreal
CN	Carolyn Nielsen, Mouth of Keswick, NB
COH	Clifford O. Hunt, Toronto
CP	Claude Paradis, Rock-Forest, Que
CPr	Céline Prévost, St-Bruno, Que

†Deceased

CPt	Cécile Petit, Thetford Mines, Que
CV	Claire Versailles, Montreal
CVl	Claire Villeneuve, Montreal
CW	Christopher Weait, Toronto
CWt	Carolyn Whitley, Ottawa
DA	Denis Allaire, Montreal
DB	Dorothy Bee, Regina
DBr	Diana Brault, Hanmer, Ont
DBS	Dorothy Blakey Smith, Victoria, BC
DBW	D. Barry Waterlow, Moncton, NB
DC	Dorith Cooper, Toronto
DD	David Duke, Red Deer, Alta
DF	David Falk, Kitchener, Ont
DFC	Donald F. Cook, St John's, Nfld
DJR	D. Jay Rahn, Toronto
DK	David Kaplan, Saskatoon
DM	Denise Ménard, Ottawa
DMk	Donald McKellar, London, Ont
DP	Dennis Patrick, Toronto
DPl	Denise Pilon, Montreal
DPr	Digby Peers, Vancouver
DR	Dorothy Ryder, Ottawa
DRA	Doreen R. Allison, Mississauga, Ont
DRM	Donald R. MacKay, Brandon, Man
DS	Don Sedgwick, Toronto
DSl	David Sale, Acton, Ont
DSm	David Smith, Kingston, Ont
DSr	Dorothy Sherick, Regina
DSt	Doris Stanley, North Bay, Ont
DW	David Waterhouse, Toronto
DWt	Donald Wetmore, Halifax County, NS
EAC	Earl A. Charboneau, Kitchener, Ont
EBM	†Edward B. Moogk, London, Ont
EC	Emilia Comisel, Bucharest, Rumania
EDI	Edward D. Ives, Orono, Me
EF	Edith Fowke, Toronto
EFks	Elizabeth Filipkowski, Edmonton
EFr	Edward Farrant, Montreal
EHR	Ernest H. Ronnenberg, Kitchener, Ont
EK	Elaine Keillor, Ottawa
EKd	Edith Kidd, Guelph, Ont
EKv	Edward Kovarik, Windsor, Ont
EL	Elizabeth Lampard, St Catharines, Ont
EM	Eric McLean, Montreal
EMD	Ellen M. Drewery, Saint John, NB
EMl	Eugene Miller, Toronto
EMn	Elizabeth Mullin, Hamilton, Ont
EMr	Elizabeth Murray, Halifax, NS
ERM	Eleanor Ritcey May, Dartmouth, NS
ES	Ezra Schabas, Toronto
ESn	Eleanor Sniderman, Toronto
EW	Elliot Weisgarber, Vancouver
FAH	Fred A. Hall, Hamilton, Ont
FB	†François Brassard, Quebec City
FC	Frances Campbell, Toronto
FCR	Francean Campbell Rich, Milliken, Ont
FEC	Frank E. Churchley, Victoria, BC
FF	Fred Foran, Hull, Que
FG	Flora Matheson Goulden, Ottawa
FH	Florence Hayes, Ottawa
FL	Fernand Lindsay, Joliette, Que
FM	Florence Musselwhite, Calgary
FMB	F. Michael Barnwell, Montreal
FM-G	France Malouin-Gélinas, Montreal
FRCC	F.R.C. Clarke, Kingston, Ont
FSC	Floyd S. Chalmers, Toronto
FVE	Florrie V. Elvin, Saskatoon
GA	Gaston Allaire, Moncton, NB
GAP	George A. Proctor, London, Ont
GB	Gilles Beaudet, Montreal
GBm	Gwen Beamish, Sarnia, Ont
GBr	Giles Bryant, Toronto
GDS	George D. Sawa, Toronto
GG	Guy Gallo, Montreal
GGrg	Graham George, Kingston, Ont
GGrv	Gertrude Greaves, Saskatoon
GH	Gary Hayes, Ottawa
GHn	Guy Henson, Halifax, NS
GHr	Glen Harrison, Winnipeg
GJ	Gordon Jocelyn, Toronto
GK	George Kidd, Toronto
GKG	Gordon K. Greene, Waterloo, Ont
GKr	Gary Karr, Hartford, Conn
GP	Gilles Potvin, Montreal
GPr	Gerald Pratley, Toronto
GPz	Geoffrey Payzant, Toronto
GR	Godfrey Ridout, Toronto
GS	George Smale, Brantford, Ont
GW	Garnet Ward, Toronto
GWt	Gladys Whitehead, Dundas, Ont
GZ	George Zaduban, Ottawa
HC	Helen Creighton, Dartmouth, NS
HCs	Harvey Chusid, Ottawa
HD	Helen Dahlstrom, Rossland, BC
HD-G	Hélène Dion-Gauthier, Lorraine, Que
HDn	Hélène Dion, Ste-Thérèse, Que
HG	Hazel Goldenberg, Toronto
HK	Helmut Kallmann, Ottawa
HL	Helen Livingston, Hamilton, Ont
HM	Helen McNamara, Toronto
HMr	Helen Martens, Waterloo, Ont
HO	Harvey Olnick, Toronto
HP	Hélène Plouffe, Montreal
HPd	Hélène Pednault, Montreal
HPl	Hélène Paul, Montreal
HPln	Henri Pilon, Toronto
HPn	Hélène Panneton, Montreal
HR	Harold Redekopp, Winnipeg
HS	Hiram Silk, Grand Falls, Nfld
HW	Henry Whiston, Montreal
HWH	†H. William Hawke, Gananoque, Ont
HWr	Harold Wright, Halifax, NS
IA	István Anhalt, Kingston, Ont
IB	Irène Brisson, Quebec City
IBr	Ian Barrie, Prince Albert, Sask
IF	Iris French, Toronto
IG	Ian Grant, London, Ont
IH	Ida Halpern, Vancouver
IM	Irene Markoff, Toronto
IMG	Ilhami M. Gökçen, Toronto
IMM	Isabelle M. Mills, Saskatoon
IP	Isabelle Panneton, Montreal
IP-C	Isabelle Papineau-Couture, Montreal
IR	Irene Rowlin, Winnipeg
JA	Jeffrey Anderson, Toronto
JB	John Beckwith, Toronto
JBk	John Berke, Toronto
JBl	Joan Baillie, Toronto
JBM	James B. McPherson, Toronto
JB-T	Juliette Bourassa-Trépanier, Quebec City
JBu	Janice Butler, Vancouver
JC	Jean Chatillon, Trois-Rivières, Que
JCB	John C. Bird, Toronto
JCl	Josèphe Colle, Montreal
JCm	June Countryman, Kitchener, Ont
JCr	Jean Crittall, Thunder Bay, Ont
JD	Josée Destrempes, Montreal
JDn	Joanne Dorenfeld, Vancouver
JDS	J. D'Arcy Shea, Vancouver
JE	Jack Edds, St Catharines, Ont
JF	John Fodi, Toronto
JH	John Hare, Ottawa
JHn	Jens Hanson, Windsor, Ont
JK	Jack Kopstein, Oromocto, NB
JLF	John L. Field, Niagara-on-the-Lake, Ont
JLm	Jacques Lamoureux, Montreal
JMc	Joseph Macerollo, Toronto
JMlt	Juliette Milette, Montreal
JMn	James Manchip, Fredericton
JMr	Jaroslav Mráček, San Diego, Cal
JMs	James Manishen, Brandon, Man
JP	Joseph Petric, Toronto
JPG	J. Paul Green, London, Ont
JPr	Jamie Portman, Calgary
JR	Jeani Read, Vancouver
JRH	Jorgen R. Holgerson, Edmonton
JRl	Joyce Rawlings, Vancouver
JRz	Jeanne Rizzo, Plantation, Fla
JS	Jacob Siskind, Ottawa
JSM	John S. McIntosh, London, Ont
JSn	Janet Schnell, Saskatoon
JSr	Jack Sorenson, Halifax, NS
JSw	Jean Southworth, Ottawa
JSz	John Szwed, Philadelphia, Pa
JT	Jacques Thériault, Montreal
JTs	Jack Thiessen, Winnipeg
JVM	John V. Mills, Toronto
JW	Joseph Wearing, Peterborough, Ont
JWl	Josephine Walton, Vancouver
JWS	John W. Searchfield, Calgary
KB	Keith Bissell, Toronto
KBr	Kenneth Bray, London, Ont
KC	Kendrick Crossley, Toronto
KM	Keith MacMillan, Ottawa
KMr	Kenneth Murphy, Banff, Alta
KN	Kenneth Nichols, Brandon, Man
KP	Kenneth Peacock, Ottawa
KS	Kenneth Scott, Toronto
KSg	Karl Signell, College Park, Md
KV	Klaas Vangraft, Toronto
KW	Kenneth Winters, Toronto
LB	Lorne Betts, Hamilton, Ont
LB-M	Louise Bail-Milot, Duvernay, Que
LC	Lawrence Cluderay, Westbank, BC
LCf	Lenore Crawford, London, Ont
LCk	Lawson Cook, Toronto
LD	Laurent Duval, Montreal
LD-B	Louise Dulude-Bennett, Montreal
LF	Laure Fink, Montreal
LFP	Leona F. Paterson, Calgary
L-GA	Louis-Gérard Alberti, Ottawa
LH	Lorna Hassell, Toronto
LHv	Lynne Hoover, Ottawa
LI	Leonard Isaacs, Winnipeg
LL	Linda Litwack, Toronto
LO	Louise Ostiguy, Montreal
LP	Lucien Poirier, Loretteville, Que
LRH	Leslie R. Hall, Toronto
LR-L	Lyse Richer-Lortie, Montreal
LS	Lorraine Saab, Toronto
LT	Lorraine Thibeault, Montreal
LV-L	Louise Valois-Liessens, Tracy, Que
LW	Lorne Watson, Brandon, Man
MB	Madeleine Bernier, Winnipeg
MB-L	Madeleine Bodier-Little, Quebec City
MBn	Martin Boundy, London, Ont
MC	Maria Calderisi, Ottawa
MCa	Margaret Campbell, Halifax, NS
MCK	Millicent C. Kavanagh, Fredericton
MCk	Melville Cook, Toronto
M-CL	Marie-Claire Lefebvre, Montreal
MCr	Marcelle Corneille, Montreal
MCv	Maria Corvin, Toronto
MD	Margaret Daly, Toronto
MDr	Margaret Drynan, Oshawa, Ont
MF	Marc Fortier, St-Bruno, Que
MFr	Margaret Frazer, Toronto
MG	Melva Graham, Halifax, NS
MH	Marjorie Hale, Toronto
MH-D	Michèle Hogue-Doré, Montreal
MHl	Margaret Holden, Ottawa

†Deceased

MIM	M. Ian Mail, Toronto
MK	Michael Koerner, Toronto
MKl	†Mieczyslaw Kolinski, Toronto
MKz	Metro Kozak, Sudbury, Ont
ML	Mabel Laine, Toronto
MM	Mark Miller, Toronto
MMl	Maud McLean, Toronto
MMV	Margery M. Vaughan, Victoria, BC
MN	Margaret Nelson, Lethbridge, Alta
MP	Mimi Poirier, Laval, Que
MPr	Michelle Proulx, Montreal
MS	Marc Samson, Quebec City
MSh	Michael Schulman, Toronto
MSm	Marie Smyth, Halifax, NS
MSr	Morris Schumiatcher, Regina
MSt	Michael Strutt, Montreal
MT	Micheline Tessier, Montreal
MW	Max Wyman, Vancouver
MWl	Marlene Wehrle, Ottawa
MWM	Mary Willan Mason, Toronto
MY	Margaret Young, Halifax, NS
M-YL	Ming-Yueh Liang, Vancouver
NJ	Nazir Jairazbhoy, Windsor, Ont
NK	Natalie Kuzmich, Toronto
NM	Nancy McGregor, Toronto
NR	Neil Rosenberg, St John's, Nfld
NT	Nadia Turbide, Montreal
NTr	Nicole Trudeau, St-Lambert, Que
NV	Nancy Vogan, Sackville, NB
OM	Ogreta McNeill, Toronto
PAS	Peggy A. Sharpe, Brandon, Man
PB	Patricia Beharriell, Kingston, Ont
PD	Paule Daunais, Montreal
PFB	Peter F. Bishop, Victoria, BC
PG	Peter Goddard, Toronto
PGD	Philip G. Downs, London, Ont
PJ	Philip Johnson, Moose Jaw, Sask
PJT	Philip J. Thomas, Vancouver
PK	Patricia Kellogg, Toronto
PL	Philippe Laframboise, Montreal
PM	Paul McIntyre, Windsor, Ont
PMr	Paul Murray, Halifax, NS
PMW	Philip M. Wults, Toronto
PP	Paul Pedersen, Huntington, Que
PPr	Percival Price, Ann Arbor, Mich
PPrn	Peter Perrin, New York, NY

†Deceased

PR	Pierre Rochon, Montreal
PRB	Phyllis R. Blakeley, Halifax, NS
PRl	Patricia Rolston, Hamilton, Ont
PS	Patricia Shand, Toronto
PSm	Peggie Sampson, Toronto
PSr	Patricia Sauerbrei, Toronto
PW	Patricia Wardrop, Toronto
RA	Raffi Armenian, Waterloo, Ont
RAK	Ralph A. Kidd, Guelph, Ont
RB	Robert Bell, Toronto
RBr	Rolland Brunelle, Joliette, Que
RC	Richard Cooke, St James, Man
RCB	Robert C. Bayley, Fredericton
RD	Raymond Daveluy, Montreal
RDM	R. Dale McIntosh, Victoria, BC
RF	Richard Flohil, Toronto
RG	Ronald Gibson, Winnipeg
RGg	Richard Gagné, Cap-Rouge, Que
RGn	Richard Green, Manotick, Ont
RH	Richard Henninger, San Mateo, Cal
RJ	Richard Johnston, Calgary
RK	Robert Klymasz, St John's, Nfld
RM	Rick MacMillan, Toronto
RMh	Renée Maheu, Montreal
RMr	Ruby Mercer, Toronto
RN	Ronald Napier, Toronto
RP	Ross Pratt, Montreal
RPl	Ramón Pelinski, Ottawa
RPn	Ruth Pincoe, Toronto
RPv	Rémi Potvin, Montreal
RPy	Ron Paley, Winnipeg
RQ	Regula Qureshi, Edmonton
RR	Robert Richard, Ottawa
RRs	Rhoda Resnick, Toronto
RS	Robert Skelton, London, Ont
RSl	Rodriguez Steele, Antigonish, NS
RSm	Raymond Simpson, Halifax, NS
RSr	Ross Stuart, Toronto
RSt	Robert Stangeland, Edmonton
RT	Roman Toi, Toronto
RTr	Rex Trotter, Toronto
RVW	Robert Van Wyck, Montreal
RW	Robert Witmer, Toronto
RWJ	Robert W. Judge, Toronto
SAB	Shirley A. Blakeley, Halifax, NS
SC	Stephen Chenette, Toronto
SL	Sam Levine, Toronto
SLH	Sharyn Lea Hall, Hamilton, Ont

SLO	Stanley L. Osborne, Oshawa, Ont
SO	Steven Otto, Toronto
SP	Shirley Penner, Steinbach, Man
SPl	Stella Plante, Rimouski, Que
SRM	S. Roy Maley, Winnipeg
SS	Stanley Saunders, Guelph, Ont
SSl	Sonia Slatin, New York, NY
ST	Suzanne Thomas, Montreal
SW	Stephen Willis, Ottawa
SWl	Susan Wilson, Toronto
TB	Terence Bailey, London, Ont
TC	Tim Classey, Toronto
TCB	Thomas C. Brown, Toronto
TC-C	Thérèse Charbonneau-Conquer, Triel-sur-Seine, France
TDN	Thomas D. Northwood, Ottawa
TJ	Thomas Johnston, Fairbanks, Alaska
TJO	Thelma Johannes O'Neill, Edmonton
TM	Timothy McGee, Toronto
TR	Timothy Rice, Toronto
TRL	Thelma Reid Lower, Vancouver
TRl	Thomas Rolston, Edmonton
TS	Terry Smythe, Winnipeg
TT	Tom Taylor, Winnipeg
VGD	Vega G. Dawson, Halifax, NS
VH	Vernon Huggins, Regina
VR	Vivienne Rowley, Castlegar, BC
VS	Veronica Sedivy, Toronto
VW	Victoria Woods, Toronto
WA	William Aide, Toronto
WB	William Bartlett, Charlottetown
WHK	Walter H. Kemp, Halifax, NS
WK	Walter Klymkiw, St Boniface, Man
WL	Wallace Laughton, St Catharines, Ont
WLB	William L. Brandhagen, Saskatoon
WLk	William Lock, La Mirada, Cal
WM	Wayne Miller, Brandon, Man
WS	William Schabas, Montreal
WU	Walter Unger, Winnipeg
WV	William Vaisey, Toronto
WW	Walter Williamson, Victoria, BC
WWGD	Walter W.G. Deller, Brandon, Man
WWt	Winston Wuttunee, Winnipeg
YC	Yves Chartier, Ottawa
YL	Yvan Lemay, Montreal
YR	Yolande Rivard, Montreal

Guide to Using the Encyclopedia

Alphabetical arrangement

Compound headings are treated as one continuous word and are alphabetized, ignoring spaces, hyphens, apostrophes, accents, and quotation marks, up to the first comma. For names of persons or corporate entities the rule is applied following the comma: eg,

Musical Union precedes Music boxes;
Gagnon, Alain precedes Gagnon, André.

However, the prefixes Mac and Mc both are treated as though spelled Mac and entered accordingly. The ampersand (&), all numbers, and St / Ste (Saint / Sainte) are alphabetized as though spelled in full.

Form of name for entry

The professional, or best-known, or (in general) most recent form of a name has been used as the form of entry. Any other form of a name follows immediately after the heading. When two or more names are familiar, 'see' references direct the reader to the main entry.

The religious name of a priest or nun has been used when that is the best-known or professional name. Religious names are entered, without inversion, under the first letter of the given name: eg,

Sister Marie-Stéphane under M.

Family entries that treat more than one generation are entered first in a list of like names: eg,

Gagnon family precedes Gagnon, Alain.

French surnames that include the definite article L', Le, or La are entered under L, and those beginning with Du under D.

Normally French surnames that include the preposition 'de' are entered under the word following. However when professional usage dictates, such French names may be entered under D: eg,

de Foras, Odette under D.

A compound name containing a surname is entered, without inversion, under the surname: eg,

Frederick Harris Music Co Ltd under H;
Floyd S. Chalmers Foundation under C.

The name of a pop group which is a compound of an individual and a group name is entered under the individual's surname, without inversion: eg,

Mart Kenney and His Western Gentlemen under K.

Other compound names are entered under the first word of the compound: eg,

John Adaskin Project under J;
Leslie Bell Singers under L;
Rebecca Cohn Auditorium under R.

The entries for most Quebec and other French-Canadian subjects appear in *EMC* under the French names: eg,

Académie de musique de Québec;
Société de musique contemporaine du Québec.

In a few instances English-language versions of French names have come into wide use in English-speaking Canada, and for each of these the English-language form of entry, marked by a dagger, is given first, followed by the French-language form: eg,

University of Moncton† / Université de Moncton;
Quebec Symphony Orchestra† / Orchestre symphonique de Québec.

Many national organizations have proper names in both languages; these are entered under the English-language name, followed by the French-language one: eg,

Canadian Music Centre / Centre de musique canadienne.

Types of entry

In addition to biographical or topical entries, there are three other types of entry in *EMC*.

The family entry. When members of more than one generation of a family are given individual biographies these are arranged in chronological order in a subdivided entry under the family name.

'See' references. This type of entry has been provided to direct the reader from one familiar form of a name to another form under which the entry appears in *EMC*.

The reader's guide. This type of entry is designed to provide the reader with a list of *EMC* entries related to its subject: eg,

Composition, topical;
Education;
Religions and music.

It also often will notify the reader of entries normally not found in a music encyclopedia: eg,

Wars, rebellions, and uprisings (listed in Composition, topical);
Inventions and devices (listed in Education);
The Amish (listed in Religions and music).

Cross-references

Within an entry an asterisk has been used before a subject to indicate the existence of an entry on that subject in *EMC*. Such cross-references usually are made only at the first mention of the subject within the entry. However, in very long or subdivided entries and family entries the asterisk may be repeated at the first mention in any subsequent subsection. In the recording information given in a list of compositions the asterisk is used before the name of a performer (or performing group) to indicate that fuller discographic detail may be found in the entry for that performer or group.

'See' or 'see also' references have been provided in bibliographies and discographies, to avoid undue duplication of information.

Usages

Dates. '1964–76' should be read as 'from 1964 to 1976.' '(1903–81)' should be read as 'begun in 1903 and concluded (or dispersed or ceased operating) in 1981' or 'born in 1903, died in 1981.' A date followed by a dash and a space, eg, '1965– ', should be read as 'beginning in 1965.'

The abbreviation 'fl' used before a date indicates the span of years in which a person or organization is known to have flourished.

Place. Place-names have been used that were current at the time under discussion in the article, with the modern or familiar name given in parentheses: eg,

Berlin, Upper Canada (Kitchener, Ont).

A Canadian city or town named after an old-country city or town is given a qualifying provincial designation. London, Ont, is always so designated unless the context makes the designation unnecessary. London, unqualified, means the original city of that name in England.

Ranks, titles, specializations. In ordinary references within the text, military, religious, and academic titles are used only rarely. Academic promotions (assistant professor, professor, etc) have not been noted for reasons of space. At the beginning of a biographical article the subject's main specializations are listed in the approximate order of their importance in his or her career.

The term 'educator' usually is applied to the teacher whose sphere of activity extends or has extended beyond the studio or classroom (ie, into the formulation of educational theories or methods, the writing or editing of textbooks, etc).

Degrees. Standardized forms have been used for academic degrees and applied irrespective of the forms used by the granting institutions. These forms are listed under 'Abbreviations and Acronyms' beginning on p xxii.

Translations. When French-Canadian churches, concert halls, streets, or other such entities are referred to in *EMC*, the French form of the descriptive part of the name has been retained, but the generic part of the name has been translated: eg,

l'église Notre-Dame becomes Notre-Dame Church;
rue Ste-Catherine becomes Ste-Catherine St.

Abbreviations and acronyms

Abbreviations and acronyms have been used extensively throughout *EMC*. An annotated list of all such forms is provided in one alphabetical sequence beginning on p xxii.

Bibliographies and writings

The bibliographies and lists of writings following the text of *EMC* articles are selective. Such lists are ordered chronologically, not alphabetically. Some large bibliographies have been arranged in classified order.

Frequently cited works, which are given full citation in the 'General Bibliography' beginning on p xxi, are given in abbreviated forms when cited in the text or in individual bibliographies. Two publications originally in English – *Aspects of Music in Canada* and *Contemporary Canadian Composers* – were published later in French-language editions that updated or added additional information. Both English and French titles may be cited therefore, and in several instances only the French-language edition is given.

Lists of compositions

The majority of the lists of compositions in *EMC* are selective. Lists of compositions have been classified by genre and are ordered chronologically within each classification (or alphabetically if the chronology is unknown). The meanings of the abbreviations used for instrumentation, publishers, and recording information are given in 'Abbreviations and Acronyms' beginning on p xxii. French-language composition titles of generic type (Quatuor, Sonate, Symphonie) have been translated (Quartet, Sonata, Symphony).

The following examples illustrate some of the short forms used in the lists of compositions. Each example is followed by a prose elucidation which will serve as a guide in reading similar items in the lists.

Example

Sonata. 1946 (Tor 1947). Vn, pf. CMCentre. 1952. RCI 73 (M. Adaskin vn, M. Bernardi pf)/CBC SM-211 (*Fenyves vn)

Meaning. *Sonata* (by Murray Adaskin and listed in his entry under Compositions: Chamber), composed in 1946 and premiered in Toronto in 1947. For violin and piano. The score is held at the Canadian Music Centre. A 1952 Radio Canada International recording by Murray Adaskin, violin, and Mario Bernardi, piano, was released as RCI 73. Full discographic details of another CBC recording (CBC SM-211) may be found in the entry for the violinist Lorand Fenyves.

Example

Paysage (Saint-Denys-Garneau). 1968 (Zagreb 1969). 8 singers, 8 spkr, sm orch. CMCentre. RCI 299 (*SMCQ)

Meaning. *Paysage* (by Jean Papineau-Couture and listed in his entry under Compositions: Soloist and orchestra), with words by Hector de Saint-Denys-Garneau, was composed in 1968 and premiered in 1969 in Zagreb. Scored for 8 singers, 8 speakers, and small orchestra. The score is held at the Canadian Music Centre. A recording of the work by the Société de musique contemporaine du Québec has been issued by Radio Canada International (RCI 299). Full discographic details may be found in the entry for the SMCQ.

Example

Two Sketches for Strings 'based on French-Canadian Airs.' 1927. Str orch (str quar). OUP 1928. CBC IS Canadian Album No. 2 (*TSO)/RCI 238 and CTL M1030 (*Hart House O)/Col MS 6962 and Col M2S 276 (TSO)/('À Saint-Malo') Dom S-1372 (Tor Philharmonia O, *Feldbrill cond)/(str quar) RCI 236 and DG 139900 (Amadeus Quar)

Meaning. (Composed by Sir Ernest MacMillan and listed in his entry under Compositions: Orchestra), *Two Sketches for Strings*, 'based on French-Canadian Airs,' was completed in 1927. The work is scored in alternative versions for string orchestra and string quartet. Both versions were published by Oxford University Press in 1928. The orchestral version has been recorded by the Toronto Symphony Orchestra (CBC IS Canadian Album No. 2) and by the Hart House Orchestra (RCI 238, also released on Canadian Talent Library M1030). See the entries for the Toronto Symphony Orchestra and for the Hart House Orchestra for full discographic details. A later recording by the Toronto Symphony was released as Columbia MS 6962 and also as Columbia M2S 276. A recording of one section, 'À Saint-Malo,' was made by the Toronto Philharmonia Orchestra, conducted by Victor Feldbrill (see his entry for full discographic details), and released by Dominion under the number S-1372. A Radio Canada International recording by the Amadeus String Quartet of the string quartet version was released as RCI 236 and also was issued by Deutsche Grammophon under the number DG 139900.

Discographies

Pop and jazz recordings are listed chronologically in discographies. All other discographies are ordered alphabetically.

Labels and catalogue numbers are largely those used in the Canadian catalogues of the international companies.

Player-piano rolls and 78-rpm and 45-rpm recordings are so designated; all others are 33⅓-rpm LPs.

Citations that include the works of several composers list the composers but may limit the listing of titles of works to those that are by Canadians.

The contents of a record are listed in one citation. An *EMC* discography does not give a separate citation for each work on a recording. Discographic citations provide the title of the recording and/or the name(s) of the composer(s) and title(s) of works performed; the performers; the year of the recording (or, when not available, the year of copyright or release, in parentheses); the label and catalogue number; and subsequent release on other labels, subject to the availability of that information.

The following examples from *EMC* discographies have been chosen to illustrate the forms used and the type of information presented therein. The explanation which follows each example is intended to demonstrate for the reader the full extent of the information given in the example.

Example

Glick . . . *i never saw another butterfly* . . . – Freedman *Poems of Young People* – Beckwith *Five Songs*. Newmark pf. 1970. CBC SM-77/Sel CC-15.073

Meaning. This recording (by Maureen Forrester as listed in the Discography at the end of her entry) of vocal works by Srul Irving Glick, Harry Freedman, and John Beckwith, with the pianist John Newmark, was made in 1970 by the CBC (CBC SM-77), and was released also on Select CC-15.073.

Example

Mozart *Così fan tutte*. Strasbourg Phil, Lombard cond, Stratas (Despina). (1978). 3-RCA FRL 3-2629

Meaning. On the recording of Mozart's *Così fan tutte* (listed in the Discography at the end of the entry on Teresa Stratas) by the Strasbourg Philharmonic, conducted by [Alain] Lombard, Stratas sings the role of Despina. The three-record RCA set (FRL 3-2629) was released in 1978.

To avoid undue duplication of information, recordings normally have been given a full citation in only one entry, and that is in the entry for the main performer or performing group. Cross-references to this full citation are found under the entries for the other performers. For instance, the main entry for the Beaver recording of Pierné's *The Children's Crusade* is given in the discography of the Toronto Mendelssohn Choir. Entries on Beaver Records, Walter Susskind (conductor), and Mary Morrison (soprano) include cross-references to the discography at the end of the entry on the Toronto Mendelssohn Choir.

Filmographies

Any list of films includes titles, producers (or Canadian distributors), and dates.

Index

The index lists those persons, organizations, companies, radio and TV stations, churches, periodicals, schools, some subjects, titles of works, etc, that do *not* have entries in *EMC*. Bibliographies, discographies (with the exception of some discographies for jazz/pop performers), and lists of writings and of compositions are not indexed, nor is the introductory matter.

The index concentrates on the Canadian material in *EMC*. Non-Canadian performers, teachers, composers, places of performance, publishers, organizations, etc, have not been indexed throughout *EMC* unless there is a strong Canadian connection. For instance, Beethoven is indexed in the article on T.F. Molt, but not necessarily in the article on a performer who played one of his concertos.

The principles used to determine the form of an entry and alphabetization for the text have been used in compiling the index.

A separate 'Index of Illustrations' can be found beginning on p 1024.

General Bibliography

The following are short forms of the titles used most often in bibliographic citations throughout *EMC* and the corresponding full citations. This should not be regarded as a comprehensive list of the basic literature on music in Canada. Pertinent literature relating to specific topics (eg, Bibliography, Folk music, Discography) is given in the entries for those topics.

Amtmann *Music in Canada*
Amtmann, Willy. *Music in Canada 1600–1800*. Montreal: Habitex Books 1975

Amtmann *Musique au Québec*
Amtmann, Willy. *La Musique au Québec 1600–1875*, transl Michelle Pharand. Montreal: Les Éditions de l'Homme 1976. Transl, rev, enl edn

Aspects de la musique au Canada
See *Aspects of Music in Canada*

Aspects of Music in Canada
Aspects of Music in Canada, ed Arnold Walter. Toronto: University of Toronto Press 1969 / *Aspects de la musique au Canada*, ed Maryvonne Kendergi and Gilles Potvin. Montreal: Centre de psychologie et de pédagogie 1970. Transl, rev, enl edn

Axes, Chops & Hot Licks
Yorke, Ritchie. *Axes, Chops & Hot Licks*. Edmonton: M.G. Hurtig 1971

Baker's
Baker's Biographical Dictionary of Musicians, ed Nicolas Slonimsky. 5th and 6th edns. New York: G. Schirmer 1971, suppl 1971, 1978

Bands Canadians Danced To
McNamara, Helen, and Lomas, Jack. *The Bands Canadians Danced To*. Toronto: Griffin Press 1973

Bio-Bibliographical Finding List
A Bio-Bibliographical Finding List of Canadian Musicians and Those Who Have Contributed to Music in Canada. Compiled by a committee of the CMLA. Ottawa: Canadian Library Association 1961. *Musicians in Canada: A Bio-Bibliographical Finding List / Musiciens au Canada: index bio-bibliographique*, ed Kathleen M. Toomey and Stephen C. Willis. Ottawa: CAML/ACBM 1981

Blow up
Maillé, Michèle. *Blow up des grands de la chanson au Québec*. Montreal: Les Éditions de l'Homme 1969

Canadian Folk Culture
Communique: Canadian Studies: Canadian Folk Culture Issue, vol 3, August 1977. Scarborough, Ont: Association of Canadian Community Colleges

Canadian Music of the Twentieth Century
Proctor, George A. *Canadian Music of the Twentieth Century*. Toronto: University of Toronto Press 1980

Catalogue de la chanson folklorique française
Laforte, Conrad. *Le Catalogue de la chanson folklorique française*. 6 vols. Quebec: Les Presses de l'université Laval 1977– : vol 1 *Chansons en laisse* (1977); vol 2 *Chansons strophiques* (in progress); vol 3 *Chansons en dialogue* (in progress); vol 4 *Chansons énumératives* (1979); vol 5 *Chansons brèves* (in progress); vol 6 *Chansons sur les timbres* (in progress)

Catalogue of Canadian Composers
Kallmann, Helmut. *Catalogue of Canadian Composers*. Toronto: CBC 1952. Repr, St Clair Shores, Mich: Scholarly Press 1972

La Chanson au Québec
Cormier, Normand; Houle, Ghislaine; Lauzier, Suzanne; and Trépanier, Yvette. *La Chanson au Québec 1965–1975*. Montreal: Bibliothèque nationale du Québec 1975

La Chanson française
Charpentreau, Jacques, et al. *La Chanson française*. Montreal: Les Éditions Bellarmin 1965

Chansonniers du Québec
Larsen, Christian. *Chansonniers du Québec*. Montreal: Beauchemin 1964

Compositeurs canadiens contemporains
see *Contemporary Canadian Composers*

Contemporary Canadian Composers
Contemporary Canadian Composers, ed Keith MacMillan and John Beckwith. Toronto: Oxford University Press 1975 / *Compositeurs canadiens contemporains*, ed Louise Laplante, transl Véronique Robert. Montreal: Les Presses de l'Université du Québec 1977. Transl, rev, and enl edn

Coup d'oeil
Morisset, Gérard. *Coup d'oeil sur les arts en Nouvelle-France*. Quebec: self-published 1941

Creative Canada
Creative Canada: A Biographical Dictionary of Twentieth-century Creative and Performing Artists. Reference Division, McPherson Library, University of Victoria, BC, compiler. 2 vols. Toronto: University of Toronto Press 1971, 1972

DCB
Dictionary of Canadian Biography. 20 vols. Toronto: University of Toronto Press 1966– / *Dictionnaire biographique du Canada*. 20 vols. Quebec: Les Presses de l'université Laval, 1966–

Dictionary of Contemporary Music
Dictionary of Contemporary Music, ed John Vinton. New York: E.P. Dutton & Co 1974

Directory of Musical Canada
Gilpin, Wayne. *Directory of Musical Canada*. Edmonton: Canadian Music Press 1978

Discopaedia
Creighton, James. *Discopaedia of the Violin 1889–1971*. Toronto: University of Toronto Press 1974

Encyclopedia Canadiana
Encyclopedia Canadiana. 10 vols. Ottawa: Grolier of Canada 1957–8. Later rev edns, Toronto 1972, 1975

Encyclopedia of Jazz
Feather, Leonard. *Encyclopedia of Jazz*. New York: Bonanza Books 1960
– *Encyclopedia of Jazz in the Sixties*. New York: Bonanza Books 1966
– and Gitler, Ira. *Encyclopedia of Jazz in the Seventies*. New York: Horizon Press 1976

Encyclopedia of Popular Music and Jazz
Kinkle, Roger D. *The Complete Encyclopedia of Popular Music and Jazz 1900–1950.* 4 vols. New Rochelle, NY: Arlington House 1974

Grove's
Grove's Dictionary of Music and Musicians, ed Eric Blom. 5th edn. 9 vols. London: Macmillan 1954. Suppl, 1961. See also *The New Grove Dictionary*

Harvard Dictionary
Apel, Willi. *Harvard Dictionary of Music.* 2nd edn. Cambridge, Mass: Belknap Press of Harvard University 1969

Jesuit Relations
The Jesuit Relations and Allied Documents. Travels and Explorations of the Jesuit Missionaries in New France, 1610–1791, ed R.G. Thwaites. 73 vols. Cleveland, O: Burrows Bros 1896–1901

Kallmann *History of Music in Canada*
Kallmann, Helmut. *A History of Music in Canada 1534–1914.* Toronto: University of Toronto Press 1960

List of Canadian Copyright Compositions
Complete List of Canadian Copyright Musical Compositions (1868–1889) compiled from the official register at Ottawa. Np 1889?

MGG
Die Musik in Geschichte und Gegenwart, ed Friedrich Blume. 16 vols. Kassel & Basel: Bärenreiter Verlag 1949–79

Musical Canadiana
Musical Canadiana: A Subject Index. Canadian Music Library Association, compiler. Ottawa: Canadian Library Association 1967

Musical Red Book
Sandwell, Bernard K. *The Musical Red Book of Montreal.* Montreal: F.A. Veitch 1907

Musiciennes de chez nous
Gingras, Claude. *Musiciennes de chez nous.* Montreal: Éditions de l'École Vincent-d'Indy 1955

Musiciens canadiens
Soeurs de Sainte-Anne. *Dictionnaire biographique des musiciens canadiens.* Lachine, Que: 1935. Repr, Ann Arbor, Mich: University Microfilms 1972

Music in Canada
Music in Canada, ed Sir Ernest MacMillan. Toronto: University of Toronto Press 1955

Musique et Cinéma
La Cinémathèque canadienne. *Musique et Cinéma: filmographie des compositeurs canadiens ayant signé des partitions musicales dans des films produits par l'ONF 1940–1964.* Montreal: 1965

The New Grove Dictionary
The New Grove Dictionary of Music and Musicians, ed Stanley Sadie. 6th edn. 20 vols. London: Macmillan 1980

Pionniers du disque folklorique
Labbé, Gabriel. *Les Pionniers du disque folklorique québécois 1920–1950.* Montreal: Les Éditions de l'Aurore 1977

'Review of records'
Stone, Kurt. 'Review of records,' *Musical Quarterly*, vol 53, July 1967

Roll Back the Years
Moogk, Edward B. *Roll Back the Years: History of Canadian Recorded Sound and its Legacy, Genesis to 1930 / En remontant les années: l'histoire et l'héritage de l'enregistrement sonore au Canada des débuts à 1930.* Ottawa: National Library of Canada 1975

Selected Bibliography of Musical Canadiana
Bradley, Ian L. *A Selected Bibliography of Musical Canadiana.* Rev edn. Toronto: GLC Publishers 1976

Sources in Canadian Music
Proctor, George A. *Sources in Canadian Music: A Bibliography of Bibliographies / Les Sources de la musique canadienne: une bibliographie des bibliographies.* Sackville, NB: Mount Allison University 1975, 1979

Thirty-four Biographies
Thirty-four Biographies of Canadian Composers / Trente-quatre Biographies de compositeurs canadiens. Montreal: CBC 1964. Repr, St Clair Shores, Mich: Scholarly Press 1972

'Toronto's pre-confederation music societies'
Sale, David John. 'Toronto's pre-confederation music societies, 1845–1867.' Unpubl MA thesis, University of Toronto 1968

La Vie musicale
Lasalle-Leduc, Annette. *La Vie musicale au Canada français.* Quebec: ministère des Affaires culturelles, 1964 (2nd printing dated 1964 is slightly augmented)

Willan Catalogue
Bryant, Giles. *Healey Willan Catalogue.* Ottawa: National Library of Canada 1972. Suppl in progress 1980

Abbreviations and Acronyms

A&R	Artist and Repertoire
ABC	American Broadcasting Corporation
AB of the RSM	Associated Board of the Royal Schools of Music 1889– (London)
AC	Alberta Culture 1975– (Cultural Development Branch 1946–71; Department of Culture, Youth and Recreation 1971–5)
ACA	Alberta Composers' Association / Association des compositeurs de l'Alberta 1977–
a cap	a cappella
acc	accordion(s)
ACCO	Associate, Canadian College of Organists 1909–59 (ARCCO 1959–)
ACME	Academy of Country Music Entertainment 1976–
ACO	Association of Canadian Orchestras / AOC, Association des orchestres canadiens 1972–
ACRA	Association of Canadian Radio Artists 1943–63 (ACTRA 1963–)
ACTRA	Association of Canadian Television and Radio Artists 1963– (ACRA 1943–63)
adap	adapter / adapted
ad lib	ad libitum / at pleasure
AF of M	American Federation of Musicians 1896–1901; American Federation of Musicians of the United States and Canada 1901–
AGSM	Associate, Guildhall School of Music
Ala	Alabama
Algord	Algord Music Ltd (publisher, Toronto)
Alta	Alberta
AMA	Associate in Music, Alberta 1936–
AMEA	Alberta Music Educators' Association 1957–69
AMM	Associate in Music, Manitoba 1936–
AMP	Associated Music Publishers, Inc (New York)
AMQ	Académie de musique de Québec 1868–
AMS	Associate in Music, Saskatchewan 1936–
A MUS	Associate in music

Ang-Can	Anglo-Canadian Music Publishers' Association 1885–1921; Anglo-Canadian Music Co 1921–ca 1943 (Toronto)
Anglo-Canadian	see Ang-Can
anon	anonymous
A of D	Ace of Diamonds (record label)
Apogee	Apogee Press, Inc (publisher, Cincinnati, O)
approx	approximately
ARAM	Associate, Royal Academy of Music
ARCCO	Associate, Royal Canadian College of Organists 1959– (ACCO 1909–59)
Arch	Ed Archambault Inc (publisher, Montreal)
ARCM	Associate, Royal College of Music
ARCO	Associate, Royal College of Organists
ARCT	Associate, Royal Conservatory of Music of Toronto 1947– (ATCM 1896–1947)
Ariz	Arizona
Ark	Arkansas
ARMCM	Associate, Royal Manchester College of Music
ARMTA	Alberta Registered Music Teachers' Association 1932–
arr	arranged / arrangement(s) / arranger(s)
ARSCM	Associate, Royal School of Church Music 1945– (School of English Church Music 1927–45)
ASCAP	American Society of Composers, Authors, Publishers 1914–
Assn(s)	Association(s)
Associated Music	Associated Music Publishers, Inc (New York)
ATCL	Associate, Trinity College of Music, London
ATCM	Associate, Toronto Conservatory of Music 1896–1947 (ARCT 1947–)
Augsburg	Augsburg Publishing House (Minneapolis, Minn)
Ave	Avenue
AWCM	Associate, Western Ontario Conservatory of Music
b	born
B (plus number)	Bryant's numbering system for Willan compositions (see *Willan Catalogue* in 'General Bibliography')
BA	Bachelor of Arts / AB artium baccalaureus
B&B	Bote & Bock (publisher, Berlin)
B&H	Boosey & Hawkes (Canada) Ltd (publisher, Toronto)
Banff SFA	Banff Centre School of Fine Arts 1933–
bar	baritone(s)
Bar	Baroque (record label)
Bar & Bar	Barger & Barclay (publisher, Fort Lauderdale, Fla)
BBC	British Broadcasting Corporation 1927–
BBG	Board of Broadcast Governors / BGR, Bureau des gouverneurs de la radiodiffusion 1958–68 (CRTC 1968–)
BC	British Columbia / Colombie britannique
BCCP	British Columbia Cultural Program 1967–76 (Cultural Services Branch, Department of Culture and Heritage, Ministry of Recreation and Conservation 1976–8, Ministry of Provincial Secretary and Government Services 1978–)
b cl	bass clarinet(s)
BCMEA	British Columbia Music Educators' Association 1957–
B COM	Bachelor of Commerce
BCRMTA	British Columbia Registered Music Teachers' Association 1932–
B ED	Bachelor of Education / ED B
Ber	Berandol Music Ltd (publisher, Toronto 1969– , see BMIC 1947–69) Ber (record label)
Berandol	see Ber
BES	Brevet d'enseignement spécialisé (teaching diploma)
BFA	Bachelor of Fine Arts
b guit	(electric) bass guitar(s)
Birchard	Summy-Birchard Co (publisher, Evanston, Ill)
B LITT	Bachelor of Letters
BLS	Bachelor of Library Science
BMA	Bachelor of Musical Arts
BMI	Broadcast Music Inc 1938– (performing rights society, USA)
BMIC	BMI Canada Ltd / Ltée 1947–77 (publisher, Toronto 1947–69, see Berandol 1969– ; performing rights society 1947–77, see PRO Canada 1977–)
B MUS	Bachelor of Music / MUS B, MUS BAC musicae baccalaureus
B MUS ED	Bachelor of Music Education
bn	bassoon(s)
BN du Q	Bibliothèque nationale du Québec, Montreal 1967– (Bibliothèque St-Sulpice 1915–30, 1940–67)
Boston	Boston Music Co (publisher, Boston, Mass)
Boucher	A.J. Boucher, Enr'g (publisher, Montreal)
B PAED	Bachelor of Pedagogy
B PH	Bachelor of Philosophy
BRH	*Le Bulletin des recherches historiques* (Lévis, Que: 1895–1956)
B SC	Bachelor of Science
B TH	Bachelor of Theology
ca	circa / around
Cal	California
Cam	Camden (record label)
CAML	Canadian Association of Music Libraries 1971– (CMLA 1956–71) / ACBM, Association canadienne des bibliothèques musicales 1956–
CAMMAC	Canadian Amateur Musicians-Musiciens amateurs du Canada 1953–
CanB	*The Canadian Bandsman* (Toronto, Waterloo, Ont: CBA 1942–9; *The Canadian Bandmaster*, Kilworthy, Ont: CBA 1949–67)
CanComp	*The Canadian Composer / Le Compositeur canadien* (Toronto: CAPAC 1965–)
CanJM	*Canadian Journal of Music* (Toronto: 1914–19)
Cap	Capitol (record label)

CAPAC	Composers, Authors and Publishers Association of Canada Ltd / Association des compositeurs, auteurs et éditeurs du Canada Ltée 1945– (CPRS 1925–45)
CAPEM	Certificat d'aptitude pédagogique à l'enseignement de la musique (teaching certificate)
CARAS	Canadian Academy of Recording Arts and Sciences 1975– (Toronto)
CAUSM	Canadian Association of University Schools of Music / ACEUM, Association canadienne des écoles universitaires de musique 1964–
CAUSM J	*CAUSM Journal / Journal ACEUM* (Vancouver, Ottawa, Calgary: CAUSM 1971–)
Caveat	Caveat Music Publishers (Toronto)
CBA	Canadian Bandmasters' Association 1931–69 (CBDA 1969–)
CBC	Canadian Broadcasting Corporation / SRC, Société Radio-Canada 1936– (CRBC 1932–6) CBC (record label)
CBC Hal Chamb O	CBC Halifax Chamber Orchestra 1963–
CBC IS	CBC International Service / Service international de la Société Radio-Canada 1945–72 (RCI 1972–)
CBC Mtl chamb orch	CBC Montreal chamber orchestra
CBC Mtl orch	CBC Montreal orchestra
CBC Mtl str orch	CBC Montreal string orchestra
CBC Que Chamb O	CBC Quebec Chamber Orchestra / Orchestre de chambre de la SRC à Québec 1964– ('Les Petits Concerts' 1954–64)
CBC SO	CBC Symphony Orchestra 1952–64 (Toronto)
CBC Van Chamb O	CBC Vancouver Chamber Orchestra 1938–
CBC Wpg O	CBC Winnipeg Orchestra 1947–
CBDA	Canadian Band Directors' Association 1969– (CBA 1931–69)
cbn	contrabassoon(s)
CBS	Columbia Broadcasting System (US network 1927– CBS (record label 1976–)
CCA	Canadian Conference of the Arts / Conférence canadienne des arts 1958– (Canadian Arts Council / Conseil canadien des arts 1945–58)
CCO	Canadian College of Organists / Collège canadien des organistes 1909–59 (RCCO 1959–)
Cegep(s)	Collège(s) d'enseignement général et professionel
cel	celesta(s)
cello(s)	violoncello(s)
CFMJ	*Canadian Folk Music Journal* (Toronto: CFMS 1973–)
CFMS	Canadian Folk Music Society / SCMF, Société canadienne de musique folklorique 1956–
CFMTA	Canadian Federation of Music Teachers' Associations / FCAPM, Fédération canadienne des associations de professeurs de musique 1935–
chamb	chamber / chambre
Chanteclair	Chanteclair Music (publisher, Toronto)
Chap	Chappell & Co Ltd (publisher, Toronto, London)
Chappell	see Chap
chor	chorus(es)
Cie	Compagnie
cl	clarinet(s)
CLComp	Canadian League of Composers / Ligue canadienne de compositeurs 1951–
cm	centimetre(s)
CMB	*The Canada Music Book / Les Cahiers canadiens de musique* (Montreal: CMCouncil 1970–6)
CMCentre	Canadian Music Centre 1959– / Centre musical canadien 1959–73; Centre de musique canadienne 1973–
CMCouncil	Canadian Music Council / Conseil canadien de la musique 1946–
CME	*The Canadian Music Educator* 1959– / *L'Éducateur de musique au Canada* 1976–8 / *Le Journal des éducateurs de musique au Canada* 1978–9 / *Le Musicien éducateur au Canada* 1979– (Toronto, Montreal, Victoria: CMEA)
CMEA	Canadian Music Educators' Association / ACEM, Association canadienne des éducateurs de musique 1959–
CMJ	*The Canadian Music Journal* (Sackville, NB, Toronto: CMCouncil 1956–62)
CMLA	Canadian Music Library Association 1956–71 (CAML 1971–) / ACBM, Association canadienne des bibliothèques musicales 1956–
CMM	Conservatoire de musique du Québec à Montréal 1943–
CMPA	Canadian Music Publishers Association / Association canadienne des éditeurs de musique 1949–
CMQ	Conservatoire de musique du Québec à Québec 1944–
CMS	Canadian Music Sales Corporation Ltd (publisher, Toronto)
CMTJ	*Canadian Music Trades Journal* (Toronto: 1900–33)
CNE	Canadian National Exhibition 1879– (Toronto)
CNR	Canadian National Railways / Chemins de fer nationaux du Canada 1923–
Co	Company
COC	Canadian Opera Company 1958–
Col	Columbia (record label)
coll	collected / collection(s)
Col Master	Columbia Masterworks (record label)
Colo	Colorado
cond	conductor
Conn	Connecticut
Cons	Conservatory / Conservatoire / Conservatorium
ConsB	*The Toronto Conservatory of Music Bulletin* (Toronto: TCM 1935–47); *Royal Conservatory of Music of Toronto Monthly Bulletin* (Toronto: RCMT 1948–64); *The Bulletin* (Toronto: RCMT 1964–74)
Cor	Coronet (record label)
CPR	Canadian Pacific Railway Company 1880s–1968 (Canadian Pacific Limited / Canadien Pacifique Ltée 1968–)

CPRS Canadian Performing Rights Society / Société canadienne des droits d'auteurs 1925–45 (CAPAC 1945–)

CQR *Conservatory Quarterly Review* (Toronto: TCM 1918–35)

CRBC Canadian Radio Broadcasting Commission / CCR, Commission canadienne de la radiodiffusion 1932–6 (CBC 1936–)

Crémazie J. & O. Crémazie (publisher, Quebec City)

CRI Composers' Recordings, Inc (record label)

CRIA Canadian Recording Industry Association / Association de l'industrie canadienne de l'enregistrement 1972– (CRM Assn 1963–72)

CRMA *Canadian Review of Music and Art* (Toronto: 1942–8)

CRM Assn Canadian Record Manufacturers' Association 1963–72 (CRIA 1972–)

CRTC Canadian Radio-Television and Telecommunications Commission / Conseil de la radiodiffusion et des télécommunications canadiennes 1968– (BBG 1958–68)

CSM Les Concerts symphoniques de Montréal 1934–53 (MSO 1953– ; see also SCSM)

CTI Creed Taylor Inc (record label)

CTL Canadian Talent Library 1962– CTL (record label)

Curwen J. Curwen & Sons (publisher, London)

d died

Daf Daffodil (record label)

db double-bass(es)

DCB *Dictionary of Canadian Biography / DBC, Dictionnaire biographique du Canada* (see 'General Bibliography')

DCL Doctor of Civil Law

DD Doctor of Divinity

DDS Doctor of Dental Surgery

D ED Doctor of Education

Del Delaware

Dept Department

DG Deutsche Grammophon (record label)

dir(s) director(s)

Ditson Oliver Ditson Co (publisher, Boston, Mass)

D LITT Doctor of Letters

D LITT S Doctor of Sacred Letters

DMA Doctor of Musical Arts

D MUS Doctor of Music / MUS D, MUS DOC musicae doctor

Dom Dominion (record label)

Drakkar Drakkar Music Publishing (Toronto)

D TH Doctor of Theology

EBU European Broadcasting Union / UER, Union européenne de radiodiffusion

E.C. Schirmer E.C. Schirmer Music Co (publisher, Boston, Mass)

ed(s) edited / editor(s)

edn(s) edition(s)

eg exempli gratia / for example

elec electronic / electric

elec pno electric piano

EMC *Encyclopedia of Music in Canada / Encyclopédie de la musique au Canada*

Emp Empire Music Publishers Ltd (New Westminster, BC)

Empire see Emp

Eng England / English-language

eng hn english horn(s)

enl enlarged

ens ensemble(s)

ESM Eastman School of Music, University of Rochester 1919–

et al et alii / and others

etc et cetera / and so forth

facsim(s) facsimile(s)

FAMEQ Fédération des associations de musiciens éducateurs du Québec 1966–

Fass A. Fassio Publications (Lachute, Que)

Fassio see Fass

FCCO Fellow, Canadian College of Organists 1909–59 (FRCCO 1959–)

FCMF Federation of Canadian Music Festivals 1926–

FGSM Fellow, Guildhall School of Music

FH Frederick Harris Music Co Ltd (publisher, Oakville, Ont)

fig figure(s)

Fischer Carl Fischer, Inc (publisher, New York)

fl floruit/flourished; flute(s)

Fla Florida

flhn flügelhorn(s)

Folk Folkways (record label)

45(s) 45-rpm recording(s)

FRAM Fellow, Royal Academy of Music

FRCCO Fellow, Royal Canadian College of Organists 1959– (FCCO 1909–59)

FRCM Fellow, Royal College of Music

FRCO Fellow, Royal College of Organists

FRHCM Fellow, Royal Hamilton College of Music 1965–80

FRMCM Fellow, Royal Manchester College of Music (honorary only)

FTCL Fellow, Trinity College of Music, London

Ga Georgia

Gav Gavotte (record label)

gl glockenspiel(s)

gp(s) group(s)

Gray The H.W. Gray Co, Inc (publisher, New York)

GRSM Graduate, Royal Schools of Music

G. Schirmer G. Schirmer, Inc (publisher, New York)

GSM Guildhall School of Music 1880– (London)

guit guitar(s)

GVT Gordon V. Thompson Ltd (publisher, Toronto)

Hal Halifax

H&H The Hawkes & Harris Music Co Ltd (publisher, Toronto)

Har Hargail Music Press (publisher, New York)

Hargail	see Har
Harms	T.B. Harms Inc (publisher, New York)
Harmuse	Harmuse Publications (Oakville, Ont)
Harris	Frederick Harris Music Co Ltd (publisher, Oakville, Ont)
Heintzman	Heintzman & Co Ltd 1866–1978 (piano builder, publisher, Toronto); Heintzman Ltd 1978–81 (piano builder, Hanover, Ont)
Helio	Heliodor (record label)
Herbert	J.W. Herbert & Co (publisher, Montreal)
Hist Soc	Historical Society
hmca	harmonica(s)
HMV	His Master's Voice / La Voix de son maître (record label)
hn	horn(s)
hon	honorary
hp	harp(s)
hpd	harpsichord(s)
I	Idaho
Ia	Iowa
I&G	Imrie & Graham (publisher, Toronto)
ibid	ibidem / in the same place
ie	id est / that is
IFMC	International Folk Music Council / Conseil international de musique folklorique 1940–
Ill	Illinois
Ind	Indiana
instr	instrument(s) / instrumental
ISCM	International Society for Contemporary Music / SIMC, Société internationale pour la musique contemporaine 1922–
ISME	International Society for Music Education / SIEM, Société internationale pour l'éducation musicale 1953–
J	*Journal*
JAF	*Journal of American Folklore* (Lancaster, Pa: 1888–)
Jar	Jarman Publications Ltd (Scarborough, Ont)
Jarman	see Jar
Jay	Jaymar Music Ltd (publisher, London, Ont)
Jaymar	see Jay
JM	Jeunesses musicales (Belgium and France 1940–)
Jmc	*Journal des Jeunesses musicales du Canada* 1951–3; *Le Journal musical canadien* 1954–61 / *Musical Youth Magazine* 1955–7?; *J.M.C. Musical Chronicle* 1958–61; *Jeunesses musicales* 1962; *Journal des Jeunesses musicales du Canada / Jeunesses musicales Chronicle* 1962–71 (Montreal: JMC)
JMC	Jeunesses musicales of Canada / du Canada 1949– JMC (record label)
Job	Jean Jobert (publisher, Paris)
Jobert	see Job
Jr	Junior
Kan	Kansas
Kerby	E.C. Kerby Ltd (publisher, Toronto)
keybd	keyboard(s)
km	kilometre(s)
Ky	Kentucky
La	Louisiana
LAB	Licentiate, Associated Board of the Royal Schools of Music 1889–1933 (LRSM 1933–)
Laur	Laurentian (record label)
LCM	London College of Music 1887–
LCSC	Licentiate in Sacred Composition, Pontifical School of Sacred Music (Rome)
Leeds	Leeds Music (Canada) a Division of MCA Canada Ltd (publisher, Willowdale, Ont)
Leslie	Leslie Music Supply (publisher, Oakville, Ont)
LGSM	Licentiate, Guildhall School of Music
LLB	Bachelor of Laws
LLCM	Licentiate, London College of Music
LLD	Doctor of Laws
L LITT	Licentiate in Letters
LLL	Licentiate in Laws
LMA	Licentiate in Music, Alberta 1936–
LMM	Licentiate in Music, Manitoba 1936–
LMS	Licentiate in Music, Saskatchewan 1936–
L MUS	Licentiate in Music / licence / licencié(e) en musique
Lon	London (record label)
Lou	Louisville (record label)
LP(s)	33⅓-rpm recording(s)
L PH	Licentiate in Philosophy
LRAM	Licentiate, Royal Academy of Music
LRCT	Licentiate, Royal Conservatory of Music of Toronto 1947–52 (LTCM 1914–47)
LRSM	Licentiate, Royal Schools of Music 1933– (LAB 1889–1933)
L SC	Licentiate in Science
LTCL	Licentiate, Trinity College of Music, London
LTCM	Licentiate, Toronto Conservatory of Music 1914–47 (LRCT 1947–52)
L TH	Licentiate in Theology
LWCM	Licentiate, Western Ontario Conservatory of Music
m	married; metre(s)
MA	Master of Arts / AM artium magister
MAC	Manitoba Arts Council 1965–
Maclean	*Le Magazine Maclean* (Montreal: 1961–72); *Le Maclean* 1972–6 (*L'Actualité* 1976–)
Maclean's	*Maclean's Magazine* (Toronto: 1905–)
MACQ	Ministère des Affaires culturelles du Québec 1961–
Man	Manitoba
mand	mandolin(s)
Manitou	Manitou Music, a Division of MCA Canada Ltd (publisher, Willowdale, Ont)
mar	marimba(s)
Mass	Massachusetts
MBS	Mutual Broadcasting System (USA)
MCA	Music Corporation of America (see Leeds, Manitou)

Mcan	*Musicanada* (Toronto: CMCentre 1967–70; Ottawa: CMCouncil 1976–)
MCan	*Musical Canada* (Toronto: 1906–28; Waterloo, Ont: 1928–33)
MCG	Magisterium in Gregorian Chant, Pontifical School of Sacred Music (Rome)
McKee	Peter McKee Music Co (publisher, Waterloo, Ont)
MCour	*Musical Courier* (Philadelphia, Pa: 1880–1962)
MD	Doctor of Medicine
Md	Maryland
Me	Maine
M ED	Master of Education
med	medium
Mel	Melbourne (record label)
MENC	Music Educators' National Conference 1907– (USA)
Mer	Mercury (record label)
mezzo	mezzo soprano(s)
MFA	Master of Fine Arts
MG	Manuscript Group
MGG	*Musik in Geschichte und Gegenwart* (see 'General Bibliography')
Mgr	Monseigneur / Monsignor
Mich	Michigan
MIDEM	International Record and Music Publishing Market / Marché international du disque et de l'édition musicale (Cannes)
Minn	Minnesota
misc	miscellaneous
Miss	Mississippi
MIT	Massachusetts Institute of Technology
MJ	*The Musical Journal* (Toronto: 1887–90?)
M LITT	Master of Letters
mm	millimetre(s)
MMA	Master of Musical Arts
MMEA	Manitoba Music Educators Association / AMEM, Association manitobaine des éducateurs de musique 1959–
M MUS	Master of Music / MUS M musicae magister
Mo	Missouri
Mont	Montana
MQ	*The Musical Quarterly* (New York: G. Schirmer 1915–)
MRMTA	Manitoba Registered Music Teachers' Association 1939–
ms(s)	manuscript(s)
MSc	*The Music Scene / La Scène musicale* (Don Mills, Ont: BMI Canada 1967–77, PRO Canada 1977–)
MSO	Montreal Symphony Orchestra / OSM, Orchestre symphonique de Montréal 1953– (CSM and SCSM 1934–53)
MT	*Musical Times* (London: 1844–)
Mtl	Montreal / Montréal
Mus H Soc	Musical Heritage Society (record label)
Music	*Music Magazine* (Toronto: 1978–)
mvt(s)	movement(s)
NAC	National Arts Centre / CNA, Centre national des arts 1969– (Ottawa)
NACO	National Arts Centre Orchestra / OCNA, Orchestre du Centre national des arts 1969– (Ottawa)
narr	narrator(s)
NB	New Brunswick / Nouveau-Brunswick
NBRMTA	New Brunswick Registered Music Teachers' Association 1950–
NC	North Carolina
nd	no date
N Dak	North Dakota
Neb	Nebraska
NET	National Educational Television (USA)
Nev	Nevada
New Valley	New Valley Music Press (publisher, Northampton, Mass)
NFB	National Film Board of Canada / ONF, Office national du film du Canada 1939– (Ottawa, Montreal)
Nfld	Newfoundland / Terre-Neuve
NH	New Hampshire
NJ	New Jersey
NL of C	National Library of Canada / Bibliothèque nationale du Canada 1953– (Ottawa)
NMC	New Music Concerts 1971– (Toronto)
N Mex	New Mexico
No./no.	Number(s) / number(s)
Nord	A. & S. Nordheimer Ltd 1844–95; Nordheimer Piano & Music Co Ltd 1895–1927 (piano builder, publisher, Toronto)
Nordheimer	see Nord
Novello	Novello & Co (publisher, London)
np	no publisher; no place of publication
ns	new series
NS	Nova Scotia / Nouvelle-Écosse
NSMEA	Nova Scotia Music Educators' Association 1960–
NSRMTA	Nova Scotia Registered Music Teachers' Association 1937–
NVMP	New Valley Music Press (publisher, Northampton, Mass)
NWT	Northwest Territories / Territoires du Nord-Ouest
NY	New York
NYO	National Youth Orchestra of Canada / ONJ, Orchestre national des jeunes du Canada 1960–
O	Ohio; Orchestra / Orchestre
OAC	Ontario Arts Council / CAO, Conseil des arts de l'Ontario 1970– (POCA 1963–70)
ob	oboe(s)
OBE	Officer, Order of the British Empire
OCan	*Orchestra Canada / Orchestres Canada* (Toronto: OFSO and ACO 1973–)
OECA	Ontario Educational Communications Authority / OTEO, Office de la Télécommunication éducative de l'Ontario

OFSO	Ontario Federation of Symphony Orchestras / FOSO, Fédération des orchestres symphoniques de l'Ontario 1954–
OISE	Ontario Institute for Studies in Education (Toronto)
Okla	Oklahoma
OMEA	Ontario Music Educators' Association 1919–
ondes M	ondes Martenot
Ont	Ontario
Op	Opus
OpCan	*Opera Canada* (Toronto: 1960–)
orch	orchestra(s) / orchestrated
Ore	Oregon
org	organ(s)
Orme	J.L. Orme & Sons (publisher, Ottawa)
ORMTA	Ontario Registered Music Teachers' Association 1936–
ORTF	Office de la radiodiffusion-télévision française 1964–74 (RTF 1959–64, Radio France 1975–)
Ott	Ottawa
OUP	Oxford University Press (London, New York, Toronto, etc)
p	page / pages
Pa	Pennsylvania
PAC	Public Archives of Canada / APC, Archives publiques du Canada 1872– (Ottawa)
Para	Paramount (record label)
Parnasse	Le Parnasse musical (publisher, Montreal)
PBS	Public Broadcasting Service (USA)
PDA	Place des arts 1963– (Montreal)
Peer	Peer International Corp (publisher, New York); Peer-Southern Organization (Canada) Ltd (publisher, Toronto)
PEI	Prince Edward Island / Île-du-Prince-Édouard
PEIMEA	Prince Edward Island Music Educators' Association 1962–
perc	percussion
perf	performer(s) / performance(s)
Peters	C.F. Peters Corp (publisher, Frankfurt, Germany, and New York)
pf	piano(s)
PfAC	*Performing Arts in Canada* (Toronto: 1961–)
PH D	Doctor of Philosophy / D PHIL, D PH
PH D ED	Doctor of Philosophy in Education
Phil / phil	Philharmonic / philharmonique
picc	piccolo(s)
POCA	Province of Ontario Council for the Arts 1963–70 (OAC 1970–)
Poly	Polydor (record label)
Presser	Theodore Presser Co (publisher, Bryn Mawr, Pa)
priv publ	privately published
PRO Canada	P.R.O. Canada, Performing Rights Organization of Canada Ltd / S.D.E. Canada, Société de droits d'exécution du Canada Ltée 1977– (BMIC 1947–77)
pseud	pseudonym
P-T	*Le Passe-Temps* (Montreal: 1895–1935, 1945–9)
publ	published
Q	*Quarterly*
QMEA	Quebec Music Educators' Association 1940–
QMTA	Quebec Music Teachers' Association / APMQ, Association des professeurs de musique du Québec 1942–
Qual	Quality (record label)
quar	quartet(s)
Que / Qué	Quebec / Québec
quin	quintet(s) / quintette(s)
R	*Review / Revue*
RAM	Royal Academy of Music 1822– (London)
RCAF	Royal Canadian Air Force / ARC, Aviation royale du Canada
RCCO	Royal Canadian College of Organists / CRCO, Collège royal canadien des organistes 1959– (CCO 1909–59)
RCI	Radio Canada International 1972– (CBC IS 1945–72) RCI (record label)
RCM	Royal College of Music 1873– (London)
RCMP	Royal Canadian Mounted Police / GRC, Gendarmerie royale du Canada 1873–
RCMT	Royal Conservatory of Music of Toronto 1947– (TCM 1886–1947)
RCN	Royal Canadian Navy / MRC, Marine royale du Canada
RCO	Royal College of Organists 1864– (London)
rec	recorder(s)
Rep	Reprise (record label)
repr	reprint(s) / reprinted
rev	revised / revision(s)
Rev	Reverend
RG	Record Group
RHCM	Royal Hamilton College of Music 1965–80 (Hamilton Conservatory of Music 1897–1965)
RI	Rhode Island
Ric	G. Ricordi & Co (Canada) Ltd (publisher, Toronto)
Ricordi	see Ric
RMCM	Royal Manchester College of Music 1893–
RMSM (Kneller Hall)	Royal Military School of Music (Kneller Hall) 1857– (Twickenham, England)
Rob	Roberton Publications (Aylesbury, England)
Roberton	see Rob
Rou	Roulette (record label)
rpm	revolutions per minute
RSAM	Royal Scottish Academy of Music 1929– (Glasgow)
RSCM	Royal School of Church Music 1945– (Croydon, England) (School of English Church Music 1927–45)
RSM	Royal Schools of Music 1889– (London)
RTF	Radiodiffusion-Télévision française 1959–64 (ORTF 1964–74, Radio France 1975–)
SAB	Saskatchewan Arts Board 1948–

Sack	Sackville (record label)
Sala	Éditions Salabert (publisher, Paris, New York)
Salabert	see Sala
Sask	Saskatchewan
SATB	4-part mixed chorus
SatN	*Saturday Night* (Toronto: 1887–)
sax	saxophone(s)
SC	South Carolina
SCSM	Société des Concerts symphoniques de Montréal 1934–53 (MSO 1953– ; see also CSM)
S Dak	South Dakota
Sel	Select (record label)
self-publ	self-published
SemRC	*La Semaine à Radio-Canada* (Montreal: SRC 1950–66)
Sera	Seraphim (record label)
78(s)	78-rpm recording(s)
sm	small
SMCQ	Société de musique contemporaine du Québec 1966– (Montreal)
SMEA	Saskatchewan Music Educators' Association 1957–
SO	Symphony Orchestra
Soc	Society / Société
sop	soprano(s)
South	Southern Music Publishers Co (Canada) Ltd (Toronto)
Southern	see South
spkr	speaker(s)
Sr	Senior
SRC	see CBC
SRMTA	Saskatchewan Registered Music Teachers' Association 1925–
St	Street; Saint
Stainer	Stainer and Bell (publisher, London)
Ste	Sainte
str	string(s)
Summit	Summit Music Ltd (publisher, Toronto)
suppl	supplement
Supra	Supraphon (record label)
synth	synthesizer(s)
TCL	Trinity College of Music, London 1872–
TCM	Toronto Conservatory of Music 1886–1947 (RCMT 1947–)
ten	tenor(s)
Tenn	Tennessee
Tex	Texas
Thompson	Gordon V. Thompson Ltd (publisher, Toronto)
tim	timpani
TNorth	True North (record label)
Tor	Toronto
tpt	trumpet(s)
trad	traditional
transcr	transcribed / transcription(s)
transl	translated / translation(s) / translator(s)
trb	trombone(s)
TS / TSO	Toronto Symphony 1967– ; Toronto Symphony Orchestra 1927–67 (New Symphony Orchestra 1922–7)
TUTS	Theatre Under the Stars 1940–63 (Vancouver)
TV	television
U	University / Université
U Artists	United Artists (record label)
UDA	Union des artistes 1937– (Montreal)
UE	Universal Edition (publisher, London, Vienna)
Universal	see UE
unpubl	unpublished
UQAM	Université du Québec à Montréal 1969–
UQATR	Université du Québec à Trois-Rivières 1969–
US	of or from the USA
USA	United States of America
USSR	Union of Soviet Socialist Republics
Ut	Utah
v(s)	voice(s)
va	viola(s)
Va	Virginia
Van	Vancouver
vc	violoncello(s)
v da gamba	viola(s) da gamba
vib	vibraphone(s)
Vic	Victrola (re-release record label)
VM	*Vie musicale* (Quebec City: MACQ 1965–71)
vn	violin(s)
vol(s)	volume(s)
Vt	Vermont
Warner	Warner Bros (record label)
Wash	Washington
Wat	Waterloo Music Co (publisher, Waterloo, Ont) Waterloo (record label)
Waterloo	see Wat
WBM	Western Board of Music 1936–
West	Westminster (record label)
Western	Western Music Co Ltd (publisher, Vancouver, Toronto)
WIM	Western International Music (publisher, Los Angeles)
Wisc	Wisconsin
WLSM	World Library of Sacred Music (World Library Publishers Ltd, Cincinnati, O)
WOCM	Western Ontario Conservatory of Music 1934– (London, Ont)
Wpg	Winnipeg
WR	Whaley, Royce & Co Ltd (publisher, Toronto)
W Va	West Virginia
ww	woodwind(s)
Wyo	Wyoming
xyl	xylophone(s)
YMCA/YWCA	Young Men's Christian Association / Young Women's Christian Association
YMHA	Young Men's Hebrew Association
YT	Yukon Territory / Territoire du Yukon
Zouche	C.C. De Zouche (publisher, Montreal)

A.A.A. (Albert Alexander Alldrick). Critic, editor, b Coventry, England, 21 Jul 1894, d Winnipeg 7 May 1972. An amateur pianist and violinist, he was critic in England 1912–16 for the *Coventry Standard* and in Canada 1921–8 for the Winnipeg *Tribune* and 1938–55 for the *Winnipeg Free Press*. His reviews bore the byline 'A.A.A.' He was the publisher-editor of *Musical Life and Arts*, a semimonthly magazine devoted to the arts and published briefly (15 Sep 1924–1 Jan 1925) in Winnipeg. He was regional adjudicator 1945–55 for CBC radio's competition *'Singing Stars of Tomorrow.'

A & M Records of Canada Ltd. Canadian subsidiary of A & M Records, a US company founded in 1962 by the trumpeter Herb Alpert (then leader of the Tijuana Brass) and the producer Jerry Moss. A & M (Canada) was established in 1970 under the direction of a vice-president, Gerry Lacoursiere, with a head office in Toronto and branch offices opened in Montreal in 1972 and in Calgary in 1976. Though the company has engaged mostly in the Canadian promotion of non-Canadian pop artists, it has released some LPs by Canadians, including the singers Bim, Charity Brown, Lucille *Starr, Ian *Tyson, *Valdy, and Gino *Vannelli, and by the rock groups Cano, *Chilliwack, *Offenbach, and Symphonic Slam. The company also distributes several affiliated US labels and controls the Canadian publishing firms Irving Music (PRO Canada) and Almo Music (CAPAC).

ABBOTT, Eric (Oscar). Bandmaster, cornetist, pianist, organist, composer, arranger, b St John's, Nfld, 4 Aug 1929; ATCL 1949, LTCL 1950, L MUS (Acadia) 1951, B MUS (Acadia) 1952, L MUS TCL 1955, M MUS (Acadia) 1956, D ED (Boston) 1969, FTCL 1970. His teachers included Edwin *Collins, Janis *Kalejs, Hugo Norden, and Gardner Read. His doctoral thesis was 'The evolution of the Canadian festival movement as an instrument of music education.' He began teaching music in St John's schools in 1948 and became band director for the Avalon Consolidated School Board in 1968. His broadcasting career, which began in 1949, has included several hundred piano, organ, and cornet recitals. He was choral arranger and conductor for eight years on CBC radio's 'Come All Ye Round' and music director 1960–2 for CJON radio and CJOX-TV, St John's. He led *Salvation Army bands in St John's and in Massachusetts and became director of the Booth Memorial Brass Band in 1968. His compositions include the choral fugues *Exalt the Lord* (Boston Music 1962) and *Alleluia* (Boston Music 1964), the marches *Invitation* (1963) and *St John's Citadel* (1977) published by the Salvation Army, the cornet solo *Supplication* (1977, Eastern Territory Music Bureau), other brass band works (including one based on Canadian folk songs), three overtures for orchestra, two double fugues for solo violin and string orchestra, a sonatina for violin and piano, and anthems. He is an affiliate of PRO Canada.

DISCOGRAPHY

Songs of the Anchor Watch. L. Meehan v, R. Clarke guit, Abbott org, arr. 1961. Citadel CTL-111

Spring Concert. Band and Glee Club, Abbott composer, arr, and cond. 1968. RCA St-55876

ABBOTT, O.J. (Oliver John). Folksinger, b Enfield, England, 1872, d Hull, Que, 3 Mar 1962. He was hailed by Edith *Fowke as 'undoubtedly one of the finest traditional singers found on the continent.' Abbott worked on several farms in an Irish community in the Ottawa Valley and in lumber camps in northern Ontario and Quebec before settling in the vicinity of Hull. Between 1957 and his death he recorded some 120 songs for Edith Fowke, most of them learned in the 1880s and 1890s from the Irish farm families and shantyboys. Some of his recordings were issued on an LP (see Folk music, Anglo-Canadian: 4 / Ontario and the Prairies), and songs from his repertoire have been performed by singers in North America and Great Britain. Abbott sang in 1958 at the National Museum of Man, in 1959 with Pete Seeger in Ottawa, in 1960 on the CBC and with Seeger at the Newport Folk Festival, and in 1961 at the *Mariposa Folk Festival and before the IFMC in Quebec City.

BIBLIOGRAPHY

Fowke, Edith. 'The passing of a great traditional singer,' *Sing Out!*, vol 12, 1962

– *Traditional Singers and Songs from Ontario* (Hatboro, Pa 1965) (EF)

ABDUL AL-KHABYYR, Al-Hajj Sayyd (Muslim name adopted in 1971; b Russell Linwood Thomas). Soprano, alto, and tenor saxophonist, clarinetist, flutist, composer, b Harlem (New York) 22 Mar 1935, naturalized Canadian ca 1965. He studied in New York with Cecil Scott (clarinet and saxophone) and with a Mr Klotzman (clarinet). After travelling with Snub Mosley's band he settled in 1954 in Montreal, working until 1956 with Al Cowans and then forming his own band. In 1957 he went to Ottawa and was a member of the Canadian Jazz Quartet (with Richard Wyands, piano, Wyatt Ruther, bass, and Doug Johnston, drums), of the Ottawa Saxophone Quartet (playing soprano), and of studio or dance bands led by Champ Champagne, Buster Monroe, and others. He led his own big band 1959–65 in the Ottawa area. He also taught 1965–70 in high schools in Ottawa and in Hull, Que. In 1970 he began teaching at the *U of Montreal. He played jazz regularly 1971–8 at his own restaurant-club, the Café Mo-Jo, first with the percussionist Dido, then with the flutist-percussionist Amin, and later with his own sons, Muhammad (trombonist, b 14 Nov 1959), Nasyr (percussionist, b 5 Sep 1958), and Zayd (pianist). He has played on occasion with the *SMCQ Ensemble and in 1977 he was a founder of the chamber group Trio 3 with the soprano Pauline *Vaillancourt and the guitarist Michael Laucke. (Among his compositions is *Bis-mil-lah!*, played by TRIO 3.) He has been a soloist with jazz groups and with *Dionne-Brégent, and a member of studio and pit orchestras in Montreal. His discography includes recordings with Sadik *Hakim, *L'Infonie, and TRIO 3. A skilled technician, Abdul Al-Khabyyr is at home in most genres from jazz (to which he brings a bebop conception) to contemporary concert music. With his own groups he plays music characterized by a devotional quality. His pupils have included his sons Muhammad and Nasyr (who have distinguished themselves in the *Canadian Stage Band Competitions of 1978 and 1979), the flutist Jennifer Waring, the trumpeter Chris Place, and the saxophonist Marie-Jo Leman-Rudolf. (CGa, MM)

Aberfan. Forty-three-minute TV opera by Raymond *Pannell to a libretto by himself and his wife, Beverly. Commissioned by the CBC, produced and directed by John Thomson, and conducted by the composer, *Aberfan* was premiered 20 Aug 1977 at the competition for the TV Opera Prize of the City of Salzburg and was awarded the $8600 first prize the following day. It was telecast in Canada 26 Oct 1977. The cast included the soprano Mary *Morrison (mother), the tenor Glyn Evans (Charlie), the baritone Gary *Relyea (father), the boy soprano John Maxwell (Tommy), and the Toronto Boys' Choir. The opera concentrates not on the 1966 Welsh disaster itself but on the larger themes of neglect and waste that destroy needlessly. Praised by the Salzburg judges for its emotional intensity and its 'economical, colourful scoring,' it uses a 20-member instrumental group – strings, woodwinds, and percussion – and electronic effects. The composer has given the singers 'extended vocal sequences to reflect on what happened, without trying to turn out a conventional operatic structure of recitatives and arias. His is a looser structure, idiomatic to television ... the effect is direct, honest and uncluttered' (William Littler, *Toronto Star*, 25 Oct 1977). *Aberfan* won a 1978 ACTRA award as the best TV program of the year.

BIBLIOGRAPHY

'Raymond Pannell wins top honours for CBC Television,' *CanComp*, Oct 1977

Pannell, Raymond. 'Don't let them forget the children,' *Toronto Star*, 21 Oct 1977 PW

ABERNETHY, Norma (Kathleen) (m Petrie). Pianist, teacher, b Vancouver 11 Jun 1914, d there 26 Apr 1973; LRSM 1931, ATCM 1933. A pupil in Vancouver of Della Johnston, Isabel Campbell, Gertrude *Huntley Green, Olga Steel, and others, she was known particularly as an accompanist and soloist on radio, first on CNRV and then on CBR (later CBU). She was a soloist with the *CBC Vancouver Chamber Orchestra, the CBR SO under Arthur *Benjamin, other radio orchestras under Jean *de Rimanoczy and Albert *Steinberg, and also, in 1947, with the *Victoria SO. Among the concertos she performed were the Schumann, the Armstrong Gibbs, and the *Rapsodia Sinfonica* of Turina. She was occasionally the orchestra pianist with the CBC Vancouver Chamber Orchestra (late 1930s to early 1940s) and the *Vancouver SO (ca 1940–7, ca 1952–64) and also performed as a duo-pianist with John *Avison. She was an accompanist for the BC Music Festival in the late 1930s and early 1940s, for *TUTS (including productions requiring piano solos, eg, *Song of Norway* in 1953), and for visiting singers such as the English Duo (Viola Morris and Victoria Anderson) and Alexander Kipnis. BNSG

Académie de musique de Québec (AMQ). Nonprofit association whose teacher-members are among the most representative Quebec musicians in the various disciplines. Founded in Quebec City in 1868 by Ernest *Gagnon, Damis *Paul, Louis S. Pfeiffer, Albert Rochette, Gustave *Gagnon, and A. Desrochers, its objectives were to promote an interest in music, raise the level of musical studies, and bring order to them by establishing programs, setting examinations, and granting diplomas and certificates in all branches of music teaching. It was incorporated in December 1870. At first, the AMQ was financed by the founders and their friends, the Quebec government supplying only a token amount of $100 a year, although that sum increased substantially when the AMQ began to administer the *Prix d'Europe in 1911, a service it continued in 1980. In the 1970s it was receiving annual subsidies from the *MACQ. The AMQ is administered by a board of directors consisting of an elected president, vice-president, treasurer, and secretary; an officer in charge of examinations; and five directors appointed for one-year renewable terms. To become a member of the AMQ a musician must be proposed by the board and accepted by a majority vote of the general assembly. There were about 50 members in 1979. The AMQ is independent of all political parties and schools of music and thus has the freedom to pursue its objectives. Each year several hundred students take examinations in instruments, voice, and theory. These are held in the main cities of the province. Each discipline is divided into from 6 to 10 classes: preparatory, elementary (one or two levels as required), secondary (several levels), advanced ('supérieur'), and graduating ('Lauréat'). The minimum requirement for a diploma ('Lauréat' only) or a certificate (other categories) is a 60 per cent average mark on all practical courses after a minimum of 50 per cent has been obtained in theory. Only the pieces that appear in the syllabus for each level are accepted for the performance examinations. The AMQ was the first private institution to award music diplomas in the province of Quebec. The first examinations in Quebec City were held 24 Aug 1871; the first in Montreal, 16 Jul 1872. The academy's records were deposited with the Archives nationales in Quebec City. Its presidents have been:

Gagnon, Ernest 1868–71, 1874–6, 1887–8, 1889–90
*Mills, Frederick William 1871–2
*Lagacé, Pierre-M. 1872–4
*Lavallée, Calixa 1876–7, 1879–80
*Jehin-Prume, Frantz 1877–8
Gagnon, Gustave 1878–9, 1881–2, 1883–4, 1885–7, 1893–4, 1895–6, 1897–8, 1899–1900, 1901–2
MacLagan, P.R. 1880–1
*Letondal, Paul 1882–3, 1888–9
*Pelletier, Romain-Octave 1884–5, 1894–5, 1902–4, 1909–10, 1915–16
Maffré, L.-A. 1890–1
Bishop, Edward Arthur 1891–2
*Lavigne, Émery 1892–3, 1900–1
*Ducharme, Dominique 1896–7
*Letondal, Arthur 1898–9, 1905–6, 1913–14, 1920–3
*Lavigne, Arthur 1904–5, 1906–7, 1908–9
*Saucier, Joseph 1907–8, 1911–12
*Bernier, J.-Arthur 1910–11, 1912–13
*Vézina, Joseph 1914–15
*Laurendeau, Arthur 1916–18, 1926–9
*Gilbert, J.-Alexandre 1918–20, 1941–4
Dessane, Léon J. 1923–6
*Gagnon, Henri 1929–32
*Pelletier, Frédéric 1932–5
*Létourneau, Omer 1935–8
*Descarries, Auguste 1938–41
*Trudel, Edmond 1944–7, 1950–2
*Bélanger, Edwin 1947–50, 1953–6, 1963–5, 1971–4
*Cusson, Gabriel 1952–3, 1956–9
Turgeon, Joseph 1959–62
*Papineau-Couture, Jean 1962–3
*Daveluy, Raymond 1965–71
*Arel, Gaston 1974– (CH)

Academy of Music / Académie de musique. Name given to several 19th-century theatres. The best-known were those in 1 / Montreal and 2 / Quebec City. Several theatres of the same name existed in other cities, notably in Halifax, Sherbrooke, and Sorel.

Academy of Music, Montreal, 1875

1 MONTREAL. A 2100-seat theatre opened in 1875 on the east side of Victoria St, a little north of Ste-Catherine St. It was demolished in 1910 to allow the expansion of the Goodwin department store (which later became Eaton's). Calixa *Lavallée directed performances of Gounod's *Jeanne d'Arc* there in 1877 and of Boieldieu's *La Dame blanche* the following year. Emma *Albani and her troupe presented *La Traviata* and *Lucia di Lammermoor* in 1890 and *Lohengrin* and *Les Huguenots* in 1892. The premiere of Victor Herbert's *Cyrano de Bergerac* was presented there 11 Sep 1899. *Goulet's *MSO began to perform at the academy in the 1903–4 season.

2 QUEBEC. Theatre constructed in 1852 and opened the following year. Built according to Charles Baillargé's plans, the Académie de musique de Québec was located on St-Louis St and for a long time was considered one of the most beautiful halls in North America. All the major events of the old capital were held there until 1900, when the theatre was destroyed by fire. Emma Albani appeared before capacity audiences 1 and 5 Feb 1889.

Academy String Quartet. Group associated with the *Canadian Academy of Music, Toronto, and led by Luigi von *Kunits. It performed at academy functions as early as 1912, and accompanied the academy's Madrigal Society in 1913. With Milton Blankstein (later Blackstone) as second violin, Alfred Bruce as viola, and George Bruce as cello, the quartet gave its inaugural series of three concerts during February and March 1914 at the academy recital hall. The group gave between four and six concerts each season, often with guest pianists, one of whom was Ernest *MacMillan. As the personnel of the group changed, succeeding second violins were Arthur Ely 1914–18, Moses Garten 1918–19, Harry *Adaskin 1919–21, and, again, Blackstone. Violist Frank Converse Smith succeeded Alfred Bruce 1922–3, and cellist Leo *Smith replaced George Bruce 1916–18 while the latter was on military service.

The US composers Leo Ornstein and Mrs H.H.A. Beach performed their works with the quartet in 1916 and 1918. Other programs offered works by Goossens, Vaughan Williams, Schoenberg (*Op 7*), Beethoven (the late quartets), and in 1915 von Kunits himself. When the academy amalgamated with the *TCM in 1924, the quartet ceased to exist. That same year von Kunits joined the Conservatory String Quartet, whose other members were Louis Gesensway (violin), Eugene Hudson (viola), and Leo Smith (cello). When Hudson and Gesensway left in 1927, the quartet disbanded. A second *Conservatory String Quartet was formed in 1929 with different personnel.
RPn

Acadia University. Non-denominational, predominantly undergraduate institution in Wolfville, NS, with some graduate programs at the master's level (not in music). Founded in 1841 as Acadia College by the Baptists of Nova Scotia and originating from Horton's Academy (founded 1828) and Queen's College (1838), it awarded its first degrees in 1843 and became Acadia U in 1891.

The Grand Pré Seminary, a residential girls' academy founded in 1858, which became the Acadia Ladies' Seminary in 1860, had a music program. Carl Farnsworth was its last director 1923–6. When it closed, its music courses were transferred to the university, thus creating the School of Music. The three-year course leading to the L MUS (Applied, Education, offered 1919–72) was completed first in 1927 by Irene Card (piano) and Melba Roop (voice). The four-year course leading to the B MUS, which was offered in 1911, was completed first in 1928 by Irene Card. Dorothy Wilson was the first recipient (1930) of the M MUS (Composition). The M MUS was discontinued in 1966.

Deans of the School of Music have been Edwin A. *Collins 1927–63, Russell *Green 1963–5, Janis *Kalejs 1966–73, and Felicita *Kalejs (acting dean) 1973–4. Vernon *Ellis assumed the deanship in 1974. The degree programs offered in 1977–8 were BA (Music) and B MUS ED – both begun in 1970 – and B MUS. In 1977–8 the school had 75 students and 22 teachers (14 full- and 8 part-time). Recipients of honorary doctorates have included Joseph Szigeti (1933), William L. *Wright (1947), Ralph A. Harris (1948) – the latter two were music graduates of Acadia – E. Power Biggs (1963), and Edwin A. Collins (1963).

In 1970 the music school moved into Harvey L. Denton Hall, which has 10 teaching studios, 19 practice rooms, and a 400-seat auditorium. Besides the Fine Arts Concert Series there are performances by the Acadia U Choir, Orchestra, Band, and Jazz Ensemble, which draw audiences from within a 50-km radius.

The school has two *Casavant organs as well as two practice organs and an organ for the professors' studio. All three are among the last built by the *Hallman Co of Kitchener. The Acadia Light Opera Society, organized in the early 1950s by Roy Watson, gave annual presentations until 1962. In 1967 Acadia initiated a three-week instrumental summer music camp.

Basil C. Silvers' manuscript 'Music at Acadia University' is deposited in the university's library.

See also College songs; Conferences and congresses. (JCm)

Accordion. Portable free-reed bellows-operated instrument patented in Austria in 1829 by Cyril Demian. It is held at lower-chest level against the player's body by a shoulder strap and played by means of manuals – a buttonboard bass manual for the left hand and a piano-keyboard or buttonboard manual for the right. (The right hand arrangements gave rise to the names 'piano accordion' and 'button accordion.') Owing to extensive modifications to the left-hand manual two basic types of accordion have emerged: 1 / the stradella or standard-bass accordion, on which each button of the left-hand manual represents a fixed chord, and the buttons (or chords) commonly are arranged in six rows; and 2 / the free-bass accordion, on which the left-hand manual has no chords at all, its buttons (usually in three rows) representing single pitches chromatically graduated in a range up to six-and-a-half octaves. The stradella accordion is the most widely played and traditionally has been associated with ethnic, folk, and pop music. The free-bass accordion has been developed mainly as a concert-music instrument, its repertoire consisting for the most part of transcriptions of the classics and original works by contemporary composers.

The first accordions produced in Canada probably were those built ca 1865–80 by Roch *Lyonnais. In the 1970s in Canada, however, most instruments were imported from Germany and Italy, though increasing numbers have come from the USSR, China, and Brazil.

It was in the mid-1960s that the free-bass accordion began to gain recognition in Canada. The instrument's foremost Canadian protagonist, Joseph *Macerollo, premiered *Surdin's *Concerto* for accordion and strings at *Expo 67, and – also in 1967, at the *RCMT Summer School – established the first accordion classes in Canada within a major government-supported music school. He worked on the first free-bass accordion syllabus for the RCMT in 1969, established programs of free-bass accordion studies at *Queen's U in 1970 and at the *U of Toronto in 1972, and has encouraged composers to write for the instrument. Among those who, at his instigation, have contributed to the growing repertoire are *Barnes, *Buczynski, *Camilleri (one of Macerollo's teachers and himself a leading stradella player in Toronto in the 1960s and a composer of music for both types of accordion), *Dolin, *Fiala, *Fleming, *Kenins, *Klein, *Kolinski, *Pentland, *Schafer, and *Wuensch.

Macerollo was the prime organizer of the International Accordion Symposium sponsored jointly by the RCMT and the *Contemporary Showcase Assn in 1975 in Toronto. Leading foreign free-bass accordionists who appeared as guests of the symposium were Alain Abbott of France, Hugo Noth of West Germany (who returned in 1976 and 1979 to teach at the RCMT Summer School), and Yuri Kazakov of the USSR. Among the works commissioned for performance at the symposium were Dolin's *Adikia*, Wilfred Mellers' *White Bird Blues*, and Klein's *Invention, Blues and Chase*. Symposium participants also gave a concert jointly with *NMC, featuring premieres of works by Alain Abbott, Jan Kapr, and Mauricio Kagel.

The number of free-bass accordionists in Canada still was relatively small in the late 1970s. Among graduates of Macerollo's courses, the US players Joseph Natoli, Richard Romiti, and John Torcello returned to the USA, but the Canadians Eugene Laskiewicz, Joseph Petric, Glen Sawich, and Frank Baggetta remained active in Ontario. Petric (b Guelph, Ont, 8 Oct 1952) studied for a year in Germany with Hugo Noth and gave the German premiere of Samuel Dolin's *Sonata*. Petric has commissioned pieces by Daniel Foley and Marjan *Mozetich and in 1978 he prepared accordion syllabi for the *RHCM and the *WOCM. Laskiewicz and Sawich joined the staff of the RCMT. Iona Reed, a free-bass player who won the top award at the Confédération internationale des accordéonistes, was a pupil of Karl *Pukara of Sudbury, a noted teacher who plays stradella accordion but teaches both stradella and free-bass. Reed has continued to teach and play in Sudbury.

Algerian-born Christian Di-Maccio gave the first classes in free-bass accordion at the Schola cantorum in Paris in 1971 and moved to Canada in 1974, teaching and performing in Montreal, where he also has played on CBC radio and TV and has toured for the *JMC. His repertoire ranges from Bach to Messiaen and also includes folk music and jazz. Harold McKenzie, a Canadian player who graduated from the U of Houston, began teaching free-bass accordion at the *U of Calgary in 1973.

Active teachers in midwestern and western Canada in 1980 included Ted *Komar, with two schools in Winnipeg at which both stradella and free-bass were taught; Ron Komar, also with a school in Winnipeg providing tuition in both types of accordion; Everett Larson in Saskatoon; and Mona Drury and Larry Thiessen in Vancouver. During the early 1970s Tony Mergel began developing a program at Humber College, Toronto, but this was not sustained in the late 1970s, nor was a similar project at *York U.

The Canadian Accordion Teachers' Assn, formed in 1952, has maintained a national executive, but by 1979 the membership stood at about 120 and was drawn mostly from Ontario. A Western Accordion Assn, organized by players and teachers in Alberta, Manitoba, and Saskatchewan, was founded in 1977. It has been estimated that in 1980 some 400 young people in southern Ontario and 600 in Canada as a whole were engaged in the study of free-bass accordion.

The button accordion (ie, stradella type with a buttonboard right hand) has played a major role (with the fiddle and the harmonica) in French-Canadian folk music. Drawing on the traditional repertoire of reels, jigs, and other dance pieces, several accordionists attained wide popularity in Quebec through their performances and recordings: Alfred Montmarquette (b Montreal 1870, d there 1944), who performed 1923–32 at the Soirées du bon vieux temps and made some 45 78s for *Starr; Arthur Pigeon (b Quebec City 1884, d 1966), who learned to play from Montmarquette and recorded for Starr and Bluebird (30 78s in all); Joseph Plante, who recorded for Victor; Joseph Guilmette (b Natashquan 1886, d 1950) and Joseph Latour (b Montreal 1888, d 1932), who recorded as soloists for Victor; and Donat Lafleur (b Ste-Croix 1892, d 1973), who performed with Conrad *Gauthier and Isidore *Soucy and recorded for Columbia. Adélard Lebrun (ca 1867–1931) and his wife, Mélissa Vadeboncoeur (ca 1868–1953), were popular as an accordion duo and made nine 78s for Starr, Apex, and Columbia. Other significant accordionists in this tradition, playing either button right hand or piano right hand instruments, have included René Alain (who played with the Trio Soucy and as a soloist in Montreal), Tommy Duchesne, and the younger Philippe *Bruneau and Denis Coté. The button accordion has been heard in the traditional music of Newfoundland in the hands of such players as Jack Fleming, Harry *Hibbs, Jack Kennedy, and Minnie White. The concertina, an instrument of the reed-organ family similar to the accordion (without a keyboard and with hexagonal rather than rectangular ends) also has been heard in traditional music. One of the first accordionists to establish himself in a large way in Canada was the German-born stradella player and teacher Eric *Mundinger, who settled in Toronto in 1929, performed widely, and in 1935 founded a school which for 37 years enforced high playing standards in the stradella tradition. The school also boasted a 125-piece accordion orchestra. In Montreal in the mid-1930s Pat Marrazza established a school that was still an active teaching centre in 1980. Rolande *Désormeaux was a Marrazza pupil.

The accordion has been played in country and ethnic music in Canada by such musicians as Gaby *Haas, Ted Komar, Ron Komar, Olav *Sveen, and Marc Wald (*Rhythm Pals). It has been played in Canadian jazz groups by Vic Centro (with Ray Norris in Vancouver in the 1940s, Phil *Nimmons and CBC groups in the 1950s and 1960s, and in Reno, Nev, orchestras in the 1970s); Gordie Fleming (in Montreal and, after 1977, in Toronto), who has recorded with Al *Baculis, Buddy DeFranco, and others; and Gary Gross (also with Nimmons). Eddie Allen (see Happy Gang), Ned Ciaschini, Dixie *Dean, and Les Foster (see Happy Gang) became popular through their studio work and appearances on CBC radio and in Toronto nightclubs. Matt DeFlorio (of the CBC's 'Holiday Ranch') and Tommy Renzeth (of the CBC's 'Hayloft Hoedown') were active in Toronto studio groups from the 1930s to the 1950s. In Montreal Émilia Heyman and Saturno Gentiletti were popular CBC performers (see 'Les Joyeux Troubadours'). See also Scotland: 2 / Traditional Scottish music.

BIBLIOGRAPHY

Bizier, Hélène-Andrée. 'On les appelait les musiciens de la misère,' *Perspectives*, 8–17 Sep 1977

Macerollo, Joe. *Accordion Resource Book* (Willowdale, Ont, 1980)

Rosenberg, Neil J. 'A preliminary bibliography of Canadian old time instrumental music books,' *CFMJ*, vol 8, 1980

Les Pionniers du disque folklorique

JMc, MM

Acoustics research in Canada. Acoustics is the science of sound, and the study of its production, accommodation, uses, and effects. After the days of Lord Rayleigh (1842–1919) acoustics as a subject failed to command much academic attention; even in the 1970s the record of acoustics research was highly fragmented, and its findings divided among many disciplines, from oceanography to medicine. Very often an acoustical process provides a way of investigating non-acoustic phenomena; for instance, the velocity of sound propagation in a material or a structure may be a sensitive indicator of its elastic properties. Such secondary uses of sound lead to interesting analogies between widely disparate problems.

Oswald *Michaud was a pioneer acoustician and teacher of acoustics at the *Cons national in Montreal, beginning in 1928. However, the first acoustics research in the field of ultrasonics (mechanical vibrations above the range audible by the human ear) began in the 1920s at the *U of Alberta under the direction of R.W. Boyle, and moved to the National Research Council ca 1930 when Boyle became director of the Division of Physics and Engineering. Studies continued at the research council on such topics as building acoustics, audiometry, machinery noise, muffler development, outdoor sound propagation, structural effects of high intensity sound, guidance devices for the blind, and electronic music. By the 1970s research in acoustics was taking place at several universities and also at other government agencies.

An illustration of the interdisciplinary nature of acoustics is the use of echo-ranging techniques, in which a pulse of sound is sent into a medium and returning echoes, reflected from obstacles or discontinuities in the path, are analysed. The principle has been utilized by the Defence Research establishments on the two coasts, and by the Bedford Institute of Oceanography at Dartmouth, to study properties of the sea and to detect underwater objects such as submarines and fish. Similar techniques, but applied to the atmosphere, have been used in meteorological studies at the *U of Toronto and *Acadia U. In the ultrasonic frequency range the same principle is being applied to the delineation of internal parts of the human body. An instance is the development at *Lakehead U of a device for determining the internal dimensions of the heart.

In room acoustics a somewhat similar technique has been applied, using impulsive signals that simulate the transient sounds of speech and music. The objective is to study the effect of the room surfaces on the sounds ultimately heard by the listener. The technique is useful, both in small-scale models and in the full-scale, in determining the nature of the transient sounds that will be perceived, for example, by an audience in a concert hall. Studies of this sort, by the National Research Council and others, have been applied to hall design and to the solution of common problems in existing halls, for example, the conveyance of comprehensible speech in over-reverberant spaces and the effective performance of music in over-absorptive spaces.

With increased understanding of transient sounds in halls electroacoustic equipment, traditionally frowned on by performers and acousticians, has earned increased acceptance as a means of enhancing theatre and concert hall acoustics. The extreme example is the modern recording studio in which the musicians perform in acoustic isolation and achieve ensemble by way of signals fed back to them through earphones by the recording engineer.

Inverse to the search for ways of achieving better communication is the attempt to find ways of reducing the propagation of intelligible speech and other 'noises' in open-plan offices and schools. The techniques employed combine judicious use of acoustical screens and sound absorbing surfaces with the use of relatively innocuous 'background noise' designed to mask more distracting sounds. Considerable effort by the National Research Council, Ontario Hydro, and other groups has been devoted to finding the best (or least undesirable) solutions to the design of such 'open' spaces.

Of greatest interest, perhaps, are topics involving the interaction of sound waves and people. At the medical level are concerns relating to human speech and hearing. Studies of speech processes and related psychophysiological problems have been pursued at *Dalhousie U, *McGill U, the *U of Saskatchewan, the *U of Western Ontario, and the *U of Calgary. Studies of hearing defects and, more particularly, development of audiometric testing procedures are of increasing importance in relation to industrial environments, where noise-induced deafness may be a hazard. Several federal and provincial regulatory agencies were active in this area in the 1970s, and research was being done at the National Research Council, various universities, and the Defence and Civil Institute of Environmental Medicine, Downsview, Ont.

An important psychoacoustic question is the relation between noise, its intensity, duration, and spectral properties, and the annoyance or disturbance it engenders. The question is basic to all noise problems, and throughout the 1970s answers were being sought at the National Research Council in connection with building acoustics and noise studies, and at the U of Calgary and *McMaster U.

Noise as a pollutant has come under wide scrutiny, with study projects in almost every Canadian university, several government agencies, and private consulting firms. Some have surveyed urban noise climates, notably those in Montreal, Toronto, Woodstock, Calgary, and Vancouver. A project of special interest, the *World Soundscape Project organized by R. Murray *Schafer at *Simon Fraser U, has produced among other items a survey of community noise bylaws in Canada. Studies of noise near airports and major roadways have been undertaken by the National Research Council in association with the Central Mortgage and Housing Corporation and the Ministry of Transport. University groups and government agencies have collaborated with manufacturers to find means of silencing mechanical devices such as power lawnmowers and power station transformers.

In the construction field, sound insulation, with respect to both indoor and outdoor noise, has remained a major concern. Other projects in the 1970s have related to the propagation of structure-borne noise, especially impact noises and the vibration of mechanical and plumbing equipment in buildings. These topics have been under study at the Ontario Hydro Research Centre, the Domtar Research Centre, the U of Western Ontario, *Concordia U, and the National Research Council.

In 1949 at the *CMM Jean *Papineau-Couture introduced courses which related acoustics directly to composition. He also gave classes along those lines 1953–70 at the *U of Montreal; he was succeeded by Louise Gariépy. Speaking generally, however, research in musical acoustics has been limited to those few whose interest transcends the problem of finding funds for such work. Typical are the studies made by T.W.W. Stewart, at the U of Western Ontario, of some aspects of the performance of string instruments. In the 1970s electronic music became a major activity. Stimulated by Hugh *Le Caine's pioneering work at the National Research Council, and especially his development of electronic instruments in the early 1950s, work was undertaken at several universities (see Electronic music). At the National Research Council itself the computer has been utilized as a tool for the composer, facilitating the assembly, playback, and revision of thematic material.

Closely related to research in acoustics is the development of standard methods of acoustical measurement, the development of subjective criteria of 'noisiness,' and the establishment of noise limits. Much of Canada's work in this field has been done in collaboration with US and international groups, co-ordinated through the Canadian Advisory Committee on ISO (International Standards Organization). A Canadian Standards Assn Committee on Acoustics and Noise Control has been formed.

The international nature of the acoustical research community makes the identification of exclusively Canadian projects practically impossible. Typically, Canadian researchers have maintained close contact with workers in the USA, Great Britain, and elsewhere; they report their work at meetings of the Acoustical Society of America; and they publish in the journal of the society or in one of the international journals of acoustics. Communication among Canadian acousticians, however, is fostered by the recently developed Canadian Acoustical Assn, which has met annually and has begun publishing a journal, *Acoustics and Noise Control in Canada / L'Acoustique et la lutte antibruit au Canada*. In 1972 James Parrott, a librarian at the U of Waterloo, began the preparation of *Bibliotheca Harmonicorum*, a bibliography on acoustics and other sciences in their relation to music.

BIBLIOGRAPHY

Leong, Kwok Onn. 'Acoustic power measurement in a reverberant room,' unpubl PH D thesis (McGill 1964)

Schafer, R. Murray. *The Book of Noise* (Vancouver 1970)

Tremblay, Gilles, et al. *Le Bruit, 4e pollution du monde moderne* (Montreal 1970)

Doelle, L.L. *Environmental Acoustics* (New York 1972)

A Survey of Community Noise By-Laws in Canada. Soundscape Document no. 4 (Vancouver 1972)

Northwood, T.D., ed. *Benchmark Papers in Architectural Acoustics* (New York 1977)

JOURNALS

J of the Acoustical Soc of America (New York)

J of Sound and Vibration (London)

Acustica (Stuttgart)

TDN

ACTRA. See Unions.

ADAMS, (Douglas) **Ernest**. Baritone, administrator, b Winnipeg 17 Dec 1920. Raised in Vancouver, Adams sang there as a boy soprano and later studied voice with Isabelle *Burnada. In 1945 he won the first scholarship awarded by the British Columbia Institute of Music and Drama (see TUTS) and studied there with Glyndwr Jones. A leading baritone in Vancouver during the 1940s, he began his career in nightclubs, appeared at TUTS, starred 1945–8 on CBC radio's 'Ernest Adams Show,' gave recitals, sang with the *Vancouver SO, and continued voice studies with William Fife. Adams was a winner in the 1947–8 and 1948–9 *'Singing Stars of Tomorrow' and moved to Toronto in 1948 for studies at the *Royal Cons Opera School with Ernesto *Vinci. That year he was the soloist in Walton's *Belshazzar's Feast* with the *Toronto Mendelssohn Choir and performed with the *CBC Opera. He returned to Vancouver (summers 1950–2) to sing at TUTS. An original member of the *COC, he sang 1950–61 in over 30 Toronto and touring productions, making his debut as Marcello in the company's first production (1950) of *La Bohème* and also singing Almaviva in *The Marriage of Figaro* in 1951 and other roles. After serving as COC tour manager in 1958 and assistant to Herman *Geiger-Torel 1959–68, Adams retired from performance to become full-time tour administrator 1962–9 and publicity co-ordinator 1967–9. He was general administrator of the *U of Toronto Opera School 1969–71. He joined the *Ontario Place Corporation in 1973 as stage manager and program assistant and in 1974 became operations manager and later program co-ordinator for its presentations at the Forum. BNSG

Adanac Quartet(te). Name of two related male-voice quartets, active in turn 1915–19 and 1921–7. (Adanac – 'Canada' spelled backwards – has been a popular trade name for many years.) Little is known about the first, save that it gave its first concert 1 Jan 1915 at Columbus Hall, Toronto, was active in Ontario during World War I on behalf of various patriotic causes such as the sale of war bonds, and comprised Redferne *Hollinshead (tenor), George Dixon (tenor), Arthur *Blight (baritone), and Ruthven Macdonald (bass). The tenor J. Elcho Fiddes also is said to have sung in this first Adanac Quartet, which was disbanded at war's end. Reorganized on a professional basis in 1921 by Macdonald with Riley Hallman (tenor), Ernest Bushnell (tenor, pianist), and Joseph O'Meara (baritone), the second quartet performed widely on Chautauqua vaudeville circuits in the USA and Canada from 40 to 45 weeks each year and made two 78s of Scottish songs for the Apex label, the first released in 1923. In 1926 Bushnell, a pupil of Arthur Blight and later a major figure in Canadian broadcasting, was succeeded by another Blight pupil, Lawrence Dafoe. Various other singers, including Charles Shearer and Cavan Jones, have been mentioned in connection with the quartet. It disbanded in 1927 after its style of singing had gone out of fashion.

BIBLIOGRAPHY
Stursberg, Peter. *Mister Broadcasting: The Ernie Bushnell Story* (Toronto 1971)

ADASKIN, Harry. Violinist, teacher, broadcaster, b Riga, Latvia, 6 Oct 1901, naturalized Canadian 1909; hon LLD (Dalhousie) 1978, hon LLD (British Columbia) 1980. The elder brother of Murray and John *Adaskin, he was an infant when his parents emigrated to Canada and settled in Toronto. He studied 1913–18 with Bertha *Drechsler Adamson at the *TCM, 1918–22 with Luigi von *Kunits at the *Canadian Academy of Music, in the summer of 1922 with Leon Sametini in Chicago, and 1922–3 with Henri Czaplinski at the *Hambourg Cons. He also took advanced training privately in Paris and Seignelay with Marcel Chailley (summers 1930, 1931) and attended interpretation classes given by Jacques Thibaud and Georges Enesco in 1931 in Paris. He taught violin 1915–22 privately in Toronto, 1938–41 at Upper Canada College, and 1941–6 at the TCM. Among his pupils were his brother Murray, Adolph *Koldofsky, Maurice *Solway, and Harold *Sumberg. He moved to Vancouver in 1946 to establish music courses at the *U of British Columbia, enlisting the composers Barbara *Pentland and Jean *Coulthard as teachers. He also instituted a course in music appreciation based on his lifelong interest in music, painting, and literature. He retired as head in 1958 but continued to teach there until 1973.

His performing career began in Toronto theatre orchestras and 1917–18 with the *Welsman TSO. He was second violin of the *Academy String Quartet in 1920 and first violin 1920–2 in Milton Blackstone's quartet before serving 1923–38 as second violin in the *Hart House String Quartet, with which he performed and toured until 1938 in Canada, the USA, Great Britain, and continental Europe. In 1923 he formed a duo with the pianist Frances (Alice) Marr (b Ridgetown, between Windsor and London, Ont, 23 Aug 1900, a pupil of Paul *Wells at the TCM and, in the summers of 1930 and 1931, of Céline Chailley-Richez in Paris) and in 1926 married her. The couple gave the premieres of several Canadian works, including *Gratton's *Réminiscence* (Toronto 1928, dedicated to the duo); *Willan's *Sonata No. 1* (Toronto ca 1930); *Blomfield Holt's *Pastorale and Finale* (Toronto 1936) and *Suite No. 2* (Toronto 1940); *Weinzweig's *Sonata* (Toronto 1942); Pentland's *Concerto* for violin and small orchestra (Toronto 1945, arr for violin and piano), *Vista* (Vancouver 1948), and *Duo* (Vancouver 1960, commissioned by the duo); Coulthard's *Two Sonatinas* (Toronto 1946) and *Poem* (Vancouver 1948, dedicated to the duo); *Turner's *Sonata* (Vancouver 1956, commissioned by the duo); and Murray Adaskin's *Divertimento No. 1* (Vancouver 1956, dedicated to the duo, premiered with the composer as second violin). The Adaskins also took Canadian music abroad with them, performing, for example, Gratton's *Danses canadiennes No. 1 and 2* and *Réminiscence*; Willian's *Sonata No. 1*; Leo *Smith's *Tambourin*; and *Champagne's *Danse villageoise* on BBC radio 22 Aug 1930. The Adaskins' repertoire also included the standard works, much French music, and a wide selection of US and European 20th-century music, including the Ives *Sonatas* and the Hindemith *Concerto*, which latter they introduced to Canada in a violin and piano arrangement. They toured Canada several times 1944–54, gave New York recitals in 1948 and 1949 and performed often for CBC radio. Frances Marr Adaskin appeared as duo-recitalist or guest pianist with many other leading instrumentalists and singers, eg, Esther Glazer, Frances *James, Boris *Hambourg, the Hart House Quartet, John Loban, Oscar Natzke, Kathleen *Parlow, Hans-Karl Piltz, Albert *Steinberg, Ernesto *Vinci, and Cornelius Ysselstyn. She also gave piano-duo recitals with Robert *Rogers and Dale *Reubart respectively. In 1930 she and her husband performed the Sibelius *Violin Concerto* in a violin and piano arrangement.

Harry Adaskin's 'third career' – that of commentator-raconteur-host for CBC – began in 1938 with a lecture series, 'Musically Speaking,' which continued with interruptions until 1946. He also was the Canadian intermission commentator 1943–6 for the New York Philharmonic Sunday broadcasts and the host 1970–ca 1973 for CBC radio's 'Tuesday Night' series. In 1976 and 1977 he was the host for the *Vancouver SO's concert series (live, not broadcast), which also bore the title 'Musically Speaking.' He was made an Officer of the *Order of Canada in 1975. Frances Marr was made a Member of the order in 1975.

WRITINGS
'Music and the university,' *CMJ*, vol 1, Autumn 1956
A Fiddler's World (Vancouver 1977)
'Imagination: the human gift,' *Recorder*, vol 20, Mar 1978

(JDn)

ADASKIN, John. Conductor, radio producer, administrator, cellist, b Toronto 4 Jun 1908, d there 4 Mar 1964; Fellow, Royal Society of Arts 1961. The younger brother of Harry and Murray *Adaskin, he studied 1924–9 at the *Hambourg Cons with George Bruce and Boris *Hambourg (cello) and 1930–3 at the *TCM with Leo *Smith (cello and theory) and Luigi von *Kunits (conducting). He played cello 1926–35 in broadcasting orchestras and 1928–38 in the *TSO and was a producer 1934–43 for the CRBC and its successor, the CBC. As head of John Adaskin Productions 1943–61 he continued to produce CBC programs, including the popular series *'Singing Stars of Tomorrow' and *'Opportunity Knocks.' He also conducted the orchestra for the latter. For a brief period ca 1950 he organized and taught courses in radio and TV production at Toronto's Ryerson Institute of Technology. In 1961 he succeeded Jean-Marie *Beaudet as executive secretary of the *CMCentre, an office he held until his sudden death. A tireless promoter of Canadian music, he developed the centre's library, edited the magazine *Music Across Canada* in 1963, and commissioned several composers to write works for school use. The *John Adaskin Project continues his work in promoting Canadian educational composition.

His wife was the pianist Naomi Yanova (b Granatstein, Toronto, 6 May 1908, a student at the Hambourg Cons, the TCM, and the *U of Toronto and a pupil 1928–38 of Mona *Bates and 1941–4 of E. Robert Schmitz). She accompanied her husband in recitals 1929–38 and was known for her work 1929–38 as part of the two-piano team Yanova and (Etta) Coles, which made its debut in Toronto and played with orchestras in New York, Montreal, Buffalo, and Rochester. Naomi Yanova Adaskin taught 1939–44 at the TCM, wrote articles 1957–60 for the *Star Weekly*, *Chatelaine*, the *Globe and Mail*, and the *Toronto Daily Star*, and edited school music texts 1965–9 for Ginn and Co and 1970–2 for McGraw-Hill Ryerson. She married the pianist Reginald *Godden in 1979.

WRITINGS
Adaskin, John. 'Radio production in relation to symphony broadcasting,' *CRMA*, vol 1, Apr 1942
– 'MacMillan as conductor,' *Music Across Canada*, Jul–Aug 1963
Adaskin, Naomi. 'Evenings with Benjamin Britten,' *Mayfair*, Dec 1957

(HK)

Murray Adaskin

ADASKIN, Murray. Composer, teacher, violinist, conductor, b Toronto 28 Mar 1906; hon LL D (Lethbridge) 1970, hon D MUS (Brandon) 1972. A brother of Harry and John *Adaskin, he studied with Harry and with Luigi von *Kunits in Toronto, with Kathleen *Parlow in New York, and with Marcel Chailley in Paris. He met and married the soprano Frances *James in 1931. For many years he lived as an orchestral and chamber musician, playing 1923–36 with the *TSO and 1938–52 with the Royal York Hotel Trio. In 1944, however, he began to study composition with *Weinzweig, and soon composition became his prime interest. He studied further with Darius Milhaud at Aspen (summers 1949, 1950, 1953) and 1949–51 with Charles Jones in California.

In 1952 he was named head of music at the *U of Saskatchewan in Saskatoon. During his tenure, 1957–60, as conductor of the *Saskatoon SO he insisted that the orchestra commission a Canadian work annually. He also included Canadian works in the program of the Summer Festival of Music which he organized in 1959 and in Six Exhibition Concerts (1967) which combined performances with an exhibition documenting the composers' careers. A charter member of the *CLComp, he also served 1966–9 on the *Canada Council. In 1966 at the U of Saskatchewan he became composer-in-residence, the first such position created by a Canadian university. In 1972 he retired, and in 1973 he moved to Victoria, where he continued to compose and teach.

A modernist without being a radical, Adaskin in his compositions developed a consistent and recognizable technique which exploits three main textures: counterpoint of two melodies, rhythmic activity under melody, and rhythmic activity alone. The rhythmic activity, often syncopated, is given characteristically to staccato woodwinds or strings. The form evolves from short motions repeated either sequentially or in rhythmic transformation, with frequent changes in texture and timbre. Phrase lengths also are short, often spanning only two bars. Adaskin has used folk material occasionally, extracting from it short motives similar to those that appear in his other music and using them in a similar way. His *Saskatchewan Legend* and *Algonquin Symphony* contain examples of this procedure.

His style is marked by a French-influenced civility and pleasantness of expression, attained through a personal mixture of neoclassic and folk-derived elements. Some works employ quasi-serial procedures, but strict dodecaphonism and its descendants would find no comfortable place in his utterance.

A great many of his works have been commissioned, including several (the opera *Grant,*

Warden of the Plains, the *Rondino for Nine Instruments*, the *String Quartet No. 1*, etc) by the *CBC, the *Diversion for Orchestra* by the *NACO, *In Praise of Canadian Painting in the Thirties* by the *Chamber Players of Toronto, the *Adagio for Cello and Orchestra* by the *Victoria Cons, *Nootka Ritual* by the Nanaimo SO, *Divertimento No. 4* by the Saskatoon SO, *Cassenti Concerto* by the *Cassenti Players, *Saskatchewan Legend* by the Golden Jubilee Committee of the U of Saskatchewan, *Divertimento No. 2* by the U of Saskatchewan at Regina, the *Bassoon Concerto* by George *Zukerman, *Fanfare* by the *Saskatchewan Centre of the Arts, and *Rondino* by the *CMCentre.

Adaskin's work as teacher, conductor, and advocate of Canadian music and musicians ranks with his work as composer. His benign and positive attitude towards Canadian music is expressed in his genial Saskatchewan reports in the 'Canadian Chronicles' of issues 1 to 4 of the *Canada Music Book* (1970–2). He was one of the first to leave the Toronto-Montreal concentration and contribute in a real way to the decentralization of Canadian musical activity. His pupils have included Andrew *Dawes, Paul *Pedersen, Boyd McDonald (see Beckett and McDonald), and Neil *Harris. He is an associate of the CMCentre and a member of CAPAC. He has begun to deposit his papers at the *NL OF C. Adaskin was made an Officer of the *Order of Canada in 1981.

See also Amati String Quartet.

SELECTED COMPOSITIONS

OPERA

Grant, Warden of the Plains (M.E. Bayer). 1967 (Wpg 1967). CMCentre

ORCHESTRA

Suite. 1948. CMCentre. RCI 17 (R. *Leduc)
2 *Marches* (1950, 1953). Both CMCentre
Ballet Symphony. 1951. CMCentre. RCI 71 (*TSO)
Coronation Overture. 1953. CMCentre
Serenade Concertante. 1954. Summit 1956. RCI 129 (*TSO)/Col MS 6285 (*CBC SO)
Algonquin Symphony. 1958 (Tor 1958). Summit 1962. (3rd mvt) Dom S 1372 (*Feldbrill cond)
Saskatchewan Legend. 1959 (Saskatoon 1959). Summit 1961
Rondino. 1964 (Tor 1965). CMCentre
Diversion for Orchestra. 1969 (Ott 1969). CMCentre
Qalala and Nilaula of the North. 1969. Sm orch. CMCentre. CBC SM-294 (*Edmonton SO)
Fanfare. 1970. CMCentre. CBC SM-163 (*CBC Wpg O)
There Is My People Sleeping. 1970. CMCentre
Essay for Strings. 1972. CMCentre
Nootka Ritual. 1972 (Nanaimo 1974). CMCentre
In Praise of Canadian Painting in the Thirties. 1975 (Tor 1976). Str orch. CMCentre
Three Tunes for Strings. 1976. CMCentre
Also a work for band, *Night Is No Longer Summer Soft*. (1972). CMCentre

SOLOISTS WITH ORCHESTRA

Concerto. 1956 (Tor 1956). Vn, orch. CMCentre
Concerto. 1960 (Van 1961). Bn, orch. CMCentre. CBC SM-143 (*Zukerman)
Capriccio. 1961 (Tor 1963). Pf, orch. CMCentre
Divertimento No. 4. 1970, 2 tpt (1 player), orch. CMCentre
Adagio for Cello and Orchestra. 1975 (originally for vc, pf 1973). CMCentre

CHAMBER

Sonata. 1946 (Tor 1947). Vn, pf. CMCentre. 1952. RCI 73 (M. Adaskin vn, Bernardi pf)/CBC SM-211 (*Fenyves vn)
Canzona and Rondo. 1949. Vn, pf. CMCentre. RCI 221/RCA CCS-1015 (*Hidy vn)
Sonatine Baroque. 1952. Vn. Summit 1961. 1952. RCI 73 (M. Adaskin)
3 *Divertimentos* for various instr. (1956, 1964, 1965). CMCentre. (No. 3) RCI 405 (*Zukerman bn)
Introduction and Rondo. 1957 (Saskatoon 1959). Pf quar. CMCentre
Rondino for Nine Instruments. 1961 (Tor 1962). Ww quin, str quar. CMCentre. RCI 215/RCA CCS-1009 (chamb ens of the *Wpg SO)
Cassenti Concertante. 1963 (Saskatoon 1964). Ob, cl, bn, vn, pf. CMCentre
Quiet Song. 1963. Vn, pf. Leeds 1964
Trio. 1970. Fl, vc, pf. CMCentre
Two Pieces for solo viola da gamba. 1972. CMCentre
Two Portraits. 1973. Vn, pf. CMCentre
Music for Brass Quintet. 1977. CMCentre
Nocturne. 1978. Cl, pf. CMCentre
Also *String Quartet No. 1* (1963), 5 short pieces for vn, pf (1963–74), and *Quintet for Winds* (1974). All CMCentre

CHOIR AND VOICE

A Hymn of Thanks (A.E. Haydon). 1953. Unison choir. B & H 1954
The Shepherd (Blake). 1934. High v, pf. Ms
Epitaph (G. Apollinaire, transl Bertha Ten Eyck James). 1948. V, pf. CMCentre. RCI 74 (F. James)
The Prairie Lily (H. Blakeney). 1967. V, pf. CMCentre

WRITINGS

'The university and audience training,' *Music Across Canada*, Jun 1963; extract in *CanComp*, 11, Oct 1966
'Contemporary music: composers, teachers, performers and audiences,' *CanComp*, 34, Nov 1968

BIBLIOGRAPHY

Savage, Richard. 'Murray Adaskin: composer, professor, gentleman,' *CanComp*, 10, Sep 1966
'Murray Adaskin – a portrait,' *Mcan*, 1, May 1967 (JHn)

Adaskin Project. See John Adaskin Project.

ADDISON, L.F. (Laidlaw Fletcher) or '**Puff**.' Bandmaster, bassist, composer, b Hamilton, Ont, 4 Jul 1878, d Toronto 19 Aug 1949. Though he studied violin with his father (euphonium soloist of Hamilton's 13th Royal Regiment for 46 years) and with W. Anderson, as a string bass player he was mainly self-taught, beginning at 10. He studied theory with Arthur W. *Hughes. He lived 1898–1900 in the USA and 1900–2 in New Westminster, BC. He joined the Canadian Kilties Band and toured North America with that organization until 1906, latterly as conductor. He played in and conducted bands in the USA and led the Savoy Theatre Band in Hamilton before settling in 1909 in Toronto, where he was a member of the *Welsman TSO 1910–14, the New SO 1923–7, and the *TSO 1929–46. After 1910 he directed bands in Barrie, Brantford, Trenton, New Toronto, and Belleville. He was music director of the 86th Machine Gun Battalion Band (later the Canadian Machine Gun Corps Band) and conducted it in Europe during World War II. He also directed the Brass and Flute Bands of the Royal Grenadier Regiment 1929–32. In 1935 he reorganized the *Toronto Symphony Band, which had its origins in a group of theatre and symphony musicians who played under Addison in the early 1920s at Ontario resorts. The Toronto Symphony Band performed at the *CNE and on CBC radio but had reduced its activities by 1945. Addison was a founding member of the *CBA and served 1944–5 as its president. His compositions (listed in *Catalogue of Canadian Composers*) include two waltzes for orchestra and several marches for band.

BIBLIOGRAPHY

'The president,' *CanB*, Feb 1945 (FH)

ADENEY, Marcus. Cellist, writer, teacher, b London 1 Jul 1900, naturalized Canadian 1904. He studied cello in Hamilton with J. Bartmann 1912–14, in Toronto with Leo *Smith 1915–16 and Boris *Hambourg 1919–22, in Detroit with Philip Abbas 1922–4, in London with Arnold Trowell 1924–5, in Vienna with Wilhelm Jeral in 1925, and in New York with Percy Such 1925–6. After working 1919–22 in theatre orchestras in Richmond, Va, Toronto, and Detroit, he joined the Detroit SO in 1922. He was a cellist 1928–44 with the *TSO, founder and conductor 1947–50 of the Beaches Concert Orchestra in Toronto, and a member of the *Solway String Quartet 1948–58 and the *CBC SO 1952–63. With Hyman *Goodman, Berul *Sugarman, and Eugene Hudson he formed the Marcus Adeney String Quartet, which performed in Toronto during the 1950s. He taught at the *Hambourg Cons 1928–51 and the *U of Toronto 1953–63, and was founder and director 1957–61 of the Inverness Music Camp in Muskoka, Ont. He began teaching at the TCM (*RCMT) in 1944 and was still on staff in 1980. A *Canada Council fellowship in 1962 allowed him to study teaching methods of master cellists and to complete *Tomorrow's Cellist* (1973), a work on technique. He has composed cello pieces and songs. Adeney pupils are or have been members of the TS, the *NACO, and the Rochester Philharmonic. Adeney was music critic 1930–2 for *Saturday Night*, program annotator 1947–67 for the TSO, and a frequent contributor to *Strad*; he also wrote book reviews and features for *Canadian Forum* and *The Canadian Bookman* and poetry for US, English, and Canadian publications and *The Book of Canadian Poetry* (Chicago 1943). He was poetry editor (1946) of the *Canadian Review of Music and Art*. In 1944 he collaborated on a brief to Parliament which led to the formation of the Canadian Arts Council (*CCA) and the *CMCouncil. He wrote an article on 'Music in post-war Canada' for the *Canadian Forum* (June 1945) and the chapter 'Chamber music' for *Music in Canada*. Adeney's wife, Jeanne, was chairman of the TSO committee which inaugurated the orchestra's public-school concerts and the first in-school CBC music broadcasts. (ES)

AGLAÉ (b Jocelyne Deslongchamps, m Roche). Singer, actress, b L'Épiphanie, near Montreal, 13 May 1933. She took piano lessons in Montreal. At 16 she was persuaded to take part in the amateur competition 'Reine d'un soir'; she placed first, singing 'Départ express' by Pierre Roche and Charles Aznavour. An admirer of these two songwriter-performers, she was heard by them at Au Faisan doré, the Montreal night club where, in 1950 as Josette France, she made her professional debut followed by a three-month engagement. That same year she married Pierre Roche and went to Paris, where, still as Josette France, she obtained an unexpected engagement at the Échelle de Jacob. Her success brought work in other Parisian cabarets. Her colleague Monique *Leyrac introduced her to the song 'Aglaé' by Lionel *Daunais. Such was her success with the song that, on Félix *Leclerc's suggestion, she adopted Aglaé as her professional name. She recorded the song (45 rpm) with Michel Legrand's orchestra, and its popularity in France and the success of a subsequent three-month tour of the country in 1950 very quickly made her an acknowledged star. After appearing at the Olympia she made her operetta debut during the 1955–6 season at the Théâtre du Châtelet in the role of Juliette in *Méditerranée* by Raymond Vincy and Francis Lopez, singing opposite Tino Rossi. In his *Histoire de l'opérette en France* (Lyons 1974), Florian Bruyas wrote, 'The vivacious and irrepressible Aglaé was the joy of the evening.'

Aglaé later toured often, not only in France but also in Switzerland, Belgium, Luxembourg, Holland, Algeria, Morocco, and Tunisia. She received top billing at numerous gala shows, singing in the presence of President Coty of France, Prince Rainier of Monaco, and the Ismaili Prince Ali Khan. In the meantime she frequently returned to Canada, where she appeared on such CBC TV programs as 'Music Hall,' 'Club des autographes,' and 'Les Grands de la chanson.' In Paris she appeared in top variety theatres, such as the Bobino, and in 1960 distinguished herself in Guy Magenta's operetta *Coquin de printemps* at the Théâtre de l'ABC.

Wherever she went, her attractive voice and dynamic personality made her a great success with audiences. In 1962 in Paris she made her acting debut in Anita Loos' *Gentlemen Prefer Blondes*. In 1963, after the birth of her second son, she decided to continue her career in Canada and devote more time to family and business interests.

Aglaé made many 45s, including some Canadian songs such as Raymond *Lévesque's 'Les Trottoirs,' and her voice is heard in the films *Les Nuits de Montparnasse* and *À la manière de Sherlock Holmes*. Her performances of excerpts from *Méditerranée* were released on an LP (Philips B77.722L). Another LP, *Aglaé* (Alouette ALP 255), combined several of her hits, including the Canadian songs *'Vlà l'bon vent,' *'Ah! Si mon moine,' 'Rapide blanc,' 'Sur l'perron,' and 'La Bastringue.' Aglaé also recorded for Pergola, Ricordi, and Dinamic.

BIBLIOGRAPHY

'L'infatigable Aglaé,' Quebec *Le Soleil*, 26 Feb 1966

Lemelin, Mireille. 'La 2e carrière d'Aglaé,' *Châtelaine*, Mar 1970

AGOSTINI. Family of musicians of Italian origin: 1 / Giuseppe, 2 / his son Lucio, and 3 / his daughter Gloria.

1 **Giuseppe**. Conductor, arranger, composer, b Fano, Italy, 20 May 1890, naturalized Canadian 1926, d Montreal 9 Dec 1971. After studying oboe, harmony, and composition 1901–9 with a Professor Calestini at the Rossini Cons in Pesaro, Italy, he taught and led bands in Fano and Cartoceto. In 1915 he took his family to Montreal, where he became principal clarinet in (Peter) Van der Meerschen's Band. He also conducted his own band in Montreal and others in Beauharnois, Trois-Rivières, and Valleyfield, Que. After serving eight years as music director in Montreal theatres – first the Palace, then the Capitol – he worked as an arranger and conductor 1933–6 for the CRBC; his programs included the popular 'One Hour with You,' broadcast nationally from the Mount Royal Hotel. He was an arranger and conductor 1936–71 for the CBC, responsible for such shows as 'Appointment with Agostini' and *'Nos Futures Étoiles.' In 1937 he was a guest conductor of the *SCSM. His published compositions (listed in the *Catalogue of Canadian Composers*) include 'Ave Maria' for voice and piano or orchestra, *Eternamente* for four violins and organ, and 'Griserie' and 'Reviens' for voice (all Parnasse musical), *The Three Trumpets* for band (Belwin), and *Marcia funebre* for organ (*Le Passe-Temps*). He also wrote pieces for band and orchestra.

BIBLIOGRAPHY

'Rencontre avec Giuseppe Agostini,' *SemRC*, Apr 1951

2 **Lucio**. Conductor, composer, arranger, b Fano 30 Dec 1913, naturalized Canadian 1926. He began his studies at 5 with his father (woodwinds) and continued with Louis Michiels and Henri *Miro (harmony and composition), and Peter Van der Meerschen (cello). At 15 he played tenor saxophone, bass clarinet, and cello in his father's theatre orchestra, and at 16 he played cello in Eugène *Chartier's Montreal Philharmonic. He conducted the *Red and White Revue* at *McGill U in 1929 and 1930, and soon afterwards conducted his first radio show on CFCF. In 1932 he began composing film scores for Associated Screen News, continuing until 1944 (though he moved to Toronto in 1943), latterly as music director. He completed scores for some 150 shorts, including monthly instalments for the *NFB's 'Canada at War' and 'The World in Action' series. He began conducting for the CRBC radio network in 1934, and for the CBC

Lucio Agostini

later. Among the programs were 'Mantilles et castagnettes,' 'The Little Review,' and 'Carnival in Venice.' In Toronto he composed and conducted incidental music for Andrew Allan's CBC radiodrama series 'Stage' 1944–55, for 'CBC Wednesday Night' Shakespeare productions (which inspired his *Shakespearean Suite for Strings* 1948), for CBC radio's 'Ford Theatre' 1949–55, and for several variety programs, including his own 'Strictly for Strings' (1951, 1952) and 'Appointment with Agostini' (1954–5). After a year in Hollywood he became conductor and arranger for CBC TV's 'Front Page Challenge,' a position he has held for over 20 years. His 'Appointment with Agostini' was resumed in 1958 for three seasons and was followed by 'Music Album' (1968), 'Collage' (1969), and 'Music to Remember' (1970). Agostini's compositions include three musical comedies (still unperformed in 1980), *Willie the Squowse* (1968), *Gibraltar* (1975), and *Divorce* (1976); scores for the feature films *Inside Out* (1975), *Ragtime Summer* (1977), *The Little Brown Burro* (1978), and *Ichabod Crane* (1978); a *Piano Concerto* (1948); a *Flute Concerto* (1960, recorded by Nicholas *Fiore with the Albert *Pratz orchestra); and *Trio Québécois* (1970, Boosey & Hawkes, written for Avrahm *Galper). An opera based on the life of the Haitian president 'Papa Doc' Duvalier was in preparation in 1980. Agostini has written arrangements for recordings by the singers Alys *Robi and Tony Ziccardi, by the guitarist Giovanni Liberatore, and by his own orchestra. Agostini's value as a composer of incidental music lies in his command of an orchestra and its colours, his ability to satisfy the dramatic requirements at hand, his speed and precision, his effectiveness as a conductor, and his efficiency as a workman. He is a member of CAPAC. His manuscripts are deposited at the *NL of C.

DISCOGRAPHY

Lucio Agostini and His Orchestra. 1963. CTLS 5013

Action with Agostini. 1964? Cap ST 6087

Mucho Lucio. 1965. CTLS 5065

Once Upon a Hundred Years. 1967. CBC LM-56

Mas Mucho Lucio. 1968. CTL 477-5019. Also issued as *Cold Shoulder and Hot Brass*. RCA CTLS 5019

BIBLIOGRAPHY

'The many-faceted career of Lucio Agostini,' *CanComp*, 21, Sep 1967

'Agostini and Surdin,' *CanComp*, 38, Mar 1969

McNamara, Helen. 'Lucio Agostini: amazing productivity, enthusiasm,' *CanComp*, 92, Jun 1974

McLarty, James. 'Appointment with Agostini,' *Motion*, vol 4, no. 2, 1975

3 **Gloria**. Harpist, teacher, b Montreal 30 May 1923. After receiving a harp at 12 as a Christmas gift from Senator Lawrence Wilson, she studied the instrument with Mother St Roméo at the Villa Maria Convent in Montreal. On a scholarship from the Quebec government she went to New York at 15 for studies with Marcel Grandjany. She joined the ABC (radio) SO in New York at 16. She returned to Canada in the early 1940s to perform on her brother's radio shows, was harpist 1941–2 with the *CSM, and in 1942 was the soloist with that orchestra in Ravel's *Introduction and Allegro*. She made her career in New York, however, playing in studio (radio and recording) and chamber orchestras, and in recital. Specializing in contemporary music, she has participated in the premieres of Pierre Boulez' *Explosante Fixe* (1973), Alberto Ginastera's *Serenata* (1974), and Barbara Kolb's *Soundings* (1973) with the Chamber Music Society of Lincoln Center, and also in the first performances of works by Henry Cowell (*Triple Rondo* for flute and harp 1965; *Concerto* for flute and harp 1965?), Paul Creston (*Symphonic Poem* for harp and orchestra 194?), Igor Stravinsky (*Epitaphium*, North American premiere, 1959), and Charles Wuorinen (*Harp Variations* 1971). She is a soloist in the recording of Frank Martin's *Petite Symphonie Concertante* under Leopold Stokowski (Cap SP 8507), and is the partner of Ruggiero Ricci in the recording of Saint-Saëns' *Fantaisie* for violin and harp (Decca DL 710177). In 1977 she began teaching at Yale U. (MCv, HM)

AHRENS, Cora B. (Bell). Teacher, lecturer, pianist, b Stratford, Ont, 23 Jan 1891, d there 26 Aug 1964; LTCM 1910, B MUS (Toronto) 1926. Her teachers included Viggo *Kihl at the TCM. With Leon Vera and Avram Pratz she played in a trio which accompanied silent movies at Stratford's Theatre Albert. During the 1930s she was one of the first itinerant rural school music teachers and taught throughout Perth County, Ont. A co-founder in 1926 with W.B. Rothwell and Margaret Stevenson Grant of the Perth County Music Teachers' Federation (see Stratford), Ahrens also served as secretary 1936, 1940–2 and president 1944–6 of the *ORMTA. She lectured in pedagogy at the *U of Western Ontario, the *U of Toronto, and *McGill U, conducted summer workshops in piano pedagogy in most major Canadian cities, and taught privately in Stratford. Her pupils included Irene *Bird, Paul *Helmer, and Campbell *Trowsdale.

WRITINGS

Mother Goose Rhymes in Rhythm (Waterloo 1937)

Daily Sight Playing Excercises for Piano, 4 vols (Waterloo 1937, rev 1963)

Rudiments of Music, 9 vols (Toronto 1943–6)

Ear Training, 6 vols (New York 1947–50)

– and Atkinson, G.D. *For All Piano Teachers* (Oakville 1955)

– and Younger, J.B. *Hints on Harmony* (Oakville 1963)

(GJ)

'Ah! Si mon moine voulait danser.' Folksong, believed to have been sung in France before the 17th century. The title is a play on words: 'moine' means both a 'spinning top' and a 'monk.' To encourage him to dance, our monk is offered – in fun – now a hood or cap, now a rosary: this is the version published in Ernest *Gagnon's *Chansons populaires du Canada* (Quebec 1865). The text was published in *La Lyre canadienne* (Quebec 1886), a work compiled by W.H. Rowan. The French words and their English translation appear in various publications, including *Chansons de Québec / Folk Songs of Quebec* (Waterloo 1957) and Edith *Fowke's *Penguin Book of Canadian Folk Songs* (Harmondsworth, England, 1973). Marius *Barbeau, in *Alouette* (Montreal 1946), claims to have collected another version, with similar music, in which the monk is bedecked with various inappropriate baubles, such as a necktie. However, he did not publish this variant. Popularized in 1927 by Charles *Marchand and his Bytown Troubadours at the first of the *CPR Festivals at the Château Frontenac in Quebec City, the song was recorded in 1928 by that ensemble for a Victor 78. Among the many other recordings are those on LPs by Louise *Forestier (RCI / RCA CS 100-9) and by Alan *Mills, accompanied by the fiddler Jean *Carignan and the guitarist Gilbert Lacombe (Folk FG 3532). HP

AIDE, William (John). Pianist, teacher, b Timmins, Ont, 27 Mar 1938; LRCT 1959, Artist Diploma (Toronto) 1959, B SC music (Juilliard) 1962. He studied piano with Alberto *Guerrero in Toronto and Beveridge Webster in New York, and in 1962 won first prize in the *CBC Talent Festival and the Canada Council Award for Young Performing Artists. After teaching 1963–4 at *Mount Allison U and 1964–5 at *Acadia U he joined the School of Music, *U of Manitoba. He was active 1965–74 as a performer in Winnipeg, both in chamber music (eg, Schoenberg's *Pierrot Lunaire* in 1969 at the U of Manitoba) and in concerto performances with the *Winnipeg SO and the *CBC Winnipeg Orchestra. In 1974 he began teaching at the *U of Western Ontario and in 1978 he joined the faculty at the *U of Toronto. He has appeared as soloist with the TS. A specialist in Canadian music, he has premiered works of Walter *Buczynski, S.C. *Eckhardt-Gramatté, and Srul Irving *Glick. He toured the USSR with the mezzo-soprano Phyllis *Mailing in 1971 and has been the recital partner of Lois *Marshall, Otto *Armin, and others. He has recorded works for piano by Haydn and Brahms (ca 1966, CBC SM-16) and by Chopin and Debussy (1971, CBC SM-91), as well as works for horn and piano by Beethoven, *Polson, Glière, and Françaix with Gloria Johnson (1969, CBC SM-79) and for violin and piano by Brahms, Leclair, and Polson with Arthur Polson. (KN)

AITKEN, Robert (Morris). Flutist, composer, teacher, b Kentville, NS, 28 Aug 1939; B MUS (Toronto) 1961, M MUS (Toronto) 1964. He studied flute as a child in Pennsylvania and 1955–9 with Nicholas *Fiore at the RCMT. He served 1958–9 as principal flute of the *Vancouver SO (at 19 the youngest principal in the orchestra's history) and at the same time studied composition with Barbara *Pentland at the *U of British Columbia. After 1959, while studying electronic music with Myron Schaeffer and composition with John *Weinzweig at the *U of Toronto, he participated in several Marlboro (Vermont) Music Festivals and served 1960–4 as second flute of the *CBC SO and 1962–4 as principal flute of the *Stratford Festival Orchestra. He considers Marcel Moyse, with whom he studied intermittently for nine years in Europe and at Marlboro, his most significant flute teacher. However, he also studied with Jean-Pierre Rampal (Paris, Nice), Severino Gazzelloni (Rome), André Jaunet (Zurich), and Hubert Barwähser (Amsterdam) during a 1964–5 European sojourn on a Canada Council grant.

In 1964 Aitken, with the pianist Marion Ross (his wife) and the soprano Mary *Morrison, formed the *Lyric Arts Trio. He also served 1965–70 as co-principal flute of the *TS, but in 1971 he gave up orchestral work to devote himself to solo performances and to appearances with the trio and with the harpsichordist Greta *Kraus. He won third prize at the 1971 Concours international de flûte de Paris and was a winner at the first Concours international de flûte pour la musique contemporaine, in 1972 at Royan, France. During the 1960s and 1970s in Canada he was a soloist with the *Edmonton, *Regina, Toronto,

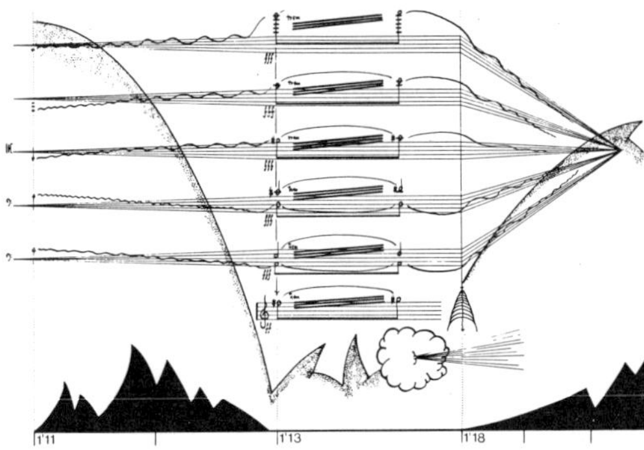

A page from *Kebyar* by Robert Aitken

Vancouver, *Victoria, and CBC SOs, the *CBC Vancouver Chamber Orchestra, the *NYO, and the *Hamilton Philharmonic. He has performed often in Europe, especially in Scandinavia, and in 1970 he toured Japan, Thailand, Ceylon, and India. From 1970 to 1972 Aitken was in charge of the 'Music Today' series at the *Shaw Festival, Niagara-on-the-Lake, and in 1971, with Norma *Beecroft, he co-founded *New Music Concerts, Toronto, serving thereafter as artistic director. In 1977 he was one of 12 instrumentalists invited to present a series of 38 solo recitals at Boulez' Institut de recherche et de coordination acoustique musique (IRCAM) in Paris. He chose his own program of solo flute pieces by Takemitsu, Morthensen, Fukushima, Globokar, Sigurbjörnsson, Y. Matsudaira, Heinz Holliger, and himself.

Aitken approaches composition through his experience as a skilled solo, chamber, and orchestral player. To a broad and practical knowledge of instrumental uses he applies a keen intuition for the effective combining of sounds. In an interview (*Music Scene*, Jul–Aug 1969) he said, 'I still compose aurally, and though I enjoy the intellectual stimulation of organization, and acknowledge, in most cases, the necessity of it, if a conflict arises between my preconception and the preference of my ear I generally give in to the ear.' His orchestral work *Spectra*, described by the interviewer as 'four chamber groups interacting in strange and sonically intoxicating ways,' exploits sound with a sensuality rooted more in harmony and antiphony than in polyphony, either old (fugue) or new (serialism). He also retains an unabashed weakness for the pretty music of the 19th-century conservatoire. Consequently, though the works following his neo-classic *Concerto for Twelve Solo Instruments and Orchestra* (1965) are in most aspects idiosyncratic and extremely free, they appeal directly – if not conventionally – to the ear. In *Kebyar* (1971), one of several works written after a four-month eastern tour in 1970, Aitken goes further by entrusting parts of the score (where notation is replaced by vivid drawings) to the performers, whose improvisations reflect the meaning of the title: an explosion of spontaneous activity.

Aitken taught 1957–64 and 1965–8 at the RCMT and 1960–4 and 1965–75 at the U of Toronto. He also taught 1974–7 at the *Shawnigan Summer School of the Arts and (with the Lyric Arts Trio) was artist-in-residence in 1971 at *Simon Fraser U and in 1976 at the *U of Saskatchewan. He has been engaged for several short residencies as well, and has taught master classes at the Musikskolan, Ingesund (Sweden), at the Bergens Konservatorium (Norway), and at the Swedish Radio Music School, Stockholm. His pupils have included Kathryn Cernauskas, Douglas Stewart, and Suzanne *Shulman. A member of the *CLComp, he received that organization's *Canada Music Citation in 1969. Aitken is an associate of the *CMCentre and an affiliate of PRO Canada.

Aitken gave the premieres of the following Canadian works:

Aitken *Kebyar* 1973, *Shadows II: Lalitá* 1973, *Plainsong* 1977
*Applebaum *Essay* 1970, *Algoma Central* 1976
*Baker *Concerto* 1974
*Barnes *Nocturne* 1963, *Sonata* 1970
*Beecroft *Improvvisazioni Concertanti No. 3* 1973, *Piece for Bob* 1975, *Collage '76* 1976
*Buczynski *Four Arabesques and a Dance* 1966
*Collier *Waterfront, Night Thoughts* 1970
Coulter, Richard *Sonatine* 1962
Felice, John *Pastoral* 1958
*Fleming, R. *Almost Waltz* 1970
*Freedman *Toccata 1967, Soliloquy* 1970
*Hawkins *Trio* 1975
*Joachim, O. *Expansion* 1963
*Kemp *Two Folksongs* 1957
*Kenins *Concertante* 1967
*Morawetz *Suite* 1974
*Morel *Nuvattuq* 1967
*Papineau-Couture *Verségères* 1975
*Pentland *Trance* 1979
*Schafer *Five Studies on Texts by Prudentius* 1963, *The Enchantress* 1972
*Symonds *A Small Concerto for Flute and Others* 1971
*van Dijk *Concertante* 1964
*Weinzweig *Riffs* 1974
*Wuensch *Sonatina* 1970, *Cameos* 1970
*Wyre *Snowflake* 1979
*Zuckert *Little Spanish Dance* 1970

In addition Aitken has participated in premieres of works by *Beckwith, *Garant, *Heard, *Hodkinson, Jaeger, *Laufer, *Mather, *Pauk, *Saint-Marcoux, *Tremblay and others (see Lyric Arts Trio), and by foreign composers including Larry Austin, Warren Benson, Attila Bozay, Lukas Foss, Haflidi Hallgrimsson, Hikaru Hayashi, Jo Kondo, Nikos Mamangakis, Pall Palasson, Thorkell Sigurbjörnsson, and Atli Sveinsson.

COMPOSITIONS

ORCHESTRA

Rhapsody. 1961. Ms
Concerto for Twelve Solo Instruments and Orchestra. 1965 (Tor 1968). Kerby (Caveat) 1974
Shadows I: Nekuia. 1971 (East Lansing, Michigan, 1971). Orch. CMCentre
Spectra for Four Chamber Groups. 1968 (Tor 1969). Ricordi 1973
Spiral. 1975. Med orch. Ms

CHAMBER

Suite. 1960. Vn, pf. Ms
Quartet. 1961. Fl, ob, va, db. Ms
Kebyar. 1971. Fl, cl, trb, 2 db. Editions Salabert 1974
Shadows II: Lalitá. 1972. Fl, 3 vc, 2 perc, 2 hp. Editions Salabert 1976
Shadows III: Nira. 1974–6. Vn, fl, ob, va, cb, pf, hpd. Ms
Icicle. 1977. Solo fl. Transatlantique Editions 1977. See Discography.
Plainsong. 1977. Solo fl. Ms. See Discography.

ELECTRONIC

Music for Flute and Electronic Tape. 1963. Ms, tape
Music for Hamlet. 1964. Tape
Noesis. 1963. Tape. Folk FM 3436 (U of Toronto Electronic Music Studio)

DISCOGRAPHY

Aitken *Icicle; Plainsong* – Tremblay '... *le sifflement des vents porteurs de l'amour* ...' – Fukushima – J.W. Morthenson – T. Sigurbjörnsson. Hartenberger perc. 1978. Mel SMLP 4037
Bach *Sonatas Nos. 1, 2*. Kraus hpd. 1977. Sine Qua Non UMDD8
Complete Flute Works of Kazuo Fukushima. Y. Takahashi pf. 1977. Columbia-Denon OX-7136-ND

François and Charles Doppler: The Complete Music for Flute and Piano. Øien fl, Henningbraaten pf. 1978–9. 3-Bis LP-128, 145, 146
From the Age of Elegance: Bach – Bodinus – Telemann – Quantz. Kraus hpd. 1969. CBC SM-102
Gellman *Mythos II.* Husaruk vn, M. Goodman vn, Kudlak va, J.-L. Morin vc, Garant cond. RCI 401
Krumpholtz – Lasala – Lauber – Inghelbrecht. Goodman hp. 1971. CBC SM-156
Nielsen *Concerto* for flute and orchestra. CBC Vancouver Chamb O. 1971. CBC SM-189
Telemann – Vivaldi – Hotteterre. Kraus hpd. 1968. CBC SM-62
Weinzweig *Divertimento No. 1* – McCauley *Five Miniatures* – Pépin *Quatre Monodies* – Kenins *Concertante* – Freedman *Soliloquy* – Fleming *Almost Waltz* – Collier *Waterfront, Night Thoughts* – Glick *Petite Suite* – Zuckert *Little Spanish Dance* – Wuensch *Cameos* – Beecroft *Tre Pezzi Brevi* – Applebaum *Essay No. 1.* Ross pf, str orch conducted by the composers. 1972. Dom S-69006/(*Five Miniatures*) CRI SD-317
Yuasa – Takemitsu – Fukushima – Y. Matsudaira – Y.A. Matsudaira – Noguchi fl. 1970. CBC Sony Sonc 16019-J

BIBLIOGRAPHY
Winters, Kenneth. 'Robert Aitken,' *MSc*, 248, Jul–Aug 1969
'Canada Music Citation 1969,' *Mcan*, 24, Nov 1969
Colgrass, Ulla. 'Aitken solos with the best,' *Fugue*, Aug–Sep 1977
MacMillan, Rick. 'Aitken's artistic side still hampered by administration,' *MSc*, 301, May–Jun 1978
Schulman, Michael. 'Interview,' *Music Market Canada*, Nov–Dec 1978
BMI Canada / PRO Canada Ltd. 'Robert Aitken,' pamphlets (1976, 1979)
Contemporary Canadian Composers / Compositeurs canadiens contemporains (LL)

'À la claire fontaine.' Sung to several melodies and with different refrains, this song is known by two titles: 'À la claire fontaine' and 'En revenant des noces.' It is said to have been sung as early as 1608 by Champlain's men. The oldest version was collected by J.-B. Christophe Ballard in his book *Brunettes et petits airs tendres* (Paris 1704). James Huston, in his *Répertoire national* (Montreal 1848), says that 'the tune and the words appear to have been composed by one of the first Canadian explorers,' while Marius *Barbeau, in *Alouette* (Montreal 1946), suggests that it probably was composed by a 15th- or 16th-century juggler. The most familiar melody is that presented by Ernest *Gagnon in *Chansons populaires du Canada* (Quebec City 1865). F.-A.-H. LaRue, in *Le Foyer canadien*, vol 1 (Quebec 1863), was the first to compare the text with a version from Brittany. In his speech at the unveiling in 1885 of the statue of Sir George-Étienne Cartier (who had sung the refrain in the presence of the Prince of Wales) the prime minister, Sir John A. Macdonald, inserted the famous line from the song: 'Il y a longtemps que je t'aime, jamais je ne t'oublierai' (I've loved thee long, I'll ne'er forget thee). 'À la claire fontaine' was chosen as national song by the St Jean-Baptiste Societies in 1834 and charmed the French writer H. Leblanc de Marconnay, who included it in a comic play published in Montreal in 1836. In Quebec City in 1865 the Louisiana pianist-composer Louis-Moreau Gottschalk improvised variations on the melody during a recital which he describes in his memoirs, *Notes of a Pianist* (Philadelphia 1881). Several arrangements and harmonizations have been made of the song, among them those by *Archer, Anthony Petti, *Sénart, and *Willan. It was recorded by Joseph *Saucier (HMV XX008) and Eva *Gauthier (Victor 69273), and later included on LPs by *Les Cailloux (Cap ST 70012), Bruno *Laplante (RCI 393), and many others. A songbook entitled *À la claire fontaine* was published in Quebec City in 1950.

BIBLIOGRAPHY
D'Harcourt, Marguerite and Raoul. *Chansons folkloriques françaises au Canada* (Quebec 1956)
Laforte, Conrad. *La Chanson folklorique et les écrivains du XIXe siècle* (Montreal 1973) HP

ALARIE, Pierrette (Marguerite) (m Simoneau). Soprano, teacher, b Montreal 9 Nov 1921. The daughter of Sylva Alarie, the Montreal choirmaster and assistant conductor of the *Société canadienne d'opérette, and the soprano and actress Amanda Alarie (b Plante), she studied voice and acting with Jeanne *Maubourg and Albert *Roberval and made her debut on radio at 14, first as an actress, then as a singer of popular music. While studying voice 1938–43 with Salvator *Issaurel she met Léopold *Simoneau, and in 1946 she married him. She made her debut (1938) at the *Monument national with the *Variétés lyriques in a supporting role in *The White Horse Inn*. She sang Barbarina in *The Marriage of Figaro* (1943) under Sir Thomas Beecham who at that time was living in Montreal, Marie in *La Fille du régiment* (1945), the title role in *Mireille* (1947), Rosina in *The Barber of Seville* (1949), and Violetta in *La Traviata* (1951). On a scholarship to the Curtis Institute, Philadelphia, she studied 1943–6 with Elisabeth Schumann.

Alarie won the 'Metropolitan Opera Auditions of the Air' in 1945 and made her *Metropolitan Opera debut 8 Dec 1945 as Oscar in *Un Ballo in Maschera*. She spent three seasons (1945–7) with that company, and in 1949 with her husband she was engaged by the Paris Opera and the Opéra-Comique and sang there the title roles of such works as *Lakmé* and *Lucia di Lammermoor* and Olympia in *The Tales of Hoffmann*. As a team Simoneau and Alarie gained celebrity in both Europe and North America, appearing at a number of festivals, including that at Aix-en-Provence, where both performed a variety of roles and where Alarie in 1953 premiered two concert arias, *Chanson* and *Romance du Comte Olinos*, written for her by Werner Egk. She also appeared at the Edinburgh, Glyndebourne, Vienna, Munich, Baden-Baden, and Würzburg festivals and in 1959 sang Isotta in Richard Strauss' *Die schweigsame Frau* at Salzburg.

Alarie had an important career in North America, appearing in opera with the San Francisco, Philadelphia, New Orleans, American, and Vancouver companies, and in recital, alone, in duo with her husband, and in the Bel Canto Trio with Simoneau and the baritone Theodor Uppman. In 1961 her recording of Mozart arias, made with Simoneau, won the Grand Prix du disque of the Académie Charles-Cros, Paris. She appeared as a soloist with several orchestras and starred in CBC radio and TV productions, including those of Arthur *Benjamin's *Prima Donna* (1956), Gounod's *Mireille* (1957), Offenbach's *La Grand Duchesse de Gérolstein* (1958), Ravel's *L'Heure espagnole* (1959), Sauguet's *Les Caprices de Marianne* (1959), and Poulenc's *La Voix humaine* (North American premiere, 1959). For the *Montreal Festivals she sang Susanna in *The Marriage of Figaro* (1956) and Constanze in *The Abduction from the Seraglio* (1960), a role which she had sung with the *COC in 1957. With the Montreal *Opera Guild, she sang Blonda in *The Abduction from the Seraglio* in 1947, Juliette in *Roméo et Juliette* in 1961, and Zerlina in *Don Giovanni* in 1964. Her last stage role was *The Merry Widow* (1966) in Quebec City and Montreal with the *Théâtre lyrique de Nouvelle-France. Her farewell concert appearance (with Léopold Simoneau) was in Handel's *Messiah* with the *MSO, 24 Nov 1970. During the 1960s she taught at the *École Vincent-d'Indy. In 1972 she moved with her family to San Rafael, Cal, and began teaching and

Pierrette Alarie

staging opera. She began teaching also at the *Banff SFA in 1973.

In the course of a 32-year career, Pierrette Alarie was eulogized by the international press. Her name ranked high among the most celebrated singers from Quebec who preceded her – *Albani, *La Palme, *Edvina, and *Donalda. An accomplished musician and talented actress, she established her command of the light and the lyric soprano repertoires before undertaking more dramatic assignments such as Constanze and the arduous single role in *La Voix humaine*. On stage, as in concert, her crystalline voice, admirably produced, easily focused, and artfully handled, was a constant joy to the most exacting critics and music lovers. She and Simoneau were awarded the 1959 *Prix de musique Calixa-Lavallée, and in 1967 she was made an Officer of the *Order of Canada.

DISCOGRAPHY
Airs d'opéras français. O des Concerts Lamoureux, Dervaux cond. 1953. Philips NOO 663R
Coloratura Arias. O des Concerts Lamoureux, Dervaux cond. 1956. Decca (catalogue no. unknown)
Couperin *Trois Leçons de ténèbres.* Retchitzka sop, Recassens vc, Geoffroy-Dechaume org. 1954. Ducretet-Thomson London DTL 93077
Debussy *Songs.* A. Rogers pf. 1959. West XWN 18778
Falla *Psyché.* Jamet Quin. 1959. Ducretet 260-C-088
Fauré *Requiem.* Chorale Élisabeth Brasseur, Lamoureux O, Fournet cond. 1953. Epic LC 3044
Mozart *Exsultate, jubilate* – Vivaldi *Gloria.* Pro Musica O, Jouve cond, T. Cahn alto. 1952. Ducretet-Thomson LPG 8556
– *Recital.* O du Théâtre des Champs-Élysées, Jouve cond. 1955. Ducretet-Thomson London DTL 93089
Music at the Canadian Pavilion: Haydn – Strauss – Papineau-Couture. Newmark pf. 1967. CBC Expo 32
Papineau-Couture *Quatrains* – Pépin *Cycle-Eluard* – Beckwith *Five Lyrics of the T'ang Dynasty.* Newmark pf. (1958). RCI 148
Ravel *Songs.* A. Rogers pf. 1956. West XWN 18789
Verdi *Un Ballo in Maschera.* Metropolitan Opera, Walter cond, Alarie (Oscar). 1945. Classic (catalogue no. unknown)
Vivaldi *Gloria.* Ens Vocal de Paris, Paris Cons O, Jouve cond. 1952. Ducretet-Thomson London DTL 93080
For recordings made with Simoneau see Discography for Simoneau II.

BIBLIOGRAPHY
Bergeron, Raymonde. 'Pierrette Alarie: un exil volontaire mais passionnant dans les collines de San Francisco,' *Perspectives*, 6–24 Sep 1977
Creative Canada vol 1
See also Bibliography for Simoneau. GP

ALBANI, (Marie Louise Cécile) **Emma** (b Lajeunesse, m Gye). Soprano, teacher, b Chambly, near Montreal, 27 Sep or 1 Nov 1847, d London 3 Apr 1930. She was the eldest daughter (the sec-

Emma Albani

ond child) of Joseph *Lajeunesse and Mélina Mignault. On her father's side she belonged to the seventh Canadian generation of the Lajeunesse family; the first of that name to arrive in Canada, Étienne Charles, called Lajeunesse and born in Brittany in 1649, had married Madeleine Niel in Trois-Rivières, Que, in 1667. On Albani's mother's side her grandmother, Rachel McCutcheon, was descended from a family of Scottish origin established over many years in Plattsburgh, NY. The exact date and year of Albani's birth have not been established with certainty to this day (see below).

She began studying the piano with her mother before she was four, but in her fifth year her father took charge, teaching her piano, harp, and singing. The family lived in Plattsburgh from 1852 until 1856, the year of Madame Lajeunesse's death, after which he and his three children settled in Montreal. In September 1856 Emma performed for the first time in public as a singer and pianist at the *Mechanics' Hall in Montreal, and later she made several other appearances in the area. In 1858 she and her younger sister Cornélia became resident students at the Sacré-Coeur Convent in Sault-au-Récollet, on the outskirts of Montreal, where their father taught music. Emma's voice and her talent for music soon drew the attention of her teachers and companions. In August 1860 she sang on the occasion of the visit of the Prince of Wales, who had been invited to attend the inauguration of the Victoria Bridge. On 13 Sep 1862 she and her sister participated in a 'grande soirée musicale' at the Mechanics' Hall. Emma performed as singer, pianist, harpist, and composer. The concert was presented under the auspices of high-ranking civil and military authorities for the purpose of 'helping the Misses Lajeunesse to meet the expenses of their forthcoming trip to Paris, where they intend to study at the Conservatoire.' In *La Minerve* of 16 September an anonymous review spoke of 'a voice that seemed sent from heaven' and predicted an international career for her. Unable to raise the necessary amount to send his two daughters to Europe Joseph Lajeunesse, after their graduation in July 1865, took them to the USA, interrupting the journey to give concerts at towns along the way and staying rather longer at Albany, NY, where Emma soon was engaged as a soloist at St Joseph's Catholic Church. For three years she sang the great masses of the classical repertoire, played the organ on occasion, and even conducted the choir. In 1868, assisted by the congregation and with the encouragement of the parish priest, Mgr J.J. Conroy, she left at last for Europe.

In Paris she studied singing with Gilbert-Louis Duprez and organ and harmony with François Benoist. Eight months later she went to Milan to work with Francesco Lamperti, who taught her the Italian method and arranged for her debut in Messina in the spring of 1870 as Amina in *La Sonnambula*. At the suggestion of her elocution teacher, she then adopted Albani as her stage name, borrowing it from an old Italian family. Her success in Messina was considerable and brought her immediate engagements in Acireale, Cento, and Florence, and also in Malta, where she sang for the whole 1870–1 winter season. Besides *La Sonnambula*, her repertoire included *Lucia di Lammermoor, Rigoletto, Martha, The Barber of Seville, L'Africaine* (the role of Inez), Romani's *Il Mantello*, and *Robert le Diable*. From Malta, echoes of her success reached London, and the impresario James Henry Mapleson, through the intercession of his Maltese colleague Zimmelli, invited her to join the Italian opera troupe at Her Majesty's. Albani arrived in London in June 1871, but her carriage took her, apparently by mistake, to the rival Royal Italian Opera at Covent Garden, which was directed by Frederick Gye. Diplomatically, Gye made her aware of opportunities – including a debut the following spring in *La Sonnambula* – which would be available to her should she choose to join Covent Garden instead of Mapleson's troupe. A contract with Covent Garden signed and sealed, the singer returned to her teacher, Lamperti, at Lake Como to study some new parts, including the title role in *Mignon*, which she was scheduled to sing in Florence in the coming winter. Anxious to perfect Mignon, she went to Paris, where the publisher Heugel introduced her to the opera's composer, Ambroise Thomas, who coached her in the role. In December she enjoyed another success in Florence, at the Teatro della Pergola, where, in addition to her regular roles, she sang Adèle in Rossini's *Le Comte Ory*. Her *Mignon* was so well received that she was obliged to give 9 performances in 10 days. For her London debut, 2 Apr 1872, she sang Amina in *La Sonnambula*, yet another triumph for the young singer, who immediately became one of the stars of Covent Garden. That same season she performed in *Rigoletto* (Gilda) and sang the title roles in *Martha, Lucia di Lammermoor*, and *Linda di Chamounix*, establishing the great London house as her home base; she sang in it every season until 1896, except for four.

In the autumn of 1872 her first appearances at the English festivals were followed by successes in Paris at the Théâtre-des-Italiens in *La Sonnambula, Lucia di Lammermoor*, and *Rigoletto*. The 1873 London season brought her fresh triumphs in Auber's *Les Diamants de la couronne*, Thomas's *Hamlet*, and *The Marriage of Figaro* (as the Countess). After triumphs in Moscow and St Petersburg she returned in 1874 to Covent Garden, where for the first time she sang Elvira in *I Puritani*. A contract with the impresarios Maurice and Max Strakosch took her to the USA for a tour 1874–5. On 21 Oct 1874 she made her debut in *La Sonnambula* at the New York Academy of Music and went on to sing Lucia, Mignon, Gilda, Martha and then Elsa (*Lohengrin*), her first Wagnerian role, learned in 15 days. The Strakosch tour lasted until February 1875, whereupon she went to Venice to sing Lucia with Tamagno, the future creator of the title role of Verdi's *Otello*.

On her return to Covent Garden she sang Elsa in the English premiere of *Lohengrin* in addition to her usual roles. The following season saw the London premiere of *Tannhäuser*, with Albani as Elisabeth. After a tour of England and Ireland she took part in the festivals of Birmingham and Leeds, then sang another season in Paris at the Théâtre-des-Italiens, where this time her success as Linda, Lucia, Elvira, Gilda, and Amina was conclusive. She was received by President MacMahon and sang at the Élysée Palace. In London her 1877 season was marked by her performance of the role of Senta in *The Flying Dutchman* and by her participation in the Handel Festival at Crystal Palace before an audience of 20,000. In the spring of 1878 she sang in *La Traviata* in Paris, then gave the first performance of an opera written for her by von Flotow, *Alma l'incantatrice*. On August 6 she married Ernest Gye, who had just taken over the management of Covent Garden from his father. The marriage produced a son, Frederick Ernest, born 4 June 1879. (In 1955, after a distinguished diplomatic career, Albani's son, who lived 1941–52 in Montreal, died a bachelor in London. In 1934 he had established at the RCM the Albani prize, which has continued to be awarded annually to a young singer.)

During the ensuing years, Albani sang again in Russia (1878), as well as in Belgium and Monte Carlo. In 1882 in Berlin she was the Elsa in a performance of *Lohengrin* before Kaiser Wilhelm I, who received her in his royal box and bestowed on her the honour of Hofkammersängerin (court singer). Two years previously, her appearance at La Scala in Milan had produced one of the rare failures of her career. Though ill, she insisted on singing Lucia and Gilda before hostile audiences. Her failure to complete a performance of *Lucia di Lammermoor* created a resounding scandal. In London in 1881 she added Rubinstein's *The Demon* to her repertoire, singing under the composer's direction. The following year she sang in Boito's *Mefistofele* and Gounod's *La Rédemption* at the Birmingham festival, with Gounod himself conducting. Gounod later wrote *Mors et Vita* for her, and she premiered it in 1885. In January 1883 she revisited New York to sing with the Symphony Society of Walter Damrosch. She went to Albany and then embarked on a long tour of the USA, sharing star billing with Adelina Patti in a troupe provided by Mapleson. She made her debut in Chicago in *I Puritani*, then visited Washington, Baltimore, New York, Toronto, and Brooklyn. Toronto, where she sang Lucia at the Grand Opera House, was the first Canadian city she had visited after an absence of almost 20 years.

At the end of March 1883 she returned at long last to Montreal, to give three concerts at *Queen's Hall. A delirious public gave her a tumultuous welcome. Newspapers estimated the number of admirers who turned out to greet her on her arrival at 10,000. She was the guest of honour at a civic reception, during which the poet Louis-Honoré Fréchette recited a long poem he had composed in her honour.

In London she then presented another season at Covent Garden and sang in festivals. In 1884 she sang the title role in Reyer's *Sigurd*, and Juliette in Gounod's *Roméo et Juliette*. She spent the summer in Scotland, near Balmoral, where Queen Victoria, who had become her friend and confidante, visited her on several occasions. In the autumn she made another tour of Holland and Belgium. In London she sang Dvořák's cantata *The Spectre's Bride*. The Czech composer was the conductor the following year when Albani performed the title role of his oratorio *Saint Ludmilla*. She also sang in Arthur Sullivan's *The Golden Legend* in London and Berlin under the composer's direction.

In 1886 Franz Liszt came to London, and in his presence Albani sang the leading role in his oratorio *The Legend of Saint Elisabeth*, earning the composer's congratulations. Then followed a new season in Berlin (*Lohengrin* and *The Flying Dutchman*) and tours of Belgium, Holland, Scotland, and Scandinavia. The Canadian diva was welcomed enthusiastically everywhere and received several honours from the royalty of the countries she visited. She returned to Canada early in 1889, performing in Montreal, Quebec, Toronto, Hamilton, and London, then went to the USA. In the fall, after a brief sojourn in London, she returned again to sing in the USA, Canada, and Mexico. In May 1890 she made her Montreal operatic debut in *La Traviata* and *Lucia di Lammermoor* at the *Academy of Music. On 10 May 1890, at the Victoria Rink at a benefit concert for the Notre-Dame hospital, 6000 people acclaimed her along with the pianist-composer Salomon *Mazurette, the violinist Alfred *De Sève, and the *Bande de la Cité conducted by Ernest *Lavigne. In March 1890 she sang Desdemona in Verdi's *Otello* at the *Metropolitan Opera as a member of the troupe of Abbey and Grau. This was her first appearance in that theatre. On 23 Dec 1891 she made her official debut as a member of the Metropolitan troupe. After *Rigoletto* she sang in several other operas during the 1891–2 season, including *Faust*, *Les Huguenots*, *Don Giovanni* (the role of Elvira), *Otello*, *Lohengrin*, *Die Meistersinger*, and finally *The Flying Dutchman*. In January 1892 she visited Montreal with her company to perform in *Les Huguenots* and *Lohengrin* at the Academy of Music.

She spent 1893 and 1894 giving concerts in Europe with such illustrious musical colleagues as Sarasate and Paderewski and appeared in Vienna with an orchestra under Hans Richter. In 1895 she inaugurated the Covent Garden season, singing Desdemona opposite Tamagno and Maurel, the creators of the roles of Otello and Iago. She sang also in the premiere of *Harold*, an opera by Frederick Cowen. Early in 1896 she returned to Canada for a short tour in which the violinist Frantz *Jehin-Prume also participated. Her last season at Covent Garden was marked by an unprecedented triumph in four performances of *Tristan und Isolde* with the de Reszke brothers, Jean and Édouard. Describing the duo from Act II, Herman Klein wrote in the *Sunday Times*: 'Never before at Covent Garden has the wondrous beauty of this scène d'amour been so totally realized. To hear the difficult music sung perfectly in tune was alone a treat that was well-nigh a revelation' (cited by Rosenthal in *Two Centuries of Opera at Covent Garden*). On 23 July, for the first and only time in her career, she sang Donna Anna in *Don Giovanni*. The next day she sang Valentine in *Les Huguenots*. These performances marked her farewell to the stage where she had made her debut 24 years earlier. In November 1896 she arrived in Canada with assisting artists to undertake a transcontinental tour which took her from Halifax to Vancouver. Everywhere she went, Canadians crowned her their 'queen of song.' She then undertook long tours in Australia and New Zealand (1898, 1907), South Africa (1898, 1899, and 1904), and Ceylon and India (1907). In England she continued her career as a performer of oratorios and gave recitals. In 1901 she had the signal honour of being asked to sing at the private family funeral service for Queen Victoria in the chapel at Windsor Castle. She made her farewell tour of Canada in 1906 with a company which included Éva *Gauthier.

On 14 Oct 1911, at the Royal Albert Hall, she gave her last public recital before a deeply moved audience. Several of her colleagues were on stage, including Adelina Patti and Nellie Melba. The same year she published her memoirs, *Forty Years of Song*, and retired to her property on Tregunter Road in Kensington. Subsequent reverses of fortune suffered by Albani and her husband compelled her to resort to teaching, and she even sang for a time in music-halls. In 1920 the British government granted her an annual pension of £100. When they were approached for assistance, the governments of both Canada and Quebec declined. On the death of her husband in 1925, Emma Albani's financial situation was most insecure. At Melba's initiative a grand benefit concert was arranged at Covent Garden on 25 May, in which Melba, Elgar, and the Canadian soprano Sarah *Fischer took part, among others. In Montreal a similar event (28 May at the *St-Denis Theatre) along with a public subscription provided the artist, by then in dire straits, with a little over $4000, which enabled her to end her days in relative comfort. She died peacefully at her home on 3 Apr 1930. The funeral was held two days later at the Servite Church on Fulham Road. Her remains were taken to the neighbouring cemetery of Brompton, where they were placed next to those of her husband.

In 1897 the Royal Philharmonic Society awarded her its gold medal, also known as the Beethoven Medal, previously bestowed on such distinguished artists as Gounod, Joachim, von Bülow, Patti, and Brahms (Paderewski received the award the same year as Albani). In 1925 George V conferred on her the title of Dame Commander of the British Empire (DBE). In 1939 the Canadian Commission for landmarks and historic monuments unveiled a commemorative plaque in Chambly on the site of her birthplace on rue Martel. In 1977 the plaque was replaced by a stele surmounted by an inscription outlining her career. The parish hall of the church of Chambly bears the name Albani. In Montreal her name was given to a street in the west of the city during the 1930s, but the name disappeared when the street became the extension of another avenue. In 1969 the name Albani was given to a new artery in the northeast part of the city. In Quebec City the Musée du Québec possesses a portrait of Emma Albani in the costume of Lucia di Lammermoor. It was painted in 1877 in Paris by the US artist Will Hicock Low and was unveiled the same year at the Salon du printemps. The museum also possesses a marble bust, the work of Prince Victor Hohenlohe of Langenburg.

In her lifetime and even to this day expressions of admiration concerning the singer have been numerous and varied. Guillaume *Couture, Ernest *Gagnon, Alexis *Contant, and Salomon Mazurette dedicated songs to her, and the Quebec composer Georges McNeill wrote an *Albani Galop* for concert band or piano (Lavigne 1875) and dedicated to her *Fleurs du printemps*, a waltz played by the *Septuor Haydn and transcribed for piano by J.A. Defoy (Lavigne 1875). An *Albani Caprice Polka* for violin and piano by Max Bachmann was published in 1897. In 1883 periodicals reported an Albani hat for ladies and published a recipe for an Albani cake. In 1972 Jean Patenaude founded, in Chambly, Les Éditions Albani, Inc, devoted chiefly to pedagogical works, and in 1975 three young Quebec singers founded the Trio Albani. In 1980 a postage stamp bearing her likeness was released to commemorate the 50th anniversary of her death.

In the course of a career spanning four decades Emma Albani became the first Canadian-born artist to achieve international fame. Her exceptionally beautiful voice, the solid musical and vocal training she acquired in her youth and later developed in conjunction with the best teachers, her mastery of French, English, Italian, and German, and her quickness in assimilating a new score all contributed to her strong appeal to conductors and composers and made her one of the most sought-after singers of her time.

Countless press articles and other testimonials paid tribute to her talent. While he was in London in 1886, the Viennese critic Eduard Hanslick wrote, 'By far the best singer at Covent Garden this season, if not the only important one, (in the absence of Patti, who was not engaged), is Madame Albani' (*Music Criticisms 1846–99*, translated and revised by Henry Pleasants, Harmondsworth, England, 1963). There are numerous written testimonies from famous musicians including Liszt ('admiration and thanks'), Charles Gounod ('my dear and great interpreter'), Hans von Bülow ('the most brilliant singing star of our era'), Hans Richter ('the master singer'), etc. On the other hand, George Bernard Shaw found her art too calculated and often charged her with a lack of spontaneity. With the years Emma Albani's soprano changed from a coloratura to a 'spinto' and even to a dramatic towards the end of her career, and this accounts for her exceptionally diversified repertoire: in 40 operas, 43 different roles ranging from Amina to Isolde. Her reputation as a performer of oratorios also was exceptional. To her musical talents were added personality, charm, and presence which did not fail to impress most critics.

The precise year of Albani's birth is still disputed; by 1980 no corroborating documents had been found. The year 1847, adopted by one of her biographers, Hélène Charbonneau, is accepted generally. In her memoirs the singer states that she was born 1 Nov 1852. The stone marking her grave claims 1 Nov 1850. Her first biographer, Napoléon *Legendre, suggests that she probably was born in 1848 and baptized later, in Plattsburgh, NY. Other sources have suggested 27 Sep 1847 and the years 1849 and 1851.

WRITINGS

Forty Years of Songs (London, Toronto 1911; New York 1977) transl and annotated by Gilles Potvin as *Mémoires d'Emma Albani* (Montreal 1972)

DISCOGRAPHY

As early as 1888 or 1889 the voice of Emma Albani is said to have been recorded on a rudimentary apparatus belonging to Thomas Edison at a Handel festival at the Crystal Palace in London. If so, no trace of the experiment has been found. Between 1904 and 1907 Albani recorded at least nine titles for the Gramophone and Typewriter Company and Pathé. Some of the titles were reissued in the USA about 1940 (IRCC label) and again in 1950 (HRS label). In Canada in 1967 *Rococo reissued eight titles on one side of an LP (5255): 'Angels Ever Bright and Fair' (*Theodora*), 'Sweet Bird' with flute obbligato (*Il Penseroso*) and 'Ombra mai fù' (*Serse*) by Handel; 'Souvenirs du jeune âge' (*Le Pré aux clercs*) by Hérold; 'L'Été' by Chaminade; 'Home, Sweet Home' by Bishop; 'Robin Adair'; and the Bach-Gounod 'Ave Maria' with violin obbligato. It is known that she also recorded the song 'Ma Normandie' by Bérat.

BIBLIOGRAPHY

David, L.O. 'D[emois]elle. Emma Lajeunesse,' *Opinion publique*, vol 1, 23 Apr 1870
Legendre, Napoléon. *Albani, Emma Lajeunesse* (Quebec 1874)
The Mapleson Memoirs (London 1888, 1966)
Maurault, Olivier. 'Albani,' *La Musique*, vol 1, Jun, Jul, Aug, Sep 1919
Klein, Herman. 'Emma Albani: Canada's famous songstress,' *Great Women Singers of My Time* (London 1931)
Thompson, Oscar. 'Emma Albani,' *The American Singer* (New York 1937)
Charbonneau, Hélène. *L'Albani, sa carrière artistique et triomphale* (Montreal 1938)
Gour, Romain. 'Albani (Emma Lajeunesse), queen of song,' *Who?*, vol 1, Mar 1949
Clément, Marie-Blanche. 'Albani,' *BRH*, vol 65, Oct, Nov, Dec 1949
Campbell, Marjorie Wilkins. 'When Albani was queen of song,' *Maclean's*, 15 Jun 1953
Rosenthal, Harold. *Two Centuries of Opera at Covent Garden* (London 1958)

Ridley, N.A. *Record Collector*, issue devoted to Albani, vol 12, Feb–Mar 1959
McPherson, Jim. 'In the beginning,' Toronto *Telegram*, 4 Oct 1969
Potvin, Gilles. 'Une Canadienne à Moscou en 1873,' *Bulletin* of the Centre de recherche en civilisation canadien-français, U of Ottawa, 19, Dec 1979
– 'La carrière canadienne d'Emma Albani à l'opéra,' *Aria*, vol 3, Spring 1980
Catalogue of Canadian Composers GP

ALBARDA, Jan (Horatius). Harpsichord builder and designer, b The Hague 7 Jun 1910, naturalized Canadian 1973. An architect 1937–51 in the Netherlands and 1951–74 in Canada, Albarda in 1962 became the second harpsichord builder to begin production in Canada. Working alone in Toronto and, after 1974, in Elora, Ont, he had made 65 instruments by 1977, including one- and two-manual harpsichords, spinets, virginals, pedal harpsichords, and clavichords for players throughout North America. Though he has restored 18th- and 19th-century instruments, he has not built replicas, preferring to concentrate on new design, development, and improvement. In 1977 he completed the first two-manual harpsichord with sympathetic (non-playing) choirs of strings in the second overtone. He named the new instrument 'cembalo marina,' following the precedent of the tromba marina and the violetta marina (viola d'amore), which also had sympathetic strings. Albarda is the author of a layman's book about harpsichords, *Wood, Wire and Quill* (Toronto 1968; Willowdale, Ont, 1976).

See also Harpsichord building.

Alberta College Music Centre. The music department of Alberta College, founded in 1903 in Edmonton by the Methodist Church under the principalship of the Rev J.H. Riddell. The oldest non-denominational private school in the province, the college offered some music studies from the outset. Vernon *Barford was the first music teacher engaged. Teachers – eight by 1907 – were not salaried, however, but rented studios from the college and taught there on commission. By 1913, full courses in instruments and voice were being offered. There was steady growth over the years, but in 1973 the staff was increased in a major expansion, the department was renamed the Alberta College Music Centre, and Robert Cook was installed as the first dean. The student enrolment reached over 1000 in 1977, and a teaching faculty of over 50, including Perry *Bauman, Audrey *Farnell, Thelma Johannes *O'Neill, Robert *Pounder, and Ranald *Shean, offered instruction in orchestral and keyboard instruments, guitar, voice, theory, and history, preparatory to examinations by either the *WBM or the *RCMT. There also were *Kodály and *Orff classes for children and for adults, and a high-school students' program which, in correlation with other college programs, led to full matriculation. Master classes and workshops, introduced in the 1970s and funded partly by *Alberta Culture, have been given by Böszörmenyi-Nagy in 1973, Lucien *Needham in 1974, György Sebok in 1976 and 1979, Paul Rolland in 1977, *Camerata in 1978 and 1979, and Maureen *Forrester in 1979. Malcolm Smith succeeded Cook as dean in 1975. In 1980 the centre still did not grant diplomas, and the regular teaching staff continued to pay studio rent and work on commission, but under the successive deans facilities and administration had been improved, the centre's prestige increased, and several bursaries established by Edmonton citizens. (TJO)

Alberta Composers' Association / Association des Compositeurs de l'Alberta (ACA). Founded at Edmonton in September 1977 upon the advice of an ad hoc committee comprising the composers Violet *Archer, Dean Blair, David Duke, Ronald Hannah, and Richard *Johnston, with the assistance of John *Weinzweig. Johnston was the founding president and continued in that position in 1980. The association was formed to further the interests and promote the activities of Alberta composers, with membership open to both senior and student Alberta composers, whether resident in or living outside the province. Categories of membership were established also for interested non-composers (associate) and for conferring distinction (honorary). In 1977 John Weinzweig was named the first honorary member.

The first objectives of the ACA were to assist in the establishment of a prairie regional branch of the *CMCentre and to found an annual Alberta Composers' Festival. Both were achieved quickly. The first festival, conceived as a showcase for young and established Alberta composers and performers, was held at Edmonton in April 1979; the second, honouring the opening of the CMCentre (Prairie Region) at the *U of Calgary, took place in February 1980. Other ACA activities have included the initiation of a commissioning program for Alberta composers (administered by the Alberta Fund for the CMCentre); the co-sponsorship with the Alberta Choral Directors' Assn of a choral composition competition; and, in 1980, an Alberta Song Competition, co-sponsored by *Alberta Culture, in honour of the province's 75th anniversary. In 1980 the ACA also presented its first Janvier Awards (bronze medals designed by the Alberta artist Alex Janvier) for outstanding contributions to musical life in Alberta. The recipients were Horst A. Schmid and Senator Donald Cameron.

In February 1978 the association began issuing the *ACA Newsletter*, a quarterly edited by Robert Rosen and Brian Baillie at the U of Calgary. The periodical was renamed *Composers West* later that year.

BIBLIOGRAPHY

Johnston, Richard. 'Alberta Composers' Association formed,' *Mcan*, 35, Apr 1978
Dawson, Eric. 'Alberta's composers sell the avant-garde to audiences content with tradition,' *PfAC*, Fall 1979

(RJ)

Alberta Culture. Department established in 1975 by the government of the province of Alberta. Prior to that date the development of the arts in the province had been the responsibility of the Alberta Cultural Development Branch, established in 1946, and its successor, 1971–5, the Cultural Development Branch of the Dept of Culture, Youth and Recreation, which in October 1971 helped establish the Alberta Music Conference. The conference was designed to act as a liaison between the music community and the provincial government, advising the latter in matters of legislation and programs relating to music. It also published six issues of an informative quarterly bulletin, *Music in Alberta*, edited by Gerald Moran. Presidents of the conference, which became inactive in 1974 and dissolved in 1978, were Richard *Johnston and Robert Cook.

Horst Schmid, Alberta minister of culture 1971–9, was succeeded by Mary LeMessurier.

The ensuing description, though given in the present tense, applies to the state of the department in 1979. The activities of Alberta Culture are funded entirely by the provincial government. Through its Cultural Development Division the department provides groups and individuals with opportunities and resources. Regional representatives in Calgary, Edmonton, Grande Prairie, Medicine Hat, St Paul and Wetaskiwin, as well as a Native Programs Co-ordinator, meet with arts and community organizations, including municipal councils, recreational boards, and schools, to provide information and assistance to local cultural programs. The division's Performing Arts Branch (whose director in 1979 was Robert M. Cook) contributes to dance, drama, and music in the province through a number of programs. This branch provides educational consultants to local groups and sponsors clinics, workshops, conferences, and special summer courses such as those offered at the Provincial Music School at Camrose. It publishes an annual catalogue of performing artists in Alberta, maintains an inventory of artists and sponsoring organizations, provides assistance in the co-ordination of tours, and runs an artists-in-the-community program which often includes clinics and concerts for schools. Financial assistance is offered in the form of operational grants to provincial festival associations and to amateur and professional performing groups; 'Cultural Assistance' awards to individuals for further study and improvement of skills; grants to provincial representative organizations, to national organizations which benefit Alberta artists (such as the *ACO, the Canadian Assn of Youth Orchestras, the *CMCentre, the *CMCouncil, and the *NYO) and to national projects such as *EMC*; touring and travel grants to groups and individuals and to communities wishing to sponsor series of performances; subsidies to educational institutions; and grants to artists wishing to participate in national and international competitions, conferences, and festivals. Special project grants and loans also are available. In addition, through its financial assistance to the *Alberta Composers' Assn (established in 1977 with Richard Johnston as president), the department is involved indirectly in the commissioning of works by Alberta composers.

Annually, in recognition of outstanding contributions, Alberta Culture bestows Alberta Achievement Awards. Among those whose activities in the field of music have been so honoured are the Alberta All-Girls Band, the Anne *Campbell Singers, Violet *Archer, Hugh *Bancroft, Tommy *Banks, James *Campbell, Dick Damron, the Edmonton Youth Orchestra, Gaby *Haas, John *Hendrickson, Leonard *Leacock, Clarence 'Big' Miller, *One Third Ninth, Leona Paterson, Nelly Peruch, Robert *Pounder, Thomas *Rolston, Ranald *Shean, Hank Smith, R. Harlan Smith, Olaf *Sveen, Huguette *Tourangeau, and Bernard *Turgeon. In 1977, in conjunction with the Canada Council Touring Office, the department sponsored the first annual 'Alberta Showcase,' a conference of workshops and performances attended by artists, managers, and sponsors.

Alberta Culture publications include annual reports, the first of which appeared in 1976, and *Performing Arts Newsletter*, which began in September 1975 and appears several times a year.

In addition to the support provided by existing Alberta Culture programs, assistance to the arts is available through the Alberta Foundation for the Performing Arts. Established by the provincial government in 1978, with Tommy Banks as chairman, the AFPA is funded by the Western Canada Lottery (Alberta Division). It offers aid to those projects which do not fall into categories set by Alberta Culture and is interested particularly in programs which will increase awareness of the performing arts, conduct research into the performing arts and arts administration, provide opportunities for performers to gain national and/or international recognition, and encourage co-ordinated and/or co-operative administrative support of performing arts activities. It assisted in the first annual Alberta Composers' Festival, held in Edmonton in 1979. Applications are judged by the foundation's board of directors.

Alberta Jubilee Auditoriums, Northern (Edmonton) and Southern (Calgary). Built between 1955 and 1957 as a memorial to Alberta's pioneers. These identical auditoriums were designed by the Alberta Dept of Public Works in consultation with Canadian and foreign acoustical and architectural specialists and were inaugurated 28 Apr 1957 by the Hon E.C. Manning, then premier of the province. In each, the fan-shaped main hall, with a seating capacity of 2731, includes a large (36 m by 13.8 m) stage and a 36-m fly loft. The orchestra pit holds 60 musicians and when fully raised increases the size of the stage by 81 square m. The auditorium proper is surrounded by a chamber auditorium (seating capacity 500), a banquet facility, an assembly hall, a club room, and offices. There is also a practice stage (identical in size to the main stage) with an audience capacity of 100. Among the installations are fully equipped workshops, an integrated closed-circuit TV system, and a computerized stage lighting system. The buildings have been rated high among their kind, with acoustics that have been compared with those of the Royal Festival Hall and Kleinhans Music Hall (Buffalo, NY). The combined cost of the buildings was $12 million, and their operation was subsidized in the 1970s by grants amounting to $250,000 a year from municipal and provincial governments. The auditoriums are the homes of the *Edmonton SO and the *Calgary Philharmonic, the *Edmonton Opera and the *Southern Alberta Opera, and the Edmonton Choral Society and the Calgary Philharmonic Chorus. Among Canadian and foreign artists and ensembles who have performed in these halls are Victor Borge, Liona *Boyd, Van Cliburn, Ferrante and Teicher, Ella Fitzgerald, John *Hendrickson, Byron Janis, Gordon *Lightfoot, Anne *Murray, the *NACO, the National Ballet of Canada, Leontyne Price, the Royal Winnipeg Ballet, the *TS, and Paul Williams.

Alberta Jubilee Auditorium, Edmonton

BIBLIOGRAPHY
George, Graham. 'Three Canadian concert-halls,' *CMJ*, Winter 1960 (RDM)

Alberta Music Educators' Association (AMEA). Founded in Edmonton in April 1957 at the instigation of Leslie *Bell and Alan S. Rumbelow, the latter at that time supervisor of music for Edmonton public schools. At first limited to school music teachers, in 1963 membership was broadened to include private teachers and those in the music trade. In 1962, to keep teachers abreast of new teaching materials and methods, the association began to sponsor workshop demonstrations on series of music books (eg, W.J. Gage's *Music for Living* and Ginn's *Our Singing World*). In 1963 it affiliated with the *CMEA. The AMEA was incorporated in August 1964. It held annual conferences which included joint meetings in 1964 and 1968 with the *ARMTA, in 1965 with the CMEA, and also with the Fine Arts Council of the Alberta Teachers' Assn. It published (ca 1962–4) a newsletter edited by Frank *Churchley, and (1965–8) seven issues of the magazine *Alberta Music Educator* edited by Malcolm Brown and later by Elizabeth Filipkowski. In May 1969 the AMEA was dissolved; members who were school teachers had the option of joining the Alberta Teachers' Assn Fine Arts Council. AMEA presidents included A.S. Rumbelow 1957–8 and 1959–60, Rev Leo Green 1958–9 and 1960–1, Cyril *Mossop 1961–2, Frank Churchley 1962–3, Elizabeth Filipkowski 1963–4, Ronald Stephens 1964–5, Isabella Kennedy 1965–6, Paul Bourret 1966–8, and Marilyn Perkins 1968–9. (EFks)

Alberta Music Festival Association. Umbrella organization formed ca 1964 to represent and coordinate the competition festivals of the province of Alberta. It was established through the initiative of a committee comprising Florence Musselwhite of Calgary, Alan Walker of Drumheller, Ken Crockett and Cora Molstad of Edmonton, and Seyward Smith of Lethbridge. Its initial funding was provided by the government of Alberta, which, through its Cultural Development Branch, continued to assist both the competition festivals in individual cities and towns and the provincial association.

The first competition festival in Canada and, it is said, in North America, was held in Edmonton in 1908. Acting in response to the wish of the governor-general, Earl Grey, to see provincial festivals established in Canada, Howard Stutchbury, Vernon *Barford, and Jackson Hanby of Edmonton drew up a syllabus and organized the Alberta Music Festival. That first festival, 5 May 1908, drew 30 entries, and a Mr Matthews and Rhys Thomas of Winnipeg were adjudicators. The festival was held annually in Edmonton until 1917, with participants converging there from all parts of the province. In 1918 Calgary, Lethbridge, and Edmonton agreed to follow a common syllabus, to rotate the provincial festival year about among the three cities, and also to hold local festivals in the two intervening years. Lethbridge established its local festival in 1923 (after 1952 the Lethbridge Kiwanis Music Festival), and Calgary its local festival in 1931 (after 1953 this was called the Calgary Kiwanis Music Festival). The Alberta Music Festival joined the competition festivals of the other western provinces in the *FCMF in 1926.

More local associations were formed throughout Alberta over the years, but the provincial association established ca 1964 was the first formal federation of these groups. By 1980 it had 22 member festivals, each represented on the board of directors. In May of 1967 the association organized the first of what were to be annual provincial finals, held alternately in Edmonton and Calgary, in which winners of classes in the member festivals were brought together to compete for provincial standings, scholarships, and trophies. The provincial winners in turn competed for the first time at a national level in 1972 when the FCMF inaugurated its *National Competitive Festival held each fall in Toronto at the *CNE.

The Alberta Music Festival Assn has published annually a syllabus for use by its member festivals. The association's scholarship fund was initiated by a contribution from the Nickle Foundation of Calgary. The papers of the original Alberta Music Festival were deposited at the Edmonton City Archives.

BIBLIOGRAPHY
Wodell, F.W. 'The Alberta musical competition festival at Edmonton,' *Musician*, no. 16, 1911
Moore, Louise A. deW. 'Progressive Alberta,' *CanJM*, Jul–Aug 1915
Coutts, George. 'Music festivals of western Canada,' *CRMA*, Oct 1943 (FM)

Alberta Registered Music Teachers' Association (ARMTA). Founded in Edmonton 15 Dec 1932 by Clara King, Florence Teets, and other teachers. Its immediate goals were to promote and support instruction by qualified music teachers within the province, to organize musical events, and to entertain visiting performers and adjudicators. It was incorporated in 1934 as the Alberta Music Teachers' Assn, its name until 1947 when 'Registered' was added. In 1935, along with fellow associations from British Columbia, Saskatchewan, and Manitoba, it helped found the Federation of Music Teachers' Associations (later the *CFMTA). In 1978 the ARMTA had 365 members, chapters in Calgary, Edmonton, Lethbridge, Medicine Hat, and Red Deer, and another chapter catering to members-at-large. It participates in the CFMTA's Young Artists Series and Creative Music Writing Competition and in 1977 it established its own Provincial Scholarship Competition. The ARMTA holds annual conventions and publishes the quarterly *ARMTA Newsletter*. Presidents were Florence Teets 1932–3, Ella Walker 1933–6, Eliza A. Hamilton 1936–8, 1939–40, 1942–3, Phyllis Chapman Clarke 1938–9, Brenna Reed 1940–1, Helen K. Robinson 1941–2, 1947–8, 1956–7, Aileen Jones 1943–4, 1955–6, Leonard H. Nichols 1944–5, G. Alex Kevan 1945–6, Velva Pickett Brough 1946–7, Mollie Pierce Hamilton 1948–9, Elsie Wright 1950–1, Thelma Osborne 1952–3, J.S. Peter *Bach 1953–4, Arthur Newcombe 1954–5, Robert *Pounder 1957–9, Joyce Hackett 1959–61, A.K. *Putland 1961–3, Florence Gillespie 1963–5, Anne *Campbell 1965–7, Thelma *O'Neill 1967–9, Betty Ferguson 1969–71, Anna Bray 1971–5, Eileen Daly 1975–6, Betty-Lou Beatty 1975–7, and Heddy Klaus 1977–9.

BIBLIOGRAPHY
Ford, Phyllis Chapman. 'History of the Alberta Registered Music Teachers' Association,' *CFMTA News Bulletin*, vol 16, April 1962
Kennedy, Jessie. 'The Alberta Registered Music Teachers' Association,' *Music in Alberta*, May–Jun 1972 (EFks)

ALBION, Edouard. See Meek, Harold.

ALDOUS, J.E.P. (John Edmund Paul). Organist, teacher, conductor, composer, b Sheffield, England, 8 Dec 1853, d Hamilton, Ont, 23 Jan 1934; BA (Trinity, Cambridge) 1876. He was organist at the chapel of the British Embassy in Paris before moving in 1877 to Hamilton, Ont, as organist-choirmaster of Central Presbyterian Church. He subsequently held posts in St Thomas, Ont, and at St Mark's and St Thomas' churches in Hamilton, returning to Central Presbyterian in 1884. In 1885 he founded and became the conductor of the Hamilton Orchestral Club, one of the city's earliest orchestras, and in 1890 he succeeded Clarence *Lucas as conductor of the Hamilton Philharmonic Society. He was head of music 1882–5 at Brantford Ladies' College and 1885–8 at the Woodstock Baptist College. He founded, and directed 1889–1908, the Hamilton School of Music and then became a director of the Hamilton Cons (*RHCM).

He was an examiner for the *U of Toronto and president (1894) of the *Canadian Society of Musicians. His pupils included Ada Twohy *Kent, Mona *Bates, and H.J. Allen. He composed four operettas: *Ptarmigan* or *A Canadian Carnival* (1895; excerpts were published by *Anglo-Canadian and the libretto was included in *Canada's Lost Plays*, vol 1, Toronto 1978), *A Golden Catch*, *Nancy* or *All for Love*, and *The Poster Girl* (ca 1902). He also wrote many shorter pieces for piano, organ, choir, and voice, several published by *Suckling, Grossman, *Ashdown, Vincent, and *Whaley Royce. Two unpublished preludes and fugues are preserved at the Hamilton Public Library and the *NL of C respectively. Aldous contribited articles to the *Organist's Quarterly Journal* and *The Violin*.

BIBLIOGRAPHY

'J.E.P. Aldous,' *MJ*, vol 2, 15 Jun 1888 (FAH)

Aleatoric music. Music in which either composition or method of performance is determined by elements of chance or unpredictability. Terms such as chance music, indeterminate music, or aleatoric music are applied to many works written after World War II, the pioneers being Cage, Lutoslawski, Stockhausen, and Xenakis, each of whom has approached the technique in his own way. Stochastic music – a term coined by Xenakis to describe music determined by the mathematical laws of chance such as the theory of probability or the games theory – is, in a sense, an outgrowth of total serialization. Although serialization is a predetermining procedure for each musical parameter (dynamics, rhythm, articulation, etc), the combination of all parameters is often subject to random ordering. Boulez' *Structures* is an attempt at total serialization. Serge *Garant modified this idea in *Asymétries I and II* by leaving some of the choices within each parameter to his intuition to give apparent, if not actual, randomness. This was a frequent compositional procedure both internationally and in Canada in the late 1950s and early 1960s in works by *Fodi, *Hodkinson, *Huse, *Joachim, *Somers, and others. Many composers have approached electronic composition by applying some indeterminate techniques with, for example, the use of voltage-controlled equipment. By setting up a simple program to allow the equipment to run almost automatically (the Moog, Arp, and Putney synthesizers, etc), the composer generates musical material determined by random combinations of various electronic units and is able to interrupt the program at will to change any result.

More often, however, aleatoric music refers to the method of performance rather than to compositional procedure. In Cage's *Music of Changes* or Stockhausen's *Zyklus* for percussion the musical components are in some way predetermined, leaving to the performer the choice of which components to play or in what order. A major exponent of 'Cagean' chance music in Canada is Udo *Kasemets, who uses performance charts or other controlled-improvisation means. In *Trigon*, he calls for 1, 3, 9, or 27 participants playing in various media, musical and non-musical, up to 81 in number, each performance being a new realization which he has notated precisely. The same is true of *Cascando*, which has spawned the precisely notated pieces *Stereosonic Vocophony*, *Synersonic Octet*, and *Synersonophony: Vocosonic Poem: Sonophonic Interlude: Stereosonovocophony*. In his desire for greater indeterminacy, Kasemets uses as material 'any dictionary, any subject in any language' for his work *Wordmusic / Interface*. Other composers who have written in this genre are Claude *Vivier, Don *Druick, and Alex *Pauk.

The majority of composers, however, have allowed for some choices in an otherwise precisely notated score. R. Murray *Schafer, in such works as *Threnody*, for chorus, narrators, orchestra, and electronic tape, and *Divan i Shams i Tabriz*, for orchestra and electronic tape, uses graphic notation, a visual representation of the sound desired, without predetermining either the pitch or the exact duration. Often electronic tape is used in conjunction with this type of instrumental or choral music, in which case the overall or macro-time is predetermined by the material on tape but with some freedom in the micro-time of events and the pitch. In a sense, the indeterminate compositional procedure applied to the creation of the tape is carried over to the instrumental writing, sometimes including some choices to be made by the performers or conductor. Composers who have used this technique extensively with tape include *Anhalt, *Aitken, *Ford, *Tremblay, and *Truax. Composers who generally have excluded tape but otherwise call for the same techniques include *Beckwith, *Beecroft, *Buczynski, *Cherney, Fodi, Garant, *Hawkins, Huse, and Joachim. Later works of *Weinzweig (*Around the Stage* and after) and *Pentland (*Trio con Alea* and after) show a trend toward the use of these procedures. (CF)

Algoma Fall Festival. Held at Sault Ste Marie, Ont, for three weeks each fall so that between performances visitors may enjoy the rich colours of the changing leaves for which northern Ontario is famous. The festival began in 1973, organized by the Algoma Arts Assn, a citizens' group formed in February of the previous year. It has been supported by funds from private donors, corporations, the *OAC, the *Canada Council, and the city of Sault Ste Marie. Music, dance, theatre, films, workshops, and school concerts have been regular features. Performances are held at local churches and schools and at the Civic Centre, the James Norris Centre, and the White Pines Auditorium. Among those who appeared at the first festival were Elyakim *Taussig, Jean *Bonhomme, Maria *Pellegrini, Dinah *Christie and Tom Kneebone, the *Festival Singers, and the Interfaith Choir of Sault Ste Marie. Another regular feature of the festival is the Algoma Festival Choir, founded by Nicholas *Goldschmidt in 1974. Established as a permanent choir in 1975, it also performs throughout the year, independent of the festival. *Canadian Brass, Maureen *Forrester, the *Hamilton Philharmonic, Pauline *Julien, Moe *Koffman, Anton *Kuerti, Maple Sugar, *Nexus, *Nimmons 'N' Nine Plus Six, the *Orford Quartet, Arthur *Ozolins, Oscar *Peterson, *Quartet Canada, and Jon *Vickers are among those who have performed at the festival. In 1976 it presented Britten's *Noye's Fludde*, with Ingemar *Korjus and Barbara Ianni, and in 1977 it offered two Menotti operas, *The Telephone*, with Eleanor *Calbes and Mark Pedrotti, and *The Old Maid and the Thief*, with Barbara Ianni, Patricia Horton McCord, Gary *Relyea, and Kathy Terrell. It has premiered several commissioned works, including Milton *Barnes' *Serenade* and Spanish-born Arsenio Giron's *Idols* in 1974, Larry *Crosley's *Variations on a Canadian Folksong* in 1975, Louis *Applebaum's *Algoma Central* in 1976, and John *Arpin's *Summer Suite* in 1977. Presidents of the festival have included Harriet Black 1973–5 and Judith Robertson 1976–7, succeeded by Robert G. Martin. Artistic directors have been Thomas Hahn 1973–4 and Nicholas Goldschmidt, who became associated with the festival at its inception, serving as consultant 1973–6 and assuming the position of artistic director in 1977. (NM)

ALLAIRE, (Joseph Georges-Émile) Gaston. Musicologist, teacher, organist, pianist, composer, b Berlin, NH, 18 Jun 1916; B MUS (Montreal) 1947, MA (Connecticut) 1956, PH D musicology (Boston) 1960. In 1918 his family settled in Danville, Que, where he took up organ and piano as a child. After further studies in Victoriaville, Que, in 1934 and in Quebec City in 1936, he continued 1940–7 at the *Cons national in Montreal with Eugène *Lapierre (organ) and Auguste *Descarries (piano) and 1948–50 in Philadelphia with George Rochberg (fugue, orchestration, composition). He also studied composition and the history of music 1953–6 at the U of Connecticut. His doctoral thesis was 'The masses of Claudin de Sermisy.' Assisted by bursaries (1961–2 from the *Canada Council, 1962 from the Fulbright Foundation, and 1965 from the *MACQ) he undertook research in musicology in Europe and the USA while also teaching 1962–7 at Loyola College in Montreal. He taught 1966–7 at the *U of Montreal and in 1967 joined the *U of Moncton, where 1969–73 he served as research officer. Between 1967 and 1970 he gave several organ and piano recitals on CBC radio in Moncton and on the national network. A long-standing interest in folk music led him to serve 1968–71 as president of the *CFMS and 1969–71 as editor of that organization's *Newsletter / Bulletin*. He received a leave fellowship from the Canada Council in 1973 for musicological research in Spain.

Allaire is the author of many articles, published mainly in the *Revue de musicologie* (Paris), the *Music Scene*, the *Boston University Journal*, and the journal of the U of Moncton. In 1969 he obtained a Canada Council grant for a modern edition of Claudin de Sermisy's *Magnificats* (American Institute of Musicology 1970) and *Holy Week Music* (ibid 1972). He composed a *Suite laurentienne* for orchestra (the Poème and the Menuet from which were premiered by the *Quebec SO in 1949), an organ work on French carols (H. W. Gray 1951), the music for the film *The Man on the Beach* (The Medallion Picture 1953), *Noël! Noël! Noël!* for mixed choir and organ (Presser, English-language edition 1959, French-language edition 1960), a *Marche* and a *Petite Suite* (1964–5) written for the Royal Canadian Ordnance Corps Band, and several preludes for organ, some motets, a communion service, a prelude and fugue for string orchestra, and a polyphonic mass.

WRITINGS

'Les messes de Claudin de Sermisy,' *R de musicologie*, vol 53, no. 1, 1967

'La rythmique de notre langue parlée,' *R de l'U de Moncton*, vol 1, no. 2, 1968

'L'essor de l'imprimerie musicale en France sous François 1er,' ibid, vol 2, Sep 1969

The Theory of Hexachords, Solmization and the Modal System (American Institute of Musicology 1972) ST

ALLAN, N. (Norman?) Fraser. Songwriter, pianist, fl Toronto 1911–40. Known to have been a pupil of W.O. *Forsyth, Allan played piano for the *Dumbells and, with his partner, the comedian Stanley Bennett, participated in some of that troupe's later productions. He wrote many songs, including some with Bennett ('Music in Canada,' 'Oh You Canadian Town,' and 'The Made in Canada Campaign Song') published 1914–16 by *Musgrave. Other collaborators (lyricists) were Kenneth McInnis and Katherine Smith. Songs entirely by Allan included 'Oh! You Harem Skirt' (Bell Piano 1911, the earliest traced), 'Canada, I Hear You Calling' (A. Cox 1916, from the musical *Belles of Boo Loo*), 'Gee! I Wish I Was a Kid Once More' (Feist 1942, featured in the Dumbells' revue *Ace High*), and 'Forever Pals We'll Be' (Harris

1942, the last-known published piece). A photo of Allan and Bennett, originally published in the *Canadian Music Trades Journal* (Mar 1923), appears in *Roll Back the Years*.

ALLAN PARK, Dorothy (Isobel) (b Allan, m Park). Soprano, teacher, choir director, b Aberdeen, Scotland, 3 May 1896, d Toronto 11 Aug 1978. She began musical studies with her father, a professional musician, and continued in London with Giovanni Celrici. The family moved to Toronto in 1908. After her debut in 1912 she continued voice lessons for six years with Dalton *Baker and appeared often with chamber music groups throughout Ontario and as soloist with the *Toronto Mendelssohn Choir and the *TSO. She lived in Peterborough from 1917 to 1941 and there formed the Madrigal Singers (1928–41), who toured extensively in Ontario. Allan Park continued to sing in Toronto, however, as soloist 1926–38 at the Church of the Redeemer and 1938–50 at St Paul's Anglican Church. In 1931 she joined the faculty of the TCM (*RCMT), where she taught singing and served as an examiner until her death. Among her pupils were Garnet *Brooks, Marie Gauley, Margo *MacKinnon, Jean *Macleod, Robert *Reid, Catherine *Robbin, and Lillian Smith Weichel. (MWM)

ALLARD, Émilien. Carillonneur, pianist, clarinetist, composer, b Montreal 12 Jun 1915, d Ottawa 18 Nov 1977; lauréat (Laval), L MUS (Montreal), carillonneur diploma (Beiaardschool te Mechelen, Belgium) 1948. He played the clarinet in the concert band of Grand-Mère, Que, and later conducted the band; he also worked as a church organist in the town. He studied piano and theory with J.-Antonio *Thompson and Father J.-G. Turcotte at the Trois-Rivières seminary, and organ and harmony with Eugène *Lapierre at the *Cons national in Montreal. He served 1942–5 as a clarinetist in the RCAF Central Band at Rockcliffe, Ont, then went to Mechelen to the Beiaardschool, where, 1946–8, he studied bell ringing with Staf Nees and composition with Jef van Hoof. While there he gave a recital for Queen Elisabeth of Belgium, who accepted the manuscript of one of his works. He continued his studies at the Paris Cons with Eugène Bigot (conducting), Maurice Duruflé (orchestration), and Olivier Messiaen (aesthetics). Before leaving Europe he took part in a 1949 Paris performance at the École normale of his *Pastorale et finale* for violin, clarinet, and piano.

On his return to Canada Allard went through a difficult time prior to his appointment in 1955 as the regular carillonneur at St Joseph's Oratory in Montreal – a position he was to hold for 20 years. In 1958 he won the International Carillonneurs' Prize at Mechelen at the time of the Brussels World Fair, and he also gave a series of recitals at the fair. From 1959 to 1976 he made annual tours in the USA. He left the oratory in 1975 to serve as carillonneur of the Peace Tower in Ottawa, and continued in that position until the year of his death. As carillonneur and organist, and with the organist Eugène Lapierre, Allard made the LP *Carols at the Carillon of Saint Joseph's Oratory* (RCA Victor LCP.1024), for which he also wrote the arrangements.

Allard composed some 50 works for carillon and made more than 700 transcriptions. Among his compositions are *Légende* for orchestra and *Poème bucolique* for piano and orchestra broadcast on CBC radio in 1946; a *Divertissement* for clarinet and orchestra performed in 1947 at a festival of Canadian music in Paris; a *Sonata a quattro* for oboe, clarinet, horn, and bassoon, played at the 1960 *Montreal Festivals; and a *Sonata* for carillon premiered in 1968 at Springfield, Ill. He also wrote a triptych for carillon based on three poems taken from *Le Jardin de nuit* by the Quebec poet Jacques Brillant (pseudonym Jabry). The Howard *Cable Band recorded his *Marche du maréchal* and his *Marche H.I.C.*, and Gordon *Slater recorded for the LP *Bells and Brass* his *Notule No. 1* and his *Profil canadien no 2*. Some of his works still are performed in Holland, Belgium, France, and the USA. The carillonneur Jacques Lannoy paid tribute to Allard in an article in *La Musique périodique* (Jan – Feb 1977): 'Couperin, Ravel, Olivier Messiaen ... these three famous musicians, whose pupil and disciple he was, sum up and typify that French musical culture of which Émilien [Allard] possessed all the finesse, all the sensibility.'

WRITINGS

'Le carillon et l'art companaire,' *La Musique*, vol 2, ed Norbert Dufourcq (Paris 1965)

BIBLIOGRAPHY

Bull, Rob. 'Ring in the new ...,' *Ottawa Journal*, 12 Apr 1975

Taylor, John. 'La vie et la mort d'un carillonneur,' *Musique périodique*, vol 1, Jan–Feb 1977 DM

ALLARD, Joseph. Violoneux, composer, b Woodland, Me, 1 Feb 1873, d near Montreal 14 Nov 1947. The son of a violoneux, he was taken as a child to Quebec and at 9 began fiddling. He returned to the USA at 16 and during the next 28 years won fiddling championships in New Hampshire, Rhode Island, Connecticut, and Massachusetts. In 1917 he settled in Ville St-Pierre, near Montreal. Allard won competitions in the Montreal area and in 1926 appears to have placed second in a major contest held in Lewiston, Me. Thereafter he enjoyed a growing reputation in eastern Canada and northeastern USA. He began recording for Victor's Bluebird label in 1928 and over the next 18 years made 75 78s. The most successful, according to the discographer Gabriel Labbé (in whose *Pionniers du disque folklorique québécois* Allard's recordings are listed), were *Reel de l'Aveugle*, *Reel de Chateauguay*, *Reel de Jacques Cartier*, and *Reel du voyageur*. Allard also appeared on six 78s for Bluebird under the name Maxime Toupin in the late 1930s.

From an appraisal of Allard's recordings Labbé concluded: 'This violoneux had developed a remarkable technique, influenced by both Irish and US music. He was known as "the prince of violoneux" because he had a supple and light bowing stroke and inimitable finger dexterity.' Allard's repertoire comprised many hundreds of folk melodies and about 60 of his own pieces. Jean *Carignan, who studied with Allard 1927–31 in Montreal, is the leading exponent of this repertoire and of Allard's style. Carignan has recorded many Allard pieces and in 1976 made the LP *Jean Carignan rend hommage à Joseph Allard*. Allard's music has been played and recorded by many other French-Canadian folk instrumentalists, and his style has been learned by fiddlers elsewhere in Canada, among them Graham *Townsend. Allard was the most important violoneux of the early 20th century and has attained legendary status. Yet, despite the popularity of his recordings and the extent of his influence during his later years, he lived in relative obscurity, working for most of his life as a fisherman.

ALLDRICK, Alexander A. See A.A.A.

ALLEN, Les or **Leslie**. Singer, saxophonist, actor, b London 29 Aug 1902. He was brought to Canada as an infant and played clarinet as a boy alongside his father in the *Queen's Own Rifles Band. One of the first Toronto saxophonists, he played in the dance bands of Burton Till and Luigi *Romanelli and in 1922 worked briefly in New York. He went to England in 1924 with a nine-piece co-operative band which also included Alfie *Noakes. As the New Princes' Toronto Band (named for the London restaurant where it performed) it recorded 16 78s for English Columbia. As Dave Caplan's Toronto Band, under the banjoist Caplan's direction, Allen and several members performed 1926–7 in Germany. Though a vocalist only occasionally with New Princes', Allen sang on 16 of Caplan's 28 78s for Polydor. (See *Roll Back the Years* for both bands' discographies.) Returning to England in 1927, he played and sang with such leading British dance orchestras as those of Carroll Gibbons, George Melachrino, and Geraldo before joining the BBC Dance Orchestra in 1932. He began his solo career in 1934 with the hit record 'Little Man You've Had a Busy Day' on English Columbia, then starred in the musical film *Heat Wave*. In 1937 he formed a vocal group, the Canadian Bachelors, with fellow countrymen Jack Curtis (lead), Herbie King (tenor), and Cy Mack (baritone and arranger). One of the most popular singers in Britain during the 1930s, he made several hundred recordings and in 1938 gave a royal command performance at the London Coliseum. He was described by Chris Lane as 'suave, immaculate and cultured, with a smooth melodic voice.' In 1945 he toured Britain in the musical *Miss Hook of Holland*, and in 1948 he retired to private business in Toronto. His son Mark (b London 1928) studied at the RAM (clarinet, piano) and with Harry Hayes (saxophone) before moving with the family to Toronto. He followed music as an avocation there and, after 1968, in Ottawa. In the mid-1970s he played saxophone with the Friars at the NAC's Café Terrasse. He made the LP *Every Little Breeze* (T-Bow 1) in 1977. The singer Eddie Allen of the *Happy Gang is a nephew of Les Allen.

BIBLIOGRAPHY

Lane, Chris. 'Memories of Les Allen,' *Memory Lane* magazine (1975) (EMI)

ALLEN, Ward (Warden Ambrose). Fiddler, composer, b Kirkton, near London, Ont, 11 May 1924, d Hull, Que, 3 Aug 1965. He began fiddling at 12, often with his brother Lorne, from whom he learned much of his repertoire. After working as a harvester in Manitoba and as a logger in British Columbia, he returned in the late 1940s to western Ontario, where he was heard on the *'CKNX Barn Dance' from Wingham. He won several competitions at this time, including the open class of the 1953 *Canadian Open Old Time Fiddlers' Contest. He toured Canada with Wilf *Carter 1954–6 and in 1958 and performed in Ottawa with the Happy Wanderers 1955–64, first on CFRA radio and then, until his death, on CFRA TV. Allen began recording for *Sparton in 1954, completing three volumes of *Ward Allen Presents Maple Leaf Hoedown* (SP 203, SP 210, SP 213), posthumously reissued in part as *Best of Ward Allen* (2-GRT 2230-1031). His fiddle tune *Maple Sugar*, which he recorded in 1957 for Sparton, was a hit in Canada and the USA. A classic of the Canadian fiddling repertoire, it has been recorded by many performers. Other popular tunes by Allen include *Frank Ryan's Hornpipe*, *C.N.E. Breakdown*, *Frisco Waltz*, *Maple Leaf Two-Step*, *Ken's Favourite*, *Back Up and Bush*, *Fishing Rod Reel*, and *Blue Pacific Hornpipe*. Two volumes of *Ward Allen Canadian Fiddle Tunes* were published (1956, 1961) by BMI Canada. Allen was inducted into the Country Music Hall of Fame, Nashville, in 1965.

Lorne (Amber) Allen (fiddle, b Kirkton 1914), by trade a construction worker, also played on

CKNX and for dances in the Ottawa area. His son Jimmy (James Lindsay) Allen (fiddler, b Kirkton 9 Mar 1946) played 1960–2 on CFRA and CJET (Smiths Falls, Ont) and has continued to perform regularly in the Ottawa area. By 1978 he had made three LPs, including *A Tribute to the Late Ward Allen* (Banff RBS 1253). (FH, MM)

Alliance chorale canadienne. Begun in 1961 by Pierre Fréchette, Father Yvon Préfontaine, and François Provencher to bring together choirs in Quebec City and the Beauce region. In 1966 it received a government of Canada charter under the name Alliance chorale canadienne. By 1980 it had expanded into an alliance of six provincial federations (Alberta, Manitoba, New Brunswick, Nova Scotia, Ontario, and Quebec) representing some 300 French-language choirs and 8500 choristers, and participation by federations from British Columbia, Saskatchewan, and Newfoundland was imminent. The alliance has striven to develop choral singing in Canada by encouraging the growth of new choirs, by providing conductors with means of perfecting their skills, by initiating young people in choral singing, and by organizing mass gatherings on a national and international scale. Presidents have been Pierre Fréchette 1961–7, Edmour Bélanger 1967–9, Marc Bernier 1969–71, and Richard Ducas 1971–4, succeeded by Guy Saint-Jean in 1974. In 1974 the provincial federations began to look after their own choirs and collect their own dues. *Le Bouscueil*, a periodical issued about three times a year and distributed to all members of the alliance, began publication in 1971.

The national office, located in Montreal, has a library of books, records, and music (single copies of more than 20,000 choral publications) and a sales department for scores, teaching manuals, and the alliance's publications. The alliance also has maintained an instructors' department with a team of choir conductors to direct workshops at the regional level or give specialized instruction in technique and repertoire. The alliance entered into a publishing sub-contract with À Coeur Joie, a French choral movement with which it has collaborated, especially in preparing the Choralies internationales, a triennial world congress of choirs in Vaison-la-Romaine (France). Begun in 1950 by À Coeur Joie at the instigation of César Geoffray, the congress has attracted as many as 6000 choristers in one year.

The alliance has organized the Choralies internationales canadiennes, also held every three years (Trois-Rivières 1967, Quebec City 1970, Edmonton 1973, Sherbrooke 1976, Moncton 1979), and special projects such as the cruise on a 'singing ship' from Montreal to the French islands of St-Pierre and Miquelon during the summer of 1975. The alliance has been financed by dues from the provincial federations, by subsidies from the secretary of state and the *Canada Council, and, where possible, by profits from choral gatherings and other ventures. Recordings issued by RCA Canada and under the ACC's own label were made during the 1966 Choralies nationales and also the 1967 and 1976 Choralies internationales canadiennes.

See also Nova Scotia Choral Federation; Ontario Choral Federation. (MB-L)

ALLISON, (Alice) Catherine. Educator, b Vankleek Hill, east of Ottawa, 1 Apr 1902; hon MA (St Francis Xavier) 1957, hon LL D (Dalhousie) 1971. She earned a teacher's certificate ca 1921 from the College of Education, *U of Toronto, and later obtained an Ontario supervisor's certificate in school music. She moved to Nova Scotia and made a significant contribution to school music in that province, teaching in Yarmouth schools during the late 1930s and later organizing the school music program in Sydney. She also helped revise the provincial music curriculum and organized – and directed for some 20 years – a course for classroom teachers and music specialists at the Nova Scotia Summer School. She inaugurated the first course in school music at the Nova Scotia Teachers' College in Truro in 1957 and taught there until her retirement in 1966.

Allison was a founder of the *CMEA and a founder and first president of the *NSMEA. She was living in retirement in Ottawa during the 1970s but was active there in competition festival associations. Her pupils have included Robert Angel, J. Chalmers *Doane, and Frances Tyrrell. She has contributed to *EMC*.

See also School music. (SAB)

ALLWORTH, (Robert Holmes) Christopher. Instrument builder, musicologist, organist-choirmaster, teacher, b Toronto 9 Oct 1940; BA (Mount Allison) 1966, M MUS (Illinois) 1974. After studies at *Mount Allison U he researched English medieval church music, iconography, and historical instrument-making 1968–70 at Jesus College, Oxford. He returned to Canada in 1972 and eventually settled in Yarmouth, NS, where he became organist-choirmaster at Beacon United Church and established an early-instrument workshop. There he has built replicas of medieval instruments such as fytheles, gitterns, harps, hurdy-gurdies, liras, psalteries, and viols. A few of these are housed at the Canadian Centre for Folk Culture Studies of the National Museum of Man. Others are owned by private collectors in Canada and England.

Allworth has given lectures and lecture-recitals on medieval instruments and has performed on early wind, keyboard, and string instruments. In 1973 in Ottawa he addressed the first Canadian Conference of Musical Instrument Makers. He displayed samples of his work at Festival Canada (*Festival Ottawa) in 1973 and at the Craftsmanship Exhibition (Royal Festival Hall, London) in 1974. In 1977 Allworth was the subject of the CBC TV documentary *A Way Out*.

WRITINGS

'The medieval processional,' *Ephemerides liturgicae*, vol 84, 1970

'Musical instruments in Nova Scotia,' *The Occasional*, vol 4, no. 3, 1977

BIBLIOGRAPHY

'Christopher Allworth: musical instrument maker,' *Craftsman / L'Artisan*, vol 6, no. 1, 1973

'Alouette!' The most popular Canadian folksong. It also has become a symbol of French Canada for the world, an unofficial national song identifiable from the first few measures of its lively chorus in 2/4 time. Marius *Barbeau is of the opinion that 'Alouette' originated in France, but James J. Fuld, in *The Book of World-Famous Music* (New York 1966), points out that the first written version, 'Alouetté,' appeared in *A Pocket Song Book for the Use of Students and Graduates of McGill College* (Montreal 1879). The song was published later as 'Alouette' in the *McGill College Song Book* (Montreal 1885). The first known printed version in France dates from 1893: it appeared in Julien Tiersot's *Revue des traditions populaires*, vol 8 (Paris). The words and music are found in many anthologies and collections in Canada, the USA, and even Europe, notably in William Parker Greenough's *Canadian Folk-life and Folk-lore* (New York 1897). Several versions exist in Canada. Marius Barbeau summarizes the different texts in a work appropriately named *Alouette* (Montreal 1946). However, in all versions of the song, with its enumerations and frequent recapitulations, the idea remains the same: the lark's feathers are plucked from its head, wings, back, tail, and so on.

Composers in both Canada and France have made use of the song – eg, the Frenchman H. Maurice Jacquet in his *Rhapsodie sur un chant canadien* for piano (Édition Belgo-Canadienne 1925) and Eldon *Rathburn in his *Variations and Fugue on Alouette* (1953) for small orchestra. Several arrangements and harmonizations have been made for vocal and instrumental ensembles. Charles W. *Sabatier's song 'L'Alouette,' however, has no connection with the folksong, nor do the various *Alouette Reels*. As is only fitting, the *Alouette Vocal Quartet has recorded the song (issued as a 78 on Bluebird B-1256 and reissued on the LPs RCA 1032 and RCA CGP 140). Other recordings have been made by *Aglaé, the Choeurs des chanteurs d'Acadie, the *Chorale de l'Université St-Joseph, Éva *Gauthier, Jacques *Labrecque, Charles *Marchand and his Bytown Troubadours, and Alan *Mills. In 1978 the Quebec group Garolou recorded it for an LP (London LFS 9027). Edith *Fowke included it in *The Penguin Book of Canadian Folk Songs* (Harmondsworth, England 1973).

The name Alouette has continued to be used extensively for commercial purposes, among others as a record label and as the name of Montreal's Canadian Football League team. HP

Alouette Vocal Quartet / Quatuor Alouette. Unaccompanied male ensemble whose repertoire consisted entirely of French and French-Canadian folksongs. It was founded in 1930 by Roger *Filiatrault, baritone, and André Trottier, bass, who were joined by Jules *Jacob, tenor, and Émile Lamarre, bass, and by Oscar *O'Brien, who served the quartet as arranger and artistic director. Its name was derived from the title of the most popular of French-Canadian folksongs. The quartet's first concert, 29 May 1932 in Montreal, was an immediate success, and the ensemble soon was called upon to fill engagements in Canada and abroad. In 1934 it was Canada's official delegate to France for the celebrations marking the fourth centenary of the discovery of Canada. In 1937 the quartet gave 35 concerts on a tour of France and Belgium. It frequently performed in the USA, mainly in New York, Washington, Detroit, Cleveland, Chicago, and Philadelphia. In 1945 it went to Brazil, where it drew an enthusiastic response both from the public and from musicians, including the composer Heitor Villa-Lobos. The quartet's radio broadcasts numbered in the hundreds. It was heard over both the CBC and private stations, especially CKAC, in whose popular weekly series 'Les Amours de Ti-Jos' it took part for about 10 years. In 1955 it celebrated its 25th anniversary with several TV appearances, notably on the CBC's 'Porte ouverte.' Filiatrault succeeded O'Brien as artistic director in 1945, and there also were some changes in personnel. The quartet's activity gradually decreased until it dissolved in the mid-1960s.

The group's repertoire consisted of hundreds of French and Canadian folksongs, some from the repertoire of Charles *Marchand and the Bytown Troubadours. The harmonizations or arrangements were made by Roger Filiatrault, Pierre *Gautier, Oscar O'Brien, Geoffrey *O'Hara, Amédée *Tremblay, and others. The quartet's performance was remarkable for its vocal consistency, striking a balance between the authentic expression of folk song and the aesthetic control of art song. The ensemble aroused the admiration of Arturo Toscanini, Désiré Defauw, and Wilfrid

Alouette Vocal Quartet: (left to right) Jules Jacob, André Trottier, Roger Filiatrault, Émile Lamarre

*Pelletier. The last-named, in a letter dated 26 Dec 1949, declared: 'For me, you are the roots of all that is most beautiful in our land. Our history, our old homes, our mountains live in your interpretations of our folklore.'

The Alouette Quartet made several recordings for Victor and Bluebird; a list appears in *Pionniers du disque folklorique*. A number of these were reissued on an LP, *Quatuor Alouette* (RCA LCT-3002). Six songs from *La Légende dorée* were released in 1948 on three 78s (RCA CP-6).

BIBLIOGRAPHY

Monpetit, Édouard. *Le Front contre la vitre* (Montreal 1936)
Hurtubise, Elzéar. 'Le "Quatuor Alouette",' *R du Québec industriel*, vol 4, no. 2, 1939
'La tournée triomphale du Quatuor Alouette au pays du café,' *P-T*, 895, Feb 1946
'Quatuor Alouette 1930–55,' brochure (Montreal 1955)
Lawless, Ray M. *Folksingers and Folksongs in America* (New York 1960) GP

AMADIO, Norm (Albert Norman Benedict). Pianist, b Timmins, Ont, of Italian-US parents, 14 Apr 1928. In Timmins he studied piano for seven years with the Grey Nuns and at 16 began playing in Gene Crocco's danceband at the Riverside Pavilion. He went to Toronto in 1947 for studies with Boris *Berlin at the *RCMT and began his professional career in 1948, in Rouyn, Que, with a country band. Playing jazz under the influence of bebop (Lennie Tristano, Bud Powell, and others), Amadio was a prominent figure in the late 1940s and early 1950s at the House of Hambourg in Toronto and became one of the city's leading accompanists. After working in the early 1950s in the cocktail-lounge groups of Jim Younger, Chico *Valle, and Jimmy Amaro, he led the houseband (with the drummer Archie Alleyne and a succession of bassists) at the Town Tavern, accompanying such US jazzmen as Roy Eldridge, Stan Getz, Bill Harris, Coleman Hawkins, and Lester Young and such singers as Carmen McRae and Mel Torme. Amadio later led the resident trios at several Toronto lounges, including those at the Regency Towers and the Four Seasons Sheraton Hotel. He was a member of many studio orchestras and also music director for CBC TV's 'Music Hop' (1963-7) and for several CBC pop and country-music specials. In 1977 he became the pianist and an occasional soloist for the syndicated TV series 'Nashville Swing.' His discography includes *The Norman Amadio Trio* (1963, CTLS 037), with Alleyne and the bassist Bill Britto, and other records as accompanist to Tommy *Ambrose, Moe *Koffman, and Phyllis *Marshall. MM

The Amati String Quartet. Founded in 1968 by Murray *Adaskin and three other faculty members of the U of Saskatchewan: Norma Lee Bisha, second violin, Michael Bowie, viola, and Edward *Bisha, cello. It gave its first concert 2 Feb 1969. Later that same year, Robert Klose was named second violin and Norma Lee Bisha replaced Michael Bowie. The personnel remained stable until the group was supplanted in 1971 by the *Canadian Arts Trio after fewer than 10 formal concerts. The quartet was too short-lived to develop a wide repertoire or a distinctive style. The instruments, however, are the only set in Canada built by the Amati family of Cremona – one violin and the viola in 1607, the other violin in 1670, and the cello in 1690. The viola's back bears the painted crest of the Borghese family which commissioned it. All were purchased by the Saskatchewan collector Stephen Kolbinson and sold to the university in 1959.

See also Instrument collections.

BIBLIOGRAPHY

'The Amati Quartet,' *CanComp*, 40, May 1969 (GW)

AMBROSE. Hamilton, Ont, family of musicians: 1 / Charles, 2 / Robert, son of Charles, and 3 / Paul, son of Robert.

1 **Charles**. Organist, teacher, b England 1791, d Hamilton 17 Feb 1856. After serving as organist at Chelmsford Cathedral in England, he emigrated to Canada in 1837 and settled on a farm near Guelph, Ont. In 1845 he became organist-choirmaster at Christ Church Cathedral in Hamilton. He also taught piano and organ there. He was the composer of *Three Grand Sonatas* for piano (Royal Harmonic Institution 1825).

2 **Robert** (Steele). Organist, choirmaster, composer, teacher, b Chelmsford, Essex, 7 Mar 1824, d Hamilton 30 Mar 1908. When the family moved to Hamilton from Guelph in 1845 he remained behind to work the farm, but in 1847 he joined his brother, Charles Jr, who was a music teacher and organist-choirmaster at St George's Cathedral in Kingston. Robert Ambrose was organist-choirmaster 1863–83 at the Church of the Ascension in Hamilton and also taught 1864–88 at the Wesleyan Female College (later Wesleyan Ladies College, still later Hamilton Ladies College). He was president in 1891 of the *Canadian Society of Musicians. During this period he composed extensively. Among his approximately 80 songs, 14 part-songs, and 25 instrumental pieces were *Claridine* (T.W. White 1872) for piano; 'Abide with Me' (Suckling 1882) for voice and piano; 'May God Preserve Thee, Canada' (Suckling 1886), written for chorus though recorded many years later (Columbia R4034) by the tenor Charles *Harrison; and 'The Contrite Heart' (Suckling 1881), an anthem. *Nordheimer issued a series of songs and part-songs, including at least seven for accompanied solo voice and three for quartet. Ambrose's most famous composition, the sacred song 'One Sweetly Solemn Thought' with words by Phoebe Carey, was published by Nordheimer in 1876, and has been included in numerous song collections. It was recorded many times by a variety of performers: as a vocal solo by Ernestine Schumann-Heink, as a duet by Alma Gluck and Louise Homer, as a harp solo, an organ solo, and a trombone solo, and on at least five piano rolls. (See *Roll Back the Years*.)

3 **Paul**. Organist, teacher, composer, b Hamilton 11 Oct 1868, d there 1 Jul 1941. He studied piano in Hamilton with his father and in New York with Albert Ross Parsons and Kate Sara Chittenden,

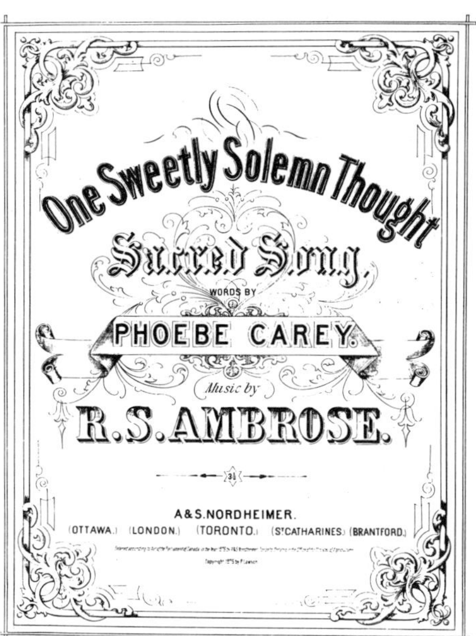

and composition and orchestration in New York with Bruno Oscar Klein and Dudley Buck respectively. In New York he was organist-choirmaster 1886–90 at Madison Ave Methodist Episcopal Church and in Trenton, NJ, he held the same position 1890–1917 at St James Methodist Episcopal Church and 1917–34 at First Presbyterian Church. He taught music history at several schools, including the Institute of Applied Music in New York, and in 1904 was appointed music director at the New Jersey State Normal School in Trenton. Retiring to Hamilton in 1934, he was guest organist at Christ Church Cathedral. He served four terms as president of the National Assn of Organists in the USA and in 1939 was elected president of the CCO. Paul Ambrose composed over 200 songs, choral pieces (including the anthem 'Saviour, Breathe an Evening Blessing'), and piano and organ pieces, many published by John Church, Ditson, Lorenz, Wm A. Pond, Presser, A.P. Schmidt, J.H. Schroeder, Silver Burdett, C.F. Summy, and White-Smith. His anthems were known throughout North America.

A cousin, Ellen Ambrose, was the founder of the *Duet Club of Hamilton.

BIBLIOGRAPHY

Hall, Frederick A. 'Hamilton: 1846–1946: a century of music,' *CAUSM J*, vol 4, Autumn 1974 (EMn)

AMBROSE, Tommy. Pop singer, composer, b Toronto 19 Oct 1939. At 5 he began singing at 'Youth for Christ' rallies at *Massey Hall and *Maple Leaf Gardens and elsewhere. Until he was 16 he performed on gospel radio shows on CKEY and CFRB. Turning to popular music he made his CBC TV debut in 1957 on 'Cross-Canada Hit Parade' and was host for 'While We're Young' (summers 1960, 1961) and for 'The Tommy Ambrose Show' 1961–3. After several years of nightclub work, accompanied in the late 1960s by Norm *Amadio, Ambrose became host for the CBC's gospel series 'Celebration' on radio 1971–4 and TV 1975–6. In the late 1970s he performed in clubs and concerts with an orchestra led by Doug *Riley. For Trudel Productions, which he formed in 1971 with Larry Trudel, he has composed 'People City' (the theme song, sung by Ambrose, of CITY-TV in Toronto), 'A Point of View' (theme song of the Global TV network in Ontario), and many successful jingles, usually in collaboration with the lyricist Gary Gray and the arranger Doug Riley. He has recorded many jingles. His other recordings include singles for the Warner Brothers and RCA Victor labels, the LPs *Fuzzy Love* with Bruno Gerussi (Kanata 4) and *Sweet Times* (1978, New Ventures NV 5005), and contributions to recordings by Jimmy *Dale and the CBC Song Market of 1967 and 1968. Blaik Kirby in the Toronto *Globe and Mail* (8 Dec 1971) wrote: 'His lean-sounding voice is invariably in tune, his notes beautifully sustained and focussed. There is a marvelous feeling of security as you listen.' Ambrose is a member of CAPAC.

BIBLIOGRAPHY
Flohil, Richard. 'Tommy Ambrose bounces back into the big time,' *CanComp*, 67, Feb 1972
Blackburn, Bob. 'Just like a celebration,' Toronto *Sunday Sun*, 18 Feb 1979

Les Amis de l'art. A non-profit society founded in Montreal in 1942 by Mesdames Aline Hector Perrier and J.-E. Perrault with the dual aim of facilitating students' access to presentations of all the arts and of encouraging young talents. The society was formed after 23,000 students – through the initiative of the Montreal Catholic School Commission – attended a large exhibition of masterworks of the classical painters at the Museum of Fine Arts. The volunteer organizers were impressed with the response to the exhibition and felt it was important to instigate other such activities and to investigate all means of giving young people free or inexpensive access to the arts on a continuing basis. The society was the result. It was registered in 1942 and incorporated in 1950. By 1953 it had 22,000 supporters. Until it became a foundation in 1953, however, its principal musical activity was to offer concert tickets at reduced prices, in collaboration with the impresarios and the schools. After that time subscription campaigns were organized, and the proceeds enabled the society to organize educational concerts and to grant numerous scholarships, available through competition.

Shortly after its founding, the society became a member of the International Federation of JM and sent a representative to the 1949 congress at Rotterdam, but this affiliation ended in 1950 when the *JMC joined the international federation. In 1956 Les Amis de l'art instituted special scholarships of $2500 and also began to award substantial prizes, bearing the names of their donors, at various important competitions such as the *MSO Concours and the *Canadian Music Competitions. Among the scholarship winners have been the soprano Nicole *Lorange, the pianist Louis-Philippe *Pelletier, the organist Monique Gendron, the cellist Denis *Brott, and the composer André *Prévost.

Mme Perrier (b Paiement; administrator, patron, b Montreal 1 Mar 1898) studied piano and voice but for reasons of health had to give them up. After her marriage to Hector Perrier, provincial secretary of Quebec and later a judge, she devoted herself to the promotion of music and the arts, particularly among the young. She was president of the society until 1967. She was succeeded by Mme Geneviève B. Deslauriers in 1967, and Mme Deslauriers by Mme Gisèle D. Larivière in 1971. In recognition of her devotion, Mme Perrier was named an Officer of the Academy by the government of France in 1951 and a life member of the Canadian Arts Council (later *CCA) in 1955 and of the UDA in 1956. She was made an Officer of the *Order of Canada in 1968. (CH)

Les Amis de l'orgue de Québec. Founded in 1966 by Antoine *Bouchard, with Pierre *Boutet as president, to present organ recitals and to sponsor lecture demonstrations on important organs in the vicinity of Quebec City. Chartered as a non-profit organization in 1972, the AOQ have received grants from the *MACQ and *Casavant Frères. In 1968 they began issuing a *Bulletin des Amis de l'orgue* approximately three times yearly. During their fifth season, 1971–2, they presented Paul-Émile *Talbot in concert with the *CBC Quebec Chamber Orchestra under Sylvio *Lacharité. In 1974 they collaborated in the dedication of the rebuilt organ at the Quebec Basilica, presenting André Marchal in recital. To mark the tricentenary of the Quebec diocese, they sponsored 1974–6 an integral presentation by various organists of the organ works of Bach. A program of avant-garde music was offered in 1975 by Xavier Darasse. Among those who have performed for the AOQ are the Canadians Antoine Bouchard, Raymond *Daveluy, Kenneth *Gilbert, Bernard and Mireille *Lagacé, Claude *Lagacé, Frederick Mooney, and Antoine *Reboulot and the visitors E. Power Biggs, Kamiel D'Hooghe, Anton Heiller, Geraint Jones, Jean Langlais, Gaston Litaize, Robert Noehren, and Lionel Rogg. Some of the recitals have been broadcast by CBC radio. (MB-L)

Amish. Branch of the *Mennonite Church, formed in Alsace in 1694 under the leadership of Jakob Amman and distinguished from other Mennonite congregations by extremely conservative dress and the shunning of technological advances and of 'the world' in general. The Amish of Canada settled in southwestern Ontario, having come from the USA after 1815 and directly from Europe in 1822; they numbered about 1000 baptized persons in 1975. They have preserved their German dialect. The music in their twice-weekly services consists solely of unaccompanied unison congregational singing; no instruments are used. Some congregations use the 'thick' Anabaptist hymnal entitled *Ausbund* (Mennonite Publishing House, Scottdale, Pa, but first published in Germany in 1564); others use the 'thin' *Unpartheyische Liedersammlung* (Mennonite Publishing House 1972), which contains songs from *Ausbund* and *Unpartheyisches Gesang-Buch* (Johann Bärs' Söhne, Lancaster, Pa, 6th edn 1854). The melodies are not notated in either of these books. Throughout centuries of aural transmission the melodies of the *Ausbund* hymns (ie, Gregorian melodies, reformation hymn tunes, and sacred and secular folk tunes of the 16th century) have become highly ornamented.

At the Sunday evening 'singings,' which offer the traditional opportunities for courting, Amish young people sing from their 'thin' book and *Church and Sunday School Hymnal* (Mennonite Publishing House 1902). In some Amish schools the children sing from the *Church and Sunday School Hymnal* and *Das* [sic] *Neue Kinder-Lieder* (Pathway Publishers, rev ed 1972). Some research has been done on the music of the US Amish but virtually none on that of the Canadian Amish. Most Amish neither dance nor sing secular songs.

BIBLIOGRAPHY
Jackson, George P. 'The American Amish sing medieval folk tunes today,' *Southern Folklore Q*, vol 10, Jun 1945
'The strange music of the Old Order Amish,' *MQ*, vol 31, Jul 1945
Umble, John. 'Recent research in Amish hymn tunes,' *Mennonite QR*, Jan 1950
Burkhardt, Charles. 'Church music of the Old Order Amish,' *Mennonite QR*, vol 27, Jan 1953
Mennonite Encyclopedia, 4 vols, ed Cornelius Krahn and Harold S. Bender (Scottdale, Pa, 1955) HMr

AMTMANN, Willy. Violinist, historian, musicologist, b Vienna 10 Aug 1910; B MUS (Toronto) 1950, M MUS (ESM, Rochester) 1952, D LITT musicology (Strasbourg) 1956. He studied 1924–30 at the Vienna Academy and arrived in Canada in 1940. While in charge of instrumental music 1947–68 for the Ottawa Board of Education he prepared his master's thesis on Bruckner's chamber music and in 1955 obtained a bursary from the Royal Society of Canada to complete his doctoral thesis on 'Musical life in New France.' He also played in the *Ottawa Philharmonic Orchestra and served 1957–9 as concertmaster. He received further grants from the Royal Society in 1965 and the *Canada Council in 1966. He joined the music department of *Carleton U in 1968 and taught music history there, specializing in Quebec, until 1976. He became a guest lecturer at the *U of Ottawa in 1976. Amtmann has contributed to several publications, including the *New Grove Dictionary*, and is the author of *Music in Canada 1600–1800* (Montreal 1975) and an amplified version in French, *La Musique au Québec 1600–1875* (Montreal 1976). Amtmann is one of the pioneers of historical writing on the music of Canada under the French regime.

ANDERSON. Winnipeg musical family: 1 / W.H. Anderson; 2 / Jeffrey, his son; and 3 / Evelyne, his daughter.

1 **W.H.** (William Henry). Composer, choir director, tenor, voice teacher, b London 21 Apr 1882, d Winnipeg 12 Apr 1955. He studied in London, first with Battistini and Garcia, then at the Guildhall on scholarship. He became lay tenor at several London churches, notably St Stephen's Walbrook and later St Paul's Knightsbridge. He also sang for a time at St Paul's Cathedral. He was the tenor in the London premiere of Messager's *Véronique* (5 May 1903) under the composer's baton, and sang with the Moody-Manners Opera company. He appeared briefly under the name Wallace Anderson, reverting to William but retaining a predilection for pseudonyms. (His compositions bear three signatures: W.H. Anderson for his most serious work; Hugh Garland for his ballads; and Michael Bilenko for his arrangements of European folksongs.) Chronic bronchitis interrupted his London singing career and forced him to seek a dry climate. He emigrated to Canada in 1910, settling in Winnipeg, where he made a name as a singing teacher, choir director, and composer. His choirs included the Canadian National Railways Choral Society, which he founded; several church choirs (his last, 1934–54, was St Andrew's River Heights United); and a 14-voice madrigal choir formed in 1936 as the Oriana Singers and transformed in 1942 into the 16-voice (later 20-voice) *Choristers, which 2 Jun 1942 began a series of CBC national broadcasts which continued uninterrupted for nearly 30 years, more than 12 of these under Anderson's direction.

W.H. Anderson was a prolific composer of songs (more than 150), carols, and anthems (more than 40), and these were published in Canada, the USA, England, and Australia. He also arranged a large number of Ukrainian, Czech, and Icelandic folksongs for the Winnipeg choir director Walter Bohonos, using particularly those variants developed among European settlers in Manitoba. For his songs he sought Canadian verse, choosing more often from among the local and the modest than from international anthologies. He set words of the Victoria poet Audrey Alexander Brown, for instance, and the Winnipeg poets R.H. Grenfell, Nan Emerson, Constance and Sheila Barbour, and Noreen Moore. He had been struck by a comment of Sir Ernest *MacMillan, who, after attending an early session of the

W.H. Anderson

*Manitoba Music Competition Festival, had said he thought Canadian children should have the chance 'to sing of their own flora and fauna.' W.H. Anderson's large output is the more remarkable in view of his daytime work as a CNR draftsman, his evening teaching and conducting, and his Sundays at church. His music is remarkable, too, for the amount which has persisted in the repertoire, for though it has no pretensions beyond usefulness, a natural lyricism, and an appreciation of what is idiomatic vocally and chorally, young singers and volunteer choirs are grateful for these qualities and for the music's effectiveness and durable charm. The success of his works in church is mildly ironic, for though W.H. Anderson was an austere moralist and a religious thinker, his beliefs were not conventional and he subscribed to theories of evolutionary reincarnation. New voice pupils were surprised to be told that good singing only began with technique, and that wide reading, a developed morality, and a constantly challenged philosophy were integral to the performing art. Among his pupils were Herbert Belyea, Lorne *Betts, Lloyd Blackman, Ronald Dodds, James Duncan, Reginald *Hugo, Wallace Lewis, Morley *Meredith, Maxine Miller, Gladys *Whitehead, and Phyllis Worth.

Perhaps W.H. Anderson's finest choral piece is the serene short motet 'Come, I Pray Thee.' Notable also are the songs 'Hospitality' and 'To Immortality'; the trio for female voices 'Sea Blue Gardens'; and the Christmas pieces 'Ane Song for the Birth of Christ,' 'Carol of the Little Angels,' and 'The World's Desire,' all of which demonstrate his happy turn of melody and sensitivity to words. Lists of his works are published in the *Catalogue of Canadian Composers* and *Contemporary Canadian Composers / Compositeurs canadiens contemporains*. His publishers include Arnold, C.C. Birchard, Boosey & Hawkes, C. Fischer, Galaxy, Gray, Oxford, Presser, G. Schirmer, Stainer and Bell, Thompson, and Western.

BIBLIOGRAPHY

Doyle, Patricia. 'W.H. Anderson: his life and contribution to music education through his compositions for the young voice,' unpubl M MUS thesis, U of Western Ontario 1977

2 **Jeffrey** (William). Radio producer, critic, b Winnipeg 26 Apr 1928; BA (Winnipeg) 1951; M PH history (London) 1960. Though not a practising musician, he studied organ and piano with Hugh *Bancroft and became an authority on British composers. He deputized for Kenneth *Winters 1959-60 as music critic for the *Winnipeg Free Press* and succeeded him in 1966, continuing in the position until 1968. His main career has been with the CBC, which he joined in 1960 as a music producer for radio and TV. For TV he produced the series 'Recital' and in 1963 Gustav Holst's opera *Savitri*. He was the CBC's program representative in England 1968-72, supervisor of radio program evaluation in Toronto 1973-4, and national supervisor of radio arts 1975-7. He became an executive producer of serious music for CBC radio in 1977. He planned and produced three two-hour musical documentaries: 'Ralph Vaughan Williams' in 1972; 'Gustav Holst, Planetmaker' in 1974 (winner of an Ohio Award in 1975); and 'Michael Tippett: A Composer for Our Time' in 1975.

3 **Evelyne** (Louise). Soprano, actress, b Winnipeg 24 Dec 1929. She studied voice with her father and Gladys *Whitehead in Winnipeg, and for a time with Jan van der Gucht in England. She was Meg Brockie in *Brigadoon*, the first full-scale production at Winnipeg's *Rainbow Stage. She returned from England for the 1956 season of Rainbow Stage to sing the title roles in *Annie Get Your Gun* and *Kiss Me Kate*. In Bristol her portrayal of Laurie in a 1957 production of *Oklahoma!* led to a London West End engagement as Susie in Bernard Slade's *Free as Air* (1957), another personal success for the young singer. For family reasons, however, she changed her career ambitions and returned in 1958 to Winnipeg where, over the next 20 years, her firm soprano, clear diction, and serene stagecraft made her virtually the leading lady of Rainbow Stage. Her most popular role has been Anna in *The King and I*, which she has sung in four separate productions there (1958, 1963, 1969, and 1979), as well as in Memphis, Tenn, in 1964 and in Fredericton for Theatre New Brunswick in 1970. Among other roles with which she has had notable success at Rainbow Stage are Madame Dubonnet in *The Boy Friend* (1961 and 1975), Marian in *The Music Man* (1962 and 1968), Eliza Doolittle in *My Fair Lady* (1966, repeated in Sydney, NS, in 1968), and Maria Trapp in *The Sound of Music* (1967). She also sang Agnes in *I Do, I Do* at the Neptune Theatre in Halifax, NS, in 1970, and Maggie in *Johnny Belinda* at the *Charlottetown Festival in 1974. An accomplished actress, she has appeared in some 20 plays during these same years, and in 1978 she read the Sitwell poems for the *Manitoba Chamber Orchestra's performance of Walton's *Façade*.

BIBLIOGRAPHY

Keys, Janice. 'Rainbow's pot of gold is music,' *Winnipeg Free Press*, 7 Jul 1979 KW

ANDRÉ, Louise (b Jeanne Baril). Soprano, teacher, b St-Tite, near Trois-Rivières, Que, 26 Feb 1913; B MUS (Montreal) 1938, MA (Montreal) 1940, L MUS (Montreal) 1942, D MUS (Montreal) 1957. She studied piano and singing with Alfred *Lamoureux and Rodolphe *Plamondon and composition with Claude *Champagne, pursuing her musical and academic studies at the Pensionnat Mont-Royal, the *École Vincent-d'Indy, and the *U of Montreal. She was a member, 1932-67, of the order of the Holy Names of Jesus and Mary under the name of Sister Louise-Andrée. Her university studies were centred on the development of the voice. 'L'éducation de l'artiste chanteur' is the title of her doctoral thesis. She received a diploma from the Pius XII Institute of Florence where she studied 1953-4 with Roberto Lupi. Her life has been devoted to the teaching of the vocal arts, beginning at the École Vincent-d'Indy in 1935 and at the U of Montreal in 1965 and continuing at both in 1980. She also taught 1967-72 at the Cons de Chicoutimi and 1971-6 at the *U of Ottawa. In her teaching she has been able to impart a sure grasp of various styles through her mastery of five languages and a personal technique resulting from study and experimentation in diverse schools. Among her pupils have been Paul-André Bourret, Josephte Clément, Claire *Grenon-Masella, Christine *Harvey, Marie *Laferrière, Andrée Lescot, Nicole *Lorange, Gloria *Richard, Roland Richard, and Sylvia *Saurette. (NTr)

ANDREW, Milla (Eugenia) (m Koyander). Soprano, b Vancouver of Russian parents; BA (British Columbia) 1952. A pupil of Avis *Phillips and Phylis *Inglis in Vancouver (where she sang in the *TUTS productions of *Song of Norway* and *The Merry Widow*) and of Irene *Jessner in Toronto, she made her *COC debut in 1954 in the role of The Foreign Woman in *The Consul*. Further COC roles included Marcellina in *The Marriage of Figaro* (1955) and Rosalinda in *Die Fledermaus* (1955, 1969) and the Witch in *Hansel and Gretel* (1957). In 1957 she won the San Francisco Opera auditions and sang in *Aida* and *Der Rosenkavalier*. She was Elvira in *Don Giovanni* at the 1958 *Vancouver International Festival and Musetta in *La Bohème* with the *Vancouver Opera. She won the *Metropolitan Opera western regional auditions in 1958. After a successful career in Vancouver radio, TV, oratorio, and opera, she moved to England where a sensational unrehearsed Sadler's Wells debut 27 Jan 1965 as Madama Butterfly led to such roles as Rosalinda, Lady Rich in Britten's *Gloriana*, Tosca, and Senta in *The Flying Dutchman*. She also sang the title role in Donizetti's *Anna Bolena* at the 1968 Glyndebourne Festival. Her Covent Garden debut 18 Apr 1969 as the Player Queen in the premiere of Humphrey Searle's *Hamlet* was followed by a succession of Strauss, Verdi, and Wagner roles. She has appeared with the Scottish, Irish, and Welsh national operas, in the USA, New Zealand, Argentina, Belgium, and Spain, and at the *Guelph Spring Festival. Her voice was described by the critic John *Kraglund as 'big and exciting' (Toronto *Globe and Mail*, 16 Sep 1969) after her appearance in the COC production of *Die Fledermaus*.

DISCOGRAPHY

Donizetti *Gabriella di Vergy*. Geoffrey Mitchell Choir, Royal Phil O, A. Francis cond, Andrew (Gabriella). (1979). 3-Opera Rara OR3

BIBLIOGRAPHY

Slater, Clare. 'Profile: Milla Andrew,' *OpCan*, Feb 1969
Kirby, Blaik. 'Canadian soprano a hit in Argentina,' Toronto *Globe and Mail*, 11 May 1979

Anerca. Inuit word for 'soul,' also the root of the verb 'to breathe' or 'to make poetry.' *Anerca* was chosen by Edmund Carpenter as the title of his edition (Toronto 1959, 1972) of Inuit verse translations by Knud Rasmussen, William Thalbitzer, and himself. Three Canadian composers have used the title for works inspired either by the verse or by the concept.

Serge *Garant's *Anerca* (1961, revised 1963, BMI Canada 1967), is a setting of two of the poems for soprano, woodwinds, strings, harp, and percussion. It was premiered 3 Aug 1961 during the *International Week of Today's Music in Montreal. The soprano was Claire *Grenon-Masella and the performance was conducted by Mauricio Kagel. Mary *Morrison is the soprano on the subsequent recording (RCI 217/RCA CCS 1011/RCI AMC 2).

Harry *Freedman's *Anerca* (1966, commissioned by Lois *Marshall) is a setting of three of the poems – one ('Great Sea') in common with the Garant – for soprano and piano. It also had its premiere in Montreal, by Lois Marshall and the pianist Weldon *Kilburn in 1966.

Victor *Davies' *Anerca* (1969, subtitled *Three Eskimo Chants: A Ballet*) uses only the title for what essentially is a mood achieved by a soprano vocalise against a background of violins, percussion, and piano or celeste. A choreographed version by the Contemporary Dancers of Winnipeg was filmed by CBC TV in 1969. KW

ANGÉ, Denyse (b Angers, m Kay). Singer, b Quebec City 31 Oct 1936. She began singing at 15 at the Château Frontenac in Quebec City with Gilbert *Darisse's orchestra. In 1955 she was named Miss CFCM TV in Quebec City, took part in the Miss Canada Competition as Miss Quebec, reached the semi-finals of the CBC competition 'Pick the Stars,' and won an ACTRA award as 'outstanding newcomer in Canadian TV.' In the next 10 years she appeared on all the major Canadian TV variety programs. She toured the West Indies for the Canadian government in 1959 and made tours of the Middle East for the Canadian armed forces in 1960 and 1961. The United Nations presented her with a medal in 1961 'for her contribution to the cause of peace as the first woman to make the trip twice to the Gaza Strip.' She appeared 13 Mar 1960 on 'The Ed Sullivan Show' (CBS TV) and won a prize in 1960 from *Liberty* magazine as 'Canada's best female vocalist.' She made tours of the Middle East and South America in 1962 and Australia in 1964. After living 1965–72 in New York, where she appeared at supper clubs and on TV, she returned to Montreal, performing on TV and in cabaret, and continuing to tour until 1976. Angé sang in three languages (French, English, and Spanish) and possessed, according to Frank Morriss, 'a slightly husky voice and a good sense of phrasing; she knows how to colour her words and she can shape a pop ballad, or a French number, to her own requirements' (*Globe and Mail* 18 Nov 1959). She made an LP with the Jimmy *Dale Orchestra for *CTL and others for Columbia. She is the sister of Danièle *Dorice and of the drummer Georges Angers.

BIBLIOGRAPHY

Angé, Denyse, and Walker, Dean. 'My starcrossed road to stardom,' *Liberty*, Nov 1962 CV

ANGER, (Joseph) Humfrey. Teacher, composer, organist, conductor, b Berkshire, England, 3 Jun 1862, d Toronto 11 Jun 1913; B MUS (Oxford), hon D MUS (Trinity, Toronto) 1902. Before being appointed head of the theory department of the *TCM in 1893, he had been conductor of the Ludlow (Shropshire) Choral and Orchestral Society, a school teacher, and a church organist. He had enjoyed some success as a composer: his cantata *A Song of Thanksgiving* (Psalm 96, Novello 1897) had won the Jubilee Prize of the Bath Philharmonic Society, and in 1890 his madrigal *Bonnie Belle* (Novello) had won the London Madrigal Society Prize. While at the TCM, Anger wrote the widely used textbooks *Form in Music* and *A Treatise on Harmony*. In Toronto he was organist-choirmaster 1894–6 at the Church of the Ascension and later at the Old St Andrew's Presbyterian Church. After 1902 he was at Central Methodist Church. He conducted the Toronto Philharmonic 1896–8, served 1895–6 as president of the *Canadian Society of Musicians and was dean of the Ontario chapter of the American Guild of Organists. He was for many years an examiner for the University of Trinity College (Toronto). In Canada Anger composed mostly church music and pieces for piano and organ, including *A Concert Overture* for organ (Whaley Royce 1895), a patriotic song, 'Hail Canada' (ibid 1911), and *Tintamarre, Morceau de Salon* (ibid 1911).

WRITINGS

Church Music (Toronto 1893)
Form in Music (Toronto 1898, rev ed Boston 1900)
Elements of Harmony (Toronto 1902)
A Treatise on Harmony, 3 vols (Toronto 1905, Boston 1906–12); ed rev by H. Clough-Leighter based on posthumously incorporated annotations by the author (Boston 1919)
The Modern Enharmonic Scale (Boston 1907)
A Key to the Exercises in Part I and II of A Treatise on Harmony, 2 vols (Boston 1909, 1913) (WLk)

Anglican church music. Music employed in the rituals and services of the Anglican Church of Canada, known until 1955 as the Church of England in Canada. There were nearly two million Anglicans in Canada in 1976.

The Church of England was among the first churches to establish a presence in Canada. The first service was held in October 1710, at the French chapel in Port Royal, NS, after the capture of that settlement by the English, who renamed it Annapolis Royal and made it the seat of the Nova Scotia government 1710–49.

The first Church of England church built in Canada (and in fact the first non-Roman Catholic church) was St Paul's, Halifax, erected in 1750. It introduced a choir during the early 1760s and an organ, possibly of Spanish origin, in 1765. Early organists at St Paul's were a Mr Evans 1765–6, Richard *Bulkeley 1767–8, and Viere Warner 1768–ca 1770. Conflict arose in July 1770 when Warner was censured by the vestry of St Paul's for displaying 'a light mind in the Several tunes he plays, called Voluntaries, to the great Offence of the Congregation.' At the same time the church's choir was accused of singing anthems whose words and music were not understood by the congregation. The wording of the remonstrance, strangely familiar to students of English church music, may refer to the choir's use of so-called 'fuguing tunes,' examples of which appear in *Humbert's (Methodist) **Union Harmony or British America's Sacred Vocal Musick* (Saint John, NB, 1801). Despite the criticism of Warner's elaboration of church music, it is noteworthy that in 1769, while he was still at St Paul's, an oratorio was performed there by the Philharmonic Society and officers of the army and navy; and in 1789, at a service celebrating George III's recovery from 'insanity' (now thought to have been a breakdown caused by an inherited metabolic defect), the final chorus of *Messiah* and a coronation anthem by Handel were performed at the church.

The first surpliced choir in Canada is said to have sung (under John *Bentley) at the consecration of the Cathedral of the Holy Trinity in Quebec City in 1804. In 1819 a choir was established in Toronto at St James' Cathedral, but that city's first surpliced choir – at Holy Trinity Church – was not formed until 1868.

Before the middle of the 19th century most services were accompanied by such instruments as were available, eg, string bass, bassoon, clarinet, and horns. However, in 1801 the Cathedral of the Holy Trinity in Quebec City ordered an organ from England; in 1802 Trinity Church in Saint John, NB, imported one; and ca 1833, ca 1843, and ca 1850, in turn, St James' Cathedral (Toronto), Christ Church Cathedral (Hamilton), and Christ Church (Ottawa) acquired organs.

The Roman Catholic church and the Church of England were the first in Canada to employ trained musicians. Stephen *Codman, in 1816, succeeded John Bentley as organist-choirmaster at the Cathedral of the Holy Trinity in Quebec City. Edward Hodges, an organist with a D MUS from Cambridge, served briefly in 1838 at St James' Cathedral in Toronto. J.P. *Clarke was organist 1844–5 at Christ Church Cathedral, Hamilton, and 1848–9 at St James' in Toronto; and John *Carter served 1854–6 at Holy Trinity, Quebec City, and 1856–78 at St James', Toronto.

Bishops who greatly encouraged the development of church music during the 19th century were Jacob Mountain (1749–1825) of Quebec, John *Medley (1804–92) of Fredericton, and A.W. Sillitoe (1841–94) of New Westminster.

Publications of the time give an idea of what was sung in the Church of England in the 19th century. *A Selection of Psalms and Hymns* (Toronto 1834 without music, 1835 with music; compiled by William Warren, first organist at St James' Cathedral, Toronto) offered metrical psalms, hymn-tunes, and chants for the canticles. A later edition (1842) added words for anthems by composers such as Arnold, Attwood, Boyce, Callcott, T. Clarke, Handel, and Kent and adaptations of music by Haydn, Mozart, and Pergolesi. A sixth edition appeared in 1857, proving the popularity of this collection. *Canadian Church Psalmody* (Toronto 1845, compiled by J.P. Clarke) added to the repertoire a greater selection of chants, some Gregorian melodies, and two Te Deums and seven other pieces by the compiler. *A Church Hymn Book* (Toronto 1862) offered 254 hymns with tunes.

On the basis of these publications and other oblique references, one may attempt a general chronology of the growth of service music. Until 1835, the standard fare was Tate and Brady or similar metrical psalms, with some anthems in 'fuguing-tune' style. After 1836 there was a gradual growth in the use of general hymns and in the chanting of the canticles and later the psalms, in non-metrical forms. The 1857 appointment of W.S. Vail to Holy Trinity Church, Toronto, contributed to a wider use of Gregorian chants and melodies. Vail was a pupil of Thomas Helmore (an English champion of plainsong), and under his direction the choral service was sung in its entirety for the first time in Toronto in 1869.

During the latter half of the 19th century the musical practices in the Church of England in Canada parallelled those in the mother church in England, though they were tempered always by the essentially pioneer character of Canadian life, with sharp differences between urban and rural areas. In the urban churches larger organs were installed, choirs were expanded in size, and paid solo quartets appeared. The works of Joseph Barnby, John Dykes, Gounod, Mendelssohn, Spohr, and Stainer and the anthems of John Henry Maunder and Caleb Simper were played and sung regularly. The custom of seasonal church performances of oratorios and other major choral works grew and has continued to this day. In large cities the repertoire and even the ordering of the musical sections of the service began to imitate the English cathedral tradition.

In the early decades of the 20th century, mainly owing to the practical scholarly efforts of Richard Terry and Edmund Fellowes, the cathedral tradition started to regain its long-lost vigour in England, restoring to the repertoire in some quantity the music of the Tudor polyphonists (Taverner, Tallis, Byrd, Tye, Morley, Mundy, Farrant, Gibbons, and others) and such restoration composers as Croft, Greene, and Boyce. The church in Canada followed suit, if at a slight distance. Symptomatic of this revival was the growth of interest in the forgotten art of unaccompanied singing – A.S. *Vogt's choirs were pioneers in the 1890s. There also was an interest in music by early 20th-century traditionalists such as Parry, Stanford, and Charles Wood. In this period one can see the beginnings of a reaction against what has been called 'the sensational, sentimental and meretricious.' Parry's 'I Was Glad' was sung in Christ Church Cathedral, Frederiction, in 1913, though in company with works by Smart and Eyre. *The*

Book of Common Praise (Toronto 1908) was a strong influence in Anglican church music.

An increase in the number of male choirs was another direct result of the influence of English cathedral tradition. Two such choirs which enjoyed considerable success were those of the Church of St Simon-the-Apostle, Toronto, led by Eric Lewis, and St George's Cathedral, Kingston, Ont, led by George *Maybee; St George's sang at Westminster Abbey services in 1954. Other outstanding Anglican church musicians of the 20th century include Gerald *Bales, Hugh *Bancroft, Vernon *Barford, Edward Bishop (Cathedral of the Holy Trinity, Quebec City), Frederick *Chubb, Frederick *Egener, Arthur *Egerton, Maitland *Farmer, Fred *Geoghegan, Donald *Hadfield, Albert *Ham, Godfrey *Hewitt, Norman *Hurrle, Kenneth *Meek, Catherine *Palmer, Charles *Peaker, Patrick *Wedd, Gerald *Wheeler, Alfred *Whitehead, and Leonard *Wilson.

The work of Healey *Willan, who came to Canada in 1913, led to a greater appreciation of Gregorian music and renaissance polyphony, and to a further rejection of sentimentality and display in church music. This is evident in 'high' (ie, 'Anglo-Catholic') church services such as those at the Church of St Mary Magdalene in Toronto, for which Willan directed the music for many years, and those at St Barnabas in Victoria, BC, and at St James in Vancouver.

British-trained musicians have joined US and a growing number of Canadian-born organists and choirmasters to bring a cosmopolitan breadth to the repertoire of major churches today. English cathedral music is supplemented by Palestrina, Josquin, Schütz, Bach, Handel, Haydn, and Mozart. The anthems and settings of Herbert Howells, Kenneth Leighton, and William Matthias are performed along with those of Alan Hovhaness, Gerald Near, and Leo Sowerby and those of the Canadians Bancroft, *Bissell, *Fleming, *Holman, *Naylor, *Ridout, Whitehead, and Willan.

The Anglican Congress held in Toronto in 1963 demonstrated vividly the growth of church music in Canada. The revised edition of *The Book of Common Praise* (Toronto 1938), while naturally drawing heavily on earlier hymnals, had provided a further unity for the Canadian church, and its successor, *The Hymn Book* (Canada 1971), is the product of a rapprochement with the United Church of Canada. *The Parish Psalter* has been replaced as the standard book by *The Canadian Psalter* (both Anglican and plainchant versions, Toronto 1963), based upon the version of the psalms in *The Canadian Book of Common Prayer* (1959).

In the 1970s many churches began raising funds through sales of recordings made by their choirs and organists, a certain sign of confidence in improved standards. The influence of the Royal School of Church Music had grown, particularly through choir festivals. Diocesan choir schools flourished, and several Canadian church choirs sang in Europe.

See also Choir schools; Hymnbooks; Plainsong; Religions and music.

BIBLIOGRAPHY

Reed, Thomas Arthur. 'Church music in Canada,' unpubl ms, Baldwin Room, Metropolitan Toronto Library

Fox, D. Arnold. 'Music in the Maritime provinces,' *Year Book of Canadian Art*, compiled by the Arts and Letters Club of Toronto (London and Toronto 1913)

Etherington, Charles L. *The Organist and Choirmaster* (New York 1952)

Peaker, Charles. 'Church Music II,' *Music in Canada*

MacMillan, Sir Ernest. 'Choral music,' *Music in Canada*

Peaker, Charles. 'Church music,' *Encyclopedia Canadiana* (Ottawa 1957)

MacMillan, Sir Ernest. 'The organ was my first love,' *CMJ*, vol 3, Spring 1959

Kallmann *History of Music*

Locke, William. 'Ontario church choirs and choral societies 1819–1918,' unpubl DMA thesis, U of California 1973

(GBr)

Anglo-Canadian Leather Company Band, or **Anglo-Canadian Concert Band**. Built on the nucleus of a small band formed by Italian immigrant workers at a Huntsville, Ont, tannery established by Charles Orlando Shaw in 1900. Shaw, an amateur cornetist and a wealthy man, encouraged the development of the band by providing a suitable rehearsal room, music, instruments, and uniforms. He also had a bandstand built. The band, made up of about 40 tannery employees, was led by Vincent Crosso until Shaw, while on a visit to Chicago for cornet lessons with Herbert L. *Clarke, was able to persuade Clarke to become the director of the band, which he did in 1918. Clarke in turn recruited a large number of musicians from other noted Canadian and US bands. He also acted as cornet soloist, although in rehearsal Shaw often would assume this role. Upon moving to Huntsville, the new recruits took regular jobs with the Anglo-Canadian Leather Co as clerks, machinists, electricians, etc, and were paid an additional salary and provided with housing. There were 69 bandsmen.

About 1922 Herbert *Barrow was assistant conductor, and in 1923 Clarke resigned. He was succeeded briefly by Frank *Welsman (summers 1923, 1924) before the US musician Ernest Pechin, a solo cornet under Sousa, was appointed.

The band was featured at the *CNE for about 10 years and was one of the first organizations of its kind in Canada to do a radio broadcast (CFRB, Toronto, 1926). In an article in *Musical Canada* (March 1929), Alfred *Zeally described it as 'one of the finest industrial plant bands in the world.' It toured very little, mainly in southern Ontario, and made no recordings. The band ceased to function ca 1927.

BIBLIOGRAPHY

West, Bruce. 'Music on the barge likely to be special,' Toronto *Globe and Mail*, 16 Aug 1979

The Anglo-Canadian Music Company. Publishing firm founded 1885 in London by a group of British publishers and established in Toronto later that year under the name Anglo-Canadian Music Publishers' Assn. The purpose was the printing, publication, and sale of British music copyrights in Canada, counteracting cheap US reprints of such copyrights, which were being exported to Canada and hence to Britain. This protectionist policy was based on the Canadian Copyright Act of 1875, which empowered the copyright owner, upon printing and publication in Canada, to stop all importation of pirated reprints from the USA. The firm bought the Canadian copyrights for songs and piano pieces from the composers for 20 shillings each and paid one penny royalty for every copy sold in Canada. By the beginning of 1889, 600 Canadian copyright editions had been issued

The composers, all British or continental European, included Stephen Heller and Arthur Sullivan besides such writers of salon pieces as Stephen Glover, Caroline Lowthian, Theodore Marzials, Ciro Pinsuti, and Sydney Smith. The number of publications decreased somewhat in the 1890s, but songs and dances by Canadians such as Carl *Martens, Angelo *Read, and J.D.A. *Tripp now were included in the catalogue. The series 'Octavo Choir Music for mixed voices' made its appearance (1891) with *Torrington's 'Abide with Me' and featured music by Ernest R. Bowles, Albert *Ham, W.H. *Hewlett, H.E. *Key, Herbert *Sanders, Charles E. *Wheeler, and others. It also included Edward *Broome's arrangement of 'O Canada' (1910).

The first manager of the company was Frank Howe, a veteran of the London music trade. By 1890 Sydney Ashdown had succeeded Howe, and until 1920 the Anglo-Canadian Music Co (as it became known about 1895) and *Ashdown's Canadian branch shared premises. The firm continued alone, keeping its licence even after a bankruptcy in 1941. During the period 1921–41 it specialized in church music and acted as agent for J.B. Cramer, J.H. Larway, and other London publishers. Its own publications included music by W.O. *Forsyth, Bertha Louise *Tamblyn, and Healey *Willan (B242), and Canadian editions of George Gershwin and Cole Porter. About 1943 it was acquired by *Canadian Music Sales, which continued to sell Anglo-Canadian publications under the Anglo-Canadian name.

BIBLIOGRAPHY

Americus. 'Trade notes from Europe,' *American Art J*, vol 44, 28 Mar 1885

HK

ANHALT, István. Composer, teacher, b Budapest 12 Apr 1919. He studied 1937–41 with Kodály at the Royal Hungarian Academy of Music. After service 1942–5 in the army he was briefly assistant conductor of the Hungarian National Opera and then studied 1946–9 in Paris with Louis Fourestier (conducting), Nadia Boulanger (composition), and Soulima Stravinsky (piano). A recipient of a Lady Davis Foundation Fellowship, Anhalt was able to emigrate to Canada in 1949, and immediately joined the theory department of the music faculty at *McGill U. A growing interest during the 1950s in electronic music led him to work at the Electronic Music Laboratory of the National Research Council in Ottawa and at the Columbia-Princeton centre in New York. A 1959 concert of his works at McGill U is thought to have been the first in Canada to include electronic music, and he established (and directed 1964–71) McGill's Electronic Music Studio. He commuted in 1969 to Buffalo as Slee Visiting Professor at the State U of New York. Appointed head of the music department at *Queen's U in 1971, Anhalt took a short leave in April 1972 to lecture on contemporary composition for voice at the Franz Liszt Academy in Budapest. As a teacher at McGill U and Queen's U he has guided such younger-generation composers as William Benjamin, John *Fodi, Clifford *Ford, Hugh *Hartwell, John *Hawkins, Alan *Heard, Jack *Sirulnikoff, and Alexander Tilley.

Anhalt's early compositional technique was based on a disciplined application of serialism. Constant transformation of ideas and variation of presentation replaced traditional procedures of sequence and development. This systematic approach to pitch relationships might be seen as a link to his subsequent (1960s) interest in electronic music. There is, however, a strong personal and intuitive element in Anhalt's work which has enlivened what otherwise might have been doctrinaire serialism. The same element has governed his sound sense, and he has continued to mix traditional instrumental sounds with electronic ones to produce enrichments of texture and sonority.

Anhalt's first large-scale instrumental piece was the *Symphony*, the premiere of which he conducted in Montreal in November 1959 at a concert organized to commemorate the 200th anniversary of the establishment of the first Jewish community in Canada. The pitch material of the

István Anhalt

Symphony centres on a four-note group which appears throughout the work both melodically and harmonically. Other aspects of the work, however – duration, dynamics, timbre – were freely composed. In form the work is a set of variations in 13 sections. The effect of the music is broadly romantic with a lyricism and intensity reminiscent of the manner, but not the sound, of the music of Alban Berg. A second large-scale work, the *Symphony of Modules* (completed in 1967, still unperformed in 1980), requires a large orchestra with augmented percussion, two tapes, and four-part chorus and includes controlled improvisatory sections as well as a fully notated score.

In his frequent use of the human voice, whether solo or in ensemble, Anhalt has been concerned less with conventional lyricism than with the range and variety of sounds which can be produced vocally. Similarly, a text often is important less for its words and meaning than for its sounds and types of articulation which can be manipulated as materials for musical composition. Anhalt's analysis of Berio's *Sequenza III* is as much a guide to his own thinking as an explication of Berio's work.

In *Comments* the text is miscellaneous newspaper clippings, interesting for their combined non-sense rather than for the manner of setting, which is conventional. Quite different is the treatment of Eldon Grier's poem 'An Ecstasy' in *Cento*, 'Cantata Urbana.' The very long poem by Grier is reduced by Anhalt to 25 lines. The text is fragmented and the words themselves broken up so that recognition of sense is blurred and meaning becomes uncertain. Something of the same technique is used in *Foci*, where words from a number of sources in a variety of languages form an important part of the texture of a piece to be performed in a planned visual environment. Once again in *La Tourangelle*, vocalism is a dominant element in a complex texture, the text providing a source of sound as well as meaning. Anhalt's keen interest in the extension of the functions of vocal music in the 20th century resulted, in 1978, in the completion of his manuscript *New Music for Voice*, a series of 'essays on contemporary innovative vocal and choral composition.' Anhalt is a member of the *CLComp, an associate of the *CMCentre, and an affiliate of *PRO Canada.

See also Electronic music.

COMPOSITIONS

ORCHESTRA

Interludium. 1950. Sm orch. Ms

Funeral Music. 1951 (Mtl 1954). Sm orch. CMCentre

Symphony. 1958 (Mtl 1959). Full orch. BMIC 1963

Symphony of Modules. 1967. Full orch, tape. CMCentre

La Tourangelle, musical tableau (Anhalt, Marie de l'Incarnation). 1975 (Tor 1975). 3 sop, ten, bass, sm orch, tape. Ber 1977

CHAMBER

Trio. 1953. Pf trio. CMCentre. RCI 229/RCA CCS-1023 (*Brandon U Trio)

Comments (*Mtl Star* clippings). 1954. Alto, pf trio. CMCentre

Sonata. 1954. Vn, pf. CMCentre. RCI 220/RCA CCS-1014 (*Bress vn)

Chansons d'aurore (Verdet). 1955. Sop, fl, pf. CMCentre

Foci (various). 1969. Sop, chamb ens, tape. Ber 1972. RCI 357 (*Mailing)

PIANO

Arc en ciel, ballet. 1951 (Mtl 1952). 2 pf. Ms

Sonata. 1951. CMCentre

Fantasia. 1954. Ber 1972. Col 32 11 0046 (*Gould pf)

CHOIR

Three Songs of Love (de la Mare, anon). 1951. SSA. CMCentre

Three Songs of Death (Davenant, Herrick). 1954. SATB. CMCentre

Cento 'Cantata Urbana' (Grier). 1967. 12 spkrs (SATB), tape. BMIC 1968. RCI 357 (*Tudor Singers of Mtl)

VOICE

Six Songs from Na Conxy Pan (Sandor Weöres). 1941–7. Bar, pf. CMCentre

Psalm XIX 'A Benediction' (A.M. Klein). 1951. Bar, pf. Ms

Journey of the Magi (Eliot). 1952. Bar, pf. CMCentre

Also *Electronic Composition* nos. 1–4. (1959–62). (no. 3, 4) Marathon MS 2111

WRITINGS

'The making of *Cento*,' *CMB*, 1, Spring–Summer 1970

'Foci,' *Artscanada*, vol 28, Apr–May 1971

'La musique électronique,' 'L'histoire de *Cento*,' *Musiques du Kébèk*, ed Raoul Duguay, Montreal 1971

'Luciano Berio's *Sequenza III*,' *CMB*, 7, Autumn–Winter 1973

'New Music for Voice: Essays on Contemporary Innovative Vocal and Choral Composition,' ms, 1978

Record and book reviews in *CMJ* (1959–61), including a review of Varèse recordings, Winter 1961

BIBLIOGRAPHY

Beckwith, John. 'Recent orchestral works by Champagne, Morel, and Anhalt,' *CMJ*, vol 4, Summer 1960

Schallenberg, Robert. 'Anhalt's *Symphony No. 1*,' *Notes*, vol 21, Fall 1964

Rivard, Yolande. 'L'enseignement de la composition à l'université McGill,' *VM*, 8 May 1968

'Istvan Anhalt – a portrait,' *Mcan*, 15, Nov 1968

BMI Canada Ltd. 'Istvan Anhalt,' pamphlets, 1970, 1976

Beckwith, John. 'Vocal usage frontier pushed back in new Anhalt works,' *MSc*, 281, Jan–Feb 1975

Thompson, Leslie. 'Anhalt takes musical cues from history,' *Music*, Mar–Apr 1980

'Review of records'

Kasemets, Udo. 'Istvan Anhalt,' *Contemporary Canadian Composers / Compositeurs canadiens contemporains* CM

ANKA, Paul. Singer, songwriter, of Syrian descent, b Ottawa 30 Jul 1941. Though Anka's rise to pop music stardom at 15 with his recording of 'Diana' seemed sudden, he had begun to perform in Ottawa at 10, in amateur shows and on radio. His formal music studies were brief: piano with Winnifred Rees and theory with Frederick *Karam (in whose St Elijah Syrian Orthodox Church choir he sang). While in school he formed a vocal trio, the Bobby Soxers, and also performed alone. At 13 he went to Hollywood and recorded one of his own songs, 'Blauwildesbestfontein.' Returning to Canada he appeared on CBC TV's 'Pick the Stars' and 'Cross-Canada Hit Parade.' At Easter 1957 he went to New York and signed a recording and composing contract with ABC-Paramount. His first single, 'Diana,' with sales eventually exceeding five million, became one of the most successful records in pop music history. In December 1957 he embarked on a 91-city tour of Britain, the USA, and Canada, attracting – as he would for several years – audiences largely of screaming teenage girls. Later in 1958 he travelled to Japan and Australia.

Paul Anka

As one of the leading teen idols of the day, Anka was as popular in Europe as he was in North America. A Parisian reviewer (quoted by David Cobb in *Canadian Magazine*) commented: 'A finger of Johnnie Ray, a touch of Frankie Laine, the zest of Elvis Presley, several drops of the Platters – shake and serve. That's the Paul Anka cocktail.' An acclaimed *NFB production, *Lonely Boy* (the title taken from one of his 1960 hits), documented Anka's rise to stardom. In 1960 he became the youngest performer ever to appear at the Copacabana in New York; the LP *At the Copa* (ABC S-353) was made at this time. Though his records were no less popular in Canada, Anka made only rare Canadian appearances over the next dozen years, and his family made New York its home in 1961.

Anka's 20 singles released 1957–62 by ABC-Paramount included: 'You Are My Destiny,' 'Put Your Head on My Shoulder,' 'It's Time to Cry,' 'Puppy Love' (a hit again in 1972 as recorded by Donny Osmond), 'My Home Town,' and 'Dance on Little Girl.' Several of these were million-sellers and with other popular singles were reissued on the LPs *Vintage Years (1957–61)* (Sire K-6043) and *Anka Gold – 28 Original Hits* (2-Sire 3704). During this period his songs also were recorded by Annette, Connie Francis, Johnny Nash, Patti Page, Bobby Rydell, and others.

Anka's career waned in the mid-1960s, the inevitable result of the change in popular tastes coinciding with the rise of the Beatles. In those years he recorded for RCA and only 3 of some 12 singles 1962–9 were hits of any size in North America: 'Love Me Warm and Tender,' 'A Steel Guitar and a Glass of Wine,' and 'Eso Besso.' His 'Ogni Volta' was a million-seller in Italy in 1964. Concentrating on songwriting, he wrote 'My Way' to the melody of a French song 'Comme d'habitude' for Frank Sinatra. 'My Way' became Sinatra's personal philosophical statement on the closing years of his career and was recorded by many other singers. 'She's a Lady' was a major hit in 1971 as recorded by Tom Jones. At about 30, Anka found new popularity as a ballad singer. He began to include 'My Way' in his performances, leading to predictions that he might become the next Sinatra. His career by then was centred in Las Vegas, where, in 1971, he began performing from six to eight weeks annually at Caesar's Palace. He also resumed his Canadian appearances: at the *CNE (1975, 1977), *Maple Leaf Gardens (1976), and *O'Keefe Centre (1978, 1979) in Toronto; at the Central Canadian Exhibition (1972) and the *NAC (1974) in Ottawa; and at *PDA (1979) in Montreal.

Anka's records from this period include the hits 'Do I Love You,' (Buddah 1971), 'Let Me Get to Know You,' (Fame 1973), and, 1974–5 for United

Artists, '(You're) Having My Baby,' 'One Man Woman, One Woman Man' (sung with Odia Coates), 'I Don't Like to Sleep Alone,' and '(I Believe) There's Nothing Stronger than Our Love.' Anka has made more than 25 LPs, among them 5 for ABC-Paramount, more than a dozen for RCA, and others for Buddah, Barnaby, and United Artists. Collections of his most popular records also have been released by RCA, United Artists, Buddah, and K-Tel. Anka is an affiliate of BMI; his songs have been published by Spanka Music Corp and Paulanne Music, Inc.

BIBLIOGRAPHY

Sonin, Ray. 'Anka's away,' *Music World*, 1 Aug 1957
Gardner, Paul A. 'Tin Pan Alley at fifteen,' *Maclean's*, 4 Jan 1958
McDermott, Claire. 'Paul Anka takes Europe by storm,' *Star Weekly*, 28 Feb 1959
Mair, Shirley. 'Paul Anka: the world's reigning juvenile,' *Maclean's*, 1 Dec 1962
Sinclair, Catherine. 'What's the secret of Paul Anka's appeal?' *Chatelaine*, Jan 1963
Trent, Bill. 'Paul Anka and the girl he left behind,' *Weekend*, 26 Jun 1965
Cobb, David. 'I'm the youngest top ballad singer in the business,' *Canadian Magazine*, 22 Jan 1972
Goddard, Peter. 'Paul Anka: I have a 20-year history in show business. I've seen it all happen,' *Toronto Star*, 9 Oct 1976

MM

Anne of Green Gables. Musical play, the mainstay of the *Charlottetown Festival during the 1960s and 1970s. Based on Lucy Maud Montgomery's 1908 girls' novel which tells the adventures of a high-spirited, adolescent Prince Edward Island girl, it was adapted for TV by Don Harron (book and lyrics), Norman *Campbell (music), and Phil *Nimmons (orchestrations). This version was premiered 4 Mar 1956 on 'CBC Folio' with Toby Tarnow as Anne Shirley and John Drainie as Matthew (Tarnow had played the role in an earlier CBC radio dramatization). A second CBC TV production 18 Nov 1958 starred Kathy Willard. In 1965 the Charlottetown Festival commissioned Harron and Campbell to expand the TV version into a full-length musical. Elaine Campbell and Mavor *Moore supplied additional lyrics, and John *Fenwick prepared the orchestrations. *Anne of Green Gables* was premiered 27 Jul 1965 at the Charlottetown Festival, with Fenwick conducting, and became an annual feature. It has toured several times in Canada, has been taken to Expo 70 at Osaka, and played 21 Dec 1971–2 Jan 1972 at the New York City Center. A British production ran nine months 1969–70 at the New Theatre in London and was named best new musical by the London critics (*Plays and Players* magazine). At Charlottetown Anne has been portrayed by the US actress Jamie Ray 1965–8, by the Prince Edward Island actress Gracie Finley, and, beginning with the 1974 Canadian tour, by Malorie-Ann Spiller. Susan Cuthbert assumed the role with the 1979 season. *Anne of Green Gables* was recorded by the London cast (1969, Col ELS 354) and selections were included on an LP by the Al *Baculis Singers. The music, published by Chappell, has been issued in a song album in 1969 and in a vocal score in 1973.

BIBLIOGRAPHY

Mungall, Constance. 'Anne of Green Gables comes home,' *Star Weekly*, 2 Jul 1966
Adilman, Sid. 'Anne of Green Gables,' *Toronto Star Week*, 2–9 Nov 1974
King, Paul. 'Canada's orphan Anne was once probed by FBI,' *Toronto Star*, 12 May 1979

Anthems, motets, psalms. The anthem has been described as the English-language protestant counterpart, and a derivation, of the Latin motet.

Susan Cuthbert (Anne Shirley) and George Merner (Matthew) in the 1979 Charlottetown Festival production of *Anne of Green Gables*

Anthems (usually accompanied) and motets (usually unaccompanied) are choral pieces sung during church services but are not a part of the prescribed liturgy or of the congregational music represented by hymns and responses. Like motets they are the province entirely of the music director and choir. Their function is partly decorative – eg, to dispel tedium and enhance contemplation during the collection of the offering – and partly provocative, useful at points of rest or suspension in the liturgy to engage the congregation's religious imagination at the highest musical level. They encapsulate some of the finest poetry of the church in some of its most unfettered, succinct, and inspired music.

If anthems and motets are a decoration of the service, the psalms in their basic use are fundamental to it, and their broad place in it is prescribed. In this prescribed use they are sung antiphonally or spoken responsorially. There is nothing, however, to prevent the setting of words of the psalms to music for use as anthems. Many psalms have been employed in concert settings of cantata proportions. The Book of Psalms is the oldest song (word) book in use.

In France forms related to the motet have been called antiennes and require three or four vocal parts, often with additional solo voice and organ and/or two or three instruments. The motet itself came into use in France after 1600, largely due to the works of Henri (Henry) Du Mont for large choir and often on psalm texts. Over the next 150 years the form was perpetuated by Lully, M.-A. Charpentier, Lalande, Campra, and others. Charpentier, in particular, was associated with the efforts of the Jesuits to ensure that music would be religious in inspiration and pious in character, and it is not surprising that music by this 17th-century master of church music accompanied Jesuit missionaries to Canada. Father René *Ménard (1605–61) is supposed to have written motets in Canada, but it is not certain whether he wrote words, or music, or both (*Les Ursulines de Québec*, vol 1, Quebec 1863, p 39).

An 18th-century reference to choral performance in Canada, probably of New England-style fuguing tunes, was made in the vestry records of St Paul's Church, Halifax, 24 Jul 1770, when complaints were made about unintelligible anthem texts ('the Major part of the Congregation do not understand either the Words or the Musick & cannot join Therein'). Canadian publications of such works, however, did not appear until the 19th century. The first Canadian 'longboy' (ie, wider than high) tunebook to include such three- and four-part works, the *Union Harmony* published in Saint John, NB, by Stephen *Humbert in 1801, contains 12 works attributed to Humbert himself as well as 4 fuguing tunes.

The first tunebook to contain anthems in addition to psalms and hymns was *The Harmonicon* of 1836. Its third edition contains an extended verse anthem on the 40th Psalm as well as five full anthems.

In Upper Canada, performance of part music followed the organization of York's first choir, that of St James' Cathedral, in 1818. Mrs Anna Jameson noted in 1837 that 'psalms and anthems are very tolerably performed' there under the organist William Warren. Two years earlier, Warren had compiled *A Selection of Psalms and Hymns for Every Sunday*, which included several of his own chant melodies, a Samuel Arnold anthem, and elaborate hymn settings of anthem-like proportions. The 1842 edition added texts of 50 anthems, almost exclusively European oratorio excerpts and works of the English cathedral tradition which presumably constituted the repertoire of the day.

The *Union Harmony*, mentioned above, contained some Canadian anthems. Another of the early collections to incorporate Canadian anthems was that issued in Toronto in 1845 by James Paton *Clarke. The nine items by Clarke himself in the *Canadian Church Psalmody* include two full anthems. There is also an anthem by Edward Hodges (1796–1867, an Englishman who spent part of 1838 in Toronto as organist at St James' Cathedral).

Anthems by Clarke and by his colleague Dr John *McCaul, then president of King's College (later *U of Toronto), enjoyed considerable vogue. McCaul's setting of Psalm 41, 'Blessed be the Man,' later internationally popular, was performed by the *Toronto Philharmonic Society 23 Mar 1846. The choir's final concert of 27 Apr 1847 included Clarke's eight-part anthem, 'Arise O Lord God,' the first Canadian B MUS exercise.

As church choirs were formed in Upper Canada in the first half of the 19th century, their labours were devoted primarily to hymn- and psalm-singing, with anthems occasionally included for festive occasions. By mid-century, however, more sophisticated materials were circulating across Canada. Performances of anthems from *Parish Choir* (an English journal) were reported in Labrador and Newfoundland in its June 1849 issue.

John *Medley, enthroned as bishop of Fredericton in 1845, introduced ideals of the Oxford Movement to New Brunswick and published many of his own anthems. One of these was included in George *Carter's *Selection of Anthems as Sung in the Cathedrals of Montreal, Toronto and Quebec*. This board-book of 1865, probably designed for congregational use of the texts, bears witness to an extensive performance practice.

At this time various denominations issued their own tunebooks 'to improve and elevate' the music of their adherents. The *Presbyterian Psalmody* (Montreal 1851) included some tunes by the US composer Lowell Mason and was among the earliest to place the tune (heretofore in the tenor) in the treble of its English and Scottish metrical psalms. *The Canadian Church Harmonist* of 1864, intended for Methodist churches, contained psalm and hymn tunes as well as anthems, sentences, and introits by European and US composers. *Hymns for the Worship of God*, printed by John *Lovell of Montreal in 1863, included 30 doxologies and anthems for the Church of Scotland.

The Seraph is the earliest extant collection devoted exclusively to anthems and set pieces. It was printed in Toronto by the Wesleyan Book Room, probably in 1863. C.W. Coates published the *Canadian Anthem Book* in 1873 to 'elevate and improve taste but meet the wants of the average choir.' Composers represented included McCaul, Warren, Edward Mammatt, and Thomas Turvey.

In the late 19th century, both performance and composition of choral works were limited by the enormous popularity of quartet choirs and 'semi-sacred' solos. However, well-established choirs in larger centres persisted in more ambitious endeavours. At All Saints Church, Toronto, Percy Greenwood was leading anthems and choral services in the style of the Oxford Movement. At the Church of the Redeemer, E.W. *Schuch's 50-voice mixed choir performed English Victorian anthems and operatic excerpts set to sacred texts.

At Jarvis St Baptist Church, Toronto, A.S. *Vogt began in 1888 to introduce unaccompanied motets. His use of unaccompanied works in the *Toronto Mendelssohn Choir concerts set a new standard for church choirs. Vogt published several motets of his own and edited the *Standard Anthem Book*, volume 1 of which appeared in 1894. This 'high class of music of but medium difficulty' consists of more than 40 full and several verse anthems by Buck, Shelley, and their contemporaries. Horace *Reyner is the only Canadian represented.

By the end of the century several Canadian church musicians had attained international repute. Albert *Ham had many anthems published by Novello, Oliver Ditson, and H.W. Gray. His sturdy harmonies were fairly chromatic but not overly complex. Contrasts of metre, texture, and key enhanced the ternary forms often used in his anthems. Works by Charles A.E. *Harriss, published by G. Schirmer, rely on heavy chromaticism and a more operatic style. Clarence *Lucas, considered the outstanding Anglo-Canadian composer of his generation, and Edward *Broome had many anthems among their published works. The *Anglo-Canadian Music Company at this time began to bring into print larger numbers of octavo-size anthems by the Canadians Ernest Bowles, Charles *Wheeler, and John Adamson, among others.

Healey *Willan's 44 full and verse anthems, 30 hymn-anthems, and 38 motets must be cited as the first to have achieved widespread popularity while providing dignified, serviceable materials for varied choral forces throughout the church year. His later works in particular considered the needs of volunteer choirs and a wider practice than the high liturgical tradition of his own experience. His diatonic melodic outlines provided choral parts with interest for all, and his convincing triadic harmonies, while simpler than contemporary English style, were appealing and useful.

The work of Alfred *Whitehead, who published more than 30 anthems in the 1930s and 1940s, provides some evidence of new directions in its use of free metre suiting the text and of non-dominant seventh chords. In his verse anthem 'If Ye Then Be Risen with Christ,' changes of key and metre point up the sectional structure, and voices often are paired low against high before spreading to four-part texture.

Before considering the works of living Canadian composers, it must be noted that the distinction between the anthem, the motet, and the psalm became increasingly tenuous after the 1930s. Contemporary anthems may use entire psalm texts or may contain fragments of psalms, hymn stanzas, or sacred poetry, alone or in combination.

The full text of the 150th Psalm has been treated by several major Canadian composers. Jean *Papineau-Couture's *Psaume CL*, one of his most striking large works, calls for choir, soloists, and instruments including two organs (the second one optional), while Barrie *Cabena's 'Psalm 150: O Praise God' offers alternatives and can be sung by a four-part mixed choir, a double mixed choir, a two-part women's choir, or a two-part men's choir, with organ or piano. Violet *Archer and John Fearing have published settings of the same psalm for four-part mixed choir with organ accompaniment (though Fearing's has optional brass quartet).

Psalm 100 (Jubilate Deo) has been set for similar forces by Cabena, Henry Clark, and, earlier, Arthur *Egerton. Gerald *Bales' setting includes a brass choir. Bernard *Naylor's is for unaccompanied mixed choir, and his 'Deus Miseratur' (Psalm 67) and 'Cantate Domino' are for divided sopranos and organ.

Canadian-trained Joseph *Roff has published settings for mixed choir of portions of six psalms and a large body of English motets (post-Vatican II) for use in the Roman Catholic liturgy.

Otto *Joachim's 'Psalm' uses mixed choir in its treatment of a Klopstock poem and the Lord's Prayer rather than words from traditional psalmody. André *Prévost's large work *Psaume 148* is scored for mixed choir, trumpets, trombones, and organ. R. Murray *Schafer's *Psalm* sets a text from Psalm 148 for mixed choir, four soloists, and percussion to be played by choir members. A challenging set of *Nine Motets* to English texts and another of *Three Motets* to Latin texts have been published by Bernard Naylor. Cabena's *Three Motets* were commissioned by the Bach-Elgar Singers of Hamilton, Ont.

Unpublished (1980) psalm settings of note include Bales' *Psalm Cantata*, Tibor *Polgar's *Lord, How Long Shall the Ungodly Triumph* (Psalms 94, 54, 69, and 44), Cabena's verse anthems on Psalms 23, 81, and 130, and Robert *Fleming's and Talivaldis *Kenins' settings of Psalm 150.

Keith *Bissell has contributed four books of anthems for treble and 3-part choirs to Canadian church repertoire. Most notably in *O Come, Let Us Sing* (18 anthems for junior choir), Bissell provides vital rhythms and modal or pentatonic melodies to suit the needs of younger ensembles. His 'Christ, Being Raised from the Dead' is a good example of his polymetric writing, which fits speech rhythm, and employs challenging harmonic devices such as parallel triads, non-dominant seventh chords, and modality. Bissell's anthems are practical chorally and make moderate use of 20th-century techniques.

William *France has provided a large number of carefully made anthems for varying choral forces. 'Unto Thee, O Lord' shows clearly the interesting part writing, economy of text usage, and solid triadic harmonies which have ensured him a large performing public.

Newer directions in anthem composition can be found in the work of Derek *Holman, whose strong rhythms, virile counterpoint, and unconventional harmonies provide challenges of a new standard. Among Violet Archer's nine published anthems, 'O Lord, Thou Hast Searched Me' shows how her use of dissonance approached by stepwise motion can bring newer idioms within the capabilities of amateur choirs.

Derek *Healey has been one of the first Canadians to include aleatoric techniques in anthem literature. His setting of 'There Is One Body' exploits the possibilities of non-traditional notation and adds synthesizer or tape accompaniment. The nine Healey anthems published by 1980 provide imaginative examples of the new directions available to Canadian composers for the church.

Among the numerous other Canadians who have contributed anthems, motets, and psalm settings to the repertoire are W.H. *Anderson (many), Hugh *Bancroft, Lorne *Betts, Allanson *Brown, F.R.C. *Clarke, Jean *Coulthard, Richard *Eaton, Graham *George, David *Ouchterlony, Godfrey *Ridout, Charles *Wilson, and S. Drummond Wolff.

See also Hymnbooks, protestant.

BIBLIOGRAPHY

Wienandt, Elwyn and Young, Robert. *The Anthem in England and America* (New York 1970)
CMCentre. *Catalogue of Canadian Choral Music* (Toronto 1970, rev enl edn 1978)
'Canadian church music composers,' *RCCO Q*, Jun 1974; suppl listing, Jun 1976
Catalogue of Canadian Composers
MG, KW

'The Anti-Confederation Song.' Sung during the heated 1869 election in which Newfoundland was to decide whether or not to join the newly formed Dominion of Canada. Pro-Confederationists argued the advantages of lower prices for goods; Anti-Confederationists countered with the prospect of high taxes on fishermen's boats and gear and played on the Newfoundlanders' pride in being Britain's oldest overseas colony.

> Her face turns to Britain, her back to the Gulf,
> Come near at your peril, Canadian Wolf!

The traditional tune is possibly a variant of the widespread 'Villikens and His Dinah.' The song was published first by Gerald S. *Doyle in *The Old-Time Songs and Poetry of Newfoundland* (1940) and is included in the *Fowke-*Johnston *Folk Songs of Canada* (Waterloo 1954). Alan *Mills recorded it (Folk 3000). EF

Apex. See Compo Company Ltd.

***An Apostrophe to the Heavenly Hosts*, B584.** One of Healey *Willan's most famous and frequently performed choral works, composed in 1921 for the *Toronto Mendelssohn Choir and premiered in 1923. A text drawn from translated Eastern Orthodox liturgies is set for unaccompanied double chorus with brief contributions from two 'mystic' choruses. It was published 1921 by the Composer's Publication Society and reprinted 1936 by Harris. It has been recorded by the Toronto Mendelssohn Choir (1968, RCA LSC 3054) and the *Festival Singers (1973, RCI 207/Cap ST 6248).

APPLEBAUM, Louis. Composer, administrator, conductor, b Toronto 3 Apr 1918; hon D LITT (York) 1979. At the *TCM and the *U of Toronto 1928–40, studying piano with Boris *Berlin and theory with Healey *Willan, Leo *Smith, and Sir Ernest *MacMillan, Applebaum completed the work towards a B MUS but did not take the examinations. Instead, he went to New York to study composition 1940–1 on scholarship with Roy Harris and Bernard Wagenaar. First a film composer, Applebaum produced some 250 scores for the *NFB between 1942 and 1960. He also established early his usefulness as conceptual thinker, practical planner, and resourceful negotiator. Appointments with the NFB (music director 1942–8, consultant 1949–53) and in New York with World Today films (music director 1946–9) and the National Film Council (member, advisory committee) set the pattern for a succession of practical or consulting assignments, all with essentially the same purpose: the efficient relating of musicians' professional functions to the needs and capacities of a burgeoning economy.

When in 1955 Applebaum established the music wing of the two-year-old *Stratford Festival, he designed each new program (opera and jazz, 1956; folk music, 1958; workshops with famous instrumentalists for the newly formed National Festival Orchestra, 1959; the *International Conference of Composers, 1960) as an unaccustomed

Louis Applebaum

confrontation of musicians and audiences. Applebaum resigned from administrative duties at Stratford in 1960 (though he would continue for many years to provide incidental music for festival productions) and embarked on the first private enterprise of his life, serving 1960–6 as president of Group Four productions, makers of documentaries and TV shows for market. Even during those years, however, his advisory skills were in demand. He was music consultant 1960–3 for CBC TV; chairman 1963–6 of the music, opera, and ballet advisory committee for the *NAC; and the author in 1965 of *A Proposal for the Musical Development of the Capital Region*, the government-commissioned report which led to the formation of the *NACO and of a plan for the establishment of a department of music at the *U of Ottawa. He then served 1965–70 as chairman of the *CAPAC-Canadian Assn of Broadcasters committee for the promotion of Canadian music. He also sat 1966–9 on the advisory arts panel and was an arts-award jury member 1970–1 for the *Canada Council, served 1967–8 on the planning committee for *Coordinated Arts Services, and was consultant 1968–70 for the *St Lawrence Centre. He was the music executive person of CAPAC 1968–71 and was still a director of the organization in 1980. He became the trustee of the John *Adaskin Memorial Fund and was a regular consultant for the POCA (see OAC).

In 1971 POCA appointed Applebaum its executive director – a position which brought into play all facets of his experience in the administration and politics of the arts, and in the arts themselves, and which gave him a major role in the phenomenal acceleration of cultural development in Ontario in the 1970s. He retained the position until 1980, when he took up new duties as chairman of the Advisory Committee on Cultural Policy to the federal government.

Applebaum's career as a composer proceeded steadily despite the heavy demands of his other activities. In 1953, with most of his several hundred film scores behind him (including *The Story of G. I. Joe*, 1946, which was nominated for an Academy Award) and with incidental music to his credit for CBC radio productions of *Hamlet*, *Le Médecin malgré lui*, *Peer Gynt*, *Antigone*, *Oedipus*, and *The Madwoman of Chaillot*, Applebaum became a kind of staff composer for the first Stratford Festival. He wrote the 'foyer fanfares' which became a tradition there and composed incidental music for the inaugural productions, *Richard III* and *All's Well that Ends Well*. Each year thereafter he turned out at least one incidental score for Stratford (36 by 1976).

Applebaum composed many scores for plays produced by Esse Ljungh on CBC radio, by Tyrone Guthrie (*Tamburlaine the Great* – adapted from Marlowe – 1956) and Michael Langham (Max Frisch's *Andorra*, 1963) on Broadway, by the Royal Shakespeare Co (*Much Ado About Nothing*, 1961), and by the Manitoba Theatre Centre (Brecht's *Mother Courage* and William Kinsolving's *Nicholas Romanov*, the latter revised by Michael Bawtree for Stratford, 1966, as *The Last of the Tsars*).

Applebaum's three ballets were commissioned: *Dark of the Moon* (revised as **Barbara Allen*) by the National Ballet of Canada, *Legend of the North* by the Janet Baldwin Ballet of Toronto, and *Homage* for performance by the National Ballet at the opening ceremonies of the NAC. He also composed the electronic curtain-music used on this occasion.

For CBC TV Applebaum has composed 8 episodes of *The National Dream* (1973), 14 of the *Purple Playhouse* (1973), and 5 of the *Images of Canada*, and has produced scores for many other series, as well as for the specials *Mother Courage* (1964), *Next Year in Jerusalem* (1974), *Homage to Chagall* (1976), and *Sarah* (1976).

Like his theatre music, Applebaum's concert pieces usually are written to order, the commissioners as various as the assignments (eg, Canadian Jewish Congress: 'Cry of the Prophet'; *Edmonton SO: *Concertante for Small Orchestra*). In this field, also, the size of Applebaum's output is remarkable considered in relation to the complexity of his administrative life, particularly if it is remembered that he conducted many of the Stratford and CBC performances of his own music, Stratford opera productions (including Guthrie's stagings of *H.M.S. Pinafore* and *The Pirates of Penzance* on tour in England and the USA, 1962–3), and Eldon *Rathburn's soundtrack (later issued as a recording, Dominion LAB-650S, conducted and produced by Applebaum) for *Expo 67's *Labyrinth*.

Though the two branches of Applebaum's career may seem divergent, to him they are confluent. In an interview in the *Canadian Composer* (January 1974) he said: 'Essentially I'm working to improve the lot of my colleagues and I have been doing that for many years – at the same time staying on ... as a functioning artist ... Though I was a composer [there], the Film Board was the kind of operation that made one part of a great social force ... And when I got into other kinds of musical activities, like the theatre at Stratford, it was a Stratford that was changing the theatrical life of our country. When the Canada Council was formed, I was there, helping in whatever way I could, and also with the League of Composers and the Canadian Music Centre, the Music Council and the National Arts Centre ... No matter where I am or in what medium I am working, my life always seems to be pointing in the same direction.'

True to his time and to his idea of his function as an artist, Applebaum is an enlightened pragmatist among composers. His scores are aware of trends without being a prey to them, perhaps because of the particular imperatives – the timing restrictions and expressive duties – of theatre and film scores. His writing is muscular, discreet, sparingly but purposefully coloured, and as strictly to the point as his commissions are prompt to deadline.

In addition to the aforementioned Academy Award nomination, Applebaum won a special Hollywood Writers' Mobilization award (1945) for his score for *Tomorrow the World*, a citation (1950) from the New York National Board of Review for *Lost Boundaries*, the Flaherty Award (1952) for *And Now Miguel*, Canadian Film Awards for *Paddle to the Sea* (1958), *Wheat Country* (1959), and *Athabasca* (1968), and a Wilderness Award (1973) for *Folly on the Hill*. He gave special courses 1974–6 on music for film, theatre, and TV at *York U, Toronto. Applebaum is a founding member of the *CLComp, a member of CAPAC, an associate of the *CMCentre, and an Officer (1977) of the *Order of Canada.

SELECTED COMPOSITIONS

STAGE

Suite of Miniature Dances, ballet. 1953. Sm orch. Ms
Legend of the North, ballet. 1957. Pf, perc. Ms
Ride a Pink Horse, musical comedy (Jack Gray). 1959. Ms
Homage, ballet. 1969. Full orch. Ms
Over 50 incidental scores and many songs for plays in Canada, USA, England
See also *Barbara Allen*.

FILM

Tomorrow the World (1945); *The Story of G.I. Joe* (1946); *Dreams that Money Can Buy* (1947); *Lost Boundaries* (1949); *Teresa* (1950); *Walk East on Beacon and Whistle at Eaton Falls* (1951); *All My Babies*, *And Now Miguel*, *End of the Long Day*, *Royal Journey*, *Varley* (all 1952); *Stratford Adventure* (1954); *Krieghoff* (1955); *Canadian Profile* (1957); *Paddle to the Sea* (1966); *Athabasca* (1967); *Energy* (1975)

RADIO, TV

Scores for ca 400 documentaries and TV films and ca 200 incidental scores for TV and radio plays

ORCHESTRA AND BAND

East by North. 1947. Full orch. Ms
Suite of Miniature Dances. 1964. Band. Kerby 1972. RCA PCS-1004 (*Cable cond)
'Revival Meeting and Finale' from *Barbara Allen*. 1964. Med orch. CMCentre. Col MS-6763 (*Susskind cond)/CBC SM-273 (*Atlantic SO)
And others

FANFARES AND CEREMONIAL MUSIC

Three Stratford Fanfares. 1953. Brass, perc. Leeds 1966. (No. 1 and 2) RCA PCS-1004 (*Cable cond)
Joy to the World, pageant (Daniel Lord). Ca 1954. Soli, SATB, orch. Ms
Fanfare to Welcome a Queen. 1958. Brass, perc. Ms
Fanfare – Royal Ceremonial. 1967. Brass, perc. CMCentre
Song for the National Arts Centre (Birney). 1967. SSA, band. CMCentre
Terre des hommes / Man and His World. 1967. Ww, brass, perc. Ms
Place Setting. 1973. Orch. CMCentre
And others

MISCELLANEOUS

'Cry of the Prophet' (biblical). 1951, rev 1952. Bar, pf. CMCentre. RCA LSC-3092 (*Fine bass)
Four English Carols. 1953. SATB, pf. Ms
Two Maritime Carols. 1958. SATB. Leeds 1971. ('Cherry Tree') Poly 2917 009 (*Festival Singers)
Touch Wood. 1969. Pf. GVT 1969. Dom S-69002 (*Mould)
Essay. 1971. Fl. Leeds 1971. Dom S-69006 (*Aitken)
Keep Moving. 1973. Pf. Wat 1973
Algoma Central (railroad timetables). 1976. Sop, pf, fl. Ms
Inunit, 5 episodes for voice and orchestra (Inuit text). 1977. CMCentre
North (Inuit). 1977. Full orch, v. Ms
And others

WRITINGS

'Film music,' *Music in Canada*.
'Musical creation in an age of technology; with discography,' *Proceedings and Transactions of the Royal Soc of Canada*, vol 4, 1961
'Introduction,' *The Modern Composer and His World*, ed Beckwith and Kasemets (Toronto 1961)
A Proposal for the Musical Development of the Capital Region (Ottawa 1965)
'Stratford's musical festival,' *The Stratford Scene 1958–68*, ed Peter Raby (Toronto 1968)
Toronto's Orchestral Resources: A Study Prepared for POCA and the Canada Council (Toronto 1968)
'Creating a climate for creativity,' Dunning Trust Lectures, Queen's U 1977
'The paradox and puzzle of music on Canadian television,' *CanComp*, 137, Jan 1979
Notes on film music in *J of Aesthetics and Art Criticism* and reviews for *Film Music Notes*

BIBLIOGRAPHY
Abel, E. 'He makes movie music,' *Maclean's*, May 1946
Berton, Pierre. 'He sets Shakespeare to music,' *Mayfair*, May 1954
'Louis Applebaum,' *Composers of the Americas*, vol 10, 1964
'From NFB and Hollywood to arts administrator,' *CanComp*, Jan 1974
'Interview: the League of Composers: how hard work paid off,' *CanComp*, 119, Mar 1977
Creative Canada, vol 1
Contemporary Canadian Composers KW

APPLEYARD, Peter. Vibraphonist, percussionist, composer, b Cleethorpes, Lincolnshire, England, 26 Aug 1928. After drumming in British dance bands and in the Central RCAF Band, he moved in 1949 to Bermuda and in 1951 to Toronto, where he began playing vibraphone. He performed with Billy *O'Connor and, 1954–6 at the Park Plaza Hotel and on CBC radio, with the US jazz pianist Cal Jackson. In 1957 he formed his own group which, though based in Toronto, travelled widely in North America (accompanying the singer Gloria DeHaven for a year) and appeared on US TV. Appleyard was co-host 1961–2 with the singer Patti Lewis for CBC radio's 'Patti and Peter' and in 1969 with Guido *Basso for CBC TV's 'Mallets and Brass.' A popular performer in Toronto nightclubs throughout the 1960s and 1970s, Appleyard has served as music director for several of them and for the cocktail lounges in the Park Plaza and Sutton Place hotels and at the Toronto-Dominion Centre. He also has been a leading percussionist in theatre, radio, TV, and recording orchestras. He travelled on four occasions to the Middle East on tours co-sponsored by the CBC and the United Nations.

Appleyard came to international notice in the early 1970s as a member of Benny Goodman's sextet, with which he has performed around the world, touring in Europe in 1972 and 1974 and in Australia in 1973. In 1975 he joined an orchestra, which included the Count Basie band, for a short engagement on Broadway accompanying Frank Sinatra. He appeared in concert annually 1976–9 at *Ontario Place with a group of US and Canadian jazzmen. In 1977 he became the host for 'Peter Appleyard Presents,' a TV jazz and variety program produced in Toronto and syndicated in North America. Of Appleyard's vibraphone playing, Jack Batten wrote (Toronto *Globe and Mail* 2 Oct 1975): 'He's most reminiscent of Red Norvo in style, given the impeccable taste and the easy rhythmic lift he displays as he glides over his vibes. He maintains wonderful control and fits every little passing nuance into perfect place.' Appleyard has written some incidental music for radio shows and some themes for his jazz groups. He is a member of CAPAC.

DISCOGRAPHY
Anything Goes. Helbig or Dale pf, Curry or Lander db, Alleyne or Rully drums. 1956, 1957. RCA Camden CAL 773
Vibe Sound. With US quartet. 1958. Audio Fidelity DFS 5901
per-cus-sive Jazz. With US orch. 1957. Audio Fidelity DFS 7002
The Vibraphone of Peter Appleyard. R. Toth or Moss pf, Bickert guit, Britto db, J. Niosi perc, Smith perc, Fearon drums. 1963. CTLS 5022
The Vibraphone of Peter Appleyard. Downes pf, Bickert guit, Britto db, Fearon drums. 1963. CTLS 5040
Polished Appleyard. With orch. 1969. RCA CTLS 1112
The Lincolnshire Poacher. With orch. 1972. CTL 477-5167
Peter Appleyard Presents. Wilkins arr, soloists including Amaro ten sax, Basso flhn, Bickert guit, Koffman fl and bar sax, McConnell trb, Young db. 1977. Salisbury SALS D2D-001
Peter Appleyard. Laurie Bower Singers, Gross or Mountford pf, Mann or Bickert guit, Young db, Fuller drums, Acevedo perc. GLS 5222/New Ventures NV 5007
Appleyard also appears as a soloist on LPs with Cal Jackson (*Cal Jackson Quartet*, 1954, X LXA-1005; *Cal Jackson Quartet*, 1954, Col CL-756; *Rave Notice*, 1955, Col CL-824), Guido Basso, Benny Goodman (*Benny Goodman into the 70s*, vol 5, 1971, Time Life STA 354; *On Stage*, 1972, 2-Lon 44182), and Peanuts Hucko (*Peanuts Hucko with the Pied Piper Quintet Featuring Peter Appleyard*, 1979, World Jazz WJLP 5-15)

BIBLIOGRAPHY
'Peter Appleyard in an interview with Roger Feather,' *Music World*, vol 1, Aug 1–5 1957
McNamara, Helen. 'King of swing opens up new world for Appleyard,' *CanComp*, 76, Jan 1973 MM

April Wine. Rock band formed in Halifax in 1970. It moved to Montreal a few months later. Founding members were the singer and guitarist Myles Goodwyn, the guitarist Dave Henman (replaced by 1974 by Gary Moffet), the bass guitarist Jim Henman (replaced in 1972 by Jim Clench, and Clench replaced in 1975 by Steve Lang), and the drummer Richie Henman (replaced by 1974 by Jerry Mercer). The guitarist Brian Greenway was added in 1977. Goodwyn (b Woodstock, NB, 23 Jun 1948) emerged as the band's leader.

The band's repertoire, mainly composed by Goodwyn, has combined the basic hard rock so successful with young Canadian audiences of the 1970s and ballads performed in a gentler style suited to pop radio. Except for the single 'You Could Have Been a Lady' (a minor hit internationally in 1972) April Wine's recording successes in the 1970s were limited largely to Canada. The singles 'Bad Side of the Moon' (1972), 'Lady Run, Lady Hide' (1973), 'I Wouldn't Want to Lose Your Love' (1974), 'Oowatanite' (1975), 'The Whole World's Going Crazy' (1976), 'You Won't Dance with Me' (1977), and 'Rock and Roll Is a Vicious Game' (1978) were national hits, and most of the band's LPs have received gold-record sales awards in Canada. Perhaps the country's leading touring band of the 1970s, April Wine has appeared annually in most major centres. Its tour after the release in 1975 of *Stand Back*, for example, included some 80 stops. In March 1977 it shared the stage for two nights at the Toronto nightclub El Mocambo with the Rolling Stones (the British band using April Wine to conceal – until the last moment – this rare club appearance). Recordings were made of both bands' performances. The resulting April Wine LP included new versions of the band's Canadian hits, intended for the international audience, whose interest had been piqued by the association of the two bands. April Wine made its first US tour later in 1977.

DISCOGRAPHY
April Wine. (1971). Aquarius AQR 502
On Record. (1972). Aquarius AQR 503
Electric Jewels. (1974). Aquarius AQR 504
Live! 1974. Aquarius AQR 505
Stand Back. (1975). Aquarius AQR 506
The Whole World's Goin' Crazy. (1976). Aquarius AQR 510
Forever, for Now. (1977). Aquarius AQR 511
Live at the El Mocambo. 1977. Aquarius AQR 515
First Glance. (1978). Aquarius AQR 517 MM

ARAB, John (Joseph). Tenor, b Halifax, NS, of Lebanese parents, 15 Jul 1930. He studied 1950–3 at the *Maritime Cons in Halifax with Teodor Brilts, summers 1953–60 at the *Banff SFA, 1954–60 at the *RCMT with Ernesto *Vinci, and 1954–60, while a member of the St Michael's Cathedral Choir in Toronto, with Mgr John *Ronan. First singing Almaviva in the *COC's touring production of *The Barber of Seville* in 1958, he made his formal debut in 1959 in its production of *The Love of Three Oranges* and appeared subsequently as a leading tenor with the COC and the Goldovsky Opera Theatre (USA), mainly in operas of Mozart and Puccini. In 1967 he created the roles of O'Donoghue and Lemieux in the COC's **Louis Riel* and in 1968 he sang the Tempter in the North American premiere of Britten's *The Prodigal Son* at the *Guelph Spring Festival. He has performed at the *Stratford Festival, with the Banff Opera, in CBC radio and TV productions, in oratorios and concerts, and as soloist with Canadian orchestras. (RSm)

Arabic music. In 1976 there were 100,000 people of Arabic extraction in Canada. The first immigration, in 1882, brought only Syrians and Lebanese who, even in the 1970s, formed a majority of Arab-Canadians, though 17 nations were represented to some degree in the total. (See also Egypt; Lebanon; Syria.) Arab-Canadians are of both urban and rural origin and include blue- and white-collar workers. The majority have settled in Montreal and Toronto. This article will discuss 1 / secular music and 2 / sacred music.

1 SECULAR MUSIC. Because of the diversity of Arab-Canadians' backgrounds, commercialized music – whether pop, or folk, or classical – with its supra-regional appeal, forms the core of most public performances intended for their enjoyment. The musicians for such performances generally include a solo singer accompanied by 'ud (lute) and darabukkah (drum). Qanun (zither), violin, or nay (flute) are used when available. The usual concert format is an uninterrupted sequence of solo songs of different types. The audience invariably dances the 'dabkah' (a Lebanese folk dance) and claps with the main beat. Such concerts may include non-Arabic dance music provided by a 'Western' band. Frequently, however, there is belly dancing, either by a professional dancer or by individual members of the audience. The belly dance also has become widely practised in Canada outside the Arab community. In private gatherings (weddings, birthdays, etc) authentic folk singing may take place, with or without instrumental accompaniment, among people from a particular locality who wish to invoke their common heritage. Authentic Arabic classical music generally is included in concerts for Syrian-Canadians as well as in those intended for Canadian audiences. The Classical Arabic Music Quintet of Toronto, led by George Sawa, is noted for its performances of this repertoire. In Montreal B. Mobayed, J. Sarwa, and G. Sawaya perform on the violin, the qanun, and the 'ud respectively.

BIBLIOGRAPHY
Qureshi, Regula. 'Ethnomusicological research among Canadian communities of Arab and East Indian origin,' *Ethnomusicology*, vol 16, Sep 1972
Sawa, George D. 'Musical acculturation of the Arab-Canadian in Toronto,' unpubl report, National Museum of Man, Ottawa 1975

2 SACRED MUSIC. Arab-Canadians come from a wide variety of religious backgrounds. Among them are Muslims, Jews, and Christians of the Coptic, Syrian Orthodox, Syrian Greek Orthodox (Byzantine), Greek Catholic, Maronite, Melkite, and other sects. Most Syrian and Lebanese immigrants (the majority of Arab immigrants to Canada) are Christians. Muslims of Lebanese extraction erected the first mosque in North America in Edmonton in 1938.

The tradition of Qur'anic chanting in the mosque has remained intact under the supervision of trained Imams from the Arab world, who also lead occasional congregational singing. In the Christian churches, chant is performed by both priest and choir, and there is congregational singing of hymns. The sacred music of some churches (eg, Syrian Greek Orthodox) shows a high degree of acculturation in the use of organ, the four-part harmony of the chorale, and the English language. That of some others (eg, the Coptic and Syrian Orthodox Churches) has avoided Western influence largely through the retention of original languages. (RQ, GDS)

Ed Archambault Inc. Business concern established in Montreal in 1896 by Edmond Archambault. It began as a sheet music store at the corner of Ste-Catherine and St-Hubert streets and moved later to Ste-Catherine and St-Denis. Archambault (b St-Paul-L'Ermite, near Montreal, August 1872, d Montreal 8 Jul 1947; in his youth a student of piano and organ in Montreal) added *Bell pianos to the store's merchandise around 1900. The success of this expansion allowed him in 1904 to lease two additional floors, containing studios and a concert hall. During World War I he took over his neighbour's business, the Hurteau music store. He became the agent for several Canadian and US pianos (*Pratte, David & Michaud, *Lesage, Baldwin) and organs (*Thomas, Baldwin). He also sold Archambault pianos, made by his firm except for the sounding board, which was imported from the USA. He was the sole agent for Paul Kaul violins (placing that department under the supervision of the Belgian Ulysse Salme) and also represented Holton, Kohn, and Selmer brass instruments. Around 1928 the firm was incorporated, and in 1930 Archambault moved into a seven-storey building which he had erected on Ste-Catherine St East. There he worked until struck down by illness in April 1946.

He was succeeded by two nephews, Edmond and Rosaire Archambault, assisted by Camille Duquette (b Montreal 19 Aug 1900, d there 5 Dec 1978, a pupil of Jean-Noël *Charbonneau at the *Schola cantorum). Duquette had been in charge of the religious music department at Archambault's 1917–19, then had worked for A.J. *Boucher, among others, before returning in 1925 to Archambault, where he served 1929–42 as general manager. After a period, 1942–8, with C.W. *Lindsay & Co, he returned again to Archambault, where he served 1948–77 as head of music and publishing and of the sheet music department. Concurrently he was choirmaster 1919–36 at the Très Saint Sacrement Church in Lachine and 1936–66 at the St-Jacques-le-Majeur Church.

In 1901 Archambault began to publish works by Canadian composers. He acquired the rights for the Édition de la Schola cantorum in 1917 and the Édition Belgo-Canadienne in 1929. Among the composers published by Archambault were *Brassard, *Champagne, *Contant, *Dela, J.-J. *Gagnier, *Gratton, Eugène *Lapierre, Albert Larrieu, Ernest *Lavigne, Léo-Pol *Morin, Émiliano *Renaud, Georges-Émile *Tanguay, and Éthelbert *Thibault. The firm also published instruction materials by Oswald *Michaud, Albertine *Morin-Labrecque, Al Stoupanse, and several others. Plate numbers were used occasionally. In the late 1970s Archambault began to publish works by Clermont *Pépin and Micheline *Saint-Marcoux. Works by composers who are members of CAPAC are published under the imprint of Archambault itself, and those of affiliates of PRO Canada are published under the imprint L'Industrie musicale. Archambault also established in 1952 the Alouette recording label, which offers LPs of a variety of music at popular prices, and in 1959 the Select label, whose catalogue features classical, popular, and religious music as well as educational recordings. Both labels have been distributed in Quebec by Archambault and in the rest of Canada by *London and others.

In the monthly *Entre-Nous* (1929–31) the chief editor, Frédéric *Pelletier, has given an account of the history and activities of the Archambault firm. Recorded therein are the founder's efforts on behalf of music education. Archambault assisted the *Cons national of Montreal from the time of its foundation (1905), placing some rent-free premises at the disposal of Alphonse *Lavallée-Smith for classes and administration. Moreover, in 1928 he ceded all his shares in this establishment to Eugène Lapierre, who at that time took over its reorganization. The firm also founded the *Prix Archambault (1940–63).

The Ed Archambault store in Montreal, 1930

BIBLIOGRAPHY

Pelletier, Frédéric. 'Le Maison Ed. Archambault,' *Entre-Nous*, vol 1, Dec 1929

Denis, Louis. 'De progrès en progrès La Maison Edmond Archambault,' *Notre Temps*, vol 1, 6 Dec 1945

Saint-Gelais, G. 'Rosaire Archambault co-propriétaire Ed. Archambault Inc.,' *Commerce*, vol 67, Oct 1965 CH

ARCHER, Thomas. Critic, broadcaster, bass, b Ely, Cambridgeshire, England, 24 Jul 1899, d Cowansville, Que, 28 Aug 1971. He began music studies at the St Paul's Cathedral Choir School in London and in 1911 received a Coronation Medal for his singing at Westminster Abbey. His war service in France earned him three medals. He emigrated to Canada in 1919 and resumed formal music studies in Montreal with Walter D. Clapperton, Percival J. *Illsley, and Frank H. *Rowe. He was the first Peterson Memorial Scholar at *McGill U. Later he was a bass soloist at St James the Apostle, Erskine, and St James Methodist (now United) churches.

In November 1929 Archer gave up singing and began to write reviews for *The Gazette*, Canada's oldest newspaper. In January 1930 he became its first staff music and drama critic. For nearly 40 years he wrote reviews of concerts, opera, ballet, drama, recordings, and films. His weekly columns earned him a large and faithful audience. He published interviews with such people as Chaliapin, McCormack, Medtner, and Rachmaninoff. In 1940 and for some seasons thereafter he was the intermission commentator of the New York Philharmonic Sunday afternoon broadcasts for CBC. At one of these, in 1945, Stravinsky, who was in Montreal, was his guest in a rare radio interview. Archer was commentator for the CBC series 'Canadian Music in Wartime.' For several years he was program annotator for the *MSO, the *Montreal Festivals, the *Casavant Society, and the *Opera Guild. He contributed to publications in Canada and abroad. In 1959 he travelled to Vienna for the first time and wrote an illuminating series of articles on the Viennese masters from Mozart to Bruckner.

Archer was always at the forefront of the Montreal music scene, fostering new talent and promoting public support for worthwhile projects. He once wrote: 'None of the decisions reached by the critic ... can be regarded as final judgment. The whole history of criticism is strewn with the corpses of critical opinions that have been put forward as judgments.' His large personal library included full scores of all of the operas of Wagner and most of those by Richard Strauss. His extended essay on the latter's music has remained in manuscript. It has been deposited at the CMM. In 1956 he was honoured at a special dinner by the Society of Friends of Music in Montreal, along with Claude *Champagne, Maureen *Forrester, George *London, and Wilfrid *Pelletier.

WRITINGS

'Claude Champagne,' *CMJ*, vol 2, Winter 1958

'Functions of a musical critic,' Montreal *Gazette*, 20 Dec 1930, repr 23 Jul 1966

'The season of music 1930–1931,' *Montreal Music Year Book 1931* (Montreal nd)

BIBLIOGRAPHY

'Critic's life,' Montreal *Gazette*, 10 Jan 1959

Siskind, Jacob. 'Former Gazette critic dies,' Montreal *Gazette*, 30 Aug 1971 GP

ARCHER, Violet (b Balestreri). Composer, teacher, pianist, organist, percussionist, b Montreal 24 Apr 1913; L MUS (McGill) 1934, B MUS (McGill) 1936, ACCO 1938, B MUS (Yale) 1948, M MUS (Yale) 1949, hon D MUS (McGill) 1971. She attended the *McGill Cons to study piano with J.J. *Weatherseed and composition with Claude *Champagne and Douglas *Clarke, and was a percussionist 1940–7 with the *Montreal Women's SO. She commuted to New York in 1942 for private study with Bartók and taught 1944–7 at the McGill Cons. Assisted by the Bradley-Keeler Memorial Scholarship (1947), Quebec government scholarships (1948, 1949), and, for her *Passacaglia*, the Charles Ditson Fellowship (1948; the companion *Fanfare* followed in 1949), she studied composition with Hindemith at Yale U. There she won the Woods-Chandler prize (1949) for her large choral-orchestral work *The Bell* (to words from the *Sermons* and *Devotions* of John Donne; it was premiered in 1953 by the *Montreal Bach Choir). Her *Fanfare and Passacaglia* was premiered at the 1949 International Student Symposium of Music, Boston. Archer was percussionist 1947–9 with the New Haven SO and taught in 1948 and 1949 at the *U of Alberta Summer School. An award in 1949 from the *Ladies' Morning Musical Club of Montreal enabled her to spend some time in 1950 in musical reconnaissance in England. She performed her piano works there and in France, Switzerland, and Italy. Composer-in-residence 1950–3 at North Texas State College, she also taught at Cornell U in 1952 and at the U of Oklahoma 1953–61, giving a series of radio lectures 1960–1 on WNAD, Norman, Okla, and acting as a state judge 1953–61 and national judge 1959–61 for various US young-composer competitions. On a Canada Council Senior Fellowship and with a year's leave 1958–9 from the university she completed four works, including *Apocalypse* and the *Violin Concerto*. Following her return to Canada for doctoral studies at the *U of Toronto in 1961, she joined the faculty at the U of Alberta in 1962, becoming chairman of the theory and composition department.

Archer is a methodical composer, working efficiently and comfortably in the western tradition but absorbing serial procedures, parallelism, and folk influence into her music occasionally. Her acceptance of the Gebrauchsmusik ethic is reflected in much of her large output. Among her early works, those for piano were the most skilful, but her command of orchestration soon improved, particularly after deliberate study of clarinet, strings, and brass, and of composition with Hin-

Violet Archer

demith. Her augmented skills are on full display in the *Piano Concerto* with its brilliant solo part and transparent orchestral writing. Adroit counterpoint and strong formal organization are hallmarks of her work. An interest in the rhythmic freedom of folk music dates from 1938 but has become highly developed and abstracted in the sonatas and the *String Trio No. 2* (1961). A growing interest in dramatic and evocative sonorities led to the expressionism of the *Prelude-Incantation* (1964). In keeping with the medieval nature of its carol texts the *Cantata sacra* favours the intervals of fourth and fifth. The comic opera *Sganarelle* exploits the basso buffo tradition and elements of Sprechstimme to convey the wit of Molière. Without making a policy of novelty Archer is not afraid of new means, and in the 1970s her *Haiku* and *Episodes* have used electronic sounds. Archer received an Alberta Achievement Award in 1970 and the Creative and Performance award (1972) from the City of Edmonton, and she was elected to the council of the *CLComp in 1975. She is a member of PRO Canada and an associate of the *CMCentre.

SELECTED COMPOSITIONS

STAGE

Sganarelle, opera (Molière, S. Eliot, Archer). 1973. Ber (rental)

ORCHESTRA

3 early works (1930–40). All ms
Poem for Orchestra. 1940. Ber (rental)
Scherzo Sinfonico. 1940. Ber (rental)
Britannia – A Joyful Overture. 1941. Ms
Fantasy on a Ground. 1946 (rev 1956). Ber (rental)
Symphony. 1946. Ber (rental)
Fanfare and Passacaglia. 1948. BMIC 1964. RCI 130 (*CBC SO)
Divertimento. 1957. BMIC 1968
Three Sketches. 1961. BMIC 1966. CBC SM-119 (*CBC Wpg O)
Prelude-Incantation. 1964. CMCentre
Sinfonietta. 1968. Ber (rental). CBC SM-226 (*CBC Van Chamb O)
Sinfonia. 1969. Ber (rental)
Little Suite for String Orchestra. 1970. Ms

SOLOIST(S) OR CHOIR WITH ORCHESTRA

Fantasia Concertante. 1941. Fl, ob, cl, str. CMCentre
Fantasy for Clarinet and Strings. 1942. CMCentre
Concertino for Clarinet and Orchestra. 1946 (rev 1956). Ber (rental)
Lamentations of Jeremy (Bible). 1947. SATB, orch. Ms
The Bell (Donne). 1949. SATB, orch. Ber (rental). RCI 130 (*CBC SO)
Piano Concerto No. 1. 1956. Ber (rental)
Apocalypse 'Revelations.' 1958. Sop, SATB, brass, tim. CMCentre
Violin Concerto. 1959. Ber (rental)
Cantata sacra (medieval dialogues). 1966. 5 soli, sm orch. CMCentre

CHAMBER

4 *String Quartets* (1940–9). All ms
Sonata. 1944. Fl, cl, pf. CMCentre
Fantasy for Violin and Piano. 1945. CMCentre
Quartet. 1945. Fl, ob, cl, bn. Ms
Two Pieces for Flute Solo. 1947. Ms
Divertimento. 1949. Ob, cl, bn. CMCentre. RCI 192 (*Berman)
Fantasy in the Form of a Passacaglia. 1951. Chamb ens. CMCentre
2 *String Trios* (1953, 1961). Both CMCentre
Trio No. 1. 1954. Pf trio. CMCentre. RCI 112 (*Bress)
Prelude and Allegro. 1954. Vn, pf. BMIC 1958. RCI 136 (*Le Blanc)
Three Duets for Two Violins. 1955. Peer 1960
Sonata for Cello and Piano. 1954. CMCentre. RCI 139 (W. *Joachim)
Sonata No. 1. 1956. Vn, pf. CMCentre. RCI 196 (M. *Goodman)
Trio No. 2. 1957. Pf trio. Wat 1977. RCI 196 (*Bress vn) / RCI 241/CBC SM-5 (*Brandon U Trio)
Divertimento No. 2. 1957. Ob, vn, vc. CMCentre
Divertimento for Brass Quintet. 1963. Ber 1974
Sonata. 1965. Hn, pf. CMCentre. RCI 412 (*Maiste)
Sonata. 1970. Cl, pf. Wat 1973. RCI 412 (*Campbell)
Three Little Studies for Violin and Piano. 1970. CMCentre
Suite for Four Violins. 1971. CMCentre
Sonata for Alto Saxophone and Piano. 1972. Ber 1973. RCI 412 (*Brodie)
Sonata for Oboe and Piano. 1973. Ber 1978
Little Suite for Trumpet and Piano. 1975. CMCentre
Simple Tune for Soprano Recorder and Piano. 1975. CMCentre
Sonata. 1976. Va, vc, pf. Ms
Suite for Solo Flute. 1976. CMCentre
Sonatina for Oboe and Piano. 1977. CMCentre

PIANO

Sonata for Pianoforte. 1945 (rev 1957). CMCentre
3 *Sonatinas* (1945, 1946, 1973). (No. 2) B & H 1948. (No. 2) RCI 132 (*Pratt pf)
Six Preludes. 1947. CMCentre
Suite for Piano. 1947. CMCentre
Ten Folk Songs for Four Hands. 1953. BMIC 1955. RCI 113 (P. *Beaudet pf, G. *Bourassa pf)
Eleven Short Pieces. 1960. Peer 1964. CCM-1 (*Cavalho)
Four Little Studies for Piano. 1963. Wat 1964
Theme and Variations for Piano. 1963. Wat 1964
Three Miniatures. 1963. Wat 1965. CCM-1 (*Cavalho)
Improvisations for Piano. 1968. CMCentre. Mel SMLP 4031 (*Kubalek)
Two Miniatures. 1970. Wat 1972 ('Little March')
Lydian Mood and A Quiet Chat. (1971). Wat 1973
Three Inventions. 1974. CMCentre
Four Bagatelles for piano. 1977. CMCentre

ORGAN

Sonatina. 1944. GVT 1971
Two Chorale Preludes. 1948. Peer 1962
Chorale Improvisation on 'O Worship the King.' 1967. CMCentre. All Saints' Cathedral Edmonton ST-56722/23 (*Bancroft)
4 other preludes. All CMCentre

CHOIR

Landscapes (T.S. Eliot). 1950. SATB. Wat 1973. CBC SM-274 (*Festival Singers)
'Proud Horses' (Sampley). 1953. SATB. CMCentre. RCI 189 (*Mtl Bach Choir)
Three French Canadian Folk Songs. 1953. SATB. BMIC 1962. Vox STPL 511-860 (*Mtl Bach Choir)
Two Songs for Women's Voices (A. Bass). 1955. SSA, ob, pf. GVT 1972
Introit and Choral Prayer (liturgical). 1961. SATB, org. BMIC 1963
'I Will Lift up Mine Eyes' (Psalm 121). 1967. SATB, org. Wat 1969
'Sweet Jesu, King of Bliss' (anon). 1967. SATB. Jay 1967
'O Lord Thou Hast Searched Me and Known Me' (Psalm 139). 1968. SATB, org. Wat 1969
'O Sing Unto the Lord' (Psalm 96). 1968. SA, org. Wat 1969
The Glory of God (Bible). 1971. SSAA. CMCentre
'Sing a New Song to the Lord' (Psalm 98). 1974. SATB, org. Wat 1974
'Three Sailors from Groix' arr (French sea shanties, transl Cockshott). 1975. SSA, pf. CMCentre
'Shout with Joy' (Psalm 100 from *The Living Bible*). 1976. SATB, org. Wat 1977

VOICE

Under the Sun (Bourinot). 1949. Mezzo, pf. CMCentre. CBC SM-79 (*Forst)
'April Weather' (A.B. England). 1950. Alto, pf. CMCentre. RCI 108 (*Forrester)
'Cradle Song' (England). 1950. Alto, pf. FH 1959. RCI 108 (*Forrester)
'The Twenty-Third Psalm.' 1952. Alto, pf. BMIC 1954. RCI 108 (*Forrester)
'I Corinthians, 13.' 1976. Mezzo, pf. CMCentre
Moon Songs. 1976. Mezzo, pf. CMCentre
'Separation.' 1976. Alto (bar), pf. CMCentre
'In Just Spring' (e.e. cummings). 1977. Med v, pf. CMCentre
Plain Songs (D. Livesay). 1977. Mezzo, pf. CMCentre

ELECTRONIC

Episodes. 1973. Electronic tape. Ms. Melbourne SMLP 4024

FILM SCORE

Someone Cares. U of Alberta documentary

WRITINGS

'Alberta and its folklore,' *Canadian Folk Music Soc Bulletin*, vol 2, Jul 1967
'Music of Canada as related to its composers,' *Pan Pipes*, vol 51, Mar 1959
'Alberta and its folksongs,' CFMS *Newsletter*, vol 2, Jul 1967

BIBLIOGRAPHY

'Violet Archer,' *Pan Pipes*, vol 45, Jan 1953
PRO Canada Ltd / BMI Canada Ltd. 'Violet Archer,' pamphlets (1970, 1979)
Byron, E., and Ashwell, K. 'Doctor Violet Archer: prominent Alberta composer,' *Music in Alberta*, vol 1, Sep–Oct 1972
Ashwell, Keith. Review of *Sganarelle*, *Edmonton Journal*, 6 Feb 1974
Creative Canada, vol 1
Contemporary Canadian Composers

EK

Archives. Repositories of documents of historical interest, usually in written, sound-recorded, or pictorial form. A distinction must be made between archival *institutions* such as the Public Archives of Canada in Ottawa and the several provincial archives, and archival *collections*, which may be found in libraries, musical organizations, monasteries, museums, and elsewhere. In Canada, as in many other countries, archival institutions have been preoccupied with the preservation of official records and have paid more attention to political than to cultural history, although items of musical interest may be found in some of their non-musical collections. Several such institutions have become interested in the creative arts in recent years, but in the late 1970s a major share of archival holdings in music belonged to university and public libraries and the *National Library of Canada.

In Canada the safeguarding of musical documents began very late. In folk and aboriginal music archival deposits date back to the late 19th century, but at least three quarters of the collections listed at the end of this article passed into public hands after 1969. In that year the NL of C purchased the papers of Healey *Willan, thus affirming the concept of public responsibility for preserving the documents of Canada's musical history. It has been possible in these years to trace the papers of a number of Canadian musicians long since deceased, but many important documents, such as the bulk of the manuscripts of Calixa *Lavallée, may be considered lost forever. Undoubtedly other papers survive scattered among descendants and friends, many of whom are unaware of their value or have no contacts with archival circles. When papers have been given to public institutions in the past, they often have received nothing but storage space since specialist care has been unavailable and regular work has had higher priority. The growth of musical archives during the 1970s has been stimulated by (and in return has encouraged the introduction of) Canadian music courses at many universities and by the research activities engendered by the preparation of *EMC*.

In contrast to published materials, which exist in many copies and which libraries classify by subject, archival materials are unique and are kept together in units, each named after the person or organization that produced or collected them.

The *produced* collections encompass the papers and memorabilia accumulated by individual musicians as products or by-products of their careers and by associations as records of their activities. They may include composers' manuscript scores, whether sketches or fair copies; performers' programs and reviews (often placed in scrapbooks); musicians' personal and business correspondence, diaries, lecture notes, speeches, diplomas, medals, photos and other souvenirs; musical societies' business correspondence, minute books and financial records; privately made recordings; and other types of material.

The *collected* collections are results of deliberate effort by researchers in special subject areas. They include the archival holdings of folk music and of 'oral history' obtained through recorded and transcribed interviews. Such collections form the backbone of ethnomusicology studies. They represent the oldest type of archival activity in music carried out under governmental auspices. (See also Marius Barbeau; National Museums of Canada; Archives de Folklore.)

To supplement these 'residual' and 'assembled' collections, archivists will acquire single items or small groups of items from a variety of sources, such as autograph dealers, auctions, and rummage sales, or through the copying of relevant documents preserved in other institutions.

Archival collections are of supreme importance to historians, biographers, broadcasters, filmmakers, exhibition planners, and other researchers because they provide the first-hand evidence of primary source material. Their usefulness depends on the archivist's skill in preparing inventories, indexes, and other finding aids. Musical societies who cannot afford to hire a professional archivist may obtain advice regarding the maintenance of their papers from some of the larger institutions. Archival help is available also from *Co-ordinated Arts Services of Toronto.

The *Union List of Manuscripts in Canadian Repositories / Catalogue collectif des manuscrits des archives canadiennes* published by the PAC (Ottawa, rev edn 1975; 1st suppl 1976) lists many holdings of musical interest but is not organized by subject. The following list should be regarded as a sampling only. It is arranged by province and city, and the items listed in each case are not necessarily the most significant ones. Excluded are 1 / active organizations maintaining their own archives, 2 / musical items incidental to non-musical collections, 3 / so-called archival holdings in libraries such as old recordings or sheet music in dead storage, and 4 / library materials organized according to archival principles, as are some of the printed music holdings at the BN du Q. Names entered do not necessarily correspond to the name of the collection they are housed in: eg, the Achille *Fortier manuscripts at the Archives nationales du Québec (Centre régional de Montréal) are part of the Claude *Champagne Collection.

ALBERTA

Calgary

*U of Calgary – *Calgary Philharmonic Society; Morris *Surdin

Glenbow-Alberta Institute – miscellaneous items

Edmonton

City of Edmonton Archives – *Alberta Music Festival; Women's Musical Club (records for 1936–66)

Provincial Museum and Archives of Alberta – *ARMTA

BRITISH COLUMBIA

Vancouver

City of Vancouver Archives – *Friends of Chamber Music; *Vancouver Woman's Musical Club; files on 'Music in Vancouver,' 'BC Philharmonic Orchestra' (1950), 'Men's Musical Club' (1917–29), *'Vancouver Symphony Society,' 'J.D.A. *Tripp,' 'The *Philharmonic Music Club,' etc

Victoria

British Columbia Archives – Philip *Thomas collection of ca 500 songs recorded in BC; files on music and musicians in British Columbia and in particular Victoria, including 19th-century compositions in manuscript

MANITOBA

Winnipeg

Provincial Archives of Manitoba – Margaret Arnett *MacLeod, Peter *Zvankin

Ukrainian Cultural and Educational Centre – Oleksander Koshetz

NEW BRUNSWICK

Fredericton

Christ Church Cathedral – church music manuscripts (19th century)

Moncton

*U of Moncton, Centre d'études acadiennes – folksong and folklore

Sackville

*Mount Allison U – Trevor Morgan Jones

Saint John

New Brunswick Museum – Ladies' Morning Musical Club (Saint John, 1926–59); Saint John Opera House; *manuscript books of Jonathan Odell and Jeremiah Regan

NEWFOUNDLAND

St John's

*Memorial U, Folklore and Language Archives – folk music

NOVA SCOTIA

Halifax

*Dalhousie U – J.D. Logan collection of 57 autograph letters; Ellen *Ballon (includes ms of Liadov and Villa Lobos, letters from famous musicians)

Provincial Archives of Nova Scotia – Helen *Creighton (folksongs); Don *Messer; *NSRMTA; Halifax, Lunenburg and other NS musical societies

ONTARIO

Hamilton

*McMaster U – Havergal Brian; Sir Robert Mayer; Sir Charles Hubert Hastings Parry (79 letters); Klaus Pringsheim (much of the material is related to Mahler); Dame Ethel Smythe; Eric Walter White (history of English opera); letters by Tchaikovsky, Clara Schumann, and others

Hamilton Public Library – Robert S. and Paul *Ambrose

Jordan

Jordan Museum of the Twenty – *manuscript books, early 19th century

Kingston

*Queen's U – H. William Hawke

London

*U of Western Ontario – Alfred *Rosé (much of the material is related to Mahler); 18th-century manuscript copies of operatic and other compositions; autographs of Cimarosa, Grétry, Jommelli, Lully, Méhul, Paisiello, Piccinni, and others

Ottawa

*National Library of Canada

- Large collections: Murray *Adaskin; Lucio *Agostini; George M. *Brewer; *CAML; *CLComp; Claude *Champagne; Alexis *Contant; Pauline *Donalda; S.C. *Eckhardt-Gramatté; Robert *Fleming; W.O. *Forsyth; Herman *Geiger-Torel; Hector *Gratton; C.A.E. *Harriss; Luigi von *Kunits; Alan *Mills; *Ottawa Philharmonic Orchestra; Pro Musica Society of Ottawa; Eldon *Rathburn; R. Murray *Schafer; Leo *Smith; Gordon V. *Thompson, Ltd; Arnold *Walter; Alfred *Whitehead; Healey *Willan
- Smaller collections: Emma *Albani; J.H. *Anger; Gena *Branscombe; Edward *Broome; John *Carter; A.T. *Cringan; Ernest *Dainty; Juliette *Gaultier de la Vérendrye; Joseph *Gould; *Hambourg family; Richard *Hayward; Emmy *Heim; Percival *Illsley; Frantz *Jehin-Prume; Henri K. *Jordan; Joy D. Kennedy; Calixa *Lavallée; Frederic *Lord; Clarence *Lucas; Ettore *Mazzoleni; Dorothy J. McCurry (includes Annie Lampman *Jenkins and F.M.S. Jenkins); T.B. Richardson; Welford *Russell; C.W. *Sabatier; Herbert *Sanders; Gustave *Smith; Toronto Choral Society (1884–92); Heinz *Unger; and others
- Non-Canadian holdings: Tadeusz Baird (autograph score); Beethoven (see T.F. *Molt); Rosy Geiger-Kullmann (Geiger-Torel collection); Nikolai Medtner (Gratton collection); Percy Scholes; Harold D. Smith (*RCA Victor and sound-recording history); letters or postcards from Elgar, Liszt, Milhaud, Clara Schumann, Vaughan Williams, and many other famous musicians

National Museum of Man – Collections of *Indian and *Inuit music at Canadian Ethnology Service / Service canadien d'ethnologie; collections of folk music at Canadian Centre for Folk Culture Studies / Centre canadien sur la culture traditionelle; see also Ethnomusicology

Public Archives of Canada

- Large collections: Louis-Honoré *Bourdon; Sarah *Fischer; Edward *Johnson
- Smaller collections: Emma Albani; Violet *Archer; J. Edgar *Birch; *CFMTA; Éva *Gauthier; Juliette Gaultier de la Vérendrye; H.H. *Godfrey; C.A.E. Harriss; Oskar *Morawetz; *Morning Music Club of Ottawa; Ottawa Amateur Orchestral Society; Toronto Musicians' Association (minute book 1874–7)
- Other: manuscript compilation of liturgical chant by François-X. Borel (1767); manuscript book of Étienne Claude Lagueux (ca 1805–18); letters by Joseph *Quesnel to John *Neilson; letters by Elgar, de Pachmann, and others

Sudbury

University of Sudbury, Centre franco-ontarien de folklore (see Germain *Lemieux)

Toronto

*CBC, Program Archives – recordings and videotapes of CBC programs

Metropolitan Toronto Library – scrapbooks on Canadian musicians and musical life, 1860s–1950s

Ontario Department of Public Records and Archives – Alexander Muir

Royal Ontario Museum – R.S. *Williams collection of musical instruments also includes autographs of Auber, Beethoven (doubtful), Bellini, Czerny, Berlioz, Donizetti, Liszt, Meyerbeer, Rossini, and others; Italian and French liturgical ms, 13th–15th centuries

*U of Toronto – *Hart House String Quartet, Edward Johnson, Kathleen *Parlow, *RCMT, Frank S. *Welsman

*York U – Mavor *Moore

Waterloo

*Wilfrid Laurier U – *RCCO

QUEBEC

Chicoutimi

Archives de la Société historique du Saguenay – local music history

Joliette
Les Clercs de St-Viateur – Roméo-Clément *Larivière; Calixa Lavallée
Montreal
Archives nationales du Québec, Centre régional de Montréal
– Large collections: Jean *Deslauriers; Jules *Dubois; Achille *Fortier; Pierre *Mercure; Isabelle and Jean *Papineau-Couture; Wilfrid *Pelletier; *SMCQ
– Smaller collections: Dantès Belleau; Gabriel *Cusson, Omer *Dumas; Howard *Fogg; Joseph-I. Pâquet; Amédée *Tremblay; various ms of church music
Bibliothèque nationale du Québec – Eugène Caron; Lionel *Daunais; José *Delaquerrière; Jean-Josaphat *Gagnier; Alphonse *Lavallée-Smith
CBC Program Archives – Recordings and videotapes of CBC programs
*Conservatoire de musique de Montréal – Autograph scores by Italian composers from A. Scarlatti to Ponchielli; autographs by Alban Berg and Francis Poulenc
Grand Séminaire de Montréal – church music
Montreal City Library – Alfred *De Sève; J.T. Leblanc and E.-Z. *Massicotte transcriptions of folksong texts; etc
*McGill U – Kelsey *Jones; Julius Schloss (includes Alban Berg items)
*U of Montreal – Guillaume *Couture
Quebec
Archives nationales du Québec, Centre régional de Québec – *AMQ; Marius *Cayouette; Club musical des dames 1926–56; *Concerts Couperin; Alain *Gagnon; Raoul *Jobin; *Quebec SO; letters by Joseph Quesnel; Edmond *Trudel
Conservatoire de musique de Québec – Joseph *Vézina
Petit Séminaire de Québec – Joseph Quesnel (*Colas et Colinette, *Lucas et Cécile*)
*Laval U – Henri *Gagnon
Laval U, Archives de folklore – Folk music and folklore
Trois-Rivières
Archives nationales du Québec, Centre régional de la Mauricie et des Bois-Francs – Anais Allard-Rousseau
U du Québec à Trois-Rivières – Raymond *Daveluy

SASKATCHEWAN
Regina
Provincial Archives Board of Saskatchewan – *SRMTA
Regina Public Library – local history
Saskatoon
Provincial Archives Board of Saskatchewan – local musical societies; Lyell *Gustin; Marjorie Wilson
Saskatoon Public Library – George Palmer; Marguerite *Spencer

UNITED STATES OF AMERICA
New York
Columbia U – Laura Boulton collection of aboriginal and folk music of Canada
New York Public Library – Gena Branscombe; Éva Gauthier
Washington
Library of Congress – Canadian folk music HK

Archives de folklore. Research centre at *Laval U for the gathering and study of the oral traditions of the French-speaking inhabitants of North America and the collection of specialized writings in this field. On 28 Feb 1944 Laval entrusted its new chair of folklore to Luc *Lacourcière and thus launched a research centre whose findings were to be disseminated later through teaching, publications, and other means of communication. This act gave official recognition to the instruction in folklore and research begun as early as 1939 by Lacourcière in the university's summer program, in which the anthropologist Marius *Barbeau and the writer Félix-Antoine Savard subsequently participated.

Following in the footsteps of Barbeau, who had been collecting songs, stories, and legends since 1914, Luc Lacourcière and Mgr Savard conducted research into folklore, gathering the over 5000 sound recordings which formed the archives' basic collection. The number subsequently increased owing to the help of many collectors. The 1979 statistics reported 506 collections of sound recordings on 5236 discs and magnetic tapes and as many music manuscripts and transcriptions; all this material was obtained from the French-speaking inhabitants of Quebec, New Brunswick, Nova Scotia, Prince Edward Island, Ontario, Manitoba, and Louisiana. The archives also held by 1972 some 50,000 artefacts and other items, including folk costumes and dance patterns. The accumulation of recorded and manuscript music and printed material led Conrad *Laforte (librarian-archivist 1951–75) and his assistants to devise a practical classification system and to establish catalogues for oral-tradition subjects. The principal catalogue – a shelf-list – is complemented by cross-indexes of informants and locations. Of particular interest to musicians and ethnomusicologists are the descriptive catalogue of more than 2000 instrumental pieces and the French-language folksong catalogue, which in 1980 contained more than 86,000 card entries. Archive facilities also include an electronic laboratory offering transcription and dubbing facilities from magnetic tapes. In addition to Luc Lacourcière, director 1944–77, and the others mentioned previously, collaborators of special interest for ethnomusicology have included François *Brassard, Marguerite Béclard d'Harcourt, Dominique Gauthier, Rosette *Renshaw, Sister Marie-Ursule, and Russell Scott Young. Roger *Matton collaborated with the archives department 1956–76 as a researcher and ethnomusicologist, specializing in the musical notation of the oral data. The Archives de folklore were host to the 1961 IFMC convention. That year, the American Assn for State and Local History presented the archives with an Award of Merit 'for outstanding work in gathering and disseminating much of the folklore and music of French Canada.'

The Archives de folklore retain autonomy despite integration with CELAT (Centre d'études sur la langue, les arts et les traditions populaires des francophones en Amérique du Nord), founded in 1976 by Jean Hamelin. The centre combines the Archives de folklore, the linguistic atlas of eastern Canada (in catalogue form), and the Trésor de la langue française au Québec. Several researcher-teachers are part of CELAT; Jean-Claude Dupont was appointed director in 1977.

The publications of the Archives de folklore, issued irregularly, began to appear in 1946. The first four volumes deal with articles on songs and the next two contain over 115 songs with music. Volumes 7 and 16 include a selection of songs from the Russell Scott Young collection and songs from Shippagan respectively; volume 17 is entitled *Poétiques de la chanson traditionnelle française*. Volume 18 begins the *Catalogue de la chanson folklorique française*, which was set up by Conrad Laforte and which in 1980 numbered more than 86,000 entries. The Archives de folklore has been assisted by the Quebec government, the *National Museums of Canada, and the *Canada Council, as well as private donations.

DISCOGRAPHY
Acadie et Québec: songs of New Brunswick and Quebec prepared by Lacourcière and Matton. RCA LCP-1020/RCA Gala CGP-139
Cible. Radio-Québec RQ-128
C'est dans la Nouvelle-France. Le Tamanoir TAM-27005

BIBLIOGRAPHY
Annuaire général de l'Un. Laval, 88 (1944–5), 89 (1945–6), and others
Les Archives de folkore, vols 1–4 (Montreal 1946–9), 5–19 (Quebec 1951–79)
Lacourcière, Luc. 'The present state of French-Canadian folklore studies,' *JAF*, 74, Oct–Dec 1961
J of the IFMC, vol 14, 1962
Brassard, François. 'French-Canadian folk music studies: a survey,' *Ethnomusicology*, vol 16, Sep 1972
CELAT-Information (Quebec 1976–9) CL

Arc Records. Subsidiary of Arc Sound Company Ltd, which was established in Toronto in 1958 by Philip G. Anderson and William R. Gilliland. At first a record distributor, Arc Sound began releasing Arc records in 1959 and purchased the Precision Pressing Co in 1961. It purchased Bay Music Publishers (PRO Canada) in 1962 and operated an artists' promotion agency ca 1962–76. In 1969 Arc Sound and its subsidiaries came under the control of a Canadian-owned holding company, the Ahed Music Corporation Ltd, Toronto, which became known in the mid-1970s for its record-merchandizing campaigns on Canadian TV. Among the earliest Arc LPs were those by the popular Newfoundland singers, Omar *Blondahl and Dick *Nolan. Later LPs, some for Arc's Caribou and International Artists labels, presented other Newfoundlanders, including Burt Cuff, Harry *Hibbs, Gordon Pinsent, Ray Walsh, and John White. Arc also produced singles by several Toronto rock bands of the mid-1960s, some of them for its Yorkville label. Other artists or groups who have recorded for Arc or its affiliated labels include the Abbey Tavern Singers, Bill Amesbury, the *Brothers-In-Law, the Majestics, Fred *McKenna, Catherine *McKinnon, Anne *Murray, Pat *Riccio, the cast of CBC TV's 'Singalong Jubilee,' and the *Travellers. By 1979 the company had released some 400 LPs.

AREL, Gaston. Organist, teacher, b Trois-Rivières, Que, 10 Sep 1928; lauréat in organ (AMQ) 1948. He began piano studies at five with Cécile Dufault (Sister Saint-Gaston, Présentation de Marie) in St-Hyacinthe, Que, and continued with Conrad *Letendre (piano 1941–7, organ 1945–54) in both St-Hyacinthe and Montreal. He was the organist 1945–53 at the cathedral in St-Hyacinthe. He studied piano 1947–8 at the *CMM and 1947–51 privately with Arthur *Letondal. A scholarship from the Quebec government made it possible for him to study organ 1953–4 with André Marchal in Paris. On his return he became the organist at the Immaculée-Conception Church in Montreal, serving in that position until 1974. In 1955 he married Lucienne *L'Heureux. In 1960, on scholarships from the Canada Council, the couple went to Hamburg for training with Charles Letestu (with whom they studied again in 1964).

In 1955, Arel began to be heard frequently on the French and English networks of the CBC, notably in the series 'Organ Works of Bach' and 'Organists in Recital.' He also has been a regular guest of the *Amis de l'orgue de Québec, *Ars Organi (of which he was a founding member), the Concerts spirituels of St-Joseph Oratory, the *JMC, *Pro Organo Society, and other concert-giving organizations. He has accompanied Léopold *Simoneau and Pierrette *Alarie (1952) and Maureen *Forrester (1953) as well as many other singers and instrumentalists.

A teacher at the Séminaire de St-Hyacinthe 1951–64 and at the Cons de Trois-Rivières 1964–9 and 1976–7, Arel joined the staff at the CMM in 1964 and at the *JMC Orford Art Centre in 1973 and continued teaching privately.

Arel was president 1946–9 of the Compagnons de l'art of St-Hyacinthe, first national president 1949–50 of the JMC, and president 1949–53 of the St-Hyacinthe Centre. He became president of the *AMQ in 1974. He served in 1975 on the jury of the *Canada Council and 1975–6 as vice-president of the Montreal centre of the *RCCO.

One of the leaders in the revival of the mechanical traction organ, Arel advised on the installation of several organs in Quebec, notably those at the Immaculée-Conception Church in Montreal and the Trappist monastery at Oka. PD

Argentina. See South and Central America, Mexico, the West Indies.

Arion Male Voice Choir. In 1980 possibly Canada's oldest existing male choir devoted to the singing of secular music. It was founded in February 1893 as the Arion Club of Victoria (BC) and gave its first concert on 17 May at Institution Hall. The variant of the name still in use in the 1970s was adopted ca 1940. Following a fashion instigated in 1854 by the New York Arion Society (a German-American male choir), it was named for Arion, the poet-singer of ancient Greece, who symbolized good fortunes for travelling musicians. (Other 19th-century Canadian Arion Club choirs were located in Halifax, Hamilton, and London.)

In April 1894 the choir gave a performance of *The Mikado*, and in June of the same year it presented its first open-air concert, an event repeated annually until the early 1930s. The choir's early repertoire included Rhenish, Norse, and American songs. In 1898 the Arions sang at the opening of the British Columbia legislative buildings in Victoria. By 1903 fraternal exchange visits with US choirs had begun. In 1905 the group joined several other choirs in a performance of Haydn's *The Creation* at Tacoma, Wash. In 1906, in a similar exchange held in Victoria, it took part in a birthday program honouring the US composer Dudley Buck. In May 1906 it joined other local choirs and two noted guests, Emma *Albani and Éva *Gauthier, in a performance of Frederick Cowen's *The Rose Maiden*.

The group's membership has fluctuated between 23 and 60, and on occasion (depending on the works to be sung, and particularly during its earlier years) it has been augmented by women singers. There is an auxiliary boys' choir.

The Arion Male Voice Choir has sung before visiting royalty, government officials, and departing and returning armed forces. It also has performed at boating concerts and the famous Swiftsure Sailing Races. It was, in effect, Victoria's ceremonial choir. In its early days it also gave benefit concerts for families bereaved by sea disasters. In 1973 the choir toured Scotland, northern England, and Wales, where it was well-received for its performance of Newfoundland sea shanties at the Llangollen Eisteddfod. In Victoria it has sung regularly at Christ Church Cathedral (which was designed by J.C.M. Keith, a choir member), at the McPherson Theatre, and at outdoor park concerts.

Choir members have included Sir Matthew Begbie, Ira *Dilworth, Beverley *Fyfe and Herbert Kent, the club historian who also was conductor 1912–13, 1918–20, and 1926–9 and sang regularly with the Arions 1893–1955. Other conductors have been William Greig 1893–8, E. Howard Russell 1898–1912, 1913–14, and 1920–6, Frank Sehl

(Behold how good and how pleasant it is for brethern to dwell together in unity.)—Psalm 133:1.

Since 1892 every rehearsal, concert, and meeting of the Arion Male Voice Choir of Victoria has opened with the singing of this motto.

1915–18 and 1930–5, Stanley Bulley 1929–30, W.C. Fyfe 1935–40, Philip Hughes 1940–4, B.C. Bracewell 1944–7, Eric Hulatt 1947–8 (concurrently with) Frank Tupman 1947–50, 1953–5, 1959–67, Graham Steed 1950–1, Peter Copeland 1951–3, Art Lewis 1955–6, Harry Dutton 1956–9, and Bert Storar 1968–78. Storar was succeeded in 1978 by Anthony Nicholas.

BIBLIOGRAPHY

Provincial Archives of British Columbia. Arion Club records. (TRL)

Armdale Chorus. Female choir of about 25 members. It began as a rhythm band, formed during the 1930s at *Mount Saint Vincent College, Halifax. Founded and conducted by Mary Dee – m Girroir, b Halifax 28 Sep 1915, d there 19 May 1981, B MUS (Mount Saint Vincent) 1935 – it evolved into a music club and then into a junior glee club which gave its first concert in 1938. It performed as the Armdale Chorus throughout the Maritimes during the 1940s and was incorporated as the Armdale Choir in 1953, though it continued to be known popularly as the Armdale Chorus. It was heard nationally over CBC radio 1947–58, and some of the broadcasts were sent via short wave to Europe and South America and were rebroadcast over the BBC. During the late 1950s it was seen on CBC TV in a performance of Britten's *Ceremony of Carols* and in the six-week series 'Journey into Melody.'

Its repertoire, accompanied and unaccompanied, includes music of Palestrina and Bach, religious, popular, art, and folk songs, and songs from musicals, mostly in arrangements by Mary Dee Girroir, who also has composed pieces for the choir. The group has made two LPs for London: *The Armdale Chorus* (NA 3502) and *Noel* (NA 3507), both recorded ca 1962–3. It remained active in 1980. (MSm)

Armenia. Beginning about 1900, but mostly from 1950 to 1965, some 20,000 Armenians emigrated to Canada from the Middle East. Their musical activity in their adopted country has centred around the Armenian Apostolic (Gregorian) Church and ethnic clubs where choral and folk singing occur for celebrations of the mass and the commemoration of national tragedies such as the Turkish massacre of Armenians, 24 Apr 1915. One such club, the Association culturelle arménienne 'Hamazkain' of Montreal, celebrated its 50th anniversary in 1978. Among Canadian-Armenian musicians who have achieved recognition are the violinist Gerard *Kantarjian, the teacher Maryvonne *Kendergi, the conductor Raffi *Armenian, and the pop musician Raffi Cavoukian. The contralto Selma Keklikian has sung with the *MSO and the *Opéra du Québec and for CBC TV and radio. The pianists Norair Artinian of Montreal and Anahid Alexanian of St Catharines, Ont, are active as recitalists and in chamber music. RA

ARMENIAN, Raffi. Conductor, pianist, composer, b Cairo 4 Jun 1942, naturalized Canadian 1971; Piano Diploma (Vienna Academy) 1962, B SC (London) 1965, Conducting Diploma (Vienna Academy) 1968, Composition Diploma (Vienna Academy) 1969. In Cairo he studied piano with Ettore Puglisi and theory with Minatto Pompeo, and at 15 he played Mozart's *Concerto in A*, K488, with the Cairo SO under Franz Litschauer. In 1959 he went to Vienna to study piano with Bruno Seidlhofer. After graduating he set music aside and attended the U of London 1962–5, majoring in metallurgy. He returned to music and studied 1965–9 at the Vienna Academy with Hans Swarowsky (orchestral conducting), Reinhold Schmidt and Ferdinand Grossmann (choral conducting), and Alfred Uhl (composition). In 1968 he was one of two finalists in the International Competition for Young Conductors at Besançon, France. He had visited Canada in 1962, and when the opportunity arose after his graduation from Swarowsky's class he moved to Halifax, NS, to become assistant conductor 1969–71 of the *Atlantic SO. During those years he also conducted the Maritime performances of the *COC Touring Company's *The Barber of Seville* and led the Dalhousie Chorale 1970–1. Armenian became conductor of the *Kitchener-Waterloo SO in 1971, and that community orchestra's emergence by 1977 as one of the most vital in Canada outside the major 11 is attributed to his shrewd assembling of players, his resourceful programming, and his growing reputation as a conductor and pianist in a wider context. As music director 1973–6 for the *Stratford Festival he conducted such works as Charles *Wilson's masque-opera *The Summoning of Everyman* and Schoenberg's *Pierrot Lunaire* (1974). The Stratford Festival Ensemble, which he founded in 1974 to accompany such performances, served also as a professional nucleus in the Kitchener-Waterloo SO. Armenian made guest-conducting appearances with the *Quebec SO in 1974 and the *TS and *NACO in 1975 and conducted *Wozzeck* for the COC in Toronto and Ottawa in 1977. He helped to establish the Centre Opera Studio in Kitchener in 1977, serving also as its adviser and guest conductor. He was the pianist, with Gerard *Kantarjian and Gisela *Depkat, in the Ararat Trio (1971–4). His compositions, all deposited at the *CMCentre, include a *Passion Cantata* (1969) for solo tenor, choir, and orchestra and *Progressions I* (1972) for flute, cello, and piano. He is an associate of the *CMCentre and a member of CAPAC.

DISCOGRAPHY

Prokofiev *Sonata* for flute and piano. Michalska fl. 1970. CBC SM-114

See Discography for Gisela Depkat. KW

ARMIN. Family of string players: 1 / Jay and his children, 2 / Otto, 3 / Paul, 4 / Richard, and 5 / Adele.

1 **Jay** (James). Teacher, violinist, b Dnepropetrovsk, Ukraine, 11 Jan 1915; BA (Manitoba) 1947, A MUS PAED (Western Ontario) 1953. His family emigrated to Canada ca 1922 and settled in Manitoba, where he learned to play the violin in his late teens. He taught strings in high schools in Plum Coulee and Lowe Farm, Man, and in Leamington, Windsor, Stratford, and Toronto, Ont. He was head of the music department at Stratford Central High School 1963–5 and Burnamthorpe Collegiate in Etobicoke, Ont, 1965–75. In Leamington he founded the Mennonite Male Voice Choir in 1948 and conducted it 1950–2. He was principal and singing teacher at the Mennonite Educational Institute. He was an administrator with the *NYO in 1962 and 1963 and was president 1970–3 of the *Canadian String Teachers' Assn. In 1975 he became a string consultant for the North York Board of Education and an occasional

teacher in Toronto schools. Among his pupils were his children, Otto, Paul, Richard, and Adele, whom he coached as members of the Armin String Quartet, and George Willms and Larry Pojhola.

2 (John) **Otto**. Violinist, teacher, b Winnipeg 22 May 1943. He studied 1946–54 with his father, 1954–61 with Carl Chase in Detroit, 1962–4 with Josef Gingold at Indiana U, and 1967–70 with Lorand *Fenyves in Toronto. As first violin with the Armin String Quartet 1955–63 he made two Canadian tours and often performed on CBC radio and TV. In 1961 the quartet studied on scholarship at Indiana U, serving also as resident quartet. Individually, all four members also played several seasons with the *NYO. Otto won the first prize in the *CBC Talent Festival (1965) and took third place in the Jan Sibelius International Violin Competition (Helsinki 1971) and sixth place in the Carl Flesch International Competition (London 1972). He taught 1967–70 at the *CMM, 1968–74 at *McGill U and 1974–8 for the NYO. After his professional debut, with the *Victoria SO in 1964, he played 1964–5 in the Cleveland Orchestra and the *Stratford Festival Orchestra and 1966–9 in the *MSO, and was concertmaster 1967–9 with the CBC Montreal orchestra and 1974–7 with the *Hamilton Philharmonic. He became first concertmaster with the Hamburg Philharmonic in 1977. A concerto soloist with several Canadian orchestras, he has given recitals in Europe, and in 1976 with his wife, the pianist Marie-Paule Hudon, he made a cultural exchange tour of Belgium and France.

Armin has played many 20th-century works – eg, Schoenberg's *Phantasy*, Prokofiev's *Suite, Op 6*, and *Sonatas* No. 1 and 2, Stravinsky's *Divertissement*, Berg's *Violin Concerto*, and *Pépin's *Monade IV: Réseaux* (the premiere, with his wife, at Redpath Hall, McGill U, in 1974). He also, however, has shown a predilection for short 19th-century pieces for violin and orchestra (Chausson's *Poème*, Saint-Saëns' *Introduction and Rondo Capriccioso* etc), which he feels have been losing their rightful place on symphony programs. In 1976 with his brothers and sister he founded the Armin Electric Strings, an ensemble which has performed music ranging from baroque to avant garde on electric instruments built for them by Otto Erdész of Toronto.

DISCOGRAPHY

A. Brott *Concerto* for violin and chamber orchestra. Hamilton Philharmonic Virtuosi, B. Brott cond. 1975. CBC SM-291

Miniatures: Rossini-Paganini – Chopin-Sarasate – et al. M.-P. Hudon pf. 1974. Sel CC-15.104

See also Discography for Orford Quartet.

3 **Paul** (Erich). Violist, b Winkler, Man, 13 Aug 1944. He studied violin 1948–55 with Jay Armin and viola 1955–61 with Morris Hochberg at Wayne State U, David Dawson 1961–3 at Indiana U, and Lillian Fuchs 1964–5 in New York. After the demise of the Armin String Quartet he gave solo recitals in New York and at the *Stratford Festival in 1964 and 1965. He played 1965–6 with the Sadler's Wells Opera and 1967–9 with the *MSO. Following a brief period 1970–1 as electronic violist and violinist with *Lighthouse, he began working in 1972 as a studio musician (sometimes in a trio with Richard and Adele Armin for David *Clayton-Thomas and Ringo Starr). He was heard as a soloist and chamber musician on CBC radio and played 1974–6 with *Camerata. He worked with Otto Erdész on the design of the instruments played by the Armin Electric Strings, which he co-founded with his brothers and sister in 1976. He premiered David Bedford's *Spillipnerak* in 1974 and Marjan *Mozetich's *Disturbance* in 1977 and can be heard on a recording with the Armin Electric Strings (1979, Unison 7903).

4 **Richard**. Cellist, b Winkler, Man, 13 Aug 1944 (Paul's twin); performance certificate (Indiana) 1963. He studied cello 1957–61 with Thaddeus Markevitch in Detroit, in 1961 with Luigi Silva in New York, and 1962–4 with János Starker at Indiana U. He played with the Joffrey Ballet orchestra in 1963, toured 1964–5 in Canada and the USA with the Don Shirley Trio, and played 1965–9 in the *TS. He toured and recorded 1969–74 with *Lighthouse. He became a freelance cellist in 1974. Based in Toronto, he is a member of the Armin Electric Strings.

5 **Adele** (m Riley). Violinist, b Morris, Man, 2 Dec 1945. She studied 1958–61 with Carl Chase in Detroit, 1962–5 with Josef Gingold (violin) and János Starker and Menahem Pressler (chamber music) at the U of Indiana, summers 1961 and 1962 with Joseph Fuchs at Blue Hill, Me, and 1968–70 with Lorand *Fenyves at the *U of Toronto. She won first prize in the 1970 *CBC Talent Festival and in the 1971 Cosmopolitan Violin Competition in New York (for which the prize included two performances of the Prokofiev *Concerto in G Minor* with the Cosmopolitan Young People's SO at Philharmonic Hall) and was a bronze medalist in the 1970 Geneva International Violin Competition. She made her professional debut with the *TS in 1968, playing the Prokofiev. She has been a concerto soloist with the *NYO (Mendelssohn's *Concerto in E Minor*) and the *MSO, and in 1973 was a founding member of *Camerata. With this group she has appeared throughout Canada and in Cuba and South America, and has recorded and performed on radio and TV. In 1974, at Town Hall, the St Lawrence Centre, Toronto, with her brother Otto she played Prokofiev's rarely heard *Sonata* for two violins. With Elyakim *Taussig she recorded sonatas of Brahms and Mendelssohn (1971, CBC SM-145). She is a member of the Armin Electric Strings and is married to the pianist Doug *Riley. NM

The Army Show. At first a musical revue produced during World War II for the Canadian army, and later the operational name for entertainment units serving with the army. Through the perseverance of Brig James Mess, the Dept of National Defence sanctioned the creation of a radio series produced in Montreal by Rai Purdy and known generally as the 'Canadian Army Radio Show.' The CBC broadcast the show from 13 Dec 1942 until 5 Sep 1943. Among the cast were the comedians Johnny Wayne and Frank Shuster (who wrote much of the material), Jimmie *Shields, Raymonde Maranda, and others. The orchestra and chorus were conducted by Geoffrey *Waddington. The radio show's success prompted a touring stage version to entertain the troops, promote recruitment by enhancing the army's image, increase the sale of war bonds, and bolster civilian morale.

Work on the touring show began during the winter of 1943 in Toronto. Wayne and Shuster wrote most of the skits, tunes, and lyrics, and Robert *Farnon, as music director, arranged and orchestrated the music and, with Freddie *Grant, wrote some of the original music. (These and other arrangements were recorded ca 1946 by Farnon in England and still are studied as models of the arranger's art.) The cast included Wayne and Shuster, Peter Mews, and Mildred Morey, and the singers Roger *Doucet, Jimmie Shields, Gordon Blythe, and Lois (Hooker) Maxwell. Aida Broadbent (of Vancouver and Hollywood) was the choreographer. The orchestra, which included the violinists Frank Fusco, Jacob *Groob, and Eddie *Sanborn, the bassists Jean Dansereau and Murray Lauder, the saxophonists Lew Lewis and Morris Weinzweig, the trombonists Murray Ginsberg and Ted *Roderman, the celeste player Denny *Vaughan, and the percussionist Freddie Powell (who later became famous as a woodcarver in California), again was conducted by Waddington. The production was supervised by the veteran showman Jack *Arthur.

The Army Show opened at the Victoria Theatre in Toronto 2 Apr 1943 and was an outstanding success. *Time Magazine*, 19 Apr 1943, described it as 'a high-spirited, always likeable, often lavish soldier show.' Two of the songs, 'That's an Order from the Army' and 'H'ya Mom,' enjoyed considerable popularity. The show toured Canada that spring and summer, visiting major army camps and urban centres and giving a special performance at the historic Anglo-American War Conference, 10–24 Aug 1943 at Quebec City.

While the show was in Vancouver being refurbished for a projected run on Broadway, the Dept of National Defence decided to split the troupe into five units to be sent overseas, two as musical revue groups and three as variety groups. Wayne and Shuster prepared the material. The five units reached England 21 Dec 1943 and there became part of the Canadian Auxiliary Services Entertainment Unit, with Rai Purdy as commanding officer. The units also were subdivided into small concert parties which could perform in hospitals. Tony *Bradan, music director for all units, recruited additional musicians and provided arrangements. Stationed first at Aldershot and then at Guildford, these units entertained the troops throughout Britain and, after the 1944 Allied invasion of western Europe, at the front lines in Holland, France, Belgium, and Germany. (Unit B, with Sanborn as music director, was assigned to duty in Italy after the Allied invasion of that country in November 1943.)

A Saturday night variety show by unit musicians was broadcast by the BBC. Farnon was conductor/arranger, and Gerry Wilmot was master of ceremonies. After the Allied victory in Europe, the function of the units was to entertain troops awaiting repatriation and others serving in the occupation forces. A new show called *Rhythm and Rodeo* was presented outside London in a gigantic tent before some 5000 servicemen and women. More than 20 entertainment units of *The Army Show* remained on active duty until 1947. JBk

ARPIN, John (Francis Oscar). Pianist, singer, composer, arranger, collector, b Port McNicoll, near Midland, Ont, 3 Dec 1936; ARCT 1953. He studied piano in Port McNicoll, in Midland, and 1950–3 at the *RCMT. Working first (1957–9) with the bands of Howard *Cable, King *Ganam, Leo *Romanelli, and Stanley *St. John in Toronto, he has performed subsequently with his trio or alone in many of the city's nightclubs. He has arranged music for LPs by Keath Barrie, the *Carlton Showband, Dick Damron, George Hamilton IV, Tommy *Hunter, Roy Payne, and others, and was music director 1968–9 for CTV's 'River Inn' (later 'The Catherine *McKinnon Show') and 1969–70 for CTV's 'Diamond Lil's.' In 1975 he became the first Canadian to record by the 'direct-to-disc' process. An internationally acclaimed ragtime pianist, Arpin was introduced to the genre by Bob Darch, in 1963 made the first of his regular appearances at the annual 'Ragtime Bash' in Toronto, and has performed at the St Louis Ragtime Festival and 1969–75 at the *Mariposa Folk Festival. In the 1960s he was chairman and then president of the

Toronto-based Ragtime Society and editor of its publication, *The Ragtimer*. Arpin's compositions include some piano rags, about 100 songs, and *Summer Suite* (1976) commissioned by *Nexus. He has recorded his own *Centennial Rag* (1965, BMI Canada), *Toronto Blues* (1965, John Arpin Music), and *Cumberland Stroll* (1969, John Arpin Music). A collector of sheet music, opera scores, and piano rolls, Arpin has developed a particular interest in Canadiana and in 1976 appeared on CBC radio's 'Morningside' performing neglected songs by early-20th-century Canadian composers. He is an affiliate of PRO Canada.

See also Ragtime.

DISCOGRAPHY

Concert in Ragtime. Joplin – Scott – Lamb – Arpin – Morton – et al. 1965. Scroll 101

The Other Side of Ragtime: Joplin – Lamb – Synder – Arpin – et al. 1966. Scroll 102

They All Play Ragtime: Marshall – Lamb. Jazzology JCE 52 (anthology)

Ragtime Piano: Wellinger – Arpin – Waller – Joplin – et al. 1969. Harmony HES 6026

Love and Maple Syrup ... John Arpin Plays Gordon Lightfoot. 1971. CTL 477-5148

Barroom to Baroque. 1972. CTL 477-5165

Direct to Disc. 1975. RCA KPL1-0125

Solo Jazz Piano: J.P. Johnson – Ellington – Confrey – Arpin– Tatum – et al. 1976. EBM 10

I Write the Songs. 1977. RCA KKK1-0258

BIBLIOGRAPHY

McNamara, Helen. 'John Arpin,' *MSc*, 247, May–Jun 1969 MM

ARRAY. Toronto organization founded to promote and present new music. It was founded in 1971 by the composers (all *U of Toronto graduates) Robert *Bauer, John *Fodi, Clifford *Ford, Gary *Hayes, Marjan *Mozetich, and Alex *Pauk, to present new works by young Canadians. The first concert, 20 Apr 1972, comprised compositions by the founders. Other concerts followed: three each year 1972–5 and four each year in 1976 and 1977 in Toronto, and one 4 Mar 1973 in Montreal. Several have been broadcast by the CBC. In 1976 concerts were given under ARRAY's auspices by the *Festival Singers and the *York Winds. Changes in membership brought changes in aim: by 1977 ARRAY's program had widened to admit all contemporary music, and performance had assumed definite priority over promotion. In 1973 the violist Michael Parker and the soprano Billie Bridgeman became the first performer-members, forerunners of an ARRAY ensemble established in 1976: Allen Beard (percussion), Robert Bick (flute), Henry Kucharzyk (piano), Douglas Perry (viola), Paul Pulford (cello), and Cameron Walter (trombone). (Bick, Perry, and Pulford also are members of the Galliard Ensemble.) Of the founders, Bauer, Ford, Hayes, and Pauk had left ARRAY by 1975. Robert Daigneault was a member 1975–6 and Elma Miller in 1977. With the departure of Mozetich in 1977 and of Fodi in 1978 control of ARRAY passed to the performing ensemble. ARRAY has commissioned works from Thomas Baker (*Triptych*), Bauer (*Viola Concerto*), John Chong (*?Who?*), Thomas Dusatko (*Nomas II*), Fodi (*Iz ist in der Werlt*), Ford (*Alliances for Winds*), Mozetich (*In the Air*), David Nichols (*Tone Surge*), Parker (*Cholê*), and Ann *Southam (*Networks*) and has premiered works by many other composers. Four issues of an *ARRAY Newsletter* were published irregularly 1972–4.

BIBLIOGRAPHY

Geddes, Murray. 'ARRAY,' *Musicworks*, 6, Winter 1979

(CF, FH)

ARSENAULT, Angèle. Singer-songwriter, b Abrams Village, PEI, of Acadian parents, 1 Oct 1943; BA (Moncton) 1965, M LITT (Laval) 1968. She started performing in Moncton in 1963, accompanying herself on the guitar and the piano, and also began collecting and singing Acadian folksongs. After 1966 she lived in various parts of Quebec, sang in clubs and cabarets and on radio and TV, and subsequently toured Canada. However, it was not until 1973 that she began writing and singing her own songs (in French and English). Among these were 'Évangéline, Acadian Queen,' 'Le Monde de par chez nous,' 'La Cuisine,' and 'L'Homme et la femme.' For TV Ontario, Toronto, she was a host for 'True North' (1973–5, with Roy Payne) and for the educational program 'Avec Angèle,' which won a Gold Hugo Award at the Chicago Film Festival in 1974. Arsenault has sung at several folk festivals, including the *Mariposa and the Milwaukee, and has participated as author and performer in some *NFB films, including Anne-Claire Poirier's *Le Temps de l'avant* (1975). In May 1977 the Quebec Ministry of Education recommended her collection of songs and poetry, *Première* (Collection Mon Pays, mes chansons, Montreal 1975), for use in teaching French to students in the province's senior high schools. She has made four LPs for SPPS-Disques (Société de production et de programmation de spectacles, the company she founded with the impresario Lise Aubut and the singers Edith *Butler and Jacqueline *Lemay). Three are in French (*Première*, 1975, PS-19901, *Libre*, 1977, PS-19903, and *Angèle Arsenault*, 1979, PS-19907), and one is in English (*Angèle Arsenault*, 1976, PS-19908). (See also Discography for Edith Butler.) Her 'Mic Mac Song' was recorded by *Stringband and *Libre* won a 1979 ADISQ recording and showbusiness award for best-selling record. In *La Presse* Pierre Beaulieu summarized her art in these terms: 'Angèle Arsenault may denounce the status of women, demand freedom for everyone, or attack the consumer society, but she always does so jokingly and optimistically, to rhythmic tunes rooted in the folk and the country, and accompanied simply and effectively.' She is a member of CAPAC.

BIBLIOGRAPHY

Champagne, Jane. 'A liberated songwriter finds serene happiness,' *CanComp*, 93, Sep 1974

Vézina, Marie-Odile. 'Ces chanteuses venues d'Acadie,' *Perspectives*, vol 18, 6 Mar 1976

Johnson, William. 'Angèle looks like a schoolmarm, but sings like her name,' Toronto *Globe and Mail*, 8 Apr 1978

Beaulieu, Pierre. 'Angèle ou l'optimisme,' Montreal *La Presse*, 2 Dec 1978

Petrowski, Nathalie. 'Angèle Arsenault libre,' Montreal *Le Devoir*, 2 Dec 1978

– 'This composer makes it with laughter and optimism,' *CanComp*, 138, Feb 1979

Lanken, Dane. 'Voice of an Angele hits a high note,' Toronto *Globe and Mail*, 31 Dec 1980 ST

ARSENEAULT, Raynald. Composer, b Quebec City, 9 Jun 1945; premier prix (CMM) 1973. He studied 1968–73 at the *CMM with Gilles *Tremblay (composition), Françoise *Aubut (organ), and Jean-Louis Martinet (orchestration). He won the *Prix d'Europe in 1973 and enrolled that autumn at the Metz Cons. There he worked under Claude Lefebvre and in 1976, on completing his studies, received the gold medal of the city of Metz. He also studied with Fernand Vandenbogaerde (electronic music) and Michel Decoust (conducting) at the Pantin Cons on the outskirts of Paris. The Société des auteurs, compositeurs et éditeurs de musique (SACEM) awarded him a prize in 1976. The following year, with his wife, the poetess Lyette Yergeau, he conducted 'Music and Poetry,' a symposium organized by the *Canadian Cultural Centre in Paris.

The organ is significant in Arseneault's works, as the following indicate: *Ode pour la mort d'un ami, Op 1* (1969, revised 1974) for solo organ; *Concerto de chambre, Op 6* (1974) for flute, clarinet, harmonium, piano, violin, cello, and double-bass; *Canzoni* (1975) for four trombones and organ; *Sept pièces pour grand orchestre, Op 8* (1976), requiring up to 130 performers, including an organ; and *Pâques, Op 9* (1976) for female solo voice, brass quintet, organ, bells, and Balinese gongs. Commissioned by the Centre européen pour la recherche musicale, *Pâques* was premiered 19 Nov 1976 as part of the fifth Rencontres internationales de musique contemporaine in Metz. Starting with the *Canzoni*, in which the organ is given virtuoso treatment, Arseneault (according to an interview in *Musicanada* 32) began to conceive his scores as 'large graphic schemas using colour as instrumental reference points, a method which presents the possibility of working in almost visual terms.' He also wrote a cantata-ballet, *Ia, Op 4* (1973), for soprano, contralto, and two small orchestras; *Quatre Miniatures, Op 3* (1973, revised 1975) for large orchestra, premiered 20 Jun 1976 by the Radio France Philharmonic Orchestra conducted by Edgar Cosma; and *Dunes, Op 5* (1974) for flute and piano. In addition, he composed three pieces for piano dedicated to Louis-Philippe *Pelletier: the *Sonate, Op 2* premiered at the Canadian Cultural Centre in 1976, *Deux Études, Op 10* (1976–7), and *Recueil, Op 11* (1976–7), a suite of 11 pieces. Arseneault is a member of CAPAC and an associate of the *CMCentre. In 1980 he was pursuing his career in France.

BIBLIOGRAPHY

Proulx, Michelle. 'Words about music,' *Mcan*, 32, May 1977 MPr

Ars Organi. Society founded in Montreal in 1960 by a group of young organists to 'contribute to a renewal of interest in the organ in Montreal by presenting recitals in which the programs, the choice of instrument and the style of performance bear witness to the highest traditions of organ music.' The founding coincided with the first installations in Montreal of tracker organs in the classical style. These organs were used for all the society's recitals: first at Queen Mary Rd United Church, then at St-Joseph Oratory and the Immaculée-Conception Church, where the complete works of J.S. Bach were presented in May 1967. The six founders – Gaston *Arel, Raymond *Daveluy, Kenneth *Gilbert, Bernard and Mireille *Lagacé, and Lucienne *L'Heureux-Arel – gave most of the recitals, but Ars Organi also arranged for numerous foreign organists of international reputation (eg, Anton Heiller, Lionel Rogg, Marie-Claire Alain, Xavier Darasse, André Isoir, Michel Chapuis) to perform in Montreal, often for the first time in North America. The society invited several Canadian artists (eg, Antoine *Bouchard, Jean Leduc) to give recitals and commissioned others (eg, Daveluy, François *Morel) to compose works. Ars Organi stimulated the renewal of organ building in Canada and created a larger public for organ music. Once this cause was won, the society's founders became concerned more with the development of their individual careers, and the society's activities came to a close with the May Festival of 1973. HPn

Members of Ars Organi: (left to right) Gaston Arel, Bernard Lagacé, Raymond Daveluy, Kenneth Gilbert, (seated) Lucienne L'Heureux-Arel

'Vivace,' bronze sculpture by Yves Trudeau at the JMC Orford Art Centre

Art, visual

1 Parallels and contrasts in the visual arts and music
2 Some compositions inspired by visual art
3 Some visual art inspired by music and musicians

1 PARALLELS AND CONTRASTS IN THE VISUAL ARTS AND MUSIC. A comparative study of the development of the two sister arts in Canada had not been published by 1980. The author of such a study would have to examine achievements and chronological priorities, trace the relative impacts of foreign models and local environments, and search for evidence of mutual contacts and cross-fertilization.

In colonial Canada both arts had primarily utilitarian functions – visual art in church decoration and in the depiction of topography, music in the liturgy and in military exercises. They moved through various phases in the 19th century when the rising middle classes strove for the 'finer accomplishments of life,' the earliest evidence being the itinerant portrait painters (eg, Louis *Dulongpré) and *singing school masters. In the second half of the 20th century both arts have flourished at various levels of sophistication and in a wide variety of genres, styles, and functions.

Despite these parallels it appears, at least on the surface, that the visual arts have developed at a faster rate. There is no abundance of compositions to match the wealth of ex voto church paintings and wood carvings of New France, although it might be fairer to compare lay craftsmen with gifted folksingers. But where are the composers contemporary to such immigrant painters as Paul Kane (1810–71) and Cornelius Krieghoff (1812–72), whose depictions of Indian and habitant scenes are famous, and to such native Canadians as Antoine Plamondon (1804–91) and Théophile Hamel (1817–70), whose expert portraits won wide admiration?

In our own century, the distinctive painting style of the Group of Seven (formed in 1920) gained international recognition at a time when Canadian musical composition was at a low ebb in both quantity and originality. Did the earlier maturing of visual art have pedagogical reasons? Bishop Laval, at Cap Tourmente (Saint-Joachim near Quebec) about 1668, established a school where the ecclesiastical arts and handicrafts were taught but where nothing was done, apparently, to train church musicians. A professional painter from France, Jacques Leblond de Latour (1671–1715), imparted instruction at the school after 1690, but there was no professional musician to guide the talented young Charles-Amador *Martin.

Sir Ernest *MacMillan offered a more basic explanation: 'The painter finds in all parts of the Dominion types of landscape peculiar to the country, and paints them as he sees them in their bold outlines and through their own distinctive atmosphere ... But the musician has little to go on. His is a more introspective art than any other. As a rule, musical self-expression matures more slowly in any nation than does self-expression in the other arts' ('Musical composition in Canada,' *Culture*, vol 5, June 1942).

Further investigation may show however that the time-lag is more apparent than real. The visual arts and music have unequal abilities to ensure their own survival. Sound is fleeting, art has a physical permanence. Church decorations of New France, unless destroyed by fire, survive as proof of their period's creative energy. The paintings of the first important Canadian-born painter, François de Beaucourt (1740–94), can be seen in the National Gallery of Canada and other museums, but the music for the odes written in 1776 and 1791 (see Cantatas) is lost, as are most of Joseph *Quesnel's compositions.

Another factor is the lack of historical interest among Canadian musicians. Through exposure in museums and exhibitions, and through discussion in books of biography and history, Canadian visual art of more than three centuries has become familiar to a large sector of the public. The personal styles of a Krieghoff, an Emily Carr, or a Jean-Paul Riopelle are recognized instantly by thousands of laymen. Music has had no comparable advocacy. Canadian performers, music publishers, and recording companies have been very negligent in exploring early Canadian compositions. The 1963 revival of Quesnel's **Colas et Colinette* (1790) and the work's subsequent recording and publication, and the recordings of Calixa *Lavallée's **The Widow* and of some late-19th-century piano music by Josephte *Dufresne and Linda Lee *Thomas, are notable but exceptional. If it were brought to light again through rediscovery and publication, concert performance, or recording, some of the music of *Bentley and Quesnel, *Dessane and Lavallée, *Codman and J.P. *Clarke might be found to stand comparison with the pictures of Kane, Krieghoff, and Plamondon.

Lastly, it has to be recognized that the major share of musical energy has been channelled not into creation but into *re*-creation. Such a division of function does not exist in the visual arts. In comparing past achievement perhaps one should seek the equivalent of the international recognition given to such painters as Antoine Falardeau (1822–90), Homer Watson (1855–1936), and Horatio Walker (1858–1938) not only in the music of a Lavallée or a Clarence *Lucas, but also in the singing of an Emma *Albani, a Louise *Edvina, or a Béatrice *La Palme, and the piano performances of a Waugh *Lauder, a Salomon *Mazurette, or an Émiliano *Renaud.

It is too early to compare the status of music and that of visual art in the middle of the 20th century. Both arts have experienced a vast upsurge of practitioners and expansion of audiences, both have teemed with talent and opportunities, and both have reflected international currents as well as regional concerns.

Contacts between artists and musicians have been largely on the levels of sociability (eg, the *Arts and Letters Club of Toronto, the *Canadian Institute of Music, and the *Institut canadien), of political action (*CCA), and of education (common departments of fine arts and music at several universities). On the creative level the *Mixed media music phenomenon of the 1960s has produced some interesting associations (eg, Sightsoundsystems, a festival organized in 1968 by Udo *Kasemets; and Kasemets' engagement in 1970, as lecturer on music and mixed media, by the Ontario College of Art). Other points of contact are stage design (eg, Louis de Niverville for *Beckwith's **Night Blooming Cereus*) and the illustration of record jackets.

There have been visual artists who make music, and musicians who paint or sculpt. Louis Dulongpré and Richard *Coates were early 19th-century musicians and portrait painters. Kane, Napoléon Bourassa, Krieghoff, and Antoine Plamondon were keen amateur musicians. M.-A. Suzor-Côté studied voice in Paris in addition to painting. Wilson MacDonald, poet, illustrator, and songwriter, illustrated the covers of his sheet music and poetry publications. Gustave *Smith, the musician, also painted water-colours and worked as a cartographer. More recently Mary *Bothwell, Guylaine *Guy, Jimmy *Namaro, John *Newmark, Christina *Petrowska, and Alfred *Whitehead have exhibited successfully in art galleries, while Harry *Freedman and R. Murray *Schafer went through periods of visual art studies before concentrating on music. Reginald *Godden has done expressionistic visual representations of elements of Bach's music and has developed a technique of 'spore painting,' a kind of 'chance art.' Joni *Mitchell has illustrated some of her record albums. The painter and sculptor Michael *Snow is also an accomplished jazz musician (see Artists' Jazz Band), while Greg Curnoe, a London, Ont, painter, is leader of the Nihilist Spasm Band and Émile *Normand is both a painter and a jazz musician.

2 SOME COMPOSITIONS INSPIRED BY VISUAL ART

Adaskin, Murray *In Praise of Canadian Painting in the 1930s*. Orchestra. 1975. The artists: Paraskeva Clark, Louis Muhlstock, and Charles Comfort

Coulthard, Jean *The Pines of Emily Carr*. Soprano, narrator, string quartet. 1969. Based on Carr's journals

Freedman, Harry *Tableau*. Strings. 1952. Inspired by a painting of an Arctic landscape

– *Images*. Orchestra. 1958. Impressions of Lawren Harris' *Blue Mountain*, Kazuo Nakamura's *Structure at Dusk*, and Jean-Paul Riopelle's *Landscape*

– *Klee Wyck*. Orchestra. 1970. Based on the work and the persona of Emily Carr

McIntosh, Diana *Paraphrase #1*. Piano. Inspired by Lawren Harris' *Maligne Lake*

– *Paraphrase #2*. Piano. 1977. Inspired by an abstract painting by Marcel Barbeau

'The Woolsey Family' by William Berczy, 1809

Morel, François *L'Étoile noire (Tombeau de Borduas)*. Orchestra. 1962. Inspired by a painting by Paul-Émile Borduas
Pépin, Clermont *Guernica*. Orchestra. 1952. Based on Picasso's painting
Somers, Harry *Picasso Suite*. Small orchestra. 1964. Nine-movement suite depicting various aspects, periods, or specific works of the artist
Healey, Derek *Arctic Images*. Orchestra. 1971. Inspired by Inuit prints

3 SOME VISUAL ART INSPIRED BY MUSIC AND MUSICIANS. In view of the lack of a complete inventory of Canadian works of art the following representative list has been compiled from personal observations (museums, books, periodicals, calendar reproductions, etc) and supplemented by a selection from 100 items in 10 museums brought to the editors' attention by the National Inventory Program of the *National Museums of Canada, a computerized stock-taking in process of preparation (1980). The list is selective mainly in a negative sense: the data are hard to find. No consideration has been given to period, to the reputation of the artist, or to the importance of the subject.

An aspect of musically inspired visual art which has seemed beyond the reach and competence and, perhaps, the courage of this article, and with which it and its lists consequently have made little attempt to deal, is the abstract. This is regretted because music itself is fundamentally an abstract art, and it and its performance have called forth strong responses from abstractionists in visual art – for instance Jean-Paul Riopelle in his 'La Bolduc,' hung in the main lobby of the *PDA. In a sense, such manifestations (and there have been many in the 1960s and 1970s) are the converse of impressionism in music (see Impressionism). In 1980, along with some other aspects of the relationship of the two arts, visual abstractions of musicians, musical performances, and musical essences deserved study in some depth. At this stage of investigation, generalizations are impossible.

Work of a foreign artist has been included when it has portrayed a Canadian musician, or a musician later to settle in Canada. Such artists are identified by nationality.

The list employs these abbreviations for museums and other owners. In some instances the location of the work is not known.

AGH Art Gallery of Hamilton
AGO Art Gallery of Ontario, Toronto
ALC Arts and Letters Club of Toronto
AN du Q Archives nationales du Québec, Montreal
CAG Centennial Art Gallery, Halifax
CCAB Canada Council Art Bank, Ottawa
JPL Jewish Public Library, Montreal
M du Q Musée du Québec, Quebec City
MTL Metropolitan Toronto Library, J. Ross Robertson Historical Collection
NBM New Brunswick Museum, Saint John
NGC National Gallery of Canada, Ottawa
NL of C National Library of Canada, Ottawa
PAC Public Archives of Canada, Ottawa
PDA Place des Arts, Montreal
RCMT Royal Conservatory of Music of Toronto
ROM Royal Ontario Museum, Toronto
U of T University of Toronto, Faculty of Music
VAG Vancouver Art Gallery
VMM Vancouver Maritime Museum
Items marked with a double dagger are reproduced in *EMC*.

Portraits

Artist / Subject and date / Medium / Owner or reference
Adelstein, Hattie / Pauline Donalda / oil / private
Alfsen, John Martin / Cellist (Tom Stone) 1925 / crayon / AGO
Allard, Delvico / Claude Champagne 1963 / relief / Salle Claude-Champagne, Montreal
Clark, Paraskeva / Murray Adaskin 1930s / oil
Collier, Alan Caswell / The Guitar Player / oil / NGC
– David Ouchterlony / drawing / ALC
Comfort, Charles F. / Alexander Chuhaldin ca 1928 / water-colour / AGH
– Sir Ernest MacMillan
– Ettore Mazzoleni / water-colour / RCMT
Cook-Endres, Barbara / Marilyn Duffus as the Mother in *Amahl and the Night Visitors* / oil / private (catalogue *150 Years of Art in Manitoba*, 1970)
Daoust, Sylvia / Soeur Marie-Stéphane / bronze / Salle Claude-Champagne, Montreal
Delfosse, Georges / Alexis Contant / oil / NL of C
– Fleurette Contant / oil / NL of C
– Émiliano Renaud 1910 / oil / M du Q
Dick, Dorothy / Hector Charlesworth / bronze / ALC
Dingle, Adrian / Healey Willan / oil / ALC
Dulongpré, Louis / Joseph Quesnel ca 1800 / oil / Château Ramezay
Eaton, Wyatt / Man with Violin (Timothy Cole) / oil / AGO
Epstein, Sir Jacob (English) / Ellen Ballon / bronze / McGill U and Dalhousie U
Fairley, Barker / series of musicians / oil / U of T
Forbes, Kenneth / Sir Ernest MacMillan / oil / U of T
– Norman Wilks / oil / RCMT
‡Forster, J.W.L. / F.H. Torrington 1899 / oil / U of T
Frankenberg, E. / Sarah Fischer / plaster bust / JPL
Gage, Frances / Sir Ernest MacMillan / relief / H. Spencer Clark
– Healey Willan / relief / H. Spencer Clark
Gramatté, Walter (German) / numerous portraits of S.C. Friedman-Gramatté (S.C. Eckhardt-Gramatté) 1920–9 / various / various
Grier, Wyly / A.S. Vogt 1917 / oil / RCMT
Hahn, Emmanuel / F.H. Torrington / plaster / ALC
‡Hamel, Théophile / Antoine Dessane ca 1859 / oil / M du Q
Hamilton, Ruby Harkness / Edward Johnson / bronze / U of T
Hébert, Adrien / Léo-Pol Morin 1925 / drawing / L.-P. Morin, *Musique* (Montreal 1944)
Hébert, Henri / Rodolphe Mathieu 1918 / drawing / *Le Nigog* (May 1918)
Hohenlohe, Prince Victor (German) / Emma Albani / marble / M du Q
Holgate, Edwin Headley / The Cellist 1923 / McMichael Canadiana Gallery, Kleinburg, Ont
Horne, Cleeve / Sir Ernest MacMillan / oil / Massey Hall, Toronto
Hunt, Dora de Pedery / Leo Smith / drawing / U of T
– Geza de Kresz / medal
Hunt?, J[ohn] P[owell] / Edward Fisher / oil / RCMT
Kokoschka, Oskar (Austrian) / Emmy Heim 1916 / lithograph / ?
Law, S.G. / Luigi von Kunits / drawing / *German-Canadian Yearbook*, vol 2 (Toronto 1975)
Lemieux, Marguerite / Salvatore Issaurel 1935 / drawing / M du Q
Low, Will Hicock (USA) / Emma Albani as Lucia di Lammermoor 1877 / oil / M du Q
Macdonald, J.E.H. / Arthur Friedheim at the Arts and Letters Club 1912 / oil / AGO
Mallory, Robert / Clement Hambourg / oil / NL of C
Manson, J.B. / Michael Hambourg / oil / NL of C
Massicotte, Edmond-Joseph / F. Jehin-Prume / drawing / M du Q
McKenzie, Robert Tait / Kathleen Parlow / sculpture / Mill of Kintail (Almonte, Ont)
McLaren, Jack / Augustus Bridle / drawing / ALC
Mendelson, Joe / multicultural series of portraits of popular musicians 1978
Middleton, Holly / Boris Roubakine / oil / Banff SFA
Moravec, Hella / Marius Barbeau / sculpture / ?
Oldham, E. / Sarah Fischer / silhouette / JPL
Plamondon, Antoine / Mme Papineau et sa fille Ezilda 1836 / oil / NGC
Pollack, Harry / Alexander Brott / bronze / PDA
– series of musicians / sculpture / private
Reynolds, J.M. / Healey Willan ca 1970 / sculpture / NL of C et al
Russell, John Wentworth / Boris Hambourg 1932 / oil / AGO
St-Mars, Alonzo / Calixa Lavallée / relief / Eugène Lapierre, *Calixa Lavallée* (Montreal 1936, etc)
Sampson, J.E. / Hector Charlesworth / drawing / ALC
Sargent, John Singer (USA) / Éva Gauthier / two drawings / one in Museum of Fine Arts, Boston
Speicher, Eugene / Edward Johnson 1950 / oil / U of T

Stephens, Anaït (USA) / Zubin Mehta 1968 / bronze / PDA
Stevens, Dorothy / The Cellist pre-1914 / NGC
Tregor, Nison (USA) / Luigi von Kunits ca 1926 / bronze / Toronto Symphony
Varley, Frederick H. / Percival Price (2) / P. Price
– Miriam Kennedy / chalk / private
Webster, H. / Sarah Fischer / oil / JPL
Weiss, Felix / Boyd Neel / bronze / U of T
Willer, James S. / W.H. Anderson / terracotta bust / private
Wilson, York / Ettore Mazzoleni / collage / ALC
‡Wyle, Florence / The Cellist – La Violoncelliste / NGC
anon / James Dodsley Humphreys / water-colour / MTL (item 3697)
? / Charles Wugk Sabatier / AN du Q

Groups, still lifes, etc
Artist / Subject and date / Medium / Owner or reference
‡Berczy, William von Moll / The Woolsey Family – La Famille Woolsey ca 1809 / oil / NGC
– Domestic Scene / private (*German-Canadian Yearbook*, vol 2, Toronto 1975)
Borduas, Paul-Émile / La Femme à la mandoline / oil / Musée d'art contemporain, Montreal
– Cello / collage / Musée d'art contemporain, Montreal
Bouchard, Simone Mary / Les Trois Rois mages – The Three Kings / oil / private
Caiserman, Ghitta / Concert / private
Cardinal, Marcellin / Cello 1971 / collage / CCAB
Colville, Alex / Child with Accordion 1954 / tempera / private
Curnoe, Greg / The Camouflaged Piano, or French Roundels – Le Piano camouflé, ou Tourteaux français 1966 / oil and damar / NGC
Dahl, Chris / The Sam Wooding Orchestra (1925) 1973 / silkscreen / CCAB
Duncan, James / Celebrated Blind Fiddler ca 1850 / drawing / ROM
Fortier, Michel / Harmonica 1973 / silkscreen / CCAB
Freiman, Lillian / Street Musicians / drawing
– Orchestra / oil / Dominion Gallery, Montreal
Gaucher, Yves / Hommage à Webern I, II, III 1963 / prints / artist
Harris, Lawren / Quintet 1962 / oil / CAG
‡Harris, Robert / The Chorister – L'Enfant du choeur ca 1881 / oil / NGC
– Harmony/ Harmonie ca 1887 / oil / NGC
– Village Choir 1888 / oil
Heriot, George / Dance at the Chateau 1801 / water-colour / PAC
– La Danse ronde / Circular Dance of the Canadians 1807 / water-colour/ PAC and also in G. Heriot, *Travels through the Canadas* (London 1807)
‡– Minuets of the Canadians / water-colour / PAC and also as above
Holzworth, T. / The Toronto Symphony Orchestra 1959 / oil / Toronto Musicians Association
Jobin, Louis / Angel with Lyre / wood / AGO
– Angel with Trumpet / wood? / ROM
Jullien, Henri / Country Dance Mid-19th Century / pen and ink / McCord Museum, Montreal and also in *Cornelius Krieghoff* by Barbeau (Toronto 1934)
Krieghoff, Cornelius / Interior at Old Pocane's ca 1894 / *Cornelius Krieghoff* by Barbeau (Toronto 1934)
– Indians Dancing 1855 / PAC
– After the Ball 1856
– Merrymakers 1860 / *Cornelius Krieghoff* by Barbeau (Toronto 1934)
– Breaking up a Sleigh Party ca 1860
Kurelek, William / Manitoba Party – Réunion au Manitoba 1964 / oil / NGC
– Handel's Messiah at Massey Hall / *O Toronto* by Kurelek (Toronto 1973)
– Ukrainian Christmas Eve Supper 1973 / lithograph / AGO
– The Barn Dance / *Kurelek's Canada* (Toronto 1978)
Larose, Ludger / Intérieur 1907 / ?
Leclair, Michel / Chez Fada – Chanteur dansant 1973 / silkscreen / CCAB and also Montreal Museum of Fine Arts
Leduc, Ozias / L'Enfant au pain – The Boy with a Piece of Bread 1890s / oil / NGC
Lismer, Arthur / Le Joueur de violon / pen and ink / Montreal Museum of Fine Arts
MacLaughlan, Donald Shaw / Song from Venice No. 2, 1912 / etching / NGC
Massicotte, Edmond-Joseph / Le Violoneux 1912 / drawing / Conte de Fréchette
– Une Veillée d'autrefois 1915 / drawing / *Pionniers du disque folklorique*
Masson, Henri / Baroque Trio 1956 / water-colour / VAG
– Les Enfants de choeur / pen and ink
Milne, David / The Concert at the 'Y,' Concentration Camp, Kinmel 1918 / drawing / NGC
Nichols, Jack / Musicians 1942 / turpentine wash / CAG
Paquet, André / Trophée de musique / Trophy of Music and Musical Instruments 19th century / wood-gilt / NGC
Pootagok / Woman with Musical Instrument 1959 / stone / AGO
Racine, Soeur Cécile / Music in Retrospect (18 plastic-coated collages) / ?
Raphael, William / Derrière le marché Bonsecours – Behind Bonsecours Market, Montreal 1866 / oil / NGC
Reed, George Agnew / Music 1900 / oil / Ontario College of Education (study for above, a drawing, AGO)
‡Seavey, Julian Ruggles / Music – La Musique ca 1890 / oil / NGC
Shaw-Rimmington, Barrie / series including Pianissimo; Rock Drummer; Classical Guitarist; etc / bronze / *Globe and Mail* (12 May 1969)
Staples, Owen / Sonata 1914 / drawing / NGC
Turner, Thomas / Great Bell of Montreal / lithograph / *Catalogue* Christie Auction 3, part 2, #354
Villeneuve / La Danse du carnaval / ?
Warre, Sir Henry James / Great Bell at Fort Victoria 1845 / PAC
Watson, Sydney H. / The Music Shop – Le Magasin à musique / oil / NGC
Wood, W.J. / Memories Melodies 1919 / U of T (Hart House)
Yarwood, Walter / Guitar 1945 / oil / AGO

HK (GP, PW)

ARTHUR, Jack. Producer, conductor, arranger, violinist, b Glasgow 10 Jun 1889, d Toronto 30 Mar 1971. He was a child prodigy of the violin and toured at 7 with his mother (the opera singer Jean Gifford) in the company of the Scottish tenor Harry Lauder. Arriving in Toronto at 13, Arthur entered the *Toronto College of Music on a scholarship. His work in minstrelsy and vaudeville in the USA in the early 1900s culminated in a position as music director for the Canadian-born minstrel George Primrose. Arthur returned to Toronto ca 1910; he played in the *Welsman TSO and studied with Jan *Hambourg at the *Hambourg Cons (where he also taught ca 1914). He conducted the Winter Garden theatre orchestra in 1915 and moved to the Regent Theatre in 1916. Arthur has been credited by Leslie *Bell (*Music in Canada*) with the introduction of pop concerts to Toronto, during intermissions at the Regent Theatre. He was appointed music director for the Famous Players Theatres chain in Canada in 1918. He also was the music director for a number of movie theatres in Toronto – eg, the Uptown, the Imperial, Shea's Hippodrome – until the late 1930s. Artists introduced at these shows included the boy soprano Bobby Breen, Phyllis *Marshall, John *Moncrieff, Jackie *Rae and the baritone Douglas Stanbury. Arthur also conducted at the Imperial Theatre and was a producer 1933–6 of CRBC broadcasts and music director for that network's 'Serenade to Summer.' Arthur produced *The *Army Show* in 1944 and perhaps was best known as the producer 1952–67 of the Grandstand shows at the *CNE. The CBC program 'Mr. Showbusiness,' 1952–4 on radio and 1954–5 on TV, dramatized events of a career during which Arthur emerged as one of the most powerful men in the Toronto entertainment world.

Artists' Jazz Band (AJB). A pioneering Canadian free-jazz group composed of Toronto visual artists initially associated with the abstract-expressionist movement of the late 1950s. Collectively self-taught, it was formed in 1962 in a studio over the First Floor Club by Dennis Burton, saxophone, and Richard Gorman, bass (both members only briefly), with Graham Coughtry, trombone, Nobuo Kubota, saxophones, Robert Markle, saxophone and piano, and Gordon Rayner, drums. It has included on a casual basis many other artists and musicians – including Michael *Snow and the guitarist Gerald McAdam – sympathetic to its unique and adventurous style of spontaneously composed music. Although public performances, usually at galleries or universities, have been rare, the group has made the LPs *Artists' Jazz Band* (1973, 2-Gallery Editions ST 57427-30) and *Live at the Edge* (1976, 2-Music Gallery Editions no. 3) and has had a marked, if controversial, influence on the development of free jazz in Toronto.

BIBLIOGRAPHY
Gallagher, Greg. 'The Artists' Jazz Band: musical mind-bender in jazz,' *CanComp*, 108, Feb 1976

Arts and Culture Centre, St John's, Nfld. Public building opened 22 May 1967. It was designed by Cummings and Campbell of St John's and Lebensold, Affleck, their Montreal associates, with acoustic design by Russell Johnson Associates. It comprises a 1017-seat theatre (regarded as one of Canada's finest auditoriums), an art gallery, a Maritime museum, libraries, and meeting and rehearsal rooms. The home of the St John's SO after 1970, the centre was the site in 1976 – a typical season – of performances by the *TS, Hank *Snow, the *Salvation Army Canadian Staff Band of Toronto, and a Provincial Folk Festival in addition to dance, theatre, film, and community-oriented presentations.

The Arts and Letters Club of Toronto. Club for men engaged in or interested in the arts (literature, architecture, music, painting, sculpture). It was founded in 1908 largely through the efforts of Augustus *Bridle. A performance 23 Mar 1908 by the *Toronto String Quartette at the club's first meeting established the place of music in its activities. Of some 92 founding members, 18 were from the field of music: J. H. *Anger, Frank *Blachford, Bridle, Hector *Charlesworth, F. H. Coombs, H. C. Cox, A.T. *Cringan, Albert E. Davies, Dr T.A. Davies, W.O. *Forsyth, J.G. Galloway, Fred Killmaster, R.S.V. Piggot, Richard *Tattersall, F.H. *Torrington, J.D.A. *Tripp, A.S. *Vogt, and Frank *Welsman.

First housed in a garret opposite the King Edward Hotel, the club moved in 1910 to the Assize Court and in 1919 to St George's Hall, which remained its home in 1980. In 1912 a constitution (set to music – B625 – by Healey *Willan in 1922 and performed annually thereafter) was adopted and in 1920 the club was incorporated. Musicians among the club's presidents were Bridle 1913–4, Willan 1923–4, Ernest *MacMillan 1930–2, Ettore *Mazzoleni 1945–7, and David *Ouchterlony 1959–61. In 1910 Jan *Hambourg (accompanied by Welsman) gave his first Toronto recital for the club. The annual Boar's Head procession (possibly the oldest in North America) was begun at Christmas 1910. Willan added carols (1921, B422) and the Choral March (1922, B626) to the ceremony, which was conducted by MacMillan and Reginald *Stewart on later occasions.

The club was the site of informal performances by amateur and professional musicians (often jointly until the AF of M forbade such interaction) and concerts by the *Hambourg Trio, the *Academy String Quartet, the *Adanac Quartet, and the New World Chamber Orchestra (all of these groups being composed of club members) and by many guest artists. The *Canadian Academy of Music and the Toronto Chamber Music Society are but two organizations whose origins may be traced to the club's activities. *The Chester Mysteries* with Willan's incidental music (1919, B3) were presented by members in 1931 and repeated in 1933, 1942, 1943, 1951, and 1954. In 1934 St George's Hall was the site of weekly CRBC orchestral broadcasts. A spring revue, begun in 1930 by Napier Moore, continued annually until 1939, then sporadically (1941, 1945, 1948) until annual presentations were resumed in 1954. Book, lyrics, and music were prepared by members, including T.J. *Crawford, MacMillan, Frederick *Silvester, and Harry *Somers. Accompaniment, usually on two pianos, was provided by Reginald *Godden and Scott Malcolm, Gordon *Hallett and Clifford *Poole, and others. A version of **Theatre of Neptune*, with incidental music (1954, B31) by Willan, was produced several times.

In 1944 Marcus *Adeney, John Coulter, and Herman Voaden presented the advisory board's report to the federal government's Turgeon Committee (for post-war reconstruction and re-establishment). This report had a direct bearing on the formation of the *CMCouncil and the Canadian Arts Council (later *CCA).

PUBLICATIONS

The Yearbook of Canadian Art (London, Toronto 1913)
The Lamps, intermittent 1919–39
The Monthly Letter, Nov 1942–
Bridle, A. *The Story of the Club* (Toronto 1945)

BIBLIOGRAPHY

Archives of the Arts and Letters Club
Jones, Donald. 'Club provides a meeting place for writers, artists, musicians,' *Toronto Star*, 14 Apr 1979

MWM, PW

Art song. Setting of a poem, typically for voice and piano and of a high aesthetic intent. As can be seen from the *CMCentre catalogue *Canadian Vocal Music / Musique vocale canadienne* or the *Catalogue of Canadian Composers* and *Contemporary Canadian Composers / Compositeurs canadiens contemporains*, most Canadian composers have written art songs.

Perhaps the earliest report indicating that the art song was cultivated in Canada appears in August Ludwig von Schlözer's *Vertrauliche Briefe aus Kanada und Neu-England vom Jahre 1777 und 1778* (Göttingen 1779). In his fourth letter Schlözer describes a party (for the queen's birthday, 20 Jan 1777) given in Trois-Rivières by Baron von Riedesel, the commander of the loyalist mercenaries: 'You should know, dear sir, that the Canadian belles sing Italian and French *chansons* at dinner; and that several *chansons* already have been written and set to music in honour of General von Riedesel and frequently are sung in Trois-Rivières.' Unfortunately, neither the music nor the name(s) of its composer(s) has survived. Late-18th-century newspapers show that music teachers taught 'vocal music,' that dealers imported vocal sheet music, and that performers gave concerts of vocal music, usually, however, operatic.

The earliest Canadian art songs surviving in print are the two canzonets by Stephen *Codman, published ca 1827. Both are elaborate display pieces for coloratura soprano and piano. James P. *Clarke had published some songs in Scotland before coming to Canada in 1835. His *Lays of the Maple Leaf or Songs of Canada* (*Nordheimer 1853), consists of an opening glee, four solo songs, one duet, and closing choruses. The first song cycle published in Canada, it aims at simplicity and employs Canadian subject matter.

Canadians of French origin in the 19th century generally wrote for church use and copied French models in the forms of chansons, chansonettes, romances (love poetry), and mélodies. Most early chansons populaires and dance-songs (valses chantées, polkas) were short compositions with many verses. While the piano parts often doubled the voice line, there were pianistic colourings, adroit rhythms, and sometimes considerable resourcefulness in word-painting and mood-setting. Composers of such pieces included Charles W. *Sabatier, Jean-Baptiste *Labelle, Célestin *Lavigueur, and Napoléon *Crépault. Antoine *Dessane wrote several art songs, though in a partriotic vein. Calixa *Lavallée, the composer of *'O Canada,' may be considered the first Canadian-born songwriter of note. His earlier songs (to texts in English and composed for US publishers – eg, 'Leaving Home and Friends' 1869) are parlour songs, in the genre designed for the multitude of voice students and amateur singers produced by an expanding middle-class society, and hover between art song and popular ballad. Lavallée's later songs, such as 'Nuit d'été,' 'Violette,' 'Harmonie,' and 'L'Absence' (in French and mostly from his Canadian period 1875–81) show much progress towards piquant harmony and melodic expressiveness. Mention also must be made of the *Seize Mélodies* (A. Lavigne 1879) by the Count of Premio-Real, consul general of Spain for Canada. This work was the largest album of one composer's songs published in Canada up to that time. The count was an amateur, and his music was edited by Lavallée, whose preface, dated 25 Sep 1878, declares, 'The parlour song – which reigned supreme for so many years and left its much too languorous and naïve sounds echoing through our drawing-rooms – has had its day.' Lavallée's vision of a trend towards serious song proved premature, however, for publishers and magazines turned out large quantities of sentimental ballads and parlour songs well into the 20th century.

Ernest *Lavigne is not far behind Lavallée in importance. His many published songs, which include settings of poems by Alphonse Daudet, Alfred de Musset, Théophile Gautier, Victor Hugo, and Armand Silvestre, are characterized by Gallic lightness of texture, charm, and piquancy and have more developed accompaniments than have Lavallée's. Alexis *Contant also left examples of rather effective melodies with smooth bass lines and telling harmonies. His settings include poems by J. Barbier, Alonzo Cinq-Mars, Gustave *Comte, Alphonse Daudet, L.O. David, Albert Ferland, Louis Fréchette, Victor Hugo, J.N. Legault, and Albert Lozeau.

Ernest *Whyte is credited with some 270 songs, 24 of which were published during his lifetime. A further 26 were published posthumously by his Ottawa friends. The songs, which make up almost his whole oeuvre, have elaborate Schumannesque piano parts and easily flowing, if not memorable, voice lines. Two other art-song composers prominent in English Canada at the turn of the century were W.O. *Forsyth and Clarence *Lucas. The former's songs (some 50 published and more in manuscript) were based on poetry by J.D. Logan, Marjorie Pickthall, A.D. Watson, and Turgenev, among others. Lucas, who composed some 70 songs, spent only a few of his mature years in Canada.

Anglo-Canadian composers such as Albert *Ham, Susie Francis *Harrison (composing under the pseudonyms 'Seranus' and 'Gilbert King'), Charles A.E. *Harriss, and Frank *Welsman followed European (especially German) models. Like Whyte and Forsyth, who had studied in German conservatories, they modelled their work on Schumann and Mendelssohn, and some set to music words by Goethe, Heine, and other German poets. Other composers of the first half of the 20th century who saw their songs in print included Paul *Ambrose, W.H. *Anderson (many to verses by Canadian poets published in the newspapers of the day), Charles Baudouin, Gena *Branscombe, John Mais Capel, Ernest *Dainty, Achille *Fortier, Alfred *Laliberté, Omer *Létourneau, Ernest *MacMillan, Rodolphe *Mathieu, Henri *Miro, Léo-Pol *Morin, Geoffrey *O'Hara, Émiliano *Renaud, Léo *Roy (who set to music 62 poems of Émile Nelligan), Leo *Smith, and Healey *Willan. Songs have continued to be composed by Canadians to words by poets of international fame (Hillaire Belloc, Emily Dickinson, Paul Éluard, A.E. Housman, James Joyce, Mallarmé, Jacques Prévert, Shelley, Shakespeare, Verlaine, and others) and also by Canadian poets (see Literature set to music).

Canadian composers of the 1930s and 1940s gradually absorbed new influences which liberated their music from European moulds. Polytonality, serialism, modal and exotic scales, and the rich Canadian heritage of folk material (both European and native) have been integrated in the modern Canadian song. *Weinzweig and *Somers have written their own words, on occasion. Somers, notably in *Evocations*, has explored in some depth new vocal techniques, as have *Anhalt and others. Indeed, much writing in the 1970s tended to eschew or subdue the human and literary elements of the art song in favour of more abstract and exotic tendencies.

True song cycles, rarely composed by Canadians before the 1920s, subsequently became more frequent. Laliberté's 15-song cycle *La Chanson d'Ève*, to words by the Belgian poet Charles van Lerberghe, was perhaps the first major cycle by a Canadian. Composers in the 20th century have seemed more responsive to the challenge of uniting word and music over the extended span which characterizes the cycle. Among 20th-century Canadians who have published sets or cycles of songs with piano or other instruments are Anhalt (*Foci*, Berandol 1972), *Beckwith (*Five Lyrics of the T'ang Dynasty*, BMIC 1949; *Four Songs from Ben Jonson's 'Volpone,'* Berandol 1967), *Bissell (*Hymns of the Chinese Kings*, Waterloo 1968), *Blomfield Holt (*Three Songs of Contemplation*, Berandol 1970), *Daunais (*Fantaisie dans tous les tons*, Archambault 1974), *Fleming (*The Confession Stone*, Leeds 1968), *Glick (*... i never saw another butterfly ...*, Leeds 1972), *Johnston (*The Irish Book*, Waterloo 1971), *Naylor (*Speaking from the Snow*, Robertson 1974), *Schafer (*Minnelieder*, Berandol 1970; *Kinderlieder*, Berandol 1970), and Somers (*Five Songs for Dark Voice*, Berandol 1972; *Twelve Miniatures*, BMIC 1965; *Evocations*, Bernadol 1970).

Others in the mid- and late-20th century who have contributed significantly to the literature of solo songs with piano or instrumental accompaniment include V. *Archer, L. *Betts, *Blackburn, Maurice Boivin, *Brott, *Buczynski, *Charpentier, *Coulthard, *Dela, *Duncan, *Eggleston, *Freedman, Alain *Gagnon, *Garant, *Gayfer, *Gratton, *Healey, J. *Hétu, *Jeannotte, *Klein, *Komorous, *MacNutt, B.*Mather, *Morawetz, *Morel, *O'Brien, *Papineau-Couture, *Pépin, *Prévost, W. *Russell, J. *Vallerand, *Vivier, Weinzweig, *Weisgarber, and *Wilson.

See also Folk-music-inspired composition.

The number of Canadian art songs and art-song cycles recorded by 1980 was small in relation to the repertoire. The following list of recordings, while not claiming to be comprehensive, nevertheless provides coverage representative at the time of compilation.

Adaskin *Epitaph* (RCI 74); *Of Man and the Universe* (CBC SM-27)
Applebaum *Cry of the Prophet* (RCA LSC 3092)
Archer 'April Weather,' 'Cradle Song,' 'The Twenty-Third Psalm,' 'First Snow' from *Under the Sun* (RCI 108): *Under the Sun* (CBC SM-79)
Beckwith *Serenade* (RCI 36); *Five Lyrics of the T'ang Dynasty* (RCI 148); 'Drimindown,' 'L'Amant Malheureux,' 'The Saint-John's Girl' from *Four Love Songs* (CBC SM-11)
Betts 5 of *Six Songs*, 1951 (RCI 74)
Bissell *Two Songs of Farewell* (CBC SM-79)
Blackburn 'Winter Serenade,' 'The Parrott,' 'The Idiot in the Belfry' (RCI 36)
Brott, A. *Songs of the Central Eskimos, Indian Legends* (RCI 391); *Songs of Contemplation* (RCI 116)
Coulthard *Spring Rhapsody* (RCI 203); 'All Day Long I Hear the Noise of Waters,' 'Rain Has Fallen All the Day' from *Three Songs* for medium voice, 1946 (RCI 20); *Three Songs*; 'Lean Out of the Window, Goldenhair' (RCI 109)
Daunais 'D'Amour et de Fantaisie' – album title (Sel CC 15.087); 2 selections from *Cinq Poèmes d'Éloi de Grandmont, Quatre Ballades de Paul Fort*, 'Le Coeur oublieux,' 'À ma cousine,' 'Voici qu'un jour,' *Fantaisie dans tous les tons, Sept Éphitaphes plaisantes* (RCI 294); 'Les Beaux Yeux clairs,' (RCI 107, RCI 294); 'L'Hirondelle,' 2 selections from *Cinq Poèmes d'Éloi de Grandmont*, 'Chansons du gars heureux,' 'L'Innocente,' 'Chansons de Mathilda,' 'Simone,' 'L'Astronome,' 2 selections from *Quatre Ballades de Paul Fort* (RCI 107); *Le Vent des forêts* (CBC Expo 23)
Dela 'Ronde' (RCI 35); *Les Saisons* (CBC Expo 33, RCI 470)
Eggleston 'Armenian Lullaby,' 'Jewish Lullaby,' 'Norse Lullaby' (RCI 247)
Fleming *The Confession Stone* (RCI 246), 4 songs from *Coulter Songs* (RCI 248)
Freedman *Poems of Young People* (CBC SM-77 / Sel CC 15.073)
Gagnon, Alain 'Que je t'accueille,' 'Tristesse' (RCI 393)
Garant 'Et je prierai ta grâce,' *Concerts sur terre, Caprices* (RCI 201)
Glick ... *i never saw another butterfly* ... (CBC SM-77 / Sel CC 15.073); *Two Landscapes* (CBC SM-180)
Hamer 'Marigolds' (RCI 35)
Hétu *Les Clartés de la nuit, Op 20* (RCI 483)
Jeannotte *Propos intimes* (RCI 470)
Jones *To Music* (RCI 203)
Lavallée 'L'Absence,' 'Nuit d'été' (RCI 426)
Mathieu, Rodolphe 'L'Automne' and 'L'Hiver' from *Saisons canadiennes* (RCI 365); 'Un Peu d'ombre,' 'Les Yeux noirs,' *Deux Poèmes* (L'Oiseau-Coeur OC S-02)
McIntyre, Margaret 'Lost Lagoon' (RCI 35)
McIntyre, P. *Four Poems of Walter de la Mare* (RCI 74)
Mercure *Dissidence* (RCI 201, Allied ARCLP 4)
Morawetz 'To the Ottawa River' (RCI 121); 'Elegy: "I am so tired" ' (RCI 121, CBC SM-180); 'The Grenadier' (RCI 121, CBC SM-42); 'The Chimney Sweeper,' 'Mad Song' (RCI 121, CBC Expo 22); 'Piping Down the Valleys Wild' (CBC SM-8, CBC SM-180) ; 'I Love the Jocund Dance' (CBC SM-8); 'Father William' (RCI 391)
Morel *Les Rivages perdus* (RCI 201)
Papineau-Couture *Quatrains* (RCI 148)
Pentland 'Wheat' and 'Mountains' from an untitled song cycle, 1945 (RCI 20)
Pépin *Cycle-Éluard* (RCI 148, RCI 426)
Prévost *Geôles* (Allied ARCLP 4); *Musiques peintes* (RCI 426)
Russell 'Come Hither You that Love' and 'Waly, Waly Up the Bank' from *Sixteen Songs*, 'My Lute Awake,' 'Over the Mountains' (RCI 333)
Schafer *Kinderlieder* (CBC SM-141)
Somers *Five Songs for Dark Voice* (CBC SM-73, RCI 286 / RCA LSC 3172); *Evocations* (CBC SM-13, CBC SM-108); *Twelve Miniatures* (RCA 217 / RCI CCS 1011)
Vallerand *Quatre Poèmes de Saint-Denys Garneau* (RCI 393, Allied ARCLP 4)
Weinzweig *Dance of the Massadah* (RCA LSC 3092); *Of Time and the World* (RCI 20); *Wine of Peace* (RCI 182)
Willan 'At Dawn,' 'To Blossoms' from *Ten Songs*, 'Sonnet "To Sleep" ' from *Song Album No. 1*, 'The Lake Isle of Innisfree' from *Song Album No. 2* (CBC SM-144)
See also Discography for David Mills. HK (GP)

'À St-Malo, beau port de mer.' In his collection *Alouette* (Montreal 1946) Marius *Barbeau says that this work song 'bears the name St-Malo only in Canada. In France it is known under the title "Bateau du Blé et la dame trompée" and the towns that figure in the first couplet are Nantes and Bordeaux.' In Canada 'C'est à Bordeaux, beau port de mer' also is sung. Of a bright and lively character, the song comes from the northwest of France and is thought to have become popular because of the 1837 rebellion, when St-Malo and patriotism were synonymous. The words appear to have been published for the first time by F.-A.-H. LaRue in *Le Foyer canadien*, vol 1 (Quebec 1863), and the music in the *Chansons populaires du Canada* (Quebec 1865) by Ernest *Gagnon. É.-Z. *Massicotte collected a variant of the song in which the refrain appears as follows: 'J'ai vu le loup, le renard, le lièvre; j'ai vu le loup, le r'nard passer' (I've seen the wolf, the fox, the hare; I've seen the wolf, the fox pass by). The song served as an inspiration for the second of Ernest *MacMillan's *Two Sketches* for string orchestra (1927), and the melody provides the theme for the third movement of Morley *Calvert's *Suite from the Monteregian Hills / Suite des collines montérégiennes* (1962) for brass quintet. Claude *Champagne and Hector *Gratton have made four-voice arrangements of it. The song was recorded by Édouard *LeBel on a 78 (HMV 63402) and subsequently on LPs by Jacques *Labrecque (Pathé AT 1029) and Alan *Mills (Folk FW 3000), among others.

BIBLIOGRAPHY

Barbeau, Marius, and Sapir, Edward. *Folksongs of French Canada* (New Haven 1925) HP

Ascher Duo (1970–5, Aschers Three 1975–7). Formed by the bass Kenneth Asch (b Montreal 26 Jun 1934) and his wife, the soprano Henriette Platford (b Winnipeg 23 Sep 1937). Platford was a pupil in Winnipeg of Doris Mills *Lewis and in Montreal of Bernard *Diamant, and Asch also was a Diamant pupil. They both studied further in Munich, he with Karl Schmitt-Walter and she with Adele Kern. Asch made his debut in 1963 at the Municipal Opera in Detmold, then became a leading bass 1963–6 with the Oldenburg and Bremerhaven opera companies, appearing also 1965–8 with the Bavarian State Opera in Munich, in 1968 with the Zurich Opera, and in 1970 with the Venice Opera and with the Royal Philharmonic Orchestra. Platford made her debut in 1959 with the *Montreal Elgar Choir in a CBC broadcast and subsequently sang in recital in 1959 and 1961 in Montreal and Munich and in opera in 1965 and 1966 in Mannheim and Augsburg, Germany.

In 1971 the couple moved to Toronto and opened a teaching studio, the Toronto Academy of Performance, with Bernard Diamant. The duo performed at Wigmore Hall, London, in 1972, appeared in 1973 in Montreal and Calgary, and sang again in 1974 and 1975 at Wigmore Hall. Works written for the duo by Alexander *Brott (*Songs of the Central Eskimos* and *Indian Legends*) and Oskar *Morawetz (*Father William*) were premiered at Wigmore Hall and, with John *Newmark at the piano, were recorded with pieces by Rossi, Blow, and Purcell (1975, RCI 391). In 1976 the German composer Werner Egk wrote for the duo *La Tentation de St Antoine* (for string quartet or orchestra and two voices).

With the addition of the soprano Burnetta Day, the duo became Aschers Three in 1975 and gave a command performance before the prime ministers of Canada and Belgium in 1976 in Ottawa. Before it disbanded in 1977, Aschers Three also broadcast on CBC radio, toured annually for *Community Concerts and *Overture Concerts, and performed with the *Hamilton Philharmonic Orchestra, the *MSO, and the *McGill Chamber Orchestra. Asch formed another trio, The Perfect Mix, with the soprano Janet Kudelka and the baritone Michael Crossman in 1977.

Edwin Ashdown Ltd. London music-publishing firm established in 1825 by C.R. Wessel as Wessel and Stodart, and known 1860–84 as Ashdown & Parry before taking its current name. Its catalogue has emphasized piano and vocal music. Ashdown had a Canadian retail store for a short time (ca 1878) in Toronto. A later Ashdown's Music Store, which sold music of many publishers, was managed (ca 1888–ca 1920) by Edwin's son Sydney. By 1890 the son also managed the * Anglo-Canadian Music Publishers Assn in Toronto, and the two firms operated jointly. In its first four years Ashdown's Canadian branch issued some 60 'Canadian Copyright Editions of Standard Music Compositions' but later did very little music publishing. Prominent among the composers published were Stephen Heller, Gustav Lange, and Sydney Smith and the Canadians A.E. *Fisher, W.H. *Hewlett, and Clarence *Lucas.

ASSALY, Edmund (Philip). Pianist, composer, arranger, teacher, b Rosetown, Sask, of Syrian parents, 4 Jan 1920; ATCM 1934, LRSM 1938. He began studying piano at eight, and when his family moved to Saskatoon he continued 1937–45 with Lyell *Gustin. He was organist at St James' Church and played on CBC radio. During World War II he took part in entertainment tours for the troops and began to compose. With Thelma Johannes *O'Neill he formed a two-piano team which performed 1943–50 on radio and popularized his *Suite* for two pianos. In Winnipeg 1945–7 he gave recitals on radio and worked as an arranger preparing, among other such occasional pieces, a piano-and-orchestra arrangement of *Red River Valley* for 'Canadian Party,' a CBC special presentation. He then settled in Montreal and took lessons 1947–50 from Michel *Hirvy. In addition to his activities as pianist and arranger, he composed other works, including *Mount Royal Fantasy* for piano and orchestra (1948) and *Carrefour*, the winning work of the Montreal Ballet Festival (1950). In 1954 he recorded (RCI 115) two of his piano pieces – *Romance* and *Habanera* – and his *Sonata in A* for violin and piano, as well as Alexander *Brott's *Invocation and Dance* with the violinist George Lapenson. Assaly was music director and orchestrator 1957–8 for the revue **My Fur Lady* and wrote several ballet scores 1960–2 for stage and TV. Using themes by Calixa *Lavallée, he composed the music for the ballet *Pointes sur glace*, premiered in 1967 by Les Grands Ballets Canadiens at *PDA, conducting the *MSO for the performance. He moved in 1970 to Milwaukee to teach orchestration, arranging, and harmony at the U of Wisconsin. He has composed and arranged for the summer concerts of the Milwaukee SO and served as music director of an opera company. Among his works are another ballet, *Daytracks* (1970), two compositions commissioned by the Milwaukee SO – *Salute to Black America* (1973) and *Trade Winds* (1978) – and musical comedies and revues. ST

ASSELIN, (Paul) André. Pianist, composer, writer b Montreal. He began piano study with Auguste *Descarries and, on scholarships from Underwood in 1945 and the TCM (*RCMT) in 1946, continued at the TCM with Ernest *Seitz and Lubka *Kolessa. In 1948 he toured South America as pianist-conductor for a dance company from the Paris Opéra. He also appeared in recital on that continent, in Canada, and then in France. In the early 1950s he settled in Paris. He has given many hundreds of recitals to favourable notices in France and elsewhere in Europe, playing the classical repertoire and works by several Canadian composers including *Archer, *Champagne, Descarries, André and Rodolphe *Mathieu, *Pentland, *Pépin, *Somers, and *Willan. He has composed *Danse*, *Fantaisie*, and *Conte* for piano and is the author of *Panorama de la musique canadienne* (Paris 1962).

The Associated Board of the Royal Schools of Music. Founded in 1889 to serve as the examination body of the RAM, the RCM, and, in 1947, the Royal Manchester College of Music and the Royal Scottish Academy of Music. It conducts or has conducted examinations annually throughout Great Britain and her dominions and colonies. It began these in Canada in 1895 and continued them until 1953. John Bayne Maclean of Montreal (president of Maclean Publishing Co) was the AB's first honorary general representative and Montreal the Canadian administration centre. *Nordheimer Piano & Music Co was the first agent for AB publications. During the years 1902–9 the AB operated in conjunction with *McGill U, with Charles A. E. *Harriss as director of examinations, but when McGill in 1909 set up its own system of examinations, the AB continued independently, establishing secretariats in eastern Canada (a Montreal office serving Quebec, New Brunswick, Nova Scotia, and Prince Edward Island), Toronto, Manitoba-Saskatchewan, Alberta, and British Columbia. By the 1930s 3500 candidates were being tested annually by British examiners. The number declined with the increase of activity by Canadian music examination systems – notably those set up by the *RCMT and the *WBM – and in 1953 the Canadian secretariats were closed. From the beginning the AB's presence in Canada was a subject of criticism. Some teachers, particularly in French Canada, chafed under policies which they felt were inapplicable to the Canadian situation and objected to the 'sheet-music traffic' in AB-approved and AB-supplied editions. Later, however, musicians appreciated the AB's high standards, well-devised syllabus, experienced examiners, scholarly editions of basic repertoire (notably the Tovey-Craxton annotated editions of Bach's *Well-Tempered Clavier* and the Beethoven *Piano Sonatas*), and the substantial scholarships which enabled as many as four Canadian students a year to complete their training in London. Of 104 Canadians awarded AB scholarships from 1909 to 1953, 77 accepted the awards.

1909 Gladys McElvie *Egbert, Calgary
1910 Jaroslav Bauer, Calgary
1911 Grace Trotter, Montreal
1912 Freda Sweet, Calgary
1913 Philip Shadwick, Winnipeg
Caroline Fotheringham, St Andrews, Toronto
1916 Odette *de Foras, Calgary
1918 Marion O'Neail, Winnipeg
1919 Ben Loban, Winnipeg
1920 Dorothy Browne, Calgary
1921 Mary Pierce, Calgary
1922 Hugo *Rignold, Winnipeg
1923 Jean Cotton, Calgary
1924 Barbara *Custance, Vancouver
1925 Mary Graham, Winnipeg
1926 James Wright, Winnipeg
Betty Bateson, Calgary
Nancy Reed, Vancouver
1927 Frederick *Grinke, Winnipeg
Smyth *Humphreys, Chilliwack
Molly Mooney, Port Arthur
1928 Mike Kucyer, Winnipeg
David *Martin, Winnipeg
1929 Elizabeth Emery, Victoria
Elizabeth Harrison, Nova Scotia
John Cuchmy, Winnipeg
1930 Sara Bakum, Winnipeg
Evelyne Pearson, Calgary
Kathleen Tierney, Calgary
1931 Aubrey Arthur, Edmonton
Beatrice Hodgson, Vancouver
Clifford McCormick, Toronto
1932 Sylvia Cates, Winnipeg
Eugene Nemish, Winnipeg
1933 Verdun Leigh, Calgary
Ross *Pratt, Winnipeg
1934 Norma Gallia, Vancouver
Mary Shortt, Calgary
Billy *Waterhouse, Winnipeg
1935 Geraldine Paget Mellor, Victoria
Violet Paget Mellor, Victoria
Noel Taylor, Calgary
Gordon Watson, Winnipeg
1936 Patricia Norris, Edmonton
Clelio Rietagliati, Winnipeg
Mary Tierney, Calgary
1937 Harold Clark, Calgary
Jean Gilbert, Calgary
Maxwell Ward, Vancouver
1939 Daphne Sandercock, Ontario
1940 Samuel Margolian, Halifax
1941 Ida Vivienne Smith, Toronto
1942 Sydney *Humphreys, Vancouver
1943 Carol Jutte, Vancouver
Robin *Wood, Esquimalt
1944 Irene Bubniuk, Saskatoon
Winifred Scott, Winnipeg
1945 Barbara Draper, Calgary
Mary Gillard, Vancouver
Elsie Jensen, Winnipeg
1946 Zonia Lazarowich, Winnipeg
1947 Mae Broadbent, Windsor
Arthur *Davison, Montreal
Walter Money, Winnipeg
1948 Eileen Graham, Kelowna
Gerald Jarvis, Vancouver
Hugh *McLean, Vancouver
Patricia Rundle, Vancouver
1949 Andrew Babynchuk, Winnipeg
Thomas *Rolston, Vancouver
1950 Carlina Carr, Calgary
1951 Marion E. Gibbs, Victoria
Lila Wong Git Sen, Nanaimo
1952 B. Dale *Bartlett, Lethbridge
Donald M. *Bell, Burnaby
1953 H. Daryl *Irvine, Toronto
Constance M. Voth, Winnipeg

BIBLIOGRAPHY

Canadian Protesting Committee. *An Account of the Canadian Protest against the Introduction into Canada of Musical Examinations by Outside Examining Bodies* (Toronto 1899)

Sandwell, B.K. *The Musical Red Book of Montreal* (Montreal 1907)

Montreal Music Year Book, 2 vols (Montreal 1931, 1932)

The Associated Board of the Royal Schools of Music 1889–1948 (London nd) NT, KW (PW)

Associated Manitoba Festivals. Co-ordinating body for Manitoba community arts festivals. It was established in 1961 by R.W. *Cooke, J.P. Redekopp, William Sonnichen, and Vi Streuber, and by 1977 it administered some 35 competition and non-competition festivals in the province. Though several of these (the *Manitoba Music Competition Festival and those in Brandon, Dauphin, Portage la Prairie, and elsewhere) have retained local autonomy, each has benefited from the association's resources. It has promoted workshops and concerts in the province's smaller centres and initiated new festivals. A 'provincial highlights' concert has been established as an annual feature. The association is funded by the province and governed by an elected executive and appointed regional representatives. A paid executive director has offices (opened in 1973) in Steinbach.

Association chorale Brassard. Male-voice choir founded in Montreal in 1915 by Joseph-Arsène Brassard. It gave its first concert at the Salle St-Sulpice 20 Nov 1916. In 1918 it performed works by Frédéric *Pelletier and Amédée *Tremblay and an excerpt from Liszt's *Saint Elizabeth*. Women's voices were added in 1919, increasing the membership to 190. The mixed-voice choir made its first appearance at the *Monument national 24 Feb 1921 in Franck's *Les Béatitudes*. The choir also took part in the celebrations for the Franck centenary at *His Majesty's Theatre in 1922 and sang twice at Aeolian Hall, New York, in 1923. The same year it won the C.W. *Lindsay and Birks trophies at the Montreal Musical (competition) Festival. It sang often for charitable causes and participated in the benefit concert at the *St-Denis Theatre, 28 May 1925, for Emma *Albani. Occasionally the choir was accompanied by an orchestra in large works, eg, Haydn's *The Creation* in 1925, Brahms' *A German Requiem* (with the baritone Lionel *Daunais) in 1926, and Dvořák's *Stabat mater* in 1931. The soloists usually were members of the choir or pupils of Brassard.

Brassard (baritone, b Pointe-St-Charles, Montreal, 15 Jul 1889, d Côteau-Landing, near Montreal, 10 Jul 1959) had studied with Jean-Noël *Charbonneau, Guillaume *Couture, Arthur *Letondal, Arthur *Plamondon, Jean *Riddez, Joseph *Saucier, and, in Paris, with Yan Ruben. In Montreal he taught singing at the St-Léon, St-Paul, and St-Thomas d'Aquin schools and voice and piano privately. He was choirmaster 1914–28 with the Pères du St-Sacrement and 1928–35? at the Ascension Church in Westmount and conductor of the St-Jean-Baptiste Society choir in Montreal.

BIBLIOGRAPHY
'L'hommage à Albani s'inscrira dans notre histoire de l'art,' Montreal *La Presse*, 16 May 1925 AP

L'Association chorale Saint-Louis-de-France. Male-voice choir founded in 1892 to serve in the church of that name in Montreal. It was incorporated in 1897. Its conductors were Charles *Labelle 1892–1902, Alexandre M. *Clerk 1903–27, Joseph *Saucier 1927–36, and Charles *Goulet 1936–68.

Female voices were added for performances with orchestra at the *Monument national of such works as Massenet's *Marie-Madeleine* in 1907 and *Ève* in 1908, Pierné's *La Croisade des enfants* and Dubois's *Sept Paroles du Christ* in 1909, scenes from Grieg's *Olaf Trygvason* with the New York Symphony Society under Walter Damrosch in 1910, Saint-Saëns' *Samson et Dalila* in 1911, Dubois's *Paradis perdu* in 1913 and 1919, Berlioz' *La Damnation de Faust* in 1914, 1915, and 1918, Alexandre Georges's *Les Chants de guerre* in 1917, Lefebvre's *Judith* in 1920, Félicien David's *Le Désert* in 1923, and Massenet's *Terre promise* in 1924. After 1924 the choir's activities were limited mainly to participation in church services.

BIBLIOGRAPHY
Gélinas, Simone. 'Les 70 ans de la chorale de Saint-Louis-de-France,' *Notre Temps*, 8 Apr 1961

L'Association des Chanteurs de Montréal. A 150-voice mixed choir which began, and sang 1918–20, as a men's chorus and was directed successively by Armand *Renaud and Hercule Desjardins. From 1920 until it disbanded in the mid-1930s it was conducted by Jean *Goulet and performed such works with orchestra as La Tombelle's *Crux* in 1922; **Jean le Précurseur*, twice in 1923 and again in 1928; Mendelssohn's *Elijah*, Planchet's *Les Mystères douloureux*, and Frédéric *Pelletier's *Stabat mater* in 1925; Tinel's *Franciscus* and Berlioz' *L'Enfance du Christ* in 1926; Berlioz' *La Damnation de Faust* in 1927; Honegger's *Le Roi David* in 1928; Massenet's *Hérodiade* and Henri *Miro's **Vox populi* in 1929; Massenet's *Ève* in 1930; and Handel's *Messiah* in 1932.

Association of Canadian Orchestras / Association des orchestres canadiens. Umbrella federation of orchestral entities, initiated in 1971 and formally constituted in 1972; not to be confused with the Organization of Canadian Symphony Musicians, for which see Unions. The member orchestras – major, community, and youth – represent all provinces of Canada. ACO has shared premises and administration with the Ontario Federation of Symphony Orchestras, although each organization has its own board, activities, and projects. For discussion of the development and activities of ACO see Ontario Federation of Symphony Orchestras. See also Orchestras; Youth orchestras.

ASTOR, David. Tenor, teacher, b Vancouver 24 Apr 1926. A pupil in London of Parry Jones and Manlio di Veroli, Astor sang in England with the Royal Opera and at the Glyndebourne and Aldeburgh Festivals and in the USA with the Chicago, Dayton, and Toledo operas. His *COC roles have been Hoffmann in *The Tales of Hoffmann* in 1967, Donald Smith and General Middleton in **Louis Riel* in 1968 and 1975, and the Fourth Jew in *Salome* in 1975. Astor has appeared with many Canadian orchestras, with the BBC, Milwaukee, and Chicago SOs, and with the Royal Philharmonic, and has been heard in recital and on CBC and BBC radio. He sings the title role in the recording of **The Fool*. He taught voice 1968–75 at the U of Wisconsin and joined the faculties at the *Banff SFA in 1974 and Grant MacEwan Community College, Edmonton, in 1975. (RM)

ATKINS, William (Thais). Bandmaster, teacher, composer, b London 29 Jul 1907, d Toronto 7 Mar 1979; ARCM 1935. After studies at the RMSM (Kneller Hall) and the RCM he was a bandmaster 1935–46 in the British army, then moved to Toronto where he was music director 1947–68 of the *Queen's Own Rifles of Canada, retiring with the rank of captain. He became music director for the city of Brampton, Ont, in 1947 and conducted the Brampton Citizens' Band for over 30 years. During that time the band won 28 firsts in national and provincial competitions. Atkins was honoured by the city at the band's 90th-anniversary concert in 1975. He began teaching conducting, composition, and woodwinds for the Ontario Dept of Education in 1953 and was principal 1968–72 of the department's summer school for teachers. He was president 1955–6 of the *CBA and adjudicated bands at many Ontario festivals. Atkins' compositions include the official march of the (British) Royal Army Physical Training Corps, *Keep Fit* (Boosey & Hawkes), and various unpublished works. He also arranged Healey *Willan's *Élégie Héroïque* for band (Boosey & Hawkes 1971). (JK)

ATKINSON, George Douglas. Educator, organist-choirmaster, b Carp, near Ottawa, 1878, d Toronto 14 Sept 1964. A pupil in Toronto of George Fairclough, W.J. McNally, F.H. *Torrington, A.S. *Vogt, and Frank *Welsman, he also studied briefly in Leipzig, in London with Tobias Matthay, and in New York with Rosina Lhévinne. After being organist-choirmaster in several Toronto churches he moved to Sherbourne St Methodist (later United) in 1911 and remained there until his retirement in 1950. His choirs won many honours. In 1922 he conducted the first Toronto performance of the complete *St Matthew Passion* at Sherbourne St Methodist Church, and in 1927 he prepared a 450-voice choir for a spring festival concert with Florence *Easton and the New SO under Luigi von *Kunits. He taught for a few years at the *Toronto College of Music and 1910–56 at the *TCM, where his subjects were piano and pedagogy. His pupils included Samuel *Dolin, Muriel *Gidley, and George *Ziegler. His studio club was among the largest and longest-lived in Canada. He also wrote many articles 1918–35 for the *Conservatory Quarterly Review*, about piano teaching, playing, and examinations and was co-author with Cora B. *Ahrens of *For All Piano Teachers* (Oakville 1955). He was music master 1912–50 at the Ontario Ladies' College, Whitby. Atkinson composed the songs *A Lullaby* (Nordheimer 1902) and *A Christmas Nocturne* (London YWCA 1903). (MHI)

Atlantic Symphony Orchestra / Orchestre symphonique de l'atlantique. Canada's first full-time regional orchestra, formed 12 Jun 1968 with the support of committees in Halifax and Sydney, NS, and Saint John, Moncton, and Fredericton, NB. The orchestra is based in Halifax but is governed by a board drawn from the above-named committees, each of which has retained responsibility for the orchestra's appearances in its own city. Klaro M. *Mizerit was music director and conductor until 1977, when he was succeeded by Victor Yampolsky (b USSR 1943), a violin pupil of David Oistrakh and assistant conductor 1971–3 of the Moscow Philharmonic.

Until 1968 the *Halifax SO and the *New Brunswick SO enjoyed the part-time services of woodwind and brass players from the Maritime military bands. However, when the Dept of National Defence dispersed the bands in 1968 the players were no longer available. Faced with these drastic depletions in their orchestras and the expense of repairing them, the Atlantic communities agreed on the fiscal advantage of disbanding the Halifax SO and the New Brunswick SO and lending joint support to a single paid regional orchestra designed to tour Atlantic centres. The Atlantic SO (48 players, mostly from elsewhere in Canada and the USA) was the result. It gave its first concert 14 Oct 1968 at St Patrick's High School, Halifax. During its first season it offered 39 subscription concerts, of which 32 were broadcast by the CBC. By 1977 the orchestra had grown to 65 players, with an operating cost which had increased (from the inaugural year's $380 thousand) to slightly over $1 million, of which the *Canada Council provided about one third, the province and municipalities between 15 and 20 per cent, and private donors and the box office the remainder. During that season the orchestra gave 110 concerts (subscription, school, community, and CBC) in various New Brunswick, Nova Scotia, and Prince Edward Island centres. (Tours in Newfoundland were discontinued when financial support from that province failed.) Ordinarily, after a performance in Halifax at the *Rebecca Cohn Auditorium, the orchestra has presented the same program on tour in three or four other centres.

Under Mizerit's direction the orchestra played the standard repertoire and some 20th-century works, notably by Stravinsky and Canadian composers. It premiered Patric Stanford's *Saracinesco* (1969), Jean *Coulthard's *Endymion* (1970) and *Malamalke* (1974, commissioned), Wolfgang *Bottenberg's *Sinfonietta* (1970), Edward *Laufer's *Variations Part II* (1971), Adrian Hoffmann's *Time Did Emit Cool Dense Cities* (1971, with the James Davis jazz ensemble), Michael R. *Miller's *Capriccio on the Seven Ages of Man* (1974), and Mizerit's *Suite No. 4 for Winds* (1976). Under Yampolsky the orchestra continued to play standard and modern repertoire including, 1978–9, *Turner's *Symphony for Strings* and *Matton's *Symphony No. 2*. With the Atlantic Choir (established in 1968 by Mizerit to complement the orchestra in major choral works) the orchestra has performed Beethoven's *Ninth Symphony*, Verdi's *Requiem*, Orff's *Carmina burana*, Handel's *Messiah*, Mozart's *Requiem*, and Bach's *St Matthew Passion* and *B-Minor Mass*. The orchestra toured major New Brunswick centres 1972–3 presenting Beethoven's *Ninth Symphony* with a choir formed by Robert Edwards from the Saint John High School Choir. During the 1970s the orchestra engaged an increasing number of Canadian soloists, eg, 1977–9, the guitarist Liona *Boyd, the soprano Gaelyne *Gabora, the cellist Vladimir *Orloff, and the pianists Robert *Silverman and William *Tritt. The orchestra's executive director in 1979, Lionel Smith of Fredericton, assumed the post in 1970, succeeding Robert Dietz, who had been manager of the Halifax SO. Smith was succeeded in 1980 by Mark Warren.

DISCOGRAPHY
Coulthard *Song to the Sea* – Elgar – Arnold. Elloway cond. 1972. CBC SM-215
Handel 'Suite' from *The Water Music*. Mizerit cond. 1971. CBC SM-215
Schumann – Mercure *Kaléidoscope* – de Falla – Dela *Scherzo*. Mizerit cond. 1970. CBC SM-132
Somers *The Picasso Suite* – Mizerit *Two Maritime Aquarelles* – N.McKay *Fantasy on a Quiet Song*. Mizerit cond. 1975. CBC SM-241

BIBLIOGRAPHY
Ball, Walter. 'The Atlantic Symphony Orchestra,' *CanComp*, 40, May 1969
Bierman, Helmer. 'The Atlantic Symphony Orchestra,' *Atlantic Advocate*, vol 63, Nov 1972
Cameron, Donald. 'Going down the road with the Atlantic Symphony,' *Maclean's*, May 1974
Coleman, Thomas. 'Down east it's a bus that brings the sound of music,' Toronto *Globe and Mail*, 20 Mar 1976
Tilley, Alexander. 'An orchestra with a special mission,' *Mcan*, Feb 1977 (SAB)

AUBIN, (Aimé Nicolas) **Napoléon**. Conductor, composer, editor, journalist, printer, poet, chemist, diplomat, b Chêne-Bougeries, near Geneva, 9 Nov 1812, d Montreal 12 June 1890. Nothing is known of his youth or musical studies. He arrived in New York in 1829 and in Montreal in 1835, and settled in Quebec City in the autumn of the same year as a correspondent for *La Minerve*. A supporter of the 'patriote' cause which culminated in the Rebellion of 1837, Aubin founded, managed, and wrote for a large number of periodicals, including *Le Fantasque* 1837–45. On 1 Jan 1836, *Le Canadien* published 'Chant patriotique du Canada,' words by M.F.R.A. (Mr François-Réal Angers), music by N.M. Aubin, in six stanzas, beginning with the words 'Canada, terre d'espérance.' In 1840 Aubin became associated with the printer W.H. Rowan and published his own composition, *Le Dépit amoureux*, and two waltzes by Charles *Sauvageau, whose sister he married in 1841. He also published and printed Sauvageau's *Notions élémentaires de musique* (1844). In 1839 he founded a theatrical company, Les Amateurs typographes. In May 1846 – *LeVasseur gives the 16th as the date and Alfred Loewenberg, in *Annals of Opera* (Geneva 1955) gives the 26th – with the Société des amateurs canadiens he presented Rousseau's *Le Devin du village* at the Sewell Theatre. According to LeVasseur he prepared the parts for soloists, chorus, and orchestra, trained the forces, and conducted the performance. Aubin lived in the USA 1853–63 and again in Quebec City 1863–6. In 1866 he settled in Montreal. He served as honorary consul of Switzerland in Montreal from 1875 until his death.

BIBLIOGRAPHY
Darveau, L.-M. *Nos Hommes de lettres* (Montreal 1873)
LeVasseur, L.-Nazaire. 'Musique et musiciens à Québec,' *La Musique*, vol 1, Sep 1919
Tremblay, Jean-Paul. *À la recherche de Napoléon Aubin* (Quebec 1969)
– *Napoléon Aubin* (Montreal 1972) JH, GP

AUBUT, (Marie Marcel Gilberte) **Françoise** (m Pratte). Organist, educator, b St-Jérôme, Que, 5 Sep 1922; premier prix organ (Montreal) 1935, teaching diploma organ and piano (Montreal) 1937, B MUS organ and piano (Montreal) 1938, Soloist Diploma (New England Cons) 1938, grand premier prix (Paris Cons) 1944. Descended from a second cousin of Calixa *Lavallée, she began her piano studies at about six with her sister Rachel. At the *Cons national in Montreal she studied organ with Eugène *Lapierre and harmony and piano with Antonio *Létourneau. She gave her first recital 23 Aug 1936 at St-Stanislas Church in Montreal. That same year she was awarded an organ diploma from the *Schola cantorum, playing from memory Bach's six trio sonatas. She continued her studies 1937–8 at the New England Cons in Boston, with Carl McKinley (organ), Jesús María Sanromá (piano), and Marian Mason (harmony). At the entrance examination, noticing that two notes of the organ refused to speak, she transposed the set piece a semitone higher.

One of the first pieces of sheet music published in Canada, Napoléon Aubin's *Le Dépit amoureux*, 1840

In Paris, 1938–44, Aubut's teachers were Olivier Messiaen (harmony), Marcel Dupré (organ and improvisation), Simone Plé-Caussade (counterpoint and fugue), Norbert Dufourcq (history), Nadia Boulanger (theory), Alfred Cortot (piano); and Henri Busser (composition). Despite the war and an eight-month internment in Besançon, she won an exceptional Grand premier prix covering all the courses taken at the Paris Cons. She was the first North American to receive this honour. Aubut was organist at the Église de l'Assomption in Passy and played also at the Palais de Versailles (on one occasion before General Dwight D. Eisenhower), at the Palais de Chaillot, at the Église St-Sulpice, and elsewhere. Following her concert at Chaillot, Messiaen wrote, 'She has shown us the measure of her immense qualities' (letter of 11 June 1946).

After her return to Canada in 1945 Aubut was one of the first Canadians to play widely the works of Dupré and Messiaen, and at her many recitals she won much respect both as an interpreter and as an improviser. She performed in 1958 at the Brussels World Fair and at *Expo 67 and took part 1955–65 in numerous seminars and conferences in Europe. She has inaugurated organs throughout Quebec (eg, those at Le Cap-de-la-Madeleine and in Louiseville) and has taught at the *Institut Nazareth, the *CMQ, the Collège de musique Ste-Croix and, 1957–74, the *CMM. She began teaching organ and theory at the U of Montreal in 1951 and organ at the *École Vincent-d'Indy in 1967. Among her pupils have been Françoys *Bernier, Victor *Bouchard, Marthe Lesage, and Denis *Regnaud. In Montreal she became the organist at St-Édouard Church ca 1950, leaving to assume a similar position at Notre-Dame-des-Neiges Church ca 1955. To the latter position she added that of organist at St-Albert-le-Grand Church ca 1968 and continued to serve in both in 1980. In 1955 she participated in the premiere of *Papineau-Couture's *Psaume CL* for CBC radio. She has been heard regularly on CBC's 'Organists in Recital.' At the request of French radio in 1963 she performed, among other works, Roger *Matton's *Suite de Pâques*. She was a jury member in 1956 for the *Prix d'Europe and in 1962 and 1978 for the examinations at the Paris Cons. She received the 1961 *Prix de musique Calixa-Lavallée. Françoise Aubut made two LPs in 1956, one (RCI 122) consisting of Franck's *Chorale No. 3* and Dupré's *Pange lingua, Ave maris stella*, and *Symphonie-Passion* and the other (RCI 128) containing Papineau-Couture's *Psaume CL* with the *Montreal Bach Choir.

BIBLIOGRAPHY
Musiciennes de chez nous HP

Auditorium de Québec. Designed by the US architect Walter S. Painter and built 1902–4 at 972 St-Jean St, Quebec City, on the initiative of the mayor, S.N. Parent. It replaced the *Academy of Music, which had been destroyed by fire in 1900. Considered at the time to be 'the most perfect of its kind,' the amphitheatre measured 23 by 29 m and could hold more than 1600 spectators, while the stage had a surface area of 74 square m. The hall was inaugurated 31 Aug and 1 Sep 1903 by two concerts featuring the Société symphonique de Québec, a choir conducted by Joseph *Vézina, and a team of soloists which included Rosario *Bourdon, Paul *Dufault, Bernadette Dufresne, J.-A. *Gilbert, Georges Haseneier, Eileen Millett, Émiliano *Renaud, and Joseph *Saucier.

The management of the building initially was entrusted to professional administrators, whose program, dictated by too great a concern for profit, favoured foreign artists over opera and concert performances organized by local citizens. Some 20 years later, Nazaire *LeVasseur was to draw up a gloomy balance-sheet of artistic life in the capital, stating that theatre in Quebec City, 'starting with the Auditorium, has become ... a means of financial exploitation, totally devoid of skill, knowledge and moral teaching.' In 1927 the architect H. Laberge remodelled the auditorium, and a 64-stop *Casavant organ was installed. A second mortgage was required to cover the cost of the renovations; this was guaranteed by the Famous Players film distribution company, which became responsible for the administration of the theatre and changed its name to the Capitol Theatre. The theatre became mainly a cinema after 1971.

From the beginning of the 1950s until 1971 the auditorium had been, as Claude Paulette has stated, 'host to all the principal manifestations of Quebec life.' Besides the debuts of the Opéra français de Québec and the *Théâtre lyrique de Nouvelle-France, it has presented performances by itinerant theatre companies, Canadian and foreign dance troupes, the *TS, the *MSO, and symphony orchestras from the USA and Europe. The *Quebec SO has continued to give gala soirées in it, as well as concerts for young people and symphony matinées. The orchestra also performed there in the 1975–6 season during a strike by employees of Quebec City's *Grand Théâtre. Many solo recitals have been presented at the auditorium in the Soirées classiques, the Grands Classiques, and other such series, on the initiative of the Quebec impresarios Arthur *Lavigne, J.-Albert Gauvin, and Émile Caouette. Among the distinguished recitalists have been Eugène Ysaÿe, Ovide Musin, Leopold Godowsky, Marcel Grandjany, Ernestine Schumann-Heink, and Witold Malcuzynski.

BIBLIOGRAPHY
Programme Souvenir de l'inauguration officielle de l'Auditorium de Québec (Quebec 1903)
LeVasseur, Nazaire. *Réminiscences d'antan* (Quebec 1926)
Paulette, Claude. 'Les grands théâtres de Québec,' *Culture vivante*, 17, May 1970 LPr

Australia and New Zealand. As long-time sister dominions, Canada, Australia, and New Zealand have many parallels. They also have striking differences: eg, the relative geographical and social isolation of the two dominions as compared with Canada's proximity to the USA and Canada's two European cultures, English and French. Though Australia and New Zealand were colonized somewhat later than Canada, Australia, in particular, has parallelled Canada in its contribution of world-class musicians to the international scene. If only the few names which leap immediately to mind are cited (the Canadians Emma *Albani, Maureen *Forrester, Glenn *Gould, Oscar *Peterson, Jon *Vickers; the Australians Nellie Melba, Percy Grainger, Joan Sutherland), the danger of a claim to pre-eminence by either country quickly becomes apparent.

Possibly the first Australian to tour in Canada was Melba, who sang in Toronto in 1903 and 1913 and in Montreal in 1922 and probably earlier. Percy Grainger gave many recitals in Canada, established friendships and corresponded with several Canadians (Douglas *Clarke, Ernest *MacMillan, Lyell *Gustin, and others), and taught Alma *Brock-Smith, Muriel *Kerr, Éva *Plouffe, and Marshall *Sumner. An early guest of the *Musical Art Club of Saskatoon, he also served it as honorary president from 1924 until his death.

Arthur *Benjamin resided and taught 1939–47 in Vancouver and Max *Pirani taught 1941–8 at the *Banff SFA and in London, Ont. Reciprocal visits saw Sir Ernest MacMillan guest conducting in Australia in 1945 and Sir Bernard Heinze in Canada 1946–7; Heinze also conducted the *CBC SO, the *TSO, and the *MSO in 1952, and the MSO again in 1960, also preparing a report that year on the orchestral situation in Canada for the *Canada Council. Heinze returned to Australia after his first visit with scores by *Brott, *Champagne, MacMillan, *Morawetz, *Walter, *Willan, and others. In 1958, works of *Archer, *Coulthard, *Freedman, Morawetz, *Pépin, *Rogers, *Weinzweig, and Willan were performed at the U of Western Australia as part of the Commonwealth Festival, and in the ensuing years, works by other Canadians have been introduced to Australian audiences.

The noted Australian jazz clarinetist Don Burrows lived in Toronto in 1950. Joan Sutherland (whose husband, Richard Bonynge, also Australian, was artistic director of the *Vancouver Opera 1974–9) made her North American debut as Donna Anna in *Don Giovanni* at the 1958 *Vancouver International Festival and has sung in several subsequent Vancouver Opera productions, besides appearing in recital in Montreal and Toronto. The Melbourne SO, under Willem van Otterloo and with the Australian soprano Marie Collier, performed at *Expo 67. In pop music, the singer Helen Reddy, the Bee Gees, the Little River Band, and Sherbet performed in Canada during the 1970s. The singer Rolf Harris, who recorded 'Tie Me Kangaroo Down, Sport,' first performed in Vancouver in 1961, has been a program host for CTV and has performed with the *Vancouver SO.

Musicians of Australian birth resident in Canada include (years given are those of immigration): Rachel *Cavalho (1948), Jack Lander (1950, a leading jazz bassist in Toronto during the 1950s and early 1960s at the House of Hambourg, who also worked with the *Travellers and later led groups in that city's dinner clubs), Marshall Sumner (1950), Howard *Leyton-Brown (1952), Harry *Mossfield (1952), John Peter Lee *Roberts (1955), Barrie *Cabena (1957), John Capek (1973, a Toronto-based studio arranger, composer, and producer), and Sir William McKie, former music director of Westminster Abbey, who retired to Ottawa in 1963. The CBC music program producer Diana Brown (b Hutson) moved to Canada in 1955. The rock-music journalist Ritchie Yorke arrived in 1967.

Among musicians of New Zealand birth who have lived or spent some time in Canada are Maria Bauchope *Hambourg, Jean *Macleod, the baritone Donald Rutherford (who studied at the *RCMT 1966–9 and sang with the *COC), the pianist Gloria Saarinen of *One Third Ninth, and the composer Ronald Tremaine (who in 1970 joined the music department at *Brock U, St Catharines, Ont).

Canadians who have toured in Australia include Emma Albani (1898, 1907), Edmund *Burke (1911–12), Paul *Dufault (1913 with Lilian Nordica), Éva *Gauthier (1914), Ross *Pratt (ca 1946), Lois *Marshall and Weldon *Kilburn (1960), Maureen Forrester and John *Newmark (1962), Denyse *Angé (1964), the *Irish Rovers (1969 and 1974), George *Zukerman (1972 and 1978), Paul *Brodie (1977), Arthur *Ozolins (1978), the *Canadian Electronic Ensemble (1978), and Robert *Silverman (1979). Don *McManus and Huguette *Tourangeau have sung with companies in Australia. Cornelis *Opthof and Joseph *Rouleau toured there with Joan Sutherland in 1965, and the organist Martin James directed musical theatre in Sydney in the 1970s. Anna *Russell toured in Australia and recorded in the Sydney Opera House in 1973. The Toronto blues band Mainline toured in 1970. The Canadian-trained Australian-born saxophonist Doug Foskett and the Canadian-born trumpeter Jack Feyer (both pupils of Gordon *Delamont) have composed for Australian radio and TV. The pop singer Gloria Kaye, Canada's representative to the 1978 Pacific Song Contest telecast from Christchurch, New Zealand, was chosen best performer in the festival.

Austria. The pre-1914 Austrian-Hungarian Empire created a socio-political mix which has made it difficult to estimate the number (probably close to 50,000 in 1960) of true Austrians in Canada. For the purpose of this article an attempt has been made to regard Austria in its modern definition, as the German-speaking republic lying within the borders established in 1919. In considering the contribution to Canadian culture, it is difficult to distinguish between the Austrian and the German. Much of the 'Austrian' music (which, as a body, constitutes the largest contribution of any country to the standard concert repertoire) was written by Beethoven and Brahms, who lived in Vienna but were not Austrians; while much of the Vienna-born Schoenberg's music was written in Germany or the USA. Moreover, the Germanic surnames of many Canadian musical pioneers, whose biographies are fragmentary, could indicate German or Swiss descent as well as Austrian.

Perhaps the first Austrian musicians to perform in Canada were Tyrolean 'families,' whose yodelling and Ländler were popular in 19th-century North America. The Rainer Family, four brothers and a sister from the Zillerthal in Tyrol, toured North America 1839–43 and performed in Toronto in 1840, in Halifax in 1841, and in other Canadian towns.

Probably the first Austrian musicians to stay in Canada were Louis (Ludwig) *Waizman(n) in 1893 and Luigi von *Kunits and George *Heinl in 1912. The most important immigration of Austrian musicians followed the 1938 Nazi invasion of Austria and included Emil Gartner and Greta *Kraus in 1938, the violinist and teacher Joseph Berljawsky and Ida *Halpern in 1939, and Franz *Kraemer and Willy *Amtmann in 1940. Hans Gruber, the conductor 1948–63 of the *Victoria SO, also moved to Canada in 1939. Among other Austrian-born musicians who moved to Canada were Emmy *Heim (1947, although she made her Canadian recital debut in 1934); Alfred *Rosé (1948, via the USA); Erwin *Marcus (1949); the cellist and viola da gambist Wolfgang Grunsky (1951), who taught at the *RCMT and specialized in renaissance music; Eli *Kassner (1951); Irene *Jessner (1952, via the USA); the composer and string bassist Paul Ruhland, who lived ca 1952–64 in Vancouver; Ernst and Marie *Friedlander (1958); Haymo Taeuber, the conductor 1963–8 of the *Calgary Philharmonic; Gerhard *Wuensch (1964); and Anton *Kuerti (1965, via the USA). Walter Kanitz (1944) was the host for light-classical-music radio shows in turn on the CBC, CHUM, CFRB, and CHFI in Toronto. The guitarist Norbert Kraft, 1979 *CBC Talent Festival winner, was born in Austria and received his early musical training at the RCMT and the *U of Toronto.

Among Austrian-Canadian ensembles are the Junior Edelweiss Choir ('Kinderchor') founded in the mid-1960s, and the Mixed Edelweiss Choir founded in 1963, both sponsored by the Austrian Club Edelweiss in Toronto. The Austrian community in Edmonton in 1967 began providing scholarships to young Albertans (eight by 1977) for musical studies in Austria.

The first musical visitor to Austria from Canada may have been T.F. *Molt. In 1825 the Quebec music teacher visited Beethoven, who dedicated to him the canon 'Freu Dich des Lebens.' The composer Arthur *Dumouchel studied ca 1870–2 in Vienna, and some Canadian pianists of note studied in Austria with Theodor Leschetizky (Jan *Cherniavsky, Jeannette Durno, J.D.A. *Tripp), Julius Epstein (W.O. *Forsyth), and Richard Epstein (Gladys *Egbert). Douglas *Haas, Bernard and Mireille *Lagacé, and Denis *Regnaud had lessons with the Viennese organist Anton Heiller, and Hubert *Bédard, Bernard Lagacé, and Regnaud took tuition from the Viennese harpsichordist Isolde Ahlgrimm. Other Canadians who have studied in Austria include Victor *Feldbrill, Anna-Marie *Globenski, the musicologist Warren Kirkendale, the pianist Sharon Krause, Percival *Price, R. Murray *Schafer, and Robert *Silverman. S.C. *Eckhardt-Gramatté lived in Vienna 1939–51 with her Austrian husband Ferdinand Eckhardt (who later served as Austrian consul in Winnipeg).

The first major Canadian artist to perform in Austria was Emma *Albani, who gave two concerts (1893) in Vienna with an orchestra under Hans Richter. Among Canadian singers who have appeared with the Vienna and Salzburg operas are Pierrette *Alarie, Kenneth Asch (*Ascher Duo), Colette *Boky, George *London, Norman *Mittelmann, Dodi *Protero, Louis *Quilico, Léopold *Simoneau, Lilian *Sukis, and Jon *Vickers. Other Canadians who have performed in concert and recital in Austria include Mona *Bates; Victor *Braun, who won the International Mozart Competition in 1963; John *Boyden, who made his recital debut in Vienna in 1961 and also recorded there; Maureen *Forrester, who, in addition to concert performances, made many recordings in Vienna; Glenn *Gould; and Flora *Goulden. During European tours the *MSO performed in Vienna's Grosser Musikvereinssaal in 1962 and the *TS gave concerts there and in Linz in 1974. Ingemar *Korjus won the International Hugo Wolf Lieder Competition in 1973, and Raymond *Pannell's opera **Aberfan* was awarded the TV opera prize of the City of Salzburg in 1977.

Among the Austrian musicians who have performed in Canada are the violinist Fritz Kreisler, the pianists Paul Badura-Skoda, Rudolf Buchbinder, and Friedrich Gulda, the sopranos Hilda Gueden and Rita Streich, the baritone Paul Schoeffler, the K & K Experimental Studio and Pupodrom, the Trapp Family Singers, the Trio Vienna, and the Vienna Boys' Choir. The *JMC sponsored tours of the Ebert Trio (1959–60, 1962–3) and the Eichendorff Quintet of Vienna in 1964 and 1965. The Vienna State Opera made its North American debut at *Expo 67 and the Vienna Philharmonic also performed. Carl Boehm and Josef Krips conducted. (The Vienna Philharmonic also played in Toronto under Carl Schuricht.) Boehm had appeared previously in Canada as the conductor of the Berlin Philharmonic in 1961, as the conductor for a CBC TV Festival Orchestra in 1963, and with the TSO and Jon Vickers for CBC TV in 1965. Krips conducted the MSO, the *CBC SO and, in 1963, the TSO. (HK)

AVISON, John (Henry Patrick). Conductor, pianist, b Vancouver 25 Apr 1915; ATCM 1929, BA (British Columbia) 1935, B MUS (Washington) 1936. He studied piano with J.D.A. *Tripp in Vancouver and attended the U of British Columbia and the U of Washington. After World War II service he resumed music studies at the Juilliard School in 1946, at Columbia U 1946–7, and with Paul Hindemith at Yale U in 1947. He began performing with orchestras in Vancouver in 1936 and toured western Canada and the USA as accompanist to such performers as Lauritz Melchior, Szymon Goldberg, and Joseph Szigeti. In 1938 he became the first conductor of the *CBC Vancouver Chamber Orchestra. Though he continued to conduct that orchestra until his retirement in 1980, he appeared with many others, including the London Philharmonic (1959) and orchestras in Toronto, Ottawa, Montreal, Quebec, Winnipeg, Edmonton, Calgary, and Seattle. In 1956 he declined an invitation from William Steinberg to become associate conductor of the Pittsburgh SO. In 1971 as conductor of the Vancouver Radio Orchestra (the touring name of the CBC Vancouver Chamber Orchestra) he directed the first orchestral concerts given in the Canadian Arctic. In 1966 he became the regular conductor for the *CBC Talent Festival.

Avison has appeared as a solo pianist, as a duo pianist with Norma *Abernethy and with Victor Babin, and as an accompanist to such performers as Maureen *Forrester, Lois *Marshall, and, on an RCI series of folk recordings, Emma *Caslor. He has composed and arranged music for CBC radio and TV programs, including 'River of the Clouds' and 'The Journey' in 1965. He was associate director 1952, 1954, and 1956 of the Aspen, Colo, Music Festival, a part-time lecturer 1967–9 in orchestration at the *U of Victoria, and a member 1968–71 of the *Canada Council's arts advisory committee. A versatile conductor especially proficient in 18th-century music, Avison has conducted as well a vast quantity of 20th-century music, and in 1961, jointly with the CBC Vancouver Chamber Orchestra, he received from the Institute of Contemporary Arts, London, a commendation for services to contemporary music. In 1970 he was the recipient of the *Canada Music Citation of the *CLComp, and in 1979 he was made a Member of the *Order of Canada. He was awarded the *CMCouncil Medal in 1980. His wife is Angelina Avison (b *Calangis), principal second violin of the *Vancouver SO.

DISCOGRAPHY

See CBC Vancouver Chamber Orchestra.

BIBLIOGRAPHY

Hughes, Doug. 'A time to play and time to go,' Vancouver *Province*, 9 Mar 1980

MW

John Avison

Awards. A broad term encompassing 1 / Honours bestowed; 2 / Scholarships; 3 / Competition prizes, Canadian; and 4 / Competition prizes, foreign. (Several of the major awards cited under these headings have entries of their own in *EMC*, and details will be found in those entries.)

1 HONOURS BESTOWED. Honours which have not been applied for or competed for, but which have been bestowed in recognition of extraordinary merit, achievement, leadership, or munificence. This is the kind of honour typified at the highest level by knighthood in Great Britain, and in fact knighthoods were bestowed in Canada (until 1919, when the granting of titular honours to Canadians was abolished, by which time, however, no musician had been so honoured). The practice was resumed briefly (1933–5) during R.B. Bennett's term as prime minister, and at that time one Canadian musician – Sir Ernest *MacMillan – was knighted. After 1935, when this honour was no longer possible, other means of demonstrating recognition assumed new significance, and new means were invented. In 1967 the *Order of Canada was created, the first distinctly Canadian honour recognizing achievement and service. By 1981, 87 musicians (of some 1531 recipients) had been honoured. Among traditional means, the granting of honorary degrees by universities has continued (see Degrees), and by 1980 some 100 had been awarded to persons in the music field. The ensuing list cites some bestowed honours for which Canadians are or were eligible.

Alberta Achievement Awards. Begun in 1969; provincial, given annually in recognition of achievement in several areas including music. See Alberta Culture.

**Alberta Composers' Association Awards*. Begun in 1980; medals, designed by Alex Janvier, are used to recognize important contributions to the art of music in Alberta by individuals and/or groups. The first medals were presented to Horst A. Schmid and the Hon Donald Cameron.

Big Country Awards. Begun in 1975. See Country music.

**Canada Council Medal*. Begun in 1961; combined in 1968 with the *Molson Prizes, which were begun in 1963.

**Canada Music Citation*. Begun in 1967; awarded by the *CLComp.

**Canadian Conference of the Arts Diplôme d'Honneur*. Begun in 1954; annual; to persons outstanding in service to the arts.

**Canadian Federation of Music Teachers' Assn Centennial Citation Award*. 1967 only.

**Canadian Music Council Awards*. Begun in 1977. Annual in various categories:

- *Special Award* to individuals or bodies in the public or private sector providing assistance to music in Canada; awarded to Floyd S. *Chalmers (1977), Alberta Culture (1978), Jean-C. *Lallemand (1979), and the *du Maurier Council for the Performing Arts (1980).
- *Artist of the Year*: Huguette *Tourangeau (1977), Kenneth *Gilbert (1978), André *Laplante (1979), and Teresa *Stratas and Louis-Philippe *Pelletier (special mention), both in 1980.
- *Composer of the Year*: R. Murray *Schafer (1977), Gilles *Tremblay (1978), no award in 1979, and Harry *Freedman (1980).
- *Ensemble of the Year*, for 1978, to the *Quebec SO.
- Also media awards for TV, radio, and recording.

**Canadian Music Council Medal*. Begun in 1971.

Canadian Woman of the Year. Begun in 1951; annual; winners chosen, in various categories including music and entertainment, by a poll of Canadian newspaper women's editors. Recipients in music have been Lois *Marshall (1958–60, 1964), Teresa Stratas (1959, 1961–3, 1965), Joan *Fairfax (1961), Maureen *Forrester (1964), Monique *Leyrac (1966–9), and Anne *Murray (1970–3).

Centennial Medals. 1967. Musicians were among the many Canadians awarded medals marking the centennial of Canada.

*Floyd S. *Chalmers Foundation Award*. Begun in 1974. Annual cash prize of $1500 to promising artists under 30 years of age.

Jean A. Chalmers Award for Opera. Begun in 1965. See Floyd S. Chalmers.

Festival du disque. Founded in 1965 in Montreal by Jacqueline Vézina to promote and stimulate the recording industry in Quebec by means of a week-long exhibition and an awards gala presentation. Held annually 1965–9 (with the exception of 1967); awards in various categories. Winners have included Léon *Bernier, *Bouchard and *Morisset, *'CA-NA-DA,' Robert *Charlebois, Neil *Chotem, Paul *de Margerie, Georges *Dor, Jean-Pierre *Ferland, Claude *Gauthier, Marc *Gélinas, Gilles *Manny, Roger *Matton, Pierre *Mercure, André *Prévost, and Gilles *Vigneault.

Financial Post Awards for Business in the Arts. Begun in 1978 to encourage corporations' involvement in the visual and performing arts. In several categories; the annual prizes offered are sculptures. Imperial Oil, DOFASCO in Hamilton, Ont, and Federated Cooperatives of Saskatchewan received the first awards in 1979; Texaco Canada, Imperial Oil, and Sunwapta Broadcasting of Edmonton the second awards in 1980.

Gala de l'industrie du disque et du spectacle québécois (ADISQ recording and showbusiness awards). Begun in 1979; annual; sponsored by the Assn du disque et de l'industrie du spectacle Québécois (ADISQ) to honour the best contributions to Quebec's record industry. Prizes for the record of the year in several categories, for song of the year, and for best female and male singers of the year, as selected by a panel of journalists, commentators, and industry representatives.

Tyrone Guthrie Awards. Begun in 1953; in conjunction with the *Stratford Festival; annual cash prizes to promising artists. The first award to a musician was made in 1965 to Maurice *Brown. Other recipients have included Gwenlynn *Little (1967), Peter Milne and Renée Rosen (1968), Donald Rutherford and Margaret Zeidman (1969), Robert Martin (1970), and Berthold Carriere (1975).

**Juno Awards*. Begun in 1964; annual awards of the Canadian recording industry.

LaFlèche Trophy. Fl mid-1940s; given in recognition of contributions to Canadian radio. Winners include Alys *Robi (1944), Evelyn *Gould (1945, 1946), Samuel *Hersenhoren (1945–7), and Marguerite *Pâquet (1949).

Moffat Awards. Begun in 1967 in memory of Lloyd E. Moffat. Awards were made annually for the best recordings in four categories: 'beat,' middle-of-the-road, folk or country, and the record which, regardless of category, best demonstrated Canadian talent and originality. Bobby *Gimby's recording of 'CA-NA-DA' won the first year as best middle-of-the-road and as best example of Canadian talent and originality.

Wm Harold Moon Award. See *PRO Canada Awards.

Prix Anik Awards. Begun in 1976; annual; incorporate the Wilderness Awards (independent 1964–76). Under CBC sponsorship, these awards fall into three categories: the Wilderness Award, for a TV documentary (won in 1973 by Louis *Applebaum for his score for *Folly on the Hill* and in 1975 by the 1974 CBC Vancouver production *Jon Vickers – A Man and His Music*); and two Prix Anik, for drama and music respectively. The winner of the music award in 1977 was the CBC Toronto production of Raymond *Pannell's **Aberfan*.

**Prix de musique Calixa-Lavallée*. Begun in 1959; annual.

**Prix d'Europe*. Begun in 1911; annual.

Quebec government awards. Include the Prix David for literature (begun in 1923; bestowed in 1931 upon J.M. *Gibbon for his book *Melody and the Lyric*, and in 1937 upon Eugène *Lapierre for his book *Calixa Lavallée, Musicien national du Canada*); and the Prix Denise-Pelletier (begun in 1977, $15,000 in cash, a certificate, and a medal, to a Quebec artist; Félix *Leclerc was a recipient in 1977 and Bernard *Lagacé in 1978).

Remeny [Remenyi] *Award*. Re-established in 1974 by the music firm House of Remenyi in conjunction with the Faculty of Music, *U of Toronto; an award granted 1902–50 at the Franz Liszt Academy in Budapest. Judges awarded newly built string instruments to the student violinists Edward LeCouffe in 1975, John Lowry in 1976, Mark Friedman in 1977, and Wendy Rose in 1978, and to the student cellist Elizabeth Dolin in 1979. The 1980 competition was for quartets.

Silver Jubilee Medals. 1977. Musicians were among the many Canadians awarded medals marking the silver jubilee of Elizabeth II.

**University of Alberta National Award in Music*. Begun in 1951; to Canadians for distinguished contribution to the development of 'Letters, Music and Painting and the Related Arts.' Recipients of the gold medal have included Healey *Willan (1951), Sir Ernest MacMillan (1952), Wilfrid *Pelletier (1953), Ettore *Mazzoleni (1954), Lyell *Gustin (1955), Kathleen *Parlow (1956), Claude *Champagne (1957), Arnold *Walter (1958), Geoffrey *Waddington (1959), Marius *Barbeau (1965), Maureen Forrester (1967), Herman *Geiger-Torel (1970), and Harry *Somers (1973).

2 SCHOLARSHIPS. Including fellowships, bursaries, study grants. These usually are applied for or competed for either actively through performance or passively through marks received in set examinations. They also often are decided by adjudication of submitted materials. (For those that are prizes won in competition, see section 3.) A complete list of available music scholarships would number in the hundreds, ranging from modest amounts granted from funds established in memory of individual teachers to the often substantial money awards cited below. The ensuing list claims only fractional and random coverage of the vast and fluctuating scholarship situation. For instance, systems designed by the provinces to support university or post-secondary studies are not included, and anyone seeking information about them is directed to individual provincial departments of education. Conservatories and schools of music across the country also award scholarships (often named in honour of donors or teachers). The 1977/8 Calendar of the *RHCM, for example, lists 18 available scholarships, and the 1977/8 Calendar of the *Community Music School of Greater Vancouver lists 12. Such institutions should be consulted directly for scholarship information.

Arthur S. Barnstead Memorial Award. Begun in 1968. Initially worth $1500. One of the *Nova Scotia Talent Trust awards.

*Murray *Adaskin Scholarship*. Founded in 1970 by the School Music Teachers' Assn of Saskatoon; for composition.

**Associated Board of the Royal Schools of Music scholarships*, Awarded 1909–53 to Canadians.

*Leslie *Bell Scholarship*. Begun in 1973; annual; for young choir conductors.

**Canada Council Victor M. Lynch-Staunton Award*. Begun in 1972. Chosen by the Canada Council from among the successful candidates for Senior Arts Grants, recipients have included Marius Barbeau (1973), Bruce *Mather (1975), John *Weinzweig (1975), Micheline Coulombe *Saint-Marcoux (1977), Mireille *Lagacé (1977), Norma *Beecroft (1978), and Jacques *Hétu (1979).

Canadian Amateur Hockey Assn Award. 1949–ca 1952. Scholarships of $2000. Among the winners were Harry Somers (1949), John *Beckwith (1950), Clermont *Pépin (1951), and Paul *McIntyre (1952).

**Canadian Opera Company Women's Committee scholarships*. Begun in 1952. They include the Josephine Harper Award; the Lillian Steinberg Award; the John Eros Scholarship; the Samuel Sorbara Scholarships; the Laxer Scholarship; the Vida H. *Peene Scholarship; the Herman Geiger-Torel Scholarship; and the Mariss Vetra Memorial Scholarship of $1000, begun in 1977, available to any Canadian singer working towards a diploma in operatic performance at the *U of Toronto.

Eaton Graduating Scholarship. Begun in 1947; annual; $2000 to the top graduating student, Faculty of Music, U of Toronto, for assistance in beginning a career. Recipients have been Tova Boroditsky (1947), Clermont Pépin (1949), Lois Marshall (1950), Betty-Jean *Hagen (1951), Ray *Dudley (1952), Margot Rowland (1954), Sheila *Henig (1955), Paul *Helmer (1958), Teresa Stratas (1959), John McIntyre (1960), Mona Kelly *Bernardi (1962), Aurelle Biggs (1963), Jeannette *Zarou (1964), Lillian *Sukis (1965), Mary-Nan Dutka (1966), Nancy Greenwood (1967), Renée Rosen (1969), Patrick Li (1970), Kathryn Wunder (1971), Janis Orenstein (1972), Eleanor James (1973), Kirk Laughton (1974), Joel Quarrington (1975), Caralyn Tomlin (1976), Steven Dann (1977), John Lowry (1978), Dorothy Lawson (1979), and James McLean (1980).

*William Erving *Fairclough Scholarship*. Begun in 1966. Administered by the U of Toronto and valued at $1200. For organ or advanced composition studies in the USA or Europe. Winners have included David Low (1966), Fred Graham (1967), Patrick *Wedd (1970), David Paul (1971), Mark McDowall (1972), Bruce Pennycook (1973), Dennis Patrick (1974), Kristi Allik (1975), Patricia Magahay and Elma Miller (1975), and Alastair Boyd and Randolph Seaby (1979).

*Sarah *Fischer Scholarship*. Begun in 1947.

*W.O. *Forsyth Memorial Scholarship*. Begun in 1968.

Inco of Canada Scholarships. 1967. Six centennial awards of $2500 each; to three instrumentalists, two singers, and one dancer.

Luella McCleary Award. Begun in 1974 by the Women's Art Assn of Canada. It has been won by Deborah Jeans (1974), Janet *Stubbs (1975), Rosemarie *Landry (1976), Alison Melville (1977), and Heather Wilberforce (1978).

**Nova Scotia Registered Music Teachers' Assn Scholarship*. Begun in 1975. Originally valued at $200.

Peace River Pioneer Memorial Scholarship. Begun ca 1962; annual; administered by the U of Alberta; $300 to a music student who has shown interest in teaching music in rural areas.

*Lord *Strathcona Scholarships*. (Montreal Scholarship 1886–95, Lord Strathcona Scholarship thereafter.)

*Portia *White Memorial Award*. Begun in 1968. See Nova Scotia Talent Trust.

Bruce Yarnell Award (USA). Begun in 1975; annual; $1000, to a baritone of 32 or younger, resident in California, Oregon, New York, or Massachusetts, or in the Canadian cities of Montreal, Ottawa, or Toronto. Winners have included Charles Long (1975) and Peter *Barcza (1976). See Joan Patenaude.

3 COMPETITION PRIZES, CANADIAN. Cash awards, scholarships won in active competition, performance opportunities, and trophies. Prizes of this kind won by composers are treated separately in the entry Composition competitions. See also Competition festivals.

Leslie Bell Memorial Trophy. Begun in 1964; originally sponsored by the CBC and the *CMEA. In 1979 it was accompanied by a $300 prize. It has been awarded biennially to the winner of the Leslie *Bell Memorial Choir Competition.

Canadian Church Choir Competition. Begun in 1978; annual; sponsored by Maclean-Hunter Cable TV; $12,000 in prizes in 19 categories. Grand prize winners have been the junior choir of St James Islington United Church and the adult choir of Christ Church Cathedral, Hamilton (1978), the Cathedral Singers of Ottawa (1979), and St Paul's Cathedral Choir of London, Ont (1980).

**Canadian Music Competitions / Concours de musique du Canada*. Begun in 1970; annual.

**Canadian Open Old-Time Fiddling Contest*. Begun in 1951.

CBC / Canada Council National Radio Competition for Amateur Choirs. Begun in 1976; biennial; categories for school, junior and youth choirs, equal- and mixed-voice choirs, large choirs and, in 1980, multicultural, traditional, and chamber choirs. Prizes of $1000 and $500 have been offered in each category, and one of $500 has been presented to the choir in any category which gives the best performance of a Canadian work.

**CBC Talent Festival* (later CBC Radio Talent Competition). Begun in 1959; annual to 1979, then biennial.

**du Maurier Search for Stars*. Begun in 1977; annual.

Earl Grey Trophy. 1909–? Awarded by the governor-general for performances in music and drama. See Sovereigns, statesmen, and other public figures.

*S.C. *Eckhardt-Gramatté Competition*. Begun in 1974; annual; held at *Brandon U. Prizes of $2500, $1500, and $1000 for performances of Canadian music. Instrument category changes each year. Winners have been David Swan, piano (1976), Gwen Hoebig, violin (1977), Jackie Parker, piano (1978). The competition was cancelled in 1979 but resumed in 1980 with a voice competition won by the soprano Nancy Herbison.

**JMC Centennial Competitions*. 1967. Held in three cities, Guelph, Ont (voice), Quebec City (piano), and Vancouver (strings). The winners were Annon Lee *Silver, Jeannette Zarou, Maurice Brown, and André Lizotte (voice); Andrew *Dawes, Sharon McKinley, and Denis *Brott (strings); and Robert *Silverman, William *Aide, and Claude *Savard (piano). First prize $5000; second $2000; and $500 from Les *Amis de l'art for the best interpretation of a Canadian work in each category.

*Manitoba Music Competition Festival. Begun in 1919. Many trophies awarded annually.

*Montreal International Competition. Begun in 1966.

*MSO Concours. Begun in 1965.

*National Competitive Festival of Music. Begun in 1972; annual; prizes include the national choir awards, the City of Lincoln Trophy (begun in 1949, administered elsewhere until 1972), the George S. Mathieson Trophy (begun in 1952, administered elsewhere until 1972), and the Rose Bowl (begun in 1974).

National Vocal Competition. Two contests, the first organized in 1967 by the Edward *Johnson Music Foundation at the request of the Centennial Commission and the JMC, and held in Guelph (see JMC above); the second held at the *Guelph Spring Festival in 1977. In 1977 the soprano Michèle Boucher won the $5000 Timex of Canada Prize and an opportunity to perform with the *TS, the bass-baritone Ingemar *Korjus received the $3000 Shell Canada Merit Award, and the soprano Sophia Alexandrova won the $2000 Friends of Edward Johnson Award.

*'Nos Futures Étoiles.' Competition for singers, 1947–55; succeeded in 1955 by the *'Concours de la chanson canadienne.'

*'Opportunity Knocks.' 1947–57.

*Prix Archambault. 1946–63.

Prix Paul Baby. 1975, 1977; administered by the *CMCentre, Montreal; open to individuals and groups interested in analysis and the didactic aspects of music education, study to be based on music of Quebec composers. The first category carried a prize of $250; the second, prizes of $500 and $250. Winners included Gaby Billette (1975, using *Tremblay's Kékoba); and Danielle Jasmin, Mireille Gagné, and Michel Beaulieu (shared award, 1977, using *Vivier's Prolifération). There was no award in 1976.

*RCCO National Organ Playing Competition. Biennial after 1975; $400 and a CBC recital to a first-prize winner; $200 to a second-prize winner. Winners have been Patricia Snyder (1975), Keith Sadko (1977), and Michael Bloss (1979). The RCCO has sponsored other competitions, including one held in conjunction with the 1967 International Congress. First prize for improvisation that year was won by Andrew Davis (see TS). In 1980 the RCCO held a National Organ competition to mark the Healey *Willan Centennial Celebration in association with the Guelph Spring Festival. Michael Bloss won the first prize, John Vandertuin the prize for improvisation.

*'Singing Stars of Tomorrow.' 1943–56.

Heinz *Unger Award. Begun in 1968; annual; founded by the York Concert Society and the *OAC. $1000 (in 1979) available through competition to a young orchestra conductor qualified to continue study at a professional level. Winners have been Wilson Swift (1968), Voltr Ivonoffski (1969), Harvey Sachs (1970), John Barnum (1971), Brian Jackson (1972), Dwight Bennett (1973), David Gray (1974), Bruce McGregor (1975), Bruce Richardson (1976), Stephen A. Rickes (1977), and Robert De Clara (1978).

*Vancouver Symphony Orchestra Women's Committee scholarships. Begun in 1956; annual; competition open to advanced students of orchestral instruments; a scholarship of $1000 is offered as first prize.

4 COMPETITION PRIZES, FOREIGN. A number of Canadians have won prizes in international competitions held in foreign countries. A sampling follows.

Major Armstrong Awards, USA. Begun in 1964; for excellence and originality in FM broadcasting. CBL-FM Toronto, 'Glenn Gould Plays Bach,' runner-up in 1971; CJRT-FM Toronto, 'Speaking of Organists,' runner-up in 1972; CBL-FM, 'Computer Music' runner-up in 1975; CFMO-FM Ottawa, 'Gord Atkinson's The Crosby Years,' runner-up in 1975.

Johann Sebastian Bach International Piano Competition, Washington, DC. Canadian winners have included Mari-Elizabeth *Morgen in 1968; and Marilyn *Engle (first), Mimi Poirier (second) in 1969.

Bach International Organ Competition, Bruges. Hélène Dugal placed third in 1970, and Pierre-Yves Asselin was a prize winner in 1976.

Benson & Hedges International Competition for Concert Singers, Great Britain. Catherine *Robbin, Gold award in 1979.

Harriet Cohen International Music Awards. Fl ca 1952–68; medals awarded to musicians of the British Commonwealth. Canadian winners were Betty-Jean Hagen (1952), Ray Dudley (1953), Hugh *McLean (1955), Malcolm *Troup (1955), Robin *Wood (1958), Glenn *Gould (1959), William *Stevens (1960), Lois Marshall (1961), Alexander *Brott (1961), Hyman *Bress (1961), Neil Van Allen (1962), and Maureen Forrester (1968).

Concertino Praga (Czechoslovak radio competition for young musicians), Prague. Louis *Lortie was third in 1973, and, in a duo with violinist Chantal Juillet, a prize-winner in 1975.

Concours international de chant de Paris. Édith *Tremblay won first prizes in opera and art song in 1972, Liette Juneau won a second in 1974, and Catherine Robbin a first in 1978.

Concours international de chant de Toulouse, France. Claude *Corbeil won a second in 1969; Édith Tremblay won a third in 1971; Mariana *Paunova won a second in 1972.

Concours international François-Couperin, Paris. Martha Brickman was second in 1969 (no first awarded).

Concours international Marguerite Long-Jacques Thibaud, France. Biennial. Calvin *Sieb was a winner in 1951 and André Laplante was third in 1973.

Concurso Internacional de Guitarra, Alicante, Spain. Michael *Strutt was a prize winner in 1974.

Emmys, USA. Awards for excellence in TV programs. The CBC has won seven, including those for productions of The Barber of Seville (1965), Cinderella (1970), Sleeping Beauty (1973), and L'Oiseau de feu (1980).

European Broadcasting Union competition for string quartets, Stockholm. *Orford String Quartet shared first prize in 1974.

Flanders Music Festival, Brussels. Geneviève *Lagacé, honourable mention, harpsichord (1977).

Carl Flesch International Violin Competition, London. Steven *Staryk was second-prize winner in 1956.

Grammys. US recording awards. See 'Both Sides Now'; Percy Faith; Robert Goulet; Galt MacDermot (Hair); Joni Mitchell; 'Snowbird.'

Grand Prix du disque. Given by the Académie Charles-Cros, Paris. The first Canadian winner, Félix Leclerc in 1951, was followed by John *Newmark (with Kathleen Ferrier) in 1952, Pierrette *Alarie and Léopold *Simoneau in 1961, Jean-Pierre *Ferland in 1968, Pauline *Julien and Gilles Vigneault in 1970, and Bruno *Laplante in 1977.

Grand Prix Paul Gilson. Awarded by the Communauté radiophonique des programmes de langue française. Otto *Joachim was a winner in 1969.

International carillonneurs' prize, Mechelen, Belgium. Émilien *Allard won in 1958.

International Chopin Competition, Warsaw. John *Hendrickson won third prize and a special critics award in 1975.

International Competition for Musical Performers, Geneva. Winners have included Charles *Reiner (1948), Rafael *Masella (1949), Steven Staryk (1956), James *Milligan (1957), Rudolf *Komorous (1957), Micheline *Tessier (1957), Gabrielle *Lavigne (1969), Marie *Laferrière (1975), Mark Widner (1975), Edith Wiens (1976), John MacDonald (1976), André Laplante (1976), Ick Choo Moon (1977), Philip Thomson (1977), and Joel Quarrington (1978).

International Competition for Singers, 's-Hertogenbosch, Holland. Marie Laferrière won a second in 1975; Ingemar Korjus won a first in 1978.

International Competition for Young Conductors, Besancon, France. Pierre *Hétu was a winner in 1961 and Raffi *Armenian in 1968.

International Music Competition, ARD broadcasting stations of the Federal Republic of Germany, Munich. The *Duo Pach won a prize in 1960; Denis Brott, cello, a second in 1973; Ingemar Korjus, voice, and John MacDonald, french horn, both second prizes in 1978.

International Music Competition, 'G.B. Viotti,' Vercelli, Italy. Angela *Hewitt, piano, won first prize in 1978.

International Tchaikovsky Competition, Moscow. André Laplante, piano, won the second prize in 1978.

Leventritt Foundation Awards, USA. Betty-Jean Hagen was a winner in 1955 and Anton *Kuerti in 1957.

*Metropolitan Opera Regional Auditions, USA and Canada.

Naumburg Foundation Awards, USA. Ida *Krehm was a winner in 1937, Lorne *Munroe in 1949, Betty-Jean Hagen in 1950, and Lois Marshall in 1952.

Ohio State Awards for excellence in international educational broadcasting, USA. See School music broadcasts and general index.

Prix Italia. Begun 1948; Radiotelevisione Italiana. Les Grands Ballets Canadiens performing *Freedman's *The Shining People of Leonard Cohen won honourable mention 1976.

Queen Elisabeth of Belgium Competition. Gerard *Kantarjian, violin, won eleventh place in 1959; Frans *Brouw, piano, fourth place in 1952; Ronald *Turini, piano, second place in 1960; Anton Kuerti, piano, fourth place in 1964; Hidetaro *Suzuki, violin, tenth place in 1963 and fifth in 1967; and Douglas Finch, piano, fifth place in 1978.

Rotterdam Schoenberg Competition. Louis-Philippe Pelletier, piano, won first place in 1979.

Artur Rubinstein International Piano Master Competition, Israel. Janina *Fialkowska won third prize in 1974.

Schubert Memorial Award, USA. Ida Krehm was the winner in 1937.

Schumann Competition, Zwickau, East Germany. Edith Wiens won first place in voice and Angela Hewitt won fourth place in piano in 1977.

Wieniawski Competition, Poland. Begun 1935. Ida *Haendel won the Polish prize in 1935.

BIBLIOGRAPHY

CMCentre. Canadian and International Competitions / Concours canadiens et internationaux (Toronto 1976)

(NM, GP, CV, PW)

Ayorama Wind Quintet / Quintette à vent Ayorama. Formed in 1969 by five members of the newly established *NACO, who selected the Inuit word 'Ayorama' ('So be it') as the name of their quintet: Jean-Guy Brault, flute; Lawrence Cherney, oboe (later replaced by Stewart Grant, and Grant by Francine Schutzman); Peter Smith, clarinet; Evan Philpotts, french horn; and Michael Namer, bassoon. The ensemble is distinguished by the nature of its programs, which feature the works of many contemporary composers. It has been coached by Samuel Baron of the New York Wind Quintet and by the Australian french horn player Barry Tuckwell.

The quintet has appeared at the *NAC, at the Kawartha Lakes Music Camp near Peterborough, Ont, in Kingston, Ont, at the Hull Cons in Quebec, and at Dartmouth College, Hanover, NH. It has participated in the 1971 Orford Festival and the 1975 *U of New Brunswick Chamber Music and Jazz Festival, and has performed on CBC radio and TV. In April 1976 it premiered Bruce *Mather's *Eine Kleine Bläsermusik* at the NAC. It has recorded works by Jacques *Hétu, André Souris, Brian *Cherney, and Darius Milhaud (1972, RCI 364) and by Barber, Hodgson, Villa-Lobos, and Ibert (1977, CBC SM 261). The quintet also has conducted workshops for winds in Ontario high schools.

DM

AYOUB, Nick (Nicholas). Tenor-and-soprano saxophonist, oboist, english hornist, composer, b Trois-Rivières, Que, of Lebanese parents, 7 Sep 1926; premier prix (CMM) 1953. Raised in Montreal he took up in turn clarinet, tenor saxophone, oboe, english horn, and flute, and studied with Arthur *Romano at the *CMM. Studies in oboe followed with Harold Gomberg of the New York Philharmonic. Ayoub began his professional career in 1943, soon playing saxophone in the dance or jazz bands of Johnny *Holmes, Maynard *Ferguson, the saxophonist Freddie Nichols, and the trombonist Butch Watanabe. Though a leading studio musician in Montreal by the 1950s and occasionally an oboist (and less frequently a saxophonist) with the *MSO after 1954, he remained active in jazz. In 1963 his quintet – whose other members were the trumpeter Al Penfold, the pianist Art Roberts, the bassist Michel *Donato, and the drummer Émile *Normand – performed at the Montreal Jazz Festival and recorded *The Montreal Scene* (RCA PC 1042). Ayoub's later groups have appeared in clubs, in concerts, and on various CBC radio jazz programs; his repertoire includes many of his own tunes. In 1977, with Penfold, Roberts, Vic Angelillo (bass), and Jacques Masson (drums), he made the LP RCI 455. Previously, as a member of the Romano Saxophone Quartet he had made the LP RCI 91. Ayoub also recorded pop instrumentals issued on three LPs in the mid-1960s: *Dance to the Saxophone* (RCA Camden CAL 935), *Nick Ayoub Plays Bossa Nova* (Trans Canada TCA 74), and, with the Denny *Vaughan orchestra, *Nick Ayoub* (CTL 5068). In 1968, at the CMM, he began teaching saxophone and directing the jazz ensemble. He also taught 1974–8 at the *JMC Orford Art Centre. His pupils have included Michel Ethier, Guy McDougall, and Martin Fournier of the Ensemble international de saxophone. Ayoub's son Jimmy (b Montreal 18 Aug 1953) became the drummer with Frank *Marino and Mahogany Rush.

BIBLIOGRAPHY
Dobbin, Len. 'The Nick Ayoub quintet,' *Coda*, Feb 1965

B

BABIAK, Walter (Andrew). Conductor, violist, composer, b Saskatoon 11 Oct 1933; B MUS (Toronto) 1955. After lessons 1939–51 at the TCM (*RCMT) with John Montague (violin) and Louis Murch (piano), he studied at the *U of Toronto with Nicholas *Goldschmidt, Oskar *Morawetz, Godfrey *Ridout, John *Weinzweig, and others. Babiak was a violist in the *Hart House Orchestra, the *CBC SO 1959–60, and the *TSO 1957–60. He studied conducting with Boyd *Neel and, in 1962 at the U of Amsterdam, with Franco Ferrara. In 1964 Babiak attended a conducting symposium at Florida State U, and in 1966 he was a semi-finalist in the Dimitri Mitropoulos International Competition. He was associate conductor 1960–7 for the National Ballet of Canada and music director of the Canadian Chamber Orchestra 1968–72, the Brantford SO 1968–74, the *Stratford Festival theatre orchestra in 1969, and the North York (Toronto) SO in 1970. In 1971 he was guest conductor of the Vienna State Opera Ballet during its first North American tour, and in 1979 he performed a similar service for the Stuttgart Ballet, conducting for the premiere of a new production of *Swan Lake*. In 1976 he became the associate director of the Shevchenko Musical Ensemble. Babiak has composed over 40 works, including *Three Songs of Time* (a setting of verses by Ogden Nash) and a *Sinfonietta for Strings* which won a 1957 CAPAC award. He was commissioned to compose a work for the Marijan Bayer Dance Company's 1977–8 season. Babiak is a member of CAPAC. (JBk)

BACH, John (Sebastian Peter). Teacher, performer, conductor, b Winnipeg 30 Jul 1908; LRAM 1930, ARCM 1931, ARAM 1943. He studied violin and viola privately 1916–28 with Philip Shadwick, winning an RAM scholarship to study violin, viola, and conducting 1928–32 in England and to attend summer courses in 1930 and 1931 in Leipzig and Paris. He was superintendent 1932–7 for Beresford's School of Music, Calgary. After teaching, playing in orchestras, and conducting 1937–47 in Australia, he was a teacher 1948–64 at the *Mount Royal College Cons and its director 1964–74. He played 1948–55 in the *Calgary SO and served 1956–73 with the *Calgary Philharmonic Orchestra. For the latter his duties included the positions of principal violist 1956–63 and personnel manager 1962–6. He claims descent from J.S. Bach through Bach's fifth son, Johann Christoph Friedrich, and grandson, Wilhelm Friedrich Ernst (1759–1845).

Bach-Elgar Choir of Hamilton. A 100-voice mixed choir established in 1946 as an amalgamation of the Elgar Choir (founded by Bruce *Carey, who led the first concert in 1905, and subsequently conducted by G. Roy *Fenwick, W.H. *Hewlett, and Edward Stewart) and the Bach Choir (founded 1931 by Graham *Godfrey). Both choirs had disbanded during World War II. The Bach-Elgar Choir made its debut in 1947 in Handel's *Messiah* under Charles *Peaker at the Centenary United Church in Hamilton. The choir has been conducted by Cyril *Hampshire 1948–55, John *Sidgwick 1955–60, Frank *Thorolfson 1960–2, Charles *Wilson 1962–74, and Donald Kendrick 1974–8, succeeded by Philip David Morehead. Its repertoire, accompanied and unaccompanied, has ranged from the baroque era to the 20th century. In 1910 the original Elgar Choir gave what is thought to have been the Canadian premiere of the Verdi *Requiem*. Its successor, the Bach-Elgar Choir, commissioned Charles Wilson's *The Angels of the Earth*, which it premiered 20 Jun 1967, and *Dona nobis pacem*, premiered 22 Nov 1970. It also commissioned Wilson's *A Choral Invitation* and premiered it 22 Nov 1970. The choir made a private recording (BEC 70) of the latter work. (LB)

Bachman-Turner Overdrive. See BTO.

BACULIS, Al (Alphonse). Alto and tenor saxophonist, clarinetist, composer, arranger, teacher, b Montreal 21 Nov 1930; L MUS clarinet (McGill) 1951. He studied clarinet 1948–51 at *McGill U and theory and composition privately 1952–6 with Istvan *Anhalt and Marvin *Duchow. During the 1950s he was active in jazz, leading the Canadian All-Stars – Gordie Fleming (accordion), Yvan *Landry (piano), Hal Gaylor (bass), Billy Graham (drums) – who made the LP *Canadian Jazz All-Stars* (1955, Discovery DL 3025), and winning CBC radio's 'Jazz Unlimited' poll as best clarinetist for five years running. After 1958 he turned to studio work – playing, composing, and arranging for the CBC ('Vedettes en direct,' 'Music Hall,' 'Let's Go,' etc) and composing scores 1961–5 for four *NFB productions. Parts of the score for the NFB's *Le Sport et les hommes* (1961) also were performed by Baculis' octet at the 1962 Montreal Jazz Festival. He led the Al Baculis Singers ca 1965–ca 1972. This studio group – comprising his wife (Margo *MacKinnon), Renée Beaumier, Raymond Berthiaume, René *Lacourse, Giselle Poitras, Rudy Pontano, Jean-Pierre Rondeau, and Nicole Scott – sang frequently for CBC radio and TV and made the LPs *The Al Baculis Singers* (1966, CTLS 1084/Birchmount BM528), *Back to Baculis* (1967, CTLS 1095/Allied Paragon ALS 228), and **Anne of Green Gables* (1967, Dom 1368). Four of Baculis' jazz themes were recorded by the US clarinetist Buddy De Franco, Fleming, and others (*Waterbed* Choice CRS 1017). In 1977 Baculis began teaching arranging and composition at the Vanier Cegep, Montreal; in 1978 he began teaching those same subjects at McGill U. He is a member of CAPAC.

BAERG, William. Choir conductor, educator, b Bassano, southeast of Calgary, 24 Feb 1938; ARCT 1961, BA (Goshen College) 1962, M MUS (Peabody Cons) 1971. After conducting studies 1963–6 with Kurt Thomas and Martin Stephani in Germany, he taught 1966–70 at the *Mennonite Brethren Bible College and College of the Arts and, after graduate studies 1970–2 at the Peabody Cons, returned to the college to become chairman of the music department and conductor of the college's Oratorio Choir and A Cappella Choir. The latter has been heard over CBC radio and has toured in Canada. Baerg also lectured 1973–5 at the *U of Manitoba and was the founder and conductor 1973–8 of the CBC Winnipeg Singers. He became one of the two regular guest conductors of the Mennonite Community Orchestra in 1978.

BAGNALL, John. Music dealer, piano manufacturer, b Staffordshire, England, 1828, d Victoria, BC, February 1885. He worked as a piano builder and cabinet maker for Collard & Collard in London, and came to Canada in 1862. The pioneer music dealer on the west coast, he sold music and instruments and tuned, regulated, and repaired pianos and harmoniums in Victoria at a store located first on Fort St and later on Government St. He built a number of pianos, probably the first to be made in British Columbia, and in 1871 announced his intention to establish a piano factory. It is doubtful that this plan came to fruition, although in 1882 the city directory listed his business as 'manufacturers of pianos, organs, and harmoniums, established in 1863.' None of his pianos is known to exist today. Following Bagnall's death, in 1885, his business was taken over by Charles Goodwin, who formed a partnership ca 1887 with G.W. Jordan, with premises on Fort St. This firm built upright pianos, several of which were shipped to San Francisco. In 1890 Goodwin and Jordan built their first grand piano, for a clothing merchant, A.G. McCandless of Victoria. The firm ceased activities during the early 1890s. No Goodwin and Jordan pianos appear to have survived.

BIBLIOGRAPHY

Kent, Herbert. 'Musical chronicles of early times,' *Victoria Daily Times*, series 3, 21 Dec 1918

Nesbitt, James K. 'On the track of Baby Grand,' Victoria *Daily Colonist*, 13 Mar 1960 (FH, HK)

Bagpipe, Great Highland (piob mhor)

1 General

2 The instrument and its music

3 Teaching, solo playing, and competitions

See also Bands: 7 / Highland pipe bands; Scotland. For reference to other kinds of bagpipe see Croatia; Macedonia; Serbia.

1 GENERAL. The Highland bagpipes, which have become the most familiar of all types of bagpipe, must have been introduced to Canada by the earliest Scottish settlers in Nova Scotia and Upper Canada. Positive data, however, are lacking, and until quite recent times the story has to be told as a series of footnotes to the history of piping in Scotland. Furthermore, although undoubtedly there was much activity, it was difficult for players in isolation from the fountainhead of their tradition to maintain or improve standards, even if their enthusiasm was undimmed. The names are recorded of some Canadian pipers and of Scottish emigré pipers active around World War I; but there is no way of ascertaining their standards of performance, and no one seems to have investigated whether they may have handed down unusual variants of traditional tunes.

2 THE INSTRUMENT AND ITS MUSIC. The Highland bagpipe has a single eight-holed chanter with conical bore and a double reed, producing nine notes on a basically Mixolydian scale, and three drones with single reeds (two tenor, one bass), sounding octave intervals below low A on the chanter. The chanter, drones, and stocks usually are made of African blackwood, with ivory or silver mounts (often both), and their manufacture is a skilled business for which, in Scotland, an apprenticeship of five years is required. At least two makers in Canada are so qualified: Jack Dunbar (St Catharines, Ont) and a more recent arrival, Matt Marshall (Bowmanville, Ont). Both have introduced their own chanter patterns, and Dunbar has experimented with new materials (impregnated beech and maple, and even plastic). Elsewhere in Ontario and in British Columbia there are good makers of practice chanters and of reeds, but in 1980 most Canadian pipers still played instruments from Scotland.

The extensive repertoire of the Highland pipes includes marches (2/4, 4/4, 6/8, 3/4), strathspeys, reels, jigs, hornpipes, slow airs, and, above all, piobaireachd (pibroch), the classical variation form. Few piobaireachdan have been composed in the late 20th century, but much light music has been written for pipes. Several published collections contain tunes by Canadian pipers. Two familiar to pipers everywhere, *Colonel Robertson* and *The Mid-Lothian Pipe Band*, were composed by Farquhar Beaton, third pipe-major of the *48th Highlanders of Canada. More recent Canadian composers whose tunes have been published include John Wilson (Toronto), George Grant (St-Hubert, Que), W.J. Wyatt (Winnipeg), A.M. Cairns (Rockcliffe, Ont), Neil Sutherland (Winnipeg), Donald MacNiven (Kirkland Lake, Ont), Sam Scott (Manotick, Ont), William Gilmour (Toronto), Angus Graham (Prince George, BC), Reay Mackay (Toronto), and John Knox MacKenzie (Vancouver). John Wilson's three books of pipe music contain many of his own compositions and settings, and his third volume especially includes many Canadian compositions.

3 TEACHING, SOLO PLAYING, AND COMPETITIONS. Pipe bands have a long history in Canada, but good solo players have been slower to appear, partly because there have been few teachers (especially of piobaireachd). A noted Toronto teacher in the years before and after World War II was Murdo MacLeod, and other influential teachers in southern Ontario were Walter Rose and George Duncan (who both lived in Detroit but taught many Canadians). In the Montreal area leading teachers have been George Grant and Alex McNeill (still active in 1979); in the Ottawa area Sam Scott and A.M. Cairns; in the Vancouver area Malcolm Nicholson, Ian Duncan, Jimmy MacMillan, and Ed Esson (still active in 1979). However, much of the credit for the improvement of standards after World War II must go to John Wilson (1906–79), one of the most distinguished players and bagpipe composers of his generation, who emigrated from Scotland and settled in Canada in 1948 and who taught nearly all the best soloists in Ontario and elsewhere. His best-known pupils include William Gilmour, Reay Mackay, Chris Anderson, James McGillivray, James Thomson, William Livingstone, and Robert Worrall. Between 1974 and 1979 the last four, and another Ontario piper, Edward Neigh, won or placed in the most senior professional competitions in Scotland. Particular heights were reached in 1977, when the first prizes at Inverness, the most important of all Scottish solo competitions, went to Canadians: Livingstone won the gold medal for piobaireachd; and Worrall won the march and the strathspey and reel competitions. Livingstone also has won the North American solo championship three times, and Worrall four times.

British Columbia has produced good solo pipers, such as Donald Cameron, Donald MacIver, James Watt, Willie Barrie, John A. MacLeod, Archie MacIndewar, Hal Senyk, Jamie Troy, and Jack Lee; but activity there has been on a smaller scale and somewhat isolated, and more emphasis has been given to pipe-band playing. Other provinces have lagged far behind, but in general the outlook for Canadian piping was bright in 1980. In the late 1970s John Wilson, Reay Mackay, and other instructors formed the Ontario School of Piping in Toronto, and William Connell (a former Clasp winner at Inverness) began teaching (in London, Ont) and judging at competitions. In various parts of Canada, notably in Nelson, BC, Fort Qu'Appelle, Sask, Brockville, Ont, and Antigonish, NS, summer schools of piping have been held regularly, and Canadians often have been engaged as instructors, together with pipers from Scotland or the USA. It is only a matter of time before the art of piping is recognized as a regular university music option.

Meanwhile, good solo players in Canada can be heard most readily at the annual competitions held in every province in conjunction with Highland games (see Bands: 7 / Highland pipe bands) and at the regular meetings of local piping societies, where the best soloists give recitals. At the 1973 Highland games in Ottawa a gold medal, the first of its kind in North America, began to be offered annually by the Piobaireachd Society; the set tunes for this competition are the same as those for Inverness.

SELECTED DISCOGRAPHY

Abercairney Highlanders; Cameronian Rant; et al. Pipe Major S. MacKinnon. Victor 216534

Bagpipe Music. William Gilmour. Dom LP 1232

The Cock o' the North. Pipe Sergeant David Ferguson. Berliner 811

Caller Herrin. Pipe Sergeant David Ferguson. Berliner 812

Pipe Major John Wilson Visits the British Columbia Pipers' Assn. Ara-Mac AML-1

Ross *Farewell to the Black Watch March; Elspeth Campbell*; et al. Pipe Major Kenneth McKenzie Baillie. 1923. Victor 19107

BIBLIOGRAPHY

MacKinnon, Pipe Major Stephen. 'The bagpipe in Canada,' *Canadian Geographical J*, April 1932

Wilson, John. *John Wilson's Collection of Highland Bagpipe Music*, 2 books, self-publ, vol 1 (Edinburgh 1937, Toronto n.d.); vol 2 (Toronto 1957)

– *The Canadian Centennial (1867–1967) Collection of Highland Bagpipe Music. John Wilson's Collection*, vol 3 (Toronto 1967)

'Dunbars,' *North American Scotsman*, vol 3, Aug 1972

Wilson, John. 'The great breakthrough,' *Piper and Dancer Bulletin*, vol 30, Jan 1975

Worrall, Robert. 'Canadian overseas – 1975,' ibid, vol 31, Feb–Mar 1976

'The Glencoe bagpipes,' *North American Scotsman*, vol 4, Aug 1976

Connell, Willie. 'Toronto indoor games. Judging impressions,' ibid, vol 4, Aug 1976

Wilson, John. *A Professional Piper in Peace and War: The Autobiography and Memoirs of Pipe Major John Wilson of Edinburgh, Scotland and Toronto, Canada* (Toronto 1978) DW

BAILEY, Terence (William). Musicologist, b Toronto 12 Jul 1937; B MUS (Toronto) 1958, MFA (Princeton) 1960, PH D (Washington) 1968. As a student he received a Woodrow Wilson fellowship in 1958 and a *Canada Council pre-doctoral fellowship for the years 1961–3. He played clarinet in CBC studio orchestras in 1962 and with the *Regina SO 1963–4. A specialist in early music of the Western world, especially Gregorian chant, Bailey has taught 1963–4 at the *U of Saskatchewan and 1964–74 at the *U of British Columbia. In 1974 he joined the Faculty of Music at the *U of Western Ontario, and in 1976 he began editing the journal *Studies in Music from the U of Western Ontario*. He served 1969–71 as secretary of *CAUSM and 1971–3 as editor of the *CAUSM Journal*. His wife, Kathryn Bailey (pianist, musicologist, b Des Moines, 28 Mar 1939), joined the faculty in 1974. Her articles have appeared in the *CAUSM Journal, The Canada Music Book*, and *Current Musicology*.

WRITINGS

The Fleury Play of Herod (Toronto 1965)

'The ceremonies and chants of the processions of the Western church,' unpubl PH D thesis, U of Washington 1968

The Processions of Sarum and the Western Church (Toronto 1971)

'Baïf, Ronsard and neo-classical music,' *Bulletin of the Canadian Humanities Association*, vol 23, Spring 1972

The Intonation Formulas of Western Chant (Toronto 1974)

'The intervention of scholarship on Gregorian chant,' *CAUSM J*, vol 5, Spring 1975

'Accentual and cursive cadences in Gregorian psalmody,' *J of the American Musicological Soc*, vol 29, Fall 1976

'Modes and myth,' *Studies in Music from the U of Western Ontario*, vol 1, Fall 1976

'Ambrosian psalmody: an introduction,' ibid, vol 2, Fall 1977

'Gerbert's *De modis*: a new explanation and edition,' *Kirchenmusikalisches Jahrbuch*, 61, 1978

Commemoratio Brevis (Ottawa 1979) (GKG)

BAILLARGEON. Montreal family of instrumentalists: 1 / Hervé and his twin sons 2 / Gilles and 3 / Marcel.

1 **Hervé**. Flutist, teacher, b L'Acadie, near Montreal, 30 Sep 1899. He began to study flute at Farnham College and continued privately in Montreal with Francis Boucher. As early as 1920 he performed at the Place Viger Hotel. Later he was a member of the *Canadian Grenadier Guards Band and 1923–30 of the radio orchestra at CKAC, Montreal. He was principal flute 1930–41 of the *Montreal Orchestra, 1935–65 of the *MSO, 1941–52 of the *Little Symphony of Montreal and other orchestras and was a soloist or chamber musician in numerous concerts for *Pro Musica, the *Ladies' Morning Musical Club, and other organizations. He played flute obbligatos for the sopranos Pierrette *Alarie, Jean Dickenson, and Lily Pons. In 1949 he recorded (RCI 8) Jean *Coulthard's *Quiet Song* and Saeverud's *Divertimento* for flute and strings with a CBC Montreal orchestra under Jean-Marie *Beaudet. He taught 1935–65 at *McGill U, 1943–70 at the *CMM, 1946–57 at the *CMQ, and at various times at other institutions. His pupils include his son Marcel, Robert Cram, Jean-Paul *Major, and Gail Grimstead. In 1945 he was made an honorary member of the Toronto Flute Club.

WRITINGS

'La flûte traversière ou flûte d'orchestre,' *Musique et musiciens*, Dec 1953

BIBLIOGRAPHY

Prévost, Roland. 'La flûte enchantée,' *P-T*, Mar 1946

2 **Gilles**. Violinist, teacher, b Montreal 6 Oct 1928. A pupil of Lucien *Sicotte 1942–3, Lucien *Martin 1943–4, and (at the CMM) Louis *Bailly 1944–7 and Noël *Brunet 1947–50, he won a Sarah *Fischer Concerts Scholarship in 1948 and the *Prix Archambault in 1949. Also in 1949 he was soloist with the Montreal Youth SO. On a scholarship from the Quebec government he studied 1950–2 at the Paris Cons with René Benedetti and in 1952 in London with Max Rostal. In 1954 he toured England as concertmaster of the Montreal Junior SO. He has been a member of various CBC orchestras (including that of the radio program 'The *Little Symphonies'), the *McGill Chamber Orchestra, the Jean-Philippe-Rameau Ensemble, the Quatuor canadien, the *Classical Quartet of Montreal, and other organizations. He also played 1953–64 with the *MSO, rejoining it in 1970 for a tour of Japan. He has been heard frequently as a soloist on radio and TV. In 1970 he began teaching violin at the Bourgchemin Cegep, where he is responsible also for orchestra and chamber music classes. He also taught 1974–5 at the UQATR. He is a member of the National Committee for the Recording Arts, USA.

See also Discography for C. Corbeil.

3 **Marcel**. Flutist, teacher, b Montreal 6 Oct 1928. He studied piano with Oscar *O'Brien and at 15 entered the CMM, where his teachers were Auguste *Descarries and Yvonne *Hubert. In 1945 he began to concentrate on the flute, studying with his father and with René Le Roy, and won several prizes. A scholarship from the *Ladies' Morning Musical *Club allowed him to study at the Paris Cons with Roger Cortet, Gaston Crunelle, and Lucien Lavaillotte. For the CBC he has given many recitals and was a soloist in the programs 'The Little Symphonies' and *'Heure du concert.' With Kenneth *Gilbert he toured Quebec 1958–9 for the *JMC. He has assisted in recitals by the sopranos Claire *Gagnier, Miliza Korjus, Marthe *Létourneau, and others. A leading Montreal studio musician, he has played in orchestras conducted by Neil Chotem, Paul de Margerie, Lee Gagnon, Gaston Rochon, and others, and on LPs by Edith Butler, Les Cailloux, Jean-Pierre Ferland, Paolo Noël, Raoul Roy, Gilles Vigneault, and others. He has been a member 1959–62 of the Ted Elfstrom Jazz Octet (and soloist on its LP *Surprise! Surprise!* 1960, Laur JL 3001), principal flute 1973–4 of the CBC Montreal orchestra, and an occasional performer in 1968 and 1971 with the *SMCQ and 1975–6 at the U of Montreal Nocturnales (late evening concerts). He taught at the CMM 1972–4 and joined the staff at the *École Vincent-d'Indy in 1972 and at the *U of Montreal in 1973. IP-C

BAILLARGEON, Hélène (Marie) (m Coté). Folklorist, singer, b St-Martin-de-Beauce, south of Quebec City, 28 Aug 1916. She studied voice in Quebec City 1935–8, in New York 1939–40 with Mrs Franz Rupp, and in Montreal 1940–4 with Alfred *Laliberté, who introduced her to folk music. She was a researcher 1950–5 with Marius *Barbeau at the National Museum of Man, Ottawa, and, as a singer and host, participated in many CBC French and English radio and TV broadcasts, including the series 'Le Réveil rural' 1951–5, 'Songs de Chez nous' 1952–5 with Alan *Mills, 'Cap aux Sorciers' 1955–8, and the popular children's program 'Chez Hélène' 1959–73. She attended international congresses in folk music in Rumania in 1959, Quebec City in 1961, and Czechoslovakia in 1962. Her vitality and her faith in the value of the Quebec heritage have contributed greatly to the popularity and status of folk music. She compiled *Vive la Canadienne* (Éditions du jour 1962), a collection of 77 folk songs, and recorded *French Canadian Folk Songs* (two LPs: 1953, RCI 97; and 1954, RCI 98), *Christmas Carols of French Canada / Chants de Noël du Canada français* (1956, Folk FC-7229), and *Chantons un peu* (Dom 48003), and made other LPs with Alan Mills. She became a Member of the *Order of Canada in 1973 and was appointed a Canadian citizenship court judge the following year. (HPn)

BAILLY, Louis. Violist, teacher, b Valenciennes, France, 13 Jun 1882, naturalized Canadian 1950, d Cowansville, near Sherbrooke, Que, 21 Nov 1974; premier prix (Paris Cons) 1899, hon D MUS (Curtis) 1930. He studied violin and viola at the Paris Cons. After playing in the orchestras of the Opéra, the Opéra-Comique and the Concerts Colonne, he became a founding member in 1903 of the Capet Quartet, with which he toured in Europe, and a member of the Geloso and Elman quartets. He joined the Flonzaley Quartet in the USA in 1917 and toured in North America and Europe until 1924. He played as a soloist with several large US orchestras and gave the premiere (1920) of Ernest Bloch's *Suite* for viola and orchestra with the National SO of New York; the preceding year he had given the premiere of the viola and piano version with Harold Bauer in Pittsfield, Mass. He was a teacher 1925–41 (latterly head of the chamber music department) at the Curtis Institute in Philadelphia, where Stanley *Solomon was one of his pupils. He taught violin, viola, and chamber music 1943–57 at the *CMM, where his pupils included Maurice *Durieux and Laflèche Robitaille, members of the *MSO; Fernand Robitaille, subsequently a member of the *Quebec SO; Stephen *Kondaks; and Lucien *Robert. Bailly was the coach 1944–5 of a CMM string quartet formed by Noël *Brunet, Lionel Renaud, Lucien Robert, and Roland *Leduc, and sometimes performed himself with chamber music ensembles at the CMM. He was a Knight of the Legion of Honour. GP

Hélène Baillargeon

BAKER, Carroll (m Beaulieu). Singer-songwriter, b Bridgewater, NS, 4 Mar 1949. Her father, Gordon Baker, was a country fiddler. She was raised in Port Medway, NS, but moved to Toronto at 16. After singing briefly on a casual basis with a band in a bar in Oakville, Ont, at 19, then at fairs and jamborees in southern Ontario, she began recording in 1970. Her first single, 'Mem'ries of Home,' for the Gaiety label (owned by Don Grashey, her manager and the co-composer of some of her songs), was a minor hit. Appearances followed in Ontario bars until, in 1975, she recorded Conway Twitty's 'I've Never Been This Far Before.' That record and a sensational appearance on the CBC's 1976 *Juno Awards telecast won her stardom. Other hit singles 1975–8 (for *RCA beginning in 1976) included her songs 'Hungry Fire of Love,' 'One Night of Cheatin' (Ain't Worth the Rea-pin'),' 'Tonight with Love,' 'Little Boy Blue,' 'Ten Little Fingers,' 'Portrait in the Window,' and 'I'm Getting High Remembering.' Though she has made some of her records in Nashville, she had not, by 1980, achieved substantial popularity in the USA. She did, however, appear to great acclaim at the Wembley (England) Country Music Festival in 1977 and 1978 and returned to perform in England in 1979. One of the most popular Canadian country singers in Canada during the mid-1970s, Baker received the ACME's Big Country Award in 1975, 1976, 1977, and 1978 as top female vocalist, a Big Country Award in 1976 for the album of the year (*Carroll Baker* RCA KPL1-0171), a second in 1978 as entertainer of the year, and Juno Awards in 1976, 1977, and 1978 as top female country singer. Writing of Baker, Ken Waxman observed in *Saturday Night*: 'She's brought a new sense of feminine sensuality to country music ... the honest toughness of the songs she writes pinpoints the sometimes aggressive sexuality and determination of many women.'

BIBLIOGRAPHY

Waxman, Ken. 'Impromptu invitation leads to career in country music,' *MSc*, 291, Sep–Oct 1976

MacGregor, Roy. 'The good part begins,' *The Canadian*, 20 Nov 1976

Base, Ron. 'Sex in the heartland,' *Maclean's*, 5 Sep 1977

Waxman, Ken. 'The lady sings what women feel,' *SatN*, Nov 1977

Goddard, Peter. 'The sensuality of Carroll Baker,' *Toronto Star*, 26 May 1979

BAKER, Dalton. Baritone, teacher, choir conductor, organist, b Merton, Surrey, England, 17 Oct 1879, d Vancouver 22 Mar 1970; ARAM 1903. He was a choirboy at All Saints, Margaret St, London, and a student at the RAM. He was organist-choirmaster at the Chelsea Barracks 1894–6 and at St Mary Magdalen's, Munster Square, 1896–1903.

After 1902, when he sang at a St James Hall Ballad Concert in London, he became known as a baritone of rare musicianship. In 1905, along with Mary Garden, Nellie Melba, and Giovanni Zenatello, he was commanded by Edward VII to sing at Windsor Castle at a state concert in honour of the King of Greece. He toured the USA in 1908 and, with *Albani, the British Isles in 1909, and was described as Great Britain's greatest baritone.

Baker emigrated to the USA in 1913 and moved to Canada in 1914 as the first organist-choirmaster at Timothy Eaton Memorial Church, Toronto, and singing instructor at the *TCM. The critic of *The World* described his singing after a Toronto recital with Healey *Willan at the piano, 1 Dec 1915: 'His voice is fine in timbre, his presentation sincere and unaffected, and his technical attack precise and accurate.' With Ernest *Seitz, Baker began a series of Sunday musicales in 1916. He founded the 100-voice Orpheus Society in 1920 and was its director for the three years of its existence, disbanding it (after a final concert, 15 Mar 1923, at which the young Richard Crooks was guest artist) to open a studio in New York. He fell ill in New York and returned to Toronto in 1924. He was soloist that November in a performance – then thought to be the first in North America – of Bach's *Watch Ye, Pray Ye*. That same year he rejoined the faculty of the TCM, retaining the post until 1932. During those years he was organist-choirmaster at St Peter's Church, where his 40-voice boys' choir specialized in Gregorian chant, and was singing master at Bishop Strachan School. In 1934 he moved to Vancouver, where he taught privately and was organist-choirmaster 1935–9 at St James' Anglican Church. He was conductor of the CBC programs 'Vesper Hour' and 'Eventide' from 1939 until his retirement in 1956.

Though primarily a performer and conductor, Baker also composed music for choirs. His compositions include a *Sanctus*, a *Kyrie and Sanctus*, a choral setting of 'Ave, verum corpus,' and various anthems, one of which – 'Shadows of Evening' – is published by *Western Music. MWM

BAKER, Michael (Conway). Composer, teacher, b West Palm Beach, Fla, 13 May 1941; B MUS (British Columbia) 1966, MA (Western Washington State) 1972. Moving to Canada in 1958, he studied with Jean *Coulthard and Elliot *Weisgarber at the *U of British Columbia, with Malcolm Arnold at the *Shawnigan Summer School of the Arts in 1971 and 1972, and with Lennox Berkeley in England in 1975. Baker's music exhibits a facile technique and blends neoclassical and neo-romantic idioms. He has received commissions from Robert *Aitken, the *Canadian Arts Trio, the National Ballet of Canada, the Okanagan SO, Robert *Silverman, the Toronto Dance Theatre, and the *Vancouver SO, and many of his compositions have been performed in the USA, Europe, the Orient, and the South Pacific. A 1975 concert of his music in London, under the patronage of the Canadian High Commission, was recorded by the BBC and broadcast 28 Jul 1975 by the CBC. Baker became a teacher in Vancouver elementary schools in 1972. He is an associate of the *CMCentre and an affiliate of PRO Canada.

SELECTED COMPOSITIONS

STAGE

The Letter, ballet. 1974. Fl (picc), cl, str trio, cel, perc. CMCentre

Washington Square, ballet. 1979. Ms

ORCHESTRA

Okanagan Landscapes. 1971. Pf, orch. CMCentre

Dialogues (Bible). 1972. Bar, SATB, orch. CMCentre

Contours. 1973. Db, hpd, str. CMCentre

Concerto for Flute and String Orchestra. 1974. CMCentre

A Struggle for Dominion. 1975. CMCentre

Concerto. 1976. Pf, orch. CMCentre

Duo Concertante. 1976. Va, vn, str. Ms

Symphony. 1977. CMCentre

CHAMBER

Sonata. 1963. Fl, pf. CMCentre

String Quartet No. 1. 1968. CMCentre

Concert Piece for Organ, Piano and Timpani. 1970. Ms

Piano Trio. 1972. Pf, vn, vc. CMCentre

Music for Six Players. 1973. Fl, ob, str trio, hpd. CMCentre

En rapport. 1974. 2 guit. CMCentre

Four Views from a Nursery Tune. 1975. Vn, hn, pf. CMCentre

Fanfare for Brass. 1976. 4 tpt, 4 hn, 2 trb, bass trb, tuba. CMCentre

PIANO

Capriccio for Two Pianos. 1964. FH 1975. CBC SM-278 (*Taussig)

Sonata. 1975. FH 1977

VOICE

Five Canadian Folk Songs. 1973. V, pf. CMCentre

Two Lyric Songs (Webb, Baker). 1973. High v, pf. CMCentre

Six Songs (Sappho). 1975. Mezzo, pf. CMCentre

WRITINGS

'Bearding the lion,' *MSc*, 286, Nov–Dec 1975

BIBLIOGRAPHY

LaMarche, Phillip G. 'Michael Baker off to England to study,' *MSc*, 279, Sep–Oct 1974

Hossie, Linda. 'The musical equivalent of a very good read,' *Maclean's*, 5 Feb 1979

Mertens, Susan. 'Michael Baker's music is made-to-measure for a full-length Washington Square,' *PfAC*, Spring 1979

PRO Canada Ltd. 'Michael Conway Baker,' pamphlet, 1979 (DD)

'Bal chez Boulé.' The text of this chanson en laisse (a type of French ballad or epic song) appears for the first time in the supplement to the *Chansonnier des Collèges* (1851). The appendix to Conrad *Laforte's *La Chanson folklorique et les écrivains du XIXe siècle* (Montreal 1973) lists versions and publications. Onomatopoeic sounds or in some versions the set phrase 'Vogue, beau marinier' make up the refrain. This diversity indicates clearly the song's antiquity and its wide distribution. The text of the verses tells the story of a servant, Louison Blé or in other versions José Blai(s), who goes off to a dance at Boulé's place (chez Boulé) with his sweetheart, having completed his daily chores around the farm and changed his clothes. His talents as a dancer – evaluated differently in different versions of the song – lead to his ejection (or not) from the ball. In *Les Anciens Canadiens* (Quebec 1863) Philippe-Joseph Aubert de Gaspé places the origin of the song in the region of Montmagny, Que (where the name of Boulé is widespread), and identifies the José in question as the author. The latter assertion, however, is questioned by Laforte. The melody, of which a version is included in Ernest *Gagnon's *Chansons populaires du Canada* (Montreal 1865), may have been borrowed (according to Edith *Fowke's *Folk Songs of Canada*, Waterloo 1954) from an old sea shanty. 'Bal chez Boulé' has been recorded several times. It has appeared on 78s by Charles *Marchand, alone and with his Bytown Troubadours, and on LPs by Robert *Savoie (RCA Victor LCP-1035), the *Alouette Vocal Quartet (RCA LCT 3002), the *Montreal Bach Choir (Vox STPL 511.860), Jacques *Labrecque (RCI/RCA CS 100-9), and others.

BIBLIOGRAPHY

Laforte, Conrad. 'Le Bal chez Boulé,' *Dictionnaire des oeuvres littéraires du Québec*, vol 1, ed Maurice Lemire (Montreal 1978) HP

BALES, (Albert) Gerald. Organist, choirmaster, composer, teacher, b Toronto 12 May 1919; ATCM 1936, FRCCO 1974. Taught first by his mother, he gave a piano recital at 7 and an organ recital at 13. He studied 1936–40 at the *TCM – piano and organ with Albert Procter, theory with Leo *Smith and Healey *Willan, and conducting with Herbert A. *Fricker. Bales' formal piano and organ debut, in 1937 at *Eaton Auditorium, included some of his own works. He was organist-choirmaster 1937–41 at St Anne's Anglican Church and 1941–3 at Rosedale United Church. After service in the RCAF during World War II he spent 1945 as organist-choirmaster at Brantford United Church, Brantford, Ont, then returned to Toronto, where he was organist-choirmaster 1946–56 at St Andrew's Presbyterian. In 1948 he played his *Fantasy* for piano and orchestra with the Chicago Philharmonic Orchestra. During the 1950s on CBC radio he conducted his St Andrew's Singers (formed in 1953) in Handel oratorios and performed many of Handel's organ works. He was organist-choirmaster 1956–9 at the Anglican Cathedral of the Redeemer in Calgary, where he also founded the Calgary Orchestra and Chorus Assn. He was the *RCCO delegate to the first International Congress of Organists, in London in 1957, and gave a recital at Westminster Cathedral during his visit. He was organist-choirmaster 1959–71 at the Cathedral Church of St Mark in Minneapolis and established there a series of concerts which introduced to the US public a number of Canadian works, including Godfrey *Ridout's *Ascension*, Keith *Bissell's *Advent Cantata*, Eugene *Hill's *Concertino* for organ and orchestra, and his own *Song of Creation* (1974, a commission from St Mark's). In 1971 he began teaching organ and choral and orchestral conducting at the *U of Ottawa and became organist-choirmaster at Trinity Anglican Church. Bales is an affiliate of PRO Canada. His works, of which there are over 120, reflect the influence of Willan.

SELECTED COMPOSITIONS

Prelude in E Minor. 1936. Org. BMIC 1947

Nocturne. 1937. Orch. Ber (rental)

Fantasy. 1939. Pf, orch. Ms

Lazarus. 1940. Solo v, choir, org. Ms

Summer Idyll. 1940. Orch. Ms

Toccata. 1946. Pf. BMIC 1947

Essay for Strings. 1947. Str orch. Ber (rental). RCI 6 (J.-M. *Beaudet cond)

Concerto for organ. 1950. Org, str. Ber (rental)

Te Deum laudamus. 1962. SATB, org, 3 tpt, tim. Wat 1968. Mastertone Recordings. Record also includes Bales *Festival Fanfare* (1952); *Jubilate Deo* (1965); and *Fanfare for Easter Day* (1964). See Discography.

Petite Suite. 1963. Org. BMIC 1965. Sears SR 101568. See Discography.

Psalm Cantata. 1965. SATB, org, 3 tpt, tim. Ms

Éclat for Orchestra. 1968. Ms

Song of Creation. 1974. SATB, orch. Ms

Also a number of film and radio scores, other works for pf, org, and choir, and songs

DISCOGRAPHY

Bales – Willan – Bach. Choir of the Cathedral Church of Saint Mark, P. Emch org, Bales cond. (1965). Mastertone Recording Co

Gerald Bales at the Organ: Willan – France – Hill – Bales – Buxtehude – Walter – Stanley. 1964. Sears SR 101568

Karam – Willan – et al. 1957. Mirrosonic DRE 1001-3

BIBLIOGRAPHY

Thistle, Lauretta. 'Organ virtuoso now concentrates on composing and teaching,' *MSc*, 275, Jan–Feb 1974 YC

Ballads. Narrative songs which form a very important part of the Anglo-Canadian folksong heritage. They fall into three groups:

1 Old popular ballads

2 British broadsides

3 Native North American ballads

1 OLD POPULAR BALLADS. The most prized in the first category are those published in *The English and Scottish Popular Ballads* (1882–98), the compilation of 305 ballads (words only) commonly called Child ballads after the scholar Francis James Child of Boston, who assembled and classified them, working mainly at the library of Harvard U. B.H. Bronson edited the complementary four-volume work *The Traditional Tunes of the Child Ballads* (Princeton 1959–72). Early British immigrants brought many of the popular ballads to eastern Canada, where they took root and survived, handed down through the generations. Half of the 305 Child ballads have ceased to be sung; of the rest, at least 70 have been noted in Canada in the 20th century.

Nova Scotia has proved the best repository of the old ballads. Helen *Creighton has found no fewer than 49, and earlier W. Roy Mackenzie found 16, including 4 not in Creighton's collection. In Newfoundland Maud Karpeles found 12, Elisabeth Greenleaf and Kenneth *Peacock each found 19, and MacEdward Leach noted 8 in Labrador. In New Brunswick Louise *Manny noted 6, Creighton 7, and Phillips Barry 10; and in Ontario Edith *Fowke found 22. Few have been reported from the other provinces.

These older ballads told dramatic stories in a vivid and objective style, concentrating on the crucial situation. Of the 70 reported in Canada, at least 14 have been established in tradition. The most popular by far, here as throughout the English-speaking world, is 'Barbara Allen,' with over 30 different versions. Three others have turned up at least 20 times: 'The Gypsy Laddie,' 'The Cruel Mother,' and 'Young Beichan.' Next in order, with between 10 and 20 known versions, are 'Sweet William's Ghost,' 'The Sweet Trinity,' 'Hind Horn,' 'Lady Isabel and the Elf Knight,' 'Sir James the Rose,' 'Little Musgrave and Lady Barnard,' 'Captain Wedderburn's Courtship,' 'Katharine Jaffray,' 'The Farmer's Curst Wife,' and 'Willie o'Winsbury.'

2 BROADSIDES. With the advent of printing, writers composed many ballads which were printed on the single sheets known as broadsides and sold to the public. By the 19th century, when most British immigrants arrived in Canada, these broadside verses had largely displaced the older popular ballads in public favour, with the result that all Anglo-Canadian folksong collections contain many more broadsides than Child ballads.

The broadsides are more prosaic than the popular ballads, dealing with less dramatic events and with ordinary people rather than lords and ladies. They include tales of war, the sea, and crime, but by far the most numerous are love stories: of family opposition to lovers, faithful and unfaithful lovers, and lovers' disguises and tricks. In the most popular single plot a lover returns after seven years' absence and tests his sweetheart's fidelity before revealing himself – a story retold in dozens of slightly different forms including 'The Pretty Fair Maid,' 'The Dark-Eyed Sailor,' 'The Mantle So Green,' and 'The Plains of Waterloo.'

3 NORTH AMERICAN BALLADS. The native ballads are less romantic: they deal largely with real events in a style not far removed from newspaper journalism. Where the old-world ballads stressed tales of love, the native ones feature adventures of soldiers, sailors, cowboys, lumberjacks, and criminals. The largest groups of native Canadian ballads spring from the men who earned their living on the sea or in the woods (see Occupational songs). Others tell of crimes like 'The Murder of F.C. Benwell' or 'The Prince Edward Island Murder,' or of tragedies and disasters like 'The Miramichi Fire' and 'The Halifax Explosion' (see Disaster songs). A few that originated in the USA drifted up to Canada, the most popular being 'The Jealous Lover,' 'The Little Mohea,' 'The Lake of Pontchartrain,' and 'The Lonesome Scenes of Winter.' A few others, like 'Brave Wolfe,' 'The *Chesapeake* and the *Shannon*,' and 'The Battle of the Windmill' memorialize historical events.

Although in French Canada some composers and chansonniers occasionally have referred to some of their songs as 'ballades,' the ballad as such has not been developed in French-Canadian song, and related forms go by other names such as 'romances,' 'mélodies,' 'chansons narratives,' or simply 'chansons.'

See also Folk music; Folk music, Anglo-Canadian. EF

Ballets. The composition of ballet scores came into its own in Canada with the rise of the major dance companies in the middle of the 20th century, notably the Royal Winnipeg Ballet (founded in 1938 as the Winnipeg Ballet, the prefix 'Royal' granted in 1953), the National Ballet of Canada (founded in 1951), and Les Grands Ballets Canadiens (founded in 1952), all of which have commissioned numerous original ballets. Other companies, including the Volkoff Canadian Ballet of Toronto (founded in 1939), the Ballets Ruth Sorel of Montreal (founded in 1946), the Montreal Ballet (founded in 1949), and the Toronto Dance Theatre (founded in 1968) have commissioned scores from Canadian composers, and the last-named deserves particular mention as perhaps the only widely known Canadian dance company to have resident composers in the persons of Ann *Southam, Milton *Barnes, and Robert Daigneault.

Among the earliest ballets scored for large instrumental forces and duly choreographed and performed were two for the Winnipeg Ballet: Walter *Kaufmann's *Visages* (1948) and Robert *Fleming's *Chapter 13* (also 1948, contrary to information in *Contemporary Canadian Composers*, which gives the date as 1950; Fleming's score supplanted Gershwin's *Concerto in F*, to which the Gweneth Lloyd choreography had been danced first in 1947). The next major pieces in this category were John *Weinzweig's *The Red Ear of Corn*, composed for and premiered by the Volkoff Canadian Ballet in 1949, and Jean *Papineau-Couture's *Papotages / Tittle-Tattle* composed in 1949 and premiered in 1950 by the Ballets Ruth Sorel. Pierre *Mercure wrote four ballets during those same years, beginning with *Dualité* (1948, not danced), but all were for very small forces. His *La Femme archaïque* and *Lucrèce Borgia* were solo pieces composed in 1949 and danced by Françoise Sullivan in Montreal. Barbara *Pentland's *Beauty and the Beast* was composed in 1940 and danced by the Winnipeg Ballet in 1941, antedating all the above, but was scored for two pianos. Numerous other original ballets written by Canadians in the 1950s or earlier were not choreographed and performed until later, if ever. The following list names only some original works written as ballets by Canadians (with the names of composers, and the year of composition or the year performed, when that information was available). It does not attempt to encompass ballet adaptations by Canadians of existing music by other composers or Canadian scores used for ballet but written as concert pieces, such as R. Murray *Schafer's *String Quartet No. 1* and *Adieu Robert Schumann* (Les Grands Ballets Canadiens), André *Prévost's *Évanescence* (Groupe Nouvelle-Aire), and Michael *Baker's *String Quartet No. 1* (Toronto Dance Theatre).

See also entries on individual ballets: *Barbara Allen* (*Applebaum); *The Fisherman and His Soul* (*Somers); *L'Horoscope* (*Matton); *L'Oiseau-phénix* (*Pépin); *La Prima Ballerina* (*Ridout); *Red Ear of Corn* (Weinzweig); *Rose Latulippe* (*Blackburn, *Freedman, and Michael McLean); *Shadow on the Prairies* (Fleming); *The Shining People of Leonard Cohen* (Freedman); *Tétrachromie* (Mercure).

Abbreviations are used here for five companies: GBC, Les Grands Ballets Canadiens; GPR, Groupe de la Place royale; NBC, National Ballet of Canada; RWB, Royal Winnipeg Ballet; and TDT, Toronto Dance Theatre.

Agostini, Giuseppe *La Petite Canadienne* Montreal Ballet 1949
Anhalt, István *Arc-en-ciel* 1951
Baker, Michael *The Letter* TDT 1974
– *Washington Square* NBC 1979
Barnes, Milton *Rhapsody in the Late Afternoon* TDT 1971
– *The Amber Garden; The Last Act; Three Sided Room* TDT 1972
– *A Flight of Spiral Stairs* TDT 1973
Benoist, Marius *Great Bear* nd
– *Grain; Kilowatt Magic* RWB 1939
Betts, Lorne *Music for a Ballet* 1960
Brabant, Pierre *La Gaspésienne* Ballets Ruth Sorel 1949
Brott, Alexander *La Corriveau* GBC 1966
Carignan, Jean / arr Patriquin *Suite Carignan* GBC 1978
Charpentier, Gabriel *Artère* GBC 1976
Clouser, Jim *Recurrence* RWB 1961
– *Golden Phoenix* RWB 1962
– *Out of Lesbos* RWB 1966
– *Riel* RWB 1966
Collier, Ron *Aurora Borealis* CBC TV 1976
Conte, Michel *Un et un font deux* RWB 1961
– *Cantique des cantiques* GBC 1974
Coulthard, Jean *Excursion* 1940
– *The Devil's Fanfare; Four Bizarre Dances* 1958
Daigneault, Robert *Dark of Moon; The Silent Feast* TDT 1971
– *4 Walk in Time* TDT 1973
– *Bugs; Atlantis* TDT 1974
– *Field of Dreams* TDT 1975
Davies, Victor *Anerca* Contemporary Dancers of Winnipeg 1969
Dionne, Vincent *Danse pour sept voix; La Dernière Paille; Les Nouveaux Espaces; Vues parallèles* GPR 1976–7
– *En Mouvement* Entre-Six 1977
Duplessis, Paul *Hip and Straight* GBC 1970
Fleming, Robert *Chapter 13* RWB 1948
Freedman, Harry *Five Over Thirteen* RWB 1969
– *Romeo and Juliet* (originally *Star Cross'd*) RWB 1973
Gagnon, André *Nelligan* Ballet Ys 1975
– *Mad Shadows* NBC 1977
George, Graham *Jabberwocky* Bettina Byers 1947
– *Peter Pan* Bettina Byers 1948
– *The King, the Pigeon and the Hawk* Bettina Byers 1949
– *The Queen's Jig* Bettina Byers 1950
Gillis, Don *Les Whoops-de-Doo* RWB 1959
Glick, Srul Irving *Heritage Dance Symphony* New Dance Group of Canada 1967
Gratton, Hector *Marie Madeleine* Ottawa Classical Ballet Company 1957
– *Les Feux Follets* 1952
– *La Légende de l'arbre sec* nd
– *Le Pommier* NBC 1952–3
Hinton, Michel *On est 00016 pour assurer votre confort (À la recherche de la lumière)* GBC 1970
Hoffert, Paul *Ballet High* RWB 1970
Humphrey and the Dumptrucks *Goose!* Regina Modern Dance Works 1977
Jackson, Calvin *The Loon's Necklace; Maria Chapdelaine* Willy Blok Hanson Dance Group 1953

Kaufmann, Walter *Visages* RWB 1948
Kunz, Alfred *Moses* 1965
Lachapelle, Guy, with Micheline St-Marcoux and Pierre Béluse *Épisodies I, II, III* Groupe Nouvelle-Aire 1972–3
Lavallée / arr Assaly *Pointes sur glace* GBC 1967
Léveillée, Claude *Fleur de lit* (sic) Les Ballets-Jazz 1976
Macdonald, Fraser *Earth* 1941
Margolian, Samuel *Alice in Wonderland* 1945
Martineau, Michel *Communion* Compagnie de Danse Eddy Toussaint 1975
Mercure, Pierre *Dualité* 1948
– *Lucrèce Borgia; La Femme archaïque* Françoise Sullivan 1949
– *Emprise* Studio Françoise Riopelle 1950
– *Structures métalliques I; Incandescence; Structures métalliques II; Improvisation* Studio Françoise Riopelle 1961
– *Surimpressions* Studio Françoise Riopelle 1964
Mills-Cockell, John *January Tree; For Internal Use Only* NBC 1971
– *Starscape* TDT 1971
Morin-Labrecque, Albertine *Les Rives au Danube; Au Petit Trianon; Russe Bohémien*
Mortifee, Ann *The Ecstasy of Rita Joe* RWB 1971
– *The Grey Goose of Silence* North Carolina Dance Theater
– *Klee Wyck: A Ballet for Emily Carr* Anna Wyman Dance Theatre 1975
– *Yesterday's Day / Variations pour une souvenance* GBC 1975
Pannell, Raymond *Masque* 1977
Papineau-Couture, Jean *Papotages / Tittle-Tattle* Ballets Ruth Sorel 1950
Pépin, Clermont *Les Portes de l'enfer* 1953
– *Le Porte-rêve* CBC 1958 'L'Heure du concert'
Pentland, Barbara *Beauty and the Beast* RWB 1940
Perrault, Michel *Commedia del arte* 1958
– *Sea Gallows* GBC 1959
– *Bérubée* GBC 1960
– *Suite canadienne* GBC 1965
– *Rigaudon* (excerpt from ballet *Ti-Jean*) GBC 1966
Plant, John *The Collector of Cold Weather* GPR 1980
Rea, John *Les Jours / The Days* 1969
Royse, Anthony *Alice in Wonderland* Oakville Junior Ballet 1975
Savaria, Georges *Médée* GBC 1960
Somers, Harry *Ballad* NBC 1958
– *The House of Atreus* NBC 1963
– *And* CBC TV 1969
Southam, Ann *Momentum* New Dance Group of Canada 1967
– *Mito; The Recitation; Trapezoid* TDT 1968
– *3 + 3* CBC 1968
– *Against Sleep; Bernarda Alba; Encounter; Voyage for 4 Male Dancers* TDT 1969
– *Continuum; Portrait; A Thread of Sand; Untitled Solo* TDT 1970
– *Legend; Prospect Park* TDT 1971
– *Boat, River, Moon* TDT 1972
– *Figure in the Pit* TDT 1973
– *Antic Eden; Harold Morgan's Delicate Balance; Mythic Journey; A Summer Song; Walls and Passageways* TDT 1974
– *Arrival of All Time; L'Assassin menacé; Me and My Friends; The Reprieve* TDT 1975
– *Nighthawks; Rude Awakening* TDT 1976
Surdin, Morris *Petite Ballet* (sic) 1955
– *The Remarkable Rocket* NBC 1961
Symonds, Norman *Tensions* CBC TV 1964
Tremblay, Georges *Ni plus ni moins qu'une variation* Compagnie de Danse Eddy Toussaint 1976
Vigneault, Gilles / arr Assaly *Tam Di Delam* GBC 1974
Wild, Eric *The Shooting of Dan McGrew* RWB 1950
Wyre, John, and Craden, Michael *Study for a Song in the Distance* TDT 1970

Composers who wrote ballets before coming to Canada include S.C. *Eckhardt-Gramatté, Theo *Goldberg, Derek *Healey, Lothar *Klein, Mieczyslaw *Kolinski, and Gerhard *Wuensch.

KW, PW

BALLON, Ellen (m Bullock). Pianist, b Montreal, of Russian parents, 1898, d there 21 Dec 1969; hon D MUS (McGill) 1954. She was a child prodigy and at the age of six, in the inaugural year of the *McGill Cons (1904), won the first director's scholarship awarded at that school. She studied there with Clara *Lichtenstein. As a child Ballon was praised by Josef Hofmann (whose pupil she became later, in Switzerland), Adele aus der Ohe, and Raoul Pugno. Artur Rubinstein is said to have declared her 'the greatest pianistic genius I have ever met.' Following a farewell recital at Royal Victoria College in Montreal 27 Dec 1906 she was sent to New York to study with Rafael Joseffy (her patrons were the Canadian prime minister, Sir Wilfrid Laurier, and the principal of McGill U, Sir William Peterson). She was a child when she made her New York debut in March 1910, playing concertos of Mendelssohn (G minor) and Beethoven (C major) with the New York Symphony under Walter Damrosch. In 1912 President Taft invited her to perform at the White House (she returned to play for President Roosevelt in 1934 and for President Eisenhower in 1954). She continued her studies in New York with Josef Hofmann and in Vienna with Wilhelm Backhaus, and when she returned from Europe to play with the New York Philharmonic under Josef Stransky (Saint-Saëns *Concerto No. 4*, 31 Jan 1921), she was a fully developed concert pianist. However, she continued her studies with Alberto Jonas in New York until at least 1925 and appeared again with the New York Philharmonic in the 1925–6, 1929–30, and 1932–3 seasons. She began her first major European tour in 1927, appearing with the Berlin Philharmonic, the Vienna Philharmonic, and the Amsterdam Concertgebouw orchestras, and then settling in London. A resident of England until World War II, she gave private recitals for Princesses Beatrice and Helena Victoria at Kensington Palace, appeared in public recital (eg, International Celebrity Series, 1936–7), and toured in Great Britain and Scandinavia. She returned to North America before the war and eventually settled in Montreal.

Long a friend and admirer of the Brazilian composer Heitor Villa-Lobos, she performed many of his works and commissioned his *Concerto No. 1*, giving the premiere (1946) in Rio de Janeiro under the composer's direction. She also gave the US premiere (Dallas SO under Antal Dorati) and the Canadian premiere (*CSM under Désiré Defauw) in 1947, repeating the work in 1951 with the CSM and in 1953 with the *TSO. Her other Canadian appearances – those made in the 1920s during North American tours – include recitals in 1928 for the Montreal *Ladies' Morning Musical Club and the *Women's Musical Club of Toronto and, later that same year, a performance with the TSO. She also performed with both the CSM in 1939 (Sir Ernest *MacMillan was guest conductor) and 1951 and the TSO in 1942 and appeared on CBC TV's *'Heure du concert.'

Ballon's playing was rhythmically secure and, at its best, full of excitement. If her concert career fell somewhat short of the promise shown by her prodigious childhood, it may have been that she was not under pressure to prove herself – a stimulus which most successful pianists experience. She became a person of considerable wealth and was popular in social and artistic circles. In later life she made important contributions to the Faculty of Music at *McGill U (where she established a piano scholarship in her own name in 1928) as a philanthropist, as a fund-raiser, and, for a short time, as a teacher. In the 1950s she initiated and sponsored a series of lectures by musicians of renown such as Gian-Carlo Menotti, Lotte Lehmann, and Deems Taylor. Epstein did a bust of Ballon. Her papers are deposited at *Dalhousie U.

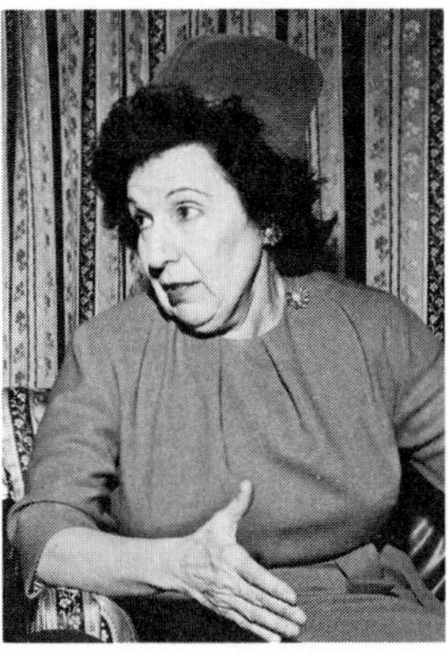

Ellen Ballon

DISCOGRAPHY

Chopin *Concerto No. 2*. London SO, Ansermet cond. (1950). Decca LX 3035
Piano Music by Villa-Lobos: solos. 1940s. Decca LX 3075 (includes works previously issued by Decca on 78s)
Piano Solos by Ellen Ballon: Bach/Siloti – Schubert – Liszt – Beethoven. (1951). Lon LPS 306
Villa-Lobos *Concerto No. 1*. O de la Suisse romande, Ansermet cond. (Ca 1949). Lon LL 77
– *Piano Music*: selections. Lon LS-531
– *Piano Music*: selections. Lon LD-9095
Ballon made a piano roll 'Were I a Bird' for Aeolian ca 1927.

WRITINGS

'Problems of the prodigy analyzed by pianist who was one,' *MCour*, 10 Jan 1945

BIBLIOGRAPHY

W.S. ' "Give us this day our daily Bach" is the prayer of Ellen Ballon, pianist,' *Musical America*, 30 May 1925
Bauer, John. 'Ellen Ballon,' *CRMA*, vol 2, Oct–Nov 1943
Hill, H. 'Prodigy's progress,' *SatN*, vol 68, 11 Apr 1953
Musical Red Book
Musiciennes de chez nous
Musiciens canadiens

EM

BANCROFT, (Henry) Hugh. Organist, choirmaster, composer, b Cleethorpes, Lincolnshire, England, 29 Feb 1904; FRCO 1925, B MUS (Durham) 1936, hon FRCCO 1976, hon D MUS (Cantuar) 1977. He studied with E.P. Guthrie and J.S. Robson in Grimsby before moving in 1929 to Canada, where he served 1929–38 as organist-choirmaster at St Matthew's Anglican Church, Winnipeg. At All Saints Church, Winnipeg, 1938–46 he developed a boys' and men's choir of national renown which specialized in the singing of chants. After two years, 1946–8, as organist-choirmaster at Christ Church Cathedral in Vancouver, conductor of the *Vancouver Bach Choir, and instructor at the British Columbia Institute of Music and Drama, he was organist-choirmaster 1948–53 at St Andrew's Cathedral in Sydney, Australia. There he performed several times with the Sydney SO under Sir Eugene Goossens and was a founding member of the Australian College of Organists. He returned to All Saints Church in Winnipeg 1953–7, went briefly to Christ Church Cathedral in Nassau, then in 1958 became organist-choirmaster at All Saints Cathedral, Edmonton. He designed the *Casavant organ installed there in 1960. He began

Hugh Bancroft

teaching theory and organ at the *U of Alberta in 1968.

In nearly 50 years of teaching, Bancroft's pupils have included Barry Anderson, Douglas *Bodle, Harold *Brown, Elwyn Davies, Donald *Hadfield, Clayton Lee, Hugh *McLean, Barbara *Pentland, Herbert *Sadler, and Winnifred *Sim. Bancroft broadcast frequently 1938–67 for the CBC, notably on the series 'Organ and Strings' in 1961, and was one of four organists from western Canada to appear at *Expo 67, where he premiered Violet *Archer's *Chorale Improvisation on 'O Worship the King.'* His compositions, mostly published by *Western Music and Novello, include anthems, motets, carols, some organ music, and a *Mass of St Thomas* (Waterloo 1974). Perhaps the best known is the Easter Carol 'Good Christians Now Let All Rejoice.' In 1938 his *Intermezzo* and *Marching Tune*, both for strings, were premiered in Winnipeg by the Minneapolis SO under Dimitri Mitropoulos. Two other large works, *Pavan* (1958) and *Concerto* (1967) for organ and strings, remained unpublished in 1980. On 18 Apr 1977 Bancroft became one of the few Canadians and one of 10 living musicians to hold the Lambeth Degree (hon D MUS) conferred by the Archbishop of Canterbury. Bancroft is a member of CAPAC. (JA)

The Band. Rock group, internationally popular in the late 1960s and the 1970s. First known as The Hawks, it evolved from a US group taken to Ontario in 1958 by Ronnie *Hawkins. The original members, except drummer Levon Helm (b Marvell, Ark, 26 May 1935), were replaced gradually by Ontario-born musicians – the guitarist Jamie Robbie Robertson (b Toronto 5 Jul 1943), the bass guitarist Rick Danko (b Simcoe, near Hamilton, 29 Dec 1942), the organist Garth Hudson (b London 2 Aug 1937), and the pianist Richard Manuel (b Stratford 3 Apr 1943). This personnel remained relatively stable for over 15 years, making the group – under its various names – one of the longest-lived in rock music. As The Hawks they worked with Hawkins during the early 1960s in Toronto and on tour, their expressive blues-rock influencing several other Canadian bands, including Luke and the Apostles, *Mandala, and *Sparrow.

Leaving Hawkins, the group continued to perform in southern Ontario and, as Levon and the Hawks or the Canadian Squires, recorded a few singles for Ware and Atco, including Robertson's song 'The Stones That I Throw (Will Free All Men),' a minor hit in Canada. They moved in 1965 to the USA, where they became Bob Dylan's back-up group, The Crackers, during his transition from folk music to rock – on tour 1965–6 in the USA, Europe, Australia, and Asia, and in seclusion 1966–8 at Woodstock, NY – an important period in the development of their music. While they continued to tour with Dylan until 1974, they released their first album, *Music From Big Pink*, in 1968 and made their 'debut' as The Band in 1969 at the Winterland Ballroom in San Francisco.

The Band's popularity grew through its subsequent LPs, although a series of singles also met with success: 'The Weight,' 'Up on Cripple Creek,' 'Rag Mama Rag,' 'Life Is a Carnival,' 'Don't Do It,' 'Ain't Got No Home,' and 'Georgia.' Other popular songs by The Band include 'We Can Talk About It Now,' 'The Night They Drove Old Dixie Down' (of which a version by Joan Baez was a hit single in 1971), 'Stage Fright,' and 'Chest Fever.' Based in Woodstock until 1974 and thereafter in Los Angeles, The Band performed throughout North America and in Europe and appeared at some of the largest rock festivals, including Woodstock (1969), the Isle of Wight (1970), and Watkins Glen, NY (1973). In Canada it performed at the Toronto Pop Festival (Varsity Stadium 1969), on two cross-country tours in 1970, at the 1976 *CNE, and in several concerts with Dylan. The Band gave its final concert ('The Last Waltz') 25 Nov 1976 at the Winterland Ballroom with Hawkins, Dylan, and many other rock stars, including Joni *Mitchell and Neil *Young. (A movie and a recording of the concert were released in 1978.) Thereafter The Band continued to record, though Helm and Danko completed solo LPs in 1977 and began to tour with groups of their own in 1978.

Perhaps as a result of the association with Hawkins and Dylan, The Band in its later period assumed an essentially US identity – one stronger than most US groups have cultivated – to the extent that it was the subject of a chapter in *Mystery Train* ('Images of America in Rock 'n' Roll') by the US critic Greil Marcus. It has drawn on the many US popular-music genres, creating 'a unique, consistent style – high wailing voices, odd chugging rhythms ... unusual instrumentation and unpredictable harmonies that had neither the prettiness nor the shrill sound most groups sought when they put their voices together' (Charlie Gillet *The Sound of the City*, New York 1972). All members sing – Danko, Helm, and Manuel are The Band's individual voices – and each has come to play several instruments, giving The Band a saxophonist (Hudson), a fiddler (Danko), two drummers (Helm, Manuel), and various guitarists. Though Robertson has been hailed as one of rock's finest players, such is The Band's constitution that it rarely is dominated by an individual. Robertson, The Band's chief songwriter, shares with Dylan a love for the narrative song form, often metaphoric and always full of images, sacred and profane. Some of The Band's songs (including 'We Can Talk about It Now' and 'Acadian Driftwood') reflect the experience of the Canadian expatriate.

DISCOGRAPHY

Music from Big Pink. (1968). Cap SKAO-2955
The Band. (1969). Cap STAO-132
Stage Fright. (1970). Cap SW-425
Cahoots. (1971). Cap SMAS-651
Rock of Ages. 1971–2. 2-Cap SAB-11045
Moondog Matinee. (1973). Cap SW-11214
Northern Lights, Southern Cross. (1975). Cap ST-11440
The Best of the Band. (1976). Cap ST-11553
Islands. (1977). Cap SW-11602
The Last Waltz. 1976 (1978). 3-Warner 3WS-3146P
Helm *Levon Helm and the RCO All Stars*. (1977). ABC 9022-1017
Danko *Rick Danko*. 1977. Arista AB 4141
With Dylan: *The Basement Tapes*. 1967 (1975). 2-Col C2-33682
– *Self-Portrait*. 1969. Col C2X30050
– *Planet Waves*. 1973. Asylum 1003
– *Before the Flood*. 1974. Asylum 201
Robertson also participated on Dylan's *Blonde on Blonde* (1965, Col C2S 841), with Danko on blues singer John Hammond's *I Can Tell* (1965, Atlantic 8152), and with Helm on Jesse *Winchester's first LP.
See also Discography for Ronnie Hawkins.

BIBLIOGRAPHY

Gladstone, H. "Robbie Robertson,' *Rolling Stone*, 48, 13 Dec 1969
Bender, William. "Down to Dixie and back,' *Time*, 12 Jan 1970
Marcus, Greil. 'The Band: pilgrim's progress,' *Mystery Train* (New York 1976)
Ward, Ed. 'The Band,' *The Rolling Stone Illustrated History of Rock & Roll* (New York 1976) MM

Bande de la Cité. Known also as the Musique de la Cité, Fanfare de la Cité, or Montreal City Band, this concert band was formed in Montreal about 1870. Little is known of its activities prior to the arrival of Ernest *Lavigne as director in 1876, when the ensemble won a grand prize at a competition in Philadelphia marking the centenary of US independence. In June 1878 at the Victoria Rink the band was featured at the Montreal Musical Jubilee, a competition in which some 20 Canadian, US, and English civilian and military bands participated. In 1879, or a little later, Lavigne and his musicians inaugurated free open-air concerts at the Viger Gardens and boat excursions 'under electric lights' on the St Lawrence river.

With the opening of *Sohmer Park in 1889, Lavigne made the Montreal City Band its official concert band. It gave two concerts daily during the summer. In 1890 it had 50 members, including Joseph *Gagnier and Alexandre *Laurendeau. In addition to its functions as the official band of the 65th regiment, it participated in such events as the arrival in Montreal of Emma *Albani in March 1883 and in three gala concerts at the Victoria rink in May 1890 in aid of Notre-Dame Hospital. Charles *Lavallée conducted the ensemble on several occasions. Its repertoire consisted of marches, overtures, quadrilles, and medleys and included Lavigne's own quadrille *Les Chevaux légers* (E. Lavigne 1882) and his *13th Regiment March* (ibid 1883). After Lavigne's death, in 1909, the ensemble survived briefly, but the players gradually dispersed into other playing activities. GP

Band festivals. Festive gatherings, usually for competition, of civic, military, and youth bands. Canada's first band festival probably was the one held in 1877 in Berlin (Kitchener), Ont. In June of the following year a Montreal competition attracted 19 entrants, including bands from distant Stratford and Waterloo, Ont. The *Waterloo Musical Society held a 16-band tournament in 1885, and other Ontario cities held festivals in later years. However, it was not until 1921 that an organized annual band competition on a national level was begun.

At that time, as part of the first Music Day at the *CNE, military bands played set pieces for adjudicators and were awarded prizes. This competition remained an integral part of the annual Toronto exhibition's music program. In later years brass or silver bands were admitted to the competition. The first annual *Waterloo Band Festival was held in 1932 in Waterloo, Ont, under the auspices of the Waterloo Musical Society, with Captain Charles *O'Neill as chief adjudicator. At this festival, which continued, except during the war years, until 1958, competition was extremely keen, with half-marks sometimes separating the first and second-place bands. In the 1970s numerous other band festivals flourished in Canada. The annual competition sponsored by the Alberta chapter of the *CBDA in different cities of the province offered three days of clinics and concerts and a competition. The CBDA in Ontario inaugurated an annual non-competition festival for elementary and high school bands in 1972. The Moose Jaw annual International Band Festival, begun in 1949, continued to feature competitions (including some for pipe bands), instrumental solos, band drill, and concert performances. In 1970 the City of Moncton, NB, sponsored its first band festival, a two-day competition for Maritime bands. In 1973 Truro, NS, was host to the first Nova Scotia Provincial Band Festival and Workshop, an entirely non-competition festival devoted to clinics, discussions of technique, rehearsals, and concerts. The *Canadian Stage Band Festival, an annual competition for bands from Canadian universities, community colleges, and high schools, began in 1973.

See also Bands; Competition festivals; Festivals. (JK, PW)

Bands. Large instrumental ensembles consisting mainly of brass, woodwind, and percussion instruments. Traditionally bands are associated with outdoor activities or ceremonies, eg, to accompany marching, add cheer to festivities, and contribute to the pomp of state occasions. The symphonic (concert) band is a modern refinement; the jazz and dance band are distant relations.

1 Exordium
2 Volunteer militia bands
3 Regular armed forces bands
4 Authorized marches
5 Police bands
6 Civilian bands
7 Highland pipe bands
8 School and youth bands

See also Canadian Forces School of Music; Dance bands; Salvation Army.

1 EXORDIUM. Military music under the French regime appears to have been limited to the sound of fifes, drums, and trumpets. When Pierre de Voyer d'Argenson, the governor of New France 1658–61, announced the intra missam on the main holy days, he had the fifes and tambours play, much to the annoyance of Bishop Laval, so Auguste Gosselin relates (*Vie de Mgr de Laval*, vol 1, Quebec 1890, p 220). In the Carignan-Salières regiment (which arrived in 1665, the first regular troops in Canada), each company had two tambours and one fife along with its 50 officers and soldiers. 'The drums placed at the head of each company were used to keep the marching in order, to quicken it, to slow it down, and to rally to the flag all the scattered men' (Régis Roy and Gérard Malchelosse, *Le Régiment de Carignan*, Montreal 1925). A few of the 'tambours' (drummers), Canada's earliest military musicians, are known by name: François du *Moussart, Gugnot dit Le Tambour, and Jean Casavan (sic), a trumpeter and an ancestor of the *Casavant organ builders. After three years of frontier warfare the regiment returned to France, but some 400 men stayed in Canada.

It was only under the British regime, in the late 18th century, that larger regimental bands were sent to Canada. For about 150 years bands remained the basis of instrumental ensemble performance in Canada, and band musicians (along with church organists) were the backbone of the musical profession. Their military employment provided a basic income that could be supplemented by teaching, playing church organs, dealing in musical merchandise, or perhaps repairing instruments. The predominance of bands over orchestras and chamber ensembles was due also to the fact that band instruments can be learned more quickly than string or keyboard instruments. Furthermore, the extrovert music and vigorous sound of bands, their suitability for rousing patriotic emotions, and their usefulness in enhancing non-musical events made them popular.

The activities of the British regimental bands in Canada are documented amply in the travel literature and the diaries of the late 18th and early 19th centuries. A few quotations will suffice to draw a picture. On 2 Mar 1792 Mrs Simcoe, the wife of the first lieutenant-governor of Upper Canada, 'gave a dance to forty people [at Quebec]. The Prince was present ... The Fusiliers ... are all musical and like dancing, and bestow as much money as other regiments usually spend in wine, in giving balls and concerts, which makes them very popular in this place where dancing is so favourite an amusement' (*The Diary of Mrs. John Graves Simcoe, 1791–1796*, ed J. Ross Robertson, Toronto 1911, p 79). Elsewhere Mrs Simcoe reveals just how much was spent on the band. On 21 Nov 1791 she attended a subscription concert in Quebec. 'Prince Edward's band of the 7th Fusiliers played, and some of the officers of the Fusiliers. The music was thought excellent. The band costs the Prince eight hundred [pounds] a year' (ibid, p 55). The program was mostly of Pleyel's music, including a symphony, a string quartet, and a concertante, and the *Gazette* (28 Nov 1791) reported that 'Beauty and Elegance partook of the most delightful Musical Fete ever remembered in this country, it being the first Winter Concert for the season. A more numerous band has not been seen together, nor a more numerous assemblage of ladies and gentlemen could not be well gathered together.' As in most such concerts, the band musicians were joined by civilian amateurs. Thus John Lambert, in his *Travels through Canada and the United States of North America in the Years 1806, 1807, & 1808* (London, 3rd ed, 1816) confirms that at the occasional private concert in Quebec 'the performers are some gentlemen of Quebec, assisted by a part of the regimental bands in the garrison.' Indeed, the Quebec subscription concerts of the 1790s, the tentative Montreal orchestras of the 1890s, and the orchestras of many medium-sized cities in the mid-20th century would not have been able to function had they been unable to 'borrow' band musicians.

Similar instances are documented in other cities. In Montreal the first battalion band of the 60th, or Royal American, Regiment played 'generally ... for a couple of hours' on summer evenings on a public promenade ('Canadian Letters ... 1792 and '93,' *Canadian Antiquarian and Numismatic Journal*, series 3, vol 9, 1912, p 106). Seventy years later Samuel Phillips Day reported from Montreal, 'The appearance of the troops on parade afforded much pleasure to the citizens; and when the military band performed on stated occasions in the Champ de Mars, the public was generally attracted thither' (*English America*, vol 1, London 1864, p 170).

Bands outside the British regiments came into existence about 1820; early examples are the band of the *Children of Peace in Hope (Sharon, Ont) and the *Musique Canadienne of Quebec City. Within a few decades most towns and cities had bands, often associated with local fire brigades, temperance societies, or volunteer militia. Later in the century bands were sponsored by municipalities, by such associations as the *St-Jean-Baptiste and the Orange societies, or by manufacturers for their employees, eg, the Taylor Safe Works Band of Toronto. About the turn of the century full-time Canadian military bands came into existence, and after that time the variety of ensembles grew: kiltie bands, Salvation Army bands, concert bands, broadcast and recording studio bands, Canadian Legion bands, football bands, cadet bands, and other varieties. Bands have been prominent among Canadian ambassadors of goodwill. Year after year Canadian bands have toured the USA, Europe, and other parts of the world, to participate in ceremonies, to enter contests, or to appear in festivals.

Bandmasters. The following are among the more prominent band directors, active in the periods shown, who are entered or mentioned (see Index) in *EMC*:

1800–50 J.-C. Brauneis I, Richard Coates, F.-H. Glackemeyer, Charles Sauvageau, Adam Schott, François Vézina, James Ziegler Sr

1850–1900 John Bayley, Peter Grossman, Edmond Hardy, Charles Lavallée, Ernest Lavigne, George R. Robinson, Joseph Vézina

1900–50 L.F. Addison, Giuseppe Agostini, Fred A. Bagley, Edwin Bélanger, S.J. Chamberlain, H.L. Clarke, H.C. Ford, J.-J. Gagnier, René Gagnier, J.-L. Gariépy, J.-J. Goulet, Richard B. Hayward, François J.-A. Héraly, E. Reginald Hinchey, Charles O'Neill, Paul Pratt, Émile Prévost, Léon Ringuet, William F. Robinson, Spurgeon Sheppard, Henry Slatter, John Slatter, Charles F. Thiele, Alfred E. Zealley

1950– William T. Atkins, B.G. Bogisch, Martin Boundy, Howard Cable, Morley Calvert, Leonard Camplin, Frank Connell, Arthur Delamont, Armand Ferland, A.C. Furey, Gérald Gagnier, J.M. Gayfer, Clifford Hunt, Ronald MacKay, F.M. McLeod, Jean-François Pierret, John Schoen, W. Bramwell Smith, Derek Stannard, Charles Villeneuve

Composers and arrangers. In addition to bandmasters themselves, other Canadian composers have written for band, especially Kenneth *Campbell, Claude *Champagne, Donald Coakley, Maurice *DeCelles, Gordon *Delamont, Robert *Fleming, Harry *Freedman, Graham *George, Sidney *Hodkinson, A.W. *Hughes, Lothar *Klein, L.-P. *Laurendeau, Calixa *Lavallée, William *McCauley, Paul *McIntyre, Jack *Sirulnikoff, Morris *Surdin, John *Weinzweig, Healey *Willan, and Gerhard *Wuensch.

Associations. Perhaps the earliest was the Assn des corps de musique, founded by Edmond Hardy in 1887. A.L. Robertson and Charles *Thiele were the main founders of the Ontario Amateur Bands' Assn in 1924 and the Canadian Bandmasters' Assn in 1931. The latter was succeeded in 1973 by the *Canadian Band Directors' Assn. The members of the Assn des fanfares amateurs de la province de Québec, founded in 1928, appear to have been from middle Quebec (the area between Montreal and Quebec City, not those cities themselves). In 1946 40 member bands representing 16 towns met in Montreal for a combined concert. J.-Arthur Vinet of Valleyfield was president of the association at that time. (See also Fédération des harmonies du Québec.) The International Military Music Society (formed in 1977) established a Canadian branch with over 100 members, branch headquarters in Toronto, a monthly newsletter, and quarterly meetings in Toronto. A Canadian band research project was set up by the society.

Festivals and competitions. Band festivals can be traced back to at least 1877 in Berlin (Kitchener), Ont, and the following year 19 military and civilian bands, from as far away as Stratford and Waterloo in the west and Quebec City in the east, competed in Montreal. The *Waterloo (Ont) *Musical Society in 1885 held a 16-band tournament, and this was followed by others in Ontario.

Later competitions included those begun at the *CNE in Toronto in 1921 and the *Waterloo Band Festival, begun in 1932. See also Band festivals.

2 VOLUNTEER MILITIA BANDS. Bands attached to reserve military units and made up completely of spare-time musicians. The growth of Canadian volunteer militia bands reflects the growth of the country's reserve forces. The Militia Act of 1855, which set up a volunteer force of up to 5000, is considered the foundation of the modern Canadian armed forces. The volunteer militia had a strength of 43,500 by 1869, and the last British regular units were withdrawn in 1871 (except for naval stations in Halifax and Esquimalt, BC), the same year the first Canadian regular units were formed.

Prior to Confederation military music was provided by British army regimental bands garrisoned in Canadian towns. These bands achieved immense popularity through their appearances in concerts and parades. When the British regiments and their bands returned to England and were replaced by the Canadian volunteer militia a void was created in band music because of the difficulty in obtaining qualified musicians and bandmasters. Fortunately some remained in Canada and became active in training and organizing militia bands. Of the many ensembles formed during the next 100 years, only a few examples can be named here. The first enlisted band in Canada was that of the Independent Artillery Company of the militia in Hamilton, Ont, under the bandmaster Peter Grossman in 1856. In 1886 Grossman also formed the 13th Battalion Band, which later became known as the *Royal Hamilton Light Infantry Band. By 1869 there were some 46 bands in the Canadian militia. A contemporary inspection report reveals the number of musicians and comments on their proficiency, eg: '29th Battalion Band: A fair band of 11 musicians; 45th Battalion Band: One of the best bands in the district, 21 performers; 65th Battalion Band: Brass band, 15 musicians, just organized.'

Canadian bands had a part in military action before World War I. From the time of the Fenian Raids in the late 1860s comes this account of the militia leaving to defend their homes: 'The Volunteers of Peel [county, Ont] had been called out to help fight the Fenian invasion. The fife and drum struck up the tune of "Tramp, Tramp, Tramp, the boys are marching," the men began to cheer and sing and the train pulled out of Toronto and as we feared, toward the front' (William P. Bull, *From Brock to Currie*, Toronto 1935). During the Northwest (Riel) Rebellion 'the brass band [90th Regiment, Winnipeg], particularly during the last few months of the campaign, improved wonderfully and was the pride and joy of the force' (Ernest J. Chambers, *A Regimental History of The 90th Regiment Winnipeg Rifles*, np, 1906?). One of Canada's oldest and most famous bands, the band of the *Queen's Own Rifles, was formed in 1862 in Toronto. Another early militia band was that of the *Royal Regiment of Canada.

Among the volunteer militia bands associated with the outstanding 19th-century Quebec bandmaster Joseph *Vézina were those of the 9th Battalion Quebec Rifles, which he led 1869–79, and the band of the 'B' Battery of the Royal Canadian Artillery, which he led 1879–1912 (see *Musical Canada*, Feb 1932). The *Governor General's Foot Guards Band of Ottawa was established in 1872 and continued to function through the two world wars and successive reorganizations of the post-war militia.

The Band of the 19th St Catharines (Ont) Regiment was formed at the turn of the century under Lieut William Peel and later became the Lincoln and Welland Band. In 1964 it performed at Bergen-Op-Zoom in the ceremonies marking the 20th anniversary of the liberation of Holland. During the centennial celebrations in 1967 the band toured northern Ontario. In 1979 in St Catharines' Montebello Park under the direction of Chief Warrant Officer Wilfred E. Higgins it marked its 81st year of park concerts.

	ca 1866	ca 1896	ca 1910	ca 1915	ca 1925	ca 1976
Picc	1	1	1	1	1	1
Fl		1	2		2	1
E-flat cl		2	2		1	
Ob		1	1		1	1
Bn		1	2		1	1
B-flat cl	4	10	10	3	12	8
Alto cl			1		1	2
Bass cl		1	1		1	1
Alto sax		1	1	1	2	2
Ten sax		1	1	1	1	1
Bar sax			1		1	1
Sop sax			1			
B-flat cornet	6	6	8	7	5	
E-flat cornet	1					
B-flat tpt		2	2	1	2	5
B-flat flhn	1		1			
E-flat hn (natural hn)	3			3		
E-flat hn (valved)		4	4	2		
F-hn (french hn)					3	3
Trb	2	4	4	2	2	2
Bass trb	1	1	1	1	1	1
Euphonium		1	2	1	1	1
Bar hn	2	2	2	3	1	
Bass (tuba)	2	3	4	1	3	2
Bass drum	1	1	1	1	1	1
Side drum	1	1	2	3	1	1
Timpani		1	1		1	

Instrumentation of volunteer militia bands

Outstanding volunteer militia bands in Winnipeg have been the Royal Winnipeg Rifles, formed in 1883 and still active (1980), and the 106th Winnipeg Light Infantry Band, organized in 1912. During World War I the bandmaster Thomas William James took the latter to England, where it merged with the 10th Battalion Band of the Canadian Expeditionary Force. It became the first Canadian band to serve on French soil.

The regimental band of the *48th Highlanders of Canada was formed in Toronto in the fall of 1892 under John Griffin and achieved fame under Capt John *Slatter, its director 1896–1946. The band of Hamilton's 91st Highlanders was formed by Harry Stares in 1903. The regiment changed its name in 1904 to the 91st Regiment Canadian Highlanders, and in 1920 it became the Argyll and Sutherland Highlanders of Canada. The band was active in the 1920s and 1930s. Another prominent ensemble was the *Canadian Grenadier Guards Band under Capt J.-J. *Gagnier, which numbered as many as 60 performers during the 1920s and 1930s. It was disbanded in 1970.

At the beginning of World War I the Dept of Militia and Defence made no provision for regimental bands, but many militia units formed thrir own on an unofficial basis. In 1914 the establishment of every Canadian Expeditionary Force battalion was increased optionally by one bandmaster and 24 bandsmen. Many militia units were fortunate in securing the services of civilian bands enlisted as groups, eg, the 157th Battalion Band of Orillia, Ont. This type of patriotism was not confined to the Dominion; in Newfoundland almost the entire Ayr Burg Band joined the Newfoundland Regiment under its bandmaster, L.L. Worthington. At the military site of Camp Borden, Ont, in August 1916, 28 bands were present among over 40,000 soldiers. At that time the first evening tattoo ceremony took place in Camp Borden.

Following World War I the Westminster (later Royal Westminster) Regiment Band came into being. Under Sgt Harry Moss it became important in the musical life of New Westminster, BC. The band appeared before George VI and Queen Elizabeth during their visit in 1939, has given summer concerts in the Queen's Park bandshell, and has played at numerous openings of the British Columbia Legislature and at the Peace Arch ceremonies in Blaine, Wash. The director in 1976 was Sgt Michael Grier. Other noted bands of the 1920–39 period included the 1st British Columbia Regiment Band in Vancouver (Lieut C.J. Cornfield), and the London (Ont) Fusiliers (later no. 4 Royal Canadian Regiment Band).

At the outbreak of World War II militia units were not authorized to enlist their bands for overseas service. However by 1940 it was decided to recruit musicians for training centres across Canada for the purpose of forming bands. Lieut A.L. Streeter was appointed music director for reinforcement units in England.

After the war a reorganization of militia bands was begun, and by 1951 106 30-piece military bands had been authorized. In 1980 authorization extended to 8 naval reserve bands, 3 air reserve bands, and 32 militia bands, all employed in unit parades and at formal dinners, in community concerts, and in a variety of musical support duties. In 1976 the Governor General's Foot Guards Band (Ottawa) and the Royal Regiment of Canada Band (Toronto) appeared in Philadelphia as a contribution to the US bicentennial celebrations. The Montreal Garrison band under Capt G. Lebrun was created in May 1972 from several former bands, including the Régiment de Maisonneuve and the Fusiliers Mont-Royal.

The table above, which was compiled by Jack Kopstein, indicates the number of instruments shown in photographs of volunteer militia bands at intervals from 1866 to 1976. Some of the instruments used in the early bands are entered under modern substitutes: eg, E-flat sax horns under Alto saxophones, B-flat sax horns under Tenor saxophones, and Sarrusophones under Bass (tuba).

DISCOGRAPHY

Centennial Salute. Lincoln and Welland Regimental Band, W.E. Higgins cond. Private recording

15th Field Artillery Regiment Band. Capt P.M. Erwin cond. Private recording

Toronto Signals Trumpet Band. 1974. Private recording

3 REGULAR ARMED FORCES BANDS. The first regular armed forces bands were formed in Canada in 1899. Their main purpose has been to provide music for military or public functions. Prior to the unification of the Canadian forces in 1968, 17 regular military bands of the navy, army, and air force were authorized. After unification they were reorganized into nine larger bands with a total personnel of over 300.

Army bands. The first full-time army band was that of the Royal Canadian Garrison Artillery formed in 1899 at Quebec Citadel with Joseph *Vézina as bandmaster. It was led later by Charles *O'Neill. The Royal Canadian Horse Artillery Band was organized in 1905 in Kingston, Ont, with Maj Alfred Light as its leader. The first unit to receive authorization for a full-time band was the Royal Canadian Regiment. The band was formed in 1900 in Halifax by the British bandmaster Michael Ryan, was officially recognized in 1905, and took part in the coronation ceremonies for George V in 1911 and in the dedication of the Cross of Sacrifice at Washington, DC, in 1927. Lieut L.K. Harrison was appointed music director in 1924 and Lieut John Proderick in 1940. The *Princess Patricia's Canadian Light Infantry Band was established in 1919, when the regiment became a permanent force unit. The band was recruited by Capt Thomas William James in Toronto and later moved to Winnipeg. In 1922 the newly organized French-Canadian Regiment, the *Royal 22nd (called the Van Doos because of its French name, Royal Vingt-deuxième) received authorization to establish a military band, and Capt Charles O'Neill became its conductor.

After the outbreak of World War II nine bands were authorized for fighting units overseas and in Canada. Lieut A.L. Streeter, formerly of the Princess Patricia's Canadian Light Infantry Band, was given the task of organizing military bands for the Canadian army. John *Slatter was supervisor of army bands at Camp Borden, Ont. In 1942 there were 136 authorized active force bands in Canada and 69 overseas. The authorized band personnel numbered 5535. However, not all bands were operating or were up to strength. In 1944 10 full-time bands were maintained overseas, and 33 full-time bands and a nucleus of permanent bandsmen in spare-time bands were employed in Canada. In March 1947 all active or regular force bands were discontinued, and three bands were reconstituted – those of the Royal Canadian Horse Artillery (stationed in Manitoba, first at Camp Shilo, then in Winnipeg), the Royal Canadian Regiment, and the Van Doos. In 1950 the Princess Patricia's Canadian Light Infantry Band was re-established. The Royal Canadian Regiment Band was reorganized in 1947 in London, Ont, under Warrant Officer William Armstrong. Capt Joseph Purcell was appointed music director in 1953 and Maj Derek *Stannard in 1963. The latter instituted the very popular 'Interlude for Music' concert series in Ontario high schools. With the 1968 unification of the forces the band was augmented, and its 65 players represented Canada in Paris at the 50th anniversary of the signing of the 1918 Armistic. In 1969 Capt John Collins became music director, and a year later the band moved from London, Ont, to Camp Gagetown, NB. It has performed in schools and public concerts across New Brunswick.

When the Korean war, coupled with the demands of NATO, brought about a great expansion of the army, full-time military bands were increased in size, and several new bands were authorized for the active force. They included the following (with year of authorization and name of first music director; rank given is not necessarily that held at the time):

1951 The Canadian Guards Band, Camp Borden, Ont, later Petawawa, Ont / Capt James *Gayfer
1952 The Royal Canadian Corps of Signals Band, Kingston, Ont / Capt B. Lyons
1952 The Royal Canadian Artillery Band (Coastal), Halifax, NS / Capt E.R. Wragg
1953 The Royal Canadian Engineers Band, Vedder Crossing, BC / Maj A. Brown
1955 Royal Canadian Dragoons Band, Camp Borden, Ont / Capt E. Spooner
1955 Royal Highland Regiment of Canada (Black Watch) Band, Halifax, NS / Lieut D. Start
1956 Royal Canadian Ordnance Corps Band, Montreal / Lieut G. *Gagnier
1956 Lord Strathcona Horse (Royal Canadians) Band, Calgary / Capt F.N. *McLeod

After the 1968 unification four army bands kept their identities: the Royal Canadian Regiment, the Princess Patricia's Canadian Light Infantry Band in Calgary, the Royal 22nd Band in Quebec City, and the Royal Canadian Artillery Band in Montreal. The Royal Canadian Artillery Band evolved from the Black Watch Band, which had been disbanded in 1968. Officially recognized in 1969, the band appeared regularly under Maj Charles Villeneuve at Man and His World, Dominion Square, and the *PDA and toured Europe and the Middle East. Capt Onil Leblanc succeeded Villeneuve in 1978. (See also Campbell Free Band Concerts.) The Royal Canadian Corps of Signals Band in Kingston, conducted by Capt Maurice Ziska, became known first as the Air Transport Command Band and later as the Vimy Band. It has performed as a ceremonial band and a symphonic concert band and has appeared in major concert halls of the world, including the Concertgebouw in Amsterdam.

Navy bands. Prior to World War II bands in the Royal Canadian Navy were voluntary and part-time. In 1939 a permanent force navy band was recruited in Toronto under the direction of Lieut Alfred E. *Zealley, who had been music director for the RCN during World War I. This band moved to HMCS Stadacona naval land base in Halifax, NS, and proved so successful that in 1940 a second naval band was approved for the base at Esquimalt, BC, under the direction of Lieut H.G. Cuthbert. By the end of the war 14 naval bands had been formed. In their place, late in 1945, naval bands were authorized for HMCS Stadacona at Halifax and HMCS Naden at Esquimalt, and Lieut S. Sunderland and Lieut-Cdr Cuthbert were appointed to recruit the two bands. The Naden band gave several performances during the British Columbia centennial celebrations in 1958 and has appeared at Grey Cup celebrations when these have been held in Vancouver.

Two additional bands were formed later, one at the naval air station HMCS Shearwater, at Shearwater, BC, and another at HMCS Cornwallis, at Cornwallis, NS, the new entry training base. The bandsmen were trained at the Royal Canadian Navy School of Music in HMCS Naden (see Canadian Forces School of Music), Esquimalt. Following unification in 1968 only two navy bands remained, the Canadian Forces Naden Band (then at Victoria, BC) and the Canadian Forces Stadacona Band at Halifax under Maj J.F. McGuire and later under Maj B.G. *Bogisch and Capt George L. Morrison. The Stadacona band absorbed the Royal Canadian Artillery Band and members of the HMCS Cornwallis Band. The 40-member band has participated in the International Festival of Military Music in Maps, Belgium, in Canada Day celebrations in Brunssum, Holland, in 1972, and in the NATO festival in Stuttgart in 1974. In 1973 the band toured in Australia, New Zealand, and Samoa, and in 1976 it performed in the USSR. In Victoria the Naden Band performs the traditional Sunset Ceremony at the Legislative Buildings. In 1975 Capt A.C. *Furey assumed direction.

Air force bands. An Air Force Band was formed at Camp Borden under Frank Tucker in 1929. During World War II several Royal Canadian Air Force bands were created from volunteer ensembles and from the ranks of professional musicians. The largest was the Central Band of the RCAF, established in 1940 and maintained at Ottawa under Flying Officer E.A. Kirkwood. Other bands included the Tactical Air Command Band, under Flight Lieut Carl Friberg, which served in Gander, Nfld, Montreal, and Edmonton. The first contingent of air force musicians – the RCAF Overseas Headquarters Band – arrived in England in 1942 under the direction of Sqn Ldr Martin *Boundy. It was followed shortly afterwards by the No. 6 Bomber Group Band under Warrant Officer Clifford *Hunt and the Bournemouth band directed by Flight Sergt Vowden. An extremely popular dance orchestra, the Streamliners, drawn from the headquarters band, appeared throughout England.

The cessation of hostilities in 1945 brought about a reduction in personnel in air force bands, but the Central Band of the RCAF continued to flourish. The RCAF Tactical Air Command Band was known briefly as the Northwest Air Command Band and was stationed at Winnipeg in 1946. In 1947 it moved to Air Force Headquarters in Edmonton and reverted to the old name. In 1946 the Training Command Band was organized by Flight Lieut Clifford Hunt in Toronto. It was renamed the Air Transport Command Band in 1949 while a new Training Command Band was organized in Winnipeg. By 1964 only the Central Band of the RCAF in Ottawa and the Training Command Band in Winnipeg remained in service. After the unification of the armed services in 1968 the Training Command Band was joined by members of the Royal Canadian Horse Artillery band in Winnipeg, and in 1975 it was renamed the Air Command Band (director, Capt Terence Barnes).

The Central Band of the RCAF in Ottawa was renamed the National Band of the Canadian Armed Forces in 1968 and the Central Band of the Canadian Forces in 1970. On frequent tours of Europe the band has appeared at the Bern International Music Festival and at the NATO Music Festivals in 1968 and 1969. In Canada the band has appeared at the *Manitoba Centennial Concert Hall and the *NAC under its music director, Derek Stannard. The Central Band traditionally has played each summer on Parliament Hill for the changing of the guard.

Ceremonies. Canadian regular force bands have travelled extensively throughout the world, appearing in concerts, parades, and tattoos, often before Canadian service personnel stationed abroad. In 1962 six bands performed at the World's Fair in Seattle, Wash, for a massed band tattoo. During Canada's centennial year (1967) several bands played an active role in the 147 performances of the Canadian Armed Forces Tattoo in 40 cities across Canada.

DISCOGRAPHY

Air Transport Command Band 50. Westmount Records WSTM 7321
The Band of / La Fanfare du Royal Canadian Ordnance Corps Salutes the Canadian Armed Forces / Salut les Forces Armées Canadiennes. Cam CAS 2565
The Band of Her Majesty's Canadian Ship 'Discovery.' Victor Crewe cond. Private recording
Canadian Centennial Celebrations. Lon TW 91407
Canadian Forces Tattoo. Dom LP 1357
The Canadian Tattoo. Hartley Records HRS 555
The Canadian Tattoo. Centennial CST 6050
The Central Band of the Canadian Forces *The Canadian Forces Presents The Central Band.* Marta Sound (unnumbered)
– *Martial Music of Canada*: vol 1 *Les Français*, Lon SW-99558. vol 2 *The British*, Lon SW-99559. vol 3 *Canada 1867*, Lon SW-99560.
– *Showstoppers for Band.* Marc Production MP-26
The Guns. Royal Canadian Artillery Band, Maj C.A. Villeneuve cond. Private recording
The National Band of the Canadian Forces. Cap ST 6334
The Royal Canadian Regiment. Lon SW 99544
The Royal Canadian Signals Band in Concert. J-Mar J-6104
The Royal Military College Pipes and Drums, Brass and Chorus. D.M. Carrigan, N.G. Jackson conds. Private recording

A Salute to the RCR. Wonderland RCR-A/RCRB
The Stadacona Band of the Maritime Command. Audat 477-4013
The Training Command Band on Parade and In Concert. Century 21 TCB-0015
See also Discographies for 2 / Volunteer militia bands (above); 7 / Highland pipe bands (below); 48th Highlanders of Canada; Princess Patricia's Canadian Light Infantry Band; Royal 22nd Regiment Band. See also Canadian Grenadier Guards Band; Royal Regiment of Canada.

BIBLIOGRAPHY

Madden, John R. 'The History of Bands in the Canadian Army,' unpubl report no. 47, historical section, Army Headquarters, 6 Feb 1952
'Canadian Armed Forces Tattoo: Canadian music on parade,' *CanComp*, 18, May 1967
McGuire, Frank R. 'Bands in the Canadian army,' *The Instrumentalist*, Feb 1971
Flohil, Richard. 'This military band moves in some new directions,' *CanComp*, 62, Sep 1971

FILMOGRAPHY
Tattoo 67 (NFB 1967)

4 AUTHORIZED MARCHES. The following list indicates the marches associated with particular regiments, units, bases, formations, or other groups of the Canadian forces.

Commands
Air Command *RCAF March Past*
Canadian Forces Training Systems *Century of Progress*
Communications Command *Communications*
Maritime Command *Heart of Oak*
Mobile Command *Celer paratus callidus*
Northern Region *Canada North*

Colleges
Royal Military College of Canada *Precision*
Royal Roads Military College *Standard of St George*; slow march *Goin' Home*
Collège militaire royal de Saint-Jean *La marche du Collège militaire de Saint-Jean*; slow march *La Gaillarde*
Military and civilian academic staff of Canadian Military Colleges 'March of the Peers' from *Iolanthe*

Branches
Air Operations Branch *RCAF March Past*
Armoured Branch *My Boy Willie*
Artillery Branch *British Grenadiers; Royal Artillery Slow March*
Chaplain Branch *Onward Christian Soldiers*
Communications and Electronics Branch *The Mercury March*
Dental Branch *March Past of the Royal Canadian Dental Corps*
Land Ordnance Engineering Branch *REME Corps March Past*
Logistics Branch *March of the Logistics Branch*
Medical Branch and the Canadian Forces Medical Branch *The Farmer's Boy*
Military Engineering Branch *Wings*
Naval Operations Branch *Heart of Oak*
Security Branch *Thunderbird*

Miscellaneous
Canadian Airborne Regiment 'CA-NA-DA'
1 Combat Group *Sons of the Brave*
5th Groupement de combat *Allons-y*
1st Canadian Signal Regiment *Corps March of the Royal Canadian Corps of Signals*
Service Battalions *Duty Above All*
Canadian Forces Leadership Academy *Our Challenge*
Canadian Forces Officer Candidate School *Ut duces sint*
CFB Gagetown Technical Services *With Equal Pace*
CFB Montreal *Servir*
Royal Canadian Army Cadets *Cadet*

Land regiments and units
Royal Canadian Dragoons *Monsieur Beaucaire; Light of Foot*
Lord Strathcona's Horse (Royal Canadians) *Soldiers of the Queen*
8th Canadian Hussars (Princess Louise's) *The Galloping 8th Hussars*
12th Régiment blindé du Canada *Marianne s'en va-t-au moulin*
Governor General's Horse Guards *Men of Harlech*
Elgin Regiment (RCAC) *I'm Ninety-Five*
Ontario Regiment (RCAC) *John Peel*
The Queen's York Rangers (lst American Regiment) (RCAC) *Braganza*
Sherbrooke Hussars *Regimental March of the Sherbrooke Hussars*
1st Hussars *Bonnie Dundee*
Prince Edward Island Regiment (RCAC) *Old Solomon Levi*
Royal Canadian Hussars (Montreal) *Men of Harlech; St Patrick's Day*
British Columbia Regiment (Duke of Connaught's Own) (RCAC) *I'm Ninety-Five*
South Alberta Light Horse *A Southerly Wind and a Cloudy Sky*
Saskatchewan Dragoons *Punjaub*
King's Own Calgary Regiment (RCAC) *Colonel Bogey*
British Columbia Dragoons *Fare Ye Well Inniskilling*
Fort Garry Horse (Militia) *Abanico; St Patrick's Day*
Régiment de Hull *La Marche de la victoire*
Windsor Regiment *My Boy Willie*
Lorne Scots (Peel, Dufferin and Halton Regiment) *The Campbells Are Coming*
Brockville Rifles *Bonnie Dundee*
Lanark and Renfrew Scottish Regiment *The Highland Laddie*
Stormont, Dundas and Glengarry Highlanders *Bonnie Dundee*
Régiment de la Chaudière *Sambre et Meuse*
Fusiliers Mont-Royal *The Jockey of York*
Princess Louise Fusiliers *British Grenadiers*
Royal New Brunswick Regiment *A Hundred Pipers; The Old North Shore*
West Nova Scotia Regiment *God Bless the Prince of Wales*
Nova Scotia Highlanders *The Sweet Maid of Glendaruel*
Régiment de Maisonneuve *Sambre et Meuse*
Cameron Highlanders of Ottawa *The Piobaireachd of Donald Dhu; March of the Cameron Men*
Royal Winnipeg Rifles *Old Solomon Levi; Keel Row*
Essex and Kent Scottish *The Highland Laddie; A Hundred Pipers*
48th Highlanders of Canada *The Highland Laddie*
Régiment du Saguenay *Le Régiment du Saguenay*
Algonquin Regiment *We Lead, Others Follow*
Argyll and Sutherland Highlanders of Canada (Princess Louise's) *The Campbells Are Coming*
Lake Superior Scottish Regiment *The Highland Laddie*
North Saskatchewan Regiment *The Jockey of York*
Regina Rifle Regiment *Lutzow's Wild Hunt*
Rocky Mountain Rangers *The Meeting of the Waters*
Royal Edmonton Regiment (4th Battalion, Princess Patricia's Canadian Light Infantry) *Bonnie Dundee*
Queen's Own Cameron Highlanders of Canada *The Piobaireachd of Donald Dhu*
Royal Westminster Regiment *Warwickshire Lads; The Maple Leaf For Ever*
Calgary Highlanders *The Highland Laddie; Blue Bonnets over the Border*
Seaforth Highlanders of Canada *The Piobaireachd of Donald Dhu*
Canadian Scottish Regiment (Princess Mary's) *Blue Bonnets over the Border*
Royal Montreal Regiment *Ça ira*
Irish Regiment of Canada (Sudbury) *Garry Owen*
Toronto Scottish Regiment *Blue Bonnets over the Border*
Royal Newfoundland Regiment *The Banks of Newfoundland*

DISCOGRAPHY
Canadian Regimental Marches. Chotem cond. 1958. RCI 158
Marches of the Canadian Armed Forces: Traditional and Contemporary. Princess Patricia's Canadian Light Infantry Band. (1978). Westmount WSTM 7813

5 POLICE BANDS. The Royal Canadian Mounted Police was organized in 1873 as the North West Mounted Police to provide protection for the settlers in Manitoba, the areas further west, and the Yukon. In 1876 its first band was formed at Swan River, Man. The instruments were purchased by the 20 players themselves and shipped from Winnipeg by dog-team. The band made its debut 24 May, Queen Victoria's birthday, under the direction of Sergt-Maj Thomas Horatio Lake. This volunteer band flourished intermittently until the outbreak of the South African War in 1899. Approximately seven other bands existed during the first 30 years of the force's history. The band at Fort Qu'appelle under Sergt-Maj Fred A. Bagley performed at a notable event in 1881, the signing of the treaty between the federal government and the Indians of the Blackfoot confederacy, the Assiniboine, and other tribes, on the banks of the Bow River near Calgary. In 1886 at Calgary Bagley founded the North West Mounted Police 'E' Division band, which achieved excellence. In addition to its regular concerts in Calgary it also played on special occasions at the Banff Springs Hotel, which was opened in 1888. The 'E' Division band dispersed on Bagley's retirement from the force in 1899. Both the Calgary and the Regina station police bands participated in one of the most glittering local events of that era, the grand ball held in 1889 on the occasion of Governor-General Stanley's visit to the Territories. As the West grew, so did the duties and responsibilities of the force. The North West Mounted Police became the Royal North West Mounted Police in 1904, and this in turn was merged into a new national police force, the Royal Canadian Mounted Police, in 1920. The earliest attempt to establish an official RCMP band was made in 1934. However, owing to the Depression, approval for a part-time band was granted only in 1938.

The director of this band, located first in Regina and later in Ottawa, was Staff-Sergt J.T. Brown (formerly of the *Governor General's Foot Guards Band of Ottawa). One of the band's first performances occurred 25 May 1939 during the visit of George VI and Queen Elizabeth to Canada. The band also appeared in New York at the 1939 World's Fair. Throughout the war years it played in many concerts and parades across Canada in connection with the Victory Loan program and the war effort; in 1944 it was on duty during the Quebec Conference. In 1949 Sergt E.J. Lydall (its leader on its Prairie tour the previous year) replaced the retiring Inspector Brown as music director. A second part-time RCMP band was organized in 1949 in Regina under Cpl C.C. Bryson. Both units continued to be active in their respective areas, and they merged for special occasions.

In 1951 the Ottawa band played an important role at performances during the visit of Princess Elizabeth and Prince Philip. In 1953 Coronation ceremonies in Canada's capital were co-ordinated by Inspector Lydall, and the massed bands were led by the RCMP Ottawa Band on Parliament Hill in a dazzling display of pomp and pageantry.

The RCMP bands flourished throughout the 1950s, but operation on a part-time basis was difficult. Government approval of a full-time band was granted in December 1958. This band, with headquarters in Ottawa, began extensive tours of Canada and the Territories. In 1961 it covered over 11,000 km by land, appearing in cities from Dawson Creek, BC, through the Prairie provinces, to Thunder Bay, Ont. The following year the band toured the Maritimes and Quebec and introduced a popular series of concerts and retreat ceremonies at the Supreme Court building in Ottawa during the summer months. The band made two CBC TV appearances in 1964 and took part in the International Band Festival in Moose Jaw, Sask, in 1965. Canada's centennial year, 1967, was a busy one, as the band joined the RCMP Musical Ride and toured Canada. The majority of Musical Ride performances (which originated in the 1880s) have used recorded music or employed local bands when the troupe is on tour in Europe or North America. In 1967 Superintendant E.J. Lydall retired, and Inspector W. Bramwell *Smith was appointed supervisor of music for the force and served as music director of the band until 1975. After a successful tour of the USA in 1968 the band was featured in a CBC TV Christmas special. In 1970 it made a memorable series of appearances at Expo 70, Osaka. In the course of nine days it was heard live by over half-a-million people and was viewed on TV by millions of Japanese and Canadians. In 1968 the band began an annual winter concert series at the NAC. In 1973, with the RCMP Centennial Review, it appeared in some 20 cities across Canada. During 1974 it appeared at the *Ontario Place Forum, Toronto. The band has maintained a heavy performance schedule in support of its role of musical ambassador of Canada's national police force. Kenneth Moore was appointed music director for the RCMP 1 Dec 1975. See also Mounties.

Municipal police bands. Many municipal police forces also have maintained their own bands and some continued to do so in 1980. A notable example, the Toronto Police Band, was founded in 1926 by Richard *Hayward and later conducted by Herbert *Barrow.

DISCOGRAPHY

Dynamic Sound. RCMP Band, W. Bramwell Smith cond. 1972. Poly 2917 008

BIBLIOGRAPHY

RCMP Band brochure

FILMOGRAPHY

The Musical Ride (NFB 1955)

Precision (NFB 1966)

6 CIVILIAN BANDS. The documentation of early Canadian civilian bands was incomplete at this writing, and the choice of examples is therefore unavoidably haphazard.

The *Children of Peace at Hope (renamed Sharon), Ont, formed a band in 1820; Toronto had an amateur band by 1824; Hamilton, by 1837; Fredericton, Guelph, and Niagara-on-the-Lake, in the 1840s. A former regimental band musician, Jean-Chrysostome *Brauneis I, organized a civilian band at Quebec City in 1831, but on his death in 1832 its activities ceased until Charles *Sauvageau revived it in 1836 with some 15 players. It was known thenceforth as the *Musique Canadienne. A German musician named Kästner organized the band of the Antigonish, NS, Musical Society in 1844. By Confederation nearly all towns in eastern Canada had one or several bands; town band, temperance band, fire brigade band, and musical society band were typical. The band movement began to spread westward to the newly settled Prairies and British Columbia. Winnipeg had a city band in 1874; Victoria, in 1878; and in the mid-1880s even the small settlement of Whitewood, Sask, had one, composed of a dozen French aristocrats who had immigrated in the hope of living the life of noblemen. Calgary's first civilian band was formed in 1885 and, sponsored by the Odd Fellows, existed until 1890, when its instruments, music, and uniforms were presented to the newly established Calgary Fire Brigade Band.

The Orangeville Band, 1878

One remarkable phenomenon of cross-cultural fertilization was the establishment of Indian brass bands among the Tsimshian and other west coast Indians of British Columbia under the influence of Anglican and Roman Catholic missionaries. The bands were particularly numerous in the Prince Rupert area, and several have survived into the late 20th century. The first is said to have been formed by the pioneer lay missionary William Duncan at the Tsimshian settlement of Metlakatla in 1879. Duncan picked up a set of instruments in San Francisco and pressed a German bandmaster from Victoria into service as an instructor. During the 1880s and 1890s several dozen bands were formed, and British bandmasters provided much of the training. Twelve bands participated at the 1905 Dominion Exposition in New Westminster, coming from such points as Lillooet, Squamish, Bella Coola, Port Simpson, and Kitimat. The repertoire included marches, waltzes, operetta tunes, and popular songs. In 1910 Sir Wilfrid Laurier was greeted in Prince Rupert to the sound of 'The Maple Leaf For Ever' and 'Rule Britannia,' and a year later seven bands competed in the presence of the Duke of Connaught at a band competition there. Indian brass bands frequently were invited to play in parades, at fairs and religious celebrations, or on ceremonial occasions. A somewhat similar encouragement of instrumental music on the Atlantic coast, where a small brass band survived at Nain, Labrador, in the 1970s, is discussed under *Moravian Missions in Labrador.

Edmond *Hardy founded the Montreal Concert Band in 1874 and was its conductor for over 50 years. It performed at the Foreign Exhibition in Boston in 1883. The Montmorency band of St-Gregoire-de-Montmorency, Que, was founded earlier and celebrated its 100th anniversary in 1972. In 1876 Ernest *Lavigne created the popular *Bande de la Cité, which became a principal attraction in the Montreal parks during the 1880s, and later specifically at *Sohmer Park. The Philharmonic Society Concert Band of St-Hyacinthe was directed 1880–1930 by Léon *Ringuet. In Ontario the Belleville Band in 1877 imported a 'quartet' of saxophones (soprano, alto, tenor, bass) from a manufacturer in Paris. By 1882 the *Waterloo Musical Society Band was appearing regularly in the parks of Kitchener-Waterloo and the surrounding area. The Forest Excelsior band of Forest, Ont, and the Brampton Mechanics Band, both founded in 1884, have had long histories. The latter was renamed the Brampton Citizens' Band in 1903, and the summer concerts initiated then were still being given in 1980. W. Emerson Dowens succeeded the first bandmaster, J.M. Crawford, in 1903, and under his direction the band won one third, one second, and four first awards at the *CNE's Ontario Amateur Bands Assn competitions between 1922 and 1927. In 1927 the band changed its name to the Peel and Dufferin Regimental Band under the direction of Capt J.J. Buckle, but later the old name was resumed. Capt Buckle retired in 1945. Between 1945 and 1947 temporary bandmasters carried on, and in 1947 Capt William T. *Atkins assumed the leadership of the band, serving for over 30 years. Under his direction the band by 1976 had gained 28 first awards at national and provincial music festivals. The Newmarket (Ont) Citizens' Band, established in the 1870s, continued to flourish in 1980.

By the 1880s many manufacturing firms had company bands. Examples are the Taylor Safe Works Band (1888) and the *Heintzman Company Band (1890), both directed by Herbert L. *Clarke in Toronto. Clarke was associated later with the *Anglo-Canadian Leather Company Band. The Calgary Citizens' Band was established in 1903 by A.L. Augade. He was succeeded as conductor in 1907 by Fred A. Bagley, who served until 1920. In 1921 the band became the official band of the Benevolent Protective Order of Elks and, as the Elks' Concert Band, was conducted 1921–4 by Bagley and subsequently by George Eltherington, H.C. Ford (a member of the Sousa Band 1923–7), Jack Bullough, and William McVeigh. The band ceased to function during World War II.

One of the first Canadian bands to gain international renown was the Belleville (Ont) Kilties Band, organized in Toronto in 1902 to assume some of the touring commitments which the *48th Highlanders Band could not fulfil. Its first bandmasters were Thomas P.J. Power and William F. Robinson. At least half of this new group, of 40 to 50 musicians had belonged to the 48th Highlanders Band. The band, supplemented by four dancers and singers, performed in the summer in parks and at fairs and during the winter on the vaudeville circuit. It travelled through 20 countries. Highlights abroad included an appearance in August 1904 at the Louisiana Purchase Centennial Exposition in St Louis and two command performances 1904–5 before Edward VII of England. The band ceased being a professional group in 1911. From 1918 to 1920 and again in 1923 it was under the direction of Alfred E. *Zealley. It disbanded in 1933.

A new type of band about the turn of the century was the studio band, organized for the specific purpose of recording (see *Roll Back the Years*). The Canadian Military Band and the Canadian Dominion Band were examples. When civilian bandsmen joined the armed forces in World War I, many of their bands were unable to continue. Some, however, as mentioned in section 2 of this article, joined as complete units. The end of that war saw the dawning of a golden age of bands in Canada. In 1918 the Nanaimo (British Columbia)

Nelson's Cornet Band, members of the Tsimshian tribe, Port Simpson, BC, 1900

Concert Band performed at the city's first Armistice service. This became an annual function of the band and continued to be in 1980. The main catalyst of the concert band movement was the organization of the CNE national band contest in 1921. Bands from almost every community in Canada competed, and as a result the Ontario Amateur Bands' Assn (1924–41) and the Canadian Bandmasters' Assn (1931, see Canadian Band Directors' Assn) were created. The first women's band was formed in 1925 in Kitchener by Lieut George *Ziegler and numbered 94 musicians at its zenith. With the formation of the *Waterloo Band Festival in 1932 that city became a focus of band activity. The old Waterloo Musical Society band flourished under Charles *Thiele. In 1927 the community of Chatham, Ont, formed the Chatham Kiltie Band, led by Sydney Chamberlain for over 20 years. In 1922 the railway porters of Winnipeg organized a band which became an instant success. Another prominent Winnipeg group of the period was the Legion Band (1926–ca 1955), led by Albert Henry Yetman. In Toronto Walter *Murdoch directed the Imperial Concert Band. Richard *Hayward directed the Toronto Concert Band, a 50-member ensemble that performed on radio, at *Massey Hall, and with the *Toronto Mendelssohn Choir until 1939. A *Toronto Symphony Band was formed in 1915 and flourished until 1959. The Philharmonie De La Salle, founded in Trois-Rivières, gave its first performance 6 Sep 1920. By 1945 the band had 70 members, and its conductors had included Ivanhoe Trudel, Antonin Corbeil, Giuseppe *Agostini, and J.-Antonio *Thompson. Philippe Filion was the conductor in 1945 of the 50-member Union musicale de Shawinigan Falls, which had been founded in 1924. This band also functioned as a symphony orchestra by adding string players. Arvida's band, established in 1930, was conducted after 1937 by J.-W. Boily and numbered 42 by 1947. Other civilian bands were active (ca 1946) in Grand-Mère (Fanfare du Sacré-Coeur, 120 members) and in Sherbrooke (L'Harmonie de Sherbrooke, 74 members). One of the finest bands in western Canada was the Vancouver Parks Board Band, formed in 1925 by Lieut C.J. Cornfield.

When their members were called up for service in World War II, many civilian bands were forced to disperse, as they had been in similar circumstances 25 years before, and it was not until 1946 that they flourished again. A few examples of post-war bands follow.

The Calgary Concert Band was organized in 1947 by W.A. Leggett, and from 1950 to the early 1960s it served also as the band of No. 403 Reserve Squadron RCAF. Capt F.M. *McLeod was the conductor in the 1970s. In 1948 the Burlington (Ont) Musical Society was organized, with three concert bands: senior, training, and junior. Phil Murphy in 1948 formed the Windsor (Ont) Federation of Musicians Concert Band, which performed in Jackson Park and later became the 'Music Under the Stars' concert band sponsored by the Ford Motor Co of Canada. This same concert series was perpetuated in London, Ont, by Phil Murphy Jr in the 1960s. On 29 Apr 1951 under the direction of Martin *Boundy, from the Victoria Bandshell in London, Ont, the first of a series of band concerts was presented over the London radio station CFPL and the Dominion network of the CBC. A new type of organization appeared in Winnipeg in 1955 when the Winnipeg Concert Band was organized as a co-operative and a limited company under the direction of Capt Albert Henry Yetman. The Fred Willett concert band, organized in 1961, performed for many years at the Brock Memorial in Queenston Park near Niagara Falls, Ont. The Howard *Cable Concert Band of Toronto was organized in the late 1950s and gave many broadcast performances heard in Canada and the USA between 1960 and 1968.

See also articles in *EMC* on individual Canadian cities and towns.

DISCOGRAPHY

The Concert Band of Cobourg. R.G. White cond. Private, cassette

BIBLIOGRAPHY

Coutu, Maurice, 'L'union musicale de Shawinigan,' *P-T*, 887, Jun 1945

Gaucher, Albert. 'La philharmonie De La Salle des Trois-Rivières,' *P-T*, 888, Jul 1945

Joly, Antoni. 'La fanfare d'Arvida,' *P-T*, 910, May 1947

Hewlett, Mrs A.E.M. 'France on the prairies,' *The Beaver*, Mar 1954

Drew, Leslie A. 'Indian concert bands,' *The Beaver*, Summer 1971

FILMOGRAPHY

Goodbye Sousa (NFB 1973)

7 HIGHLAND PIPE BANDS. As a musical unit, a pipe band usually consists of a pipe corps and a drum corps, the latter comprising side drums, a bass drum, and tenors (the last optional). The earliest organized pipe bands in Canada were probably those of Highland regiments.

The first Scottish regiments to see service in Canada (mainly in Quebec and Nova Scotia) were Montgomery's Highlanders (1759), the 42nd Highlanders or Black Watch (1759), and the Fraser Highlanders (1761). This was before the days of pipe bands in the modern sense, but the Fraser Highlanders at least had 30 pipers and drummers. (This musical unit was revived in 1967 for the Canadian centennial.) In the later 18th century Highland regiments began to be raised in Canada itself, the earliest being the Royal Highland Emigrants (1775; later called the 84th Highlanders) and the Argyle, or 74th, Highlanders (1778). These, together with the Highland companies of various Canadian regiments and Highland regiments from Scotland stationed in Canada, helped to keep bagpipe playing alive, as they did in Scotland itself, at a time when private playing and the wearing of the kilt were proscribed.

Most Canadian Highland regiments were volunteer reserve units (militia), of which the oldest (5th Highland Regiment of Hamilton) was founded in 1816. Of these, the most influential musically came to be the *48th Highlanders of Canada, founded in 1891. Other prominent military pipe bands in Canada in the late 19th and 20th centuries have been those of the Seaforth Highlanders (Vancouver), the Canadian Scottish Regiment (Victoria), the Canadian Black Watch (Gagetown, NB, a regular unit), the Argyll and Sutherland Highlanders (Hamilton, Ont), the Calgary Highlanders, the Highland Light Infantry (Galt, Ont), the Cameron Highlanders (Ottawa), and the Black Watch Royal Highlands Regiment (Montreal). Many other reserve units have had or still have pipe bands. In 1916 Piper James Richardson, of the Canadian Scottish (16th Battalion Canadian Expeditionary Force), was awarded the Victoria Cross posthumously for his gallantry at Regina Trench.

After the 1950s the pipe band scene in Canada was transformed by the development of civilian competition bands, and standards of playing improved dramatically. There also have been new developments in drumming, in which George Pryde (Pipes and Drums of Powell River, BC) and John Kirkwood Sr (d 1972; Clan MacFarlane Pipe Band, St Catharines, Ont) have played an important part and have influenced bands throughout the world. The City of Toronto Pipe Band (founded 1950) and Clan MacFarlane (founded 1958) dominated Canadian competitions during the 1960s and early 1970s, but their supremacy has been challenged increasingly. The leading civilian bands in the 1970s in Ontario were Macnish Distillery (formerly St Thomas Police Band or St Thomas Legion Band, known however as 'the St Thomas,' founded there 1921), Clan MacFarlane, Guelph, Windsor, Erskine (Hamilton), Toronto and District Caledonia Society, and General Motors (Oshawa). In British Columbia, leading bands are Triumph Street (Vancouver, founded 1971) and the City of Victoria (founded 1972).

For competition, pipe bands are classified by the provincial pipe band societies into four grades, all those mentioned in the previous paragraph being grade 1 (highest proficiency) bands. Most of these bands are heard by the general public only in the competitions at annual Highland Games, of which there are many in each province. Canadian bands also compete at games in Scotland and the USA. Some of the Canadian Highland Games are quite old; but the most important annual pipe band competitions have been established in Ontario, at Maxville (the largest in North America), Ottawa, and Toronto. The last-mentioned was begun 1972 as part of the Scottish World Festival at the *CNE, and many of the best bands in Scotland have flown over for it. On these occasions the international panel of judges several times has placed Canadian bands in the prize list, and in 1976 the grade 1 competition was won by Guelph. As long ago as 1966 the City of Toronto Pipe Band was placed 5th in the World Pipe Band Championship at Inverness (and 2nd in piping); it is fair to say that by 1980 all the grade 1 Canadian pipe bands were on a level with the best in Scotland.

See also Bagpipes, Great Highland; Scotland.

DISCOGRAPHY

MILITARY PIPE BANDS

The Black Watch R.H.R. of Canada. Lon TW 91353

The Black Watch: War Pipe and Plaid. Lon SW 99407

Canadian Centennial Celebration (Black Watch). Lon SW 99432

The Pipes and Drums of the Toronto Scottish Regiment. Arc 657

See also Discography for 48th Highlanders of Canada.

CIVILIAN PIPE BANDS

Clan MacFarlane Pipe Band, vol 1. World Records WRC 192

The Pipes and Drums of Powell River. Aragon ALP 125

Play the Sweet Music: City of Victoria Pipe Band. Iona 77-018

The Sounds of Macnish Distillery Pipe Band. World Records WRC 210

The Triumph Street Pipe Band. Ensemble Productions EPN 228

Vancouver Ladies' Pipe Band. Ara-Mac Records AML-2

A band at Nanton, Alta, ca 1915

BIBLIOGRAPHY
Malcolm, C.A. *The Piper in Peace and War* (London 1927)
MacKinnon, Pipe Major Stephen. 'The bagpipe in Canada,' *Canadian Geographical J*, Apr 1932
Grant, George. *The New Highland Military Discipline of 1757*, Historical Arms Series no. 10 (Ottawa 1967)
Doig, John. 'The music factory: Macnish marches to a different drummer,' *The Canadian*, 9 Jun 1979

FILMOGRAPHY
Pipers and A' (NFB 1963)

8 SCHOOL AND YOUTH BANDS. Bands came into favour in Canadian schools at the beginning of the 20th century. Wind and percussion instruments and colourful uniforms exerted a strong attraction on teenagers, and educators, parents, and civic leaders recognized very early the worth of the band as an adjunct to school games, dances, and other events. They also saw in it not only an attractive music-teaching device but an excellent means of building co-operative and co-ordinated behaviour and stimulating school spirit. Many Canadian school bands have undertaken tours in North America and Europe, winning awards and recognition.

For the first half of the 20th century, school bands functioned mostly as extracurricular performing organizations, and they often were dependent for members upon students who had lessons with private teachers or training from the *Salvation Army or other community organizations with a strong interest in music. Several youth bands were formed outside the school systems in the early part of the century. One or two may be mentioned as examples. Capt John *Slatter organized a Toronto Cadet Band, and his brother, Henry Arthur Slatter, tutored and directed the Boys' Band of New Westminster ca 1919–28. Arthur *Delamont formed the *Kitsilano Boys' Band of Vancouver in 1928. The Winnipeg Sea Cadet Band under William Cramp toured Ontario in 1941 as part of a Navy League recruiting program.

After World War II the youth band movement took a new lease on life. A nationwide groundswell of interest in instrumental instruction in schools was reflected by the degree program in school music established at the *U of Toronto in 1946. Techniques for group instruction introduced into the program by Robert *Rosevear did much to refine and systematize youth band teaching methods generally. Educators in the other provinces also showed a new concern with instrumental training and applied new ingenuities to the solving of its problems. The efforts of these educators were opportune, coming as they did at a time when there was a growing demand for ensembles in which young musicians could participate; hundreds of such ensembles were formed.

Detailed and balanced coverage of this vast scene is impossible in the context of this general article. By 1979 approximately 8000 Quebec young people were members of youth bands grouped in the province's *Fédération des associations musicales du Québec. Norman Draper's *Bands by the Bow, A History of Band Music in Calgary* (Calgary 1975) mentions 15 high-school bands, 100 junior-high-school bands, and an All Girl Drum and Bugle Corps flourishing in Calgary in the mid-1970s. The periodical *Tripper* in September 1979 listed well over 100 high-school and junior-high-school bands, from all parts of Canada, interested in making tours or exchange trips with other youth bands. Such figures can only indicate the great numbers of other such bands that existed in Canada at the beginning of the 1980s. Among summer camps for teen-age players may be mentioned 'Bandberg,' the *Waterloo Music Camp for Boys, established by Charles F. *Thiele at Bamberg, Ont, in 1946; and also the Salvation Army camps. In 1978 the *CBDA established the National Youth Band of Canada.

See also Barrie Central Collegiate Band; Canadian Stage Band Festival; School music.

DISCOGRAPHY
The National Youth Band of Canada '78 – Premier Performance. M. Boundy cond. 1978. Private recording

FILMOGRAPHY
Boy Meets Band (NFB 1961)

GENERAL BIBLIOGRAPHY
Logan, John Daniel. *Canada's Champion Regimental Band: A Critical Study of the Musicianship of the Band of the 85th Overseas Battalion, C.E.F., Nova Scotia Highlanders*, pamphlet (1916); held at U of Toronto, Ontario Archives
Zealley, Alfred E., and Hume, J. Ord. *Famous Bands of the British Empire* (London 1926)
Massicotte, E-Z. 'La musique militaire sous le régime français,' *BRH*, vol 39, Jul 1933
Hobday, Kathleen. 'Survey of the musical resources of the province of Ontario,' unpubl MA thesis, Toronto 1946
Berger, Kenneth. *Band Encyclopedia*, self-published, USA (1960)
Stewart, Charles H. *The Service of British Regiments in Canada and North America*, Dept of National Defence Library (1962)
Rosevear, Robert. 'Composing for concert band,' *CanComp*, 39, Apr 1969
Senior, Elinor. 'The British garrison in Montreal in the 1840's,' *J of the Society for Army Historical Research*, vol 52, Summer 1972
Pille, John M. *Catalogue of Band Music by Canadian Composers*, typescript (Lennoxville Que, 1973)
Draper, Norman. *Bands by the Bow* (Calgary 1975)
PERIODICALS
Canadian Bandsman and Musician, monthly, published by R.S. Williams Jun 1913–19; renamed *The Canadian Bandsman and Orchestral Journal* 1919–24. Absorbed by *Musical Canada* in 1924
Canadian Bandsman, Canadian Band Directors 1942–9; *Canadian Bandmaster* 1949–67
CBDA Journal

HK, JK, PW

Banff Centre School of Fine Arts (Banff School of Fine Arts, 1933–71). One of four divisions of the Banff Centre for Continuing Education and Canada's oldest extant major summer school of the arts, located on Tunnel Mountain in Banff National Park, Alberta. It began in August 1933 as an experimental theatre school, with a grant of $30,000 over three years from the Carnegie Foundation of New York to the *U of Alberta in support of adult education fine arts programs. Some of that sum was used by the extension department of the university (then under the direction of A.E. Corbett) to establish a training centre at Banff for community theatre leaders. Creative writing and painting were added to the curriculum in 1935, and a master class in piano under Viggo *Kihl followed in 1936.

Donald Cameron – b Devonport, England, 6 Mar 1903; B SC (Alberta) 1930, M SC (Alberta) 1934, LLD (British Columbia) 1959; appointed to the Senate in 1955 – was the driving force behind the efforts to establish a permanent school. As director 1936–56 of the extension department he developed the Banff SFA into a centre for continuing education which he hoped would become the Salzburg of North America. The first permanent building was erected in 1947. Cameron was director of the Banff SFA until 1969. He was succeeded by acting director Donald F. Becker and in 1970 by David S.R. Leighton.

The centre is financed by grants from the Alberta government, the *Canada Council, and foundations, by corporate and private donations, and by tuition fees. Stewardship of the school was transferred from the U of Alberta to the *U of Calgary in 1966; in 1978 a provincial act established the school as an autonomous body administered by its own council. In 1978, facilities included the 1000-seat Eric Harvie Theatre, the 250-seat Margaret Greenham Theatre, the Roubakine Auditorium, the Walter J. Phillips Art Gallery; studio, practice, and teaching facilities; and administrative and residential buildings. Annual auditions are held in major Canadian and US cities in February and March to select prospective students.

Music became an integral part of the program in 1936 and has remained so. Instruction in choral music was begun in 1937, initially under Glyndwr Jones of Calgary. Jacques Jolas of the Juilliard School joined the faculty as piano instructor in 1940 and was succeeded in 1941 by Max *Pirani, whose presence at the Banff SFA attracted an increasing number of music teachers and senior students in the next six years. Boris *Roubakine served 1957–73 as director of the piano department. Richard S. *Eaton, who joined the U of Alberta in 1947 to establish a music department, also became a choral instructor at the school. Clayton *Hare initiated a program in strings at about the same time. Oratorio performances employing the resources of the choral and instrumental divisions became regular end-of-term events. In 1949 Ernesto *Vinci initiated a voice (later voice and opera) department, and by 1951 an opera company was touring Alberta for 10 days after each term. The productions were combined efforts of the opera, orchestra, drama, and ballet divisions and included *The Barber of Seville, Madama Butterfly, Die Fledermaus, La Traviata, The Marriage of Figaro, Tosca, Falstaff, The Old Maid and the Thief, Gianni Schicchi*, and *The Abduction from the Seraglio*. The orchestra program developed rapidly after 1965 under Thomas *Rolston. In 1972 the School of Fine Arts, which had operated as a single unit for 40 years, became two units – the year-round Visual Arts program and the summer Performing Arts program (extended that year to 14 weeks). By 1979 the latter included studies in musical theatre, voice and opera, instrumental performance (piano, strings, brass, woodwinds, percussion, and classical guitar), chamber music, and jazz, and a chamber orchestra training program.

Many Canadians and many distinguished foreign musicians have taught at the school. In 1977, for example, the faculty included Kazuyoshi Akiyama, Pierrette *Alarie, Rose Bampton, Ada *Bronstein, George *Brough, Howard *Cable, the members of *Canadian Brass, Alirio Diaz, Lorand *Fenyves, Alexander *Gray, Marek *Jablonski, Claude *Kenneson, Thomas *Monohan, Phil *Nimmons, Marie-Thérèse *Paquin, William Primrose, Dodi *Protero, György Sebök, Léopold *Simoneau, Zoltán Székely, Gerald *Stanick, Henri Temianka, Tsuyoshi *Tsutsumi, Bernard *Turgeon, David *Zafer, and George *Zukerman.

The Banff Festival of the Arts, established in 1971 as an extension of the school, has offered performances by members of the faculty and has mounted teacher-student productions of operas and musicals, including Carlisle Floyd's *Susannah* in 1971; *Willan's **Deirdre* in 1972; *The Magic Flute* in 1973; *Don Pasquale* and Bob Merril's *Carnival* in 1975; *La Cenerentola*, Porter's *Kiss Me Kate*, and a workshop production of Copland's *The Tender Land* in 1976; *La Bohème* and Lerner and Loewe's *Gigi* in 1977; and *Così fan tutte*, *Archer's *Sganarelle*, and Lerner and Loewe's *Brigadoon* in 1978.

The Summer Showcase provides students and faculty with the opportunity to perform in recital on a regular basis. The Banff SFA was the subject of the NFB productions *Holiday at School* (1945) and *Campus in the Clouds* (1966); the latter title was used by Donald Cameron for his history of the school (Toronto 1956).

In 1978 the Banff Centre received formal approval in principle from the Alberta government to develop the music program into a year-round professional training conservatory. The first syllabus announcing the realization of this program was issued in the summer of 1979 under the title *Advanced Music Studies*. Courses in 1979–80 in strings, piano, chamber music, and composition were offered under a resident faculty of four – the violinists Thomas Rolston (director) and Zoltán Székely, the bassist Stuart Knussen, and the pianist Isobel Moore – and a distinguished visiting faculty of 19 solo performers or composers and three chamber groups, each scheduled to spend from three to eight days at the school.

BIBLIOGRAPHY

'Banff School of Fine Arts offers summer courses for musicians,' *CanComp*, 26, Feb 1968

Boyle, Harry J. 'The Banff School of Fine Arts ... "I've pleaded, begged and panhandled $11,000,000 to build ... this place," ' *Globe Magazine*, 17 Oct 1970

Edinborough, Arnold. 'The magic of Banff inspires excellence in its students,' *PfAC*, Summer 1975

Zwarun, Suzanne. 'The hills may come alive with the sound of music,' *Maclean's*, 11 Dec 1975

Edds, Jack. 'Music at Banff,' *OCan*, vol 6, May 1979

(GKG)

BANKS, Tommy (Thomas Benjamin). Pianist, conductor, arranger, composer, TV personality, b Calgary 17 Dec 1936. He studied piano as a child and began his career at 14 in the band of the jazz saxophonist Don *Thompson. Banks was music director 1954–8 of the Orion Musical Theatre in Edmonton and also led his own groups in performances in western Canada and the USA. He accompanied many pop performers 1960–8 as a pianist or orchestra conductor, rising to the forefront of pop music in Alberta and becoming a major force in western Canada. In 1967 he led his jazz quintet at *Expo 67 and produced and directed the revue *Klondike Follies*, starring Paul *Anka and others. In 1968 he became host, pianist, arranger, and conductor for 'The Tommy Banks Show,' a TV talk show seen 1968–71 on CBC TV in Edmonton, nationally 1971–4 on the CBC network, and briefly after 1974 in private syndications originating from CITV, Edmonton. Banks has been the co-ordinator (and occasional guest conductor) of *Edmonton SO pop programs featuring such performers as Vicki Carr, Aretha Franklin, Engelbert Humperdinck, and Tom Jones, filmed by CITV for syndication throughout North America. In 1979 Banks filled a similar role for a series starring the US singer Jack Jones with the *Hamilton Philharmonic Orchestra. Banks conducted the Edmonton SO in the premiere and recording of Rod McKuen's orchestral suite *Ballad of Distances* (1973, 2-Stanyon 2731).

Banks has been heard on the CBC's 'Jazz Radio-Canada' with his jazz quartet, with his big band, and occasionally as a host. With such soloists as P.J. *Perry (soprano and alto saxophones), Pete Thompson (tenor saxophone and flute), Earl Seymour (baritone saxophone), Bob Stroup (trombone), Rick Tait and Bob Tildesley (trumpet and flugelhorn), and the singer Clarence 'Big' Miller his band performed at the 1978 Montreux Jazz Festival in Switzerland; a double LP of its concert won the *Juno Award as jazz recording of 1978, thus establishing its reputation as one of the leading big bands in Canada. Banks has written or arranged music for the big band (other works have been contributed by Curt Watts), and composed the musical fantasies *The Lady That's Known as Kate* and *The Gift of the Magi* (heard on the CBC and subsequently performed again by the Edmonton and *Regina SOs), and the score for the CBC production of Pierre Berton's *Klondike* (see Klondike).

Through his company, Century II, Banks has written, and produced recordings of, many jingles, and has conducted orchestras for recordings by several pop artists. In 1972 he received the Alberta Achievement Award from the provincial government. In 1978 he assumed the chairmanship of the Alberta Foundation for the Performing Arts. Banks operates his own publishing company (Tommy Banks Music) and is an affiliate of PRO Canada. (RDM)

'The Banks of Newfoundland.' At least six different folk songs have this title, but the most widely known is an old Irish broadside ballad that gives a colourful description of the hardships of sailing across the north Atlantic in winter: 'Beware of the cold nor'westers on the banks of Newfoundland.' It was particularly popular on the sailing ships carrying emigrants from Britain to America during the 19th century, and was preserved by maritime singers in both Newfoundland and Nova Scotia. It is related to an earlier British ballad describing the sufferings of convicts transported to the penal colony of Van Diemen's Land (after 1853, Tasmania). It was published first in Canada in W. Roy Mackenzie's *Ballads and Sea Songs from Nova Scotia* and is also in the *Ballads and Sea Songs of Newfoundland* (Cambridge, Mass 1933) by E.B. Greenleaf and G.Y. Mansfield. Alan *Mills recorded it for Folkways (*Songs of the Maritimes*).

EF

BARBAN, Andreas. Pianist, teacher, b Leipzig 5 Feb 1914. He studied 1934–6 at the Leipzig Cons with Robert Teichmueller and Max Hochkofler and privately with G. Stieglitz, Tania Zunser-Ury, and Erich Liebermann-Rosswiese. He also studied theory with Wolfgang Fraenkel. After teaching piano 1939–47 in Shanghai, he moved in 1947 to St John's, Nfld. There he has been heard for many years in weekly radio recitals as soloist or as accompanist. He has given recitals with Joseph Berljawsky, Eileen Stanbury, Jack Glatzer, Lynn Channing, Elizabeth Benson *Guy, and others. An important figure in the development after 1952 of the festival movement in Newfoundland, Barban has served as adjudicator, adviser (preparing syllabi), and accompanist. He has taught music appreciation and piano privately and music appreciation 1960–1 at *Memorial U. His pupils include the pianists Karen Quinton (*Prix d'Europe 1972) and David Stone. He was conductor 1963–6 of the St John's SO. (HS)

Barbara Allen. Ballet in nine scenes by David Adams to music by Louis *Applebaum and based on the folksong and legend of the same name. It was premiered 26 Oct 1960 at the Palace Theatre in Hamilton, Ont, by the National Ballet of Canada (with George *Crum conducting and Angela Leigh as Barbara Allen) and was taken on tour during the 1960–1 season. The Revival Scene and Finale from *Barbara Allen* were recorded by the Toronto Philharmonia under Walter *Susskind (*Scored for Ballet*, Col MF 6763). An earlier ballet, *Dark of the Moon*, choreographed by Joey Harris to a previous draft of the Applebaum score, was premiered 15 Nov 1953 by the National Ballet (with Crum conducting and Celia Franca as Barbara Allen) at the Capitol Theatre in Halifax and was taken on tour during the 1953–4 and 1954–5 seasons. The CBC TV presentation of this earlier ballet – on 'Scope,' 24 Apr 1955 – used the title *Barbara Allen*, probably because *Dark of the Moon* infringed copyright.

BARBARIN, Lazare-Arsène. Choirmaster, teacher, b Marseilles 6 Nov 1812, d there 14 Mar 1875; LL L (Faculté d'Aix-en-Provence) 1833. He was a member of the illustrious Italian family Barberini and descended from the family of Pope Urban VIII. In 1838 he studied theology at the St-Sulpice seminary in Paris, and in 1841 he was ordained a priest of St-Sulpice. He arrived in Montreal 24 Jun 1842 and soon was teaching senior courses in rhetoric and philosophy at the Collège de Montréal. Later he taught Holy Scripture at the Grand séminaire. He called upon the 11-year-old Calixa *Lavallée to accompany funeral services and predicted a brilliant future for the young musician. Barbarin served 1854–61 as the first official choirmaster of Notre-Dame Church in Montreal. He resumed those duties 1866–74, after a leave of some five years during which J.-J. *Perrault substituted for him. He filled the same function at St-Joseph Church and adapted liturgical texts to such works as Rossini's *Moses in Egypt* and Félicien David's *Le Désert*. He had sung with David at the choir school in the archdiocese of Aix-en-Provence. Barbarin and Perrault collaborated on a four-part harmonization of the plainsong *Messe des morts*.

While not himself an accomplished musician, Barbarin commanded attention through his strong personality; he was known familiarly as Messire Barbarin. In addition to his qualities as a singer he could play several string instruments. After praising his knowledge of literature and his prodigious memory Auguste Achintre wrote in *L'Opinion publique*: 'Remembering the choirmaster, we marvel afresh at the keen intellect, the astonishing cerebral facility, which could make sport of the difficulties of art. Composition, harmony, fugue, sacred song and secular song, he was familiar with them all; and also with instruments, and the works of the masters' (15 Apr 1875). In the autumn of 1874, his health failing, Barbarin returned to his native city.

BIBLIOGRAPHY

'Feu Messire Barbarin,' *Canada musical*, vol 2, 1 Jun 1875
Blanchet, L.J.N. *Une Vie illustrée de Calixa Lavallée* (Montreal 1951) HP

BARBEAU, (Charles) **Marius**. Anthropologist, ethnologist, folklorist, b Ste-Marie-de-Beauce (later Ste-Marie), Que, 5 Mar 1883, d Ottawa 27 Feb 1969; BA (Laval) 1903, LL L (Laval) 1907, B SC (Oxford) 1910, Anthropologist diploma (Oxford) 1910, hon D LITT (Montreal) 1940, hon Fellow (Oriel College, Oxford) 1941, hon D LITT (Laval) 1952, hon D LITT (Oxford) 1953. He studied music as a child with his mother and took his classical studies at the Collège de Ste-Anne-de-la-Pocatière. After receiving a Rhodes Scholarship in 1907, he studied anthropology, archeology, and ethnology at Oriel College, Oxford (1907–10). He also took summer courses in Paris at the École des hautes études de la Sorbonne and at the École d'anthropologie. In Paris he met Marcel Mauss, who encouraged him to study Indian folklore, and Raoul and Marguerite d'Harcourt, who aroused his interest in the musical culture of early Indian civilizations.

On his return to Canada in 1911, Barbeau was hired as anthropologist and ethnologist to the Museum Branch of the Geological Survey of Canada (which in 1927 became the *National Museum). In the spring of 1911, on a Huron Indian reserve in Notre-Dame-de-Lorette, near Quebec, he began a series of recordings on Edison wax cylinders. During his three years of research with the Hurons he undertook, in 1912, an expedition that led him to the Thompson and Lillooet rivers, where he recorded some 60 songs of the Salish, a British Columbia tribe. During the course of another excursion, he visited (and grew interested in the mythology of) other tribes, among them the Iroquois and Wyandots. Through these encounters with the Indians he came across aspects of French folklore, and the mixture of French-Canadian and Indian tales stimulated his studies of French-Canadian folklore. His 1914 meeting with the US anthropologist Franz Boas encouraged him to pursue his researches in this vein.

In 1916 Barbeau set off on a recording expedition along the St Lawrence River, determined to refute the assumption that Ernest *Gagnon, in his *Chansons populaires du Canada* (Quebec 1865), had published all the traditional French songs there were to be found. In the counties of Charlevoix and Chicoutimi he gathered, in notation and recordings, more than 500 songs as well as several folk legends – enough material to prove his point. Barbeau later made several trips, travelling as far as the Rockies and the Pacific Coast with a few colleagues, among them Edward Sapir, É.-Z. *Massicotte, Adélard Lambert, and Ernest *MacMillan. Sapir and MacMillan taught him how to set down folk tunes in musical notation. After 1910 and throughout the 1920s, Evelyn Bolduc, Gustave Lanctot, Lambert, and Massicotte were inspired largely by Barbeau. With Massicotte Barbeau established the Soirées du bon vieux temps in 1919, held at the Bibliothèque St-Sulpice (BN du Q). François *Brassard, Luc *Lacourcière, and Joseph-Thomas Leblanc were his principal disciples in the 1930s.

In 1918 Barbeau became president of the American Folklore Society, of which he had been a member since 1911. He became co-editor of the *Journal of American Folklore* in 1916. That same year he was elected to membership in the Royal Society of Canada, and in 1933 he became president of

Marius Barbeau

its francophone section; in 1950 he was named a Fellow. In 1917 he reconstituted the Canadian Society of Folklore in two divisions, so as to serve more effectively the separate needs of the provinces of Quebec and Ontario in the collection and preservation of their individual traditions.

On three occasions – 1925, 1929, 1945 – Barbeau received the Prix David for his literary works. In 1937 he was named president of the National Consulting Committee for the Protection of Canadian Wildlife. By 1939 he was a member of the Washington Academy of Sciences, the Canadian Authors Assn, and the Société des écrivains canadiens. He gave his first series of courses in human geography at the *U of Ottawa in 1942. In 1945 he joined the faculty of letters at *Laval U, where in 1942 he had begun lecturing during the summer. The *Archives de folklore at Laval U had been established in 1944.) He retired from the National Museum in 1948 but kept up his private research; for many more years he devoted himself to the transcription and publication of the folk tunes and texts he had collected during his expeditions. He served 1956–63 as president of the *CFMS, which he also had helped to found. In 1946 he received the Parizeau Medal at the 14th congress of the Association canadienne-française pour l'avancement des sciences; in 1962, the *Canada Council medal; in 1965, the *U of Alberta National Award; and in 1968, the Diplôme d'honneur from the *CCA. He was made a Companion of the *Order of Canada in 1967. In 1963, on the French network of the CBC, he presented his reminiscences and findings in a series of eight programs called 'Le Rossignol y chante' for the 'Images du Canada' series. His interests were wide-ranging and covered not only music, folklore, and ethnology but also art in general – sculpture, architecture, embroidery, culinary arts, and painting. He also was interested in the origin and history of the west-coast Indians as revealed in their totem poles. In linguistics he revealed the relationship between the Huron and Iroquois languages. He contributed articles to many periodicals, among them *La Revue canadienne*, *La Revue populaire*, *Scientific American*, the *Bulletin of the Geographical Society of Philadelphia*, *Le Canada français*, *Culture*, *La Revue de l'Université d'Ottawa*, *Journal of American Folklore*, *Saturday Night*, the *Beaver*, and the *Canadian Forum*.

'A tireless seeker, he was the first to open up the field of scientific research in the realm of folklore' (Réginald Hamel et al, *Dictionnaire pratique des auteurs québécois*, Montreal 1976); that is, Barbeau was the first in Canada to document precisely the location and the date of collection and the singer's name for each song gathered; the first to transcribe the tunes in a precise manner and to comment on the structure, semantics, and prosody of the verse. He left 13,000 original texts and variants of Indian and French songs, 8000 with tunes. He transcribed in syllabic notation the lyrics of more than 3000 Indian songs and invented a system of notation for their music.

Considering that he was virtually self-taught, his ability to transcribe the music recorded on his cylinders and to sing Indian songs authentically was remarkable. Most of his archives can be found at the Salle Marius Barbeau, in the Canadian Centre for Folk Culture Studies, a division of the National Museum of Man in Bell's Corners, near Ottawa. A branch of the municipal library of Laval, Que, was named after Barbeau, and in 1969 the highest mountain in the Canadian Arctic was christened Barbeau peak. In 1971 Barbara *Cass-Beggs organized Les Amis de Marius Barbeau to perpetuate recognition of his work.

WRITINGS

'How the folksongs of French Canada were discovered,' *Canadian Geographical J*, vol 49, Aug 1954
See also Bibliographies for Christmas; Ethnomusicology; Folk music; Folk music, Franco-Canadian; Indians.

DISCOGRAPHY

My Life in Recording Canadian-Indian Folklore. 1957. Folk FG 3502

BIBLIOGRAPHY

Savard, Félix-Antoine. 'Marius Barbeau et le folklore,' *R de l'U Laval*, vol 1, Nov 1946
Cardin, Clarisse. 'Bio-bibliographie de Marius Barbeau,' *Archives de folklore*, vol 2, Montreal 1947
MacMillan, Ernest. 'Marius Barbeau – his work,' *Canadian Author and Bookman*, vol 37, Winter 1962
– 'Some reminiscences of Marius Barbeau,' *Mcan*, 18 Apr 1969
Luchaire, André. 'Le grand folkloriste canadien de XXe siècle: Marius Barbeau,' Montreal *La Presse*, 12 Apr 1969
Katz, Israel J. 'Marius Barbeau,' *J of the Society for Ethnomusicology*, vol 14, Jan 1970
Saint-Martin, Fernande. 'L'oeuvre de Marius Barbeau, nord- américain,' Montreal *Le Devoir*, 21 Dec 1974
(DM)

BARBINI, Ernesto. Conductor, b Venice 15 Jul 1907; baccalaureate piano and organ (Benedetto Marcello Cons) 1925, master of organ 1927, baccalaureate theory 1928, master of piano 1929, and master of composition 1930 (all at Cesare Pollini Cons), hon D LITT (York) 1980. His studies 1913–26 with Gino Tagliapietra (piano) and Oreste Ravanello (organ) at the Benedetto Marcello Cons, Venice, and 1926–30 with Ravanello at the Cesare Pollini Cons, Padua, led to a 1934 conducting debut in Boito's *Mefistofele* at La Fenice. He joined the staff of the Chicago Opera School in 1938 and toured South America in 1940. After service in the US Army in World War II and engagements with the Cincinnati Civic Opera in 1945 and the Chicago Civic Opera in 1946, he served 1946–52 as an assistant conductor at the *Metropolitan Opera. He toured Canada in 1949 with a cast from the Met and made his formal Met debut conducting *Cavalleria Rusticana* in 1952. Recommended by Edward *Johnson, he was invited to join the *RCMT, where he founded the Collegium Musicum in 1953 and was coach and conductor 1953–69 of the *Royal Cons Opera School; his appointment continued when in 1969 the school became a department of the *U of Toronto Faculty of Music and lasted until his retirement in 1975.

Opera School productions under Barbini's direction have included Prokofiev's *The Love of Three Oranges* (1965), Stravinsky's *Oedipus Rex* (1967), Debussy's *Pelléas et Mélisande* (1968), and Verdi's *Falstaff* (1973). In 1954 at Edward Johnson's instigation he established the Guelph Civic Symphony and Chorale and the Barbini String Orchestra, which performed intermittently in Toronto until 1965. For the *COC he has conducted *Madama Butterfly* (1953, 1956, 1962, 1967), *La Traviata* (1955, 1964, 1966, 1970), *Tosca* (1957, 1961, 1968, 1972), *La Forza del Destino* (1959, 1969), *Rigoletto* (1962, 1965, 1973), *Aida* (1963, 1964, 1968, 1972), *Turandot* (1965, 1969), *Macbeth* (1966, 1971), *The Barber of Seville* (1967, 1973), and *Faust* (1970, 1974). He has also conducted concerts by the *CBC SO (1958, 1959) for CBC radio, *Otello* (1962) and *Rigoletto* (1964) for CBC TV, *Messiah* (1964) with the *TSO and *Toronto Mendelssohn Choir, *Cavalleria Rusticana* (1964) with the *Edmonton Professional Opera, and Mercure's *Triptyque* with the Belgrade Philharmonic (1965). In 1975 he became music director of the *Manitoba Opera but continued his work with the COC. He is respected widely for his affectionate and idiomatic readings of the Italian repertoire and his memorable *Faust*.

DISCOGRAPHY

Bass Arias and Monologues: Verdi – Rimsky-Korsakov – Verykivsky – Fomenko. Canadian SO, Hoshuliak bass. 1975. Boot BMC 3005

Verdi *Aida*. Chor and Orch des Teatro dell'Opera, Rome. 1958. 3-Musical Masterpiece Society MMS-2157

BIBLIOGRAPHY

Graham, June. ' "Cav" and Tosca are red-letter operas for maestro Barbini,' *OpCan*, Sep–Oct 1961

'Maestro Ernesto Barbini,' *Crescendo*, Jan 1971

BARCLAY, Robert Lenard (b Basham, Leonard Edwin). Composer, writer, b Penticton, east of Vancouver, 2 Feb 1918, naturalized US 1951; ATCM 1941, d Fort Lauderdale, Fla, 11 Mar 1980. He studied in Vancouver (with Arthur *Benjamin) and Toronto and won two CPRS composition prizes (1938, 1939) before moving to the USA to study 1944–7 at the Juilliard School. There, under Bernard Wagenaar and Frederick Jacobi, he received what he considered to be his main musical education. Barclay's works from his Canadian years, 1938–51, (listed in *Catalogue of Canadian Composers*) are tonally oriented and include works for orchestra and for strings, and duos for violin and piano and for clarinet and piano. His *Set of Five* (1938) and *Sonatine* for piano (1947) were recorded by John *Newmark. His *Symphony in One Movement* (1950 Boosey & Hawkes – rental) had its European premiere in Baden-Baden over the Südwestfunk and has been performed in West Germany, Switzerland, and the USA. His works 1954–9 include three piano pieces, a violin-piano duo, and a pavan for harp and strings, all published by Barger and Barclay. His atonal *Variations for Orchestra* (1975) were premiered by the Indianapolis SO under Oleg Kavalenko at the 1976 Contemporary Music Festival at Indiana State U, where Barclay was artist-in-residence. Barclay was a contributor during the 1950s to *Music and Musicians* and *Records and Recordings*. He was a member of CAPAC. (BNSG)

BARCZA, (Joseph) Peter. Baritone, b Stockholm, of Hungarian parents, 23 Jun 1949, naturalized Canadian 1957; diploma, opera performance (Toronto) 1971. While a pupil of Howell *Glynne and Louis *Quilico, studying 1968–71 on scholarship at the Opera Dept of the *U of Toronto, he sang in several of the department's public productions. After his professional debut as Thomas in Schenk's *The Village Barber* at the 1970 *Guelph Spring Festival he studied in Florence (summer 1971) with Tito Gobbi, then sang supporting roles in the *COC's 1971 productions of *Madama Butterfly* and *Macbeth*. He won the 1971 Jean Chalmers Award as the most promising young member of the COC. In 1972 he sang Charles de la Tour in the premiere of Norman *Symonds' *The Spirit of Fundy*. Other COC roles have included Cascada in *The Merry Widow* in 1973, Valentin in *Faust* in 1974, Silvio in *I Pagliacci* in 1975, and Papageno in *The Magic Flute* in 1977. Barcza has sung with the *Manitoba Opera Assn, the *Southern Alberta Opera, and the *TS.

BARETTE, Yvon. Pianist, accountant, b Hull, Que, 1 Aug 1910. After taking private lessons 1917–20 he studied 1928–38 with Harry *Puddicombe at the Canadian Cons, Ottawa. Though he made his living as an accountant with the Hull School Board, he gave several solo recitals in Ottawa 1929–35, in particular for the *Morning Music Club. He also played, among other works, Grieg's *Piano Concerto* in 1935 with the La Salle Symphonic Ensemble of Ottawa, Dohnányi's *Variations on a Nursery Song* in 1939 with the Cercle philharmonique de Québec, and Liszt's *Concerto No. 1* in 1940 with the La Salle ensemble and in 1941 (its orchestral premiere in Quebec City) with the Cercle philharmonique. With a CBC Montreal orchestra under Jean-Marie *Beaudet he premiered and on 13 Feb 1949 recorded (RCI 2) Maurice *Blackburn's *Concertino* for piano and wind instruments. Barette also gave many private recitals 1931–5 at the residence of the governor-general, Lord Bessborough, at the French, US, and Argentinian embassies, and for the Société des conférences at the *U of Ottawa.

BIBLIOGRAPHY

Musiciens canadiens (DM)

BARFORD, Vernon (West). Organist, choirmaster, teacher, b Wellington College, Berkshire, England, 10 Sep 1876, d Edmonton 22 Apr 1963; Associate American Guild of Organists 1912, hon MA (Alberta) 1924, hon FCCO 1945. He began piano lessons at four and attended the choir school of Worcester Cathedral 1887–92. Having failed preliminary examinations for Oxford, he emigrated to Canada in 1895 to homestead in the Qu'Appelle district of Saskatchewan. He soon was engaged as organist at the pro-cathedral in Qu'Appelle and one year later gave up farming to teach piano at Qu'Appelle, Fort Qu'Appelle, Indian Head, and Sintaluta. In 1900 he was engaged as organist-choirmaster at All Saints Church (Cathedral 1945), Edmonton, where he stayed until 1956. He also taught piano privately. In a career which spanned effectively more than half a century of the musical development of Edmonton, perhaps Barford's most distinctive pioneer achievement was the establishment, with the help of Howard Stutchbury, of Canada's first provincial competition festival 5 May 1908. His abilities as a conductor came to the fore in the early 1900s, when with the Edmonton Amateur Operatic Society, which he founded in 1904, he conducted Planquette's *The Chimes of Normandy* (1904) and Gilbert & Sullivan's *Trial by Jury* (1905) and *The Pirates of Penzance* (1906). In 1912 he organized the first *U of Alberta Glee Club. In 1920 he conducted the Mendelssohn Chorus of Edmonton in the city's full-scale choral-orchestral performance of *Messiah* and for the 1924–5 season he served as conductor of the *Edmonton SO. He was in charge of music for the inauguration ceremonies of Alberta as a province in 1905 and for the golden jubilee in 1955. In 1958 he conducted the RCAF Band and a chorus organized for the occasion at the opening ceremonies of the *Alberta Jubilee Auditorium in Edmonton.

Barford's style as a lecturer, described by Graham *George as 'fluent and persuasive ... with a solid array of factual information,' was epitomized in a series of talks he gave over radio station CKUA in 1932 and 1933. His compositions – more than 50 songs, short choral works, and piano pieces – achieved, according to George, 'unpretentiousness, clarity and expressive accuracy, not always by very simple means.'

Barford served 1907–14 as the first president of the Edmonton Musicians' Union. He was made an Honorary Fellow of St John's College, Winnipeg, in 1950.

See also Edmonton; Competition festivals.

WRITING

'Music in Alberta,' *Alberta Golden Jubilee Anthology* (Toronto 1955)

BIBLIOGRAPHY

Provincial Archives of Alta. Vernon Barford interview, tape 67.182; papers 67.277

George, Graham. 'Vernon Barford,' *CMJ*, vol 5, Winter 1961 RDM

BARKIN. Family of Abraham Barkin (1882–1939), a graduate of the Warsaw Cons who taught piano and voice in Ukraine and Poland before moving in 1923 to Canada as cantor of Goel Tzedec (Beth Tzedec) Synagogue in Toronto. Of his five children, three pursued careers in music: 1 / Leo, 2 / Sara, and 3 / Jack.

1 **Leo.** Pianist, teacher, coach, b Warsaw 18 May 1905, naturalized Canadian 1931. As a child in Ukraine he studied with his father and at 8 he began accompanying the elder Barkin's voice pupils. At 12 he performed as a soloist and accompanist in Ukraine and Poland. He joined his father in Toronto in 1926, and at first played for silent films and vaudeville at the Rialto Theatre. Subsequently he began broadcasting on CKNC, on various other private radio stations, and on the CRBC (CBC). In the first 50 years of Canadian radio he was heard on more broadcasts than any other pianist. He also taught piano until 1953 and continued to coach singers and instrumentalists after that time.

Barkin's adaptability and gifts as a sightreader earned him recognition as one of Canada's leading accompanists. He has accompanied such string players as Mishel Piastro, Gregor Piatigorsky, William Primrose, Ruggiero Ricci, Joseph Szigeti, and Zara *Nelsova and such singers as Igor Gorin, Dorothy Maynor, Jarmila Novotna, Jan Peerce, Leontyne Price, Lawrence Tibbett, and Richard Tucker. He has recorded with Hyman *Bress, John *Dembeck, Avrahm *Galper, Betty-Jean *Hagen, Marta *Hidy, Charles *Jordan, Kathleen *Parlow, Albert *Pratz, and others (see Discographies for aforementioned). He has given support to many fledgling artists and has performed with the *Parlow String Quartet and other groups. He played orchestral keyboard parts with the *Promenade Symphony, the *CBC SO, and, for more than 25 years, the *TSO. He was soloist in many performances of Gershwin's *Rhapsody in Blue* including one (1941) under Paul Whiteman. Barkin has appeared at the *Stratford Festival and in other Ontario centres, but rarely outside the province. In 1971 he was awarded the *CMCouncil Medal. On 17 Jun 1976 he was honoured by the CBC in a radio documentary, in the course of which he claimed that 'to be an accompanist is to be somebody else's mind,' and his long-time associate Albert Pratz described him as 'a complete musician.'

2 **Sara** (m Sandler). Pianist, soprano, b. Uman, Ukraine, 6 Sep 1908, naturalized Canadian 1934. She studied piano at five with her father and on arriving in Canada in 1925 began several years of study on scholarship at the *TCM with W.O. *Forsyth and Mona *Bates in piano and Nina *Gale

Leo Barkin

Brian Barley

in voice. She also studied voice in New York with Maria Kurenko and Frank LaForge. As a singer she appeared 1934–7 with orchestras in Toronto and was a soloist 1937–42 in the annual TCM performance of the *St Matthew Passion*. She gave recitals throughout Ontario and on radio and was the soprano soloist 1943–73 with the choir of the Holy Blossom Temple in Toronto. She also performed 1940–73 as a concert and radio accompanist.

3 **Jack** (Jacob). Tenor, b Uman, Ukraine, 23 Apr 1914, naturalized Canadian ca 1930. He studied voice with his father and subsequently at the TCM, the ESM, and with Euphemia Giannini and Giuseppe Boghetti in Philadelphia. He was coached during the mid-1950s by Fausto Cleva of the Metropolitan Opera, but declined an offer to join the company. He was a cantor for 17 years in synagogues in Washington, DC, and continued that vocation in Pittsburgh, Philadelphia, San Francisco, and 1967–9 at the Holy Blossom Temple, Toronto, before moving in 1969 to Sharrey Zedec Synagogue, Detroit. He has sung in concert with the Israel Philharmonic.

BIBLIOGRAPHY

Kraglund, John. 'Barkin finally returns to sing in Toronto,' Toronto *Globe and Mail*, 13 Mar 1965

1 / HK, 2 / CF, 3 / MM, PW

BARLEY, Brian. Saxophonist, clarinetist, composer, b Sarnia, Ont, 10 Dec 1942, d Toronto 8 Jun 1971. He began playing the clarinet at 11 and, inspired by Lee Konitz, took up the saxophone at 13. His clarinet teachers were Avrahm *Galper and Ezra *Schabas at the U of Toronto and Robert Marcellus at the Cleveland Cons. He played saxophone with the New Jazz Quartet (Toronto 1964) and was principal clarinet with the *NYO in 1963 and 1964. He also played clarinet in the Cleveland orchestra and the *Vancouver SO. In Montreal 1966–70 Barley played in jazz groups led by Pierre *Leduc, Ron Proby, Herb *Spanier, and others. About 1968 he formed the adventurous jazz trio Aquarius Rising (Barley, tenor and soprano saxophone and bass clarinet; Claude *Ranger, drums; Daniel Lessard, bass guitar, or Michel *Donato, double-bass), which made an LP under the title *The Brian Barley Trio* (1970, RCI 309) and performed in Montreal and Quebec City. The LP (with Lessard) included Barley's compositions *Plexidance*, *Schlucks*, *Three by Five*, and *Oneliness*. Barley also recorded in Montreal as sideman to Maynard *Ferguson and Leduc. Shortly before his death (of complications from an automobile accident some years before) Barley returned to Toronto and was reunited with Ranger and Donato for a brief appearance in March 1971 at the jazz club Meat and Potatoes.

In a review of one of the two Ferguson LPs on which Barley played, Doug Ramsey wrote: 'Barley ... would undoubtedly have become a giant of the tenor saxophone ... There was enough of Sonny Rollins in Barley to be recognizable, but he was a distinctive stylist whose legacy of recorded work ... is rich with humour, a thorough knowledge of jazz tenor history, and awesome musicianship' (*Down Beat*, 12 Apr 1973). Barley's later work also reflected the influence of Eric Dolphy. Bernie *Senensky's theme *BB* was dedicated to Barley. He was an affiliate of BMI (PRO) Canada.

BARNES, Milton. Conductor, composer, b Toronto 16 Dec 1931. He studied composition and conducting at the *RCMT 1952–5 and graduated from the Vienna Academy of Music in 1961. He was conductor of the Toronto Repertory Ensemble 1964–70, the *St Catharines SO and Chorus 1964–72, and the Philharmonic Orchestra of Niagara Falls, NY, 1965–73. He became the conductor for the Toronto Dance Theatre in 1968. His compositions are tonal in idiom and romantic in style. He has received commissions from Robert *Aitken, Paul *Brodie, the *CMCentre in collaboration with *OFSO, Joseph *Macerollo and John *Perrone, the New Chamber Orchestra of Canada, and the St Catharines Symphony Assn. He is an associate of the *CMCentre and a member of CAPAC.

SELECTED COMPOSITIONS

STAGE AND FILM

Byron the Wonderful Bandit, musical (Jack Oldfield, Helen Conway-Marmo). 1965. CMCentre

Blood and Guts, film. 1977. Ms

Several ballet scores, including *Masque of the Red Death* (1970), *Rhapsody on a Late Afternoon* (1971), *Amber Garden* and *Three-Sided Room* (1972), and *The Spiral Stairs* (1973)

ORCHESTRA

Symphony No. 1. 1964. CMCentre

Children's Suite. 1966. CMCentre

Pinocchio. 1966. CMCentre

Sonata for flute and string orchestra. 1970. CMCentre

The Classical Concerto. 1973. Pf, orch. CMCentre

Concert Overture. 1973. CMCentre

Psalms of David. 1973. Sop, bar, SATB, orch. CMCentre

Shebetim. 1974. Str orch. CMCentre

Concerto for saxophone and strings. 1975. CMCentre

Concerto for violin and strings. 1975. CMCentre

Chamber Concerto. 1976. Ww quin, str orch. CMCentre

Symphony No. 2. 1976. Str orch. CMCentre

Concerto for viola and orchestra. 1977. CMCentre

Maid of the Mist. 1977. CMCentre

Concerto No. 1 for flute and string orchestra. 1978. CMCentre

CHAMBER

Several works including *Concerto Grosso* (1973), *Serenade* (1973) for guit and acc, *Fantasy for Guitar* (1975), *Nocturne* (1976) for solo acc, *The Dybbuk* (1977) for ten and instr ens, *Ladino Suite* (1977) for brass quin and *Poème juif* (1977) for vn, va, vc, pf. All CMCentre

CHOIR

Thespis, cantata (Michael Sanquillet, French transl Curt Reis). 1956 (rev 1973). Ten, narr, SATB, 2 pf. CMCentre

Madrigals (medieval Sephardic texts). 1975. SSAA, 2 tpt, 2 trb. CMCentre

Shir Hashirim, cantata (Song of Solomon). 1975. Mezzo, ten, unison female chor, chamb ens. CMCentre

Also several works for v, some for pf

DISCOGRAPHY

(all with Barnes cond, Tor Repertory Ens)

Kenins *Septet*. 1970. CBC SM-135/RCI AMC 1

Weinzweig *Concerto* for harp and chamber orchestra. Loman hp. 1967. CBC SM-55

Weinzweig *Divertimento No. 4*. Morton cl. 1969. CBC SM-134

BIBLIOGRAPHY

Goddard, Peter. 'A conductor goes through changes,' *CanComp*, 67, Feb 1972

Schulman, Michael. 'Two films, two music scores, two less-than-happy composers,' *CanComp*, 138, Feb 1979

CF

BARNUM, Marion (Phyllis). Pianist, teacher, b Vancouver 12 May 1926, naturalized US 1959; diploma, piano (Juilliard) 1949, post-graduate diploma, piano (Juilliard) 1951, MFA (Iowa) 1966, DMA (Iowa) 1971. She studied privately 1938–45 with May Pout Henderson, at Juilliard 1945–9 with Arthur Newstead and 1949–51 with Rosina Lhévinne, and at the U of Iowa 1962–71 with John C. Simms. Ida *Halpern was an adviser in her performing and academic career after 1952. Barnum taught 1961–4 at Knoxville College in Tennessee and 1967–71 at the U of Missouri, and became chairman of the piano division at Iowa State U in 1971. She has given concerts and recitals in Canada, the USA, Europe, and the USSR and has been heard on radio with the *CBC Vancouver Chamber Orchestra. She has given Canadian premieres of Easley Blackwood's *Three Fantasies*, Dallapiccola's *Quaderno Musicale di Annalibera*, d'Alessandro's *Toccata*, Jacques de Menasce's *Toccatina*, M. William Karlins' *Sonata No. 2* and William Schuman's *Voyage*. In addition she has given premieres of works by David Van Vactor, Eugene Harzell, Thomas McKenney, and others. She has specialized in the music of Hummel (the subject of her doctoral research), has revived his *Sonata Op 81*, and has performed entire programs of his works. Barnum has conducted workshops and given lecture-recitals and concerts for children in Nelson, BC, and in the USA and has adjudicated at competition festivals. Her pupils include Scott McCoy. NM

Baroque Records. See Canada Baroque Records Ltd.

The Baroque Strings of Vancouver. Founded in 1966. They made their debut at the opening of the *JMC national string competition in June 1967 and performed with the harpsichordist George Malcolm at the 1967 *Vancouver International Festival. Besides broadcasting frequently, they have presented series of concerts at the Vancouver Art Gallery and the *Community Music School of Greater Vancouver and have performed throughout British Columbia. Leaders and first violinists of the 14-member ensemble have been Norman *Nelson (1966–72, 1976), Vaclav Benkovic (1972–6), and Gwen *Thompson (1977–).

DISCOGRAPHY

Corelli – Vivaldi – Geminiani – Pergolesi – Albinoni. Nelson dir. 1971. CBC SM-151

Handel – Purcell – Avison. Nelson dir. 1970. CBC SM-137

Stamitz – Stanley – Pergolesi – Vivaldi. Benkovic dir. 1973. CBC SM-244

Telemann *La Lyra Suite; Suite in G Major; Concerto in E Flat for Two Horns*. Nelson dir, McLean hpd. 1970. CBC SM-136
See Discography for Vancouver Chamber Choir. MW

Baroque Trio of Montreal / Trio baroque de Montréal. Formed in 1955 by Melvin *Berman (oboe), Mario *Duschenes (flute and recorder), and Kelsey *Jones (harpsichord and organ) to perform works chiefly of the baroque period. The group also, however, played 20th-century pieces suitable for its combination of instruments. Its first concert took place in 1955 at the *Ermitage in Montreal. It subsequently performed on CBC radio, at McGill U's Redpath Hall, and in 1957 at the *Montreal Festivals. It toured Quebec, Alberta, Manitoba, Saskatchewan, and the Maritimes and performed at *Expo 67. Among numerous musicians who appeared as guests with the trio were Walter *Joachim, the *Masella brothers, Mildred *Goodman, Kenneth *Gilbert, and Jean-Pierre Rampal. It commissioned and premiered several works by Canadians, including Jones' *Sonata da Camera* (1957), Jacques *Hétu's *Trio* (1961), *Pentland's *Canzona* (1962), and *Schafer's *Trio* (1964). In 1973, following a concert at the *Eaton Auditorium in Toronto and a CBC broadcast, the trio ceased its activities after having given close to 1000 concerts and radio broadcasts.

DISCOGRAPHY

Bach 4 *Trio Sonatas*. 1962. Vox STDL 500.920
Fasch *Trio in D Major* – Telemann *Trio in C Minor* – K. Jones *Sonata da Chiesa*. 1968. CBC SM-56/RCI 335/RCA LSC 3091
Handel *Sonatas and Trios*. 1960. Vox STDL 500.930
K. Jones *Sonata da Camera* – Telemann *Sonata in G Minor*. (1963). RCI 192
Music and Musicians of Canada, vol 7: Morawetz *Trio* – Freedman *Variations*. 1966. RCA CCS-1013/ RCI 219
Music of the Italian Baroque: Frescobaldi – Samartini – Vivaldi – Albinoni – Bononcini. 1960. 3-Vox VBX 65 HP

Barrel organs. Mechanical instruments featuring a barrel-and-pin mechanism turned by a crank which activates a set of organ pipes or metal tongues. Those with pipes usually are stationary, the others portable. Although known in the 16th century and possibly earlier, barrel organs enjoyed their greatest vogue in Great Britain in the late 18th and early 19th centuries. Some 500 were used in British churches about 1850 and several were installed in Canadian churches, since their player mechanisms provided psalm and hymn singing with an accompaniment more reliable than that of the amateur instrumentalist. Thus St John's Church, York Mills, Toronto, preserves an organ with three interchangeable barrels of 10 hymn tunes each. It was purchased in London in 1847 and until 1864 provided the only accompaniment for congregational singing. The only known Canadian-built instruments are those of Richard *Coates, two of which survive. One with 20 tunes on two interchangeable barrels was built ca 1818 for the *Children of Peace. It was still on display in 1980 at the Temple in Sharon, Ont.

Not all barrel organs were intended for use in church. This is probably true of 'a compleat new chamber organ, with two barrels and the most favorite new tunes' advertised in the Quebec *Gazette* of 12 Jul 1787 and of the 'barrel organ that cost sixty guineas in London' auctioned in the same city 3 Apr 1797. It certainly is true of the barrel organ carried by the English explorer William Edward Parry (later Sir) on his arctic expeditions (1819–20, 1921–3, 1924–5) and used to entertain, to accompany physical fitness exercises, and to amuse the Inuit children. Parry's instrument survives in Cambridge and has been recorded (Saydisc SDL 234).

Baroque Trio of Montreal: (left to right) Mario Duschenes, Kelsey Jones, Melvin Berman

Another English instrument had found its way to Victoria by 1859, and one with 30 hymn tunes on three barrels, built in London ca 1845, was for some time in St Stephen's Anglican Church, Chambly, Que, but was sold in 1856 or 1857 to St Thomas' Anglican Church, Rougemont, Que, where it still could be seen in 1980. An instrument with 15 tunes (9 of them secular), presented by King George III to the famous Indian chief Joseph Brant (1742–1807), was acquired by the Château de Ramezay museum of Montreal. No inventory of barrel organs preserved in Canada had been undertaken by 1980.

The 'hurdy-gurdy' of the organ grinder, common on Canadian streets and at fairs during the late 19th and early 20th centuries, is of the type using metal tongues. HK

Barrie Central Collegiate Band. High school band of approximately 90 members, founded in 1939 at Barrie, Ont, by W. Allen *Fisher. Originally a student orchestra, it was converted to a band in 1941. Under Fisher it established its reputation as one of Canada's leading school bands, touring extensively in Canada and the USA and twice in Europe, and winning over 100 first prizes in competitions such as those at the World Music Festival at Kerkrade, Holland, where it placed first in 1970. In 1972 its leadership was assumed by Morley *Calvert, under whom it has won more than 25 first and second prizes, including gold medals at Kerkrade in 1974 and 1978 and the Major Brian S. *McCool Trophy annually 1974–6 and in 1978 at the *Kiwanis Festival in Toronto. In 1975 the band represented Canada at the inaugural International Festival of Youth Brass and Symphonic Bands held at Cardiff and London. Its repertoire contains works of Robert Russell Bennett, Bernardus *Bogisch, Morley Calvert, Norman Dello Joio, Robert *Fleming, Alexander Goedicke, Vaclav Nelhybel, and Alfred Reed, as well as Frescobaldi, Kabalevsky, Mozart, Tchaikovsky, Walton, and Wagner. A parents' advisory committee traditionally has raised funds for the band and sponsored annual series of four evening concerts and four student matinees featuring the band and guest performers. The *Hamilton Philharmonic Orchestra, the *London (Ont) SO, the *NACO, *Nexus, the *Ontario Youth Choir, Oscar *Peterson, the Shevchenko Musical Ensemble, and the touring company of the *COC have been presented at these concerts. Recordings by the band were issued privately in 1969, 1971, and 1975. NM

BARROW. Toronto family of french horn players: 1 / Herbert, 2 / Reginald, his son, and 3 / Mary, Reginald's wife.

1 (Benjamin) **Herbert**. B London 22 Sep 1875, d Toronto 31 Dec 1955. The son of a musician, Barrow studied viola and french horn at the GSM, winning the school prize for viola in 1898. After 12 years with His Majesty's Scots Guards he moved in 1913 with his family to Toronto, where he played viola in the *Royal Alexandra Theatre orchestra and, until 1918, french horn in the *Welsman *TSO. He was principal horn 1927–32 of the TSO. He served 1914–18 as bandmaster of the *Queen's Own Rifles and in 1922 was assistant conductor of the *Anglo-Canadian Leather Company Band in Huntsville, Ont. In Toronto he owned and operated Barrow Music Supplies.

2 **Reginald** (Herbert). B London 12 Apr 1907, d Toronto 10 Dec 1973. He studied in Toronto with his father and in England with Aubrey Brain. In 1927 he joined the TSO, succeeding his father as principal for one year in 1933 and continuing with the orchestra until 1958. He also taught 1944–72 at the *RCMT. His library and instrument collection are held by the *U of Toronto.

3 **Mary** (b Robb, m Barrow, m Rogers). B Aberdeen 28 Sep 1918. Taken to Canada in 1920, she studied in Toronto with Herbert and Reginald Barrow and began playing professionally at 15. In 1938 she became the principal horn for the *Promenade Symphony Concerts. A member 1939–51 of the TSO (and principal 1939–45), she played the important horn part in the North American premiere (1945) of Britten's *Serenade*. She was a member 1952–62 of the *CBC SO. GR

BARTLETT, Dale. Pianist, teacher, accompanist, b Lethbridge, Alta, 10 Aug 1936. He studied 1941–53 in Lethbridge with Margaret Stevens and later with Beatrice Foster. During these years he received the silver medal of the *RCMT eight times in succession.

On a scholarship from the *AB of the RSM he worked 1953–8 with Vivian Langrish at the RAM, and received the Macfarren gold medal in 1958. The following year he studied at the Accademia Chigiana in Siena with Guido Agosti and Alfred Cortot. He won first prize at the 1961 G.B. Viotti International Competition in Vercelli, and also was a prizewinner at the 1962 Busoni International Piano Competition in Bolzano. He made several tours for the JM in Europe, playing in Berlin, Munich, Hamburg, Brussels, and Paris. He also toured for the *JMC in Canada, as a soloist 1964–5 and 1965–6, and with the violinist Hyman *Bress 1966–7. Winner of the grand prize in the 1964 JMC national competition, he also received the prize for the best interpretation of the prescribed Canadian work, Jacques *Hétu's *Variations*. He performed Liszt's *Concerto No. 1* in 1964 with the *MSO, and the Khatchaturian *Concerto* 26 Feb 1968 with the *Calgary Philharmonic. Besides appearing frequently 1964–8 with the *CBC Winnipeg Orchestra, he was the soloist on two notable occasions with CBC Montreal orchestras: in Rachmaninoff's *Rhapsody on a Theme of Paganini* in 1964 on the TV program *'Heure du concert' and in Liszt's *Hungarian Fantasy* in 1977 on 'Les Beaux Dimanches.' He has accompanied several singers and instrumentalists, including Donald *Bell, Hyman Bress, Anna *Chornodolska, and Arthur *Garami. Bartlett began teaching at the Cons de Hull in 1967 and became a member of the *Hertz Trio in 1977. With the trio he has performed in Quebec, Alberta, and British Columbia.

DISCOGRAPHY
Beethoven *Sonatas, Op 14*. 1968. CBC SM-57
Schumann *Carnaval* – Debussy *Pour le piano* – J. Hétu *Variations*. 1964. CD-JMC-4
See also Discography for Donald Bell. ST

BARTLEY, Ewart. Organist, choirmaster, teacher, composer, b Toronto 4 Jan 1909. He studied piano in Woodstock, Ont, and at the *TCM with Albert *Jordan (organ), Ernest *Seitz (piano), and Healey *Willan (composition). In 1943 he became music director of Knox's Presbyterian Church, Galt (Cambridge), Ont. He often has served as an examiner for the RCMT. Of his more than 60 compositions many are for piano, including *The Whistling Boy* and *River Song* (Harris 1966), *Suite for Children* (Jarman 1950), and *Two Dances for Piano* (Harris 1960). The dances have been recorded by John *Newmark (RCI 134). Bartley published a choral work, 'Blessed is the Man,' in 1975. He is an affiliate of PRO Canada. RM

BROTHER BASILE (b Simon Néron). Ethnomusicologist, teacher, b Roberval, near Chicoutimi, Que, 18 Apr 1906, d Roma, Lesotho, Southern Africa, 5 Sep 1973; L MUS (Montreal) 1941, D MUS (Montreal) 1946. He joined the order of the Brothers of the Sacred Heart at St-Hyacinthe in 1918 and took his perpetual vows in 1928. He studied African music during his assignments as a missionary 1933–7 in Sudan, 1937–9 in Madagascar, and 1939–49 and 1954–71 in Lesotho. He obtained a licentiate for his thesis, 'Le symbolisme en musique' (Symbolism in Music), and a doctorate for his work 'La musique chez les Noirs d'Afrique' (Music in Black Africa), published under the title *Au rythme des tambours* (Montreal 1949). Recognized as a specialist in African music, Brother Basile contributed articles on the subject to European and South African publications including *African Music* (vol 1, 1957, vol 2, 1958), *La Revue musicale* (no. 239–40, 1958), *Worldmission* (vol 10, 1959), and *Journal of the International Folk Music Council* (vol 11, 1959). He was a poet, entomologist, philatelist, and educator. GP

Bass. See Double-bass.

BASSO, Guido. Flugelhornist, trumpeter, arranger, composer, conductor, b Montreal 27 Sep 1937. He began playing trumpet at nine, studied at the *CMM, and in his teens played in dance and show bands led by Al Nichols, Maury *Kaye, and others. He was known as 'Stubby' Basso at this time. At 18, while playing at the club El Morocco with Kaye, he was heard by Vic Damone, who took him on the road for six months. Basso subsequently worked 1957–60 throughout North America with the singer Pearl Bailey and the orchestra led by her husband, the drummer Louis Bellson. In 1960 Basso settled in Toronto, becoming a first-call studio musician and leader. He was music director 1963–7 for CBLT's 'Nightcap' and 1968–9 for CBC TV's 'Barris and Company.' He also co-starred in 1969 with vibraphonist Peter *Appleyard on CBC TV's 'Mallets and Brass,' was music director 1969–71 for CBC radio's 'After Noon,' and led orchestras for two CBC TV series devoted to the big band era: 'In the Mood' (1971–2) and 'Bandwagon' (1972–3). In 1975 he organized big bands for concerts at the *CNE by Dizzy Gillespie and Benny Goodman. He also has performed in Toronto nightclubs and hotel lounges with his own groups – several bringing together jazz and latin music – and has been a soloist with the *Boss Brass, *Nimmons 'N' Nine Plus Six, and the big bands of Ron *Collier and others.

Reviewing a Basso performance, David Lancashire (Toronto *Globe and Mail*, 10 Aug 1978) observed: 'His tone and technique are stupendous, and on the bossa nova tunes and the bop standards he played ... he floats through long, intricate embellishments with all the fluency of a saxophone player, occasionally colouring the effect with a few deep rasps and flutters. Indeed, like so many studio musicians, he is so glib and polished that one suspects he may be dipping at times into a collection of stock phrases from a vast repertoire, instead of truly improvising.' Basso has been credited with the theory that one attacks the trumpet and makes love to a flugelhorn. Lancashire noted: 'He evidently forgets the rule when he plays: there is a lot of gentle legato in his flugelhorn choruses and his vibrato on a ballad can be so wide it almost sounds like he is doing a duet, but there is an attack in some of the phrases hard enough to chop down a tree.'

Basso has made several pop instrumental LPs: *It's Happening with Guido Basso* (1967, CTLS 5088/Birchmount BM 527), *Christmas Today* (1968, CBC LM 52/ RCA CAS 2289), *Love Talk* (1970, Kanata KAN 1/CTLS 6002), and *Guido Basso and All That Latin Jazz* (1978, CTLS 5216). He also was the nominal leader for *All-Star Jazz*, a CBC recording (LM 300) made by Appleyard, Ed *Bickert, Terry *Clarke, Bruce Harvey (piano), Moe *Koffman, Rob *McConnell, Gary Morgan (baritone saxophone), Phil Nimmons, and Don (W.) *Thompson at the CNE Bandshell in 1973. Basso has written several songs; his 'My Sicilia' was recorded by Keath Barrie. Basso is an affiliate of PRO Canada.

BIBLIOGRAPHY
Norris, John. 'Guido Basso,' *MSc*, 246, Mar–Apr 1969
Topalovich, Maria. 'Human experience is source of Guido Basso's music,' *MSc*, 286, Nov–Dec 1975
Adilman, Sid. 'Guido Basso,' *(Toronto Star) Star Week*, 7–14 Jan 1978 MM

BATES, Arthur L. Organist, b Hanley, Staffordshire, England, 21 May 1894, d Saskatoon 20 Nov 1939. He came to Canada in 1911 and lived in Saskatoon, where he was organist-choirmaster at St Thomas-Wesley United Church 1920–5 and organist at Third Avenue United Church 1926–30 and Knox United Church 1931–9. He studied with Lynnwood *Farnam. Bates served as president of the *Musical Art Club in 1933 and the *Saskatchewan Music Festival Assn in 1934. WLB

BATES, Mona (Hazelwood). Pianist, teacher, b Burlington, Ont, 31 Oct 1889, d Toronto 29 Mar 1971; ATCM 1908. She studied with J.E.P. *Aldous in Hamilton (giving her first recital there at seven), and with Edward *Fisher, A.S. *Vogt, and, after 1913, Viggo *Kihl in Toronto. She became a teacher at the *TCM in 1912. While studying with Kihl, she appeared 30 Apr 1914 at Massey Hall in a performance of Liszt's *Hungarian Fantasy* with the *Welsman *TSO and was praised in the *Canadian Journal of Music* for 'a legitimate reading and confident technique.' After giving a benefit recital in Toronto 23 Mar 1916 for the Canadian Army Medical Corps, she published her receipts (gross: $251.50, expenses: $50.90, donation to the corps: $200.60), thus setting a local precedent.

Mona Bates met Ernest Hutcheson at Chautauqua in 1916, became his pupil, and served also as his assistant 1917–20 at Chautauqua and the Juilliard School. Later, she studied with Sigismund Stojowski, also in New York. Her New York debuts were 21 Aug 1919 at Lewisohn Stadium (*Conservatory Quarterly Review*, vol 2, Nov 1919), where, with an orchestra, she repeated the Liszt *Fantasy*, and in 1920 at Aeolian Hall (*Who is Who in Music* 1951), where she gave a recital, her program including Beethoven's *'Waldstein' Sonata*.

Mona Bates, ca 1931

She was soloist 28 Feb 1921 with Damrosch and the New York SO at a *Massey Hall concert in Toronto, and her performance was described by Lawrence *Mason in *The Globe* as 'a remarkable example of finished, fluent execution.' Her London debut, 9 Nov 1922 at Aeolian Hall, earned praise from *The Times* ('fresh, sincere and genuinely musical') and the *Daily Telegraph*. She then toured Europe, playing in Prague, Vienna, Budapest, and Paris. While in Paris she studied with Isidor Philipp; while in Budapest, with Zoltán Kodály. Her name was considered too plain for Europe, so she reversed the spelling and toured as the exotic Anom Setab. However, her publicity stressed her Canadian birth and was full of information about wheat and mineral resources. She recorded for Victor and for Duo-Art Piano Rolls.

In 1925 Bates gave up her concert career and opened a studio on Jarvis St, Toronto, where she taught piano for the next 40-odd years. Among her pupils were Elsie Bennett, Madeline Bone, Margaret Miller *Brown, Etta Coles, George *Crum, Erica *Goodman, Marian *Grudeff, Gordon *Hallett, John Knight, Warren *Mould, Patricia *Parr, Clifford *Poole, and Naomi Yanova *Adaskin. In 1931, inspired by a benefit concert conducted by Walter Damrosch, Mona Bates organized the Ten-Piano Ensemble to raise funds for the needy. The ensemble comprised the best-known Bates pupils and was conducted by her. During World War II the ensemble became part of her Musical Manifesto Group, gave numerous performances, and raised thousands of dollars for the war effort. In 1967 she was one of six recipients of the *CFMTA Centennial Citation. In 1976 several of her pupils set up a scholarship fund in her name at the RCMT. The first winners were Erica Goodman and Lawrence Pitchko in 1978.

BIBLIOGRAPHY
'Mona Bates gets bouquets,' *MCan*, vol 16, Aug 1920
'Famous Canadian pianist's success in Austria and Hungary,' *MCan*, vol 6, Jul 1925
Hamilton, H.C. 'Canadian musician of the month,' *MCan*, vol 12, Jul–Aug 1931
Dempsey, Lotta. 'Money will help the music sound sweeter,' *Toronto Star*, 8 Nov 1978 (MWM)

BATTLE, Rex. Pianist, conductor, composer, b London 4 Jan 1892 (1895?), d Toronto 27 Jan 1967. A child prodigy, he had his first piano lessons with Vlahol Budmani, who presented him at Buckingham Palace. Battle later studied organ with E.H. Thorne. After several tours in Australia he settled in New York, where he assisted Sigmund Romberg in the production of operettas. He resumed his career as a pianist with a series of broadcasts in 1921 on WWJ, Detroit, then played 1922–9 at the Mount Royal Hotel, Montreal. He was conductor 1929–38 of the Royal York Hotel

Concert Orchestra, Toronto, which was heard in the USA on the NBC network for several years, and he also conducted an orchestra, chorus, and soloists for broadcast 1930–1 on the CPR network. He formed in 1934 one of Canada's first (jazz) big bands, which performed in the summer of 1935 at Bob-Lo Island near Detroit. After three years in New York, playing, conducting, and studying piano with Moriz Rosenthal and Hedwig Kanner-Rosenthal, Battle appeared in 1941 as pianist with the *Promenade Symphony Concerts in Toronto. Soon afterwards he returned to live in Toronto, where he served 1943–56 as music director and conductor of CBC radio's *'Singing Stars of Tomorrow.' In 1962 he began performing with young operatic singers of his choice at Toronto's Gaslight Restaurant. Battle composed morceaux for piano, violin, and voice and a short orchestral piece, *Simon Says 'Thumbs Up'* (Thompson). His recordings as pianist, accompanist, and soloist with the Mount Royal Orchestra are listed in *Roll Back the Years*.

BIBLIOGRAPHY

Sinclair, Gordon. column, *Toronto Daily Star*, 15 Jan 1955
'Still king of the keys, Rex boosts young talent,' Toronto *Telegram*, 6 Apr 1964 RPn

Battle music. A genre of descriptive program music originally known as Battaglia and very popular from the 15th to the early 19th centuries. Beethoven's *Wellington's Victory* (1813) is a late example. Although Canada never has been the scene of major wars, there are at least three descriptive battle pieces of Canadian interest.

1 *Siege of Quebec*. Franz Koczwara (ca 1750–91), a Czech composer who was living in London at the time of his death, had had a great success with his *The Battle of Prague* (ca 1788). In consequence he began another work of the sort, but it remained to W.B. de Krifft to complete it after Koczwara's death. *Siege of Quebec* (Bland ca 1791) is a 'sonata for the harpsichord or pianoforte with accompaniments for a violin, violoncello & tympano ad libitum' dedicated to 'the Officers &c Engag'd in that Glorious Service, Sept 10th 1759.' The work begins with a favourite song of General Wolfe, one which was sung for him the evening before his death. After a slow march, trumpets and drums give the signal for the attack, the British soldiers intone a national air (from Purcell's *Bonduca*), and the attack begins. De Krifft took over the composition at the point where 'the heavy artillery ascends the rocks.' Further directions in the score describe the effects meant to be achieved: cannons fire and there is fighting with swords, the wounded are lamented, and another skirmish follows, but the trumpets announce a 'flag of truce for a capitulation.' The deaths of General Wolfe and his men are lamented; then follows a march of victory and 'General Rejoicing.' Before a performance in Quebec 1 Jul 1806 the work was described in the *Mercury* as a 'splendid and grand piece (told in action).' *Ten Centuries Concerts revived *The Siege of Quebec* 9 Dec 1962 in an arrangement by *Beckwith, *Kallmann, and *Schafer. The performance was accompanied by colour slides of historical paintings. The Trio Nouvelle France also revived the original score, minus percussion, for a *JMC tour 1978–9. For a subsequent recording (RCI 500) the percussion was restored.

2 *The Charge at Batoche*. 'A descriptive song' by J.W. Bengough (words) and Barton Browne. The fighting between Louis Riel's Métis forces and the government troops under General Middleton, 11 May in the Northwest Rebellion of 1885, is the subject of this musical scena, in which the battle is

An excerpt from *The Siege of Quebec* (ca 1791) by Koczwara and de Krifft

illustrated graphically in the piano part. The printed lyrics and an abbreviated recorded version are included in the Jackdaw kit *Riel* issued by Clarke Irwin, Toronto, in 1967.

3 *The Battles of Lake Champlain and Plattsburg*. A grand sonata for piano by Francesco Masi (Boston 1812), which celebrates a US victory in the War of 1812.

It is not known whether F.H. *Glackemeyer's *Chateauguay March* (1813, lost) includes descriptive music.

See also History of Canada in music; Wars, rebellions and uprisings. HK

BAUER, Robert (Paul). Composer, guitarist, b Port Colborne, south of Niagara Falls, Ont, 24 Jan 1950; B MUS (Toronto) 1972. Studies in Port Colborne with Norma Kowalchuk (guitar) and Mark Fairchild (saxophone) preceded training at the *U of Toronto with John *Beckwith and John *Weinzweig (composition), Eli *Kassner (guitar), and Paul *Brodie (saxophone). Bauer won the 1971 *CLComp Prize with *Filaments* (1971) for two guitars and *Water Colours* (1971) for two flutes and string orchestra. A founding member of *ARRAY in 1971, he also began teaching that year at the Brodie School of Music. He became a technician in 1976 and a producer in 1979 for CBC radio. Most of his works have used a freely modified 12-tone technique. His *Sokasodik* (1974, Berandol 1976) and *Willy Rag* (1973) were recorded by Paul Brodie, who also commissioned ... *a sincere and earnest appeal* ... (1974) and *Three Pieces for Soprano Sax and Guitar* (1975). *Mao* (1973, for mandolin, guitar, voice, and wind chimes), *White Line on a Green Fence* (1976, Berandol 1976, for solo guitar), *Filaments*, and *Extensions II* (1975, for guitar and tape) have been recorded by the composer with William *Kuinka on *Guitar Extensions* (1975, Mel SMLP 4028). Bauer's *Episode I* and *Episode II* for solo horn were premiered in a *Contemporary Music Showcase Assn concert in Toronto in 1978. A guitar duo which Bauer formed in 1976 with Douglas Virgin has performed on CBC radio, has appeared with the *Canadian Electronic Ensemble and with the *CJRT Orchestra, and has commissioned works from Robert Daigneault, Gary *Hayes, and David Jaeger. Bauer is an affiliate of PRO Canada.

WRITINGS

'Guitar music in Canada,' *ARRAY Newsletter*, vol 1, Spring 1974

BIBLIOGRAPHY

MacMillan, Rick. 'Robert Bauer is activist for today's music,' *MSc*, 290, Jul–Aug 1976
BMI Canada Ltd. 'Robert Bauer,' pamphlet, 1977 (RM)

BAUMAN, Perry. Oboist, b Erie, Penn, 22 Jul 1918; performance diploma (Curtis) 1942. He moved in 1920 with his family to Dorset, O, where at 10 he played saxophone in the school band and went on to play in a number of other bands. His main formative studies were pursued 1937–41 at the Curtis Institute with the French oboist Marcel Tabuteau. He moved to Canada in 1940 to take up a position as principal oboe of the *TSO and continued in that capacity until 1956. He rejoined the orchestra in 1964, serving as co-principal until 1971. Bauman also served 1952–64 as principal oboe of the *CBC SO and played and recorded 1955–71 with the *Toronto Woodwind Quintet. A highly respected musician, regarded as one of the leading oboists in Canada, he was in great demand in radio, TV, and other orchestras. He toured with the Philadelphia Orchestra in 1955 and 1958 and with the Cincinnati Orchestra in 1957. He participated in many chamber and orchestral concerts at the *Stratford Festival. After a performance as soloist with the *Hart House Orchestra, Bauman was praised for his 'warm tone' and 'technical brilliance' (Toronto *Globe and Mail*, 25 Jan 1965). He taught oboe 1944–71 at the *RCMT. Among his pupils were Lawrence *Cherny, Harry *Freedman, and Stan Wood. Bauman joined the *Edmonton SO in 1971 and was principal oboe 1974–9. In addition, he taught summers 1972–9 at the *Banff SFA and main terms 1974–8 at *Alberta College. In 1979 he joined the Faculty of Music, *U of Western Ontario. He premiered in 1948 and recorded in 1952 (RCI 86) *Weinzweig's *Divertimento No. 2* for solo oboe and strings. The recording was re-released in the *Weinzweig Anthology* in 1979 (RCI ACM 1).

BAUMANN, Joseph W. Violinist, teacher, b Berlin (Kitchener), Ont, 29 Oct 1847, d Hamilton, Ont, 3 Apr 1905. He was self-taught until at 21 he departed for Vienna to study with Adolf Brodsky. Two years later he went to Berlin for private study with Joseph Joachim. Returning to Canada, he taught in a succession of Ontario towns – Walkerton, Berlin, Toronto – before settling in Hamilton in 1882. About 1888 he appeared frequently in recital with the pianist D.J. O'Brien, founder of the Hamilton Musical Institute (see Royal Hamilton College of Music). Baumann's playing was noted for its full tone and robust technique, both of which were imparted to his students. Among his pupils were George *Fox and Nora *Clench. HL

BAYEUR, Rosario. Violin maker, b St-Pauline-de-Maskinongé, near Trois-Rivières, Que, 21 Aug 1875, d Montreal 1 Jun 1944. He worked first as a cabinet-maker. He travelled extensively 1895–1900 in the USA and during a stay in Providence, RI, became interested in string instruments and made his first violin. He then studied with the master violin maker Bohmann in Chicago. He had several instruments to his credit by the time he settled in Montreal, where he spent his evenings making and repairing violins and tuning pianos. In 1916, with his brother Albert (b St-Paulin-de-Maskinongé 3 Aug 1885, d Montreal 24 Aug 1965), he established Bayeur Frères, Luthiers. The brothers enrolled in correspondence courses with the British Violin Makers' Guild of London and earned certificates of competence.

Rosario travelled in 1921 and 1926 to Europe to complete his training with Émile Germain of Paris and other noted violin makers. In a competition organized in 1921 by the Parisian journal *Le Monde musical* and open to ancient and modern instruments, judged according to tone and sonority, one of his violins placed third in the modern class. Made of spruce and maple-à-Giguère (Negundo, sometimes called Manitoba maple or box elder), the violin was owned by Claude *Champagne. Other Bayeur instruments were owned by Isaac Braunstein, Albert *Chamberland, Alfred *De Sève, and Lucien *Sicotte. In 1923 a Bayeur violin, commissioned by the Canadian government and fashioned from indigenous wood, was displayed at an exhibition at Wembley, England, as proof that a Canadian wood could be used for this purpose. During his career Bayeur made 54 signed and numbered violins, three violins signed but not numbered, one viola, and three cellos. His models were instruments by Amati, Stradivarius, Guarnerius, Maggini, and LeLyonnais.

BIBLIOGRAPHY

Ayotte, Alfred. 'Les violons Bayeur d'érable canadien,' *Technique*, vol 14, Nov 1939

Bourdages, François. 'Stradivarius n'a pas emporté dans sa tombe le secret de son art,' Montreal *La Patrie*, 21 Jan 1951

Henley, William, ed. *Universal Dictionary of Violin and Bow Makers* (Brighton, Sussex 1959–60)

Vannes, René. *Dictionnaire universel des luthiers* (Brussels 1972)

Huot, Cécile. 'Rosario Bayeur, luthier, 1875–1944,' *CMB*, 9, Autumn–Winter 1974 CH

BAYLEY, John. Bandmaster, clarinetist, violinist, organist, b Windsor, England, ca 1847, d USA? 1910. His father, also John Bayley, who was trained in Chelsea (London) at the Royal Military Asylum for boys, became a cornet soloist and conductor and took his family to Philadelphia ca 1850, to San Francisco ca 1857, and, in the excitement of the Fraser River gold rush, to Victoria, BC, in 1859. While inspector of police there, he conducted the Victoria Philharmonic Society in the first concerts given in that city. At the opening one 6 May 1859 the younger Bayley played a clarinet solo that was 'enthusiastically encored' (Victoria *Gazette*, 10 May 1859). Bayley returned to England in November 1860, in part to provide his son with a musical education. The boy studied violin with Leopold Jansa and harmony with Henry Wylde at the London Academy of Music. He was bandmaster of the 46th Regiment for seven years (part of the time possibly in Canada), then returned to Canada, living 1877–9 in Montreal and, as bandmaster 1879–1901 of the *Queen's Own Rifles, in Toronto. He was also second violin 1884–7 of the *Toronto String Quartette and first violin of the 1894 TSQ, and formed a Citizens' Band which performed for a season (1887) on Toronto's Centre Island. Bayley was described by Herbert L. *Clarke (in his autobiography *How I Became a Cornetist*) as 'a finished musician of high order; he was a remarkable organist ... and one of the best clarinetists I have ever heard in my life.' When Bayley resigned from the Queen's Own Rifles he moved to Buffalo, NY.

BIBLIOGRAPHY

Musical Journal, 17, 15 May 1888

Smith, Dorothy Blakey. 'Music in the furthest west a hundred years ago,' *CMJ*, vol 2, Summer 1958 HK

BAYLEY, Robert Charlton. Educator, organist, choir conductor, composer, b Buctouche, near Moncton, NB, 4 Apr 1913; B SC (New Brunswick) 1934, LTCL 1935, L MUS (McGill) 1938, B ED (New Brunswick) 1970. His teachers included Sister M. Gabriel, William Smith, and (in England 1938–9) Ernest Bullock, Harold Darke, and Sydney Nicholson. He was supervisor of school music in Fredericton 1945–6 and in Moncton 1946–63 before joining the New Brunswick Teachers' College in 1963 and the *U of New Brunswick in 1973. He was music editor 1947–50 of the *New Brunswick Educational Review*. Bayley has been organist-choirmaster in various New Brunswick churches, and also the founder and conductor 1933–9 of the Cecilian Singers in Fredericton and conductor of the CNR Glee Club, the New Brunswick Teachers' College Choir, and the U of New Brunswick Faculty of Education Choir. He has composed over 40 works in a conservative idiom, mainly for church choir and for voice and piano. His publishers are BMI Canada (now *Berandol), *Harris, and Hope. He is an affiliate of PRO Canada.

See also School music. (RM)

BEARDER, John (William). Organist, composer, b Bradford, Yorkshire, England, 26 Dec 1873, d Toronto 6 May 1958; FRCO 1895, D MUS (Bishop's College) ca 1930. At 12 he held the first of many positions as organist-choirmaster in English churches. In Canada he was organist 1907–13 in Sherbrooke, Que, at St Peter's Anglican Church, and 1913–50 in Ottawa, successively at All Saints Anglican Church and St Matthew's Anglican Church. Bearder was president 1926–7 of the CCO (later *RCCO) and for several years chairman of the CCO Ottawa Centre, and he gave over 200 recitals in Ottawa churches during his career. He founded the Ottawa Collegiate Institute orchestras in 1915 and supervised several other school orchestras until ca 1950. He was an examiner ca 1928–37 for *Bishop's U and the *Dominion College of Music. For a time he was music editor of the *Ottawa Journal*. Bearder composed and arranged many songs and choral pieces for church use and also wrote for violin and piano. Most of his works remain in manuscript, though his *Communion Service in B Flat, Morning Service*, and *Evening Service* were published by Woodward, London. Several of his songs, including 'Canadian Born,' 'When I Survey,' and 'Be Thou My Vision,' received public performance.

BIBLIOGRAPHY

Hamilton, H.C. 'Dr. John W. Bearder,' *MCan*, vol 12, Sep 1931 (FH)

BEATTIE, Mac (John McNab). Singer-songwriter, b Arnprior, near Ottawa, 1916. While in high school he organized his first country band, which performed fiddle tunes and US hits of the day, especially those of Jimmie Rodgers. Beattie sang and played harmonica and washboard; the sound of the latter instrument has lent a distinctive sound to Beattie's music over the years. After playing hockey in western Canada and serving during World War II, Beattie returned in 1948 to Arnprior and began performing professionally. With his oldtime music group, the Ottawa Valley Melodiers, he performed regularly on CFRA radio, Ottawa, until the late 1950s and on CHOV, Pembroke, until the early 1960s. He has continued to perform at local fairs, dances, and clubs. The Melodiers have included at various times Beattie's daughter Bonnie, the steel guitarist Garnet Scheel, and the noted fiddler Reg Hill. Beattie's first 78, 'The Log Driver's Song,' released by *Rodeo Records in the early 1950s, was followed by nine LPs on Rodeo's various labels by 1976. Many of his songs are based on Ottawa Valley events, people, and places. Beattie is a member of CAPAC. (RGn)

BEAUCHAMP, (Marie Berthe) **Fleurette** (m Huppé). Pianist, teacher, soprano, b Montreal 12 Dec 1907. She studied piano with Alice McCaughan 1915–22 and with Romain-Octave *Pelletier, Arthur *Letondal, and Romain *Pelletier 1922–32. She also studied singing with Albert *Roberval, stage deportment with Jeanne *Maubourg, and harmony with Henri *Miro and Rodolphe *Mathieu. She appeared as a singer in the productions of the *Société canadienne d'opérette. As a pianist she won the first prize of the *Canadian Institute of Music in 1930, 1931, and 1932, and its Prix de Paris in 1933. In Paris 1933–4 she studied piano with Victor Staub, Edith Lang-Laszlo, and José Estrada. On her return to Canada she gave recitals and was a soloist with orchestra on CBC and CKAC radio, performing works by François *Brassard, Alexis *Contant, R. Mathieu, Miro, Georges *Savaria, and other Canadians, some of whom dedicated works to her. In 1945 she was the *MSO's soloist in *Les Djinns* by Franck. In her long and fruitful teaching career, notably 1945–75 at the *CMM, her pupils included Monique Marcil and Paul and Rafael *Masella. She has written several pieces (unpublished) for piano. She accompanied Yohadio (Adrienne *Roy-Vilandré) for the recording *Popular Songs of French Canada*. Beauchamp is a life member of the *AMPQ and Les *Amis de l'art.

BEAUDET, Jean-Marie or **Jean**. Conductor, pianist, administrator, organist, b Thetford Mines, south of Quebec City, 20 Feb 1908, d Ottawa 19 Mar 1971; BA (Séminaire de Québec) 1928, diplôme de virtuosité (Fontainebleau) ca 1930. He studied piano and organ at the Collège de Lévis with Father Alphonse *Tardif, and at the *Séminaire de Québec with Henri *Gagnon and Robert *Talbot. After winning the *Prix d'Europe for piano and organ in 1929, he studied 1929–32 at the Paris Cons with Yves Nat (piano), Marcel Dupré (organ), and Louis Aubert (harmony), and during the summers at the American Cons at Fontainebleau with Pierre Lucas. Upon his return to Canada he taught at *Laval U and became organist at St-Dominique Church in Quebec City. He also began a career as a pianist, playing Beethoven's *Concerto No. 3*, the Schumann *Concerto*, and other works in appearances 1935–7 with the *CSM orchestra and in 1937 with the Cercle philharmonique de Québec. Responding to his interest in conducting, Wilfrid *Pelletier invited him to share certain concerts in the 1936–7 season of the CSM orchestra, and Beaudet distinguished himself in Jacques Ibert's *Escales*, the Franck *Symphony*, and other works, and conducted some summer concerts.

Beaudet relinquished his posts in Quebec City and accepted a position with the CBC where, successively 1937–47, he was program director for the Quebec region, national music director, program director for the French network, and that network's representative in the Pacific region. In addition he assisted in the compilation of the 1947 *Catalogue of Canadian Composers* (see Dictionaries). He also, 1936–46 for CBC radio, conducted several major works including Berlioz' *L'Enfance du Christ*, the Fauré *Requiem*, Honegger's *Le Roi David*, and Pierné's *Les Enfants à Bethléhem*. He was responsible for bringing about the considerably larger role of music in CBC programming and for the decisions leading to the first operas commissioned by the CBC: *Willan's **Transit through Fire* (1942) and **Deirdre of the Sorrows* (1945). In the summer of 1944 the NBC invited the CBC to take part in its series 'Music of the New World.' Beaudet prepared and conducted eight programs under the title 'Canadian Music in Wartime,' featuring major works by Lucio *Agostini, Arthur *Benjamin (at that time living in Canada), *Blachford, *Blackburn, *Brott, *Champagne, *Coulthard, *Farnon, *Fleming, J.-J. *Gagnier, *Gratton, *Walter, *Weinzweig, and

Jean-Marie Beaudet

Willan. He also conducted a 1943 performance of *Carmen* at the *St Denis Theatre with singers from the *Metropolitan Opera and gave a 1946 recital of piano music of Debussy at the *Ermitage. His European conducting debut, 13 May 1946 at the Prague Festival, was in a concert of Canadian works (Blackburn, Brott, Champagne, *MacMillan, *Tanguay, and Willan) by the Czech Philharmonic Orchestra. Beaudet left the CBC in 1947 to free himself from administrative duties and devote himself to music. Even so, when the CBC IS was formed after World War II, he was responsible for the series 'Music and Musicians of Canada' (1948–9), which promoted Canadian music abroad. For it he selected works by *Archer, Blackburn, Brott, Champagne, Coulthard, *Matton, *Mercure, *Morel, *Papineau-Couture, *Pentland, *Somers, Weinzweig, and others.

He taught at the *CMM (orchestra class 1947–52) and also at the École supérieure de musique (*École Vincent-d'Indy), where Jocelyne *Binet, Josephte *Dufresne, and Elayne Julien were among his pupils. He also accompanied Raoul *Jobin, Marjorie Lawrence, Ezio Pinza, Georges Thill, Ninon Vallin (1947), and others in Canadian recitals, and appeared as a duo-pianist with Jeanne *Landry. Continuing his conducting career, in 1949 he directed *Tosca* for the *Montreal Festivals, Bizet's complete incidental music for Daudet's *L'Arlésienne* for a production in St-Laurent, Que, and Milhaud's opera *Le Pauvre Matelot* for Montreal's *Minute Opera. For the CBC in 1951 he conducted the *MSO and the *Quebec, *Vancouver, and *Winnipeg SOs, and directed a performance of *Faust*.

With the aid of a grant from the Royal Society of Canada he went to Paris in 1952. Returning in October 1953, he conducted 16 performances of *Madama Butterfly* for the *Variétés lyriques before moving to Toronto where he served 1953–7 as director of production and program planning for CBC radio. During those years he conducted many of the major programs both on radio ('CBC Wednesday Night') and on TV (*'Heure du concert' and 'CBC Folio'), presenting Pierné's *Les Enfants à Bethléhem* and Dvořák's *Requiem* in 1954; Puccini's *La Bohème*, Ravel's *L'Heure espagnole*, Debussy's *Pelléas et Mélisande*, and Gluck's *Alceste* in 1955; Martinu's *Comedy on the Bridge* and Massenet's *Werther* in 1956; and Rameau's *Hippolyte et Aricie*, Gounod's *Mireille*, and Bizet's *Carmen* in 1957. He also 1953–64 frequently conducted the *CBC SO, often in Canadian premieres (eg, the Dukas *Symphonie* and Messiaen's *Turangalîla-Symphonie*), and once (1955) in a rare public concert, part of a summer festival in Montreal.

After serving 1957–9 as the CBC's representative in Paris, Beaudet returned to Canada as executive secretary of the *CMCentre. He conducted again for the CBC, notably Sauguet's *Les Caprices de Marianne* (1959, radio) and Poulenc's *Dialogues des Carmélites* (1960, TV). While he was assistant vice-president in charge of programming at the CBC, 1961–4, Beaudet conducted Rameau's *Les Fêtes d'Hébé* for TV. For the Montreal Festivals he conducted eight performances of Offenbach's *Barbe-bleue* in 1959 and operas by Blackburn (**Silent Measures*), Somers (**The Fool*), and *Vallerand (**Le Magicien*) in 1962. Leaving the CBC for the last time in 1964, he became music director for the *NAC and served in that position until his death. Among his responsibilities at the centre was the assembling of the permanent orchestra (*NACO) which made its distinguished debut in 1970 under its conductor Mario *Bernardi.

Both as a competent and sensitive conductor and as a bold and enlightened administrator Jean-Marie Beaudet played a notable role in the development of Canadian music. He conducted CBC orchestras in several first recordings of symphonic works by Canadian composers, including Blackburn, Champagne, Gagnier, *Pépin, and Willan. In 1971, posthumously, he was awarded the *CMCouncil Medal. The same year the Jean-Marie Beaudet Fund for aspiring conductors was created by the Music Dept of the *U of Ottawa.

WRITINGS

'Composition,' *Music in Canada*

DISCOGRAPHY (as orchestra conductor)

Blackburn *Concertino in C* for piano – Mercure *Pantomime*. Barette pf, CBC Mtl orch. 1949. RCI 2

A. Brott *Concordia; Cradle Song* – Tanguay *Lied*. CBC Mtl orch. Ca 1949. RCI Canadian Album No. 3 (4 78s)

Champagne *Suite canadienne* – Willan *Concerto in C Minor* for piano. Butcher pf, La Cantoria, CBC Mtl orch. 1945. RCI Canadian Album No. 1 /RCA DM 1229 (4 78s)

– *Symphonie gaspésienne*. CBC Mtl orch. 1967. RCI 216/RCA CCS-1010

Gratton *Coucher de soleil* – Bales *Essay for Strings* – Champagne *Danse villageoise*. CBC Mtl orch. 1949. RCI 6

Mercure *Cantate pour une joie* – Pépin *Le Rite du soleil noir*. Lavergne sop, CBC Mtl chor and orch. 1958. RCI 155

Morawetz *Serenade* – A. Brott *Lullaby* – Martinu *Tre Ricercare*. CBC Mtl orch. Ca 1949. RCI 5

Morel *Suite* for small orchestra – H. Gagnon *Deux antiennes; Mazurka* – M. Perrault *Les Fleurettes*. CBC Mtl orch. Ca 1950. RCI 7

Pépin *Variations symphoniques* – Blackburn *Rigaudon* – J.-J. Gagnier *Le Vent dans l'érable effeuillé*. CBC Mtl orch. Ca 1949. RCI 1

Tanguay *Pavane*. CBC Mtl orch. (1946). RCI Canadian Album No. 2 (78)

See also Hervé Baillargeon and Discographies for Kuerti and Simoneau II.

As a pianist Beaudet accompanied N. *Brunet (RCI 92).

BIBLIOGRAPHY

'Profile: Jean Beaudet,' *CBC Times*, 4–10 Mar 1951

Sauvé, Wilfrid P. 'L'orchestre du Centre national des arts,' *JMC*, vol 15, Apr 1969

Arthur, Gérard. 'Jean Beaudet,' *CMB*, 2, Spring – Summer 1971

Thériault, Jacques. 'Portrait d'un musicien Jean-Marie Beaudet,' *Culture Vivante*, Summer 1971 GP

BEAUDET, Pierre (Hugues). Pianist, producer, b Thetford Mines, south of Quebec City, 20 Jan 1924, brother of Jean-Marie *Beaudet. He first studied piano with Léo-Pol *Morin in Montreal. At the *CMM 1943–6 his teachers were Germaine *Malépart and Gilberte *Martin (piano) and Louis *Bailly (chamber music). He studied privately with John *Newmark. In 1947 he worked in Paris with Jean Batella (piano) and Paul Bazelaire (ensemble) and spent the summer at the American Cons at Fontainebleau with Robert Casadesus (piano) and Nadia Boulanger (interpretation). Returning to Montreal, he formed a duo with Guy *Bourassa and presented several series of four-hand piano recitals on CBC radio and in public. Beaudet has accompanied and coached several singers, has taught piano, and has arranged and directed the music for numerous radio and TV programs – 'Tour de chant,' 'Sur les ailes de la chanson,' 'Noblesse oblige,' etc. In 1958 he joined the *CBC as record librarian, and in 1962 he became a producer of musical broadcasts. He has composed several songs and has had poems published in the magazine *Gants du ciel*.

DISCOGRAPHY

Archer *Ten Folk Songs* – Beckwith *Music for Dancing*. G. Bourassa pf. 1954. RCI 113 (CH)

Beau Dommage. Leading Quebec rock band of the mid-1970s, its name an old Quebec expression meaning 'most certainly' or 'why not.' Formed in 1973 by participants in mixed-media and theatrical productions 1970–3 at the *UQAM, Beau Dommage at first comprised the composer-singer-guitarist Michel Rivard, the composer-keyboardist-flutist Robert Léger, and the lyricist Pierre Huet. They were joined in turn by the composer-guitarist Pierre Bertrand, the singer-keyboardist Marie-Michèle Desrosiers, and in March 1974 the drummer Réal Desrosiers. Though Léger continued to compose for Beau Dommage he was replaced as a performer by Michel Hinton in 1976.

Beau Dommage made its debut in Otocber 1973 at Luducu (UQAM) and, through appearances at various Cegeps, boîtes à chansons, and concert halls, rose quickly to the front rank of Quebec pop groups. Sales in Canada (almost exclusively in Quebec) of the LPs *Beau Dommage* (1974, Cap ST 70.034) and *Où est passée la noce?* (1975, Cap SKAC 70.037) exceeded those of all other Canadian artists of the mid-1970s. The second LP (which included the long vocal-instrumental work 'Un Incident à Bois-des-Filion') won the 'Jeune Chanson 1976' prize (presented by the secretary of state and culture of France) at the MIDEM trade convention in Cannes. Other Beau Dommage LPs have been *Un autre jour arrive en ville ...* (1976, Cap ST 70.048), *Passagers* (1977, Cap ST 70.055) and the compilation *Les Grands Succès de Beau Dommage* (Cap SKAO 70.058) released in 1978. (In 1977 Rivard recorded his own LP – *Méfiez-vous du grand amour*, Cap ST 70.053.) In 1976 the group wrote and recorded the score for the Michel Tremblay–André Brassard film *Le Soleil se lève sur la rue Bélanger*. It made annual tours of Europe (France, Belgium, Luxembourg, and Switzerland) 1975–8 and performed in the major venues in Quebec and in several English-Canadian centres. With Contraction, *Harmonium, and *Octobre, Beau Dommage headlined the 1976 St-Jean-Baptiste celebrations (on Mount Royal, Montreal), which attracted some 400,000 people. Beau Dommage's most popular songs include 'La Complainte du phoque en Alaska' (released on LP and as a 45, and also recorded by Félix *Leclerc), 'Le Blues d'la métropole,' and 'Amène pas ta gang.' The group's composers – Bertrand, Huet, Léger, and Rivard – are members of CAPAC. The lyrics and music to some of their songs have been published by the Éditions Bonté divine in the folios *Beau Dommage Volume I* (1976) and *Beau Dommage Volume II* (1977).

According to Georges-Hébert Germain (*La Presse*, 20 Sep 1975) each of Beau Dommage's songs 'recreates ... a kind of drama. Dramas of loneliness, of boredom, of love and of disillusion.' Bruno Roy, in his *Panorama de la chanson au Québec* (Montreal 1977), adds: 'Beau Dommage is very "Montreal." There is in its songs a poetic and musical study of adolescence in Montreal's east end ... Beau Dommage belongs mainly to the tradition

Beau Dommage: (left to right) Pierre Bertrand, Marie-Michèle Desrosiers, Michel Rivard, Réal Desrosiers, Robert Léger

of the chanson and the musicians claim to have been influenced by the Beatles and the chansonniers.' In 1978 the band suspended its activities.

BIBLIOGRAPHY

Germain, Georges-Hébert. 'Beau Dommage et l'histoire d'un down de rêve,' Montreal *La Presse*, 20 Sep 1975

Jasmin, Hélène. 'Beau Dommage: Canada's most successful new pop group proves that being true to yourself pays off,' *CanComp*, 106, Dec 1975

Freeston, David. 'Chez Beau Dommage,' *Montreal Scene*, 12 Feb 1977

Petrowski, Nathalie. 'Beau Dommage ... dans le corridor de France,' Montreal *Le Devoir*, 16 Apr 1977 (BLH)

BEAUDRY, (Joseph René) **Jacques** (André). Conductor, b Sorel, Que, 10 Oct 1924; BA (Montreal) 1945. After studying piano and organ with Lucien Jolicoeur at the Collège de Montréal 1938–43 and performing there as organist 1940–3, he studied 1944–7 under Alfred *Laliberté (piano) and Séverin *Moisse (harmony, counterpoint). He continued his studies 1947–54 at the Brussels Royal Cons with Marcel Maas (piano), André Souris (harmony), Jean Absil (counterpoint), Maurice Raskin (chamber music), and René Defossey (conducting), obtaining diplomas in these subjects. He then decided to concentrate on conducting and attended the classes of Willem van Otterloo in Hilversum, Holland, and those of Paul van Kempen at the Accademia Chigiana of Siena.

Beaudry made his debut as a conductor in 1955 on the CBC radio program 'Petit Concert.' Since that time he has conducted numerous concerts by the *Quebec SO, the *MSO, the *TSO, and the *NACO, as well as the *CBC SO and other CBC orchestras. His visits to the USSR in 1957 and 1959, at the invitation of the Soviet ministry of cultural affairs, were possibly the first by a North American conductor and included appearances with several orchestras, including the Moscow SO and the Leningrad Philharmonic. He frequently conducted concerts in Europe, including some by the Czech Philharmonic Orchestra (Prague Spring Festival 1961) and others in Poland, Norway, Greece, Belgium, Switzerland, Italy, and Holland. When the MSO visited the USSR in 1962, performing for the first time abroad, Zubin Mehta and Beaudry shared the conducting duties. Beaudry conducted the orchestra in four of its Soviet appearances, as well as in one of its two concerts in Paris. He was also the first Canadian to conduct at the Paris Opera, giving a total of more than 150 performances in that theatre between 1967 and 1972, including *Aida, Carmen, Don Carlos, Lucia di Lammermoor*, and *Tosca*. Following his debut in *Lucia di Lammermoor*, Bernard Gavoty (Clarendon) wrote in *Le Figaro* (Paris, 15 Nov 1967): 'Now's there's a conductor indeed! It's not a common breed. This one has bearing and presence, fine craftsmanship, dash, subtlety when required and a sense of choral balance, and he's a painstaking accompanist of soloists. I found the same Beaudry in the operatic field that I had known and enjoyed in the symphonic: poised, a perfect musician, able to command the esteem and respect of those he conducts – in short, I repeat, a conductor.'

Beaudry was guest conductor at the inauguration of the new opera house in Warsaw in 1969. Though he resides in Paris, he has returned frequently to Canada; he has conducted, among other works, concert versions of Verdi's *La Traviata* and *Aida* on the CBC in 1971 and Puccini's *La Bohème* in a production by the *Opéra de Québec at the *PDA and the *Grand Théâtre in Quebec City in 1975. He also conducted performances given by the dancers Margot Fonteyn and Rudolph Nureyev in New York and Washington in 1974 and 1975. With the Stuttgart Opera Ballet he performed in 1973 and 1975 in New York, Washington, Philadelphia, Stuttgart, and elsewhere. Between 1962 and 1980, he conducted more than 200 performances as a regular guest conductor with the opera houses of Mulhouse, Lyons, Strasbourg, Nice, Toulouse, and Lille.

Beaudry has conducted several works by Canadian composers, including François *Morel's *Esquisse* (USSR 1960), Roger *Matton's *Mouvement symphonique No. 1* (*Montreal Festivals 1961, Athens 1961, Paris 1966, Brussels 1967, Quebec City and Thetford Mines 1973), Pierre *Mercure's *Kaléidoscope* (USSR 1957, Canada 1958, Guatemala 1959), and, Jean *Vallerand's *Cordes en mouvement* (Paris 1972) and *Le Diable dans le beffroi* (Poland and Czechoslovakia 1960, Norway and Canada 1961, USSR 1962, France 1962 and 1972). He premiered some 10 works by the French composer André Casanova, including the opera *Le Bonheur dans le crime*, at the Théâtre du Capitole in Toulouse in 1973, a work that received the grand prix de la Création lyrique in France. The St-Jean-Baptiste Society awarded him the 1960 *Prix de musique Calixa-Lavallée.

DISCOGRAPHY

Papineau-Couture *Pièce concertante No. 3* – J. Hétu *Symphony, Op 2* – O. Joachim *Concertante No. 1*. Bress vn, CBC Mtl str orch. 1971. RCI 293

BIBLIOGRAPHY

Prévost, Pierre. 'Jacques Beaudry ambassadeur de la musique,' *Maclean*, Aug 1961 (TC-C)

BEAULIEU, Joseph. Teacher, folklorist, composer, b Mattawa, Ont, 21 May 1895, d North Bay, Ont, 1 Oct 1965; B MUS (Montreal) 1942. He settled in Ottawa in 1915 and studied piano with Oscar *O'Brien and Amédée *Tremblay, and later with Harry *Puddicombe at the Canadian Cons, where he subsequently joined the teaching staff. He also taught at the *U of Ottawa (piano, singing, business) and at the same time participated in musical evenings with Charles *Marchand, O'Brien, and Tremblay. He made his first folk music tours with Marchand. In the course of his travels in Quebec and Ontario he collected numerous folksongs and harmonized them for the Petits Chanteurs céciliens, which he founded and directed 1931–43. His song collections include *Gerbes de chansons nouvelles, Chantez petits et grands, Chantez, les petits* (Thompson 1960), and the eight-volume series *Mon École chante* (La Bonne Chanson 1956–64).

Beaulieu served 1942–65 as assistant director in charge of the teaching of music for the Ontario Ministry of Education. In 1942 the Benedictines of St-Benoît-du-Lac engaged him to teach voice. He moved to North Bay in 1946 and for nearly 20 years spent his summers at nearby Lake Talon,

where he taught music, particularly singing, to boys. Beaulieu wrote some 200 religious and folk-inspired songs, of which many were published by La *Bonne Chanson and *Thompson. He composed the operetta *Le Trésor du pauvre* and the *Messe Vatican II* for four mixed voices. In 1967 the Joseph Beaulieu Camp for the study of music was opened on the Ile-aux-Chênes in Lake Nipissing, and in October 1968 North Bay inaugurated the Joseph Beaulieu Centre, which includes a library and a theatre. DM

Beaver. As an emblem of Canada the beaver goes back at least as far as the 17th century. The industrious, flat-tailed, rich-pelted animal was the staple of the fur trade which prompted Europe's first keen commercial interest in the new world; one was depicted on a coat of arms granted in the early 1600s to Sir William Alexander (who held Nova Scotia) by Charles I of England. It also appeared on the coat of arms of the newly incorporated city of Montreal in 1832 and on the first Canadian postage stamp in 1851. In 1865 in Montreal the anonymous 'Sam Scribble' wrote a musical satire with the title *King of the Beavers*. In song titles and sheet music cover illustrations, however, the beaver appears rarely by comparison with the ubiquitous maple leaf. The earliest-known instance is the cover of Joseph *Maffré's *Original Canadian Quadrilles* (J.W. Herbert 1847), where it appears with the maple leaf, as it does on C.H. Moody's song 'Here's to the Land of the Beaver' (1900), N. McLeod's song 'Maple Leaf and Beaver' (1915), and N. Fraser *Allan's 'Made in Canada Campaign Song' (1915). *Le Castor* (polka patriotique), by Fleury D'Eschambault, published by J. W. Herbert, was advertised in 1857, and sheet music of the same composer's 'La Frontière' (chant national) and 'Nos Jours de gloire' (chanson Canadienne) had cover designs that featured the beaver. *Danse du castor Canadien* was recorded by the accordionist Tommy Duchesne for *Starr in the 1930s. Gilles *Vigneault's story 'Le Dict de l'aigle et du castor' was set to music by Claude *Léveillée in what the composer called a 'spoken concerto.' Songs which have some reference to the beaver include Charles *Harrison's 'My Own Dear Canada' (1917), the campfire favourite 'Land of the Silver Birch,' and *Stringband's 'Show Us the Length.' Boosey & Hawkes published (nd) *The Land of the Maple and the Beaver* by Charles *O'Neill.

Garth Beckett (right) and Boyd McDonald

Beaver Records Ltd. Company established in 1950 by the Toronto lawyer, musical patron, and supporter of the *Toronto Mendelssohn Choir F.R. MacKelcan (1882–1962), with the purpose of recording the choir. Beaver released, in 1952 and 1953 respectively, the first Canadian LP recordings of *Messiah* and the *St Matthew Passion*, followed by recordings of Handel anthems in 1953 and Pierné's *The Children's Crusade* in 1956. In 1953 the company issued its only purely orchestral recording – a performance of Tchaikovsky's *Symphony No. 5* by the *TSO in *Massey Hall. A recording of Lalo's *Symphonie espagnole* by the same orchestra, with the violinist Betty-Jean *Hagen, was not released. Pressed in Toronto by Victor, Beaver records were issued in the USA on Victor's Bluebird Classics label.

BECKETT, Garth. See Beckett and McDonald.

Beckett and McDonald. Two-piano team formed in 1966 at the U of Saskatchewan by Garth Beckett and Boyd McDonald. In 1967 both players joined the faculty of music at the *U of Manitoba and, besides teaching there, had intensive coaching in the two-piano literature from Alma *Brock-Smith. At first the team performed throughout western Canada and on the CBC, giving the premieres of Bruce *Mather's *Sonata* in 1970 at the U of Manitoba and Robert *Turner's *Concerto for Two Pianos and Orchestra* in 1972 with the *Winnipeg SO. Its 1972 recital at Wigmore Hall, London, led to four more there over the next five years, to other appearances in the United Kingdom (eg, the 1973 Cheltenham Festival) and to performances in London and Amsterdam in 1979. It made its New York debut at Alice Tully Hall in 1978. Both players in the meantime (1976) had joined the teaching staff at *Wilfrid Laurier U.

Beckett and McDonald both originally were pupils of Lyell *Gustin. Beckett (b Easton, Sask, 22 Dec 1933) also studied 1954–6 in England with Geoffrey Tankard and James Ching and in 1957 in Italy with Arturo Benedetti Michelangeli. He served 1964–6 as president of the *Musical Art Club of Saskatoon. McDonald (b Tuberose, Sask, 28 Sep 1932) studied composition in Saskatoon with Murray *Adaskin and 1957–60 in Paris with Darius Milhaud and Nadia Boulanger. He studied piano in Paris with Jean Casadesus. McDonald's compositions include *Suite for Nine Solo Instruments* (a commission for the 1959 Saskatoon Summer Festival) and *Fantasy for Piano* (1975), for the Winnipeg Centennial Committee.

DISCOGRAPHY

Berkeley *Concerto for Two Pianos and Orchestra*. London Phil, Del Mar cond. 1974. Lyrita SRCS 80

Stravinsky – Mather *Sonata for Two Pianos* – Bartok. 1971. RCI 354

BIBLIOGRAPHY

Burt, Eric O. 'Former Saskatoon pianists keep hectic pace,' Saskatoon *Star-Phoenix*, 25 May 1979 (JA)

BECKWITH, John. Composer, writer, educator, pianist, broadcaster, b Victoria, BC, 9 Mar 1927; B MUS (Toronto) 1947, M MUS (Toronto) 1961, hon D MUS (Mount Allison) 1974, hon D MUS (McGill) 1978. His paternal forebears settled in Nova Scotia in 1760. Both parents were musical and encouraged the development of his talent. In Victoria he sang in the Anglican Cathedral choir directed by Stanley Bulley and studied piano at the age of six with Ogreta *McNeill, then with Gwendoline Harper. In 1945 he went to Toronto to study on a TCM scholarship with Alberto *Guerrero, who was his most influential teacher. In Toronto he became a member of a circle of musicians and writers that included the poet James Reaney, with whom he began a collaboration that has lasted over 25 years (he has collaborated occasionally with other poets: Jay Macpherson, Margaret Atwood, Dennis Lee). At university he was the arts editor 1947–8 of *The Varsity*. Upon graduation he undertook a broad range of professional activities: composing, acting, coaching, and public relations for the conservatory (by then *RCMT) among others. In 1950 he married the actress and stage director Pamela Terry; that same year he won the Canadian Amateur Hockey Assn award, which enabled him to study composition 1950–2 with Nadia Boulanger in Paris.

Beckwith wrote occasional concert reviews 1948–9 and 1952–3 for the *Globe and Mail* and was a regular critic 1959–62 and 1963–5 for the *Toronto Daily Star*. He also wrote program notes 1966–71 for the *TSO. He was on staff 1953–5 at the CBC, and remained associated with the corporation as a regular freelance until 1963. During these years he planned and wrote the radio series 'Music in Our Time' (1953–6) and 'The World of Music' (1956–63). Later, with the producer Diana Brown, he planned 'The Music of Chopin,' serving as writer-narrator for that series. He also prepared the radio documentaries 'The Legacy of Paul Hindemith' (1964), 'The Boulez View' (1965), 'A Bartók Microcosm' (1966), and 'Berlioz after a Century' (1969). He was an associate editor (1957–62, record reviews) of the *Canadian Music Journal*. In 1965 he received a *Canada Council fellowship to study electronic music and write an opera.

Beckwith began lecturing part-time at the *U of Toronto in 1952, taught full-time 1955–70, and was dean of the Faculty of Music 1970–7. His deanship ushered in a new emphasis on Canadian studies and correlation of disciplines. He served with 'characteristic patience, fairness and wisdom' (U of Toronto Faculty of Music *News*, Spring – Summer 1977), and during his term the faculty 'enhanced its reputation and remained stable' (ibid). It well may be Beckwith's class teaching, however – with its extraordinary wit, erudition, and breadth of reference and its easy and authoritative passage through the linked yet separate worlds of composition, performance, and scholarship – that ultimately will be regarded as his main contribution to the university. When he retired from the deanship he continued on staff as composer, teacher, and co-ordinator (performance). William *Aide, Robert *Aitken, Gustav *Ciamaga, Edward *Laufer, and Bruce *Mather are among those who attended his classes, and Clifford *Ford, prior to joining them, was a private student. A perceptive, outspoken critic, Beckwith has commented on Canadian music and other

John Beckwith

musical topics in numerous publications, and it was his article on Canadian coverage in international music encyclopedias, 'About Canadian music: the P.R. failure,' which suggested to Floyd *Chalmers the need for a Canadian reference work on the subject, thus contributing to the genesis of *EMC* (for which Beckwith has written several articles).

As a composer Beckwith has received commissions from the CBC (*Canada Dash – Canada Dot, Five Love Songs, Four Love Songs, The Journals of Susanna Moodie, The Killdeer, Message to Winnipeg, Montage, Night Blooming Cereus, The Trumpets of Summer, Twelve Letters to a Small Town, Wednesday's Child*); *Canadian Brass (*Taking a Stand*); the *Festival Singers (*Jonah*); Forest Hill Community Centre, Toronto (*Music for Dancing*); the Leslie *Bell Competition Committee (*Papineau*); Lois *Marshall (*Four Songs to Poems by e.e. cummings*); Ewen McQuaig (*Upper Canadian Hymn Preludes*); the National Ballet of Canada (*Music for Dancing*); the *Orford String Quartet (*Quartet*); St George's United Church, Toronto (*The Sun Dance*); the TS (*All the Bees and All the Keys, Musical Chairs*); the *Toronto Mendelssohn Choir (*Place of Meeting*); the U of Toronto Faculty of Music Alumni Assn (*Fall Scene and Fair Dance*); the *Vancouver International Festival (*Circle, with Tangents*); the Vancouver Junior Symphony (*Concertino*); the *Victoria SO (*Flower Variations and Wheels*); the Waterloo Lutheran University Choir (*Sharon Fragments*).

Beckwith's knowledge, objectivity, and experience have made him a respected and sought-after committee member, and he has served on the program committee for *CAUSM (chairman 1973–4); the music task force of the advisory committee on academic planning, Council of Ontario Universities (chairman 1973–4); the board of directors of the *COC (planning committee 1970–7); the board of directors of the *CMCentre, 1970–7 (publication committee chairman 1972–7); and the board of directors of *EMC*. He was secretary 1952–5 and 1961–3 of the *CLComp. In 1972 he received the *CMCouncil Medal. In 1978, in London, Ont, he gave the keynote address – 'Music: The Search for Universals' – at the 13th Congress of ISME.

The persistent theme in Beckwith's oeuvre (a search for a Canadian voice through music) and the preferred mode of construction (a quilt-like design) were present even in 1949 in *The Great Lakes Suite*, which suggests, as if through the perception of an imaginative child, familiar sights, people, attitudes, actions, and the resulting feelings and thoughts. Witty, spiky, or gently weaving melodies and brisk, clipped, or flowing and simple rhythms invoke a 1920 music hall, a Victorian ballroom, a rowing excursion, a patter song heard long ago, or a half-forgotten joke, all sewn together with a light hand into a harmonious whole. The last movement, turning introspective, observes 'My voice is soft while theirs is loud ... I am one, they are a crowd.' (This theme, the pull between public and private worlds, was still engaging Beckwith 20 years later in *Place of Meeting*.) Returning from Paris in 1952, secure in technique and conscious of the objective, Beckwith evolved with Reaney the theme of the opera **Night Blooming Cereus*. The work became a parable told as an Ontario village tale of an old woman mourning the long absence of a prodigal daughter and of a granddaughter who comes seeking a heritage and love. The event of their finding each other is shared by a few townspeople, who also live lonely lives sustained by yearning and timid hope. All are portrayed simply and compassionately in vernacular song, sung prayer, and hymns. The local nurseryman (perhaps a male reincarnation of Ceres) suggests the possibility of happiness through self-renewal, parallelling nature, and the blooming of the cereus coincides with a rebirth of love in the hearts of these people.

After completing the *Concerto Fantasy*, a work at once abstract and colourful but isolated in his output, Beckwith collaborated again with Reaney in three collages laden with referential content and experimenting with loose juxtaposition (and superposition) of elements of strong and contrasting individualities. The largest of these collages is *Canada Dash – Canada Dot*, a panoramic triptych conveying an image of a country and its people through the intricate weave of a disparate assemblage: stylized morse code, a country fiddler, enumerations of names (Whitmanesque in incantational effect), a transmuted *Lavallée galop (very *Variétés Lyriques in character), railway lore, hawking, the song of a footloose pop singer, and hymns. At one point the journey turns north and into the past, to Sharon, Ont, home of the *Children of Peace, a place of symbolic significance for Beckwith. The movement from place to place and from period to period is not linear; subtle modes of perception and recall ensure a more complex and evocative progression. *The Trumpets of Summer*, commissioned for the Shakespeare quatercentenary, 'illuminate[s] the ways in which Shakespeare has become part of the Canadian experience' (program notes). In Margaret Atwood's text life and theatre are merged into a perception of the 'world around us' with one's own chair conceived as 'the centre [holding] the earth and skies.' A life unfolds: memories of childhood torments (a serial, bi-metric, contrapuntal web based on a seven-note, six-pitch diatonic row); a sendup of 'culture consumption' in high school (an expertly gauche semi-operatic scene using two 12-tone rows each divisible into two diatonic hexachords); a spoof of pseudo-scholarly debate (in which serial polyphony, pompous declamation, and patter song coalesce into satire); and an introspective Epilogue. As in other works, Beckwith uses instrumentation frugally to imply the extreme resourcefulness of Canada's early settlers, who had to do so much with so little.

Beckwith's second opera, *The Shivaree*, again on a libretto by Reaney, achieves a high-powered dramatic sweep through a rapid succession of short scenes in two acts which expertly paint an early-20th-century southwestern Ontario farming district and the two protagonists, Quartz, a rich storekeeper, and Daisy, the desperate and resisting young woman whose soul and body he attempts to purchase. The story is given depth by the emotive force of the music and the implied dichotomies: ancestors/descendants, old/young, rich/poor, organic/inorganic, gentleness/roughness, the innocence of the individual/the wisdom of the group, etc. This poignant story of a group of archetypes, whose lives in a crisis are affected by a dialectic between personal desire and the ethos of their small society, culminates with a triumph of common sense which, in turn, provides a sanctioned fulfilment for all. Besides the penetratingly clear local colour the work also has broad relevance and appeal. Echoes from a similar past permeate the five miniatures of Beckwith's delightful *Upper Canadian Hymn Preludes*.

Jonah, a lesson in 'forgiveness and tolerance,' blends in a syncretistic whole a Hebrew tale, a serial melos patterned after biblical cantillation, early protestant hymn style, and echoes of Purcell and serial Stravinsky. *Jonah* is the first of Beckwith's works to reveal the force of his ethical, societal, and ontological concerns. The same evangelizing urge informs later works of otherwise different characters. *Sharon Fragments* are eight short movements exquisitely wrought from serializations of two hymn tunes on texts by David Willson, the leader of the Sharon sect. The work evolves through flexible declamation and subtle textural transformations, achieving a perfect balance among the parts and a rare, fresh euphony.

Place of Meeting depicts life in a large city ('Niniveh-Toronto' perhaps) burdened and hardened by trivia and aggression. Three male solo voices represent a countervailing spirit, and their search, poignantly castigating, is for a 'Civitas Dei.' The original (later discarded) title was, in fact, Civitas. *The Sun Dance* descends into the distant past, probing for spiritual roots, using words from Plains Cree, first-century-BC Chinese, and other sources. A mood of ritual is invoked by a pentatonic melos, percussion, singing and declaiming chorus, spatial play, and flexible time relationships. In *Circle, with Tangents* and in the *Quartet* Beckwith has refined further his collage techniques. Both are major works which in their own ways use, in a carefully controlled manner, complex and subtle time organizations that highlight the simultaneous deployment of different periodicities and the interplay of various densities of texture. *Taking a Stand* (the title has two senses) and *Musical Chairs* add a new dimension to his quest for musical allegory and show the same sense of fun as his (and Reaney's) children's tale *All the Bees and All the Keys*.

Beckwith is a composer of magic eclecticism. The influences and borrowings in his works give up a part of their identity and take on new roles assigned by him. His is, perhaps, the most characteristically English-Canadian voice in composition. In him, composer and teacher are inseparable, both powered by an inquisitive, sensitive, informed, and intelligent mind. He is an associate of the CMCentre and an affiliate of PRO Canada.

COMPOSITIONS

STAGE

Night Blooming Cereus, chamb opera (Reaney). 1953–8 (Tor 1959). Ric (rental)

The Killdeer, incidental (Reaney). 1959. Ms

The Shivaree, chamb opera (Reaney). 1965–78. Ms

ORCHESTRA AND BAND

Music for Dancing (orch from pf, 4 hands). 1948 (pf), orch 1959 (Ott 1959). BMIC 1961. CBC SM-47 (*CBC Van Chamb O)

Montage. 1953, rescored 1955 (Tor 1953). Med orch. CMCentre

Fall Scene and Fair Dance. 1956 (Tor 1956). Vn, cl, str. BMIC 1957

Concerto Fantasy. 1959 (Mtl 1962). Pf, orch. Ber (rental)

Flower Variations and Wheels. 1962 (Victoria 1963). Med orch. Ber (rental)

Concertino. 1963 (Tor 1964). Hn, orch. Ber (rental)

Jonah, cantata (various). 1963 (Tor 1963). BMIC 1969

Place of Meeting (Dennis Lee). 1967 (Tor 1967). Spkr, ten, blues singer, SATB, orch. CMCentre

Elastic Band Studies. 1969, rev 1975 (Tor 1976). Concert band. Ms.

All the Bees and All the Keys (Reaney). 1973 (Tor 1973). Narr, orch. (Orch) Ber (rental), (pf score) Press Porcépic 1976

CHAMBER

The Great Lakes Suite (Reaney). 1949. Sop, bar, cl, vc, pf. CMCentre

Five Pieces for Brass Trio. 1951. CMCentre

Five Pieces for Flute Duet. 1951. BMIC 1962

Four Pieces for Bassoon Duet. 1951. CMCentre

Quartet for Woodwind Instruments. 1951. CMCentre

Three Studies for String Trio. 1956. CMCentre

Circle, with Tangents. 1967. Hpd, 13 str. BMIC 1968

Taking a Stand. 1972. 8 brass, 14 music stands, 5 players. Ber 1975

Musical Chairs. 1973. Str quin. CMCentre

Quartet. 1977. Str quar. CMCentre. Mel SMLP-4038 (*Orford Str Quar)

PIANO

Four Conceits 1945–48. 1945–8. CMCentre. RCI 228/RCA CCS-1022 (*Troup)

Music for Dancing. 1948. Pf: 4 hands. CMCentre. RCI 113 (P. *Beaudet, G. *Bourassa)

The Music Room. 1951. FH 1955. RCI 134 (*Newmark)

Novelette. 1951. BMIC 1954

Six Mobiles. 1959. BMIC 1960. CCM-2 (*Cavalho)

Interval Studies. 1962. BMIC 1962

Suite on Old Tunes (arr). 1966. BMIC 1967. CCM-2 (*Cavalho)

Variation Piquant sur la 'Toronto Opera House Waltz.' 1967. 2 pf. CMCentre

New Mobiles. 1971. Wat 1972

Also a work for org and prepared tape, *Upper Canadian Hymn Preludes* (1977). CMCentre

CHOIR

The Trumpets of Summer (Atwood). 1964. Soloists, SATB, narr, chamb ens. Ber (rental). CBC SM-81/ Cap ST-6323 (*Festival Singers)

Sharon Fragments (Willson). 1966. SATB. Wat 1966. Cap ST-6258 (*Festival Singers)

The Sun Dance. 1968. SATB, spkr, org, perc. CMCentre

Three Blessings (Fisher, Burns, Wesley). 1968. SATB, instr (optional in No. 2). BMIC 1968. CBC SM-81/Cap ST-6323 (*Festival Singers)

Gas! (Beckwith). 1969. 20 spkrs. CMCentre

1838 (Lee). 1970. SATB. Novello 1970

Papineau (2 Lower Canada folk songs). 1977. 2 equal vs. GVT 1978

VOICE

Five Lyrics of the T'ang Dynasty (various). 1947. High v, pf. BMIC 1949. RCI 148 (*Alarie)

'Serenade' (Thibaudeau). 1949. Med v, pf. CMCentre. RCI 36 (C. *Jordan)

'The Formal Garden of the Heart' (Thibaudeau). 1950. Med v, pf. CMCentre

Four Songs to Poems by e.e. cummings. 1950. Sop, pf. Wat 1975

Four Songs from Ben Jonson's 'Volpone.' 1961. Bar, guit. BMIC 1967

A Chaucer Suite. 1962. Alto, ten, bar. CMCentre

Ten English Rhymes (anon). 1964. Young vs, pf. BMIC 1964

Four Love Songs (Canadian folk songs). 1969. Bar, pf. Ber 1970. (Nos. 1, 3, 4) CBC SM-111 (*Bell)

Five Songs (arr). 1970. Alto, pf. Wat 1971. CBC SM-77/Sel CC-15073 (*Forrester)

COLLAGE

A Message to Winnipeg (Reaney). 1960 (Tor 1960). 4 spkrs, vn, cl, pf, perc. Ms

Twelve Letters to a Small Town (Reaney). 1961 (Tor 1961). 4 spkrs, fl, ob, guit, pf-harmonium. Ms

Wednesday's Child (Reaney). 1962 (Tor 1962). 3 spkrs, sop, ten, fl, va, pf, perc. Ms

Canada Dash – Canada Dot (Reaney). 1965–7 (Tor 1967). 5 vs, 4 spkrs, chamb ens. Ms

The Journals of Susanna Moodie, incidental (Atwood). 1972 (Tor 1973). 2 kybd plyers, perc. Ms

WRITINGS

'Recordings,' *Music in Canada*

'Composers in Toronto and Montreal,' *U of Toronto Q*, vol 26, Oct 1956

'Music,' *The Culture of Contemporary Canada*, ed J. Park (Cornell 1957)

'Music,' *The Arts in Canada*, ed M. Ross (Toronto 1958)

– and Kallmann, Helmut. 'Musical instrument building,' *Encyclopedia Canadiana* (Ottawa 1958)

'Music Education,' ibid

'Young composers' performances in Toronto,' *CMJ*, vol 2, Summer 1958
'Jean Papineau-Couture,' *CMJ*, vol 3, Winter 1959
'Recent orchestral works by Champagne, Morel and Anhalt,' *CMJ*, vol 4, Summer 1960
– and Kasemets, Udo, eds. *The Modern Composer and His World* (Toronto 1961)
'Notes on a recording career, (the work of Glenn Gould),' *Canadian Forum*, vol 40, Jan 1961
Review of *A History of Music in Canada 1534–1914* by Helmut Kallmann, *U of Toronto Q*, vol 30, Jul 1961
'Schoenberg ten years after,' *Canadian Forum*, vol 41, Nov 1961
'Stravinsky triptych,' *CMJ*, vol 6, Summer 1962
'The Bernstein experiment,' *Canadian Forum*, vol 43, Apr 1964
'Notes on *Jonah*,' *Alphabet*, 8 Jun 1964
Review of *British Composers in Interview*, ed R. Murray Schafer, *U of Toronto Q*, vol 33, Jul 1964
'A "Complete" Schoenberg,' *Canadian Forum*, vol 46, Jan 1967
'About Canadian music: The P.R. failure,' *Mcan*, 21, Jul–Aug 1969; reprinted with postscript, *AGO / RCCO Music*, vol 5, Mar 1971
'What every U.S. musician should know about contemporary Canadian music,' *Mcan*, 29, final issue 1970
'Music in Canada,' *MT*, vol 111, Dec 1970
'Trying to define music,' *ConsB*, Christmas 1970
'Aims and methods for a music-theory program,' *CAUSM J*, vol 1, Spring 1971
'Healey Willan,' *Canadian Forum*, vol 52, Dec 1972
'Teaching new music: What? How? Why?' *MSc*, 270, Mar–Apr 1973
'Canadian music,' 'Harry Somers,' *Dictionary of Contemporary Music* (New York 1974)
– and MacMillan, K., eds. *Contemporary Canadian Composers* (Toronto 1975)
'Istvan Anhalt,' *MSc*, 281, Jan–Feb 1975
'A big song-and-dance,' *CME*, vol 18, Spring 1977
'Reflections on Ives,' *An Ives Celebration*, ed H. Wiley Hitchcock and Vivian Perlis (Urbana, Ill, 1977)
'A festival of Canadian music,' *Musicanada: A Presentation of Canadian Contemporary Music* (Ottawa 1977)
Articles on Anhalt, Gould, Kasemets, Kolinski, MacMillan, Marshall, and L. Smith in *The New Grove Dictionary*

BIBLIOGRAPHY

Reaney, James. 'An evening with Babble and Doodle,' *Canadian Literature*, vol 12, Spring 1962
Wilson, M. 'John Beckwith's new cantata "Jonah,"' *Alphabet*, 7, Dec 1963
'John Beckwith: a portrait,' *Mcan*, 6, Nov 1967
Winters, K. 'How Beckwith influence will be felt in new task,' Toronto *Telegram*, 8 Jan 1970
Read, Gardner. *'Circle, with Tangents,' Notes*, vol 26, Jun 1970
Littler, William. 'Beckwith works unique in their sensitivity,' *MSc*, 261, Sep–Oct 1971
Such, Peter. *Soundprints* (Toronto 1972)
Carson, Susan. 'I compose in spite of the fact that it costs me money,' *Weekend*, 11 Mar 1972
BMI Canada Ltd/PRO Canada Ltd. 'John Beckwith,' pamphlets (1970, 1976, 1978)
Contemporary Canadian Composers / Compositeurs canadiens contemporains
Dictionary of Contemporary Music
The New Grove Dictionary IA (KW)

BECKWITH, (Robert) Sterling. Teacher, musicologist, b New York, 14 Aug 1931; BA (Harvard) 1954, MA (Harvard) 1955, PH D (Cornell) 1969. After studies in Europe 1952–6, notably 1952–3 with Nadia Boulanger in Paris, he taught 1956–7 at the Juilliard School, 1959–62 at Emory U, and 1962–9 at the State U of New York, Buffalo. He then initiated in 1969 and directed until 1971 the program in music, Faculty of Fine Arts, *York U, Toronto, and thereafter continued to teach the history and literature of music there. He received grants from the Ford Foundation in 1962 and the British Council in 1971, and, on an Inter-University Committee on Travel Grants research fellowship, was the first American exchange scholar to study in 1963 at the Leningrad Cons. Specializing in Russian music, he has edited the series *Russia's Choral Heritage* (MCA 1965–) and many pieces by 15th- and 16th-century European composers. He has written articles and reviews for *Notes* (1966, 1967, 1968, 1971, 1974), the *American Choral Review* (1967, 1968), and the **Canada Music Book* (1974). Another of his interests is the use of electronics and computer devices in music. He was host on the Ontario Education Communications Authority's *Imagery of the New Medium: Sound* in 1971, a TV series on electronic and experimental music.

BÉDARD, Denis. Organist, harpsichordist, b Quebec City 13 Jan 1950; deuxième prix harmony (CMQ) 1966, premier prix counterpoint (CMQ) 1970, premier prix fugue (CMQ) 1971, premier prix organ (CMQ) 1972, premier prix harpsichord, premier prix chamber music (CMQ) 1973. He began piano lessons with a private teacher at seven and continued with Tania Krieger at the *CMQ in 1961, also at that time beginning organ with Claude *Lavoie and harpsichord with Donald Thomson. Bédard also studied with André *Mérineau (harmony) and Magdeleine *Martin (counterpoint and fugue). On three consecutive *Canada Council grants he studied 1973–4 in Paris with André Isoir (organ) and Laurence Boulay (harpsichord and keyboard harmony), and 1974–5 in Montreal with Mireille and Bernard *Lagacé (organ and harpsichord). He won the *Prix d'Europe for his harpsichord playing in 1975 and studied 1976–7 for short, intensive periods with the organist-harpsichordist Gustav Leonhardt in Holland.

Bédard served 1969–78 as organist at the Church of Notre-Dame de la Nativité in Beauport (near Quebec City) and in 1978 he became the regular organist at the Church of Saint-Coeur-de-Marie in Quebec City. As his reputation as an organ and harpsichord recitalist grew, he appeared in Quebec City for the *Amis de l'orgue and the *Concerts Couperin and at Cap-de-la-Madeleine, Que, for the *Pro Organo Society, and played regularly on CBC radio. After a Bédard performance of works by Messiaen, Mozart, de Grigny, Buxtehude, and Bach, Marc *Samson wrote, 'Moreover, he displays musical ideas which, while they may be debated from some points of view, never leave us indifferent' (*Le Soleil*, 6 Mar 1975).

WRITINGS

'La musique sera tonale ou ne sera pas,' *VM*, 15 Mar 1970 HP

BÉDARD, Hubert (François). Restorer of old keyboard instruments and maker of replicas, harpsichordist, organist, b Ottawa 28 Dec 1933. After medical studies in Ottawa he decided to devote himself to music. He studied 1957–9 in Montreal with Kenneth *Gilbert (harpsichord) and Bernard *Legacé (organ) and completed his harpsichord training 1960–1 in Vienna with Isolde Ahlgrimm and Eta Harisch Schneider. The idea of researching the authentic sounds of earlier musical eras came to him while he was working with Gustav Leonhardt in Amsterdam in 1961. To put his idea into practice, he studied harpsichord manufacture 1962–6 in Boston with Frank Hubbard. When the latter was asked in 1967 to assess the work required to restore the instruments at the museum of the Paris Cons, he took Bédard with him, and Bédard remained in France as director of the museum's restoration workshop.

The Brussels Museum of old instruments and similar museums in Amiens, Besançon, Chartres, and Antwerp, have entrusted Bédard with the repair and restoration of their priceless holdings. Laurence Boulay, Huguette Dreyfus, Huguette Grémy-Chauliac, and the conservatories of Brussels and Paris have commissioned harpsichords from him. For the publishing house Heugel he designed a spinet, a French harpsichord, and an Italian harpsichord according to the style and work methods of the 17th century. In addition he has given numerous lecture demonstrations throughout Europe on the building of string instruments and on medieval and renaissance music, and has participated in radio programs. Belgian, Canadian, and French TV have recorded programs in his workshop, set up in 1975 at the Château de Maintenon. Bédard is considered an authority on the restoration of harpsichords, clavichords, etc (he had restored more than 50 by 1980) and an expert in the manufacture both of authentic copies of such instruments and of 'do-it-yourself' kits. He is a member of a Unesco international commission for the preservation of old instruments. He received the medal of Antwerp in 1970. He has recorded the *Suites* no. 4, 7, 8, and 11 by Georg Boehm and those in G minor and F by Louis Couperin (1964, Pirouette S-19019). He is a cousin of Gilles *Potvin.

WRITINGS

'La restauration des clavecins anciens,' *VM*, 12, Jun 1969

BIBLIOGRAPHY

Conquer, Thérèse. 'Hubert Bédard: à la recherche de sons d'antan,' *CMB*, 8, Spring–Summer 1974 TC-C

BÉDARD, Yves (Raymond). Violist, educator, administrator, b Quebec City 11 May 1929. He began violin lessons at 16 in Joliette with Father Rolland Brunelle and studied 1948–53 at the *CMQ with Lucien *Robert (viola) and Gilbert *Darisse and Calvin *Sieb (violin). He completed his training 1953–5 at the Paris Cons with Pierre Pasquier (chamber music) and Alexis Roland-Manuel and Marcel Beaufils (aesthetics). He was a violist 1956–8 in the Buffalo SO under Josef Krips. He resumed studies 1958–61 in Paris with the violist Micheline Lemoine. Returning to Quebec City in 1961, he lectured in music history at *Laval U and in 1962 became adviser on the pedagogy of music. In the latter capacity he helped formulate programs in music education for the Province of Quebec, and in 1964 at Laval U he began pedagogical lectures based on those programs. He was appointed assistant director of the Music School in July 1977. In the 1960s and 1970s he also played in the *Quebec SO and the *CBC Quebec Chamber Orchestra. His name is associated mainly, however, with the various school music reports on which he collaborated (notably the Parent and *Rioux reports), and with the translation into French of several US pedagogical works. He is the author of *Oeuvres commentées à l'usage des professeurs d'éducation musicale* (Montreal 1968) and several pedagogical tracts and essays on music education. IB

BEDDOE, Mabel (Beatrice). Contralto, b Hamilton, Ont, 18 Aug 1880, d New York 15 Feb 1959. Her father, Thomas Davis Beddoe (1853–1933), was known as an amateur tenor in Toronto. She studied in Toronto with Edward *Schuch, Boston with Albert Baker Cheney, Chicago with William Lawrence Tomlins, and Dresden with Frau Auer-Herbeck. Her career (ca 1910–40) was confined exclusively to concert and oratorio, and her many engagements throughout North America included annual participation for several years in the famous Bach Festivals at Bethlehem, Pa. After a Montreal concert of uncertain date the *Star* reported: 'Miss Beddoe has a contralto voice of individual timbre, unusual range and richness, and remarkable sonority in the upper register. She uses it with an art that is partly the result of careful training and partly instinctive. She clearly understands what an all-important thing interpretation is.' In 1929 at St Paul's Church, Toronto, she participated in a performance of Bach's *B-Minor Mass* on the occasion of the dedication of a memorial window to A. S. *Vogt. JBM

BEDFORD, Reginald. See Bedford and Eby.

Bedford and Eby. Duo pianists and teachers: Reginald Bedford (b London, Ont, 13 Dec 1909; ATCM 1924) and Evelyn Eby (b Outlook, near Saskatoon, 12 May 1909; ATCM 1923). Both were pupils of Lyell *Gustin in Saskatoon; Bedford also studied in the USA with Percy Grainger, Edwin Hughes, Alfred Madeley Richardson, and Carl Friedberg and on scholarship at the American Cons at Fontainebleau, France, with Robert Casadesus; and Eby on scholarships in the USA with Jeannette Durno and Josef Lhévinne. They made their debut as a team in 1938 in Chicago. Their career included an appearance with the *TSO in 1945, weekly recitals 1945–6 on CBC radio, and concerts in New York at Town Hall in 1949 and in London at Wigmore Hall in 1956. They were married in 1948. A recital at *Eaton Auditorium in 1954 brought the following comment in *Saturday Night* (5 Nov 1944): 'They have a broad and beautiful tone, superb execution; their interpretations are brilliant, thoughtful and imbued with musical feeling. Their mastery of the bravura style was especially apparent in a dazzling rendering of the Saint-Saëns *Scherzo*; and their interpretation of Brahms' *Variations on a Haydn Theme* was noble and impressive. Their profound rhythmical sense was revealed in a *Barcarolle* and *Valse* by Rachmaninoff.'

Bedford was an examiner 1940–2 for the *WBM and briefly was head of the piano department at the Halifax Cons (*Maritime Cons) and organist at All Saints Cathedral, Halifax, prior to serving 1944–8 as principal of the Hamilton Cons (*RHCM). He first examined for the TCM (*RCMT) in 1944. In 1948 he and Eby opened the Reginald Bedford Piano Studios in Hamilton. He began teaching also at the Ontario Ladies' College, Whitby, in 1968 and at *McMaster U in 1972. His pupils have included Bob *Hahn, Gordon *Hancock, Elaine *Keillor, and Marjan *Mozetich. Bedford was president 1931–3, and 1939–41 of the *Musical Art Club of Saskatoon, 1957–9 of the *ORMTA and 1959–63 of the *CFMTA. Eby was president of the Musical Art Club 1937–9. The bass James Eby is her brother.

BIBLIOGRAPHY
'Prairie pianistic prodigy,' *Maclean's*, vol 41, 1 Jan 1928
(IF, EK)

BEE, Dorothy (Williamina). Piano teacher, editor, b Lemberg, near Regina, 1 Nov 1910; ATCM 1928, LAB 1931. She studied 1928–31 with William M. Buckley and in 1936 with Lyell *Gustin, and took master classes in 1940 with Rosalyn Tureck, several times 1944–8 with Max *Pirani, in 1960 with Victor Babin, and in 1970 and 1971 with André Previn. As head of the *WBM's piano syllabus committee 1968–74 she introduced to the current syllabus more than 1000 new pieces, many by little-known composers. Also for the WBM she was co-editor, with Gordon Wallis, of *Explorations* (Leeds 1969, three volumes of piano studies designed to resolve specific technical problems), and editor-in-chief of eight graded volumes of piano repertoire (Waterloo 1976). She pioneered workshops for rural Saskatchewan piano teachers, was president 1955–7 of the *SRMTA (becoming a life-member in 1968), and has been a vice-president of the *CFMTA. Bee became a faculty member of the *Regina Cons in 1946 and began teaching at the *U of Regina in 1949, retiring in 1979 as associate professor emeritus. She has been an adjudicator and piano consultant for the *Saskatchewan Music Festival Assn and the *SAB and an examiner for the WBM and *Mount Royal College, Calgary. She played string bass 1943–71 in the *Regina SO. Donald Bohlen, Joan Gabriel, Sylvia Howell, Deanne Parker, Joyce Reddell, Glenna Syse, and Barry Wells have been among her piano pupils. (WLB)

BEECROFT, Norma (Marian). Composer, producer, broadcaster, administrator, b Oshawa, Ont, 11 Apr 1934. Her father, Julian Balfour Beecroft, was a musician, an inventor, and a pioneer in the development of electronic tape. Her mother, Eleanor (Chambers) Beecroft (b Norton) was trained in music and dance and was an actress. A sister, Jane Beecroft (poet, painter, b Toronto 1932), has collaborated with Norma, as writer or translator, on several works (*From Dreams of Brass, Rasas II, The Living Flame of Love*).

Norma Beecroft took piano lessons, first 1950–2 privately with Aladar Ecsedy, then 1952–8 at the *RCMT with Gordon *Hallett and Weldon *Kilburn, and at the same time studied composition with John *Weinzweig. She also took flute lessons 1957–8 with Keith Girard and continued composition studies (summer 1958) on scholarship at the Berkshire Music Center, Tanglewood, with Aaron Copland and Lukas Foss, and 1959–61 at the Accademia Santa Cecilia, Rome, with Goffredo Petrassi. She took private flute lessons 1959–62 in Rome with Severino Gazzelloni. She attended the lectures given by Bruno Maderna in 1960 and 1961 at Darmstadt, Germany, and the Dartington School, England, and the electronic music classes of Myron Schaeffer 1962–3 at the *U of Toronto and of Mario Davidovsky in 1964 at the Columbia-Princeton Electronic Music Center, New York.

Beecroft's first musical employment had been with the CBC as a script assistant 1954–7 for TV music programs and as a music consultant 1957–9. After her European studies she returned to the CBC, working as a script assistant 1962–3, then successively as talent relations officer 1963–4, national program organizer for radio 1964–6, and producer 1966–9 of such series as 'Music of Today,' 'Organists in Recital,' and 'RSVP' and such programs as 'From the Age of Elegance,' which dramatized the music of the baroque period. When she resigned as a producer in 1969 she remained as host and commentator for 'Music of Today.' In 1976 her documentary 'The Computer in Music,' a freelance production, received a Major Armstrong Award for excellence in FM broadcasting. Another freelance project was the preparation in 1975 of 13 broadcast records, 'Music Canada,' from tapes in the libraries of RCI and *CAPAC. Assiduous in the service of Canadian music, Beecroft has been president 1956–7 of *Canadian Music Associates (the Toronto concert committee of the *CLComp); president 1965–8 of *Ten Centuries Concerts; and co-founder (in 1971 with Robert *Aitken), president, and manager of *NMC. She is an associate of the *CMCentre and a member of CAPAC.

About two-thirds of Beecroft's small but significant compositional output has been commissioned – by the *Charlottetown Festival (*Pièce Concertante No. 1*), Ten Centuries Concerts (*Elegy* and *Two Went to Sleep*), the puppeteers Dora and Leo Velleman (*Undersea Fantasy*), Waterloo Lutheran U (*Wilfrid Laurier U) choir (*The Living Flame of Love*), the *SMCQ (*Rasas I*), the *NACO (*Improvvisazioni Concertanti No. 2*), the CBC (*Rasas II, 11 and 7 for 5+, Piece for Bob*), the *TS Junior Women's

Norma Beecroft

Committee (*Improvvisazioni Concertanti No. 3*), the Ontario Youth Choir (*Three Impressions*), NMC (*Rasas III*), the *OAC (*Collage '76*), and the *Canadian Electronic Ensemble (*Consequences for Five*).

The character and variety of Beecroft's work proceed from her strong responses to specific stimuli, whether the musical influences of her childhood, the successive effects of her several main teachers, the virtuosities of individual friends in the performing world, or the challenge of commissions.

Basic and persistent among the influences, however, is the music of Debussy, which she experienced as a child and which, with its sensuality and subtle colours, continued to affect her aesthetic predispositions despite the intrusion of four strong subsequent influences: the resilient counterpoint of Weinzweig; the new academism of Petrassi (founded on analyses of the scores of Stravinsky, Hindemith, and Bartók); the modified-12-tone precepts of Maderna; and the allure of the new electronic hardware. Each of these enlarged her horizons, altered her vocabulary, or increased her skills, but her choice and blending of timbres remained neo-Debussyan even in her 12-tone and electronic pieces. She has used electronically produced or altered sounds as an extension of vocal and instrumental sounds rather than as an alien alternative (*From Dreams of Brass* is the obvious example). It is probable that her assurance in handling this kind of mix has stemmed from her early acceptance of electronic sounds in her father's workshop.

COMPOSITIONS

STAGE

Undersea Fantasy, puppet show. 1967 (Mtl 1967). tape

ORCHESTRA

Fantasy for Strings. 1958 (Tor 1958). CMCentre

Improvvisazioni Concertanti No. 1. 1961 (Rome 1961). Fl, med orch. Leeds 1973. Audat 477-4001 (*Fiore fl)

From Dreams of Brass (J. Beecroft). 1963–4 (Tor 1965). Sop, narr, SATB, orch, tape. CMCentre. RCI 214/RCA CCS-1008 (*CBC SO)

Pièce Concertante No. 1. 1966 (Charlottetown 1966). CMCentre

Improvvisazioni Concertanti No. 2. 1971 (Ott 1971). Leeds. RCI 382 / RCA KRL 1-007 (*NACO)

Improvvisazioni Concertanti No. 3. 1973. Fl, orch. UE 1976

CHAMBER

Tre Pezzi Brevi. 1960–1. Fl, hp (guit or pf). UE 1962. Dom S-69006 (*Aitken fl)

Contrasts for Six Performers. 1962. Ob, va, xylorimba, vib, perc, hp. CMCentre

Elegy and *Two Went to Sleep* (Cohen). 1967. Sop, fl, perc (pf), tape. CMCentre. RCI 404 (*Lyric Arts Trio)

Rasas I. 1968. Fl, hp, str trio, perc, pf. CMCentre. RCI 301 (*SMCQ)

Rasas II and *III* (J. Beecroft and others). 1973 (rev 1975), 1974. V, chamb ens, tape. CMCentre

11 and 7 for 5+. 1975. Brass quin, tape. CMCentre

Piece for Bob. 1975. Fl, tape. CMCentre

Collage '76. 1976. Fl, solo fl, ob, hn, vc, db, 3 perc, hp, pf, prepared tape. CMCentre
Consequences for Five. 1977. Pf, synth, live electronics
Collage '78. 1978. Bn, pf, 2 perc, tape. Ms
CHOIR
The Living Flame of Love (St John of the Cross, Eng version J. Beecroft). 1968. SATB. Wat 1969. Poly 2917 007 (*Festival Singers)
Also *The Hollow Men* and *Three Impressions* (1956, 1973). Both CMCentre

WRITINGS
'Two musical adventures in Italy: a Canadian composer reports back,' *CanComp*, 76, Jan 1973

BIBLIOGRAPHY
"'From Dreams of Brass," ' *CBC Times*, 19–25 Feb 1966
'Miss Norma Beecroft: well-travelled composer,' *CanComp*, 9, May 1966
'The new world of electronic music,' *CanComp*, 22, Oct 1967
'Norma Beecroft,' *Mcan*, 19, May 1969
Winters, Kenneth. 'A composer who doesn't wear music like a straight jacket [sic],' *CanComp* 64, Nov 1971
Such, Peter. 'The suspended sounds of Norma Beecroft,' *Soundprints* (Toronto 1972)
CAPAC. 'Norma Beecroft,' pamphlet and recording (1975).
Kieser, Karen. 'Norma Beecroft's open mind,' *Fugue*, vol 1, Feb 1977
Contemporary Canadian Composers KW

BEHRENS, Jack. Teacher, composer, b Lancaster, Pa, 25 Mar 1935; B SC (Juilliard) 1958, M SC (Juilliard) 1959, PH D (Harvard) 1973. His composition teachers were William Bergsma, Vincent Persichetti, and Peter Mennin at the Juilliard School and Leon Kirchner and Roger Sessions at Harvard U. He also received instruction from Darius Milhaud at the Aspen Music Festival (summer 1962) and from Stefan Wolpe and John Cage at the Emma Lake Composers-Artists Workshop (summers 1964, 1965) in Saskatchewan. In Regina 1962–6 he taught at the *U of Saskatchewan and was head of the theory department at the affiliated conservatory. He taught 1966–70 at *Simon Fraser U and 1970–6 at California State College, and became chairman of the department of theory and composition in the Faculty of Music, *U of Western Ontario, in 1976, and dean of the faculty in 1980. He has given many lectures and lecture-recitals on 20th-century music. His compositions include commissions from several Saskatchewan organizations. He conducted the premiere of his chamber opera *The Lay of Thrym* (a Canadian Centennial commission, with libretto by C.K. Cockburn) 13 Apr 1968 at *Darke Hall, Regina. Based on an Icelandic legend, the four-scene work is atonal and employs aleatoric and improvisational techniques. Behrens is a member of ASCAP and the *CLComp and an associate of the *CMCentre. His wife, the pianist Sonja Peterson – b Oregon 1938; M MUS (Juilliard) 1962 – taught 1962–6 at the *Regina Cons.

SELECTED COMPOSITIONS
STAGE
The Lay of Thrym, opera (Icelandic 'Thrymskvitta,' transl C. Keith Cockburn). 1968. CMCentre
ORCHESTRA
Trumpet Concerto. 1955. Ms
Introspection. 1956. Str orch. CMCentre
Declaration. 1964. CMCentre
The Sound of Milo (Jack Wasserman). 1970. Narr, orch. Ms
Concerto for clarinet, violin, piano, and orchestra 'Triple Concerto.' 1971. Ms
Fantasy on Francis Hopkinson's 'My Days Have Been So Wondrous Free.' 1976. Sm orch. Ms
New Beginnings. 1976. Ms
A Greeting. 1977. CMCentre
CHAMBER
Quartertone Quartet. 1960. Str quar. CMCentre
Early Song (Ted Godwin). 1965. Ten (bar), fl, ob, hn, vn, va. CMCentre
Serenades. 1969. Fl, cl, pf, vn, vc. Ms
Happy Birthday John Cage I and II. 1972. Solo instr in C, A, G, E flat. Ms
Clarinet Quintet. 1974. Cl, str quar. Ms
Bass Variants. 1977. db. Ms
KEYBOARD
Passacaglia. 1964 (rev 1976). Pf. CMCentre
Music for a New Arrival. 1970. Hpd. Ms
Taos Portraits. 1976. Pf. CMCentre
Others, including a film score, *The Old Order Amish* (1959); many works for v, choir (SW)

BÉIQUE, Alcibiade. Organist, teacher, b St-Jean-Bapitiste-de-Rouville, near Montreal, 20 Oct 1856, d Montreal 20 Jun 1896. After organ lessons with Romain-Octave *Pelletier, he studied 1877–8 at the Liège Cons and travelled in Italy, France, and England. He then lived for five years in the USA before returning in 1885 to St-Hyacinthe, where he taught and was organist 1886–91 at the cathedral. He studied further 1887–8 at the Paris Cons with Eugène Gigout and Alexandre Guilmant. Upon being introduced by the *Casavant brothers to the priest at Notre-Dame Church, Montreal, he was offered charge of the church's great organs, succeeding J.-B. *Labelle. His official appointment began 24 Jan 1891, the same day the new organ was inaugurated by the US organist Frederick Archer. Béique became known for his virtuosity and for his skill as an accompanist and improviser. A member of the *AMQ, he enjoyed some success as a teacher of organ, piano, and harmony. His pupils included Amédée *Tremblay.

BIBLIOGRAPHY
'Alcibiade Béique,' *Canadian Album*, vol 4, 1895 CG

BÉIQUE, Pierre. Administrator, b Montreal 7 Sep 1910; B COM (McGill) 1935. After classical studies at Ste-Marie and Jean-de-Brébeuf colleges and courses in commerce at McGill U, he joined the Montreal company Vinant Ltd. He devoted part of his free time to the new SCSM, serving as assistant treasurer, then as honorary treasurer. In 1939 he was appointed administrator and in that capacity directed the destinies of the SCSM (*MSO) until his retirement in 1970. As special adviser to the president of the MSO 1970–5, musical adviser to the delegated administrator in 1977, and special assistant to the artistic director 1978– , Béique stands as the prime architect of the MSO as we know it today, and it is to him that the Montreal public owes the early visits of conductors of the calibre of Walter, Klemperer, Munch, Szell, Markevitch, and Monteux, and the later ones of Bernstein, Leinsdorf, Abbado, Ozawa, and Mehta, whom Montrealers were able to meet at the same time as were US and European centres. Concurrently with the early years of the orchestra Béique's private enterprise, Les Concerts Pierre Béique (1940–5), presented in Montreal a large number of world-famous artists, among them Horowitz, Anderson, Serkin, Casadesus, and Melchior. In November 1978 Béique was named 'the Great Montrealer' of the last 20 years in the field of music by the Queen Elizabeth Hotel on the occasion of its 20th anniversary. His prognosis on the immediate future of the MSO is contained in the chapter 'Allegro ma non troppo' that he wrote for *Montréal: la prochaine décennie* (Montreal 1980). In 1979 he was made a Member of the *Order of Canada. PR

Pierre Béique

BÉLANGER. Quebec family of musicians comprising 1 / Edwin and his sons 2 / Marc and 3 / Guy.

1 **Edwin.** Orchestra and band conductor, violinist, violist, arranger, teacher, b Montmagny, near Quebec City, 18 Nov 1910. He studied violin first at the Brothers of the Sacred Heart College in Montmagny, then at the *Séminaire de Québec with J.-Alexandre *Gilbert. He also studied harmony there with Omer *Létourneau, one of whose daughters he later married. He was a member 1928–31 of the Société symphonique de Québec (*Quebec SO) and in 1933 won the *Prix d'Europe for violin. He took violin lessons 1933–4 with Carl Flesch in Paris and subsequently studied conducting with Ernest Read in London. On his return to Canada in 1935 he began working for the CBC in Quebec City as instrumentalist, conductor, and arranger. He also helped found the Cercle philharmonique de Québec (see Quebec SO) and conducted it until 1942. In 1937, with the rank of captain, he succeeded Charles *O'Neill at the head of the *Royal 22nd Regiment Band, touring with the band in the Far East, Europe, and the USA and serving in the post until 1961. He made several arrangments for concert band.

Edwin Bélanger was artistic director of the Quebec SO 1942–51 and later frequently a guest conductor; he returned to serve 1966–75 as a first desk player in the second violins, 1975–7 as principal viola, and thereafter as a member of the second violins. He began teaching viola and directing orchestral classes at the *CMQ in 1973 and became music director of the *Concerts Couperin in 1977. He was president of the *AMQ 1947–50, 1953–6, 1963–5, and 1971–4. In 1966 he became the proprietor of the music retail and publishing firm the *Procure générale de musique de Québec.

BIBLIOGRAPHY
Falardeau, Sergt Victor. *La Musique du Royal 22e régiment, 50 ans d'histoire (1922–1972)* (Quebec 1976)

2 (Joseph Charles) **Marc.** Violinist, violist, arranger, composer, teacher, b Quebec City 30 Jul 1940; premier prix harmony, chamber music (CMQ) 1960. He began violin lessons with his father at six, and studied 1948–61 at the *CMQ with Claude *Létourneau and Calvin *Sieb. He also studied conducting with his father and, in the summer of 1965, with Hermann Scherchen at the Accademia Chigiana in Siena. He was a conductor and arranger for the CBC in Quebec City, and played in CBC orchestras 1956–71 in Quebec and 1972–6 in Montreal and in the *Quebec SO 1958–72, the last three years as principal viola. He taught viola and chamber music 1973–9 at the *U of Montreal. He has composed a number of instrumental works including a *Divertissement* (1969) for string quartet.

The Groupe Marc Bélanger, which he founded in 1976, recorded several of his compositions for the LP *Les Cordes en liberté* (Kébec-Disc KD-931). The 10-musician ensemble performs on electrified instruments, in particular the violin (vi-tar), which can be made to achieve effects akin to those produced by percussion instruments. Marc Bélanger orchestrated André *Gagnon's music for the ballet *Mad Shadows* (1977) and made several arrangements for Gilles *Vigneault, also playing 1966–79 in the ensemble that accompanied the author-composer. In the summer of 1979 Marc Bélanger taught at the Domaine Forget in St-Irènée, Que, and conducted a 50-piece orchestra in performances of his works at Montreal's Expo Theatre. He is a member of CAPAC.

3 (Joseph Gabriel) **Guy**. Tenor, choir conductor, teacher, b Quebec City 24 Nov 1946; B MUS (Laval) 1973. He studied 1965–6 at the *CMQ with Guy Lepage and 1966–72 at *Laval U with Marthe *Létourneau (singing) and Françoise *Aubut (theory). He also studied privately with Rolande *Dion. He became music director of the *Société lyrique d'Aubigny in 1968, and in the society's productions he sang the title role in *Faust* (1969) and Nadir in *Les Pêcheurs de perles* (1974). He conducted *Faust* in 1978, and *Carmen* and *The Land of Smiles* in 1979 at the *Grand Théâtre in Quebec City. He was appointed director of the choir Étoile au grand large in 1974. He taught 1972–5 for the Chauveau Regional School Board and 1975–6 for the Externat St-Jean-Berchmans. (CH)

BELCOURT, Émile (Adrien). Tenor, b Laflèche, near Regina, 27 Jun 1926; B SC (Saskatchewan) 1949. Though trained as a pharmacist, Belcourt studied during the 1950s at the Academy of Music in Vienna with Editha Fleischer. After appearances in Germany and France he made his English debut at Covent Garden 19 Jun 1963 as Gonzalve in *L'Heure espagnole* and in the same year joined Sadler's Wells (later English National Opera). He made his debut as Pluto in *Orpheus in the Underworld* and has sung Eisenstein in *Die Fledermaus*, the title role in Offenbach's *Bluebeard and His Six Wives*, and Raoul in *La Vie parisienne*. His *COC debut 8 Sep 1973 as Bernard of Clairvaux in the premiere of Charles Wilson's **Heloise and Abelard* was followed by performances as Camille in *The Merry Widow* in 1973, Shuisky in *Boris Godunov* in 1974, Gonzalve in 1974, and Dr Falke in *Die Fledermaus* in 1975. He has sung Shuisky with the Scottish Opera, Macheath in Britten's *The Beggar's Opera* at the 1976 *Guelph Spring Festival, and Eisenstein with the *Edmonton Opera. He has been described by the critic of the *Financial Times*, London, as 'a character tenor of great accomplishment.'

DISCOGRAPHY

Delibes *Lakmé*. Monte Carlo Opera, Bonynge cond, Belcourt (Hadj). (1969). 3-Lon 1391/1-Lon 26201 (excerpts)

Wagner *Das Rheingold*. English National Opera, Goodall cond. Belcourt (Loge). (1975). 4-Angel S-3825 (JBl)

Belgium. European country whose musicians have made a significant contribution to the development of skill and style in the performance of instrumental music in Canada. The Belgian conservatories were turning out large numbers of highly trained young players around 1890 when Ernest *Lavigne, the dynamic leader of the *Sohmer Park band and orchestra, visited Europe seeking instrumentalists to play in those ensembles. As a result, numerous Belgian musicians settled in Canada, especially in Montreal, in the late 19th century. Their teaching of string instruments brought to Canada the great traditions of the Franco-Belgian school. They also demonstrated a mastery of wind instruments.

Guillaume *Mechtler, who arrived in Montreal in 1789, probably was the first Belgian musician to settle in Canada. Jules *Hone (second prix violin, Liège Cons, and one of the first qualified violin teachers in Montreal) arrived from New York ca 1865. Another more famous Belgian violinist, Frantz *Jehin-Prume, was an important figure in Quebec music from 1870 until his death in 1899 and worked effectively to raise the level of interpretation and teaching. In 1871 he formed Montreal's first professional string quartet. Jean-Baptiste *Dubois was appointed principal cello and assistant conductor of the Sohmer Park Orchestra in 1890 and was joined by two compatriots, the violinists J.-J. *Goulet and Jean-Julien *Clossey, in 1891. After 1894 Clossey served in the first violins of the *Couture MSO and then of the Goulet *MSO. (His son Émile, a cellist, conducted the Montreal Municipal Orchestra ca 1935–45.)

Lavigne was equally determined to improve the quality of wind playing and brought gifted performers from Belgium to play in his ensembles and teach young Canadians. Jacques Vanpoucke (b Ghent 25 Oct 1865, d Montreal ?), Lavigne's principal clarinet, also directed the Collège St-Louis Band and taught at the Collège Ste-Marie. Oscar Arnold (b Liège 1 Nov 1862, medal winner, clarinet and saxophone, Liège Cons, and a member of the Spa Brass Band in 1881) joined his compatriot in the woodwinds in 1892, along with Léon Medaer, clarinet (b Tournemont 1864) and Charles Dom, oboe (b Brussels 3 May 1863). In 1893 Louis Vanpoucke (b Ypres 1873, d Montreal ?, a former principal trumpet with the Rotterdamsche Schuttery) arrived in Montreal. Among other Sohmer Park Belgian musicians, Albert Dehairs, Eugène Devaux, Théo Mahy, and Jean Moermans should be mentioned.

For his own orchestra J.-J. Goulet brought to Canada his brother Jean and other Belgian musicians, eg, the clarinetists Georges Haseneier and Émile Quiquemberg, the trumpeter Van Camp, the cellist Peter (?) Van der Meerschen, and the bassist Léon Wathieu. Charles *Goulet, Jean's son, founded the *Disciples de Massenet in 1928 and the *Variétés Lyriques in 1936.

Other Belgians arrived in Montreal early in the 20th century: François *Héraly, the bandmaster, whose wife taught piano to the young Wilfrid *Pelletier; Léon Kaster, the oboist, and his son Jean, a cellist (*Prix d'Europe 1918); Auguste *Liessens, the organist and composer, who settled in Sorel in 1913; Louis Michiels, the french hornist and theoretician who founded the publishing house *Édition Belgo-Canadienne in 1925; Charles *Tanguy, the teacher and composer; Benoît *Verdickt, the organist and choirmaster; and Joseph and Henri *Vermandere (Brother Placide and Brother Séverin), a composer and a choirmaster respectively. In Toronto Frederic Nicolai (b Liège) was active as a cellist 1903–14 and as a member of the *Toronto String Quartette 1906–14. César Borré (conductor, composer, and authority on Gregorian chant, b Belgium 1880, d Toronto 1950) founded the London (Ont) Ladies' Choir and the London Philharmonic Union and the Toronto Opera Company. After emigrating to Canada in 1921, the harpist Frank J. Simons was a member of the *Winnipeg SO and taught in Winnipeg. The violinist Maurice *Onderet arrived in Montreal in 1927 to fill a position at the McGill Cons.

Désiré Defauw (conductor, violinist, composer, b Ghent 5 Oct 1885, d Gary, Ind, 25 Jul 1960) began conducting the CSM orchestra in 1940 and remained its artistic director until 1948. A conductor of international reputation, he had been acquainted with the composers Richard Strauss and Ravel and ardently promoted their works and those of his fellow countrymen Peter Benoît, César Franck, and Théodore Ysaÿe. He conducted the premieres of several Canadian works, eg, *Vallerand's *Le Diable dans le beffroi*, *Blackburn's *Symphony in One Movement*, *Pépin's *Variations symphoniques*, and Alexander *Brott's *War and Peace*.

Other Belgians arrived after 1920, including Ria *Lenssens (soprano), Arnold Becker (bass), Séverin *Moisse (pianist and composer), Henri Weber (clarinetist), and Armand Weisbord (violinist). Several Belgian pianists made careers in Canada, notably Jenny *Lerouge LeSaunier, a teacher 1922–71 in Edmonton, Frans *Brouw, and Nadia Strycek, a teacher at the Cons de Trois-Rivières and at the *JMC Orford Art Centre. The cellist Charles *Houdret arrived in Canada in 1952 and, inspired by the Queen Elisabeth of Belgium International Music Competition, instigated the *Montreal International Competition. René Thomas, the jazz guitarist, lived in Montreal 1958–63 and worked in collaboration with another Belgian, the saxophonist Bobby Jaspar. The Belgian composer Henri Pousseur (who taught Michel *Gonneville) visited Montreal to give some lectures, and his *Icare apprenti* was performed by the *SMCQ in 1973. In 1979 the Centre lyrique de Wallonie presented a season of opera and ballet at the *PDA, performing *Carmen*, *Roméo et Juliette*, *Les Indes galantes* (North American premiere), *La Vie parisienne*, and *Swan Lake*. The Canadian singers Céline *Dussault, William Pirie, and Ronald Bermingham were part of the company.

The sterling example set by Belgian musicians in Canada prompted a number of Canadians, particularly string players, to complete their training in Belgium. The violinist Eugène Ysaÿe, who made his first Canadian appearance 22 Apr 1895 at the *Monument national, taught, among others, Nora *Clench in 1891, Flora Matheson *Goulden 1927–8, Adolph *Kodolfsky, Geza *de Kresz, Maurice *Solway 1926–8, and Émile *Taranto. The violinist Noël *Brunet, Alfred *De Sève, Chambord Giguère, J.-Alexandre *Gilbert, Oscar *Martel, and Roland Poisson and the cellists Rosario *Bourdon, Raoul *Duquette, and Roland *Leduc also trained at Belgian conservatories. Camille *Couture, while enrolled for violin lessons at the Liège Cons, studied violin making with Émile Heynberg. Alcibiade *Béique, Arthur *Letondal, Marie-Thérèse *Paquin and the singers Roger *Filiatrault and Céline *Marier also studied in Belgium. Émilien *Allard, Robert *Donnell, Percival *Price and Leland *Richardson attended the École royale de carillon de Malines (Beiaardschool te Mechelen).

Among the Canadian artists whose visits to Belgium attracted particular attention were Emma *Albani and Pauline *Donalda, who sang in Brussels at the Théâtre de la Monnaie and in other cities. The tenor Jacques *Gérard studied in Brussels and made his debut in Liège in 1927, and Jacques *Beaudry worked at the Brussels Cons. The impresario Bernard *Laberge was decorated in 1951 with Belgium's Croix de chevalier de la Couronne for having presented numerous Belgian artists in North America, eg, the Musique royale des Guides, the Pro Musica Antiqua Ensemble, the Belgian Keyboard Quartet, and the organist and composer Flor Peeters, with whom Patrick *Wedd studied. The pianists Glenn *Gould, Marek *Jablonski, and William *Tritt, the *Orford String Quartet, and the *Hart House Orchestra have visited Belgium. Kenneth *Gilbert was invited to teach 1971–4 at the Royal Flemish Cons in Antwerp. Winners in the Queen Elisabeth International Music Competition have included Frans Brouw (4th prize 1952), Ronald *Turini (2nd prize 1960), Anton *Kuerti (4th prize 1964), Hidetaro *Suzuki (5th prize 1967) and Douglas Finch (5th prize 1978). A number of chansonniers have distinguished themselves at the Festival de la chanson française at Spa.

BIBLIOGRAPHY

'Les musiciens du Parc Sohmer,' *P-T*, 31, 2 May 1896
Huot, Cécile. 'Musiciens belges au Québec,' *CMB*, 8, Spring – Summer 1974
Solway, Maurice. 'Ysaÿe – gentle giant of the violin,' *Music*, May 1980
Potvin, Gilles. 'Les Belges et la musique à Montréal,' Montreal *Le Devoir*, 11 Oct 1980 (CH)

BELL, Donald. Bass-baritone, b South Burnaby, BC, 19 Jun 1935. In 1948, while still a pupil of Nancy Paisley *Benn in Vancouver, he sang with the *Vancouver SO. While on scholarship 1952–4 at the RCM he won a Harriet Cohen Award (the 1954 Arnold Bax Memorial Medal) as the outstanding student from the Commonwealth. Studies followed 1955–7 with Hermann Weissenborn in Berlin. In 1955 he sang with the Glyndebourne Opera and the Berlin Staatsoper and in 1958 he appeared in Bach's *St Matthew Passion* with the Berlin Philharmonic and in Blacher's *Abstrakte Oper* at the Berlin Festival. After his recital debut 22 Apr 1958 at London's Wigmore Hall and a Bayreuth Festival engagement to sing Amfortas in *Parsifal* (which he repeated annually until 1961) and a minor role in *Die Meistersinger*, he made his first tour of Canada in the fall of 1958. During the late 1950s and early 1960s he was often a soloist in choral-orchestral works (eg, in 1957, *Messiah*, in Lucerne under Beecham and in Berlin under Sargent, and Beethoven's *Ninth Symphony* with the *Toronto Mendelssohn Choir) and in recital and was heard on various CBC radio programs, including 'Distinguished Artists' and 'CBC Wednesday Night.' He was Ford to Louis *Quilico's Falstaff in the 1961 CBC TV production of the Verdi opera.

Bell toured Israel in 1959 and 1964, and the USSR in 1963, made his Carnegie Hall debut in 1959, sang with the New York Philharmonic under Leonard Bernstein 28 Sep 1962 in the inaugural concert of Lincoln Center's Philharmonic (Avery Fisher) Hall, and appeared there in 1963 in a concert performance of Strauss' *Intermezzo* with the Concert Opera Society. He took up European residence in 1964 to fulfil a three-year contract with the Deutsche Oper am Rhein in Düsseldorf. There he sang leading roles in operas of Mozart (Don Giovanni, Almaviva), Wagner (Wolfram, Amfortas, Kurwenal), and Gounod (Mephistopheles). He also appeared with other European opera companies and orchestras under the direction of Krips, Sawallisch, Barbirolli, Klemperer, Knappertsbusch, and others.

Bell's Canadian engagements have included tours 1964–8 and performances of *Messiah* (1968, 1974, 1975 with the Toronto Mendelssohn Choir; 1968, 1975 with the *MSO) and other choral works and cantatas (Bach's *Ich habe genug*, 1973 with the *McGill Chamber Orchestra; *Schafer's cantata *Brébeuf* with the Vancouver SO; Beethoven's *Mass in C*, 1975 with the *Vancouver Bach Choir; Szymanowski's *Stabat mater*, 1975 with the Vancouver Bach Choir; the Verdi *Requiem*, 1977 with the *Quebec SO). He gave the Canadian premiere in May 1975 of Peter Maxwell Davies' *Eight Songs for a Mad King* and was the Speaker in the 1975 Festival Canada (*Festival Ottawa) production of *The Magic Flute*, the Prince in the premiere (*Guelph Spring Festival 1977) of Derek *Healey's *Seabird Island*, and the First Soldier in the premiere (Toronto 1977) of Harry *Somers' *Inkadu*.

Noted for his proficiency in the contemporary repertoire, Bell was Alfred '3' in the 1973 British premiere of Von Einem's *The Visit of the Old Lady* at the Glyndebourne Festival and Catiline in the premiere in 1974 of Iain Hamilton's *The Catiline Conspiracy* at the Scottish Opera (a role he re-

Donald Bell

peated there in the fall of 1978). He also sang the title role in the 1969 British premiere of Dallapiccola's *Ulisse* on the BBC, and sang in 1974 in a BBC SO performance of Henze's *Der Vorwurf* conducted by the composer. In 1973 he toured the USSR under the auspices of the *Canada Council. He returned to Canada to live in 1976 and settled in Ottawa in 1977 as Community Artist at *Carleton U and the *U of Ottawa on a grant from the Canada Council.

DISCOGRAPHY

Bach *St Matthew Passion*. Collegiate Chorale, Transfiguration Church Boys' Choir, New York Phil, Bernstein cond. 1962. 3 Col M3S-692
Beethoven *Songs*. Newmark pf. (1962). RCI 200
Symphony No 9. BBC Chor, London SO, Krips cond. 1960. Everest 3110
– *Symphony No 9*. Cleveland O and Chor, Szell cond. 1963. 2 Epic BSC 112
Bissell *Folk Songs of Canada: Six Maritime Folk Songs* from sets 1 and 2. Helmer pf. 1971. CBC SM-168
Brahms *Liebeslieder Waltzes, Op 52*. Vronsky pf, Babin pf. 1959 Cap SG-7189/Sers 60033
Fleming – Dargomiszhsky – Tosti. Bartlett pf. 1972. CBC SM-259
Haydn – Barber – Beckwith – Beethoven. Newmark pf. 1969. CBC SM-111
Herrmann *Wuthering Heights*. Elizabethan Singers, Pro Arte O, Herrmann cond, Bell bar (Heathcliff). 1964. Unicorn UNB 400
Purcell – Strauss – Mussorgsky. Newmark pf. Ca 1967. CBC SM-33
Scarlatti – Monteverdi – et al. Newmark pf. 1968. CBC SM-87/A of D SDD 2161
Serenade: Donald Bell Sings Schubert and Loewe. J. Wustman pf. 1961. Col MS-6343
Stainer *The Crucifixion*. Leeds Phil Choir, Bardgett cond. 1961. Angel S-35984/(1962) HMV ALP 1885
Vaughan Williams *Serenade to Music*. New York Phil, Bernstein cond. 1962. Col MS-7177
Walton *Belshazzar's Feast*. Philharmonia O and Chor, Walton cond. 1958. Angel S-35681 (HCs)

BELL, H.P. (Hugh Poynter). Critic, composer, b Kew, London, 1872, d Montreal 28 Jan 1961. Though he belonged to a family active in the arts (his mother, Clara, with whom he began his music training, made the first English translation of Spitta's *Johann Sebastian Bach* in collaboration with J.A. Fuller-Maitland; Rudyard Kipling was a cousin), Bell decided to become a chemist. He attended Clare College, Cambridge, where his studies included music, and the universities of Kiel and Bonn. He moved to Canada in 1912, working first for the federal department of information, then at *Hart House, U of Toronto (secretary-treasurer 1921–3), before succeeding Philip King in 1923 as music critic of the *Montreal Daily Star*. He held this position, along with that of art critic, for the next 26 years. For some years afterwards he contributed a weekly column to the Montreal daily *The Herald*, which ceased publication in 1959.

Bell considered himself little more than a cultivated amateur, but he brought to his writing a high level of perception and a richness of experience that few people in the field could match at that time. He had met Tchaikovsky and had heard performances by Clara Schumann, Liszt, Brahms, Saint-Saëns, and others. An ardent Savoyard, he had attended all the premieres of the Gilbert & Sullivan operas from *The Mikado* on. In another person, such a background could have led to a patronizing attitude towards the less-developed musical life of Montreal in the years after World War I. Bell's writings, however, did not condescend, and he missed no opportunity to praise merit, even while discerning faults. No choir was so small, no organist so obscure, that he would dismiss them. It is probable that Bell composed throughout his life. However, those compositions of which a record was kept postdate World War II. Like his gentle watercolours, these were done for the pleasure of doing: he had no ambitions as either composer or painter. In spite of this, 'Love's Philosophy' (1945, one of his 16 known songs) was published by BMI Canada, and his *Sonata* for violin and piano (1946) was performed by Ethel *Stark and John *Newmark for the CBC IS. Bell also composed eight *Interludes* for piano in the 1950s.

WRITINGS

'The Montreal Orchestra,' *Montreal Music Year Book 1931*
'Review of 1931,' ibid 1932
'Quebec musicians meet in festival,' *Curtain Call*, 11, Apr 1940 EM

BELL, Leslie (Richard). Choir conductor, educator, writer, arranger, composer, b Toronto 5 May 1906, d there 19 Jan 1962; BA (Toronto) 1930, MA (Toronto) 1931, D MUS (Montreal) 1946. While studying 1917–25 with Frederick *Horwood at the *TCM and with Louis *Waizman, he played clarinet and saxophone in the orchestras of Luigi *Romanelli and Joe DeCourcy and later led his own dance band. He taught English, history, and music 1935–9 at Parkdale Collegiate Institute (where his pupils included Howard *Cable, later an associate at the CBC) and founded a girls' choir there, the Alumnae Singers – later the *Leslie Bell Singers. He was president of the music section of the Ontario Education Assn (*OMEA) 1938–41. He was chairman 1939–48 of the music department at the Ontario College of Education and also taught summers 1940–6 at *Queen's U and 1946–52 at the *U of Toronto.

Later in the 1950s Bell divided his time between conducting (he also formed the short-lived Leslie Bell Gleemen in 1957), writing, and broadcasting. His broad musical interests were reflected in his work as music columnist 1946–62 for the *Toronto Daily Star*, associate editor in charge of music education 1958–62 for the *Canadian Music Journal*, contributor to many other publications, and radio commentator for CBC ('Music Won't Hurt You' and 'Speaking of Music') and CFRB, Toronto. He was the co-founder in 1959 and first executive director of the *CMEA and editor 1959–62 of its journal, the *Canadian Music Educator*. In the *Canadian Music Journal* (Spring 1962), Geoffrey *Payzant wrote: 'It was his driving ambition to close the gap between the art of music and the minds of the many. He took the view that there is popular music good and bad and art music good and bad, and that the best of each had more in common than is generally thought to be the case.'

Bell's compositions included *Variations on a French Noël* for string quartet, several choral works for female and mixed groups published by *Canadian Music Sales and Mills, and many folk song arrangements published by Canadian Music Sales, G.V. *Thompson, Shawnee Press, and Summy. After Bell's death, the CBC and the CMEA sponsored the Leslie Bell Memorial Choir Competition in 1963–4 and 1965 (won by the *Tudor Singers of Montreal and the Acadia Chapel Choir of Wolfville, NS, respectively). The Leslie Bell Scholarship Competition was established in 1973 to assist a choir conductor in post-graduate training. Administered by the *Ontario Choral Federation, it has been awarded to Edward F. Moroney (1973), Robert Cooper (1974), David Christiani (1975), Carole Boyle (1976), and Jean Ashworth-Gam (1977). Bell was a member of CAPAC.

WRITINGS

The Chorister: Theory and Sight Reading for Vocalists, 2 vols (Toronto 1947–50)

'Popular music,' *Music in Canada*

'The failure of music appreciation,' *CMJ*, vol 2, Spring 1958

'An experiment in National Broadcasting,' *CMJ*, vol 5, Winter 1961

BIBLIOGRAPHY

Benson, Nathaniel. 'Choir conductor extraordinary,' *U of T Alumni News*, May 1952

'Leslie Bell: 1906–1962,' *Toronto Daily Star*, 19 Jan 1962

(AHC)

BELLAND, Jean. Cellist, teacher, b Le Mans, France, 16 Jun 1895, d Montreal 7 Jan 1965; premier prix cello (Cons du Mans) 1911, premier prix (Paris Cons). After studies in his native city, he entered the Paris Cons in 1914. He was conscripted for national service before graduating and served 1915–18 in the Corps expéditionnaire d'Orient. When armistice was declared he settled in Constantinople, where he taught at the conservatory and gave many concerts, especially for the entourage of the Sultan of Turkey, who awarded him the distinguished decoration of the Medjidié.

On his return to Paris, in 1919, Belland resumed cello study at the conservatoire with Louis R. Feuillard. He gave recitals at the Salle Gaveau and the Trocadéro and became known as an artist of distinction and a master of his instrument. For four years he was principal cellist for the Assn des concerts spirituels of the Sorbonne. He also was a member of the Pelletier String Quartet.

At the suggestion of the pianist Edmond *Trudel, Belland moved in 1926 to Montreal, where he taught at *McGill U and played in both the first *McGill String Quartet, ca 1930, and the second one, 1939–42. In addition he was principal cellist of the *Montreal Orchestra 1930–41, the *CSM 1936–40, the *Little Symphony of Montreal 1942–52, and the Orchestra of the *Montreal Festivals 1939–46. Belland gave many recitals in Canada on CBC radio and TV. He also taught 1946–60 at the *CMM. Among his pupils were his son Ary, Jean Charbonneau, Raymonde *Martin, André *Mignault, Suzanne Perrault, and Brahm Sand.

GP

BELLAVANCE, Ginette (m Sauvé). Composer, b Lévis, near Quebec City, 30 Jun 1946; BA (Collège Basile-Moreau) 1966. She studied music at the *U of Montreal, where her composition teacher was Serge *Garant. On a *Canada Council grant she did research in auditory perception which provided material for her teaching at the U of Montreal and the UQAM. She was also interested in song, working with the experimental music group YUL, which she directed 1969–74. She composed incidental music for Tirso de Molina's *Le Timide au palais* in 1971, Molière's *Don Juan* in 1972, Marcel Godin's *Julien* in 1973, Rostand's *Cyrano de Bergerac* in 1974, and other plays. Most of her incidental music was written for productions by the Théâtre populaire du Québec, the Théâtre du Nouveau-Monde, and the Nouvelle compagnie théâtrale. Her *Match en coordonnées* (1971) for percussion, two electric guitars, and tape (prerecorded tape, soundtrack) has been conducted by Serge Garant. In 1974 she began collaborating on CBC productions, as composer or as organizer-researcher. She is a member of CAPAC.

BIBLIOGRAPHY

Jasmin, Hélène. 'A constant musical voice in Quebec's theatre scene,' *CanComp*, Apr 1976

Bell Piano and Organ Co. Instrument-manufacturing firm. Established in 1864 in *Guelph, Canada West (Ontario, 1867) by the brothers William and Robert Bell with a staff of three, it produced 25 four-legged 'Diploma' melodeons in its first year. William Bell assumed management in 1865 and, as W. Bell and Co, opened a factory on Market Square in 1871. By 1881 nearly 200 employees produced annually over 1200 melodeons and reed organs, some of which were exported as far as Australia. In 1884 (at which time the company claimed to have produced 26,000 instruments to date) Bell formed a partnership with his son W.J. Bell (1863–1925), Mrs. W.B. Kennedy, and A.W. Alexander. The younger Bell sold the firm to an English syndicate in 1888, at which time the name was changed to the Bell Organ and Piano Co, Ltd, and the manufacture of pianos was begun. The company's production reached 600 reed organs and 200 pianos per month. The first grand pianos were built in 1901. Bell pianos were exported extensively, and some of the handsomer models were sent to the palaces of Queen Victoria, Queen Frederica, the kings of Italy and Spain, and a Turkish sultan. The instruments also enjoyed success in trade exhibitions and competitions. When piano sales out-stripped organ sales and seemed likely to continue doing so, the company in 1907 changed its name to the Bell Piano and Organ Co, Ltd. Agencies were established across Canada (one of which, in Toronto, became in 1913 a separate organization – the Bell Music and Piano Co – and also sold records, phonographs, and sheet music). A trade magazine was published in the years before 1913. By 1920 the company had begun to produce player pianos, electric reproducing pianos, phonographs, piano benches, radio tables, and cabinets. Over 170,000 pianos and organs had been built by 1928, when the company was sold to a syndicate headed by John S. Dowling of Brantford, Ont. The manufacture of organs was discontinued and the company renamed Bell Pianos Ltd. In 1934 the company was sold to *Lesage Pianos, which perpetuated the Bell design.

FH

Bells. Percussion instruments which, by virtue of their material and shape, emit, when struck, sounds characterized by many partial tones (not overtones). The highest tones fade away almost immediately, while the lowest continue to sound for an appreciable time. Most bells are made of bronze, an alloy of copper and tin, though they may be of other hard alloys, and some are made of clay. Generally they are of two shapes: the cup (the common, 'open' bell) and the pod (the closed sleigh bell or crotal). Sound is produced when they are struck with a hard (usually metal) object and then left to vibrate freely. In the case of open bells, this striking object may be an outside hammer (as in stationary clock bells) or a clapper, ie, a rod-like member attached inside (as in swinging bells and carillons). Crotal bells contain a loose pellet which strikes the inner surface of the bell when it is shaken.

No instrument varies so greatly in size as the bell. Cup-shaped bells may range from 5 millimetres to 3 metres in diameter, though a few are over 5 metres in diameter and weigh over 20 tonnes. Crotals vary from less than 5 millimetres to approximately .3 metres in diameter. The larger the bell, the further its sound carries. The low frequencies of very large bells cause them to be heard farther than any other instrument, and they diffuse their sound in all directions.

Bells can be used individually or in scale series, as in *carillons, *chimes, and handbells. Crotals are chiefly rhythm instruments and sometimes are worn by dancers to emphasize their movements. Crotals of definite pitch have been introduced into orchestral works, eg, Mozart's *German Dances* and Percival *Price's symphony *The Saint Lawrence*. While some Russian and French orchestras use large, open bells, most others use tubular kinds to suggest real bell sounds. (Tubular bells sometimes are used instead of real bells, in pseudo-carillons in church towers, and the instruments are operated electronically by keyboards located elsewhere in the churches.)

One of the oldest musical instruments, the bell was found in most prehistoric metal-working cultures. In modern times it is found throughout the world. Historically its widest use has been to ward off harm. Tuned series of bells were used first about 500 BC, in Confucian musical ensembles. Large bells intended to be heard far away were used first at Buddhist temples ca 300 AD, and Christians began to use tower bells ca 1000 AD.

Early European explorers found small bells in use in South and Central America, but not as far north as Canada. The Hudson's Bay Company hung large European bells at its trading posts as early as 1683 to call servants in from work and to sound an alarm. It also introduced crotal bells to western Canadian Indians.

PPr

SOME BELLS IN CANADA. An early reference to bells in Quebec appears in the *Jesuit Relations*, vol. 27 (p 101): 'On the 25th [November 1645] a larger bell was placed in the parish church, instead of the small one which was there.' A bell from the France of Louis XIV was given to the church at Beauport, Que, by Robert Giffard in 1666. The first bells of Canadian origin, however, were installed at Quebec in 1664. According to the 18th-

The Peace Tower bells arriving at Ottawa, 1927

century Quebec parish priest Bertrand de la Tour (quoted in E. *Gagnon's *Louis Jolliet*, 3rd ed, p 33), 'At year's end ... the Bishop blessed the three first bells of Canada, bells of a kind that had not existed until then: these bells were cast in Canada.' It is known that the parish church of Montreal, which dates back to 1656, had a tower with two bells, but the bells could have been installed later. Bells are mentioned in historical records in 1672 and again in 1683. In 1710 Queen Anne of England gave a church bell to a group of Iroquois living in what became New York State. The bell later was brought to Canada by the Mohawk Princess Catherine (the future wife of Joseph Brant) and in 1786 was installed in a church built in Upper Canada, at what was to become Brantford, Ont. In British Columbia Russian bells arrived via Alaska while Mexican bells were brought by Spanish traders and pirates who ventured that far north. One of the biggest bells in North America (11,240 kg) was installed in the west tower of Notre-Dame Church in Montreal in 1843. This bell, a 'Jean-Baptiste' or Gros Bourdon, cracked six months after it was rung for the first time but was replaced six months later by a second bell of the same size. It is said that 12 men were needed to pull the ropes to ring it. Later electrically operated, and rung only on special occasions, it was still in use in 1980.

In 1862 the Bishop of (British) Columbia received a chime of eight bells as a gift from an English lady, Angela Georgina Burdett Coutts. It was installed in 1865 in a specially built tower of Holy Trinity Church, New Westminster, BC. Some time later, a bell ringers' club was started at the church by Private Howse of the Royal Engineers. All but the tenor (the lowest) bell of this chime were destroyed in the devastating fire of 1898. The surviving bell was used again when the cathedral reopened in 1899. The first bell installed in Vancouver (1873) was placed in the cupola of the Indian Wesleyan Methodist Church, located on the edge of the beach at the foot of Abbott St (later Water St). The City of Victoria was presented with a .9-tonne bell by the Chinese community. Cast in 1627 in China, it originally was the property of the Lew family; it was installed in Beacon Hill Park in 1904.

The three bells in Toronto's old city hall were rung first on 31 Dec 1900 and were still in use in 1980. They weigh 5400 kilograms, 1504 kilograms, and 857 kilograms respectively. The quarter-hour is rung on the small B-flat bell; the half-hour on the middle E-flat bell and the small bell together; the three-quarter-hour by the same two in sequence; and the hour by the large B-flat bell. In 1911 St John's Church in Peterborough, Ont, installed 13 bells which came to be known as the People's Chimes and were played daily until 1967. In October 1977 a Japanese temple bell was presented to Ontario in celebration of the 100th anniversary of the Japanese in Canada. The bell, which weighs nearly .9 tonne, was hung in a pagoda located on the west island of *Ontario Place.

A bell foundry was established by Carl Stoermer in 1931, at Breslau, Ont.

In the latter part of the 20th century bells seldom were rung manually; keyboards and clockwork systems for the most part had supplanted the rope and the bell ringer. But bells themselves, however rung, continued to play a prominent role in town and village life, hung in churches, townhalls, schools, and firehalls to ring church hour, noonhour, schooltime, or fire warning. Edward Lye (of the *Lye Organ Co) and his descendants rang the bells of St James' Cathedral in Toronto for 96 years (1867–1963).

Bell ringers often practise with small handbells, and in 1980 handbell choirs still could be found throughout the country, among them the Harriet Clark Memorial Handbell Choir in Fredericton, NB, and the group led by Ted Eames of Prince George, BC, which played at Expo 70 in Osaka, Japan, at the invitation of the Japanese government.

Among Canadian musicians who have collected bells are Percival Price and John *Wyre. Price became an authority on all aspects of bells and bell-ringing. Wyre has put his collection to active use in performances by himself and by the group *Nexus, and has composed a work called *Bells* on a commission arranged by Seiji Ozawa for the Contemporary Music Festival at Expo 70.

BIBLIOGRAPHY

Gormely, Sheila. 'Tongues of bells tell many tales,' *London Free Press*, 10 Feb 1962

'The bellfounders of Breslau,' (*Toronto Daily Star*) *Canadian Weekly*, 23 Jun 1962

Fletcher, Elva. 'His home is a bell-ringer's paradise,' *Country Guide*, Dec 1972

Atkinson, Corday Mackay. 'Beacon Hill's Chinese bell,' Victoria *Daily Colonist*, 15 Jul 1973

Graham, Melva Treffinger. ' "Play, sing and ring," a parish musician looks beyond the keyboard,' *RCCO Q*, Apr 1978

Bell Singers. See The Leslie Bell Singers.

BÉLUSE, Pierre. Percussionist, teacher, b Lachine, near Montreal, 21 Jul 1935. He played 1953–65 in several Montreal nightclubs and studied 1957–9 at the *CMM with Saul Goodman and Louis *Charbonneau. Béluse was one of the leading jazz drummers in Montreal in the early 1960s and worked with Paul *Bley, Pierre *Leduc, Galt *MacDermot, and René Thomas, among others, and with such distinguished US musicians as Jimmy Heath. In 1961 he toured in Quebec with the Double-Six vocal ensemble from Paris. He made LPs with MacDermot and Armas *Maiste.

Béluse joined the *MSO in 1959 and the *SMCQ Ensemble in 1967. With the latter he participated in the ninth Festival d'art contemporain (1972) in Royan, France. He also has played in CBC orchestras and, with percussionists Guy *Lachapelle and Robert Leroux, has been a member of the Ensemble Polycousmie founded by Micheline Coulombe *Saint-Marcoux in 1972. He began teaching at *McGill U in 1967 and at the St-Laurent Cegep in 1975. He is a founder-member and the director of the McGill Percussion Ensemble, established in 1969, and he toured Quebec with the ensemble for *JMC in 1978. In 1977 the group recorded works by Andrew Culver, Serge *Garant, Alcides *Lanza, and François *Morel (McGill U Records 77003) and, under the name of Concept Neuf, works by Walter *Boudreau, Vincent *Dionne, and Claude *Vivier (RCI 478).

See also Dorothy Morton and the discographies for Patricia Rideout and Gilles Tremblay. Béluse has composed works for percussion and recorder. He is a member of CAPAC.

Béluse is married to the pianist Édith Boivin – b St-Odilon de Dorchester, near Quebec City, 14 Feb 1947; B MUS (Montreal) 1968; M MUS (Montreal) 1969; premier prix, piano, Cons de Hull, 1972. She studied with Sister Lucille Brassard at the *École Vincent-d'Indy and with Anisia Campos at the Cons de Hull, where she became rehearsal pianist and coach in 1973. She also works with pop groups. She premiered the *Concerto in A* by François *Dompierre, a work commissioned by the CBC and presented on TV 25 Dec 1978 in the program series 'Les Beaux Dimanches.' She gave the concert premiere of the work with the MSO under Charles Dutoit in the Maurice-Richard Arena in July 1979. A subsequent recording with the same performers was produced by Deutsche Grammophon (2531 265) for international distribution.

ST

BENDER, Garfield (Lloyd). Administrator, teacher, choir director, b Listowel, near Stratford, Ont, 23 May 1912; LTCL 1947, hon D MUS (Wilfrid Laurier) 1973. He studied music in Listowel and Toronto. In 1947 he became a Canadian member of Great Britain's Royal Society of Teachers. He taught choral methods at the *U of Saskatchewan (summer 1947) and at the *U of Toronto (summer 1948) and teaching methods at *Dalhousie U (summers 1949–64). His main post was supervisor of music for the Waterloo County Board of Education, from which he retired in 1972. He was president of the *OMEA 1951–2 and of the *CMEA 1965–7. He conducted two 1200-voice children's choirs in Kitchener 1959–66. These were open to all the school children in the city, and the two choirs alternated in performance. In 1973 Bender became founding president of the Ontario Federation of Concert Assns.

BENJAMIN, Arthur. Pianist, composer, teacher, b Sydney 18 Nov 1893, d London 10 Apr 1960. Having established an international reputation as a pianist and composer in Australia and then in England (where he lived after 1921), Benjamin first visited Canada in the 1930s as an adjudicator. In 1939 (the year after he wrote his famous *Jamaican Rhumba*) he settled in Vancouver following his adjudication of the 17th *Kiwanis Music Festival. Remaining there throughout World War II, he gave recitals and conducted the *Vancouver Sun*'s Promenade Symphony Concerts 1941–2, the CBR SO (radio 1941–6), and, as a guest, the *Vancouver SO. He performed with William Primrose for the *Ladies' Morning Musical Club in 1942 and also played that year with the *McGill String Quartet. Among the compositions he completed during his Vancouver years were the rondo for orchestra *Prelude to Holiday* (chosen for performance at the 1942 ISCM festival in San Francisco), the *Oboe Concerto after Cimarosa* (premiered in Vancouver at a 1941 promenade concert), *Sonata, 'Elegy, Waltz and Toccata'* (premiered by the composer and the violist William Primrose in Vancouver, 14 Oct 1942; the date given in *Grove's* is incorrect), and *Symphony No. 1*. An accomplished pianist, Benjamin was also an outstanding teacher. His Canadian pupils included Robert *Barclay, Jean *Coulthard, Robert *Fleming, Hugh *McLean, Gregory *Millar, Phyllis *Schuldt, and Ira *Swartz. Benjamin returned to England in 1946. (BNSG)

BENN, (Anne) Nancy (b Paisley). Teacher, conductor, b London 7 Dec 1894, d Vancouver 20? Oct 1972; LRAM ca 1911. She studied and taught piano and voice in England before coming to Canada about 1920 with her husband, also a pianist. In Vancouver she continued to teach voice and piano, but it was chiefly in the vocal field that she made her name. Her voice pupils were consistently successful in the Vancouver *Kiwanis Festival and elsewhere. They include Audrey Glass, Lilli Washimoto, Donald *Bell, Ralph Lear, and Jack Ringham. She was an adjudicator (vocal and instrumental) at competitions throughout British Columbia and was a founding member of the *BCRMTA. She was active in the Welsh musical community in Vancouver and ca 1931–50 directed the St Cecilia Choristers. During the 1940s and 1950s she led Music Makers (a children's choir). The Vancouver Kiwanis Festival awards a Nancy Paisley Benn Scholarship for accompanists and performers of art songs and a Mrs Paisley Benn Cup for boy soloists aged nine and younger. BNSG

BENOIST, Marius. Conductor, choirmaster, composer, administrator, customs broker, b Ste-Anne-des-Chênes, near Winnipeg, 1 Oct 1896. He studied piano with Rodolphe Pépin in St-Boniface, Man, and took courses at the *Schola cantorum in Montreal. Returning to St-Boniface he served as organist-choirmaster at the Roman Catholic cathedral of that city for nearly 40 years (until 1965) and as a musical leader for several generations of Franco-Manitobans. An ardent champion of French music, he founded the Société lyrique Gounod, which presented Gounod's *Mireille* and *Roméo et Juliette*, and Berlioz' *L'Enfance du Christ*. He also organized a youth orchestra, the Cercle Calixa-Lavallée, and a Sinfonietta which, under his direction, performed *L'Arlésienne* with the Cercle Molière and *Peer Gynt* with the Winnipeg Little Theatre. He served 1974–5 as administrator of the St-Boniface Museum.

Benoist has composed more than 100 scores for radio plays produced by CBC Winnipeg. He also

Marius Benoist

has written three operas (*Le Secret des Amati, La Rencontre dans l'escalier, Saint-François d'Assise*), the oratorio *Mère d'Youville*, and the lyric drama *La Légende du vent* (libretto by Léo Brodeur). *La Légende* was telecast in 1974 by the CBC, earning Benoist the Prix Anik of that year, and was shown also in Poland and Hungary. Among his works – all unpublished – are the ballet *Great Bear; Erivadnus* for voice and orchestra; *La Fin du maître-chantre* and *La Vérendrye* for choir and orchestra; an *Ode to Spring* (1949) for voice, chorus, and orchestra; and *Sérénade* (1953) for small orchestra. In November 1977 Benoist's opera *Onadéga ou la tragédie du lac des bois*, adapted from the English libretto by Milway Filion, was premiered at St-Boniface Cathedral with Napoléon *Bisson as Onadéga, and with local singers and the Chorale des intrépides. At another concert that year the same choir, conducted by Marcien *Ferland (a former instrumentation pupil of Benoist), performed the composer's 1938 *Te Deum*. (MB)

BENSON GUY, Elizabeth. See Guy, Elizabeth Benson.

BENTLEY, John. Organist-choirmaster, harpsichordist, composer, b England 1754, d Quebec City 10 Nov 1813. Resident in London until about 1781, Bentley moved to the USA and in 1783 founded the City Concerts in Philadelphia. In 1785 he joined Lewis Hallam's touring theatre company, participating in its fall season in New York as harpsichordist, orchestra director, and occasional actor. He composed pantomime music for the production *The Cave of Enchantment* (or *The Stockwell Wonder*), presented 26 Oct 1785 in New York, and for others, *The Genii of the Rock* and *Touchstone* (or *Harlequin Traveler*), mounted the same year. While similarly associated 1785–6 with the Allen-Moore Company, Bentley travelled to Albany, Montreal, and Quebec City and wrote music for *The Enchanters* (or *The Triumph of Genius*) staged 12 May 1786 in Montreal.

After a brief residence in Montreal Bentley settled in 1787 in Quebec City, participating in theatrical activities and in vocal and instrumental concerts. After 1797 he also held municipal positions such as high constable and surveyor of roads. Appointed organist in 1801 and choirmaster in 1802 by the Church of England, he served 1804–7 and 1810–13 as organist-choirmaster at the new Cathedral of the Holy Trinity, providing the consecration ceremonies 28 Aug 1804 under Bishop Jacob Mountain with a full choral service (13 boys, 4 men) and organ accompaniment. In a letter (22 Nov 1814) to Jonathan *Sewell, Bishop Mountain remarked: 'Mr. Bentley was paid £40 a year for teaching singing to the Choir and a Dollar each time for playing the organ. It should be known that the service is not daily' (Anglican Church of Canada Archives). He was also organist-choirmaster 1810–13 at Notre-Dame Cathedral, where his duties included training a successor. Two of Bentley's chants appear in F.H. Andrews' *Collection of Original Sacred Music* (Lovell & Gibson 1848), and he composed an ode (text printed in *Quebec Gazette* 5 Jan 1792) and sang it at the constitutional meeting, 26 Dec 1791, which divided British North America into Upper and Lower Canada. DR

Berandol Music Limited. Toronto publishing company formed in 1969 by Andrew *Twa with the acquisition of the music-publishing division of BMI Canada (*PRO Canada). Ralph Cruickshank (who joined BMI Canada in 1966 and became head of its publishing division in 1969) served as vice-president of Berandol until he purchased the company and succeeded Twa as president in 1972. Berandol has continued to publish in the areas developed by BMI Canada and also has expanded in new directions. It has maintained a large catalogue of concert music and a rental library of orchestral material by François *Morel, Jean *Papineau-Couture, R. Murray *Schafer, Harry *Somers, Gilles *Tremblay, Healey *Willan, and others. The education catalogue includes recorder music by Mario *Duschenes and Hugh *Orr, books and multi-media performance materials by Schafer, and *What to Do Until the Music Teacher Comes* (1978) by Louise Glatt. Berandol's pop music catalogue was taken over by Broadland Music in 1972; a second pop catalogue was developed in subsequent years. In addition Berandol has created MUSIcache, a collection of the standard repertoire on microfiche produced by Bell and Howell. Berandol Records, established 1975, have released LPs by the pianish-organist Harold Clayton, the Toronto Baroque Trio, the *Toronto Consort, and, in the pop field, the pianist Rob Liddell. A second label, Bear 'n' Doll, was introduced in 1978 with the first of several LPs by the singer Sandy Offenheim. Berandol has acted as agent for Hargail Music Press and *Jaymar Music and for some years also represented Universal Edition. Most of Berandol's publications are printed by the W.R. *Draper Co. Plate numbers are not used. A PRO Canada affiliate, Berandol also operates Cee and Cee Music, a CAPAC affiliate. The name Clark & Cruickshank also appears on the imprint of some Berandol publications.

BIBLIOGRAPHY
'"Canada first" is Berandol policy,' *MSc*, 251, Jan–Feb 1970

Cruickshank, Ralph. 'The Berandol story,' *MusicJ*, vol 28, Jan 1970

Linden, J.J. 'Berandol Music – ten years of publishing and recording high quality Canadian music,' *RPM*, 21 Apr 1979 (MWI)

BERGINK, Herman. Carillonneur, organist, b Enschede, the Netherlands, 15 May 1924; organ-and-choir-training diploma (Utrecht Cons) 1955. He studied organ with Adriaan Schuurman, piano and organ with Dick van Wilgenburg, and carillon with Leen 't Hart. In 1957 he emigrated to Canada, settling in Victoria where he was organist-choirmaster 1957–8 at Victoria West United Church, 1958–9 at First Baptist Church, and 1962–8 at the Church of St David-by-the-Sea, Cordova Bay; he resumed duties at the last-named church in 1977. Bergink was appointed British Columbia's provincial carillonneur in 1968, assigned to the Netherlands Centennial Carillon at Victoria. The carillon's bells were a gift from the province's Dutch community (see also Carillons).

In 1979 Bergink maintained his custom of regular performances on the Victoria carillon, also appearing elsewhere as a guest performer. In 1979 he gave a recital at the U of California at Riverside. He may be heard on *The Sound of Victoria*, a 1971 recording of his performances on the Netherlands Centennial Carillon. His pupils include Tobias Yenney and the US carillonneurs Randall Jay McCarty and John Barg. Bergink is a member of the *Guild of Carillonneurs in North America.

BIBLIOGRAPHY

Baird, Ron. 'The music man,' *Victoria Post*, 20 Dec 1978

BERLIN, Boris. Piano teacher, composer, b Kharkov, Russia, 27 May 1907, naturalized Canadian 1931. He studied at the Sebastopol Cons, at the Cons de Genève 1923–5, and with Mark Hambourg and Leonid Kreutzer at the Berlin Hochschule für Musik. Although he began his career as a pianist, performing in Germany and Switzerland, he soon concentrated on piano pedagogy. While visiting Canada in 1925 he toured Ontario in a concert trio and held a position as piano teacher 1925–7 at the *Hambourg Cons. He began teaching at the TCM (*RCMT) in 1928 and at the *U of Toronto in 1970.

Disturbed by the lack of Canadian material for music students, Berlin has written over 20 pedagogical works, beginning with *The Modern Piano Student* (Harris 1930), the first of a number of collaborations with Ernest *MacMillan. Other widely used manuals and teaching pieces were published by Boosey & Hawkes, Harris, Heintzman, Jarman, and Thompson in Canada, and by other publishers in England and the USSR. These include *20 Lessons in Ear Training* (with MacMillan, Harris 1939), the eight-volume *Four Star Series in Sight Reading* (Harris 1939–55), and the *ABC of Piano Playing* (Harris 1941), also issued in French under the pseudonym René Saint-Jean. Some of his pieces are published under the pseudonym Lawrence London. He has given workshops for teachers and, with Warren *Mould, prepared a teachers' manual, *Basics of Ear Training* (Toronto 1968), published in a translation by Juliette *Milette as *Rythme et son* (Toronto 1969). Milette also translated Berlin's *Keys to Music Rudiments* (*Principes élémentaires de la musique*), both published in Toronto in 1968. Berlin's pupils have included Louis *Applebaum, Dorothy Sandler *Glick, Gwen Beamish *MacMillan, Bernadene Blaha, Adrienne *Shannon, Christina *Petrowska, and the jazz pianists Rudy *Toth and Norman *Amadio. Berlin is a member of CAPAC.

BIBLIOGRAPHY

Schulman, Michael. 'Boris Berlin: music for all our children,' *CanComp*, 88, Feb 1974 (MH)

Berliner Gramophone Company. First record company in Canada and the manufacturer of 'Gram-O-Phone' records and talking machines. It was established in Montreal by Emile Berliner (b Hanover, Germany, 20 May 1851, d Washington, DC, 3 Aug 1929), the inventor of the gramophone and co-founder (in Germany, 1898, with his brother Joseph) of Deutsche Grammophon. Berliner took out a Canadian patent on his invention 24 Feb 1897 and in the Bell Telephone factory on Aqueduc St established manufacturing facilities. He also set up retail store on Ste-Catherine St. Production of seven-inch records, made from masters recorded by Berliner's European and US companies and bearing the inscription 'E. Berliner, Montreal,' began 2 Jan 1900. In 1901, 10-inch single-sided discs called Concert Grands were introduced, followed in 1903 by the 12-inch Deluxe

Boris Berlin

Records, and finally in 1908 by double-sided records.

The Berliner Gramophone Co of Canada was chartered 8 Apr 1904 and was reorganized as the Berliner Gramophone Co in 1909. A recording studio was opened on Peel St, and in 1906 a factory was built at the corner of St-Antoine and Lenoir, to be supplemented in 1921 by a plant at St-Antoine and Lacasse. The company's subsidiary, His Master's Voice, was operating distribution outlets in six Canadian cities in 1924. Emile Berliner remained president of Berliner Gramophone until 1924. His son Herbert (Samuel) (b Cambridge, Mass, 13 Sep 1882, naturalized Canadian, d Montreal 9 Aug 1966) was the company's vice-president and general manager until he resigned in 1921 to devote his time to another company, *Compo, which he had founded in 1918. He was succeeded at the Berliner Gramophone Co by his brother Edgar (b Washington 25 Jul 1885, naturalized Canadian, d Beverly Hills, Cal, 20 Jul 1955), previously the company's secretary-treasurer. It was Edgar who in 1924 relinquished the controlling interest in Berliner to the Victor Talking Machine Co of Camden, NJ, a company whose records and equipment Berliner had distributed in Canada since 1901. The Berliner Gramophone Co was renamed the Victor Talking Machine Co of Canada (after 1929, *RCA Victor), and Edgar was its president until 1930.

In its 20 years of production, the Berliner company pressed and distributed several record series, mostly of non-Canadian origin, including those bearing the Berliner labels. Artists included the Canadian expatriates Harry McClaskey (Henry *Burr) and Arthur Pryor. The Berliner x label appeared on recordings of Pauline *Donalda, Berliner xx on those by Joseph *Saucier. Of musicological interest are 12 ancient tribal songs recorded by the Iroquois chief Ho-nu-ses for Emile Berliner in 1904. Some Victor lines offered other Canadian performers (Mark *Hambourg, the *Hart House String Quartet), as did the HMV 21600 series, introduced in 1916. HMV's 263000 series, begun in 1918, was devoted to French-Canadian performers. Both HMV series were recorded in Montreal and continued after the Victor takeover. The 21600 line offered recordings of, among others, the tenors Paul *Dufault and Henri *Prieur, the violinist Albert *Chamberland, the fiddler J. B. Roy, the cellists J.-B. *Dubois and Raoul *Duquette, the Hawaiian guitarist Ben Hokea, the conductor Henri *Miro (who was music director 1916–21 of the BGC), the trios of Willie *Eckstein and Harry *Thomas, and the *Canadian Grenadier Guards Band. The 263000 line presented, among others, the soprano Camille *Bernard, the tenors Charles Dalberty, José *Delaquerrière, Paul Dufault, Ludovic Huot, Émile *Larochelle,

Emile Berliner, ca 1915

and Roméo Mousseau, the baritones Hector *Pellerin, Charles *Marchand (and his Bytown Troubadours), and Jean *Riddez, the fiddler Joseph *Allard, the harmonica player Henri Lacroix, the monologuist Elzéar Hamel, and the vocal groups Quatuor canadien and Quatuor franco-américain. Most of the recordings released by Berliner are listed in *Roll Back the Years*. (EBM)

BERMAN, Melvin. Oboist, teacher, b Hartford, Conn, 28 Feb 1929; B MUS (Hartford) 1949, M MUS (Hartford) 1950. He studied oboe with Clement Lenom and Harold Gomberg. He has played principal oboe with the *MSO, the orchestras of the *NFB and the CBC, the Hartford Symphony, the New Orleans Philharmonic, the Boston Pops Orchestra, and Ballet Theatre of New York. A founder of the *Baroque Trio of Montreal and the Pro Arte Woodwind Quintet, Berman became a member of the *Toronto Winds in 1971. He was a woodwind teacher at the U of Hartford in 1950, the *CMM 1956–70, and *McGill U 1956–64. In 1971 he began teaching at the *U of Toronto.

Berman has composed a *Quintet for Brass* (1962, Berandol 1974). His film, *The Oboe Reed* (U of Toronto Media Centre), was completed in 1972.

WRITINGS

'The power of pops,' *Fugue*, May 1979

DISCOGRAPHY

Archer *Divertimento*. Iacurto cl, Moisan b cl. 1962. RCI 192
A Baroque Bouquet: Bach – Telemann – Handel – et al. Weait bs, Gaylord pf. 1976. Berandol BER 9009
Jones *Wind Quintet*. Pro Arte Wind Quintet. 1971. RCI 355.
Sammartini – Jacob – Fleming – Hindemith. Gaylord pf. 1974. CBC SM-268
Telemann *Sonatas*. Jones hpd. 1963. Vox STPL 514020
Vivaldi *Il Pastor fido*. Jones hpd, Joachim vc. 1973. Orion 73115
See Discographies for Baroque Trio of Montreal; Toronto Winds. (WS)

BERNARD, Camille. Soprano, diseuse, teacher, actress, b Joliette, Que, 25 Feb 1898. After a year (1907) in Paris she began studying singing in Montreal with Béatrice *La Palme and Salvator *Issaurel. The Quebec Ladies' Musical Club invited her to perform on several occasions, the first in 1917, and in 1923 offered her a bursary to study in Paris where, ca 1924, she obtained the diploma of the professional union of French singing teachers. She later completed her training in France with Pauline *Donalda, the famous diseuse Yvette Guilbert, and others. She sang in Paris theatres and with operetta troupes in Monte Carlo, Le Touquet, and Vichy. At the Casino in Vichy she gave a recital which the *Lyon républicain* (26 Aug

1927) deemed 'exceptionally attractive in its program and highly artistic in its performance.'

Bernard's stage repertoire in Paris and for the *Société canadienne d'opérette included the roles of Betly in Adam's *Le Chalet*, Saffi in Strauss' *The Gypsy Baron*, L'Institutrice in Ibert's *Angélique*, Suzette Janville in Hahn's *Le Droit d'aimer*, and Lisette in Poise's *L'Amour médecin*. In Montreal in 1929 she founded the Théâtre des petits, a school of diction and music which presented a program of the same name on radio station CKAC, and shortly afterwards the École nouvelle, which gave courses for children with language difficulties. These two establishments later merged to form the Institut Camille-Bernard. She made a 78 of the songs 'Hum Humm' and 'La mort du mari' (HMV-263158). She appeared in the role of Mme Tassy in the film *Kamouraska*. (IP-C)

BERNARDI, Mario (Egidio). Conductor, pianist, b Kirkland Lake, northern Ontario, 20 Aug 1930; hon D MUS (Laurentian) 1972, hon D MUS (Ottawa) 1974, hon FRHCM 1978, hon D MUS (Windsor) 1978. Sent at six to Italy, he studied piano, organ, and composition 1938–45 with Bruno Pasut at the Manzato Cons at Treviso and took his examinations at the Venice Cons. He obtained the highest marks possible and was the youngest student to graduate that year. Returning to Canada in 1947, he studied 1948–51 at the *RCMT with Lubka *Kolessa (piano) and Ettore *Mazzoleni (conducting), supporting himself as the organist at St Vincent de Paul Church, Toronto. He was soloist in the Grieg *Concerto* in the *Melody Fair production (1951) of *Song of Norway* and also played that work on CBC radio.

Though his career as a conductor and coach began in 1953 with the *Royal Cons Opera School, his work as a pianist and accompanist continued unabated during the next 10 years. His playing in a Brahms concert with Lea *Foli (violin) and Peggie *Sampson (cello) drew these comments from Kenneth *Winters: 'Brahms' lack of consideration for the human hand is legend, yet Bernardi met his rudest demands with absolute poise, never-failing intelligence and a physical competence which made them seem positively polite ... He is a joyous and skilful man, a credit to his profession' (*Winnipeg Free Press*, 15 Jan 1963). Bernardi has been a soloist with the *CBC SO (*Pentland's *Piano Concerto*, premiere, 1958), the *TSO (Strauss' *Burleske*, 1960), the (Stratford) National Festival Orchestra (*Papineau-Couture's *Pièce Concertante No. 1*, 1960), and the *MSO (*Beckwith's *Concerto Fantasy*, premiere, 1962), and accompanist on occasion to Donald *Bell, Margo *MacKinnon, Jean-Pierre Rampal, Janos Starker, and others. Bernardi played the Fauré *Quartet* with members of the *Parlow String Quartet in 1957 and, at the *Stratford Festival, two works of Bartók: the *Sonata for Two Pianos and Percussion* with William *Aide in 1963 and *Contrasts* with Oscar Shumsky and Benny Goodman in 1965.

Bernardi made his *COC conducting debut 25 Feb 1957 in *Hansel and Gretel* and subsequently directed that company's *Carousel* (1957), *The Merry Wives of Windsor* (touring production 1960), *I Pagliacci* (1961), *La Bohème* (1963), *Don Giovanni* (1963), *The Barber of Seville* (1965), *Mavra* (1965), *Rigoletto* (1969), and *Carmen* (1970). He also conducted *Gianni Schicchi* and Mavor *Moore's *The Optimist* for CBC TV in 1957, operas for the Stratford Festival and the Vancouver and Edmonton opera associations in the 1960s, and four performances each of *La Bohème* in 1966 and *The Marriage of Figaro* in 1967 for the *Opera Guild in Montreal. In the summer of 1959 he studied with Erich Leinsdorf at the Mozarteum in Salzburg. Appointed coach and assistant conductor at Sadler's Wells,

Mario Bernardi

London, in 1963, he made his conducting debut there 19 December as a replacement for Colin Davis in *Hansel and Gretel*. In 1966 he was named music director of one of the two Sadler's Wells companies. He held this position until 1968, conducting *Don Pasquale*, *The Flying Dutchman*, *I Pagliacci*, *The Queen of Spades*, *A Masked Ball*, an acclaimed revival of Britten's *Gloriana* (which he also conducted on the continent), *Don Giovanni*, and *The Italian Girl in Algiers*. While in London he appeared in recital with Steven *Staryk at Wigmore Hall and in 1968 he guest-conducted the London SO and the Royal Philharmonic Orchestra. He made his US debut in 1967 in *La Bohème* with the San Francisco Opera.

In 1968 Bernardi became the first conductor of the newly formed *NACO and, with Jean-Marie *Beaudet, was responsible for the selection of musicians. Bernardi alone, however, may claim credit for the shaping of the orchestra into an organization of extraordinary distinction, noted for its clean attack, transparent sound, and fine tuning. With that orchestra he has conducted premieres of works by *Adaskin, *Beecroft, *Fleming, *Freedman, *Gellman, Pentland, *Prévost, *Ridout, *Schafer, *Tremblay, and *Wilson. With the NACO, Bernardi has performed as a soloist in concertos of Mozart and Ravel, conducting from the keyboard. In 1971 he became general music director for the *NAC and artistic director for the centre's Festival Canada (renamed *Festival Ottawa in 1978), subsequently conducting the major Mozart operas and a lengthening list of other works including *Le Comte Ory* (1974), *The Queen of Spades* (1976), *Ariadne auf Naxos* (1977), and Britten's *A Midsummer Night's Dream* (1978). Other conducting engagements have taken him to *PDA (*La Bohème* 1970), the New York City Opera (*The Abduction from the Seraglio* 1971), the Chicago and Pittsburgh SOs (1972), and the Warsaw Philharmonic (1975). He also conducted the BBC SO in works of *Aitken, Beecroft, Freedman, *Hétu, and Schafer 4 Nov 1977 during *Musicanada. Among the premieres Bernardi has conducted with orchestras other than the NACO are Ridout's *The Dance* (CBC SO 1960) and *Folksongs of Eastern Canada* (CBC Toronto orchestra 1967), Adaskin's *Rondino for Nine Instruments* (Toronto 1962), Norman *Symonds' TV ballet *Tensions* (CBC Toronto 1962), Harry *Somers' *Movement for Orchestra* (CBC Toronto orchestra 1962), Papineau-Couture's *Contraste* (MSO, *Montreal International Competition, 1970), Malcolm *Forsyth's *Sagittarius* (Canadian Chamber Orchestra and *Canadian Brass 1975), and Rudi *van Dijk's *The Shadow Maker* (TS and Victor *Braun 1978).

For its particular distinction Bernardi's conducting relies on a keenly tuned orchestra, the strings lightly bowed and deft rather than deeply sonorous, yielding buoyant and elegant performances of the classics, particularly Mozart, for whom his affinity is marked. Bernardi can illumine the sheerly musical elements – as distinct from the romantic or connotative or broadly dramatic – of whatever he chooses to interpret. While this tendency could be a drawback in opera, it paradoxically is not, possibly because the listener is grateful for the musical redress afforded by performances which are transparent in texture, rhythmic, and proportionate, not sacrificing musical values to histrionics. Perhaps the outstanding Canadian conductor of his generation and blessed with an orchestra of unique privilege and subsidy (the NACO is Canada's only state orchestra), Bernardi, by the discipline of his work and the conscientiousness of his program, proved himself worthy of both his gifts and his good fortune prior to announcing his resignation from the NACO in the summer of 1980.

Bernardi was made a Companion of the *Order of Canada in 1972. His wife, the mezzo-soprano Mona Kelly – b Port Arthur, now Thunder Bay, Ont, 4 Sep 1940; Artist Diploma (Toronto) 1962 – studied with Irene *Jessner, Aksel *Schiøtz, and, in England, Otakar Kraus, and has sung such roles as Hansel in *Hansel and Gretel* (COC 1962), Nancy in *Albert Herring* (Stratford Festival 1967), and Oreste in *La Belle Hélène* (Festival Canada 1973, 1975).

DISCOGRAPHY

Humperdinck *Hansel and Gretel*. Sadler's Wells Opera, Bernardi cond. 1966. Cap GBO 7256

Mozart *Quartet* K478. Bernardi pf, Prystawski vn, Sternic va, Whitton vc. 1971. CBC SM 170

Papineau-Couture *Pièce Concertante No. 1*. CBC SO, Susskind cond, Bernardi pf. Col MS-6285

Pentland *Concerto*. CBC SO, Feldbrill cond, Bernardi pf. 1958. RCI 184

See also Compositions for Murray Adaskin; Discographies for Frances James: NACO; Robert Silverman; and Steven Staryk.

BIBLIOGRAPHY

Olver, Michael. 'Famous musicians: featuring pianist Mario Bernardi,' *Sharps & Flats*, Jan 1963

Slater, Clare. 'Profile: Mario Bernardi,' *OpCan*, May 1968

Hale, Barrie. 'A conductor for all seasons,' Toronto *Globe Magazine*, 27 Mar 1971

Hale, Barrie. 'The sound of Mario Bernardi,' *Maclean's*, Apr 1972

Van Vlasselaer, Jean-Jacques. 'Mario Bernardi: a true professional,' *Musicanada*, Jan 1978

O'Toole, Lawrence. 'Flying with trumpets and strings,' *Maclean's*, 10 Sep 1979 (FF)

BERNIER. Quebec City family of musicians comprising 1 / Joseph-Arthur, his sons 2 / Maurice and 3 / Conrad, his daughter 4 / Gabrielle, and Maurice's children 5 / Françoys, 6 / Madeleine, and 7 / Pierre.

1 **Joseph-Arthur**. Organist, pianist, teacher, composer, b Lévis, near Quebec City, 10 Mar 1877, d Quebec City 28 Apr 1944; hon D MUS (Washington College of Music) 1931. He received his early musical education from his mother and continued his musical studies in Quebec City with Gustave *Gagnon and Philéas *Roy (organ and piano) while completing his general education at Lévis. He was organist 1892–1908 at St-Sauveur Church and 1908–17 at Notre-Dame-de-Jacques-Cartier Church in Quebec City. He completed his training 1902–3 in Paris with Alexandre Guilmant (organ) and Félix Fourdrain (composition). The cellist Jean Gérardy, the violinist Ovide Musin, and other musicians sought his services as an accompanist. In 1903 he became a member of the Société des auteurs et compositeurs de Paris. In Montreal

Conrad Bernier

he inaugurated the organs of the churches of St-Pierre in 1908, St-Jean-Baptiste in 1915, and Sacré-Coeur in 1917, and several US churches invited him to perform the same service. He gave recitals in Buffalo in 1901, Worcester in 1905, Springfield, Mass, in 1910, Phoenix in 1915, and Woonsocket in 1917. He also played in Toronto in 1914, in Cap-St-Ignace, Que, in 1918, and with the Union musicale of Quebec City in 1919. In 1917 he became organist at St-Jean-Baptiste Church in Quebec City, a post he held until his death. At *Laval U 1922–44 he taught, among others, Charles-Eugène Albert, Dantès Belleau, Clotilde Coulombe, Rolland-G. *Gingras, and Omer *Létourneau.

Joseph-Albert Bernier's compositions include four masses for female voices; several motets published chiefly by Quebec City's *Procure générale de musique; pieces for organ, violin (*Berceuse*), oboe (*Pastorale*), and cello (*Cantilène*), published in Paris by A. Débert (1903); a *Mazurka* for piano (Lavigueur et Hutchinson 1906); and some other secular music. He served 1910–11 and 1912–13 as president of the *AMQ.

2 **Maurice**. Cellist, critic, b Quebec City 17 Apr 1900. He studied piano with his father and Henri *Gagnon, and cello 1912–20 with J.-Alexandre *Gilbert and Paul Robitaille. He played in the *Quebec SO under Joseph *Vézina in 1915. He was music critic 1922–32 with *L'Événement* of Quebec City, and subsequently became a parliamentary reporter, continuing in that vocation until 1972. On the 75th anniversary of the Quebec SO (1978) he wrote a number of articles for *Le Mois à Québec*.

3 **Conrad**. Pianist, organist, composer, teacher, b Quebec City 9 May 1904; hon D MUS (St Francis, Loretto, Pa) 1962. His father was his first teacher of solfège, organ, and piano. He continued piano study with Berthe *Roy. At 13 he inaugurated the organ of the church at Bienville, and the following year in Quebec City he inaugurated that of St-Sacrement Church, where he served 1920–3 as organist, while he was also assistant organist at St-Jean-Baptiste. Winner of the 1923 *Prix d'Europe for organ, he studied 1923–6 in Paris with Sylva Hérard and Simone Plé-Caussade (piano), Georges Caussade (theory), and Joseph *Bonnet (organ). For Bonnet he substituted on occasion at the organ of St-Eustache. Returning to Canada in 1926, he went on a concert tour and spent a few months in Detroit as organist at the Church of the Visitation. He then taught for nearly 50 years, 1927–74, as director of the organ department of the music college of the Catholic U of Washington, which named him professor emeritus in 1974. He was organist 1935–69 at the church of Ste-Anne in Washington and also became the regular organist of the National Sanctuary of that city. He returned to Canada to give courses 1943–7 at the *CMM and the *CMQ and performed in recital for the *Casavant Society.

Conrad Bernier was the author of two textbooks, *Harmonie moderne* and *Traité d'improvisation à l'orgue* (1962, both unpublished) and *Organ Method / Méthode d'orgue* (Toledo, O, 1962). He composed *Croquis petit-capiens* (Édition Belgo-Canadienne) and *Variations et fugue* for two pianos; *Esquisse* and *Prière* for organ; a *Mass* for mixed-voice choir and two organs; two songs, 'Les Colombes' and 'Les Berceuses'; and several motets, published mainly by Quebec City's *Procure générale de musique.

WRITINGS

'Joseph Bonnet (1884–1944),' *VM*, 9, Oct 1968

4 **Gabrielle**. Pianist, b Quebec City November 1906. She began studying piano with her father and continued at *Laval U. She gave a performance of a Mozart concerto with the Cercle philharmonique de Québec 25 Nov 1938. After her marriage to a US citizen she moved to California.

5 **Françoys** (Joseph Arthur Maurice). Pianist, conductor, producer, administrator, b Quebec City 12 Jul 1927. He began his musical studies as a child with his grandfather. Towards the end of his academic studies 1939–47 at the seminary in Quebec City he began his mature musical studies, most of which he completed 1945–50 at the *CMQ, with Hélène *Landry, Françoise *Aubut, Ria *Lenssens, Henri *Gagnon, and Alphonse *Tardif. He continued to study 1949–50 at *Laval U with Marius *Cayouette and Lucien *Brochu. From 1950 to 1953 he taught music at the college of Gravelbourg, Sask, and served as program director of CFRG, the radio station of that town. He joined the French network of the *CBC in 1953 as a radio producer of music programs, including 'Premières,' and in 1954 he took over the production of the TV shows 'Concerts pour la jeunesse' and *'Heure du concert.' Among the works he produced were Stravinsky's *L'Histoire du soldat* (1955) and *Les Noces* (1956), Ravel's *L'Enfant et les sortilèges* (1956, 1957), Gounod's *Faust* (1957), Puccini's *Madama Butterfly* (1958), Leoncavallo's *I Pagliacci* (1958), Massenet's *Manon* (1960), and Poulenc's *Dialogue des Carmélites* (1960). He also directed the Laval U Choir 1956–9 and served 1957–9 as music director of the *Montreal Festivals. With Gilles Potvin he presented Wilhelm Kempff 1961–4 in recitals in Canada.

During his terms as general director 1960–6 and artistic director 1966–8 of the *Quebec SO Françoys Bernier emphasized French and Canadian music and also championed other contemporary music, presenting important works by Messiaen and Berg. On *Canada Council grants, 1962 and 1963, he studied scores and conducting in Europe with Sergiu Celibidache (Siena) and Hermann Scherchen (Salzburg). He conducted the Quebec SO in the premieres of *Matton's *Mouvement symphonique no. 1* (1960) and *Te Deum* (1967), and *Garant's *Ouranos* (1963). He served 1969–76 as the first director of the Music Dept of the *U of Ottawa and was a board member 1970–6 and president 1973–5 of the *CMCouncil. He became the director in 1976 and president in 1977 of the Charlevoix École de Musique, a non-profit corporation which is a part of the Domaine Forget in St-Irénée, Que. From September to May the school receives mostly music students from the region, whereas during the summer the accent is more on the socio-cultural character of the Domaine Forget, and the school becomes a community centre featuring all the arts, especially music. (See Summer camps and schools.) Françoys Bernier has guest-conducted in France, his assignments including the Orchestre des Concerts Colonne in Paris and the philharmonic orchestras of Bordeaux and the ORTF, the last-named in 1969 in the European premiere of Matton's *Te Deum*. (See also Discography for Robert Savoie.)

6 **Madeleine** (m Magnan). Pianist, b Quebec City 26 Aug 1929; deuxième prix piano (CMQ) 1953, B MUS (Laval) 1953, teaching diploma (Institut Jacques-Dalcroze, London) 1957. She studied 1950–3 at the *CMQ with Guy *Bourassa and Henri *Gagnon (piano) and Ria *Lenssens (solfège) and at *Laval U with Jeanne *Landry (theory). She completed her studies 1953–6 in Paris with Antoine *Reboulot, and also took courses in *Dalcroze eurythmics in Paris, London, and Geneva. She taught 1959–60 at the School of Education and the School of Music of Laval U, and became accompanist at the CMQ in 1960. She was accompanist in 1973 for the classes of Jean-Pierre Rampal (flute), Mady Mesplé (opera), and Hans Sittner (lieder) at the Académie internationale d'été in Nice, and also accompanied the Italian opera classes at the Mozarteum in Salzburg during the summer of 1979. She is the wife of François Magnan, who became the general director of the Quebec SO in 1972.

7 **Pierre** (Marie Honoré Edmond). Cellist, choir director, teacher, b Quebec City 19 Aug 1933. He studied 1948–54 at the CMQ with Walter *Joachim, Lucien *Plamondon, and Paul *Létourneau. He served 1956–66 as a cellist with the *Quebec SO and the *CBC Quebec Chamber Orchestra, and in 1957 he began teaching philosophy at the Petit Séminaire. In October 1972 in Quebec he founded and became the conductor of La Cantate, an amateur choir. He served 1969–79 as teacher of cello and director of the orchestra for the *Société musicale Le Mouvement Vivaldi. (CH)

BERNIER, Alfred. Teacher, musicologist, choirmaster, composer, b Montreal 26 Oct 1896, d there 25 Apr 1953; BA (Montreal) 1919, PH D (Montreal) 1925, L TH (Montreal) 1932, D Sacred Music (Pontifical Institute of Sacred Music, Rome) 1939. He studied voice with Arthur *Laurendeau and harmony with Louis Michiels. He joined the Jesuit order in 1921 and took on administrative responsibilities. Nevertheless, he remained active musically throughout his life. He studied liturgical music 1934–8 in Rome, after which he taught voice, choral conducting, and theory for the Jesuits in Montreal and at the Gregorian Institute of America in Toledo, O. With his thorough knowledge of polyphony and of vocal style he was ideally equipped to found in 1938, and direct until 1944, the *Petite maîtrise de Montréal. In 1948 he became the director of the Caughnawaga Choir.

Bernier in 1950 helped found the Faculty of Music, *U of Montreal. He also taught at the faculty and served 1951–3 as dean. He was author of an important study, *Saint Robert Bellarmin de la Compagnie de Jésus et la musique liturgique* (Paris and Montreal 1939), and of other writings on music of the church. He was regarded by Jean *Vallerand as 'an alert and informed musicologist whose writings are recognized as authoritative in all the serious musical circles of the world' (Montreal *Le Devoir*, 2 May 1953) and his artistic and religious integrity gave weight to his opinions and made him a strong and determining influence on musical education in Montreal at the university level.

His compositions, all vocal, follow the tradition of the Roman Pontifical Institute. They often appear under the pseudonym J. Bernal. His cantata

Ode à Marie, reine de Montréal (*Le Messager canadien* 1942) was written for the Montreal tricentenary. It was premiered 12 Jan 1942 at the Gesù Church, Montreal, and was repeated 10 May on CBC radio, performed with orchestra by the choir of the Petite maîtrise. Other choral works by Bernier also were published in *Le Messager canadien*. (IP-C)

BERNIER, Léon. Pianist, accompanist, conductor, arranger, composer, b Hull, Que, 6 Sep 1936; premier prix piano (CMQ) 1954. He studied with Hélène *Landry at the CMQ. He won several awards during the early 1950s and appeared at young people's concerts with the *Quebec SO and the *MSO. He won the 1955 *Prix d'Europe and studied until 1958 at the Santa Cecilia Cons of Rome with Renzo Silvestri. After his return to Quebec City he conducted and worked as an arranger for radio and TV orchestras. In 1962 he founded the 98-member drum and bugle corps Les Diplomates (which won several competitions) and an 18-member jazz band. He was music director 1964–72 for Ginette *Reno, and his arrangements for the singer's LP *Ginette Reno* (GPS-3301) won a prize at the Festival du disque in 1968.

Moving in 1969 to Montreal Bernier continued his work as conductor, arranger, music director, or pianist on the CBC TV series 'Les Coqueluches,' 'Boubou,' and 'Zoum.' He also directed summer concert series 1970–2 at the *PDA. In 1974 he reorchestrated (for 12 players) Claude *Léveillée's musical play *Il est une saison* (1965) and wrote scores for the CBC TV dramas *Edna, Le Vélo devant la porte, Pâques, Le Misanthrope*, and *Coup de sang*. He wrote incidental music for Jean Duceppe's productions of *Who's Afraid of Virginia Woolf?, Le Dernier des Don Juan*, and *Les Après-midis d'Émilie*. Bernier composed the music for *Un Simple Mariage double*, a musical play by Louis-Georges Carrier and Georges *Dor premiered (Jun 1978) at the Marjolaine Theatre, Eastman, Que. He is a member of CAPAC. (CH)

BERTRAND, Félix-R. (Routhier). Organist, pianist, choirmaster, composer, b Montreal 12 Oct 1909, d Moncton, NB, 28 Jul 1978; D MUS (Montreal) 1948. He was the grand-nephew of Sir Adolphe-Basile Routhier. He began his academic studies at the Collège séraphique in Trois-Rivières, where he became organist at 12. He studied organ with Hervé Cloutier, Raoul *Paquet, and Georges-Émile *Tanguay, piano with Rose *Goldblatt, and Gregorian chant with Jean-Noël *Charbonneau, Dom Lucien David, and Dom Georges Mercure. In 1938 he was the official organist for the National Eucharistic Congress in Quebec. He held posts as organist at the cathedral in Chatham, NB, and 1948–50 at St-Louis-de-France in Montreal, and was organist-choirmaster 1961–74 at Notre-Dame-de-l'Assomption Cathedral in Moncton. Bertrand founded and directed the Choeur mixte de Montréal, and was organist for the programs 'Sweet Hour of Prayer' on CBM radio, 'Jean Narrache' on CBF, and 'Le Vagabond qui chante' on CKAC. He was a regular recording artist for Polydor, Victor, and (for several Tante Lucille albums) *RCA Victor. He gave numerous organ recitals in Canada and the USA and inaugurated about 50 instruments. He was president of the *Casavant Society of Montreal and president 1953–7 and secretary-archivist for the *QMTA. His doctoral thesis, *La Musique à la radio*, was published in 1948 in Montreal. His compositions include a cantata (*Peace*, 1944), some motets, a string quartet, several vocal works, and numerous arrangements published by Le Parnasse musical.

BIBLIOGRAPHY

'Le petit-neveu de l'auteur d'O Canada au grand orgue de Saint-Louis-de-France,' Montreal *Petit Journal*, 21 Nov 1948 GP

BERTRAND, Jacques. Producer, administrator, b Montreal 7 Nov 1923. He studied violin and theory 1935–43 with Albert *Chamberland and also worked 1946–8 with Claude *Champagne. As producer-announcer 1948–52 on CHLP radio, Montreal, he was host for the program 'Studio d'art.' He was a producer 1952–3 and 1955–9 for the CBC French network, responsible for the radio series *'The Little Symphonies' and *'Le Petit Ensemble vocal.' In Ottawa 1954–5 he represented the French network within the CBC national radio network. He became head of production for the CBC French network in 1959 and succeeded Jean *Vallerand as head of music programming in 1966, retaining the position in 1980.

BETTS, Lorne. Composer, critic, organist-choirmaster, b Winnipeg, 2 Aug 1918; ACCO 1940, LRSM 1941, hon FRHCM 1968. After piano, organ, voice, and theory tuition in Winnipeg with Filmer *Hubble, W.H. *Anderson, and Hunter Johnston he attended the *RCMT, studying composition 1947–53 with John *Weinzweig and, during successive summers 1950–3 with Ernst Krenek, Alan Rawsthorne, and Roy Harris. He was music director 1950–64 at St Paul's Presbyterian Church in Hamilton, Ont, and became organist-choirmaster at Melrose United Church in 1964. He served 1953–9 as principal of the Hamilton Cons (*RHCM) and 1965–79 as music critic for the Hamilton *Spectator*. Betts' compositions, listed in *Contemporary Canadian Composers*, include the operas *Riders to the Sea* (1955) and *The Woodcarver's Wife* (1960), two symphonies (1954, 1961), two piano concertos (1955, 1957), three string quartets (1950, 1951, 1970), and such other large works as *Joe Harris, 1913–42* (1951), *Music for Orchestra* (1963) commissioned by the *Hamilton Philharmonic Orchestra, *Kanadario: 'Music for a Festival Occasion'* (1966), and a *Mass for St Thomas* (1973). He has written many songs, works for soloist and orchestra and voice with instruments, and choral pieces. Some keyboard works have been published, eg, *8 Recital Pieces for Young Pianists* (1959, MCA 1963) and *Suite Brève* (1967 MCA). Except in his *Music for Orchestra*, which uses a 12-tone series, Betts has shown little interest in dodecaphony and its heirs and successors, but his fastidious use of chromatic tonality with a spice of dissonance, his sparse textures, and his resourceful rhythms lend his music personality and life. He has recorded as accompanist with his wife, the contralto Jean *Macleod. He is an associate of the *CMCentre and a member of CAPAC.

BIBLIOGRAPHY

'Lorne Betts – a portrait,' *Mcan*, 28, Apr 1970 (EK)

BETTS, W. (William) **Seemer**. Choir director, teacher, adjudicator, bass singer, b London 27 Jan 1864, d Saskatoon 2 Aug 1960. On leaving school he joined the staff of the publishers J.S. Curwen and Sons, London, and became their choral consultant. In London he also taught at the Tonic Solfa College and directed, for 25 years, the choirs of Regent Street Polytechnic School and the Lavender Hill Congregational Church and for 9 years the National Temperance Union 5000-voice children's choir at Crystal Palace. He emigrated to Canada in 1920, settling in Saskatoon, where he taught voice and was choir director at St John's Church until his retirement in 1949. He also conducted the Kinsmen's Boy's Choir and Male Chorus and the Saskatoon Philharmonic Society. Robert *Fleming and Doreen Hayes were among his pupils.

BIBLIOGRAPHY

Walls, A.H. 'City's grand old man of music,' *Saskatoon Star-Phoenix*, 28 Jan 1954 WLB

BEY, Salome (m Matthews). Singer, actress, songwriter, b Newark, NJ. Salome, her brother Andy, and her sister Geraldine sang 1957–66 throughout the USA as Andy and the Bey Sisters. She made her first appearance in Toronto in 1961 and settled there in 1966, singing jazz, blues, and spirituals in nightclubs and on radio and TV, appearing as a featured performer at the *CNE grandstand in 1969, and enjoying a particular success in musicals. After a stage debut in 1969 at the Global Village (theatre) in Robert Swerdlow's *Blue S.A.* she appeared there in 1970 in Swerdlow's *Justine*. She received an Obie Award in 1972 for her performance 1971–2 in the New York production of *Justine* (renamed *Love Me, Love My Children*). Leading roles followed in Galt *MacDermot's *Dude* (New York 1972), in *Don't Bother Me, I Can't Cope* (Toronto 1973, Washington 1974), and in *Your Arms Too Short to Box with God* (New York 1975–7). Her performance on the cast recording (ABC 1004) of the last-named production brought a nomination for a 1977 Grammy Award.

Bey wrote and starred in *Indigo*, a history of the blues which enjoyed two successful runs (4 Oct 1978 to 1 Jul 1979, and 17 Jan to 29 Mar 1980) at the Toronto cabaret Basin Street. She also has continued her concert, club, radio, and TV work, often appearing with her daughters Tuku and Saidah. She sang in CBC TV's Canada Day celebrations at *Ontario Place in 1977 and on Parliament Hill in Ottawa in 1978. She has become known for her interpretation of *'Mon Pays,' a song she sang first in the 1970 *Spring Thaw. Her recordings include the LPs *Salome Bey* (1970, CTLS 5140 / Qual SV-1852) and *Songs from Dude* (1972, Kilmarnock 72003). She is an affiliate of PRO Canada.

BIBLIOGRAPHY

LeBlanc, Larry. 'Black artists crave opportunities for free expression,' *MSc*, 276, Mar–Apr 1974

Blackadar, Bruce. 'Lady serenity,' (Toronto *Star*) *The City*, 19 Mar 1978

Bronstein, Martin. 'Salome Bey returns with her history of the blues,' Toronto *Globe and Mail*, 27 Sep 1978

Livingstone, David. 'Bey makes hay, and how,' *Maclean's*, 12 Feb 1979

Bibliography

1 Introduction
2 The growth of bibliographical research
3 The state of music bibliography by 1980
4 Canadian contributions to international music bibliography

1 INTRODUCTION. Bibliography may be described as the listing, in descriptive detail, of items of printed literature; in a wider sense the term embraces the research and the theories employed towards this end. No distinct term exists to describe the listing of scores; bibliography, within the context of this entry, includes notated music. (For the listing of sound recordings see Discography.) A bibliography may be compiled for the publications of a specific author or a publisher; or for items owned by a private collector or a library; or for material produced in a time period or in a country; or – probably the most frequently encountered type – around a subject. The items may include books and periodicals (or chapters and articles therein), pamphlets, catalogues, and theses. The descriptive detail ought to include author, ti-

tle, city of publication, publisher, date, pagination, and series title, as well as information about physical format, collation, successive editions, prefatorial sections and appendices, notes on the origin of the work and its publishing history, and other details, as applicable. Many of the available sources of information about Canadian music and musical life, however, are no more than rudimentary checklists and indexes, many of which provide little more descriptive detail than author, title, publisher, and date.

The arrangement of the individual items in a bibliography can vary, but it is commonly alphabetical, by author's surname, or chronological, by date of publication. *EMC* has adopted a chronological order to enable the reader to trace the growth of research and the development of opinion from one author to another (or, in the case of a composer, the progress from one composition to another). It also makes it possible to identify the latest publication quickly.

On p xxi *EMC* provides a bibliography of basic sources of information about music in Canada and the abbreviated names used to refer to them throughout *EMC*. There also are selective bibliographies appended to many of the individual entries. See especially Archives; Biography; Canadian Association of Music Libraries; Canadian Music Centre; Canadian Music Library Association; Dictionaries; Discography; Hymnbooks; Lande Collections; National Library of Canada; Periodicals; Publishing; School songbooks; Theory textbooks. The abbreviations and acronyms and rules of style used in bibliographies and lists in *EMC* entries are explained on p xx and p xxii.

2 THE GROWTH OF BIBLIOGRAPHICAL RESEARCH. The earliest documents of bibliographical interest are the lists of copyright registrations appended annually to the *Sessional Papers* of the House of Commons 1868–1900 and printed in the Patent Office Records 1901–29. The copyright records provide information on an estimated two-thirds of Canadian music published between 1868 and 1929. The more than 42,000 items registered include much of musical interest, especially information on sheet music but also on songbooks and hymnbooks. Each entry contains a brief statement of the composer's name, the item's title, the name of the copyright owner or publisher, and the date of registration. The entry number provides a chronology of copyright music publications. An enterprising group of music publishers issued an extract of the musical items: *Complete List of Canadian Copyright Musical Compositions (entered from 1868 to January 19th, 1889) compiled from the Official Register at Ottawa* (np 1889?). This is a unique example in Canada of a bibliography based on a copyright list.

Interest in musical bibliography, though sporadic and often incidental to other pursuits, was apparent first in the province of Quebec. The writings of Ernest *Gagnon, Nazaire *LeVasseur, and Ernest *Myrand contain bibliographical references to musical literature, and Philéas Gagnon's *Essai de bibliographie canadienne* (Quebec 1895; supplement Montreal 1913; the collection is in the Montreal City Library) lists many music publications. Early bibliographies relating to individual musicians include a list of *Jehin-Prume's compositions (*Une Vie d'artiste*, Montreal, ca 1900), a list of writings about Calixa *Lavallée (*Le Passe-Temps*, 864, August 1933) and, at a more general level, Mary Smitherman's bibliography of 61 composers in 'Canadian composers' (*Ontario Library Review*, vol 15, August 1930). However, true musical bibliography in Canada may be said to have begun with Jean Ross MacMillan's 'Music in Canada: a short bibliography' (*Ontario Library Review*, vol 24, November 1940), a list of some 190 books, song collections, and articles by Canadians. Supplements were provided in the same journal by Lucille May (vol 33, August 1949) and Nancy J. Williamson (vol 38, May 1954).

The stocktaking of Canadian composers and their works became a necessity to the CBC in the fulfilment of its mandate to seek out and provide exposure for Canadian music. The *Catalogue of Canadian Composers* (see also Dictionaries), issued in 1947, provides basic information about the works of 238 living composers. It revealed for the first time the quantity and identity of Canada's composers and provided performers and program planners with a great incentive. A revised edition, expanded to include newer names as well as composers from the 17th to early 20th centuries, contained full treatments of 356 composers and brief treatments of over 100. Compiled 1950–1, it was issued in 1952.

The 1950s witnessed the appearance of several institutions and associations with a strong interest in musical bibliography. The Canadian Bibliographic Centre (1950) and its successor, the National Library of Canada (1953), have issued *Canadiana*, a monthly bibliography of new Canadian publications. This bibliography listed only books when it was begun in 1950 but added scores in 1953 and recordings in 1970. The NL of C also is responsible for compiling a retrospective 19th-century Canadian bibliography in all subject areas and for supplying bibliographical services through its national union catalogues and its reference, music, and other divisions. The Bibliothèque nationale du Québec in 1968 began to issue a monthly *Bibliographie du Québec*, listing Quebec and Quebec-related publications, including printed but not recorded music. The *CLComp and, after 1959, the CMCentre assumed the main responsibility for compiling and publishing detailed catalogues of the works of composers of concert music. Both *Canadiana* and the CMCentre catalogues were computerized in the 1970s. The *U of Montreal's MUSCADØC project of storing data, including bibliographical ones, on Canadian music (see Lyse Richer-Lortie) also was computerized. Owing to a lack of funds the project was suspended in 1975.

The CMLA and its successor, the CAML, have devoted much of their members' energy to the preparation of several useful bibliographies and related projects, from *Musical Canadiana: A Subject Index* (1967) to *Canadian Music: A Selected Checklist 1950–73 / La Musique canadienne: une liste sélective 1950–73* (ed Lynne Jarman, 1976). The organizations' largest project, begun in 1966, is the detailed cataloguing of early Canadian music publications. The records from this project are deposited at the NL of C as a union catalogue of Canadian music publications to 1950 and provide descriptions of approximately 12,000 items found in some 25 libraries and 20 private collections or listed in copyright entry lists or publishers' advertisements. Access is by composer, title, date of publication, and name of publisher.

Another organization seriously concerned with bibliography is the *Canadian Folk Music Society, whose *A Reference List on Canadian Folk Music*, compiled by Barbara *Cass-Beggs and Edith *Fowke, has gone through three editions (1966, 1973, 1978, the last two appearing also in the *Canadian Folk Music Journal*, vols 1, 1973, and 7, 1978) and is one of the most useful and practical tools available to the student of Canadian music. Its first section lists books, pamphlets, and articles; its second lists compositions based on folksong; and its third is a discography. The society also embarked on a more exhaustive bibliographical project, which remained incomplete in 1980. It includes information about 1600 items (literature, songbooks, folk music arrangements and compositions, recordings, and iconography) and the files have been deposited at the NL of C. Two members of the CFMS, Edith Fowke and Carole Henderson, published the comprehensive 'Bibliography of Canadian Folklore in English' (*Communique: Canadian Studies*, August 1977) which includes a section on folk music and dance.

The *Archives de Folklore of *Laval U also have issued important bibliographical publications, beginning with Clarisse Cardin's 'Bio-bibliographie de Marius Barbeau' (*Archives de Folklore*, vol 2, 1947) and continuing with Conrad *Laforte's *Le Catalogue de la chanson folklorique française* (1958). A new edition of the latter work, planned in six volumes, began to appear in 1977 (vol 1, *Chansons en laisse*). Vol 2, *Chansons énumeratives*, was published in 1979. The Bibliothèque nationale du Québec issued *La Chanson au Québec 1965–1975* (Montreal 1975) as no. 3 in its series of Bibliographies québécoises. Holdings of specific folk music collections are listed in *Catalogue of Canadian Folk Music in the Mary Mellish Archibald Library and Other Special Collections* (*Mount Allison U, Bell Library Publications in Music, no. 1, Sackville, NB, 1974) and in *Songs Sung by French Newfoundlanders*, compiled by Gerald Thomas and itemizing the material at the Folklore and Language Archive at *Memorial U (St John's, Nfld, 1978). Marie-Françoise Guédon and Beverley *Cavanagh prepared bibliographies of Indian and Inuit music, respectively, for the Canadian issue of *Ethnomusicology* (vol 16, Sep 1972).

Essentially, bibliographical initiative belongs to individuals rather than institutions. Among these was Helmut *Kallmann who, having edited the revised edition of the CBC's *Catalogue of Canadian Composers*, went on to compile a general bibliography of music in Canada (unpublished but largely integrated into *EMC*), 'A check-list of Canadian periodicals in the field of music,' (*CMJ*, vol 1, Winter 1957), and the CLComp's *Catalogue of Orchestral Music* (Toronto 1957). His private research formed the basis of CMLA's *Bio-bibliographical Finding List of Canadian Musicians* (Ottawa 1961, rev edn in progress, 1980) and the listing of pre-1951 music imprints which has remained his responsibility over the years. His *History of Music in Canada* offered the first generally available bibliography arranged by broad subject. Kallmann also was entrusted with devising the CFMS's large-scale bibliography mentioned above.

Giles *Bryant compiled the first book-length listing of a Canadian composer's works, the *Healey Willan Catalogue* (Ottawa 1972 – a detailed description of 784 works followed by extensive bibliographical and discographical sections.

In the field of general surveys of the literature about Canadian music, Victor Legendre's *Musique canadienne* (Séminaire Saint-Augustin, Cap-Rouge, Que, 1970, mimeographed, about 400 items, mostly in French) had its English counterpart in *A Basic Bibliography of Musical Canadiana*, compiled by Frederick and Sharyn Hall, Bruce and Kathryn Minorgan, and Nadia Turbide (Toronto, 1970, mimeographed, about 700 items in English and French). Ian Bradley of the *U of Victoria took up the initiative and in his *A Selected Bibliography of Musical Canadiana* (Victoria BC, rev edn 1976) provides dramatic proof for the growth of the literature about Canadian music – listing 10 times the number of items contained in Jean MacMillan's 1940 pioneer effort. Neither MacMillan nor Bradley has been able, however, to cover adequately the large amount of 19th- and early 20th-century literature. Although as yet unpublished, significant work in this area has been done by

Elaine *Keillor of *Carleton U, listing articles and notices in Canadian and foreign turn-of-the-century magazines. A fine example of detailed bibliography is Barclay McMillan's 'Tune-book imprints in Canada to 1867: a descriptive bibliography' published in *Papers of the Bibliographical Society of Canada / Cahiers de la Société bibliographique du Canada* (vol 16, 1977).

3 THE STATE OF MUSIC BIBLIOGRAPHY BY 1980. A sound bibliographical basis is the sine qua non of the writing of musical history and biography and indeed of any serious research. Surveys of the state of bibliographical work related to Canadian music were conducted in 1974 independently by Kallmann and George *Proctor. The former, in the chapter on 'Subject bibliography – music' in *Proceedings, National Conference on the State of Canadian Bibliography, Vancouver, Canada, 22–24 May 1974* (Ottawa 1977) contrasted existing work with the categories and quantities that should be covered in an ideal complete bibliography. He concluded that progress was considerable in several areas (eg, the listing of current publications, of Canadian compositions, of biographical and folk music literature), but that many valuable projects remained unpublished (eg, Keillor's analytical indexes, the exhaustive bibliography undertaken by the CFMS in the late 1960s, the union list of Canadian music publications to 1950 and the index of biographical articles maintained at the NL of C's Music Division, and Joachim Sandvoss' list of 496 music theses of Canadians).

Proctor's *Sources in Canadian Music / Les Sources de la musique canadienne* (Sackville, NB, 1975, 1979; also in *CAUSM J*, vol 4, Autumn 1974) provides a useful examination of the source materials under such headings as 'General bibliography,' 'Periodicals,' 'Biography,' 'Bio-bibliography of individual composers,' 'Scores,' 'Music education,' 'Theses and papers' and includes a list of 167 pertinent bibliographies. His conclusions are similar to Kallmann's: that there are more scores, recordings, and printed materials in the field of Canadian music than is realized generally, and certainly enough to nourish university courses on the subject.

In 1980 much work remained to be done, especially in the way of indexing articles in Canadian and non-Canadian music magazines before 1950 and in non-musical Canadian magazines. Unfortunately the *Canadian Periodical Index* (Windsor, Ont, 1928–32; Toronto 1938–47; Ottawa 1948–63; and, under the title *Canadian Index to Periodicals and Documentary Films*, Ottawa 1964–), *the Music Index* (Detroit 1949–), and *RILM* (Répertoire international de la littérature musicale, New York 1967–) provide limited coverage of Canadian music. To encourage Canadian bibliography in all fields, the Committee on Bibliographical Services for Canada was set up in 1975 (an outcome of the 1974 conference already referred to) with its secretariat in the NL of C, and a joint bibliography committee was established in 1977 by CAML and CAUSM to identify needs, co-ordinate individual efforts, and advise on standards of bibliographical technique.

4 CANADIAN CONTRIBUTIONS TO INTERNATIONAL MUSIC BIBLIOGRAPHY. Outstanding examples are Andrew *Hughes' *A Bibliography of Medieval Music: The Sixth Liberal Art* (Toronto 1974) and Lowell Cross' *Bibliography of Electronic Music* (Toronto 1967, 1970). (Cross is a US citizen who compiled his bibliography while doing graduate studies in electronic music and musicology at the *U of Toronto.) James Parrott in 1972 began to compile a bibliography on acoustics, *Biblotheca harmonicum*, the first volume of which was ready for publication in 1980.

Canada participates in several projects undertaken by the International Assn of Music Libraries (and several co-sponsors), RISM (Répertoire international des sources musicales; see Libraries), RILM, and RIdIM (Répertoire international d'iconographie musicale; see Iconography). HK

BICKERT, Ed (Edward Isaac). Guitarist, b Hochfeld, south of Winnipeg, 29 Nov 1932. Raised in Vernon, BC, he took up the guitar at 11 and first played with his father, an oldtime fiddler, and his mother, a pianist, in a country dance band. He moved in 1952 to Toronto, working until 1955 as a radio engineer on CFRB while playing at such after-hours jazz clubs as the House of Hambourg. His few lessons with Tony *Bradan were his only formal training. A member in the 1950s of Norman *Symonds' jazz octet, Bickert also appeared with Ron *Collier's groups 1954–65, Phil *Nimmons' big band 1957–70, and, intermittently beginning in the late 1950s, with Hagood *Hardy and Moe *Koffman. He was a leading studio musician in Toronto until the early 1970s, when he began to devote more time to jazz. In the 1970s he was a regular member of Koffman's quintet and of the *Boss Brass. He also played in a duo with the bassist-pianist-vibraphonist Don *Thompson and in one of Thompson's quartets. Bickert and Thompson's LP of duets received the *Juno Award for best jazz recording of 1979. Around 1974, he began to appear with his own trio – usually Thompson (bass) and Terry *Clarke (drums) – in various Canadian centres and on CBC radio. The trio played in Europe in 1979 as part of a tour sponsored by *RCI.

Bickert's work 1974–6 as sideman to the US saxophonist Paul Desmond brought him international acclaim, drawing praise for 'an understated eloquence matched only by such masters as Jim Hall' (Chuck Berg, *Down Beat*, 7 Oct 1976) and for the ability to 'combine in his solos the logic of a mathematician and the grace of an angel' (Jack Batten, *Globe and Mail*, 7 Jul 1976). Besides recording with Desmond he appeared in Toronto and San Francisco clubs and at the 1976 Monterey Jazz Festival. Bickert has performed in Toronto clubs with such US musicians as Chet Baker, Red Norvo, Milt Jackson, and Frank Rosolino. With Jackson he toured Japan in 1979. His playing, rooted in bebop and influenced by Tal Farlow, Barney Kessel, Jimmy Raney, and others, is characterized by an intuitive harmonic sense and a mellow sound. Bickert taught in the early 1960s at the Advanced School of Contemporary Music, Toronto, and resumed teaching in 1978 at the *U of New Brunswick Chamber Music and Jazz Festival and at the *Banff SFA.

DISCOGRAPHY

Ed Bickert. Thompson db, Clarke drums. 1975. PMR-010

I Like to Recognize the Tune. Orch with G. Williamson keybds, Thompson db and pf, Clarke drums, and others. 1977. CTL 5206/United Artists UALA 747G.

Ed Bickert/Don Thompson. Thompson db. 1978. Sack 4005

WITH OTHERS

Desmond *Pure Desmond*. 1974. CTI 6059

– *The Paul Desmond Quartet Live!* Also with Thompson db, *Fuller drums. 1975. 2-Horizon 850

– *Paul Desmond*. With Thompson and Fuller. 1975. Artists House AH2

Others with Peter *Appleyard, Guido *Basso, Collier, Koffman, Kathryn *Moses, Nimmons, Oscar *Peterson, Thompson, the Boss Brass, and many as a studio accompanist

BIBLIOGRAPHY

Miller, Mark. 'Ed Bickert,' *Down Beat*, 20 May 1976

Waxman, Ken. 'Ed Bickert guitarist,' *Audio Scene Canada*, Jun 1976

Batten, Jack. 'Playing it safe,' *The Canadian*, 31 Dec 1978

Miller, Mark. 'Ed Bickert,' *Guitar Player*, Sep 1978

BIGGAR, Marjorie (May). Mezzo-soprano, b Vancouver ca 1938; LRAM 1960, ARAM 1965. She studied with Scott Robertson in Vancouver, Jennie Tourel in Aspen, Colo, and Astra Desmond and Olive Groves at the RAM, London. She sang in England with the Glyndebourne Festival Opera, the Sadler's Wells Opera, the English Opera, the Handel Opera Society, and the Royal Opera, Covent Garden, and in Brussels at the Théâtre royal de la Monnaie; her roles included Amneris in *Aida*, Dido in *Dido and Aeneas*, Emelia in *Otello*, Idamante in *Idomeneo*, Larina in *Eugene Onegin*, Lucretia in *The Rape of Lucretia*, and the title role in Granville Bantock's *The Seal Woman*. She also toured in Great Britain with the Royal Philharmonic Orchestra as soloist in Beethoven's *Ninth Symphony*. She has been heard over the BBC, the CBC, and the Belgian, German, and Swiss radio networks. She has given recitals in Europe and Canada and performed with major orchestras in London and with the *NACO in Canada. In 1973 she toured the USA as a soloist with the Royal Choral Society. Returning to Canada in 1976, she settled in Vancouver. She has given concerts with the Amity Singers of Victoria, the *Vancouver Chamber Choir, and the *Vancouver Bach Choir.

W.H. Billing. Toronto retailer and publisher established in 1880 by Willimott H. Billing. A listing under *Strange & Billing in 1881–2 city directories implies a short-lived partnership. About 100 songs and pieces of dance and march music were published in the period 1880–1903, and also such volumes as the *Giant King Folio* (nd) and Theodore Lamotte's *How to Vamp* (1894). The sheet music, though mostly by foreign composers, includes Carl *Martens' 'Toronto's Jubilee' (1884) and W.T. Diefenbaker's 'Rush to the Klondike' (1897) as well as pieces by Edwin *Gledhill and A.W. *Hughes. Mrs. Adeline White was president of the firm after 1911. Directories list it until 1925. It went bankrupt at that time, and the Atwell Fleming Printing Co (1904–), Billing's printer, retained the stock and plates, printed music, and filled orders under the Billing name (which appeared again in city directories 1950–7) until demand had dwindled.

BILODEAU, Léonard (Albert Joseph). Tenor, b Quebec City 11 Jul 1935. He studied singing ca 1955 with Louis *Gravel and 1957–61 on scholarship with George *Lambert and Irene *Jessner at the *RCMT. He was soloist in the Verdi *Requiem* at the RCMT under Ernesto *Barbini and gave a recital in Toronto for the Alliance française in 1958. Winner of an award from the Martha Baird Rockefeller Fund for Music, he sang the roles of Nadir (*Les Pêcheurs de perles*), Roméo, Werther, Vincent (*Mireille*), and Bénédict (*Béatrice et Bénédict*) at the Manhattan School of Music, New York, where he continued his training ca 1962–ca 1965 with John Brownlee and the stage director Carlton Gold. He sang in Spontini's *La Vestale* with Régine Crespin at Philharmonic Hall, New York, and in *Mignon* at the 1963 summer festivals in Central Park. In Quebec he appeared with the *Théâtre lyrique de Nouvelle-France in *La Bohème* (Rodolphe) in 1962, *Madama Butterfly* (Pinkerton) in 1964, *La Traviata* (Alfredo) in 1965, *Lakmé* (Gérald) in 1965, and *Mignon* (Wilhelm Meister) in 1966.

After winning a government of Quebec scholarship he studied in Paris ca 1965–ca 1967 with Mme Georges Philippot, Maurice Fauré, and Georges Jouatte and in Milan with Gennaro Barra. He made his French debut in Lille, singing Gérald in a production of *Lakmé* with Mady Mesplé in the title role, and gave recitals in Austria. On his return to Canada he undertook a *JMC tour in 1965 as a member of an operatic trio. In 1967 he sang *Les Pêcheurs de perles* in New Orleans, drew critical praise in Canada for his performance in the *COC touring production of *Don Pasquale*, and sang on CBC radio and TV. He gave up singing in 1970 to pursue a career in business.

BIBLIOGRAPHY
Lesage, Marthe. 'Profile: Léonard Bilodeau,' *OpCan*, Feb 1968 AP

BINET, Jocelyne. Composer, pianist, teacher, b East Angus, near Sherbrooke, Que, 27 Sep 1923, d Quebec City 13 Jan 1968; B MUS (Montreal) 1943, L MUS composition (Montreal) 1946. She studied at the École supérieure de musique in Outremont (*École Vincent-d'Indy), where her teachers were Claude *Champagne (theory and composition) and Jean *Dansereau and Jean-Marie *Beaudet (piano). In 1946 she obtained a CAPAC prize for composition. She studied at the Paris Cons 1948–9 on a bursary from the French government and 1949–51 on another from the Quebec government. Her teachers were Tony Aubin (composition), Noël Gallon (counterpoint and fugue), and Olivier Messiaen (analysis). On her return to Canada she taught formal analysis and counterpoint 1952–8(?) at the École Vincent-d'Indy and 1958?–68 at *Laval U and also gave private lessons. Serge *Garant, Gilles *Tremblay, and Monique *Vachon were her pupils in counterpoint.

Among Binet's works are three pieces for orchestra, *Evocation* (1948), *Danse* (1949), and *Un Canadien à Paris* (1951), as well as some chamber music, including a *Trio* for violin, cello and piano (1945) and a *Suite* for flute, piano, and strings (1946). She wrote several songs 1949–50. Her earlier *Petite Suite vocale* (1945, words by Jean-Henri Fabre, for solo voice, female choir, and piano) was dedicated to Champagne. The manuscript is deposited with the *CMM. Her works have been performed on radio and in concert in Brazil, Canada, and France. GP

BINNINGTON, Doreen. Musicologist, educator, b Vermillion, east of Edmonton, 24 May 1929; B ED (Saskatchewan) 1952, M ED (Portland) 1968, PH D (California) 1973. Her teachers included Marjorie Wilson (piano, Saskatoon), and Mantle Hood, Klaus P. Wachsmann, Charles Seeger, and David Morton (ethnomusicology, U of California). She taught at the U of California, Los Angeles, while preparing her doctoral thesis, 'The development of an interdisciplinary curriculum based on an integration of ethnomusicology and the social studies.' Her research involved the study of music of the Inuit of Barrow, Alaska.

Binnington undertook further field study of *Inuit music in 1973 at Coppermine, NWT, sponsored by the *National Museum of Man, Ottawa. She joined the faculty of education at the *U of British Columbia in 1970, and has directed a research project, 'Identity with our mineral resources, people and processes,' under the aegis of the university, the Canadian Mining and Metallurgical Foundation, the *U of Toronto, and school districts in British Columbia and Ontario. Binnington's doctoral research attempted to define the processes of ethnomusicological study and to incorporate these into a school curriculum. Her more recent work has extended this principle of curriculum development to such areas as social studies. (BAC)

Biography. A survey of 1 / biographies and autobiographies of Canadian musicians, and 2 / biographies of non-Canadian musicians by Canadian authors.

1 Biographies are of importance not only because they document careers and achievements but because they bring to the public consciousness many composers and performers who otherwise would remain mere names attached to scores, recordings, and concert programs. No matter how logical the claim that 'only the music matters,' the desire to know public figures as people seems to be ingrained deeply in the human psyche. One might say that the public's awareness of a Beethoven, a Berlioz, a Liszt, or a Wagner owes almost as much to the facts and legends spread by their biographers as to knowledge of their music. The imagination is kindled by legends (keeping in mind that truth usually is more fascinating than fiction), and those legends are given shape by biographers.

That the most successful Canadian musicians are not better known may be attributed in part to the dearth of biographical writing about them; and what there is, moreover (see list below) has not always chosen its subjects from among the top echelons. In 1979 there still were no major treatments of Marius *Barbeau, Claude *Champagne, Guillaume *Couture, Lynnwood *Farnam, Sir Ernest *MacMillan, A.S. *Vogt, or Healey *Willan, but at least Emma *Albani, Glenn *Gould, Edward *Johnson, Calixa *Lavallée, and Wilfrid *Pelletier had received due biographical attention.

The following list of biographical and autobiographical writings is arranged chronologically by publication date and does not include article-length studies, such as those in the Montreal periodical *Qui?*:

1874
Legendre, Napoléon. *Albani / Emma Lajeunesse* (Quebec City). An account of the early years of the singer, then 27 years old

1900?
Jehin-Prume, Jules. *Une Vie d'artiste* (Montreal). The life of Frantz Jehin-Prume by his son

1911
Albani, Emma. *Forty Years of Song* (London, Toronto). Memoirs of the famous singer. Translated into French and annotated by Gilles Potvin as *Mémoires d'Emma Albani* (Montreal 1972) with added chronology, discography, and bibliography

1923
Mercier, François-Xavier. *Souvenirs de ma carrière artistique* (Quebec City); reissued as 'Gerbe de Souvenirs' in his book *Technique de musique vocale* (Quebec 1928). Memoirs of the Quebec operatic tenor and teacher

1934
Clarke, Herbert Lincoln. *How I Became a Cornetist* (St Louis). Autobiographical sketch of the US virtuoso, who spent significant portions of his life in Canada

1936
Lapierre, Eugène. *Calixa Lavallée* (Montreal, rev and enl 1950, and 1966). The first major study of a Canadian musician; based on extensive though incomplete research

1938
Charbonneau, Hélène. *L'Albani, sa carrière artistique et triomphale* (Montreal). A fairly well researched book but far from being a definitive biography

1948
Gour, Romain. *La Palme-Issaurel* (Montreal). A critical biography of the soprano and of her husband, a tenor and renowned teacher

1951
Cook, Lyn. *The Little Magic Fiddler* (Toronto). The career of the young Donna Grescoe

1955
Leclerc, Félix. *Moi, mes souliers* (Montreal, Paris). Autobiography of the chansonnier; with chronology, bibliography, and critical opinions

1956
McCarthy, Pearl. *Leo Smith, A Biographical Sketch* (Toronto). A portrait rather than a researched piece

1957
Marcoux, Albertine. *Musicien et Paysan, fatal destin d'un agriculteur-musicien* (Quebec). The story of Joseph-Désiré Marcoux, a late-19th-century small town Quebec band musician

McDowell, Louise. *Past and Present, A Canadian Musician's Reminiscences* (Kirkland Lake). Memoirs of a piano teacher, with fascinating accounts of her student days at the TCM and in Leipzig

1959
Benoît, Réal. *La Bolduc* (Montreal). Life story of the French-Canadian pop star of the 1930s

1964
Brousseau, Serge. *Le Beau Roman d'amour de Rolande Désormeaux* (Montreal). Life story of a pop singer who died in 1963

Herndon, Booton. *The Sweetest Music This Side of Heaven* (Toronto, New York, London). The Lombardo family story, with emphasis on Guy

1967
French, Maida Parlow. *Kathleen Parlow: A Portrait* (Toronto). By the virtuoso's cousin; a description rather than an analysis of the career

1968
Robitaille, Aline. *Gilles Vigneault* (Montreal). French-language account of the career of the chansonnier

Sylvain, Jean-Paul. *Félix Leclerc ou mes 25 années dans l'intimité de Félix Leclerc par Andrée Leclerc* (Montreal). The chansonnier seen through the eyes of his former wife

1969
Berimont, Luc. *Félix Leclerc* (Montreal, Paris). With a selection of songs, a discography, a bibliography, and photographs

Matti, Jacques. *Michèle Richard raconte Michèle Richard* (Montreal). Life of the Quebec pop star as told by herself; photographs and an interview

Rioux, Lucien. *Gilles Vigneault* (Paris). Pocket-size book in the collection 'Poètes d'aujourd'hui'

Sellick, Lester B. *Canada's Don Messer* (Kentville, NS). Career of the country musician

1970
Haendel, Ida. *Woman with Violin* (London). Autobiography written in mid-career. Few references to Canada

1971
Boucher, Jacqueline. *Jean-Pierre Ferland jaune ou...* (Ottawa). Short, illustrated book about the chansonnier

L'Herbier, Benoît. *Charlebois, qui es-tu?* (Montreal). An illustrated book about the pop star

The Welsman Memoranda (Toronto). Researched by Mary E. Jolliffe, this compilation of facts and press notices deals largely with Frank S. Welsman as the first conductor of the TSO.

1972
Fournier, Roger. *Gilles Vigneault, mon ami* (Montreal). An intimate study by the close friend and novelist

Pelletier, Wilfrid. *Une Symphonie inachevée...* (Montreal). The conductor's detailed autobiography

1973
Rioux, Lucien. *Robert Charlebois* (Paris). Selection of songs, with discography and articles; in the collection 'Chansons d'aujourd'hui'
1974
Calvet, Louis-Jean. *Pauline Julien* (Paris). Writings about the Quebec singer; with discography and photographs
Gagné, Marc. *Propos de Gilles Vigneault* (Montreal). A revealing book in question-and-answer form
Gagnon, Claude. *Robert Charlebois déchiffré* (Montreal). Analytical study of the chansonnier
Richard, Ti-Blanc. *Ti-Blanc super-violoneux* (Montreal). Written in collaboration with Jean-Paul Sylvain and Jean Laurac; emphasis on anecdotes
1975
Brotman, Ruth C. *Pauline Donalda* (Montreal). Well-documented account of the prima donna's career and brief history of the Opera Guild of Montreal, which she founded
Cherney, Brian. *Harry Somers* (Toronto). The first in a series of monographs issued under the auspices of the CMCentre; the first Canadian biography to include an analysis of compositions
Creighton, Helen. *A Life in Folklore* (Toronto). The first book of memoirs written by a Canadian folksong collector
Duncan, Chester. *Wanna Fight, Kid?* (Winnipeg). Memoirs and essays of the musician, English professor, and critic; based on broadcast scripts
LeSerge, Diane. *Willie Lamothe, trente ans de Showbusiness* (Montreal). The career of the Quebec country singer
Lombardo, Guy, with Jack Altschul. *Auld Acquaintance* (New York). Memories of his family and friends by the bandleader
1976
Racicot, H. et al. *Diane Dufresne* (Montreal). Well-illustrated, large-size book on the singer, with discography; in the collection 'Les Gens de mon pays'
Fleischer, Leonore. *Joni Mitchell* (New York). Mid-career life story of the singer-songwriter by a US journalist
Hone, François. *La Fascinante Histoire de nos familles – Jules Hone-Antoine Gérin-Lajoie* (Montreal). Private edn. A compilation of documents and notes on the two families, including the Belgian-born violinist Jules Hone
Mercer, Ruby. *The Tenor of His Time* (Toronto). Life of Edward Johnson
Rudel-Tessier, J. *André Mathieu, un génie* (Montreal). A hastily written and incompletely documented biography of the composer, pianist, and child prodigy
1977
Adaskin, Harry. *A Fiddler's World: Memoirs to 1938* (Vancouver). Devoted in equal parts to autobiography, reflections, and anecdotes; to be followed by a second volume
Gagné, Marc. *Gilles Vigneault* (Quebec City). A 1000-page compilation of material on the Quebec chansonnier, including descriptive and critical bibliography, discography, filmography, inconography and chronology
1978
McCullagh, Harold. *The Man Who Made New Brunswick Sing* (St Stephen, NB). The story of David Thomson, provincial supervisor of school music 1949–65
Payzant, Geoffrey. *Glenn Gould: Mind and Music* (Toronto). A philosophic approach to the art of this Canadian artist; with discography
Dufiechou, Carole. *Neil Young* (New York). Singer-songwriter's story by a US author
Ravel, Ginette. *Je vis mon alcoolisme* (Montreal). Autobiography of a Montreal pop singer and the story of her addiction to alcohol and subsequent recovery
André Gagnon (Montreal). Collected views and sayings; compiled by Lucie Rozon
Wilson, John. *A Professional Piper in Peace and War* (Toronto). Recollections of a Scottish-Canadian piper
1979
Gabiou, Alfrieda. *Gordon Lightfoot* (Toronto). Subtitled 'The first biography of the legendary singer / songwriter'
Huot, Cécile. *Entretiens avec Omer Létourneau* (Montreal). Memoirs of Létourneau, with bibliography, list of works, notes on Quebec musical organizations (AMQ, Quebec SO, choirs in Quebec City area, etc)
1980
Robi, Alys. *Ma Carrière et ma vie* (Montreal)
Savaria, Georges. *Hors De Portée* (Mandeville, Que). Story of the Prix d'Europe winner's years in France and his imprisonment and escape during World War II

Among musicians who have left unpublished autobiographical sketches are Gustave *Smith and Sir Ernest MacMillan. An account of Ernest *Dainty's life was written by his widow, Gertrude Dainty. A study of Lynnwood Farnam was completed by H. W. Hawke. Other such manuscripts may be assumed to exist.

Theses have been written about Claude Champagne, Wilfrid Pelletier, Rodolphe *Mathieu, Healey Willan, and others. Most deal with the works rather than the lives of their subjects.

Volumes uniting biographical sketches of several musicians range in treatment from thumbnail portraits to fairly substantial discussions. Examples of the two extremes are Claude *Gingras' *Musiciennes de chez nous* (Montreal 1955) which deals with 19 women musicians on 93 pages of text and Peter Such's *Soundprints* (Toronto 1972), which gives six composers (*Beckwith, *Beecroft, *Buczynski, *Schafer, *Somers, and *Weinzweig) an average of 24 pages each. James McPherson has written a book of short biographies of 100 Canadian singers, past and present (unpubl 1980). Other works of this type are Louise G. McCready's *Famous Musicians* (Toronto 1957), including Edward Johnson, Sir Ernest MacMillan, Wilfrid Pelletier, and Healey Willan; Augustus *Bridle's *Sons of Canada* (Toronto 1916), which includes biographic pieces on Couture, *Torrington, and Vogt; Christian Larsen's *Chansonniers du Québec* (Montreal 1964); Michèle Maillé's *Blow up des grands de la chanson au Québec* (Montreal 1969); Ritchie Yorke's *Axes, Chops and Hot Licks* (Edmonton 1971); and Gabriel Labbe's *Les Pionniers du disque folklorique québécois 1920–1950* (Montreal 1977). There also are biographies treating persons marginally involved in music or domiciled only briefly in Canada – Leonard *Cohen, Marie Dressler, Louis *Jolliet, Beatrice *Lillie, John *Medley, Eva Rose *York, and others.

2 Among biographies by Canadians of foreign musicians are:
Goddard, Peter. *Frank Sinatra* (Don Mills, Toronto 1973)
Ondaatje, Michael. *Coming through Slaughter* (Toronto 1976). An account of the life of the legendary New Orleans jazzman Buddy Bolden
Ouellette, Fernand. *Edgard Varèse* (Paris 1966), transl Derek Coltman (New York 1968)
Pinsonneault, Bernard. *Nicolas Medtner, pianiste, compositeur (1879–1951)* (Montreal 1956)
Robinson, Paul. *Karajan* (Toronto 1975)
– *Stokowski* (Toronto 1977)
– *Solti* (Toronto 1979)
Sachs, Harvey. *Toscanini* (London 1978; French transl by W.C. Cuvillier and G. Zeisel, Paris 1980)

Unpublished works include Luigi von *Kunits' 'The Hero as Musician' (1913) about Beethoven, and James McPherson's biography of Ernestine Schumann-Heink.

See also Dictionaries.

BIRCH, (John) Edgar. Organist, conductor, teacher, b Reading, England, 25 Aug 1854, d Ottawa 23 Oct 1931. He was a chorister in the Chapel Royal and studied in London. He emigrated to Canada to teach at Trinity College School, Port Hope. From there he moved to Montreal as organist-choirmaster at Christ Church Cathedral. In 1894 he was one of the founders of the *Dominion College of Music. In 1895 he settled in Ottawa as principal of the Canadian College of Music and organist-choirmaster of All Saints Church. Birch also became the music director of the Schubert Club that year and in 1897 organized the *Ottawa Choral Society, conducting the latter's first concert 11 Jan 1898. He remained conductor until 1914. He was an organist and teacher in Ottawa until his death.

BIBLIOGRAPHY

Morgan, Henry J., ed. *The Canadian Men and Women of the Time* (Toronto 1898)

BIRD. Ontario family of musicians: 1 / Charles and his sons, 2 / Bailey and 3 / John.

1 **Charles** (Albert). Conductor, administrator, french hornist, b Beccles, Suffolk, England, 31 Jul 1890, d Stratford Ont, 8 Dec 1961. He joined the British army in 1906, studied at the RMSM (Kneller Hall), and served in India with the Second Norfolk Regiment. In 1924 he took his family to Stratford, Ont, where he became a shop foreman for the CNR. He conducted the CNR Employees' Band and Orchestra until the early 1950s. He was cofounder in 1926 of the Perth County Music Teachers' Federation, president 1930–40 of the Stratford Music Festival, and secretary and president of local 418 of the AF of M.

2 (William Thomas) **Bailey**. Administrator, publisher, b Belgaum, India, 17 Mar 1917. A violin pupil of Elie *Spivak in Toronto, he was a founder in 1936 of the Aeolian Trio in Stratford. He joined Gordon V. *Thompson Ltd in 1937 and became general manager in 1946. He served 1953–60 as head of the publications division of *BMI Canada. With Wallace Young he founded Concert Assns. of Canada, which in the 1950s presented Maureen *Forrester, Glenn *Gould, Lois *Marshall, James *Milligan, and others in recitals throughout southern Ontario. In 1960 Bird joined *Leeds Music (Canada) as general manager and vice-president, becoming in 1970 president of MCA (Canada) and a vice-president of MCA, which had purchased Leeds in 1967. He has been president of the *CMPA 1958 and 1959 and of the *NYO 1968–9 and was appointed a director of *CAPAC in 1966. His wife, Irene (May) Bird (b Jocelyn) (b Stratford 6 Feb 1915; ATCM 1933, LTCM 1936, LRSM 1937) studied piano with Cora B. *Ahrens in Stratford and Mona *Bates and Viggo *Kihl in Toronto. She founded and conducted 1936–46 the Orpheus Girls' Choir in Stratford and was the official accompanist in the 1930s and 1940s for the Stratford Music Festival. In 1971 she became personal assistant to Maureen *Forrester.

3 **John** (Charles). Publisher, b Belgaum, India, 2 Nov 1923. After World War II service as a euphonium player in the RCAF Band he joined Gordon

V. Thompson Ltd in 1946 and served as sales manager 1950–5 and general manager 1955–65. He became president in 1965 on the death of G.V. Thompson. He was president 1969–71 of the *Festival Singers, chairman 1962–3 and president in 1976 of the CMPA, and president 1976–7 of the *Ontario Choral Federation. He became vice-president of CAPAC in 1975. (MMI)

BIRD, (Charles) Laughton. Educator, b Toronto 4 Mar 1914, d Halifax 6 Jan 1979; LTCL piano 1947, B MUS (Toronto) 1951. He held posts as an elementary and secondary school teacher, then as supervisor of music 1937–43 in Orillia, Ont, and 1943–8 in St Catharines, Ont, as a staff member in Radio and TV Arts 1951–2 at Toronto's Ryerson Polytechnical Institute, as music director 1953–8 for the South Peel Board of Education, as president 1954–5 of the *OMEA, and as co-ordinator of music 1963–73 for the North York Board of Education in Metropolitan Toronto; in all these capacities Bird consistently advocated new approaches to music in schools, latterly with much emphasis on creativity. With the composer Harry *Somers he assisted in the development of the first phase (1963) of the *John Adaskin Project and in the perpetuation of the principles evolved by that project. In that connection and under Bird's direction the music program at North York employed Somers in 1963 and 1968–9, R. Murray *Schafer 1963–4, Harry *Freedman 1971–3, Udo *Kasemets in 1972, Ann *Southam 1971–5, and other composers on an occasional basis, inlcuding Norma *Beecroft, Robert *Aitken, Walter *Buczynski, Milan *Kymlička, and Norman *Symonds. Bird also gave classes at summer schools of the Ontario Dept of Education 1941–50 and at the *U of British Columbia in 1959 and the *RCMT in 1962. 'A Festive Concert celebrating the life of C. Laughton Bird' took place at MacMillan Theatre, Toronto, 30 Sep 1979. Sponsored by *NMC, it featured John *Arpin, the dancer Patricia Beatty, the Elmer *Iseler Singers, the *Lyric Arts Trio, the Music Builders' Chorus of North York, and *Nexus, with Harry Somers as master of ceremonies. Proceeds helped establish a Laughton Bird Scholarship for young musicians.

See also School music.

BIBLIOGRAPHY

Wood, Glen. 'In memoriam: C. Laughton Bird,' *Recorder*, vol 21, Spring 1979 (PS)

BIRKETT, Madame Alicia. Teacher, soprano, b England, d Consett, County Durham, England, 31 Oct 1965. After a youthful career in opera and oratorio in Great Britain she emigrated to Canada and taught voice at the *Regina Cons from the late 1920s until 1954. She also taught privately in Moose Jaw, Sask. In Regina she was for some years the soloist at Metropolitan Church and was the founder and the conductor ca 1932–40 of the Elizabethan Singers, a 15-voice choir which sang on CRBC and CBC radio. Among her pupils were Ann Nancy Goodfellow, June *Kowalchuk, David *Mills, Helen and William *Morton, and Irene *Salemka. She returned in 1954 to England and taught there until her death. WLB

BIRSE, Berythe. Choir conductor, teacher, b Rossburn, north of Brandon, Man, 25 Jul 1904; BA (Manitoba) 1924. After teaching music in public and private Winnipeg schools for over 20 years, she was music supervisor 1944–8 for suburban Winnipeg schools. She was music instructor 1952–3 and 1956–7 at the Manitoba Teachers' College and 1967–71 at the faculty of education, *U of Manitoba. She founded the Young Women's Musical Club Choir in 1939 and the Winnipeg Ladies' Choir in 1940. During World War II she also directed the Carollers on CBC radio.

In 1954 Birse formed the Oriana Singers, a 25-voice female choir which appeared with the *Winnipeg SO in works requiring female voices (eg, the Debussy *Nocturnes*, 17 Jun 1963) and gave many concerts on its own from a repertoire of Britten (*A Ceremony of Carols*), Debussy (*The Blessed Damozel*), Vaughan Williams (*Magnificat*), and others. The Oriana Singers premiered Bernard *Naylor's *Kubla Khan* in 1960. They disbanded in 1966.

For Winnipeg service organizations Birse produced several chamber operas, including Britten's *Let's Make an Opera* (1952) and Menotti's *Amahl and the Night Visitors* (1953, 1954) in their first Canadian performances. Other works she produced included *The Impresario* (1956), *Noye's Fludde* (ca 1957), *Cox and Box*, and *La Serva Padrona* (1958) for the *Wednesday Morning Musicale. (RG)

BISHA, Edward (Russell). Cellist, b Louisville, Ky, 26 Aug 1927, naturalized Canadian 1973. He studied 1947–9 at the Cincinnati Cons, 1950–4 at the Juilliard School with Felix Salmond and Bernard Greenhouse, and privately with Janos Starker. He won the Piatigorsky Award in 1949 and later was a member of the American Chamber Orchestra and the Harp Trio (New York) and gave solo recitals. He moved to Canada where he served 1956–66 as principal of the *Halifax SO and 1956–67 as a member of the Halifax Trio (later *Brandon University Trio). He taught 1966–8 at *Brandon U and 1968–75 at the *U of Saskatchewan (Saskatoon campus), where he was a member 1969–71 of the *Amati String Quartet and 1971–5 of the *Canadian Arts Trio. He was a member 1975–6 of the *NACO.

Bisha's wife, Norma Lee Eskey – b Andersonville, Va, 3 Sep 1926, naturalized Canadian 1973; B MUS (North Carolina) 1947, M MUS (Cincinnati Cons) 1949 – was principal viola 1956–66 in the CBC Halifax Orchestra, taught 1966–8 at Brandon U and 1970–5 at the U of Saskatchewan, and was second violin, then viola, of the Amati String Quartet. GW

Bishop Strachan School Chapel Choir. Toronto girls' school choir. Variable in size, it numbered 52 members in 1980. A school choir existed at the time of World War I under J.W. Galloway (the composer of the school's first anthem, 'Gaudeamus') and 1921–6 under H.A. *Fricker, but the chapel choir was formed in 1925 for service in the newly added chapel. It also sang for other school functions and, at its conductor's initiative, in other contexts. Conductors have included John *Hodgins 1949–65 and 1972–4, Derek *Holman 1965–70, and Edgar Hanson 1970–2, succeeded by Maureen Hall in 1974.

In May and June 1953 the choir participated in the Coronation festivities in Great Britain. A second British tour in 1958 included a performance at the Llangollen International Eisteddfod. On invitation, the choir sang at the Seattle World's Fair (in 1962, also touring that year in western Canada), at the New York World's Fair in 1964, at Expo 74 in Spokane (again coupled with a tour of western Canada), and at the 1977 International Festival of Youth Orchestras and Performing Arts in Aberdeen and London. In Toronto the choir has performed with the *Toronto Mendelssohn Choir (*St Matthew Passion* 1957, *Children's Crusade* 1960), with the *TSO (*Joan of Arc at the Stake* 1958, Mendelssohn's *A Midsummer Night's Dream* 1965), with the *Orpheus Choir of Toronto (*Elijah* 1966), with the Concord Singers (Britten's *St Nicholas* 1975), and with the *Festival Singers in 1976. It gave the Canadian premiere 19 Apr 1961 of Britten's *Missa brevis in D* and the premiere 3 May 1972 of a commissioned work, Harry *Freedman's *Keewaydin*. The choir made two 78s for Hallmark in 1957 and an LP (CHL 603, which included Healey *Willan's *Magnificat*) for Canterbury in 1958. (PW)

Bishop's University. Founded in 1843 in Lennoxville, near Sherbrooke, Que, by George Jehoshaphat Mountain, the third Anglican bishop of Quebec, as a liberal arts college. Its foundation was ratified by an act of the Quebec Legislative Assembly. Established as a university by royal charter in 1853 and affiliated to Oxford and Cambridge universities, it first bore the name University of Bishop's College. By its charter it was empowered to grant degrees in theology, law, medicine, and fine arts, including music. The university was under the control of the Church of England until 1947, after which time its business affairs have been tended by a corporation made up of Anglican bishops from the dioceses of Quebec and appointed trustees, and academic matters have been dealt with by a senate. Instruction began in 1845, and the first degrees were granted in 1854. Bishop's was one of the first universities to offer the B MUS and D MUS degrees; the first graduate was Percival J. *Illsley (B MUS 1894, D MUS 1913). In 1895 the *Dominion College of Music became affiliated to Bishop's U, which ceased to grant university degrees in music in the 1950s.

In 1980 the director of the music department and its only teacher was Howard *Brown. No music courses were given when he arrived there in 1967. A BA with a minor in music was introduced then. A BA with a major in music was initiated in 1978, concentrating primarily on the history and literature of music. Among the examiners at different periods were John *Bearder, G.F. Garrett, Albert *Ham, and Healey *Willan. Graham *Godfrey and Herbert *Sanders were among the teachers and occasional lecturers. In 1933 Ham received an hon DCL from Bishop's. The University Singers were formed in 1977. That same year the university sponsored a series of musical and other cultural events at the Centennial Theatre.

BISSELL, Keith (Warren). Composer, educator, conductor, b Meaford, near Owen Sound, Ont, 12 Feb 1912; B MUS (Toronto) 1942. While teaching 1934–48 in Toronto schools he studied composition at the *U of Toronto with Leo *Smith. He was assistant supervisor in 1948 and supervisor 1949–55 of school music in Edmonton, where he was organist-choirmaster at Christ Church and founder ca 1952 of the Edmonton Junior SO. In 1955 he was appointed supervisor of school music in Scarborough (part of Metropolitan Toronto). After studies in 1960 in Munich with Gunild Keetman and Carl Orff he introduced the *Orff Schulwerk method to the Scarborough school system. Using Canadian folk music and his own compositions Bissell effected the transition from the German idiom to the English, thereby increasing the method's usefulness to music educators across the country. He has lectured at universities in British Columbia, Alberta, Ontario, Wisconsin, and Iowa. He also founded and conducted the Scarborough Teachers' Chorus (1956–70) and the Scarborough Orff Ensemble (1960–73). He has encouraged educators to use music by Canadian composers. With John *Adaskin he organized the first Canadian composers' seminar in music education, held in Toronto in 1963. He has been president of the *OMEA 1957–8, the *NYO 1970–1, and the *CMCentre 1975–7 and a vice-president of the *CMCouncil. Bissell has received commissions from the American Orff-Schulwerk Assn, *CAMMAC, ISME, and the *NACO Assn. His compo-

Keith Bissell

sitions bring to traditional forms a modest but graceful sense of renewal and many reflect his interest in music for young people and his belief that writing for amateurs can be more rewarding than writing for professionals. His folksong arrangements for voice and piano and for choir are among the simplest and subtlest by a Canadian, recalling those of Britten in a nearness to artsong that would be risky in a treatment less appreciative of the natural contours and honest expression of the original material. After a concert 1 Jun 1976 of Bissell's works when he retired from the Scarborough Board of Education, John *Kraglund wrote in the *Globe and Mail*: 'There were startling dissonances in the *Mass*, particularly in treble lines and in the fortissimo climax of the Sanctus. And, as in the setting of the Psalm 90, there was a strong emotional undercurrent – too rare in new Canadian music – as well as a feeling that the music was a personal response to the text.' In 1976 a trust fund was established in Bissell's name to commission annually a Canadian choral work written for school use. In 1978 he was awarded the *CMCouncil Medal. He is an associate of the CMCentre and an affiliate of PRO Canada.

SELECTED COMPOSITIONS

STAGE

His Majesty's Pie, operetta (K. Bissell). 1964. Wat 1966

Incidental Music to 'The Centennial Play' (Davies, Mitchell, Murphy, Thériault). 1967 (Ott 1967). Ms

ORCHESTRA

Three Pieces. 1960 (Tor 1961). Str. Kerby 1972

Under the Apple Boughs. 1961. Hn. Str. Ber (rental)

Adagio for Small Orchestra. 1963. Ber (rental)

Little Suite for Trumpet and Strings. 1963. Ber (rental)

Divertimento. 1964 (Hal 1965). Str orch. Kerby 1972

A Bluebird in March. 1967 (St Catharines 1967). SATB, orch (pf). Wat 1969 (pf version)

Andante e Scherzo. 1971. Chamb orch. Kerby 1972. 1972. Silver Crest Mid-72-2 (New Trier East SO, Ackerman cond)

The Passion According to St Luke. 1971 (Tor 1971). Soli, SATB, orch. Wat 1973. See also Oratorios, Canadian (composition and performance) 1.

Three Commentaries on Canadian Folk Songs. 1973. Str Orch. CMCentre

Variations on a Canadian Folk Song. 1973 (Tor 1973). Str. CMCentre. CBC SM-289 (*Chamber Players of Toronto)

A Celebration of the Nativity (Milton, Hardy, M.E. Coleridge, anon). 1978, Sop, bar, SATB chor, chamb orch. CMCentre

CHAMBER

Ballad 1949. Vn, pf. BMIC 1950

A Folk Song Suite for Woodwinds. 1960. B & H 1963

Little Suite. 1962. Tpt, pf. BMIC 1968

Overheard on a Saltmarsh (H. Monro). 1968. Mezzo, fl, pf. Kerby 1972

How the Loon Got Its Necklace. 1971. Narr, str quin, perc. CMCentre. RCI 388 (*Czech Quar, R. Coneybeare narr)

Serenade for Five Winds (1972) and *Trio Suite* (1973). Brass. Both CMCentre

Cantate Domino. 1977. SSA, chamb orch. CMCentre

Suite for bassoon, string quartet, and percussion. 1977. CMCentre

Suite for brass quintet. 1977. CMCentre

Sonata for french horn and piano. 1978. CMCentre

Suite for winds. 1978. CMCentre

CHOIR

Publ by Wat: 'In April'; 'I Was Glad When They Said unto Me'; 'Christ Is Risen from the Dead'; 'God Be Merciful unto Us'; 'Laudate Dominum'; 'O Holy Spirit'; 'Old Adam, the Carrion Crow'; 'The Three Princes'; 'None Other Lamb'; 'Full Fathom Five'; *People, Look East*; 'Canada, Dear Home'; 'Requiem'; 'A Summer Evening'; 'Gloria in Excelsis Deo'; 'Early Spring'; 'Song for Fine Weather'; 'In Canso Strait'

Publ by GVT: 'Lullaby'; *Two Christmas Songs*; 'Christ Being Raised from the Dead'; 'Hear Thou My Prayer'; 'Christ, Whose Glory Fills the Skies'; 'Lord, Dismiss Us with Thy Blessing'; *Let There Be Joy*; 'A Song of Longing'

Publ by BMIC: 'The Earth Is the Lord's'; 'The Dark Hills'; 'Dream River'; 'The Plowman'; *Ten Short Pieces*

Also works publ by West, FH, and Kerby; also some in ms, including *The Gracious Time* (1972), recorded 1973 on J Mar Electronics J13153 (Choir of St Simon's Church, Hanson cond); *Canadian Folk Song Suite* (1976); *A Musical Play* (1977); *Anniversary Cantata* (1978). All CMCentre

Over 20 arr of folksongs for choir

VOICE

Two Songs of Farewell (C. Bissell). 1961. V, pf. Wat 1963. CBC SM-79 (*Forst)

Six Maritime Folk Songs arr (traditional) 1969. V, pf. Ber 1970. CBC SM-168 (D. *Bell)

Six Folk Songs from Eastern Canada arr (traditional). 1970. V, pf. B&H 1971. CBC SM-144 (*Forrester)

Ten Folk Songs of Canada, arr (traditional). 1970. V, pf. Wat 1972. CBC SM-168 (D. *Bell)

Plus others publ by Wat and Manitou

Also 3 works for pf publ by Wat and Harmuse; 3 works for org publ by BMIC and Wat

WRITINGS

'The Canadian composer and the public,' *PfAC*, vol 1, Oct 1961

Singing in Schools (Don Mills 1962)

'What's wrong with music educators,' *Music Across Canada*, Mar 1963

'School music to-day and tomorrow,'' *MSc*, 238, Nov–Dec 1967

'The Canadian Music Council – a symposium,' *CME*, vol 10, Nov– Dec 1968

Singing and Playing / Chantons et jouons (Wat 1968)

– and Schabas, Ezra. *Choral Music in Ontario* (Toronto 1970)

'R.M. Schafer's books,' *CMB*, 2, Spring – Summer 1971

Let's Sing and Play, 2 vols (Wat 1973, 1975)

BIBLIOGRAPHY

Schulman, Michael. 'Keith Bissell,' *MSc*, 268, Nov–Dec 1972

Sweetman, Paul. 'A tribute to Keith Bissell,' *Recorder*, vol 18, Jun 1976

BMI Canada Ltd. 'Keith Bissell,' pamphlet (1976)

Contemporary Canadian Composers (MDr)

BISSETT, Billy (William) (after 1942, Bishop). Pianist, bandleader, b Buffalo, NY, 24 Aug 1907. He was taken as a child to St Catharines, Ont. There in 1925, with the saxophonist Duart McLean, he formed the dance band Bissett, McLean and Their Orchestra, which played in vaudeville throughout New England and in New York, Syracuse, and Cleveland. In the early 1930s he assumed sole leadership of the band and appeared in Montreal, at the Seigniory Club in Montebello, Que, and 1933–6 at the Royal York Hotel in Toronto. Billy Bissett and his Orchestra, which included Dave *Bowman, Eric *Wild, and Bissett's wife, the singer Alice Mann, went to Monte Carlo, then to England, where it played at the Savoy Hotel, the Mayfair, and the Café de Paris in London, and at the Royal Bath Hotel in Bournemouth. It also appeared in the movies *Dinner at the Ritz*, *The Divorce of Lady X*, and *The Sidewalks of London* and made some 78s for HMV. Rivalling Guy *Lombardo in international popularity at the time, Bissett organized a new band in Chicago in 1940, playing at the Trianon and Aragon ballrooms. He took the name Billy Bishop in 1942 and continued to lead his band in US nightclubs until 1953. Thereafter he worked in California as a stockbroker. He retired to Poway (near San Diego) and in the late 1970s served there as organist at St Michael's Catholic church.

BIBLIOGRAPHY

Bands Canadians Danced To MM

BISSON, (Joseph Georges) **Napoléon**. Baritone, b Montreal 17 Dec 1922; premier prix (CMM) 1953. He studied 1946–50 under Adelina Czapska and continued his training 1950–3 at the *CMM, working with Dick Marzollo, Martial Singher, Rachele Maragliano-Mori, and Jacqueline *Richard. He made his debut in 1951 as Mercutio in *Roméo et Juliette* on the CBC radio program 'Théâtre lyrique Molson.' After hearing him in *Parsifal*, Jean *Vallerand wrote, 'The surprise of the performance, however, is Napoléon Bisson who sings Klingsor with the finish and the style that one would expect from a Wagnerian of international reputation' (Montreal *Le Devoir*, 13 Apr 1954). In 1955 he was Amonasro in a New Orleans production of *Aida*. He sang at Covent Garden for two seasons, notably as Donner in *Das Rheingold*, in the title role of *Rigoletto*, and as Balducci in *Benvenuto Cellini*. He took the leading role in the Canadian premiere (CBC radio 1959) of Humphrey Searle's *The Diary of a Madman*. He also toured for the *JMC with the pianist Jacqueline Richard during the 1958–9 season. For the *Opera Guild of Montreal he sang Ford (*Falstaff*, 1958), Morales (*Carmen*, 1960), Mercutio (*Roméo et Juliette*, 1961), Germont (*La Traviata*, 1962), Valentin (*Faust*, 1963), Schaunard (*La Bohème*, 1966), Bartolo (*The Barber of Seville*, 1968), and the Bonze (*Madama Butterfly*, 1969). For the *Montreal Festivals, he sang Don Inigo in Ravel's *L'Heure espagnole* (1961), Antonin in *Blackburn's **Silent Measures*, and the title role in Vallerand's **Le Magicien* (1962). He toured in *Le Magicien* for the JMC in 1961–2. Bisson made his debut with the *Vancouver Opera in *La Bohème* (1962) and appeared with the *Edmonton Opera in the title role of *Rigoletto* and with the *COC as Amonasro in *Aida* in 1964. He sang Bartolo in *The Barber of Seville* on the CBC TV program *'L'Heure du concert,' a production which won an Emmy Award in 1965. In 1966–7 he returned to the Royal Opera House, London, appearing in Wagner's *Ring* cycle (as Alberich), Strauss' *Die Frau ohne Schatten* (the blind brother), *Carmen* (Morales), *The Bartered Bride* (the father), and *Benvenuto Cellini* (Balducci). He sang the title role of *Rigoletto* at the Royal Opera of Copenhagen in 1967. He was heard with the *Southern Alberta Opera in *Rigoletto* (1973) and with the *Manitoba Opera in *Tosca* (1974). For the Pittsburgh Opera in 1974 he portrayed Michele (*Il Tabarro*), Tonio (*I Pagliacci*), and Sulpice (*La Fille du régiment*). In the same year he played in *Don Quichotte* on CBC TV. With the *Opéra du Québec he performed the title role of *Gianni Schicchi* (1971) as well as the High Priest (*Samson et Dalila*, 1971), the Bonze (*Madama Butterfly*, 1974), and Schaunard (*La Bohème*, 1975). He also sang in *La Belle Hélène* (Agamemnon) at the *NAC with Festival Canada (*Festival Ottawa) in 1973 and on the CBC in 1975.

Napoléon Bisson excels in tragi-comic roles in which he makes use of his powerful, resonant voice and acting skills. He was particularly outstanding in *Tosca* with the Edmonton Opera in November 1978, singing the role of the Sacristan which he had recorded the previous year with Nicole *Lorange, Jaime Aragall, and Louis *Quilico. Bartolo, however, remains one of his best roles. In

Napoléon Bisson

the USA he regularly performs in Boston, Cincinnati, Dallas, Los Angeles, New Orleans, Philadelphia, and Pittsburgh.

BIBLIOGRAPHY
Maître, Manuel. 'Du pic et de la pelle à la gloire de Covent Garden,' Montreal *La Patrie*, 12 Nov 1967 (CB)

BIZONY, Celia. Musicologist, soprano; British citizen, b Berlin of Hungarian parents in 1904. A specialist in early music, particularly the medieval repertoire, she studied at Columbia U in 1948 prior to settling in Montreal in 1949. She taught musicology and music history 1949–54 at *McGill U and also 1949–50 directed the Schola cantorum there. She commuted to Kingston 1950–4 to teach at *Queen's U. In Montreal she founded, and directed 1951–5, *Musica Antica e Nuova, a society similar to one she had co-founded and co-directed 1942–8 with Boris Ord at Cambridge U, England. She also taught voice at *Mount Allison U before returning to England in 1955. She then began teaching at the GSM and was a lecturer until 1970 at Morley College. She also taught 1967–9 at the U of London. Her Canadian pupils included the bass-baritone James Bechtel. She is considered the initiator of authentic early music performances in Montreal.

BIBLIOGRAPHY
Musiciennes de chez nous

BLACHFORD, Frank (Edward). Violinist, teacher, conductor, composer, b Toronto 28 Dec 1879, d Calgary 24 Jun 1957; ATCM 1897. He studied at the TCM with Bertha *Drechsler Adamson, graduating in 1897, and continued at the Leipzig Cons with Hans Sitt and Carl Reinecke. After graduating in 1901 with the Helbig prize he studied in Geneva with Henri Marteau and in Berlin. He returned to Canada in 1901 and taught at the *TCM until his death. He was concertmaster of the Conservatory Orchestra 1906–8, continuing 1908–18 with the *Welsman *TSO, and was in the first violins of the *TSO 1932–46. His solo career, in concerts and broadcasts, included tours of Ontario and Canada and appearances with the Welsman orchestra and in 1923 with the New SO. He was the founder in 1907 and first violin of the *Toronto String Quartet, a member 1902–5 of the Schumann Trio and 1926–8 of the Conservatory Trio, and conductor 1914–25 of the TCM String Orchestra and 1920–30 of the Victoria College Orchestra. In the late 1920s he produced and conducted programs for local radio and in 1932 he formed the Blachford String Symphony, a group of 16 TSO musicians which performed in concert and on the CRBC (later CBC) network. He was president of the *ORMTA 1936–7. In later years he concentrated on teaching, at the TCM and in public schools. His pupils included Albert Aylward, Jack Montague, and Harvey *Perrin. Blachford died during an examining trip for the TCM. His compositions include violin teaching pieces and transcriptions for quartet or orchestra of baroque and romantic music. Concert works included *Idylle* and *Romance* for solo violin and strings and *Suite from the Ontario Northlands* for orchestra. He also wrote a number of songs, a 'Serenade' for men's voices, and an anthem, 'He Was Despised.'

WRITINGS
First 20 Lessons (F. Harris 1929)
Blachford Violin Class Book (GVT 1949)
Tunes for Strings (F. Harris 1953)

BIBLIOGRAPHY
'Musical bibliographies of Canadian composers – Blachford,' Toronto *Globe*, 17 Oct 1936
'Conservatory Portrait Gallery – Mr. Frank Blachford,' *CQR*, vol 15, Aug 1933 (RPn)

BLACKBURN, (Joseph Albert) Maurice. Composer, b Quebec City 22 May 1914; lauréat piano (Laval) 1939. He studied with Jean-Marie *Beaudet (piano, composition), Henri *Gagnon (organ, improvisation), Robert *Talbot (theory), and J.-Arthur *Bernier (organ, piano) at *Laval U 1937–9, and privately with Claude *Champagne (composition) and Georges-Émile *Tanguay (harmony, counterpoint) in Montreal. In 1938 his work *Les Petites Rues du vieux Québec* won second prize in the Jean *Lallemand composition competition. Recipient of a scholarship from the Quebec government, he studied 1939–41 at the New England Cons, Boston, with Quincy Porter (composition, counterpoint) and Francis Findlay (orchestration, conducting). His *Sonatina* for piano earned him the George Allan prize in 1940 and the same year he conducted the *Quebec SO in his *Fantaisie en mocassins*. Also in 1940 he attended the lectures given by Stravinsky at Harvard U.

Blackburn embarked on a long career, 1942–6, 1948–53, and 1955–78, as a composer with the *NFB. It was there, along with Norman *McLaren, that he developed the process of etching sound and picture directly onto film. In *The Canadian Composer* (March 1969), Blackburn recounts the nature of this music which he describes as 'semi-improvised': 'McLaren and I had discussed a way of recording music without a score, from just a very rough sketch of the score, in which the musicians could choose the notes they wanted – either low, middle or high – but the rhythm was fixed. We recorded many short things – a chorale, fast things – and from that, after I left, McLaren chose what appealed to him and made a film called "Blinkity Blank".' That 1954 film received 12 awards, including the Palme d'or at the Cannes International Festival. (See also Film scores.)

During Blackburn's early association with the NFB his symphonic works were being performed in concert. His symphonic poem *Charpente* was premiered on the CBC by Jean-Marie Beaudet in the 1944 series 'Canadian Music in Wartime' and was performed again by Beaudet at the 1946 Prague Festival. The work was repeated in 1946 by the London Philharmonic Orchestra and in 1948 by the Montreal Youth Orchestra.

With the help of a second Quebec government scholarship Blackburn continued his studies in composition 1946–8 with Nadia Boulanger in Paris. In 1951 his *Ouverture pour un spectacle de marionnettes* won first prize for composition on the CBC program *'Opportunity Knocks.' A scholarship from the Royal Society of Canada enabled him to spend a second sojourn 1954–5 in Paris, where he associated with the Groupe de recherches de musique concrète directed by Pierre Schaeffer at the RTF, and allowed him to pursue his studies in composition. He was invited by Unesco to take part in a convention of composers of film music in 1954 at Cannes.

Maurice Blackburn

Blackburn's operas **Pirouette* and **Silent Measures* were given more than 100 performances 1960–1 by the *JMC. Blackburn wrote the music for films presented at several of the *Expo 67 pavilions including those of Quebec and the JMC. He was awarded a *Canada Council study grant in 1967.

'The works of Blackburn, such as the *Concertino in C* for piano and winds (1948), possess some of the characteristics – especially the propulsive rhythm – of French music in the early 20th century (particularly that of Honegger and Poulenc)' (*Contemporary Canadian Composers*). Léo-Pol *Morin described him as 'imaginative, impulsive, a vibrant and caustic poet, one whose chief concern is to give expression to the responses of his mind through music. A creator of images, he has a gift for colour and design, and the stories he tells are original, vivid and spontaneous' (*Musique*, Montreal 1945).

Blackburn is a member of CAPAC and of the *CLComp and an associate of the *CMCentre.

SELECTED COMPOSITIONS
STAGE
Rose Latulippe, ballet. 1953. Ms
La Chasse au corbeau (E. Labiche), incidental music. 1962. Ms
Hyménée (Gogol), TV. 1964. Vs, balalaika, acc, pf. Ms
Other incidental music
See also *Pirouette* and *Silent Measures*.
FILM
Blackburn has composed the music or sound tracks for more than 100 NFB films, full-length and short, documentaries, and animated films, including *La Poulette grise* (arr 1947), *Blinkity Blank* (1954), *J.A. Martin, photographe* (1976), *Mourir à tue-tête* (1979), and *Cordelia* (1979).
ORCHESTRA
Les Petites Rues de vieux Québec. 1938. Ms
Fantaisie en mocassins. 1940. Ms
Symphonie en un mouvement. 1942. Ms
Charpente 'Canadian Forest.' 1944. Ms
Suite from Le Gros Bill. 1949. Ms
Bal à l'huile. Ca 1950. Str orch. Ms
Pantomime. Ca 1950. Str orch. Ms
Petite Suite. Ca 1950. Ms
Ouverture pour un spectacle de marionnettes. 1951. Ms
Promenade. 1951. Ms
Suite. 1960. Str orch. Ms. CBC Expo-15 (*Hart House O)
SOLOIST WITH ORCHESTRA
Concertino in C. 1948. Pf, ww. Edn CMCentre. RCI 2 (*Barette)
Rigaudon. 1949. Vn, chamb orch. Ms. RCI 1 (J.-M. *Beaudet)
Nocturne. Ca 1950. Fl, str orch. Ms

CHAMBER MUSIC

Marine. Ca 1950. Str, hp. Ms

Six Formes musicales (M. Maurisset Blackburn). 1967. Narr, ww quar, str trio, pf, org. 1967. CD-JMC-7 (J.-P. Major fl, Berman ob, Rafael Masella cl, Rodolfo Masella bn, Sieb vn, Malowany va, André Mignault vc, Stevens pf, Gilbert org, J. Faubert, Y. Roy, and J. Houde narr, Blackburn cond)

PIANO

Cinq Digitales. 1940. FH 1955 (no. 2 and 5). 1974. RCI 397 (J. Holtzman)

Sonatina. 1940. Ms

Trois Danses. 1949. Ms

Étude. Ca 1950. Ms

Polka. Ca 1950. Ms

Marionnettes. Ca 1950. Ms

Valse ivre. Ca 1950. Ms

CHOIR OR VOICE

Messe. 1949. Children's vs. Ms

Trois poèmes d'Émile Nelligan. 1949. V, pf. Ms

'Notre Père' (traditional, arr). Ca 1950. SATB. Ms

'L'Âne de p'tit Jean' (Blackburn). Ca 1951. SATB. Alliance des chorales du Québec 1977

'Chanson du gars perdu' (É. de Grandmont). 1953. V, pf. Publ in *Plaisirs*, Montreal 1953

'Mon oncle a bien mal à sa tête' (traditional, arr). 1954. SATB. Ms

'La Rose blanche' (traditional, arr). 1954. SATB. Ms

'Garde notre amour' (É. de Grandmont). 1957. V, pf. Jacques Labrecque 1957

'Ramenez-moi chez moi' (É. de Grandmont). 1957. V, pf. Arch 1958

Several other songs for v and pf to poems by Aimé Plamondon, Éloi de Grandmont, and others

BIBLIOGRAPHY

Trente-Quatre Biographies (DA)

'The Black Fly Song.' Words and music by Wade *Hemsworth. It was written in 1949 while he was visiting northern Ontario with an Ontario Hydro Electric Commission survey party studying the feasibility of a dam on the Little Abitibi River, which flows north towards James Bay. Like most visitors to Ontario's northland in summer, the survey party suffered from the toxic attentions of 'the little black flies.' The song was published by Southern Music (Canada) in 1957 and was included in *Canada's Story in Song* (Toronto 1960), compiled by Edith *Fowke, Helmut *Blume, and Alan *Mills. The composer sings it on his LP *Folk Songs of the Canadian North Woods*; other versions have been recorded by the *Travellers and, as 'The Black Flies of Ontario,' by Omar *Blondahl. It was heard in the film *Tempo Canada 66*. EF

BLACKLEY, Jim (James David). Teacher, drummer, b Edinburgh 4 Mar 1927. He was the solo soprano in a youth choir and at 13 took up pipe-band drumming, studying with James Catherwood and George Pryde, and becoming a leading drummer in Scotland before moving to Montreal in 1952. While a drumming instructor 1953–6 at the RCAF base in Ottawa, Blackley visited Toronto and, on hearing the US drummer Max Roach perform there, took up jazz. He lived 1957–67 in Vancouver, teaching privately and playing jazz with Dave *Robbins and others. In New York 1967–73 he operated a studio (also commuting 1971–3 to Toronto to give lessons) and worked with the jazzmen Jim Hall, Richie Kamuca, Wynton Kelly, and Clarence Hutchenrider. Settling in Toronto in 1973, Blackley continued to teach and also made rare appearances with his own band of young musicians. He came to be recognized as the leading teacher of jazz drumming in Canada and has numbered among his pupils his son Keith, Mel Brown, Terry *Clarke, Barry Elmes, Jerry *Fuller, Jake Hanna, Duras Maxwell, Bob McLaren, Stan Perry, and Howie Silverman. Blackley has published two volumes of *Syncopated Rolls for the Modern Drummer* (Vancouver 1961, 1962).

Keith Blackley (b Edinburgh 11 Aug 1950) has worked in Vancouver with rock bands, in New York in jazz groups and Broadway pit orchestras, and in Toronto with the jazz groups of Sonny *Greenwich, Don (W.) *Thompson, and others. In Toronto he formed a duo with the saxophonist Michael Stuart in 1974, later expanding it to a quartet with pianist Frank Falco (replaced by George McFetridge) and bassist Steve Wallace. The Stuart-Blackley Quartet made the LP *Determination* (Endeavour 1001) in 1979.

BIBLIOGRAPHY

Freedman, Adele. 'The Sufi and the jazz drummer,' Toronto *Globe and Mail*, 24 Aug 1977 MM

Black (Afro-American or Negro) **musicians**. The first black in Canada was Matthew da (de) Costa, a former Portuguese slave and fisherman, who sailed to Port Royal in 1605 (or 1606) to serve as a translator for Champlain. The holding of slaves was legal under French and British law during the colonization of Canada, and the first slaves were introduced to Canada as early as 1628 (post-dating the first slaves in the southern colonies of the USA by nine years). Some 5000 blacks migrated to Canada (specifically Nova Scotia and New Brunswick) during the US War of Independence, 3500 as freemen (who became tenant-farmers) and 1500 as slaves. In the late 19th century, however, 1200 blacks sailed from Halifax for Sierra Leone.

With the abolition of slavery in Canada by 1833 (and the de facto abolition in Upper Canada as early as 1793) Canada became a haven for blacks escaping from the southern USA by means of the 'underground railway' which had terminal points at several border locations in southwestern Ontario along the Detroit and Niagara rivers. It would appear that several thousand, perhaps tens of thousands, of the fugitives availed themselves of the opportunity to live in freedom under British law, but that a very large percentage returned to the USA after 1865. Nevertheless, many communities of their descendants survive in the area between Windsor and Niagara Falls, and several black musicians were born in Ontario towns in the late 1800s and early 1900s: the trumpeter Arthur Briggs in St George, the songwriter Shelton Brooks and the pianist Lou *Hooper in North Buxton (the most famous of all black communities in Ontario), the composer Nathaniel *Dett in old Drummondville (which became part of Niagara Falls), and the jazz pianist Kenny Kersey in Harrow.

In 1871 there were 21,000 blacks in Canada; by 1890, however, the number had declined to 15,000. Not until 1940, with the substantial influx from the West Indies, did this figure increase. In the 1970s the number of blacks in Canada was estimated to be 300,000 (census figures are not broken down according to such criteria), and the largest number, 150,000, resided in Toronto, the rest in other urban centres, notably Montreal and Halifax, with some still living in the rural areas of the Maritimes settled by their ancestors 200 years before.

The earliest documented instance of a black musician in Canada is a notice in the *Quebec Gazette* of 30 Nov 1775 for a runaway slave named Lowcanes who spoke French but little English, 'et jouant très bien du violon.' A water-colour from 1807, G. Heriot's *Menuet des Canadiens*, shows a black musician playing a tambourine for a group of dancers.

Music in the black communities of the Maritimes and Ontario was centred in the church. It is known, for example, that blacks in *Oakville, Ont, had their own British Methodist Episcopal Church, established in 1875, and that one of their ministers often was invited to gatherings in Hamilton and Toronto because of his ability to sing spirituals. However, few songs have survived in the older black communities of Canada. Arthur Huff Fauset's *Folklore of Nova Scotia* (Philadelphia 1931) includes 20 song texts, most either collected from blacks or of black origin. (Fauset cites a white Nova Scotian, Carrie B. Grover, who had in her repertoire 'songs from slavery days,' all of which she had learned from her father.) Helen *Creighton and Doreen H. Senior's collection, *Traditional Songs from Nova Scotia* (Toronto 1950) includes some songs of black origin, and Creighton reports (*Ethnomusicology*, Sep 1972) that she collected at least 81, including some singing games. Paul *McIntyre, in *Black Pentecostal Music in Windsor*, notes many African survivals in the music at a Black Pentecostal church attended by descendants of the North Buxton settlers and other blacks in the Windsor area. Francis Henry, however, found little evidence of black musical activity in the Maritimes in the 1970s; in 'Black Music in the Maritimes' (*Canadian Folk Music Journal*, 1975) he concluded: 'there is no really viable folk-music tradition remaining in these communities. Most religious music revolved around hymns and social music is heavily influenced by pop and country and western.'

Black choirs usually have been church or social groups. Two of the best-known are the (Toronto) British Methodist Episcopal Church Choir, which under Grace Trotman was active for many years and developed several successful Toronto entertainers, and the Montreal Black Community Youth Choir, connected to the Union United Church in St-Henri. The latter is directed by the former rhythm and blues singer Trevor Payne, who has called it 'a phenomenon, coming as it does from a city where the black population is almost non-existent and the members don't even live in the black community which is fast disappearing' (Montreal *Gazette*, 25 Oct 1978). The choir has made LPs of spirituals for RCI (LP 424) and the Presqu'ile label (*Goin' Up Yonder*, PE 13501).

Afro-American music of the 20th century – jazz and its outgrowths – has enjoyed considerable popularity in Canada, and some, though by no means the majority, of its practitioners in Canada are blacks. (See also Blues; Ragtime.) Black dance bands were active in the 1930s: throughout Ontario and Quebec the Canadian Ambassadors, led by Myron Sutton; in Toronto the Rhythm Aces (later Rhythm Knights), led by Harry Lucas, a pianist from Chatham, Ont, and, most notable in the late 1930s, the Cy McLean Orchestra, led by pianist McLean from Sydney, NS. However, discrimination – social and professional (the latter by unions) – made it difficult until the mid-1940s for black bands to perform in Toronto in any but local halls catering to black audiences; further, blacks were not admitted to performances in Toronto by black bands (eg those visiting from the USA) when white audiences were in attendance. (See also Dance bands.)

The careers of Eleanor *Collins and Phyllis *Marshall began in the late 1930s; both singers were popular on CBC radio and TV.

Among the earliest black jazz musicians resident in Canada were Lou Hooper and the US trumpeter Louis Metcalf. Metcalf worked in Montreal briefly in the 1930s and again 1946–50, when he led the International Band (so named for the various nationalities of its members) at the Café St Michel. The pianist Argonne Thornton (Sadik *Hakim) and the bassist Al King were members of this band. The pianists Oscar

Members of the choir of Stewart Memorial Church, Hamilton, Ont, 1962

*Peterson and Milt Sealey began their careers in Montreal during the 1940s, and Peterson's sidemen late in that decade were the US musicians Ozzie Roberts and Clarence Jones. In the 1950s many other black US jazzmen made Canada their home, if only temporarily. Among them were the bassist Charles Biddle in Montreal, the bassist Wyatt Ruther and the saxophonist Russell Thomas (Sayyd *Abdul Al-Khabyyr) in Ottawa, and the pianist Cal Jackson in Toronto. The MINC Club in Toronto was operated ca 1960 for and by black musicians, including the newly emerging Canadian-born players Sonny *Greenwich, Connie Maynard (piano), and Doug Richardson (tenor saxophone). Other important black jazz musicians in Canada include the guitarists Nelson and Ivan *Symonds; the pianists Linton Garner (brother of Erroll) and Elmer Gill (both US-born), Wray *Downes, Oliver Jones, Joe Sealy, and Steep Wade; the drummers Archie Alleyne, Charlie Duncan, Clayton Johnston, Billy McCant, and Norman Villeneuve; the saxophonists Bucky Adams and Michael Stuart; and the singers Salome *Bey, Olive Brown, and Jodie Drake.

Black folk and blues performers in Canada include Leon Bibb and Fred Booker in Vancouver (both US-born), Al Cromwell and Jackie Washington in Toronto, Beverly Glenn-Copeland (b Philadelphia 1944) in Montreal and Toronto, and Lucie Guanel (b Martinique) in Montreal. (See also Blues.)

In the 1960s a number of black musicians contributed substantially to the popularity of rhythm and blues in Canada – Dianne Brooks, Shawne and Jay Jackson, Eric Mercury, Bobby Taylor and the Vancouvers, Davy Wells, and others. In the 1970s they contributed to funk – Crack of Dawn, Rick James, the Mighty Pope, and George Thurston (Boule Noire of Montreal) – and to disco – Claudja Barry, Alma Faye Brooks, and others. The influx of West Indians to Canada in the 1960s and 1970s shifted the focus of black music to styles popular in the Caribbean, in particular reggae. 'Caribana,' an annual week-long festival begun in 1967 and held each August in Toronto, has recreated activities held in Trinidad, with fancy balls and dance and music contests, culminating in a parade down University Ave to the sounds of steel bands (eg, the Steltones and Dick Smith's Syncona) and reggae and calypso ensembles. Reggae was heard in many clubs around Toronto in the late 1970s, and its audiences were not only black. The Jamaican singer-guitarist Ernie Smith led the most popular band, Roots Revival. Other bands and individuals included Ishan People, Earth Fire and Water, Leroy Sibbles, and the Tropical Energy Experience. The organist Jackie Mittoo, who moved from Kingston, Jamaica, to Toronto in 1969, has made several LPs of reggae in Canada (for CTL) and in his homeland. Reggae has spawned white imitators in Canada, notably the groups Chalawa and Limbo Springs (Toronto) and Heaven's Radio (Ottawa).

Black musicians also have had some impact on the concert world. The contralto Portia *White had a successful, if limited, career as a recitalist and teacher; the tenor Garnet *Brooks has performed in North American and European opera companies; and the soprano Burnetta Day performed often in Toronto with her husband Warren *Mould and with the *Ascher Duo, before she moved to Germany in the late 1970s. Several black US musicians have contributed to music in Canada, among them the conductor James De Preist (nephew of the famous contralto Marian Anderson), who became artistic director of the *Quebec SO in 1974, and the cellist Anthony Elliott, who played 1970–3 in the *TS and became principal of the *Vancouver SO in 1978. Other US musicians in Canada include the pianist Monica *Gaylord (who has given recitals devoted to the music of black composers) and the counter-tenor Theodore Gentry. The West Indian composer Edford Providence, while studying at *York U, Toronto, sponsored a concert of his own works, played by the *Hamilton Philharmonic Orchestra, at *Massey Hall in 1979.

In Montreal a Société de recherche et de diffusion de la musique haïtienne was formed in 1978, and by 1980 it had presented three concerts of works by Haitian composers some of whom were residents in Montreal.

BIBLIOGRAPHY

Winks, Robin. *The Blacks in Canada: A History* (Montreal 1971)

Henry, Francis. *Forgotten Canadians: The Blacks of Nova Scotia* (Don Mills, Ont 1973)

McIntyre, Paul. *Black Pentecostal Music in Windsor*, Canadian Centre for Folk Culture Studies Paper no. 15 (Ottawa 1976)

Spellen, Suzanne. 'Black music in Canada: A search for Afro-Canadian music (with a special emphasis on sacred music),' undergraduate essay (Yale 1977)

Johnson, B. Derek. 'Backbeat for Jah Jah,' Toronto *Globe and Mail*, 5 Apr 1978

Richmond, Norman. 'The uphill struggle of our black musicians,' Toronto *Star*, 14 Apr 1979

Harry, Isobel. 'Reggae,' *Can Comp*, 152, Jun 1980

(MM, PM, JSz)

BLAIN DE ST-AUBIN, Emmanuel-(Marie). Translator, song-writer, tenor, teacher of music and languages, b Rennes, France, 29 Jun 1833, d Ottawa 9 Jul 1883; B LITT (Rennes) 1851. He completed his education in Paris. After brief sojourns in 1857 on St-Pierre and Miquelon and Prince Edward Island he settled in Quebec City. He was a government translator in Quebec and after 1865 in Ottawa. He wrote the words and music of many songs, including some on political and religious subjects, and developed a personal style of performance. In effect an early chansonnier, he performed in the salons of Sir George-Étienne Cartier and Sir Adolphe Caron, at the *Institut canadien, and elsewhere. He also did much to make the music of the French song-writer Gustave Nadaud popular in Canada. His published songs include 'L'Exilé de là-bas' (words by H. Violeau) in *L'Echo du Cabinet de lecture paroissial* (1 Jul 1862) and 'Le Chemin des amoureux'/'The Lovers' Walk' and 'Vir' de bord, mon ami Pierre' in *L'Album Musicale*, 1882. He was the author of the poem 'La Mère canadienne,' which was set to music by Antoine *Dessane. His series of essays 'De l'enseignement de la musique' were published in the Montreal *Journal de l'instruction publique* (February, March, April 1860). He was the grandfather of Charles and Blain *Mathé.

BIBLIOGRAPHY

LeVasseur, N. 'Musique et musiciens à Québec,' *La Musique*, vol 3, Apr, May, Jun 1921 HK, DM

BLAIR, Frederick H. (Harold). Organist-choirmaster, pianist, teacher, b Chatham, NB, 10 Jan 1874, d at sea, near the Hebrides, 3 Sep 1939. At 12 he was a chorister and at 14 the organist at St Mary's Anglican Church in Chatham, where he studied piano and organ with A.W.S. Smythe. At 15 he became the organist at St George's Anglican Church in Saint John, NB, and he studied in Saint John for three years with Thomas Morley. In 1897 he began studies at the RCM with Sir Walter Parratt. He returned to Canada to take a position as organist at St John's Church in Moncton, but moved shortly to Christ Church Cathedral in Fredericton. He was subsequently organist-choirmaster 1900–39 at the Church of St Andrew and St Paul in Montreal. An original staff member 1904–13 of the *McGill Cons, teaching piano, organ, and accompaniment, he regularly studied abroad during the summers. In 1913 he was appointed director of the *Canadian Academy of Music in Montreal. He was briefly (1908) the conductor of the *Montreal Oratorio Society, and piano accompanist to such noted artists as Edmund *Burke, bass, and Lucien *Martin, violinist. He served as president of the English section of the *Casavant Society in Montreal. Thomas *Archer wrote in *The Gazette* (23 Sep 1950): 'Due to [Blair's] initiative ... Montreal had already become a centre for organ music in North America. But with [his] death in 1939 the position deteriorated.' His death had occurred when the ship *Athenia*, on which he was a passenger, was torpedoed by a German submarine. (NT)

BLAQUIÈRE, Arthur. Baritone, choir conductor, b Salem, Mass, 7 Dec 1896. He studied 1914–15 at the seminary in Joliette with his uncle, Father Phi-

lippe Dubé, and in 1916 in Quebec City with François-Xavier *Mercier. While he was a soloist with the Jesuits at the Villa Manrèse, he also sang leading roles in performances of Gilbert & Sullivan's *The Pirates of Penzance* and *The Gondoliers* conducted by Charles *O'Neill. At Spencer Wood, the residence of the lieutenant governor of Quebec, he gave a concert 4 Feb 1919 in collaboration with other artists, among them the organist Omer *Létourneau. He also took part in joint concerts in Victoriaville, St-Basile, and St-Casimir. In Quebec City he performed in 1920 at the fifth concert of the Institut d'art vocal and sang at the Allen Film Theatre. In 1921 he studied in Montreal with Arthur *Laurendeau (voice), Jean-Noël *Charbonneau (harmony and Gregorian chant), and Paul *Doyon (piano), giving some concerts with Doyon. He also sang for the *Ladies' Morning Musical Club. Blaquière was soloist 1923–6 at the Montreal cathedral and subsequently with the Dominicans at Notre-Dame-de-Grâce. He founded, and directed 1929–31, the choir of St-Antonin parish in Montreal.

In 1934 he and 6 of his 11 children founded the Blaquière Septet, also known as the Petit Septuor de la Bonne Chanson, with whom he made five 78s, one of which presents a performance, with Anna *Malenfant, of A.T. Bourque's 'Évangéline' and 'Le Pêcheur acadien' (Bluebird B-1230). In the 1930s and 1940s the septet travelled several times across Quebec, the Maritimes, and the main Franco-American centres of New England. The ensemble, which had a repertoire of about 300 songs, sang at the Festival of Lewiston, Me, and the Festival de la Bonne Chanson at the Montreal *Forum and was invited to perform on CBC radio.

BIBLIOGRAPHY

Le Voisin. 'Le "Petit Septuor de la Bonne Chanson",' *L'Oeil*, 15 May 1941

'Les Rossignolets de la montagne,' *P-T*, 906, Jan 1947

Musiciens canadiens

HP

BLEY, Paul. Pianist, synthesizist, composer, b Montreal 10 Nov 1932. He began violin studies at five and piano at eight and attended the *McGill Cons as a youth. As 'Buzzy' Bley he led his first group at the Chalet Hotel 1945–8 and followed Oscar *Peterson at the Alberta Lounge in 1949. While he was studying composition and conducting at the Juilliard School 1950–3, he occasionally performed in New York nightclubs with such leading jazzmen as Charlie Parker, Sonny Rollins, and Ben Webster. On a 1953 return visit to Montreal he founded the short-lived Montreal Jazz Workshop with the pianist Keith White, presenting and accompanying Parker on CBC TV and Rollins and other New York jazzmen at the Chez Paree and the Cavendish Cafe. After 1953 Bley worked with his own groups in New York, touring briefly in 1955 with the trumpeter Chet Baker before moving in 1957 to Los Angeles. There he met the composer-pianist Carla Borg (later Carla Bley) and eventually formed a quintet which included the then-unknown saxophonist Ornette Coleman. On Bley's return to New York in 1959 the remaining quartet, under Coleman's leadership, became the saxophonist's first influential band.

In 1959 Bley's collaboration in New York with pianist Bill Evans for the recording of George Russell's *Jazz in the Space Age* preceded five years as a sideman with Charles Mingus, Jimmy Giuffre, Don Ellis, and Rollins. His time with Rollins included a 1964 Japanese tour. A central figure in the 1964 'October Revolution' of avant-garde jazz in New York, Bley became a charter member (1964–5) of the resulting Jazz Composers' Guild. Thereafter he performed, exclusively with his own groups, to particular acclaim in Europe, as a concert and recording artist. He formed a number of influential trios and, after taking up the synthesizer and electric piano in 1968, joined the composer-vocalist-keyboardist Annette Peacock in the Bley-Peacock Synthesizer Show 1969–73. He has appeared with his quartet Scorpio 1972–5, with the New Jazz Piano Quartet (Paris 1975), and on a 1976 Japanese tour, again with a trio. He also has performed extensively as a solo pianist. In 1975 he formed the New York-based record company Improvising Artists Incorporated (IAI). Although internationally respected, Bley has appeared only occasionally in Montreal after the early 1960s, and has been generally unrecognized in Canada, although he gave solo concerts in Ottawa (1978) and Toronto (1979).

Bley moved easily and precociously in bebop circles, serving an 'apprenticeship' 1950–3 in New York and Montreal with Parker, Rollins, and others. Under Coleman's influence he was drawn away from song-form composition structures and initiated by Giuffre into collective improvisation; by the mid-1960s Bley developed a reflective, romantic, and emotionally impulsive jazz style. Jon Balleras has described him in *Down Beat* (23 Oct 1975): 'He thinks in melodic shapes and rhythmic thrusts, rather than key signatures, meters and conventional harmonic cadences ... Time is implicit ... Tonality is implied only. Music as process, flux, momentum.' Bley has been an acknowledged influence on Chick Corea and an attributed influence on several other young jazz pianists, including Keith Jarrett. Performing his own epigrammatic compositions (over 25 recorded) and those of Carla Bley, Coleman, and Peacock, a repertoire which has survived his pioneering experiments in electronically modulated sound in improvisation, Bley has developed a highly personal body of work, unique in contemporary music.

DISCOGRAPHY

Introducing Paul Bley. 1953. Debut DLP-7

Paul Bley. 1954. Wing MGW 60001

Solemn Meditation. 1957. GNP Crescendo GNPS 31

The Fabulous Paul Bley Quintet. 1958 (1976). Inner City IC 1007

Footloose. 1962; 1963. Savoy MG 12182/BYG 529.114

With Gary Peacock. 1963; 1968. ECM 1003

Barrage. 1964. ESP Disk' 1008

Turning Point. 1964, 1968 (1976). IAI 373841

Closer. 1965. ESP Disk' 1021

Copenhagen and Haarlem. (1975). 2-Arista Freedom 1901 (reissue of *Touching*, 1965, Fontana S 688.60ZL; and *Blood, Paul Bley in Haarlem*, 1966, Poly S 623258)

Ramblin'. 1966. BYG S 529.313

Blood. 1966. Fontana S 883.911CY

Virtuosi. 1967 (1976). IAI 373844

Ballads. 1967. ECM 1010

Mr. Joy. 1968. Limelight SLS-86060/Trip TLP 5587

Paul Bley Trio. 1968. RCI 305

Bley-Peacock Synthesizer Show: Revenge: The Bigger the Love, the Greater the Hate. 1969. Poly 2425.043

Improvisie. 1970. America 30 AM 6121

Dual Unity. 1970, 1971. Freedom SFLP 40 109

The Paul Bley Synthesizer Show. 1970, 1971. Milestone MSP 9033

Open, to Love. 1972. ECM 1023

Scorpio. 1972. Milestone MSP 9046

Paul Bley NHØP. 1973. Steeplechase SCS 1005

Alone Again. 1974. IAI 373840

Pastorius/Metheny/Ditmas/Bley. 1974. IAI 373846

Quiet Song. (1976). IAI 373839

Japan Suite. 1976. IAI 373849

Axis. 1977. IAI 373853

Bley's earliest recordings (1952) for the Silver and Stinson companies in Montreal and New York respectively were not released.

WITH OTHERS

Parker *On the Road*. 1953 (1975). Jazz Showcase 5003

Russell *Jazz in the Space Age*. 1959. 2-MCA 4017

Mingus *Revisited*. 1960. Mer 60627

– *Mingus*. 1960. Candid 9021

Giuffre *Fusion*. 1961. Verve 6839

– *Thesis*. 1961. Verve 68402

– *Free Fall*. 1962. Col CS 8764

Ellis *Essence*. 1962. Pacific Jazz S-55

Rollins *Sonny Meets Hawk*. 1963. 2-RCA Victor (France) 741074/5

Jazz Composer's Orchestra *Communication*. 1964, 1965. Fontana S 881.011ZY

Peacock *I'm the One*. 1971. RCA LSP 4578

Marion Brown *Sweet Earth Flying*. 1974. Impulse 9275

A detailed discography prepared by Ib Skovgaard Petersen and Laurent Goddet appears in the Apr–May 1979 issue of *Coda*.

BIBLIOGRAPHY

Heckman, Don. 'Paul Bley,' *Down Beat*, vol 31, 12 Mar 1964

Dobbin, Len. 'Paul Bley,' *Coda*, vol 7, Jun–Jul 1965

Merceron, G. 'Pudique Bley,' *Jazz Hot*, 219, Apr 1966

Knox, Keith. 'Paul Bley,' *Jazz Monthly*, vol 12, Dec 1966

Cuscuna, Michael. 'Paul Bley: being together,' *Down Beat*, vol 35, 7 Oct 1968

Goddet, Laurent. 'Un canadien bien tranquille,' *Jazz Hot*, 276, Oct 1971

Klee, Joe and Smith, Will. 'Focus on Paul Bley,' *Down Beat*, vol 41, 17 Jan 1974

Duluth, Alex. 'Paul Bley: Lecture d'une photographie,' *Jazz Hot*, 334, Feb 1977

– 'Interrogation,' *Jazz Hot*, 335, Mar 1977

Lyons, Len. 'Paul Bley improvising artist,' *Contemporary Keyboard*, vol 3, May 1977

Smith, Bill. 'Paul Bley,' *Coda*, 166, Apr–May 1979

MM

BLIGH, Stanley (Arthur). Critic, b Luton, England, 9 Sep 1883, d Harpenden, England, 11 Nov 1975. Bligh was raised in Yorkshire, where he served as organist-choirmaster in his local parish; he moved in 1911 to Taber, near Lethbridge, Alta, then in 1922 to Winnipeg, and finally in 1924 to Vancouver. In 1934 he joined the staff of the Vancouver *Sun* and included music criticism among his duties. Although he retired in 1961, he continued to write occasional pieces for the *Sun* until he returned to England in 1971. One of his great loves was choral music, and he conducted ensembles in Vancouver until the early 1950s. In 1936 he co-produced *A Midsummer Night's Dream* with E.V. Young at the outdoor Brockton Oval, and later he conducted a full orchestra and 200-voice choir in Coleridge-Taylor's *Hiawatha* at the same location. These events set a precedent for *TUTS. Through his writings he encouraged young musicians, urged impresarios to bring in first-rate performers, and campaigned for the construction of suitable concert halls.

BNSG

BLIGHT, Arthur (Howard). Baritone, teacher, b Keokuk, Ia, 1874, d Toronto 2 Sep 1928. He arrived in Canada as a child and lived in Orono, near Bowmanville, Ont. He studied music in Toronto, concentrating on voice, and became director of vocal studies at the Toronto Junction College of Music in 1900. In 1904 he took further voice lessons with William Shakespeare in England. Returning to Toronto in 1905 he served as soloist at a succession of churches and was the baritone in the North American premiere of Max Bruch's cantata *The Cross of Fire*, 21 Nov 1907, with the Festival Chorus at *Massey Hall. The Blight Male Quartette (Joseph Twigg and J. Elcho Fiddes, tenors; Blight, baritone; James R. Milne, bass) was active during the first years of the new century. During the second decade Blight became music director at the Ontario Ladies' College, Whitby, and was a member 1915–19 of the *Adanac Quartet. He taught 1919–22 at the *TCM, though with a leave of absence in 1921 to study in Italy. Among his pupils were Lady Eaton, Anne Jamison, Grace McKenzie, Mabel Palen, Clara Stiles, and the tenors Ernest Bushnell and Lawrence Dafoe. Blight introduced the Ernest *Seitz-Gene Lockhart song *'The World Is Waiting for the Sunrise' at a Massey Hall concert in September 1922. Though reluctant to record as a soloist, he did so for Edison and Victor. He was music director for the Toronto radio station CKNC in the last few years of his life. (EBM)

The blind. Though a blind person is not by definition either more or less talented in music than one who can see, his condition causes greater reliance on his hearing, which, in response, may grow more acute or more perceptive than that of a similarly talented person with sight. For a blind person music has traditionally been considered an ideal activity, whether pastime or profession, performance or trade (eg, piano tuning). Popular music and folk music, which can be assimilated by ear, are perhaps the genres most easily mastered by blind musicians. However, Braille notation, which can be used for reading and memorizing, has made it easier for the blind to enter the concert field – though orchestral playing, which demands constant sight-reading, remains impractical. Of the approximately 32,000 blind Canadians living in 1980, only a small number were blind from birth.

The Canadian National Institute for the Blind (CNIB) / Institut national canadien pour les aveugles, the country's chief agency working on behalf of the visually handicapped, was incorporated in 1918, with headquarters in Toronto, as an administrative, co-ordinative, and educational organization. In 1939 it appointed a research committee to consider the needs of blind musicians and piano tuners in Canada. The committee's findings resulted in the creation of a separate CNIB music department; in 1946 the committee itself was established permanently as the National Advisory Committee on Music to the CNIB. With assistance from this body the music department has run a music library; set training standards for musicians, teachers, and piano tuners; organized conferences for music teachers and musicians every five years and for piano tuners and technicians every three years; and employed a music consultant.

The CNIB's National Music Library has printed and maintained a *Catalogue of Braille Music* to assist blind musicians in selection. Its music transcription service – which has made available Braille transcriptions for instruments and for small choirs and orchestras – began as an independent program for blind musicians in Quebec and was taken over by the CNIB in 1943. With the

A poster announcing a concert by blind performers in Montreal

encouragement of the Quebec Braille Music Society (established in 1949) the CNIB extended the service to other parts of the country and in 1955 it became known as the National Braille Music Transcription Service of the CNIB. Its office has remained in Montreal, which has come to be considered the centre of activity for blind musicians in Canada. Braille transcriptions of popular music have been made readily available, and musicians who have subscribed to the service have received automatically all 'hit parade' numbers in Braille as soon as printed copies reach the market.

In the course of duties the national music consultant for the CNIB has carried out much of the organizational work of the advisory committee on music and provided counselling to musicians, arranged concerts and workshops, and acted as secretary to the committee. The consultant also has served as researcher and editor for the CNIB's quarterly publication, *Mouthpiece*, which has provided information for those interested in music and the blind. With a circulation of 1500 in 1980, this journal continued to be published in both inkprint and Braille. Ernest Whitfield, secretary of the music committee 1942–6, was succeeded by Edith Dymond Simpson, national music consultant 1946–67, and Simpson was succeeded by William M. Vaisey.

Another organization which has worked for the blind is the Montreal Assn for the Blind, incorporated in 1910. It began in 1908 as a body founded on the individual initiative of Philip E. Layton (d 1939), a blind organist, composer (his *Dominion March*, 1898, was dedicated to Lord Strathcona), piano tuner, and piano dealer, whose Peel St firm, Layton Bros, flourished in Montreal in the late 1880s and has survived as a high-fidelity record equipment business. The association's aim was to advance the social and economic welfare of the blind.

A number of residential schools for the blind have established music curricula which include classes in ear-training, rhythmic development, sight-singing, instrument identification, music history, and choral singing, and instruction in voice and instruments. Some also have provided facilities for studies in piano tuning and technology. Sighted as well as blind musicians have been trained at such schools. In chronological order of establishment Canadian residential schools have included Montreal's *Institut Nazareth, which was founded in 1861 and established a music department in 1876; the Halifax School for the Blind, which began in 1863 (or 1871?); the W. Ross Macdonald School in *Brantford, Ont, founded in 1871 as the Ontario School for the Blind (Frederic *Lord was music director 1923–45); the school of the Montreal Assn for the Blind, opened in 1912; the British Columbia School for the Blind, founded in Vancouver in 1915; and the Institut Louis-Braille, founded in Montreal in 1952, with piano-tuning classes and apprenticeship workshops established by Raphaël Brilotti in 1954. The last-named amalgamated with the Institut Nazareth in 1975, continuing thenceforth as the Institut Nazareth et Louis-Braille.

Blind or visually handicapped persons in the concert music field in Canada have included Ann *Burrows, Édouard *Clarke, Hervé Cloutier, Gabriel *Cusson, Paul *Doyon, Pierre *Gautier, Antonin *Kubálek, Alfred *Lamoureux, Conrad *Letendre, Paul *Letondal, Auguste *Liessens, Charles William *Lindsay, Mary *Munn, Antoine *Reboulot, Denis *Regnaud, and Jeannine *Vanier. Among those in the pop music field are Gilles Losier (fiddler and pianist with Jean *Carignan), Fred *McKenna, and the pianist Joel Shulman. Nicole Trudeau, a contributor to *EMC*, is blind. Armand Pellerin – b Ste-Sophie-d'Halifax, near Sherbrooke, Que, 1 Nov 1899, d Montreal 6 Aug 1961, B MUS (Montreal) 1921 – who lost his sight at the age of two, was organist at several Montreal churches, taught at the Institut Nazareth, and was librarian 1951–61 for the CNIB in Montreal. Eugénie Tessier (soprano, pianist, b Montreal 1872, d ?) a pupil of Rosalie Euvrard and Paul Letondal at the Institut Nazareth, had a successful concert career in Canada and the USA.

There appears to have been a markedly higher number of blind musicians of French-Canadian origin, a fact which may be attributed to the music training available at the Quebec schools for the blind.

BIBLIOGRAPHY

Johnson, Robin. 'Music and the blind child,' *Recorder*, vol 14, Dec 1971

Larose, Jacques. 'L'enseignement de la musique aux déficients visuels,' unpubl L MUS thesis, U of Montreal 1973

Vaisey, William. 'Notes,' *Music*, Nov–Dec 1978

Roberge, Huquette. 'À 78 ans, le roi des accordeurs de pianos du Québec, accroche sa clé d'accordage,' Montreal *La Presse*, 6 Dec 1980 (WV)

BLOMFIELD HOLT, Patricia (b Blomfield, m Holt). Composer, teacher, pianist, b Lindsay, Ont, 15 Sep 1910. She studied and taught concurrently 1929–39 at the *TCM, where her teachers included Norman *Wilks, Hayunga *Carman, Norah *de Kresz, and Healey *Willan, and rejoined the staff in 1954 to teach piano, composition, theory, and history. Her compositions, mainly for small ensembles, include *Two Lyric Pieces for Cello* (1937, 1938), *String Quartet* (1937), *Suite No. 1* for violin and piano (1936; winner of the 1938 *Vogt Society award for the best Canadian composition), and *Suite No. 2* for violin or viola and piano (1939, BMI Canada 1952). Her *Songs of My Country* (1950) for baritone, string orchestra, harp, and french horn are based on three poems, Duncan Campbell Scott's 'The Winter Lakes,' Susannah Moodie's 'The Canadian Herd Boy,' and Marjorie Pickthall's 'Quiet.' Harris published 'Quiet' in 1966. Her *Three Songs of Contemplation* (Berandol 1970) use texts by E.J. Pratt, Marcus *Adeney, and Amy Lowell. Her works have been performed widely in Europe, the Soviet Union, the USA, and

Canada. Of her *Suite No 2* London's *Musical Times* stated: 'the language is frankly of the 19th century, and the forms are reminiscent of Schumann, but the material is handled with certainty and a nice sense of texture' (Aug 1953). She is an affiliate of PRO Canada. (MWM)

BLONDAHL, Omar. Folksinger, b Wynyard, east of Saskatoon, of Icelandic parents, 6 Feb 1923. He studied piano and violin as a child and voice later in Winnipeg. After singing country music in Edmonton on radio and in California (sometimes using the name 'Sagebrush Sam'), he moved in 1955 to Newfoundland. There he developed a repertoire of local folk songs, some of which he had collected himself. Adopting a Newfoundland accent and performing in a refreshingly simple manner (though employing a non-traditional style of guitar accompaniment), Blondahl preferred to sing for local rather than national audiences. However his radio and TV appearances helped popularize Newfoundland songs throughout Canada. He made eight LPs 1955–67 of Newfoundland songs and other material for the Rodeo, Arc, and Melbourne labels (see Michael Taft's *A Regional Discography of Newfoundland and Labrador 1904–1972*, St John's 1975). He also edited *Newfoundlanders Sing!: A Collection of Favourite Newfoundland Folk Songs* (St John's 1964).

See also Folk Music, Anglo-Canadian: 1 / Newfoundland. (RGn)

'The Blooming Bright Star of Belle Isle.' Newfoundland adaptation of an old Irish love song, 'Loch Erin's Sweet Riverside.' It tells the familiar story of a lover who returns after a long absence and tests his sweetheart's fidelity before revealing himself. The fine Mixolydian tune has been used as well for another Newfoundland love song, 'The Green Shores of Fogo.' First published in Greenleaf and Mansfield's *Ballads and Sea Songs of Newfoundland* (Cambridge, Mass, 1933), 'The Blooming Bright Star of Belle Isle' is also included in *The Penguin Book of Canadian Folk Songs* (London 1973) by Edith *Fowke and has been recorded by Waterloo (*Folk Songs of Canada*, Wat CS3). EF

'The Blue and White.' In the fall of 1908 the *U of Toronto student newspaper *Varsity* proclaimed the need for a new college song to succeed H.H. *Godfrey's 'Pride of the North.' In response Clayton Bush, an engineering student and leader of a male chorus that sang at rugby games, wrote 'The Blue and White' to words by a University College student, C.E. Silcox. J.D.A. *Tripp arranged the music. The song was sung first 11 Feb 1909 and was made popular through performances at sports events by the *48th Highlanders Band under Captain John *Slatter.

See also College songs.

BIBLIOGRAPHY

'He wrote "The Blue and White",' *Varsity Graduate*, Spring 1962

Montagnes, Ian. 'Silcox, Bush and dignity of spirit,' *The Graduate*, vol 8, Sep–Oct 1980

'Bluebird on Your Windowsill.' Popular song by the Vancouver nurse (Carmen) Elizabeth Clarke (b Winnipeg 1911, d Vancouver 1960). The words (1947) were inspired by a small bird which perched on a windowsill of Vancouver's Hospital for Sick and Crippled Children. The melody was added later. The *Rhythm Pals, who introduced the song on radio station CKNW, New Westminster, made an unsubstantiated claim that they contributed something to the final version. The song was published in 1948 by *Empire Music and recorded first by Don Murphy for Aragon. Many other country artists recorded the song, and versions in 1949 by Doris Day and Tex Williams were hits in the US pop and country markets respectively. Clarke turned over all royalties to children's hospitals in Canada. The song was chosen as the theme for the 1949 US March of Dimes.

Blues. Afro-American folk/pop music with a vocal and instrumental tradition; also a song form. Though by origin and nature a folk music, the blues have enjoyed wider popularity dating from the advent of commercial recording. 'Race records,' as 78s made in the 1920s and 1930s by blues singers were known, were among the earliest pop records. The basic elements of blues have remained constant – the tonic, sub-dominant, dominant-seventh, tonic harmonic structure; the preponderance of 'blue notes' (flattened thirds and sevenths); and the highly emotional content of the music, predominantly a personal expression of the grievances and frustrations of US blacks in terms ranging from despair to humorous irony. Performance styles, however, have undergone significant change with the migration of segments of the black population within the USA. Two distinct styles resulted, and both survived in the 1970s: the earlier, country (one or two musicians accompanying themselves on acoustic instruments), and the later – after World War II – urban (usually a small band employing amplified instruments). There also are many sub-styles defined in most cases geographically, eg, Mississippi blues, Chicago blues. Further refinement in performance style led in the 1950s to rhythm and blues, which has enjoyed greater popularity than either traditional blues style.

Many US blues musicians have appeared in Canada, the country musicians generally in coffee houses or at folk festivals, and the urban musicians (usually from Detroit or Chicago) at nightclubs which otherwise present jazz or rock. Many of the music's most important figures appeared in a 90-minute CBC program, 'The Blues,' telecast 28 Dec 1966 on 'Festival.' Few resident Canadian blues performers have been black. Among these are the legendary US singer-guitarist Lonnie *Johnson, who spent his last years in Toronto, and the singer-pianist-guitarist Jackie Washington (b Hamilton, Ont, 12 Nov 1919), who enjoyed particular popularity in the 1970s, making the LP *Blues and Sentimental* (K 2001) and appearing at folk festivals and in nightclubs. Some black folk performers (eg, Al Cromwell, b Finny's Cove, NS, and active in Toronto's Yorkville district in the 1960s and 1970s) and jazz singers (eg, Eleanor *Collins, Phyllis *Marshall, and the US-born singers Jodie Drake and Clarence 'Big' Miller) have made blues a part of a larger repertoire.

The growth in popularity of blues among Canadian performers – almost all young (born in the 1940s or 1950s) and white – coincided with the rise ca 1965 of such British bands as the Rolling Stones, the Animals, and the Yardbirds, which had considerable success with recordings copying classic US blues performances. Initially Canadian bands followed the example of the British groups; the Ugly Ducklings, for example, took the Rolling Stones as their model. Later bands, however, turned to the original musicians – usually of the urban school – for their influence. Bands and musicians active in Canada during this period (mid-1960s through the 1970s) and devoted exclusively or in large measure to blues, include Dutch Mason of Halifax; Minglewood of Cape Breton; the Stephen Barry and Albert Failey blues bands, *Offenbach, *Ville Émard, and West End, all of Montreal; Heaven's Radio of Ottawa; *Crowbar, *Downchild, Lick 'n' Stick with Paul James, Luke (Gibson) and the Apostles, the *King Biscuit Boy, (Michael) McKenna (Joe) Mendelson Mainline, Whisky Howl, and David Wilcox, all of Toronto; Houndog of Winnipeg; Hot Cottage of Edmonton; and the Black Snake Blues Band, the Al Foreman-Jim Byrne Band, the Powder Blues Band, and Hans Staymer, all of Vancouver. (See also Guitar; Harmonica.)

Only a few blues songs of note have been composed by Canadian musicians. Two by Don Walsh of Downchild – 'I Got Everything I Need (Almost)' and 'Shotgun Blues' – were recorded by the Blues Brothers ('Jake and Elwood Blues,' of whom 'Elwood' was Dan Ackroyd of Toronto) for the million-selling LP *Briefcase Full of Blues* (1978, Atlantic KSD-19217). Moe *Koffman's **Swinging Shepherd Blues* is a blues in form only.

Rhythm and blues (R and B, also known as soul or funk) was popular in Canada during the 1960s. Among several other nightclubs, the Blue Note was the centre of R and B in Toronto; the music itself was played in that city by such local (and often racially mixed) bands as Diane Brooks and Jack Hardin and the Silhouettes, Brooks and Eric Mercury and the Soul Searchers, Shawne and Jay Jackson and the Majestics, Jon and Lee and the Checkmates, *Mandala, and groups led by George Olliver and Grant Smith. Montreal musicians such as Trevor Payne, Walter *Rossi, and the Soul Mates specialized in R and B, and the Vancouver group Bobby Taylor and the Vancouvers had an international hit in 1968 with the single 'Does Your Mama Know About Me?,' released by the Motown (Detroit) label Gordy. In the 1970s R and B (by then known as funk, exhibiting only superficial changes in style) was performed in Canada by such bands as Crack of Dawn and Sweet Blindness and by the singers Shawne Jackson and the Mighty Pope. The late 1970s saw the influence of reggae and disco music draw R and B further from its blues roots.

Among Canadian R and B musicians, Mercury, R. Dean Taylor, and Rick James (b Buffalo, NY) have had success with careers in the USA in the 1970s, Taylor as a singer-songwriter and producer with Motown and its 'white' label, Rare Earth (for which his 'Indiana Wants Me' was a major hit in 1970), and James as a writer and producer for Motown and as leader of the Stone City Band, whose single 'You and I' and LP *Come Get It!* (Gordy 7-981) were hits in North America in 1978. MM

BLUME, Helmut. Pianist, broadcaster, administrator, educator, b Berlin 12 Apr 1914, naturalized Canadian 1945. He studied 1932–3 at the U of Berlin, with Hindemith at the Hochschule für Musik, Berlin, and in England with Louis Kentner. He moved to Canada in 1940, and in 1942, while continuing his studies with Alberto *Guerrero at the TCM, he was appointed head of the piano department of the *Hambourg Cons. During this period he gave radio and public recitals. He was associated 1944–6 with the German section of CBC IS in Montreal, first as editor-broadcaster, then as head. Subsequently he became music consultant to CBC IS and produced many music programs, including the radio series 'International Concert' 1953–62. He prepared various programs for 'CBC Wednesday Night' in the late 1950s, including those on Haydn, Berlioz, and Mahler, and performed and commented in the six radio lectures entitled 'Form in Music' (1959, published in 1960 by CBC Toronto as a two-record album). Some of his other radio programs were 'Opera Stars and Stories,' 'Music and the Church,' and 'The Musical Mind.' In 1958 the CBC won an Ohio State U award for Blume's eight-lecture TV series 'Music to See' (1957).

Helmut Blume

In the late 1950s Blume was associated with Edith *Fowke and Alan *Mills in the preparation of *Canada's Story in Song* (Gage 1960). He was supervising editor of *Thirty-Four Biographies of Canadian Composers*. He joined the Faculty of Music at *McGill U as an instructor in 1946 and became dean in 1964. In 1955, while chairman of the department of keyboard and vocal music, he opened the opera workshop. During his tenure as dean he initiated changes in course structure and established an electronic studio under the direction of Istvan *Anhalt. Plans for the Pollack Concert Hall in McGill's Strathcona Music Building were completed during Blume's deanship. He was co-founder in 1964 of *CAUSM, and in 1976, the year of his retirement from McGill U, he began a study of music training in Canada for the *Canada Council. The study was published in 1978 as *A National Music School for Canada*.

To a rare degree Blume has combined skills as musician, administrator, scholar, and public personality. Through the media he has reached the population at large, and through his work as a teacher and administrator he has affected the lives of a generation of McGill graduates.

BIBLIOGRAPHY

'Helmut Blume – professor emeritus,' *Music McGill*, 6, Autumn 1979 (NT)

BMI Canada Ltd. See P.R.O. Canada Ltd.

BODLE, (George Talbot) Douglas. Organist, harpsichordist, pianist, b Winnipeg 7 Aug 1923; LRSM piano 1946, ACCO 1951, AAGO 1957. His teachers included Bernard *Naylor (general music studies), Gwendda Owen *Davies (piano), Greta *Kraus (harpsichord), and Hugh *Bancroft (organ). He served 1963–6 as organist-choirmaster at St Andrew's Presbyterian Church, Toronto, resuming duties there in 1969 and becoming organist-choirmaster also at Holy Blossom Temple that year. He commissioned the composition of Walter *Buczynski's *Mass with Outside Prayers* (1976).

Bodle has given organ and harpsichord recitals in major cities in Canada and eastern USA. As a soloist and a member of the St Andrew's Consort he has performed often on CBC radio, his engagements including a performance 15 Feb 1959 of Bach's *Concerto for Two Harpsichords* with Greta Kraus and the *CBC SO. He has accompanied many solo performers (eg, the baritone Aksel *Schiøtz in 1959; the flutist Suzanne *Shulman in 1979) during more than 30 years in that branch of the profession. He has accompanied the *Toronto Mendelssohn Choir and the *Festival Singers, has performed in chamber works with the *York Winds, and has been orchestral pianist with the CBC SO and the *TS.

He has had a notable career as a teacher, beginning in 1959 at the *RCMT, continuing 1966–8 at the school of music, *U of Manitoba (during which time he also toured in Ontario, British Columbia, and California as a member of the *Manitoba University Consort), and joining the Faculty of Music at the *U of Toronto in 1969 as a teacher of piano, harpsichord, and organ. Among those who have studied with Bodle in Winnipeg and Toronto are John Derksen, Donald *Hadfield, and Peter McCoppin (organ), Audrey *Cooke Belyea, John Kruspe, and R. Murray *Schafer (piano), and numerous singers whom he has coached and taught piano. After an organ recital at St James' Cathedral in Toronto John Fraser described Bodle's technique as admirable and his style as 'impeccably sharp and clean' (Toronto *Globe and Mail*, 13 Mar 1974). (DS)

BOGISCH, Bernardus G., 'Ben.' Bandmaster, composer, teacher, b The Hague 2 Nov 1932; ARCM 1965, LTCL 1965, Associate LCM 1965. He emigrated to Canada in 1953 and joined the Canadian armed forces. As a clarinetist with the Royal Canadian Artillery Band he travelled extensively in Europe and Korea, and as a pianist he toured 1956–9 in Europe with a gypsy ensemble. Returning to Canada, he served 1959–62 with the *Princess Patricia's Canadian Light Infantry Band in Edmonton. After taking courses in band conducting 1962–5 in England at the RMSM (Kneller Hall) he was briefly (1965) music director of the Royal Canadian Dragoons Band in Gagetown, NB. Later that year he was appointed musical training officer at the *Canadian Forces School of Music in Victoria, BC. In 1970 he became music director for the Naden Band, Victoria, which he led in hundreds of concerts at home and abroad. In 1975 he was posted to the Canadian Forces Stadacona Band in Halifax, NS. A major in the Canadian armed forces, Bogisch has composed pieces for band, including the overture *Chebucto* (1968) and *Huronian Episode* (1971), both published by Boosey & Hawkes. He is a member of CAPAC. (JK)

BOHNER, Charles. Composer, arranger, teacher, fl Toronto 1882–98. Bohner, who is known to have had a music studio on Yonge St, wrote songs and piano pieces, of which the earliest extant, *Aesthetic Valse* and *Claxton's Grand March* (1882, both for piano), were published by T. *Claxton. Other piano pieces included an arrangement of Chas. K. Harris' popular song 'After the Ball' (1893) and various waltzes and polkas published by *Whaley Royce, *Suckling, and *Williams. He collaborated with several lyricists, including the popular singer James ('Jimmie') Fax, on many songs published by Whaley Royce. The same publisher issued several of Bohner's 'Canadian' pieces – 'Sounds of Toronto' (1890), *Sir John Macdonald's Funeral March* (1891), *The Osgoode* (1894) – and his compilation of non-Canadian popular music, *The Elite Song Folio* (nd).

BOHRER. Family of musicians originally of Mannheim. The third generation included Max (1785–1867), in his day one of the foremost cellists in Europe. He visited Quebec City in 1843. The fourth generation included Max's sons 1 / Henri and 2 / William, both of whom emigrated to Canada. William's son 3 / Max was born in Canada.

1 **Henri** (b Heinrich). Pianist, teacher, b Paris 1829; d Victoria, BC, 1889. He was a pupil of Ignaz Moscheles and Peter Joseph von Lindpaintner and settled in Montreal in 1877 as a music teacher. His performance that year of Bach's *Chromatic Fantasy and Fugue* possibly was the work's premiere in Montreal. About 10 years later he moved to Victoria. His wife Josephine, née Chatterton, was the daughter of a noted British harpist and a harpist herself. After Henri's death she established a music school in Chicago.

2 **William** (b Wilhelm). Pianist, teacher, b Stuttgart, 1830s, d Montreal ca 1908. He studied in Stuttgart under Siegmund Lebert and Dionys Pruckner and in Vienna under J.A. Pacher and Simon Sechter. Active in Montreal and Ottawa after 1860, he taught piano, voice, and theory. Montreal directories of the mid-1870s describe him as the manufacturer of an automatic hand guide for pianists. After a sojourn in London 1878–82, William returned to Canada to become the founder and only principal of the Montreal School of Music (ca 1886–ca 1899) and eventually the bursar of the *Dominion College of Music. His compositions include a waltz, *Fabiola* (Laurent, La Force 1867; dedicated to Mme George-Étienne Cartier), and *Souvenir de Montréal* (Novello nd), both for piano. Among his pupils were his son Max and Caroline *Racicot.

3 **Max** (Alfred Edward Maximilian). Pianist, teacher, b Montreal 25 Feb 1860, d there 24 Apr 1942. He was taught by his father and was auditioned by Anton Rubinstein during the latter's visit to Montreal in 1873. A music teacher in Montreal for some 57 years, Max was vice-principal of the Montreal School of Music and succeeded his father, ca 1908, as bursar of the Dominion College of Music, a position he still held at the outbreak of World War II. His playing was noted for a singing quality, said to have been a characteristic of his father's playing as well. His pupils included J.-Adélard Brunet. He willed his extensive piano-music collection of nearly 1300 volumes to the Fraser (later Fraser-Hickson) Institute of Montreal.

BIBLIOGRAPHY

MGG, vol 15 HK

Boîtes à chansons. Name given to the intimate rooms which sprang up in the mid-1950s outside the normal entertainment circuits and in which most young Quebec chansonniers made their start. Usually seating 50 to 100 on uncomfortable chairs, these smoke-filled rooms were casually decorated, often with fishing nets. Coffee and occasionally beer – rarely liquor – were served on rickety tables which were bare or sometimes covered with checkered cloths. The audience generally was made up of students, and despite the surroundings great enthusiasm was generated. In these intimate rooms young singer-songwriters such as Pierre Calvé, Claude *Gauthier, Sylvain Lelièvre, Pierre Létourneau, Raymond *Lévesque, and Monique *Miville-Deschênes were discovered.

Several people claim to have opened the first boîte à chansons. Some consider nightclub owner François Pilon the probable inventor of the term. In the early 1950s he opened a boîte à chansons beside the Café St-Jacques in Montreal. In 1959 six young chansonniers (Les Bozos) founded the boîte Chez Bozo, and its success prompted Gilles Mathieu to open one in Val-David in the Laurentians. La Butte à Mathieu provided several young artists with an opportunity to try out and gave chansonniers like Raymond Lévesque the chance to perform regularly. In Quebec City, Renée *Claude drew her first audiences in 1960 at the room which actually bore the name Boîte à chansons, and Gilles *Vigneault sang his first song for the patrons of L'Arlequin. These first clubs spawned a movement that spread over the entire province. Their proliferation represented an artistic, cultural, and social phenomenon. Boîtes closed regularly only to be replaced immediately by others; most had only brief existences. Claude *Léveillée opened at least 50, including Le Chat noir in Montreal. Other chansonniers who became owners of boîtes are Tex *Lecor (La Poubelle) and Raymond Lévesque (Le P'tit caporal) in Montreal, as well as Raoul *Roy (Le Pirate) at St-Fabien-sur-Mer. Félix *Leclerc, who had introduced the idea of performing his songs alone on stage accompanied by guitar or piano, also sang in boîtes à chansons.

In its original form the phenomenon gradually lost momentum and for all practical purposes petered out in 1967. Once they became stars, the chansonniers needed larger halls and more complex sound equipment. Yet it was towards the end of the boîtes à chansons era that Le *Patriote began operating in Montreal's east end. Larger than most, this boîte in 1980 continued to feature the big names of Quebec song, both early chansonniers and newcomers. However, it had not preserved the charm and intimacy of the earlier clubs.

Over the years the raison d'être of the boîtes has been broadened. Jazz ensembles, folk groups, singer-instrumentalists, and others, as well as the originating singer-songwriters, may be heard in them. In 1980 there were numerous boîtes à chansons, cafés chantants, and venues of the newer type in Quebec. The following, with seating capacities of between 50 and 300, are representative: L'Évêché and L'Imprévu (Montreal); Le Créneau, Le Gaulois, and L'Ostradamus (Quebec City); Le Café Virgule (Sherbrooke); Le Théâtre de l'Île (Hull); Le Chat gris (Eastman); La Lucarne (Rimouski); Le Café Carcajou (Baie-Comeau); Le Mouton noir (Baie St-Paul); and L'Épave (Cap-aux-Meules). Most Cegeps and universities have similar places. The coffeehouse in English Canada is to some extent the counterpart of the boîte à chansons. See Coffeehouses.

BIBLIOGRAPHY
Beaulieu, Pierre. 'Le renouveau des boîtes à chansons,' Montreal *La Presse*, 23 Dec 1978
Guide du spectacle et du disque (MACQ 1978) (BLH)

BOKY, Colette (Marie-Rose Élisabeth) (b Giroux). Soprano, b Montreal 4 Jun 1935; premier prix voice (CMM) 1962. In 1953 Jean *Deslauriers heard her at an amateur competition and advised her to study voice, which she did 1953–5 at l'*École Vincent-d'Indy, and later privately with Laurette Bailly. She won first prize in a 1958 competition organized by the Montreal radio station CKVL, then studied in the summer of 1959 at the *RCMT opera workshop and 1959–62 at the *CMM with Raoul *Jobin, Roy *Royal, Otto-Werner *Mueller, Dick Marzollo, and Rémus *Tzincoca. In May 1961 she made her stage debut in Chicoutimi, Que, as Rosina in a *Théâtre lyrique de Nouvelle-France production of *The Barber of Seville*. She sang the title role in *Lakmé* in Quebec City with the same company the following year. After winning the 1962 *Prix d'Europe she continued her studies in Paris with Janine Micheau and Jobin, and the same year won second prize and a medal at the Geneva International Competition for musical performers. She made her European debut in 1964 in Haydn's *L'Apothicaire*, performed first in Versailles and then at the Théâtre de France in Paris.

At the Bremen Opera 1964–5 Boky sang Despina in *Così fan tutte* and the title role in Stravinsky's *Le Rossignol*. In 1965 she was Sandrina in

Colette Boky as Adèle in *Le Comte Ory*

Mozart's *La Finta giardiniera* at the Salzburg Festival and took the leading soprano role in Rossini's *La Scala di seta* at the Munich Festival (the latter production repeated at the Schwetzingen festival). In the same year she sang Frau Fluth in a film version of Nicolai's *The Merry Wives of Windsor* and the leading soprano role in Gounod's *Le Médecin malgré lui*, directed by Jean-Pierre Ponnelle at the Cuvilliés Theatre in Munich. She also was a soloist in orchestral concerts on Bavarian Radio.

In 1966 Boky sang several roles with the Volksoper in Vienna and appeared in Carl Orff's *Carmina burana* with the Vienna Philharmonic Orchestra. She also appeared that year in Haydn's *The Creation*, with the Munich Bach Choir and Orchestra under Karl Richter (performing not only in Munich but also, on tour, in Montreal and New York), and in the title role in Offenbach's *La Belle Hélène* at the *PDA with the Théâtre lyrique de Montréal.

Boky's 1967 *Metropolitan Opera debut, as Queen of the Night in *The Magic Flute*, made her an international star. In 1967 she also sang her favourite role, Manon (in the Massenet opera), with the Théâtre lyrique de Nouvelle-France in both Quebec City and Montreal, and the roles of Rosina (*The Barber of Seville*) and Olympia (*The Tales of Hoffmann*) with the *COC in Toronto and Montreal. She was a guest of numerous symphony orchestras in Canada and the USA. In 1973 she repeated Manon with the *Opéra du Québec and sang the title role in *La Belle Hélène* for *Festival Ottawa. She returned to Festival Ottawa the following year to sing Adèle in Rossini's *Le Comte Ory*, and in 1976 for the company's revival of *La Belle Hélène*, with performances in Ottawa and, in honour of the US bicentenary, in Washington, DC. That same year she sang the title role in *Thaïs* in Nice. Meanwhile, her career had flourished at the Metropolitan Opera. By 1978 she had sung more than 25 leading roles there, notably Juliette in *Roméo et Juliette*, Marguerite in *Faust*, Violetta in *La Traviata*, Gilda in *Rigoletto*, Lucia in *Lucia di Lammermoor*, Sophie in *Der Rosenkavalier*, the four soprano roles – Olympia, Giulietta, Antonia, and Stella – in *The Tales of Hoffmann*, and Adina in *L'Elisir d'Amore*. She has repeated her best roles with companies in Hartford, Conn, Miami, New Orleans, Pittsburgh, and San Francisco, has appeared in numerous concerts and opera performances on CBC and BBC TV and has given radio recitals, particularly of French song and Lieder, in which she excels.

Boky has recorded music of Johann Strauss (RCA CCS 1002), Karl Weigl (1963; Turnabout TV-S34522), Bizet (Frasquita in *Carmen*, with the Metropolitan Opera, 1973, DG 2740-101), and Fauré and Debussy (with pianist Janine *Lachance, 1977, RCI 463).

Boky was awarded the 1971 *Prix de musique Calixa-Lavallée. In 1974 on CBC TV she was the subject of 'Portrait d'une artiste,' a program distributed internationally to French TV networks. She also appeared in the Metropolitan Opera's 1978 live telecast of *The Bartered Bride*.

BIBLIOGRAPHY
Gingras, Claude. 'Colette Boky vent refaire son image,' Montreal *La Presse*, 24 Feb 1975
Fitzgerald, John. 'Boky builds bridge of songs,' Montreal *Gazette*, 17 Sep 1977
Dawson, Eric. 'Realization of a 10-year dream fulfilled with the Merry Widow,' *Calgary Herald*, 13 Jan 1979
(NT)

BOLDUC, Madame or **La** (b Marie or Mary-Rose-Anne Travers). Singer, songwriter, harmonica player, 'violoneuse,' b Newport, Gaspésie, Que, 4 Jun 1894, d Montreal 20 Feb 1941. Born into a large family of English descent, she left home at 13 to earn her living in Montreal. A gifted child, she had learned easily to play the violin, the harmonica, the button accordion, and the jew's-harp. To pay for her trip to Montreal she played the violin in the main street of Newport while selling Red Pills – a patent medicine. In Montreal she worked as a domestic. She married Édouard Bolduc, a plumber, on 17 Aug 1914; they produced a large family. She began to perform publicly out of economic necessity.

After she accompanied the singer Ovila *Légaré in a recording session, she was recommended to Conrad *Gauthier, organizer of the Veillées du bon vieux temps at the *Monument National. She was engaged at first as a violoneuse, but in 1927 Gauthier encouraged her to sing for the first time in public. Such was her success that Gauthier suggested that she compose some songs. Though she was scarcely known, her recordings of 'La Cuisinière' and 'La Servante,' issued on a Starr 78, quickly sold some 12,000 copies – a success unprecedented in Quebec at the time. There followed other songs and recordings which enjoyed great popularity because of their humour, frankness, and inimitable style of embellishment, with 'turlutages' or comic ritornelles produced by clicking the tongue against the palate. She performed tirelessly in Canada and the USA and continued to record, completing 29 two-sided 78s and 16 one-sided 78s for Starr before her death. Apex has reissued 24 of her songs on two LPs (ALF 1505, ALF 1515). MCA Coral reissued another two albums: CB 33015 and CB 33021.

This illiterate woman, likeable, joyous, and dynamic, composed her songs as she lived, wilfully, intuitively, guided by an uncommon sense of observation. She was Canada's first chansonnière in the true sense of the word, in that her verses deal with real life and, seen as a whole, reflect vividly the particular climate of the 1930s in Quebec. The daily problems and the material difficulties of ordinary people are reflected in her songs: 'Le Commerçant des rues,' 'L'Enfant volé,' 'Les Cinq Jumelles,' 'Les Colons canadiens,' 'La Grocerie du coin,' 'Les Agents d'assurance,' 'Les Conducteurs de chars,' and others. La Bolduc has had a definite influence on the evolution of the chanson in Quebec and, though she has had many imitators, she has had no equals. She has become a legend, and her work may be considered a prototypical and permanent part of Quebec's legacy of song. According to Réal Benoit, Marius *Barbeau has said: 'Her songs have struck me for their reckless verve and unique twist of the tongue in the manner of the singers of the true soil. Her repertoire certainly deserves to be safeguarded or given a revival.'

La Bolduc

LPs celebrating the music of La Bolduc have been made by Jeanne D'Arc Charlebois and Jean *Carignan (*Hommage à Madame Bolduc*, issued by Philo), by Marthe Fleurant (*La Bolduc '68*, issued by Vedettes on VD 801), and by André *Gagnon (his variations on 11 of her songs, *Les Turluteries*, issued by Columbia). A prize bearing her name was awarded to Claude *Léveillée at the 1966 Festival du disque in Montreal. Jean-Paul Riopelle's painting 'La Bolduc' hangs in the foyer of the *PDA's Salle Wilfrid Pelletier. La Bolduc's musical estate is administered by CAPAC.

BIBLIOGRAPHY

Benoit, Réal. *La Bolduc* (Montreal 1959)

Leclerc, Monique. 'Les chansons de "la Bolduc": manifestation de la culture populaire à Montréal (1928–40),' unpubl MA thesis, McGill 1974

Larouche-Nadeau, Olivette. *Le Forillon (du turlutage au gogo)* (Ottawa 1977)

Gaulin, André. 'Chansons, de Madame Édouard Bolduc,' *Dictionnaire des oeuvres littéraires du Québec*, vol 2, ed Maurice Lemire (Montreal 1980) (PL)

BOLYER, Maurice (Joseph) (b Beaulieu). Banjoist, composer, b Edmundston, NB, of Acadian parents, 1 Dec 1920, d Toronto 18 Aug 1978. Bolyer, who was to become known as King of the Banjo, began playing the instrument in his late teens with a country band in Edmundston after attaining proficiency on various other string instruments and piano. He played on radio station CKCW, Moncton, NB, with Hank *Snow in the early 1940s, and was heard regularly on the *'CKNX Barn Dance,' from Wingham, Ont, in the late 1940s. He also performed on 'Main Street Jamboree' (CHML, Hamilton, Ont), on various US TV shows before joining CBC radio's 'The Tommy *Hunter Show' in 1963, and from 1965 until his death as a regular on Hunter's CBC TV show. A virtuoso of the banjo, Bolyer attempted in his last years to extend its stylistic range. He was interested, for example, in exploiting it as a solo (rather than rhythm) instrument in jazz. Seven of his own tunes are included on his LPs *King of the Banjo* (Arc 252), *Country Banjo* (Banff SBS 5324), *Golden Banjo Classics* (Cachet 1005), and *Pure Gold Banjo Favourites* (RCA KNL-0108). He also may be heard on LPs by Hunter, Graham *Townsend, and others.

BIBLIOGRAPHY

Hyde, Steve. 'Maurice Bolyer: King of the banjo,' *World of Country Music*, vol 2, Mar 1973

BONHOMME, Jean (Robert Gérard Joseph). Tenor, b Ottawa 14 Feb 1937; BA (Ottawa) 1957. He studied 1961–4 with Raoul *Jobin privately and 1962–4 with George *Lambert at the RCMT. He continued his studies 1965–6 in Geneva with Maria Carpi and in Rome with Luigi Ricci, under the sponsorship of the Royal Opera House, Covent Garden. In 1964 he won the top vocal award in the *CBC Talent Festival, the Senior Silver Tray as best male singer in the Toronto *Kiwanis Music Festival, the Canadian Opera Women's Committee Scholarship, and the Richard Tucker Search for Talent award.

In 1964 he sang the title role in the *Royal Conservatory Opera School production of Milhaud's *Le Pauvre Matelot*, made his debut at the *Stratford Festival (as Basilio in *The Marriage of Figaro*), and joined the Sadler's Wells Opera, London. With that company he performed 1964–5 in *Attila* (Verdi), *Madama Butterfly*, *The Marriage of Figaro*, and *Orpheus in the Underworld*. In 1965 he returned to Canada to sing the role of Fatty in Weill's *Rise and Fall of the City of Mahagonny* at Stratford and made his *COC debut as Rodolfo in *La Bohème*. From 1965 to 1969 he was a principal tenor at the Royal Opera House, Covent Garden, where he sang leading roles in *Carmen*, *A Masked Ball*, *Madama Butterfly*, *Tosca*, *La Traviata*, and *The Trojans* (as Aeneas, alternating with Jon *Vickers). He sang Rodolfo on the 1968 recording *Royal Opera House Covent Garden – Covent Garden Opera Anniversary Album* (2-Lon OS 26088-26089). He again returned to Canada in 1969.

Bonhomme has sung in COC productions (*Faust* 1966, 1974; *Carmen* 1970) and with several European and US companies, including the Budapest, Marseilles, Netherlands, and Paris operas and the Houston Grand Opera and New Orleans and Santa Fe operas. In 1969 he made his Paris Opera debut as Aeneas in *The Trojans*. In 1971 he made his US debut with the Santa Fe Opera Association in Verdi's *Don Carlo* (title role) and Wagner's *The Flying Dutchman* (Erik). The critic for the *Houston Chronicle*, reviewing (6 Oct 1971) his Houston debut as Don José in *Carmen*, called him 'unquestionably the star of the occasion' and praised his 'superb voice ... fine articulation, perfect clarity and projection' and added that his 'Flower Song' in act II 'was more than a traditional high point. Bonhomme, in keenly enunciated French, drove home the intensity of his feelings in this aria which thus was made luminous and triumphant.' With the *Opéra du Québec he sang the roles of Luigi in *Il Tabarro* (1971) and Turiddu in *Cavalleria Rusticana* (1973). In 1972 he appeared as Don José in Johannesburg and Pretoria, South Africa, and in 1975 he sang the title role in *Faust* with the *Southern Alberta Opera Assn.

He has given recitals (including one at *Expo 67), has appeared as soloist with the London and Los Angeles Philharmonic Orchestras and with the *MSO, the *TSO, the *NACO, and the *Quebec, *Winnipeg, and *Vancouver SOs, and has been heard on CBC radio. His outstanding role has been that of Don José (over 30 performances in two different productions at Covent Garden; 12 performances in South Africa in 1972, etc). He also has performed as soloist in Bach's *St John Passion*, Beethoven's *Ninth Symphony* and *Missa solemnis*, Dvořák's *Stabat mater*, the Mozart and Verdi *Requiems*, and other major choral works. (JSw)

'Bonhomme! Bonhomme!' Traditional audience-participation song. 'Voleurs de pois et vieille chanson' ('Peashooters and old song'), a droll article by Ernest *Gagnon – written after he had discovered a document preserved in the legal archives of Quebec City – maintains that this song was sung in Quebec City as early as 1638. In France the words consist of a mixture of French and patois. As Gagnon states in his *Chansons populaires du Canada* (Quebec 1865), two versions are known in Canada. The first asks the Bonhomme (to whom the song is addressed) whether he can play knee-on-the-ground. When he touches the ground with his knee the song continues specifying the elbow, then other parts of the anatomy. The second version asks the Bonhomme (or the audience) if he can play a musical instrument. He then is required to mime the playing of several instruments. In Gagnon's volume the melody is found in the minor mode, differing from the better-known melody in the major mode published by La *Bonne Chanson in *Chantons en choeur* (St-Hyacinthe 1945). Talivaldis *Kenins arranged the song for choir (Harris 1962). Recorded in the 78 era by Conrad *Gauthier and others, the song later appeared on LPs by André Bertrand (Franco-Elite 6901) and Paul-Émile *Corbeil and les Gais Copains (Fonorama MF-5).

BIBLIOGRAPHY

Gagnon, Ernest. 'Voleurs de pois et vieille chanson,' *Nouvelle-France*, vol 7, Nov 1908 HP

La Bonne Chanson. A publishing company dedicated to the dissemination of French and French-Canadian songs of quality. It was founded in St-Hyacinthe, Que, after the 1937 French Language Congress in Quebec City, which emphasized the value of song as a vehicle for the preservation of culture and language. Father Charles-Émile *Gadbois, the company's founder, began publishing the words and music of songs of France and Quebec in albums of 50. Ten albums (500 songs) were published in this manner. La Bonne Chanson also prepared the series *Madeleine et Pierre* for young people and adapted several programs of solfège and singing for the schools: *La Bonne Chanson à l'École*, a collection of 50 sacred and secular songs for Christmas; *Chants pour le temps des Fêtes*; and finally *Cent plus belles chansons*. A collection entitled *Vingt choeurs à voix égales* enjoyed considerable success, as did books of accompaniments for many songs.

In 1939 for the Bluebird label Father Gadbois produced some 50 78s for the record series issued under the name La Bonne Chanson. Performers for the series included François Brunet, P.-É. *Corbeil, Marthe *Létourneau, the *Alouette Vocal Quartet, David Rochette, and Albert *Viau. The radio program 'Le quart d'heur de la Bonne Chanson,' on CBC and CKAC in Montreal 1939–52, contributed to the popularity of the newly restored heritage of song. Les Amis de la Bonne Chanson, founded in 1942 and 12,000 strong by 1945, also assisted in the promotion and distribution of the published songs. La Bonne Chanson published 16 issues of the periodical *Musique et Musiciens* 1952–4. In 1955 the company's administration was assumed by Les Entreprises culturelles Enr, La Prairie, Que.

BIBLIOGRAPHY

'Quinzième anniversaire de la Bonne Chanson,' *Musique et Musiciens*, vol 1, Feb 1953

Gervais, Albert. 'Nouvelles rampes de lancement pour La Bonne Chanson,' *Le Magister*, Oct 1977

Pionniers du disque folklorique (CH)

BONNET, Joseph (Élie Georges Marie). Organist, teacher, composer, b Bordeaux 17 Mar 1884, d Ste-Luce, near Rimouski, Que, 2 Aug 1944; premier prix (Paris Cons) 1906. He studied organ with Guilmant, Tournemire, and Vierne and was organist at St-Eustache Church in Paris from 1905 until the beginning of World War II. He toured Europe often and visited North America for the first time in 1916. He taught for several years at the ESM, Rochester. In 1920 he inaugurated the organ of St-Stanislas Church in Montreal during a Canadian tour. When the *CMM opened in 1943, he was appointed to its teaching staff. Conrad *Bernier, Henri *Gagnon, Magdeleine and Marcelle *Martin, and D'Alton *McLaughlin are among his Canadian pupils. He edited numerous classical works for Durand, Sénart, G. Schirmer, and Fischer. He is buried in the cemetery of the Benedictine Abbey in St-Benoit-du-Lac, Quebec. His *Année liturgique au grand orgue* was published by Fides (Montreal 1948).

BIBLIOGRAPHY
Bernier, Conrad. 'Joseph Bonnet,' *VM*, 9, Oct 1968 GP

BONSALL, Bessie (m Barron). Contralto, b Ottawa 30 Aug 1870, d Paris, Ont, 15 Dec 1963. She studied with W. Elliott *Haslam at the *Toronto College of Music and at 18 was soloist at St James' Cathedral. After touring 1893–5 as assisting artist to the Belgian violinist Ovide Musin, she continued her studies in England with Charles Santley and was a member of the Savoy Theatre company under the direction of Gilbert and Sullivan. In 1898 she became a soloist at New York's Temple Emanu-El. Later she toured North America with Sousa's Band, the Banda Rossa, and the Redpath Grand Opera Concert Company. Her public appearances dwindled following her marriage in 1906. She is known to have made trial recordings at about the turn of the century, but these have not survived. JBM

Boosey & Hawkes (Canada) Ltd. Canadian branch of the British publishing firm. After the merger in 1930 in London of (Thomas) Boosey & Co (founded 1816) and (William) Hawkes & Son (founded 1865), the Canadian branch was opened in Toronto in 1935 and has remained a wholly owned subsidiary of the parent company. (Hawkes & Son and Frederick Harris, though not affiliated in England, had operated together 1912–23 in Toronto.) Boosey & Hawkes (Canada) Ltd was managed 1939–47 by Harry Jarman and 1947–76 by Will (William J.I.) Croombs, who joined Boosey & Hawkes in his native England at 14, was also a board member of various Canadian organizations including *CAPAC, and took a special interest in elementary music education. On Croombs' death in 1976 a scholarship was established in his name at the *U of Toronto. He was succeeded by George Ullmann.

Boosey & Hawkes' Canadian publications include, among much other material, choral and vocal music by Keith *Bissell, Morris *Surdin, and Bernard *Naylor, piano music by Violet *Archer and Oskar *Morawetz, band and orchestral works by James *Gayfer, Kelsey *Jones, Talivaldis *Kenins, John *Weinzweig, and Healey *Willan, and the educational works of Cora *Ahrens and Boris *Berlin. The Boosey & Hawkes booklet *Canadian Composers* (Toronto 1973, rev 1974) lists the Canadian publications of the firm, with brief biographies of the composers. The catalogue of the parent firm includes music by Bartók, Britten, Copland, Prokofiev, Rachmaninoff, Stravinsky, Richard Strauss, and many others. Boosey & Hawkes (Canada) is the Canadian agent for Edwin Ashdown, Faber-Curwen, and Roberton of Great Britain, Fearon of the USA, Artia of Czechoslovakia, and Kultura of Hungary, and handles the rental materials of Novello, Oxford University Press, and D'Oyly Carte of Great Britain and Supraphon of Czechoslovakia.

The sale of orchestral instruments manufactured by Boosey & Hawkes London and instrument repairs became a large part of the company's business in 1947. Another supplementary activity is the distribution of recordings of background music produced by the parent company. Boosey & Hawkes (Canada) are affiliated with CAPAC.

BIBLIOGRAPHY
'Boosey & Hawkes celebrates 150th anniversary in 1966,' *CanComp*, vol 13, Dec 1966 (MWI)

Boot Records Ltd. Country-music label formed in 1971 in Toronto by Stompin' Tom *Connors and his manager Jury Krytiuk. At first an outlet for Connors' recordings (16 LPs by 1977, including several reissues of his earlier Dominion records), Boot soon began to add other Canadian country artists, including Con Archer, the instrumental group The Emeralds, *Humphrey and the Dumptrucks, Dick *Nolan, Stevedore Steve, and Ted Wesley. Boot's budget label, Cynda, has reissued Boot LPs by Connors and has released LPs by artists of various ethnic backgrounds, including the popular Irish-Canadian group Larry McKee and the Shandonairs. The Boot Master Concert series, which was established in 1973, initially under the direction of Eleanor *Sniderman, has released LPs by Liona *Boyd, *Canadian Brass, the pianist Monica *Gaylord, and the Ukrainian-born bass Yosyp Hoshuliak.

The president of Boot, Jury Krytiuk (b Neunhaus, Germany, 1948), has written several songs, including 'Goofie Newfie' (co-composed and popularized by Roy Payne) and the often recorded 'Maritime Farewell.' Krytiuk in 1971 established the country-music publishing company Morning Music Ltd and he has managed other music publishing ventures as well.

BIBLIOGRAPHY
Flohil, Richard. 'One man's impact,' *Canadian World of Country Music*, Jun, Jul 1973
'Interview Jury Krytiuk,' *CanComp*, 128, Feb 1978

Border Scottish Choir of Windsor. A mixed-voice choir of 130, founded in 1924 by H. Whorlow Bull (b London 27 Mar 1872, d Windsor, Ont, 12 Oct 1938) who was founder of the Windsor and Walkerville Choral Society in 1905, choirmaster in a number of Windsor and Detroit churches 1905–35, and supervisor of music in Windsor schools 1909–38. The choral society's large repertoire of English and Scottish music contained both original unaccompanied compositions (including several by Healey *Willan) and arrangements. The society presented concerts twice yearly in the Windsor area and also appeared in Chatham and Leamington and many times in Detroit with the Detroit SO. After Bull's death the choir was reorganized by one of its members – Willis Martin – as the Scottish Choir of Windsor. Martin expanded the choir's repertoire to include *Judas Maccabaeus* and other oratorios. In 1956 the Scottish Choir and the Schubert Choir of Windsor (founded in 1926) amalgamated to form the Windsor Choral Society, which was disbanded in 1958 and succeeded by the Graham Steed Chorale (fl 1959–60).

BORNOFF, George. Violinist, educator; b Winnipeg 5 Nov 1907; LAB 1926, BA (Manitoba) 1933, MA (Columbia) 1946, D MUS (Montreal) 1949. His studies were in Winnipeg: 1916–18 with Gus Hughes, 1919–20 with John *Waterhouse, 1922–4 with I.S. Garbovitsky, and ca 1925–8 with Jean *de Rimanoczy. Bornoff was concertmaster of the Winnipeg String Orchestra during the early 1930s and a member of the *Winnipeg SO during the late 1930s. A staff orchestra member 1934–43 for the radio stations CKY and CJRC, he also played regularly 1935–43 for the CRBC and CBC orchestras, and in 1937 gave weekly recitals on CKY. As a soloist he performed widely throughout western Canada.

In 1937 he prepared eight successful candidates for the LRSM, something that astounded the examiner. He founded the *Bornoff School of Music that same year and served as director until 1947. In 1945 he began to teach violin and chamber music at the Teachers' College, Columbia U. He lectured in music education and was in charge of string development 1953–73 at Boston U. In 1973 he began teaching violin at the Boston Cons. He has been an adjudicator and consultant to music schools and departments of education in Canada, the USA, and Mexico, and has presented string demonstrations and given workshops throughout North America. He is the author of many articles, of *Bornoff's Finger Patterns for Violin* (Thompson, C. Fischer 1948), and of other instruction treatises. Bornoff has emphasized group study. In 'A word to the teacher' (*Bornoff's Finger Patterns for Violin*) he states: 'The key to this approach lies in the introduction of the instrument as a whole. Definite objectives for the mastery of the whole violin, from the beginning will offer a purposeful meaning to a student's practising and will replace the tedious isolation of certain skills and techniques with a musical experience and a sense of accomplishment.'

Bornoff has received several honours, including, in 1974, a Distinguished Service award from the American String Teachers' Assn. His wife is the Canadian pianist and contralto Mary Baron Bornoff. His pupils have included J. Chalmers *Doane, Donna *Grescoe, Stanley Kolt, and Gerald *Stanick. (JTs)

Bornoff School of Music and Associated Arts. Founded in Winnipeg by George *Bornoff. It opened on Bannatyne Ave on 1 Sep 1937, offering instruction in violin, piano, clarinet, voice, theory, sculpture, fine arts, and public speaking. The staff during the early years included Bornoff, principal and head of the violin department; Leonard Dunelyk, Stanley Kolt, and John *Konrad, violin; Mary Baron Bornoff, Gordon *Kushner, and Frans *Niermeier, piano and theory; W. H. *Anderson, Doris Mills (*Lewis), John *McTaggart,and Gladys *Whitehead, voice; Stephen Krawetz, violin and theory; and Hugh *Bancroft, organ and theory.

The school offered both a general and a graded course of study, the latter for those who exhibited distinct ability. Students in the graded stream underwent rigorous training and were examined by the principal monthly. There were also piano classes for preschool children and adult 'Music hobbyists.' The initial student enrolment of 70 expanded in the 1940s to over 600. In-house recording facilities were provided, school orchestras and choirs were formed, and senior students were encouraged to give recitals in the school's own small concert hall. Annual concerts, in auditoriums about the city, were open to the public. In 1938 a day school was established under Clive von Cardinal, so that both academic and musical training could be offered on the premises, and in 1941 this school came under the official supervision of the Manitoba Dept of Education. The day school did not survive into the 1950s.

Donna *Grescoe, Anne *Pomer James, Gerald *Stanick, and Mary *Morrison are among the school's many noted alumni. George Bornoff remained as director until 1947. The school was operated 1947–9 by Bernard Stanick (father of Gerald), and was taken over in 1949 by John Konrad, who renamed it the Konrad Cons of Music in 1950. (JTs)

Boss Brass. Toronto jazz orchestra (big band) led by Rob *McConnell. Composed of the city's leading studio musicians, it was formed in 1968 as a 16-piece band to record arrangements of pop

Boss Brass

songs of the day for *CTL. It took its name from its instrumentation at that time – trumpets, trombones, french horns, and a rhythm section. (Five saxophones were added in 1970, and a fifth trumpet in 1976.) The Boss Brass made its first public appearance in January 1969 at the Toronto nightclub the Savarin. Although public performances have been rare, there have been concerts at *Ontario Place and longer engagements (one or two weeks) at the Savarin, the Colonial Tavern, and Basin Street. The band has been heard on CJRT-FM (Toronto) and on the CBC's 'Jazz Radio-Canada,' and it appeared in 1975 in a CBC TV special, 'The Best Damn Band in the Land.' Having built a challenging and largely original repertoire of jazz compositions by McConnell and other members, by the mid-1970s the Boss Brass had become the leading big band in Canada, and one of the finest in the world.

In 1978 the Boss Brass accompanied the vocal groups Singers Unlimited and the Hi-Los on recordings for the German label MPS. Soloists include Eugene Amaro, Guido *Basso, Ed *Bickert, Jimmy *Dale, Moe *Koffman, Ian *McDougall, Sam Noto, Jerry *Toth, and Rich *Wilkins. Jack Batten in the Toronto *Globe and Mail* (21 Jan 1976) called the music of the Boss Brass 'as disciplined, varied and imaginative as anything you'll hear this side (that's the better side) of Woody Herman and Maynard Ferguson.' The direct-to-disc two-album set *Big Band Jazz* won a *Juno Award as jazz recording of 1977, and was nominated for a Grammy Award (big band instrumental) in 1979.

DISCOGRAPHY

The Boss Brass. 1968. CTL 477-5015/RCA CTLS 1015
Boss Brass Two. 1969. CTL 477-5118/RCA CTLS 1118
The Sound of the Boss Brass. 1970. CBC LM-73
Rob McConnell and the Boss Brass. 1971. CTL 477-5143. Reissued as *Down to Brass Tacks*. Pickwick PC 40013
Rob: Rob McConnell's Boss Brass 4. 1972. CTL 477-5159. Reissued as *Odds and Ends*. Pickwick PC 44007
The Best Damn Band in the Land. 1974. CTL 5182/U Artists UALA 309G
The Jazz Album. 1976. Attic LAT 1015
Big Band Jazz. 1977. Umbrella 2-UMB-DD4
Rob McConnell and the Boss Brass Again! 1978. 2-Umbrella UMB GEN 1-12
Singers Unlimited with Rob McConnell and the Boss Brass. 1978. MPS 0068.238
Present Perfect. 1979. MPS 0068.249
Are Ya Dancin' Disco. 1979. New Ventures NV 5008 MM

'Both Sides Now.' Song, sometimes known as 'Clouds,' by Joni *Mitchell. Written ca 1968, it was recorded in 1968 by the US folksinger Judy Collins and by the US pop group Harper's Bizarre. Collins' single (Elektra 45639) eventually was a million seller, and her LP of the same name won the 1968 Grammy Award for best folk performance. A philosophical song ('I've looked at love [or life] from both sides now ... '), it also has been included on LPs by Bing Crosby, Catherine *McKinnon (as the title song), Dave van Ronk, Frank Sinatra, and many others; van Ronk's was popular and, according to Leonore Fleischer's *Joni Mitchell* (New York 1976), was regarded by the composer as the most successful interpretation to that date. Instrumental arrangements have been recorded by the Paul Winter Consort and Tom Scott. Mitchell herself included versions on her second LP, *Clouds*, and the live recording *Miles of Aisles*. 'Both Sides Now' is published by Siquomb Music, and was included in the *Joni Mitchell Songbook* (vol 1, songs 1966–70, Warner Brothers 1970), Edith *Fowke's *Canadian Vibrations* (Macmillan 1972), and the *Judy Collins Songbook* (Grosset & Dunlap 1976).

BOTHWELL, Mary. Soprano, painter, b Hickson, near Woodstock, Ont, 28 Nov ca 1900. At the *Canadian Academy of Music, Toronto, she studied singing with Otto *Morando and piano with Peter Kennedy. She sang 1920–9 as a contralto in opera and oratorio, appearing opposite Douglas Stanbury, Edmund *Burke, and others in Toronto and Buffalo. In 1937 she undertook further studies at the Mozarteum in Salzburg, continuing with Paul Althouse in New York in 1938, and again with Morando in Los Angeles. Bothwell made her New York debut 1 Nov 1938 at Town Hall and continued to appear there until the early 1960s. In 1947 she made the first of several European tours, specializing in Lieder and German opera and drawing praise from even the German critics. Notable successes included her Marschallin (*Der Rosenkavalier*) at the 1947 Scheveningen Festival, Holland, and Isolde (*Tristan und Isolde*) with the BBC SO under Sir Adrian Boult in 1948. She performed on radio in New York, Paris, London, and Basel. She gave her first Toronto recital at *Eaton Auditorium 29 Nov 1948. Among her recordings for Royale are *An Hour of Lieder: Hugo Wolf Sung by Mary Bothwell* (1310), *An Hour of Concert Songs* (1318), and *Bless This House* (1538). She also made a *Richard Strauss Album* for Allegro (4069). As president of the Canadian Women's Club of New York she has encouraged the careers of young Canadian performers. Bothwell became known also for her paintings of flowers.

BOTTENBERG, Wolfgang (Heinz Otto). Composer, teacher, b Frankfurt-am-Main 9 May 1930, naturalized Canadian 1964; B MUS (Alberta) 1961, M MUS (Cincinnati) 1962, DMA composition (Cincinnati) 1970. He trained as a carpenter before entering the Jesuit order in 1952. Self-taught in the rudiments of theory and organ, he did not study music formally until 1958. He graduated in 1957 from the Theologische Hochschule Vallendar, and moved to Canada in 1958. He produced a number of chamber works while attending the *U of Alberta and the U of Cincinnati. He taught 1963–5 in Alberta and British Columbia schools and 1965–73 at *Acadia U, Wolfville, NS, and joined the music teaching staff of *Concordia U, Montreal, in 1973.

Bottenberg has been influenced by Hindemith and medieval music. He employs strict contrapuntal control within an expanded tonal-modal idiom but never at the expense of expressive values. The *Triptych* for organ and the *Fantasia Serena* for chamber orchestra, for instance, evince a sustained introspective lyricism. He shares with Hindemith an interest in composing for the gifted amateur, and his works in this manner include parts for such instruments as harpsichord and recorder. His interest in early instruments led him to form in 1971 and direct until 1973 the Acadia Medieval Ensemble of Wolfville and to found the Collegium Ferialis in Montreal in 1974. He is a member of CAPAC and an associate of the *CMCentre.

SELECTED COMPOSITIONS

ORCHESTRA

Sinfonietta. 1961 (orch 1970). CMCentre
Duino Cantata (Rilke). 1962. Bar, SATB, orch. CMCentre
A Suite of Carols. 1963–7. Med orch. CMCentre
Fantasia. 1966. Tpt, sm orch. CMCentre
Ritual (Bottenberg). 1970. SATB, orch. CMCentre
Fantasia Serena. 1973. Sm orch. CMCentre

CHAMBER

Quartet. 1960. Fl, 2 cl, bn. CMCentre
Three Amerindian Songs (Eskimo, Peruvian, Hopi Indians, transl Clavert, Astrov). 1961 (rev 1968). Ten, alto and ten rec, guit or fl, cl, hpd (pf). CMCentre
Trio for Flute, Clarinet and Bassoon. 1963. CMCentre
Trio. 1963–4. Fl, cl, pf. CMCentre
Trio for Three Recorders. 1964. Ber 1972
Divertimento for Flute Quartet. 1968. CMCentre
First String Quartet. 1968. CMCentre
My Funny Little Clock (Beissel). 1969. V, alto rec (fl), hpd (pf). CMCentre
Variables. 1969. Rec, ww quar, str quin. CMCentre
Dialogue. 1971 (rev 1972). Alto rec (fl), hpd (pf). CMCentre
Octet. 1972. Ww quar, tpt, 2 hn, trb. CMCentre
Fa So La Ti Do Re. 1972. Sop sax (cl), str quar. CMCentre
Eine Weihnachliche Hausmusik (trad, Rilke, Möricke). 1973. V, 2 alto rec, pf. CMCentre
Ciacona. 1977. Alto rec, hpd. CMCentre
Partita. 1978. Rec quar, guit, v da gamba (vc). CMCentre

KEYBOARD

Sonata for Piano Duet. 1961 (rev 1967). CMCentre
Moods of the Modes. Ca 1967. Pf. Wat 1975
Triptych. 1967. Org. CMCentre
6 other works for organ. 1963–9. WLSM
Piano arrs of *Three English Carols* (Wat 1973) and other pf works

CHOIR AND VOICE

The World Is a Rainbow (Beissel). 1968. Sop, ten, SATB, ww quin. CMCentre
'The Law of Love' (Evers). 1969. 2 vs, org. Apogee 1969
'The Power of Prayer' (Evers). 1969. 2vs, org. Apogee 1969

WRITINGS

'Music and creativity in school,' Halifax *J of Education*, vol 17, Feb 1968 (AF)

BOUCHARD, Antoine (Rodrigue Albert). Organist, teacher, b St-Philippe-de-Néri, near Quebec City, 22 Mar 1932; BA (Laval) 1952, L TH (Laval) 1956. He studied 1942–3 with Yvette Michaud, 1944–9 and 1952–6 with Claude *Lavoie, and 1950–2 with Father Léon *Destroismaisons. After ordination as a priest in 1956 he continued his studies 1958–61 in Paris with Gaston Litaize, Antoine *Reboulot, and Simone Plé-Caussade. Upon his return to Canada in 1961 he began teaching at the Collège de Ste-Anne-de-la-Pocatière and at *Laval U. He became director of the School of Music at Laval in 1977. Bouchard has performed as an organist in the USA, France, and especially eastern and central Canada. In 1974 he took part in the recording of *Hommage à Henri Gagnon* (ALPEC A-75008) at the basilica in Quebec City.

In 1975–6 he was heard on the French network of the CBC in a series of concerts given on 20 historical organs in 6 European countries. A founder-member of the *Amis de l'orgue de Québec, he wrote on the subject for numerous music journals, and helped re-establish the Canadian organ-building industry through his activities as a consultant in the construction of several organs in eastern Canada. He has written for *EMC*. Reviewing his recording 'Noëls français' Jacob *Siskind wrote in the Montreal *Gazette* (11 Jun 1977): 'These are all by their very nature short pieces, few taking more than five minutes, and it is here that Bouchard is most effective. The charm of these folksy miniatures has been captured with great effectiveness and the variety of sound possible on the organ has been highlighted very cleverly.' Bouchard became a member of the board of the *CMCouncil in 1978.

WRITINGS

'Casavant Frères,' *Forces*, 2, Spring–Summer 1967

'Dix ans d'orgue au Québec,' *VM*, 17, Sep 1970

'300 ans d'orgue au Canada,' *Mcan*, 35, Apr 1978

Record jacket notes for *Anthologie de l'organiste*, vol 1 (see Discography)

DISCOGRAPHY

Anthologie de l'organiste, vol 1: 23 works from the classical period. 1976. ALPEC A-76001

Antoine Bouchard, organiste: Buxtehude *Passacaglia in D Minor* and other works – Dandrieu *Suite in A* and other works. 1971. Micro Art AB-100

Antoine Bouchard, orgue: Noëls français de D'Aquin – Corette – Dandrieu – Balbastre. 1977. RCI 402

Antoine Bouchard, orgue: Pachelbel *Prelude, Fugue and Chaconne in D Minor* – Bach *Trio Sonata No. 3; Toccata, Adagio and Fugue in C*. 1977. RCI 401

Hommage à Henri Gagnon: Bouchard, H. Gagnon, D'Aquin, L. Couperin. 1974. ALPEC A-75008 HPn

BOUCHARD, Joe or **Jos** (Joseph). Violoneux, composer, b Pointe-au-Pic, near La Malbaie, Que, 6 May 1905, d Île d'Orléans, Que, 12 Jun 1979. At eight he began playing the violin and was taught the folk repertoire by Élie Sioué; by 14 he was a competent violoneux. Though fiddling was largely an avocation during the 32 years he worked in Quebec City for the CNR, Bouchard participated in local festivals (winning the contest for violoneux held at the Salle paroissiale de Limoilou in 1934, for example), was heard with the accordionist Théodore Duguay's Montagnards laurentiens on CHRC radio in 1948, and also performed in the Lac St-Jean region. In 1938 he began recording for *RCA Victor's Bluebird label, completing 13 78s; the most popular of the tunes recorded, according to the folklorist Gabriel Labbé, were his *Lancier 5ème partie*, *Reel Pointe-au-Pic*, the four-part *Quadrille Bouchard*, and versions of *Les Joyeuses Québécoises* and *Reel de Rimouski* by the older violoneux Fortunat Malouin. Other Bouchard recordings from this period have served as models for performances by later Quebec folk instrumentalists, Philippe *Bruneau and Jean *Carignan among them. Bouchard also recorded in 1948 for Columbia and in later years for Carnaval (the LP *Reel Carnaval* CS 530) and for Tamanoir (*Portrait du vieux Kébec*, vol 13, TAM 513) and its Opus label (*Jos Bouchard: Violoneux Île d'Orléans* OP-221). In 1975 he performed at the *Mariposa Folk Festival.

BIBLIOGRAPHY

Pionniers du disque folklorique québécois

BOUCHARD, Victor. Pianist, administrator, b Ste-Claire-de-Dorchester, near Quebec City, 11 Apr 1926; LLL (Laval) 1948, premier prix piano (CMQ) 1950. He took his first sustained music studies 1941–6 at the Collège de Lévis with Father Alphonse *Tardif, and continued 1946–50 at the *CMQ with Tardif (harmony), Hélène *Landry (piano), and Françoise *Aubut (theory). In 1949 he received the piano prize of the Rotary Club. He married the pianist Renée *Morisset in 1950. After completing his training 1950–2 in Paris with Alfred Cortot and Antoine *Reboulot he returned to Canada and in October 1952 in Quebec City, he and his wife gave a two-piano recital, followed shortly afterwards by a performance of Mozart's *Concerto* K365 for two pianos and orchestra. These programs marked the arrival before the public of a two-piano team whose reputation soon extended across Canada, the USA, and Europe.

A second study period 1952–3 in Paris with Reboulot also gave rise to numerous public recitals by Bouchard and Morisset, as well as radio and TV appearances. They toured in Canada 1955–6, 1957–8, 1961–2, and 1962–3 for the *JMC, and 1956–7 in France for the JM, and in Belgium, Holland, and Italy. They also appeared with the *Quebec SO, the *MSO, the *TS, the *McGill Chamber Orchestra, and the leading orchestras of Ottawa, Vancouver, Victoria, and Winnipeg. After an appearance at Carnegie Recital Hall in New York they gave numerous recitals 1965–70 in the USA and Canada.

Bouchard and Morisset have a large repertoire both for two pianos and for one piano four hands. They have premiered, and have played both in Canada and abroad, several works written especially for them, including *Pépin's *Nombres* (1963) for two pianos and orchestra, *Matton's *Concerto* (1964, performed with the Quebec SO 17 Jan 1971 at the inauguration of Quebec City's *Grand Théâtre), and Jacques *Hétu's *Sonata* (1965). Their 1965 recording of the Matton won the Prix Pierre-Mercure at the 1966 Festival du disque, Montreal. As Jacob *Siskind wrote in the Montreal *Gazette* (7 Mar 1977), the duo is 'the most distinguished piano team that Canada has ever produced,' and its stylistic authority and virtuosity has earned it the 1964 *Prix de musique Calixa-Lavallée.

While pursuing his career as a pianist Bouchard also served 1955–66 as a teacher and music director at the *JMC Orford Art Centre. In 1967 he joined the *MACQ, where he held the positions of general director of the *Cons de musique et d'art dramatique du Québec 1967–71, director of the music section 1971–5, and adviser 1975–8. He resumed his former duties as general director of the Cons de musique 1978–80. He served 1957–9 as national president of the JMC, and in 1961 as vice-president of the *AMQ and has sat on numerous juries including, in 1976, that for the *Montreal International Competition. Bouchard has composed

Bouchard and Morisset

a string quartet, a *Danse canadienne* for violin and piano (1945, Presser 1950; also transcribed for two pianos), a *Toccata* (1953), and about 100 harmonizations of French-Canadian folksongs, some of which have been performed by Maureen *Forrester, Gaston *Germain, Jacques *Labrecque, and (on RCI 393) Bruno *Laplante.

DISCOGRAPHY (Bouchard and Morisset)

Évolution de la musique pour deux pianos: Mozart – Brahms – Schumann – Bartók – Milhaud. Ca 1952. Club national du disque CND 28

Évolution de la musique pour piano à quatre mains: Bach – Brahms – Fauré – Poulenc – Stravinsky. Ca 1952. CND 50?

Matton *Concerto*. TS, Susskind cond. 1965. Cap SW 6123/CRI SD 317

Mozart – Soler – Pépin – Debussy. 1968. CBC SM-61

Mozart *Sonata No. 3* K497 – Schubert *Rondo, Op 138; Fantasy, Op 103*. 1976? Sel CC-15.080

Muethel *Sonata duetto* – Bouchard *Toccata; Danse canadienne* – Hétu *Sonata*. (1967). RCI 227/RCA CCS 1021

BIBLIOGRAPHY

'Victor Bouchard et Renée Morisset,' *Variations*, vol 1, Feb 1978 AP, GP

Bouchard and Morrisset. See Bouchard, Victor.

BOUCHER. Montreal family of musicians, devoted for three generations to the business, publishing, and performance of music. Dominated by 1 / Adélard Joseph Boucher, the family includes his wife Philomène, his sons 2 / François and 3 / J.-Arthur, and the latter's daughter Marie-de-Lourdes.

1 **Adélard Joseph** (François-Arthur). Publisher, importer, choirmaster, organist, conductor, writer on music, numismatist, b Maskinongé, near Trois-Rivières, Lower Canada (Quebec), 28 Jun 1835, d Outremont, near Montreal, 16 Nov 1912. He began his studies in Montreal. Orphaned in 1845, he was placed in the College at Emmitsburg, Md, where he spent six years. A teacher by the name of Henry Dielman introduced the boy to the organ, the piano, singing, the flute, and the violin, and he showed obvious talent. In September 1851 his foster father, Antoine LaRocque, sent him to the Sulpicians at the Séminaire d'Issy-les-Moulineaux, near Paris, to ensure his receiving a good religious education. He joined the Jesuits in Amiens in March 1852, but returned to Canada the following August and became interested in business. Still attracted by the religious life, he spent six more months with the Jesuits before beginning law studies. He was employed in October 1853 by the Montreal and Bytown Railway, and had become secretary-treasurer by 1854. He served 1855–8 as registrar for the Commission seigneuriale, and 1855–9 as a

Adélard Joseph Boucher, 1894

broker for the Trust & Loan Co. He thought of going into politics but was more interested in music, numismatics, and genealogy.

In 1861, in order to overcome the difficulty that existed in obtaining French music at that time, Adélard Boucher joined *Laurent et Laforce, a Montreal publishing and importing house. The following year he bought a controlling interest in this company and, in association with a Mr Manseau, established a new business 1862–4. In 1865 he founded the company bearing his own name, A.J. Boucher, Enr'g, and in May 1867 he took over the vast stocks of Gould & Hill at 130 Grande Rue St-Jacques, maintaining, however, his own establishment at 260 Notre-Dame St. In 1868, in collaboration with Arthur *Lavigne, he opened a store in Quebec City. In 1878 he expanded his sheet music business to include instruments, entrusting that department first to René Hudon, who later married his oldest daughter, Philomène, and the following year to Napoléon (L.-É.-N.) *Pratte, who married his daughter Cécile. In 1882 Adélard Boucher opened a store in Ottawa with his son François.

In the course of four trips to Europe before 1890 and several trips to the USA Adélard Boucher reached understandings with several publishers. La Maison Boucher published the works of numerous Canadian composers (Calixa *Lavallée, Alexis *Contant, C.W. *Sabatier, Ernest *Gagnon, J.-J. *Perrault, J.-B. *Labelle, Albertine *Morin-Labrecque, Alfred *Mignault, Roméo *Larivière, Eugène *Lapierre, and others), as well as works in the international repertoire, teaching pieces, and reprints of other Canadian publications which he took over. In 1863, with Manseau and Gustave *Smith, he founded a monthly magazine, *Les Beaux-Arts*, which lasted a year. In 1866 he founded **Le Canada Musical*, which also disappeared after a year but was revived in May 1875 and continued until 1881 when, with Napoléon Pratte, Boucher brought out *Boucher & Pratte's Musical Journal* (1881–2).

Despite his activities in business and journalism, Adélard Boucher was able to pursue an active career as a musician. He taught piano and voice at several institutions, including the Collège Ste-Marie and the Villa-Maria Convent. He became the organist in 1853 at St Patrick's Church and moved in 1858 to St-Pierre Church, where he founded and directed a renowned choir school. He also was organist 1860–3 and choirmaster 1865–8 at St-Jacques Church, then choirmaster at the Gesù Church, where he remained 1868–88, and at St-Jean-Baptiste Church 1890–?. Boucher championed sacred and secular music with equal vigour. He founded the Société Ste-Cécile in 1860 and the Orphéon canadien and the Société Mozart later. He conducted numerous works with orchestra, including Rossini's *Stabat Mater* (1860, 1868), Sabatier's *Cantata* (1862), David's *Le Désert* (1866), selections from Bellini's *La Sonnambula* and Balfe's *The Bohemian Girl* (1867), Donizetti's *The Daughter of the Regiment* (1867, 1882), and Gounod's *Gallia* (1879), as well as masses and other choral works. In December 1870 Boucher conducted a choir of 100 and an orchestra of 30 in a concert at St-Patrice Hall to commemorate the centenary of Beethoven's birth.

Adélard Boucher's wife, Philomène Rousseau, whom he had married in 1854, was a soprano who often took solo roles in his concert presentations, notably as Amina in *La Sonnambula*. They had 15 children.

Adélard Boucher composed several works for piano, most of which were published before 1866 (including *Coecilia*, a mazurka caprice; *Les Canotiers du St-Laurent*, 'quadrille canadien'; *Jolly Dogs Galop*; and *Souvenir de Sabatier*, a suite of waltzes), and the song 'Que je voudrais avoir des ailes.' Boucher was an enthusiastic coin collector. In 1862 he founded the Société de numismatique de Montréal, serving also as its first president. His collection, which he sold in 1866, contained 1600 coins.

After Adélard Boucher's death the firm was managed first by his oldest daughter, Philomène (Mme René Hudon, later Mme Deligny Boucher), then by her daughter Mme Joséphine Boucher-Ouimet, who died in April 1975. In May of that year the firm, then located on Amherst St, closed its doors after 113 years of service to musicians and to the public.

BIBLIOGRAPHY

Mauraut, Olivier. 'Adélard Boucher 1835–1912,' *La Musique*, vol 2, Jan 1920
– 'Adélard Boucher,' *Entre-Nous*, vol 1, Sep 1930
– 'Adélard Boucher 1835–1912,' *Mémoires et comptes rendus de la Société Royale au Canada*, vol 32 (Ottawa 1938)
Kallmann, Helmut. 'A century of musical periodicals in Canada,' *CMJ*, vol 1, Autumn 1956, Winter 1957
Potvin, Gilles. 'L'édition musicale est morte,' Montreal *Le Devoir*, 29 Mar 1975
Calderisi, Maria. 'Music publishing in Canada: 1800–1867,' unpubl MMA thesis (McGill 1976)

2 **François**. Violinist, teacher, b Montreal 1860, d Kansas City ca 1936. He studied the violin with Jules *Hone and Frantz *Jehin-Prume. In 1876, before going to Belgium to study with Massart at the Liège Cons, he gave a farewell concert at which Calixa *Lavallée played a galop, *Bon Voyage!* 'for François Boucher.' In 1881 François Boucher played the Mendelssohn *Concerto* in Montreal. In 1882, with his father, he opened a music store in Ottawa and established himself as a teacher (notably of the Marchioness of Lansdowne, the governor-general's wife) and as the first violin of a string quartet. He began teaching at the *TCM in 1887 and at the *Toronto College of Music in 1889. In 1893 he played the Bruch *Concerto* with the *Toronto Philharmonic Society. Emigrating ca 1894 to the USA, he taught 1906–23 at the Kansas City Cons. His wife, whom he met in the USA, taught piano at the same institution. They both retired in 1923. Their daughter Alice taught voice at the conservatory in Kansas City.

3 **Joseph-Arthur**. Bassist, conductor, choirmaster, bandmaster, b Montreal 2 Apr 1869, d there 20 Dec 1927. It is likely that his father was responsible for the main part of his musical education. He is credited with being the first person (1887) to bring together and conduct an instrumental ensemble under the name of Symphonie de Montréal. He also founded the Montreal Band, which gave concerts in the parks. Choirmaster for 23 years at St-Jean-Baptiste Church and for three years at St-Michel Church, he also conducted the Shamrock Club Orchestra. His daughter Marie-de-Lourdes (b Montreal ca 1895, d there 20 Jul 1975) was a pianist renowned for her virtuosity and for her sight-reading ability.

BIBLIOGRAPHY

B.G. 'M.-J.-Arthur Boucher,' *La Lyre*, 57, Jan 1928 GP

BOUCHER, Lise (m Reboulot). Pianist and teacher, b Montreal 21 May 1941; premier prix (CMM) 1957. She was a piano pupil of Germaine *Malépart at the CMM. In 1958 she was awarded the *Prix d'Europe, and for the following six years she studied in Paris with Antoine *Reboulot, whom she later married. She won second prize in the 1961 *JMC National Competition and toured in 1962, 1964, and 1965 for JMC. She also reached the finals of the 1965 International Competition in Munich. She has appeared regularly on the CBC in 'Les grands concerts' and 'Récital.' She also has given numerous recitals for the *Pro Musica Society and has performed with the *McGill Chamber Orchestra, the CBC *'Little Symphonies' Orchestra, and other CBC orchestras. In 1965 she was pianist and coach at the *CMM, and she has accompanied several instrumentalists, including Steven *Staryk, Arthur *Garami, and Jacques Verdon. She began to teach at the CMM in 1967. Pierre Prévost, in a review in Montreal's *Le Jour* (25 Nov 1977), wrote: 'She is a very engaging pianist and plays with authority, delicacy and taste. The instrument always responds beautifully to her touch and the maturity acquired over twenty years as a performer is everywhere in evidence.' In 1966 she recorded five sets of *Variations* by Mozart (K353, K460, K500, K573, and 'Unser dummer Poebel meint' K455) for Baroque (BC 2872). See also Discography for Staryk.

BIBLIOGRAPHY

'Brahms par Lise Boucher,' *Musique périodique*, vol 1, Nov 1976 (PR)

BOUCHER, Lydia (Sister Marie-Thérèse). Teacher, composer, b St-Ambroise-de-Kildare, near Montreal, 28 Feb 1890, d Montreal 5 Mar 1971; lauréat (AMQ) 1914, diplôme académique (AMQ) 1916, B MUS (Montreal) 1931. She joined the Soeurs de Ste-Anne in 1907 and took her vows in 1909. She studied with Auguste *Descarries (piano and composition), Claude *Champagne and Louis Michiels, (composition), Rodolphe *Mathieu (harmony), Raoul *Paquet (organ), J. Alexandre Delcourt (violin), and Fleurette Contant (voice). She taught piano, voice, violin, and organ 1909–69 at various schools and institutions, notably the Maison-Mère Mont-Ste-Anne in Lachine and the École de musique Wilfrid-Pelletier in Montreal. All her compositions were written between 1923 (*Ave Maria*) and 1971 (*Hommage à Mère Marie-Anne*). They include an oratorio, *L'Oeuvre d'Esther Blondin* (1949), and several other works for choir (unison or SSA) with organ or piano accompaniment, some of which were published by *Édition Belgo-Canadienne, Musica Enrégistré, and Éditions canadiennes. She wrote works for piano, including *Trois Préludes* (1928–30) and *La Ronde des aiguilles* (Éditions canadiennes 1950), and also an *Alleluia* for organ (1958). ST

BOUCHER, Richard-Gaudreault. Composer, b Montreal 8 Oct 1946. He studied 1968–74 at the *CMM with Gilles *Tremblay (analysis and composition), Françoise *Aubut (counterpoint), and Gaston *Arel (harmony). He visited electronic music studios in Europe in 1973 on a *Canada Council grant and studied 1975–7 at the *McGill U studios. His *Angoisse des fuyantes créations* for ondes Martenot and two percussion, which won one of four first prizes in the 1973 *CBC National Radio Competition for Young Composers, was performed in Paris in 1974 at the Tribune internationale des compositeurs. Besides electronic pieces and environmental scores for various exhibitions Boucher's works include: *Esquisse* (1971) for 16 musicians; *Zones* (1972); *Études* (1973); *Sonde I* and *Sonde II* (1975); *Solo* (1975) for clarinet; *Action rouge* (1975) for 30-voice unaccompanied choir; and *Begonia Rex* for four ondes Martenot, premiered in 1977 by the *SMCQ. Boucher wrote the music for the CBC TV documentary 'Depuis la mer du Nord,' broadcast in 1977. In November of that year he participated in the *CAPAC-organized Canadian Music Festival in Europe; his *Angoisse des fuyantes créations* was played at Bonn and at Leverkusen, and was broadcast by Cologne radio. The CBC commissioned his Cantata *Anges maudits, veuillez m'aider* as a submission for the 1979 Prix Italia.

(IP)

BOUDREAU, Walter. Composer, saxophonist, b Montreal 15 Oct 1947. Although he studied piano for several years in Sorel, Que, he virtually taught himself to play the various saxophones and to compose. At 15 he became a member of a jazz band conducted by Arthur *Romano. He directed 1966–8 his own jazz group which, for the LP *Jazz Walter Boudreau +3=4* (1968, Phono PHS 5007), was made up of Pierre *Leduc (piano), Jacques Valois (bass), and Richard Provençal (drums). During *Expo 67 Boudreau led various jazz groups at the Youth Pavilion. There he met Raôul *Duguay, with whom he founded the *Infonie in 1969. He took part in the group's concerts and recordings until 1973. In 1969, commissioned by the CBC, he wrote *Pain-beurre*, on a poem by Duguay, based on the opposition of the male (Yang) and female (Yin) principles of Chinese philosophy. Selections from Duguay's tract *Manifeste de l'Infonie* inspired *Ysengouronnie* (1971), a double concerto for wind instruments and two pianos.

Wishing to further his education, Boudreau studied analysis 1968–70 with Bruce *Mather at *McGill U and analysis and composition 1970–3 with Gilles *Tremblay at the *CMM and with Serge *Garant at the *U of Montreal. From the *Canada Council he received several grants which enabled him to attend summer courses given by Boulez in Cleveland in 1971 and by Kagel, Ligeti, Stockhausen, and Xenakis in Darmstadt in 1972. He participated 1973–6 in the activities of the research team Informatique-musique at the U of Montreal. In 1975 he took a summer course at the Centre for Communications and the Arts at *Simon Fraser U, and in August 1978 he studied at San Diego U.

Boudreau has composed music for the films *Les Maudits Sauvages*, *L'Infonie inachevée*, *Rejeanne Padovani*, *Ultimatum*, and *Une Nuit en Amérique*. Some of the music from the last named was used in *Variations I* (1973, for chamber ensemble). After winning a first prize in the 1973 *CBC National Radio Competition for Young Composers *Variations I* was presented in a second version on a CBC broadcast in 1974. A final, hour-long version (called *Variations*) was conducted by Boudreau at an *SMCQ concert in 1976. Gilles *Potvin (*Le Devoir*, 22 Mar 1976) described it as 'a sound labyrinth populated by phantasms,' and emphasized the composer's 'inexhaustible imagination.' Boudreau has composed other works for chamber ensemble, including *Ubiquital III* (1972), *Dans les champs il y a des bibittes* (1973), *Les Sept Jours* (1977, commissioned by the McGill Percussion Ensemble), and *Cercle gnostique I* (1977, commissioned by the TRIO 3). In 1973 he began playing baritone sax-

Manuscript page from *Les Sept Jours* for eight percussionists by Walter Boudreau

ophone in the Quatuor de saxophones de l'Infonie, and also directed the group, touring the Maritimes with it 1977–8 for the *JMC. Boudreau is an associate of the *CMCentre and an affiliate of PRO Canada.

WRITINGS

'Ma vision du toutarbel,' *Musiques du Kébèk*, ed Raoul Duguay (Montreal 1971)

BIBLIOGRAPHY

'Saviez-vous que nous avons aussi des compositeurs de musique "sérieuse"?' *Perspectives*, vol 17, 21 Aug 1976

Gingras, Claude. 'Un orchestra populaire du Québec,' Montreal *La Presse*, 23 Dec 1978

(PR)

BOUDREAULT (or Boudreau), **Louis 'Pitou.'** Violoneux, raconteur, b Chicoutimi, Que, ca 1906. He began fiddling at 11, learning his repertoire from his father, Pius Boudreault, and grand-uncle, Thomas Vaillancourt, among other violoneux. He performed in the Saguenay–Lac-St-Jean region of Quebec in the 1920s and 1930s and then retired from music for 35 years.

While attending a fiddling contest at the Gesù Hall in Montreal in 1973 Boudreault was encouraged to perform; he did so, reluctantly, and won the contest. Appearances at the 1974, 1976, and 1977 *Mariposa Folk Festivals followed and Boudreault developed a substantial following in eastern Canada and northeastern USA among folk music fans who considered him a rare practitioner of an earlier, purer strain of Quebec traditional music. His concerts and recordings mix fiddle-playing with stories of life in rural Quebec. Describing his LP *Portrait du vieux Kébec*, vol 2 (1974, Opus OP-219), Larry Sandberg and Dick Weissman have commented on the 'joyful, thoroughly delightful fiddling' and noted that 'Boudreault is a unique player in the old self-contained solo style, accompanying his own melodies with a judicious use of drones and double stops, as well as with his own highly rhythmic clog dancing' (*Folk Music Sourcebook*, New York 1976). Boudreault also has made the LP *Portrait du vieux Kébec*, vol 12 (Tamanoir TAM 512). He is the subject of the documentary film *Pitou Boudreault, violoneux* (1975) by Michel Brault, made as part of the NFB series *Le Son des français d'Amérique*.

BIBLIOGRAPHY

Beaulieu, Michel. 'Le retour des violoneux,' *Le Maclean*, Feb 1975

BOUHIER, (Joseph Marie Emmanuel) **Louis.** Teacher, choirmaster, b La Marne, France, 8 Nov 1867, d Magog, near Sherbrooke, Que, 22 Jun 1949. Ordained a priest 29 Jun 1893, he joined the Sulpicians. He studied in Nantes, in Paris, and at the Benedictine monastery in Solesmes. He arrived in Canada in 1896, and his appointments as music teacher at the Collège de Montréal in that year and at the Notre-Dame choir school in 1906 shaped his career and made him one of the best-informed pioneers in the use of Gregorian chant in Montreal. He was rector 1929–39 at Notre-Dame Church, and later chaplain. He was renowned as a lecturer, and his effectiveness lay in his self-effacing but whole-hearted commitment to the cause of music.

Bouhier's publications include *Quatre-vingt Motets en chant grégorien et en musique moderne pour les saluts du Saint-Sacrement* (Montreal 1907) and *300 Cantiques anciens et nouveaux* (Montreal 1907, 1916, 1931), a work known throughout America (over 100,000 copies were printed). It was Bouhier who initiated the Théodore Botrel concerts in Montreal, presented in collaboration with L.-H. *Bourdon, and who arranged for the distribution of the best works of this 'Bard of Pont-Aven,' collected in the volume *Chansons de Botrel pour l'école et le foyer* (Montreal 1903). The collection was immensely successful and enriched the repertoire of popular ballads in French Canada. Bouhier was named Chevalier de la légion d'honneur, Officier d'Académie, and Officier de l'Instruction publique de France.

BOUNDY, Martin. Conductor, organist, b Southwick, Durham, England, 2 Oct 1911. In 1923 he left England and, with his parents, settled in Stratford, Ont, where he studied organ with W.T. Baird and played trumpet, trombone, and euphonium with the *Salvation Army band. He was supervisor of school music 1933–9 in Tillsonburg, Ont, and then was appointed organist-choirmaster at Wesley United Church in London, Ont.

After enlisting in the RCAF in 1941 he became the first permanent conductor of the RCAF Central Band. He was commissioned and posted overseas in 1942 and thereupon was appointed music director for the RCAF. He conducted the RCAF Headquarters Band at Buckingham Palace in 1944 and 1945 and after VE Day he directed the Overseas Service Band on a six-week tour of the Continent.

After returning to Canada in 1946 Boundy was named supervisor of music in London, Ont, schools and directed the London Tech Concert Band and the Police Boys' Band, leading both to many prizes in music festivals. He was conductor 1949–69 of the London Civic Symphony (later the *London SO) and was music director 1969–78 at Fanshawe College and conductor of the college's Four Counties Choir. Honoured 24 Apr 1962 with the Bene Merenti Medal by Pope John XXIII, Boundy conducted the Band of the London, Ont, Catholic Central School before Pope Paul VI in Rome in 1964. Boundy has served 1950–1, 1969–72, and 1973–4 as president of the Ontario chapter of the *CBDA and 1968–9 as president of the *Canadian Music Festival Adjudicators' Assn.

BIBLIOGRAPHY

Crawford, Lenore. 'Maestro of the oompah,' *SatN*, 20 Oct 1951

(PD)

BOURASSA, Guy. Pianist, teacher, b St-Raymond-de-Portneuf, near Quebec City, 30 Jul 1923. He began his musical training with Alphonse *Tardif at the Collège de Lévis, then studied until 1944 with Germaine *Malépart at the

CMM, and 1944–6 with Robert Casadesus in New York and for several summers at the American Cons at Fontainebleau. He began giving radio and TV recitals in 1946 and appeared as a soloist with the *MSO and the *Quebec SO. He began teaching at the *CMQ in 1948. A sought-after accompanist, he has played for the tenors Pierre *Boutet and Raoul *Jobin, the violinist Christian Ferras, and the cellist Pierre Fournier. In 1954 Bourassa gave the first performance of Serge *Garant's *Variations pour piano* on the CBC radio program 'Premières.' In the same year he presented a series of piano duet recitals with Pierre *Beaudet, and, also with Beaudet, recorded John *Beckwith's *Music for Dancing* and Violet *Archer's *Ten Folk Songs* (1954 RCI 113). At the inauguration of the *Salle Claude-Champagne, 22 Nov 1964, he was the soloist in the *Champagne *Concerto*. Bourassa has recorded Rodolphe *Mathieu's *Sonata* (1956, RCI 123). MB-L

BOURDON, Louis-Honoré. Impresario, b Longueuil, near Montreal, 13 Sep 1890, d Montreal 8 Jun 1974. He studied cello and solfège at the Ghent Cons, following in the footsteps of a musical family which included several cellists: his mother Caroline Derome; his stepfather Jean-Baptiste *Dubois; his brother, the conductor Rosario *Bourdon; and his half-brother Jules Dubois, later director of solfège for the province of Quebec. On his return to Montreal Louis-H. Bourdon became an impresario. In 1910 he presented the *Dubois String Quartet in its first concert. The first foreign artist he presented was Mary Garden, 9 Apr 1912 at the *Montreal Arena, paying her a fee of $2000 and himself suffering a loss of $300 despite the immense banners, carrying the singer's name, which he had placed at the principal intersections in the city. By contrast, it is reported that he must have broken the world record at that time for the sale of tickets for a single concert, taking in $28,888 when he presented Enrico Caruso 27 Sep 1920 at the Aréna Mont-Royal, and giving the artist the highest fee he had ever paid anyone, a reported $20,544. He was the first Canadian impresario to bring a French artist to North America, the tenor Edmond Clémont, whom in 1921 he presented on tour in Canada and the USA. On his own initiative, and without subsidy, he presented to the Canadian public the stars of the day – Kreisler, Paderewski, Rachmaninoff, Ravel, Heifetz, la Argentina, Melba, and Calvé. He volunteered his services to organize several recitals in aid of war victims. At the *St-Denis Theatre 28 May 1925 he arranged a large benefit concert for Emma *Albani. He retired in 1947 after 40 years of activity. For him the hiring of an artist was based primarily on intuition. If he had to choose among several who were his friends, he invariably chose the one who, more than the others, seemed to him best equipped to serve the artistic ideal.

WRITINGS

'Réminiscences,' *VM*, vol 9, Oct 1968

BIBLIOGRAPHY

Béraud, Jean. 'Le métier d'impresario: Louis Bourdon,' Montreal *La Presse*, 25 Nov 1961 YR

BOURDON, (Joseph Charles) Rosario. Conductor, cellist, arranger, composer, record company executive, b Longueuil, near Montreal, 6 Mar 1885, d New York 24 Apr 1961; premier prix cello (Cons of Ghent) 1898, hon D MUS (Montreal) 1944. He was a brother of Louis-Honoré *Bourdon and a halfbrother of Jules Dubois. At nine he began to study the cello with J.-B. *Dubois (later his stepfather).

Rosario Bourdon as a child, *La Presse*, 1 Dec 1900

In 1897 he joined the class of Édouard Jacobs at the Royal Cons of Ghent. He studied also in Brussels and toured Europe as a child prodigy (billed as 'Rosario') before returning to Canada in 1900 to give successful recitals in Quebec and Montreal. He was a member 1902–3 of the Cincinnati SO, and during that time returned to perform Servais's *Le Désir* with the Société symphonique de Québec (*Quebec SO) at the inauguration (31 Aug 1903) of the *Auditorium de Québec. He was a member 1904–8 of the Philadelphia Orchestra. At some time in the mid-1900s he studied conducting in Europe, returning to join the St Paul (Minn) SO, serving 1908–11 as cellist and assistant conductor.

In 1909 he began recording for the Victor Talking Machine Co, and eventually he became the company's house cellist. In 1911 he was appointed music director for Victor, a position he shared with Joseph Pasternak. He was the conductor for recordings by the Victor Concert and Symphony orchestras, by Sousa's Band, and by many Victor solo artists including Mary Garden. His recordings as conductor and cellist are listed in *Roll Back the Years*. He also played cello obbligatos on records made by such singers as Frances Alda, Enrico Caruso (1917, *Sancta Maria* by Fauré), Mabel Garrison, John McCormack, and Alma Gluck, and piano accompaniments for many Victor artists including his fellow cellist Victor Herbert. In 1923 Bourdon began a parallel and equally successful career as music director on NBC radio; he was responsible for 'Cities Service Concerts' (1927–38) and other series. After leaving the Victor company in 1931 he worked with other recording organizations, including Brunswick, NBC, Thesaurus, and Muzak.

On 14 Jan 1935 Bourdon conducted the opening concert of the *SCSM at *Plateau Hall; the program included his arrangement of *Lavallée's *Le Papillon*. Bourdon returned to conduct the orchestra on subsequent occasions, his programs including Saint-Saëns' *Symphony No. 3* (the 'Organ' Symphony) and Poulenc's *Concert champêtre*, with Léo-Pol *Morin as soloist, as well as works by Beethoven, Tchaikovsky, and Wagner. For the critic Marcel *Valois, 'the principal quality of this conductor lay in the relation – that is to say, the balance – between the cultivation and the gift. He was an exemplary musician because he had both authority and discrimination. There was no seeking after personal success, no desire to impose his tastes, only a constant wish to make the voices of the composers heard.' Three of Bourdon's compositions in light style were recorded: *Is There a Santa Claus?*, *Ginger Snaps* (T.B. Harms), and *Danse bagatelle* (Feist) the latter two by the Victor Novelty Orchestra. His *Poème élégiaque* for cello and orchestra was performed by Roland *Leduc in 1943 at the *CMM.

BIBLIOGRAPHY

Valois, Marcel. 'Rosario Bourdon était un musicien exemplaire,' *Au carrefour des souvenirs* (Montreal 1965)

(EBM)

BOURQUE, Pierre. Saxophonist, teacher, b Plessisville, Que, 27 Jan 1938; premier prix (Paris Cons) 1961. A member of the Sainte-Cécile concert band 1948–55 while at the Collège de Lévis he continued his musical studies 1955–8 at the *CMQ with Maurice *DeCelles and 1958–61 at the Paris Cons in the class of Marcel Mule. He toured 1960–1 as a recitalist for the *JMC and in 1962 as a soloist with the *Quebec SO. In 1963 he founded the *Pierre Bourque Saxophone Quartet. He began teaching saxophone and wind chamber music classes at the CMQ in 1962 and also taught 1961–72 at the *JMC Orford Art Centre and 1962–5 at Ste-Anne-de-la-Pocatière College. Among his pupils are Jean Bouchard, Claude Brisson, and Rémi Ménard. Bourque served 1972–3 as director of the Cons de musique de Chicoutimi. He has performed frequently with the Quebec SO and the *CBC Quebec Chamber Orchestra. SW

Bourque Saxophone Quartet. See Pierre Bourque Saxophone Quartet.

BOUTET (Sieur de Saint-Martin), **Martin**. Choirmaster, violinist or viol player, teacher, soldier, tailor, carpenter, b Sceaux, France, ca 1612, d Quebec City ca 1683. He enlisted 7 Apr 1643 at La Rochelle to serve three years in Canada as a soldier and labourer. Taking up residence in Quebec City in 1645, he remained there except for a trip to France in 1677. He is thought to have been attached to the Fort St-Louis garrison until his wife's death sometime between 1661 and 1664, at which time he offered himself to the Jesuits, whom he served as business agent. He started a mathematics course at the Jesuit college, also teaching surveying, hydrography, and piloting, and this earned him an engineer's certificate, awarded in 1678 by Louis XIV.

An artist as well as an engineer and a scholar, Boutet played an important role in the musical life of Quebec, especially with regard to church services. It is known that he played the viol (or violin?) at Christmas Mass in 1645 and at a wedding in the same year. According to a notarized document of 2 Sep 1651, he was appointed as both singer at the services and director of the children's choir in the parish church in Quebec City. He also taught reading, writing, plainchant, and the forms of worship. He even provided the money for the purchase of singing books. One of his two pupils at that time, Louis *Jolliet, became one of the first organists in New France, and it is likely that Boutet initiated his organ studies. Charles-Amador *Martin also was one of his pupils. Boutet has earned a place in the history of the new colony as the first schoolmaster and mathematics teacher, the first secular singer, and the first choirmaster.

BIBLIOGRAPHY

Gosselin, Amédée. *L'Instruction publique au Canada sous le Régime français* (Quebec 1911)

Roy, Antoine. *Les Lettres, les sciences et les arts au Canada* (Paris 1930)

Massicotte, Édouard-Z. 'Violons et luthiers,' *BRH*, vol 41, Apr 1935

Lachapelle, Ch.-E. 'Martin Boutet (1616–1686), ingénieur, savant et artiste,' *Mémoires de la Société généalogique canadienne-française*, vol 15, Summer 1964

Amtmann *Music in Canada*

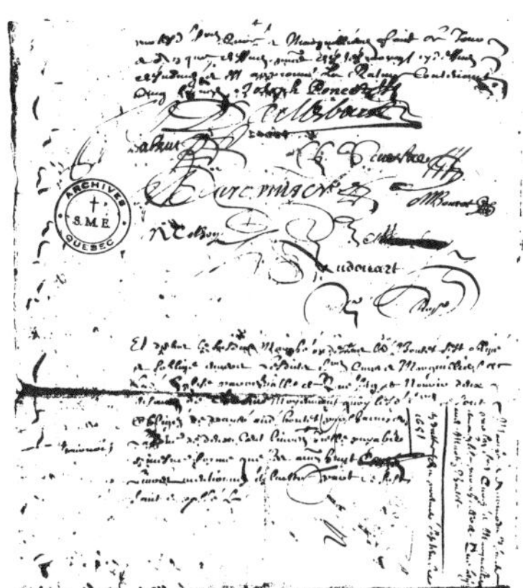

Excerpts from a contract between the 'sieurs et marguilliers de Québec' and Martin Boutet. Signed on 2 Sep 1651, this is one of the earliest documents in which music is mentioned.

Burke-Gaffney, M.W. 'Boutet de Saint-Martin, Martin,' *DCB*, vol 1

Jesuit Relations LP

BOUTET, Pierre (André). Tenor, radio producer, b Quebec City 6 Nov 1926; LRCT 1951. He began vocal studies in 1943 with Émile *Larochelle and attended regular music classes 1947–8 on scholarship at Columbia U. He also studied 1948–51 at the *RCMT with George *Lambert (voice) and Herman *Geiger-Torel (staging). He won several competitions, sang in oratorio performances in Toronto (notably the *St Matthew Passion* with the *Toronto Mendelssohn Choir), and in 1950 made his debut with the Opera Festival (*COC) as Ottavio in *Don Giovanni* and sang the title role in *Faust*. After his performance in the *St Matthew Passion* for the *Montreal Festivals Marcel *Valois wrote: 'the voice is rich, the singer already seasoned' (*La Presse*, 9 Jul 1950). Boutet was the tenor soloist with the Toronto Mendelssohn Choir in its 1950 performances of Beethoven's *Missa solemnis* and Verdi's *Manzoni Requiem*. A winner in 1950 (fourth place) and 1951 (second place) of the radio competition *'Singing Stars of Tomorrow,' he continued his training 1951–3 in New York with Paul Althouse and Cesare Sturani. In 1953 he took part in the Canadian premiere of *Jeanne d'Arc au bûcher* at the Montreal Festivals. After winning the CBC French-network competition *'Nos Futures Étoiles' in 1955 he performed with the *MSO, the *Quebec SO, the *TSO and the *Vancouver SO. On a scholarship from the Quebec government he studied 1957–8 in Rome with Manfredi Palverosi and Rachele Maragliano-Mori, and on a *Canada Council grant he continued his studies 1958–60 in Paris with Giuseppe Boralevi and Simone Tillard. He also made recital tours throughout Europe and North Africa. His performance in Haydn's *The Creation* (Théâtre des Champs-Élysées, Paris, 1959) and Bach's *B Minor Mass* (Notre-Dame de Paris, 1960) earned him much praise from the critics and confirmed his aptitude for oratorio.

Returning to Quebec in 1960, Boutet sang in recitals across Canada as well as on CBC radio and TV. He was Jean in the premiere, 30 Jul 1960, of *Blackburn's *Pirouette* and sang excerpts from that work on a recording produced by the *JMC. Also for the JMC he appeared on tour in Blackburn's *Pirouette* 1960–1 and in the stage version of Debussy's *L'Enfant prodigue* 1961–2. During the 1962–3 season at the *Théâtre lyrique de Nouvelle-France he sang the role of Count Almaviva in *The Barber of Seville*. In 1963 he began to work as a producer for the CBC FM network, preparing in particular the programs 'Les petits concerts' and 'Recital.' Nevertheless, he has continued to appear regularly as soloist with the Quebec SO, the MSO, the *Orchestre de chambre Pierre-Morin, the Montreal Elgar Choir, and other organizations.

In addition, Boutet taught 1965–72 at the municipal centre in Rimouski and privately in Quebec City, and became choirmaster at the Quebec City churches of Charlesbourg in 1968 and Ste-Odile in 1974. In 1966 he became president of the *Amis de l'orgue in Quebec. He also has served 1972–5 as artistic consultant to the *Opéra du Québec and, at different times, as an adjudicator of the examinations for the *CMQ, *Laval U, the *MSO concours, and the *CBC Talent Festival.

Boutet has made five LPs in the series *La Bonne Chanson présente nos plus belles chansons* (RCA Victor) and the LPs *Chansons d'hier ... chansons d'aujourd'hui* (1957, RCA Victor LCP 1021), *Noël Noël Noël* (RCA Victor CGP 109), *Chants pascals et religieux* (Radio-Marie NDC 336306) and *Chants de Noël* (Radio-Marie NDC 336318). In addition, he is the soloist on the recording of the *Messe solennelle pour le jour de Pâques* (BML 10) with the choir of St-Dominique Church in Quebec City. (IB)

La Boutique d'opéra. Studio founded in Montreal in 1960 by Jacqueline *Richard, pianist, André Bisson, baritone, and Paul Landry, administrator, with the aim of training operatic performers and technical staff. At first a travelling company, its initial production, Ferdinando Paer's *Le Maître de chapelle*, was presented in St-Georges-de-Beauce and in Montreal. In 1962 the group became a stationary company, enlisting singers, dancers, a chorusmaster (Claude *Létourneau), rehearsal pianists (Janine *Lachance and Monik *Grenier), a director (Charlotte Boisjoli), and supplementary staff (electricians, costumers, and people working on stage properties). A small theatre with 99 seats was opened in the former Égrégore Theatre on Clark St, and nearly 70 performances of six chamber operas were given in less than six months: Hugo Weisgall's *The Stronger* (Montreal premiere); Menotti's *The Medium*; Mozart's *The Impresario* and *L'Oca del Cairo*; Offenbach's *Le Mariage aux Lanternes*; and Menotti's *Amahl and the Night Visitors*. The group included about 30 singers, notably Napoléon *Bisson, Fernande *Chiocchio, Clarice *Carson, and Cécile *Vallée. In March 1964, when the necessary subsidies could not be raised and the theatre was reclaimed by its owner, the company ceased its activities. DA

BOWER, Laurie (Lawrence Wayne). Arranger, singer, trombonist, b Kirkland Lake, Ont, 31 Aug 1933; B MUS ED (Toronto) 1957. He studied at the *U of Toronto with Charles *Peaker (choral technique), Robert *Rosevear (music education), and Harry Stevenson (trombone) and played in the dance bands of Benny Louis, Ozzie Williams, and Mart *Kenney before pursuing a dual career as a trombonist in Toronto studio orchestras and as a singer and choral arranger. He sang with several CBC vocal groups and in 1969 formed the Laurie Bower Singers. The singers have worked in Toronto studios, recording many jingles, and in concert and on TV, accompanying other performers. Original members were Bower, Tommy *Ambrose, Kathy Collier, Vern Kennedy, and Patty Van Evera; in 1979 they were Bower, Cal Dodd, Bill Misener, Colina Phillips, Judy Tate, and Stephanie Taylor. By that time the singers had made 10 LPs of pop songs (arranged by Bower) for the *CTL. Five of these were issued commercially: three under the title *The Laurie Bower Singers* (1969, RCA CTLS 1114; 1973, RCA KXL 1-0020; 1974, U Artists 391G) and two under separate titles – *Got a Feelin' for Love* (1976, U Artists 640G) and *You* (1979, New Ventures NV.5006). MM

Liona Boyd

BOWMAN, Dave (David). Pianist, b Buffalo, of Canadian parents, 8 Sep 1914, d Miami 28 Dec 1964. Raised in Hamilton, Ont, he played piano at four, later studying at the Hamilton Cons (*RHCM) and the Pittsburgh Institute of Music. He worked in Hamilton with singer Ken Steele, went to London with Billy *Bissett in 1936, and joined Jack Hylton's orchestra 1936–7. He performed in New York with dixieland stars Bobby Hackett 1937–9, Bud Freeman 1939–40 and 1954–5, Jack Teagarden in 1940, and Muggsy Spanier 1941–2, and was a radio staff-pianist 1943–54. He freelanced in Florida from the late 1950s until his death there in an automobile accident. Described as 'a continually inspired and very adaptable player who never deserted his love of swing' (*Decca Book of Jazz*, London 1958), Bowman recorded as a leader for Signature and with Freeman, Hackett, Spanier, Sidney Bechet, Yank Lawson, and others, including various singers. MM

BOYD, Liona (Maria). Guitarist, composer, b London 11 Jul 1950, naturalized Canadian 1975; B MUS (Toronto) 1972. Brought to Canada as a child, she began studies with Eli *Kassner at 14. After attending the U of Toronto she lived 1972–4 in Europe, studying in Paris with Alexandre Lagoya (of whom she had been a pupil in 1971 at the *JMC Orford Art Centre). She also has taken master classes with Julian Bream, Alirio Diaz, and Narciso Yepes. In 1974 she began recording for *Boot's Master Concert Series, completing three successful LPs. She made her New York debut 22 Mar 1975 at the Carnegie Recital Hall and in 1976 began to tour North America with Gordon *Lightfoot, performing at the opening of his programs and thus introducing classical guitar to a new and substantial audience. She herself was the object of the attention usually accorded a pop performer. By 1978 she had performed througrout Canada (including the Yukon) and in the USA, South America, New Zealand, and Australia.

Boyd made her orchestral debut 7 Jan 1977 in Toronto, playing Vivaldi's *Concerto in D* with the New Chamber Orchestra. Her recital repertoire includes her own compositions *Cantarell* and *Llanto de Gaviota*, her transcriptions of Bach, Beethoven, Cimarosa, Debussy, and Satie, and works by Milton *Barnes, Robert Feuerstein, and Godfrey *Ridout. She has premiered Barnes' *Fantasy for Guitar*, Ridout's *Capriccio*, and several works by Carlos Payet. Boyd is a member of CAPAC.

DISCOGRAPHY

Bach – Albinoni – Marcello – Cimarosa – Vivaldi. English Chamb O, A. Davis cond. 1979. Col M 35853

The First Lady of the Guitar: Barnes – Barrios – Payet – et al. (1978). Col M 35137
The Guitar: Bach – Albeniz – D. Scarlatti – et al. 1974. Boot BMC 3002
Liona: Cimarosa – Feuerstein – Boyd – et al. (1976). Boot BMC 3006
Miniatures for Guitar: Tarrega – Carcassi – Sor – et al. (1977). Boot BOS-7181

BIBLIOGRAPHY

Cobb, David. 'Scarlatti in Nashville,' *The Canadian*, 28 Jun 1975
Shubin, Cindy. 'Liona Boyd: Canada's first lady of classical guitar,' *Guitar Player*, vol 12, Oct 1978
Kennedy, Paul. 'Eclectic guitar,' *Fugue*, Feb 1979

BOYDEN, John. Baritone, b Woodstock, Ont, 22 Nov 1935. In 1939 his family moved to Stratford where at eight he began singing as a boy soprano. He joined the *Elizabethan Singers and studied with their conductor, Gordon D. Scott. During the first official Stratford Music Festival (summer 1955) he participated in a workshop directed by Elisabeth Schwarzkopf. Her encouragement and a scholarship raised by Stratford people enabled Boyden to study 1956–7 in London with Henry Cummings at the RAM. In the summer of 1956 he placed fifth in the international voice competition at Salzburg. In 1958 he received a *Canada Council scholarship to study with Schwarzkopf, Bernard *Diamant, and John *Newmark. On a scholarship from the Mozarteum he was coached by Erik Werba during the summer of 1961. He continued his studies with Diamant in Montreal until 1963.

Boyden returned to the *Stratford Festival in 1957 to sing the Canadian premiere of Gerald Finzi's *Let Us Garlands Bring* with the *CBC SO. In the Montreal premiere of *Somers' opera *The Fool* (15 Mar 1959) Boyden sang the role of the King. Also in 1959 he made his Montreal recital debut for the *Ladies' Morning Musical Club. After his Vienna recital debut at the Konzerthaus the *Express* (7 Nov 1961) referred to him as 'a singing poet from Canada'; it added: 'The last debut of an almost unknown recitalist who made a similar deep and strong impression took place about ten years ago. At that time a young German baritone sang *Winterreise* in the same hall. His name was Dietrich Fischer-Dieskau. This time an equally young baritone, Canadian, sang an exclusively German program. His name is John Boyden. Comparisons come immediately to mind.'

In 1962 Boyden appeared at the Spoleto Festival of Two Worlds, where he sang Schumann's *Dichterliebe*. He also made appearances that year with the New York Philharmonic and the *TSO, and at the Vienna Festival. He made his New York recital debut 22 Apr 1963 at Judson Hall. Commenting on his interpretation of Schumann's *Dichterliebe*, the reviewer for the *New York Herald-Tribune* wrote: 'the work assumed the noblest kind of expression. Each song was conveyed with extraordinary sensitivity ... It was lieder singing of consummate skill.' That same year Boyden sang the Christus in the NBC telecast of Bach's *St Matthew Passion*, and in Hamburg in May 1964 he gave a recital and sang in Monteverdi's *Orfeo* and Orff's *Carmina burana*. At the Vienna Festival he also gave a recital and sang in Mahler's *Des Knaben Wunderhorn* and Bach's *St John Passion*. He returned to the Stratford Festival to sing Aeneas in Purcell's *Dido and Aeneas* with Lois *Marshall and Elizabeth Benson *Guy. In 1964 his other engagements included appearances at the Caramoor Festival in New York State and with the Detroit and Pittsburgh SOs. He toured Europe in 1965, giving recitals in Amsterdam, Vienna, London, Berlin, Lisbon, Milan, and Munich, and performing with orchestras in Bern and Zurich. With John Newmark at the piano Boyden gave the US premiere, 18 Jan 1967 at New York's Town Hall, and the Canadian premiere, 19 Feb 1967 at *York U, Toronto, of Britten's *Songs and Proverbs of William Blake*. In 1968, accompanied by the pianist Mikael Eliasen, he toured the USSR, performing in Leningrad, Moscow, Minsk, and other cities. He studied opera 1969–70 with Eugénie Ludwig. Unfortunately illness cut short his career in the early 1970s.

DISCOGRAPHY

Bach *Cantata No. 42*. Stich-Randall sop, Forrester alto, Young ten, Vienna Academy Chamb choir, Vienna Radio O, Scherchen cond. 1964. West WST 17080/West 8303.
Beethoven and Schumann Songs. M. Eliasen pf. 1970. CBC SM-88/AofD SDD-2158
Brahms *A German Requiem, Op 45*. Yeend sop, Handel and Haydn Soc Chor. 1963. 2-Boston 221-2/1022-3
– *Liebeslieder Waltzes*. Tyler sop, Sarfaty mezzo, Bressler ten, Gold and Fizdale pfs. 1963. Col MS6461
F. Martin *Six Monologues from 'Jedermann'* – R. Fleming *Four Songs* – F. Poulenc *Le travail du peintre*. Newmark pf. 1969. RCI 248
Songs of Franz Schubert. P. Helmer pf. 1970. CBC SM-149
Wolf – Debussy – Dowland – Ravel: songs. Newmark pf. 1965. RCI 202

BIBLIOGRAPHY

Goddard, Peter. 'A home-coming for John Boyden,' Toronto *Telegram*, 17 Aug 1970 (SW)

BRABANT, Pierre. Pianist, composer, b Montreal 26 Aug 1925. Aside from some lessons with J.-Élie *Savaria he was self-taught. While he was very young he gave a public recital, and in 1942 he appeared on the CBC program 'Young Artists of Tomorrow.' Shortly afterwards he won first prize in the CBC radio competition 'Les Talents de chez-nous,' and was invited to play on the CBC programs 'Mosaïque musicale' and 'Radio-Carabin.' After a sojourn 1947–8 in Paris he undertook a 78-recital tour of Canada, playing many of his own compositions – *Sonatine en do*, *Caprice laurentien*, *Cinq Cantilènes*, *Cinq Églogues*, *Berceuse*, and *Souvenir d'un musicien polonais* (Éditions de l'Aube 1947). After his recital at *Plateau Hall in Montreal Jean *Vallerand wrote: 'Pierre Brabant is a splendid pianist and a fine artist. He also is a very intelligent, sensitive composer, with a solid technique and something to say' (*Le Devoir*, 20 Nov 1952). Brabant composed the music for Ruth Sorel's ballet *La Gaspésienne* (1949), premiered in Montreal and performed in Toronto, New York, and at the Warsaw Opera in 1950. He appeared as a solo pianist on the CBC TV programs *'L'Heure du concert' in 1954 and 'Fantasies canadiennes' in 1955.

Later Brabant became interested in light music and, to words by Jean-Pierre *Ferland, wrote the song 'Feuilles de gui,' which was awarded prizes on the CBC's 'Chansons sur mesure' and at an international competition held in Brussels in 1962. He composed the soundtracks for several CBC children's programs, and participated as pianist and composer in the recordings *Maman Fonfon raconte et chante* (RCA Victor LCP 1023), *La Souris verte* (Caparo CO-502), *Au jardin de Pierrot* (Caparo CO-503 and Pantin PTN 48 M59-60), and Tante Lucille's *20 Contes pour enfants* (RCA Gala KTL 2-7020-1-4). Brabant was music director and arranger for recordings by Georges *Dor and Félix *Leclerc and also composed the music for 'La Semaine verte' and 'Rue des pignons,' a popular TV series for which he recorded the theme song (Sel SSP 24161) and played the background music 1967–78. He is a member of CAPAC.

BIBLIOGRAPHY

Scarpaleggia, Cherubina. 'Pierre Brabant,' Montreal *Le Samedi*, 10 Jan 1953 GP

BRADAN, Tony or **Anthony** (Antonio Alfredo), (b Bradanovich). Teacher, guitarist, arranger, b Ladner, south of Vancouver, of Yugoslavian-Canadian parents, 6 Oct 1913. Though his formal training was limited, he did study banjo and guitar with Roy Barry; harmony, counterpoint, and composition with Pasquale *Fiore in Vancouver; and harmony with John *Weinzweig in Toronto. He began his career at 14 in Percy Smith's dance orchestra and was a member 1937–42, in Vancouver and Toronto, of Mart *Kenney's Western Gentlemen. During World War II he served as music director of the *Army Show, recruiting and arranging for some 15 orchestras, and also was an arranger for the Canadian orchestra of the Allied Expeditionary Forces. After the war he played in CBC Toronto orchestras under Lucio *Agostini, Bert *Niosi, Ivan *Romanoff, Geoffrey *Waddington, and others. He also has taught privately in Toronto for over 30 years, becoming one of the leading guitar instructors in Canada. His pupils have included Neville Barnes, Ed *Bickert, Art DeVilliers, Bobby Edwards, Peter Harris, Andy Krehm, and Lorne Lofsky, all prominent studio or jazz players in Toronto. On his retirement in 1979 Bradan began a series of books on the playing of fretted instruments.

Bradan's wife, the singer Judy Richards (b Calgary 15 Oct 1922), appeared 1940–3 with Kenney and later with the Toronto dance bands of Frank Bogart, Trump *Davidson, Ellis *McLintock, and others, retiring in the 1950s.

BRADSHAW, (John) Lloyd. Choir conductor, teacher, b St Mary's, near Stratford, Ont, 21 Feb 1929. He studied music in Stratford, in London, Ont, intermittently 1958–61 at the U of Toronto, and in 1965 with David Willcocks in Cambridge, England. A graduate (1948) of the Stratford Teachers' College, he taught, until 1963, in turn in rural Ontario, Stratford, and Toronto schools. He was editor 1959–62 of the *OMEA journal *The Recorder*.

Bradshaw was a member 1954–60 and music director 1960–2 of the *Festival Singers. As organist-choirmaster 1960–70 at St George's United Church Bradshaw conducted several choirs, including the St George's Youth Choir, which toured in England (1964), Canada (1967, with appearances at *Expo 67), and Europe (1970). His St George's Boys' Choir took part in the Toronto premiere (*TSO under Heinz *Unger 4 Feb 1964) of Mahler's *Third Symphony*. Bradshaw was supervisor of music and assistant co-ordinator of music education 1963–8 for North York (Toronto) schools and special lecturer in choral music 1968–73 at the *U of Toronto, where he also conducted the university choir and was chorusmaster for the opera department. Concurrently he was chorusmaster of the *COC and founding conductor of the *Canadian Children's Opera Chorus. At a Massey Hall concert 19 Dec 1969 he conducted three St George's choirs, the university choir, and the opera chorus in a program of Christmas music. He prepared most of the choirs for TS performances while Seiji Ozawa was conductor. He was the founder in 1970 and director until 1973 of the Toronto Youth Choir, of which a part, the Sound Company, performed regularly in 1971 at *Ontario Place. In 1975 he became music director at Trinity United Church, Toronto, and of the *Orpheus Choir. He retained the latter position until 1980. After an Orpheus Choir concert he was praised by John *Kraglund for 'a rare ability to get clarity of both musical line and texts from his singers' (Toronto *Globe and Mail*, 3 Jun 1976). (AHC)

BRAND, Oscar. Folksinger, composer, guitarist, b Winnipeg 7 Feb 1920, naturalized US; B SC psychology (Brooklyn College) 1942. Though he was taken as a boy to the USA – where he lived in Minneapolis, Chicago, and New York – and established himself as one of the most popular US personalities in folk music, Brand has maintained his ties to Canada. He was host for the TV hootenany 'Let's Sing Out' (filmed before audiences at Canadian colleges and universities, and seen on CTV 1963–6 and on CBC 1966–7) and for CTV's 'Brand: New Scene' 1966–7. He has performed at the *Charlottetown Festival (1969, a concert heard on the CBC's 'Showcase'), at *O'Keefe Centre, at the Calgary Stampede, in coffeehouses, and at folk festivals. Brand has made some 60 LPs in the USA for Audio Fidelity, Elektra, Riverside, Tradition, and other labels, and has prepared several collections of folksongs for US publishers. His compositions include over 300 songs – the best known is 'A Guy Is a Guy,' an adaptation of an army song – and collaborations on several musical comedies produced in New York.

BIBLIOGRAPHY

Lawless, Ray. *Folksingers and Folksongs in America* (New York 1960) (LHv)

BRANDON, Tom. Folksinger, b Midland, Ont, 1927. He learned many Irish songs from his parents and uncles and, after he began working at 16, picked up others from the sailors on Great Lakes boats in the smmer and the men in lumbercamps in winter. In 1951 he became a leverman for the CPR, first in Toronto and later in Peterborough, where his songs were recorded in 1957 by Edith *Fowke. Some of them have been released on the Folkways, Prestige, and Folk Legacy labels (see Discography for Folk music, Anglo-Canadian: 4 / Ontario and the Prairies). Brandon appeared at the 1961 conference of the IFMC in Quebec City and at the *Mariposa and Philadelphia folk festivals. EF

Brandon. Manitoba city on the Assiniboine River, 200 km west of Winnipeg. The first settlers arrived in 1878. Named after Brandon House, a one-time Hudson's Bay Co depot, the settlement received railway service (CPR) in 1881 and was incorporated as a city in 1882. Brandon had in its vicinity in 1975 over 60 industrial firms, although it continued to be an agriculturally based community. Its population had reached 40,000 by 1978.

As Manitoba's second largest city Brandon is the cultural centre of western Manitoba. The city's major musical institution is the School of Music at *Brandon U. The school maintains ensembles, notably the Brandon U Chamber Orchestra and the *Brandon U Trio, which perform publicly throughout Manitoba. It is the site of the annual S.C. *Eckhardt-Gramatté competition for the performance of Canadian music. Many of the school's graduates are teachers in the city's elementary and secondary schools, several of which present annual productions of musicals.

Developing out of the Musical Nomads, the Brandon Operatic Society (mid-1920s–ca 1940) performed musicals on the auditorium stage of the city hall. Mme Marjorie Johnson (b Tyson, her maiden name rearranged to create her British stage name, St Oyn) directed and starred in operetta productions such as Howard Talbot and Lionel Monckton's *The Arcadians*, Edward German's *Merrie England*, Monckton's *The Country Girl* and *The Runaway Girl*, Harold Fraser-Simson's *The Maid of the Mountains*, and Sidney Jones' *The Geisha*. Other performers included Lillian Edmundson, Humphrey and Eric Davies, and Sidney Wrightson. Casting problems brought on by wartime conditions caused the company to dissolve: 'The eight army and air force camps in a radius of 50 miles changed the atmosphere forever. The young men left and the pretty girls quickly married and took off ... *The Geisha* wavered in rehearsals for two seasons and tip-toed into oblivion' (*Brandon Sun*, 26 Nov 1971).

Brandon's annual Festival of Music and Speech Arts began as a competition festival as early as 1928, one of the network of such festivals visited by British adjudicators. William Neale (b ca 1887), a clarinetist, school music teacher, and bandmaster active in Brandon after 1910, founded an amateur orchestra that appeared regularly at the festival before the war. After the war the festival was perpetuated by a civic committee and came to include non-competition classes and a workshop approach to student performance.

The great Emma *Albani sang in Brandon in 1897. Probably the first major choral concert was given 1 May 1903 by the 150-voice Festival Chorus, prepared by Frank B. Fenwick for the *Cycle of Musical Festivals of the Dominion of Canada. Church and secular choirs have involved citizens in choral activity throughout the century. The 70-voice Western Manitoba Philharmonic Choir (1965–76), whose conductors have been Lucien *Needham 1965–7, Leonard *Mayoh 1967–73, Derek Morphy 1973–5, and Peter Allen 1975–6, gave two concerts annually, performing *Messiah*, the Mozart and Brahms *Requiems*, and similar works with the visiting *Winnipeg SO. Brandon has been visited by artists touring under the auspices of the *Overture Concerts organization, the *CFMTA, and the *JMC. After 1969 major musical presentations have been given in the *Western Manitoba Centennial Auditorium. Notable Brandon-born musicians include the singer Arlene Meadows, the pianist Louise Chapman Needham, and the pianist, teacher, and administrator Peggy Sharpe. (WM)

Brandon University. Established in Brandon, Man, in 1899 as Brandon College by the Baptist Union of Western Canada. In 1938 it became non-denominational when the Baptist Church severed its links with it for financial reasons. The college affiliated itself with the *U of Manitoba in 1938 and became Brandon U in 1967.

When the Dept of Music was founded in 1906, it offered only conservatory instruction. As an affiliate of *McMaster U it at first attracted Canadian singers and pianists who worked towards the Graduate Diploma of Music. After a decline during the Depression and World War II the department gradually recovered in the 1950s and was offering university credit courses by 1953. In 1963 Brandon College offered the first B MUS program in Manitoba and the department became the School of Music in its own new building.

In the 1970s its facilities included an electronic music studio. A Steinway concert grand was provided for the J.R.C. Evans Theatre in a bequest from Abbie Helmer Vining, the first director, 1906–7, of the college's music department. W.L. *Wright was Vining's successor 1907–47. The acting director 1947–8 was Peggy A. Sharpe (b Brandon 26 Jul 1914), who in 1963 became the first supervisor of the school's Conservatory Dept. Lorne *Watson, who had succeeded Sharpe as director of the department in 1948, stayed as director of the school after the 1963 move.

Emphasizing music education and performance (strings in particular), Brandon U offers the B MUS (education, applied, and general) and the BA (music major, minor) degrees. The Music School's first graduate (1966) was Jack Spalding. Honorary doctorates have been awarded to W.L. Wright (1969), S.C. *Eckhardt-Gramatté (1970), Murray *Adaskin (1972), and Jon *Vickers (1976).

The establishment of the school as a centre of string pedagogy dates from Albert *Pratz' appointment to the faculty in 1964. Pratz' work was carried on and expanded by Edward and Norma Lee *Bisha, Francis *Chaplin, and Malcolm *Tait. Brandon graduates (string and other) have entered many Canadian and foreign orchestras. In 1978–9 the school consisted of 102 students and 32 teachers (18 full-time). Many of the teachers have given concerts and workshops and acted as adjudicators throughout Manitoba.

As its centennial project in 1967 the Wawanesa Insurance Co set up a program of scholarships for string players. Brandon also has administered the Carl and Lyle Sanders Grant and the Arthur and Abbie Vining Memorial Graduate Scholarship.

Besides the School of Music's regular recitals by students, faculty, and visiting artists, there is an annual opera production. The university also has co-sponsored (with the Western Manitoba Philharmonic Choir) an annual presentation of a major work with the *Winnipeg SO and (with the *MMEA) an annual January workshop which attracts up to 300 music educators from Manitoba, Ontario, and Saskatchewan. Guests have included Victor *Feldbrill, George *Little, Wilfrid *Pelletier, and R. Murray *Schafer.

The Brandon U Chamber Orchestra (known during its first season, 1962, as the Brandon Civic Orchestra) consists of about 40 students and teachers. Between September and April each year it presents two concerts, makes tours, and participates in opera performances. Its conductors have been David Sublette 1962–5, Walter Hekster 1965–71, Gordon *Macpherson 1971–4, James Manishen 1974–5, and Macpherson again after 1975. Other ensembles include the *Brandon U Trio, Concert Band, Chorale (conducted by Leonard *Mayoh), Jazz Band, and Chorus. The Collegium Musicum, established in 1973 and directed by James Mendenhall, had a collection of over 50 replicas of early instruments by 1978.

In 1967 the school became a member of the *WBM. The annual S.C. Eckhardt-Gramatté Competition for the Performance of Canadian Music was inaugurated in 1976 at Brandon U.

BIBLIOGRAPHY

Sharpe, Peggy. 'Sixty years of music at Brandon College,' *Sharps & Flats*, vol 6, Apr 1966

Watson, Lorne. 'Small-school spirit enlivens Brandon's music program,' *MSc*, 269, Jan–Feb 1973 (LW)

Brandon University Trio (formerly Halifax Trio). One of Canada's longest-lived chamber ensembles. A piano trio, it was founded in 1955 in Halifax as the Halifax Trio by Francis *Chaplin, violin, Edward *Bisha, cello, and Gordon *Macpherson, piano, and established a national reputation through its many CBC broadcasts. Aided by a *Canada Council grant the members of the trio moved to *Brandon U in 1966 as artists-in-residence and remained there as the Brandon University Trio. Bisha was succeeded in 1968 by Malcolm *Tait. A repertoire of over 100 trios includes the standard works, as well as compositions by Violet *Archer, S.C. *Eckhardt-Gramatté, Michel *Perrault, Robert *Turner, and Arnold *Walter. In 1963 a work by Barbara *Pentland was commissioned for the group by the CBC.

DISCOGRAPHY

Archer *Trio No. 2* – Turina *Trio No. 2 in B Minor*. 1967. RCI 241

Arensky *Trio in D Minor* – Turina *Piano Trio No. 1*. 1973. CBC SM 245

Contant *Trio* – Anhalt *Trio*. 1966. RCI 229/RCA CCS-1023

KN

BRANDT, Gordie (Gordon Edward). Guitarist, b Regina 20 Jun 1924. Raised in Saskatoon, Brandt began playing guitar at 12. Although he was interested in jazz in his mid-teens, he first worked professionally 1940–1 as a member of a country group, Sleepy and Swede and the Tumbleweeds (see also the *Rhythm Pals), who toured in western Canada. While playing 1941–8 in Vancouver dance and jazz bands (with Carl DeSantis, Wilf Wylie, Arnie Molar, and others), he was guided informally by the guitarist Ray Norris and by the pianists Wylie and Alan McNab. Brandt spent four years in Toronto, where he studied in 1950 with Gordon *Delamont, worked in clubs with Vic Centro, Phil *Nimmons, and Rudi *Toth, and played in CBC orchestras under Johnny *Burt and Bert *Niosi. Brandt returned to Saskatoon in 1952. As that city's leading jazz musician he appeared 1954–60 on CFQC TV's 'Gordie Brandt Show' and performed in concerts and in clubs. After he opened a retail and teaching centre in 1961 he became less active as a performer. Though not widely known outside western Canada, Brandt has become a legend among his peers as one of Canada's finest jazz guitarists.

Brandt's son Kim (b Saskatoon 24 Nov 1953), a bassist 1969–73 with the *Saskatoon SO, moved in 1973 to Toronto, where he has worked as bass guitarist in Ian *Tyson's band, the Great Speckled Bird, and with Sylvia Tyson. MM

BRANSCOMBE, Gena (m Tenney). Composer, choir conductor, teacher, pianist, b Picton, near Kingston, Ont, 4 Nov 1881, d New York 26 Jul 1977; BA (Chicago) 1900, hon MA (Whitman) 1932. She studied 1897–1903 at the Chicago Musical College with Felix Borowski (composition), Alexander von Fielitz (songwriting), and Florenz Ziegfeld, Arthur Friedheim, Hans von Schiller, and Rudolph Ganz (piano), winning gold medals in composition in 1900 and 1901. She taught piano in Chicago 1903–7 and then became director of the piano department of Whitman College, Washington, DC, leaving in 1909 to study with Humperdinck in Berlin.

Though she often revisited Canada, Branscombe lived and worked in the USA for more than 75 years. Publishers in both countries accepted her piano pieces, songs, and choral and orchestral works. An opera, *The Bells of Circumstance*, with a text written by the composer and treating 16th-century French settlers in Canada, was never completed, but an orchestral work, *Quebec Suite*, was extracted from it in 1928 and was premiered in 1930 by the Chicago Women's SO, conducted by the composer. Her large choral drama *Pilgrims of Destiny*, also to her own words and on a pioneering subject (the voyagers on the Mayflower), was awarded the 1928 League of American Pen Women annual prize for the finest work produced by a woman. The orchestral work *A Festival Prelude*, first played in 1914 at Peterboro, NH, had several later performances including one at the San Francisco Exposition.

Branscombe's greatest successes, however, were in the vocal and choral field. *Coventry's Choir*, with words by Violet B. Alvarez, was performed at Coventry in 1962 and several times afterwards in Great Britain and North America. In 1960 her hymn 'Arms that Have Sheltered Us' was adopted by the Royal Canadian Navy. The *Introit, Prayer Response and Amen*, commissioned by Riverside Church, New York, and premiered in 1973, testified to the astonishing vigour of a composer active at 92. Gena Branscombe enriched the repertoire especially in the area of short choral works for women's voices. Characteristically these works suspend vocal lines of individual shape over and within an accompaniment of shift-

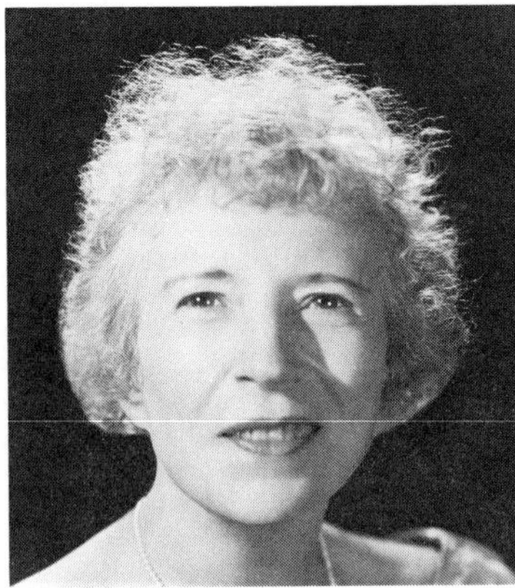

Gena Branscombe

ing chromatic harmonies, though bitonality and parallelism are used occasionally. Many of her vocal works use her own texts.

Branscombe was often a guest conductor at performances of her works in Canada, England, and the USA, and was leader of various choirs in New Jersey during the 1930s and 1940s. She founded in 1934 and conducted for 20 years the Branscombe Chorale of New York. She received numerous non-academic honours, particularly from US women's organizations, many of which she had served. She was president of the Society of American Women Composers during the 1940s and vice-president and director (1950) of the National Assn of American Composers and Conductors. She was a member of ASCAP.

SELECTED COMPOSITIONS

OPERA

The Bells of Circumstance (Branscombe). Unfinished. Ca 1928. Ms

ORCHESTRA

Festival Prelude. 1913 (Peterboro, NH, 1914). Orch. Ms
Quebec Suite. (Branscombe, from *Bells of Circumstance*). 1928 (Chicago 1930). Ten, orch. Ms
Baladine. 1935. Chamb orch. Ms
Procession. 1935. Orch. Ms
Elegie. 1937. Orch. Ms
Just in the Hush before the Dawn, *Pavane*, *Rigaudon*, and *Wings*. (1946). All ms
French Suite. 1960. Str orch. Ms

CHOIR WITH ORCHESTRA

The Morning Wind (Banning). Ca 1913. Female vs, orch. Schmidt 1913
Dear Lad O'Mine (Hale). Ca 1915. Female vs, orch. Schmidt 1915
Spirit of Motherhood (Driscoll). Ca 1924. Female vs, orch. Schmidt 1924
A Wind from the Sea (Longfellow). Ca 1924. Female vs, orch. Schmidt ca 1924
The Dancer of Fjaard (Branscombe). Ca 1926. Soli, female vs, orch. Schmidt 1926
The Phantom Caravan (Banning). Ca 1927. Male vs, orch. Presser 1927
At the Postern Gate (Banning). Ca 1927. Male vs, orch. Schmidt 1927
Pilgrims of Destiny (Branscombe). 1919. Soli, SATB, orch. Ditson 1926
Youth of the World (Branscombe). Ca 1932. Female vs, orch. Witmark 1932
Sun and the Warm Brown Earth (Henderson). Ca 1935. Female vs, orch. Birch 1935
Coventry's Choir (Alvarez). Ca 1944. Sop, female vs, orch. G. Schirmer 1944

CHOIR

Publ by Schmidt: 'In Arcady by Moonlight'; 'ol' Marse Winter'; 'Roses in Madrid'; 'God of the Nations'; 'Hail Ye Tyme of Holie-Days'
Publ by others: 'In Granada'; 'Afar on the Purple Moor' (G. Schirmer); 'Into the Light'; 'Wreathe the Holly, Twine the Bay' (Fischer); 'Mary at Bethlehem'; 'Prayer for Song' (Ric); 'Our Canada from Sea to Sea'; 'Arms that Have Sheltered Us' (GVT)
'A Joyful Litany' (Branscombe). 1967. Female vs. Ms
Introit, Response, Amen (Branscombe). 1973. SATB. Ms
Over 100 arr of folk songs, traditional and modern works.

VOICE

Publ by G. Schirmer: 'Hail, Bounteous May'; 'Love in a Life'; 'Starlight'; 'With Rue My Heart Is Laden'; 'An Epitaph'; 'Just in the Hush before the Dawn'
Publ by Schmidt: 'Old Doctor Ma'Ginn'; 'Hail Ye Tyme of Holie-Days'; 'A Lute of Jade'; 'The Sun-Dial'; 'The Morning Wind'; 'Laughter Wears a Lilied Gown'; 'I Bring You Heartsease'; 'Changes'; 'My Love Is Like a Tempting Peach'; 'Bluebells Drowsily Ringing'; 'Songs of the Unafraid'; 'By St Lawrence Water'
Other works publ by WR, Ditson, Chappell, Galaxy
6 works for vn and pf, 4 publ by Schmidt (1911–20); *American Suite* (1959) for hn, pf
13 works for pf publ by WR, Teller, G. Schirmer, Schmidt

WRITINGS

'The sound of trumpets,' *Showcase*, vol 61, no. 3, 1962

BIBLIOGRAPHY

Britten. 'Gena Branscombe,' *CMJ*, vol 1, Jun 1914
Hodgins, J. Herbert. 'Canadian composer has two selves,' *Maclean's*, 1 Jun 1925
'Musical bibliographies of Canadian composers: no. 8,' Toronto *Globe*, 12 Sep 1936
'Gena Branscombe,' *Picton Gazette*, 10 Aug 1977 (EK)

BRANT, Saul. Violinist, choirmaster, teacher, b Savannah, Ga, 1882, d ?. In his youth he spent eight years in Europe, studying the violin with Henri Marteau and Carl Flesch. He arrived in Canada around 1910 and taught at *McGill U, where for several years he was director of violin classes. Audrey Cook, André *Durieux and Ethel *Stark were among his pupils. Brant took part in many chamber-music recitals with Boris *Hambourg, George M. *Brewer, and others. As the conductor of the *Mendelssohn Choir of Montreal he directed *Elijah* and *Messiah* in April 1927. He emigrated to the USA in 1929.

Around 1923 Saul Brant also taught his son Henry Dreyfus Brant (composer, pianist, flutist, arranger, b Montreal 15 Sep 1913), who was enrolled 1926–9 at McGill U before studying composition in New York with Rubin Goldmark, George Antheil, Aaron Copland, and Wallingford Riegger. Winner of many prizes, Henry Brant is a prolific composer and an important figure in contemporary music in the USA. Jack *Sirulnikoff and Morris *Surdin studied composition with him. As an audacious and inventive creator Brant is fascinated by esoteric instruments and the spatial possibilities of sound. He is the author of 'Space as an essential aspect of musical composition,' published in *Contemporary Composers on Contemporary Music* (edited by E. Schwartz and B. Childs, New York 1967). See also *Dictionary of Contemporary Music*. GP

Brantford. Ontario settlement established in 1805 on the Grand River. It was named in 1827 in honour of the Mohawk chief Joseph Brant, and incorporated as a city in 1877. The population, under 10,000 in 1867, had increased to over 66,000 by 1975. Brantford's first musical organizations of record (fl 1850s) were two choral groups, Gideon's Band and the Brantford Choral Union, the latter conducted by A.W. Smith and accompanied by military band musicians from the British garrison there. Civilian brass bands (the Keller, the Philharmonic, the City, and the Grand Trunk) first appeared in the 1860s. The Brantford Philharmonic (choral) Society was founded in the 1870s with E.C. Kimpton as conductor and was reorganized in 1893 under Frederic Rogers. In 1881, with the opening of Stratford's Opera House in Brantford, the first theatre orchestra was formed. Other organizations active before World War I included the Dufferin Rifles Band (formed 1882); the Brantford Mendelssohn Society (1880s); the Brantford Operatic Society (1880s); the Brantford Musical Society (1896); the Brantford Male Chorus, founded in 1902 by A.D. *Jordan and conducted 1903–6 by H.K. *Jordan before assimilation into the newly formed *Schubert Choir; and the Women's Musical Club, founded ca 1902 and renamed the Brantford Music Club in 1934. This club has presented many important performers in Brantford, eg, Maureen *Forrester, Glenn *Gould, Alberto *Guerrero, Viggo *Kihl, Luigi von *Kunits, Winifred *Lugrin Fahey, Lois *Marshall, Ernest *Seitz, and Jon *Vickers. The Ontario School for the Blind (later the W. Ross Macdonald School) was opened in 1872. B.F. Cheesbro of Vincennes, Ind, the school's first music director, devised musical notation in New York Point characters in 1874. With Frederick *Lord's 1923 appointment as music director light opera became a part of the school's music program. Lord was followed by George S. *Smale in 1945 and Smale by William Murphy in 1970. See also the Blind.

It was in Brantford in 1874 that Alexander Graham Bell invented the telephone: hence the city's popular name, 'Telephone City.' Bell's interest in sound took him to concerts at the Brantford Ladies' College and Cons of Music. Chartered in 1874 and thus one of the earliest conservatories in Canada, it was renamed the Brantford Cons in 1900 and affiliated with the *U of Western Ontario in 1911. It flourished under the successive principals W. Norman Andrews, Frederick C. Thomas, and Arthur G. Merriman until the building's sale in 1935 and then continued in the home of Merriman's widow for a few years. Other schools included the D.L. Wright Academy of Music (1908–20) and the (F.C.) Thomas School of Music (1920s).

Music in Brantford schools was organized in 1936 by G.A. Smale, who also in that year, with H.B. Jones and the Brantford Home and School Council, organized the Brant County Musical Festival, a competition designed to stimulate musical accomplishment in public, separate, and secondary schools. Its successor, the Brantford Music Festival, began in 1945 under the auspices of the local Music Teachers' Assn and the Kiwanis Club.

Performing groups active after World War I included the Brantford Oratorio Society formed in 1917 and conducted in turn by J.W. Schofield and F.C. Thomas; a Brantford SO, formed in 1923 and briefly active under Thomas; the Canadian Choir (1928–45), founded and conducted by Frederick Lord; the Cockshutt Male Choir (1935–60, sponsored by the Cockshutt Plow Co), conducted by Frank Holton, G.A. Smale, and Lansing *MacDowell; Smale's Varié Singers (1937–45); and the Frank Holton Mixed Choir and Ladies Choir. The Brantford SO (see Orchestras) was established in 1949.

Brantford is the birthplace of the lyricist Alfred Bryan (1871–1958), who wrote 'Peg O' My Heart' and 'Come Josephine in My Flying Machine'; the conductor composer Morley *Calvert; the educator Philip Cady Hayden; the songwriter Wade *Hemsworth; and the soprano Phyllis *Mailing. In October 1909 a meeting in Brantford between Albert *Ham and several of the city's organists led to the founding in December of the Canadian Guild of Organists (subsequently the CCO and later the *RCCO). On an island in the Grand River, in an outdoor concert held 3 Aug 1978 to raise money for the renovation of the Capitol Theatre (site of Brantford SO concerts), the Boston Pops Orchestra, conducted by Arthur Fiedler, made its first Canadian appearance in 20 years to play for an estimated audience of 30,000.

BIBLIOGRAPHY

Mason, Lawrence. 'Backgrounds and horizons in Ontario's music and drama: IX Brantford,' Toronto *Globe*, 22 Aug 1925

Slack, Lyle. 'How they brought the Pops from Boston to Brantford,' *Maclean's*, 19 Mar 1979 (GS)

Brass. Brass instruments are the first instruments mentioned in Canadian history. When Jacques Cartier and the Indians at Hochelaga (Montreal) had their first ceremonial meeting, 3 Oct 1535, 'the captain next ordered the trumpets and other musical instruments to be sounded, whereat the Indians were much delighted' (H.P. Biggar, *The Voyages of Cartier*, Ottawa 1924, p 166). Besides fulfilling traditional military and ceremonial functions, brass instruments have accompanied services in churches lacking organs, summoned farm workers for lunch (see Dinner horn), played a pioneer role in the development of ensemble playing (the brass band being the instrumental group most easily trainable in a short time), participated in orchestral performances, and simply displayed their own gleaming brand of virtuosity, notably in the cornet solos that were a feature of wind band concerts in the late 19th and 20th centuries, and later in jazz ensembles. Despite the wide use of brass instruments the concert repertoire for soloists has remained small.

There are documentary references to trumpets in 17th-century New France: one occurs in a letter written by Mother Marie de l'Incarnation 4 Oct 1658; Jean Casavan (sic), a 17th-century ancestor of the organ builders *Casavant, is supposed to have been a fine trumpeter (Ernest Gagnon, *Louis Jolliet*, Montreal 1926, p 135); E.-Z. *Massicotte, in 'La musique militaire sous le régime français' (*BRH*, vol 39, July 1933), mentions that an expedition to Lake Ontario included two trumpeters; and Baron de Lahontan, in letter XVI, 28 May 1689, in *New Voyages to North America / Nouveaux Voyages dans l'Amérique septentrionale* (1703, in English and French editions), advises the would-be explorer to carry with him some 'trumpeters and fiddlers, both for animating his retinue, and for raising the admiration of the savages.' However, the military band in New France seems to have excluded brass: the Carignan-Salières Regiments, which arrived in Canada in 1665, had two tambours and one fife in each company of 53 men.

An inscription on an early copy of Campra's *Motets* (1710), preserved at *Laval U, reveals that the copy belonged to Jean-Baptiste Savard, 'joueur de serpent de la cathédral [sic] de Québec.' Henri Têtu's article 'Le chapitre de la cathédrale de Québec ...' (*BRH*, vol 13, August 1907) mentions a Sieur Perin, who was a serpent player there in 1718. Graham *George (in *Culture*, Dec 1955), quoting Frère Pierre-Alphonse, says that the viol (la viole), bass viol, flute, and bugle (clairon) were the instruments used in churches before 1760. In 1842, before church organs were customary in Anglo-Canadian settlements, a 'horn' was used in Christ Church, Hamilton, Ont.

Late-18th-century newspaper advertisements in Canada usually offered violins, flutes, and harpsichords for sale, but no brass instruments. Presumably the brass players in the concert ensembles of the day (eg, horn in chamber music) were military bandsmen not required to supply their own instruments. With the growth of numerous towns in Lower and Upper Canada ca 1830 came the formation of municipal (temperance, parish, fire-brigade, town-police, company bands, etc) brass or mixed bands (see Bands 6; Children of Peace; La Musique Canadienne), and soon there were hundreds of such bands across Canada. Thus, there was a considerable demand

for brass and woodwind instruments which had to be imported from England, France, and later the USA. In 1888 the music firm *Whaley Royce made the first Canadian cornet and soon established the brand names 'Imperial' (top line) and 'Ideal' (a less expensive line). Probably Canada's only maker of brass instruments, it ceased production in 1974, though it continued sales and repairs.

ENSEMBLES

The bands of the *Salvation Army and more particularly those of the armed forces, patterned on British prototypes, contributed significantly to the development of brass playing in Canada. In his book *The Cultural Connection* (Toronto 1978) Bernard Ostry points out that until after World War II federal government aid to the arts was 'the result of isolated initiatives,' rather than of any consistent cultural policy or even attitude, except in the Dept of National Defence. There, he says, 'the importance of music and theatre was recognized early, not only in relieving the tedium of military routine but in promoting a corporate spirit and sense of pride, and in fostering cheerful relations between garrisons and civilian populations. For years the Department of National Defence was alone among federal departments in developing a conscious, consistent and imaginative cultural policy and providing the funds to make it work.' Standards in brass playing certainly improved during World War II, when substantial monies were made available for the establishment of service entertainment groups using professional players; and the personnel from these groups, many re-entering the musical community after the war as players or teachers in high schools or universities, supplemented the work of private teachers and conservatories, developing bands, bugle corps, and skilled individual players who joined orchestras and ensembles.

In the 1960s the Montreal Brass Quintet (James Ranti and Jean-Louis Chatel, trumpets; Aimé Lainesse, horn; Joseph Zuskin, trombone; and Robert Ryker, tuba) gave many concerts and commissioned Morley *Calvert's *Suite from the Monteregian Hills* and François *Morel's *Quintette de cuivres*. It disbanded shortly after appearing at *Expo 67. Numerous other brass groups were formed in the 1960s and 1970s: the Atlantic Brass Ensemble, which recorded Charles *Wilson's *Concerto 5 X 4 X 3* (CBC SM 195); *Canadian Brass; the Canzona Brass Ensemble, Calgary; the Dalhousie Brass Trio, Halifax; the Mount Royal Brass Quintet, Montreal; the City Brass, the Ontario Brass Quintet, the Brass Company, and the Toronto Brass Quintet, all of Toronto; the London (Ont) Brass Quintet; and the Vancouver Brass Quintet, which recorded the Calvert suite and other pieces for release on CBC SM 252. However, only Canadian Brass was a full-time ensemble in 1980.

PLAYERS, TEACHERS

It was not uncommon for the professional musician at work in Canada in the years bounded by 1875 and 1950 to play a brass instrument (usually cornet) and a string or keyboard instrument – one with at least proficiency, the other with some degree of virtuosity. Calixa *Lavallée played piano, organ, violin, and cornet in Canada and the USA, while Herbert L. *Clarke, born in the USA but raised in Canada, played the violin and the viola in addition to being the outstanding cornet virtuoso of his time. The horn player Herbert *Barrow also played the viola. Other excellent cornet/trumpet players of that era were Lavallée's brother Charles; Ernest *Lavigne; Édouard L'Africain, a Canadian who became principal trumpet with the Boston SO; the Belgians Louis Vanpoucke and Theodore Van der Meerschen; Charles de la Casinière; and O.D. Joiner. Thomas H. King (b Hamilton, Ont, 15 Jan 1868, d Chicago 27 Mar 1926) was trombone soloist with the Innes Band, the 7th Regiment Band of New York, Victor Herbert's band, and others. He was known as one of the greatest technicians on the instrument and was also a trombone designer. Other trombonists at the turn of the century were G. Arless, E. Laberge, Télesphore Laliberté, and John *Slatter. Laliberté and Slatter also played the euphonium. Joseph-Laurent Gariépy, bandmaster of the Victoria Rifles of Montreal, was a prominent trumpet and cornet teacher in the 1930s and 1940s.

Players and teachers of note who were active at some time during the period 1930–80 include the trumpeters George Anderson, Martin *Boundy, Steven Chenette, John *Cowell, Robert *Farnon, Jerold Gerbrecht, Theodore Gorshkoff, George Jones, Jacques *LeComte, Ellis *McLintock senior and junior, Henry Meredith, Fred Mills, Robert Oades, Ramon Parcells, Bill *Phillips, Ronald Romm, Albert Simoens, W. Bramwell *Smith, Jeffrey Stern, Douglas Sturdevant, John Tickner, and Joseph Umbrico; the trombonists Joseph Bell, Gordon Cherry, Albert Devito, H.C. 'Wick' Ford, E.J. Fowler, Seymour 'Red' Ginzler, Harry Hawe, Herbert *Jeffrey, R. Pezzella, David *Robbins, Ted *Roderman, Emil Subirana, James Thompson, Eugene Watts, and Alfred Wood; the tuba players Charles Daellenbach, J.P. *Hamilton, John Leonard, Hubert Meyer, Dennis Miller, David Otto, Ted Robbins (also euphonium), Robert Ryker, Gurney Titmarsh, and Ellis Wean; and the french-hornists Reginald *Barrow, Mary Robb *Barrow, Robert *Creech, Guillaume *Gagnier, Jean Gaudreault, Daniel Gress, Martin Hackleman, James and John MacDonald, the brothers Joseph, Giulio, and Paul *Masella, Graeme Page, Eugene *Rittich, and John Scecina.

Among outstanding players of traditional or dixieland jazz have been James 'Trump' *Davidson, Ken Dean, Charlie Gall, and Mike White (cornet), Stew Barnett and Paul 'Slim' Chandler (trumpet), and Jim Abercrombie, Jack Fulton, Bud Hill, Bob Livingston, and Peter Sagermann (trombone). Important soloists in modern jazz include the trumpeters and/or flugelhorn players Guido *Basso, Bruce Cassidy, Don Clark, Bobby *Hales, Mike Malone, Sam Noto, Al Penfold, Herbie *Spanier, Fred *Stone, and Roger Walls; and the trombonists Ron *Collier, Ross Culley, Ted Elfstrom, Russ *Little, Rob *McConnell, Dave Pepper, Ray Sikora, and Butch Watanabe. Lead trumpeters, distinguished by their range, tone, and sight-reading ability, are essential to studio orchestras and big bands; in Canada they include Bix Belair, Arnie Chycoski (considered among the finest in North America), Gordon *Delamont (whose father, Arthur, led the *Kitsilano Boys' Band, an important west-coast training ground for brass players), Graham Topping, and Erich Traugott. Johnny Frosk of Winnipeg became an important lead trumpeter in New York. Belair and Bobby *Gimby have had success in the pop music or dance band fields. Other players, including the trumpeters Chico Alvarez, Maynard *Ferguson, Max Goldberg, Alfie *Noakes, Jimmy Reynolds, and Ken *Wheeler and the trombonist Murray *McEachern, have had careers outside of Canada. (See also Boss Brass.)

The *CMCentre *Catalogue of Chamber Music* and its 1976 supplement list 39 Canadian composers who have written music for brass solo or brass ensemble. Some of these are Ovid Avarmaa, *Archer, *Beckwith, A. *Brott, M. *Forsyth, *Freedman, *Legrady, *McCauley, *Papineau-Couture, *Prévost, Winston Purdy, A. *Rae, *Rathburn, and *Weinzweig. Louis *Applebaum has written a number of fanfares and Alfred *Kunz, Sir Ernest *MacMillan, Clermont *Pépin, and Gerhard *Wuensch also have composed in this genre.

See also Bands; Canadian Band Directors' Association; Fédération des harmonies du Québec; Jazz.

BRASSARD, François (Joseph). Composer, ethnomusicologist, organist, critic, teacher, pianist, b St-Jérôme (Métabetchouan, Saguenay), Que, 6 Oct 1908, d Quebec City 26 Apr 1976; BA (Laval) 1928, hon D MUS (Laval) 1961. He studied piano at the Chicoutimi Seminary with Father H. Fortin. Continuing his piano studies with Rolland-G. *Gingras, he also studied organ with Omer *Létourneau and began harmony with J.-Robert *Talbot. A scholarship student at the *AMQ in 1930, he also studied in Montreal with Léo-Pol *Morin (piano) and Claude *Champagne (counterpoint and fugue). He supplemented his studies 1933–4 in Paris with Albert Bertelin and Guy de Lioncourt and in 1935 at the RCM with Ralph Vaughan Williams. Appointed the organist at the Church of St-Dominique de Jonquière in 1930, he maintained that position intermittently until 1970. He began teaching at *Laval U in 1946 and was appointed to the publications committee of the university's *Archives de folklore that same year. He joined that department in 1971.

In 1940 Brassard began his important work in the research, compilation, editing, and harmonization of French-Canadian folksongs. He collected some 1200 songs or variants during trips in Quebec, New Brunswick (Acadia), Ontario, western Canada, New England, the upper Mississippi, and Louisiana and wrote numerous articles, essays, and analyses which were published in Canada and abroad. His harmonizations were heard on the CBC 1959–61 in the series of programs presented by the *Petit ensemble vocal and 1965–7 in the series 'Au bois du rossignolet,' for which he prepared the scripts and served as animateur.

Brassard's compositions are rooted in tradition. He believed, to use his own words, 'in renewal through simplicity,' and acknowledged certain influences, particularly from polyphony, the language of tonality, and folk and liturgical song. In 1942 his *Panis angelicus* was awarded a prize by the Société des musiciens d'église de Québec. A member of the *CFMS and of the IFMC, he was the Canadian delegate in 1949 at the latter organization's conference in Venice. He received grants 1961–2 from the *Canada Council and 1965–6 from the *MACQ. In 1964 he began appearing as a guest professor at the *U of Montreal, and in 1966 he de-

François Brassard

livered lectures at the Museo del Pueblo Espanol in Madrid. In 1965 the new concert hall of the Collège de Jonquière was named Salle François-Brassard. In 1974 he received the *CMCouncil medal. He contributed to *EMC*. He was a member of CAPAC.

COMPOSITIONS

ORCHESTRA

Marche fantasque et Festival. 1949. CMCentre

Poème d'amour et de joie (H. Dumont). 1967. Bar, orch. CMCentre

Matapédienne (1969?) and *Vigile* (1973). Both ms

KEYBOARD

Sonatine. 1936. Org. Arch 1938

Luminures. 1938. Pf. MCA 1969

Orléanaises. 1939. Pf. BMIC 1953 ('Les Noisettes' and 'Oratoire à la croisée des chemins'). ('Oratoire ... chemins') RCI 134 (*Newmark)

Basilicale No. 1 (1962) and *No. 2* (1969). Org. Ms

CHOIR OR VOICE

Panis angelicus. 1942. V, org. Procure générale de musique 1942

Chansons populaires de l'Amérique française

I: 1946. V, pf. Ms

II: 1947. SATB. MCA 1973

III: 1956. V, pf. Ms

IV: 1959. SATB. MCA 1969

V: 1959. SATB, pf. Ms

II and IV were recorded on Vox STLP-511.860 (*Mtl Bach Choir).

Petites Chansons populaires de l'Amérique. 1972. 2 and 3 equal vs. Ms

Also *Suite villageoise*. 1948. Vn, pf. CMCentre

WRITINGS

'Étude monographique sur les orgues de la cathédrale,' *Progrès du Saguenay*, 14 Oct 1937

'La musique en Nouvelle-France acadienne,' *Horizons*, May, Sep 1939

'Où l'on fond nos cloches,' *R dominicaine*, Mar 1940

'Chansons de la Louisiane,' *Action nationale*, Apr 1940

'Naissance d'une chanson,' *Ensemble*, Apr 1941

'Léo-Pol Morin et la composition canadienne,' *Canada français*, Mar 1942

'La chanson acadienne,' *Action nationale*, Apr 1942

'Quand m'y marierai-je?' *Canada français*, Mar 1944

'Chansons folkloriques,' *20e siècle*, 4 instalments, Jun 1944, Apr 1945, Jun, Nov 1946

'Le miroir d'argent,' *Canada français*, Sep 1944

'La résurrection des chansons d'Acadie,' *R de l'U Laval*, Nov 1946

'Chansons d'accompagnement,' *J of the IFMC*, vol 2, Mar 1950

'Le retour du soldat et le retour du voyageur,' *JAF*, 248, Apr–Jun 1950

'Une date pour la musique canadienne,' *R de l'U Laval*, Apr 1951

'Une date pour la musique canadienne: la Symphonie gaspésienne de Claude Champagne,' *Vie musicale*, Oct 1952

'La chanson folklorique du Saguenay,' *Progrès du Saguenay*, 5 Sep 1953

'A même une réserve sans fond,' *Bon Temps*, Mar–Apr 1958

'Les thèmes d'emprunt,' *Musicien amateur*, Winter 1966
'French-Canadian folk music studies: a survey,' *Ethnomusicology*, vol 16, Sep 1972
'Le canot d'écorce – formation d'une grande chanson du fonds canadien,' *CMB*, 9, Autumn – Winter 1974
Also many articles in *La Lyre* (1928–30), *Progrès du Saguenay* (1928–53), *Le Béret (1929–30), Musical America* (1929–31), *Action catholique* (1933, 1937), *P-T* (1934–5), *Alma Mater* (1936–53), *Archives de folklore* (1946–9), and *Le Réveil* of Jonquière (1946–58), of which certain ones were signed Braz Arpiani or Thibaut de Champagne

BIBLIOGRAPHY
Joly, Antoni. 'François Brassard: compositeur,' *P-T*, 907, Feb 1947
'Un quart d'heure de folklore avec François Brassard,' *Semaine de Radio-Canada*, Mar 1967
Béliveau, André. 'François Brassard, de Jonquière, compositeur,' Montreal *La Presse*, 6 Jul 1968 GP

BRASSARD, Henri. Pianist, teacher, conductor, b St-Siméon, near Quebec City, 16 Jan 1950. He began his first piano studies at the *École Vincent-d'Indy with Lucille Brassard (Sister Rachel-Yvonne) and continued 1960–8 with Yvonne *Hubert. At 12 he won his first honours in competition – at the Quebec Kiwanis Festival and the Quebec Music Festivals. For the latter he played the first movement of the Schumann *Concerto* with the *Quebec SO, and the $250 scholarship was presented to him by Queen Elizabeth, the Queen Mother. He then gave some recitals in Quebec and New Brunswick, appearing also on the CBC TV programs 'Jeunesse oblige' and '20 ans express.' He won first prize in the *MSO Concours in 1965 and second prize in the *CBC Talent Festival in 1966. After his recital in the spring of 1966 at the *Salle Claude-Champagne in Montreal, Jean *Vallerand wrote, 'Henri Brassard, in addition to being a promising pianist, possesses a very fine, very sensitive personality which comes through in the freshness of his playing' (*La Presse* 5 Apr 1966). In 1967 Brassard appeared as a soloist with the *MSO, the *TS, and the Erie Philharmonic.

On his graduation from the École Vincent-d'Indy, Brassard studied for some time in New York with Nadia Reisenberg, but it was in Vienna, 1972–5 with Dieter Weber, that he completed his education. Although he gave about 30 recitals 1974–5 for the *JMC, he began his professional career on his return from Vienna in 1975. That same year his recital at Toronto's *St Lawrence Centre won him an enthusiastic press and the Floyd S. *Chalmers Foundation Award given annually to the most promising young artist of the season. Brassard's engagements subsequently multiplied. He appeared with the *Ladies' Morning Musical Club of Montreal and the *Pro Musica Society / Goethe-Institute in 1976, the MSO in 1977 (Beethoven's *Fantasia in C Minor*) and 1978 (Chopin's *Concerto No. 2*), the Quebec SO in 1977 (Beethoven's *Concerto No. 1*), and the *CBC Quebec Chamber Orchestra in 1977 (Mozart's *Concerto No. 20*) and 1979 (Haydn's *Concerto in D*). He also gave recitals in Salmon Arm, BC, in 1978, at the St Lawrence Centre and the Festival de Lanaudière, near Joliette, Que, in 1979, and elsewhere. He appeared for the first time with the *NACO in 1979. In December 1978 he began a European tour which included six appearances in the USSR and recitals at the *Canadian Cultural Centre in Paris and at Canada House in London; his program included Harry *Somers' *Three Sonnets*.

After his performance of the Beethoven *Fantasia* with the MSO, Claude *Gingras wrote: 'The technique is irreproachable, the sound is exceptionally powerful and is entirely justified because the piano is, after all, competing with an orchestra and a choir. There also is a lovely musicality and an interesting texture, indicating that Brassard had given his interpretation careful and lengthy consideration' (Montreal, *La Presse*, 18 May 1977). Brassard began teaching at *Laval U in 1978 and became conductor of the Orchestre régional du Saguenay-Lac-St-Jean in 1979. For the LP RCI 410 (1977) he recorded Mozart's *Variations on a Minuet of Duport* K573 and *Sonata in B Flat* K281 and Schubert's *Sonata in A Minor, Op 164*. He contributed the article 'Libres propos d'un pianiste' to the *Bulletin des JMC* of January 1975.

BIBLIOGRAPHY
Harvey, Jacques. 'Les 10 prochaines années sont importantes pour le pianiste Henri Brassard,' *Musique périodique*, vol 1, Mar 1977
Ward, John. 'Pianist not the best-known, but he's among the busiest,' *Calgary Herald*, 10 Feb 1979 GP

BRAULT, Cédia (m Desautels). Mezzo-soprano, b Ste-Martine, near Montreal, 4 Jan 1894, d Montreal 27 Jun 1972. The sister of Victor *Brault, she studied voice 1911–18 with Céline *Marier and 1918–19 with Salvator *Issaurel and harmony 1918–20 with Rodolphe *Mathieu. She made her debut in the title role of *Carmen* on 19 and 21 Nov 1918 at the *Monument national, singing with Sarah *Fischer (Micaela), Ulysse *Paquin (Escamillo), and Victor Desautels (Don José). She married Desautels in 1920. In *Le Canada musical* of 7 Dec 1921 C.-O. *Lamontagne wrote: 'In her debut Cédia Brault has established herself immediately as an actress of talent and an artist of rare promise. Her voice is more than sufficient in the lower register, very powerful on top – certain notes being prominent – and of a beautiful timbre in the middle. Her diction is very clear. Mlle Brault had some excellent moments; she sustained the role of Carmen to the end, with no weaknesses.'She performed the role frequently, both in Canada and the USA. In Montreal she appeared in the title role of *Mignon*, as Charlotte in *Werther* (1919), and in other roles. She sang Dalila in a 1922 Montreal concert performance of *Samson et Dalila* with the tenor Émile *Gour, and repeated the role the following year in Worcester, Mass, with the Boston SO conducted by Pierre Monteux. In 1923 she sang Hérodiade in the premiere of *Couture's *Jean le Précurseur*. She participated in the performances of the Manhattan Opera Company and the Russian Opera Company in New York and other cities in the USA with marked success, particularly in the role of Carmen.

Brault's career made similar progress on the concert platform. In 1918 in Quebec City she gave the Canadian premiere of Debussy's *Proses lyriques* with Léo-Pol *Morin at the piano; the following year she gave the Montreal premiere. She was one of the first to perform, in Canada, songs of Ravel, Casella, and Milhaud, notably Milhaud's *Poèmes juifs*, which in 1926 she sang with the composer at the piano. Upon hearing her in Montreal in 1928 Ravel exclaimed: 'I'm delighted to discover in Canada such a faithful performer of my *Chansons madécasses*.'

With Morin and Robert Imandt, violinist, she participated in a 1927 Debussy Festival at the Windsor Hotel in Montreal. She also took part in the 1927 and 1928 *CPR Festivals in Quebec City. Her recitals took her all over Canada as well as to Paris (Salle Pleyel) and London (Aeolian Hall) in June 1931. At her farewell performance, 13 Jul 1939, she sang Carmen outdoors at the Chalet atop Mount Royal in Montreal before more than 6000 spectators.

Brault's husband, Victor Desautels (b Montreal 23 Mar 1893, d 11 Apr 1970), was a pupil of Salvator Issaurel and a very active tenor in Montreal in the 1920s. He was an impresario and organized many operatic shows and concerts with singers. Their daughter is the musicologist Andrée *Desautels. GP

BRAULT, Pierre (Florent). Composer, arranger, record producer, b Montreal 3 Aug 1939. He was largely self-taught but did study harmony with Michel *Perrault and fugue and counterpoint with Françoise *Aubut. He began his career in 1961 as an accordionist in boîtes à chansons. Attracted to composition, he wrote several scores for the theatrical group Les Apprentis Sorciers. While he was arranger 1964–7 (he resumed the function in 1978) for Clémence *Desrochers, he composed the music for many of her songs and for her *Le Vol rose du flamant* (1964), considered to be Quebec's first musical comedy.

Brault produced his first film music for Claude Jutra's *Roulis-roulant* (1966). The following year *The Animal Movie*, an NFB cartoon for which he composed the score, won the Gold Plaque of the Festival of Motion Pictures for Children at Mardel Plata, Argentina, and first prize in the Gottwaldov Children's Film Festival in Czechoslovakia. With the aid of a grant (1968) from the *MACQ he visited Paris, Prague, and Zagreb to further his training in the theory and practice of sound-on-film. He taught these subjects, along with music history, 1971–6 at the National Theatre School in Montreal. By 1978 Brault had composed the music and produced sound tracks for more than 70 animated cartoons, shorts, and full-length feature films by Quebec producers. In 1972 his score for *La Vraie Nature de Bernadette*, a feature film by Gilles Carle, earned him the prize (an Etrog) for best original music at the Canadian Film Festival.

Brault also has composed an instrumental suite, *Adjuration*, and has been music director and arranger for recordings by several chansonniers including Robert *Charlebois, Clémence Desrochers, and Claude *Gauthier. Brault became president of Productions Imagination Inc in 1970, and of the recording studio Poly-Sons Inc in 1973. In 1976 he began to devote his energies to record production, and among his projects were two series of recordings (29 LPs) for the Quebec Ministry of Education. His arrangements of songs by *Vigneault and songs of early Quebec have been performed and recorded by the *Ensemble Claude-Gervaise. Brault is a member of CAPAC. See also Film scores.

BIBLIOGRAPHY
Boucher, Denis. 'Pierre Brault: Notre pays est le meilleur endroit du monde pour la création,' Montreal *Petit Journal*, 17 Apr 1966 (DM)

BRAULT, (Robert) **Victor.** Baritone, choir conductor, teacher, b Ste-Martine, near Montreal, 1899, d Montreal 1963. The brother of Cédia *Brault, he studied piano in Montreal with Alexis *Contant and voice and theory 1919–24 in Paris with A. Landély Hettich and André Gedalge respectively. He also studied voice with the tenor Edmond Clément and appeared in concerts with him. In Paris he was deputy soloist at the Madeleine Church, sang the role of Peter in Beethoven's *Christ at the Mount of Olives* with the Assn des concerts spirituels de la Sorbonne, and was a soloist in the Concerts Touche. In recitals 1922–3 at Salle Gaveau and Salle Pleyel he sang works of Honegger, Roussel, and Tansman with the composers at the piano. Fauré was his accompanist in *L'Horizon chimérique* and he premiered *Un Peu d'ombre* by Rodolphe *Mathieu at Salle Gaveau in 1922. Brault made his London debut at Wigmore Hall in 1923 in a recital of French songs, and sang Ravel's *Trois Poèmes de Mallarmé* at Queen's Hall shortly afterwards under the composer's direction. Ernest Newman wrote of him: 'One would not have missed the beautiful diction for words, and one does not often hear such thorough understanding of poet and composer' (*The Times*, 19 Oct 1923). Brault later repeated the work in Brussels and at The Hague.

Back in North America Brault performed in New York, Boston, and Montreal. He participated in the benefit concert for Emma *Albani at the *St-Denis Theatre in 1925, then opened studios in Montreal and Boston. He also taught at the *Cons national of Montreal, at *McGill U and at the Trafalgar Institute. With his sister he took part in the *CPR Festival in Quebec City in 1928. He served 1930–1 as managing director of the Canadian Opera Company of Montreal and directed individual productions of *The Marriage of Figaro* in 1933, and Honegger's *Le Roi David* and Debussy's *Le Martyre de saint Sébastien* in 1934. He was active as a conductor of choirs on CBC radio, and founded the vocal ensemble La *Cantoria. Brault was commentator and artistic director of the series of radio broadcasts 'Le Chant du monde' presented 1944–5 on CBC as part of Radio-Collège. Also at this time he was given the job of rehearsing the choirs for performances of the *Metropolitan Opera in Montreal.

Brault made harmonizations of Canadian folksongs and composed some works under the pseudonym of Laurent Winter. Among his students were Marcelle *Gagné, Gérard *Gélinas, Claude *Létourneau, Gabrielle Parrot, and Albert *Viau. Andrée *Desautels is his niece. GP

BRAUN, Victor (Conrad). Baritone, b Windsor, Ont, of Mennonite parents, 4 Aug 1935. He studied 1954–7 with Lillian Wilson in London, Ont, and also 1956–8 at the RCMT, where his teachers were George *Lambert and Weldon *Kilburn. After a year in the *COC chorus he made his solo debut in 1957 as Sciarrone in *Tosca*. For the next five years he sang secondary roles, but was admired particularly as Escamillo in *Carmen* (1961 and again in 1964) and as Monterone in *Rigoletto* (1962). These roles marked a new phase in his development. In May of 1963 he was the Grand Prize winner at the Vienna International Mozart Competition. This brought him to the attention of Wieland Wagner who invited him to audition for Bayreuth. Wagner felt Braun's voice was too young for Wagnerian roles, but recommended his engagement as leading baritone with the Frankfurt Opera. He made his debut as Count Almaviva in *The Marriage of Figaro* and appeared in a variety of roles, including Ottone in Monteverdi's *L'Incoronazione de Poppea*.

Despite a heavy schedule of performances in Germany Braun returned to Canada several times in the 1960s, most often to sing with the COC (Amonasro in *Aida*, 1963; Germont père in *La Traviata*, 1964; the Count di Luna in *Il Trovatore*, 1967), but he also was the baritone soloist with the *TSO in the Canadian premiere (1964) of Britten's *War Requiem*, and appeared in special *MSO productions as Escamillo in *Carmen* (1964, with Shirley Verrett) and as Amonasro in *Aida* (1965, with Jon *Vickers and Virginia Zeani). He sang Mahler's *Lieder eines fahrenden Gesellen* in 1968 with the TS for CBC TV, and he gave a CBC radio 'Celebrity Recital' in 1969.

Braun was a regular guest, as well, with several European companies – Cologne 1965–6, Düsseldorf 1966–8, La Scala 1967 (as Wolfram in *Tannhäuser*), Stuttgart 1967–9. In 1967 he toured with the Israel Philharmonic under Zubin Mehta as a soloist in Beethoven's *Symphony No. 9*, and shared with soprano Gundula Janowitz the solos in Mahler's *Das Knaben Wunderhorn* at the Vienna Festival. Braun's Almaviva (1968) in *The Marriage of Figaro* at the Bavarian State Opera in Munich in-

Victor Braun

itiated a long tenure as leading baritone with that company. At the same time his career became increasingly international in scope. He made debuts with the San Francisco Opera in 1968 (as the Count di Luna and as Enrico in *Lucia di Lammermoor*) and at Covent Garden in 1969 (singing the title roles in *Eugene Onegin* under Solti and Humphrey Searle's *Hamlet*, in its English premiere). His repertoire had expanded to include the title roles in *Don Giovanni* and *Rigoletto*, the roles of Scarpia in *Tosca*, Golaud in *Pelléas et Mélisande*, and Ford in *Falstaff*, and the main baritone roles in Wagner and Strauss.

In the 1970s, still based in Munich, Braun divided his time among the opera houses and concert platforms of Europe, the USA, and Canada. In Europe he made his Paris Opera debut in 1974 in *Il Trovatore*. At the Cologne Opera he had an outstanding success as Mandryka in *Arabella* in 1976 and as Jokanaan in *Salome* in 1977. That same year at Cologne he sang the General in Henze's *We Came to the River*. In 1979 at Lyons he created the title role in Jean Prodromides' *Ulysses*. In the USA he has appeared with the Portland Opera (title role in the US premiere, 1975, of Krenek's *Life of Orestes*; and Ford in *Falstaff*, 1977), the Boston Opera (Russlan in *Russlan and Ludmilla*, 1977), and in concert with the Los Angeles Philharmonic and the San Francisco SO.

In Canada Braun has continued to appear with the COC (*Eugene Onegin*, 1972; Jokanaan, 1975; Rodrigo in *Don Carlos*, 1977), and has sung with the *Manitoba Opera (Germont père, 1973) and the *Edmonton Opera (Marcello in *La Bohème*, 1976; Jokanaan, 1977). In 1978, with the TS under Mario *Bernardi, he premiered Rudi *van Dijk's *The Shadowmaker*, commissioned by Braun with a grant from the *Canada Council.

Braun's voice is a flexible lyric baritone, at once mellow and carrying. He has been praised equally for his musicianship, his sensitivity as an actor, and his competence in mastering roles in contemporary works as well as those of greater difficulty and less currency in the established repertoire.

A brother, Richard Braun (an actor and also a baritone), sang supporting roles 1964–72 with the COC and studied 1969–70 with Martial Singher in California.

DISCOGRAPHY

Schubert *Winterreise*; Helmer pf; 1972; 2-CBC SM-196
Wagner *Tannhäuser*; Vienna Phil O, Solti cond, Braun (Wolfram); 1971; 4-Lon 1438
See also Discography for CBC SO.

BIBLIOGRAPHY

Morrow, Marianne. 'Victor Braun,' *OpCan*, Dec 1964
Mercer, Ruby. 'Victor Braun,' *OpCan*, Feb 1976 (HCs)

BRAUNEIS. Father (bandmaster) and son (teacher), both known as Jean (or John) Chrysostome, and both prominent in 19th-century Quebec.

BIBLIOGRAPHY

Brassard, T.-L. and Massicotte, E.-Z. 'Les deux musiciens Braunies (sic),' *BRH*, vol 41, Nov 1935

1 **Jean-Chrysostome** I. Bandmaster, teacher, composer, b Darmstadt 1785, d Quebec City 15 Sep 1832. He settled in Quebec City in or before 1814 as a musician with a British army band. He left the 70th regimental band in 1818 to teach piano. Five years later he obtained a shop licence and advertised instruments for sale. In 1831 he became director of the first Canadian militia band in Quebec and was also associated with an artillery battalion band. He died a victim of the 1832 cholera epidemic. On 27 Feb 1819 the band of the 60th regiment played Brauneis' *Grand Overture of Quebec* as the Duke of Richmond, the governor-in-chief, entered Government House in Quebec City. The work was dedicated to the duke's daughter, Lady Mary Lennox. Brauneis advertised copies of this piece and also, in September 1819, of one in memory of the duke, who had died in August. The speed of production suggests that these are early instances of Canadian sheet music printing, but no copies have yet been located.

2 **Jean-Chrysostome** II. Teacher, organist, composer, b Quebec City 26 Jan 1814, d Montreal 11 Aug 1871. He studied with his father and was perhaps the first Canadian to study music in Europe, 1830–3. He was the organist at two Montreal churches – Notre-Dame Church 1833–44 and St James Cathedral 18??–57, both at St Denis Street and, after the 1852 fire, at its other locations. He taught music at the Institut des Soeurs de la Congrégation Notre-Dame for 30 years and also at other schools and privately. The Société de Musique which he founded in 1837 was short-lived, but later in 1842 he offered courses in vocal music patterned after a German method. He introduced his pupils to the classical repertoire and the piano studies of Clementi, Cramer, and Czerny. A versatile musician, Brauneis taught guitar, harp, violin, voice, and theory, led a band, composed, tuned pianos, and imported instruments. A mass with orchestral accompaniment, though performed with only five instruments on 12 Jul 1835, earned an admiring review in *La Minerve*. A few pièces d'occasion were published by Lovell & Gibson (*Marche de la St. Jean Baptiste*, 1848, and probably *The Montreal Bazaar Polka*, ca 1848), by A. Fiot (*Monklands Polka*, 1849; also published by Dubois and by Mead Brothers), and by Brauneis himself (*The Royal Welcome Waltzes*, 1869, dedicated to Prince Arthur, with individual waltzes named after Canadian cities). Other dance music is known by title only. Highly regarded as a teacher, Brauneis has been described as a humble and industrious person who was very devoted to his pupils. The young Calixa *Lavallée was introduced to Brauneis but did not study with him.

BIBLIOGRAPHY

Kallmann, Helmut. 'Jean-Chrysostome Brauneis,' *DCB*, vol 10
PAC. *Quebec Gazette*, Index HK

BRAUSS, Helmut (Friedrich Ludwig). Pianist, teacher, b Milan, of German parents, 19 Oct 1930. This prominent European pianist (pupil of Elly Ney, Hans Ehlers, and Edwin Fischer) moved to Canada in 1966 to teach at the *U of Saskatchewan, Regina campus. He was a member 1967–9 of the Regina Cons Trio, has been a soloist with CBC orchestras in Winnipeg and Vancouver and with the *Edmonton SO, and has continued to tour regularly in Europe. He was an examiner 1966–7 for the *WBM and an adjudicator 1966–70 for the *Saskatchewan Music Festival Assn, and he also initiated and administrated Beethoven '70, a province-wide festival in Saskatchewan. In 1969 he began teaching at the *U of Alberta. His pupils include Thelma Johannes *O'Neill and Catherine Vickers. With the Harlan Green Players of the Edmonton SO Brauss recorded Poulenc's *Sextet for Woodwind Quintet and Piano* (1974, CBC SM 253).

(RDM)

Brave Belt. See BTO.

'Brave Wolfe.' The first and one of the finest of the native Anglo-Canadian ballads, 'Brave Wolfe' describes the British victory on the Plains of Abraham in 1759. Composed soon after the battle, it seems to have been patterned on an old British love lament called 'The Blacksmith.' It circulated widely throughout the British colonies, appearing in many New England broadsides and songbooks of the 18th and 19th centuries, and survived in oral tradition in both Newfoundland and Nova Scotia well into the 20th century. Elisabeth Greenleaf, who collected it in Newfoundland in 1929, described it as a martial and moving song whose 'stately measures linger in one's memory with some of its striking lines. Mackenzie testifies to the fervor with which it is sung in Nova Scotia, and it is sung in the same mood in Newfoundland.' It was first published in Elisabeth Greenleaf and Grace Mansfield's *Ballads and Sea Songs of Newfoundland* (Cambridge, Mass 1933) and is also in E. *Fowke and R. *Johnston's *Folk Songs of Canada* (Waterloo 1954) and on a recording of the same title (Waterloo CS3). Another song, usually entitled 'Bold Wolfe' or 'General Wolfe,' describes the same battle; it is better known in England than in North America. EF

BRAY, Kenneth (Ira). Educator, bassoonist, arranger, b Chaffey Township (Muskoka), Ont, 24 Feb 1919; B MUS (Toronto) 1949, M MUS (ESM, Rochester) 1957. Bray was a rural supervisor in Muskoka, Ont, schools, and a tuba player and arranger 1940–6 for the RCAF. He taught 1950–7 and was head of the music department 1957–61 at Riverdale Collegiate, Toronto. He was appointed head of the music department at the Ontario College of Education, Toronto, in 1961. He joined the faculty of the *U of Western Ontario, London, in 1969 and also played bassoon 1969–75, and thereafter on a casual basis, with the *London SO. He joined the London Woodwind Quintet in 1969. Many of his arrangements for band and for chorus are published by G.V. Thompson, Leeds, and Waterloo. He was president of the *OMEA 1959–60 and of the *CMEA 1973–7, and edited *The Canadian Music Educator* 1963–9.

WRITINGS

– et al. *For Young Musicians*, 4 vols (Waterloo 1961, 1967, 1972, 1974)

– et al. *Music for Young Canada*, 8 vols (Gage 1967–9)

'A Canadian adaptation of Kodály's music education principles,' *CAUSM J*, vol 1, Spring 1971

'The arts in education (a need or a luxury),' *Recorder*, vol 19, Jun 1977

'Donald F. Cook: a distorted view from the mainland,' *CME*, vol 19, Fall 1977 WL

BRAZIL, (E.) Jules. Songwriter, arranger, entertainer, fl Toronto 1910–25. Known to have been a music teacher 1910–25 in Toronto, Brazil also was the composer or arranger (rarely the lyricist) of many songs published 1915–21 by *Whaley Royce, Gordon V. *Thompson, *Anglo-Canadian, Feist, *Chappell, and others. He composed music for 'Remember Nurse Cavell' (1915) and 'Dreaming of Home' (1916), both with lyrics by their publisher G.V. Thompson. His other collaborators included Florence Benjamin, Edith S. Butler, P.L. MacDonald, Private T. Pritchard of the 'Princess Pats,' and Fred Sims. Brazil also arranged several patriotic songs by Will J. White for publication by *Musgrave. His setting of Lillian Waters McMurtry's 'Our Canada' was published by Chappell, and his 'Lord Byng, Canada Welcomes You' (Feist 1921) was recorded by baritone Fred Patton (Brunswick), the Canadian Military Band (Apex), and the *Starr-Gennett Military Band. In 1923 he was advertised as 'The Pianistic Humorist.'

BRAZIL. See South and Central America, Mexico, the West Indies.

BREAU, Lenny. Guitarist, singer, composer, b Auburn, Me, 5 Aug 1941. His parents are Hal 'Lone Pine' Breau (b Harold John Breau in Peacove, Me, 1916) and Betty Cody (b Auburn, Me), country singers who lived in the Maritimes during the late 1940s and early 1950s, singing on CFBC radio, Saint John, NB, and, after a sojourn back in the USA, in Winnipeg in the mid-1950s. 'Lone Pine' recorded for Banff and RCA and composed such songs as 'I Hear the Prairies Calling' and 'Prince Edward Island Is Heaven to Me.' He is a member of CAPAC and has had songs published by *Canadian Music Sales. Betty Cody was known especially as a yodeler.

As a child Lenny Breau began singing and playing guitar with his parents under the name Lone Pine Jr. In Winnipeg he received informal guidance from the jazz pianist Bob Erlendson. (The *BTO guitarist Randy Bachman later received similar help from Breau.) Influenced also by the jazz pianist Bill Evans, Breau developed a unique guitar style which exploited the instrument's harmonic potential to a point at which it rivalled, and even in some particulars surpassed, the range of a keyboard instrument. He performed in the early 1960s with the singer Don *Francks in Toronto (where they appeared in the NFB production *Toronto Jazz* in 1962) and in the USA, and then returned to Winnipeg, where he appeared frequently on radio and TV and in nightclubs. During a nomadic career he divided his time between Winnipeg and Toronto and was inactive for long periods. His own trio or quartet was heard on the CBC, and he accompanied jazz musicians (eg, Peter *Appleyard, Glenn McDonald) and folk and pop singers (eg, Beverly Glenn-Copeland, George Hamilton IV, Gene *MacLellan, *Malka, and Anne *Murray). His own sidemen included such bassist-and-drummer combinations as Reg Keln and Ron Halldorson, Billy Meryll and Dave Lewis, Don *Thompson and Terry *Clarke, and Michel *Donato and Claude *Ranger; the saxophonist Ron *Park was a member 1970–1. In 1975 Breau returned to the USA and gradually resumed his career in Nashville, New York, and Los Angeles.

An eclectic musician, virtuosic at his best and accomplished in folk, flamenco, and country idioms, Breau is at his most original as a jazz player. Alastair Lawrie wrote: 'The jazz element finds its expression in modern terms mostly – the rich, sophisticated chords that are dropped in with cool understatement behind a melody line that swings softly along until it bursts suddenly into a passage of rapid-fire brilliance' (Toronto *Globe and Mail*, 12 Feb 1969). Breau has composed pieces for guitar in several idioms, including *Taranta* and *Spanjazz*, both recorded.

DISCOGRAPHY

Guitar Sounds from Lenny Breau. Keln b guit, Halldorson drums. 1968. RCA LSP-4076

The Velvet Touch – Lenny Breau Live! Keln b guit, Halldorson drums. 1969. RCA LSP-4199

Five O'Clock Bells. solo guit. 1977, 1978. Adelphi AD 5006

With Copeland *Beverly Glenn-Copeland*. Copeland v and guit, Breau guit, Riley pf, Thompson db, Clarke drums. 1970. GRT 9233-1001

With Chet Atkins *Me and My Guitar*. 1977. RCA CPL 1-2045

With Buddy Emmons and Buddy Spicher *Buddies*. 1977. Flying Fish 041

With Buddy Spicher *Yesterday and Today*. Direct Disk DD 102

Others with Don Francks, Moe Koffman, and Anne Murray

BIBLIOGRAPHY

Webb, Martin K. 'Lenny Breau: Atkins-style jazz on a 6-string 12!' *Guitar Player*, Sep 1974 MM

***Brébeuf*, B29**. Healey *Willan's setting, for two narrators, choir, and orchestra, of E.J. Pratt's poem 'Brébeuf and His Brethren' (Toronto 1940), which tells the story of the 17th-century missionary (1593–1649) among the Hurons. It was commissioned by the CBC and first broadcast 26 Sep 1943 in a performance conducted by Ettore *Mazzoleni. A public presentation, entitled *The Life and Death of Jean de Brébeuf*, by the *Toronto Mendelssohn Choir and the *TSO under Sir Ernest *MacMillan followed on 18 Jan 1944 at *Massey Hall. A second version for choir and organ, revised for a projected performance in 1947 at the Brébeuf Festival in Midland, Ont, finally was heard in 1967 under Willan's baton in Timothy Eaton Memorial Church in Toronto. Some excerpts (*Fugue in G Minor* for organ, B161, Harris 1954; *Ave verum corpus*, B328, Harris 1948; and *Jesous Ahatonhia*, B424, Harris 1927) are performed separately.

BRÉGENT, Michel-Georges. Keyboard player, composer, b Montreal 29 Jan 1948. He studied at the *CMM 1967–70 with Gilles *Tremblay (composition), Jean *Laurendeau (ondes Martenot), Raoul *Sosa (piano), and Irving *Heller (sight reading). Among the instruments he has mastered are organ, electric piano, vibraphone, Mellotron, and synthesizer. Accompanied by a few musicians, he performed in 1972 with his brother Jacques (who recited poems and texts of songs by Cocteau, Ferré, *Leclerc, and Prévert set to his brother's music) at Le *Patriote, which awarded them a prize for performance. The brothers made the LP *Poussière des regrets* (RCA PCS 4021) in 1972 and staged rock music shows in Montreal in 1973. They resumed their activities in 1978, setting to music works by the Quebec poets Paul Chamberland, Michel Lamarre, Gaston Miron, and others, and making the LP *Partir pour ailleurs* (CAM CML 2003). Brégent went to Paris on a *Canada Council grant in the fall of 1973 and lived there until 1978, working as accompanist for shows by Lewis *Furey in 1974 and in the Dionne-Brégent Duo, formed with Vincent *Dionne, in 1975.

In 1965, prior to his composition studies, Brégent had undertaken the first part, for organ, of a vast four-part biblical fresco entitled *Testaments*, the composition of which was to continue by stages over the next 12 years. In the meantime he composed the piano work *Hommage à l'impressionnisme et au romantisme* (comprising *Paysage* and *Toccate-Sonate*) in 1967, and the following year completed five *Portraits* for piano, which he had begun in 1965. In 1968 he began writing *Conjugaison*, a work whose structure is inspired by the conjugation of the verb, and completed three works described as 'manifestations of free will': *Introspection*, for organ and instrumental ensemble; *Liage 5*, for organ; and ... *des restreintes de l'espace*, for 'feedback' and solo instrument. To this series he added *Geste* (1970, for five pianos, lighting, and public) and *Xaryt Shtryben* (1972, for organ, blacksmith, and gong). *Geste* subsequently was adapted for piano and was played in 1976 at the *SMCQ and recorded by Brégent's wife, Christina *Petrowska. In 1975 on a commission from the English network of the CBC, Brégent composed *Between Innocence and Experience* for bass, percussion, and keyboards. In 1978 he wrote *Contes pour enfant* for harmonica and guitar, in collaboration with the harmonicist Claude Garden. In 1979 he completed *Sapho* [sic] (1979) for soprano, flute, and guitar and *Sur Mesure* for violin and guitar. Brégent is an affiliate of PRO Canada.

BIBLIOGRAPHY

Petrowska-Brégent, Christina. 'The concept of "Geste",' *CMB*, 9 Autumn–Winter 1974

L'Heureux, Christine. 'Brégent seeks to broaden consciousness through music,' *MSc*, 301, May–Jun 1978

AP

BRESS, Hyman. Violinist, b Capetown 30 Jun 1931, naturalized Canadian 1952. He took his first lessons with his father, making his debut with the Capetown Municipal Orchestra at nine and performing extensively in South Africa afterwards. At the Curtis Institute in Philadelphia he studied 1946–51 with Ivan Galamian. In 1951 he moved to Montreal, where he appeared in recital and on CBC radio. Chamber music performances with Otto and Walter *Joachim led to the founding of the *Montreal String Quartet, in which he played first violin 1955–63. He was concertmaster of the *MSO for a single season (1958–9). At that time he won several awards as a solo performer: the 1956 New York Concert Artist Guild Award, the 1957 Jascha Heifetz Award at Tanglewood, and the 1961 Harriet Cohen Commonwealth Medal.

Bress has premiered, among other Canadian works, Otto Joachim's *Concertante No. 1* (the second part in Montreal in 1957, and the complete work in Paris in 1958), Kelsey *Jones' *Introduction and Fugue* (1959), Violet *Archer's *Concerto* (1960) on the CBC's *'Little Symphonies,' and Udo *Kasemets' *Concerto* (13 Apr 1967) with the CBC Festival Orchestra. He has given recitals in the world's major cities and has appeared with leading Canadian and US orchestras, the London SO, and the Berlin Philharmonic. In 1973 he made a tour of the Far East. He has revived and in some instances recorded unusual or seldom played works like the Joseph Joachim and Bloch concertos. He has broadcast in Canada largely for the CBC. Bress has recorded his own *Fantasy* (1961–2, Presser) for violin, piano, and electronic tape, and has performed the work in New York and elsewhere while the score was being projected page by page on a screen behind the performers. He has divided his time between Europe and North America. In 1975 he attracted the attention of the British and North American press with his plans for a transatlantic tunnel for undersea transportation.

Of his playing the London *Times* wrote in March 1961: 'Bress's phrasing was always significantly and expressively shaped, and to the exacting 20th-century works he brought a wide range of tone colour and dynamics ... His tone – mellow and rich in its lower register and silky up at the top – in Mozart's *Adagio*, for instance, was beautiful in its cantabile line.' He plays a 1739 Guarnerius del Gesù violin.

WRITINGS

'The role of electronic music in relationship to the violin,' *Musical Events*, Apr 1962

DISCOGRAPHY

Archer *Trio No. 1* – Leclair *Sonata*. W. Joachim vc, Newmark pf. 1954. RCI 112
– *Trio No. 2*. W. Joachim vc, Newmark pf. 1962. RCI 196
Bach *Concerto* BWV1052 – Mozart *Concerto* K271a (cadenzas by Bress). MSO members, Bress cond. 1964. Mode MDINT 9246
– *Ein Musikalisches Opfer* BWV1079. Duschenes fl, O. Joachim va, W. Joachim vc. 1953. RCI 95
– *3 Solo Sonatas; 3 Solo Partitas* BWV1001 –6. (1966–7). 3-Mace MCS 9056-9058
– Also accompanied versions. K. Bergemann pf. CBS Set 77325
Bartók *Sonatas No. 1 and 2*. Reiner pf. (1965). Victor LSC 2853
Beethoven *Romance No. 2*. London Phil O, Boult cond. World Record Club ST 730
Beethoven – Mozart – Schubert – Paganini. Reiner pf. 1962. Folk 3352
Bloch *Concerto in A; Suite Hébraïque*. Prague SO, Rohan cond. (1968). Crossroads 22 16 0212
– *Sonata* for violin and piano. Reiner pf. (1964). Folk 3357
– *Baal Shem No. 2*. Reiner pf. (Ca 1962). Folk 3354
Brahms – Fauré – Wieniawski – Tchaikovsky – Sarasate – Kreisler – Dvořák. Reiner pf. (Ca 1962). Folk 3353
Bress – Haba – Sessions – Webern. Reiner pf. (Ca 1962). Folk 3355
Busoni *Sonatas No. 1 and 2*. B. Johnsson pf. (1967). Oiseau S-2916
Debussy – Schoenberg – Bloch – Bartók. Reiner pf. (Ca 1962). Folk 3554
O. Joachim *Concertante No. 1*. CBC Mtl str orch, Beaudry cond, Charbonneau perc. (1971?). RCI 293
Jones – Anhalt – Brahms. Reiner pf. 1966. RCI 220/RCA CCS-1014
Leclair *Sonata No. 3* – Mozart *Concerto No. 4; Serenade No. 7* 'Haffner' (4th mvt). English Chamb O, Gibson cond and pf. World Record Club T106
Magnard *Sonata, Op 13* – Ropartz *Sonata No. 3*. O. Alain pf. Alpha CL4018
R. Mathieu *Quintet No. 1*. Sieb vn, O. Joachim va, W. Joachim vc, Reiner pf. 1956. RCI 123
M. Perrault *Trio*. W. Joachim vc, Newmark pf. RCI 125
Prokofiev *Sonatas No. 1 and 2*. Reiner pf. 1969. CBC SM-117
Reger *Sonatas No. 1, 3, 7, Op 91*. (1966). Dover HCR ST 7016
Sarasate *Zigeunerweisen*. London Phil O, Boult cond. World Record Club ST 728
Schoenberg *Concerto, Op 36* – Stravinsky *Concerto in D*. Prague SO, Rohan cond. 1968. Supra SUAST 50878
Schubert *Sonatina in G Minor; Rondo Brilliant in B Minor; Fantasia in C*. A. Holecek pf. 1971. Supra III 1039
Schumann *Sonatas No. 1 and 2*. Reiner pf. (1964). Bar BC 2833
Spohr *Concertos No. 8 and 9*. Symphony O, Beck cond. (1966). Oiseau S-278
Stravinsky *Duo Concertant; Suite Italienne*. Reiner pf. (1964). Folk 3356
Tartini – Corelli – Bach. Reiner pf. (1962). Folk 3351
Tchaikovsky *Concerto, Op 35*. London Phil O, Boult cond. (1968). Crossroads 22 16 0224
Vallerand – Weinzweig – Kenins – Morawetz. Pratt pf. Masters of the Bow MBS-2002
Veracini *Sonatas 1–12, Op 1*. J. Schrick v da gamba, O. Alain hpd. (1965). 3-Lyrichord LLST 7138-7140
Vivaldi *Concertos, Op 3, No. 6 and 12*. Mtl Sinfonia. 1963. Bar BC 2832
Ysaÿe *Sonatas 1–6, Op 27*. 1967. Alpha DB 132

(NT)

BREWER, George MacKenzie. Organist, pianist, teacher, composer, lecturer, b London, Ont, 30 May 1889, d Montreal 18 May 1947; Associate (Dominion College of Music) 1903, Fellow (American Guild of Organists) 1910. Though he studied in Montreal with Percival J. *Illsley in his childhood, he was largely self-taught and was an avid reader on all subjects. He was organist at Bethlehem Congregational Church in 1908, and by 1912 he had moved to the Church of the Messiah where he stayed until his death. He also served as organist at Temple Emanu-el, Westmount (Montreal), and as accompanist 1923–31 for the *Montreal Elgar Choir. He was the pianist 1922–9 with the *Dubois String Quartet in many concerts, he accompanied the violinist Saul *Brant, and he later gave organ recitals for the *Casavant Society.

Brewer was an examiner 1907–47 at the *Dominion College of Music and taught 1944–7 at the *CMM, under whose auspices he gave series of recitals demonstrating the history of organ music. He also taught piano, organ, and theory privately. Brewer travelled widely 1913–35, his interest in the native musics of various countries taking him as far as Eastern Europe and North Africa. His experiences made him an able lecturer on exotic and contemporary music and on visual art and philosophy, as well as on dramatic music, organ history, and Bach. He was a reviewer for the *Montreal Daily Star* and wrote program notes 1943–7 for the *CSM. His compositions (itemized in *Catalogue of Canadian Composers*) include choral works, short piano pieces, and many songs, some published by *Édition Belgo-Canadienne, Boston Music, and in *La Lyre*. He also composed incidental music for Montreal Repertory Theatre productions, in some of which he appeared as an actor. With his broad culture and many skills he contributed significantly to Montreal's cultural development in the first half of the 20th century. A memorial concert was held in his honour on 25 May 1948 at the Church of the Messiah under CMM auspices. The *NL of C holds many of his papers.

SW

Bridge music. Term used by musicians in the 1970s to describe an approach to music that seeks to unite the strong rhythmic roots of the native Indian culture and the folk appeal of a Bob Dylan. This 'native sound' (an alternative designation) was developed by the Métis nation. Bridge music is sung and accompanied by the instrument of the artist's choice, usually guitar. It is meant to be understood easily and to be appreciated by native and non-native alike for its melodic beauty and its strong message. An example is 'See the Arrow' by Winston Wuttunee, an Indian from Red Pheasant, Sask. Recordings have been made by Shannon Two Feathers (for WSM and Kanata), David Campbell (Development Education Centre, Noona, Columbia Special Productions), Shingoose (CBC, Native Council of Canada), Willy Dunn (Summus, Kot'ai), and Duke Redbird (CBC). The Native Country Performing and Film Arts Ltd company was formed in 1976 to cultivate bridge music and to foster native and other Canadian talent.

See also Indians; Powwow singers.

BRIDLE, Augustus (John). Critic, writer, editor, b East Stour, Dorsetshire, England, 4 Mar 1868, d Toronto 21 Dec 1952. Of illegitimate birth and orphaned in infancy, he became a ward of the Rev T.B. Stephenson, founder of the National Children's Home in London. Bridle was sent to Hamilton, Ont, in 1878. Details of his early childhood are not clear, but it is believed that he lived and worked with a shoemaker, a Mr Stewart in Merlin, Ont, in 1880, and moved in 1882 to the farm of Richard Smith in Dealtown, Ont. He received his teaching certificate in 1887 and began teaching in 1889 in Blenheim, Ont. He taught later in Edmonton and in Stratford, Ont. In 1903 he took up newspaper work, writing for the Stratford *Herald*, the Toronto *News*, and the Edmonton *Bulletin*. He was associate editor 1908–16 and editor 1916–20 of the weekly *Canadian Courier*, then briefly editor of *Musical Canada*. In 1922 he joined the staff of the *Toronto Daily Star*, which he served for 30 years as music critic, book reviewer, and film and drama editor. In 1935 he began to review films for the *Star Weekly* also.

The moving force behind the formation (1908) of the *Arts and Letters Club of Toronto, Bridle was its secretary 1908–13 and president 1913–14, and was referred to as 'Perpetual Grand Secretary' for the rest of his life. He instigated the

Yearbook of Canadian Art in 1913, and was a staunch champion of the Canadian painters known as the Group of Seven. He sang briefly in the bass section of the *Toronto Mendelssohn Choir.

Bridle was responsible for devoting an entire issue (12 Oct 1912) of the *Canadian Courier* to Canadian music and musicians. In one of the articles, 'Music in two cities' [Toronto and Montreal], he revealed a shrewd grasp of the problems of isolation and regionalism and declared that 'if Canada is ever to achieve anything national in music, the people who make music, as well as those who listen to it, must at least find out what has been and what is being done in other parts of the country than their own.' His article 'Who writes our music?' (*Maclean's*, 15 Dec 1929) was the first attempt to survey contemporary Canadian musical composition on a comprehensive scale. During the early 1920s, under the auspices of the *Star*, Bridle organized over 100 free 'Good Music' concerts (these later became the Star Fresh Air Fund concerts) and several free 'famous music' and carol concerts, and participated in the creation of the *Canadian National Exhibition Chorus. In 1927 in Toronto he staged his symbolic pageant 'Heart of the World' at the *CNE for an international meeting of the World Federation of Teachers.

Bridle was the author of several books, including *A Backwoods Christmas* (Toronto 1910), *Sons of Canada* (Toronto 1916; it includes biographies of Guillaume *Couture, F.H. *Torrington, and A. S. *Vogt), *Masques of Ottawa* (Toronto 1921), a novel, *Hansen* (Toronto 1925), and *The Story of the Club* (Toronto 1945). In later years his reviews were known for their epigrammatic and telegraphic style. (MMI)

William Briggs. Trade-publishing operation of the Methodist Book and Publishing House (later Ryerson Press), Toronto. It was directed by William Briggs (b Banbridge, Ireland, 1836, d Port Credit, Ont, 1922), a clergyman who served 1879–1919 as book steward of the Methodist Book and Publishing House. Briggs' musical copyrights – some 40 pieces of sheet music and 10 volumes – date from the years between 1883 and the turn of the century and are all religious. The volumes include Canadian editions of E.O. Excell's *Triumphant Songs* (various dates), *Revival Hymns* (1889), *Canadian Hymnal* (1889, rev 1894), and the *Methodist Hymn and Tune Book* (1894). In its field Briggs' production was among the largest and highest-ranking in Canada. HK

BRIMSON, Florence (Anne) (m Graff). Soprano, b Newmarket, near Toronto, 2 Oct 1873, d Santa Barbara, Cal, 4 Oct 1953. After initial study with W. Elliott *Haslam at the *Toronto College of Music she spent four years with Mathilde Marchesi in Paris, and the latter is said to have suggested the singular *nom de théâtre* under which she pursued her professional career: Mlle Toronta. Although she had sung publicly as a student in Toronto and Paris, her official debut was at the Philadelphia Academy of Music, 29 Nov 1897, as Siebel in *Faust*, under the auspices of the Damrosch-Ellis Opera. With that company she toured for two seasons, her repertoire including Stéphano in *Roméo et Juliette*, Philine in *Mignon*, Micaela in *Carmen*, Lola in *Cavalleria Rusticana*, and the Forest Bird in *Siegfried*. In 1899 she sang with great success in Toronto performances of *Elijah* and *Messiah*. In that year she married Clarence Graff of New York and retired from the stage. After many years in England the Graffs settled in Santa Barbara, where Clarence Graff became a founding member (1946) and first president (1947) of the Music Academy of the West. JBM

BRISSON, Gaston. Pianist, composer, arranger, actor, b Pointe-au-Père, near Rimouski, Que, 5 Dec 1940; BA (Bathurst) 1962, B MUS (Montreal) 1964, M MUS (Montreal) 1966. Son of Ernest Brisson, a popular fiddler in the Rimouski region, he studied piano in Bathurst, NB, and with Yvonne *Hubert at the *École Vincent-d'Indy in Montreal. He won third prize in 1963 and first prize in 1964 at the Quebec Festivals (*Canadian Music Competitions), playing a Bach concerto with the *Quebec SO under Wilfrid *Pelletier in the 1963 competition. Though he has retained an interest especially in Chopin, and his compositions and arrangements reflect a classical influence, he turned to popular music in 1967, and worked in the years following as accompanist to Jacqueline Barrette, Clémence *Desrochers, Georges *Dor, Pauline *Julien, and others. While accompanist 1974–5 to Yvon Deschamps, he collaborated on the music for some of the monologuist's songs. Brisson played Tony Panneton in the premiere (1974) of **Les Hauts et les bas dla vie d'une diva: Sarah Ménard par eux-mêmes*, and appeared in all performances of that musical through 1978. He was composer of *Heureux celui qui meurt de rire* (1976), a show starring Jacqueline Barrette, and he opened his own one-man show 19 May 1976 at Le *Patriote (Montreal). He played his *Concertino* for piano and orchestra 1 Apr 1978 with the *MSO. His recordings include the LPs *Corridor* (1975, Cap ST-70.040), *Gaston Brisson* (1976, Kébec-Disc KD-915), and *Filigranes* (1977, Kébec-Disc KD-936), each a collection largely of his compositions and arrangements (folk songs and dances) for instrumental ensemble. Brisson is a member of CAPAC.

BIBLIOGRAPHY
Jasmin, Hélène. 'An accompanist from the Gaspé becomes a star on his own,' *CanComp*, 111, May 1976
(HPd)

British Columbia Cultural Services Branch. Established in 1975 as an agency of the provincial government operating under the Ministry of Provincial Secretary and Government Services. Known at first as the British Columbia Cultural Program, it functioned 1975–6 under the auspices of the Dept of the Provincial Secretary and 1976–8 within the Dept of Culture and Heritage in the Ministry of Recreation and Conservation. The director, Thomas G. Fielding, was appointed in 1975. Among other duties the Cultural Services Branch administers the British Columbia Cultural Fund and acts as secretariat for the British Columbia Arts Board.

The British Columbia Cultural Fund was established 1 Apr 1967 as a perpetual endowment fund of $5 million (increased in 1969, 1972, and 1974 to $20 million), from which the interest was to be used for cultural development within the province. In 1975 the fund began to be augmented with revenue from the provincial lottery. The fund was administered through the office of a provincial minister and grants were made with the assistance of a government-appointed advisory committee.

The British Columbia Arts Board, set up in 1974 to replace the advisory committee and representing all regions of the province, is a 15-member consultative body that advises the Provincial Secretary on the formulation of comprehensive arts policies for the province. Appointments to the board are made by the province and are for three-year terms. In 1978–9 the Cultural Services Branch expended more than $3.5 million. In the field of music grants were made to students (through a scholarship assistance program, and tuition and summer study awards), to professional arts organizations (eg, the *Vancouver SO, the *Victoria SO, the Okanagan SO, the *Vancouver Opera, the *Purcell String Quartet, *Days Months and Years to Come, etc), to training organizations (eg, *Community Music School of Greater Vancouver, *Shawnigan Summer School of the Arts, Courtenay Youth Music Centre, *Victoria Cons of Music, etc), to special service organizations (eg, BC Choral Federation, *BCRMTA, *Overture Concerts, etc), and to organizations for special projects (eg, Amity Singers, Kamloops Symphony, *Vancouver Bach Choir). It has provided touring subsidies to assist in the presentation of musical events throughout the province, and has continued the annual grants to community arts councils, as well as assisting them through a Community Arts Projects program established in 1979. The projects program is open also to non-profit recreation commissions and community-oriented arts organizations. The Cultural Services Branch has supported national organizations or projects such as the *CCA, the *Canadian Music Competitions, *EMC*, and the *NYO. The Cultural Services Branch began to issue the quarterly bulletin *Arts B.C.* in 1975 and its supplement *Interim News* in 1979. It also publishes an annual report.

BIBLIOGRAPHY
Wyman, Max. 'British Columbia,' *CMB*, 9, 10, Autumn–Winter 1974, Spring–Summer 1975

British Columbia Music Educators' Association. Organization founded in 1957 with Sherwood *Robson as president. Its objectives at that time were to unite the various groups teaching music in the schools and to encourage the creation of a curriculum in music education at the *U of British Columbia. In 1962 the BCMEA amalgamated with the Secondary Instrumental Teachers' Assn, thus becoming affiliated with the British Columbia Teachers' Federation. This affiliation gave the BCMEA a greater voice in curriculum development and in-service training in the schools. The BCMEA's principal forum has been its yearly conference, which emphasizes new trends and materials and features important personalities in music education. The association's journal, the *B.C. Music Educator* was begun in 1958, with issues emerging irregularly but on the average twice a year. Although not affiliated with the CMEA, the BCMEA has maintained a close liaison with that organization and was the host for the 1979 CMEA national conference held in Vancouver. Presidents include Lloyd *Slind in 1958, W. Karren in 1959, E. Davies 1960–1, M. Rose 1961–3, Allen Clingman 1963–4, P. Kinvig 1964–5, G. McKinley 1965–6, G. Lapthorne 1966–8, R. Featherstonhaugh 1968–70, O. Whitcutt 1971–3, V. Haslin 1973–5, Dennis Tupman 1975–7, succeeded by L.J. White in 1977. MMV

British Columbia Music Festival Association. Provincial umbrella organization founded in 1964 (after informal discussions held as early as 1961) at a meeting of representatives of urban competition festivals. The meeting was initiated by Elise White, at that time secretary of the Vancouver Kiwanis Music Festival, and Phyllis *Schuldt, a Vancouver music teacher. The association has worked to further the competition festival movement, acting as a link between local festivals and exploring possible sources of financial support for them. By 1979 25 individual festivals throughout British Columbia had become members. Both the association and the festivals themselves have received regular financial assistance from the British Columbia Cultural Fund (*British Columbia Cultural Services Branch).

In 1972 the association organized its first provincial competitions, open to winners from the member-festivals. Solo instrumentalists, instrumental ensembles, singers, and choirs competed for provincial standings, trophies, and money prizes, and also for eligibility to compete at the national level in the *FCMF's recently established annual *National Competitive Festival of Music at the *CNE, Toronto. The provincial competitions continued annually, held in a succession of British Columbia cities, including New Westminster, Prince George, Terrace, Vernon, and Victoria. In 1979 65 member-festival winners performed in the provincial competitions. Adjudicators from outside the province (eg, from the universities of Alberta or Washington State) have been favoured for the provincial assignments. The 25 member-festivals have been autonomous in British Columbia, each preparing its own syllabus, unlike those in Alberta, which in 1918 adopted a common syllabus prepared by their provincial association. For the British Columbia provincial finals the syllabus of the National Competitive Festival of Music has been used.

British Columbia Registered Music Teachers' Association (BCRMTA). Founded in 1932 as the British Columbia Music Teachers' Federation, incorporating the Vancouver Music Teachers' Assn (formed in 1920 with H. Roy Robertson as president) and other provincial groups. It changed its name to the British Columbia Music Teachers' Assn in 1935. That same year, with fellow associations from Alberta, Saskatchewan, and Manitoba, it helped to found the Federation of Music Teachers' Assns (later *CFMTA). In 1947 it received a provincial charter and was renamed the British Columbia Registered Music Teachers' Assn. In 1978 the BCRMTA had 533 members. Those without access to one of its 19 branches are designated 'provincial members.' Funded by the provincial government, the BCRMTA sponsors workshops in remote areas of the province. It also helps its smaller branches to obtain competent guest lecturers and promotes their Student Teachers' Auxiliaries. It awards prizes to British Columbia winners of the Canada Music Week Writing Contest and scholarships to the winners of the Young Artists' Competitions held at its biennial conventions. It has been host to CFMTA conventions in 1936, 1941, 1955, and 1969. In 1972 it began publishing a quarterly, the *Provincial Newsletter*. BCRMTA presidents have included H. Roy Robertson 1932–7, Reginald Cox 1937–40, 1944–6, and 1955–7, May James 1940–2, Ida Verrall 1942–4, Charles E. *Findlater 1946–55, Alf Carlson 1957–69, Morris Dean 1969–70, Helen *Dahlstrom 1970–2, Rodney R.A. Webster 1972–4, Joyce Horner 1974–8, succeeded by Ernest Schneider in 1978.

BIBLIOGRAPHY

'History of the British Columbia Registered Music Teachers' Association,' CFMTA *Newsletter*, Winter 1980 FH, NM

Broadcasting. Vast distances and the isolation of communities have posed major problems for Canada. Radio and TV therefore have contributed immensely to the nation's cultural life, particularly radio in the case of music.

1 Introduction
2 Canadian Broadcasting Corporation / La Société Radio-Canada
3 Early history of Canadian broadcasting
4 The era of CBC Radio 1936–52
5 CBC Television
6 CBC Radio 1952–79
7 CBC International Service / Radio Canada International
8 Change and reassessment
9 The private sector
10 TV changes and radio's survival

CKAC radio orchestra under Edmond Trudel, Montreal 1930 (*La Lyre*, Feb, Mar, and Apr 1930)

1 INTRODUCTION. In 1980 Canada's broadcasting system was the world's most complex, being an aggregation of many privately owned profit-motivated stations, one nationally owned system, and three provincially operated systems (Alberta, Ontario, and Quebec), broadcasting for the most part in one or the other of the two official languages, English and French (and locally in some others as well), through longitudes spanning seven time zones and over a land area (10 million square kilometres) second only to that of the Soviet Union. Moreover some 80 per cent of Canadians have chosen to live along the southern fringe, within easy electronic reach of the world's most clamorous broadcaster, the USA. Broadcasting undoubtedly has been a unifying force for Canada. At the same time it opened electronic channels which facilitated penetration by foreign cultures, particularly the USA. The general status and objectives of this publicly-cum-privately owned system are prescribed by the Broadcasting Act of 1968; it is to be 'owned and controlled by Canadians so as to safeguard, enrich and strengthen the cultural, political, social and economic fabric of Canada.' The principal interpreter of the Act is the Canadian Radio Television and Telecommunications Commission (*CRTC), set up in 1968 to report to Parliament through the secretary of state (the minister of communications beginning in 1980), and thus to be under the control of Parliament itself rather than the ruling party of the day. By 1970 the CRTC had begun to draft and to implement regulations to ensure that Canadian broadcasters would use 'predominantly Canadian creative and other resources,' as required by the Act. Since for many years most broadcasting of music on radio had consisted of playing records, and since the Canadian recording industry until recently (with the partial exception of the Province of Quebec) had been an importing enterprise only, such regulations were bound to encourage Canadian recording, though probably more of popular than of serious music. (See also CRTC; RPM MAPL logo).

2 THE CANADIAN BROADCASTING CORPORATION (CBC) / LA SOCIÉTÉ RADIO-CANADA (SRC). Publicly owned, and the largest single component of the system, reaching 98.5 per cent of Canadians, the CBC braodcasts not only through its own networks of stations and transmitters (by 1979 497 TV and 538 radio) but also through privately owned 'affiliate' stations and transmitters with which the CBC has retransmission contracts (243 TV and 87 radio). The problem of covering vast territories has been formidable, and in 1973 the system was extended by use of the Anik satellite; by the end of the 1970s at least 62 TV and 25 radio stations drew their national service signals from Anik, many in turn feeding other transmitters in their areas. Most of the CBC's radio broadcasting has been of programs originated by the CBC itself. On TV, however (especially English-language), the foreign-produced content has been extensive. Moreover, in the late 1970s on TV less than 1.5 per cent of total air time was devoted to 'Music and Dance,' while on CBC radio, serious music might have accounted for some 15 per cent on AM (Amplitude Modulation: a wide-band far-reaching signal suitable for information broadcasting) and more than 60 per cent on FM (Frequency Modulation: a narrow-band short-reach signal carrying sounds with high fidelity, usually in two-channel stereo, and thus suitable for music broadcasting). The CBC opened FM stations in Toronto, Montreal, and Vancouver in 1946 and a tape-exchange FM 'network' in 1960. The network was suspended 1962–4 as a government economy measure. On its reopening in 1965 as a microwave-linked network, an FM station – CBW-FM – was installed at Winnipeg, the first CBC station to begin regular multiplex stereophonic broadcasting. CBU-FM Vancouver and CBUF-FM, the Vancouver outlet for French AM network service, followed in 1967, CBO-FM Ottawa in 1969, CBL-FM Toronto in 1970, and CBF-FM and CBM-FM Montreal in 1971.

It has been to CBC radio, therefore, and particularly its FM stations, that the listener has turned for serious music. Throughout the 1940s (and for many years later) it also was to CBC radio that performers of serious music turned for employment, whether regular, frequent, or occasional. There was justice in Geoffrey *Waddington's retrospective comment in 1952, after he had assumed the directorship of music for the CBC's English-language radio network, 'The CBC has been the dominant factor in providing some measure of economic security for the Canadian musician.' He might have added that the CBC also was the most effective champion of the Canadian composer, through commissions, public performances, payment of royalties, etc. The foregoing no longer would be true by the mid 1970s. Nonetheless, the story of the broadcasting of serious music in Canada virtually begins and ends with the CBC.

3 EARLY HISTORY OF CANADIAN BROADCASTING. As befits a nation so dependent on long-range communications, Canada has an honourable place in the early development of radio. The Italian engineer Guglielmo Marconi is credited with accomplishing in 1901 the first trans-Atlantic 'interrupted code' transmission, from St John's, Nfld, but it was a Canadian, Reginald A. Fessenden, who developed the principle of continuous-wave transmission upon which all modern broadcasting depends; Fessenden first transmitted the sound of the voice in 1900 over a distance of 50 miles, and in 1906 from Boston to Scotland. Fessenden was bitterly disappointed that the Canadian government granted Marconi's company, rather than his own Wireless Telegraph Company of Canada, exclusive rights to build the first transmitting stations in Canada. Fessenden's aim had been to make Canada a world centre for long-range radio transmission, but he never again chose to live in his native country. His name as one of the great radio pioneers has remained largely unknown, even to Canadians.

Regularly scheduled radio broadcasting did not begin until after World War I, however, and to the Canadian Marconi Company station XWA (now CFCF) in Montreal went the distinction of giving, 20 May 1920, the first scheduled broadcast in North America, possibly in the world.

In the USA radio broadcasting boomed in the early 1920s, as businesses and corporations vied with each other to pay for air-time advertising, but in Canada commercial messages at first were forbidden (although sponsor identification was permitted), and commercial interest in radio lagged. Nor did the government help to develop the medium.

Initiatives were many and varied in these uncoordinated early days, and many an amateur appeared on local radio in the spate of ever-popular (and inexpensive) 'amateur hours.' Public service was the order of the day, and the beginnings of educational broadcasting soon appeared. In 1925, for example, Canada's earliest French station, CKAC (founded in 1922 by the Montreal newspaper *La Presse*), presented a 30-week radio series of piano and theory lessons, apparently a first for Canada, by Émiliano *Renaud, the broadcasts including many of his own pieces, some written for the purpose. Probably the first successful systematic school broadcasts were given over CNRV, the CNR radio station (see below) in Vancouver in 1927; the Vancouver School Board prepared the series, the musical portions of which were organized by the assistant supervisor of music for Vancouver schools, Miss A. Roberts. (See School music broadcasts.)

CKAC Montreal – and on occasion its affiliated stations in the province of Quebec – carried an early example (1929–38) of provincially sponsored broadcasting: 'L'Heure provinciale,' broadcasts devoted mainly to the work of Quebec composers and performers and directed by Henri *Letondal (later succeeded by Alfred *Mignault).

Reginald A. Fessenden

Individual stations provided many enterprising programs. In 1924, however, Sir Henry Thornton, the farsighted president of the recently formed Canadian National Railway system, was thinking on a larger scale. He decided that transcontinental passengers should be able to listen to radio on their long journeys, so receivers were installed on CNR trains, an attractive travelling novelty. At that time the available listening fare would have been largely of US origin, so Thornton decided to build Canadian transmitting studios, the first in Ottawa (CNRO, 27 Feb 1924) and another in Moncton (CNRA, 7 Nov 1924), and this initiative culminated five years later in a trans-continental network of CNR 'landlines' (which, with those of the CPR, provided the mainstay of inter-city radio linkage until the establishment of the Bell System's microwave network in 1962). In 1924 the airwaves were relatively uncrowded, and some transmitters could be heard for hundreds of kilometres, especially over the prairies. Radio audiences were growing swiftly.

Although 'public service' programming (news, weather reports, local announcements, etc) was of prime importance, music was not neglected. In October of 1925, for example, from CNRT in Toronto not only was a complete studio performance of *The Yeomen of the Guard* given (under Reginald *Stewart), but so also was a special series, 'The Music Makers,' by J. Campbell *McInnes, one program of which was devoted to Bach; two months later *The Mikado* was broadcast from CNRM in Montreal. That same year the CNR signed an exclusive contract with the *Hart House String Quartet, who two years later made a trans-Canada tour, broadcasting Beethoven quartets over each of the CNR's radio stations in honour of the Beethoven centenary.

By 1927 a new method of multi-channel transmission was being developed for long-distance lines, and it became evident that broadcasting 'networks' of interconnected stations could be contemplated. To mark in a spectacular way the Diamond Jubilee of Canada's Confederation, 1 Jul 1927, a broadcast of trans-continental scope was suggested by the Assn of Canadian Clubs. The engineers pronounced it feasible, and on 1 July, after months of planning and two weeks of testing, the broadcast emanated from Parliament Hill in Ottawa, with a 1000-voice choir (augmented by 10,000 children singing in English and French) and the new Peace Tower carillon (its inauguration) played by Percival *Price; also participating were Éva *Gauthier, the Hart House String Quartet, the Bytown Troubadours under Charles *Marchand, and the Chateau Laurier Orchestra under James McIntyre, who included among his selections a *Suite* by the governor-general, Lord Willingdon (see Sovereigns, statesmen, and other public figures). The governor-general also spoke, as did Prime Minister W.L. Mackenzie King and other dignitaries. The broadcast was given in three segments, the first beginning at 10:45 am and the last at 9:30 pm. The daring experiment's success was due in no small measure to the contribution of the musicians. Thereafter, in the minds of public and politicians alike, it was clear, for the first time since early colonization, that the vast land that had coalesced into Canada indeed could function as one nation.

Two years later (20 Oct 1929) Thornton inaugurated North America's first series of trans-continental symphonic broadcasts, the 'All-Canada Symphony Concerts,' with Luigi von *Kunits conducting 55 members of the *TSO. The last concert was entirely of music by Canadian composers, another 'first' for the burgeoning broadcasting system.

In September 1929 Thornton added to his broadcasting staff Esmé Moonie, of a distinguished Edinburgh family of musicians. As program director, particularly for music, it was the bilingual Moonie's task to present the best of Canadian and foreign talent not only on the existing English network but also on the new French network. By the end of her tenure in 1932, studio productions of condensed versions of great operas had become regular fare on network programs (particularly those on the French network, which were conducted mostly by Henri *Miro).

Meanwhile the CPR also had been developing a chain of hotels and broadcasting outlets, and in 1930 it began its own series of music broadcasts, including an orchestra series from Montreal under Douglas *Clarke, and the Concert Orchestra broadcasts under Rex *Battle from the CPR's new Royal York Hotel in Toronto. Imperial Oil sponsored another imposing series broadcast from the Royal York, with Reginald Stewart conducting a 55-piece orchestra and internationally known soloists.

With the Depression, the CNR in 1931 and the CPR the following year were forced to abandon broadcasting, and a public clamour grew for a reorganization and consolidation of public broadcasting. Especially vocal was the public-spirited Radio (later Canadian Broadcasting) League, headed by Graham Spry and Alan Plaunt, to whom Canadian music-lovers of later generations were to owe tremendous gratitude. In September of 1929 the government's Royal Commission on Broadcasting (the Aird Commission) advocated strongly a publicly owned broadcasting system. In consequence the Canadian Radio Broadcasting Commission was formed in 1932 and began operations in May 1933 under the chairmanship of Hector *Charlesworth, the music critic of *Saturday Night* magazine. However, owing to a combination of underfinancing, lack of government support, and administrative ineptitude, in 1936 the CRBC was superseded by the Canadian Broadcasting Corporation, which was organized as a Crown Corporation and which swiftly set about establishing the necessary basic physical and technical facilities, at the same time expanding its contractual links with private stations hitherto active only locally, thus extending the national service. In order to develop an integrated national broadcasting system the CBC's board of governors had been given the basic regulatory powers over private broadcasting as well as its own. This later was to prove an embarrassment, and in 1958 such powers were given to the independently created Board of Broadcast Governors. These powers were weak and philosophically unclear, and in

1968 a new Broadcasting Act was promulgated and the CRTC created.

4 THE ERA OF CBC RADIO (1936–52). From the first, the presentation of good music was given high priority in CBC broadcasting, and the musical public became indebted to the work of such early producers as Albert *Chamberland, Morris 'Rusty' *Davis, Georges *Dufresne, Guy Mauffette, and R.-O. *Pelletier II in Montreal; John *Adaskin, Norbert Bauman, John Kannawin, and Ernest Morgan in Toronto; and Norman Lucas in Winnipeg. In 1936 J.-J. *Gagnier was appointed director of music for the Quebec region. He had fulfilled that function for the CRBC since 1934, and he continued to do so for the CBC until his death in 1949. In 1938 Jean-Marie *Beaudet was appointed the first overall director of music. That same year in Montreal a regular symphonic series, 'L'Heure symphonique,' was inaugurated, and the 'Chalet' concerts from Montreal and the 'Prom' concerts from Toronto became standard summer fare, as did regular broadcasts by chamber groups, choirs, and soloists. By the 1940–1 season, for example, the CBC national, regional, and local schedules encompassed no fewer than 45 programs of opera (including the *Metropolitan Opera from New York), more than 600 symphony concerts (including relays of broadcasts by the major US orchestras), over 2000 programs of chamber music, and over 3000 of 'semi-classical' music. These were mostly 'live,' recordings not yet being in regular use; in fact, until 1958 the use of recordings and transcriptions during the evening hours was banned, so as to encourage the use of 'live' talent.

The musical pace set in the late 1930s was continued during the war years (notably in the 'Canadian Music in Wartime' series conducted by Beaudet, and broadcast also on NBC's University of the Air), with special attention being paid to Canadian music, through Samuel *Hersenhoren's series 'Tribute to Young Canadians,' through the music of many Canadian composers for radio dramas and documentaries (John *Weinzweig lists about 100 such scores, mostly from the 1940s), and through other commissions, such as Healey *Willan's radio operas **Transit through Fire* in 1942 and *Deirdre of the Sorrows* (*Deirdre*) in 1945. From 1943 to 1956 the popular nation-wide talent-hunt series *'Singing Stars of Tomorrow' and its French-language equivalent *'Nos Futures Étoiles' played their parts in the emerging careers of many Canadian singers. Other wartime series of exceptional interest included one 1943–4, under Sir Ernest *MacMillan, devoted to the oratorios of Handel and another (1943, with Wanda Landowska and conducted by Adolph *Koldofsky) featuring several comparatively unknown keyboard concertos of Carl Philipp Emanuel Bach.

This also was a period of program exchange with the USA, in which Canadian orchestras and musicians were heard widely over the NBC, the CBS, and the MBS. The weekly broadcasts of the TSO and the CSM (*MSO) were carried regularly by the MBS, and in the early 1940s the *Promenade Symphony Concerts from Toronto were carried by the NBC. In 1939 the *Toronto Mendelssohn Choir under Herbert *Fricker broadcast Bach's *Mass in B Minor* throughout Canada and also was heard in the USA over the NBC. Roland Leduc's *'The Little Symphonies' from Montreal began its durable series of broadcasts over MBS in 1948.

Proportionately more US programs were imported into Canada, however, including several series – 'The Longines Symphonette,' 'The Firestone Hour,' and the Fine Arts Quartet, Metropolitan Opera, and the New York Philharmonic Orchestra broadcasts. (The Metropolitan continued to be heard on the CBC English and French AM and FM networks, after 1960 by arrangement with the continent-wide Texaco Radio Network, of which the CBC became a member.) This was a period in which commercial sponsorship played a vital part in musical broadcasting on both sides of the border, although neither the CBS's New York Philharmonic broadcasts, nor those by the NBC SO (Toscanini) were sponsored. This also was a time when certain Canadian stations were affiliates of large US networks. (For example, CFRB in Toronto and CKAC in Montreal were affiliates of CBS.)

By 1944 the broadcasting obligations of the English-language radio network (the 'Trans-Canada,' whose anchor station was CBL in Toronto) were pressing heavily on available time. Therefore a second and alternative English-language network, the 'Dominion,' was inaugurated coast-to-coast, 2 Jan 1944, to provide deliberately alternative programming for the evening hours only. Its anchor station was the CBC-owned CJBC in Toronto, all others being affiliates but not owned by the CBC. Programming tended to be lighter than on the Trans-Canada, although the TSO and the MSO alternated live on the Dominion on Tuesday nights and were followed immediately by the half-hour recital series 'CBC Concert Hall.' The Dominion Network provided its service until 1962. In 1947 the Trans-Canada Network instituted 'CBC Wednesday Night' – an entire evening of substantial fare each week, unsponsored and including much serious music and many musical documentaries, often markedly esoteric, the whole being integrated with advance commentary by the legendary James Bannerman (b Jack McNaught). This distinguished series and its successors ('CBC Sunday Night,' 'CBC Tuesday Night') continued until 1976, with commentary, after Bannerman's death, by Harry *Adaskin and others. *'Opportunity Knocks,' another widely popular young talent series, produced for its 10-year duration by Adaskin's younger brother John, also was begun in 1947. That year, too, Geoffrey Waddington was appointed music adviser to the CBC, succeeding Jean-Marie Beaudet. (Waddington became director of music in 1952. Beaudet returned to assume other executive positions within the CBC.) In 1948, in collaboration with the *Royal Cons Opera School, the *CBC Opera Company was formed under the dynamic leadership of Terence *Gibbs, who had arrived in Canada from England that same year. Gibbs studio-produced the North American radio premieres of Britten's *Peter Grimes*, Dallapiccola's *The Prisoner*, and Arthur Benjamin's *A Tale of Two Cities*. *Don Giovanni, Fidelio, Turandot*, Stravinsky's *The Rake's Progress*, and many others also were presented by the company – by 1952 some 25 major opera productions in all.

During this period several CBC studio orchestras were active – the Halifax Symphonette, Montreal's 'The Little Symphonies' (under Roland Leduc), the *CBC Quebec Chamber Orchestra, various CBC Toronto and Montreal orchestras, the *CBC Winnipeg Orchestra (Eric *Wild), and the *CBC Vancouver Chamber Orchestra (John *Avison); the latter's programming, produced by the composer Robert *Turner, pointedly included much new music by Canadian and foreign composers. The existence of these orchestras, especially in cities other than Toronto and Montreal, was of crucial importance in enabling musicians to remain and work in these cities.

Producers of radio drama, a genre extremely popular before the TV era, enlisted composers to provide incidental music, often on a regular basis over a number of years in the case of long-running serials. Lucio *Agostini, Louis *Applebaum, and Morris *Surdin in Toronto and Neil *Chotem, Hector *Gratton, and Jean *Vallerand in Montreal were among those composers most often employed. (See also Incidental music.)

Although the French radio network did not develop its own opera company, its schedule did evolve a distinctive musical personality with such programs as 'Adagio,' 'Chefs d'oeuvre de la musique,' 'Heure du concert,' 'Radio-concerts canadiens,' 'Sérénade pour cordes,' the sponsored 'Théâtre lyrique Molson,' 'Radio-Carabin,' and 'Festivals européens' (the last-named with Mary-vonne *Kendergi as host).

While the dreams of some of the earlier broadcasters for French-English exchange programming never were realized adequately, a few series exchanges did prove successful – for example, the alternating broadcast concerts of the Montreal and Toronto SOs and other large-scale orchestral and choral concerts. Some other series, live or recorded, did have more or less direct counterparts – or perhaps equivalents would be a more accurate term – on the other network, notably:

Distinguished Artists / Artistes de renom
Sunday Morning Recital / Récital du dimanche matin
Music of Today / Musique de notre siècle
(TV) Music to see / Son et Image
Jazz Unlimited / Jazz en liberté
International Concert / Concert international
The Happy Gang / Les Joyeux Troubadours
Opera Time / L'Heure de l'opéra
Singing Stars of Tomorrow / Nos Futures Étoiles

5 CBC TELEVISION. The first CBC telecasts were seen in September of 1952. The impact of the powerful new medium on the patterns of radio music was, however, far from immediate. At first the TV medium itself was explored by imaginative producers (and in fact the CBC Montreal studios quickly became the second-largest producers of French-language programs in the world). From Toronto the opera productions of Franz *Kraemer were particularly noteworthy, as were Norman *Campbell's of ballet and light opera. The names of Vincent Tovell and Eric Till also are among those associated with outstanding productions in the first decade. One series of youth programs, 'Junior Magazine' (seen on both English and French TV networks in the 1961–2 season), was produced by Paddy Sampson with Louis Applebaum as executive producer. (One program in the series was devoted to Prokofiev's *Peter and the Wolf*, conducted and also narrated, in English and French, by Mario *Bernardi.) In 1962 Stravinsky came to Toronto to mark his 80th birthday with two documentaries on his life and work – one of two hours for radio (produced by Keith *MacMillan with the composer Harry *Somers as musical guide and host), the other produced by Kraemer for TV, with notable scenes of Stravinsky rehearsing as well as conducting *L'Histoire du soldat* and *Symphony of Psalms*. Both documentaries subsequently were seen or heard world-wide.

A particularly distinguished musical series also was seen in 1962. 'Concert' was presented on Sunday afternoons for 37 weeks on the English and French TV networks, 20 of these originating in Montreal, 11 in Toronto, 4 in Vancouver, and 2 in Winnipeg. These series included orchestral concerts (eg, the CBC SO in 'Portrait of an Orchestra'; the *Winnipeg SO with Victor *Feldbrill), operas (Vaughan Williams' *Riders to the Sea* and Bartók's *Bluebeard's Castle*), recitals (Elizabeth Benson *Guy, the Juilliard String Quartet), and lecture-recitals (Glenn *Gould, Elliot Carter, Benjamin Britten).

The CBC Symphony Orchestra and the Toronto Mendelssohn Choir being conducted by Sir Ernest MacMillan in a studio broadcast, 1953

Probably the most breathtaking musical series on all Canadian TV was *'L'Heure du concert' (1954–65) from Montreal, mostly to the French network but occasionally appearing on the English as well. In its first five years (1954–9) its programming included 88 operas, or segments thereof, and 82 ballets; of the more than 7250 artists engaged, only 244 were not Canadian (among them Pierre Boulez, who was seen in a memorable rehearsal and performance of *Le Sacre du printemps*). The series included much Canadian music. Two members of its production team, Pierre *Mercure and Gabriel *Charpentier, were noted composers; *Schafer's *Loving* and *Pépin's *Le Porte-rêve* were among the works seen. Also among the producers of 'L'Heure du concert' were Françoys *Bernier, Noël Gauvin, Jean-Yves *Landry, and Pierre Morin. Morin's production of *Le Barbier de Seville* for this series won a 1965 Emmy Award for the outstanding program produced outside the USA.

By the late 1960s the presence of serious music on TV, especially English-language TV, had diminished markedly. Even so, Norman Campbell's production of Prokofiev's *Cinderella* with the National Ballet of Canada did win an Emmy Award in 1966; similarly outstanding was Kraemer's production (telecast 29 Oct 1969) of Harry Somers' opera **Louis Riel*. (R. Murray Schafer later prepared a 'case study' of televised music in Canada, with particular reference to *Louis Riel*; the study was published in Vienna in 1972.)

By the end of the 1960s there remained the occasional 'special,' the modest series 'Music to See,' and the largely imported 'Musicamera' (English-language) and 'Son et Image' and the hardy 'Les Beaux Dimanches' (French-language). However, for all practical purposes, by the 1970s the TV medium had ceased to have any influence on the development of music in Canada, let alone of Canadian music.

6 CBC RADIO 1952–79. Although TV's programs in the 1950s and 1960s contained many riches, music on radio remained the mainstay of fulfilment for the listener and of employment in broadcasting for the musician. The period from the late 1940s to the mid-1960s could be called the 'golden age' of music on Canadian radio, with a sumptuous variety of programming ranging over the entire repertoire from early to modern, presenting both Canadian and foreign musicians, and paying much attention to the music of Canadian composers. Programs of serious arts criticism ('Critically Speaking,' 'Revue des arts et des lettres,' 'CJBC Views the Shows,' etc) played an important role, as they and others continued to do in the ensuing decades. It was due in no small measure to the CBC that the serious Canadian composer at this time began to come into his own, through performances, through commissions, and in general through the CBC's acceptance of the composer as a serious working professional. Programs of orchestral, choral, recital, and chamber music were presented from CBC studios across the country in startling abundance, not only for adult audiences but also in many broadcasts tailored to the special needs of school classrooms. The nation-wide *'CBC Talent Festival' series, initiated in the late 1950s under the travelling baton of Sir Ernest MacMillan, carried on the work of its predecessors 'Singing Stars' and 'Opportunity Knocks' and continued throughout the 1970s (latterly as 'CBC Talent Competition'). For the English network this was the era of the musical directorship of Geoffrey Waddington and subsequently (after 1964) music broadcasts under the supervision of John Peter Lee *Roberts, whose chapter on broadcasting in *Aspects of Music in Canada* (Toronto 1969) details many of the outstanding programs and series prior to 1968 (updated to 1970 in the French translation).

Successive directors of music for the French-language network were Roy *Royal 1959–62 (the first appointment to the position since the death of Gagnier 10 years previously), Hugh *Davidson 1962–5, Jean Vallerand 1965–6, and Jacques *Bertrand, appointed in 1966. During the eras of Royal, Davidson, and Vallerand the French-network programmers were particularly conscious of the need to encourage Canadian composers. Even earlier, in the 1950s, that network inaugurated the 'Premières' series which made a feature of works by Canadians, especially French-Canadians.

In 1952 the CBC SO was founded, broadcasting from Toronto, mostly with guest conductors, and produced first by Terence Gibbs, later by Carl *Little, then by Keith MacMillan. It survived the NBC SO to become the only full radio symphony orchestra in North America. Under the musical directorship of Waddington, its programming was eclectic, but at least 40 per cent of its repertoire was composed after 1900, and much of it was Canadian. The orchestra acquired an enviable reputation among many visiting conductors (including Stravinsky and Beecham) for its phenomenal sight-reading ability. By 1964, heavy financial and other pressures forced the 'suspension' (in fact, the demise) of the CBC SO. The CBC's Toronto studio needs were served for a period thereafter by the TSO.

Some of the more prominent music producers of that era (in addition to those mentioned previously) were Ira Stewart (Halifax); Pierre *Boutet (Quebec); Jacques Bertrand, André Clerk, Jean-Yves Contant, Claude Garneau, Kit Kinnaird, Earl Pennington, Armand Plante, Gilles Poirier, Pierre Rainville, and Paul *Roussel (Montreal); James Kent and John Reeves (Toronto); Norman Lucas and Tom Taylor (Winnipeg); Duncan McKerchar (Edmonton); and Robert *Chesterman and Robert Turner (Vancouver).

After 1952 not only the competition of TV (especially following the introduction of colour with its higher costs) but also certain other technical developments persuaded the CBC to reshape its radio music policies. For one thing, radio had become the poor sister. In the 1950s, too, the adoption of tape as a broadcast tool tended more and more to encourage producers to modify the traditional 'studio broadcast' techniques of the 1930s and 1940s towards the more careful (and more artificial) recording and tape editing techniques of the recording studio. (In other words, delayed broadcasting instead of live.) By the mid-1960s the SM (Serious Music) and LM (Light Music) series of Broadcast Recordings, issued first in mono then in stereo disc form, were being produced by the English Services division for broadcast use (some later for limited public sale), to the point where by the mid-1970s the producers and broadcast executives had virtually abandoned the studio-produced integral 'programs' in the swing towards the program manipulation of disc and pre-taped material delivered by the program series 'host.' There is, of course, nothing new in programs of recorded material presented by a 'host' of either special knowledge or charismatic personality. Allan Sangster's ambitious and long term series 'The Music of Mozart' over many years presented virtually all the recorded works of that great composer and was followed by similar series on Handel, Schubert, Chopin, Mendelssohn, Berlioz, Mahler, Holst, Britten, and Tippett, prepared by Sangster and others. 'The World of Music,' prepared by John *Beckwith; 'Music of the 20th Century' by Beckwith, Harry Somers, and Norma *Beecroft; Clyde *Gilmour's perennial 'Gilmour's Albums,' and many others have been staple radio fare. But with the demise of the live program and with virtually every musical note being pre-processed through tape or disc, the entire music schedule during the 1970s became systematically reorganized as a succession of 'hosted' shows ('Arts National,' 'Mostly Music,' etc) in which the personality of the host was as important as the musical content of the series. As a universal, almost axiomatic, technique of broadcasting its very uniformity tended to discourage imagination and initiative.

More subtly perhaps, under such a system the producer working directly with his musicians, in Vancouver for example, all too often had little if any control over the final format of the program as it may have been packaged weeks later in Toronto. Moreover, a host frequently might have no contact with the artists themselves. To a final-stage production staff, music becomes in effect a commodity to be agreeably studio-packaged. This casual attitude is picked up unconsciously by the listener, to whom the daily spate of music becomes simply a component of the familiar daily environment. Music on radio ceases to matter. Against such an attitude it is all the more difficult for the radio producer of imagination and originality to make his own demands on the time and special attention of his potential audience. True, in the late 1970s some hosts and executive producers became aware of this and strove to minimize the deadening effect of the lack of contact with the artists themselves. Nonetheless the 'hosted package' technique did seem to have diminished the sense of importance of music as a great art, at least on radio. The will to create, to experiment in imaginative and significant radiophonic forms, indeed to provide musical services as only radio can, seemed to be far less influential than formerly.

The increasing use of recordings grew hand-in-hand with the growing independence of FM programming, especially during the 1960s, culminating in the establishment of the coast-to-coast English language FM stereo network and the extended French-language FM stereo network late in 1975. FM, with its superior sound, even after transcontinental transmission, became the most important broadcasting medium for music, although the initial eight English transmitters at that time could reach no more than some 56 per cent of the population of Canada's vast territory. A remarkable series of CBC public festivals was presented in several cities across the country in the late 1960s and early 1970s and tape-recorded before audiences for later presentation as delayed broadcasts. These were discontinued in 1975, when preparation for the 1976 Olympics in Montreal made heavy demands on staff, equipment, and funds. By the end of the 1970s, after fitful regional revivals, there seemed little likelihood that the festivals or their like would be continued on a similar scale in future years.

7 CBC INTERNATIONAL SERVICE / RADIO CANADA INTERNATIONAL. Whereas the foregoing has dealt with CBC music broadcasting within the country, Canada's musical image abroad had long been projected most ably by the CBC's International Service (in 1972 renamed Radio Canada International – RCI), operating first, in 1945, as the 'voice' of the federal government's Department of External Affairs, but functioning after 1968 as a department of the CBC. Although most IS / RCI voice transmissions are beamed to Europe and the Americas by short-wave from Sackville, NB, quality music from the first has been distributed to foreign national broadcasting services through the medium of disc recordings, initially (briefly) on 78 rpm albums, then on the standard 16-inch broadcast transcription discs, in the early 1950s on LP discs, and subsequently on stereo discs. These albums, more than 500 by 1980, virtually all representing Canadian artists and Canadian music of all types, constituted at that time by far the largest single repository of recorded Canadian music, whether licensed for broadcast only or whether for public sale as well. Moreover the production staffs, headed successively by Gérard Arthur, Patricia Fitzgerald, Roy Royal, Gérard Poupart, Hugh Davidson, Gilles *Potvin, Edward Farrant, and Gilbert Lemieux, had been meticulous in the making of these discs, much more so than have been the production teams of the domestic service's Broadcast Recordings (See CBC recording.)

For many years it was part of the mandate of RCI to represent the CBC and Canada generally in the international forums of such agencies as the EBU, the Unesco International Rostrum of Composers, and the Communauté radiophonique des programmes de langue française, promoting many forms of international exchange through which Canadian music and musicians are heard throughout the world. In the mid-1970s international representation was arranged through foreign relations departments of the CBC.

8 CHANGE AND REASSESSMENT. In May 1976 Robert *Sunter succeeded John Roberts as head of music for the English radio networks, thus heralding new directions for those networks' music broadcasting policies. Earlier that year the CBC English Services division had released a 'Report of the CBC Radio Study Group on Programming of and about Arts, Music and Drama,' compiled (somewhat hastily) by an in-house group consisting of Doug Field (chairman of the group), John Douglas, and Harold Redekopp. Field subsequently was promoted to the CBC radio head office, and Redekopp became executive producer of a highlighted series, indicating that the essential recommendations of the report were to be followed. The overriding concern of the report was the recapturing and enlargement of audiences. In music, at any rate, mostly on FM, the new policy was successful in that aim, but very much at the cost of imagination and distinction in broadcasting. Rarely indeed in the late 1970s did the CBC initiate a musical event which demanded the attention of the serious music-lover. Virtually all its broadcasting had come to serve a 'pipeline' function, providing useful reportage on (or rebroadcasts of) existing musical events across the country, but initiating little on its own. To be sure the initiative functions (experimentation, commissioning, etc) had been taken over increasingly by universities, orchestras, and contemporary music groups, subsidized by the *Canada Council and the Provincial Arts Councils; and undoubtedly the CBC's new policies recaptured as listeners a large number of music-lovers who blessed the CBC, especially in smaller centres, for a radio diet which at least provided a welcome respite from the clamour of mindless inanity dominant elsewhere on the North American airwaves. However, as a musical creator and innovator the CBC, even CBC Radio, had become relatively inactive.

9 THE PRIVATE SECTOR. The contribution made to serious music by commercial TV by 1980 was virtually nil. ('Quebec sait chanter' telecast by the TVA network in Quebec and 'Inside the Toronto Symphony' by CFTO were exceptions.) As to private radio, over the years many stations had provided their listeners with small helpings of serious music from time to time. These might take the form of a 'Concert Hour' of recorded music with a locally prominent musician as host, or perhaps a broadcast of the community orchestra; but these would constitute a very small percentage of the station's broadcasting time or budget. In the early years of FM (1960s) several FM stations attempted to carve out programming niches as commercial 'good music' stations, but by the mid-70s few of these remained, most having 'gone pop.' A very few might be said to have made something of a specialty of the classics and/or light classics. Some by intention became avowedly educational, and a very few of these, notably CJRT in Toronto, have presented their programming (mostly of commercial recordings, but occasionally of live concert fare under CJRT's music program director Paul *Robinson) with care and imagination. However, Robinson's concerts excepted, there is little, even on these stations, which the listener could not buy conveniently from a good record store.

One enterprising organization deserves special mention – the *Canadian Talent Library of broadcast recordings, initiated in CFRB in Toronto and developed over the years by the veteran broadcaster Lyman Potts, its royalties accruing to the CTL Trust. The CTL has functioned as a syndicated series to which private stations could subscribe, featuring Canadian performers and, in part, Canadian repertoire. Basically the repertoire is light, 'middle of the road' music. Nonetheless the intention always has been to buck the supposition, rampant among the private broadcasters of Canada, that Canadian talent is better ignored. By the mid-1970s many of the CTL discs also were available in record stores.

10 TV CHANGES AND RADIO'S SURVIVAL. One other development in the late 1970s which appeared to contain the germ of good TV broadcasting was the emergence of provincial government educational TV program services, transmitting principally through cable (Canada at the time being the most heavily 'cablized' country in the world). It seemed possible that such services as those for Alberta, Quebec, and Ontario might venture successfully where only the CBC had not feared to tread.

The possibilities inherent in Pay-TV, multi-channel satellite reception, etc, defy foresight at the time of writing, although it is difficult to see how the Canadian voice can continue to be heard above the rising clamour of the shouting, shrinking world at large.

By the end of the 1970s, therefore, it seemed that the bold, innovative days and the commanding importance of Canadian music broadcasting were forever past. Certainly television, at least English-language television, had become musically quite irrelevant.

Radio on the other hand, for all its easy-listening formats, familiar as wallpaper, and for all that it, too, lacked the creative zest of yesteryear, had extended among its public, coast to coast, a sense of national musical community (rather than merely of Toronto and Montreal) – a sense extraordinarily difficult to achieve in this far-flung land – while at the same time providing for the public a ready listening resource of a variety and quality undreamed of scarcely half a century before.

See also CBC; 'CKNX Barn Dance'; Country music; Dance bands; Jazz; Recorded sound; Rock.

BIBLIOGRAPHY

'Broadcast famous string quartette,' *Canadian National Railway Magazine*, Sep 1925
'World record broadcast made,' ibid, Aug 1927
'Starring a national network,' ibid, Dec 1929
' "All-Canada Symphony" opens,' ibid, Oct 1930
Spry, Graham. 'A case for nationalized broadcasting,' *Queen's Q*, Winter 1931
Bertrand, Félix-R. *La Musique à la radio* (Montreal 1948)
'Music on the air in Canada,' *MCour*, Mar 1948
Waddington, Geoffrey. 'Music and radio,' *Music in Canada*
Bell, Leslie. 'An experiment in network broadcasting,' *CMJ*, vol 5, Winter 1961
Weir, E. Austin. *The Struggle for National Broadcasting in Canada* (Toronto 1965)
'CKFH uses Canadian music as valuable part of format,' *CanComp*, 18, May 1967
Roberts, John. 'Communications media,' *Aspects of Music in Canada* / 'Les moyens de diffusion,' *Aspects de la musique au Canada*
Irwin, Joan. '1919–1969: fifty years of broadcasting,' *CanComp*, 44, Nov 1969
Stursberg, Peter. *Mister Broadcasting: The Ernie Bushnell Story* (Toronto 1971)
Proulx, Gilles. *Pour une radio civilisée* (Montreal 1972)
Schafer, R. Murray. *The Public of the Music Theatre: Louis Riel, A Case Study* (Vienna 1972)
Proulx, Gilles. *Pour une radio réformée* (Montreal 1973)

Weinzweig, John. 'Making Canadian music known – the CBC,' *CMB*, 6, Spring–Summer 1973
CRTC. *Bibliography: Some Canadian Writings on the Mass Media* (Ottawa 1974)
Stewart, Sandy. *A Picture History of Radio in Canada* (Toronto 1975)
Allard, T.J. *The C.A.B. Story 1926–1976: Private Broadcasting in Canada* (Ottawa 1976)
Hallman, Eugene, Hindley, H., and Blackwood, R. *Broadcasting in Canada* (Toronto 1977)
Jack, Donald. *Betty, Sinc and the Morning Man: the Story of CFRB* (Toronto 1977)
Shepherd, Philip R. 'CJRT-FM: profile of a radio station,' *Onion*, 28 Feb 1977
MacMillan, Keith. 'Music on the CBC: the English Service Division of CBC radio,' *Mcan*, 31, Feb 1977
Gingras, Claude. 'Music on the CBC: the French network: a mountain to be moved,' *Mcan*, 32, May 1977
Twomey, John E. *Canadian Broadcasting History Resources in English: Critical Mass or Mess* (Toronto 1978)
Applebaum, Louis. 'The paradox and puzzle of music on Canadian television,' *CanComp*, 137, Jan 1979
Proulx, Gilles. *L'Aventure de la radio au Québec* (Montreal 1979)
CBC Times, 1948–69
La Semaine à Radio-Canada, 1950–66
Ici Radio-Canada, 1966–
CBC program schedules, 1939–48
Annual Reports of the Canadian Broadcasting Corporation / Rapports annuels de la Société Radio-Canada KM

BROADFOOT, Jean (McNeill). Teacher, pianist, b Winnipeg 29 Apr 1920; LRSM 1946, LMM 1948. Her studies were in Winnipeg with Leonard *Heaton, in London with Harold Samuel, and in Minneapolis with Bernard Weiser. She began teaching privately in Winnipeg in 1940, and her consistent success led to frequent engagements as a competition-festival adjudicator and a *WBM examiner. Though she has not appeared often as a solo performer, she has been active as an accompanist, especially for singers and for the choirs and operatic productions of Berythe *Birse. She taught 1964–9 at the school of music, *U of Manitoba. Among her pupils have been Emanuel Ax, Audrey *Cooke Belyea, Douglas Finch, Sheila *Henig, Ailsa Lawson, Sydney *Young McInnis, and Patricia Shand. She became president of the *MRMTA in 1978.

BROCHU, (Joseph-Pierre) Lucien. Administrator, teacher, choirmaster, librarian, b Drummondville, Que, 2 Oct 1920; BA (Montreal) 1942, B MUS (Montreal) 1952, M MUS (Laval) 1955. He began teaching at *Laval U in 1947 and served 1962–77 as director of the École de musique. He also taught 1948–62 at the *CMQ and was choirmaster 1948–66 at Notre-Dame-du-Chemin Church in Quebec City. He served 1959–60 as chairman of the *CMLA and 1971–3 as president of *CAUSM. He has been a member of the board of the *CMCouncil and vice-director-general of the *EMC*.

BIBLIOGRAPHY

'Entrevue avec M. Lucien Brochu, directeur de l'école de musique de l'Université Laval,' *Musicien éducateur*, vol 3, no. 1, 1969–70

BROCK-SMITH, (Mary) Alma (b Sheasgreen, m Harrington, m Brock-Smith). Pianist, teacher, b Concord, Mass, 21 Feb 1908, naturalized Canadian 1971; ATCM 1927. As a young woman she lived in Saskatoon. She taught there privately 1924–34 and studied 1927–38 with Lyell *Gustin. She also studied on scholarship at the Chicago Musical College in 1928 with Percy Grainger, in New York in 1930 with Edwin Hughes, and in Seattle in 1935 and Los Angeles 1944–5 with Heifetz's accompanist Emmanuel Bay, and attended the master classes of Egon Petri 1958–9 and Rosina Lhévinne in Berkeley 1960–1. With the *Saskatoon SO she played Bach and Mozart concertos in 1929 and the Schumann concerto in 1930. During the 1930s she and Virginia Johnson performed as a piano team on Vancouver, Seattle, and San Francisco radio. She was also staff pianist 1934–5 at CKMO radio, Vancouver. After teaching at the San Francisco Cons 1947–62 and at the U of California 1953–62 she moved to Winnipeg in 1962 and began teaching at the *U of Manitoba in 1965. She has specialized in the coaching of duo-piano teams, notably (Garth) *Beckett and (Boyd) *McDonald and Paulette Price and Claudette Caron. Other pupils include Marjorie Beckett, Karen Redekopp, Alice Enns, Doreen Oiens, Margaret Turner, and John Clarke. Her husband, Harding St John Brock-Smith, was a board member 1972–4 of the *ACO and president 1973–4 of the *Winnipeg SO. (JA)

Brock University. Non-denominational university founded in St Catharines, Ont, in 1964 with undergraduate programs in arts, sciences, and administration, and master's degree programs in some scientific areas.

Ronald Tremain, appointed in 1970, introduced music courses and organized a chamber choir and a collegium musicum. He was chairman of the Music Dept 1973–6 and was succeeded by Thomas McGary. In 1973 music became eligible for choice as one of two majors in three-year combined-major programs. In 1978–9 there were three full-time and four part-time teachers in the department. Among the facilities is a modest electronic studio. Two continuing ensembles in 1979 were the University Singers and the Chamber Choir. Students and faculty present lunch-hour and evening concerts in the university's Thistle Theatre, and the *St Catharines SO (Niagara SO) also performs there. Brock U has awarded honorary degrees to Elmer *Iseler and Léopold *Simoneau. (JPG)

BRODIE, Paul (Zion). Saxophonist, teacher, b Montreal 10 Apr 1934; M MUS (Michigan) 1958. He studied saxophone 1953–8 with Larry Teal at Ann Arbor and in 1959 with Marcel Mule in Paris, and made his New York debut at Town Hall in 1960. He taught woodwinds 1959–60 at the *RCMT and 1968–73 at the *U of Toronto. In 1961 he became the founder and director of the Brodie School of Music and Modern Dance, Toronto. In 1969 he helped found the *World Saxophone Congress, and in 1972 he formed the Paul Brodie Saxophone Quartet with his pupils Lawrence Sereda, Robert Pusching, and John Price; members of the quartet in 1978 were Brodie, Price, Marino Galluzzo, and John Salistian.

Possibly Canada's foremost proponent of the classical saxophone, Brodie performs and has recorded original works and transcriptions of baroque, classic, romantic, and modern works on the alto, soprano, and sopranino saxophones. He has persuaded *Bissell, *Henninger, *Klein, *McCauley, *Morawetz, *Polgar, *Weinzweig, and others to compose for the saxophone. His playing – flexible, restrained, strong technically, and fine tonally – has been a factor in the success of his crusade. Brodie has toured as soloist and with the quartet throughout Canada, the USA, Europe, and Mexico and has appeared with the *Halifax SO, the *Hamilton Philharmonic, the *TSO, and the Vancouver Chamber Orchestra. In 1976 the quartet represented Canada at the World Saxophone Congress in London, and in 1977 Brodie became the first concert saxophonist to tour Australia. A selection from his recording of Handel's *Sonata No. 3* (Golden Crest RE 7049) was heard in the film *Heaven Can Wait*. His pupils include Robert

Paul Brodie

*Bauer, Jean-Guy Brault, Bob Brough, Karen Goldberg, Glen Montgomery, Ramon Ricker, Bill *Smith, Michael Stuart, and John Tank.

DISCOGRAPHY

A Recital with Soprano and Sopranino Saxophone: Glick – Telemann – Vrana – Handel. Kubalek pf. 1972. Golden Crest RE 7049
A Solo Saxophone Recital: Britten – Debussy – Bach-Londeix. 1977. Golden Crest RE 7071
Alto Saxophone Recital: Badings – Creston – Lantier – Mather – Van Delden. Schechter pf. 1970. Golden Crest RE 7037
Archer *Sonata* for saxophone. Brough pf. 1973. RCI 412
Baroque and Classical Music for Soprano Saxophone: Tartini – Leclair – et al. Kubalek pf. 1971. Golden Crest RE 7041
Duets for saxophone: Telemann – Leclair-Londeix. J.-M. Londeix sax. 1974. Golden Crest RE 7062
Koechlin *Etudes* for saxophone and piano. Kubalek pf. 1973. Classic Editions 16
Music for Alto Saxophone and Soprano Saxophone: Hindemith – Gershwin – Vivaldi – C.P.E. Bach – Schumann. Kubalek pf. 1973. Golden Crest RE 7056
The Saxophone in Concert: Bach – Bozza – et al. Brough pf. 1969. Cap W6066
Saxophone Recital: Tcherepnin – Debussy – et al. Brough pf. 1969. Golden Crest RE 7028
THE PAUL BRODIE QUARTET
A Recital with the Paul Brodie Saxophone Quartet: Pierné – Bach – et al. 1975. Golden Crest GC 4143
Paul Brodie Saxophone Quartet: Dubois – Glazounov – et al. 1973. Golden Crest CRS 4131
The Paul Brodie Saxophone Quartet in Concert: Rimsky-Korsakov – Wiedoeft – McPeek *Audubon Suite* – Debussy – Jacob. 1977. Golden Crest CRSQ 4164
The Paul Brodie Saxophone Quartet on Tour: Scarlatti – Boccherini – et al. 1976. Golden Crest CRSQ 4154
Also, educational and instructional records, including 4 in the Music Minus One series (MMO 8021, 8023, 8025, 8027), and a Clinician Album Golden Crest CR 1010

BIBLIOGRAPHY

'The saxophone in concert,' *JMC*, Jun 1964
Schulman, Michael. 'Brodie's saxophone: triumph through joy,' *PfAC*, vol 13, Spring 1976
Fetherling, Doug. 'Sax appeal,' *The Canadian*, 27 Aug 1977

The Broken Ring. Folk opera in one act by Trevor Morgan Jones with a libretto by Donald Wetmore. The Saladin Mutiny (1844, off the coast of Nova Scotia) provides the background for a story of lovers reunited by means of a ring they had halved on parting. The opera is based on six ballads chosen from the collection of Helen *Creighton and harmonized by Jones. It was premiered in Halifax, on 15 Aug 1953 by the *Nova Scotia Opera Assn, with Ray Simpson as narrator, Keith Barrie, tenor, and Gladys Dickson, soprano; Trevor Jones conducted. Revised in 1954, it was telecast 29 Feb 1956 by the CBC with Karen Mills and Bernard *Johnson in the leading roles and Thomas Mayer as conductor. A third production was staged at the *Banff SFA in August 1958, and a fourth, mounted by Dartmouth (NS) High School, was seen at *Expo 67.

BIBLIOGRAPHY
'"The Broken Ring" – Nova Scotian folk opera,' *CBC Times*, 26 Feb–3 Mar 1956 SW

BRONSTEIN, Ada (b Lvoff). Pianist, accompanist, teacher, b Harbin, China, 1916, naturalized Canadian 1957. She studied piano in Harbin and Shanghai with Boris Lazareff, pupil and son-in-law of Alexander Siloti. She made her debut at 20, playing the Schumann *Concerto* with the Shanghai SO and appeared with the orchestra annually 1936–52. She participated 1948–52 in many concerts of British and French chamber music. She taught privately and 1950–2 at the National Cons in Shanghai, numbering among her pupils the internationally known concert pianist Fou Ts'ong.

Bronstein came to Canada in 1952, settling in Winnipeg. By 1954 her career was re-established, and over the next 20 years in Winnipeg she performed – as soloist, chamber musician, or accompanist – in more than 300 public, radio, and television concerts. She has toured western Canada as the piano partner of Yi-Kwei Sze, Richard *Verreau, Donald *Bell, Marta *Hidy, Hyman *Bress, Tsuyoski *Tsutsumi, George *Zukerman, and others. Bronstein joined the *Banff SFA in 1969 as accompanist for the strings division, and has given several two-piano recitals there with George *Brough. With Dirk *Keetbaas she has recorded Leslie *Mann's *Five Improvisations* for flute and piano. (SRM)

BROOKS, Garnet. Tenor, b London, Ont, 4 Sep 1937. His voice studies began in his native city and continued 1960–4 in Toronto at the *RCMT, where his teachers were Mary Raze, Dorothy *Allan Park, John *Coveart, and Douglas *Bodle. He made his *COC debut in September 1963 as von Faninal's major-domo in *Der Rosenkavalier*. In 1966 he studied with Robert Weede in San Francisco. In 1967 a *Canada Council travel grant enabled him to audition at opera houses in England, Germany, and Switzerland. He was a member of the Glyndebourne Touring Company in 1968, the Western Opera Theatre (the touring branch of the San Francisco Opera) 1968–9, and the Staatstheater of Bern 1974–6. For the COC he has sung Alfredo in *Die Fledermaus*, Arturo in *Lucia di Lammermoor*, Don Ottavio in *Don Giovanni*, Malcolm in *Macbeth*, Narraboth in *Salome*, Pang in *Turandot*, and Pinkerton in *Madama Butterfly* and has appeared in supporting roles in the premieres of *Somers' **Louis Riel* and *Wilson's **Heloise and Abelard*. He sang the title role in the premiere (Halifax, 1973) of Wilson's *The Summoning of Everyman* and repeated the role in the 1974 *Stratford Festival production. Brooks has performed in oratorio, in recital, and on CBC radio and TV. He has appeared several times at the *Guelph Spring Festival, where his assignments have included the title role in the North American premiere (1969) of Britten's *The Prodigal Son* and a major role in the premiere (1977) of *Healey's **Seabird Island*. He also toured with the latter production in 1978. Brooks possesses a genuine high tenor, lyric rather than heroic, clear and vibrant in sound and effortlessly produced. In 1976 he settled in Vienna.

BIBLIOGRAPHY
Forner, Jane. 'Profile: Garnet Brooks,' *OpCan*, May 1970
Kirby, Blaik. 'Garnet Brooks lives by singing – but abroad,' Toronto *Globe and Mail*, 19 Jul 1975 (SW)

BROOKS, Norman (Joseph) (b Arie). Singer, songwriter, actor, b Montreal of Lebanese parents, 19 Aug 1928. Possessing a voice naturally similar to that of Al Jolson, Brooks began his career in his late teens, singing in the Jolson style in small Montreal nightclubs, often in duet with his sister Annie (who as Anne Brooks has sung in Canadian and US nightclubs). During his career he has returned frequently to Jolson routines, but he also has sung in a more personal style. By the early 1950s he had graduated from clubs to theatres – the Seville in Montreal and the Casino in Toronto. He made two 78s for Canadian Victor at this time. In 1953 he went to New York where he appeared in nightclubs and recorded 'Hello Sunshine,' a substantial hit that year for Zodiac, a label set up expressly for Brooks. He was a popular nightclub and TV performer in the USA during the 1950s and 1960s, appearing, for example, for 44 weeks 1959–60 at The Sands Hotel, Las Vegas. He also performed frequently in Canadian nightclubs and on CBC TV, and was host for CTV's 'Musical Showcase' in 1966. After working extensively in Florida, he went to New York, where he appeared in 1975 on Broadway in *The Magic of Jolson* and then sang and played piano in nightclubs. He has continued to tour, and in 1979 performed in Montreal at the *PDA.

Brooks' other recordings include singles for Zodiac and for RCA's 'X' label, LPs of Jolson material for Spin-O-Rama, Coronet, Diplomat, and Sutton, and LPs of pop songs for Verve, Sure, and Promenade (see Kinkle's *Encyclopedia of Pop Music and Jazz* for details). He has recorded some of his own songs. Brooks played Jolson in the film *The Best Things in Life Are Free* (1956) and dramatic roles in *The Block* (1963) and *Ocean's Eleven* (1965).

BIBLIOGRAPHY
Lazarus, Charles. 'Norman Brooks returns,' *Montreal Star*, 3 Mar 1979

BROOME, (William) **Edward**. Choir conductor, organist, composer, teacher, b Manchester 3 Jan 1868, d Toronto 28 Apr 1932; piano diploma RAM 1884, Fellow (Guild of Organists) 1889, B MUS (Trinity College, Toronto) 1901, D MUS (Toronto) 1908. He grew up in Wales, where he studied organ and piano 1876–90 with Roland Rogers and conducting with Jules Riviere. He went to the USA to conduct the Penryhn Male Chorus at the Chicago Exposition in 1893 and afterwards accepted a position as organist-choirmaster at the First Presbyterian Church in Brockville, Ont. He was organist-choirmaster 1895–1906 at Douglas Methodist Church, Montreal, and 1906–25 at Jarvis Street Baptist Church, Toronto, where he succeeded A.S. *Vogt. He began teaching voice and choir techniques at the *TCM in 1907, but he was best-known for his work with choirs. He was the founder and sole director 1910–25 of the *Toronto Oratorio Society. The New York Philharmonic and Cleveland and Detroit SO's were among those he brought to Toronto to perform with the Society. He was also organist-choirmaster 1926–7 at Knox United Church in Calgary.

A mainly self-taught composer, Broome won eight first prizes in composition at the Welsh Eisteddfods. The most notable of his winning compositions was the dramatic cantata *The Siege of Cardiff Castle* (1908; ms at *NL of C). Another cantata, *A Hymn of Trust* (Psalm 18), was published (1910) by G. Schirmer. Approximately 100 of his works, primarily for church, were published by G. Schirmer, Ditson, Boston Music Company, and Schmidt. His arrangement of *'O Canada' was published in *The Home Journal* (Dec 1907) and by *Anglo-Canadian in 1910. His pupils included Allan *Burt and Isabel Lloyd. He was president of the Toronto Clef Club in 1910. FH

BROOMER, Stuart (Charles). Pianist, bassist, composer, writer, b Toronto 26 Dec 1947. He studied piano, trumpet, and guitar as a child, bass in high school, and electronic music at the *RCMT 1967–8 with Samuel *Dolin. An early exponent in Toronto of the 1960s' new jazz, Broomer played professionally first in 1965 as bassist with trumpeter Ric Colbeck and 1966–7 as pianist and bassist with the Toronto New Music Ensemble and his own Kinetic Ensemble. Inactive for several years, he returned to performance in 1974 as a pianist – often working with a 'prepared instrument' – giving solo concerts, playing 1975–6 with the Avant Garde Jazz Revival Band, and in 1975 beginning an association with the saxophonist Bill *Smith, his partner on the LP *Conversation Pieces* (1976, Onari 1002). Broomer has aligned himself with the avant garde of both jazz and concert music, and his playing is characterized by 'an incredible energy and wealth of techniques ... His "open" work is fierce or rhapsodic in turn, and his prepared piano is simply a sound machine which blurs lines, chords and clusters into a great percussive roar' (Mark Miller, *Down Beat*, 12 Aug 1976). His compositions include a musical-dramatic work, *The Conquest of Winnipeg*, and several programmatic pieces. His writings include reviews 1964–7 in **Coda*.

BIBLIOGRAPHY
Garber, Lloyd. 'Stuart Broomer,' *Coda*, Aug 1977
Miller, Mark. 'Stuart Broomer,' *Down Beat*, 18 May 1978

Brothers-in-Law. Satirical singing group formed (1963) in Windsor, Ont, its name reflecting the vocations of its founding members – the banjoist Alec Somerville, the guitarists Howard Duffy and Larry Reaume, and the bassist Ken Clarke, all policemen. Clarke left the group in 1965 and was replaced by Bob Lee (a school teacher). Duffy left in 1966. Inspired by the Kingston Trio, which was popular at the time, the group gave its first performance 22 Nov 1963 at a police banquet in Sandwich West (Windsor). Its popularity grew as Somerville began to write satirical lyrics to music by Duffy (and later Lee) or to traditional and classical melodies. Its subjects, which ranged from North American cultural and political institutions to sexual mores, limited the number of platforms available to the group. 'What they [the Brothers-in-Law] do, to the sound of a reasonable facsimile of traditional folk music, is pure contemporary satire ... much of the Brothers' material is amusing if a bit collegiate, some of it absolutely blunt; rarely is any of it as skilfully sharp and as directly aimed as true satire ought to be' (Arthur Zelden, *Toronto Star*, 4 Nov 1966). The group's first and most successful LP, *Oh! Oh! Canada* (1965, Arc Sound 636), sold more than 100,000 copies and was followed by five others for *Arc Sound, including *The Brothers-In-Law Strike Again*, *Expose 67*, and *Total Lewdity*. Despite their success the Brothers-in-Law maintained their jobs outside the field of music and gave only 12 to 20 concerts each year, mostly in Ontario. The group dispersed in the early 1970s.

BIBLIOGRAPHY
'The Brothers-In-Law: Canada's court jesters,' *CanComp*, 12, Nov 1966
Cobb, David. 'What's a nice cop like you doing in an act like this?' *The Canadian*, 21 Feb 1970 MM

BROTT. Montreal family of musicians: 1 / Alexander, 2 / Lotte, his wife, and 3 / Boris and 4 / Denis, their sons.

The Brott family in 1968

BIBLIOGRAPHY
Heller, Zelda. 'The Brott family,' *Jmc*, Aug 1966; repr as 'The Alexander Brott family: music, rare instruments and the sound of the telephone,' *CanComp*, 12, Nov 1966
Schulman, Michael. 'The Montreal family Brott and its musical ramifications,' *PfAC*, vol 13, Winter 1976
Waller, Adrian. 'Bravo for the musical Brotts,' *Reader's Digest*, vol 42, Jan 1978
Bailey, Bruce. 'First family of music,' Montreal *Gazette*, 15 Sep 1979

1 **Alexander**. Conductor, composer, violinist, teacher, b Montreal 14 Mar 1915; L MUS (McGill) 1932, lauréat (AMQ) 1933, Diploma orchestration, composition (Juilliard) 1938, Diploma interpretation (Juilliard) 1939, hon D MUS (Chicago Cons College) 1960, hon LLD (Queen's) 1973. He studied violin with Alfred *De Sève, then entered the *McGill Cons which granted him five bursaries 1929–34; his teachers were Maurice *Onderet (violin) and Douglas *Clarke (composition). He continued his studies 1934–9 at the Juilliard School, where his teachers were Sascha Jacobsen (violin), Willem Willeke (chamber music), Bernard Wagenaar (composition), and Albert Stoessel (conducting). He received the Loeb Memorial Award for chamber music performance in 1938 and 1939 and the Elizabeth Sprague Coolidge prize for orchestral composition in 1938 (*Two Symphonic Movements*) and 1939 (*Oracle*). He also received the 1939 *Strathcona Scholarship in composition, granting him three years of study at the RCM, but he was unable to avail himself of the opportunity because of World War II. He then embarked on a fruitful career in Montreal as violinist, composer, conductor, and teacher.

Alexander Brott had played 1930–4 and 1939–41 in the *Montreal Orchestra, and in 1934 he began giving solo recitals across Canada and on CRBC radio. In the early 1930s, also, he had been a member of the Montreal Trio with Edmond *Trudel and Jean *Belland. In 1939 he began teaching at McGill U, and the same year he founded the *McGill String Quartet, in which he played first violin. He taught violin, orchestration, and conducting and in 1955 assumed responsibility for the department of orchestral instruments. He was appointed teacher of conducting and musical literature in 1965 and conductor-in-residence in 1974.

Brott made his conducting debut in March 1939 with the Montreal Orchestra, premiering his own symphonic poem *Oracle*, a work that was repeated by the *TSO under Sir Ernest *MacMillan in 1942, by the Seattle SO under Sir Thomas Beecham in 1942, and again under Beecham at the *Montreal Festivals in 1944. The work established Brott's reputation as a composer and presaged what was to become, over the years, a large orchestral output, ranging from broad symphonic frescos like *War and Peace* (CAPAC award 1945), *Concordia*, and *From Sea to Sea* to lighter works such as the overtures *Delightful Delusions* and *Martlet's Muse* (1962), via such works for soloist and orchestra as *Songs of Contemplation* and the *Violin Concerto* (played at Carnegie Hall in 1953 by Noël *Brunet under Stokowski's direction).

Nevertheless, Brott's foremost concern was a conducting career. He guest-conducted in Europe as early as 1948 and returned there on several occasions, mainly with the *McGill Chamber Orchestra, which he founded in 1945. He has conducted in England, Belgium, France, Holland, Israel, the USA, Luxemburg, Mexico, Scandinavia, Switzerland, Hungary, Czechoslovakia, Poland, and the USSR. With the *MSO he was concertmaster 1945–58 and assistant conductor at different times 1948–61. Several series of pop concerts, in particular at the Mount Royal Chalet and at the Maurice-Richard arena, were presented at his initiative, as were certain performances of oratorios at Notre-Dame Church and Marie-Reine-du-Monde Cathedral where, among other works, he conducted Beethoven's *Missa solemnis* and *Christ at the Mount of Olives*. His admiration for that composer led him to compose *Paraphrase in Polyphony*, based on a two-part canon that Beethoven had dedicated to the Canadian musician T.F. *Molt in 1825, and to make adaptations for orchestra of unpublished youthful works by the great composer: *The Young Prometheus* (1970 see Discography) and *Seven Minuets, Six Canons* (1971). The latter work was recorded by the McGill Chamber Orchestra, of which, by 1980, he had been the sole artistic director and conductor for 35 years. He has guest-conducted most Canadian symphony orchestras, including the *CBC SO, and has led the orchestras on the CBC TV programs *'Heure du concert' (20 times), 'Concerts populaires,' and others. In addition to his heavy schedule in Montreal, he assumed the artistic directorship of the *Kingston Symphony in 1965 and retained it in 1980.

Considering the volume of his production, the abundant variety of his means, and the ever changing nature of his inspiration, it is not easy to discern and define the real personality of Alexander Brott the composer. After the solemnity and even austerity of his early works, of which certain passages call to mind Richard Strauss, Bloch, and Shostakovitch, he gradually adopted a style at once more relaxed and less affected, affording a large place to humour and satire, an attitude reflected in the titles of the works, if not their content. Some have deduced from this that Brott has not taken his creative role sufficiently seriously. Others have reproached him with too frequent lapses into facility. However, it is acknowledged that Brott possesses a mastery of form and structure along with the techniques of composition, a remarkable aptitude for work, and considerable effectiveness in his vocal and instrumental writing. From the perspective of four decades of creative activity his work may be viewed as an immense kaleidoscope of changing forms and colours, an aspect which well may constitute one of its chief attractions.

To those who would accuse him of conservatism Alexander Brott replies: 'I take exception to this business of whether one does or does not write contemporary music. We are all of our time ... I do not particularly favour the mainstream of today for a variety of reasons ... Either we choose to express emotions and feelings and sensations which are common sensations, which most people have and share, or else a form of escapism into a remote area where a few of the more experimental composers feel they can impress other experimental composers' (*Canadian Composer*, November 1976).

In 1961 Alexander Brott was named a Fellow of the Royal Society of Arts of London and received the Arnold Bax Commonwealth Medal. Bronze medals for composition were conferred on him at the Olympiads of London in 1948 and Helsinki in 1952. In 1974 he received the prize of the Concert Society of the Jewish People's Schools and Peretz Schools, awarded annually to a personality of the Canadian artistic world. He was awarded the Pro Mundi Beneficio medal of the Brazilian Academy of Human Sciences in 1975. He received the *CMCouncil medal in 1976 and was made a Member of the *Order of Canada in 1979. He is a member of CAPAC and the *CLComp and an associate of the *CMCentre.

SELECTED COMPOSITIONS

ORCHESTRA

Oracle. 1938. Full orch. Ms
Laurentian Idyll. 1940. Str orch (band). CMCentre
Lullaby and Procession of Toys. 1943. Str orch (str quar). CMCentre. (*Lullaby*) RCI 5 (J.-M. *Beaudet)
War and Peace. 1944. Full orch. CMCentre
Concordia. 1946. Full orch. CMCentre. RCI: Canadian Album no. 3 (J.-M. *Beaudet)
From Sea to Sea. 1947. Full orch. CMCentre
Delightful Delusions. 1950. Full orch. CMCentre
A Royal Tribute to Queen Elizabeth II. 1953. Full orch. CMCentre
Analogy in Anagram. 1955. Full orch. CMCentre
Three Astral Visions. 1959. Str orch. Summit 1973. RCI 188 (*McGill Chamb O)
Spheres in Orbit. 1960. Full orch. CMCentre. Bar BC 1831. See Discography.
Circle, Triangle, Four Squares. 1963. Str orch. CMCentre. RCI 216/RCA CCS-1010 (*McGill Chamb O)
Paraphrase in Polyphony. 1967. Ms. RCI 235/RCA CCS-1029/Sel CC-15.088. See Discography.
H.B.S. 1975. CMCentre
Bacchi – Annus – Handle. 1976. Ms
E Dai P Milo. 1976. Str orch. CMCentre
Also a ballet, *La Corriveau*. 1966. Ms

SOLOIST(S) AND ORCHESTRA
Characteristic Dance. 1940. Vn, orch. CMCentre
Songs of Contemplation (Houghton, Tennyson, anon, Rossetti). 1945. High v, str orch. CMCentre. CBC SM-6 (G. *Gabora)/RCI 116 (L. *Marshall)
Concerto. 1950. Vn, chamb orch. CMCentre. (1952). RCI 71 (Dembeck vn, TSO, Waddington cond)/CBC SM-291 (O. *Armin)
Israël (A. Brott). 1956. SATB, strs. Ms
Arabesque. 1957. Vc, chamb orch. CMCentre. RCI 187 (*Nelsova)
The Vision of Dry Bones (Bible). 1958. Bar, strs. CMCentre
From the Hazel Bough (E. Birney). 1959. Med v, strs (pf). CMCentre
Profundum praedictum. 1964. Db (vn or vc), strs. CMCentre. RCA LSC 3128/Sel CC-15.088 (*Karr)
Centennial Cerebration(sic) (A. Brott). 1967. Narr, SSAA, strs. CMCentre
Centennial Colloquy. 1967. Ww, brass, perc. CMCentre
The Emperor's New Clothes (H.C. Anderson, adap G. Whalley). 1970. Narr, orch. Ms
Cupid's Quandary. 1975. Vn, strs, perc. CMCentre
Evocative Provocations. 1975. Vc, orch. Ms

CHAMBER MUSIC
Invocation and Dance. 1941. Vn, pf. CMCentre. RCI 115 (E. *Assaly pf)
Ritual. 1942. Str quar (strs). CMCentre
Critic's Corner. 1950. Str quar, perc. CMCentre
Sept for Seven (E. Birney, E.J. Pratt, G. Douglas, M. Pickthall, A.S. Bourinot). 1954. Narr, cl, sax, vn, va, vc, pf. CMCentre. RCI 131. See Discography.
Mutual Salvation Orgy. 1962. Brass quin. CMCentre
World Sophisticate (A. Brott). 1962. Sop, brass quin, perc. CMCentre
Three on a Spree. 1963. Fl, ob, hpd (or various combinations of 3). CMCentre
Mini-Minus. 1968. Cl, bn, tpt, trb, vn, db, perc. Leeds 1971
Toute de suite. 1970. Vc. Ms
Spasms for Six. 1971. 6 perc. Ms
How Thunder and Lightening Came to Be (Inuit legend). 1972. Narr, perc, pf, chamb ens; rev 1973 for sop, bass, spkr, children's choir, orch. CMCentre
Psalmody. 1973. Vc. CMCentre
Shofar. 1976. Vc. Ms
3 works for sax quar: *Three Acts for Four Sinners* (1961), *Berceuse* (1962), and *Saxi – foni – saties* (1972), all ms
2 str quars, and *Saties – Faction* (1973) for str quar or strs and *Double Entente* for str quar (1976), all ms

PIANO
Suite. 1941. FH 1955 (only 'Sacrilège')
Berceuse. 1947. *P-T*, May 1971
Vignettes en caricature. 1952. CMCentre. 1974. RCI 397 (J. Holtzman)
Also *The Prophet* (1960) for sop, ten, pf; *Indian Legends* (1973) and *Songs of the Central Eskimo* (1973) for sop, bar, pf, recorded by the *Ascher Duo (RCI 391); *Israël* (1952); *Elie, Elie Lama Sabachtani* (1964); *Fun-Ethics-S* (1968); and *Time's Trials Triumph* (1976), all for chorus, and all ms

WRITINGS
'My most successful work,' *CanComp*, 24, Dec 1967

DISCOGRAPHY (as conductor)
Bach *The Art of Fugue* (excerpts arr Isaacs). CBC str & ww ens. Ca 1955. RCI 126
Brott *Paraphrase in Polyphony* – Papineau-Couture *Concerto* for piano and orchestra. CBC Mtl orch, G. Manny pf. 1967. RCI 235/RCA CCS-1029/(*Paraphrase in Polyphony*) Sel CC-15.088
– *Sept for Seven*. Chamb ens, D. McGill narr. Ca 1955. RCI 131
– *Spheres in Orbit* – Respighi *The Pines of Rome*. Soviet Radio O. 1961. Bar BC 1831
– *The Young Prometheus* (arr). CBC Festival O. (1971). RCI 310/Sel CC-15.038
K. Jones *Miramichi Ballad*. CBC Mtl orch. 1967. RCI 291
Mercure *Divertissement*. CBC Mtl chamb orch. Ca 1957. RCI 154
See also Discography for Anton Kuerti; McGill Chamber Orchestra.

BIBLIOGRAPHY
Potvin, Gilles. 'Alexander Brott compositeur,' *P-T*, 910, May 1947
'Europe hears Canadian music,' *CBC Times*, 16 Oct 1949
'Alexander Brott follows some very sound advice,' *CanComp*, 28, Apr 1968
'Alexander Brott: a portrait,' *Mcan*, 17, Mar 1969
Grobin, Michael. 'Our composers on microgroove. Part III: Montreal composers of non-French origin,' *Mcan*, 29 (final issue 1970)
Schulman, Michael. 'Brott: a total musician,' *CanComp*, 115, Nov 1976
– 'Our salute to a most distinguished composer-conductor,' ibid, 149, Mar 1980
Contemporary Canadian Composers/Compositeurs canadiens contemporains
Creative Canada, vol 2

2 **Lotte** (b Charlotte Goetzel). Cellist, administrator, b Mannheim, Germany, 8 Feb 1922, naturalized Canadian 1943. Her parents were musicians and she began studying the cello at eight. Her family moved to Switzerland in 1933 and she continued her studies with Karl Reitz at the Zurich Cons, where she obtained a diploma in 1939. She also studied with Emanuel Feuermann. Rejoining her parents in Montreal, she worked with Jean *Belland, then on scholarship with Zara *Nelsova at the *TCM. She was a member of the CSM orchestra 1941–53 and joined the *MSO in 1953. In 1942 she succeeded Jean Belland as cellist of the *McGill String Quartet, a position she held until its disbandment in 1954. She married Alexander *Brott in 1943 and continued to play as a freelance musician, particularly with the CBC, the *McGill Chamber Orchestra, and, 1946–52, the *Little Symphony of Montreal. She has taught at *McGill U and has organized concerts and managed public relations, especially for the McGill Chamber Orchestra and other organizations of which her husband has been artistic director. She became the manager of the *Kingston Symphony in 1978.

3 **Boris**. Conductor, violinist, b Montreal 14 Mar 1944. He studied violin with his father and performed at the age of five with the orchestra of the *CSM at a young people's matinee. He took courses at the *CMM and the *McGill Cons, and 1956 studied conducting at the summer school of Pierre Monteux. The latter engaged him as assistant for concerts in Europe. He next studied with Igor Markevitch by means of a grant from the Mexican government and six months later won first prize at the 1958 Pan-American conducting competition. In 1959 he founded the Philharmonic Youth Orchestra of Montreal and led it in his conducting debut. His first international success came in June 1962, when he won third prize at the Liverpool Competition. He served 1963–5 as the assistant conductor of Walter *Susskind with the *TSO and then embarked on a career in England as the first conductor 1964–8 of the Northern Sinfonia at Newcastle-on-Tyne. He made several tours with this chamber orchestra, including one in Canada, with concerts at the World Festival of *Expo 67. During the 1965–6 season at Covent Garden he conducted performances of the Royal Ballet, including the first production at that theatre of Stravinsky's *The Soldier's Tale* (1966). He won one of the four first prizes at the sixth Dimitri Mitropoulos International Music Competition in 1968 and served 1968–9 as one of the assistant conductors of the New York Philharmonic Orchestra.

Boris Brott was artistic director of the Lakehead SO (*Thunder Bay SO) 1967–72 and of the *Regina SO 1971–3. In Thunder Bay he was music consultant on the four school councils for the region. In 1969 he became the artistic director and conductor of the *Hamilton Philharmonic Orchestra; under his leadership it has made considerable progress, increased its number of concerts, and made tours. In 1972 Brott was appointed conductor of the BBC Welsh Orchestra, and in 1975 he assumed directorship of the *CBC Winnipeg Orchestra (maintaining, along with both, his position with the Hamilton Philharmonic).

In addition to being invited to conduct the major Canadian orchestras, Boris Brott has guest-conducted in England (London Philharmonia, Royal Philharmonic Orchestra, BBC Symphony Orchestra, Liverpool Philharmonic, BBC Northern Orchestra, etc), France (Orchestre des Concerts Colonne), and Italy (Italian Radio Orchestra, Rome). He also conducted the Orquesta Sinfonica d'El Salvador in 1973, and has appeared in the USA, notably at Chautauqua, NY, and Greensboro, NC. In November 1977 he conducted works by *Kenins, *Symonds, and *Weinzweig with the orchestra of the Beethovenhalle in Bonn as part of CAPAC's 'Rendezvous with Canada.' A few weeks earlier he had made his opera debut, conducting Donizetti's *Daughter of the Regiment* for the *COC.

DISCOGRAPHY
Corelli *Concerto Grosso No. 1, Op 6* – Vivaldi *Concerto Grosso No. 8, Op 3*. CBC Tor str orch, Zafer vn, Benac vn. 1966. CBC SM-3
Fiala *Montréal*. CBC Mtl orch. 1970. RCI 291
Gounod *Petite Symphonie* – Beethoven *Rondino* for winds. CBC Tor chamb ens. 1966. CBC SM-2
Canadian Music in London, Paris and Bonn: Norman Symonds *Impulse* – Kenins *Beatae voces tenebrae* – Weinzweig *Dummiyah/Silence*. Beethovenhalle O. 1977. RCI 477
See also Discographies for Edmonton SO; Hamilton Philharmonic O.

BIBLIOGRAPHY
Bisbrouck, Noël. 'Un jeune chef de 18 ans dirige l'orchestre de "concert" à la télévision,' *SemRC*, vol 13, Jan 1963
'Pour sa dernière émission de la saison "L'Heure du concert" présente trois jeunes musiciens canadiens,' ibid, vol 16, Mar–Apr 1966
Graham, June. 'Boris Brott,' *CanComp*, 51, Jun 1970
Littler, William. 'Canada's mobile music man,' *En route*, Mar 1973
'CBC Winnipeg Orchestra appoints Boris Brott,' *PfAC*, Summer 1975
Schulman, Michael. 'The arts have always been an easy political football to bounce, both pro and con ...' *CanComp*, 142, Jun 1979
Creative Canada, vol 1

4 **Denis**. Cellist, b Montreal 9 Dec 1950. He first studied 1959–67 at the CMM with Walter *Joachim and in the summers 1963–8 with Zara *Nelsova at the Aspen Festival in Colorado. Subsequent teachers were Janos Starker 1968–71 at the U of Indiana and Gregor Piatigorsky 1971–5 at the U of Southern California. Brott served for a time as Piatigorsky's assistant. With the aid of bursaries from the Canada Council he also spent some time completing his training with Leonard Rose in New York, Maurice Gendron in Paris, and André Navarra in Siena.

In 1967 Denis Brott won first prize in the Merriweather Post competition in Washington and placed first in the *MSO Concours, making his debut with the orchestra in November in the Dvořák *Concerto*. In 1969 he won another first prize at a competition for young artists in Odessa, Texas; and in 1973 in Munich, at the 22nd International Music Competition of the radio organizations of the Federal Republic of Germany, he obtained second prize in the cello category. He made his Zurich debut 23 Apr 1976, and the following day the *Neue Züricher Zeitung* reported 'a new star in the cello sky.' In Canada Brott has performed frequently with the orchestras of Montreal and Toronto, in recital, on *JMC tours 1967–8 and 1969–70, and on CBC TV and radio. Abroad he was soloist with the Los Angeles Philharmonic (1974), the Orchestre de la Suisse romande, and the BBC Welsh Orchestra. In 1974 at the *Salle Claude-

Champagne in Montreal he premiered *Psalmody*, a work for solo cello dedicated to him by his father. In 1976 he played with the *Hamilton Philharmonic Orchestra in Montreal as part of the Arts and Culture program of the Olympics. During the 1978–9 season he performed works of Schubert with the violinist Charles Treger and the pianist André Watts on a North American tour.

Denis Brott taught 1975–7 at the U of North Carolina at Winston-Salem, and began teaching at the RCMT in 1978. He was appointed the cello in the *Orford String Quartet in 1980. He has recorded works of Richard Strauss, Schubert, and Debussy with the pianists Rebecca Penneys and Charles *Reiner (1971, 1973, CBC SM-185) and Tchaikovsky's *Variations on a Rococo Theme* with the *NACO.

BIBLIOGRAPHY

'Denis Brott,' *Variations*, vol 1, Oct–Nov 1977

1/GP, (CV), 2/(NT), 3/GP, 4/(NT)

BROUGH, George. Pianist, organist, harpsichordist, opera coach, b Boston, Lincolnshire, Eng; ARCM 1938, FRCO 1938, LRAM 1943, D MUS (Oxford) 1943. He studied 1937–40 at the RCM with Kendall Taylor (piano) and George Thalben-Ball (organ). Moving in 1945 to Halifax, NS, he was organist-choirmaster at All Saints Cathedral and taught at the Halifax Cons (*Maritime Cons). He became an examiner for the *RCMT in 1947 and first worked with the *CBC Opera Company in 1949, later acting as coach and assistant conductor. He also worked 1958–61 at the *Vancouver International Festival and in 1965 began teaching each summer at the *Banff SFA. He was assistant conductor and accompanist 1958–66 with the *COC and in 1972 became opera coach at the *U of Toronto. He has been organist with the *Toronto Mendelssohn Choir and the *TS and harpsichordist with the *Chamber Players of Toronto. Brough is recognized widely as one of Canada's most skilful, reliable, and versatile accompanists. He has provided secure support for hundreds of performers, from students in competitions to professional artists such as Heinz Holliger, Gervase de Peyer, Henri Temianka, Bernard *Turgeon, and Jon *Vickers.

DISCOGRAPHY

Handel – Haydn – Berg. I. Kombrink sop. Ca 1961. RCI 204

Leclair *Sonata No. 3* – Bloch *Baal Shem Suite*. Kathryn Wunder vn. 1967. CBC SM-55

Martinu – Ferguson – Arnold. John Rapson cl. 1970. CBC SM-146

Pergolesi *Stabat Mater*. St Augustine Boys' Choir, D. Hansen cond. 1968. PRS 11669S

See also Discographies for P. *Brodie; *Chamber Players of Toronto, CBC SM-289; *Festival Singers *Make We Merry*; G. *Depkat; F. *James; C. *Weait; D. *Zafer.

BROUW, (Florent Robert) **Frans**. Pianist, teacher, b Furnes, Belgium, 31 Jan 1929, naturalized Canadian 1975; premier prix piano (Brussels Cons) 1948, diplôme de virtuosité (Brussels Cons) 1951. He studied piano with Marcel Maas and Jenny Solheid 1946–52 at the Brussels Cons. A prizewinner in the Queen Elisabeth International Music Competition in Belgium in 1952, he made his debut that same year performing Beethoven's *Concerto No. 4* with the Orchestre national de Belgique conducted by Franz André.

Following this, Brouw gave some 60 concerts a season, many in Europe, but also in Africa in 1953, 1958, and 1959, the USA in 1959, the USSR in 1960 and 1962, and Canada for the first time in 1953 during a *JMC tour. Under the same auspices he toured during the 1958–9 season in a duo with the violinist Clemens Quataker, and in the 1960–61 season alone. He won a Harriet Cohen Award (London) in 1957. In December 1959 he appeared at Carnegie Hall in New York. He taught piano 1962–4 at the Ghent Cons, and then settled in Quebec City. He began teaching at *Laval U in 1964. Brouw has toured Canada in 1957, 1959, and 1960 and the USA regularly 1964–70. He has performed frequently for CBC radio and TV, broadcasting from Quebec City, Montreal, Toronto, and Vancouver. He is a jury member for Quebec conservatories and universities and for the *Canada Council. He recorded Raymond Chevreuille's *Concerto* for piano and orchestra for Decca (BA 143210) in 1956. (BM)

BROWN, Allanson (Gordon Yeoman). Organist, choirmaster, composer, b York, England, 31 May 1902, naturalized Canadian 1951; FRCO 1926, FRCCO 1940. He studied piano, organ, and theory for two years with F.T. Stout and Sir Edward Bairstow in York, but is primarily self-taught. He has been organist-choirmaster in England and Ireland, and in Canada at the Dominion United Church 1932–50 and St Matthew's Anglican Church 1950–4 in Ottawa. He assumed the same position at the Leamington (Ont) United Church in 1954. He has conducted choral and instrumental societies in England and Canada. His compositions include a one-act opera, *Legend of Grand-Pré* (1949), at least 40 choral pieces, 11 works for organ, and 7 orchestral pieces. Many are published by F. *Harris, H.W. Gray, *Waterloo, C. Fisher, Lorenz, Presser, A.P. Schmidt, and others. Brown is an affiliate of PRO Canada.

BROWN, Harold (Douglas). Pianist, coach, b Wynyard, near Saskatoon, 28 Oct 1917; ATCM 1935. After studies in his home town he moved in 1936 to Vancouver, where his teachers included J.D.A. *Tripp, Barbara *Custance, Phyllis *Schuldt, and Hugh *Bancroft. A leading ensemble pianist in Vancouver, Brown has toured with various chamber groups including the *Cassenti Players in the mid-1950s. He was accompanist for the BC (later *Kiwanis) Music Festival, the *Vancouver Opera 1960–70, and *TUTS 1958–63, and pianist 1964–7 for the *Vancouver SO. In 1972 he became an accompanist and coach at the *Banff SFA. He has accompanied John Alexander, Judith *Forst, Arthur *Polson, Marie *Schilder, George *Zukerman, and others. After 1974 he limited his work solely to the accompaniment of singers. MW

BROWN, Howard (Fuller). Pianist, teacher, b Arkona, near London, Ont, 24 Jul 1920; ATCM 1939, BA (Toronto) 1943, B MUS (Toronto) 1946, Artist Diploma (RCMT) 1949, MA, music literature (Michigan) 1954. After completing his ATCM he studied at the U of Toronto with Healey *Willan and Leo *Smith and at the RCMT with Lubka *Kolessa and Boris *Roubakine (piano) and Arnold *Walter (history). He was in charge of piano teaching 1949–50 at the Halifax Cons (*Maritime Cons of Music) and 1950–3 at *Mount Allison U and served 1953–67 as head of the Dept of Music at Mount Allison U. He spent the summers of 1951–4 studying music literature at the U of Michigan. In 1957, on an award from the Royal Society of Canada, he studied in England with the pianist Harold Craxton and the harpsichordist Valda Aveling. He was appointed head of the Dept of Music at *Bishop's U in 1967. Brown has appeared in recital and as an orchestral soloist in the Atlantic provinces and has been heard in broadcasts from CBC Halifax. In recent years he has been working with the poet Ralph *Gustafson to transfer to tape Gustafson's collection of rare early piano recordings. (CF)

BROWN, Margaret Miller. Pianist, teacher, b Owen Sound, Ont, 22 Apr 1903, d there 15 Feb 1970. Born into a musical family, she studied in her hometown, in Toronto with Frank *Welsman and Mona *Bates, and in New York with Ernest Hutcheson. She made her Toronto debut 1 Mar 1927 at the TCM concert hall and her London debut 15 Jun 1936 at Aeolian Hall. Her concert career, which continued into the 1950s, included Canadian tours and appearances with the *TSO and in Mona Bates' Ten-Piano Ensemble. With the *Promenade Symphony Concerts, Toronto, she gave the Canadian premiere 13 Jun 1940 of Ulric Cole's *Divertimento*. In 1951 she toured in Europe. She taught 1924–69 at the TCM (*RCMT) and for many years at the *U of Toronto. Her pupils include Brian *Cherney, John *Coveart, Anna Drake *Dembeck, Sheila *Henig, Gordon *Macpherson, Clifford *Poole, Sydney *Young McInnis, Doug *Riley, and Clifford *von Kuster. (WS)

BROWN, Maurice. Bass, b Toronto 1 Jan 1940; LRCT 1962, Artist Diploma (Toronto) 1962. He studied voice with Jeanne *Pengelly, Irene *Jessner, and Ernesto *Vinci. He made his *COC debut in 1960 as Francesco in *A Night in Venice* and continued to sing in the company's productions until 1970, creating the Judge in Somers' **Louis Riel* in 1967 and the Priest in Raymond *Pannell's *The Luck of Ginger Coffey* in 1967. He was a soloist with the *Festival Singers (singing in 1963 the title role in the premiere of *Beckwith's *Jonah*), with the *Toronto Mendelssohn Choir, and with several Canadian orchestras. He sang Squire in the CBC radio premiere 5 Sep 1967 of **Sam Slick* by Kelsey Jones. A *CBC Talent Festival winner in 1967 and 1968, he was enabled to study in Pasadena, Cal, with Beatrice Rowe. He won second prizes in the 1969 Geneva Competition and the 1970 *Montreal International Competition. He sang 1970–2 with the Musiktheater im Revier, Gelsenkirchen, Germany, and in 1973 joined the Landestheater in Coburg, Germany, concurrently studying in Cologne with Josef Metternich. In Germany Brown has appeared most notably as Figaro in *The Marriage of Figaro*. He may be heard on recordings of **The Fool* and, with John *Newmark at the piano, of music by Oskar *Morawetz and Brahms (1967, CBC SM 42). He was married to the mezzo-soprano Geneviève *Perreault. (SLO)

BRUNEAU, Philippe (Georges). Accordionist, b Montreal 22 Sep 1934. His father was an amateur accordionist. Bruneau took up the instrument at 15 and joined a folk music ensemble at the Trinidad Ballroom in Montreal at 19. Playing a three-row button accordion, he worked weekends with the group for six years and with the help of one of its violoneux, Lionel Simard of La Malbaie, Que, developed his fluency in the style and repertoire of Quebec folk music. In 1960, at the violoneux Jean *Carignan's suggestion, he turned to the single-row button accordion. At this time he began performing as a soloist, and with Carignan and others, in concerts and festivals and on radio and TV. It was not until 1969, however, that he relinquished his job of 13 years with a Montreal surveying crew to play music full-time.

Bruneau has appeared throughout Quebec and, as music director 1968–75 of the Danseurs du St-Laurent, has performed in Toronto at the *Mariposa Folk Festival and in the USA at the National and Fox Hollow folk festivals. The dancers were seen regularly in 1975 on CTV's 'John Allan *Cameron Show.' Bruneau also appeared at Mariposa as a soloist in 1975 and 1978. A virtuoso devoted to the perpetuation of the authentic instrumental tradition of Quebec folk music, and also of the music of the US accordionist John Kimmel, Bruneau has made the LPs *Philippe Bruneau* (1973, Philo FI-2003) and *Danses pour veillées canadiennes* (1974, Philo FI-2006), each comprising his arrangements of dance music from the repertoires of Kimmel, the fiddlers Joseph *Allard, Joe *Bouchard, Carignan, Simard, and Isidore *Soucy, the older accordionist Alfred Montmarquette, and others. Bruneau plays single- and three-row accordions on each LP. He also has recorded as an accompanist to Carignan. He is a member of CAPAC.

BRUNELLE, Paul. Singer-songwriter, guitarist, b Granby, Que, 10 Jun 1923. He was introduced to music at the age of seven, when he became a member of the *Petits chanteurs de Granby. In 1939 he formed his own country group and performed with it for eight years at weddings and receptions. He took part in various amateur programs and was a prizewinner in 1943 and 1944 in the CKAC Montreal radio competition 'Living Room.' One of the first country and western singers in Quebec, Brunelle has written his own songs (words and music), performing them in both French and English, and accompanying himself on the guitar. His first 78, for *RCA Victor in 1944 ('Femmes que vous êtes jolies' and 'Les Filles des prairies'), was very popular. After touring Quebec in 1949 with Laurent Lacroix and 1950–1 with Antoine Grimaldi he established his own troupe in 1951. For 10 years he performed in the cabarets, theatres, and arenas of Quebec, Ontario, New Brunswick, Prince Edward Island, and New England. He also was a radio program host for CKAC (ca 1946) and CKVL ('Paul Brunelle et ses troubadours du Far West,' 1955–7) and a regular guest on the TV series of Lévis Bouliane, Willie *Lamothe, Marcel *Martel, and Ti-Blanc *Richard in Montreal or Sherbrooke.

Brunelle has been compared to Ernest Tubb, and hailed by Roger Charlebois as a writer of authentic country songs and a performer whose vocal style rings true (*Country Music News*, Dec 1973). He has many hit singles among his recordings, including 'Par Une Nuit d'étoiles,' 'Mes Chers Vingt Ans,' 'Le Train qui siffle,' 'Destin cruel,' and, more recently, 'Ma Belle Poupée d'amour' and 'Ma Petite Maison.' He recorded 1944–61 for RCA Victor and 1961–75 for London. In 1975 he began recording for Bonanza. By 1979 he had made some 50 78s, 40 45s, and over 40 LPs. He is a member of CAPAC.

BIBLIOGRAPHY

Godin, Gérald. 'Ils ont inventé le cowboy québécois,' *Maclean*, Dec 1965

AP

BRUNET, Noël (Armand). Violinist, teacher, b Montreal 25 Dec 1916, d Chicoutimi, Que, 11 Aug 1973; premier prix (Royal Cons of Brussels) 1939. After violin study as a child with his brother Henri he trained with Alfred *De Sève. Brunet was five times a scholarship winner at the *McGill Cons, where his studies continued with Maurice *Onderet (violin) and Claude *Champagne (solfège). He studied harmony privately with Hector *Gratton. At 19, after concert and broadcast performances, Brunet won the *Prix d'Europe in 1936 and studied at the Royal Cons in Brussels with Alfred Dubois, a pupil of Ysaÿe. Further study in Brussels was supported by a scholarship in 1938 from the *AMQ. In the conservatory examinations of 1939 Brunet won the Adolphe Canler Prize and, after a performance of the Brahms and Sibelius concertos, a prize for virtuosity. He also received the gold medal of King Léopold III. He made his professional debut in the same year in a performance of the Beethoven concerto with the

Noël Brunet

Royal Cons orchestra. He then gave recitals throughout Belgium and in the Netherlands.

Returning in 1939 to Montreal, he began an active career in Canada and the USA, at the same time studying further with Theodore and Alice Pashkus in New York and with Joseph Szigeti in California. Brunet opened the 1944–5 SCSM season with the Glazunov *Concerto*, and in 1945 he played the 19 mature Mozart sonatas with John *Newmark for CBC broadcast. He made *JMC tours 1949–50, 1954–5.

Several composers wrote major works for Brunet, and he in turn guaranteed their compositions a premiere, a recording, and performances in Canada and abroad. Such works included Jean *Papineau-Couture's *Sonata in G* and *Concerto*, Alexander *Brott's *Concerto*, and Jean *Vallerand's *Sonata*. After he played the Brott *Concerto* at Carnegie Hall on 16 Oct 1953 under Stokowski, during a concert of Canadian music, critic Miles Kastendieck of the New York *Journal-American* described Brunet as 'a first-class fiddler.' In 1953 Brunet gave numerous concerts in European centres, including Paris, London, Rome, and Bonn, and in 1953 and 1954 he took part in chamber music concerts at the *Montreal Festivals. In 1955 he joined the Los Angeles Philharmonic and the faculty of the California Institute of the Arts. He visited Montreal as a juror for the 1966 International Violin Competition and taught violin 1967–9 at the Cons de Trois-Rivières and 1969–73 at the Cons de Chicoutimi, where he was acting head 1972–3. His students included Gilles *Baillargeon, Langis Breton, John Charuk, Jasmine Perron, Gérald Sergent, and Jacques Verdon.

DISCOGRAPHY

Brahms *Trio in E Flat*. J. Masella hn, Newmark pf. 1949. RCI 1

Papineau-Couture *Concerto for Violin and Chamber Orchestra*. CBC Mtl orch, Waddington cond. 1954. RCI 117

– *Sonata in G* – Vallerand *Sonata*. J.-M. Beaudet pf. 1953. RCI 92

Veracini *Sonata No. 7*. Pratt pf. Archambault 8604-1

GP

Brunswick. Trade name of phonographs and records, the former introduced to Canada in 1917, the latter in 1920, by Brunswick-Balke-Collender of Canada, Ltd, a Toronto-based subsidiary of the US firm of the same name. The company originally manufactured bowling and billiard equipment; and after 1934, when it left the record business, it returned exclusively to billiards. Brunswick phonographs featured the Ultona tone-arm designed for vertical-cut discs, Edison diamond discs, and the now customary lateral-cut recordings. Brunswick's own records initially were of the vertical-cut type, but soon were replaced by the lateral-cut variety. In 1924 (US) Brunswick took over the Aeolian-Vocalion label of the (US) Aeolian Piano Co. After Victor and Columbia signed a production agreement for electrically-recorded discs with Western Electric in 1925, Brunswick – with the co-operation of the Radio Corporation of America (RCA), General Electric, and Westinghouse – met the competition by being the first to introduce an all-electric phonograph (known as the Panatrope) and to release discs made by the complicated light-ray system (which later was abandoned). In 1926 Brunswick interchanged its masters with Polyphonwerke and Deutsche Grammophon. With the 1932 takeover of the Brunswick operation by the American Record Company an agreement was signed with the *Compo Co to manufacture and sell the Brunswick and Melotone lines in Canada. Subsequently many of Brunswick's popular artists were lured away to the newly formed Decca company in New York, and Brunswick was reduced simply to a name which passed through the hands of several major US record companies and survived into the LP era.

Canadian musical organizations which recorded for Brunswick in the 1920s and 1930s include the *Toronto Mendelssohn Choir under H.A. *Fricker (recorded at the TCM with portable equipment brought in from Chicago), Jack Denny and his Mount Royal Hotel (Montreal) Orchestra, Lloyd Huntley and His Orchestra (in the USA), Guy *Lombardo and His Royal Canadians (in the USA), and the Ukrainian National Chorus of Winnipeg. Among individuals who recorded for Brunswick were Louis *Chartier, Herbert L. *Clarke (his last recordings), Florence *Easton, the harmonica player Henri Lacroix, Charles *Marchand, the baritone Frank Oldfield, and Irene *Pavloska. EBM

Brunswick String Quartet. Quartet-in-residence at the *U of New Brunswick. It was formed in 1970, with the assistance of the Canada Council, as the U of New Brunswick Pach String Quartet. Members of the original group were Joseph Pach (see *Duo Pach) and Andrew Benac, violins, James Pataki, viola, and Ifan *Williams, cello. In 1972, with the departure of Benac and the enlistment of Arlene Nimmons Pach, they performed for a year as a piano quartet. In 1973 Pach and Pataki, with Paul Campbell, second violin, and Richard Naill, cello, formed the group which came to be known as the Brunswick String Quartet. By 1976 the group had given over 40 school concerts in New Brunswick and several concert series in Fredericton and Saint John. It has performed frequently for CBC radio and has given a series of concerts, 'Music East,' heard monthly on the Maritime network. The BSQ, which has performed throughout Canada, made its London debut at Wigmore Hall in February 1977 and performed again in England in 1978.

DISCOGRAPHY

Brahms *Piano Quintet, Op 34*. Nimmons Pach pf. 1975. CBC SM 250

Mendelssohn *Octet, Op 20* – Shostakovich *Octet, Op 11*. Purcell Str Quar. 1976. CBC SM-304

BRUYÈRE, (Marie Anne) **Germaine** (m Haserot). Soprano, b Montreal 20 Sep 1905. She studied theory with *Champagne, and dramatic art and languages, then voice, with Salvator *Issaurel and Rodolphe *Plamondon. In New York her teachers were Edgar Schofield, Florence *Easton, and Ivan Ivantzoff. After her 1930 Montreal debut she was seen in the Canadian Opera Company of Montreal productions of *The Marriage of Figaro* in 1933, and Honegger's *Le Roi David* and Debussy's *Le Martyre de saint Sébastien* in 1934. Edward

*Johnson arranged a six-month scholarship for her to study in New York, and while she was there she sang on the NBC, the CBS, and the MBS radio networks. After further study on a Quebec government scholarship in 1936 she performed in numerous Canadian and US radio broadcasts, and in September 1938 she sang the title role in three Montreal performances of Xavier Leroux's opera **Évangéline*. She made her Carnegie Hall debut in December of that year singing Christmas carols with the New York Philharmonic, and appeared again with that orchestra in February 1939 as the soloist in Vaughan Williams' *Symphony No. 3*, the 'Pastoral,' under Barbirolli. She was Beauty in a performance of Vittorio Giannini's opera *Beauty and the Beast* at Carnegie Hall in 1940. Among her numerous song recitals those featuring Debussy and Mussorgsky were notable. She took part in CBC broadcasts of such works as Berlioz' *L'Enfance du Christ*, Massenet's *Hérodiade*, and Pierné's *Les Enfants à Bethléem*. Following her marriage in 1941 she settled first in Virginia and later in Florida, gradually abandoning her public career. GP

BRUYÈRE, Jules. Baritone, b Murray Bay, near Quebec City, 18 Apr 1928. After studying voice 1946–7 with Louis *Gravel in Quebec City he went to Montreal to work 1947–50 with Albert *Cornellier. He also studied with Martial Singher in the summer of 1948 in Aspen, Col, and 1948–51 at the CMM. With the aid of a Quebec government scholarship he continued with Singher 1952–7 at the Mannes College in New York. He took stage training 1957–8 with Paul Cabanel at the Paris Cons, and in 1959 received honourable mention at the International Competition for Musical Performers. Returning to Canada, he made two *JMC tours, performing in *Blackburn's **Silent Measures* and **Pirouette* (1960–1), Debussy's *L'Enfant prodigue*, and *Vallerand's **Le Magicien*. He gave recitals on CBC radio and TV and in 1962 was awarded the Grand Prix d'excellence at the 6th Concours international de la mélodie française in Paris and the Croix de chevalier du ministère de l'Éducation nationale de France. At Covent Garden 1963–7 he sang supporting roles in Gluck's *Iphigénie en Tauride* and Berlioz' *Benvenuto Cellini*, appeared in Stravinsky's *Les Noces*, and was Hortensius in Donizetti's *The Daughter of the Regiment* with Joan Sutherland and Luciano Pavarotti. In 1967 Bruyère toured Quebec with the *Théâtre lyrique de Nouvelle-France, singing the title role in *The Barber of Seville*. With Charles *Reiner at the piano he made an LP (1963, RCA L3C 2658) of music by Berthomieu, Donaudy, Duparc, Durante, Gounod, Tosti, and Verdi. While he was with Covent Garden he sang Hortensius for the recording of *The Daughter of the Regiment* (2-Decca SET 372-373/Lon 1273) which appeared in 1968. He can be heard on the LP *La Bonne Chanson présente chansons d'hier ... chansons d'aujourd'hui ...* (RCA Victor LCP-1021). After 1968 he gave up his career to devote himself to business. (DM)

BRYANT, Giles (Bradley). Organist-choirmaster, tenor, editor, b Weybridge, Surrey, England, 20 Jun 1934; BA (University College, London) 1957, ARCO 1978, with the John Brook Prize. After rising from boy chorister to assistant organist at St George's College in Weybridge Bryant served 1954–9 as cantor and assistant organist at St James' Spanish Place, London. He emigrated to Canada in 1959, settling in Toronto where he became assistant organist (and later was organist) at Grace Church on-the-Hill and was a member until 1970 of the *Festival Singers. He served as organist-choirmaster at St Mary the Virgin Anglican Church and later at St Andrew's Presbyterian Church and in 1968 succeeded Healey *Willan at St Mary Magdalene Anglican Church, assuming also the directorship of the *St Mary Magdalene Singers. He was music director of several CBC radio and TV dramas and in 1971 prepared a CBC radio documentary about the *TS in honour of its 50th anniversary. He was organist 1965–75 at Massey College, *U of Toronto, and organist-choirmaster 1973–5 at Trinity College, University of Toronto. He taught 1971–2 at *York U and was music director 1972–5 at Upper Canada College. Returning to England in 1975, he was director of music 1975–8 at Cranborne Chase school, near Salisbury, and was a free-lance lecturer and broadcaster for the BBC. He returned to Canada in September 1978 to become music director of the Festival Singers, and led them until they ceased operations in 1979. In 1979 he assumed duties as organist-choirmaster at St James Cathedral, Toronto, and founder-conductor of the Sine Nomine Singers. Bryant has edited six verse anthems published in the *Massey College Series of Verse Anthems* (Leeds 1967, 1968, 1969) and composed several liturgical works, including 'Advent Responsory and a Wedding Psalm' (Boosey & Hawkes 1971) and settings of the *Magnificat* and *Nunc dimittis* (Waterloo 1968). He edited the *Catalogue of Canadian Choral Music* (1966, 1970) for the *CMCentre and the *Healey Willan Catalogue* (Ottawa 1972) for the *NL of C. He has contributed articles to magazines and to *EMC*.

DISCOGRAPHY

Evensong from Trinity. Bryant org-chm, Trinity College Choir. 1975. TCC 75-1

See also Discography for St Mary Magdalene Singers.

(MDr)

Bachman-Turner Overdrive (BTO)

BTO (Bachman-Turner Overdrive 1970–7). Rock band, internationally popular in the mid-1970s. It was formed in 1970 in Winnipeg as a country-rock band, Brave Belt, by lead guitarist Randy Bachman and the singer-keyboardist-guitarist Chad Allan (one-time members of the *Guess Who) with the drummer Bob Bachman. The band recorded the LPs *Brave Belt I* (1970, Reprise RS 6447) and, adding the singer and bass guitarist C.F. (Fred) Turner, *Brave Belt II* (1971, Reprise MS 2057). A single, 'Dunrobin's Gone,' was a minor hit in Canada. In 1972, with the departure of Allan and the addition of the guitarist Tim Bachman, the group assumed the name Bachman-Turner Overdrive and adopted an aggressive hard-rock style. Tim Bachman was succeeded as co-lead guitarist by Blair Thornton in 1974, after the LPs *Bachman-Turner Overdrive I* (1972, Mer SRM 1-673) and *Bachman-Turner Overdrive II* (1973, Mer SRM 696) were made.

Though based in Vancouver after 1972, Bachman-Turner Overdrive built its career mainly in the USA, appearing in concert as an opening act for other bands and achieving top billing by late 1974 on the strength of a high-powered stage show and the hit singles 'Blue Collar,' 'Let It Ride,' and 'Takin' Care of Business.' The single 'You Ain't Seen Nothin' Yet' was a million-seller in 1974 and was followed by other hits, including 'Roll On down the Highway,' 'Hey You,' and 'My Wheels Won't Turn.' Canadian appearances included annual concerts 1975–7 at the *CNE and performances in other major venues. Tours were also made in Europe (1975) and Japan (1976). Other LPs issued 1974–7 were *Not Fragile* (1974, Mer SRM 1-1004), *Four Wheel Drive* (1975, Mer SRM 1-1027), *Head On* (1976, Mer SRM 1-1067), *Freeways* (1976, Mer SRM 1-3700), *Japan Tour* (1976, Mer SRM 1-3703), and the compilation *The Best of BTO (So Far)* (Mer SRM 1101). Describing the group's music, Larry LeBlanc wrote: 'They've merged a hard-edged Memphis country/rock instrumental sound with the sweaty 1956–7 rock and roll and the hardness of the earliest days of British Mod. Overall, it's an unabashedly commercial hard-rock framework' (*MSc*, Nov–Dec 1974). At its peak (1974–6) the group won many polls and honours from US trade publications, as well as seven *Juno Awards in six categories. The first four LPs received platinum or gold record-sales awards in Canada and the USA.

In 1977 Randy Bachman (b Winnipeg 1946) left the group to resume his solo career as a guitarist and made the LP *Survivor* (Poly PD 16141). He previously had made the LP *Axe* (1970, RCA ISP 4348) and was active also in record production. In 1979 he formed Iron Horse, making an LP of the same name (Scotti Bros. SB 7103). In BTO Turner became co-lead guitarist with Thornton, and the bassist Jim Clench (once of *April Wine) was added. The name BTO (the acronym which had been in popular use for some time) was adopted officially in 1978. The new group recorded *Street Action* (1977), Mer SRM 1-3713) and gave its first concert in February 1978 in New Orleans. The LP *Rock 'n' Roll Nights* (Mer SRM-1-3748) followed in 1979.

BIBLIOGRAPHY

Melhuish, Martin. *Bachman-Turner Overdrive* (Toronto 1976) MM

BUCK, Gary. Singer-songwriter, administrator, recorder producer, b Thessalon, near Sault Ste Marie, Ont, 21 Mar 1940. His career began in Sault Ste Marie where he sang on CKCY radio (at first with Ray Kovisto's band The Country Caravan) and recorded in 1959 for the Canatal label. In 1963 Buck's recording of his song 'Happy to Be Unhappy' became an international hit and he was hailed as 'newcomer of the year' by the US trade magazine *Cashbox*. Other hit records followed, including 'Close As We'll Ever Be' and 'The Wheel Song' in 1964 for Petal, and 'Calgary, Alberta,' 'Sorry About That Chief,' and 'Mr. Brown' in 1968 for Capitol. Though he was based in Toronto after 1963, Buck appeared on various US and Canadian country music TV shows and starred 1967–9 in 'The Gary Buck Show' from CKCO-TV, Kitchener, Ont.

Buck later divided his time between performance and administration. He was general manager 1970–1 of *Capitol Records' BMI publishing affiliate, Beechwood Music, and in 1971 he established his own publishing and recording company, Broadland Music, which has included on its roster Dick Damron, Dallas Harms, Orval *Prophet, and Ian *Tyson. The label was taken over by *Quality Records in 1976. Buck was a director 1971–5 of the Nashville-based Country Music Assn and a founder of ACME. He has been the producer for recording sessions by Tommy *Hunter, The *Mercey Brothers, and others, and his songs have been recorded by such pop and country artists as Bobby *Curtola, Prophet, and Donna Darlene. His own recordings include four LPs for Capitol, two for *RCA, and over 20 singles. Buck won the *Juno Award in 1964, 1965, and 1966 as 'best male country singer.' At the 1975 Big Country Awards he was named 'top male singer' and 'top producer,' and Broadland was proclaimed 'top record company.'

BIBLIOGRAPHY

Batten, Jack. 'Gary Buck: the country singer is all business,' Toronto *Globe and Mail*, 29 Apr 1972 (RGn)

BUCZYNSKI, Walter (Joseph). Composer, pianist, b Toronto 17 Dec 1933; ARCT, 1951, LRSM 1953. He studied piano with Earle *Moss and theory with Godfrey *Ridout. He won second prizes in *CAPAC competitions in 1952 and 1953 for his student compositions *Seven Songs* and *Piano Sonata* and a first in 1954 for his *Pianoforte Trio*. He later studied composition with Darius Milhaud (Aspen, 1956) and Nadia Boulanger (Paris, 1960–1) and piano with Rosina Lhévinne (New York, 1958–9) and Zbigniew Drzewiecki (Warsaw, 1959–61). In 1962 he joined the *RCMT as teacher of piano and theory. He began teaching at the *U of Toronto in 1969. Much of his music reflects an irreverent puckishness, kept under control by the technical discipline of the professional pianist. He has given piano recitals in New York, Paris, and Warsaw, as well as in Canadian cities, and has recorded. A recital of his piano music by Antonin *Kubalek was broadcast 20 May 1979 on CBC-FM. He was president 1974–5 of the *CLComp and is an associate of the *CMCentre and a member of CAPAC.

SELECTED COMPOSITIONS

DRAMATIC WORKS

Mr. Rhinoceros and His Musicians, children's opera (Lilly Barnes). Sop, bar, narr. Ms

Do Re Mi, children's opera (Lilly Barnes). Sop, ten, bar, 2 actors, instr ens. Ms

From the Buczynski Book of the Living, chamb opera (Buczynski). 1972. Sop, ten, cl, pf, perc. CMCentre

Naked at the Opera, chamb opera (Tom Hendry). 1978. 2 sop, 3 ten, bar, bass, vn, va, vc, acc. CMCentre

ORCHESTRA

Beztitula. 1964. Pf, orch. CMCentre

Four Arabesques and Dance. 1964. Fl, str orch. CMCentre

Three Thoughts for Orchestra. 1964. CMCentre

Triptych for Orchestra. 1964. CMCentre

Four Movements. 1969. Pf, str orch. CMCentre

Seven Miniatures for Orchestra. 1970. CMCentre. CBC SM-308 (*CBC Van Chamb O)

A Work for Dance. 1970. Cl, perc, str. CMCentre

Zeroing In No. 2 'Distractions and Then.' 1971. Full orch. CMCentre

Zeroing In No. 4 'Innards and Outards.' 1972. Sop, fl, pf, orch. CMCentre

Three against Many. 1973. Fl, cl, bn, orch. CMCentre

Zeroing In No. 3. 1973. Str quar, orch. CMCentre

Ars Romantica. 1976. Chamb orch. CMCentre

Lyric for Piano and Orchestra. 1976. Ms

Rhapsody for two horns and string orchestra. 1976. CMCentre

Three Serenades. 1976. orch. CMCentre

Legends for String Orchestra. 1977. CMCentre

4 learning pieces for str orch (1964–5). All CMCentre

CHAMBER

Trio, Op 4. 1954. Vn, vc, pf. CMCentre

Divertimento for Four Solo Instruments, Op 15. 1957. Vn, vc, cl, bn. CMCentre. 1968. CBC SM-74 (Van Symphony Chamb Players)

Elegy for Violin and Piano 'In Memoriam Kathleen Parlow.' 1963. CMCentre

Six Miniatures for String Quartet. 1963. CMCentre

Four Corners of Gregory. 1966. Guit. CMCentre

Milósc / Love (J. Beecroft). 1967. Sop, fl, pf. CMCentre

Trio / 67. 1967. Mand, cl, vc (cb). CMCentre

Duo. 1974. Db, pf. CMCentre

Trio / 74. 1974. Hp, b cl, db. CMCentre

Two Pieces for Woodwind Quintet. 1975. CMCentre

Olympics '76. 1976. Brass quin. CMCentre

3 *Serenades* for chamber ensemble. 1976. Ms

The Tales of Nanabozho (D. Reid). 1976. Ww quin, narr. Ms

The First Symphony. 1977. Ms

Missa brevis. 1977. SATB, str quar, brass quar. CMCentre

Sonate Belsize. 1977. Solo Acc. CMCentre

Suite Capricorn. 1978. Guit. Ms

PIANO

Aria and Toccata for piano. 1963. CMCentre. CBC SM-162. See Discography.

Amorphus. 1964. CMCentre. CBC SM-162. See Discography.

Suite 1-2-3. 1964. CMCentre. Marie Currie Sklodowska Presents CGA 654369. See Discography.

Ten Piano Pieces for Children. 1965. CMCentre. ('Happy' and 'Solitude') Dom S-69002 (*Mould)

Sonata for piano 'Dzieki.' 1967. CMCentre. CBC SM-162. See Discography.

Eight Epigrams for Young Pianists (contains pieces from *Seven Pieces for Piano*, 1965). 1967. B & H 1969. ('Canon') Dom S-69002 (*Mould).

Burlesque. 1970. 1 perf: pf, spkr, tape. CMCentre. CBC SM-270. See Discography

Three Piano Pieces. FH 1970

Zeroing In. 1971. 1 perf: pf, spkr, tape. CMCentre. CBC SM-270. See Discography.

Zeroing In No. 5 'Dictionary of Mannerisms.' 1972. CMCentre. Marie Currie Sklodowska Presents CGA 654369 (Book II). See Discography.

Twenty-Seven Pieces for a Twenty-Seven Minute Show. 1973. CMCentre. CBC SM-270. See Discography.

Zeroing In – Zeroing Out. 1977. Pf, prepared tape. CMCentre Also 3 works for v and pf (1954, 1955, 1966); *Mass with Outside Prayers* for SATB, ww quin (1976); and *Psalm for Organ*. All CMCentre

DISCOGRAPHY

Buczynski *Burlesque; Zeroing In; Twenty-Seven Pieces for a Twenty-Seven Minute Show*. 1974. CBC SM-270

Buczynski – Pentland – Somers – Weinzweig – Tremblay. 1971. CBC SM-162

Buczynski Plays Chopin and Buczynski. 1973. Marie Currie Sklodowska Presents CGA 654369

See also Discography for Mary Morrison.

BIBLIOGRAPHY

'Walter Buczynski,' *CanComp*, 33, Oct 1968

Such, Peter. *Soundprints* (Toronto 1972)

Schulman, M. 'Walter Buczynski, a composer whose music reflects his life,' *CanComp*, Dec 1975

'Walter Buczynski: sabbatical symphony,' *CanComp*, 125, Nov 1977

Contemporary Canadian Composers MSh

Bulgaria. In the mid-1970s there were approximately 7000 Bulgarian-Canadians, concentrated mainly in Ontario and specifically in Toronto. The most substantial influx from this Balkan country took place 1901–31. The immigrants who arrived after World War I were mostly from rural backgrounds and became blue-collar workers; immigration after World War II brought many professionals of urban origin who were assimilated easily into Canadian society. The religious affiliation of most Bulgarian-Canadians is Eastern Orthodoxy.

The major contribution of Bulgarians to Canada's cultural pluralism has been the transmission of a rich heritage of folksong and folkdance. Ritual-ceremonial, calendric, occupational, and dance songs, as well as those sung at evening social gatherings, still are remembered, although they have lost their traditional context of expression and thus their original function. Nevertheless, at private gatherings and weddings these traditional songs assume a new collective function: that of entertainment. Because of the diversity in the regional origins of singers and songs, there is little stimulus for sharing in performance. Consequently a major portion of the repertoire remains in Canada in a form of stasis. The songs shared most enthusiastically by the Bulgarian-Canadian community are town songs (gradski pesni) whose wide popularity in the homeland sustained them in their transition to the new land. Their appeal has been patriotic and national (rather than regional) in character.

Folkdancing binds Bulgarian-Canadians together much more strongly than does singing. At most social occasions there are performances of one or another of the traditional forms of the horo or round dance: the pravo (straight) in 2/4 time; the teshkoto (heavy) in 2/4; the Eleno mome (meaning 'Dear Helen') in 7/16; or the Daichovo (dance for Daicho) in 9/16. The first thorough study of the folk music traditions of Bulgarian-Canadians was completed in 1974 by Irene Markoff for the *National Museum of Man. She found 7 instrumental pieces and 201 songs.

Outstanding Bulgarian-born musicians in Canada include the conductor and teacher Zanko Zankov of Hamilton; the Rev R.G. Katsunov, composer and choral conductor, active in Winnipeg and Montreal in the 1920s and 1930s; the concert pianist Slavka Nikolova of Toronto, reputed to have been an authoritative interpreter of Chopin; and Chris (Christo) Dafeff, a violin instructor 1941–69 at the *RCMT, where his pupils included Joseph Pach (see Duo Pach) and Steven *Staryk. Dafeff was the founder and conductor of massed folk choirs and orchestras. Later emigrés from Bulgaria include Anastas Fotev, an expert violin-maker in Toronto, and Blago Simeonov, who began teaching clarinet and composition at the RCMT in 1973. The pianist Marion *Grudeff and the contralto Mariana *Paunova are of Bulgarian descent. The Bulgarian violinist Luben Yordanoff toured in Canada 1959–60 under *JMC auspices. In 1979 the *Leamington Choral Society performed in Bulgaria after winning first place in one section of the International Choral Competition at Varna.

BIBLIOGRAPHY

Balikci, Asen. 'Remarques sur la structure du groupe ethnique bulgare et macédonien de Toronto,' unpublished report for the National Museum of Man, Ottawa 1956

Markoff, Irene. 'Folk music traditions of Bulgarian-Canadians resident in Southen Ontario,' unpublished report for the National Museum of Man, Ottawa 1973–4

Pelinski, Ramon. 'Music of Canada's ethnic minorities,' *CMB*, 10, Spring–Summer 1975 IM

BULKELEY, Richard. British army officer, provincial secretary of Nova Scotia 1758–92, amateur organist, b Dublin 26 Dec 1717, d Halifax, NS, 7 Dec 1800. He came from London in 1749 as aide-de-camp to Governor Edward Cornwallis at the time of the founding of Halifax. A wealthy man with a wide cultural background, Bulkeley promoted music in the Charitable Irish Society and at St Paul's Anglican Church (the oldest non-Roman-Catholic church on the Canadian mainland, boasting a beautiful Spanish organ installed in 1765). Bulkeley was a vestryman at St Paul's for many years and was the organist 1767–8 (or, according to the *DCB*, 1759–60). He was described by Archdeacon Armitage in the Halifax *Acadian Recorder* (16 Jan 1913) as 'the father of music in English-speaking Canada.'

BIBLIOGRAPHY
Macdonald, James S. 'Richard Bulkeley,' *Collections* of the NS Hist Soc, vol 12 (Halifax 1905)
'Richard Bulkeley,' *DCB*, vol 4 PRB

BURCHELL, (Henriette) **Louise**. Organist, teacher, composer, b Sydney, NS, 13 May 1882, d Falmouth, NS, 6 Jan 1962; ARCM, LTCL, B MUS (Oxford) 1908, MA (Radcliffe) 1929. She studied organ, piano, and theory with Peter LeSueur in St John's, Nfld, and then had special coaching in London from C.W. Pearce of the TCL. In 1908 she was the first woman from the dominions to qualify for a B MUS from Oxford U. She was assistant director and teacher of organ and theory 1915–19 at the Mount Allison Cons (*Mount Allison U) and taught subsequently at Dakota Wesleyan U and Milwaukee-Downer College, and 1934–42 at the Halifax Cons (*Maritime Cons). Organist in many churches, she held her final post until July 1953 at Trinity United Church in Windsor, NS. She composed many vocal pieces on sacred subjects, as well as chamber and orchestral works. A list of her compositions, some of which received CBC performances, is published in the *Catalogue of Canadian Composers*. The Public Archives of Nova Scotia hold a file of her personal papers. SAB

BURKE, Edmund (Arbuckle). Bass, b Toronto 12 July 1876, d Flintridge, near Pasadena, Cal, 19 Feb 1970. After attending McGill U he studied voice with Alberto Visetti in London and Edmond Duvernoy in Paris. His debut, at Montpellier in 1905, was followed by operatic appearances 1906–7 in Algiers, 1907–9 at The Hague, and 1910–11, 1919–20 at Covent Garden; his principal roles were Méphistophélès in *Faust*, Nilakantha in *Lakmé*, Athanaël in *Thaïs*, Scarpia in *Tosca*, and Rodolfo in *La Sonnambula*. He toured Australia 1911–12 with the Melba-Williamson Grand Opera Company. His *Metropolitan Opera career, 1922–5, was curtailed by the effects of a chest wound, suffered while serving in World War I. His later years were spent in private business. The possessor of a rich dark bass, which extended well into the baritone range, he made two rare records for HMV in 1913.

BIBLIOGRAPHY
Moran, William R. 'Edmund Burke,' *The Record Collector*, vol 19, Jun 1970 JBM

BURNADA, Isabelle (b Boyer de la Giroday). Mezzo-soprano, teacher, b Curepipe, Mauritius, 15 Feb 1899, d Vancouver 13 Mar 1972. Her parents emigrated to Canada when she was a child and settled in Mission, BC, in 1909. In 1919 she moved to Vancouver. Her talent greatly impressed Senator Patrick Burns, who for six years sponsored her studies with Mme Courso, Charles Panzéra, and Marcel Boudouresque in Paris and Maestro Piccoli in Milan. (Her professional name, Mme Burnada, was derived from 'Burns' and 'Canada.') Her first major success (ca 1924) came when she substituted for an ailing colleague in the title role of Gluck's *Orfeo* in Orange, France. After performances 1927–8 in Toronto, New York, Boston, and Chicago, she made her London concert debut in April 1928. She appeared in Vancouver in October 1929 and subsequently toured in Canada and the USA. Mme Burnada was best known for concert performances of operatic arias and Lieder. Ill health curtailed her concert career, and from the mid-1930s until 1957 she devoted herself to teaching in Vancouver. Her pupils included Ernest *Adams, Douglas McKay-Smith, and Robert Heath. BNSG

BURNETT, (George) **Jennings**. Organist-choirmaster, composer, impresario, b Stogumber, Somerset, England, 21 Dec 1867, d Victoria, BC, 10 Jan 1941. His first important teacher was J.R. Kelway Toms in Wellington, England. Burnett emigrated to the USA and in 1889 held a church position in Chicago. In 1890 he went to New Westminster, then to Victoria, BC. A leading musician in that city for five decades, he was organist-choirmaster 1890–1903 at St Andrew's Presbyterian Church and then, until shortly before his death, at St John's Church. He brought outstanding concert artists (Alfred Hollins, T. Tertius Noble, Marcel Dupré, Clarence Eddy, and others) to Victoria and organized performances of Handel's *Messiah* in 1894, Rossini's *Stabat Mater* in 1917, and other choral works. For several years the choir director at Victoria High School and a piano-organ-theory teacher, Burnett was a founding member of the *BCRMTA. Of his compositions – over 100 anthems, chants, and services, and piano, organ, and orchestral works – some were published by Novello, Weekes, Summy, *Nordheimer, *Whaley Royce, and Derek. DBW

BURR, Henry (b Harry McClaskey). Tenor, b St Stephen, southwest of Saint John, NB, 15 Jan 1885, d New York 6 Apr 1941. The most prolific recording artist of his day, he recorded not only as Henry Burr (for Emerson, Aeolian-Vocalion, Starr, and Lyric) and under his own name, Harry McClaskey (for Monarch, Victor, Columbia, and Pathé), but as Irving Gillette (for Edison), and as Harry Haley, Alfred Alexander, and Shamus McClaskey for any company able to pay his fee; he may have used other names as well. McClaskey began singing as a child, and at 13 was a boy soprano with a Saint John, NB, concert band. The Metropolitan Opera baritone Giuseppe Campanari heard him and suggested that he be sent to the USA for study. McClaskey's teachers in New York were Ellen Burr (from whom he took one of his professional names) and John D. Meehan. He sang at Grace Methodist Episcopal Church in New York and, still in his teens, began recording for Columbia in 1902.

Burr joined in 1906 and managed 1910–28 a vocal group which recorded for Columbia as the Columbia Male Quartet and for Victor as the Peerless Quartet. A member of the quartet was Albert Campbell, a tenor with whom Burr recorded many duets. The two sang also as members of the Heidelberg Quintette and the Sterling Trio. In 1915 McClaskey organized the Paroquette Record Manufacturing Co, and for a few years he operated a music publishing firm under his own name in New York. He wrote the words of Ray Perkins' 'Stand Up and Sing for Your Father an Old-Time Tune.' Burr began his radio career in the early 1920s on the Goodrich Zippers and Cities Service programs from New York. After his recording career waned, he was a great favourite singing old-time ballads on WLS' 'National Barn Dance' from Chicago. In all, Burr recorded some 12,000 titles, of which about 3000 are listed in *Roll Back the Years*.

BIBLIOGRAPHY
Walsh, Ulysses. 'Favourite pioneer recording artists,' *Hobbies Magazine*, Apr, May, Jun 1943 EBM

BURRITT, Lloyd (Edmund). Composer, educator, b Vancouver 7 Jun 1940; B MUS (British Columbia) 1963, M MUS (British Columbia) 1968. In his teens he took piano lessons from Elaine Korman and Annette Atlee. He studied in Canada at the *U of British Columbia with Jean *Coulthard (composition) and Donald Brown and Marie *Schilder (voice), and in England at the RCM 1963–5 with Herbert Howells and Gordon Jacob (composition). At Tanglewood (summers 1965, 1966) he studied conducting with Leonard Bernstein, Erich Leinsdorf, and Gunther Schuller. Returning to the U of British Columbia, he worked 1966–8 in electronic music under Courtland *Hultberg. In 1964 he began teaching in schools in the Vancouver area. He has composed on commission for the *Vancouver SO (*Assassinations*, *Fanfare*, and *Electric Tongues*), the CBC (*Spectrum* and incidental music for *Peer Gynt*), the *NACO (*Overdose*), the *RCCO (*Memo to RCCO*), and Hugh *McLean (*Icon*). Burritt uses sounds colouristically and patterns repetitiously to produce a freely structured expressionist music. He is a member of CAPAC and an associate of the *CMCentre.

SELECTED COMPOSITIONS

DRAMATIC WORKS

– *'Once Again ... Pop!,'* pantomime (Burritt). 1969. SATB, tape. Ms

Electric Chair, pantomime. 1971. Actress, alto sax, tape. Ms

Others including *Moby Dick Rehearsed* (1969), *Tiny Alice* (1969), *Peer Gynt* (1972). All ms

ORCHESTRA

Song (Burritt). 1963. Mezzo, chamb orch. Ms

Symphony in One Movement. 1963. Orch. Ms

Three Autumn Songs (R. Frost, F.R. Scott, A. MacLeish). 1965. Mezzo, pf, orch. Ms

Hollow Men (T.S. Eliot). 1968. SATB, orch, tape. Ms

David (E. Birney). Ca 1977. Ten, bar, SATB, orch. Ms

Several other works for orch and tape: *Assassinations* (1968), *Electric Tongue* (1969), *Cicada* (1970), *New York* (1970), *Overdose* (1971), *Spectrum* (1972). All ms

KEYBOARD

Sonata. 1962. Pf. ms

Memo to ———. 1972. Org, tape, typewriter. Ms

Memo to FATC. 1972. Keyboard, tape. Ms

Memo to RCCO. 1972. Org, tape. Ms

CHOIR AND VOICE

Works for choir: 'In Time of the Breaking of Nations' (1963), Kyrie (1967), 'Rocky Mountain Grasshopper' (1970). All ms

Works for voice 'October' (ca 1965), 'Winter Is Another Country' (1965), 'Landscapes' (1968), *Haiku* (1969). All ms

ELECTRONIC AND MIXED MEDIA

Acid Mass (T.S. Eliot). 1969. SATB, dancers, film. Ms

Fanfare. 1969. Brass, tape, film. Ms

Electric Soul. 1970. Tape, dance

Also *Sonata* (1963) for vn, pf. Ms

WRITINGS

'Musique concrète,' 'Electronic music,' *This is Music for Today 7*, ed Paul J. Bourett and Sherwood Robson (Toronto 1971)

'Transpersonal psychology in the music room,' *BCMEA J*, Spring 1977

BIBLIOGRAPHY
'Electronic ... ? Baroque ... ?,' *CanComp*, 45, Oct 1969
'Lloyd Burritt: electronic music,' *CanComp*, 55, Dec 1970
Contemporary Canadian Composers (BNSG)

BURROWS, (Barbara) **Ann.** Teacher, critic, b Entrance, west of Edmonton, 16 Jul 1922; ARCM 1945, M MUS (Indiana) 1964. Her teachers included Frank Merrick and Frank Howes at the RCM 1942–6, Boris *Roubakine in Banff, and Raymond *Dudley and György Sebök at Indiana U. Although Burrows lost her sight in childhood, she pursued an active career, teaching piano, theory, and history 1948–52 at Downe House School for Girls in Berkshire, England, and privately from 1952 onwards in Edmonton, and working as a CBC broadcast writer and commentator 1960–5 and as music critic 1965–71 for the Edmonton *Journal*. She began broadcasting as a reviewer for CBC Edmonton in 1971. RDM

BURT, (William) **Allan.** Baritone, b Toronto 11 Aug 1897, d there 6 Sep 1957. After study with Edward *Broome in Toronto, he won a scholarship to work with Vladimir Rosing in the Opera Department of the ESM. He made his professional debut in July 1926 in the first season of opera ever presented at Chautauqua, NY, his roles including Alfio in *Cavalleria Rusticana*, Silvio in *I Pagliacci*, and Captain Corcoran in *H.M.S. Pinafore*. Thereafter, for two seasons 1927–9, he was a member of the American Opera Company, touring the USA and Canada in a repertoire that included Silvio, Valentin in *Faust*, and Plunkett in *Martha*. Subsequently Burt was active in concerts and on CBC radio until he joined the Canadian armed forces at the advent of World War II. After the war he taught at the Maritime Academy of Music (*Maritime Cons of Music). JBM

BURT, Johnny (John Edward). Arranger, composer, pianist, b London 31 Mar 1914, d Toronto 21 Sep 1980. Taken to Toronto as an infant, he studied piano as a child and later composition, briefly, with John *Weinzweig. He was a pianist in the 1930s with the dance bands of Luigi *Romanelli, Jack Slatter, George *Wade, and others, and he was heard on CFRB radio, Toronto, with his own jazz trio (Murray *McEachern, clarinet and saxophone; Danny Perri, guitar). As a member of the Trump *Davidson band, led by Ray Noble, he travelled to Great Britain in 1939, and there he was a pianist-arranger for Billy *Bissett's orchestra. He played with Joe DeCourcy's dance band after returning to Toronto in 1939. Later, after working 1941–2 in the USA as an arranger for Paul Whiteman's orchestra, he spent three years as an RCN bandsman at HMCS York, Toronto. Subsequently he became an arranger for CBC Toronto, writing for the orchestras of Geoffrey *Waddington, John *Adaskin (*'Opportunity Knocks'), Jean *Deslauriers, Samuel *Hersenhoren, Paul *Scherman, and others. His own trio (Stan Wilson, guitar; Sam Levine, bass) was heard on CBC radio 1946–8, and his orchestra on 'Johnny Burt and Company' (1952) and other shows starring Elwood Glover, Wally *Koster, and Gisèle (*MacKenzie).

Burt was music director 1962–72 for the *CTL, in which capacity he chose the artists and supervised their recordings for the label. He himself made eight LPs of pop songs in orchestral, big band, and choral arrangements for CTL (including the label's first album), and others for RCA. Among the LPs are two by big bands (RCA CTLS 1100, RCA CAS 2406), *Dance to the Trombones* (RCA CAS 997), and *Around the World* (RCA PCS-1199). His compositions include three commissions from 'Opportunity Knocks,' *Theme for Susan* (his orchestra's theme song), pieces recorded for the CTL by Henry Cuesta, John *Perrone, Nat Raider, and others, and several *NFB scores. Over 20 of Burt's songs have been recorded for the Chappell Library of Background Music. He was a member of CAPAC.

BIBLIOGRAPHY

'Opportunity keeps knocking at Johnny Burt's door,' *CanComp*, 5, Jan 1966

'Johnny Burt: a Canadian point of view,' *CanComp*, 32, Sep 1968

Hickman, Jim. 'Johnny Burt's up-dated middle-of-the-road music,' *CanComp*, 74, Nov 1972 (HM)

BUSHBY, Arthur Thomas. Amateur musician, civil servant, b London 2 Mar 1835, d New Westminster, BC, 18 May 1875. Bushby's 1856 diary shows that he played violin and sang in musical societies in London. He spent the summer of 1856 in Italy, studying voice, piano, and Italian. On Christmas Day 1858 he arrived via Panama in Victoria (colony of Vancouver Island), and two months later, on 8 Feb 1859, he entered the civil service in New Westminster (capital of the mainland colony of British Columbia), where he became registrar-general, postmaster-general, and county court judge.

This versatile and public-spirited young Englishman did much to foster music in the two colonies. He was a founding member on 26 Jan 1859 of the Victoria Philharmonic Society, the first amateur musical organization in what is now British Columbia. As honorary secretary he organized the society's first concert, 6 May 1859. Even after his headquarters were in New Westminster, he continued to sing at the society's charity concerts. According to Mrs Israel Wood Powell, a contemporary amateur musician, Bushby 'possessed a tenor voice of beautiful quality and his solos and duets were rendered with true artistic skill" (N. de Bertrand Lugrin, *The Pioneer Women of Vancouver Island, 1843–1866*, Victoria 1927). In New Westminster Bushby played violin, piano, cornet, and drum at dances in support of worthy causes, and he trained the choir of Holy Trinity Church. In the Cariboo he took part in the concerts of the miners and on one occasion 'favored the audience with an original composition containing many local hits' (Barkerville *Cariboo Sentinel*, 15 Feb 1873). The manuscripts of a dozen or so of Bushby's occasional pieces 1856–74 are held by the Provincial Archives. One of these, the *British Columbia March*, 1874, is reproduced in *The Canadian Music Journal* (Summer 1958).

BIBLIOGRAPHY

Provincial Archives of BC. Bushby Journals (1856, 1858–9, 1860, 1864, 1872–4); music (1856–74)

Smith, Dorothy Blakey, ed. 'The journal of Arthur Thomas Bushby, 1858–59,' *BC Hist Q*, vol 21, Jan–Oct 1957–58

– 'Music in the furthest west a hundred years ago,' *CMJ*, vol 2, Summer 1958

– 'Bushby, Arthur Thomas,' *DCB*, vol 10 DBS

BUSSIÈRES, Jean-Marie. Organist, b Pont-Rouge, near Quebec City, 4 Jun 1910, d Quebec City 8 Nov 1978. He studied 1932–6 at *Laval U with Henri *Gagnon (piano and organ) and Robert *Talbot (harmony and counterpoint). In Montreal he studied organ with George M. *Brewer. He was organist 1931–78 at Quebec City's St-Sacrement Church, and he also taught 1959–62 at Laval U and the *CMQ. He gave more than 40 recitals on the CBC and for the *Casavant Society in Montreal and Quebec City, and gave the inaugural recitals on some 20 organs, including that of the Moncton cathedral. His repertoire included works by Canadian composers. He gave the first performance (1946) of Andrée Paduci's *Symphonie No. 1* for large organ, and in 1970 composed a mass in French for four-voice choir. He became the cultural officer for the *MACQ in 1967, and was the editor 1968–71 of *Vie musicale*, a periodical issued by the ministry. He was a member of the Research Institute (fine arts section) of De Paul U in Chicago from 1961 until his death. YC

BUTCHER, Agnes (m Searle). Pianist, teacher, b Edmonton 11 Apr 1914; LTCM piano 1936. She moved to Hamilton in 1925 and began studies with W.H. *Hewlett. She later studied in Toronto with Viggo *Kihl and Charles *Peaker. In 1933 she began teaching at the Hamilton Cons (*RHCM). She made her professional debut in 1935 in a performance of Saint-Saëns' *Concerto No. 2* at Toronto's *Massey Hall. The following year she won both the Eaton Scholarship and the Dominion Gold Medal of the *TCM. From 1938 to 1940 she lived in Hungary, where she studied with Bartók, assisting him as copyist and English translator at the same time. While there she also appeared in recitals and broadcast performances under the supervision of Dohnányi, who was director of Hungarian radio. After her return to North America in 1940 she performed throughout Canada and in the USA, actively promoting the music of Bartók, and was on the teaching staff at the TCM. In August 1944 she premiered Healey *Willan's *Concerto in C Minor* (a work dedicated to her) in a broadcast performance from CBC Montreal with an orchestra under Jean-Marie *Beaudet. (The same performers later recorded it for release on the CBC IS Canadian Album No. 1 / RCA DM 1229.) Butcher gave the first public performance of the work in November 1944 with the *TSO under *Mazzoleni. (FAH)

BUTLER, (Marie Nicole) **Edith.** Singer-songwriter, b Paquetville, near Caraquet, NB, 27 Jul 1942; BA (Moncton) 1964, L LITT (Laval) 1969. She began singing in cafés in Moncton while studying 1960–4 at the Collège Notre-Dame d'Acadie. Between 1962 and 1967 she performed mainly at festivals and on Halifax TV, drawing on a repertoire of Acadian folksongs which she sang to her own guitar accompaniment. She took the leading role in the film *Les Acadiens de la dispersion*, produced by the NFB in 1964. After teaching 1964–6 in Bathurst, NB, she did ethnographic research 1966–9 at *Laval U and continued to perform in boîtes à chansons in the Quebec City area. At Expo 70 in Osaka, Japan, she was a featured performer at the Canadian Pavilion for six months. That same year she took part in the *Mariposa Folk Festival and other festivals in Toronto and Washington. She toured Ireland in 1971 and continental Europe in 1973.

In 1973 Butler began composing her own songs, usually to lyrics by Lise Aubut. On stage Butler plays several instruments (banjo, dulcimer, guitar, harmonica, drum, violin), most of which she makes herself. She has given recitals at the *PDA (1974, 1979), at the *Grand Théâtre in Quebec City (1974), at Le *Patriote (1975, 1977, 1978, and 1979), at Camp Fortune, north of Ottawa (1976), and, with the French singer Serge Reggiani, at the Spa Festival in Belgium (1977). She also sang in Toronto and Paris in 1976 and was the host for 'Veillée de Noël' on CBC TV in 1977. In 1978 she was featured in a show presented to mark the 370th anniversary of the founding of Quebec City.

After her appearance at the *NAC the critic for *Le Droit* (Ottawa, 12 Apr 1979) wrote: 'Tall and regal,

Edith Butler

dressed all in white, Edith Butler sparkles on stage. She sings the songs and legends of her native Acadia so forcefully that you simply can't resist the artful invitation of their rhythm and melody ... her performances of laments and old folk songs, unaccompanied for the most part, have great strength and invoke haunting memories that you would like to retain for ever.' Her show, entitled 'Asteur qu'on est là,' is also the title of a song. 'Avant d'être dépaysée,' 'Marie Caissie,' 'Mon Arcadie,' 'L'Acadie s'marie,' 'Je vous aime, ma vie recommence,' and 'Le Fil de la rivière' are among her best-known songs.

In 1975 with her agent Lise Aubut she founded les Éditions de l'Arcadie and l'Acalf (Aide à la création artistique et littéraire de la femme). In 1976 she became the managing director of the record company SPPS (Société de production et de programmation de spectacles) which with Lise Aubut, Angèle *Arsenault, and Jacqueline *Lemay she had founded in 1974. She has published a collection of songs, *L'Acadie sans frontières* (Montreal 1974), and a calendar for the year 1979 (Montreal 1978).

A collection of Butler's songs was published by Intermède Musique in 1978. Awarded the Ordre du Mérite de la culture française in 1971 by the Canadian Senate, she also was made an Officer of the *Order of Canada in 1975, and named a Chevalier de l'Ordre de la Pléiade, an honour bestowed by New Brunswick, in 1978 in recognition of her contribution to the dissemination of Acadian culture. Edith Butler became a member of the board of directors of CAPAC in 1979.

DISCOGRAPHY

Chansons d'Acadie. Ca 1969. RCI 390
Avant d'être dépaysée. 1973. CBS FS 90156.
L'Acadie s'marie. 1974. CBS FS 90274
C'est la récréation, with Arsenault, Lemay. 1977. SPPS EP-990-0
Edith Butler. 1977. SPPS PS-19909
L'Espoir. 1978. SPPS PS-19904
Asteur qu'on est là. 1979. SPPS PS-19905

BIBLIOGRAPHY

Kroll, Stephen. 'A singer, composer and folklorist from Acadia,' *CanComp*, 83, Sep 1973
Vézina, Marie-Odile. 'Ces chanteuses venues d'Acadie,' *Perspectives*, vol 18, 6 Mar 1976
Jasmin, Hélène. 'The lady knows and loves – the Quebec music business,' *CanComp*, 118, Feb 1977
Beaulieu, Pierre. 'L'Âme de l'Acadie,' Montreal *La Presse*, 10 Mar 1979
Petrowski, Nathalie. 'Le pays intérieur d'Edith Butler,' Montreal *Le Devoir*, 19 Mar 1979
– 'Edith Butler: the voice from Acadia,' *CanComp*, 148, Feb 1980 ST

BUTLER, Roma (m Riddell). Soprano, b St John's, Nfld, 30 Apr 1931; Artist Diploma voice (Toronto) 1953. she moved to Toronto in 1949 to study voice with Ernesto *Vinci at the *RCMT. In the 1950s she won four *Kiwanis scholarships, the Kiwanis Rose Bowl in 1952, and the second female award in the 1954 *'Singing Stars of Tomorrow.' In 1953, as that year's grand award winner of CBC's *'Opportunity Knocks,' she was given a 13-week radio series. For three years during the 1950s she was heard on CBC summer radio in the Maritimes. She participated in CBC TV productions of *The Marriage of Figaro*, *The Pirates of Penzance*, *The Mikado*, and *Darling Cory*, and sang with the *COC in *The Marriage of Figaro* (Susanna, 1955) and *The Consul* (Anna Gomez, 1954). In 1956, with Paul *McIntyre at the piano, she gave the first Toronto performance in public of Hindemith's *Das Marienleben*. In 1962 she sang in a Toronto production of *Orpheus and Eurydice*. She has appeared with the *TSO and the Detroit SO. During the 1960s she gave two 13-week series of recitals over radio station CBE in Windsor, Ont. She was a member of the Detroit Opera Theatre, where her roles included Zerlina (1962) in *Don Giovanni*. She began teaching voice in 1977 at the *U of Windsor.

BYATT, Irenee (Irene). Contralto, actress, b Vancouver 3 May 1926. After lessons in Victoria, BC, she studied 1948–50 with Albert Whitehead at the RCMT, and 1950–4 with Roy Henderson in England. In 1953 she sang in *Messiah* at Albert Hall with the London SO under Sir Malcolm Sargent. Later in London she was Buttercup in *H.M.S. Pinafore* at Her Majesty's Theatre, and Mrs Botting in *Half-A-Sixpence* at the Cambridge Theatre. In Canada she sang at first in recitals, drawing praise on one such occasion from George Kidd, who described her in the Toronto *Telegram* (11 Nov 1954) as 'one of Canada's foremost contraltos. The voice is big and strong, with wonderful control, beautiful concentration on diction and an admirable range.'

In 1959 Byatt was a soloist in the York Concert Society presentation of Beethoven's *Ninth Symphony*. She appeared in several Gilbert & Sullivan operettas, including *Patience*, *The Mikado*, *H.M.S. Pinafore*, and *Iolanthe*, on CBC TV, and in *H.M.S. Pinafore* (1960, as Buttercup) and *The Pirates of Penzance* (1961, as Ruth) at the *Stratford Festival. She also sang in several presentations by the *Ottawa Choral Society (eg, Rossini's *Petite Messe solennelle* in 1961), participated in the radio (1959) and stage (1960) premieres of John *Beckwith's *Night Blooming Cereus*, and performed in musical comedy at Melody Fair (Buffalo) and Music Fair (Toronto). In 1965 she moved to the USA, appearing there in several touring productions of musical comedies, and in *South Pacific* (1967, as Bloody Mary) at Lincoln Center, New York. In the USA she has appeared as an actress on TV and in movies. In 1976 she returned to Canada to sing Mrs Trapes in *The Beggar's Opera* at the *Guelph Spring Festival. She played Emily Carr in the 1972 CBC TV production 'The Wonder of It All.' In 1978 she was living in Los Angeles.

Cabaret. See Musical theatre.

CABENA, (Harold) Barrie. Organist, composer, b Melbourne, Australia, 12 Aug 1933, naturalized Canadian 1966; ARCM organ 1955, ARCM teacher's

Barrie Cabena

1956, FRCO 1956, FTCL 1959, hon FRCCO 1973. He studied 1954–7 at the RCM with Sir John Dykes Bower (organ), W.S. Lloyd Webber (theory), Herbert Howells (composition), and Eric Harrison (piano). As music director 1957–75 at First St Andrew's Church, London, Ont, he began a regular series of recitals and presentations of church opera culminating in 1969 in the festival (which became annual) called The Church and the Arts. He has done some private teaching, and his best-known pupil probably is Jan *Overduin. In 1970 he joined the department of music at *Wilfrid Laurier U to teach organ and church music. He was president 1967–9 of the *RCCO. A practising concert organist, he has given recitals and broadcasts in Canada, the USA, Australia, and Great Britain. He gave a series of recitals in the Canadian pavilion at *Expo 67. His secure technique and resourceful use of registration are particularly effective in the 19th- and 20th-century repertoires. His compositions for organ, cast in various tonal-modal schemes, are distinguished by clear design, lucid counterpoint, and incisive rhythm. Within the same stylistic idiom, but of varying degrees of difficulty suitable to the purpose of each piece, he has written anthems, masses, service music, carols, and hymns. In 1972 for services to French music, he received the silver medal of the Académie française. Cabena is a member of CAPAC.

SELECTED COMPOSITIONS

CHOIR

'Praise to the Lord,' Op 7a. 1958. SATB, org. Gray 1964
Mass in the Dorian Mode, Op 20 (liturgical). 1965. SATB, org. OUP 1967
'Introit for the New Year,' Op 37 (Minnie Louise Hoskins). 1968. Ten (bass), SATB, org. Jay 1971
'Psalm 150,' Op 39. 1968. SATB (double 2-part choir), org. Jay 1971
Twelve Benediction Amens, Op 45 (liturgical). 1969. Various comb of vs. Jay 1971
'Let Your Light Shine Before Men,' Op 63 (Bible). 1974. SATB, org. Wat 1975
Others publ by Jay, GVT, Wat

ORGAN

Cabena's Homage 'Ten Portraits for Organ.' 1967. Wat 1967
Sonata da Chiesa. 1968. Jay 1971. (3rd mvt) RCI 481(McLean)
Other publ works: *Sonata for Manuals* (1966), *Sonata Festiva* (1969), *Sonata IX* (1971). All Jay 1971
Also an opera for children, *The Selfish Giant*. (Ca 1970). Ms
Catalogue of Cabena's church music, *RCCO Q*, 12, Jun 1976

BIBLIOGRAPHY

'*The Selfish Giant* by Barry Cabena,' *CanComp*, 51, Jun 1970 WHK

Howard Cable

CABLE, Howard (Reid). Conductor, arranger, composer, b Toronto 15 Dec 1920; ATCM conducting and bandmastership 1939. He studied piano but played clarinet and oboe in the Parkdale Collegiate Institute orchestra of Leslie *Bell. While leading a dance band, the Cavaliers, 1935–41 in Toronto and at southern Ontario summer resorts, he studied at the TCM with Sir Ernest *MacMillan, Ettore *Mazzoleni, and John *Weinzweig. He began his radio career in 1936 on CFRB, Toronto, as a programmer and scriptwriter, and began working for the CBC in 1941 as a composer of incidental music, soon succeeding Percy *Faith (who had moved to Chicago) as CBC Toronto's leading conductor-arranger-composer. In the 1940s Cable was responsible for such radio shows as 'Music by Cable,' 'Canadian Cavalcade,' and 'Jolly Miller Time.' He was music director 1948–53 for 'Canadian General Electric Hour' and 1954–7 for TV's 'Showtime.' His concert band was heard 1952–4 on the CBC and in the USA on the MBS network. It was the nucleus of his orchestra at the *CNE Grandstand, where he was music director 1953–67 and assistant producer to Jack *Arthur 1963–7. In 1968 he became Arthur's successor and produced *Sea to Sea*, a pageant based on Canadian history. Cable was music director 1954–8 and executive producer 1958–66 for General Motors' automobile shows in Canada. During the early 1960s he collaborated on many jingles with Dolores *Claman and Richard Morris and worked in New York as a studio conductor. He was civilian assocciatiate conductor and arranger 1962–6 for the NORAD Command Band in Colorado Springs and has been guest conductor of the RCMP Band. He conducted many clinics and established a reputation as a band arranger throughout North America. He has conducted pop concerts with several Canadian orchestras. In 1974 he became music director at the Royal York Hotel, Toronto, a position he still held in 1980.

Cable's compositions include many scores for CBC radio and TV and 10 1946–51 for *NFB productions. He has written *Newfoundland Sketches* for string orchestra (1948, Canadian Music Sales) and *Newfoundland Rhapsody* for concert band (1956, Chappell; recorded by Cable's Concert Band, by the Toronto Philharmonia under Victor *Feldbrill, and by the *Barrie Central Collegiate Band), both works inspired by a trip Cable made with Leslie Bell to collect folksongs in the province in 1947; the score for *Sea to Sea* (recorded by the CNE cast for Arc – CNE 68); and several band pieces published by Chappell. Cable's musical play *Mary* (libretto by Christopher Gore, based on the life of Mary Queen of Scots) was staged in 1971 and 1972 at the *Charlottetown Festival. With Peggy Feltmate, his third wife, Cable has written children's works such as *Your Work with Love Surrounds You* (Boston Music 1973; an oratorio based on the Creation) and *Rana's Pond* (Thompson 1975; a musical about ecology). Cable's arrangements include music from Broadway shows (eg, *The Sound of Music* and *State Fair*) adapted for band and choral use and published by Chappell, other band and choral music for Leeds and Southern Music, pieces for *Canadian Brass, and several French-Canadian folksongs for orchestra, band, or choir published by Chappell. Cable is a member of CAPAC, of which he was president 1969–71.

DISCOGRAPHY

Music by Cable. 1962. CTLS 5002
Howard Cable Conducts. 1962. CTLS 5010
Howard Cable's Orchestra. 1964. CTLS 5056
Souvenir de Québec: DeCelles – O'Neill – Allard. Cable Concert Band, DeCelles cond. 1965. RCA PCS 1003
Music in the Round: Cable – Weinzweig – Applebaum – Gayfer – K. Campbell – O'Neill. Cable Concert Band, Cable cond. RCA PCS 1004
Also, as conductor, two LPs of pop songs for the CBC in 1950 (RCI 13 and 14), and a recording of Serge *Garant's *Anerca* with a chamber ensemble and soprano Mary *Morrison. See also Discography for Feldbrill.

BIBLIOGRAPHY

Flynn, Bob E. 'Getting acquainted with Howard Cable,' *Radio World*, 8 Dec 1945
Frayne, Trent. 'Howard Cable,' *Liberty*, 2 Feb 1946
Callwood, June. 'Arrangements by Cable,' *Maclean's*, 15 Jun 1949
'Musician for all seasons,' *CanComp*, 27, Mar 1968
Kirby, Blaik. 'Good bands, no debt – Cable's bounced back from fall in fortunes,' Toronto *Globe and Mail*, 2 Nov 1974 (FH, GH)

CADORET, Charlotte (Augustine) (Sister St Jean du-Sacré-Coeur, Congregation of Notre-Dame). Educator, composer, pianist, b Newark, NJ, of Canadian parents, 29 Feb 1908; teaching diploma (Montreal) 1928, B MUS (Montreal) 1931, L MUS (Montreal) 1941. She studied piano with E. Robert Schmitz, harmony, composition, counterpoint, and orchestration with Claude *Champagne, harmony and composition with Rodolphe *Mathieu, Gregorian chant with Clément *Morin and Jules *Martel, and Gregorian chant accompaniment with Eugène *Lapierre. She also earned a diploma in Gregorian chant from the *Schola cantorum. After her studies, she served 1942–54 as director of the *École normale de musique (where she had studied) and in 1954 she became the general director of musical studies of the Congregation of Notre-Dame in Montreal. A member of the Comité d'Initiation à la musique of the Quebec Dept of Public Education 1945–65, she also played an important role in music education through her contributions to the pedagogical magazine *L'École* and through the establishment of programs of study. Because of her interest in folk music she joined the *CFMS shortly after its inception in 1956 and became vice-president in 1976. She has composed choral works, masses, cantatas, songs, folksong arrangements, and a *Messe à Notre-Dame* for two medium voices and organ (BMI Canada 1950). Among her published art songs are 'Lorsque je mourrai' (BMI Canada 1951) and 'A Cradle Song' (G. Schirmer 1944). The latter was performed, among others, at the Canadian Pavilion at *Expo 67 by Louis *Quilico, and was recorded by him. Sister Cadoret is an affiliate of PRO Canada. (DPI)

Les Cahiers canadiens de musique. See *The Canada Music Book*.

Les Cailloux. Vocal quartet – Jean Fortier, Jean-Pierre Goulet, Robert Jourdain, and Yves *Lapierre – popular from 1963 to 1968. Les Cailloux met at St-Paul College in Montreal and made their debut there in 1963. The four members accompanied themselves on the guitar and occasionally the banjo. To their initial repertoire of folksongs of various countries, they gradually added Quebec folksongs arranged by Lapierre. The quartet appeared in boîtes à chansons and made the LPs *Les Cailloux* (Pathé SPAM 67.142) and *Ohé le vent!* (Pathé SPAM 67.146) in 1964. Both were released in France by Pathé in 1965 under the title *Escale au Canada*. The LP *Ce soir Les Cailloux* (Cap ST 70000) was the result of a live recording at the *École Vincent-d'Indy in 1965. The group also performed at the Comédie-Canadienne and the *PDA and at the boîtes à chansons Le *Patriote in Montreal and La Butte à Mathieu in Val David, Que. In 1967 the quartet toured Europe, Africa, and Asia. A fourth LP (Cap ST 70015) was released in April of the same year. Les Cailloux also appeared in a show at the Olympia in Paris with Quebec performers Gilles *Vigneault, Louise *Forestier, and Clémence *Desrochers. The quartet starred in the series 'Les Cailloux' on CBC TV during the summer of 1966 and again during 1967–8 and gave a farewell concert at the end of that season at the Expo theatre. A reissue of the hits from the first three LPs, *Les Cailloux Salut!* (Cap ST 70012), preceded the group's dissolution. Another reissue, *Les Titres d'or des Cailloux* (Cap ST 70029), appeared as late as June 1972, an indication of the group's popularity. 'Canot d'écorce' and 'Au Chant de l'alouette' were among its best-known songs. (BLH)

Caïn. Oratorio by Alexis *Contant on a text by Brother Symphorien (Christian Brothers), inspired by the biblical story of Cain and Abel. Begun in 1904, the work was premiered by a 250-voice choir and a 45-piece orchestra conducted by J.-J. *Goulet 12 Nov 1905 at the *Monument national in Montreal, in the presence of Sir Wilfrid Laurier, prime minister of Canada. The soloists were Ellsworth Duquette, bass (Caïn), Édouard *LeBel, tenor (Abel), Joseph *Saucier, baritone (Adam), Antoinette Landry, mezzo-soprano (Ève), and Mme A. Desmarais (Messager céleste). The work is in three parts: La Haine (the Hatred), Le Sang (the Blood), and La Promesse (the Promise), preceded by an overture. Part of the work was repeated at the Monument national 25 Oct 1906. Selections were performed on CBC radio in 1958 and 1977, and the first public performance outside Quebec was given 27 Sep 1980 in Victoria, BC, by the *Victoria SO, the Amity Singers, and soloists, under the direction of Paul Freeman. According to Romain *Gour, 'the work shows striking polyphonic contrasts in the manner of Verdi or Berlioz ... A certain influence of Wagner can be found, too, and a very strong predisposition toward opera' (*Qui?*, December 1953). The original 300-page manuscript is deposited at the *NL of C. See also Oratorios, Canadian 4. GP

CALANGIS, George. Conductor, mandolinist, banjoist, b Vancouver 14 Jun 1916, d there 1 Jul 1966. As a boy he performed in vaudeville in an ensemble with his five sisters – Geneva, Angelina, Mary, Helen, and Ethel – playing mandolins and banjos of various registers. They were billed as the Musical Calangis Family. George studied violin in Vancouver with George Brailey, although he was especially skilled on the mandolin (he was able, for example, to play on it violin pieces of Sarasate and an adaptation of Mendelssohn's E-minor *Violin Concerto*). The sisters also became proficient in string instruments and piano. Managed by an uncle, Andrew B. Chrest, the family ensemble performed 1929–32 in Seattle, San Francisco, and, for a period, on KNX radio and in leading nightclubs in Los Angeles. It specialized in light music with a continental flavour, to which it added Mexican music during its US sojourn. Returning to Vancouver the group became the staff orchestra 1933–43 on CKCD radio, and in 1934, augmented by other musicians, began performing on CBC radio for such shows as 'Music from the Pacific,' 'Continental Varieties,' and 'Music from the Riviera.' After service in World War II as music director of the *RCAF Blackouts, George led the orchestra at the Commodore Cabaret until the early 1950s. He conducted CBC radio shows ('Calangis and Co,' 'Continental Varieties,' and others) and TV shows ('Bamboula,' 'Meet Lorraine,' and 'Lolly Too Dum') until the mid-1950s, but by then music had become secondary to a career in business. Of the Calangis sisters, three remained active in music after the mid-1950s. Angelina, the wife of John *Avison, had studied violin with Arthur Gramm, Wilfred Rutley, Jean *de Rimanoczy, and Gregori *Garbovitsky and became a member, and later principal second violin, of the *Vancouver SO. Mary (m Dennis), a cellist, joined the Vancouver SO in 1950, and Geneva (m Cameron), a pianist and pupil of Helen Devlin, taught privately and assisted teachers of dance.

BIBLIOGRAPHY

Wedman, Les. 'Music by Calangis,' *Vancouver Province BC Magazine*, 26 Dec 1953

Smith, Bob. 'Remember?' Vancouver *Sun*, 28 Jul 1967

(BNSG)

CALBES, Eleanor (m Wickes). Soprano, b Aparri, Cagayan, the Philippines, 20 Feb 1944, naturalized Canadian 1967; teacher's diploma (Philippines) 1961, Diploma, opera performance (Toronto) 1965. She was a singer and dancer with the touring Bayanihan Dance Company when Nicholas *Goldschmidt heard her and arranged two scholarships at the *Royal Cons Opera School, where she studied with Irene *Jessner. She made her *COC debut in 1963 as an orphan in *Der Rosenkavalier*, sang Fifi in *Die Fledermaus* in 1964 and Musetta in *La Bohème* in 1965 and alternated with Colette *Boky as Olympia / Stella in *Tales of Hoffmann* in 1967. Appearances followed on Broadway in *The King and I* (New York City Center, 1967) and *West Side Story* (Lincoln Center, 1968). She was Liat in *South Pacific* at *O'Keefe Centre in 1964, at New York City Center in 1965, and on the recording (1967, Col OS 3100) and was Lotus Blossom in the 1970 premiere of the musical version (*Lovely Ladies, Kind Gentlemen*) of *Teahouse of the August Moon*. She sang in opera in Germany and Austria, 1972–5. Her roles at the Klagenfurt Stadttheater included Gilda, Papagena, and Olympia. She also performed at Wuppertal and Kaiser Lautern. She has appeared at the *Stratford and *Guelph festivals, on CBC radio and TV, and with the *TS and the *Hamilton Philharmonic. (LL)

Calgary. Alberta city founded on or near the site of Fort la Jonquière which was built in 1751 at the junction of the Bow and Elbow rivers and was abandoned after 1785. Fort Brisebois, established there by the Northwest Mounted Police in 1875, was renamed Fort Calgary a year later. Calgary, with a population of 500, was incorporated as a town in 1884 (a year after it had been reached by the Canadian Pacific Railway) and as a city in 1893. By the 1970s, with a population of more than 500,000 and an economy founded particularly on oil, ranching, and tourism, Calgary had become a major Canadian financial centre.

Mrs John McDougall's recollections of the early days, noted in Norman Kennedy's thesis on music in Calgary, include references to the incessant drumming of tom-toms and chanting by the Indians, the playing of fiddles by métis traders at the fort, and the singing at the mission – the Indians listening to 'Nearer My God to Thee,' 'All Hail the Power of Jesus' Name,' and other hymns. The McDougall family presented a portable organ to the mission church in 1873. Governor-General the Marquis of Lorne is said to have written the words for the hymn 'Unto the Hills around Do I Lift up My Longing Eyes' in 1881 while leading a surveying party on the site of Calgary. By 1883 the *Calgary Weekly Herald* (first issued in August of that year) began to document local musical activity. One item described a program which consisted of 'instrumental music, dialogues, comic and sentimental songs ... and a dance after the concert'; another, a piano recital by a Mrs Millward.

Bands provided most of Calgary's instrumental music in the pioneer years. The first band of the Northwest Mounted Police 'F' Division was formed in 1877 and performed until 1881; the second, led by Fred A. Bagley from 1886 until his retirement in 1899, participated in many community events. The first civilian band, the Calgary Brass Band, was formed in 1885. The Salvation Army Band followed in 1887, and the Calgary Fire Brigade Band in 1890. In 1907 the 15th Light Horse Band, conducted by Bagley, became the first Canadian regimental band to tour the British Isles.

Church choirs, directed by such enthusiasts as J.J. Young (leader of the Methodist Church Choir 1894–1908), were the focus of early choral activity, with accompaniment by vocalions, harmoniums, or reed organs. By the turn of the century churches began to appoint trained organists and choirmasters (eg, Wilfred V. Oaten, F.B. Cooper, Mme Ellis Browne, Annie *Glen Broder, who later taught Odette *de Foras, and Frank Wrigley) and to install pipe organs: a *Karn in 1905, followed by a *Casavant in 1917 in Central Methodist Church, a Casavant in Knox Presbyterian in 1905, and an organ built by the Canadian Pipe Organ Co in Wesley Methodist in 1912.

Church choirs formed a basis for amateur choral societies. Col J.S. Dennis conducted Gaul's *Holy City* in the early 1890s and later (26 Apr 1904), aided by Annie Glen Broder, presented the Canadian premiere of Coleridge-Taylor's oratorio *The Atonement*. As a result the Calgary Philharmonic Society was founded. The society was the first attempt to establish a permanent choral organization, but it functioned only until 1908.

The Apollo Choir (1908–18) made its debut 7 Apr 1908 under P.L. Newcombe in Haydn's *The Creation*. The Calgary SO, assembled for the choir's performance of Stanford's choral ballad *The Battle of the Baltic*, also played Elgar's *Pomp and Circumstance No. 1* under A.P. Howells. In its 1911–12 season, the Apollo Choir sponsored a visit by the St Paul SO. Max *Weil, a violinist with that orchestra, became the conductor of a second *Calgary SO (1912–14) which, along with other concerts at the Sherman Grand Theatre, presented a school children's matinee series featuring local artists. Though secular choral music was less popular than oratorio, the local Methodist church choir gave a Wagner centennial concert in 1913.

In 1928 Gregori *Garbovitsky, who had led the Palace Theatre Orchestra, became conductor of the third Calgary SO, sponsored by the Calgary Choral and Orchestral Society, which flourished until 1939. In 1947 Clayton *Hare founded the Mount Royal College Orchestra, renamed the Calgary SO, and in 1955 Henry Plukker amalgamated it with the recently formed Alberta Philharmonic to create the *Calgary Philharmonic Orchestra, which remained the city's major orchestra in 1980. The (Southern) *Alberta Jubilee Auditorium became the orchestra's home in 1957.

Musical theatre in Calgary dates back to the 1890 production of *Trial by Jury* at the Calgary Opera House. J.S. Dennis was active in operetta production as was Mrs W. Roland Winter, who both directed and acted. Mrs Winter was influential in the Calgary Operatic Society which, in addition to its many productions of Gilbert & Sullivan, in 1899 presented Sidney Jones' *The Geisha*. The society continued annual operetta productions until 1920. Operettas were produced at Hull's Opera House, erected in 1893, remodelled in 1905, and reopened under the new name Sherman's Opera House. The Sherman Grand Theatre, which opened in 1912, had at the time the largest stage in Canada and attracted such touring ensembles as the *San Carlo Opera Co and the D'Oyly Carte Co.

Calgary became the headquarters of the *Chautauqua in 1917. In 1972 Alexander *Gray and several Calgary citizens founded the *Southern Alberta Opera Association to bring Calgary regular grand opera productions of professional calibre.

Clifford Higgin (organist, choirmaster, b Manchester 1876, d Calgary 1951) arrived from Brantford, Ont, in 1920 and was active in the city's musical life for three decades. He conducted the Knox United Church choir, the Calgary Light Opera Society, and the Institute of Technology Chorale and in 1931 was instrumental in founding the Calgary Music Competition Festival which later became the Calgary Kiwanis Music Festival. Calgary's involvement in competition festivals began in 1918, when it became active in the *Alberta Music Festival Assn and took its turn as the site of the rotating provincial festivals. Higgin's wife Eileen, a singing teacher, has directed the annual musical productions of the Calgary Theatre Singers.

Under the sponsorship of the *Calgary Women's Musical Club (1904–64), the Calgary branch of the Canadian Concert Assn (1938), the Calgary Chamber Music Society (1964–8), Celebrity Concerts, and *Community Concerts (introduced in 1969) many performing artists have visited Calgary, among them Emma *Albani (who first sang there in 1897), Clara Butt, Amelita Galli-Curci, Fritz Kreisler, Nellie Melba, and the Calgary-born violinist Kathleen *Parlow.

Informal music instruction began at the Calgary public school under Ada Dowling Costigan in 1887. (Gladys *Egbert later was one of her pupils.) The first full-time music teacher, Frank Fenwick, was appointed in 1892. Shortly after 1900 A.O. MacRae became the local representative of the *AB of the RSM, whose examiners visited the city annually.

The short-lived Calgary Cons of Music (1909–10) was succeeded by the *Mount Royal College Cons, established in 1910 by the Methodist Church. (In 1972 Mount Royal named a hall in honour of one of its outstanding teachers – Leonard *Leacock.)

The *U of Calgary, founded in 1945 and offering the B MUS in the 1960s, has provided a home for local instrumental and choral ensembles and has sponsored numerous concerts and recitals. In 1969, with the local *RCCO branch, it established the Cecilian organ recital series.

The *CMCentre established an office at the university in 1980. The Glenbow-Alberta Institute is located in Calgary (see Archives; Instrument collections; Libraries). Leif Karlsson of Calgary has specialized in building and repairing string instruments.

Among the city's musicians and performing groups active in the 1960s and 1970s were *One Third Ninth, the Calgary Youth Orchestra conducted by Frank Simpson, and the Calgary Festival Chorus conducted by John *Searchfield. The last-named was the author of the regular Alberta reports in the *Canada Music Book* 1971–4. Pop groups active in the city in 1980 were the Stardells and the *Stampeders.

In 1967 Lloyd *Erickson (appointed supervisor of music for the Calgary public schools in 1972) became the first choral director of the Young Canadians, who have appeared regularly in the Stampede grandstand show and have performed throughout Canada and in the USA. Erickson has conducted the Calgary Philharmonic Choir as well.

The annual Calgary Stampede traditionally has included among its musical attractions the nightly grandstand show which features international entertainers, a parade with many of the city's bands (eg, the Cavalier Drum and Bugle Corps, the Calgary School Patrol Band), and outdoor performances by the *Rhythm Pals, the fiddler Al *Cherny, and others. The *Princess Patricia's Canadian Light Infantry Band, stationed in Calgary in 1968, took part in the 1975 Century Calgary celebrations and also has appeared in the Stampede parade.

Besides Kathleen Parlow, musicians born in Calgary include Tommy *Banks, Donna-Faye *Carr, Constance *Channon, Arthur *Crighton, Marilyn *Engle, Jerry *Fuller, Clyde *Gilmour, Sylvia *Grant, Minuetta *Kessler, Ian *McDougall, Diana *McIntosh, Cyril *Mossop, Alexandra *Munn, the composer Stephen Pedersen, P.J. *Perry, Doug *Randle, Eugene *Rittich, Dick *Todd, and the noted US accompanist Yehudi Wyner.

BIBLIOGRAPHY

Kennedy, Norman. 'The growth and development of music in Calgary, 1875–1920,' unpubl MA thesis, U of Alberta 1952

Draper, Norman. *Bands by the Bow: A History of Band Music in Calgary* (Calgary 1975)

Ward, Tom. *Cowtown: An Album of Early Calgary* (Calgary 1975)

Calgary Philharmonic Orchestra. An amalgamation (1955) of the *Calgary SO and the Alberta Philharmonic, the latter established earlier in 1955 under the Dutch conductor Henry Plukker (b Dornbirn, Austria, 14 May 1908). Plukker served as the CPO's conductor until 1961. Initially the CPO presented 10 concerts annually at the Palace Theatre and some school programs. Later the orchestra played in the *Alberta Jubilee Auditorium. By 1963, when Haymo Taeuber became conductor, attendance had grown from an average of 900 per concert to over 2500. Under Taeuber (b Graz, Austria, 1 Jan 1908; a pupil of Felix Weingartner and a former conductor of the Vienna Boys' Choir and of orchestras in Austria, Turkey, and Iran), junior, intermediate, and senior youth orchestras were established to encourage and train young musicians. Taeuber was succeeded in 1968 for one year by the noted pianist José Iturbi (b Valencia 28 Nov 1895), during whose term the orchestra for the first time augmented its ranks with 27 full-time musicians (increasing that number to 45 by the 1977–8 season). After Iturbi and a year of guest conductors, Maurice Handford (b Salisbury, Wiltshire, England, 29 Apr 1929) led the orchestra 1969–75, followed again by guest conductors; Franz-Paul *Decker was artistic adviser and principal guest conductor 1975–7. Arpad Joo (b Budapest 1948, a protégé of Kodály) became music director in 1977. By the 1978–9 season the orchestra offered a 10-concert main series, a 5-concert *du Maurier pop series, a 5-concert chamber orchestra series, a 3-concert 'special favourites' series, and school recitals by small ensembles. The orchestra has accompanied *Southern Alberta Opera Assn productions. Though it has not toured widely, it has appeared in Red Deer and Medicine Hat.

Guest conductors have included Kazuyoshi Akiyama, Raffi *Armenian, John *Avison, Mario *Bernardi, Boris *Brott, Harman Haakman, Pierre *Hétu, the Soviet conductor Yuri Lutsiv (on exchange with Plukker in 1961), and the orchestra's concertmaster (1975–) Cenek Vrba. Guest performers have included Carlina Carr, Constance *Channon, Van Cliburn, Janina *Fialkowska, Leon Fleisher, Maureen *Forrester, Ida *Haendel, Betty-Jean *Hagen, Eugene Istomin, Marek *Jablonski, Louise *Lebrun, Lois *Marshall, Allan *Monk, Sandra *Munn, Igor Oistrakh, Albert *Pratz, Jan *Rubeš, Janos Starker, Steven *Staryk, Henryk Szeryng, Bernard *Turgeon, Ronald *Turini, and George *Zukerman.

Among works commissioned by the orchestra are Richard *Johnston's *Portraits* (1972, premiered 29 Jan 1973) and Harry *Freedman's *Nocturne No. 2* (1975, premiered 24 Apr 1977). Other Canadian works performed by the orchestra include 1958–9, *Champagne's *Paysanna;* 1963, Leonard *Leacock's *The Lonely Lake;* 1974–5, *Pentland's *Ave atque vale* and *Eckhardt-Gramatté's *Capriccio Concertante;* 1975–6, *Pépin's *Rite du soleil noir;* 1976–7, *Ridout's *Frivolités canadiennes*, *Archer's *Sinfonia*, *Applebaum's *Place Setting*, and Champagne's *Hercule et Omphale;* and 1977–8, *Kenins' *Violin Concerto*, *Somers' *Five Songs for Dark Voice*, *Mercure's *Triptyque*, and *Weinzweig's *Divertimento No. 1*.

The orchestra has been managed by Mrs E.R. Deutsch 1960–3, Mrs John R. McKay in 1963, Max L. Malden 1966–70, N.N. Herrington 1970–2, Kurt Trachsel 1972–7, and Alan Graham 1977–9, succeeded by John Shaw.

BIBLIOGRAPHY

'Calgary Philharmonic on the map,' *CanComp*, 53, Oct 1970

Musselwhite, Bill. 'The philharmonic (in one form or another) has been around since 1928,' Calgary *Herald Magazine*, 12 Mar 1971

The Calgary Philharmonic History, souvenir program (Calgary 1975)

Edds, Jack. 'Calgary's indomitable link with our eastern cities: the Symphony Orchestra,' *OCan*, vol 4, May 1977 (RDM)

Calgary Symphony Orchestra. The name of four organizations in Calgary. The first was formed in 1910 to accompany the Apollo Choir led by P.L. Newcombe and was directed in public concerts by a local violinist, A.P. Howells. Its success led to the formation of a second Calgary SO in 1912 with Max *Weil as conductor. This orchestra made its debut 27 Jan 1913 at the Sherman Grand Theatre before more than 700 people in a program which included the overture to Mozart's *The Magic Flute* and other works for orchestra and/or choir by Wagner, Tchaikovsky, Dvořák, and Elgar. Under Weil the orchestra numbered 55 musicians (amateur and professional, including 12 US players) and according to the *Canadian Courier*, 13 Dec 1913, brought to Calgary the distinction of being 'the only city in Canada outside Toronto which supports a professional symphony orchestra.' (The term 'professional' may be an exaggeration in this context. See discussion in Orchestras.) This Calgary SO was one of the first orchestras in Canada to give concerts for school children. By 1914, however, enthusiasm had waned, financial problems beset the organization, and at the outbreak of World War I the orchestra was disbanded. A third Calgary SO was formed in 1928, under the auspices of the Calgary Choral and Orchestral Society, by Colonel John Drummond, with Gregori *Garbovitsky as conductor. At first comprising only 50 musicians, it grew to 75 and gave many public concerts and a series of CBC broadcasts. It also appeared in outdoor concerts at Banff. This third Calgary SO was disbanded in 1939 because of the outbreak of World War II. In 1949, by which time the orchestra still had not been revived, the directors were invited to transfer its charter, funds, musical instruments, and library to the *Mount Royal College SO, an orchestra of young adults which had grown out of the college's pre-war 'Baby Symphony,' with Clayton *Hare as its conductor. The transfer was effected and the new organization was chartered as the Calgary SO in 1949. Under the direction of Hare it continued until 1955, when it amalgamated with the Alberta Philharmonic as the *Calgary Philharmonic Orchestra.

Calgary Women's Musical Club. Formed in 1904 to provide Calgary women with the opportunity to hear music on a regular basis. Mrs Scott Dawson was the first president, and concerts were given by local performers. Though interest flagged and the club ceased functioning, it was revived in 1912 by Mrs H.E. Anderson, who also served as president. This second club arranged concerts by local and internationally known artists. The first concert was held 5 May 1913 at Unity Hall and subsequent concerts at Nolan's Hall, the Isis Theatre, and halls in various schools, churches, and hotels. Mrs. H.H. Sharples, the local RSM representative, who became president of the club in 1916, was responsible for beginning a September-to-June concert series. In 1921 she organized a concert of music by local composers; such events became annual and continued for over 25 years under her direction. Among the composers were Jeanne Ackland, Clifford Higgin, Minuetta *Kessler, Leonard *Leacock, and Robert Spergel. Mrs Sharples was instrumental also in the establishment of a student scholarship fund (financed in the early 1920s by the receipts from club-sponsored recitals by such artists as Amelita Galli-Curci).

Other club members of note were Beatrice Chapman, Elaine Dudley Smith, and Mrs W. Roland Winter. After World War II the club concentrated on the presentation of Canadian performers, including Maureen *Forrester, Glenn *Gould, Lois *Marshall, and Jon *Vickers. In 1964, however, faced with declining interest and rising costs, it transferred its assets to the scholarship fund of the Kiwanis Music Festival and discontinued its activities.

BIBLIOGRAPHY

'The Women's Musical Club,' Calgary *Herald*, 10 Sep 1938 (FM)

CALVERT, Morley. Bandmaster, conductor, composer, b Brantford, Ont, 11 Jun 1928; LRSM 1948, A MUS (McGill) 1950, B MUS (McGill) 1956. He taught instrumentalists and choirs 1950–72 in Montreal high schools and was director 1954–6 of the Imperial Singers and 1960–70 of the Montreal Citadel Band of the *Salvation Army. He also founded and was the director 1960–70 of the *McGill U Concert Band and 1967–72 of the Lakeshore Concert Band. In 1958 at Ayers Cliff, Que, he founded the Monteregian Music Camp, which offered summer training for high school students. He remained active in this project until its end in 1970. In 1972 he became the conductor of the *Barrie Central Collegiate Band. Calvert has composed and arranged many works for band (some for the Salvation Army) and a few for brass quintet and for choir. His *Suite from the Monteregian Hills* (1961, self-published 1962, based on French-Canadian folksongs and named for the eight mountains which range in an arc from Mount Royal to the American border) was commissioned by the Montreal Brass Quintet. It has been performed in London and Paris and recorded (Boot BMC-3001) by *Canadian Brass. It also has been recorded by the Vancouver Brass Quintet (1973, CBC SM-252) and, in the USA, by the Baldwin-Wallace Quintet, the New England Brass Quintet, and the United States Army Band Brass Quintet. *An Occasional Suite*, a centennial commission, was premiered at *Expo 67 by the Montreal Brass Quintet and published in 1967 by BMIC. *Romantic Variations* (1976) was commissioned and privately recorded by the Youth Band of Ontario. Calvert served 1959–61 as president of the *QMEA. He is a member of CAPAC. NM

Camerata. Chamber ensemble formed in Toronto in 1972 by the pianists Elyakim *Taussig and Katherine Root, the flutist Suzanne *Shulman, the clarinetist James *Campbell, the cellist Coenraad Bloemendal, the violinist Adele *Armin, and the violist Paul *Armin. (The Armins later left the group.) Camerata covers a wide area of the chamber music repertoire, adding or subtracting players and inviting guest players as needed. It has appeared often at *St Lawrence Centre and Casa Loma, Toronto, at the *Shaw and *Stratford Festivals, the *Guelph Spring Festival and the *Algoma Fall Festival, at the Orford and CBC Summer Music Festivals, and at *Festival Ottawa. Camerata has devised special 'concert theatre' presentations, eg, *Soirée-musicale* (the re-creation of a 19th-century salon concert) and, for children, versions of Oscar Wilde's story *The Canterville Ghost* and Prokofiev's *Peter and the Wolf*, and an amalgam of Saint-Saëns, Rimsky-Korsakov, Prokofiev, and a stage gorilla, entitled *Camerata Zoo*. These have been featured at the Shaw Festival, the Art Gallery of Ontario, the *PDA (during the 1976 Olympics), and the *NAC. Camerata specializes also in chamber music workshops. Classes for young musicians often are co-ordinated with its playing engagements, particularly during its 'residences' at the Shaw, Algoma, and Orford festivals and its visits to Canadian colleges and universities.

Camerata toured Cuba, Mexico, and Venezuela in 1976 and made its first European tour in 1977, performing in England at the Harrogate Festival in Yorkshire and the Three Choirs Festival in Gloucester, and in London. On the continent it gave concerts in Rumania and in Paris. During the tour it was heard on Dutch, French and British radio. The group has toured Canada, performing in British Columbia in 1977 and 1979, Newfoundland in 1978, and the Yukon, Alberta, Saskatchewan, and Manitoba in 1979.

Mary Lou *Fallis, Maureen *Forrester, Fujiko Imajishi, Moe *Koffman's jazz quartet, Victor Martin, and others have made guest appearances with Camerata. Members of the group have appeared with Glenn *Gould on his CBC TV program 'Music for Our Time.'

DISCOGRAPHY

Beethoven *Trio, Op 11* – Martinu *Madrigal Sonata* – Mozart *Trio* K548 – Baker *Capriccio for Two Pianos*. A. Armin, Bloemendal, Campbell, Shulman, Root, Taussig. 1974. CBC SM-278

Schoenberg *Kammersymphonie, Op 9* – J. Strauss (arr Schoenberg) *Emperor Waltz* – Berg *Adagio from the Chamber Concerto*. 1975. CBC SM-313

Camerata Canada: Fanny Mendelssohn *Trio, Op 11* – Saint-Saëns *Tarantella, Op 6* – Paganini (arr Taussig) *Paganiniana*. Bloemendal, Campbell, V. Martin, Shulman, Root, Taussig. 1977. Crystal S642

Camerata members: (left to right) James Campbell, Adele Armin, Kathryn Root, Elyakim Taussig, Suzanne Shulman, Coenraad Bloemendal

CAMERON, Dan (Daniel) **A.** Teacher, journalist, choirmaster, b Ottawa, of Scottish parents, 7 Aug 1880, d Regina 13 Nov 1963. Although his childhood was spent in Winnipeg he studied in New York with Herbert Witherspoon, Oscar Saenger, and others, began singing in Ottawa church choirs in 1919, and first taught voice at Albert College, Belleville, Ont. He was head of the voice department 1923–39 and director 1939–51 of the *Regina Cons. Under the pseudonyms Simon the Jester and Alan Brandt he wrote music and world affairs columns for the Regina *Leader-Post* 1923–54, and on his retirement from the conservatory in 1954 became a full-time editorial writer and music columnist. He was music director at Knox-Metropolitan Church, Regina, for over 25 years, conducted the Regina Bach Ladies' Choir, and founded and conducted 1926–46 the *Regina Male Voice Choir. Appointed the Saskatchewan director of the *WBM in 1951, he was also a member of the Regina Music Festivals Board, a founder of the Regina Music Teachers' Assn (later *SRMTA), and president 1951–3 of *CFMTA and editor 1946–53 of its news bulletin. (DSr)

CAMERON, John Allan. Singer, guitarist, fiddler, b Inverness, Cape Breton, NS, 16 Dec 1938; BA (St Francis Xavier) 1966, B ED (Dalhousie) 1967. His uncle, Dan R. (Rory) MacDonald, was a prolific composer of fiddle music in the Cape Breton tradition. His mother and brother (John Donald Cameron) are fiddlers, and at 12 he began playing guitar accompaniments for his brother at local dances. He studied 1957–63 for the priesthood with the Order of the Oblate Fathers in Ottawa. Though he took his final vows he received papal dispensation in 1964 to become a performer. While studying subsequently at St Francis Xavier U he performed on CJFX radio, Antigonish, NS. A performer on CBC Halifax TV ('Singalong Jubilee,' summer 1967), he has appeared also on other country and pop music TV programs and starred 1975–6 on his own CTV show and in 1979 on a CBC summer series. He was host in 1976 for the CBC's telecast of the *Juno Awards ceremonies. He has performed at the *Mariposa, Newport, and Atlantic folk festivals, at the Grand Ole Opry (Nashville), in coffeehouses in various Canadian centres, and with Tommy Makem and Anne *Murray in concert and on TV. He also toured with Makem in Ireland. Cameron's repertoire includes Cape Breton fiddle tunes and 'mouth music,' Scottish and Irish folk songs and stories, bagpipe music adapted for 12-string guitar, and songs by Bruce *Cockburn, Bob *Ruzicka, and others. Cameron made two LPs for Apex in 1967, three for Columbia 1971–6, and one, *Freeborn Man*, for his own Glencoe label in 1979. The Cape Breton Symphony – the fiddlers John Donald Cameron, Winston 'Scotty' *Fitzgerald, and Wilfred Gillis and the pianist-accordionist Bobby Brown – began in 1975 to accompany Cameron frequently and in 1978 recorded the LP *Fiddle* for Glencoe. With the group, Cameron made his second visit to Ireland in 1978. He is an affiliate of PRO Canada.

BIBLIOGRAPHY

LeBlanc, Larry. 'Folk purism not for John Allan Cameron,' *MSc*, 274, Nov–Dec 1973

Howell, Bill. 'The thinkin' man's Stompin' Tom,' *Maclean's*, Dec 1973

Brown, Dick. 'For the love of it,' *Canadian Magazine*, 20 May 1976

FILMOGRAPHY

Celtic Spirits (NFB 1978) (RGn)

CAMILLERI, Charles (Mario). Composer, accordionist, b Hanrun, Malta, 7 Sep 1931; B MUS (Toronto) 1965, hon FRHCM 1978. He resided 1959–65 in Toronto after working for the Maltese, Australian, and British broadcasting systems and composing for British films and London West End musicals. In Toronto he taught (Joe *Macerollo was a pupil) and played the accordion in nightclubs and on CBC radio's 'Camilleri and Company' (1961–2) and 'Variety Showcase.' He studied 1961–5 at the *U of Toronto with John *Weinzweig, who introduced him to the 12-tone technique (which, however, remained only an influence, not a strict method, in his work). His style usually has been described as agreeably eclectic rather than doctrinaire or avant garde. Compositions premiered in Toronto (by the *CBC SO, the Toronto Chamber Orchestra, the Toronto Repertory Ensemble, etc) include *The Silent Giant – A Canadian Portrait* (1962), *Six Biblical Dances* (1962), *Rhapsody for Violin and String Orchestra* (1963), *Concerto for Accordion and Strings* (1963), *Concertante for Violin and String Orchestra* (1964), *Fantasy Fugue for Strings* (1964), *Quintessa* (1966), *Fantasia Concertante No. 5* (1977, Ramsey / Roberton 1978, a work for solo guitar which won the *Guitar Society of Toronto Prize in 1977), and *Rite of Wild Dawn* (ca 1978). He also composed a *Missa brevis* (1971, Roberton 1975). Camilleri returned to Malta in 1965, then became a visiting lecturer at universities in Great Britain and the USA. In 1975 he gave a course in 'word music' at the RCMT Summer School and in 1977 he became music consultant for the *RHCM and resumed Canadian residence. In 1979 he moved to England. Camilleri is an associate of the *CMCentre.

BIBLIOGRAPHY

Palmer, Christopher. *The Music of Charles Camilleri* (Malta 1975) MH

CAMMAC (Canadian Amateur Musicians / Musiciens amateurs du Canada). Non-profit organization founded in Montreal in 1953 by the brothers Georges and Carl *Little and their wives, Madeleine and Frances, with the aim of encouraging amateur musicians at all levels. First established as a summer camp, accessible to all without distinction of age, sex, or musical competence, it was called the Otter Lake Music Centre (Centre musical du Lac-à-la-Loutre) and was situated at Huberdeau in Argenteuil county to the northwest of Montreal. During the last two weeks of August about 20 participants took courses in solfège, choral music, and recorder with Carl and Georges Little, Mario *Duschenes, and Ruth Blanchard. At the end of the week a mini-festival of three concerts by professional musicians was later added to the program of studies. In 1959 Canada's first conference of amateur musicians was held at the Otter Lake centre.

In 1961 an amendment to the charter obtained from the Quebec government in 1954 conferred the name CAMMAC on the organization. In 1957 a special program was added for children from 4 to 12 in order to allow entire families to make music together (a feature uncommon, if not unique, in North America). In response to the wishes of the participants, winter courses were begun in Montreal, and regional committees were established. In a short time a veritable 'people's conservatory' of some 400 students emerged. With the development of 'continuing education' and leisure programs by the education authorities in Quebec, CAMMAC courses were abandoned in 1975. However, the regional committees continued to function effectively, those of Montreal, Toronto, and Ottawa being particularly active.

In February 1959, the periodical *CAMMAC* was launched. Mimeographed at first, it appeared 1964–9 as a printed quarterly titled *Musicien amateur / Amateur Musician*. With Madeleine Little as its editor it offered news, editorials, and articles by professional and amateur musicians, an international column, and unpublished works by Canadian composers. In 1966 5000 copies of a special issue on music education were printed. Georges Little helped found the CAMMAC music library in 1959 by donating his personal collection of choral music. The library of the defunct *Little Symphony of Montreal, another contribution, is located at the national office in Montreal. The CAMMAC library is operated on the general principles of the Drinker (choral) Library in the Free Library of Philadelphia, and its lending service is open to all Canadian members of CAMMAC. A catalogue and supplements are issued. During the winter season, depending on the wishes of its members, CAMMAC organizes readings of cantatas and other choral works under the direction of guest conductors. The acquisition in 1968 of the splendid Domaine des Bouleaux on Lake MacDonald, some 50 kilometers northwest of Montreal, has made it possible to accommodate larger numbers of participants. In 1974 the summer session was extended to seven weeks, and there were 350 participants, 28 teachers, 22 different courses, and seven public concerts. Besides accommodating the regular activities, the centre is available for rental by various member groups, choirs, orchestras, etc. In 1978 a nine-day summer program, along the lines of that at Lake MacDonald, was initiated in Ontario at the Rousseau Lake School for Boys in the Muskoka region, north of Toronto between Parry Sound and Huntsville.

CAMMAC has been subsidized from the outset by the *MACQ and the ministère de l'Éducation du Québec. Later the *Canada Council and the *OAC also contributed. From 1962 to 1968, in collaboration with the Goethe-Institute, CAMMAC invited German string quartets for four-week residencies at the MacDonald Lake camp. In 1972 a special subsidy from the secretary of state made it possible for some 30 French-speaking Canadians from outside Quebec to take part for 15 days in the camp's activities. This feature became annual and was still in effect in 1980.

Through its public concerts CAMMAC has assisted the early careers of artists who later have achieved fame, including Maureen *Forrester, Frans *Brouw, and Louis *Quilico. The *Montreal Bach Choir, directed by Georges Little, for several years gave its services free of charge. Among the professional musicians who have participated in CAMMAC activities as teachers or performers have been Jan *Simons (appointed director in 1969), Walter and Otto *Joachim, Hyman *Bress, Bernard and Mireille *Lagacé, John *Newmark, R. Murray *Schafer, and John W. Taber.

BIBLIOGRAPHY

Howe, Margaret. 'Otter Lake music camp,' *Recorder*, vol 3, Oct 1960
Little, Madeleine. 'CAMMAC,' *MSc*, 239, Jan–Feb 1968
Thompson, Ilse M. 'The CAMMAC approach to music education,' *CME*, vol 16, Fall 1974
'Les amateurs de musique du lac MacDonald,' *Musique Périodique*, vol 1, Oct 1977
Cohen, Judy. 'Teaching folklore at CAMMAC,' *Canada Folk Bulletin*, vol 2, May–Jun 1979

FILMOGRAPHY

Harmonie (NFB 1977) (MB-L)

Cammie Howard and His Western Five. See Howard.

CAMPBELL, Anne (b Cowie). Choir conductor, b Sutherland, near Saskatoon, 16 Jun 1912; ATCM piano 1930, L MUS (Saskatchewan) 1932, ATCM voice 1934. A pupil of Lyell *Gustin (piano) and Elizabeth *Morrison (voice) in Saskatoon, she studied further with Ernesto *Vinci at the *Banff SFA in 1950 and with Filmer *Hubble in 1951. She began training choirs at 14 in Sutherland. From her youth choir, formed in 1943 in Lethbridge, Alta, she developed the Teen-Clefs in 1963 and the Anne Campbell Singers in 1968, winners of the George S. Mathieson Trophy in 1968 and 1970 respectively. The Anne Campbell Singers appeared at *Expo 67, the Dominion Music Festival, Saint John, NB, in 1967, and Expo 70 in Osaka. They toured Great Britain, Germany, and Holland, winning firsts in competition at the Tees-Side Eisteddfod in 1968 and at the Llangollen International Festival in 1972. The record *The Anne Campbell Singers* (1973, CBC SM 230) draws on folk and popular songs, hymns, and Lieder. The group has recorded as well for Westmount, Souvenir Sounds, Sound Box Records, and Big Chief Records. In 1977 Anne Campbell became an Officer of the *Order of Canada. (RDM)

CAMPBELL, James (Kenneth). Clarinetist, b Leduc, near Edmonton, 10 Aug 1949; B MUS (Toronto) 1971. He studied at the Music Academy of the West, Santa Barbara, Cal, and in Paris 1971–3 with Yona Ettlinger. A semi-finalist in the Budapest International Clarinet Competition in 1970, he also won the *CBC Talent Festival and the JM International Clarinet Competition in Yugoslavia in 1971. He has been a member 1967–9 of the *Hamilton Philharmonic and, in 1968 and 1969, of the *NYO; has toured as a soloist in Canada, the USA, and, in 1972, in Yugoslavia; has performed on BBC and CBC radio; and has appeared with Glenn *Gould on CBC TV. In 1972 he represented Canada at the 26th Congress of the International Federation of JM at Augsberg. With his partner for that occasion, the English pianist John York, he later made three recordings. He was a founding member of *Camerata that same year and of the Arioso Trio in 1976. He played Copland's *Clarinet Concerto* with the *TS under the direction of the composer 16 and 17 May 1978, and again 10 Aug 1979.

DISCOGRAPHY

Archer *Sonata*. Brough pf. 1974. RCI 412
Debussy – Saint-Saëns – Freedman *Lines* – Symonds *Quintet* for clarinet and synthesizers. York pf, Canadian Electronic Ensemble. 1978. RCI 484
Poulenc – Mather – Lutoslawski. Cavanagh pf. 1972. CBC SM-184
Schumann – Berg – Vaughan Williams – Poulenc – Jeanjean. York pf. 1974. Crystal S331
Weber – Lefèvre – Martinu – Wellesz – Arnold. York pf. 1977. Crystal S333

BIBLIOGRAPHY

Kraglund, John. 'Busy time ahead for clarinetist Campbell,' Toronto *Globe and Mail*, 8 Aug 1979

CAMPBELL, Kenneth. Arranger, composer, conductor, b Port Arthur (Thunder Bay), Ont, 1922. He was a clarinetist and arranger with the *Princess Patricia's Canadian Light Infantry Band during World War II. After the war he worked in Toronto as an arranger for Ellis *McLintock and Bert *Niosi, and for radio and later TV. In Ottawa he was staff arranger for the RCAF Central Band during the 1960s and wrote scores for a number of *NFB films, including *Blades and Brass* (1966) and *Flight in White* (1968) and arrangements for his 16-piece dance band, which broadcast locally over the CBC. During the late 1960s and early 1970s he lived in England, where he composed for the BBC and arranged for the Scots Guard Band. He returned in the 1970s to Ottawa and continued to freelance. Among Campbell's compositions are *Capital City Suite* (G.V. Thompson 1962) and *Puppet Parade* (G.V. Thompson 1963). He has composed and arranged for the *Orpheus Operatic Society of Ottawa, the NORAD Band, and the comedian Rich Little and for official Ottawa functions, including the 1967 centennial celebrations on Parliament Hill. Two of his works, *River by Night* and *Confusion Square*, have been recorded by Howard *Cable's Concert Band (RCA PCS 1004). He is a member of CAPAC.

BIBLIOGRAPHY

Thistle, Lauretta. ' "Adaptable" is probably the best word to describe Ken Campbell, Ottawa composer and arranger,' *CanComp*, 46, Jan 1970 (FH)

CAMPBELL, Norman (Kenneth). Producer, composer, b Los Angeles, of Canadian parents, 4 Feb 1924; BA mathematics and physics (British Columbia) 1944. He joined CBC Vancouver as a radio producer in 1948, moving to Toronto in 1952 to produce some of the first CBC telecasts. His reputation was built as a producer of ballet for TV, notably with the National Ballet of Canada, beginning with *Swan Lake* 12 Dec 1956. He received the Prix René Barthélemy in 1966 for *Romeo and Juliet* and Emmy awards in 1970 for *Cinderella* and in 1972 for *The Sleeping Beauty*. His other CBC TV productions have included the Royal Winnipeg Ballet's *The Nutcracker* (1975), the National Ballet's *Giselle* (1976), and the music specials 'Percy *Faith: Off the Record' (1966), 'Robert *Farnon' (1970), and 'Music East, Music West – The Toronto Symphony in China' (1978). For the exchange programs of CBC, BBC, and NET he has produced the operas *Hansel and Gretel* (1970) and Puccini's *La Rondine* (1972). In 1963 for the *Stratford Festival he directed a production of *The Mikado* which later was telecast on CBC's 'Festival.' He composed music for the CBC musical comedies *Take to the Woods* (1955), *The Gay Deceivers* (1958), and *The Wonder of It All* (1972). His CBC TV musical *Anne of Green Gables* (1956) was adapted for a stage production (1965) at the *Charlottetown Festival and became an annual presentation there. It also has been produced frequently in the USA and England. Campbell was made a member of the Royal Canadian Academy in 1975 and an Officer of the *Order of Canada in 1979.

WRITINGS

'Scrambled scores, solid sets and sandpaper soles,' *OpCan*, 65, Dec 1975
'Conquering China,' *The Canadian*, 30 Sep 1978

BIBLIOGRAPHY
'Norman Campbell and television,' *OpCan*, Fall 1972
'Notes on a career in musicals and television,' *CanComp*, 89, Mar 1974
Batten, Jack. 'Cool hand Campbell,' *The Canadian*, 30 Sep 1978

CAMPBELL, Wishart. Baritone, songwriter, b Oro Station, near Lake Simcoe, Ont, ca 1905; ATCM voice 1927. A church organist, then movie-house and dance-band pianist in his youth, Campbell became a school principal in Haliburton and Galt, Ont, before studying voice at the *TCM. After his radio debut in 1927 on CKGW, Toronto, he sang 1928–32 on the CNR network from Jasper Park, Alta, apparently the first singer to be heard from coast-to-coast in Canada. He also appeared in 1930 on the CNR's 'All-Canada Symphony Hour' under Luigi von *Kunits, sang as a church soloist in Ontario, and performed on many of Toronto's commercial radio stations. Known as 'The Golden Voice of the Air' he joined the CRBC in Toronto as a staff artist in 1933, then sang 1938–42 on CBC and CFRB after a brief period in New York. During World War II he performed in the *RCAF Blackouts. His composition 'The Airman's Prayer,' with words by G.L. Creed, was adopted as a hymn by the RCAF. Campbell was music director 1945–60 for CFRB, then retired to private business in the Hebrides. He made singles for the Gavotte label in the 1950s and an album of his own songs, *A Campbell Comes Home*, for RCA in 1960. (EMB)

Campbell Free Band Concerts / Concerts Campbell. Annual summer series begun in 1924 in Montreal parks (Lafontaine, Jarry, Jeanne-Mance, etc) and public squares (eg, Dominion) 'to encourage bands to play on summer evenings ... in public places handy to overcrowded parts of the city.' The concerts were established with a bequest of $230,000 by Kingston-born corporation lawyer Charles S. Campbell (1858–1923). Numerous Montreal-based bands such as the *Canadian Grenadier Guards, the Victoria Rifles, the Fusiliers Mont-Royal, the *Salvation Army, the Black Watch, the Harmonie Métropole, and the Royal Montreal Regiment have appeared in an estimated 4000 concerts since the inception of the series, which is to be perpetuated. As a tribute to the philanthropist, the Montreal composer Maurice *Zbriger has written *Campbell Memorial March* and *Campbell 50th Anniversary Overture*. In 1970 the program began to include popular, folk, and ethnic entertainment.

BIBLIOGRAPHY
Moore, Brian. 'Campbell bands play on,' *Montreal Scene*, 9–15 Aug 1975 GP

CAMPLIN, Leonard. Bandmaster, conductor, oboist, b London 16 Aug 1928. He attended the RMSM (Kneller Hall) and upon graduation became bandmaster (1955–9) of the North Staffordshire Regiment. He moved in 1959 to Canada as music supervisor in the Sturgis School Unit, Saskatchewan. While music consultant to the *SAB and an examiner for the *WBM he adjudicated at several festivals in Alberta and British Columbia. He was principal oboe 1959–61 of the *Regina SO. He joined the Canadian armed forces in 1961 and has been music director 1961–8 of the Royal Canadian Engineers Band and 1968–70 of the Canadian Forces Naden Band, Victoria, BC, musical training officer 1970–2 of the *Canadian Forces School of Music, Victoria, BC, and music director 1972–8 of the *Princess Patricia's Canadian Light Infantry Band, Calgary. In 1979 he was appointed music director for Militia Area Pacific, representing all militia bands in British Columbia and co-ordinating their performances. He became music director and conductor of the Okanagan SO in 1964 (a position he continued to fill in 1980) and also conducted the Vancouver Metropolitan Orchestra 1967–72, the New Westminster Orchestra 1964–5, and the Calgary Promenade SO 1972–4. He is the conductor on the recording *A Salute to the Royal Canadian Engineers Band* (private 1968). (JK)

Camps. See Summer camps and schools.

'CA-NA-DA.' A centennial song by Bobby *Gimby. Composed with French and English text as a children's marching-song for a CBC TV documentary, 'Preview '67,' it was adopted by Canada's Centennial Commission as a theme song for the centenary. A recording by the Young Canada Singers (Quality SE 1967), two groups of ten-year-old children, one conducted in Montreal by Raymond Berthiaume and the other in Toronto by Laurie *Bower, became the most popular Canadian single of 1967. Recordings also were made by Jim *McHarg, the *Sugar Shoppe, and others. Published in 1967 by G.V. *Thompson, by 1976 'CA-NA-DA' had been recorded by over 75 artists, including the composer, and had sold over 75,000 copies of sheet music. Rights to the song were given by the composer to the Boy Scouts of Canada in January 1971.

Canada Baroque Records Ltd. Recording company established in Montreal in 1962 by Giveon (Jim) Cornfield (b Montreal ca 1926), who studied musicology in Israel before returning to Montreal in 1952. His intent was to establish a balance between the surfeit of recorded versions of well-known masterworks and the virtual absence of recordings of interesting works by little-known composers. His initial capital of $5000 was used to produce five LPs with a total run of 2000 copies. It took the company two years to break even. However, in 1965 sales of 4500 discs pressed in Canada and 70,000 pressed in the USA and abroad brought in $160,000. In 1966, of 92 LPs in the Baroque catalogue, 52 offered works not to be found on other North American labels. Some 14 new LPs of music by such little-known composers as Johann Gottfried Walther and Friedrich Kuhlau were issued in August 1966. At the end of the 1960s Baroque was taken over by the US-based Everest group, and about 1973 the label expired.

The technical quality of the recordings and the diversity of the repertoire account for the continued demand around the world. Among the Canadian musicians who recorded for the Baroque label are Lise *Boucher, Hyman *Bress, Alexander *Brott with the Soviet Radio Orchestra, Mario *Duschenes, Kenneth *Gilbert, Charles *Houdret, Gilles *Manny, Monique Marcil, the *McGill Chamber Orchestra (with Jean-Pierre Rampal as soloist), Steven *Staryk, Marie-Aimée *Varro, and Jacques Verdon. Works by Canadian composers – Brott, *Papineau-Couture, and *Prévost – also were recorded.

Cornfield was music director for radio station CKVL-FM before emigrating to Los Angeles in the early 1970s. For the Everest Record Group he reissued certain items from the Baroque catalogue under the Orion label. ST

The Canada Council / Conseil des arts du Canada. A crown corporation constituted 28 Mar 1957 by an act of the federal government, its principal task being 'to encourage and support the arts, humanities and social sciences' in Canada. It was designed to provide artists and cultural organizations with a wide range of subsidies and services, to supply administrative services to the Canadian Committee for Unesco, and to play a role in the dissemination of Canadian culture abroad. Headquarters were established in Ottawa.

The origin of the council may be traced back to the period following the end of World War II, when a volunteer organization, the Canadian Arts Council, consisting of personalities from the artistic world, patrons of the arts, and cultural groups, came into being. This council sought the creation of a royal commission into the development of arts, literature, and science, and such a commission in fact was established by the Canadian government in 1949 under the chairmanship of Vincent Massey. It was called the Royal Commission of Inquiry into the Advancement of the Arts, Literature and Science in Canada (*Massey Commission). Its report, submitted in 1951, recommended that a state-supported arts council be formed. (In 1958 the aforementioned Canadian Arts Council, an advisory and investigative body, took the name *Canadian Conference of the Arts, not to be confused with the Canada Council that was created in 1957 in response to the Massey Commission's report and that is the subject of this article.)

The Canada Council as it exists at the time of this writing (1980) is governed by a 21-member board of directors appointed by the government of Canada, and its decisions are implemented by a staff headed by a director and an associate director. The board and its staff work in close liaison with the Advisory Arts Panel and with representatives from diverse cultural milieus. The latter are consulted either individually or as members of juries and selection committees. In addition, the council is in close contact with federal and provincial cultural organizations and with the Bureau of International Cultural Relations of the Dept of External Affairs. Within the terms of reference laid down by the act, the council as a crown corporation is free to set its own guidelines, independent of government, and to act autonomously. It does, however, give account of its activities to Parliament through the Minister of Communications and report periodically to the House of Commons' Standing Committee on Broadcasting, Films and Assistance to the Arts.

Financially the council relies mainly on subsidies voted each year by Parliament. To these are added revenues from an endowment fund of $50 million, voted by Parliament in 1957, as well as various gifts and legacies issuing from the private sector and reserved, in most cases, for specific purposes.

The Arts Division provides several specific programs and services – in visual arts (including film and television), literature, publishing and translation, dance, music and opera, and theatre – besides the more general Explorations and Killam programs, the Arts Awards Service, and the Touring Office.

In the fiscal year 1978–9, from a total amount of some $42.5 million allotted in subsidies and arts programs, music and opera received $10,444,000. This sum was divided as follows: orchestras, 40 per cent; opera, 19 per cent; bursaries, 12 per cent; Touring Office, 7 per cent; chamber music, 5 per cent; youth programs, 5 per cent; support groups, 5 per cent; choirs, 4 per cent and miscellaneous, 3 per cent.

The council grants subsidies to institutions and professional groups such as orchestras, opera companies, instrumental and vocal ensembles, schools, and associations. It assists amateur choirs by giving them subsidies to pay for the services of professional instrumentalists, conductors, soloists for special concerts, and workshop leaders. Grants are available also to artists or companies for the commissioning of works from Canadian composers, to cover composition fees and copying costs. The publishing of Canadian music is encouraged through subsidies to publishing firms established in Canada or with a majority Canadian participation, to cover part of the publishing costs. Canadian record companies may receive subsidies to issue performances of works by Canadian composers. The council allocates monies to cultural or community centres, municipalities, music festivals, schools, or conservatories, as part of a program to enable them to engage professional musicians and organizers to assist with their activities. Subsidies are given to groups and professional organizations to cover travel expenses incurred by their members for the purpose of consultation and exchange of views. In the 1978–9 fiscal year the council provided individual artists with five categories of grants: senior arts grants or arts grants 'A,' to a maximum of $17,000, intended for artists well on in their careers; arts grants 'B,' up to $10,000, available to those whose basic training has been completed or who are considered professional; short-term grants offered to professionals to allow them to devote themselves to specific projects for a maximum of three months; project cost grants; and travel grants. All requests for grants are examined by juries separate from the council and then are submitted for its approval.

Other programs have been concerned with visits to Canada by foreign artists and the allocation of studios at the Cité international des arts in Paris. The Explorations program was set up to finance original projects of a cultural nature. The purpose of the Killam grants is to enable outstanding researchers to undertake large-scale scholarly projects. In 1978–9 the Humanities and Social Sciences division was replaced by a new Social Sciences and Humanities Council responsible for the allocation of grants in areas such as musicology.

The Canada Council Touring Office was created in 1973 to assist in making the performing arts accessible to the greatest number of Canadians and to help artists and groups to perform widely. The office has collaborated in strengthening the support structure of tours by offering specialized services to tour organizers and promoters, and to localities. It has published an annual (after 1978–9, biennial) *Touring Directory of the Performing Arts in Canada*, as well as a quarterly *Bulletin*. In 1978–9 the office allocated 19 per cent of its estimated $2,446,100 to music, including the agency Concerts Canada, which provided career management 1973–6 for a group of young Canadian performing artists. After that time it turned its assistance towards the financing of a program of encouragement for Canadian agents and impresarios. The council has worked in co-operation with the *CBC National Radio Competition for Young Composers and the CBC / Canada Council National Radio Competition for Amateur Choirs, and has conferred the *Canada Council Medal (integrated in 1968 with the *Molson Prizes).

Chairmen of the council have been Brooke Claxton 1957–60, Claude Bissell 1960–2, Douglas B. Weldon 1962–4, Jean Martineau 1964–9, John G. Prentice 1969–74, Brian Flemming (interim) 1974–5, and Gertrude M. Laing 1975–8, succeeded by Mavor *Moore. Directors have been Albert W. Trueman 1957–65, Jean Boucher 1965–9, Peter M. Dwyer 1969–71, Robert Élie (interim) 1971–2, and André Fortier 1972–5, succeeded by Charles A. Lussier. Associate directors have been Eugène Bussière 1957–65, Dwyer 1965–9, and Élie 1969–72, succeeded by Timothy Porteous. Dwyer was responsible for music during his term 1957–65 as director of the Arts Division. The post of head of music services, created in 1966, was held by Gilles *Potvin in 1966, Guy *Huot 1966–73, and Hugh *Davidson 1973–8, succeeded by Franz *Kraemer. The first general manager of the Touring Office, John Cripton, was followed briefly in 1980 by Jean-Claude l'Espérance, and Hugh Davidson assumed the post in 1981. Among those who have represented music on the council are Murray *Adaskin 1966–9, Andrée *Desautels 1967–70, Nicholas *Goldschmidt, appointed in 1980, Raoul *Jobin 1961–4, Luc *Lacourcière 1962–5, Annette *Lasalle-Leduc 1964–7, Howard *Leyton-Brown 1971–4, Sir Ernest *MacMillan 1957–63, Eric *McLean 1970–7, Élise Paré-Tousignant, appointed in 1978, Vida *Peene 1957–61, and Ignatius *Rumboldt 1965–8.

Over the years, the policies of the Canada Council often have been subject to criticism and discussion in the public forum and in the media. Considering the relatively limited funds at its disposal, pressure groups have questioned and have continued to question the criteria governing the allocation of grants to individuals or subsidies to organizations. Some have reproached the council, claiming that it has encouraged the arts only at the highest professional level, that it has practised a certain elitism, and that it has not been sufficiently interested in artistic activity at the regional level and among the masses. Others have defended the council on its record, pointing to the extraordinary stimulus it has provided, manifest in the vast increase in the products and activities of all the arts since its creation in 1957. In 1980 the debate was far from over; indeed, it continued to play a useful role in the evolution and continual revaluation of the principles of state support of the arts in a democratic society.

Many *EMC* articles contain references to grants, subsidies, and commissions by the Canada Council. It remains to be mentioned that without the generous support of the Canada Council this encyclopedia could not have been produced.

PUBLICATIONS

STATEMENTS AND SPEECHES

Fortier, André. *Is There a Future for the Symphony Orchestra in Canada? / L'Orchestre symphonique a-t-il un avenir au Canada?* (1974)

– *Careers and Markets in the Arts / Carrières et débouchés dans le monde des arts* (1975)

– *The Canada Council and the Francophone Community in the North American Context / Le Conseil des arts et la francophonie canadienne dans le contexte nord-americain* (1975)

Lussier, Charles A. *Music Development in a Restrained Economy / Développement musical et restrictions financières* (1976)

– *Public-Private Partnership in the Arts / Mécénat privé et mécénat public* (1976)

Porteous, Timothy. *The Arts in Canada: A Better Way? / Les Arts au Canada sont-ils plus favorisés qu'aux États-Unis?*

– *The Canada Council and the Arts in Saskatchewan / Le Conseil des arts et la vie artistique en Saskatchewan* (1976)

Lussier, Charles A. *The Canada Council: The Principle of Excellence and Its Implications in a Democratic Society / Le Conseil des arts du Canada, en quête d'excellence dans une société démocratique* (1977)

Porteous, Timothy. *The Arts in the Canadian Community / Les Arts dans la communauté canadienne* (1977)

– *Culture and Confederation / Culture et confédération* (1978)

STUDIES, BRIEFS, OTHER TEXTS

Canada Council Information Service. *Readings on the Governing Boards of Arts Organizations / Glanures sur les conseils d'administration des entreprises artistiques* (Mar 1971)

Pasquill, Frank T. *Subsidy Patterns for the Performing Arts in Canada / Modes d'assistance financière aux arts du spectacle au Canada* (Feb 1973)

Dept of Manpower and Immigration. *An Analysis of Selected Performing Arts Occupations / Analyse de certains emplois dans le domaine des arts du spectacle* (Jul 1974)

Urwick, Currie and Partners Ltd. *An Assessment of the Impact of Selected Large Performing Companies upon the Canadian Economy / Incidence de certaines grandes compagnies de spectacle sur l'économie canadienne* (Sep 1974)

Cameron, Duncan. *The Arts in Canada 1975: Viewpoint / Les Arts au Canada en 1975* (May 1975)

Twenty plus Five / Vingt et cinq (Nov 1977)

Blume, Helmut. *A National Music School for Canada / Une École nationale de musique pour le Canada* (Mar 1980)

BIBLIOGRAPHY

CMJ, vol 1, Spring 1957, issue devoted to music and the Canada Council

Canada Council. *Annual Reports* (1958–)

Leopold, Douglas. 'The Canada Council views the arts: an interview with Charles Lussier,' *OpCan*, Sep 1976

Gwyn, Sandra. ' "The Canada Council had the right people in the right places at the right time",' *SatN*, Jun 1977

Fraser, John. 'A cheerless celebration for the arts,' Toronto *Globe and Mail*, 24 Sep 1977

Ostry, Bernard. *The Cultural Connection* (Toronto 1978)

Aspects of Music in Canada

The Canada Council Medal. Annual award established in 1961 by the *Canada Council 'for outstanding achievement in the arts, humanities or social sciences.' The first medals were awarded 19 Feb 1962 to Marius *Barbeau, Wilfrid *Pelletier, and Healey *Willan and to seven persons in other fields. Among the 24 later recipients were Claude *Champagne in 1963, Sir Ernest *MacMillan in 1964, Norman *McLaren in 1966, and in 1967 the first foreigner, Igor Stravinsky. The award was combined in 1968 with the *Molson Prizes, continuing under the latter name. The medal, cast in bronze, was designed by Dora de Pedery Hunt.

Canada in European and US music. Works by European and US composers have treated Canada as a subject or found it an inspiration in various ways, discussed here under these headings:

1 Stage works
2 Canadian battles
3 Visits to Canada
4 British imperial patriotism
5 Settings of Canadian folk tunes
6 Other

1 STAGE WORKS. Rameau's *Les Indes galantes* (1735) and Grétry's *Le Huron* (1768) have only a fanciful and non-realistic relationship to the native peoples of North America. In Rameau's opera-ballet only one section – 'Les Sauvages,' in which a peace festival is enacted – is of North American interest, and even that, with its setting 'close to the French and Spanish settlements,' suggests the southern USA rather than any part of Canada. The plot of the Grétry opera deals with the visit of an Indian to France. Rossini's first opera, *La Cambiale di Matrimonio* (1810), was translated into German as *Der Bräutigam aus Kanada*. Though it lacks a Canadian setting the work includes among its four characters a Canadian businessman, Slook. (The opera has been performed in Canada by the Piccolo Teatro Musicale di Roma at *PDA in 1968 and by the *McGill Opera Studio.) Mozart may have been the first of the great composers to set the word 'Canada' to music, in 'Rivolgete a lui lo sguardo' ('Turn your eyes towards him'), the supplementary aria (K584) for *Così fan tutte*, which includes the phrase 'che gli uguali non si trovano da Vienna al Canada' ('whose like you won't find from Vienna to Canada'). Donizetti's *Rita* (1840) also contains a reference to Canada. Rudolf Friml's **Rose Marie* (1924), on the other hand, has a genuine (though romanticized) Canadian setting of rocky mountains and a cast featuring mounted policemen. Ivan Caryll's musical *The Pink Lady* (1911) includes the song 'By the Saskatchewan.' The *Evangeline story has inspired several operas, including two by non-Canadians – France's Xavier Leroux and the USA's Otto Luening. During one of his expeditions to the Canadian Arctic in the 1820s, Sir Edward William Parry

The Canada Herald, published in 1899

was the co-author of a small opera, *The North West Passage* or *Voyage Finished*, that was performed on board ship.

2 CANADIAN BATTLES. A manuscript, 'Not unto us, Lord' – subtitled a 'Thanksgiving Anthem, for the taking of Montreal and making us Masters of all Canada' and attributed to the Chapel Royal composer James Nares – is held in the British Library. Franz Koczwara, whose descriptive instrumental piece *The Battle of Prague* was widely popular, began another, *Siege of Quebec* (for harpsichord or piano and violin, cello and timpani ad lib), which after his death in 1791 was completed by W.B. de Krifft and in 1806 was performed in Quebec. *The Battles of Lake Champlain and Plattsburg* (where the US forces defeated the Canadian in 1812) was the title of a grand sonata by the Boston musician Francesco Masi. (See also Battle music.)

3 VISITS TO CANADA. Probably the first composer to write music inspired by a visit to Canada was Ole Bull, the Norwegian violinist who wrote *Niagara* (for violin and piano) ca 1845. (See also Niagara Falls in music.) Oliver King, an Englishman who served in Ottawa as the pianist to Princess Louise (wife of the governor-general, the marquis of Lorne) wrote an overture (*Among the Pines*, Novello 1883?) which won a prize offered by the London Philharmonic Society in 1883. Louis Victor Saar, a Dutch-American, wrote *From the Mountain Kingdom of the Great North-West* (*Aus der kanadischen Alpenwelt*) for orchestra in 1922 and a Canadian song cycle, 'Four Seasons,' to words by John Murray *Gibbon in 1926. Among other 20th-century orchestral works inspired by visits to Canada are Quinto Maganini's *The Lake at Sunset, A Canadian Idyll* (1938, inspired by Lake Timagami in northern Ontario), Benjamin Britten's *Canadian Carnival* (1939), Arthur *Benjamin's *North American Square-Dance* (1951, a suite based on fiddle tunes from Canada and the USA), and Alan Shulman's *Laurentian Overture* (1952).

4 BRITISH IMPERIAL PATRIOTISM. At the invitation of the governor-general, the marquis of Lorne, Arthur Sullivan wrote a Dominion hymn (1880) to Lorne's text 'God bless our wide Dominion.' C.H.H. Parry wrote a Newfoundland hymn in 1902, and Edward German composed a patriotic hymn, 'Canada,' in 1904. None of these composers had visited Canada save Sullivan, who was a guest of the governor-general in 1880. Gounod's 'Notre Dame du Canada' seems to be simply an adaptation of his 'Notre Dame de France, hymne de la patrie.'

5 SETTINGS OF CANADIAN FOLK TUNES. Arrangements of Canadian folk material for choir or voice and instrument(s) were written by Joseph Canteloube, Paul Creston, Louis Victor Saar, Lazare Saminsky, Arthur Somervell, and Ralph Vaughan Williams. Of instrumental pieces by non-Canadian composers, Paul Gilson's *Fantaisie canadienne* was written by 1898 and Alexander Mackenzie's *Canadian Rhapsody* (1905) for orchestra is perhaps the most ambitious. For smaller combinations there are Eugène Gigout's *Rhapsodie sur des airs canadiens* (organ, late 19th century) and Maud Wyatt Pargeter's *String Quartet on Canadian Themes* (which received an honourable mention in the E.W. Beatty Competition at the 1928 Canadian Folksong and Handicraft Festival – see CPR Festivals). There are several other works of this type, including H. Maurice Jacquet's *Suite canadienne* (Birchard 1927). *Tres preludios sobra temas canadenses* (1943) by the Brazilian composer Francesco Mignone have been recorded by André-Sébastien *Savoie (RCI 418).

6 OTHER. Romualdo Marenco's ballet *Sport* (1897) includes a Montreal episode 'Valzer dei pattinatori.' Scott Joplin's ragtime classic *The Maple Leaf Rag* (1899) is said to have had indirect Canadian inspiration (see Ragtime). Among songs, 'Canadian Capers' (1915) by the US writers Gus Chandler, Bert White, and Harry Cohen (music) and Earl Burtnett (lyrics) and 'Canadian Sunset' (1956) by the US bandleader Eddie Heywood have been especially popular, and in French-speaking countries 'Ma Cabane au Canada' (1947), by Louis (Loulou) Gasté to lyrics by Mireille Broccy, had a success, particularly as sung by the French chanteuse Line Renaud. The musical *Foxy* (1962), set in the *Klondike, was conceived by a team of US writers, including the Canadian expatriate Robert Emmett Dolan. HK, GP

Le Canada musical. Name of two unconnected periodicals published in Montreal.

1 Published monthly, 1 Sep 1866–1 Aug 1867 and (numbered vols 2–7) 1 May 1875–1 Apr 1881, by its owner A.J. *Boucher. Labelled a 'revue littéraire et artistique,' a typical issue had 16 pages. It reported news of musical interest from Canada (mainly Montreal and other Quebec cities but also Ottawa and Winnipeg) and from France. It took much interest in the careers of young musicians such as *Albani (biography by *Legendre), *Couture, *Lavallée, *Jehin-Prume, François *Boucher, and Oscar *Martel. Activities of Roman Catholic church choirs, particularly at Easter and Christmas, often were reported in detail. Some of the material (eg, essays on famous composers) was reprinted from French periodicals. Of considerable interest to the historian are listings and reviews of new publications (mostly if not always Boucher's) and teachers' advertisements. Beginning with the 1875 revival it featured short piano pieces and songs, practically all by non-Canadians (eg, Frédéric Boissière, Gustave Nadaud, C. Kinkel). Both suspensions of publication were intended to be temporary. The first was due to overwork and preoccupation with his business interests as an importer and retailer of music, and the second to financial problems. An 1879 advertisement claims *Le Canada musical* to be 'the only musical review published in the Dominion, also the

LE
ANADA MUSICAL
REVUE ARTISTIQUE ET LITTÉRAIRE
PARAISSANT LE 1er DE CHAQUE MOIS.
MONTREAL, 1er. JUILLET, 1867. No. 11

CANADA MUSICAL,
Publié le 1er de chaque mois
PAR ADELARD J. BOUCHER,
Editeur-Propriétaire.
Bureau, à Montréal,
Rue Notre Dame, No. 260.
BONNEMENT, avec PRIME,
$1.00 par année,
Rigoureusement payable d'avance.
10 centins le Numéro.

PRIME EXCEPTIONELLE
présentée aux Abonnés du
ANADA MUSICAL.

SOMMAIRE.—Gaétano Donizetti, par Léon Escudier.—Correspondance québecquoise.—Mozart et l'accordeur, (*suite*), par Charles Barbara.—Catalogue des publications musicales de la maison Boucher.—Description générale de l'orgue (*suite*).—Une lettre de Boïeldieu, par G. Héquet.—La musique dans les salons de l'imperatrice Joséphine, par C. Robert.—Liste d'abonnés au Canada musical, (*suite*).—Conseils de Robert Schumann aux jeunes musiciens, (*suite*).—Calendrier.—Annonces.

GAETANO DONIZETTI.
Ce n'est pas sa biographie que nous donnons

Part of the first page of the 1 Jul 1867 issue of *Le Canada musical*

only one published in the French language in America.' In 1881, it was followed briefly by *Boucher & Pratte's Musical Journal*, essentially a US magazine with a Canadian title and back page ('Le Journal musical, nouvelles artistiques canadiennes'). It appeared monthly, and the numbering (vol 3, no. 6, July 1881, to vol 4, no. 11, Dec 1882) may be explained by its US connection.

2 Published bimonthly 5 May 1917–19 Apr 1924 (vol 1 to vol 7, no. 24) and semi-monthly 6 Sep 1930–20 Dec 1930 (vol 8, no. 1–8), edited by C.-O. *Lamontagne. Lamontagne's aim was to present news of music and to stimulate interest in and understanding of the art. Articles usually were short; news items covered Quebec and at times the rest of Canada. The editor's particular interest in opera is reflected by detailed reports on performances at the *Metropolitan Opera, New York, and at the Opéra and Opéra-Comique in Paris. Correspondents were maintained in both cities. The magazine is a valuable source of information and pictorial documentation relating to Quebec's musical life. It also featured regular reports on activities in the French-Canadian centres of New England. Some articles dealt with history: eg, Lamontagne on Guillaume Couture, 6 Dec 1930, and Frédéric *Pelletier on the *AMQ, 18 Oct 1930. The suspension in 1924 was due to an intended 4-month trip by the editor to Europe, but the publication was revived only six years later. HK

The Canada Music Book / Les Cahiers canadiens de musique. Bilingual periodical published by the *CMCouncil and edited by Gilles *Potvin. The editorial board was made up of directors of the CMCouncil. From issue 7 to issue 10 Adrian Waller acted as assistant editor. Articles were in either English or French and most editorial matter and announcements in both. The first year of publication yielded only one issue (Spring–Summer 1970). Subsequent years yielded two (Spring–Summer and Autumn–Winter) until 1975. Autumn–Winter 1975 was delayed and combined with Spring–Summer 1976, after which publication went into abeyance. Each issue had about 200 pages, and the individual cover colours of issues 1 to 8 added up to a rainbow spectrum which began again at issue 9.

Some issues contained as many as 10 major articles, while others were devoted largely to the council's conferences (issues 2, 3, 5, and 9) and the International Music Council's 16th General Assembly and *World Music Week (issue 11 / 12). There was strong emphasis on the analysis and discussion of contemporary music and musical issues, but historical subjects of Canadian interest were dealt with occasionally. Besides a large review section there was a regular series of 'Canadian Chronicles,' arranged by province or region, which will be invaluable for the future historian. Two issues were devoted to special subjects: a 'Dossier Stravinsky-Canada 1937–1967' (issue 4) and a 'Dossier John *Weinzweig' with tributes on the composer's 60th birthday (issue 6).

Besides a wide range of Canadian writers on music, contributors included such foreign musicians as Pierre Boulez, Maurice Fleuret, and Yehudi Menuhin, apart from the many visitors to World Music Week (issue 11 / 12). The *CMB* published historical articles about R. *Bayeur (no. 8), J.-M. *Beaudet (no. 2), Beethoven (no. 2), J.P. *Clarke (no. 1), W.O. *Forsyth (no. 7), R. *Mathieu (no. 5), and Scriabin (no. 3); on musical life in *Quebec 1840–5 (no. 7) and in *Winnipeg 1900–7 (no. 8); and on the *CLComp (no. 2). There also are musicological articles on Boulez (no. 2), Britten (no. 1), Kierkegaard (no. 2), Messiaen (no. 1), Schütz (no. 5), and Webern (no. 5) and a comparison of Wagner and R. Murray *Schafer as men of letters (no. 2). Sterling *Beckwith (no. 9) and L. Beaudet-Léonard (no. 8) contributed pieces on music education. There also are miscellaneous articles about the *CMCentre (no. 4), music *criticism in Canada (no. 7), 'Radio as music,' by Glenn *Gould (no. 2), 'Muscadet,' a computer data bank on music in Canada (no. 8), and Canadian composition and the music of Canada's ethnic minorities (no. 10). HK

The Canada Music Citation. Established in 1967 by the *CLComp to recognize a musician (not a CLComp member) 'who has shown dedication and outstanding achievement in the performance of Canadian music.' The conductor Victor *Feldbrill, the first recipient, was presented with one of a limited series of lithographs by the Canadian artist John Gould 11 Oct 1967 at the Montreal performance of **Louis Riel*. The citation, which is not awarded annually and is granted only at the discretion of the council of the CLComp, has been given to the soprano Mary *Morrison 14 Jan 1969, the flutist Robert *Aitken 30 Nov 1969, and the conductor John *Avison 17 Sep 1970. In recognition of outstanding service to Canadian music through commissioning and programming, John Peter Lee *Roberts, then head of music of the English Services Division of CBC radio, received a special tribute in 1972. Norma Dickson and Henry Mutsaers were presented with lithographs in 1979 to mark their long and dedicated service to the *CMCentre. PW

Canada Packers Operatic Society (Canada Packers Maple Leaf Choir 1942–3). Amateur group formed 1942 in Toronto under the patronage of J.S. McLean, president of Canada Packers (a meat processing company) and a supporter of the arts. After its first public presentation – *The Gondoliers*, 10, 12, and 15 May 1943 at *Eaton Auditorium – it changed its name to the CPOS and continued to mount annual productions until 1955. At first the society concentrated on the most familiar works of Gilbert & Sullivan (*Iolanthe, H.M.S. Pinafore, The Pirates of Penzance*), but in its fifth season, with *Utopia (Limited)*, it began to present the lesser-known pieces and also popular works of other composers (eg, Edward German's *Merrie England*). With a membership almost exclusively of Canada Packers employees and their families, the CPOS featured as its soloists James Green and Mary Black and one regular guest artist, Arthur Sclater. W. Richard Curry served as producer and music director. Productions were discontinued with J.S. McLean's death in 1955. (DS)

Canadian Academy of Music. Toronto school founded and financed by Col Albert *Gooderham, its president during its entire existence, 1911–24. Established for the purpose of keeping gifted students in Toronto and bringing outstanding teachers from Europe, it was known, during its first year in the Heintzman building on Yonge St, as the Columbian Cons of Music. In 1912 the school became the Canadian Academy of Music, moved to a spacious building at 12–14 Spadina Road, and absorbed the *Metropolitan School of Music, which became its Parkdale branch. Peter C. Kennedy was director until 1918. In that year, the academy took over the *Toronto College of Music, and until 1923 the school featured both names. In 1918, also, a musical directorate was formed, with Kennedy, Frank S. *Welsman, and Alfred Bruce, the latter serving as managing director. W.O. *Forsyth, Albert *Ham, and Ernest *MacMillan later joined the directorate, and in 1922 Welsman assumed the role of music director. Among the outstanding teachers were Luigi von *Kunits (who also founded the *Academy String Quartet) 1912–24, Walter Kirschbaum 1912–14, Ham 1919–24, Welsman 1918–24, Forsyth 1919–24, MacMillan 1920–4, and Arthur Friedheim 1921–4. The school awarded associate and licentiate diplomas (ACAM, LCAM).

A Columbian Cons of Music in Montreal on Sherbrooke St, directed by J.F.H. Wallace, is less well documented. It is known that Salvator *Issaurel taught there 1911–14 and that Paul-G. Ouimet, Fleurette Contant, and Ulysse *Paquin were among the pupils. In 1913 a group of teachers from this conservatory founded the Canadian Academy of Music of Montreal, with Frederick H. *Blair as artistic director and W.D. Birchell as president. Other teachers at the academy were Albert *Chamberland, J.-B. *Dubois, Théo Henrion, Frank *Rowe, and F. Whitely. The relationship, if any, between the Toronto and Montreal institutions of the same names has not been established.

BIBLIOGRAPHY
'Canadian conservatories plan for a successful year,' *CanJM*, Sep 1914
Charlesworth, Hector. 'The Canadian Academy of Music is amalgamated with the Conservatory,' *CQR*, Aug 1924
Gour, Romain. *La Palme-Issaurel* (Montreal 1948)
HK, PW

Canadian Academy of Recording Arts and Sciences (CARAS). Organization of representatives of the recording industry, formed in Toronto in 1975 'to foster the development of the Canadian music and recording industries and to contribute towards higher artistic standards.' On its formation CARAS became the co-governing body of the *Juno Awards (sole governing body after 1977), responsible for the nomination and voting procedures – only members of the academy are eligible to vote – and for the CBC TV presentation of the awards ceremony. Founders of the academy included 11 of the major record companies in Canada. Its first president was Mel Shaw, who was succeeded in 1978 by Brian Robertson. Governed by a board of seven directors drawn from the production and retail spheres of the recording industry, a seven-man (six in 1980) advisory board (which included, in 1980, Alan Wood of the AF of M in Canada, J.T. Meisel of *CRTC, John Mills of *CAPAC, and Jan *Matejcek of *PRO Canada), and eight regional representatives, CARAS in 1979 had a membership of about 900 from the fields of performance, recording, publishing, broadcasting, and retailing. CARAS shares offices in Toronto with *CRIA. MM

Canadian Amateur Musicians / Musiciens amateurs du Canada. See CAMMAC.

Canadian Artistic Society / Société artistique canadienne. Founded in Montreal and incorporated 24 Dec 1894 to 'develop the taste for music and encourage artists.' More specifically, its aim was to 'establish a national conservatory of music.' A bi-monthly lottery was held to raise funds for the conservatory, and Edmond *Hardy was requested to found it, which he did in 1896, and to serve as director. It was known simply as the Cons of the Canadian Artistic Society. For his teaching staff, Hardy retained the services of Achille *Fortier (voice and harmony), Charles *Labelle (solfège), Arthur *Letondal (piano), and Oscar *Martel (violin). Courses were free, and each teacher received a monthly salary of $25. The conservatory accepted several hundred students but was obliged to close in 1901 when the federal government prohibited lotteries. Among its students were the soprano Rose MacMillan, the pianist Éva *Plouffe, and the violinists Henri Arnoldi and Chambord Giguère.

BIBLIOGRAPHY
'La Société artistique canadienne,' Montreal *Le Samedi*, 6 Apr 1895
Musical Red Book
GP

Canadian Arts Trio. Formed in 1971 at the *U of Saskatchewan. Supplanting the *Amati Quartet and using two of four Amati instruments owned by the university, it comprised Robert Klose (violin), Robin *Harrison (piano), and Edward *Bisha (cello). In addition to giving concerts in Saskatoon, the trio toured Ontario for the *JMC in 1972 and gave six concerts in Great Britain in 1973. Harrison was replaced in the fall of 1974 by Mary Lou Kolbinson, but the trio ceased its activities in 1975 when Klose moved to Vancouver and Bisha to Ottawa. GW

Canadian Association of Music Libraries (CAML) / **Association canadienne des bibliothèques musicales** (ACBM). A reconstitution in 1971 of the *Canadian Music Library Assn. In order to avoid a proliferation of affiliations and membership fee payments, the new organization affiliated with the International Assn of Music Libraries rather than the Canadian Library Assn and became the former organization's Canadian branch. Membership, individual and institutional, surpassed 100 in 1978. Presidents have been Marjorie Hale 1971–2, Cheryl Osborn 1972–3, Dale Ward 1973–4, 1975–6, Keith *MacMillan 1974–5, Maria Calderisi 1976–8, and Isabel Rose 1978–80, succeeded by Kathleen McMorrow. Annual meetings have been held concurrently with those of CLA or *CAUSM, and regional workshops take place several times a year. CAML played host to the first Canadian conference of IAML, held in Montreal in 1975. Besides a *Newsletter / Nouvelles* issued four times a year, CAML has published Lynne Jarman's *Canadian Music: A Selected Checklist 1950–73 / Le Musique canadienne: une liste sélective 1950–73* (Toronto 1976) and the revised edition of the *Union List of Music Periodicals in Canadian Libraries* (London, Ont, 1981), edited by Larry Lewis.

Canadian Association of University Schools of Music (CAUSM) / **Association canadienne des écoles universitaires de musique** (ACEUM). National organization of university schools, faculties, or departments of music and of university music teachers. Proposed in July 1964 at a meeting of representatives from Toronto, Montreal, and McGill universities, CAUSM was established at a general meeting 5 Feb 1965 in Ottawa under the auspices of the Centennial Commission. Subsequent annual meetings, held in different cities each June, have featured discussion and the presentation of papers on music education and related matters. Objectives of the founding constitution (drafted by Helmut *Blume and Arnold *Walter and revised in 1971 by Donald McKellar and Lorne *Watson) are to facilitate the exchange of views between heads and faculty members of music schools, to set minimum standards for music programs at universities, to maintain and strengthen the position of music study in universities, to serve as a consultative and advisory body for all Canadian university music schools, to enlist the co-operation of member departments in matters relating to common concert and lecture projects, to initiate worthy musical projects and actions, and to stimulate scholarship and improve instructional methods at Canadian universities (and in the wider sphere of music teaching in the country) by scholarly papers, symposia, and publications. Initially CAUSM membership was restricted to institutions themselves, represented by a council of senior administrators from those institutions. The revised constitution established a category of individual membership for university music teachers. CAUSM has published *Curriculum Standards for Canadian University Music Departments* (1969) edited by G. Welton *Marquis, the annual and occasionally biannual *Journal* (Ottawa 1971–) and the *CAUSM Annual Directory* (Moncton 1974–). CAUSM presidents have been Arnold Walter 1965–7, Clément *Morin 1967–9, Welton Marquis 1969–71, Lucien *Brochu 1971–3, Lorne Watson 1973–5, Brian *Ellard 1975–7, Donald A. McKellar 1977–9, succeeded by Armand *Ferland. DMk

Canadian Band Directors' Association 1973– (Canadian Bandmasters' Association 1931–73). Established in September 1931 by 35 bandmasters meeting in Toronto at the *CNE, in the culmination of efforts by the first president, Capt John *Slatter, who since 1918 had advocated the need for such an organization.

Chartered in 1934, the association had as its purpose 'to improve band conditions and to provide better educational facilities for band leaders.' While it showed some interest in school music programs, its orientation was towards community bands, and in 1937 it was instrumental in getting the Ontario Band Tax Law passed. This law enabled municipalities to vote funds towards the support of community bands. In 1948 the association absorbed the Ontario Amateur Bands' Assn and assumed administration of the CNE band contests. By 1949 there were 268 members.

In 1955, at the request of Alberta members, the association established a provincial chapter in Alberta. Other regional or provincial chapters were initiated in 1956 in Ontario-Quebec and British Columbia, and in 1957 in Manitoba, Saskatchewan, and the Maritime provinces. In 1956 a National Council was formed to act as a governing body and serve as a liaison with other national or international musical organizations and with federal government departments. Specifically, the council was created to administer the CNE band contests (founded in 1921 through the efforts of A.L. Robertson and others and administered 1924–56 by the Ontario Amateur Bands' Assn – see C.F. Thiele); to serve as co-host, with one of the chapters, of the biennial national convention; to solicit federal government assistance; and to act as a lobby.

During the 1960s interest in the association waned, and several chapters became inactive, although an independent Quebec chapter was created in 1964. However, in the 1970s, with a shift of emphasis from the community bandmaster to the school band director, it was revitalized. In 1973 the CBA changed 'Bandmasters' to 'Band Directors' in its name and increased its activities to include band clinics and workshops, summer band camps, provincial and national band festivals, and the commissioning of original Canadian works (eg, Malcolm *Forsyth's *Colour Wheel*, commissioned in 1978 by the Alberta chapter). Also in 1973, a scholarship was established in memory of Alexander L. Robertson (b Scotland ca 1894, d St Petersburg, Fla, 1967), secretary-treasurer of the CBA for 25 years and editor of its periodicals 1942–67. In 1976 the association created the CBDA National Music Award, presented at its biennial national meetings. Recipients have been Martin *Boundy in 1976 and Wilfred L. Manning and Harry Pinchon in 1978. The National Youth Band of Canada was formed in 1978, with Boundy as music director. In the same year the CBDA had some 400 members in four provincial chapters (Ontario, Alberta, Manitoba, and British Columbia).

The CBA published a newsletter 1933–4? and, edited by A.L. Robertson, *The Canadian Bandsman* 1942–9 and *The Canadian Bandmaster* 1949–67. The *CBDA Journal*, a quarterly, is edited by Keith Mann, and the *CBDA Festival Syllabus* was published in 1976. The Ontario and Alberta chapters also issue provincial newsletters.

Presidents of the CBA were John Slatter 1931–3, J.-J. *Goulet 1933–4, C.F. *Thiele 1934–5, S.J. Chamberlain 1935–6, W.E. Brush 1936–8, J.A. Cowie 1938–9, Robert Moore 1939–40, Percie Cox 1940–1, Fred Jobson 1941–2, T.E. Jackson 1942–3, R.H. Chappell 1943–4, L.F. *Addison 1944–5, W.I. Baxter 1945–6, J.C. Lougheed 1946–7, Charles M. Allan 1947–8, E. Reginald *Hinchey 1948–9, Spurgeon *Sheppard 1949–50, Martin Boundy 1950–1, W.H. Peryer 1951–2, W.L. Manning 1952–3, Peter C. Allan 1953–4, C.O. *Hunt 1954–5, W.T. *Atkins 1955–6, E. Von Ayres 1956–8, T. Vernon Newlove 1958–9, C.O. Hunt 1959–61, K.A. *Elloway 1961–2, H.O. Lomnes 1962–3, W.L. Manning 1963–5, Albert M. Culham 1965–8, Horace Beard 1968–9, and Martin Boundy 1969–73. Presidents of the CBDA have been Martin Boundy 1973–4 and Keith Mann 1974–7, succeeded by F. Ralph Kennard.

See also Band festivals; Bands; Fédération des harmonies du Québec.

BIBLIOGRAPHY

Atkins, W.T. 'The Canadian Bandmasters' Association,' *CMJ*, vol 2, Winter 1958

Beard, Horace. 'Musical milestone,' *Recorder*, vol 8, Jan–Mar 1966 (JPG, FH, PW)

'Canadian Boat Song.' A song composed by the Irish poet Thomas Moore during a visit to Canada in 1804 – not to be confused with the 'Canadian Boat Song' known also as 'The Lone Shieling' (1829), which is not Canadian, even in implication, and is not a boat song, either. Moore's verses began:

Faintly as tolls the evening chime
Our voices keep tune and our oars keep time.

The tune was inspired by a voyageurs' song 'Dans mon chemin j'ai rencontré,' which Moore heard and noted down while being rowed down the St Lawrence from Kingston to Montreal. However, Moore's tune resembles the voyageurs' only in its opening bar. In effect, it was a new composition, and the verses had little resemblance to those of any genuine voyageur song. In the preface to the second volume of his verse (London 1840), Moore printed the voyageur tune, and wrote, 'I departed in almost every respect but the time from the strain our voyageurs had sung to us, leaving the music of the glee nearly as much my own as the words.' The song was published first in London (Carpenter 1805) in a three-voice setting. US editions soon appeared, and by 1825 there were at least 12 (most for three voices, a few for solo voice, many under the title 'The Rapids'). Later (probably before 1865) Louis Moreau Gottschalk made arrangements of the song, and these were published by Reed Meyer in 1870. Arrangements have appeared in *Folk Songs of Canada* (Waterloo 1954) and numerous other collections. (EF)

The first page of music of the first edition of 'Canadian Boat Song'

Canadian Brass. Quintet formed in 1970 as the Canadian Brass Ensemble by Stuart Laughton (b St Catharines 19 Aug 1951) and William *Phillips, trumpets, Graeme Page, french horn (b Toronto 8 Sep 1947), Eugene Watts, trombone (b Warrensburg, Mo, 22 Feb 1936), and Charles Daellenbach, tuba (b Rhinelander, Wisc, 12 Jul 1945). The name was abbreviated to Canadian Brass in 1971, and that same year Ronald Romm (b New York 4 Dec 1946) replaced Laughton. In 1972 Fred Mills (b Guelph 15 Mar 1935) replaced Phillips.

Canadian Brass toured Ontario for *Prologue to the Performing Arts in 1970 and became artists-in-residence with the *Hamilton Philharmonic Orchestra in 1971. Though the players moved to Toronto in 1976 they continued to be members of the Hamilton orchestra until 1977. They were artists-in-residence in 1975 and 1976 at the *Banff SFA. First touring Europe in 1972 with the *Festival Singers, the quintet also performed under the auspices of the Dept of External Affairs at the 1974 Festival estival in Paris, at the Kennedy Center in Washington in 1976, and on tour in China, where in 1977 it gave 10 concerts before a total of 15,000 people and played in six broadcasts over Radio Peking. Later that year it performed in England, France, Germany, Italy, and the USSR. It has performed on CBC TV in the children's show 'Canadian Brass' (29 Mar 1976), the special 'Brass-A-Ma-Tazz' (28 Nov 1976), the popular children's program 'Sesame Street' (1979), and other shows. In the summer of 1976 it opened the *JMC Orford Art Centre festival.

For its *TS debut in 1978, Canadian Brass performed Gary Kulesha's transcription of Handel's *Organ Concerto in F, Op 4, no. 4*. For its New York debut, 6 Feb 1979 at the Alice Tully Hall, Lincoln Center, it premiered *Flashbacks* by Michael *Colgrass. On other occasions it has premiered works written for it by Peter Schickele (*Hornsmoke*, 1976; *Five of a Kind*, 1979). It has appeared in concerts across Canada and in 1976 gave a special performance before the governor-general at Rideau Hall, Ottawa. In the summer of 1980 it made its first appearances at the Edinburgh Festival.

Canadian Brass in China in 1977

Combining disciplined performance and informal deportment in a repertoire encompassing several centuries and styles as disparate as renaissance and ragtime, Canadian Brass quickly won wide audiences of both children and adults, and by the latter half of the 1970s was established as one of Canada's most popular touring groups. As the Pucker and Valve Society Band, it extended its range in 1977 with an LP of novelty compositions and arrangements by Ben *McPeek. The matched gold-plated instruments on which Canadian Brass plays were made by Renold Schilke. Between 1971 and 1976 Canadian Brass commissioned, and premiered in the years given, the following works from Canadian composers, all of whom have biographies in *EMC*.

Beckwith *Taking a Stand* 1972
Beecroft *11 and 7 for 5 +* 1975
Buczynski *Olympics '76* 1976
Crosley *Variations on a French Canadian Theme* 1975
Forsyth, M. *Sagittarius* 1975, *Quinquefid* 1977
Freedman *Five Rings* 1977
Glick *Deborah* 1972
Hayes *Convolutions* 1975
McCauley *Miniature Overture* 1973, *Concerto Grosso* 1973
Morawetz *Improvisations* 1977
Rathburn *Nomadic V* 1974, *Three Ironies* 1975
Symonds *A Diversion* 1971
Weinzweig *Pieces of Five* 1976

DISCOGRAPHY

Bells and Brass: Handel – Emberley – Joplin – Brahms – J. Strauss – et al. G. Slater carillon. 1978. Tapestry GD 7371
Canadian Brass: Calvert – Scheidt – Bach – McCauley – G. Gabrieli – Joplin – et al. 1973. Boot BMC 3001
Canadian Brass: Bach – Peuerl – G. Gabrieli – Freedman – Beecroft – Symonds. 1976. CBC SM-320
Canadian Brass in Paris: Bach – Purcell – McCauley – Forsyth – Dahl – Handel – et al. 1974. Boot BMC 3003
Mostly Fats. 1978. RCA XRL-1-3212
Music Canada VI. RCI/CAPAC RM 222
Pucker and Valve Society Band. 1977. Attic LAT 1030
Rag-Ma-Tazz. Joplin – McPeek – Crosley – Debussy – Fillmore – Rathburn. 1974. RCI 403/Boot BMC 3004
Scheidt – Reicha – Morel – Gesualdo. 1971. CBC SM-216
Traditional Christmas Songs 'Westminster Carol.' 1976. CBC LM-440
Unexplored Territory: Gillis – Satie – Bach – Handel – Gilbert/Ory – Melrose/Rappolo. 1978. CBC LM 453
See also Discographies for Festival Singers; Hamilton Philharmonic; NACO.

BIBLIOGRAPHY

Schulman, Michael. 'Opening the kids' eyes,' *PfAC*, vol 10, Spring 1973
Levich, Gerald. 'The Canadian Brass: taking the stuffiness out of music,' *CanComp*, Apr 1976
Orchard, Pat. 'Canadian Brass,' *Adagio*, vol 1, Apr 1976
'Sour notes at the Globe and Mail or what really happened to the Canadian Brass in China,' *PfAC*, vol 14, Summer 1977
'Bells and brass combine to make unique recording,' *CanComp*, 139, Mar 1979
'Canadian Brass charms the Sesame Street set,' *Music*, vol 2, Mar–Apr 1979
Bradbury, Patricia. 'The Canadian Brass,' *Fugue*, Apr 1979
Waller, Adrian. 'Des musiciens pas comme les autres,' *Sélection du Reader's Digest*, Feb 1980 (SC)

Canadian Broadcasting Corporation. See CBC.

Canadian Bureau for the Advancement of Music. National organization chartered in 1919 to encourage and promote interest in music and music education throughout Canada. A non-profit organization, the bureau's work has been financed by its fee-paying members – individuals, organizations, and companies – who elect a board of volunteer directors. Headquarters, under a managing director, were established in Toronto.

The bureau evolved from the *Canadian Piano and Organ Manufacturers' Assn's 'Music in the Home' campaign, developed and directed by John A. Fullerton who became the bureau's first managing director in 1919. Fullerton was succeeded in 1922 by Capt J.A. Atkinson.

The bureau's long association with the *CNE began in 1921 when it organized the first of the exhibition's Music Days. It functioned then as the music department of the CNE, organizing the annual competitions and recitals. In 1954, when its headquarters were established in the exhibition grounds, it expanded its activities to include co-administration, with the *CBDA, of the band competitions.

In the 1920s the bureau inaugurated essay contests, community music weeks, and local music festivals. In 1922 in Toronto it held the first of its teacher-training courses in the techniques of group or class piano instruction. These were to become its major and continuing project. By 1926 class piano instruction was being given as an extracurricular activity in public schools. At first a two-year basic program that included theoretical rudiments, it later increased to a three-year course, using a syllabus prepared by the bureau.

After World War II class instruction in violin was begun. In 1955 51,000 students were enrolled in the piano classes, 10,000 in the violin, and adult classes were established in association with the *U of Toronto's Extension Dept. Piano teacher training courses have been conducted in centres across Canada, with supervisors located in all the major cities in which the program functions.

As a member of the *FCMF, the bureau has given regular assistance to the annual *National Competitive Festival of Music.

Following Atkinson's death, Richard Edmunds became the managing director in 1954, and Edmunds was succeeded by Clifford *Hunt in 1969. Hunt's continuing work as director of the music department of the CNE perpetuated and focused the close relationship between the department and the bureau.

BIBLIOGRAPHY

Edmunds, Richard. 'Promoting music,' *Recorder*, vol 8, Nov–Dec 1965 PW (COH, FH)

The Canadian Centennial Choir / Le Choeur du centenaire canadien. Mixed 200-voice choir founded in 1966 by Nicholas *Goldschmidt on behalf of the Canadian Centennial Commission to perform at Ottawa's 1967 ceremonies. It sang first 31 Dec 1966 on Parliament Hill for the lighting of the flame, then participated in the July 1967 ceremonies and gave three programs of oratorio and opera selections that year. With a core of 60 voices the CCC was incorporated 1 Aug 1968, thereafter presenting a large-scale choral work each year with Ottawa orchestras and touring smaller Ontario centres. Although the Ottawa soprano Doris Parker has been its most frequent soloist, the CCC has also performed with the singers Gwenlynn *Little, Rhoda Pendleton, Roxolana *Roslak, Léopold *Simoneau, and Jeanette *Zarou and the organist Godfrey *Hewitt. Goldschmidt was succeeded in 1973 by Fred K. Graham, who introduced seldom-performed unaccompanied works. Graham was followed by Gerald *Wheeler 1975–9. During Wheeler's absence 1977–8, John Laing directed the choir. The CCC gave the Canadian premiere 29 May 1973 of Haydn's *Missa brevis Sancti Joannis de Deo*. Other works performed include Bruckner's *Te Deum*, Cherubini's *Requiem Mass in C Minor*, Schubert's *Deutsche Messe*, and Vaughan Williams' *Festival Te Deum*.

Canadian Children's Opera Chorus. A paid, autonomous, 45-voice children's choir, the first of its kind in Canada. Initiated by Ruby *Mercer, who also became the first president of its governing board, it was formed in 1968 in Toronto as a 32-voice ensemble under the direction of Lloyd *Bradshaw and was hired later that year for the first time by the *COC for productions of *La Bohème* and *Tosca*. It made its concert debut 1 Dec 1968 at St Paul's Roman Catholic Church in Toronto. Further performances with the COC have included *Turandot* in 1969, *Boris Godunov* in 1974, and *Wozzeck* in 1977. For its own use the chorus commissioned Charles *Wilson's opera *The Selfish Giant* and gave its premiere 20 Dec 1973 at Town Hall, *St Lawrence Centre, Toronto, under the composer's direction. Part of a later performance was broadcast in 1974 on CBC radio. The chorus presented Richard Rodney Bennett's *All the King's Men* and Britten's *The Golden Vanity* in 1977 and commissioned Gian-Carlo Menotti's children's opera *Chip and His Dog* and premiered it in 1979 at the *Guelph Spring Festival. Besides appearing with the *TS, the *Hamilton Philharmonic, the *Chamber Players of Toronto, and the *Toronto Mendelssohn and *Bach-Elgar choirs, the chorus has sung in concert throughout Ontario. Conductors have been Bradshaw 1968–73, Donald Kendrick 1974–5, and Derek *Holman 1975– .

DISCOGRAPHY

Menotti *Chip and His Dog* – Britten *Friday Afternoons*. D. Bate pf, D. Kent perc, D. Holman cond. 1979. Aquitaine MS 90567

BIBLIOGRAPHY

Glasgow, Jane, and Gilbert, Amy. 'The Canadian Children's Opera Chorus performs at the London workshop,' *Recorder*, vol 18, Dec 1975
Mercer, Ruby. 'Opera's inspiration and challenge in the International Year of the Child: Canada,' *OpCan*, Spring 1979
Schulman, Michael. 'Spring operas beguile with fairytales old and new,' *PfAC*, Summer 1979 (ML)

Canadian College of Organists. See Royal Canadian College of Organists.

The Canadian Composer / Le Compositeur canadien. Periodical published monthly (except July and August) in Toronto for *CAPAC by the Creative Arts Company. Numbering is consecutive, by issue rather than volume. Publication commenced in May 1965 with Richard Robinow as editor. No editor's name appeared on the masthead, however, until February 1968, when Donald Schrank took the position, holding it until December of that year. Ronald Hambleton succeeded Schrank in 1969, and Richard Flohil succeeded Hambleton in 1970. Assistant editors have been Dean Grosart 1969–70, Gundi Jeffrey in

The first issue of *The Canadian Composer*

1970, Joan Meredith 1970–1, Jane Champagne 1971–8, and Nicola Timmerman 1978–80, succeeded by Isobel Harry. Bruno Dostie, named to the new position of Quebec editor in 1977, was succeeded by Nathalie Petrowski in 1978.

The text is bilingual and publicizes the activities of composers, authors, and publishers affiliated with CAPAC. It gives space to concert music, pop music, folk music, and other genres. In addition to articles on the affiliates, it prints stories and news on such related areas as copyright, publishing, recording, and education. There have been series of articles on Canadian music publishers and Canadian orchestras. Reports on conferences inside and outside Canada are frequent. With issue 87, January 1974, articles on individual CAPAC members began to appear, often in the form of interviews. At times the composers themselves have written articles expressing their views. The pages devoted to 'CAPAC Members in the News' and lists of new members and new recordings by CAPAC affiliates are regular features of the periodical. Primarily a promotional vehicle, the magazine is profusely illustrated and avoids technical or critical analysis of compositions.

Canadian Concerts & Artists Inc. Corporation founded in Montreal by Nicolas *Koudriavtzeff (president and general director 1943–76) with the aim of presenting artists, concerts, and shows in Canada. The company collaborated 1943–5 in the Vendredis artistiques at the *St-Denis Theatre and during the same years presented open-air concerts which attracted audiences of up to 15,000 people to Molson Stadium. In the 30 years of its existence it is estimated that the company presented 385 different artists or groups (soloists, symphony orchestras, ballet and folkdance presentations, operas and operettas, theatre, variety shows) in 147 visits to, or tours of, Canada. Notable among these were the *Metropolitan Opera and the Peking Opera; the Moscow Circus; the major orchestras of Berlin, Vienna, Paris, Boston, and Warsaw; the Bolshoi and Paris Opera ballets, the Kirov Ballet of Leningrad and the Maurice Béjart Ballet; the solo artists or entertainers Gilbert Bécaud, Maria Callas, Maurice Chevalier, Fernandel, Jascha Heifetz, Luis Mariano, David Oistrakh, Renata Tebaldi; the Comédie française; and the Renaud-Barrault company. At first on its own initiative, and later in the framework of official Canada-USSR exchanges, the company organized tours in the Soviet Union for numerous Canadian solo artists, including Hyman *Bress, Ida *Haendel, Monique *Leyrac, Lois *Marshall, Louis *Quilico, Joseph *Rouleau, Teresa *Stratas, Micheline *Tessier, Bernard *Turgeon, Ronald *Turini, and Richard *Verreau, as well as the *MSO, the *McGill Chamber Orchestra, and the Royal Winnipeg Ballet. In 1947, the company presented the *Montreal Women's SO at Carnegie Hall, the first Canadian orchestra to play in the famous hall.

Canadian Concerts & Artists Inc declared bankruptcy in the summer of 1976, and Koudriavtzeff then formed the company Concerts & Artistes Canadiens Inc, which supervised the presentation of recitals and shows at the *PDA. Its international exchange program was taken over by the Touring Office of the *Canada Council in 1976. Some months after Koudriavtzeff's death in 1980, Concerts & Artistes Canadiens ceased its activities.

GP

Canadian Conference of the Arts (Canadian Arts Council 1945–58) / **Conférence canadienne des arts** (Conseil canadien des arts 1945–58). Founded by 16 national cultural organizations 5 Dec 1945 at a meeting in Toronto. It developed as an independent, non-profit umbrella organization comprising arts organizations, artists, friends, and patrons; its concerns extended to all areas of arts activity, including film, theatre, music, dance, literature, painting, sculpture, design, graphics, crafts, museums, and art education. In 1978 the membership exceeded 1100, including the Canadian Assn of Youth Orchestras, the *CLComp, the *CMCentre, the *CMCouncil, the *ACO, the *JMC, most of Canada's leading operas, ballets, and symphony orchestras, several foundations, provincial arts boards, educational institutions, etc. From its inception the CCA has worked, on behalf of its total membership, for increased government funding and recognition of the arts, greater public awareness of the arts, and the protection of the professional interests of the arts community. Indeed, analysis and documentation of the current needs of the larger arts community and of the public which that community serves, and a consequent lobbying of government and private funding agencies to help meet those needs, may be described as the CCA's main activities.

The CCA contributed directly to the creation of the *Canada Council and the Canadian Commission for Unesco (1957), and during the 1960s and 1970s it campaigned for arts funding agencies on provincial and municipal levels as well. It has sponsored seminars, regional conferences, and its own national conferences, and has established task forces on the arts and education, broadcasting and the arts, censorship, taxation, etc. Though not ordinarily involved in performance or the presentation of performances, in 1962 it presented five Toronto performances (28 May–2 Jun) of Gluck's *Orpheus and Euridice*, with Roma *Butler, Maureen *Forrester, and Arlene Sanders. The production (designed originally for the *Vancouver International Festival) was conducted by Nicholas *Goldschmidt and directed by Hanya Holm.

CCA publications include the periodicals *Communiqué* (Dec 1970–May 1975) and *Arts Bulletin* (May 1973–), a series of handbook directories, and occasional papers and reports, all in both French and English. Besides an elected board of governors and an executive committee the CCA has a salaried national director – Duncan Cameron 1968–71, succeeded by John Hobday. With the appointment of Cameron offices were established in Toronto. Previously the conference had used the address of the current president or secretary of the organization. In 1979 the offices were moved to Ottawa. Presidents have included Herman Voaden 1945–8, Jean Bruchési 1949–51 and 1957–8, Claude Lévis 1952–3, Roland Charlebois 1954–5, John Parkin 1956–7, Robert Ellis in 1959, Arthur Gelber 1959–68, Jean-Louis Roux 1969–71, Gilles *Lefebvre 1971–2, Pauline McGibbon 1972–3, Richard Courtney 1973–6, Elizabeth Lane 1976–8, and Micheline Legendre 1978–80, succeeded by Lister Sinclair. In 1954 the CCA began to award, annually, a Diplôme d'honneur to individuals outstanding in their service to the arts in Canada. Among the recipients have been Marius *Barbeau (1968), Floyd S. *Chalmers (1974), S.C. *Eckhardt-Gramatté (posthumous, 1975) Maureen Forrester (1980), Arthur Gelber (1979), Glenn *Gould (1976), Yvonne *Hubert (1979), Félix *Leclerc (1976), Gilles Lefebvre and Norman *McLaren (1978), Wilfrid *Pelletier (1970), Barbara *Pentland (1977), Oscar *Peterson (1975), and Wayne *Riddell (1962).

BIBLIOGRAPHY

Duval, Paul. 'Canadian Arts Council,' *Canadian Art*, vol 3, Summer 1946

Hobday, John. 'The Canadian Conference of the Arts: what has been accomplished and what remains to be done,' *OpCan*, Summer 1979

NM

Canadian Cultural Centre / Centre culturel canadien. Established in Paris by Canada's Department of External Affairs to foster the dissemination of Canadian culture. The centre is housed in an 18th-century private mansion at 5 rue de Constantine in the seventh arrondissement. Since the centre's establishment, in April 1970, music has been an important part of its activities. Its first director, Guy Viau, was assisted by the conductor Jacques *Beaudry in arranging musical events. After Viau's death in 1971, Jacques Asselin carried on until the arrival of Gilles *Lefebvre, who served 1972–8 in the position. Under Lefebvre's direction Michelle Proulx, responsible 1972–6 for music at the centre, established a music and record library representing Canadian composers and performers. The *CMCentre and the CBC IS donated scores and recordings. A system was installed in the 150-seat auditorium to allow audiovisual transmission of public events in three other adjoining rooms. In October 1970 the centre inaugurated its musical activities with a concert by the Ars Nova Ensemble conducted by Marius Constant and Jacques Beaudry and later broadcast by the ORTF. Canadian works on the program were *Freedman's *Fantasy and Allegro*, *Weinzweig's *Divertimento No. 1*, *Joachim's *Concertante No. 2*, *Papineau-Couture's *Pièce concertante No. 3*, and *Prévost's *Scherzo*. Concerts and recitals were given at an ever-increasing rate by Canada's major performers, eg, the duo pianists Victor *Bouchard and Renée *Morisset, Maureen *Forrester, Kenneth *Gilbert, Joseph *Rouleau, Hidetaro *Suzuki, George *Zukerman, and the *Orford String Quartet. Informal encounter sessions were held with the composers Serge *Garant, Bruce *Mather, Jean Papineau-Couture, Clermont *Pépin, André Prévost, and R. Murray *Schafer and with the tenor Jon *Vickers. The centre also welcomed many chansonniers, notably Robert *Charlebois, Félix *Leclerc, Claude *Léveillée, and Gilles *Vigneault. In May 1971, a concert by the Groupe international de musique électroacoustique of Paris presented *Trakadie* and *Arksalalartôk* by Micheline Coulombe *Saint-Marcoux. In January 1973, the *SMCQ Ensemble gave a concert of works by Gilles *Tremblay, John *Hawkins, Robert *Aitken, Bruce Mather, and Serge Garant, with the latter conducting. In 1976 in homage to Pierre *Mercure on the 10th anniversary of his death, the Paul Kuentz Orchestra performed his *Divertissement*, and Lyse *Richer-Lortie presented an illustrated lecture and an exhibition of his scores and other documents. In 1973 Gilles Lefebvre instituted 'Musicroissants,' a series of concerts for parents and children devised along the lines of the successful 'Sons et Brioches' concerts in Montreal in 1972. The centre also has invited French hosts such as the critics Jacques Bourgeois and Maurice Fleuret. The centre was among the organizations which helped coordinate the *Musicanada project of November 1977 in Paris and London. In 1979 Aline Legrand was appointed director of the centre.

BIBLIOGRAPHY
Hambleton, Ronald. 'Canada's Cultural Centre in Paris,' *CanComp*, 57, Feb 1971
– 'Jacques Asselin: Canada's new-breed cultural counsellor at work in Paris,' ibid, 59, Apr 1971
Campbell, Francean. 'Music at the Canadian Cultural Centre in Paris,' *CMB*, 3, Autumn–Winter 1971
Bouchard, Jacques. 'La vie qu'on mène après cinq ans au Centre culturel canadien à Paris,' Montreal *Le Devoir*, 18 Jan 1976
Leblond, Jean-Claude. 'Paris: Centre culturel et ... politique culturelle,' Montreal *Le Jour*, 21 Jan 1976
Maheu, Renée. 'Our Canadian Cultural Centre gives Canadian music and musicians a high profile,' *Mcan*, 31, Feb 1977 RMh

Canadian Electronic Ensemble. Composer-performers' group founded in Toronto in 1971 'to promote the live performance of electronic music and thereby the composition of new repertoire for this medium.' Members are David Grimes (b Salem, Mass, 9 Mar 1948; B MUS Berklee College of Music 1970, M MUS Toronto 1972; composer of *Increscents*, which won a prize in the 1976 *CBC National Radio Competition for Young Composers), David Jaeger (b Green Bay, Wis, 19 Nov 1947; B MUS Wisconsin 1970, M MUS Toronto 1972; joined CBC as a radio music producer in 1973), Larry Lake (b Greenville, Penn, 2 Jul 1943; B MUS Miami 1966, M·ED Miami 1968, M MUS Miami 1970; CBC radio music producer 1972–5), and James Montgomery (b Ravenna, O, 6 Feb 1943; B MUS Baldwin-Wallace College 1966, M MUS Toronto 1972: joined the U of Toronto in 1976 as a lecturer in electronic music; prizewinner in the 1977 Paris Film Festival for his score for *Deep Blue Sleep*; president 1978–9 of the *CLComp).

The ensemble gave its first concert with the *NMC in 1972. In 1976 it established a regular concert series. It has performed throughout Canada and in Europe, the USA, Australia, and New Zealand. It has appeared at the CBC's Toronto Festival, the Okanagan Festival for Composers, and at *World Music Week (1975) and has given concerts for *NOVA MUSIC in Halifax, and the *Vancouver New Music Society. Members of the group were artists-in-residence at *York U in 1976, acted as music consultants for the Structured Sound Synthesis Project of the Computer Systems Research Group of the *U of Toronto, and in 1978 became co-ordinators of a research project on the life and discoveries of the electronic-music pioneer Hugh *LeCaine. In fulfilling its schedule of concerts, demonstrations, lecture-recitals, and workshops, the ensemble has given premieres or Canadian premieres of over 200 works, including compositions by Robert *Bauer, Norma *Beecroft, John Cage, Patrick Carpenter, Gustav *Ciamaga, Derek *Healey, Mauricio Kagel, Udo *Kasemets, David Keane, Yori-aki-Matsudaira, Karlheinz Stockhausen, Norman *Symonds, Steve Tittle, Barry *Truax, and Gayle Young. It has commissioned several of these works and its members have collaborated on over 25 compositions and have recorded three of these (*Whale Oil, Arnold*, and *Piano Quintet*, the last named with the pianist Karen Kieser) for Music Gallery Editions (MGE 8).

In *Fugue* magazine Karen Kieser described the ensemble's manner of performing: 'All sit around a large table crowded with apparatus and trailing wires, and listen intently to each other and to themselves. Turning knobs, twisting dials and playing various keyboards, the composer-performers interact somewhat in the manner of jazz musicians.' The members all play brass instruments as well, and some of the works in their repertoire (eg, Norma Beecroft's *Consequences for 5* and Udo Kasemets' *David and David and Larry and James*) require them to play these (trumpets, horn, and trombone) while also performing on their electronic equipment. The ensemble has performed several of its works for radio broadcasts in Canada, the USA, France, Sweden, and West Germany.

See also Electronic music.

BIBLIOGRAPHY
Littler, William. 'The search continues for ideal way for group to communicate,' *Toronto Star*, 16 Apr 1977
Kieser, Karen. 'The excitement of that plug-in music,' *Fugue*, Sep 1977

The Canadian Federation of Music Teachers' Associations (CFMTA) / **Fédération canadienne des associations de professeurs de musique** (FCAPM). An umbrella organization encompassing provincial registered music teachers' associations including *Alberta Registered Music Teachers' Assn, *British Columbia Registered Music Teachers' Assn, *Manitoba Registered Music Teachers' Assn, *New Brunswick Registered Music Teachers' Assn, *Nova Scotia Registered Music Teachers' Assn, *Ontario Registered Music Teachers' Assn, *Quebec Music Teachers' Assn, and *Saskatchewan Registered Music Teachers' Assn. The CFMTA and its members should not be confused with the *CMEA; the latter is an association of institutional educators and teachers.

The CFMTA was established in 1935 by the British Columbia, Alberta, Saskatchewan, and Manitoba associations, joined in 1942 by Ontario, in 1944 by Nova Scotia, in 1945 by Quebec, and in 1954 by New Brunswick. It was incorporated in 1961. Its purpose was to lobby for school credits for grades achieved in private music study. Latterly, in addition, its objectives have been to improve the standards of music education, to promote provincial music teachers' associations, and to foster public appreciation of music.

The federation is governed by an executive council of elected provincial representatives. It serves approximately 90 branches in Canada and a membership of about 3000. Roy Robertson was the first president 1935–6, followed by Minnie Boyd 1937–9, May James 1939–41, Lyell *Gustin 1941–6, Edna Marie *Hawkin 1946–51, Dan A. *Cameron 1951–5, Violet Isfeld 1955–9, Reginald *Bedford 1959–63, Robert *Pounder 1963–7, Flora *Goulden 1967–71, Helen *Dahlstrom 1971–5, and Thelma *Wilson 1975–9, who was succeeded by Kathleen Fensom. Conventions are held biennially and feature master classes, workshops, and concerts. In alternate years the CFMTA has organized charter tours of world cultural centres. The CFMTA has published the *Canadian Music Teacher* (1937–46), *News Bulletin* (1946–71), and the *Canadian Music Teacher* (1971–5). It began publishing its *Newsletter* in 1975. In 1942 it initiated the Young Artist Series, under the successive direction of Lyell Gustin, Minna McCrea, Charles *Findlater, Gertrude Greaves, and Thelma *O'Neill, to provide touring experience for talented student performers. Among these have been Garth *Beckett, Neil *Chotem, Andrew *Dawes, Elaine *Keillor, Boyd McDonald, Morley *Meredith, Kenneth Perkins, Arthur *Polson, Winifred Scott, and Malcolm *Tait. It also established in 1960 the annual Canada Music Week under the chairmanship of Leonard *Wilson 1961–2, Sister Rodriguez Steele and Eleanor Harkness 1963–9, and Helen Dahlstrom 1970– , to support Canadian composers and performers, to introduce Canadian contemporary music to students, and to sponsor competitions for student composers. In 1967 Centennial Citation Awards for outstanding teaching were made to Mona *Bates, Gladys *Egbert, Lyell Gustin, Edna Marie Hawkin, Jenny *Lerouge LeSaunier, and John *Waterhouse. CFMTA is affiliated with the *CMCouncil and the Canadian committee of the International Society for Music Education (ISME).

BIBLIOGRAPHY
'The music education structure in Canada,' *Mcan*, 6, Nov 1967 (HD)

Canadian Folk Music Society / Société canadienne de musique folklorique. Established on the initiative of Maud Karpeles and Marius *Barbeau at a meeting in the National Museum in Ottawa 20 Sep 1956 as the Canadian branch of the International Folk Music Council. The name Canadian Folk Music Society was adopted soon afterwards, and in 1957 the society became autonomous, though retaining affiliation with the international council. It was incorporated in 1966. The presidents have been Marius *Barbeau 1956–63, Carmen Roy 1963–5, Graham *George 1965–8, Gaston *Allaire 1968–71, Michael Cass-Beggs 1971–6, and John *O'Donnell 1976–9, succeeded by Jon Bartlett. Membership grew from 80 in the first year to 220 in 1961, to 303 individuals and 93 institutions in 1979. The first annual meeting took place at Fort Qu'Appelle, Sask, in 1957. Subsequent meetings have been held most frequently in Ottawa. Among the original aims were the encouragement of research, the utilization of folk and Indian song, and the representation of the profession vis-à-vis the Canada Council, then recently established. The basic aims were redefined later as the encouragement of 'the study, appreciation and enjoyment of the folk music of Canada in all its aspects' and the promotion of 'publication and performance of Canadian folk music.' During its first years, the society's main project was the organization of the international council's 14th annual conference in Quebec, 28 Aug–3 Sep 1961, the theme being the meeting of the old and new worlds. Later, the society concentrated on problems of research and publication and for some years was successful in obtaining grants from certain provinces to send scholars on field trips. In 1967 it co-sponsored a Centennial Workshop on Ethnomusicology at the *U of British Columbia (19–23 June), organized by Ida *Halpern. The *Canada Council enabled the society to undertake a 'National Bibliography of Canadian Folk Music,' but in 1980 the compilation, consisting of some 1600 articles, treatises, songbooks, arrangements, recordings, and films, remained incomplete as a card file housed at the *NL of C, with entries being added only occasionally. A less ambitious but useful bibliography is *A Reference List on Canadian Folk Music*, compiled by Edith *Fowke and Barbara *Cass-Beggs (1966, 1973, and revised in 1978). The society also issued Kenneth *Peacock's *A Practical Guide for Folk Music Collectors* (1966). In July 1965 a *Newsletter* / *Bulletin* began appearing irregularly (usually twice a year), and in 1973 the *Canadian Folk Music Journal*, edited by Edith Fowke, began its annual appearances. Volume 1 contains the 1973 version of the Fowke / Cass-Beggs bibliography, and volume 6 the 1978 revised version. HK

Canadian Forces School of Music / École de musique des Forces canadiennes (Royal Canadian Navy School of Music / École de musique de la

Marine royale du Canada 1954–68). Established in 1954 in Victoria, BC, to provide musicians for Canadian navy bands. In 1961 it expanded to accommodate trainees for army and air force bands. With the unification of the navy, army, and air force in 1968, it became the CFSM. The school in 1980 offered a two-year program for male and female students aged 17 to 24, providing individual and ensemble instrumental instruction leading to qualification for positions in Canadian forces bands. An average of 100 students are enrolled annually in the school, and 150–200 students attend the annual summer program. The school also in 1980 offered a one-year program for experienced forces musicians wishing to become bandmasters, with classes in conducting and related musical subjects, as well as band administration and management, and provision for graduates' return to Canadian forces bands as assistant music directors. The school in 1980 was made up entirely of service musicians (23 being the normal complement). CFSM commandants have been: Lieut-Cdr Harry Cuthbert 1954–6, Lieut-Cdr Stanley Sunderland 1956–66, Lieut-Col Clifford *Hunt 1966–8, and Lieut-Col Edmund T. Jones 1968–75, succeeded by Maj Tom Milner in 1975.

BIBLIOGRAPHY

'The Canadian Forces School of Music,' *The Lookout*, 11 Jul 1974 (JK)

Canadian Grenadier Guards Band. Regimental band founded 26 Apr 1913 in Montreal by J.-J. *Gagnier, who became its conductor. At that time it consisted of about 40 players, half of whom were professionals, including six members of the Gagnier family. Formed at the request of F.S. *Meighen, His Majesty's Canadian Grenadier Guards Band was intended to accompany parades and other regimental activities. However, as early as 1919 its reputation as a concert band began to grow. It gave four concerts 1919–20 at the *Orpheum Theatre and five Sunday concerts annually 1920–3 at *His Majesty's Theatre. It played works by Beethoven, Wagner, Meyerbeer, Saint-Saëns, Berlioz, and Massenet and the *Marche héroïque* by Alexis *Contant – an unusual repertoire for a regimental band of that era. The band also presented, at Meighen's expense, Canadian and foreign solo artists such as Joseph *Saucier, Blanche Gonthier, Émile *Gour, Edmund *Burke, Hipolito Lazaro, Robert Couzinou, Louis Graveure, and Jean *Riddez. The music critic Philip King wrote, 'It is safe to assert that no concert organization in North America, even among the symphony orchestras, is doing more in the matter of program-making, within the limits of its power, than the band of H.M. Canadian Grenadier Guards' (*Montreal Daily Star*, 31 Jan 1921).

In 1921 and 1929 the band performed at the *CNE. Acclaimed from the Atlantic to the Pacific, it toured the Maritime provinces in 1928. Some of its numerous radio broadcasts 1931–2 and 1940–1 on CFCF and CKAC were relayed nationally, and several of those made in 1931 were heard in the USA as well, on the CBS and NBC networks. The band was heard on CBC radio about 1945 in a series of Sunday concerts. At the beginning of World War II it remained in Montreal as a part of the second battalion. (The first battalion, mobilized in 1940, formed its own musical group conducted by Sergt H.E. Finlayson.) Gagnier was director of the band until 1947, by which time he bore the rank of captain. His last appearance with his musicians was at the Montreal *Forum at a meeting of the United Nations Organization. A new ensemble was created in 1952 under the direction of Lieut Norman Mouland. Regimental Sergt-Maj Joe Miceli succeeded Mouland in 1959. In 1974 the Dept of National Defence decided to form a single ensemble, the Montreal Garrison Band.

Under Gagnier the grenadiers made seven 78s for HMV (the list is found in *Roll Back the Years*), one 78 (not commercially available) for Victor (PR 659–60), and in 1964 with Miceli the LP *On Parade* for RCA (LPM 2599). Claude *Champagne composed the *Ballade des lutins* for the grenadiers in 1914; like Hervé *Baillargeon and Francis Boucher, Champagne for a time was a member of the band. HP

Canadian Institute of Music / Institut canadien de musique. Organization founded in Montreal in 1929 and directed by Rodolphe *Mathieu; its aim was to create an intellectual milieu enabling 'young artists and literary talents to perform before an elite audience.' In 1930 the institute claimed to possess 22 studios in the city and styled itself as 'the largest institution for general music instruction in Canada.' In 1930 the institute presented its first Soirées Mathieu. These concerts, given at first monthly and then at irregular intervals, continued until 1952 and took place successively at the Windsor and Ritz-Carlton hotels and at the Cercle universitaire. The first concert (28 Oct 1930), devoted to works by Mathieu, was given by Hortense Lord (*Sonata* for piano), Paul Trottier and the Durieux String Quartet (*Deux Poèmes*), and Lucien *Plamondon and Ulysse *Paquin, accompanied by the composer (*Sonata* for cello and piano and *Saisons canadiennes*). After that the soirées usually took the form of informal lecture-concerts, during which one or two speakers might address literature, art, philosophy, science, psychology, or politics, as well as music. Among the guest artists were George M. *Brewer, Paul *Doyon, Jean *Leduc, Roland *Leduc, Anna *Malenfant, and the young André *Mathieu, who presented his own compositions in 1935. The proceeds from the soirées were used to provide scholarships for the winners of an annual competition for advanced performers initiated by the institute in 1930. The winners also had the privilege of performing in recital at a Mathieu soirée. Fleurette *Beauchamp, who appeared as a winner on three occasions, was also the first recipient of the institute's Prix de Paris (1933). The activities of the institute ceased around 1956. AP

The Canadian League of Composers / La Ligue canadienne de compositeurs. An organization formed in 1951, with headquarters in Toronto, to promote the music and advance the professional interests of composers. It was the result of the appearance during the 1940s of a wave of young composers expressing themselves in contemporary idioms. They decided to take collective action because of resistance to their music, on the one hand by publishers and concert and orchestra managers who thought it bad for business, and on the other by conservative performers and audiences who prejudged it as meaningless and ugly and were suspicious of homegrown art. The composers had no desire to issue a credo of aesthetic convictions or to forge a distinct Canadian style of music; on the contrary, CLComp members have followed a great variety of styles and techniques. Their main objectives were to end the composers' isolation from each other, challenge the public's apathy towards contemporary music, and establish composition as a recognized profession in Canada.

The idea of a league grew out of an informal discussion 3 Feb 1951 between Samuel *Dolin, Harry *Somers, and John *Weinzweig at the Toronto home of the last-named. After the recruitment of several other sympathetic Toronto composers (Murray *Adaskin, Louis *Applebaum, Harry *Freedman, Phil *Nimmons, and Andrew *Twa) the first organizational meeting was held 1 Apr 1951. John Weinzweig, the true father of the CLComp, was chosen president, and a concert of his music, presented 16 May 1951 by soloists and a string orchestra under Ettore *Mazzoleni at the *RCMT Concert Hall and broadcast on 'CBC Wednesday Night,' introduced the young organization to the public. By the end of 1951 it had close to 20 members. A charter was obtained in 1952.

The group's first move was to arrange hearings for its members' compositions by organizing a series of concerts. The first symphonic program was presented 26 Mar 1952 under Geoffrey *Waddington at *Massey Hall, Toronto. Other performances were organized in Toronto and, with league support, in 1953 in Stratford, Ont, and Vancouver. A concert committee in Montreal arranged a performance 3 Feb 1954 under Waddington at *Plateau Hall. However, the chores of organizing concerts proved too taxing for a small number of composers, so subsidiary organizations – of supporters rather than composers – were set up: the *Canadian Music Associates (Ontario) in 1954 in Toronto and the *Society of Canadian Music / La Société de musique canadienne (Quebec) in 1959 in Montreal. Two to four concerts and film showings were held each season in Toronto until 1958, including two short operas, 17 Nov 1956: *Blackburn's **Silent Measures* and Somers' **The Fool*. Three more concerts were held in 1963. Individual events took place in Hamilton in 1954 and Ottawa in 1956, and CBC radio carried some of the music on its networks. By 1966 some 200 works had been presented in about 40 concerts. At this point the performance of Canadian music had grown to such a degree that special concerts seemed pointless and ineffective. Responsibility for the performance of contemporary Canadian music was assumed and shared, gradually, by other organizations (*ARRAY, *Days Months and Years to Come, Musique de notre temps / Music of Our Time of Montreal, *NMC, *NOVA MUSIC, *SMCQ, *Ten Centuries Concerts, and, to a degree, the various avant-garde series of Udo *Kasemets).

Meanwhile the CLComp itself sought other ways to promote knowledge of Canadian music. It selected for publication *Fourteen Piano Pieces by Canadian Composers* (Harris 1955) and prepared a *Catalogue of Orchestral Music* (1957) listing 233 works written between 1918 and 1957. It built up a small library of scores by its members, but soon recognized the need for an independent agency for the circulation of unpublished Canadian scores and performance materials and of information and propaganda. A plan to this purpose was formulated by John *Beckwith and John Weinzweig and submitted to the *CMCouncil in 1957 (see *CMJ*, Spring 1957) for inclusion in a submission to the new *Canada Council. The result was the opening in 1959 of the *CMCentre, on the board of which the league has kept a strong presence.

The original battle for recognition of Canadian music having been fought with much success (and with much support from the CBC), and the CMCentre having been launched, the league was able to turn more of its attention to the protection of composers' professional interests in the legal, economic, and administrative spheres. It has concerned itself with questions of copyright, mechanical licences, norms for commissioning and rental fees, publishing and recording contracts, Canadian broadcast content, and university courses on Canadian music. Among the briefs it has submitted are those to the Royal Commission on Broad-

Twentieth-anniversary meeting of the Canadian League of Composers, Victoria, BC, 1971

casting (ie, the Fowler Commission 1955–7), the Fowler Committee (1964–5), the Interdepartmental Committee on Copyright in 1970, and the *CRTC in 1970.

The CLComp has concerned itself also with Canadian representation in international competitions and festivals. It submitted scores for the 1952 Olympiad in Helsinki and was the Canadian chapter of the ISCM from 1953–6, and after a hiatus of some years it has taken up liaison with that body once more. International relations were fostered through the league's joint sponsorship with the *Stratford Festival of the *International Conference of Composers in Stratford, Ont, in 1960. In recognition of the contributions made by performers to the interpretation of Canadian music, the league created the *Canada Music Citation. To assist young composers it established a scholarship (worth $250) in 1968. The first recipient of this award was John *Fodi, who won it again in 1970. Other winners have been Denis *Lorrain (1970), Robert *Bauer and Paul *Crawford (1971), Michel *Vinet (1973), Dennis Patrick (1974), Michel *Longtin (1975), and Denis Gourgeon (1977). In 1976 the competition was made biennial, with a $500 scholarship.

Another landmark in the CLComp's history was the 20th-anniversary celebration, held at the *U of Victoria in February 1971 and consisting of concerts and panel discussions.

Membership in the CLComp has been regarded as an honour. Initially it was by invitation (requiring nomination by a member); later, applications could be made directly as well, but applicants had to have a certain number of works and performances to their credit and had to submit scores to a selection committee. Another qualification is that new members must be under 65 years of age. Membership grew from 20 in 1952 to 107 in 1979. Healey *Willan and Claude *Champagne were made honorary members in 1955. All member composers automatically are members of the CMCentre. Apart from a small Canada Council grant matching members' fees, the CLComp has never sought governmental subsidies to aid in its activities, and all of those involved have worked voluntarily.

Presidents have been John Weinzweig 1951–7, 1959–63, Jean *Papineau-Couture 1957–9, 1963–6, Srul Irving *Glick 1966–9, Samuel Dolin 1969–73, Talivaldis *Kenins 1973–4, Walter *Buczynski 1974–5, Harry Freedman 1975–8, and James Montgomery 1978–9. Victor *Davies succeeded Montgomery in 1979. The CLComp's archives are preserved at the *NL of C.

Although by 1980 the organization no longer was in the public limelight as frequently as it had been in its 'heroic' early years, it remained an effective lobby and a forum for the exchange and generation of new ideas. The league by then had gone far towards realizing its principal aim of giving contemporary Canadian composition a vital position in musical life, but its greatest achievement probably had been and continued to be its moral support and encouragement to the individual composer, member and non-member alike.

BIBLIOGRAPHY
Kallmann, Helmut. 'First fifteen years of Canadian League of Composers,' *CanComp*, 7, Mar 1966
– 'Chronology,' *CMB*, 2, Spring-Summer 1971
MacMillan, Keith. 'Report from Victoria,' ibid
'The League of Composers: 20 years on, what progress?' *CanComp*, 59, Apr 1971
'The League of Composers: how hard work paid off,' *CanComp*, 119, Mar 1977
Schulman, Michael. 'The Canadian League of Composers on the warpath,' *Mcan*, 35, Apr 1978
Timar, Andrew. 'Talk with Victor Davies,' *Musicworks*, 10, Winter 1980
HK

Canadian Mennonite Bible College. School of theology, liberal arts, and music, founded in 1947 in Winnipeg by the Conference of Mennonites in Canada. The music department was established under the direction 1947–54 of John *Konrad and continued under George Wiebe. Courses lead to a Bachelor of Theology or a Bachelor of Church Music; cross-registration has allowed students to obtain credit towards a BA in music at the *U of Manitoba or an ARCT. In 1978 the focus of the department – which that year enrolled 36 music students served by three full-time and four part-time instructors – was on the training of organists, conductors, church choir directors, educators, and teachers, and this had not changed by 1980. The college has a chamber choir and an oratorio choir, the latter merging in 1965 with the *Mennonite Brethren Bible College Oratorio Choir for annual concerts accompanied by members of the *Winnipeg SO. Graduates of the school include the choral director Henry Engbrecht, the tenor Arthur Janzen, the church musician Neil Matthies, the music director Bernie Neufeld, the choral director Henry Peters, the music director John Poettcker, and the bass William Thiessen.

See also Mennonites.

Canadian Music Associates (Ontario). Formed in 1952 as the concert arm of the *CLComp. Made up of laymen, musicians, and CLComp members, it was incorporated in 1954. Acting on the CLComp's behalf the group organized, financed, and promoted from two to four concerts a year and several *NFB film nights. The league itself was responsible for program content, and the CMA made a point of engaging Canadian artists. By 1957 it had arranged for the performance of 80 Canadian compositions, including the premieres 17 Nov 1956 of *Somers' **The Fool* and *Blackburn's **Silent Measures*. CMA presidents have included David Catton, Stewart Sutton, John Osler, and Norma *Beecroft. With the formulation of plans for a *Canadian Music Centre and the *Canada Council's decision to shift its financial support to that organization alone, the CMA chose to dissolve in 1958.

Canadian Music Centre / Centre de musique canadienne (Centre musical canadien 1959–73). A non-profit, non-governmental central library and information centre for the dissemination and promotion of Canadian concert, operatic, educational, and church music. It was founded 1 Jan 1959 by the *CMCouncil with grants from the recently formed *Canada Council and *CAPAC. The first office was in Toronto; a Montreal office was opened in 1973. Continuing support from the Canada Council and CAPAC has been supplemented by grants from the *OAC, the *MACQ, *PRO Canada, and the governments of British Columbia and Alberta. Presidents of the centre have been Arnold *Walter in 1959 and again in 1970, Sir Ernest *MacMillan 1959–70, John Peter Lee *Roberts 1971–3, Jean *Papineau-Couture 1973–4, and Keith *Bissell 1974–7, succeeded by Paul Baby in 1977. Keith *MacMillan was executive secretary of the centre 1964–77 and was succeeded by John Peter Lee Roberts. Previous incumbents were Jean-Marie *Beaudet 1959–61 and John *Adaskin 1961–4. In 1973 Louise *Laplante became associate executive secretary responsible for the Montreal office. Early in 1976 the centre underwent a restructuring preparatory to the development of regional centres. The original centre (Toronto) became the national headquarters with Keith MacMillan as general manager. The Montreal centre became the Quebec regional centre with Louise Laplante as regional manager. In 1977 a British Columbia regional office was opened in Vancouver with Christine Callon as manager, succeeded in 1978 by Colin Miles; in 1980 a Prairie regional office, managed by Christine (Callon) Purvis, was established in Calgary to serve Alberta, Manitoba, and Saskatchewan.

Though the centre's main task is the promotion of Canadian music, it also provides a variety of information services, administers several organizations' scholarships to young composers, and offers services in copying and reproduction to professional composers. Norma Dickson became the centre's resource person in 1961 and received the *CMCouncil Medal in 1980 in recognition of her work on behalf of Canadian composers. The centre's main promotional tools are its library and its collection of reference recordings. In 1963 Henry Mutsaers (b Naarden, Holland, 19 Mar 1919, naturalized Canadian 1972) was appointed full-time librarian for the Toronto centre, responsible for score copying, reproducing, binding and recording and for establishing and maintaining contact with composers. From the 300-odd scores collected and catalogued by the *CLComp and a small library contributed by the CMCouncil, the Toronto centre's circulating library of published and unpublished scores grew by 1980 to nearly 6500, of which the most significant are reproduced as the foundation of the regional libraries. The Toronto, Montreal, and Vancouver libraries contain extensive reference collections of discs, tapes, and cassettes. These do not circulate but may be listened to at any of the centres. The centres also keep files of program notes and dossiers on composers.

The associate composers of the CMCentre have special status and are chosen by a selection committee appointed by the board of directors. The associateship is applied for, and the applicant must be demonstrably a serious career composer and a Canadian citizen living in Canada or, if living abroad, doing so for not more than five years. If not a Canadian citizen the applicant must have been resident in Canada for at least five years. The centre also grants associate status to deceased composers whose works it holds. In 1979 there were 159 associate composers, all but 18 living. The centre's library and catalogues do not, however, represent associates exclusively and in fact include many works by non-associates. The centre makes photocopies of unpublished works of associate composers for its libraries; it may in some instances pay copying costs to ensure first performances and will act as a composer's rental agent for unpublished works. As a precaution it microfilms unpublished scores (with the composer's permission), and the microfilms can be made available to libraries and others.

The centre is not a music publisher, though the Quebec regional centre has published *Garant's *Offrande II* (1978) and *Vivier's *Lettura di Dante* (1979). The centre does, however, act as a liaison between composers and publishers, commissioning agencies, performing organizations, and recording companies. In addition it has helped develop guidelines for a Canada Council music publication subsidy program. In 1967 – Canada's centennial year – it negotiated 44 of the more than 100 commissions of Canadian works. In 1963 it began to select and commission Canadian music for school use through its *John Adaskin Project. It also co-operates with such organizations as *Contemporary Showcase and the *CMEA which promote Canadian music for students. The centre advises several award-granting bodies, presents displays and lectures (in Canada and abroad), and has participated in international exchanges of contemporary music, especially through the International Group of Music Information Centres (a working commission of the International Assn of Music Libraries), of which the centre's former executive secretary, Keith MacMillan, was named secretary in 1964 and president in 1976. The centre's efforts have contributed to a marked increase in the performance of Canadian music and to a growing recognition of Canada's composers.

PUBLICATIONS

Report on the John Adaskin Project Policy Conference (Toronto 1968)
John Adaskin Project: Towards New Music in Education (Toronto 1968)
Reference Sources for Information on Canadian Composers (Toronto 1970, suppls 1974, 1975)
Contemporary Canadian Composers, ed John Beckwith and Keith MacMillan (with OUP, Toronto 1975)
Cherney, Brian. *Harry Somers* (with U of Toronto Press, Toronto 1975)
Billette, Gaby. *À l'Écoute de la musique d'ici: Kékoba de Gilles Tremblay* (Montreal 1976)
Compositeurs canadiens contemporains, ed Louise Laplante (with U of Quebec Press, Montreal 1977)
Shand, Patricia. *Canadian Music: A Selective Guide List for Teachers* (Toronto 1978)

BROCHURES

Compositeurs au Québec: Gilles Tremblay (Montreal 1974), *François Morel* (Montreal 1974), *Jean Papineau-Couture* (Montreal 1974), *Bruce Mather* (Montreal 1974), *André Prévost* (Montreal 1975), *Serge Garant* (Montreal 1975), *Micheline Coulombe Saint-Marcoux* (Montreal 1975), *Roger Matton* (Montreal 1975), *Pierre Mercure* (Montreal 1976), *Jacques Hétu* (Montreal 1978), *Claude Champagne* (Montreal 1979), *Otto Joachim* (Montreal 1980)
14 British Columbia Composers (Vancouver 1978)

CATALOGUES

ORCHESTRAL AND BAND

Catalogue of Orchestral Music at the Canadian Music Centre / Catalogue des oeuvres disponibles au centre musical canadien (Toronto 1963, suppls 1968, 1971)
Catalogue of Canadian Music Suitable for Community Orchestras, compiled by Jan Matejcek (Toronto 1971)
Canadian Compositions for Band (Toronto 1973)
Catalogue of Canadian Music for Orchestra / Catalogue de musique canadienne pour orchestre (Toronto 1976, suppl 1979)

CHAMBER

Catalogue of Chamber Music / Catalogue de musique de chambre (Toronto 1967, suppls 1971, 1976; 2nd edn 1980)

INSTRUMENTAL

Catalogue of Canadian Keyboard Music / Catalogue de musique canadienne à clavier (Toronto 1971, suppl 1976)
Canadian Music Featuring Saxophone (Toronto 1972)

CHORAL

Catalogue of Canadian Choral Music (Toronto 1966, enl 1970)
Catalogue of Canadian Choral Music / Catalogue de musique chorale canadienne (Toronto 1978)

VOCAL

Canadian Vocal Music / Musique vocale canadienne (Toronto 1971, 1976)
Canadian Vocal Music / Musique vocale canadienne, rev edn (Toronto 1976)

OTHER

Catalogue of Microfilms of Unpublished Canadian Music (Toronto 1970)

PERIODICALS

Music Across Canada, Feb–Aug 1963
Newsletter / Bulletin de nouvelles, Sep 1964–Dec 1965
Musicanada, May 1967–Jun 1970
Newsletter, British Columbia CMCentre, Jan 1978–

DISCOGRAPHY

Canada on Records: Some Recordings of Works by Canadian Composers, special issue *Musicanada*, 26, Jan–Feb 1970; suppls 1974, 1976

LISTS

Canadian Chamber and String Orchestras / Orchestres de chambre et orchestres à cordes canadiens, Oct 1971
Various Canadian Music Publishers, annual listing, Oct 1971–
Canadian Symphony Orchestras / Orchestres symphoniques du Canada, Oct 1971
Youth Orchestras in Canada / Orchestres des jeunes au Canada, Nov 1971
Summer Music Courses / Cours d'été en musique; National Youth Orchestra / Orchestre national de la jeunesse du Canada, 1972
List of Music Critics, Columnists, etc, Sep 1972
Women's Musical Clubs: 1972–73 season, Sep 1972
List of University Schools of Music, Conservatories and Music Schools in Canada / Liste des écoles universitaires de musique, conservatoires et écoles de musigue au Canada, Oct 1975
Canadian and International Competitions / Concours canadiens et internationaux, Apr 1976, Jul 1976
Canadian Operas Available from the Canadian Music Centre, 1979
Canadian Music Inspired by the Music, Poetry, Art and Folklore of Native Peoples, 1979

BIBLIOGRAPHY

Winters, Kenneth. 'Canadian Music Centre's 10th Anniversary,' *CanComp*, 38, Mar 1969
Thériault, Jacques. 'Le Centre musical canadien,' *CMB*, 4, Spring–Summer 1972
MacMillan, Keith. 'Canadian Music Centre: information supplier,' *CanComp*, 74, Nov 1972
Littler, William. '20-year-old centre is music to ears of composers,' *Toronto Star*, 26 May 1979
Canadian Music in the 1960s and 1970s: A Chronicle, program for the concert honouring the 20th anniversary of the CMCentre presented by New Music Concerts 20 Oct 1979 (Toronto 1979)
MacMillan, Rick. 'Recordings are missing in musical life,' *MSc*, 310, Nov–Dec 1979 (PS)

Canadian Music Competitions, Inc / Concours de musique du Canada, Inc. Umbrella organization founded in 1970 in Montreal and Toronto by Claude Deschamps, Hélène M. Stevens, and Denyse Raymond to establish and co-ordinate high-level performance competitions in each province of Canada (leading to national finals), with the dual aim of discovering young musicians of exceptional talent and achievement and of preparing them for international careers through the provision of bursaries and performing opportunities. A national office was established in Montreal with Deschamps as managing director and incorporation was achieved in 1971.

The Quebec Music Festivals / Festivals de musique du Québec, founded in 1960 by Deschamps, Pierre Émond, and Charles Charrère, were the prototype for the national organization. Observing their development over a 10-year period as their director, and convinced of their worth, Deschamps had come to realize that a provincial boundary was a limitation in a program which hoped to prepare musicians for international careers. It was this realization which led him to approach advisers and patrons in Montreal and Toronto in 1970 in order to enlist support for a national organization.

In 1971 the Quebec Music Festivals – which continued under Deschamps's direction but henceforth functioned as the Quebec branch of the Canadian Music Competitions, changed their name to Quebec Music Competitions. An Ontario branch had been established at the same time as the national organization (1970), and branches followed in Alberta, British Columbia, and Manitoba in 1972, and in the Atlantic Provinces in 1978. The governments of these provinces and the *Canada Council have subsidized the regional and provincial competitions held annually in April and May, and have contributed, along with the municipalities involved, to the national finals held each year in June in a different city.

The syllabus provides for competition in voice, piano, guitar, recorder (in Quebec), and any orchestral instrument. The candidates, Canadians or landed immigrants, may be from 7 to 23 years old (grouped in categories by age) for the initial competitions, and from 15 to 28 years old (instrumentalists) or 18 to 30 (singers) for the International Stepping Stones (Tremplin international), the highest level of the competition. This section, created in 1971, allows the best candidates to prepare for the rigours of international competition, both in repertoire and standards of participation. By the time a candidate reaches the national finals he has prepared two complete recitals. The bursaries come from government subsidies and from private and corporate donations. In 1978 the first prizes for the competitions were $500 (7 to 14 years) and $1000 (15 to 23 years). The first prize of the International Stepping Stones section, awarded to the winning instrumentalist, was $3000. A special prize of $300 was awarded to the best performer of a prescribed, unpublished Canadian piece. The juries have been composed of foreign artists and of Canadians living abroad.

The competitions have drawn between 800 and 3000 participants annually, of which about 50 have reached the Stepping Stone level. Among the winners, of whom some already have acquired national or international reputations, are the pianists William *Aide, Suzanne Blondin, Henri *Brassard, Gaston *Brisson, Jane *Coop, Jacinthe *Couture, Marc Durand, Janina *Fialkowska, Douglas Finch, John *Hendrickson, Angela *Hewitt, André *Laplante, Stéphane Lemelin, Louis *Lortie, John Mackay, Denise Massé, Diane Mauger, Lorraine Prieur, Claude *Savard, Robert *Silverman, Elyakim *Taussig, and William *Tritt; the violinists Martin Foster, Gwen Hoebig, and Chantal Juillet; the cellists

Denis *Brott and Marcel St-Cyr; the oboist Bernard *Jean; the horn player Jean Gaudreault; the singers Michèle Boucher, Clarice *Carson, Céline *Dussault, Marie *Laferrière, and Nicole *Lorange; and the guitarist Liona *Boyd. In 1979 the first National Composers' Competition was initiated.

BIBLIOGRAPHY

Samson, Marc. 'Claude Deschamps: éliminer toute compétition va contre la vie elle-même,' Quebec *Le Soleil*, 21 Jun 1975

Epstein, David. 'The Canadian Music Competition,' *Musical America*, Feb 1976

Novak, Barbara. 'Canadian Music Competitions,' *Arts Bulletin*, Oct–Nov 1976 (CH)

Canadian Music Council / Conseil canadien de la musique. Umbrella organization established in 1944 as a 'music committee.' It adopted the present name in 1945, received a federal charter in 1949, and set up a permanent secretariat in Ottawa in 1976. Its membership consists of organizations and individuals. It aims 1 / to provide information about music in Canada, 2 / to generate discussion of musical issues of general concern, 3 / to represent the musical community to governments and international organizations, and 4 / to assist the development, and concern itself with the protection, of music in Canada.

1 Origin
2 The early years – waiting for the Canada Council
3 1957–65
4 1965–79

1 ORIGIN. A national music council is a response to the mid-20th-century need to co-ordinate musical activities within a country and to provide liaison with other countries in a variety of subjects from financing to copyright, from publicity to scholarly projects. Among the oldest such councils are those of Germany (Allgemeiner Deutscher Musikverein 1861) and Britain (British Music Society 1918). In Canada there was no organization to speak on behalf of all musicians when in 1944 the House of Commons' Committee on Post-War Reconstruction was ready to listen to spokesmen from all walks of life. Urged by interested persons, Sir Ernest *MacMillan hastily assembled a committee and presented a report on the problems and hopes of the musical community, endeavouring henceforth to maintain contact with musicians concerned about the future. He asked Charles *Peaker to take over the chairmanship of the committee, and Peaker invited John *Cozens to help with the organizing. A few months later 20 persons gathered for a discussion in Toronto, and the name Canadian Music Council was adopted. Soon afterwards, Peaker resigned, and MacMillan was elected chairman, a position he held (as chairman or president) for 20 years. Cozens served as voluntary secretary for 30 years.

2 THE EARLY YEARS – WAITING FOR THE CANADA COUNCIL. As chartered in 1949, the CMCouncil had a board of 12 directors. In practice the number was smaller – the first directors included Jean-Marie *Beaudet, William St Clair Low, and Arnold *Walter. As work was voluntary and there were no funds for travel, the council was essentially a Toronto group despite a fair national representation on the membership list. Three to five membership meetings took place in Toronto each year; the first elsewhere was one in Montreal 7 Feb 1959. Membership was by invitation (upon approval by the preceding meeting) and included representatives of the main university music departments, distinguished individuals, and specialists in various fields. In 1953 there were 40 individual members and three organizations: *CAPAC, *CFMTA, and CCO (*RCCO). The CBC at first was an observer but later was a member. The following organizations of national scope became members during the 1950s: the *CLComp, BMI Canada (*PRO Canada), the *CMLA (replaced later by *CAML), *JMC, *CMPA, *CFMS, *CBA, *FCMF, *Canadian Bureau for the Advancement of Music, and the Canadian Music Educators' Conference (soon changed to *CMEA). Much of the time at council meetings was taken up with the exchange of news between these organizations.

Financial resources (donations from CAPAC and later also BMI Canada, and nominal membership fees) being limited, no projects of any size could be undertaken. Many of the council's meetings were spent in monotonous alternation of the questions 'How can we find money for what should be done?' and 'If we had money, what should we do with it?' The CMCouncil was waiting for the establishment by the Canadian government of the rumoured Canada Council, which might delegate the music group to implement its policy in the field of music.

When the *Canada Council became a reality in 1957, however, it did not appoint the CMCouncil its music arm. It did appoint Sir Ernest to the Canada Council (he served 1957–63) and provide subsidies, increasing over the years, to many of the CMCouncil's (proposed) projects. Meanwhile, however, the council had completed many worthwhile projects without subsidies. For the 1948 Olympics it helped to collect scores by Canadian composers for submission to a music competition. (One of these, *Weinzweig's *Divertimento No. 1*, was the winner in the chamber music class.) The council also assembled, largely upon donation by the publishers, a library of some 700 printed Canadian compositions; prepared a brief for the Royal Commission on Patents, Copyright, Trademarks and Industrial Design in 1954; selected five orchestral works and, with the help of the federal Dept of External Affairs, printed and distributed them in Canada and overseas in 1955. The same year, the council published *Music in Canada*, edited by MacMillan, with 18 chapters on specific aspects contributed by specialists. A year later the council launched the **Canadian Music Journal* (1956–62), the country's first high-quality music periodical of national scope. One of the early issues of the *CMJ* (Spring 1957) was devoted to 'Music and the Canada Council' and presented a summary of proposals that had been worked out by members who were specialists in various fields, together with an examination of the problems of patronage by Arnold Walter.

3 1957–65. The establishment of the Canada Council in 1957 did not change the status of the CMCouncil as an 'unofficial' voice of Canadian musicians, but at least it enabled the organization to reimburse its members' travel expenses and to ask for funds for some major projects. The largest and most far-reaching was the *CMCentre (1959) for the promotion of Canadian compositions. Until 1965 the centre remained under the direct control of the council, which received and passed on the Canada Council's annual grants.

The CMCouncil became the Canadian committee of the International Music Council in 1952 and of CIDEM (the Inter-American Music Council) in 1959. In the next few years it welcomed several new organizations to its own ranks: *CAMMAC, *NYO, and *CAUSM.

4 1965–80. The mid-1960s brought change. The main burden of discussion and decision shifted from the frequent general meetings to single annual meetings with an emphasis on trends and themes, the meetings combined with conferences (every two years after 1979), a focal point for the exchange of ideas and the meeting of minds. Their topics and locations were

1965 The Pros and Cons of the Competitive Festival (Toronto)
1966 Music in Canada, Its Resources and Needs (Ottawa)
1967 Music and Media (Toronto)
1968 Music Education in Canada (Montreal)
1969 Contemporary Music and Audiences (Montreal)
1970 The Musician in 2001 (Ottawa)
1971 Music and Youth in Canada (Quebec City)
1972 The Development of a Music Policy for Canada (Banff, Alta)
1973 Music Criticism in Canada (Montreal)
1974 Folk Music in Canada (Halifax, NS)
1975 Music in Canada: Survey and Perspective (Ottawa); Music as a Dimension of Life (Ottawa and Montreal – in collaboration with the International Music Council, Paris, and the International Institute of Music, Dance and Theatre, Vienna)
1976 Music in a Restrained Economy: From Proliferation to Consolidation (Guelph, Ont)
1977 Music in the Community (Vancouver)
1978 Music and Television (London, Ont)
1979 For All Children, Their Daily Music (Quebec City)

After Sir Ernest's retirement and his appointment as hon president in 1966, the headquarters shifted frequently, and directors were elected from a larger geographical area. The incoming president 1966–7 was Arnold Walter, who had been vice-chairman for many years. During his presidency the CMCouncil played host to the CIDEM conference in Toronto in 1967. Subsequent presidents have been Jean *Papineau-Couture 1967–8, John P.L. *Roberts 1968–71 and 1975–7, Françoys *Bernier 1971–3, Ronald *Napier 1973–5, and Maryvonne *Kendergi 1977–80. George Laverock succeeded Kendergi. Wilfrid *Pelletier was appointed hon president in 1969.

In 1970 performing groups (non-national organizations) began to be admitted as members, and 13 had been accepted by the end of that year. Membership in 1979 was 22 national organizations, 55 non-national organizations, and 108 individuals. In 1969 a category of honorary membership was established.

The special projects in these years have included the publication of *Aspects of Music in Canada* (Toronto 1969), edited by Arnold Walter, with chapters by the editor and seven contributors, translated and brought up to date in a French edition, *Aspects de la musique au Canada* (Montreal 1970) under the supervision of Maryvonne Kendergi and Gilles *Potvin. The latter was appointed editor of the council's new periodical, **The Canada Music Book*, in the same year. Also in 1970, the council saw to the formation of a Canadian committee to ensure Canadian participation in the selection of music for performance at the annual festivals of the ISCM. In 1971 the *CMCouncil Medal was established, and in 1977 several other awards were created: artist of the year, composer of the year, a special award, and a number of media awards for achievements in radio, TV, and recording. (The pop field is not included.) The main energy of the CMCouncil during the early 1970s, however, was brought to bear on the preparation of the 16th General Assembly of the International Music Council and its first *World Music Week, 24 Sep–5 Oct 1975. This assembly surpassed in scope and attendance all previous such meetings in Canada.

Soon after this successful meeting the CMCouncil, with the help of the Canada Council, was able to realize one of its oldest dreams, a permanent secretariat, which opened in Ottawa in 1976 with Guy *Huot as secretary-general and John Cozens as hon secretary. (A secretariat opened in 1949 and run by Kenneth Ingram had been premature and was short-lived.) One of the first projects after the establishment of this office was the publication of *Musicanada*, a revival and adaptation of the CMCentre's discontinued magazine.

In 30 years the CMCouncil has gone through changes of structure and role, growing from a Toronto-centred organization into a truly national one. It has looked inwards to take stock of the weaknesses and strengths of music in Canada, and outwards to ensure Canadian recognition abroad. Activity has ranged from lobbying to publicizing, from awarding to co-ordinating. Not all activities have been effective, and not all potentials of a national umbrella organization have been realized, but the accomplishments are impressive, and the dedication to a variety of worthy causes has yielded historic results.

PUBLICATIONS

Music in Canada, ed Sir Ernest MacMillan (Toronto 1955)
Canadian Music Journal (Sackville NB and Toronto 1956–62)
Reports of CMCouncil Conferences: *Music in Canada: Its Resources and Needs* (1966), *Music and Media* (1967), *Music Education and the Canadians of Tomorrow* (1968), *Contemporary Music and Audiences / La Musique contemporaine et la publique* (1969)
Aspects of Music in Canada, ed Arnold Walter (Toronto 1969)
Aspects de la musique au Canada, eds Maryvonne Kendergi and Gilles Potvin (Montreal 1970)
The Canada Music Book / Les Cahiers canadiens de musique (1970–6)
Musicanada, quarterly (1976–)

BIBLIOGRAPHY

Walter, Arnold. 'The Canadian Music Council,' *TSO News*, Dec 1954
MacMillan, Sir Ernest. 'The Canadian Music Council,' *CMJ*, vol 1, Autumn 1956
MacMillan, Keith. 'National organizations,' *Aspects of Music in Canada*
Roberts, John. 'A word about the Canadian Music Council,' *CMB*, vol 1, Spring–Summer 1970 HK

The Canadian Music Council Medal. Instituted in 1971 and awarded for outstanding service to music in Canada. The medal was designed by the Canadian sculptor Charles Daudelin. Recipients, nominated by members of the council and selected by its directors, have been

1971 Leo *Barkin, Jean-Marie *Beaudet (posthumously), Serge *Garant
1972 John *Beckwith, Lionel *Daunais, Lois *Marshall, R. Murray *Schafer, Léopold *Simoneau
1973 Lyell *Gustin, Sir Ernest *MacMillan (posthumously), Eric *McLean, Soeur *Marie-Stéphane SNJM, Jean *Papineau-Couture, Gilles *Tremblay
1974 François *Brassard, Helen *Creighton, Luc *Lacourcière
1975 Elmer *Iseler, Yehudi Menuhin, Wilfrid *Pelletier
1976 Alexander *Brott, John *Cozens, Nicholas *Goldschmidt
1977 Helmut *Kallmann, Phyllis *Mailing, André *Prévost
1978 Keith *Bissell, Mario *Duschenes, Keith *MacMillan, Olivier Messiaen, John *Weinzweig
1979 Richard W. *Cooke, Yvonne *Hubert, John *Newmark
1980 John *Avison, Norma Dickson, Nicholas *Koudriavtzeff

The Canadian Music Council Medal

The Canadian Music Educator 1959– / ***L'Éducateur de musique au Canada*** 1976–8; ***Le Journal des éducateurs de musique au Canada*** 1978–9; ***Le Musicien éducateur au Canada*** 1979– . Official journal of the *CMEA. A quarterly, it began publication in June 1959 and includes essays, feature articles, and reviews of music and books. It served also as a news publication until 1968, when the CMEA established a separate newsletter. CMEA convention news, however, continued to appear in the *CME*. With an eye to becoming a fully bilingual publication, in 1975 it began to increase its French-language content, and a bilingual title appeared on the fall 1976 issue. Editors have been Leslie *Bell 1959–62, Ezra *Schabas 1962–3, Kenneth *Bray 1963–9, Alfred *Garson 1969–73, and Duane Bates 1973–9. Barbara Keane was interim editor while Bates was on sabbatical leave in 1976. Margery Vaughan succeeded Bates.

Canadian Music Educators' Association (CMEA) / **Association canadienne des éducateurs de musique** (ACEM). National organization representing the music educators' associations of the provinces: *Alberta Music Educators' Assn, *British Columbia Music Educators' Assn, *Manitoba Music Educators' Assn, *Music Education Council of the New Brunswick Teachers' Assn, *Music Council of the Newfoundland Teachers' Assn, *Nova Scotia Music Educators' Assn, *Ontario Music Educators' Assn, *Prince Edward Island Music Educators' Assn, *Quebec Music Educators' Assn (see also FAMEQ), *Saskatchewan Music Educators' Assn. The CMEA and its members, which represent school music educators and teachers, should not be confused with the *CFMTA and its provincial associations, which represent private music teachers.

The CMEA was formed in Toronto at the April 1959 convention of the OMEA. The spade-work for the association is attributed to several Canadians who met under the chairmanship of Leslie *Bell while attending the 1957 Music Educators' National Conference in Atlantic City. Forty delegates from nine provinces attended the 1959 inauguration and elected G. Roy *Fenwick president. The first executive committee comprised Fenwick, an executive director (Leslie Bell), a secretary-treasurer (Keith *Bissell), and three regional representatives (Richard *Johnston, Lloyd *Slind, and David *Thomson). Fees from the 69 charter members, a contribution from the *Canadian Bureau for the Advancement of Music, and a gift of the profits from the International Festival held in Montreal in 1950 gave the new organization a healthy financial base. Formal incorporation as a professional association took place in 1972, and in 1979 individual members numbered 1844. The Alberta MEA disbanded in 1969, and by 1979 the BC, Manitoba, and Ontario MEAs still had not assumed affiliate status in the CMEA, though participating as members of the organization.

The CMEA's chief aim – unifying and informing Canada's musicians and music educators – has been carried out mainly through publications and conventions. Its quarterly, the *Canadian Music Educator*, began in June 1959, and in the fall of 1976 began to appear also as a bilingual publication (*L'Éducateur de musique au Canada*, 1976–Fall 1978; *Le Journal des éducateurs de musique au Canada*, Winter 1978–9, *La Musicien éducateur au Canada*, 1979–). In addition, an English language *Newsletter*, begun in 1968, has been issued three or four times a year. In 1980 the *Newsletter* continued to be edited by Wallace Laughton (b Vancouver 17 Nov 1914), the founder and director of the CMEA Resource Centre. This centre, established in St Catharines, Ont, in 1968, has provided CMEA members with reprints of articles, general information and reference service, materials for non-commercial displays for conventions and workshops, etc. During the mid-1970s a publications committee was formed to evaluate and select outstanding Canadian monographs on music education, to prepare lists of these, and occasionally to circulate copies of them among the membership. Biennial national conventions have been held in Calgary, Charlottetown, Edmonton, Halifax, London, Montreal, Ottawa, Regina, Toronto, Vancouver, and Winnipeg. Guest speakers, from the fields of education and publishing, have included N. Scarth of the *U of British Columbia (1962), Louis Wersen of the MENC (1967), and C. Leonhard (1969, 1971). Clinics and performances by Canadian ensembles have been regular features. The Leslie Bell Memorial Choral Award, a trophy and cash prize initiated by the CMEA and the CBC in 1964, has been presented at each subsequent convention to a choral group from the host province and presentation continued in 1980. Two commissioned works were premiered at the CMEA 1967 convention – *Fleming's *Four Fantasias on Canadian Folk Themes* and *Ridout's *When Age and Youth Unite*. The CMEA has been responsible for the formation of the *Canadian String Teachers' Assn (1965), the *Canadian Music Research Council (1973), and the Music Teacher Education Council (1973). The two last-named are adjuncts of the CMEA. The *John Adaskin Project has been a joint CMEA / *CMCentre venture, and together the two organizations also published Patricia Shand's *Canadian Music: A Selective Guidelist for Teachers* (Toronto 1978).

The CMEA is a member organization of *CAUSM, the *CCA, and ISME. Its presidents have included G. Roy Fenwick 1959–60, Gifford *Mitchell 1960–2, Lloyd Slind 1962–3, Lola *MacQuarrie 1963–5, Garfield *Bender 1965–7, Frank *Churchley 1967–9, Vernon *Ellis 1969–71, Allen Clingman 1971–3, Kenneth *Bray 1973–7, and Paul *Murray 1977–9, succeeded by Winnifred Voigts.

BIBLIOGRAPHY

'The music education structure in Canada,' *Mcan*, 6, Nov 1967 (MMV)

Canadian Music Festival Adjudicators' Association. An informal movement during the 1930s, its chief aim was to promote, encourage, and assist Canadian adjudicators, thus counterbalancing the predominance of British adjudicators in Canadian competition festivals. Early participants included Leslie *Bell, Garfield *Bender, Eldon Brethour, G. Roy *Fenwick, Reginald *Geen, Harvey *Perrin, and George *Smale. Owing to

Bell's determined efforts the association was established formally in 1960. Membership (approximately 100 in 1980) is open to those whose experience qualifies them to adjudicate music or speech arts. Lists of members are sent to the 250 festivals operating annually across Canada. During its early years the CMFAA was allied closely to the *CMEA; in 1968, however, it became separate. Its executive meets three to four times a year, and there are occasional workshops. In 1974 the association published a *Festival Handbook* which provides guidelines for prospective adjudicators and for festival organizers. Presidents have included G. Roy Fenwick 1960–1, Reginald Geen 1961–8, Martin *Boundy 1968–9, Harvey Perrin 1969–71, Clifford McAree 1971–3, George Smale 1973–5, Gladys *Whitehead 1975–6, and Lansing *MacDowell 1976–9. H. Alex Clark succeeded MacDowell. (NM, GWt)

The Canadian Music Journal. A quarterly, published 1956–62 by the *Canadian Music Council. Twenty-four issues appeared from autumn 1956 to summer 1962. Geoffrey *Payzant was the editor, Arnold *Walter the chairman of the editorial board, and beginning with the Winter 1958 issue John *Beckwith, Leslie *Bell, and Marvin *Duchow were associate editors for record reviews, music education, and book reviews respectively. Among other contributors were Thomas *Archer, Marius *Barbeau, Alan *Detweiler, Chester *Duncan, Peter Garvie, Graham *George, Glenn *Gould, Helmut *Kallmann, Udo *Kasemets, William *Krehm, Hugh *Le Caine, Sir Ernest *MacMillan, Kathleen *Parlow, Charles *Peaker, Godfrey *Ridout, R. Murray *Schafer, and Kenneth *Winters. The CMJ was the most consistently scholarly music periodical to appear in Canada until that time and did much to document historical and current events, to plead urgent causes, to stimulate discussion, and to develop writers on music. It featured six essays on Canadian composers (*Champagne, *Pentland, *Papineau-Couture, *Willan, *Somers, and *Weinzweig) and special issues on music and the Canada Council (Spring 1957), music in education (Spring 1958), music in British Columbia (Summer 1958), and organs and organ playing in Canada (Spring 1959). Unfortunately few contributions were in French. Although the journal achieved a subscription rate of about 1200, publication ceased because of economic pressures.

BIBLIOGRAPHY

Falle, George. *'The Canadian Music Journal,' Canadian Forum*, Sep 1958

Canadian Music Library Association (CMLA) / **Association canadienne des bibliothèques musicales** (ACBM). Founded in 1956 as a section of the Canadian Library Assn, to establish contact between music librarians and carry out projects of interest to them. The membership grew from 37 in the 1950s to about 100 in 1970. Annual meetings coincided with those of the Canadian Library Assn. Newsletters appeared in certain years and the CLA issued a number of important bibliographical publications (see list). A brief regarding the role of the *NL of C in the area of music was submitted to the national librarian in 1957. CMLA chairmen have been Ogreta *McNeill 1956–7, 1964–5, Helmut *Kallmann 1957–8, 1967–8, Helen Sinclair 1958–9, Lucien *Brochu 1959–60, Melva J. Dwyer 1960–1, Auguste Morisset 1961–2, Laurie Allison 1962–3, Jean Lavender 1963–4, Ronald *Napier 1965–6, James Pilton 1966–7, Laura Murray 1968–9, Rhoda Baxter 1969–70, and Lynne Jarman 1970–1. In the absence of a Canadian branch of the International Assn of Music Libraries CMLA kept the international association's Canadian membership records and appointed Helmut Kallmann to serve 1959–71 as its delegate. In 1971 the CMLA was reconstituted as the *Canadian Assn of Music Libraries.

SELECTED PUBLICATIONS

Standards for Music Collections in Medium-Sized Public Libraries (Ottawa 1959)

A Bio-bibliographical Finding List of Canadian Musicians and Those Who Have Contributed to Music in Canada (Ottawa 1961)

Union List of Music Periodicals in Canadian Libraries (Ottawa 1964, suppl 1967)

Musical Canadiana; a Subject Index (Ottawa 1967)

The Canadian Music Publishers Association / Association canadienne des éditeurs de musique. Organization formed in 1949 to safeguard and advance the interests of the composer and publisher in accordance with the Canadian Copyright Act (1921), to encourage fair trade practices, and to maintain high standards of workmanship and services. In the beginning the association, with an all-Ontario membership of 10, was affiliated with the Board of Trade of Metropolitan Toronto. It opened its own offices in 1975 with a membership of 30, including firms from British Columbia, Alberta, and Quebec, comprising most of the companies which publish music by Canadian composers and which, as agents, represent some 650 foreign firms. There are two types of membership, full and associate, and the association maintains four committees to handle copyright legislation, copyright infringement, popular music, and music festivals and exhibits.

Active as a lobby at both provincial and federal levels, the Canadian Music Publishers' Assn has been responsible for the exemption of music from the Ontario sales tax; the exemption of training methods, voice or instrument studies, and liturgical music from import duties; and the formation in 1975 of the Canadian Musical Reproduction Rights Agency to administer, in Canada, mechanical rights, synchronization rights, and other reproduction rights (see Copyright) on behalf of the owners of those rights. Association chairmen have been T. St Clair Low 1950–1, Harry Jarman 1952–3, C.C. Devereux 1954–5, Edward Hough 1956–7, Bailey *Bird 1958–9, William J.I. Croombs 1960–1, John *Bird 1962–3, Freda Ferguson 1964–5, Ron *Napier 1966–7, Matthew Heft 1968–9, Bruno Apollonio 1970–1, and Ray Stephens 1972. In 1973 the office of chairman became that of president and has been held by Ray Stephens in 1973, Franco Colombo 1974–5, John Bird 1976–7, William Brubacher in 1978, and Matthew Heft in 1979. The association has submitted briefs to government concerning the new Canadian copyright act, and has published a *Directory* (Toronto 1975) of its members and exclusive agancies. JCB

Canadian Music Research Council. Adjunct of the *CMEA, organized by Frank *Churchley (U of Victoria) and G. Campbell *Trowsdale (U of British Columbia) and founded at the 1973 CMEA convention in Ottawa. Its primary goal has been the collection and dissemination of information concerning music research activity in Canada, taking into consideration education (see Music education research), *musicology, *ethnomusicology, and *bibliography. The council undertook 1974–5 an initial survey of such research and supplemented its findings in 1977. It has published the twice-yearly *Music Research News*, which includes abstracts, reviews of new material, announcements, and conference reports. Deane Jensen (U of Saskatchewan at Regina) was chairman 1973–4, and Margery Vaughan (U of Victoria) succeeded him.

Canadian Music Sales Corporation (after June 1977 Boddington Music Publishing Ltd). Established in the late 1920s as the Canadian affiliate of Warner Brothers' Music Sales Corp (USA), which controlled music from the newly invented sound movies. This music was distributed in Canada by syndicated stores (eg, the Kresge and Metropolitan chains). In the financial crisis of 1929 Warner Brothers relinquished control and within a few months Canadian Music Sales went bankrupt. A Toronto chartered accountant, William St Clair Low, took over the business as a trustee paid by Warner Brothers. In 1934, having liquidated all debts, he assumed full control of the company and remained its manager until 1947. He was succeeded by his brother T. (Thomas) St Clair Low, who had joined Canadian Music Sales in 1933 and retired in 1971. The latter sold the corporation in 1971 to Terry Regan who remained its manager until 1977, by which time it was under the ownership of a holding company.

In the early 1940s Canadian Music Sales purchased (and subsequently expanded) the *Anglo-Canadian Music Co Ltd catalogue, which included a large amount of church music. The resulting enlarged choral catalogue included folk-song arrangements by Leslie *Bell and Howard *Cable and church music. Canadian Music Sales also published several band arrangements by Maurice *DeCelles and country music by Hal 'Lone Pine' *Breau, Stu *Davis, Earl *Heywood, Don *Messer, and the young Hank *Snow and distributed publications of such US companies as Warner Brothers (Hollywood), Alfred Music (Port Washinqton, NY), Rubank (Miami), and Beacon Music, Columbia Pictures Music, Harms Inc, Pietro Deiro Publications, Shapiro, Bernstein & Co, and M. Whitmark and Sons (all of New York).

Canadian Music Sales entered the recording field in the 1930s as the Canadian distributor of Columbia Records. In 1950 it established its own label, Dominion; recorded the country and folk performers Isidore *Soucy, Stompin' Tom *Connors, Earl Heywood, and others; and became the Canadian distributor of the Music Minus One instructional series, the Dewolfe library of sound effects, and the US folk, jazz, and blues labels Arhoolie and Yazoo. In June 1977 Boddington Music Publishing Ltd, a newly established affiliate of Fred Boddington Music, took over all Canadian Music Sales copyrights and holdings. Under the management of Gary Wadsworth the company planned to specialize in educational material.

BIBLIOGRAPHY

'Canadian Music Sales promotes Canadian compositions,' *CanComp*, 9 May 1966

'T. St. Clair Low: away from it all,' *CanComp*, 64, Nov 1971 MWl

Canadian Music Trades Journal. Magazine of the instrument, recording, and publishing industries, issued in Toronto from 1900 to January 1933. Under its original owner, Dalton C. Nixon & Co., it was called *Canadian Music and Trades Journal*; it featured reports on musical life in Canadian cities and published pieces of music (usually of US origin) as well as trade news. In 1905 ownership passed to Fullerton & Shaw (later the Fullerton Publishing Co), and for a few years the magazine appeared twice a month. The rapid growth of musical commerce (and, probably, the establishment of another periodical, **Musical Canada*) led the publishers to concentrate entirely on matters related to the industry, although from time to time the journal continued to report on school music,

An early issue of *Canadian Music and Trades Journal*, March 1901, featuring a photograph of Samuel Nordheimer

festivals, organ inaugurations, and other events of interest to the music trade. The journal's owner was John A. Fullerton (b ca 1878, d 1957); its editor during most of its later years was Harvey A. Jones. The circulation reached over 1000 but only two libraries have important holdings: the New York Public Library (19 issues for 1907–9) and the *NL of C (one issue from 1900, four issues from 1901, and the volumes August 1912–January 1933). Most of the early issues have not been located.

Coinciding in time with the peak of the Canadian instrument-building trade and with the burgeoning of the recording industry, *Canadian Music Trades Journal* covered its field in great detail, giving space to technical discussion as well as news. Lavishly produced and illustrated, the issues from 1912 to the late 1920s have from 50 to over 120 pages each, including much advertising. Special features included monthly listings of new records (from at least 1912 to March 1927 and again from December 1928 to February 1930) and of 'New music copyrights entered at Ottawa' (from at least 1912 to February 1919). Major sections were 'Music and Musical Merchandise' and 'Talking Machines and Records.' Some issues have a 'Tuner's Corner.' The journal continued to cover the record trade even after Fullerton established the *Phonograph Journal of Canada* about October 1919. The latter was absorbed by the senior publication in April 1926; no copies have been found in any library. The Depression years sharply curtailed music trade, and even an expanded coverage, revealed in the change of title (January 1931) to *Canadian Music and Radio Trades*, could not save the enterprise: the last issue, January 1933, has a mere 16 pages. HK

Canadian National Exhibition (CNE). World's largest annual exposition, held mid-August to Labour Day (first Monday in September) in the 140-hectare permanent grounds on Toronto's waterfront; in 1976 an attendance record of 3.85 million was established. The CNE was opened 5 Sep 1879 under the auspices of the city council and local trade and arts associations. At first it was called the Industrial Exhibition of Toronto, but the name was changed to CNE in 1904.

From the early 1920s until the CNE Music Dept was established, the *Canadian Bureau for the Advancement of Music helped to organize CNE music events, which were of three main kinds: 1 / entertainment, 2 / exhibition, and 3 / competition. The music department evolved gradually in co-ordination with the bureau and remained linked to it in the person of a common managing director, Lieut-Col Clifford *Hunt, who assumed that position with the department in 1968 and the bureau in 1969.

The cover of the sheet music of *The Exhibition Lancers!* 1881

1 ENTERTAINMENT. The CNE's annual Music Day, organized by the bureau and traditionally attended by large audiences, dates back to 1921. Military bands were the main musical attraction until the mid-1920s and retained their popularity throughout most of the 20th century. Canadian bands (eg, *Anglo-Canadian Leather Co Band, *Canadian Grenadier Guards Band) and celebrated international ensembles played at a number of bandstands on the site; in 1928, for example, 19 bands played 108 two-hour concerts on the two bandstands then in use. In 1936 the open-air Bandshell was built to house band and variety-show presentations and the official opening and closing ceremonies. Other venues for music have been the 23,500-seat open-air Grandstand, the 1300-seat Queen Elizabeth Theatre, auditoriums in other buildings, bandstands, a small Music Building, and the large arena in the Coliseum, designed for horse shows and livestock judging but used as the concert hall for the *Canadian National Exhibition Chorus for some years from 1922 onwards.

The original 5000-seat Grandstand, built in 1879, was replaced in 1906 by a 16,400-seat structure; and that in turn was supplanted in 1948 (with some additions later) by a building combining enclosed display space with steeply raked bleachers seating 23,500. For about 50 years the Grandstand presented vast spectacles with hundreds of participants in tableaux with music; typical were *Ivanhoe* (1906), *Cleopatra* (1923), *Arabia – An Oriental Spectacle* (1926), *Montezuma* (1933), and celebrations of Canadian and British history (1921, 1927, 1938) or stirring patriotic sentiment (during World War I). The pageants were combined with vaudeville and variety entertainment and community singing and were climaxed by dazzling fireworks displays; they were presented on a huge stage with scenery 210 metres long and 15 metres high and with casts as large as 1500 supplemented by horses and chariots, floats, motorcars, and even helicopters.

When the CNE reopened in 1947 after the six-year hiatus caused by World War II, the Grandstand show reflected the growing influence of US pop culture upon Canada. Jingoistic pageants gave way to variety shows featuring US film and radio stars such as Olsen and Johnson, Danny Kaye, Jimmy Durante, and Victor Borge. In 1952 Jack *Arthur, a Canadian impresario of long experience, took over as producer of the shows, with Howard *Cable as music director and Alan Lund and Midge Arthur as choreographers. While still featuring US stars, the shows thenceforth presented more Canadian performers in supporting roles. Arthur continued as producer until 1967, to be succeeded by Cable in 1968. Cable was followed in 1969 by Billy *O'Connor, who instituted a policy, continued throughout the 1970s, of presenting one- or two-night appearances by pop stars, rock bands, country-western groups, comedians, and other entertainers. Most of these were from the USA, but Canadian performers have included Paul *Anka, Bachman-Turner Overdrive (*BTO), Burton Cummings, Patsy Gallant, the *Guess Who, Hagood *Hardy, the *Irish Rovers, Catherine *McKinnon, Anne *Murray, and René *Simard. In 1972 a partial return to large-scale spectacle came in the form of the Scottish World Festival Tattoo, which became an annual four-day feature presenting massed pipe and military bands, highland dancers, and variety entertainment with a total cast of about 1300.

In the 1930s, when swing music was at the height of its popularity, the Automotive Building for two years (1934–5) contained the Ballroom, where the dance bands of Duke Ellington, Rudy Vallee, Guy *Lombardo, and others played to overflow crowds. Later in the 1930s a large marquee with a dance floor was erected to house the bands and their audiences. Dance bands have continued to appear at the Bandshell and other locations, and in the 1960s and 1970s the Automotive Building again became a site of musical activity, mainly of youth-oriented rock concerts; in 1977 it served as the Canadian Recording Industry Pavilion to mark the centenary of recorded sound. This was appropriate, since one of the world's oldest surviving speech recordings (11 Sep 1888, of Governor-General Lord Stanley) was made in connection with the CNE (see *Roll Back the Years*, p 11). In 1975 the Bandshell was the location of a reunion performance of the *Happy Gang.

The small Music Building, built as the Railways Building in 1907, has housed recitals and chamber-music concerts. Recitals by outstanding *RCMT pupils were given for many years in an auditorium in the Grandstand. Other musical events have been held in the Queen Elizabeth Theatre, which opened in 1957. Music also has been used in connection with product displays and on the games, rides, and sideshows of the Midway. In 1974 the Carlsberg brewery installed a 50-bell carillon in the Carlsberg Bell Tower.

Many concerts have been presented by groups of players and singers in the open air. In the 1920s and 1930s these 'troubadours' were clad in national costumes and presented many varieties of ethnic music on Music Day; in 1923 one act of Flotow's *Martha* was a part of the free entertainment. Strolling performers have included The Little Singers from Tokyo, the Royal Hawaiian Band, barbershop quartets, and a bizarre one-man band named Werner Hirzel.

2 EXHIBITION. The CNE has been the site of displays by piano, organ, phonograph, and musical-instrument manufacturers and distributors. *Heintzman & Co began exhibiting as early as 1879. The Disk Talking Machine Co and several piano manufacturers exhibited in 1903 in the newly opened Manufacturers' Building. The *Canadian Piano and Organ Manufacturers' Assn negotiated the conditions under which their members would exhibit in 1906 and leased space

soon afterwards. A building for musical instrument display existed in 1905 and a Phonograph Building was in operation in 1922. For the most part, however, musical displays were mounted in the Manufacturers' Building until it burned down in 1961. Thereafter they were set up in the Better Living Building. In earlier years exhibitors emphasized prestige and presented impressive or informative displays about their industries; after World War II the emphasis shifted towards selling products to CNE visitors.

3 COMPETITION. In 1919, as an adjunct to its product displays, the phonographic division of the music industry in Canada arranged singing competitions which proved popular with the public. In 1921 the Canadian Piano and Organ Manufacturers' Assn presented a one-day festival of piano recitals, each pianist sponsored by an exhibitor in 'Piano Row' of the Manufacturers' Building. That same year, through the initiative of A.L. Robertson, the first band competition was held. The success of these undertakings convinced the CNE directors that music activities and programs increased attendance. Also begun in 1921, the CNE Music (competition) Festival and the Annual Music Day (on which the piano exhibitors again presented continuous concerts) both had their official inaugurations in 1922. By 1924 the Ontario Amateur Bands Assn (and later the *CBDA) assumed the organization and administration of the band competitions, which drew entries from across Canada, first for military bands, then for all categories of bands including brass and silver. In 1954 the Canadian Bureau for the Advancement of Music began to administer the band competition. The CNE Music Festival has attracted competitors ranging in age from six to adult, in solo and group instrumental and vocal categories. It has scheduled classes not only for the usual instrumentalists and groups but also for harmonica bands, bagpipes, old-time fiddlers, and drum-and-bugle corps. Adjudicators have been appointed from across Canada, and for prizes the CNE has awarded medals and, beginning in 1940, scholarships. In 1975 the first annual *National Competitive Festival of Music was held during the CNE at the Queen Elizabeth Theatre.

The CNE has inspired several compositions. Richard *Hayward composed the *Golden Jubilee Marching Song* for the exhibition's 50th anniversary in 1928. The US bandmaster Edwin Franko Goldman wrote the *Canadian National Exhibition March* to mark the first appearance at the CNE of his famed Goldman Band in 1929. J.-J. *Gagnier wrote *Ca-Na-Ex* for band. Léo *Roy's *Hail to the Exhibition* was performed in 1930.

In the 49 weeks each year when the CNE is not operating, the grounds are open to the public as parkland, and some of the buildings are leased from time to time by entrepreneurs for the presentation of concerts and other activities.

BIBLIOGRAPHY

Hamilton, H.C. 'Music day at the Exhibition,' *MCan*, Sep 1928

White, Alvin C. 'Toronto notes,' 'Band news from the Canadian National Exhibition,' ibid

Withrow, O.C.J. 'Music,' *The Romance of the Canadian National Exhibition* (Toronto 1936)

Lorimer, James. *The Ex: A Picture History of the Canadian National Exhibition* (Toronto 1973)

Gallo, Nancy, and Linden, J.J. 'The CNE: a centennial celebration,' *RPM Weekly*, 26 Aug 1978

Lancashire, David. 'Grandstand show: the bogeyman Canadians fear,' Toronto *Globe and Mail*, 10 Aug 1979

TCB

Canadian National Exhibition Chorus. A mixed choir of approximately 2000 voices, founded in Toronto in 1922 under the sponsorship of the Toronto *Star* and organized by that daily newspaper's music critic Augustus *Bridle. Sometimes referred to as the 'Pageant Chorus,' by 1925 it was possibly the largest choir in North America. Its singers were drawn mainly from other choirs in the Toronto area. It performed annually 1922–34 under Herbert *Fricker at the *CNE and gave between two and four performances each season with groups such as the Toronto Concert Band and the Goldman Band of New York. In August 1927 it sang in *The Heart of the World*, a pageant organized by Bridle and staged at the Coliseum for the Second Biennial Conference of the World Federation of Education Assns. Its repertoire included arrangements of folksongs and waltzes, operatic selections, religious pieces, and patriotic songs. Its three recordings made for Victor in 1928 are listed in *Roll Back the Years*. The chorus ceased activities in 1934.

In 1940 a similar chorus was formed, again through the efforts of Bridle and the *Star*. Known as the Coliseum Chorus, it was led by Charles *Peaker. Fricker was honorary conductor and made some guest appearances. This chorus, accompanied by the Goldman Orchestra from New York, gave its first concert 29 Aug 1940 at the CNE and sang with the *TSO under Ernest *MacMillan in the fall of that year at Toronto's *Maple Leaf Gardens. It appeared there again in 1941 with the US Navy Band. Altogether, the chorus gave six concerts and raised several thousand dollars for war charities. It made a recording for RCA Victor. A Healey *Willan composition entitled *The Trumpet Call* (B55) was written especially for the chorus. With the increasing mobilization of Canadians for war work in 1942 the chorus was forced to disband. MH, NM

Canadian Open Old Time Fiddlers' Contest. Most important annual competition of its kind in Canada (see Fiddling). Begun in 1951 to raise funds for charity, the contest has been held on two days each August at the arena in Shelburne (northwest of Toronto) under the joint sponsorship of the Rotary Club and the CBC. Latterly informal music-making also has taken place in nearby Highland Park. By the mid-1970s, with more than 150 fiddlers competing (amateur and professional, Canadian and other), seven classes had been established: the open, the women's, the novelty (in which emphasis is placed on showmanship), and four divided according to age (eg, under 12, over 65). A competitor is judged in a waltz, a jig, and a reel, all played within a three-minute period. Victory in the open class carries the greatest honour. Winners have been Mel Lavigne of Honey Harbour, Ont, 1951, 1952; Ward *Allen of Ottawa, 1953; Wayne (Sleepy) Marlin of Louisville, Ky, 1954; Victor Pasowisty of Winnipeg, 1955; Ned *Landry of Saint John, NB, 1956, 1957, 1962; Ed Gyurki of Woodstock, Ont, 1958, 1959, 1967, 1971, 1974, 1976, 1978; Al *Cherny of Toronto, 1960, 1961; Graham *Townsend of Toronto, 1963, 1968, 1969, 1970; Johnny Mooring of Springhill, NS, 1964, 1965, 1966; Rudy Meeks of Orillia, Ont, 1972, 1973, 1975, 1977; and Eleanor Townsend of Toronto, 1979. Winners are heard on the final night (Saturday) in a concert broadcast by CBC radio. Cash prizes and trophies are awarded.

BIBLIOGRAPHY

Proctor, George A. *Old-Time Fiddling in Ontario* (Ottawa 1963)

Teitel, Jay. 'Miracle at Shelburne,' *Toronto Life*, Dec 1976

MM

Canadian Opera Company (COC). Leading producer of opera in Canada during the 1960s and 1970s. (An earlier COC, Montreal 1931, mounted only one production, Gounod's *Roméo et Juliette*.)

1 History
2 Repertoire
3 Performers

1 HISTORY. The COC emerged as a direct result of the establishment in 1946 of the *Royal Cons Opera School under Arnold *Walter, with Nicholas *Goldschmidt as music director and conductor, and with Felix Brentano as stage director, succeeded by Herman *Geiger-Torel in 1948. By 1949 the school had presented opera excerpts at *Hart House Theatre and seven complete operas at *Eaton Auditorium. Public interest and support encouraged the school's directors to form the Royal Conservatory Opera Company and to present the first Opera Festival – *Don Giovanni*, *Rigoletto*, and *La Bohème* – at the *Royal Alexandra Theatre in February 1950. Although the singers and most of the technical and musical staff were from the Opera School, this festival marked the true beginning of the COC.

In November 1950 the Opera Festival Assn was incorporated to sponsor the annual presentations of the company and, by assuming all administrative and financial responsibility for the productions, to absolve the *RCMT of direct costs while providing an opportunity for the school's students and staff to exercise their talents. Torel, stage director and producer, was named artistic director in 1956 and Goldschmidt remained music director until 1957. Ernesto *Barbini had begun his long association as a conductor with the COC when he joined the RCMT staff in 1953. With the 1954 season the Opera Festival Assn began to mount its own productions under the name Opera Festival Company of Toronto. Casting and preparation were independent of the RCMT and personnel were hired under contract. After a successful fall season of operetta in 1957 the main season was shifted to the fall, where it remained for many years (locked there 1968–77 by the availability of the *TS). Ettore *Mazzoleni, director of the Opera School 1952–66, remained honorary general director of the Festival until 1957, when the last official links with the school were broken. Although the increased use of professional casts and the limiting of the season to the fall precluded Opera School participation on more than a supportive basis, the COC continued to use the school's facilities and many of its graduates, and to co-operate, through mutual employment agreements with the school, in ensuring the year-round availability to both organizations of competent stage directors.

During 1958, with the beginning of the first tours, the name Canadian Opera Company came into use and has remained the popular and operative name of the organization. The appointment in 1959 of Geiger-Torel as general director and Barbini as music adviser preceded the letters patent of 20 Sep 1960 which changed the old name (Opera Festival Assn of Toronto) to The Canadian Opera Assn, which has remained the legal name.

Ancillary to the COC but important as supporting organizations have been the Canadian Opera Women's Committee, which originated in the Opera and Concert Committee of the RCMT, founded in 1947 with Mrs Floyd *Chalmers as its first president; and the Canadian Opera Guild, formed by Vida *Peene in 1959. The Guild began to publish **Opera Canada* in 1960.

Although securely based in Toronto, with *O'Keefe Centre as its home after 1961 and the TS

Ernest Adams, Herman Geiger-Torel, and Ruby Mercer with cast members from the Canadian Opera Company's touring production of *Così fan tutte*, 1963

as its accompanying orchestra 1968–76, the company justified the inclusion of 'Canadian' in its title by its intention to tour. Indeed, a 1958 tour which took 19 performances of *The Barber of Seville*, with George *Brough as accompanist and music director, to cities in eastern Canada was the beginning of regular tours by a special COC touring company which has travelled some 10,000 miles each year, visiting virtually every urban area of Canada and parts of the USA. At first performing with only piano accompaniment, the touring company began travelling with its own orchestra in 1968. Supplementing the touring company's performances outside Toronto, the main company has appeared in London, Ont (1950, 1954, 1957), Kitchener, Ont (1954, 1955, 1956), Hamilton, Ont (1954, 1955, 1956), Ottawa (1956, 1957, and annually beginning in 1969 at the *NAC), Montreal (1957), and Washington, DC (1975). The main company of the COC performed at *Expo 67, and in 1972 COC singers began to appear in operatic excerpts annually at *Ontario Place. Geiger-Torel continued as general director of the COC until his retirement in 1976. He was succeeded by Iranian-born Lotfi Mansouri, but continued as general director emeritus until his death.

In 1977, under Mansouri, the COC introduced the stagione system, under which single operas have intensive runs at different times throughout the year, instead of (as formerly) several operas being given concurrently in a mingled program in one large annual 'season.' Since the TS, because of its heavy concert commitments, could reserve only September for the COC, continued collaboration became impractical under the new system, and the COC began working with its own orchestra. A transitional step toward the adoption of the stagione principle was the presentation of a major Toronto run of the company's touring productions in a spring season at the Royal Alexandra Theatre in 1978.

2 REPERTOIRE. By 1977 the COC had given over 600 performances of 54 different operas, while the touring company had presented more than 1200 performances. In contrast to the RCMT Opera's first season in 1950 (three operas totalling 10 performances), the COC in 1975 presented a total of 36 performances of *I Pagliacci*, *Il Tabarro*, *Madama Butterfly*, *Die Fledermaus*, *Louis Riel*, *Manon Lescaut*, and *Salome*. However, financial problems forced the curtailment of the 1976 season, when only four productions were mounted. Although the COC repertoire has leaned heavily on the most popular of the standard works, such as *La Bohème* (1950, 1954, 1958, 1963, 1965, 1968, 1972, 1976), *Madama Butterfly* (1951, 1953, 1956, 1962, 1964, 1967, 1971, 1975), *The Barber of Seville* (1959, 1965, 1967, 1973), and *Aida* (1963, 1964, 1968, 1972), it occasionally has staged less-heard and more difficult standard works, such as *Turandot* (1965, 1969), *Salome* (1965, 1968, 1975), *Elektra* (1969), *Siegfried* (1972), *Die Götterdämmerung* (1973), *Boris Godunov* (1974), *Die Walküre* (1962, 1971, 1976), *Wozzeck* (1977), *Don Carlos* in the original French (1977), Tchaikovsky's *Joan of Arc* (1978, the Canadian premiere), Britten's *Peter Grimes* (1980), and Berg's *Lulu* (1980, the Canadian premiere). The COC performed *Willan's *Deirdre* in 1966 and commissioned three other Canadian operas: Harry *Somers' critically acclaimed **Louis Riel* (performed 1967, 1968, 1975), Raymond *Pannell's *The Luck of Ginger Coffey* (1967, with libretto by Ronald Hambleton after the Brian Moore novel of the same name) and Charles *Wilson's **Heloise and Abelard* (1973). In 1967 the COC began its participation in *Prologue to the Performing Arts, mounting, among other productions, two operas written for Prologue: Norman *Symonds' *The Spirit of Fundy* (1972) and Tibor *Polgar's *The Glove* (1975). The latter production was televised by the CBC.

3 PERFORMERS. Close though no longer formal ties with the RCMT, and later with the U of Toronto Opera Dept, have given the COC a ready supply of young singers for solo roles and for the chorus. Many of Canada's leading singers have risen within the RCMT and COC ranks, including John *Arab, Peter *Barcza, Alexander *Gray, Peter Milne, Patricia *Rideout, Jan *Rubeš, Heather *Thomson, and Bernard *Turgeon. Others, including Victor *Braun, Alan *Crofoot, Don *Garrard, Robert *Goulet, Gwenlynn *Little, Ermanno *Mauro, Morley *Meredith, James *Milligan, Cornelis *Opthof, Maria *Pellegrini, Irene *Salemka, Teresa *Stratas, Jon *Vickers, and Jeannette *Zarou benefited from early COC experience and became leading artists on the international stage. Important singers of French-Canadian origin have appeared in COC casts (Pierrette *Alarie, Colette *Boky, Claude *Corbeil, Marguerite *Gignac, Jean *Bonhomme, Pierre *Duval, Louis *Quilico, Joseph *Rouleau, Léopold *Simoneau, Richard *Verreau, etc), as have leading US and European singers: Grace Bumbry, Richard Cassilly, Marilyn Horne, Marina Krilovici, Astrid Varnay, Mignon Dunn, Jerome Hines, Patricia Kern, Regina Resnik, etc.

Among conductors frequently engaged by the COC (besides Barbini and Goldschmidt) have been Mario *Bernardi, James *Craig, Victor *Feldbrill, Ettore Mazzoleni, and Walter *Susskind. From abroad Bryan Balkwill and Heinrich Bender have specialized in the Italian and German repertoire respectively. John *Fenwick and Errol Gay (b Pouce Coupé, BC, 8 Feb 1941) have conducted many touring productions. The company's stage directors have included Geiger-Torel (who was responsible for over 70 productions of some 40 different operas), Mansouri, Carlos Alexander, Peter Ebert, Constance *Fisher, Irving *Guttman, Leon Major, and Mavor *Moore, and among its designers have been Hans Berends, Murray Laufer, and Lawrence Schäfer (sets), Marie Day, Warren Hartman, and Suzanne Mess (costumes), and Wallace Russell (lighting).

The COC has emphasized the employment of Canadian artists, a reflection largely of Geiger-Torel's philosophy that the cost of importing international stars would be, and indeed has been, more profitably spent raising the standards of the company's productions. In the 10-year period 1967–77 the COC's annual budget rose from $1.1 million to $3.7 million, the funds assembled from production revenue (50 per cent), federal and provincial grants (37 per cent), fund-raising drives (10 per cent), and business sponsorship (3 per cent).

Canadian Opera Assn presidents have been R.H. Lorimer Massie 1950–1, J.D. Woods, Jr 1952–4, R.S. Van Valkenburg 1955–6, Floyd S. *Chalmers 1957–60, Frank F. McEachren 1961–2, W. Preston Gilbride 1963–4, Russell T. Payton 1965–6, W.A. Curtis 1967–8, Rodney J. Anderson 1969–70, Robert L.T. Baillie 1971–2, Montague Larkin 1973–4, Douglas A. Sloan 1975–6, Rodney J. Anderson 1977–8, Lionel C. Mohr in 1978, James M. Robertson 1978–9, and Walter G.D. Strothers 1979–80, succeeded by Albert E. Bates.

Business managers of the COC have worked traditionally in the shadow of the artistic director, but as the operation increased in complexity so did the manager's duties, and by the 1970s the post had become one of considerable, and sometimes shared, responsibility. Over the years, beginning with Ernest Rawley 1950–6, the COC management team has included Edwin De Rocher 1957–8, Rawley again 1958–9, Ernest *Adams 1959–68, Margot Murray 1961–4, Warren Hughes 1965–7, Ehrhard Nowack 1967–71, Bruce Chalmers 1972–5, and Gary Adamson in 1976. John Leberg succeeded Adamson in 1977.

BIBLIOGRAPHY

Reviews in *CMJ* by William Krehm (vol 1, Spring 1957; vol 2, Winter 1958; vol 3, Winter 1959; vol 4, Summer 1960) and John Kraglund (vol 5, Winter 1961)

Hecht, Maurice. 'Building a business in opera – Toronto,' *Executive*, Oct 1959

Mercer, Ruby. 'Canadians like opera,' *Music Across Canada*, vol 1, May 1963

McNiven, Elina. 'History of the Canadian Opera Company,' *OpCan*, Sep 1965

Geiger-Torel, H. 'The director,' and Winters, Kenneth. 'The critic,' Toronto *Telegram*, 10 Sep 1966

'Canadian Opera Company tours looking back: 1958–1968,' *OpCan*, Sep 1968

McPherson, Jim. 'Please Mr. G-T can you do one for opera lovers,' Toronto *Telegram*, 7 Sep 1968

Carson, Neil. 'The Canadian Opera Company's 20th anniversary,' *Commentator*, vol 12, Oct 1968

Potvin, Gilles. 'Seule une formule régionale rendrait ici l'opéra viable,' Montreal *La Presse*, 26 Oct 1968

Winters, Kenneth. 'In defence of opera,' Toronto *Telegram*, 4 Oct 1969

McPherson, Jim. 'Did you see ... ?' Toronto *Telegram*, 12 Oct 1969

Morey, Carl. 'The Canadian Opera Company,' *PfAC*, vol 8, Winter 1971

Kraglund, John. Reviews in 'Canadian chronicles: Ontario,' *CMB*, Autumn-Winter 1971–4

Smith, P.J. 'The Canadian Opera Company,' *High Fidelity/Musical America*, vol 22, Feb 1972

Mercer, Ruby. 'The Canadian Opera Company: a 150-year history,' *OpCan*, Fall 1973

Geiger-Torel, H. 'Toronto's Opera School and Opera Company,' *Opera J*, vol 6, Sep 1973

Rey, Anne. 'Vingt-cinq ans d'art lyrique à Toronto – les super-stars sont pour demain,' *Le Monde*, 5 Oct 1973
Geiger-Torel, H. 'Canada an operatic desert?' *German-Canadian Yearbook*, vol 2 (Toronto 1975)
Remembered Moments of the Canadian Opera Company 1950–1975 (Toronto 1976)
Schulman, Michael. 'Rescue fund bailing out sinking COC,' *PfAC*, vol 13, Fall 1976
McVicar, William. 'The COC on the road,' Toronto *Globe and Mail*, 12 Feb 1977
Mansouri, Lotfi. 'A "first" in Canada: the story of the launching of the new Canadian Opera Company Ensemble,' *OpCan*, Summer 1980
Canadian Opera Company. Four handbooks: *Canadian Opera Company 1950–1974, 1950–1975, 1950–1976, 1950–1977* (Toronto 1974–7)
Opera Canada 1960–
COC Archives (CM)

Canadian Piano and Organ Manufacturers' Association. Established, with a secretariat in Toronto, to provide co-operative action in the promotion, regulation, and protection of the piano and organ manufacturers of Canada. Its first constitution and by-laws were dated 1899.

During the 76 years of its existence the association appeared before the federal and provincial governments regarding the imposition of tariffs, excise taxes, sales taxes, import taxes, freight rates, etc, and to that end it systematically collected statistical data from its members to support its submissions and briefs.

Membership fluctuated, reflecting conditions in the industry, and included at various times companies in Nova Scotia, Quebec, and Ontario, the majority of members coming from the last-named province. Piano manufacturers outnumbered organ manufacturers and included such companies as Amherst; Craig; *Doherty; *Evans Bros; *Gourlay, Winter & Leeming; *Mason & Risch; *Nordheimer; *Pratte; Stanley; *Williams; and *Weber.

There were 23 member-companies in 1914 and 17 in 1927. However, following the curtailment of activities and loss of members during the Depression, membership was broadened first to include firms who manufactured supplies and parts for the industry and later to include distributors of pianos and/or organs in Canada. Yet in 1965 only 10 companies were members, and by 1973 only 4 of these were manufacturers – *Heintzman, *Lesage, *Sherlock-Manning, and *Willis.

Presidents were elected annually and all meetings were held in Toronto except in 1923 and 1930 when the annual meetings took place in Montreal.

The **Canadian Music Trades Journal* reported the activities and meetings of the association 1900–33. In 1924 its editor, John A. Fullerton, became the permanent secretary of the organization, succeeding James G. Merrick. Fullerton retired in 1954 and was replaced by Richard Edmunds (who combined the job with his position as secretary of the *Canadian Bureau for the Advancement of Music).

The association negotiated agreements with the *CNE, beginning in 1906, to administer the allocation, regulation, and supervision of the industry's display space at the annual exhibition.

In 1917 the association, under the guidance of James Fullerton, launched a promotional and educational campaign – 'Music in the Home' – which in 1919 resulted in the founding of the Canadian Bureau for the Advancement of Music. Beginning in 1920 annual financial support for the bureau was provided through a levy on each association member, based on the number of pianos sold. This form of support for the bureau continued for the life of the association and agreement to the assessment became a condition of membership. The association was represented on the bureau's board.

In 1975 the members recommended that the association be dissolved and reconstituted as the Keyboard Committee of the Music Industries Assn of Canada (MIAC), a national umbrella organization for all facets of the music business. Headquarters were established in Toronto in 1972. The Keyboard Committee has perpetuated the functions of its predecessor.

BIBLIOGRAPHY
CMTJ issues PW

Canadian Recording Industry Association (CRIA) / **L'association de l'industrie canadienne de l'enregistrement.** Formed 9 Apr 1963 as the Canadian Record Manufacturer's Assn by 10 companies. It was renamed CRIA in 1972 when membership was opened to individuals (eg, producers) as well as other companies. In 1978 the 35 members produced over 95 per cent of the sound recordings sold in Canada. CRIA has served as a lobby on matters pertaining to copyright and importation and as a liaison with music and recording organizations in other countries. It has maintained an office in Toronto, which in 1975 it began to share with *CARAS. Brian Robertson was executive secretary 1973–7 (Bert Betts had served the CRMA in a similar capacity 1968–72) and permanent president thereafter. In 1975 CRIA introduced a program for the certification of 'gold' and 'platinum' records according to sales (see Recorded Sound 5 /); in 1978 it began compiling a bi-weekly chart of best-selling records (50 singles and 50 LPs) based on statistics supplied by retailers across Canada. This chart has appeared in various publications. A quarterly newsletter, *CRIA News*, was published 1975–8. In 1977, at the *CNE, CRIA sponsored a pavilion where exhibits, demonstrations, and concerts were mounted in celebration of the first 100 years of recorded sound. MM

Canadian Society of Musicians. One of the earliest professional musical societies in Canada, it was founded in 1885 as the Ontario Music Teachers' Assn. At its second annual convention, December 1886 in Toronto, the name Royal Canadian Society of Musicians was proposed, but the prefix 'royal' was not approved by the Ontario government. The aim of the society was to encourage musical art in all its forms, and to promote the higher interests of the profession, the interchange of ideas, and the cultivation of fraternal feeling among its members. The annual conventions, all but two (London 1887, Hamilton 1890) in Toronto, featured concerts and discussions of essays read by members. Out of some emerged resolutions on such issues as the licensing of teachers, the improvement of public-school music, and the standards of church singing.

In 1886 several compositions were submitted under noms de plume for a contest; those composers who obtained 'the marks necessary to pass' included A. E. *Fisher, F.J. Hatton, Davenport *Kerrison, and G.W. *Strathy. The presidents of the society were Charles A. *Sippi 1885–7, St John Hyttenrauch 1887–8, Edward *Fisher 1889–90, R.S. *Ambrose 1891–2, F.H. *Torrington 1892–3, J.W.F. *Harrison in 1893, J.E.P. *Aldous in 1894, and Humfrey *Anger 1895–6. Membership was between 150 and 200 and appears to have been made up primarily of southern Ontario musicians, though all Canadian music teachers were eligible. The society was described as prosperous by W.O. *Forsyth in 1895, yet it seems to have come to an end within a year, perhaps because of rivalry between groups of musicians and music schools. This was reflected in the formation in 1894 of two new societies in Toronto, the Musical Art Club and the Toronto Clef Club, which had objectives similar to the Canadian Society of Musicians.

BIBLIOGRAPHY
NL of C. Ontario Music Teachers' Assn Program, 2nd annual convention (Toronto 1886)
'The Canadian Society of Musicians,' *The Week*, vol 6, 12 Jul 1889
Hamilton Public Library. Canadian Society of Musicians, Report, 6th annual meeting (Toronto 1890)
Metropolitan Toronto Library. A.E. Fisher scrapbook
Keillor, Elaine. 'Wesley Octavius Forsyth 1859–1937,' *CMB*, 7, Autumn–Winter 1973 HK

Canadian Stage Band Festival. Annual competition for student and non-professional stage (or big) bands. The major force in the development of the stage band movement in Canadian schools, the festival was initiated in 1972 by Toronto musicians Robert Richmond (president), Gary Wadsworth (vice-president) and Paul Miner (secretary-treasurer). The number of participating bands from high schools, community colleges, and universities across Canada increased from 18 at the first festival, in 1973, to over 240 by 1977. After regional competitions, the national finals have been held, with commercial sponsorship, each May 1973–7 in Toronto, in April 1978 in Winnipeg, and in May 1979 in Vancouver. Bands in junior, senior, and open classes are adjudicated by leading jazz and studio musicians. Concerts have been given by the big bands of Maynard *Ferguson, Woody Herman, and others, and by the *Boss Brass. The closing concert of winners was televised by TV Ontario in 1975, by CTV in 1976 and 1977, and by the CBC in 1978. Under Miner's direction the 1974 CSBF Allstar Band made an LP, *Northern Lights*, of works by Ron *Collier, Gordie Fleming, Rob *McConnell, Phil *Nimmons, Wadsworth, and others, for the Music Minus One Instruction series (MMO 2000–MMO 2008). MM

Canadian String Quartet. First quartet-in-residence (1961–3) at the *U of Toronto, established jointly by the university and the CBC to teach advanced students, coach string groups, and give concerts. Members were Albert *Pratz and Bernard Robbins, violins; David Mankovitz, viola; and George Ricci (replaced in 1962 by Laszlo Varga), cello. The founding of the group was a project of Pratz and Geoffrey *Waddington, who hoped to develop in Canada a quartet of international stature. The quartet gathered to rehearse on 1 Jul 1961 and gave its first public concerts on 18 and 21 Jan 1962 in Toronto. It was heard in 1962 in a CBC series playing quartets of Haydn. It gave its final concert on 4 Jul 1963 and disbanded soon afterwards because the dream had not materialized. Despite the high skills of the performers the quartet did not stimulate the continuing support and patronage that gave security and longevity to the earlier *Hart House Quartet and later *Orford String Quartet. It nevertheless in its brief existence performed some 150 works and premiered *Weinzweig's *Quartet No. 3* (which it had commissioned), *Morel's *Quartet No. 2*, *Adaskin's *Quartet No. 1*, and *Somers' *Quartet No. 2*.

An earlier Canadian String Quartet, founded by Eugene Hudson in Regina in 1930, also was short-lived.

DISCOGRAPHY
Pentland – Pépin – Vallerand – Weinzweig. 1962. Col MS 6364

BIBLIOGRAPHY
Pratz, Albert. 'Canada's Campus Quartet,' Toronto *Globe and Mail*, 17 Jun 1961
Schafer, Murray. 'The Canadian String Quartet,' *CMJ*, vol 6, Spring 1962 (BJE)

Canadian String Teachers Association. Organization dedicated to the improvement of string playing and teaching in Canada. It was formed in Regina in 1967 and its initial membership, from across Canada, numbered 120. At first it was affiliated with the *CMEA and the American String Teachers Assn, but after a hiatus 1974–5 it was reorganized as an autonomous body 2 Apr 1975 at a meeting in Edmonton. The membership, comprising professional performers, university, school, conservatory, and private teachers, and students, reached 160 by 1978. A news sheet, edited 1975–7 by Lawrence Fisher, developed into the periodical *Notes* (vol 1, no. 1, Winter 1977), issued thrice yearly, and edited by Patrick Burroughs. CSTA presidents have been Lloyd Blackman 1967–9, Jay *Armin 1970–2, and Alfred *Garson 1973–4, succeeded by Robert Skelton. The location of the secretariat changes with the home location of the current elected secretary. (RS)

Canadian Talent Library (CTL). A non-profit trust formed in 1962, with offices in Toronto, to provide a major series of recordings by Canadian artists and of Canadian compositions. It was conceived by J. Lyman Potts (b Regina 11 Nov 1916, a broadcast executive, who began his career in 1938 in Regina and worked at stations in Hamilton, London, and Montreal before joining Standard Broadcasting Corporation in Toronto in 1963 and becoming vice-president of Standard Broadcasting Productions in 1966; he was general manager of the CTL until 1978, when he was succeeded by Jackie *Rae) and was initiated by the Standard Broadcasting radio stations CFRB (Toronto) and CJAD (Montreal). The veteran US recording executive and artist Ben Selvin acted as a consultant, and the arranger Johnny *Burt was music director until 1972, when his position was assumed by Mal Thompson, the CTL's manager of music services.

Initially the CTL distributed its recordings only to subscribing broadcast stations, but in 1966, with its 80th project, it began leasing its masters to *RCA, Columbia (*CBS), *Capitol, *GRT, *Quality, and United Artists for use in the production of records for sale. By 1979 it had released over 200 LPs of popular and light classical music in formats suitable for AM broadcast. When in 1970 the *CRTC introduced its regulations requiring the increased use, on radio, of music composed and/or performed by Canadians, the CTL assumed fresh significance as a ready source of such broadcast material. Its roster has included Peter *Appleyard, John *Arpin, the pianist Bill Badgley, the singer Keath Barrie, the *Boss Brass (formed specifically for a CTL recording), the Laurie *Bower Singers, Ron *Collier, the clarinetist Henry Cuesta, Trump *Davidson, the singer Vic Franklyn, the *Hamilton Philharmonic, the *Hart House Orchestra, Yves *Lapierre, William *Stevens, and several orchestras and choirs under the direction of Johnny Burt.

BIBLIOGRAPHY
Guettel, Alan. '15 years and 200 albums later,' *RPM*, vol 25, 18 Sep 1976
'The musicians pay tribute to the Canadian Talent Library,' *RPM*, vol 25, 18 Sep 1976
Conlon, Patrick. 'The birth of album number 211,' *Toronto Life* 'Audio Guide,' Autumn 1977 (EBM)

Canadian Vitaphone Company. Phonograph manufacturer located in Toronto 1913–16. Its product, the Vitaphone, was devised by the US inventor Clinton B. Repp and featured a wooden tone-arm and stationary sound-box. The company, headed by W.R. Fosdick (former manager of His Master's Voice Ltd in Toronto), also imported Columbia recordings for release on the Vitaphone Label, from masters leased from Columbia in the USA. Artists included the popular Canadian tenors Henry *Burr and Harold *Jarvis, the Columbia Male Quartette (renamed the Maple Leaf Male Quartette), and Prince's Band (renamed the Vitaphone Military Band). The Vitaphone series is listed in *Roll Back the Years*. EBM

'Un Canadien errant.' There are numerous versions of the story of this song's origins, but few that are not distorted by sentimentality. In his manuscript 'Souvenirs de collège' Antoine Gérin-Lajoie (1824–82; a lawyer and journalist) describes his tailoring of his verse to an existing folk tune: 'I wrote it in 1842 when I was taking my classical exams at Nicolet. I did it one night in bed at the request of my friend Cyp Pinard, who wanted a song to the tune of "Par derrière chez ma tante" ... It was published in 1844 in the *Charivari canadien* with my initials (A.G.L.).' However, in that publication the song bore the title 'Le Proscrit' and the tune was said to be 'Au bord d'un clair ruisseau.'

Ernest *Gagnon in his *Chansons populaires du Canada* (Quebec 1865) says the original tune was 'J'ai fait une maîtresse' of which the words of the variant 'Si tu te mets anguille' 'are only rather altered fragments.' The Gagnon analysis is considered definitive.

The Penguin Book of Canadian Folk Songs, edited by Edith *Fowke (Harmondsworth, England, 1973) notes that after the political turmoil of 1837–8 several rebels were imprisoned, deported to Tasmania, or hanged, and those who escaped reprisal had to go into exile in the USA. Fowke writes: 'Their plight inspired a young student, M. A. Gérin-Lajoie, to write "Un Canadien errant," setting it to the tune of a popular French folk song, "Si tu te mets anguille." Soon after the song appeared in 1842, French Canadians were singing it from Acadia on the east coast to the distant reaches of the North-West Territories.'

The Acadians' adoption of the words as the basis for their national song in 1844 is explained by the history of their expulsion and dispersal in the previous century. After refusing to swear allegiance to the British crown many Acadians, between 1749 and 1755, fled inland in Acadia (following the Saint John River), or to Île St-Jean (known later as Prince Edward Island), or to Cape Breton. Fearing they might join the French during the war, Charles Lawrence, the governor of Nova Scotia, decided in 1755 and 1758 to deport the Nova Scotian Acadians to New England and the Atlantic coast. When peace was restored in 1760 several of the exiles settled in Louisiana; others returned to Acadia and Quebec. It was the descendants of these Acadians who, finding the words of 'Un Canadien errant' appropriate to their own situation, changed the opening line to 'Un Acadien errant' and sang the resulting variant to the Gregorian tune 'Ave Maris stella,' adopting it as their national song.

There is an English version of the song in *Canadian Folk Songs, Old and New* by John Murray *Gibbon (London 1927, 1949). A *Fantaisie* on the tune of 'Un Canadien errant' was played at the *Monument national by its composer Albert *Chamberland on 13 Apr 1926. Morley *Calvert also used the melody for a movement in his *Suite from the Monteregian Hills / Suite des collines montérégiennes* (1962). Jean-François *Sénart made an arrangement of the song for four-part choir (Alliance des chorales du Québec 1975). Joseph *Saucier's 78 (HMV XX007) was one of the first recordings of the song in Canada. Several LPs subsequently appeared, including those by Jacques *Labrecque (RCI and RCA CS 100-2), Alan *Mills with Hélène *Baillargeon (as 'Si tu te mets anguille' RCI and RCA CS 100-1), and Nana Mouskouri, who made the song well known outside Canada.

BIBLIOGRAPHY
Charivari canadien, vol 1, 4 Jun 1844
Gérin, Léon. 'Note sur l'écrit de "Un Canadien errant" (d'un cahier manuscrit de Gérin-Lajoie, "Souvenirs de collège"),' *Antoine Gérin-Lajoie: La Résurrection d'un patriote canadien*, ed Léon Gérin (Montreal 1925)
Grenon, Hector. *Us et coutumes du Québec* (Montreal 1974)
Hone, François. *Un Siècle et demi de documents historiques*, priv publ (Montreal 1976)
Laforte, Conrad. 'Un Canadien errant,' *Dictionnaire des oeuvres littéraires du Québec*, vol 1, ed Maurice Lemire (Montreal 1978) (HP)

Cantata. A sung composition usually in several movements and from 10 to 30 minutes long, accompanied by orchestra, and intended for church or ceremonial use. It may employ biblical verses but more typically sets a text by one author, often a contemporary of the composer. The 19th- or 20th-century church cantata, unlike that of the 18th century (which reached its zenith in J.S. Bach's 295 [nearly 200 extant] examples of the genre), seldom is based on a congregational hymn.

The earliest composition of the cantata type to be mentioned in Canadian historical documents was an ode performed in Quebec City on 31 Dec 1776 to mark the first anniversary of the repulsion of US invaders. Written especially for this anniversary, the work contained airs, an arietta, recitatives, a march, and a chorus. The English text is printed in the *Quebec Gazette* (2 Jan 1777). Its composer's name was not reported and the music has not been found. Another work inspired by a historical occasion was John *Bentley's *Ode*, performed in Quebec on 26 Dec 1791 at the constitutional meeting which marked the partition of the colony into Upper and Lower Canada.

In the period 1860–1920 the cantata was favoured, even above the light opera and the mass, among the forms used for large-scale Canadian compositions. Choral singers were abundant, and the instrumental accompaniment could be played on an organ. Many British, French, and German works also were performed and served as models for Canadian works. The popularity of the cantata form is attested by the fact that nearly all of the following were published:

1860–9

*Sabatier, Charles W. *Cantata in Honour of H.R.H. the Prince of Wales on the Occasion of his Visit to Canada / Cantate en l'honneur de son altesse royale le prince de Galles à l'occasion de son voyage au Canada* (1860; Boucher & Manseau ca 1862–4 excerpts); *Les Beaux Arts* (1864 excerpts)

*Labelle, J.-B. [but two sections composed by an unidentified other]. *Cantate 'La Confédération'* (ca 1867; score lost)

1870–9

*Lavallée, Calixa. *Cantate en l'honneur du Marquis de Lorne et de la Princesse Louise* (ca 1879; score lost)

1880–9

Labelle, J.-B. *La Croisade canadienne* 'cantate aux Zouaves pontificaux' (1886; score lost)

1890–9

*Harriss, C.A.E. *Daniel before the King* (1890; G. Schirmer 1890)

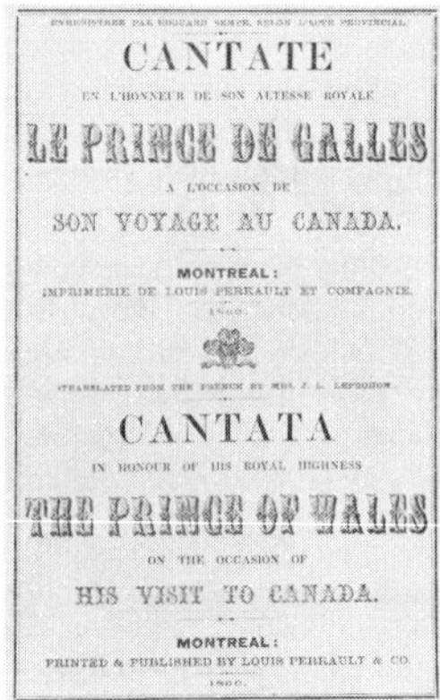
CANTATE
EN L'HONNEUR DE SON ALTESSE ROYALE
LE PRINCE DE GALLES
A L'OCCASION DE
SON VOYAGE AU CANADA.
MONTREAL:
IMPRIMERIE DE LOUIS PERRAULT ET COMPAGNIE.

CANTATA
IN HONOUR OF HIS ROYAL HIGHNESS
THE PRINCE OF WALES
ON THE OCCASION OF
HIS VISIT TO CANADA.
MONTREAL:
PRINTED & PUBLISHED BY LOUIS PERRAULT & CO.

*D'Auria, Francesco. *The Sea King's Bride* (performed Toronto 1890); *Gulnare* or *The Crusader's Ransom* (Suckling 1891)
*Fisher, Arthur E. *The Wreck of the Hesperus* (ca 1893)
*Illsley, Percival J. *Ruth* (1894; Whaley Royce 1894)
*Read, Angelo. *A Song of the Nativity* (G. Schirmer 1899)
1900–9
*Lucas, Clarence. *The Birth of Christ* (Chappell 1901)
Read, A. *David's Lament* (G. Schirmer 1902)
Harriss, C.A.E. *Pan* (Novello 1904)
Charlebois, J.A. *Cantate à Saint Viateur* (Recueil de cantiques ca 1906)
*Broome, Edward. *A Hymn of Trust* (G. Schirmer 1910)
1910–19
*Reed, William. *The Message of the Angels* (Ditson 1910); *The Resurrection and the Life* (Ditson 1911); *The Burden of the Cross* (Ditson or Presser 1912)
*Ham, Albert. *The Solitudes of the Passion* (ca 1917; Novello 1917)

Others who composed cantatas during this period include Octave *Chatillon, Guillaume *Couture, Napoléon *Crépault, Antoine *Dessane, Ralph *Horner, Alphonse *Lavallée-Smith, and Charles *Wheeler.

After World War I the cantata lost its pre-eminent position among extended compositions, possibly because the emergence of professional orchestras and chamber groups enticed composers to write instrumental works. Only a few composers, and those few mainly traditionalists, perpetuated the form in Canada between the wars: Gena *Branscombe, with *The Dancer of Fjaard* and *The Phantom Caravan* (both 1926); Bjorgvin Gudmundsson, with *Adveniat regnum tuum* (1924–5); Omer *Létourneau, with *Dieu te garde mon Canada* (1934); Henri *Miro, with **Vox populi* (1928); and Healey *Willan, with *The Mystery of Bethlehem* (ca 1923), *All Hail the Queen* 'A Canadian Ode' (1936), and **Brébeuf* (1943).

During the second half of the century, however, the cantata came into favour again. Canadians who have written cantatas after World War II include:

*Anhalt, István. *Cento* 'Cantata urbana' (1967)
*Archer, Violet. *The Bell* (1949); *Cantata sacra* (1966)
*Barnes, Milton. *Thespis* (1956–73); *In Our Time* (1968); *Psalms of David* (1973); *Shir Hashirim* (1975)
*Beckwith, John. *Jonah* (1963)
*Beecroft, Norma. *From Dreams of Brass* (1964)
*Bissell, Keith. *Christmas Cantata* (1949); *Let There Be Joy* (1965); *People Look East* 'An Advent Cantata' (1965)
*Brott, Alexander. *The Prophet* (1960)
*Coulthard, Jean. *Pastorale Cantata* (1967)
*Dolin, Samuel. *Marchbankantata* (1971)
*Ferland, Marcien. *La Basilique de Saint Boniface* (1977)
*Fleming, Robert. *Prairie Sailor* (1970)
*Freedman, Harry. *The Flame Within* (1968)
*Grégoire, Richard. *Cantate* (1968)
*Kaufmann, Walter. *Coronation Cantata* (1953)
*Kenins, Talivaldis. *Cantata 'To a Soldier'* (1953); *Sawan-oong 'The Spirit of the Wind'* (1973); *Cantata Baltica* (1974)
*Mather, Bruce. *The White Goddess* (1960–2)
*McIntyre, Paul. *Judith* (1957, rev 1958)
*Mercure, Pierre. **Cantate pour une joie* (1955); *Psaume pour abri* (1963)
*Naylor, Bernard. *The Living Fountain* (1947–63); *King Solomon's Prayer* (1953); *Sing O My Love* (1963); *Resurrection According to St Matthew* (1965); *The Armour of Light* (1967)
*Pedersen, Paul. *Cantata and Narrative for Good Friday* (1972)
*Pépin, Clermont. *Hymne au vent du Nord* (1960)
*Prévost, André. *Terre des hommes* (1967)
*Schafer, R.M. *Brébeuf* (1961); *The Judgement of Jael* (1961)
*Turner, Robert. *The Third Day* (1962)
*van Dijk, Rudi. *Christmas Cantata* (1967)
*Walter, Arnold. *For the Fallen* (1949)
Willan, Healey. *Coronation Suite* (1952)
*Wilson, Charles. *On the Morning of Christ's Nativity* (1963)
*Wuensch, Gerhard. *Laus sapientiae* (1977)

In a general list of Canadians who composed cantatas between 1920 and 1980 these names also would appear: Raffi *Armenian, Gerald *Bales, Alfred *Bernier, Felix-R. *Bertrand, Maurice Boivin, Wolfgang *Bottenberg, Charlotte *Cadoret, J.C.E. Caron, F.R.C. *Clarke, Gabriel *Cusson, Reine *Décarie, Léon *Destroismaisons, Clifford *Ford, Jon Fridfinnsson, J.-J. *Gagnier, Graham *Godfrey, Theo *Goldberg, Frank *Haworth, Janis *Kalnins, Minuetta *Kessler, Lothar *Klein, Alfred *Kunz, Lucienne Lafleur, Leslie *Mann, John *McTaggart, Michael *Miller, Juliette *Milette, Kornelius *Neufeld, Oscar *O'Brien, Charles *O'Neill, Stanley *Osborne, David *Ouchterlony, Tibor *Polgár, Arthur *Semple, Ben *Steinberg, A.D. *Thompson, Roman *Toi, Elliot *Weisgarber, and Leon *Zuckert. (HK)

The Cantata Singers of Vancouver. A 40-voice mixed choir founded in 1958 by Hugh *McLean. It made its debut 8 Feb 1959 in Bach's *Mass in B Minor* at Christ Church Cathedral and soon established a reputation for performances scrupulously authentic in language, instrumentation, and style. Works of composers as different as Josquin, Buxtehude, and Bach were performed with correct accompaniments, using instruments of the period. McLean was succeeded as conductor in 1967 by John Wiebe (b Killarney, near Brandon, Man, 7 Jan 1932, educated at the Mennonite Education Institute at Clearbrook, BC, and the Nordwestdeutsche Musik-Akademie, Detmold, Germany). Wiebe's Motet Singers, founded in 1962, were absorbed into the Cantata Singers. James L. Frankhauser followed Wiebe as conductor in 1973. The Cantata Singers have performed mainly in Vancouver and the Fraser Valley. They have sung often with the *Vancouver SO, on CBC radio, and at the *U of British Columbia.

Cantate pour une joie. Cantata in seven sections for soprano, chorus, and orchestra, composed in 1955 by Pierre *Mercure. The poems by Gabriel *Charpentier (English version by Harold Heiberg) express modern man's search for the happiness of faith. The work incorporates four previous works by Mercure, the choral piece *Ils ont détruit la ville* (1950) and the three songs, *Dissidence* (1955). The cantata's premiere, 1 Feb 1956 by Marguerite *Lavergne and a CBC chorus and orchestra, was part of a *CLComp concert conducted by Jean-Marie *Beaudet at Montreal's *Plateau Hall and was broadcast by CBC. A recording (RCI 155) features the same performers. Under Mercure's direction the cantata was telecast later in 1956 on CBC. Notable among many subsequent performances have been those by Lois *Marshall, the *Toronto Mendelssohn Choir, and the *MSO under Elmer *Iseler in Montreal in 1967; by the Société Chorale À Coeur Joie de Lyon under Chantal *Masson at Vaison-la-Romaine, France, in 1968; by the *NACO under Alexander *Brott in 1970 and under Mario *Bernardi in Ottawa in 1974; by Clarice *Carson and an orchestra under Alexander Brott in the presence of Queen Elizabeth II at the Olympics in Montreal in 1976; by the *Thunder Bay SO under Dwight Bennett in 1976; and by university groups under Françoys *Bernier in Jerusalem and Tel Aviv in 1976.

The music, in the lyrical-muscular manner of the 28-year-old Mercure (who was indebted to Ravel and Honegger), has served also as the score of a Brian Macdonald ballet which was performed 15 Mar 1976 at *PDA by Les Grands Ballets Canadiens. A vocal score of the cantata was published in 1960 by Ricordi.

La Cantoria. Montreal choir with a nucleus of about 30 voices, founded ca 1939, and directed by Victor *Brault. It performed choral works with one or two pianos as well as operas and oratorios. Its aim was to promote Canadian music and part-songs and folksongs from other countries. Four CBC radio series, 'Le Chant du monde' 1939–42, were very successful and later were broadcast in Latin America. La Cantoria, under Jean-Marie *Beaudet's direction, also sang for the CBC Honegger's *Le Roi David* in 1941, Pierné's *La Croisade des enfants* in 1942, and the same composer's *Les Enfants à Bethléem* in 1946. In September 1943 the choir, a member of the *Metropolitan Opera Guild, took part in Metropolitan performances of *Aida, Lohengrin,* and *Boris Godunov* at the St-Denis Theatre. It also performed operas such as *Orphée et Eurydice* and *Carmen* with Victor Brault.

Brault commissioned original works by several renowned composers, including Alexandre Tansman, whose *Deux Chants anciens religeux de Pologne*, for choir and piano, La Cantoria premiered on CBC radio in 1945. With the co-operation of Nadia Boulanger and Jean Françaix La Cantoria appeared in 1947 at the École normale in Paris, singing Lili Boulanger's *Vieille prière bouddhique* and works by Canadian composers, notably Claude *Champagne (*Suite canadienne*, its first performance in Paris since it had been premiered there in 1928), James Callihou (Léo-Pol *Morin), Laurent Winter (Victor Brault), and Andrée *Desautels. The honorary board of La Cantoria included Sir Ernest *MacMillan, Claude Champagne, Darius Milhaud, Vladimir Golschman, Alexandre Tansman, and Arthur Honegger. La Cantoria recorded Champagne's *Suite canadienne* (78 rpm) with the CBC Montreal orchestra conducted by Beaudet (1945, RCI Canadian Album no. 1 / RCA DM 1229). The choir disbanded in the early 1950s.

Another ensemble, La Cantoria de Montréal, directed by Pierre Albrech, flourished briefly in 1926. AD

CAPAC (Composers, Authors and Publishers Association of Canada Limited / Association des compositeurs, auteurs et éditeurs du Canada Ltée). An organization established in 1925 as the Canadian Performing Rights Society (CPRS). A subsidiary of Great Britain's Performing Rights

Society (PRS), CPRS was created to administer the royalties of composers and/or lyric writers whose works were performed in Canada. In 1930 the US performing rights society ASCAP became part owner of CPRS. In 1945 by Supplementary Letters Patent CPRS became CAPAC. In 1963 PRS and ASCAP transferred their legal ownership of shares in CAPAC to the Canada Permanent Trust Co in trust for the members of CAPAC.

In 1921 the Canadian Copyright Act established performing rights of musical works as a constituent part of copyright. Thus the owner of the copyright of a musical work, as the owner of the performing right, must authorize any use of that work. A composer/author or publisher member of CAPAC assigns the legal ownership of his performing right to CAPAC (see also Copyright). CAPAC collects fees from those who make public or broadcast use of music (over radio and TV stations, in concert halls, theatres, and cinemas, etc) and distributes them (less administration costs) to those whose music is performed. In order to ascertain proper payments CAPAC establishes a number of distribution pools of money (eg, 'broadcast general' and concert hall, TV, etc), which then are divided among those who own rights in the works performed within that sector, according to the number of performances logged, the lengths of the works, and other criteria. Thus the composer of an unpublished instrumental work would receive a virtual 100 per cent of the amount earned by that work's performances, while the fees for a published work with lyrics would be divided: publisher 50 per cent, composer 25 per cent, lyricist 25 per cent.

CAPAC has its head office in Toronto and branch offices in Montreal (established in the late 1940s) and Vancouver (established in 1974). It administers the performing rights of works performed in Canada on behalf of approximately 9000 Canadian members and an estimated 250,000 members of 34 affiliated foreign societies. In return, the foreign societies administer the rights of Canadian works performed in their countries. Wholly controlled by its Canadian members, CAPAC has a board of 16 directors elected annually by the membership. The directors – eight composers and authors and eight publishers – are responsible for the appointment of CAPAC management and for the formulation and amendment of CAPAC policies. General managers have been Harry T. Jamieson 1925–47 and William St Clair Low 1947–68, succeeded by John Mills, QC. (Mills was made an Officer of the *Order of Canada in 1980.) Presidents have included Sir Ernest *MacMillan 1947–69, Howard *Cable 1969–71, Rosaire Archambault 1971–3, John *Weinzweig 1973–5, C.C. Devereux 1975–7, and Stéphane *Venne 1977–9. John *Bird succeeded Venne.

In addition to its primary functions of licensing performances and collecting and distributing royalties, CAPAC provides support to the Canadian music community in other ways. Its bilingual monthly magazine *The Canadian Composer / Le Compositeur canadien* (published by Creative Arts Co, Toronto) began to appear in May 1965. In 1938 the CPRS inaugurated a competition for composers with a first prize of $750 for study at the TCM. In 1941 it added a junior division. Among those who won awards were Louis *Applebaum 1938, Robert *Barclay 1938, 1939, Robert *Fleming 1941, 1942, Graham *George 1943, 1947, Paul *McIntyre 1949, 1950, 1951, Oskar *Morawetz 1945, 1946, Clermont *Pépin special junior award 1937, regular awards 1946, 1947, 1948, Eldon *Rathburn 1938, and Charles *Wilson 1951.

In 1970 these scholarships were replaced by the Sir Ernest MacMillan and William St Clair Low Fellowships, the former awarded for compositions for 12 or more players, the latter for chamber music compositions for up to 12 players, or for electronic music or mixed media compositions. At first the fellowships were $2000 each, and were available only to composers who were graduates of Canadian universities and were intending to take up post-graduate studies in Canada. In 1976 the fellowships were increased to a total of $6000; students at the *RCMT and the *Cons de musique du Québec became eligible to compete for them; and winners were permitted to continue their studies either in Canada or abroad. Winners of the Sir Ernest MacMillan and the St Clair Low Fellowships respectively have been Clifford *Ford and John *Fodi 1970, David Paul 1971, Myra Grimley and Edward Dawson 1972, Bruce Pennycook and Christian L'Ecuyer 1973, Dennis Patrick and David Tanner 1974, Thomas Dusatko and Patrick Cardy 1975, Myke Roy 1976, Marjan *Mozetich and Gilles Bellemare 1977, Patrick Cardy and Michael Maguire 1978, and Stephen Klein and Hope Lee 1979. CAPAC grants to the RCMT helped fund the MacMillan (later CAPAC-MacMillan) Lectures, given annually 1963–77 as part of the RCMT Summer School. The inaugural lecturer was Glenn *Gould. Subsequent lecturers were Sir Ernest MacMillan, Jean *Vallerand, Zoltan Kodály, Welton *Marquis, Peter Maxwell Davies, Ravi Shankar, Wilfrid *Pelletier, Aaron Copland, Galt *MacDermot, György Ligeti, Maureen *Forrester, Luciano Berio, Arthur Schwartz, and Iannis Xenakis.

CAPAC was a founder-sponsor of the *CMCentre and for many years provided financial assistance to the *CMCouncil. One of the first orchestral concerts of Canadian music ever given – the *TSO under MacMillan in works by *Champagne, *Dela, *Ridout, Leo *Smith, Vallerand, Weinzweig, and *Willan, on 27 Jan 1948 at *Massey Hall – was sponsored by CAPAC.

In 1963, with the Canadian Assn of Broadcasters, CAPAC formed the CAPAC-CAB Committee, under the chairmanship of Louis Applebaum, for the promotion of Canadian music. Originally CAPAC set aside an annual fund of $50,000 for use by this committee, which at first devoted the money primarily to subsidizing recordings of music by CAPAC composers. The recordings appeared in the commercial record market on many labels, including Capitol, Columbia, RCA, Decca, Dominion, Select, etc. Sponsored by CAPAC alone after 1972, and with a much larger budget, the project continued under the direction of two committees, one concentrating on pop music, the other on concert music.

In Paris on 19 Mar 1974 CAPAC presented a concert of music by Norma *Beecroft, John *Hawkins, Alan *Heard, Micheline Coulombe *Saint-Marcoux, Norman *Symonds, and John Weinzweig. In November 1977, in co-operation with the Dept of External Affairs and the Canadian Embassy in Bonn, it sponsored 'Rendezvous with Canada,' a week of concerts which included premieres of works by A. *Brott, *Kenins, and Morawetz, and performances of compositions by Richard-Gaudreault *Boucher, *Freedman, *Garant, Michel *Gonneville, *Holman, Rathburn, Saint-Marcoux, Donald Steven, Symonds, Weinzweig, and Wilson. Performers included Janina *Fialkowska, the *Festival Singers, the *SMCQ, *Canadian Brass, Robert *Aitken, and Boris Brott, who conducted the Beethovenhalle Orchestra.

CAPAC grants are made to member composers to assist in the preparation of demonstration tapes, and in 1976 a series of Musical Portraits began to be issued. These are small-disc recordings circulated in pamphlet-envelopes; each recording contains short excerpts from a composer's works and the envelope provides concise biographical information. The editor for the series has been Norma Beecroft. CAPAC has published John V. Mills' *You and the Music Business / L'Industrie musicale et vous* (Toronto 1974), which explains copyright law.

To mark its 50th anniversary in 1975 CAPAC sponsored two TV specials: 'Superfleurs' on the CBC French network and 'Festival of Canadian Song' on the CBC English network. In 1978 CAPAC was host, in Toronto and Montreal, to the 31st Congress of CISAC, the International Conference of Societies of Authors and Composers.

BIBLIOGRAPHY

Jamieson, H.T. 'Protecting the author and composer,' *Canadian R*, vol 5, Dec–Jan 1947
'The many activities of the CAPAC-CAB committee,' *CanComp*, 11 Oct 1966
Mills, John. 'Some questions and answers about CAPAC,' *CanComp*, 19, Jun 1967
CAPAC. Special 50th-anniversary edition, *CanComp*, 105, Nov 1975
The Canadian Composer / Le Compositeur canadien, May 1965–

Capitol Records – EMI of Canada Limited / Disques Capitol – EMI du Canada Limitée. Company established in Canada in 1954 by the US parent firm, Capitol Records, which had been founded in 1942 by the songwriters Buddy DeSylva, Johnny Mercer, and Glenn Wallachs. Prior to 1954 Capitol records were pressed and distributed in Canada 1946–7 by Musicana Records (which also had its own roster of Canadian performers – the young Gisèle *MacKenzie, Bert *Niosi, the Howard *Cable Orchestra, and others) and 1947–54 by its successor, Regal Records, both of London, Ont. In 1947 an associate firm, Capitol Records of Canada, headed by W. Lockwood Miller, was set up in London. When the British firm Electrical and Musical Industries (EMI) took over Capitol in 1955, Capitol Records of Canada Ltd became Capitol Records – EMI of Canada Ltd. Head offices were established in Toronto.

In Canada Capitol has distributed classical recordings on the Angel and Seraphim labels and pop music on Capitol, Chrysalis, EMI, and other labels. It has recorded many Canadian performers, especially in the pop field: Bill Amesbury, *Beau Dommage, Wes Dakus and the Rebels, *Edward Bear, Lee *Gagnon, *Maneige, Anne *Murray, the Staccatos (*Five Man Electrical Band), Suzanne Stevens, and many country artists. Among Canadian concert performers Lois *Marshall recorded folksongs for Capitol in England, and other singers have participated in opera or oratorio recordings for Angel.

BIBLIOGRAPHY

Stephens, Robert. 'Capitol Records' alchemists can turn those plastic disks into gold platters,' Toronto *Globe and Mail*, 6 May 1978 (EBM)

Capitol Theatre (Quebec City). See Auditorium de Québec.

Caravan. Annual multicultural festival founded in Toronto in 1969 by Leon and Zena Kossar. Billed as a nine-day 'trip around the world,' it features the arts, crafts, foods, music, and entertainments of nearly 50 cultures. 'Pavilions' named after cities and towns of the world (29 in 1969, 58 in 1978, 50 in 1979) are set up throughout the city in rented halls, clubs, and church basements, and admission to each is gained through the purchase of a single Caravan 'passport.' Music has played a large role in the festival. Most of the pavilions present floor shows daily, and the performers range from solo singers and instrumentalists through divers small groups to pipe bands, steel bands, balalaika orchestras, folk choirs, and dance ensembles. One might hear classical Arabic music at the Kuwait pavilion, Maori songs at the Auckland pavilion, or watch a 'pearly king' host in an old music-hall setting at the London pavilion. Most groups, such as the Kolmaya Dance Ensemble and Bandurists (Ukrainian), the Glen Echoes (Scottish), and Zrinski and Frankopan (Croatian), are local. There also are guest performers, however, such as the Dare Singers, a 24-man choir from Wales, which appeared at the Cardiff pavilion in 1978.

Canada itself has been represented in Caravan by various pavilions over the years. In 1978 there were five: Discovery (NWT), 'Neekaunisi-Kaun' (native Canadian Indian), Quebec, St John's (Nfld), and Toronto. The Quebec pavilion featured the singing group Les Fantaisistes; the Discovery pavilion, Moe *Koffman and his jazz group and a group which performed Inuit music. The Toronto pavilion has been devoted to musical theatre. Organized in 1977 by the *COC, it displays COC props, sets, and costumes and has presented members of the company in selections from musicals and operettas and in abridged versions of *Hansel and Gretel* and *The Barber of Seville*, etc. *Gallantry*, a half-hour comic 'soap opera' by the US composer Douglas Moore, was staged for Caravan by Lotfi Mansouri in 1978. Also of musical interest is the New Orleans pavilion, which in 1978 featured Jim *McHarg and the Midnight Special, Peter *Appleyard, Phyllis *Marshall, and the Excelsior, Silver Leaf, and Climax Jazz bands in programs of jazz, dixieland, and ragtime. NM

CARBONI, Giuseppe (Angelo). Teacher, b Venice 1866?, d Toronto 9 Feb 1934. After study in Vienna and Paris Carboni conducted opera in Germany and Austria and then served six years as a coach at the Opéra-Comique in Paris. In 1915 he settled in Toronto, where he became voice director at the *Hambourg Cons. In 1915, too, he presented the first of many amateur operatic productions, among them such rarely heard works as Paer's *Le Maître de Chapelle*, Adam's *Le Chalet*, and Gounod's *Philémon et Baucis*. In certain lean years these student performances provided the only opera to be heard in Toronto. After leaving the Hambourgs Carboni opened his own studio; among his many pupils were Jeanne *Dusseau, J. Elcho Fiddes, Redferne *Hollinshead, Ivy Dale, Kenneth *Sakos, Mabel Manley Pickard, and Jeanne *Pengelly. JBM

CARDINAL, Réjane (m Goosens). Mezzo-soprano, b Montreal 25 Dec 1926. She studied with Roger *Filiatrault, privately 1941–3, and then for five years at the École supérieure de musique in Outremont (*École Vincent-d'Indy). In 1945 she was the singing voice for Jeanne *Maubourg's dramatic portrayal of Emma Calvé in the CBC radio program 'Sous tous les ciels j'ai chanté.' Cardinal received a bursary in 1947 from the Sarah *Fischer Concerts and another in 1948 from the Montreal Social Club. She was coached 1949–51 in Paris by Charles Panzéra and also appeared in recital during her stay in France. Returning to Montreal, she studied opera with Raoul *Jobin. She toured 1951–2 for *JMC in Quebec, and in 1953 sang Suzuki in *Madama Butterfly* with the *Variétés lyriques. For the radio program 'CBC Wednesday Night' she sang Marie in Berlioz' *L'Enfance du Christ* (1953) and Geneviève in Debussy's *Pelléas et Mélisande* (1955), and for CBC TV's *'L'Heure du concert' she appeared in Poulenc's *Dialogue des Carmelites* (1960) and Puccini's *Suor Angelica* (1964). She toured Europe as soloist with the *Disciples du Massenet in 1960. At the Congrès du spectacle in Montreal she won the trophy for best operatic artist for her portrayal of the Mother in the CBC TV production (1961) of Menotti's opera *Amahl and the Night Visitors*. She sang Dorabella in six performances of *Così fan tutte* at the 1962 *Montreal Festivals. Another JM tour, 1962–3, took her to southwestern France, Brittany, and Normandy. She was soloist with the *Quebec SO in Beethoven's *Symphony No. 9* in 1963, Handel's *Messiah* in 1964, and Mozart's *Requiem* in 1966. For the *Théâtre lyrique de Nouvelle-France she sang Taven in *Mireille* in 1965 and Charlotte in *Werther* during the 1968–9 season. Of her Taven, Louise Lasnier wrote in *Le Soleil* (Quebec City, 26 Apr 1965): 'Réjane Cardinal unquestionably deserves full praise for her magnificent portrayal ... She has shown herself to be a great interpreter, and an intelligent and subtle actress.' Cardinal appeared 1970–4 in the series 'Québec sait chanter' on Télé-Métropole. ST

CAREY. Family of Millgrove and Hamilton, Ont. Its members by 1980 had been active as singers, choir directors, and teachers for four generations: 1 / Whitfield, his brother Abiathar, and his sister Olive; 2 / Bruce, oldest son of Whitfield; 3 / Edith, daughter of Whitfield, and Ellen, granddaughter of Edith; 4 / Clara, daughter of Whitfield; 5 / Vernon, son of Whitfield; 6 / Bertha, daughter of Whitfield, and Elizabeth, daughter of Bertha; 7 / Talbert, brother of Whitfield, and Lorne and Roy, sons of Talbert; 8 / Flora, daughter of Roy, and Earlene, daughter of Flora; and 9 / Estelle, daughter of Abiathar.

1 (George) **Whitfield**. Businessman, baritone, b Millgrove, near Hamilton, Ont, 9 Jul 1851, d Hamilton 13 Mar 1922. At first a farmer, he and his brother Abiathar (b Millgrove 1864, d there 1949) established a music and instrument store in the 1880s on King St in Hamilton. In 1905, in the hall above the George W. Carey Piano House (as it was known then), the Elgar Choir was founded. With their brother Talbert, Whitfield and Abiathar formed a vocal trio that performed locally. Their sister Olive (b Millgrove 1876, d New Rochelle, NY, m Filman, m Chapman) took singing lessons in Hamilton before going to New York to study. She sang in opera in New York in the early 1900s under the name Dorothy Hunty, but retired to Toronto following her second marriage.

2 **Bruce** (Anderson). Choir conductor, baritone, teacher, b Millgrove 16 Nov 1876, d Hamilton 8 May 1960; hon D MUS (Moravian College, Pa) 1936. He studied piano with J.E.P. *Aldous and voice with Mrs Bruce Wickstrom in Hamilton and voice with W. Elliott *Haslam in Toronto. In 1900 he went to London where he studied voice with Albert Visetti and choral and orchestral conducting with William Cummings at the GSM. He later continued his studies of opera (summers, 1908 and 1913) with Isidore Braggiotti and Carlo Carrobbi (or Corelli) in Florence and of Lieder with Heinrich Neidhardt in Munich. After his return from London in 1901 he was choirmaster at a succession of Hamilton churches (Erskine Presbyterian, St Thomas' Anglican, Knox Presbyterian, St Paul's Presbyterian) and in 1905 he established the Elgar Choir (later *Bach-Elgar Choir), which he directed until 1922. Carey was one of the triumvirate of administrative officers 1907–17 of the Hamilton Cons (*RHCM) and supervisor of music 1918–22 for Hamilton schools. He taught during the summers 1918–22 at Cornell U, Ithaca, NY and served 1922–43 as director of vocal music at Girard College for Boys, Philadelphia. In 1926 in Philadelphia he led the Festival Chorus of 6300 voices in several performances during the six-month celebration of 150 years of US independence. He was director 1926–34 of the Mendelssohn Club, working in association with Leopold Stokowski and the Philadelphia Orchestra. A US delegate at the Anglo-American Music Educators conference in Lausanne, Switzerland, in 1931, he directed the conference's mixed-voice choir. Carey was director 1933–8 of the renowned Bach Choir of Bethlehem, Pa. He was the national organizer of music for the United Service Organization in 1943. After his retirement (1945) he lived in Florida.

BIBLIOGRAPHY

Bartlett, George. 'He blended 6,300 voices into one,' *St Petersburg Times*, 3 Mar 1957

3 **Edith** (Marsella) (m Smythe). Contralto, b Millgrove 31 Jan 1878, d Brockville, Ont, 13 Mar 1941. She was contralto soloist in the early 1900s at St Giles United Church, Hamilton. With her husband, Frederick, she was one of the group of singers that formed the Elgar Choir. Her granddaughter Ellen (b Smith, m Wetherill; mezzo-soprano, b Morrisburg, Ont, 1937) studied voice with Bertha Carey Morrow in Hamilton and Jean *Létourneau in Edmonton and became a member of the *Richard Eaton Singers.

4 **Clara** (Mable) (m Allan). Contralto, b Millgrove 8 Aug 1879, d Hamilton 26 Dec 1974. She taught singing privately and was a soloist at Centenary United Church in the early 1900s. She was a founding member of the Elgar Choir, as was her husband, George Allan, who was noted also as a recitalist in Hamilton and the area.

5 **Vernon** (Talmage). Tenor, choirmaster, b Millgrove 11 Jun 1885, d Hamilton 3 Nov 1948. He studied singing with his sister Clara and in New York for a short time in 1906. He was tenor soloist in Hamilton churches, choirmaster and soloist ca 1909–11 at Central Presbyterian Church in Erie, Pa, and then choirmaster until the 1940s at Hamilton's Ryerson United Church. He was a member of the Elgar Choir and appeared as a soloist throughout southern Ontario, often performing with his sister Bertha and cousin Estelle.

6 **Bertha** (Roxena) (m Morrow). Contralto, teacher, b Millgrove 25 Jun 1887, d Hamilton 12 Jul 1970; hon FRHCM 1966. She studied voice at the Hamilton Cons and, during the summers of 1908 and 1910, in Florence with Isidore Braggiotti. At first a soloist at Hamilton's Hannah Street Methodist Church, in 1905 she took a similar position at the First Methodist Church and became a founding member of the Elgar Choir. After a recital in Erie, Pa, her 'full rich contralto of power and beauty' was praised by the reviewer in the Erie *Evening Herald* 1 Jun 1910. She was a member of the *Duet Club for more than 60 years and president in 1928. She joined the Hamilton Cons in 1932 and taught voice there until 1966. She examined for the RCMT in the 1960s. Her pupils included her daughter Elizabeth Morrow (m McNairn) (soprano, b Hamilton 1921) and Phyllis *Mailing. Beth Morrow McNairn studied further in Italy with Mme Lala and has appeared as a soloist with the *Cantata Singers and the *Vancouver Bach Choir, as well as in Vancouver churches. Bertha Morrow also taught her granddaughter, the soprano Margaret Hutchinson, of Hamilton.

7 **Talbert**. B Millgrove 16 Jun 1856, d 20 Jan 1909. The choirmaster at Carlisle United Church in Flamborough Township, he and his wife and their twin sons Roy (b Millgrove 17 Nov 1884, d 29

Apr 1918) and Lorne (d 9 Mar 1955) performed as a vocal quartet and were members of the Millgrove Choral Group and the Carlisle Church choir. Lorne and Roy toured as bell-ringers with the Musical Eckhardts, a vaudeville troupe, in the early 1900s. Lorne presented the first silent films in Hamilton and played the accompanying piano.

8 **Flora** (m Everett). Pianist, soprano, teacher, b Hamilton 1914; ATCM voice 1940, ATCM piano 1942. The daughter of Roy Carey and the organist Florence Green, she studied piano with Marion Begg Hope and Eileen MacManamy at the Hamilton Cons and singing with Bertha Morrow and Ernesto *Vinci. She taught piano and voice 1938–48 at the Hamilton Cons and was an accompanist for Bertha Morrow. She taught privately 1948–68 in Waterdown, Ont, and after 1968 in Hamilton. Her pupils have included the tenor John Keane and her daughter Earlene (pianist, b 1938; M MUS Carleton).

9 **Estelle** (m Allen, m Riegel). Soprano, b Hamilton 1890, d there 1 Mar 1963. The oldest of Abiathar Carey's seven children, she studied voice with her cousin Bruce Carey and in 1908 in Italy with Isidore Braggiotti. She was soloist ca 1907 at Centenary United Church in Hamilton. She appeared in concert and recital throughout southern Ontario, often with her cousins Vernon and Bertha, and in 1912 sang with the *Welsman *TSO in Chatham. She toured western Canada in 1913, singing in Fort William, Winnipeg, Regina, and Edmonton, and also Calgary, where she was soprano soloist in Gounod's *Gallia* and Rossini's *Stabat mater* with the Central Methodist Church choir led by Wilfred V. Oaten. She pursued her career in the USA during the 1920s, performing in Chicago, Detroit, and New York. During her 52-week engagement in 1923 at the Strand Theater, New York, her sweet but powerful coloratura voice earned her the sobriquet 'The Little Brown Thrush of Broadway.'

Other members of the Carey family have been active in Hamilton's musical life: Bertha's son George as chairman of the RHCM board in the 1960s and Vernon's son William as president of the Bach-Elgar Choir in the 1970s. EMn, PW

CARIGNAN, Jean or **'Ti-Jean.'** Violoneux, b Lévis, near Quebec City, 7 Dec 1916; hon D MUS (McGill) 1977. His father, a bricklayer, also was a violoneux. At 4 Carignan began playing and at 5 he was performing on street corners in Lévis. At first he learned his father's repertoire of traditional tunes, but at 7 he heard a recording of Joseph *Allard, and after the family moved to Montreal he studied 1927–31 with Allard and began to learn the recorded repertoires of the Irish fiddler Michael Coleman and the Scotsman J. Scott Skinner. He continued to perform in the streets but was harassed by the police and at 11 or 12 became a shoemakers's apprentice.

In his mid-teens Carignan joined George *Wade and his Toronto oldtime band, the Cornhuskers. He played violin and occasionally clarinet and saxophone for about five years with the band and participated in the Cornhuskers' Victor recordings. (In later years he occasionally would include a Wade medley on his concert programs.) Returning to Montreal he led a small dance band at the St-André Dance Hall until 1954 and imtermittently worked in factories. He then played for two years with Bob Hill's dance band in the Montreal area. In 1956 he began driving a taxi, choosing to perform only in concert and at folk festivals until, in 1978 increasing deafness forced his retirement from music.

Ti-Jean Carignan

Carignan's performing association with Alan *Mills took him to the 1960 Newport Folk Festival and to the earliest of the *Mariposa Folk Festivals, at which he continued to perform regularly until 1977. He appeared at many other folk festivals in North America and in Europe. In 1960 he performed with Mills and others at Carnegie Hall. The film *Jean Carignan violoneux* was produced by the *NFB in 1975. In the later years Carignan's accompanist was Gilles Losier (b Tracadie, NB, 1936), a pianist and fiddler who studied at the Halifax School of the Blind and has been active in both traditional and popular (rock) music. At the Théâtre Maisonneuve (*PDA) in 1976, Carignan led an orchestra (which included his twin brothers Marcel and Rodolphe, also violoneux) in *Veillée québécoise*, a program of traditional songs and dances. In 1976 André *Gagnon composed the *Petit Concerto pour Carignan et orchestre*, a work with roles for two soloists – a violoneux and a classically trained violinist – that draws a witty analogy between the traditional style of the great country fiddler and the violin writing of Vivaldi or Bach. Carignan and Yehudi Menuhin were the soloists in a performance of the work in an episode of the CBC's TV series 'The Music of Man' (1979). In 1978 Carignan played for *Suite Carignan*, a ballet based on his music, scored by Donald Patriquin, choreographed by Brian Macdonald, and danced by Les Grands Ballets Canadiens. Acclaimed by folklorists and fellow violinists (from Louis 'Pitou' *Boudreault to Yehudi Menuhin), Carignan has been the leading exponent of the Celtic traditions (especially of Coleman's Sligo style) in French-Canadian fiddling. He adopted an uncompromising approach to his repertoire of some 7000 reels, jigs, and other dance tunes learned from Coleman, Skinner, Allard, Wellie *Ringuette, and many others and strove for strict authenticity in his performances. According to *The Folk Music Sourcebook* (New York 1976), 'Carignan's technique is amazing, but more so the joy and energy with which he applies it. There are few players in any music who reach his degree of virtuosity without sacrificing feeling or orginality.' In 1973 400 fiddlers from the USA and Canada gathered at Ascot Corner, south of Montreal, in tribute to Carignan, and a bust by the woodcarver Georges Morisette was unveiled. In 1974 Carignan was made a Member of the *Order of Canada and in 1977 he was awarded the 1976 *Prix de musique Calixa-Lavallée.

DISCOGRAPHY

For London (ca 1952–6): *Ti-Jean ... Le Violoneux*. Ruff pf, Romandini guit, A. Morin caller. MB 4

– *Valses, reels et gigues*. Bruneau acc. MB 32

– *En hommage à l'atelier folklorique*. Ruff pf, A. Morin clogging and spoons. MB 52

– *Jean Carignan ... Le Violoneux*. Bruneau pf. MB 78

Old Time Fiddle. Bruneau acc, M. Roy pf, R. Carignan guit, J. Ferland db. Elektra 266. Reissued as Legacy LEG 120

For Folkways: *Old Time Fiddle Tunes*. FG 3531

– *Songs, Fiddle Tunes and Folktales from Canada*. Mills v, Lacombe guit. FG 3532

For Philo (1973–6): *Jean Carignan*. Losier pf. FI 2001

– *Hommage à Joseph Allard*. Losier pf. FI 2012

– *Hommage à Madame Bolduc*. Jeanne d'Arc Charlebois v, Losier pf and db. FI 2014

– *Coleman, Morrison and Skinner*. FI 2018

Ti-Jean Carignan, violoneux. Losier cond. 1975. Totem TO 9221

Patriquin *Fantasy* and *Hommage*. McGill Chamb O, A. Brott cond. 1977. Sel CC15128

Carignan also appears on recordings of the Newport Folk Festival (1960, Vanguard VSD 9083; 1963, Vanguard VSD 79149) and on the collections *La Veillée des Veilées* (1975, 2-Kébec Disc KD 928-929) and *Soirée québecoise* (Promoson JPA-7503)

BIBLIOGRAPHY

Hresko, Phil. *Jean Carignan*, record liner notes, Philo FI 2001

Beaulieu, Michel. 'De Carnegie Hall au poste de taxi,' *Perspectives*, 16 Jun 1973

Scott, Gail. 'The cab driver who may save a musical tradition,' *CanComp*, 92, Jun 1974

Lanken, Dane. 'Finally, Jean Carignan makes another record,' Montreal *Gazette*, 3 May 1974

Forest, Jean. 'Quand parle le violon,' Montreal *Télé Presse*, 8–15 Nov 1975

Dostie, Gaëtan. 'Ti-Jean Carignan violoneux et ... Québécois,' Montreal *Le Jour*, 19 Feb 1976

Beaulieu, Pierre. 'Jean Carignan ou l'instinct de la musique,' Montreal *La Presse*, 18 Sep 1976

L'Heureux, Christine. 'Jean Carignan enfin reconnu publiquement,' Montreal *Le Devoir*, 25 Sep 1976

Lanken, Dane. 'Farewell of a genius,' Toronto *Globe and Mail*, 23 Nov 1977

Petrowski, Nathalie. 'Jean Carignan, musicien,' Montreal *Le Devoir*, 3 Jun 1978

Begin, Carmelle. 'La musique traditionnelle pour violon: Jean Carignan,' unpubl D MUS thesis, U of Montreal 1979 (RGn)

Carillon. A set of at least 23 bells encompassing, in half-tones, two or more octaves, and playable manually or automatically or both. It originated in the 17th century in the Low Countries, in ranges of from two to three octaves. In the 20th century a range of four octaves is common; five or more is exceptional. The carillon usually is an outdoor instrument, its bronze cup-shaped bells hanging stationary in a tower bell-chamber or, in some modern examples, on an open frame. The bells vary in size: those of the large carillon range from 16 cm in diameter and 5 kilograms in weight to over 2 m and 10 tonnes. The carillon is played manually from a keyboard of large round wooden keys and short pedals which are connected to the bell clappers by simple tracker action. The keys and pedals are depressed with full arm and leg stroke, and require considerable physical exertion. Dynamics vary with touch, and there are no dampers. Automatic playing (in which there is virtually no control of expression and dynamics) formerly was rendered by a rotating cylinder, with pegs (set according to the music) moving the bells. Latterly electric magnets have been used to move the hammers or clappers, the music being encoded on a paper band or cassette. Automatic playing is limited mostly to European carillons.

The carillon came into use as an adjunct to the newly perfected Dutch tower clock, serving to announce the time at frequent intervals with pleasing melodies, and to provide hand-played open-air music on festive occasions. The carillon's rarity may be attributed to the difficulty in tuning the partial tones in the bells so that chords and complex passages may be sounded accurately. After the mid-18th century there was a lapse of 150 years before well-tuned carillons were built again; in the 19th century about 15 instruments of infe-

The Dominion carillonneur, Gordon Slater, at the Peace Tower console, 1978

rior quality were installed in Europe and 3 in the USA. At the beginning of the 20th century two English founders, Gillett & Johnston of Croydon and John Taylor & Co of Loughborough, developed sufficient skill in casting and tuning to produce satisfactory carillons, and prior to 1922 about eight appeared in Europe. The first carillon to be installed in Canada, a 23-bell set commissioned from Gillett & Johnston by Chester D. *Massey in memory of his wife, was placed in Metropolitan United Church, Toronto, in 1922. It was followed by instruments in the USA and in many other parts of the world. By 1974 there were 11 carillons in Canada, all of European (especially Dutch) origin:

Metropolitan United Church, Toronto (installed 1922 with 23 bells, increased to 35 in 1960 and to 54 in 1971)
Norfolk War Memorial, Simcoe, Ont (1925; 23 bells)
St George's Church, Guelph, Ont (1926; 23 bells)
Hart House, Soldiers' Tower, *U of Toronto (1927; 23 bells, increased to 42 in 1952, renovated and enlarged to 51 bells in 1975)
Peace Tower, Parliament Buildings, Ottawa (1927; 53 bells)
Cathedral of Christ the King, Hamilton, Ont (1933; 23 bells)
St-Jean-Baptiste Church, Ottawa (1940; 47 bells; inactive)
Rainbow Tower, Niagara Falls (1947; 55 bells)
St Joseph's Oratory, Montreal (1955–6; 56 bells)
The Netherlands Centennial Carillon, Victoria, BC (1967; 49 bells, increased to 62 bells in 1971)
Carlsberg Carillon, *CNE, Toronto (1974; 50 bells)

The playing of the carillon in Canada rests in very few hands. The pioneer in the field and a world authority is Percival *Price; other carillonneurs include Émilien *Allard, Claude Aubin, Herman *Bergink, Robert *Donnell, Sydney Giles, Charles Hogg, Gordon Johnston, Douglas *Millson, J. Leland *Richardson, Jack Skillikorn, June Somerville, and James and Gordon *Slater and their pupil Heather Spry. Eight Canadians, Price among them, were founding members of the *Guild of Carillonneurs in North America, and Ontario was the guild's base for its first seven years (1938–45). For the most part Canadians have trained in Belgium at the Beiaardschool te Mechelen. Recordings have been made on the Peace Tower carillon by Price and Gordon Slater, on the Netherlands Centennial Carillon in Victoria by Herman Bergink, on the carillon at St Joseph's Oratory by Émilien Allard, on the Soldiers' Tower by Leland Richardson, and on the Rainbow Tower by Gordon Slater.

In 1966 the Province of Alberta installed a 'Centennial Carillon' in Edmonton. This device is not a true carillon as it does not use bells. Rather, the sounds, produced from tiny cast alloy rods, struck by playing a two-manual organ console and pedal board, are electronically picked up, amplified one million times, and played through loudspeakers.

See also Bells; Chimes.

The Peace Tower bourdon in Ottawa

BIBLIOGRAPHY
'Bell music invades Canada,' *CMTJ*, vol 22, May 1922
Belford, Margaret S. 'Victoria's singing tower,' Victoria *Daily Colonist*, 3 May 1970 (PPr)

Carleton University, Ottawa. Non-denominational university founded in 1942 as Carleton College (evening classes). It granted its first degrees in 1946, in journalism and public administration, and was incorporated in 1957 when it moved to the Rideau River campus. A wide range of undergraduate and graduate degrees has been developed by faculties of arts, science, engineering, and graduate studies. The Institute of Canadian Studies, within the graduate division, brings a multi-disciplinary, cross-departmental approach to the investigation of Canadian topics.

Carleton's Music Dept was founded in 1967 with John *Churchill as its first chairman; he was succeeded by Alan *Gillmor in 1976, and Gillmor by David Piper in 1980. Besides establishing the B MUS program (Carleton was one of the first Canadian universities to offer a course in Canadian music history) Churchill introduced Canadian music as a subject in the graduate studies program in 1975. In 1978–9 Carleton offered the following music degrees: BA (music major, general), B MUS (honours, musicology, composition), and MA (Canadian studies). In the same year there were 34 teachers (6 full-time and 28 part-time) and 138 undergraduates.

In 1979 Willy *Amtmann, Robert *Fleming, Elaine *Keillor, and David Piper were or had been staff members and Anne *Eggleston and Ross *Pratt were among the part-time staff. The Carleton U Choir, directed by Churchill, and the Madrigal Singers and Collegium Musicum, directed by Bryan Gillingham, were the department's main performing ensembles. The department also presented an Annual Chamber Music Series.

BIBLIOGRAPHY
Churchill, John. 'Rumours now Carleton reality,' *MSc*, 251, Jan–Feb 1970
'Early music at Carleton,' *Continuo*, Dec 1979 (JPG, PMW)

Carlton Showband. Houseband 1967–77 for CTV's 'Pig and Whistle,' a variety show ostensibly taking place in an Irish pub of that name. The group was formed ca 1964 in Toronto. Members in 1966 were Chris O'Toole (leader, drum, and spoons), Mike Feeney (vocals), Seamus Grew (transichord), Chris McLaughlin (button accordion, harmonica, vocals), Sean McManus (guitar, vocals), and Freddy White (guitar, vocals); in 1976 this group was augmented by Johnny Paterson and Bob Lewis. All are Irish-born, save White (b New Waterford, NS) and Lewis (b Sydney, NS). The group began its career playing in Canadian and US dance halls. However, the success in 1967 of its recording of 'The Merry Ploughboy' (also known as 'The Green on the Green') for the Casl company brought it wider popularity, culminating in its years on the Toronto-produced 'Pig and Whistle.' The Showband colours the traditional Irish repertoire with some country-music performance styles, and in 1975 it won a *Juno Award as top country group and a Big Country Award as top vocal group. Among its recordings are 'Up Went Nelson,' a minor hit in Canada, and LPs for RCA, including *Best of the Carlton Showband* (Camden CAS 2483). (MD)

CARMAN, (Bertram) **Hayunga**. Pianist, teacher, b Morrisburg, near Cornwall, Ont, 22 Feb 1875, d Toronto 6 Jun 1965. His teachers were J.D.A. *Tripp in Toronto, Tobias Matthay in London (where Carman was the dedicatee of the English composer York Bowen's *Second Suite*), and Isabelle Vengerova and Xaver Scharwenka in Europe. Deciding against a concert career, Carman joined the faculty of the *TCM on his return to Canada in 1910. In the next 45 years he developed a reputation as one of Canada's leading piano teachers. His pupils included Edna (Victoria) Baggs, who continued to teach in his tradition at the *RCMT after his retirement in 1957, Patricia *Blomfield Holt, George *Haddad, Bruce Harding, Margaret Ann *Ireland, Muriel *Kilby, Patricia *Perrin Krueger, Percival *Price, Mary *Syme, and Gordon Wallis. (LCk)

CARON, Gérard. Organist, pianist, b St-Martin-de-Beauce, Que, 2 Apr 1916. At the age of nine he became organist at the church in Mansonville, Que, where his parents lived. At the *Cons national of Montreal and the *U of Montreal, where he enrolled in 1933, he studied organ with Eugène *Lapierre and Raoul *Paquet and piano and composition with Albertine *Morin-Labrecque. Later he became regular organist of the churches of Notre-Dame-des-Victoires and St-Jean-Berchmans in Montreal. On a grant from the Quebec government in 1942 he worked in New York with Charles-Marie Courboin, and in 1944 he became organist-choirmaster of the church of St Vincent de Paul in New York. He also was Courboin's assistant at St Patrick's Cathedral. He decided to make New York his home in 1945. In 1952 he went to Rome to work with Fernando Germani. He performed in Florence, Turin, and Rome and trained for a period at the Accademia Chigiana of Siena. Caron gave many recitals in Montreal under the aegis of the *Casavant Society, and played also in Quebec City and several other cities in Canada and the USA. As a pianist he frequently accompanied singers, including Pierrette *Alarie, John Brownlee, Nicola Moscona, and Léopold *Simoneau. Caron became organist-choirmaster at the Church of St John the Baptist in New York in 1964.

DISCOGRAPHY
Noëls aux grandes orgues. 1963. RCA Gala CGPS 148
Noëls a l'orgue / Christmas Carols at the Organ . 1963. RCA Camden CAS 788
Music for Meditation: Schubert *Ave Maria* – Franck *Panis angelicus* – et al. 1963. Mirosonic 137 GP

CARON-LEGRIS, Albertine. Pianist, composer, teacher, b Louiseville, near Trois-Rivières, Que, 1906, d Montreal 1972; B MUS (Montreal) 1942. In Montreal she studied piano with Romain-Octave *Pelletier and later with Michel *Hirvy, singing with Rodolphe *Plamondon, and composition with Canon Élysée Panneton and Eugène *Lapierre. After her marriage to Dr J.-A. Legris, ca 1918, she began teaching in Montreal and giving piano recitals throughout Quebec. She was known mainly, however, as a composer. She wrote songs, piano music, and harmonizations of folksongs. Her best-known work is probably 'La Berceuse de Donalda' (Musica Enr 1947) featured on the CBC radio (later TV) program 'Un Homme et son péché.' A *Canada Council grant made possible the publication of *Mes Plus Belles Chansons* (Montreal 1962), a collection of song melodies arranged for children to play on the piano. Other compositions included *Poème pastorale* for the piano (BMI Canada 1948) and two songs – 'Soir d'hiver' (BMI Canada 1948) and 'Ceux qui s'aiment sont toujours malheureux,' published in *Le Passe-Temps* (Mar 1947). Among singers who have performed Caron-Legris songs are Raoul *Jobin, Nicholas *Massue, Marthe *Létourneau, Maureen *Forrester, and Albert *Viau. Caron-Legris was an affiliate of BMI Canada.

BIBLIOGRAPHY

Barbeau, Marius. 'Au service de notre folklore: Mme Albertine Caron-Legris,' *P-T*, Mar 1947 (LF)

CARR, Donna-Faye. Soprano, b Calgary 4 Jan 1945; ARCT voice 1964. After studying voice and piano 1953–63 with E.E. Hooper in Calgary, she continued her voice training 1965–6 with Roy Henderson at the RAM and 1967–8 with Henderson and Maria Carpi at the London Opera Centre. As a leading soprano 1968–71 at Sadler's Wells, London, she made her debut on 21 Aug 1968 as Donna Anna in *Don Giovanni* and sang Micaela in *Carmen*, Marzelline in *Fidelio*, Mimi in *La Bohème*, and other roles. She was heard as Lady Macbeth in Verdi's *Macbeth* with the Haddo House Choral Society, Aberdeen, Scotland, in 1969, and sang in productions of *Albert Herring* and Verdi's *Giovanna d'Arco* in England, as well as in Mozart's oratorio *La Betulia Liberata*. She has appeared in concerts and operas on the BBC and in Europe. Representing Great Britain, she was a finalist at the 1973 Madama Butterfly Competition in Tokyo and Nagasaki. In Canada she has sung Kathleen in *Riders to the Sea* and the Mother in *Hansel and Gretel* at the *Banff SFA (1970), Tosca with Opera East at *Dalhousie U, Halifax (1976), and Ortlinde in *Die Walküre* with the *COC (1976).

'Carry On.' Patriotic song popular during World War II. The music was written by Ernest *Dainty as part of the orchestral accompaniment to the Canadian silent feature film *Carry On Sergeant*. Extracted from the score, the tune was given lyrics by Gordon V. *Thompson and sung at the film's premiere 10 Nov 1928 in Toronto. 'Carry On' was published in 1928 by Leo Feist, for which Thompson was the Canadian manager. The film, released at the beginning of the 'talkies' era, was not a success, and the song did not become popular until it was revived by Thompson at the beginning of World War II. Stanley Maxted provided new verses, and Térèse Rochette wrote a French-language version, 'En avant.' The new version, published by Thompson in 1940, became a kind of theme song for the war effort and was included by the *Happy Gang in its programs. Although a test recording was made by the Happy Gang for *Compo, 'Carry On' was not recorded commercially. FH

Clarice Carson

CARSON, Clarice (b Katz, m Ornstein, m Ktsanes). Soprano, b Montreal 23 Dec 1936. Her teachers were Pauline *Donalda and Jacqueline *Richard (in Montreal) and Julia Drobner (in New York). She made her public debut at a Sarah *Fischer Concert in Montreal in 1956. Her first operatic roles were with the *Opera Guild of Montreal: the Lady-in-Waiting in *Macbeth* in 1959, Micaela in *Carmen* in 1960, and Siebel in *Faust* in 1963. A season with the New York City Opera 1965–6 (where she made her debut as the Countess in *The Marriage of Figaro*) and a tour 1966–7 with the *Metropolitan Opera National Company (as Violetta in *La Traviata*, the Countess, and the Female Chorus in Britten's *The Rape of Lucretia*) led to three seasons 1967–70 at the Metropolitan Opera, where she made her debut as Pamina in *The Magic Flute*. One of her most successful roles there was Musetta in *La Bohème*. Since then she has sung widely in opera in the USA (Chicago, Pittsburgh, Cincinnati, Houston, San Francisco), Canada (Montreal, Toronto, Vancouver, Quebec, Edmonton, Stratford), and Europe (Barcelona, Glasgow, Amsterdam, Rouen, Nice, Tel Aviv). She returned to the Metropolitan 1975–6 to portray Fiordiligi in *Così fan tutte*. She sang the title role in *Tosca* for CBC TV in 1970 and for the *COC in 1972, and was Elisabeth deValois in *Don Carlos* for the COC in 1977. She has sung several leading roles for the *Opéra du Québec: the title role in *Suor Angelica* and Giorgietta in *Il Tabarro* in 1971, Desdemona in *Otello* in 1973, and Donna Anna in *Don Giovanni*, Cio-Cio San in *Madama Butterfly*, and Alice Ford in *Falstaff* in 1974. In New York she has appeared in concert versions of such seldom heard operas as Berlioz' *Les Troyens* in 1972 and Pfitzner's *Palestrina* in 1973. Her bright lirico-spinto encompasses a wide repertoire ranging from Constanze in *The Abduction from the Seraglio* to Elsa in *Lohengrin*, Maddalena in *Andrea Chenier*, and the title roles in *Aida*, *Salomé*, and *Turandot*. Her second husband is Philon Ktsanes, a Greek-American basso and vocal coach.

BIBLIOGRAPHY

Zachary, Ralph. 'Best foot forward,' *Opera News*, 14 Feb 1970

Billington, Dave. 'Clarice Carson: eloquent museum keeper,' Montreal *Gazette*, 22 Sep 1973 (JBM)

CARTER. English-born brothers, 1 / John, 2 / George, 3 / Henry, and 4 / William, all musicians, sons of the English organist John Carter.

BIBLIOGRAPHY

Brown, J.D., and Stratton, Stephen S. *British Musical Biography* (Birmingham 1897)

LeVasseur, N. 'Musique et musiciens à Québec,' *La Musique* (1919–22)

'Toronto Pre-Confederation Music Societies, 1845–1867'

1 **John**. Choir conductor, organist, b London 7 Jul 1832, d Port Dalhousie (St Catharines), Ont, 1916. He arrived in Canada ca 1853 and lived at first in Quebec City, where he was organist 1853–6 at the Anglican Cathedral of the Holy Trinity. In 1856 he moved to Toronto, where he founded and conducted, ca 1857–9, the Sacred Harmonic Choir, whose presentation of *Messiah* on 17 Dec 1857 is thought to have been the first complete oratorio performance in Upper Canada (Ontario). He was the organist 1856–78 at St James' Cathedral and in 1861 founded the *Musical Union. He gave piano recital series in Toronto in 1865 and 1866, and during the early 1870s he directed his brother William's cantata, *Placida, the Christian Martyr*, at St James' Schoolhouse. No evidence has been found of professional activities after 1878.

BIBLIOGRAPHY

'The Late John Carter,' *Musical Canada*, Feb 1917

2 **George**. Organist, composer, b London 26 Jan 1835, d ?. A pupil of Sir John Goss in London, he gave recitals in England, continental Europe, and the USA. He emigrated to Canada ca 1861 and was the organist for nearly 10 years at Christ Church Cathedral in Montreal. In the 1862–3 season he organized a series of five 'Concerts classiques' of chamber music in Montreal. After his return to England in 1870, he was the organist for several years at Royal Albert Hall. He was the compiler of *A Selection of Anthems as Sung in the Cathedrals of Montreal, Toronto and Quebec* (John Lovell 1865). His compositions include operas, cantatas, organ works, songs, and miscellaneous pieces.

3 **Henry**. Organist, composer, choir conductor, b London 6 Mar 1837, d ?. He studied with Sir John Goss, Ernst Pauer, and Charles Steggall in London and with August Haupt, Ferdinand Hiller, and Friedrich Kiel in Germany. He arrived in Canada during the 1850s and was organist 1857–61 at the Anglican Cathedral of the Holy Trinity in Quebec City. He is said to have founded one of Canada's earliest oratorio societies there, and to have presented the first performance in Canada of *Messiah* (Quebec 1857). At this time he was the English choirmaster of the *Quebec Harmonic Society. In 1864 he moved to the USA, where he was a church organist and a teacher 1880–3 at the College of Music in Cincinnati. He was best known as a recitalist and as a composer of church music, as well as two string quartets and an anthem for soloists, chorus, and orchestra. He also wrote several songs.

BIBLIOGRAPHY

Grove's *American Supplement* (New York 1935)

Dwight's Journal of Music (Boston 1864, 1866)

4 **William**. Choir conductor, organist, pianist, composer, b London 7 Dec 1838, d ?. He studied organ with his father and Ernst Pauer and later was organist at several churches in England. For one year (1859) he exchanged positions with his brother Henry, organist at the Anglican cathedral in Quebec City. While there he conducted what possibly was the largest Handel festival held in Canada up to that date; it included a performance of *Judas Maccabeus* on 13 Apr 1859, the centenary of Handel's death. His compositions include the cantata *Placida*, anthems, songs, part-songs, and choral arrangements. (FH, NM, JRz)

CARTER, Wilf (Wilfred Arthur Charles). Singer-songwriter, guitarist, b Port Hilford, on the Atlan-

Wilf Carter

tic coast of Nova Scotia, 18 Dec 1904. Inspired by a touring Swiss yodeller, Carter began singing as a boy. After working as a lumberjack in the mid-1920s he went to Alberta and became a cowboy, but he also entertained at dances and performed for tourist parties travelling in the Rockies. In 1930 he made his radio debut. Later he was heard on stations CFCN and CFAC in Calgary, and nationally on the CRBC. About 1932 he recorded for *RCA Victor in Montreal. His first 78, of his songs 'My Swiss Moonlight Lullaby' (displaying his yodelling style, which had come to be influenced by the US singer Jimmie Rodgers) and 'The Capture of Albert Johnson,' was popular – indeed, the first hit record by a Canadian country performer. Other records followed, some reissued on the LP *The First Five Sessions* (CMH 111). Many of Carter's songs were published by *Thompson between ca 1933 and 1949, in several volumes individually titled *Cowboy Songs*, *More Cowboy Songs*, *New Cowboy Songs*, etc. In 1935 Carter went to New York, where, as 'Montana Slim,' he was host until 1937 for a CBS radio country music show. He then returned to Canada (purchasing a ranch near Calgary) and was heard on CBC radio. Before 1940, however, he had two other US radio shows, on the CBS and NBC networks. An automobile accident in 1940 left him inactive for nine years; his popularity was sustained by the periodic release of new recordings.

In 1949 Carter resumed live performance with tours in Canada and the USA. In 1950 he attracted 70,000 people during a week at the *CNE Bandshell, Toronto. For several years he performed with his daughters Sheila and Carol; his tours also introduced such country artists as the *Rhythm Pals and Orval *Prophet to audiences across Canada. His popularity began to wane in the 1960s in the face of changing styles in country music. Nevertheless Carter continued to tour in the 1970s from a home in Florida, appearing annually in Canada and on CBC TV's 'Tommy *Hunter Show.' In 1976 he made the LP *Have a Nice Day* (RCA KXL1 0157). His other LPs – over 15 for RCA, two each for Decca, Apex, and Starday – include *The Best of Wilf Carter* (RCA Camden CAS-2286), *By Request* (RCA Camden CAL 701), *32 Wonderful Years* (RCA Camden CAL 787), *Wilf Carter's Best Wilf Carter's West* (Apex AL71635/MCA Coral CB 35016), and *Living Legend* (Starday SLP 300).

Carter is known for his simple, straightforward singing and guitar style. He has written several hundred songs, many as much in the folk tradition of the Maritimes as in a country vein. These include 'The Fate of the Old Strawberry Roan' and several with references to life as a cowboy. Carter has been acknowledged the father of country music in Canada, a distinction based on his prominence as Canada's first country star, on his influence on Canadian performers, and on his assistance with the careers of others. If the distinction does not belong solely to Carter, he shares it only with Hank *Snow. Carter is a member of CAPAC.

WRITINGS

The Yodelling Cowboy, autobiography (Toronto 1961)

BIBLIOGRAPHY

Callwood, June. 'The singing cowboy from Nova Scotia,' *Maclean's*, 1 Dec 1951

Flohil, Richard. 'Wilf Carter: calling the shots himself these days,' *CanComp*, 59, Apr 1971

Grigsby, Wayne. 'Wilf Carter: 40 years on the country music road,' *CanComp*, 85, Nov 1973

Brown, Dick. 'Wilf Carter can't sing,' *Canadian Magazine*, Dec 1973 (MD)

CARTIER, Victoria (Prudença Victorine). Pianist, organist, teacher, b Sorel, Que, 4 Apr 1867, d Montreal 1 Jan 1955. She was a niece of Sir George-Étienne Cartier. She took her academic studies with the Sisters of the Congregation of Notre-Dame in Sorel and was a pupil of Romain-Octave *Pelletier in piano and organ. She gave her first recital in Sorel, where she also taught piano and was the organist at St-Pierre Church. In 1896 she went to Paris to study organ with Eugène Gigout, piano with Élie Delaborde, theory with Louis-Albert Bourgault-Ducoudray, and pedagogy with Hortense Parent. While in Paris she met Théodore Dubois, Raoul Pugno, and Camille Saint-Saëns. On her return to Montreal in 1898 she founded the École de piano Paris-Montréal, at which the teaching methods of her French masters were to be propounded for some 25 years. On 27 Oct 1898 at Karn Hall she gave the Canadian premiere of the *Rhapsodie sur des airs canadiens* for organ (Durand ca 1898), which Gigout had dedicated to her.

Cartier broadened her knowledge of the workings of European institutions during several other trips. Her contribution to music education was remarkably stimulating at the time, as was her participation in the numerous concerts produced at her school, in public, and later on the radio. She taught in several institutions, such as Villa Maria Convent and the Institut pédagogique de Westmount. Among her pupils were Alfred *Lamoureux, Jean *Leduc, Éva *Plouffe, and Esther *Wayland. In addition to her own teaching and her work in education she was the organist at several Montreal churches – first at St-Louis-de-France, then at St-Viateur d'Outrement where she inaugurated the Casavant organ in 1913, and finally at Immaculée-Conception. In Paris she was named an officer of the French Académie in 1901 and of the Instruction publique in 1912.

BIBLIOGRAPHY

Gleason-Huguenin, Madeleine. *Portraits de femmes* (Montreal 1938) DPI

Casavant Frères, Limitée. Illustrious and pre-eminent Canadian organ-building firm which celebrated its centenary in 1979. It was founded in St-Hyacinthe, Que, by the Casavant brothers Joseph-Claver (b 10 Sep 1855, d 10 Dec 1933) and Samuel-Marie (b 4 Apr 1850, d 23 Nov 1929), both sons of Joseph Casavant (b 23 Jan 1807, d 9 Mar 1874), the first Canadian-born organ builder of note.

It was probably an unfinished organ by the builder Jacotel (from France, 1821) that Casavant père discovered on his arrival at Father Charles-Joseph *Ducharme's college in Ste-Thérèse-de-Blainville in 1834. At 27, a blacksmith by trade, Joseph Casavant went there to study Latin. But it was the half-built organ rather than declensions and the rigours of Latin composition that became the focus of the belated student's interest. With the help of *L'Art du facteur d'orgues* (Paris 1766–78), a classic treatise by Dom François Bédos de Celles, he managed to complete the instrument. The news spread throughout the region, and the vestry of St-Martin-de-Laval ordered an organ from him. Thereupon, Casavant appears to have dedicated himself entirely to his new trade, so that the organ was completed and delivered in 1840. He persevered in this field and by 1866, when he retired from business, he had built 17 organs, including two of considerable importance in the Roman Catholic cathedrals of Bytown (Ottawa) in 1850 and Kingston, Ont, in 1854. Nothing of his work remains, unfortunately, except some pipes of the organ of the church of Mont-St-Hilaire, which subsequently was rebuilt by his sons. The testimonies of his comtemporaries tell us little about the instruments themselves.

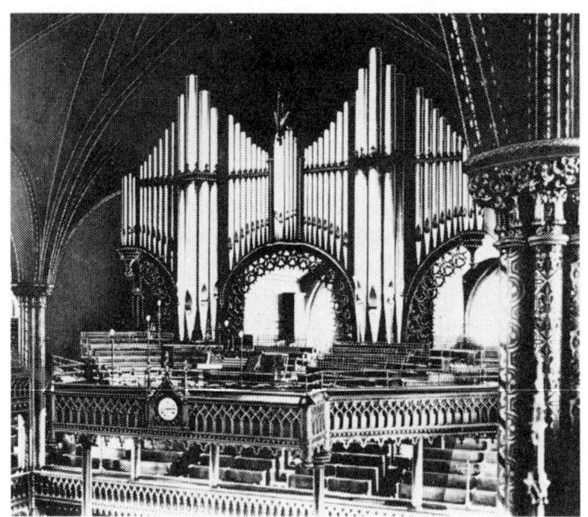

The Casavant organ installed at Notre-Dame Church, Montreal, in 1890

It was with the builder Eusèbe Brodeur, to whom their father had handed over his establishment in 1866, that the Casavant brothers began learning the details of organ building while pursuing their academic studies at the St-Hyacinthe Seminary. Claver worked full-time 1874–8 with Brodeur. In 1878 he began a 14-month apprenticeship with John Abbey in Versailles. He then was joined by Samuel, and the brothers travelled western Europe inspecting organs and visiting workshops.

On their return to Canada in 1879 the brothers adopted the name Casavant Frères and established themselves in the very spot where their father had installed his modest workshop 30 years earlier. In a circular letter in November of the same year the two brothers declared: 'We are honoured to inform you that we have just opened a workshop for the building of Pipe Organs for Churches, Chapels, Concert Halls, Salons, etc.' In 1980 Casavant organs still were being manufactured at the original location.

Claver excelled at voicing and Samuel was skilled in mechanics and a gifted adminstrator. In 1880 they installed their first instrument in the chapel of Notre-Dame-de-Lourdes in Montreal. While the design of this 16-stop organ did not constitute a radical departure from current trends, the four pedals with adjustable combinations were a novelty indeed, the product of the inventive genius of Dr Salluste Duval (a collaborator of the Casavant brothers from the beginning; see Inventions and devices) and, apparently, the first of their kind. The firm made a further innovation when it employed tubular traction as early as 1884 for its seventh instrument, built for the chapel of the St-Hyacinthe Seminary.

Fascinated by new ideas, the brothers also sought a means of using electricity to operate the organ and were assisted in their research by Duval and Father P.-A. Choquette, a physics professor at their alma mater. One of the brothers returned to Europe in 1886 to investigate the latest advances and probably to seek advice on the enormous 32-foot pipe they were in the process of building for Notre-Dame Church in Montreal. The Notre-Dame organ was completed in 1890; its adjustable-combination pedals were the first to be operated by electricity. In 1892, in the basilica organ in Ottawa, electricity was used for an electro-pneumatic traction. The invention, by the Frenchman Albert Peschard, had run into problems when put into actual construction by Peschard himself and by the US builder Hilbourne Lewis Roosevelt. At Ottawa, for the first time, the system gave results which appeared to satisfy the tastes of the period. The instrument installed in St Patrick's Church in Montreal in 1895 was 'all-electric,' including the functioning of the stops.

The reputation of Casavant organs grew quickly in Canada and then abroad and rose steadily over the first 50 years. By 1914 Casavant Frères had completed their 600th instrument, by 1929 their 1355th. Most of their early clients were in Quebec, but soon they began receiving orders from other areas: Ontario (1887, first assignment for the parish church of Tecumseh, near Windsor), the Maritimes (1891), the USA (1895, first order delivered to Holyoke, Mass), Manitoba (beginning of the 20th century), the Yukon (1901), and British Columbia (1907).

Until World War II, sales were limited mainly to Canada and the USA. There was even a branch in South Haven, Mich, managed by J. Pépin, a former St-Hyacinthe employee who in the interim had opened a bellows plant in Montreal. A total of 52 instruments were built at South Haven between 1912 and 1918. The war brought production to a halt, but the employees who remained turned for a time to the manufacture of phonograph cabinets for *RCA Victor; the subsidiary then closed its doors.

Besides the many fine organs on the North American continent, those installed in Paris, the West Indies, South America, and as far afield as South Africa, India, and Japan, constitute a legitimate source of pride. The firm's archives abound in testimonials from famous organists – eg, Alexandre Guilmant, Louis Vierne, Charles-Marie Widor, Joseph *Bonnet, and Marcel Dupré – who have played on Casavant instruments.

Until 1897 the majority of Casavant organs had tracker action. From 1898 to 1924 pneumatic action took over, electro-pneumatic action being confined chiefly to large-scale instruments. In 1905, after completion of the organ built for Sayabec, near Matane, Que, tracker action was abandoned. Electricity and pneumatic action were employed about equally 1925–9. In 1930 the founders were awarded the Grand Prix at an international exhibition held in Antwerp, Belgium. From that time on the electric action prevailed, far outstripping the tubular, which disappeared completely in 1944. Among the instruments built prior to 1930 should be noted, if only for their size, those in the churches of Notre-Dame in Montreal (83 stops), St-Nom-de-Jésus in Montreal (90 stops), St Paul's Anglican Church in Toronto (106 stops), Royal York Hotel in Toronto (107 stops), and Emmanuel Church in Boston (137 stops). Lynnwood *Farnam was the organist at the last-named. Metropolitan United Church, Toronto, commissioned the largest Casavant instrument in Canada; it had 5 keyboards and 125 stops and was installed in 1930. For quite different reasons, mention may be made of the organs of Lacolle in Quebec (1885) and of St-Eugène in Ontario (1893), which have preserved their original charm and the qualities of their tracker action. Many other instruments which have withstood the ravages of time and the vagaries of fashion deserve mention as examples of that fresh and clear-cut design that characterized the Casavant organs of the early decades.

In 1931 Casavant acquired the equipment of the Compagine d'orgues canadiennes, which had closed down. During the 1930s, however, the firm went through difficult times: the death of the founders and the economic crisis had serious repercussions. Many organs were built, but their musical quality suffered increasingly from the standardization of certain stops. Even the design of the instruments occasionally lapsed into a strange confusion. This caused concern among an increasing number of organists but went unnoticed by management for quite some time, since there remained a clientele apparently satisfied with the poor instruments of this period. In 1938 it became necessary to diversify production, and a department of church furnishings was created. In about 1964 production was restricted to component parts for all kinds of furniture, but in 1978 Casavant marketed two collections inspired by traditional Quebec furniture.

In 1956 the promotion to the management ranks of Charles Perrault, a Montreal-born metallurgical engineer who had joined Casavant in 1954, gave rise to a really spectacular recovery. With the help of Lawrence I. Phelps, from the US firm of Aeolian-Skinner and appointed tonal director in 1958, and later of Phelps's successor (1972–9) Gerhard Brunzema, Perrault set about restoring to the old firm the spirit of initiative that had characterized its founders. Thus by 1958 a well-ordered system of stops again was in production (eg, those of the organ of Saints-Martyrs-canadiens Church in Quebec City). In 1961, owing to the contribution of Karl *Wilhelm, a recruit from Germany, Casavant made its first modern instrument with tracker action. In 1964 the team, augmented 1963–5 by Hellmuth *Wolff, restored to the three keyboards of St-Pascal Church, Que, the tonal quality enjoyed by New France in 1753 when the Parisian organ was installed in Quebec Cathedral.

In 850-or-so instruments delivered between 1960 and 1980 have enabled the firm to maintain the predominant position it has long held on the North American market. Their numbers apart, it is primarily their aesthetic and musical qualities that have earned these instruments a select place on the continent. Experts agree that a fair number of them would bear comparison with the best anywhere in the world. Among the finest are those in the Marie-Reine-des-Coeurs sanctuary in Montreal (1965); the chapel of the Soeurs de l'Hôtel-Dieu in Gaspé, Que, (1966); the parish church of St-Pascal-de-Kamouraska in Kamouraska, Que (1964); the church of Notre-Dame-des-Sept-Douleurs in Edmunston, NB (1966); the St-Pie X Church in Rimouski, Que (1969); the *Acadia U in Wolfville, NS (1963); the *U of British Columbia in Vancouver (1970); Our Lady of Sorrows Church in Toronto (1964); the *U of Western Ontario in London, Ont (1972); and the Maison St-Joseph in Edmonton (1963). In addition to these tracker-action organs, the list of which could be lengthened considerably for both Canada and the USA, there are several notable electro-pneumatic traction instruments which, like those of the Cap-de-la-Madeleine Basilica or the St-Zéphirin Church at La Tuque, Que, accommodate the full so-called 'symphonic' organ repertoire, at least in so far as the quality and allotment of timbres is concerned.

Company presidents after Claver (1879–1933), were Samuel's son Aristide 1933–38, Fred N. Oliver 1939–59, Samuel's son-in-law Jules Laframboise 1959–61, Charles Perrault 1961–71 and 1972–4, Lawrence I. Phelps 1971–2, and Paul Falcon 1974–6, succeeded by Bertin Nadeau.

Output increased over the years at an impressive rate: 100 instruments in 1899, 200 in 1904, 500 in 1912, 1000 in 1923. In 1980 total output reached the remarkable figure of 3500 instruments of all sizes. In that same year 207 employees (111 in the organ department, 66 in furniture, and 30 in the offices) worked for Casavant. By 1980 it still was the only Canadian firm to manufacture its own metal pipes.

Casavant became a joint-stock company in 1919, incorporated under the name of Casavant Frères Ltée. At the same time, the new company acquired the former Société Casavant Frères and became incorporated as the Compagnie de phonographes Casavant Ltée. The latter, which was dissolved in 1927, had been created in the Casavant plant for the purpose of diversifying production. La Société Nadeau Ltée acquired the firm in 1976.

In 1945 the *NFB produced a film on the Casavant firm, *The Singing Pipes / Le Vent qui chante* (in its shortened form *Music in the Wind*). A Montreal street was named for Joseph Casavant in 1959, and the Place Casavant, nearby, was named in 1963. To celebrate the firm's centenary (1979) the French organist André Isoir presented a recital in 1978 at Notre-Dame Church in Montreal. Casavant Frères also received a special mention from the *CMCouncil in 1979.

In addition to the voluminous archives preserved by the firm, the Société d'histoire régionale de St-Hyacinthe and the St-Hyacinthe Seminary, hold papers and materials relating to the company.

See also Casavant Society; Organ building.

BIBLIOGRAPHY

Élie, Frère. *La Famille Casavant* (Montreal 1914)

'Les débuts de la facture d'orgues au Canada' (extraits d'un discours prononcé par Samuel Casavant le 17 août 1905 à une fête champêtre donnée à l'occasion du 25e anniversaire de la maison Casavant), *La Musique*, vol 3, Sep 1921

Casavant Frères. *Les Grandes Orgues de la basilique de Québec* (Montreal 1927)

Bingham, Seth. 'The new Casavant organ in New York,' *The Organ*, vol 7, 1927–8

'The organ at the Royal York Hotel, Toronto, Canada,' ibid, vol 9, 1929–30

'S.S.' 'Electro-pneumatic pallet and pressure transformer by Casavant Frères,' ibid, vol 25, 1945–6

Kemp, Hugh. 'Musical frères,' *Maclean's*, 15 Oct 1947

White, Herbert D. 'Casavant Frères,' *The Organ*, vol 34, 1954–5

Dufourcq, Norbert. ' Au Canada: Beckerath et Casavant,' *L'Orgue*, 102, 1966

Bouchard, Antoine. 'Casavant Frères,' *Forces*, 2 Spring–Summer 1967

Perrault, Charles. 'La facture moderne de l'orgue à tuyaux,' ibid

Bouchard, Antoine. 'Dix ans d'orgue au Québec,' *VM*, 17, Sep 1970

Dubuc, Madeleine. 'Chez Casavant, la tradition d'abord,' Montreal *La Presse*, 23 May 1977

Lapointe, Laurent. *Casavant Frères 1879–1979* (St-Hyacinthe 1979)

Potvin, Gilles. 'L'Aventure de Claver et de Samuel Casavant,' Montreal *Le Devoir*, 5 Jan 1980 AB

Casavant Society / Société Casavant. Two societies, one formed in Montreal and the other in Toronto in the mid-1930s, for the purpose of presenting recitals by the best Canadian and foreign organists. The name was chosen in honour of

*Casavant Frères, the noted organ builders, but the societies were affiliated in no way with the company; they did, however, use its instruments exclusively and receive various subsidies from it.

While pursuing the same objectives – ie, to promote the organ as an instrument in its own right, not necessarily associated with religious services; to make known its rich repertoire from all periods by means of performances of the highest calibre; and, whenever possible, to grant bursaries to young organists – the Montreal and Toronto societies were autonomous in their administrations. They collaborated, however, in the engagement of foreign organists, chiefly through Bernard R. *Laberge whose New York office had become specialized in acting as the North American agent for organists of repute.

1 Montreal
2 Toronto

1 MONTREAL. The Casavant Society / Société Casavant was founded in 1936 by Mme Roger Maillet (b Corinne Dupuis) with the help of francophone and anglophone organists. The French and English chapters each had an honorary president and regular president, while George M. *Brewer acted as joint secretary. The French chapter contained such organists as Eugène *Lapierre, Arthur *Letondal, Raoul *Paquet, and Benoît *Poirier. The English chapter counted among its members Frederick H. Blair and Alfred *Whitehead. Mme Maillet handled the administration in an office provided free of charge by Ed *Archambault.

Marcel Dupré inaugurated the first season, 1936–7, of seven recitals before 750 season-ticket holders at Notre-Dame Church. Later, Joseph *Bonnet and André Marchal were heard, as well as Canadians including Sir Ernest *MacMillan. The second season took place in the Church of St Andrew and St Paul, but the number of recitals was reduced by half and the number of season-ticket holders fell to 350. Activities were suspended after a third season because of the war and the death of Blair, who had been one of the mainstays as well as president of the English section.

Through the initiative of Georges-Armand Robert (organist, b St-Alexis, Maskinongé, Que, ca 1910, d Montreal 20 Sep 1950; a pupil of Lapierre, Hervé Cloutier, and M.-T. *Paquin) the Casavant Society was reorganized in 1942; while retaining its bilingual name, it now had a single board of directors. Robert expanded the range of activities, adding to the organ recitals concerts involving choirs and other instruments. *Messiah* was presented each year beginning in 1948. A Quebec City chapter, established in 1945, was short-lived. Robert was administrator until his death. Under his direction, recitals were given by many distinguished foreign virtuosi, including E. Power Biggs, Claire Coci, Charles Courboin, Dupré, Rolande Falcinelli, Virgil Fox, Fernando Germani, Hugh Giles, Alexander McCurdy, Flor Peeters, Alexander Schreiner, Clarence Watters, and Carl Weinrich and many of the foremost Canadians including Françoise *Aubut, Maurice Beaulieu, Félix-R. *Bertrand (who became administrator after the death of Robert), Jean-Marie *Bussières, Gérard *Caron, Raymond *Daveluy, Arthur *Egerton, Claude *Lavoie, Georges *Lindsay, Sir Ernest MacMillan, Marcelle *Martin, Kenneth *Meek, Phillips Motley, and Charles *Peaker. The recitals were held in churches such as Notre-Dame, St Andrew and St Paul, and St James and in St James Cathedral (renamed Marie-Reine-du-monde).

Winners of the Prix Casavant, a competition instituted in 1949 but not continued, were André *Mérineau (first), Jeanne *Vanier (second) and Gaston *Arel (third), who performed at the end of the 1948–9 season. In 1948 the society added chamber music concerts to its program (including the cycle of 17 Beethoven quartets performed by the Loewenguth Quartet) as well as other events, unfortunately incurring substantial losses. After Robert's death only organ recitals were presented, but the society was unable to recover from its precarious financial situation. It ceased its activities after the 1952–3 season.

BIBLIOGRAPHY
Archer, Thomas. 'George A. Robert,' Montreal *Gazette*, 23 Sep 1950
Lapierre, Eugène. ' Feu Georges-Armand Robert, organiste et impresario,' Montreal *Le Devoir*, 25 Sep 1950

2 TORONTO. After playing in Montreal as a guest of the society Sir Ernest MacMillan conceived the idea of establishing a similar endeavour in Toronto. In the spring of 1938 with several colleagues, including Charles Peaker who became president, he formed a Casavant Society with Mrs V. A. Hooper as secretary. An opening season, 1938–9 at *Eaton Auditorium where the society subsequently was to present all of its recitals, featured in succession, André Marchal, Sir Ernest, Maitland *Farmer, Virgil Fox, Frederick *Silvester, Arthur Egerton, D'Alton *McLaughlin, and Charlotte Lockwood. Dupré inaugurated the 1939–40 season. McLaughlin became president of the committee in 1940–1, a season inaugurated by Ernest *White. McLaughlin was succeeded by David *Ouchterlony in the 1941–2 season, of which the opening recital was given by Virgil Fox. In addition, special opportunities for young organists to be heard in recital were arranged by the society. In 1942–3 five concerts were presented with the participation of choirs; also heard in succession were Claire Coci, McLaughlin, Farmer, Schreiner, and Muriel *Gidley. McLaughlin was president until the 1945–6 season (during which, 12 Dec 1945, Glenn *Gould made his debut as an organist). Later presidents were Muriel Gidley 1946–8, John J. *Weatherseed 1948–50, and Frederick Silvester 1950–2. A marked drop in the number of subscribers brought about the society's dissolution after a final concert, 16 Jan 1952, with Peaker and the *Toronto Mendelssohn Choir.

See also Organ playing and teaching.

BIBLIOGRAPHY
T. Eaton Co, Toronto. Archives (CH, HP, PW)

CASLOR, Emma (b Carmichael, Enid Maude, m Finn, m Watson, performed until 1948 as Nina Finn). Folksinger, pianist, b Chilliwack, BC, 18 Dec 1913, d there 25 Dec 1977. She began piano lessons as a child in Chilliwack, and in her teens she studied voice in San Francisco with a Mr Jaffe(y). She also studied voice in Vancouver and with Colin Ashdown in Halifax, where she had settled in 1931 after her first marriage. She became acquainted with folk music after she was the piano accompanist for the English singer Eve Maxwell Lyte in 1938 in a recital which included songs collected by Helen *Creighton. Known at this time as Nina Finn, she sang on Creighton's CBC radio program in 1939 and travelled with her on field trips. In *A Life in Folklore*, Creighton wrote of Finn: 'Hers was the only trained voice that satisfied the folk singers. When she was through there was no singing them [the folksongs] over again "right," for they [the folksingers] could tell she loved them as much as they did.' Creighton recorded Finn's versions of several songs for the (US) Library of Congress. While working 1943–7 in Ottawa for the music and sound department of the *NFB Finn incorporated in movie soundtracks much folk material from the board's recorded collection. She also collaborated with Marius *Barbeau at this time.

In 1948, as Emma Caslor – the names were taken from her ancestors – she began a professional career as a singer in Vancouver, performing on CBC radio and TV and recording many songs for CBC IS (LPs 22, 65, 66, 67, 68, 103, 104, 105, 160, 161). John *Avison often served as her accompanist. She appeared at the 1958 *Stratford Festival. She continued broadcasting until the early 1960s. Her repertoire, initially drawn from Gaelic and Anglo-Saxon songs, eventually embraced music from many other folk cultures in Canada, including that of the west coast Indians. She also sang Elizabethan songs.

Caslor taught singing to her daughter Gretchen (Joan Bartley) Grinnell (b Finn, in Prince Rupert, BC, 23 Dec 1932), who also studied voice with Colin Ashdown and piano 1946–7 with B. Gunn in Washington, DC. As a child Grinnell sang for the soundtracks of NFB productions. Later, though by profession a psychotherapist, she gave concerts of folk music in Vancouver.

See also Folk music, Anglo-Canadian; Gaelic.

MM (FH)

CASS-BEGGS, Barbara (b Cass, m Beggs). Teacher, folksong collector, singer, b Nottingham, England, 10 Nov 1904; ARCM 1927, LRAM 1928. She studied voice, piano, pedagogy, and composition at the RCM, where her teachers were Basil Allchin, Percy Buck, C.C. Collier, Reginald Jacques, and Herbert Howells. She taught music to young people 1929–39 and gave song recitals in London and Oxford. Moving to Canada in 1939, she continued her work with youth as director 1945–52 of the University Settlement Music School in Toronto. While teaching 1955–64 at the *Regina Cons she founded the Regina (later *Saskatchewan) Junior Concert Society, of which she became honorary president for life. Also during this period she began collecting Canadian folk songs for teaching purposes. The recording *Folksongs of Saskatchewan* (Folk FE 4312), released in 1963, reflects her findings. She initiated music courses for teachers of pre-schoolers at Algonquin College, Ottawa, in 1969, and taught music to children privately 1972–6 in Vancouver and thereafter in Ottawa, where she also lectured at Algonquin College. Her method, which uses principles established by Orff and more especially Kodály, attempts to help children discover the relation of music to the other arts. It also is concerned with basic training in pitch and rhythm. Cass-Beggs was vice-president 1968–71 and 1972–4 of the *CFMS. Her son, Michael, a CBC producer, was president 1971–7.

WRITINGS
'Junior Concerts,' *CMJ*, vol 6, Spring 1962
Eight Songs of Saskatchewan (CMS 1963)
A Festival Pageant (Waterloo 1964)
Seven Métis Songs of Saskatchewan (BMIC 1967)
– and Cass-Beggs, Michael. *Folk Lullabies* (Oak 1969)
– and Fowke, Edith. 'A reference list on Canadian folk music,' CFMJ, vol 1, 1973
To Listen, To Like, To Learn (Toronto 1974)
Canadian Folk Songs for the Young (Douglas 1975)
Your Baby Needs Music (Vancouver 1978) CF

Cassenti Players. Chamber group of varying instrumentation first organized as a woodwind quintet in 1954 by George *Zukerman. The name Cassenti was derived from two types of composition characteristic of the repertoire they would play: cassations and divertimenti. Since Zukerman wished to extend the repertoire beyond that for wind ensemble the original quintet – Kenneth

Helm (flute), Roland Dufrane (oboe), John Arnott (clarinet), Zukerman (bassoon) and Douglas Kent (french horn) – was supplemented by string players and other musicians as required, including the pianists John *Avison, Harold *Brown, and Robin *Wood; the violinists Lea *Foli, Esther Glazer, Jack *Kessler, Arthur *Polson, and David *Zafer; the violist Smyth *Humphreys; the cellist James Hunter; the flutists Conrad Crocker and Lanny Pollet; the oboist Warren Stannard; the clarinetists Ronald *de Kant and Henry Ohlemann; and the trumpeters Martin Birenbaum and Kenneth Hopkins.

At first the players made brief tours of British Columbia and the northwestern USA. They gained a national reputation through CBC broadcasts, however, and during the 1963–4 season, with *Canada Council assistance, they gave 26 concerts on a tour stretching from Thunder Bay, Ont, to Uranium City, Sask, where they premiered Murray *Adaskin's *Cassenti Concertante*. They represented Vancouver at *Expo 67 and participated in the opening concerts at the *NAC in 1969. Another Canada-Council–sponsored Cassenti venture 1974–5 brought musicians from across Canada for rehearsal at the *Banff SFA followed by a major tour. These players were Zukerman, Robert *Creech (French horn), Taras *Gabora (violin), Paul Grice (clarinet), Sydney *Humphreys (violin), Robert Meyer (double-bass), Gerald *Stanick (viola), and Malcolm *Tait (cello). By 1977 the players had given over 160 concerts in Canada and the USA (including engagements in Los Angeles, San Francisco, and Honolulu).

DISCOGRAPHY

Casella *Serenata* – Rieti *Sonata (1924)*. 1969. CBC SM 97

Telemann *Concerto in D Minor* – Turner *Diversities* – Milhaud *Suite*. 1967. RCI 239 BNSG

CAUSM. See Canadian Association of University Schools of Music.

CAVALHO, Rachel. Pianist, teacher, lecturer, b Queensland, Australia. She went to England as a child and studied with Arthur Alexander, Louis Kentner, John Nowell, and Priaulx Rainier. She performed in concert and on radio in England and later in Canada. She moved to Canada in 1948 to teach at the *Hambourg Cons, Toronto. She presented CBC radio's weekly 'Music for Young Musicians' 1955–6 and 'Music for Young Pianists' 1956–7, has taught privately in Toronto, and has lectured frequently on contemporary music. Her efforts to promote the teaching and performance of Canadian music include the publication *Scale Patterns for Young Pianists* (BMI Canada 1968) and the article 'Canadian Piano Music for Teaching' (*Musicanada*, Jun–Jul 1968). She became a director of *Contemporary Showcase in 1970 and has served on the contemporary music selection committee of the *ORMTA. She is the player and commentator on *Music for Young Pianists* (Hallmark RS-8), an educational recording based on her radio series, and a pianist on the 1969 Waterloo-BMI recordings *Contemporary Canadian Music for Young Pianists* (CMM-1, CMM-2). She is a contributor to *EMC*. EK

CAVANAGH, Beverley (Anne) (b Diamond). Ethnomusicologist, pianist, b Kitchener, Ont, 8 Jun 1948; ARCT 1964, B MUS (Toronto) 1970, MA musicology (Toronto) 1971, PH D (Toronto) 1979. Her teachers at the *U of Toronto included Mieczyslaw *Kolinski and Clifford *Poole. A specialist in the music of the Inuit, Cavanagh has made field trips to the North West Territories (Gjoa Haven, Spence Bay, and Pelly Bay in 1972, Gjoa Haven in 1975, and Pelly Bay in 1978) to collect songs and other lore. She has presented papers before the 41st International Congress of Americanists, the Society for Ethnomusicology, the *CMCouncil, and CAUSM. A book of Inuit animal, game, and story songs for children was in preparation in 1980. Cavanagh taught 1973–5 at *McGill U before joining the Dept of Music at *Queen's U in 1975 to teach musicology and ethnomusicology. She has written articles for *EMC*.

See also Inuit.

WRITINGS

'Annotated bibliography: Eskimo music,' *Ethnomusicology*, vol 16, Sep 1972

'Imagery and structure in Eskimo song texts,' *CFMJ*, vol 1, 1973

'Some throat games of Netsilik Eskimo women,' *CFMJ*, vol 4, 1976

'Music of the Netsilik Eskimo: a study of stability and change,' unpubl PH D thesis (Toronto 1979) RPn

CAYOUETTE, Marius. Organist, teacher, composer, b Ste-Justine de Dorchester, Que, 3 Nov 1904. He began his musical studies with the Sisters of Notre-Dame-du-Perpétuel-Secours at the parish school, and continued with Father Alphonse *Tardif (piano) and Father Henri Raymond (aesthetics) at the Collège de Lévis, and with Henri *Gagnon (piano and organ), J.-Robert *Talbot (theory), and Joseph Turgeon (piano) in Quebec City. He devoted himself to 'the defence and illustration' of church music, especially in his capacity as a member of the Diocesan Commission on Sacred Music. He became the organist at Saint-Grégoire-le-Grand Church at Montmorency, near Quebec, in 1924, and continued in that position well into the 1970s. In addition to his private teaching he occupied the chair of musical aesthetics 1946–52 at *Laval U and has taught music history and aesthetics at the *CMQ. He has contributed effectually, albeit modestly, to the renaissance of organ-building in Quebec. Among his compositions are some pieces for organ – *Deux Ex-voto* ('Ave maris stella,' 'Victimae paschali'), *Offertoire* on 'Hodie Christus natus es,' *Thèmes grégoriens* for Easter, *Deux Miniatures* (Christmas and Easter), and *Prélude sur un cantique à Ste-Anne* – and an 'Ave Maria' for soprano (Recueil Rancourt). CH

CBC. Canadian Broadcasting Corporation / La Société Radio-Canada. Publicly owned national broadcasting system created in 1936 by the Broadcast Act to succeed the Canadian Radio Broadcasting Commission established in 1932. *EMC* traces the history of the organization and its music and variety programming in the entry on Broadcasting. It also treats individual CBC institutions and programs in the entries on CBC National Radio Competition for Young Composers, CBC Opera Company, CBC Quebec Chamber Orchestra, CBC Recording, CBC Symphony Orchestra, CBC Talent Festival, CBC Vancouver Chamber Orchestra, CBC Winnipeg Orchestra, the Choristers, 'Concours de la chanson canadienne,' Clyde Gilmour ('Gilmour's Albums'), 'Happy Gang,' 'Heure du concert,' 'Joyeux Troubadours,' 'The Little Symphonies,' 'Nos Futures Étoiles,' 'Opportunity Knocks,' School music broadcasts, and 'Singing Stars of Tomorrow.'

Among CBC executives concerned primarily or entirely with music have been Louis *Applebaum, John Barnes, Jean-Marie *Beaudet, Jacques *Bertrand, Hugh *Davidson, Ira *Dilworth, J.-J. *Gagnier, John P.L. *Roberts, Roy *Royal, Robert *Sunter, Jean *Vallerand, and Geoffrey *Waddington.

A number of CBC music-broadcast producers

Discussing a CBC Opera Company production, ca 1950: (left to right) Nicholas Goldschmidt, Geoffrey Waddington, Arnold Walter, Terence Gibbs

have *EMC* entries. These include John Adaskin, Jeffrey Anderson (see Anderson family), Pierre Beaudet, Norma Beecroft, Françoys Bernier, Pierre Boutet, Norman Campbell, Albert Chamberland, Gabriel Charpentier, Robert Chesterman, André Clerk (see A.-M. Clerk), Morris C. Davis, Georges Dufresne, Denys Gagnon (see Gagnon family), Terence Gibbs, Srul Irving Glick, Denis Harbour, Gary J. Hayes, Benjamin Horch, Margaret Ann Ireland, Franz Kraemer, Jean-Yves Landry, Carl Little, Fraser Macdonald, Keith MacMillan (see MacMillan family), Pierre Mercure, Pat Patterson, R.-O. Pelletier, Gilles Potvin, Jackie Rae, Peter Symcox, and Robert Turner; the list contains a number of composers and performers.

Among other CBC music producers of note are or have been Norbert Bauman, Jean Bissonnette, Jacques Blouin, Jacques Boucher, Diana Brown, Fred H. Brown, Jean-Yves Contant, Richard Coulter, Drew Crossan, Ken Dalziel, Roger Daveluy, Ian Fellows, Patricia Fitzgerald, Jane Forner, Claude Garneau, Noël Gauvin, Marcel Henry, Keith Horner, Don Hudson, David Jaeger, John Kannawin, James Kent, Karen Kieser, Don Kowalchuk, Berthe Lavoie-Fortin, Norman Lucas, Guy Mauffette, Duncan McKerchar, Ernest Morgan, Jean Morin, Pierre Morin, Norman Newton, Huguette and Pauline Paré, Digby Peers, Armand Plante, Gilles Poirier, Mario Prizek, Pierre Rainville, Guy Rajotte, Harold Redekopp, John Reeves, Claude Routhier, Peter Shaw, Pauline Sincennes, Tom Taylor, Oleg Telizyn, and Lucien Thériault. Concerned with CBC recordings (including the RCI series) have been Gérard Arthur, Edward Farrant, George *Fiala, Mark Goldman, Monique Grenier (see Hélène Grenier), Dirk *Keetbaas, Anton Kwiatkowski, Gérard Poupart, and several of the aforementioned producers.

The CBC's numerous and considerable music and record libraries and program archives are mentioned in *EMC's* entries on Libraries and Archives. Among the librarians have been Perry W. Teale in Halifax; Marie Bourbeau, Claude Gagnon, Térèse Rochette, and Conrad Sabourin in Montreal; Sabourin and Jeannette Trépanier in Ottawa; Helmut *Kallmann, Pat Kellogg, Edgar Knapp, John Lawrence, and Erland Misener in Toronto; Laurie E. Thompson in Winnipeg; and Ruth Levy in Vancouver.

The CBC was created as a crown corporation, ie, subsidized by the federal government and required to report to Parliament through the secretary of state (beginning in 1980, the Dept of Communications), yet independent in its operation. That operation has struck a compromise between the US and Canadian free-enterprise broadcasting systems, in which size of audience and profits dictate program policy, and the public ownership system common in Europe, where quality and variety of programming is the prime consideration. Some of the CBC's revenue does come from the sale of advertising air space.

The CBC's importance in the cultural and social fabric of Canada is incalculable, whether it is engaged in the quick dissemination of news across the world's second-largest country, in the spreading of cultural nourishment to outlying areas hundreds of kilometres from the amenities of urban life, in creating and supporting the employment of musicians, or in commissioning and providing exposure to Canadian compositions. No other single organization has played so large a role in making Canadians and the outside world aware of Canadian cultural pursuits and in helping these to flourish. It is no surprise that throughout *EMC's* biographies of mid- and late-20th century musicians no other organization is acknowledged as often as the CBC, whether as a performance medium, an employer, a sponsor, or a discoverer of talent.

The corporation's varied role, of course, has changed over the years, in music to some extent from that of an initiator to that of a pipeline, as is argued in the Broadcasting entry. Certainly the emphasis has shifted, in the 1970s, from studio broadcasts to the carrying of public performances – *TS and *MSO and other orchestral concerts, live CBC-organized festivals (eg, in 1980, those devoted to Mendelssohn, Dvořák, and Tippett), recitals, etc. But the CBC has remained the primary purveyor of Canadian music and performance to the largest possible part of the population. The somewhat more passive role in recent years as a musical catalyst is due to many factors, among them the arrival of TV (with its primarily visual concerns), the increasing quantity of recorded music – which in some ways has made the live performance of standard classics unnecessary – and the growing support of musical activity by concert-giving organizations of all kinds and by universities, arts councils, and other governmental agencies.

BIBLIOGRAPHY
See also Bibliography for Broadcasting.
Roberts, John. 'CBC and the Canadian composer,' *CanComp*, 1, May 1965
– 'CBC Centennial commissions investment in musical future,' ibid, 19, Jun 1967
– 'Music in Canadian broadcasting – yesterday and today,' *Music and Media*, CMCouncil conference (1967)
'Music and television ... an interview with John Barnes,' *PfAC*, Winter 1972
Litwack, Linda. 'Music and the CBC / SRC / RCI,' *CMB*, 10, Spring–Summer 1975
Roberts, John. 'What the CBC does for Canadian orchestras,' *OCan*, vol 3, Jul 1976
CBC Public Relations. *CBC: A Brief History of the Canadian Broadcasting Corporation* (Ottawa 1976) / *Radio-Canada: Un Bref Historique de la Société Radio-Canada* (Ottawa 1977)
MacMillan, Rick. 'Composers find additional roles in CBC,' *MSc*, 306, Mar–Apr 1979
Music in Canada
Aspects of Music in Canada

CBC National Radio Competition for Young Composers (CBC Radio Canada Council Awards for Young Composers 1973–4; National Competition for Young Composers 1975–6) / **Concours national des jeunes compositeurs**. Biennial awards established to promote the composition of concert music by Canadians, and to ensure a performance of such music. A total of $19,000 was awarded in 1974 from monies provided by the *CBC, the *Canada Council, the *OAC, and the *MACQ. The amount had increased to $26,000 by 1977 as a result of allocations from the British Columbia Cultural Fund in 1975 and from the *MAC and *Alberta Culture in 1977. The competition is administered by the *CMCentres in Toronto and Montreal, and jurors are drawn from the ranks of established Canadian and foreign composers (eg, for the 1977–8 competition, the US composer Earle Brown and the Canadians Malcolm *Forsyth, Otto *Joachim, and Jean *Papineau-Couture).

To be eligible a work must be composed by a Canadian citizen or in Canada by a landed immigrant 29 years of age or younger; it may be from 6 to 10 minutes in length; and as many as three works may be submitted by a composer. 190 works by 133 composers, mainly from Quebec, Ontario, and British Columbia, were submitted to the 1977–8 competition. Deadlines are in the fall of odd years and awards are made in the spring of even years. In 1977 three separate categories were introduced: electronic works; works employing from 2 to 12 instruments or voices; and works for solo instrument or voice, unaccompanied or accompanied. Awards have been announced in February or March of the award years (1974, 1976, 1978, 1980) and the winning compositions performed on CBC radio.

AWARDS

1973–4
Bruce *Davis, *String Quartet;* Walter *Boudreau, *Variations;* David J. Nichols, *Slant;* Richard-Gaudreault *Boucher, *Angoisse des fuyantes créations*
OAC award: Gary *Hayes, *Pythian I*
MACQ award: Pierre *Trochu, *Orange*

1975–6
1 / Pierre Trouchu, *Eros;* 2 / Patrick Carpenter, *Touch-Stone I;* 3 / David Grimes, *Increscents;* 4 / Philippe Ménard, *Reel-à-Phil*, and 4 / Michael Parker, *Chôle;* 6 / Michel *Gonneville, *Rôle*
BC Cultural Fund award: Patrick Carpenter, *Touch-Stone I*

1977–8
Chamber: 1 / John Thrower, *Recitatives, Arias;* 2 / John Burke, *Spectre*
Electronic: 1 / Jean Piché, *La Mer à l'Aube;* 2 / John Thrower, *Suite from Atma*
Solo: 1 / Anthony Genge, *Eleven Steps;* 2 / John Burke, *Six Regions*

1979–80
Chamber: 1 / John Burke, *Interface;* 2 / Mark Hand, *Soliloquy*
Electronic: no awards
Choral: 1 / no first awarded; 2 / John Burke, *Diffusa est gratia*, and 2 / Denis Gougeon, *Berceuse*

CBC Opera Company. Founded in 1948 to perform on the radio series 'CBC Wednesday Night.' Under the chairmanship of Charles Jennings the company was administered by Harry Boyle, Terence *Gibbs (producer), Nicholas *Goldschmidt (conductor), Geoffrey *Waddington (music adviser), and Arnold *Walter. Herman *Geiger-Torel occasionally acted as coach. Auditions were held in Toronto the first year and in Toronto and Montreal the following year. The company made its debut 20 Oct 1948 in *La Bohème*, with Mary *Morrison (Mimi), Jimmie *Shields (Rodolfo), Beth Corrigan (Musetta), and Edmund *Hockridge (Marcello). The production won the Best Music Program award in the 1949 Canadian Radio Awards Competition (sponsored by the Canadian Assn for Adult Education). Other operas in the first season were *Orpheus and Eurydice*, *La Traviata*, and *Don Giovanni*.

The second season opened 12 Oct 1949 with the Canadian premiere of Britten's *Peter Grimes* with William *Morton as Grimes, Edmund Hockridge as Captain Balstrode, Frances *James as Ellen Orford, Eric *Tredwell as Swallow, and Gordon *Wry as Bob Boles. The opera was so well received that it was performed and broadcast a second time one week later over 'CBC Wednesday Night.' The production won a Best Music Program award in the 1950 Canadian Radio Awards Competition.

The company made its first public appearance 14 Dec 1949 in a concert performance of *Carmen* conducted by Goldschmidt at *Massey Hall. In the spring of 1951 it made its first Montreal broadcast, a production of *Faust* with Pierre *Boutet (Faust), Dolorès Drolet (Marguerite), and Denis *Harbour (Mephistopheles). On 14 May 1953 it performed *Don Giovanni* for the inauguration of the Toronto-Montreal TV network.

The company presented many of the most popular operas, including *Così fan tutte*, *Madama Butterfly*, *The Marriage of Figaro*, *Rigoletto*, and *Tosca*. It also was heard, however, in less frequently performed works, such as Beethoven's *Fidelio*, Benjamin's *A Tale of Two Cities*, Britten's *Albert Herring*, Dallapiccola's *The Prisoner* (Canadian premiere), Debussy's *Pelléas et Mélisande*, Puccini's *Gianni Schicchi* and *Turandot*, Stravinsky's *The Rake's Progress* (Canadian premiere), Verdi's *Falstaff* and *Otello*, and Wolf-Ferrari's *The School for Fathers*. Canadian operas presented were *Willan's **Deirdre* in 1951, conducted by Waddington, and *Kaufmann's *Bashmachkin* in 1952 (Canadian premiere), conducted by the composer.

In addition to the singers mentioned above, Ernest *Adams, Pierrette *Alarie, Trudy Carlyle, Earl Dick, Don *Garrard, Esther *Ghan, Marguerite *Gignac, Yoland *Guérard, Elizabeth Benson *Guy, Joan *Hall, Bernard *Johnson, Alphonse Ledoux, Lois *Marshall, James *Milligan, Louise *Roy, Jan *Rubeš, Mary *Simmons, and Jon *Vickers sang with the company.

In its last regular season (1954–5) the company presented five productions; thereafter opera performances continued to be broadcast (later telecast) but only on an occasional basis. Among these later presentations were Walton's *Troilus and Cressida* with Mary Simmons, Jon Vickers, and Harry *Mossfield in the lead roles, and Rameau's *Hippolyte et Aricie* with Elizabeth Benson Guy, André *Turp, Louis *Quilico, and Robert *Savoie, both in 1956–7, and the Canadian chamber operas **Night Blooming Cereus* and **Silent Measures* during the 1958–9 season.

Also popular during the late 1940s and early 1950s was the CBC Light Opera Group, founded ca 1947 to perform the operettas of Gilbert & Sullivan. The 30-piece orchestra, 16-voice chorus, and soloists were under the direction of Geoffrey Waddington. The producer and narrator was Ernest Morgan and the soloists were Jean Haig and Doreen *Hume (sopranos), Nellie *Smith and Margaret Evans (contraltos), Edmund Hockridge and Eric Tredwell (baritones), and William Morton (tenor). In 1948 this group presented a 13-week Gilbert & Sullivan series with such success that it was repeated the following year. The English radio network continued to present Gilbert & Sullivan and other light operas from time to time.

BIBLIOGRAPHY
Gibbs, Terence, 'New CBC opera season,' *CBC Times*, 11 Sep 1949
NM

CBC Quebec Chamber Orchestra / Orchestre de chambre de la SRC à Québec. Radio ensemble of as many as 38 players, including a permanent nucleus of 24 strings, founded in Quebec City in 1954 as the regular orchestra for 'Les Petits Concerts,' an annual series of 33 programs broadcast

from September to May on the CBC's French network FM stations. Sylvio *Lacharité, the conductor and music director, was assisted 1954–64 by Edwin *Bélanger. The repertoire at that time comprised baroque and preclassical works (Couperin, Handel, Lully, etc) and arrangements made by Lacharité. In 1964 the ensemble became the CBC Quebec Chamber Orchestra and the title of the program was changed to 'Orchestre de chambre de Québec.' Winds and percussion were added to the strings, permitting the performance of a larger repertoire, including contemporary music. In 1971 the conducting duties were divided. Lacharité continued to direct half the programs, and guests (Alexander *Brott, Françoys *Bernier, James De Preist, Pierre Dervaux, Jean *Deslauriers, Raymond *Dessaints, Pierre *Morin, Antoine Padilla, Wilfrid *Pelletier, Armando *Santiago, and others) were engaged for the remainder. Soloists, mainly from Quebec City, included the duo-pianists Victor *Bouchard and Renée *Morisset; the soprano France *Dion; the violinists Angèle Dubeau, Chantal Juillet, Malcolm Lowe, Jean-Louis Rousseau (concertmaster), and Hidetaro *Suzuki; the oboist Jacques *Simard; and the flutist Barbara Todd. Though by 1979 the CBC Quebec Chamber Orchestra (as reconstituted in 1964) had broadcast nearly 40 programs a year for 15 years, it had appeared only rarely in public.
MB-L

CBC recordings. It was in 1945 in Montreal that the Canadian Broadcasting Corporation produced its first music recordings intended for broadcast abroad and in Canada. The venture gave rise in 1947 to the Music Transcription Service of the CBC International Service (renamed Radio Canada International in 1972, at which time its record album numbers began to be prefixed by the initials RCI). In 1966 the English Services Division embarked on a program which was similar but was intended primarily to serve CBC stations and affiliates. The resulting serious music recordings are numbered and bear the initials CBC-SM ('serious music'); the light music ones have the initials CBC-LM ('light music').

1 RCI label
2 CBC-SM and CBC-LM labels

1 RCI LABEL. Before 1945 very little music by Canadian composers existed on disc, and the number of Canadian performers represented on disc, while much more considerable, was not representative. For this reason CBC IS, shortly after its creation in 1945 as 'the voice of Canada abroad' with a mandate, among others, to be 'the continuing reflection abroad of Canadian culture,' resolved to correct this deficiency while meeting its own needs.

In March 1945, under the impetus of its program director, Gérard Arthur, and the conductor Jean-Marie *Beaudet, it produced a *Canadian Album No. 1* made up of five 78-rpm discs comprising *Willan's *Concerto* for piano and orchestra and *Champagne's *Suite canadienne*. The orchestra, a CBC Montreal ensemble, was conducted by Beaudet. La *Cantoria and the pianist Agnes *Butcher also participated in the recording. This first album aroused warm interest among foreign radio organizations and Canadian diplomatic missions. A *Canadian Album No. 2* (works of *Coulthard, *MacMillan, and *Weinzweig by the *TSO under Sir Ernest MacMillan, and a work of *Tanguay by the Montreal orchestra under Beaudet) appeared in 1946, and a *Canadian Album No. 3* (works of *Brott and Tanguay, again by the Montreal musicians) some years later.

The success of the first two albums led in 1947 to the creation of a Music Transcription Service. Patricia Fitzgerald, the first director of the service, was succeeded in 1952 by Roy *Royal, and Royal in 1959 by Gérard Poupart. In the mid-1960s the service gradually became integrated with the CBC IS Recorded Programs. The successive heads of music production were Hugh *Davidson, Gilles *Potvin, Edward Farrant, and Gilbert Lemieux, with Monique Grenier and Mark Goldman as producers.

By 1955 about 100 transcription discs (in the 40-cm size) had been produced, featuring prominent Canadian soloists and ensembles and presenting a substantial selection of concert works by Canadians. In 1956 the 40-cm format was supplanted by the standard 30-cm LP format, and eventually stereo recordings began to be produced.

In 1980 the RCI catalogue listed more than 500 recordings bearing programs which represented almost 200 years of musical creativity in Canada, from Joseph *Quesnel's comic opera **Colas et Colinette* (1790) to the most recent works by a virtual 'who's who' of the country's leading composers. The performers' list was similarly comprehensive, consisting of all the large orchestras, a wide variety of smaller ensembles, and such soloists as Pierrette *Alarie, Maureen *Forrester, Glenn *Gould, Frances *James, Jacques *Labrecque, André *Laplante, Gisèle *Mackenzie, Lois *Marshall, Oscar *Peterson, and Léopold *Simoneau.

RCI's policy has been to distribute its recordings free of charge on request to radio organizations around the world, CBC stations, Canadian diplomatic missions, conservatories, schools of music at the college level, and libraries. In order to meet a persistent public demand for recordings, RCI in 1967 initiated a series of co-productions with the commercial labels *RCA, *Capitol, *London, Select, Deutsche Grammophon, Madrigal, and Harmonia Mundi. In this way several ambitious collections and individual discs were released, including *Music and Musicians of Canada* (1967, 17 LPs), *Canadian Folk Songs* (1967, 9 LPs), *JMC 20* (1969, 10 LPs), and the *Complete Harpsichord Works of François Couperin* performed by Kenneth *Gilbert (1970–1, 16 LPs). With a view to presenting in an ordered format the wealth of material accumulated over 35 years, RCI in 1978 launched the *Anthology of Canadian Music*, a mammoth undertaking to gather together in boxed sets the works of individual composers recorded over the years. The first phase of the project, representing 36 composers, was scheduled for completion by 1983.

In addition to transcriptions, which are of a permanent nature and have unlimited broadcast use, RCI began recording relays in 1960; these are identical in appearance to transcription discs, but their broadcast use is tied to an expiry date. Such relays afford an international dimension to music programs presented on the CBC national networks as well as to important events occurring in Canada, such as the *International Conference of Composers (held in Stratford, Ont, in 1960 and broadcast in 52 countries), the *Montreal International Competition, and the most important concerts presented during *Expo 67, not to mention certain special events occurring at festivals in Vancouver, Stratford, Montreal, Ottawa, and the *JMC Oxford Art Centre.

2 CBC-SM AND CBC-LM LABELS. The considerable use of foreign commercial discs on CBC stations, in part because there was no substantial alternative catalogue of recordings by Canadian soloists and ensembles, led the English Services Division of the CBC under John P.L. *Roberts to begin in 1966 a program of more deliberately competitive phonograph recordings, also known as broadcast recordings. These were confined exclusively to Canadian performers, though with no particular emphasis on Canadian music. The further intent was to increase the Canadian content of radio programs of international concert music in order to satisfy *CRTC requirements in this regard. Two numbered series were initiated: CBC-SM and CBC-LM.

The first 40 discs of the SM series were produced in co-operation with the CBC IS. The project was co-ordinated by Dirk *Keetbaas, and when it was discontinued in 1980 the CBC-SM catalogue comprised more than 350 discs, mostly works from the current repertoire, performed by Canadian orchestras – the TS, the *Vancouver SO, the *Winnipeg SO, the *Edmonton SO, the *Hamilton Philharmonic, the *NACO, and others; by ensembles such as the *Orford, *Purcell, and *Vaghy string quartets, the *Toronto Mendelssohn Choir, and the *Festival Singers; and by instrumentalists and singers of the calibre of Robert *Aitken, *Bouchard and *Morisset, Marek *Jablonski, and Jon *Vickers – again a veritable register of leading Canadian artists.

In 1980 the CBC's English Services Division put on the market four LPs in a new series, SM 5000, featuring Canadian orchestras. These discs and a selection from the SM and RCI collections, listed in *The 1980/81 CBC Classical Record Reference Book*, were produced to meet high standards and, like the two prior series, could be purchased through a mail order system.

The CBC-LM series has assembled the top names in light music, jazz, and pop music in Canada. As in the SM series the first 40 discs were produced in collaboration with CBC IS. Beginning in 1968, certain recordings were co-productions and appeared on such commercial labels as RCA, Capitol, London, Kanata, Apex, *Nimbus 9, Columbia (*CBS), Dominion, Kilmarnock, and Warner Bros. In 1970 the standard LP format was abandoned in favour of 45 rpm, but there was a return to the 30 cm LP in 1974. Among the soloists and ensembles listed in the CBC-LM catalogue are Tommy *Ambrose, Peter *Appleyard, Guido *Basso, Salome *Bey, the *Boss Brass, Neil *Chotem, Sonny *Greenwich, *Juliette, Moe *Koffman, Ann *Mortifee, *Pacific Salt, and the *Travelers. The orchestras of Johnny *Burt, Trump *Davidson, Johnny *Holmes, Milan *Kymlicka, Vic *Vogel, and others are represented as well. In 1980 the LM catalogue comprised more than 450 discs.

CBC recordings, from both the RCI collection and the CBC-SM, CBC-LM, and CBC-SM 5000 collections, have enriched the record libraries of broadcasting organizations in Canada and around the world and those of many individual music lovers, carrying the achievements of Canada's leading performers and ensembles to a wider public than they could have reached by any other means.

BIBLIOGRAPHY
Ardoin, John. 'CBC chronicle,' *Musical America*, vol 82, Jul 1962
Renner, Karl D. 'The CBC International Service and music in Canada,' *CanComp*, 3, Oct 1965
'A playable feast,' *Time*, 13 Jan 1967
Klein, Howard. 'You can stay home and still hear the music of Canada,' *New York Times*, 7 May 1967
Ashley, Patricia. 'Music and musicians of Canada,' *Saturday R*, 29 Apr 1967
Potvin, Gilles. '180 years of Canadian music,' *MSc*, 244, Nov–Dec 1968
Farrant, Ted. 'RCI disseminating Canadian music since 1940s,' *MSc*, 284, Jul–Aug 1975
Gingras, Claude. 'Une anthologie de la musique canadienne,' Montreal *La Presse*, 6 Jan 1979
Biermann, Helmer. 'Canadian music put on world map,' Saint John *Telegraph-Journal*, 10 Mar 1979
'Weinzweig works featured by CBC in premiere of Anthology series,' *CanComp*, 139, Mar 1979

Littler, William. 'Anthology of Canadian music will make history,' *Toronto Star*, 5 May 1979
Aspects of Music in Canada
Music in Canada
'Review of records' GP

CBC Symphony Orchestra. Broadcasting orchestra formed in Toronto in 1952 under the musical direction of Geoffrey *Waddington and maintained until 1964. It made its broadcast debut 29 Sep 1952 playing the overture to Rossini's *La Cenerentola* and Sibelius' *Symphony No. 3*. The orchestra's weekly broadcasts under Waddington and various guests were produced first by Terence *Gibbs, then by Carl *Little, and finally (until its dissolution in 1964) by Keith *MacMillan. Of its 80 members, from 30 to 50 were *TSO players.

Famous for its sight-reading abilities, the CBC SO established also a particular reputation for its performances of contemporary works, Canadian and other. Almost half its repertoire post-dated 1900. It premiered many CBC commissions, including Roger *Matton's *L'Horoscope*, Harry *Somers' *Symphony No. 1, Passacaglia and Fugue*, and *Piano Concerto No. 2*, Norman *Symonds' *Concerto Grosso*, and John *Weinzweig's *Violin Concerto* and *Wine of Peace*. Specific programs were broadcast in honour of Sir Ernest *MacMillan and Healey *Willan. Other highlights included the Canadian premiere of Carl Nielsen's *Symphony No. 4* under Heinz *Unger during the 1953–4 season, the premiere of Violet *Archer's *Piano Concerto* under Victor *Feldbrill in 1958, with the pianist William *Stevens, and performances of Beethoven's nine symphonies under Efrem Kurtz in 1959.

Primarily a radio orchestra, the CBC SO made a public debut 16 May 1955 under Waddington at *Massey Hall. Concerts followed at the *Montreal Festivals in 1955, at the 1955 *Stratford Festival, at CBC Toronto's Carlton Theatre studios (where a 1958–9 series boasted the North American conducting debuts of Colin Davis and Zubin Mehta), and at the *International Conference of Composers 12 Jul 1960 under Walter *Susskind. In 1961 the CBC SO travelled twice to the USA; under Waddington it gave the premiere 28 April of Harry *Freedman's *Symphony No. 1* at the Inter-American Music Festival in Washington, and under MacMillan it performed 23 and 24 October at the United Nations in New York. As a result of its role in CBC radio's 1962 documentary 'Igor Stravinsky, Inventor of Music' the CBC SO began an association with Stravinsky and with the conductor Robert Craft, which included a concert 29 Apr 1962 at Massey Hall and participation in the celebrated series of Columbia recordings of Stravinsky and Schoenberg.

The orchestra's last public concert was given at the official opening 7 Mar 1964 of the Edward Johnson Building at the *U of Toronto. By that time it had given some 380 concerts, 50 of them under Waddington, 72 under foreign conductors, the remainder under Canadians. The roster included John *Avison, Sir John Barbirolli, Sir Thomas Beecham, Jean-Marie *Beaudet, Pierre Boulez, Alexander *Brott (20 times), Aaron Copland, Josef Krips, Roland *Leduc, Charles Mackerras, Ettore *Mazzoleni (31 times), Pierre Monteux, Boyd *Neel (27 times), Edouard van Remoortel, Sir Malcolm Sargent, Paul *Scherman (16 times), Heinz Unger (24 times), Heitor Villa-Lobos, and others. Soloists included Hyman *Bress, Van Cliburn, Reginald *Godden, Glenn *Gould, Greta *Kraus, Albert *Pratz (the orchestra's concertmaster after 1953), Mary *Simmons, and Jon *Vickers.

The CBC SO was disbanded in 1964 after an agreement to recruit CBC Toronto orchestras from TSO ranks. Several of these later contract orchestras recorded or broadcast under the name CBC SO, CBC Orchestra, or CBC Toronto Orchestra.

DISCOGRAPHY

CANADIAN COMPOSERS

Archer *The Bell; Fanfare and Passacaglia* – Somers *Where do We Stand, Oh Lord*. CBC Chorus, Waddington cond. 1955. RCI 130

Beecroft *From Dreams of Brass*. CBC Chorus, Avison cond. 1964. RCI 214

Dolin – Somers – Twa – Weinzweig. Loman hp, Galper cl, Bauman ob, Waddington cond. 1952. RCI 86

Matton *L'Horoscope*. Waddington cond. 1958. RCI 185

Morawetz – Morel – Somers. Waddington cond. 1957. RCI 180

Morawetz *Piano Concerto No. 1*. Kuerti pf, Susskind cond. 1963. RCI 212

Pentland *Concerto for Piano and Strings*. Bernardi pf, Feldbrill cond. 1958. RCI 184

Somers *North Country*. Scherman cond. RCI 154

Somers – Adaskin – Papineau-Couture. Loman hp, Susskind cond. 1962. Col MS 6285

Symonds *Concerto Grosso*. Feldbrill cond, Ron Collier Quintet. 1957. RCI 181

Turner *Opening Night* – Champagne *Altitude*. (1962). RCI 179

Weinzweig *Concerto for Violin and Orchestra*. Waddington cond, Pratz vn. 1958. RCI 183 / RCI ACM 1

– *Divertimento for Flute and Strings*. Feldbrill cond, Day fl. 1958. RCI 182/RCI ACM 1

– *Wine of Peace*. Susskind cond, Simmons sop. 1958. RCI 182

Willan *Coronation Suite*. Mazzoleni cond, CBC Chorus. 1954. RCI 118

OTHER COMPOSERS

Mozart *Piano Concerto No. 24*. Gould pf, Susskind cond. 1961. Col MS 6339

Schoenberg *Kol Nidre; Chamber Symphony No. 2* – Bach-Schoenberg *Prelude and Fugue 'St Anne.'* Festival Singers, Braun bar, Craft cond. 1962. Col M2S-709

– *Modern Psalm, Op 50C*. Festival Singers, Foldi bass, Craft cond. 1964. Col M2S-780

– *Piano Concerto*. Gould pf, Craft cond. 1961. Col MS-6339

– *Piano Concerto; Violin Concerto*. Gould pf, Baker vn, Craft cond. (1967). Col MS-7039

– *Prelude to the Genesis Suite*, etc. Festival Singers, Craft cond. 1962. Col M2S-694

– *Survivor from Warsaw; Violin Concerto*. Festival Singers, Baker vn, Craft cond. 1962. Col M2S-679

Stravinsky *Favorite Short Pieces; 4 Etudes for Orchestra*, etc. Stravinsky cond. 1962. Col MS-6648/ (1972) Col M31729/MT31729

– *Mavra; Le Faune et la bergère*. Belink sop, Simmons sop, Rideout alto, Kolk ten, Stravinsky cond. 1964. Col MS 6991

– *Nine Masterpieces Conducted by the Composer*. (1970). Col D3S 775

– *Recent Stravinsky Conducted by the Composer*. Verrett mezzo, Driscoll ten, Festival Singers. (1967). Col MS 7054

– *Scènes de ballet*. Stravinsky cond. 1963. Col MS 6649

– *A Sermon, a Narrative and a Prayer*, etc. Stravinsky cond, Festival Singers, Verrett mezzo, Driscoll ten, Horton narr, Colicos reciter. 1962–3. Col MS-6647

– *Spectacular Sound of Stravinsky: Scherzo Fantastique*. Stravinsky cond. 1962. MS-7094

– *Stravinsky Conducts: Four Norwegian Moods*. 1963. Col M30516

– *Stravinsky Conducts Stravinsky*: choral selections. Festival Singers, Iseler cond. 1963. Col M31124

– *Symphony of Psalms; Symphony in C*. Festival Singers, Stravinsky cond. 1962–3. Col MS-6548

BIBLIOGRAPHY

'The CBC Symphony Orchestra,' *CBC Times*, 11–17 Apr 1954
McNamara, Helen. 'The unseen symphony,' *Mayfair*, Jul 1957
Brown, Thomas. 'The CBC Symphony Orchestra,' *PfAC*, Mar 1961
Roberts, John. ' Stravinsky and the CBC,' *CMB*, 4, Spring–Summer 1972

FILMOGRAPHY

Stravinsky (NFB 1965) (CF, PW)

CBC Talent Festival (1959–76; CBC Talent Competition 1976–) / **Concours National de Radio-Canada**. Radio competition – a successor to *'Opportunity Knocks' – initiated by Geoffrey *Waddington and Terence *Gibbs in 1959. The first finals were broadcast in 1960 from Toronto. Open to performers aged 15 to 30, the competition has attracted over 200 contestants annually. Semi-finalists are selected at auditions in major cities across Canada, and from these, two finalists are chosen in each performance category. The competition is carried in French and English on the CBC networks, and the finals, while generally held in Ottawa (with the *NACO) or Quebec City (with the *Quebec SO), also have taken place in Edmonton, Montreal, Toronto, and Vancouver.

During the first five years only singers and pianists competed, and the winner in each category received $1000, the runner-up singer $250. The categories then were increased to four and in 1978 to five: piano, voice, strings, winds, and a rotating 'speciality' category – harpsichord in 1978 and guitar in 1979. By 1978 prize money had increased to $500 for all finalists, $2500 for the winners in each category, and a $5000 grand prize. Winners have appeared in special broadcasts or telecasts. In addition, beginning in 1978 first-prize winners received scholarships to either the *Banff SFA or the *JMC Orford Art Centre. During the broadcast of the 1979 finals it was announced that the competition henceforth would be biennial.

Contestants perform with an orchestra. Conductors for the competitions have included Sir Ernest *MacMillan, John *Avison, Mario *Bernardi, and James De Preist. Among the judges have been Murray *Adaskin, Robert *Aitken, Victor *Bouchard, Marius Constant, Lorand *Fenyves, Kenneth *Gilbert, Leonard *Isaacs, Alexandre Lagoya, Sir Ernest MacMillan, Phyllis *Mailing, Franco Mannino, Mary *Morrison, Arthur *Ozolins, Jan *Rubeš, Léopold *Simoneau, Gerald *Stanick, Steven *Staryk, Malcolm *Troup, Ronald *Turini, and George *Zukerman.

First prize winners have been as follows:

1960 Gordana *Lazarevich, piano; Cornelis *Opthof, baritone

1961 Michel *Dussault, piano; Heather *Thomson, soprano

1962 William *Aide, piano; Claude *Corbeil, bass-baritone

1963 Irene *Weiss, piano; Joan *Patenaude, soprano

1964 Constance *Channon-Douglass, piano; Jean *Bonhomme, tenor

1965 Otto *Armin, violin; Peter Smith, clarinet; Louis *Lebrun, soprano

1966 Marilyn *Engle, piano; Hélène *Gagné, cello; Alban Gallant, clarinet; Jeannette *Zarou, soprano

1967 Elsbeth Coop, piano; Kathryn Wunder, violin; Robert Cram, flute; Carrol Anne *Curry, soprano, and Maurice *Brown, bass, both second prizes (first not awarded)

1968 Arthur *Ozolins, piano; Osher Green, viola; Gloria Coleman, horn, and Jadwiga Michalska-Bornyi, flute (tied); Judith *Forst, mezzo-soprano

1969 Janina *Fialkowska, piano; Gisela *Depkat, cello; Jean Lavoie, clarinet; Sonia Rohozynsky, soprano, second prize (first not awarded)

1970 Jane *Coop, piano; Adele *Armin, violin; John Rapson, clarinet; Gabrielle *Lavigne, mezzo-soprano

1971 William *Tritt, piano; James *Campbell, clarinet; Lynne Cantlon, soprano

1972 Linn Hendry, piano, second prize (first not awarded); Malcolm Lowe, violin; Anna *Chornodolska, soprano

1973 Robert Mayerovitch, piano; Angela Cavadas, violin; Douglas Stewart, flute; Mary Lou *Fallis, soprano, and Mariana *Paunova, mezzo-soprano (tied)
1974 Jacinthe *Couture, piano; Denise Lupien, violin; Marcel Saint-Jacques, flute; Ingemar *Korjus, bass-baritone (also 15th anniversary special prize)
1975 Louis *Lortie, piano; Gwen Hoebig, violin; Timothy Maloney, clarinet; Micheline Dinel, soprano
1976 Sharon Krause, piano; Joel Quarrington, double-bass; Richard Stewart, trumpet; Rosemarie *Landry, soprano
1977 Jamie Syer, piano; Philippe Djokic, violin; John MacDonald, horn; Marion Harvey, soprano
1978 Angela *Hewitt, piano; Chantal Juillet, violin; Harcus Hennigar, horn; Gina Fiordaliso, soprano; Valerie Weeks, harpsichord (grand prize)
1979 David Swan, piano; Angèle Dubeau, violin; Ellis Wean, tuba; Ben Heppner, tenor, and Norbert Kraft, guitar (tied for grand prize)

BIBLIOGRAPHY

Schulman, Michael. 'CBC's Talent Festival is exactly that,' *PfAC*, Summer 1976 (NM, GP, CV, PW)

CBC Vancouver Chamber Orchestra. Longest-lived regularly performing Canadian radio orchestra, founded in 1938 by Ira *Dilworth, who appointed John *Avison conductor.

Similar orchestras in Vancouver antedated the CBC VCO: the CNRV Concert Orchestra (pre-1934) under Percy Harvey; another, heard around 1935 on CRCV's 'Jewels of the Madonna,' with Jean *de Rimanoczy as conductor; and the CBR Concert Orchestra. The CBR SO, founded also by Dilworth and conducted by Arthur *Benjamin, flourished in the early 1940s.

The CBC Vancouver Chamber Orchestra, however, comprising 25 players (increased to 35 in 1952), was still being heard regularly on the CBC in 1980, 42 years after its inception. Its broadcasts have been produced by Ernest Morgan 1938–42, David S. Catton 1942–3, James Finlay 1943–4, John Barnes 1944–8, Robert Allen 1948–52, Robert *Turner 1952–66, and Don Campbell 1967–8, succeeded by Norman Newton in 1968. Its repertoire encompasses the baroque, classic, and romantic periods, the full complement of Canadian works suitable for its instrumentation, and such European and US 20th-century composers as Berio, Britten, Carter, Copland, Dallapiccola, Fricker, Hartmann, Henze, Maderna, Nono, Piston, Schoenberg, and Stravinsky, to name only a few. It has premiered works by *Adaskin, *Baker, *Bales, *Beckwith, *Betts, *Dela, *Glick, *Goldberg, *Healey, *Hétu, *Kasemets, *Kenins, *Mather, *Papineau-Couture, *Pentland, *Ridout, *Schafer, *Symonds, Turner, *Weinzweig, *Weisgarber, and *Wuensch. In 1960, for service to contemporary music, Avison and the orchestra received a commendation from the ISCM.

Over the years guest conductors have included Victor *Feldbrill, Serge *Garant, Milton Katims, Sir Ernest *MacMillan, Ettore *Mazzoleni, Harry Newstone, and Heinz *Unger. Most of Canada's leading concert artists have appeared as soloists. Because most of the orchestra's players are members of the *Vancouver SO, public concerts and tours have been difficult to schedule. Nevertheless, the orchestra appeared annually 1958–60 at the *Vancouver International Festivals, gave five concerts in 1961 at the Vancouver Art Gallery, toured Saskatchewan in 1967, and performed in communities in the northern part of Vancouver Island 1967–8.

In 1969 a 26-member ensemble, drawn from the orchestra and governed by a separate board, began to tour as the Vancouver Radio Orchestra. Under Avison the smaller ensemble has performed in western Canada, the Arctic, the USA (Alaska and Montana), and as far east as Ottawa. John Eliot Gardiner (b England 6 Dec 1928) was named Avison's successor in 1980.

DISCOGRAPHY

Arnold – Felton – Mozart – Brixi. McLean org, Avison cond. 1970. CBC SM-129
Beckwith *Music for Dancing* – Ives *Symphony No. 3*. Avison cond. 1966. CBC SM-47
Contemporary Canadian Compositions for Orchestra: Turner *Eidolons* – Healey *Arctic Images*. Avison cond. 1974. CBC SM-265
Copland *Concerto* for clarinet and string orhcestra – Weinzweig *Divertimento No. 3* for bassoon and strings. de Kant cl, Zukerman bn, Avison cond. 1976. CBC SM-317
Dittersdorf *Four Ovid Symphonies*. Avison cond. 1972. CBC SM-198
Dvořák *Legends, Op 59*. Avison cond. 1974. CBC SM-283
Haydn *Orlando Paladino Overture; Symphonies No. 67 and 68*. Avison cond. 1970. CBC SM-126
Haydn – Galuppi – Boccherini – Moeran. Avison cond. ca 1966. CBC SM-20
Haydn – Méhul – Mozart. Avison cond. 1971. CBC SM-191
Haydn – Somers – Mozart. Mailing mezzo, Avison cond (?). 1968. CBC SM-73
Martin y Soler *Una Cosa Rara*. Newstone cond. 1973. CBC SM-217
McPhee – Morawetz – Buczynski. Avison cond. 1975. CBC SM-308
Mozart *Serenade K320; Two Marches K408*. Avison cond. 1970; CBC SM-128
Music and Musicians of Canada II: Turner *Symphony for Strings*. Avison cond. (1967). RCI 214/RCA CCS 1008
Music by Talivaldis Kenins: Violin Concerto; Fourth Symphony. Staryk vn, Avison cond. 1975. CBC SM-293
Music by the Sons of Bach: C. P. E. Bach – J. C. Bach – W. F. Bach. Avison cond. 1971. CBC SM-164
Music from Spain: Arriaga *Symphony in D Major* – Falla *Three Cornered Hat*. Avison cond. 1973. CBC SM-232
Ravel – Milhaud – Roussel. Avison cond. 1970. CBC SM-127
Revueltas – Respighi – Mendelssohn. Avison cond. 1971. CBC SM-166
Ridout *Frivolités canadiennes* – Archer *Sinfonietta*. Avison cond. 1974. CBC SM-226
Rossini – Grétry – Cherubini – Cimarosa. Avison cond. 1971. CBC SM-165
Schubert *Symphony No. 3* – Dvořák *Czech Suite*. Avison cond. 1974. CBC SM-266
Six Orchestral Overtures: Mozart – Schumann – Mendelssohn – Schubert – Weber – Cherubini. Avison cond. 1971. CBC SM-190
Strauss – Chabrier-Françaix – Purcell – Champagne – Holst. Avison cond. 1972. CBC SM-214
Tippett – Schoeck – Elgar. CBC Van Chamb O strings, Avison cond. 1970. CBC SM-124
Three Modern Romantics: Nielsen – Moeran – Delius. Aitken fl, Avison cond. 1971. CBC SM-189
Turner *Variations on the Prairie Settler's Song* – Healey *Primrose in Paradise* – Mather *Musique pour Rouen*. Avison cond. 1976. CBC SM-331
Weinzweig *Divertimento No. 3 for Bassoon and Strings* – Schafer *Partita for String Orchestra*. Zukerman bn, Avison cond. Ca 1965. CBC SM-15
Willan – Adaskin – Mather – Healey. Healey org, Zukerman bn, Avison cond. 1970. CBC SM-143
Willan *Concerto in C Minor* – Schumann *Overture, Scherzo and Finale, Op 52*. Henig pf, Avison cond. 1973. CBC SM-205 (BNSG, MW)

CBC Winnipeg Orchestra. Radio orchestra founded in 1947. Preceded by a CBC concert orchestra conducted by Geoffrey *Waddington in 1940 and a succession of string orchestras conducted by Martin Fleisher ca 1940, Albert *Pratz 1941–3, Eugene Hudson 1943–4, Marius *Benoist 1943–5, Roy Locksley and Ronald *Gibson in 1946, and Percy Harvey 1946–7, the CBC Winnipeg Orchestra became a permanent ensemble under Eric *Wild in 1947. When Wild retired 27 years later the orchestra was conducted for a year by its concertmaster (appointed 1966), Arthur *Polson. Boris *Brott became the conductor in 1975.

From 1947 to 1980 the orchestra has been heard virtually weekly on CBC radio. It has been contracted, however, not on an annual basis but for 13-week or 26-week series, and its programming has varied according to the various CBC program directors' wishes and in relation to the product of CBC orchestras in other centres (Montreal, Toronto, Vancouver, etc). The orchestra was the main participant in the live public concerts of the 1962 CBC Winnipeg (summer) Festival which was the initiator of similar CBC festivals across Canada in the 1960s and 1970s. The festivals were held first at the *U of Manitoba Summer School and later at the Basilica in St Boniface, at the *Manitoba Centennial Concert Hall, and elsewhere.

Among guest performers with the orchestra have been William *Aide, Evelyne *Anderson, *Beckett and McDonald, Clarice *Carson, Anna *Chornodolska, Chester *Duncan (with whom it gave the North American premieres of Gordon Jacob's *Concerto No. 2* and George Dyson's *Concerto Leggiero*), Janina *Fialkowska, Alexander *Gray, Elizabeth Benson *Guy, Diedre *Irons, Lois *Marshall, Joan *Maxwell, Diana *McIntosh, Sylvia *Saurette, Bernard *Turgeon, Ronald *Turini, and the *Choristers. Guest conductors have included Aaron Copland, Victor *Feldbrill, Ruben *Gurevich, Harman Haakman, Pierre *Hétu, and Sir Ernest *MacMillan. Concertmasters of the orchestras prior to 1947 were Valberg Leland 1937–9, Joseph Sera 1939–40, Albert Pratz 1940–2, and Richard Seaborn 1942–7. Seaborn continued with the Wild orchestra until 1957. Marta *Hidy succeeded Seaborn in 1957, and Arthur Polson succeeded Hidy in 1966. The repertoire has centred on standard light classics scored for medium-sized orchestra (some 50 players) and as well contains many contemporary Canadian works. The orchestra has premiered compositions by *Adaskin, *Archer, *Davies, *Fiala, *George, *Keetbaas, *Mann, *Naylor, and *Zuckert. It also participated in the first recording of selections from *Lavallée's comic opera **The Widow*. Tom Taylor succeeded Norman Lucas to serve as producer of the majority of the orchestra's concerts from the 1950s to the early 1970s. Taylor was followed in the 1970s by Harold Redekopp, Leslie Uyeda, and Randy Barnard.

DISCOGRAPHY

(Wild is the conductor, except where another is indicated)
Archer *Three Sketches for Orchestra* – Rathburn *Images of Childhood* – et al. 1969. CBC SM-119
Farnon *À la claire fontaine* – Weber – et al. 1972. CBC SM-210
Farnon – *Scherzo for Trumpet and Orchestra* – Litolff *Scherzo* – Wild *Repartee* – Polson *Improvisation* for violin and orchestra – et al. Parcells tpt, Aide pf, Polson vn. 1968. CBC SM-68
Galuppi – Rameau – et al. 1969. CBC SM-130
Light Orchestral Classics: Lavallée *The Bridal Rose* – Couture *Rêverie, Op 2* – Vézina *Souffle parfumé* – Lucas *As You Like It* – J.-J. Gagnier *Journey* – L. Smith *A Summer Idyll*. Ca 1967. RCI 233/Cap ST 6261
Mann *Symphony No. 1* – Byrd – Vaughan Williams. Wild cond (Mann), Neel cond (Byrd, Vaughan Williams). 1974. CBC SM-281
Music of Old Vienna: Strauss – Stolz – von Suppé. O.-W. Mueller cond. 1975. CBC SM-285
Prokofiev – Graener – et al. 1973. CBC SM-231
Turner *Opening Night Overture* – Adaskin *Fanfare* – Jones *Miramichi Ballad* – Weinzweig *Edge of the World* – et al. 1971. CBC SM-163
See also *The Widow*.

BIBLIOGRAPHY

CBC Winnipeg Orchestra spotlights Canadian compositions,' *CanComp*, 31, Jul–Aug 1968 NM (TT)

CBS Records Canada Ltd / CBS Disques Canada Ltée (until 1976 Columbia Records of Canada).

Established in Toronto in 1904 by the Columbia Graphophone Company. The company name in Canada had several variants: Columbia Phonograph 1904–13, Columbia Graphophone 1914–22, Columbia Gramophone 1923–4, and Columbia Phonograph 1925–3?. The US parent company was created in 1894 by the merger of the American Graphophone Co, manufacturer 1886–94 of playback machines (graphophones) and cylinder recordings, and the Columbia Phonograph Company, manufacturer of cylinder recordings and, after 1902, of disc recordings. By 1912 Columbia had established a factory in Toronto for record pressing and graphophone assembling, expanding in 1919 into the former plant of the Canadian Aeroplane Company. In 1923, however, Columbia declared bankruptcy for various reasons, including an unmanageably high inventory and the rapid advance of radio. The following year Columbia was reorganized as the Columbia Phonograph Company and its Canadian operation taken over by Montreal financiers, who maintained the head office in Toronto and distribution centres in Vancouver, Winnipeg, and Montreal. The Canadian operation did not survive the depression. Control of (US) Columbia passed through various hands until it was purchased in 1938 by CBS, which in 1939 contracted *Sparton records as Canadian presser and distributor for the Columbia line. The arrangement lasted until Columbia itself moved again into Canada in 1954. A head office and plant were located in Toronto, and by 1978 offices also were located in Vancouver, Calgary, and Montreal. In 1971 a manufacturing plant was opened in Don Mills, Ont, with the capacity to press 100,000 discs a day.

Columbia had Canadian artists on its roster in its earliest years, beginning with the concert performers Pierre-A. Asselin, Craig Campbell, Louis *Chartier, Paul *Dufault, Eduardo *Ferrari-Fontana, Jeanne *Gordon, Émile *Gour, Kathleen *Parlow, and Joseph *Saucier, some of whom recorded for the US company, others for the French-Canadian catalogue established after 1910 by L.-R. (Louis-Richard) Beaudry. After Columbia's 33⅓-rpm recordings took command of the LP revolution in 1948, the company's roster of world artists expanded greatly. In subsequent years the classical roster – the Masterworks series – has included Donald *Bell, John *Boyden, the *Canadian String Quartet, Don *Garrard, Glenn *Gould (who has recorded exclusively for Columbia), Raoul *Jobin, Lois *Marshall, James *Milligan, Léopold *Simoneau, the *TS, and André *Turp. Between 1962 and 1964 many of the Stravinsky recordings using Canadian artists (notably the *Festival Singers) and conducted by the composer were made in Canada. CBS Records became the international distributors for Eleanor *Sniderman's Aquitaine label in 1976.

In the pop field the Quebec folk instrumentalists Joe *Bouchard, Wellie *Ringuette, and Isidore *Soucy, among others, recorded for Columbia, as did the folklorists Conrad *Gauthier, Ovila *Légaré, and Charles *Marchand. In later years the pop roster included Leonard *Cohen, Maynard *Ferguson (who recorded for US Columbia), *Harmonium, Frank *Marino and Mahogany Rush, *Mashmakhan, *Octobre, Michel *Pagliaro, Les *Séguin, and Gilles *Valiquette. CBS Records also has distributed Portrait (Burton Cummings and Heart) and *True North recordings. (EBM)

CCMC. 'Free music orchestra' formed in 1974 in Toronto as the Canadian Creative Music Collective. Only the acronym was in use by 1978. Defining itself as 'a composing ensemble ... united by a desire to play music that is fluid, spontaneous, and self-regulating,' the CCMC, by its instrumentation, by the backgrounds of several of its members, and by the improvised nature of its music, has been aligned most readily with the free jazz community. Its original members were Peter Anson (guitar and later synthesizer), Graham Coughtry (trombone), Larry *Dubin (percussion), Greg Gallagher (saxophones), Nobuo Kubota (saxophones), Allan Mattes (bass, bass guitar, electronics), Casey Sokol (piano), Bill *Smith (saxophones), and Michael *Snow (trumpet and piano). With the departure of Gallagher, Coughtry, and Smith 1976–7, the death of Dubin in 1978, and the departure of Anson in 1979, the group was reduced to a quartet. The CCMC has toured widely: Dubin, Smith, and Snow in western Canada in 1976, and the full ensemble across Canada in 1977 and in Europe in 1978 and 1979.

In 1975 the CCMC opened its own performance venue, the Music Gallery, in a converted downtown Toronto warehouse, and began performing there twice weekly. The Music Gallery also has served as the focus of other activities in the avant garde of Canadian music, providing a platform for concerts by many ensembles and performers. Electronic music and solo piano festivals were presented there in 1979.

Music Gallery Editions, 'a record company devoted to new Canadian music,' was started in 1976. By 1980, under the direction of Marvin Green, it had released eight LPs of the CCMC (MGE 1, 2, 6, 15, 22 and 31, MGE 15 comprising a three-LP memorial set, *Larry Dubin and the CCMC*) and others by the *Artists' Jazz Band, the *Canadian Electronic Ensemble, the Glass Orchestra, Interspecies Music, the Nihilist Spasm Band, the Duos John Oswald and Henry Kaiser and Casey Sokol and Eugene Chadbourne, and the solo performers James MacDonald, James McKay, Lubomyr Melnyk, David *Rosenboom, Peggie *Sampson, Casey Sokol, and others. The company has also released LPs by the Six Nations Singers Society, the Inuit throat singers, and folk musicians from Tadoussac, Que. The Music Gallery began publishing the quarterly newspaper *Musicworks* in 1978, edited by Andrew Timar.

BIBLIOGRAPHY

Snider, Norman. 'Call it frontier music,' Toronto *Globe and Mail*, 22 Jun 1977 MM

Cegeps (Collèges d'enseignement général et professionel). Introduced in the Province of Quebec in the late 1960s, Cegeps have supplanted a whole stratum of autonomous schools and colleges (including the classical colleges) whose only common ground was their situation between the secondary level and university. In 1968 23 Cegeps opened their doors. The number had increased to 30 by 1969 and 41 by 1979. The Cegeps may be regarded as the Quebec counterpart of English-speaking Canada's *community colleges.

In the Cegeps certain basic disciplines are offered in the compulsory program. In order to undertake or complete his professional training the student selects a 'block' of such courses corresponding to his specialty. He chooses additional courses reflecting his tastes and aptitudes. The duration of the program is two or three years depending on whether the student intends to attend university or enter the labour market.

In 1978 there were seven Cegeps offering specialized courses in music: in Montreal the Cegeps of St-Laurent (beginning in 1968) and Vanier (anglophone, 1972); in Quebec City the Ste-Foy Cegep (1968); in the St-Maurice region the Cegep of Trois-Rivières (1969); in Drummondville the Bourgchemin Cegep (1971); in Le Saguenay the Alma Cegep (1972); and in the Eastern Townships the Cegep of Sherbrooke (1972). Four private teaching institutions also offered specialized courses in music: the colleges of Vincent-d'Indy (*École Vincent-d'Indy), Marguerite-Bourgeoys, and Marianapolis (anglophone) in Montreal and of Nicolet. Four Cegeps (St-Laurent, Vanier, Alma, and Drummondville) offered an alternative third year oriented towards popular, commercial, and folk music. The objective of a specialized course is to give the student, in addition to basic courses enabling him to pursue specialized studies at university or complete the popular music program, a general musical background which will allow him to grasp the human value of music.

In 1978 11 public and private colleges were offering complementary courses in music: Valleyfield, Thetford Mines, Gaspé, Shawinigan, Joliette, Dawson (Montreal), John Abbott (Ste-Anne-de-Bellevue and Kirkland), Lionel-Groulx (Blainville), Notre-Dame-de-Foy (Cap Rouge), Lévis, and Rimouski. In the 1978–9 school year Sept-Îles Collège began to offer the Diplôme d'études collégiales (DEC) in arts. Complementary courses are devised for students who take music studies within the framework of a general course in arts or humanities, or for those who are pursuing studies in another field.

The music specialization program was offered for the first time in 1968 following efforts by the Ministry of Education to democratize this area of instruction, previously the exclusive domain of private institutions and conservatories. Subsequently, music training at the collegiate level has been offered, at no cost, to all students whose preparatory training is deemed adequate. Only the quota system may restrict access. A student who specializes in music at the college level must take ear training (four courses), musical literature (four courses), and main instrument, second instrument, and ensemble playing (four courses).

The complementary courses pursue different objectives, allowing the student to enter into contact with music through musical literature, ear training, or the playing of an instrument (preferably in a group).

In the Cegeps and colleges which offer music there is a great variety of musical activity: concerts, jazz bands, chamber orchestras, concert bands, choirs, classical orchestras, contemporary music workshops, etc.

In 1978 close to 1200 pupils were enrolled in the specialization courses in the Cegeps; there were some 390 teachers, 60 full-time, 80 part-time, and 250 remunerated on a per-lesson basis. In the complementary courses there were close to 700 students. The six colleges offering both specialization and complementary courses had a total enrolment of some 500. There have been 1450 music graduates from the time the Cegeps were established to December 1978.

The overall direction of musical studies in the Cegeps has been maintained by a music subcommittee made up of the directors of the colleges which offer music specialization – in 1978 Adrienne Milotte (St-Laurent), Claude *Lagacé (Ste-Foy), Raymond Laliberté (Vanier), Claude Parenteau (Trois-Rivières), Gilles Fortin (Drummondville), Normand Laprise (Alma), and Laurette Brunelle (Sherbrook) – along with Claude Poirier (Gaspé) representing the colleges offering complementary courses, Micheline *Tessier the private colleges, and Clément Paré, the Ministry of Education. Cécile Petit acted as co-ordinator of the subcommittee.

See also Classical colleges and seminaries in Quebec; Universities.

BIBLIOGRAPHY

Lagacé, Claude. 'Un être soudainement surgi du néant,' *Cégépropos*, Oct 1978 CPt

Celebrity Concerts. See Gee, Fred M.

Cello. The bass of the violin family ('basso di violino') was made in the early 1600s, but it was not until the 18th century that it was recognized as a potential solo instrument, ideal string quartet bass, and orchestral instrument. By the late 18th century, the growing popularity of string quartets and quintets by composers such as Boccherini, Haydn, Mozart, and Pleyel created a demand for cellists. George Gibsone, Fréderic *Glackemeyer, Narcisse Hamel, J. Harvicker, and Adam *Schott were worthy cellists active in Canada from the late 18th to the mid-19th centuries. Two professionally trained French cellists arrived in Canada mid-century – Antoine *Dessane in 1848 in Quebec City and Paul *Letondal in 1852 in Montreal. At a recital in 1854 Letondal performed works by the cello virtuoso Auguste Franchomme, as well as a fantasy of his own composition.

Other cellists who visited Quebec City during the 19th century were Henri Billet (in 1842, billed as the 'premier violoncelle de la musique privée de l'Empereur de Russie') and Léon Jacquard, who lived a few years in Montreal in the early 1870s. Jean-Baptiste *Dubois arrived from Belgium in 1891, settled in Montreal, and propagated the traditions of the Franco-Belgian school of cello playing. Dubois's pupils included Rosario *Bourdon, Suzette Forgues, Gustave *Labelle, Roland *Leduc, Brahm Sand, and Dubois's son Jules. A Montreal-born pioneer of the instrument was Louis *Charbonneau, a pupil of Alwin Schroeder of Boston and the teacher of Rodolphe *Plamondon and of Charbonneau's son Maurice. Plamondon's son Lucien also became a noted cellist, in France and Canada. Labelle's pupils included Gabriel *Cusson, Raoul *Duquette, and Yvëtte *Lamontagne. The German cellist Ernst Doering taught in Halifax in the 1890s and was a member of the Leipzig Trio with Charles *Porter and Heinrich *Klingenfeld.

Active in Toronto during the 19th century were John Ellis (ca 1840s), a keen amateur, and Giuseppe Dinelli, a London-born teacher (fl 1897). In the early part of the 20th century several cellists who made significant contributions as teachers and performers arrived in Canada. The Hungarian cellist Dezsö *Mahalek, a pupil of David Popper and Julius Klengel, settled in Winnipeg ca 1912 and moved to Vancouver in 1936. His Canadian pupils included Isaac *Mamott, Lorne *Munroe, Zara *Nelsova, and Malcolm *Tait. George Bruce, Paul *Hahn, Boris *Hambourg (a pupil of Hugo Becker), and Leo *Smith (a pupil of Carl Fuchs) all lived in Toronto in the early 1920s, and the English cellist Lionel Bilton (a pupil of Popper) appeared with Jack *Arthur's orchestra. Bruno Schmitt and Janet Palmer taught cello in Saskatoon in the 1920s. In 1926 the French cellist Jean *Belland (a pupil of Louis R. Feuillard) moved to Montreal, where he had an active career as both soloist and teacher. Among his pupils were Paul *Létourneau, Raymonde *Martin, André *Mignault, Brahm Sand, and Belland's son Ary. Cornelius Ysselstyn (b The Hague 9 Dec 1904, d Toronto 3 Apr 1979) arrived in Toronto in 1936. A member of the *Dembeck and *Parlow quartets and, for some years, of the *TSO and *CBC SO, he also taught at the RCMT, where his pupils included Donald Whitton and Michael *Kilburn. The Polish cellist Martin Hoherman lived in both Toronto and Winnipeg during the 1950s.

Herbert Coulson, an Englishman who pioneered as a farmer near Dauphin, Man, in the early years of the 20th century, played in string quartets and had a good library. However, as a rule, the cello has been an 'urban' instrument, which has flourished as symphony orchestras and chamber ensembles grow and as conservatories offer instruction. As the 20th century progressed, talented players and teachers could be found in many centres: Marcus *Adeney, Isaac Mamott, Vladimir *Orloff, and Philip Spivak in Toronto, James Hunter in Victoria, Walter *Joachim (a Klengel pupil) in Montreal, Claude *Kenneson in Winnipeg and Edmonton, Peggie *Sampson (a Suggia and Alexanian pupil) in Winnipeg and Toronto, Malcolm Tait in Brandon, Man, and Tsuyoshi *Tsutsumi (a Starker pupil) in London, Ont, and at Banff, Alta.

'The Cellist' by Florence Wyle

In some centres the *Suzuki method has lowered the starting age for cello students, but such methods have not had wide acceptance among cello teachers, who tend, on the whole, to be empirical individualists. Marcus Adeney has written a treatise on the history of cello methods and the philosophies which motivate them. The *Vancouver Cello Club has helped to focus interest in all matters pertaining to the cello, its literature, and its performance. The *Canadian String Teachers Assn has published articles and information for teachers in its newsletter, *Notes*.

Canadian cellists who have pursued major international careers are Rosario Bourdon, Lorne Munroe, and Zara Nelsova. Other noted cellists and teachers active during the 20th century include Dorothy Bégin (*CMM), Klara Benjamin Belkin (principal of the *Winnipeg SO), Edward *Bisha, Lotte *Brott and her son Denis, Marthe *Delcellier, Gisela *Depkat, Daniel Domb (principal of the TS), Anthony Elliott (principal of the *Vancouver SO), Mary *Evens, Guy Fouquet (principal of the *MSO), Ernest *Friedlander, Hélène *Gagné, Ian Hampton (of the *Purcell String Quartet), Talmon Hertz (Calgary), Edward Culbreath (Montreal), Pierre (principal of the *Quebec SO) and Huguette *Morin, Rowland *Pack, Audrey *Piggott, Marcel St-Cyr (*Orford String Quartet), Joyce *Sands, Peter Schenkman (former principal of the TS), Kurt Trachsel (former principal with both the Calgary and Edmonton orchestras), Yuli Turovsky (CMM and *McGill Chamber Orchestra), Donald Whitton (principal, *NACO), Ifan *Williams, and Eric *Wilson.

*Archer, Bourdon, Alexander *Brott, *Fiala, *Hétu, *Miro, *Morawetz and *Prévost have written works for cello and orchestra, and Archer, *Contant, *Coulthard, *Eckhardt-Gramatté, Fiala, Otto *Joachim, *Kenins, *Lavallée, R. *Mathieu, *O'Brien, *Pentland, Prévost, and *Weinzweig have composed pieces for cello and piano.

See also Instruments: medieval, renaissance, and baroque: 2 / Playing and teaching. GP, PSm

Centennial celebrations, 1967. Events which marked the 100th anniversary of Canada's Confederation. Undoubtedly the most concentrated and imposing of these were the epoch-making *Expo 67 and its companion World Festival, both in Montreal. But other celebrations of that year, diffused throughout the country under the name Festival Canada and less easy to summarize, nevertheless mobilized Canada's creative and performing arts, and particularly music, to an unprecedented degree.

The Centennial Commission, formed in January 1963 under the Secretary of State, Judy LaMarsh, appointed John Fisher as its commissioner and Nicholas *Goldschmidt as chief of its performing arts division. It was the performing arts division which planned and subsidized Festival Canada (not to be confused with the later annual Ottawa summer festival which began as Festival Canada but was renamed *Festival Ottawa in 1978).

Under the Festival Canada umbrella national tours were organized for **Anne of Green Gables*, Les Feux-Follets, Don *Messer and His Islanders, the *MSO, the National Ballet of Canada, the *NYO, the New York Philharmonic Orchestra, and the singers Gordon *Lightfoot and Ian and Sylvia *Tyson. These artists also appeared at Expo 67.

A year-long festival was held in Ottawa, featuring performances by the aforementioned groups and individuals, by the *COC, and by the *Canadian Centennial Choir, which had been formed by Goldschmidt for the festivities. An entertainment entitled 'Centennial Spectacle,' with words by Robertson Davies and music by Louis *Applebaum, was scheduled for presentation on Parliament Hill 1 Jul 1967, but never took place.

Financial assistance was made available to performing arts groups across Canada for productions and commissions; the *CMCentre alone received a grant of $60,000, which it used to help in the commissioning of some 45 works, each of which was to have at least one public performance in Canada during 1967.

Professional and amateur entertainments were organized on a regional basis, by means of grants to local groups for performances within their communities. Choral groups, opera companies, symphony orchestras, and chamber ensembles were encouraged to give special performances. This resulted in presentations of works such as Britten's *War Requiem* by the *Vancouver SO, Verdi's *Requiem* by the *Victoria SO, Orff's *Carmina burana* by the *Winnipeg SO, Messiaen's *Turangalîla-Symphonie* by the *TSO, and Verdi's *Otello* and Gounod's *Faust* by the MSO. Operas, premiered or otherwise presented in conjunction with the program, included *Somers' **Louis Riel* and *Pannell's *The Luck of Ginger Coffey* (by the COC), *Rigoletto* (*Vancouver Opera Assn), and *Faust* (*Edmonton Opera Assn).

Other organizations assisted by Centennial Commission grants included the *FCMF, for a national competition held in Saint John, NB; and the *JMC, for competitions in Quebec City, Guelph, and Vancouver, and a concert by the national winners at the *PDA in Montreal.

The Canadian Folk Arts Council (Counseil canadien des arts populaires), founded in 1964, was assisted by the Centennial Commission in the presentation of 100 folk festivals across Canada during 1967. Many musical groups were among the 35,000 participating in provincial and regional festivals that demonstrated the varied cultural heritage of Canada.

Among grants given to assist individuals were those awarded to Edward B. *Moogk of London, Ont, to assemble the nucleus of a collection of Canadian recordings for deposit at the *NL of C; and to Arnold *Walter of Toronto to assist in the preparation of the book *Aspects of Music in Canada / Aspects de la musique au Canada* (Toronto 1969, Montreal 1970).

Among numerous works written for the centennial year (see also list of composers and commissioners below) were the official thanksgiving 'Centennial Hymn' / 'Hymne de centenaire' (Leeds, 1967; music by Rex *LeLacheur, English words by Rev Kenneth Moyer and French words by Ronald Duprès), commissioned directly by the Centennial Commission, and *Willan's 'Anthem for the Centennial of Canadian Confederation' / 'Hymne à l'occasion du Centenaire de la Confédération canadienne' (B611). The Willan anthem, commissioned by the Canadian Inter-Faith Conference and known also as the 'Centennial Anthem,' was a setting of words by Robert Choquette, adapted into English by John Glassco, and published by BMIC in 1966. Other national songs composed for centennial year were Bobby *Gimby's *'CA-NA-DA' and Raymond Gould and Frederick Sheffield's 'My Canada' (Chappell ca 1967).

As a joint centennial project *RCA Victor and the *CBC released the 17-album series *Music and Musicians of Canada / Musique et musiciens du Canada* (RCA CCS 1007–1023/RCI 213–229), containing 42 compositions by 32 Canadians, performed by a wide variety of Canadian musicians and the 9-album series *Canadian Folk Songs: A Centennial Collection / Chansons folkloriques du Canada: Collection du Centenaire* (RCA/RCI CS 100), containing 120 selections.

The appended list of composers commissioned to write works for the centenary, and of their commissioners, was extracted from the December 1967 issue of *Musicanada*:

Composer / Commissioner(s)

Murray Adaskin / CBC (2)
István Anhalt / Simon Fraser U; U of British Columbia Chamber Singers
Louis Applebaum / Centennial Commission; Edmonton SO; Expo 67; federal government; NAC (2)
Violet Archer / CBC; RCCO; Hugh Bancroft; two others
Milton Barnes / OFSO
John Beckwith / Vancouver International Festival; Toronto Mendelssohn Choir; CBC
Norma Beecroft / Ten Centuries Concerts; Dora and Leo Velleman (puppeteers); Waterloo Lutheran U
Jack Behrens / U of Saskatoon
Lorne Betts / OFSO
Keith Bissell / Centennial Commission; St Catharines SO; Confederation Centre, Charlottetown
François Brassard / CAMMAC
Alexander Brott / CBC; Canadian Pavilion, Expo 67; Les Grands Ballets canadiens; Lawrence Lande; McGill Chamber Orchestra
Barrie Cabena / RCCO
Morley Calvert / Montreal Brass Quintet
Jean Coulthard / Rolston-Moore Duo; Vancouver SO
Edgard Davignon / La Chorale de la Vallée de l'Or
Roger Deegan / Strathcona Composite High School
Maurice Dela / MSO
Gordon Delamont / Ten Centuries Concerts
Samuel Dolin / Stratford Festival; Toronto Repertory Ensemble
S. C. Eckhardt-Gramatté / CBC; Marta Hidy Trio; U of Manitoba
Robert Fleming / Canadian Pavilion, Expo 67; OMEA; Ottawa Music Festival Assn; Dora and Leo Velleman
Harry Freedman / CBC; Lois Marshall; NYO; Saskatoon SO; Stratford Festival
Serge Garant / Youth Pavilion, Expo 67
Srul Irving Glick / Toronto Chamber Orchestra; New Dance Group of Canada
Theo Goldberg / Vancouver SO
Frank Haworth / Sudbury Arts Guild
Jacques Hétu / Duo Pach; JMC; Quebec Woodwind Quintet
Otto Joachim / TSO
Kelsey Jones / CBC; Baroque Trio of Montreal
Janis Kalnins / Halifax Trio; New Brunswick SO
Talivaldis Kenins / Saskatoon SO
Edward Laufer / Halifax SO
Rex LeLacheur / Centennial Commission
Sir Ernest MacMillan / CBC
Bruce Mather / CBC; Ten Centuries Concerts
William McCauley / Dora and Leo Velleman
Oskar Morawetz / Donald Bell; Festival Singers
François Morel / CBC; Edmonton SO
Bernard Naylor / U of Manitoba; U of Manitoba Chamber Music Group; Choristers of Winnipeg
Raymond Pannell / COC/Centennial Commission; London SO
Jean Papineau-Couture / CBC (2); Festival Singers; Steven Staryk
Barbara Pentland / ARCT Assns of British Columbia; Hugh McLean Consort; U of British Columbia Chamber Music Ensemble
Clermont Pépin / MSO; NAC
Michel Perrault / CBC; Victoria SO
André Prévost / Expo 67
Eldon Rathburn / NFB
Godfrey Ridout / CBC; CMEA; National Ballet of Canada; Toronto Board of Education
R. Murray Schafer / Berkshire Music Festival; CBC; Pavilion of the Chemical Industries, Expo 67; St John's Brass Consort; Vancouver Alumni of RCMT
Harry Somers / CBC (2); COC/Floyd S. Chalmers Foundation; Institut international de musique du Canada (see Montreal International Competition)
Ann Southam / New Dance Group of Canada
Morris Surdin / Hart House Orchestra; 'Mac 14' Theatre Society (Calgary)
Norman Symonds / CBC; Ten Centuries Concerts; Winnipeg SO
Robert Turner / Cassenti Players; CBC
John Weinzweig / CBC; Judy Loman and the Toronto Repertory Ensemble
Healey Willan / Centennial Commission

BIBLIOGRAPHY
Goldschmidt, Nicholas. 'The performing arts in Canada's centennial,' *CanComp*, 3, Oct 1965
Hicklin, Ralph. 'Cultural workers in the centennial garden,' Toronto *Globe and Mail*, 15 Oct 1966
Festival Canada: A Report Prepared by the Performing Arts Division, Centennial Commission / Festival du Canada: programme ... Un rapport de la Division des Arts d'interpretation, Commission du Centenaire (Ottawa 15 Nov 1966)
MacMillan, Keith. ' Canadian notes for NOTES,' *Notes*, vol 23, Dec 1966
'Festival Canada highlights,' *OpCan*, Feb 1967
Stone, Kurt. 'Review of records,' *MQ*, vol 53, Jul 1967
'Centennial collection of Canadian folk songs issued,' *CanComp*, 23, Nov 1967
MacNiven, Elina. 'CBC radio: centennial review,' *OpCan*, Dec 1967
Moyer, Kenneth A. ' My most successful work: The Centennial Hymn,' *CanComp*, 30, Jun 1968
Proctor, George. *Canadian Music of the Twentieth Century* (Toronto 1980)

The Centennial Hall. Located on Wellington St in downtown London, Ont. Built as the city's centennial project, it is a multi-purpose concert and entertainment hall, designed by Phillip Carter Johnson. It opened 21 June 1967 with a concert by the *London SO. The hall is rectangular, with 1854 seats on three levels (orchestra, mezzanine, and balcony) backing on three walls. There is no curtain, orchestra pit, or fly gallery. A second room, below the hall, is used for a variety of purposes. Centennial Hall is the home of the London SO and the annual *Kiwanis Music Festival. In the years 1970–5 it accommodated an annual average of 400 bookings. GKG

'C'est la belle Françoise.' Song originating in France and sung in Canada as early as 1650 by the French soldiers who fought the Iroquois. It describes a soldier's farewell to his fiancée. Ernest *Gagnon in *Chansons populaires du Canada* (Quebec 1865) gives three versions, as different in their music as in the turns of phrase in their verse – in one instance 'ma luron lurette'; in another 'blanc loup-marin, ma lon la'; in a third 'ma dondaire.' The text appeared among others in *La Nouvelle Lyre canadienne* (Montreal 1882) under the title 'La Belle Françoise.' Text and music are found in several collections, notably *Canadian Folk-Life and Folk-Lore* by William Parker Greenough (New York 1897). The tune has been harmonized by Alfred *Laliberté (*Le Passe-Temps*, July 1945), Claude *Champagne (Waterloo 1960), and others. For the LP MB 7899–7900 Champagne directed the Petit ensemble vocal of the *École normale de musique of Montreal in a performance of his arrangement. Among the numerous LPs of other arrangements is one by Alan *Mills and Hélène *Baillargeon (RCI/RCA CS 100–4). HP

'C'est l'aviron.' These words, taken from the refrain of the voyageur song 'M'en revenant de la joli' Rochelle,' have come to be recognized as the song's surrogate title. Certain phrases in the song have been traced back to 15th-century France, where it originated. It is found in several textual and melodic variants. In *Chansons folkloriques françaises au Canada* (Quebec 1956) Marguerite and Raoul d'Harcourt give three versions based on incomplete minor scales. One of these uses a refrain different from that of 'C'est l'aviron.' Still another version with different words is given by Ernest *Gagnon in *Chansons populaires du Canada* (Montreal 1865), and in a Montreal newspaper, *Le Canard*, of 13 Nov 1897. François *Brassard compares 'C'est l'aviron' to a refrain known in Canada, 'Mon joli champ d'avoine,' and to the French refrain of 'Allons voir nos vignes.' Edith *Fowke in *Folk Songs of Quebec* (Waterloo 1957) and *The Penguin Book of Canadian Folk Songs* (Middlesex 1973) presents a version collected by E.-Z. *Massicotte in 1927, probably the best-known version in the 1970s. Several singers have made LPs of the song, notably André Bertrand, Jules *Bruyère and the Choeurs de la Bonne Chanson, Alan *Mills (Folk FP 29), and Raoul *Roy (RCI and RCA CS 100-7).

BIBLIOGRAPHY
Barbeau, Marius. *Alouette* (Montreal 1946)
Brassard, François. 'Refrains canadiens de chansons de France,' *Archives de folklore*, vol 1 (Montreal 1946) HP

CFMTA. See Canadian Federation of Music Teachers' Associations.

CHADWICK, Berkley E. Choir conductor, b Saint John, NB, 19 Nov 1880, d Hudson, near Montreal, 1964. He spent most of his life in Montreal and for several years was choirmaster at Erskine and American United Church. At the request of the United Church of Canada the choir there carried out an assignment of unusual interest: the recording of hymns in the Umbundu dialect for use by missionaries in Angola. Chadwick became director of the Apollo Glee Club in 1921 and served 1923–51 as conductor of the *Montreal Elgar Choir, the product of a merger of the all-male glee club and the Elgar Women's Choir. In 1926 he participated in the formation of the Chamber Music Society, later known as the Montreal String Quartette. During the 1930s he taught music at Lower Canada College and Trafalgar School. For 14 years he conducted the School for Crippled Children's choir and rhythm band, leading both to many honours at the Quebec Music Festivals. For many years Chadwick was the chorus master for works conducted at the *MSO and the *Montreal Festivals by Sir Thomas Beecham, Emil Cooper, Sir Ernest *MacMillan, Bernard *Naylor, Eugene Ormandy, Wilfred *Pelletier, and Lazar Weiner. He retired in 1951, settling in Hudson, but was organist-choirmaster of St James' Anglican Church there until his death in 1964. CB

CHALMERS, Floyd (Sherman). Publisher, administrator, editor, patron, b Chicago 14 Sep 1898 of Canadian parents; hon LLD (Western Ontario) 1962, hon LLD (Waterloo Lutheran) 1963, hon D LITT (Trent) 1968, hon BFA (York) 1973. He attended school in Orillia, Ont, and Toronto, and joined the Bank of Nova Scotia at 16. While he was overseas during World War I with the First Canadian Tank Battalion, he edited the *Battalion News*. He joined the *Financial Post* in 1919 and became Montreal editor in 1923 and editor in 1925. He was appointed to the board of the TCM (*RCMT) in 1935 and served on it as vice-chairman for nearly 20 years. He was appointed executive vice-president of the publishers Maclean-Hunter Ltd, in 1942, and was president of the firm 1952–64 and chairman 1964–9. A director of numerous corporations, Chalmers also was founder and president 1929–30 of the Ticker Club, president 1932–3 of the Canadian Club of Toronto, president 1947–9 of the Periodical Press Assn of Canada, president 1965–7 of the *Stratford Shakespearean Festival Foundation, and chancellor 1968–73 of *York U, Toronto.

Chalmers has been accorded many honours reflecting the variety of his endeavours. In 1957 he was named a Liveryman of the Worshipful Company of Stationers and Newspaper Makers, England, a Freeman of the City of London, and a Fellow of the International Institute of Arts and Letters. He was made an Officer of the *Order of Canada in 1967 and received the first Special Award of the *CMCouncil in 1977.

He is the founder and chairman of the Floyd S. *Chalmers Foundation, the original sponsor of *EMC*. Chalmers first conceived the idea of an encyclopedia of music in Canada upon reading John *Beckwith's critical essay 'About Canadian music: the PR failure' (*Musicanada*, Jul–Aug 1969). After consultation with several experts he initiated the *EMC* project, assembling a board of governors, appointing a triumvirate of editors, and providing, through the Chalmers Foundation and personally, some $328,000 towards the preparation of its manuscript. In 1979 he transferred to the *OAC the assets and administration of the Chalmers Foundation. The assets represented the OAC's first major capital holding.

Chalmers' wife (b Jean A. Boxall, Toronto, 18 Aug 1899) has been a patron of music in her own right, helping to promote the *Promenade Symphony Concerts in the 1930s and the Five O'-Clocks (an RCMT chamber music series) in the late 1940s, and forming the *COC's first women's committee. In 1965 she established the Jean A. Chalmers Award for Opera, given annually to the most promising young member of the COC in performance or production. The award – dispensing the income from a gift of shares – increased from $500 at the outset to $1000 by 1978. Musician-winners have included Danielle Pilon, soprano, 1967; Donald Rutherford, baritone, 1968; Renée Rosen, mezzo-soprano, 1969; Peter *Barcza, baritone, 1971; Eleanor James, mezzo-soprano, 1973; Derek Bate, conductor-coach, 1975; and Theodore Berg, baritone, 1978.

BIBLIOGRAPHY

Colgrass, Ulla. 'Patronage is hard work,' *Music*, May–Jun 1979

KW

The Floyd S. Chalmers Foundation. Fund, incorporated in 1964, in the Province of Ontario, to make grants in the fields of theatre, music, opera, dance, and mime (and in related educational areas) from monies provided by Floyd S. *Chalmers, his wife Jean A., his son Wallace G., and his daughter M. Joan. By the end of 1975 the foundation had made grants of some $600,000, of which more than half had gone to music, opera, and dance.

Though annual grants have been made to the *COC, the *TSO, and the *MSO, and other major organizations, emphasis during the 1970s shifted away from repeated assistance with operational expenses to specific assistance with individual projects. Instances of the latter are: funds to the COC for the commissioning in 1967 of the opera *Louis Riel* as a Canadian centennial project; $100,000 to the *Stratford Festival towards the cost of rebuilding the Avon Theatre for music and drama; $25,000 to Toronto Arts Productions to help build the *St Lawrence Centre; $157,875 towards the cost of writing, editing, and translating this book, the first *Encyclopedia of Music in Canada*; $5000 to the Fathers of Confederation Building Trust to recostume the Canadian musical **Anne of Green Gables* for its visit to Expo 70, Japan; $4200 to the *St Catharines SO to furnish its teaching, workshop, and office building, Symphony House; and $2500 to *York U to launch an opera workshop. Smaller grants have been made to the *Guelph Spring Festival to commission a libretto for a Canadian opera; to the *Toronto Mendelssohn Choir to help finance a European tour; to the *U of Toronto for opera productions; and to other establishments for like purposes. Funds for awards and scholarships have been given to the *JMC, the *Canadian Music Competitions, York U, and Toronto Arts Productions (which has been granted $1500 annually for a promising young Canadian performer; among the recipients of its award have been the Winnipeg violinist Victor Schultz in 1974, the Montreal pianist Henri *Brassard in 1975, the duo-pianists Adrienne *Shannon and Jane *Coop in 1976, the clarinetist James *Campbell in 1977, the Dalart Trio in 1978, and Ingemar *Korjus in 1979).

In 1979 the assets of the Chalmers Foundation were given outright to the *OAC. These funds were matched by a Wintario grant, thereby establishing for the arts in Canada a $2-million foundation which will be augmented by bequests from members of the Chalmers family. KW

CHAMBERLAND, Albert. Violinist, conductor, producer, teacher, composer, b Montreal 12 Oct 1886, d there 4 Apr 1975. He studied violin with Jean *Duquette and later at the *McGill Cons with Alfred *De Sève, and made his debut as a soloist in 1904. A member of the *Goulet *MSO, the Beethoven Trio 1907–10, and the *Dubois String Quartet 1910–20, he was one of the founders in

Albert Chamberland

1920 of the Montreal Philharmonic Orchestra, and was the first violin 1920–5 of the Chamberland String Quartet (Norman Herschorn, violin, Eugène *Chartier, viola, Raoul *Duquette, cello). He joined the *Montreal Orchestra in 1932 and was concertmaster 1934–9 and assistant conductor 1939–48 of the *SCSM orchestra. A music producer 1937–52 for the CBC French network, he was responsible for such programs as 'The *Little Symphonies' and 'Récital.' He taught at several schools, including the *Cons national and the Villa-Maria Convent in Montreal, and served on several competition juries. Among his pupils were Alexander *Brott, Norman Herschorn, and Lucien *Martin.

Chamberland's compositions included an *Allegro militaire* for band, a *Sérénade* for violin and piano, an *Étude de concert d'après Rode* (Édition Belgo-Canadienne ca 1925), and a *Fantaisie* on the tune 'Un *Canadien errant,' played by him at the *Monument national 13 Apr 1926. His recordings as soloist and with his trio, four 78s (seven songs) for His Master's Voice, are listed in *Roll Back the Years*.

Chamberland's sister Luce, a pianist, married the basso Ulysse *Paquin. (GG)

Chamber music. The term applies to composition for from 2 to about 12 parts, intended for one performer per part. Its older implications, of leisure music-making for the delight of performers and a few cultivated listeners, may be largely anachronistic, but chamber music in that sense may be exemplified in Canadian cities starting in the mid-18th century. However, from early mentions, such activities fostered European chamber-music literature rather than adding to it. The creative musicians of the late 18th to late 19th centuries contributed rather to other forms – concert-hall music, parlour music, church music, theatre music, parade-ground music. There is no known early-Canadian counterpart to Johann Friedrich Peter, the gifted 18th-century Pennsylvanian composer of string quintets.

If chamber-music composition was slow to emerge, its first Canadian manifestations, in the early decades of the 20th century, align with a decidedly conservative view of the genre. The composers seem intent on preservation of classical ideals, maintaining an 'academic' interpretation of Mozart and Beethoven comparable to that found in the works of Daniel Gregory Mason in the USA, the Cobbett movement in England, and the Schola Cantorum circle in France. *Contant's *Trio* (1907), *MacMillan's *String Quartet* (1914), and the *Quartet* (1920) and the *Trio* (1921-2) of Rodolphe *Mathieu, may be classed legitimately as 'academic,' not in a pejorative sense but rather because of the reasoned and idealized view of classical chamber-music forms which they represent.

Thus the MacMillan work is notable for its busy textures and its confidently handled four-movement form, including a neat, classically shaped scherzo and a weighty slow introduction to the vigorous finale. However, Mathieu's *Trio* reveals symptoms of a less orthodox approach: the three movements bear titles ('Discussion,' 'Reflection,' 'Pantomime') and, despite the conventional textures, one finds frequent dramatic relationships of the three instruments, and tension stemming from unusually harsh dissonances is often left unresolved. The titles and the deliberate maintenance of dissonant tension are both qualities which link Mathieu in a curious way more with an independent New-World figure, Ives, than with his composition teacher, d'Indy.

These early-20th-century works have been revived and in some cases recorded, and they form an interesting basis of the Canadian chamber-music literature. While they were not the only examples produced before the 1930s, the catalogue is admittedly sparse. *Lavallée is thought to have composed two string quartets and a trio, and J. P. *Clarke 'a number of chamber trios and quartettes' but the scores have not survived. A like fate befell George F. *Graham's *Piano Quintet in F*, played in Toronto in 1858, and A.E. *Fisher's *String Trio*, reportedly performed there in 1888. *Couture and W.O. *Forsyth showed little interest in chamber music beyond an early string quartet each; *Lucas none at all. It should be added that the Couture, called *Quatuor-fugue*, was performed and published in Paris in 1876 and possibly is the earliest extant chamber work by a Canadian. Von *Kunits, the composer-violinist, and Leo *Smith, the composer-cellist, each produced a few pieces: von Kunits' early *String Quartet* (1890), written before he emigrated to Canada, has proved its charming qualities in revival, while Smith's *Quartet in D* (1932) is the largest item in a fair-sized list of original works and arrangements, including also a few neo-Elizabethan pieces for viols and voices.

The experience of *Willan seems typical for the period. Chamber music forms a minor part of his output. He confided to students how hard he found the string-quartet medium and never completed a work in this form, though several fragments exist. The *Trio in B Minor* (1907), written before his emigration to Canada, formed part of a full program of his music given in Toronto in 1916. The E.W. Beatty (see CPR Festivals) and CPRS prizes of the late 1920s and 1930s often drew attention to new compositions for chamber groups, suggesting a slow but noticeable growth in that period (see also Leo Smith's reviews of new scores in the *Canadian Review of Music and Art* in the early 1940s). Quentin *Maclean's neo-romantic *Quartet* (1936) and *Trio* (1937) are typical. That was the heyday of the *Hart House String Quartet; its repertoire included only a few samples of new music (quartets by Bloch, Honegger, Schoenberg's First, Bartók's First, works by English contemporaries such as Bax, Delius, and Goossens) and none by Canadian composers beyond such brief, light pieces as MacMillan's *Two Sketches* (1927) and similar folk-music derivations.

Mathieu's return to a large chamber-music form in his *Piano Quintet* (1942) is marked by originality and seriousness. The work is a strongly sustained abstract design whose two movements are integrated through cyclic thematic relationships. A parallel to this example of special, isolated integrity in the Canadian chamber-music repertoire may be found in one of the late works of Claude *Champagne: his *String Quartet* (1956) incorporated surprising, even daring, reflections of his awareness of such 20th-century figures as Schoenberg and Messiaen. It may be regarded as a turning point towards the modernism of Champagne's last compositions. It is notable that for Champagne (a violinist by training) this turning point should take the form of a venture into the time-honoured chamber-music medium of the string quartet.

The newer composing personalities, the young professionals of the 1940s, used chamber-music media in their early works by habit – a distinctly new phenomenon. Exceptions were those closest to Willan – *Fleming and *Ridout, for example – who, like their mentor, seemingly gave little priority to the genre. Others not only contributed to the standard media – string quartet, woodwind quintet – but went beyond them to discover novel instrumental groupings and mixtures of sounds (such as percussion) seldom found in traditional chamber-music scores.

If those standard media took on new life and new guises in this period, such external factors as the growth of radio broadcasting (for which chamber music was a natural and handy form) and the rise of more permanent professional playing ensembles may be cited as possible reasons. The following is a brief survey of the Canadian string trio, string quartet, piano trio, piano quartet, and woodwind quintet repertoires:

1 STRING QUARTET. The production of new string quartets is considerable on the part of leading Canadian composers of recent times. One can enumerate *Pépin with five, *Morawetz, *Pentland, *Somers, *Turner, *Weinzweig, and *Wilson each with three, and *Archer, *Brott, *Cherney, *Ford, *Morel, *Papineau-Couture, *Prévost, and *Schafer each with two, to note only a few of the more prominent names. Morawetz' *Second Quartet* (1953–4) sets a model of conservative and thoughtful chamber-music discourse. In the *Quartet* (1956) of Otto *Joachim, a new appreciation of sonority and a more explosive musical expression become apparent; significantly, the work was introduced by the *Montreal String Quartet, of which Joachim was the violist. An unusual contribution to the repertoire, in terms of style, is the highly contrapuntal *Quartet* (1953–5) of Glenn *Gould, its long one-movement structure evidently suggested by Schoenberg's *Quartet No. 1*, its idiom (the composer said) by the string quintet of Bruckner.

Elegiac and prayerful feelings, for which the string-quartet sound often has provided a vehicle, mark works as different as Pentland's *Quartet No. 2* (1953), Weinzweig's *Quartet No. 3* (1962), and Prévost's *Quartet No. 2* (1972, subtitled *Ad pacem*). Weinzweig's composition is notable further for the variety it extracts from a succession of predominantly slow tempi in three of its five movements. Somers' dynamic *Quartet No. 3* (1959), in one movement, is based on material from his short opera *The Fool*. William *Douglas' *Quartet* (1968) is a concise and unusually showy rhythmic study.

Cherney's *Second Quartet* (1970) employs theatrical action, silent gesturing, and quotations from other music, and *Freedman's *Graphic II* (1972) and *Beckwith's *Quartet* (1977) both employ altered tunings for particular open-string and natural-harmonic effects; the former introduces, as the title suggests, new graphic forms of notation, as well as humming, recitation of texts to given rhythms, and shouting by the players, while the latter evokes traditional string-instrument sonorities of Canada, especially fiddle music, in the course of an abstract variational structure. Schafer's *Second Quartet* (1976, first winner of the Jules Léger Prize for chamber-music composition) is subtitled *Waves*, and as an integral feature of its musical structure (rather than as a purely 'programmatic' element) it employs rhythmic recurrences actually found in ocean waves measured by the composer.

2 PIANO TRIO, PIANO QUARTET, STRING TRIO. Though the medium of violin, cello, and piano is an uneven and acoustically awkward one, its traditional attraction for composers continues in Canada, as elsewhere. However, in the later 20th century it is a less obligatory staple for composers of chamber music than it was a couple of generations previously. The later additions to be set alongside the works by Contant, Mathieu, Willan, and others already noted are the trios by Archer, *Buczynski, *Coulthard, *Eckhardt-Gramatté, Pentland, Pépin, *Perrault, and Turner.

The piano quartets of Pentland (1939), *Eggleston (1954–5), Coulthard (*Sketches from a Medieval Town*, 1956), and *Kenins (1958), together with *Kasemets' *Sonata concertante* (1957), are notable additions to repertoire for piano with string trio. For string trio alone, special importance in their respective composers' outputs attaches to two unusually advanced works: the *Trio con Alea* (1966), first of Pentland's several forays into limited aleatorism, and Papineau-Couture's *Slano* (1975), with its consistent sharp dissonances, its lively counterpoint, and its wide range of timbral contrasts indicated by different specific bowing locations.

3 WOODWIND QUINTET. The 1960s and 1970s were remarkable for the increased cultivation of this medium, spurred perhaps by the presence of a number of Canadian professional and student groups for whom it became a specialty. Weinzweig's three-movement *Quintet* (1964) sums up in dry and neatly poised fashion the rhythmic and constructional concerns found in his earlier divertimenti and sonatas; it has been much played. Among other quintets are those by *Adaskin, *Dela (*Petite Suite maritime*), Buczynski, *Fiala, Freedman, Hawkins, *Hétu, *Mather (*Eine kleine Bläsermusik*), Papineau-Couture (*Fantaisie*), and *Weisgarber. The Mather work is inventive in the timbral changes of its opening unisons, and its final section includes two passages in which the instruments are both unmetred and uncoordinated. The chorale-like conclusion of Hawkins' rhythmically complex *Quintet* (1977) corresponds somewhat to the solemn tonal fragments at the end of Cherney's *Notturno* (1974, woodwind quintet with piano). In the latter, all performers are called on to double on percussion instruments and to produce humming and whispering sounds at times; three of the wind players also switch to alternative instruments now and then. In the same composer's *Group Portrait with Piano* (1979) the piano is a stage property only, played into, but not upon, by the quintet members, who, in period costume, end by posing for a photograph against the piano, to a lengthy Schubert quotation. Similar in technique, though not in attitude, is *Saint-Marcoux's *Genesis* (1975), calling for widespread spatial separation of the players, improvised sections scored in chart form, and auxiliary vocal and percussion sounds produced by the quintet.

Derivative of the standard groupings are instrumentations which add to or subtract from the quartet or quintet base. Thus Brott's *Critics' Corner* (1950) adds percussion to the string quartet, *Gellman's *Mythos II* (1968) a flute, Pentland's *Interplay* (1972) an accordion, *Kolinski's *Encounterpoint* (1973) an organ, Adaskin's *Quintet*

(1977) a bassoon, and Gilles Bellemare's *Osmose* (1978) a bass trombone. Thus also a rare chamber-music excursion by Ridout, his *Introduction and Allegro* (1968), joins a violin and a cello to the standard woodwind quintet; the ideas and their treatment in fact suggest a miniature orchestra. Subtraction (ie, using fewer than the standard 4 or 5 parts), of which the string trios noted above are examples, may be found also in variously grouped woodwind trios – two by Pedersen and one each by Archer (*Divertimento*), Michael *Baker (*Five Epigrams*), and Michael *Miller (*In-Talk*).

Brass quintets as self-sufficient chamber-music statements are a relatively new phenomenon, separate from the functional ceremony-music for a handful of brass players epitomized in *Applebaum's *Stratford Festival fanfares (surely the most frequently heard in live performance of any ensemble music in the country). The ceremonial and processional associations of brass are retained to some extent in Beckwith's *Taking a Stand* (1972), for 'five players, eight brass instruments, fourteen music stands, and one platform,' and both this work and Weinzweig's *Pieces of Five* (1976, 'a series of short-long, fast-slow, soft-loud actions') incorporate inflections familiar from jazz playing. The brass quintets of Fleming, Freedman (*Five Rings*), Gellman, Morel and Pentland (*Occasions*) also may be noted.

In the 1960s and 1970s Canadian composers paid markedly greater attention to 'odd' or special groupings in their one-to-a-part instrumental ensembles – in the modern tradition associated with Stravinsky's *Octet for Winds*, Webern's *Concerto, Op 24*, or, more pertinently, postwar European pieces such as Boulez' *Le Marteau sans maître* and Berio's *Circles*. Rather than deriving from the fixed 18th- and 19th-century ensembles, the resultant works aim to create new statements beginning with the choice of a perhaps unique instrumentation.

Some of the new groupings, unique and odd at first, become established by the presence of performing groups seeking new repertoire. Just as the Montreal, *Orford, *Vaghy, and *Purcell string quartets, the *Quebec Woodwind Quintet and the *York Winds, and *Canadian Brass and the Mount Royal Brass Quintet all inspired (and sometimes actually commissioned) new works, so also did the more specialized performing ensembles. To take two examples only, the *Baroque Trio of Montreal inspired, commissioned, and introduced works for the combination of harpsichord, flute, and oboe by Freedman, Hétu, *Jones, Morawetz, Pentland, Schafer, and others, and the *Lyric Arts Trio stimulated a comparable extensive production for flute, voice, and piano, including Weinzweig's action-piece *Trialogue* (1971), the even-more-theatrical *A Tea Symphony* (1972) of *Charpentier, and Freedman's *Pan* (1972). The *Cassenti Players and *Camerata also were responsible for bringing about new works.

Sometimes unique groupings have united several instruments of the same kind, augmenting a perhaps sparse repertoire and providing an experience of shared learning (such works are in demand for students in instrumental classes) and also the hope of an original musical expression. Examples are Malcolm *Forsyth's two trombone quartets, Freedman's bassoon quartet, the clarinet quartets of *Fodi and Weinzweig, *Bottenberg's large number of works for various assemblages of recorders, and – a special case indeed – *Schudel's *Richter 7.8* (1979) for 12 tubas arranged in three antiphonal quartets.

Pioneer works calling for special chamber-music mixtures include Papineau-Couture's *Suite* (1947) for four wind instruments and piano (characteristic of this composer's neoclassic phase), Pentland's *Octet* (1948) for four woodwinds and four brass, and Somers' *Trio* (1950) for flute, violin, and cello. Recollections of the contrasts of sonorities in baroque chamber music are discernible in Kenins' *Concerto a cinque* (1968) for flute, oboe, violin, viola, and piano, although its harmony, linear style, and range of colours are modern features. Buczynski has contributed a number of works introducing novel chamber-music sounds, among which may be cited his *Trio/67* for mandolin, clarinet, and double-bass, with its unusual two-movement structure and the jazz touches of its finale, and his *Quartet/74* for flute, clarinet, cello, and harpsichord and *Trio/74* for harp, bass clarinet, and double-bass, both containing aleatoric devices and passages in a free time-notation; the latter work is distinguished also by its succession of sustained quiet moods. Hawkins' *Remembrances* (1969), for brass trio, harp, and piano, composed in nine segments each based on a verbal phrase, is exceptional in its range of effects, many of them again subtle and quiet; the images and allusions suggested in these sounds and the work's external references (a loon's cry, a fragment from the last piano sonata of Bethoven) lend a meaning which is private and oblique – though nonetheless intense – and more common in poetry than in music.

Schudel's *Set No. 2* (1967) is a double quintet (woodwind quintet plus brass quintet) introducing an original concept of cumulative density in the sequence of 'free' phrases for one, two, four, six, and eventually all ten instruments in the third of its four movements. To this work may be compared (in terms of deliberate contrasts between instrumental sub-groups) Papineau-Couture's *Sextuor* for the combination of woodwind trio and string trio and Pentland's *Septet* for brass trio, string trio, and organ (both 1967). Wilson's *Concerto 5 x 4 x 3* (1970) realizes this tendency more fully, incorporating a string quintet (quartet plus double-bass), a woodwind quartet, and a brass trio in a loose, mobile-like structure containing 'three expositions and three developments for each of the [ensembles]' and conceived to be performed optionally by each ensemble separately or with either or both of the other ensembles. The expositions are strictly notated, while the developments are free and improvisatory. In the full version, acoustic separation of the ensembles is called for, as well as a conductor – the latter representing a borderline situation between chamber music and hall music which, however, for practical reasons is fairly often encountered in the more recent compositions.

Some of the larger mixed-chamber-music groupings prefer arrangements which oppose a solo instrument to a group. This concerto-like feature may not negate, however, chamber music's traditional independence and separateness of each part in the score. Schafer's early (1954) *Concerto* for harpsichord and eight winds, Beckwith's *Circle, With Tangents* (1967) for harpsichord and 13 solo strings, and Cherney's *Chamber Concerto* (1975) for viola and 10 players are examples. Mather's *Ausone* (1978–9), for solo flute with string sextet, two guitars, and two harps, introduces microtonalism as an integral quality: five instruments are tuned a quarter-tone lower than the rest, and the flute part also calls for many quarter-tones; the concerto-like structure helps towards aural clarity. (A precedent in earlier chamber music is Jack *Behrens' *Quartertone Quartet* – composed in 1960, shortly before his emigration to Canada – in which two instruments similarly are tuned slightly apart from the remaining two.)

In newer trends of the 1960s and 1970s, while the stock media are far from neglected, three areas formerly less well established as belonging within chamber music's province – percussion, electronics, and voices – become more and more attractive to composers.

Percussion, a stranger to the classical chamber-music forms, is cultivated extensively in the newer mixed-ensemble groupings. This tendency is seen in such works as *Tremblay's *Champs I* (1965), for piano and two percussionists, and may be traced to the rediscovery in the late-1950s of the music of Varèse, as well as to the strong development in percussion performance, especially in Montreal, around that time. Later, the same tendency intensified through the programs of the new-music societies, the first of which sprang up in the mid-60s, almost always including an exceptionally gifted percussionist or two among their available performers. Moreover, as will be seen with electronics and with the newer vocal techniques, percussion offers the composer an extraordinary range of timbral possibilities.

*Hodkinson's *Interplay* (1966, an award-winner in the JM International Competition for Composers in 1967 provides a typically resourceful illustration, not only in its percussion part but also in the flexibility of the other parts, calling for doublings of piccolo/alto flute and clarinet/alto saxophone, with a double-bass as the fourth member of the ensemble. *Beecroft's *Rasas* (1968) for flute, harp, string trio, percussion, and piano, *Aitken's *Shadows II: Lalitá* (1973) for flute, three cellos, two harps, and two percussion, and *Garant's *Offrande III* (1971) for three cellos, two harps, two percussion, and piano may illustrate the influence of new-music-society programming on instrumentation. The close similarity of the ensembles called for by the two last-named is explained by their initial appearance on the same program. Their musical approaches are quite different, however. Aitken's work conjures up a sensuous oriental atmosphere through its glissandi, flute multiphonics, and fluid treatment of time, and Garant's explores in a more abstract way various time-factors and conglomerates of pitches derived from Bach's *Musical Offering*. Tremblay's *Champs II (Souffles)* (1968) and *Champs III (Vers)* (1969) adopt larger groupings of 13 and 12 instruments respectively, in which percussion is a dominant factor. His *Solstices ('Les Jours et les saisons tournent')* (1971) is scored for flute, clarinet, horn, double-bass, and two percussion, and is both technically advanced and highly visionary in the associations afforded between its chart-notation and the seasonal and geographic conditions of individual performances.

Music for prepared tape has been defined by one Canadian practitioner (Gustav *Ciamaga) as a form of chamber music – on the grounds that its individual strands, while they may be amplified electronically for performance, do not envision the sort of doublings found in orchestral music, the special aural effect of the same line played by 20 violins in unison being in fact virtually impossible to synthesize in an electronic-music laboratory. With prepared-tape, synthesizer, and computer techniques may be combined the various electronic performance aids – for example, the use of amplification, filtering, ring modulation, etc, with live instruments. *Mercure's *Tétrachromie* (1963), for four instruments and prepared tape, represents the first stage of this development with astonishing maturity. Saint-Marcoux's *Episodie II* (1972) for percussion trio with prepared tape and Coulthard's *The Birds of Lansdowne* (1972) for piano trio with taped birdsongs are contrasting examples, the one experimental in its treatment of sonority, the other impressionistically related to the nature paintings of the noted west-coast Canadian artist J. Fenwick Lansdowne. In John *Rea's

... *Wings of Silence* ... (1978), for six instruments and tape, inspired by Milton's *Comus*, the presence of the tape part is to be disguised in performance, with the speakers hidden from the audience. The use of electronic guitar, electronic keyboard, and similar sounds is found in chamber works by Walter *Boudreau, James Montgomery, Allan *Rae, Donald Steven, and others.

Chamber-music combinations including one or more solo voices have a slightly longer history, in which Mathieu's *Deux Poèmes* (1928) for tenor and string quartet, to his own texts; Papineau-Couture's *Eclogues* (1942) for alto voice, flute, and piano, to poems by Pierre Baillargeon; Beckwith's early *The Great Lakes Suite* (1949) for soprano, baritone, clarinet, cello, and piano, to poems by James Reaney; and *Anhalt's *Comments* (1954) for alto voice and piano trio, to clippings from a daily newspaper, give a fair cross-section. More demanding vocally are two quite different works on religious texts – Charpentier's *Trois Poèmes de St-Jean de la Croix* (1954) for alto voice, violin, and cello, and Schafer's *Five Studies on Texts by Prudentius* (1962) for soprano and four flutes. The former develops a non-repetitive diatonic continuity in chant-like melodic lines, long and of an ascetic expression; the latter wraps a florid voice part in a texture of complex canons. An earlier piece by Schafer may be mentioned: his *Minnelieder* (1956) for mezzo-soprano and woodwind quintet, on medieval German poems.

Garant's **Anerca* (1961, rev 1963) for soprano and eight instruments, on English translations of Inuit texts, may be seen in retrospect as establishing a style for works of the succeeding 10-to-15-year period, particularly in the work of composers such as Mather, Tremblay, Beecroft, and Schafer. The trademarks of this style are the wide-ranging expressive devices in the voice parts, by no means confined to conventional singing, and, in the instrumental parts, the dominance of sounds from the harp and mallet-percussion. Major additions to the literature in this period include Mather's *Orphée* (1963) for soprano, piano, and percussion (text, Paul Valéry), his series of five *Madrigals* (1967–73), for one or two voices with various instrumental forces (texts, Nos. 1–4, Saint-Denys-Garneau; No. 5 without text), including (in No. 4) a prepared tape, and his *Musique pour Champigny* (1976) for three voices (again textless) and four instruments; Tremblay's *Kékoba* (1965–7) for three voices, percussion, and ondes Martenot (phonemic text by the composer, adapted from various religious sources) and *Oralléluiants* (1975) for soprano and eight instruments (text, first alleluia for Whitsunday); Beecroft's *Rasas II* (1973, rev 1975) for contralto, six instruments, and tape (text, various sources) and *Rasas III* (1974) for soprano, four instruments, and tape (phonemic text by the composer); and Schafer's **Requiems for the Party-Girl* (1966, later incorporated in his opera *Patria II*) for mezzo-soprano and nine instruments and *Arcana* (1972) for voice and 10 instruments, both to texts by the composer.

Somers' *Twelve Miniatures* (1964) touch on this style at times but achieve an original shape and a particular poignancy of expression. The texts, English translations of Japanese haiku, are arranged in a seasonal order, and the recurrence in the last of phrases from the first provides an effective comment on human perceptions of time. The scoring, for soprano, flute, cello, and harpsichord, the economy of musical means, and the adroit use of silences all provide sonorous correspondences to the intensity and brevity of the oriental poems. Further exploration is indicated in Alain *Gagnon's *Les Oies sauvages* (1973) for voice and seven instruments, including intricate parts for both harpsichord and piano (text, Guy de Maupassant), and in *Vivier's *Lettura di Dante* (1974) for soprano and seven instruments (texts, Dante Alighieri).

In Joachim's *Illumination I* (1965) and *Illumination II* (1969) and in Anhalt's *Foci* (1969), refined concepts of vocal and instrumental chamber music are fused with theatre and mixed media in novel ways. Joachim's two works, notated in free chart form, include live electronics and lighting effects which are integral to performance in determining specifics of dynamics, texture, and duration. *Foci* embraces not only a multi-channel prepared-tape part made up of voices speaking and singing in a variety of languages, but also slide-projections and a scheme of ritualistic entrances and exits for the performers (10 instrumentalists, with a solo soprano in the extended finale only).

Finally, in this summary, a few typical works of the late 1970s – Fodi's *Western Wynde* (1979), Alexina Louie's *Lotus I* (1978), and various pieces by *Druick – may indicate future preoccupations: detailed reference to historical musical models, sonorities imitative of far-eastern music, and concentration on the thorough working-out of small motives and rhythms, ie, minimalism.

This summary has been sketched by examples, selected to illustrate highlights and main trends. The chamber music catalogue of the *CMCentre, arranged by instrumentation, indicates the considerably fuller extent of the repertoire.

BIBLIOGRAPHY
Bridle, Augustus. 'Chamber music in Toronto,' *The Year Book of Canadian Art 1913*, compiled by the Arts and Letters Club (Toronto, London 1913)
Laurendeau, Arthur. 'Chamber and church music in Montreal,' ibid
Loudon, J.S. ' Reminiscences of chamber music in Toronto during the past forty years,' *CanJM*, Jul–Aug 1914
Adeney, Marcus. 'Chamber music,' *Music in Canada*
CMCentre. *Catalogue of Chamber Music* (Toronto 1967; suppls 1971, 1976; 2nd edn 1980)
Skelton, Robert A. 'Weinzweig, Gould, Schafer: three Canadian string quartets,' unpubl D MUS thesis, Indiana U 1976
JB

The Chamber Players of Toronto. A 15-piece string ensemble formed in 1968 by the players themselves and directed until 1977 from the first chair by the violinist Victor Martin. The success of the first two concerts (20 Feb and 10 Apr 1969 at *St Lawrence Hall) led to a three-concert subscription series 1969–70 at Walter Hall, *U of Toronto. In the 1973–4 season they doubled the number of concerts in their series by repeating each program, and in the 1975–6 season they tripled it by scheduling an alternative series. The main series was devoted to the baroque and classical repertoires, the alternative series to a mixture of baroque, romantic, and contemporary works. The players have performed in other Ontario centres and in Quebec City, have broadcast on CJRT FM (Toronto) and CBC radio and TV, and have given concerts in schools and at summer music camps.

The Chamber Players of Toronto commissioned and premiered Lothar *Klein's *Passacaglia of the Zodiac* 15 Apr 1972, Keith *Bissell's *Variations on a Canadian Folk Song* 24 Feb 1973, Srul I. *Glick's *Symphonic Elegy* 20 Apr 1974, Godfrey *Ridout's *Concerto Grosso* 18 Jan 1975, and Murray *Adaskin's *In Praise of Canadian Painting in the Thirties* 24 Jan 1976. Soloists have included Robert *Aitken, Martin Berinbaum, André Bernard, Lorand *Fenyves, José-Luis Garcia, Victor Martin, Miguel Rubio, Tsuyoshi *Tsutsumi, and Narciso Yepes. In 1977 Martin returned to Spain. Marta *Hidy, who conducted 1977–9, was succeeded by Winston Webber. The managers of the Chamber Players of Toronto have been Mabel H. Laine 1969–79 and Barbara Mancktelow and Pat Carter, who became joint managers in 1979.

During his nine years in Canada Victor Martin (b Elne, France, of Spanish parents, 24 Sep 1940; a pupil of Antonio Arias, Lorand Fenyves, and Max Rostal) taught at the U of Toronto and toured regularly in Europe, where as a soloist he made more than 10 LPs, listed in *Discopaedia*. He also recorded for the CBC (1975, CBC SM-289) and the Masters of the Bow series (1978, MBS 2003).

DISCOGRAPHY
Glick *Gathering In*. 1972. RCI 389
Ridout *Concerto Grosso* – Rodrigo – Bissell *Variations on a Canadian Folk Song* – Leclair-Ysaye. Martin vn, Brough pf. 1975. CBC SM 289

BIBLIOGRAPHY
'In the shadow of the giants,' *OCan*, vol 5, May–Jul 1978
PS

CHAMPAGNE (b Desparois dit Champagne), **Claude** (Adonaï). Composer, educator, b Montreal 27 May 1891, d there 21 Dec 1965; hon D MUS (Montreal) 1946. Little is known about his early life, except that his family nurtured the growth of his musical talents. His father, born Desparois and descended from a Parisian family, encouraged him to participate in various musical activities. His mother was Irish and is said to have taught him hymns. His grandfather, a fiddler well known in the Repentigny region, exercised an influence on his aural development, as is seen later in his appreciation of the modal sounds of Canadian folk music.

Champagne began piano and theory at 10 with Orpha-F. *Deveaux and continued with Romain-Octave *Pelletier. At 14 he studied the violin with Albert *Chamberland, and this became his favourite instrument. He earned his diplomas from private institutions: the *Dominion College of Music (theory and piano, 1906) and the *Cons national of Montreal (piano, 1909) where the teaching, he later said, left something to be desired (letter to Doctor Grondin, director of the Maison des étudiants canadiens in Paris, 17 Feb 1928). Between 1910 and 1921 he taught piano, violin, and other instruments at the Varennes and Longueuil colleges; extended his knowledge of instruments (particularly the viola and the saxophone) through his participation in the *Canadian Grenadier Guards Band directed by J.-J. *Gagnier; gave private lessons in theory and harmony; became the accompanist of choirs such as that of the Maisonneuve district, and furthermore, played violin during the intermissions at the National, a variety theatre.

Champagne was already composing. He wrote *Ballade des lutins* (1914) for the Grenadier Guards and background music for *Ils sont un peuple sans histoire* (1917), a 'historical scene' by Brother Marie-Victorin performed at Varennes College and later in Montreal (1918). A meeting with Alfred *Laliberté, arranged by Rodolphe *Mathieu, was a turning point for him as a composer. The rough manuscript of *Hercule et Omphale* (1918) moved Laliberté, who saw in it the evidence of a major talent for composition, to find the funds necessary to underwrite Champagne's studies in Paris 1921–8.

Champagne went first to Brussels, with the intention of studying with the composer Paul Gilson. The latter, however, persuaded him to look in Paris for an atmosphere more conducive to the full development of his talent. He acquired the essentials of his craft there. At the Paris Cons he studied counterpoint and fugue first with André Gedalge, then with his successor, Charles Koech-

Claude Champagne

lin, and composition and orchestration with Raoul Laparra. The influence of these teachers and the advice of Paul Dukas, among others, account for the definitely French flavour of Champagne's writing. He continued violin studies with Jules Conus. At the Schola cantorum – where he met Vincent d'Indy – he joined the choir and, on occasion, coached the trio. He exercised his talents as an accompanist at the Babaïan Concerts. In between these numerous activities he enjoyed moments of leisure at the Café Dreher, filling numerous notebooks with musical ideas, and he also did cataloguing work on behalf of the Public Archives of Canada. *Hercule et Omphale* was performed 31 Mar 1926 by the symphony orchestra of the Artistes du conservatoire conducted by Juan Manen, and the *Suite canadienne* 20 Oct 1928 by the Concerts Pasdeloup orchestra directed by Rhené-Baton at the Champs-Élysées Theatre. (The *Suite* won an E.W. Beatty prize ($750) in the 1928 *CPR Festivals, and Champagne himself conducted the *Montreal Orchestra in its Canadian premiere 5 Mar 1933.)

Champagne returned to Montreal in December 1928 with his wife, Jeanne Marchal of Liège, whom he had married in 1922 in Paris. In Montreal the needs of the community had changed. The needs were greater on the organizational and administrative levels, and particularly in teaching. Champagne, nearing 40, therefore found it necessary to divide his time between teaching, administration, and composition. In the unstable period 1930–7 he undertook the most diverse tasks, among them appointments to the staffs of new schools of music where women's religious orders such as the Sisters of the Holy Names of Jesus and Mary (*École Vincent-d'Indy), the Congrégation Notre-Dame (*École normale de musique), and the Sisters of St Anne (École supérieure de musique de Lachine) laid the foundation of a more structured musical training. He also taught harmony and composition 1932–41 at *McGill U and worked 1934–42 for the Catholic School Commission in Montreal as director of musical instruction, training primary school teachers and editing five solfège teaching manuals.

In 1942 he left the commission to become assistant director of the new *CMM, of which he had been a major proponent. His specific duties included those of director of studies and curriculum planning. Champagne played an important part in the development of many composers – students at the CMM and McGill who benefited as much from their informal apprenticeships with him as from the formal classes. Among those who worked under his direction were Violet *Archer, Jocelyne *Binet, François *Brassard, Maurice *Dela, Marvin *Duchow, Richard *Eaton, Serge *Garant, Rhené *Jaque, Roger *Matton, Pierre

A page from *Altitude* by Claude Champagne

*Mercure, François *Morel, Clermont *Pépin, Gilles *Tremblay, Robert *Turner, and Jean *Vallerand. Champagne came to be recognized as an influential and respected musician, involved in a variety of activities in addition to his composition and teaching. He served as chief editor for BMI Canada's department of publication for Canadian works 1949–65, as an adjudicator or juror for many competitions, and as a Canadian representative at international conferences (eg, in 1946 the Cons of Rio de Janeiro invited him to give a series of lectures, and during his stay he conducted the Brazil SO in his *Symphonie gaspésienne*; in 1948 he represented Canada at the International Conference of Folk Music in Basel, Switzerland). Naturally these numerous tasks lessened his musical production. Between the *Symphonie gaspésienne* (1945) and *Altitude* (1959) only three or four important works appeared.

In 1964 a 'Claude Champagne Year' was celebrated, dedicated partly to Champagne the composer and even more to Champagne the servant of music, concerned about the development of the art in a young country and willing to do his utmost to meet the requirements of that development. As part of the celebration, the *NFB produced *Bonsoir Claude Champagne* and CBC TV presented 'Hommage à Claude Champagne' in recognition of this important figure. That year also saw the inauguration of the *Salle Claude-Champagne at the École Vincent-d'Indy.

Champagne's art cannot be understood entirely without considering cultural context of his environment and his era. He worked and matured in a Quebec environment which affirmed its adherence to French civilization, deferring to France as the final arbiter of thought, and in a musical era in which a return to cultural roots made a reconsideration of folk music and indigenous popular art appear to be the only means of investing the arts of modern Canada with a really homegrown flavour (on this subject see the writings of Eugène *Lapierre). In this area as well, France influenced the apprenticeship of musicians (the early years of the 20th century were particularly favourable for studies in France) because of the efforts of French composers and scholars to revitalize outworn themes and harmonies through a return to modality. (Solesmes reform, Niedermeyer school). Champagne entered this stream naturally. Clarity, order, discipline, all the traditional earmarks of French art are reflected in his musical language. No one knew better than Léo-Pol *Morin how to describe the charm and subtlety of this music: 'A refined art, extremely civilized, with rounded corners, which seeks a beautiful outline, beautiful forms, precision and conciseness. No waste, no rough edges, no hesitancy ever interferes with the style of this musician, one of the best informed and most balanced of his generation' (*Papiers de musique*). Champagne was not affected by constraints. He left to his intuition the job of defining the impressions that he perceived around him. Further, although he may not have felt the need to abandon his music's continuing over-reliance on 19th-century procedures, he at least developed it with true mastery. The inspiration which he drew from folk music did not lead him to forge a specific idiom in the sense that Bartók did. When he borrowed themes from folk music, they were used unaltered. Occasionally, in the *Suite canadienne* for example, an interesting curtailment of the phrasing puts into relief a countermelody introduced with care and seeming naturalness. His instrumentation is classical and creates a transparency that closely unites the medium to the content. His harmony is assimilated naturally into the lyricism of the melody and becomes songlike itself, in the sense of Franck, Fauré, and even Debussy. The *Symphonie gaspésienne* is a long symphonic poem which, in 1945, attested to Champagne's fondness for a kind of melody not infinitely prolonged as in Debussy (the unstable cadence of the Debussyan tonic, the whole-tone scale, the combining of keys and modes, resulting in a chromaticism which gives his melody the effect of endlessness) but unceasingly renewed as in Schumann (the established diatonic organization in which, among other things, the harmonic steps may be discerned, as well as the forthrightness, the alternation of episodic structures, and the relaxed combining of motifs). Over harmonies of superimposed fifths, the shape of the phrase links one cadence to the next, in major and natural-minor tonalities (with frequent use also of the Dorian and Aeolian modes), creating fleeting impressions on pillars of sound, which like the long-held notes of a medieval cantus firmus lend the whole a calm serenity. The *String Quartet*, a terse work of an admirable polyphonic texture with bold discords, is a remarkable example of synthesis and at the same time a foretaste of a new departure in Champagne's writing, surprising at this ripe stage of his career. *Altitude*, an extended fresco in sound and the composer's last major work, stands at the threshold of a new acoustic world, a vast and promising horizon which Champagne's style seems ready to move towards as it attains a renewed maturity. Claude Champagne's works were to epitomize for a certain time the musical and artistic aspirations of French-speaking Canadians.

Champagne was honorary president of the Canadian Arts Council (later *CCA) and, in this capacity, a member of the International Music Council of Unesco. He became an honorary member of the *CLComp in 1956. In 1963 he was awarded the *Canada Council Medal. The town of Outremont in Montreal gave his name to the avenue adjacent to the École Vincent-d'Indy. Large portions of his personal documents and manuscripts were deposited in the *NL of C and at the Archives nationales du Québec. The *CMCentre has granted him the associate status reserved for deceased composers whose work the centre holds. The musical rights of his estate are administered by PRO Canada.

COMPOSITIONS
ORCHESTRA
Hercule et Omphale. 1918 (Paris 1926). Full orch. Ber (rental)
Berceuse. 1933. Sm orch. Ber (rental)
Évocation. 1943. Sm orch. Ms
Symphonie gaspésienne. 1944 titled *Gaspésia*, rev 1945 with present title (Mtl 1944, rev Mtl 1947). Full orch. BMIC 1956. RCI 216/RCA CCS-1010 (J.-M. *Beaudet)
Concerto in D Minor. 1948 (Mtl 1950). Pf, orch. Ber (rental). RCI 17 (*Chotem)
Paysanna. 1953. Sm orch. Ber 1979. RCI 90 (R. *Leduc)/CBC SM-214 (*CBC Van Champ O)
CHORUS AND ORCHESTRA
Suite canadienne. 1927. SATB, sm orch. Durand 1929 (v, pf). RCI: Canadian album No. 1/RCA DM 1229 (*Cantoria)
Images du Canada français. 1943 (Mtl 1947). SATB, full orch. Ber (rental). RCI 152 (R. *Leduc)
Altitude. 1959 (Tor 1960). SATB, full orch. BMIC 1961. RCI 179 (*CBC SO)
CHAMBER MUSIC
Danse villageoise, 4 versions: 1 / 1929. Vn, pf. Fassio 1949. Ber (rental). Acadia 300CB (*LeBlanc). 2 / Ca 1936. Str quar. 3 / nd. Str orch, hp, pf. BMIC 1961. RCI 6 (J.-M. *Beaudet)/CTL S 5030 (*Hart House O). 4 / After 1954. Orch. Ber 1974. Dom S-1372 (*Feldbrill). A version for hmca and pf arranged and recorded by Claude Garden, with Richard *Gresko, pf (RCI 443)
Habanera. 1929. Vn, pf. CMCentre
String Quartet. 1954 (Mtl 1954). Ber 1974. RCI 143 (*Mtl Str Quar)
Suite miniature, 2 versions: 1 / 1958. Fl (vn), vc (v da gamba), hpd (pf). CMCentre. 2 / Titled *Concertino grosso*. 1963. Str quin. CMCentre
8 (early) works of his youth (waltzes, incidental music, etc) for instr ens
Several untitled educational pieces for vn
KEYBOARD
Prélude et Filigrane. 1918. Pf. BMIC 1960. 1974. RCI 397 (J. Holtzman)
Quadrilha brasileira. 1942. Pf. BMIC 1951. RCI 252 (J. *Dufresne)/(1974) RCI 397 (J. Holtzman)
Tocane pour un clown. 1962. Pf. Ms
Prière 'à la mémoire d'Henri Gagnon.' 1963. Org. Ms. RCI 254 (*Mérineau)
Educational pieces for pf, including *Exercises pratiques de lecture à vue / Practical Sight Reading Exercises for Piano Students*, compiled by Boris Berlin and published by GVT
VOICE
1 *Arrangements of folksongs*
'À St-Malo.' TTBB. Orphéon 1939
'C'est la belle Françoise' / 'Lovely Frances' (transl A.B. England). SSAA or TTBB. Wat 1960
'Dans Paris' / 'In Paris' (transl A.B. England). V, pf. FH 1961
'En roulant ma boule.' SATB. CMCentre
'Gai lon là, gai le rosier.' SSAA or TTBB. Orphéon 1939
'Isabeau s'y promène' / 'Isabel Went Walking' (transl A.B. England). SSAA or TTBB. Wat 1960
'Le Nez de Martin' (transl A.B. England). SS or AA, guit (hp or pf). Wat 1962
'Marianne s'en va-t-au moulin' / 'Marianne Went to the Mill' (transl A.B. England). V, pf. FH 1959
'Noël Huron.' SATB, sm orch. CMCentre
'Petit Jean' (transl A.B. England). V, pf. FH 1959
'The Rosebush' (transl A.B. England of 'Gai lon là, gai le rosier'). SSAA or TTBB. Wat 1960
'Une perdriole.' SATB. CMCentre
'V'là l'bon vent' / 'Fair Wind' (transl A.B. England). SSAA or TTBB. Wat 1960
'Voici le temps et la saison' / 'This Is Time and Season' (transl A.B. England). SS or SA, guit (hp or pf). Wat 1962
19 unpubl arr of folksongs
2 *Other works*
'Ave Maria.' 1924. TBB BMIC 1954. RCI 206 (*Mtl Bach Choir)
'Easter' (transl A.B. England). V, pf. Peer 1966
'La Laurentienne' (A. Plouffe). V, pf. Arch 1938
Missa brevis. 1951. 3 vs, org. BMIC 1954
'Scoutisme' (A. Plouffe). V, pf. Arch
'For the Christ Child'; 'Frost in the Air'; 'Thanksgiving' (A.B. England). V, pf. Peer 1966
6 unpubl works for soloist or choir; 8 educational pieces, 5 of which are publ by Arch
Also 5 instr works listed in catalogues but unlocated

WRITINGS
Initiation pratique au solfège (Montreal 1938)
Solfège pratique (Montreal 1939)
Solfège scolaire (Montreal 1940)
Solfège pédagogique (Montreal 1948)
Solfèges manuscrits à changements de clefs: 44 leçons pour voix moyennes, vol 1 (Montreal 1958)
'Leçons à Radio-Collège,' ms

DISCOGRAPHY
Several of Champagne's harmonizations of folksongs are included on the LP *Folklore du Québec* by the Petit Ensemble vocal of the École normale de musique, conducted by Champagne.

BIBLIOGRAPHY
INVENTORIES COMPILED BY MARVIN DUCHOW
'An auxiliary collection of books and scores in the library of Claude Champagne ...' ms 1972, U of Montreal library
'Claude Champagne: inventory of his manuscripts and other documents,' ms 1972, NL of C
'Inventory list of the compositions of Claude Champagne,' *CAUSM J*, vol 2, Autumn 1972
'Detailed inventory of the Claude Champagne archive,' ms 1973, NL of C
'A selective list of correspondents drawn from the personal documents of Claude Champagne,' *CAUSM J*, vol 3, Autumn 1973
'Melodies from André Gedalge's *L'Enseignement de la musique par l'éducation méthodique de l'oreille* in the undated Claude Champagne workbook: an index and thematic catalogue,' ms 1974, NL of C
'Some early Champagne documents in the National Library collection,' paper, CAUSM meeting, U of Toronto, 3 Jun 1974
'A summary account and partial inventory of the Claude Champagne collection,' *CAUSM J*, vol 4, Autumn 1974
'A summary account and partial inventory of the Claude Champagne collection – section IV: recorded materials,' ibid, vol 5, Spring 1975
'Thematic index of Claude Champagne's pedagogical material,' card file 1977, NL of C
THESES
Pilote, Gilles. 'L'enseignement du solfège dans les écoles élémentaires de la CECM: Claude Champagne et ses contributions,' unpubl MMA thesis, McGill 1970
Provost, Marie-Paule. 'Claude Champagne, l'un des nôtres,' unpubl L MUS thesis, U of Montreal 1970
Bail-Milot, Louise. 'L'oeuvre et les procédés de composition chez Claude Champagne,' unpubl M MUS thesis, U of Paris, Sorbonne 1972
Walsh, Anne. 'The life and works of Claude Adonaï Champagne,' unpubl PH D thesis, Catholic U 1972
ARTICLES
Morin, Léo-Pol. 'Le retour de M. Claude Champagne,' *La Lyre*, vol 6, Jan 1929
'Notre portrait, Claude Champagne,' ibid, vol 8, Aug–Sep 1930
Morin, Léo-Pol. 'Claude Champagne,' *Papiers de musique* (Montreal 1930)
– 'Claude Champagne,' *Musique* (Montreal 1955)
Clopoys, Andrew. 'Claude Champagne, a distinguished Canadian composer,' *CRMA*, vol 5, Dec–Jan 1946–7
Brassard, François. 'Une date pour la musique canadienne,' *R de l'U Laval*, Apr 1951
Tour Fondue, Geneviève de la. 'Claude Champagne,' *Interviews canadiennes* (Montreal 1952)
Bisbrouck, Noël. 'Portrait de compositeur canadien, Claude Champagne,' *Jmc*, Nov 1954
Archer, Thomas. 'Claude Champagne,' *CMJ*, vol 2, Winter 1958
Desautels, Andrée. 'Claude Champagne, maître d'oeuvres,' *Jmc*, Apr 1963
'Hommage à Claude Champagne,' *Jmc*, Jan 1965
Duchow, Marvin. 'Claude Champagne,' *MSc*, 243, Sep–Oct 1968
'Composer's widow collecting manuscripts,' *MSc*, 265, May–Jun 1972
Desautels, Andrée. 'The history of Canadian composition 1610–1967,' *Aspects of Music in Canada*
Bail-Milot, Louise. 'Claude Champagne,' *Contemporary Canadian Composers / Compositeurs canadiens contemporains*
CMCentre. *Compositeurs au Québec: Claude Champagne* (Montreal 1979)
Dictionary of Contemporary Music LB-M

CHANNON, Constance (m Douglass). Pianist, b Calgary 20 Dec 1937; ARCT 1956, diplomas (Juilliard) 1962, 1963. After studies with Gladys *Egbert in Calgary and a *JMC tour in 1959 she attended the Juilliard School 1960–4 for training with Irwin Freundlich. A winner in the 1964 *CBC Talent Festival, she made her New York debut in 1965 at Town Hall, then studied in Rome with Guido Agosti. She has made solo appearances with the *Calgary SO and the *Calgary Philharmonic, the *CBC Winnipeg and Toronto orchestras, the *Quebec SO, the *MSO, and the Bayerischer Rundfunk in Munich. She has performed frequently on CBC radio's 'Distinguished Artists' and has recorded works by Mozart, Prokofiev, Scriabin, and Schumann (1969, CBC SM 109). JS

Chanson in Quebec. It is through the oral folk tradition, deriving its essential qualities from European folkore, that the Quebec chanson has carved out its privileged position. Perhaps one Canadian folksong in 20 originated in Canada; the rest were imported: Irish and Scottish rhythms thus merged with French ones, and popular songs with folksongs. Despite their continual battle with the present, folksongs were the great forerunner of the Quebec chanson (formerly known as 'la chanson de l'expression française').

Popular artists such as La *Bolduc, Paul-Émile *Corbeil, Eugène *Daignault, Lionel *Daunais, Conrad *Gauthier, Ovila *Légaré, Charles *Marchand, and the *Alouette Vocal Quartet continued the folksong tradition in an urban and industrial context, seeking to entertain people at a time (1920–45) when living conditions were difficult.

La Bolduc and Lionel Daunais were among the first to seek inspiration in the reality of Quebec life. Drawing on both folk music and the chansonnette, the art of Daunais changed the face of the popular song, stamping it with a new delicacy and optimism. In his book *La Chanson québécoise* Benoît L'Herbier relates the singer's words: 'I wanted to do Canadian songs, not French ones. I tried to give them local colour by using words or expressions from these parts but without slipping straight into folk music. I used the structure of folk music because I wanted there to be something "québécois" about them.'

The humour, the jig-like rhythms, and the vulgar doggerel of La Bolduc were in sharp contrast to the out-and-out sentimentality, the maudlin radio serials, of the 1930s. Alain Sylvain wrote in *La Chanson française*: 'La Bolduc not only has an innate and probably unconscious sense of verbal fantasy; she manages to surprise us still, after several hearings of the same song, by her off-hand alignment of words, and by the most hilarious juxtapositions, all of which most certainly would delight a Jacques Prévert, for example, presuming, of course, that the author of *Paroles* was familiar with her recordings.'

The Veillées du bon vieux temps, 1921–41 at the Monument national in Montreal, made folk music and popular song a part of the traditional background. French and US songs had dominated radio and cabaret since 1930. Fernand Perron (pseudonym Le Merle rouge) was the counterpart of Tino Rossi, and Jean Sablon, of Bing Crosby. Wishing to be universally recognized, Quebec artists performed their pop songs in a Paris or New York manner.

With an altogether different idea in mind, in 1937 Father Charles-Émile *Gadbois determined, through La *Bonne Chanson, to popularize folksongs and songs of religious and patriotic inspiration, both those of French origin and those of Quebec.

From Albert Larrieu to Théodore Botrel (two French composer-performers who toured Quebec several times between 1910 and 1925), the chanson served as a guide to popular values, as the beauty of the most-favoured works attests. Then in 1938 came the French singer-composer Charles Trenet, who was to become famous and whose influence in Quebec was enormous. His songs, eg, 'La Route enchantée,' 'Le Grand Café,' and 'Les Oiseaux de Paris,' were a familiar part of the Quebec singer's repertoire.

A little later, Fernand Robidoux organized the competition 'La Feuille d'érable' (Maple Leaf) to sound a Canadian note in the songs heard on the radio. Radio station CKVL Verdun's 'Parade de la chansonnette française,' with the Quebec singer and entertainer Jacques Normand as host, helped re-establish the French popular song, whose progress in Quebec had been interrupted by World War II. However, the desire to produce something original, either in the chanson or elsewhere, was non-existent, despite the US hits sung by Robidoux in French translations and certain of Robert *L'Herbier's compositions in a style borrowed directly from the chanson of France.

The advent of TV in the early 1950s, which introduced the new chansonniers to the public, brought a fresh outlook to the Quebec scene. Radio began to broadcast programs devoted to the so-called 'Canadian chanson,' including 'Baptiste et Marianne' with Guy Mauffette in 1951. The CBC's *'Concours de la chanson canadienne,' organized in 1956, gave the Quebec chanson an important initial impetus. As the host at Montreal cabarets such as the Au Faisan doré and the Au St-Germain-des-Prés, Jacques Normand promoted the emerging talents of *Aglaé, Clémence *Desrochers, Serge Deyglun, Raymond *Lévesque, and Monique *Leyrac. Combining the formulae of the chansonniers of Montmartre and the pop singers of North America, the singers at the Faisan doré attracted an audience different from that of the more traditional cabarets.

In another connection entirely, the country song should be viewed as the perpetuation of a certain circumstantial lyricism whose first and last representative was Rolland (Le Soldat) *Lebrun. In Lebrun's wake, in the sombre post-war period, came the western music phenomenon with its essentially US influences. With Willie *Lamothe, country and western music in Quebec came into its own; it subsequently was to acquire considerable industrial power (see also Country music).

The particular achievement of the chansonnier of Quebec – the Quebec chanson – was a synthesis, stemming from the union of folk music and poetry, influenced by the songwriters of France. In 1959 new voices already were making themselves heard: Aglaé, Hélène *Baillargeon, Jacques Blanchet, Lionel Daunais, Jacques *Labrecque, Ovila Légaré, Raymond Lévesque, Monique Leyrac, Pierre Pétel, and, the most distinguished of all, Félix *Leclerc. It was through Leclerc that the newly created Quebec chanson was to serve as the natural channel for the collective identity of the people of Quebec. While taking diverse approaches individually, the Bozos (see Chansonniers) were among the first chansonniers whose songs tended to introspection, coupled with a penchant for pseudo-lyricism. They were the aesthetes of the chanson, Claude *Léveillée contributing to the genre a melodic breadth not previously attained, and Jean-Pierre *Ferland also emerging as a melodist.

After 1960 the *boîtes à chansons and the chansonniers increased in number concurrently with the socio-political ferment known as Quebec's Quiet Revolution. At the same time the popular song – which through the efforts of Michel *Louvain had reached a turning point in 1957 – was on the rise, sung by Joël Denis, Fernand Gignac, Pierre *Lalonde, Donald *Lautrec, Margot Lefèbvre, Ginette *Ravel, Ginette *Reno, Michèle *Richard, Ginette Sage, and Pière Sénécal.

Rhythms novel in the world of pop music shook traditional thinking in several ways, and the arrival on the scene of the Beatles in 1964 transformed popular music around the world. Along with many other places, Quebec experienced a rash of musical and vocal groups. Most of these groups, however, lacked composers to provide them with material, and though they tried to compensate for lack of musical originality with sartorial disguises (Les Gants blancs, Les Classels, César et ces Romains, Les Sultans, and others) they did not survive.

The mixing of genres that occurred in the USA was not lost on Robert *Charlebois, who took up both the music and the language. His outlandish stage show *L'Osstidcho* (1968), in which Louise *Forestier and others participated, hastened the end of one era and the beginning of another. After that, the gates were opened wide to musical experimentation, usually by the group seeking to establish its own music in the face of foreign imports and cultural stagnation.

Some groups, such as Les *Séguin, *Beau Dommage, Jim (Corcoran) et Bertrand (Gosselin), subjected the music to a prolonged poetical treatment. Taking a fresh approach to folk music, Jocelyn Bérubé, Breton-Cyr, Louise Forestier, Garolou, Les Karricks, Le clan Murphy, Le Rêve du diable, Raoul *Roy, and Quebreizh have endeavoured to return to the source while maintaining a modern approach. By 1980 a new folk movement, involving such performers as Jim et Bertrand, François Guy, Plume Latraverse, Paul Piché, Fabienne Thibeault, Guy Trépanier, and Gilles *Valiquette, was being built around North American rhythms.

The Quebec chanson has absorbed a mixture of electronics and tradition. Some singers have performed light rock with simple lyrics in the vernacular. Their songs are spontaneous, anecdotal, dealing with city life (like those of Beau Dommage), and recall the idealism of the early chansonniers (as in the lyricism of Jean Lapointe). A product of the *Cegeps, Paul Piché has seemed a successor to Louise Forestier musically, while following more in the footsteps of Félix Leclerc in the realm of nationalistic ideas. Others, such as Marie-Claire Séguin, Jim Corcoran, and Michel Rivard, have derived originality from the group experience. Their slightly more aggressive music has explored the fields of rock and jazz.

Describing pop groups in *La Presse*, 29 Mar 1975, Georges-Hébert Germain wrote: 'Their music is effecting a radical and fundamental transformation of all popular music, for the very reason that it appeals to the musicians and chansonniers themselves in precisely the same way as pure science appeals to the applied sciences.' While expressing themselves differently and with quite distinct philosophies, groups such as Aut'Chose, *Harmonium, Héritage, *Maneige, *Octobre, and *Offenbach, along with a number of English and US groups, have engaged in highly original research at the level of language, rhythm, timbre, and sonority, while assimilating existing genres into their own individual styles to varying degrees.

At the outer limit of this trend the instrumental duo Dionne-Brégent, the most radical of all those using the musical material of the chanson, is concerned with its sound possibilities and its use in purely musical invention, in an attempt to touch the highest spheres of consciousness. Though contemporary and experimental in treatment, the duo's music also seeks to synthesize various musical styles: jazz, rock, and classical.

In his book *Québec, chant des possibles* Guy Millière presents Raoul *Duguay as the inspiration behind the broad trends leading to the ascendancy of author-composers in the late 1970s. Their music places the Quebec chanson in the hour of peace, stripped of the artifices of fashion. Their combined strength brought about the abolition of clichés, including the traditional concept of the Quebec artist, along with a return to the source in the direction of a certain anonymity calling for the individual to withdraw in favour of a collective approach.

As early as 1965 Stéphane *Venne observed in *Liberté*: 'The Quebec chanson has been loaded down with an impossible burden; that of being for Quebeckers what jazz is for the American blacks, opera for the Italians and so forth. A pivot of Quebec culture; a passport to all the countries in the world.' By 1980 the Quebec chanson had emerged from that cultural framework and from the restrictions it had imposed upon musical possibilities. It had acquired the prerequisites for an international existence. It was thus that the Quebec chanson enabled Quebec to see herself as she was, to open herself to the world, and to leave her mark on it.

Various movements have sprung up to promote the cause of the chanson in Quebec as well as the professional status of its performers. One of these, Action-Chanson, began publishing the review *Pourquoi chanter?* in 1977. In the late 1970s the Quebec chanson became involved anew in rebuilding a French culture in Quebec with the people of Quebec as custodians. In finding an authentic resonance for the language of Quebec it assumed a representative character, articulating the cultural values for which the Québécois have stood in North America, and its birth and evolution reaffirmed the dignity of the Quebec people. 'We are interesting,' explained Gilles *Vigneault, 'as a symbol of America's cry of liberty and, in an exactly opposite sense, of the people she oppresses' (*Propos de Gilles Vigneault*, Marc Gagné, Montreal 1974).

See also Folk music, Franco-Canadian; Rock.

BIBLIOGRAPHY
Belleau, André et al. 'Pour la chanson,' *Liberté*, vol 8, Jul–Aug 1966
Gagnon, Lysiane. 'La chanson,' *Culture vivante*, 5, Jan–Feb 1967
L'Herbier, Benoît. *La Chanson québécoise* (Montreal 1974)
Normand, Jacques. *Les Nuits de Montréal* (Montreal 1974)
Germain, Georges-Hébert. 'Maneige: la musique, c'est un monde en soi,' Montreal *La Presse*, 29 Mar 1975
Dor, Georges. *Si tu savais ...* (Montreal 1977)
Roy, Bruno. *Panorama de la chanson au Québec* (Montreal 1977)
Millière, Guy. *Québec, chant des possibles* (Paris 1978)
Blow up
La Chanson au Québec
La Chanson française
Chansonniers du Québec
Pionniers du disque folklorique

BR

Chansonniers. Singer-songwriters of the indigenous popular songs of Quebec, especially after World War II. Their songs served a common social ideal and shared a style of utterance and manner of performance whose simplicity and intimate character were conducive to poetic expression.

Félix *Leclerc and Raymond *Lévesque were the originators of this new species and of the movement it generated, though some historians point to La *Bolduc and even Rolland (Le Soldat) *Lebrun as its predecessors. Even the singer Emmanuel *Blain de Saint-Aubin, who came to Canada in 1857 and composed his first song, words and music, in 1865, could be considered a chansonnier. As early as 1842 T.F. *Molt, through newspaper announcements, called upon 'the chansonniers of Canada to send him Canadian chansons' for inclusion in an anthology.

In the years following what is known as Quebec's Quiet Revolution, which began in the 1960s, the chansonniers remained an inspiration to the collective phenomenon of writer-composer-performers whose outlook was aesthetic before it was social or political. 'We were voices,' declared Gilles *Vigneault, 'it was their hands that changed everything' (*Passer l'hiver*, Paris 1978). Jacques Blanchet, Hervé Brousseau, Pierre Calvé, Clémence *Desrochers, Georges *Dor, Jean-Pierre *Ferland, Jean-Paul Filion, Claude *Gauthier, Sylvain Lelièvre, Pierre Létourneau, Claude *Léveillée, Raymond Lévesque, Monique *Miville-Deschênes, Marie Savard, Gilles Vigneault – all these and many others were preceded, and in many cases influenced, by Félix Leclerc. Leclerc had prepared the way for this popular vogue of the solitary singer who would play his or her own accompaniment on the guitar.

In its initial sense of a writer of popular songs, the word 'chansonnier' (ie, 'songer' or 'songmaker') has retained over the years a meaning closely linked to the spirit of the poet-singers of the time of the Crusades – the troubadours and trouvères. In France, the term has designated performers in cellar bars who have based their lyrics on current events.

In the 1940s Jacques Normand continued this Montmartre tradition in the Montreal cabarets, assuming the role of a singing commentator, and treating the events of the day in a style marked by political and social satire. In the same way, certain other chansonniers subjected everyday events to close scrutiny, notably Jean-Pierre Ferland ('Les Journalistes'), Robert *Charlebois ('Marche du président'), and Gilles Vigneault ('Lettre de Ti-Cul Lachance à son sous-ministre'). Others, such as Raymond Lévesque, Jean-Guy Moreau, and Yvon Deschamps, also developed an alert and incisive style in both their songs and their monologues.

The 1950s, with Charles Trenet in France, invested the word 'chansonnier' with a more particular meaning, one which affected Quebec: that of an individual who becomes identified with his or her own works. The CBC French network's *'Concours de la chanson canadienne' (1956), in reality a competition for Canadian popular songs in French, allowed the Quebec public to hear compositions by its own writers on a considerable scale.

In 1959, Jacques Blanchet, Hervé Brousseau, Clémence Desrochers, Jean-Pierre Ferland, Claude Léveillée, and Raymond Lévesque formed a group, Les Bozos, and inaugurated in Montreal the boîte à chansons Chez Bozo, where they performed regularly. Their commitment, like that of all the chansonniers of that time, was at first apolitical. The commitment, if indeed there was one, was personal, founded on traditional human values: freindship, love, justice, freedom, communication, and so on.

The rise of the poetic song was chiefly the work of the early chansonniers. Its proliferation, its quality, its performers (Renée *Claude, Louis *Forestier, Pauline *Julien, Monique *Leyrac, Danielle Oderra), and the themes found in its lyrics made it the vehicle, however, for a young generation eager for community and liberation. A brief survey, conducted in 1965 among owners of clubs and *boîtes à chansons, revealed that at one time or another some 2000 young persons had requested auditions as chansonniers.

Stéphane *Venne in *Parti-Pris* draws a vivid picture of the typical would-be chansonnier about to make his debut: 'The chansonnier must be young, must not have chosen to sing for a living but rather to have a kind of vocation for it. He must perform "without artifice," in the plainest of surroundings, with a minimum number of musicians, ideally with no other accompanist but himself, on the guitar or the piano. He appears somewhat clumsy on stage and, above all, he must have composed the words and music of the songs he performs and in them display a preference for the first person.'

The role of the chansonniers, in view of the profound changes that society was undergoing, was essential to social evolution and gradually assumed a collective meaning: that of presenting the spirit of one's native environment in song. As Gaston Miron says when speaking of Georges Dor, for example, the chansonnier 'is a new person that we are all struggling nowadays to become' (preface to *Si tu savais* ...). The chansonniers of the 1960s and 1970s represented a new instance of the self-assertion of the people of Quebec, one linked to the discovery of their own identity. Thus the chansonniers were in the forefront of a general historical process: from that time on, most inhabitants of Quebec would see themselves no longer only as French (or English) Canadians but as québécois. In 1960 the chansonniers were tangible evidence of an exclusively 'québécois' phenomenon. They represented a peculiarly 'québécois' point of view and life-style. The boîtes à chansons where they played offered the first evidence and were the first symbols of this new approach; they sprang up everywhere in Quebec. The chansonnier vogue arose from a need for self-expression and self-recognition on the part of the poet-songwriters. Their rise created a new force, a market corresponding to a cultural reality and given unconditional support by the CBC, which broadcast almost all the chansonniers of the day. The movement then took on an unexpected dimension: lyricists and musicians such as Paul Baillargeon, Paul *de Margerie, François *Dompierre, André *Gagnon, Marcel Lefebvre, Pierre Nolès, Luc Plamondon, and Stéphane Venne entered its ranks.

The chansonniers with something to say could find no outlet on the commercial circuit. A cold war had developed between them and the popular singers who employed a style borrowed for the most part from the French or US song tradition. In about 1967–8 came the realization that the boîtes à chansons and the old chords repeated over and over were no longer sufficient. To lessen the differences between the two groups, such writer-composers as Marc *Gélinas and Stéphane Venne turned to such performers as Renée Claude, Emmanuelle, Pierre *Lalonde, Donald *Lautrec, Isabelle Pierre, Ginette *Ravel, and Ginette *Reno. It was thus that the pop movement became aware of more pressing realities than the contemplation of self. Of the writer-composer-performers on the scene, Robert Charlebois was the one most disposed to musical change. His delineation of a genuinely contemporary and québécois chanson, starting with *L'Osstidcho* (1968), remains the major achievement in the genre in the 1970s. He was the first chansonnier, acknowledged as such, to be accompanied by the electric guitar or to sing with a group, and he was succeeded in this by Claude *Dubois, Jean-Pierre Ferland, and Jacques *Michel.

Stimulated by the demands of the recording industry, whose involvement occurred at the same time as the opening of the large concert halls (Comédie-Canadienne, *PDA), the chansonniers moved from a cultivated amateur status to a professional one. Several of them, unable to write music, sought the services of professional musicians. The French school of song-writing was the matrix of the first generation of chansonniers. The influence of certain Californian currents, however, became apparent in the second generation: Charlebois, Dubois, Francoeur. Younger chansonniers of the group type, such as *Harmonium, Les *Séguin, Jim et Bertrand, *Beau Dommage, and Garolou, recalled the early chansonniers by their vitality and abundant skills in performance.

The poetic and musical creativity of the chansonniers preserved the essential qualities of Quebec folk music while at the same time serving to bring about its revival. Some never moved in the direction of rock. What Georges Dor, Claude Gauthier, Félix Leclerc, Raymond Lévesque, and Gilles Vigneault were offering their audiences in 1980 was similar in style to what they had presented 10, 15, or 20 years earlier, and songs such as the 'Hymne au printemps,' *'Mon Pays,' or *'Quand les hommes vivront d'amour' continued to be performed in many countries, defying fashion.

Indigenous and unsubsidized, the chansonnier movement was initiated by the public, which nourished and supported it. According to Georges Dor in his book *Si tu savais* ..., 'The people here were looking for new songs and the poet-chansonniers delivered them by the cartload ... though some were, admittedly, very rough-hewn. This all coincided with the arrival in Quebec of the consumer society and the chansonniers quickly became the standard-bearers for art in Quebec; they even at one point summarized the whole of Quebec art.' All contributed in an original way to the creation in Quebec of what is generally known as the 'chanson d'auteur.' Moreover, as the sociologist and chansonnier Pierre Bourdon believes, the chansonniers raised the lid of a political conscience in Quebec. They enabled the people of Quebec to identify themselves, to reveal themselves to one another, and, through a personal means of expression, to become fully aware of who they are. To conclude with the words of Roger Fournier, 'the chansonniers are all that can be done to save a country' (*Liberté*, July–August 1966).

See also Chanson in Quebec.

DISCOGRAPHY

Noël de nos chansonniers: Gisèle Bonin, Brousseau, Renée Claude, Dompierre, Ferland, Létourneau, Miville-Deschênes, Raoul Roy, Venne. Sel SSP 24.122

The Singer-Composers of Quebec: Brousseau, Desrochers, Dor, Filion, Louise Forestier, Gauthier, Julien, Lévesque, Bruce Mackay. GM 502

5 Chansonniers: le disque d'or: Charlebois, Létourneau, Lévesque, Miville-Deschênes, Venne. 1969. Sel S-398.151

Les Chansonniers du Québec (26 selections): Blanchet, Dor, Ferland, Julien, Leyrac, Vigneault. 1970. 2-RCI 360-361

J'ai vu le loup, le renard et le lion: Vigneault, Leclerc, Charlebois. 1974. Les Productions du 13 août enrg. VLC 13

1 fois 5: Charlebois, Deschamps, Ferland, Léveillée, Vigneault. 1976. 2-Kébec-Disc KD 923-924

BIBLIOGRAPHY

Venne, Stéphane. 'La chanson d'ici,' *Parti-Pris*, vol 2, Jan 1965

Gagnon, Lysiane. 'Chansonniers à gogo,' *Perspectives*, 8 Jan 1966

Belleau, André et al. 'Pour la chanson,' *Liberté*, vol 8, Jul–Aug 1966

Gagnon, Lysiane. 'La chanson,' *Culture vivante*, 5, Jan–Feb 1967

Brien, Lucien. 'Les chansonniers,' series of 4 articles, *CanComp*, 35–48, Dec 1968–Mar 1969

Bernard, Monique. *Ceux de chez nous: auteurs-compositeurs* (Montreal 1969)

Daigneault, Yvon. 'La chanson poétique,' *Archives des lettres canadiennes*, vol 4 (Montreal 1969)

Hermelin, Christian. *Ces Chanteurs que l'on dit poètes* (Paris 1970)

Dillaz, Serge. *La Chanson française de contestation* (Paris 1973)
Robidoux, Fernand. *Si ma chanson ...* (Montreal 1974)
Dor, Georges. *Si tu savais ...* (Montreal 1977)
Roy, Bruno. *Panorama de la chanson au Québec* (Montreal 1977)
Royer, Jean. *Pays intimes* (Montreal 1977)
Roy, Bruno. *Et cette Amérique chante en québécois* (Montreal 1979)
Blow up
La Chanson au Québec
La Chanson française
Chansonniers du Québec BR

Chanteurs de Ste-Thérèse et du cégep Lionel-Groulx. Mixed choir founded in 1962 (under the name Chanteurs de Ste-Thérèse) at the request of Mgr Laurent Pressault, priest of the parish of Ste-Thérèse de Blainville, near Montreal. In 1970 the choir of the Cegep Lionel-Groulx was integrated with it and the new name adopted. Jean-Pierre Guindon, a former student at the *CMM and the *École normale de musique, was the choir's founding conductor and remained in that position in 1979. A traditional repertoire was established. The choir presented its first broadcast, 'Chorales du Canada français,' on the CBC in 1964. In 1969 it joined the *MSO and the MSO choir for two performances of Mahler's *Symphony No. 2* ('Resurrection') in Montreal, and for another performance a few weeks later at the opening festival of the *NAC in Ottawa. Also with the MSO the choir has performed de Falla's *La Vida Breve* and Beethoven's *Fidelio* and *Christ on the Mount of Olives* in 1970, Orff's *Carmina burana* and Brahms' *A German Requiem* in 1972, and other such works. The choir numbered 125 members in 1979. It has received subsidies from the city of Ste-Thérèse, the *MACQ and the *Canada Council. ST

Les Chanteurs Saint-Coeur-de-Marie. Choir founded in Quebec City in 1973 by its conductor Claude Gosselin. The 12 male voices perform Gregorian chant and polyphonic music at the St-Coeur-de-Marie Church and are augmented by some 20 female voices for large polyphonic works performed during religious holidays and at three concerts annually. The choir's regular accompanist is Sylvain Doyon, organist at the St-Coeur-de-Marie Church.

While dedicated primarily to sacred music, the choir also performs secular pieces from several periods, sung either unaccompanied or with organ or instruments. Among the works given in concert have been Mozart's *Coronation Mass*, Bach's *Cantata No. 21*, and Handel's *Judas Maccabeus*. In a review in *Le Soleil* Marc *Samson commended a performance of the Handel work for its 'blend of fervour, musical sense, and fine judgment of pitch and tonal nuance.' In 1975 the choir took part in a performance of *Messiah* with the *Quebec SO under Otto-Werner *Mueller. It also sang at the *Institut canadien in Quebec City in 1975, the *Concerts Couperin in 1976, the ninth convention of *FAMEQ in 1976, and the tricentenary celebrations in St-Jean-Port-Joli, Que, in 1977. On tour during the 1975-6 season it gave concerts in Ottawa, Quebec, and Chicoutimi. The choir is financed by receipts from concerts and by grants from the *Canada Council, the Quebec High Commission for Youth, Recreation and Sports, the *MACQ, and the Musicians' Assn of Quebec City.

DISCOGRAPHY
Le Mariage: chants liturgiques. Doyon org. 1975. Alpec A-74003
[J.] Strauss Musical Festival. 1975. Nada 3-1075-A
Veni creator spiritus. 1975. Alpec A-76009 MB-L

CHAPLIN, Francis (Eugene). Violinst, b Newcastle, NB, 30 Dec 1927; hon D MUS (Mt Allison) 1974. He studied violin with Hans Graae in Newcastle and with Clayton *Hare 1940-5 at Mount Allison Academy in Sackville, NB, and then privately in Calgary. He continued at the Juilliard School with Louis Persinger 1946-9 and Ivan Galamian 1949-53, and upon graduation received the Loeb Prize. He moved in 1953 to Halifax, where he was concertmaster of the CBC Halifax Orchestra and the *Halifax (now *Atlantic) SO. He was a member of the Halifax (later *Brandon U) Trio and the Halifax String Quartet. The trio moved to *Brandon U in 1966 and Chaplin began teaching there in 1967. He has recorded for the CBC with the Brandon Trio, and with Judy *Loman and the Johnny *Burt Orchestra (1966, CTLS 5075). KN

Chappell & Co Ltd. British publishing firm established in London in 1810 and opened for business 1 Jan 1811. A Canadian branch of Chappell's New York office opened in Toronto in 1912 and closed in 1920. A second Canadian branch opened in Toronto in 1946. Cyril C. Devereux, a director 1947-77 of *CAPAC and chairman 1954-5 of the *CMPA, was general manager of Chappell's Canadian branch until 1975, when he was succeeded by Jerry Renewych. Chappell by that time was a part of the Polygram Group – the worldwide entertainment conglomerate, owner of Intersong music publishers and *Polydor and Phonogram records. The publisher of many works for the musical stage, Chappell's first such success came with an English version of Gounod's *Faust*. It has published the Gilbert & Sullivan operettas and many later operettas and musicals, including *Rose Marie, The Desert Song, The Student Prince, My Fair Lady*, and *The Sound of Music*.

Clarence *Lucas did editorial work in the London office in the 1890s and Chappell published some of his compositions, as well as many songs and piano pieces of John Mais Capel (b Lennoxville, Que, 1 Nov 1862). Other Canadians on the Chappell roster are Johnny *Burt, Howard *Cable, Wishart *Campbell, Robert *Farnon, Harold *Ramsey, and Godfrey *Ridout. One of Chappell's best-selling popular songs was Ernest *Seitz' *'The World Is Waiting for the Sunrise.'

In 1980 the Canadian branch remained primarily a distributor of British and US popular music, representing, among others, the catalogues of Bregman, Vocco & Conn, Famous Music, Edwin H. Morris, Screen Gems, and Twentieth Century Music (all of New York), and Hansen Publications of Miami. The company also distributes the Chappell Recorded Music Library of Sound Effects. Chappell became a member company of CAPAC. Its subsidiaries Belinda Canada Ltd, Canadiana Music, and Intersong Canada became affiliate companies of PRO Canada.

BIBLIOGRAPHY
Devereux, C.C. 'The romance of Chappell's,' *CanComp*, 2, Aug 1965
'Music publisher predicts bright future for composers,' *CanComp*, 21, Sep 1967 MWl

CHARBONNEAU. Montreal family of instrumentalists: 1 / Louis; 2 / Maurice and 3 / Roger, his sons; and 4 / Louis, Roger's son.

1 **Louis**. Cellist, teacher, b Montreal 23 or 24 Feb 1864 or 1865, d Quebec City 23 Nov 1927. His father was the organ-builder Raymond Roger Charbonneau, who worked at *Casavant Frères. Louis began studying violin at 12 but transferred to cello when he was 20 and studied in Boston with the German virtuoso cellist Alwin Schroeder. Considered a pioneer of his instrument in Montreal, he was a member of the *MSO under *Couture and later under *Goulet. About 1890, with Frantz *Jehin-Prume and Émery *Lavigne, he founded the Trio de Montréal. The quartet he formed with Alfred *De Sève, Émile *Taranto, and Otto Zimmerman performed some of the Beethoven *String Quartets*. Charbonneau performed 1899-1900 in the Sunday Concerts at Karn Hall as a member of various trios and quartets and during the 1911-12 season in the National Theatre orchestra with the young pianist Wilfrid *Pelletier. Rodolphe *Plamondon was a pupil.

BIBLIOGRAPHY
Men of Canada (Toronto, Brantford 1896)

2 **Maurice**. Cellist, teacher, b Montreal 22 Jun 1903. He began studying cello at 12 with his father and made his debut with the Société symphonique de Québec (*Quebec SO). About 1929 he joined the *MSO, under *Gagnier, and the orchestra of the *Cons national of Montreal, where he had begun teaching in 1928. He also taught at the *Institut Nazareth. While playing 1929-39 in the orchestra at *His Majesty's Theatre he became a member of the *Montreal Orchestra and a founding member of the *CSM Orchestra (MSO), in which he played for 35 years, serving ca 1937-57 as principal cello. He was a member of the *McGill Chamber Orchestra and the Chartier Quartet. He took part in numerous CBC broadcasts.

3 **Roger**. Bassist, teacher, b Montreal 18 May 1908, d there 20 Oct 1964. He studied solfège with J.-J. *Goulet and cello with his father before taking up the double-bass with, in turn, Léon Wathieu, Warren Bentfield, and, at the *CMM, Anselme Fortier of New York 1943-8. After Fortier's death, he attended classes in interpretation with Gaston Dufresne of Boston. He taught 1943-64 at the CMM and the *CMQ. Roland R. Desjardins, Jean-Paul *Major, and Rénald St-Pierre were among his pupils. He was principal double-bass in the *MSO 1953-63 and also gave several recitals on CBC radio.

4 **Louis**. Timpanist, percussionist, teacher, b Montreal 29 Jun 1932; premier prix percussion (CMM) 1950. After studying piano for four years with Françoise D'Amour and Hector *Gratton, he entered the *CMM in 1947 to study solfège with Isabelle *Delorme and percussion with Louis Decair and Saul Goodman. In 1950 he began teaching at the CMM and also at the *CMQ, where he established the percussion class. By 1974 he had trained a great many young instrumentalists, including Ian Bernard, Paul Duplessis, Vincent *Dionne, Jean-Normand Iadeluca, Roger Juneau, Serge Laflamme, Robert Leroux, and Jean-François Roch. Appointed timpanist of the CSM Orchestra (*MSO) in 1950, he appeared frequently as a soloist with the orchestra, notably in a 1959 performance of Milhaud's *Concerto* for percussion and small orchestra under Igor Markevitch, after which the conductor invited him to take part in the 1960 US tour by the Orchestre Lamoureux of Paris. For the MSO's Matinées symphoniques Charbonneau was soloist in Adolphe Schreiner's *The Worried Drummer* in 1950, Kurt Striegler's *Concerto* in 1961, and Carlos Chavez' *Toccata* in 1962. In 1963 he played the Werner Thaerichen *Concerto* with the orchestra under Zubin Mehta. For the opening of the Salle Port-Royal, *PDA, he was soloist with the *McGill Chamber Orchestra in Alexander *Brott's *Critic's Corner*. In 1976, with the same ensemble, he played Franco Donatoni's *Concertino*, and his artistry led the critic Claude

*Gingras to write (*La Presse*, 27 Jan 1976): 'Charbonneau is ... capable of the greatest strength and the greatest refinement at the same time ... He's a kind of "poet of the timpani".' Among premieres of Canadian works in which Charbonneau has participated are *Mercure's *Pantomime* (1949), *Joachim's *Concertante No. 1* (second movement) (1957), and *Matton's *Concerto* for two pianos and percussion (1958). In September 1977 at the PDA he conducted the Percussions de Strasbourg, six additional percussionists from Montreal, and Gilles *Tremblay, piano, in a performance of Varèse's *Ionisation*, a work which his CMM percussion class had given its Canadian premiere in February 1969 in Toronto. Charbonneau was a member of the juries for percussion competitions at the Metz Cons and the Strasbourg Cons in 1972 and at the Paris Cons in 1973, and was a coach for the JM World Orchestra in Israel in 1973. He was founder (1972) and director of the Percussions du Québec and has performed frequently on CBC radio and TV. He taught 1974–8 at the *École Vincent-d'Indy.

See also Discographies for Hyman Bress (RCI 293); Josephte Dufresne.

BIBLIOGRAPHY
Berger, Paul. 'Je lui dois ma carrière ... percutante,' *Culture vivante*, 11, Dec 1968 (GP)

CHARBONNEAU, Jean-Noël. Teacher, choirmaster, Gregorianist, b Montreal 5 Jun 1875, d there 26 Jan 1945; D MUS (Montreal) 1932. He took his classical education at Ste-Thérèse and continued his musical studies in Montreal under Guillaume *Couture and Achille *Fortier. He also studied with Arthur *Letondal, Joseph-Daniel *Dussault, and Pascal Deremouchamps, and in 1910 travelled to Europe for studies with René Moissenet in France and with Dom Lucien David at the St Anselme Abbey in Rome. While choirmaster 1900–33 at St-Charles Roman Catholic Church in Montreal, he founded the *Schola cantorum in 1915, the year he became president of the *Cons national. He became a director and teacher at the conservatory in 1917 and remained there until 1922, when he organized the Institut musical du Canada, which in 1938 became affiliated with the U of Montreal. In 1934 he went to Valleyfield, Que, to establish the Schola Ste-Cécile, a diocesan school of liturgical singing. He also became choirmaster at the Valleyfield Cathedral. At this time he organized summer courses and Gregorian chant competitions. In 1942 he was elected president of the Commission diocésaine de musique sacrée in Montreal.

Charbonneau's writings (all unpublished) include *Solfège des écoles* (three volumes), *Traité d'harmonie*, and his doctoral thesis, L'histoire musicale de l'église.' He composed motets, fauxbourdons (on psalms, graduals, and tracts), and cantatas. A distinguished educator, he worked in several areas for the advancement of the study of music and gave many lectures.

Charbonneau's sons were both musicians. Jean (1911–55) was his successor in 1933 at St-Charles Church, founded an orchestra in the Notre-Dame-de-Grâce district, and was choirmaster at the cathedral in Chatham, NB. Also a voice teacher, Jean conducted the Lavallée-Smith Choir in Montreal. CMr

CHARLEBOIS, Robert. Singer, actor, songwriter, guitarist, pianist, b Montreal 25 Jun 1945. After studying piano for six years and acting 1962–5 at the National Theatre School in Montreal, he divided his early career between music and theatre. In 1965 CBC TV's 'Jeunesse oblige' named him 'discovery of the year' in the chansonnier category, and his first LP, *Ma Boule*, received a jury award for debut recordings in the Festival du disque. In 1966 he appeared at the *Monument national in Labiche's play *Le Plus Heureux des trois*, performed in several CBC téléromans (television serials), and starred in Michel Brault's film *Entre la mer et l'eau douce* before going to France to sing in Paris boîtes. Combining the two interests, he performed in 1966 in Louis-Georges Carrier's musical comedy *Ne ratez pas l'espion* and, with the actor Jean-Guy Moreau and the singer Mouffe (Claudinen Monfette), wrote and presented in 1967 the revue *Terre des Bums*. An LP of the revue (whose title is a word play on the theme of *Expo 67, Terre des hommes) was issued by Phonodisc (PHL 5006). In 1968, with Mouffe, Louise *Forestier, Yvon Deschamps, and le *Quatuor de jazz libre du Québec, he performed in the revue *Peuple à genoux* at the Théâtre de Quat' Sous. The revues *L'Osstidcho* (1968, at the Comédie-Canadienne) and *L'Osstidchomeurt* (1969, at the *Palais Montcalm) followed with the same cast. In 1968 Charlebois represented Quebec at the fifth International Festival of French song, at Spa, Belgium, winning the grand prize with 'Lindberg,' which he wrote with Claude Péloquin. His recording of 'Lindberg,' a brash, electrifying performance in which Forestier also sings, was very popular and won him the Prix Félix-Leclerc in the 1969 Festival du disque.

Robert Charlebois

Charlebois continued to sing with Mouffe or Forestier as his partner in concert and on records. A tour of France in April 1969, with Forestier and le Jazz libre, was curtailed after a riotous performance at the Olympia in Paris. Nevertheless, Charlebois's image as 'Superfrog,' an outlandish figure in a Montreal Canadiens hockey sweater who sang in joual to the accompaniment of a jazz-rock group, soon became a novelty in French pop music; amusement at the novelty gradually gave way to an appreciation of the originality and energy of his music. Charlebois returned to France in 1970 and performed at the Olympia in 1972 (twice), 1973 (for three weeks), and 1974.

In 1969 Charlebois also made his first significant appearance in Canada outside Quebec, at the Toronto Pop Festival (Varsity Stadium); in 1970 he was a member of the Festival Express, a concert party of the most popular rock performers in North America, which travelled across Canada by train for concerts in Ottawa, Toronto, Winnipeg, and Calgary. (In later years he gave occasional concerts elsewhere in Canada – eg, at *Ontario Place in 1978. He also was seen nationally on such TV specials as 'Outer Places with Robert Charlebois' in 1974.)

Charlebois's second major success, 'Ordinaire,' written by Charlebois and Mouffe with, and about, their pianist Pierre Nadeau ('le gros Pierre ... un gars ordinaire'), was introduced in 1970. Representing the CBC at the 10th Sopot International Festival in Poland that year, Charlebois won first prize with 'Ordinaire.' His other most popular songs to 1974 included 'CPR Blues,' 'Avril sur Mars,' 'Le Mur du son,' 'Conception,' 'Fu Man Chu,' 'California,' 'Entre deux joints,' 'Entre Dorval et Mirabel,' 'Que-can blues,' and 'Cauchemar.'

By this time the outstanding figure in Quebec pop music and a radical force in the musical development of the chansonnier movement, Charlebois performed frequently in the province's major venues: at the *Forum (1969, 1970), at *PDA (in recital and in pops concerts with the *MSO, 1970, 1971, 1972, 1974), at the Bastille in Quebec City (1973), and elsewhere in Cegeps and at festivals. In 1974 Charlebois announced a two-year sabbatical, which began after he participated with *Leclerc and *Vigneault in the 'Superfrancofête' held 13 August on the Plains of Abraham, Quebec City – a historic gathering (telecast on the CBC's French-language network and later in France) of the three men who have shaped the tradition of the chanson in Quebec – and gave concerts at the Olympia in Paris.

During his sabbatical Charlebois appeared in the French film *Sombre Vacances* (for which he wrote the music, 1975) and in Sergio Leone's Italian-made western *Un génie, deux associés, une cloche* (1976); he also wrote scores for the Quebec films *Jusqu'au coeur* (in which he performed, 1969), *A soir, on fait peur au monde* (1969), *Deux Femmes en or* (1970), and *Bulldozer* (1971).

In 1976 he returned to the concert stage with performances at the St-Jean-Baptiste day celebrations on Montreal's Mount Royal, at the Olympic Village in Montreal alongside Gordon *Lightfoot, on tour in Quebec, and on tour in France, where he played 10 nights at the Palais des Congrès in Paris. He received the Prix de l'Académie Charles-Cros for his recording *1 Fois 5* (see Discography for Chansonniers). In 1978, with the LP *Swing Charlebois Swing*, he turned from the raucous style of his heyday to a form of crooning which resulted in his being compared with Sinatra or Montand. The change in style did not take over his entire presentation, however; his concerts in the late 1970s included material from his early years. Although his popularity waned in Quebec, it continued to grow in France. In 1979 he performed for three weeks at the Palais des Congrès with Nanette Workman as his partner, then toured the country.

Charlebois's impact on the broadening of style of the Quebec chanson cannot be overestimated. He brought to his early work an awareness of the pop musics of Great Britain and the USA; he was possibly the first in the chansonnier tradition to use an electric guitar (and later a full band) for accompaniment; he introduced into his presentations panache and a sense of the theatre and its applicability to pop music. Referring to Charlebois as the standard by which the Quebec chanson and its artists are measured, Benoît L'Herbier (*La Chanson québécoise*, Montrel 1974) continued: 'He has become the epicentre – the nerve centre around which all the others gravitate ... We can find traces of the French and Anglo-Saxon influences that have contributed to the present originality [of his music]. But let's not forget, above all, the poetry, his own or others', that he has transmitted and communicated. With the help of Claude Péloquin, Marcel Sabourin, Mouffe and Réjean Ducharme in particular [among his songwriting collaborators], Charlebois has created a universe of his own – both poetic and musical, complete ... If Michel Tremblay has revolutionized and revitalized the theatre of Quebec, Charlebois has done the same for the chanson. Like Tremblay he belongs to this new generation which wants to sing about, to project a Quebec as it is, without artifice, with candour, but also with colour, poetry, humour and intelligence ... *Joual* has served Charlebois to enhance an already extraordinary music and augment the incalculable impact generated by his appearance.'

Music heard on Charlebois's LPs has been arranged and/or conducted by Jean-Marie Benoît, Paul *de Margerie, Pierre Nadeau, Art Philips, Vic *Vogel, and others. Charlebois's music has been published by Éditions Gamma and Éditions Conception. He is a member of CAPAC.

DISCOGRAPHY (by label)

Select (to 1966): *Robert Charlebois*, vol 1. SSP-24.131
- *Robert Charlebois*, vol 2. SSP 24-147

Gamma (1968–72): *Robert Charlebois*. GS-115
- *Lindberg*. GS-120
- *Québec Love*. GS-136
- *Un Gars ben ordinaire*. GS-146
- *Les Grands Succès de Robert Charlebois*. GS-144.
- *Robert Charlebois*. G-2-1003

L'Histoire de Robert Charlebois. G-3-601

Barclay (1973–4): *Charlebois*. 80123
- *Solidaritude*. 80173
- *Charlebois*. 80200
- *Les Grands Succès Barclay: Robert Charlebois*, vol 21. 2-75021

Solution/Kébec-Disc (1976–9): *Longue Distance*. SN 905
- *Live de Paris*. 2-SN 925/926
- *Swing Charlebois Swing*. SN 939
- *Disque d'or*. SNX 945
- *Disque d'or*. SNX 926
- *Cauchemar*. Solet SNA 947/948
- *Solide*. SNL 964

See also Discography for Chansonniers.

BIBLIOGRAPHY

L'Herbier, Benoît. *Charlebois, qui es-tu?* (Montreal 1971)

Lefèbvre, Jean-Pierre. 'Charlebois ... c'est pour ça ...,' *Musiques du Kébèk*, ed Raoul Duguay (Montreal 1971)

Rioux, Lucien. *Robert Charlebois* (Paris 1972)

Gagnon, Claude. *Robert Charlebois déchiffré* (Montreal 1974)

Rodriguez, Juan. 'Charlebois at a turning point,' *Montreal Star*, 26 Jan 1974

Petrowski, Nathalie. 'Charlebois contre son image,' Montreal *Le Devoir*, 1 Apr 1978

Germain, Georges-Hébert. 'Un golfeur bien ordinaire,' *Actualité, Apr 1978*

Beaulieu, Pierre. 'C'est devenu à la mode d'être anti-Charlebois,' Montreal *La Presse*, 23 Jun 1978

Radz, Matt. 'Charlebois' battery is charged to go,' *Montreal Star*, 23 Jun 1979

CHARLESWORTH, Hector (Willoughby). Writer, critic, editor, b Hamilton, Ont, 28 Sep 1872, d Toronto 30 Dec 1945. In his teens he studied piano and theory (with Arthur E. *Fisher) and submitted poems and articles to *Saturday Night* using the pseudonym 'Touchstone.' In 1891 he joined the staff of *Saturday Night* for a year. His interest in music and theatre was reinforced by his marriage in 1897 to the singer and pianist Katherine Ryan (d 1944). He was a reporter 1892–1904 for various Toronto papers and city editor and music critic 1904–10 for the *Mail and Empire*. He then became assistant managing editor 1910–26 and editor 1926–32 of *Saturday Night*. Most of his music criticism was published in *Saturday Night*, English Canada's most influential weekly in the first half of the 20th century. Charlesworth served a controversial term 1932–6 as chairman of the CRBC. His book *I'm Telling You* (Toronto 1937) details those years. He returned in 1936 to *Saturday Night* as music critic and also contributed music and drama reviews to the *Globe and Mail* until his death.

Charlesworth's memoirs, *Candid Chronicles* (Toronto 1925) and *More Candid Chronicles* (Toronto 1929), include anecdotes of musical interest. His writings also appeared in *Musical Canada*, the *Conservatory Monthly*, the *Canadian Journal of Music*, the *Conservatory Quarterly Review*, the *Yearbook of Canadian Art*, and others. Charlesworth adjudicated many performance and composition competitions. MMI

Charlottetown. The capital of Canada's smallest province, Prince Edward Island. Established by 300 French colonists as Port-la-Joie in 1720, it was renamed Charlottetown in 1768, and was incorporated as a town in 1855 and as a city in 1875. The site of the 1864 conference which drew up the first plans for the union of British North America, Charlottetown is known as 'the cradle of Confederation.' With a population of 18,000 in 1979, Charlottetown is the island's academic, cultural, and administrative centre.

Because of Charlottetown's island isolation its early musical activity depended on amateurs and a few visiting professionals. *Singing schools for instruction in church music were organized from time to time, and in the 1840s Miss Charlotte McCormick and a Mrs Jamieson gave piano lessons. Visiting musicians included the Rainer family of Tyrolean singers in 1841 and Baron Rudolph de Fleur, a pianist from Russia, in 1847. About 1850 Watson Duchemin, a local lumber dealer, built and installed in St Paul's Church what was then probably the only pipe organ on the Island. The Charlottetown Brass Band and the Sons of Temperance Band were active at this time. New bands continued to appear throughout the 19th century, some attached to military units, others to fraternal organizations such as the Knights of Columbus.

'Professor' Vinnecombe, an immigrant from England, conducted an instrumental group as early as 1877. His orchestra accompanied the Gilbert & Sullivan operettas (*H.M.S. Pinafore* in 1885) presented by S.N. (Sammy) Earle at the Market Hall Stage, using local performers. By the end of the century Charlottetown had its own "opera house," in which Earle staged *The Pirates of Penzance*, *The Mikado*, and other operettas.

Henry Watts, an organist who taught music in the schools and directed a massed choir from all the Charlottetown churches in a memorial service in 1901 for Queen Victoria, continued the city's Gilbert & Sullivan tradition with school productions of *Trial by Jury*, and their other operettas. In 1926 Roberta Spencer Full came to Charlottetown and will a colleague (E. Lillian MacKenzie, like herself a church organist and music teacher) mounted Gilbert & Sullivan productions with singers from the local schools and colleges. The Women's Musical Club (1926–42) brought in visiting artists such as Rose Bampton, Nelson Eddy, and a trio from Winnipeg, the Nelson Sisters, one of whom later became known as Zara *Nelsova. In 1940 the club formed a 32-voice choir which, with the help of local male soloists, performed opera excerpts. Roberta Full and Helen Lawson helped establish the *Community Concerts Assn, which sponsored four (later three) concerts annually 1931–77.

In 1946 the Women's Institute of Prince Edward Island (first president, Jessie Beck) founded the Prince Edward Island Music Festival, a competition which has grown to include a week of sessions in Summerside, Montague, and Charlottetown, with adjudicators from outside the province.

In 1955 Prince of Wales College (established in 1834 and amalgamated in 1969 with St Dunstan's U to form the *U of Prince Edward Island) presented *The Mikado*, led by E. Lillian MacKenzie,

A song printed in Charlottetown in 1861

music director at the college. This was the beginning of an annual spring festival of Gilbert & Sullivan productions that in subsequent years included *Trial by Jury*, *The Pirates of Penzance*, and *H.M.S. Pinafore*.

Choral groups in Charlottetown have included, in addition to church choirs, the Serenaders, a women's choir directed by Roberta Full; the Charlottetown Chorale; and the *Confederation Choir and its successors, the Confederation Madrigal Choir and the Confederation Boys' Choir. The singers and teachers Raoul and Marguerite Raymond, the organist Flora Rogers, the singer Barbara Roper, and the violinist Kathleen Hornby were among individuals who contributed to musical activity in the city.

During the 1960s standards in musical education and in performance increased apace. Christopher *Gledhill, music director of the Prince Edward Island Dept of Education 1961–77, directed choirs, was organist-choirmaster at the Kirk of St James, and was the first president of the *PEIMEA. Others active in music education were Royston Mugford and Gerard Rutten. The establishment of the Music Dept at the U of Prince Edward Island in 1969 provided a stimulus and focus for many musical activities in the city. The university undertook the training of qualified music instructors for schools and sponsored series of faculty and student recitals and concerts by its performing groups (chorus, band, chamber ensembles, etc). The *Confederation Centre, completed in 1964, became the home of the *Charlottetown Festival and of the popular stage musical *Anne of Green Gables*, and is the location of performances by local and visiting artists. The Prince Edward Island SO, a community orchestra of 40–50 players, has been conducted 1967–70 by Thomas Hahn, 1970–6 by Alan *Reesor, and 1976–9 by William Bartlett. Czeslaw Gladyszewski succeeded Bartlett in 1979.

Oldtime music also has enjoyed great popularity in Charlottetown, as it has throughout the island. The city's radio station CFCY was the original home of Don *Messer and His Islanders.

Two natives of Charlottetown who have achieved distinction as composers are William Keith *Rogers and Walter *MacNutt.

BIBLIOGRAPHY

Koko. 'Opera in P.E.I.,' *OpCan*, Feb–Mar 1961 (CGl)

Charlottetown Festival. Established to present original Canadian musical theatre in the summer, it opened 27 Jul 1965 with the premiere of *Anne of Green Gables*. The first season also included productions of **Spring Thaw* and *Laughing with Leacock* and a revue featuring the comedians Wayne and Shuster. Other productions, three or four each season in repertory at the *Confederation Centre of the Arts, included Charlottetown premieres of Mavor *Moore's *The Ottawa Man* and *Private Turvey's War* (later **Turvey*) in 1966; Pierre Berton's *Paradise Hill* in 1967; John *Fenwick and Mavor Moore's **Johnny Belinda* and Moore's *Sunshine Town* in 1968; Marion *Grudeff and Ray Jessel's *Life Can Be Like Wow* in 1969; the British musical *Jane Eyre* in 1970; Howard *Cable and Christopher Gore's *Mary, Queen of Scots* in 1971; Michel Conte and Arthur Samuels' *Ballade* in 1972; Helen Porter and Ben *McPeek's *Joey* in 1973; Cliff *Jones' **Kronberg: 1582* in 1974; *By George*, a salute to George Gershwin, and Cliff Jones' *Rowdyman* in 1976; Alan Lund's *The Legend of the Dumbells* in 1977; and David Warrack's *Windsor* in 1978. *Anne of Green Gables* has been performed each year, and *Johnny Belinda* also has received many productions. Several Charlottetown productions have toured in eastern Canada (appearing at the *NAC in Ottawa, and the *O'Keefe Centre and the *Royal Alexandra Theatre (in Toronto).

Mavor Moore was artistic director of the festival until 1967 and was succeeded by Alan Lund. John Fenwick was the founding music director, a position he retained in 1978. Errol Gay served 1967–9 and in 1971 as assistant director. The festival's orchestra in the 1970s was drawn largely from the *Atlantic SO. Prince Edward Island performers at the festival have included Gordon Crozier, Gracie Finley (who played Anne 1969–74), Glenda Landry, and Esther Pletch. In conjunction with the musicals, the festival has offered recitals and concerts by noted performers and groups, such as Maureen *Forrester, Félix *Leclerc, Lois *Marshall, Alan *Mills, and the *NYO in 1965; and John Allan *Cameron, Anne *Murray, and other Canadian and US pop performers in 1977.

BIBLIOGRAPHY

Smith, Rebecca, and Peake, Linda. 'Prince Edward Island is not just the Charlottetown Festival,' *PfAC*, vol 13, Winter 1976 (CGl)

CHARPENTIER, Gabriel. Composer, poet, artistic consultant, teacher, b Richmond, near Sherbrooke, Que, 13 Sep 1925. He studied piano with Estelle Letarte in Richmond and J.-Antonio *Thompson in Trois-Rivières, and 1940–4 with Hervé Cloutier and Fernand *Graton at Jean-de-Brébeuf College in Montreal, and with Jean *Papineau-Couture. While pursuing his academic studies he discovered the music of Berg, Debussy, Schoenberg, Stravinsky, and Webern, and during a stay 1945–7 with the Benedictines of St-Benoît-du-Lac he studied Gregorian chant with Dom Bergeron. He completed his studies in Paris 1947–53 with Andrée Bonneville, Nadia Boulanger (composition), Annette Dieudonné (solfège), and Norbert Dufourcq.

Charpentier served 1953–79 as programming co-ordinator and artistic consultant for the CBC's musical shows on French-language TV. In this dual capacity he collaborated with Françoys *Bernier, Pierre *Mercure, Pierre Morin, and other producers on the development and production of such series as 'Concerts pour la jeunesse,' 'L'*Heure du concert,' 'Musiques folles des années sages,' and 'Les Beaux Dimanches.' The last-

Gabriel Charpentier

named series presented many contemporary works, and one of its programs – 'Loves,' featuring Serge *Garant's ... *chant d'amours* and the Brian Macdonald-Harry *Freedman ballet **The Shining People of Leonard Cohen* – received honourable mention in the 1975 Prix Italia competition. During the summers of 1955 and 1956 Charpentier gave courses in the history of music at *McGill U. He also taught music history and rhythm 1962–4 at the National Theatre School. In 1979 he became the artistic director of the *Pro Musica Society.

Charpentier's vocal and instrumental scores reveal his contrapuntal skills and his profound attachment to Gregorian melisma, a consequence of his time with the Benedictines of St-Benoît-du-Lac. He himself has said: 'This [Gregorian chant] is my folklore; this is the basis of all my work. Chant, for me, is a line. If an actor or a singer can trace a line that lives and is meaningful, it is perhaps the most beautiful thing that can happen to a man' (*Montreal Star*, 18 Jan 1969).

In Charpentier all of the performing arts converge. He divides his musical ability into three categories: vocal and instrumental music, musical theatre, and music for the theatre. Equally drawn to music and to poetry, he has written, among other verse, the words for Pierre Mercure's **Cantate pour une joie* and *Dissidence* and for Jocelyne *Binet's *Trois Poèmes*. His collection of poems *Aire* (Paris 1948) won the Prix de la poésie moderne. He wrote both music and words for his miniature operas *An *English Lesson*, 'opera-happening'; *A Tea Symphony or The Perils of Clara*, 'kitsch opera in nine drinks'; *Clara et les philosophes*, 'opera cocktail'; *Clarabelle-Clarimage*, 'une opération'; and *La Ballade du Fils de l'homme*, 'opera seria.' These remarkable small works (parts of a projected series to be called *A Night at the Opera*) reflect Charpentier's creative imagination, his sense of humour and of detail, and his mastery of composition; they also illumine his passionate love for the theatre. In *Orphée I*, commissioned for the inauguration of the *NAC in 1969, and *Orpheus II*, an English-language adaptation for the 1972 *Stratford Festival, Charpentier combined voices, instruments, and 12 actors. He understands actors; a one-time member of the theatrical troupe the Compagnons de St-Laurent, he defines himself as a 'theatre musician.' In more than 50 productions, mostly at the Théâtre du Nouveau-Monde (where he served 1959–72 as music director) and the Stratford Festival, he developed a personal concept of the role of music in theatre. He felt it should be not 'incidental' but integral to the production. He requires his actors to sing, beat out rhythms, and play instruments. For example, in Euripides' *Electra* and Shakespeare's *Pericles* he asked the actors to produce extremely complex rhythmic counterpoints that created a mood favourable to a better understanding of the profound nature of these tragedies. On 14 Feb 1965 in Montreal's *Orpheum Theatre, the Théâtre du Nouveau-Monde premiered *Klondyke* (book by Jacques Languirand, music by Charpentier). It was presented in the same year in London's Old Vic for the Commonwealth Festival of the Arts.

Francean Campbell wrote of Charpentier: 'He has never embraced serialism or any other strict system but welcomes new sounds and techniques whether natural in origin, or electronic' (*Canadian Composer*, November 1970). In Toronto in 1979 the *NMC presented three of his works, including the premiere of *Clarabelle-Clarimage*. Charpentier serves on the administration council of Comus Music Theatre Foundation of Canada in Toronto, and in 1971 he became a member of the artistic committee for MUDRA, a performing artists' improvement and research centre directed by Maurice Béjart in Brussels. Charpentier is an associate of the *CMCentre and a member of the *CLComp and of CAPAC.

SELECTED COMPOSITIONS

OPERA

Orphée I / Orpheus II (Charpentier). 1969, 1972 (Ott 1969, Stratford 1972). 7 perfs, 12 actors, solos, chor, band. Ms

A Tea Symphony or The Perils of Clara (Charpentier). 1972 (Banff 1972). P, fl, Sop. CMCentre

Clara et les philosophes (B. Char). 1976. Pf, fl, cl, sop, mezzo, alto, bar, bass. CMCentre

La Ballade du Fils de l'homme (Charpentier). 1979. Elec org, bar. Ms

Clarabelle-Clarimage (B. Char). 1979 (Tor 1979). 2 fl, cl, 2 pf, 2 sop, bar. CMCentre

See also *An English Lesson*.

FILM

Lumières. 1953

La Chute de la maison Usher. 1955. For 1929 Epstein silent film

Histoires extraordinaires (Balzac, Poe, et al). 1962

La Courte Échelle. 1964

CHAMBER MUSIC

Debout Joseph! (A. Césaire). 1955. V, guit. Ms

Trois Poèmes de saint Jean de la Croix (transl A. Godoy). 1955. Alto, vn, vc. CMCentre

Trois Ricercars. 1966. Hpd, ob. Ms

Trois Oraisons. 1971. Sop, hpd, pf, hp, vib. Ms

Processionnal (Charpentier). 1974. Spkr, speech chor, men's chor, brass, hpd, hp, gl, bells, org. Ms

CHOIR AND VOICE

Sept Chansons d'enfants (R. Radiguet, Charpentier, et al). 1952. 4 vs. Ms

Messe I. 1952. CMCentre. (Gloria, Credo) RCI 189 (*Mtl Bach Choir)/Poly 2917009 (*Festival Singers)

'L'Avenir' (H. Michaux). 1962. Speech chor. Ms

Permutation 1 2 3 4. 1962. 1, 2, 3, or 4 chors. Ms

'Jamais' (Charpentier). 1963. Sop, mezzo, ten. CMCentre

'Veni creator spiritus.' 1973. 2 vs. Ms

'Artère' (Charpentier). 1976. Bar. Ms

KEYBOARD

Suite d'après la musique du Bourgeois gentilhomme. 1964. Hpd. Ms

Grande Chaconne d'après la musique de Galileo Galilei. 1971. Hpd. Ms

Also the music for more than 50 theatrical productions, including *Tartuffe* (Molière) recorded on Caedmon TRS-332 in 1969

WRITINGS

Cantate pour une joie (Montreal 1955)

'Labyrinthe 4,' *CMB*, 11, 12, Autumn–Winter 1975, Spring–Summer 1976

BIBLIOGRAPHY

Doré, Fernand. 'La musique n'est qu'un élément du grand tout,' *Maclean*, Aug 1968

'Un petit opéra from Stratford,' *CBC Times*, 3–9 Aug 1968

McLean, Eric. 'Gabriel Charpentier – man of music and man of the theatre,' *Montreal Star*, 18 Jan 1969

Desjardins, P.W. 'Orphée,' *Vie des arts*, 57, Winter 1969–70

Littler, William. 'Cymbeline music man invents new sound,' *Toronto Daily Star*, 8 Jul 1970
Kraglund, John. 'Gabriel Charpentier: master of incidental music for theatre,' Toronto *Globe and Mail*, 23 Oct 1971
Littler, William. 'Composer explains why his opera is not opera,' *Toronto Star*, 8 Jul 1972
Laplante, Louise. 'Gabriel Charpentier,' *Mcan*, 35, Apr 1978
Malouin-Gélinas, France. 'Gabriel Charpentier,' *Contemporary Canadian Composers / Compositeurs canadiens contemporains* (FM-G)

CHARTIER, Eugène. Violinist, violist, conductor, teacher, b Montreal ca 1893, d Beaconsfield (Montreal) 1 Nov 1963. He studied violin with Cyril Cartier, then with Oscar *Martel and Alfred *De Sève. He was second violin 1917–22 with the *Dubois String Quartet and viola 1920–5 with the Chamberland String Quartet, and he also played viola with the orchestras of the *CSM and the *Montreal Festivals and with the *Montreal Orchestra. He founded in 1922 and directed the orchestra of the *Cons national of Montreal (later Montreal Philharmonic Orchestra), and in 1925 he began to teach regularly at the conservatoire. He also taught at the colleges of Terrebonne and Berthier, and at the convent of Ste-Émilie de Viauville. Roméo *Mastrocola and Lucien *Robert were among his pupils. In 1932 he was appointed director of the Maisonneuve regimental band, and in 1933 he was a founding member of the Euterpe Music Society. He was invited to conduct the CSM orchestra on several occasions, notably in 1935, and again in 1937 in a performance of Beethoven's *Symphony No. 3* 'Eroica.' Of the latter Marcel *Valois wrote in *La Presse* (9 Jan 1937): 'The second movement, the Marche funèbre, was played in a most interesting manner and in it M. Chartier showed that he possesses a sense of values and of true emotion.' Chartier also conducted on several broadcasts of 'Concert estival' on CBC radio. At the *Monument national in December 1942 he conducted the premiere of Eugène *Lapierre's *Père des amours*, a comic opera in five acts and six tableaus inspired by the life of Joseph *Quesnel.
HP

CHARTIER, Louis. Baritone, teacher, fl 1914–30. In 1914 he was one of the students at the *La Palme-Issaurel studio. He was a soloist at Notre-Dame Church in Montreal, and he gave a concert in December 1916 with Hercule Lavoie in Verdun, near Montreal. He sang 1920–1 in the USA, notably in Detroit, Burlington, Fall River, Springfield, and Worcester, and also in the large theatres and cinemas (Loew's, Capitol) of Montreal. A member of the *Société canadienne d'opérette, he distinguished himself in *Cavalleria Rusticana* with this company at the *Monument national. It is known that in April 1923 he was a soloist in two performances of Franck's *Les Béatitudes* with the *Assn chorale Brassard at Aeolian Hall in New York. That summer he gave several concerts in Quebec City. He also sang 20 Sep 1923 at *Windsor Hall in Montreal with the cellist Yvette Lamontagne and the pianist Wilfrid *Pelletier. At about the same time he gave a concert on the ship *Saguenay* in memory of President Harding. In 1924 he performed again at Aeolian Hall with the harpist Flora Adler. The impresario J.-A. Gauvin presented him in recital in September 1926 at the *Auditorium de Québec, after which Léo *Roy wrote in *La Lyre*: 'M. Chartier has a solidly-produced voice: his sound "carries," rather than being strained or choked, his breathing is perfectly controlled, his diction is excellent, and his interpretation intelligent.' Chartier then moved to Montreal and opened a voice studio. He gave a concert 19 Jan 1930 at the cabaret Le Matou botté. Louis Chartier recorded 38 songs, arias, and duos for *Brunswick, 2 for Melotone, and 38 for *Columbia, including several duos with Blanche Gonthier and Madeleine Cardinal. Details may be found in *Roll Back the Years*.

BIBLIOGRAPHY
'Concert Louis Chartier le 20 septembre,' *La Lyre*, vol 1, Aug 1923
Roy, Léo, 'Louis Chartier à Québec,' ibid, vol 4, Sep 1926
Gour, Romain. *La Palme-Issaurel* (Montreal 1948) HP

CHATILLON. Quebec family of musicians. Four generations are considered here: 1 / Octave Hardy, known as Octave Chatillon; 2 / Édouard and Edmond, sons of Octave; 3 / Robert, son of Édouard; and 4 / Jean, son of Robert.

1 **Octave**. Violinist, pianist, organist, composer, playwright, b Quebec City 12 Apr 1831, d Nicolet, near Trois-Rivières, Que, 18 Jan 1906. He took his academic studies at the *Séminaire de Québec while also studying music, probably with Antoine *Dessane. After spending two years with the Jesuits, he taught music 1855–62 at the Ste-Thérèse-de-Blainville College near Montreal and for the remainder of his life at the Séminaire de Nicolet. Alphonse *Lavallée-Smith and Arthur *Lavigne were among his pupils. Chatillon was organist at the Nicolet Cathedral. He composed six masses, five cantatas, some motets and other short choral pieces, and a variety of works for small combinations of instruments and for band. Most of his music was written for the Séminaire de Nicolet or for convents, and none has survived in use. Chatillon also wrote the plays *Le Lion de Flandre, La Délivrance de Batavia*, and *La Prise de Québec* (the last-named staged in Quebec City in 1902).

2 **Édouard**. Organist, teacher, composer, b Nicolet 1866, d there 1947. A pupil of his father, he succeeded him as organist at the Nicolet Cathedral in 1896 and remained in the position until his death. At the Séminaire de Nicolet for 35 years he taught voice, piano, and organ and directed the bands for several stage shows with music. He also directed the Nicolet Band. He composed two patriotic songs, 'Le Baiser de la langue française' (Boucher nd) and 'Reviens Dollard.' His brother Edmond (Joseph-Edmond-Hardy) (b Nicolet 1865, d ?), doubtless also a pupil of his father, was ordained a priest in 1893. He served 1896–1918 as choirmaster at the Nicolet Cathedral.

3 **Robert**. Bandmaster, teacher, b Nicolet 1904, d there 1973. A pupil of his father, he, too, taught at the Séminaire de Nicolet. Shortly before his father's death, he succeeded him as director of the Nicolet Band and also of the seminary band. He produced several stage shows in the Nicolet region.

4 **Jean**. Composer, theoretician, teacher, administrator, b Nicolet 13 Sep 1937; B PED (Montreal) 1967, Teacher's Diploma (Montreal) 1967. His first music lessons, from Gilles Fortin, were followed by studies 1957–67 in Montreal with Conrad *Letendre (composition) and Michel *Perrault (theory and orchestration). At the request of the *MACQ, he conducted research 1968–9 on early Quebec music publications. He founded in 1969, and directed until 1974, the music department of the UQATR. In 1976 he returned to teach composition and counterpoint there. He founded the Club artistique de Nicolet (1959–63) and in 1974 established the group Art-Nicolet. He has composed some 300 works, including the piano suites *La Fête* and *Valses pour Marie Vetsera* (recorded by Michel *Dussault); *Rue du Trésor*, for orchestra; a *Sonata* for violin and piano, and another for alto saxophone and piano; the *Suite Pantomime* for organ, premiered in 1967 by Lucienne *L'Heureux-Arel; about 20 songs (11 of which have been recorded by the soprano Marie *Daveluy and the pianist Diane Mauger); and some works for recorder including *Duos folkloriques* (Montreal, Centre de psychologie et de pedagogie, 1971) and *Duos de Noël* (Richelieu, Centre de la flûte à bec, 1974). A recital of his songs was presented in 1972 at the UQATR by Marie Daveluy and Diane Mauger. Some 20 of his works have been published by UQATR. Several of his theoretical and instructional works – *Le Procès des clefs* (1969), *Initiations aux structures de la musique pantonale* (3 vols, 1969–75), *L'Emploi des accords ascendants par les grands compositeurs* (1971), *Précis de contrepoint* (1972), *L'Architecture musicale* (1975), and *Le Style modal* (1975) – have been published by UQATR. He is a member of CAPAC.

WRITINGS
'À la recherche de l'ancienne musique québécoise,' *VM*, 9, Oct 1968
'Le cas Letendre,' *VM*, 14, Dec 1969
'Une nouvelle nomenclature pour les intervalles,' *Carnet musical*, 2 Oct 1971

BIBLIOGRAPHY
'Jean Chatillon compose pour les salles pleines,' *Musique périodique*, vol 1, Oct 1977 1–3 / GP, 4 / RD

CHATTOE, Thomas C.. Organist, choirmaster, teacher, b Stafford, England, 15 Sep 1890. After studies in piano and organ in Stafford he went to the Midland Institute in Birmingham and on to the university there, taking in 1913 the course work for a B MUS under Granville Bantock. During World War I he served in France. For 10 years following the war he was an organist-choirmaster in Liverpool and Birkenhead. Before moving to Canada he conducted numerous small orchestras for silent movies and for passenger entertainment on Mediterranean and South American ocean cruises. In 1929 he was appointed music director at the Metropolitan United Church, London, Ont, a position he held for 30 years. In Canada in 1931 he completed the B MUS (Birmingham) he had begun in 1913. His thesis, 'Music in Canada,' described the festival movement, composition, choral societies, organs, and organ builders of Canada. A copy of the thesis is on file at the *U of Western Ontario. After 1934 Chattoe devoted much energy as examiner and teacher to promoting and developing the *Western Ontario Cons, and at the age of 90 he continued to serve it as an examiner. He was president of the *ORMTA 1965–6. GKG

Chautauqua. The name given to travelling tent shows which originated in the USA and flourished in Canada 1917–35. Of Senecan Indian origin, the word 'chautauqua' has been translated variously as 'place of mists,' 'place of easy death,' and 'where the fish was taken out.' A summer school, established in 1874 on Lake Chautauqua, NY, with an eye to combining adult education and morally uplifting recreation, adopted the name from its location, and gradually the name came to represent the type of recreation offered. In Canada a similar type of organization – a Methodist camp – had been established in 1859 at Grimsby Park in Lincoln County, Ont, but by 1900 interest had declined and by 1909 it had ceased. In the USA, however, 'chautauquas' flourished. By 1900 there were some 200 independent chautauquas serving 31 of the United States, almost all held in permanent pavilions close to lakes and offering lectures, plays, and concerts of religious, classical, and popular music.

Chautauqua orchestra at Gainsborough, Saskatchewan, 1926

The notion of making the chautauquas more accessible by sending them on the road was conceived by the US entrepreneurs Keith Vawter and J.R. Ellison, and in 1904 the first of the 'circuit' chautauquas, housed in portable brown tents, began its tour in the mid-west. The second circuit took place in 1907, and from then until 1932 the tours were annual. Tours were promoted in advance, and the chautauquas stayed in each town for five or six days. In addition, short autumn and winter chautauquas carried entertainment to remote areas missed by the regular circuits. Charles F. *Thiele and his family performed on the US circuit. In 1912 Ellison left the Redpath-Vawter Chautauqua Co and with Clarence H. White established the Ellison-White Chautauqua System, which brought the first travelling chautauqua to Canada in 1917. Canadian headquarters were set up in Calgary under the direction of John and Nola Erickson, both from the USA.

In 1917 the Canadian branch of Ellison-White (known from its inception as Dominion Chautauquas) booked tours in all four western provinces, playing in 40 towns during the summer and 108 towns in the autumn. In 1918 chautauquas took place in 294 Canadian towns, again all in the West. A chautauqua offered different programs for each day of its stay at a given location. Music might be supplied by any combination of soloists, small vocal groups (such as the *Adanac Quartet), choirs, instrumental ensembles, or orchestras. Song and dance acts were popular, as were ethnic music groups. Examples of the latter were the Elias Tamburitza Serenaders of Croatia, various Hawaiian ensembles, the Russian Cossack Chorus, Umberto Serrentino and his Venetian Strollers, the Serbian Tamburica Orchestra, and the Scotch(sic)-Canadian Concert Party which featured the comedian Walter Henderson singing Harry Lauder songs. Novelty acts were booked regularly for tours. These included the Carlyle Novelty Trio, the Rainbow Novelty Co, and Robert S. Herrick, who sang humorous songs and imitated female singers including Galli-Curci and Ernestine Schumann-Heink. Among orchestras which appeared on the tours were the Canadian Overseas Orchestra, Leake's Orchestra, and Lieurance's Symphonic Orchestra, coached by Thurlow Lieurance, a composer and 'highest authority on Indian music.' Soloists included the Toronto baritone Ruthven McDonald, the Edmonton soprano Edna Reed, the Australian violinist Ernest Toy, the soprano Mable Markle, and the Metropolitan Opera baritone J. Horace Smithey.

Although the chautauqua phenomenon had its greatest success in western Canada, independent chautauquas flourished in Ontario from time to time, including one said to have been active in Niagara-on-the-Lake during the 1890s. Dominion Chautauquas had offices in London, Ont, ca 1917–18 and in Toronto during the 1920s. By 1926 there were two circuits operating in Ontario. Other Ontario circuits were managed by the US-based Coit-Alber organization. In the Maritimes and Newfoundland over 50 towns were served by a US company known as Swathmore Chautauqua.

By the early 1930s the demise of the chautauqua seemed inevitable. The Depression was a contributing factor. More significant, however, was the new availability of radios and automobiles, which meant that people could stay at home or travel distances to be entertained. Dominion Chautauquas, which became independent of the Ellison-White organization in 1926 and changed their name to Canadian Chautauquas, remained in business under John and Nola Erickson until 1935, when the Ericksons returned to the USA.

BIBLIOGRAPHY

Mugan, Monica. 'When culture came in tents,' *Maclean's*, 15 Jul 1952

Jameson, Sheilagh S. *Chautauqua in Canada* (Calgary 1979)

Pettigrew, Eileen. 'Remember when Chautauqua was the only show in town,' Imperial Oil *Review*, vol 64, no. 4 1980

NM, PW

CHERNEY, Brian. Composer, teacher, b Peterborough, Ont, 4 Sep 1942; ARCT 1961, B MUS (Toronto) 1964, M MUS (Toronto) 1967, PH D (Toronto) 1974. His interest in composition began in childhood. He commuted weekly to study at the *RCMT: piano with Margaret Miller *Brown and Jacques Abram, composition with Samuel *Dolin. His *Variations for Orchestra* were composed for the M MUS under the supervision of *Weinzweig. He taught theory and composition at the *U of Victoria 1971–2 and began teaching the same subjects at *McGill U in 1972. His extensive writings include the only major biography (1975) about Harry *Somers published by 1980.

Cherney's early compositions, eg, the *Quintet*, are doctrinaire, using the 12-tone system to discipline a dense polyphonic texture. His four *Mobiles* (1968–9) depart from such absolutes of craft and use graphic (instead of traditional) notation and variations of rhythm and instrumental colour to stretch and turn note patterns for a constantly changing perspective. Without being radical his recent works have continued to seek a reconciliation of serial procedures and visual or spatial concepts which bend or interrupt them. In 1979 his *String Trio* (1976) tied for top position on the International Rostrum of Composers list of recommended works. Cherney is an affiliate of PRO Canada and an associate of the *CMCentre.

Cherney's brother Lawrence oboist, is a member of the *York Winds.

SELECTED COMPOSITIONS

ORCHESTRA

Two songs (Rilke). 1963. Sop, chamb orch. CMCentre
Concerto. 1964. Vn, orch. CMCentre
Variations for Orchestra. 1967. CMCentre
Six Miniatures. 1968. Ob, str. CMCentre
Seven Images for 22 Players. 1971. CMCentre

CHAMBER

2 *String Quartets*. 1966, 1970. Both CMCentre
Quintet. 1962. Alto sax, str quar. CMCentre
Interlude and Variations. 1965. Ww quin. Jay 1970. RCI 364 (Ayorama WW quin)
Suite. 1965. Va, pf. Ms lost. 1968. ('Largo') CBC SM-78 (O. Green va, Barkin pf)
Woodwind Quintet. 1965. CMCentre
Mobile II. 1968. Vc. CMCentre
Kontakion 'Quiet Music for Eleven Players.' 1969. Ww quin, str quar, db, pf. CMCentre
Mobile IV (Tu Fu, transl K. Rexroth). 1969. Sop, chamb ens. Jay 1970
Eclipse (B. Hendersen). 1972. Sop, fl, pf. CMCentre
Notturno. 1974. Ww quin, pf. CMCentre
Chamber Concerto for Viola and Ten Players. 1975. CMCentre
Tangents I. 1975. Vc, tape. CMCentre
Tangents II. 1975–6. Ob, tape. CMCentre
String Trio. 1976. CMCentre
Group Portrait – with Piano. 1978. Ww quin. Ms
Études. 1979. Solo ob. Ms
The Garden of Earthly Delights. 1979. Ten, ww quin, optional hpd or spinet, optional chimes, offstage pf. Ms

PIANO

Sonata. 1966. CMCentre
Intervals, Shapes, Patterns. 1968. Wat 1970
Pieces for Young Pianists. 1968. Jay 1971–2
Elegy for a Misty Afternoon. 1971. WBM 1973
Mémoires, reflets et rêves d'ailleurs ... 1977–9. Ms

WRITINGS

'The Bekker-Pfitzner controversy (1919–1920): its significance for German music criticism during the Weimar Republic (1919–1931),' unpubl PH D thesis, U of Toronto 1974
Harry Somers (Toronto 1975)
Articles on Somers for *Contemporary Canadian Composers*, *The New Grove Dictionary*, *EMC*

BIBLIOGRAPHY

'Stratford music,' *CBC Times*, 26 Jul–1 Aug 1969

Morgan, Kit. 'Good performance means more than acclaim to Cherney,' *MSc*, 264, Mar–Apr 1972

PRO Canada Ltd. 'Brian Cherney,' pamphlet, 1980

(JF)

CHERNIAVSKY, Jan. Pianist, b Uman, Ukraine, 25 Jun 1892, naturalized Canadian 1922. He was the second of three brothers (Leo, violinist, b 30 Aug 1890, d 1974; Mischel, cellist, b 1893) who performed together as the Cherniavsky Trio from childhood (1901) until 1934, touring Europe 1901–6, South Africa, Egypt, Australia, and New Zealand in 1908, and North America 1915–17. They disbanded in 1934 after a concert in Salt Lake City. (Leo went to Australia, where he performed and broadcast, and then to South Africa. Mischel moved to London, where he pursued a solo career; he eventually settled in France.) Jan, after early studies in the Ukraine, had his most significant tuition from Leschetizky, first when the family moved to Vienna in 1905 and then between 1910 and 1915.

Though all three brothers became Canadian citizens in 1922, only Jan actually lived in Canada, but not permanently until 1934, when he settled in Vancouver. (He lived there briefly before 1920, married a Vancouver woman, and did some teaching.) He continued to give concerts throughout North America, and in 1958, with his brothers, briefly revived the trio for a tour of South Africa. In Vancouver he has involved himself in the musical life of the city, promoting opera, giving concerts in aid of the Vancouver Endowment Trust Foundation, and contributing to opera and theatre for children. He also played an important part with Allard de *Ridder in the re-establishment of the *Vancouver SO in 1930, en-

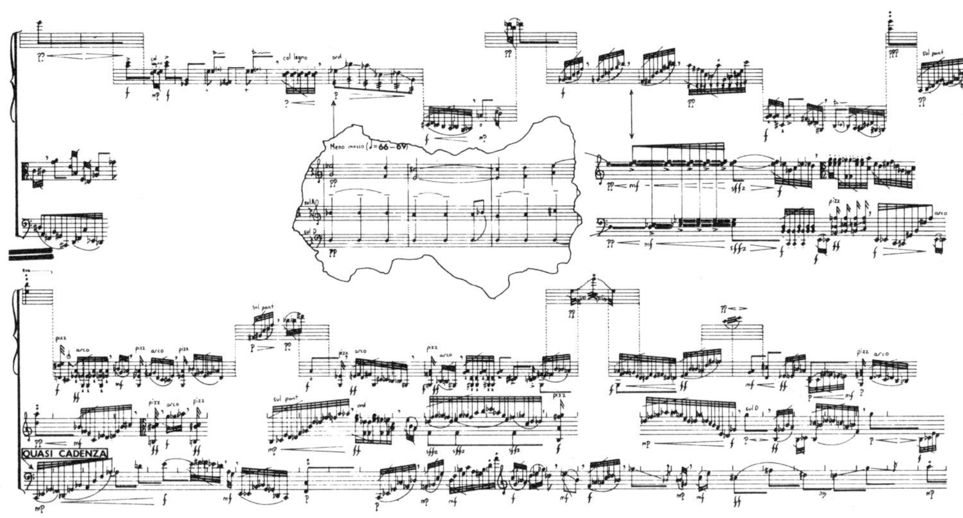

Part of a manuscript page from *String Trio* By Brian Cherney

couraging patrons and helping to inaugurate the orchestra's Sunday concerts. JBu

CHERNY, Al (Alexander Peter) (b Chernywech). Fiddler, b Medicine Hat, Alta, of Ukrainian parents, 1 Nov 1932. As a youth he studied violin with Frank Nowak and in his teens he played country music on CHAT radio, Medicine Hat. in 1951 he joined Vic Siebert and his Sons of the Saddle, cowboy music group in Calgary, and he was a featured performer 1952–9 on *'"CKNX Barn Dance' from CKNX radio, Wingham, Ont. At the *Canadian Open Old Time Fiddlers' Contest he won the novelty class in 1959, 1960 and 1961, and the open class in 1960 and 1961. Cherny was a regular performer on CBC TV, first 1963–5 on 'Country Hoedown' and thereafter on 'The Tommy Hunter Show.' He also appeared with *Hunter on CBC radio's 'Country Holiday' and on tour for the CBC during the 1960s in Europe and the Middle and Far East. Considered one of Canada's finest professional fiddlers, Cherny by the early 1970s had become a leading studio musician, recording as a sideman with Gary Buck, Dick Damron, Hunter, Sylvia Tyson, Jesse Winchester, and others. Under his own name Cherny had recorded seven LPs for *RCA by 1977. One, exclusively of Ukrainian music, was reissued by Tee Vee Records. He received a Big Country Award in 1978 as top country instrumentalist. He is an affiliate of PRO Canada. Dunbar Music has published several of his fiddle tunes.

BIBLIOGRAPHY

Buck, Gary. 'Al Cherny Canada's all time fiddle champion,' *World of Country Music*, Dec 1972 MD

CHESTERMAN, Robert (Paul). Radio producer, b Purley, Surrey, England, 17 Dec 1931, naturalized Canadian 1976. He studied piano in England with Percy Taylor and George Oldroyd. In 1957 he moved to Vancouver, and in 1959 he joined the CBC there as a producer. He was the host 1960–74 for 'Music Diary' and the producer 1961–6 of Dave *Robbins' broadcasts on 'Jazz Workshop.' His feature program on the Benedictine Monastery in Mission, BC, 'The Church at Work,' and his 26-program series 'Masters of the Keyboard' won Ohio State Awards in 1960 and 1961. Though in 1963 Chesterman began working in radio drama, he also produced 1964–72 radio profiles of eminent conductors (Ansermet, Bernstein, Boult, Klemperer, Ormandy, von Karajan, and Walter), and from his interviews for this series he prepared the book *Conversations with Conductors* (London 1976). His dual interest in music and theatre led him to produce radio dramatizations of the lives of Mahler, Bruckner, Haydn (the London period), Mozart (the last years), and Beethoven (an eight-part series, 1970). His documentary on the history of the choir at King's College, Cambridge, was a 1976 highlight of 'CBC Tuesday Night.' BNSG

CHIASSON, Warren. Vibraphonist, percussionist, pianist, composer, b Cheticamp, Cape Breton, NS, 17 Apr 1934. Raised in Sydney, NS, he studied at *St Francis Xavier U in Antigonish and at the *Maritime Cons in Halifax. He was a member 1954–9 of the Royal Canadian Artillery bands in Halifax (trombonist in the military band, violinist in the string orchestra, pianist and guitarist in the dance band), and he played also 1957–9 in CBC Halifax orchestras. Chiasson toured 1959–61 in the USA and Canada as vibraphonist in the pianist George Shearing's group. In 1962 he settled in New York, where he studied with the pianist Lennie Tristano and the composer George Russell. Besides leading his own groups from the vibraphone in various New York jazz clubs and, beginning in 1976, on tour in the USA and Canada, he has played with the jazzmen Chet Baker, Art Blakey, Tal Farlow, Benny Golson, Roland Hanna, and others. He has appeared occasionally in Halifax (he was artist-in-residence 1977–8 at St Mary's U), and was heard in 1978 on the CBC's 'Jazz Radio Canada,' and was seen 1978–9 on CBC TV's 'Denny's Sho*.' His recordings include the LPs *Quartessence* (1973, Van Los VLM 3608) and *Good Vibes for Kurt Weill* (1977, Monmouth-Evergreen MES 7083), several as sideman to Shearing, and one each with the US saxophonists Harold Vick and Frank Strozier and the US guitarist Chuck Wayne. Chiasson's small compositional output includes *Bossa Nova Scotia* and *A Shanty for Peggy* (inspired by Peggy's Cove). He has written 'The Contemporary Vibist,' an unpublished teaching manual. He is a member of ASCAP. MM

Children and music. Articles in *EMC* that deal directly and indirectly with music by and for children include:

Bands: 8 / School and youth bands
CAMMAC
Children's concerts
Children's songs, traditional
Choir schools
Choral singing (a list of choirs with *EMC* entries is appended to that entry and includes several children's choirs and youth choirs)
Competition festivals
Composition for ensemble teaching
Dalcroze Eurythmics
Educanima
Fletcher Music Method
Jeunesses musicales of Canada
John Adaskin project
Kelly Kirby Kindergarten method
Kodály method
Lullabies
Martenot method
National Youth Orchestra
Orff-Schulwerk
Pantonal
Piano playing and teaching
Prodigies
Prologue to the Performing Arts
School music
School music broadcasts
School song books
Summer camps and schools
Suzuki method
Violin and viola playing and teaching
Ward method
Woodwinds
Youth Orchestras

See also *EMC* articles on individual conservatories and music schools, as listed under Education.

The Children of Peace. A religious sect active in the area of Sharon (known as Hope until the 1860s), south of Lake Simcoe, Ont, from the second to the ninth decade of the 19th century. Maintaining a membership of a few hundred, the community rose and declined with its leader, David Willson (b Dutchess County, NY, 7 Jun 1778, d Sharon 19 Jan 1866), a self-made theologian and charismatic leader; indeed the members of the sect were known also as the Davidites. Of Irish descent and Presbyterian background, Willson had little formal education. He was a joiner and sailor before settling on Upper Canada crown land in 1801. A few years later he became a member of the Society of Friends (Quakers), but his independent interpretation of the Bible and his passion for music led to his secession, along with a few friends. In reaction to the austerity of the Quaker meetings, the Children of Peace expressed their Christianity in diverse and imaginative ways: through the symbolism of their architecture, their emphasis on equality, and their cultivation of both vocal and instrumental music.

Four communal buildings were erected in Hope, the first a Meeting House (1819–93) which later became a Music Hall for band practice, entertainments, and Sunday school. Two buildings have survived (they both were purchased in 1918 by the York Pioneer and Historical Society and converted in that same year to a museum): they are Willson's study (1829), and the Temple (built 1825–31), a structure square-shaped to express square dealing, in three tapered storeys to symbolize the Trinity, and supported by 12 pillars, one for each apostle. The York (Toronto) painter-musician Richard *Coates supplied paintings for the Temple and built three organs: a barrel organ (ca 1820) with 133 pipes and two barrels with 10 sacred tunes each, another barrel organ (18??)

Sharon Temple

with three barrels of sacred and secular tunes, and a keyboard instrument (1848) for the second Meeting House (1842–1913).

The first organ (if not the first built in Canada then almost certainly the oldest preserved) has charmed the ears of visitors to the Temple for many years but in the 1970s came to be demonstrated by means of a replica of the original barrel, which had become too fragile to be operated. Geoffrey *Payzant was engaged in the mid-1970s as a consultant on the preservation of the organs. (Payzant restored the playing mechanism, and the organ builder Steward Duncan restored the pipework and wind chest). In a sense the barrels are the oldest sound recordings in Canada – they provide exactly the same sounds as they did to Canadians in the early 19th-century. By plotting the graph of the pins which activate the passage of air through the pipes Don F. Wright of Dundas, Ont, transcribed the tunes in 1967; Keith *MacMillan made a tape-recording in 1963 that is used in the Temple, and with John *Beckwith and Helmut *Kallmann identified all but one of the tunes. Most are of British origin (eg, Old Hundredth, St Ann's, Shirland), but at least one (China) is by the New England composer Timothy Swan and one has a secular origin (In My Cottage Near the Wood). The 30 tunes of the second barrel organ are said to have included 'Blue Bells of Scotland,' 'Henry's Cottage Maid,' 'Lochaber No More,' and 'Water Painted by the Sea,' in addition to some hymn tunes. This instrument was placed in Willson's study but has not survived. The keyboard organ, though preserved in the Temple, is beyond complete restoration, lacking some of the pipes and other parts.

Whereas many Presbyterian, Methodist, and Baptist clergymen in 19th-century Canada bitterly opposed secular music and even instrumental accompaniment of church singing, the Children of Peace cultivated music wholeheartedly both in and outside their Temple, recognizing its educational and community-building value. Singing classes began about 1819, and a band was formed in the following year under one of the Davidites, Patrick Hughes. Richard Coates succeeded Hughes and for some years coached the individual players. According to William Lyon Mackenzie, the instruments in 1831 included 'three or four clarionets, two French horns, two bassoons, besides German and octave flutes, flageolets, &. They have also violins and violoncellos, and are masters of their delightful art' (*Sketches of Canada and the United states*, London 1833). Elsewhere in this book Mackenzie mentions bass-viols and trombones.

Although both men and women sang and played instruments, the white-clad 'chorus of virgins' was the mainstay of singing. 'The women [singers] ... assemble previous to entering the temple, and march thither for public worship, two abreast, with as much regularity as a file of soldiers' (Isaac Fidler, *Observations on Professions, Literature, Manners and Emigration, in the United States and Canada, Made during a Residence there in 1832*, New York 1833). They would climb up the steep 'Jacob's ladder' to the gallery of the Temple and, with the instruments and the organ, join in hymns of praise, the sound floating down to the congregation below. Mackenzie considered their music 'unequalled in any part of the Upper, and scarcely surpassed even by the Catholics in the Lower province.'

The musicians were the delight not only of neighbouring villages but of the citizens of Toronto, where Willson would travel from time to time to present a petition or press for a reform. 'King David frequently goes to a great distance, in order to edify the people of other townships by his music and eloquence ... He never performs such religious errantry without being accompanied by his virgins, six in number, selected from among the females of his household, for their superior voices. These virgins are conveyed in the same wagon with himself over which there is an awning, to shelter them from the inclemency of the weather, and from sultry rays. In one of the other wagons follow as many youths, who form an accompaniment to the damsels, and swell the anthems and hosannahs by vocal and instrumental music. In the remaining wagon are transported ... their musical instruments ... He never fails to attract a large assemblage of people ... The music of his sacred band is considered curious; and the oddity of his manner, and his condemnation of the Established Church, and of the government, are approved by many' (Fidler). One such occasion was reported in Mackenzie's newspaper, *The Advocate* (Toronto, 20 Feb 1834) under the heading of Grand Procession: 'We understand that David Wilson of Hope, with his friends will walk in procession from their hotel to the Old King's Bench Court House ... on Wednesday the 26 inst., being the day preceding the meeting of the General Convention of Delegates for the several townships of the county. They will be accompanied by music and bands, as on the occasion of the county election ... The band of the township of East Gwillimbury [the location of Hope] is one of the most splendid and complete we have ever listened to ...' At home, on festive occasions the band would march 'up and down the streets of Hope, playing cheerful and enlivening airs' (Mackenzie), and monthly concerts were held in the Temple, for charitable aims.

The zest for music continued throughout the years, as young people would come on horseback or ox-drawn sleighs from their villages and farms to attend rehearsals at the Music Hall. A Boston singing teacher, Daniel Cory, was engaged in 1846 for two years; and a set of silver instruments was purchased in Boston for a reputed $1,500 in the 1860s. The bandleaders, Jesse Doan and from 1866 his nephew John Doan Graham (probably the only Sharonite to have compositions published), were of local stock. The Sharon Silver (or Temperance) Band, a dozen players in blue uniforms, not only entertained nearby villagers and townsfolk but on occasion appeared on Lake Simcoe steamers and in Toronto. Trewhella even asserted: 'It is on printed record that the Silver Band of Sharon competed at the great Philadelphia Centennial in 1876, and that there they won the First Prize as the best band in North America,' but the records of that event do not furnish the proof. The repertoire of the band was primarily secular and consisted largely of medleys of US tunes 'of martial swing and ... sentimental appeal' (Trewhella), as well as overtures and potpourris. 'Popular music was ... whistled in Sharon a year before first heard in Old Toronto' (Pearson).

As a sect the Children of Peace began to decline even before Willson's death. Yet some of the old spirit endured, and in September 1883 the choir was heard once more at the Feast of Harvest. In August 1886 the Children of Peace held their last meeting, ending one of the most colourful chapters in Canada's early music history. The music in Sharon proves that musical excellence can be found outside wealthy and sophisticated urban centres, given inspired leadership and a prominent place in the social fabric.

In 1966 John Beckwith wrote his *Sharon Fragments* (for SATB) to words of David Willson.

See also Hymnbooks.

BIBLIOGRAPHY

Pearson, A. Helen. 'The passing of the Children of Peace,' *SatN*, 30 Nov 1912

Trewhella, Ethel Willson. 'The story of Sharon,' Newmarket *Era and Express*, 42 instalments, 14 June 1951–27 Mar 1952

McFaddin, Charles E. 'A study of the buildings of the Children of Peace, Sharon, Ontario,' unpubl MA thesis, U of Toronto 1953

Reaney, James. 'David Willson,' *DCB*, vol 9

Kallmann *History of Music* HK

Children's concerts. Symphony concerts for children in North America began in 1883 under Theodore Thomas in New York. His programs were built around established light concert works such as the *William Tell Overture* or *The Blue Danube Waltz*. This set a pattern adhered to in the USA, Canada, and ultimately Great Britain during the following 75 years. Children attended the concerts independently or in organized gorups. Admission prices were nominal, and transportation often was provided. In Canada after 1950 children's and youth concerts have included comments by the conductor or an assistant; program notes, adapted to the age group they serve, sometimes have been supplied, and literature and recordings sent to classroom teachers in advance for preparation of the young audience. Radio and TV have been used to supplement classroom work. The CBC has co-operated in producing and transmitting national and provincial radio programs during school hours (see School music broadcasts). The *NFB and educational TV stations sponsored by some provincial departments of education have produced programs on music for the young. However, symphony orchestras in Canada, whether the major ones or the community orchestras, remain the main purveyors of children's concerts and devote up to 10 per cent of their time to them (see also Orchestras). It has become common, too, for small groups of performers from the local orchestra to make informal appearances in school classrooms, gymnasiums, and public libraries, to play and also to discuss music and instruments with the children. Active participation and involvement by the children are sought through techniques of inductive teaching. The organization and administration of these programs usually is carried out by volunteer groups associated with the orchestras, working with local boards of education and public library boards.

The *Calgary Symphony Orchestra gave its first young people's matinée concert 25 Nov 1913, performing works by Grétry, Haydn, Delibes, Schumann, Dvořák, and Waldteufel for a public-school audience, each of whom paid 15 cents to attend. The *TSO gave its first children's concerts in 1925 and 1926. However these lapsed until 1930, when regular series began to be presented annually.

The *Montreal Orchestra, the CSM Orchestra (*MSO), and the Cercle philharmonique de Québec (*Quebec SO) all initiated children's concerts during the 1930s. The *Ottawa Philharmonic Orchestra followed during the 1940s and the *Vancouver SO ca 1950. During the 1960s the *Hamilton Philharmonic began sending chamber groups selected from the orchestra into school classrooms to give hundreds of concerts each year. With the MSO in the 1974-5 season Mario *Duschenes, known as one of Canada's foremost directors of symphony concerts for children, gave a series based on three motifs: 'So You Want to Be a Conductor? Let us define the conductor's task,' 'Say It with Music. How the composer conveys his message to us,' 'Instrumental Technique. From the first music lesson to the first recital ... quite a long way!' Duschenes has given series in Quebec City also, has made guest appearances in Ottawa, Toronto, Vancouver, and other cities, and has conducted series of such concerts on CBC TV. Other noted conductors of children's symphony concerts have included Boris *Brott (Hamilton), Victor *Feldbrill (Winnipeg and Toronto), Eugene *Kash (Ottawa), Sir Ernest *MacMillan (Toronto), and Wilfrid *Pelletier (Montreal, Quebec City).

Among chamber groups, *One Third Ninth has prepared and presented programs for children throughout Alberta, and the five members of *Canadian Brass, not only in Hamilton but in many other centres, have given zestful in-school concerts which have been emulated widely by other chamber groups. The *JMC and *Educanima present or sponsor concerts for school children. See also Les Amis de l'art; Prologue to the Performing Arts; Société musicale Le Mouvement Vivaldi.

Compositions that have been written for children's concerts (many commissioned by the sponsoring organizations) include Milton *Barnes' *Children's Suite* (1966), *Beckwith's *All the Bees and All the Keys* (1973), *Beecroft's *Improvvisazioni Concertante No. 3* (1973), Alexander *Brott's *Thunder and Lightning (1973)*, *Buczynski's *Three Against Many* (1973), Howard *Cable's *Sing Sea to Sea (Five Canadian Folksongs)* (1979), *Dela's *Le Chat, la belette et le petit lapin* (1950, rev 1965), *Freedman's *March?* (1970) and *Tikki Tikki Tembo* (1971), Kelsey *Jones' *Jack and the Beanstalk* (1954), Alfred *Kunz' *The Song of the Clarinet* (1961), Michel *Perrault's *Fête et Parade* (1952), Eldon *Rathburn's *Waltz for Winds* (1949, rev 1956), *Ridout's *Music for a Young Prince* (1959), *Surdin's *Eine kleine 'Hammer-Klapper' Musik* (1976), and Christopher *Weait's *The Merry Raftsmen (1979)*. Rathburn's four pieces – *Miniature, Pastorella, Parade,* and *Second Waltz for Winds* – were composed to illustrate the use of various instruments in the NFB film *Children's Concert* (1949). Ridout's *Kids' Stuff* (1978) was 'composed as a jeu d'esprit because Eric Woodward complained that Roger Quilter's *Children's Overture* was too expensive to rent' (CMCentre, *Catalogue of Canadian Orchestral Music: Supplement*, Toronto 1979). Musical plays and operas for children have been composed by Milton Barnes, Keith *Bissell, Barrie *Cabena, Alan *Detweiler, Pat *Patterson, Tibor *Polgar, and Charles *Wilson. The *Canadian Children's Opera Chorus commissioned and performed a children's opera by Menotti in 1979.

Concerts of the folk and pop repertoire, tailored for children, also have been successful in Canadian schools and (under independent sponsorship) concert halls. The *Mariposa Folk Festival established the Mariposa in the Schools program in 1970, and by 1979 had some 20 performers or groups under its aegis in the Toronto area. Two of these, the singer Raffi (son of the noted Canadian portrait photographer Cavouk), and the trio Sharon (Hampson), Lois (Lilienstein), and Bram (Morrison), have made their careers performing for children. Each has recorded, Raffi for Troubadour, the trio for Elephant (its first LP, *One Elephant, Deux Éléphants*, sold over 50,000 copies 1978-9). Other children's presentations (concerts and/or recordings) have been conceived by Alan *Mills, Sandy Offenheim (Toronto), Jan *Rubeš, and the *Travellers.

In 1979, in celebration of the International Year of the Child, the Canada Council Touring Office produced 'The Greatest Little Travelling Supershow for Young People,' which, in addition to mime, dance, and theatre, featured visits to some centres on the tour by the US musician David Amram, Canadian Brass, Alain Lamontagne, Raffi, and Sharon, Lois and Bram. The show travelled across Canada.

BIBLIOGRAPHY

'Symphony orchestra children's concert,' Calgary *Albertan*, 26 Nov 1913
Armstrong, A.H. 'Ottawa children's concerts,' *Canadian Welfare*, 23 Dec 1950
Dugan, James. 'Big music for small people,' *Maclean's*, 15 Feb 1951
Davies, Doris, 'Children's concerts – music for the young,' *Over the Years* [Toronto 1961]
Syme, Mary. 'Music for children offers opportunities for composers,' *CanComp*, 4, Dec 1965
Samson, Marc. 'The world's largest little orchestra,' *Mcan*, 39, Jun 1979
Schulman, Michael. 'Sandy, Raffi, Sharon, Lois and Bram,' *PfAC*, Summer 1979
'The expanding world of children and music,' *Music*, Oct 1979
Sedgwick, Don. 'Sharon, Lois and Bram: new music for children,' *CanComp*, 146, Dec 1979
Linton, Marilyn. 'A looking-glass view of staging symphonies for youngsters,'' *PfAC*, Winter 1979 (ES)

Children's songs, traditional. Songs which children learn from each other – chants passed on orally from one generation of children to the next. They may be rigmaroles, used for games or to accompany skipping, ball-bouncing, or clapping, or simply songs sung for fun. Most of them are old – even centuries old – and came originally from Britain or France: very few actually were composed in Canada, although some of the older ones have acquired Canadian twists or local references.

Formal singing games used to be common but now children sing the game songs to unstructured activities like the twirling of skipping ropes or the bouncing of balls. However, most children still know some bridge games ('London Bridge' or 'Trois fois passera'), ring games ('The Farmer in the Dell' or 'Nous n'irons plus au bois'), line games ('Nuts in May' or 'J'ai un beau château'), and action games ('Oats, Peas, Beans, and Barley Grow' or 'Quant le bonhomme a semé son avoine').

The chants for skipping are particularly numerous and varied: two common Anglo-Canadian ones begin 'On yonder mountain stands a lady' and 'The wind, the wind, the wind blows high.' The English 'Mother, mother, I am ill' is paralleled by the French 'Salade, salade, je suis malade.' Perhaps the most widespread ball-bouncing chant begins 'Are you coming out, sir?' which has its French-Canadian counterpart, 'Allo, allo, monsieur. Sortez-vous ce soir, monsieur?'

In addition to the songs that circulate among children in the playground, others are picked up at summer camps. These usually originate with adults but soon become part of the children's repertoire. In this group are rounds ('Row, Row, Row Your Boat' and 'Frère Jacques'), cumulative songs ('The Green Grass Grows All Around' and 'Alouette'), parodies ('Found a Peanut' to the tune of 'Clementine'), and nonsense songs ('Il était un petit navire').

Edith *Fowke's *Sally Go Round the Sun* and *Ring Around the Moon* (Toronto 1969 and 1977) include many Anglo-Canadian children's songs, while Marius *Barbeau's *Roundelays: Dansons à la ronde* (Ottawa 1958) gives some French-Canadian examples. The folksong collections of Helen *Creighton, Arthur Fauset, and Kenneth *Peacock contain some children's songs. Robert Cosbey's 'Down the Okanagan: skipping songs from Regina' appeared in the *Canadian Folk Music Journal* (1973). Two Inuit children's game songs are included on the recording *The Eskimos of Hudson Bay and Alaska* (Folk FE 4444), and Sam *Gesser recorded *Game Songs of French Canada* for Folkways (FC 7214). There also is a recording of some of the songs from *Sally Go Round the Sun* (McClelland and Stewart).

BIBLIOGRAPHY

Posen, Ira Sheldon. 'Song and singing traditions at children's summer camps,' unpubl MA thesis, Memorial 1975 EF

Chile. See South and Central America, Mexico, the West Indies.

Chilliwack. Vancouver-based rock band, formed in 1964 as the Classics and first popular as the Collectors. The Classics – singer Howie Vickers, keyboardist-saxophonist Claire *Lawrence, singer-guitarist Bill Henderson, bass guitarist Glenn Miller, and drummer Ross Turney – worked as the house band at a strip club, the Torch. As the Collectors, 1966-70, they recorded their own songs 'Looking at a Baby' and 'Fisherwoman' for New Syndrome in 1967 and 'Lydia Purple' for Warner Brothers in 1968 (all minor hits), and wrote and performed music for George Ryga's play *Grass and Wild Strawberries*, for the *NFB production *Don't Let Angels Fall*, and for the multi-media presentation at the Canadian pavilion at Expo 70 in Osaka. The Collectors also gave concerts in San Francisco, Los Angeles, and western Canadian cities. Their extended work *What Love Suite* was especially successful in live performance, and reflected the influence of 'psychedelic' rock, popular among west coast US bands at the turn of the decade. The name Chilliwack was adopted in 1970. After several personnel changes 1970-3 the band was set at Henderson, Turney, Miller, and guitarist Howard Froese. Chilliwack's singles 'Rain-O' (1970, Parrot), 'Lonesome Mary' (1971, Parrot), and 'Crazy Talk' (1974, Goldfish) were hits in Canada. 'Baby Blue' (1977) and 'Fly at Night' (1977) and two LPs, all for Mushroom recordings, brought the group success on the US record market. In 1977 keyboardist-guitarist Brian MacLeod was added to the band, and in 1978 Froese was replaced by Jamie Bowers. Also in 1978 Turney and Miller were replaced for tours by other musicians, but remained associated with the band.

Chilliwack has toured widely in Canada, and also has performed in the USA. During 'a career full of interesting, sometimes quirky, but always original hard rock' (Alan Niester, *Globe and Mail*, 5 Aug 1978) Chilliwack gradually developed in its recordings a popular blend of well-harmonized voices (in support of Henderson's high-pitched lead) and skilfully arranged instrumentation, a style given a harder edge in live performance. The band's composers are affiliates of PRO Canada.

DISCOGRAPHY

The Collectors. 1967. New Supreme WS 1746
Grass and Wild Strawberries. 1968. New Syndrome WS 1774
Chilliwack. 1970. Parrot PAS 71040

Chilliwack. 1971. A & M SP 3509
All Over You. 1972. A & M SP 4375
Riding High. 1974. Goldfish CA 1003
Rockerbox. 1975. Casino CA 1006
Dreams, Dreams, Dreams. 1976. Mushroom MRS 5006
Lights from the Valley. 1978. Mushroom MRS 5011

BIBLIOGRAPHY

Read, Jeani. 'The character of the west reflected in Chilliwack's music,' *MSc*, 282, Mar–Apr 1975
'Chilliwack gaining international momentum,' *RPM*, 5 Aug 1978 (JR)

Chimes. A set of bells, large or small, located in or out of doors, played by hand or, if stationary, automatically. A simpler and older instrument than the *carillon, chimes are used primarily for sounding melodies. The bells are in diatonic sequence, ranging up to two octaves; they may, however, number only two to four bells if they are intended for mere snatches of melody. The best-known melody for chimes was composed by William Crotch in Cambridge, England and uses just four bells. Though properly called the *Cambridge Quarters*, it has come to be known as *The Westminster Chime* since the clock at Westminster, London, was fitted to sound the tune. The oldest known chimes, the Chinese pien-chung, date from the fifth century BC. Similar but later instruments have been used in central Africa and western Europe. In North America a particular type of tower chimes, played from a row of large levers, was developed in the 19th century primarily for playing hymns as people came to church. Their popularity waned with the introduction of the carillon, but some 50 such sets of bells (the leading example of which is the set at St Mary's Cathedral in Halifax) have remained in Canada.

See also Bells.

BIBLIOGRAPHY

'From the archives: the chimes of New Westminster,' *CMJ*, vol 2, Summer 1958 PPr

China. The migration of Chinese to Canada began in 1858 as a result of the Fraser River Gold Rush in British Columbia. Most of the 19th-century migrants, including those contracted for CPR labour from 1882 to 1885, came from Kwangtung (Canton) Province, some via the USA. These immigrants were men, mostly of peasant background, many of whom had left families behind: their primary goal in Canada was to make their fortunes and return to China. In contrast, the later arrivals, particularly after 1960, have been highly trained, women as well as men, representing all areas of China and Hong Kong. In the 20th century most of the over 118,000 (1971 census) Chinese Canadians have lived in and around the large cities of Ontario, Alberta, and British Columbia. (In British Columbia in 1904 the Chinese-Canadian residents of Victoria presented the city with a 2000-pound bell cast in 1627 in China. The bell hangs in Beacon Park.)

Recorded evidence of music among the first Chinese Canadians is scarce for many reasons. What little is known has been gathered piecemeal from a variety of sources. Canadian Chinese music is predominantly Cantonese and may be classified in four genres: folk-street-work songs; Cantonese operas; Cantonese ensemble music; and traditional music other than Cantonese. That in the first two categories was perhaps the earliest heard in Canada. Presumably the Chinese, though possessing and patronizing an endless variety of music, perpetuated their folksongs and other traditional music in Canada to entertain and comfort themselves in a new land. Popular arias from Cantonese opera, a deeply rooted folk – rather than high-art – tradition, also were widely sung among the people. By the 1870s there were three Cantonese operatic clubs established in Victoria, BC: Yuen-t'ien-lo, Yao-t'ien-lo, and Tan-feng-shang. These and similar organizations filled a great need for social contact and entertainment and were encouraged by the merchant class in the rising 'Chinatowns.' Opera clubs from San Francisco, and in at least one instance from Hong Kong, also were invited to perform.

The production of Cantonese opera required about six instrumentalists, and this led to the founding of music clubs apart from opera clubs. The music associations, as exemplified by the Ching Won Musical Society (founded in Vancouver in 1936), engaged in such activities as the celebration of traditional Chinese festivals, banquets, and Chinese chess. The musical instruments typically found in the Cantonese ensemble for both opera and pure instrumental music are yang-ch'in (dulcimer), yueh-hu and ban-hu (two-string violins), and yueh-ch'in, ch'in-ch'in, and p'i-p'a (plucked lutes), as well as percussive instruments. It is not unusual, however, for Cantonese ensembles to include Western instruments such as the violin, the guitar, the clarinet, the saxophone, or the double-bass.

With the arrival in Canada of substantial numbers of immigrants originating from Chinese provinces other than Canton and from Hong Kong, many with broader education, Chinese musical fare in Canada has expanded to include the traditional, non-Cantonese repertoire. However, as Chinese-Canadians adopt Canadian living patterns, language, professions, and education, there is a decrease in the practice of traditional Chinese music. In fact, it has become common for Chinese-Canadian youngsters to study Western musical instruments, and many achieve a high level of proficiency.

Chinese-born musicians in Canada include Ada *Bronstein (of European parents), Ming-Yueh Liang, a teacher at the *U of British Columbia, and the pianist Thomas Wong (who was a pupil of Garth *Beckett in Winnipeg). Several other musicians, later active in Canada, spent periods in China. They include Andréas *Barban, Ida *Halpern, Otto and Walter *Joachim, Rudolf *Komorous, Erwin *Marcus, and Herbert *Ruff. Toronto-born Jo-Anne Chong was a child star in 1947 on CBC radio's 'Microphone Moppets.'

Prior to the establishment of diplomatic relations between the People's Republic of China and Canada in 1972 formal cultural exchanges did not take place, although the Peking Opera toured Canada in 1960. However, in 1973 Ida *Haendel toured in China with the London Philharmonic Orchestra and in 1976 the Men of the Deeps choir from Cape Breton visited China, followed in 1977 by *Canadian Brass, and in 1978 by the *TS under Andrew Davis, with Maureen *Forrester and the pianist Louis *Lortie as soloists. The CBC TV special 'Music East, Music West,' produced by Norman *Campbell, documented the tour. In turn, Canada was host for performances by the Shanghai Ballet in 1977, the Peking Opera in 1979, and other organizations. Lai Tak-ng, conductor of the Toronto Chinese Chamber Orchestra, conducted the *Vancouver SO 15 Jun 1979 in a program of post-1950 Chinese music that featured as soloists Adrian Chiu, a violinist with the Vancouver SO, and the pianist Vance Hoy, a teacher at the *U of Calgary.

BIBLIOGRAPHY

Lee, David T.H. *Chia-na-ta-hwa-ch'iao-shih* [History of Chinese in Canada] (Vancouver, Toronto 1967)
Davis, Morris, and Krauter, Joseph F. *The Other Canadians – Profiles of Six Minorities* (Agincourt, Ont 1971)
Norris, John. *Strangers Entertained – A History of the Ethnic Groups of British Columbia* (Vancouver 1971)
Rittich, Eugene. 'Brief impressions of China,' U of Toronto *News*, from the Faculty of Music, vol. 12, Spring–Summer 1978 M-YL

CHIOCCHIO, Fernande. Mezzo-soprano, pianist, teacher, b Montreal 29 May 1929; B MUS piano (Montreal) 1950. She studied piano at the École supérieure de musique in Lachine and voice 1950–5 with Pauline *Donalda and Sister Rolande Ouimet. In 1951 she received the *Prix Archambault. She also studied voice with Rachele Maragliano-Mori and Philon Ksanes and stage skills with Jan Doat. With the *Opera Guild she made her debut in 1952 at *Her Majesty's Theatre in Prokofiev's *The Love of Three Oranges*. She subsequently performed some 12 roles with the company, notably Mercédès in *Carmen* (1960), Flora in *La Traviata* (1962), Dame Marthe in *Faust* (1963), and Suzuki in *Madama Butterfly* (1965, 1969). She was a member of a vocal quartet which made a 50-concert JM tour in France in 1958. In 1963 she formed the Trio vocal de Montréal with Josèphe *Colle and George Morgan, performing primarily on CBC radio. For CBC TV she appeared in Ravel's *L'Enfant et les sortilèges* (1957), and was Mère Jeanne in *Dialogue des Carmélites* (1960) and Bertha in *The Barber of Seville* (1965). She sang Suzuki with the *COC in 1964 and with the *Vancouver Opera in 1965. On grants from the *Canada Council in 1966 and 1967 she studied with Pierre Médecin and Iris Corradetti at the Académie internationale d'été de Nice. For the *Montreal Festivals she sang in Stravinsky's *Les Noces* and was the Queen in Harry *Somers' **The Fool*, Charlotte in *Werther* (1963), and Mara in Gilbert Bécaud's opera *Aran* (1965). At the *Opéra du Québec she sang the Mistress of the novices in *Suor Angelica* (1971), Maddelena in *Rigoletto* (1972), and Emilia in Verdi's *Otello* (September 1973 – a role she had performed at *Expo 67 with the *MSO). She participated in the recording of Gilles *Tremblay's *Kékoba* and Serge *Garant's *Phrases I* (RCI 240/RCI ACM 2). In 1977 she sang the Marquise de Berkenfield in *The Daughter of the Regiment* in Vancouver; and in the autumn of 1978 she appeared in Charpentier's *Louise* and Jacques Bondon's *I 330* at the Opéra de Nantes. After a Chiocchio recital at the U of Montreal Jean *Vallerand wrote: 'This singer, capable in opera of attaining that kind of dramatic intensity which reveals itself in vocal amplitude, knows, in recital, how to adjust her interpretive powers so that they function on a plane of the most delicate and human intimacy' (Montreal *La Presse*, 11 Dec 1963). Chiocchio taught voice 1967–77 at the Cons de Hull. ST

Choeur Kattialine. Choir founded in 1962 in Montreal by its conductor Jean-François *Sénart. Made up of some 30 young amateurs, it made its name in a repertoire of Renaissance madrigals and motets and of folksongs of all countries. The name Kattialine is the Basque equivalent of Catherine. The group was engaged to give a 'tour of song' in 12 languages at *Expo 67, was heard often on CBC radio, and in 1968 won a first prize at the Quebec Music Festivals (*Canadian Music Competitions). In its later years it expanded its repertoire to include unaccompanied music of the 19th and 20th centuries. It toured Canada in 1968 and Europe in 1969 and 1971. A 1969 private recording (MS 7236) included works by Lassus, Sermisy, Janequin, and others. A 1972 CBC recording, *Noël nouvelet* (RCI 372), offered carols of several countries and four motets for Christmas by Poulenc. The choir ceased activities in January 1974. PR

Le Choeur Pie X. Founded in Montreal in 1936 by its first director, Éthelbert *Thibault, and Eugène *Lapierre. It was the regular choir on the CKAC radio program 'L'Heure catholique,' but was disbanded after less than two years. Restored and reorganized in 1955 by Clément *Morin, the choir resumed performance at a concert presented by the Diocesan Commission for Sacred Music at *Plateau Hall. The choir brought together again about 40 choirmasters from the metropolitan region who wished to improve their knowledge of Gregorian chant and polyphony in order to serve the liturgy more effectually. Its repertoire was limited to Gregorian chant and Renaissance polyphony. The choir performed often in concert and on the CBC. In 1959 it joined the Ensemble vocal of the *École normale de musique to record *Chants à la Vièrge*. The liturgical reforms of Vatican II brought about the disbanding of the choir in 1965. ADV

Choeur V'la l'bon vent. Founded in Quebec City in 1958 by Gilles Julien, president, and François Provencher, music director 1958–73. (Diane Lapierre succeeded Provencher in 1973.) In 1960 the choir became affiliated with the French choral movement À Coeur Joie. The choir maintains 80 to 100 members, and its constitution stipulates that 60 per cent of its repertoire must be Canadian. The stipulation is met mainly by arrangements of pop songs (Gilles *Vigneault, Félix *Leclerc etc) and to a degree by folksongs. The group also includes dancers and an instrumental trio (piano, percussion, double-bass) directed by Gilles Breton. The choir gives a large annual concert and has participated in several congresses. It was the first Canadian choir at the Choralies de Vaison-la-Romaine in France, where its particular style (choreography and movement with singing) captured attention. It participated in *Expo 67 in Montreal, at the Canada Week at Expo 70 in Osaka, Japan, at the Choralies internationales in Morocco, etc. Its tours have taken it to Belgium, Italy, Switzerland, Tunisia, and most parts of Canada. It has made three LPs entitled *Le Choeur V'la l'bon vent*, one for the Radio-Marie label (1962, RM NDC 336217) and two for the label using its own name (1972, VBV 100; and 1975, VBV 200). MB-L

Choir schools, church. Institutions set up to train young musicians in the literature and performance of church music and to enable them, through the presentation of such music, to worship in a manner at once spiritual and artistic. Prototypes are the English choir schools at Canterbury Cathedral, King's College, Cambridge, and Westminster Abbey, where the program combines academic and musical training with obligatory participation in church services. In Canada various attempts have been made to duplicate or at least approximate the traditional choir school, but changes in tradition and limited funds have resulted in some broad adaptations and variations. It is only in Ontario and Quebec that some full-time schools exist. St Michael's Roman Catholic Cathedral in Toronto has a day school (founded in 1937 by Mgr J.E. *Ronan) where, along with a full academic program, choristers are trained for the cathedral choir and some students are trained for larger musical responsibilities in the church. Similar schools in Quebec include the Maîtrise des *Petits Chanteurs du Mont-Royal (in Montreal), the *Maîtrise du chapitre de Québec, the Maîtrise Notre-Dame-du-Cap (in Cap-de-la-Madeleine), the Manécanterie des Petits Chanteurs de Tracy, the Maîtrise des *Petits Chanteurs de Granby, and the Maîtrise des Petits Chanteurs de Trois-Rivières. Two others, no longer in operation, were the Maîtrise des *Petits Chanteurs à la Croix de Bois (1933–61) and the *Petite Maîtrise de Montréal (1938–44). Some of these Quebec schools provide full academic and musical training; others offer only the latter.

There are (1980) no full-time choir schools connected with Canadian Protestant churches. The traditional choir school is most nearly approximated in Ontario, where the English influence is strongest. Independent schools affiliated with the Anglican Church offer a broader educational approach than do their English prototypes. *Bishop Strachan School and St George's College (Toronto), St John's School (Elora), Ridley College (St Catharines), and Trinity College School in Port Hope provide a general education with extra music for some students. In the early 1950s, the Anglican Church began to sponsor a number of summer choir schools offering intensive training in church music. The first of these was the Toronto Diocesan Choir School, founded in 1954 under the directorship of Healey *Willan and conducted at Trinity College School until 1977, when the school was relocated at St Andrew's College, Aurora. Similar Anglican schools were established in Wallacetown, Ont, and in New Brunswick, Prince Edward Island, and Quebec. A girls' summer choir school was established in 1975 at the Ontario Ladies' College in Whitby, Ont.

BIBLIOGRAPHY
Ronan, J.E. 'Toronto's Cathedral Choir School,' *Culture*, vol 7, Sep 1946
Martel, Jules. 'Church music I,' *Music in Canada* (KS)

Choral composition. On 14 Nov 1606 the first choral work either written or arranged in Canada was performed on the waters before Port Royal (Annapolis Royal, NS) – the four-part song 'Great God Neptune' in the masque **The Theatre of Neptune* by Marc Lescarbot.

The main influence on choral music in succeeding years was the church, Roman Catholic at first, later also Anglican, Presbyterian, and Methodist. Unfortunately facts are scarce – it was not an age given to recording its own cultural history. In the late 18th century *singing schools flourished; there were concerts – often featuring operatic arias and ensembles; oratorio was performed (St. Paul's Church, Halifax, in 1769), as was opera (Gretry's *Richard Coeur-de-Lion* at Halifax, in 1798); but of original choral composition there was little.

A Sanctus by the composer-priest Charles *Ecuyer, possibly written before 1800, and restored by Gustave *Smith in 1877 (from two surviving choristers' memory of it) as a duet with organ accompaniment, has an oblique claim to being the oldest surviving Canadian choral composition.

Joseph *Quesnel is said to have written motets, and his operas contained trios and finales, but there is some indication that the church music of this blithe late-19th-century spirit was too cheerful and dramatic for the church of his day, and there is no evidence that he persevered in the genre or wrote any major choral works. Church musicians are traditionally conservative and while there was probably a trickle of original anthems from Quesnel and others, most choirmasters, having been educated in Europe, brought with them the repertoire with which they were familiar.

Later, publication begins to give a clue to activity. The earliest printed works to appear were editions of service books for Roman Catholic use. The first choral compositions by Canadians appeared in the church music collections of *Humbert (**Union Harmony*), Mark Burnham (*Colonial Harmony*, 1832), and J.P. *Clarke. Clarke's six hymn-tunes and two anthems in his *Canadian Church Psalmody* (1845) are notable. He composed an eight-part anthem, 'Arise, O Lord God, Forget Not the Poor.' In Montreal J.-C. *Brauneis wrote a *Mass* (1835; for choir, violin, flute, bass viol, bassoon, and organ) which was highly praised. Antoine *Dessane was a prolific composer of church music, as were Joseph-Julien *Perrault, whose *Messe de Noël* (1860) was performed and much admired, and Jean-Baptiste *Labelle.

The next generation produced more native-born composers. Guillaume *Couture wrote an oratorio, **Jean le Précurseur* (1909), which has been described as 'one of the monuments of Canadian music,' and composed a setting of the *Requiem Mass*. Alexis *Contant wrote two oratorios, **Caïn* (1905) and **Les Deux Âmes* (1909), three large-scale masses, and other, shorter choral works.

Other composers of choral music in this period were Achille *Fortier and Amédée *Tremblay. Angelo *Read wrote a cantata, *David's Lament* (1903), and other church music. The contribution of Clarence *Lucas included the cantata *The Birth of Christ* (1902) and a *Requiem Mass*. William *Reed and A.S. *Vogt (the latter one of Canada's most famous choral conductors) each wrote a number of short choral pieces.

English-born musicians who contributed to the repertoire in this period include Charles A.E. *Harriss, who wrote a cantata *Daniel before the King* (1890), a *Festival Mass* (1901), a *Coronation Mass* (1902), and other large-scale choral-orchestral works; Percival *Illsley, composer of the cantata *Ruth* (1894); Albert *Ham who wrote a cantata, *The Solitudes of the Passion*, and an *Advent Cantata*; and Edward *Broome who composed several major choral works.

A slightly later arrival, Healey *Willan, exercised a profound effect on later musicians and made a vast contribution to the literature. Both his performances and his style of choral writing, a subtle blend of sinuous lines, warm harmony, and fastidious counterpoint, became models for composers of the next generation. His most influential works are undoubtedly the shorter liturgical pieces – in particular a group of 11 liturgical motets, 14 masses, and a series of hymn-anthems. There is choral music in several major works including the opera **Deirdre* (1945, revised 1962) and some music-dramas. Also of note are the large-scale motet **An Apostrophe to the Heavenly Host* (1921) and the *Coronation Suite* (1953).

Writing in a similar vein, but at a more modest level, were W.H. *Anderson and Alfred *Whitehead. Anderson specialized in music for less sophisticated choirs, both church and secular, and Whitehead's work reflected his career as a cathedral organist.

Meanwhile, in Quebec, a native strain flourished, though there is an impression that choral music was not the chief manifestation. There are a few works by Claude *Champagne, including the major piece for choir and orchestra *Altitude* (1959) and some shorter liturgical pieces, and there is the *Te Deum* (1945) of Joseph *Vermandere, but little from their contemporaries.

The next generation, however, produced Jean *Papineau-Couture who made a striking setting of Psalm 150 (1954) for choir, instruments, and organ and composed the very advanced *Viole d'amour* (1966); Pierre *Mercure whose **Cantate pour une joie* (1955) and *Psaume pour abri* (1963) are distinctive; and Roger *Matton who in *L'Escaouette* (1957) and *Te Deum* (1967) showed a predilection for choral writing employing very large forces. Notable also is Jacques *Hétu's *Les Djinns*.

Among composers of the younger generation in Quebec, Claude *Vivier has attracted attention with his *Chants* (1972–3) and his *Festival Singers commission *Journal*, for choir, soloists, and percussion. Otto *Joachim produced an outstanding choral piece, *Psalm* (1960). Kelsey *Jones has written extensively for voices. Among his major works are *Songs of Time* (1955), *Songs of Experience* (1958), and *The Prophecy of Micah* (1963). André *Prévost's *Terre des Hommes* (1967), a massive work for three choirs, orchestra, and narrators, was composed for the opening of the World Festival at *Expo 67.

Toronto-born or -educated composers have been perhaps particularly 'choral minded,' partly because of Willan and partly because of a very strong local choral tradition which stretches back to *Torrington and Vogt. Godfrey *Ridout, with such works as *Esther* (1952), *Pange lingua* (1960), and *The Dance* (1960), and Robert *Fleming, who has written several small-scale works and a cantata *Heirs through Hope* (1968), represent this influence most clearly. Ben *Steinberg's *Pirchay Shir Kodesh* (1963) is one of several settings he has composed for synagogue services.

Keith *Bissell has a large list of choral works to his credit, intended mostly for school or amateur choirs, and a growing list of longer works, including the Advent cantata *People Look East* (1966), *The Passion According to St Luke* (1971), *God's Grandeur* (1975), and *Famous Men* (1976) and a few more complex works written for commissions.

John *Beckwith has written in a more modern vein, exploiting the possibilities of serial techniques in *Jonah* (1963) and of vocal collage in *The Trumpets of Summer* (1964) and, to a lesser degree, *Sharon Fragments* (1966). The work of Harry *Somers also exploits more adventurous techniques ranging from the comparatively simple contrasts in *God the Master of This Scene* (1962) and *Gloria* (1962) through the bonhomie of *Five Songs of the Newfoundland Outports* (1969) to the complications of *Kyrie* (1972).

Harry *Freedman has composed a few choral works – *The Tokiado* (1964) and *The Flame Within* (1968) are important. Talivaldis *Kenins' *Chants of Glory and Mercy* (1970) is a large and effective work. Oskar *Morawetz' few and short choral pieces are valuable. R. Murray *Schafer has written a few pieces designed to lift school choirs out of traditional ruts and expose them to modern devices and effects; the best known is *Epitaph for Moonlight* (1968). Clifford *Ford's *Mass* (1976), commissioned by the Festival Singers, is an unaccompanied setting of varying polyphonic density, ranging from four-part to 16-part writing.

Mention must be made of three composers living in the west. Violet *Archer has written a great deal of very challenging music for choirs. Among her chief works are *The Bell* (1949), *Landscapes* (1950), *Songs of Prayer and Praise* (1953), and *Sing, the Muse* (1964), and there are interesting smaller pieces for church choirs. Jean *Coulthard is particularly successful in her short works for younger singers, but she also has written a cantata, *Quebec May* (1948), and several longer works. Bernard *Naylor, who has divided his time between Canada and England, has written a large body of challenging music, chiefly for skilled church choirs. Particularly interesting are a set of *Nine Motets*, another of *Three Latin Motets*, several cantatas, and a *Missa da camera* (1966).

In general, a study of programs by choral organizations reveals a repertoire largely European. This is not surprising when one considers the sheer volume of music available and the hundreds of years of history involved. There is the advantage of both education and inspiration that can be drawn from such exposure. However, Canada has encouraged native composers to a certain degree, and, with ever-improving standards of performance and the healthy growth in the number of choirs during the 1970s, more composers became encouraged to think of choral music as a logical and idiomatic outlet for their important work.

Among the Canadians who have compsed choral works are Hugh *Bancroft, Milton *Barnes, Leslie *Bell, Lorne *Betts, Wolfgang *Bottenberg, Alexander *Brott, Barrie *Cabena, F.R.C. *Clarke, Lionel *Daunais, William *France, James *Gayfer, Graham *George, Srul Irving *Glick, Frank *Haworth, Derek *Healey, Harry *Hill, Derek *Holman, Richard *Johnston, Lothar *Klein, Alfred *Kunz, Quentin *Maclean, Sir Ernest *MacMillan, Michael *Miller, David *Ouchterlony, Welford *Russell, Robert *Turner, and Charles *Wilson.

During the late 19th and early-to-mid-20th century, Canadian publishers issuing choral series often mixed non-Canadian and Canadian music together. These series of choral works included the Octavo Choir Music, The Lute series of anthems, both by *Anglo-Canadian; The Canadian Part Singers Treasury by *Harris; *Nordheimer's Octavo Edition; *Western Music's Western Choral Series and Western Folk Song Series; and *Whaley Royce's Octavo Choruses and Quintettes, and Select Choruses and Part Songs.

In 1980, recent or current series included Alliance des chorale du Québec's Turlurette; Harris's Harris Sacred Choral Series, Harris Secular Choral Series, and Folk Songs of Canada; *Leslie Music Supply's Leslie Choral Series; *Thompson's The Festival Singers of Canada Choral Series; and *Waterloo's four: the F.R.C. Clarke Sacred Choral Series, the Hymn Sing Choral Series, the Waterloo Folk Music Library, and the Waterloo Sacred Choral Library. Most of the other 20th-century Canadian publishers have issued some choral music.

See also Anthems, motets, psalms; Cantata; Choral singing; Christmas; Easter, Lent, the Passion; Folk-music-inspired composition; Masses; Oratorios, Canadian; and Te Deum laudamus.

BIBLIOGRAPHY

CMCentre. *Catalogue of Canadian Choral Music* (Toronto 1966, enl 1970)

– *Catalogue of Canadian Choral Music* (Toronto 1978)

(GBr)

Chorale de l'Université St-Joseph. Male choir founded by Father Léandre Brault in 1946 in Memramcook, NB, with the aim of developing interest in Gregorian chant. In 1950 the choir received the City of Lincoln Trophy, awarded annually by the *FCMF to the best amateur choir in Canada. In 1952 for the *NFB Father Brault made three documentary films on the university and its choir. Father Brault was succeeded by Father Roland Soucie in 1953, when he left the choir to assist in the organization of the *Petits Chanteurs du Mont-Royal choir school. Father Soucie was succeeded by Father Neil Michaud in 1955. The Chorale de l'Université St-Joseph won the City of Lincoln Trophy again in 1956, 1957, and 1958. Its name was changed to the Chorale de l'Université de Moncton in 1963 when St-Joseph U became the *U of Moncton. The choir began making annual tours in 1965, including one across Canada in 1968 and one in France in 1973, performing arrangements of old French and English songs and standard pieces from the male-choir concert repertoire. Female voices were added to the original male choir in 1975 to form a mixed choir that represented New Brunswick in the Olympic Games in Montreal in the following year.

DISCOGRAPHY

En montant la rivière. (1974). Son Excellence Sound 101

Folklore canadien. (1959). Col FL 234

Tournée Trans-Canada. (1960). Col FL 259

The University of Moncton Male Choir. (1968). Harmony HES 6008

The Voyageurs and Their Songs. (1967). Minnesota Hist Soc

GA

Choral singing. Canada's choirs have contributed significantly to religious, educational, and concert activities within the country, and several have earned high reputations abroad. Choral singing in Canada became immensely popular in the second half of the 19th century, reached its first peak – unsurpassed, certainly, in the quantity of choristers – in the years preceding World War I, and entered a new period of vigour and expansion after the middle of the 20th century. From the turn of the century until the serious onset of the 'television era' after World War II, voluntary church choirs were the centres of regular musical activity in innumerable towns and small cities of Canada, and many of the larger cities' concert choirs in the 19th and early 20th centuries were extensions or amalgamations of church choirs, favouring names such as philharmonic society or choral union (usually prefaced by the name of the city). These large-scale choirs strove to master the choral-orchestral literature, especially oratorios and cantatas. Other choral groups, such as the *Montagnards in Montreal, had their roots in the love of operatic and folk music. Still others made a specialty of unaccompanied music (eg, the *Mendelssohn Choir of Montreal, though it also sang accompanied works) or were made up entirely of male voices (eg, the *Arion Male Voice Choir of Victoria, the *Winnipeg Male Voice Choir). Church and school choirs have remained the most numerous, but other types came into prominence in the mid-20th century: the children's choir (eg, the *Canadian Children's Opera Chorus, the *Mennonite Children's Choir), the female choir (eg, the *Leslie Bell Singers), the folk or ethnic choir (eg, the *Toronto Jewish Folk Choir, the *Jeunes Chanteurs d'Acadie), the small studio ensemble for broadcast performance (eg, the *Choristers, the Carl Tapscott Singers), the 'barbershop' quartet and its female counterpart the Sweet Adelines, and many others. While most have remained amateur, a few choirs have turned professional, in the sense that their members earn a basic livelihood from choral singing; the first of these was the *Festival Singers in 1968.

Visits to other countries began about the turn of the century – the *Toronto Mendelssohn Choir visited the USA in 1905 – and have continued. Many have expanded into tours, not only of the USA but of Europe, Japan, and other parts of the world. Some of the touring choirs have participated in competitions and festivals (eg, the Eisteddfods in Wales and England), and others have made a specialty of concert appearances, notably the *Elgar Choir of British Columbia, the Winnipeg Male Voice Choir, the Toronto Mendelssohn Choir, the *Disciples de Massenet, the *Montreal Bach Choir, the Festival Singers, the *Tudor Singers of Montreal, and the *Vancouver Chamber Choir.

Important associations of choirs are the *Alliance chorale canadienne, founded in 1966; the *Ontario Choral Federation, established in 1971; the *Nova Scotia Choral Federation, formed in 1975; the Saskatchewan and the British Columbia choral federations founded in 1978; and the New Brunswick and Prince Edward Island choral federations, both founded in 1979.

Important meetings, festivals, and competitions specifically for choirs have included the *Cycle of Musical Festivals, the various

'The Chorister' by Robert Harris, 1880

*Sängerfeste, the annual gatherings of choirs sponsored by provincial choral federations (eg, Ontario's Choirs in Contact and the British Columbia Choral Conference), and the Choralies internationales canadiennes, organized every three years by the Alliance chorale canadienne.

Competitions include the CBC/Canada Council National Radio Competition for Amateur Choirs / Concours radiophonique national des chorales d'amateurs, established in 1976 and held every two years, and that sponsored by the *FCMF for the George S. Mathieson and the City of Lincoln trophies.

Important Canadian composers of choral music are treated in the entries on Anthems, motets, psalms; Cantatas; Choral composition; Christmas; Easter, Lent, the Passion; Masses; Oratorio performance (international repertoire); Oratorios, Canadian (composition and performance); and Te Deum laudamus. Important choral conductors are mentioned in Conductors and conducting. See also CAMMAC; Choir schools; Competition festivals; Hymn singing; Oratorio performance; Plainsong; Schola cantorum; Singing schools.

The appended list names those choirs which have entries in *EMC*. Some others are noted briefly in the entries for cities and for countries.

Anne Campbell Singers (see Campbell, Anne)
Arion Male Voice Choir
Armdale Chorus
Association chorale Brassard
Association chorale St-Louis-de-France
Association des chanteurs de Montréal
Bach-Elgar Choir of Hamilton
Bishop Strachan School Chapel Choir
Border Scottish Choir of Windsor
Brunswick Singers (see Thomson, David)
Canadian Centennial Choir
Canadian Children's Opera Chorus
Canadian National Exhibition Chorus
Cantata Singers of Vancouver
Carl Tapscott Singers (see Tapscott, Carl)
Carriden Choir (see Thomson, David)
Chanteurs de Ste-Thérèse et du cégep Lionel-Groulx
Chanteurs St-Coeur-de-Marie
Choeur Kattialine
Choeur Pie X
Choeur V'la l'bon vent
Chorale de l'Université St-Joseph
The Choristers
Confederation Choir
Disciples de Massenet
Dofasco Male Chorus
Don Wright Chorus
Elgar Choir of British Columbia
Elizabethan Singers
Ensemble vocal Chantal-Masson
Festival Singers
Gallery Singers
Halifax Choral Society
Halifax Harmonic Club
Hart House Glee Club
Jeunes Chanteurs d'Acadie
Kingston Choral Society
Kitchener-Waterloo Philharmonic Choir
Leamington Choral Society
Leslie Bell Singers
Madrigal Singers
La Maîtrise du chapitre de Québec
Men of the Deeps (see O'Donnell, John)
Mendelssohn Choir of Montreal
Mennonite Children's Choir
Montagnards
Montreal Bach Choir
Montreal Elgar Choir
Montreal Oratorio Society
Montreal Philharmonic Society
Musical Union (Toronto)
National Chorus of Toronto
Ontario Youth Choir
Orpheus Choir of Toronto
Orpheus Club (Halifax)
Orpheus Club (Regina)
Ottawa Choral Society and Union
Palestrina Choir
Petite Maîtrise de Montréal
Petits Chanteurs à la Croix de Bois
Petits Chanteurs de Granby
Petits Chanteurs du Mont-Royal
Regina Male Voice Choir
Les Rhapsodes
Richard Eaton Singers
St David's Welsh Male Voice Choir
Schubert Choir
Société musicale Ste-Cécile
Toronto Bach Choir
Toronto Jewish Folk Choir
Toronto Mendelssohn Choir
Toronto Men Teachers' Choir
Toronto Oratorio society
Toronto Philharmonic Society
Tudor Singers of Montreal
University of British Columbia Chamber Singers
Vancouver Bach Choir
Vancouver Chamber Choir
Winnipeg Male Voice Choir
Winnipeg Oratorio Society
Winnipeg Philharmonic Choir

BIBLIOGRAPHY

The Church Choir, fl 1907 (Toronto) a periodical of which but a single copy of a single issue has been located in any library – the NL of C

Middleton, J.E. 'Choral music in Ontario,' *The Year Book of Canadian Art*, compiled by the Arts and Letters Club (London, Toronto 1913)

Hesselberg, Edouard. 'A review of music in Canada,' *Modern Music and Musicians* (New York, Toronto 1913)

'Choral music in Canada,' *CanJM*, June 1914

Peaker, Charles. 'Choral music in Canada,' 'La musique chorale au Canada,' *CRMA*, vol 4, Oct–Nov 1945

Hobday, Kathleen Maude. 'A survey of the musical resources of the province of Ontario,' MA thesis, U of Toronto 1946

MacMillan, Sir Ernest. 'Orchestral and choral music in Canada,' *Proceedings of the Music Teachers' National Assn* (1946)

– 'Choral music,' *Music in Canada* (Toronto 1955)

Aspects of Music in Canada / Aspects de la musique au Canada

Bissell, Keith, and Schabas, Ezra. *Choral Music in Ontario* (Toronto 1970)

Lock, William Rowland. 'Ontario church choirs and choral societies, 1819–1918,' unpubl DMA thesis, U of Southern California 1972

Saunders, Vernon S. 'Choral music in Saskatchewan,' OCF *Newsletter*, vol 6, Aug–Sep 1976

1979 Canadian Choral Records List, compiled by Jon Washburn for CBC 'Choral Concert' (Vancouver 1979) HK

The Choristers. Winnipeg chamber choir founded by W.H. *Anderson in 1936 as the Oriana Singers, a 14-voice madrigal choir which in 1942 expanded to 16 (later to 20) voices and took the name the Choristers for broadcast purposes. The Choristers achieved a national reputation for their fine choral blend and sense of style and for many years were among the few Canadian choirs reaching a large audience regularly. On occasion during World War II the choir sang under the name the Cathedral Singers for semidramatic broadcasts with the John Holden Players (eg, 'Tudor Manor,' 'Under the Lofty Towers of Westminster,' 'Western Saga'. Also on occasion Anderson augmented and prepared the Choristers for performances of choral-orchestral works such as the Fauré *Requiem* and large pieces by Holst and Vaughan Williams; the combined forces were conducted by Geoffrey *Waddington or later Eric *Wild.

The Choristers as such, however, began weekly broadcasts under Anderson's direction on the national network of the CBC 2 Jun 1942. Gordon *Kushner and later Roline Mackidd were among the regular piano accompanists associated with the choir during the first 10 years, when the program consisted of a mixture of sacred and secular partsongs, madrigals, motets, and folksong arrangements. In 1952 the name of the broadcast became 'Sunday Chorale' and the format of the program changed, becoming devoted exclusively to church music – hymns, anthems, motets – with organ accompaniment, first by Hugh *Bancroft, then by Herbert *Sadler and Filmer *Hubble. Anderson chose the music and conducted the choir until a few months before his death in 1955. At that time the directorship was assumed by Hubble. The choir, though it remained the Choristers, gradually became known by the name of the program. Hubble conducted 'Sunday Chorale' until his death in 1969, when he was succeeded by Herbert Belyea, a tenor in the choir. Belyea conducted the choir in several public concerts, but broadcasts were only intermittent in the early 1970s and it disbanded in 1974.

Gladys *Whitehead, May *Lawson, Reginald *Hugo, and Lorne *Betts were among the original Choristers, along with many other leading Winnipeg singers of the day. The personnel changed over the years but several of the original singers continued with the choir until well into the 1960s. Among other noted singers who sang with the group are Evelyne Anderson, Devina Bailey *Duggan, Kathleen Morrison Brown, Joan *Maxwell, and Phyllis *Cooke Thomson. JA, KW

CHORNODOLSKA, Anna. Soprano, b Vienna, of Ukrainian parents, 21 Apr 1946, naturalized Canadian 1956; premier prix (CMM) 1970, BA (McGill) 1970. Taken to Montreal in 1948, she studied voice 1965–70 at the CMM with Bernard *Diamant, Léopold *Simoneau, and Daniel Ferro, and made her debut 28 Sep 1970 with the *MSO in Mahler's *Fourth Symphony*. Under the auspices of *JMC she made three tours 1971–4 in Canada and one in November 1977 in France. She made her New York debut at Carnegie Recital Hall 18 Jan 1972; (the *New York Times*, 20 Jan 1972, said of her: 'She entered into each song deeply and fully, dramatizing its uniqueness with great temperament, taste and intelligence.') She made a Washington, DC, debut with the Canadian harpsichordist Martha Brickman in that same year, and was a winner of the 1972 *CBC Talent Festival.

Chornodolska's operatic debut as Micaela in *Carmen* at *PDA was followed by roles with the *Opéra du Québec (*La Traviata*, 1972; *Manon*, 1973), with the NAC's Festival Canada (as Blonda in *The Abduction from the Seraglio*, 1974; see *Festival Ottawa), and with the *McGill Chamber

Orchestra in 1976 in the North American premiere of Antonio Sacchini's *Olimpiade*. In Toronto in 1977 she was Monica in the Comus Music Theatre production of Menotti's *The Medium*; John *Kraglund in the *Globe and Mail* (9 Jul 1977) wrote: 'Her scenes with Toby ... were among the most sensitive moments in the production.' She has appeared in leading roles in CBC TV productions of *The Merry Widow* and *West Side Story*. The dedicatee of George *Fiala's *Five Ukrainian Songs*, she premiered the work 24 May 1973 with the *Winnipeg SO. She has sung with other leading Canadian orchestras, including the MSO (*St Matthew Passion*, 1975) and the *TS (Mozart concert arias, 1976), and with the National Orchestra of Mexico (Strauss' *Four Last Songs*, 1977). In 1978 she recorded Jacques *Hétu's *Les Clartés de la nuit* and songs of Schubert and Spohr (RCI 483).

CHOTEM, Neil. Pianist, composer, arranger, conductor, teacher, b Saskatoon, of Russian parents, 9 Sep 1920. In Saskatoon he began his piano studies at the Palmer School of Music at five and continued with Lyell *Gustin 1930–8. He made his debut in 1933 in Saint-Saëns' *Concerto No. 2* with the *Regina SO. The following year he studied in Chicago with the Canadian pianist Jeannette Durno. His family moved to Winnipeg, where he gave many recitals 1935–9 on the CBC and premiered his *Scherzo Tarantelle* for piano and orchestra. He also played 1940–2 as a duo-painist with Gordon *Kushner and gave solo recitals in several western Canadian cities. He joined the RCAF as a musician in 1942. While stationed overseas he discovered jazz, and he retained this interest throughout his subsequent career as a composer, conductor, and arranger. He settled in Montreal in 1945 and studied 1946–50 with Michel *Hirvy. In 1946 he accompanied the tenor Richard Tauber on a Canadian tour. The following year he appeared in the film *La Forteresse*, and in its English version, *Whispering City*, playing André *Mathieu's *Concerto de Québec*. Chotem made his Montreal recital debut 3 Mar 1947. Invited by Sir Ernest *MacMillan to play with the *TSO, he appeared 4 Apr 1947 in Rachmaninoff's *Concerto No. 2* and Franck's *Variations symphoniques*. He was heard by Artur Rubinstein, who predicted a brilliant future.

Chotem led a jazz trio (of which the variable complement included, for a time, the bassist Lucien Gravel and the drummer Donat Gariépy) 1946–8 in a series of CBC radio broadcasts. In 1952 another Chotem trio and the singer Yvonne Lanauze made the LPs RCI 79 and RCI 80. Soloist on the CBC programs 'Radio-Carabin,' 'The Sunday Night Show,' 'Stardust Serenade,' and 'CBC Star Time,' he also composed and conducted for several CBC radio plays (among them 'The Dybbuk,' 'The World's Illusion,' 'The Trial,' 'A Tribute to Eugene O'Neill,' and the series 'The Iliad' and 'The Odyssey') and wrote music for the radio dramas directed 1948–50 byRupert Caplan for 'CBC Wednesday Night.' Between 1950 and 1960 he played several times with the *'Little Symphonies' orchestra and the CSM Orchestra (*MSO) and again with the TSO. He also performed Beethoven's *Concerto No. 4* with the *CBC SO, played with the *McGill Chamber Orchestra, and toured 1950–1 and 1959–60 for *JMC. He premiered and recorded Claude *Champagne's *Piano Concerto* with the CBC Montreal orchestra (1950, RCI 17), and made three other LPs as a conductor with that orchestra, two (1951, RCI 31; 1950, RCI 32) of pop song arrangements, and one (1950, RCI 46) of national anthems. As arranger, conductor, and pianist he took part 1955–60 in the CBC broadcasts 'Music from Montreal,' often performing Canadian works (by Robert *Farnon, Robert *Fleming,

Neil Chotem

Michel *Perrault, Eldon *Rathburn, etc). In the 1960s he performed on radio and TV with Maureen *Forrester, Claire *Gagnier, Félix *Leclerc, and Monique *Leyrac. In 1968 Chotem shared a Montreal Festival du disque prize for his contribution to *3 12* (Sel SSP 24.1555), an LP for which he, = Paul *de Margerie, and Marcel Lévêque alternated as conductors and arrangers, and the flutist Marcel *Baillargeon was soloist. In 1968 he received a prize from the same organization for his arrangement of Jacques Brel's song 'Ne me quitte pas,' as recorded by Renée *Claude. In 1967 he resumed his career as a pianist. Later, however, he continued to write arrangements for pop groups and singers: *Harmonium, Paul Piché, Michel Rivard, and Les *Séguin. He wrote *Fantaisie sur des airs de Gilles Vigneault* (1973), and also orchestrated *Le Dict de l'aigle et du castor* (text by *Vigneault, music by Claude *Léveillée).

Chotem appeared as a guest conductor of the MSO in the summers 1969–72, of the *Quebec SO 1970–2, and of the *NACO. He conducted the CBC Montreal orchestra for recordings of songs from the Maritimes (RCI 152) and selections from Dolores *Claman's musical comedy *Timber!!* (RCI 119), and he directed orchestras for LPs of Canadian regimental marches (RCI 158) and of pop song arrangements (RCI 176, 177, 178, 259, and 346, the last exclusively of music by Gordon *Lightfoot). With an orchestra and with Baillargeon as flute soloist he recorded Marc Huard's *Thèmes et mélodies* (Céleste MA 2224) in 1974.

A teacher of orchestration 1955–6 at *McGill U, where his pupils included Hugh *Davidson, Marcel Lévêque, Galt *MacDermot, and Art Phillips, he also taught orchestration, arranging, and composition 1970–2 at the *École Vincent-d'Indy and the *U of Montreal, 1970–6 at McGill U, and 1973–6 at the *CMM.

Of his work with the pop group Harmonium, which resulted in the acclaimed LP *L'Heptade*, Chotem remarked: 'at the moment it's hard to say where I'm going as a composer. I'm looking around, as are all composers, and I'm exploring without committing myself to a particular route. I'm aware there are categories: classical music, contemporary music, jazz, Harmonium. But it's a real mistake to think only in terms of labels. In the long run, if you succeed in ignoring the existing categories, you end up creating a new one' (*Canadian Composer*, Oct 1978). He is a member of CAPAC and an associate of the *CMCentre.

SELECTED COMPOSITIONS

THEATRE

The Song of Solomon, oratorio for radio. 1951. SATB, soli STB, orch. Ms. 1951. RCI 85 (CBC Mtl orch and chor, Chotem cond)

Camera on Canada, TV. 1967. Orch. Ms

Lysistrata, musical comedy (Aristophanes, adap M. Tremblay). 1969. Orch. Ms

Raven, radio. 1971. Orch. Ms

Pythagore 1 à 7, TV ballet. 1975. Orch. Ms

ORCHESTRA

Scherzo Tarantelle. 1936. Pf, orch. Ms

Rhapsody on El Vito, spanish folk tunes. Arr 1963. Pf, tim, perc, str orch. Ms

Salute to Expo, chansons by S. Venne and tunes by Chotem. Arr 1967. Ms

Son et lumière / Sound and Light. 1967. Ms

Saskatoon Berry Rock. 1975. Ms

PIANO

Prelude in E Flat Minor. 1932. Ms

Prelude in B Flat Minor. 1935. Ms

Prelude in A Minor. 1946. Ms

Fuguey Wooguey. 1947. Ms

3 Slow Waltzes. 1972. Ms

Pterodactyl. 1974. Pf (pf, orch). Ms

Ad infinitum. 1978. Ms

JAZZ

Bleuets verts. 1970. Orch. Ms

Narcisse. 1971. Orch. Ms

Le Jazz et la Java, arr of Brubeck. Nd. Honky-tonk pf, hpd, pf, orch. Ms

Opus minus. Nd. Pf, orch. Ms

Slow Rock. Nd. Orch. Ms

Snake Eyes. Nd. Orch. Ms

Also 3 works for v and instr ens on texts by Michel Conte: *Et bye bye; Je resterai tout seul; Je veux*

BIBLIOGRAPHY

Campbell, Francean. 'Neil Chotem,' *CanComp*, 47, Feb 1970

Petrowski, Nathalie. 'How helping Harmonium inspired this composer,' *CanComp*, 134, Oct 1978

Beaulieu, Pierre. 'Neil Chotem: l'émotion d'abord,' Montreal *La Presse*, 25 Nov 1978

Petrowski, Nathalie. 'Neil Chotem, le huitième ... ,' Montreal *Le Devoir*, 26 Jan 1980

FILMOGRAPHY

Music Master NFB 1952

PR (MM, ST)

CHRISTIE, Dinah (Barbara). Singer, comedienne, b London 29 Dec 1942. Daughter of the British-Canadian actors Robert and Margot Christie, she was taken to Canada at two. She began her career at 17, singing to her own guitar accompaniment in Toronto folk clubs and night spots. Later she studied voice with Portia *White. In the early 1960s she acted at the *Stratford Festival and on CBC TV, and in 1965 she starred in *Ding Dong at the Dell* at Toronto's Theatre in the Dell. This was the first of several revues in which she has appeared with Tom Kneebone. She then appeared in *The Decline and Fall of the Entire World as Seen through the Eyes of Cole Porter, Revisited* in 1965 in Toronto and Montreal, and in *Spring Thaw* in 1967 on tour. She also was hostess 1965–6 for CBC TV's controversial public-affairs program 'This Hour Has Seven Days.' Further nightclub engagements followed, interspersed with roles in Mavor *Moore's *The Best of All Possible Worlds* (CBC TV 1968), *Your Own Thing* (New York, off Broadway, 1968), and Stanley Silverman's *The Satyricon* (Stratford 1969). In 1973 she played Annie in *Annie Get Your Gun* at *Rainbow Stage. Her revues with Kneebone have included *Oh Coward!* (1970, in Toronto and in the USA), *Non-Stop Britain* (1971–3, for the British Tourist Authority), and *The Apple Tree* (1973, at Niagara-on-the-Lake and in Toronto). Christie and Kneebone's *Evening with Noel Coward and Cole Porter* was premiered 24 Sep 1973 at *Massey Hall and toured Canada under the auspices of the *Canada Council, appearing with the *Edmonton SO, the *Hamilton Philharmonic, and the *London (Ont) SO in the home cities of those orchestras. A later revue, *An Evening with Tom Kneebone and Dinah Christie*, which was premiered 25 Jan 1977 at the Theatre in the Dell, included music by many US composers and lyricists (eg, Sondheim, Rodgers and Hart) and was presented in other centres and in part on CBC radio. Kneebone and Christie made an LP, *The Apple Tree* (Trillium TR 2000), in 1974.

BIBLIOGRAPHY
Shields, Roy. 'Dynamic is the word for Dinah,' *Star Weekly*, 25 Jan 1964
Allison, Peter N. 'What makes Dinah so special?' *The Canadian*, 20 Nov 1964
Peredo, Sandra. 'Dinah Christie: the image may change but the soul goes on forever,' *Star Week*, 30 Dec 1972–6 Jan 1973 MM

Christmas. Of all Christmas music Handel's *Messiah* has been the major work most frequently performed during the Christmas season across Canada. Christmas portions of *Messiah* were performed as early as 30 Dec 1793 at Quebec, though the complete oratorio probably was not given until 1857 in Quebec and Toronto. In 1645, nearly 100 years before *Messiah* was premiered in Dublin, the Noël 'Chantons tous à la naissance' ('Chantons Noël') was sung at Midnight Mass in New France.

Several carols of French origin, such as 'Ça Bergers' and 'Les Anges dans nos campagnes' are sung widely, particularly as harmonized for SATB and organ by Ernest *Gagnon in his *Cantiques populaire pour le Fête de Noël* (Boucher 1922). Of composed Christmas songs the most popular in Quebec has been Adolphe Adam's 'Minuit, chrétiens,' also known as 'Cantique de Noël' or simply 'Noël' ('O Holy Night'). Gagnon heard it in 1857 at the church of Saint-Roch in Paris and claims to have introduced it to Quebec the following year. It has become a custom in Quebec to have it sung (preferably by a tenor) on the stroke of midnight, just before the Midnight Mass. Its enduring popularity is confirmed by the large number of recordings made over the years by such Canadian singers as Louis *Chartier, Émile *Gour, Raoul *Jobin, Arthur Lapierre, J.-M. Magnan, Rodolphe *Plamondon, Albert Quesnel, Joseph *Saucier, and Richard *Verreau. Also widely popular in Quebec is Gounod's 'Jésus de Nazareth.' (A detailed study of carols and other Christmas music sung in French Canada throughout the centuries has been made by Ernest *Myrand.)

Of Christmas music written in Canada probably the most ancient is the so-called Huron Carol (*'Jesous Ahatonhia') attributed to Jean de Brébeuf. There is conjecture that the motets sung at Midnight Mass in 1642 at Quebec were composed in Canada by René *Ménard, but this cannot be proved (see Amtmann *Music in Canada*). The earliest Canadian carol to be published was probably J.P. *Clarke's 'A Canadian Christmas Carol,' in the *Anglo-Canadian Magazine*, January 1853. In Nova Scotia the early English settlers created variants of older English carols, such as 'The Seven Joys of Mary' and 'The Cherry Tree Carol' (the tune of the latter being different from that used in England). Despite these early efforts by Canadians traditional carols and songs from the old countries continued to dominate.

Large-scale Christmas works began to appear in the latter half of the 19th century. In Montreal various messes de Noël were written – notably those of Joseph-Julien *Perrault and Romain-Octave *Pelletier. Perrault's *Messe de Noël: 'Deo infanti,'* his most popular work, incorporates 15 traditional carols. The Kyrie, Gloria, Sanctus, and Agnus Dei were written 1859–60, the Credo and Magnificat in 1865 for a Christmas performance at Notre-Dame Church. The mass was published posthumously in 1870. The Pelletier mass did not survive, but his *Quatre Noëls anciens* (1893) were printed. Among those who composed messes de Noël in the 20th century were J.-Antonio *Thompson and Alexandre d'Aragon. Clarence

'Christmas Party,' a drawing by W. Scheuer (*Canadian Illustrated News*, 27 Dec 1873)

*Lucas composed a cantata, *The Birth of Christ*, and Arthur *Poynter a full-length sacred opera, *The Birth of Our Lord*. Geoffrey *O'Hara's operetta *The Christmas Thieves* (1943) was published by Gamble Hinged. A short Christmas opera, Clifford Crawley's *The Slaughter of the Innocents*, appeared in 1974. Godfrey *Ridout's Christmas TV opera, *The Lost Child*, was telecast by the CBC in 1976.

Other significant Christmas works with orchestral accompaniment include Graham *George's *Hymn for Christmas Day*, Violet *Archer's *Cantata sacra* (Christmas portions), and Robert *Turner's *Johann's Gift to Christmas*. Of the Christmas cantatas for choir and organ Healey *Willan's *Mystery of Bethlehem* is performed widely, and there are similar works by Keith *Bissell, F.R.C. *Clarke, Albert *Ham, and Charles *Wilson. Also noteworthy is Paul-Émile *McCaughan's motet *Hodie Christus natus est* (1949) for choir and organ.

Works requiring voices and small instrumental ensembles include Sir Ernest *MacMillan's *Two Christmas Carols*, R. Murray *Schafer's *City of Bethlehem*, Harry *Somers' *Gloria*, David *Ouchterlony's *Carol Cantata*, and Wolfgang *Bottenberg's *Eine Weihnachtliche Hausmusik*. Outstanding in the field of writing for unaccompanied voices, Healey Willan's work ranges from his *Missae brevi Nos. 4 and 12* (both based on Christmas plainsongs) through motets and anthems (eg, 'Hodie Christus natus est' and 'Here Are We in Bethlehem') to arrangements of traditional carols (eg, his popular setting of 'The Twelve Days of Christmas'). Christmas anthems, carols, motets, and arrangements by other composers are too numerous to mention, but specimens of high calibre have been written by W.H. *Anderson, Hugh *Bancroft, Louis Bédard, Leslie *Bell, Keith Bissell, Claude *Champagne, S.C. *Eckhardt-Gramatté, William *France, Robert *Fleming, Ernest Gagnon, Graham George, Eugene *Hill, Derek *Holman, Talivaldis *Kenins, Ada Twohy *Kent, Lucienne Lafleur, Eugene *Lapierre, Roméo *Larivière, Walter *MacNutt, Kenneth *Meek, Alfred *Mignault, Bernard *Naylor, Godfrey Ridout, Bertha *Tamblyn, and Alfred *Whitehead. Udo *Kasemets' *Choreolae gaudia* contains settings outside the usual 'church' style.

Canadian composers have not overlooked the Christmas season in the realm of purely instrumental music. For orchestra there are works such as Jean *Coulthard's *The Bird at Dawning Singeth* and *Canadian Fantasy* (partially based on the Huron Carol), Sir Ernest MacMillan's *Medley of Carols*, Glen *Morley's *Christmas Overture*, Wolfgang Bottenberg's *Suite of Carols*, and F.R.C. Clarke's *Pastorale and Fugue on Puer nobis*. For organ there are numerous preludes based on Christmas tunes: Healey Willan's preludes on 'Puer nobis' and 'Quem pastores' are played frequently, and others of good quality have been written by John Cook, George *Coutts, Marvin *Duchow, Arthur *Egerton, Walter MacNutt, Kenneth Meek, Eric *Rollinson, and Alfred Whitehead.

In the area of pop music the Christmas season has occasioned many pieces, some of which have quaint titles (eg, 'Honky the Christmas Goose,' by Chip Young and Orville Hoover).

SELECTED DISCOGRAPHY

CANADIAN CHRISTMAS MUSIC

Anne Campbell Singers. 'The Indian Christmas Carol.' CBC SM-230
Armdale Chorus. 'Jesous Ahatonhia.' London NA 3507
Hélène Baillargeon and l'équipe des Bouttes en Train. *Christmas Carols of French Canada / Chants de Noël du Canada français*. Folk FC 7229
The Concordia Choir (Moorhead, Minnesota). Willan 'Hodie Christus natus est.' Concordia CDLP-4
Festival Singers of Canada
Choral Music of Healey Willan; includes several Christmas pieces. RCI 207/Cap ST-6248
– Applebaum 'Cherry Tree Carol' – Holman 'Mary Is a Lady Bright'; 'Make We Joy.' Polydor 2917 009
– Willan (arr) 'Twelve Days of Christmas'; 'The First Nowell' (with the Toronto Mendelssohn Choir). RCI 331
– Willan 'Hodie Christus natus est'; (arr) 'The Twelve Days of Christmas'; 'Welcome Yule.' Hallmark ChS-4
– Willan 'Make We Merry'; Iseler (arr) 'Away in a Manger' CBC SM-80/RCA LSC-3174
Gentlemen and Boys of St Simon-the-Apostle Church, Toronto
– Willan 'Hodie Christus natus est' – Ketchum 'Not One Candle in the Stall' – Holman 'Make We Joy.' St Simon's T-55562-3
– Willan 'Make We Merry.' Canterbury CHL 605
John Alldis Choir. Naylor 'Christmas Day' motet from *Nine Motets*. Argo ZRG 5426
Kelvin High School Choir of Winnipeg. Bray 'A Christmas Folk Song.' CBC SM-219
Mennonite Children's Choir. 'Jesous Ahatonhia.' CBC SM-171
Mormon Tabernacle Choir
– Willan 'The Three Kings.' Col MS 6019
– Willan 'Hodie Christus natus est.' Col ML 5592
St Mary Magdalene Singers. Willan 'Christmas Song of the 14th Century'; 'Hodie Christus natus est'; 'Here We Are in Bethlehem.' Church of St Mary Magdalene QC 982
St Michael's Choir School. 'A Canadian Christmas Carol / Un chant de Noël canadien.' Abitibi Paper Co Ltd QC 392 E
Gordon Slater. *Peace Tower Christmas*: 'Huron Carol.' Tapestry GD 7373
Timothy Eaton Memorial Church Choir. Ouchterlony *Carol Cantata*. F. Harris FHR 1
Toronto Mendelssohn Choir (see also Festival Singers above)
– Willan (arr) 'The Twelve Days of Christmas,' 'The First Nowell,' 'The Son of Righteousness.' CBC SM-80/RCA LSC-3174
– Somers *Gloria*. RCA LSC 3043
Tudor Singers of Montreal. Somers *Gloria*. CBC SM-53

CHRISTMAS MUSIC RECORDED BY CANADIANS

Anne Campbell Singers. *A Snow Legend*. Big Chief Records BCS-5002
Bank of Montreal Choral Society. *Christmas Recital*. Bank of Montreal CT 25183-84; CT 26835-36
Guido Basso. *Christmas Today*. CBC LM-52/RCA CAC 2289
Maurice Boivin. *Christmas Time Is Here*. London SDS 5080
Antoine Bouchard. *Antoine Bouchard, orgue*: noëls français de D'Aquin, Corrette, Dandrieu, Balbastre. RCI 402
Laura Boulton. *Ukrainian Christmas Songs*. FW 6828
André Collin. *Noël au Québec*. RCA Gala CGPS-307
Carl Tapscott Singers. *Carols for a Family Christmas*. CBC LM-54/Cap SN 6297
Wilf Carter. *Christmas in Canada*. RCA Camden CAS 889
Bishop Strachan School Chapel Choir, Toronto. 'Silent Night'; 'O Little Town of Bethlehem.' Hallmark Chs-1001
Choeur Kattialine. *Noël nouvelet*. RCI 372
Christ Church Cathedral Choir, Vancouver. *Music for Christmas*. KVP Records KVP 603F
Croxton Trio. Christmas Hymns. Apex 4207-A
Da Camera Singers. *Da Camera Singers of Edmonton*. CBC SM-256
Bob Davis, cond. *Christmas in the Maritimes*. Dane LP-7605
Les Disciples de Massenet
– *Cantiques de Noël* (with Raoul Jobin). RCA LSC 2503
– *René Simard et les Disciples de Massenet à l'église Notre-Dame*. NOBEL NBL 511
– *Richard Verreau à l'église*. RCA CCS 1003
Ensemble vocal de Montreal. *Noël de la Paix*. RCI 435
Gentlemen and Boys of St Simon-the-Apostle Church, Toronto
– *Christmas Music, Medieval to Modern*. Canterbury CHL 604
– *The Gracious Time – Christmas Music*. J-13153
Hamilton Phil O. *Christmas Brott to You*. CTL 477-5153
Lucien Hétu. *Joyeux Noël*. RCA Gala CGPS-240
Ivan Romanoff Male Chorus. *Ukrainian Christmas*. CBC SM-67/Cap ST 633
Jeunes Chanteurs d'Acadie. *Revivre nos noëls / Christmas Reflections*. Inter-Media WRC 203
Johnny Burt Singers and Orchestra. *A Christmas Wish*. CTL 477-5154
Ray Johnson. *Christmas with Ray and His Friends*. Audat 477-4015
Juliette, Jimmy Dale Swingers and Orchestra. *Juliette's Christmas World*. CBC SM-51/RCA CAS 2279
Diane Leigh. *Christmas at Home*. Marathon TX-1002
Leslie Bell Singers
– *Carols and Traditional Songs*. RCI 166
– *The Story of the Nativity*. RCA LCP 3001
Claude Leveillée. *Noël avec Clo-Clo*. Col HFL 8008
Little Mountain Singers, Vancouver. *Christmas at the Planetarium*. London PS 724
Judy Loman. *Make We Merry*: traditional carols arr by Loman for solo harp. CBC SM-80
Magee Secondary School, Vancouver. *Wolcum Yole!* Ensemble EPN 129
Maple Leaf Singers. *Christmas with the Maple Leaf Singers*. KVP Records KVP 107
Catherine McKinnon. *The Catherine McKinnon Christmas Album*. Arc
Hugh McLean. *Music for Christmas*. CBC SM-209
McLeod-Stewarton United Church Choir, Ottawa. *A Christmas Musicale* ... McLeod-Stewarton United Church QCS 1027
Montreal Bach Choir. Britten *Ceremony of Carols*. RCI 89
Newfoundland Showband. *Christmas in Newfoundland*. Marathon DX 5141
The Peaches. *Christmas with the Peaches*. Realistic 68-8100
Les Petits Chanteurs de Granby. *Minuit, Chrétiens*. RCA Gala CGPS 278
St John's Church, Shaughnessy (Vancouver). *A Procession with Carols and Lessons for Advent Sunday*. Ensemble EPN 187
St Mary Magdalene Singers
– *Hodie*: Motets and Carols for the Advent of the Christ Child. St Mary Magdalene QC 982
– *Rorate Coeli – Plainsong for Advent and Christmas*. SMM 7506
– *Veni: Music for Advent and Christmas*. World Records WRC 452
St Matthias' Church, Westmount. *Noel*. SMC 1001
Pete Schofield and the Canadians. *Christmas Is Love*. P.S. Records 1002
George Beverly Shea. *Christmas, Christmas*. RCA Victor 20-6315
The Singing Post Family. *Christmas Time in the Country*. Marathon DX 5144
The Stringbusters. *Christmas in the Maritimes*. Marathon DX 5148
Toronto Mendelssohn Choir. Handel's *Messiah*. Beaver LPS 1001
Vancouver Chamber Choir. *Christmas Carols from Many Lands*. CBC SM-338
Richard Verreau (see also Disciples de Massenet above). *Chantons Noël*. RCA LSC-2390
Westmorland Singers. *Christmas in Canada with the Westmorland Singers*. Rodeo RBS 1065
Rick Wilkins and the Mutual Understanding. *Peace*. CBC LM-80
Winnipeg Mennonite Children's Choir. *Christmas Songs*. RCA KXL-1-6028/CTL-175

BIBLIOGRAPHY

Myrand, Ernest. *Noëls anciens de la Nouvelle-France*, 2nd ed (Quebec City 1907)
Gagnon, Ernest. 'Une page d'Adolphe Adam'; 'La musique et les Noëls populaires,' *Pages choisies* (Quebec City 1917)
Barbeau Marius. 'Christmas carols on the St Lawrence,' *Canadian Geographical J*, vol 41, Dec 1960
Covert, Mary E. 'Canada's Christmas music,' *Montreal Star*, 24 Dec 1966
Creighton, Helen. 'Carols and other songs for Christmas,' *CanComp*, 45, Dec 1969
Morgan, Kit. 'Christmas music: on the air ... on records,' ibid
'Songs for Christmas,' *CanComp*, 55, Dec 1970
Amtmann *Music in Canada 1600–1800* (FRCC)

CHUBB, (John) Frederick. Organist, choirmaster, teacher, composer, b Hastings, England, 16 Apr 1885, d Vancouver 6 Mar 1966; ARCO 1904, FRCO 1904, BA (Cambridge) 1909, B MUS (Oxford) 1909. After studies with A.W. Wilson at St John's Choir School, Upper St Leonards, he became Wilson's assistant at Ely Cathedral in 1903. He became organist-choirmaster at Christ Church, Harrogate, in 1910. In 1912, following an unnecessary confinement resulting from the incorrect diagnosis of asthma as tuberculosis, he accepted a position in Canada – that of organist-choirmaster at Christ Church, Vancouver. His last position was that of organist 1946–62 at St John's Church, Victoria.

A brilliant performer in the Edwin Lemare tradition, Chubb gave 200 recitals on the Hope-Jones organ of Christ Church, introducing much symphonic music (through transcriptions) and many major organ works to Vancouver. He also gave four recitals at the 1915 San Francisco Exhibition and performed widely throughout the Pacific Northwest. He brought to Vancouver such organists as Sir Hugh Percy Allen, Marcel Dupré, Herbert A. *Fricker, Alfred Hollins, Tertius Noble, and Louis Vierne. Chubb taught privately in Vancouver, his students including his son George, who was a Montreal organist and teacher, Jean *Coulthard, and Arthur Cleland Lloyd. Chubb made the Christ Church Cathedral choir one of the finest in western Canada. He participated in diocesan activities, founding Purcell Hall (1935–41), a large store rented and converted for use as a school and auditorium for church music. Although some of Chubb's church music has been published (Waterloo, Novello), his major works, including *Rhapsody* for piano and orchestra and an *Organ Sonata*, remain in manuscript. (DBW)

CHUHALDIN, Alexander. Violinist, teacher, conductor, composer, b Vladikavkas, Crimea, 27 Aug 1892, d Victoria, BC, 20 Jan 1951. At eight he entered the Imperial Cons of Moscow, studying violin with Jules Conus, and at nine he appeared in public. He joined the Imperial Grand Opera (later the State Opera) orchestra in 1913 and became concertmaster in 1922. In 1923 he began teaching violin at the State Cons, and in 1924 he toured Asia, Australia, and New Zealand. He moved to Toronto in 1927, and later joined the staff of the *TCM, where his pupils included Murray *Adaskin, Harry Bergart, Isidor Desser, Betty-Ann Fischer-Byfield, Hyman *Goodman, Blain *Mathé, and Albert *Pratz. A radio conductor for the CRBC and then for the CBC ('Symphonic Strings,' 'Melodic Strings,' and 'CBC Strings'), Chuhaldin gave the premiere of Britten's *Young Apollo*, which was written for 'Melodic Strings' and dedicated to the conductor, in a broadcast performance with the composer at the piano 27 Aug 1939. He was a guest conductor of the W.P.A. Civic Symphony in New York in 1936 and of the *TSO in 1941. In 1948 he became conductor of the newly formed Forest Hill Community Orchestra in Toronto. Chuhaldin wrote five pieces for solo violin, published by Paling & Co (Australia) or Thompson, several works for string orchestra (listed in *Catalogue of Canadian Composers*), and over 30 transcriptions for string orchestra (some published by C. Fischer). He was a member of CAPAC.

BIBLIOGRAPHY

Mason, Lawrence. 'Musical bibliographies of Canadian composers,' Toronto *Globe*, 29 Aug 1936 EK

CHURCHILL, John. Educator, conductor, b London 29 May 1920. He studied at the RCM and the U of London, taught theory and pedagogy 1947–67 at the RCM, and was master of music 1948–67 at the Royal Church of St Martin-in-the-Fields, London. He conducted the Westminster Choral Society 1956–64 and the Croydon Philharmonic Choir 1959–62 and was a founder-member of the Academy of St Martin-in-the-Fields in 1956. Churchill commissioned Vaughan Williams' last work, *The First Nowell, a nativity play* (1958), and Malcolm Arnold's *The Song of Simeon, a nativity masque* (1960), and premiered them at Drury Lane Theatre. He moved to Canada and served 1967–76 as chairman of the new Dept of Music at *Carleton U, where he established a B MUS program, fostered the study of Canadian music, and directed the university choir. His writings include *Congregational Singing* (London 1966). In 1970 he began writing program notes for the *NACO. He edited the facsimile edition of Nicolo Pasquali's *Thorough-Bass Made Easy* (London 1974), and has arranged *Three Songs from Eastern Canada* (Lengnick 1973). AHC

CHURCHLEY, Frank (Franklin Eugene). Educator, author, pianist, b Oshawa, Ont, 15 Jun 1930; B MUS (Toronto) 1950, LRCT 1952, MA (Columbia) 1957, D ED (Columbia) 1959. His thesis was 'The piano in Canadian music education.' He taught music in high school, studied piano in the summer of 1954 with Nadia Boulanger and Robert Casadesus at Fontainebleau, and served 1959–64 as head of the Dept of Fine Arts, *U of Calgary. He joined the faculty of *McGill U in 1964, and moved in 1966 to the *U of Saskatchewan at Regina, and in 1969 to the *U of Victoria, specializing in music education. He was president 1967–9 of the *CMEA. He has given papers at seminars on music education. In addition to many articles, his published works include an eight-volume series (with six LP recordings) *Basic Goals in Music*, a program for primary grades (Toronto 1964–72) which he co-edited with Lloyd *Slind.

WRITINGS

'Contemporary approaches in music education,' *McGill J of Education*, vol 11, Spring 1967
'New developments in music education,' *The Education of Elementary School Teachers*, ed R.D. Armstrong (Edmonton 1967)

'Music education and the prairie provinces,' *Music Education and the Canadians of Tomorrow*, CMCouncil conference report (Ottawa 1968)
Music Curriculum and Instruction (Toronto 1969) (WL)

Church music. See Religions and music.

CIAMAGA, Gustav. Composer, teacher, writer, b London, Ont, 10 Apr 1930; MFA (Brandeis) 1958. He attended the *U of Western Ontario 1951–4 while studying privately with Gordon *Delamont. He studied composition 1954–6 with John *Weinzweig and John *Beckwith at the *U of Toronto and composition and musicology at Brandeis U in Waltham, Mass, where his composition teachers were Arthur Berger, Harold Shapero, and Irving Fine. He continued his studies in Waltham until 1963, and also organized an electronic studio. He joined the Faculty of Music, U of Toronto, in 1963 and became director of the Electronic Music Studio in 1965 and chairman of the theory and composition department in 1968. He was appointed dean of the faculty in 1978. On sabbatical in 1970 he worked in several European electronic studios.

Ciamaga has written a number of non-electronic works, including a mass and a string quartet, but most of his compositions in the latter half of the 1960s and in the 1970s employed electronic tape. In co-operation with Hugh *Le Caine of the National Research Council, Ciamaga has developed apparatus, such as the Serial Sound Structure Generator, for use in the creation of electronic music. Many of his *Two-Part Inventions* employ this equipment. His experiments with the application of computer control to music (in the PIPER Project at the U of Toronto during the mid-1960s) have included an arrangement for computer (1969) of Bach's *Brandenburg Concerto No. 1*. He has worked, as well, with electrical level controls such as a modified Hamograph and a two-channel alternator. Ciamaga's works have been performed in Canada, the USA, and Europe. He has provided scores for films, the theatre, and TV documentaries. *Curtain Raiser*, composed with Louis *Applebaum, opened the *NAC in 1969, and *Solipsism While Dying* was premiered in 1973 by the *Lyric Arts Trio. Ciamaga is a member of the *CLComp, an associate of the *CMCentre, and a member of CAPAC.

See also Electronic music.

SELECTED COMPOSITIONS

TELEVISION AND FILM

Phone-phugue (with Cross). 1965. TV
Margaree (with Tony Gnazzo). 1966. TV
Mosaic (film by Jack Chambers). 1966
Music for the Film 'Dizziness' (film by U of T Faculty of Medicine, with Talivaldis *Kenins). 1968–9
Other non-elec works include pieces for jazz or stage band, a *Mass*, a *String Quartet*, short pieces for orch.

ELECTRONIC TAPE

One Part Invention. 1965
Two Part Inventions No. 1–8. 1965–70
Scherzo. 1966
Ottawa 1967 (with Louis Applebaum). 1966. Tape sections for outdoor theatre production
Fanfare for Computer. 1967
Four Part Invention No. 1. 1967
Ragamuffin No. 1, 2 (with Lowell Cross). 1967
Bach Brandenburg Concerto No. 1 (movement 3, transcr). 1969. Computer
Curtain Raiser / Lever de rideau (with Applebaum). 1969
Canon for Stravinsky. 1972. Computer
A Greeting for J.W. 1973. Computer. *CMB*, 6, Spring/Summer 1973
Solipsism While Dying (Atwood). 1973. V, fl, pf, tape. Ms
Ars nova (medieval and 20th-century theorists). 1976. Synths, tape, narrs. Ms

Gustav Ciamaga

WRITINGS

– and Gabura, James. 'Digital computer control of sound generating apparatus for the production of electronic music,' *J of the Audio-Engineering Soc*, vol 16, 1967
– and Le Caine, Hugh. 'A preliminary report on the serial sound structure generator,' *Perspective of New Music*, vol 6, Fall–Winter 1967
'Some thoughts on the teaching of electronic music,' *Inter-American Institute for Musical Research Yearbook*, vol 3, 1967
– and Le Caine, Hugh. 'The sonde: a new approach to multiple sine wave generation,' *J of the Audio-Engineering Soc*, vol 18, 1970
'The training of the composer in the use of new technological means,' *Music and Technology* (Paris 1971)
'The tape studio,' *The Development and Practice of Electronic Music*, ed Jon A. Appleton and Ronald C. Perera (New York 1975)
Unpubl papers; book and record reviews for the *CMJ*

BIBLIOGRAPHY

Le Caine, Hugh. 'Some applications of electrical level controls,' *Electronic Music Review*, 4, Oct 1967
Contemporary Canadian Composers EK

CJRT Orchestra. Concert and broadcasting ensemble formed in Toronto in 1975 by Paul *Robinson for the independent non-commercial educational radio station CJRT-FM (which receives 70 per cent of its funding from the Ontario government and 30 per cent from private donors). By 1980 the orchestra had given five annual subscription series of from six to nine concerts in the Ryerson Theatre. A program usually was planned around a theme ('Music of Beethoven,' 'Bach and His Sons,' etc), often contained chamber works as well as orchestral ones, and was preceded by a talk by Robinson. The concerts were recorded for later broadcast. On the day of a concert, however, CJRT broadcast commercial recordings of music illustrating the same program theme. The orchestra, consisting of members of the *TS and leading freelance players, has varied in size from 25 to 60. It has premiered *Buczynski's *Lyric for Piano and Orchestra* (January 1977) and *Schafer's *Hymn to Night* (January 1978), and has given the Canadian premiere of Britten's *Suite on English Folk Tunes* (January 1979). The orchestra also has presented such rarely heard works as Schumann's *Violin Concerto* (1975), Weber's opera *Abu Hassan* (concert performance, 1976), Arriaga's *Symphony in D* (1976), and Gounod's *Symphony No. 2* (1977). In the fall of 1980 it mounted a full-scale festival of the symphonies and concertos of Beethoven.

Robert *Aitken, Jorge Bolet, Liona *Boyd, Maureen *Forrester, James Galway, Greta *Kraus, Antonin *Kubalek, Anton *Kuerti, Gérard Souzay, Steven *Staryk, Janet *Stubbs, Tsuyoshi *Tsutsumi, and Barry Tuckwell are among the solo artists who have performed with the orchestra.

'CKNX Barn Dance.' 'Canada's Largest Travelling Barn Dance,' a radio show heard Saturday nights 1937–63 on CKNX, Wingham, Ont. At the initiative of W.T. 'Doc' Cruickshank, owner of CKNX and also a fiddler, barn dances began in the CKNX studio in the early 1930s. Broadcasts from outside locations on a circuit in west-central Ontario began in 1937. The earliest performers included the Gully Jumpers and George *Wade and the Cornhuskers. By the late 1940s three bands were associated with the show: the CKNX Ranch Boys (led by Don and Cora Richardson), the Golden Prairie Cowboys, and the CKNX Barn Dance Gang (featuring Earl *Heywood). Many stars in Canadian country music appeared on the show early in their careers, including Ward *Allen, Maurice *Bolyer, Al *Cherney, Tommy *Hunter, and the *Mercey Brothers. Though the program ended in 1963, it was revived in 1967 when 10 barn dances were held in honour of the Canadian centenary. Annual reunions began in 1975 and have been held in various Wingham-area centres. Patterned after the barn dances first heard on US radio in the 1920s (see Country music), the CKNX Barn Dance was the longest-lived show of its kind in Canada.

MM

CLAMAN, Dolores (Olga) (m Morris). Composer, pianist, b Vancouver 6 Jul 1927. She studied in Vancouver and at the U of Southern California; then, encouraged by the baritone Lawrence Tibbett (who heard some of her songs), she attended the Juilliard School of Music (New York), where her teachers were Rosina Lhévinne and Edward Steuermann (piano) and Vittorio Giannini and Bernard Wagenaar (composition). Among her first major works were the ballet *Le Rêve fantasque* (1950) and the musical comedy **Timber!* (1952), the latter written with Doug Nixon and David Savage and produced at *TUTS. In 1953 she went to London, where she composed music for the ITV network and collaborated on songs for the West End revues *Airs on a Shoestring* (1953), *From Here to There* (1955), *Fresh Airs* (1956), and *Pieces of Eight* (1957).

In London Claman met and married the writer Richard Morris (b London 13 Oct 1931, naturalized Canadian 1975), who wrote the lyrics for most of her subsequent work. They moved to Toronto in 1958 and by the mid-1960s had become one of Canada's most successful jingle-writing teams, winning some 40 awards internationally 1962–78. They also have written *Mr. Scrooge* (1963, with Ted Wood), a musical based on Dickens' *A Christmas Carol* and produced at the Crest Theatre, Toronto, in 1963 and on CBC TV in 1964; *In the Klondike* (1968, with Michael Leighton), a musical telecast 6 May 1968 by the CBC; *Graffiti* (1979), a musical written for the London stage; scores for the feature films *The Man Who Wanted to Live Forever* (1970) and *Captain Apache* (1972); and themes for the CBC TV programs 'Hockey Night in Canada' and 'House of Pride.' Claman and Morris also wrote the score for the film *A Place to Stand*, which was made for the Ontario Pavilion at *Expo 67 and which won an Oscar. The title song (Thompson 1967), known popularly as 'Ontar-i-ar-i-ar-i-o,' is probably their best-known work. Claman and Morris are members of CAPAC.

BIBLIOGRAPHY

'New Canadian musical based on Robert Service's poetry,' *CanComp*, 19, Jun 1967
Carroll, Joy. 'Claman and Morris,' *CanComp*, 51, Jun 1970 MM

CLAPPÉ, Arthur A. Bandmaster, composer, writer, b Cork, Ireland, 1850; d 22 Nov 1920. The son of a British army colonel, he studied at the TCL and the RMSM (Kneller Hall). He served in Canada as director of the *Governor General's Foot Guards Band 1877–84. He then moved to the USA, where he became prominent as a bandmaster and in 1918 founded the US Army Music School. He was the editor for some years of *Metronome* and later of another magazine, *Dominant*. *Canada's Welcome*, a masque 'as shewn before his Excellency The Marquis of Lorne and H.R.H. The Princess Louise on February 24 1879 at the Opera House, Ottawa,' with words by Frederick A. Dixon, was not only the largest work Clappé wrote in Canada but also, with 102 pages of music, one of the largest scores published (J.L. *Orme, Ottawa, 1879) and printed in Canada up to that time. Typical of Clappé's other Canadian works are such titles as *United Empire Valse, Farewell Waltzes* (dedicated to the Earl and Countess of Dufferin), and the song 'Softly Round Thy Pillow,' all published or advertised in 1878. Clappé's publications also include *The Band Teacher's Assistant* (New York 1888), *The Wind Band and Its Instruments* (London 1912), *The Principles of Wind-Band Transcription* (New York 1921), and others. See also Sarnia.

CLARE, Eva. Pianist, teacher, b Neepawa, Man, 1884, d Winnipeg 29 Mar 1961. She studied piano in Winnipeg, for five years in Berlin with Madame Varet-Stepanoff and Josef Lhévinne, and during World War I in New York with Ernest Hutcheson and Howard Brockway. She taught in Regina, and her Eva Clare Studio Club, founded there in 1915, has survived as the *Orpheus Club of Regina and provided material for her book *Musical Appreciation and the Studio Club* (New York 1924). She settled in Winnipeg in 1918. In 1922, at a concert in Winnipeg by the Minneapolis SO, she was soloist in the Grieg *Concerto*. The *Canadian Annual Review* (1927–8) reported that 'Eva Clare, pianist, won the highest praise from European critics when playing at Prague, Munich, Vienna and Budapest in December 1927 and January 1928.' From 1918 until her retirement Clare was a force in Manitoba as teacher and reformer. A prime mover in the *MRMTA, she was its first president and was honoured with a life membership in 1955. With Leonard *Heaton and Gladys *Egbert she assembled the first graded books for *WBM piano examinations. In 1933 in Winnipeg – as earlier in Regina – she formed a studio club from her private pupils and friends, and this club too developed into a permanent organization, the *Wednesday Morning Musicales. In 1937 she became music director at the *U of Manitoba and on her retirement in 1949 director emeritus. The recital hall of the U of Manitoba music building is named in her memory. Among her many pupils were Beth Cooil, Phyllis *Holtby, Anna *Moncrieff Hovey, Barbara *Pentland, Helga and Snjolaug *Sigurdson, Frank *Thorolfson, and Moira Wilson. (RG)

CLARK, LaRena (b LeBarre, later changed to LeBarr). Folksinger, b Pefferlaw, near Lake Simcoe, Ont, of French and English-Irish parents, 1917. Raised in various northern Ontario centres (her father and grandfather were hunters), she learned many songs from her family and developed a large and varied repertoire which included British ballads and music hall songs, country and western songs, and Canadian lumbering songs. For the collector Edith *Fowke she sang a number of these songs in the early 1960s. Some of these were published in Fowke's collections and issued on the LP *LaRena Clark: A Canadian Garland* (Topic 12T140). Appearances followed on local radio stations and at folk festivals in Canada and the USA. She lived near Orillia, Ont, in the 1970s. She had made seven LPs of folksongs for her own Clark label by 1979.

BIBLIOGRAPHY
Sarjeant, William A.S. 'Canada's traditional queen of song,' *Canada Folk Bulletin*, vol 2, May–Jun 1979 EF

CLARKE. 1 / James P., and 2 / his son Hugh, both associated with the beginnings of academic musical life in Canada and the USA.

1 **James P.** (Paton). Organist-choirmaster, composer, conductor, teacher, b Edinburgh? 1807 or 1808, d Toronto 27 Aug 1877. The son of a musician, Clarke was first remarked as a music dealer's assistant in Edinburgh. By 1829 he had become the leader of psalmody at St George's Church in Glasgow, and two years later he signed the second edition of his *Parochial Psalmody* as 'Leader of the Music [at that church] and Professor of the Piano Forte and Singing.' In 1834 he became the organist at another Glasgow church, but in the following year he emigrated to Canada, settling in Elora, some 85 km west of Toronto, presumably as a farmer. He had established contact with St James' (Anglican) Cathedral, Toronto, by 1842 (the records mention his being paid for organ and piano tuning), and in 1844 he became the organist at Christ Church (Anglican) in Hamilton. Toronto continued to attract Clarke, and in 1845 he attended the founding meeting of the Toronto Choral Society, conducted one of the two concerts organized by John *McCaul to celebrate the King's College Triennial Commemoration, was invited to move to the city, and became conductor of the newly formed *Toronto Philharmonic Society, as well as a teacher of piano, guitar, and singing. In Clarke McCaul apparently found the right person to help realize his ambitions for the performance of music by the great masters from Handel to Mendelssohn. The two men collaborated until 1855 as president and conductor of a succession of musical societies, and again in 1872 in the revival of the Philharmonic Society, for which 28 Feb 1873 Clarke conducted his first and last full-scale performance of an oratorio in Toronto, Handel's *Messiah*.

During his first eight years in Toronto Clarke rose to musical prominence. Under the influence of McCaul he programmed some of the first Toronto performances of Beethoven and Mozart symphonies in 1846 and 1847. He submitted an 8-part anthem, 'Arise, O Lord God, Forget Not the Poor,' to King's College in 1846 and received for it the first B MUS degree issued by a Canadian university. Though not on the staff of the college, he may have been employed as an adjunct teacher. He was the organist at St James' Cathedral for the year prior to its destruction by fire in 1849. At about the same time Clarke taught at the Toronto Normal School and the Toronto Academy, a boys' school. His compositions were published by *Nordheimer and in the *Anglo-American Magazine*, and won three prizes offered by King's College in 1848.

Fortune reversed itself about 1853. A Mr Paige, who had appeared with his daughters in one of Clarke's concerts, won such popular favour that the Toronto Vocal Music Society appointed him conductor in Clarke's place in 1853, an action that split the membership and destroyed the society. In the same year Clarke's application for a teaching position at Trinity College was turned down in favour of G.W. *Strathy's, while a year later the *Daily Leader* of Toronto (31 May 1854) attacked Clarke's songs as being 'below mediocrity' and 'sadly deficient in both design and originality,' and argued, rather unfairly, that 'the meretricious

THE JANUS MINUET.
By J. P. CLARKE, Mus. Bac., K. C., Toronto.
TEMPO DI MINUETTO.

The Janus Minuet by James P. Clarke (*Musical Times*, New York, 25 Apr 1852)

drapery of the accompaniment' served to hide poor melody.

Whether Clarke received a musical doctorate (the first to be granted by a Canadian university) is likely to remain a mystery (see Degrees). The *U of Toronto's program for commencement, 1 Jul 1856, listed Clarke among those who were to receive degrees. On the copy now in the University Archives, however, Clarke's name is crossed out and a delete symbol is marked in the margin, suggesting a last-minute withdrawal. Other university records and a number of respectable dictionaries credit him with the doctorate, yet even after 1856 Clarke identified himself only as a B MUS. After his death it was asserted, incorrectly, that he held a doctorate from Oxford.

Despite the apparent reverses in fortune which affected his career Clarke seems to have been held in high respect. In his first Toronto advertisement (*British Colonist*, 11 Nov 1845) he called himself a piano teacher with 20 years' experience and a pupil of Domenico Crivelli, a voice teacher at the RAM in London. Clarke was an exponent of Johann Bernard Logier's system of piano teaching which, despite its pitfalls, represented progress in its emphasis on class instruction. Thus it probably was not incompetence but only illness, intrigue, or bad luck that caused Clarke, between his Philharmonic Society concert in May 1855 and the early 1870s, to play a very minor role in the musical life of Toronto. If he was absent from the city for a while, he certainly had returned by 1861; yet no record exists of any conducting, church, or teaching appointment after 1855. In 1861 Clarke edited, with John *Carter and G.W. Strathy, *A Selection of Chants and Tunes* for the Church of England's Toronto diocese (Toronto 1861). The same year he directed a gala concert to celebrate the opening of Toronto's first streetcar line and an inaugural concert in a New Music Hall. The directories for the 1860s list him as a music teacher; it was only with the revival of the Philharmonic Society in 1872 that Clarke rose again to prominence, and failing health soon curtailed his activity.

Clarke is not only the earliest musician in Canada who has found his way into the standard music dictionaries (which, alas, perpetuate as many errors as truths), but also the first musician in English-speaking Canada to have written and published a sizable number of compositions. In addition to the *Parochial Psalmody* and *A Selection of Chants and Tunes* which he co-edited, his compilations include *The Choir* (Glasgow? 1835, a selection of choruses, anthems, etc, co-edited with A. Thomson) and *Canadian Church Psalmody* (Toronto 1845, with two *Te Deums* and seven other pieces by Clarke). Before emigrating from Scotland Clarke had published songs in such publications as *Border Garland* (ca 1829), *The Western Garland* (ca 1832), *The Harmonicon* (1832, 1833), and *Chameleon* (1833). The most interesting of these, 'Away to Loch Long' (in the *Chameleon*), is a through-composed song with an interesting accompaniment, displaying rhythmic and harmonic variety. This song suggests that the simplicity of Clarke's other vocal pieces was deliberate, not involuntary. Echoing tendencies of his time, Clarke strove, both in Scotland and in Canada, to write 'for the people' and to build a national literature. His Canadian titles provide a mirror of the country – 'The Wild Stream Leaps' (performed 1851); 'The Maple Leaf' (Nordheimer ca 1852); 'The Trapper's Song' (*Anglo-American Magazine*, September 1852); 'A Forest Home' (ibid, October 1852); 'A Canadian Christmas Carol' (ibid, January 1853); and, above all, his *Lays of the Maple Leaf, or Songs of Canada* (Nordheimer 1853), a cycle of seven songs for solo voice, duet, and chorus, which won immediate acclaim and deserves a modern revival.

Only two instrumental pieces have been traced, *The Janus Minuet* (*Musical Times*, New York, 25 Apr 1852), a contrived piece that sounds alike when played forward or backward, and the jolly *Favorite Toronto Air*, 'arranged as a Rondo for the piano forte,' and dedicated to Mrs John McCaul (Nordheimer, before 1853). A younger contemporary of Clarke's reported, however, that 'during the latter portion of his career he composed a number of chamber trios and quartettes of an original and pleasing character, and constructed on the best classical models' ('Music in Toronto,' *The Mail*, 21 Dec 1878). That instrumental rather than vocal works are meant is suggested also by the same writer's report that in his later years Clarke played second violin or viola in chamber ensembles.

See also Inventions and devices.

BIBLIOGRAPHY

Kallmann, Helmut. 'James Paton Clarke – Canada's first Mus. Bac.' *CMB*, 1, Spring–Summer 1970

– 'James Paton Clarke,' *DCB*, vol 10

'Toronto's pre-confederation music societies'

2 **Hugh** (Archibald). Educator, composer, organist, conductor, b Upper Canada (Ontario), 15 Aug 1839, d Philadelphia 16 Dec 1927. His birthplace has been cited variously as Toronto, Hamilton, and 'near Toronto'; it is not known where his parents resided in 1839. His father, James P., was his principal teacher. Hugh Clarke grew up in Toronto, where he made his debut as a pianist in 1854. In 1859 he went to Philadelphia with his bride, the singer Jane Searle, and established himself as an organist and teacher. As his father had made musical-academic history in Canada, so did Hugh Clarke in the USA: in 1875 he was appointed professor of music at the U of Pennsylvania, one of the first two such in the USA. (The other, John Knowles Paine, was appointed at Harvard in the same year.) Clarke remained at Pennsylvania for over 50 years and in 1920 was made head of its new School of Fine Arts. He was one of the earliest specialists in music theory in North America. Among his pupils were the composer William Wallace Gilchrist, the musicologist Otto Albrecht, and his own daughter Helen Clarke (1860–1926, a poet and composer and the editor of *Poet Lore* magazine). Clarke formed and led the university's Abt Male Chorus. His music to Aristophanes' *Acharnians*, of which he himself published the vocal score in 1886, is considered his best work; it earned him an hon D MUS (Pennsylvania 1886). Other major works were the cantata *The Music of the Spheres* (self-publ 1880), the oratorio *Jerusalem* (Presser 1890), and incidental music for Euripides' *Iphigenia in Tauris* (1903). He also wrote chamber and choral music, piano pieces and songs.

See also Oratorios, Canadian 3.

WRITINGS

– ed. *Songs of the University of Pennsylvania* (Philadelphia 1879)

Harmony on the Inductive Method (Philadelphia 1880, Boston 1908)

The 'Scratch Club' (Philadelphia 1889)

Theory Explained to Piano Students (Philadelphia 1892)

Pronouncing Dictionary of Musical Terms (Philadelphia 1896); student ed, *Pronouncing Musical Dictionary* (Philadelphia 1896)

A System of Harmony Founded on Key Relationships (Philadelphia 1898, 1926)

Music and the Comrade Arts (Boston 1899)

The Elements of Vocal Harmony (New York, Boston 1900)

Key to Harmony (Philadelphia 1901)

Counterpoint Strict and Free (Philadelphia 1901, 1929)

Highways and Byways of Music (New York, Boston 1901)

– ed. *Songs of Bryn Mawr College* (Philadelphia 1903)

– ed. *The Amateur*, a periodical (Philadelphia 1870–5)

BIBLIOGRAPHY

Mahoney, John D. 'Dr. Hugh A. Clarke, musician,' *General Magazine and Historical Chronicle*, vol 48, Apr 1941

HK

CLARKE, Douglas (William). Conductor, educator, organist, pianist, composer, b Reading, Berkshire, England, 4 Apr 1893, d Warwick, England, 14 Nov 1962; FRCO 1920, BA (Cambridge) 1926, B MUS (Cambridge) 1926, MA (Cambridge) 1930. Clarke served 1930–5 as dean of the Faculty of Music at *McGill U, but it was in his role as a founder and the regular conductor 1930–41 of the *Montreal Orchestra that he had the greatest impact upon the musical community.

Educated in England, Clarke studied 1909–12 under Sir Hugh Allen at Reading U College. After holding a commission in the Royal Navy during World War I he resumed his musical studies at Cambridge U, where his teachers were Gustav Holst, Ralph Vaughan Williams, and Charles Wood. Three of the compositions resulting from these studies were performed by the London SO. He was appointed organ scholar at Christ's College, Cambridge U, in 1923, and was conductor of the university's musical society. He moved to Canada in 1927 as conductor of the *Winnipeg Male Voice Choir and the *Winnipeg Philharmonic Choir and organist at Holy Trinity Church. In 1929 he succeeded Harry Crane *Perrin as director of the McGill Cons. In 1930 he became dean of the Faculty of Music, McGill U, and was invited to lead the newly formed Montreal Orchestra. He occupied the position without remuneration for 11 years, until the orchestra's dissolution after the 1940–1 season, and created a competent ensemble out of which grew the *MSO.

Apart from the generous contribution of his services to the Montreal Orchestra, Clarke's importance as a conductor lay in his pioneer programming. Many works now regarded as part of the standard repertoire were heard in Montreal for the first time under his direction: to name only a few of the more obvious, Brahms' *First* and *Fourth Symphonies*, *Second Piano Concerto*, *Violin Concerto*, and *Variations on a Theme of Haydn*, Berlioz' *Symphonie fantastique*, and Sibelius' *First*

Douglas Clarke

Symphony. He also conducted the Canadian premiere of Rachmaninoff's *Variations on a Theme of Paganini*. He was especially interested in British music, and introduced pieces by Bax, Bridge, Butterworth, Delius, Elgar, Holst, Vaughan Williams, Walton, and Warlock. He conducted his own *Three Pieces* in 1931 and *Piece for Full Orchestra* in 1936. An exceptionally gifted sight reader, Clarke could reduce an unfamiliar full orchestral score at the keyboard. He was an eloquent organist and pianist; in the latter capacity he performed during the 1940–1, 1944–5, and 1945–6 seasons with the *McGill String Quartet. For a time he gave lecture recitals on radio station CFCF prior to each of the orchestra's concerts.

Though he was not a great conductor, Clarke's very high qualifications as a musician were incontrovertible, and he assisted significantly in the rapid development of the orchestra while opening new avenues of experience to both musicians and the public. The *Montreal Festivals sponsored a concert 29 Mar 1946 at His (*Her) Majesty's Theatre in public recognition of Clarke's achievements. Many of his composition students at McGill U have attested to the fact that he was an inspired teacher whose lessons might range far beyond music to include a variety of related subjects – poetry in particular. His pupils included Violet *Archer, Alexander *Brott, Eric *McLean, Robert *Turner, and Octavia Wilson (whom he married upon his retirement to England in 1955). Most of his compositions are in manuscript, but some works for choir – 'Domine Deus,' 'A Late Lark,' *The Passion*, a 'Magnificat,' and 'Nunc dimittis,' and various liturgical pieces and introits – were published by Stainer & Bell. EM

CLARKE, Édouard. Pianist, organist, teacher, b Montreal 4 Nov 1867, d Biddeford, Me, 2 Feb 1917. He studied 1874–88 with Rosalie Euvrard, Paul *Letondal, and Dominique *Ducharme at the *Institut Nazareth in Montreal. Despite his blindness Clarke was a gifted interpreter, a brilliant technician, and a fine accompanist. While organist at St-Henri Church, he also taught in several Montreal schools. In 1901 he moved to Biddeford, where he pursued various musical activities.

CLARKE, F.R.C. (Frederick Robert Charles). Organist-choirmaster, composer, teacher, b Vancouver 7 Aug 1931; ARCT piano 1948, ARCT organ 1951, B MUS (Toronto) 1951, FCCO 1952, D MUS (Toronto) 1954. His teachers included Kenneth Ross (piano) in Vancouver, Eric *Rollinson (organ) at the *RCMT, and Healey *Willan, S. Drummond Wolff, and George Laughlin (theory and composition) at the *U of Toronto. Clarke was organist-choirmaster 1950–8 for several churches in Toronto and St Catharines. He also taught 1956–8 at the Hamilton Cons (*RHCM) and conducted 1957–8 the St Catharines Civic Orchestra (renamed *St Catharines SO). In 1958 he became organist-choirmaster at Sydenham Street United Church in Kingston, Ont, and conductor of the *Kingston Choral Society. He lectured 1959–69 at Queen's Theological College and joined the faculty of music at *Queen's U in 1964 to teach theory and other subjects. There he founded and conducted 1965–9 the Queen's Chamber Players Ensemble. Of his numerous compositions in the English tradition, *Bel and the Dragon* (1954; see Oratorios, Canadian 2) was written for his D MUS, *Sing a New Song to the Lord* (1960) was composed for the United Church of Canada in commemoration of the 400th anniversary of the Scottish Reformation, and *Psalm 145* (1966) won the CBC (Ottawa) Choral Composition Prize in 1967. Clarke was chairman of the music subcommittee for *The Hymn Book* of the Anglican and United Churches (1971), to which he contributed 7 tunes and 18 arrangements. He is a member of CAPAC.

SELECTED COMPOSITIONS

ORCHESTRA AND BAND

Bel and the Dragon, cantata (Apocrypha). 1954. Sop, ten, bar, 2 SATB, orch. CMCentre
Festival Overture. 1955. Orch. CMCentre
Sonata for Organ and Strings. 1958. CMCentre
Mini-Suite. 1971. Orch. CMCentre
Festival Te Deum. 1972. SATB, orch. CMCentre
Pastorale and Fugue on a Christmas Hymn. 1975. Str orch. CMCentre
Some works for band

KEYBOARD

Six Hymn Tune Voluntaries. Ca 1950–60. Org. Wat 1964
Simple Siciliano. 1954 (rev 1974). Pf. Wat 1974
Prelude. 1968. Org. GVT 1968
William Boyce Suite. 1970. Org. Nov 1973
Meditation on 'Primrose.' 1971. Org. GVT 1972
Also 2 suites for org (1956, 1966), both ms. Other works for pf, including *Five Easy Variations on a Theme*, *Ostinette*, and *Three Easy Pieces*, all publ by Wat

CHOIR AND VOICE

Christmas Cantata. 1955 (rev 1963). Sop, ten, bass, SATB, org. Ms
Choral pieces published by Wat: 'Breathe on Me, Breath of God'; 'Blessed Art Thou, Lord God of Our Fathers'; 'Glory to God on High'; 'Hail Our Monarch, Son of David'; 'Hail, Thou Source of Every Blessing'; 'Let Every Soul Be Subject'; 'Lord of All Hopefulness'; 'Lord of Our Life'; *Missa brevis*; 'O Father, on Our Festal Day'; 'O Father We Praise Thee'; 'O Sing a New Song to the Lord'; 'With Joy We Go Up to the House of the Lord'
9 works for v, pf (org). 1950–75. All ms
Also several works for chamb ens, including a *String Quartet* (1951), *Sonata* for vc, pf (1952), and works for brass and for other instr, all ms

WRITINGS

'Schubert's use of tonality: some unique features,' *CAUSM J*, vol 1, 1971
'The structure of Vaughan Williams' Sea Symphony,' *Music Review*, vol 34, Feb 1973 RPn

CLARKE, Herbert L. (Lincoln). Cornetist, bandmaster, violinist, violist, composer, b Woburn, Mass, 12 Sep 1867, d Long Beach, Cal, 30 Jan 1945. His father, William Horatio Clarke (1840–1913), was appointed organist-choirmaster at Jarvis St Baptist Church, Toronto, in 1880. Three sons, Ernest, Edwin, and Will, joined the regimental band of the *Queen's Own Rifles. Herbert, the youngest son, envied their accomplishments and taught himself to play the cornet by studying the Arban method. He organized a small orchestra which played at church socials. He practised the violin and viola and joined the orchestra of the *Toronto Philharmonic Society. He also played in string trios and quartets, and at 14 occupied the last chair in the 12-man cornet section of the Queen's Own Rifles Band. After a year in Minneapolis, he returned in 1886 as solo cornet to the Rifles band. That same year he joined the Citizens' Band of Toronto. He later organized the *Heintzman Piano Company Band and in 1888 he was engaged to teach and conduct the newly formed Taylor Safe Works Band. Also in 1888 he became an instructor at the new *Toronto College of Music.

Herbert L. Clarke

By the 1890s Clarke was recognized as one of the leading cornetists of the time. In 1891 or 1892 he became cornet soloist in the famous 22nd Regiment (US) Band under Patrick Sarsfield Gilmore. In April 1893, seven months after Gilmore's death, he played with that band under Victor Herbert, and then joined John Philip Sousa's Band, where he was first a cornet soloist and eventually an assistant director. He maintained his contact with Herbert until 1897 and with Sousa until 1917. Clarke returned to Canada, where he served 1918–23 as leader of the *Anglo-Canadian Leather Company (later Anglo-Canadian Concert) Band of Huntsville, Ont, and then moved to Long Beach, Cal. There he conducted the Municipal Band until shortly before his death.

Clarke recorded most of his 50-odd solo cornet compositions, including *Bride of the Waves* (recording date 1904), *Sounds from the Hudson* (1904), *Caprice Brilliante* (1908), *Southern Cross* (1911), *Stars in a Velvety Sky* (1911). He also composed more than 50 marches and 10 overtures for band. He wrote three volumes of *Studies for the Cornet: Elementary, Technical*, and *Characteristic* (Huntsville 1909–15; rev ed New York 1934–6), *Setting-Up Drills for Calisthenic Exercises*, and a short autobiography, *How I Became a Cornetist* (St Louis, Mo, 1934). Publishers of his compositions included *Whaley Royce, C. Fischer, Witmark, Fillmore, and Belwin. As a soloist Clarke recorded for *Berliner, Victor, Columbia, *Brunswick, and other companies; he also conducted the Sousa Band for Edison (cylinders) and Victor. His recordings are listed in *Roll Back the Years*.

BIBLIOGRAPHY

Bridges, Glenn D. *Pioneers in Brass* (Detroit 1965, 1968, 1972) (EBM)

CLARKE, Terry (Terence Michael). Drummer, b Vancouver 20 Aug 1944. While a pupil 1960–5 of Jim *Blackley in Vancouver, Clarke performed with Chris *Gage, David *Robbins, and others, then toured with US performers John Handy 1965–7 and the Fifth Dimension 1967–9. In 1970 he settled in Toronto, at first working with Lenny *Breau, and soon became the city's leading studio drummer. An exuberant and versatile player, equally skilled in jazz and rock, Clarke has performed in clubs and concerts and on radio and TV, and has recorded with Guido *Basso, Ed *Bickert, Sonny *Greenwich, Moe *Koffman, the *Boss Brass, Kathryn *Moses, Ted *Moses, Doug *Riley (Dr Music), Don *Thompson, and many others. He has played in Vancouver and Toronto clubs with many major US jazzmen, including Jim Hall, Thad Jones, Barney Kessel, Don Menza, Blue Mitchell, Art Pepper, and Frank Rosolino. Besides recording with Handy, Hall (see Discography for Thompson), and Beverly Glenn-Copland (see Discography for Breau), Clarke is heard on many pop LPs. MM

CLARKSON, (George) Austin (Elliott). Musicologist, administrator, b London 9 Aug 1932, naturalized Canadian 1940; BA science (Toronto) 1953, MA (ESM Rochester) 1955, PH D (Columbia) 1970. While studying science at the U of Toronto, Clarkson had private lessons from Oskar *Morawetz and Richard *Johnston (harmony and composition) and from Greta *Kraus and Alberto *Guerrero (piano). Other teachers were Louis Mennini at the ESM, Paul Henry Lang and Erich Hertzmann at Columbia U (Clarkson's doctoral thesis was 'On the nature of the medieval song'), and Stefan Wolpe privately in New York. Clarkson taught at the *U of Saskatchewan 1955–8, Columbia U 1964–7, and Yale U 1967–72, and in 1972 he joined the faculty of *York U, where he was chairman of the Music Dept until 1975 and then an associate professor. Founding editor of and contributor 1965–7 to Columbia U's *Current Musicology*, he also has reviewed books, music, and records for such publications as the *Canadian Music Journal*, the *Musical Quarterly*, *Notes*, and the *Yale Journal of Music Theory*, and has written biographies of several US composers for *The New Grove Dictionary of Music*. He was one of the editors of Hans Tischler's *A Complete Edition of the Earliest Motets ca. 1190–1297* for Yale U Press. RRs

Classical colleges and seminaries in Quebec. Teaching institutions run by Roman Catholic religious communities providing a program of studies termed 'classical.' These studies include the humanities, sciences, and philosophy, and prepare the students for university with a view to a career in the professions, or, for boys, for studies in theology to prepare for the priesthood. A classical college for boys, located in an episcopal town was called a seminary or a 'petit séminaire' in order to distinguish it from the 'grand' seminaries devoted to studies in theology and canon law. There are usually separate establishments for boys and girls, though certain colleges became coeducational during the 1960s. This article is concerned specifically with the boys' colleges (those for girls are described in the article on Ladies' colleges).

These institutions have always been numerous in Quebec and have exerted considerable influence on Quebec society. Most of them gave optional courses in music. The first in North America was the Jesuit college founded in Quebec City in 1635 under Samuel de Champlain. Martin *Boutet taught mathematics and music there, and Louis *Jolliet and Charles-Amador *Martin were probably among his pupils. The Petit Séminaire de Québec was founded in 1668; Ernest, Gustave, and Henri *Gagnon, Célestin *Lavigueur and Philéas *Roy all taught there at different periods. The Petit Séminaire or Collège de Montréal was set up in 1767; its distinguished teachers have included L.-Arsène *Barbarin, Alexis *Contant, J.-J. *Gagnier, J.-B. *Labelle, Alphonse *Lavallée-Smith, Joseph-Julien *Perrault, and Benoît *Poirier. Most of the founders of classical colleges strongly recommended the study of music, even in the early

19th century. They equipped their institutions with large music rooms, auditoriums for plays and concerts, and chapels where liturgical music was provided almost daily. Considerable sums of money also were invested in the purchase of pianos, organs, and orchestral and band instruments. Even when music was not incorporated into the academic program, it held a prime place among extracurricular activities. Depending on the availability of trained teachers, these schools made honest efforts to offer introductory courses in music and courses in solfège during regular class periods. Provision also was made for sectional rehearsals and for ensemble drill for choirs and concert bands, which occurred during study periods, recreation, or free periods. In addition, the students could work at their instruments individually for at least two 30-minute periods a day. Since most colleges were also boarding schools, there was ample opportunity for group rehearsals, individual instruction, sessions of listening to records, and educational concerts. Religious festivals, birthday celebrations, student theatre performances, and lectures or visits from well-known guests were all occasions for students' musical performances. The auditoriums or school halls of these establishments, with the balconies reserved for the pupils, were often the only concert halls in the region for such cultural activities as those of the *JMC, the *Community Concerts, and the Société des Amis du collège.

This encouragement to study music occasionally produced musicians of professional calibre such as Alphonse Lavallée-Smith, a student at the Collège de Nicolet (founded 1803), Calixa *Lavallée and L.J. Oscar *Fontaine at St-Hyacinthe (1811), Charles *Marchand at L'Assomption (1832), Clément *Morin and Ernest Gagnon at Joliette (1846), Arthur and Édouard *Dumouchel at the Collège Bourget in Rigaud (1850), and Alphonse *Tardif and J.-Alexandre *Gilbert at Lévis (1853). To guide the young musicians, two categories of teachers were required. In the first were members of the institution's teaching staff who were asked to conduct the choir, orchestra, or concert band while continuing to teach academic subjects; a priest occasionally would go to one of the major music schools to study so that he then could teach all the instruments and conduct the concert band and the choir. In the second category were lay professional musicians who were engaged to teach piano and violin classes. These teachers spent one or two days a week giving private lessons and assisting the resident conductors. Professional musicians, after graduation or on their return from European studies, found in the classical colleges a means of practising their art while obtaining additional income. The complete list of these teachers is too long to enumerate here, but notable besides those already mentioned are Octave, Édouard, and Robert *Chatillon at Nicolet; Abbé Charles-Joseph *Ducharme, founder of the Collège de Ste-Thérèse (1825); Guillaume *Dupuis at the Collèges St-Laurent (1847) and Notre-Dame (1869) in Montreal; Hervé Cloutier, J.-B. Labelle, Charles-Hughes *Lefebvre, Paul and Arthur *Letondal, and Paul Wiallard at the Collège Ste-Marie (1848) in Montreal; Joseph-Antoine Charlebois, Lucien Jolicoeur, Roméo *Larivière, and Agostino Salvetti at Rigaud; Jean-Gers Turcotte at Trois-Rivières (1860); Armand Renaud at the Collège Loyola (1898) in Montreal; Jean *Goulet at the Collèges de Montréal and Notre-Dame; and Jean *Papineau-Couture at the Collège Brébeuf (1928) in Montreal.

Following the reform of 1967 in Quebec's educational system, the colleges and seminaries were succeeded by the *Cegeps. (RBr)

The Classical Quartet of Montreal / Le Quatuor classique de Montréal. Founded in 1968 by Arthur *Garami, violinist. Robert Verebes, violist, is the other remaining original member. Cellist William Valleau was succeeded by Ifan *Williams in 1973, while the second violin has been, respectively, Gilles *Baillargeon 1968–9, Adolfo Bornstein 1969–70, Luis Grinhauz 1971–4, Janice Baty 1974, and Claire Segal 1974– . The quartet made its debut on CBC TV ('Let's Talk Music,' Montreal, March 1969) and has broadcast over 100 programs for the CBC. The Classical Quartet of Montreal has performed at the *JMC Orford Art Centre and the *Stratford Festival. In 1974 it taped, with guest pianists, Fauré's quartets and trios for broadcast over the French network of CBC and for international broadcast on the 50th anniversary of Fauré's death. The quartet established a public concert series in 1974, playing at the Centaur Theatre.

DISCOGRAPHY

Haydn – Wolf – Schubert – Mozart – Shostakovitch. 1962. CBC SM-206

Papineau-Couture – Saint-Marcoux – Gagnon. 1972. RCI 363

See also Marie Daveluy; Michel Dussault NT

CLAUDE, Renée (b Bélanger). Singer, b Montreal 3 Jul 1939. She studied piano for eight years at the *École Vincent-d'Indy and also took singing lessons with Alphonse Ledoux. In 1955 she won first prize in the program 'Découvertes de Billy Munro' on CKVL (Verdun). She began by performing French songs, especially those of Léo Ferré and Georges Brassens. Her first TV appearance was in 1960 on the CBC program 'Chez Clémence,' and in October of that year she began singing at the Boîte à chansons in Quebec City. The first Canadian song she performed was 'Ton Visage,' written for her by Jean-Pierre *Ferland. In November 1964 she gave her first recital at *Plateau Hall in Montreal. In 1965, with the actor Hubert Loiselle, she was co-host for CBC radio's 'Pour ceux qui s'aiment.' She was invited to appear on NBC TV's Johnny Carson Show in May 1967 and later that year performed at *Expo 67, appearing at the Quebec Pavilion, the Youth Pavilion, and the Expo Theatre.

Claude's first recording success was a single of Michel Conte's 'Shippagan.' Stéphane *Venne, her record producer 1967–72, composed several songs for her, including 'C'est le début d'un temps nouveau,' 'Le Tour de la terre,' and 'C'est notre fête aujourd'hui.' In 1968 she was awarded the Méritas trophy (best performer) in Montreal's (TV) Gala des artistes organized by the weekly magazine *Radiomonde*, and in June 1970, with Michel Conte's 'Viens faire un tour,' she won first prize in the 'Concours de la clé d'or,' which leads to the international competition 'Chanson sur mesure' (See 'Concours de la chanson canadienne').

Following a two-week engagement at the Canadian Pavilion at Expo 70 in Osaka, she returned to Canada to perform with the *MSO at the *PDA in August. Her performance at the Variety Theatre of Moscow in 1971 was followed by appearances in several cities in the USSR, and she returned there the following year for a six-week tour. Her TV special 'Je suis une femme' and her single of Yvan Ouellet's 'Le Ciel du sud' were successful in 1974. She participated in the *St-Jean-Baptiste celebrations on Mount Royal in 1975. In 1976 she sang at the Place des nations (Man and His World, Montreal), at Camp Fortune (Ottawa), and at the *NAC, among other places. On CBC TV she appeared in 'Vedettes en direct' in 1973 and 1976 and in 'Superspecial' and '90 Minutes Live' in 1977. In Paris she appeared in the telecasts 'Roger Pierre et Jean-Marc Thibault' (1971), 'Spécial Québec' with Yvon Deschamps, André *Gagnon, and Gilles *Vigneault (1976), and 'Numéro un ... le Québec' produced in December 1977 and shown in Canada as part of the CBC TV series 'Les Beaux Dimanches.'

Renée Claude represented Canada at the 1966 Sopot Festival in Poland with 'Tu es noire' by François *Dompierre and Stéphane Venne; in Paris in the 1969 competition 'Chansons sur mesure' with the song 'Le Geste' by Jacques Blanchet; at the 1970 Olympiades de la chanson in Athens; at the 1972 World Festival Ondo Nueva in Caracas; and, as a guest, at the 1976 International Song Festival in Spa, Belgium.

She has given many recitals in Montreal (at the Comédie-Canadienne in 1966, 1967, and 1970, at *Le Patriote in 1967, at the PDA in 1971, 1972, 1973, and 1974, at the *St-Denis Theatre in 1974, at the Méridien Hotel's Boîte à chansons in 1976) and in Quebec City (at the *Palais Montcalm in 1971, at *Laval U and the *Institut canadien in 1972, and at the *Grand Théâtre in 1974). She has toured in Quebec (1967 with Jacques Brel; and 1968, 1970, 1971, and 1975), in Ontario (1967 and 1972), and elsewhere. Among those who have composed music or lyrics for her songs are Jacqueline Barrette, Michel Conte, Clémence Desrochers, François Dompierre, Jean Fugère, André Gagnon, Mouffe, Luc Plamondon, Stéphane Venne, and the musicians of the *Ville Émard Blues Band.

Claude's natural elegance and her refined, tender, and sensuous voice have combined to produce an exceptional performer, especially of love songs. 'There is no mystery; this woman is an artist as assuredly as others will never be, for no sooner does she make the songs she performs her own than she restores them to us as filled with emotion and meaning as they can be, whereupon we understand them to a point at which, for one brief moment, we all become artists.' These words by Stéphane Venne were reported in *La Tribune* (Sherbrooke 12 Dec 1970). The Montreal boîte à chansons Le Patriote established a Renée-Claude trophy and awarded it to numerous performers between 1965 and 1972. Renée Claude is a member of CAPAC.

DISCOGRAPHY

Renée Claude, vol 1. 1963. Sel S 398.024
Renée Claude, vol 2. 1964. Sel S 398.071
Renée Claude, vol 3 *'Il y eut un jour.'* 1965. Sel SSP-24130
Renée Claude, vol 4. 1966. Sel SSP-24146
Renée Claude: Le Disque d'or. Sel S 398.150
Renée Claude 'Shippagan.' 1967. Col FS 673
Renée Claude. 1968. Barclay 80038
Le Tour de la terre. 1969. Barclay 80065
Le Début d'un temps nouveau. 1970. Barclay 80087
Tu trouveras la paix. 1971. Barclay 80116
Je reprends mon souffle. 1972. Barclay 80141
Ce Soir je fais l'amour avec toi. 1973. Barclay 80177
Les Grands Succès, vol 1. 1973. Barclay 75008
Chansons d'amour. 1974. Barclay 85012 (with J.-P. Ferland)
Les Grands Succès, vol 2. 1975. Barclay 75018
Je suis une femme. 1975. Lon LFS-9012
L'Enamour / Le Désamour. 1976. Lon LFS-9019
Bonjour. 1979. Solset Solt 1001
See also Discography for Chansonniers.

BIBLIOGRAPHY

Belleau, Massue. 'Renée Claude: "Je ne suis pas une fille triste",' *Maclean*, Apr 1965
Brouillé, Jean-Louis. 'Renée Claude en face de Renée Claude,' *L'Actualité*, Nov 1970
'Two singers try to cross the pop music culture gap,' *CanComp*, 63, Oct 1971
Grégoire, Daniel. 'Cette mystérieuse Renée Claude,' *Madame*, vol 1, Sep 1974
Beaulieu, Pierre. 'Renée Claude aux prises avec son image,' Montreal *La Presse*, 23 Jun 1979 BLH (DM, ST)

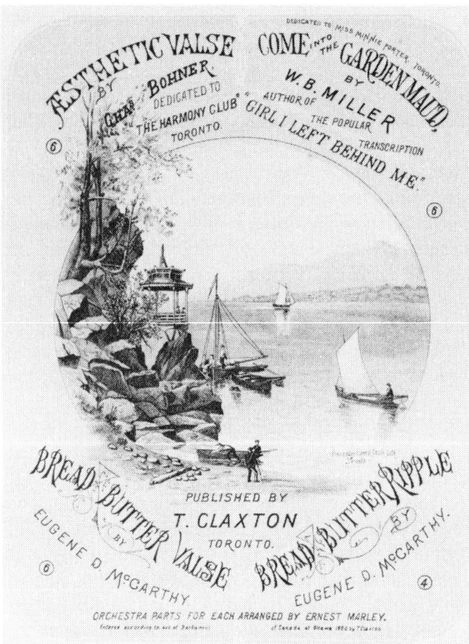

CLAXTON, Thomas. Publisher, instrumentalist, bandmaster, b Norfolk, England, 15 Mar 1837, d Toronto 19 Jan 1923. He came to Kingston, Canada West (Ontario), in 1850 and joined the *Queen's Own Rifles Band, Toronto, in 1863 as a player and temporary bandmaster. A few years later he apprenticed as an organ tuner and instrument repairman with R.S. *Williams, and in 1869 he began to import band and orchestral instruments. He established a store on Yonge St, had added a sheet music and mail order business by 1882, and later claimed to have been the first in Toronto to sell Edison phonographs and Berliner talking machines. After his retirement (ca 1911) the store was operated under a different management until about 1931. Claxton also established (ca 1885) Claxton's Celebrated Orchestra, a group of 30 to 35 theatre musicians (highly regarded by H.L. *Clarke who played in it 1887–8) and Claxton's Military Band. He was the first president of the Toronto Musical Protective Assn. Claxton's publishing output consists mostly of dances, marches, and songs, dating from the period 1879–87. Some 30 are known; they include *The Regimental March of the Queen's Own Rifles*, Charles *Bohner's *Claxton's Grand March*, pieces by J.F. *Davis, Edwin *Gledhill, and G.W. *Strathy, and several works by non-Canadians.

BIBLIOGRAPHY
'Trade notes,' *MJ*, vol 2, Jul–Aug 1888
'Pioneer merchant dies at ripe age,' Toronto *Globe*, 20 Jan 1923
'Thomas Claxton deceased,' *CMTJ*, vol 23, Feb 1923 HK

CLAYTON-THOMAS, David (b Thomsett). Singer, songwriter, producer, b Surrey, England, of British-Canadian parents, 13 Sep 1941. He was taken to Canada at six, and later raised in Toronto. He began playing the guitar in his late teens, during a series of terms in Ontario prisons. He began performing in Toronto nightclubs in the early 1960s, and developed a reputation as a tough, brawling blues singer. As Sonny Thomas (later David Clayton-Thomas) he led the Fabulous Shays, the rhythm and blues band which recorded 'Walk That Walk' (1965, Red Leaf) and 'Out of the Sunshine' (1965, Roman), and then formed the Bossmen, one of the first rock bands to incorporate elements of jazz. The Bossmen recorded several songs, including the 1966 hit 'Brainwashed,' written by Clayton-Thomas and the jazz pianist and band member Tony Collacott. These and other early recordings were re-issued on LPs in the 1970s to capitalize on Clayton-Thomas' popularity.

Clayton-Thomas went to the USA in 1966 and was the lead singer and figurehead 1968–72 of the New York jazz-rock group Blood, Sweat and Tears, with which he recorded such international hits as his own songs 'Spinning Wheel' (a million seller in 1969) and 'Lucretia MacEvil' (1970), as well as 'And When I Die' (1969), 'You Make Me So Very Happy' (1969), and 'Hi-De-Ho' (1970). The band toured widely in North America and Europe, and in 1971 performed in Moscow and Warsaw. Leaving Blood, Sweat and Tears in 1972, Clayton-Thomas made the LPs *David Clayton-Thomas and the Magnificent Sanctuary Band* (1972, Col KC-31000), *Tequila Sunrise* (1972, Col KC-31700), and *David Clayton-Thomas* (1973, RCA APLI 0173) and worked often in Las Vegas. He rejoined Blood, Sweat and Tears in 1974 as co-leader with Bobby Columby and by 1976 had assumed sole direction of the band. He made several LPs 1968–76 with the band for Columbia. After a two-year hiatus he re-formed the band in Toronto with local musicians, embarked on a cross-Canada tour, and made the LP *Nuclear Blues* (1979, MCA 3227). Clayton-Thomas has produced recording sessions for the Toronto reggae band Ishan People.

BIBLIOGRAPHY
Brown, Dick. 'The respectable Mr. David Clayton-Thomas,' *Weekend Magazine*, 17 Aug 1974
Gormely, Sheila. 'Gone nice,' *Canadian*, 31 Jul 1976
MM (PG)

CLENCH, (Esther Leonora) **Nora** (m Streeton). Violinist, b St Marys, near Stratford, Ont, 6 May 1867, d Toorak, Australia, 17 May 1938. She began violin lessons with her father, a lawyer and amateur violinist, and also studied with J.W. *Baumann, at first intermittently, but later, when she boarded at Loretto College in Hamilton, regularly for two years. She was a pupil 1884–9 of Adolf Brodsky at the Leipzig Cons and graduated with a diploma and a prize for excellence. From 1889 to 1891 she performed in Canada and the USA, and was principal violin of an orchestra in Buffalo, NY. In 1891 she studied with Ysaÿe and appeared in several concerts in Europe. In 1892 she moved to London, where she gave many successful recitals and a command performance before Queen Victoria. She toured briefly in Canada in the fall of 1893, and accompanied Emma *Albani on tours of Australia and South Africa in 1898. In 1904 she organized the Nora Clench Quartet, a female string quartet, which performed new works as well as standard repertoire and in 1907 premiered Max Reger's *Quartet in D Minor* in England. She retired in 1908 when she married the Australian painter Sir Arthur Streeton (1867–1943). She returned with him to Australia in 1924. Morgan's *Canadian Men and Women of the Time* (1898) describes Nora Clench's playing thus: 'tone broad, pure, resonant; style severely classical and correct.' SLH

CLERK, Alexandre-M. (Marie). Choirmaster, teacher, b Montreal 31 Aug 1861, d there 27 Jul 1932. In 1896 he succeeded R.-O. *Pelletier as choirmaster at the Gesù Church. Under his direction the choir gave many concerts, performing such works as Dubois's *Le Paradis perdu*, the choral portions of Mendelssohn's *Athalie*, Massenet's *La Vierge* and *Marie-Magdeleine*, and *The Sun-Worshippers* by the English composer Arthur Goring Thomas. In 1903 Clerk succeeded Charles *Labelle as choirmaster at Saint-Louis-de-France Church and took over the direction of the *Assn chorale Saint-Louis-de-France. He conducted the latter, with orchestra, in many oratorios and concert performances of opera. He harmonized four plainsong masses and composed other music. Most of his works later were destroyed by fire. His grandnephew, André Clerk, is a producer of music programs for the CBC. GP

CLERK-JEANNOTTE, Albert. Tenor, teacher, administrator, b St-Hilaire (now Mont-St-Hilaire), near Montreal, 15 Jan 1881, d New York 21 Jul 1945. He began music study with his uncle, Alexandre-M. *Clerk, and with Achille *Fortier. In 1898 he went to Paris, where he studied harmony with Xavier Leroux and voice with Jacques Bouhy, Fidèle Koenig, Victor Maurel, and Pauline Viardot-Garcia. He returned to Canada in 1900, but poor health forced him to give up singing and he became a journalist. He went again to Paris, nevertheless, to attend 1902–4 the opera classes of Jacques Isnardon and Victor Capoul. He auditioned successfully for Albert Carré, director of the Opéra-Comique, but health problems intervened again and he returned to Montreal, where he became a teacher at the *McGill Cons. During several subsequent summers he journeyed to France for study with Jean de Reszke, and during this period he sang Danilo in *The Merry Widow* in Vienna with Lina Abarbanell. He lived 1906–9 in New York.

Returning to Montreal, Clerk-Jeannotte founded, with the financial assistance of Frank S. *Meighen, the Montreal Musical Society, which became the *Montreal Opera Company, and 1910–13 he presented three seasons of grand opera in four Canadian cities. In the autumn of 1916 he left Montreal for Paris with his brother-in-law Wilfrid *Pelletier. In 1917 he tried unsuccessfully to revive the Montreal Opera Company, and opened a voice studio in New York. His pupils included Georges *Dufresne, Hope Hampton, Ludovic Huot, Fabiola Poirier, Henri *Pontbriand, the pop singer Hildegarde, and the actor Cary Grant.

BIBLIOGRAPHY
'M. Albert Clerk-Jeannotte,' *Montréal Musical*, 34, 26 Jan 1913
Pelletier, Wilfrid. *Une Symphonie inachevée ...* (Montreal 1972)
Musical Red Book GP

CLOSSEY, Jean-Julien. Violinist, organist, pianist, conductor, teacher, b Pepinster, Belgium, 3 Jun 1866, naturalized Canadian 1918, d Montreal 16 May 1926. He studied piano and cornet 1873–82 at the Liège Cons while also taking private violin lessons. At 15 he gave a violin recital in Verviers and then went to France, where he worked 1886–90 as violinist, rehearsal pianist, and conductor. At the invitation of Ernest *Lavigne he came to Canada in May 1891 and was a member of the first violins at *Sohmer Park 1891–4, with the *Couture MSO 1894–6, with the *Goulet MSO 1897–1901, and with the Assn artistique 1891–6. He taught and was organist at Mont-St-Louis College from 1891 until his death. Clossey was organist at the Orpheum and Imperial theatres and a founding member of the *Société canadienne d'opérette. He composed some light music for orchestra, piano, and violin as well as choral pieces and songs. None of his works has been published.

Clossey had eight children; the eldest, Émile (b Montreal 29 Mar 1897, d 30 Jul 1955), studied cello in Montreal and 1910–12 in Liège. A pianist and conductor as well, he founded and conducted the

Montreal Municipal Orchestra (ca 1935–45), which was composed mainly of civic employees like himself (he worked as a civil engineer for the City of Montreal). GP

CLOUTIER, Jean-Marie. Teacher, composer, b Quebec City 8 Aug 1923; B MUS (Montreal) 1953, L MUS Sacred Music (Montreal) 1954, L MUS (Montreal) 1955. After studying at the *U of Montreal with Jean *Papineau-Couture (composition), Georges-Émile *Tanguay (harmony), and Jean *Vallerand (orchestration) he wrote incidental music for the troupe the Jongleurs de la montagne, the theatre group the Apprentis sorciers, and the Théâtre de l'Égrégore. For the last-named group his most notable assignment was the music for Tennessee Williams' *Summer and Smoke*. He worked with various directors, including Paul Buissonneau, for whom he was pianist and actor in La Roulotte, a children's theatre. He composed the sound track for Pierre Perrault's film *Le Règne du jour* (NFB 1967), and also the incidental music, performed by computer, for the Nouvelle Compagnie théâtrale's 1971 production of Euripides' *The Trojan Women*. In 1971 his *Hypothèses* for *ondes Martenot was premiered at the Nocturnales (late evening concerts) at the U of Montreal. In 1977 excerpts from his opera *Pour qui pour quoi* (libretto by Roland Laroche) were performed by l'Atelier d'art lyrique. His incidental music for Roland Lepage's play *Le Temps d'une vie* was produced that same year by the Théâtre d'aujourd'hui.

Cloutier taught 1960–3 at Ste-Marie College, 1962–3 for the Pointe-Claire School Board, and 1964–5 at St-Denis College. In 1968 he began teaching counterpoint and fugue at the Faculty of Music, U of Montreal. He was secretary of the faculty 1969–76. His pupils have included Michel *Longtin, Denis *Lorrain, and Pierre *Trochu. His work 1973–6 with children in the elementary and secondary grades at Notre-Dame-des-Rapides school provided the material for *Découverte des sons* (Quebec City 1976), a teaching guide on which he collaborated; it deals with a child's creativity with respect to the aural world and music. (PR)

Club musical de Québec. Non-profit organization founded in 1891 by women of the English and the French élite of Quebec City, with the aim of organizing morning concerts and making more widely available musical experiences which hitherto had been reserved for the privileged. Among the founders were Mrs E.A. Bishop, Mme Jules Tessier, Mme Fred Gaudet, Mrs W. Sharples, Cécile Gagnon, and Josephe Anderson. The group at first was called the Quebec Ladies' Morning Musical Club. The name was changed to the Club musical des dames de Québec in 1896 and later was amended to the Club musical de Québec.

The initial formula, which provided for a committee of 16 members divided equally between English-speaking and French-speaking members, was maintained for 50 years, but after 1940 French-speaking members predominated. The by-laws were drafted in 1894, but some documents bear witness to the activities of the first members as early as the autumn of 1891. The first official season, however, was in 1895–6 and included 12 morning concerts. As the society grew it changed its concert time from morning to afternoon (ca 1913) and then to evening. Concerts were presented in the YMCA hall until 1908, at Morrin College 1909–12, in Chevaliers de Colomb hall 1912–24, in the Château Frontenac ballroom 1924–71, and in the Louis-Fréchette and Octave-Crémazie halls of the *Grand Théâtre 1972–6. They moved to the *Institut canadien in 1976.

Local artists were engaged at first, and on occasion foreign artists who were passing through Quebec City. The pianists Léo-Pol *Morin and Wilfrid *Pelletier appeared there after 1909. The club has presented many famous artists, but it also has remained conscious of the importance of providing opportunities for young artists. The club's program developed greatly from 1920 to 1937 under the direction of two of its presidents, Mrs H.H. Sharples and Mme Paul Robitaille. During those years negotiation with New York impresarios produced visits from a succession of the greatest artists, Artur Rubinstein, Rudolf Serkin, Robert Casadesus, Elisabeth Schwarzkopf, and the Budapest Quartet among them. The popularity of the concerts reached a peak between 1936 and 1942 when there were more than 1000 subscribers. Though later it faced increasing competition, the club nevertheless maintained its level of quality. It has enhanced the artistic life of Quebec City and has presented a succession of such Canadian artists as Lionel *Daunais, Janina *Fialkowska, Maureen *Forrester, Yvonne *Hubert, Alfred *Laliberté, Arthur *LeBlanc, Louis *Lortie, André *Mathieu, and Ronald *Turini. PD (MS)

Club musical et littéraire de Montréal. Founded in 1933 by the pianist and teacher Gérard Gamache (b Trois-Rivières, Que, 25 Jan 1903) after a public concert by his pupils and a lecture by Philippe Aubé at St-Sulpice Hall. The club's dinner-discussions, six each year at the Viger Hotel during the mid-1930s, became lecture-recitals after 1941. The meetings were held 1936–8 at *Tudor Hall, 1938–41 and 1973–5 at the Windsor Hotel, and 1941–72 at the Ritz-Carlton Hotel. In 1975 they returned to St-Sulpice Hall in the BN du Q. In the 42 years of the club's existence prior to that time the membership had varied between 63 and 850. Musicians who have participated in the club's meetings include the pianists Aline van Barentzen, Alfred *Laliberté, Charles *Reiner, and Ronald *Turini, the violinists Hyman *Bress, Albert *Chamberland, and Arthur *LeBlanc, the soprano Colette *Boky, and others. Jean *Vallerand gave a series of lectures 1940–2 on music history. Lecturers who talked about Canadian musicians include Félix Desrochers ('Calixa Lavallée' in 1942), Arthur *Letondal ('Guillaume Couture' 1934–5), and Gilles *Potvin ('Emma Albani' in 1974). In 1979 the club was one of the oldest of its kind still active in Canada. It has published (non-commercially) most of the lectures given 1940–61.

BIBLIOGRAPHY

Bergeron, Raymonde. 'Un goût du beau qui me veut pas vieillir,' *Perspectives*, 16 Feb 1980 (NT)

Clubs. See the following *EMC* articles:
Arts and Letters Club of Toronto
Club musical et littéraire de Montréal
Hart House
Junior Musical Club of Winnipeg
Men's Music Club of Winnipeg
Musical Art Club, Saskatoon
Record collector clubs
Sir Ernest MacMillan Fine Arts Club
Vancouver Cello Club
Women's musical clubs

CLUDERAY, Lawrence (Rushby). Organist, choir conductor, critic, b Leeds 1 Dec 1907; FRCO, ARCM. He studied in England with H.P. Richardson and Sir Edward Bairstow. He emigrated to Canada in 1947 and settled in Vancouver, where, save for a short stay 1960–1 in Calgary, he remained. He served as organist-choirmaster at St Andrew's-Wesley United Church and at St John's (Shaughnessy) and St Stephen's Anglican churches in Vancouver, and at Christ Church, Elbow Park, in Calgary. He reviewed concerts for the Calgary *Herald* and *Albertan* and 1966–73 for the Vancouver *Province*. He contributed 1954–73 to the CBC programs 'Music Diary,' 'Critics at Large,' and 'Record Review.' He served 1950–9 as director of the *Vancouver Bach Choir, and the English traditions he maintained had a lasting effect on the choir's repertoire and style of performance. Notable among his achievements were the Easter performances of Bach's *St Matthew Passion* at St Andrew's-Wesley Church and his preparation of the choir for the CBC's 1957 broadcast of Elgar's *The Dream of Gerontius*. He retired in 1973. TRL

Richard Coates

CMEA. See Canadian Music Educators' Association.

CNE. See Canadian National Exhibition.

CNR. See Broadcasting; Concerts.

COATES, Richard. Bandmaster, music teacher, organ builder, painter, sawmill operator, b Thornton Dale, Yorkshire, England, 30 Nov 1778, d Aldborough Township, southwest of London, Ont, 29 Jan 1868. Little is known about Coates' youth. His mother is supposed to have been a relative of the painter Sir Joshua Reynolds (1723–92). As a young man Coates played in a British army band and is said to have served as a bandmaster at the battle of Waterloo. He moved to Canada in 1817 and after a year in Quebec City settled in York (Toronto). He painted oil portraits and became associated with the *Children of Peace (though not necessarily as a member of the sect), painting the pictures 'Peace' and 'Plenty' for their temple at Sharon, building several organs, and coaching their choir and band. Coates was reported by William Lyon MacKenzie to be the 'concert horn' player in 1829 in the small Sharon orchestra (*Sketches of Canada and the United States*, London 1833).

The first of Coates' three Sharon organs was built ca 1820. Preserved at Sharon and restored to playing condition in 1979, it became probably the oldest organ still in use in Ontario, and certainly the oldest surviving organ built in Ontario. According to Geoffrey *Payzant it was not restored prior to that date because of the delicate condition – and the historical significance – of the original barrels, which were fashioned from a soft wood. It was felt unwise to risk operating them until replicas had been made. Coates' second organ, like the first a barrel-operated rather than a keyboard organ, was not preserved. The third Sharon organ, Coates' largest, was built in 1848 and has a keyboard. From 1831 to about 1861 Coates operated a sawmill and a thrashing mill east of *Oakville, Ont. Though he was prosperous for some time, the depression of the early 1860s caused his last move, to a farm in Aldborough Township, near what became the village of Rodney. Of seven organs he is said to have built, one has been preserved by a descendant, Paul Shippey of Chatham, Ont, and two survive at Sharon. His last organ, built when he was 79, was used at St Jude's Church in Oakville until about 1899. No account survives of the other two organs.

BIBLIOGRAPHY
Kallmann, Helmut. 'Richard Coates,' *DCB*, vol 9
Harper, J.R. *A People's Art* (Toronto 1974) HK

COCKBURN, Bruce. Singer-songwriter, guitarist, pianist, b Ottawa 27 May 1945. Raised on a farm near Pembroke, west of Ottawa, and in Ottawa itself, he began playing guitar and piano in his teens. After working as a street musician in Paris he studied theory, composition, and arranging ca 1964–6 at the Berklee College of Music, Boston. Though he was introduced in Boston to the urban folk music movement and also to jazz (which had an increasing influence on his work in the mid-1970s), he played in several rock bands, including the Esquires and the Children, on his return to Ottawa. In 1967 he sang alone in coffee houses and made his first appearance at the *Mariposa Folk Festival. His solo career continued, though he was a member of the folk-rock band *Three's A Crowd when it was revived 1968–9 for a CBC TV series.

With the critical and popular acclaim accorded his score for the film *Goin' Down the Road* (1970) and his early LPs Cockburn rose to national prominence, making his first cross-country tour in 1972. He received *Juno Awards as folksinger of the year for 1970, 1971, and 1972, and again for 1979. One of the few English-Canadian performers to enjoy success in Quebec, he has sung several of his songs in French, and has had the lyrics to his songs translated for publication on the covers of his LPs, beginning with *Sunwheel Dance*. His 'Prenons la mer,' a bilingual song, was a hit in 1978 in Quebec.

Cockburn has performed rarely in the USA (where his LPs have had limited exposure), but he appeared at the Philadelphia Folk Festival in 1974 and at Alice Tully Hall, New York, in 1977. He shared the stage with Murray *McLauchlan on a tour of Japan in 1977, and returned there alone in 1979. Cockburn has performed alone (playing guitar, piano, banjo, and dulcimer) and with such accompanists as the guitarist Eugene Martynec (the producer of Cockburn's LPs), the bassists Dennis Pendrith and Robert Boucher, the keyboardist Pat Godfrey, and various percussionists. After two of Cockburn's many *Massey Hall concerts – he recorded *Circles in the Stream* in that hall in 1977 – Bryan Johnson called him 'one of the few folk guitarists with both a good-time bounce and amazing virtuosity' (Toronto *Globe and Mail*, 13 Feb 1976); and Katherine Gilday wrote: 'His songs have the coherence and the conviction of a body of poems ... and are virtually all fueled by one dominant emotion, a yearning for purity and wholeness. Images of stars and streams and blue space abound in his pieces – and for the most part, it is this mystical sort of longing that comes through in his voice and vaguely ethereal melodic lines ... Underneath the ... delicacies of his instrumental and vocal musings, however, there is an earthy

Bruce Cockburn

rhythmic substructure deriving from a variety of folk sources that declares his human rootedness' (Toronto *Globe and Mail*, 30 Oct 1978). Cockburn's best-known songs include 'Goin' Down the Road,' 'Goin' to the Country,' 'Musical Friends,' 'Laughter,' 'Mama Just Wants to Barrelhouse All Night Long,' and 'Burn, Baby, Burn.'

Cockburn's songs are published by Golden Mountain Music and also have been recorded by John Allan *Cameron, George Hamilton IV, Anne *Murray, Tom Rush, *Valdy, David *Wiffen, and others. Cockburn has produced LPs for Wiffen and for the poet Paul Stoddard; on the latter's *Day Coach Rider* (TNorth TN 15) he also played guitar, bass guitar, and percussion. Cockburn is an affiliate of PRO Canada.

DISCOGRAPHY
Bruce Cockburn. 1969. TNorth TN 1
High Winds White Sky. 1970–1. TNorth TN 3
Sunwheel Dance. 1971. TNorth TN 7
Night Vision. 1973. TNorth TN 11
Salt, Sun and Time. 1974. TNorth TN 16
Joy Will Find a Way. 1975. TNorth TN 23
In the Falling Dark. 1976. TNorth TN 26
Circles in the Stream. 1977. TNorth TN 30
Further Adventures of Bruce Cockburn. 1978. TNorth TN 33
Dancing in the Dragon's Jaws. 1979. TNorth TN 37

BIBLIOGRAPHY
Lewis, Lee. 'Bruce Cockburn,' *MSc*, 254, Jul–Aug 1970
Batten, Jack. 'From Bruck Cockburn to youth – a very private message,' *Maclean's*, Jan 1971
Kotash, Myrna. 'The pure unadulterated spaces of Bruce Cockburn,' *SatN*, Jun 1972
Holtz, Patricia. 'Success without compromise,' *The Canadian*, 3 Apr 1976 MM

Coda. Jazz magazine started in May 1958 by John *Norris and initially and briefly under the auspices of the Traditional Jazz Club of Toronto. In June 1959 it took the subtitle 'The Canadian Jazz Magazine'; with the August–September 1964 issue it became 'Canada's Jazz Magazine,' and in October 1976 'The Jazz Magazine.' Frequency of publication has varied from monthly to bimonthly. By May 1978, 160 issues had been published and circulation was about 5000. Norris was editor 1958–76. In 1963 he was joined by Bill *Smith, who served until 1976 as art director and then became co-editor with David Lee. Norris continued with Smith as the magazine's copublisher, and remained with the umbrella organization, Coda Publications, in a business capacity.

Frequently referred to as the finest jazz magazine in the English language, *Coda* includes feature articles, record, concert, and club reviews, and news columns. Coverage of Canadian musicians' activities was extensive in the early years when Norris and Len Dobbin provided comprehensive reports of jazz in Toronto and Montreal respectively, and various correspondents intermittently served other Canadian cities. By the mid-1970s, however, coverage of Canadian activity had decreased.

Coda Publications have operated the Jazz and Blues Centre (a record store and mail-order business at two successive downtown Toronto locations) and Sackville Records. Sackville was established by Norris, Smith, and others in 1968, and by 1979 had released LPs by Jim *Galloway, Sonny *Greenwich, the US drummer and Toronto resident Pete Magadini, Phil *Nimmons, and Don (W.) *Thompson (one with a quintet, a second of duets with Ed *Bickert), and over 25 others by leading US traditional, mainstream, and avant-garde musicians. Sackville also distributes the Onari label (see Smith, Bill).

BIBLIOGRAPHY
Lees, Gene. 'You want U.S. jazz recordings? Try Toronto,' *High Fidelity and Musical America*, Jul 1973
Waxman, Ken. 'How jazz came up the Humber River and settled on Yonge Street,' *Toronto Life*, Dec 1975
Weiner, Andrew. 'The hip shrine on Yonge Street – for Smith and Norris, jazzing up Toronto is a labor of love,' (*Toronto Star*) *The City*, 26 Mar 1978 MM

CODMAN, Stephen. Organist, composer, teacher, b Norwich, England, ca 1796, d Quebec City 6 Oct 1852. He obtained a solid grounding in music with John Christmas Beckwith and William Crotch before crossing the Atlantic in 1816 at the invitation of Bishop Jacob Mountain to take a position as organist of the (Anglican) Cathedral of the Holy Trinity in Quebec City, probably succeeding John *Bentley. The outstanding events of Codman's career were a 'Grand Concert of Sacred Music' 26 Jun 1834 for the benefit of the Emigrants' Society (Codman not only served as chairman of the organizing committee and music director of the 174 performers, but also performed as soloist and accompanist) and two concerts, in April 1841, of excerpts from *Messiah, The Creation*, and *Christ on the Mount of Olives*. It seems likely that he was responsible for the replacement of the cathedral's original organ in 1847.

Codman's known works, all for solo voice or vocal ensembles, appear to have been written before 1835. Two of them, 'The Fairy Song' and 'They Are Not All Sweet Nightingales,' published in London at Goulding, D'Almaine, and Co and highly praised in an article in the *Quarterly Musical Magazine and Review* (London 1827), are among the oldest published Canadian compositions. Certain occasional religious pieces, such as the anthem 'I Heard a Voice in Heaven' (performed 20 Jun 1825 at the funeral of Jacob Mountain) and the invocation 'O Most Merciful' (which opened the concert in 1834) well may have exemplified Codman's best work, but copies have not survived. The only manuscripts preserved in the archives of the catehdral contain some adaptations and orchestrations of fragments of works by Webbe, Spohr, Crotch, and others; a novelty piece, 'Brothers'; and a collection of some 40 psalm-chants for four voices with organ accompaniment, in the manner of many English church composers of the end of the 18th century. Although the reputation of this learned organist did not travel very far beyond the parish, it appears that in upholding high standards of liturgical singing he was able to implant in Quebec City the musical tradition exemplified in the religio-dramatic music of Handel, Boyce, Haydn, Mozart, Cherubini, and Beethoven, his spiritual masters. His piano teaching, moreover, introduced to the city the methods of Cramer and Kalkbrenner. A plaque at the Anglican cathedral commemorates his services as organist.

Letters and documents in the archives of Notre-Dame parish reveal that Codman also took an interest in the musical standards at the Catholic cathedral. In appreciation of their efforts in this direction he sent the churchwardens in 1837 a volume of his accompaniments (published in London), and in 1838 he acted as an adviser, advocating a systematic course of study and recommending the services of his pupil Bender. The same year the churchwardens were instructed to 'enquire of Messrs Codman and Binder [sic]' as to their availability 'to undertake to play the organ ... and to form a lay choir on a solid foundation.' In a letter of 9 Jun 1839, 'remaining under consideration,' Codman offered his services as organist and choirmaster to the parish church; he was, however, not appointed to the post.

BIBLIOGRAPHY

Quebec Gazette, 12 Dec 1816; 23 Jun 1825; 23, 27 Jun 1834
Quebec Mercury, 28 Jun 1834 LP

Coffeehouses. Cafes which in English Canada and English-speaking areas of Montreal have provided performance venues for folk and pop musicians (Bruce *Cockburn, Bonnie *Dobson, Gordon *Lightfoot, Murray *McLauchlan, among many other), as in French Canada *boîtes à chansons have for chansonniers. Like the boîte à chansons, the coffeehouse – often in a converted house or a church basement – is characterized by its limited seating capacity (an average of less than 100), informality, and intimacy. As its name suggests, it is not licensed to sell liquor.

As centres for music the coffeehouses date from the late 1950s, when they began to proliferate throughout North America, at first in the larger US cities. Many have been located in areas of cities populated by young people – on or near university campuses (eg, the Yellow Door, opened in 1967 near *McGill U, Montreal, and the Cuckoo's Nest, opened in 1973 on the campus of the *U of Western Ontario, London) or in 'bohemian' communities (eg, Yorkville in Toronto and Gastown in Vancouver, which in the late 1960s were the sites of many coffeehouses popular with members of the 'hippy' movement). The Gerrard Street Coffee House and Club 71 (the latter in Yorkville), both of which opened in Toronto in the late 1950s, were among the first in Canada. Others followed in the 1960s, including the Bohemian Embassy, the Fifth Peg, the Penny Farthing, the Pornographic Onion, and the *Riverboat in Toronto; the Bunkhouse and the Classical Joint in Vancouver; the Depression in Calgary; the Second Stage in Winnipeg; the Black Swan in Stratford, Ont; and Le Hibou in Ottawa. In the late 1960s several Yorkville coffeehouses – Boris's, El Patio, the Gaslight, and the Night Owl among them – departed from the folk tradition and were homes to Toronto's most innovative rock bands. Jazz was heard at the Penny Farthing.

While the boîtes à chansons continued as a platform for the Quebec pop performer after the passing of the era of the chansonnier in the late 1960s, coffeehouses had all but disappeared by the mid-1970s for several reasons, among them the failure of revenues (especially in the absence of the liquor license) to keep pace with the rising costs of operation and performers' fees, and the changing tastes of audiences. In Toronto, moreover, the 1970s redevelopment of the Yorkville area put rents there well beyond the budgets of the coffeehouses. As the commercial feasibility of coffeehouses diminished, those that remained often were adjuncts to folk societies (eg, the Green Cave, opened by the Vancouver Folk Song Society in 1977) which presented performers one or two nights a week. Among other coffeehouses still open in 1979 were the Classical Joint (Vancouver), Change of Pace (previously Smale's Place, in London, Ont), Fiddler's Green (in fact a folk club operating one night a week, with a liquor license, in Toronto), and the Yellow Door (Montreal). MM

COHEN, Leonard (Norman). Poet, singer-songwriter, novelist, b Montreal 21 Sep 1934; BA English (McGill) 1955. One of the most controversial Canadian literary figures of the 1960s, Cohen has been quoted as saying: 'everytime I pick up a pen to write something, I don't know if it's going to be a poem, a song or a novel' (Toronto *Globe and Mail*, 22 Feb 1969). At 15, under the influence of country and western music, he began playing guitar. While studying at McGill U he worked in a country band, The Buckskin Boys. He gave his earliest poetry readings in a Montreal nightclub to the accompaniment of jazz. In the years following he wrote the poems collected in *Let Us Compare Mythologies* (1956), *The Spice-Box of Earth* (1961), *Flowers for Hitler* (1964), and *Parasites from Heaven* (1966), and the novels *The Favourite Game* (1963) and *Beautiful Losers* (1966).

In March 1966, during a poetry reading at the YMCA in New York, Cohen sang two of his poems, *'Suzanne' and 'Stranger.' His readings soon evolved into concerts, and his songs became increasingly popular through performances by other artists. In Toronto the folk-rock group the Stormy Clovers sang some of his songs in local coffeehouses and for the soundtrack of the *NFB film *Angel* (1966). In New York Judy Collins sang and recorded several of his songs and introduced Cohen himself to some of her audiences. In 1967 Cohen performed at the *Mariposa and Newport folk festivals and *Expo 67. In that same year Norma *Beecroft based two works – *Elegy* and *Two Went to Sleep* – on Cohen verses. After three years of relative inactivity Cohen appeared in 1970 in Europe (where his popularity as a singer has been greatest) at London's Royal Albert Hall, Paris' Olympia Music Hall, and the Isle of Wight rock festival. Thereafter he continued to perform somewhat less frequently in North American and European concert halls. Though he made an LP in 1977, he was relatively inactive in music by the late 1970s. He turned again to poetry and to a novel, writing songs only on occasion and without the commercial success he enjoyed earlier. His most popular songs include: 'Suzanne,' 'Dress Rehearsal Rag,' 'So Long Marianne,' 'Hey, That's No Way to Say Goodbye,' and 'Sisters of Mercy.' His 'Bird on a Wire,' as recorded by Joe Cocker, was popular in 1970. Cohen himself sang 'Stranger' in the NFB film *The Ernie Game* (1967) and for the soundtrack of the US film *McCabe and Mrs. Miller* (1971).

During his career as a singer-songwriter Cohen has received praise for his gifts as a lyricist, but has suffered some criticism of his abilities as a musician. In a favourable review of *Death of a Ladies' Man* (an LP produced and co-composed by Phil Spector), Ken Waxman in *Saturday Night* (Mar 1978) expressed a common sentiment about Cohen's earlier work: 'Too often airborne imagery was shackled to a pedestrian tune, while Cohen compounded the problem by singing in an off-hand, droning monotone.' Some of Cohen's songs have been published by his own company, Stranger Music, in folios corresponding to his LPs. He is a member of PRO Canada.

Cohen's literary publications include *Selected Poems 1956–1968* and *The Energy of Slaves* (1972). Brian Macdonald's ballet **The Shining People of Leonard Cohen* interprets verses of the poet incorporated in an electronic score by Harry *Freedman. A musical, *Sisters of Mercy*, put together by Gene Lesser from Cohen's writings about women (utilizing poems, songs, fiction, letters, and fragments of unpublished manuscripts), was produced in 1973 at the *Shaw Festival.

DISCOGRAPHY

Songs of Leonard Cohen. 1967. Col CS 9533
Songs from a Room. 1968. Col CS 9767
Songs of Love and Hate. 1971. Col C303103
Live Songs. 1970–2. 2-Col CK31724
New Skin for the Old Ceremony. 1974. Col KC 33167
The Best of Leonard Cohen. (1975). Col ES 90334
Death of a Ladies' Man. (1977). Col PES-90436
Recent Songs. (1979). Col JC 36264

BIBLIOGRAPHY

Ruddy, Jon. 'Is anyone in the world ready for Leonard Cohen?' *Maclean's*, 1 Oct 1966
Brown, S. 'King of the now people,' *SatN*, Feb 1968
Grescoe, Paul. 'Poet writer singer lover,' *The Canadian*, 10 Feb 1968
Ondaatje, Michael. *Leonard Cohen* (Toronto 1970)
Morley, Patricia A. *The Immoral Moralists: Hugh MacLennan and Leonard Cohen* (Toronto 1972)
Saltzman, Paul. 'Famous last words from Leonard Cohen,' *Maclean's*, Jun 1972
MacDonald, Ruth. 'Leonard Cohen, a bibliography, 1956–73,' *Bulletin of Bibliography*, vol 31, Jul–Sep 1974
Gnarowski, Michael, ed. *Leonard Cohen: The Artist and His Critics* (Toronto 1976)
Waxman, Ken. 'Rebirth of a ladies' man,' *SatN*, Mar 1978 MM

Cohn Auditorium. See Rebecca Cohn Auditorium.

Colas et Colinette ou le Bailli Dupé. 'Comedy in prose intermixed with ariettas,' text and music by Joseph *Quesnel, probably the first operatic work with original music to be written on Canadian soil (and most likely in North America), and the first to be performed. Composed about 1789, it was premiered in Montreal 14 Jan 1790 at the Théâtre de Société and drew a flattering unsigned notice in the *Gazette de Montréal* (21 Jan 1790): 'the work pleases first, then charms, then delights ... The applause was duly merited and did credit both to the author and to the audience ... it is one of those works which decis repetita placent.' A second performance was given at the same place 9 February 'in aid of the poor.'

The work was performed again 15 years later, at the Théâtre Patagon in Quebec City 29 Jan and 23 Feb 1805, and the *Gazette* (31 Jan 1805), after pointing out that 'this is perhaps the first piece of the kind that has been written and performed in this province,' added: 'as a colonial production, it possesses considerable merit. It is rare that poetry and music are composed by the same person.' The work was performed again in Quebec City 7 and 21 Feb 1807. Although it is only presumed that Quesnel attended his work's premiere, it seems that he did hear at least one of the Quebec performances, and that it was not to his liking. In a letter to the publisher John *Neilson in April 1807 he said that it had given him 'very little pleasure,' that it 'doubtless was very unpleasant for the gentlemen and ladies of Quebec that the music, which in this work is as necessary to success as the words ... was murdered so cruelly,' and that it 'would have been a hundred times better to have left out the instruments and let the well-rehearsed voices sing alone, than to make them sing to screeching clarinets and deafening horns.'

Inspired by Rousseau's philosophy, the plot centres on Monsieur Dolmont's ward, the shepherdess Colinette, who would rather have Colas, a simple and honest young shepherd, as a husband than le Bailli, who claims to be well established but is old and cranky. The score consists of 14 musical pieces, comprising arias for each character, duos, and a final chorus. The libretto and music are of French inspiration and recall certain works by Quesnel's contemporaries Grétry, Monsigny, and Philidor. The tunes are suited to the personalities of the characters, vivacious or noble according to the situation. Occasionally the style is even dramatic. The score does not state the type of voice required for each role, but the tessitura assigns a soprano to Colinette, a tenor to Colas, and basses to le Bailli and Monsieur Dolmont. The ABA form used in several pieces applies rather to the harmonic and metric proportions than to melodic reprise.

Research done in 1952 by Helmut *Kallmann brought to light the manuscript parts for the voices and the second violin at the Archives of the *Séminaire de Québec (MG Verreau). It is possible thus to verify that the work was performed with instrumental accompaniment, as Quesnel states in his remarks to Neilson. We know from Quesnel's letters to Neilson that those responsible for the Quebec performance failed to follow the original instrumentation. Quesnel emphasized that the accompaniment was 'intended exclusively for violins, viola, and cello' and that he could not 'tolerate those wretched clarinets.'

The overture which Quesnel planned to 'put at the beginning of the work's music according to custom' was never written by him and did not appear until 1963, when Godfrey *Ridout, using themes from the work and reconstructing the orchestration after a study of extant manuscripts, composed an overture for a revival of *Colas et Colinette* 6 Oct 1963 by *Ten Centuries Concerts in Toronto. The performance, in costume but without staging, brought together Geneviève *Perreault as Colas, Judith Lebane as Colinette, Peter Dimuantes as le Bailli, and Howard *Mawson as Monsieur Dolmont. John Walker was the narrator and Ridout conducted. CBC Radio broadcast the work on its French network in March 1965 and on its English network in May of that year. It was performed again in English (in a translation by Micheline *Tessier) 25 Mar 1969 on CBC TV with Perry Price as Colas, Claire *Gagnier as Colinette, Claude *Corbeil as le Bailli, and David Geary as Monsieur Dolmont. Peter *Symcox was the director and producer. Other performances were given at the *U of Ottawa in January 1972, the orchestral parts in a two-piano reduction; and in Milan in 1977 as part of I Pomeriggi Musicali, with a cast which included Janis Orenstein and Janos Vaskenicius, under the direction of Harvey Sachs. An abridged version, but staged, costumed, and accompanied by an orchestra, was given in 1976 at Dundurn Castle in Hamilton, Ont, by the Mohawk College Opera Theatre. Lee *Hepner conducted, and Giuseppe *Macina directed the staging.

The libretto of *Colas et Colinette ou le Bailli dupé* was published in Quebec City in 1808 by Neilson, who also wanted to print the music. He exchanged about a dozen letters on this subject with Quesnel, who made several recommendations (for instance, 'having all the music printed in separate parts and the play in a booklet in the same format as those that are printed in Paris or Toulouse'), adding that publication of the complete score would be less profitable, 'seeing that few people in this country have the desire or the means to make such an expenditure.' Quesnel deplored that 'the taste for music, which for three-quarters of Europeans is the source of their greatest pleasure ... lags in Canada, by a century or more, behind the taste for literature.' Quesnel was unable to finish correcting the proofs before his death and the project was never pursued.

The libretto was printed again in James Huston's *Le Répertoire national* (Montreal 1848). Neilson's original edition appeared in facsimile (Réédition Québec 1968). The text was published also in *Anthologie thématique du théâtre québécois du XIXe siècle* by Étienne-F. Duval (Montreal 1978). The vocal score of Godfrey Ridout's reconstruction, with English translation by the latter and Michel S. Lecavalier, was published by Gordon V. *Thompson in 1974. An abridged recording (12 excerpts, RCI 234/Select CC.15.001 and SSC-24.160) was made in 1968 by the CBC IS, with Léopold *Simoneau as Colas, Pierrette *Alarie as Colinette, Claude Corbeil as le Bailli, and Claude *Létourneau as Monsieur Dolmont; Pierre *Hétu directed.

BIBLIOGRAPHY

Kallmann, Helmut. 'Joseph Quesnel, pioneer Canadian composer,' *CanComp*, 3, Oct 1965

Potvin, Gilles. 'Joseph Quesnel, le premier Canadien à composer un opéra, fut un contemporain de Mozart!' Montreal *La Presse*, 23 Mar 1968

Haworth, Frank. '*Colas et Colinette*: a character larger than life,' *CanComp*, 31, Jul–Aug 1968

Chartier, Yves. 'La reconstitution musicale de *Colas et Colinette* de Joseph Quesnel,' *Bulletin* du Centre de recherche en civilisation canadienne-française, vol 2, Apr 1972

Kallmann, Helmut. Introduction to the Thompson edition of *Colas et Colinette* (Toronto 1974) and for the Select recording

Du Berger, Jean. 'Colas et Colinette ou le Bailli dupé,' *Dictionnaire des oeuvres littéraires du Québec*, vol 1, ed Maurice Lemire (Montreal 1978) (DM, AP)

COLEMAN, Francis (Arthur). TV producer, conductor, writer, b Montreal 12 Jan 1924. He studied viola and conducting at the *CMM and was a pupil 1948–50 of Pierre Monteux in Maine. In 1949 he was co-founder with Noël Gauvin and Gilles *Potvin of the *Minute Opera Theatre in Montreal and conducted many of its productions. He was music director 1949–52 of the newly formed Royal Winnipeg Ballet. In 1952 he became a producer and program director for CBC TV in Montreal. In 1958 he moved to London, where he produced arts programs for the BBC and for the various independent TV companies. His production of Britten's *St Nicholas* cantata in 1976 for Thames TV received the coveted Prix Italia in 1977. Coleman has written articles about music, ballet, and opera for several Canadian, British, and US periodicals, and is the author of *Bluff Your Way in Opera* and *Bluff Your Way in Ballet* (London 1969). He also has written music criticism for *Inside London* and for the *Montreal Star* and in 1978 was London correspondent for **Musicanada*. GP

COLGRASS, Michael. Composer, percussionist, b Chicago 22 Apr 1932; B MUS (Illinois) 1956. His teachers at the U of Illinois included Paul Price (percussion) and Eugene Weigel (composition). He also studied composition in 1953 with Darius Milhaud in Aspen, in 1954 with Lukas Foss at Tanglewood, and 1958–62 with Wallingford Riegger and Ben Weber in New York. He supported his composing activities by working 1956–66 in New York as a freelance percussionist, playing with the New York Philharmonic, Stravinsky's Columbia Recording Orchestra, various ballet, film, musical theatre, and opera orchestras, modern dance groups, and new music ensembles. He began to compose on a full-time basis in 1967. He moved to Canada in 1974 and settled in Toronto.

Among Colgrass' compositions, over 30 of which have been published by Fischer, MCA, Plymouth Music, and G. Schirmer, are works for orchestra, chamber ensemble, solo instruments, and voice. Much of his work reflects a life-long interest in jazz. He has received commissions from the Boston and Detroit SOs, the Chamber Music Society of Lincoln Center, the Musica Aeterna Orchestra of New York, the New York Philharmonic, the Corporation for Public Broadcasting, and the Ford Foundation in the USA; the Brighton Festival in England; and the *CBC and the *NACO in Canada. Works written in Canada include *Concertmasters* (1975) for three violins and orchestra; *Wolf* (1975) for solo cello; *Best Wishes U.S.A.* (ca 1976) for choruses, jazz band, soloists, folk instruments, and orchestra; *Letter from Mozart* (1976) for orchestra; *Déja vu* (1977) for orchestra; *Flashbacks* 'A Musical Play for Five Brass' (1978), a CBC commission premiered in New York by *Canadian Brass in February 1979; *Night of the Racoon* (ca 1979) for soprano and four chamber players; and *Delta* (1979) for violin, clarinet, percussion, and orchestra, commissioned and premiered by the NACO. *Déja vu* was written for the New York Philharmonic Orchestra and received the 1978 Pulitzer Prize in music.

Several of Colgrass' works have been recorded, including *As Quiet As*, by the Boston SO under Leinsdorf (RCA Victor LSC-3001); *Concertmasters*, by the American SO under Akiyama (Turnabout 34704); *Earth's a Baked Apple*, by the New Orleans Philharmonic-SO under Torkanowsky (Orion 7268); *Fantasy Variations*, by the New Jersey Percussion Ensemble (Nonesuch 71291); *Three Brothers*, by the American Percussion Society (Urania 1007) and by another percussion group (Golden Crest 4004); and *Variations* for four drums and viola, by the MGM Band under Winograd, and with the composer as percussionist (MGM 3174). In March 1978 CBC radio presented a concert devoted entirely to Colgrass compositions as part of its Contempo series at St Andrew's Presbyterian Church, Toronto.

Colgrass has given lecture-demonstrations on a variety of performance techniques, some based on classes with the Piccolo Teatro di Milano and with Jerzy Grotowski of the Polish Theatre Laboratory. He also has written a regular column for the monthly magazine *Music*, introduced in February 1978 and edited in Toronto by his wife Ulla Colgrass. Colgrass is a member of CAPAC. NM

COLLE, Josèphe (m Fonder). Soprano, teacher, b Nancy, France, 24 Aug 1929, naturalized Canadian 1958; premier prix, analysis and musical aesthetics (Cons national, Paris) 1956. At the *CMM she studied choral conducting in 1953 with the visiting Father Émile Martin of St-Eustache Church, Paris, and voice 1953–4 with Martial Singher and 1954–5 and 1956–8 with Bernard *Diamant. Also at the CMM, with the composer at the piano, she gave the premieres of François *Morel's *Quatre Chants japonais* in 1954 and *Les Rivages perdus* in 1955. She went to Paris on two occasions, studying analysis and musical aesthetics 1955–6 with Olivier Messiaen and choral conducting 1958–9, again with Father Martin. During the second visit she sang under the pseudonym Florence Hébert and the critics praised her 'pure voice ... of rare beauty' (Paris *La Croix*, 25 Mar 1959).

In Montreal, after attending Ruzena *Herlinger's singing classes 1961–2, Colle was co-founder in 1963 with George Morgan and Fernande *Chiocchio, and director 1963–8, of the Trio vocal de Montréal. The trio gave the premiere of Gabriel *Charpentier's *Jamais*, Gilles *Tremblay's *Kékoba* (RCI 240), and folksong arrangements by Claude *Champagne and Lionel *Daunais. Co-founder in 1965, with Maryvonne *Kendergi, of the Group rencontres musicales, she served as director of the group until 1968 and took part in the premieres of a number of Canadian works, including Serge *Garant's *Cage d'oiseau* in 1967. After teaching dictation and solfège 1965–8 at the CMM she was engaged to assist 1968–73 in the reorganization of the Tunis Cons, and took advantage of her stay in Tunisia to study the lute for a year on a *Canada Council grant. She returned to Canada and taught solfège and singing 1973–5 at UQAM. In 1974 she began teaching solfège and choral singing at the Cons de Trois-Rivières. Josèphe Colle became known to CBC listeners both as a singer and, after 1961, as the hostess or commentator for such radio programs as 'Chronique du disque,' 'Café des arts,' 'Art aujourd'hui,' and 'Documents.' (DA)

Collections. See the following:
Archives
Archives de folklore
Gustafson, Ralph
Instrument collections
Lande collections
Libraries
Manuscript books
National Museums of Canada
Record collector clubs

College songs. In a wide sense the term refers to songs popular among university and college students, such as those sung at rallies, sports events, or other gatherings. They often are associated with college glee clubs and include internationally popular songs such as 'Gaudeamus igitur' and 'The Whiffenpoof Song.' In Canada many universities have compiled their own songbooks and several have adopted, by tradition or official sanction, specific songs as their own. The following alphabetical list cites examples from universities across Canada. It lists textual and musical sources and first lines of first verses and choruses where available.

*ACADIA U. The first Acadia songbook, *Songs of Acadia College*, containing 105 songs, was compiled by the university's Athenaeum Society and published in 1902. It was revised in 1907 and again in 1910. *Acadia Songs*, edited by Basil C. Silver, was published in 1966. Individual Acadia songs include the following:

1 'The Acadia Clan Song.' Words, Charles W. Williams; music, Lila P. Williams (both 1880s graduates); verse: 'Tell us how our songs run'; chorus: 'Here we're gathered, hail the Clan'
2 'Alma Mater – Acadia.' Words, L.D. Cox (a 1903 graduate); tune, 'Massa's in the cold, cold ground'; verse: 'Where the Minas Basin stretches'
3 'Alma Mater Acadia.' Composed 1938. Words, Dr J.H. MacDonald (an 1891 graduate); tune, 'Austria' (Haydn's 'Emperor's Hymn'/ 'Deutschland über Alles'); verse: 'Hail Acadia's sons and daughters'
4 'The Acadia Centennial Song.' Written 1938. Words, Marietta Silver (a 1924 graduate of the Acadia Ladies' Seminary); music, Basil C. Silver (a 1932 graduate); verse: 'A century has rolled away'; chorus: 'O Alma Mater dear'
5 'Alma Mater Song.' Commonly thought of as Acadia's official school song. Tune is a Cornell U song; verse: 'Far above the dykes of Fundy'

*BISHOP'S U

1 'Alma Mater.' Words, Rev Sidney Mead; tune, an old German folksong, adapted by Mead; verse: 'Bishop's we pledge to thee'
2 'Bishop's University Marching Song.' Words, Phil Townsend and/or John Mortland; music,

John Piper; verse: 'Drink a toast to Bishop's University'

*DALHOUSIE U. Songbooks include *Dalhousie Songs* (1921), printed for the Students' Council of Dalhousie, and *Dalhousie University Song Book* (nd), compiled by Charles B. Weikel, published by T.C. Allen and Co.

MACDONALD COLLEGE (OF *MCGILL U)

1 'All Hail MacDonald.' Printed in the McGill U songbook. Words, anon; verse: 'All Hail MacDonald, we sing to thee'
2 'Braw MacDonald.' Words, J.L. Dashwood; music, G.A. Stanton; verse: 'You may talk to me of Cambridge with its Gothic soup tureens'; chorus: 'Then clear your throats my hearties'

*MCGILL U

McGill College Song Book, published by J.L. Lamplough in 1885:

1 'A Health to Old McGill.' Words, R.W. Huntingdon (an 1874 law graduate); music, Mrs W.C. Baynes
2 'L'Enfant du McGill.' Words, L. Fréchette; music, Guillaume *Couture

Other songs in this book include 'Alma Mater McGill' (words, J. McDougall), 'McGill's Student Song' (words, W.N. Evans), 'The Student of McGill' (words, R.D. McGibbon).

McGill University Song Book, published by William Foster Brown in 1896:

1 'God Save McGill.' Words, W.M. Mackeracher (an 1894 arts graduate); tune, 'God Save the Queen'
2 'McGill.' Words, C.W. Colby; tune, 'The Gay Cavalier'
3 'McGill Revisited.' Words, Professor John Cox; music, a / a German air, and b / original, written for this edition

There were editions of McGill U songbooks in 1879, *A Pocket Song Book for the Use of the Students and Graduates of McGill College*, and in 1921, the latter published by the McGill Students Council.

*MCMASTER U

1 'The McMaster Hymn.' Words, Rev D.A. McGregor, principal of the Toronto Baptist College (precursor of McMaster U); tunes, a / 'Franconia,' and b / 'McMaster,' by A.S. *Vogt; verse: 'Jesus, wondrous saviour'
2 'McMaster Song.' The school song until 1935. Verse: 'Thy praises, McMaster'
3 'The Alma Mater Song.' Written 1935. Words, Mrs A.A. Burridge; music, Hugh Brearley; verse: 'To thee, oh McMaster, we sing with heart and voice'
4 'Alma Mater.' Written during the 1940s. Words and music, Donald Tapscott (a 1943 graduate); verse: 'God hath inspired within McMaster hearts a friendship true'
5 'The McMaster March.' Words, Claire Senior Burke and others; music, A.A. Burridge; verse: 'Shout! Shout! Shout! for Mac Mas Tar'

*MOUNT ALLISON U. *Mount Allison Songs* first appeared in 1908 and was revised in 1926 by William B. Perry (a 1925 graduate). Published for the Eurhetorian Society of the U of Mount Allison, it contains a number of songs written by students and an 'Alma Mater Song' which still was sung in the 1970s. A collection of songs (1859–92) by Mount Allison teachers is preserved at the university.

*QUEEN'S U. The *Queen's University Song Book* was published for the General Alumni Assn of Queen's U by *Whaley Royce in 1903, and included the official college song 'Queen's College Colours.' Composed in 1891, its original title was 'Our University Yell.' It was written for the class dinner of 1891. Words, A.E. Lavell; tune, 'John Brown's Body'; verse: 'Queen's College Colours we are wearing once again'; chorus: 'Oil thigh na Banrighinn a' Banrighinn gu brath'

ROYAL MILITARY COLLEGE OF CANADA, KINGSTON, ONT

1 'The College Hymn.' A traditional hymn; verse: 'Fight the good fight with all thy might'
2 'The RMC March.' After 1933 subtitled 'Precision,' the title of a 1933 Associated Screen News feature film on the RMC gentlemen cadets in training. Words, Lieut-Col T.F. Gelley; music, Mme C.A. Chabot (wife of RMC staff member Lieut-Col C.A. Chabot; verse: 'Heads up and swing along'

RYERSON POLYTECHNICAL INSTITUTE, TORONTO

'The School Song.' Composed ca 1950. Words, Rennie Charles (English Dept staff member); music, A. Sauro; verse: 'Ryerson, our faith, our pride'

*U OF ALBERTA

1 'The Evergreen and Gold.' Published in *The Gateway*, graduation issue 1915. Words, William H. Alexander (dean of arts and sciences 1936–8); tune, Tsarist Russia National Anthem; verse: 'Hail, Alma Mater dear! We sons and daughters true'
2 'Alberta.' Published in *The Gateway*, graduation issue 1920. Words and music, Emma Newton (wife of Robert Newton, later president of the university); verse: 'A-L-B-E-R-T-A, herald of a greater day!'
3 'Quaecumque vera' (motto of the U of Alberta). Published by The Rooters Club 1926. Words and music, Ewart W. Stutchbury (a 1922 graduate); verse: 'Fair Alberta, now to thee we sing'
4 'Alberta Cheer Song.' Words, R.K. Michael; music, Chester Lambertson (a graduate of 1936); verse: 'Ring out a cheer for our Alberta'; chorus: 'Shout it out! Come on you Aggie'
5 'Alberta.' A revision of the 'Alberta Cheer Song.' Verse: 'Ring out a cheer for our Alberta'; chorus: 'Green and Gold! Quaecumque vera!'

*U OF BRITISH COLUMBIA

1 'Hail, U.B.C.' Words and music by Harold King (a 1932 graduate); verse: 'We wear the blue and gold of the victors'; chorus: 'Hail, U.B.C.'

2 'High on Olympus.' Convocational anthem; words by D.C. Morton (a 1949 graduate), music by J.C.F. Haeffner; verse: 'High on Olympus, where dwelt Athene'

Both songs are included in the *U.B.C. Song Book* (Vancouver 1948), published by the Alma Mater Society.

*U OF MANITOBA

'The Brown and the Gold.' Official theme song of the U of Manitoba Students' Union; written ca 1934. First performed by the U of Manitoba Glee Club in 1934. Words, Charles McCulloch; music, W.J. MacDonald; verse: 'We are proud to boast of Manitoba U'; chorus: 'On Manitoba, glory now unfold'

*U OF NEW BRUNSWICK

1 'Alma Mater.' Published in a leaflet of song texts, *Carmina Universitatis Novi Brunsvici* (1904). Anon; verse: 'The old college rises where the free winds sport their will'; chorus: 'Glory, glory, glory, shout we Alma's worth'
2 'UNB Anthem.' Not official. Words, A.G. Bailey (former dean of arts); music, D.V. Start; verse: 'The hillside campus Douglas chose'

*U OF TORONTO

1 'Honour Old Varsity.' Published in the *U of Toronto Songbook* (*Suckling 1887). Words, adapted by E.C. Acheson (an 1889 graduate); tune, Norwegian National air; verse: 'Minstrels awaken the harp from its slumbers'
2 'Hurrah! For the Blue and White.' Published in *New Songs of the U of Toronto* (*Whaley Royce 1899). Words, G.W. Ross (an 1899 graduate); music, Elmer H. Smith (an 1899 graduate); verse: 'The best of men you'll find at U of T'; chorus: 'Then cheer boys cheer'
3 'Varsity.' Published in *New Songs of the U of Toronto* (1899). Words and music (?), A.E. Wickens (an 1895 graduate); verse: 'Let all who 'neath her sombre walls now roam at will'; chorus: 'Here's to Varsity'
4 *'The Blue and White.' Published in the *U of T Songbook* (*Anglo-Canadian 1918). Words, Rev Claris E. Silcox (a 1908 graduate); music, Clayton E. Bush (a 1907 graduate), arranged by J.D.A. *Tripp; verse: 'Old Toronto mother ever dear'; chorus: 'Toronto is our university'

*U OF WATERLOO

'The Black and White and Gold.' The official school song. Words, K.D. Fryer and H.F. Davis; music, Alfred *Kunz; verse: 'We are proud of Waterloo'; chorus: 'Waterloo we hail thee'

*U OF WESTERN ONTARIO

'Western University Song.' Words, Margaret Ovens (a 1929 graduate); verse: 'Western, Western, Western U, College fair and square'; chorus: 'This "U" is our 'U" and for her we'll strive'

VICTORIA U (*U OF TORONTO)

'On the Old Ontario Strand.' Adapted from the school song of Rutgers College, now Rutgers U, and used by Victoria since the 19th century. Verse: 'My father sent me to Victoria'; chorus: 'On the old Ontario strand, my boys'

*YORK U

'York Song.' Not official. Written for the 'Yeowomen' (York U's women's athletic teams). Tune, 'Harvard'; verse: 'Cheer, cheer for old red and white' HK, NM

COLLIER, Barbara (Jean) (m Tessényi). Soprano, b Stratford, Ont, 27 Feb 1940; ARCT 1959, BA anthropology (Trinity, Toronto) 1962. She studied voice 1956–9 with Gordon D. Scott in Stratford and coached 1960–1 with Douglas *Bodle in Toronto, where she won the rose bowl at the 1960 *Kiwanis Festival and for two years was a member of the *Festival Singers. She continued her studies in London 1962–5 with Rodolfo Mele, in Cologne 1963–4 at the Conservatory Opera School on a German-Academic Exchange scholarship, and in Salzburg in 1963 at the Mozarteum with Erik Werba. She made her operatic debut in 1965 as Liu in *Turandot* at Oberhausen, Germany. She began coaching occasionally with Kálmán Hetényi in Budapest in 1967 and established residence in Munich in 1968. She has appeared in concert and oratorios in Germany, Hungary, and Canada; has broadcast frequently over the CBC; and has sung with the *COC (Gutrune in *Gotterdämmerung*, 1973; Fiordiligi in *Così fan tutte* with the touring company 1972–3 and 1973–4; Mimi in *La Bohème* with the touring company 1974–5 and 1975–6; Sara in *Louis Riel* in 1975; and Gerhilde in *Die Walküre* in 1976). She married the Munich Opera bass János Tessényi.

COLLIER, Ron (Ronald William). Composer, conductor, trombonist, b Coleman, near Lethbridge, Alta, 3 Jul 1930. He received his early training 1943–50 in Vancouver, where he played trombone in the *Kitsilano Boys' Band. He also studied in Toronto 1951–4 with Gordon *Delamont (composition) and (on the first *Canada Council grant given to a jazz composer) in New York 1961–2 with George Russell (the Lydian chromatic concept of tonal organization) and Hall Overton (orchestration). Collier played trombone in the 1950s with Toronto dance bands, including Mart *Kenney and His Western Gentlemen, and, on a freelance basis, with the *TSO, the National Ballet and *COC orchestras, and CBC radio and TV groups. While he was a member of Norman *Symonds' jazz octet, he formed his own jazz group – at first (1954–7) a quartet without piano, then a quintet (which performed at the *Stratford Festival in 1957), a dixtuor (formed in 1960), and, on occasion in the 1960s (eg, *Expo 67), a big band. His quintet participated with the *CBC SO in the premiere and recording of Symonds' *Concerto Grosso* for jazz quintet and symphony orchestra, and in subsequent performances of the work with other orchestras.

During the late 1950s Collier, like Symonds, was a central figure in the Third-Stream movement in Canada. In that idiom he composed such works as *Sonata* (pre-1956, played with Norm *Amadio) for piano and jazz quintet. In the 1960s he worked also with the spoken word, completing *The City* (1960, for orchestra and narrator-singer, an evocation of life in a city, with readings by Don *Francks), *Hear Me Talkin' To Ya* (1964, for octet and narrator-singer; a collaboration with Francks, whose libretto was taken from the book of the same name, comprising remarks on the subject of jazz made by musicians), and *Carneval* [sic] (1969, libretto by Gwendolyn MacEwen, premiered by Collier's orchestra, with Bruno Gerussi as narrator and Fred *Stone as flugelhorn soloist, premiered 2 Jul 1969 at the Detroit-Windsor International Freedom Festival). Collier also wrote scores for the play *The Mechanic* (1965), for the ballet *Aurora Borealis* (1966, Almitra; seen 1 Jan 1967 on CBC TV), and for several industrial films 1967–71. His *Waterfront, Night Thoughts* (1965, Almitra) has been recorded by Robert *Aitken.

In 1966 Collier conducted a big band and string orchestra for a *CAPAC-sponsored recording of *Aurora Borealis* and *Silent Night, Lonely Night* (the latter from a CBC TV drama score of the same name) and two works each by Symonds and Delamont, with the pianist Duke Ellington as soloist. Subsequently Collier collaborated as an orchestrator (and, though unacknowledged, as the co-composer) with Ellington on *Celebration* (1972, a commission from the Jacksonville SO) and other works; on occasion he conducted the Ellington orchestra.

In 1972 Collier became the composer-in-residence at Humber College in Toronto, and in 1974 he began teaching composition and arranging there. He also helped establish the college's stage band program as Canada's foremost in the late 1970s. His pupils include Pete Coulman, Alistair Kay, and Ilmars Sermulis. He directed the college's stage band to victory at the 1975 *Canadian Stage Band Festival and in that same year, with graduates and senior students, he formed the Humber Extension big band for concerts and TV appearances in the Toronto area.

Collier's other compositions include scores for CBC radio and TV shows and for the feature films *Face Off* (1971), *A Fan's Notes* (1972), and *Paperback Hero* (1973), as well as the big band works *Requiem for JFK* (1964, Almitra 1971), *Humber Suite* (1973, in three movements, of which the first was recorded under his direction by the Humber College Big Band), and *Jupiter* (1974, written for and recorded by Moe *Koffman). He also composed many other, and earlier, pieces for jazz groups of varying sizes. He is a member of the *CLComp, an associate of the *CMCentre, and a member of CAPAC.

DISCOGRAPHY

Symonds *Concerto Grosso* for jazz quintet and symphony orchestra. CBC SO, Feldbrill cond, Collier trb, Piltch alto sax, Bickert guit, Bray db, Rully drums. 1957. RCI 181

Ron Collier Tentet. Collier trb and cond, Stone and Basso flhn and tpt, Piltch alto sax, Bickert guit, and others. 1965. CTLS 5059

Duke Ellington 'North of the Border' in Canada. Jazz and str orch, Collier cond, soloists Ellington pf, Bickert guit, Piltch alto sax and cl, Watanabe trb. 1967. Decca DL 75069

Reissued as *Collages*. (1973). MPS BASF 21704

Ron Collier Jazz Orchestra. 1967. CBC Expo 25

Carneval. Jazz orch, Collier cond, Stone solo flhn, Gerussi narr. 1970. CBC LM-92

First Take. Humber College Big Band, Collier cond. 1977. Privately recorded

BIBLIOGRAPHY

'The accent is on finesse,' *CBC Times*, 5–11 Sep 1959

Norris, John. 'Jazz composing in Canada,' *CanComp*, 4, Dec 1965

'Ron Collier: a serious approach to jazz,' *CanComp*, 18, May 1967

Creative Canada, vol 2

Contemporary Canadian Composers MM (HM)

COLLINGWOOD, Arthur. Educator, conductor, organist, composer, b Halifax, Yorkshire, England, 24 Nov 1880, d Montreal 22 Jan 1952; FRCO, hon FTCL. He studied piano with Claude Pollard and Tobias Matthay, organ with W.H. Garland and Kendrick Pyne, and theory with Charles Pearce and Ebenezer Prout. He moved to Aberdeen where he was the organist-choirmaster 1898–1930 of the Free West Church, conducted the Choral Union and Male Voice and Madrigal choirs, and lectured at Aberdeen U. He emigrated to Canada as the head 1931–47 of the newly formed Dept of Music at the *U of Saskatchewan. In 1932 he unified an informal group of Saskatoon musicians, thereby establishing the *Saskatoon SO, which he conducted until his retirement in 1947. He was chairman 1934–6 of the first *WBM syllabus committee, gave radio lectures for Saskatchewan schools, and adjudicated music festivals across Canada. He retired to Montreal in 1947 as dean emeritus of the U of Saskatchewan. The university holds his library. Collingwood's compositions (listed in the *Catalogue of Canadian Composers*) include choral, vocal, and piano works published by Paterson, J. Curwen, and *Thompson. His essay 'Music in education' (*Queen's Quarterly*, vol 44, Winter 1937) reflects his experience in the field. IBr

COLLINS, Edwin (Alec). Organist, choirmaster, composer, teacher, b Debenham, Suffolk, England, 25 Apr 1893; FRCO 1911, B MUS (Cambridge) 1923, MA (Cambridge) 1923. In 1911 he became assistant organist-choirmaster of Ely Cathedral. After World War I he conducted army bands in Italy, Austria, and Egypt and lectured at the Imperial School in Cairo. He attended Cambridge U 1921–3, studying with C.V. Stanford, Charles Wood, and Cyril Rootham. He then became organist at the Kidbroke Church in London. He emigrated in 1926 to Canada, living a year in Saint John, NB, and then moving to Wolfville, NS, as dean of *Acadia U's newly established School of Music. He remained there 36 years. Watson Kirkconnell wrote: 'He was known to asseverate that early training in an organ factory and the management of army mules in World War I had not been wholly irrelevant to his tasks at Acadia.' Among Collins' pupils are Dorothy Wilson, Elsa Noble, and Phyllis MacLennan, instructors of piano and theory at Acadia, and Vernon *Ellis, appointed dean of music there in 1974. Collins' son Paul, violinist and teacher, is a graduate of the school.

In addition to teaching and administrating Collins trained the University Chorus, which gave two concerts each year, accompanied by the University Orchestra. Typical programs included Mendelssohn's *Elijah* and *The Hymn of Praise* and Haydn's *The Creation*. Collins made Acadia a musical centre for the towns of the Annapolis Valley. Music lessons were available to children and concerts to the public. While president of the *NSRMTA he persuaded the Department of Education to accept music credits for matriculation.

Collins' compositions include such large pieces for choir and orchestra as *Song of the Indian Maid, Memorial Ode, Psalm 90*, and *Graduation Anthem* (1949), as well as other vocal, chamber, and orchestral music. *A Night Rhapsody* and *A Dance Fantasy*, both for violin and piano, won *CAPAC awards in 1947. His light opera *The Mod at Grand Pré* (words by Watson Kirkconnell) was performed in 1956 by the Acadia Light Opera Society. In 1963 Acadia U conferred upon Collins an honorary MUS D and he retired to England.

BIBLIOGRAPHY

Acadia Bulletin, vol 49, Jun 1963
Kirkconnell, Watson. *The Fifth Quarter-Century: Acadia University, 1938–1963* (Wolfville 1968)
Silver, B.C. 'Music in Acadia University,' unpubl ms, Acadia U 1972 SAB

COLLINS, Eleanor (Elnora Ruth) (b Procter). Singer, actress, b Edmonton 21 Nov 1919. At 15 she won an amateur contest in Edmonton and subsequently sang with Joe Macelli's dance band, with the Three 'E's, and on radio station CFRN. She moved to Vancouver in 1938, performing in 1938 and 1940–7 with Ray Norris' jazz quintet and 1940–2 on CBC radio with a gospel group, the Swing Low Quartette. Her only recordings (RCI 57 and 58) were made with Norris. After a brief retirement 1948–52 she appeared at *TUTS in *Finian's Rainbow* in 1952 and 1954 and *Kiss Me Kate* in 1953 and made her TV debut in 1954 on CBC Vancouver's 'Bamboula.' For many years Vancouver's leading jazz singer, she appeared on various CBC TV variety shows and starred in CBC TV's 'Blues and The Ballad' in 1960, in 'Eleanor' in 1964, and, with Chris *Gage, in 'Quintet' in 1962. She also starred on CBC Vancouver radio's 'Eleanor Sings the Blues' in 1960 and sang in other shows, in clubs, and in concert, with Gage, Lance *Harrison, Doug Parker, and Dave *Robbins. Continuing to perform occasionally in concert and on TV in the 1970s, she starred in the 1975 Canada Day celebrations on Parliament Hill. MM

Columbia Records of Canada Ltd. See CBS Records Canada Ltd.

'Come Back, Old Pal.' Waltz ballad, music and words by Merton W. Plunkett of the *Dumbells. It was sung by Plunkett in the Dumbells' 1922 production *Carry On*, and was published that year by Leo Feist. A French-language version, 'Reviens, petite amie,' prepared by Richard Beaudry, was recorded by the Canadian tenor José *Delaquerrière. Two Montreal dance bands, Andy Tipaldi's Melody Kings and the Jazzbo Band, recorded instrumental versions of the song, and the US tenors Harold Harvey and Reese Williams recorded it in English. (See listing in *Roll Back the Years*.) According to *Al Plunkett, the Famous Dumbell* (New York 1956), the song enjoyed some currency among English dance bands as late as the 1950s. FH

COMMON, Tommy. Singer, b Toronto 21 Sep 1934. A boy soprano, he made his radio debut at eight and was a regular on the CBC's 'Microphone Moppets' at 11. Later he sang as a tenor with Percy Morgan's dance band in Toronto and made his TV debut (1955) on the CBC's 'Pick the Stars.' While a regular performer 1956–65 on CBC TV's 'Country Hoedown,' he sang on several other CBC Toronto shows, including 'The Common Touch,' and a number of times in 1956 and 1957 in New York on Arthur Godfrey's CBS TV show. In the 1960s he began performing in nightclubs, but later he returned to TV as co-star 1971–2 with Vanda King of CTV's 'Diamond Lil's' and as the successor 1972–3 to Charlie Chamberlain on 'Don *Messer's Jubilee.' Early in Common's career his style was compared to that of the US singer Eddie Fisher. Common recorded the LPs *The Common Touch* (1961, Columbia FL 271) and *Tommy Common* (1965, CTL 061), the latter with the Bert *Niosi orchestra.

BIBLIOGRAPHY

Sonin, Ray. 'Meet Mr. and Mrs. Tommy Common and Jamie,' *Music World*, 15 Aug 1957 MM

Community Arts Council of Vancouver. Advisory body established in Vancouver in 1946, the first organization of its kind in North America. A model for many later community arts organizations, the council has helped to initiate the construction of the *Queen Elizabeth Theatre and Playhouse, the planning of the *Vancouver International Festival, the development of a music department at the *U of British Columbia, the founding of the *Vancouver Opera Assn, the establishment of the *Community Music School of Greater Vancouver, and the preservation of the *Orpheum Theatre. In these and other cases the projects have been completed under the supervision of other organizations. Financed by membership fees, grants, and donations, and operated by its volunteer members, the council has undertaken to act as a clearing-house for information on the arts in Vancouver, publish a monthly calendar of events, act as liaison between arts and government bodies, oversee the distribution of city and provincial grants to small and non-professional arts organizations, and display the work of city artists at its Gastown premises. (MW)

Community colleges. Post-secondary, non-university educational institutions in English-speaking Canada (for Quebec, see Cegeps). Community colleges do not grant degrees, although some offer university transfer credit. A concept of the educational surge of the 1960s, the colleges have taken over the roles formerly played by the technical institutes and the business, agricultural, and art colleges and have added courses and programs of their own. The community colleges are neither technical schools nor junior universities. Rather, they represent a new approach to education, valid in its own right, and directed to a population hitherto unserved by higher education.

In addition to performing a formal post-secondary function, the community college serves the educational needs of the general populace in the surrounding community by offering courses, programs, and activities of a professional, vocational, cultural, and recreational nature through Continuing Education or Community Service departments. Music plays a varied role in both purpose and quality, and the extent of musical activity in each ranges from nothing whatever to sophisticated and often innovative programs. In 1976 the Assn of Canadian Community Colleges, representing a national membership of community colleges and Cegeps, began publishing the nine-times-yearly periodical *College Canada*.

1 British Columbia
2 Alberta, Saskatchewan, Manitoba
3 Ontario
4 The Atlantic provinces

1 BRITISH COLUMBIA. The 20 post-secondary institutions in British Columbia in 1980 included 14 community colleges, 1 privately funded college, and 5 institutes of technology. British Columbia community colleges offer one or two years of university transfer credits. Six of the 14 have maintained music departments with at least one full-time faculty member and a fairly comprehensive selection of courses. For example, Vancouver Community College offers vocal, instrumental, and ensemble training, composition, and jazz and commercial music courses. The one private college, Trinity Western in Langley, also has maintained a music department. In addition to the transfer program, several of the colleges have offered a two-year music program leading to an Associate diploma. Choirs, bands, orchestras, theatre groups, etc, as well as instructional courses, have been a part of the evening school activities.

2 ALBERTA, SASKATCHEWAN, MANITOBA. While no music has been offered in either of Alberta's two major institutes of technology or in its three agricultural colleges, a good deal has been carried on in four of the six community colleges and the three private colleges. Grande Prairie Regional College, Alberta's northernmost conservatory, has become a focal point for community musical life. It has offered a two-year music transfer program, as have Medicine Hat College, *Mount Royal College in Calgary, and Grant MacEwan Community College in Edmonton. The private Camrose Lutheran College, offering a music transfer program, has maintained a music faculty of three. The Red Deer College continuing education program includes support of the Central Alberta String Orchestra.

St Peter's College of Muenster, Sask, a private institution directed by the Order of Saint Benedict, offers a one-year music university transfer program and a community orchestra, band, and choir. By 1980 there had been no music in the other 15 Saskatchewan community colleges or technical institutes.

Almost no music had been introduced by the three community colleges of Manitoba by 1980, although one service course (see explanation in next section) has been offered at Red River Community College, Winnipeg, and sacred music has been taught at the private *Mennonite Brethren Bible College and College of Arts, Winnipeg.

3 ONTARIO. Of 29 colleges in Ontario in 1980 22 were colleges of applied arts and technology and 5 were agricultural colleges. The remaining 2 were the Ontario College of Art and the Niagara Parks Commission School of Horticulture. Over half of the 29 have offered music programs, courses, ensembles, concerts, or combinations of these. Humber College in Toronto, Mohawk College in Hamilton, and Cambrian College in Sudbury all have established three-year, post-secondary programs in Applied Music. Graduates of these programs receive a Colleges of Applied Arts and Technology diploma. George Brown College, Toronto, in 1978 became the first college in Canada to initiate a piano technicians' department.

Music studies designed to fill various needs have been offered throughout the college system as 'service' courses in Early Childhood Education, Communication Arts, Child Care Work, Fine Arts Administration, Recreation Leadership, Library Techniques, Musical Theatre, etc. Music courses as 'electives,' open to the entire student body, also have been prominent in the colleges' curricula.

Most popular have been the 'listening' courses in music appreciation and the 'applied' music electives such as band, choir, class recorder, class piano, and class guitar.

The majority of Ontario's colleges which have offered music courses also have fostered some kind of musical activity in their evening school offerings. Bands, orchestras, choirs, musical theatre, clinics, workshops, and concerts have functioned in numerous colleges throughout the system. Opera has been a specialty at Mohawk College; stagebands at Humber College (see Ron Collier). Northern College in South Porcupine, Mohawk College in Hamilton, Sheridan College in Oakville, George Brown College in Toronto, and Georgian College in Barrie all have established music summer schools and/or camps.

4 THE ATLANTIC PROVINCES. Nova Scotia's college musical activity has been centered at Le Collège Sainte-Anne, Church Point. In co-operation with the Nova Scotia Dept of Education this college has offered class and private music instruction and maintains a choir and band. Atlantic Baptist College in Moncton, NB, has offered courses in church music. The French St-Louis-Maillet College, Edmundston, has introduced music courses as electives, and the local concert association has scheduled events on its campus. In 1980 Prince Edward Island's one community college still had initiated nothing in music. In 1980 the Western Regional College of *Memorial U, St John's, Nfld, had made plans to include music in its future activities.

Although the community college concept still was relatively new in 1980, the idea of music had taken a strong hold in the majority of the colleges and promised development. By providing outlets for creativity and performance and opportunities for developing musical understanding, the colleges have made a significant contribution to the growth of music in Canada. (PRl)

Community Concert Associations. Autonomous concert associations organized by individual communities and affiliated with Community Concerts, Inc, a subsidiary of Columbia Artists Management Inc, New York.

The concept of organized audiences began in the 1920s in the USA as the Civic Music Assn, an attempt to bring the best possible performing artists to medium-sized cities and small towns without involving financial risk to the organizers. Previously, whereas larger cities usually could be assured of good audiences and thus no deficit when important musicians were engaged for performances, smaller communities frequently were faced with discouraging losses if they were to make up the difference between an artist's fee and ticket sales. Following the efforts of Harry P. Harrison and Dema Harshbarger in 1920, a young US musician, Ward French, developed the Organized Audience Movement in 1922, establishing a new plan which would avoid such losses and yet would encourage volunteers within the community to participate in the organizing of concerts. The plan was based on the principle of the local community gathering the audience first, through a one-week membership campaign, and then engaging such artists as the proceeds of that campaign would allow. In this way the community would hire only the artists it could afford, and at the same time everyone interested in the community's music could be involved in the membership campaign.

The idea was so successful that in 1928 it was taken up in New York by Columbia Concerts Corporation, which in 1948 became Columbia Artists Management Inc. A subsidiary company, Community Concerts, Inc, began working with local communities to help them form their own Community Concert Assns. Representatives from New York visited the local community, bringing information about available artists. In return, the associations were required to agree to book all their performers through Community Concerts, Inc, in New York. Once the local association had chosen the artists, the New York office arranged contracts, provided the local association with publicity material, and subsequently forwarded program information in printed form ready for distribution at the time of the performance. A Community Concert Assn was free to choose any available artist it could afford, and the New York office made the arrangements. However, in some cases the New York office contracted artists or groups of artists to do Community Concert tours, from which local associations also could benefit, if geographically appropriate. Fees were assessed on the basis of an amount agreed to by the artist, plus a margin fee to Community Concerts, Inc. These fees were paid directly by the local association to Community Concerts, Inc, New York, who in turn paid the artist his or her share.

The success of Community Concert Assns in US cities and towns encouraged Canadian interest in similar ventures. The first Canadian city to become affiliated with Community Concerts, Inc, was *Kitchener, Ont, which in 1930 organized its own Community Concert Assn. The success of the Kitchener series encouraged *Hamiltom to organize in 1931, and within the next few years cities and towns throughout Ontario and subsequently the Maritimes and Quebec were forming their own associations. In French Canada the associations were known and operated as Sociétés des concerts. By the 1940s the Community Concert movement had spread across Canada, and as a result many towns and smaller cities enjoyed performances by artists many of whom were, or later became, world-renowned. Pierrette *Alarie, Licia Albanese, Marian Anderson, Rose Bampton, Robert Casadesus, Richard Crooks, Nelson Eddy, Betty-Jean *Hagen, Denis *Harbour, Sheila *Henig, Alexander Kipnis, John Knight, Arthur *LeBlanc, Lois *Marshall, Yehudi Menuhin, Ezio Pinza, Artur Rubinstein, Teresa *Stratas, Gladys Swarthout, Ronald *Turini, Leonard Warren, and many others have performed in Canada for Community Concert Assns. This came about because the operation, both within the community itself and at the head office in New York, was organized so that artists could avoid long journeys between engagements and could include small communities in their tours.

In 1955 Community Concerts of Canada, Inc, was incorporated as a subsidiary of Community Concerts, Inc, and was based in Ottawa with a Canadian board of directors. However, local Community Concert Assns are required to conduct their business negotiations with the head office in New York. In the early days of the associations US performers were most often engaged, but as local organizers became more sophisticated musically and better acquainted with Canadian talent, increasing numbers of Canadian musicians were engaged to perform for Community Concert towns and cities in both Canada and the USA.

At the peak of activity, in the 1950s, Community Concert Assns in Canada numbered 75. However, in the 1970s the number declined, largely because many provincial arts councils have established their own touring divisions to assist communities in planning, financing, and organizing their own independent concert series. The increase in the early 1970s of Canadian artists' managers has stimulated communities even further to engage Canadian musicians directly rather than through an intermediary organization, thus saving the additional margin cost.

In 1980 there were 35 Community Concert Assns in Canada. Though this reduction in numbers demonstrates a turning away from the service provided by the US-based agency and symbolizes indirectly the growth of Canada's own concert industry, it would be a mistake to construe it as a deprecation of the pioneering contribution of the Community Concerts movement. Indeed, in breaking the ground for the wide diffusion of concerts in the small cities and towns of Canada the movement achieved what probably could not have been achieved in any other way and made it possible for thousands of Canadians living outside the major centres to hear performances they might never have heard otherwise.

BIBLIOGRAPhY

French, Ward. 'Canada's community towns,' *CRMA*, vol 4, Aug-Sep 1945

Potvin, Gilles. 'Les sociétés des concerts aident la diffusion de la bonne musique,' Montreal *Le Canada*, 21 Jun 1950

Smith, Cecil. 'The world of the organized audience,' *Worlds of Music* (Philadelphia, New York 1952) ML

Community Music School of Greater Vancouver (1969-79; renamed Vancouver Academy of Music in 1979). The result of a five-year study, by the non-profit *Community Arts Council, of Vancouver's expanding needs. Founded in 1969 and situated at first on West 12th Ave, the school moved in May 1976 to the Music Centre in Vanier Park, a former RCAF warehouse, reconstructed at a cost of $1.8-million. The centre comprises classrooms, practice studios, a library, rehearsal rooms for orchestra and choir, 36 teaching studios, and the 284-seat Koerner Recital Hall. The rehearsal facilities and auditorium are shared with other performing groups. Administered by a Board of Trustees and an Advisory Committee of leading

Vancouver musicians, the school is funded by foundations and federal, provincial, and civic grants, individual donations, membership fees, and tuition fees.

The Community Music School began with *Orff, *Suzuki, and *Kodály classes for young children and in fact was a pioneer in the development of the Suzuki and Kodály concepts in Canada. Following the appointment of Jerold Gerbrecht as music director, a full non-degree program of private instruction was added, covering all band and orchestra instruments, piano, composition, history, theory, chamber music, voice, and ballet. The Academy Strings for advanced students, the Symphonic Band and Kodály Choir, master classes in violin, voice, and piano, and teacher training in the Kodály method also were established.

Some of Canada's leading instrumentalists and singers have taught at the school/academy, including Robert *Creech, Ronald *de Kant, Jacob Hamm, Ian Hampton, Lee Kum-Sing, Phyllis *Mailing, Leslie Malowany, Norman *Nelson, Audrey *Piggott, Gerald *Stanick, Steven *Staryk and Gwen *Thompson. In 1979 there was a faculty of 70. Enrolment has grown from 50 students in 1969 to 1500 in 1979. Reflecting the change of name to the Vancouver Academy of Music, a four-year diploma course in performance, accommodating 80 students, was scheduled to begin in the autumn of 1980. A newsletter, *Keynote*, is issued jointly with the Junior Symphony Society of Vancouver.

JWl

Competition festivals. Public, graded competitions for student and amateur musicians; school, amateur, and church choirs; and school, amateur, and civic instrumental ensembles. Contestants are adjudicated publicly by trained professionals who give them comparative marks.

Non-competition festivals, developed in reaction against the practice of giving comparative marks, are little different in other respects (for instance, though marks are not given, adjudications are), but in some instances they allow time for workshops conducted by the adjudicators. The competition type has remained the more numerous and widespread.

Both types are operated by volunteers – often a local music or service club, eg, the *Men's Music Club in Winnipeg or the Kiwanis clubs in Toronto and many other cities – and are largely self-supporting, their economies based on the fees of contestants and supplementary monies raised by the sponsoring organizations. Syllabi defining classes and setting test pieces are published months in advance to allow competitors ample preparation time. There are usually some 'open' (ie, ungraded) classes to permit competition by performers who, for one reason or another, are not readily gradable. These classes often attract performers at the highest level.

In 1980 every province in Canada had annual competition festivals, usually lasting from two days to two weeks and also had established some form of co-ordinating 'umbrella' organization.

For a guide to other *EMC* articles which treat competition festivals see Competitions.

The competition festival movement as it has taken root in Canada originated in Great Britain, and the earliest of the general type was held in Edmonton in 1908 (see Alberta Music Festival Assn), although a competition for fiddlers had taken place in Montreal in 1867, and band tournaments had begun during the 1870s in Berlin (Kitchener), Ont, and in Montreal (see Band festivals). Governor-General Earl Grey is credited with being the first to advocate strongly the development of competition festivals in Canada.

The Edmonton festival, which had 30 participants in 1908, was followed by festivals in Regina (1909, 25 participants, see Saskatchewan Music Festival Assn), Winnipeg (1918, see Manitoba Music Competition Festival), Vancouver (1923, BC Music Festival), and Nanaimo, BC (1928, Upper Island Musical Festival). Festivals are said to have been held in British Columbia and Manitoba as early as 1909, but these did not become annual.

Support for the festival movement was especially strong in the West, where it contributed to the development of musical activity both in the educational system and in a wider social context and helped to lessen the sense of 'musical isolation.' By 1914 265 participants were competing at the festival in Regina. After World War I Alberta, Saskatchewan, and Manitoba began to co-ordinate their festivals, avoiding conflicts in dates, sharing adjudicators, and so on. British Columbia joined this arrangement in 1923, and in 1926 representatives from the four provinces established the *Federation of Canadian Music Festivals.

In Montreal in 1922 the Delphic Study Club of Canada founded a competition festival known as Music Week. In 1923 the Metropolitan Choral Society of Montreal initiated a competition for choirs and vocal quartets, singers, and instrumentalists. Local school boards in Ontario began sponsoring competition festivals in the early 1920s (see School music). In 1923 and 1924 the Ontario Musical Assn held a competition at Toronto's *Massey Hall, and in 1927 the North Western Ontario Musical Competition Festival (in 1967 the Lakehead Music Festival) and the Stratford (Ont) Music Festival were established; for several years the Stratford festival was the largest in the province.

The Halifax Cons sponsored that city's first competition festival in 1936; Yarmouth, NS, established a festival in 1938; and the Cape Breton Competitive Musical Festival began in 1939. The Saint John, NB, Competition Festival of Music was founded in 1936 (although non-competition festivals had been part of the city's school music program for a number of years prior to this).

Manitoba claimed to have held in 1937 the largest competition festival in the British Empire. In the same year more than 5400 competed in Montreal at the first Festival-concours de musique du Québec. Father Alfred *Bernier, Léon David, Louis Hasselmans, Bernard *Naylor, Sir Hugh Roberton, Thomas Salignac, and Steuart Wilson were among the adjudicators during the four years of its existence, and in 1939 12,000 competed. The Prince Edward Island Music Festival was established in 1946, and the first annual competition festival in Newfoundland took place in St John's in 1952.

Not all teachers and performers have approved of competition. Many have argued that there is little value and even possible harm in young musicians vying with one another for marks and awards. Others have maintained that competition is a part of living and that competition festivals are a benign ordering of this natural tendency. In any case they have survived and increased. By 1980 the FCMF could list more than 220 affiliated festivals. In *Music in Canada* Richard *Cooke spoke out in favour of the movement, calling it 'the most potent factor in operation today ... [The] competition festival reaches all ages and nationalities ... talented and less gifted performers ... It sets a high standard ... and in an age beset with many attacks on authentic values it is inspiring to find so many responding to the challenge' (p 206).

For many years Canadian music festivals employed British adjudicators almost exclusively, and among them were distinguished performers and educators whose knowledge, platform experience, and tact justified their near monopoly. With the development of Canada's own musical maturity, however, especially in the years after World War II, Canadian adjudicators came to be used more frequently and with increasingly satisfactory results, and the trend was reinforced by the efforts of the *Canadian Music Festival Adjudicators' Assn.

Kiwanis Clubs International have made perhaps the most significant contribution of any service club to the competition festival movement. The first Canadian Kiwanis Music Festival took place in Toronto in 1944. *Kiwanis festivals were established later in British Columbia, Alberta, Ontario, Nova Scotia, and Newfoundland, and the responsibility for many competitions begun by other organizations has been assumed by the Kiwanis clubs. Several of the Kiwanis festivals named in the appended list are the largest in their provinces.

Some of the main Canadian competition festivals flourishing in 1980 were:

BRITISH COLUMBIA
Greater Victoria Music Festival
Okanagan Valley Musical Festival
Upper Island Musical Festival, Nanaimo
Vancouver Kiwanis Music Festival

ALBERTA
Alberta Music Festival (annual; location rotates among Calgary, Edmonton, and Lethbridge)
Kiwanis festivals (annual; in Calgary, Edmonton, and Lethbridge)
Medicine Hat Rotary Music Festival

SASKATCHEWAN
Saskatchewan Music Festival (provincial festivals held annually in Regina and Saskatoon)

MANITOBA
Brandon Festival of Music, Speech Arts and Dance
Manitoba Music Competition Festival, Winnipeg

ONTARIO
Belleville-Trenton Rotary Music Festival
Lakehead Music Festival, Thunder Bay
Ottawa Music Festival
Peel County Music Festival, Brampton
Kiwanis festivals in Brantford, Chatham, Hamilton, London, North Bay, Oshawa, Owen Sound, Peterborough, Sudbury, and Toronto

QUEBEC
Quebec Music Competitions (Quebec Music Festivals 1960–71)

NEW BRUNSWICK
Festival de musique de la régionale, Tracadie
Fredericton Festival of Music
Greater Moncton Music Festival
New Brunswick Competitive Festival of Music, Saint John

NOVA SCOTIA
Bridgewater Area Music Festival
Lunenburg and District Music Festival
Kiwanis festivals in Halifax and Sydney

PRINCE EDWARD ISLAND
Prince Edward Island Music Festival, held at Charlottetown, Summerside, and Montague

NEWFOUNDLAND
Central Newfoundland Kiwanis Festival, Grand Falls
St John's Kiwanis Music Festival
Stephenville Rotary Music Festival

BIBLIOGRAPHY

Higgin, Clifford. 'Musical festival competition movement,' *CQR*, vol 1, Feb 1919
Bantock, Granville. 'The festival movement in Canada,' *Musical News and Herald*, 2 articles, 11, 18 Aug 1923
Greene, H. Plunkett. 'A trip to the Canadian festivals,' *Music and Letters*, vol 4, Oct 1923
MacMillan, Ernest. 'Competition festivals in western Canada,' *CQR*, vol 11, Summer 1929

Greene, H. Plunkett. 'Another trip to the Canadian festivals,' *Music and Letters*, vol 13, Jan 1932
Coutts, George. 'Music festivals in western Canada,' *CRMA*, vol 2, Oct–Nov 1943
Peaker, Charles. 'Canadian competitive musical festivals,' Music Teachers National Association *Proceedings* (1946)
Duncan, Chester. 'Competition festivals,' *Northern R*, vol 3, Aug–Sep 1950
Cooke, Richard W. 'Competition festivals,' *Music in Canada*
Payzant, Geoffrey. 'The competitive music festivals,' *CMJ*, vol 4, Spring 1960
'Forum: the music festival controversy,' ibid, Summer 1960
Collier, R.F. 'Music festivals in Canada,' *CanComp*, 22, Oct 1967
'Music festivals in Quebec involve 40,000 young musicians,' *CanComp*, 26, Feb 1968
MacFarlane, Dalton. 'Music festivals and the Canadian composer,' *MSc*, 243, Sep–Oct 1968
Abbott, Eric. 'The evolution of the Canadian festival movement as an instrument of musical education,' unpubl D ED thesis, Boston U 1969
Fiske, Dr. H.E. 'Adjudication: are we doing it all wrong?' *Recorder*, vol 18, Mar 1976
The Federation of Canadian Music Festivals. *Digest Report*, annual

FILMOGRAPHY
Listen to the Prairies (NFB 1945); shorter version titled *A City Sings*

Competitions. See the following:
Alberta Music Festival Association
Associated Manitoba Festivals
Band festivals
British Columbia Music Festival Association
Canadian Music Competition / Concours de musique du Canada
Canadian National Exhibition
Canadian Open Old Time Fiddlers' Contest
Canadian Stage Band Festival
CBC Talent Festival
Competition festivals
Composition competitions
'Concours de la chanson canadienne'
du Maurier Council for the Performing Arts
Granby Song Festival
Kiwanis Festivals
Manitoba Music Competition Festival
Metropolitan Opera Company
Montreal International Competition
MSO Concours
National Competitive Festival of Music
'Nos Futures Étoiles'
'Opportunity Knocks'
Prix Archambault
Prix d'Europe
Saskatchewan Music Festival Association
'Singing Stars of Tomorrow'

See also Awards; Canadian Music Festival Adjudicators' Association; CAPAC; Federation of Canadian Music Festivals; PRO Canada Awards.

Compo Company Ltd. First Canadian independent record pressing plant; also the largest of its day. Established in 1918 as a pressing plant at Lachine, near Montreal, by Herbert S. Berliner (then vice-president and general manager of the *Berliner Gram-O-Phone Co), it initially handled US labels such as Phonola and Starr-Gennett. Berliner resigned from the Berliner Gram-O-Phone Co in April 1921, taking many of that company's senior staff to Compo; the two companies became bitter rivals as a result. Compo's first house label, Sun, based in Toronto, was introduced in May 1921. It was supplanted in September by Apex, a name which continued in use for over 50 years, passing through the control of several companies. Other labels were adopted (at one time Compo had over 20), among them Domino, Microphone, Sterling, and Lucky Strike. In 1924 Apex phonographs were introduced. As Herbert Berliner had a great personal interest in radio and its ramifications, Compo was the first Canadian company to issue microphone recordings (in 1924) and records taken from radio broadcasts (in 1925). It was one of only two recording companies in Canada to survive the depression of the 1930s, diversifying its activities to include the manufacture of cylinder records (for dictation machines) and radio transcriptions.

In 1935 Compo became the Canadian licensee for pressing and distributing the US Decca line. In 1950 Decca purchased Compo, retaining Berliner as its president until his death in 1966. Decca in turn was purchased by MCA, which, besides maintaining the Lachine pressing plant until the early 1970s, established a plant in Cornwall, Ont, which operated until 1976. The Compo and Apex labels were in use until 1971.

Compo always recorded Canadian performers, mostly from the pop field, though in the 1920s such concert performers as Rex *Battle, J.-B. *Dubois, Paul *Dufault, Ruthven McDonald, and Rodolphe *Plamondon were on its roster. In addition to the performers on Compo's *Starr line (the name taken over from Starr-Gennett in 1930), Compo also recorded, for Apex, the *Adanac Quartet(te), Willie *Eckstein, Vera *Guilaroff, Al and Bob *Harvey, Léo *Le Sieur, the accordionist Joseph Latour, Don *Messer and His Islanders, the pianist Billy Munro, the fiddler Sid Plamondor and his Western Pals, Wellie *Ringuette, and the Andy Tipaldi Orchestra. Compo distributed in Canada many records made by expatriate Canadians for Decca. A number of Compo's production ledgers and masters have been deposited at the *NL of C. In 1979 MCA revived the Apex label for LPs and 45s by Canadian performers. (EBM)

Composers, Authors and Publishers Association of Canada Limited. See CAPAC.

Composition. See the following:
Anthems, motets, and psalms
Art song
Ballets
Brass
Cantata
Cello
Choral composition
Chamber music
Christmas
Composition competitions
Composition for ensemble teaching
Composition, instrumental solos and duos
Composition, topical
Concertos and concertante music
Double-bass
Easter, Lent, the Passion
Electronic music
Film scores
Folk-music-inspired composition
Guitar
Harp
Harpsichord composition
Incidental music
Jingles
Librettos
Literature set to music
Lullabies
Masses
Musical theatre
Operas
Oratorios, Canadian (composition and performance)
Orchestral composition
Organ music
Songs
Te Deum laudamus
Woodwinds

See also Aleatoric music; Impressionism; Mixed media; Neoclassicism; Twelve-tone technique.

Composition competitions. Increasingly numerous after 1950, sponsored by governmental, professional, educational, and other organizations. Prizes may be in the form of medals, scholarships, commissions, performances and cash, or cash alone.

In 1886 the *Canadian Society of Musicians sponsored a composition contest, awarding 'the marks necessary to pass' to J.D. *Kerrison and G.W. *Strathy. Later, the E.W. Beatty Competition (1928), named for the chairman and president of the CPR, was open to Canadian and foreign composers and offered $3000 in prizes for the best settings of, or compositions based on, French-Canadian folksongs. Winners were Arthur Cleland Lloyd ($1000 for his *Orchestral Suite*); Claude *Champagne ($750 for *Suite canadienne*); George Bowles ($500 for *Suite for String Quartet*); and Ernest *MacMillan ($250), Alfred *Whitehead ($150), and Irvin *Cooper ($100), all of whom had arranged folksongs for choir. Honourable mentions were awarded to Bowles, Maud Wyatt Pargeter, and Pierre *Gautier. Some of the prize-winning compositions were performed in May 1928 at the *CPR Festival in Quebec City. That same year the journal *Musical Canada* sponsored a pianoforte composition contest which offered prizes of $100, $50, and $25. First prize was won by Leslie *Grossmith's *Air de ballet*, published in *Musical Canada* in June 1929. During the 1930s prizes were offered by Jean *Lallemand (Prix Jean-Lallemand, 1936–8) and by the *Vogt Society (Vogt Society Competition for Canadian Composers 1938–9).

In 1938 the CPRS (*CAPAC) initiated an annual competition. The first prize was a $750 scholarship for study at the TCM. In 1941 a junior division was added, offering scholarships for composers under the age of 18. These were replaced in 1970 by the Sir Ernest MacMillan Fellowship of $2000 and the William St Clair Low Fellowship of $2000 (the name changed in each case from 'Fellowship' to 'Award' in 1978). The former was for compositions scored for 12 or more players; the latter for compositions for up to 12 players. By 1978 the awards had a combined value of $6000 (see CAPAC).

In 1951 the US-based Broadcast Music Inc began to sponsor a student composers' competition; several Canadians have been among the winners. BMI Canada (*PRO Canada) established centennial scholarships for student composers in 1967 and annual songwriters' awards in 1969. In 1979 it initiated a major composition competition, the PRO Canada Student Composer Awards (See PRO Canada Awards).

The Jewish Women's Musical Club of Winnipeg began a composition competition in 1950, and winners have included Kenneth *Winters, Lionel Greenberg, and Aaron Rosenthal. Several organizations have sponsored single competitions. In 1955 the Canada Foundation and the *Ottawa Philharmonic Orchestra offered a $500 prize for a short symphonic composition to be performed at the Ottawa Centenary Festival Concert 5 May 1955. The winner was Neil McKay. In 1958 CAPAC, in conjunction with the *Vancouver International Festival, awarded a $1000 prize to Paul *McIntyre for his cantata *Judith*, subsequently premiered at the festival. In 1963 the Montreal Brass Quintet offered a prize for the best brass quintet; the winner was Thomas *Legrady for his *Suite*. The Second-Century Week Composition Competition, sponsored by the *U of Alberta and the *U of Calgary in 1967, was won jointly by John *Hawkins (for *Eight Movements*, 1966) and Hugh *Hartwell (for *Matinée d'ivresse*, 1966).

By the late 1950s the Junior Committee of the *MSO had begun an annual composition competition. The *TSO Junior Women's Committee sponsored two student composers' competitions for which the prizes were $500 and $700 respectively and performance of the chosen works. The first, in 1972, was won by John Chong for *Continuum*, the second in 1976 by Jean-Claude Paquet for *Metamorphosis – Beauty and the Beast – Fantasia for Orchestra*.

The CBC has provided encouragement for both composers and pop-song writers through a number of competitions: the CBC International Service Song contest in 1950 for art songs, ballads, and pop songs; *'Opportunity Knocks' (which included a composition category); *'Concours de la chanson canadienne,' 1956–ca 1961; CBC Ottawa's Original Music Competition for Composers, 1964–70; CBC Song Market, 1967–72; and the *CBC National Radio Competition for Young Composers begun in 1973.

Other competitions for song composition include the *Granby Song Festival established in 1969 and the annual Multicultural Songwriting Competition, which began in 1974, supported by the multicultural radio stations CHIN, CJVB, CFMB, and CKJS and by PRO Canada and CAPAC. The winner receives $1500 and the Douglas McGowan Award for the best song written in a language other than French or English.

In 1968 the *CLComp established a $250 annual scholarship to assist young composers; after 1975 the competition became biennial and the prize was doubled.

The *CMCentre became the administrator for three awards. The John *Adaskin Memorial Award, first offered in 1964, took the form of a $500 commission for a chamber work. Winners have included John Hawkins (1968), John *Rea (1970), Edward Dawson (1972), and Thomas Dusatko (1975). The Canadian Federation of University Women's Creative Arts Award, established in 1969, has offered a $750 commission annually for a chamber work by a young composer chosen through an adjudication of his or her completed works. Winners have been Hugh Hartwell 1970, Paul *Crawford 1971, Donald Steven 1972, Denis *Lorrain 1973, Peter Paul *Koprowski 1975, Patrick Cardy 1976, James Hiscott 1977, Michael Maguire 1978, and Kristi Allik 1979. Whenever possible the CMCentre has arranged for premieres and CBC radio broadcasts of the works commissioned for the Adaskin and University Women's awards. The third award administered by the centre, the Alberto *Guerrero Memorial Prize of $2000 for an original piano composition by a Canadian citizen under 35, was begun in 1978. The first recipient was Edward Arteaga.

The *CFMTA's annual Canada Music Week Writing Contest, begun in 1970, has been limited to pupils of CFMTA members. It has awarded $25 to a composer 11 years and younger, $50 to a composer 15 years and younger, and $200 to a composer 19 years and younger, with the winners announced during the CFMTA Canada Music Week and the winning compositions reproduced in the CFMTA *Newsletter*.

The Robert *Fleming Award for Young Composers was begun in 1979 as a memorial to the composer and open to one graduating candidate from each university and conservatory in Canada. It was to be administered by the *CMCouncil, with the winner to receive the interest earned in one year on a $10,000 endowment fund established by friends of the composer. It was won in 1979 by André Lamarche and in 1980 by Denys Bouliane both of Quebec City.

Other annual competitions established during the 1970s were the Okanagan Festival for Composers, begun in 1973, and the Jules Léger Prize for New Chamber Music, named for the man who served as Canada's governor-general 1974–9. The Léger prize, begun in 1978, open to all Canadians and to landed immigrants of at least one year's residence, carries a $5000 prize and includes a performance and a CBC broadcast by a leading Canadian chamber group. The prize was won in 1978 by R. Murray *Schafer for his *String Quartet No. 2, 'Waves'* (1976), by Bruce *Mather in 1979 for *Musique pour Champigny* (1976), and by Serge *Garant in 1980 for *Quintette* (1978). The Arthur *Romano Saxophone Prize was established in Montreal in 1978. The *Canadian Music Competition launched a National Composers' Competition in 1979.

The appended list cites some Canadian winners of foreign competitions:

1928 Gena *Branscombe. League of American Pen Women; annual award for the finest work by a woman. For *Pilgrims of Destiny*

1938 and 1939 Alexander *Brott. Elizabeth Sprague Coolidge Awards for orchestral composition. For *Two Symphonic Movements* (1938); for *Oracle* (1939)

1941 André *Mathieu. New York Philharmonic Centennial Competition. For *Concertino No. 2*

1948 John *Weinzweig. The Olympic Games composition competitions. Silver medal for *Divertimento No. 1*

– Alexander Brott. The Olympic Games composition competitions. Bronze medal for *War and Peace*

1949 Lionel *Daunais. Polydor-Marly Competition. First prize for 'Chanson du maître cordonnier'

1955 Clermont *Pépin. Radio-Luxembourg. Second prize, for *Le Rite du soleil noir*

1961 S.C. *Eckhardt-Gramatté. GEDOK International Competition for Women Composers, Mannheim. Shared first prize for *Triple Concerto*

1965 Pierre *Mercure. International Competition of Symphonic Music, Cava dei Tirreni. First prize for *Tryptique*

– Harry *Somers. International Competition of Symphonic Music, Cava dei Tirreni. Critics' award for *Movement for Orchestra*

1966 Oskar *Morawetz. International Competition of Symphonic Music, Cava dei Tirreni. Critics' award for *Sinfonietta* for winds

– S.C. Eckhardt-Gramatté. GEDOK International Competition for Women Composers. A prize for *String Quartet No. 3*

– Hector *Gratton. Brussels Radio Competition for Marches. For *Les Draveurs* for brass band

1967 Sydney *Hodkinson. Prince of Monaco Award. For *Caricatures*

1969 Marc *Fortier. Ferdinando Ballo Composition Competition (Milan). First prize for *Un Doigt de la lune*

– Otto *Joachim. Paul Gilson Prize of the Communauté radiophonique des programmes de langue française. For *Illumination II*

– John *Rea. Concours de musique de ballet, Geneva. Third prize for *The Days / Les Jours*

1972 Thomas *Schudel. Premio Città di Trieste. First prize for *Symphony No. 1*

1974 José *Evangelista. Confederación Española de Cajas de Ahorros (Madrid). First prize for *En guise de fête*

1976 Marjan *Mozetich. Gaudeamus International Composers' Competition, Holland. Second Prize for wind quintet *It's in the Air*

1977 Denis *Lorrain. Prométhée Special Composition Prize (Lourdes, France). For *Extrema*

– Raymond *Pannell. TV Opera prize of the City of Salzburg. First prize for **Aberfan*

1980 R. Murray Schafer. Prix musical international Arthur-Honneger for *String Quartet No. 1*

See also PRO Canada Awards for BMI composition awards.

BIBLIOGRAPHY

CMCentre. *Canadian and International Competitions / Concours canadiens et internationaux* (Toronto 1976)

Composition for ensemble teaching. Some Canadian composers have been loth – or insufficiently experienced – to work within the constraints imposed by writing for student performers. Others, whose experience is in no doubt and whose ingenuity might be stimulated by such constraints, bristle at the prospect of their work being labelled 'educational music,' with the attendant connotations of academism. Nevertheless, the need for a Canadian repertoire of technically pertinent and aesthetically engrossing works composed out of firsthand experience with teachers and students has been recognized. Through a pioneer commissioning program the *John Adaskin Project has placed composers in classrooms with the benefits of reciprocal experience in mind: a chance for the composer to explore students' concerns and needs in exchange for an opportunity for students to find out something about the human creative process. Other organizations have commissioned works: the *CBC, the Alliance for Canadian New Music Projects (*Contemporary Showcase), some of the provincial music educators' associations (the *BCMEA, the *SMEA, the *OMEA, the *NSMEA, and the *Music Education Council of the New Brunswick Teachers' Assn), the *Guelph Spring Festival, the *NYO, the women's committees of symphony orchestras, and others. Financial aid for commissioning programs has been supplied by the *Canada Council, the *OAC, the *Nova Scotia Dept of Culture, Recreation and Fitness, and other government arts-support agencies. The interaction of composers, students, and educators has been productive of works devised for various combinations of instruments and geared to difference levels of playing competence.

1 Orchestral music
2 String music
3 Wind music
4 Other

1 ORCHESTRAL MUSIC. The NYO has commissioned orchestral works with specific educational objectives in mind. Harry *Freedman's 12-tone work *Tangents*, commissioned in 1967 and scored for full orchestra, is a set of symphonic variations whose three sections are played without pause; the work contains an aleatoric section for percussion. The atonal work *Offrande II* by Serge *Garant, scored for full orchestra, was performed in 1970. *Shadows – Part 1: Nekuia*, by Robert *Aitken, is scored for full orchestra. The Japanese word 'Nekuia' refers to the calling up of ancestors from the past somewhat in the style of a séance. The composition, first performed by the NYO in 1971, is based upon Japanese musical idioms and employs many contemporary techniques, including graph notation, tone rows, aleatoric effects, instrument exploration, and conductor's prerogative. *North / White*, by R. Murray *Schafer, premiered by the NYO in 1973, is inspired by 'Canadian identity and by the rape of the Canadian North that is being carried out by the nation's governments in conspiracy with business and industry; the instruments of destruction are pipelines, airstrips, highways and snowmobiles.' This work,

which correlates music with social feelings and ideas, is written for full orchestra, snowmobile, and other accessory equipment. The piece is committed to the idea of the splendid and indestructible North. *Big Lonely*, by Norman *Symonds, takes its title from the phrase used by Canadian hobos to describe the country and the great distances between cities. The work is large in scale and features a taped soundscape (eg, children laughing, the cry of a loon) and narration. The narration is deleted in a revised (1979) short version. The composer was in residence for three weeks discussing his travels and his feelings with the NYO players while completing the work. *Bells*, first performed in 1970 in Tokyo by the Japan Philharmonic Orchestra, was rescored for the NYO by the composer, John *Wyre. In its original form it may be performed by any number of players from 11 to a full string section, harp, and percussion. In its rescored form for full orchestra it employs a blend of soloists, improvisation, contrasting timbres, and, in an effort to break down the psychological barriers that some instrumentalists have in relation to creating music as opposed to re-creating music, all orchestral players double with various types of bells.

Other composers have written for student performers in addition to those mentioned above. Barbara *Pentland composed her *Symphony No. 2*, a work for orchestra in four short movements in which contrapuntal writing dominates, for the Vancouver Junior SO in 1950. Robert *McMullin was commissioned by the OMEA to write a work primarily for high school orchestra; the result was *Prairie Sketches* (1958). Violet *Archer composed *Three Sketches for Orchestra* in 1961 for the Montreal Junior SO. Alfred *Kunz, who has composed a number of works for university forces, wrote *Behold the Beauty of the Sky* for high school chorus and orchestra in 1961, and, on commission, a *Concerto* for percussion and orchestra for the Kitchener-Waterloo Junior SO in 1973. For the *CMCentre's Graded Educational Music Plan Murray *Adaskin composed *Rondino (1964) for Orchestra*. Talivaldis *Kenins wrote *Folk Dance Variations and Fugue* in 1964 for use in Canadian schools and two works for summer music camps – *Sawan-Oong* (a symphonic cantata for chorus and orchestra, 1973) and *Naačnaača* (a ballade for orchestra, 1975) – as well as the *CMEA-commissioned one-movement *Simfonietta* (sic) in 1976. Also for the CMEA Robert *Fleming (who had composed *Three Contrasts* for school orchestra in 1964) wrote *Four Fantasias on Canadian Folk Themes* for high school orchestra in 1966, and Godfrey *Ridout wrote *When Age and Youth Unite* for chorus and orchestra in 1967. The BCMEA commissioned Lloyd *Burritt's *David* for soloists, school chorus and orchestra, and prepared tape in 1977. Contemporary Showcase requested orchestral works for school performers by Allan *Rae (*Celebration* 1974) and Schafer (*Train* 1976, for string orchestra, piano, woodwinds, and optional brass). Schafer's compositions for schools include *Statement in Blue* (1964, a 'controlled "compose-it-yourself" piece,' recorded by the Lawrence Park Collegiate orchestra and members of the North Toronto Collegiate orchestra on Melbourne SMLP 4017) and *Threnody* (1967, an anti-war work based on texts from children who survived the Nagasaki bombings; it was commissioned for the Vancouver Junior SO and is scored for orchestra, speakers, chorus, and prepared tape; it is recorded on Melbourne SMLP 4017).

Other composers who have written specifically for school or youth orchestras include Milton *Barnes (*Concert Overture* 1973, *Maid of the Mist* 1977); Keith *Bissell (*Andante e scherzo* 1971, *God's Grandeur* 1975); Wolfgang *Bottenberg (*Fantasia* 1966); F.R.C. *Clarke (*Mini-Suite*, 1971, for the Kingston Youth Orchestra): Sydney *Hodkinson (*Drawings: Set No. 7* and *Set. No. 8* 1974); and Bernard *Naylor (*Resurrection According to Saint Matthew* 1965).

2 STRING MUSIC. Commissioned in 1955 by the U of Toronto Faculty of Music Alumni Assn, Harry *Somers composed a work for amateur and school orchestras – *Little Suite for String Orchestra on Canadian Folk Songs*. More than 20 years later the John Adaskin project commissioned Somers to explore with a grade 9 class such matters as string sonorities and effects (glissando, etc). A composition for junior string orchestra was the result, and *Variations* was premiered at a Toronto workshop of the OMEA in November 1979.

The CMCentre Graded Music Education Plan commissioned works for string orchestra from Anne *Eggleston (*On Citadel Hill*, a theme and six variations, 1963), from Robert Fleming (*'You Name It' Suite*, 1964), from Clermont *Pépin (*Three Miniatures for Strings*, 1963), and from Kenins (*Nocturne* of his *Nocturne and Dance*, 1963). Murray Adaskin's *Essay for Strings* was commissioned by the Oak Bay Junior-Senior High School orchestra in 1972; his *Three Tunes for Strings* by the Oak Bay Junior Strings in 1976. Walter *Buczynski has received commissions to compose for youthful string groups from the Contemporary Showcase (*Legends for String Orchestra*, 1976) and from the Courtenay Youth Music Centre (*Rhapsody for Two Horns and String Orchestra*, 1976). In 1977 Morris *Surdin composed three works for school string orchestra – *Five for Four*, *A Group of Six*, and *Who's on Bass?* The Saskatchewan Dept of Culture and Youth provided funds to commission Thomas *Schudel's *Prairie Wildflower*, premiered by the SMEA Honour Orchestra at the SMEA convention in the fall of 1979.

3 WIND MUSIC. In 1949 Eldon *Rathburn composed *Waltz for Winds* for flute, oboe, clarinet, and bassoon and designed for young players. Keith Bissell's *A Folksong Suite for Woodwinds* (1960) was composed for the Scarborough (Ont) Public School Woodwind Ensemble of six players. Through its 1963 Graded Educational Music Plan the CMCentre commissioned Alfred Kunz to compose *Fun for Two* and *Fun for Three* for woodwinds and *Three Fanfares* for brass, and John *Weinzweig to write his *Clarinet Quartet*, four pieces in the 12-tone idiom. Several Canadians have written educational music for the recorder – among them *Dela, *Duschenes, *Fiala, Kenneth *Meek, Hugh *Orr, Antoine Padilla, *Papineau-Couture, and Suzanne Sieber.

Presser published Sydney Hodkinson's *A Contemporary Primer for Band* in 1973. These three progressive volumes are graphically notated miniatures suitable for band or a smaller ensemble of wind and percussion. Suggestions are provided for supplementary listening and for original compositions and projects including work with electronic tape. Harry Freedman discussed and rehearsed his *Monday Gig* (1978, for woodwind quintet) with the performers of a school ensemble; both the students and their teacher suggested possible changes in the score to alleviate serious technical problems. A new work by Donald Coakley for junior wind ensemble – *Songs for the Morning Band* – was commissioned by the John Adaskin Project and premiered at the OMEA Toronto workshop in November 1979.

4 OTHER. Compositions suitable for advanced student string soloists, wind or brass soloists, chamber groups, string orchestras, and orchestras have been written by Murray Adaskin, Louis *Applebaum, Robert *Bauer, John *Beckwith, Norma *Beecroft, Morley *Calvert, Albert *Chamberland, Claude *Champagne, Brian *Cherney, Jean *Coulthard, Quentin Doolittle, Robert Evans, Steven *Gellman, Derek *Healey, Rhené *Jaque, Kelsey *Jones, Leslie *Mann, Oskar *Morawetz, Glenn *Morley, Paul *Pedersen, André *Prévost, Healey *Willan, Gerhard *Wuensch, Leon *Zuckert, and others.

Other educational music projects have included Norman Symonds' two stage works developed for public school classes, *Laura and the Lieutenant* (1974) and *Sam* (1976), and his music drama *Episode at Big Quill* (1979), commissioned by the CBC and scored for narrator, elementary school children, other children at play, choral sections taped by a choir of teenagers, percussion, and synthesizer. The work is based upon the story of a group of pioneer families in Saskatchewan. Raymond *Pannell's *The Downsview Anniversary Song Spectacle Celebration Pageant* was written for Downsview Secondary School in North York, Ont. Clifford Crawley's *The Miracle Child*, scored for chorus, band, and strings, was performed in 1979 by students of the Frontenac County (Ont) Board of Education. The children's operetta *Song of the Wood*, by Michael *Miller, is based on New Brunswick history and was commissioned by the Music Council of the New Brunswick Teachers' Assn in 1979.

See also Brass; Violin and viola; Woodwinds.

BIBLIOGRAPHY

Musique symphonique de 1880 à 1950, vol 1 of series *Repertoires internationaux de musique contemporaine à l'usage des amateurs et des jeunes* (New York 1957)
Somers, Harry. 'Composer in the school. A composer's view,' *Mcan*, May 1969
Canadian Music Suitable for Community Orchestras, compiled by Jan Matejcek (Toronto 1971)
Shand, Patricia Martin. *Canadian Music: A Selective Guidelist for Teachers* (Toronto 1978)
Special issue: children and music, *Mcan*, 39, Jun 1979
Orr, Colleen. 'Commission a work!' *Recorder*, vol 22, Fall 1979
Alliance for Canadian New Music Project. Syllabus of Contemporary Showcase (1972–) (SS)

Composition, instrumental solos and duos

1 Introduction
2 Piano solos
3 Piano duos
4 Instrumental duos with piano
5 Solos and duos without piano

1 INTRODUCTION. One may consider the repertoire of Canadian compositions in these categories in two ways. First, 'repertoire' may indicate those works which are played repeatedly. From the late 19th century *Lavallée's *Le Papillon* for piano would be an internationally recognized example; a generation or two later *Champagne's *Quadrilha Brasileira*, also for piano, offers an instance of wide use. From the mid-20th century *Pentland's *Studies in Line*, *Morawetz's *Scherzo*, and *Hétu's *Variations* for piano, *Adaskin's *Canzona and Rondo* and *Beecroft's *Tre Pezzi Brevi* for flute all could be cited as appearing with regularity in concert programs, broadcasts, and (sometimes) recordings. Further pieces could be added.

But one may broaden the lists much more by using a second meaning of 'repertoire': that by which one may indicate *all* compositions which have been completed and have proved themselves in performance (though perhaps on only a few occasions or at the hands of only one performer or pair of performers). The available repertoire in this sense is surprisingly large, and includes older compositions deserving revival as

Souvenir de Vénise for piano by Ernest Gagnon

well as newer and perhaps more experimental ones as yet not assimilated.

More frequently than in other compositional categories, in solos and duos one feels the impact of the performer-composer who writes for his/her own instrument, bringing a ready acquaintance with its idiomatic nature which the generalist composer must gain by more external effort. When Murray Adaskin composes for the violin, Ernest *Friedlander for the cello, Robert *Aitken for the flute, Leslie *Mann or Blago Simeonov for the clarinet, Christopher *Weait for the bassoon, Robert *Bauer or Davis *Joachim for the guitar, the musical statement relates with ease and assurance to the instrument's capabilities. The same is true of the piano music of composers who are accomplished pianists (as distinct from those who 'play the piano like composers') – among them *Buczynski, *Eckhardt-Gramatté, *Garant, *Mather, Morawetz, Pentland, *Pépin, *Somers, and *Tremblay.

Little use has been made in this genre of borrowings from folk music, compared to that found in the orchestral and choral categories. Ernest *Gagnon's *Stadaconé*, 'danse sauvage' for piano; Léo-Pol *Morin's *Suite canadienne* and *Three Eskimos* for piano; and from a later generation *Kenins' *Fantasy-Variations on an Eskimo Lullaby*, for flute and viola, may be mentioned. In the string category, where the violoneux and fiddle traditions are well developed and ripe for compositional comment, one can point to only a few examples from the 1920s and 1930s – Champagne's *Danse villageoise* (a 'repertoire' piece in the first sense, in its several arrangements) and the five *Danses canadiennes* for violin and piano by *Gratton. These works sometimes dress the borrowed idioms in rather flowery harmonic garb, and even introduce programmatic touches, but in Gratton's second *Danse* the pitches remain faithful to a single mode almost throughout, and concentration centres on the characteristic fiddling rhythms.

In the 1940s and 1950s a remarkable crop of longer concert pieces appeared. These works often adopted the abstract, neoclassic shape of the sonata in several movements, whether for a solo instrument or, more frequently, for a duo consisting of piano and one other instrument. Following the Gebrauchsmusik example of her one-time teacher Paul Hindemith, Violet *Archer has been notably productive in this field, composing duo-sonatas for piano with violin, cello, oboe, clarinet, horn, and alto saxophone. This lively series, though it may adopt Hindemith's outward example, does not always emulate his style. Other Canadian solo and duo sonatas of the period are dependent even less on specific international models, though individual works or single movements may evoke comparisons.

The 1960s and 1970s revealed a trend away from the abstract utility sonatas, and also from the concurrently cultivated 'showcase' genre (as seen in the exuberant concertante pieces for various instruments by Kenins, Eckhardt-Gramatté, and others), and towards sonorous experiment. *Morel's *Deux Études de sonorité*, with their post-impressionist colourings and freer structures, may be regarded as a prophetically titled early symptom of this tendency. Garant's *Cage d'oiseau*, Tremblay's *Deux Pièces* (*Phases* and *Réseaux*), and the *Five Piano Pieces* of *Hawkins represent later stages in works for the solo piano; other works, including those from other instrumental areas, will be noted at appropriate points below, where the trend will be seen to link by natural consequence with the particular subcategory of the duo for instrument and prepared tape.

In the 1970s a further new direction arose in the form of theatrical elements – applied with special emphasis, for example, by *Weinzweig in a cycle of interrelated works starting with the percussion solo *Around the Stage in Twenty-Five Minutes*. Here the scores give indications of physical attitudes and gestures alongside the symbols for musical sounds, but the results, in Weinzweig's case at least, are often interior and personal rather than theatrical in the melodramatic sense, while such traits as whimsy, humour, and even nostalgia are often present.

2 PIANO SOLOS. The largest body of Canadian instrumental music from the 19th century is for solo piano. The waltzes, galops, and quadrilles (often based on French-Canadian tunes) followed the prevailing facile entertainment-music fashions of the USA and Europe and were designed almost exclusively for the parlour upright piano rather than the concert hall grand. Exceptions occurred with increasing frequency as professionalism and concert life developed. C.W. *Sabatier, in the late 1850s, probably was the first Canadian to write the kind of showy salon piece taken a stage further by Calixa Lavallée. Lavallée's graceful and idiomatic piano works occasionally reached beyond the conventional requirements of their variational or dance forms, as in *Le Papillon*, a Mendelssohnian character-piece with the unusual shape ABAC, the C-section being an extended emergence into the major from the minor. This work, once highly popular and internationally anthologized, remains a true Canadian piano classic. Like Lavallée, his contemporary Salomon *Mazurette produced a large body of short genre pieces. In the generation after Lavallée, *Lucas and *Forsyth, and later Émiliano *Renaud, wrote more extended pieces with a more personalized expression, using Chopinesque forms and titles (prélude, impromptu, etc). Their music may be compared to that of such interesting minor US piano composers of the day as William Mason; indeed, in common with great quantities of junior and intermediate piano pieces by L.J. Oscar *Fontaine, G.A. *Grant-Schaefer, Cedric Lemont, and Léon *Ringuet, their work was published and performed more often in the USA than at home. More innovative, perhaps daring for the early decades of the 20th century, were *Anger's *Tintamarre*, with its echoes of the Celtic dreaminess of Bax, Cyril Scott, or perhaps MacDowell, and the effective short *Preludes* of Colin *McPhee, composed and published in Toronto in his early Wunderkind period.

By the 1930s and 1940s – in the *Sonata* of Rodolphe *Mathieu, the *Trois Pièces brèves* of Georges-Émile *Tanguay, the young Robert *Fleming's tuneful and Poulenc-like *Sonatina*, and the first items in Pentland's distinguished piano list – a sense of greater variety in the forms and styles and of a deeper artistic commitment (even in short and light-textured movements) may be felt. Pentland's *Studies in Line*, *Variations*, and *Sonata-Fantasy* show this commitment in their careful structuring and stark piano colours. The four *Studies*, with geometrical figures as their titles, exhibit especially well-devised contrasts between their brief neoclassic explorations of characteristic motives. Her later piano music – such as the lighter *Sonatinas No. 1 and 2*, the *Suite Borealis*, and the *Toccata* – reveals the same approach applied to different problems (shorter or longer forms, evocative aspects, leaner textures, etc). Other strong representatives of this era are the concise, Stravinskian *Sonata* of Weinzweig, the eloquent *Passacaglia* of *Duchow, Arnold *Walter's *Sonata*, *Suite*, and *Études*, and various pieces by Pépin, notably his three-movement *Suite*, with its showy finale, *Danse frénétique*, often played separately.

Indications of change were apparent in several other works of the later 1940s and early 1950s. A notable isolated example is Otto *Joachim's *L'Éclosion*, with its then-novel approach to duration, and its characteristic intensity. Just as original and as isolated is *Anhalt's imposing and eruptive *Fantasia*. The piano music of Somers, however, has a special importance, for its extent and concentration as well as for its quality: the first four of his five sonatas belong to the era mentioned, as do his *12 × 12* (a set of 12 short fuges on 12-tone subjects) and a number of shorter compositions. Taking the keyboard almost for granted in their ease of idiomatic treatment, these works develop a personal rhetoric and a sense of musical space through their application to various kinds of writing – romantic in *Sonata No. 1*, virtuosic in *Sonata No. 2*, linear in the fugues, etc. Though suggesting models (conscious or unconscious) as diverse as Mozart, Liszt, Ives, Debussy, Krenek, and Weinzweig, the pieces always demonstrate Somers' own profile most of all. Another sensitive, though smaller, output for piano from the 1960s is that of Bruce Mather, whose *Smaragdin*, *Like Snow*, *Mystras*, and (especially) *Fantasy* are all worthy of greater circulation than they have enjoyed so far. *Kolinski's *Sonata*, four *Suites*, and especially *Four Dances in Étude Form* – composed before his arrival in Canada – are fluent and rhythmically intriguing.

The sonorous experimentation already referred to, which is exemplified in the well-imagined piano harmonies of Tremblay's *Phases* and *Réseaux*, continued into the 1970s in such works as *Papineau-Couture's *Complémentarité*, with its structured use of knocks on the side, key-lid, and keys, and its chromatic glissandi produced by lowering the key-lid partway and passing a rod along the inside, behind the black keys, and *Gellman's *Veils*, with its use of the three pedals simultaneously, two to be depressed by the left foot, the third by the right. In *Douglas' *Celebration* one sees an affinity successfully struck with classic-jazz piano idioms, while Kristi Allik's *Fragments* is an even later product, by a younger composer, showing strongly confident ideas and interesting durational subtleties. At the same time one well may register surprise at the freshness of Weinzweig's mid-1970 *Impromptus*; with their fragmented and interrupted continuity, their conscious self-quotations, and their humourous stage gestures they move to a world quite apart from his earlier *Sonata*.

3 PIANO DUOS. The list of concert works for four hands at one piano is small. The main items are Archer's *Ten Folk Songs for Four Hands*, *Beckwith's

early suite *Music for Dancing*, *Kasemets' puzzle-piece called *Squares*, and Pentland's *Three Duets after Pictures by Paul Klee*.

There are more, and more varied, works for two pianos, the more customary concert medium in modern times. *Willan's *Theme and Variations* is a solid late-romantic entry. Kenins' *Concertino* and Michael *Baker's *Sonata* cultivate the mechanical brilliance of much mid-20th-century two-piano writing, while the *Sonata* of Jacques Hétu, the *Sonata* of Mather, and the *Études* of Hawkins explore different sonorous and rhythmic possibilities.

See also Piano teams.

4 INSTRUMENTAL DUOS WITH PIANO. Sonatas for violin and piano from the early and mid-20th century include Willan's flamboyantly romantic *Sonata No. 1*, his deliberately Handelian *Sonata No. 2*, and the incomplete, posthumously discovered *Sonata No. 3*; the two robust sonatas of Somers; *Coulthard's two sonatas; *Vallerand's example modelled on Fauré and Poulenc; and the crisply neoclassic example by Papineau-Couture. Shorter pieces include André *Mathieu's and Maurice *Dela's *Sonatas*, Morawetz's one-movement *Duo*, pieces by Adaskin and *Brott, Pépin's *Monade IV (Réseaux)*, Somers' *Rhapsody*, and *Freedman's *Encounter*.

The cello has been, perhaps surprisingly, more richly supplied than the violin by Canadian composers over the years. *Contant's *La Charmeuse*, *Méditation*, *Romance sans paroles*, and *Tarantelle* represent early styles. A program of Canadian cello and piano sonatas might range from the early-20th-century examples of Rodolphe Mathieu, Oscar *O'Brien, and Leo *Smith, through Weinzweig's passionate yet not overblown *Sonata* 'Israel,' to the broad gestures of *Prévost and Otto Joachim. Eckhardt-Gramatté's *Duo Concertante*, of sonata dimensions, embodies concerto principles of display-dialogue and technical extension. Smith's *Four Pieces in Old English Style* and Pentland's *Mutations* represent a similarly wide range of expression and style in shorter cello works. Buczynski's *Duo* with contrabass is a successful answer to a special challenge few composers have tackled.

Pieces for solo wind instrument with piano may be exemplified by Beecroft's Webernian *Tre Pezzi Brevi* (for flute, the accompaniment alternatively for piano, guitar, or harp), Eckhardt-Gramatté's ingeniously constructed *Ruck-Ruck Sonata* and Garant's sonorously innovative *Asymétries No. 2* (both for clarinet), Mather's *Elegy* (for alto saxophone), and sonatas for horn by *Wuensch, for flute by Baker and *Saint-Marcoux, and for bassoon by *Weisgarber, in addition to those of Archer already referred to. The trumpet list begins with the leisurely showpieces (perhaps originally for cornet) by Lavallée and Herbert L. *Clarke and also includes the effective and much played *Little Suite* by *Bissell. Francis Chan's *Three Movements* (1978, for clarinet) is an absorbing study employing yet newer resonances.

5 SOLOS AND DUOS WITHOUT PIANO. Rodolphe Mathieu's *Douze Études Moderne, 'Monologues'* for solo violin were written in 1924, but the composition of instrumental solos is more characteristic of the period after 1940, when several serious and challenging solo works emerged, eg, Eckhardt-Gramatté's *Suite for Violin Solo No. 4, 'Pacific'* (written for Marta *Hidy), Papineau-Couture's *Suite* (written for Szeryng), and Somers' *Music for Solo Violin* (written for Menuhin). For solo cello Kasemets' *Sonata da camera* achieves an illusory double fugue by interlocking the two subjects at points where they are broken by rests, while Donald Steven's *Illusions* is marked by wide contrasts of 'distant' harmonics and floating arpeggios with chordal gestures typical of the cello's traditional rhetorical voice.

*Klein's *Six Exchanges* for saxophone and *Eclogues* for guitar are both idiomatic and exploratory. The guitar is enriched further by Somers' *Sonata* and Morel's *Me Duele España*, and the various pieces of Bauer. *Dolin, Kolinski, and Wuensch have contributed useful and original works for the free-bass accordion, and Weait has composed neat and resourceful *Variations* for the bassoon. Other notable solo compositions for woodwinds include Pépin's *Quatre Monodies* for solo flute and Bruce Mather's *Étude* for solo clarinet. A full-blooded and colourful solo work for harp, with electronics and auxiliary percussion (including anklet bells) to be played by the soloist, is *Schafer's suite *The Crown of Ariadne*. Robert *Turner's *Little Suite* and *Fantasy and Festivity* are other additions to the repertoire for solo harp.

Some instrumental duos have that sense of sharing brief musical thoughts between equals that is so common in four-handed piano music – examples are Simeonov's *Studies* for two clarinets and Beckwith's *Five Pieces* for two flutes. In other cases the musical intentions are expanded further, as in Hawkins' sonorously varied *Eight Movements* for flute and clarinet, *Bottenberg's *Sonata* for the same combination, Morel's *Étude en forme de Toccate* for two percussionists, or the *Music for Violin and Viola* of Otto Joachim. Tremblay's '... *le sifflement des vents porteurs de l'amour* ...' occupies a unique place by its sophisticated rapport between amplified flute and percussion, and by its poetic treatment of an exceptionally wide dynamic range.

The special case of the instrumental solo with tape shows a fair number of Canadian examples, all from the 1960s and 1970s. Among these may be mentioned *Healey's *Lieber Robert* for piano and tape, partly based on quotations from the keyboard music of Schumann; Saint-Marcoux's delicate *Miroirs* for harpsichord and tape; and the three one-movement *Sonatas* of Dolin (the first for violin, the second for flute, the third for cello). The solo part for each contains four pages of score in a free style – free, that is, of dynamics, articulation marks, or tempo indications: these aspects are to be determined by the performer, the given parts providing characteristic gestures and idioms of each instrument as a framework. The free-form concept extends further, in that the three tapes are interchangeable, so that 'three different performances of each sonata can be realized.'

BIBLIOGRAPHY

CMCentre. *Catalogue of Canadian Keyboard Music* (Toronto 1971; suppl 1976)
– *Catalogue of Chamber Music* (Toronto 1967; suppls 1971, 1976)
Chapman, N.B. 'Piano music by Canadian composers, 1940–1965,' PH D thesis (Case Western Reserve U 1973)
Butler, E.G. 'The piano sonatas of Harry Somers,' DMA thesis, U of Rochester 1974 JB

Composition, topical. See the following:
Anerca
Battle music
Beaver
Christmas
College songs
Confederation and music
Coronations
Disaster songs
Easter, Lent, the Passion
Flag songs
History of Canada in music
Klondike
Lakes
Maple leaf
Mountains
Mounties in music
National and royal anthems
Niagara Falls in music
Occupational songs
Patriotic songs
Political songs
Rivers
Sports
Sovereigns, statesmen, and other public figures
Trade union songs
Transportation
Wars, rebellions, and uprisings
Winter

See also *Brébeuf*; Canada in European and US music; *Evangeline*; *Louis Riel*.

COMTE, Gustave. Critic, teacher, librettist, b Montreal 30 Mar 1874, d there 14 Feb 1932. He abandoned his legal studies to devote himself to music and theatre journalism, and wrote for several dailies in Montreal (*La Patrie*, *La Presse*, *Le Canada*) and Ottawa (*Le Temps*). He was one of the first regular contributors to *Passe-Temps*, for which he wrote many articles and a regular column 'L'Art et les artistes.' He also wrote articles in such magazines as *Le Samedi*, *La Quinzaine musicale*, and *La Revue Moderne*. He began teaching music history at the *Cons national of Montreal in 1905, but it is not known how long he continued. Comte also performed as an amateur tenor and was active ca 1910 as an impresario. In 1927 he was appointed secretary of the Montreal Tramways Commission. Comte's writings are a valuable source of information on the musicians and musical activity of Montreal from the end of the last century to the early 1930s. He wrote some librettos for operettas, including the one for *Sandwich* by Émiliano *Renaud. His first marriage, in 1900, was to Blanche Duquette, daughter of Jean-A. *Duquette and niece of Calixa *Lavallée.

WRITINGS

'Calixa Lavallée – notes biographiques inédites sur le chantre de la nation,' *P-T*, 374, 24 Jul 1909
'La première troupe canadienne d'opéra et Calixa Lavallée,' *Quinzaine musicale*, 26 Dec 1931 GP

Concert halls and opera houses. Perhaps the oldest reference to a venue for musical performance is the one found in the *Quebec Gazette* of 29 Nov 1764 which advertises a dance to be held at the Concert Hall. However, the building, or at least the name, did not last very long, and concert performances in Quebec in the last two decades of the 18th century took place at such a variety of places as the Thespian Theatre, Marchant's Coffee House, Frank's Tavern (Taverne de Frank), Ferguson's Hotel (Hôtel de Ferguson), and the Nouvelle Salle des Spectacles. The Théâtre Patagon was the scene of the first Quebec City performance (1805) of *Quesnel's *Colas et Colinette*. The names of places where Montreal concerts were held suggest similar makeshift arrangements: Mr Cushing's long room, Mr Frank's Assembly Room, Dillon's Hotel, and the Salle de Spectacle. The *Theatre Royal and the Masonic Hall were centres of public entertainment in early-19th-century Montreal. There was a Halifax Theatre in the 1790s, and from the end of the century until at least Confederation that city boasted a Theatre Royal. St. John's, Nfld, had its Amateur Theatre and Globe Tavern. No doubt some of these halls were little more than wooden sheds, and fire was a great danger – eg, the blaze that destroyed the Théâtre Saint-Louis of Quebec during

Quebec, 24th December, 1764.

A QUEBEC, *le 27 de Decembre*, 1764.

TOUS les nouveaux ſujets de ſa Majeſté, réſidens dans le département de Québec, qui ont été avertis le 20 courant, que ceux d'entre eux qui ont des requêtes à préſenter relativement à l'Ordonnance du 4 d'Octobre dernier, &c. iront pendant l'abſence de Monſieur Panet, chez Monſieur Saillant, Notaire, pour les faire répondre ; ſont avertis par le préſent de differer juſqu'à nouvel avis, à cauſe de certains arrangemens que le tems et les circonſtances n'ont pas encore permis de prendre.

A PUBLICK BALL,

WILL be held To-morrow, being the 28th Inſtant, at the CONCERT-HALL, where Tickets are to be had of Mr. DIENVAL.

[*Price One Dollar.*]

N. B. No Body will be admitted without a Ticket.

IL ſera tenu demain, 28 du Courant, un BAL PUBLIC à la Salle du Concert, ou l'on peut avoir des Billets de Monſr. DIENVAL.

[*Le Prix de chaque Billet ſera d'une Piaſtre.*]

N. B. On n'admettra Perſonne ſans être pourvuë d'un Billet.

Quebec Gazette, 24 Dec 1764

a performance in 1846 and that which razed Montreal's Masonic Hall during a song recital in 1833.

The growth of population and of wealth in the second half of the 19th century led to auditoriums of more solid construction and, usually, a good measure of elegance (eg, Toronto's *St Lawrence Hall, 1850, restored to its erstwhile splendour and original function in 1967); and though by modern standards these were recital halls rather than symphony orchestra halls, some were of considerable size.

The most frequent name for such halls was Academy of Music. One of these, built in Quebec City in 1852 by Charles Baillargé, one of the architects of the original Parliament Buildings in Ottawa, was counted among the most beautiful halls in North America. It burned down in 1900. The name also was used in Ottawa, Sorel, Que, Toronto, Montreal, and Halifax (see Academy of Music for details on those in Montreal and Quebec). Following the model of London, both Toronto and Montreal erected Crystal Palaces, in 1858 and 1860 respectively. St Patrick's Hall (1867) in Montreal and *Shaftesbury Hall (1872) in Toronto frequently resounded to music. These halls, and many similar ones in other cities, were used not only for music but also for political rallies, balls, plays, lectures, minstrel shows, vaudeville, and, on occasion, even operetta and opera.

Although opera was rare (see Opera performance), the name stood for the ultimate in elegant entertainment, and many opera houses in which opera would never be heard were erected. The name thus was a deliberate euphemism. 'Opera houses' were opened in Ottawa (by 1874), Toronto (1874), Montreal (1875), Kingston (1879), Winnipeg (1883), and Vancouver (1891). Indeed the name was attached to new theatre buildings even in smaller towns, from Nelson, BC (600 seats), to Yarmouth, NS (850 seats), including such remote places as Dawson City, Yukon; Canmore, Alta; and Indian Head, Sask. The 43 Canadian 'opera houses' listed in *Julius Cahn's Official Theatrical Guide 1905–1906* include those in Nanaimo, BC; Portage-la-Prairie, Man; Arnprior, Gananoque, Mount Forest, and Petrolia, Ont; and Charlottetown, PEI. (The book does not list any Quebec province opera houses.) 'Grand' opera houses existed in Barrie, Brockville, Chatham, Collingwood, Hamilton, Kingston, London, Ottawa, Port Hope, St Catharines, and Toronto, Ont, while St Thomas, Ont, had a 'Grand' as well as Dunscombe's New Opera House. The largest ones listed by Cahn – Kingston, London, Stratford, and Toronto, Ont – had between 1500 and 1900 seats.

While most of these late-19th-century opera houses and music halls have been demolished,

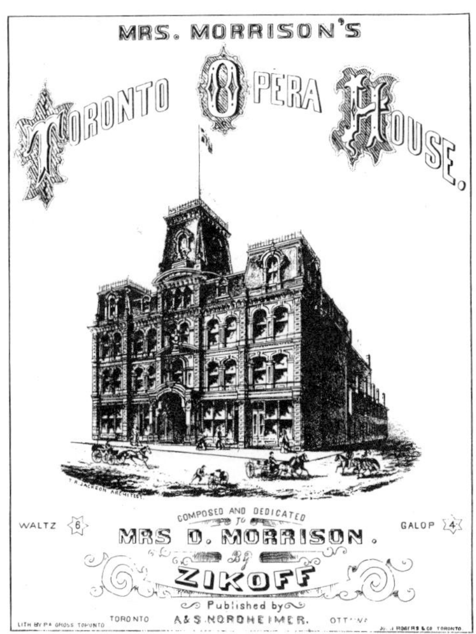

The Toronto Opera House was opened in 1874.

The Opera, National Arts Centre, Ottawa

destroyed by fire, or converted to movie houses (with appropriate name changes), the occasional one has been restored to its old magnificence and given back its name of 'opera house,' eg, the one at Barkerville, BC, in 1958. In Cobourg, Ont, Victoria Hall, with its 300-seat auditorium, had its 1860 elegance returned to it by 1980, and in Petrolia, Ont, another of Canada's several Victoria Halls was restored during the 1970s. Two which have retained their names throughout the decades are the Gravenhurst (Ont) Opera House – its style suggests 1915 – and the *Haskell Opera House.

A new era began with Massey Music Hall (*Massey Hall) opened in Toronto in 1894, built expressly for orchestral and massed choral performances and deliberately unsuited for theatrical fare, though it was used also for rallies and other assemblies. An example of private munificence, Massey Hall for many years remained unique among Canadian auditoriums, the envy of other centres because of its size, suitability, and acoustic properties. (Montreal had a hall built especially for concerts: *Queen's Hall, 1880; but it was much smaller, became a theatre in 1891, and was destroyed by fire in 1899. The same city's *Monument national, however, built 1891–4 and not intended primarily for concerts, became the site of many, and was still standing in 1980.)

Massey Hall unfortunately did not set a pattern. On the contrary, despite the prosperity of the opening years of the 20th century the construction of auditoriums languished. One exception was the *Auditorium de Québec, opened in 1903 and surviving in 1980 as the Capitol Theatre, a movie house. As old forms of entertainment, such as vaudeville, gave way to the movies, many theatres and opera houses that had been homes to orchestras and choirs were converted to movie houses – eg, the *Orpheum in Vancouver, which, built as a vaudeville theatre in 1927, was transformed into a movie palace in the 1930s. (In what may be regarded as a step up the musical ladder, however, the Orpheum was transformed into a concert hall in 1977, as the new home of the *Vancouver SO.) Other halls were torn down – eg, the *Russell Theatre in Ottawa, which was demolished in 1928. For some 50 years – from World War I until the 1960s – many, if not most, concert and opera performances in Canada were given in halls inadequate in seating capacity, stage dimensions, acoustical properties, and rehearsal facilities. Some orchestras performed in movie houses on Sundays when movies were not allowed to be shown (*Ottawa Philharmonic Orchestra in the Capitol Theatre); the *CSM played in the high-school auditorium, *Plateau Hall; and among other more improbable solutions to the problem were the *Metropolitan Opera guest performances in those famous hockey arenas the *Forum of Montreal and the *Maple Leaf Gardens of Toronto, and a recital by Nelson Eddy in Osborne Stadium, Winnipeg. In smaller cities churches, community halls, movie theatres, and high-school auditoriums have been the mainstay of performances in the 20th century. The discouragement to orchestral and operatic performance caused by the lack of proper halls is one of the blots on Canada's musical history. Among the positive events were the opening of a splendid recital hall, *Eaton Auditorium, in Toronto in 1931, and the construction of identical halls in Calgary and Edmonton, the *Alberta Jubilee Auditoriums, opened in 1957. Others erected 1920–60 include *Darke Hall auditorium, Regina (1929), the *Winnipeg Auditorium (1932), the *Queen Elizabeth Theatre, Vancouver (1959), and the *O'Keefe Centre, Toronto (1960).

The relative prosperity of the 1960s and the wave of initiative and civic pride engendered by preparations for Canada's centenary in 1967 are the main reasons for the construction of many fine buildings all across Canada. Many of these embodied a new concept: the performing-arts or cultural centre, a group of connected buildings designed as an architectural unit, with two or more halls, differing in size and varying in function from recital and lecture to concert, theatre, and opera. Such complexes often included museums, art galleries, libraries, planetariums, and restaurants. The most famous examples are Montreal's *Place des Arts (opened 1963, 1967), Charlottetown's *Confederation Centre of the Arts (1964), the *Arts and Culture Centre in St John's, Nfld (1967), the *Manitoba Centennial Concert Hall, Winnipeg (1968), the *Saskatoon Centennial Auditorium (1968), Ottawa's *National Arts Centre (1969), and the *Grand Théâtre de Québec (1971). Other fine concert halls opened in the 1970s include the *Saskatchewan Centre of the Arts in Regina (1970), the *St Lawrence Centre in

Toronto (1970), the concert hall in the Winnipeg Art Gallery (1971), and the *Rebecca Cohn Auditorium (*Dalhousie U Arts Centre) (1971). Elsewhere as well, universities have built halls that are focal points for the musical life of their cities, eg, MacMillan Theatre and Walter Hall at the *U of Toronto, Pollack Hall at *McGill U, *Western Manitoba Centennial Auditorium at *Brandon U, and the Concert Hall at the *U of Victoria. The Centre in the Square in Kitchener, Ont, was inaugurated in the fall of 1980. In 1980 in Toronto construction was under way on a new Massey Hall, scheduled for completion early in 1982.

See also Centennial Hall (London, Ont); Concerts; Ermitage; Grand Theatre (Kingston); Hamilton Place; Hart House; Her (His) Majesty's Theatre; JMC Orford Art Centre; Malkin Bowl; Mechanics' Hall / Salle des artisans; Mechanics' Hall (Toronto); Montreal Arena; Ontario Place Forum; Orchestras; Palais Montcalm; La Poudrière; Rainbow Stage; Royal Alexandra Theatre; St-Denis Theatre; Salle Claude-Champagne; Sohmer Park; Tara Hall; Théâtre de Société; Orpheum Theatre, Theatre under the Stars; Tudor Hall; and Windsor Hall.

EMC articles on individual cities should be consulted for references to concert halls and opera houses. Many universities have concert facilities. These are noted in the *EMC* articles on individual universities (see Universities directory).

See also Boîtes à chansons; Canadian National Exhibition; Coffeehouses; George's Spaghetti House; Jazz; Riverboat.

BIBLIOGRAPHY

Godfrey, H.H. *A Souvenir of Musical Toronto* (Toronto 1897, 1898–9)

Talbot, Hugo. *Musical Halifax* (Halifax 1903–4)

Julius Cahn's Official Theatrical Guide 1905–1906 (New York 1905)

Massicotte, E.-Z. 'Les théâtres et les lieux d'amusements à Montréal pendant le XIXe siècle,' *L'Annuaire théâtral* (Montreal 1908)

LeVasseur, Nazaire. 'Musique et musiciens à Québec,' *La Musique*, vol 1, Sep 1919

Colgate, William. 'Toronto theatres in the 80s,' *Canadian Magazine*, May–Oct 1921

Jewett, A.R. 'Early Halifax theatres,' *Dalhousie R*, Jan 1926

Pierre Key's Music Year Book, annual (New York 1925–1938)

Blakeley, Phyllis R. 'Theatre and music in Halifax, 1787–1901,' *Dalhousie R*, Apr 1949

'The Grand Opera House, 1894–95,' (London, Ont) *Western Ontario Historical Notes*, vol 9, Sep 1951

Harper, J. Russell. 'The Theatre in Saint John, 1789–1817,' *Dalhousie R*, Autumn 1954

Irwin, Mrs D.D. 'Behind the footlights,' (Indian Head Opera House, Sask) *Saskatchewan History*, Winter 1956

Béraud, Jean. *350 ans de théâtre au Canada-français* (Montreal 1958)

George, Graham. 'Three Canadian concert halls,' *CMJ*, vol 4, Winter 1960

Sangwine, Jean. 'Squire Sowden's Opera House,' (Souris, Man) *Beaver*, Spring 1960

'Theatre in Canada: a bibliography,' *Canadian Literature*, Autumn 1962

Johnson, Sydney. 'Montreal's theatres of the past,' program of PDA's opening (Montreal 1963)

Miller, Orlo. 'Old opera houses of Western Ontario,' *OpCan*, May 1964

Karr, Jack. 'The Avon: an old theatre is re-born' [Stratford, Ont], ibid

Edwards, Murray D. *Stage in Our Past: English-speaking Theatre in Eastern Canada from the 1790s to 1914* (Toronto 1968)

Paulette, Claude. 'Les grands théâtres de Québec,' *Culture vivante*, 17, May 1970

Morriss, Frank. 'Theatre has flourished since city was born,' Winnipeg *Tribune*, 31 Jul 1971

The History of Theatre in Saskatoon 1897–1955, 2 vols, index prepared by U of Saskatchewan students (Saskatoon 1973, 1974)

Ward, Tom. *Cowtown: An Album of Early Calgary* (Calgary 1975)

Portman, Jamie. 'Alberta's gutsy theatre in a pioneer setting,' (Canmore, Alta) *PfAC*, Summer 1976

'The ghost theatre of Yonge Street,' (Toronto *Star*) *The City*, 3 Jun 1978

Harris, Marjorie. 'Travels with Maureen,' *The Canadian*, 6 Jan 1979

Becker, Ken. 'New life for a grand old lady,' (Victoria Hall, Cobourg) *Maclean's*, 24 Dec 1979

Amtmann *Music in Canada; Musique au Québec*

Kallmann *History of Music in Canada*

Musical Red Book

HK (GP, PW)

Concertos and concertante music. The 19th-century virtuoso vehicle for soloist and orchestra is represented in Canada by the two violin concertos (1860, 1874) of Frantz *Jehin-Prume, two violin concertos (1891, ?) by von *Kunits, and a cello concerto (1887) by *Lavallée (played first by cello and piano, and the piano part never written down; *Canada artistique*, July 1890). Of these only Jehin-Prume's *Concerto No. 2* was composed in Canada. Émiliano *Renaud's *Concertstück*, performed in Montreal in 1900 and 1903 with the composer as soloist, appears to be the first Canadian piano concerto. Continuing the virtuoso concept into the early 20th century are works by Donald *Heins, Allard de *Ridder, Frederic *Lord, and Rosario *Bourdon (*Poème élégiaque*, cello and orch).

There is a considerable gap in time between this small cluster of titles of works either lost or forgotten and the next period of cultivation of the concerto form. Colin *McPhee's *Piano Concerto No. 2* (1924) was an isolated attempt whose initial performance in Toronto was regarded, because of the work's modernity, as just short of scandalous. But the *Ballade* (1938) for viola and string orchestra by the 20-year-old Godfrey *Ridout and the *Concerto* (1939; earlier title, *Capriccio*) for the unexpected medium of timpani and orchestra by the 26-year-old Violet *Archer were harbingers of a sudden increase of interest in concerto writing. The new impetus in creative life after 1945 was an obvious factor in maintaining this increase, and the expansion of performing outlets, broadcasting, and recording at that time were challenges for which many composers evidently found the concerto an attractive and exuberant response.

The 1940s and 1950s were especially productive of new works. A full chronology would show, for example, performances of 13 new piano concertos between *Willan's (1944) and *Pépin's second (1949). While further works for piano were added in the 1950s, attention seems to have shifted to the violin, with premieres of nine new concertos for the latter instrument between Alexander *Brott's (1950) and Murray *Adaskin's (1956).

The concertante principle – soloist(s) versus ensemble – seems in fact to have had a special attraction for several of the most prominent composers of the generation born 1910–20. One notes major works in the genre by Adaskin (three), Archer (four), *Coulthard (three), *Morawetz (three), and *Pentland (three), and in the work of two other composers the attraction had a deeper hold, resulting in series of works of fundamental importance in their output – *Papineau-Couture's five variously scored *Pièces concertantes*, as well as his two concertos: and *Weinzweig's seven *Divertimentos* for solo wind instruments, as well as his three concertos. These are referred to in more detail below.

The piano concertos of the 1940s revived with gusto the romantic and vehicular concepts of this instrument's traditional literature. The most immediately successful specimen was the *Quebec Concerto* (published in 1948) of André *Mathieu. It was an abridgement of the third work written in this form by a composer then in his mid-teens. It was a stormy and exhibitionistic piece and was introduced with the composer as soloist: comparable cases are the *Alberta Concerto* (1947) by Minuetta *Kessler, *Somers' *First Concerto* (1947), and the two by Pépin (1946 and 1949). The concertos in this group by older and more established composers also adopted the conventional three-movement form and the rhetorical solo style with heavy octave underlining and bravura runs. They tended towards minor rather than major keys: Willan's in C minor and *Champagne's (1948) in D minor. The former is Franckian in its melodic flavour, turning rather stiffly to the major near the end of the finale; the latter shows a few bolder and more dissonant harmonies amid a prevailing Rachmaninoff-like continuity. Exceptional in this flurry of piano showpieces is Maurice *Blackburn's *Concertino* (1948) written for an ensemble of 14 winds only. Despite its subtitle 'en do majeur,' tonality is treated freely; motives are more diatonic than was usual in the predominantly chromatic pieces of the period. The music has a Poulenc-like wit and freshness to which the wind-instrument support gives an appropriate clarity. Perhaps because it, too, has a 'period' character, the composer has withdrawn this work from circulation for performance purposes, although the score and an early recording exist as reminders.

Later piano concertos expand on the 'grand tradition' approach, with somewhat more original compositional ideas and resources. Three in particular may be mentioned – Archer's (1956; called by Kenneth *Winters 'possibly the best concerto by a Canadian' – *Contemporary Canadian Composers*, p 14), Morawetz's (1962), and *Eckhardt-Gramatté's (*Symphony-Concerto*, 1966–7). The latter two were made more widely known through recordings with Anton *Kuerti as soloist. Gerhard *Wuensch's *Piano Concerto* (1971), with chamber orchestra, revives the neoclassic approach with special smoothness. That of Jacques *Hétu (1969) has been played frequently.

The violin concertos of the 1950s represent a stronger, more original, and more professional level of achievement than the previous works for piano, although, like them, they seldom depart from traditional structure. Brott's *Concerto* (alternatively titled *Concertino*) uses a chamber orchestra of classical size. Its frequent scale motion with augmented-second gaps suggests an influence from the string music of composers such as Bloch; its motor rhythms are akin to those of Stravinsky. After a New York performance the US composer Henry Cowell described this work as 'skillfully written, the work of a sophisticated conservative modern' (*Musical Quarterly*, vol 50, January 1954). The *Concertante 1* (1955) of Otto *Joachim, however, sets a quite different course – mildly radical for the time – by its less developmental mode of construction and by its unusual basic timbre, a string orchestra with solo drums as a co-ordinate to the solo violin.

More ambitious pieces of those decades were the *Second Piano Concerto* (1954–6) of Somers and the *Violin Concerto* (1955) of *Kasemets. Both represented attempts to infuse the standard forms with greater depth of expression by means of contrapuntal textures rather than sheer rhetoric and bombast. Both were longer than usual – the Somers 43 minutes, the Kasemets 35. Neither is as completely successful as other works by these two composers, but they remain interesting pointers.

Among later concertante pieces with solo violin may be cited Lothar *Klein's *Paganini Collage* (1967), a novel treatment of themes from the Paganini *Caprices*, and Pépin's *Monade III* (1972). The latter is in three continuous movements but resembles the traditional concerto in few respects. Its first movement is a recitative, begun by the soloist alone, and its third is a dialogue between the soloist and some prerecorded bird-calls. In between is a long movement of driving energy; its many-layered pizzicatos for the orchestral strings are an especially well-developed feature.

Papineau-Couture's *Pièces concertantes* highlight a remarkable concentration on structural experiment in his work of the late 1950s and early 1960s. It is significant that he chose concertante media for this purpose. Each of the five *Pièces* has a different instrumentation, and each focuses on a unique formal idea: retrogradation of a large continuous structure in *No. 1* for piano ('Repliement'), fanning-out of motives in *No. 2* for cello ('Éventails'), constant metamorphosis in *No. 3* for five soloists ('Variations'), and additive rhythmic procedures somewhat à la Messiaen in *No. 4* for oboe ('Additions'). These four pieces all belong to the same year, 1959. *No. 5*, composed in 1963 and subtitled 'Miroirs,' is a study in musical inversions and applies concertante treatment to the full orchestra.

Weinzweig's *Divertimentos*, by contrast, represent a form in which he has shown recurrent interest over a period of 30-odd years involving several style-changes in his work. *No. 1* (1946) for flute and strings and *No. 2* (1948) for oboe and strings are deft, transparent mini-concertos in a three-movement pattern of fast-slow-fast, clear, unpretentious, and engaging in their handling of timbre (for example, the oboist plays against only low strings in the first movement, only upper strings in the second, and full string orchestra in the third). Their suggestions of quirky, jazz-like rhythmic motion (perhaps derived from some of Stravinsky's neoclassic ballet scores) were more fully apparent in *No. 3* (1960) for bassoon and strings, with its references to 'swing' in the tempo directions. *No. 5* (1961), for trumpet and trombone with wind ensemble, is consistent with this style, despite its different background instrumentation. In *No. 4* (1968) for clarinet and strings a more radical view of solo-timbre possibilities results in an abandonment of the three-movement framework in favour of a freer continuity. The tendency toward a wide gamut of timbral effects continues in *No. 6* (1972) for saxophone and strings and *No. 7* (1979) for horn and strings; both are marked by cadenzas of an exploratory rather than merely brilliant sort and by passages in free-form notation – while both occasionally recall the composer's rhythmic trademarks.

An interesting point of comparison between Papineau-Couture and Weinzweig may be made in their piano concertos, written a year apart, in 1965 and 1966 respectively. These works share two traits: an exceptional economy, amounting almost to pointillism, in the solo writing; and a freshness of structural design. Conventional octaves and 'passagework' for the piano are spurned; few chords have more than four notes. Papineau-Couture's work is in one movement, a long rondo-like form which he has called a fantasy. The Weinzweig is in five continuous sections, alternating slow and fast tempi, and – an exception for a piano concerto indeed – it actually ends softly. But a basic difference is to be noted in the rhythmic character of the two pieces. Papineau-Couture's is marked by busy, motoristic passages, while Weinzweig's deliberately evokes jazz, bebop, and swing in its rhythms (as well as in its melodic elements).

These characteristic major works by two leading composers deserve far more performances than they have enjoyed so far. The same may be said, to be sure, for several other Canadian concertos. Few works in the literature, in fact, survive more than an initial two or three concert performances, a fact which discourages performers from devoting time to their preparation.

Several composers have turned their attention to instruments other than the piano and the violin – notably the flute (William *McCauley, *Five Miniatures*, 1958; Norma *Beecroft, *Improvvisazioni concertanti no 1*, 1961); the clarinet (Archer, 1946/56; Robert *Turner, 1948); the bassoon (Eckhardt-Gramatté, 1950; Adaskin, 1960); the horn (McCauley, 1959; *Beckwith, *Concertino*, 1963; Michel *Perrault, 1967); the tuba (Robert *Fleming, 1966); the double bass (Brott, *Profundum praedictum*, 1964, alternatively playable by viola or cello; Allan *Rae, 1977); the mandolin (Morris *Surdin, 1966); and the organ (Pentland, 1949; Gerald *Bales, 1957; Derek *Healey, 1960; and Wuensch, 1979).

The cello, romantic soloist par excellence, has been less cultivated, but major compositions appear in late years from Ernst *Friedlander (1959), Coulthard (*Symphonic Ode*, 1965), Morawetz (*Memorial to Martin Luther King*, 1968), Eckhardt-Gramatté (*Konzertstück*, 1974), André *Prévost (1976), and Donald Steven (*For Madmen Only*, 1978). The harp has drawn characteristic pieces from Somers (*Suite*, 1949), Weinzweig (1967), and Morawetz (1976). Works with solo accordion, nearly all composed for Joseph *Macerollo, include two concertos by Surdin (1966 and 1977) and one work each by George *Fiala (*Sinfonietta concertata*, 1971), Klein (*Invention, Blues, and Chase*, 1975), and Wuensch (*Concerto Grosso*, 1979); all are with string orchestra, the Fiala adding also a harpsichord.

Concertante pieces with multiple soloists are more frequent in the later decades, corresponding perhaps to composers' increased appreciation of timbre and to their greater freedom in instrumental mixtures in chamber music. The concertante principle in fact becomes applied at times to works for a soloist with a small one-to-a-part ensemble (see Chamber music for some examples). Works for two pianos and orchestra have been contributed by Pépin (*Nombres*, 1962), *Matton (1964), and Turner (1971); works for solo string quartet and orchestra by Pierre *Mercure (*Divertimento*, 1957/8), Joachim (*Concertante 2*, 1961), and Prévost (1978); and one for brass quintet and orchestra by Morawetz (1968). In this group, Matton's *Concerto for Two Pianos* has been much played, especially by *Bouchard and Morisset; indeed it may be the most often performed of all Canadian concertos. Double concertos for different instruments are those of Hétu (1962) for violin and piano, and Talivaldis *Kenins (1965) for violin and cello with strings only; the latter's *Sinfonia concertante* (1967, subtitled *Symphony No. 2*) for flute, oboe, and clarinet also may be mentioned. A particularly assured treatment of a complex plan of textures and contrasts is found in Robert *Aitken's *Concerto for Twelve Soloists and Orchestra* (1968), essentially a 'concerto for orchestra' with a fixed, rather than flexible, solo component.

There are several Canadian examples of the 'popular' concerto – ie, either a / one which strives deliberately for a familiar style, in romantic or folk-like vein, or b / one which applies the principle by juxtaposing the sounds of popular music and those of symphonic music. Sometimes thought of as a new phenomenon, in reality it dates in Canada from Quentin *Maclean's *Concerto Grosso in Popular Style* (1942), subtitled *Electric Concerto*, a work calling for electronic organ, electric guitar, solovox, and theremin, among other instruments, and reflecting the composer's experience as a theatre and broadcast organist. The concerto-grosso format is adopted again in Norman *Symonds' 1958 work of that name for jazz quintet and symphony orchestra. A companion-piece is his *Democratic Concerto* (1967) for the same combination. Steven *Gellman's *Odyssey* (1971) co-ordinates a rock group and a solo piano with the symphony orchestra and uses free improvisation in the rock idiom in some sections, culminating in a vocal refrain. Similar influences are seen in François *Dompierre's *Piano Concerto* (1978) and Paul *Hoffert's *Violin Concerto* (1979), both composed specifically for discs, recorded by sophisticated new techniques. Popular in a different sense are the folk-derived works *Steelhenge* (1974) by Eldon *Rathburn, for steel band and orchestra; the *Piano Concerto* (1979) by Ben *McPeek, based on Canadian folksong material; and André *Gagnon's *Petit Concerto pour Carignan* (1976), with its juxtaposition of fiddling and baroque style. Serious in a different sense are Gagnon's four piano concertos *Mes Quatre Saisons* (late 1960s) which reconceive pop tunes by leading chansonniers in terms of the Vivaldian namesake.

Bearing in mind the original early-baroque application of the term 'concerto' to works for solo *voice* with instrumental ensemble, brief mention is made of a few Canadian concert works for voice and orchestra. A strong streak of what the German critic H.H. Stuckenschmidt calls 'music of commitment' is found in this category – a significant number of composers choosing texts which express firm religious, ethical, or political views. Examples are Ridout's three *Cantiones mysticae* (1953, 1962, and 1972), Somers' *Five Songs for Dark Voice* (1956), Weinzweig's *Wine of Peace* (1957), R. Murray *Schafer's *Protest and Incarceration* (1960), Morawetz's *From the Diary of Anne Frank* (1970), and Pentland's *News* (1970). More purely lyrical in outlook are Brott's *Songs of Contemplation* (1945, with string orchestra only), Fleming's *Our Mind Was the Singer* (1972), and two pieces by Coulthard, *Night Wind* (1951) and *Spring Rhapsody* (1958). Klein's *The Philosopher in the Kitchen* (1974) is a whimsical combination of classical music and classical gastronomy. Textural experiment occurs in Bruce *Mather's *Au Château de Pompairain* (1976), with its phonetic text, and in Schafer's *Arcana* (1972) with its text from middle Egyptian hieroglyphs.

Schafer's works for voice and orchestra constitute a sizeable portion of his repertoire and cover a variety of types. One may add as further examples the dramatic solo cantata *Brébeuf* (1961) on texts from the *Jesuit Relations* and *Adieu Robert Schumann* (1976) on texts from the diaries of Clara Schumann dealing with Schumann's last illness. The former contains an imaginative orchestral depiction of the Canadian north woods (the insects, the ice breaking up on the lakes, and so on), while the latter is bound together with numerous fragmentary quotations from the piano music and songs of Schumann, a composer for whom Schafer has felt a close sympathy.

In 1965 the *Montreal International Competition began commissioning short works for soloist and orchestra to be performed by its finalists. François *Morel, Papineau-Couture, Pentland, Prévost, and Jean *Vallerand are among the composers who have responded. In this way, the competition has provided an incentive for additions to the concerto and concertante repertoire.

BIBLIOGRAPHY

Papineau-Couture, Jean. *Analysis of 'Pièce Concertante No. 1 for Piano and String Orchestra' (Repliement) / Notes sur la Pièce concertante No. 1'*, CMCentre Study Course No. 1 (Toronto 1961); French text reprt in *Musicien éducateur du Québec*, vol 5, no. 1 1974

Somers, Harry. *Analysis of 'Suite for Harp and Chamber Orchestra'*, CMCentre Study Course No. 1 (Toronto 1961)

Owen, Stephanie O. 'The piano concerto in Canada since 1955,' unpubl PH D thesis, U of Washington 1969

Webb, D.J. 'Serial techniques in John Jacob Weinzweig's five divertimentos and three concertos,' unpubl PH D thesis, U of Rochester 1973

CMCentre. *Catalogue of Canadian Music for Orchestra* (Toronto 1976, suppl 1979) JB

Concerts. Performances given by one or more artists before audiences which have assembled, and usually paid admission fees, primarily for the purpose of hearing and contemplating music as music, distinct from music performed as an adjunct to other activities such as worship, ceremony, dining, or theatre. See also Bands; Broadcasting; Centennial celebrations; Children's concerts; Choral singing; Concert halls and opera houses; Conductors and conducting; Criticism; CRTC; Electronic music; Expo 67; Festivals; Mixed media; Opera performance; Oratorio performance; Oratorios, Canadian; Orchestras; Profession of music; Sängerfeste; Women's musical clubs; Youth orchestras. See also *EMC* articles on individual cities.

This article will study some of the social, economic, and organizational aspects of the concert as an institution and as a vehicle for the diffusion of musical literature: who brings concerts about, how they have been financed, who participates, the changing tastes of performers and public, the introduction of the music of the great foreign composers, and the emergence of Canadian compositions on concert programs. In the absence of a comprehensive book on the subject, this article will attempt to marshall available data but does not claim completeness.

1 1534–1799
2 1800–99
3 1900–14
4 1914–50
5 1950–80
6 Programming of Canadian music

1 1534–1799

New France. European music was used first in Canada by the French explorers under Jacques Cartier in 1534 in religious services and ceremonial meetings with the native people, and as early as 1606 as an adjunct to masques or plays; but no evidence has been found of formal, organized concerts prior to the late 18th century. This is hardly surprising, for even in contemporary Europe music was an aristocratic entertainment or a domestic diversion, and public concerts were rare. Moreover, the colonies were remote from the great centres, their population small and widely scattered. Much spontaneous music-making no doubt filled the hours of work, travel, and leisure, but education was needed to produce the skilled performers and receptive listeners who would justify and demand formal concerts. A severe lack of instruments also hampered early attempts: it is reported that only one piano existed in Quebec City as late as 1783.

There are some early references to 'concerts,' but it is likely that the term meant simply 'playing together' or 'consorts.' For instance, *Jesuit Relations* (vol 47, Feb 1662, p 275) mentions: 'This month commenced the concerts of four viols, first at the ceremony of the first prizes, then at the 40 hours' devotion; the rest was just as it was last year.' Religious music probably was performed outside the church services – the Indians apparently found it entrancing – on informal occasions or as part of some ceremony; some volumes of French music (eg, Campra motets) in early-18th-century editions surviving in Quebec libraries have led some scholars to believe that such music was performed in a secular setting. Another mention of 'concerts' concerns Jacques Raudot, who was intendant of New France 1705–11. Mother Juchereau de Saint-Ignace, in *Histoire de l'Hôtel-Dieu de Québec* (Montauban 1751, p 463) says, 'His entertainment was a mixed concert of voices and instruments. He was so obliging, he was resolved we should hear this symphony, and several times he sent his musicians to sing motets in our church.' Elisabeth Bégon, the widow of another intendant, whose correspondence from Montreal 1748–50 refers to many dances, balls, masquerades, and other entertainments, never mentions a concert. However, in a letter of 7 Nov 1757 to the Chevalier de Lévis, the Marquis de Montcalm states: 'We are going to have some concerts. Of all the pleasures of Quebec, I like best chatting with M. le chevalier de Lévis ... There is good company here, and more to do of an evening than in Montreal.' On 16 Dec 1757 Montcalm wrote, 'On Sunday there is to be a huge supper for 80, many ladies, a concert, lansquenet [a card game] with nine cutters ... ' (*Journal du Marquis de Montcalm*, ed H.R. Casgrain, Quebec 1895). These were, of course, the entertainments of the nobility and upper classes, not concerts in the modern sense.

FIRST CONCERT.

TUESDAY EVENING, 26th JANUARY, 1886.

Programme.

1. QUARTETTE, Op. 12 . . . . *Mendelssohn*
Adagio non troppo—Allegro Canzonetta.
Andante espressivo: Finale L'istesso tempo.
Ottawa String Quartette Club.

2. SONG . . . "Should He Upbraid" . *Sir Henry Bishop*
Miss Clara Code.

3. PIANO SOLO . "Phantaisie in C" . . *Schumann*
(a) Durchaus phantastisch und leidenschaftlich vorzutragen.
(b) Massig-Durchaus energisch.
Miss Annie Lampman.

4. QUARTETTE, Op. 17, "The Mill" . . . . *Raff*
Ottawa String Quartette Club.

5. VIOLIN SOLO . "Zigeunerweisen" . . *Sarasate*
Mr. F. Boucher.

6. SONG . . . "Sans Adieu" . . *Blumenthal*
Miss Clara Code.

7. QUARTETTE, Op. 18, No. 2 . . . . . . *Beethoven*
Allegro—Adagio Cantabile—Scherzo.
Allegro Molto quasi presto.
Ottawa String Quartette Club.

A program of the Ottawa String Quartette Club, 1886

The English regime. After 1759 a new element, the British regimental band, augmented the existing elements of spontaneous folk music and church music. Until Canada's Confederation (1867) British home regiments served in rotation, bringing with them their bands, which included some of the best instrumentalists in Britain. The French had had military musicians as well, of course, but the British bands brought with them a tradition of music-making which exercised an influence far beyond the military sphere. Bands assisted at theatrical performances or provided players for the orchestras in the few concerts that were given; gala balls were popular and frequent in garrison towns such as Halifax, Quebec, Montreal, and Niagara during the long winters, and Saturday morning promenade concerts were given by bands in many towns. Moreover, the military officers often were proficient in music and, as time hung heavy during peacetime in the colonies, they frequently would take part in musical activities, or would engage the bands to play for their guests at social affairs. Upon retiring from military service, some of the bandsmen and bandmasters (many of whom were German) settled in Canada, where they later wielded considerable influence as teachers and performers.

Quebec City appears to have been the cradle of concert life in Canada. The Quebec *Gazette* of 29 Nov 1764 carried an advertisement for a dance being held at the Concert Hall, and that of 14 Feb 1765 announced a concert there 16 February for the benefit of Sieur Dienval, M.M. (probably maître de musique) (Amtmann p 204). A 1770 notice announced that the Gentlemen's Subscription Concerts henceforth would begin at six o'clock. The other garrison towns enjoyed the benefits of the bands' efforts also: in April of 1769 an oratorio was performed at St Paul's Church in Halifax by the 'Philharmonic Society' assisted by officers of the army and navy. (That society is the first noted in Canada; a hundred years later there were to be Philharmonic Societies, ie, choirs with available instruments, in almost every city and town.) Elizabeth Simcoe, the wife of the first lieutenant-governor of Upper Canada, recorded in her diary in November 1791 that she had attended a Halifax subscription concert by the band of the Seventh Fusiliers, and five years later in Toronto she wrote about concerts given by the regimental band in that city. In Montreal in 1792 the band of the 60th Regiment played 'generally for a couple of hours' on summer evenings, for the delectation of the public promenading on the Parade. Such events provided an impetus to the cultivation of secular art music for which the military officers' patronage was largely responsible.

The musical content of these concerts was variable, to say the least; anything from the latest popular songs to symphonic excerpts might be heard. A concert in Quebec, 21 Feb 1792, was presented in two parts with 13 separate numbers and offered music by Gluck and Grétry for 'orchestra,' arias with harp and guitar accompaniment, a concerto for hunting horn, a clarinet-bassoon duet, and other items. In Halifax in 1783 a certain Mrs Mechtler gave a concert which included some arias sung by herself, a harpsichord concerto played by the local bandmaster, and an overture (played by his band) which probably was by Johann Christian Bach. But from these relatively informal concerts, often given in taverns, coffee houses, or church halls, grew the first subscription series, such as the 24 Monday-evening performances given in Quebec during the winter of 1790–1, and with continuity came the possibility of improved quality. Indeed, the musical content of many of the concerts ca 1790–1815 reflects a remarkably sophisticated taste. The programs included symphonies, overtures, and concertos by leading European composers of the time such as Haydn, Mozart, Pleyel (by far the most frequently performed composer in Quebec City), J.C. Bach, Gluck, Grétry, Gyrowetz, and Jean-Baptiste Davaux, and much of the music was quite new: Mozart's *String Quintets*, K515 in C and K516 in G minor were played in Quebec in 1793, six years after their composition.

2 1800–99. The early years of the 19th century were plagued with the same problems encountered in the previous period: inadequate halls, inability to assemble a complement of instruments, and financial hardships. Much of the musical activity depended on the efforts of a few tireless and devoted individuals; a society revolved around its leader and often dissolved when he left. (The Toronto musician John *Carter was described by the *Globe* in an 1866 performance of *La Sonnambula* as 'pianist, director, conductor, chorus leader and prompter.') Nevertheless, it was through the societies that music grew in Canada during the early decades. After the relative sophistication of the 1790s, however, taste seemed to slip back to the popular and banal. Mélanges of sacred and secular music, usually described as 'Grand Concert of Vocal and Instrumental Music' persisted from about 1820 to 1870, and later than that in small centres. Public taste of the time accepted the overture to *The Marriage of Figaro* on the same program as a song entitled 'I Would I Were a Fairy'; at a To-

ronto Choral Society concert on 23 Oct 1845 Beethoven's *Prometheus Overture* was reported as giving 'general satisfaction' while Topliffe's song 'Consider the Lilies' was encored. Vocal novelties and instrumental stunts played an important part in the lighter Promenade concerts (as, indeed, they did in concerts in Europe and the Americas during this period), and it is doubtful that the original instrumentation was used in the overtures and symphonic movements that were played.

Kallmann (*History of Music*, p 107–8) has summarized this period: 'Concerts, other than oratorio and opera performances, were not yet specialized into the choral, orchestral, chamber, and solo types that we know today. The majority of musical organizations were choirs; instrumentalists were assembled hurriedly for each concert. Most concerts, in fact, displayed all the musical talent that happened to be available at the moment. A typical concert might feature an augmented church choir, an orchestra of from 15 to 50 players built around the core of a local brass band, the local music teacher performing first on the violin then on the cornet, a talented lady amateur and her daughter attempting an operatic duet, and on rare occasions a famous guest artist. Good performers were scarce and everybody who was willing to face an audience was welcome to have a try. At many concerts amateurs alternated with professionals, making for a very uneven quality of performance.'

Only in the 1860s and 1870s did the musical societies emerge as regular institutions with any kind of stability and continuity, eg, the *Mendelssohn Choir of Montreal (1864–94), the *Toronto Philharmonic Society (1872–94), the *Montreal Philharmonic Society (1875–99), and the *Orpheus Club (1882–1917) of Halifax. During the period of growth, each element of the process enriched the others and in turn was enriched by them: local societies took the lead in musical evangelism, which whetted the appetite of the public for music, resulting in more concerts which, reciprocally, could create an attractive working environment and thus encourage professional musicians to emigrate to Canada, and guest performers would set new standards for local musicians to strive for.

Some of the musical societies were very exclusive, selling no tickets at the door and being supported entirely by the subscriptions of their members; an example is the Philharmonic Society which existed 1845–7 in Toronto. Some other organizations, like the Germania Singverein that flourished in Victoria in 1861, were popular groups (some grew out of sporting clubs) that placed as much emphasis on eating, drinking, marching, and socializing as they did on music. Although most of the societies were primarily choral organizations, several did attempt to create and maintain permanent instrumental ensembles. From Halifax to Victoria such societies made possible the performance of large-scale choral works, sometimes with impressively massive forces. A sacred-music program in Quebec, 26 Jun 1834, involved more than 100 singers and 60 instrumental musicians; Toronto's Metropolitan Choir could boast of 308 singers, 31 instrumentalists, and 150 subscribing members by 1858. Such ventures could be risky; if things went awry a conductor or impresario could lose his life savings on one concert, and there were no arts-support agencies to soften the financial blow.

While the societies continued to carry music to an ever-widening public, another element was being introduced: the indigenous militia or civilian bands which were the main source of entertainment in the summer, and which took over the public role of the British regimental bands after Confederation. However, though both the choral societies and the bands were obliged to recruit additional performers from nearby communities in Canada (or the USA) for special performances, there was no national cohesion to musical activities and little exchange between major centres many hundreds of kilometers apart. Exceptions were Sängerfeste and band tournaments in the late decades of the century; but this kind of activity did not extend to the choral societies. Halifax and Montreal and Toronto had their own musical leaders and stars, who generally were little known in the other centres.

Concerts often served purposes other than musical ones. Band performances were excellent for stirring patriotic fervour or political partisanship and concerts often were held to raise funds for charity, as in Toronto in 1852 for the benefit of black fugitives from the USA, and in 1855 for victims of the Crimean War.

By the middle of the century populations had grown to a size that made concerts by international musical celebrities economically feasible, while railways and steamships made Canadian cities increasingly accessible. In both respects, Canadians benefited from their proximity to the larger population centres of the USA. Visits by such troupes as Hermann and Co of Munich, which in the 1830s gave concerts in the Maritimes, were well received and well attended, while a solo artist of the stature of Jenny Lind could draw 1000 people to a Toronto performance at *St Lawrence Hall in 1851 and command press attention for weeks. By the 1850s visits by such celebrities had become fairly frequent in eastern Canada: the violinists Ole Bull and Henri Vieuxtemps, the pianist Sigismund Thalberg, the singers Henriette Sontag and Adelina Patti, and the Germanians Orchestra. While this development no doubt tended to raise standards of taste to some extent, the musical literature of the programs remained variable, and an entire evening of one type of music (vocal, piano, chamber, or orchestral) was almost unknown. Jenny Lind's 1851 farewell concert in Toronto, for example, included not only her arias and songs but also solo offerings by a pianist, a violinist, and a clarinetist. Some historians have claimed that the true solo recital did not come until around 1900, when it was cultivated by the pianist Émiliano *Renaud; however, as early as 1865 in Montreal a pianist, writer, and composer named James Pech presented lecture-recitals of his works and those of Bach, Chopin, Mendelssohn, and Doehler, while another exponent of the lecture-recital, Waugh *Lauder, by 1889 had given about 300 such recitals in Ontario alone. Johanna van Beethoven, wife of the grandnephew of Ludwig, gave a piano recital in Montreal in 1872.

Musical life had gained a good deal of stability and confidence after the middle of the century. Choirs and orchestras were strong enough to perform entire oratorios and symphonies, and concerts generally became more ambitious. Reportedly, by 1860 in Canada there had been performances of the overtures to *The Marriage of Figaro, La Clemenza di Tito, The Magic Flute, The Creatures of Prometheus, A Midsummer Night's Dream, William Tell, An Italian Girl in Algiers*, and *Semiramide*; Haydn's *Surprise* and *Toy* symphonies, Mozart's *Symphony No. 40*, and Beethoven's *First* or *Second Symphony*. Many concerts contained music of Mozart, Haydn, Beethoven, and Handel; excerpts from the operas of Bellini, Donizetti, and Rossini were popular, and so were the works of Mendelssohn and Weber. Chopin, Schumann, Liszt, and Berlioz as yet were little known. Sonatas and string quartets were played rarely, though Beethoven's 'Moonlight' and 'Pathetique' sonatas may have had some vogue. Bach was heard almost never except when played on the organ by such high-minded church musicians as R.-O. *Pelletier and F.H. *Torrington. (See Organ playing and teaching.) Operatic medleys and light overtures were more usual in the repertoires of other organists. The main emphasis still was on choral music; oratorios and cantatas became so pervasive that a Montreal music critic of 1866 uttered a cry of joy when a sacred-music concert for once presented something other than *Messiah* or *The Creation*. Chamber music may have had a place in the private homes of some Canadians, but there is little record of public activity in that sphere (though, of course, the hodge-podge 'orchestral' concerts often included works for small forces). There were notable exceptions to the foregoing generalization. The *Septuor Haydn, an ensemble comprising string quintet, flute, and piano, was founded in Quebec City in 1871 and lasted 30 years, giving hundreds of concerts throughout the province. The *Toronto String Quartette presented 12 bi-weekly concerts in the 1885–6 season (one concert drawing 1300 listeners) and its programs included several whole (not excerpted) works of Mozart, Haydn, and Beethoven. The violinist Frantz *Jehin-Prume, his singer-wife, Rosita *del Vecchio, and the pianist-composer Calixa *Lavallée gave recitals in Canada and the USA. In 1871 Jehin-Prume organized a series of six classical concerts, and in 1891 he founded the Assn artistique de Montréal, an ensemble of four strings and piano which presented 30 concerts in the following five years.

The last decades of the 19th century were characterized by performances on the grand scale, reflecting a world-wide worship of bigness in musical and other endeavours. These were presaged by a concert held in Montreal 24 Aug 1860 to celebrate the opening of the Victoria Bridge by the Prince of Wales. R.J. Fowler conducted the 400 voices of the Montreal Musical Union, with an orchestra and the soloists Adelina Patti and Emma *Albani, before an audience of 6000. The main work was a specially written cantata by C.W. *Sabatier. At a great festival in Quebec City in October 1883 several bands combined to form a huge orchestra, with choirs and soloists, the whole massive enterprise organized by Arthur *Lavigne. Toronto's Philharmonic Society (1872–99), not to be outdone, in 1886 created an enormous ensemble for a series of four performances by 1000 adult choristers, 1200 children's voices, an orchestra of 100, and visiting soloists (one of whom, Lilli Lehmann, described the whole affair as 'extremely ludicrous'). Other mammoth music festivals were held in Hamilton, Ont, in 1887 and at the opening of Toronto's *Massey Hall in 1894. Though these spectacles may have been somewhat gross musically, the public enthusiasm generated by them no doubt supported many musical developments in succeeding years. As a result, it became the practice of some choirs to import leading orchestras from New York or Boston to accompany them.

3 1900–14. The 1900s ushered in a vital new era of concert life in Canada. Larger numbers of people than before had the leisure time to pursue musical activities and the money to support them, and the pioneer work of earlier decades began to bear fruit in wide public awareness of music. Because radio had not arrived and the phonograph was in its infancy, music was less a spectator's recreation than an active amateur's or professional's, and a much larger proportion of the population took part in music than was the case later. Increasing numbers

of European musicians arrived to find employment with Canadian musical organizations, and visits by international celebrities no longer were unusual. These developments brought about major changes in musical life. The old amateur-based musical societies were replaced by two kinds of groups: amateur choirs and associations whose purpose was to create and support professional ensembles. The Musicians' Union began to exert its influence, and, to serve as the 'broker' between the public and the artists, a concert-management and impresario function began to develop. The Toronto Philharmonic Society disbanded in 1894, the Montreal Philharmonic Society in 1899, and the Septuor Haydn of Quebec in 1903. All were supplanted by new organizations: the *Toronto Mendelssohn Choir and the *Couture MSO in 1894; an orchestra at the *TCM in 1906 organized by Frank *Welsman; another in Montreal under the aegis of J.-J. *Goulet in 1898; and the Société symphonique de Québec in 1903 (*Quebec SO).

While the orchestral organizations were building their professional skills the amateur choral groups were in their heyday. Towns as small as Lethbridge, Alta, St-Hyacinthe, Que, Truro, NS, and Sherbrooke, Que, had their own choral societies, while in the major centres the taste for bigness remained. The Mendelssohn Choir was only one of five large choirs in Toronto by 1910 (besides great numbers of church choirs) and a choirmaster named Herbert M. Fletcher had three choirs whose combined membership reached about 1000.

The impresario-management activities were carried out both by professionals and by talented amateurs. Among the latter were the *women's musicals clubs, which undertook to arrange concerts by visiting artists and occasionally by Canadian performers. Such clubs existed in a great many cities (and some continued to flourish in 1980). Their sustained activity perhaps was the most important element in the presentation of concerts in Canada in the 20th century. The work of individual impresarios, managers, promoters, and organizations must not be deprecated, however. Concerts were arranged, prior to 1914, by Charles A.E. *Harriss in Ottawa and Montreal; Louis-Honoré *Bourdon in Montreal; Arthur Lavigne and J.-A. Gauvin in Quebec City; the *Hambourgs, M.L. Solman (manager of the Mutual St Arena), the TCM, and Norman Withrow (manager of Massey Hall) in Toronto; and George J. *Dyke and his brother Fred in British Columbia.

The massive concert festival continued to be popular during the first years of the 20th century, one of the most notable events being a country-wide series of concerts arranged by the aforementioned Charles A.E. Harriss. In 1903 Harriss invited the Scottish conductor Sir Alexander Mackenzie to conduct the *Cycle of Musical Festivals, emphasizing British music, in 18 cities during five weeks. The *Winnipeg Oratorio Society began its Western Canada Musical Festival in 1908 and gave an annual series of six concerts with the Minneapolis SO, besides presenting many artists of international reputation. Some chamber-music ensembles also gave concerts: the *Dubois String Quartet in Montreal (1910), the *Toronto String Quartet (1907), the *Academy String quartet (1912) and the *Hambourg Trio in Toronto. Their programs, however, were restricted in the main to movements from quartets and arrangements of familiar songs and to performances by guest soloists.

4 1914–50. With the outbreak of World War I the male sections of many choirs were depleted and many orchestras reduced as the men went into the armed forces, while funds were diverted to wartime purposes. Recovery took a long time, and in some cities it was 1930 (when cinema orchestras became unnecessary with the introduction of sound movies) before concert orchestras were revived to provide employment for musicians. In the 1920s there was a shift in taste from vocal to instrumental music, and, at least in the cities, concerts had become standardized into specific categories: choral concert, orchestral concert, chamber concert, solo recital, and so on, with few mixtures of genre. An exception was the *CPR Festivals, a series presented across the country from 1927 to 1931. In these, singers and chamber ensembles combined in presenting folk-song arrangements and other music.

Though leading international artists toured regularly, and Montreal, Toronto, Winnipeg, and Vancouver had competent orchestras, serious music still was offered in fairly small doses. A Fritz Kreisler or Mischa Elman recital of the 1920s probably would consist of one classical sonata and a number of trifles; and the main orchestras had to educate their audiences to Bach and Brahms as much as to Sibelius and Debussy (although radio broadcasts from the USA usually offered a wider repertoire). Avant-garde music rarely was performed, and 'modern' usually implied Richard Strauss, Delius, Sibelius, Ravel, or even Elgar, rather than Stravinsky, Schoenberg, Hindemith, or Bartók.

Gradually, repertoires and audience tastes developed in historical depth. Sir Ernest *MacMillan pioneered in presenting the music of Bach and in 1937 invited Stravinsky to conduct the *TSO; a Beethoven quartet cycle was done in Toronto in 1927, and the TSO's Sunday afternoon one-hour broadcasts were initiated that same year; Healey *Willan, the Halifax Madrigal Society (founded 1923), and others cultivated interest in renaissance music; the guitar and harpsichord were rediscovered; Mozart, Schubert, and other composers who earlier had been represented by a handful of works now were explored more fully. Important in this process of discovery were recordings and broadcasts, both by privately owned radio stations and, from 1936 onwards, by the CBC. Radio took performances by major ensembles even to small towns, while Canadian performers' broadcasts made their names known to potential concert audiences. The restrictions imposed by the economic Depression of the 1930s imposed a handicap. Nevertheless the period is remembered as one when groups like the *Hart House String Quartet (Toronto), the *Winnipeg Philharmonic Choir, the *Schubert Choir of Brantford, and the *Canadian Grenadier Guards Band (Montreal) achieved exceptionally high standards of performance. Impresarios active in this period were the *Tremblays of Ottawa; Dorothy Parnum, Catharine Whetham, *Hart House at the U of Toronto, and later Walter *Homburger, in Toronto; Edouard Blouin, Samuel *Gesser, and Nicolas *Koudriavtzeff in Montreal; the *Men's Music Club and Fred M. *Gee in Winnipeg, the Prairies, and western Ontario; the *Musical Art Club in Saskatoon; the *Chautauqua organization in the mid-west; and Lily Laverock, the *Philharmonic Music Club, Gordon *Hilker, and (later) George *Zukerman (*Overture Concerts) and J.J. *Johannesen (*Festival Concert Society) in British Columbia. Another element was the *Community Concerts system (a division of Columbia Artists Management, Inc., USA) founded in Chicago in 1920 and introduced to Canada in 1930. After World War II Canadian universities began to play an important part in concert activity. The *JMC also began in 1949 to develop its country-wide network of centres, presenting young artists from Canada and abroad. The rise of these impresarios ensured that important foreign artists appeared with reasonable regularity on Canadian concert stages.

5 1950–80. Most musical organizations were more firmly founded at the time of World War II than they had been when World War I unseated them so summarily, and consequently most of the orchestras and other ensembles were able to continue throughout the war or resume operations shortly after hostilities ceased. There were some changes on the horizon, though. In the 1950s and 1960s there was a gradual loosening of the tight categorization of concert types which had prevailed from the 1920s onwards. Perhaps these new varieties of event were a response to the threat posed to traditional concerts by the increase of broadcasts and recordings. In any case, widely differing types of music were to be found bundled together, in such summer festivals as those at Stratford, Montreal, Vancouver, and Niagara-on-the-Lake and in the concerts organized by CBC Radio (see Broadcasting) in cities all across the country. A conscious effort to shake up traditional concert formats and program-content was made by Montreal's *Musica Antica e Nuova in the 1950s and Toronto's *Ten Centuries Concerts in the 1960s, the latter mixing all kinds of music from plainchant to jazz. In attempts to enlarge the popular base of support for serious music, some orchestras and other ensembles gave concerts in shopping plazas and factories, arranged concerts combined with wine-and-cheese parties, co-operated closely with schools and universities in presenting music to young people, and employed various 'gimmicks' to make the classics more approachable for the musically uneducated potential concert-goer. Smaller specialized audiences were served by organizations such as *NOVA MUSIC in Halifax, *SMCQ in Montreal, *NMC in Toronto, and the *Vancouver New Music Society, as well as by other historically oriented or experimental groups. (In the latter category were the Isaacs Gallery concerts in Toronto, organized by Udo *Kasemets.) Some observers, notably the pianist Glenn *Gould, prophesied the demise of the live concert in the face of the competition provided by the electronic media, but that gloomy prospect was averted. Indeed, the concert season, extended by several summer festivals, became year-round.

During the 1970s Canada's numerous orchestras – full-time, chamber, radio, community, and school – perhaps were the country's most active and continuous purveyors of concerts, live and broadcast, in main series and supplementary series, in schools, at festivals, and on tour. By 1980 the three busiest orchestras – the *MSO, the *TS, and the *Vancouver SO – each were giving more than 130 concerts a year.

In 1969 the *Canada Council established the *National Concert Bureau, under the direction of Edith Binnie at the U of Toronto, in an effort to begin meeting the need for representation felt by Canadian performing artists in the absence in Canada of agencies like Columbia Artists and Sol Hurok in the USA. The bureau's modest initial undertaking was the promotion and management of six young solo artists and the *Orford String Quartet. It continued until its function was absorbed by the National Touring Office, established by the Canada Council in 1973. Prior to this, in 1970, the *OAC had initiated its Concerts and Artists Program (see James Norcop), which in January of 1971 distributed to musical employers its first catalogue of Ontario solo performers. The response, particularly from orchestra conductors, led to a series of auditions in Toronto of specific performers whom conductors had asked to hear. After a similar series of opera auditions early in 1972 the OAC's first large-scale bringing together of employers and performers from all parts of Canada took place that same year in Toronto under the name Contact 72. Its success led to its annual repetition (and development) in Ontario.

In 1974 the OAC (whose Concerts and Artists program had been transformed into its Ontour Dept) and the Canada Council Touring Office – the latter by then in its second year – encouraged the arts agencies of the other provinces to establish similar audition systems, and one by one they did: Pacific Contact in British Columbia was followed by Contact East in the Atlantic provinces; then came Alberta Showcase, Contact Québec, and similar events on alternating years in Saskatchewan (first in 1978) and Manitoba (first in 1979). The effect of these programs was to heighten concert-giving organizations' awareness of the remarkable amount of Canadian talent available to them, and in fact to cause a major turnabout in the proportions of Canadian and foreign artists appearing on Canadian concert platforms.

For this and other reasons, Canadians in the 1970s were acquainted increasingly with their nation's performers, including chamber groups, which enjoyed a particular surge in popularity. Groups like *Camerata, *Canadian Brass, the Dalart Trio, *One Third Ninth, the Orford String Quartet, and *Quartet Canada became familiar to a wide public. Individuals and organizations continued in the 1970s to promote such chamber-music series as those of the Vancouver East Cultural Centre, the *Vancouver Society for Early Music, and the Northstars series (Toronto) of Anton *Kuerti.

Live performances undoubtedly received their greatest single stimulus through the 1967 centennial celebrations, during which the federal government contributed about $91 million for activities of all kinds in cities and towns from coast to coast. In the wake of that boom, however, arts funding became less plentiful, and financial problems continued to plague performing groups and creative artists. The Canada Council, the provincial arts agencies (notably those in Ontario, Quebec, Alberta, and Saskatchewan), and municipal funding bodies like those of Montreal and Toronto have helped the situtation; but private and corporate assistance to the arts remained minimal in the 1970s, despite organized efforts to stimulate it. The performing repertoire, meanwhile, became entirely cosmopolitan. Few countries have displayed so little prejudice as Canada in the presentation of and reception of music and performers from all parts of the world. This tolerant attitude has been decried by nationalists, who would wish to see greater enthusiasm for the performance by Canadians of works by Canadians.

6 PROGRAMMING OF CANADIAN MUSIC. Little is known about Canadian music performed in the 19th century, though programs show that many bandmasters conducted their own marches, and solo performers often played small-scale pieces of their own composition. *EMC*'s entry on *Cantatas lists a fair number of performances from about 1860 onwards (and even two in the 18th century). The first all-Canadian concert of record, in Toronto in 1889, was devoted to the works of the teacher and composer W.O. *Forsyth (1859–1937). The first opportunity to hear the works of an entire group of Canadian composers was in October 1903 in Montreal, when a concert of music by 10 Montreal composers was presented. Concerts devoted to the works of one Canadian composer, or of several, were held every few years throughout the first three quarters of the 20th century. Highlights included a CNR network radio program by the All-Canada Symphony in April 1930, a Lavallée concert in Montreal in July 1933, a BBC broadcast of Canadian works in 1935, and concerts in New York in 1942 and 1953, in Prague in 1946, and in Paris in 1956. The vogue for all-Canadian concerts reached its height in the 1950s and early 1960s under the influence of the *CLComp, whose first offering was a *Weinzweig concert in 1951. By the 1970s Canadian music had become a familiar component of concert fare, integrated into programs as a matter of course. The need to emphasize it as something unique and separate seemed to have lessened. However, many Canadian composers would reject the suggestion that there is room for complacency in promoting their efforts, and their continuing concern was demonstrated by the major concerts organized in Paris and London in 1977 under the name *Musicanada and those in France and Germany in the same year under the name Rendezvous with Canada.

GENERAL BIBLIOGRAPHY

The Canadian Courier, issue devoted to music in Canada, 12 Oct 1912

The Year Book of Canadian Art 1913, compiled by the Arts and Letters Club of Toronto (London, Toronto 1913)

Mason, Lawrence. 'Ontario's vistas: journeyings into the rich field of provincial music and drama,' Toronto *Globe*, 11 instalments, 4 Jul–26 Sep 1925

Gould, Glenn. 'The prospects of recording,' *High Fidelity Magazine*, Apr 1966

Morey, Carl. 'Canada's first opera ensemble,' *OpCan*, Sep 1970

Thompson, J.-Antonio. *Cinquante Ans de vie musicale à Trois-Rivières* (Trois-Rivières 1970)

Payzant, Geoffrey. 'Non-take-twoness,' *Glenn Gould: Music and Mind* (Toronto 1978)

Amtmann *Music in Canada; Musique au Québec*

Kallmann, Helmut. 'Historical background,' *Aspects of Music in Canada*

Potvin, Gilles. 'Performance,' ibid

Walter, Arnold. 'Introduction,' ibid

Kallmann *History of Music in Canada*

Musical Red Book

Music in Canada

'Toronto's Pre-confederation Music Societies'

La Vie musicale

TCB, HK, DSI

Concerts & Artistes canadiens Inc. See Canadian Concerts & Artists Inc.

Les Concerts Couperin. Established in 1956 in Quebec City on the initiative of Gérard Morisset (curator of the Musée du Québec), Judge Thomas Tremblay, and the musicians Victor *Bouchard and Sylvio *Lacharité. Sponsorsed by the *MACQ, the Concerts Couperin have presented between four and eight free recitals and chamber music concerts each year at the Musée, at Notre-Dame-des-Victoires Church, in the chapel of the Ursulines' convent, and in the chapel of the Petit séminaire de Québec, among other places. The society has encouraged numerous Quebec musicians, among them Pierre *Boutet, Jean-Louis Rousseau, and Donald Thomson. In 1967 the program of the Concerts Couperin, originally baroque as the name indicates, began to include modern works, some by Quebec composers such as Serge *Garant, Jacques *Hétu, and Bruce *Mather. Judge Tremblay was president 1956–67 and Jacques Boulay succeeded him in 1968. Lacharité was music director 1956–77; he was succeeded by Edwin *Bélanger. Paul-Eugène Jobin became administrator in 1967. By 1980 the Concerts Couperin had presented over 125 performances. IB

Concert Society of Ottawa. See Morning Music Club.

Concerts Symphonique de Montréal. See Montreal Symphony Orchestra.

Concordia University. Created in August 1974 by a merger of Sir George Williams U and Loyola College, located respectively on Maisonneuve and Sherbrooke streets in Montreal's west end. Both of those institutions offered music courses within regular programs. Concordia U in the 1970s had faculties of arts and science, commerce and administration, engineering, and fine arts, as well as the faculty of graduate studies and the Simone de Beauvoir Institute devoted to women's studies. In the 1978–9 academic year some 23,000 students took classes from 1600 teachers.

Growing out of the YMCA's educational work in Montreal, Sir George Williams U began evening classes at the university level in 1929. Day courses in arts, science, and commerce were inaugurated in 1932. Non-specialized courses in the history of music and theory were given at that time to arts students. The university was granted a special charter by the Quebec government in 1948. Following a thorough investigation in 1969 by Philip Cohen, music officially became a division of the Dept of Fine Arts in 1970. The preparatory music school opened that year and led to the creation of courses in continuing education in 1972. In conjunction with these courses various workshops were held, such as music for children (recorder, the *Orff method), instrument repair and manufacture, piano tuning, and chamber ensembles.

Loyola College was incorporated in Quebec in 1899. Administered by the Jesuits, this classical college was dependent at first on *Laval U and later on the *U of Montreal for the granting of its diplomas. After 1968 it offered practical music courses (instruments) as part of its student services, and music-theory courses within the Dept of Fine Arts. Father William Brown, music director in 1966, encouraged the formation of instrumental and choral groups, including the Loyola Symphonette (renamed the Loyola Orchestra in 1970), the Loyola Concert Band (conducted 1967–9 by Henry Rzepus and 1969–72 by Thomas *Legrady), and the Loyola Choral Society.

Concordia U began in 1974–5 with about 400 predominantly English-speaking music students, 300 from Sir George Williams U and 100 from Loyola College. In 1979, however, 70 per cent of the students were French-speaking. Courses were given in the two languages according to demand. The music section became a department in 1975 when the Dept of Fine Arts obtained faculty status. A BA with a major in music was offered in 1974–5. After that, Concordia U granted the BFA in four areas of concentration: a major in 'studio music' (involving all aspects of popular music), performance, theory and composition, and special studies (a program established according to a student's particular aptitudes, which must meet stringent criteria).

Philip Cohen, who joined the staff in 1970 and served 1975–7 as the first director of the Music Dept, developed, on a basis of individualized teaching, a flexible, innovative program which allowed a student, even one without extensive prior training, to attain a high level of competence. Cohen was succeeded in 1977 by Sherman Friedland, a clarinetist who also was artist-in-residence along with Christopher *Jackson (organ, harpsichord), Bernard *Lagacé (organ), and Douglas Walter (saxophone). Friedland in 1976 initiated a student orchestra of about 65 players and in 1977 began a chamber group (Concordia Chamber Ensemble) of 3 to 10 professional musicians (including Lauretta Milkman, piano, and Donald Pistolesi, cello), most of them teachers at Concordia. A jazz ensemble, founded in 1976, brought together some 30 students under the direction of Douglas Walter and Andrew Homzy. Christopher Jackson conducted a choir of 50 students after 1978.

All these groups have performed in the Loyola chapel, established as a concert hall by the college before the merger. The music library is part of the Vanier Library. The Dept of Music in 1979 continued the summer sessions (theory courses and individual lessons in various instruments) begun at Sir George Williams in 1950. In 1977 Concordia U was host to the conference of the Canadian Assn of Music Therapy. Subsequently it planned to introduce a program of studies in that subject. During 1978–9 some 160 full- and part-time students were enrolled in the Dept of Music, which had eight regular and five part-time teaching staff and several assistants. (NT)

'Concours de la chanson canadienne.' Songwriting competition organized in 1956 by the CBC at the instigation of Robert *L'Herbier, to encourage the composition of original songs in French and to promote the Canadian recording industry. That year a series of radio broadcasts introduced the songs to the public; 1200 had been submitted, and several semifinals had to be programmed. The five-member jury, which included Félix *Leclerc and Jean *Deslauriers, ultimately chose 12 songs, and the composer-authors were awarded gold or silver records. The songs were premiered 22 Feb 1957 at a radio and TV gala. Among the songs were Jacques Blanchet's 'Le Ciel se marie avec la mer,' Camille Andréa's 'Su'l perron,' Lionel *Daunais's 'Voyage de noce' and 'Perceurs de coffres-forts,' Lucien *Hétu's 'Parc Lafontaine,' Lucien Brien's 'Les Étoiles,' and Rolland *D'Amour's 'La Croix du Mont-Royal.' The 12 songs were recorded by Electric Musical Industries (EMI) in New York for the Pathé-Marconi label.

The competition deteriorated in the ensuing years, and it was reorganized in 1961 as 'Chansons sur mesure' by the countries (Canada among them) of the Communauté radiophonique des programmes de langue française. Jean-Pierre *Ferland won a prize in the reorganized contest in Brussels in 1962 with his 'Feuilles de gui,' and other Quebec composers have been successful in subsequent years. (BLH)

Conductors and conducting

1 Introduction
2 To World War I
3 The 1920s and 1930s
4 After 1940

1 INTRODUCTION. The practice of beating time with hand, foot, stick, bow, or rolled-up sheet of paper to help co-ordinate group performance is centuries old. The entrusting of that responsibility to an individual as his sole function, however, was not established until the early 19th century. Until then the dominant performer in an instrumental group directed from his position at the head of the violin section, at the keyboard of the harpsichord, or at the console of a church organ.

Most of the first stand-up conductors, in the modern sense, were composers (eg, Weber, Mendelssohn, Berlioz, and Nicolai) whose instrumental and vocal writing was of a complexity requiring careful direction for its effective representation. By the end of the 19th century, probably in response to the enormous expansion of the orchestra and its literature and the popularity of opera and ballet, a new breed of virtuoso had sprung up: the full-time interpreter-conductor of orchestra, choir, or opera who either had given up or never had undertaken a career as composer or performer.

Because Canada has been slow in developing major orchestras and opera companies, it has been slow in producing major conductors. Marching bands and church choirs, because of the regularity of their functions, did require leaders and these were forthcoming (though closer to the old than the new tradition in conducting). But high-budget symphony orchestras and choirs regularly and frequently before the public were too few in Canada, even after the mid-20th century, to stimulate the emergence or support the ambitions of a native school of career conductors.

A very few Canadian musicians, due to innate ability, strong ambition, and particular opportunity were able, without specific training or experience as conductors, to assume major conducting positions – Ernest *MacMillan and Wilfrid *Pelletier being prime examples. And conversely, the proliferation after 1956, particularly in Ontario, of community orchestras (Canada's nearest approximation to the small opera houses which spawned the great European conductors) began to provide young conductors with platforms for the testing of their gifts and the development of their skills.

But self-made giants have been too few; and the products of the community orchestra system have seemed too modest in the eyes of orchestra boards shopping for box-office-stimulating charisma in their leaders. In 1980 the conductors of the 11 major symphony orchestras in Canada still were predominantly foreign, the exceptions being Mario *Bernardi of the *NACO and Boris *Brott of the *Hamilton Philharmonic Orchestra, although also at that time Pierre *Hétu was principal guest conductor (having resigned as artistic director) and Peter McCoppin resident conductor of the *Edmonton SO.

2 TO WORLD WAR I. The surviving printed programs and concert announcements of pre-Confederation Canada reveal mixtures of orchestral and solo performances and identify the featured soloist more often than the conductor. The first Canadians who may be considered conductors (always part-time) of a band, a choir, or an orchestra included Jean-Chrysostome *Brauneis I, James Paton *Clarke, Richard *Coates, Stephen *Codman, Antoine *Dessane, F.-H. *Glackemeyer, and at least two Canadian-born musicians, Charles *Sauvageau and François *Vézina. For most, conducting was an occasional, if glamorous, emergence from a modest existence as organist, choirmaster, and music teacher.

This is true also of the many bandmasters and leaders of musical societies in the later decades of the 19th century. The most distinguished bandmasters included John *Bayley, Edmond *Hardy (active until the 1930s), Charles *Lavallée, Ernest *Lavigne, George R. Robinson, and Joseph *Vézina; outstanding leaders of philharmonic societies and choirs were A.-J. *Boucher and Guillaume *Couture of Montreal, John *Carter of Toronto, Edward *Fisher of Ottawa and Toronto, Charles H. *Porter of Halifax, F. H. *Torrington of Montreal and Toronto, and Theodor *Zoellner of Berlin (Kitchener). Calixa *Lavallée, equally skilled as bandmaster, choirmaster, and opera conductor, both in Canada and the USA, was in a class by himself.

The beginning of the 20th century was one of musical expansion and prosperity; large choirs flourished in many cities, and orchestras had at least precarious existences. Among the great choral leaders of this period were Edward *Broome, Bruce *Carey, Alexandre-M. *Clerk, Albert *Ham, Charles A.E. *Harriss, and A.S. *Vogt; among the pioneer orchestra conductors J.-J. *Goulet, Max *Weil, and Frank *Welsman, and two previously known mainly as bandmasters, Ernest Lavigne and Joseph Vézina. Among the first women conductors were Bertha *Drechsler Adamson of Toronto, Gertrude *Huntley Green of Victoria, and Gena *Branscombe, an emigrant to the USA.

3 THE 1920S AND 1930S. In surveying conductors and conducting from World War I to the present, emphasis will be placed on describing the varieties of professional outlets and on naming representative figures, with whom conducting formed a main or major activity and the basis of their reputation. Most will be named only once, even though their work spanned several categories. It is impossible to list here all of the more than one hundred orchestra conductors, bandmasters, and choir directors who have entries in *EMC*, and the several hundred others whose names are found in entries on individual performing ensembles, cities, universities, ethnic minorities, etc.

Professional or semi-professional orchestras after World War I usually were entrusted to (or established by) European-born musicians. Many of these were string or keyboard players who became conductors only in Canada: Luigi von *Kunits and Reginald *Stewart in Toronto, Douglas *Clarke in Winnipeg and Montreal, Donald *Heins in Ottawa, Allard *de Ridder in Vancouver and Ottawa, Gregory *Garbovitsky in Calgary, Graham *Godfrey in Hamilton, and W. Knight *Wilson in Regina.

Among the few Canadian-born symphony-orchestra conductors embarking on careers between the two wars were Jean-Marie *Beaudet, Eugène *Chartier, and J.-J. *Gagnier in Montreal, Ernest MacMillan in Toronto, and Edwin *Bélanger and Robert *Talbot in Quebec.

Far more numerous outlets for orchestra conducting were provided by the theatre, movie, and hotel orchestras and by a new and developing type, the broadcast-studio orchestra. Notable conductors in these areas (many still active after World War II) were Giuseppe *Agostini, Jack *Arthur, Rex *Battle, Alexander *Chuhaldin, Henri *Delcellier, Percy *Faith, Howard *Fogg, Bruce *Holder, Armand and Maurice Meerte, Henri *Miro, Marjorie *Payne (considered the first woman to conduct on radio), Luigi *Romanelli, Joseph Shadwick, Jerry *Shea, Herbert *Spencer, Edmond *Trudel and Geoffrey *Waddington.

Among the most gifted choral conductors may be counted W.H. *Anderson, J.-Arsène Brassard, Dan A. *Cameron, H. Whorlow Bull, Berkley E. *Chadwick, Harry *Dean, Charles E. *Findlater, H.A. *Fricker, Charles and Jean *Goulet, Filmer *Hubble, H.K. *Jordan, Frederic *Lord, Bernard *Naylor, Hugh Ross, Alfred *Whitehead, and Healey *Willan; the names of Ernest MacMillan and Reginald Stewart deserve to be repeated here.

Outstanding bandmasters included J.-J. Gagnier, Charles *O'Neill, and John *Slatter (for a longer list see *Bands 1 / Introduction).

A few Canadian conductors made names for themselves in the USA: Rosario *Bourdon as a recording-studio conductor for RCA Victor, Bruce Carey as a choral director, and Wilfrid Pelletier at the *Metropolitan Opera in New York (though assuming an important role in Montreal after 1934 and in Quebec City later).

4 AFTER 1940. Despite the difficulties mentioned earlier, after World War II a number of young Canadians persevered in making conducting their major or only specialization. Unlike the many musicians of the previous generation whose conduct-

ing ventures never quite got the upper hand over their orchestral occupations – one thinks of John *Adaskin, Samuel *Hersenhoren, Eugene *Kash, Paul *Scherman, and Albert *Steinberg – the younger ones often succeeded, aided undoubtedly by better educational facilities and the wider opportunities offered by the expanding needs of the CBC and by orchestras, choirs, and music festivals all over the country.

Prominent among the Canadian-born symphony orchestra conductors of the post-war period have been Jacques *Beaudry, Mario Bernardi, Françoys *Bernier, Boris Brott, Raymond *Dessaints, Victor *Feldbrill, Pierre Hétu, Sylvio *Lacharité, and Ethel *Stark, the last-named the first Canadian woman to guest-conduct major orchestras in Canada and abroad.

Orchestra conductors whose centre of activity has been the radio, TV, or film studio have included Lucio *Agostini, Louis *Applebaum, John *Avison, Jean-Marie Beaudet, Howard *Cable, Neil *Chotem, Morris *Davis, Jean *Deslauriers, André *Gagnon, William *McCauley, Neil *Harris, Robert *McMullin, Art *Morrow, Albert *Pratz, Ivan *Romanoff, Geoffrey Waddington, and Eric *Wild.

Chamber orchestra conductors of note, Canadian-born and immigrant, have included Raffi *Armenian, Milton *Barnes, Alexander *Brott, Ruben *Gurevich, Marta *Hidy, Brian *Law, Victor Martin, Boyd *Neel, and Bill *Phillips.

Conductors who have made a specialty of contemporary music have been relatively few. The Canadians Victor Feldbrill and Serge *Garant are the notable exceptions.

Conductors with reputations based on the excellence of their work with community orchestras include Leonard Atherton, Martin *Boundy (also a bandmaster), Leonard *Camplin, Clifford *Evens, Harman Haakman, Matti Holli, and Stanley *Saunders.

In the 1970s, with the growing emphasis on youth orchestras as serious training arenas for professional orchestra musicians, a number of Canadians came to be regarded as specialists in the field. Notable among these were Patrick Burroughs (Guelph Youth Orchestra), Jacques Clément (Montreal Civic Youth Orchestra), James Coles (Kingston Youth Orchestra), Victor Feldbrill (U of Toronto SO), Ermanno Florio (TS Youth Orchestra), Brian Law (Ottawa Youth Orchestra), Glenn Mallory (Hamilton Philharmonic Youth Orchestra), Michael Massey (Edmonton Youth Orchestra), Uri Mayer (Orchestre des jeunes du Québec), Frank Simpson (Calgary Youth Orchestra), James White (London Youth SO), and Carlisle *Wilson (Winnipeg Youth Orchestra).

Among Canadian-born conductors George *Crum has specialized in ballet, John *Fenwick in theatre music, Mario Bernardi, James *Craig, and Jean Deslauriers in opera. A number of former Europeans also have specialized in opera, notably Ernesto *Barbini, but also Emil Cooper, Nicholas *Goldschmidt, and Alfred *Strombergs. Raffi Armenian has done a steadily increasing amount of opera conducting.

Prominent bandmasters are listed under Bands: 1 / Introduction.

Choral conductors after World War II, in addition to several still active from the pre-war era, have included Hugh *Bancroft, Leslie *Bell, Lloyd *Bradshaw, Richard *Eaton, Marcien *Ferland, Emil Gartner, Fernand *Graton, Elmer *Iseler, René *Lacourse, Marcel *Laurencelle, Brian Law, Georges *Little, Victor *Martens, Chantal *Masson, Leonard *Mayoh, Glenn *Pierce, Wayne *Riddell, Sherwood *Robson, François *Senart, John *Sidgwick, Karel ten *Hoope, Stewart *Thomson, Jon *Washburn, and Don *Wright. A number of Mennonite conductors made significant contributions in the choral field (see Mennonites).

A few Canadians, among them Arthur *Davison, Harry Newstone, and Hugo *Rignold, have entered conducting careers in other countries, Mario Bernardi and James Craig have been regular conductors at Sadler's Wells, and Gregory *Millar has conducted many ensembles in the USA and in Mexico, but all three have returned to Canada.

A few Canadians have won honours in foreign conducting contests. Alexander Brott won the Pan-American Competition (Mexico) in 1957 and Boris Brott won it in 1958, with Otto-Werner *Mueller second. Boris Brott placed third in the Liverpool Competition in 1962 and was one of four winners in the Mitropoulos Competition in New York in 1968. In the Besançon Competition, Pierre Hétu was first in the professional category in 1961 and Raffi Armenian was a winner in 1968.

It would be superfluous to list the many international star conductors who have visited Canada as guests. Suffice it to mention a few of the earliest to visit: Wilhelm Gericke, Victor Herbert, André Messager, Emil Mollenhauer, Artur Nikisch, Emil Paur, Anton Seidl, Theodore Thomas (1873), and Arturo Toscanini, most from the USA and with their regular orchestras.

Perhaps the earliest visit by an important choral conductor was Sir Alexander Mackenzie's, to lead the *Cycle of Musical Festivals in 1903. Mackenzie also was the first visitor to conduct Canadian orchestras and choirs.

A few foreign conductors have lived in Canada for limited periods. Among them were Sir Thomas Beecham ca 1940–1 (*Montreal Festivals, *Vancouver SO), Emil Cooper 1944–60 (*Opera Guild of Montreal), Meredith Davies 1964–71 (Vancouver SO), Désiré Defauw 1940–52 (*CSM, Montreal), Pierre Dervaux 1968–75 (Quebec SO), Irwin Hoffman 1952–64 (Vancouver SO), Charles *Houdret 1952–64 (Montreal Festivals, etc), Walter *Kaufmann 1947–56 (*Winnipeg SO), Otto Klemperer 1961–3 (*MSO), Lawrence Leonard 1968–73 (Edmonton SO), Igor Markevitch 1957–61 (MSO), Thomas Mayer 1955–60 (*Ottawa Philharmonic Orchestra), Zubin Mehta 1961–7 (MSO), Otto-Werner Mueller 1951–73 (*Victoria SO), Seiji Ozawa 1965–9 (*TSO), Henry Plukker 1955–62 (Calgary Philharmonic), Brian Priestman 1964–70 (Edmonton SO), Jacques Singer 1947–50 (Vancouver SO), Walter *Susskind 1956–65 (TSO), and Haymo Taeuber 1963–8 (Calgary Philharmonic).

Conductors who have settled in Canada (if not deceased by 1980, only arrival year indicated) include Kazuyoshi Akiyama 1972 (Vancouver SO), Karel Ančerl 1968–73 (TS), Leonard Atherton 1972 (*St Catharines SO), Ernesto Barbini 1953 (*Royal Cons Opera School), Andrew Davis 1975 (TS), Franz-Paul *Decker 1967 (MSO), Charles Dutoit 1978 (MSO), James De Preist 1976 (Quebec SO), Piero Gamba 1971 (Winnipeg SO), Laszlo *Gati 1957 (Victoria SO), Nicholas Goldschmidt 1946 (Royal Cons Opera School), David Gray 1973 (Newfoundland SO), Arpad Joó 1977 (Calgary Philharmonic), Vladimir *Jelinek 1965 (Les Grands Ballets Canadiens), Janis *Kalnins 1948 (*New Brunswick SO), David *Kaplan 1960 (*Saskatoon SO), Howard *Leyton-Brown 1952 (Regina SO), Ettore *Mazzoleni 1929–68 (Royal Cons Opera School), Klaro *Mizerit 1968 (*Atlantic SO), Boyd Neel 1953 (*Hart House Orchestra), Alfred Strombergs 1948 (*Nova Scotia Opera Association), Remus *Tzincoca 1959 (*CMM), Heinz *Unger 1948–65 (York Concert Society), and Victor Yampolsky 1977 (Atlantic SO).

In summary, despite the existence of countless choral societies and numerous amateur orchestras that have been part of Canadian musical life from the mid-19th century, training opportunities have been and in 1980 remained inadequate for the aspiring professional. Far fewer Canadians have made a mark as conductors than as specialists in almost any other branch of music, either in or outside Canada, and at the beginning of the 1980s nearly all the top conducting positions in Canada continued to be occupied by musicians from abroad.

Conducting classes have been established at some universities. These have proved valuable for aspiring school teachers and church musicians, but rarely have shown decisive influence on a born conductor, who benefits less from conducting lessons than from score study and the opportunity to advance from modest to more sophisticated assignments.

Major professional opportunities have been all but withheld from Canadian-born conductors – and only in part because of a shortfall in Canadian talent or the inadequacies of Canadian training. The international network of artist managers and orchestra managers takes into consideration many factors besides talent and training in the shrewd and competitive marketing and placement of conductors in such desirable positions as become available. Symphony boards have abetted in this, dazzled by the allure of exotic talent and sure their audiences will be dazzled too, and excited by the adventure of assisting at a choice made from the world's talent and not just from their own country's. In 1980 Canadians continued to find it difficult to be as impressed by the home-grown as by the imported. It perhaps was significant that the only Canadian-born conductors then in major positions – Mario Bernardi and Boris Brott – had demonstrated that their skills were admired abroad before they won their Canadian postings.

Among incentives to young conductors have been the Heinz Unger Award administered by the *OAC; a conductor's workshop at the *U of Toronto, set up in 1968; and the TS Apprenticeship program, established in 1976.

See also Orchestras; Youth orchestras.

BIBLIOGRAPHY

ACO / OFSO. *Directory of Conductors in Canada / Annuaire des Chefs d'Orchestre au Canada* (Toronto [1977])

HK, GP, KW

Confederation and music. Confederation is the popular term for the federal union in 1867 of the provinces of Upper and Lower Canada (henceforth Ontario and Quebec), New Brunswick, and Nova Scotia under the name Dominion of Canada. Manitoba joined the dominion in 1870, British Columbia in 1871, Prince Edward Island in 1873, and Newfoundland in 1949. Alberta and Saskatchewan, which had been territories or districts, were created provinces in 1905.

Confederation did not occur without much debate, and the popular sentiments for and against union occasionally were expressed in music. An advertisement for Sergeant H. Dixon's *Confederation Galop*, published in 1865 in 'The New Brunswick Minstrel' series, claimed that this 'stirring composition ... ought of itself to impel every one to vote for Confederation.' Léon Casorti's *La Confédération Quadrille*, however, was subtitled 'danse nationale, inaugurée en 1840, coup de grace en 1865' and dedicated to George Brown (who resigned from the government in 1865, but was to become one of the 'fathers of Confederation') in the following words: 'Son Excellence le Vicomte Georges Diocletien de Braun, Chevalier du gros Castor, Ministre des Cultes.' An *'Anti-Confederation Song' from Newfoundland, typical of the 19th-century campaign songs, is included in Edith *Fowke's *Canada's Story in Song*. Three 1867 publications owed their origins to the birth of the new dominion: *'The Maple Leaf for Ever' (by Alexander *Muir), 'This Canada of Ours' (words by J.D. Edgar, music adapted and arranged by E.H. Ridout), and 'Our Dominion' (words by G.R. Kingsmill, music by J. Holt).

The largest composition inspired by Confederation undoubtedly was Jean-Baptiste *Labelle's *Cantate: la Confédération*, to a text by Auguste Achintre, dedicated to George-Étienne Cartier and performed 7 Jan 1868 at the city hall in Montreal. The cantata included Labelle's song *'O Canada! mon pays! mes amours!' Labelle also composed an 'opérette comique' with words by Elzéar Labelle. *La Conversion d'un pêcheur de la Nouvelle-Ecosse* has only two protagonists – a Nova Scotia fisherman and a Quebec farmer, who argue the merits of Confederation. *Boucher published a piano score ca 1867.

Anniversaries of Confederation have been celebrated by A. Pleau's *Marche Confédération* (1919), by Albert E. MacNutt's 'The Birthday of Confederation' (1927), and by various works written for the centenary in 1967.

See also Centennial celebrations; Expo 67; *Louis Riel*; *La Prima Ballerina*; *Requiems for the Party Girl*.

BIBLIOGRAPHY

La Minerve, 11 Jan 1868

Hare, John. 'La Cantate de la Confédération,' *Papers of the Bibliographical Society of Canada*, vol 5 (1966)

'Comprehensive catalogue of new Canadian music written in honour of Canada's centennial year, 1967,' *Mcan*, 7, Dec 1967

Moisan, Clément. 'La Confédération, cantate d'Auguste Achintre,' *Dictionnaire des oeuvres littéraires du Québec*, vol 1, ed Maurice Lemire (Montreal 1978) HK

Confederation Centre of the Arts (correctly, The Fathers of Confederation Centre of the Arts), Charlottetown, Prince Edward Island. Arts complex declared open 6 Oct 1964 by Queen Elizabeth II. The centre's design, by architect Dimitri Dimakopoulos and theatre theorist George Izenour, was selected by a jury of internationally distinguished architects from among 47 submissions. The centre consists of a 1070-seat theatre, an art gallery and museum, a 300-seat lecture hall, libraries, a restaurant which looks out on a sculpture court, and an 18-metre-square Memorial Hall. In 1974 the Mackenzie Building (formerly the Capitol Theatre) was acquired for smaller productions. The theatre in the centre has a permanent proscenium stage, but the auditorium itself is flexible. Mobile wall panels and ceiling baffles permit acoustic modification. The first five rows of seats in the orchestra section can be lowered hydraulically.

Like the *NAC, the Confederation Centre of the Arts was chartered federally, its national significance evident in the funding formula for its construction: of the total cost of $5.6 million, the federal government contributed $2.8 million, the provinces $0.15 per capita. The centre was to belong to Canada, with Prince Edward Island as custodian. However, no financial provision had been made for upkeep and operation. By 1975 the centre was carrying a deficit of $600,000 and needed repairs at an estimated cost of almost $1 million. The deficit was alleviated by a federal operating grant of $800,000 in 1976, and another of $900,000 in 1977. In 1978 the federal government allotted a capital grant of $1.25 million over a three-year period for renovations and repairs.

The *Charlottetown Festival, held annually at the centre, is devoted particularly to Canadian

The Confederation Centre of the Arts, Charlottetown

musical theatre, and the program of the winter season has had a high concentration of pop entertainments from the USA. The centre also has presented, however, the *COC, the Royal Winnipeg Ballet, Les Grands Ballets Canadiens, the National Ballet, the *NYO, the *TS, the annual seasons of the *Atlantic SO and the Prince Edward Island SO, and appearances by such accomplished individual performers as Maynard *Ferguson, Maureen *Forrester, Lois *Marshall, and Oscar *Peterson.

BIBLIOGRAPHY

Morrow, Marianne. 'Overture to Canada's centennial,' *OpCan*, May 1964 (PMW)

Confederation Choir, Charlottetown. Mixed-voice group formed in 1963 from the nucleus of the Charlottetown Chorale, which had functioned since 1951 under William Keith *Rogers and Christopher *Gledhill. The Confederation Choir survived integrally until February 1974, conducted successively by Royston Mugford, Margaret Hall, and Mark LeRoux. In 1974 it was succeeded by the Confederation Madrigal Choir of 16 voices. This, with the Confederation Boys' Choir of 70 to 90 voices in 1972, continued under the direction of LeRoux, who was succeeded by Neil Houlton in 1978. In addition to standard major works, the choirs occasionally have performed contemporary pieces. The boys' choir has sung Christopher Gledhill's *Abegweit Suite* and Keith *Bissell's *Christmas in Canada*, as well as many of Bissell's folksong arrangements.

Conferences and congresses. Canada has played host with increasing frequency to meetings of worldwide and North American musical organizations. This has been the result of a number of factors: the growth of international organizations in all fields of music after World War II, the effective participation of Canadians in such organizations, the improvement of conference and concert facilities in Canada, and encouragement and support from agencies such as the *Canada Council, the Dept of External Affairs, the Secretary of State, the *CBC, the *NFB, and the provincial governments.

Groups concerned with composers and composition, contemporary music, folk music, musicology, ethnomusicology, libraries, education, orchestra personnel, youth orchestras, and the playing and teaching of specific instruments have gathered in Canada. The following list cites the more important of these gatherings.

1 WORLDWIDE

1955

FIJM (Fédération internationale des Jeunesses musicales), 10th general assembly. Montreal. Host: *JMC

1960

*International Conference of Composers. Stratford, Ont. Sponsors: *CLComp, CBC, the Canada Council, the *Stratford Festival, and others. Directed by Louis *Applebaum

1961

International Folk Music Council, 14th annual conference. Quebec City. Host: *CFMS

*International Week of Today's Music. Montreal. Sponsor: the *Montreal Festivals. Organized by Pierre *Mercure

1962

International *Orff-Schulwerk Conference. Toronto. Host: *U of Toronto. Attended by Orff

1967

CIDEM (Inter-American Music Council). Toronto. Host: *CMCouncil. Directed by Arnold *Walter

FIJM, 22nd general assembly. Montreal. Host: JMC

International Congress of Organists. Toronto, Montreal, Ottawa. Host: *RCCO

1972

*World Saxophone Congress (the third). Toronto. Directed by Paul *Brodie

1975

'Guitar '75.' Toronto. Host and sponsor: *Guitar Society of Toronto

International Association of Music Libraries. Montreal. Host: *CAML. Chairman of the organizing committee: Kathleen Toomey

International Free-Bass Accordion Symposium (the first). Toronto. Co-sponsors: *RCMT and *Contemporary Showcase. Organized by Joseph *Macerollo

International Music Council, 16th general assembly. Calgary, Toronto, Ottawa, Montreal, Quebec City. Host: CMCouncil. Chairman of planning committee: John *Roberts. Included *World Music Week in its framework

1976

FIJM, 31st general assembly. Magog, Que. Host: JMC, at the *JMC Orford Art Centre

International Double-Reed Society (fifth meeting). Toronto. Host: U of Toronto. Program chairman, Christopher *Weait

1977

International Kodály Symposium (the third). Wolfville, NS. Host: *Acadia U

1978

CISAC (International Conference of Societies of Authors and Composers), 31st congress. Toronto and Montreal. Host: *CAPAC

'Guitar '78.' Toronto. Host and sponsor: Guitar Society of Toronto

International Clarinet Congress and Clinic. Toronto. Host: U of Toronto. Directed by Ezra *Schabas

ISME (International Society for Music Education), 13th biennial international conference. London, Ont. Host: *U of Western Ontario. Directed by Donald McKellar

2 NORTH AMERICAN

1947
Women's Association for Symphony Orchestras. Toronto. Host: *TSO Women's Committee

1960
Music Library Association. Montreal. Hosts: Canadian Library Association and American Library Association

1962 and ff
Ragtime Society, Inc, annual meetings. Toronto

1970
American Musicological Society and the College Music Society, joint annual meeting. Toronto. Host: U of Toronto

1971
American Bandmasters' Association, 37th annual convention. Toronto

1972
Society for Ethnomusicology, 17th annual convention. Toronto. Host: U of Toronto

1973
American Federation of Musicians of the USA and Canada. 76th annual convention. Toronto
Women's Association for Symphony Orchestras. Montreal. Host: *MSO Women's Committee

1975
Major (Orchestra) Managers' Conference. Toronto. Host: TS manager Walter *Homburger

1979
Society for Ethnomusicology. Montreal. Host: *U of Montreal
Central Opera Service, National Conference. Toronto. Host: *COC

Canadian organizations which hold regular meetings, conventions, or conferences of national scope include the *Association of Canadian Orchestras, the Canadian Association of Music Libraries, the *Canadian Association of University Schools of Music, the *Canadian Federation of Music Teachers' Associations, the CMCouncil, the *Canadian Music Educators' Association, the Canadian Association of Music Therapy, the *Canadian Folk Music Society, the *Federation of Canadian Music Festivals, the Jeunesses musicales of Canada, and the Royal Canadian College of Organists. In the area of popular music **RPM* magazine sponsors an annual three-day convention prior to the announcement of the *Juno Award winners. In collaboration with ACME *RPM* also sponsors an annual 'Big Country Awards' weekend.

CONNELL, Frank (Joseph). Bandmaster, b Shotts, Lanarkshire, Scotland, 24 Jun 1920. A graduate of the RMSM (Kneller Hall), he was a soloist with the BBC Scottish Orchestra, royal trumpeter at the Edinburgh Festival, and director 1948–58 of a Royal Artillery Band. He moved to Canada in 1958. The Moose Lions Junior bands, which he directed 1958–73, came to be regarded as models of their kind during his tenure. With them he made two recordings (Lumby Productions 1965, 1967), one of which (LP 1135) contains a performance of his own *Tri-State Festival March*. He also composed a *Scottish Folk Rhapsody*. He founded and directed 1962–72 the Saskatchewan Summer School of the Arts at Fort San, and has been director of the Red Deer (Alta) Community Band Assn.

CONNORS, 'Stompin' Tom.' Singer-songwriter, guitarist, b Saint John, NB, 3 Feb 1936. At 11 he wrote his first song, 'Reversing Falls Darling,' and at 15 he began playing the guitar. The influences of Wilf *Carter and Hank *Snow date from this period. Music remained an avocation as Connors worked for 10 years at various jobs across Canada, often in the company of Steve Foot (later 'Stevedore Steve,' the Boot Records recording artist). Connors began singing professionally in 1964 at the Maple Leaf Hotel in Timmins, Ont, where he remained for 14 months. In the absence of amplification Connors pounded the floor with his foot to establish the rhythm of his songs (partly sung and partly recited) above the noise of the crowd, thereby earning the name 'Stompin' Tom.' Also in Timmins he sang daily on CKGB radio. He recorded his first single, 'Carolyne,' in 1965 and distributed his other early recordings (for the Revel label) while touring in northern Ontario. In 1969 he moved to Toronto and began recording for Dominion. His first Dominion single, 'Bud the Spud,' was a national hit; it was followed by 'Sudbury Saturday Night,' 'Big Joe Mufferaw,' 'To It and At It,' and others.

The subject of two films, *This is Stompin' Tom* (Marlin 1972) and the feature *Across This Land with Stompin' Tom* (Cinepix 1973), Connors starred 1974–5 on CBC TV's 'Stompin' Tom's Canada' and has enjoyed country-wide popularity in club and concert appearances. By 1977 he had written over 500 songs, many based on actual events, others in honour of the locales in which he was performing. 'Consumer Song,' performed by the composer, became the theme for CBC TV's 'Marketplace.' Connors' songs are published by Crown Vetch Music, Morning Music, and Broadland Music. By 1979 he had made 29 LPs released by Boot Records (which he founded in 1971 with his manager Jury Krytiuk), including two five-volume sets, *Stompin' Tom Sings 60 Old Time Favourites* (STC 1) and *Stompin' Tom Sings 60 More Old Time Favourites* (STC 2). Four LPs received gold-record sales awards from the *CRIA – *Bud the Spud* (1969, Dom LPS 21002/Boot BOS 7114), *Stompin' Tom Connors Meets Big Joe Mufferaw* (1970, Dom LPS 21007/Boot BOS 7123), *My Stompin' Grounds* (1971, Boot 7103), and *Live at the Horseshoe* (1971, Dom LPS 21016/Boot BOS 7128).

Robert Martin wrote (Toronto *Globe and Mail*, 22 Jun 1973): 'Connors appeals to a parochial form of nationalism and to a rather class conscious working man's pride. Neither of these appeals is sophisticated but both are important, if not vital, to a large number of people who live in rural and small town Canada.' Connors won the *Juno Award annually 1970–4 as male country singer, and his LP *To It and At It* (Boot BOS 7127) received a Juno as the country album of 1973. Connors is a member of CAPAC.

BIBLIOGRAPHY

Clausen, Oliver. 'Yoo-hoo-hoo! It's Stompin' Tom,' *Globe Magazine*, 31 Jan 1970
Brown, Dick. 'Tom started stompin' when he was 5 cents short of a beer,' *Canadian Magazine*, 25 Mar 1972
Nowlan, Alden. 'What's more Canadian than Stompin' Tom?' *Maclean's*, Aug 1972
Flohil, Richard. 'Stompin Tom: Canada's unlikely national symbol,' *CanComp*, 85, Nov 1973 (RGn)

Conservatoire de musique de Chicoutimi. See Conservatoire de musique du Québec.

Conservatoire de musique de Hull. See Conservatoire de musique du Québec.

Conservatoire de musique de Montréal. See Conservatoire de musique du Québec.

Conservatoire de musique de Québec. See Conservatoire de musique du Québec.

Conservatoire de musique de Rimouski. See Conservatoire de musique du Québec.

Conservatoire de musique de Trois-Rivières. See Conservatoire de musique du Québec.

Conservatoire de musique de Val-d'Or. See Conservatoire de musique du Québec.

Conservatoire de musique du Québec. A network of seven provincial music-teaching institutions established in stages over the years, beginning in 1942, with branches located in 1 / Montreal, 2 / Quebec City, 3 / Trois-Rivières, 4 / Hull, 5 / Chicoutimi, 6 / Val-d'Or, and 7 / Rimouski.

Central administration of the seven music schools and of theatre schools in Montreal and Quebec City, became the responsibility of the Conservatoire de musique et d'art dramatique de Québec, an *MACQ division reporting directly to the minister. The founding director, Wilfrid *Pelletier, was succeeded by Roland *Leduc (see section 1), and the division has been directed subsequently by Victor *Bouchard 1967–71, Jean *Vallerand 1971–8, and Uriel G. Luft for a few months in 1978. Bouchard returned to succeed Luft in 1978, and he in turn was succeeded by Pierre Genest in 1980. According to statute, the aim of the conservatoire is to 'coordinate the professional training of composers, singers, instrumentalists and actors.' Provincial standardization of curricula, of levels of achievement necessary for student admission and advancement, and of criteria for the selection of teachers, has produced a remarkable equality in the calibre of teaching and the availability of advanced musical training throughout Quebec. The establishment of full-time staff appointments in 1961 and the opening of preparatory or pre-conservatory schools in Trois-Rivières, Sherbrooke, and Arvida (Chicoutimi) in 1963–4 were important landmarks in the institution's development. In 1978–9 the seven schools of the Cons de musique du Québec served about 1100 students and employed more than 200 teachers either full-time or on contract. The operation of the seven establishments has been governed by two broad principles: admission to its courses by competition and the training of professional musicians through specialized cost-free instruction. The study program leads to tests in the final year, following which two kinds of certification are awarded: 1 / premier prix, deuxième prix, and mention, for voice, individual instruments, harmony and counterpoint, history, analysis, composition, chamber music, and orchestra conducting; and 2 / first and second medals for solfège and dictation. Through an agreement between the Ministry of Education and certain *Cegeps, the conservatoire also is able to offer the Diplôme d'études collégiales (DEC) and the Diplôme d'études supérieures (DES), which qualify holders for admission to the faculties of education in the universities.

BIBLIOGRAPHY

Venne, Stephen. 'The Quebec Conservatory of Music is wholly state-supported,' *CanComp*, 4, Dec 1965
Potvin, Gilles. 'Le premier conservatoire de musique public en Amérique,' Montreal *La Presse*, 24 Aug 1968
Pelletier, Wilfrid. *Une symphonie inachevée…* (Montreal 1972)
Vallerand, Jean. 'Le conservatoire dans la cité,' *Culture vivante*, 11, Dec 1968
La Vie musicale

1 CONSERVATOIRE DE MUSIQUE DU QUÉBEC À MONTRÉAL. The first entirely state-subsidized institution of higher learning for music in North America. It was founded by the Quebec government following a report by Claude *Champagne on the teaching of music. (It may be recalled that in the late 1870s Calixa *Lavallée had tried unsuccessfully to obtain funds from an earlier government of the province in order to open a conservatory.) A bill entitled 'Loi du conservatoire' (The Conservatory Act) was passed by the Legislative Assembly 29 May 1942; a budget of $30,000 was provided. Directly inspired by the European conservatories, especially the one in Paris, the new institution began offering courses in January 1943. In October of that year, with an enrolment of 175, it embarked on its first full academic season, occupying space in the St-Sulpice library (now the BN du Q) on St-Denis St.

Wilfrid *Pelletier, director 1942–61, assembled a staff which included the Quebec musicians Noël *Brunet, Albert *Chamberland, Camille *Couture, Maurice *Onderet, and Ethel *Stark (violin); Fleurette *Beauchamp, Jean *Dansereau, Auguste *Descarries, Yvonne *Hubert, Arthur *Letondal, Germaine *Malépart, and Edmond *Trudel (piano); George M. *Brewer (organ); Jean *Belland and Roland *Leduc (cello); Roger *Charbonneau (double bass); Hervé *Baillargeon (flute); and Joseph Moretti (clarinet). Roger *Filiatrault taught singing, a discipline added in 1951 to the instrumental classes and to those in theory, solfège, and dictation given by Gabriel *Cusson, Isabelle *Delorme (who was responsible also for the harmony and counterpoint courses), Ria *Lenssens, Alfred *Mignault, and Jean *Papineau-Couture, among others. Claude Champagne combined the functions of assistant director and teacher as early as 1942; Clermont *Pépin taught composition before his appointment as director in 1967. For several years Jean *Vallerand served as both general secretary and a member of the teaching staff. Among artists from abroad who joined the staff were Isidor Philipp (piano), Joseph *Bonnet (organ), Dick Marzollo (opera), Rachele Maragliano-Mori and Martial Singher (singing), Marcel Grandjany (harp), Louis *Bailly (viola, chamber music), Anselme Fortier (double bass), René Le Roy, Arthur Lora, and Marcel Moyse (flute), Harold Gomberg, Bruno Labate, and Michel Nazzi (oboe), Simon Kovar and Louis Letellier (bassoon), Harry Berv (horn), Bernard Baker (trumpet), Charles Gusikoff (trombone), Saul Goodman (percussion), and Léon Barzin and Charles *Houdret (orchestra). A string quartet, the Quatuor du Conservatoire, under Louis Bailly's direction, comprising Noël Brunet, Lionel Renaud, Lucien *Robert, and Roland Leduc, enjoyed a brief existence in 1944–5.

In addition to the Montreal region, the CMM serves all regions of Quebec, attracting students from Granby, Joliette, St-Jean, St-Jérôme, Sherbrooke, Valleyfield, and elsewhere. Located 1956–64 on Ste-Catherine St West and 1964–75 on Berri St, the conservatoire moved in 1975 into the former Palais de Justice on Notre-Dame St East, which provided 38 teaching studios, 11 practice studios, three rehearsal rooms, and two electroacoustic studios. In 1980 the conservatoire's libraries contained some 48,000 books and scores, 7500 recordings, and 150 periodical titles, 30 of which were current publications. Two small halls, the Salle Gabriel-Cusson (200 seats) and the Salle Germaine-Malépart (125 seats), accommodated public student recitals and concerts and also chamber concerts by the ensemble classes. Formed in the 1950s, the 65-player Orchestre du Conservatoire gave about 10 concerts in 1978–9. Its conductors have been Charles Houdret, Roland Leduc, Rémus *Tzincoca, and Raymond *Dessaints, who succeeded Tzincoca in 1968.

Heads of the CMM after Pelletier have been Roland Leduc 1961–7, Clermont Pépin 1967–73, Gilberte *Martin (interim) 1973–4, Raymond *Daveluy 1974–8, and Gilles Gauthier (interim) 1978–9; Albert *Grenier assumed the position in 1979. In June 1979 there were 232 students and 63 teachers, including Lise *Boucher (piano), Bernard *Lagacé (organ), Dorothy *Weldon (harp), Lina Narducci (singing), John Charuk (violin), Walter *Joachim (cello), Jean-Paul *Major (flute), Bernard *Jean (oboe), Rafael *Masella (clarinet), Jean *Laurendeau (ondes Martenot), Andrée *Desautels (history of music), Micheline Coulombe *Saint-Marcoux (harmony and counterpoint), and Gilles *Tremblay (composition, analysis).

2 CONSERVATOIRE DE MUSIQUE DU QUÉBEC À QUÉBEC. The CMQ opened its doors 17 Jan 1944. It was directed 1944–6 by Wilfrid *Pelletier until Henri *Gagnon was appointed in 1946. Gagnon was succeeded by Raoul *Jobin in 1961, Jobin by Paul-Émile *Talbot in 1970, and Talbot by Armando *Santiago in 1978. Located on Quebec City's Langelier Blvd, and later, for more than 22 years, on St-Denis St (beside the Citadel), the CMQ moved 29 Oct 1972 to new premises in the building of the *Grand Théâtre de Québec. In addition to 49 classrooms and 22 practice studios, they provided the advantage of proximity to the Louis-Fréchette and Octave-Crémazie halls, in which the conservatory could present its public activities, including the 'Lundis du Conservatoire' in which both teachers and students have participated. In 1979–80 some 25 recitals or concerts were organized and master classes were given for conservatory students and guests from *Laval U's Music School. In the same school year the CMQ curriculum covered some 50 subjects, ranging from baroque instrumental music to electroacoustic techniques, from vocal chamber music to the techniques and writing of jazz. The program also allowed participation in an orchestra, a choir, and a variety of ensembles (woodwinds, brass, percussion, saxophones, guitars). The CMQ library in 1980 held 7400 books, about 100 periodical titles, 24,000 scores, and 6000 discs.

Several CMM staff members travelled back and forth between Montreal and Quebec City in the early years. The Quebec staff, under the directorship of Gagnon (who also taught organ) included Alice Duchesnay, Hélène *Landry (piano), Gilbert *Darisse (violin), René *Gagnier (clarinet, trombone), Maurice *DeCelles (oboe), Olga Gosselin (harp), and Robert *Talbot (theory). In 1978–9, 278 students were enrolled, and the teaching staff of 74 included Guy *Bourassa (piano), Claude *Lavoie (organ), Donald Thomson (harpsichord), Rolande *Dion and Marguerite *Pâquet (voice), Claude *Létourneau and Hidetaro *Suzuki (violin), Edwin *Bélanger (viola, chamber music), Pierre *Morin (cello), Jacques *Simard (oboe), Pierre *Bourque (saxophone), Pierick *Houdy (composition, orchestration), and Irène Brisson (history, musicology).

3 CONSERVATOIRE DE MUSIQUE DU QUÉBEC À TROIS-RIVIÈRES.
Opened 1 Apr 1964 under the direction of the pianist Czeslaw Kaczynski as a preparatory school with 35 students and three teachers, it became the Cons de musique du Québec à Trois-Rivières 1 Apr 1967. Under Kaczynski's direction 1967–70 the teaching staff of 13 included Gaston *Arel (theory), Hervé *Baillargeon (flute), Raymond *Daveluy (harmony/counterpoint), Réal *Gagnier (oboe), and Rafael *Masella (clarinet). Most of the students come from the St-Maurice region. The conservatoire moved in 1970 from Laviolette St to new quarters in the building of the Centre culturel and the former École Ste-Marie. That year the institution, headed by a new director, Raymond Daveluy, had 200 students and 23 teachers. Daveluy, who served 1970–4, consolidated the recently formed string orchestra and appointed Jean *Deslauriers as its director. Daveluy was succeeded in 1974 by Armando *Santiago but remained as a teacher. Jacqueline *Martel inaugurated instruction in singing in 1974. The teaching staff also has included Michel *Dussault, Christiane Sénart, and Nadia Strycek (piano), Noëlla Genest (organ), Bernard *Jean (oboe), Jean *Laurendeau (clarinet), Joseph *Masella (horn), Joseph Zuskin (trombone), Jacques Larocque (saxophone), and Josèphe *Colle (theory).

In October 1978 the conservatoire moved into new Radisson St premises containing 40 studios, a concert hall, an electroacoustic laboratory, and a recording studio. In the 1978–9 school year some 39 concerts were given by the students either at the conservatoire itself or in the Anaïs-Rousseau Hall at the Centre culturel. Classical guitar classes, sight-reading at the keyboard, and chamber music were added to the previous courses of study in the autumn of 1979. Preparatory training for entrance to the conservatoire continued to be offered by the school of St-Gabriel du Cap-de-la-Madeleine. Georges *Savaria was director of the Cons de Trois-Rivières in 1979 and was succeeded by Roger Bédard in 1980.

4 CONSERVATOIRE DE MUSIQUE DU QUÉBEC À HULL. Located on Alexandre-Taché Blvd, the conservatoire was opened 15 Oct 1967, enrolling 168 pupils from the Ottawa region. Its directors have been Fernand *Graton 1967–77, Jean Charron (acting) 1977–8, and Aimé Lainesse 1978–80. Josephte *Dufresne, who had been assistant director 1977–8, succeeded Lainesse. The teaching staff has included Dale *Bartlett and Anisia Campos (piano), Jean-Louis Chatel (trumpet), Fernande *Chiocchio (voice), Josephte Dufresne (piano), Gaston *Germain, Claire *Grenon-Masella and Yaëla *Hertz (violin), Paul *Masella (who also conducts the 35-to-40-player Conservatoire Orchestra), and Pietro *Masella (oboe). Facilities in 1980 included an auditorium, 23 teaching studios, 11 practice studios, and a rehearsal room for ensembles. The students have tended to give about 25 concerts a year at the Alexandre-Tiché school and the Outaouais Cegep – the latter institution also providing requisite courses for the Diplôme d'études collégiales. In 1976 the conservatoire organized a violin class for children aged three to five, employing the *Suzuki method.

5 CONSERVATOIRE DE MUSIQUE DU QUÉBEC À CHICOUTIMI. Housed in the same cultural complex as the Chicoutimi Cegep, the Saguenay museum, and other related institutions, the conservatoire was designed to serve the population of the Saguenay-Lac-St-Jean region. Courses for 172 students began 16 Oct 1967 under 13 teachers, including Louise *André, Lise DesRosiers (piano), Aimé Lainesse (horn) and Maurice *Onderet (violin). Noël Brunet (violin), Rolande Dion (singing), Robert Girard (organ), and Jean Morin (flute) subsequently joined them. Directors of the conservatoire have been Georges *Lindsay 1967–71, Noël Brunet (interim) 1971–2, Pierre Bourque 1972–3, Sylvio *Lacharité (interim) 1974–7, and Aimé Lainesse (interim) 1977–8, succeeded by Jean Charron. In 1980 facilities included 24 teaching studios, a 300-seat hall, and a library of books, scores, and recordings. Sunday concerts have been pre-

sented by teachers and students in the Sacré-Coeur Church in Chicoutimi. During the summers, conservatoire staff members have taught at the Lac-St-Jean Music Camp.

6 CONSERVATOIRE DE MUSIQUE DU QUÉBEC À VAL-D'OR. Designed for the population of northeastern Quebec (Abitibi, Témiscaming), the Conservatoire de Val-d'Or was opened in September 1967, enrolling 45 pupils in its temporary quarters at the Édifice provincial. Edgard Davignon, first director of the conservatoire and instructor in flute and theory, retained both duties in 1980. Other instrumental disciplines have been taught by Monique Collet-Samyn (piano), Luiz Rebelo (violin), Hélène Martineau (cello), and Noël Samyn (clarinet, saxophone). Some 85 students were enrolled in 1978. In 1980 facilities included practice studios and a library of books and scores. Students give concerts regularly in the hall of the Comprehensive High School in Val-d'Or.

7 CONSERVATOIRE DE MUSIQUE DU QUÉBEC À RIMOUSKI. The most recently established of the conservatories, on three floors of Rimouski's Civic Centre building, and containing an 1100-seat concert hall and a 275-seat second hall. Opened in 1973, its official inauguration, in June 1974, was marked by a concert by staff members which later was broadcast by the CBC. The Cons de Rimouski was established to serve students from the lower St Lawrence, Gaspé, the Magdalen Islands, and the North Shore. Directors have been Gilles Gauthier 1973–8 and Geneviève Paradis 1978–9, succeeded by Stella Plante. The enrolment in 1978 was 73. Facilities in 1980 included 43 rooms, including 35 studios and a music library. Bérengère Pasquier (piano), Jacques Montgrain (organ, theory), Marcel St-Jacques (flute), Jean Bouchard (saxophone), and Roger Bédard (harmony/counterpoint, analysis) have served on the teaching staff. The Rimouski Cegep and the U du Québec's Rimouski branch have provided courses leading to the Diplôme d'études collégiales (DEC) and the teaching certificate issued by the Ministry of Education. In collaboration with the La Neigette School Commission, the Cons de Rimouski in 1975 set up a preparatory music school in which advanced students from the conservatoire have served as teachers. ST

Conservatoire de musique et d'art dramatique du Québec. See Conservatoire de musique du Québec.

Conservatoire national de musique. At first called the Conservatoire national de musique et de l'élocution, it was founded in Montreal in 1905 by Alphonse *Lavallée-Smith. Letters patent in 1906 from Canada's secretary of state officially gave it the right to teach music, diction, elocution, drawing, and painting and to grant diplomas. It later was named the Cons national Ltée (National Cons Ltd). The conservatory benefited from the support of religious institutions which taught music in conjunction with the academic courses. Its program and the opportunity to present examination candidates prepared according to that program were available to teachers across the country. At the time of its founder's death in 1912, 250 diplomas had been conferred.

From 1921 to 1951, the conservatory was affiliated with the *U of Montreal. In 1928, Eugène *Lapierre (secretary 1922–7, director 1927–70), wishing to make the conservatory a school of music rather than just an examining body, reorganized it along the lines of European conservatories he had visited and studied 1924–7, obtaining financial support from Edmond *Archambault and Joseph Versailles. Lapierre was assisted by his brother Albert, by Alexandre d'Aragon, and by Antonio *Létourneau, and enlisted a teaching staff made up of (in his own words) 'our own specialists,' among whom were Sylva Alarie, Victoria *Cartier, Albert *Chamberland, Claude *Champagne, Jean-Noël *Charbonneau (president and director 1915–22), Eugène *Chartier, Camille *Couture, Charles Delvenne, Auguste *Descarries, Orpha-F. *Deveaux, Camille Duquette, Alfred *Laliberté, Arthur *Laurendeau, Arthur *Letondal, Germaine *Malépart, Rodolphe *Mathieu, Léo-Pol *Morin, Albertine *Morin-Labrecque, Frédéric *Pelletier, Benoît *Poirier (president 1923–5), Marcel *Saucier, Joseph-Élie *Savaria, and Benoît *Verdickt. Among the musicians who studied at the conservatory were Émilien *Allard, Françoise *Aubut, Eugène Caron, Gérard *Caron, Albertine *Caron-Legris, Ferrier Chartier, Georges Codling, Marguerite Lesage, Colombe *Pelletier, and Paul *Pratt. The official publication of the institution, *La Quinzaine musicale,* appeared twice monthly from September 1930 to March 1932. Works by French-Canadian composers which appeared in its pages later were issued separately by Éditions du Conservatoire. The conservatory came under independent management again in 1951. On Lapierre's death in 1970, Élise Chapdelaine, who had been secretary since 1940, served 1970–1 as interim director. Édouard *Woolley, a graduate of the institution, was director 1971–5, succeeded by Chapdelaine.

BIBLIOGRAPHY
'Conservatoire de musique et d'élocution,' *Album universal,* 1139, 20 Feb 1906
Lapierre, Jos.-Eugène. 'Feu Joseph Versailles,' *Quinzaine musicale,* vol 1, 27 Jun 1931 (CH, AP)

Conservatory of Music, University of Regina (Regina Conservatory of Music 1911–74). Established at the founding of Regina College as that college's music school and housed in the college building until 1928, when it moved to the newly completed *Darke Hall. It survived the subsequent phases of the evolution of the college (a junior college of the *U of Saskatchewan 1934–61, though still called Regina College; the Regina campus of the U of Saskatchewan, and so called, 1961–74; the autonomous *U of Regina thereafter). Early directors of the conservatory included F.G. Killmaster 1920–7, George *Coutts 1927–8, Cyril *Hampshire 1928–34, and Dan A. *Cameron 1939–51.

The college was re-organized in 1950 and Richard Watson was appointed the conservatory's first full-time director in 1951. The *Regina Cons Opera was established at this time and continued until 1968. Howard *Leyton-Brown, head of the string department 1952–5, became director of the conservatory in 1955 and gradually assembled a full-time staff of Canadian, European, and US teachers. In 1978 there were 13 full-time and 47 part-time instructors. The conservatory prepared students 1964–8 for the university's B MUS degree. In 1968 the academic program and the granting of the B MUS were taken over by the university's newly created Dept of Music, but the conservatory continued to prepare students in the practical requirements towards the degree and in *WBM requirements, including those leading to the AMS and LMS diplomas. Enrolment in 1975 was about 1150.

Darke Hall's facilities include a 700-seat main auditorium, a 140-seat recital hall, a library, studies, and practice rooms. The conservatory owns a chest of Dolmetsch viols. In addition to regular courses and individual lessons in voice, instruments, ballet, and speech, there are children's classes conducted according to the *Kodály, *Orff, and *Suzuki systems. In the 1970s a junior choir and baroque and junior orchestras were active. (WLB)

Conservatory String Quartet. Founded in 1929 at the *TCM by Elie *Spivak at the request of the conservatory's principal, Ernest *MacMillan. It made its debut 26 Oct 1929 with MacMillan as pianist, beginning a series of six concerts with Alberto *Guererro, Norah Drewett *de Kresz, Florence Singer, and Viggo *Kihl as assisting artists. It did not perform under its proper name until November 1930. The original members of the quartet were Spivak and Harold *Sumberg (violins), Donald *Heins (viola), and Leo *Smith (cello). Heins was replaced in 1934 by Tom Brennand, who in turn was replaced in 1937 by Cecil Figelski. Smith left the quartet in 1942 and Zara *Nelsova took his place. In 1944 Joyce *Sands succeeded Nelsova and Harold Carter succeeded Figelski. In early 1946 the members of the quartet were Pearl Palmason, Goldie Bell, Carter, and Sands.

During its existence the quartet played regularly in Toronto, made an appearance during the 1942–3 season in Montreal, and toured in Ontario, appearing in Guelph, Hamilton, Kingston, London, Ottawa, Sarnia, and elsewhere. In addition to the standard quartet repertoire it presented the Franck *Piano Quintet* with Reginald *Stewart (November 1932), and Vaughan Williams' *On Wenlock Edge* with Hubert Eisdell, tenor, and Ernest MacMillan, piano. It also made a point of performing works by Canadians – eg, Patricia *Blomfield Holt, Walter *MacNutt, John *Weinzweig, and Leo Smith, whose *Quartet in D* it premiered in January 1932. The group gave concerts on the Hart House viols in 1936. Though it was heard over CBC radio, it made no recordings. In 1946 the quartet's members (all of whom were on staff at the conservatory) faced increased teaching demands which, combined with illness within the group, led to its disbandment.

The quartet is not to be confused with an earlier all-female Conservatory String Quartette whose members included Bertha *Drechsler Adamson. NM

CONTANT, (Joseph Pierre) **Alexis**. Composer, organist, teacher, pianist, b Montreal 12 Nov 1858, d there 28 Nov 1918. The son of an amateur violinist, he took piano lessons from his mother, who was born in Chambly and had studied the instrument with Emma *Albani. He next worked with the organist and pianist Joseph A. *Fowler and first performed in public at 13. When Calixa *Lavallée returned from Paris in 1875, he accepted Contant as a pupil. Over the next few years Contant accompanied several artists in recital, including the violinist *Jehin-Prume, who advised him to go to Europe to study. The young man's father feared such a journey would endanger his son's religious faith, however, and refused to let him go. From September 1880 to February 1881 Contant taught at the Collège de l'Assomption. Anxious to learn more of musical theory, Contant joined Lavallée in Boston in January 1883 and studied harmony, counterpoint, and composition. Besides substituting occasionally for his ailing master in concerts, he attended many operas and concerts; a performance of Gounod's oratorio *La Rédemption* made a deep impression on him. Discovering that he was given to uncontrollable attacks of stage-fright, he decided to devote himself to the organ, to composition, and to teaching. He returned to Montreal that June and had several consultations with Guillaume *Couture, but left him following a disagreement. To further his

Alexis Contant

knowledge of composition he began to study and analyse the masterworks of Bach, Gounod, Wagner, Saint-Saëns, Massenet, and Franck. He became organist at St-Jean-Baptiste Church in Montreal in 1885 and held the position until his death. But for the rest of his life his teaching duties were to take most of his time and energy; he taught 1883–90 at the Collège de Montréal, ca 1885 at the convent of Hochelaga, 1900–18 at the Collège de Mont-St-Louis, and 1905–17 at the *Cons national, as well as giving private lessons. His studio was attended by numerous pupils, notably Victor *Brault, Claude *Champagne, Orpha-F. *Deveaux, J.-J. *Gagnier, Rodolphe *Mathieu and Wilfrid *Pelletier.

Contant had to reconcile his creative activity with his duties as organist and teacher and his family responsibilities, and until 1900 he had written relatively little. *La Lyre enchantée, Op 2*, a 'fantaisie-nocturne' for piano in the style of Chopin, was popular on the concert stage and in the salons. Of his four masses with orchestra, the third was premiered 1 Feb 1903 at the *Monument national by a choir of 180 voices and an orchestra of 50 players conducted by Edmond *Hardy. A *Marche héroïque* and two pieces for cello, *Romance sans paroles* and *Méditation*, were also on the program. The concert was a great success and established the composer's reputation; it was repeated in substance in the same hall on 8 November following. Contant soon undertook what was to be his major work and one of the first oratorios composed by a Canadian, *Caïn*, premiered 12 Nov 1905 at the Monument national under J.-J. *Goulet, in the presence of Sir Wilfrid Laurier, the prime minister of Canada. Contant then began to compose a second oratorio, **Les Deux Âmes*, to a text by Henri Roullaud. It was not completed until 1909 and not performed until 1913 (see Oratorios, Canadian 4, 5). In the mean time, Contant turned to chamber music and produced a *Trio* for violin, cello, and piano, played first in 1907 and repeated often. His patriotic cantata for baritone, chorus, and orchestra, *Le Canada*, also was performed that year. In 1912 he completed a symphonic poem, *L'Aurore*, which displays greater craftsmanship and an increased resourcefulness in both composition and instrumentation. He orchestrated his *Méditation* for the conductor Agide Jacchia, who performed it at a Sunday concert at *His Majesty's Theatre. Wishing to attempt an opera, Contant for his libretto chose *Veronica*, a play by Louis Fréchette. However, he had only completed the prelude to the first act and sketched the third act when a paralytic stroke cruelly interrupted his activities. From 1914 until his death he wrote little except the song 'Sur Un Crucifix,' to a poem by Albert Lozeau.

Contant was the first Canadian composer of note to receive all his training in Canada. Though he did spend six months in Boston, he worked there with his mentor Lavallée. Largely self-taught, by necessity rather than choice, he worked at his craft by studying the scores of the masters he admired. Such training, acquired only after tremendous effort in a somewhat unfavourable environment, kept him isolated from new ideas. In form and aesthetic, his works resemble those of Gounod, Dubois, or Saint-Saëns, while the elegance of his melodic line often calls to mind Fauré. Although naturally reserved, he felt compelled to compose: 'I write not for glory but rather to satisfy an irresistible need' (Jean-Yves Contant, *VM*).

Immediately after the premiere of Contant's *Messe No. 3*, Achille *Fortier described it as 'a solidly structured work; a composition of merit whose inspiration reveals itself in an elegant and expressive melody, sustained by a harmony that is both scholarly and discreetly refined' (Montreal *La Patrie*, 2 Feb 1903). Léo-Pol *Morin, on the other hand, was much more severe in his assessment: 'Although ... Alexis Contant has always had a certain facility, or better still, a certain fecundity, he has always lacked taste and judgment ... his oratorios represent the serious efforts of a musician who is conscientious but bereft of originality of thought or form and with an immature grasp of his craft. *Caïn* and *Les Deux Âmes* reveal a lack of craft and an imagination at once generous and in questionable taste' (*Papiers de musique*, Montreal 1930). Morin went on to charge that Contant's works had 'been written half a century too late' and displayed 'a pretentious and lacklustre verbiage rather than real inspiration.'

Contant was a pioneer whose vision was on a large scale, and although the results of his efforts do not equal his ambitions, he displays a sincerity and honesty worthy of admiration. His works were published in Paris by Hamelle, Haussman, and L. Grus and in Montreal by *Archambault, Beauchemin, J.E. Bélair, A.J. *Boucher, L. Cardinal, *Édition Belgo-Canadienne, and J.-C. Yon and in *Le Passe-Temps*. Of his major pieces, the *Trio* for violin, cello and piano is the one most often performed.

On the centenary of Contant's birth, the CBC presented, 13 Nov 1958, a special program of his works under the direction of Roland *Leduc and broadcast from St-Jean-Baptiste Church in Montreal, where he was organist for more than three decades. An avenue in Montreal was named for him in 1962. His manuscripts and personal papers were acquired in 1971 by the *NL of C and an exhibition of them was mounted in Ottawa in 1979.

Contant's sister Marie (Alida), Mme Eugène L'-Africain (b Montreal ca 1860, d ?), studied voice with Rosita *del Vecchio and Achille Fortier and beginning in 1897 with Romain Bussine at the Paris Cons. His brother Joseph-Albert (b Montreal 1 Oct 1877, d Joliette Que, 16 Apr 1942), organist-choirmaster, was a pupil of Alexis and of Alcibiade *Béique. He held posts in Granby, Chambly, Beauharnois and Joliette and composed some religious works. In 1918 he founded the Zouaves Band in Joliette, which he was still conducting in 1935. A daughter of Alexis, Fleurette (b Montreal 3 Dec 1892), studied voice in Montreal with Albert *Clerk-Jeannotte in 1912 and Salvator *Issaurel, and then with Félia Litvinne in Paris. Returning to Montreal because of the war, she continued her studies with Béatrice *La Palme and began to teach in 1918.

Contant's grandson Jean-Yves Contant (b Montreal 28 Mar 1918) was a CBC radio producer 1938–79 and was responsible for such music programs as 'Adagio' 1945–55 and 'Les Grands Concerts' 1975–7. As part of the latter series, excerpts of *Caïn* were performed in 1976 in the *Salle Claude-Champagne under the direction of Jean *Deslauriers.

COMPOSITIONS

ORCHESTRA

Fantaisie sur des airs canadiens. 1900. Ms
Marche du sacre de Pie X. 1903. Ms
Marche héroïque 'Les Alliés.' 1903?. Orch (band or pf). Arch? 1914 (pf)
L'Aurore, symphonic poem. 1912. Ms
Veronica, overture of an unfinished opera. 1914?. Ms

CHOIR AND ORCHESTRA

Mass in D Minor. 1884. Ms
Mass No. 2. 1897. Choir, orch, org. Ms
Tantum ergo. 1897. Ms
L'Angelus. 1898. Choir, orch, org. Ms
Mass No. 3. 1903. Choir, orch, org. Ms
Le Canada, patriotic cantata (O. Crémazie). 1906?. Bar, choir, orch. Ms
Mass in B Flat. Ms
See also *Caïn* and *Les Deux Âmes*.

CHORAL

Messe brève. 1894. TTBB, org. CMCentre
Messe des morts. 1908?. TBB. Ms
Messe brève. 1910. TBB, org. Ms
Messe des anges. SATB. Ms

CHAMBER MUSIC

Méditation. 1897. Vc (vn), pf or orch. Édn Belgo-Canadienne 1925, CMCentre (vc and pf)
Romance sans paroles. 1900?. Vc, pf. Édn Belgo-Canadienne 1925, CMCentre
La Charmeuse. 1903. Vc, pf. Édn Belgo-Canadienne 1925, CMCentre
Trio. 1907. Vn, vc, pf. Ms. RCI 229/RCA CCS-1023 (*Brandon U Trio)

PIANO

La Lyre enchantée Op 2. 1875. Boucher?, Hardy 1896. RCI 252 (J. *Dufresne)
La Cavalcade. 1883. Pf-4 hands (pf-2 hands). Ms
Vive Laurier. 1897. Pf (band). J.G. Yon, Boucher
Also variations on 'Un Canadien errant' (1896) and 'God Save the King' (1907?). Ms
Other works including songs for voice and pf and motets for choir and organ

BIBLIOGRAPHY

Lapierre, Eugène. 'Alexis Contant,' *Action musicale*, 17 Sep 1932
Gour, Romain. 'Alexis Contant, pianiste-compositeur,' *Qui?* vol 5, Dec 1953
Contant, Jean-Yves. 'Un pionnier de la musique canadienne,' *VM*, 7, 1967
Robin, Étienne. 'Alexis Contant,' *Information médicale et paramédicale*, 16 Jul 1968 GP

Contemporary music. The mid-20th century in Canada saw the rise of several societies devoted to public performances of contemporary music in general or music by contemporary Canadian composers in particular, or, in a few cases, to an emphasis on both these repertoires in a varied context of older music. After 1960 such organizations increased in number and became geographically more widespread. At the same time there appeared individual performers and small ensembles for whom the newest styles and techniques became a specialty. The existence of these sponsoring societies and specialist performers influenced the work of many composers. Contemporary music societies and performing ensembles include the following (those with only a founding year indicated were still in existence in 1980):

*ARRAY Toronto 1971
Assn de musique actuelle de Québec Quebec City 1978
Assn pour la création et la recherche électroacoustique du Québec Montreal 1977
*Canadian Electronic Ensemble Toronto 1971
*Canadian Music Associates Toronto 1952–8
*CCMC Toronto 1974

Comus Music Theatre Toronto 1975
*Days Months and Years to Come Vancouver 1975
Edmonton New Music Series
Espace musique Ottawa 1979
Les Événements du neuf Montreal 1978
*GIMEL Quebec City 1974
Gropus 7 Montreal 1975
*Infonie Montreal 1969–73
Isaacs Gallery Mixed Media Ensemble Toronto 1965–7
*Lyric Arts Trio Toronto 1964
McGill Percussion Ensemble Montreal 1969
*Musica antica e nuova Montreal 1951–5
Music Inter Alia Winnipeg 1977
Musique de notre temps Montreal 1956–?
Musique en vie Montreal 1979
*New Music Concerts Toronto 1970
New Music Co-operative Toronto 1974
*Nexus Toronto 1971
*NOVA MUSIC Halifax 1971
Quatuor de saxophones de l'Infonie Montreal 1973
*Société de musique contemporaine du Québec Montreal 1966
*Society of Canadian Music Montreal 1953–69
*Ten Centuries Concerts Toronto 1962–7
TRIO 3 Montreal 1977
*Vancouver New Music Society Vancouver 1973
*Vogt Society Toronto 1936–45

See also Canadian League of Composers; Canadian Music Centre; The Canada Music Citation; Electronic music; First Symposium of Canadian Contemporary Music; International Conference of Composers; International Week of Today's Music.

BIBLIOGRAPHY
CMCouncil. *Contemporary Music and Audiences / La Musique contemporaine et la public*, brochure (Toronto 1970)
Schulman, Michael. 'Contemporary music groups thriving across Canada,' *MSc*, 303, Sep–Oct 1978
CMCouncil. 'Contemporary music in Canada: a selective list of contemporary music societies: performing groups interested in contemporary music,' pamphlet [Ottawa 1980]

Contemporary Showcase. Week-long festival held approximately biennially at the *U of Toronto, 1970, 1972, 1974, 1976, and 1979, to promote the use of contemporary music in teaching and performance. In 1976 it became concerned exclusively with Canadian music. The first showcase, in November 1970, was organized by the Contemporary Music Selection Committee of the Central Toronto Branch of the *ORMTA. The members of this committee (Rachel *Cavalho, Patricia Elliott, Ralph Elsaesser, and Terry Levis) already had worked together throughout the late 1960s, preparing the graded lists of Canadian piano works which appeared in **Musicanada* (Jun–Jul, Aug–Sep 1968) and ensuring that recordings of such works were made by Cavalho on CCM 1 and 2 and by Warren *Mould on Dominion S 69002. The showcase presents student performances of selected contemporary Canadian music, premieres of Canadian works commissioned for the festival, workshops, and guest speakers. Winning student performers appear in a public concert on the last day of the festival. A student composer competition also is featured. Guest speakers have included Lukas Foss, Wilfred Mellers, Geoffrey *Payzant, and R. Murray *Schafer. Scholarships (totalling $6500 in 1979) are awarded to promising student performers and composers.

After the first showcase in 1970 the Contemporary Music Showcase Assn, founded to take responsibility for the organization of future festivals, began to work in collaboration with the *CMCentre. In 1978 the association changed its name to the Alliance for Canadian New Music Projects. By that time, supported by the *OAC, the *Canada Council, and private donors, the association had commissioned works by *Bauer, *Buczynski, *Calvert, *Cherney, *Freedman, *Gellman, *Healey, *Morley, *Pentland, *Rae, Schafer, *Symonds, and *Wuensch. It has published a graded syllabus of contemporary music along with each of its festival programs. Showcase/Alliance presidents have included Terry Levis 1970–2 and Joseph *Macerollo 1973–7, the latter succeeded by Mary Gardiner in 1977.

BIBLIOGRAPHY
Gyokeres, Nancy. 'Contemporary Showcase '70: teachers encouraged to use new Canadian music,' *MSc*, 258, Mar–Apr 1971
Littler, William. 'Canadian composers get to sound off,' *Toronto Star*, 27 Feb 1979 (NM)

COOK, (Alfred) **Melville**. Organist, choir conductor, teacher, b Gloucester 18 Jun 1912; ARCO 1931, FRCO with the Harding Prize, 1931, B MUS (Durham) 1934, D MUS (Durham) 1940. He studied in England with Sir Herbert Brewer, Herbert Sumison, and Sir Edward Bairstow. At 25 he became the youngest organist ever appointed to Leeds Parish Church, remaining there 19 years, except for five years in East Africa with the Royal Artillery. He subsequently was organist-choirmaster 1956–66 at Hereford Cathedral and conducted the Three Choirs Festival there in 1958, 1961, and 1964. He moved to Canada in 1966 as director of the *Winnipeg Philharmonic Choir and organist-choirmaster at All Saints Anglican Church. In 1967 he became the organist-choirmaster at Metropolitan United Church, Toronto, where he has organized series of organ recitals, chamber concerts, and choral performances, and presented a number of oratorios with the Metropolitan Festival Choir and orchestra. He became teacher of organ at *McMaster U, Hamilton, in 1974. Among his published choral compositions are 'I Love All Beauteous Things' (Stainer & Bell 1935), 'West Sussex Drinking Song' (Curwen 1956), and 'Antiphon of Darkness and Light' (Novello 1973), commissioned for the Dayspring Festival at Metropolitan United Church. He gives recitals and adjudicates in Canada and abroad. He has made recordings at Hereford Cathedral (EMI CSD 3565, RCA LVLI 5019) and Leeds Parish Church (RCA VICS 1624). (MMI)

COOKE. Winnipeg family: 1 / Richard (Westall) Cooke, his daughters, 2 / Audrey (Belyea) and 4 / Phyllis (Thomson), and his son-in-law 3 / Herbert Belyea, husband of Audrey.

1 **Richard** (Westall). Business executive, volunteer-administrator, choirmaster, b Leeds 28 Apr 1903. Brought to Canada at seven, he sang as a child in Manitoba church choirs. In the years prior to 1964 he served as choirmaster in four Winnipeg Anglican churches successively. He joined the *Men's Music Club of Winnipeg in 1924, becoming secretary in 1944, and at the same time secretary for the club's main project, the *Manitoba Music Competition Festival. He retained that dual post for 16 years, then served three years as the club's president. In the 1940s he was secretary of the Winnipeg Civic Music League, which was responsible for the revival of the *Winnipeg SO. With the incorporation in 1949 of the *Federation of Canadian Music Festivals, he became secretary-treasurer of that organization and remained responsible for the selection of adjudicators for competition festivals across Canada until 1978. Before his retirement from the business world in 1968 he was secretary-treasurer and director of the Winnipeg printing firm Saults & Pollard. In 1972 he became secretary for the *National Competitive Festival of Music. A trophy, to be awarded to the best public-school choir, was named in his honour in 1978. He received the *CMCouncil Medal in 1979.

2 **Audrey** (Cecilia) (m Belyea). Pianist, organist, b Winnipeg 1 Aug 1930; ARCT 1966. She studied during the 1940s with Gwendda Owen *Davies, and in the 1960s with Jean *Broadfoot, Douglas *Bodle, Leonard *Isaacs, and Donald *Hadfield. In 1949 she became an accompanist for the Manitoba Music Competition Festival. She has been an organist 1957–76 in Winnipeg churches and has taught privately. Her pupils include the pianist Duncan Campbell.

3 **Belyea,** (Warren) **Herbert**. Teacher, choir conductor, composer, b Winnipeg 22 Dec 1917; BA (St John's College, Winnipeg) 1948, B ED (Manitoba) 1953, M ED (Manitoba) 1961. He taught music in the schools before joining the Faculty of Education at the *U of Manitoba in 1967. He served 1952–66 as choirmaster at St Jude's Anglican Church, Winnipeg, and assumed the same position at St Andrew's United Church in 1971. Some of his vocal and choral pieces have been published by Frederick *Harris.

4 **Phyllis** (Angela) (m Thomson). Soprano, b Winnipeg 14 May 1934. She studied voice in Winnipeg with Doris Mills *Lewis and won top honours (Tudor Bowl 1952, Rose Bowl 1956) in the Manitoba Music Competition Festival. Later studies were with Lucien *Needham and Victor *Martens. She was a member of the CBC *Choristers and a soloist with Berythe *Birse's Oriana Singers. She has been soloist with the *Vancouver SO (*St Matthew Passion*, 1963), the *Winnipeg Philharmonic Choir (*Judas Maccabaeus*, 1958; *St John Passion*, 1963; *St Matthew Passion*, 1965; *The Creation*, 1966), the Winnipeg SO (Mahler's *Symphony No. 4*, 1969; Beethoven's *Symphony No. 9*, 1969; Vaughan Williams' *Serenade to Music*, 1972), and the *Calgary Philharmonic (Mozart's *Requiem*, 1974). She was a member 1964–9 of the *Manitoba University Consort. She has adjudicated across Canada. Her clear soprano is particularly suited to renaissance and baroque music, oratorio, and the song repertoire. She has given many public and CBC recitals with her husband, the pianist Stewart *Thomson. (RG, SRM)

COOP, Jane (Austin). Pianist, b Saint John, NB, 18 Apr 1950; B MUS (Toronto) 1972, M MUS (Peabody Cons) 1974. She grew up in Calgary, where her teachers included Alexandra *Munn and Gladys *Egbert. She studied 1968–72 with Anton *Kuerti in Toronto and was awarded the 1971 W.O. *Forsyth Memorial Scholarship. She also studied 1972–3 with Peter Feuchtwanger in London, and 1973–4 with Leon Fleisher in Baltimore. She was Kuerti's teaching assistant 1974–80 and joined the Dept of Music at the *U of British Columbia in 1980. She won first prize in the *CBC Talent Festival in 1970 and in the Washington International Competition in 1975, the Baldwin Prize in the Maryland International Piano Competition in 1972, and the only piano prize given in the New York Concert Artists' Guild Competition in 1975. In 1977 she placed fourth in the Munich International Piano Competition.

Coop has appeared in concert and recital throughout Canada and in the USA, and has been heard over CJRT radio and CBC radio and TV. She was a member 1975–6 of the Harvard Summer School Chamber Players in Cambridge, Mass. She has been a guest soloist with several Canadian orchestras, including the *CBC Vancouver Chamber Orchestra, the *Calgary Philharmonic, the *NACO, the *TS, and the *Thunder Bay, *Vancouver, and *Victoria SOs, and with chamber groups such as the *Orford String Quartet and the *York Winds. Not only a solo performer, Coop has collaborated with the singers Ingemar *Korjus, Rosemarie *Landry, and Janet *Stubbs in recitals of lieder and art songs; and in 1976 with Adrienne *Shannon in a duo-piano debut at the *St Lawrence Centre, Toronto. She has recorded works by Bach, Mendelssohn, and Berg (1971, CBC SM-146).

BIBLIOGRAPHY

Marchant, Janet. 'The passion of a concert pianist,' *Today Magazine*, 6 Sep 1980

(FH, NM)

COOPER, Irvin. Composer, conductor, pianist, b Nelson, Lancashire, England, 16 Aug 1900, d Florida Nov 1971; ARMCM 1922, B MUS (McGill) 1925, D MUS (Montreal) 1945. He studied 1919–23 at the RMCM with Max Meyer (piano), Walter Carroll (composition), Marie Brema (opera), and Sir Hamilton Harty (conducting). He moved to Canada in 1923 and settled in Montreal, where he was music director 1923–38 at West Hill High School and a lecturer in music education in 1926 at *McGill U. In 1939 he initiated and served as first president a group that became the *QMEA. Other positions included supervisor of music in 1938 for the Montreal Protestant schools, director 1947–8 of the Eastern Townships Cons, Stanstead, Que; president in 1947 of the International Festival of School Music; and educational director 1948–50 for Gordon V. *Thompson Limited. During the years 1948–50 he also appeared as a conductor of choirs, orchestras, and bands, and as a guest speaker at state festivals and conferences in the USA. In 1945 he won the Order of Merit (Quebec) for outstanding service to education. In 1950 he was engaged by Florida State U to give courses in the teaching of music. His compositions, mostly vocal works, have been published by Boston, Carl Fischer, Remick, Curwen, McLaughlin & Reilly, and of course Thompson, and many are listed in the *Catalogue of Canadian Composers*. His *Circle of Fifths* (Toronto 1933) is a textbook on the rudiments of music. (See also School music.) CWt

Co-Ordinated Arts Services. Non-profit organization founded in Toronto in 1968, under the sponsorship of the *Canada Council and the *OAC, to help arts organizations increase revenues cooperatively and cut costs through a system of shared services. On behalf of its members (which by 1978 included the *COC, the National Ballet of Canada, the *Shaw and *Stratford Festivals, Toronto Arts Productions, and the *TS) the organization has taken responsibility for the allocation of subscription seating and the mailing of publicity and other materials. Besides maintaining and renting out a mailing list of over 100,000 addresses of subscribers to the member organizations, CAS has revised press and board lists regularly. In 1977 it mailed more than two million brochures, flyers, press releases, and newsletters on behalf of its members.

CAS developed a portable pension plan for the salaried artistic and administrative personnel of member companies, and in 1975, with financial assistance from the OAC, it instigated a program which provides a trained person to advise on the development and maintenance of archives for each of the companies. In addition, CAS Productions have provided a common scenery-building and storage facility for the COC and the National Ballet. In 1971 and 1972, as a forerunner to Wintario (Ontario's lottery program), CAS organized two fund-raising lotteries (Lottario I and II); the proceeds of the lotteries were divided among participating CAS members.

Initially funded by the Canada Council (through grants to member organizations) and the OAC, CAS was self-sustaining by 1973, financed solely by the users of its services. Its board of directors comprises one administrative representative and one board representative from each of its members. Executive directors of CAS have included James *Norcop 1968–70, Norman Walden 1970–3, and Ruth Cox and Barbara Tiede jointly 1973–7, succeeded by Barbara Tiede alone in 1977. CAS offers associate membership to other non-profit arts organizations. An associate member organization does not delegate a member of its board and a member of its administration to the CAS board, but is entitled to use its choice of the CAS services at the fees stipulated for each. In 1978 such associate members numbered over 50, including the *CCA, the *Festival Singers, the *Guelph Spring Festival, the *Hamilton Philharmonic, the *Southern Alberta Opera Assn, and the *Vancouver Opera Assn.

BIBLIOGRAPHY

Adler, Stephen. 'C.A.S.: a united front for the performing arts,' *Toronto Symphony News*, Jan–Feb 1976

(NM, PW)

Copyright. The legal protection given to creators of literary, musical, and artistic works.

1 Copyright proper
2 Performing rights
3 Mechanical and synchronization rights
4 International conventions
5 Historical notes

1 COPYRIGHT PROPER. The owner of the copyright for a particular literary, dramatic, musical, or artistic work has the sole right to reproduce such a work or any substantial part of it in any form, and to perform it or authorize the performance of it in public. The right to reproduce includes the right to make copies of notated music by means of handwriting, printing, photocopying, photography, or other process. While registration is not a requisite of copyright protection, a composer, arranger, or publisher of music may register, for a fee, a work with the Copyright Office of Consumer and Corporate Affairs Canada, in Ottawa. For international protection, however, it is recommended to place a *c* (for 'copyright') inside a small circle (©) at the bottom of the first page of music, followed by the name of the copyright owner and the year.

If a piece is published, the publisher usually acquires the copyright from the composer in return for the payment of a royalty on each copy sold. Canadian publishers (and self-publishing composers) are obliged to deposit copies of each work immediately after publication in the *NL of C (and also, in the province of Quebec, in the BN du Q). The proof-of-publication date indicated by deposit receipts, the listing in the current bibliographies *Canadiana* and *Bibliographie du Québec*, and the accessibility to library patrons are obvious benefits of 'legal deposit.' The copyright on a published work extends for 50 years after the composer's death, at which time the composition enters the 'public domain,' ie, it no longer enjoys protection. There are special provisions for works of joint authorship and anonymous or pseudonymous works.

Canadians wishing to protect their copyrights in the USA must realize that it is essential to register a composition with the Copyright Office of the Library of Congress, Washington, DC.

2 PERFORMING RIGHTS. The Canadian Copyright Act guarantees to the copyright owner the sole right to authorize public performances, as do the copyright acts of virtually all other developed countries. These rights are divided into two basic categories, small rights and grand rights.

Small rights cover performances of all musical works unaccompanied by stage action (as opposed to grand rights, which cover performances of dramatico-musical works). In order to administer small rights effectively in view of the wide diversification of methods of performance throughout the world, the creators of musical works and the publishers have established special organizations which operate as non-profit collectives for the administration of their rights. These 'performing rights societies,' *CAPAC and *PRO Canada in Canada, collect revenue for the live public performances and cinema, radio, and TV performances of their members' music; they distribute this revenue on the basis of performance frequency and other criteria. Revenues are collected through the licensing of concert halls, dance halls, other places of entertainment, broadcasting stations, cinemas, etc. Licensing also embraces the public performance of certain recordings. Annually, for the various types of performance, both CAPAC and PRO Canada propose tariffs which must be approved by the Copyright Appeal Board. Certain exemptions are allowed for performances for educational, religious, and charitable purposes.

Grand rights cover performances of dramatico-musical works such as operas, operettas, musical shows, oratorios, or ballets. Grand rights must be obtained for each production directly from the copyright owner rather than from his performing rights society which, however, usually is authorized to administer the rights for the performance of individual excerpts from such works.

3 MECHANICAL AND SYNCHRONIZATION RIGHTS. These terms relate to the sole right to authorize or make any device by which copyright musical works may be performed mechanically. Any person or company wishing to produce a recording of such music must obtain a licence from the owner authorizing the mechanical reproduction. It should be noted, however, that once a licence for a recording has been issued by the copyright owner to one person or organization, any person or organization wishing to produce another recorded version of the same composition may do so under a statutory licence. Few such licences are issued pursuant to the statutory rules, but an industry custom has developed whereby most compositions under five minutes in duration are licensed at two cents per recording sold, subject to negotiation.

Permission from the copyright owner also must be obtained for the synchronization right, ie, the right to use recorded music protected by copyright in conjunction with a visual medium. The fees vary according to the length of the music and other factors.

In 1976 the *CMPA set up the Canadian Musical Reproduction Rights Agency (Agence canadienne des droits de réproduction musicaux limitée) to administer mechanical and synchronization rights. Most copyright musical works could be cleared through this organization thereafter.

4 INTERNATIONAL CONVENTIONS. The two international copyright agreements in force in 1980 were the Berne Convention (1886, various revisions 1896–1971) and the Universal Copyright Convention (1952, revised 1971). Nearly all countries have subscribed to one or the other, and many, including Canada, to both. Basically each subscribing

country undertakes to apply its national copyright laws to the nationals of each other signatory country.

As a result of these two conventions authors are assured of worldwide protection and, inasmuch as the domestic copyright laws of most countries are similar in nature, the creative person is assured of adequate protection on a worldwide scale. Most countries observe a term of copyright for the life of the composer and 50 years following his death.

5 HISTORICAL NOTES. Since British statutory copyright law goes back to 1710, it is not surprising to find that as early as 1832 the *Provincial Statutes of Lower-Canada* provided that authors and composers (and their executors, administrators, and legal assigns) had the sole right to print, reprint, publish, and sell their works for a term of 28 years. In 1841 this statute was extended to Upper Canada. In the following year Canadian copyright was extended to residents of the United Kingdom, provided that their works were printed and published in Canada; but it was not until 1850 that Canada imposed a duty on the import, from the USA or continental Europe, of reprints of British copyrights. The registration of a Canadian publication through deposit in the Office of the Registrar of the lower and upper provinces and in the Legislative Library, together with a statement of copyright on the publication itself, was introduced in 1859. (Up to that year only seven musical publications, all hymnbooks, bore copyright notices.) According to Calderisi, Martin Lazare's 'Canadian National Air' (Nordheimer 1859) is the first sheet music with a Canadian copyright notice (many Nordheimer publications had US notices). Maria Stisted's *The Rose of Ontario Waltz* (Nordheimer 1868) is the first musical item – number seven – in the numerical register of copyrights. The numbering system continued to 42,462 in 1924 and included a large proportion of music. Many of the deposit copies have found their way from the Dept of Agriculture, the first to be charged with copyright administration, to the NL of C (see Bibliography entry for information about copyright lists). The fact that only about two-thirds of Canadian music publications of the late 19th century bore copyright notices may be the result of one publisher's trust in his colleagues and in some cases of ignorance of the benefits available.

After the Berne Convention of 1886 a British publisher no longer had to print copies of his music in Canada to prevent US publishers from selling the reprints in Canada. (See Anglo-Canadian Music Company.) The revised Berne Convention of 1908 resulted in the United Kingdom copyright legislation of 1911 (which had some bearing on Canadian practice) and in similar Canadian legislation in 1921. This act protected copyright during the lifetime of an author and for 50 years after his death for published works, and copyright until publication and 50 years thereafter for unpublished works (regardless of whether the author died before publication). The 1921 legislation also introduced the provision for compulsory licensing for the mechanical reproduction of musical works on sound recordings, discussed above. Substantially the 1921 legislation remained unchanged in 1980, but during the 1970s much discussion took place to initiate a revision of the copyright laws, particularly in view of the many new technologies for duplicating and distributing music. The act was scheduled for revision in the 1980s.

BIBLIOGRAPHY

'Copyright,' *Encyclopedia Canadiana*, vol 3 (Ottawa 1958)
Mills, John V. 'Music and the copyright law,' *CMJ*, vol 5, Spring 1961
Henderson, Gordon F. 'Copyright: protection for originality,' *MSc*, 252, Mar–Apr 1970
Boncompain, Jacques. *Le Droit d'auteur au Canada* (Montreal 1971)
Mills, John V. *You and the Music Business / L'Industrie musicale et vous* (Toronto 1974)
Calderisi, Maria. 'Music publishing in Canada: 1800–1867,' unpubl MMA thesis (McGill 1976)
Keyes, A.A., and Brunet, C. *Copyright in Canada. Proposals for a Revision of the Law.* (Ottawa 1977) (JVM)

CORBEIL. Quebec singers: 1 / Paul-Émile and 2 / Claude, his son.

1 **Paul-Émile**. Bass, radio producer, actor, producer, b Montreal 5 Oct 1908, d there 10 Jan 1965. He studied with Salvator *Issaurel and in 1928 distinguished himself at a concert given by Issaurel's pupils in Lindsay Hall. He received a grant that year from the Delphic Study Club as well as trophies in 1928 and 1929. He was a soloist with the *Assn des chanteurs de Montréal, sang in 1928 in Henri *Miro's **Vox populi* at the Delorimier stadium, and made his operatic debut in 1929 in Massenet's *Hérodiade* at the *St-Denis Theatre. *La Lyre* (May 1929) remarked on 'the impressive debut of this extraordinary bass' in the role of Phanuel. He performed 1932–4 in Canada and the USA with a vocal quartet, the Imperial Grenadiers, which he had founded with the tenors François Brunet and Gaston Nolin and the baritone Albert *Viau. In the spring of 1934 Wilfrid *Pelletier presented the quartet in two *Metropolitan Opera Sunday concerts. It performed on the NBC network at Radio City Music Hall and for Bluebird (La Bonne Chanson collection) made three 78s whose titles appear in *Pionniers du disque folklorique*. Corbeil produced several programs for NBC, including 'Hands across the Border.' He returned to Montreal in 1935 as chief producer for radio station CRBC. In 1937 he became the first director of radio station CJBR in Rimouski, Que, and in 1941 he was appointed artistic director at CKAC. In September 1941 at the St-Denis Theatre he sang supporting roles in the Metropolitan Opera's productions of *Mignon*, *La Bohème*, and *Madama Butterfly*.

The writings of the popular poet Jean Narrache, whom he had met about 1927, inspired Corbeil to create the character of an old storyteller, presented 1941–9 on radio station CKAC as 'Le Vagabond qui chante' and revived in 1961 on CFTM TV as 'Le Vieux Vagabond.' He and Paul Langlais were partners in an agency called Radio Programme Producers, and Corbeil maintained his own radio production office. He produced the program 'Les *Joyeux Troubadours' 1941–53 for CBC radio and played the title role in 'L'Oncle Paul' ca 1948–55 on radio station CKAC. In 1962 he recorded the poetry of Narrache on three LPs (Musirac): *Le Temps de Noël puis du jour de l'An*, *Le Temps de Pâques*, and *Le Temps des semences pis des vacances*. He also recorded *Chansons à répondre avec Paul-Émile Corbeil et les gais copains* (Fonorama MF-5) and one 78 (Victor 55-5226). Besides his son Claude, his pupils have included Jean-Pierre Comeau, Dolorès Drolet, Guylaine *Guy, and Lise Roy.

2 (Paul) **Claude**. Lyric bass, b Rimouski, Que, 17 Apr 1940; premier prix (CMM) 1958. He studied 1955–8 at the *CMM under Dina Maria Narici and Ruzena *Herlinger, and at 18 made his debut as Schaunard in *La Bohème* with the *Quebec SO conducted by Wilfrid *Pelletier. He won the 1962 *CBC Talent Festival, received a scholarship in 1967 from the International Nickel Co of Canada, and

Claude Corbeil

in 1969 won the second prize at the International Singing Competition of the City of Toulouse. He made his Covent Garden debut in 1965 as Silvio in *I Pagliacci* and appeared also in Britten's *Billy Budd*. Reviewing the latter Arthur Jacobs commented, 'Among the newcomers Claude Corbeil brought a fine voice and dignity to the small part of the Novice's Friend' (*Opera*, June 1965). The same year Corbeil sang Mac Jorry in the premiere of Gilbert Bécaud's *Opéra d'Aran* at the *PDA. His roles with the *Théâtre lyrique de Nouvelle-France included Nilakantha in *Lakmé* (1965), Don Andres in *La Périchole* (1966, 1967), Colline in *La Bohème* and the Count in *Manon* (1967), Raimondo in *Lucia di Lammermoor* (1968), and Guglielmo in *Così fan tutte* (1970). He also toured Quebec in 1967 as Basilio in *The Barber of Seville*. For his 1970 debut with the *COC he sang Masetto in *Don Giovanni*, and in 1974 for that company he sang Zuniga in *Carmen* and Bluebeard in Bartók's *Bluebeard's Castle*. He repeated the Count (1973), Colline (1975), and Basilio (1976) with the *Opéra du Québec and sang supporting roles in *La Traviata* and *Salomé* in 1972. He appeared with the *Vancouver Opera in 1970, 1971, and 1974, the *Edmonton Opera in 1971 and 1975, the *Manitoba Opera in 1975, and *Festival Ottawa in 1975 and 1978.

Claude Corbeil's lyric bass, mellow and resonant, is adaptable equally to the lightness required in the Rossini operas and to the heavier demands of oratorio or the recital repertoire. He has sung with the *MSO, the Quebec SO, the *TS, and the *NACO. Among his roles on CBC TV have been the Grand Inquisitor in *Don Carlo* (1968) and le Bailli in **Colas et Colinette* (1969). He sang in Lausanne in 1965 and 1967 and appeared in Mulhouse and several other cities in France in 1969. He sang the title role of *Don Giovanni* in 1968 in Chautauqua, NY, and appeared in *Samson et Dalila* in 1968 in Pittsburgh and in *Manon* in 1969 with the New York City Opera and in Los Angeles. He sang in *Tosca* (1969), *Lucrezia Borgia* (1969), and *Otello* (1971) with the Philadelphia Lyric Opera. In 1970 he made the first of regular appearances in Miami, New Orleans, and Hawaii, and in the summer of 1977 he sang in Santa Fe, New Mexico.

DISCOGRAPHY

Rameau *Aquilon et Orithie*: Lyman v da gamba, G. Baillargeon vn, M. Lagacé hpd – Fauré *L'Horizon chimérique*, *Op 118* – Ropartz *4 Poèmes d'après l'Intermezzo de Henri Heine*. J. Lachance pf. 1970. RCI 296
See also *Colas et Colinette*.

BIBLIOGRAPHY

'Canadian bass Claude Corbeil: a CBC "Opera Time" interview,' *OpCan*, Fall 1978 1 / ST, 2 / SW

CORMIER, Paul. See Pointu, Monsieur.

CORNEILLE, Marcelle (Sister Saint-Armand-Marie). Administrator, educator, b Montreal 27 Jan 1923, B MUS (Montreal) 1952, L MUS (Montreal) 1960. She entered the order of the Congregation of Notre-Dame in 1943 and in the same year obtained a diploma in religious studies from the Institut Pie X in Montreal. She became interested in the music-education methods of *Martenot, Corneloup, *Dalcroze, *Orff, and *Kodály and later studied these intensively in the USA and Europe. She taught 1949–76 at the *École normale de musique in Westmount and became the school's director in 1957. She also served 1969–78 as administrator of the music section of *UQAM and, beginning in 1976, of UQAM's preparatory school of music. She was a consultant to numerous committees and organizations concerned with music education and secretary 1965–75 of the provincial executive committee and vice-president 1971–3 of *FAMEQ. She has taught music education at the Thomas More Institute and at Sir George Williams U (*Concordia U), Montreal. She has contributed to several periodicals, including *L'École* 1965–9, and has given lectures at the international Kodály symposium in 1973, 1975, and 1977, at the fourth annual convention of the Canadian Association of Music Therapy in 1977, and at the Congress of ISME in London, Ont, in 1978.

WRITINGS

'Esquisse sur la méthode Jacques-Dalcroze,' *Musicien amateur*, special issue by CAMMAC, 1969

'La formation des spécialistes en musique,' *Musicien éducateur*, vol 3, 1971 (NT)

CORNELLIER, Albert (Joseph). Baritone, teacher, b St-Rémi-de-Napierville, near Montreal, 28 Mar 1900; premier prix, light opera, Paris Cons. At five he sang in a church choir. After beginning law studies at the U of Montreal, he studied singing with Salvator *Issaurel, Arthur *Laurendeau, and Jean *Riddez and earned his living as a cinema pianist. In 1922 he gained special admission as a regular foreign student at the Paris Cons and studied there with Albert Carré. He was engaged as a lyric tenor by the Opéra-Comique, and made his debut 14 Jan 1927 as Beppe in Leoncavallo's *I Pagliacci*. He lived in Paris until 1947, singing in Charpentier's *Louise*, Thomas's *Mignon*, Puccini's *Tosca*, Falla's *La Vida breve*, and Wagner's *Tristan und Isolde*, as well as in numerous premieres at the Opéra-Comique, notably of Messager's *Béatrice* (1927), Lévadé's *La Peau de chagrin* (1929), and Zandonai's *Conchita* (1929). He taught, sang in churches, gave recitals in Paris and the provinces, studied with Simone Sorelli, and gained a certain renown as an interpreter of Fauré and Franck.

In 1947, singing by then as a baritone, Cornellier settled in Montreal and gave a recital in the Ritz-Carlton Hotel for the *Ladies' Morning Musical Club. He taught 1948–64 at the *École normale de musique, and was the director 1951–9 of the first vocal art class at the Faculty of Music of the *U of Montreal. In 1964 he moved to San Francisco, where he was still teaching in the late 1970s. Cornellier sang Remendado in a recording of *Carmen* with the orchestra and choirs of the Opéra-Comique directed by Piero Coppola (Gramophone HMV G-L695/711, reissued on RCA Camden CCL-100). His pupils have included Jules *Bruyère, Yoland *Guérard, Jean-Pierre *Hurteau, Guy Martin, Gérard *Paradis, Joseph *Rouleau, and Huguette *Tourangeau.

BIBLIOGRAPHY

Wolff, Stéphane. *Un Demi-siècle d'Opéra-Comique* (Paris 1953) HD-G

Cornhuskers. See Wade, George.

CORON, Charles-François. Organist, tailor, notary, b St-François-de-Sales (Ile Jésus, later part of Laval, near Montreal) 21 Dec 1704, d there 13 Feb 1767. A comparison of extant documents suggests that there may have been two persons by this name. The tailor and notary were the same person, but the identity of the organist is not beyond doubt. The organist is believed to have held a position 1722–34 at the Montreal parish church of Notre-Dame. Documents described by Lapalice provide interesting light on a 17th-century musician's salary: for 20 months of work 1722–3 Coron was paid 83 livres and 15 sols. In 1725 and 1726 he received a 'capot' and a 'veste de Mazamet' (Mazamet: French town renowned for its leather and wool production), and in 1727 he was given a choice between 45 livres in cash or 50 livres in merchandise.

BIBLIOGRAPHY

Lapalice, Ovide. 'Les Organistes et maîtres de musique à Notre-Dame de Montréal,' *BRH*, vol 25, Aug 1919

Kallmann, Helmut. 'Charles-François Coron,' *DCB*, vol 3 HK

Coronations. Canadian compositions for coronations and other ceremonial occasions are not numerous, but the genre has had among its practitioners composers of distinction, including C.A.E. *Harriss and Healey *Willan.

Harriss wrote a *Coronation Mass for Edward VII* (1902) and an ode, *The Crowning of the King* (for the coronation of George V, 1911). For the crowning of George VI in 1937 Willan wrote *A Coronation Ode* (B52) to words by Frederick *Harris, a *Te Deum laudamus* (B53), and a *Coronation March* for orchestra (B71), the last two works premiered under Reginald *Stewart in Toronto. The coronation of Queen Elizabeth II in 1953 in Westminster Abbey included the singing (in the composer's presence) of Willan's 'O Lord, Our Governour' (B56, words from Psalms), the first piece of music commissioned for the coronation ceremony of a British monarch from a composer not resident in Great Britain. For the same occasion the CBC invited Willan to write his *Coronation Suite* for choir and orchestra (B57; words from Milton, James Edward Ward, and the Bible), premiered on Coronation Day in Toronto under Geoffrey *Waddington. Other CBC commissions were Alexander *Brott's *Royal Tribute* (orchestra), Jean *Coulthard's *A Prayer for Elizabeth* (strings), Bernard *Naylor's cantata *King Solomon's Prayer*, Jean *Papineau-Couture's *Prélude* (orchestra), and William Keith *Rogers' *A Coronation Tribute* (orchestra). The coronation of Elizabeth also prompted Walter *Kaufmann's *Coronation Cantata* to words by James Reaney. 'Elizabeth the Queen,' a song for young people by Claire Senior Burke, was published for the coronation in 1953 by G.V. *Thompson.

See also Sovereigns, statesmen, and other public figures. HK

CÔTÉ, Hélène. See Sister Marie-Stéphane.

COULOMBE SAINT-MARCOUX, Micheline. See Saint-Marcoux, Micheline Coulombe.

COULTHARD. Vancouver family notable musically for the careers of 1 / Mrs. Walter Coulthard and 2 / Jean Coulthard, her daughter.

1 **Mrs Walter Coulthard** (b Jean Blake Robinson). Pianist, teacher, patron, b Moncton, NB, 13 Aug 1882, d Vancouver 16 Jul 1933. She studied piano with Charles Dennée at the New England Cons, Boston, and graduated in piano and singing. Settling in Vancouver in 1905, she was a founding member (and president 1910–12) of the *Vancouver Woman's Musical Club. She performed frequently as soloist and accompanist and became known ca 1908 as a champion of contemporary music, particularly that of Debussy. A Vancouver press notice in 1910 commended her brilliant rendition of *Jardins sous la pluie*. She taught voice, and among her outstanding pupils were Maxine Castleton of the San Francisco Opera and Joan (Brownie) *Peebles. In the early 1920s she was an organizer of the British Columbia Music Teachers' Federation.

Jean Coulthard, a drawing by F. André

2 **Jean Coulthard** (m Adams). Composer, teacher, b Vancouver 10 Feb 1908; ATCM 1926, LRSM 1930. She studied with her mother and 1924–8 with Jan *Cherniavsky (piano) and Frederick *Chubb (theory). On a scholarship from the *Vancouver Woman's Musical Club she attended the RCM 1928–30, studying with Kathleen Long, R.O. Morris, and Vaughan Williams. In Vancouver she was head of the music departments at St Anthony's College 1934–6 and Queen's Hall School 1936–7 and was lecturer in composition 1947–57 and senior instructor 1957–73 at the *U of British Columbia. Intermittently she returned to compositional studies, working with Arthur *Benjamin in 1939, Bernard Wagenaar in 1945 and 1949, and Gordon Jacob 1965–6. She submitted her work for criticism to Copland in 1939, Schoenberg and Milhaud in 1942, Bartók in 1944, and Nadia Boulanger in 1955.

Coulthard's early compositions – eg, 'Cradle Song' and 'Threnody' – were mostly for voice and piano. On the advice of Arthur Benjamin she turned to orchestral composition in 1939 and during the next four years produced four works – *Canadian Fantasy*, *Excursion*, *Ballade (A Winter's Tale)*, and *Song to the Sea* – which established her reputation in Canada. She experimented 1945–50 with larger forms and more diverse instrumentation, eg, *Music on a Quiet Song* for flute and strings, *Sonatas* for cello and piano, oboe and piano, and piano solo, *String Quartet No. 1*, and *Symphony No. 1*. When compared to the sonatas, with their looser formal structure and more overt romanticism, her *Variations on B-A*-C-H*, *Duo Sonata*, and especially *String Quartet No. 2: Threnody* reveal broadening tonal material, conciseness, and an increasing mastery and intensity of expression. In 1953 the CBC commissioned *A Prayer for Elizabeth* to mark the coronation of Elizabeth II.

While Coulthard was in France in 1955 on a Royal Society of Canada Scholarship, she came

Manuscript opening page from *Night Wind* (1951) by Jean Coulthard, to a text by Douglas LePan

under the influence of Nadia Boulanger. She had planned to write an opera but instead, at Boulanger's suggestion, she began the *Violin Concerto*, a *Canada Council commission premiered in 1959 by Thomas *Rolston and the *Vancouver SO. *Lyric Suite: Sketches from a Medieval Town* and *Aegean Sketches* also reflect Boulanger's influence. In 1958 the *Vancouver International Festival commissioned the song cycle *Spring Rhapsody* for Maureen *Forrester. During the 1960s Coulthard not only wrote increasingly complex works for a variety of ensembles, many on commission, but also produced significant teaching material. The Vancouver SO commissioned *This Land* and *Canada Mosaic* and performed the latter on its Japanese tour in 1974. *The Pines of Emily Carr*, based on the journals of the west coast painter, introduces aleatoric elements, and *Music for Saint Cecilia* and *The Birds of Lansdowne* explore the uses of electronic tape.

Coulthard is the first west coast composer to have gained wide recognition. Her music, though in several styles, is unified and characterized by an integral lyricism and romanticism within a distinctly personal and contemporary framework. She was made an Officer of the *Order of Canada in 1979. She is an associate of the *CMCentre, a member of the *CLComp, and an affiliate of PRO Canada.

SELECTED COMPOSITIONS

STAGE

Excursion. Ballet. 1940. CMCentre

The Devil's Fanfare 'Four Bizarre Dances,' ballet. 1958. CMCentre

ORCHESTRA

Ballade (A Winter's Tale). 1940 (Van 1942). Str orch. Ber (rental). CBC IS Canadian Album No. 2 (*TSO)

Song to the Sea, overture. 1942 (Van 1942). CMCentre. CBC SM-215 (*Atlantic SO)

Symphony No. 1. 1951 (Tor 1954). CMCentre

A Prayer for Elizabeth. 1953 (Tor 1953). Str. BMIC 1961

Rider on the Sands. 1953. CMCentre

Serenade 'Meditation and Three Dances.' 1961 (Van 1962). Str. CMCentre

Endymion. 1964 (Hal 1970). CMCentre

Kalamalka 'Lake of Many Colours.' 1974. CMCentre

SOLOIST(S) WITH ORCHESTRA

Night Wind (LePan). 1951. Sop, orch. CMCentre

Fantasy. 1961 (Victoria 1963). Vn, pf, orch. CMCentre

The Bird of Dawning Singeth All Night Long. 1962 (Van 1964). Vn, hp, str. CMCentre

Concerto for Piano and Orchestra. 1963; rev 1967 (Ott 1967). CMCentre

Choral Symphony 'This Land' (Canadian poets). 1966–7. Soli, SATB, orch. CMCentre

Two Visionary Songs (Monro, de la Mare). 1968. Sop, fl, str. CMCentre

Music for Saint Cecilia. 1969. Org, tape, str. CMCentre

Lyric Symphony 'Symphony III.' 1975. Bn, orch. CMCentre

Burlesca. 1977. Pf, orch. CMCentre

Symphonic Ode for Viola and Chamber Orchestra. 1977. CMCentre

CHAMBER

Music on a Quiet Song. 1946. Fl, str. CMCentre. RCI 8 (Hervé *Baillargeon)

Sonata for Cello and Piano. 1947. Novello 1968. Col MS-6542 (*Friedlander)/CBC SM-305 (*Orloff)

String Quartet No. 1. 1948. CMCentre

Sonata for Oboe and Piano. 1948. CMCentre. RCI 4 (Perrier and *Newmark)

Duo Sonata for Violin and Piano. 1952. BMIC 1963

String Quartet No. 2: Threnody. 1954; rev 1969. CMCentre. RCI 386 (*U of Alberta Str Quar)

Lyric Suite: Sketches from a Medieval Town. 1957. Pf quar. CMCentre

Two Night Songs (Monro, Belloc). 1960. Bar, pf quin. CMCentre

Sonata Rhapsody. 1962. Va, pf. CMCentre

Correspondence (Sonata No. 2). 1964. Vn, pf. CMCentre

Ballad of the North. 1965–6. Vn, pf. CMCentre

Divertimento. 1968. Hn, bn, pf. CMCentre

Lyric Trio. 1968. Pf trio. CMCentre

Lyric Sonatina. 1969. Bn, pf. Wat 1973. Mel SMLP 4032 (*Weait)

The Pines of Emily Carr. 1969. Sop, narr, str quar. CMCentre

Lyric Sonatina. 1971. Fl, pf. Wat 1976

The Birds of Lansdowne. 1972. Pf trio, tape. CMCentre

Octet '12 Essays on a Cantabile Theme.' 1972. 2 str quar. CMCentre

Songs for the Distaff Muse. 1972. Sop, alto, vc. CMCentre

Music on a Scottish Folk Song. Ca 1974. Vn, guit. CMCentre

Lyric Sonatina. 1976. Cl, pf. CMCentre

Serenade (E. Gourlay). 1977. Alto, vn. CMCentre

Three Sonnets of Shakespeare (Shakespeare). 1977. Alto, str quar. CMCentre

PIANO

Four Études. 1945. BMIC 1952 (1, 2), 1954 (3, 4). (No. 1 and 2) Bar BC 2837 (*Varro) / RCI 93 (*Pratt), (no. 4) RCI 134 (*Newmark)

Sonata. 1947. BMIC 1953. 1969. RCI 289 (Ogdon)

Music on a Quiet Song. 1948. Pf. RCI 93 (*Pratt)

Three Dances. 1950. FH 1957 (3)

Variations on B-A-C-H. 1951. Novello 1972. 1969. RCI 289 (Ogdon)

Twelve Preludes. 1954–64. Ber (1, 2, 3)

Aegean Sketches. 1961. BMIC 1964. Mel SMLP 4031 (*Kubalek)

Noon Siesta. 1964. BMIC 1966. CCM-1 (*Cavalho)

Pieces for the Present. 1973. Wat 1974

Many early educational pieces (1917) at the CMCentre

CHOIR

'Cradle Song' (Padraic Colum). 1927. SA, pf. BMIC 1960. RCA CCS-1020 (CBC Van Chorus, H. *McLean)

'Threnody' (Herrick). 1935. SATB. BMIC 1961. RCA CCS-1020 (CBC Van Chorus, H. *McLean)

'Sea Gulls' (Pratt). 1954. SA, pf. Jay 1967

'More Lovely Grows the Earth' (Helena Colman). 1957. SATB. CMCentre. RCI 189 (*Montreal Bach Choir)

'Auguries of Innocence' (Blake). 1963–5. CMCentre. RCA CCS-1020 (CBC Van Chorus, H. *McLean)

'Soft Fall the February Snows' (W. Campbell). 1958. TTBB, pf. CMCentre. RCA CCS-1020 (CBC Van Chorus, H. *McLean)

'Hymn of Creation.' 1975. SATB (SATB, perc.) CMCentre

Others at CMCentre

VOICE

Two Songs (J. Joyce). 1946. Bar, pf. RCI 109 (*Diamant)

Three Songs (L.A. McKay). 1946. Bar, pf. RCI 109 (*Diamant)

'Cradle Song' (arr). 1927. Mezzo, pf. BMIC 1960. WST-17137 (*Forrester)

Six Medieval Love Songs (Latin, trans P. Waddell). 1962. Bar, pf. CBC SM-180 (*Vickers)

Spring Rhapsody (various). 1958. Alto, pf (orch). BMIC 1968 (4). RCI 203 (*Forrester)

'Ecstasy' (D.C. Scott). Ca 1969. V, pf. BMIC 1969

Several others at CMCentre

BIBLIOGRAPHY

Ridout, Godfrey. 'Two west coast composers,' *CRMA*, vol 3, Dec 1944–Jan 1945

Cluderay, Lawrence. 'Jean Coulthard,' *MSc*, 240, Mar–Apr 1968

BMI Canada Ltd / PRO Canada Ltd. 'Jean Coulthard,' pamphlets (1970, 1979)

Rowley, Vivienne W. 'The solo piano music of the Canadian composer Jean Coulthard,' unpubl DMA thesis, Boston 1973

Duke, David. 'Coulthard's career intensifies since "retirement",' *MSc*, 299, Jan–Feb 1978

Contemporary Canadian Composers

1 / JBu, 2 / VR

Country music. Popular music genre of southern US origin, also called 'hillbilly' (1920s and 1930s) and 'country and western' (1940s and 1950s). Its roots have been traced to the folksongs and ballads brought to North America by Anglo-Celtic immigrants and preserved especially in the southern USA. (See Bill C. Malone, *Country Music, U.S.A.*, Austin, Texas, 1968, for further discussion of the folk background of country music. See also Folk music; Folk music, Anglo-Canadian, for a discussion of this tradition in Canada.) With those folksongs and ballads country music shares a melodic and harmonic simplicity. Initially it was sung in the high, nasal voice characteristic of the traditional singer of the southern USA, although in later years country singing styles have diversified under the influence of other pop music genres. The addition and evolution of instrumental accompaniment (guitar, banjo, fiddle, string bass, steel guitar, dobro guitar, and drums) was a major factor in the transition of the music from a folk to a pop form.

1 Early history in Canada
2 Growth of popularity and diversification of style
3 Media
4 Canadian characteristics

1 EARLY HISTORY IN CANADA. Country music was introduced to Canadian audiences by US radio. Early shows on WBAP, Fort Worth (beginning in 1923), WLS, Chicago ('WLS Barn Dance' 1924), and WSM, Nashville ('Grand Ole Opry' 1925), as well as the later (1933) and influential WWVA, Wheeling, WV, were heard in many parts of Canada. Country music soon was presented on Canadian radio, beginning with George *Wade and His Cornhuskers on CFRB, Toronto, in 1928, and Don *Messer on CFBO, Saint John, NB, in 1929.

The US fiddlers Eck Robertson and Henry Gilliand are said to have been among the first US hillbilly performers to be recorded (Victor, 1922) for commercial release. However, French-Canadian traditional instrumentalists had recorded as early as 1918 (eg, the violoneux J.B. Roy for Victor). By 1925 the Apex label (see Compo) carried 78s of several English-Canadian traditional musicians, including the fiddlers Percy Scott, Dennis O'Hara, and Jock McDonald, and the harmonica and ukulele player Billy Russell. In the USA the music underwent its first period of transformation into a commercial product in the late 1920s, as evident in the great success of such performers as Vernon Dalhart, Jimmie Rodgers ('The Singing Brakeman,' country music's first star, and an influence on Wilf *Carter and especially Hank *Snow), the (US) Carter Family, and several instrumental groups. In 1932 Wilf Carter was recorded in the new commercial style by A. Hugh *Joseph for Canadian Victor. His 'My Swiss Moonlight Lullabye' was a national hit, the first in Canada recorded by a Canadian. His success prompted Victor to record other Canadians, including George Wade (1933), Hank Snow (1936), and Hank LaRiviere (1941). However, the Canadian records had not the success of the US ones because the Canadian market was small and unfocused. Thus for many years personal appearances and radio work sustained Canadian country performers, including such regionally popular bands as the Gully Jumpers, Charlie Hannigan and His Mountaineers, Billy Hole and the Livewires (Toronto), Bert Anstice and His Mountaineers (Montreal) who were heard on the CRBC, and Andy *DeJarlis' Red River Mates (Winnipeg).

2 GROWTH OF POPULARITY AND DIVERSIFICATION OF STYLE. Several factors (discussed in Malone, chapter 6) led to the music's increased popularity in the USA: the social upheaval of the Depression and of World War II, which brought people of varying backgrounds together and resulted in a mixing and levelling of musical tastes; the rise of movies starring such 'singing cowboys' as Gene Autry, Tex Ritter, and Roy Rogers, whose styles were tempered purposely to appeal to an urban audience; and the adoption of some superficialities of the country genre by Tin Pan Alley songwriters. Canada reflected these trends, which lasted into the 1950s.

Carter, Snow, and Earl *Heywood continued to be popular, and new performers emerged, including the Bunkhouse Boys (Maritimes), the Hillbilly Jewels (including Joe and Vivian Brown of Amherst, NS; Joe later became the patriarch of the Family Brown), Sid Plamondor and His Western Pals (Ontario), Jim *Magill and the Northern Ramblers (Toronto), Sleepy and Swede and the Tumbleweeds (Saskatoon, later to become the *Rhythm Pals), Vic Siebert and His Sons of the Saddle (Calgary), and King *Ganam and His Sons of the West (Edmonton). Singers included Stu *Davis, Bob ('Mr Sunshine') King, Myrna *Lorrie, Bev Monro, Jimmy Arthur Ordge, Stu *Phillips, Keray Regan, and Lucille *Starr and Bob Regan ('The Canadian Sweethearts'). Several of Canada's leading fiddlers began their careers during this period (see Fiddling). Western swing, a hybrid of country music and jazz, popularized in the 1930s in the USA by Bob Wills, Milton Brown, and others, had its Canadian followers during the 1940s in Siebert, Ganam, and Plamondor (and in the 1970s, during a revival associated with country rock, in the Toronto band Prairie Oyster).

In Quebec the rise in popularity of country music (based on US styles rather than traditional French-Canadian music) was marked by the first recordings (mid-1940s) of Paul *Brunelle and Willie *Lamothe. Previously the songs of Le Soldat (Roland) *Lebrun bore some resemblance, in feeling and topic, to those of country music. In *La Chanson québécoise* (Montreal 1974) Benoît L'Herbier wrote: 'country music's popularity in Quebec is easily explained. Like the average American, Quebecers, many of them farmers, country folk, and close to the soil, experienced the same feelings in the face of life, existence and the world ... Their world of simplicity mourned the loss of the La *Bolduc and lingered over Le Soldat Lebrun. Country music seemed to them a logical continuation. Moreover, "cowboy songs" possessed a certain folk flavour adapted to a "modern" climate.' Other pioneers of country music in Quebec, many of whom were still popular in the 1970s, include Bobby Hachey, Marcel *Martel, Paul Ménard, Roger Miron, and Ti-Blanc *Richard. Later popular performers have included Lévis Bouliane, Armand Desrochers, Elaine, André Hébert, Renée *Martel, Claude Patry, Larry Robichaud, Jerry and Jo'Anne (Robitaille), and especially Marie King. Songs in French are either original or translations of US hits. Evidence of country music's popularity in Quebec is the success of the Festival of St-Tite.

As country music's popularity grew across Canada, its focus began to shift from local musicians playing for social gatherings in village or town halls to professional performers who toured regionally or nationally, appearing in taverns and bars. (In Canada the most famous of these 'honky tonks' – as they are known in the USA – was the 400-seat Horseshoe Tavern, Toronto, which presented US and Canadian stars 1950–77.) George Wade probably was the first to tour nationally – in the 1930s, from the Maritimes to the prairies; others generally did not begin to tour until the late 1940s, the most popular over the years being Wilf Carter, Tommy *Hunter, Myrna Lorrie, Don Messer, and Hank Snow, each with a troupe.

However, much of Canadian country music has remained regionalized. The Maritimes and Newfoundland in particular support many performers whose songs draw on local topics and regional folk traditions and on the work of other eastern Canadian country artists. These include Omar *Blondahl (Newfoundland) and Charlie MacKinnon (Cape Breton). Some eastern Canadian performers of the 1970s ('Stompin' Tom' *Connors, Harry *Hibbs, Dick *Nolan, Roy Payne, Michael T. Wall, and others) have capitalized on their backgrounds and have enjoyed popularity elsewhere in Canada where migrants from eastern Canada have settled.

The popularity of country music declined in the mid-1950s – in part as a result of the rise of rock 'n' roll – but it recovered ground in the 1960s by annexing elements of other pop styles. Several artists (in Canada Tommy Hunter, the *Mercey Brothers, Stu Phillips, the Rhythm Pals, and others) turned from traditional to more sophisticated accompaniment and to a less characteristically country style of singing. Conversely, Shirley *Eikhardt, Ian and Sylvia (*Tyson), Murray *McLauchlan, Anne *Murray, R. Harlan Smith, and others, though not specifically country performers, show country influence and have been popular with country audiences in the 1970s.

Bluegrass, the style developed in the late 1940s by Bill Monroe (see Neil V. *Rosenberg's *Bill Monroe and His Blue Grass Boys*, Nashville 1974) and characterized by high-pitched singing in harmony and virtuosic banjo, fiddle, and mandolin playing, gathered new Canadian followers in the 1970s (attendant to the urban folk revival of the 1960s). These included Big Redd Ford, the Good Brothers, the Humber River Valley Boys, (fiddler) Rudy Meeks and Station Road, and Saltspring Rainbow (all of Toronto), the Dixie Flyers (London), the White River Bluegrass Band (Quebec), Eddy Poirier (New Brunswick), Vic *Mullen and Meadowgreen, and *Humphrey and the Dumptrucks. Several bluegrass festivals have been staged, including the annual Bluegrass Canada, which began in 1973 near Carlisle, Ont, and the Waterford Bluegrass Festival which began in 1974 at Waterford, Ont. The fusion of country songs and instrumentation with rock rhythms and attitudes, a US development during the late 1960s in the music of the Byrds, Poco, Neil *Young, and others, was foreshadowed by Ian and Sylvia's Great Speckled Bird and was adopted in Canada by the Good Brothers, Danny Hooper, Murray McLauchlan, Colleen Peterson, and Prairie Oyster. Mainstream country music also has flourished in the hands of established performers and of such newer artists as Carroll *Baker, the Family Brown, Country Edition, Fjellgaard, Mike Graham, Dallas Harms, Chris Nielson, Jerry Palmer, Ronnie *Prophet, Donna Ramsey, and Lee Roy.

Evidence of country music's growth in Canada was the formation in 1975 of the Canadian Academy of Country Music Advancement during *RPM*'s first annual 'Big Country Awards.' It was renamed the Academy of Country Music Entertainment (ACME), with Hank Smith (a Munich-born, Edmonton-based singer and songwriter) as interim president 1975–7, and the announcer Dave Charles of Toronto as first elected president. ACME members vote for the 'Big Country Awards' (patterned after the *Juno Awards, with competition in performance, composition recording, and other categories). Award ceremonies have been held in Toronto in 1975, Edmonton in 1976, Ottawa in 1977, Regina in 1978, and Toronto in 1979, and have become major events for the Canadian country music industry.

3 MEDIA. (recording, publishing, radio, TV, films, and publications). Though the major recording companies in Canada, beginning with Victor (*RCA Ltd) and Compo (on its Apex and Point labels), have included country performers on their rosters (see also Capitol, CBS Records, London, and Quality), only the smaller and often regionally oriented companies have devoted themselves exclusively to the genre. These include Al Reusch's Aragon Records (founded New Westminster, BC, 1947), which recorded Stu Davis, Keray and Bob Regan, the Rhythm Pals (with *Juliette), Vic Siebert, and others; George Taylor's *Rodeo Records (1951), which later brought forth the Banff label and took over the Celtic line started in 1933; Jack Hosier's Marathon Records (Toronto 1970, taken over in 1975 by Lonnie Salazar's Condor Music), with a roster including Dick Damron, Tommy Hunter, Julie Lynn, and Marg Osburne; Gary *Buck's Broadland Records (Toronto 1971); 'Stompin' Tom' Connors' *Boot Records (Toronto 1971); the impresario and songwriter Don Grashey's Gaiety Records (Thunder Bay 1971), with such artists as Carroll Baker and Jerry Palmer; and the singer-songwriter R. Harlan Smith's Royalty Records (Edmonton 1974), which has recorded Fjellgaard, Danny Hooper, Chris Nielsen, and Jimmy Arthur Ordge. In Quebec Bonanza and Trans World have had large country rosters. Among Canadian publishers, *BMI Canada, *Canadian Music Sales, *Empire Music, *Jarman, and G.V. *Thompson have included country musicians in their catalogues.

Radio remained a valuable performance medium for country artists until it turned in the mid-1950s to the extensive use of records (largely of US origin, although the *CRTC Canadian content regulations introduced in 1970 altered the balance of programming to some extent). Besides shows starring Don Messer, King Ganam, Cammie *Howard, and later Tommy Hunter on the CBC network, many country music shows were heard on independent stations. These included the announcer W.D. 'Billy' Hassell's program (1930s) on CJOR, Vancouver; 'Bill Rae's Roundup' (1940s) on CKNW, New Westminster, BC; 'Fiddler's Fling' (1940s; see Orval *Prophet) and 'The Happy Wanderers' (1950s, with Joe Brown and Bob King) on CFRA, Ottawa; 'Saturday Night Barndance' (1940s and 1950s; see Earl Heywood) on CKNX radio and TV, Wingham, Ont; and 'Main Street Jamboree' (1960s, with the comedian Gordie Tapp, later a star on NBC TV's 'Hee Haw' from Nashville) on CHML, Hamilton. One result of live broadcasts was the phenomenon of announcer-singers – Ted Daigle (CKBY, Ottawa), Earl Heywood and Ray Kovisto (CKCY, Sudbury, Ont), Stu Phillips, and others. In 1976 the syndicated program 'Opry North' (originating from CFGM, Toronto) reintroduced the live-broadcast format to independent radio, emulating the long-running 'Grand Ole Opry' from Nashville. A survey of Canadian AM and FM radio stations in 1976 (*RPM Canadian Music Industry Directory*, Toronto 1976) found over 110 of the 450 stations programming some percentage of country music; 15 stations presented it exclusively, the first – CFGM, Richmond Hill, Ont – beginning in 1963.

Country music has had a small place on Canadian TV from the outset, beginning in 1952 with the CBC's 'Holiday Ranch.' Other CBC shows followed, drawing on the established artists – Messer, Phillips, Ganam, Hunter, and Lorrie – for their stars. The later CTV network has presented several short-lived series, including 'Cross Canada Barndance' from Halifax, and programs starring King Ganam and Ronnie Prophet. Privately syndicated programs have included Harry Hibbs' 'At the Caribou' (1968–74), 'Don Messer's Jubilee' (1969–73), and 'The George Hamilton IV Show' (begun in 1973), all from CHCH TV, Hamilton, and 'Family Brown Country' (begun as 'Call It Country' in 1972) on CJOH, Ottawa. Many performers have had local series: Louis Bilodeau ('Soirée canadienne' on CHLT TV, Sherbrooke, Que, 1960), Gary Buck, Jerry and Jo'Anne (a biligual program begun in 1977 on CHLT, Sherbrooke), Willie Lamothe, Tex *Lecor, André Lejeune ('À la canadienne' on CFTM, Montreal, 1972–7), Lorrie, Ti-Blanc Richard, and others.

Documentary films have been made about Jean *Carignan, Stompin' Tom, Lamothe, Messer, Anne Murray, Monsieur *Pointu, and others. Documentary surveys include *Country Music, Montreal '71* and the NFB's *Every Saturday Night* (1973, about the Badlanders from Drumheller, Alta, a band formed in the 1930s). The country music milieu has served as the background for the Canadian dramatic film *The Hard Part Begins* (Cinepix 1973), based on the career of singer-songwriter Cliff Carroll, and for other films starring Lamothe and Marcel Martel.

Press coverage of country music was limited for many years to occasional newspaper and magazine articles. Canadian columns have appeared in US publications, though significantly a column published in the 1950s in *Country Song Roundup* often referred to the Canadian music as 'folk music.' Latterly some Canadian publications have specialized in the subject – *Country Gentlemen* (Toronto 1965), *Country Music Vanguard* (originally *The Underground*; Montreal 1967–69, 1971–), *World of Country Music* (Toronto 1972–3), *Country Music News* (Langley, BC, 1972–4), *Down Home* (Orangeville, Ont, begun in 1976), *Country Music Connection* (Edmonton, begun in 1976), *Canadian Blue Grass Review* (Waterdown, Ont, begun in 1978) and *Fan Fair Country Music Magazine* (St Catharines, Ont, begun in 1980 and retitled *Jamboree Country Music* that year) – all dividing their coverage between Canadian and US performers. *RPM* publishes a weekly list of hit records and has included, over the years, columns by Grant Nelson Hewlett, Johnny Murphy, and others. A column by Dave Mulholland (Ottawa *Citizen*) has been syndicated (late 1970s) in several other newspapers. Books have been written about Lamothe, Messer, and Richard. Though some scholarly consideration has been given to country music in the USA, in Canada only *Memorial U – through its Folklore and Language Archive – has included country music in its research and publications program.

4 CANADIAN CHARACTERISTICS. Canadian country music generally has followed the US model, though it has developed some distinctive characteristics. Because ethnic cultures in Canada have maintained their individuality and preserved their languages and customs to a greater degree than have their counterparts in the USA, European folk and popular musics have had an influence, especially in the West. These influences are evident in the music of the accordionists Gaby *Haas (Czechoslovakian) and Olaf *Sveen (Norwegian), of the fiddlers Al *Cherny and Victor Pasowisty (Ukrainian), and of the groups the *Carlton Showband and Larry McKee and the Shandonnairs (Irish), and the Emeralds, the Polka Dots, the Western Senators, and D-Drifters-5 (eastern European).

Canadian country vocal styles also differ from US ones in their reflection of Canadian regional speech accents. Canadian singers generally have a lower -pitched, less nasal sound than their US counterparts, with clearer enunciation, and less drawling and slurring. The Canadian style, in turn, particularly that of Hank Snow and Wilf Carter, has influenced several US singers, including Johnny Cash. The subjects common to US country songs – what George Hamilton IV has called 'cheating songs about booze, broads and slippin' around' (Toronto *Globe and Mail*, 4 May 1974) – are not absent from Canadian songs. However, a greater number of Canadian songs follow in the ballad tradition of North American folk music. As many of these songs also appeal to a non-country audience, there is in Canada a unique group of performers and composers (without a US counterpart) which is popular with both country and urban folk audiences. Among this group are the Good Brothers, Ian and Sylvia, Gordon *Lightfoot, Murray McLauchlan, Colleen Peterson, and Bob *Ruzicka.

Songs by these and other Canadian writers (Willie P. Bennett, Dick Damron, Stu Davis, Ray *Griff, Dallas Harms) have been recorded by US artists. The most popular country songs written by Canadians (and recorded by performers on both sides of the border) include Elizabeth Clarke's *'Bluebird on Your Windowsill,' Ray Griff's 'Canadian Pacific,' Ian Tyson's *'Four Strong Winds,' Charlie MacKinnon's *'The Ghost of Bras d'Or,' Hank Snow's *'I'm Movin' On,' Dallas Harms' 'Paper Rosie,' and Bob Nolan's *'Tumbling Tumbleweeds.'

Among Canadian-born country performers who have had successful US careers are Wilf Carter (as 'Montana Slim'), Ray Griff, the steel-guitarist Ernie Hagar (once sideman to Roy Rogers and in the mid-1970s a member of Commander Cody's Lost Planet Airmen), Bob Nolan, Stu Phillips, Ronnie Prophet, Bob Regan and Lucille Starr, and Hank Snow. Other Canadians have had hit records in the USA, but their homeland has remained their base. These include Carroll Baker, Gary Buck, Myrna Lorrie, Orval Prophet, and Joyce Smith ('Leave It on Your Mind' 1961). US-born performers who have lived or worked extensively in Canada include Harold 'Lone Pine' *Breau and his wife Betty Cody and North Carolina-born George Hamilton IV, who has been, through his recordings and TV show, one of the most ardent supporters of Canadian country music.

BIBLIOGRAPHY

Elliott, Kate. 'Country music ends decade on a high note,' *MSc*, 309, Sep–Oct 1979

Beaulieu, Pierre. 'Le western, blues des Nègres blancs ...,' Montreal *La Presse*, 1 Dec 1979

'Les 500 géants de la musique country de tous les temps,' ibid, 15 Mar 1980

Rosenberg, Neil J. 'A preliminary bibliography of Canadian old time instrumental music books,' *CFMJ*, vol 8, 1980

RGn, MM

COUSINEAU, Jean (Bernard). Violinist, educator, composer, b Montreal 6 Nov 1937; BA (Montreal) 1958; brother of François and Luc *Cousineau. He began studying violin with Marcel *Saucier at eight. With the aid of grants from the *MACQ 1958–61 and the *Canada Council 1961–2 he worked in Paris with René Benedetti (violin) and Renée Jamet-Hansen (harmony and counterpoint). On his return to Canada he taught violin 1962–5 at the Institut des arts du Saguenay. After developing a violin method specifically for young people, he submitted it to the educator Shinichi Suzuki, whom he visited when he was in Japan in the summer of 1965. While in Tokyo he published – in English and Japanese – *Canadian Music*, a teaching manual adapted to the *Suzuki method. He returned to Montreal in the autumn, and founded the École des petits violons and in January 1974 the ensemble Les *Petits Violons. He made numerous arrangements of works by Bartók, Corelli, Mozart, Paganini, and others, for the ensemble, and conducted it in concerts and recordings. He also composed film scores for *Pour la suite du monde, Taureau, À tout prendre, Ada, Mon Oncle Antoine* (which won the prizes for best film music at the Canadian Film Awards and the International Film Festival in Bergamo in 1971), and *Dream Speaker* (which won the film-music prize at the Canadian Film Awards in 1977). Cousineau also has contributed 1962–5 to the CBC radio series 'Histoire du jazz' and has composed music for TV serials. He is a member of CAPAC. AP

COUSINEAU, Luc. Singer-songwriter, producer, b Montreal 19 Sep 1944. He studied cello 1949–54 in Sherbrooke, saxophone for two years with Arthur *Romano in Montreal, and double-bass 1964–6 with Roland Desjardins at the *École Vincent-d'Indy. There he met the singer Lise Vachon (b Montreal 9 Jun 1944), who later became his wife. Cousineau and Vachon formed the singing duo Les Alexandrins and made their debut in 1965, with Cousineau accompanying them on the guitar. Their songs whimsically explored all aspects of everyday life, especially the themes of love and comradeship, typified in their first single, 'Les Copains' (Capitol). They gave shows all over Canada and toured Quebec several times. They were selected by the CBC to be sent by the Canadian government to represent Canada at the 1970 Festival of Popular Song in Rio de Janeiro. Les Alexandrins performed 1970–3 under the name of Luc et Lise and worked with other musicians. The elegant melodies and counter-melodies of their love songs recall the age of minstrels yet emcompass the idioms of the 1970s. During their eight-year association, they made four LPs for Capitol and the same number for Polydor, including *Les Alexandrins* (1966, CAP ST 70001), *Laisse un temps à l'amour* (1970, Poly 2424.046), *Tout le monde est heureux?!* (1971, Poly Medium 2907.006), and *Cousineau* (1972, Poly 2424.074).

Lise worked as singer and composer 1973–4 with the *Ville Émard Blues Band and 1974–7 with the group Toubabou, consisting of Michel Séguin and other musicians. After 1977 she devoted herself mainly to composing. She performed her own songs for the LP *Moi, Lise Cousineau* (1979, Le Tamanoir TAM 27017). After 1973 Luc pursued a career as composer, writing the music for the play *Double-Jeu* by Françoise Loranger, for several *NFB films, including *Le Bonhomme* and *L'Absence*, and for about 30 documentary films. He also wrote the music for numerous commercial jingles and in 1978, to market these, founded Les Productions Luc Cousineau. His fame as a writer-composer-performer grew through such LPs as *Cousineau* (1973, Clic SCN 1001), *Vivre en amour* (1975, Airedale LUL.500), *Schlack ...* (1976, Airedale LUL.506), and *Luc Cousineau* (1979, Telson AE 1520). He is a member of CAPAC and the brother of Jean *Cousineau and François Cousineau. François has been the accompanist of several Quebec singers, including Diane *Dufresne and Pauline *Julien.

BIBLIOGRAPHY
Basil, Lydia. 'Luc and Lise Cousineau: part of an incredible future for Quebec music,' *CanComp*, 73, Oct 1972 (BR)

COUTTS, George (James). Organist, pianist, conductor, composer, teacher, adjudicator, b Aberdeen 6 Aug 1888, d Toronto 28 Apr 1962. At 14 he was organist in a church in a small town near Aberdeen. He moved in 1911 to Toronto, where he held church positions and taught at the Academy of Music and at Woodstock (Ont) College. In 1921 he became head of the piano department at the *Regina Cons and concurrently held church positions, conducted the Regina Operatic Society and Regina Choral Society, and gave many piano and organ recitals, some with the violinist W. Knight *Wilson. Following studies in England 1928–9 with Sir Henry Wood (conducting) and Benjamin Dale (composition), he composed the *Sonata in the Olden Style* which in 1930 won the music prize in Governor-General Willingdon's Arts Competition. He moved in 1931 to Vancouver as organist at Chalmers United Church and conductor of the Brahms Choir and the Little Symphony (later the Vancouver Junior Symphony). He returned to Toronto and was organist-choirmaster 1940–8 at Walmer Road Baptist Church, 1948–56 at St Stephen's in-the-Fields and 1956–9 at Kew Beach United. He adjudicated and examined throughout Canada and taught at the *RCMT and the *U of Toronto. He wrote for organ, piano, violin and piano, choir, and solo voice. He arranged *Douze chansons canadiennes* for voice and piano (Waterloo 1958). MMI

COUTURE, Camille. Violinist, teacher, violin maker, b Loretteville, near Quebec, 23 Feb 1876, d Montreal 27 Jun 1961. An aunt started him in music, and he studied violin for seven years with Jean *Duquette in Montreal. In 1899 he went to Europe to continue his training and to study violin making, which particularly attracted him, perhaps because he was at once a violinist and the son of a sculptor. Studying at the Liège Cons with Jean Quintin and Ovide Musin, he also attended the school of the master luthier Emile Heynberg. He made his debut as a solo violinist in Chaud-Fontaine and gave several concerts in Liège. His shyness, however, made him prefer teaching to playing as a career. On his return to Canada it was as a teacher that he worked 1903–16 in Winnipeg, and thereafter in Montreal, where he also became an examiner for the *AMQ and was a juror for the *Prix d'Europe. His pupils included Gladys and Russell Chester in Winnipeg, and John Charuk, Georges Codling, Arthur *Davison, Jean *Deslauriers, Conrad *Letendre, Lucien *Martin, Roland Poisson, Ruth Pryce (Prix d'Europe, 1920), Marielle Provost, and Rhoda Simpson in Montreal.

Violin making was Couture's hobby, and he copied the instruments of such famous violinists as Jacques Thibaud (a Stradivarius), Adolfo Betti, Jan Kubelík, Max Rosen, and Eugène Ysaÿe. These artists all praised the high quality of Couture's work, and his talent was recognized at the Wembley Exposition in England, where he won bronze medals in 1924 and 1925. Couture used European and indigenous materials – maple-à-Giguère (Negundo, sometimes called Manitoba maple or box elder), beech, pine, and fir – carefully selected and treated with his own varnishes. He signed more than 200 violins, all of which were sold. These handmade Canadian instruments were admired by Kreisler and Thibaud; the latter wrote to Couture: 'I had the pleasure this morning of playing one of your recent violins and am delighted to re-affirm how well you have understood the art of violin making. The varnish is of great beauty and the resonance is extraordinary. Bravo and thank you!' (Montreal, 23 Feb 1921).

WRITINGS
'La Mémoire,' *Quinzaine musicale et artistique*, vol 1, 25 Apr 1931

BIBLIOGRAPHY
Tanguay, Yves. 'Chez Camille Couture, violoniste et luthier,' *P-T*, 883, Feb 1945 (CH)

COUTURE, Guillaume (William). Teacher, conductor, choirmaster, composer, organist, baritone, critic, b Montreal 23 Oct 1851, d there 15 Jan 1915. He studied solfège in primary school and at 13 became choirmaster at the church of Ste-Brigide in his native parish. He also served 1867–73? as choirmaster at St-Jacques Church, while teaching solfège at the École normale Jacques-Cartier. In the spring of 1873, with the support of Léon A. Sentenne, Sulpician and curé of St-Jacques, he went to Paris and on June 20 successfully completed the entrance examinations for the Conservatoire. There, in the foreign students' section, he studied voice with Romain Bussine and harmony with Théodore Dubois. In one year he covered a program normally spread over three, and by the end of the second year he had mastered counterpoint, fugue, and orchestration and had begun composition. In a letter to Sentenne (27 Jun 1874), Dubois wrote: 'I am happy to express my complete satisfaction with him. In the year in which he has studied with me, he has displayed assiduousness, eagerness and an intelligence worthy of the highest praise.' In March 1875 Couture's *Memorare* was sung at the Salle Pleyel, and the following 15 May the premiere of his *Rêverie* for orchestra was given by the Société nationale de musique under Édouard Colonne, at a concert which also offered works by the leading composers of the day, Duparc, Fauré, Franck, and Lalo.

Couture returned to Montreal in the summer of 1875, resumed teaching, and became a critic for *La Minerve*. Penetrating in his perception of true musical values and lucid and articulate in praise of them, he made very high demands on himself in all that he undertook and vigorously berated ignorance, mediocrity, and charlatanism wherever he found them, to the point of arousing violent animosities towards him. In July 1876 the attitude of his compatriots caused him to return to Paris, where his erstwhile teachers and musician friends gave him a sympathetic welcome.

Establishing himself in the French capital, he taught, composed, and had some works published by Girod. When Dubois succeeded Saint-Saëns in 1877 as organist of the Madeleine, Couture replaced Dubois as choirmaster at Ste-Clotilde Church, where César Franck presided over the great organ and Charles Bordes over the choir organ. Though esteemed by his Paris colleagues – Bussine, Delibes, Dubois, Fauré, Franck, Massenet, Saint-Saëns, and Vincent d'Indy – and secure in a position which inevitably would lead to increasing success and prestige through his industry, professional conscience, integrity, and worth as an artist, Couture nevertheless decided to return to Canada. His decision probably was influenced by feelings of indebtedness towards his patron, M. Sentenne, but even more by a sense of having something to contribute to the musical life of his own country. In December 1877 'it was with a clear purpose that he turned homeward,' according to his grandson, the composer Jean *Papineau-Couture, 'knowing

Guillaume Couture, 1888

full well he would meet with incomprehension, jealousy, artistic ignorance ... and the bondage of a heavy workload.' With characteristic pertinacity he set about the task of training and reconstruction he believed to be necessary in Montreal, applying all his skills as teacher, orchestra conductor, and choir director. His demands brought frequent clashes with his employers; he went from one choir to another, from Trinity Church to Christ Church Cathedral, to the Gésu Church, to Notre-Dame Church, and finally, in 1893, to St-Jacques Cathedral, where he remained until his death.

Couture taught at several establishments – Villa-Maria, the Hochelaga Convent, the High School for Girls, the Protestant High School, and the *McGill Cons – and in 1896 he even took on duties at the New England Cons in Boston. Among his Canadian pupils were Guillaume *Dupuis, Lynnwood *Farnam, L.J. Oscar *Fontaine, Achille *Fortier, Henri *Gagnon, George Alfred *Grant-Schaefer, Arthur *Laurendeau, Édouard *LeBel, Léo-Pol *Morin, Ada Moylan, Rodolphe *Plamondon, and Caroline *Racicot. Alexis *Contant also took some lessons with him.

Couture was extremely active as a conductor – at the helm of the Société des Symphonistes which he organized in 1878, and after 1880 as conductor of the *Montreal Philharmonic Society, a position he retained for 19 years. He also conducted the orchestra for some concerts by Emma *Albani. He acquainted the public with the oratorios and operas of the great classical and romantic composers including Wagner. After 1890 he founded in succession the Montreal Amateur Operatic Club (first concert in 1892), the Montreal Ladies Vocal Society, and, in 1894, the first *MSO, which he conducted for two seasons. To ensure the quality of some events he went to the length of importing players from Boston, or even, on occasion, the whole Boston Festival Orchestra. As a critic he wrote for the *Revue de Montréal* in 1877, for *La Patrie* ca 1879–84, and for the *Montreal Daily Star* 1889–90 under the pseudonym 'Symphony.' His many activities did not always run smoothly. While the US critics appreciated his worth and paid tribute to the Canadian conductor, in his own city regular campaigns of denigration and slander were unleashed against him, particularly in *L'Étendard* and the *Montreal Daily Witness*. Resolutely Couture rode out the storms and made his mark by dint of his talent, personality, and artistic merit.

His intense activity left him little time for composing. At the request of his wife, Mercédès Papineau, he wrote a *Requiem Mass*, performed in 1906 at the funeral services for the federal minister and former mayor of Montreal Raymond Préfontaine (and later at his own). At the request of a group of friends and through the intervention of the Archbishop of Montreal, Mgr Paul Bruchési, who granted him the necessary free time, he spent the years 1907–9 on his major work, the three-part oratorio *Jean le Précurseur*, based on the life of John the Baptist. Its premiere was planned for November 1914 but was postponed because of the onset of World War I. Couture never had the pleasure of hearing a public performance of the work into which he had poured all his heart and talent. It was premiered in February 1923. (See Oratorios, Canadian 6.)

According to Léo-Pol Morin, Couture 'was one of the most eminent composers of his generation, the greatest master of harmony in Canada ... an almost universal musician and the first great one in the history of Canadian music.' If some aspects of his work may seem disappointing, he nonetheless was responsible for manoeuvring Canadian music vigorously towards those standards of quality which characterize it today. Couture deserves unbounded admiration above all for his pioneer achievements and his contribution as an educator. It is in those areas, perhaps, that his claim to fame is strongest.

France honoured Couture in 1900 by naming him Officier d'Académie and Officier de l'Instruction publique et des Beaux-Arts. Montreal named a square in the Notre-Dame-de-Grace district after Couture in November of 1951, the 100th anniversary of his birth, and an avenue in the northeast part of the city in December 1962. The *CMCentre has granted him the associate status reserved for deceased composers whose work the centre holds. Several of his manuscripts and other signed documents have been deposited at the *U of Montreal. The *Répertoire numérique du fonds Guillaume-Couture (P14)* by Francine Pilote and Jacques Ducharme, with a preface of Papineau-Couture, was published by the Service des archives of the university in 1979.

COMPOSITIONS

VOCAL

Memorare 'Prière à la très sainte Vierge,' Op 1. Before 1875? Soli, chor, orch (org). Girod

Trois chorals 'Salut pour les doubles majeures et mineures,' Op 5. 1875. Chor. Girod

'Salut de la Fête-Dieu,' Op 6. Chor. Girod

'O salutaris.' 1875? Chor. Girod 1875, Breitkopf & Härtel?

'Ave verum.' 1877. Sop, bar (bass), org. Ms

'Sub tuum.' 1877? Sop, chor, org. Ms?

'Épanchement' (Turquety). 1884. Sop (ten), pf. Ms?

'Le Drapeau rouge et noir,' 'Chanson des étudiants.' Hardy ca 1890

'Rêverie.' V, pf. *Piano-Canada* 1894

Messe de requiem. 1900. Soli, SATB, orch (org). Ms

'Le Souvenir' (L. Nastorg). 1907. V, pf. Ms

Many works in mss (date of composition unknown); 'Hymne national': 'O Mon Pays, terre adorée,' Op 4 (L. Fréchette, trans J.T. Lesperance); *Atala*, cantata for soli and orch (pf); 'Three Horsemen Rode Out' for v and pf; 'Antiphono beata Maria virginis'; 'Modus respondendi in missa'; 'Modus respondendi in officium'; 'Tantum ergo,' 4 unequal vs

See also *Jean le Précurseur*.

INSTRUMENTAL

Rêverie, Op 2. 1875. Orch. Girod. RCI 233/Cap ST 6261 (*CBC Wpg O)

Quatuor-Fugue, Op 3. 1876? Str quar. Girod

Grande fugue for organ. 1876? Ms?

Berceuse. 1884. Vc, pf. Ms

Petit Menuet. 1884. Pf. Ms

Souvenir de couvent. 1906. Pf. Ms

WRITINGS

'Une oeuvre canadienne,' *Canada artistique*, vol 1, Aug 1890

'Emery Lavigne,' ibid, vol 1, Oct 1890

'Le nouvel orgue de l'Église de Notre-Dame de Montréal,' Montreal *Le Monde*, 4 Jul 1891

Laval U, Guillaume Couture letters (May 1962)

Many articles in *La Minerve*, *Revue de Montréal*, *La Patrie*, *Montreal Daily Star*

BIBLIOGRAPHY

Bridle, Augustus. 'Two pères de musique,' *Sons of Canada* (Toronto 1916)

Morin, Léo-Pol. 'Guillaume Couture,' *Papiers de musique* (Montreal 1930)

Laurendeau, Arthur. 'Guillaume Couture,' *Entre-Nous*, vol 1, June 1930

Lamontagne, Charles-O. 'Guillaume Couture,' *Canada musical*, vol 13, 6 Dec 1930

Laurendeau, Arthur. 'Musiciens d'autrefois: Guillaume Couture,' *Action Nationale*, 2 instalments, vol 36, Sept, Oct 1950

Gour, Romain. 'Guillaume Couture, compositeur,' *Qui?* vol 3, Sep 1951

Royer, Henri. 'Guillaume Couture,' *R Saint-Grégoire*, May 1952

Maheux, Mgr Arthur. 'Guillaume Couture, musicien canadien, 1851–1915,' *R de l'U Laval*, 2 instalments, vol 16, May, Jun 1962

Papineau-Couture, Jean. 'Guillaume Couture,' unpubl lecture to the Société St-Jean-Baptiste, 2 Jun 1962

Potvin, Gilles. '40 ans après sa création, reprise de Jean le Précurseur,' Montreal *Le Devoir*, 13 Jun 1964

Papineau-Couture, Jean, and Potvin, Gilles. MSO program notes, 22 Jun 1964

McLean, Eric. 'Guillaume Couture – patriarch of Canadian music,' *Montreal Star*, 27 Jun 1964

– '77 years ago the Star's music critic conducted the local premiere of Beethoven's oratorio,' ibid, 2 May 1970

Musical Red Book ADV

COUTURE, (Marie Jeanne Henriette) **Jacinthe**. Pianist, b St-Gédéon, near Chicoutimi, Que, 4 Nov 1950; M MUS piano (Laval) 1971. She studied piano 1967–71 at *Laval U with Anna-Marie *Globenski and Robert *Weisz. For her participation in the *Canadian Music Competitions she won a bursary from the Quebec Ministry of Education and continued her studies 1972–5 at Indiana U in Bloomington with György Sebök (piano) and Joseph Gingold and Janos Starker (chamber music). She returned to Indiana in 1978 to take courses in performance with Jules Herford and on occasion worked again with Sebök. She won first prize in the *MSO Concours in 1973, and won the *CBC Talent Festival, the Civic Orchestra of Chicago prize, and the *Prix d'Europe in 1974. She was assistant to Sebök at the Sibelius Academy in Finland in 1976 and in Bloomington in 1977, and also taught 1976–8 at the U of Massachusetts in Amherst. She played Liszt's *Concerto No. 2* with the *MSO in 1973 and with the *Atlantic SO in 1974, Ravel's *Concerto for Left Hand* with the Belgian Radio Orchestra in 1976, and Beethoven's *'Emperor' Concerto* with the Civic Orchestra of Chicago in 1975. Hearing her in the Beethoven, the critic Robert C. Marsh wrote: 'Her tone is large and richly colored without being percussive, and in quiet passages it commands attention as much as in climactic passages' (Chicago *Sun-Times*, 12 Apr 1975). In 1977 Couture performed at Carnegie Recital Hall as part of the exchange program of *JMC, for which organization she also toured Quebec 1976–7. She has recorded the fugues *12 x 12* by Harry *Somers (1975–7, RCI 452). HP

COVEART, John. Pianist, accompanist, vocal coach, teacher, b Toronto 14 Sep 1924; ATCM 1943. He studied for two summers 1943–4 with Gerald Moore. Coveart became a piano teacher and vocal coach at the *RCMT in 1948 and at the *U of Toronto in 1960. He taught at the *U of British Columbia summer school 1958–60 and at various times has been a coach and accompanist for the *COC. He spent the summers of 1969 and 1970 studying repertoire with the French baritone Martial Singher. He accompanied the Danish baritone Aksel *Schiøtz in western Canada, and Anna *Russell on tour in Canada and the USA and on her recording *Anna Russell Sings! Again?*. He has recorded with Jeannette *Zarou (CBC SM-8) and with Stephanie Fedchuk (*Ukrainian Songs Recital*, RCA SF 1000). (WS)

COWAN, Don (Donovan Frankland). Educator, composer, b Outlook, Sask, 22 Jun 1919; B MUS (Saskatchewan) 1948, MA (Minnesota) 1962, ED D (Northern Colorado) 1971. He taught music 1948–59 at various British Columbia and Saskatchewan high schools and 1959–61 at the Saskatchewan Teachers' College. In 1961 he joined the faculty of the *U of Saskatchewan at Regina. He has composed *Impressions* (Boosey & Hawkes 1968), *Morceau de Genre* (ibid 1968), and *Reflections* (ibid 1969) for saxophone and piano, *Charm Bracelet* (ibid 1972) for flute and piano, and *Shadows* (ibid 1975) for solo saxophone. He has written articles for *The Instrumentalist*, the *Modern Instructor*, and other periodicals and is the author of *Search for a New Sound* (Toronto 1967), *The Sounds of Music* (Toronto 1970), *Classroom Recorder Method* (Toronto 1973), and *Guides to the Recorder* (New Westminster 1969). He has edited a collection of recorder trios (Empire 1965) and arranged pieces for recorder by Maspurg, Clementi, and Scarlatti (BMI Canada).

COWELL, Johnny (John Marwood). Trumpeter, composer, arranger, b Tillsonburg, near London, Ont, 11 Jan 1926. His father and three uncles were members of the Tillsonburg Town Band, with which Cowell played his first trumpet solo at six. Largely self-taught, he did study briefly with Edward Smeale in Toronto on joining the *Toronto Symphony Band as solo trumpet in 1941. After serving during World War II with the RCN in Victoria, BC, and playing first trumpet 1943–5 with the *Victoria SO, he studied composition at the *TCM with Oskar *Morawetz and John *Weinzweig. He played trumpet with the dance band of Stanley *St John, and in 1952 joined the *TSO. In the mid-1970s he resumed his solo work, appearing with the TS and Ontario community orchestras.

With his song 'Walk Hand in Hand' (1956) Cowell became one of Canada's most successful songwriters. Introduced by George *Murray and recorded by Denny *Vaughan, Tony Martin, Andy Williams, and others, the song was a major hit in both Britain and North America. By 1977 almost 150 of Cowell's 200 songs had been recorded, including the hits 'Just My Luck To Be 15' (1957), 'Stroll Along with the Blues' (1958), 'Our Winter Love' (recorded in orchestral arrangements by André Kostelanetz, Lawrence Welk, and Hugo Winterhalter, and a major hit of 1963), and 'These Are the Young Years' (1963). By 1978 Cowell had made eight LPs of his songs and arrangements, two with orchestra and chorus for the Scope and *CTL labels, and others of varying instrumentation for Cascade, Stone, Ampersand, Audat, and Broadland. Cowell also has composed *Girl on a Roller Coaster* (1969), an encore performed by the TS, the New York Philharmonic, the Boston SO, and other orchestras; *Anniversary Overture* (1972), a CBC commission for the TS's 50th anniversary; *Sangre de Toro Bravo* (1974) for trumpet and orchestra; and a *Trumpet Concerto* (1978) premiered 18 Jul 1978 by the composer with the TS at *Ontario Place. He has arranged works by Bach, Beethoven, Handel, and Satie for soloist and orchestra. Cowell is an affiliate of PRO Canada, and has received six BMI Canada certificates of honour for his most popular songs.

BIBLIOGRAPHY
Hilliard, Harold. 'Story of a song,' *Star Weekly Magazine*, 9 Mar 1957
Ferry, Antony. 'Canada's gift to Tin Pan Alley,' *Canadian Weekly*, 17–23 Aug 1963
Duff, Maurice. 'Johnny Cowell,' *MSc*, 242, Jul–Aug 1968
Kirkland, Bruce. 'Self-taught musician pens pop hits, classical concerto,' *Toronto Star*, 15 Jul 1978

(MM, PW)

A. Cox & Co. Toronto music store and publishing firm, established by Arthur Cox and operated ca 1892 to ca 1931. Cox specialized in cheap editions of popular music. About half of his more than 150 publications are undated reprints of US and other music at that time unprotected by copyright in Canada. These range from 10-cent sheet music to collections such as *Songs That Never Die*, *Easy Pieces in Easy Keys*, and *Old Favorite Songs*. Cox' own copyrights include Robert Todd's translation of *'O Canada' (1909), H.H. *Godfrey's 'Canada's Hymn of Empire' (1899) and N. Fraser *Allan's 'Canada I Hear You Calling' (1916), and such albums as *Songs of the British Empire* (1909), *Songs for the Little Folk* (1910), and *National Songs of All Nations* (1914). Cox' publishing seems to have stopped after World War I, presumably because the copyright act of 1921 made this type of 'pirating' operation illegal. (HK)

COZENS, John. Administrator, choir conductor, tenor, b Tottenham, near London, 27 Apr 1906, naturalized Canadian 1950. He emigrated to Canada in 1913 and studied voice in Toronto. He was a church soloist in Toronto 1918–1950 and also lectured on sacred music. In the 1940s he conducted the Tallis Choir, which specialized in polyphonic music. He served 1945–9 as publicity director for the *TCM and 1949–52 as manager of the Toronto branch of the *Western Music Co. He then worked for the Ontario government, 1960–72 as its chief of protocol. In 1951, with S. Drummond Wolff, he founded a Toronto Orpheus Choir which sang for four seasons. Cozens was secretary 1944–76 of the *CMCouncil and retired as honorary secretary with the *CMCouncil Medal for outstanding service to Canadian music. He has edited choral music for Concordia, Stainer & Bell, *Thompson, and Western Music and composed two patriotic songs (Harris). He compiled *Uncommon Christmas Carols* (Schmitt, Hall & McCreary 1941) and *Six Christmas Carols* (Thompson 1948). (HK)

CPR Festivals. A series of music and folk arts festivals held 1927–31 under the auspices of the Canadian Pacific Railway and organized by the railway's publicity agent, John Murray *Gibbon, to explore the variety of Canada's cultural resources. The festivals were of particular significance in the evolution of music in Canada, representing as they did an early and happy instance of support for the arts by a major corporation, an early attempt to promote serious composition by Canadians, taking into account, moreover, the folk material of the country as a source for such composition, and one of the early concerted attempts to acquaint Canada's many different musical communities and audiences with each other. The festivals, whose activities were centred in CPR hotels in Banff, Calgary, Quebec City, Regina, Toronto, Vancouver, Victoria, and Winnipeg, also used *Darke Hall in Regina, the Walker Theatre in Winnipeg, and the Basilica and the *Auditorium in Quebec City for some of the concerts. The following chronological list cites dates, locations, cosponsors, the names of the major individual and group participants, and the highlights of the programs, where such information has been available.

1927

Quebec City, 20–2 May. Canadian Folk Song and Handicraft Festival. Other sponsors: the National Gallery, *National Museum, and Public Archives of Canada. Participants: Cédia *Brault, Jeanne *Dusseau, Juliette *Gaultier de la Verendrye, J. Campbell *McInnes, Charles *Marchand, Rodolphe *Plamondon, the Bytown Troubadours of Ottawa, the Ensemble of Spinners and Folk Singers, the Music Makers of Toronto, Johnny Boivin (champion fiddler of Canada), and the *Hart House String Quartet, which played Ernest *MacMillan's *Two Sketches for String Quartet* (which, along with the first movement of the *Sonata* for cello and piano by Oscar *O'Brien, had been composed for the occasion). After the success of this festival the CPR announced the E.W. Beatty Competition (Beatty was the president of the CPR), offering $3000 in prize money for compositions based on French-Canadian folksongs; winning pieces were to be heard at the next Quebec festival.

Banff, Alta, 3–5 September. Highland Gathering / Scottish and Music Festival. Participants included J. Campbell McInnes, Jeanne Dusseau, Davidson *Thomson, Ruth Matheson, and the Canadian Pacific Calgary Male Choir. Highland dancing and bagpipe competitions were included.

1928

Quebec City, 24–8 May. Canadian Folk Song and Handicraft Festival. Other sponsors: the National Gallery, the National Museum, and the Public Archives of Canada. Participants: many of those who took part in the 1927 festival, as well as Alexandre d'Aragon, Philéas Bédard, Gérard *Gélinas, Léon Rothier, the Canadian Singers, and Les *Disciples de Massenet. Special features included the 13th-century comic opera *Le Jeu de Robin et Marion*, and the premiere of *L'Ordre de bon temps* (*The Order of Good Cheer*), B20, a ballad opera by Healey *Willan, based on French-Canadian folksongs. Others who contributed to the festival, as composers and arrangers, were Hector *Gratton, Alfred *Laliberté, Ernest MacMillan, Léo-Pol *Morin, Oscar O'Brien, and Leo *Smith. The ethnomusicologist Marius *Barbeau also assisted. Winning works in the E.W. Beatty Competition were an orchestral suite by Arthur Cleland Lloyd, *Suite canadienne* by Claude *Champagne, a *Suite* for string quartet by George Bowles, an arrangement for male voices by Ernest MacMillan (*Six Bergerettes du Bas-Canada*), and one arrangement each, for mixed voices, by Alfred *Whitehead (*Four French-Canadian Folksongs*) and Irvin *Cooper. The judges were Achille *Fortier of Montreal, Eric De Lamarter of Chicago, Ralph Vaughan Williams and Sir Hugh Allen of London, and Paul Vidal of Paris.

Winnipeg, 19–23 June. The New Canadian Folk Song and Handicraft Festival. Featuring songs and crafts of recent settlers of 'European Continental extraction,' this festival offered performances by 19 different national groups, including Black Forest dancers and singers and the Bellman Quartet (a vocal group named for C.W. Bellman, the 'Robert Burns of Sweden)'.

Banff, 23–8, July. Indian Week at Banff. It featured ceremonial songs and dances, handicrafts, decorated teepees.

Banff, 31 August–3 September. Highland Gathering and Scottish Music Festival. Participants included Frances *James, and also Marjory Kennedy-Fraser performing Hebridean songs. In addition to highland dancing, piping, and concerts of Scottish music, Robert Burns' 'Jolly Beggars' and other historic revivals were presented.

Victoria, December. Old English Yuletide Festival. Participants included Frances James.

1929

Vancouver, 23–6 January. Sea Music Festival. Participants: Poul Bai, Jeanne Dusseau, the English baritone John *Goss, Frances James, Ulysse *Paquin, the Hart House String Quartet, and Healey Willan, who performed in recital with Marion Copp and conducted a performance of his *Order of Good Cheer*. Two works written for the occasion were *Bound for the Rio Grande*, an operetta by Frederick William Wallace (on English shanties), and a Gaelic folk play by the Vancouver musician Ethel Bassin. Also featured were solo, choral, and instrumental pieces with connotations of the sea.

Regina, 20–3 March. Great West Canadian Folksong-Folkdance and Handicraft Festival. Participants: Poul Bai, Charles Marchand, Selma Johanson de Coster (Swedish songs), Doris Williams (English folksongs), the accompanist Cyril *Hampshire, and the music director Harold Eustace *Key. This festival featured songs and dances of almost 30 ethnic groups.

Banff, 30 August–September. Highland Gathering. Participants: Henry Button, Finlay Campbell, Herbert Hewetson, Frances James, Stanley Maxted, and Catherine Wright, all of whom appeared in the premiere of Willan's ballad opera *Prince Charlie and Flora*, B21, written for the gathering, staged by Alfred *Heather, and conducted by H.E. Key.

Toronto, 13–18 November. English Music Festival (held to mark the opening of the Royal York Hotel). Other sponsors: the Lyceum Club and the Women's Art Assn of Canada. Participants: Jeanne Dusseau, the Hart House String Quartet, the English baritone Herbert Heyner, J. Campbell McInnes (who spoke on English music), the Ottawa Temple Choir, the organist Harvey Robb, and the English cellist Felix Salmond. Special features were two performances of Vaughan Williams' *Hugh the Drover*, directed by Alfred Heather, conducted by Ernest MacMillan, and with Allan Jones in the title role; and a performance of F.W. Wallace's *Bound for the Rio Grande*.

Victoria, 23–30 December. Old English Yuletide Festival. Participants: Herbert Hewetson, Frances James, Josephine Wood. Included on the program were performances of the ballad opera *Christmas with Herrick*, music arranged by H.E. Key; and a premiere production of Willan's *Indian Christmas Play*, B24.

1930

Victoria, 15–18 January. Sea Music Festival. Participants: the Amphion Society Choir and the Graham Morgan Singers (both of Seattle), John Goss, Herbert Hewetson, Herbert Heyner, Madame F.X. Hodgson, Frances James, Ulysse Paquin, Josephine Wood. Works presented included *The Order of Good Cheer*, *Bound for the Rio Grande*, and MacMillan's *Three French-Canadian Sea Songs* which had been written for the festival.

Calgary, 19–22 March. Great West Canadian Folk-Dance, Folk-Song and Handicraft Festival. Among the participants was a choir of Welsh miners.

Banff, 29 August–1 September. Highland Gathering and Scottish Festival. This featured a performance of Willan's ballad opera *The Ayreshire Ploughman*, B22.

Quebec City, 16–18 October. Canadian Folksong and Handicraft Festival. Participants: the singers Émile Boucher and Germaine LeBel, the Bytown Troubadours, Métis dancers from Alberta, the music directors H.E. Key and Oscar O'Brien. The festival featured performances of Willan's *L'Ordre de bon temps* and Alberic Bourgeois's and Oscar O'Brien's *Une Noce canadienne-française (en 1830)*.

1931
Banff, 27–30 August. Highland Gathering and Scottish Music Festival. Participants: the Scottish baritone Robert Burnett, Jeanne Dusseau, Amy Fleming, Mary Stewart, and Theodore Webb. The program included performances of the ballad operas *Prince Charlie and Flora* and *Prince Charming* (with songs arranged by MacMillan).

While not an official part of the festivals, also worthy of note is a travelling series of six concerts of British and Canadian music organized and sponsored by the CPR 1929–30, and presented in CPR hotels in Calgary, Regina, Toronto, Victoria, Vancouver, and Winnipeg. These concerts featured John Goss, the Hart House String Quartet, Florence Hood, Winifred MacMillan and Jean Rowe, Frances James, Marjory Kennedy-Fraser, Stanley Maxted, and Lucien and Rodolphe Plamondon.

BIBLIOGRAPHY
Mason, Lawrence. 'Festival proves revelation of riches of Canadian music,' Toronto *Globe*, 23 May 1927
Charlesworth, Hector. 'Order of Good Cheer revived,' *SatN*, 9 Jun 1928
Robertson, C.B. 'Artists all!' *Canadian Magazine of Politics, Science, Art and Literature*, Jan 1930
Canadian Pacific. Corporate Archives. Festival programs

CRAIG, W. (William) **James**. Conductor, coach, b Kenora, Ont, 21 Aug 1933; ARCT 1953. He studied composition and conducting with Walter *Kaufmann in Winnipeg, then continued his training in conducting at the RAM in London, and with Luigi Ricci in Rome. He was a coach and conductor 1958–64 at the *Royal Cons Opera School, conducted 1960–70 at the *Banff SFA, and was music director 1968–9 of the *Vancouver Opera Assn Training Program. He has conducted several COC productions – *La Bohème* in 1962, *Madama Butterfly* in 1964, *I Pagliacci* in 1966, and *Eugene Onegin* in 1972 – and touring productions – *La Bohème* in 1965 and 1968, *Die Fledermaus* in 1964 and 1965, and *Don Pasquale* in 1967. He also conducted 1966–70 at Sadler's Wells, where his repertoire included *La Bohème, Don Pasquale, La Traviata, Idomeneo*, and *Così fan tutte*. In 1971 he became head coach and conductor for the *U of Toronto Opera Dept. There he conducted Stravinsky's *The Rake's Progress* (1971) and the Canadian premieres of Ward's *The Crucible* (1976) and Janáček's *Katya Kabanova* (1977). The latter productions were directed by his wife, Constance *Fisher. (MM, PW)

CRAWFORD, Bertha (May). Soprano, b Toronto 1886, d there 26 May 1937. After study with Edward Schuch in Toronto, Mme Nevosky in London, and Mme Corsi in Milan, Crawford made her debut in 1913 in Venice as Gilda in *Rigoletto*. Engagements in provincial houses throughout Italy were followed by a triumphant appearance in January 1914 in Warsaw, and thereafter she sang with great success in several eastern European centres, including Petrograd in 1915, Moscow in 1916, Helsinki in 1917, and Warsaw annually ca 1919–34. She returned to live in Toronto ca 1935. Possessor of a high lyric soprano of great beauty and agility, she was particularily admired as Rosina, Violetta, and Gilda.

BIBLIOGRAPHY
Robbins, Blanche. 'Once great singer passes in Toronto,' Toronto *Globe and Mail*, 28 May 1937 JBM

CRAWFORD, Paul (Duncan). Composer, radio producer, organist, b Toronto 21 Aug 1947; LTCL 1967, B MUS (McGill) 1971. He studied piano with William Pengelly and attended St Michael's Cathedral Choir School, Toronto, receiving a Bachelor of Gregorian Chant in 1966. In Montreal he studied with Kenneth *Meek (organ) and Harry *Freedman and Bruce *Mather (composition) at *McGill U, and with Lubka *Kolessa (piano) and Raymond *Daveluy (organ) at the *CMM. After attending St Augustine's Seminary in Toronto 1971–2 he joined the CBC, working as a radio music producer 1972–6 in Toronto and 1976–7 in Ottawa (on 'Arts National'). He also has been a church organist in Toronto, Montreal, and Hamilton. In 1977 he moved to Nelson, BC.

Though Crawford often employs serialism in his compositions, he is not attracted to avant-garde techniques. The modality in much of his writing reflects his church background. His *Féerie* (1970) was premiered by *ARRAY, *La Nuit étoilée* (1972) by the *Vaghy String Quartet, and 'O quam gloriosum est' (1976) by the *Festival Singers. Other works include a piano suite, a string trio, an étude for percussion, a brass quintet, *L'azur* for orchestra (1971), and *Lyric Piece* for orchestra (1978). He is an associate of the *CMCentre and a member of CAPAC. FH

CRAWFORD, T.J. (Thomas James). Organist, choirmaster, teacher, composer, b Barrhead, Scotland, 11 Jun 1877, naturalized Canadian 1928, d after a car accident near Barrie, Ont, 5 Jul 1955; ARCO 1892, FRCO 1902, B MUS (Durham) 1902. He studied organ and theory in Glasgow with H. Sandiford Turner and Otto Schweitzer, and in 1894 in Leipzig with Carl Reinecke and Paul Homeyer. While he was in Leipzig, he was organist at All Saints (Anglo-American) Church. He also was successful there as a composer; his *Lipsia Suite* for orchestra was performed under Reinecke (and later under Sir August Manns at the Crystal Palace in London). Returning to London in 1898, Crawford assisted Sir Frederick Bridge for seven years at Westminster Abbey. In 1911 he became the organist-choirmaster of St Michael's Church, Chester Square, London. In December 1922 he moved to Toronto to take up posts as organist at St Paul's Bloor St Anglican Church and teacher at the *TCM. He conducted the Eaton Choral Society 1925–31, transforming the group in 1931 into the *Eaton Operatic Society, and continuing as music director until 1947. Crawford also conducted 1927–42 the Victoria College Music Club, *U of Toronto. He was organist-choirmaster 1931–2 at Holy Trinity Church and 1933–46 at Timothy Eaton Memorial Church. Retiring in 1946, he continued to travel as an examiner for the RCMT and produced a book, *Keyboard Harmony and Transposition* (Toronto 1952, 1966). His last position was at St Andrew's Church, Barrie, in 1954.

Among Crawford's numerous works (listed in the *Catalogue of Canadian Composers*) a *Toccata in F* (Bosworth 1904) and *In a Great Cathedral* (Western Music 1951), both for organ, continue to be performed. A *Piano Trio* and a *Scottish Suite* for strings date from his Leipzig days. *Variations on an Original Theme*, for orchestra, dates from his early Toronto years. Bosworth has published excerpts from Crawford's children's operettas, *Dot's Dream* and *Vi's Christmas Party*. MMI

CREECH, Robert (Edward). French hornist, teacher, administrator, b Victoria, BC, 26 Sep 1928; BA history, music (British Columbia) 1954, MA history (British Columbia) 1974. He studied at the *U of Manitoba, with Mason Jones at the Curtis Institute of Music in Philadelphia, and at the *U of British Columbia. He was first horn with the *Victoria SO 1945–6, the *Winnipeg SO 1949–51, and the *Vancouver SO 1958–74; second horn with the *TSO and *CBC SO 1952–8; and a member of the *Vancouver Woodwind Quintet 1968–76. He has performed widely as a soloist in Canada and the USA. He joined the music staff at the U of British Columbia in 1959, became music director of the Courtenay Youth Music Camp in 1970, and was named chairman of the music department of Vancouver City College in 1974. He was chairman 1967–9 of the music committee of the *Community Arts Council of Vancouver, and became a director of the *CMCouncil in 1975. In 1976 he became chairman of the Arts Advisory Council of the *Canada Council and chairman of the Performance Dept of the *U of Western Ontario. He has recorded with the *Baroque Strings, the Vancouver Woodwind Quintet, and the *Purcell String Quartet. MW

CREIGHTON, (Mary) **Helen**. Collector, folklorist, b Dartmouth, NS, 5 Sep 1899; hon LLD (Mount Allison) 1957, hon D LITT (Laval) 1961, hon DCL (Dalhousie) 1967, hon D LITT (St Francis Xavier) 1975, hon D LITT (St Mary's) 1976. She received a junior diploma in music from *McGill U in 1915 and graduated from the Halifax Ladies' College in 1916. During the 1920s she worked briefly as a social worker in Halifax and taught at the American School in Guadalajara, Mexico. She was 'Aunt Helen' 1926–7 in a children's radio show on CHNS Halifax.

In 1928, inspired by the work of W. Roy Mackenzie (compiler of *Ballads and Sea Songs of Nova Scotia*, Cambridge 1928), Creighton began to collect folk songs and lore in her native province, often travelling into isolated areas on foot, pushing her melodeon in a wheelbarrow. Unskilled in the transcription of music, she would 'pick out' on this instrument the tunes that were sung to her. During the 1930s she collaborated with Doreen Senior, an English musician who acted as her transcriber. Creighton was Dean of Women at *Dalhousie U 1939–41. In 1942 she received a certificate for studies at the Summer Institute of Folklore, U of Indiana. Between 1942 and 1946 she won three Rockefeller Foundation fellowships; and in 1943 the Library of Congress, Washington, DC, supplied her with her first portable tape recorder. She collected and recorded Nova Scotia songs and folklore 1943–4 and in 1948 for the Library of Congress and 1947–67 during her years on staff at the *National Museum of Canada. In 1954 she began to collect in New Brunswick as well. The Nova Scotians Ben Henneberry, Freeman Young, Grace Clergy, Enos Hartlan, and the Redden family sang for her, as did the New Brunswicker Angelo Dornan.

During her career Creighton gathered and recorded in Nova Scotia and New Brunswick over 4000 songs and their variants, in English, French, Gaelic, Micmac, and German. Among those in English were Negro songs. Typical titles in the collection are 'He's Young but He's Daily a-Growing,' *'I'll Give My Love an Apple,' 'The Cherry Tree Carol,' 'The Farmer's Curst Wife,' 'Lost Jimmy Whalen,' and 'The Bold Pedlar,' a 15th-century folk song lost in England but preserved in Canada. The oldest of her finds is the 13th-century ballad 'The False Knight upon the Road.' The best-known is *'The Nova Scotia Song' ('Farewell to Nova Scotia'), popularized in the 1960s by Catherine *McKinnon. Several Canadian

Helen Creighton

compositions have been based on the tunes Creighton collected, including the music for the ballet *Sea Gallows* (Michel *Perrault 1958), the opera *The Broken Ring* (Trevor Jones ca 1953), Klaro *Mizerit's *Two Maritime Aquarelles* (1970), and Alex Tilley's *Maritime Folk Song Medley* (1977). In addition, many of the songs have been recorded commercially. Creighton has been heard frequently on CBC radio and has appeared on CBC TV programs such as 'Open House' (1960), 'Land of the Old Songs' (1960), 'The Lady of the Legends' (ca 1966), 'The Helen Creighton Story' ('Take 30,' 1968), and the mini-series 'Gary Karr and His Friends' (1973). In 1958 she was shown at work in the *NFB film *Songs of Nova Scotia*.

Creighton's interest has extended to the performance of folk music as well as to the music itself. In 1956 she 'discovered' Finvola *Redden-Bower, and in 1957 the Redden family sang on an episode of the CBC TV's 'Graphic' which dealt with Creighton's work as a collector. She was an organizer and conductor 1967–73 of the seven-voice Nova Scotia Folk Singers. She has lectured widely in Canada and the USA and in 1959 she addressed the International Folk Music Council in Rumania. She is an authority on Nova Scotia ghost stories. Creighton is the recipient of many honours, including a *CMCouncil Medal (1974), and she was made a Member of the *Order of Canada in 1976. In March 1980 'The Collector,' a musical tribute to her life's work, was presented by *Mount Saint Vincent U. She has been a fellow of the American Folklore Society and the American Anthropological Assn, a correspondent of the International Folk Music Council, and vice-president 1957–67 of the *CFMS. She was made honorary president of the society in 1974. A member of the board of *EMC*, she has contributed several articles. She is an affiliate of PRO Canada.

WRITINGS

BOOKS

Songs and Ballads from Nova Scotia (Dent 1932, repr Dover 1966)
– and Senior, Doreen. *Twelve Folksongs from Nova Scotia* (Novello 1940)
Folklore of Lunenburg County, Nova Scotia (Ottawa 1950, repr Toronto 1976)
– and Senior, Doreen. *Traditional Songs from Nova Scotia* (Ryerson 1950)
Bluenose Ghosts (Toronto 1957)
Maritime Folk Songs (Ryerson 1962, 1972)
– and MacLeod, Calum. *Gaelic Songs in Nova Scotia*, National Museum of Man *Bulletin*, 198 (Ottawa 1964)
Bluenose Magic (Toronto 1968)
Folksongs from Southern New Brunswick, National Museum of Man Publications in Folk Culture 1 (Ottawa 1971)
A Life in Folklore (Toronto 1975)
– and Sircom, Eunice. *Eight Ethnic Songs for Young Children* (GVT 1977)
– and Sircom, Eunice. *Nine Ethnic Songs for Older Children* (GVT 1977)

ARTICLES

'Song singers,' *Maclean's*, 15 Dec 1937
'Recording folk songs "before it's too late",' *CBC Times*, 14–20 Dec 1952
'Fiddles, folk-songs and fishermen's yarns,' *Canadian Geographical J*, vol 51, Dec 1955
'Songs for Christmas,' *Atlantic Advocate*, vol 50, Dec 1959
'Collecting folk songs,' *Music across Canada*, vol 1, Apr 1963
'W. Roy MacKenzie, pioneer,' CFMS *Newsletter*, vol 2, Jul 1967
'Carols and other songs for Christmas,' *CanComp*, 45, Dec 1969
'Capturing folklore on tape,' *Canadian Author and Bookman*, 46, Spring 1971
'Canada's Maritime provinces – an ethnomusicological survey,' *Ethnomusicology*, vol 16, Sep 1973
'Looking back on a satisfying career,' *CanComp*, 120, Apr 1977
Also articles on folklore, folk dancing, in *JAF*, *Encyclopedia Canadiana*, etc
See also Bibliography for Folk music, Anglo-Canadian: 2 / Nova Scotia and New Brunswick.

BIBLIOGRAPHY

Sclanders, Ian. 'She's collecting long lost songs,' *Maclean's*, 15 Sep 1952
Belliveau, J.E. 'She's working against time to preserve ballads out of the past,' Toronto *Star Weekly*, 7 Jul 1956
MacGorman, Harry. 'Lady of the legends,' *Nova Scotia Magazine*, vol 1, Jun 1959
Cameron, Donald. 'Thanks for the memories,' Toronto *Weekend Magazine*, 28 Sep 1974
Johnston, Richard. 'Tribute to Helen Creighton,' *CMB*, 9, Autumn–Winter 1974
Edwards, Barry, et al. 'Collecting the lore of Maritime folk,' *Fugue*, Dec 1977 NM

CREIGHTON, James. Discographer, recorded-sound archivist, b Vancouver 24 Aug 1934; BA economics (British Columbia) 1956. After violin studies in Vancouver he worked 1961–4 in England as the sound archivist of the BBC Gramophone Library prior to assuming a similar position in the *U of Toronto music library. In 1970 he received the first *Canada Council grant for recorded-sound research, to assist with the preparation of his monumental *Discopaedia of the Violin – 1889–1971* (Toronto 1974; awarded the Ysaÿe Medal of Belgium in 1976). He has lectured on discography, and in 1974 he began research on a 'tapeography' of the violin. His company, the Historic Recording Society, issues both historic and contemporary violin recordings on its Masters of the Bow label and orchestral recordings on the Baton label. It had released close to 60 recordings by 1979, perpetuating performances by violinists such as Auer, Heifetz, Kreisler, Szigeti, Ysaÿe, Zimbalist, pianists such as Backhaus, Gieseking, Richter, and Michelangeli, and conductors such as Cantelli, Hindemith, Horenstein, and Koussevitsky.

BIBLIOGRAPHY

Schonberg, Harold. 'The great names march before us,' *New York Times*, 8 Sep 1974
Schulman, Michael. 'Jim Creighton: Canada's finest fiddler finder,' Toronto *Globe and Mail*, 23 Aug 1975

J. & O. Crémazie. Quebec City booksellers and music publishers. The partnership between the brothers Joseph (1812–80) and Octave (1827–79) began in 1844 and lasted until 1862. Octave, whose spiralling debts drove him first to extravagant borrowing and then to fraud, was forced to flee the country and live in France under an assumed name (Jules Fontaine). Until its dissolution the Crémazie shop on Fabrique St had been a meeting place for literati. The firm's musical interests were concentrated in a very small amount of sheet music bearing its imprint, notably three settings of poems by Octave: *'Le Drapeau de Carillon' and 'L'Alouette' by *Sabatier, and 'Chant du vieux soldat' by *Dessane. The firm also issued *Chants canadiens* (1856?), one of the earliest Canadian collections of songs. Among the seven songs it contained were 'En roulant ma boule,' 'Ah! Qui me passera le bois,' *'À la claire fontaine,' and *'J'ai cueilli la belle rose.' None of the music so far discovered actually was printed by the publishers. Three of the pieces were produced in Paris and two others probably were printed locally by a job-printer.

BIBLIOGRAPHY

Dassonville, Michel. *Octave Crémazie* (Montreal 1956)
Calderisi, Maria. 'Music publishing in Canada: 1800–1867,' unpubl MA thesis, McGill 1976
Robidoux, Réjean. 'Octave Crémazie,' *DCB*, vol 10 MC

CRÉPAULT, Napoléon. Organist, pianist, choirmaster, composer, b Kamouraska, Que, 17 Dec 1849, d Quebec City 28 Sep 1906; lauréat (AMQ) 1871. He began to study piano and solfège in 1858 at the Collège de Ste-Anne-de-la-Pocatière and organ with Antoine *Dessane and harmony with Ernest *Gagnon in Quebec City in 1865. He was appointed organist at Notre-Dame de Lévis in 1873. In 1876 he began teaching in the parish of St-Roch, Quebec City, replacing Nazaire *LeVasseur as parish organist in 1881. As a result of knee injuries he gave up the organ in 1883, devoting himself thereafter to composition, but remaining choirmaster at St-Roch, where his *Mass in G* (1882) and his oratorio *La Communion des saints* were performed. He also composed a cantata on a text by Pamphile Lemay and the reverie *Les Voix du soir* (1900), with words by Arthur Lacasse. Several of his works were published in Quebec by A. *Lavigne and R. *Morgan, including *La Ruche harmonieuse*, a volume of about 40 songs, and *Les Joies du foyer*, some 30 pieces for piano. In 1905, with the help of his son Léonce and of Ernest and Gustave Gagnon, Crépault established a branch of the *Dominion College of Music in Quebec City.

Léonce (b St-Roch, now Quebec City, 3 Nov 1880) was organist-choirmaster 1899–1919 at St-Roch, succeeding Philéas *Roy. He gave up that position to enter the music and instrument selling trade, but later resumed his vocation as organist at St-Dominique Church, the Jesuits' Chapel, and finally St-Patrice Church. (CH)

The Crew-Cuts. Rock and roll vocal quartet. The tenors Pat Barrett and Johnnie Perkins, the baritone and arranger Rudy Maugeri, and the bass Ray Perkins, all students of Mgr John *Ronan at St Michael's Cathedral Choir School in Toronto, sang together as the Four Tones first in 1952, performing in Toronto church variety shows and on radio station CKFH. Discovered in 1954 by Mercury Records while appearing as The Canadaires in Cleveland, the group became the Crew-Cuts, adopting the then-popular hair style of that name. One of the first white groups to record rock and roll versions of black rhythm-and-blues hits, they had some success with such singles as 'Crazy 'Bout You Baby' (1954), 'Don't Be Angry' (1955), and 'Earth Angel' (1955). Their biggest hit, a version of the Chords' 'Sh-Boom,' was listed by *Cashbox* as the fifth most popular single of 1954. Before disbanding in 1964 the Crew-Cuts also made nine LPs for Mercury and Victor. Some of their hits were included in the anthology *Solid Gold Rock 'n' Roll* (2-Mercury 61371/2).

BIBLIOGRAPHY

Callwood, June. 'Sh-Boom! The crazy career of the Crew Cuts,' *Maclean's*, 1 Dec 1954
O'Neill, Dorothy. 'He relives days of crew-cut fame,' *Toronto Star*, 30 Jan 1979 MM

CRIGHTON, Arthur (Bligh). Organist, teacher, choirmaster, b Calgary 6 Jun 1917; LRSM 1938, B MUS (Toronto) 1948, LTCM 1948, ACCO 1958, M MUS (California) 1962, DMA (Southern California) 1965. His doctoral thesis treated the '*Te Deum laudamus* in 20th-century English coronations.' He began teaching music history and theory at the *U of Alberta, Edmonton, in 1949, conducted the university orchestra 1950–67, and became the university organist. In 1980 he was chairman of the history and literature division of the university's Music Dept. Crighton began giving organ recitals and *WBM broadcasts in 1958. He was organist-choirmaster at Grace United Church 1963–5, at St Faith's Anglican Church 1965–7, and at St Joseph's Cathedral 1967–74. He assumed the same position at St Paul's Anglican Church in 1974. He is the author of *A Workbook for Music Analysis* (Oakville 1977). CF

CRINGAN, Alexander T. (Thom). Teacher, administrator, conductor, ethnomusicologist, b Carluke, near Glasgow, 13 Oct 1860, d Toronto 1 Feb 1931; B MUS (Toronto) 1899. After early training in Carluke he attended John Spencer Curwen's Tonic Sol-Fa College in London (licentiate 1886) and studied voice with Emil Behnke. He visited Toronto about 1885 and settled there in 1886, teaching school music and becoming music director for city schools. He was music director 1901–31 at the Toronto Normal School and in 1918 was appointed inspector of music for Ontario. He also taught tonic sol-fa at the *Toronto College of Music and voice at the *TCM ca 1900–20. He was the first president of the music section of the Ontario Educational Assn (*OMEA) 1919–22. He was choirmaster at Central Presbyterian Church 1887–95 and Cooke's Presbyterian Church 1897–1900, a member 1900–11 of the *Toronto Mendelssohn Choir, and often the organizer of massed choirs of school children for such public events as the opening in 1894 of Massey Music Hall (*Massey Hall). His manual *The Canadian Music Course* (Toronto 1888) was the official music text of the Toronto Board of Education. Other books by Cringan include *Teacher's Handbook of the Tonic Sol-Fa System* (Toronto 1889), *The New Educational Music Course* (Toronto 1898–1907), *The Conservatory Sight-Singing Method* (Toronto 1901), and, in collaboration with P.G. Marshall, *The Canadian Song Series* (Toronto 1931–4).

Cringan also recorded ca 1897–1902 and transcribed about 100 Iroquois songs, analysing them mainly in terms of 'gapped' major and minor scales, usually pentatonic. The songs were published in a series of archaeological papers appended to the report of the minister of education of Ontario. These represented some of the earliest Canadian ethnomusicological research and pioneered the use in Canada of the phonograph for this purpose. Wax cylinders and tape recordings of the songs (about 50 minutes of music) are held at the National Museum of Man.

See also Ethnomusicology; School music.

WRITINGS

'Iroquois music,' *Report of the Minister of Education of Ontario*: Appendix (Toronto 1898)
'Pagan dance songs of the Iroquois,' ibid (Toronto 1899)
'Iroquois folk songs,' ibid (Toronto 1902)
'Indian music,' ibid (Toronto 1905)
'Aboriginal Indian songs,' in 'A review of music in Canada,' *Modern Music and Musicians* (New York 1913)

BIBLIOGRAPHY

'Mr. A.T. Cringan,' *MJ*, 19, Jul–Aug 1888
'In memoriam,' *MCan*, vol 12, Feb 1931
Brault, Diana. 'Alexander Thom Cringan, 1860–1931,' *Recorder*, vol 19, Jun 1977
Report of the reading of Cringan's paper 'Traditional songs of the Iroquois Indians' at the Imperial Institute in London, *MT*, vol 41, Feb 1900 RPn

Alexander T. Cringan

Criticism. In Canada, printed opinions on music and musical performance began to appear almost as early as the first newspapers (Halifax *Gazette*, 1752; *La Gazette de Québec*, 1764; *La Gazette du commerce et littérature de Montréal*, 1778, etc). Several categories may be noted, eg, writings in the daily press and in popular magazines, periodicals devoted to music alone, and, in later times, broadcast talks on music. Research writings, which often uphold a more deeply studied definition of criticism, are dealt with in the *EMC* entry for Musicology.

The early journalistic writings were almost exclusively reports of musical events. The audience's applause, the performers' facial expression and apparel, and the intermission refreshments were often of more account than the music:

> The opera last evening was 'Il Trovatore,' and it was rendered, in the individual singing and in the choruses in capital style. Mrs. Seguin and Miss Howson were the recipients of much favour and numerous bouquets during the evening, and at the close were called before the curtain, where they received a perfect ovation. (Toronto *Daily Globe*, 9 May 1873)

> The programme throughout was well given and was received with much applause. Miss Cambourne in response to a hearty encore sang sweetly 'Turnham Toll.' A vote of thanks was tendered the ladies at the close, for the excellent tea and entertainment. (Winnipeg *Manitoba Daily Free Press*, 14 Jan 1885)

Sometimes a strong local pride emerged:

> At last we have in Montreal a complete symphony, and, that being so, we shall have our Concerts Colonne and our Orchestre Lamoureux just like Paris ... Forty musicians – recruited from the orchestra of the Théâtre Français and among the best players from other theatres, with our local instrumental teachers – held under their spell for two hours an audience which for a début concert was relatively numerous. (Montreal *La Patrie*, 9 Nov 1894)

When essaying description and analysis of musical performances, the writers often betrayed an emotional view of music paralleling that found in much of the standard concert repertoire of the age:

> We did not hear the first part of the Concert, but the 'Laughing Song' she sang with inimitable skill and grace, and being encored she sang a plaintive ballad with such simple sweetness and such touching pathos as almost to draw tears from those who laughed so heartily with her a moment before. It was one of the most affecting songs we ever listened to, and the skill of the artist was shown in the simple and perfectly natural way in which the emotion excited by the words found expression in the music. (Saint John *Morning Freeman*, 17 Jun 1873)

However, there were some reviews which offered genuine appreciation of the performance, such as the following early notice on the appearance of the French tenor Auguste Nourrit:

> He possesses one of the truest of voices, with a very extensive range; his delivery is perfectly attuned to the operatic stage and his singing – always clear, agreeable, and gracious – allows one to observe that, assisted by action, costumes, and stage effects, M. Nourrit could expect brilliant success. What we admire most in him is that he contents himself with performing the music as written, without recourse to those *fioriture*, trills, and other needless ornaments favored by the old school, and on which superannuated singers rely, thus hiding their imperfections under a false glitter and forcing bravos from their more vulgar hearers. (Quebec City *Le Fantasque*, 15 Sep 1842)

The late 19th century was in fact not entirely devoid of informed and impassioned criticism. The outstanding case is that of Guillaume *Couture, who added criticism to his achievements in orchestra and church music performance and in composition and who is virtually unique in having written extensively in both national languages. The first of many prominent Canadian composer-critics, he began writing detailed and often analytical notices in *La Minerve* in 1875 and later wrote for *La Patrie* and the Montreal *Star* (under a pseudonym, Symphony). The following, from one of his reviews of the 1884 Wagner Festival Concerts, exemplifies his style:

> Most of all, emotion reached an extraordinary degree of intensity in the introduction to *Die Walküre*. That long and constant repeated figure of the second violins accompanied by that moaning and no less persistent double bass line, at first met with surprise, but soon after with admiration. (Montreal *La Patrie*, 27 Jun 1884)

More caustically he wrote of the soprano Christine Nilsson:

> She sang *Ah! Perfido* – which was her most successful presentation – in a careless and negligent manner; she sang the *Jewel Song* turning the innocent, fresh, pure, and chaste Marguerite into a flirting coquette, I could even say a trollop; she sang the aria from *Judas Maccabeus* ... in an impossible, unbelievable way, making constant errors in both notes and time-values, changing the text, breathing in the middle of words, introducing into Handel cadenzas in the style of Bellini! ... An artist who is only a vendor of notes. (Ibid, 30 Jun 1884)

The second half of the 19th century saw the first of a series of journals devoted to music: the *Canadian Musical Review* (1856). Of many subsequent journals before 1900, few survived more than an initial season or two; even the strongest, *Le *Canada Musical*, had a total lifespan (not uninterrupted) of only seven years. Significant journals in the later 19th and early 20th centuries include **Musical Canada*, the *Canadian Journal of Music*, the [Toronto] *Conservatory Bi-Monthly* (later revived as the *Conservatory Quarterly Review*), *L'Album musical*, *Le Passe-temps* (the longest survivor, 1895–1935 and 1945–9).

The middle and later 20th century saw the *Canadian Review of Music and Art*, the **Canadian Music Journal*, *Les Cahiers canadiens de musique* / **Canada Music Book*, and **Musicanada*. Annotated checklists are found with the articles by *Kallmann and McMorrow (see Bibliography, below), which refer respectively to 78 journals produced from 1860 to 1956 and 40 journals produced from 1956 to 1980. To the above general publications may be added more specialized ones of later years such as **Opera Canada* and **Coda: the Jazz Magazine*, both of which have continued for more than two decades. (See Periodicals.)

In the earlier period, the note of moral uplift often approximates that of the parallel Bostonian publication of the period, *Dwight's Journal*. In later years, however, descriptive and reflective commentary on music too often gives way to clipped reportage, the language of publicity; as Helmut Kallmann complained in 1968:

The chronicler will find it easy to discover what Canada's musicians were *doing* in 1968, but the future historian and biographer will be hard put to discover what our musicians were *thinking* about their art and what kind of people they were. (*Canadian Annual Review for 1968*, Toronto 1969, p 478)

The first half of the 20th century was a period of cultural expansion, reflected in the emergence of music journalists who acquired local, and sometimes national, prominence and whose articles attracted a steady readership, although their content remained by and large the descriptive chronicling of events. Thomas *Archer, H.P. *Bell, and Philip King in Montreal, Augustus *Bridle and Hector *Charlesworth in Toronto, *'A.A.A.' and S. Roy *Maley in Winnipeg, Stanley *Bligh in Vancouver, and George *Dyke in Victoria, wrote in English newspapers; Gustave *Comte, Eugène *Lapierre, Léo-Pol *Morin, Paul-G. Ouimet, and Paul *Roussel in Montreal and Omer *Létourneau and Léo *Roy in Quebec City in French. All were conscientious and lively reviewers.

Those critics most prominent in the 1960s and 1970s included in English, Kenneth *Winters, Winnipeg and Toronto; Jacob *Siskind, Montreal and Ottawa; Eric *McLean, Montreal; William *Littler, Vancouver and Toronto; Lorne *Betts, Hamilton; Jean *Southworth, Ottawa; John *Kraglund, Toronto; Lawrence *Cluderay and Max *Wyman, Vancouver; and in French, Gilles *Potvin and Claude *Gingras, Montreal; Marc *Samson, Quebec City. The CMCentre maintains an up-to-date directory of newspaper critics which is available on request.

Mention has been made of the phenomenon of the composer-critic. Besides Couture, Morin, and Betts, other examples are Leo *Smith, Jean *Vallerand, John *Beckwith, Udo *Kasemets, and R. Murray *Schafer.

Though in modern times Canada cannot be said to have established a profession of musical letters, many musical leaders have in fact been productive in their incidental writings. These exhibit at times a deeper critical tone, and a tendency to attack larger issues, suggested already in the reviews of Couture. Rodolphe *Mathieu addressed fundamental musical questions in his essays, and one thinks of Leo Smith and Luigi von *Kunits, both of whom found time to edit musical journals; of Sir Ernest *MacMillan's long bibliography of essays, talks, and critical articles; and, particularly, of the writings of Léo-Pol Morin, in whose career the role of critic was paramount rather than incidental, though balanced against others (pianist, teacher, composer).

Morin's reviews, program notes, and essays form a high-water mark in Canadian musical writing, in their security of knowledge and taste, in the span of their subjects, and in their clear, sharp honesty of view. Given the insularity and conservatism of much Canadian culture in his period, Morin's two collections of writings (*Papiers de musique*, published in 1930, and *Musique*, edited and published posthumously in 1944) show an astonishing range of topics – current European and US music, the music of Canadian composers, the musical classics, musical education, folklore, jazz.

When reviewing modern trends in Italian music, Morin welcomed the relief from the 'thick and vulgar mists' of *verismo* and found, in the 'pure air' of Pizzetti, Casella, and Castelnuovo-Tedesco, 'an excellent health precaution in a country where the Mascagnis, Boïtos, and Puccinis, though skilled and astute, have devoured musical taste' (*Papiers de musique*, p 20–1).

In comparing the indigenous view of French-Canadian folk music to the more romanticized one being purveyed in his time through the *CPR Festivals as both a patriotic movement and a spark to the hotel and railway trade, Morin frankly admitted:

They bore us somewhat, these old ballads, with their knitted, crocheted, and woven textures; we do not find in them the same artistic depths as do well-meaning amateurs and glassy-eyed old maiden ladies. We are less sentimental, and not sufficiently detached from our land to view it romantically. We are less comfortable than others when listening to these songs of traditional singers, weavers, and spinners, in manufactured 'local colour' settings such as the lounge of a luxury hotel. (Ibid, p 142)

Morin wrote on the critic's métier and pointedly wondered in 1930 whether his fellow countrymen had yet outgrown the 'naïveté, childishness, and sentimentality' of the writers on music of 50 years before (ibid, p 158). To Morin's statements of critical purpose may be compared later 'credos' such as those of *Detweiler and Winters (see Bibliography, below).

Although Canadian critics periodically have voiced their thoughts on criticism itself, it seems an unspoken rule – as in journalism generally – that critics do not criticize other critics, at least not in publications addressing the same market. The rule is virtually never broken in the daily press, but Thomas Hathaway's *Canadian Forum* commentaries in the 1970s constitute an interesting exception to it.

Regrettably, during the same period the popular magazines in English paid no attention at all to concert music or opera, only infrequently and fitfully noticing recordings and pop music. One journal, *Saturday Night*, had fairly regular music coverage by such writers as Hector Charlesworth from the 1890s until its change to less frequent publication and a more streamlined appearance in the 1950s.

The *Canadian Forum*, smaller in audience and less susceptible to commercial pressures than other journals, has included serious music in its arts coverage regularly during most of its 60-year existence. *Forum* articles, read in retrospect, give a vivid picture of how several prominent Canadians saw the changing musical world at an early stage in their own careers. For example, Ernest MacMillan in 1924:

There are here, as elsewhere, several musical publics. Few of the devotees of Dame Clara Butt or Madame Galli Curci are likely to storm the box office on the occasion of a concert by the London String Quartette; the Bach lover may be astonished, but he will hardly be charmed, by Mr. Ignaz Friedman's rendering of the *Tannhauser* Overture or Mr. Moritz Rosenthal's amazing transcription of *Fledermaus*. We have among our connoisseurs those who think of musical history as beginning with Debussy, and also those who think of it as ending with Brahms. We have those who dislike Wagner because there is too much sex in his music (whatever this may mean), and those who enjoy him for the same reason. We have the collector of old musicians – the man who can tell you everything about Ockeghem, Robert Fayrfax, and Luigi Rossi in their respective centuries; also the collector of the latest celebrities – the Bela Bartoks and the Kaikhosru Sorabjis ... In fact we have a very interesting public. ('Our musical public,' *Canadian Forum*, July 1924)

Or the even more precocious Northrop Frye in 1936:

[Delius'] importance will, I am forced to think, become increasingly historical. Composers are now impatient with the long harmonic lethargy of romantic music, and the twinges of contrapuntal conscience which have so sorely afflicted Stravinsky, Schönberg, and even Antheil in recent years may indicate that contemporary music is doing a certain amount of noisy yawning and stretching preparatory to getting up and going somewhere. ('Frederick Delius,' *Canadian Forum*, August 1936)

In the 1940s and 1950s the range of *Forum* subjects broadens beyond what was usual in the newspapers of these decades (or even later) in Milton Wilson's regular column on recordings, new music, and books on music side by side with Allan Sangster's regular column on radio, which frequently touched on music as well. Wilson's reviews of current Canadian-composed works (*Willan, *Weinzweig, *Somers), and of recorded works by Schoenberg, Bartók, Stravinsky, and other internationally influential figures were exceptional in English-speaking Canada as sensitive and well-founded commentaries by a non-musician – a corresponding case to the slightly earlier, and more professional, articles of Morin in French-speaking Canada.

Though considerable changes are seen in journalistic criticism over the years (see Littler, in Potvin, 'Newspapers and journals ...,' Bibliography below), its problems continue to be formulated in rather similar fashion. On the reviewers' side these include: lack of sufficient space; tightness of deadlines; in larger centres, the impossibility of coverage of conflicting events; in smaller centres, and sometimes in larger ones too, an obligation to take assignments in other performing arts (ballet, film) as well as music. On the readers' side are complaints about a confusion of viewpoint which arises when both advance-promotional articles and reviews appear under the same byline, and about the almost total absence of a perspective such as might be afforded by more comment on general musical questions or more reviews of books on music than are provided usually.

An exceptional case among newspaper publications was the weekly musical column of Leslie *Bell, which ran in the *Toronto Daily Star* for some 16 years (1946–62). Rather than reviewing performances, it discussed general topics, in the manner of such popularizers of the 'music appreciation' movement of the 1930s as Percy A. Scholes, Sigmund Spaeth, or Deems Taylor.

Many latter-day practitioners have become members of the US Music Critics' Association, have attended its annual conventions and seminars, and have been quoted in its (now defunct) journal, the *American Musical Digest*. The association held a two-day seminar on Canadian music in Toronto in 1975.

Criticism itself was a central concern at several national gatherings in the 1970s. In May 1973 the annual *CMCouncil Conference was devoted entirely to this topic (see Bibliography, below); in 1974 the Winter Arts Festival at the *U of Victoria included an extensive exploration of arts criticism; in the fall of 1975 criticism formed the theme for an international panel as part of the IMC's general assembly held in various Canadian cities (see Bibliography below).

*McMaster U's music department sponsored a conference on musical criticism in October 1976, with Canadian and international speakers. Alan *Walker, then chairman of the McMaster department and author of *The Anatomy of Music Criticism*, inaugurated a plan for the country's first graduate program in musical criticism, which began accepting students in 1978.

Response to critics by those criticized often employs the not very satisfactory medium of the letters to the editor column. Occasionally a controversy can be prolonged into an extended dialogue of viewpoints. Two or three characteristic examples from 1961 are noted in the *Canadian Annual Review* for that year (Toronto 1962, p 404–5). Critics referred to will not easily forget the curtain speech of the then-conductor of the *TSO, Walter *Susskind, where they were characterized as 'ill-bred little puppies yapping hysterically' at music's heels – a more original choice of metaphor at least than that of the after-dinner speaker at the

1973 CMCouncil Conference who merely classed them as 'the eunuchs in the harem.'

A more relaxed outlet for the exchange of opinions between critics, artists, and fans is the radio 'hotline,' where listeners call in by telephone and discuss (popular) recordings with the broadcast critic and, sometimes, with the performers. At the 1973 CMCouncil Conference, several participants commented that the callers were often both knowledgeable and articulate and that the approach well might be tried more widely.

Increasing prominence and space have been devoted by Canadian newspapers to jazz and pop music coverage in the 1950s, 1960s, and 1970s. Among others, Gilles Archambault, Jack Batten, Helen McNamara, Mark Miller, John *Norris, Nathalie Petrowski, Patrick Scott, and Patrick Straram have written on jazz, and Ritchie Yorke and Peter Goddard on pop music. Yorke's articles on Canadian pop music groups and their recordings resulted in a book (*Axes, Chops and Hot Licks*, Edmonton 1971) – the only example of that more permanent kind of critical publication since the collections of Mathieu and Morin in the 1930s. Jay Rahn's analytical essays, on questions associated with the popular and folk music scenes, may also be noted.

In the heyday of Canadian radio network broadcasting, the late 1930s to early 1960s, talks on music held a regular place. Personalities who gained national prominence through their radio criticisms and commentaries include Harry *Adaskin, Ian *Docherty, Chester *Duncan, and Maryvonne *Kendergi. Aside from local arts-review programs on both private and public stations, of which many continue in good health, there have been several long-running CBC networks series, among them 'Critically Speaking,' 'Music Diary,' and 'New Records' on the English networks and 'Revue des arts et des lettres' and 'Chronique du disque' on the French.

The short reviews on CBC radio's 'Arts National' had in the late 1970s a continuing effect of informing various parts of Canada about each other's musical activities. This is one of the few widespread public means of performing this important function; in print media, the wire service reviews of the Canadian Press and Southam News have a similar intention.

Reviewing of records in the daily press is confined almost exclusively to popular music, which of course constitutes the bulk of the market. When concert and opera recordings are reviewed, the coverage consists almost invariably of short and general 'squibs' in the style of consumers' reports. The level of discussion and of evident commitment is considerably lower than for the reviewing of musical events. When a reviewer 'covers' 14 discs in one 350-word review, not only are the comments superficial to the point of being worthless, but one may also well wonder if he/she actually has listened to every piece in full. *Music, Fugue, FM Guide*, and other journals of the 1970s have included more extended, and thoughtful, record reviews.

The *Canadian Music Journal* and the *Canada Music Book* hold a special place among journals of the recent past (in true Canadian tradition, each lasted only a few years) in that they regularly and at serious length reviewed not only recordings but also books on music and published scores, especially those with a particular pertinence to Canada.

A special problem of Canadian musical criticism, since it is a verbal medium, is translation. Possibly a few critics in each of the two national languages can be said to communicate information and values beyond their own regions (through broadcasting, principally); but the country's two language groups remain unaware of each other's best accomplishments in criticism.

In addition to the individual entries for those critics mentioned above, see entires for François Brassard, G.M. Brewer, Ronald Gibson, Annie Glen Broder, Ida Halpern, Karel ten Hoope, Audrey St Denis Johnson, George Kidd, Henri Letondal, Elizabeth Morrison, Frédéric Pelletier, Jamie Portman, Herbert Sanders, Edward Schuch, John Searchfield, Jean Southworth, Robert Sunter, Lauretta Thistle, Marcel Valois, A.S. Vogt ('Moderato'), and Leonard Wilson.

Among many writers on music not treated in *EMC* are some known as critics but more often as essayists or feature writers or interviewers. They range from men of fame and distinction in other fields of writing, such as Robertson Davies, to magazine journalists such as Michael Schulman of Toronto and veteran music reviewer-reporters for smaller-city newspapers such as Lenore Crawford of London, Ont. A sampling of names which might be mentioned could include Madeleine Bernier, Francean Campbell Rich, William Krehm, Dominique Laberge, Elizabeth Lampard, Paul Larose, Hugues Lefebvre, Pearl McCarthy, Renée Maheu, James Pitcher, Pierre Prévost, Robert Richard, Colin Sabiston, Hugh Thompson, J.J. van Vlasselaer, Charles H. Wheeler, and Edward W. Wodson ('Yenmita').

BIBLIOGRAPHY

Kallmann, Helmut. 'A century of musical periodicals in Canada,' *CMJ*, vol 1, Autumn 1956, Winter 1957

Detweiler, Alan. 'Musical criticism: its functions and limitations,' *CMJ*, vol 3, Summer 1959

Winters, Kenneth. 'Music criticism,' *CMJ*, vol 5, Spring 1961

Beckwith, John. 'Notes on criticism,' *MSc*, Sep–Oct 1967

McLean, Eric. 'Hanslick had it better,' *The World of Music*, vol 14, no. 3, 1972

Malouin-Gélinas, France. ' La vie musicale à Québec 1840–45,' *CMB*, 7, Autumn–Winter 1973

'Music and criticism in Canada / Musique et critique au Canada,' a record of events of the 1973 CMCouncil Conference in Montreal, ibid

Malouin-Gélinas, France. ' La vie musicale à Québec de 1840 à 1845, telle que décrite par les journaux et revues de l'époque,' unpubl M MUS thesis, U of Montreal 1975

Potvin, Gilles. 'Newspapers and journals / Journaux et revues: rapport, section I, 4,' *CMB*, 11–12, Autumn-Winter, Spring–Summer 1976

Widerman, Jane. 'For the defense: music critics state their case,' *Fugue*, Apr 1977

Littler, William. ' The critic, the community and their orchestra,' *OCan*, Jul 1977

McMorrow, Kathleen. 'Canadian music periodicals,' Music Library Assn *Notes*, vol 36, Jun 1980

JB (JCm)

Croatia. The first substantial immigration of Croatians to Canada occurred 1918–28 prior to the reconstitution of the union of the provinces of the Serbs, Croats, and Slovenes as *Yugoslavia. Most settled in the mining and industrial centres of northern Ontario – Timmins, Schumacher, and Sudbury.

After World War II Croatian tradesmen and professional people began to arrive in Canada, and in the mid-1970s Croatian-Canadians lived mainly in more southerly or larger urban centres: Hamilton, Edmonton, Calgary, Montreal, and especially Toronto and Vancouver. Each of these cities has at least one dance band (in Toronto there are four or five), consisting of accordion, electric guitar, and drums, which plays at weddings and dances and at picnics sponsored by Roman Catholic churches and social and political clubs. The repertoire comprises popular songs in English and Croatian. Usually only two traditional circle dances or kolo – drmš and seljančica – are performed at these social functions.

Alan Crofoot

Over a dozen folkdance groups, many accompanied by an orchestra of tamburicas (long-necked plucked lutes), are active across the country in Croatian communities. One such, the Tamburitzan Ensemble of Hamilton, was formed in 1944 and has performed in Ontario, New York, and Pennsylvania. The Croatian Folklore Federation, founded in 1974 with headquarters in Sudbury, has sponsored annual festivals in different cities, as well as seminars led by Croatian-Canadian experts in the fields of tamburica playing and folksong and dance. Among traditional genres which have survived in Canada are vocal polyphony from the island of Krk and the mountains of Hercegovina, Croatian patriotic songs of the 19th century, and the playing of the Hercegovinian bagpipes (mih).

The Croatian-born composer Branimar Vidmar, by trade an engineer, emigrated to Canada in 1955, settling in Timmins, Ont, where he has taught tamburica and organized and directed Croatian choirs. The Croatian-born child-prodigy Hilda Irek, a pianist, studied with Boris *Berlin and performed in Toronto before moving to the USA.

BIBLIOGRAPHY

Perkowski, Jan L. *Gusle and Ganga among the Herzegovinians of Toronto*, National Museum of Man report (Ottawa 1973–4)

Narodne Pjesme / Popular Songs, collected and arr by Božidar Vidov (Toronto 1976)

TR

CROFOOT, Alan (Paul). Tenor, actor, b Toronto 2 Jun 1929, d Dayton, Ohio, 5 Mar 1979; MA psychology (Toronto) 1953. He made his *COC debut in 1956 as Yakuside in *Madama Butterfly* and studied 1957–9 at the *Royal Cons Opera School. He married the soprano Dodi *Protero in 1961. After three years 1960–3 at Sadler's Wells, he created Mr Bumble in the Broadway production (1964) of *Oliver!*, Josiah Creach in the New Orleans Opera production (1965) of Carlisle Floyd's *Markheim*, and Clarence in the COC production of Raymond *Pannell's *The Luck of Ginger Coffey* (1967). He appeared with the New York City, Honolulu, Boston, and San Francisco operas and in the festivals at Stratford, Ont, and Glyndebourne. He also acted on stage and TV, and starred 1963–4 in the CBC TV children's show 'Mr. Piper.' His other COC roles included Alfred in *Die Fledermaus* (1957, 1964, 1969). Bacchus in the touring production of *Orpheus in the Underworld* (1961, 1970, 1971), and the parish priest in the CBC TV opera *The Lost Child* by Godfrey *Ridout (1976).

In 1978 Crofoot's career gained impetus through a contract with the *Metropolitan Opera. He made his debut there as the Circus Master in a new production of Smetana's *The Bartered Bride*, appearing also in the telecast of that production.

Also in 1978 he sang the title roles in Mozart's *La Clemenza de Tito* for Stuart *Hamilton's 'Opera in Concert' series in Toronto and in the *Guelph Spring Festival's Canadian premiere of Schubert's *Lazarus*, and was Herod in the Central City Opera (Denver) production of Strauss' *Salome*. He took his own life in 1979, while in Dayton, Ohio, to direct a production of *Salome*. Crofoot recorded as Padre in *Man of La Mancha* (1958, Decca DXSA 7203) and as John Styx in *Orpheus in the Underworld* (1961, Angel 35903). (GK)

CROFT, James. Violin maker and repairer, b Maidenhead, Berkshire, England, 10 Jun 1884, d Winnipeg 4 Sep 1968. Though he moved to Winnipeg in 1904 as an engineer, he had been taught violin making by an uncle and in 1915 he began building and repairing violins. After a partnership 1921–4 with Arthur Paulus, a violin repairer from New York, Croft devoted his time exclusively to instrument repair and restoration, establishing his name throughout North America. In 1926 he was joined by his son Henry James Croft, and in 1927 their company became the Winnipeg-area representative of the London firm W.E. Hill & Sons. After James Croft's retirement in 1965 the company, which had expanded its retail operation over the years to include pianos, organs, and band instruments, as well as violins, continued under H.J. Croft's direction. (RG)

CROSLEY, Larry (Lawrence Eugene). Composer, conductor, b Oaklandon, Ind, 19 May 1932; B MUS (ESM, Rochester), 1957, M MUS (ESM, Rochester) 1960. He lived in Ottawa as staff composer 1959–60 and music director 1961–6 for Crawley Films and then became a freelance composer-conductor, working for CBC TV in Ottawa and Toronto, Crawley Films, the *NFB, and others. He has composed music for over 100 films and TV programs, including the successful *Cry of the Wild* (NFB 1972), the Academy Award winner *The Man Who Skied down Everest* (an improvised score by *Nexus and Robert *Aitken, co-ordinated by Crosley; Crawley Films 1974), and CBC TV's *The Tenth Decade* (1971) and *The Days before Yesterday* (1973). Crosley has won two Canadian Film Awards, 'Best original music (non-feature)' for *Seasons of the Mind* (Milne-Pearson Productions 1971) and 'Best music score' for *Journey to Power* (Crawley Films 1972). He has also composed for his own jazz groups, which have performed in the Ottawa area, and for orchestra, brass, and woodwind quintets and other chamber groups. The theme *The Days before Yesterday* was recorded on *Canadian Brass' *Rag-Ma-Tazz*. Crosley is a member of CAPAC and an associate of the *CMCentre.

See also Film scores.

BIBLIOGRAPHY

Edwards, Lee. 'The vibrations were beautiful,' *CanComp*, 35, Dec 1968

Beckett, Barbara. ' Larry Crosley – dilettante,' *CanComp*, 46, Jan 1970

'NRC "music machine" helps composer Crosley,' *CanComp*, 53, Oct 1970 (CF)

Crowbar. Blues-rock band formed by Ronnie *Hawkins as a septet in Toronto under the name And Many Others in the summer of 1969. The group left Hawkins in April 1970 after it had made an LP and appeared several times in the USA. It then accompanied the individual members *King Biscuit Boy, Blake 'Kelly Jay' Fordham, and John Rutten on recordings released under their own names. Various personnel changes followed (including the departures of the pianist Ricky Bell to Janis Joplin's Full-Tilt Boogie Band and the drummer Larry Atamuniuk to the US band Seatrain), leaving Crowbar (the new name taken by the group in 1970) in 1971 with the singer-pianist-harmonica player Kelly Jay (who emerged as the group's figurehead), the lead guitarist Rheal Lanthier, the slide guitarist John Gibbard, the keyboardist Josef Chirowski, the bass quitarist Roly Greenaway, and the drummer Sonnie Bernardi. King Biscuit Boy continued to be an occasional guest. Crowbar was based in Ancaster, near Hamilton, Ont, on an estate known as Bad Manors – also the title of the group's first LP (Daf SBA 16004), from which the hit single 'Oh What a Feeling' was taken.

One of the most popular touring bands in Canada, Crowbar combined in its concerts rousing rock, blues, and boogie with an exuberant stage presentation led by Kelly Jay. A 1971 concert at *Massey Hall was recorded and released as *Larger than Life* (*And Liver than You'll Ever Be*) (2-Daf SBA-16007). Other LPs were *Heavy Duty* (1972, Daf SBA-16013), *KE32746* (1973, Epic KE32746), and *Crowbar Classics: Memories Are Made of This* (Daf SBA-16030); singles included 'Million Dollar Weekend' (1973). Despite early predictions of international success and one tour in Great Britain, Crowbar made little impact outside Canada, perhaps the result of the strong nationalistic feeling which characterized its performances. The group disbanded in mid-1975, only to re-form for a tour of eastern Canada in late 1977 and appearances in Toronto in 1978.

BIBLIOGRAPHY

Yorke, Ritchie. 'Canada's rock invasion,' *Axes, Chops and Hot Licks* (Edmonton 1971) MM

CROZIER, St George B. Teacher, conductor, composer, b Dover, England, 13 May 1814, d Belleville or Cobourg, Ont, 21 Nov 1892. The few isolated known facts of Crozier's life suggest that he was a musician of more than ordinary merit. He lived in Toronto in 1844, and two years later A. & S. *Nordheimer issued his quick march *Those Evening Bells*, one of its earliest Canadian compositions. In 1855 Crozier led an orchestra in Hamilton in a program which included Haydn's *'Surprise' Symphony* (or part of it); in this period he also held the position of inspector of revenue in that city. In 1858 he participated in several Toronto concerts, conducting the Metropolitan Choral Society on one occasion. In 1871 he was appointed organist at St Andrew's Church in Belleville and music director of Albert College. The following year he received a D MUS from Victoria U, Cobourg, Ont, the second (or third; see Clarke family) such degree conferred in Canada. Late in the 1870s the Nordheimer Co published his *Nor'West Mounted Police Waltzes*. Crozier appears to have remained a resident of Belleville for the rest of his life. In 1886 he was a vice-president of the *Canadian Society of Musicians. HK

CRTC (Canadian Radio-Television and Telecommunications Commission / Conseil de la radiodiffusion et des télécommunications canadiennes). Independent regulatory agency of the federal government. It was established in 1968 to interpret the Broadcasting Act passed that year. The CRTC succeeded the Board of Broadcast Governors (1958–68). Personnel specifications required a chairman (Pierre Juneau 1968–75, Harry Boyle 1975–7, and Pierre Camu 1977–9, succeeded by John Meisel), a vice-president in charge of broadcasting, a vice-president in charge of telecommunications, five full-time commissioners, and 10 part-time, regionally based commissioners. The CRTC assumed responsibility for the licensing of broadcasting and telecasting. In 1976 it acquired responsibility for all aspects of telecommunication (eg, telephone systems).

The CRTC at first reported to Parliament through the secretary of state, but early in the 1970s it began reporting through the minister of communications. During the 1970s the agency had a significant influence on the expansion of the music industry, especially through its regulations governing Canadian content (a mandatory 30 per cent) in radio music programming. Appended is an amending excerpt from the AM Broadcasting Regulations, reported 24 Jun 1970 and effective 18 Jan 1971. (The regulations applied in principle to FM stations as well, but were not policed directly; rather they were used as guidelines in appraising stations' applications for broadcasting licences.)

4. Section 12 of the said Regulations is revoked and the following substituted therefor:

'12. (1) At least 30 per cent of the musical compositions broadcast by a station or network operator between the hours of 6.00 a.m. and 12 midnight shall be by a Canadian and shall be scheduled in a reasonable manner throughout such period.

(2) From January 18, 1971, to January 17, 1972, a musical composition shall be deemed to be by a Canadian if it fulfils at least one of the conditions set out in subsection (5).

(3) After January 18, 1972, a musical composition shall be deemed to be by a Canadian if it fulfils at least two of the conditions set out in subsection (5).

(4) After January 18, 1973, at least 5 per cent of the musical compositions broadcast by a station or network operator between 6.00 a.m. and 12 midnight shall fulfil the condition set out in either (b) or (c) of subsection (5).

(5) The following are the conditions referred to in subsections (2), (3) and (4):

(a) the instrumentation or lyrics were principally performed by a Canadian;

(b) the music was composed by a Canadian;

(c) the lyrics were written by a Canadian; and

(d) the live performance was wholly recorded in Canada.

(6) A mechanical reproduction of a musical composition that is deemed at any time to be by a Canadian continues to be so deemed thereafter.

(7) If a station operator is able to demonstrate to the satisfaction of the Commission that the application of this section would result in a significant reduction in the quality and diversity of program service within the area normally served by his station, the Commission may vary the application of this section.

(8) For the purposes of this section, a person shall be deemed to be a Canadian if

(a) he is a Canadian citizen;

(b) he is a landed immigrant as defined in the *Immigration Act*; or

(c) his ordinary place of residence was in Canada during the six months immediately preceding his contribution to the musical composition in question.

(Canada. Broadcasting Act. Radio AM Broadcasting Regulations, amended. *Canada Gazette*, part II, vol 104, no. 12 (24 Jun 1970))

See also Broadcasting; Canadian Talent Library; RPM MAPL Logo. MM

Cruel Tears. Country-music opera by Regina playwright Ken Mitchell and *Humphrey and the Dumptrucks. Written for the Persephone Theatre Co of Saskatoon, *Cruel Tears* was premiered 15 Mar 1975 at the Mendel Art Gallery, Saskatoon. After some revision it was performed at the 1976 Habitat conference in Vancouver and at the 1976 Montreal Olympics. A production by the Arts Club of Vancouver made a 12-city tour across Canada in 1977. Excerpts from a radio version broadcast in 1976 by the CBC were issued as an LP, *Songs from Cruel Tears* (Sunflower SUNOOZ). The libretto was published in 1976 by Pile of Bones Music, Saskatoon. Allen Garr described *Cruel Tears* as 'a magnificent rendering of Saskatchewan's mail-order mosaic: a Ukrainian truck driver Johnny Roychuck is enmeshed in a plot loosely based on *Othello* and falls in love with, then kills, his Irish

Desdemona to the accompaniment of CB [Citizen's Band] radio lingo, a Ukrainian dance troupe, a Greek chorus and, of course, country and western music.' Humphrey and the Dumptrucks appeared as musician-actors in the 13-member cast in all the performances mentioned above, as did Winston Rekert in the role of Johnny Roychuck.

BIBLIOGRAPHY

Gelmon, Larry. 'The Dumptrucks: bluegrass country-opera in Saskatoon,' *CanComp*, 102, Jun 1975

Garr, Allen. 'The boys from Blackstrap Mountain,' *The Canadian*, 8 Jan 1977

Timson, Judith. 'Will it play in Saskatoon? Hell, it was born there!' *Maclean's*, 19 Sep 1977 MM

CRUM, George (Francis, Jr). Conductor, pianist, b Providence, RI, 26 Oct 1926, naturalized Canadian 1973. Taken to Canada at three, he attended Trinity College School in Port Hope, Ont, where he studied piano and organ 1938–42 with Edmund Cohu. He continued piano studies with Elsie Bennett and Mona *Bates in Toronto, and made his recital debut at 16 at the *Arts and Letters Club. At the *TCM 1943–7 he studied theory and orchestration with Barbara *Pentland and Ettore *Mazzoleni and opera coaching and conducting with Herman *Geiger-Torel and Nicholas *Goldschmidt. He also served in the opera department as a coach and assistant to Goldschmidt. Crum was the original chorus master of the *Royal Cons Opera School (later the *COC), and he made his conducting debut in 1948 in that company's production of *Faust*. He continued with the company as coach and assistant conductor 1948–51 and also worked in 1949 and 1950 with the Opera Nacional de Centro-America in Guatemala. During the 1950s he served as coach and chorus master for CBC radio opera broadcasts. In 1951, at the invitation of Celia Franca, he became music director of the newly formed National Ballet of Canada. He has guest-conducted CBC opera telecasts, and opera and symphony performances in Canada, the USA, Japan, and Europe. In 1952 he served as an opera coach at the Salzburg Festival under Furtwängler; in May 1953 he conducted the *CBC Opera Company in *Don Giovanni*, the first full-length opera telecast in North America; and in 1969 he conducted at the opening of the *NAC. In 1972 he received the Celia Award in recognition of his services to ballet in Canada. Crum married the Canadian soprano Patricia Snell in 1951.

Snell (b Leamington, near Windsor, Ont, 30 Jun 1927) studied at the RCMT, was a member in 1949 of *Geiger-Torel's Opera Backstage, and sang with the COC until 1960, where her roles included Fiordiligi in *Così fan tutte* (1953), Gilda in *La Traviata* (1954), Elvira in *Don Giovanni* (1956), and Rosina in *The Barber of Seville* (1959).

BIBLIOGRAPHY

O'Toole, Lawrence. 'George Crum: the anonymous baton down in the pit,' Toronto *Globe and Mail*, 27 Feb 1976 (TCB)

CSM. See Montreal Symphony Orchestra.

CURRY, Carrol Anne. Soprano, b Orangeville, Ont, 27 Jun 1942; Artist Diploma (Toronto) 1963, Licentiate Diploma (Toronto) 1963. She studied with Irene *Jessner at the *Royal Cons Opera School. She was a member of the *Stratford Festival company 1965–7 (Donna Elvira in *Don Giovanni*, Emmie in *Albert Herring*), and in 1969 appeared with the Scottish Opera (Despina in *Così fan tutte*). She has sung with the *COC and its touring company. On a Canada Council grant in 1971 she studied Lieder and French song in Europe, principally with Pierre Bernac. After solo and oratorio appearances in Canada and England she made a New York recital debut at Alice Tully Hall in 1973. She was affiliate artist and visiting musician at Waterloo Lutheran U (*Wilfrid Laurier U) 1969–71, 1973–4. Her interpretations of the French repertoire, including Poulenc's *La Voix humaine*, have been praised. She was affiliate artist at the Union Theater, Madison, Wis, for the 1975–6 season. WHK

CURTOLA, Bobby (Robert). Singer, b Port Arthur (Thunder Bay), Ont, 17 Apr 1944. After singing in high school with a pop group, Bobby and the Bobcats, he made his first record, 'Hand in Hand with You,' in 1959 for the Tartan label (owned by the Port Arthur songwriters Dyer and Basil Hurdon, who became Curtola's managers and wrote all of his hits). Other singles for Tartan followed, including two international hits in 1962, ' Fortune Teller' (a million-seller) and 'Aladdin,' as well as 'Three Rows Over,' 'Indian Giver,' and 'Hitchhiker.' By 1974 Curtola had made over 50 singles and 15 LPs. As English Canada's only 'teenage idol' in the early 1960s Curtola specialized in what the Hurdons called 'rock-a'ballads,' and sang in a 'silvery tenor' with 'a soft-sweet quality' (Frank Rasky, *Star Weekly*). He received a *Juno Award in 1965 as 'best male singer.' Curtola toured widely in Canada until 1967, his performances often creating hysteria among his young audiences. In 1968 he turned to a career in Canadian nightclubs, and in 1972 he began to appear six months of each year in Las Vegas. His TV career has included the lead in 1964 in the CBC play *Charlie Love from Liverpool* (by David French), and the role of host for the CTV variety shows 'After Four' 1965–6 and 'Shake, Rock and Roll' 1973–4.

BIBLIOGRAPHY

Wallace, Clarke. 'How Bobby Curtola makes a living,' *Weekend Magazine*, 11 Jan 1964

Rasky, Frank. 'Bobby Curtola: Canada's prince of wails,' *Star Weekly*, 18 Jan 1964

Ashwell, Mary. 'Bobby's beat in tune with teenagers,' *Liberty*, 31 Mar 1964

Epstein, Anita. 'Bobby Curtola's earning (boy is he ever earning) and learning too,' *The Canadian*, 22 Jul 1967 MM

CUSSON, Gabriel. Composer, teacher, b Roxton Pond, near Granby, Que, 2 Apr 1903, d Montreal 18 Apr 1972; B MUS (Montreal) 1924. He studied first at the *Institut Nazareth with Gustave *Labelle (cello), Alfred *Lamoureux (voice), Arthur *Letondal (piano and organ), and Achille *Fortier and Romain *Pelletier (harmony). Winning the *Prix d'Europe for cello in 1924, he pursued his studies 1924–30 at the École normale, Paris, with Nadia Boulanger (composition), Charles Panzéra (voice), and Diran Alexanian (cello). After Cusson's return to Canada he taught counterpoint; *Papineau-Couture was a pupil 1937–40. He also taught ear training 1943–71 at the *CMM, where his pupils included Gaston *Arel, Raymond *Daveluy, Kenneth *Gilbert, Bernard *Lagacé, Aline Letendre, Lucienne *L'Heureux-Arel, and Michel *Perrault. He served 1952–3 and 1956–9 as president of the *AMQ. Among his unpublished compositions are incidental music for the biblical dramas *Jonathas* and *Tobie*, two *Suites* for orchestra (one of which has been recorded under the direction of Roland *Leduc), and some motets. *La Bonne Chanson has published some of his folksong arrangements. Cusson also left four unpublished volumes of exercises containing the essence of his ear-training methods. His writings included 'Quelques souvenirs des années '30 et sur un sujet bien actuel' (*Vie musicale*, December 1970). His name was given to a recital hall at the CMM. JC

CUSTANCE, Barbara (m Kerr). Pianist, teacher, b Vancouver 20 Jun 1909; LAB 1923, hon ARAM 1948. After early training in Vancouver she went to England in 1924 on an AB scholarship, studying at the RAM with York Bowen, Claude Pollard, and Frederick Moore. She made her debut in 1928 at Wigmore Hall and returned to North America for further study 1929–33 with Sigismund Stojowski in New York. She made her Town Hall debut in 1943, and her first US tour (1955) culminated in her fifth recital at that same hall. She has toured widely in Europe and North America, both as recitalist and as orchestral soloist, appearing with the *TSO, the *Winnipeg and *Vancouver SOs, the *Little Symphony of Montreal, the Seattle SO, and the Buffalo Philharmonic. She has been heard on the BBC and NBC networks and has performed regularly on the CBC. She was a faculty member 1960–8 of the *U of British Columbia. In 1968 she travelled to the USSR to attend the Moscow May Festival of Music and observe Soviet teaching methods and in subsequent years returned several times to that country. Besides teaching and performing she has adjudicated many competitions. In 1974 she began to spend most of her time in New York, but in 1978 she returned to Vancouver. She has recorded works by Beethoven and Brahms (Hallmark RS-7). Her pupils include Harold *Brown, Robin Chow, Maria Pappas, and Lyn *Vernon. BNSG

Cycle of Musical Festivals of the Dominion of Canada. Series of concerts of mainly British choral and orchestral music conducted by Sir Alexander C. Mackenzie, principal of the RAM, between 31 Mar and 9 May 1903 in 15 Canadian centres, some of which had not heard before concerts of this kind and scope. Charles A.E. *Harriss was the initiator and organizer.

As 'the first general combined effort for "musical advancement" from ocean to ocean' (according to Harriss' program notes), the cycle required two years of preparation involving the formation and training of festival choruses under local associate conductors in most of the centres. Those choruses in Moncton (under George H. Brown) and Saint John, NB (James S. Ford), as well as the existing Halifax *Orpheus Club under Charles H. *Porter, were accompanied in performance by the Goulet *MSO. Those in Hamilton (under Charles L.M. *Harris), Brantford (Henry K. *Jordan), Woodstock (J.H. Chadfield), and London (Roselle Pococke), as well as the *National Chorus of Toronto (Albert *Ham) and the Festival Chorus in Montreal (Harriss and Guillaume *Couture), were accompanied by the Chicago SO. That orchestra also performed with the existing Toronto Festival Chorus (under F.H. *Torrington), the *Ottawa Choral Society (J. Edgar *Birch), and the *Montreal Oratorio Society (Horace *Reyner). The Minneapolis SO accompanied the specially formed Winnipeg and Brandon choruses under Rhys Thomas and F.B. Fenwick respectively, while the Portland and Seattle Orchestra supported choruses in Vancouver (under Fred *Dyke and H. Smith), New Westminster (A.E. White), and Victoria (George Taylor and Howard Russell). In all, over 3600 voices and nearly 500 instrumentalists were involved. Soloists included the soprano Ethel Wood, the tenor Wilfrid Virgo, the baritone Reginald Davidson, and the bass R. *Watkin Mills, all from London, and the soprano Millicent Brennan of Paris and the contralto Grace Lillian Carter of Boston.

The music performed, mostly British at the insistence of Mackenzie, included works by Sterndale Bennett, Coleridge-Taylor, Elgar, Harris, MacKenzie, Mendelssohn, Parry, Stanford, and Sullivan. 'Canadians responded with great enthusiasm to this display of imperial goodwill ... For five weeks Sir Alexander worked with superhuman energy, often conducting three times a day and leading rehearsals on Sundays as well' (Kallmann *History of Music*, p 216). Though planned as the first of an annual cycle of festivals and in fact a financial success despite the complex problems of organization, the 1903 festival was the only one realized. However, several of the new choirs, including the National Festival Chorus, continued after 1903.

BIBLIOGRAPHY

Mackenzie, Sir Alexander C. 'To the editor of the Musical Times,' series of letters, *MT*, 1 May, 1 Jun, 1 Jul 1903
– *A Musician's Narrative* (London 1927)
NL of C. C.A.E. Harriss papers (MM)

Czechoslovakia. Perhaps the first musically important immigrant to Canada from what later was to be known as Czechoslovakia was Wilhelm Labitzky (violinist, b Becov 1829, d Toronto 1871; son of Joseph Labitzky, 'the waltz king of Bohemia'). The young Labitzky, who had been trained at the Prague Cons, performed in Toronto in 1858 and settled there shortly afterwards.

A more general immigration did not begin until the 1880s, however, when Czechs and Slovaks began arriving from Bohemia, Moravia, and Slovakia (the three main regions of modern Czechoslovakia) and settled in Kolin, Sask, and later in Winnipeg, Fort William (Thunder Bay), Ont, and other centres. The German component in the backgrounds of an appreciable number of these immigrants is a reminder that until 1918, when Czechoslovakia became a republic, it had been part of the Austro-Hungarian Empire.

The unrest of the 1930s (including that among the largely German population in the northwest area known as the Sudetenland) leading to World War II, the civil strife of 1948, and the Soviet military intervention of 1968 caused major waves of Czech emigration. Around those dates (though not necessarily in all cases for those reasons) many Czechs moved to Canada.

Toronto, followed at some distance by Montreal, Winnipeg, and Vancouver, attracted the largest number of those who entered Canada immediately before and after World War II, and after the Soviet military intervention in 1968. While many of the pre-war settlers had been either industrial craftsmen or farmers, most of the later arrivals had business or professional backgrounds.

The early settlers kept alive the songs and dances of their homelands. These folk arts and the Czech and Slovak languages were passed on to the young generation in the home and at Saturday auxiliary schools sponsored by church groups and, after World War II, by the Czechoslovak National Assn of Canada, founded in 1939. Local events (tanečni zábavy) have been sponsored throughout the country by the association and by other organizations including the Masaryk Memorial Institute. Folk groups which have flourished include the Tatra Dancers and the Circle of Moravian Slovaks, both of Toronto, and the Dolma Ensemble of Montreal.

Active congregations of Roman Catholics, Baptists, and Lutherans, holding services in Czech or Slovak, were founded in several Canadian cities. Among those flourishing in 1979 were in Toronto the Czechoslovak Baptist Church, the Slovak St Paul's Evangelical Lutheran Church, the Czech St Wenceslaus Roman Catholic Church, and the Slovak Roman Catholic Church of Cyril and Methodius; and in Montreal the Slovak Roman Catholic Church of Cyril and Methodius, founded in the early 1930s, whose organist-choirmaster was the composer Michael Sinčák. In Chatham, Windsor, and Winnipeg there were also musically active Czech and Slovak church communities.

Among musicians who arrived prior to 1950 were the tenor Otto *Morando; the violinist Antoniná Dvořáková-Houston (a niece of the composer Antonin Dvořák), who was active in the 1930s and retired in Montreal; the violinist Charles Dobiáš, a pupil of Kathleen *Parlow and a graduate of the TCM; the accordionist Gaby *Haas; the mezzo-soprano Helen Hájnik; and the educator and composer Arnold *Walter. Leon Koerner and members of his family (see Koerner Foundation) settled in Vancouver in 1939; Oskar *Morawetz in Toronto in 1940; Nicholas *Goldschmidt in Toronto in 1946; Walter *Kaufmann briefly in Halifax in 1947, and in Winnipeg in 1948; Jan *Rubeš in Toronto in 1949; Ruzena *Herlinger in Montreal in 1949. Others active in Canada included the pianists Joseph Musil, František Pokorný, and František Stein, the baritone and RCI producer Walter Schmolka, and the composer George Traxler. The violin builders Anton *Wilfer and his sons-in-law Alois Fogl and Ewald Fuchs established themselves in Montreal in the 1950s. Walter *Susskind became the conductor of the *TSO in 1956. The harpsichord builders Simon and Sigurd *Sabathil settled in Vancouver in 1960.

Before and after 1968 a new wave of immigrants arrived. Among these were in Montreal the conductor Vladimír *Jelínek and his wife, the violinist Sonja Pečmanová-Jelínkova, who had graduated from *McGill U in the 1940s, and the pianist Dagmar Rydlová-Otta; in Ottawa the pianist Walter G. Haulena, the violin maker Joseph Kun, the pianist Adolfina Kun, and the violinist Michael Kun (son of Joseph and Adolfina); and in Toronto the cellist Alban Berky, the organists Michael Borov and Dagmar Ledlová-Kopecký, the pianists Antonín *Kubálek and Zdenka Helena Picha, the violinist Rudolf Kula, the composer Milan *Kymlička, the administrator Jan *Matejček, and the Janáček scholar Veronica Sedivy. The *Czech Quartet was active in the Hamilton area. The violinist Cěněk Vrba became concertmaster of the *Calgary Philharmonic; the pianists Vaclav Benkovic, Maria Benkovic, and Leo Kokes settled in Vancouver; the composer Rudolf *Komorous in Victoria. Karel Ančerl, artistic director and conductor of the TS 1969–73, made Toronto his home from 1968 until his death in 1973 (see Toronto Symphony).

Canadian musicians of Czech or Slovak antecedents include the cellist Charles E. Dojak of Winnipeg, the violinist Anthony Ginter, the musicologist Jaroslav Mráček, the violinist Joseph *Pach, and the singer-songwriter Bob *Ruzicka.

Among Czech artists who have visited and performed in Canada are the pianist Rudolf Firkušný, Boris Krajný, and Ivan Moravec, the violinist Jan and the conductor Rafael Kubelík, the violinist Josef Suk and the Suk Trio, the Prague Chamber Orchestra, and the Janáček and Smetana String Quartets. Vaclav Smetáček, conductor of the Prague Municipal Orchestra, in 1964 led the *MSO in the first complete Montreal performance of Smetana's symphonic cycle *Má Vlast* (a work repeated there in 1967 by Karel Ančerl and the Czech Philharmonic). *JMC sponsored tours by the Foerster Trio in 1965–6, by the Talich Quartet and the contralto Helena Tesarova in the 1967–8 season, and by the singer Jerzy Artysz, the pianist Michal Wesolowski, and the violinist Krzyztof Jakowicz in the 1970–1 season. Les Solistes de Prague (with the harpsichordist Zuzana Ruzickova) and the Czech Philharmonic appeared at *Expo 67. The Hamburg State Opera presented the Canadian stage premiere of Janáček's *Jenůfa* with the Czech soprano Nadeja Kniplova in the title role. The Brno Children's Choir, which had premiered the Canadian composer H. Klyne Headley's choral-orchestral work *Peace* in Brno in 1968, toured in the composer's province of British Columbia in 1969. Vaclav Neumann guest-conducted the TS in 1975 and again in 1978. The Czech Nonet appeared in Montreal in 1976.

Canadians who have appeared in Czechoslovakia include Emma *Albani, who performed in Prague at the Rudolfinum Concert Hall in March 1893; Jean-Marie *Beaudet, who probably was the first Canadian to conduct there (works by *Brott, *Champagne, *MacMillan, *Tanguay, and *Willan, at the Prague May Festival in 1946); Jacques *Beaudry, who conducted in Prague, Brno, and Bratislava in 1960; and Raymond *Dessaints, who conducted the State Radio Orchestra in 1970. The MSO appeared at the Prague May Festival in 1976; and Huguette *Tourangeau sang the title role in Handel's *Orlando* there in May 1976.

The works of Dvořák, Janáček, Martinů and Smetana are performed frequently in Canada. Beecham conducted Dvořák's *Stabat mater* at the 1942 *Montreal Festivals. In September 1950 CBC radio presented the North American premiere of Martinů's chamber opera *Comedy on the Bridge* in an English translation by Walter Schmolka. The opera department of the *U of Toronto gave the Canadian premiere of Janáček's *Katya Kabanova* in 1977. In 1978 CBC radio, the *RCMT, and the Toronto branch of the Czech National Assn of Canada presented a Janáček 50th Anniversary series. Comprising five concerts, it also featured works by Dvořák, Martinů, and Smetana. Among the performers were Antonín Kubálek, the *Vaghy String Quartet, and the *York Winds.

BIBLIOGRAPHY

Gellner, John, and Smerek, John. *The Czechs and Slovaks in Canada* (Toronto 1968)
Lower, Thelma Reid. 'Cultural exchange: children – between Canada and Czechoslovakia,' *CanComp*, 44, Nov 1969
Mráček, Jaroslav. 'The contribution of Czechs and Slovaks to music in Canada,' paper presented at the 7th congress of the Czechoslovak Society of Arts and Sciences in America, New York (Nov 1974) (JMr)

The Czech Quartet. Quartet-in-residence 1969–74 at *McMaster U, its members also principals with the *Hamilton Philharmonic Orchestra. The quartet was composed of Rudolf Kalup and Stephen Czapary (Milan Vítek after 1972), violins, Jaroslav Karlovsky, viola, and Zdenek Koniček, cello. Formed by members of the Prague Quartet who left Czechoslovakia in 1968, the Czech Quartet made its Canadian debut 16 Oct 1969 in Guelph, Ont, and divided its time 1969–71 between Canada and New Zealand, where it was quartet-in-residence at Christchurch. Assisted by the *OAC while it was at McMaster U, the quartet also toured 1971–3 twice in Europe and once with Rudolf Firkušný in eastern North America, and appeared at US and Canadian universities, on CBC TV, at *Hart House, Toronto, in 1973, and in 130 school concerts annually for the Hamilton, Wentworth County, and Halton County boards of education. With assisting artists it recorded Keith *Bissell's *How the Loon Got Its Necklace* (RCI 388) in 1972. The quartet disbanded in 1974, but Koniček continued with the Hamilton Philharmonic Orchestra until 1976 and remained on staff at *McMaster U. (IF)

D

DAHLSTROM, Helen (Arline) (b Underbakke). Teacher, pianist, organist, choir conductor, b Regina, of Norwegian-Canadian parents, 5 Jun 1917; ATCM 1930, L MUS (Saskatchewan) 1932. She studied piano 1929–35 with Cyril *Hampshire at the *Regina Cons; in the summer of 1935 with Stephen Balogh at the Cornish School, Seattle; and privately 1944–6 with Leonard *Heaton in Winnipeg and later with Boris *Roubakine in Calgary. At 16 she played the Schumann *Concerto* with the *Regina SO. She was accompanist for John *Goss on a tour in 1940 of western Canada and was heard frequently 1940–3 as a soloist on radio station CJRM, Regina. She lived 1945–7 in Winnipeg, where she often played on CBC radio. Moving to Rossland, BC, she served 1950–64 as organist-choirmaster at St Andrew's United Church and became conductor of the A Cappella Singers in 1964. She led that group in various southeast British Columbia centres for over 10 years. Over the years she has accompanied many distinguished instrumentalists in recital, including Elfreda Gleam (1965) and Reginald Kell (1969). Dahlstrom, who began teaching piano and theory in 1929, was president 1970–1 of the *BCRMTA and 1971–5 of the *CFMTA. She also inaugurated Canada Music Week in 1971 and served as federal chairman 1971– . (WL)

DAIGNAULT. Quebec singers and folklorists: 1 / Eugène and 2 / Pierre, his son.

1 **Eugène**. Actor, folksinger, b St Albans, Vt, 14 Sep 1895, d Montreal 27 Jan 1960. Arriving in Quebec in 1900, he was educated, and involved in theatre, at the St-Hyacinthe Seminary. In 1920 he began working for the Montreal Board of Health. He continued his theatre work, however, and sang 1921–41 in the Veillées du bon vieux temps at the *Monument national with Conrad *Gauthier. He witnessed the early days of radio and for station CKAC took part in several program series, including the 'Veillées canadiennes' (1940–50), on which he was joined by Isidore *Soucy, Blanche Gauthier, and Ovila *Légaré, among others. His repertoire contained thousands of folksongs. He made several recordings (Starr, Columbia, Bluebird), which are listed in *Pionniers du disque folklorique*.

Daignault often was accompanied by La *Bolduc (harmonica and accordion, before she achieved fame as a performer), Ovila Légaré (violin), and Samuel Letendre (piano). He also recorded duos with Juliette Béliveau. He played the role of Ovide, the father, in the Quebec saga 'Un homme et son péché' on radio and on film, as well as later on CBC TV in 'Les Belles Histoires des pays-d'en-haut'. The role was revived in 1960 by his son.

2 **Pierre**. Actor, folksinger, script writer, b Montreal 25 Mar 1925. He made his stage debut in 1939 and as a performer and caller of Canadian square dances was a regular member of the CBC radio folk-music program 'Soirée de chez-nous' in 1947. He was also the star of 'Swing la baquaise' with Adrien Avon and his Gais Lurons on radio station CKVL. Pierre Daignault acted in serials on several Montreal radio stations and had some film roles. On CFTM TV he was host and script writer of the programs 'Chez Isidore' (1961–6), 'Comme dans l'bon temps' (1966–71), and 'À la Canadienne' (1972–4). He collected several chansons à répondre (words and music) which have been published in the volumes *Vive la compagnie* (Montreal 1961) and *À la Québécoise* (Montreal 1973). ST

DAINTY, Ernest (Herbert). Pianist, organist, composer, conductor, b Peckham, London, 30 Sep 1891, d Toronto 30 Oct 1947. He moved to Toronto at 10 and studied piano with F. H. *Torrington at the *Toronto College of Music, touring Canada at 12 as a pianist and treble soloist. Following further study with Jaroslav de Zielinski in Buffalo 1907–10, and with Luigi von *Kunits (harmony), Dr Eggett (violin), and Peter Kennedy (piano) at the Academy of Music in Toronto 1910–11, he made a *Massey Hall debut in 1911 and studied 1912–14 in Vienna with Godowsky. After World War I service he returned to Toronto, working as a theatre organist and later giving organ and piano recitals on CKNC, CKCL, CBC, and other radio stations. He received particular praise for his interpretations of Chopin. He was a popular accompanist in Toronto and also gave many broadcasts with a trio and conducted the Canadian General Electric Orchestra on the CBC. He founded in 1929 and conducted the Toronto Hebrew Male Chorus and was organist-choirmaster in several Toronto churches. Dainty's compositions, listed in the *Catalogue of Canadian Composers*, include works for string orchestra, violin trio, and violin or cello and piano. Some piano pieces and songs were published by *Waterloo, *BMI Canada, and *Thompson. His *Nocturne for Strings* (1936), premiered in 1939 by the *TSO, received a number of performances. He also composed and arranged music for many broadcasts and for the early Canadian feature film *Carry on Sergeant* (1928). His song, *'Carry On' was a World War II hit. Some of his papers have been deposited at the *NL of C.

BIBLIOGRAPHY
Dainty, Gertrude. 'A Biography of Ernest Dainty,' private ms
FMB

Dalcroze Eurythmics. A method of music education originated at the beginning of the 20th century and developed over the next 25 years by the Swiss composer Émile Jaques-Dalcroze (1865–1950). It is based on the perception that 'from its birth, music has registered the rhythms of the human body of which it is the complete and idealized sound image.' Jaques-Dalcroze believed that a musical phrase 'revived ... the entire mental state of the period at which it was composed ... and aroused ... a muscular echo or response of the bodily movements imposed at the period in question by social conventions and necessities' (Jaques-Dalcroze, *Eurythmics, Art and Education*, London 1930). According to *Grove's* the primary objective is 'to create by the help of rhythm a rapid and regular current of communication between brain and body, and to make feeling for rhythm a physical experience.'

The first teacher of Dalcroze Eurythmics in Canada was Madeleine Boss Lasserre (b Neuchâtel, Switzerland, 1901). She arrived in Canada in 1924 and began teaching at the Margaret Eaton School, Toronto, in 1925, as a member first of the physical education department, then of the drama department. In 1927 she joined the TCM (*RCMT), where she continued to teach eurythmics, solfège, and improvisation for over 50 years. In 1927 the Dalcroze Eurythmics Assn was formed to sponsor demonstrations (the first, in Convocation Hall, *U of Toronto, 29 Mar 1928) by students and by artists such as Paul Boepple (the successor to Dalcroze and head of the New York School). The association was inactive during World War II and was terminated formally in 1949.

Though the TCM was given approval in 1934 to grant elementary certificates, many prospective teachers have sought advanced certification in Geneva and New York. Graduates such as Frances Barwick, Brenda Beament, Suzanne Brossard, Donald Himes, Louise Mathieu, Louise Milota, Elizabeth Morton, Joan Raeside, and Marie Wahli have introduced the system into the curricula of universities, teachers' colleges, settlement houses, and ballet companies across Canada.

The RCMT and *Laval U have active centres of eurythmics, but the system never has gained widespread acceptance in Canada as a music teaching method. Nevertheless its influence on their lives and its contributions to their heightened sensitivity have been rated highly by those students who have chosen to exercise its disciplines.

BIBLIOGRAPHY
Wilson, Helen R. 'Dalcroze system of rhythmic gymnastics,' *MCan*, vol 8, May 1913
'Dalcroze Eurythmics,' *CQR*, vol 9, Summer 1927
Godfrey, Stephen. 'Art of eurythmy is graceful and colourful dance spectacle,' Toronto *Globe and Mail*, 19 Nov 1978
(GJ)

DALE, Jimmy (James Edwin). Arranger, conductor, composer, pianist, organist, b London 23 Oct 1935. Taken to Canada in 1947, he studied piano for two years with Alma Allen at the *RCMT and theory and composition with Gordon *Delamont privately in Toronto. After working in Toronto dance bands and pit orchestras he joined the Peter *Appleyard quartet in 1957. He began his CBC career as a rehearsal pianist and was music director in the 1960s for 'À la carte' and 'In Person.' Dale moved to Hollywood in 1969 and, before returning to Toronto in 1972, was music director for 'The Smothers Brothers Show' (CBS TV 1969), 'The Andy Williams Show' (NBC TV, 1969–71), and 'The Sonny and Cher Comedy Hour' (CBS TV, 1971–3, commuting for the last season). For the last he received an Emmy nomination in 1972 for 'outstanding achievement in the musical direction of a variety, musical or dramatic program.' In 1975 he returned to Hollywood briefly as music director of 'The Cher Show.'

In Toronto Dale has been music director 1973–5 for CBC TV's *'Juliette and Friends,' 1976–8 for CTV's 'Bobby Vinton Show,' and, beginning in 1975, for CBC TV's 'Bob McLean Show.' Dale has written scores for films (eg, *B.S. I Love You* and *Crunch*), many jingles and TV signature songs, and arrangements for recordings by the pop singers Denyse *Angé (accompanied by a studio orchestra under his direction for CTL), Keath Barrie, Mary Lou Collins, and Bobby Vinton. His own recordings include the LPs *Soft and Groovy* (1968, CBC LM-40/Cap SN 6290), *Juliette's Christmas World* (1968, CBC LM-51/RCA CAS-2279, with the Jimmy Dale Swingers), and others as sideman to Appleyard or a member of the *Boss Brass.

BIBLIOGRAPHY
Quill, Greg. 'What it's like to work in the world of media musicians,' *CanComp*, 107, Jan 1976
MM

DALE, Terry (b Iris Hatfull, m Millar). Singer, b Vancouver 2 May 1927. At four she appeared on CJOR Vancouver's 'Big Brother Bill,' a children's radio show. Later she sang at The Cave with Earl Hill's dance band, and in 1946 she moved to Toronto and joined Art *Hallman's dance band. With the Wayne and Shuster show she sang 1948–54 on CBC radio, in several Canadian cities, and on tour in 1953 in Japan and Korea. Known as the 'Sweetheart of the Armed Forces' for her appearances 1948–9 on CBC radio's 'Comrades-in-Arms,' she also sang in the 1950s on many other

CBC Toronto and Vancouver variety shows. These included the CBC's first telecast (Toronto 1952), the premiere (Toronto 1954) of Mavor *Moore's *The Hero of Mariposa* (as Lillian Drone), and two TV series, both from Vancouver, 'Terry and Me' (1956–7, with her husband, the announcer Alan Millar) and 'The Terry Dale Show' 1957–8. CBC appearances in the 1960s included the radio show 'Terry, Joyce [*Hahn] and Bill [*O'Connor]' in 1962. Dale recorded some 78s with Hallman and two RCI LPs (171, 172) with the Albert *Pratz Orchestra. MM

Dalhousie University, Halifax, NS. Non-denominational university founded in 1818 by the ninth Earl of Dalhousie, lieutenant-governor of Nova Scotia. Dalhousie U awarded its first BA in 1866. The U of King's College (Halifax), *Mount Saint Vincent U (Rockingham), and Nova Scotia Technical College (Halifax) are affiliated with Dalhousie. Dalhousie began elective music history courses in 1961 and organized its Dept of Music in 1968. Chairmen have been David Wilson 1968–71; Ray Byham 1971–2; Vernon *Ellis, Jack Sorenson, and A.G. Scott-Savage – a three-man committee – 1972–3; James *Gayfer (interim chairman) July–October 1973; Peter Fletcher 1973–6; and William Valleau (acting chairman) January–August 1977. Walter *Kemp assumed the chair in 1977. Two music degrees are offered: the B MUS ED (Applied, General) and, beginning in 1978, the B MUS. A BA with a major in music is offered also. There are no music programs given by the faculty of graduate studies.

Music teacher training benefits from the department's use of special lecturers, such as Kay *Dimock, who are involved in the active Halifax school music program. The department also emphasizes performance. Among many student recitals are those required of all graduating B MUS ED students. Gary *Karr (double-bass) and Harmon Lewis (harpsichord) – known together as the Karr-Lewis Duo – were artists-in-residence 1972–4. William *Tritt (piano), appointed artist-in-residence in 1974, formed the Dalart Trio in 1976 with the faculty members Philippe Djokic (violin) and William Valleau (cello). The composers James Gayfer, Dennis Farrell, Steve Tittle, and Clifford *Ford are, or have been, members of the faculty. During 1978–9 there were 35 teachers (15 full-time and 20 part-time) and 100 students. About half of the part-time teachers were members of the *Atlantic SO. Dalhousie has awarded honorary LLDs to Geoffrey *Waddington in 1956 and Elmer *Iseler and Catherine *Allison in 1971.

The department is housed in the university Arts Centre, completed in 1971. Special facilities include the *Rebecca Cohn Auditorium, 20 practice rooms, a piano laboratory with 12 electronic pianos, a 24-unit listening laboratory, and a well-equipped experimental music studio. Performances are given by the Dalhousie concert band, chamber orchestra, chamber singers, chorale (which has performed with the Atlantic SO), early-music group, symphonic wind ensemble, guitar ensemble, and experimental group. In 1971 Dalhousie's Dept of Cultural Activities and Dept of Music, aided by a *Canada Council grant, established *NOVA MUSIC. The Scotia Chamber Ensemble (organized in 1972 by the pianist John *McKay) performs traditional chamber music – Haydn to Prokofiev – and employs local musicians. Dalhousie Concerts offer an evening series by visiting artists in the Rebecca Cohn Auditorium.

In the Dalhousie Opera Workshop, founded in 1966 by the English baritone Philip May, director 1965–75 of Dalhousie's voice studies, Halifax had the only opera school program in the Maritimes apart from that of Mariss Vetra at the Halifax Cons (*Maritime Cons) in the 1940s and 1950s. Between 1971 and 1978 the workshop presented *Così fan tutte*, *The Beggar's Opera* (Britten adaptation), *The Consul* (Menotti), *The Mikado*, *The Summoning of Everyman* (commissioned from Charles *Wilson in 1972 and premiered in 1973 by Dalhousie Opera; Philip May sang the role of Death in the premiere), *L'Histoire du soldat* (Stravinsky), *Gentlemen's Island* (Joseph Horovitz), *The Marriage of Figaro*, *The Barber of Seville*, *Tosca*, *Gianni Schicchi*, and a series of one-act operas.

Dalhousie Arts Centre, Halifax

University song-books include *The Dalhousie University Song Book*, ca 1905, and *The Dalhousie Song Book*, 1912–13, both containing words and music.

The Halifax Cons became affiliated with Dalhousie in 1898 and offered licentiate diplomas and B MUS degrees. The Maritime Academy also was affiliated, and the academy's successor, the Maritime Cons of Music, maintained the affiliation until 1962.

See also Archives; College songs.

BIBLIOGRAPHY
Sorenson, Jack. 'Teacher training main aim of Dalhousie department,' *MSc*, 271, May–Jun 1973 (JCm)

D'AMOUR, (Joseph Prosper Jean-Baptiste) **Rolland**. Choirmaster, actor, bass, composer, b Lac Mercier, Labelle County, Que, 26 Jul 1913. After making his debut as an actor he attended voice classes under Georges Toupin in 1948 and studied solfège and composition with Frank Mella 1951–5. He has written lyrics and music for some 50 songs, of which 'Nuage dans le bleu' won a first prize in the Marly-Polydor competition (Montreal 1949) and 'Vent d'automne' won first prize in a competition sponsored by the weekly *Radiomonde* (Montreal 1950). His songs have been recorded by Estelle Caron, Rolande *Désormeaux, Lucille *Dumont, Fernand Robidoux, and others. During the 1950s he composed some incidental music and wrote both the music and librettos for two musical comedies, *Céline* (1959) and *Gatineau* (1961), both produced successfully on CBC TV. D'Amour became a soloist at St-Viateur Church in Outremont in 1950 and choirmaster there in 1965. He has composed an 'Ave Maria,' an 'O salutaris,' a 'Pater noster,' and three masses (1969, 1970, 1972). He is a member of CAPAC. HPn

Dance bands (or orchestras). Groups of musicians which play for social dancing; more specifically those bands in North America in the period 1900–50 which enjoyed great popularity through their radio work, recordings, and public appearances. Their popularity peaked in the 1930s, despite or perhaps because of the Depression, when audiences crowded into dance halls or listened avidly at home to late-night dance band broadcasts. The radio programs gave them free entertainment and a welcome escape from the desperate times. The best-known bands were of US origin, and these were no less popular in Canada. Only one Canadian organization attained international success – Guy *Lombardo and His Royal Canadians, who in fact were among the most popular dance bands of the day.

In Canada the relatively small size of cities and towns, the distances that separated them, and the severity of the climate made impractical the kind of touring regimen which sustained many bands in the USA. A Canadian band's sole means of wide exposure was national radio – at various times the CNR and CPR networks (which broadcast bands from the ballrooms of their hotels) and the CRBC and its successor, the CBC. Mart *Kenney and His Western Gentlemen were successful in co-ordinating radio and touring and consequently became the only Canadian dance band of national significance; other bands may have been known nationally by their broadcasts but, with few exceptions, rarely performed outside their home provinces.

Over the years the bands grew to as many as 20 pieces, comprising trumpet, trombone and saxophone sections, piano and/or guitar, string bass, and drums. Most bands also featured singers. The earliest dance bands in Canada, as in the USA, were small: 5 to 10 pieces including the obligatory cornet (or trumpet), saxophone, violin, piano, tuba (or, later, string bass), and drums. Among these early bands was the 10-piece group of Charles Bodley (1885–1953), formed in Toronto in 1908. Others in the pre-1940s era were led in Toronto by Gordon *Day, Jack Evans, Fred Fralick, Charles Musgrave, the *Romanelli brothers, Stanley *St John, and Gilbert *Watson; in Montreal by Earl Melloway, Billy Munro, George Sims, Andy and Johnny Tipaldi (of the Melody Kings; Johnny a violinist and Andy a banjo player who later, 1942–69, was president of the Musicians' Guild of Montreal, AF of M local 406); and in Vancouver by Lafe Cassidy, Len Chamberlain, Les Crane, Harry Pryce, and others. Dance bands in this period recorded for Apex, *Brunswick, *Compo, Domino, HMV, *Starr, and Victor.

Most of the early bands were employed by hotels, and many bore their employers' names, eg, in Montreal, the Windsor Hotel Orchestra (Harold Leonard and his Red Jackets) and Andy Tipaldi and his Ritz-Carlton Orchestra. The largest hotels in Canada have had successions of orchestras which, by the 1950s and 1960s, also came to be used as showbands to accompany individual performers. Leaders at the Royal York Hotel (Toronto) have included Charles Bodley, Fred Culley, Don Romanelli, Billy *Bissett, Horace *Lapp, Moxie *Whitney, and Howard *Cable; at the King Edward Hotel (Toronto), Luigi Romanelli, Norman Harris, and Leo Romanelli; at the Mount Royal Hotel (Montreal), Joseph C. Smith, Rex *Battle, Jack Denny, Charlie Dornberger, Lloyd Huntley, Don Turner, all US-born save Battle, who was English-born, and Max Chamitov; at the two successive Hotels Vancouver, Lafe Cassidy, Len Chamberlain, Mart Kenney, Stan Patton, and Dal *Richards (the latter 1940–65); and at the Chateau Laurier (Ottawa), James McIntyre, Joe DeCourcy, Ozzie Williams, Len Hopkins, and Moxie Whitney. Long-term engagements were held by Gilbert *Darisse at the Château Frontenac (Quebec City), Jimmy Sadler at the Nova Scotian Hotel (Halifax), and Billy Tickle at the Empress Hotel (Victoria, BC).

Dance halls, built or converted for the purpose, were popular, among them Casa Loma (the home

1927–1950s for a succession of bands), the Palais Royale (home 1932–50 of Bert *Niosi's band), and the Palace Pier (home 1944–61 of the Trump *Davidson orchestra) in Toronto; the Brant Inn at Burlington, Ont; Victoria Hall (home 1941–51 of Johnny *Holmes' band) in Montreal; the Roseland Ballroom in Winnipeg; the Trianon Ballroom in Regina; and the Alexandra and White Rose ballrooms in Vancouver. Summer resort areas and amusement parks also had dance pavilions in season. Both US and Canadian bands appeared at Dunn's Pavilion in Bala (in the Muskoka Lakes tourist region of Ontario), but other venues were the domain of Canadian bands alone – eg, the Royal Muskoka Hotel and Bigwin Inn in Muskoka; Sylvan Lake, south of Edmonton (where Paul *Perry led a band 1945–ca 1965); Belmont Park, Montreal; and Manoir Richelieu, at Murray Bay, Que (where the Romanelli orchestras played for many years). Summer entertainment was heard also at Clear Lake, Man, Crystal Beach, Ont, and at hotels in the Banff and Waterton Lakes national parks. Boat cruises often employed dance bands as entertainment. Don Romanelli led bands on the Lake Ontario boats *Cayuga* and *Chippawa* as early as 1918; Art Brown played in the 1920s and Eddie *Sanborn in the 1930s on Canadian Steamship Lines boats on the St Lawrence River and Great Lakes; and boats of the Union Steamship Lines carried dance bands for evening excursions from Vancouver, while those of the CP and CNR took bands on longer trips along the west coast.

Individual characteristics among dance bands developed as their locales diversified and the competition for work increased. Among US bands, which set the styles for Canada, there were 'sweet' bands and 'swing' bands. Examples of the former, also known as society bands and often heard in private or club functions, were those of Stanley St John and Frank Bogart in Toronto, Eddie Alexander and Pete Nassif in Montreal, and Dal Richards and Claude Logan in Vancouver. Examples of the latter – populated by a large contingent of jazz musicians – were the bands of Benny Louis, Cy McLean, Bert Niosi, and Pat *Riccio in Toronto, Johnny Holmes and Stan Wood in Montreal, Jerry Gage in Winnipeg, Paul Perry at Sylvan Lake, and Trevor Page and Sandy DeSantis in Vancouver. Many bands fluctuated between the two styles, depending on the occasion. Others were distinguished by their repertoires (eg, the Latin-American music of Chicho *Valle e los Cubanos and the music for ice skaters played and recorded by Max Boag of Newmarket, Ont) or their instrumentation (eg, Stan Patton's band of reeds and rhythm section only). Other bands of regional popularity included those of Roy Brown and Paul Grosney in Manitoba (Grosney's heard 1948–59 on the CBC's 'Rancho Don Carlos'), Walter Budd and Ken Peaker in Saskatchewan, Trevor Page in British Columbia, the Wright Brothers (see Don Wright) and Ellis *McLintock in Ontario, Bruce *Holder in New Brunswick, and Peter Power and Don Warner in Nova Scotia.

Though some of these bands still were active in the 1950s and 1960s, the end of the 'dance band era' was signalled by the AF of M recording ban 1942–4 during which North American instrumentalists under the leadership of James C. Petrillo refused to perform for recordings until a system of remuneration to them for repeated public use of their recorded performances could be agreed to and made part of law. Because the instrumentalists were forbidden to record, singers and vocal groups (many of whom started their careers with dance bands) filled the void for recording companies. Their resulting popularity left dance bands in a secondary position in pop music after the ban was lifted. Singers also made the adjustment more readily to TV when it was introduced in the USA in the late 1940s. These factors and the increasingly high cost of touring greatly reduced the number of bands. By the 1970s only a dozen or so US dance bands (eg, the Tommy Dorsey, Guy Lombardo, and Glenn Miller orchestras under 'ghost leaders') and big (jazz) bands (eg, Count Basie, Duke Ellington, Woody Herman, and Buddy Rich) remained on the road in North America. No Canadian organization was active in this manner.

Besides the Lombardos, many Canadian musicians had careers in the USA during the dance band era. Among them were Billy Bissett (Bishop); the Bob-O-Links, a Toronto vocal group (Babs Babineau, George Dean, Jack Duffy, Ron Martin, and Babs Masters) which travelled in 1948 with the Tommy Dorsey Orchestra (Duffy continued as a soloist with Dorsey until 1950); Fred Culley, concertmaster, assistant conductor, and finally music director with Fred Waring's Pennsylvanians for some 40 years, and his brother George, a trumpeter with the same orchestra for some 25 years; the Large brothers, Freddie (leader and saxophonist), Jerry, and Ken, of Niagara Falls, Ont, whose orchestra was taken over in the USA by Jan Garber in the early 1930s and became one of the most popular 'sweet' bands of that decade; Will Osborne (b William Oliphant, Toronto 25 Nov 1906, d ?), a singer who imitated Rudy Vallee and led a popular orchestra in New York during the 1930s; and such other singers as Phyllis *Marshall and Dick *Todd. The Toronto origin of the Casa Loma Orchestra has been the subject of some confusion in dance band histories. The band, originally from Detroit, did play at Toronto's Casa Loma (a disputed point) under another name and at the time (1927–8) included several Toronto musicians. The US musicians who made up the core took the name Casa Loma Orchestra when they formed an orchestra in New York in 1929. Two Canadians (the pianist Joe Hall and the drummer Tony Briglia, both of London, Ont) were members of this new orchestra, and Murray *McEachern was a featured soloist 1938–41.

Other Canadian musicians had careers in England – those in New Princes' Toronto Band (see Les Allen), as well as the singers Allen, Paul Carpenter (b Charpentier), and Denny *Vaughan, and the instrumentalists Johnny *Burt, Art Christmas (saxophone), Max Goldberg (trumpet), and Alfie *Noakes. The Trump Davidson band of 1938 was taken over by the English bandleader Ray Noble for a British tour, and several Toronto musicians (including the pianist Dave *Bowman, Murray McEachern, the guitarist Danny Perri, and the trumpeter Jimmy Reynolds) worked for the English bandleader Jack Hylton during his years in the USA.

See also Black musicians; Jazz.

BIBLIOGRAPHY

McNamara, Helen. *The Bands Canadians Danced To* – 'Remembering the good old days and the fine old dance bands,' *CanComp*, Sep 1975 (HM, MM)

Dancing, pre-Confederation. A history of social dancing in Canada had not been written by 1980. As much research into folksong as had been accomplished, as little seemed to have been undertaken in instrumental folk music which, in the early centuries of European colonization, usually was dance music. The following lines therefore are in the nature of a sketch.

1 European observers of Indian dancing
2 Dancing in New France
3 Dancing after 1759

1 EUROPEAN OBSERVERS OF INDIAN DANCING. Dancing was one of the Indian activities that fascinated the European explorers (see also Indians). Their observations begin with the very first visit of Jacques Cartier in 1534. On the arrival of Cartier's ship at the Baie des Chaleurs, groups of Indian women and men waded into the sea, jumping, singing, and dancing and making great signs of joy at the visitors' arrival. With the Indians, as with other aboriginals, dance was not an isolated activity, but was linked with song, ceremony, and ritual, and early descriptions deal rather with their dancing's function than with its musical aspects. Marc Lescarbot in his *Histoire de la Nouvelle-France* (*The History of New France*, ed and transl W.L. Grant, Toronto 1907–14) and Gabriel Sagard-Théodat in his *Histoire du Canada* (4 vols, Paris 1636, 1866) devote considerable attention to Indian music and dancing, although their attempts at musical transcription are inadequate. A discussion of 17th-century chronicles of Indian singing and dancing is given in *Amtmann's *Musique au Québec* (p 209–56).

Among 18th-century descriptions are those in *Peter Kalm's Travels in North America* (2 vols, New York 1966). For instance, the Swedish botanist described an Indian dancing 12 Oct 1749 at Prairie à Magdal (area of Fort St Jean, Richelieu River, Que): 'A drum was lent them [the musicians] which they struck regularly, one beat after the other, singing at the same time ... Sometimes the beats of the drum were further apart, sometimes quite close, and the Indian danced accordingly. Now and then he talked to the others who sang and beat upon the drum and they answered him. Sometimes they sang continuously, for the most part these words: Here I am, Here I am, etc' (vol 2, p 556). In the *Journal du Marquis de Montcalm, 1756–1759* (ed Casgrain, vol 7 of series Collection des manuscrits du Maréchal de Lévis, Quebec 1895) a visit 21 Jan 1758 to the Hurons of Lorette is described. Mantcalm noted three kinds of dance, Chaouénons, calumet, and découverte, and observed that the Hurons were influenced by French manners.

Baron de Lahontan, in his *New Voyages to North-America* (ed Thwaites, 2 vols, Chicago 1905) distinguished several types of dances: 'The principal is that of the *Calumet*; the rest are the Chiefs or Commanders Dance, the Warriors Dance, the Marriage Dance, and the Dance of the Sacrifice ... [In a war dance certain Players] ... beat Time upon a sort of a Kettle-Drum; Every one rises in his turn to sing his Song; And this is commonly practis'd when they go to War, Or are come from it' (vol 2, p 423, 424). In September 1688 he watched some Algonquin tribes in the Green Bay region: 'The Singing and Dancing lasted for two hours, being season'd with Acclamations of Joy and Jests, which make up part of their ridiculous Musick' (vol 1, p 169). The duc de La Rochefoucauld-Liancourt described the visit in the summer of 1795 of a party of some 80 Indians to Governor Simcoe at Niagara: 'The Indians danced and played among themselves. Some of their dances are very expressive, and even graceful. A mournful and monotonous ditty, sung by one, and accompanied with a small drum, six inches high, and three in diameter, forms all their music ... They dance around the music, which they frequently interrupt by loud shrieks. The hunting and war dances are the most expressive, especially the latter. It represents the surprise of an enemy, who is killed and scalped ... The moment when the enemy is supposed to have breathed his last, a strong expression of joy brightens every face; the dancer raises a horrid howl, resumes his pantomine, and

'Minuets of the Canadians' by George Heriot (*Travels through the Canadas*, 1807)

is rewarded by universal shouts of applause. When he has thus finished his dance, another enters the stage' (*Travels through the United States of America, the Country of the Iroquois, and Upper Canada, in the Years 1795, 1796, and 1797; with an Authentic Account of Lower Canada*, transl H. Neuman, London 1799).

As early as 1806 the Indians gave 'performances' of their dances. For example, the Lorette Indians presented 'War and Fancy Dances' in Quebec City 1 Jul 1806 before a white audience.

Composers were attracted by the exotic element, but Rameau's *Les Indes galantes* (1735) has no genuine Indian music. A *Savage Dance* in Rachel Frobisher's music notebook (Montreal 1793) has little of a savage sound. *Stadaconé, Danse sauvage* by Ernest *Gagnon (Lovell 1858) is an interesting imitation of Indian music couched in 19th-century harmonies.

2 DANCING IN NEW FRANCE. One of the earliest references to dancing among the French settlers is provided by Father Le Jeune in an account dated 14 Aug 1636: the natives were 'begging that ... some of our young people should dance to the sound of a hurdy-gurdy [vielle in French], that a little Frenchman held. This was granted them, to their great satisfaction' (*Jesuit Relations*, vol 9, p 269). The Jesuits had little interest, however, in reporting on dancing; and when they did comment it was with apprehension rather than approval. 'God willing, the effects won't be lasting' (E.M. Faillon, *Histoire de la colonie française en Canada*, Montreal 1866, vol 3, p 397), exclaimed the chronicler when the first ball was held, 4 Feb 1667, on the occasion of Louis-Théandre Chartier de Lotbinière's promotion to a senior administrative position. But nothing was to stop the circle of colonial administrators and their coterie from indulging in dances and festivities. As revealed in 'La Correspondance de Madame Bégon, 1748–1753' (*Rapport de l'Archiviste de la Province de Québec pour 1934–35*), the priests kept condemning and the upper crust kept on dancing. On 26 Jan 1749 Mme Bégon reports that the curé preached against parties and balls. He felt they were 'wholly reprehensible' and that 'mothers who escorted their daughters there were adulterers.' He called the dance music 'lascivious tunes which lead only to shameful pleasures.'

François Bigot, the last intendant of New France, gave or participated in the balls, which took place several times each week during the winter season. This went on at Quebec right through the critical years of 1758 and 1759, much to the chagrin of the Marquis de Montcalm. 'Grand ball this evening at the Intendant's. Crude sport, needless to say,' he wrote, typically, 22 Jan 1758 (*Lettres du Marquis de Montcalm au Chevalier de Lévis*, ed Casgrain, vol 6 in series Collection des Manuscrits du Maréchal de Lévis). The only dance named is the minuet; thus Mme Bégon says 'one sings wildly there, and prepares oneself to go to the ball and run through one's minuet' (20 Jan 1749), or M Bigot dances only two or three minuets, 'c'est tout' (14 Feb 1749). One may say that the leaders of society were dancing minuets while Quebec burned!

3 DANCING AFTER 1759. In addition to the reports of travellers, newspaper advertisements for printed music became an important source of information about dancing in the period after 1760. The minuet remained the most frequently mentioned dance. Joseph Hadfield, in *An Englishman in America* (1785; ed Robertson, Toronto 1933), mentions an occasion at which 40 minuets were danced in an evening; but country dances also became popular. They were published in annual collections ('Country dances for the year 1790'). Pierre de Sales Laterrière in *A Political and Historical Account of Lower Canada* (London 1830) says 'Never have I known a nation which so loves to dance as do the Canadians; they still dance the minuet, spelling it off with English dances' (p 61). The mixing of dances of different national origins, referred to here, was a typical and important development of the time. Unlike songs, which were bound to specific words, dance tunes and dance steps crossed boundaries easily, and it was the Irish country dances, jigs, reels, and so on, that were to become absorbed into the repertoire of the Quebec violoneux, with some adaptations (see Fiddling).

By the end of the 18th century there were settlements all around Lake Ontario, and at the capital of Upper Canada, Niagara (Niagara-on-the-Lake), 'as in all parts of Canada, they are much attached to dancing. During winters, there are balls once a fortnight', ('Canadian Letters ... 1792 and '93,' *Canadian Antiquarian and Numismatic Journal*, series 3, vol 9, 1912, p 45). Isaac Weld, in his *Travels through the States of North America and the Provinces of Upper and Lower Canada ... 1795, 1796 and 1797* (London 1799), confirms that during the winter Canadians would visit each other for parties and 'pass the day with music, dancing, card-playing, and every social entertainment that can beguile the time' (p 225).

Other dances popular about 1800 were the new quadrilles and mazurkas and the older hornpipes, reels, jigs, clogs, and strathspeys, and the cotillon (the latter a type of dance rather than a specific musical dance form). Little is known about the instrumental accompaniment for the dances. The term 'les violons' appears to have been synonomous with dance band, just as 'les hautboys' meant the wind band. Still, violins, whether played by a cultured amateur or a village fiddler, must have been the most common instruments; dancing masters used a miniature type, the kit or pochette, small enough to be tucked away in the pocket. But pipers and flutists also were pressed into service, and singing, whistling, hand clapping, or the thwack and jingle of the tambourine led the dancers when no melody instruments were to be found.

The 'apple-bees' (described by W.L. Smith in *The Pioneers of Old Ontario*, Toronto 1923), held as the settlers harvested and prepared apples for winter storage, were occasions for music. 'Then followed a supper and after that a dance ... A wandering fiddler, usually an old soldier, would be called in. If there was no fiddler, the boys whistled, or the girls sang dance music through combs covered with paper' (p 68).

Fortunately, extant late-18th- and 19th-century manuscript books provide specific examples of dance music literature. (See Manuscript books.) The one of Rachel Frobisher of Montreal, begun in 1793, even includes directions for the dance steps. The book compiled by Allen Ash in the area north of Lake Ontario, for example, contains 13 waltzes, 7 hornpipes, 4 reels, 18 jigs, and 1 galop. The one of Havilah Jane Thorne (Bridgetown, NS, 1839) has many waltzes, as well as dances in 6/8 time. Publication of these collections would be of both practical and theoretical value. The Don *Messer collection at the Public Archives of Nova Scotia includes in notation many traditional dances that have an early-19th-century origin.

As the 19th century wore on, a distinction between the folk dances of the rural and remote regions and the ballroom dancing of urban middle-class society became apparent, but both kinds flourished. From the 1830s onwards, Canadian dance compositions began to appear. Soon they constituted one of the music publishers' most important products, second only to songs, and slightly ahead of march music. The minuet had gone out of fashion, and the waltz reigned supreme until the early 20th century, but polkas, galops, mazurkas, and quadrilles were popular with Canadian composers and publishers. There also were polka-mazurkas, lancers, redowas, and such novelty dances as the money musk (the dance may be a variant of the 18th-century Scottish strathspey 'Monymusk,' or the name may be a corruption of 'monkey musk,' the common name of the flower *mimulus luteus* which could be construed as resembling a dancer) and the brandy (yet another variant of the branle, bransle, brantle, or brawl, the dance which takes its name from the French verb 'branler,' to sway?).

To the extent that composition provided any income to the Canadian musician, dance music was the bread and butter of that income, and even the most learned musical practitioners – for example, George William *Strathy, Antoine *Dessane, or Calixa *Lavallée – wrote dance music for the larger public. Among the better-known composers of dance music in the 19th century may be listed A.J. *Boucher, Henry *Prince, Charles W. *Sabatier, and Joseph *Vézina.

BIBLIOGRAPHY

Massicotte, E.-Z. 'La valse au Canada,' *BRH*, vol 39, Apr 1933

Guillet, Edwin C. *Early Life in Upper Canada* (Toronto 1963)

Fisher, W. Allen. 'Fiddling in retrospect,' *CME*, vol 16, Winter 1975

HK

D'ANGÉ (or **d'Anger**), **François**. Musician, fl 1662–3. One of the first persons referred to as a musician in Canadian historical documents. He was accepted as a boarder at the Jesuit College in

Quebec in the fall of 1662. At Christmas the chronicle singles him out as one of the musicians who, having been treated too generously to beer and wine, were too hoarse to sing at the divine services. In December 1663 the Jesuits again fed and clothed the young man, but nothing is known of his further life.

BIBLIOGRAPHY
Jesuit Relations, vol 47, p 292–5, 310–11
Kallmann, Helmut. 'François D'Angé,' *DCB*, vol 1 HK

DANSEREAU, Jean (b Hector). Pianist, teacher, b Verchères, near Montreal, 21 Apr 1891, d Yorktown Heights, NY, 2 Nov 1974; hon PH D (Montreal) 1940. Born into a family of musicians, he received his first lessons from his mother, a cousin of Calixa *Lavallée. He also studied with Angéline Normandin-McNamara and at the *McGill Cons with Walter Hungerford. In 1913 he was soloist with the McGill U Orchestra in Tchaikovsky's *Concerto No. 1*. He was awarded the *Prix d'Europe in 1914, but the war obliged him to postpone his departure for two years. In Paris he worked with Isidor Philipp, Édouard Risler, and Charles-Marie Widor. In 1920 he began to appear as pianist for such noted singers as Mary Garden, Rodolphe *Plamondon, and Oscar Seagle, accompanying them on their European and North American tours. He was the resident accompanist 1924–5 at the studio of Jean de Reszke, whom he had befriended. Upon the latter's death in 1925 he took the Christian name of Jean at the request of the Polish tenor's widow. He pursued his career in Europe and the USA until 1936, when he went to Vienna to work with Emil von Sauer.

In 1938, after an absence of almost 20 years, he marked his return to Canada with a brilliant performance of Beethoven's *Concerto No. 3* with the Orchestra of the *CSM. Subsequent recitals, often with commentary, won him a large following in Canada and the USA and also in Brazil, where he lived 1942–3. He gave weekly radio recitals for three months in Rio de Janeiro. In several of them he accompanied his wife, the soprano Muriel Tannahill.

He began teaching in Outremont, Que, at the École supérieure de musique (*École Vincent-d'Indy) in 1941 and at the *CMM in 1943, the year of its foundation. He gave summer courses at the *RCMT. Among his pupils were Jocelyn *Binet, Auguste *Descarries, Françoise Gay-Poulin, Anna-Marie *Globenski, Clermont *Pépin, Sister Stella Plante, and Madeleine Raymond. Later he settled in the USA. His last visit to Canada was in the mid-1950s, when he played Chopin's *Concerto No. 2* on the CBC TV program 'L'*Heure du concert.'

The inspiration and sensitivity of Dansereau's playing clearly identify him with the romantic school. His repertoire, while very large, rarely departed from the traditional composers. He was known particularly as an interpreter of Chopin and Debussy, and in 1953 he recorded a program of pieces by these composers for the LP RCI 94. In 1926 and 1929 he recorded 11 songs with the soprano Mary Garden for two series of discs by Victor; two of the songs were not released.

Dansereau's brother Alphonse, a violinist and a member of the *Dubois String Quartet 1915–16, died in Montreal 13 Nov 1918. GG

Jean Dansereau

'Dans les prisons de Nantes.' One of the best-known French songs to have survived in Canada. It originated in France, probably in the 17th century. 'Dans les prisons de Nantes' (or 'de Londres,' as often heard) is known also as 'La Fille du geôlier,' and is popular especially in Quebec and the Maritimes. The words most commonly used were published in *Le Foyer canadien* (vol 1, Quebec 1863). They tell of a prisoner who is in love with the jailer's daughter, is freed by her, and thereupon proposes marriage. A version distinguished by the use of the augmented fourth appeared in Raoul and Marguerite d'Harcourt's *Chansons folkloriques françaises au Canada* (Quebec City 1956). Marius *Barbeau, in *Le Rossignol y chante* (Ottawa 1962), offers a textual variant in which the young girl dies and the prisoner is pardoned. At least 17 versions of this song were collected 1916–26. The *Sonate* (1927, for cello and piano) by Oscar *O'Brien is based on the melody. Among Canadian recordings of the song are 78s by Joseph *Saucier and Charles *Marchand and LPs by Hélène *Baillargeon and Alan *Mills (Folk FP 923) and Louise *Forestier (Gamma GS 167).

BIBLIOGRAPHY
Gagnon, Ernest. *Chansons populaires du Canada* (Quebec City 1865)
Barbeau, Marius, and Sapir, Edward. *Folk Songs of French Canada* (New Haven, Conn, 1925) HP

'Dans Paris y a-t-une brune.' A French chanson of which several variants exist in Canada. It tells the story of a serving-girl who, wishing to be as pretty as her mistress, a dark-haired beauty, buys some makeup at the apothecary's. The latter advises her not to admire herself while applying it. She follows his advice, and when she meets her suitor he laughs at her black smeared face: she had been sold shoe polish because 'a servant has no right painting her face.'

A notable early published version of the song appears in Ernest *Gagnon's *Chansons populaires du Canada* (Quebec 1865). Marguerite and Raoul d'Harcourt, in *Chansons folkloriques françaises au Canada* (Quebec 1956), give a version with similar words, 'Dedans Paris y a-t-une brune,' but which has a different ending: on Sunday the maidservant waits in vain for her beau 'because he had found her too black in the street.' In the same collection may be found two other versions of the song, one of which bears the title 'C'est dans Paris y a-t-une brune,' but with a very different story. A young wife who looks at herself in the mirror loses her temper because she does not receive the compliments she was expecting from her servant. Then the husband intervenes, reproving his wife for her silliness. There are also four versions collected by Marius *Barbeau in the *Journal of American Folklore* (vol 32, no. 123, 1919) and one by Sister Marie-Ursule in the *Archives de folklore* (vols 5–7, Quebec 1951). All versions, it may be noted, make use of a varied refrain. Claude *Champagne made an arrangement for voice and piano, 'Dans Paris' / 'In Paris' (Harris 1961). Joseph *Saucier recorded the chanson on 78 rpm (Col E2364). HP

DARISSE, Gilbert (Antoine). Violinist, conductor, music librarian, b St-André-de-Kamouraska, near Rivière-du-Loup, Que, 28 Oct 1909; B PAED (ESM, Rochester) 1932. After studying in Quebec City with Robert *Talbot and 1927–32 in Rochester at the ESM, he served 1933–60 as concertmaster, 1960–5 as manager, and subsequently as librarian of the *Quebec SO. With the orchestra he premiered a concerto by Lucien Vocelle and was a soloist in Bach's *Concerto* for two violins and orchestra, once with Edwin *Bélanger and once with Calvin *Sieb. He conducted his own dance orchestra 1935–60 at the Château Frontenac and was conductor and arranger for the CBC radio shows 'Ici l'on chante' (1936–47) and 'Variétés' (1948–56). At the *CMQ he taught violin 1944–65 and sight reading 1965–75, and also coached Camille *Couture's pupils. Among his pupils were Yves *Bédard, Raymond *Dessaints, François Magnan, and Jean-Louis Rousseau.

BIBLIOGRAPHY
Samson, Marc. 'Gilbert Darisse "l'homme-orchestre" de la musique à Québec,' *Avril à Québec*, vol 2, Apr 1978
MS

Darke Hall. Home of the Regina Cons (*Cons of Music, U of Regina) and, until 1970, the *Regina SO. The gift of Regina businessman Franklin N. Darke, the building, with its fine 740-seat auditorium, was designed by J.H. Pontin. Darke Hall opened 6 Jan 1929, 'dedicated to music and arts and the enrichment of the lives of the people of the city.' Ambrose C. Froom donated a Casavant pipe organ and Dr Hugh MacLean a large art collection more recently housed in the Norman MacKenzie Art Gallery adjacent to Darke Hall. In 1963 extra rehearsal, recording, storage, and dressing rooms were added. Darke Hall has housed performances by Jorge Bolet, Marjorie Lawrence, Nino Martini, Nan Merriman, Jan Peerce, Teresa *Stratas, Jean Watson, and Efrem Zimbalist, among others. DB

'Darktown Strutters' Ball.' A traditional-jazz classic. The words and music, by Shelton Brooks, were inspired by a ball at the 1915 Pacific-Panama Exposition in San Francisco. The music, in arrangements for band and for orchestra, was published first 18 Jan 1917 by Will Rossiter, Chicago, and a version recorded 30 Jan 1917 by the Original Dixieland Jazz Band may be the earliest commercially made jazz record. 'Darktown Strutters' Ball' has been recorded subsequently by many pop and jazz artists, including the *Six Brown Brothers (1917), Miff Mole's Molers (1928), Jimmy Dorsey (1938), and Benny Goodman (1945). It was selected in 1963 by ASCAP for its All-Time Hit Parade. Shelton Brooks (1886–1975) was born in Amherstburg, near Windsor, Ont. He was taken to Cleveland as a boy. He first worked in Detroit cafés as a ragtime pianist, later performed in vaudeville as a comedian and impersonator, and during the 1920s appeared in various all-black revues. Other Brooks hits included *'Some of These Days' (1910) and 'Walkin' the Dog' (1916). Brooks' own discography and many recordings of his songs are listed in *Roll Back the Years*. MM

DAULÉ, Jean-Denis. Teacher, composer, amateur violinist, b France 16 Aug 1765, d Ancienne Lorette, near Quebec City, 18 Nov 1852. Ordained as a priest in Paris in 1790, Father Daulé was forced by the French Revolution to take refuge for two years in England. He moved to Quebec in 1794. He was chaplain 1806–32 to the Ursulines in Quebec City and organized a student choir there. In 1819 he published *Le Nouveau Recueil de cantiques à l'usage du diocèse de Québec*, a volume of some 200 hymns of which the texts and tunes (some with accompaniment) were printed separately. (Though published anonymously, the book later was attributed to Daulé.) Nazaire *LeVasseur wrote of the collection: 'it is true that the music provided for these pious texts often was no more than a rehash of popular tunes and drinking songs ... but the words, full of religious sentiment, that he adapted to it served him as a passport to heaven' (*La Musique*, Apr 1919).

BIBLIOGRAPHY

Prince, Suzanne. 'Jean-Denis Daulé et son époque (1765–1852),' unpubl MA thesis, U of Ottawa 1965 JD

DAUNAIS, (Noël Ferdinand) **Lionel.** Baritone, composer, lyricist, b Montreal 31 Dec 1902; lauréat (AMQ) 1925. He studied singing with Céline *Marier and, later, harmony and composition with Oscar *O'Brien. In 1922 he performed in a student concert at the Académie Querbes in Outremont. A year later he won first prize at the Montreal Musical Festival, organized by the Metropolitan Choral Society. In January 1926 he made his operatic debut as Ourrias in *Mireille* at the *Orpheum Theatre, and in March he gave his first recital at the Ritz-Carlton Hotel. The same year he won a *Prix d'Europe which enabled him to continue his studies in Paris with Émile Marcellin of the Opéra-Comique. In 1929 he was engaged as principal baritone at the Opera of Algiers and sang in *Carmen, Faust, Manon, La Traviata*, and *The Barber of Seville*.

On his return to Canada in 1930 Daunais took part in the third Canadian Folk Song and Handicraft Festival (*CPR Festivals) in Quebec City with the Bytown Troubadours (an Ottawa quartet which he joined as a replacement for Charles *Marchand) and portrayed Champlain in *Willan's *The Order of Good Cheer*. Also in 1930 he appeared for the first time (singing Clément Marot in Messager's *La Basoche*) with the *Société canadienne d'opérette, a Montreal organization with which he performed regularly until 1935. He sang in 1931 with the Troupe Franco-Italienne and the Canadian Opera Company of Montreal. In 1932 he founded the *Trio lyrique, which in 1954 made an LP of his songs. In 1936, in association with Charles *Goulet, he founded the *Variétés lyriques, serving also as co-director, baritone, and producer. In 1940, Daunais, Anna *Malenfant, the *Assn chorale St-Louis-de-France, and the *Disciples de Massenet gave a concert at the Salle St-Sulpice in Montreal consisting entirely of works by Daunais. When Willan's opera **Deirdre* was premiered on CBC radio, 20 Apr 1946, he sang the role of Conochar. His 'Chanson du maître cordonnier' in 1949 won the first prize in the Polydor-Marly competition of France, and he recorded four of his songs in Paris in 1951 for Pathé.

Daunais was stage director 1958–9 of a program of operettas on CBC TV. Towards the end of 1959 he received a grant from the *Canada Council which allowed him to complete a collection of children's songs. He also went to Italy and Germany for further studies in stage production. During 1961 and 1962 he gave a series of 250 programs on CBC radio with the Trio lyrique, and in 1963 he directed a production of Audran's operetta *La Mascotte* which was given 31 times at the Théâtre de Verdure. He was artistic director of several live stage presentations sponsored by radio station CJMS and director of productions of *La Belle Hélène* in 1966, *La Margoton du bataillon* in 1966, *Valses de Vienne* in 1967, *Les Mousquetaires au couvent* in 1969, and *La Vie parisienne* in 1969 at the *PDA. The CBC presented a series of 13 programs, 1970–1, devoted entirely to Daunais's compositions for voice. He is the composer of the words

Lionel Daunais

and music for some 100 songs and 18 choral pieces and has harmonized some 40 folksongs and composed 30 songs for children.

After acquainting himself with Daunais's songs, Francis Poulenc told him: 'There is a droll spirit in your music, and if someone points it out to you, don't blush. It's a rare gift!' In 1972 Daunais was awarded the *CMCouncil Medal and was appointed to the board of directors of the *Opéra du Québec. He was awarded the 1977 *Prix de musique Calixa-Lavallée, and in 1978 he was made an Officer of the *Order of Canada. He is a member of CAPAC and an associate of the *CMCentre.

SELECTED COMPOSITIONS

SONGS

Cinq Poèmes d'Éloi de Grandmont. Arch 1974

Douze Chansons canadiennes. Arch 1954. 2nd series Arch 1957

En roulant ma boule. Dix Chansons pour les enfants. Arch 1959

Fantaisie dans tous les tons. Arch 1974

Sept Épitaphes plaisantes. Arch 1974

Turlurette 2. Alliance des Chorales du Qué 1978

Also several other songs, choral works, and a work for str orch, *Propos piquants*

DISCOGRAPHY (Daunais's songs)

Chansons de mon pays. Ens vocal Katimavik, Beaumier dir. (1978). Soc nouvelle d'enregistrement SNE-502

D'Amour et de Fantaisie. Daunais bar, Newmark pf. 1974. Sel CC-15.087

12 chansons. Daunais bar, Newmark pf. 1954. RCI 107

See also Discographies for Disciples de Massenet; B. Laplante.

BIBLIOGRAPHY

Contemporary Canadian Composers (M-CL)

D'AURIA, Francesco (Mariano). Conductor, composer, teacher, b Naples 1841, d after 1913. D'Auria was the conductor for the US tour 1881–2 of the soprano Adelina Patti, and worked in New York and Cincinnati before joining the *TCM in 1887 as a voice teacher. W.H. *Hewlett, Edith *Miller, and J.D.A. *Tripp studied with him. During the 1890s he established a Toronto Symphony Orchestra which gave several concerts but faltered because of inadequate financing. D'Auria joined the Winnipeg Cons in 1895 but by 1897 he had moved to Minneapolis. He was a teacher and choir conductor 1904–13 in Vancouver. He composed songs published 1888–93 by *Suckling and *Nordheimer and an anthem published by *Whaley Royce, and also completed the large-scale cantatas *The Sea King's Bride* (performed 1890 in Toronto) and *Gulnare, or the Crusader's Ransom* (Suckling 1891). *Gulnare*, a dramatic cantata with words by Mrs Edgar Jarvis of Toronto, is an elaborate piece with considerable variety of harmony and modulation, quite advanced for its time. It was performed 29 Mar 1892 by the Toronto Choral Society. (CM)

DAVELUY, Marie (Marguerite Cécile Alice Louise). Soprano, teacher, b Victoriaville, Que, 20 Mar 1936. She studied 1956–9 in Vienna with Ferdinand Grossmann and Viktor Graef and received a grant from the *Canada Council in 1960. After her debut at the Salzburg Opera in the role of Zerbinetta in Richard Strauss' *Ariadne auf Naxos* she sang 1959–61 with that company. At the Heidelberg Opera 1961–6 she performed about 30 roles, including the Queen of the Night, Susanna, Zerlina, Despina, and Constanza in the Mozart operas, Sophie in *Der Rosenkavalier*, Micaela in *Carmen*, Musetta in *La Bohème*, Gilda in *Rigoletto*, Anna in *Falstaff*, and the title role in Flotow's *Martha*. She continued her studies 1960–6 in Munich with Henny Schöner and Peter Schneider.

In Quebec City she sang *Lakmé* and other roles with the *Théâtre lyrique de Nouvelle-France in 1965 and was soloist with the *Quebec SO, the CBC Montreal chamber orchestra, and the *Concerts Couperin. In Montreal she participated in the noon-hour concerts at the *PDA in 1979. She began to teach singing at the UQATR in 1971 and Lieder interpretation at the CMM in 1973. She was the organizer 1972–7 of 'Musique vivante,' a series of weekly concerts in Trois-Rivières. With the pianist Diane Mauger she recorded 11 songs by Jean *Chatillon (L'Oiseau-Coeur OC S-01) in 1974 and songs by Rodolphe *Mathieu for the LP *Musique québécoise 'nos compositeurs'* (L'Oiseau-Coeur OC S-02) in 1978. She also performed *Deux Poèmes* by Mathieu with the *Classical Quartet of Montreal on the latter recording. She is the sister of the organist Raymond *Daveluy. ST

DAVELUY, (Joseph Eugène) **Raymond** (-Marie). Organist, composer, administrator, educator, b Victoriaville, Que, 23 Dec 1926. In 1938 he began studying music with his father, Lucien Daveluy, an organist and bandmaster in Victoriaville. In Montreal he studied theory 1939–45 with Gabriel *Cusson and organ 1942–8 with Conrad *Letendre. In 1948 he won the *Prix d'Europe and pursued his organ studies in New York with Hugh Giles.

In 1946 Daveluy began appearing as a recitalist in Canada, the USA, and Europe. Jean *Vallerand observed in Montreal's *Le Devoir* (24 Feb 1953): 'I admire ... the precision of his playing, the accuracy of his legato, the transparency of his contrapuntal passage work, his intelligent grasp of the various styles of the works in hand, and the musical scholarship revealed in his carefully chosen tempi and appropriate registers.' In 1959 Daveluy was the first organist from North America to be invited to participate in an improvisation competition in Haarlem, the Netherlands. He performed at the Festival de Magadino in Switzerland in 1976, and at the Royal Festival Hall in London and the international convention organized by the American Guild of Organists in Philadelphia in 1977. The following year he performed at the Festivals of Avignon, Paris, Salzburg, and Millstatt, Austria. At a recital in 1951 he played pieces by the Canadians Arthur *Letondal, Amédée *Tremblay, and Conrad Letendre. In 1975 he performed Saint-Saëns' *Symphony No. 3* with the *MSO. In Montreal he was the organist 1946–51 at St-Jean-Baptiste Church, 1951–4 at Immaculée-Conception Church, and 1954–9 at St-Sixte Church. He assumed charge of the organ at St Joseph's Oratory in 1960. Daveluy performed regularly on CBC radio's 'Récital d'orgue' and for the *Pro organo society, for which he gave the inaugural concert. He also developed remarkable improvisatory skills: 'Mr Daveluy gave a spectacular display of improvisation, full of contrasts and strange harmonies' (Gilles *Potvin, *La Presse*, 8 Aug 1968).

Daveluy has played an important role in teaching and administration: he gave organ and theory classes 1957–60 at the *CMM, taught organ and harmony 1966–7 at the Cons de Trois-Rivières, and in 1965 began giving occasional organ courses at *McGill U. He served 1965–71 as president of the *AMQ, 1967–70 as assistant director of the CMM, and 1970–4 as director of the Cons de Trois-Rivières. From 1974 to 1978 he was director of the CMM, where he later resumed teaching duties. Pierre-Yves Asselin, Paul *Crawford, Mireille *Lagacé, and Lucienne *L'Heureux-Arel were among his pupils. Daveluy was a juror at international organ competitions in London, Ont, in 1967, at Munich in 1971, and at Philadelphia in 1977.

He has written three *Sonatas* (1955, 1957, 1960), of which the third was recorded by Kenneth *Gilbert (RCA CCS 1019); four *Chorale Preludes* for organ; a *Fantaisie* for organ and string orchestra (1962); two *Masses*, one (1953) for mixed choir, soloists, and organ, the other (1970) for choir, brass ensemble, and two organs; incidental music to Molière's *Monsieur de Pourceaugnac* (1947); sundry other pieces; and harmonizations, several of which were published by La *Bonne Chanson and recorded by Les *Petits Chanteurs du Mont-Royal with Daveluy at the organ (RCA 10 PPKM 1339 and Telson AE 1517). He is the brother of Marie *Daveluy and is married to the pianist Hilda Metcalfe. In 1980 he was made a Member of the *Order of Canda. His grandfather, Adolphe Daveluy, founded Daveluyville, near Trois-Rivières.

WRITINGS

Letter to Pierre Delagrave, president of the MSO, Montreal *La Presse*, 3 Oct 1975

DISCOGRAPHY

G. Corette *Messe*. 1965. Oryx 1736/Mus H Soc MHS 1430

L. Marchand *Livre d'orgue*, vols 1 and 3 (excerpts). 1965. RCA CCS 1001

Raymond Daveluy aux grandes orgues de l'oratoire St-Joseph / on the St Joseph's Oratory Organ. Bach *Toccata and Fugue in D Minor* BWV565 – and others. Ca 1965. RCA CCS 1000

(JC)

DAVID, Madame Athanase (b Antonia Nantel). Patron, administrator, b St-Jérôme, near Montreal, 14 Apr 1886, d Montreal 6 Dec 1955. She studied piano in her native Quebec and later with Antoine-Émile Marmontel at the Paris Cons. She also studied voice in anticipation of a career in opera. However, after her marriage to the Hon Louis-Athanase David, Provincial Secretary of Quebec and later a member of the Canadian Senate, she devoted herself to the development of music in Montreal. She supported the founding in 1930 of the *Montreal Orchestra and served as a member of the orchestra's executive committee. Finding the policy of hiring soloists to be discriminatory against French-speaking musicians, she resigned in 1934 to participate with her husband in the founding of the SCSM (*MSO). Two years later she worked with Wilfrid *Pelletier to establish the *Montreal Festivals, which she served as president until 1952. CH

DAVIDSON, Hugh (Hanson). Administrator, composer, writer, b Montreal 27 May 1930. He began piano lessons at 7 and studied at the *RCMT 1945–8 with George *Crum (piano) and Godfrey *Ridout (composition). His *Three Preludes* for piano, composed at 16, won a *CAPAC award in 1946. In 1951 he continued his composition studies in English with Bernard Stevens and Humphrey Searle. Returning in 1955 he worked in Montreal as a composer and studied orchestration with Neil *Chotem. He joined CBC Montreal in 1956 as a radio producer for the English network and was supervisor of music 1962–5 for the French network. In 1965 he became music coordinator for the CBC IS, Montreal, and in 1966 he was named assistant program director of the English radio network, Toronto. He was seconded to the BBC in London in 1969 and returned in 1971 as music administrator of the *NAC in Ottawa. He was appointed head of music at the *Canada Council in 1973 and served there until 1978, when he was named cultural councillor to the Canadian High Commission in London. In 1981 he became general manager of the Canada Council's Touring Office.

Davidson has composed piano works, ballets, chamber music, songs, choral works, and incidental music for the theatre, including *His Eminence of England* (1953, for the Canterbury Coronation Festival) and *Cymbeline* (1954, for the Bristol Old Vic). His *Divertissement* for three winds is recorded (RCI 192, 1958). His writings include reviews for the Montreal newspapers and the English magazine *Music and Musicians* and program notes for the *MSO and the *Pro Musica Society of Montreal. He was assistant editor 1956–60 of the journal of the *JMC. He was music consultant for the Canadian Pavilion at *Expo 67, head of the music selection committee for Festival Canada during Centennial year, and a founding member of the *SMCQ. KMr

DAVIDSON, Jimmy (James Douglas), **'Trump'** after ca 1936. Cornetist, singer, arranger, b Sudbury, Ont, 26 Nov 1908, d there 2 May 1978. He played trumpet at 12 with the Canadian Legion Band in Sudbury and formed the Melody Five ca 1925, possibly the first jazz-styled group in Canada. Moving to Toronto, he worked 1929–36 with Luigi *Romanelli (first as a singer, then as a cornet soloist and arranger, and occasionally as a baritone saxophonist) and briefly with Rex *Battle's dance band. For Toronto's Club Esquire he organized a 12-piece orchestra in 1936, broadcasting on CKEY and in 1937 in the USA on the NBC network. The orchestra toured England in 1938 as the Ray Noble Orchestra, under Noble's direction, before disbanding in 1942. The personnel lists in Brian Rust's discography *Jazz Records 1897–1942* and on the Noble LP *The Swinging Briton* (Swing Era LP 1012) are incorrect; the Davidson band did not record under Noble's name.

After a year with Horace *Lapp's orchestra Davidson organized another dixieland big band which appeared 1944–61 at Toronto's Palace Pier. His dixieland sextet, formed ca 1936, included at different times his brother Ted (b Sudbury 21 Jun 1914, a tenor saxophonist who began playing in Toronto dance bands in the 1930s), Howard 'Cokie' Campbell (clarinet), Murray Ginsberg (trombone), Reef McGarvey (drums), and Harvey Silver (piano). It broadcast regularly on CBC radio – during the 1940s on 'Jazz Unlimited' and 'Trans-Canada Matinee' and 1950–65 on Davidson's own shows, 'Trump Davidson's Dixieland,' 'Dixieland Concert,' and 'Dixieland Downbeat.' After 1974 Davidson performed only as a vocalist, and in 1976 he re-formed his big band for special occasions. His cornet parts usually were played by the trumpeter Paul Grosney.

A singer in the relaxed manner of Jack Teagarden and a cornetist inspired by the white dixieland stylists of the 1920s and 1930s, Davidson was a pioneer and popularizer of jazz in Canada. His wife, the violinist Erica Zentner – b Regina 5 Dec 1925, Artist Diploma (RCMT) 1950 – studied with John Thornicroft in Regina and with Kathleen *Parlow at the RCMT before playing in the *TSO (TS) 1958–72, the *CBC SO, and studio orchestras. Their daughter Sarah (b Toronto 5 Dec 1958), a harpist, has studied with Judy *Loman and has been a member of the North York SO and a soloist with other orchestras (including the TS) in the Toronto area.

DISCOGRAPHY

Trump Davidson + Horn = Dixie. 1961. Chateau CLP 1009

Jimmy (Trump) Davidson and His Dixieland Band. 1963. CTL 021

In the Land of Dixie. 1969. Sound Canada SC-7701

BIBLIOGRAPHY

Scott, Patrick. 'Canada's Mr Dixieland,' Toronto *Globe Magazine*, 31 Oct 1964 MM (HM)

DAVIES, Gwendda (Dorothy Owen). Pianist, teacher, b Kettleburgh Rectory, Wickham Market, Suffolk, England, 5 Aug 1896; LRAM 1912, ARCM 1912. At 12 she received the AB of the RSM gold medal for the highest marks in advanced piano in the United Kingdom and at 15 she played Beethoven's *Emperor Concerto* with the Hull Orchestra. At the RAM her teachers were Oscar Beringer (piano) and Stewart MacPherson (theory), and her diploma examiners were Tobias Matthay and Sir Hubert Parry. She subsequently was appointed assistant to MacPherson and subprofessor of transposition and keyboard harmony. In 1916 she performed concertos by Saint-Saëns and Sterndale Bennett at Queen's Hall with the RAM orchestra under Sir Alexander Mackenzie.

Davies travelled to Canada in 1923 to teach at Rupertsland College, Winnipeg, for one year. Deciding to remain and teach privately, she also became the accompanist for the *Winnipeg Philharmonic Choir (continuing into the early 1930s), for the Young Women's Musical Club Choir, and for many singers, including May *Lawson, Gertrude *Newton, and W. Davidson *Thomson. In 1930 she studied in Paris with Nadia Boulanger and Céliny Chailley-Richez. Returning to Winnipeg she played in the 1930s in two-piano teams with Mary Scarlett Wood, Cécile Henderson, and Marjorie Dillabough. She also performed in Bach's *Concerto for Four Claviers* (with Ronald *Gibson, Filmer *Hubble, and Herbert *Sadler) in 1925 and was the soloist in Beethoven's *Concerto No. 4* for the *Women's Musical Club in 1930 and with the *CBC Winnipeg Orchestra in 1949. In over 50 years of teaching piano and theory in Winnipeg her pupils have included Audrey *Cooke Belyea, Douglas *Bodle, Esther *Ghan, Gordon *Kushner, Frans *Niermeier, Winifred Scott *Wood, Winnifred *Sim, Gordon Watson, and Kenneth *Winters.

JA

DAVIES, Victor (Albert). Composer, pianist, conductor, b Winnipeg 1 May 1939; B MUS (Indiana) 1964. He began piano and violin studies in childhood, took courses with Ronald *Gibson and Peggie *Sampson at the U of Manitoba, and studied composition at Indiana. In 1969 he attended Pierre Boulez' conducting class in Switzerland. He was organist-choirmaster in 1959 at Wesley United Church, Winnipeg, music director in 1964 of the Manitoba Theatre Centre, and composer, arranger, and conductor 1966–70 for CBC radio and TV. His compositions include the orchestral works *Variations I* (1963), *Variations II* (1964), *From Harmony* (1968), *Celebrations for Orchestra* (1969, commissioned by the *Winnipeg SO), and *A Short Symphony* (1974); the ballets *The Colour of the Times* (1966) and *Anerca (1969); the musicals *The Egg that Laid the Eagle* (1966), *Mama* (1971), and, for children, *The Magic Trumpet* (1969) and *Reginald the Robot* (1970). His multi-media work *The Beginning* *and the End of the World* (1971) has been recorded (OMNI-1001), as has his rock opera *Beowulf* (1974), with lyrics by Betty Jane Wylie (1974, Daffodil DAFF 10050).

Davies' *A Mennonite Piano Concerto*, a three-movement work (sonata, theme-and-variations, rondo) based on 11 chorales, was premiered in 1975 in Winnipeg at a Sängerfest marking the 450th anniversary of the *Mennonite faith. His *Violin Concerto*, commissioned by the CBC, was premiered in 1978 by Arthur *Polson and the *CBC Winnipeg Orchestra. Davies is a member of CAPAC and an associate of the *CMCentre. He became president of the *CLComp in 1979. JMs

DAVIS, Bruce (Gridley). Composer, sound ecologist, b Toronto 27 Sep 1946; B MUS (McGill) 1970. After studies in composition with Bruce *Mather at McGill U, Davis moved in 1971 to Vancouver to teach at *Simon Fraser U and participate in the *World Soundscape Project there. (He became the project's research officer in 1972 and collaborated on its publications; see that entry's Bibliography). He received *Canada Council grants in 1971 and 1976 and shared first prize in the 1974 *CBC National Radio Competition for Young Composers. His principal works include *How the Rhinoceros Got His Skin* (1970) for flute, two pianos, vibraphone, marimba, tape, and conductor; *Canto II* (1971) for tape; a *String Quartet* (1973), commissioned and performed by the *Purcell String Quartet; *From Night Chant* (1974) for piano; *Comp 1101011* (1976) for alto flute, english horn, vibraphone, marimba, piano, tape, and conductor, premiered by *Days Months and Years to Come; and some taped incidental music. His *Salmacis* (1977), also premiered by Days Months and Years to Come, was inspired by two months of research into aboriginal music in Australia in 1976. The *Vancouver New Music Society premiered *Shields, Shadows, Smiles* in 1978. He is an affiliate of PRO Canada and an associate of the *CMCentre.

BIBLIOGRAPHY

Mertens, Susan. 'Background in sound applied to architectural design,' *MSc*, 300, Mar–Apr 1978 (MW)

DAVIS, John Freeman. Teacher of music and dancing, b Oakville, Upper Canada (Ontario), 1835, d Toronto ca 1916. Active as a musician in Toronto after 1855, he ran a music store ca 1873–5 and later advertised himself as 'professor and teacher of dancing, deportment and calisthenics,' operating a dance studio until his death. He issued *The Modern Dance Tutor* (Toronto 1878) and between 1873 and 1896 wrote some 20 polkas, lancers, rockaways, waltzes, two-steps, and other dances published by *Nordheimer, *Claxton, *Whaley Royce, and Davis. His *Call to Arms Polka* (1885) was inspired by the North West Rebellion; *The New Premier* (1896) commemorates Sir Wilfrid Laurier's election victory.

DAVIS, Morris or **'Rusty'** (Cecil). Composer, arranger, conductor, b Ottawa 1 Mar 1904, d Montreal 13 Nov 1968; BA (McGill) 1930. He studied piano in Montreal with Nicholas Eichorn, A.E.J. MacCreary, and Alfred *Laliberté, but was self-taught in composition and orchestration. While taking courses in law at *McGill U, he wrote the university's annual *Red and White Revue* of 1926 and 1927. Also in 1927 he collaborated with Robert Emmett Dolan on *The Little Revue that Starts at 10 Past Nine*, which was staged at the *Orpheum Theatre. Davis' radio career as a pianist and conductor began in 1929 on a local station. While a producer 1937–47 with CBC Montreal he arranged music for such conductors as Lucio *Agostini, Jean *Deslauriers, and Allan *McIver. In 1948 he established his own production house in Montreal, working as a freelance composer, arranger, and conductor (one of the first active extensively in the jingles field), serving as the agent for several commercial orchestras, and assisting in the development of young performers' careers. He was music director for various stage productions in Montreal and elsewhere. His compositions include scores for over 30 films (including the features *Whispering City, La Forteresse, Tambour battant*, and *Le Curé de village*), several works for orchestra, incidental music for some 100 radio and TV programs, songs, revues, and about 200 jingles. His *Blues and Finales in G* (1942) is a jazz concerto in the manner of *Rhapsody in Blue*, and his *Serenade for Trumpet in Jazz* (written before 1948) was played by Maynard *Ferguson. In 1962 a studio orchestra under Davis' direction made an LP for CTL (M1005) with accordionist Gordie Fleming as soloist. Davis was a member of CAPAC. MM

DAVIS, Stu (b Stewart, David). Singer-songwriter, guitarist, b Boggy Creek, near Regina, of Scottish parents, 1 Jul 1921. In his youth a collector of cowboy songs and ballads, he began his radio career at 18, when he and his brother Fred sang as the Harmony Boys on CKCK, Regina. He took the name Stu Davis at this time and became known also as 'Canada's Cowboy Troubador.' After service in the RCAF he moved in 1945 to Calgary, where he performed on radio, at the Stampede, and at the Buckhorn Guest Ranch. On Wilf *Carter's recommendation Sonora in Chicago recorded his performances of several songs, including his own 'What a Fool I Was' in 1946. RCA Victor also recorded Davis performances in New York in 1948, and he later appeared on NBC radio's 'National Barn Dance' (Chicago) and 'Grand Ole Opry' (Nashville). He sang on CBC radio from Edmonton, then starred on CBC Winnipeg TV's 'Swing Your Partner' (1957–8), 'Rope Around the Sun' (1958–9, a children's show), and 'Red River Jamboree' (1960–1). In Edmonton in 1961 he headed his own 'Stu Davis Show' on CBC TV and in 1968 he narrated the 13-part CBC TV documentary history of western Canada, 'Trail-Riding Troubadour.' Some of Davis' songs appear in folios published by Gordon V. *Thompson (1946, 1956), *Empire Music (1949), and *Canadian Music Sales (1952). His 'What a Fool I Was,' recorded by US singer Eddie Arnold, was a major hit in 1948. Davis' songs also have been recorded by Wilf Carter, Ray Price, and Hank *Snow. Davis himself made 78s for Aragon and Apex in the early 1950s and 15 LPs for London 1955–67, among them two volumes of *Stu Davis Salutes the Western Stars* (Lon EB 6, Lon EB 33). In 1970 he recorded as Johnny Canuck for Quality; in 1971 an LP of his songs was released by Dominion. Duane and Derry Davis, both guitarists, have worked with their father and in other pop music contexts in Edmonton. Stu Davis is a member of CAPAC.

BIBLIOGRAPHY

Wills, Brian. '... meanwhile, back at the Lazy SD ... ' *CanComp*, 42, Sep 1969 MM

DAVISON, Arthur (Clifford Percival). Conductor, violinist, b Montreal 1919?; FRAM 1966, hon M MUS (Wales) 1974. He studied violin privately with Camille *Couture and in 1943 enrolled at the *CMM, where his teachers were Couture and Maurice *Onderet. He also attended the *McGill Cons. He was concertmaster of the Montreal Youth SO 1945–8 and during those years gave solo recitals in public and on CBC radio. In 1948 he won an AB scholarship which enabled him to study at the RAM in London. He soon began to play in London orchestras and chamber ensembles and was principal second violin of the London Philharmonia Orchestra in 1954 when it toured Europe under Herbert von Karajan. He later joined the London Philharmonic, becoming assistant concertmaster in 1964 and concertmaster later, and serving on the board of that self-governing orchestra.

Davison's interest in conducting had begun in his student days when he received advice from Wilfrid *Pelletier at the CMM. In the mid-1950s he conducted the London Youth SO and made periodic trips to the continent to study with Franco Ferrara. He visited Canada in 1955 to conduct the orchestra for an appearance of the New York City Ballet on CBC TV's 'L'*Heure du concert' and to give violin recitals on CBC radio, also recording, with Ross *Pratt, duos by Marais, Brahms, and Berkeley (RCI 138). The following year, with John *Newmark on CBC radio, he gave the premiere of *Kenins' *Sonata* for violin and piano.

During the 1960s Davison became increasingly busy as a conductor. In 1964 he was appointed director of the London Little Symphony. After a concert by that orchestra the reviewer for *The Times* remarked: 'Mr. Davison's conducting both demanded and received sophistication and stylishness from his experienced orchestra' (July 1964). He was a guest conductor of the Royal Danish Ballet that same year and became assistant conductor of the Bournemouth SO in 1965 and conductor of the National Youth Orchestra of Wales in 1966. In that year he founded in Croydon (South London) the Arthur Davison Concerts for Children. By 1970, when he was named director of the Virtuosi of England (a recording ensemble), he has ceased appearing publicly as a violinist. In 1971 he became music director and a lecturer at Goldsmiths' College, U of London, and in 1973 he was appointed a governor and served as a lecturer at the Welsh College of Music and Drama. He has appeared regularly on BBC radio and TV as a conductor and commentator, and on Scandinavian TV as a guest conductor. His 1973 conducting tour of Europe was filmed by the BBC. Davison has lectured and adjudicated in several countries. In 1974 he was made a Commander of the Order of the British Empire for his services to music, and in 1977 he was made a Fellow of the Royal Society of Arts. When the sales of his recordings exceeded one million he received in 1977 a Gold Disc from EMI.

DISCOGRAPHY (as conductor)

Albinoni – Mozart – Barber – Tchaikovsky – Bach. International Concert O. (1972). Music for Pleasure MFP 6034

Bach *The Brandenburg Concerti*, complete. Virtuosi of London. (1972). 2-Van S-313, 314/Classics for Pleasure CFP 40010

– *Concerti* for violin and strings BWV1041, 1042; *Concerto* for two violins and strings BWV1043. Bean vn, Sillito vn, Virtuosi of England. (1976). Classics for Pleasure CFP 40244

Dvořák *Symphony No. 7*. London Phil O. (1974). Classics for Pleasure CFP 40088

Handel *Messiah*, excerpts. Little Symphony O and Chor. (1967). Music for Pleasure MFP 2108

– *Music for the Royal Fireworks; Concerti Grossi, Op 3, no. 2 and 5*. Virtuosi of England. (1970). Classics for Pleasure CFP 105

– *Organ Concerti, Op 4, no. 2, 4, 7*; 'Sonata' from *Il Trionfo del Tempo*. Kynaston org, Virtuosi of England. (1973). Classics for Pleasure CFP 40044

– *Water Music*, complete. Virtuosi of England. (1974). Classics for Pleasure CFP 40092

Hoddinott *Welsh Dances; Investiture Dances; Concerto Grosso, Op 46* – Mathias *Sinfonietta; Celtic Dances*. National Youth O of Wales. (1976). REC 222

L. Mozart *Toy Symphony* – Prokofiev *Peter and the Wolf*. London Little Symphony, Daneman narr. (1969). Music for Pleasure SMFP 2126

Mozart *Concerto* K467; *Serenade* K525. Lympany pf, Virtuosi of England. (1972). Classics for Pleasure CFP 40009
– *Horn Concerti* K412, 417, 447, 495. James Brown hn, Virtuosi of England. (1970). Classics for Pleasure CFP 148
Purcell Overture to *The Indian Queen*; *Abdelazar Suite*; et al. Virtuosi of England. (1975). Classics for Pleasure CFP 40208
Shostakovich *Festival Overture* – Mussorgsky *Pictures from an Exhibition*. National Youth O of Wales. (1973). Music for Pleasure MFPS 57009
Strauss – Berlioz – Chabrier – et al. London Phil O. (1976). Classics for Pleasure CFP 40254
Vivaldi *The Four Seasons*. Sillito vn, Virtuosi of England. (1973). Classics for Pleasure CFP 40016
Vivaldi *Oboe Concerti, No. 1 and 2* – Albinoni *Concerti, Op 7, no. 3 and 6*. Sutcliffe ob, Virtuosi of England. (1971). Classics for Pleasure CFP 163
Walton – Hoddinott – Sibelius – et al. National Youth O of Wales. Music for Pleasure MFP 2129 (GBr)

DAWES, Andrew (Albert). Violinist, b High River, near Calgary, 7 Feb 1940. He studied violin 1947–55 with Clayton *Hare in Calgary and 1955–60 with Murray *Adaskin in Saskatoon. On Isaac Stern's advice he completed his training 1960–5 with Lorand *Fenyves at the Cons de Genève, where he received in 1964 the Prix de virtuosité with the highest marks awarded to that date. Previously he had won the 1962 Concours national des *JMC and, with his pianist-sister Marylou, third prize in the 1963 Munich duo competition. He also won first prize at the 1967 JMC competition in Vancouver and awards at the 1966 and 1969 *Montreal International Competitions. He has appeared in Europe with the Orchestre de la Suisse romande and the Belgrade Philharmonic, and in Canada with the major orchestras. He has given recitals in Canada, the USA, and several European countries. Dawes is the original first violin of the *Orford String Quartet and with the other members of the quartet has taught chamber music during the summers 1971–4 at the Kelso Music Centre and regularly beginning in 1972 at the *U of Toronto. In Dawes' playing, whether as soloist or as quartet leader, keen intuition and high energy are controlled by a schooled and capable musical mind.

DISCOGRAPHY
Chausson *Concert, Op 21*. Kubalek pf, Dawes vn, members Orford Str Quar assisted by O. Armin. 1974. CBC SM-246
Paganini *Sonata Concertante in A*. Lagoya guit. RCA Victor LSC 3142
See also Discography for Orford String Quartet. (WS)

DAY, Gordon (Hugh). Flutist, b Toronto 16 Oct 1914, d near Millbrook, Ont, 19 Jun 1962. After playing clarinet and saxophone with a country music band, Billy Hole and the Livewires, he led his own dance band, the Rhythm Knights, in Toronto, and in 1935 joined Horace *Lapp's orchestra as a clarinetist and saxophonist. He began playing flute with the orchestra in 1937 and studied with William Kincaid in Philadelphia that same year. He was a member of the RCN Band stationed in Toronto during World War II and also principal flute in the *Promenade Symphony Concerts and 1941–8 in the *TSO. His CBC radio show 'Flavoured with Flute' in the late 1940s was heard throughout the USA on the MBS network. He was a member of Chico *Valle's CBC ensemble for many years, of the *CBC SO 1953–62, and of other radio and studio orchestras. He was a member of the CBC Woodwind Quintet and a founder in 1955 of the *Toronto Woodwind Quintet. One of Canada's leading flutists for more than 20 years, Day premiered William *McCauley's *Five Miniatures for Flute and Strings* and Morris *Surdin's *Softly as the Flute Blows*, and recorded *Weinzweig's *Divertimento No. 1* with the CBC SO (1958, RCI 182/RCI ACM 1).

His son Bob (b Robert Gordon, Toronto 27 Aug 1946), a trumpeter and composer, who studied with Don Johnson and Gordon *Delamont in Toronto and Carmine Caruso in New York, has been a member of various commercial orchestras, of the *Boss Brass, and of the big bands of Bobby *Hales and Phil *Nimmons. Day's *Desert Walk* has been performed by *Canadian Brass. (WS)

Days Months and Years to Come. Vancouver group founded in 1974 to perform new Canadian compositions in a context of other contemporary music and to commission works. A stable core of performers was established to ensure presentations of consistent calibre and to provide a specific resource for composers. The group's conductor, the pianist-composer Alex *Pauk, was a founding member of *ARRAY in Toronto and of Array West in Vancouver. The latter group was superseded by Days Months and Years to Come, comprising Pauk, the flutist Kathryn (Birute) Cernauskas (b Hanover 15 Sep 1948, naturalized Canadian 1955; a pupil of *Aitken, Gazzelloni, Moyse, and Rampai), the percussionist Paul Grant (b Vancouver 21 May 1946, a member 1965–8 and 1970– of the *Vancouver SO), the oboist Tony Nickels (b Reno, Nev, 9 Mar 1945; a pupil of Bert Gassman, Al Goltzer, and Robert Bloom and appointed principal oboe of the *Vancouver Opera orchestra in 1977), the organist-harpsichordist Patrick *Wedd, and the cellist Lee (Alan) Duckles (b Berkeley, Cal, 9 Oct 1946; a pupil of Margaret Rowell and Colin Hampton and appointed associate principal cello of the Vancouver SO in 1976). The group became the resident new-music ensemble at the Vancouver East Cultural Centre in 1975 and has presented five subscription concerts each season and performances in high schools. Composers are encouraged to be present, to talk with the audiences. Extensive program notes are mailed to subscribers before each concert. The concerts explore various aspects of new music, including improvisation, compositional techniques, and unusual instrumentation. The ensemble is augmented as needed by guest performers, and composers often assist in their own works.

The programs have included works by such world figures as György Ligeti, Toru Takemitsu, and Elliott Carter. Prominence has been given, however, to pieces written for the group's particular combination of instruments, eg, Bruce *Davis' *Comp 1101011* and *Salmacis* (1975), Olov Franzen's *The Vancouver Piece* (1975–6), Allan *Rae's *Rainbow Sketches* (1976), Christopher Butterfield's *Trismegiste* (1976), Pauk's *Underneath the Afternoon* (1977) and *Beyond* (1978), Grant's *Year of the Horse: Three Rituals* (1978), and a collective work, *Six Bagatelles* (1978, for group and audience). With the assistance of the *Canada Council, Days Months and Years to Come have commissioned Marjan *Mozetich's *Rush-Hour Blues* (1976), John *Fodi's *Partimento: Here the Forsaken Virgin Rests* (1976), Harry *Freedman's *The Explainer* (1976), John *Rea's *Jeux de scène* (1977), Thomas Baker's *Yantra: Come Sweet Death* (1977), Rudolf *Komorous' *The Midnight Narcissus* (1977), and Alexina Louie's *Lotus* (1977). Works by Serge *Garant (*Quintette*), Donald Steven, and Claude *Vivier were commissioned for the 1978–9 season.

BIBLIOGRAPHY
Mertens, Susan. 'Taste in music: to stop at the soup is to miss the duck,' Vancouver *Sun*, 23 Oct 1976 (PSr)

DEAN, 'Dixie' (George William). Accordionist, teacher, composer, b London 25 Sep 1916. Taken to Canada in 1923, he began his career playing pop music during the 1930s on Toronto radio stations – CFRB and, after working 1933–5 in Bermuda, CBC. He also played in dance bands led by Stanley *St John and others. In 1939 he appeared with the renowned accordionist Charles Magnante in recital at *Eaton Auditorium. In 1940 he accepted a teaching post in New York with Pietro Deiro, the inventor of the piano accordion. Dean also toured with Deiro in the northern USA. During World War II he served with the RCN and played 1943–5 in *Meet the Navy*. Returning to Toronto he resumed his CBC work and also taught privately. By the late 1940s his pupils had included Eddie Allen and Les Foster (both later of the *Happy Gang) and Joan *Fairfax. In later years, Dean established the Ontario Cons of Music in Waterloo, Ont, and under its auspices edited or compiled several piano accordion instruction books published 1969–75 by Singspiration (Grand Rapids, Mich) or *Leeds. Dean composed the scores for the *NFB productions *Song of the Ski* (1947) and *Holiday Island* (1955). He is a member of CAPAC. MM

Harry Dean

DEAN, Harry. Teacher, organist-choirmaster, pianist, conductor, b Yorkshire, England, 22 Feb 1879, d Halifax, NS, 30 Oct 1955; ARCO 1898. After studies in England with Tobias Matthay and at the Leipzig Cons with Robert Teichmüller (piano) and Paul Homeyer (organ), he served 1906–8 as head of the keyboard and theory department and 1908–34 as director of the Halifax Cons. He founded (and directed 1934–54) the Maritime Academy of Music (see *Maritime Cons of Music), and examined 1909–25 and lectured 1925–32 at *Dalhousie U. An important figure in the development of music teaching in Halifax schools (see School music), Dean also served 1937–8 as founding president of the *NSRMTA and held the office again 1945–6 and 1949–51. In nearly 50 years of teaching his many pupils included Howard *Brown, Harold *Hamer, Georges and Carl *Little, Gordon *MacPherson, Jocelyn *Pritchard, and Marguerite *Spencer. One of the most versatile musicians in the Halifax of his day, Dean was organist-choirmaster 1906–53 at Fort Massey United Church, a piano recitalist, and the accompanist for many of the city's visiting soloists. He conducted the *Orpheus Club 1907–17 and its successor, the Halifax Philharmonic Society, 1919–54, and assisted in the organization of the *Community Concerts series in 1931. MSm

'Dear Old Pal of Mine.' Pop song from World War I with music by Gitz *Rice. The idea for the song, according to an editorial note on the sheet music (Ricordi 1918), was conceived by Rice while on sentry duty at the front lines at Ypres, France. The words, written by Harold Athol Robè (b USA 1881, d 1946), express the longing of a man, presumably a soldier, for his sweetheart (the 'pal' of the song's title). The universality of the sentiment may have contributed to the song's post-war popularity. The song was recorded by several tenors and baritones; one of two versions (Victor 755) by John McCormack was among the Irish tenor's most popular recordings. Among other vocal recordings were those by the Canadian singers Henry *Burr and Hector *Pellerin (the latter's in French), and instrumental versions were made by Sascha Jacobsen (violin), Sam Moore and Leroy Smeck (handsaw and guitar), and the Joseph C. Smith orchestra. Details of further recordings and discographical information are published in *Roll Back the Years*. FH

DÉCARIE, Reine (Sister Johane D'Arcie). Voice teacher, composer, b Montreal 4 Jan 1912; B MUS (Montreal) 1941, M MUS (Montreal) 1944, L MUS composition (Montreal) 1948. She joined the order of the Holy Names of Jesus and Mary in 1932 and studied at the École supérieure de musique in Outremont (*École Vincent-d'Indy) mainly with Claude *Champagne (composition), Alfred *Laliberté (voice and piano), and Rodolphe *Plamondon and Roger *Filiatrault (voice). She also studied violin and the harmonization of Gregorian chant and completed her studies in medieval music history and renaissance musical theory at the U of Boston in 1968. She began to teach singing at the École Vincent-d'Indy in 1942, and her pupils have included Réjane *Cardinal, Louise *Lebrun, Gloria *Richard, and Cécile *Vallée. In addition to psalm settings and songs for voice and piano, Décarie has set poems to music for other combinations – eg, *Le Jeu de ma subconscience* (1948) for voice, flute, and harp and *Palinods* (1950) for chorus, solo, and organ on texts by Gustave Lamarche. Her *Chanson de mon pays* (1952) is published by Les Éditions de La *Bonne Chanson. Her song cycle *Four Seasonal Poems* (1956) is dedicated to Maureen *Forrester. Décarie has composed five complete *Masses*, a *Cantate à Ste-Cécile* (1944), *Chants liturgiques* for a wedding mass (1965), a *Fugue* for organ (1947), a *Sonatine* for piano (1948), and the miniature opera *Cendrelune* (1950). All these were published by Les Éditions de l'École Vincent-d'Indy. ST

Decca. See Compo Company Ltd.

DECELLES, Maurice (Duclos). Clarinetist, oboist, bandmaster, teacher, composer, b Trois-Rivières, Que, 11 Oct 1905. After studies in music and literature 1918–23 at the Académie de la Salle at Trois-Rivières he played in a theatre orchestra for a year and then took a position with Bell Canada. He remained with that company for 40 years. He was transferred to Quebec City in 1928 and joined the *Quebec SO as principal clarinet in 1929, but in fact served until 1939 as oboist. He also conducted a number of cadet and student bands and taught clarinet 1928–30 at the Académie commerciale and 1942–63 at the *CMQ. His pupils included Pierre *Bourque and Jacques *Simard. DeCelles has composed many works for band (some listed in the *Catalogue of Canadian Composers*). Six, based on French-Canadian folk tunes, have been published by *Canadian Music Sales and recorded under the composer's direction by the Howard *Cable Concert Band. DeCelles was associate executive director 1965–8 of the Canadian Folk Arts Council. (FC, MM)

DECKER, Franz-Paul. Conductor, b Cologne 22 Jun 1923; hon LL D (Concordia) 1975. He studied 1941–4 at the Hochschule für Musik in Cologne with Philip Jarnach and Eugen Papst and took classes in conducting, composition, and pedagogy at the U of Cologne. He began his career as a choir conductor in Giessen in 1944 and was a conductor of orchestras in a succession of German cities. He was artistic director of the Rotterdam Philharmonic Orchestra 1962–8. He visited Canada in the summer of 1965 to direct the *NYO, which engaged him again for the 1968 session.

Franz-Paul Decker

Decker guest-conducted the *MSO in 1966 and succeeded Zubin Mehta as conductor and artistic director in 1967, retaining that position until 1975. The MSO made notable progress under his energetic and disciplined leadership and appeared under his direction at Expo 70 in Osaka, Japan. Decker has directed the MSO in the premieres of several Canadian works, notably *Pépin's *Quasars-Symphonie No. 3* in 1967, *Schafer's *Son of Heldenleben* and *Garant's *Phrases II* in 1968, *Saint-Marcoux's *Hétéromorphie* in 1970, Jacques *Hétu's *Passacaille* in 1971, and Pépin's *Prismes et cristaux* in 1974. At the *Opéra du Québec Decker directed *Il Trittico* (*Il Tabarro*, *Suor Angelica*, and *Gianni Schicchi*) in 1971, *Cavalleria Rusticana* and *I Pagliacci* in 1973, and *Falstaff* in 1974. After 1975 he continued to appear frequently as a guest conductor with the MSO and also with the *NACO. He served 1975–7 as artistic adviser to the *Calgary Philharmonic Orchestra. He has appeared with numerous major European orchestras and has toured South America in 1960, 1961, 1963, 1974, and 1975, Australia in 1967, 1975, and 1978, and New Zealand in 1966 and 1976. In December 1975 he was praised in Dallas, Texas, for his conducting of *Tristan und Isolde* with Jon *Vickers; and in 1978 after he led the same company in performances of *The Flying Dutchman*, John Ardoin wrote, 'His direction of *Dutchman* reaffirmed the luminous qualities of drama, style, and commitment he brought to *Tristan*, into which he had breathed life' (*Dallas Morning News*, 3 Dec 1978).

DISCOGRAPHY

Beethoven *Symphony No. 3*. Rotterdam Phil. Between 1962 and 1968. DG 135050

Brahms *Concerto No. 1*. Munich Philharmonic O, Gelber pf. 1976. EMI (HMV) HQS 1068/Connoisseur Society CS 2102

Mozart *Concerto No. 22* K482 – Haydn *Concerto, Op 21*. Berlin Radio SO, Demus pf. DG 138049

See also Discography for the *MSO. MT

de FORAS, Odette. Soprano, teacher, b Savoie, France, ca 1895, d Calgary 31 Dec 1976 or 1 Jan 1977. She spent her youth in Paris and at the Château de Thuyset, near Lake Geneva. With her family, she settled ca 1903 in High River, south of Calgary. Her father, the Count of Foras, gave her her first voice lessons, and her mother started her on the piano. She continued her studies with Annie *Glenn Broder in Calgary until 1916, when a scholarship to the RCM made it possible for her to study 1916–25 in London with Gustave Garcia. In 1924 de Foras sang Mary in the premiere of Vaughan Williams' *Hugh the Drover*. At the Royal Opera House, Covent Garden, where she sang 1927–35, her repertoire included Kundry in *Parsifal*, Sieglinde in *Die Walküre*, Musetta in *La Bohème*, Senta in *The Flying Dutchman*, and the title roles in *Aida*, *Madama Butterfly*, *Tosca*, and *Turandot*. When Ravel visited London in 1928 and 1929, de Foras gave the English premieres of most of his songs with the composer at the piano. Returning to Alberta in 1936, de Foras occupied herself with the family ranch, appearing in public only on rare occasions, notably in 1946, when at the urging of friends she appeared as guest artist with the *Mount Royal College SO, and again in 1959 when after a solo recital she recieved an ovation at Calgary's Southern *Alberta Jubilee Auditorium. On this occasion Rosemary Wood wrote in the *Calgary Herald* (17 Jan 1959), 'Her sincerity as an artist, blended with her dignity of person, captivated the house during the varied program.' Among her pupils is Lloyd *Erickson.

BIBLIOGRAPHY

Wood, Rosemary. 'Retired opera star returns to platform after 10 years,' *Calgary Herald*, 12 Jan 1959 GP

Degrees. Academic titles conferred upon individuals by universities and colleges to recognize the successful completion of particular programs of study set by those institutions, or (as honorary degrees) to recognize outstanding achievement in the arts, sciences, or humanities.

The first B MUS degree granted in Canada (and said to be the first, earned or honorary, granted in North America) was awarded in 1846 by King's College (Toronto) to J.P. *Clarke for his eight-part anthem 'Arise, O Lord God, Forget Not the Poor.' In 1856 Clarke may have received as well, from the *U of Toronto, the first D MUS granted in Canada, but the records cast some doubt on his actually having received it. George *Strathy was the recipient of the second B MUS (1853) and of a D MUS (1858), both from the *U of Trinity College (Toronto). Until 1879 Oxford U, Cambridge U, and Dublin U awarded almost all music degrees in the English-speaking countries, although US universities granted a few after 1850. Degrees for music studies were offered in Canada in the mid-1880s, but only 50 had been earned before World War I, as the first faculties of music were not founded until after the war. (See Universities.) Prior to that time degree candidates were prepared and instructed at conservatories and tested by examiners appointed by *Bishop's U, *Dalhouse U, *McGill U, the U of Toronto, and the U of Trinity College.

In 1883 the U of Trinity College devised a syllabus and set up annual examinations towards the B MUS degree, and in 1885 that college appointed a registrar in England in order that examinations might be held simultaneously in England and Canada. It is known that 193 candidates in both countries applied for Trinity music degrees between 1886 and 1891 and that 89 bachelor and doctorate degrees were awarded. In 1891, after a series of complaints by British musicians, this practice of granting degrees to English candidates 'in absentia' was discontinued.

Canadian recipients of the B MUS in the late 19th century included A.E. *Fisher and Clarence *Lucas (both Toronto 1893) and Percival *Illsley (Trinity College 1893 and Bishop's 1894). C.L.M. *Harris earned a doctorate from Trinity College in 1898. At the U of Toronto the majority of turn-of-the-century graduates were women, including A.K. Paget in 1896, Eva Taylor Nurse in 1898 (B

MUS) and 1908 (D MUS), Ethel Husband Scase in 1898, Ada Briggs McLellan in 1902, and Ada Twohy *Kent in 1906. McGill U's first music degree was a D MUS earned by Charles H. Mills in 1911. Between the two world wars McGill awarded three or four, the *U of Montreal four or five, *Laval U three, and the U of Toronto nine earned doctorates. Armand Pellerin was awarded a B MUS by the U of Montreal in 1921 following the affiliation of the *Institut Nazareth with that university. Eugène *Lapierre earned the U of Montreal's first D MUS in 1930. Laval U's School of Music granted its first B MUS degrees to Charles Lapointe and Sister Thérèse de l'Enfant-Jésus in 1929. Even after proper faculties had been formed, with many who had been examiners providing lectures and classes, attendance was rarely compulsory.

The francophone universities of Quebec functioned on a system of affiliated classical colleges, seminaries, and schools operated by various religious communities and organized on a modified Jesuit pattern. Degrees granted by the U of Montreal included the B MUS in performance (three-year program), which led to an M MUS in performance after one additional year of study. (In the 1950s this M MUS in performance led to a Diplôme d'artiste, which became Diplôme de concertiste in the 1960s.) Students wishing to continue their studies in historical or theoretical subjects would enter the Licence (L MUS) program requiring two years of study after the B MUS. At Laval U, the B MUS and L MUS were granted during this period. In the 1970s both universities changed their L MUS programs to an M MUS to bring them more closely into line with North-American practice.

It is interesting to note that until the mid-20th century earned doctorates from English-language universities always were given for 'exercises' in composition – usually symphonies or choral-orchestral works – but this rule did not apply in French-language universities, where doctorates were granted mostly, if not exclusively, for written historical or theoretical theses. Examples were Robert *Talbot's theoretical work on intervals of the fifth (D MUS Laval 1933, published Quebec City 1940), Sister *Marie-Stéphane's study on music education (D MUS Montreal 1936), Leslie *Bell's text on vocal sight-reading for adolescents (D MUS Montreal 1946), and G. Roy *Fenwick's survey of school music in Ontario (D MUS Montreal 1950). Before the major reform of education in Quebec in the 1960s, the general academic background required for a B MUS was, as elsewhere in Canada, the successful completion of grades at the secondary level (high-school matriculation). In 1967, however, Quebec became the only province in which the university-bound student must have studied at a *Cegep and obtained his or her DEC (Diplôme d'études collégiales).

Until the 1940s the programs offered in English-speaking universities were facsimiles of those offered in Great Britain and were intended primarily for composers. The possibility of earning a B MUS in performance, in history and literature (musicology), or in music education was virtually non-existent. After 1940 the overwhelming tendency in English Canada was to model university music programs on those in the USA, distinguishable from their British counterparts by compulsory attendance and a broader array of fields of concentration. The first Canadian degree course to follow the US model was instituted at the U of Toronto in 1946 and led to a B MUS in School Music. In 1949 19 individuals graduated from the course. The first Master of Music to be awarded in Canada was John *Fenwick's, in composition, from the U of Toronto in 1956.

During the late 1950s and early 1960s music degree programs expanded rapidly. By 1966, 17 Canadian universities were offering undergraduate music degrees, and of these 7 had introduced graduate programs.

In 1978, 28 Canadian universities were offering music programs leading to baccalaureate degrees: Bachelor of Fine Arts (BFA), Bachelor of Music (BM, B MUS, MUS BAC), Bachelor of Music Education (B MUS ED), and Bachelor of Musical Arts (BMA). Requirements for these degrees have varied, but certain generalizations can be made. Usually from three to five (most often four) years of residence have been required: roughly two-thirds of the courses have been in music (including performance); and concentrations have been possible in performance, theory and/or composition, and music history and literature (or musicology). In some instances no concentration has been specified (or possible), and the degree has been awarded with 'general mention.'

In addition, in 1978 more than 30 universities were offering programs of study leading to other baccalaureates (BA, B ED, etc) in which music might be stressed to a variable extent but subjects other than music predominated. The BA (Honours: Music) usually has represented an undergraduate program in which music courses predominate, but historical and theoretical subjects, rather than performance, are emphasised. In 1980, of the 28 universities which have offered programs leading to the B MUS or its equivalent, 12 (Alberta, British Columbia, Montreal, Regina, Saskatchewan, Sherbrooke, Toronto, Victoria, Western Ontario, Carleton, Laval, and McGill) also have offered master's programs with music the primary field of study: Master of Arts (MA), Master of Education (M ED), Master of Music (MM, M MUS), and Master of Musical Arts (MMA). Seven (Alberta, British Columbia, Montreal, Toronto, Victoria, Laval, and McGill) also have offered doctorate programs: Doctor of Education (D ED), Doctor of Music (D MUS, MUS DOC), Doctor of Musical Arts (DMA), Doctor of Philosophy (PH D). The requirements for these degrees are so diverse that the only possible significant generalization is that a master's or doctor's degree may be earned in Canada in any of the major branches of music. In 1950 John Reymes *King received the first Canadian PH D in music from the U of Toronto.

As is the custom in other countries (though perhaps most frequently in Canada and the USA), honorary doctorates (MUS DOC hc, hon D MUS, MUS DOC, LL D, D LITT) have been awarded in recognition of outstanding achievements in the field of music. Some 100 such doctorates have been awarded, including those to George Strathy (see above) and St George *Crozier (from Victoria U, Cobourg, Ont, in 1872). Honorary degrees have been given to musicians who have made great local contributions, such as Amy Ferguson (hon D MUS, Notre Dame, Nelson, BC, 1970); to nationally known figures such as *Applebaum, Jean *Carignan, *Champagne, Helen *Creighton, Jean *Dansereau, S.C. *Eckhardt-Gramatté, Maureen *Forrester, Glenn *Gould, Elmer *Iseler, Raoul *Jobin, Helmut *Kallmann, Gilles *Lefebvre, Gordon *Lightfoot, *MacMillan, Lois *Marshall, Anne *Murray, *Naylor, R.-O. *Pelletier, Wilfrid *Pelletier, Oscar *Peterson, Léopold *Simoneau, *Somers, *Vézina, *Vigneault, *Vogt, *Weinzweig, and *Willan; and to distinguished foreigners, including Sir Thomas Beecham, E. Power Biggs, Maud Karpeles, and Sir Alexander Mackenzie. Several Canadians have received degrees from outside the country. For instance, the Lambeth degree D MUS (Cantuar) has been conferred upon C.A.E. *Harriss (1905), Percival Illsley (1912), Healey Willan (1956), Godfrey *Hewitt (1973), and Hugh *Bancroft (1977). Alexander *Brott, Champagne, *Duchow, *Mazzoleni, *Parlow, *Papineau-Couture, and Wilfrid Pelletier are among those who have received honorary degrees from US universities.

See also Awards; Diplomas; Education, professional.

BIBLIOGRAPHY

U of Trinity College, Faculty of Music, Memorials Presented to Lord Knutsford, H.M. Secretary of State for the Colonies with Appendices, etc. (London 1890)

Joyce, F.W. *The Life of the Rev. Sir F.A.C. Ouseley, Bart* (London 1895)

'British musical degrees in Canada: the truth at last,' *SatN*, 26 Nov 1898

Reed, T.A., ed. *A History of the University of Trinity College, Toronto* (Toronto 1952)

Walter, Arnold. 'Education in music,' *Music in Canada*

MacMillan, Sir Ernest. 'Music in Canadian universities,' *CMJ*, vol 2, Spring 1958

Beckwith, John. 'Music education,' *Encyclopedia Canadiana*, vol 7

U of Toronto, Music Alumni Assoc. *Directory of Degree Graduates* (Toronto 1964)

Proctor, George A. 'The bachelor of music degree in Canada and the United States,' *CME*, vol 7, Jan–Feb 1966

Brown, A. Malcolm. *A Study of Music Curriculum in Degree and Diploma Programs Offered at Canadian Institutions of Higher Learning, 1968–1969* (Calgary 1969)

Walter, Arnold. 'Music education,' *Aspects of Music in Canada*

Ellard, Brian J., ed. *Directory of the Canadian Association of University Schools of Music*, annual (Moncton, Ottawa 1974–)

– *Inventory of Undergraduate Programs*, CAUSM conference report (1976) (BE)

Deirdre. Opera in three acts, for nine soloists, chorus, and full orchestra. The music, composed 1934–5, is by Healey *Willan, the text by John Coulter. The first full-length opera commissioned by the CBC, it was premiered 20 Apr 1946 on radio as *Deirdre of the Sorrows*, conducted by Ettore *Mazzoleni and with Frances *James as Deirdre. A preliminary version, *Conochar's Queen*, had been written by Willan in 1941. A revision for stage was given 2 Apr 1965 by the *Royal Cons Opera School at the MacMillan Theatre with Jeannette *Zarou and Lillian *Sukis alternating in the title role, and in 1966 it became the first Canadian opera produced by the *COC, with Zarou as Deirdre. A production for the 1972 *Banff Festival of the Arts was staged by Andrew Downie and conducted by Alfred *Strombergs, with Ann Looman in the title role. Drawn from an Irish saga of the Red Branch Knights of Ulster in the druidic era, the story tells of the doom of the ruthless Conochar, King of Ullah, and the tragic death of Naisi and his brothers, the Princes of Ullah, as a result of Naisi's love for the foundling Deirdre. Since much of the original text was devoted to the description of action required by radio, revisions for stage trimmed the material extensively. Willan wrote in his customary late-19th-century harmonic idiom, creating a rich polyphonic texture that is effective on radio though problematic in the theatre, where it can overwhelm the singers. Dramatically and musically *Deirdre* is a 'Wagnerian' opera, yet with a character distinctively its own. The libretto (Toronto 1944, rev 1965) and a vocal score (Berandol 1972) have been published.

BIBLIOGRAPHY

'Deirdre of the Sorrows, Canada's first full-length opera,' *CRMA*, vol 5, Feb 1946

Coulter, John. 'Words for music,' *OpCan*, Sep 1965 CM

DEJARLIS, Andy (b Joseph Patrice Ephreme Desjarlais, legally amended in 1971 to Andrew Joseph Patrick Ephreme DeJarlis). Fiddler, composer, b near Woodridge, near Winnipeg, 29 Sep 1914, d St Boniface, Man, 18 Sep 1975. Taught by his grandfather and later (1938) by W. George Rutherford in Winnipeg, DeJarlis won his first fiddling contest in 1935. One of the most popular entertainers on the Prairies, he performed 1935–43 on Winnipeg's CJRC radio and toured 1937–43 in northern Ontario, Manitoba, and Saskatchewan. His band, known then as the Red River Mates, later became the Early Settlers. Though less active 1948–54, owing to poor health, DeJarlis had won over 20 fiddling contests in western Canada by 1952. He later appeared on 'Don *Messer's Jubilee' and was featured 1962–3 on CFTM TV in Montreal. In 1965 he returned to Winnipeg. DeJarlis began recording in 1956 for *Quality Records and in 1959 for the *London label – the latter released some 25 LPs featuring many of his more than 175 songs, fiddle tunes, and dance pieces. Most of his compositions, like his various 'Red River' pieces and the BMI Canada award-winning *Manitoba Waltz* (1967), are named for specific locations. His publishers included Broadland Music and DeJarlis Music. In the *Winnipeg Free Press* (25 Jun 1966) Don Messer is reported to have called DeJarlis 'one of the greatest exponents of old time music in Canada.' DeJarlis is particularly remembered for his way with waltz music. The musical rights of his estate are administered by PRO Canada.

(RGn)

de KANT, Ronald. Clarinetist, b Lancaster, Penn, 30 Oct 1931; Artist Diploma (Juilliard) 1953. He studied with Daniel Bonade at the Juilliard School then taught for two years at the US naval school of music in Washington, DC. After a year in Toronto with the National Ballet orchestra, de Kant was principal clarinet 1955–65 with the New Orleans Philharmonic Orchestra. He became principal clarinet of the *Vancouver SO in 1965 and of the *CBC Vancouver Chamber Orchestra in 1967. He has also been a member of the New Orleans Woodwind Quintet, the *Vancouver Woodwind Quintet, the Vancouver SO Chamber Ensemble, and, occasionally, the *Cassenti Players. As soloist he has performed the major works for clarinet with the two Vancouver orchestras. He gave the premiere 22 Sep 1968 of *Weinzweig's *Divertimento No. 4* with the CBC Vancouver Chamber Orchestra and has recorded the Mozart *Quintet* with the *Purcell String Quartet, the Copland *Concerto* with the CBC Vancouver Chamber Orchestra, and other chamber works as a member of the Vancouver Woodwind Quintet. He began teaching at the *U of British Columbia in 1965 and has taught intermittently at the Vancouver City College, the *Community Music School of Greater Vancouver, and the Courtenay Youth Music Centre. In 1977 he began teaching at the *Banff SFA.

MW

de KRESZ, Geza. Violinist, teacher, conductor, b Budapest 11 Jun 1882, d Toronto 2 Oct 1959; naturalized Canadian 1930. He studied at the National Cons in Budapest with Károly Gobbi, Frigyes Arányi, and Jenö Hubay, graduating in 1900, and continued at the Prague Cons with Otakar Ševčik, receiving a second diploma in 1902. For the following three years he was a pupil of Eugène Ysaÿe in Brussels and at Godinne-sur-Meuse (where he met and played quartets with Boris *Hambourg) and also studied composition in Brussels with Théophile Ysaÿe and in Paris with Albert Lavignac.

He made his debut in Vienna in 1906, was concertmaster 1907–9 of the Vienna Tonkünstler Orchestra, and appeared as soloist with many European orchestras. In Bucharest 1909–15 he taught at the State Cons and led a string quartet at the royal court of Rumania. He went to Berlin in 1915 and was concertmaster 1917–21 of the Berlin Philharmonic Orchestra and a teacher 1919–23 at the Stern Cons. In 1918 he married the pianist Norah Drewett, with whom he gave duo-recitals after they moved – at the prompting of Boris Hambourg – to Toronto in 1923. De Kresz taught at the *Hambourg Cons, played first violin in the *Hart House String Quartet (until 1935), and founded and conducted the Little Symphony, a chamber orchestra. He spent many summers in Europe teaching at the U of Vienna and at the Mozarteum in Salzburg and performing. He remained in Budapest 1935–47, teaching at the State Academy of Music and the National Cons. As director of the latter 1941–7 he instituted one of the first high school curricula in Hungary to combine musical training with academic subjects. After World War II he adjudicated at several international competitions. In 1947 de Kresz and his wife returned to Toronto, where he taught at the *RCMT, conducted courses in violin pedagogy, and, until 1956, continued to perform.

Norah and Geza de Kresz

Ettore *Mazzoleni said of him, 'Here was a musician of vital temperament, full of zest for life, and completely selfless where music, and those he admired, were concerned' (*RCMT Monthly Bulletin*, Nov–Dec 1959). Harry *Adaskin, in *A Fiddler's World*, wrote that de Kresz had 'a good steady bow arm so that slow movements were beautifully played, very intellectually musical, and with a confident stage manner,' but added 'his most serious drawback was rhythmical unsteadiness and, since he had perfect pitch, he tended to sound out of tune.' A respected teacher, de Kresz included among his pupils Arthur *Garami, Flora Matheson *Goulden, Betty-Jean *Hagen, Clayton *Hare, Maurice *Solway, and Irene Diehl Thorolfson. Nora de Pedery Hunt designed a medallion in 1969 to mark the inauguration of the Geza de Kresz Memorial Scholarship Fund.

Norah de Kresz (b Sutton, England, 14 Jun 1882, d Budapest 24 Apr 1960), a piano pupil of Victor-Alphonse Duvernoy at the Paris Cons and of Bernhard Stavenhagen in Munich, played in recitals and with chamber groups. She taught 1928–35 at the TCM and later privately, her pupils including Patricia *Blomfield Holt and Ida *Krehm.

De Kresz' papers are deposited at the U of Toronto, the Metropolitan Toronto Library, and the *NL of C.

WRITINGS

Course in Violin Pedagogy: Introduction, Summary and First Lecture (Toronto 1949)

'Violin pedagogy,' *Strad*, 62, Oct 1951

'Some thoughts concerning progressive violin pedagogy,' *American String Teacher*, vol 7, Spring 1957

'Eugène Ysaÿe centenary 1858–1958,' *CMJ*, vol 1, Summer 1957

'Review' of *Cello Playing of Today* by Maurice Eisenberg, *CMJ*, vol 2, Spring 1958

Thoughts on Violin Teaching (Winnipeg 1969)

BIBLIOGRAPHY

Adaskin, Harry. *A Fiddler's World* (Vancouver 1977)

(RPn)

DELA, Maurice (b Albert Phaneuf). Composer, arranger, organist, pianist, b Montreal 9 Sep 1919, d Verdun (Montreal) 28 Apr 1978; BA (Montreal) 1940. He took lessons in organ and theory with Raoul *Paquet, then studied theory and composition 1943–7 at the *CMM with Séverin *Moisse and Claude *Champagne. He studied orchestration concurrently with Leo Sowerby in Chicago and J.-J. *Gagnier in Montreal. He received the *CAPAC prize in 1947 for *Petite Suite maritime* and *Ballade*, *Laval U's tri-centenary prize in 1952 for *Les Fleurs de glais*, and the *CFMTA prize in 1960 for *String Quartet No. 1*. His *Sonatine* for violin and piano has been played many times in Canada and in Europe, and his *Scherzo* was performed in 1970 by the Costa Rica SO conducted by Carlos Vargos.

After 14 years (1951–65) as an arranger and composer for the CBC – notably for the series 'L'*Heure du concert,' 'Serenade for Strings,' and 'Les Belles Mélodies françaises' – Dela was director and supervisor of music teaching 1965–78 at André-Laurendeau secondary school. He also began teaching orchestration at the *UQAM in 1973. He was organist at the Church of Notre-Dame des Sept-Douleurs in Verdun and wrote articles for the periodical *Les Carnets viatoriens*. Though the form of his later works remained classical, he often used polytonality and occasionally incorporated elements of serialism. He composed pedagogical pieces and works for recorder, organ, and piano, and harmonized popular and folk songs, including some by Gilles *Vigneault. In June 1978 the André-Laurendeau secondary school dedicated its concert hall, Salle Albert-Phaneuf, in his memory. Dela was a member of the *CLComp, an associate of the *CMCentre, and an affiliate of PRO Canada.

SELECTED COMPOSITIONS

ORCHESTRA

Ballade. 1945. Pf, orch. CMCentre

Concerto for piano and orchestra. 1946. CMCentre

Dans tous les cantons. 1949. Str orch. CMCentre. CTL 477-65137 (*Hart House O)

Ronde (Hugo). 1949. Sop, orch. CMCentre. RCI 35 (E. Benson *Guy)

Les Fleurs de glais (F. Mistral). 1951. Narr, orch. CMCentre

Scherzo. 1952. Ber (rental). CBC SM-132 (*Atlantic SO)

Adagio. 1956. Str orch. CMCentre. CTL 477-65137 (*Hart House O)

Projection. 1966. CMCentre

Symphony No. 1. 1970. CMCentre

Symphony No. 2 'Concertante.' 1972. CMCentre

Tryptique. 1973. CMCentre

Suite 437. 1977. Concert band. CMCentre

Other works for orch and various instr, in ms and at the CMCentre

CHAMBER MUSIC

Sonatina. 1945. Vn, pf. CMCentre

Petit Suite maritime. 1947. Ww quin. Ber 1979. (Excerpts) CBC Expo 11 (*Tor WW Quin)

String Quartet No. 1. 1960. CMCentre

String Quartet No. 2. 1963. CMCentre

10 Bagatelles. 1975. Sop rec. Musantiqua 1975

Gratifications I. 1976. Sop rec. Musantiqua 1976

Gratifications II, III, IV. 1977. Sop rec. Musantiqua 1977

CHOIR OR VOICE

'Xami' (A. Ferland). 1945. V, pf. Arch 1945. Master MA-275 (D. *Mills)

'Berceuse béarnaise' (anon). 1947. V, pf. *P-T*, Oct 1947. West WST 17137/West Gold W6S-8124 (*Forrester)
'Spleen' (Verlaine). 1949. V, pf. BMIC 1950
Les Saisons (Mme M. Dela). 1954. V, pf. CMCentre. CBC Expo 33 (*Simoneau)/RCI 470 (*Trépanier)
'La Lettre' (H. Barbusse). 1958. V, pf. BMIC 1958
'Le Vaisseau d'or' (E. Nelligan). 1967. SATB. CMCentre
'Le Paysage' (G. Vigneault). 1972. SATB. CMCentre
Other works, including 3 pieces for pf published by BMIC; collections of songs for children; as well as several song arrangements published by Arch and the Alliance des chorales du Québec

BIBLIOGRAPHY

Thériault, Jacques. 'Enjoyment of music Dela's chief concern,' *MSc*, 267, Sep–Oct 1972
BMI Canada Ltd / PRO Canada Ltd. 'Maurice Dela,' pamphlet (1972, 1979) (IP)

DELAMONT. Family of musicians: 1 / Arthur and 2 / his son Gordon.

1 **Arthur** (William). Bandmaster, cornetist, b Hereford, England, 25 Jan 1892. He played clarinet and later cornet with his father and brothers in a Salvation Army band in Hereford. Arriving in Canada with his family in 1908 he played in a Moose Jaw, Sask, Salvation Army band, and, after 1922, in Vancouver theatre orchestras. In 1928 he formed the *Kitsilano Boys' Band, remaining its conductor for over 50 years. Under his influence many of the band's members (see article for partial list) became professional musicians, and in 1976 he formed the Arthur W. Delamont Concert Band, which included many of these men. The concert band toured in Great Britain in 1979.

In the 1950s Delamont also began to conduct the band at the *U of British Columbia. According to Alan Daniels (*Vancouver Sun*, 28 Jan 1978), 'despite his irreverent approach and impish sense of humour, [he] is an avowed disciplinarian who commands respect at the rostrum.' He was made a Member of the *Order of Canada in 1980.

2 **Gordon** (Arthur). Teacher, author, composer, trumpeter, b Moose Jaw, Sask, 27 Oct 1918, d Toronto 16 Jan 1981. Raised in Vancouver, he studied trumpet with his father and was soloist with the boys' band. He moved to Toronto in 1939, played lead trumpet in dance bands and with CBC radio orchestras, and led his own dance band 1945–9 at the Club Top Hat, Toronto, and in other southern Ontario halls. After brief studies (arranging, composition, and pedagogy) in New York with Maury Deutsch in the summer of 1949, he opened his own studio in Toronto. In over 30 years of private teaching of harmony, counterpoint, composition, and theory he counted among his pupils Peter *Appleyard, Saul Chapman, Gustav *Ciamaga, Ron *Collier, Jimmy *Dale, John Dobson, David Elliott, Jack Feyer, Doug Foskett, Bill Goddard, Steve Gould, Hagood *Hardy, Herbie Helbig, Paul *Hoffert, Lawrence House, Don Johnson, Eddie *Karam, Moe *Koffman, Rob *McConnell, Ben *McPeek, Marek Norman, Lloyd Orchard, Bernie *Piltch, Bill Povey, Mort Ross, Fred *Stone, John Swan, Norman *Symonds, and Rick *Wilkins. His theoretical texts have been used in schools and by musicians throughout North America. Delamont led a rehearsal band ca 1953–ca 1962 in order that his students might have an outlet for their compositions. In the 1960s he directed a jazz octet which performed for *Ten Centuries Concerts and on the CBC.

A guiding figure in Canada in the third-stream movement which revolved around two of his earliest pupils, Collier and Symonds, Gordon Delamont himself composed several works applying classical forms to the jazz idiom. His compositions

Gordon Delamont

include *Allegro and Blues* (1962, for jazz orchestra), *Portrait of Charles Mingus* (1963, for octet), *Ontario Suite* (1965, Kendor 1967, a piece for soprano and orchestra performed daily at the Ontario Pavilion at *Expo 67), *Centum* (Kendor 1966, for band), *Collage No. 3* and *Song and Dance* (both 1967, Kendor 1970, recorded by the Ron Collier Orchestra with Duke Ellington as soloist), *Moderato and Blues for Brass Quintet* (1973, Kendor 1974), and *Conversation for Flugelhorn and Alto Saxophone* (Kendor 1977). His best-known work, *Three Entertainments for Saxophone Quartet* (1969, Kendor 1970), has been performed widely in North America and in Europe and was recorded by the New York Saxophone Quartet (Mark MES 32322). Gordon Delamont contributed articles to *Saturday Night*, *The *Canadian Music Journal*, jazz magazines, and newspapers. CBC radio broadcast a 90-minute documentary on his life and work, 'Gordon Delamont: Taking the Notes Where They Want to Go,' in 1979. The musical rights of his estate are administered by CAPAC.

WRITINGS

'Jazz composition: a minority report,' *Music Across Canada*, Jun 1963
Modern Arranging Techniques (Delavan, NY 1965)
Modern Harmonic Techniques, 2 vols (Delavan, NY 1965)
Modern Contrapuntal Techniques (Delavan, NY 1969)
Modern Twelve-Tone Techniques (Delavan, NY 1973)
Modern Melodic Techniques (Delavan, NY 1976)

BIBLIOGRAPHY

McNamara, Helen. 'Sweet music for a tone deaf Canada Council,' Toronto *Telegram*, 4 Oct 1969
'Gordon Delamont talks about teaching and music,' *CanComp*, 123, Sep 1977 (HM, MM)

DELAQUERRIÈRE, José (Mario Louis). Tenor, teacher, choirmaster, composer, actor, b Paris 16 Sep 1886, naturalized Canadian 1958, d Montreal 10 Apr 1978. In Paris his early musical training was provided by his father, Louis Delaquerrière, a tenor with the Opéra-Comique, and his mother, the singer Louise de Miramont. At the Schola cantorum he studied singing, theory, piano, organ, cello, and percussion. Among his teachers were Charles Bordes, d'Indy, Fauré, Amédée Gastoué, Gabriel Grovlez, and Guy de LaTombelle. At the Cons de Paris he was a pupil of Edmond Duvernoy (voice) and Émile Pessard (harmony and solfège). In addition he took courses in diction and drama. He began his career in music halls and in the leading roles of French and Viennese operetta, especially at the Gaieté-lyrique. After voluntary service in World War I he returned to operetta and the concert stage in Paris and the provinces. In January 1923 he arrived in Montreal to participate in a French operetta season at the *St-Denis Theatre, distinguishing himself in *La Mascotte*, *La Fille de Madame Angot*, *Les Cloches de Corneville*, and *Le Grand Mogol*. He opened a studio in Montreal and gave a series of broadcast recitals on the recently established radio station CKAC. In New York in 1924 he took part in International Composers' Guild concerts produced by Edgard Varèse, and was soloist in Carissimi's *Jephte* and Bliss' *The Tempest*. In 1923 he participated in the North American premiere of Stravinsky's *Renard* with the Philadelphia Orchestra under Stokowski. Returning to Europe, he pursued his career in operetta, films, and radio, and also taught. He settled permanently in Montreal in 1938 and again opened a studio. In fulfilling radio and TV engagements he attempted to make music attractive to a wide public. He founded the Cons populaire, where he taught singing and interpretation free of charge to more than 8000 young people, and he conducted the mixed choir Choeur de France. The activities of these two ventures continued until 1966. He began teaching at the *CMM in 1951.

He composed – mainly for voice – around 200 pieces, of which a dozen were published, mostly by Chapsal and Salabert. The recipient of numerous honours, Delaquerrière was made an Officier de l'Instruction publique de Paris in 1936 and a Member of the *Order of Canada in 1975. In France he was an active member of the Union professionnelle des Maîtres du chant français, and of the Société des Auteurs et Compositeurs de musique (SACEM). Excelling particularly in operetta, ballad, and popular song, he is remembered for his efforts to foster in Quebec the traditions of French song, as advocated in his book *Savoir chanter* (Montreal 1976). His recordings 1923–4 for HMV in Montreal and Pathé in Paris (see *Roll Back the Years*) consist of about 40 songs and excerpts from operettas. His papers were deposited with the BN du Q in 1976.

BIBLIOGRAPHY

Rudel-Tessier, J. 'José Delaquerrière: il faudrait écrire un livre,' Montreal *La Presse*, 20 Apr 1972
Catalogue of Canadian Composers GG

DELCELLIER. Montreal family of musicians of French origin: the brothers 1 / Henri and 2 / Joseph, both clarinetists, and the children of Henri, 3 / Henri-Aimé, clarinetist, and 4 / Marthe, cellist.

1 (Joseph) **Henri** (Jean). Clarinetist, violinist, conductor, b Béziers, France, 21 Sep 1872, d Montreal 27 Dec 1967. He began clarinet lessons with his father, Joseph Delcellier, and studied violin and theory in Paris at the École Niedermeyer, from which he graduated with a diploma. Alexandre Luigini and Léon Jehin taught him orchestra conducting. He was concertmaster at the Opéra de Paris and a member of other Parisian orchestras including that of Hasselmans and also conducted at the Casino de Paris. In 1911 he moved to Canada to assume direction of the choirs of the *Montreal Opera Company. After service in World War I he returned to Montreal in 1917. He staged dramatic works and conducted at the Imperial Theatre and the *Monument national (*Faust* and *Mignon*, presented at the latter theatre by the Canadian Opera Association in 1919). He was an instrumentalist and conductor at station CKAC ('Allo Paris') and on CBC ('Concert estival'), and he also served 1934–5 as personnel manager and 1935–52 as a clarinetist with the orchestra of the *CSM, and 1935–52 as vice-president of the Montreal Musicians Guild. He composed some works (unpublished) for orchestra and concert band.

2 **Joseph** (M.P.). Clarinetist, b Béziers 1876, d Montreal 1957. For 12 years, prior to 1914, he was a member of the noted English opera company of Carl Rosa. He later moved to Montreal and became an original member of the CSM (*MSO). For that orchestra's inaugural concert, 14 Jan 1935, Delcellier and Hervé *Baillargeon performed Rosario *Bourdon's transcription, for flute, clarinet, and orchestra, of *Lavallée's famous piano piece *Le Papillon*. Delcellier remained with the CSM until about 1948.

3 **Henri-Aimé**. Clarinetist, civil engineer, b Béziers 3 Jun 1902, d Hudson, near Montreal, 16 May 1975. A member of the Mount Royal Hotel orchestra and the *Ottawa Philharmonic, he also was a colonel in the Canadian armed forces.

4 **Marthe**. Cellist, b Laval, France, 8 May 1904. She was the wife of the violinist Pierre Iösch and the mother of the harpist Marie *Iösch-Lorcini. She joined the CSM (*MSO) in 1937 and played in that orchestra for 30 years. She also served for 10 years as principal cello of the *Montreal Women's Symphony and played on CBC radio and TV. She retired to London, Ont. AP

DELLA PERGOLA, Edith (b Leb). Soprano, teacher, b Cluj, Rumania, 12 Jun 1918, naturalized Canadian 1961. She studied voice at the Bucharest Royal Academy of Music, where her teacher was Luciano *Della Pergola, whom she married in 1935. Leaving the academy in 1939, she obtained a scholarship to study in Florence and made her Florentine debut that year as Mimi in *La Bohème* at the Teatro Comunale. She sang in numerous orchestral concerts in Florence before rejoining her husband at the Alberto Della Pergola Cons in Bucharest and teaching there 1942–7. Engaged by the Vienna Staatsoper in 1947, she sang the title role in *Aida*, followed by the title roles in *Tosca* and *Madama Butterfly* and Amelia in *Un Ballo in Maschera*. She went on to the Zürich opera and also appeared 1950–2 at the Teatro San Carlo in Naples, where she sang the role of the Amica in the Italian premiere (1950) of *Von Heute auf Morgen*, a comic opera by Schoenberg. She was a guest at theatres in Antwerp, Brussels, Frankfurt, and Munich. In 1955 she and her husband moved to Montreal, where she taught and, jointly with him, directed the *McGill Opera Studio. She continued the workshop alone in 1978 when her husband retired. Among her pupils was Jane Ellison, a noted Montreal teacher of pop singers. For CBC radio Della Pergola has given recitals and has been a soloist with the orchestra on *'The Little Symphonies.' For CBC TV she has appeared in 'L'*Heure du concert.' In 1946 she received the decoration of the Order of Cultural Merit from King Michael of Rumania. NT

DELLA PERGOLA, Luciano. Tenor, teacher, producer, b Bucharest 23 Jun 1910, of Italian parents, naturalized Canadian 1961. The son of the tenor Alberto Della Pergola, who was one of the founders of the Bucharest Opera, he studied with his father at the Bucharest Royal Academy of Music. In 1931, the year of his graduation, he made his operatic debut as Spoletta in *Tosca* and began to teach at the academy. One of his pupils, Edith Leb, became his wife in 1935. On the death of his father, Luciano and his wife founded the Alberto Della Pergola Cons, a private institution where they taught 1942–7. He made his Milan debut at the Teatro alla Scala during the 1947–8 season as the Herdsman in *Tristan und Isolde*. He joined the Teatro di San Carlo in Naples and sang there 1948–51 before returning to La Scala, where, 1951–5, he sang many roles in the standard repertoire and appeared in premieres of works by Pizzetti, Liebermann, and Milhaud, among others. He also sang in other Italian cities. Arriving in Canada in 1955, he settled in Montreal and began to teach at *McGill U. He founded the *McGill Opera Studio in 1956 and directed it with Edith *Della Pergola until 1977, after which time he continued to direct most of the productions. Among his pupils were Allan *Fine, Gina Fiordaliso, Joan *Patenaude, and Mariana *Paunova. Della Pergola sang the role of Prunier in the 1955 recording of Puccini's *La Rondine* (CBS Italiana 51147/7) and that of Malcolm, alongside Maria Callas, in a recording of Verdi's *Macbeth* (Cetra Opera Live LO 28) produced during a live performance at La Scala in 1952. NT

DELORME, Isabelle. Teacher, pianist, composer, b Montreal 4 Nov 1900. A pupil of Sister Madeleine-Marie at the École supérieure de musique in Outremont (now *École Vincent-d'Indy), she later studied piano with Arthur *Letondal and violin with Albert *Chamberland and Agostino Salvetti. She received her teaching certificate ca 1918 from the *AMQ. A composition pupil 1929–39 of Claude *Champagne, she began teaching theory and solfège in 1943 at the CMM, where she stayed for 26 years, though she also taught at other institutions, notably the Ursuline Convent in Trois-Rivières. In the summers of 1955 and 1956 she continued her theory studies with Nadia Boulanger at the American Cons in Fontainebleau. In 1967 her treatise on harmony (unpublished), a product of her teaching experience, gained Boulanger's approval. In 1969 she became an examiner for the music conservatories of Quebec and also continued to teach privately. Her pupils include Andrée *Desautels, Jacques *Hétu, Roger *Matton, François *Morel, and André *Prévost. Her compositions, written in 1940–60 in a lyrical and traditional style using classical harmonies, have been played but not published. Her works for string orchestra include *Fantaisie, Choral, et Fugue, Prélude et Fugue, Suite, Berceuse dans le style ancien* (also for piano), and *Andante*, which was premiered in 1941 and repeated several times by the CBC Montreal orchestra conducted by Jean *Deslauriers. She also wrote choral works and motets such as 'O salutaris,' organ pieces, and 'Prière à la Vierge' for solo voice. DRA

del VECCHIO, Rosita (Rosa) (m Jehin-Prume). Mezzo-soprano, actress, b Montreal 15 Dec 1846, d there 11 Feb 1881. A descendant of an Italian family which settled in Quebec in the late 18th century, she studied at the Sacred Heart Convent in Sault-au-Récollet, where she was a friend of Emma *Albani. In 1866 she married the violinist Frantz *Jehin-Prume, who had been her teacher. She studied voice with a Professor Wicart in Brussels, then toured 1869–70 with her husband in the USA and Cuba. Thereafter she went to Europe to study with Francesco Lamperti in Nice and fulfil engagements in Italy, France, Belgium, and Switzerland. In Canada she gave many concerts with Jehin-Prume and with Calixa *Lavallée. She enjoyed great success as an actress in a series of performances of Jules Barbier's *Jeanne d'Arc* in May 1877 at the *Academy of Music, Montreal. Gounod's incidental music for the play was conducted by Lavallée. In 1880 she created the role of Rose Laurier in Louis Fréchette's historical play *Papineau*. She also played in Fréchette's *Le Retour de l'exilé*. She died of bronchial pneumonia, the result of a chill caught while leaving a charity concert. Her last words, 'Laissez-moi dormir,' inspired Fréchette to write a poem. Two verses of 'Laissez-moi dormir' were set to music (Op 40) by Jehin-Prume and published by Olivier in 1881. Another poem of the same source of inspiration and title, by Tancrède Trudel, was set to music by Ernest *Lavigne (Lavigne & Lajoie). A talented singer and an outstanding actress, del Vecchio was very popular in Quebec and was called the Sarah Bernhardt of Canada. In Montreal an avenue was named in her honour in 1965.

Rosita del Vecchio

BIBLIOGRAPHY

'Feu Madame F. Jehin Prume,' *Le Canada musical*, 1 Mar 1881

Forest, Sylvain. 'Mme. Rosita Jehin-Prume,' *Le Canada artistique*, Mar 1890

Jehin-Prume, Jules. *Une vie d'artiste* (Montreal ca 1900)

Delvec, Paul. 'Nos disparus,' Appendix C, *Calixa Lavallée* (Montreal 1936, 1950, 1966) GP

de MARGERIE, Paul. Pianist, arranger, composer, b Vonda, near Saskatoon, 1931, d near Ottawa spring 1968; ARCT 1948. A pupil of Lyell *Gustin in Saskatoon, he studied also 1944–9 at the TCM (*RCMT). While attending *Laval U 1952–5 he won the Prix du gouvernement français in 1954. After serving 1955–8 as secretary to the director of the school of music at Laval U and director of the university choir, he moved in 1958 to Montreal. At first an accompanist to the visiting French singers Charles Trenet and Catherine Sauvage, in Canada and abroad, he also played for many chansonniers. He wrote arrangements and conducted studio orchestras for over 20 LPs by Robert *Charlebois, Renée *Claude, Clémence *Desrochers, Jean-Pierre *Ferland, Pierre *Létourneau, Raymond *Lévesque, Raoul *Roy, and others. He was one of three arranger-conductors who took part in making the LP *3-12* (1967, Select SSP-24. 155, an orchestral recording of songs by 12 chansonniers) which won a Festival du disque award in 1968. An admirer of Michel Legrand, he conducted several concerts of that composer's music. His own musical, *Hanger '54*, influenced by Legrand's *Parapluies de Cherbourg*, was produced in 1967 on CBFT-TV. His small output of songs includes 'Ton Visage' (of which a version was recorded by its lyricist, Jean-Pierre Ferland) and 'Les Enfants que j'aurai.' Both confirm de Margerie's self-description as a 'belated romantic.' The musical rights of his estate are administered by CAPAC. (EFr)

de MARKY, Paul (Alexander). Pianist, teacher, composer, b Gyula, Hungary, 25 May 1897, naturalized Canadian 1931. He studied in Budapest with Stephan Thomán (a pupil of Liszt), making his debut there in 1921. He moved to Canada in 1924. He first performed 9 Oct 1926 at the TCM Concert Hall, Toronto, but took up residence in Montreal. He played Franck's *Symphonic Variations* under Douglas *Clarke at the inaugural concert 12 Oct 1930 of the *Montreal Orchestra. While continuing to perform in Europe, Canada, and the USA, he taught 1929–37 at the *McGill Cons and broadcast frequently on the CBC until 1948, often on Oswald *Michaud's Sonobel piano. He retired from performance in 1950 and taught piano privately in Pointe-Claire (a suburb of Montreal) until 1972, specializing in teaching children. Robert Cram, Samuel *Levitan, Oscar *Peterson, and Doug *Riley have been among his pupils. His compositions (some listed in *Catalogue of Canadian Composers*) include works for piano and orchestra and several songs. He premiered his *Ballad* for piano and orchestra under Jean-Marie *Beaudet on a CBC broadcast 31 Aug 1944 and performed his piano concerto, *The Trans Atlantic*, under Jacques Singer at the 1950 *First Symposium of Canadian Contemporary Music in Vancouver. RVW

Dembeck String Quartet. Toronto group active 1950–61 under the leadership of the violinist John Dembeck. The members were Dembeck and Stanley Kolt (violins), Robert Warburton (viola), and Cornelius Ysselstyn (cello). In 1954 Warburton was replaced by Ross Lechow (briefly) and Jack Neilson, and Ysselstyn by Rowland *Pack. The quartet made its CBC radio debut 12 Jan 1951 playing works by Haydn and Beethoven. Though known mostly for its CBC broadcasts, the quartet gave a few public recitals in Toronto. It appeared 3 Apr 1954 at a *CLComp concert, playing *Freedman's *Five Pieces for String Quartet* and participating with the mezzo-soprano Trudy Carlyle in Alexander *Brott's *Songs of Contemplation*.

Dembeck, a native of New York and a graduate of the Juilliard School, made his Town Hall debut in 1937. He served 1941–8 and 1957–61 in the first violins of the *TSO, was the viola 1943–5 in the *Parlow String Quartet, and was concertmaster in 1945 for the*Promenade Symphony Concerts and concertmaster 1952–3 and later a violinist with the *CBC SO, with which he also was soloist in the Sibelius *Concerto*. He recorded Brott's *Violin Concerto* with the TSO (1952, RCI 71). With the quartet's demise, Dembeck became a freelance violinist in Toronto and has given duo recitals with his wife, the pianist Anna Drake Dembeck.

BIBLIOGRAPHY

'The birth of a string quartet,' *CBC Times*, 11–17 Feb 1951

(LH, MH, HK)

DEMPSEY, Nina (Gray) (b Ferguson). Teacher, soprano, b Regina 22 Jun 1893; ATCM 1930, ARAM 1931, AMM 1936. She studied voice 1917–18 with Rhys Thomas and 1920–5 with Winona Lightcap in Winnipeg (where she was a soloist ca 1922 in *Messiah* with the *Winnipeg Oratorio Society under J.J. *Moncrieff), and pedagogy (summers 1920–1) with Herbert Witherspoon in Chicago. She also attended the RAM in the early 1930s. After serving 1920–2 as assistant supervisor of music in Winnipeg primary schools, she opened her own voice studio in 1923. In over 40 years of teaching, her pupils included Devina Bailey (*Duggan), Belva Boroditsky, Donna Bouma, Heather Ireland, Nona Mari, Helly Sapinski *Jedig, Patricia Siwek, Mary Ann Taylor, Sarah Udow, and Peter *van Ginkel. Dempsey was president 1955–7 of the*MRMTA. In 1965 she retired from teaching and moved to California. (CC)

DENISET, Thérèse (m Souchon). Soprano, teacher, b St Boniface, Man, 11 Apr 1914. After studies in Montreal with Salvator *Issaurel she made her debut on radio in the 1937–8 season, then moved to the south of France to study with Ninon Vallin, remaining with the famous soprano and teacher during the war years. She also studied production with Roger Lalande and sang leading roles 1941–2 at the Opéra de Lyon and the following season at the Monte Carlo Opera. After the war (1945) she won critical praise for her recital debut in Paris at the salle Chopin-Pleyel. She participated in several broadcasts on French radio and appeared in recital and concert. Returning to Canada in 1947, she was heard on CBC radio, notably on 'Distinguished Artists,' and in public recital with the Winnipeg pianist Roline Mackidd. Five years later Deniset returned to France, where she performed especially on radio. Forced by ill health to return to St Boniface, she abandoned her performing career and took up teaching. Her recordings of eight titles appear on one side of the *Rococo LP 5354, with several by Ninon Vallin on the other. The Deniset recordings were produced in Winnipeg in 1947 and 1949. She retired to France in 1974. (MB)

Denmark. The earliest settlement in Canada from this southernmost Scandinavian country was that founded at New Denmark, NB, ca 1872. Danes also settled in Ontario, near London, and at Pass Lake, in the area of Port Arthur (Thunder Bay). By 1971 there were 75,725 people of Danish origin in Canada. Natives of Denmark who have lived in Canada and contributed to the musical life include St John Hyttenrauch (arrived 1857; see London), Viggo *Kihl (1913), Poul Bai (1927), John *Kraglund (1927), and Ulla (Mrs Michael) *Colgrass (1974), the editor of *Music Magazine*.

Bai, a baritone, taught at the TCM 1927–32 and privately until about 1960, appeared in 1929 at the *CPR's Great-West Canadian Folksong-Folkdance and Handicraft Festival and its Vancouver Sea Festival (in Willan's *Order of Good Cheer*), sang Scandinavian folksongs at *Massey Hall in a concert by the Five Piano Ensemble, and conducted a 20-member Scandinavian Male Voice Choir for several years.

Other Canadian residents of Danish origin or birth are the pianist Mikael Eliasen, a graduate of *McGill U and an accompanist of the singers John *Boyden, Joan *Patenaude, and others; Julius (Duke) Nielsen, the bassist with Don *Messer; the clarinetist Erick Nelson, who played with the Montreal City Jazz Band and Toronto's Metro Stompers during the 1960s; the Vancouver bassist Torben Oxbol; and the pop singer *Valdy (Valdemar Horseal). Ronald *Turini's mother is of Danish origin. The Danish singer Aksel *Schiøtz lived in Canada for a few years in the mid-1950s. Visitors from Denmark have included the illustrious Wagnerian tenor Lauritz Melchior, the pianist John Damgaard Madsen for the *JMC 1975–6, the Copenhagen String Quartet for the JMC 1964–5, the Copenhagen University Choir, the Danish Quartet, and the Eriksson Trio. The last-named made JMC tours in 1966–7 and 1967–8. In 1960 Vagn Holmboe represented Denmark at the *International Conference of Composers at Stratford, Ont.

Canadians who have performed in Denmark include Emma *Albani, who sang in Copenhagen in 1888 and received the order of merit from King Frederick VIII; Éva *Gauthier, who toured in 1910 and was decorated by Queen Marie; Ida *Krehm; Gertrude *Newton; the *Hart House String Quartet (1937); the *Hart House Orchestra (1966), whose conductor, Boyd *Neel, was of Danish ancestry; and the conductors Arthur *Davison, who appeared with the Royal, Tivoli, and Royal Danish Ballet orchestras, and Simon *Streatfeild and John Warren, both of whom have conducted Danish radio orchestras.

Canadian musicians have exhibited a strong interest in the works of the composer Carl Nielsen (1865–1931). The *TSO gave the Canadian premiere of his *Symphony No. 5* in February 1951 under Erik Tuxen, then conductor of the Danish State Opera. In October 1953 the *CBC SO under Heinz *Unger gave the first Canadian performance of Nielsen's *Symphony No. 4*. Nielsen was the subject of a documentary film written by Peter Haworth in 1976 and based on the composer's autobiography *My Childhood*. In 1977 the Canadian Carl Nielsen Society was founded in Toronto, with Svend Roewade as executive secretary. Roewade prepared the script for 1978 CBC radio documentary on Nielsen. By 1975 20 Danish folksongs had been recorded in Canada by the Canadian Centre for Folk Culture Studies of the National Museum of Man.

DENYS, Jean-Baptiste. Pianist, organist, choirmaster, composer, b Berthier (renamed Berthierville), near Sorel, Que, 24 Jun 1864, d Montreal 23 Mar 1947. He began piano studies with Charles-Marie *Panneton in 1873, and then was a church organist in 1879 in Montreal (St-Pierre Apôtre), 1880–2 in Belleville, Ont, 1882–5 in Rigaud, Que, in 1885 in Peterborough, Ont (St Peter's Cathedral), and 1887–94 in L'Assomption, Que. Returning to Montreal, he served as organist-choirmaster 1894–1912 at Ste-Cunégonde Church and organist 1912–ca 1942 at St-Édouard Church. He taught at Bourget College in Rigaud and in Terrebonne and Montreal. He was the first teacher of Alfred *Laliberté and Roméo C. *Larivière. He made several trips to Europe, one in the company of Samuel *Casavant. Denys' compositions include sacred music, harmonizations of popular songs, and piano pieces such as *Air varié sur O Canada* (Boucher 1909). GP

DEPKAT, Gisela. Cellist, teacher, b Königsberg, Germany, 5 Sep 1942, naturalized Canadian 1960. Her parents settled in Port Arthur (now Thunder Bay) in 1954. After studies with A. Troester in Germany in 1958, Lorne *Munroe at the 1960 International String Congress in Puerto Rico, and Eugene Eicher in Pittsburgh in 1961, she joined the class of George Neikrug in 1962. It was through Neikrug that she became an advocate of the cello method developed by Emanuel Feuermann and his physiotherapist Dr D.C. Dounis. Her work with Neikrug, to whom she was an assistant 1967–8 at the U of Texas, continued through master classes into the 1970s. She was awarded second prize for cello in the 1964 International Competition for Musical Performers in Geneva. She performed 7 Dec 1966 as the winner of a Concert Artists Guild Competition in recital at Town Hall, New York, toured in 1967 for the *JMC, and made her formal New York debut 6 Feb 1968 at Carnegie Recital Hall. In 1970 she won first prize in the *CBC Talent Festival and played the Dvořák *Concerto* with the *Winnipeg SO. With the National Orchestral Assn Orchestra under John Barnett she played Haydn's *Concerto in D* at Carnegie Hall 24 Feb 1970.

Depkat taught 1971–4 at the U of Richmond, Va, where she was a member of the university quartet-in-residence and principal cellist of the Richmond SO. She played 1972–4 in the Ararat (piano) Trio in Kitchener, Ont, and toured as soloist in 1973 with the *NACO. She was principal cellist 1974–5 of the Icelandic Broadcasting SO in Reykjavik (where she taught at the College of Music) and 1975–7 of the Stratford Festival Ensemble and the *Kitchener-Waterloo SO. She joined the faculty at *McGill U in 1976. She gave the Canadian premiere (Vancouver 29 May 1975) of Ginastera's *Serenata*.

Gisela Depkat

DISCOGRAPHY

Kodály – Neikrug – Hindemith. 1977. Aquitaine MS 90504

Schubert – Tartini – Boccherini – Bloch – Joachim *Sonata*. Brough pf. 1970. CBC SM 113

Schubert *Sonata in A Minor 'Arpeggione'* – Brahms *Sonata in F*. Armenian pf. Aquitaine MS 90354 (CF)

de RIMANOCZY, Jean. Violinist, conductor, b Vienna 4 Feb 1904, d Los Angeles 2 Mar 1958. Educated at the Academy of Music in Budapest under Jenö Hubay, Bartók, Kodály, and Leo Weiner, de Rimanoczy emigrated in 1925 to Canada, settling first in Winnipeg. He was a member 1928–33 of the *Calgary SO and performed as a soloist in western Canada. An appearance with the *Vancouver SO led to his appointment in 1934 as concertmaster and assistant conductor. He also became the first violin of the Allard de *Ridder Chamber Music Quartette. A soloist on the CRBC and CBC program 'Jewels of the Madonna' in the mid-1930s, he also conducted a string orchestra 1938–52 for CBC radio's 'Classics for Today' and a larger orchestra briefly on 'Music in the Night.' He taught privately in Vancouver, where his pupils included Angelina *Avison, *George Bornoff, Ricky *Hyslop, Gregory *Millar, and Cardo *Smalley. In 1943 he was engaged by Sir Thomas Beecham to be the concertmaster of the Seattle SO, concurrent to his Vancouver activities. In Seattle he was a string instructor 1944–9, and head of the violin department 1949–51, at the Cornish School (later Institute) of Music. In 1947 he founded the *de Rimanoczy Quartet in Vancouver. Prior to moving to Los Angeles in 1957, de Rimanoczy also conducted the Vancouver Junior SO 1952–5 and was host (1955) for CBC TV's 'Theme in Seven,' a seven-part history of chamber music. All of his activities were marked by enormous energy, sensitivity, and a demand for accuracy. Though on occasion abrasive, he got results. In music he dared to do what was difficult and to do it well. BNSG

The de Rimanoczy Quartet. First major Vancouver string quartet, founded in 1947 by Jean *de Rimanoczy (first violin), with John Chlumecky (second violin), Smyth *Humphreys (viola), and Audrey *Piggott (cello). The latter was succeeded in 1955 by Malcolm *Tait. The quartet was active until 1956, performing frequently on CBC radio and touring at least once in British Columbia and Alberta. It drew its repertoire largely from the standard works but also included pieces by Barbara *Pentland and Robert *Turner.

DESAUTELS, (Marie) Andrée (Carmen). Instrumentalist, musicologist, teacher, b Montreal 9 Oct 1923; premiers prix in history of music and aesthetics (Paris Cons) 1949. The daughter of Victor Desautels and Cédia *Brault, she studied piano with Isabelle *Delorme and later attended the École supérieure de musique in Outremont (*École Vincent-d'Indy). At the *CMM 1944–7 her teachers were Germaine *Malépart (piano), Isabelle Delorme (harmony and counterpoint), and Claude *Champagne (composition and orchestration). Also during this time she studied the history of art and literature 1945–6 at the *U of Montreal. Admitted to the Paris Cons, she took courses in the history of music with Norbert Dufourcq and aesthetics with Marcel Beaufils and Alexis Roland-Manuel. She studied composition and orchestration privately with Andrée Vaurabourg-Honegger, analysis with Nadia Boulanger, and ondes Martenot with Maurice Martenot. Three of her works, 'Bois amical,' 'Accalmie,' and 'Hymne aux étoiles,' were sung at the École normale de musique in Paris 1 Jul 1947 at a concert of French and Canadian music in which La *Cantoria took part.

In 1949 on her return from Paris Desautels began teaching the history of music and musicology at the CMM. She was an examiner for the Paris Cons in 1952. From 1961 to 1964 she taught the history of music at the U of Montreal and the École Vincent-d'Indy. She was visiting professor for three summers (1963–5) at the international sessions of the Château d'Argenteuil in Brussels. She was active in the *JMC 1949–66 as a commentator (more than 500 concerts) and 1951–6 as managing editor of the *Journal des JMC*, which in 1954 became *Le Journal musical canadien*. She was appointed associate commissioner of the JMC pavilion at *Expo 67, Man and Music, where she was responsible for both the basic concept and the programming. At the *JMC Orford Art Centre 1964–8 she was host to several conferences and offered public courses 1975–8 on the work of various composers including Bach and Ravel. For CBC radio she both wrote and introduced numerous series, including 'La Chanson de France' (1956), 'Connaissance de la musique' (1957), 'Musique nouvelle d'autrefois' (1958), 'Chronique de la vie musicale au Canada' (in collaboration with James Bannerman and Helmut *Kallmann, 1965), and 'Reflets des sources' (1972–3), besides contributing to such programs as 'La Revue des arts et des lettres.'

In 1946 Desautels wrote the incidental music for Carl Dubuc's play *La Fille du soleil*. In 1950 she brought to Canada Ginette Martenot, a virtuoso performer on the electronic instrument invented by her brother. Andrée Desautels wrote a background score for that instrument, for a Théâtre du Nouveau-Monde production (1954) of Molière's *Dom Juan* and performed it herself. She also composed the incidental music for *Antigone* by Anouilh for the CBC (1952).

In 1951 Desautels was elected a member of the Société française de musicologie. She was the founder and president of the Assn des professeurs of the *Cons de musique du Québec 1960–8 and was a member of the *Canada Council 1967–70. She has collaborated in drawing up numerous briefs, including the one submitted to the *MACQ by the association in 1962, and she has written several articles and reviews for newspapers (notably *Le Devoir*, Montreal, 1962–3) and Canadian and European periodicals. She has contributed to *EMC* and to *The New Grove*.

WRITINGS

'Les trois âges de la musique au Canada,' *La Musique*, vol 2, ed Norbert Dufourcq (Paris 1965)

'La musique' in 'Canada 4: Vie culturelle,' *Encyclopaedia universalis*, vol 3 (Paris 1968)

'The history of Canadian composition 1610–1967' / 'Histoire de la composition musicale au Canada de 1610 à 1967,' *Aspects of Music in Canada / Aspects de la musique au Canada* (Toronto 1969, Montreal 1970)

Saint-Denys-Garneau et la musique, in the series Dossiers de documentation sur la littérature canadienne-française (Montreal 1971)

'Certain aesthetic considerations on musical creation in Canada,' *Arts and Culture* (Montreal 1976)

'La création et la vie musicale au Québec,' *Dossier-Québec*, ed Claude Glayman (Paris 1979)

'Un manuscrit original de Marc-Antoine Charpentier à Québec,' *Recherches* (Paris 1980) GP

DESCARRIES, (Joseph Ernest) Auguste. Pianist, organist, teacher, composer, b Lachine, near Montreal, 26 Nov 1896, d there 4 Mar 1958; laureat (AMQ), D MUS (Montreal) 1949. He studied piano with Arthur *Letondal, Alfred *Laliberté, and Jean *Dansereau and harmony with Rodolphe *Mathieu in Montreal, and at 11 began playing the organ in the Gesù Church. After studying law, he decided on a musical career and succeeded Alexis *Contant as organist of St-Jean-Baptiste Church.

In 1921 Descarries won the *Prix d'Europe for piano but, before departing for Paris, where he was to remain for the ensuing nine years, he accompanied the tenor Edmond Clément on tour in Quebec and the USA. In 1923, assisted by a special scholarship in composition from the *AMQ, he attended the interpretation classes of Alfred Cortot and Marcel Dupré at the École normale and studied harmony and counterpoint with Alice Pelliot, piano with Léon Conus, composition with Georges Catoire, and violin with Jules Conus. He became known as a gifted improviser. In his development as a composer he benefited from contacts with Glazunov and Nicholas Medtner. With the latter he concentrated particularly on the study of rhythm. After giving a series of six well-received Paris recitals in 1929, Descarries returned to Montreal in 1930 and presented several recitals there. He also undertook numerous other assignments, serving as organist-choirmaster at the churches of St-Germain and St-Viateur and teaching piano in several institutions, notably the *Cons national de musique. He joined the teaching staff at the *CMM in 1944 and remained there until his death. His pupils included Gaston *Allaire, André *Asselin, Jean *Deslauriers, Monique *Gusset, Piere *Leduc, and Samuel *Levitan. At the *U of Montreal, he taught music history and in 1951 became assistant dean of the Faculty of Music. On his retirement from the university he was named professor emeritus.

Descarries founded (and directed 1933–5) the Société de musique de chambre Euterpe, served 1938–41 as president of the AMQ, and was a vice-president of the Commission diocésaine de chant liturgiques. He gave series of lectures at his studio, and wrote articles for *Le Devoir*, *La Lyre*, *La Presse*, and other publications. In 1945 he founded the Entraide de l'École Auguste-Descarries, which for 10 years assisted in establishing careers for his most gifted pupils. He gave a farewell recital at *Plateau Hall in 1956.

Descarries gained recognition as a composer with his *Rhapsodie canadienne* for piano and orchestra, premiered in 1936 by Helmut Baerwald and the orchestra of the CSM and subsequently repeated in New York and in Montreal. He also wrote a *Petite Symphonie*, a string *Octet*, numerous works for piano including a *Toccata* (BMI Canada) and a *Sonata*, a *Magnificat* (BMI Canada), some masses for mixed choir and some art songs. He also left numerous harmonizations of carols and Canadian folksongs, and some church music. Classical in form and romantic in content, his works did not establish themselves in the repertoire despite sound craftmanship, often genuine inspiration, and sophisticated harmony.

BIBLIOGRAPHY
L.-Descarries, Marcelle. 'Un musicien canadien à Paris 1921–1930,' *CMB*, 8, Spring-Summer 1974 GG

DESCHÊNES-HARVEY, Marcelle (b Deschênes, m Harvey). Composer, b Price, near Matane, Que, 2 Mar 1939; B MUS (Montreal) 1965, L MUS (Montreal) 1967. At the *U of Montreal she studied 1963–7 with Jean *Papineau-Couture and Serge *Garant. On grants from the French government, the Quebec government, and the *Canada Council, she continued her training 1968–9 in France with François Bayle, Henri Chiarucci, and Guy Reibel of the Groupe de Recherches musicales de Paris, and in 1969 she participated in a collective work, *Musiques éclatées*, produced by the group and presented at the Festival d'Avignon. In Paris from 1968 to 1970 she also attended Pierre Schaeffer's Conservatoire courses on music and its application to audio-visual techniques and studied analysis with Olivier Alain at the École César-Franck. She continued 1970–1 with Daniel Charles (aesthetics), Claude Laloum (analysis, ethnomusicology), and Jean-Étienne Marie (analysis) at the U of Paris and added studies in ethnomusicology at the École pratique des hautes études of the Musée des Arts et Traditions populaires in Paris. In Canada in 1971 she took part in the composition, production, and direction of a collective work *Si...longetmps* performed in 1972 at the U of Montreal.

Deschênes-Harvey taught 1972–7 at the electronic music studio of *Laval U and participated in the organization of a sound library while also carrying out research in music education. In 1973 she made two experiments in collective music with non-musicians, including a three-day creativity session for 30 women aged 18 to 75. In the autumn she produced sound tapes for the experimental video films *Amertube* and *Le phasé mou*. She participated 1974–6 in concerts by the group *GIMEL, and in 1975 she composed the sound track for the *NFB film *Le Port de Montréal*. Her most important works are 1½ (1966), premiered in 1968 by the pianist Albert *Grenier; *Voz (cantate mitrailleuse)* (1968); *7777* or *progressions sur la circonférence du jaune au rouge par l'orange ou du rouge au bleu par le violet, ou même embrassant le pourtour total* (1968); *talilalilalilalarequiem* (1970), premiered by the *SMCQ Ensemble in 1974; and *Moll, Opéra-Lilliput pour six roches molles* (1976), commissioned by the SMCQ and premiered in 1976. This work won first prize for mixed-media music at the sixth Concours international de musique électroacoustique in Bourges in 1978. Deschênes-Harvey is a member of CAPAC. (PD, HP)

De SÈVE, Alfred. Violinist, teacher, composer, b Montreal 1860, d there 1928. He began violin study at seven with Oscar *Martel and made a promising debut six months later. He also was taught by Frantz *Jehin-Prume. In 1876 De Sève went to Paris for studies, briefly with Sarasate, then with Hubert Léonard and Lambert Massart. During three years as a pupil of Henri Vieuxtemps he developed a career in Paris under the patronage of the Queen of Spain, Isabelle II, who made De Sève her court violinist. His reputation established, he returned in 1879 to Canada, where he gave many concerts. In 1880 he married the pianist Joséphine Bruneau, who also became his accompanist. Moving in 1881 to the USA he soon began teaching at the New England Cons in Boston, and in 1891, on the death of Calixa *Lavallée, succeeded him as choirmaster at Holy Cross Cathedral. De Sève was a member of the Boston SO, and his solo appearances with the orchestra – 18 Feb 1882 in Mendelssohn's *Concerto in E Minor* and 15 Dec 1883 in Saint-Saëns' *Introduction and Rondo Capriccioso* – were among the earliest by a Canadian soloist with a US orchestra. He was concertmaster of the Philharmonic Orchestra and made several tours of the USA as a member of the Boston Symphony Orchestral Club. About 1907 he returned to Montreal to teach violin, privately and at the *McGill Cons, and to manage his considerable personal fortune. His pupils included Alexander *Brott, Noël *Brunet, Albert *Chamberland, Eugène *Chartier, Marcel Saucier, and Lucien *Sicotte. De Sève wrote compositions for violin and piano, solo piano, and orchestra, published by Ditson and Arthur P. Schmidt. In 1931 a Montreal street was named after De Sève.

BIBLIOGRAPHY
'Notre violoniste canadien à Paris,' *Canada musical*, Jun 1878
'Alfred De Sève,' *Canada artistique*, vol 1, Dec 1889
Laurendeau, Arthur. 'Musiciens d'autrefois; Alfred Desève [sic],' *Action nationale*, vol 35, Mar 1950
Musical Red Book (CG)

DESJARDINS, Jeanne (m Lonergan). Soprano, teacher, b Montreal ca 1903, d 16 Apr 1961. After studies with her father (a cellist, bassoonist, and choirmaster) and Salvator *Issaurel, she made her debut in 1923 in Debussy's cantata *L'Enfant prodigue* at the Monday Concerts sponsored by Raoul *Vennat. She then worked with Henri *Pontbriand, Pauline *Donalda, Alfred *Laliberté, and the pianist Marie-Thérèse *Paquin, who collaborated with her on all her subsequent recitals. She was coached in Paris by the wife of the noted conductor Louis Fourestier. She appeared with the *Société canadienne d'opérette in 1929 at the Palace Theatre and in 1932 sang light music under the name of Jeanne Shaw over radio stations CRC and CRCM. She made her operatic debut in 1933, singing Marcellina in *The Marriage of Figaro* in a production directed by Victor *Brault. She was known as 'the Canadian Kate Smith.' In the admired series of Montreal performances conducted by Wilfrid *Pelletier, in which leading stars of the *Metropolitan Opera were supported by Montreal singers and a Montreal orchestra, Desjardins sang several roles, notably the Priestess in *Aida* in 1941 and 1943, Dame Marthe in *Faust* in 1941 and 1942, and the Innkeeper in *Boris Godunov* in 1943. She was a soloist in 1941 with the orchestra of the CSM and in 1942 with the *McGill String Quartet, and during the 1941–2 season, assisted by her accompanist Marie-Thérèse Paquin, she emerged as a distinguished performer of French song in a series of recitals with commentary, 'Les liedistes français,' at the Windsor Hotel. The critic Marcel *Valois wrote, 'Her voice...possessed a unique colour, a blend of subtle shades.' In 1945 she was heard over the CBC's Dominion network in the Canadian premiere of Ravel's *Sheherazade* under Jean-Marie *Beaudet. Desjardins premiered songs by Jean *Deslauriers, Lucien *Martin, and Jean *Vallerand on the radio series 'Sérénade pour cordes,' ca 1940–50, and was heard in numerous other radio programs.

BIBLIOGRAPHY
Valois, Marcel. 'On ne pouvait qu'aimer Jeanne Desjardins,' *Au carrefour des souvenirs* (Montreal 1965)
Gleason-Huguenin, Madeleine. *Portraits de femmes* (Montreal 1938)
Musiciennes de chez nous GP

DESJARDINS, Louis-Édouard (pseudonym 'Bon vieux temps'). Physician, folklorist, bass, choirmaster, teacher, composer, b Terrebonne, near Montreal, 10 Sep 1837, d Montreal 2 Mar 1919; MD (Victoria College, Cobourg, Ont) 1872. He took his academic studies at the Collège Masson in Terrebonne and at the Nicolet Seminary, where he taught singing and instrumental music. He settled in Montreal in 1865 and became choirmaster at the cathedral, which was then in temporary premises. He pursued medical studies in Europe in 1870 and 1872, became a surgeon at the Hôtel-Dieu Hospital in Montreal, and taught 1872–1908 at that hospital's school of medicine and surgery. In 1873 he founded the Ophthalmic Institute of the Asile Nazareth. For several years he held musical evenings at his home and in 1895 he staged and conducted Ferdinand Poise's comic opera *L'Amour médecin*. His four-voice folksong harmonizations, *Chansons populaires du Canada*, were published under the pseudonym 'Bon vieux temps' by Tremblay & Dion and were performed in 1912 at the French Language Congress in Quebec City. His *Messe de minuit*, based on Christmas airs, was published by the Compagnie d'Imprimerie moderne (Montreal 1902). He also composed some *Motets* (Montreal ca 1917) under the pseudonym 'Ancien maître de chapelle' and other choral works.

BIBLIOGRAPHY
Canadian Who's Who (Toronto 1910)
Musiciens canadiens DM

DESLAURIERS, Jean. Conductor, violinist, b Montreal 24 Jun 1909, d St-Jérôme, Que, 30 May 1978. He studied violin 1918–23 with Émile *Taranto and Camille *Couture, harmony and solfège with R.-O. *Pelletier, counterpoint and instrumentation with Auguste *Descarries, and orchestration with Claude *Champagne. He toured Canada and New England 1924–9 with the singers Paul *Dufault and Joseph *Saucier. Deslauriers was a member of the *CSM Orchestra 1935–45 and began his career as a conductor of radio orchestras in 1936, working principally for the CBC. He conducted for several important radio series: the popular 'Serenade for Strings' 1937–57, which won the 1946 LaFlèche Trophy and became a TV program in 1955; 'Radio-Concerts canadiens'; 'Théâtre lyrique Molson'; 'Concerts d'opéras'; and the TV series 'L'*Heure du concert,' 'Sérénade,' and 'Concerts populaires.' He was the conductor in 1954 for a TV opera production of *The Barber ofSeville* and the 'CBC Wednesday Night' broadcast of Messager's *Monsieur Beaucaire*. Other CBC operas he conducted on radio or TV included *Roméo et Juliette* (1971) and *Madama Butterfly* (1977).

In Quebec City, as music director 1967–70 of the *Théâtre lyrique du Québec, Deslauriers conducted *Mignon* and *Les Pêcheurs de perles* among others. He was the assistant conductor 1972–5 of the *Opéra du Québec and conducted *Samson et Dalila* (1971), *La Fille du régiment* (1972), *Manon* (1973), and *Madama Butterfly*, in which he 'brought forth all the instrumental beauty of the score' (Montreal *Le Devoir*, 1 May 1974). He also appeared as guest conductor with the *COC (*La Bohème* 1972) and the *Edmonton Opera Assn (*Faust* 1973). In 1976 he presented extracts of Alexis *Contant's **Caïn* at the CBC's Grands Concerts series at the *Salle Claude-Champagne. He was guest conductor on numerous occasions of concerts by the symphony orchestras and CBC radio orchestras in Montreal, Quebec, Toronto, Ottawa, Halifax, Vancouver, and Winnipeg. He conducted the premiere of Robert *Turner's *Three Episodes for Orchestra* with the *TS in 1966 and François *Morel's *Prismes-Anamorphoses* with a Toronto CBC orchestra in 1968. Deslauriers arranged and conducted the scores for many films immediately following World War II. Among his compositions are a *Prélude* for strings and a song, 'La Musique des yeux.' He was a member of the Rioux commission and contributed to the **Rapport de la Com-*

mission royale d'enquête sur l'enseignement des arts dans la province de Québec.

Deslauriers's daughter Yolande, a soprano, is married to the violinist Eugène *Husaruk.

DISCOGRAPHY

Dela 3 folksongs (arr) – Gratton *Quatrième Danse canadienne*. 'Serenade for Strings' O and Chor. 1962. RCI 186

Morawetz *Sinfonietta* – Morel *Prismes-Anamorphoses* – Weinzweig *Divertimento No. 5*. CBC Mtl orch. 1969. RCI 292/(Weinzweig) RCI ACM 1

Turina *Rapsodia Sinfonica* – Elgar *Serenade for Strings* – Britten *Simple Symphony*. CBC Hal Chamb O. 1968. CBC SM-85

See also Discography for *TS.

BIBLIOGRAPHY

Husaruk, Yolande. 'Jean Deslauriers, '*Le Bulletin*, vol 1, no. 4, 1978 (GG)

DESMARAIS, Gérald. Bass, choirmaster, b Montreal 30 Mar 1906, d Hardwick, Vt, 29 Jul 1950. He studied singing and theory with Alfred *Lamoureux, Paul *Doyon, and Alfred *Laliberté, and received a scholarship in 1927 from the Delphic Study Club. With Laliberté he concentrated on Wagnerian roles and Lieder. He made his *Montreal Orchestra debut in 1936 in Wotan's farewell scene from *Die Walküre*. With the Orchestra of the *CSM he was a soloist in Bach's *B-Minor Mass* in 1937 and in Beethoven's *Ninth Symphony* in 1941, 1944, and 1947. At the *Montreal Festivals he made his operatic debut in 1944 as King Mark in *Tristan und Isolde*, repeating the role that year, and also singing Hunding in *Die Walküre* at the Chicago Opera. At the Montreal Festivals he was a soloist in Mozart's *Coronation Mass* in 1945 and Bach's *St Matthew Passion* in 1946 and 1950 and sang Zuniga in *Carmen* in 1946 and 1947, the Bonze in *Madama Butterfly* in 1947, and the Comte des Grieux in *Manon* in 1949. Desmarais also sang at the *Opera Guild (the Bonze in 1947, Ferrando in *Il Trovatore*, 1949, and Colline in *La Bohème*, 1950) and at the *Variétés lyriques (Basilio in *The Barber of Seville*, 1949). Following his performance in *Tristan und Isolde* Marcel *Valois wrote: 'Gérald Desmarais's King Mark was excellent in voice, delivery, phrasing and accent...It truly was a revelation, and the whole audience responded with prolonged applause' (Montreal *La Presse*, 30 May 1944). Desmarais also gave recitals of Lieder and French songs, notably in 1948 at *Plateau Hall and on CBC radio. He sang in numerous Montreal churches; his last appointment of the kind was at St-Germain in Outremont, where he served 1938–50 as choirmaster. A few days after appearing as a soloist in the *St Matthew Passion* at the 1950 Montreal Festivals he died as the result of a road accident. GP

DÉSORMEAUX, (Marie Arsalie) **Rolande** (m L'Herbier). Singer, accordionist, b Montreal 27 Jul 1925, d Laval, near Montreal, 15 May 1963. She studied accordion at the school of Pat Marrazza and diction with Jeanne *Maubourg. She was the hostess ca 1942 for CKAC radio's 'Rolande et ses chansons' and an accordionist and singer in 1944 on CBC radio's *'Les Joyeux Troubadours.' She appeared on several other radio programs, including the CBC's 'Les Alouettes Everyday' and 'La Soirée du vieux moulin' and CKVL's 'Fresque musicale' (with her husband Robert *L'Herbier) and 'Vive la gaîté.' She was named 'Miss Radio '48' at a competition organized by the Montreal weekly *Radiomonde*. She made her first recordings in 1947 for Marly-Polydor. In a Quebec documentary which she made for Crawley Films of Ottawa she performed her own composition 'Madame la lune.' With L'Herbier she gave courses in accordion, singing, and solfège. 'Rolande reçoit' (1961–2) was her last radio series. It was as a guest on 'Jeunesse d'aujourd'hui' on CFTM-TV in November 1962 that she gave her last public performance. For *Pathé, alone and with L'Herbier, she recorded several of the songs which won prizes in the CBC French network's *'Concours de la chanson canadienne.'

BIBLIOGRAPHY

Brousseau, Serge. *Le Beau roman d'amour de Rolande Désormeaux* (Montreal 1964) HP

DESROCHERS, Clémence. Singer-songwriter, actress, b Sherbrooke, Que, 23 Nov 1933. Her work as an actress has claimed the greater part of her career, but her monologues and songs have helped bring her name before a vast public. It was Jacques Normand who introduced this Quebec chansonnière to the public 1958–9 at his Montreal cabaret, the St-Germain-des-Prés. In 1959 Desrochers was a member of the group Les Bozos with, among others, Jean-Pierre *Ferland and Claude *Léveillée. On her own she opened some boîtes à chansons in Montreal (La Boîte à Clémence and, with Yvon Deschamps, Le Fournil) and in the suburbs (at the motel-restaurant La Barre 500). In 1964 she wrote the libretto for Pierre *Brault's musical comedy *Le Vol rose du flamant*, considered the first of that genre written in Quebec. Brault subsequently composed the music of most of Desrochers's songs. In 1966 she took part, along with Claude *Gauthier, Pauline *Julien, and Gilles *Vigneault, in a show at the Olympia in Paris.

Among her works are the books and lyrics for four revues: *La Grosse Tête* (music by Brault, 1967), *Les Girls* (music by François Cousineau, 1968, her greatest success), *La Belle Amanchure* (music by Jacques Crevier, 1970), and *C'est pas une revue, c't'un show* (1971). Two songs from the latter became popular: 'La Chaloupe verchères' (music by Gaston *Brisson) and 'Je ferai un jardin' (music by Louis-Philippe *Pelletier). These shows were presented in a small hall, Le Patriote à Clémence, located above *Le Patriote in Montreal. Another of Desrochers's successful songs is 'Avec les mots d'Alfred une chanson pour Rose' (with music by Marc Larochelle, and lyrics based on a fragment from *Élégies pour une épouse en-allée*, a work by her father, the poet Alfred Desrochers). The single 'Le Monde aime mieux Mireille Mathieu' was a recording success for Desrochers in 1975.

Desrochers was inactive 1971–2 but returned in 1973 to work for CBC TV as host of the bilingual program 'Les Montréalais' and author of the script of 'À propos.' She appeared 1975–6, at Le Patriote and the Outremont cinema in Montreal, at the *Grand Théâtre in Quebec City, and at the *NAC in Ottawa. A tour took her to northern Quebec in 1976. The following year she performed at the *Institut canadien in Quebec City and again at the Outremont cinema. A volume containing several excerpts from the series of CBC telecasts 'Les Trouvailles de Clémence,' for which she was host 1976–9, was published in Montreal in 1978. She also is the author of six volumes (published in Montreal) of short stories, poems, songs, monologues, excerpts from her revues, and a play.

In her monologues and songs Desrochers handles satire and caricature zestfully, and her humour can be caustic; but she can be candid, too, and tender, even romantic. In an open letter published in *La Presse* (Montreal, 4 Mar 1976), the critic Georges-Hébert Germain paid her this tribute: 'Again, it was you who perfected the formula for the monologue and the show. You remain the most brilliant portraitist of the Quebec woman. You're like a mirror in which she can see herself, admire herself, or make herself beautiful once more as required. The soul of Quebec is revealed in your monologues and songs...our realities, our dreams, our emotions.' Desrochers is a member of CAPAC.

DISCOGRAPHY

Clémence sans pardon. 1964. Gamma GM-104

Clémence Desrochers vol 1. Sel M 298.047/ Alouette SAD-520

Le Vol rose du flamant. 1965. RCA PCS 1024

La Belle Amanchure. 1970. Tremplin TNL-2001

Il faut longtemps d'une âpre solitude pour assembler un poème à l'amour. 1972. Poly 2424 087

Je t'écris pour te dire. 1974–5. Franco FR-793

Mon dernier show. 1977. 2-Franco FR-41001

See also Discography for Chansonniers.

BIBLIOGRAPHY

Boucher, Denise. 'La fantaisie faite femme, Clémence Desrochers,' *Châtelaine*, 9 Sep 1971

Drostie, Bruno. 'Seriously speaking: Quebec's funniest lady,' *CanComp*, 126, Dec 1977 HP

DESSAINTS, Raymond. Violinist, conductor, teacher, b Quebec City 1930?; premier prix violin (CMQ) 1952. His main studies were with Calvin *Sieb at the *CMQ. The recipient of a bursary from the Quebec government in 1952, he studied 1952–4 in Paris with René Benedetti (violin) and Pierre Pasquier (chamber music) and 1954–6 in Rome with Remi Principe. On his return to Canada he taught 1956–60 at the CMQ as assistant to Calvin Sieb. He was a member of the *MSO 1960–8. He studied conducting during the summers of 1966 and 1967 with Otto-Werner *Mueller in Victoria, BC, and on a *Canada Council grant in the summer of 1968 with Hans Swarowsky in Nice. Under a cultural exchange program he toured Czechoslovakia in 1970 as a conductor with the state radio. In 1968 he began teaching violin at the CMM and conducting the CMM orchestra. He has been a guest conductor with several Canadian orchestras including the one heard on the *CBC Talent Festival. He frequently conducts the*CBC Quebec Chamber Orchestra and the MSO and in 1977 and 1978 he was music director of the summer concerts for the city of Montreal. In 1977 he made a tour of Tunisia, where he conducted André *Mathieu's *Concerto No. 3* for piano, with André-Sébastien *Savoie as soloist. Among Dessaints's pupils are Angèle Dubeau (first prize in the under-14 section of the *MSO Concours in 1976, and a violin graduate of the CMM in 1978), J.-F. *Sénart, and Raymond Thibodeau. ST

DESSANE, (Marie Hippolyte) **Antoine** (Antonin). Organist, pianist, cellist, teacher, composer, b Forcalquier, near Aix-en-Provence, France, 10 Dec 1826, d Quebec City 8 Jun 1873. He was a son of Louis Dessane, the author of a theory of music approved by Luigi Cherubini, and Marie Maurel, who came from a family of soldiers. Antoine's elder brother was his first teacher of composition. Another brother was to become the organist at St-Sulpice in Paris. Until 1837, when the Dessanes moved to Paris, Antoine received his musical education from his family. His father, who had been teaching since 1828 at the Jesuit college in Billom, in Auvergne, imposed a strict discipline on his son: at nine he was studying music nine hours a day. A few months after his 10th birthday he became one of the youngest students at the Paris Cons and was one of the few who became the favourites of its formidable director, Luigi Cherubini. Among his fellow students were César Franck and Jacques Offenbach. Dessane won two competitions at the conservatoire, one in cello and one in piano.

Antoine Dessane, by Théophile Hamel, ca 1859

Despite this, his father withdrew Antoine from the conservatoire in October 1841 and took him and his older brother on a concert tour of the French provinces, Italy, Austria, and Germany. The tour lasted a year and a half; the musicians gave concerts in many towns and several castles, including those of the duchesses of Angoulême and Berry and of the prince of Polignac. On their return Antoine taught for a year at Billom with his father. He settled in Clermont-Ferrand in 1845 and completed his musical education there with the composer George Onslow. During the next two years he discovered the fascination of composition and absorbed as much as he could of the musical heritage of the Western world. In addition, he gave lessons at several institutions and households. One of his pupils, Irma Trunel de la Croix-Nord, became his wife in 1847, a few months before the revolution of 1848. The necessities of life were rationed, and France was unable to support her artists, especially in the provinces. It was at this time that Dessane accepted the offer to succeed T.F. *Molt as the organist of Notre-Dame Basilica in Quebec City.

Dessane landed at Quebec with his wife and daughter in July 1849. Finding that the people there shared their language and religion, and deeply impressed by the city's beauty, the Dessanes integrated quickly into a milieu steeped in cultural pursuits. At first the family settled on the outskirts of the city on the Chemin-de-la-Petite-Rivière on the west of the St-Charles Cemetery. It was during a fishing excursion on the St-Charles River that Dessane heard some folk songs which were to inspire his *Quadrille sur cinq airs canadiens*. In 1850 the Dessanes gave a concert with the 79th regiment and a German violinist, Sigismond Pfeiffer. Irma Dessane sang songs by Meyerbeer, Adam, and Hippolyte Monpou. Dessane played cello and piano and presented a work of his own, *La Québécoise*, 'as a tribute to the ladies of Quebec.'

This concert marked the beginning of an active musical career in which, no doubt because of the vocal talents of Irma Dessane, opera was to play a large part. In 1852–3 the family moved to St-Vallier Street. This more central location made it possible to offer music lessons, which soon became popular among the middle-class families with which the Dessanes associated. The courses were supplemented by musical soirées. These 'Soirées Dessane' later were held in the Knights of Columbus hall. In 1855 Dessane conducted the first act of Boïeldieu's *La Dame blanche*. The same year for the *Quebec Harmonic Society he directed two concerts of works by Mozart, Beethoven, Haydn, and Weber.

The society disbanded in 1857, and 13 years passed before Dessane, with the help of Frederick W. Mills, attempted to revive it. In the meantime he formed the Septett Club, a string and wind ensemble which gave its first concert 27 Apr 1857 and flourished until 1871. The club performed classical and romantic music which before that time in Quebec had been heard only in arrangements for military band. The septet resorted to arrangements, too, but these attempted to approximate more closely the original works. The ensemble gave its concerts alone or with church choirs; in the latter case the program would consist mainly of religious music, and works by Dessane often would be sung by his wife. A disagreement between Ernest *Gagnon and Dessane on the accompaniment to plainsong – demonstrating the importance attached at that time to the manner in which music should be related to the liturgy – led to Dessane's resignation in 1860 from the post of organist at Notre-Dame. He continued his teaching and concerts, however, and formed a 60-piece orchestra, recruiting the members mainly from the regimental bands. In 1863 Dessane wrote his major work for full orchestra, the *Suite*, which has remained unpublished.

In September 1865 the family moved to New York, where the Jesuits had offered Dessane the position of organist at St Francis Xavier Church. Even though this new post was attractive financially to the musician, who now had seven children, his four-year stay in the US metropolis was rather unhappy. Moreover, Dessane's health by then was impaired. He nevertheless continued to put on concerts, especially of religious music with soloists, choir, and orchestra. On 7 Feb 1866 he performed his *Messe solennelle* in D minor at St Francis Xavier Church, with the aid of his wife, three other singers, the church choir, and an orchestra of 60. Between January and April 1868 in Steinway Hall he presented six concerts with five singers, two pianists, and a string quartet. The programs contained some of his own works. In 1869 he completed a manual on orchestration which has remained unpublished. The same year Damis *Paul left St-Roch Church in Quebec City, where he had been organist for 18 years. Through the influence of his friends Adolphe *Hamel and Nazaire *LeVasseur Dessane obtained the post and took up his new duties 1 Nov 1869. In December he founded the choir known as the *Société musicale Ste-Cécile.

In 1870 Dessane directed his efforts towards establishing a conservatory modelled on the one in Paris. Besides classes in piano, organ, singing, and theory, he planned to form an orchestra which would rehearse twice a week. An inaugural concert took place on 28 Jun 1871, but the classes scheduled to begin 3 November had to be cancelled. Dessane's health steadily worsened; in the spring of 1872 LeVasseur was obliged to replace him both as the organist of St-Roch and as the director of the Société Ste-Cécile. On 1 Jun 1873 Dessane was able to play at the Offertory of the mass, but a week later he died in his home on St-Jean Street.

Antoine Dessane had taught at the Hôpital général, and at the Collège Jésus-Marie, and privately. His compositions, many of them vocal, number about 50, secular and sacred, including several masses and liturgical hymns. His secular works consist of songs and short works for piano, flute, violin, cello, and orchestra, often quadrilles, polkas, or marches.

Several of Dessane's children also had careers in music. Léon (b Quebec 15 Dec 1863, d there 7 May 1930), a pupil of Calixa *Lavallée, was organist at St-Roch for 33 years. He was choirmaster at Manrèse, a Jesuit retreat house in Quebec City which in 1909 became the Church of Notre-Dame-du-Chemin, founded the Gounod Quartet and the Dessane Choir, and conducted several of his father's works. He was a music teacher in Quebec City and president of the *AMQ 1923–6. Irma and Antonia Dessane were singers, as was Nancy (whose son, Paul-G. Ouimet, was to become a music critic). Marie was in charge of music at the Jésus-Marie Convent in Sillery. After the father's death, teaching continued in the Dessane household. On the French side, a descendant, Albert Dessane, a pupil of Paul *Loyonnet, has pursued a career as a pianist in France.

SELECTED COMPOSITIONS

INSTRUMENTAL MUSIC

La Capricieuse, polka. Pf. J.T. Brousseau
Fantasia-Sonata. 1858. Fl, str quar
Les Gardes nobles, quick-step. 1871. Full orch
Quadrille sur cinq airs canadiens or *Quadrille canadien*. 1854. Pf. Léger Brousseau, Crémazie 1855
La Québecoise, polka. Ca 1850. Pf
Souvenir de Kamouraska 'quadrille historique pour piano.' 1854. J.T. Brousseau
Suite for full orchestra. 1863
Other works for pf, for org, for vn and pf, for vc and pf, and for orch, including a *Symphony in C* (composed before 1858)

CHOIR AND VOICE

'Chant du vieux soldat canadien' (O. Crémazie). V, pf. Crémazie 1856, *Chansonnier des Collèges* 1860 (v only)
'Chant patriotique canadien.' 1850. Bass, pf
'Hommage à la France' (O. Crémazie). 1860. *Chansonnier des Collèges* 1860
'Libera me Domine.' 1868. 4 vs, org. G. Schirmer 1868, Boucher, Morgan
'La Mère canadienne' (E. Blain de Saint-Aubin). 1862. V, pf. Eusèbe Sénécal 1862. Albert Turcotte 1862 (v only)
Messe 'La Conception.' 1862. SATB. Ms at the Séminaire de Québec
Messe de Noël. 1861. SATB. Ms at the Séminaire de Québec
Mass in E Flat. SATB, orch
Messe royale. 1864. SATB. Ms at the Séminaire de Québec
Messe solennelle in D Minor. 4 soli, SATB, orch
Messe solennelle in G. 1849. SATB
Te Deum. 4 soli, SATB
'Terra tremuit.' 1864. Bass, choir (men's choir). Ms at the Séminaire de Québec
Other sacred songs and hymns, including 4 'Regina coeli,' 3 'Tantum ergo,' 2 'Ave Maria,' 2 'Domine salvum' (1851), and 1 'Laudate' (1857). Other songs including 'Une Larme' (1860), 'La Fiancée du marin' (1860), 'Le Drapeau de carillon' (1861), 'Le Grillon'

BIBLIOGRAPHY

Smith, Gustave. 'Du mouvement musical en Canada,' *Album musical*, 1882
LeVasseur, Nazaire. 'Musique et musiciens à Québec,' *La Musique*, vols 1 and 2, 1919–20
Michaud, Irma. 'Antonin Dessane – 1826–1873,' 'Madame Dessane, née Irma Trunel de la Croix-Nord – 1828–1899,' *BRH*, vol 39, 1933
Kallmann, Helmut. 'Marie-Hippolyte-Antoine Dessane,' DCB, vol 10

JB-T

DESTROISMAISONS, Léon. Organist, teacher, composer, b St-Anne-de-la-Pocatière (now La Pocatière), near Quebec City, 2 Mar 1890. While preparing for the priesthood he studied music with Father Joseph Bourque at the Collège Ste-Anne. He also taught organ and harmony 1914–25 at the collège while continuing his own studies in organ and piano with Henri *Gagnon. In 1925 on a provincial bursary he began four years' study in Paris with Maurice Sergent and Marcel Dupré (organ), Simone Plé (piano), Georges Caussade (harmony and counterpoint), Vincent d'Indy (composition), and Henri Potiron and Auguste Leguennant (Gregorian chant). He received a diploma from the Institut Grégorien, Paris, in 1929. He then returned to his post at the Collège Ste-Anne-de-la-Pocatière (teaching there until 1965), and in 1931 he also began teaching at *Laval U. He assumed the presidency of the sacred music commission of the diocese of Ste-Anne and wrote a chronicle (to 1910) of the music at the Collège Ste-Anne. Between 1929 and 1962 he gave more than 30 concerts to inaugurate organs throughout Quebec and in New Brunswick. With Louis-Philippe Morneau he prepared *Manuel de chants sacrés* (Paris, Tournai, Rome 1940), a hymn and canticle collection intended mainly for use in colleges and seminaries. He composed songs and hymns, a cantata, and a work for organ based on the Graduation Song of the Collège Ste-Anne. Among Canon Destroismaisons's pupils were Antoine *Bouchard, Sylvain Doyon, Pierre Dusseault, André *Gagnon, and Clermont *Pépin. (CH)

DETT, (Robert) Nathaniel. Composer, educator, pianist, b Drummondville (now Niagara Falls), Ont, 11 Oct 1882, d Battle Creek, Mich, 2 Oct 1943; B MUS (Oberlin) 1908, hon D MUS (Harvard) 1924, M MUS (Oberlin) 1926, M MUS (ESM, Rochester) 1932. Many reference works mistakenly give Drummondville, Que, as his birthplace. He studied piano as a child and was a church organist 1898–1903 in Niagara Falls, Ont, where he composed *After the Cakewalk – March-Cakewalk* in 1900. His formal studies were in the USA. He gave recitals in Canada in 1925 and later studied piano with Nadia Boulanger in Paris. He performed in the USA at Carnegie Hall, Boston Symphony Hall, the Library of Congress, the Philadelphia Academy of Music, and Symphony Hall and before presidents Herbert Hoover and Franklin D. Roosevelt. He worked as a piano teacher and choir director 1908–11 at Lane College, Jackson, Tenn, and taught 1913–32 at the Hampton Institute, Hampton, Va, 1935–7 at Samuel Houston College, Austin, Tex, and 1937–42 at Bennett College, Greensboro, NC. As director of the Hampton Choir he toured Europe in 1930. He was chairman of the advisory board 1919–24 and president 1924–6 of the National Association of Negro Musicians. Prior to his death he directed musical activities for the United Service Organization, designed to build US armed forces' morale.

Dett was dedicated to the cause of black music in America and in 1920 won the Bowdoin and Francis Boott prizes from Harvard U for his paper 'The emancipation of Negro music' and for the motet 'Don't Be Weary, Traveller' (J. Church 1921) based on a Negro folk motive. He was awarded the Harmon Medal in 1927, the Palm and Ribbon of the Royal Belgian Band, and several literary prizes. He edited collections of spirituals and folksongs and composed piano suites, motets, anthems, and songs characterized by the melodies and rhythms of black folk music. His works include the oratorios *The Chariot Jubilee* (1921) and *Ordering of Moses* (J. Fischer 1937) and the piano pieces *The Magnolia Suite* (C.F. Summy 1912), *In the Bottoms Suite* (ibid 1913), which contains the popular 'Juba Dance' (a favourite of his friend Percy Grainger), *Enchantment Suite* (1922), *Cinnamon Grove Suite* (1927), and *Tropic Winter Suite* (1938). The last movement of a symphony commissioned by CBS radio was not completed. A few recordings are given in *Roll Back the Years*. 'Listen to the Lambs' was recorded by the Mormon Tabernacle Choir (COL ML5048). He discovered and helped to develop the careers of several singers, among them the soprano Dorothy Maynor.

COMPOSITIONS

– ed *The Dett Collection of Negro Spirtuals*, 4 vols (Hall & McCrean 1936)
– ed *Religious Folk Songs of the Negro* (AMS Press 1972)
The Collected Piano Works of R. Nathaniel Dett (Summy-Birchard 1973)

Nathaniel Dett

WRITINGS

'The emancipation of negro music,' *Southern Workman*, vol 47, 1918
'Negro music of the present,' *Southern Workman*, ibid
'From bell stand to throne room,' *Etude*, Feb 1934
The Development of the Negro Spiritual (Minneapolis 1936)

BIBLIOGRAPHY

'Leading negro choir's European visit,' *MT*, 1 May 1930
Pope, M. *A Brief Biography of Dr. Robert Nathaniel Dett* (Hampton, Va, 1945)
McBrier, V.F. 'The life and works of Robert Nathaniel Dett,' PH D thesis, Catholic U of America 1967
Grove's
MGG Supplement, vol 15, 1973 (FMB)

DETWEILER, Alan. Composer, b Toronto 15 Jun 1926; BA (Toronto) 1950, MA (Trinity, Dublin) 1952, PH D (London) 1956. He studied composition 1945–6 in Toronto with Godfrey *Ridout and Barbara *Pentland. His thesis was 'The aesthetics of music.' He spent 1952 in Stockholm researching the music of Franz Berwald on a grant from the Swedish government and the ensuing four years in London studying composition with Lennox Berkeley and Howard Ferguson. Detweiler's children's entertainments, including the operas *Beware of the Wolf* (1964) and *David and Goliath* (1969, the first of a projected trilogy of church operas on the theme of David and Saul), have been produced in England and broadcast in Canada, the USA, England, Australia, France, Germany, Nigeria, and Hong Kong. *David and Goliath* was filmed by CBS TV. The second in the trilogy, *King Saul*, was premiered by the Elizabethan Singers at Southwark Cathedral, England, in December 1975. Detweiler lives in London and is a member of the Performing Rights Society of England.

WRITINGS

'Musical criticism: its function and limitations,' *CMJ*, vol 3, Summer 1959

BIBLIOGRAPHY

'A Canadian composer in London,' *CanComp*, 44, Nov 1969

Les Deux Âmes. Called a symphonic poem by the composer but actually an oratorio, composed 1906?–9 by Alexis *Contant to a text by the journalist Henri Roullaud. Scored for two solo voices, narrator, choir, and orchestra, this second oratorio by Contant was premiered 16 Nov 1913 during Sunday matinee and evening concerts at the Princess Theatre in Montreal with J.J. *Shea as conductor and the baritone Joseph *Saucier and the tenor J.E.F. Monday as soloists. The story, an allegory, deals with the relationship of two lonely souls – a young orphan and his unidentified guide – who wander around the world falling prey to the temptations of good and evil. *Les Deux Âmes* was submitted to the conductor Walter Damrosch, who expressed his admiration for it in a letter to the composer dated 10 Mar 1910. The 344-page original manuscript of the oratorio was deposited at the *NL of C in 1971. See also Oratorios, Canadian (composition and performance) 5.

BIBLIOGRAPHY

Comte, Gustave. 'Les Deux Ames,' *P-T*, 488, 6 Dec 1913

DEVEAUX, Orpha-F. Organist, pianist, teacher, b Saginaw, Mich, 24 Jul 1872, d Hartford, Conn, December 1933. His teachers in Montreal were Alexis *Contant and Percival J. *Illsley. He also studied at the New York College of Music with Mat Schmidt, among others. He taught in Montreal ca 1901, and in 1905 was appointed organist at the St-Nom-de-Jésus Church. In 1914 he was named secretary of the *Cons national of Montreal, where he taught organ, piano, theory, and harmony. In 1930 his name no longer was listed among the teachers there. In Montreal in 1918 he announced the private publication of *Principes de la musique* 'based on mathematical calculations and illustrated with examples in color,' available in one volume or in sections by subscription; the work was distinctive for its use of colours to facilitate understanding. The sequel to this volume, also privately published, was *Les Principes de l'harmonie* (Montreal 1919), consisting of 25 lessons. Among Deveaux's pupils were Claude *Champagne, Paul *Pratt, and Hedwige Saint-Jacques. In 1923 Deveaux left Montreal to serve as organist with the Dominican fathers in Fall River, Mass. GP

C.C. De Zouche. Music and instrument dealer and publisher active in Montreal approx 1869–90 (after 1883, De Zouche & Atwater). The earliest-known De Zouche publication is *The Church Chant Book* (1878), edited by the Montreal organist Charles F. Davies. The other 20 publications traced by 1977 date from the years 1880–3 and include songs or dances by the Montreal organist William Powell, the Ottawa orchestra leader C.J. Arthur Marier, and others. Davies' 'The Prairie Settler's Song' (1882) provided the theme for Robert *Turner's orchestral variations of 1974. De Zouche issued Canadian editions of music by Michael Balfe, Frederick Boscovitz, 'Claribel' (Mrs Barnard), and others and published Arthur Sullivan's 'Dominion Hymn.'

See also Patriotic songs. HK

DIAMANT, Bernard. Baritone, teacher, b Rotterdam 11 Oct 1912, naturalized Canadian 1955. A son of the choir conductor and composer Bernard Diamant and the operatic soprano Marie Taverne, he began playing cello and piano as a child. Starting voice lessons at 17, he studied at the Royal Cons in The Hague and the Berlin Hochschule für Musik, and privately in Holland, Germany, and France. His most important teacher was Charles Panzéra, a leading baritone of the day and the author of several books on voice production. After singing in opera and concert in Germany, Austria, Czechoslovakia, and Holland, Diamant moved in 1950 to Montreal, where he taught at *l'École Vincent-d'Indy and *McGill U and gave recitals in Canada and the USA with John *Newmark. In the 1960s he curtailed his performing career and expanded his teaching activities, establishing in 1968 a second private vocal class in Toronto. In 1972 he joined the *U of Toronto Faculty of Music and opera department and in 1973 he took up full-time residence in Toronto. In over

25 years of teaching in Canada his pupils have included John *Boyden, Anna *Chornodolska, Jeannette Dagger, Orville Derraugh, Mary-Lou *Fallis, Maureen *Forrester, Gaelyne *Gabora, Marion Harvey, Pierre *Lalonde, Rosemarie *Landry, Louise *Lebrun, Diane Loeb, Joan *Patenaude, Princess Christina of the Netherlands (who travelled to Montreal for her studies), Finvola *Redden-Bower, Sylvia *Saurette, and Janet *Stubbs.

DISCOGRAPHY
Barber – Coulthard – Reutter. Newmark pf. 1954. RCI 109
See also Musica Antica e Nuova. LL

The Diamonds. Rock and roll vocal quartet formed in early 1954 at the U of Toronto by the lead singer Dave Somerville, the tenor Ted Kowalski, the baritone Phil Levitt (replaced in 1957 by Mike Douglas), and the bass Bill Reed. The Diamonds made their TV debut in 1955 on the CBC's 'Pick the Stars' and thereafter worked extensively in the USA. In the following six years they made six LPs for Mercury and an estimated 16 singles of varying success, including 'Why Do Fools Fall in Love?' (1956), 'Silhouettes' (1957), 'The Stroll' (1958; it precipitated a dance craze of the same name), and 'She Say (Oom Dooby Doom)' (1959). Like The *Crew-Cuts, The Diamonds made several cover-versions of black rhythm-and-blues recordings. Their biggest hit, 'Little Darlin'' (1957, previously recorded by The Gladiolas), satirized a standard rhythm-and-blues falsetto-bass vocal style. 'Little Darlin' ' and 'The Stroll' were listed by *Cashbox* as the 6th and 30th most popular singles of 1957 and 1958 respectively. Some of The Diamonds' hits were included in the anthology *Solid Gold Rock 'n' Roll* (2-Mercury 61371/2). Another Canadian, Glen Stetson, replaced Somerville in 1961. Under Stetson's direction and with changed personnel the group continued to perform in US and Canadian nightclubs into the 1970s. MM

Di BELLO, Victor. Conductor, administrator, b Toronto, of Italian parents, 11 Feb 1933. He studied piano with Jessie Blake and Madeline Bone. At 17 he began to study conducting with Heinz *Unger and formed the Pro Arte Orchestra – an amateur chamber orchestra which gave one or two concerts annually. He also studied in Toronto with Walter *Susskind (under whose auspices he made his *TSO debut, 16 Mar 1958) and at the Berkshire Music Center, Tanglewood, Mass, with Eleazar de Carvalho. In 1957 he reorganized the Pro Arte Orchestra as an ensemble of professional string players which made its debut 28 March at the Casa Loma Library. For some years thereafter the orchestra gave concert series annually, in turn at Casa Loma, Maurice Cody Hall, and St Anne's Anglican Church. With the orchestra Di Bello presented *Messiah* at St Anne's several times during the 1960s. The orchestra played for opera productions directed by Rita Ubriaco at *Hart House – Pergolesi's *La Serva Padrona* in 1962 and *The Music Master* in 1963, and Haydn's *The Apothecary* in 1964 – and appeared at the *Stratford Festival in 1967 and 1968. Di Bello was conductor 1958–62 of the *Hamilton Philharmonic, assistant conductor in 1960 and 1961 of the *NYO, and a guest conductor of the TSO and the CBC String Orchestra in the early 1960s. He served as assistant (1960) to Louis *Applebaum at the Stratford Festival, was the festival's music administrator 1962–9, and conducted the Festival Theatre Orchestra in 1972. After a year 1972–3 as assistant managing director of the Minneapolis SO, he returned to Toronto. In 1979 DiBello began conducting a reconstituted Pro Arte Chamber Orchestra of 12 players. In the 1979–80 season the orchestra gave string concerts in 20 Toronto high schools. OM (MM)

DICHMONT, William. Pianist, organist, violinist, teacher, conductor, composer, b Accrington, Lancashire, England, 3 Feb 1882, d Vancouver 17 Jul 1943. He studied piano and violin with Gerhard Kuhnel and later attended the Manchester School of Music. For a time he was assitant conductor of the Princess Theatre and Royal Theatre orchestras in Manchester. In 1903 he moved to Winnipeg, where he taught piano and violin at the College of Music and privately. Among his pupils was Russell E. Chester. By 1909 he was supplementing his income by accountancy, and later he worked in a brokerage firm. In 1915 he went overseas with the Canadian Expeditionary Force, serving until 1917, when he joined his brother in Vancouver. There he became known as a composer and voice coach and also served as organist at the Second Church of Christ Scientist. It was in Vancouver that the Winnipeg tenor George *Kent studied with him.

Nearly all of Dichmont's compositions are vocal, and most of these songs with piano accompaniment. One of them, 'Such a Li'l' Fellow,' was recorded by Alma Gluck for Victor in 1917 and also was sung by her in recital. He wrote most of his own lyrics, using the pseudonyms Arthur Rutherford and Frances Lowell, and came to be regarded as one of the most successful Canadian songwriters of the day. In 1911 in Winnipeg he wrote and produced the musical play *Miss Pepple (of New York)*, with book and lyrics by C.S. Blanchard; it was published by Wray's Music Store in Winnipeg in the same year. Approximately 40 of Dichmont's songs were issued by John Church, Ditson, Presser, Ricordi, G. Schirmer, and Wood between 1910 and 1930. A list appears in *Catalogue of Canadian Composers*. SW

Dictionaries of music. Reference books which present information in alphabetically ordered individual entries. The entires are usually in prose, although in a related type of reference work, the catalogue of compositions, lists abound. Both types will be considered here since their respective main functions – the provision of biographies and/or of information on music itself – overlap.
1 Canadian dictionaries
2 Canada in foreign dictionaries

1 CANADIAN DICTIONARIES. All Canadian music dictionaries and dictionary-sections in larger books prior to *EMC* have been biographical with the exception of *The Pocket Dictionary of Musical Terms* compiled by C.F. *Thiele and published by Waterloo (nd). The earliest examples are the biography sections in H.H. *Godfrey's *Musical Toronto* (1897, 1898–9), Hugo Talbot's *Musical Halifax* (1903–4), and Bernard K. Sandwell's *The Musical Red Book of Montreal* (1907). Edouard *Hesselberg's 'A review of music in Canada' (in *Modern Music and Musicians*, New York ca 1913) is essentially a Canadian supplement compiled in Canada, though published abroad. It offers the first nationwide coverage: 71 major and not-so-major musicians sketched on nine pages. In all these cases, the author's main purpose was to take stock of musical activity and accomplishment, and the dictionary section was only a subsidiary device.

The first true dictionary was the *Dictionnaire biographique des musiciens* published in 1922 by the Soeurs de Sainte-Anne of Lachine, Que, the anonymous work of Louise *Paquin (Sister Marie-Valentine). Some 675 non-Canadian musicians were included along with 150 Canadians. The choice was slanted towards French operetta and salon music composers of the late 19th century in the first category, and almost entirely towards Quebec musicians, both French-speaking and English-speaking, in the second. Of much greater importance was the second edition, which appeared in 1935 as *Dictionnaire biographique des musiciens canadiens* (Lachine 1935; reprint Ann Arbor, Mich, 1972). It includes 384 musicians whose careers centred in the province of Quebec but only a handful (eg, A.S. *Vogt and Annie Lampman *Jenkins) from Ontario. Coverage begins with such men as Charles-Amador *Martin and Martin *Boutet in the 17th century and includes the young generation of 1934. The book misses only a few major figures, among them Joseph *Quesnel, T.F. *Molt, Clara *Lichtenstein, and Sarah *Fischer. The work remains an indispensable tool in Canadian studies, despite its inaccuracies and imbalances which stem from a scissors-and-paste approach to compilation and an obvious dearth of original historical research.

Since one of its major responsibilities was the performance of Canadian music, the CBC, created in 1936, set out to gather information about living composers and their compositions by means of a questionnaire distributed at the beginning of World War II. The project of assembling the raw data into a *Catalogue of Canadian Composers*, begun under the direction of J.-J. *Gagnier and continued by Jean *Beaudet, was shelved for a number of years. When the work did appear in 1947 it was typed without critical editing or supplementary research and was, for many composers, out of date. Because of the shortcomings of this mimeographed edition and the phenomenal growth of Canadian composition in the late 1940s, a new edition in book format was compiled 1950–1 and issued in 1952 (reprint Ann Arbor, Mich, 1972). It was edited by Helmut *Kallmann and includes 356 composers (and some 100 others briefly listed), expanding the scope not only forward in time but also backwards to the 19th century and earlier.

The next dictionary-type book again was sponsored by the CBC. *Thirty-four Biographies of Canadian Composers / Trente-quatre Biographies de compositeurs canadiens* (Montreal 1964) provided extensive biographical sketches and lists of works. It was written by V.I. Rajewsky and edited by Helmut *Blume and Gilles *Potvin as a project of RCI. A similar format, but applied to 144 composers active after 1920, was adopted by the *CMCentre's *Contemporary Canadian Composers* (Toronto 1975) with contributions by several writers under the editorship of John *Beckwith and Keith *MacMillan. This was the first Canadian music dictionary pervaded by a strong analytical and critical element. A French translation, *Compositeurs canadiens contemporains* (Montreal 1977), incorporating recent compositions and a few corrections and increasing the number of composers to 160, was edited by Louise *Laplante, the CMCentre's regional director for the province of Quebec.

A number of other reference books, though not music dictionaries in the strict sense, supply coverage in specialized fields. The 1950 edition of the *Canadian Radio and Television Annual* (Toronto 1950) includes about 240 entries for musicians, while Edward *Moogk's *Roll Back the Years* (Ottawa 1975) features a chapter of 'Biographical notes' on over 80 recording artists and groups active up to 1930, in addition to a large discography section. Of specific Quebec interest are Michèle Maillé's *Blow up des grands de la chanson au Québec* (Ottawa 1969) and Gabriel Labbé's *Les Pionniers du* *disque folklorique québecois 1920–1950* (Montreal 1977). The following Canadian general reference books have a useful coverage of music and/or musicians: H. J. Morgan, *The Canadian Men and Women of the Time* (Toronto 1898, 1912); *The Canadian Who's Who* (Toronto 1910 –); The *DCB* (Toronto 1966–); *Encyclopedia Canadiana*, 10 vols (Ottawa 1957–8, Toronto 1970); list of music entries in *CMJ*, vol 3 Spring 1959; and *Creative Canada*, 2 vols (Toronto 1971, 1972). *L'Encyclopédie Grolier* (Montreal 1947) includes some biographical entries and a survey written by Eugène *Lapierre under 'Canada, musique.' Substantial musical coverage in special fields is provided by Jean-Baptiste-Arthur Allaire's *Dictionnaire biographique du clergé canadien-français*, 6 vols (Montreal 1908–34), and *Who's Who in Canadian Jewry* (Montreal 1965). Many others could be cited.

Dictionary-type catalogues for specific genres of composition include the *CLComp's *Catalogue of Orchestral Music* (Toronto 1957) and those of the CMCentre (see list under that entry).

2 CANADA IN FOREIGN DICTIONARIES. Before the 1930s the world had little opportunity to know of the existence of Canadian musicans. The *Musical Times* of London or the *Musical Courier* and other US magazines would carry the occasional concert review submitted by a Toronto or Montreal correspondent and the odd 'Music in Canada' article, but the interested music lover would find only one entry, Emma *Albani, in the first (1878–89) and second (1900) editions of *Grove's Dictionary of Music and Musicians* and only Joseph Quesnel in Fétis' *Dictionnaire universel des musiciens* (Suppl 1881). F.O. Jones' *Handbook of American Music and Musicians* (Canaseraga, NY, 1886, 1887) at least included five Canadians well known or active in the USA: Albani, H.A. *Clarke, Calixa *Lavallée, J. B. Sharland, and S. R. *Warren, while Brown and Stratton's *British Musical Biography* (London 1897), thanks to the collaboration of F. H. *Torrington, contained articles on six Canadian-born and seven immigrant musicians. Matters improved slowly, and *Grove's American Supplement* (np 1928) came out with entries for over 60 Canadians, the 11th edition of *Riemanns Musiklexikon* (Berlin 1929) with 18, *Thompson's International Cyclopedia of Music and Musicians* (New York 1938) with 110 biographical and 20 organizational or topical entries (Lawrence *Mason, a former *Globe and Mail* critic, acted as Canadian editor), and Wier's *Macmillan Encyclopedia of Music and Musicians* (New York 1938) with about 125 biographical entries gleaned, it appears, uncritically from other reference sources. Generous coverage was given Canadians also in J.T.H. Mize's *Who Is Who in Music* (Chicago, 4th ed 1941), the various editions of *Baker's Biographical Dictionary* (1900, 1919, 1940, 1958, etc), and *The ASCAP Biographical Dictionary* (2nd ed, New York 1952, 1966), but inclusion in non-English-language books was poor indeed. The standard dictionaries of piano, organ, and violin makers include some Canadian names.

The complaints about Canadian coverage in the major international music dictionaries should be focused not on quantity – which is reasonably generous – but on accuracy and choice. When the fifth edition of *Grove's Dictionary* appeared in 1954, entries on *MacMillan, *Mazzoleni, and *Willan remained 20 years behind the times, while Léo *Roy was able to persuade the editor to include a number of Quebec city musicians of relatively minor importance (corrections followed in the 1961 supplement). Other dictionaries were similarly slow in updating their Canadian information, principally because they did not know where to turn. Some editors, however, such as Nicolas Slominsky in his revisions of *Baker's* and *Thompson's*, went to great lengths to correct errors and present new facts. Canadians, too, began to offer assistance to foreign editors. The *CMCouncil, under the signature of Sir Ernest MacMillan, prepared a large entry on Canada for an Italian publication, *La Musica*, edited by Guido Gatti (Turin 1966). Helmut Kallmann saw to Canadian inclusion in *MGG* and the 1969 edition of the *Harvard Dictionary of Music* and supplied corrections and suggestions to Riemann, Baker's, and Scholes' *Concise Oxford Dictionary of Music*, while Andrée *Desautels wrote an essay on 'Les trois âges de la musique au Canada' for Larousse's *La Musique* (vol 2, Paris 1965). John Beckwith acted as Canadian adviser for the *New Grove Dictionary*, with Kallmann and Keith MacMillan as consultants. The latter supplied Canadian material for the 1975 edition of Thompson's *Cyclopedia* and for many other reference works. Jan *Matejcek was the Canadian consultant for a new supplement to Altmann's *Tonküstler-Lexikon* (vol 1, Wilhelmshaven 1974). Gilles Pilote prepared the entry on Canada for *Science de la musique* (Paris 1976) edited by Marc Honegger. Kenneth *Winters wrote the Canadian entry for the Swedish *Sohlmans Lexikon* (1977). An article on Canadian music by M. Yakovlev is included in the Soviet *Musical Encyclopedia* edited by Yuri Keldich (Moscow 1974). These and other instances show the recent improvements that have been effected with regard to Canadian representation. The same is true about such specialized works as Berger's *Band Encyclopedia* (Evansville, Ind, 1960), Feather's three jazz encyclopedias (New York 1960, 1966, 1976), Rosenthal and Warrack's *Concise Oxford Dictionary of Opera* (London, Toronto 1964, rev ed London 1979; French transl of 1st ed by Aziz Izzet, *Dictionnaire de l'opéra*, Paris 1974), Kutsch and Riemens *A Concise Biolgraphical Dictionary of Singers* (English ed, Philadelphia 1969), and Vinton's *Dictionary of Contemporary Music* (New York 1974).

A key to locating 2000 Canadian names in some 120 Canadian and non-Canadian reference books was provided by the *CMLA in its *Bio-bibliographical Finding List of Canadian Musicians* (Ottawa 1961). It is of interest to note the names that were found most frequently: Albani (entries in 42 dictionaries), Sir Ernest MacMillan (31), Gena *Branscombe (29), A.S. Vogt (27), Healey Willan (26), Boris *Hambourg and Calixa Lavallée (25), Nathaniel *Dett (23), H.A. *Fricker, C.A.E. *Harriss, Kathleen *Parlow, Wilfrid *Pelletier, and F.H. Torrington (22), Edward *Johnson (20).

See also Bibliography; Biography; Discography.

BIBLIOGRAPHY

Kallmann, Helmut. 'The New Grove's: disappointment to Canada,' *SatN*, 12 Mar 1955

Beckwith, John. 'About Canadian music: the P.R. failure,' *Mcan*, 21, Jul–Aug 1969 (HK)

DILWORTH, Ira. Administrator, teacher, editor, conductor, b High Bluff, near Winnipeg, Man, 25 Mar 1894, d Vancouver 23 Nov 1962; BA (McGill) 1915, MA (Harvard) 1920, LL D (British Columbia) 1948. As a child he moved with his family to the Okanagan Valley and there studied piano. He served the arts in British Columbia tirelessly, 1915–38 as a teacher of English literature, then as an administrator with the CBC, as the literary executor of the writings of the painter Emily Carr, and as the first president (1946) of the *Community Arts Council ofVancouver. He worked especially during the 1920s and 1930s for the recognition of music in the province's schools. Besides teaching English 1934–8 at the *U of British Columbia, he taught music appreciation, lectured on music throughout the province, was responsible for the university's collection of scores and records, and established its Carnegie Foundation Recorded Library. He conducted 1930–4 the Ladies' Choir of Victoria and 1935–40 the *Vancouver Bach Choir. In 1938 he joined the CBC, working first, 1938–47, in Vancouver as British Columbia regional representative and manager of station CBR, where he encouraged the development of the *CBC Vancouver Chamber Orchestra, then 1947–51 in Montreal as director of the International Service, and finally in Toronto as director of program production 1951–3 and director of radio for the province of Ontario 1953–6. In 1956 he assumed responsibility for the CBC's English network and in 1958 he became director of program evaluation.

BIBLIOGRAPHY

Luce, P.W. 'Music his passion,' *SatN*, 10 Aug 1940

DIMOCK, Kaye (Frances) (b King). Soprano, educator, b Avonport, near Kentville, NS, 3 Aug 1937; B MUS (Acadia) 1964. She studied music at *Acadia U, the *Maritime Cons of Music, *Dalhousie U, and *Mount Saint Vincent U and also, during 1975, in Esztergan, Hungary. In 1954 she began teaching in Nova Scotia public schools. She has been a teacher, a supervisor, and the director of music teacher training at Dalhousie U, a director of continuing-education choral classes in Halifax, and an adjudicator at various festivals. She has acted as consultant to the Halifax City School Board and has designed the pre-high-school music curriculum adopted for use by Halifax in 1969 and by other parts of Nova Scotia in 1973. She has sung on the CBC and has appeared as a soloist with the *Atlantic SO, the Dalhousie Chorale, the Atlantic Chamber Ensemble, and *NOVA MUSIC in performances of works such as Haydn's *Theresa Mass*, the *Requiems* of Mozart, Verdi, and Fauré, Handel's *Messiah*, *Schafer's **Requiems for the Party Girl*, Vanity's aria from Schafer's *Loving*, and Stephen Pedersen's *Three Haiku*. In 1974 she performed folksongs on a lecture-tour with Helen *Creighton and sang at the *CMCouncil convention in Halifax. In 1975 she sang at the second International Kodály Symposium in Hungary. She has been secretary 1973–7 of the Kodály Institute of Canada and 1975–7 of the *NSMEA, and was co-chairman of the third International Kodály Symposium in 1977 at Acadia U.

See also Kodály method; School music. (EMr)

Dinner horn. A crude wind instrument used by pioneer farmers in 19th-century Upper Canada to call field workers home for meals. 'In the more remote parts of the woods, where schools are unknown...a belle...will employ her leisure hours in learning to play – not the piano-forte – but the dinner-horn, a bright tin tube sometimes nearly four feet in length, requiring the lungs of that almost obsolete animal, an English mail-coach-guard; and an intriguing mamma of those parts will bid her daughter exhibit the strength of her throat and the delicacy of her musical ear, by a series of flourishes and "mots" upon her graceful "tooting-weapon," enough to deafen a whole club of bell-ringers' ('A chapter on chopping,' *The Maple-Leaf*, Toronto 1849; repeated in Samuel Thompson's *Reminiscences of a Canadian Pioneer for the Last Fifty Years*, Toronto 1884). A specimen is displayed at Upper Canada Village, Morrisburg, Ont. HK

DION, France. Soprano, b Quebec City 16 May 19??. She studied piano and voice 1953–4 at *Laval U and voice 1957–9 at the *CMM with Dina Maria Narici, Raoul *Jobin, Dick Marzollo, and Otto-

Werner *Mueller. In 1959 she made her debut in the Verdi *Requiem* and a concert performance of *Madama Butterfly* with the *Quebec SO. On scholarships from the Quebec and Canadian governments she went to Vienna to study opera with Ferdinand Grossmann and Augustin Kubizek. She settled in London, where the Sadler's Wells Opera engaged her for a tour of England and Scotland. She sang the Queen of the Night in *The Magic Flute* at the Glyndebourne Festival and, in November 1963, the title role in the English premiere of Verdi's *Giovanna d'Arco* in London. She also sang *Manon* at the Liceo in Barcelona. In 1964 she returned to Quebec to sing Fiordiligi in *Così fan tutte*. After her Wigmore Hall recital in 1965 the London critics commended the intensity and conviction of her interpretation of a Mozart aria and the charm and finesse she brought to Ravel's *Chansons grecques*. For the *JMC she made a recital tour of Quebec in 1966 and appeared in about 40 performances of the opera *L'Amante Cubista* by Roberto Hazon in 1967. Les Grands Ballets Canadiens engaged her in 1969 for their presentation of Carl Orff's *Triomphe d'Aphrodite* at the *PDA and in 1971 for the premiere of a Canadian ballet scored for soprano and percussion, Paul Duplessis's *Hip and Straight*. Dion accompanied the dance troupe on several tours of Canada and the USA. In 1972 in Quebec City she sang Messiaen's *Harawi*, appeared for the *Opéra du Québec as Flora in *La Traviata*, gave several recitals, and sang Ravel's *Shéhérazade* with the *CBC Quebec Chamber Orchestra. Among other roles for the CBC she has sung the countess in *The Marriage of Figaro* and Amor in *Orpheus and Eurydice*. She began teaching at the UQAM and the Institut Marguerite-Bourgeoys in 1971. ST

DION, (Marie Berthe) **Rolande**. Soprano, teacher, b Quebec City 5 Apr 1915. She studied singing in her native city 1931–5 with Émile *Larochelle and 1935–9 with Louis *Gravel. In 1939, on a bursary from the Quebec government, she went to New York and worked in succession with Margaret Hamill, with the rehearsal pianist Franz Rupp and his wife Stéphanie, with Greta Stauber, and with the coach Erich Itor Kahn. In 1944 she sang the role of the dew fairy in the *Opera Guild of Montreal production of *Hansel and Gretel*. On her return to Quebec City in 1950 she concentrated on teaching at her studio and performing for CBC radio and TV ('Récital conjoint,' 'Sérénade pour cordes'). In 1961 on a *Canada Council grant she spent six months in Europe attending voice-training programs. In 1972 she began teaching at the Cons de Chicoutimi and at the *CMQ. Guy *Bélanger, France *Dion, Geneviève *Perreault, and France Simard are among her pupils.

BIBLIOGRAPHY

Desparois, Lucille. 'Interview avec Rolande Dion,' *Le Film*, Dec 1945

Duval, Monique. 'Rolande Dion, soprano lyrique,' Quebec City *Le Soleil*, 5 Apr 1956 AP

DIONNE, Télesphore-Octave. Violin builder, bassist, b Quebec City 1869, d Montreal 30 Nov 1920. He began his career playing clarinet in the Montreal Concert Band, then took up the double-bass. He played 1905–6 in the J.-J. *Goulet *MSO. He was very young when he began his apprenticeship as a luthier, spending three years in Boston in the workshops of Gould and Sons. He returned to Montreal in 1890 to open his own workshop. A large part of his business was instrument repair, but he made a dozen violins and one cello, all finely finished. After his death his apprentice, Rosario *Forget, took over the business but retained Dionne's name.

Dionne's brother J.F. Raoul (b Quebec City 2 Dec 1877, d ?) sang in the choirs of the Notre-Dame, Gesù, and St-Louis-de-France churches in Montreal. In Quebec City he established a choir, the Chanteurs de Saint-Dominque, which he continued to conduct as late as 1927, appearing with it that year in the *CPR Festivals. CH

DIONNE, (Lauréat) **Vincent**. Percussionist, composer, b Chicoutimi, Que, 15 Jan 1942; premier prix percussion (CMM) 1968. He studied 1962–6 at the *CMQ with Roger Juneau and Louis *Charbonneau and 1966–8 with the latter at the *CMM. He spent the summer of 1965 at the Berkshire Music Center in Tanglewood, Mass, played on occasion with the *Quebec SO, the *MSO, and the CBC orchestras in Quebec City and Montreal, and was solo percussionist with the American Wind Symphony in Pittsburgh in 1968. He made *JMC tours 1968–9 in western Canada and in 1970 in Yugoslavia with Louise *Forand and Jean *Laurendeau. On a grant from the *Canada Council he studied 1969–70 with Jacques Delécluse at the Paris Cons. He also worked 1970–1 with the Groupe de recherches musicales de l'ORTF and 1971–3 at the Centre américain in Paris with the Baschet brothers, inventors of the Structures sonores Lasry-Baschet. During this time he played percussion with the Pasdeloup Orchestra, accompanied Mikis Theodorakis on a European tour in 1971, and played in Vienna and Hanover with the Groupe international de musique électroacoustique de Paris. In Paris Dionne composed incidental music for the Studio-Théâtre of Vitry-sur-Seine and the Théâtre national des enfants and performed at the *Canadian Cultural Centre.

On his return to Quebec in 1973 Dionne continued to give concerts and composed for the dance troupes the Groupe de la Place royale, the Groupe Nouvelle-Aire, and Entre-Six (*En mouvement*, recorded in 1977 by the Ensemble de percussions McGill, RCI 478). In Montreal he was a member 1973–5 of the Atelier de musique expérimentale. In February 1975, with the keyboard artist Michel-Georges *Brégent, he formed the duo Dionne-Brégent, a 'rock-classico-cosmique' ensemble. Until 1979 the team experimented with a 'universe of sound in perpetual movement,' seeking an expansion of consciousness by way of many instruments (suspended sheets of metal, glass jugs, etc), often of the two musicians' own design. They gave concerts in Montreal, mostly in the Piano nobile of the PDA and at the Outremont cinema, enlisting on occasion, in 1978, the assistance of other instrumentalists such as Sayyd *Abdul Al-Khabyyr. The team also made JMC tours 1975–6 in Ontario and 1976–7 in Quebec and made the LPs *...et le troisième jour / L'éveil du lieu* with the soprano Pauline *Vaillancourt (1976, Cap ST 70044) and *Deux* (1977, Cap ST 70052). Dionne is a member of CAPAC.

See also Ballets. AP

Dionysos. Rock group established in Montreal in 1969 by Paul-André Thibert (voice, recorder), Éric Clément (guitars), Jean-Pierre Legault (bass guitar), Robert Lepage (drums), and André Mathieu (electronic keyboards). Legault was replaced by Fernand Durand in 1971. Philippe Bech (flute, keyboards) also worked with the group in 1973–4, as did Jean-Pierre Forget (piano, saxophone) after 1975. Dionysos began just at the end of the 1960s, when the repertoires of most Quebec pop groups consisted mainly of French versions of US hits. Following in the footsteps of *Infonie and Robert *Charlebois, Dionysos was among the first Quebec groups to sing original rock compositions in French. In 1969 its members wrote the music for *Simon Neige*, a play staged by a student troupe from Valleyfield, Que, and undertook a series of concerts which resulted in the LP *Le Grand Jeu* (Jupiter YDS 8032), released in Janaury 1971. That June Dionysos took part in the Montreux Jazz Festival; it also made a second LP in 1971, *Le Prince croule* (Zodiaque ZOX 6001). In 1972 and 1973 it toured Quebec, New Brunswick, and Ontario, and in 1974 members of the group composed and performed the incidental music for the Montreal production of *The Tooth of Crime*, a rock opera by Sam Sheppard, presented at the Centaur Theatre. After a voluntary 18-month retirement the group re-formed in the autumn of 1975, and an LP, *Dionysos* (Deram XDEF 125), was followed by a week of concerts at the Évêché in the Nelson Hotel in Old Montreal. 'L'Âge d'or' and 'Suzie' were among the group's best-known songs. It had ceased to perform by 1978; Paule-André Thibert, however, made a solo LP, *Musique de mes amis Dionysos* (Solo SO 25507), from which 'Un Air de fête' and 'Vancouver' were especially popular.

BIBLIOGRAPHY

Kroll, Stephen. 'Quebec's heavy rock band is ready for English Canada,' *CanComp*, 88, Feb 1974 (HPd)

Diplomas. Documents certifying the successful passing of examinations. Although the terms certificate, diploma, and degree have similar or related meanings, in music certificates usually are given for achieved grades in performance proficiency below the diploma level; diplomas (most commonly the licentiate, associate, or fellow in English Canada, the premier prix or deuxième prix in French-Canadian conservatories) are given for graduation, as teacher or performer, from the most advanced courses offered or prescribed by applied-music schools or conservatories; and degrees (bachelor, master, doctor) are granted for the successful completion of post-secondary academic programs (or, more rarely, performance programs, following the US system) administered by universities, some colleges, and other such accredited institutions of higher learning (see Degrees). Some universities with developed performance departments offer diplomas as well, eg, the *U of Toronto, with its Artist Diploma (performer's) and Licentiate Diploma (teacher's).

In Canada in 1980 the pre-eminent diploma-granting institutions were the *AMQ (for Quebec), the *RCMT (for all of Canada), and the *Western Board (for Manitoba, Saskatchewan, and Alberta), and all of these toured examiners to hear students prepared by private teachers and non-diploma-granting institutions. The two English institutions which have conducted grade and diploma examinations in Canada – the *Associated Board of the Royal Schools of Music (service discontinued in 1953) and the *Trinity College of Music, London (still sending examiners in 1980) – also had granted great numbers of diplomas.

The following list provides information on the main diplomas offered in 1980 or formerly in Canada. The date at the beginning of each item is the founding date of the institution. Where possible, dates for the initiation of diplomas and certificates have been supplied. See also Community colleges; Ladies' colleges.

date institution: certificates, diplomas

1813 *McGill U: licentiate 1966– ; concert diploma 1966– ; diplôme d'études collégiales (through the Quebec Ministry of Education) 1969–74

– McGill Conservatorium 1904–66: licentiate 1904–55; associate diploma (established 1939, retroactive to 1929) 1929–66

1827 *U of Toronto (see 1886 below, Toronto Conservatory of Music): licentiate diploma 1901–21; artist, licentiate diplomas 1952– ; diploma in operatic performance 1970–
1854 Mount Allison Ladies' College; Mount Allison Conservatory of Music 1885–1937; *Mount Allison U 1937– : diplomas, first awarded in 1874, in piano, voice, violin; artist's and teacher's diplomas 1892–1937; soloist's diploma 1906–37; honours diploma 1906–37; musical leadership diploma 1934–47; licentiate in music 1937–57; associateship 1947–60
1868 *Académie de musique de Québec: certificates, diplomas (lauréat)
1872 *Trinity College of Music, London (began sending examiners to Canada in 1887): associate, licentiate, fellowship diplomas
1886 Toronto Conservatory of Music 1886–1947: associate diploma 1886–1947; fellowship diploma 1890–1914; licentiate in performance 1914–47 (TCM grants the U of Toronto licentiate diploma after 1921)
– *Royal Conservatory of Music of Toronto 1947– : associate diploma 1947– ; licentiate diploma 1947–52; artist's diploma 1947–52 (U of Toronto grants artist and licentiate diplomas after 1952)
1887 Halifax Conservatory of Music 1887–1954: certificates; associate diplomas 1898–1954; *Maritime Conservatory of Music 1954– (see also 1934 below, Maritime Academy of Music): associate diploma (performance or teaching)
1888 *Toronto College of Music (1888–1917): associate, fellow; post-graduate artist's diploma; teacher's and kindergarten teacher's certificates
1889 *Associated Board of the Royal Schools of Music (sent examiners to Canada 1895–1953): licentiate diploma 1899–1953
1892 London (Ont) Conservatory of Music 1892–1922 (London Institute of Musical Art 1934–): associate, teacher and fellow diplomas; *Western Ontario Conservatory of Music 1934– : associate, licentiate diplomas
1894 *Dominion College of Music / Collège de musique Dominion 1894–1940s. Affiliated with *Bishop's U: associate, licentiate diplomas
1897 Hamilton Conservatory of Music 1897–1965: associate diplomas; *Royal Hamilton College of Music 1965– : associate, licentiate, hon fellow diplomas
1905 *Cons national de musique (affailiated 1921–51 with the *U of Montreal): diplomas
1909 Canadian (Guild) College of Organists 1909–59: associate, fellow; *Royal Canadian College of Organists 1959– : associate, fellow
1910 *Mount Royal College Conservatory of Music: associate, licentiate diplomas 1931–
1911 *Canadian Academy of Music 1911–24; associate, licentiate
1911 *Hambourg Cons 1911–51: certificates and diplomas
1926 *École normale de musique 1926–76 (affiliated with U of Montreal 1926–67; UQAM 1969–76): certificates, teaching diplomas (brevet d'enseignement)
1932 École supérieure de musique d'Outremont 1932–51 (affiliated to U of Montreal 1933–68); to U of Sherbrooke 1970–8); *École Vincent-d'Indy 1951– : composition diploma (Montreal) 1933–70; artist's diploma (École Vincent-d'Indy) ca 1953–63; concert diploma (D'Indy) 1963–70, (U of Sherbrooke) 1970–9; brevet d'enseignement spécialisé (Quebec Ministry of Education) 1964–73; diplôme d'études collégiales (Quebec Ministry of Education) 1969– ; certificat d'aptitude pédagogique à l'enseignement de la musique (Sherbrooke) 1973–80
1934 Maritime Academy of Music 1934–54: certificates (accompanying, school music); licentiate diploma
1936 *Western Board of Music: associate diploma (performance, teaching); licentiate diploma
1937 *Bornoff School of Music 1937–49; *Konrad Conservatory 1949–62: diplomas first offered in 1941
1942 *Conservatoire de musique du Québec: premier prix; deuxième prix; diplôme d'études collégiales
1964 *Victoria Conservatory of Music: associate diploma 1978–
1969 *Community Music School of Greater Vancouver 1969–79; Vancouver Academy 1979– : diploma (performance) 1980–

For standard abbreviations used for diplomas see *EMC* List of Abbreviations and articles on individual diploma-granting institutions.

PW (FH, HK, CV)

Disaster songs. Disasters have inspired many ballads, quite a few composed in Canada. The great Miramichi fire of 1825, which raged over one-fifth of New Brunswick destroying several towns and driving 1500 people from their homes, led to 'The Miramichi Fire', the words credited to John Jardine. This song has survived in oral tradition in New Brunswick and Maine.

A later ballad, 'The Halifax Explosion' (*Creighton's *Maritime Folk Songs*, 1962), described the holocaust of 6 Dec 1917 when two ships – one laden with explosives – collided in the city's harbour. The explosion laid waste a large area of the city and killed some 1200 people.

Two mining disasters in Springhill, NS, inspired ballads. The first, an explosion in 1891, was described in 'Springhill Mining Disaster' and in the Acadian song 'La Complainte de Springhill' (*Maritime Folk Songs*). The second disaster trapped 12 men in a mineshaft for eight days in 1958. One of the men was Maurice Reddick, 'The Singing Miner,' who, by singing and leading them in song, helped his companions to keep up their spirits. He later described the experience in verses to be sung to the melody of 'I've Been Working on the Railroad.' The accident also led the folksingers Peggy Seeger and Ewan MacColl to write 'The Ballad of Springhill.'

A rockslide from Turtle Mountain, which in 1903 buried much of the little town of Frank, BC, was the subject 40 years later of Robert Gard's 'Ballad of the Frank Slide' (BMI Canada 1949). The collapse of Second Narrows bridge in Vancouver in 1958 inspired Stompin' Tom *Connors' 'The Bridge Came Tumblin' Down.'

An old sailors' song 'Lady Franklin's Lament,' recalled the loss of the Franklin expedition in the Canadian Arctic in 1845. Even more numerous disasters befall cargo and passenger vessels. Among the multitude of shipwreck ballads are those describing the loss of the *Atlantic*, the *Eliza*, the *Florizel*, the *Greenland*, and the *John Harvey*. Almost every ship that went down inspired a ballad and dozens survive in tradition. *Peacock gives more than 30 in his section 'Tragic Sea Ballads' (*Songs of the Newfoundland Outports*, Ottawa 1965), and Creighton, Greenleaf, Leach, and Mackenzie give others. A few had happier endings with lives saved through the bravery of seamen or landsmen, as in 'The Wreck of the Steamship *Ethie*' with words by Maude Roberts Simmons, 'The Loss of the *Jewel*,' and 'The Flemmings of Torbay.' *'The Wreck of the *Julie Plante*,' which supposedly took place on Lac St Pierre (part of the St Lawrence River) was sung widely by lumberjacks in the Great Lakes area.

Ballads describing disasters on the Great Lakes include 'The Loss of the Schooner *Antelope*,' 'The Wreck of the *Algoma*,' and 'The Foundering of the *Asia*.' In 1976 Gordon *Lightfoot's recording of his 'Wreck of the *Edmund Fitzgerald*' (1 Nov 1975 on Lake Superior) was popular.

Disasters in Canada also have suggested titles for instrumental compositions, including F. Dulder's 'Seven Bells Waltzes' (G.F. DeVine 1877), written in reference to the Saint John, NB, fire, and Morris Manley's 'The Ottawa Fire' (R.S. Williams 1900).

A song commemorating the Ottawa fire of 1900

See also Occupational songs. EF

Les Disciples de Massenet. A 65-voice mixed choir founded in Montreal 4 Feb 1928 by Charles *Goulet. He named it after the composer of *La Navarraise*, the opera in which he had made his 1923 debut as a baritone at the Théâtre royal, Liège. The choir gave its first public performance 17 Apr 1928, and in the autumn of 1930 it took part in the *CPR Festivals in Quebec City. Its performance in Beethoven's *Symphony No. 9* at the 1936 *Montreal Festivals initiated a long association with the festivals; over the following seasons it sang Verdi's *Requiem*, Bach's *Magnificat*, Fauré's *Requiem*, Dvořák's *Stabat mater*,etc. With the CSM orchestra the choir sang *Boris Godunov*, *The Damnation of Faust*, and Mozart's *Requiem*, as well as additional performances of the above-mentioned works under such conductors as Beecham, Busch, Defauw, Klemperer, Krips, Markevitch, Monteux, Ormandy, *Pelletier, and Stassevich. Its Fauré's *Requiem* received the American Recording Society prize for the best North American choral recording of 1942.

In 1950 the choir performed in Europe, singing, among other works, Fauré's *Requiem* at Notre-Dame Church, Paris, and it also reached the finals at a festival in Lille. The following year it won first prize at the Chicagoland Music Festival. It made a second European tour in 1960, giving 16 concerts in France, Belgium, Luxembourg, and Monaco. Goulet was succeeded by Léon Plante 1963, and Plante by René *Lacourse in 1970. The choir gave 10 concerts in France in 1974 at the invitation of the French government and took part in the opening and closing ceremonies of the 1976 Olympics in Montreal. At a 1978 concert marking its 50th anniversary the choir performed Dvořák's *Stabat mater*; on this occasion Gilles *Potvin commented in *Le Devoir* (Montreal, 27 Nov 1978), 'The time-honoured qualities of the Disciples – precision, strength and style – were present throughout this performance.' In 1979 the choir estimated at close to 1500 the number of concerts given since its foundation. Claude *Létourneau became director of the choir in 1980.

DISCOGRAPHY

De Félix à Charlebois. Lacourse cond. 1975. Nobel NBL-603

Les Disciples de Massenet: Christmas carols. Goulet cond. (1958). RCI 151

Les Disciples de Massenet parmi nous: selections including songs and arr of Daunais. Goulet cond. 1958. RCA Victor LCP 1006/RCA Gala CGP 113
Fauré *Requiem* – Mozart *Ave verum*. M. Denya sop, M. Harrell bar, Mtl Festivals O, Pelletier cond, Goulet dir. 1941. RCA Victor DM 844 (78)
French Folk Songs from Canada. Goulet cond. (1960). RCI 164
Mozart *Agnus Dei* K427. M. Denya sop, Mtl Festivals O, Pelletier cond, Goulet dir. 1941. RCA Victor V-18512 (78)
Noël autour du monde. R. Simard soloist, Lacourse cond. 1974. Nobel NBL-602
René Simard et les Disciples de Massenet à l'église Notre-Dame: Christmas songs. Lacourse cond. 1973. Nobel NBL-511
Also several other 78s for RCA Victor
See also Discographies for R. Jobin; Petits Chanteurs du Mont-Royal; Verreau.

BIBLIOGRAPHY

Laberge, Dominique. 'Les Disciples de Massenet,' *Qui?*, vol 4, Mar 1953

GP

Discography

1 Introduction
2 Canadian recordings: Source materials; Discographies
3 International

1 INTRODUCTION. A discography is a list, in descriptive detail, of sound recordings; also the research and systems employed in compiling such a list. The term has come to cover the listing of cylinder and tape recordings and other sound-retaining devices as well as discs. The detail and format of a discography tend to differ according to the musical genre being treated.

In jazz discography, perhaps the most detailed in its approach, lists usually are ordered by performer (ie, leader), then subdivided by recording session (whether studio, concert, or radio broadcast). The list would include, wherever possible and for each recorded performance (including unreleased or lost material): complete personnel divided by instrumentation and with soloists identified; city and exact date of recording; titles of works recorded and perhaps, but not ordinarily, composers; matrix numbers (the designation given by a company to a recorded performance for the purpose of in-house identification); and the label and label number of commercial release and, as applicable, of reissues. The discographies of dance bands follow similar principles.

In discographies of classical (ie, concert or operatic) music, an area not as fully covered by the late 1970s, lists usually are ordered according to composer or performer: if the former, subdivisions follow by composition and performer; if the latter, by composer and composition. The detail of such lists may include, as applicable: principal personnel (eg, name of ensemble or performing company, soloists, accompanists, conductors); date and place of recording; and date, label, and label number of commercial release or reissue.

Ultimately, however, the guidelines for each discography are set according to the subject's scope and to the limits of available information. Discographies for other genres of music (eg, folk or pop) may adopt either the jazz or the classical format, but more often list only performer, record title, label, and label number.

2 CANADIAN RECORDINGS. By definition, any annotated list of records is a discography, regardless of the limits of the annotation or the basic principle or theme underlying the list's compilation. For the purpose of this article, however, lists of Canadian recordings published in catalogues (eg, for commercial purposes), as directories to collections, as a reader service (eg, the lists of new records found in periodicals), or as charts ordered according to momentary popularity (eg, those in *RPM) will be considered, but only as source material for the preparation of the detailed discography whose purpose is historical documentation.

Source materials. The earliest regular listings of Canadian and other new records issued in Canada probably were those in the **Canadian Music Trades Journal*, published monthly from at least 1912 to February 1930 (with a gap April 1927 – December 1928). The lists were arranged by label. The magazine's publisher also issued the *Phonograph Journal of Canada* from 1919 until sometime in the 1920s; since no issues have been located its significance cannot be measured. The Montreal periodical *La Lyre* (1922–31) included occasional record lists.

Important for the study of this early period – the Canadian recording industry goes back only to about 1900 – are company files and ledgers. Such files give recording dates and other information about recordings of the day and have been exploited for discographies by Alex Robertson of Montreal (assisted by George Humble), who compiled *The Apex 8000 Numerical* (Pointe-Claire, Que, 1971, rev 1974) and *Canadian Gennett and Starr-Gennett 9000 Numerical* (ibid 1972). Robertson also published *Canadian Compo Numericals* (ibid 1978). Edward B. *Moogk, in *Roll Back the Years*, includes over 4000 entries by manufacturer's number for the *Berliner, (*RCA) Victor, HMV, *Columbia, *Compo, *Starr, Apex, Ajax, Opraphone, and *Canadian Vitaphone labels and their series. While in themselves authoritative discographies, these are invaluable sources, as well, for other discographers.

Also useful are company advertisements, catalogues, and leaflets, of the kinds issued by Victor, *Sparton, *Quality, etc. Imported and domestic items, however, usually are indistinguishable in such listings. The *CBC began issuing catalogues of its transcription series (RCI) in 1949, culminating in the 1970s in a loose-leaf binder – one page per record – indexed by composer, title, and performer in the traditional, contemporary concert music, jazz, and variety categories, and by title and performer in the folklore category. Though the complete CBC recording output (ie, the RCI, SM, and LM series) has not been documented in one location or publication, several issues of *The Canadian Collection*, a catalogue of recordings drawn from these series and for sale to the public, have been published in Toronto. The *Canadian Talent Library also has issued a catalogue in instalments for use by subscribing radio stations. *Canadiana*, a *NL of C publication first issued in 1950 and devoted to a monthly listing of 'publications of Canadian interest received by the National Library,' began in 1970 to include records with a release date of 1969 and later. The order of listing follows the Dewey Decimal system of classification, but the indexes allow access by composer, performer, some other personal and corporate names, title of music, subject headings, and album title. Coverage until 1978 was limited to LPs, cassette and reel-to-reel-cartridge tapes, and a few 45-rpm discs. Some 9580 recordings had been listed in detail by mid-1979. The *Library of Congress Catalog – Music and Phonorecords* (Washington 1953– ; title changed in 1973 to *Music, Books on Music, and Sound Recordings*) gives similar information for US releases, which may include recordings of Canadian interest. Two other international compilations containing data are the Eastman School of Music's *Sibley Library Catalogue* (Boston 1977) and Kurtz Myers' 1978 edition of *Index to Record Reviews* (New York). Two published catalogues of the *Mount Allison U library holdings are of discographical interest: *Canadian Music Scores and Records* (Sackville, NB, 1976) by Gwendolyn Creelman, Esther Cooke, and Geraldine King, a classified and indexed catalogue in which 13 of the basic subject areas (eg, secular songs, juvenile music) include reference to recordings; and the *Catalogue of Canadian Folk Music in the Mary Mellish Archibald Library and Other Special Collections* (Sackville, NB, 1974) by Eleanor Magee and Margaret Fancy, which lists 15 items by traditional singers and 55 by others.

Private collections form the backbone of original discographical research in Canada, and many collectors are themselves discographers, eg, the members of the West Mississauga Jazz Muddies and the Montreal Vintage Music Society (see Record collector clubs). Most discographical research is done at this level, and an informal network of collectors and discographers exists on an international scale, with knowledgeable Canadians assisting in the preparation of many works of international scope and helping in each other's projects.

There are other publications useful for research purposes. *RPM*, the Toronto-based periodical first issued in 1965, publishes a list of singles and LPs ranked according to their popularity and updated weekly in pop, country, and 'adult-oriented' categories. The short-lived *Record Week* published similar charts 1975–7. *A Chartology of Canadian Popular Music: January 1965 to December 1976* (Toronto 1978), compiled for *RPM* by Brendan J. Lyttle, includes, by date, title, and artist, every Canadian single and LP listed on the *RPM* charts. One issue only was published of the *Canadian LP & Tape Catalogue* (Ann Arbor, Mich, and Ottawa, Summer 1975), designed by M.J. MacArthur Wrightman along the lines of *Schwann* and *Gramophone* as 'a comprehensive reference guide to recorded music and spoken material for the dealer and home consumer.' Subdivided into sections for classical music, choral music, opera, musicals, popular music (English-language and French-language), and similar categories, with listing partly according to composer, partly by performer, it has suffered from incompleteness and from various misattributions. *Schwann* (Boston 1949–) and *Gramophone* (Harrow 1953–) include records by Canadians if released in the respective countries of their publication: the USA and England. The classical record mail-order catalogues of the Canadian record dealer André *Perrault, Ltd, also are of research value.

Several articles, general and specific, have been written about Canadian recordings. These include John *Beckwith's chapter 'Recordings' in *Music in Canada* (Toronto 1955), which looks at the history of recording in Canada, and his survey 'Canadian recordings, a discography' (in the Canadian Library Association's *Bulletin* Apr 1956), which lists 44 concert performers and eight discs of Canadian compositions and makes two references to folk singers. **Musicanada*, at the time a *CMCentre publication, presented a three-part series by Michael S. Grobin (September 1969, March 1970, final issue 1970) which discussed over 25 composers, with reference to recordings of their works. The series continued in *Performing Arts in Canada* (Summer 1971 to Spring 1973, followed by 'The Canadian collection,' Summer 1973). In the August 1972 issue of **Coda* John *Norris examines the jazz recordings of RCI. Detailed discographical information in these articles, however, is minimal. Among general lists is *Canadian Music List / Liste de la musique canadienne* (Toronto 1971, compiled and somewhat hastily edited under the auspices of the Canadian Assn of Broadcasters in response to the *CRTC's Canadian content regulations) and *A Treasury of Canadian Recordings* (Toronto nd, issued by BMI Canada to promote its composer-members).

Record reviews also are useful in the compilation of discographies, and two Canadian librarians, Andrew Armitage and Dean Tudor, have prepared an *Annual Index to Popular Music Record Reviews* (Metuchen, NJ, 1972–).

Discographies. Various guides or reference works, though limited in the range of information they provide, may be considered discographies. These include Edith *Fowke's 'A guide to Canadian folk song records,' published in *Canadian Forum* (September 1957) and her later *Reference List on Canadian Folk Music* (Toronto 1966, revised in 1973 and 1978 for the *Canadian Folk Music Journal*), compiled with Barbara *Cass-Beggs. The 1978 revision lists 38 records by traditional performers (cited by title, collector, label, and number; performers are not named) and 64 by non-traditional performers (cited by performer, record title, label, and number). The CBC radio program 'Choral Concert' issued the *1979 Canadian Choral Records List* (Vancouver 1979), compiled by Jon *Washburn, the host of the series. It lists 113 choral recordings by performing group, location, titles, label, and number. *The Great Canadian Jazz Discography* (11 editions, Winnipeg 1976–9), compiled by the CBC's 'Jazz Radio-Canada,' lists records (under performer, title, label, and number) according to current availability; 'Contemporary Canadian Jazz Recordings – a Selected Discography,' compiled by Lois Moody and published in *Jazz Ottawa* (no. 19, 1978), offers similar information. In 1980 a detailed discography of Canadian jazz, covering some 1000 recordings, was eight years in preparation by Jack Litchfield of Montreal. *Musicanada* devoted an entire issue (subtitled 'Canada on Record,' January – February 1970) to 'some recordings of works by Canadian composers' – 233 works by 99 composers on 74 LPs' a supplement (October 1972) adds 182 compositions on 72 LPs. Citations include record title, performer(s), composers and works, timings, record label, and number. For *Aspects de la musique au Canada* (Montreal 1970), Gilles *Potvin completed a 'Selection discographique de musique canadienne,' covering 64 composers and more than 130 works by title, performers, record label, and number. Wayne Gilpin's *Directory of Musical Canadiana* (Edmonton 1978) includes similar listings for 127 composers.

Three Canadian discographies have concentrated on specific areas of research. The most ambitious, Edward B. *Moogk's pioneering *Roll Back the Years* (Ottawa 1975), covers the period of recorded-sound history in Canada from its beginnings to 1930 and provides a firm foundation for all Canadian discographical work to follow. It lists some 7700 recordings ordered alphabetically by performer – the performers all either born or at some time in their careers resident in Canada – as well as some 860 recordings arranged alphabetically by composer or lyricist (some 75 in the two categories) and numerical series for several labels. There is no title index; thus one cannot refer quickly, for instance, to specific Canadian folksongs. A second volume of *Roll Back the Years*, covering the period from 1930 to the end of the era of 78-rpm recordings, was in preparation in 1979 but was not completed at the time of the author's death. A list of all known recordings of Canadian interest of the period 1931–69 is maintained at the NL of C.

Michael Taft's scholarly *A Regional Discography of Newfoundland and Labrador* (St John's 1975) is divided into two sections: 'Newfoundlanders on record' and 'Newfoundland songs recorded by non-Newfoundlanders.' There are indexes by composer, song title, and accompanist, and the book is prefaced by a short history of recorded music in the province.

Gabriel Labbé's *Les Pionniers du disque folklorique québécois 1920–1950* (Montreal 1977) includes bio-discographies for 24 performers and history-discographies for the *Alouette Vocal Quartet and *La Bonne Chanson.

Biographies or other works devoted to individual musicians or groups may include discographies. Among these are Réal Benoit's *La Bolduc* (Montreal 1959), Luc Bérimont's *Félix Leclerc* (Paris, Montreal 1969), Lucien Rioux's *Robert Charlebois (Paris 1972), Mémoires d'Emma Albani* (Montreal 1972), Giles *Bryant's *Healey Willan Catalogue* (Ottawa 1972), Jean Calvet's *Pauline Julien* (Paris 1974), Ruth C. Brotman's *Pauline Donalda* (Montreal 1975), Brian *Cherney's *Harry Somers* (Toronto 1975), Martin Melhuish's *Bachman-Turner Overdrive* (Toronto 1976), Ruby *Mercer's *Edward Johnson* (Toronto 1976, discography by J.B. McPherson and W.R. Moran), Marc Gagné's *Gilles Vigneault* (Quebec City 1977), Geoffrey *Payzant's *Glenn Gould: Music and Mind* (Toronto 1978), and Alfrieda Gabiou's *Gordon Lightfoot* (Toronto 1979). Edwin Harkin's *Maynard Ferguson: A Discography* (self publ, San Diego 1976) is perhaps the only exclusively discographical work devoted to a Canadian musician. Similar discographies for Max Boag and Mart *Kenney have been prepared by Ross Brethour of Aurora, Ont, but had not been published by 1980. Three issues of the British publication the *Record Collector* have been devoted to Canadian singers: Pauline *Donalda (November 1956, by Arthur E. Knight), Emma *Albani (February – March 1959, by W.R. Moran), and Florence *Easton (January 1974, by John *Stratton). An extensive discography of Paul *Bley, compiled by Ib Skovgaard Petersen and Laurent Goddet for *Jazz Hot*, was reprinted in *Coda* (March – April 1979). Canadian musicians have had entries in international discographies; Jorgen Jepsen Grunnet's *Jazz Records 1942–6* (9 vols, Holte, Denmark, 1962–8), for example, has detailed entries for Peter *Appleyard, Georgie Auld, Bley, Gil Evans, Ferguson, Moe *Koffman, Phil *Nimmons, Bert *Niosi, Pat *Riccio, Milt Sealey, and Mike White. J.B. Steane's *The Grand Tradition* (New York 1974), 'Seventy years of singing on record 1900–1970,' considers some recordings of Emma Albani, Pauline Donalda, Pierre *Duval, Florence Easton, Louise *Edvina, Maureen *Forrester, Don *Garrard, Edward Johnson, George *London, Louis *Quilico, Joseph *Rouleau, Léopold *Simoneau, Jennie Tourel, and Jon *Vickers.

Selected or complete discographies have been appended to many articles in *EMC*, employing different formats for classical music, jazz, and pop (see p xx for explanation and guidance).

3 INTERNATIONAL. Canadians also have made valuable contributions to the field of discography internationally. James *Creighton's monumental *Discopaedia of the Violin 1889–1971* (Toronto 1974) is the most impressive. Others include Jean-Marie Gaboury's *Mozart sur le disque* (Montreal 1949), René Girard's *Oeuvres et disques de Beethoven* (Montreal 1952), Fernand Ouellette's *Edgard Varèse* (Paris 1966), Barry Tepperman's contribution to *Eric Dolphy, A Bio-Discography* (Washington 1974), and Bruce Surtees' discographies for Paul *Robinson's books about the conductors Karajan, Stokowski, and Solti. Harvey Sachs included a discography in his *Toscanini* (London 1978). Paul *Roussel's *Votre Discothèque* and Jacques Thériault's *Une Discothèque de base* (both Montreal 1973) are general reference books devised to assist in the building of a private record library. Both deal with classical records, but Thériault has included jazz and pop sections by Gilles Archambault and Pyer Gingras respectively. Gerald Parker has compiled a discography of non-commercial recordings of Saverio Mercadante's operas and other vocal works for the Ottawa publication *Spectrum* (Vol 2, September – October 1979). HK (MM)

DOANE, J. (John) **Chalmers**. Administrator, ukulele player, string bassist, b Truro, north of Halifax, NS, 3 Nov 1938; B MUS ED (Boston) 1966. He graduated in 1961 from Nova Scotia Teachers' College and later studied string methods with George *Bornoff at Boston U. After his appointment in 1967 as supervisor of music for the Halifax School Board, he changed school music programs dramatically, using the ukulele as an inexpensive and practical teaching instrument for children and adults. Doane's unconventional methods are vindicated by the success of Halifax school bands and orchestras in concerts and competitions across Canada. He is much in demand as a consultant.

See also School music.

WRITINGS

Classroom Ukulele Method (Waterloo 1971)
Ukulele Encore (Waterloo 1975)
The Teachers' Guide to Classroom Ukulele (Waterloo 1977)

DISCOGRAPHY

Ukulele Yes! 1973. Audat 477.4012
Ukuleles on Tour. 1974. Audat 477.4016
Ukulele Magic. 1975. Halifax School Board C-142
Ukulele Solos. 1976. Wat CSPS 1015
An Introduction to Ukulele Basics with J. Chalmers Doane. 1976. Wat WR9

BIBLIOGRAPHY

'Halifax has a lot in common with Honolulu: a lot of ukuleles,' *Weekend Magazine*, 2 Feb 1974
Kimber, Stephen. 'Pied Piper of Halifax,' (*Toronto Star*) *Today*, 16 Aug 1980 (GKr)

DOBSON, Bonnie (m Beaver). Singer-songwriter, guitarist, b Toronto 13 Nov 1940. Under the influence and encouragement of Pete Seeger she began singing folk songs in her early teens. She toured in the USA 1960–2 and lived in Chicago 1962–4 and New York 1964–5, making occasional appearances in Toronto coffeehouses and performing at the *Mariposa Folk Festival. Likened at this time to Joan Baez and Carolyn Hester, she made four LPs in the USA for Prestige – *She's Like a Swallow* (13021), *Dear Companion* (7801), *Bonnie Dobson at Folk City* (13057), and *A Merry Go Round of Children's Songs* (13064) – and one for Mercury – *For the Love of Him* (MG 20987). Returning in 1965 to live in Toronto, she sang in a production (1965) of *The Emperor's New Clothes* and performed in local coffeehouses. For CBC radio she sang regularly on '1967 and All That' and was co-hostess (1968–70, with Chantal Beauregard) for 'La Ronde.' She made her London debut 3 Nov 1969 at Queen Elizabeth Hall and moved in 1970 to England, where she has performed extensively on the BBC and the ITV and has made the LPs *Bonnie Dobson* (Argo ZFB 79) and *Morning Dew* (Poly 2383 400). She has appeared throughout Europe in concert and on radio and TV. Dobson's repertoire has included music by Gordon *Lightfoot and Ian and Sylvia (*Tyson), as well as traditional and original songs. The most popular of her own songs are '(Walk Me out in the) *Morning Dew' and 'I'm Your Woman.' She is an affiliate of PRO Canada. Of her voice Barrie Hale wrote, 'It's a clear soprano – one calls it clear because it cuts, but it has a texture that brushes the ear as well' (Toronto *Telegram*, 29 Sep 1965). Dobson's other LPs (recorded in Canada) are *Bonnie Dobson* (RCI 348 / RCA LSP-4219) and *Good Morning Rain* (RCA LSP-4277). MM

DOCHERTY, Ian (Donald). Baritone, writer, b Winnipeg 25 Feb 1914. His teacher of voice, piano, and theory in Edmonton 1936–9 was Alexander Nizoff, who gave him a particular awareness of the 19th-century Russian tradition. He sang on CKUA radio and other stations and was a member of the Edmonton Male Chorus. In 1938 he was a founder and soloist of Opera Slav (a precursor of the *Edmonton Opera Assn). Continuing his studies with Marie *Schilder in Vancouver, he sang 1941–52 on CBC radio as a Lieder and oratorio soloist and as a member of the CBR Singers. He became a CBC music commentator in 1949 and served 1957–61 as music critic for the Vancouver *Province*. He became program annotator for the *Vancouver SO in 1966 and a regular columnist for the Kerrisdale *Courier* in 1970. For many years he was a contributor to the periodicals *Musical America* and *Opera*. He was the fine arts coordinator 1960–6 at the *U of British Columbia and began teaching music history at the *Community Music School of Greater Vancouver and music journalism at the Vancouver Community College in 1976. BNSG

Documentation: See the following:
Archives
Archives de folkore
Canadian Music Centre
Ethnomusicology
Libraries
Musicology
National Library of Canada
National Museums of Canada
See also Bibliography; Biography; Discography; Iconography.

Dodecaphonic music. See Twelve-tone technique.

DODINGTON, John. Bass, b Toronto 3 Jul 1945; B MUS (Toronto) 1972. His teachers included George *Lambert 1965–71 and Louis *Quilico 1971–2. In 1972 he went to England, where he studied until 1975 with Otakar Kraus and appeared in performances of *Wozzeck* during the 1974–5 season at the Royal Opera House, Covent Garden. Returning to Canada he participated 1976–7 in the *Vancouver Opera Resident Artist Program. Dodington has performed with the *Festival Singers, the *Cantata Singers of Vancouver, the Toronto Chamber Society, and the *Thunder Bay SO. During the 1979–80 season he appeared in recital with the pianist Jane *Coop for the *Women's Musical Club of Toronto; with his wife, the mezzo-soprano Catherine *Robbin, at the *U of Lethbridge; and with Coop and Robbin together in a recital at the *St. Lawrence Centre, Toronto. Dodington has sung with the *Edmonton Opera (Angelotti and Sciarrone in *Tosca* in 1978), at *Festival Ottawa (as the Marquis d'Obigny in *La Traviata* in 1978 and Narumov in *The Queen of Spades* in 1979), with the *Southern Alberta Opera (as Tom in *A Masked Ball* and the Commendatore in *Don Giovanni* in 1978), and the Vancouver Opera. For Toronto's Opera in Concert series he sang the roles of Friar Laurence in *Roméo et Juliette* (1977) and Quasimodo in Franz Schmidt's *Notre Dame* (1978). His *COC roles have included Don Basilio in *The Barber of Seville* (1977), Zuniga in *Carmen* (1979), and Doctor Grenvil in *La Traviata* (1978). NM

Dofasco Male Chorus. Choir sponsored by Dofasco (Dominion Foundries and Steel Co Ltd) of Hamilton, Ont, as a public relations project. It was founded in 1945 under the conductorship of Edward Stewart, who was succeeded in 1972 by G. Murray Hall. Most of the 60 singers are Dofasco employees. The chorus has toured in Canada and the USA and, as the Dofasco Choir (with 14 female voices added), has presented an annual Christmas program on CHCH-TV, Hamilton. Under Stewart's direction the DMC recorded the LPs *Men of Steel* (RCA PCS 1011) and *A Festival of Christmas Carols* (1969–70, Warner WSC 9010). The choir's repertoire ranges from Bach to popular songs.

DOHERTY, Denny (Dennis Gerard Stephen). Singer, b Halifax, NS, 29 Nov 1940. He began his career at 15 with the Halifax dance band of Peter Power, then sang with a succession of pop-folk groups – the Hepsters, the Colonials, and the Halifax Three. The last-named (which at one time included Toronto guitarist Zal Yanovsky, later of the Lovin' Spoonful) made the LP *San Francisco Bay Blues* (1963, Epic BN 26060) and performed in eastern Canada and in the USA. Doherty sang in New York in the Big Three (with Cass Elliott and Tim Rose) and in 1964 in the seminal folk-rock group The Mugwumps (with Elliott, Yanovsky, and James Hendricks). He was a member in Los Angeles (1965–8, with Elliott and John and Michelle Phillips) of the Mamas and the Papas, the most popular vocal group of its day. The quartet made several hit singles ('California Dreaming,' 'Monday, Monday,' 'I Saw Her Again,' and others) and five LPs for ABC/Dunhill. It re-formed briefly in 1971. Doherty then pursued a solo recording career in the USA and made the LP *Watcha Gonna Do?* (1972, ABC/Dunhill S 50096) before returning in 1977 to Nova Scotia. He sang at the 1977 and 1978 Atlantic Folk Festivals and became host for CBC Halifax TV's 'Denny's Sho*' in the summer of 1978.

BIBLIOGRAPHY
Stambler, Irwin. 'The Mamas and the Papas,' *Encyclopedia of Pop, Rock and Soul* (New York 1976)
Kimber, Stephen. 'Denny's back in town,' *The Canadian*, 3 Jun 1978 MM

Doherty Pianos Ltd (Doherty Piano and Organ Co Ltd 1875–1913). Manufacturing firm founded in 1875 in Clinton, Ont, by William Doherty (b ca 1840, d Clinton 9 Feb 1924), a furniture dealer and *Bell Organ representative. Under the name W. Doherty & Co he began the manufacture of reed organs at a factory on Rattenbury St. He was joined in partnership ca 1880–90 by John Gibbings. Doherty's company made its first pianos in 1907 and was incorporated as the Doherty Piano and Organ Co Ltd in 1908. The firm produced about 400 organs a year and increased its piano production to 1500 annually during the first 10 years. 'Organ' was dropped from the name in 1913, and production seems to have been curtailed ca 1917. Retail branches were established after about 1908, in Winnipeg, Calgary, Edmonton, and, briefly, Regina. The firm's mainstays were its piano and the Doherty Attachable Player (which converted any style or make of standard piano into a player piano). In 1913 a grand piano was introduced and also a new standard design, the 'Clinton' line. In 1915 the firm advertised that over 70,000 Doherty instruments were in use 'throughout the civilized world.' The same year Doherty closed its retail operations, planning to extend its wholesale trade. With Doherty's retirement in 1917, the firm was reorganized as Doherty Pianos Ltd under the control of a group of businessmen, and thenceforth it manufactured player, Doherty, and Clinton pianos, reed organs, benches, and stools. Bought in 1920 by *Sherlock-Manning (Sherlock and Manning were former Doherty employees) it continued to operate under its own name. Though head offices were moved to London, Ont, factories remained in Clinton and increased their production to 2500 instruments a year. B.J. Gibbings, son of the one-time partner John Gibbings, served as plant superintendent at Clinton. Contrary to figures in the *Pierce Piano Atlas*, production of Doherty pianos ceased in the early 1930s. (FH)

DOLIN, Samuel (Joseph). Composer, teacher, b Montreal 22 Aug 1917; B MUS (Toronto) 1942, D MUS (Toronto) 1958. He began his studies in Montreal and continued at the TCM and later at the *U of Toronto. In 1945, after three years as music supervisor in Ontario's Durham and Northumberland counties and visiting music master of Trinity College School, Port Hope, he joined the staff of the TCM (*RCMT) and resumed studies at the U of Toronto with Reginald *Godden and Weldon *Kilburn (piano) and John *Weinzweig (composition).

Dolin's works encompass several styles, from the chromatic, traditional *Serenade for Strings* premiered at the 1952 Olympics to the multimedia *Drakkar* for singers, dancers, synthesizers, and slides. (See also Composition, instrumental solos and duos 4 / Instrumental duos with piano.) He began using electronic sounds in his music in 1966 when, after a tour of American and European facilities, he established an electronic studio at the RCMT. Many of his pupils, including Stuart *Broomer, Brian *Cherney, Steven *Gellman, Herbie Helbig, Moe *Koffman, Michel *Longtin, John *Mills-Cockell, Allan *Rae, Ann *Southam, Ben *Steinberg, and Roman *Toi, have become successful composers. Dolin has organized public hearings of his pupils' works and has devoted much time and energy to their support and promotion. He is a founding member of the *CLComp and served 1969–73 as president. He was vice-president 1972–5 of the ISCM and chairman 1970–4 of the revived Canadian section. He is an affiliate of PRO Canada and an associate of the *CMCentre.

SELECTED COMPOSITIONS

DRAMATIC WORKS

Casino 'Greed,' opera (R. Hambleton). 1967. Ms
Machina, film (Choklakian-Schmidt). 1970. Ms
The Meeting Point, TV (L. Rampen). 1971. 6 vs, synth, org. Ms
Missionaries, radio drama (T. Findlay). 1971. Ms
Drakkar, multimedia (S. and L. Dolin). 1972. Mezzo, 2 bar, narr, 2 dancers, chamb ens, 2 synth, slides. CMCentre

ORCHESTRA

Sinfonietta. 1950. Ber (rental). ('Scherzo') RCI 171 (*TSO)
Serenade for Strings. 1951. Ber (rental). RCI 86 (*CBC SO)
Symphony No. 1 'Elk Falls.' 1956. CMCentre
Isometric Variables 'Bassooneries in Free Variations.' 1957. Bn, str. Ber (rental)
Symphony No. 2. 1957. Ber (rental)
Sonata for String Orchestra. 1962. CMCentre
Fantasy for Piano and Chamber Orchestra. 1967. Ber (rental)
Concerto for Piano and Orchestra. 1974. CMCentre
Symphony No. 3. 1976. CMCentre

CHAMBER

Sonatina and *Barcarolle* (1954, 1962). Vn, pf. Ms
Sonata for Violin and Piano. 1960. BMIC 1968. Mel SMLP 4021 (*Zafer vn)
Portrait for String Quartet. 1961. CMCentre
Concerto Grosso 'Georgian Bay.' Perc, accord, tape. CMCentre
Sonata. 1970. Accord. Wat 1971. RCI 385 (*Macerollo)
Three Sonatas. 1973. 1 vn, tape; 2 fl, tape; 3 vc, tape. CMCentre
Ricercar and Fantasy for guitar. 1974 (rev 1977). *Drakkar* 1977. (*Ricercar*) Mel SMLP 4025 (D. *Joachim)
Adikia. 1975. 1–5 accord, tape. CMCentre
Prelude, Interlude and Fantasy. 1976. vc solo. CMCentre
Duo Concertante. 1977. Free bass acc, guit. CMCentre
Sonata. 1978. Vc, pf. CMCentre

PIANO

Little Suite. 1954. FH 1955 ('Old Dance')
Little Toccata. 1959. BMIC 1961
Sonatina. 1959. BMIC 1960. CCM-2 (*Cavalho pf)
Slightly Square Round Dance. 1966. Ber (rental)
If. 1972. Wat 1972
Queekhoven and A.J. 1975. CMCentre

CHOIR AND VOICE
'Chloris' (W. Strode). 1951. V, pf. BMIC 1961
The Hills of Hebron and *Mass* (1954, 1972), both for choir. CMCentre
Marchbankantata (R. Davies). 1971. Bar, SATB, pf, synth. CMCentre
Deuteronomy XXXII (Bible). 1977. V, fl. CMCentre
3 sets of songs (1951). All ms

WRITINGS
'ISCM's 45th festival in London,' *CMB*, 3, Autumn – Winter 1971

BIBLIOGRAPHY
Morgan, Kit. 'Success of Dolin's students evidence of his teaching skill,' *MSc*, 267, Sep – Oct 1972
BMI Canada Ltd / PRO Canada Ltd. 'Samuel Dolin,' pamphlets (1972, 1978)
MacMillan, Rick. 'Instrumental clinic for composers is Dolin innovation,' *MSc*, 291, Sep – Oct 1976
Contemporary Canadian Composers

CF

Dominion College of Music / Collège de musique Dominion. Founded in Montreal in 1894 by J. Edgar *Birch, Percival J. *Illsley, and Horace *Reyner, it was incorporated in 1895 and became affiliated the same year with *Bishop's U. Initially its purpose was to set and administer practical and theoretical examinations. Its first president was W. H. Benyon. Teaching began at Karn Hall in 1896 but was discontinued in 1899 owing to financial difficulties. The college subsequently confined itself to holding examinations and granting diplomas.

Through its affiliation with Bishop's U, the college awarded the L MUS, Associate diploma, B MUS, and later the D MUS, according to requirements set by the *TCL. Gold and silver medals were awarded as well. Six candidates sat for the examinations of 1895 in the vestry of the church of St James the Apostle. In 1905 more than 350 students presented themselves for examinations, and a branch was set up in Quebec City by Napoléon *Crépault and his son Léonce along with Ernest and Gustave *Gagnon. The examinations of this bilingual college at first took place in the private schools and convents of Ontario and Quebec (in particular in the Ursulines' monastery in Quebec City) but later spread to the Maritime provinces, certain areas of the western provinces, and the USA. In 1917–18 200 diplomas were granted in the Montreal district alone.

Among the college's diploma-holders or pupils were Max *Bohrer, Marie E.G. Caron, Claude *Champagne, Germaine Daigle (L MUS), Ernest Gagnon, Caroline *Racicot, Rose MacMillan (Associate), and Mme L. Clapin (L MUS). Among the teaching staff and examiners over the years may be found the names of John W. Bearder, Max and William Bohrer, George M. *Brewer (also secretary), Dominique *Ducharme, Septimus Fraser, Percival J. Illsley, Romain-Octave *Pelletier, William *Reed, Horace Reyner, and Marguerite Sym. For some years Charles *O'Neill was the college's vice-president. The Dominion College of Music appears to have ceased its activities during the 1940s.

BIBLIOGRAPHY
Montreal Musical Year Book 1931 (Montreal 1931)
Musical Red Book

NT

Dominion Organ and Piano Co. Instrument manufacturer. Founded in 1872 in Oshawa, Ont, as Darley and Robinson (later Oshawa Organ and Melodeon Manufacturing Co) the firm relocated in Bowmanville, Ont, in 1873 and was renamed the Dominion Organ Co in 1875. It specialized in cabinet reed organs. These were distinctive for the reed-qualifying tubes which replaced tuning slides to give even-register voicing. In 1876 a 19-stop Dominion organ with 12 sets of reeds won an international medal at the Philadelphia Centennial Exhibition. Prizes in Paris, London, and Chicago followed. A piano factory was added in 1876, and two-manual organs for church use were introduced in the 1880s. The exceptional quality of Dominion's square grand and upright pianos made the company second only to *Bell as a Canadian instrument producer and exporter. As a sales promotion the firm published complimentary piano music as well as the *Dominion Organ and Piano Company's Modern Method for Reed Organ*, possibly the first such work to appear in Canada. After several changes of owner the company was taken over in 1901 by J.W. Alexander. Later models of Dominion organs displayed a declining tonal quality. Demand decreased, and the company closed during the Depression of the mid-1930s.

(MG, FH)

DOMPIERRE, (Joseph Eugène Frédéric) **François**. Composer, accompanist, conductor, arranger, producer, b Ottawa 1 Jul 1943. He studied piano with Hélène *Landry and Noëlla Vaillancourt in Ottawa and then organ with Paul Larose for four years. He continued 1959–64 at the *CMM with Françoise *Aubut (fugue, harmony, counterpoint, organ), Clermont *Pépin (composition, orchestration), and Irving *Heller (piano). He first became known in Montreal as an accompanist and a singer-songwriter with a fondness for melancholy songs inspired by jazz and slightly influenced by Michel Legrand. His appearance on the CFTM TV program 'Découverte' in 1963 was seen by John Damant, the artistic director of Select recording company, and as a result Select released his first LP, *Dompierre* (SSP 24.104).

Dompierre abandoned his career as a performer, but his songs came to be sung by Julie Arel, Pierre Calvé, Christine Charbonneau, Renée *Claude ('Tu es noire'), Emmanuelle, Louise *Forestier, Claude *Gauthier, Pauline *Julien ('Insomnie blues'), Félix *Leclerc, Monique *Leyrac, the Ménestrels, and others. Dompierre also composed film music, notably for *Délivrez-nous du mal, O.K. Laliberté, Ixe 13, Tiens-toi bien après les oreilles à papa, Yul 871* (the last in collaboration with Stéphane *Venne), and for the official Quebec film for Expo 70 in Osaka. He also composed the musical comedy *Demain matin Montréal m'attend* (with text by Michel Tremblay), and numerous commercials, one of which won him the Prix de Coq d'or in 1975. His *Sonate* for ondes Martenot and piano was premiered in 1974 and recorded by the ondist Sylvette Allard and the pianist Théodore Parasquive (Dompierre 80198). In 1975 he made the LP *Dompierre* (Dompierre 80212-213 and Philips 6311 190), devoted to his instrumental compositions, including *Ballade pour Violaine, La Chasse-Galerie, Ragtime pour plus tard,* and *Saute-Mouton.* He also organized and directed Bach concertos with soloists at *Le Patriote in 1975 and at the *PDA in 1976.

During 1976–7, a year of work and study in Paris, he composed *Harmonica Flash* for harmonica and orchestra for Claude Garden. The work was premiered in Vancouver in January 1978. On the CBC TV special program 'Dompierre,' 25 Dec 1978, he conducted the *MSO, the solo pianist Édith Boivin-Béluse, and the pop instrumentalists Jean-Marie Benoît (guitar), Michel *Donato (bass guitar), André Proulx (violin), and Richard Provençal (drums) in the premiere of his *Concerto in A.* The concerto and *Harmonica Flash* – both of which had been commissioned by the CBC – were recorded in 1979 for Deutsche Grammophon by the same soloists and the MSO conducted by Charles Dutoit. 'Although it is in classical form with the three movements and the traditional construction,' explained the author speaking of his *Concerto*, 'all the themes are drawn from the source of the popular music of our North American culture' (*Ici Radio-Canada*, 23–9 Dec 1978). He also wrote *Les Diableries*, the required piece for the 1979 *Montreal International Competition (violin). Dompierre told a *Variations* interviewer: 'I do not limit myself. I agree with the idea of breaking down divisions between styles. The great variety in means of communication in our age forces us to create for all media.' He made the arrangements and composed the music for several songs on Félix Leclerc's LPs *Mon Fils* and *Le Tour de l'Île* and for the Leclerc retrospective LP (1979).

In 1967 Dompierre founded Productions François Dompierre Inc, and in 1977 he collaborated with Intermède Québec in establishing Publications Chant de mon pays, Inc, which publishes the compositions of Quebec chansonniers and the composers Gaston *Brisson, André *Gagnon, Gaston Rochon, and Gilles *Vigneault. Dompierre is a member of CAPAC.

BIBLIOGRAPHY
''Interview: how to make your own album and succeed by really trying,' *CanComp*, 102, Jun 1975
Vézina, Marie-Odile. 'Le succès d'un travailleur de l'ombre,' Montreal *Dimanche-Matin*, 25 Jan 1976
Taschereau, Yves. 'Dompierre, créateur polyvalent,' *Variations*, vol 3, Sep–Oct 1979
Vallerand, François. 'Francois Dompierre,' *Séquences*, 100, Apr 1980
Petrowski, Nathalie. 'A Montreal writer seaks a pop audience for his symphonic music compositions,' *CanComp*, 154, Oct 1980

(MF)

DONALDA, Pauline (b Lightstone, m Seveilhac, m Léon). Soprano, teacher, administrator, b Montreal 5 Mar 1882, d there 22 Oct 1970; hon D MUS (McGill) 1954. Her parents were Jews from Russia and Poland who changed their name from Lichtenstein to Lightstone. She attracted attention as a child because of the quality of her voice, and studied on scholarship with Clara *Lichtenstein (no relation) at the Royal Victoria College. In 1902, before allowing her to go to Europe, her father insisted on having New York experts confirm her talent. Walter Damrosch refused to hear her, but the French tenor Thomas Salignac encouraged her warmly. That year she went to Paris on a grant from Donald Smith, Lord *Strathcona, and studied voice with Edmond Duvernoy, stage techniques with Paul Lhérie, speech with Pierre Berton, and Italian with Babette Rosen. In honour of her benefactor she adopted the stage-name Donalda. She auditioned for the title role in Massenet's *Chérubin* but lost it to Mary Garden. With Massenet's help, however, she made her debut 30 Dec 1904 in Nice, singing Manon. She was equally successful in the roles of Marguerite, Micaela, and Mimi. Leoncavallo was in Nice for the French premiere of *Chatterton*, in which Donalda sang Jenny, and subsequently, under his direction, she sang Nedda in *I Pagliacci*.

She made her London debut 24 May 1905 at Covent Garden, singing Micaela with Emmy Destinn and Charles Dalmorès, under the direction of André Messager. On 28 June she sang Ah-Joe in the premiere of Franco Leoni's *L'Oracolo*, with Dalmorès, Scotti, and Vanni-Marcoux as partners. Considered a rival of Melba, she often replaced her and thus sang Mimi with Enrico Caruso. Her success continued in the roles of Juliette and Zerlina. She sang Marguerite in the 1905 production of *Faust* at Covent Garden, and the French baritone Paul Seveilhac, who was to become her husband in May of the following year, was one of the cast. In the autumn of 1905 she sang Marguerite and

Pauline Donalda as Carmen

Mimi at the Théâtre de la Monnaie in Brussels, but afterwards, on medical advice, she went to the south of France for six months' rest. She returned to Brussels in March to sing Manon; later she also sang Elsa (*Lohengrin*) and Eva (*Die Meistersinger*), demonstrating her competence in these Wagnerian roles.

After the 1906 season in London, she sang again in Brussels but broke her contract and paid a fine in order to accept an offer from Oscar Hammerstein's Manhattan Opera Company. Before going to New York she made her professional debut in Canada, 16 Nov 1906, singing with her husband at a recital in the *Montreal Arena. She made her New York debut 7 Dec 1906 in *Faust* and sang in *Carmen, Martha, Don Giovanni, La Traviata, Lohengrin, and I Pagliacci* in the course of a historic season which brought together Melba, Calvé, Bonci, Ancona, Sammarco, Renaud, and Gilibert. Exhausted by the heavy season, and disappointed when offers she had expected from the Metropolitan and the Teatro Colon in Buenos Aires did not materialize, she left Hammerstein. She sang at Covent Garden during the summer of 1907 and made her debut at the Opéra-Comique in Paris 19 October singing in *Manon* with Salignac, Périer, and Fugère, and in *La Bohème* and *La Traviata*. She then divided her time between London and Paris and made concert tours which took her through Central Europe, and to Russia in 1910. She became a renowned performer of oratorio and gave concerts with the great performers of the day, including Elman, Kreisler, Paderewski, Zimbalist, Kubelik and Casals, and with many distinguished conductors, including Hans Richter and Sir Landon Ronald.

After a short visit to Canada in the spring of 1910, she opened the Covent Garden season, replacing Luisa Tetrazzini on short notice in *La Traviata* with McCormack and Sammarco. She returned for the 1912 season, singing the Page in *Les Huguenots* and Nedda in *I Pagliacci*, with her husband – now a tenor – as Canio. After being coached by Marie Roze, the famous Carmen, she recreated that role in November 1913 in an English-language version. She had a huge success with it and sang it in French in Nice in February 1914, also performing in *La Bohème*.

She was in Canada that July prior to an intended departure for a concert tour of Australia. When World War I broke out and the tour was cancelled she decided to stay in Canada, pursuing her career in concerts and even in the music-hall, often giving benefit appearances for the war effort or charity. In 1915 she organized the Donalda Sunday Afternoon Concerts in Montreal, and she also sang in New York and Boston. She returned to Paris in 1917. Her first marriage having ended in divorce, she married the Danish tenor Mischa Léon (b Haurowitz) in June 1918 in Paris. She sang with him that year in Balfe's *Le Talisman* in Nice. Covent Garden reopened in 1919, but this was her last season in this theatre. On 24 July she sang Concepcion in the English premiere of Ravel's *L'Heure espagnole*, a performance given 17 curtain calls. She began to devote herself to teaching, opening a studio in Paris in 1922. A member of the Assn professionnelle des maîtres du chant français, she taught hundreds of pupils before returning to Montreal in 1937 and opening a studio there. She founded the *Opera Guild in 1942 and directed it until 1969, presenting 29 operas, including several Canadian premieres, in 28 seasons. Some of her pupils had international careers, notably Clarice *Carson, Fernande *Chiocchio, Mary *Henderson, Eileen *Law, Germain *Lefebvre, and Robert *Savoie. She received an hon D MUS from *McGill U in 1954, the 50th anniversary of her debut, and in 1967 she was made an Officer of the *Order of Canada. During her relatively short performing career, Pauline Donalda was recognized for the purity of her exceptional voice and for her musicality, fine diction, and incomparable stage presence. Her name should be remembered also, however, for the unfailing energy with which she promoted opera in Montreal and encouraged talented young Canadian singers. Some of her personal papers were left to the *NL of C, and her music library and some 200 letters were left to McGill U. Her nine recordings include one (1914) of an unpublished aria from *Manon* and one (ca 1916) of the card scene from *Carmen*, both made for Emerson in the USA. Seven made in London in 1907 and 1908 for G & T were reissued in 1967 (Rococo 5255) with a short introduction by the singer. They are 'Vedrai carino' from *Don Giovanni*, 'Balatella' from *I Pagliacci*, 'Mi chiamano Mimi' from *La Bohème*, 'Air des bijoux' from *Faust*, Tosti's 'Love's Way,' Wynne's 'Who Can Tell Me?,' and Hahn's 'Si mes vers avaient des ailes.'

WRITINGS

'A Jewish singer's career,' *Canadian Jewish Year Book*, vol 2, 1940–1

BIBLIOGRAPHY

Northcott, Richard. *Covent Garden and the Royal Opera* (London 1924)
Issue devoted to Donalda, *Record Collector*, vol 10, Nov 1956
Cone, John F. *Oscar Hammerstein's Manhattan Opera* (Norman, Okla 1966)
Guttman, Irving. 'Pauline Donalda: a memorial tribute,' *OpCan*, Dec 1970
Salès, Jules. *Théâtre de la Monnaie* (Brussels 1971)
Brotman, Ruth C. *Pauline Donalda* (Montreal 1975)
Musiciennes de chez nous
Musiciens canadiens

GP

DONATO, Michel (André). Bassist, b Montreal 25 Aug 1942. His father, Roland, was a saxophonist. The younger Donato studied 1960–3 at the *CMM and was a member in the mid-1960s of the *MSO and a CBC Montreal chamber orchestra. Until 1969 he worked in Montreal clubs and in concerts with the jazzmen Nick *Ayoub, Brian *Barley, Lee *Gagnon, Sonny *Greenwich, Pierre *Leduc, Ron Proby, and others, and with the singers Charles Aznavour, Jacques Brel, and Carmen McRae. He then moved to Toronto, playing there in studio orchestras and in the groups of Lenny *Breau, Claude *Ranger, and others. He toured the world 1972–3 as a member of Oscar *Peterson's trio and also played frequently at the Toronto nightclub Bourbon Street with the pianists Carol Britto or Bernie *Senensky, accompanying such leading US jazz musicians as Benny Carter, Al Cohn, Milt Jackson, Don Menza, Blue Mitchell, and Zoot Sims. In 1977 he returned to Montreal and has worked there with Bill Evans and others. Donato has recorded with Ayoub, Bruce *Cockburn, Gordie Fleming, Gagnon, Greenwich, Leduc, Armas *Maiste, Pierre Nadeau, the US saxophonist Gerry Niewood (*Timepiece*, 1976, Horizon 719), Senensky, Herb *Spanier, Don *Thompson, and others. Considered one of the finest jazz bassists in the world, Donato was praised by Barry Tepperman (*Coda*, May 1974) for 'a graceful, open power, one of the most attractively rich bass sounds in existence, and an impish sense of humour.' MM

Don Messer and His Islanders. See Messer.

DONNELL, Robert. Carillonneur, composer, b Toronto ca 1910. He studied in Guelph, Ont (where he became carillonneur at the Cutten Memorial Carillon in 1926), at the *TCM, and with Jack Skillicorn on the *Hart House carillon. After studies 1934–6 with Percival *Price (Dominion Carillonneur at the Peace Tower on Parliament Hill, Ottawa), he became Price's assistant in 1936, then attended the Beiaardschool te Mechelen (Royal Flemish Carillon School) in Belgium. He graduated in 1938 and succeeded Price as Dominion Carillonneur in 1939. He later studied composition and orchestration with Bernard Wagenaar at the Juilliard Graduate School in New York. During World War II Donnell served in the RCAF as a music arranger and consultant. He was musical adviser 1946–9 and president 1950–2 of the *Guild of Carillonneurs in North America, and he has performed on instruments in North America, Australia, New Zealand, and Europe. In 1975 he retired as Dominion Carillonneur and became the official carillonneur at the Rainbow Tower in Niagara Falls, Ont. Donnell's compositions include Canada's official citizenship song 'This Canada of Ours' (Thompson 1947) and many other works and carillon arrangements for his own performance.

BIBLIOGRAPHY

Shackleton, Philip. 'Young man in a belfry,' *SatN*, 10 Jan 1950
Stephenson, Bill. 'Crash Bang Boom: the masterful touch,' *The Canadian*, 4 Mar 1967

FMB

Don Wright Chorus (CFPL Chorus until 31 Dec 1948). A 14-voice mixed choir formed in 1947 and conducted by Don *Wright at the London, Ont, radio station CFPL. Its Sunday evening broadcasts of popular and light classical music on the CBC Dominion Network 1947–56 and simultaneously in the USA 1949–50 on the Mutual network and 1955–6 on the NBC network brought the chorus considerable fame. Wright then organized the Don Wright Singers (1957–62) in Toronto for TV performances.

BIBLIOGRAPHY

Frayne, Trent. 'Neighbours who sing for Canada,' *Maclean's*, 1 Mar 1950

DOR, Georges (Henri) (b Dore). Singer-songwriter, author, b Drummondville, Que 10 Mar 1931. He worked 1948–52 in a factory, 1952–7 for private radio stations, and 1957–67 at CBC Montreal as an announcer, a news editor, and a producer. In 1954 he began to publish his poetry, novels, and plays. His song 'La Manic' brought him considerable popularity and marked his debut as a chansonnier in 1967. It was included on his first LP, *Georges Dor* (Gamma GS 108). 'Chanson pour ma femme' and 'Pour la musique' also became very popular. He won the Prix Félix-Leclerc at the 1968 Festival du disque in Montreal.

Dor gave recitals at the Comédie-Canadienne in 1968 and 1969 and at the Théâtre Port-Royal (*PDA) in 1970 and also performed at the boîte à chansons La Butte à Mathieu in Val-David (north of Montreal) and at the Art Centre in Percé. He has toured Quebec frequently and has sung in Ottawa, Toronto (1972), Vancouver, and Winnipeg. He made four other LPs for Gamma, including *Mes Ormes dans la plaine* (1968, GS 113) and *Georges Dor entre autres ...* (1969, GS 122). About 1972 he gave up his stage career but continued to record and began writing lyrics for music of the pianist Robert Séguin. Dor's later recordings include *Georges Dor au ralenti* (1972, Sillon DS-500), *Amour* (1974, Sillon DS-501), *Maudit Pays* (1975, Deram XDEF 108), *Fidélité* (1976, Sillon DS-502), and *Georges Dor chante encore* (1978, Solo 255-12). Gamma also released *Les Grands Succès de Georges Dor* (G2-1002), and Dor re-recorded some of the same songs for RCI (LPs 360 and 361). Pauline *Julien, Catherine Sauvage, and others have recorded his songs. François Cousineau, Gaston *Brisson, and Jean-Claude Tremblay have served in turn as his music director. Pierrette Robitaille wrote of him in *The Canadian Composer*: 'As a chansonnier, Georges Dor sings of tenderness, intimacy and everyday life. You have only to listen to his love songs to sense the attachment to a woman, the faithfulness in love ... He's also a philosopher who knows full well the heart and soul of Quebec, her touching failings and her enduring qualities.' Dor was the owner 1971–7 of an art gallery in Longueuil (a Montreal suburb) and in 1976 founded an arts centre and the Théâtre des ancêtres in St-Germain-de-Grantham, Que. He is a member of CAPAC.

BIBLIOGRAPHY
Gingras, Claude. 'To me, the lyrics themselves are music,' *CanComp*, 28, Apr 1968
Brien, Lucien. 'Georges Dor,' *CanComp*, 40, May 1969
Robitaille, Pierrette. 'This Quebec lyricist has found serenity,' *CanComp*, 68, Mar 1972 HPn (ST)

DORICE, Danièle (b Dorice Angers, m Skerczak). Singer, b Quebec City 23 Jul 1935. After singing in Quebec City cabarets, she placed second in the Miss Canada competition in 1957, winning a trip to London. She performed there, then toured for several years in Europe, South America, and the Far East. On her return to Canada in 1963 she performed in several cabarets and hotels, then went abroad again for a tour of 11 countries, including the USA, France, and Japan. In 1965 she made the first of many tours for the CBC, visiting stations of the Canadian armed forces in Cyprus, Egypt, and elsewhere; her seventh took place in March 1967. She was hostess for the weekly TV programs 'Comment allez-vous' (CBC, 1966–7) and 'Le Caf' Conc'' (CFCF-TV, broadcast 1969–70 on the CTV national network) and made guest appearances on several others, particularly on CBC and Télé-Métropole, Montreal. She appeared on several US TV programs, notably in 1969 and 1970, when she also performed at the St Regis Hotel in New York. She sings in nine languages, and her programs offer a variety of songs as well as imitations and comedy. 'As the situation requires it, Danièle Dorice is tender, gay or sad. Then she displays infectious energy for "Step to the Rear." Mlle Dorice becomes a whole parade in herself' (*Le Droit*, 3 Feb 1968). Les Productions Danièle Dorice Inc, a booking agency founded in 1971 in Candiac, a Montreal suburb, also established in 1974 a school where Dorice began teaching voice, dance, and staging to aspiring entertainers. In 1978 the school had 250 pupils. In the 1970s Dorice herself has concentrated on convention work and cruises. She made the LP *Danièle Dorice, la joie de vivre* (1971 Astra AS-1002) with an orchestra conducted by Nat Raider, as well as some 45s. She is the sister of Denyse *Angé and of the drummer Georges Angers, who was her music director 1972–8. CV

Double-bass (contrabass, string bass, bass viol). The largest viol and the largest bowed-string instrument. This article discusses the role of the double-bass in music in Canada.

In her book *Old-time Primitive Methodism in Canada (1829–1884)* (Toronto 1894), Mrs R.F. Hopper reiterates the commonly held belief that the fiddle was regarded as 'the devil's instrument to snare the young into the dance; but a bass viol was not in the same category because consecrated to the service of God.' The double-bass therefore was a favourite instrument to accompany hymn singing in 19th-century parish churches, but it did not come into general secular use until late in that century, when orchestras and larger performing ensembles began to be organized. Many double-bass players began by studying other instruments, developed proficiency on the string bass only later in their careers, and were self-taught. Some doubled as tuba players; several in fact have been bandmasters. Bass players active in Quebec and Montreal in the late 19th and early 20th centuries included Joseph-Arthur *Boucher, T.-O. *Dionne, C. Hardelin, and Léon Wathieu. In Calgary in the late 19th century Mrs C.W. McMillan and George Mitchell played bass in early orchestral ensembles.

In the 20th century in Canada double-bass players and teachers of note have been members of orchestras – symphony, theatre, radio, and chamber – throughout the country. In Vancouver Harold Perkins, F.W. Poole, and later J.P. 'Doc' *Hamilton and Kenneth Friedman were leading bassists. James Mackay, originally a tuba player, studied bass with Sydney D. Wells of Toronto and was principal bass with the *Victoria SO 1945–68 and a member of the *Vancouver SO 1968–78. Stanley H. Allen and Sidney Doe, English-born sons of bass players, studied with their fathers, J.J. Allen and Alfred Doe. They settled in Winnipeg in the early 20th century, were members of various Winnipeg orchestras and chamber groups, and taught there. Winnipeg-born Jack Drewrys and Paul Olynyk were violinists who became bass players during the 1930s. In Toronto Charles Greenwood and L.S. 'Puff' *Addison played in the *Welsman *TSO and in the later TSO. Other Toronto bass players and teachers were Robert Cochrane, Charles Rose, and Gurney Titmarsh. The latter, who played in the TSO and the *CBC SO was a tuba player who had studied the string bass with Rose and Cochrane. Sydney D. Wells, a member of the TSO and its principal 1942–61, was a noted teacher. Cameron McKay, Reginald Wood, Sam Levine, and Sam Davis (who studied with Alfred Doe and Harold Perkins) played in the TSO. Thomas *Monohan who became principal of the TS in 1966, has given solo recitals and has become known widely as a teacher. His pupils, including Peter Madgett and Jane McAdam of the TS and David *Young of the *Hamilton Philharmonic, have taken positions in orchestras throughout Canada. William *Kuinka, a pupil of Ray Brown and Fred Zimmerman, has been a member of several Toronto orchestras and also played with the Hamilton Philharmonic. In Montreal the Hardy brothers, Charles, Gaston, and Joseph, played in various orchestras after the turn of the century. Charles was principal of the *Montreal Orchestra and of the *CSM for many years. Players in the *MSO have included Nathalie Clair-Feldman, Jacques Beaudoin, and more recently Dennis James and Michael Leiter. Roger *Charbonneau (principal of the MSO 1953–63), who studied with Léon Wathieu, has taught string bass at both the *CMM and *CMQ. Rénald St-Pierre (principal of the *Quebec SO) and Roland Desjardins of the MSO were among his pupils. Gertrude Probyn, an original member of the Montreal Orchestra (founded 1930), was also principal double-bass of the *Montreal Women's SO. Ruth Ross Budd, who studied in Winnipeg and Vancouver, was a member of the Vancouver SO and of the TSO 1947–52 and rejoined the TSO in 1964. Alan Molitz, the original principal of the *NACO, retained the position in 1980.

Few bassists in Canada have made solo careers. Notable among those who have are the US-born Gary *Karr, who lived in Halifax and performed widely 1972–7, and Joel Quarrington (b Toronto 1955), a pupil of Peter Madgett and Thomas Monohan in Toronto and Francesco Petracchi in Rome. Quarrington won first prize in the 1976 *CBC Talent Festival and second prize (no first awarded) in the 1978 Geneva International Competition for Musical Performers. A member of the *Chamber Players of Toronto 1974–7, Quarrington also has appeared as guest artist with other Canadian orchestras and toured for the *JMC in 1979. He became principal bass of the Hamilton Philharmonic in 1979.

A few works for double-bass have been composed by Canadians, eg, *Baker's *Contours*, *Brott's *Profundum praedictum* (written for and recorded by Gary Karr), *Weinzweig's *Refrains*, and Vancouver SO double-bassist Frederick Schipizky's *Recitative* and *Theme and Variations*, the latter work premiered in 1973 by Gary Karr and Harmon Lewis. (Schipizky was a pupil of Ken Friedman.) Thomas Monohan has composed *Melodic Studies for the Double-Bass* (Harris 1973), and in 1973 he commissioned *Buczynski's *Duo* for double-bass and piano.

In Canada, as in the USA, early jazz and dance bands employed the 'brass bass' (tuba) until the late 1920s, and many double-bassists (eg, the aforementioned Gurney Titmarsh) began as tuba players. (See also Brass.) The double-bass was the mainstay of jazz, dance, and (beginning in the late 1920s) country bands, until the rise of the bass guitar in the 1960s. (See also Guitar.) Only in jazz has the double-bass remained in wide use, and by the late 1960s most jazz bassists also played bass guitar.

Canadian jazz players who achieved international reputations in the 1970s were Michel *Donato and Don *Thompson. Others of note include Stan Johnson, Torben Oxbol, and Paul Ruhland of Vancouver; Lenny Boyd, Carne Bray, Bill Britto, David Field, Terry Forster, Richard *Homme, Jack Lander, Jim *McHarg, Bob Price, Doug Willson, and David *Young of Toronto (Boyd and Lander were also prominent as teachers); and Vic Angelillo, Charles Biddle, Don Habib, Neil Michaud, and Bob Rudd of Montreal. Of economic necessity jazz bassists have been versatile musicians. The leading players usually have been among the elite of studio musicians in their respective cities. Others have worked in commercial or pop contexts (eg, dance bands, lounge groups), and some (Donato, Tom Haslett, Jack McFadden, Ruhland, and Young) have played in symphony or chamber orchestras. Some symphony musicians, in turn, have played jazz, including Sam Levine and J.P. 'Doc' Hamilton. Several Canadian-born bassists have worked successfully abroad, among them Lloyd Thompson in Europe and Hal Gaylor, Al Lucas, and Bob Rudd in the USA. (See also Jazz.) Younger Canadian players of promise in the mid-1970s included Scott Alexander (Ottawa), David Piltch and Steven Wallace (Toronto), and Neil Swainson (Vancouver-Toronto). (MM, NM, GP)

DOUCET, Roger. Tenor, b Montreal 21 Apr 1919. As a boy, he sang at the Immaculée-Conception Church. The choir director, Émile Fontaine, gave him his first music lessons 1929–33 at the École St-François-Xavier. He studied voice 1938–40 with Céline *Marier and Georges Toupin, 1940–1 with Sarah *Fischer, and 1941–3 with Albertine *Morin-Labrecque and participated during this time in amateur competitions, notably 'Nos Talents locaux' on CHLP radio. This led to engagements in several Montreal cabarets, including the Faisan bleu, the Casino Bellevue, and the Montmartre. Doucet later became a member of *The *Army Show*, with which he toured Canada twice and visited several European countries. He left the army with the rank of sergeant and on his re-establishment allowance from the Department of Veterans' Affairs studied 1946–9 with Alfredo Martino at the New York College of Music.

Doucet continued his career in cabarets and on radio, taking part in the CBC opera broadcasts called 'Théâtre lyrique Molson.' On CBC TV's 'L'*Heure du concert' he sang in excerpts from various operas, including *The Barber of Seville* (Count Almaviva), *Les Pêcheurs de perles* (Nadir), and *Roméo et Juliette* (Roméo). In 1960 he sang the Chaplain in *Les Dialogues des Carmélites*. For the *COC he was the Duke in *Rigoletto* (1950), the Prince in *The Love of Three Oranges* (1959), and Fenton in Nicolai's *The Merry Wives of Windsor* (touring production, 1960). In 1953 he sang Otello with the Civic Grand Opera of Philadelphia and the leading tenor roles in *The Magic Flute*, *La Traviata*, and *La Bohème* with the New York Opera Caravan. During a European sojourn 1955–7, he sang in *Le Comte Ory* at the Glyndebourne Festival and broadcast for the BBC in London and for the NDR in Hamburg. In Germany he studied with Dr Schmidt di Giorgi and recorded for Decca. On his return he continued his career in cabarets, on radio and TV, in Montreal's major hotels and restaurants (Au Lutin qui bouffe 1965–72 and Vita beginning in 1973), and elsewhere in Canada and in the USA, singing popular songs, musical comedy excerpts, and opera and operetta arias. In 1971 he was appointed to sing 'O Canada' at televised hockey games in the Montreal *Forum. He began doing the same for the Alouettes' football games in 1974 and the Expos' baseball games in 1977. In this capacity, he has been invited to the USA for special ceremonies, birthday celebrations, and all star sports games. In 1980 he was made a Member of the *Order of Canada.

DISCOGRAPHY

Bakaleinikov *Habe Mitleid mit mir* – Schröder-Schween *Ein Glück, dass man sich so verlieben kann*. Str orch, R. Müller cond. 1956. Decca Teldec F46300

Cette nuit ... mon amour. 1962. RCA Victor LCP-1057

Lopez-Woezel *Santa Maria* – Götz-Hellmer *Mein ganzes Leben*. 1956. Decca Teldec F46193 (78 rpm)

Roger Doucet Songs of Glory / Roger Doucet Chants glorieux: national songs and hymns. 1976. Aquarius AQE-612/Aquarius AQE-613

BIBLIOGRAPHY

Burke, Tim. 'One nation from sea to sea, tone of Roger's O Canada,' Montreal *Gazette*, 11 Sep 1975

Curran, Pat. 'To Canada with love,' *Montreal Star*, 4 Nov 1975

Bruce, Marian. 'O Canada: it still gives Doucet butterflies every time,' Montreal *Gazette*, 23 Sep 1977

Rodriguez, Juan. ' "Belter" Doucet started in the church choir,' ibid, 29 May 1978

Collie, Ashley. 'What would hockey night be without Roger Doucet?' *Maclean's*, 21 May 1979 ST

DOUGLAS, Beth (Martha Elizabeth). Educator, choir conductor, b Winnipeg 28 Apr 1913; BA (Manitoba) 1959, B ED (Manitoba) 1964. After teaching music 1943–56 at the Manitoba Teachers' College, she was assistant director of music 1956–75 in Winnipeg schools and a member 1975–6 of the faculty of education, *U of Manitoba. She became music consultant to the Winnipeg school board in 1976. With Lola Smith *MacQuarrie she prepared the elementary school music texts *Melody Makers* (two volumes), *Treasure Tunes*, and *Happy Harmonies* (Toronto 1959, 1961, 1965). With Glen *Harrison and Colin Walley she wrote the junior high school texts *Fanfare Act I* and *Act II* (Toronto 1968, 1970). For many years she has been active in Manitoba *school music broadcasts. She was conductor 1940–62 of the Winnipeg Boys' Choir (initially, 1940–3, co-conductor with Ethel *Kinley) and has been choir director at Bethesda College for over 30 years and director of the Vivace Ladies Choir. (RG)

DOUGLAS, William. Composer, bassoonist, pianist, teacher, b London, Ont, 7 Nov 1944; B MUS (Toronto) 1966. He studied bassoon with Nicholas *Kilburn at the *U of Toronto. A Woodrow Wilson Fellowship enabled him to study with Robert Bloom (bassoon) and Mel Powell (composition) at Yale U. In 1969 at Tanglewood he received a Margaret M. Grant Award for his *String Quartet* (1968). On a *Canada Council grant he studied 1969–70 in England. In 1970 he began teaching bassoon, composition, and piano at the California Institute of the Arts. Most of his works are for chamber ensemble, including *Improvisations III* (1969) for clarinet and piano and *Vajra* (1972) for any combination of instruments. Both works are recorded by Orion (ORS 73125), and the former is recorded by the CBC (RCI358). In the summer of 1976 Douglas toured as bassoonist with Peter Serkin's group, Tashi, and with the group recorded the piano and wind quintets of Beethoven and the Stravinsky Septet for RCA. In 1976–7 he toured the USA and Canada as pianist with the clarinetist Richard Stoltzman.

Doukhobors. Fundamentalist Christian sect of Russian origin. The tenets of the Doukhobors' simple faith held them apart from what they considered the idolatry, opulence, and corruption of the Russian Orthodox Church. Although the epithet Doukhobortsi (Spirit-Wrestlers) was applied to them by the church in the 18th century, many of their beliefs derive from sectarian traditions centuries older. As heretics, they were banished at various periods to distant parts of the Russian Empire, where they invariably flourished as a result of their diligence and agrarian skills. During some periods they were left relatively unmolested, but the persecutions reached such a pitch in the 1890s under Tsar Nicholas II that many decided to emigrate. Arriving in Canada in 1899, 7500 settled on the Prairies and built more than 60 communal villages in the area north of Yorkton, Sask. Internal dissension and disputes with government officials over land regulations led to a second migration beginning in 1908. Their traditional leader, Peter V. Verigin, brought many of his followers to the interior valleys of British Columbia to establish new Christian communes. Factionalism eventually split Doukhoborism into three groups: the Independents, who remained largely on the Prairies to farm individually; the moderate Union of Spiritual Communities of Christ (orthodox Doukhobors from the Verigin tradition); and the more militant Sons of Freedom. A zealot fringe of the latter group was responsible for the activities (arson, bombings, nude demonstrations) reported so sensationally

Doukhobor Singers, Grand Forks, BC, 1963

in the news media. As a result, the vast majority of peaceable, innocent Doukhobors from all groups were linked in the public mind with these radical acts. However, by the mid-1970s, as the old traditions and enmities declined, a new spirit of co-operation became manifest. Younger, educated Doukhobors, working in collaboration with sympathetic elders, sought wider application of the traditional Doukhobor beliefs and modes of conduct that had worked so well in isolated communes.

Traditional Doukhobor music is exclusively vocal. The vast literature of religious precepts, known as the Book of Life, was passed on orally from generation to generation by the choral singing of the whole community. Congregational singing of the sacred texts was, in effect, the auditory manifestation of the life-style of the Christian commune. No hymnbooks or musical notation were used. The intricacies of contrapuntal and harmonic singing were passed on with the same degree of mnemonic virtuosity as the texts.

The oldest stratum of music is found in the psalms. The texts are continuous and non-metrical. Some were composed by the Doukhobors themselves, while others were inherited or adapted from earlier texts. Staggered breathing is used quite unconsciously to produce a continuous flow of sound. The tempo is slow, the melismatic style very pronounced. In one psalm, 'The Singing of Psalms Beautifies Our Souls,' it takes almost 10 minutes to sing the first five words. In Canada only the first five words of these psalms are sung; the rest is recited. One or two psalms are monodic, but most display a primitive type of counterpoint somewhat similar to early Russian Orthodox Church polyphony. More research remains to be done, but it seems likely that the style of Doukhobor psalm singing is a polyphonic development of the znamenny chant. The znamenny chant, in turn, evolved from Byzantine chants of the sixth, seventh, and eighth centuries.

The more recent corpus of religious music comprises hymns of various types. These are metrical and set out in verses. A few early hymns are psalm-like but sung faster. Some have been borrowed from sects of similar persuasion – Molokans, Evangelical Christians, Mennonites, etc – but most are of Doukhobor origin. A sizeable group of hymns was composed in Canada, all in the old Russian style. The most prolific Doukhobor-Canadian poet and hymnist was John F. Sysoev. Doukhobor hymn singing is unlike the Western chorale style with its SATB voice spacing and the melody on top. In Doukhobor singing the melody is central, with ancillary counterpoint or harmony above and below. Over 500 hymns and psalms have survived in Canada.

Recreational music is drawn from Russian folksong tradition. Folksongs are sung in a variety of formats: choral, solo, duet, trio, quartet. Improvised part-singing is a highly developed faculty among Doukhobors. Examples of many religious and folksong genres are found in Kenneth *Peacock's *Songs of the Doukhobors* (National Museum of Man, Ottawa 1970, four recordings enclosed).

BIBLIOGRAPHY

Woodcock, George, and Avakumovic, Ivan. *The Doukhobors* (Toronto 1968)

Martens, Helen. 'The music of some religious minorities in Canada,' *Ethnomusicology*, vol 16, Sep 1972

Tarasoff, Koozma J. *Traditional Doukhobor Folkways* (Ottawa 1977) KP

'D'où viens-tu bergère?' Christmas carol in the form of a dialogue between a shepherdess who describes the scene of the Nativity (verse) and a throng which plies her with questions (chorus). Known in several European countries, it was brought to Canada in the 17th century and became a perennial favourite. William McLennan published an English version in *Songs of Old Canada* (Montreal 1886). François *Brassard, in *Les Archives du folklore*, vol 3 (Montreal 1948), quotes four versions, all differing from the familiar one included by Ernest *Gagnon in his *Chansons populaires du Canada* (Quebec City 1865). According to Gagnon the song was not sung in the church of his day. Among the first recordings were those on Victor 78s by Éva *Gauthier and by Charles *Marchand and his Bytown Troubadours. Many others have recorded it, including Hélène *Baillargeon with Alan *Mills, the *Montreal Bach Choir, the *Festival Singers (Hallmark CH 4), Jacques *Labrecque, Monique *Miville-Deschênes (Gamma GS 135), the *Petits Chanteurs de Granby, and the *Alouette Vocal Quartet. Émilien *Allard recorded it on the carillon of St-Joseph's Oratory in Montreal. Hector *Gratton arranged it for voice and strings, and *Le Passe-Temps* (December 1945) published another arrangement (for voice and piano) by Alfred *Laliberté. Sir Ernest *MacMillan made an arrangement for piano duet.

BIBLIOGRAPHY

Myrand, Ernest. *Noëls anciens de la Nouvelle-France* (Quebec City 1899, Montreal 1913) HP

DOW, Jack (March). Educator, conductor, b Dutton, near London, Ont, 17 Jul 1912; BA (Western Ontario) 1936, MA (Montreal) 1950. After teaching school 1935–7 in Ottawa and 1937–46 in Toronto he was head 1946–58 of the music department at North Toronto Collegiate, where he established the first in-school program of instrumental music in Ontario. His bands, orchestras, and choirs won many festival awards. For 25 years he also taught vocal and instrumental music at the Ontario Dept of Education Summer School, and in 1958 he became assistant director of music for the Toronto Board of Education, where he established an instrumental music program in elementary schools. He became director in 1972 and retired in 1976. In 1970 he established the annual Toronto Music Camp at Lake Couchiching. He was made a Member of the *Order of Canada in 1979.

BIBLIOGRAPHY

'The spotlight ... on Jack M. Dow,' *Recorder*, vol 7, Jan–Mar 1966 WL

Downchild (or **Downchild Blues Band**). Toronto band, named for a Sonny Boy Williamson song, 'Mr. Downchild.' Formed as a quintet in 1969 by the lead and slide guitarist, harmonica player, and singer Don ('Mr. Downchild') Walsh (b 1947), the band has undergone many personnel changes, expanding at times to a septet; in addition to Walsh, the membership has included the singers Rick ('The Hock') Walsh or (in the mid-1970s when The Hock led his own band briefly) Tony Flaim, the pianist Jane Vasey, and various brass and reed players, bass guitarists, and drummers. Downchild began its career at Grossman's Tavern in Toronto and, although it continued to work extensively in southern Ontario bars, also toured several times in Canada and appeared in the USA. Dependent on the Chicago blues repertoire and respectful of that music's traditions, Downchild made one hit single, 'Flip, Flop and Fly' (1973), sung by The Hock, and the LPs *Bootleg* (1971, Special SS001), *Straight Up* (1973, GRT 9230-1029), *Dancing* (1974, GRT 9230-1049), *Ready to Go* (1975, GRT 9230-1060), and *We Deliver* (1979, Attic LAT 1085). An anthology, *So Far: A Collection of Our Best* (Posterity PTR 13004), was released in 1978. With The Hock's departure again in 1978 to form his own band, Downchild continued with Don Walsh (or later Tony Flaim) as lead singer and, in 1979, toured in the USA. The Hock appeared (winter 1978–9) at the Cameo Room, Hotel Isabella, Toronto.

DOWNES, (Rupert Arnold) Wray. Pianist, b Toronto 14 Jan 1931. He studied 1938–50 with Anne Scott-Mumford in Toronto, and in 1949 was the first Canadian to receive the British Empire (Overseas) Scholarship to the TCL. He studied there with Kinloch Anderson and at the Paris Cons with Lazare Lévy and Henri Lauth. After turning in 1952 from classical music to jazz, he studied with Dizzy Gillespie (harmony) in France and later with Oscar *Peterson (piano) and Neil *Chotem (composition) in Montreal, also attending Peterson's Advanced School of Contemporary Music in Toronto. Downes played until 1956 in France with such leading US and European jazzmen as Sidney Bechet, Buck Clayton, Bill Coleman, and Guy Lafitte, and 1956–9 in Montreal clubs and on CBC radio and TV.

Returning to Toronto in 1959, Downes began a long association with Peter *Appleyard, performing also with the saxophonist Don *Thompson and, as leader of the house band 1963–5 at the Town Tavern, with such visiting US players as Roy Eldridge, Coleman Hawkins, and Ben Webster. For CBC TV he was music director for 'Show on Shows' (1964, 1965) and 'The Umbrella' (1966) in Toronto, music co-ordinator for 'Music Hop' (1965) in Halifax, and music director for 'Segue' (1969) in Ottawa. He accompanied various singers (Joyce *Hahn, Catherine *McKinnon, and others) in hotels in Newfoundland and Ottawa, then lived 1971–2 in the USA before returning again to Toronto, where he resumed, 1972–4, his association with Appleyard. In 1976 he formed the Downes-Young Duo with the bassist David *Young (later adding the guitarist Ed *Bickert when possible). The duo has toured twice (1977, 1978) in western Canada, appeared in Toronto and Halifax nightclubs, and performed on CBC radio. Downes and Young complete the Pete Magadini–Rick *Wilkins Quartet. A vigorous player, with a technique based on bebop tempered by the influence of Oscar Peterson, Downes is among the most impressive jazz musicians in Canada. He appears on LPs by Appleyard, Coleman (*Jazz à Pleyel*, 1952, Phillips N76.006R) and Magadini (*Bones Blues*, 1977, Sack 4004), and on other recordings (made in Europe) by Sidney Bechet and Zutty Singleton. MM

DOYLE, Gerald S. (Stanley). Businessman, folksong collector, b King's Cove, Bonavista Bay, Nfld, 26 Sep 1892, d St John's, Nfld, 12 Jul 1956. With the benefit of wealth acquired as a manufacturer and distributor of drugs and patent medicines, Doyle sought to preserve and promote the cultural heritage of Newfoundland. Beloved by his fellow islanders, he was known especially for his company's sponsorship of radio news bulletins 1932–66 on VONF (later CBN), which included personal messages of interest to those living in isolated fishing villages. In 1943 Doyle financed the first recordings of Newfoundland songs – initially contemporary material by Arthur *Scammell and later, in 1948, traditional songs sung by the Commodore's Quartet. These recordings were broadcast in Newfoundland and in the Maritime provinces on Doyle's program. Doyle's publication and free distribution of *Old-Time Songs and Poetry of Newfoundland* was perhaps his most significant contribution to the perpetuation of the lore of his province. Appearing in five editions – the first in 1927 without music and others in 1940, 1955, 1966, and 1978 – the book consisted of material collected during Doyle's travels (by yacht) to the outports. Doyle confined his publication to native Newfoundland songs, causing Kenneth *Peacock to comment in the introduction to *Songs of the Newfoundland Outports* (Ottawa 1965), 'Though the value of his collection cannot be overestimated, its wide dissemination on the mainland has created the impression that Newfoundland folksongs consist entirely of locally-composed material.' Nevertheless, Peacock credits Doyle with being 'more responsible than anyone else for making the general public aware of Newfoundland songs.' Doyle was active in many other community enterprises. In 1944 he received the OBE.

See also Folk music, Anglo-Canadian 1 / Newfoundland. FH

DOYLE, Joseph Nevin. Journalist, organist, singer, composer, b Belleville, Ont, d there 1916. Little is known about his life, but in 1895 he was city editor of the Belleville *Sun*. His works include the music for the play or operetta *Cingalee*, the libretto and music for *The Golden Age*, and the comic opera *The Enchanted Garden*, work on which was interrupted by his death. *The Golden Age* was presented in Belleville and early in 1915 at the *Royal Alexandra Theatre in Toronto. The *Canadian Journal of Music* (Feb 1915) judged it a 'creditable and meritorious effort.'

BIBLIOGRAPHY

Toronto Public Libraries. Scrapbook 125

DOYON, Paul. Pianist, organist, b Montreal 26 Mar 1903; L MUS (École normale, Paris) 1926, hon D MUS (Montreal) 1957. At two he lost his sight, and in 1908 he entered the *Institut Nazareth, where he studied violin with Camille *Couture and J.-J. *Goulet, voice with Alfred *Lamoureux, and piano and organ with Arthur *Letondal. He was appointed organist in 1922 at Notre-Dame-de-Grâce Church in Montreal. He won the 1925 *Prix d'Europe for piano and went to Paris, studying 1925–7 and 1929–30 at the École normale. His teachers were Nadia Boulanger (harmony, counterpoint), Alfred Cortot (piano), Eugène Gigout and Louis Vierne (organ, improvisation), and Raymond Gilles and Charles Panzéra (voice). In 1937 he began having occasional lessons with Sigismond Stojowski in New York. Doyon played Franck's *Variations symphoniques* for the CSM in 1936 and 1940 and performed 1942–3 on radio stations in New York, Lewiston, Me, and Bridgeport, Conn. He was heard frequently 1937–47 on

CBC radio. In a 1950 *NFB film he explained how to read music in Braille. The following year, he toured Newfoundland and in 1956 he gave concerts and lectures in the USA. With the Detroit SO in 1957 he played Mozart's *Concerto in A*, K488, and gave the North-American premiere of Marcel Dupré's *Fantaisie* for piano and orchestra. In 1958 he inaugurated the organ of the church of Ste-Trinité in Dorion, Que, and in 1948, 1950, and 1959 he was a member of the jury for the Prix d'-Europe. He was the official delegate of the blind in Canada in Paris in 1952, at celebrations marking the centenary of the death of Louis Braille, and also in Rome in 1959. In 1969 he was invited to tour India, Japan, and Taiwan giving organ and piano concerts. Eugène *Lapierre wrote of Doyon, 13 Feb 1960 in the weekly *Notre Temps* 'The artist's musicality, in his performances on the piano, the organ or the violin, is always engaging, original and personal.' In 1950 Doyon became the first French-speaking Canadian to receive the Christian Culture Medal, granted each year by Assumption College (*U of Windsor) to an 'exceptional defender of Christian ideals.'

WRITINGS

'Réponse de Paul Doyon à son éloge fait par le recteur de l'Université,' Montreal *La Presse*, 16 Apr 1957

GG (HP)

DRAPEAU, (Jean-Baptiste) **Stanislas**. Printer, publisher, journalist, b St-Roch (later a part of Quebec City), 28 Jul 1821, d Pointe-Gatineau, Que, ? Feb 1893. He was a typographer 1837–8 in the printing shop of *Le Fantasque* founded by Napoléon *Aubin. Drapeau established a number of newspapers and periodicals himself before serving 1851–6 as editor of the *Journal de Québec*. He founded, and directed 1849–59, the choir of St-Jean Church and in 1854 he directed the Société musicale des amateurs de St-Jean. He published two works by T.F. *Molt: *La Lyre sainte, recueil de cantiques, hymnes, motets, etc.*, 2 vols (Quebec 1844, 1845) and *Traité élémentaire de musique vocale* (Quebec 1845). He also published numerous works on colonization and was the colonization agent 1859–65 in St-Jean-Port-Joli before moving to Ottawa. While working there in the Dept of Agriculture he founded and published the journals *Le Foyer domestique* (1876–9) and *L'Album des familles* (1880–4), both of which contained music, and *La Lyre d'or* (1888–9). In Ottawa he was director of the choir of Notre-Dame Basilica ca 1865–ca 1891.

BIBLIOGRAPHY

Thibault, Ch. *Biographie de Stanislas Drapeau* (Ottawa 1891)

GP (DM)

'Le Drapeau de Carillon: légende canadienne.' Voice-and-piano setting (1858) by Charles Wugk *Sabatier of four stanzas from a 32-stanza patriotic poem of the same title by Octave *Crémazie. Alfred *Paré, accompanied by Sabatier, gave the first performance 15 May 1858. The song commemorates the 100th anniversary of Montcalm's victory over the British troops at Fort Carillon (Ticonderoga, NY). It was published by J. & O. Crémazie (1858) and also in the third edition of *Le Chansonnier des collèges* (1860). Later editions and reprints testify to the popularity of the song. Joseph *Saucier recorded the song twice for HMV.

BIBLIOGRAPHY

Crémazie, Octave. *Oeuvres, I – Poésies*, ed Odette Condemine (Ottawa 1972)

Condemine, Odette. 'Le Drapeau de Carillon,' *Dictionnaire des oeuvres littéraires du Québec*, vol 1, ed Maurice Lemire (Montreal 1978)

W.R. Draper Co Ltd. Toronto lithographers, in the 1970s the largest music-printing establishment in Canada. The company was established around the turn of the century by William R. Draper (b ca 1861, d Toronto autumn 1921). A member of the *Queen's Own Rifles Band, Draper also, by 1892, was manager of the Toronto branch of the Philadelphia music publisher William F. Shaw & Co. In the late 1890s Draper was associated with the Verrall and Draper Music Publishing Co, which ca 1899 became the Draper Music Publishing Co. Draper also, ca 1898–1906, was managing director of the Canadian-American Music Co in Toronto. The combined publishing output of Draper and Canadian-American consisted of fewer than 100 songs, some of them Canadian. Printing always has been the Draper company's main activity, though Draper himself composed such items as the march *Boys of the Old Brigade* (Canadian-American 1903), the song 'Only You in Dreams' (Draper 1918) with violin obbligato, and the *Veteran's March* (Draper 1920). Some publications in the popular genre were 'printed for the composer' in the 1916–30 period by the company. The company was purchased in 1922, after Draper's death, by Frederick Cecil Madill and Robert Ewart Forsythe, and was transferred from its Pearl St quarters, moving through a succession of addresses to Dee Ave in Weston, Ont, in 1944. W.R. Draper claims to be the first music printer in North America to employ the offset process. In 1978, under the direction of Harald Madill, W.R. Draper Co had a staff of 10 and printed for such music publishers as Algord (*Whaley Royce), *Boosey & Hawkes, Frederick *Harris, *Jarman, E.C. *Kerby, and *Waterloo. HK (MM, PW)

DRECHSLER ADAMSON, Bertha (b Hamilton). Violinist, teacher, conductor, b Edinburgh 25 Mar 1848, d Toronto 12 May 1924. A relative of the noted cellists Louis and Karl Drechsler she first studied music with her father, Adam Hamilton, a pianist and organist who taught at the U of Edinburgh. She and her sister Emily studied violin in Leipzig with Ferdinand David for five years and played before German nobility. She performed extensively in the UK with her father's piano quartet, which included her sister and her brother Carl Hamilton, a cellist. On marrying in 1869 she moved to Canada, settling at first in Hamilton, then moving in 1871 to Toronto, where in 1877 she became a member of the original teaching staff at the *TCM. She conducted the Conservatory String Orchestra for many years, was the first violin 1901–4 of the Toronto Conservatory String Quartette, and played 1906–18 in the Conservatory Symphony Orchestra (after 1908, Frank *Welsman's *TSO). Her pupils included Harry *Adaskin, Frank *Blachford, Julia Choate, and her daughter Lina Drechsler Adamson (b Emily Caroline Adamson, Toronto 1876, d there 28 Feb 1960), who also studied 1904–5 in Leipzig with Hans Sitt and much later in Switzerland with André de Ribaupierre. Lina played with the Toronto Conservatory String Quartette (her mother was lead violin, Lena Hayes, later the wife of Leo *Smith, was viola, and first Henry S. Sanders then Lois Winslow, cello) and made her concert debut ca 1905 at *Massey Hall with the Conservatory String Orchestra under her mother's direction. Ca 1908 she formed the Toronto Ladies Trio with Eugénie Quéhen (piano) and Lois Winslow (cello). She taught violin at the *Peterborough Cons and at the TCM. She inherited her mother's strength and intelligence as a performer.

DROST, Herbert (Mason). Lawyer, choir conductor, music dealer, publisher, b Hartney, near Brandon, Man, 19 Nov 1892, d Vancouver 20 Jan 1979. He studied music in Vancouver and took part in musical activities in Montreal while a law student at McGill U, from which he graduated in 1914. In Vancouver he founded (and conducted 1930–4) the *Vancouver Bach Choir, initiated choral broadcasts from the west coast (1934, Handel's *Messiah*), and established *Western Music Co (1930–70), which also published *Western Music News* (1934–54). TRL

DRUICK, Don. Composer, flutist, b Montreal 23 Jul 1945; B SC mathematics (McGill) 1966. In Montreal he studied flute with Hervé *Baillargeon, Jean-Charles *Morin, Harriet Crossland-Edwards, and Gail Grimstead. He moved to British Columbia where he was resident composer with the Savage God Theatre Co 1969–70, Intermedia in 1972, and Image Flow Productions in 1973 and music director of the Playhouse Theatre Co / Theatre Two in 1971 and Another Smith Productions in 1971. He has composed film scores for Keith Rodan's *Cinetude III* (1969), David Rimmer's *Cellophane Wrapper* (1970), Byron Black's *Master of Images* (1972), and Jack Darcus' feature *Wolfpen Principle* (1973) and has been commissioned to write for chamber and dance ensembles. Druick's works are highly experimental, often using graphic notation or simply an instruction sheet as a guide to an improvised performance. He has prepared many such performances for art galleries in Canada and the USA. He is an affiliate of PRO Canada.

SELECTED COMPOSITIONS

String Trio Music. 1969. Str trio. Ms

Cellophane Wrapper, film (film by D. Rimmer). 1970. Film, tape. Ms. Mel SMLP 4027

Sonatine. 1972. Vc, pf. Ms

A Sacred Mole, Sacrificed. 1973. 3 high ww instr. Ms

Mout is. 1975. 2 actors, 4 pf, fl, va, tape recorder. Ms

Public (with Martha Miller). 1975. 2 actors, 2 musician/actors, 1 singer/actor. Ms

Sweeterrainforterraine (with G. Simpson). 1975. Fl, pf, perc, video and audio tapes, ocharina. Ms

Here in The First The Endless I was Shinjuku. 1976. v (vs). Ms

27, 1, 76. 1976. Carillon. Ms

The Second Movement of the Shostakovich First Cello Concerto by Distant Memory. 1977. Solo ww. Ms

Some 10 film scores, numerous works for chamb ens, some for mixed media

CF

DRYNAN, Margaret (Isobel) (b Brown). Teacher, composer, organist-choirmaster, writer, b Toronto 10 Dec 1915; B MUS (Toronto) 1943, ARCT 1975, hon RCCO 1976. Her teachers included Arthur *Benjamin, Madeline Bone, Michael Head, E. Kelvin James, Campbell *McInnes, Molly *Sclater, and Healey *Willan. A member for 37 years of the *St Mary Magdalene church choir, she also sang in Toronto with the Tudor Singers and with Reginald *Stewart's *Toronto Bach Choir (approximately four years with each), was organist-choirmaster 1950–3 at Holy Trinity Church, Oshawa, and was founder and conductor 1953–68 of the Canterbury Singers of Oshawa. She was supervisor of music 1960–9 for the Oshawa elementary school system and in 1969 she became music consultant to the Durham Region Board of Education. She was a founding member (1963) and president 1973–5 of the Oshawa District Council for the Arts and a founder of the Oshawa Arts Centre. She has been active in other local organizations and local branches of national ones. For many years the Canadian editor of *Diapason* magazine, she also has contributed to *Music Magazine* and *EMC*. In 1978 she was a founding member of the Healey Willan Centennial Celebration Committee, which she has served as vice-president. Her compositions include a *Missa brevis* (1952), four operettas, some 40 songs and string works, folksong arrangements, carols, and plainsong settings. The *Missa brevis* and such songs and carols as 'Songs for Judith,' 'Including Me,' and 'Why Do the Bells of Christmas Ring?' have been performed in Canada and abroad. Her publishers include *Berandol, *Thompson, and *Boosey & Hawkes. TCB

DUBIN, Larry (Lawrence Jacob). Drummer, b New York 4 Feb 1931, d Toronto 25 Apr 1978. His father, Maurice (violinist, b Pinsk, Russia, 20 Dec 1907), played in Eugène *Chartier's Montreal Philharmonic after moving to Canada in 1924 and briefly in New York in the Manhattan Symphony and with one of Vincent Lopez' hotel orchestras. Shortly after his son's birth Maurice Dubin moved to Cochrane in northern Ontario and opened a department store. He went to Kingston, Ont, in 1957 and played 1958–78 in the *Kingston SO. Larry Dubin began his career in Toronto in the early 1950s, playing bebop with Jack Dale and dixieland jazz with Bud Hill, Mike White (Imperial Jazz Band), and others. He also accompanied the US players Muggsy Spanier, Rex Stewart, and Edmund Hall during Toronto appearances. Dubin led his own band, the Big Muddys, at the Last Chance Saloon, Ports of Call, 1963–6 and in 1968. The band made one LP, *The Big Muddys* (1964, Cap T 6074). In the mid-1970s Dubin turned exclusively to free improvisation, playing in a unique melodic style which he had begun to develop in the early 1960s. He was a founding member of the *CCMC in 1974 and also played with the *Artists' Jazz Band and groups led by Stuart *Broomer, Bill *Smith, and others. He appears on six LPs with the CCMC, the last three released posthumously as a set, *Larry Dubin and the CCMC* (1976–8, 3-Music Gallery Editions 15). Michael *Snow, with whom Dubin played in the Imperial Jazz Band, in Snow's quartet, and in the CCMC, wrote: 'Larry Dubin produces the most subtle range of qualities of any drummer I have heard: sprays, splashes, bursts, rustlings, flutterings, roars. His playing is orchestral ... had he emerged in New York he probably would be influential' (Toronto *Globe and Mail*, 1 Apr 1978). Dubin was the subject of a CBC radio documentary prepared by Ray Gallon and broadcast 7 Jan 1979 on 'Two New Hours.'

BIBLIOGRAPHY

Snow, Michael. 'Larry Dubin's music,' *Impulse*, vol 7, no. 1 1978

Miller, Mark. 'Larry Dubin: either you play or you don't,' *Coda*, 166, Apr–May 1979 MM

DUBOIS, Claude (André). Singer, songwriter, b Montreal 24 Aug 1947. He began his career at 12 in a country group with which he made the LP *Claude Dubois et ses montagnards* (Rigaudon TCR 1011). As early as 1966 he performed his songs at the *PDA along with Georges *Dor, Claude *Gauthier, and Donald *Lautrec; he returned there in 1973, 1975, and 1976. To mark *Expo 67 he wrote the music for *Cerveaux gelés* (Frozen Brains), a documentary film on Montreal, and also sang at the Youth Pavilion. The same year he gave a concert at the Comédie-Canadienne and sang in France on 'La Fine Fleur de la chanson,' a radio program of the ORTF. He was named 'discovery' at Montreal's *Le Patriote, thereby earning the Renée Claude Trophy. He then abandoned his career and from 1968 to 1973 travelled all over the world.

Dubois's return was marked by the LP *Touchez Dubois* (1973, Barclay 80154) and the establishment of the Éditions du Son (later Éditions Claude Dubois), his publishing company. In *La Chanson québécoise* (Montreal 1974) Benoît L'Herbier wrote, 'The music of this modern-day Québécois successfully blends Latin and Anglo-Saxon idioms in a contemporary language which soon would be popular on both sides of the Atlantic.' Dubois was host on CBC TV's 'Décibels' (1973) and CFTM-TV's 'Showbizz' (1975–6). The LP *Mellow Reggae* (1976–7, Barclay 80271), recorded in concert in Montreal, Paris, London, and Miami, reflected Dubois's growing interest in West Indian music. In 1978 he founded his own label, Pingouin, under which the LP *Fable d'espace* (UFO.1) was released, and presented the show 'Dubois deboutte' at the *St-Denis Theatre in Montreal. In Paris he sang 'Le Blues du businessman' for the recording of highlights from Michel Berger and Luc Plamondon's rock opera *Starmania* (Kébec-Disc KF 8001-02), and the recording was a success in France and Quebec. Among his other recorded hits are 'Comme un million de gens,' 'Besoin pour vivre,' 'Femmes de rêve,' and 'Le Labrador.' He has made LPs for Barclay and Columbia, and of those for the latter label *Tu sais* (FS 90080) and *Le Monde de Claude Dubois* (FS 90223-224) are notable. He was named male performer of the year at the 1979 ADISQ recording and showbusiness awards in Montreal. 'Dubois,' wrote Nathalie Petrowski, 'is possibly our last authentic bohemian as well as our first real "punk." After fifteen years of rebelliousness, he hasn't worn out yet' (*Canadian Composer*). He is a member of CAPAC.

BIBLIOGRAPHY

Vincent, Pierre. 'Coming home to settle down to become a star,' *CanComp*, 78, Mar 1973

Beaulieu, Pierre. 'Claude Dubois, entre l'Europe et l'Asie ... ' Montreal *La Presse*, 28 Oct 1978

Petrowski, Nathalie. 'This Quebec star comes back again stronger than ever,' *CanComp*, 136, Dec 1978

Lavoie, Denis. 'Claude Dubois – le souci de bien faire,' Montreal *La Presse*, 26 Jul 1980 (BLH)

DUBOIS, Jean-Baptiste (Alphonse). Cellist, conductor, teacher, b Ghent, Belgium, 19 Jan 1870, d Montreal 4 Jul 1938; premier prix cello (Ghent Cons) 1890. He studied cello at the Ghent Cons with Jean-Baptiste Rappé and Jules de Swert. While still too young to be admitted to the senior class, he performed in the competition that determined entry and obtained an honourable mention. In Ghent he was a member 1883–4 of a variety orchestra and the municipal theatre orchestra and taught 1885–91 at the conservatory. At Ernest *Lavigne's invitation, he moved to Montreal and was assistant conductor 1891–4 of the *Sohmer Park orchestra. He was principal cellist 1893–6 with the *Opéra français of Montreal, then spent a short time in Amsterdam before settling permanently in Canada in 1896.

Then began a period of intense activity during which Dubois was solo performer, chamber player, conductor, and teacher. He returned to Sohmer Park as assistant conductor and was principal cello of the *Couture MSO in 1896 and of the *Goulet MSO 1898–1910, appearing often with both as concerto soloist. He spent the 1903–4 season, however, as principal cello of the Cincinnati SO. He was a member 1896–8 of the Haydn Trio (with J.-J. Goulet, violin, and Émery *Lavigne, piano) and was the cello 1905–6 of the *Mendelssohn Trio, replacing Rosario *Bourdon. In 1907 he formed the Beethoven Trio with Albert *Chamberland and Maria Heynberg. He founded the *Dubois String Quartet three years later and remained a member until it ceased to exist in 1938. He was conductor of the Montreal Amateur Orchestral Society 1904–5, the Assn symphonique de Montréal, the *Canadian Academy of Music in 1914, and the Symphonie Dubois 1916–17. Dubois had a long teaching career in Canada, beginning at the Collège de Montréal in 1896. He taught at the *McGill Cons in 1904, the year it was founded, at the *Cons national after 1906, and at the Canadian Academy of Music in 1914. He was the founder, and the director 1893–1903, of the public solfège classes established by the province of Quebec. His many pupils included Rosario Bourdon, Hermann Courchesne, Suzette Forgues, Napoléon Dansereau, Roland *Leduc, Brahm Sand, and his own son Jules (b Montreal 1904).

Dubois's few compositions include an *Élégie* for cello and piano (ca 1925, Édition Belgo-Canadienne). The recordings he made for HMV and Starr are listed in *Roll Back the Years*. He was the stepfather of Louis-Honoré and Rosario Bourdon. His son Jules was a member of various orchestras, taught cello and solfège, and eventually was put in charge of the public classes his father had founded. Jules wrote *Théorie élémentaire de musique* (Montreal 1961) / *Elementary Music Treatise* (Montreal 1962). GP

Dubois String Quartet / Quatuor à cordes Dubois. Founded in Montreal in 1910 by the cellist Jean-Baptiste *Dubois. Its other members were Albert *Chamberland and Alphonse Dansereau (violins) and Eugene Schneider (viola). It gave its first concert 8 Nov 1910 at *Windsor Hall, performing Beethoven's *Op 18, no. 2* and Schumann's *Quintet, Op 44* with the pianist Ada L. Richardson. After a first season of six concerts the quartet enjoyed 28 seasons of activity, uninterrupted until Dubois's death in 1938. In the early 1920s it performed in the Ladies' Ordinary Room at the Windsor Hotel. In 1927 it moved to the St-Sulpice Library (now the BN du Q). Later concerts were at *Tudor Hall, where in 1938 it made its last appearance. Over the years there were many changes of personnel, but Dubois himself remained. Chamberland was replaced by Edgar Braidi in 1920, and Braidi by Maurice *Onderet in the early 1930s. Dansereau was followed by Eugène *Chartier 1915–16, Alexandre Delcourt, Eric Zimmerman ca 1923, Lucien *Sicotte 1929–36, René *Gagnier 1936–7, and Lucien *Martin 1937–8. Joseph *Mastrocola succeeded Schneider in 1920. So that duo-sonatas and piano trios, quartets, and quintets could be included in the programs, a regular pianist was engaged. George M. *Brewer and Marie-Thérèse *Paquin successively held this position. When the founder of the quartet died, Marcel *Valois wrote in *La Presse* (9 Jul 1938), 'Jean-Baptiste Dubois revealed the masterworks of chamber music to several generations of Montrealers for more than 25 years.' The quartet played the great works of the classical and romantic periods and also, as early as 1912–13, the Debussy *Quartet* (1893), repeating it 16 times in the ensuing years. At its 100th concert, 10 Feb 1927, the quartet performed works of Franck, Debussy, Saint-Saëns, and Vincent d'Indy. In April 1928, when Ravel visited Montreal, it performed his *Quartet* at the *St-Denis Theatre. The Dubois String Quartet's concerts were free from 1927–8 on, because of grants from the Quebec government. Only in the last few years was a minimal entrance fee reinstated. The quartet gave concerts around the province as well as in Montreal and played in Trois-Rivières as early as 1913. Impresario Louis-H. *Bourdon managed the group's financial affairs. GP

DUCHARME, Charles-Joseph. Teacher, b Lachine, near Montreal, 10 Jan 1786, d Ste-Thérèse-de-Blainville (Ste-Thérese), near Montreal, 25 Mar 1853. He studied music at the *Séminaire de Québec along with academic subjects and theology. He was ordained a priest in 1814, and was

vicar 1814–16 at St-Laurent (Montreal) and then curé 1816–49 in Ste-Thérèse. In 1825 he began teaching six children in his presbytery, thus founding what was to become in 1834 the Collège Jaune, in 1840 the Ste-Thérèse Seminary, and eventually the Cegep Lionel-Groulx. He was deeply interested in music, possessed a pleasant voice, and was knowledgable. According to his biographer, Father P. Dagenais, 'M. Ducharme liked to encourage talent of all kinds; what little free time he had was devoted to teaching music and thus, in what was a pastime, he was skilful and fortunate enough to train several able musicians' (F. Elie, *La Famille Casavant*, Montreal 1914). Father Ducharme taught Damis *Paul, Louis *Mitchell, and probably Joseph *Lajeunesse and Augustin *Lavallée after 1839. He also instructed Joseph *Casavant in organ construction and encouraged him to build his first instrument in 1840. Ducharme Blvd, Ste-Thérèse, was named after him.

BIBLIOGRAPHY

Dictionnaire biographique du clergé canadien-français (Montreal 1910) GP

DUCHARME, Dominique. Teacher, pianist, organist, b Lachine, near Montreal, 14 May 1840, d Montreal 28 Dec 1899. He studied piano as a child with a teacher called Andrews, an organist in Lachine, and continued in Montreal with Paul *Letondal and then for a year with Charles W. *Sabatier. In 1863 he was admitted to the Paris Cons as an auditor. There he studied piano for five years with Antoine Marmontel and harmony with François Bazin. Ducharme met Liszt at the musical soirées organized by Rossini, and Liszt's suggestions were important in developing his piano technique. He also became acquainted with Camille Saint-Saëns.

On his return to Montreal in 1868 Ducharme concentrated on teaching piano. Among his pupils were Édouard *Clarke, Achille *Fortier, Alfred *Laliberté, Ernest Langlois, Zénon Paquin, William *Reed, Émiliano *Renaud, and Joseph *Saucier. In 1889 he met Paderewski, whom he considered to be the greatest pianist of his day, and because of his influence introduced methods of piano technique characteristic of the Viennese school. Besides teaching, Ducharme held the post of organist 1868–98 at the Gesù Church. A man of retiring disposition, he rarely performed in public as a pianist, preferring to display his musical talents in the seclusion of the organ loft. According to Arthur *Letondal, Ducharme 'used great tact in compensating for the deficiencies of the often incomplete orchestras that were assembled on festive occasions. As a soloist, he played pleasant, melodic pieces exquisitely, bringing to them the stamp of his personality ... He has left the memory of a sensitive artist and a delightful man' ('Le Gesù musical,' *Album annuel du Collège Sainte-Marie*, Montreal 1939). He was president 1896–7 of the *AMQ.

BIBLIOGRAPHY

'Dominique Ducharme,' *MCour*, vol 40, 30 May 1900
Letondal, Arthur. 'Dominique Ducharme,' *La Musique*, vol 2, Nov 1920
Laurendeau, Arthur. 'Musiciens d'autrefois: Dominique Ducharme,' *Action nationale*, vol 35, Feb 1950 (CG)

DUCHOW, Marvin. Musicologist, composer, administrator, b Montreal 10 Jun 1914, d there 24 May 1979; B MUS (McGill) 1937, Diploma in Composition (Curtis) 1939, BA (New York) 1942, MA musicology (ESM, Rochester) 1951, hon D MUS (Chicago Cons) 1960. He studied theory 1933–7 with Claude *Champagne at the *McGill Cons and composition privately. He continued his studies 1937–9 at the Curtis Institute with Rosario Scalero (composition) and Samuel Chotzinoff (criticism) and 1939–42 at New York U, teaching the while at various US schools. Returning to Montreal he taught 1943–9 at the *CMM and 1944–78 at McGill U, whose music department he also served as acting dean 1955–7, dean 1957–63, and chairman of the theory department 1955–63, remaining as a professor after 1963. He was a visiting lecturer in 1964 at the *École Vincent-d'Indy and became a curriculum consultant to the *École normale de musique in 1966. Over the years he served the CMM and the *CMQ as an examiner. He was an associate editor (book reviews, 1957–62) of the *Canadian Music Journal* and in 1976 was appointed a member of the editorial board of *Musica Judaica*, the journal of the American Society for Jewish Music.

A specialist in 18th-century French music and in certain aspects of renaissance music, Duchow was one of Canada's leading musicologists and an authority on Claude Champagne. He assisted with the final revision of Gaston *Allaire's book *The Theory of Hexachords, Solmization and the Model System*. Generally conservative in style, his compositions display a solid craftsmanship and marked sensitivity. His *Sonata* for piano shows strongly the influence of Hindemith. His *Three Songs of the Holocaust* represent his first attempt at serialism; they were commissioned by the Canadian Jewish Congress and premiered 28 Sep 1978 by Pauline and Jean-Eudes *Vaillancourt. Among his private pupils for harmony and counterpoint were Alan Belkin (whose *Introduction and Fugue for Double Wind Quartet*, premiered in 1979, is dedicated to Duchow), Georges *Little, and Alejandro Enrique Planchart. Students in his theory courses included Kenneth *Gilbert, Hugh *Hartwell, Carl *Little, Roger *Matton, Pierre *Mercure, Dorothy *Morton, Wayne *Riddell, and Robert *Silverman. Among his history pupils were Gregory Butler, Fred Hall, Jacob *Siskind, and Gerrit Tetenburg. 'The Legacy: A Profile of Marvin Duchow, Canadian Musician' was broadcast on CBC radio in 1975. In 1980 the library of the Faculty of Music at McGill U was named after him. The musical rights of his estate are administered by PRO Canada.

COMPOSITIONS

ORCHESTRA AND CHAMBER

Variations on a Chorale. 1936. Orch. Ms
Quartet in C Minor. 1939 ('Scherzo' and 'Andante' rev 1942). Str quar. Ms. 2nd mvt rev 1975 as *Movement for Strings* or *Largamente*. Str orch. Ms
Badinerie. 1947. Orch, pf. Ms

PIANO AND ORGAN

Seven Chorale Preludes in Traditional Style. 1939. Org. Ber 1970
Chant intime (formerly *Prelude*). 1947. Pf. BMIC 1947. RCI-134 (*Newmark)
Sonata. 1955. Pf. CMCentre, BMIC 1961 (2nd mvt *Passacaglia*)

CHOIR AND VOICE

Songs of My Youth, song cycle (various). 1930s (4 songs rev 1975 as *A Garland of Love Songs*). V, pf. Ms
For a Rose's Sake. 1938. V, pf. BMIC 1956
Motet. 1938. SATB. Ms
A Carol Choir (arr). 1943. 2, 3, 4-part choirs. Boston 1946
Three Songs of the Holocaust / Trois Chants de l'Holocaust (German text N. Sachs). 1977. V, pf. Ms

WRITINGS

'Criticism of comic opera in the *Correspondance littéraire* (1753–1773),' unpubl MA thesis, ESM, Rochester 1951
'Musico-textual criticism in the *Correspondance littéraire*,' *CMJ*, vol 1, Summer 1957
'The International Conference of Composers at Stratford,' *CMJ*, vol 5, Autumn 1960
'Canadian music libraries: some observations,' Music Library Assn *Notes*, 2nd series, vol 18, Dec 1960
'Conference summary,' *The Modern Composer and His World*, ed John Beckwith and Udo Kasemets (Toronto 1961)
'Claude Champagne,' *MSc*, 243, Sep–Oct 1968
'Inventory list of the compositions of Claude Champagne,' *CAUSM J*, vol 2, Fall 1972
'An auxiliary collection of books and scores in the library of Claude Champagne ...' ms 1972, U of Montreal Library
'Claude Champagne: inventory of his manuscripts and other documents,' ms 1972, NL of C
'Detailed inventory of the Claude Champagne archive,' ms 1973, NL of C
'A selective list of correspondents drawn from the personal documents of Claude Champagne,' *CAUSM J*, vol 3, Autumn 1973
'Some early Champagne documents in the National Library collection,' paper, CAUSM conference, U of Toronto, 3 Jun 1974
'A summary account and partial inventory of the Claude Champagne collection,' *CAUSM J*, vol 4, Autumn 1974
'Melodies from André Gedalge's *L'enseignement de la musique par l'éducation méthodique de l'oreille* in the undated Claude Champagne workbook: an index and thematic catalogue,' ms 1974, NL of C
'A summary account and partial inventory of the Claude Champagne collection – section IV: recorded materials,' *CAUSM J*, vol 5, Spring 1975
'Thematic index of Claude Champagne's pedagogical materials,' card index, 1977, NL of C

BIBLIOGRAPHY

Siskind, Jacob. 'Cataloguing a composer,' Montreal *Gazette*, 18 Nov 1972
Karpman, I.J. Carmin ed. *Who's Who in World Jewry* (Tel Aviv 1978)
'In memoriam – Marvin Duchow,' *Music McGill*, vol 6, Autumn 1979 NT

DUDLEY, Raymond. Pianist, b Bowmanville, east of Toronto, 20 Jun 1931; ARCT 1947, LRCT 1949, Artist Diploma (RCMT) 1952. He studied piano with Alberto *Guerrero at the *RCMT and made debuts with the RCMT SO in 1949 and the *TSO in 1951. In 1952 he won the Eaton Graduating Scholarship in Toronto and a medal (awarded unanimously) at the International Competition for Musical Performers in Geneva. He made his recital debut 13 Jan 1953 at Wigmore Hall, London. He received the Harriet Cohen Commonwealth Medal in 1953, studied in Milan with Ilona Deckers, and made his New York debut 11 Dec 1955 at Town Hall, subsequently appearing with the New York Philharmonic (1957), at Carnegie Hall (1958), and at the opening (1962) of Avery Fisher Hall in Lincoln Center. He became a resident of the USA in the mid-1950s.

Dudley has toured the USA and Canada frequently and has performed throughout Europe, first as a *JMC exchange artist in 1957. In 1966 he took up the fortepiano or Hammerflügel, an 18th-century Viennese portable forerunner of the modern pianoforte, and subsequently he has made a speciality of comparative recitals on the two instruments. Although his repertoire ranges from

Bach to contemporary Canadians, he is noted as a Haydn specialist and in 1968 performed all of that composer's piano sonatas in eight recitals at the Purcell Room in London. He has recorded several Haydn sonatas for Lyrichord (1965; LLST 7149) and the CBC (1975; SM 309). His *A Coronation March* was published (1956) by *Harris and he has contributed articles on the piano and the fortepiano to *American Music Teacher* (1965), *Music Journal* (1968), and *Diapason* (1969). Dudley taught at Indiana U 1957–63 and Florida Southern College 1963–4. He joined the teaching staff at the U of Cincinnati's College-Cons in 1964. EK

The Duet Club. Oldest surviving women's musical club in Canada. Founded in Hamilton, Ont, in 1889 by Ellen *Ambrose with 10 of her pupils, it was called the 'Haydn Duet Club' because the students performed Haydn symphonies arranged as piano duets. In the early years the club was limited to 21 active members who performed for their own enjoyment and education in private concerts. A Duet Club Chorus (founded ca 1900) was conducted successively by Bruce *Carey, Mrs Harold Hamilton, Cyril *Hampshire, Reginald *Bedford, and Bertha *Carey Morrow. In 1916 the club began sponsoring public recitals by a variety of Canadian and foreign artists, including the *Baroque Trio of Montreal, Mona *Bates, *Bedford and Eby, Neil *Chotem, Jean Dickenson, Arthur *Garami, Vladimir Horowitz, Winifred *Lugrin-Fahey, Guiomar Novaes, Gladys Swarthout, Leo *Smith, and Albert Spalding. Club membership by the 1960s numbered over 200. A Student Duet Club flourished 1927–35 and was revived in 1942 and 1959. It was incorporated into the parent club in 1972. Besides the Ellen Ambrose Memorial Scholarship, established in 1940, the club has offered other scholarships and recital opportunities for young performers.

BIBLIOGRAPHY

The Duet Club of Hamilton 1889–1964 (Hamilton 1964)

FAH

DUFAULT (Du Faut), **Paul**. Tenor, b Ste-Hélène-de-Bagot, near St-Hyacinthe, Que, 10 Dec 1872, d there 20 Jun 1930. He first studied music in Montreal with a Mr Birtz, later in Boston with a Mr Dobson, then in Worcester, Mass, with a Mrs Petersen. He is also known to have studied with Hector Dupeyron of the Paris Opera and to have been active professionally by 1897. He sang with the Société symphonique de Québec (*Quebec SO) in 1903, when the program mentioned that he had been living in New York 'for many years,' making there several concert and church appearances. Barring the occasional oratorio appearance, his career was confined exclusively to the concert platform, and he should not be confused with the French dramatic tenor Jean Dufault, who sang with Hammerstein's Manhattan Opera. In his prime (ca 1906 to 1921) Paul Dufault appeared with great success in many parts of the world, including Australia (three visits), China, and Japan. During this period, too, he toured Quebec nearly every year, concentrating on the smaller towns and villages otherwise deprived of professional concert fare. In 1921 he toured Canada. His programs, comprising exclusively French classical arias and French and English songs – notably by Botrel, Gounod, Goublier, and Tosti – were served well by a sympathetic lyric tenor of somewhat limited range. Following a typical New York recital in 1911, the *Times* wrote, 'Mr. Dufault has very considerable requirements in the management of a not wholly tractable organ, in the matters of diction, style, phrasing, interpretation, which are much to his credit.' His circumscribed

Paul Dufault (*Le Canada musical*, Sept 1918)

but highly polished repertoire is well represented on records made ca 1911 to 1921 for Columbia, Edison, Victor, and Starr and listed in *Roll Back the Years*. His name was given to a Montreal street in the Rivière-des-Prairies district in 1972.

BIBLIOGRAPHY

'Paul Dufault's New York success,' *MCour*, vol 48, 20 Dec 1911
'Paul Dufault reveals a musician's El Dorado,' *Musical America*, 3 Oct 1914
'Dufault's new Canadian successes,' *MCour*, vol 51, 12 May 1915
'Paul Dufault in the Orient,' *MCour*, vol 53, 24 May 1917
'Paul Dufault finds swift growth in musical culture throughout Canada,' *Musical America*, 24 May 1919
Entre-Nous, issue devoted to Dufault, vol 1, Oct–Nov 1930
Musiciens canadiens

JBM

DUFRESNE, Diane. Chanteuse, actress, b Montreal September or October 1940 or 1944. She began singing in Montreal in her teens and took lessons in 1957 with Simone *Quesnel. From 1965 to 1967 she studied voice with Jean Lumière and dramatic art with Françoise Rosay in Paris. There she sang in such boîtes à chansons as l'Écluse, l'Échelle de Jacob, and le Caveau de la Bolée. Returning to Montreal, she appeared in 1969 in Clémence *Desrochers's revue *Les Girls* and began a well-publicized relationship with the revue's composer, François Cousineau, who later wrote the music (to lyrics by Luc Plamondon) for her most popular songs. She sang in studios (for jingles, etc), then made her first LPs, *Tien-toé ben j'arrive* (1972, Barclay 80143) and *Opéra Cirque* (1973, Barclay 80172). The song 'J'ai rencontré l'homme de ma vie' (1972) was especially popular. Attempting to capitalize on the popularity in France of such identifiable Quebec performers as *Charlebois, she opened a show for the singer Julien Clerc at the Olympia in Paris in 1973, to a mixed reception. Of her potential impact, Juan Rodriguez wrote, 'Her joual is even cruder than Charlebois's ... her costumes are legendary and her vocal style is more hysterical than anything France has ever seen' (*Montreal Star*, 29 Sep 1973). Dufresne nevertheless moved to the forefront of pop performers in Quebec in the mid-1970s, with her LPs *Sur la même longueur d'ondes* (Kébec Disc KD 703), *Mon Premier Show* (J'arrive J-909 recorded at the *PDA in 1975), and *Maman si tu m'voyais ... tu s'rais fière de ta fille* (Barclay 80270), with the hit single (1975) 'Chanson pour Elvis,' and with such shows as 'Diane' and 'Comme un film de Fellini' on the Montreal stage. In France she received a Jeune Chanson award from the French Music Exchange Assn and performed at the Élysée Montmartre in Paris in 1977. She returned 14 Mar 1978 to the Olympia to great acclaim, and her concerts there yielded two LPs for Barclay (80286 and 80288). She also appeared in several French TV specials in 1978 and 1979 and played the role of Stella Spotlight alongside several Quebec and French pop stars in the rock musical *Starmania* (with music by Michel Berger and lyrics by Plamondon), produced in 1979 in Paris. Her song 'Les Adieux au Sex Symbol' from the LP of *Starmania* (Kébec Frog KF 8001-2) was a hit in France in 1979. Other songs popularized by Dufresne and included in a 'greatest hits' package released by Barclay (75017) are 'Rock pour un gars d'bicyc,' 'Tu m'fais flipper,' 'Rill pour rire,' 'La Chanteuse straight,' 'Pars pas sans me dire bye bye,' and 'J'me sens ben.' Her LP *Strip Tease* (Barclay 80294) was released in 1979 and included many songs by Plamondon and Germain Gauthier.

BIBLIOGRAPHY

Piuze, Simone. 'La nouvelle Diane Dufresne,' *Perspectives*, 3 Feb 1973
Moore, Gilbert. 'Paris, c'est la vie! Diane,' *Montreal Star*, 18 Mar 1978
Beaulieu, Pierre. 'La garde-malade du show business,' Montreal *La Presse*, 20 May 1978
Racicot, H. et al. *Diane Dufresne* (Montreal 1978)
McDonald, Marci. 'Starmania's salad days,' *Maclean's*, 30 Apr 1979
Beaulieu, Pierre. 'Vivre à la limite de soi,' Montreal *La Presse*, 29 Nov 1980

MM

DUFRESNE, Georges (Joseph-Édouard). Tenor, radio producer, b Nicolet, Que, 21 May 1894, d Montreal 25 Jun 1973. After receiving his formal education at the Nicolet Seminary, he settled in Montreal, where he studied with Rodolphe *Mathieu and Albert *Clerk-Jeannotte. He continued his vocal studies in Paris under Jean de Reszke, Albert Dumontier, and André Paulet and learned stagecraft under Jean Fournetz. During World War I he served in the Canadian army and was decorated by the French Republic. He made his debut in 1919 at the Gaîté-Lyrique theatre, Paris, under the name 'Dufranne' and sang elsewhere in France as well as in England and later in the USA. He sang *The Merry Widow* with Mary Garden at New York's Knickerbocker Theater and then signed a four-year contract with the Keith Vaudeville. During this period he appeared with artists from the *Metropolitan Opera, singing the title role in *Faust*, Des Grieux in *Manon*, and Don José in *Carmen*. In 1927 he participated in the opening performances at New York's Paramount Theater. The following year he signed a three-year contract with the Roxy Theater, where he shared top billing in 1930 with Ernestine Schumann-Heink. For the Chicago Opera he sang leading roles in *I Pagliacci*, *Mignon*, *Manon*, *La Bohème*, and *Lucia di Lammermoor*. He returned to Canada in 1935 and appeared in recitals and on CBC radio. He also sang with the *Variétés lyriques. In 1942 he joined the staff of the CBC as a producer of concert and opera broadcasts, a position he held until his retirement in 1967.

DISCOGRAPHY

Le Chant du désert – O Doux Mystère de la vie. Victor Orthophonic 263680 (78 rpm)
En te donnant ma rose – Roses de Picardie. Victor Orthophonic 263708 (78 rpm)
Handel – Schumann – Massenet – et al. 1958. 2-CT 25810-25811
Lalo – Hue – Levadé – et al. 1960. 2-CT 29951-29952
Treize Mélodies de la belle époque: P. Bernard – D'Hardelot – Tosti – et al. 1961. CT 28473

CH

DUFRESNE, Josephte (m Landry). Pianist, teacher, b Trois-Rivières, Que, 9 Jan 1929. She studied piano in Trois-Rivières and Montreal with Jean-Marie *Beaudet and, on a *Prix d'Europe (1950), in Paris with Yves Nat. In 1955 she began performing and teaching in Montreal. A recitalist and concerto soloist on radio (CBC and CKAC) and TV, she has championed Canadian music. She gave the premiere of Jean *Papineau-Couture's *Pièce concertante No. 1* (which is dedicated to her), and in the fall of 1967 she presented 13 half-hour CBC recitals of music by some 60 Canadians. In 1975 she began work on a book about Canadian piano music. Dufresne has performed in Paris and other centres in France, in New York State, and throughout Quebec. She has toured as an accompanist to Claire *Gagnier and others and has coached singers for several CBC TV opera productions. She began teaching at the Cons de Hull in 1967, was assistant director 1972–8, and was appointed director in 1980. She married the producer and conductor Jean-Yves *Landry.

DISCOGRAPHY

Letondal – Champagne – G.-E. Tanguay – Lavallée – Contant – Renaud – Garant – Gagnon – Hétu. 1969. RCI 252

Matton *Concerto* for 2 pianos and percussion; *Danse brésilienne*. J. Landry pf, L. Charbonneau and Lachapelle perc. 1955. RCI 145

Papineau-Couture – Prévost – Mercure – Vallerand – Élie. Myette v, Millet fl. Allied ARCLP 4

Pépin – Morel – Mathieu – Tremblay – Garant – Papineau-Couture – Matton. 1955. RCI 135/ (Garant *Variations*) RCI ACM 2

BIBLIOGRAPHY

Rudel-Tessier, J. 'Josephte Dufresne, interpreter of Canadian composers,' *CanComp*, 4, Dec 1965 LF

DUGGAN, Carl. Tenor, b Leacross, Sask, 23 Jan 1935; LMM 1960, ARCT 1960, FTCL 1969, B MUS (Durham) 1974. He studied in Saskatoon with Mary Anderson (voice) and Mabel Sanda (piano) and in Winnipeg after 1955 with Filmer *Hubble (organ). During his first year in England he won a National Federation of Music Societies prize which led to a series of engagements 1962–6, including the title role in a performance of *The Dream of Gerontius* under Eric Thiman. He also had lessons with Roy Henderson and Dame Eva Turner and was coached by Peter Pears. In 1966 he joined the English Opera Group with which, in England and abroad, he sang Lysander in Britten's *A Midsummer Night's Dream*, the Madwoman in Britten's *Curlew River*, and Acis in *Acis and Galatea*, among other roles. He also taught at the U of London. He became principal of the Western Ontario Cons and a voice teacher at the *U of Western Ontario in 1974 and that same year sang in Mozart's *Requiem* with the *NACO in Ottawa and Kingston, Ont, and was aria soloist in Bach's *St Matthew Passion* with the Metropolitan Festival Choir and Orchestra, Toronto. He has given recitals in Ontario and in 1977 he sang in France and England.

Duggan's wife, the Winnipeg-born mezzo-soprano Devina Bailey (LRAM 1969, FTCL 1969), studied with Nina *Dempsey, Gladys *Whitehead, and Filmer Hubble, singing frequently in the 1950s in public and on CBC radio. After a year (1955) with Roy Henderson in England she resumed her Canadian career, of which a highlight was the solo role in the North American premiere 23 Apr 1959 of Grace Williams' *The Dancers* with the Winnipeg Ladies' Choir under Hubble. Returning to England with Duggan in 1962 she sang in recital and oratorio. In 1975 she began teaching at the U of Western Ontario. That same year she was heard in two CBC recitals. In 1977 she was soprano soloist in performances of *Elijah* and the Vivaldi *Gloria* in London, Ont. GKG

DUGUAY, Raôul or **Raoul**, pseudonym Luoar Yaugud. Poet, performer, composer, b Val d'Or, Que, 13 Feb 1939; L PH (Montreal) 1963. While studying philosophy (until 1966) this man of many artistic directions began, in 1965, to present shows throughout Quebec, and in Paris and Brussels, as a singer, guitarist, trumpeter, pianist, and storyteller. He was music critic 1964–5 for the CBC radio program 'Le Carnet des arts,' taught philosophy and aesthetics ca 1966 in various Cegeps and lectured in 1972 at *UQAM. In 1969 he founded *Infonie with Walter *Boudreau, remaining with the group until 1972 and continuing thereafter to write the texts of Boudreau's compositions, among them *Cercle gnostique I*, performed in 1978.

A prolific writer, Duguay has had published in Montreal various tracts, texts, and poems, including *Le manifeste de l'Infonie* (1970). He edited, and wrote the preface for, *Musiques du Kébèk* (1971), a collection of essays by several authors. He has written plays, creating the music and the stage design and frequently taking the leading role alongside other actors, singers, and dancers. His writings have been published in *La Barre du jour*, *Mainmise*, *Quoi*, *Parti-Pris*, and *Passe-Partout*, and he has appeared in several Quebec films, including the documentary *L'Infonie inachevée*. He produced the NFB's *Ô ou l'invisible enfant* (1976). As lyricist and performer he has participated in recordings by Infonie and in the LP *Les Porches* by *Maneige. He has made his own LPs *Alllô Tôulmônd* (1975, Cap ST 70.036), *L'Envôl* (1976, Cap SKAO 70.042), and *Raôul Duguay vivant avec tôulllmônd* (1978, Cap SWBC 70.057).

Describing himself as a multidisciplinary poet, Duguay appears above all to be a communicator. After one of his shows at the *St Denis Theatre, Montreal, Nathalie Petrowski wrote (*Le Devoir* 19 Dec 1977): 'His approach is probably the least conventional and the most unusual in Quebec show business ... His show exceeds the simple art of entertainment, exceeds the art of performance and becomes a true human happening, a meeting of hearts and minds.' He is an affiliate of PRO Canada.

BIBLIOGRAPHY

Pedneault, Hélène. 'Song is best means of communicating for Raoul Duguay,' *MSc*, 287, Jan–Feb 1976

Radz, Matt. 'Raoul Duguay: creative anarchist,' *Montreal Star*, 18 Feb 1978

Beaulieu, Pierre. 'Duguay: j'écris dans les oreilles,' Montreal *La Presse*, 10 Jun 1978 (PR)

DULONGPRÉ, Louis. Painter, teacher of music and dancing, stage manager, topographer, b St-Denis, near Paris, 1754?, d St-Hyacinthe, Lower Canada (Quebec), 1843. He came to North America on a French troopship during the American War of Independence. Later, in Albany, he was persuaded by some Canadians to move to Montreal, where he could live in a French society. In 1787 he opened a dancing school and also taught 'La Musique, ainsi qu'à jouer de plusieurs instruments' (Montreal *Gazette*, 18 Oct 1787). In 1791 he proposed to open a school for girls in which music was to be one of the subjects taught (ibid, 23 Feb 1791). Probably the project came to naught, for in November 1791 Dulongpré once more advertised a music and dancing school. In November 1789 he had been appointed the manager of the *Théâtre de Société which produced the premiere of *Quesnel's *Colas et Colinette* the following January. This position included setting up the stage, hiring musicians, advertising, and painting the scenery. Indeed, it was as a painter that Dulongpré became best known. He is reputed to have painted over 3000 portraits (including one of Joseph Quesnel) and pictures for churches, and worked as a topographer. Samples of his art are in several Canadian museums, but no specific evidence of his musicianship survives. He was '[un] homme d'ancien Régime, "grand, bien fait, d'une belle figure et d'excellentes manières" ' (Gérard Morisset, *Coup d'oeil sur les arts en Nouvelle-France*, Quebec 1941) (Morisset does not state whom he quotes). Dulongpré was one of the first known to have attempted to make a living as a music teacher in Canada. A street in Montreal was given his name in 1974.

BIBLIOGRAPHY

'Le peintre Louis Dulongpré,' *BRH*, vol 8, Apr 1902

Kallmann, H., 'From the archives: the Montreal Gazette on music from 1786 to 1797,' *CMJ*, vol 6, Spring 1962

Massicotte, E.-Z. 'Un théâtre à Montréal en 1789,' *BRH*, vol 23, Jun 1917

Amtmann *Musique au Québec* HK

DULUDE, Yolande. Soprano, b Montreal 12 Jan 1931; lauréat (Basile-Moreau College) 1948. After studying piano for a number of years, she began voice study in 1944. The following year she won CKAC radio's competition 'Le Club juvénile Excel' and in 1946 she won the CBC's 'Les Talents de chez-nous.' She made her debut with the *Variétés lyriques in *Rigoletto* in 1949 and sang with the company regularly until 1953. During these years she continued her studies under Sarah *Fischer, and in 1950 she made her recital debut at the Sarah Fischer Concerts. She studied in London 1953–4 with Dino Borgioli, Ivor Newton, and Joan Cross. In Canada she appeared on CBC TV for the first time in 1954, singing Marzelline in *Fidelio*, Musetta in *La Bohème*, and other roles. In April 1955 she sang the title role in Offenbach's *La Fille du tambour-major*, the final presentation of the Variétés lyriques.

In 1956, at the invitation of Wilfrid *Pelletier, Dulude joined the new opera class of the *CMM under the direction of Rachele Maragliano-Mori and Dick Marzollo. She sang with the *MSO at the Mount Royal Chalet and the Mountain Playhouse in Menotti's operas *The Old Maid and the Thief* and *The Telephone*. In 1959 she studied in New York with Dick Marzollo. (The Quebec government assisted her with bursaries in 1953, 1955, and 1959.) On her return in 1960 she sang Frasquita in *Carmen* for the *Opera Guild of Montreal. As soloist with the *Disciples de Massenet she toured France, Belgium, and Luxembourg and, for the *Montreal Festivals, sang 31 Aug 1960 in Vivaldi's *Gloria* and Bruckner's *Te Deum* at Notre-Dame Church. Awarded a *Canada Council bursary in 1962 she returned to London, this time to study with Edward Downes of Covent Garden. In 1965 she became hostess and music consultant for the program 'Les Grands Classiques' on radio station CJMS-FM and the same year sang Flora in *La Traviata* at the *PDA. She has appeared frequently in operetta productions – in 1968 as Simone in Louis Varney's *Les Mousquetaires au couvent* at PDA, in 1969 as Lady Mary in Messager's *Monsieur Beaucaire* with the *Théâtre lyrique du Québec, and in 1970 as the Glove Girl, the Widow, and the Brazilian in Offenbach's *La Vie parisienne*. For the *Opéra du Québec she was the Duchess of Crakentorp in a 1972 production of Donizetti's *La Fille du régiment* and the Duchesse de Berry in a 1974 production of Maurice Yvain's *Chanson gitane*.

Dulude has sung on the CBC radio programs 'Récital,' 'Mélodies,' and 'Arlequin et Colombine' and on the CBC TV programs 'Vedettes en direct' and 'Les Beaux Dimanches.' She also has appeared on the TVA network's 'Québec sait chanter' on several occasions. A perfectionist, Dulude is admired for the sensitivity of her expression and for the charm of her voice and personality. (GB)

DUMAINE, Graziella. Soprano, b Shawinigan, Que, ca 1890, fl ca 1920. She studied singing in Montreal with Salvator *Issaurel, then with Béatrice *La Palme, obtaining the *Prix d'Europe in 1916. A pupil of Jean de Reszke in Paris, she sang for the wounded in the military hospitals of France during World War I. In 1918 she created the role of Marcia opposite Tito Schipa and Marcel Journet in the premiere of Raoul Gunsbourg's *Manole* at the Monte Carlo Opéra. Reviewing the premiere in *Le Petit Monégasque* (Monte Carlo, 19 May 1918), Jules Méry wrote, 'She possesses a voice brimming with the freshness of youth, pure and steady, rich, and with a splendid brilliance in the upper register.' After her marriage Dumaine settled in Paris and gave up her career.

BIBLIOGRAPHY
Gour, Romain. *La Palme-Issaurel* (Montreal 1948) GP

DUMAS, (Joseph) Omer. Violoneux, composer, b St-Antoine-Abbé, south of Montreal, 1 Apr 1889, d Montreal 9 Jul 1980. He took up the violin in his youth and studied in Montreal after 1907. In 1912 he began playing in a small group for silent films. By this time he had started to compose; his first published piece, *Fleurette Valse*, appeared in *Le Passe-Temps* in 1913 and was recorded by Dumas and his Ménestrels du Québec in the early 1940s. The *Passe-Temps* of February 1947 published his *Danse campagnarde* and *Le Quadrille de Caraquet*. Other Dumas compositions appeared in *La Lyre*, eg, a *Romance* for violin or cello and piano in the September 1928 issue. Dumas was an affiliate of PRO Canada.

A popular old-time music ensemble of the day in Quebec, Dumas and his group were heard regularly 1938–67 on CBC radio's 'Réveil rural' and performed for other radio series and on TV. They began recording for *RCA Victor's Bluebird label in 1940, completing 32 78s by the end of that decade, and they began annual tours of Quebec and New Brunswick in 1942. Their most popular recordings, according to the discographer Gabriel Labbé (who lists Dumas's 78s to 1950 in *Pionniers du disque folklorique québécois*), were *Clog du Lac St-Jean*, *Le Reel du forgeron*, *Valse Annette*, and *La Valse de souvenir*.

Personnel of the Ménestrels included Dumas and Eugène Bastien (violins), Jean Dansereau or Stanley Widman (bass), Americo Funaro (guitar), Armand Gagné (clarinet), Saturno Gentiletti (accordion), and Ernest Décarie or Léo *Le Sieur (piano). Réal Béland and Mariette Vaillant (Dumas's wife) sang with the group, and such noted musicians as the violoneux Albert Bastarache and Isidore *Soucy, and the harmonica players Oscar and Edgar Morin, were frequent guests.

MM (GP)

du Maurier Council for the Performing Arts. Funding agency, established in 1971 by the Imperial Tobacco Co, at a time when tobacco advertising was in serious dispute, to develop Canadian talent and to broaden public interest in the performing arts. Increased from an initial allocation of $173,500 in 1972 to $307,360 in 1976, financial support totalling $3 million had been provided by February 1980 to more than 70 organizations including the *COC, the *Opéra du Québec, the *Southern Alberta Opera Assn, the *Shaw Festival, various dance groups and, for pop concerts, the *TS, the *MSO, the *Vancouver SO, the *Winnipeg SO, and other Canadian orchestras. In 1977 the council initiated an annual contest for young Canadian performers – the du Maurier Search for Talent, renamed Search for Stars in 1979 – leading to bursaries of $2000 each for 15 semi-finalists and $5000 each for five finalists and CBC telecasts of the semi-finals (three) and finals (one). Preliminary auditions are held in Halifax, Montreal, Toronto, Winnipeg, Regina, Calgary, and Vancouver. Isabelle Sauberli was appointed executive director of the agency in 1971 and retained the position in 1980. Senator Donald Cameron was chairman of the 10-member citizens' council 1971–8 and remained as honorary chairman in 1980, with the Hon Pauline M. McGibbon as chairman, André Bachand as co-chairman, and the Hon Muriel Fergusson, Albert D. Cohen, Fred Davis, Marvin Gelber, Carl O. Nickle, Gaston Pelletier, and Leonard J. Starmer as directors.

BIBLIOGRAPHY
'The corporate money tree,' *Music*, Sep–Oct 1980

The Dumbells. World War I concert party which became, after the armistice, a leading Canadian vaudeville troupe. It was formed in 1917 near Vimy Ridge, France, by 10 members of the Canadian army's third division under the direction of Merton (Wesley) Plunkett (b Orillia, Ont, 1888, d Toronto 21 Dec 1966, a YMCA entertainment director, assigned the rank of captain in the army). It took its name from the division's emblem, a red dumbell. Original members were Merton Plunkett, managing director and comedian; his brother Albert, a baritone; Ted Charters, assistant manager and comedian; Ross Hamilton ('Marjorie') and Allan Murray ('Marie from Montreal'), female impersonators; Jack Ayre, pianist and music director; Bill Tennent, tenor; Bert Langley, bass baritone; and Frank (later Jerry) Brayford and Leonard Young, actors. Shortly after the first show in August 1917 at Guoy-Servis (near Poperinge, Belgium, in the Passchendale combat sector) the Dumbells increased to 16. Other soldiers associated in various capacities with the early Dumbells included Bill Redpath, Elmer Belding, George Thorne, Andrew Catrano, J. McCormick, and D.L. Michie. With a collectively conceived program of songs of the day and skits about life in the trenches, the Dumbells entertained Canadian soldiers – often at the front lines – and played a four-week engagement in 1918 at the Coliseum in London. Highlights of their shows included the songs 'These Wild, Wild Women Are Making a Wild Man of Me' and 'I Know Where the Flies Go' (sung by Al Plunkett), 'Hello My Dearie' (a duet by 'Marjorie' and Tennent) and 'Someday I'll Make You Love Me' ('Marjorie'). Their theme was Ayre's 'The Dumbell Rag,' which eventually sold 10,000 copies.

Towards the end of the war, the Dumbells were joined by some members of the Princess Patricia's Canadian Light Infantry Comedy Co, a similar concert party (formed in May 1916, disbanded in June 1917, and re-formed in November) which had given a royal command performance in June 1918 at the Apollo Theatre in London. (Lieut Gitz *Rice is known to have played the piano occasionally for the Princess Pat's group.) The two troupes first appeared together 12 Nov 1918 (the day after armistice) as the Dumbells in Mons, Belgium, in a production of *H.M.S. Pinafore* which ran for over a month. The Dumbells also performed in other Belgian centres prior to demobilization in 1919.

The Dumbells re-formed later in 1919 in Orillia, Ont, as a vaudeville troupe, again under Merton Plunkett's direction. Members included Al Plunkett, Hamilton, Brayford, Tennent, Langley, Murray, and Ayre from the original Dumbells, Jack McLaren and Fred Fenwick from the Princess Pat's troup, and several performers from other Canadian army concert parties – Albert Edward 'Red' Newman (famed for his jocular rendition of 'Oh, It's a Lovely War') and Charlie McLean from

The Dumbells

the Y Emmas, the blackface comedian Ben Allan from the 16th Battalion Party, the female impersonator Jock Holland from the Bow Belles (a Scottish army troupe), the blackface comedian Jimmy Goode, and the baritone Tommy Young. Later additions and replacements included former army entertainers Morley Plunkett and Pat Rafferty and such professional performers as the tenor Harry Binns, the bass Cameron Geddes, the singer Stan Bennett, the pianist N. Fraser *Allan, the violinist Howard *Fogg (the conductor of the orchestra 1925–30), and the comedy team Charlie Jeeves and Fred Emney.

After rehearsals in Orillia and a 'tryout' in Owen Sound, Ont, the Dumbells opened 1 Oct 1919 at the Grand Opera House in London, Ont, with the revue *Biff, Bing, Bang*. They then spent 16 weeks (8 before Christmas and 8 after) at the Grand Theatre in Toronto before playing in Hamilton, Ottawa, and Montreal and undertaking the first of 12 (by 1932) cross-country tours. In May 1921 a revised *Biff, Bing, Bang* opened at the Ambassador Theater in New York, the first Canadian musical revue to appear on Broadway. It ran for about 12 weeks. Prior to the mounting of a new show, Al Plunkett and Hamilton left to form the short-lived Originals, then returned to the Dumbells. Many shows followed – *The Dumbells Revue of 1922*, *Carry On* (1922), *Cheerio* (1923), *Oh, Yes* (1924), *Ace High* (1924), *Lucky 7* (1925), *That's That* (1926), *Let 'er Go* (1926), *Oo-La-La* (1927), and *Why Worry?* (1928) – with the wartime references gradually being replaced by more topical material. Hit songs from these shows (most of them published by Leo Feist) included 'Canada for Canadians,' *'Come Back Old Pal,' 'Give Me a Little Cosy Corner,' 'Hahaski Hohoski Wow Wow,' 'It's Canada, the Land for Me,' 'K-K-K-Kiss Me Again,' 'Li'l Old Granny Mine,' 'Most Powerful Love,' 'She Must Be a Wonderful Girl,' 'Shufflin' Along,' 'Winter Will Come,' and 'Yum-Yum-Yum-Yum.' Some were originals; others, hits of the day. Several songs were repeated in new shows. In *Why Worry?* the Dumbells employed actresses for the first time. Financial difficulties brought on by the Depression, by the introduction of the 'talkies,' and by some poor investments (including an attempt to launch a second soldiers' revue, *The Maple Leafs*) forced the Dumbells to disband in 1932. At their peak the Dumbells made national stars of the 'crooner' Al Plunkett (b Orillia 1899, d Toronto 19 Apr 1957), Ross Hamilton (b Pugwash, NS, 1889, d Halifax 29 Sep 1965), and the comic singer Red Newman (b Dover, England, 1887, d 1952). Both Plunkett and Newman are well represented among the 27 78s the Dumbells made for HMV, of which some were reissued in 1977 on the LP *The Original Dumbells* (Aquitaine ELS 385). The Dumbells were reunited for concerts on a few occasions, including those at Lansdowne Park, Ottawa, in 1939 and *Massey Hall, Toronto, in 1955. They have been the subject of several CBC radio and TV documentaries, including 'The Dumbells' (telecast 5 Mar 1978) which combined a dramatization of the troupe's war years with scenes from a 1975 reunion at Lambert Lodge in Toronto of the last surviving members – Ayre, Brayford, McLaren, and Redpath. A musical, *The Legend of the Dumbells*, conceived by Alan Lund, was staged at the 1977 *Charlottetown Festival and seen also at the *NAC.

BIBLIOGRAPHY

McLaren, J.W. 'Mirth and Mud,' *MacLean's*, 1 Jan, 1 Mar, 15 May 1929
Braithwaite, Max. 'The rise and fall of The Dumbells,' *Maclean's*, 1 Jan 1952
Earle, Patrice. *Al Plunkett, The Famous Dumbell* (New York 1956)
Murray, Alan. 'The Dumbells,' *The Legionary*, Jan 1965
McLaren, Jack, and Franklin, Stephen. 'A funny thing happened on the way to the trenches,' *Weekend*, 25 Nov 1967
Rasky, Frank. 'When shells fell in World War I, he played on,' *Toronto Star*, 9 Nov 1974
Anglin, Gerald. 'Direct hit,' *The Canadian*, 25 Feb 1978

(HK, EBM, MM)

DuMESNIL, called la Musique, **Pierre**. Joiner, musician, b Bayeux, France, 1670, d Quebec? ca 1718–26. DuMesnil is listed in the Quebec census of 1716 (*Rencensement de la Ville de Québec pour 1716*, Quebec 1887) as 'musicien et ouvrier,' perhaps the first Canadian to indicate his profession in this way. The name 'dit la Musique' was attached to a number of other DuMesnils (also Dumesnil and Dumesny), who may have been Pierre's sons.

BIBLIOGRAPHY

Tanguay, Cyprien. *Dictionnaire généalogique des familles canadiennes* (Montreal 1871–90)

DUMONT, Lucille. Singer, teacher, b Montreal 20 Jan 1919. She received some early guidance from Léo *Le Sieur, who arranged her radio debut on CKAC with the Sweet Caporal orchestra in 1935. The same year she had her own series, 'Linger a While,' on station CFCF. Relying largely on the repertoire of the French singer Lucienne Boyer, she performed 'Parlez-moi d'amour,' 'Si petite,' and 'Prenez mes roses,' among others. Between 1935 and 1949 she participated in many radio series, eg, 'Rêverie,' 'Variétés françaises,' and 'Refrains d'hier et aujourd'hui.' In a program promoting the Victory Loan in April 1945 she premiered a song that was to become a worldwide hit, 'Insensiblement,' written by the French composer and conductor Ray Ventura, who conducted it on that occasion. In 1947 she became the first singer to be named Miss Radio by the Montreal weekly *Radiomonde*. On CBC radio she performed 1949–52 in the series 'Tambour battant,' 'Le Petit Bal des copains,' 'Les Chansons d'hier,' and 'Aux rythmes de Paris.' In 1950, on the 15th anniversary of the beginning of her career, the CKVL radio host Jean Baulu called her the 'Grande dame de la chanson,' and the name remained associated with her. She also was popular on TV in the early days of the medium, starring in 'Café des artistes' and 'Feux de joie' and serving 1956–60 as host for 'À la romance.' She was host for several other programs, including 'Entre vous et moi' 1961–2, 'Histoire d'une étoile' 1967–9, and 'Le Temps d'aimer' 1972–3 on CFTM-TV and 'Lucille Dumont' in 1965 on CBC. She was invited to appear on the CBC's 'Zoom' in 1968 and 'Vedettes en direct' in 1974.

In 1956 Dumont premiered Jacques Blanchet's 'Le Ciel se marie avec la mer,' which won first prize in the *'Concours de la chanson canadienne.' She won second prize with 'Tête heureuse' by the same songwriter in the 1962 Belgian competition 'Chansons sur mesure.' She performed in 1965 and 1970 in the boîte à chansons Chez Clairette in Montreal. Claude *Gingras described a recital at the Comédie-Canadienne: 'It's always the same warm voice, caressing, poignant, immediately recognizable ... And what Lucille Dumont sings better than ever are those tender, sentimental songs, the repertoire sometimes referred to contemptuously – though wrongly so – as "love songs" ' (Montreal *La Presse*, 22 Oct 1968). Among her principal recordings are *Mes Premières Chansons* (RCA Victor Gala CGP 243), *Lucille Dumont pour toi* (Harmonie HFS 9055), and one of popular French-Canadian songs (RCI 169, released in 1960). In 1968 she opened L'Atelier de la chanson, a school for voice and interpretation in Montreal.

ST

DUMOUCHEL, (Léandre) **Arthur**. Organist, teacher, composer, pianist, choirmaster, b Rigaud, near Montreal, 1 Mar 1841, d Albany, NY, 10 Jan 1919. Like his twin brother Édouard *Dumouchel he attended the Collège Bourget and studied with his aunt, Esther Fournier (1805–74), the organist at Rigaud. He pursued his career principally in the USA. On 11 Sep 1866 he made a debut at Carthage, NY, and on 29 November he played again at the church of St James in Carthage, also conducting a mixed choir. His brother and Emma Lajeunesse (*Albani) participated in this concert. According to *Le Canada Musical* of January 1867, 'the Dumouchel brothers' expert organ performance filled the audience with wonder.' He was in Europe 1869–72. Sources affirm that in 1872 he was the first Canadian to receive a doctorate in music; however, no document corroborates this assertion. His presence at the Leipzig Cons 1869–70 is confirmed by his teachers Ignaz Moscheles (piano), Friedrich Richter (theory), and Carl Reinecke (singing, chamber music). A diploma certifies that he also studied organ and piano with Robert Papperitz, who testified to his 'unpretentious technique, clear and elegant execution.' Returning to the USA in 1872, Dumouchel was organist at St Paul's Church in Oswego, at Rochester, and 1876–1919 at the Cathedral of the Immaculate Conception, Albany.

Although Dumouchel is known to have completed several compositions, they apparently are not extant. If, as is believed, he wrote a symphony, then – with Calixa *Lavallée, who also is supposed to have written one – he was one of the first Canadians to do so. No trace of the work or of any performance had been found by 1980, however. His *Grand Magnificat in C*, dedicated to William Bergé, and his motet 'Ecce panis' – both for mixed choir – were published by Ditson ca 1875. He also wrote masses, hymns, and piano pieces.

BIBLIOGRAPHY

Canada musical. vol 1, Jan 1867
'Nécrologie,' ibid, vol 2, Feb 1919
Musiciens canadiens

HP

DUMOUCHEL, (Alphonse) **Édouard**. Organist, pianist, teacher, b Rigaud, near Montreal, 1 Mar 1841, d Ogdensburg, NY, 21 Sep 1914. He attended college in Rigaud and studied music with his aunt, Esther Fournier. He was an organ teacher in Ogdensburg in 1867, the year in which he and his twin brother Arthur had been featured in two concerts given by 300 musicians. He participated in numerous concerts with his brother, and others with the soprano Emma Lajeunesse (the future *Albani) and her sister Cornelia, a violinist. *Le Canada musical* reported in April 1867 that the Dumouchel brothers 'are well known and have a great reputation in a large part of the United States.' In 1870 Édouard went to continue his studies in Germany. Subsequently he visited several countries, including England, Spain, and Egypt. He settled in Ogdensburg in 1883 and taught organ there for several years. Édouard and Arthur were buried at Rigaud.

BIBLIOGRAPHY

Musiciens canadiens

HP

DUNCAN, Chester (Thomas Alexander Winchester). Teacher (literature), pianist, critic, composer, b Strasbourg, north of Regina, 4 May 1913; ATCM 1930, BA (Manitoba) 1934, MA (Manitoba) 1939. He studied piano privately in Winnipeg with Beryl Ferguson and majored in literature 1930–4, 1935–9 at the U of Manitoba, and 1945–6 at the U of Toronto, specializing in 20th-century British poetry. He taught piano from 1936 to 1942. He developed his parallel interests – music and literature – to a high level, often interrelating them. A member for 35 years, 1943–78, of the Dept of English, U of Manitoba, where his lectures were noted for their civility and wit, he became known nationally for his incisive commentary – usually, though not always, on music – for CBC radio ('Critically Speaking,' 1950–63; 'Sharp, Flat and Natural,' 1954; 'Listening with Duncan,' 1958–61; 'Duncan's Diary,' 1961–3; a series of talks in 1952; special programs on the poetry of Yeats, Eliot, and Auden for 'CBC Wednesday Night' in 1959; programs on the music and letters of Brahms and Schumann in 1962; three lecture recitals on 'Jazz and the Modern Composer' in 1966, during which he also played Constant Lambert's *Sonata* and the piano part in Bartók's *Contrasts*; and a special program, 'Some Canadian Poets with Music,' in 1972 for 'CBC Tuesday Night'). Some of the material from his hundreds of broadcasts is preserved in his book *Wanna Fight, Kid?* (Winnipeg 1975).

Duncan has performed most often as a chamber musician (pianist of the *Hidy Trio, 1961–8, and sometime duo-recitalist with the violinist Frederick *Grinke, the cellist Martin Hoherman, the flutist Dirk *Keetbaas, the cellist Lorne *Munroe, and others) and as accompanist for singers (regularly Orville Derraugh and Joan *Maxwell, on occasion Belva Boroditsky, Uta Graf, Frances *James, Peter *van Ginkel, and many others). He has recorded with Marta *Hidy and Joan Maxwell for the CBC. He has also, however, given solo recitals in public and on radio and has performed many times as soloist with the *CBC Winnipeg Orchestra, in such works as Howard Ferguson's *Concerto* for piano and strings (twice), Alec Rowley's *Concertino* (twice), George Dyson's *Concerto Leggiero* (North American premiere), Hindemith's *The Four Temperaments* (twice), William Walton's *Sinfonia Concertante* (twice), Gordon Jacob's *Concerto No. 2* (North American premiere, and a repeat performance), E.J. Moeran's *Rhapsody No. 3* (three times), and Gershwin's *Concerto in F* (twice). He also played the solo part in Franck's *Symphonic Variations* for various performances of Gweneth Lloyd's *Allegory* by the Royal Winnipeg Ballet in the late 1940s.

Duncan's compositions – including his incidental music and songs for Auden's *The Ascent of F6* and *For the Time Being* – have had public performances in Winnipeg, and *For the Time Being* was broadcast by the CBC in 1965. A retrospective recital of his songs was presented 28 Jan 1973 by the School of Music, *U of Manitoba.

Duncan has contributed articles on music to *Saturday Night*, the *Dalhousie Review*, the *Tamarack*

Review, the *Canadian Music Journal*, the *Canadian Forum*, and the *Northern Review*. His wife, Ada (b Edith Margaret Elwick), is a gifted pianist and organist, and of their three children the youngest – Laurie Matthew, b Winnipeg 16 Sep 1956, B MUS (Manitoba) 1978, and a pupil in Winnipeg of Leonard *Isaacs, William *Aide, Boyd McDonald, and Merek *Jablonski, and, in London, of Phyllis Sellick – has become known as a solo pianist and accompanist of uncommon ability.

SELECTED COMPOSITIONS

INSTRUMENTAL

Incidental music for *Hassan* (James Elroy Flecker) 1944, *Coriolanus* (Shakespeare) 1950, *Elizabeth the Queen* (Maxwell Anderson) 1954, *Troilus and Cressida* (Shakespeare) 1956

Incidental music and songs for *The Ascent of F6* (Auden, Isherwood) 1945–50, *Pleasant Plain* (Margaret Stobie) 1952, *The Winter's Tale* (Shakespeare) 1953, *For the Time Being* (Auden) 1946–65, *Will Shakespeare* (Clemence Dane) 1949, *Woyzeck* (Büchner) 1962

PIANO

Entertainment (suite in 5 mvts). 1946. Ms

The Bridge, film music. 1951. Ms

Others

VOICE AND PIANO

Rhymes (limericks). 1966. Mezzo (bar). Ms

'Bed Time Prayer' (anon). 1971. Mezzo. Ms

'Exchanges' (Ernest Dowson). 1974. V. Ms

Also collections of songs: *A.E. Housman Songs* (1937–63), *Auden Songs* (1940–72), *Canadian Songs* (1944–71), *Hilaire Belloc Songs* (1974)

Several arrs of American, Australian, Canadian, and Scottish folk songs

CHOIR

Then and Now (Yeats). 1969. Sops in unison ('Then'), SSA ('Now'). Wat 1970

'Nunc dimittis.' 1970. Men and boys' choir. Ms

Three Songs (L. Carroll, Blake, Clough). 1974. Mixed chorus, pf. Ms

BIBLIOGRAPHY

Garlick, Richard. 'Duncan true Renaissance man,' Winnipeg *Tribune*, 6 Jan 1979 KW

DUNCAN, John. Harpist, harp builder, b Derbyshire, England, 2 Jan 1904. He began his study of the harp at 10 under Thomas Archibald Wragg in Derby and took further instruction from Charles Collier at the RCM. He worked for five years at the Rolls Royce plant in Derby, acquiring mechanical knowledge helpful later in the construction of harps. After playing in a Derby theatre orchestra he moved in 1927 to Canada, where he joined Reginald *Stewart's radio orchestra heard on 'Maple Leaf Symphony' on station CKGW in Toronto and, soon afterwards, the Uptown Theatre orchestra. In 1930 he formed the Old World Musicians, a group of four dedicated, though not exclusively, to the performance of medieval music. The group was heard weekly on local independent stations and, after 1932, on the CRBC and its successor, the CBC. It performed intermittently until 1965.

Duncan taught 1932–42 at the *TCM. In May 1933 he began to work for the CRBC (CBC 1936–), playing as a soloist or orchestral musician in hundreds of programs and participating in many premieres. By 1979 he had composed and played the music for CBC TV's 'The Friendly Giant' for more than 20 years. Duncan has made several cross-country tours, including one 1935–6 during which he played for the famous skater Sonja Henie. He has composed several works for harp and, for the Old World Musicians, some for violin, cello, flute, harp, and organ. Duncan has built 11 harps, one owned by the *Agostini family, the others by 'wealthy students' (his own comment) in New Zealand, Newfoundland, Vancouver, and Toronto. He has restored, rebuilt, or repaired more than 100 harps. CWt

Duo Pach. Joseph Pach, violin, and Arlene Nimmons Pach, piano. Married in 1954, the Pachs pursued solo careers until 1959, when they began studying as a sonata team in Vienna. They adopted the name Duo Pach in 1960 when they won a prize in the duo section of the Ninth International West German Radio Networks Competition in Munich. In 1961 they spent four months in London on a *Canada Council fellowship and made their BBC debut in the Respighi *Sonata*. Their Wigmore Hall debut in 1963 was followed by performances in Edinburgh, Frankfurt, and Dublin. A cross-Canada tour followed in the spring of 1964. Appointed musicians-in-residence at the *U of New Brunswick in Fredericton in 1964, they have performed frequently in that city and have toured in Canada and played for CBC broadcasts. They commissioned and premiered (at the *Charlottetown Festival, 1967) Jacques *Hétu's *Double Concerto* and performed the work with the *NACO on tour in the Maritimes in 1973.

Joseph Pach – b Toronto 8 Jan 1928; Artist Diploma (Toronto) 1947, a pupil of Chris Dafeff at the TCM 1933–45, and of Kathleen *Parlow at the U of Toronto 1945–50 – made his *TSO debut in 1947, playing the Tchaikovsky *Concerto* at a student concert. He toured the Maritimes as soloist with the *Halifax SO in 1965. In 1970 he was a founder of the U of New Brunswick Pach String Quartet (later *Brunswick String Quartet).

Arlene Nimmons Pach – b Kamloops, BC, 26 May 1928; ATCM 1945; BA philosophy (British Columbia) 1949 – sister of Phil *Nimmons, studied with Boris *Roubakine at the TCM. She has played and recorded with the Brunswick String Quartet. In 1966 she initiated the *U of New Brunswick Summer (later *Chamber Music and Jazz) Festival in which the Duo Pach and the Brunswick String Quartet have participated annually.

DISCOGRAPHY

Dohnanyi – Schubert – Walton. 1971. CBC SM-115

Morawetz *Duo* – Jones *Introduction and Fugue* – Somers *Rhapsody* – Bach. 1967. RCI 244

Duo-pianists. See Piano teams.

DUPUIS, Guillaume (Ladislas). Teacher, choirmaster, b Montreal 3 May 1887, d there 25 Apr 1954. He began his musical training under Joseph *Piché (piano and harmony) and later studied Gregorian chant with Guillaume *Couture and Henri *Garrouteigt, harmony with Romain *Pelletier, and choral conducting with Charles-Hugues *Lefebvre. He was choirmaster successively at the Ste-Philomène, Ste-Brigide, and Sacré-Coeur churches and occupied the same position 1918–49 at Notre-Dame Church. He also taught voice and solfège in several institutions, including the Ste-Croix Seminary, the Notre-Dame College, and the convents of the Sisters of the Holy Names of Jesus and Mary in Outremont and Villa-Maria. He was director of solfège classes for the province of Quebec and specialized in the development and instruction of children's choirs. He was director of the Octave-Pelletier Quartet, which consisted of the tenors Arthur Lapierre and J.-H. Thibaudeau, the baritone Rodrigue Gauthier, and the bass J.-M. Magnan. The group enjoyed considerable success, particularly in 1918. Dupuis's son Charles-O. Dupuis (b Montreal 7 Mar 1928) served 1969–78 as director of the choir *Petits Chanteurs du Mont-Royal. (CMr)

DUQUETTE. Montreal family of musicians: 1 / Jean A., 2 / Ellsworth, brother of Jean A., and 3 / Raoul, son of Jean A.

1 **Jean** (or John) **A.** (Alfred). Violinist, violist, teacher, b Oswego, NY, 15 Mar 1853, d Montreal 10 May 1902. Arriving in Montreal ca 1865, he studied violin 1865–71 with Jules *Hone. He spent the next two years at the Boston Cons, where he obtained a diploma. After teaching violin and piano 1873–80 at St Joseph College in Ottawa he taught 1880–1 in New York before returning to Montreal, where he gave lessons in violin, mandolin, and accompaniment, both privately and in several institutions. Albert *Chamberland and Camille *Couture were among his pupils. Duquette was first violin in a string quartet formed in 1890 with Isaac Silverstone (violin), Cathcart Wallace, (viola), and Louis *Charbonneau (cello). He was one of the founders of the *Couture *MSO, playing as a member of the viola section, and serving as president 1894–6. He also served as president of the Montreal Musical Union. He participated in chamber music concerts 1899–1901, at *His Majesty's Theatre and Karn Hall, as a member of a quartet with Otto Zimmermann, Herbert *Spencer, and Charbonneau. On 26 Jun 1878 he married the pianist and singer Cordélia Lavallée, sister of Calixa *Lavallée. Their daughter Blanche, a pianist, married the critic Gustave *Comte in 1900.

2 **Ellsworth**. Bass, accountant, b Phoenix, NY, 25 Jun 1862, d Montreal 18 Oct 1922. Endowed with an exceptional voice, he received some instruction from Georges W. Cornish, the organist and choirmaster of Erskine Church in Montreal, and studied solfège with his father. Throughout his life he was active as a singer in Montreal and in the USA while working as an accountant. He sang in the choirs of Notre-Dame Church and was a soloist in several churches. He was one of the soloists in the premiere of Henri *Miro's *Messe solennelle* and in a 1904 concert of works by Alexis *Contant, and he sang the title role of Contant's **Caïn* at its premiere the following year. Duquette made frequent guest appearances 1895–6 with the Couture MSO and 1904–5 with the Goulet MSO. In 1918 he was president of the *Assn des Chanteurs de Montréal. He was the grandfather of Marcelle *Gagné.

3 **Raoul**. Cellist, teacher, b Montreal 1879, d there 9 May 1962. He received a basic musical training from his father and studied cello with Gustave *Labelle. He continued his cello studies 1901–4 under Édouard Jacobs at the Ghent Cons. On the recommendation of Emma *Albani, an acquaintance of his father, he auditioned for Sir Henry Wood, who hired him; he was a member 1904–10 of the orchestra of the Covent Garden Royal Opera. After returning to Montreal he performed as a soloist and orchestral player and taught at *McGill U. He was a conductor for radio station CKAC, a member of the *Montreal Orchestra throughout its existence, and a member 1935–ca 1950 of the *CSM Orchestra. In 1917 he founded the César Franck Trio with Leon Kofman (violin) and Blanche Hardy-Laurendeau (piano) and he was a member 1920–5 of the Chamberland String Quartet. He recorded a cello transcription of the song 'Annie Laurie' for HMV (216041). GP

DURIEUX, André (Henri). Violinist, conductor, arranger, teacher, b Paris 1899, d Montreal 18 Dec 1951. His family settled in Canada in 1911. He studied at the *McGill Cons with Saul *Brant and in Chicago with Otakar Ševčík and Leopold Auer. Returning to Montreal he joined the McGill Cons and taught violin there 1923–37. In 1924 he was concertmaster of the orchestra of radio station CKAC and the Little Symphony of the Northern Electric station CHYC, as well as first violin of CHYC's string quartet. He was first violin of the Durieux String Quartet, which included his brother Maurice (second violin), Lucien *Robert (viola), and Lucien *Plamondon (cello). The pianist Léo-Pol *Morin joined the group for quintets. During its short existence (1930–2), the quartet gave numerous concerts, mainly for the *Ladies' Morning Musical Club and the Arts Club, and at the Windsor and Ritz-Carlton hotels. Along with Henri *Delcellier, Giulio *Romano, and Benny Chackelston, among others, Durieux was a founding member of the *Montreal Orchestra and was its assistant concertmaster 1930–2. In 1935 he began a long association with CBC radio, conducting orchestras for such light-music programs as 'Ici Paris' in 1935, 'Bonjour Paris' in 1938, and 'Sur les boulevards' in 1939, and for talent searches like 'Les Talents de chez-nous,' which he developed in 1946. He wrote some waltzes and chansonnettes, including 'La Java des Laurentides' and 'C'est que je t'aime.' GP

DURIEUX, Maurice. Conductor, arranger, violinist, violist, b Courbevoie, near Paris, 3 Dec 1907, d Ottawa 11 Nov 1976. He arrived in Montreal in 1911 and some time later began to study violin with his elder brother André. He was also a pupil of Maurice *Onderet (violin) and Rodolphe *Mathieu (harmony). Durieux began his career in 1924 on radio station CHYC. He was a soloist and conductor for several CBC radio light music programs and also played in the Howard *Fogg and Benny Chackelston orchestras; in 1930 he was a founding member of the *Montreal Orchestra. He was second violin in the Durieux Quartet, which was established by his brother in 1930 and played for two years. Having decided to concentrate on the viola, he studied in the 1940s at the *CMM with Louis *Bailly and William Primrose. About 1951 he was conductor for the CBC radio programs 'Rythmes de Paris,' 'En sourdine,' and 'Stringtime.' He also conducted the orchestra of the Montreal Press Club and accompanied Muriel *Millard in songs she recorded for RCA Victor. For the *Montreal Festivals he directed the concerts 'Soirée viennoise' in 1952, 'La Grande Valse' in 1953 and 1954, and 'Fête populaire dansante' in 1955. He was a member of the CBC Serenade for Strings and *'Little Symphonies' orchestras and played ca 1952–67 in the *MSO. He composed some light music, including *Isola d'amore* (*Passe-Temps*, 906, Jan 1947). GP

DUSCHENES, Mario. Flutist, conductor, teacher, b Altona, near Hamburg, 27 Oct 1923; prix de virtuosité (Geneva Cons) 1946, hon LLD (Concordia) 1979. By 1935 he had studied in turn recorder, solfège, and piano. He then became interested in the flute and studied with his father and brothers. He entered the Geneva Cons and completed his training 1943–7 with Henri Gagnebin, André Pépin, Frank Martin, and Isabelle Nef. He won an award at the 1947 International Competition for Musical Performers in Geneva. After several tours in Europe as soloist with the Ars Antiqua Ensemble, he moved to Canada in September 1948. In August 1949 he staged and narrated the Canadian premiere of Stravinsky's *L'Histoire du soldat* at *McGill U.

After settling in Montreal, Duschenes became active in musical life there, mainly as a soloist with the CBC *'Little Symphonies' orchestra, the *Pro Musica Society, the *McGill Chamber Orchestra, the *Casavant Society, and *Musica Antica e Nuova. He appears on an LP made by members of the latter society. He was co-founder in 1953 of the *CAMMAC Music Centre, where he has taught for over 25 years, and he has taught 1954–70 at McGill U and 1970–3 at the *U of Montreal. He was co-founder in 1957 of the *Baroque Trio of Montreal. Appointed conductor of young

Mario Duschenes

people's matinées for the *Quebec SO in 1969, he assumed similar positions with the *MSO in 1970 and the *NACO in 1973. He has appeared on the podium of several other Canadian orchestras, including the *TS, as guest director of children's concerts. In 1973 he also became director of the Concerts-midi at *PDA. An expert in the Carl *Orff teaching method, he became a member in 1974 of the advisory board of the association Music for Children Carl Orff Canada. His contribution to music appreciation was underlined by Jamie *Portman, who wrote in *The Gazette* (7 Dec 1978) that Duschenes 'is probably doing more for the image of young people's concerts than anyone else in Canada.' Duschenes is the author of numerous widely distributed works published by BMI Canada and later by *Berandol, notably *Method for the Recorder I* (1957) and *II* (1962) for soprano or alto (issued in French as *Méthode de flûte à bec I*, 1962, and *II*, 1968), *School Recorder Method* (1957) for soprano and alto together (issued in French as *La Flûte à bec à l'école*, 1973), and *Studies in Recorder Playing* (1960). He has edited or written easy duos and trios, studies for alto recorder, and adaptations or arrangements of works from the renaissance and baroque periods, of Bach (1960), and of Leopold Mozart. Duschenes was awarded the *CMCouncil Medal in 1978 and the prize of the Concert Society of the Jewish People's Schools and Peretz Schools in 1980.

DISCOGRAPHY

Albinoni *Sonata, Op 6, no. 6*. K. Jones hpd. 1960. Vox 514320

The Art of Mario Duschenes. 1969. Orion ORS 6911

Bach *Concerto in F*. Goldberg rec, Beckensteiner hpd, Paillard Chamb O, Paillard cond. 1958. Erato LDE 3094

Duets for Flutes and Flute and Recorder: Telemann – Bodinus – et al. Rampal fl. 1966. Bar 2855

Flute Recital: Music from the 13th to the 20th century. 1965. Sel CC 15.066

Handel *Four Flute Sonatas*. K. Jones hpd. 1960. Vox STPL 516.340

– *Eight Flute Sonatas*. K. Jones hpd. (1963). 2-Vox SVUX 52021

– *Four Sonatas*. Veyron-Lacroix hpd. 1958. Erato LDE 3126

Handel – Bach: *Flute Sonatas*. K. Jones hpd. (1973). Vox SVBX 535

Handel – Locatelli – Telemann. Rampal fl, Larrieu fl, Veyron-Lacroix hpd. (1964). Mus H Soc MHS 556

K. Jones *Rondo* for solo flute. (1967). RCA CCS 1013

Recorder Music Old and New: Byrd – Frescobaldi – K. Jones – et al. Duschenes Rec Quar. 1965. Bar BC 1857

Sammartini – Quantz – Telemann – Loeillet: *Sonatas* for flute, recorder, and harpsichord. Rampal fl, Veyron-Lacroix hpd. 1957. Erato EFM 42.037

Telemann *Concerto in E Minor*. Rampal fl, Paillard Chamb O, Paillard cond. 1957. Erato EFM 42.038

– *Two Concertos*. Fonteny vc, Paillard Chamb O, Paillard cond. 1965. Erato LDE 3352/Erato STU 70252

– *Sonatas* et al. Duschenes rec, André tpt, Rampal fl, Pierlot ob, Chambon ob, Hongne bn, Veyron-Lacroix hpd. (1965). Erato EFM 8081/Mus H Soc MHS 754

– *Sonatas* and *Trios*. Rampal fl, Veyron-Lacroix hpd. 1965. Erato LDE 3376

Trio Sonatas: Bach – Pepusch – et al. Rampal fl, Gilbert hpd. 1966. Bar 2879/Musidisc 30RC 780

Duschenes also can be heard on *The Art of Jean-Pierre Rampal* (Orion ORS 7149), *The Golden Sound of Jean-Pierre Rampal* (Orion ORS 73114), *The Art of the Flute* (4-Everest SDBR 3194-3197), *Four Centuries of the Flute* (Everest SDBR 3299), and *Thèmes musicaux avec l'oncle Hubert* (Fantel FA 39411).

See also Discographies for Baroque Trio of Montreal; Bress; Montreal String Quartet.

BIBLIOGRAPHY

Proulx, Michelle. 'Mario Duschenes began conducting as a student,' *MSc*, 304, Nov–Dec 1978 (PR)

DUSSAULT, Céline. Soprano, b Thetford Mines, Que, 14 May 1946; B MUS (Montreal) 1968, premier prix voice (CMM) 1973. She studied 1964–8 at the *École Vincent-d'Indy, concentrating first on piano under Sister Rachel-Yvonne and Yvonne *Hubert, then on singing with Louise *André, Bernard *Diamant, and Roy *Royal and opera with Pierrette *Alarie. She continued 1968–73 at the *CMM with Heinz Rehfuss, Daniel Ferro, Rose Bampton, and Pierre Héral. Her performance in the 1971 *MSO Concours won her a Women's Committee bursary, and the following year she became the first singer to win the International Stepping Stones prize of the *Canadian Music Competition. During the summer of 1972 she attended courses at Aspen Music School in Colorado.

Dussault gave a recital as part of the 1972 Young Canadian Performers series at *St Lawrence Centre, Toronto. At the *Poudrière Theatre she sang the roles of Laetitia in Menotti's *The Old Maid and the Thief* in 1973, Suzanne in Wolf-Ferrari's *Le Secret de Suzanne* in 1974 and 1976, Monica in Menotti's *The Medium* in 1974, and Laurette in Bizet's *Le Docteur Miracle* in 1975. She toured 1973–4 with the *JMC production of *The Magic Flute*, singing the roles of Pamina and Papagena, and was part of the *Ensemble Cantabile de Montréal when it was formed in August 1974. That October she sang in Janáček's *Jenůfa* at Lincoln Center, New York. On CBC radio she premiered Ginette Bertrand's *La Fugitive*, and the performance was selected for submission to the 1975 Paul-Gilson competition in Brussels. During that season she also sang the Child in Ravel's *L'Enfant et les sortilèges* with the Vermont Opera Theatre. As part of the Arts and Culture program of the 1976 Olympics she sang Nadia in the Quebec City and Montreal performances of the *Quebec SO's production of *The Merry Widow*. She was a member 1977–9 of the Centre lyrique de Wallonie in Liège, Belgium, singing several roles, including Annie in *Oklahoma*, Poussette in *Manon*, Céline in Grétry's *Richard Coeur de Lion*, Lady Lucy in Messager's *Monsieur Beaucaire*, Stéphano in *Roméo et Juliette*, and the title role of Messager's *Véronique*. In the premiere of Paul Francy's *Alice au pays des merveilles* she sang the role of Alice; Renée Maheu thought her 'a spirited performer, lively and playful' (*Musicanada*, March 1979). After her return to Canada in 1979 she taught at the UQATR. She is the sister of pianist Michel *Dussault. ST

DUSSAULT, Joseph-Daniel. Organist, teacher, b Charlesbourg, near Quebec City, 6 Jan 1864, d Montreal 1 Apr 1921. He studied organ with his father, Cléophas, an organist in Charlesbourg, and after 1879 with Gustave *Gagnon in Quebec City. At the same time he was organist at the Jesuits' church until his appointment to the parish church of Lotbinière, where he was organist 1881–9. At the suggestion of R.-O. *Pelletier he went to Paris to continue his training 1889–91 under Eugène Gigout. On his return to Canada, he was organist 1891–2 at the St-Hyacinthe Cathedral and organist-choirmaster 1892–6 at St Paul's Church in Oswego, NY. He was invited to succeed Alcibiade *Béique at Notre-Dame Church in Montreal and held that position from 1896 until his death, giving nearly 100 recitals there. He taught at *McGill U and in several other institutions, including the convents of Villa-Maria and Lachine and that of the Dames du Sacré-Coeur. His pupils included Jean-Noël *Charbonneau and Hector *Pellerin. In a program 9 Apr 1935 on CBC radio Arthur *Letondal recalled him: 'A brilliant organist both in concert and in church services, Dussault was an artist who was really absorbed in his art.'

Dussault 'revised and amplified' J.S. Eschmann's *Guide du jeune pianiste* (Montreal ca 1890). He had undertaken the compilation of an 18-volume work, *L'Organiste liturgique*, but only the first two volumes were published, appearing after 1900. Because of the church music reforms advocated by Pope Pius X's *Moto proprio* (1903; see Plainsong), the series was discontinued. (CH)

DUSSAULT, Michel (Joseph). Pianist, teacher, broadcaster, composer, b Thetford Mines, Que, 8 Jul 1943; premier prix (CMM) 1961, premier prix (Cons de Paris) 1963. He studied piano in Sherbrooke and 1955–61 at the *CMM under Yvonne *Hubert. At 13 he played the first movement of Beethoven's *Concerto No. 3* with the *Sherbrooke SO conducted by Sylvio *Lacharité and with the CBC Montreal orchestra under Wilfrid *Pelletier. In 1960 he obtained the *Prix Archambault and a scholarship from the *Amis de l'Art foundation. He was the winner of the grand prize of the *CBC Talent Festival Competition in 1961 and performed with all the principal orchestras in Canada. He was a pupil of Vlado Perlemuter 1961–2 in Paris and of Yvonne Lefébure 1962–3 at the Cons de Paris. He represented Canada at the International JM Congress in 1963, performing on that occasion with the Swiss Orchestra at Palma de Mallorca.

After a recital at the Centre social of the *U of Montreal, for which Dussault's program included Debussy's *L'Isle joyeuse* and *Étude pour les accords*, Jean *Vallerand wrote: '[Dussault's] playing was of a very fine quality, his musical sensitivity that of a magnificent artist, capable of depth of thought and subtlety in interpretation. His dynamic scheme was charmingly put forward, the phrases "sung" with sincerity and inner conviction' (*La Presse*, 31 Oct 1963).

Between 1959 and 1972 Dussault made seven *JMC tours and on one in 1968–9 he accompanied the baritone Max Van Egmond, the clarinetist Milenko Stefanovic, and the violinist Konstantin Kulka. Other tours in these years included one, sponsored in 1963 by the *Canada Council, of Canadian universities.

Dussault was one of the winners of the JMC National Competition in 1964 and was the host 1965–7 for 'Jeunesse oblige' on CBC TV. As well as playing with the Boston SO in 1958, the San Francisco SO in 1960, and the Cleveland Orchestra and the Chicago Symphony in 1965, he has appeared with the *Quebec SO on several occasions. In 1978 he performed Chopin's *Concerto No. 2* with that orchestra. In 1979 Dussault became one of the hosts of 'Au gré de la fantaisie' on CBC radio.

Dussault established the music program at the Sherbrooke Seminary in 1966–7, began teaching at the UQATR in 1969, and taught at the Cons de Trois-Rivières 1973–5.

Between 1954 and 1966 Dussault composed about 30 piano pieces as well as some chamber works. For the LP *Musique québécoise: 'Nos compositeurs'* (L'Oiseau-Coeur OC S-02) he recorded Rodolphe *Mathieu's *Sonata* and, with the *Classical Quartet of Montreal, the same composer's *Quintet*. He is the brother of the soprano Céline *Dussault. (PR)

DUSSEAU, Jeanne (b Ruth Cleveland Thom). Soprano, b Glasgow 2 Feb 1893. Taken to Toronto as a child she began voice study with M.M. Stevenson and at 16 was contralto soloist at Bloor St Baptist Church. After study with Atherton Furlong, she made a formal debut 12 Nov 1912 as a soprano in a recital at Foresters' Hall. She continued her studies with Giuseppe *Carboni, then sang 1921–2 with the Chicago Opera, her roles including the Shepherd in *Tannhäuser* and Ninette in the world premiere in 1921 of *The Love of Three Oranges*. For several years thereafter the soprano (who had married the French-Canadian baritone Lambert Victor Dusseau in 1919) confined her activities to recitals and concerts with symphony orchestras in Toronto, New York, Boston, Cincinnati, and abroad. Her contributions to the Canadian music scene were considerable at this time. During a coast-to-coast tour in 1928, presented by the Association of Canadian Clubs in co-operation with the *National Museum of Canada and the *TCM, she introduced a large number of Canadian folksongs in new arrangements by Alfred *Laliberté, Ernest *MacMillan, and Healey *Willan. In the late 1920s and early 1930s she was a participant in the *CPR Festivals. Mme Dusseau made a highly successful London debut 15 Oct 1929 at Wigmore Hall and sang 1936–40 at the Sadler's Wells Opera, her roles including Tosca, Aida, Cio-Cio San in *Madama Butterfly*, Leonore in *Fidelio*, and Rosalinda in *Die Fledermaus*. After her retirement from performance in 1942 she taught for many years in New York, then moved to Washington, DC. Her only commercial recording, for HMV in 1939, couples the Easter Hymn from *Cavalleria Rusticana* and the Barcarolle from *The Tales of Hoffmann* (with Nancy Evans and the Sadler's Wells Chorus). JBM

Dutch. See the Netherlands.

DUVAL, Pierre (b Coutu, Ovide). Tenor, b Montreal 17 Sep 1932. He took lessons from Frank *Rowe in Montreal and from Rachele Maragliano-Mori 1956–7 in Rome and in 1958 at the Accademia Santa Cecilia. He continued his studies 1958–9 at the *CMM with Dina Maria Narici. With the help of a *Canada Council scholarship he studied in Rome 1960–3 with Alberto Volonnino and made his debut in 1962 at the Teatro dell'Opera in Stravinsky's *The Nightingale*. With the Théâtre lyrique du Québec he sang Des Grieux in *Manon* in 1967, Cavaradossi in *Tosca* in 1968–9, and Nadir in *Les Pêcheurs de perles* in the 1969–70 season. He had sung Nadir in 1964 for the *Théâtre lyrique de Nouvelle-France, as well as Alfredo (*La Traviata*) in 1965. In *La Presse* (13 Jul 1966) Jean *Vallerand described a concert appearance with the *MSO: 'Pierre Duval is the consummate opera singer: he has unfailing courage, perfect technique and an amazing communicative generosity ... Last night he sang splendidly, one after another, five of the most demanding pieces in the repertoire.'

In 1968 Duval was a soloist with the Cleveland SO under George Szell in Verdi's *Requiem* in Cleveland and New York. For the *Vancouver Opera he sang the Duke in *Rigoletto* in 1967, and for the *COC he sang Rodolfo in *La Bohème* in 1968 and the Duke in 1969. For the *Opéra du Québec, he repeated the Duke in 1972 and sang Cassio in *Otello* in 1973 and Almaviva in *The Barber of Seville* in 1976. Duval's name became widely known through his Arturo opposite Joan Sutherland's Elvira in the recording of Bellini's *I Puritani*. He repeated the role at the Teatro Comunale in Bologna in March 1973 and also, during the 1972–3 season, appeared in *Roméo et Juliette* in New Orleans, *Lucia di Lammermoor* in Syracuse, and *Rigoletto* in Milwaukee. He has sung with several major US orchestras, including those of Chicago, the Hollywood Bowl, Los Angeles, Philadelphia, and Pittsburgh, and has performed in Europe, Chile, and South Africa.

Duval sang the role of Paris in the Festival Canada (*Festival Ottawa) production of *La Belle Hélène* at the *NAC in 1973, in the festival's revival of the piece in 1975, and in performances of it at the Kennedy Center, Washington, DC, and on CBC TV in 1976. He took part in a number of other CBC opera telecasts in the series 'Festival' and 'L'*Heure du concert,' appearing in the 1965 Emmy-Award-winning *The Barber of Seville* and singing Roméo in *Roméo et Juliette* in 1971, Macduff in *Macbeth* in 1973, and Pinkerton in *Madama Butterfly* in 1976. In 1978 he sang *Faust* at the *Grand Théâtre in Quebec City, Charles VII in the COC production of Tchaikovsky's *Joan of Arc*, and Alfredo in the *Manitoba Opera production of *Die Fledermaus*. After the *Fledermaus* performance Donald Gislason of the *Winnipeg Free Press* remarked (24 Nov 1978) on 'the splendour of his voice,' which he compared with that of the Italian tenor Luciano Pavarotti.

DISCOGRAPHY

Bellini *I Puritani*. Maggio Musicale Fiorentino, Bonynge cond. 1964. 3-Lon OSA 1373

Donizetti *Lucia di Lammermoor*. RCA orch and chor, Prêtre cond, Duval (Arturo). 1966. 3-RCA LSC 6170

Montemezzi *L'Amore dei tre Re*. Rome SO, Accademia Santa Cecilia chorus, R. Karp cond. 1969. 2-Sel CC 15035-15036 ST

DYDE, Henry Alexander. Lawyer, patron, b Kingston, Ont, 29 Jun 1896, d Edmonton 3 Feb 1976; BA (Alberta) 1916, BA (Oxford) 1921, BCL (Oxford) 1922, LL B (Alberta) 1923, hon LL D (Alberta) 1965. After distinguished service during World War I (he was awarded the Military Cross and Bar) he held a number of executive positions 1930–45 in the Ministry of National Defence. He was awarded the OBE in 1945. In 1949 he moved to Edmonton, where he and his wife, Dorothy Reynolds Plaunt, as volunteers and benefactors, supported the *Edmonton SO and the Society for Talent Education. Their interest in string playing in Alberta is perpetuated in the H.A. Dyde Memorial String Scholarship established at the *Banff SFA in 1977. They also supported the visual arts and ballet.

DYER, James (Edwin). Violin and viola maker, b Norfolk County, Ont, ca 1897, d Toronto? ca 1960. His interest in violins began at about 12 on receipt of an old and stringless instrument from a neighbour. It was while studying telegraphy in Toronto ca 1915 that Dyer first attempted to build a violin, using as a guide Edward Heron-Allen's *Violin Making As It Was and Is* (London 1884). Except for a year in the 1920s in the employ of the George *Heinl Co, where he broadened his skills, Dyer worked at Toronto's Union (railway) Station until retirement in the 1950s, building instruments only as a hobby. He completed about 30 violins and violas, and his work is said to have been well regarded by such performers as Jascha Heifetz, Sascha Jacobsen, and Adolph *Koldofsky. Dyer instruments have been owned by Arthur *Le-

Blanc, Stephen *Kondaks, D'Arcy *Shea, and Sigmund Steinberg.

BIBLIOGRAPHY
Anglin, R.G. 'Violin maker,' *Maclean's*, 15 Aug 1942
Zuchter, Victor. 'Of strings and things,' *TS News*, Oct–Nov 1973 CF

DYKE, George J. (John). Violinist, conductor, teacher, impresario, critic, *b St Blazey, Cornwall, England, 23 Mar 1864, d Victoria, BC, 16 Mar 1940. He studied in St Austell and in Plymouth with John Parde (violin) and W. Willoughby (organ). With his brother (Frederick William, cellist, organist, choirmaster, b St Blazey 15 Mar 1865, d Victoria 11 Jul 1928) he emigrated to Canada in 1886. After ranching near Moose Mountain, NWT (now southeast Saskatchewan), and editing the Moosomin *Courier*, he followed his brother to Vancouver in 1888. The brothers, with F.J. Painton, opened the first music shop in Vancouver, the short-lived Painton and Dyke. Several years later the brothers established a second firm, Dyke and Evans, which was operated by Fred until 1910. (It became the J.W. Kelly Piano Co in 1925.) George was also co-founder (1890s) of a violin academy which was Vancouver's first music school and a forerunner of the Vancouver Cons. In connection with the academy, the brothers (who had played in a string quartet as early as 1888) formed a trio with the pianist Francis Tuck. They also were members of a quartet with the violinist Robert Marshall and the violist J. Wyatt. George formed the Dyke Orchestra, which gave promenade concerts, served for four years as the orchestra at the Vancouver Opera House, and accompanied the Emma Juch English Opera at the opening of the CPR's Vancouver Opera House. He also played in Bishop Sillitoe's New Westminster orchestra and in the bishop's oratorio and chamber music presentations. In Vancouver Dyke was the founder of a 20-member mandolin and guitar club, the choirmaster at the Reformed Episcopal and Knox Presbyterian churches, the conductor of the 'Songs of Nations' choral concerts in Stanley Park, a participant with Carr Walton in operettas of the day (*Cinderella, Sleeping Beauty*, and *The Charming Princess*), a judge at band competitions, a representative of the *TCL, a music critic under the pen name 'Gamba' for the *Vancouver World*, the composer of an evening service, three hymns, and *Six Petites Pièces* (violin and piano), and the promoter of many concerts by Canadian and foreign performers, including the Mendelssohn Quintette, the pianist Harold Bauer, the violinist Leonora Jackson, the cellist Anton Hekking, the singer Edith *Miller, and the Channing Ellery bands. In 1913 George Dyke moved to Victoria. Though by profession a broker, he continued to organize concerts by Mark *Hambourg, Mischa Elman, Leopold Godowsky, Kathleen *Parlow, and the Los Angeles, Minneapolis, Vancouver, and Seattle orchestras, among others. To stimulate recruiting during World War I he initiated and managed Sunday evening band concerts under the bandmaster James M. Miller. In 1919 he became the music critic for the Victoria *Times* and in his writings encouraged the festival movement on Vancouver Island. He also began violin classes in the public schools and organized the George J. Dyke String Orchestra. His brother Fred conducted the Vancouver Choral and Orchestral Society, trained the Vancouver choir for the *Cycle of Musical Festivals in 1903, directed the cantata *The Haymakers* and the operetta *Patience* (the latter with the young Louise *Edvina), and served as organist-choirmaster in a succession of Vancouver churches. Fred succeeded George as supervisor of music 1919–28 in the city's schools.

BIBLIOGRAPHY
Kaye. 'Celebrates half century serving music,' *Vancouver Daily Province*, 6 Feb 1937 (BNSG)

E

Early instruments and early music. See Instruments: medieval, renaissance, and baroque.

'Early Morning Rain.' Song by Gordon *Lightfoot. Written in the summer of 1964, it recounts a lonely man's attempts to make his way back to a faraway home. It was recorded first by Ian and Sylvia (*Tyson) as the title song of their fourth LP (Vanguard VSD 79154) and was a minor hit 1965–6 as recorded by the US trio Peter, Paul and Mary (Warner 5659). Over 60 other recordings followed, including those by Harry Belafonte, Johnny Cash, Judy Collins, Bob Dylan, George Hamilton IV, the Kingston Trio, and Jerry Lee Lewis. The composer recorded the song for his LPs *Lightfoot* and *Sunday Concert*. 'Early Morning Rain' was copyrighted in 1964 and 1966 by M. Witmark, New York, and has been included in the Lightfoot folios *Anthology I* (Warner nd) and *Gord's Gold* (Warner 1976). MM

Easter, Lent, the Passion. The term 'Easter music' is used to describe all music specific to the season beginning with Ash Wednesday, through Holy Week and ending with the Ascension. Bach's *St Matthew Passion* has become a staple of the season in Canada, owing mainly to the performances given for over 30 years (1923–57, many of them broadcast) by Sir Ernest *MacMillan, first at Timothy Eaton Memorial Church, then with the *TCM chorus, and after 1942 with the *Toronto Mendelssohn Choir. The other Bach passions, Beethoven's *Mount of Olives*, Brahms' *German Requiem*, the Mozart and Fauré requiems, Spohr's *Calvary*, and Gounod's *La Rédemption* also have been sung during the Easter season in public concert and in Canadian churches, though during at least the first half of the 20th century works of somewhat less distinction – John Stainer's *The Crucifixion*, Alfred Gaul's *The Holy City*, Théodore Dubois's *Les Sept Paroles du Christ*, and John Henry Maunder's *From Olivet to Calvary* – were encountered more frequently. The Dubois has remained the single most popular Easter-season work in Quebec churches, Good Friday performances often enlisting the services of such leading soloists as Raoul *Jobin or Richard *Verreau. Many less famous works also have been performed, eg, *Messiah Victorious*, a cantata by William G. Hammond, at Trinity Methodist Church in Toronto, on Easter in 1913, and *Crux* by Fernand de La Tombelle and *Les Mystères douloureux* by Charles Planchet, performed in Montreal in 1922 and 1925 respectively.

Probably the first extended seasonal offering of the kind in Canada was the plainsong passion sung at Quebec on Good Friday 1646. A participant wrote: 'Then the service took place at which the passion was sung by three voices, – to wit, by Monsieur de St. Sauveur [Jean Le Sueur], Gospeller; by Monsieur the prior [René Chartier], who represented the synagogue; and by me' (Jérôme Lalemant, *Jesuit Relations*, vol 28, p. 177).

Easter-season works of major proportions composed by Canadians include Frédéric *Pelletier's *Stabat mater* (performed 1925) and his oratorio *La Rédemption* (ca 1930), Roberta Geddes-Harvey's oratorio *Salvator* (1907, performed in *Guelph, Toronto, and Kingston), Joseph-Julien *Perrault's *Stabat mater* and *Passion* (both composed between 1849 and 1866), Albert *Ham's cantata *The Solitudes of the Passion* (1917), J. Antonio *Thompson's *Les Sept Paroles du Christ* (1933) and *Messe de Pâques* (1941), and Arthur *Poynter's church opera *The Triumph of Our Lord* (1950). More recent are settings of *The Passion According to St Luke* by James McRae and Keith *Bissell and of the *Stabat mater* by Welford *Russell and Bernard *Naylor. Naylor also composed an Easter cantata, *The Resurrection According to St Matthew* (1965). Other significant works are Godfrey *Ridout's *The Ascension* (1962, the second of his *Cantiones mysticae*), the Easter portions of Violet *Archer's *Cantata sacra* (1966), and Paul *Pedersen's *Cantata and Narrative for Good Friday* (1972).

Among Canadian composers of anthems, carols, and motets for the Easter season are W.H. *Anderson, Keith Bissell, Barrie *Cabena, George Fox, Graham *George, Barry Gosse, Kenneth *Meek, Bernard Naylor (notably his *Victimae Paschali*, his *Three Latin Motets*, and some of his *Nine English Motets*), Alfred *Whitehead (who probably has composed a greater number of short Easter pieces of good quality than any of his colleagues, his output being exemplified by his setting of *Most Glorious Lord of Lyfe*), and Healey *Willan (*Introit and Gradual for Dedication in Eastertide*, B601, and numerous others). Willan also wrote *Responsories for the Offices of Tenebrae* (1956), *Propers for Lent*, and *Antiphon for Lent*.

There are several Easter-seasonal works for organ, eg, Willan's chorale preludes on *Gelobt sei Gott* and *Vexilla regis* (1950) and on the *Easter Hymn* and *O filii et filiae* (ca 1956), *Matton's *Suite de Pâques* (1950), *Morel's suite *Alleluia* (1964–8), *Bales' *Fanfare for Easter Day* (organ and brass, 1964), Lynnwood *Farnam's *Toccata* on 'O filii et filiae,' Bernard *Piché's *Fugue sur l'Ite missa est alliluiatique*, Benoît *Poirier's *Cloches de Pâques*, and Marius *Cayouette's *Prélude pour les Matines de Pâques*.

BIBLIOGRAPHY
Bryant *Healey Willan Catalogue*
'Canadian church music composers,' *RCCO Q*, Jun 1974; 'Supplement one,' ibid, Jun 1976
Canadian Music Centre. Catalogues and scores (FRCC)

EASTON, Florence (Gertrude) (m MacLennan, m Rogers). Soprano, b Middlesbrough, Yorkshire, England, 25 Oct 1882, d New York 13 Aug 1955, buried in Montreal. (Corrected birthdates of Easton and her first husband, and the years of her career in Hamburg, are from research by John *Stratton). The Easton family moved to Toronto ca 1888, and the young Florence sang in the choir of Parkdale Methodist Church, where her father was choirmaster and her mother organist. After her mother's death the family returned to England, where Florence attended the RAM 1900–1. She studied in Paris the following year with Elliott *Haslam. During her debut season, 1902–3 with the Moody-Manners Opera, she met the tenor Francis MacLennan (1874–1935), who had been raised in Collingwood, Ont. They were married in 1904 and together toured North America 1905–7 with the Savage English Grand Opera, with which Easton is known to have sung Butterfly in England and Norina (*Don Pasquale*) in Toronto in April 1907, as well as other leading roles. She and MacLennan also sang three performances of *Madama Butterfly* at the opening of the Walker Theatre in Winnipeg in 1907.

Easton was prima donna 1907–13 at the Hofoper, Berlin, 1913–16 at the Hamburg Opera, and 1916–17 at the Chicago Opera. She also sang Serpina in the North American premiere (1917) of *La Serva Padrona* with the Society of American Sing-

Florence Easton as Cio-Cio-San

ers, made her *Metropolitan Opera debut 7 Dec 1917 as Santuzza in *Cavalleria Rusticana*, and went on to enjoy success, during 12 consecutive seasons there, in a wide variety of roles, including Carmen, La Gioconda, Elsa, Tosca, Isolde, Turandot, Fiordiligi, and the Marschallin. In the early years of this period she sang Butterfly (1919) and Tosca (1920) with the Scotti Grand Opera in its Montreal appearances. During these years, too, she sang in several premieres, notably Puccini's *Gianni Schicchi*, Deems Taylor's *The King's Henchman*, and Edward W. Naylor's *The Angelus*. She was Fiordiligi in the first US performance of *Così fan tutte*, 24 Mar 1922 at the Metropolitan Opera, and sang in the first US performance of Krenek's *Jonny spielt auf*.

In the early 1920s Easton re-studied as a dramatic soprano with the famous voice coach Anna Schoen-René. In the 1930s she sang often in England, at Covent Garden, and with other companies. During her career she is said to have sung 150 roles. In 1936 she moved with her second husband to New York, where she continued to sing – her appearances including one at the Metropolitan Opera that year – and where, at the Juilliard School, she began teaching in the late 1930s. She retired from Juilliard in 1943, gave a farewell recital in Town Hall, New York, 6 Dec 1943, and ca 1944 moved with her husband to Montreal, where she taught privately for a few years. (She did not, contrary to other sources, teach in Toronto). She returned to New York in 1950 and there taught a very few pupils during her last years. Among her pupils, in the USA and Canada, were the English tenor Arthur Carron, the US soprano Nadine Conner, and the baritone John *Stratton.

Easton made a large number of records for Aeolian-Vocalion 1918–20, for Brunswick 1921–8, for Edison in 1928, and for HMV in the late 1920s and early 1930s. For HMV she recorded the final scene of *Siegfried* with Lauritz Melchior in 1932 and songs with Gerald Moore in 1933. Several privately made recordings of 1937–42 have been circulated. Stratton has issued a collection of arias on the Cantilena LP 6234, and his article in *The Record Collector* includes an Easton discography. Not included in the discography is the Rubini LP GV-520 containing 13 standard songs and arias from *Carmen, Gianni Schicchi, Madama Butterfly, Tosca*, and Rimsky-Korsakov's *Sadko* and *The Snow Maiden*.

WRITINGS

'The open door to opera,' *Great Singers on the Art of Singing*, ed James F. Cook (Philadelphia 1921)

BIBLIOGRAPHY

'A talk with Florence Easton,' *MCan*, vol 1, Dec 1920

Thompson, Oscar. 'Florence Easton,' *American Singer* (New York 1937)

Matz, Mary Jane. 'First ladies of the Puccini premieres: Florence Easton,' *Opera News*, 13 Jan 1968

Stratton, John R. 'Florence Easton,' *Record Collector*, Jan 1974 (JBM)

EATON, Richard (Stephen). Organist-choirmaster, educator, composer, b Victoria, BC, 16 Jan 1914, d Rhodes, Greece, 25 Jan 1968; Licentiate (McGill) 1939, B MUS (McGill) 1941. He took his first lessons in Victoria, where he was a choir boy and, 1930–5, assistant organist at All Saints' Cathedral. In 1936 he went to Montreal to study at *McGill U, where his teachers included *Champagne. In Montreal he was organist-choirmaster at St Martin's Church. In Toronto 1939–44 he was a music master at Upper Canada College. In Ottawa 1944–7 he was director of instrumental music at Ottawa Technical High School and organist-choirmaster at McLeod United Church. In 1947 he joined the *U of Alberta, Edmonton, serving as lecturer in the music division of the Dept of Fine Arts and 1948–65 as head of the division. When in 1965 it became the Music Dept, he was appointed head.

During Eaton's tenure music activities at the university were greatly expanded. In addition, he was an active director, 1947–68, of the Alberta division of the *WBM. He also was on the boards of the *Edmonton Opera Assn and the *Edmonton SO. Throughout his Alberta years he conducted the U of Alberta Mixed Chorus, which brought music to rural Alberta, the Northwest Territories, and northwestern BC. He founded the University Singers in 1951 and conducted them until 1967. In 1968 they were renamed the *Richard Eaton Singers in his memory. Eaton composed many anthems and arranged a number of folksongs including 'Blest Are the Pure in Heart' (Oxford 1943), 'O Holy Spirit, Lord of Grace' (BMI Canada 1954), and 'Three French-Canadian Folksongs' (BMI Canada 1958). BH

Eaton Auditorium. Concert hall located on the top (seventh) floor of the former Eaton's College Street store in Toronto. Designed by Jacques Carlu of Paris, with seating for 795 on the main floor and 480 in the balcony, a four-manual 90-stop *Casavant organ, and interior appointments in the art deco style, the auditorium was built in 1929 as part of the retail complex and opened 26 Mar 1931 with a recital by soprano Florence Austral and flutist John Amadio with Ernest *MacMillan at the organ. It was the site of recitals by the leading artists of the day (in 1932–3 Rachmaninoff, Sophie Braslau, Vincente Escudero, Efrem Zimbalist, and Conchita Supervia; in other years Biggs, Bjoerling, Dupré, Flagstad, Kreisler, Schnabel, Tibbett, Traubel), of the *Casavant Society organ series (in which Glenn *Gould made his recital debut 12 Dec 1945), of various CBC broadcasts, and of countless films and lectures. Eaton Auditorium also has been the home of the *Eaton Operatic Society, the *Kiwanis Festivals, the *Women's Musical Club of Toronto, and the York Concert Society. the *COC and the National Ballet of Canada staged many of their early productions there. In the late 1940s the auditorium was described by the noted English musician William Glock – then on an adjudicating tour – as one of the two finest concert halls in Canada (the other being the small concert hall of the *Winnipeg Auditorium). In 1951 permanent theatre seats were installed on a raked floor, and the auditorium lost some of its acoustic distinction. With the building of other concert halls in Toronto, its use declined in the 1960s and 1970s, and when Eaton's College Street store closed 5 Feb 1977, plans for the building's renovation included the reduction of the hall to 1000 seats and the removal of the organ.

Eaton Auditorium was managed 1931–67 by Paul Johnston, a New Yorker of Canadian parentage who had worked as an impresario before joining the auditorium as booking manager. He was succeeded by John P. Heffernan, who managed the auditorium until the College Street store closed.

BIBLIOGRAPHY

Kidd, George. 'One tradition's uncertain future,' Toronto *Telegram*, 16 Jul 1966

Hurst, Lynda. 'Eaton Auditorium: a future or just a past?' *Toronto Star*, 16 Aug 1980

Jones, Donald. 'Wrecker's hammer may toll for auditorium's golden jubilee,' ibid, 6 Sep 1980

T. Eaton Co. Archives (MH)

Eaton Operatic Society (Eaton Choral Society 1919–31). Toronto light opera group. It was founded in 1919 as a choir by employees of the T. Eaton Co department store (with a subsidy from the company) and gave its first concert 4 Feb 1920. Herbert M. Fletcher, its first conductor, was succeeded in 1925 by T.J. *Crawford. It gave annual concerts in *Massey Hall with orchestra and soloists, including the harpist Carlos Salzedo in 1923, the singers Arthur *Blight, Elizabeth Campbell, Jeanne *Dusseau, and Alfred *Heather in 1927, and Paul Althouse, Poul Bai, and Frank Oldfield in 1929. The membership had grown to 200 singers by that time.

Following a change of policy in 1931 the society began to cultivate operetta. Gilbert & Sullivan's *Iolanthe* was its first production, 2 and 3 Mar 1932 at *Eaton Auditorium, and other operettas were offered there each spring until 1965. Productions were taken to other communities in southern Ontario – Brantford, Hamilton, Kitchener, Lindsay, Peterborough, and St Catharines – and to other halls and theatres in Toronto. During World War II the society visited Ontario army bases. It presented only Gilbert & Sullivan until 1946, when Leslie Stuart's *Florodora* was performed. Several works were given repeat performances, including *Iolanthe* (1932, 1938, 1950), *The Gondoliers* (1933, 1939, 1948, 1954), *The Mikado* (1934, 1940, 1949), *The Yeoman of the Guard* (1935, 1941, 1952), and *The Pirates of Penzance* (1936, 1942, 1953). After 1954 the society turned exclusively to musicals, including *The Vagabond King* (1957, 1965) and **Rose Marie* (1959). Among the featured performers were George Aldcroft, Norman Cherrie, Leslie Mackey, Elizabeth *Mawson, Howard *Mawson, and Helen Murray. In 1945 Lois *Marshall, then an Eaton employee, was understudy to the lead in *Princess Ida* and performed in the production on 14 March. The society's music directors were T.J. Crawford until 1947, Harry Norris (listed as conductor) in 1948, Godfrey *Ridout 1949–58, Lloyd *Bradshaw 1959–61, and Horace *Lapp 1962–5. The orchestra included members of the *TSO.

BIBLIOGRAPHY

Nelligan, M. '7 floors up,' *OpCan*, May 1963 (DS)

Eaton Singers. See Richard Eaton Singers.

EBY, Evelyn. See Bedford and Eby.

ECKHARDT-GRAMATTÉ, S.C. (Sophie-Carmen, 'Sonia', (b Friedman, m Gramatté, m Eckhardt). Composer, pianist, violinist, teacher, b Moscow? 6 Jan 1899, naturalized Canadian 1958, d Stuttgart 2 Dec 1974; hon D MUS (Brandon) 1970. Her mother, Catherina de Kochevskaya, of French and Slavic ancestry, a pupil of Anton and Nicholas Rubinstein and music instructor in the household of Tolstoi, was married to Nicolas de

S.C. Eckhardt-Gramatté

Friedman, from whom she separated before Sophie-Carmen was born. (However, the child bore his name and until 1920 was known professionally as Sonia Friedman). Fearing the father would kidnap the infant, her mother sent her to England, where she spent four years with foster parents in an expatriate Tolstoian colony, Whiteway, in the Cotswold Hills, Gloucestershire.

Reunited with her mother in 1904, Sophie-Carmen was taken to Paris, and it was there that her music tuition began. Under her mother's instruction, 1906–8, her advancement at the piano was precocious. Her *Alphabet Pieces* and *Little Pieces* were composed in Paris 1905–9. In September 1909, although she had had no violin instruction of a regular nature, she was accepted as a violin student at the conservatoire, where her teachers were Alfred Brun and later Guillaume Rémy. She also studied piano there with Mme S. Chenée and chamber music under the guidance of Vincent d'Indy and Camille Chevillard. At 11 she made debuts in Paris, Geneva, and Berlin, appearing on the program alternately as pianist and as violinist. In Geneva her program included a Bach *Suite* for solo violin, the violin part of Beethoven's *Sonata in A* ('Kreutzer'), and Chopin's *Fantaisie-Impromptu*. In 1911 she gave a recital of improvisations in Paris and a recital in Berlin which included a Chopin *Étude*, the Chaconne from Bach's *Partita No. 2* for solo violin, and the Ernst *Violin Concerto in F Sharp Minor*. In 1912 her chamber work *Ein Wenig Musik* was published by the Paris firm Vieu et Vieu. She left the conservatoire in 1913. It was in 1915 in Berlin (not in 1910 as sometimes reported) that she played Beethoven's (piano) *Sonata in F Minor, Op 57*, and the violin part of the 'Kreutzer' on the same program.

Sophie-Carmen had moved to Berlin with her mother and sister early in 1914 and for a time supported them there by playing in cafés. However, the daughter-in-law of the great Joseph Joachim, Suzanne Joachim-Chaigneau (who referred to the young musician as her 'adopted wartime child'), presented her with one of Joachim's violins and arranged a scholarship from the banker Franz von Mendelssohn (a descendant of the composer) for her to study with the Polish virtuoso Bronislav Huberman, with whom she extended her bowing technique. During her first six years in Berlin she appeared in a number of recitals and private musicales. She was introduced to Busoni, D'Albert, Philipp Scharwenka, and Schnabel, and received much encouragement. A conflict developed, however. Her patrons wanted her to continue as a virtuoso, whereas her own inclination was to devote herself to composition. By 1920 she was composing larger works (eg, *Ziganka*, a pantomime ballet). She married the German expressionist painter Walter Gramatté 13 Dec 1920 and from 1922 until 1929 used Sonia Fridman-Gramatté (dropping the 'e' from Friedman) as her professional name. (From 1929 to 1936 she was to use only Gramatté).

The Gramattés' move to Spain, where they lived in Barcelona 1924–6, brought Sonia a new mentor – the cellist Pablo Casals – and yielded several works, including the *Concerto for Solo Violin*. During the years in Spain she performed frequently there and also travelled to Germany for a 1925 concert series with the eminent Swiss pianist Edwin Fischer, playing Bach's *Concerto in C Minor* for two keyboards and orchestra, Mozart's *Sonata* K526 for violin and piano, and also her own solo-violin concerto. After resuming residence in Berlin in 1926 she returned to Spain for nine concerts in 1927. News of her versatility and virtuosity had reached Leopold Stokowski, and during a visit to Paris the eminent conductor sent word that he would like to audition her. He engaged her for appearances with the Philadelphia Orchestra, but these were postponed owing to the serious illness of her husband. Gramatté died in 1929 of tuberculosis, and it was only later in that year that the young widow was able to fulfil her US engagement. In the 1929–30 season she performed her own works for piano (*Konzertstück*) or violin and orchestra with the Philadelphia Orchestra under Stokowski and the Chicago SO under Frederick Stock. The Philadelphia *Public Ledger* reported that she had 'enormous talent in all three capacities' and continued, 'she unquestionably has great possibilities as a soloist with either instrument [and] it is doubtful if any musician has ever become the equal master of two.' The *Music News*, Chicago, described 'a brilliant Chicago debut,' reporting that 'the piano concerto was stupendous – tremendously difficult, spectacularly preformed.' The *Chicago Evening Post* found the young composer-performer 'an interesting personality, businesslike and straight to the point, with none of the airs of the virtuoso.'

In 1930 Gramatté decided to give up her performing career to concentrate on composition. Stokowski recommended that she enrol as a pupil of Max Trapp at the Preussische Akademie in Berlin, but it was not until 1936 that she finally took that advice. In 1934 she married Ferdinand Eckhardt, an Austrian art historian living in Berlin, who had been interested in the graphics of her late husband. In 1939 the couple moved to Vienna, and at that time she adopted the professional name with which her works are signed: S.C. Eckhardt-Gramatté. In 1945 Eckhardt-Gramatté was one of a small group who re-established the Austrian branch of the ISCM. She was awarded the Composition Prize of the Musikverein for her *Piano Concerto No. 2* in 1948 (also performing it that year under Eugen Jochum) and for the *Markantes Stück* for two pianos and orchestra in 1949; an Austrian State Prize for the *Triple Concerto* in 1950; and first prize for the last-named work in the International Competition for Women Composers (GEDOK, Mannheim) in 1961.

In 1952 the *Violin Concerto No. 2* was commissioned by the ISCM for the Salzburg Festival of that year. In 1953 her husband became director of the Winnipeg Art Gallery, and the couple arrived in Winnipeg 24 October. Being transplanted from Vienna presented the active, ambitious musician with a challenge which she met courageously. Her first recital in Canada was for CBC radio 14 Mar 1955 on the 'Distinguished Artists' series. Winnipeg musicians became regular visitors to the house on Harrow Street for evenings of Hausmusik. She also began teaching a few gifted pupils and senior musicians interested in refreshing their ideas. Kenneth *Winters, at the time a Winnipeg critic, described her as cutting a striking figure: 'She is small but sturdy, with the large, useful hands of the virtuoso, short-cropped black hair, black snapping eyes and a voice rather like an adventurous alto saxophone with a few flute notes for excitement and some viola tones for pathos. She is friendly, volatile, restless, quick-witted, quick-tempered and altogether alive. She loves conversation and good food and is a tireless, somewhat impatient promoter of her own music and her ideas on music' (*Winnipeg Free Press*, 17 Feb 1962).

In 1959 Eckhardt-Gramatté was commissioned to write a *Duo Concertante* for cello and piano for performance at the University Music Festival in Saskatoon during the Saskatchewan Jubilee. The work was premiered by two Manitoba musicians who had become strong supporters, Peggie *Sampson and Lorne *Watson. Other commissions followed, and the resulting works included the *Symphony-Concerto* for piano and orchestra and the *Manitoba Symphony* in honour, respectively, of the Canadian and the Manitoba centenaries. The *Piano Trio* is another important work commissioned for 1967 and was premiered by the *Hidy Trio, whose founder, Marta *Hidy, also commissioned, and in 1970 premiered, the *Suite for Solo Violin No. 4, 'Pacific.'* In 1970 Eckhardt-Gramatté was awarded the title 'professor' by the Austrian government.

Eckhardt-Gramatté composed music virtually throughout her life, beginning with the *Alphabet Pieces* at six and concluding with the *Trumpet Concerto* left incomplete at her death.

The works of her childhood reflect the charm of the Parisian salon, with a considerable gesture towards virtuosity and Bach polyphony. As she performed extensively throughout the 1920s it is not surprising that the output for this decade is characterized by virtuoso repertoire for the violin (a solo concerto, three solo suites, nine original caprices, and four Paganini transcriptions) and for the piano (the *Piano Concerto No. 1* and four sonatas). The relatively small output of the 1930s is due in part to the shock of Gramatté's death and in part to her decision to write more for orchestra. To the late years of the 1930s, however, belong the development of a highly individual style of counterpoint and the composition of the *String Quartet No. 1* and *Symphony in C*. In the symphony, the Mahleresque second subject of the opening movement and other details of thematic control and instrumental colour bear witness to the conservative influence of Trapp.

Neo-classic ideas for small chamber groups characterize the music of the 1940s. The *Ruck-Ruck Sonata* (clarinet and piano) and the *Triple Concerto* (clarinet, trumpet and bassoon with chamber orchestra) are typical in their clarity of purpose, their imaginative treatment of rhythm and counterpoint, and their bi-tonal, often jazzy, good humour. The *Piano Sonata No. 5* (1950) represents Eckhardt-Gramatté's first excursion into serial music. This colourful work, imaginatively held together by a recurrent three-note pattern simulating bass gongs, ends with a movement in which the 12-tone idiom is absorbed within the composer's personal style. The metric principle associated with Messiaen and Blacher is incorporated into the *Concerto for Orchestra* (1955). Serial principles also are incorporated. As a child Eckhardt-Gramatté had come to love the unaccompanied violin works of J.S. Bach, and as a mature composer she concluded this concerto with a tribute to the master – an extremely free adaptation of one of her favourite encore pieces, the Prelude from the *Partita in E*. The concerto and other works of the composer's maturity frequently show a Bartókian concern for interval structure and a predilection for the interval of the fourth. An earlier movement that is based essentially on fourths is the slow movement of the *Piano Sonata No. 2*.

Although as a performer Eckhardt-Gramatté was trained very strictly from childhood until that time in her career when she was ready for the independence she craved, as a composer her disciplines were subservient from the beginning to her natural independence. Apart from basic theoretical studies with her mother and at the conservatoire, her writing of music was in her own hands until she was nearly 37 and spent three intensive years with Max Trapp. And while she acknowledged Trapp's important contribution to her skills in counterpoint and orchestration, there can be little doubt that her distinctive and somewhat wilful creative personality had been formed through her own investigations of the creative experience, often guided by her virtuosity as a performer. It was affected, too, by the challenge of being a woman composer, first in the highly structured, precedent-laden, intensely competitive milieu of the Europe of her day, and then in the radically contrasting frontier situation of Canada. The result was a music of marked, not to say headstrong, character, full of ideas, impulses, and technical difficulties, the whole, despite its contrapuntal skill, not invariably serene in its organization. Its worth has been recognized and its cause championed by musicians of great distinction, but it remains a music which by its very nature will divide listeners into partisans and non-partisans.

Eckhardt-Gramatté never held an official teaching appointment, yet she maintained throughout her professional life a great interest in teaching. As might be expected from a performer who had such strong personal approaches to the piano and violin, she evolved what could be termed a 'method' for each. A basic principle in the 'E-gré Piano Technique' is to utilize the natural rotary and rolling actions of all limbs, and she described her 'method' as the Natural Piano Technique. In its purest form it takes a stand exactly opposite to that of the 'finger' technique. Over a period of some years, beginning in 1959, she worked with Lorne Watson on a book (still unpublished in 1980) on the 'E-gré Technique.' Important to the evolution of this technique was Eckhardt-Gramatté's outstanding artist pupil, Diedre *Irons, who studied with her from 1957 to 1965. European master piano pupils included Erna Heiller and Luise Fischer-Thielemann.

An early supporter of Eckhardt-Gramatté in Canada was the cellist, later gambist, Peggie Sampson. Intrigued by Eckhardt-Gramatté's new approach to the violin, she worked with her, adapting principles of bowing and hand position to the cello. Another important string pupil was the violinist and teacher Gwen *Thompson. In recognition of Eckhardt-Gramatté's unique career and of her importance on the Canadian scene the CBC in November 1974 broadcast a two-hour radio documentary prepared by Lorne Watson and produced by Walter Unger. Shortly after the broadcast she departed for a European trip. During a visit to Stuttgart she fell while on a bus and was removed to hospital, where she died during a bone-setting operation. She was buried beside Walter Gramatté and her mother, in a secluded cemetery in the village of Wilhelmshagen in East Berlin.

For the last two years of her life plans had been proceeding with a dream – a competition to encourage young artists to play the works of contemporary composers. After her death the planning committee decided in 1975 to name the event the S.C. Eckhardt-Gramatté Competition for the Performance of Canadian Music. In 1975 she was awarded posthumously the *CCA's Diplôme d'honneur. She was a member of the *CLComp, an associate of the *CMCentre, and a member of CAPAC.

SELECTED COMPOSITIONS

ORCHESTRA

Skelettenspiel and *L'Île*. 1923. Ms
Weihebild and *Tanzbild*. 1924–35. Ms
Passacaglia and Fugue. 1937 (Berlin 1937). Ms
Symphony in C. 1939 (Breslau 1942). CMCentre
Capriccio Concertante. 1941 (Vienna 1942). CMCentre
Concertino for Strings. 1947 (Vienna 1948). Str orch. CMCentre
Concerto for Orchestra. 1954 (Winnipeg 1961). CMCentre
Symphony No. 2 'Manitoba.' 1970 (Winnipeg 1970). CMCentre
Also the ballet suite *Ziganka* (1920). Ms

SOLOIST(S) WITH ORCHESTRA

Concerto No. 1. 1925 (Berlin 1932). Pf, orch. CMCentre
Grave Funèbre. 1931. Vn, chamb orch. Ms
Piano Concerto No. 2. 1946 (Vienna 1948). CMCentre
Triple Concerto. 1949 (Vienna 1949). Tpt, cl, bn, orch. UE 1952. CBC SM-272 (*NACO)
Markantes Stück. 1946–50 (Vienna 1952). 2 pf, orch. CMCentre
Concerto. 1950 (Ausee 1950). Bn, orch. CMCentre
Violin Concerto No. 2. 1951 (Salzburg 1952). Vn, orch. CMCentre
Four Christmas Songs (F. Eckhardt). 1953. SSATBB, ww, brass, pf, orch. CMCentre
Symphony-Concerto. 1967 (Tor 1968). Pf, orch. CMCentre. CBC SM-107/RCA LSC 3175 (*Kuerti)
Also *Konzertstück for Cello and Chamber Orchestra* (1928, rev 1974), ms; and arrangements of several Paganini *Caprices* for vn and orch

CHAMBER

Ein Wenig Musik. 1910. Pf trio. Vieu et Vieu 1912
Suites for Violin Solo, No. 1 and 2. 1922. Simrock 1924
Suite for Violin Solo No. 3, 'Mallorca.' 1924. Eschig 1929
Ten Caprices for Violin Solo. 1924–34. Simrock 1925 (No. 1, 2, 3)
Concerto for Solo Violin. 1925. CMCentre. Odeon 0-6973-6/Masters of the Bow MB-1031 (Eckhardt-Gramatté)
Lagrima. 1926. Va (vc), pf. Ms
Februar Suite. 1934. Vn, pf. CMCentre
2 *String Quartets* (1938, 1943). CMCentre
Duo for Two Violins No. 2. 1944. Österreichischer Bundesverlag 1949
Wind Quartet. 1946. Fl, cl, bassetthorn, bass cl. CMCentre
Nicholas Trio and *Triotino*. 1947. Str trio. CMCentre
Ruck-Ruck Sonata. 1947, rev 1962. Cl, pf. CMCentre
Duo Concertante. 1956. Fl, vn. CMCentre
Duo Concertante. 1959. Vc, pf. CMCentre. RCI 224/RCA CCS-1018 (*Sampson vc)
Woodwind Quintet. 1963. CMCentre
String Quartet No. 3. 1962–4. Ber 1978 (?)
Nonet. 1966. Str quar, ww quin. CMCentre
Piano Trio. 1967. CMCentre
Suite for Solo Violin No. 4, 'Pacific.' 1968. CMCentre
Concertino. 1971. V da gamba, hpd. Ms
Fanfare. 1971. 8 brass. Ms
Also a few works for fl and pf, *Berceuse* (1925?), *Presto* (1922?), and *Improvisation* (1925?), all CNCentre; duos for 2 vn, for va and vc, and for 2 vc (all 1944); 2 str trios (1947); 2 ww trios (1947 and 1967), all CMCentre

PIANO

Alphabet Pieces. 1905–10. Vieu 1912 ('Y')
Children's Pieces. 1907–11. Vieu 1912 ('Marcelle')
Étude de concert. 1910. Mercier 1910
Danse de nègre. 1922. Simrock 1924
Sonata No. 1. 1923. Simrock 1924
Sonatas No. 2–4 (1924, rev 1952; 1925; 1928). CMCentre
Sonata No. 6 (Drei Klavierstücke). 1928–51. CMCentre. RCI 224/RCA CCS-1018 (*Irons)
Also *Kosak* (1924), *Cirque de Village* (1925), *Trepak*, (1926), *Arabesque* (1928), and *Tune for a Child* (1972). All ms. Some arrangements of pf works by Chopin and Paganini

BIBLIOGRAPHY

Winters, Ken. 'The same moon and stars: Eckhardt-Gramatté in profile,' *Winnipeg Free Press*, 17 Feb 1962

Sanguine, Jean. 'Sophie-Carmen Eckhardt-Gramatté,' *Chatelaine*, Sep 1967
Anderson, Jeffrey. 'Winnipeg composer completes four centennial commissions,' *CanComp*, 25, Jan 1968
'Eckhardt-Gramatté,' *CanComp*, 42, Sep 1969
'S.C. Eckhardt-Gramatté,' *Mcan*, 23, Oct 1969
'Manitoba composers: a collective voice,' *CanComp*, 52, Sep 1970
Watson, Lorne. 'The E-gré piano technique,' unpubl paper, Indiana U 1976
– 'S.C. Eckhardt-Gramatté,' *CME*, vol 17, Fall 1975
Smith, M. Elaine. 'The works for violoncello by Sophie-Carmen Eckhardt-Gramatté,' unpubl M MUS thesis, U of Western Ont 1978
Selected Works, 21 vols (Estate of S.C. Eckhardt-Gramatté 1980)
MGG
'Review of Records'
Contemporary Canadian Composers / Compositeurs canadiens contemporains
Eckhardt, Ferdinand. 'S.C.E.G.,' unpubl biography

LW (HK, KW)

ECKSTEIN, Willie or **Billy** (William). Pianist, composer, b Pointe St-Charles (now Montreal), 6 Dec 1888, d Montreal 23 Sep 1963. He began playing piano at 3, and at 12 was billed in New York as 'The Boy Paderewski.' After six years in vaudeville and a European tour he returned to Montreal, where he played in movie houses, notably the Strand, accompanying silent films. There he was known as 'The World's Foremost Motion Picture Interpreter.' In 1919 he accompanied the tenor Gus Hill on Montreal radio station XWA (later CFCF) in the first live performance broadcast in Canada. With the advent of talking pictures Eckstein worked in clubs, radio, then TV. A noted exponent of the novelty rag, he recorded first (1921) with his Strand trio for HMV, and later as a soloist for Apex in 1923, for Okeh 1923–4, and for Victor 1929–32. He was a prolific songwriter, and several of his collaborations with Sam Howard, including 'Lest You Forget' (1922) and 'S'Nice' (1923) were popular. He also composed the ragtime pieces *Delirious Rag* (1916) and *Perpetual Rag* with Harry *Thomas. *Roll Back the Years* lists his recordings and some of his compositions. Some of his 78s have been reissued by Folkways and Herwin on LP collections of ragtime or jazz.

(EBM)

École normale de musique. Conservatory and teacher-training institution founded in 1926. It formed part of the Institut pédagogique of Westmount (Montreal), run by the Sisters of the Congregation of Notre Dame. The other two parts of the Institut pédagogique were Marguerite-Bourgeoys College, which offered classical (ie, general academic) studies and later Cegep courses, and the École normale, which granted a class A schoolteaching diploma. This article will discuss only the École normale de musique.

Restricted to girls and women during its first 40 years, the École normale de musique began admitting boys and men in 1966. It was affiliated 1926–67 with the *U of Montreal. Thereafter until 1976 (when it ceased to exist as a private institution), it gave university-level music courses under a contractual agreement with *UQAM, the university conducting the examinations and issuing the degress.

The school was directed 1926–30 by Sister Saint-Édouard-Martyr and 1930–42 by Sister Sainte-Cécile-des-Ange (both teachers of piano), 1942–54 by Sister Charlotte *Cadoret, 1954–7 by Sister Saint-Roméo, and 1957–76 by Sister Marcelle *Corneille.

Among the members of the teaching staff over the years were: Françoise *Aubut, Eugène *Lapierre, and Lucienne *L'Heureux-Arel (organ); Alexander *Brott (conducting); Claude *Champagne (solfège, harmony); Albert *Cornellier, France *Dion, Roger *Filiatrault, Sister Louis-Raymond, Jean *Riddez, and Micheline *Tessier (singing); André *Gagnon (keyboard harmony); Henri *Garrouteigt (Gregorian chant); Luis Grinhauz, Stephen *Kondaks, and Maurice *Onderet (violin); Jean *Leduc, E. Robert Schmitz, and William *Stevens (piano); Pierre *Mollet (performance); Antoine Padilla (musical literature); Frédéric *Pelletier (history of music); and Michel *Perrault (harmony).

In 1926–7 the examiners were Victoria *Cartier, Arthur *Letondal, Rodolphe *Mathieu, and Georges-Émile *Tanguay. The school's first three teaching diplomas were granted in June 1927 to Charlotte Cadoret, Eileen Gillis, and Jeanne Turcotte. Instruction in organ began around 1930, and pupils and teachers had to travel to the Villa-Maria Convent for lessons. (The *Casavant organ in the chapel of the Institut pédagogique was not installed until 1949). The students performed regularly in recital, and in 1938 and 1940 gave concerts at *Plateau Hall.

The École normale de musique was divided into three sections.

The first section, a conservatory operation for young students, reported to the Congregation's Board of Music Studies and consisted of five two-year stages, each leading to a certificate. The program encompassed theory, harmony, solfège, instrumental or vocal technique, sight-reading, music dictation, and interpretation. The student could complete the music major at the same time as her academic grade 11 and be admitted to the baccalauréat or, later to the college-level course with specialization in music.

The second section, a college-conservatory for more advanced students, gave professional training corresponding to university degrees. Thus the four-year B MUS provided for the obtaining of the teaching diploma after the second year. The L MUS was replaced by the M MUS instrumental (reduced to one year) after the faculty of music of the U of Montreal was created in 1950. (Beginning in 1967, the pupils at the Cegep level specializing in music also belonged to this section.)

The third section was a school-music-teacher-training centre designed to equip prospective teachers with pre-school, elementary school, and secondary school pedagogical skills. The BES (music option A and B), granted by Quebec's Ministry of Education, was introduced in 1964.

Sister Marcelle Corneille took a keen interest in new music teaching methods, and in 1954 she organized practical classes reflecting this interest at the nursery school level. These courses for young children were at the same time elective classes for aspiring teachers. The École normale de musique established in 1954 a specialized music option for kindergarten teachers at the École normale of the Institut pédagogique. Summer courses in piano-teaching methodology were held 1929–64. Retraining and refresher courses in music pedagogy (taught by Jacques Chailley, Marcel Corneloup, Marguerite Croptier, Maurice Martenot, Jacquotte Ribière-Raverlat, and others) were given 1964–74 to the practising teacher who wished to obtain a university degree or the BES. After 1974 Sister Corneille continued to organize sessions with Marcel Corneloup each summer for teachers of the elementary grades. Guy Fouquet, Davis *Joachim, Chantal Juillet, Louise *Laplante, Yolande Lemarier-Catrice, and Louis *Lortie are among those who studied at the École normale de musique, which enrolled more than 600 pupils per year in the last few years of its existence.

The Ensemble vocal de l'École normale de musique was founded in 1954 and conducted 1954–60 by Ria *Lenssens. Until 1960 the group consisted of about 30 female voices. Sister Thérèse Boucher played an active role 1955–68 as director or assistant director. Among the other conductors were Roland *Leduc 1960–2, William Tortolano 1962–4, and Alexander Brott 1964–76 (assisted by Sister Jacqueline Nault 1968–76). In 1964 it was a mixed choir of some 160 voices. The ensemble obtained the lieutenant-governor's silver medal at the Quebec Music Festivals in 1961. It performed at the *Pro Musica Society that year, the Sarah *Fischer Concerts in 1964, 1965, and 1970, and on the CBC TV program 'Let's Talk Music' in 1969 and 1970. It participated in the premiere of Alexander Brott's *Centennial Cerebration* (sic) in 1967. The group also performed at Marie-Reine-du-Monde Cathedral in Beethoven's *Christ on the Mount of Olives* in 1970, Mozart's *Requiem* in 1971, and Haydn's *The Creation* in 1973; at the *PDA in Vaughan Williams' *Flos Campi* in 1973; and several times at Notre-Dame Church, notably in Verdi's *Requiem* in 1975. It made two LPs: *Chants à la Vierge* with the *Choeur Pie X conducted by Clément *Morin (1959, MRC 1001) and *Folklore du Québec* under the direction of Claude Champagne (1960, MB 7899–7900). The group ceased its activities in 1976.

The Opera Workshop, founded and directed by Micheline Tessier, presented 1967–71 several works, including Chabrier's *L'Étoile*, Delibes's *Le Serpent à plumes*, Menotti's *Amahl and the Night Visitors*, Roussel's *Le Testament de tante Caroline*, and Schubert's *La Croisade des dames* (*Die Verschworenen*).

In September 1976, after 50 years of professional and pedagogical training of teachers, the École normale de musique was integrated in UQAM as the Module de musique. At the same time it became the music department of Marguerite-Bourgeoys College (Cegep section), with Micheline Tessier as director, and the preparatory music school of UQAM for grades leading to college and university. The preparatory school has continued the annual piano competition, which began in 1935, and has attracted students from all parts of Quebec.

BIBLIOGRAPHY

Lambert, Thérèse. *L'Histoire de la Congrégation de Notre Dame de Montréal*. 1900–50 in vol 2 (Montreal 1974) ST

École Notre-Dame-d'Acadie. Music school founded in 1946 at Notre-Dame-d'Acadie College and administered by the sisters of Notre-Dame-du-Sacré-Coeur in Moncton. Affiliated 1949–63 with the U St-Joseph, this girls' college offered the B MUS degree as well as a teaching diploma in piano or singing. The choir, under the direction of Sister Marie-Lucienne, was awarded the City of Lincoln trophy (see *FCMF) four times (1952, 1954, 1955, and 1965), and a mixed choir, combining members of the *Chorale de l'U St-Joseph and the Notre-Dame-d'Acadie choir under the same conductor, won the trophy in 1962. The college's influence spread throughout New Brunswick because the nuns opened music centres in about 20 locations including Bathurst, Grand-Sault, Petit-Rocher, St-Basile, Edmundston, and Campbellton.

After the closing of the Notre-Dame-d'Acadie College in 1965, the school became a private preparatory institution, affiliated in 1972 with the *U of Moncton. Directed by Sister Claudette Melanson, the Notre-Dame-d'Acadie school in 1980 continued to offer courses in piano, singing, and flute as well as private classes in theory, solfège, dictation, harmony, introductory music history, and analysis. A certificate is granted for each of the nine grades. Summer courses for teachers were begun in 1952.

BIBLIOGRAPHY

Elliott, Carleton. 'Music in New Brunswick,' *The Arts in New Brunswick* (Fredericton 1967) (GA)

Écoles Sacré-Coeur and Mitchell of Sherbrooke. Two public schools, one elementary and the other secondary, operated by the Catholic school board in Sherbrooke, Que, and offering children an academic education conforming to the program of the Quebec education ministry as well as serious preparatory work in instrumental music. The decision to establish arts classes integrated with the regular program was made after various reports and studies, notably the **Rapport de la Commission royale d'enquête sur l'enseignement des arts dans la province de Québec*, which recommended that teaching be diversified to respond to children's needs and aptitudes.

Classes began in 1972 with 198 students divided into three groups, aged six, seven, and eight respectively. A new group of six-year-olds was added each year. In 1977 the total enrolment was 402 in the elementary school (École Sacré-Coeur) and 85 in the secondary school (École Mitchell). Aptitude tests are used to determine whether a student is a suitable prospect and can absorb both the academic and the musical instruction. Of a yearly average of 150 applicants, 66 are chosen.

The timetable allocates seven-and-a-half hours a week to music, two-and-a-half of these for classes in piano, violin and cello, theory, choral singing, rhythm, folk music, and movement. Seventeen-and-a-half hours are devoted to academic work. The methods of Claude *Létourneau for string instruments and of Zoltan *Kodály for theory and choral singing are used, as well as the works of Thomas *Legrady, Jacquotte Ribière-Raverlat, and the *Dalcroze Eurythmics approach for rhythm.

The total cost of this project has been absorbed by the Sherbrooke Catholic school board, which also established a piano teaching laboratory comprising 30 electronic pianos and a teaching console and bought 130 violins, 55 cellos, and Orff percussion instruments.

In 1980, besides offering an ideal ground for research in music therapy, these two schools, in their integration of intensive musical training with the general academic program (about one-third of the timetable is devoted to music), remained unique among publicly subsidized elementary and secondary schools in Canada. ST

École Vincent-d'Indy. Music school in Montreal, formerly called the École supérieure de musique d'Outremont. It dates back to 1920, when Sister *Marie-Stéphane was the director of a music study program for young girls in all the houses of the Sisters of the Holy Names of Jesus and Mary. In 1932 a special school was set up, called the École supérieure de musique d'Outremont; it became affiliated the following year to the faculty of arts of the *U of Montreal. Its main objectives were 'to promote the art of music, to teach music and singing in regular courses, to give lectures, concerts and recitals, to organize competitions, to set examinations and to grant certificates and diplomas.' To assist in achieving this program, the services of eminent musicians were sought from the beginning. Among the teachers were Claude *Champagne, Camille *Coutoure, Alfred *Laliberté, Léo-Pol *Morin, Raoul *Paquet, Frédéric *Pelletier, Rodolphe *Plamondon and later, Louise *André, Louis *Bailly, Louis *Charbonneau, Jean *Dansereau, Bernard *Diamant, Yvonne *Hubert, Jean-Paul *Jeannotte, Roland *Leduc, Michel *Longtin, Paul *Loyonnet, Pierre *Rolland, and Jean-François *Sénart, as well as many nuns, including Lucille Brassard, Reine *Décarie, Rhené *Jaque, Juliette *Milette, Nathalie Pépin, and Monique Pomerleau.

Sister Marie-Stéphane, who had become an admirer of Vincent d'Indy after hearing him lecture in Montreal in 1921, commemorated the centenary of his birth in 1951 by naming the school after him. During the 1950s enrolment in the school increased, and in 1960 it moved to a building specially designed for music on Bellingham Ave (Ave Vincent-d'Indy since 1972). It became co-educational at this time. The adjoining auditorium was inaugurated on 22 Nov 1964 and named *Salle Claude-Champagne in honour of the composer and teacher who had worked at the school for close to 35 years.

The school's diplomas continued to be granted by the U of Montreal until 1970, but formal affiliation had already ended in 1967 when the university received a new charter. The school thus had to reconsider its status, and in 1970 it became affiliated to the U of Sherbrooke. This affiliation was terminated in 1978, and the school assumed the status of a private Cegep. Students who had enrolled in the university program before 1978, however, were allowed to continue their courses at the school and to receive their degrees from the U of Sherbrooke. In addition to the Diplôme d'études collégiales (DEC) offered since 1969 and granted by the Quebec Ministry of Education, the latter also granted the Brevet d'enseignement specialisé (BES) 1964–73 and the U of Sherbrooke conferred the teaching certificate (CAPEM) 1973–80. The university-level program included a B MUS in performance 1933–80 and in musicology 1970–80; an M MUS in performance 1933–80; a licence (L MUS) granted by the school 1931–3, and then by the U of Montreal until 1959; and a diploma for concert performance in preparation for major national or international competitions, granted by the school 1963–70, and then by the U of Sherbrooke until 1979. In addition, a diploma for composition was granted by the U of Montreal 1933–70 and an artist's diploma was granted by the school ca 1953–63. The school provides extracurricular instruction in musical theory, including elementary and secondary courses, given part-time and in groups. Instrumental lessons are individual at all levels. Among the musicians who have graduated from the school are the singers

École Vincent-d'Indy, Montreal

Louise *Lebrun, Gloria *Richard, and Sylvia *Saurette; the pianists Henri *Brassard, Janina *Fialkowska, Anna-Marie *Globensky, Monik *Grenier, Jeanne *Landry, André *Laplante, and William *Tritt; the composer Micheline Coulombe *Saint-Marcoux; and the pianist and extempore performer Madeleine Raymond. In August 1967 Sister Marie-Stéphane was succeeded by Sister Stella Plante and in 1978 the latter was succeeded by Sister Lorraine Boulanger. In the year 1979–80 the school had some 850 pupils, including teachers pursuing advanced training programs and adults taking private lessons, and a staff of 90 part- or full-time teachers.

In 1926 the school's publishing program began, under the name Institut des Saints Noms de Jésus et de Marie, with Sister Marie-Stéphane's *Manuel d'harmonie*. Starting in 1951 it published under the name Éditions de l'École Vincent-d'Indy. Its publications were chiefly didactic works and compositions by the nuns of the school. In 1980 the U of Montreal bought the school's building, including the Salle Claude-Champagne. In 1981 the school was relocated in a convent of the Order of the Holy Names of Jesus and Mary on Côte Ste-Catherine in Outremont.

BIBLIOGRAPHY

Prévost, Roland. 'Une grande institution canadienne, l'École supérieure de musique d'Outremont,' *P-T*, 913, Oct 1947

Sorel, Anne. 'Une grande école: Vincent-d'Indy,' *VM*, vol 1, 1965

Hélène-Andrée, Sister M. [Marie-Paule Morel]. 'Une oeuvre d'éducation artistique: l'École Vincent-d'Indy,' unpubl B PED thesis, Institut de pédagogie familiale 1966

'Soeur Stella Plante a conduit Janina Fialkowska jusqu'à Rubinstein,' *Musique périodique*, vol 1, Dec 1976

Congregation of the Holy Names of Jesus and Mary. Music dept archives (CGa, BHe, CH)

ECUYER, Charles. Priest, choirmaster, composer, b Montreal 20 Nov 1758, d Yamachiche, near Trois-Rivières, Que, 29 May 1820. He was ordained in 1783. After serving in Montreal, Pointe-Claire, Que, and, for nine years, Repentigny, Que, he was the parish priest at Yamachiche from 1802 until his death. More gifted as a musician than as an orator, according to Caron, 'he preached to his parishioners through the medium of a magnificient choir which he had formed himself.' His compositions included psalms, motets, vespers, and a *Magnificat*. When Sir George Prevost, commander-in-chief of the British forces during the war of 1812, passed through Yamachiche, Ecuyer wrote the song 'Prevost le magnanime.' The melody of a *Sanctus* was still remembered in 1877 by two surviving choristers, so that Gustave *Smith was able to publish it as a duet with organ accompaniment in *Le Foyer domestique* (May 1877). The *Sanctus* is one of the oldest Canadian compositions extant.

BIBLIOGRAPHY

Caron, Abbé N. 'Notes sur Yamachiche,' *Foyer Domestique*, Apr 1877; also publ in his *Histoire de la paroisse d'Yamachiche* (Trois-Rivières 1892) HK

L'Édition Belgo-Canadienne. Music publishing house founded in Montreal in 1925, with the firm Schott Frères of Brussels as agent for Belgium. Its founder, Louis Michiels, a horn player who held a premier prix from a Belgian conservatory, arrived in Montreal before 1914 and gave lessons in solfège, harmony, and brass instruments. Among his pupils were Lucio *Agostini, Jacques *Gérard, Jean Kaster, Roland *Leduc, Marie-Thérèse *Paquin, Roland Poisson, and Ruth Pryce. By the summer of 1928 the firm had published about 40 works by Canadian composers, including Lydia *Boucher, George M. *Brewer, Albert *Chamberland, Alexis *Contant, Jean-Baptiste *Dubois, Alfred *Laliberté, Arthur *Letondal, Henri *Miro, Charles P. Rice, and Louis Valmont. Plate numbers were used in some cases. Also in the company's catalogue were treatises by the Belgian musicians Mathieu Crickboom and Paul Gilson as well as works by Belgian and French composers, including H.-Maurice Jacquet (*Rhapsodie sur un chant canadien* and *Bouquet de Noëls*). Ed *Archambault Inc acquired the firm ca 1929 but most of the stock was destroyed by fire ca 1935.

BIBLIOGRAPHY

Morin, Léo-Pol. 'La maison d'Édition Belgo-Canadienne,' Montreal *La Patrie*, 7 Jul 1928 GP

Edmonton. Capital of Alberta. Established in 1795 as a Hudson's Bay Co post, it was settled first in the mid-1860s. The population had increased to approximately 2500 by 1900 because of the Klondike gold rush. Edmonton was incorporated as a city in 1904 and was made the capital of Alberta when the province entered Confederation in 1905. By 1978, with a population of almost 600,000, Edmonton had become a centre of business, administration, and education. Its main industries are oil, meat packing, and agricultural products.

The turn-of-the-century population explosion brought an influx of musicians, one of whom, Vernon *Barford, was an Englishman who arrived in 1900 to play the organ of All Saints Anglican Church. In 1904 Barford founded the Edmonton Choral Society and the Edmonton Amateur Operatic Society, both of which he also conducted. The latter society produced operettas such as *The Chimes of Normandy* and those of Gilbert & Sullivan. In 1908 the *Edmonton Musical Club (also called the Women's Musical Club) was formed to organize concerts and lectures. One of the Edmonton area's first permanent performing groups was the band of neighbouring Strathcona, well established in 1910. The Edmonton Musicians' Assn was formed in 1907.

In 1914 the *Musical Times* could report: 'Edmonton, the capital of Alberta, is a fine city striding the hills, but music is overdone here. The number of studios opened during the past year is out of all proportion to the demand. No pianoforte teachers are required for many a long day. There may be a little more opening for qualified vocal teachers, for there are as many quacks, in proportion, ruining voices in Canada as there are in the more sophisticated European musical centres.' Among the dependable teachers, performers, and organizers who settled in Edmonton were W.J. Hendra, who arrived in 1906, Edgar Williams in 1912 (Williams played in the *Edmonton SO until 1976), Mrs J.J. Duggan (b Bessie Evans) in 1914, Arthur *Putland in 1918, Mrs J.B. Carmichael in 1919, and Jenny *Lerouge LeSaunier in 1922.

In 1920 radio station CKUA was opened, Mrs Duggan formed the Women's Musical Club Chorus, Herbert Wild founded the Kiwanis Operatic Society, and A. Weaver Winston directed the first concert (14 November) of the Edmonton SO. Although the Depression is blamed for the demise of the orchestra in 1932, it did not prevent the formation of the Edmonton Civic Opera in 1935 under Mrs. Carmichael and the Elgar Ladies' Chorus in 1936 under Hendra.

During World War II Abe Fratkin and Ranald *Shean formed the Edmonton Philharmonic, and in 1947 Lee *Hepner began the Edmonton Pops orchestra. These groups amalgamated to become the Edmonton SO in 1952, the same year that the Edmonton Junior Symphony (Edmonton Youth Orchestra) under Keith *Bissell and the *Edmonton Chamber Music Society came into being. Harry Farmer founded the Edmonton Boys' Choir in 1958, and the *Princess Patricia's Canadian Light Infantry Band was posted in Edmonton 1959–68. In 1965 the Alberta All-Girls Band was founded under the direction of Bob Nagel.

The Light Opera of Edmonton under H.G. *Turner was established in 1950. In 1963 the Edmonton Professional Opera Assn (*Edmonton Opera Assn) was organized, with Jean *Létourneau as the first artistic director.

The Women's Musical Club (1908–73) sponsored recitals 1922–8 in the 1500-seat Empire Theatre, presenting, among others, Vladimir Rosing, Florence Austral, Amelita Galli-Curci, Fritz Kreisler, Tito Schipa, Edward *Johnson, Jascha Heifetz, and Serge Rachmaninoff. After World War II, when the Empire Theatre no longer was available, the club presented concerts in McDougall Church and, after growing audiences necessitated larger quarters, in the Stock Sales Pavilion ('Cow Palace') in the exhibition grounds. Lily Pons, Jeanette MacDonald, Nelson Eddy, Jan Peerce, Marian Anderson, and Victoria de los Angeles performed there. The Cow Palace remained in use until 1957, when the Northern *Alberta Jubilee Auditorium opened.

School music took a step forward in 1911, when J. Norman Eagleson was appointed school music supervisor. Eagleson was succeeded in 1948 by Keith Bissell. *Alberta College offered music courses from its inception in 1903. Three years later, the *U of Alberta was founded but the Music Dept was founded, under John Reymes *King, only in 1945. Teachers, there or at Alberta College, have included Violet *Archer, Arthur *Crighton, Richard *Eaton, Malcolm *Forsyth, Sandra *Munn, Thelma Johannes *O'Neill, Robert *Pounder, Manus Sasonkin, Alfred *Strombergs, and Bernard *Turgeon.

The *Alberta Music (competition) Festival, first held 5 May 1908 in Edmonton, was the earliest of its kind in Canada. Acting on the suggestion of George Bulyea, Alberta's lieutenant-governor, Vernon Barford and Howard Stutchbury (1874–1957) organized and initiated it, bringing in two Winnipeg adjudicators who judged 30 groups and individual contestants the first year. So popular was the festival that by its fourth year it had 28 competition categories. With an emphasis on choral singing, the festival culminated annually with a performance by a combined chorus of around 200 singers accompanied by 50 instrumentalists before an audience of 2000.

Choral groups in Edmonton have included Les Chantamis, the Edmonton Centennial Singers, the Edmonton Columbian Girls Choir, the Edmonton Male Chorus, the Edmonton Welsh Male Chorus, the Leo Green Singers, the Orpheus Male Voice Choir, the *Richard Eaton Singers, and the *St David's Welsh Male Voice Choir.

In July 1978 Edmonton was the site of the Festival of the Arts which accompanied the 11th Commonwealth Games. The idea of Horst A. Schmid, then Alberta's minister of culture (see Alberta Culture), the festival received funding from the Western Canada Lottery and was organized by Robert Dubberly. It featured Canadian and foreign concerts and exhibitions. The *Alberta Composers' Assn was founded in Edmonton in 1977 and held its first festival there in April 1979.

Among musicians born in Edmonton are Agnes *Butcher, the composer Dorothy Cadzow, Eleanor *Collins, Avrahm *Galper, the pianist Robert Gariepy, Betty-Jean *Hagen, Lee Hepner, the guitarist Peter Higham, the violinist Robert Klose, the harpist Janice Lindskoog, Leslie *Mann, Don *McManus, Ron *Park, the singer Mona Paulee, the teacher-conductor Albert Rodnunsky, Roy *Royal, Bob *Ruzicka, Ranald Shean, and Bernard Turgeon. Among those who were raised or lived in Edmonton are Tommy *Banks, the violinist Tamara Fahlman, Robert *Goulet, the pianist John *Hendrickson, Marek *Jablonski, and Ermanno *Mauro. (RDM)

The Edmonton Chamber Music Society. Formed in 1952 with a small membership of amateurs who met to play chamber music recreationally. In 1962, it was reorganized on a subscription basis to sponsor concerts by musicians from Canada and abroad. Membership in 1977 was about 800. The season runs from October to May and consists of six concerts in Convocation Hall, *U of Alberta. The *U of Alberta String Quartet has played for the society annually since 1969. Groups presented by the society include the Juilliard, Amadeus, Hungarian, Borodin, and Cleveland string quartets. Various other small instrumental and vocal ensembles also perform. BH

Edmonton Musical Club. Founded 30 Oct 1908 as the Ladies' Musical Club of Edmonton. It underwent three changes of name (Edmonton Musical Club, 1910; Women's Musical Club of Edmonton, 1912; and back to Edmonton Musical Club, 1970–3) in 65 years of continuous existence. It was organized to promote musical activities among its members – a ladies' chorus formed by Vernon *Barford and a ladies' orchestra led by Mrs. J.B. Carmichael. As Edmonton grew, activity expanded. Between 1922 and 1928 the club presented in recital, such celebrities as Kreisler, Heifetz, Rachmaninoff, Galli-Curci, Tito Schipa, and Edward *Johnson. Proceeds from the recitals established the club's scholarship fund which by 1975 had given young Alberta musicians more than $40,000 assistance. It also initiated children's symphony concerts and worked to establish the *U of Alberta's music department. At its dissolution, 17 May 1973, the club bequeathed its scholarship trust fund to the university.

BIBLIOGRAPHY

Edmonton Musical Club records. Mrs. R.J. McClinton, Edmonton

Provincial Museum and Archives of Alta. ARMTA papers

RDM

The Edmonton Opera Association. Founded 1963 as the Edmonton Professional Opera Association; the name was shortened in 1966. Predecessors were the Edmonton Amateur Operatic Society, formed in 1904 by Vernon *Barford; the Edmonton Civic Opera (1935–46) organized by Mrs. J.B. Carmichael; and the Light Opera of Edmonton founded by Mr and Mrs Herbert G. *Turner. The EPOA's first presentation (October 1963) was *Madama Butterfly*. Jean *Létourneau was the first artistic director, 1963–6, succeeded in 1966 by Irving *Guttman. David Ker was the first president and Barry Thompson the first administrator, 1969–73, succeeded by Lorin J. Moore. There is no permanent music director.

Guest conductors have included Ernesto *Barbini, Mario *Bernardi, Richard Bonynge, George *Crum, Pierre *Hétu, Jean *Deslauriers, Lawrence Leonard, Jean *Létourneau, and Brian Priestman. A typical season offers four productions, each running for three nights, and a touring production attended by some 16,000 students. Nearly 200 school performances were given between 1970 and 1976. In 1968, with the *Vancouver Opera Assn, the EOA initiated the system later incorporated as *Opera West, collaborating in productions of *La Bohème* (1969) and *Lucrezia Borgia* (1972, with Joan Sutherland). Among other highlights of EOA productions have been the operatic debut of Ermanno *Mauro (1963, as Pinkerton in *Madama Butterfly*), Heather *Thomson's first Violetta (1968) and Butterfly (1971), Beverly Sills' Canadian operatic debut (1969, in *Lucia di Lammermoor*), Maureen *Forrester's first Ulrica (*Un Ballo in Maschera*, 1971), and appearances by Anna Moffo (*La Traviata*, 1974) and Jerome Hines (the Canadian premiere of Verdi's *Attila*, 1978). The association has sponsored operatic concerts by Teresa *Stratas (1971), Montserrat Caballé (1974), and Richard Tucker and Robert Merrill (1974). The budget for 1975 reached $350,000, aided by grants from the *Canada Council, the province of Alberta, and the City of Edmonton.

BIBLIOGRAPHY

Johnston, Richard. 'The lively state of opera,' *Mcan*, May 1977

'Edmonton Opera Association,' *OpCan*, Sep 1977 (RDM)

Edmonton Symphony Orchestra. One of Canada's 11 major orchestras. An Edmonton Orchestral Society of about 15 players is known to have flourished as early as 1913, but the first organization to use the name Edmonton Symphony Orchestra was founded in 1920 and made its debut, 52 players strong, at the Pantages Theatre 15 Nov 1920 under the direction of Alberta Weaver Winston. After Winston's departure that year, the orchestra was conducted by Henri Baron and Vernon *Barford. F. Holden Rushworth succeeded Barford about 1929 and was in charge until the orchestra's demise in 1932.

During the 1940s orchestral concerts were provided by the Edmonton Philharmonic Orchestra, founded in 1941 by Abe Fratkin (assistant conductor of the Edmonton SO 1923–6) and Ranald *Shean, and more briefly by the Edmonton Pops Orchestra, conducted 1947–ca 1951 by its founder, Lee *Hepner. Edmonton Philharmonic conductors were Fratkin 1941–8 and Edgar Williams 1948–51.

In 1952 members of these two orchestras joined to form a 60-member second Edmonton SO. A moving force behind the creation of this orchestra was Mrs Marion Mills, founding president of the Edmonton Symphony Society established in 1952 to provide support for the new orchestra. The first concert was given 30 Nov 1952 at the Capitol Theatre under Hepner, who remained as conductor until 1960. During the initial season the orchestra offered a subscription series and two children's concerts. Soloists included Lois *Marshall, Patricia Rolston, and Soulima Stravinsky. In 1957 the orchestra moved to the Northern *Alberta Jubilee Auditorium, which remained its home in 1980. After Hepner resigned, Thomas *Rolston served as acting conductor for four years. In 1964 Rolston was succeeded by Brian Priestman (b Birmingham 10 Feb 1927, founder of Birmingham's Opera da Camera and Orchestra da Camera, music director 1960–3 of the Royal Shakespeare Theatre, and, after four years with the Edmonton SO, conductor 1968–9 of the Baltimore SO and 1970–8 of the Denver SO; he was appointed conductor of the New Zealand SO in 1973.) In Edmonton Priestman was responsible for the introduction of 'main series' concerts and a 'Little Symphony' series of performances by groups drawn from the orchestra. He also helped instigate, with the assistance of the Alberta Cultural Development Branch, a National Performing Artists Competition which offered a cash prize and a contract to perform with the orchestra. The winner of the only competition (1968) was Arthur *Ozolins. Priestman conducted summer sessions of the *NYO in 1967 and 1970.

He was succeeded in Edmonton in 1968 by Lawrence Leonard (b London 22 Aug 1923, a pupil of Ansermet, Kleiber, and Fournet, a cellist at 16 with the London SO, and assistant conductor 1963–8 of the Hallé Orchestra). Under Leonard's leadership the orchestra had developed by 1971 into a full-time ensemble and one of Canada's major orchestras. It premiered two of Leonard's compositions (an adaptation of Machaut's *Grande Messe de Notre Dame* and *Group Questions for Orchestra*) in 1972 and 1973 respectively. About 1973, with the encouraging success of the *NACO as an example and the high cost of supporting a full-sized orchestra as a goad, the board of the Edmonton SO took the decision to maintain the orchestra henceforth as a full-time 'classical-sized' (45-player) ensemble. Pierre *Hétu succeeded Leonard in 1973 and served as artistic director and conductor of the newly constituted orchestra until the end of the 1978–9 season and as principal guest conductor 1979–80. Peter McCoppin, assistant conductor 1978–9, was named resident conductor in 1979.

The orchestra has toured many times in western Canada and the Northwest Territories and has performed often on CBC radio and TV. In addition to its main concert series, pop concerts, and concerts for children and young people (including in-school performances), it has accompanied the *Edmonton Opera, though necessarily augmented for such operas as *Salome*. The principals of its wind sections have performed independently as the Harlan Green Players and have recorded for the CBC (CBC SM-253).

Soloists with the orchestra have included Donald *Bell, Victor Borge, Victor *Bouchard, and Renée *Morisset, Denis *Brott, Janina *Fialkowska, Rudolf Firkusny, Maureen *Forrester, Judith *Forst, Pierre Fournier, James Galway, Horacio Gutierrez, John *Hendrickson, Byron Janis, Lili Kraus, Anton *Kuerti, André *Laplante, John Ogdon, Joseph *Rouleau, Steven *Staryk, Elyakim *Taussig, and Tamás Văsăry. Guest conductors have included Tommy *Banks, Mario *Bernardi, Boris *Brott, Victor *Feldbrill, Ruben *Gurevich, Farhad Mechkat, Jorge Mester, Peter Schenck, Walter *Susskind, and Yuval Zaliouk.

Works commissioned and premiered by the orchestra include *Applebaum's *Concertante*, *Archer's *Prelude-Incantation* and *Sinfonia*, Malcolm *Forsyth's *Symphony No. 2* '... A Host of Nomads ...' (composed for the orchestra's 25th anniversary), *Morel's *Neumes d'espace et reliefs*, and Manus Sasonkin's *Musica post prandia*. In 1973 the orchestra commissioned and premiered Rod McKuen's *Ballad of Distances, A Suite for Orchestra*.

The orchestra's first commercial recording, a 1971 collaboration with the British rock group Procul Harum, recieved a gold record sales award from NARAS (National Academy of Recording Arts and Sciences). During 1975–6 the orchestra took part in a series of internationally syndicated TV programs with such pop stars as Charles Aznavour, Vicki Carr, Roberta Flack, Tom Jones, Henry Mancini, Anne *Murray, Neil Sedaka, and Paul Williams.

The orchestra has continued to be supported by the Edmonton Symphony Society, and its women's committee has organized concert programs for students and raised funds for the Edmonton Youth Orchestra, founded by Keith *Bissell in 1952 (see Youth Orchestras). Financial backing for the Edmonton SO has been provided by the *Canada Council, *Alberta Culture, and numerous private and corporate donors.

General managers of the orchestra have included Leonard Stone 1966–7, Jorgen Holgersen (b Copenhagen 1 Nov 1932, naturalized Canadian 1964, president of ACO 1976–7) 1967–77, and Michael Engelbert 1978–9. Richard Palmer succeeded Engelbert in 1979.

DISCOGRAPHY

Haydn – Debussy – Wiren. B. Brott and Avison conds. 1973. CBC SM-284

Ibert – Françaix – Rameau. Hétu cond. 1976. CBC SM-316

Procul Harum Live in Concert. Procul Harum, Da Camera Singers. 1971. A & M SP 4335

Wolf – Purcell – Adaskin *Diversion for Orchestra* – Warlock. Hétu cond. 1975. CBC SM-294

BIBLIOGRAPHY

'Ozolins wins top prize in Edmonton competition,' *CanComp*, 28, Apr 1968

Burrows, Anne. 'The ESO – the third in Canada?' *CanComp*, 46, Jan 1970

Edmonton Symphony Orchestra Comes of Age [Edmonton 1973]

Ashwell, Keith. 'Edmonton: keeping the home fires burning,' *PfAC*, Spring 1977

Éducanima. Agency for educational concerts and entertainments, founded in Montreal in 1974 by Jean Ruest and Denis Saint-Jean. It derived its name from the words 'education' and 'animation,' and its objective was to instil a taste for the arts in young people by introducing them to different forms of expression. Musicians, dancers, mimics, and actors visited elementary and secondary schools and colleges in groups of two to five, adapting their repertoire and commentary to the average ages of their audiences. Éducanima produced records and cassette tapes as well as teaching aids.

The agency began its work in the Montreal area, where 300 concerts and workshops were presented in 1974–5, and spread rapidly through Quebec. It then moved into Ontario, where it presented some 125 events a year, especially in centres such as Windsor, North Bay, and Timmins, where French is spoken. In Ontario Éducanima operated in conjunction with *Prologue for the Performing Arts, except for the Ottawa area and in centres near the Quebec border. In 1979–80 Prologue organized some 100 Éducanima events, of which 50 were devoted to music.

By 1980 Éducanima had presented more than 1500 concerts and shows, and its tours involved vocal and instrumental ensembles (strings, woodwinds, brass, and percussion), workshops in 'musical awareness' for classroom teachers, and clinics for conductors of school bands. Éducanima's artists were mostly young professional music and drama graduates of recognized schools. Working in co-operation with local school boards, in 1980 Éducanima's continuing aim was to 'demystify the world of art' by means of a teaching method based on participation and animation. In 1980 its artistic director was Rolland Côté, and the founders, Ruest and Saint-Jean, were president and vice-president.

BIBLIOGRAPHY

Ribeyron, Marie-Thérèse. 'Éducanima,' *Perspectives*, 3 Nov 1979

GP

Education. For *EMC* articles that treat various aspects of education and music, or are directories to articles related to education, see the following:

Canadian Association of University Schools of Music
Canadian Federation of Music Teachers' Associations
Canadian Music Educators' Association
Cegeps
Choir schools
Classical colleges and seminaries in Quebec
Community colleges
Degrees
Diplomas
Education, professional
Inventions and devices
John Adaskin Project
Ladies' colleges and convent schools
Music education research
School music
School music broadcasts
School songbooks
Singing schools
Solmization
Summer camps and schools
Teaching methods
Theory textbooks
Universities

For conservatories, schools of music, examining boards, and institutions see the following:

Académie de musique de Québec
The Associated Board of the Royal Schools of Music
Alberta College Music Centre
The Banff Centre School of Fine Arts
Bornoff School of Music and Associated Arts
Canadian Academy of Music
Canadian Institute of Music
Canadian Mennonite Bible College
The Community Music School of Greater Vancouver
Conservatoire de musique du Québec
Conservatoire national de musique
Conservatory of Music, University of Regina
Dominion College of Music
École normale de musique
École Notre-Dame-d'Acadie
Écoles Sacré-Coeur et Mitchell de Sherbrooke
École Vincent-d'Indy
Hambourg Conservatory of Music
Maritime Conservatory of Music
Mennonite Brethren Bible College and College of Arts
Metropolitan School of Music
Mount Royal College Conservatory
Royal Conservatory of Music of Toronto
Royal Hamilton College of Music
Shinn Conservatory of Music
Toronto College of Music
Trinity College of Music, London
Victoria Conservatory of Music
Western Board of Music

Education, professional. The musical training needed by a performer, composer, teacher or scholar if he or she is to function at a level of adequacy or excellence both artistically and economically. The demand for professional musicians normally precedes the availability of private and institutional study facilities, but the reverse may be true. Thus, when the *U of Toronto began to produce Canada's first specialist high school music teachers and opera singers, about 1950, there was a wide market for the teachers but outlets for the singers' talents were few and an audience had to be built.

The conditions for the establishment of advanced music education include not only guarantees of living wages to master teachers but also rich opportunities for students of year-round concert and opera attendance, and well-stocked libraries. At long last, in the 1970s, such conditions obtained in the larger Canadian cities. They did not, of course, lessen the value, to the advanced student, of an experience of the teaching methods and musical climates of other countries.

1 1600–1950
2 1950–80

1 1600–1950. Until late in the 19th century there was little resembling professional training in Canada. The French missionaries in 17th-century Canada were little interested in providing musical instruction that did not have to do directly with such use as they could make of plainsong in carrying out their duties. Willy *Amtmann notes that the École des arts et métiers, founded at St-Joachim (near Quebec) in the late 17th century, helped to establish the tradition of skilled artisanship still flourishing in Quebec, but adds that 'in the brilliant mosaic of clerical initiative and cultural attainment the development of musical art alone remains a somewhat colourless, sadly neglected and insignificant segment' (*Music in Canada 1600–1800*, p 60–1). In other words, everything was taught, from theology and mathematics to weaving and shoemaking, except music!

Probably the first of the many native Canadians to obtain musical training in Europe (along with a general education) was Louis *Jolliet (1645–1700) who for a time, at the Quebec church organ, plied the keyboard skills he had learned abroad 1667–8, though he attained fame only as the discoverer of the source of the Mississippi. Jolliet never intended to become a professional musician, unlike J.C. *Brauneis II and Tom Haliburton (see Prodigies) who studied abroad 1830–3 and ca 1840–5, respectively, probably in Germany, leading the way for a stream of Canadians bound for study in Paris, Leipzig, or elsewhere in Europe. By and large, the need for professional musicians in Canada was supplied by European immigrants but only a few of these (such as Antoine *Dessane, Jules *Hone, Paul *Letondal, and Frantz *Jehin-Prume) were competent to raise their Canadian pupils to the level of professional musicians.

A generation later, Canadians who had some training abroad (*Lavallée, Guillaume *Couture, W.O. *Forsyth, Philéas *Roy, Waugh *Lauder, and others) were able to impart training to advanced pupils. Indeed, some 19th-century Canadians were trained almost entirely at home (*Contant, Amédée *Tremblay, and Joseph *Vézina), but the same educational opportunities would have permitted few of these bandmasters, church musicians, and piano teachers to reach the top level of the profession in the 20th century.

Music schools offering lessons and examinations in a variety of subjects were seen by Dessane, Lavallée, and others as an answer to the need for training professionals, but it was only with the increase of urban population and wealth that conservatories could be established in the late 1880s. Most of their students, of course, were beginners and amateurs. The curricula of the *TCM, the *Toronto College of Music, and similar institutions are impressive; an associate candidate in piano was expected to perform 10 pieces from a list which included some Bach, the Beethoven sonatas (Op 53 and later), the Chopin sonatas, and solo pieces and concertos by Schumann, Brahms, Liszt, and Grieg. Among the early graduates of Canadian conservatories were J.D.A. *Tripp, Lena Hayes Smith, and William Robinson. Yet the limitations of even the best 19th-century Canadian training are obvious from the account of Louise McDowell, one of the early piano graduates of the TCM, who had mastered concertos by Chopin and Mendelssohn but until some years later had never heard a symphony orchestra! (*Past and Present*, Kirkland Lake, Ont, 1957, p 31).

About the same time, *Trinity College, Toronto, and later the U of Bishop's College (see Bishop's U), Lennoxville, Que, and the U of Toronto established music syllabi and degree examinations without, however, providing full-fledged instruction. The subjects of these examinations – harmony, counterpoint, orchestration, analysis, fugue, and history – reflected a thoroughly British outlook and for about 60 years formed the backbone of academic music instruction. The standards were high enough; but, while offering essential skills and mental discipline, the system did little to equip a musician for a professional career – except in a perpetuation of the same academism. The harmony and counterpoint had little to do with contemporary composition, skills in orchestration were useless when orchestras were scarce and in any case gave little exposure to Canadian music, and music history was considered a subject for polite conversation rather than scholarship. Thus the universities contributed little towards fostering those branches of the profession that require advanced training; composition, scholarship, virtuoso performance, school and private teaching, conducting, and opera.

Far-seeing persons strove to improve the situation. When Ernest *Lavigne imported Belgians to play in an orchestra in Montreal in 1895, he hoped they would teach young Canadians to become orchestral players. When Col A.E. *Gooderham founded the *Canadian Academy of Music in Toronto in 1911, his purpose was to save Canadian students expensive trips overseas by bringing to Canada teachers of international rank such as von *Kunits and Otto *Morando. It is true that a few famous teachers resided in Canada in the early 20th century, but all only for brief periods (eg, Arthur Friedheim, Henri Czaplinski, Walter Kirschbaum, and Claude Biggs).

In any case, after taking bachelor degrees or associate diplomas in Canada, most serious students aspired to further studies abroad. By the second quarter of the century, in addition to the traditional study centres of Europe, the many excellent and modern music schools of the USA were an enticement. The Juilliard School attracted Paule-Aimée Bailly, Alexander *Brott, Marcelle *Martin, Phil *Nimmons, Barbara *Pentland, and William Keith *Rogers; the ESM (Rochester), *Weinzweig; the New England Cons, *Papineau-Couture and *Blackburn; the Curtis Institute, Marvin *Duchow, Pierrette *Alarie, Clermont *Pépin; the Peabody Institute, Colin *McPhee. Most French-Canadians continued to go to Paris (J.-M. *Beaudet, *Champagne, A. *Descarries, Raoul *Jobin, R. *Mathieu, Léo-Pol *Morin, and Wilfrid *Pelletier). Perhaps it was the very existence of these opportunities that retarded development of professional training at home. It was only during World War II, when it was difficult or impossible to study abroad, that the problem was faced squarely.

In response to strong proposals by Champagne and others, the Quebec government established its Conservatoire de musique et d'art dramatique in Montreal (1942) and Quebec (1944), under the direction of Wilfrid Pelletier, to provide free instruction for talented students (see Cons de musique du Quebec).

The U of Toronto and the board of the *TCM commissioned Ernest Hutcheson, the president of the Juilliard School in New York, to prepare a report on the expansion of music education in Canada. 'Report: On a Short Survey of the Toronto Conservatory of Music' (1937) recommended that a strong 'graduating and professional' department, leading to active professional occupation or to advanced university courses, be established; that advanced students take courses, with major and secondary subjects plus theory, rather than lessons in one subject; that teachers be assigned to pupils; that teachers be salaried rather than paid lesson fees; that a summer school be established for continuing education or refresher courses; and that training be geared to occupational needs (eg, musicians to teach in schools or work in broadcast studios). Hutcheson's recommendations were adopted, with some changes, in 1946 when Arnold *Walter was asked to set up a school music course, a senior school, and an opera school at the U of Toronto, under the direction of Sir Ernest *MacMillan and the TCM's board of directors.

2 1950–80. Ca 1950 an unprecedented increase in breadth and seriousness marked professional education programs. The number of Canadian university degree programs in music increased from 12 in 1955 to 17 in 1966; the CAUSM *Directory* for 1978–9 lists 31 (most are described individually under their separate institutional names). The following were adopted enthusiastically in English-speaking Canada as founding premises: school music programs require specialists, equipped to organize courses centred on instrumental ensemble performance (the band, the orchestra); professional performers should acquire degrees and should mix advanced practical studies with those in liberal arts subjects; and music is an appropriate area for graduate studies.

These premises were all based on US patterns. At the outset a notable, and also quite new, dependence on US models was seen in Canadian professional education. In music, no less than in other disciplines, the 'Americanization' of university programs came to be felt, and expressed, by the mid-1960s, a trend attributable both to the adoption of such patterns and to the importation of expert personnel. The universities of Toronto, British Columbia, and Saskatchewan, for example, appointed prominent US scholars to direct new professional programs in music. New departments followed a similar line in their appointments, for example those at the *U of Calgary and *York U. Among Canadians appointed in the same period a majority had acquired graduate degrees in US schools. (Columbia, Yale, Rochester, Michigan, Indiana, Illinois, Washington, Stanford, and Berkeley all attracted Canadian graduate students in the 1950s and 1960s.)

As departments proliferated and grew in size, their curricula became both more varied and more specialized. Whereas previously music had existed as either a liberal arts option or a 'general' professional concentration exclusive of performance, in the late 1940s instrumental school music became suddenly the program of highest enrollment, whether offered by music faculties (Toronto) or by music specialists appointed to education faculties (British Columbia, Alberta). In the 1950s musicology was introduced as a specialized discipline (Toronto, Laval, Montreal); and, as corollaries, a sudden huge expansion in music library resources was seen, and master's and doctor's programs were introduced. (Sir Ernest MacMillan had remarked in an essay at the start of the decade that there was no adequate research library in the country and that serious graduate programs would not be viable until there was at least one.)

Although cautious in adopting the US pattern of degrees in musical performance, the Canadian university departments had fostered advanced studies in this area, sometimes offering full-time professional diploma programs (Mount Allison, Toronto, McGill, Western Ontario), but stopping short of degree status. When, in the early 1960s, degree programs in performance were inaugurated, it was principally in answer to demand: the most talented Canadian students seeking professional performing careers wanted the advantages of university degrees and were going in increasing numbers to the US universities for them; the departments felt obliged to stem the 'talent drain,' and they succeeded.

The success may have been, however, partly at the expense of the independent conservatories which, because of their lack of state subsidy and their non-degree-granting character, felt a decline in their professional role. A co-operating link with a university degree program has been an effective compromise in some instances, notably that between the *Victoria Cons and the *U of Victoria's music department.

In the late 1960s and 1970s there were further diversification and specialization in the adoption of ethnomusicology as an undergraduate and graduate subject by several university departments (especially Montreal, Toronto, Ottawa, British Columbia, and York; Laval with its *Archives de folklore had pioneered in this field). Research in Canadian music began to be fostered, a leader in the area being the Faculty of Music at the U of Montreal. During the 1970s some departments added undergraduate courses in the history of music in Canada or analysis and appreciation of Canadian composers' music.

Although conference panels continued to deplore the fact that dissertation topics in the area of musical Canadiana were undertaken more often abroad than within Canada (see Musicology: 2 / Canada as a subject for musicological study), a well-attended gathering of teachers, scholars, and researchers was held in Toronto in 1970 in connection with the annual meeting of the American Musicological and College Music Societies; and in 1974, again in Toronto, CAUSM made 'Canadian Music' the central theme of its annual meeting – two encouraging examples of the nationwide attention paid to this important specialty.

Although the influence of US patterns was pronounced, this was counterbalanced to some extent in the 1950s and 1960s by other factors. US-born and -educated musicians held prominent positions, but significant numbers of mature professionals arrived from other parts of the world as well. Often these were composers, concert performers, or orchestral musicians who contributed a direct acquaintance with trends and standards from, for example, post-war England, Germany, or the USSR. At the same time also, in one important specialization – teacher-training for the elementary levels – the predominant patterns in fact were non-US ones. The *Orff, *Suzuki, and *Kodály approaches all had, in Canada, strong advocates who swiftly acquired first-hand knowledge of these methods. The English translation of Orff's *Schulwerk* was done by Canadians, and direct experience of Kodály's work was developed in the 1960s by extended visits of a number of Canadian music educators to Hungary and by Kodály's own 1964 and 1966 visits to Canada.

In the 1970s a series of issues came increasingly under discussion in informal professional circles, as well as in convention papers and journal articles, representing a questioning of the premises so heartily accepted in the immediate post-war years. Why should not choral music, or non-performance programs, be considered as valid alternatives to instrumental study for school music curricula? Does the school music program in fact require a specialist at all; can it not be entrusted instead to a good classroom teacher with a general love of music? Is a music degree an essential qualification for the supervision of a school music program and, if so, should this be pursued concurrently or consecutively with education studies (ie, who 'owns' music education – the musician or the educator)? Are the university departments producing performers in sufficient numbers and of high enough calibre to compete in the Canadian and international markets? Has the budding performance specialist sufficient time to devote to a broad study of music in its liberal arts context? Are graduate programs in danger of isolating themselves from musical life, and are there too many of them, or not enough?

These and other questions obtained no definitive answers, and their persistence indicated perhaps the departments' unrest in a period of market uncertainty, financial shortages, and declining enrollments, expected to last well into the 1980s.

To the uneasiness of their own competition for students, moreover, was added a new professional trend, the growth of short-term craft courses in community colleges. As long as these courses were offered in areas the university departments were not equipped for or were not interested in (such as, in many cases, commercial arranging), and as long as the circumscribed vocational objectives were clear, this growth was regarded as healthy and a complement to existing programs. But the same natural process by which university departments, as they grow, develop a desire to specialize and to assume a more senior role as symbolized in the adoption of a graduate program seems to ensure that community college instructors gradually yearn for a fuller professional program, perhaps even with a degree attached. Thus, one more issue was planted for the music educators of the 1980s to grapple with. (See also Cegeps; Community colleges.)

Against these points of uneasiness and uncertainty may be placed yet another phenomenon of the 1970s – the rapid spread of summer and evening courses and workshops, supplementing professional education in many special fields, especially at the preparatory and undergraduate levels. In almost every part of Canada, first class active programs became available and, while professional mastery is not obtainable part-time in an exacting discipline such as music, these played a strong adjunct role in the formation of performers and composers especially.

While in 1980 the immediate years ahead were expected to be a period of grappling with problems and issues, and of questioning premises previously agreed upon, the real achievements of Canadian professional education in music could not be ignored. That graduates of the various Canadian university programs have been able to win international contests in composition and performance, publish internationally valued scholarly writings, pursue international careers on the concert stage, in opera, in broadcasting and recording, and hold responsible positions in education, research, and music administration, and in orchestral, chamber, and vocal ensembles will be evident from other articles found in these pages.

BIBLIOGRAPHY

Mazzoleni, Ettore. 'Music teaching in Canada,' Music Teachers National Association *Volume of Proceedings* (1946)

Walter, Arnold. 'Education in music,' *Music in Canada*

Beckwith, John. 'Music education,' *Encyclopedia Canadiana*, vol 7 (Toronto 1958)

Proctor, George. 'The bachelor of music degrees in Canada and the US,' *CME*, vol 7, Jan–Feb 1966

Chartier, Yves. 'La musicologie à l'université,' *R de l'U Laval*, vol 38, Jul–Sep 1968

Walter, Arnold. 'The growth of music education,' *Aspects of Music in Canada*

Morey, Carl. 'Misalliance: the state of music education,' *PfAC*, Summer 1971

Kuzmich, N. 'A creative-affective aural approach to music learning,' *CME*, vol 15, Summer 1974

Green, Paul. 'A proposed doctoral program for Canadian universities with specific recommendations for specialization in music education,' unpubl D ED thesis, Rochester 1974

Blume, Helmut. *A National Music School for Canada: An Inquiry* (Ottawa 1978)

Corey, Gerald. 'Training and employment of Canadian musicians for Canadian orchestras,' *OCan*, vol 5, Oct–Nov 1978

Report of ACO symposium: 'Training and Employment of Orchestral Musicians in Canada,' *OCan*, vol 6, Dec [1978]–Feb 1979 1 / HK, 2 / JB

EDVINA, (Marie) **Louise** (Lucienne Juliette) (b Martin). Soprano, b Montreal 28 May 1878, d London 13 Nov 1948. She was raised in Vancouver, where she made several appearances as an amateur. Her studies were exclusively with Jean de Reszke in Paris, and her debut was at Covent Garden, as Marguerite in *Faust*, 15 Jul 1908. Her performance 18 Jun 1909 in the British premiere of Charpenter's *Louise* established her as one of London's favourite artists. Subsequently she was admired as Desdemona, Mélisande, Thaïs, Tosca, Manon, Maliella in Wolf Ferrari's *I Gioielli della Madonna*, and several other characters. Her North American debut was with the *Montreal Opera, as Louise (5 Nov 1912). Three weeks later she began the first of two highly successful seasons as a member of Henry Russell's Boston Opera. With that company she visited Paris in April 1914, singing Fiora in the French premiere of Montemezzi's *L'Amore dei tre Re*.

In her prime Edvina was also heard in Brussels, Stockholm, and Monte Carlo, at the Paris Opera and Opéra-Comique, and with the Chicago Opera. She made a single appearance at the *Metropolitan Opera (27 Nov 1915) as Tosca, with Caruso. Her operatic career was interrupted by World War I, during which period she gave her services at many benefit concerts and undertook her only concert tour (1916) of Canada. Following her farewell operatic performances in 1924 at Covent Garden, she played in 1926 in an unsuccessful musical comedy, *Hearts and Diamonds*, at London's Strand Theatre.

Edvina's three marriages – to James Matthews Buxton in 1898, the Hon Cecil Edwardes in 1901, and Major Nicholas Rothesay Stuart Wortley in 1919 – ended in widowhood. By Edwardes she had two daughters, Marie Bride and Lumena Sibyl Grace. After her third husband's death in 1926, she retired to Cannes, where she operated an antique shop until the coming of World War II.

A highly sophisticated woman of great integrity, warmth, and charm, Edvina's performances in the fiery masterworks (*Tosca, I Gioielli della Madonna, Francesca da Rimini*) of modern Italy were sometimes faulted for lack of temperament. In roles more congenial to her graceful talents (Mélisande, Marguerite, Louise), it is not uncommon to find contemporary critics preferring her interpretations to those of as celebrated a rival as Mary Garden. Quaintance Eaton, in her history *The Boston Opera Company* (New York 1965), wrote: 'Her clear vitality of spirit was one of her most attractive qualities. Her limpid and even voice with its pure sensuous quality held great charm, even though produced in the "open"

Louise Edvina (*Le Canada musical*, July 1917)

French manner. She showed expertness in shading and molding and coloring. "Very modern" as an actress, she sang too well for the ancients to flout her on that score.'

Edvina's six records (which include samples of her most admired portrayals, Louise and Tosca) were made for HMV in 1921 when she was past her prime. They are listed in *Roll Back the Years* and have been reissued (with the exception of 'Vissi d'arte' from *Tosca*) on a *Rococo LP (5254), which Edvina shares with Jeanne *Gordon and Edward *Johnson. JBM

Edward Bear. Toronto rock band formed in the late 1960s as the Edward Bear Revue, a quintet which took its name from a character in A.A. Milne's book *Winnie the Pooh*. It played at first in Yorkville coffeehouses and as a trio began recording for Capitol in 1969. Members 1969–74 were the singer-songwriter-drummer Larry Evoy, the guitarist Danny Marks until 1971, replaced by Roger Ellis, and the organist Paul Weldon until 1972, replaced by Bob Kendall. Though Edward Bear's original leanings (evident on its first LP, *Bearings*, 1969, Cap SKAO 6238) were to blues-rock, its success resulted from the wider appeal of Evoy's singing and song-writing. Three of the band's singles were international hits: 'You, Me and Mexico' (1970), the million-seller 'The Last Song' (1972), and 'Close Your Eyes' (1973). Canadian hits included 'You Can't Deny It' (1970), 'Fly across the Sea' (1971), 'Masquerade' (1972), and 'Freedom from the Stallion' (1974). Its other LPs were *Eclipse* (1970, Cap SKAO 6349), *Edward Bear* (1972, Cap ST 6387), and *Close Your Eyes* (1973, Cap SKAO 6395). The band received a *Juno Award for the outstanding performance of 1972 and appeared in many Canadian centres. In 1974 Evoy and Kendall continued as Edward Bear, accompanied by the quintet New Potatoes, then Evoy pursued a solo career under his own name. Reviewing Evoy's appearance in a Toronto nightclub, Alan Niester (*Globe and Mail*, 6 Sep 1978) referred to his 'boyish voice' and called him 'one of the finest pop ballad singers Canada has ever produced.' An LP, *Larry Evoy* (Attic LAT 1049), was released in 1978. Evoy is a member of CAPAC.

BIBLIOGRAPHY

Hambleton, Fergus. 'The Bear,' *CanComp*, 50, May 1970

'Last Song: the anatomy of a major hit record,' *CanComp*, 77, Feb 1973

Martin, Robert. 'Edward Bear's chaos all comes out honey,' Toronto *Globe and Mail*, 17 Mar 1973 MM

EGBERT, Gladys (Alma) (b McKelvie). Piano teacher, b Rapid City, near Brandon, Man, 31 Dec 1896, d Calgary 7 Mar 1968; hon FRAM 1936, hon LLD (Alberta) 1965. Her family moved to Calgary in 1903 and she began piano study with Mrs. J.R. Costigan. In 1909 she was awarded a three-year scholarship to the RAM in London. She was the youngest student and the first Canadian ever to receive this award; she did not complete her final year but instead studied 1911–14 in New York with Sigismond Stojowski, Ernest Hutcheson and Richard Epstein. Her studies with Hutcheson continued intermittently until his death in 1951. On her return in 1914 to Calgary she opened a studio, and over, the next 50 years, gained renown as a piano teacher. Indeed, English adjudicator James Gibb described her as 'one of the world's best music teachers' (*Calgary Herald*, 22 Jun 1964). Her pupils included Carlina Carr, Constance *Channon, Jane *Coop, Marilyn *Engle, Jean Gilbert, Marek *Jablonski, Minuetta Schumiacher *Kessler, Leonard *Leacock, Diana *McIntosh, Alexandra *Munn, Linda Lee *Thomas, and Irene *Weiss Peery. In the 1940s with Molly Pearce-Hamilton and Phyllis Ford, believing in the necessity of a comprehensive system of music instruction, Egbert established the Associated Studios of Music. The same convictions led to her active participation in the founding of the *WBM. In 1967 she was one of six recipients of the *CFMTA Centennial Citation.

BIBLIOGRAPHY

Reid, Eva. 'Distinguished citizen,' *SatN*, 29 Oct 1955 RDM

EGENER, Frederick (Tristram). Organist, composer, b Hamilton, Ont, 1886, d London, Ont, 17 June 1973; B MUS (Toronto) 1918, D MUS (Potomac) 1920; FCCO 1920s. His teachers were T.J. Palmer, H.A. Wheeldon, F.J. Thomas, and J. Norman in Canada and Frederick Keel and Reginald Goss-Custard in England. While organist 1905–10 at Zion Presbyterian Church, Brantford, Ont, he was a founding member in 1909 of the CCO (*RCCO). He held various church positions 1910–19 in southwestern Ontario and operated the Woodstock Cons before pursuing a concert career in the USA. He was chief organist and organ designer for the Marcus Loew Theatre Corp in New York, inaugurating theatre organs in Detroit, Minneapolis, and elsewhere.

In 1922 Egener became organist at Welland Ave United Church, St Catharines, Ont, serving also as bandmaster and music director 1928–32 of the Lincoln Regiment. He was then appointed organist (1932–51) at Cronyn Memorial Anglican Church, London, Ont, where he gave over 100 recitals and presented oratorios. By 1949 he had given some 2400 recitals in Switzerland, Canada, the USA, and England. Before his retirement in 1965 he served also at St James (Westminster) Anglican Church, London, Ont, and in nearby Sarnia and St Thomas. Egener composed five songs, a few miniatures for piano, a choral setting of 'The Lord's Prayer' (Waterloo), and *Scenes Canadian, Op 12* (Waterloo 1929), a set of 10 character pieces for organ, begun in 1918.

EGERTON, Arthur (Henry) (b Egg). Organist-choirmaster, teacher, composer, b Montreal 1891, d Hemmingford, Que, 10 Dec 1957; hon ARCM, FRCO 1913, B MUS (McGill) 1921, D MUS (Toronto) 1936. He studied organ at the *McGill Cons with Percival J. *Illsley and Lynnwood *Farnam and on a Lord *Strathcona Scholarship at the RCM 1911–13 with Sir Walter Alcock, Sir Walter Parratt, and others. On his return to Montreal Egerton succeeded Farnam as organist-choirmaster 1913–21 at Christ Church Cathedral and taught organ and theory at McGill. Moving to Winnipeg, he was organist-choirmaster 1922–7 at All Saints Anglican Church and Grace United Church successively and conductor 1926–7 of the Winnipeg Choral and Orchestral Society. He spent the next 10 years in the USA, 1927–9 as organist-choirmaster at St Paul's Episcopal Church in Duluth, Minn, and 1927–37 as head of the Music Dept at Wells College, Aurora, NY. He returned to Canada and a succession of church positions – at St Andrew's Presbyterian, Ottawa, in 1937, at Trinity Memorial in Montreal 1938–47, and again at Christ Church Cathedral 1947–51 – and to a position as supervisor of school music in Outremont, Montreal. Egerton composed anthems and organ pieces, some published by Gray, Oxford, and Western. His D MUS exercise, a setting of Bliss Carman's 'A Sailor's Wedding,' remained unpublished. (RG)

EGGLESTON, Anne (Elizabeth). Composer, b Ottawa 6 Sep 1934; Artist Diploma (Toronto) 1956, M MUS (ESM, Rochester) 1958. She studied in Ottawa with Gladys Barnes and Robert *Fleming, at the *RCMT 1953–6 with Pierre *Souvairan (piano) and *Morawetz, *Ridout, and *Weinzweig (composition), and at the ESM with Bernard Rogers (composition) and Emily Davis and Orazio Frugoni (piano), completing *Autumnal Clouds* (1958) for baritone and orchestra as her master's thesis. In 1958 she began teaching piano and composition privately in Ottawa. She has received commissions from the *CMCentre, the *Charlottetown Festival, *CAMMAC, and the *WBM. Performances of her works, mainly in eastern Canada, have established Eggleston as a serious composer, unassertive but accomplished. She is a member of CAPAC and an associate of the *CMCentre.

SELECTED COMPOSITIONS

STAGE

The Woodcarver's Wife, opera. 1961. CMCentre

ORCHESTRA

Three Pieces for Orchestra. 1956. CMCentre

Interlude for Small Orchestra. 1957. CMCentre

Autumnal Clouds (John Gould Fletcher). 1958. Bar, orch. CMCentre

On Citadel Hill. 1964. School str orch. CMCentre

Fanfaron. 1966. Orch. CMCentre

CHAMBER

Piano Quartet. 1955. Pf, vn, va, vc. Jay 1972

String Quartet. 1957. CMCentre

Also 2 works for vn and pf (1952, 1969); 2 works for pf and 2 alto recorders

CHOIR AND VOICE

Five Lullabies of Eugene Field. 1961. V, pf. Jay 1973. RCI 247. (*Patenaude).

Also other works for choir, including several arrangements of folk songs; some pieces for voice; some educational piano pieces (LI)

EGLAUCH (also Eglau or Ecclaugh), **Leonard**. Piano teacher, organist, b Germany, d Montreal? ca 1886. He is mentioned first in newspapers in 1842 as a piano recitalist-accompanist in Kingston, Upper Canada (Ontario) and Quebec City and as a teacher in Montreal. For the first eight months of 1845 he was the organist at Notre-Dame Church in Montreal. Though he was dismissed, 'having given [his employer] grave cause for dissatisfaction,' it is not known whether the 'grave cause' was musical. Indeed Gustave *Smith described him as a talented and original musician and a good pianist who enjoyed analysing the classical masterworks. He was feared, however, by his pupils for his temperamental teaching manner. He was listed in Montreal city directories as a piano teacher but he also advertised 1857–8 as a piano dealer.

BIBLIOGRAPHY

Smith, Gustave. 'Du mouvement musical en Canada,' *L'Album musical*, Feb 1882 HK

Egypt. Immigration of Egyptians to Canada first became appreciable in the 1950s. During the 1960s they formed the majority of immigrants from Arabic countries. Most Egyptian immigrants have been of urban origin, 75 per cent of them white-collar professionals. Copts account for the majority. (The Coptic church is the native Christian church in Egypt.)

In the 1970s the small size of the community as well as its recent date of settlement limited the organization of public concerts. However the Reda Folklore Dance Troup from Egypt, led by Ali Ismail, performed in Montreal, Quebec City, and Toronto in 1973, and the Egyptian Embassy, as part of an Egyptian Week Festival held in June 1978, sponsored appearances in Montreal, Ottawa, and Toronto of the 'Om Kolsoum,' an Arabic orchestra and 15-voice mixed choir. The musicians used both western and traditional instruments (Qanun, 'ud, Darabukkah, violin, and cello). Informal gatherings in the 1960s and 1970s featured commercialized popular and folk music provided by amateur musicians, the audience usually participating. In addition, there was occasional singing of Coptic and Arabic chants on religious and even secular occasions by small groups in the home. (See Arabic music.) To the limited extent that this small community engaged in cultural activites, it managed to avoid absorption of Western influences. Egyptian-born musicians in Canada include the Montreal organist George Missiha and George Sawa, a member of the Classical Arabic Music Quintet of Toronto. The pianist Paul Bempechat studied with Daphne Sandercock in Montreal. (Raffi *Armenian and Gerard *Kantarjian, though both born in Egypt, are of Armenian descent.) (GDS)

EIGER, Walter (Wladislaw). Pianist, composer, arranger, conductor, teacher, b Łodz, Poland, 6 Feb 1917, naturalized Canadian ca 1955. He received his musical training in France, at the U of Grenoble and the École normale de musique in Paris. At the end of the 1940s he appeared in Montreal as accompanist for the singers Charles Trenet and Patachou. He settled in Canada in the early 1950s and worked as conductor and arranger for the CBC TV programs 'Feux de joie,' 'Silhouette,' 'Quartiers de Paris,' 'Domino,' and 'Music-Hall.'

Among Eiger's compositions are a *Concerto grosso* for jazz ensemble and symphony orchestra, *American Youth Overture*, the overture *Hello Paris*, and an *Overture on Canadian Folk Tunes*, written before 1952, revised in 1978, and published by Peer International in 1980.

Eiger has produced orchestrations for Broadway shows and for the comedian Victor Borge's TV shows. Between 1967 and 1970 he worked in New York as an arranger at Radio City Music Hall, for whose special Canadian Centennial Show he composed an *Ouverture Canadienne* based, like his earlier work in the genre, on Canadian folk tunes. He composed the music for the *NFB film *Royal Journey*. In 1960 he began giving courses at several universities in the USA, notably at Pensacola, Fla. He began teaching at *Concordia U, Montreal, in 1978. He is a member of CAPAC. GP

EIKHARD. Family of pop musicians: 1 / June and 2 / her daughter Shirley.

1 (Marguerite) **June** (b Cameron). Fiddler, b Moncton, NB, 1 Dec 1932. Taking up the violin at 15 she led a country band, the Tantramar Ramblers, in the Maritimes during the 1950s with her husband, Cecil (Arnold) Eikhard (b Eikhoudt), a bass player. In 1959 she became the first woman participant in the *Canadian Open Old Time Fiddlers' Contest, placing fifth in the open class. After the family moved in 1963 to Oshawa, Ont, she worked with various local country bands. She has made the LPs *Canada's First Lady of the Fiddle* (1959, Rodeo RLP 78), *June Eikhard* (1960, Rodeo RBS 1076), and a second *June Eikhard* (1969, Banff SBS 5311).

BIBLIOGRAPHY
Foster, Don. 'Canada's first lady of the fiddle,' *Country Music News*, vol 1, Nov–Dec 1972

2 **Shirley** (Rose). Singer-songwriter, guitarist, pianist, b Sackville, NB, 7 Nov 1955. A songwriter at 11, she made her debut at 12 singing at a fiddler's contest in Cobourg, Ont, appeared at the *Mariposa Folk Festival at 13, and sang on CBC TV's 'Singalong Jubilee' at 14. Her early performances elicited comparisons with Anne *Murray (who was the first artist to record an Eikhard song – 'It Takes Time' in 1971), though a Toronto *Globe and Mail* reviewer later commented, 'The only thing linking Murray and Eikhard now is that low husky voice, but in a pinch, Eikhard's is far more flexible, both in range and expression' (10 Aug 1977). Her first LP, *Shirley Eikhard* (1971, Cap ST 6371), was followed by appearances across Canada in concert halls and coffeehouses. In 1975 she toured the country with Hagood *Hardy. Her later recordings – *Child of the Present* (1975, Attic LAT 1007), *Let Me Down Easy* (1976, Attic LAT 1021), and *Horizons* (1977, Attic LAT 1032) – reflect a variety of influences, especially those of jazz, and her appearances of the mid-1970s reveal a calculated change in image from a casual and folksy performer to a more sophisticated entertainer. Her most successful songs include 'It Takes Time,' 'Pickin' My Way' (recorded as the title tune of an LP by guitarist Chet Atkins), 'Let Me Down Easy,' 'I Still Believe in Love Songs' (with some lyrics by Greg Adams), 'Grey Day,' and 'Let Love Write Our Song.' Her songs have been recorded by Gary *Buck, Donna Ramsey, the Laurie *Bower Singers, and others and are published by Pondwater Music / Canvee Music. An affiliate of BMI Canada until 1973 (she received certificates of honour in 1971, 1972, and 1973), Eikhard then joined CAPAC. She also received *Juno Awards as 'female country singer' of 1972 and 1973.

BIBLIOGRAPHY
McCracken, Melinda. 'The voice, it's the voice, that warm soothing alto,' *Maclean's*, Jun 1972
Graves, Lief. 'Getting to know Ms. Shirley Eikhard,' *CanComp*, 93, Sep 1974
Beker, Marilyn. 'Packaging Shirley Eikhard,' *Weekend Magazine*, 22 May 1976 LL (MM)

Electronic music. A broadly applied term encompassing tape music (using natural acoustic sounds; or generated sound, analog or digital), live electronics (performance on electronic instruments or on-the-spot electronic processing of acoustic sounds), and combinations of the above. (*The Development and Practise of Electronic Music*, J.A. Appleton and R.C. Perera eds, New York, 1975, is a useful source of detailed information on equipment and terms.)

See also Acoustics research in Canada; Mixed media.

1 Introduction
2 National Research Council
3 UTEMS
4 McGill U
5 Simon Fraser U
6 Other studios
7 Individuals

Arnold Walter with Myron Schaeffer in the Electronic Music Studio, Edward Johnson Building, University of Toronto

1 INTRODUCTION. The development of electronic music in Canada has been characterized by a vigorous effort by many composers, scientists, and technicians. The number of uniquely designed electronic devices, published research articles, and compositions that have emanated from studios and individuals working privately attest to the productivity during the period 1955–80.

Most studios in Canada were founded and developed in educational institutions rather than being formed in conjunction with radio facilities as in Europe. However, some of the tapes for early works, including Serge *Garant's *Nucléogame* (1954) and Pierre *Mercure's *Psaume pour Abri* (1963), were produced at the CBC in Montreal, a facility not formally recognized as an electronic studio.

A precise, definitive account of this period is hardly possible because of contradictory data, failing memories, and the modesty of those involved. The material below provides one view of important early studios, later studios, and individuals.

2 NATIONAL RESEARCH COUNCIL (NRC). The establishment, in the early 1950s, of the National Research Council's Electronic Music Laboratory (ELMUS) in Ottawa was an important beginning in the development of electronic music in Canada. Over a period of about 20 years Hugh *LeCaine, its director, produced numerous instruments of original design (sine bank, serial structure generator, multitrack special purpose tape player, sonde, etc) and composed many pieces which illustrated the possibilities of these instruments. LeCaine's collaboration with the studios of the *U of Toronto and *McGill U aided their development, and the two studios provided homes for ELMUS equipment. During 1959–61 István *Anhalt produced *Electronic Compositions Nos. 1–4* at ELMUS. A computer system for use by composers was developed 1968–72 under the direction of Ken Pulfer and continued in use until 1974. It permitted composers to write their music into the computer in standard notation or by means of an organ-type keyboard. The music could be subjected to many kinds of modification and manipulation and the result then played. Composers who employed the system included Morris *Surdin, Larry *Crosley (theme music for the CBC TV series 'Weekend,' 1971), Ben *McPeek (CBC commercials), and Samuel *Dolin (*Concerto Grosso*, 1970).

3 UTEMS. The U of Toronto Electronic Music Studio was founded in 1959 by Arnold *Walter. Myron Schaeffer (1908–65), its first director, developed the Hamograph, an amplitude control

device, and produced numerous compositions (*Dance 4:3*, 1960; *Haiku Nos. 1–3*, 1962; *Lament from Jephtha*, 1963) and film music (*New Intruder*, 1962; *The Smile*, 1962). Schaeffer also collaborated with Harvey Olnick and Arnold Walter on incidental music for TV ('Summer Idyll,' 1960). During the 1960s the studio attracted many composers from Canada, the USA, and Europe. Among those who worked in this period were Robert *Aitken, Norma *Beecroft, Douglas Lilburn (New Zealand, *Four Studies*, 1963), Jean Ivey (USA, *Enter Three Witches*, 1964), Anthony Gnazzo (USA, *Music for Two Pianos* and *Electronic Sounds*, 1964; numerous works for dance), Pauline Oliveros (USA, numerous works, summer 1966), Albert Mayr (Italy), Rudolf *Komorous (*Gone*, 1969), and Richard *Henninger (*Reflections from Outer Space*, 1969).

While at UTEMS, Lowell Cross (USA), a doctoral student and research assistant, developed systems for controlling light and video images using electronic sound (*Video II*, 1965); collaborated with Gustave *Ciamaga (*Phone Phugue*, 1966, TV), Harry *Freedman (*Isabel*, 1967, film), and Harry *Somers (electronic sequences for the opera **Louis Riel*, 1967); produced electronic compositions (*Three Etudes for Hugh LeCaine*, 1965); and compiled a bibliography of electronic music (see Bibliography).

In addition to being a traditional analog studio, UTEMS has concerned itself with the development and use of computers. Gustav Ciamaga, who became director of the studio in 1965, collaborated 1963–8 with James Gabura in the development of a computer-controlled analog synthesizer (Piper II). During 1971–2, UTEMS also implemented a 'Music IV' type of program called Outperform. This was adapted by David Jaeger and is used not only for original sound synthesis but also for teaching computer techniques. In 1977, William Buxton of the Computer Systems Research Group (CSRG) of the U of Toronto, began developing a graphics-oriented digital synthesizer (Structured Sound Synthesis Project, SSSP) in co-operation with the Faculty of Music.

Composers who worked in the studio in the 1970s included members of the *Canadian Electronic Ensemble, Bruce Pennycook (*Study in Pulse Trains*, 1973), and Dennis Patrick (*Phantasy* for oboe and tape, 1976).

4 MCGILL U. The studio was founded by István Anhalt in 1964 in collaboration with ELMUS of the National Research Council. Early users included Pierre Mercure (*Forme des Choses*, 1964, film), R. Murray *Schafer (**Loving*, 1965), and Paul *Pedersen (*Phantasie*, 1967). Pedersen, the studio's director 1971–4, began using computers for sound synthesis and composition in the mid-1960s. His *Serial Composition* (1965) for violin, horn, bassoon, and harp was composed with the aid of a computer program written in collaboration with James Gabura (Toronto). Users of the McGill studio in the 1970s have included Alcides *Lanza (who became the studio's director in 1974), Michel *Longtin, Denis *Lorrain, and Otto *Joachim.

5 SIMON FRASER U. In 1967, R. Murray Schafer founded the Sonic Research Studio in co-operation with the Dept of Communications Studies and, with the assistance of Anthony Gnazzo, installed a Buchla synthesizer. Composers associated with the studio include Peter *Huse and Phillip Werren. In 1971 Schafer initiated the *World Soundscape Project, the aim of which was to bring together research on the scientific, sociological, and aesthetic aspects of the acoustic environment. Members of the project included Bruce *Davis, Peter Huse, Barry *Truax, and Howard Broomfield. Barry Truax, who became director of the studio in 1975, has developed and installed his POD (1973) computer programs. The system features interactive composition and real-time FM sound-synthesis. Micheline Coulombe *Saint-Marcoux, a teacher at the *CMM, used the equipment of the Sonic Research Studio in 1972 for *Zones* and *Alchéra*.

6 OTHER STUDIOS. In the late 1960s and early 1970s other studios emerged. At the *U of British Columbia, Courtland *Hultberg founded a studio in 1965. The *RCMT studio was established in 1966 by Samuel Dolin; Wes Wraggett, who joined the studio in 1976, took charge of its operation in 1978. Nil *Parent established the electronic music studio (SMEUL) at *Laval U in 1969 and formed *GIMEL (Groupe d'interprétation de musique électroacoustique) in 1974. The members of GIMEL have performed compositions in which the sounds from traditional instruments are transformed electronically. The Groupe informatique-musique, formed in 1971 at the *U of Montreal and directed by Eric Regener, developed a sound-synthesis program and conducted research into score analysis. Studios also have been established at *York U (1970, by James Tenney), *Carleton U (1974, by David Piper), the *U of Western Ontario (1972, by Peter J. Clements), *Queen's U (1971, by David Keane), *Dalhousie U (1971, by Steve Tittle), the *U of Calgary (early 1970s, by Warren Rowley), and the *U of Victoria (1978, by Martin Bartlett).

7 INDIVIDUALS. While most composers work in the institutional studios mentioned above, others, including David McLey, Otto Joachim, and Ann *Southam, have developed private studios. The availability, in the late 1960s and early 1970s, of packaged synthesizers – Moog, Buchla, EMS (London), etc – increased the use, by Ben McPeek, John *Mills-Cockell, and others, of electronic music in commercial and popular idioms. Keyboard synthesizers came into wide use by pop music groups. In 1977 the Assn pour la création et la recherche électroacoustique du Québec (ACREQ) was founded in Montreal by the composers Yves Daoust, Marcelle *Deschênes-Harvey, Michel *Longtin, Philippe Ménard, Jean Sauvageau, and Pierre *Trochu, to encourage creation and research and promote international exchange.

See also Norman McLaren; Morse Robb; David Rosenboom.

DISCOGRAPHY

Carrefour: electroacoustic music: Joachim – Pedersen – Saint-Marcoux – Huse – Longtin – LeCaine – Paul. 1973. RCI 373

Electronic Essays: Anhalt – J. Rea. Marathon MS 2111

Electronic Music: Aitken – LeCaine – Olnick – Schaeffer – Walter – J.D. Robb. 1967. Folk FM 34360

Electronic Music by Canadian Composers Vol 1: Southam – Archer – R. Daigneault. Mel SMLP 4024

– Vol 2: Longtin – Druick – Huse – R. Berg. Mel SMLP 4027

BIBLIOGRAPHY

LeCaine, Hugh. 'From the labs: a new music,' *Financial Post*, 29 Sep 1956

Walter, Arnold. 'Music and electronics,' *CMJ*, vol 3, Summer 1959

LeCaine, Hugh. 'Synthetic means,' *The Modern Composer and His World* ed Beckwith and Kasemets (Toronto 1961)

Schaeffer, Myron S. 'The Hamograph, a new amplitude – rhythm control device for the production of electronic music,' *Institute of Radio Engineers Transactions on Audio*, Jan–Feb 1962

– 'The creation of melodic contours from non-melodic raw material without loss of text or timbre,' *J of the Audio Engineering Soc*, vol 11, Jan 1963

– 'The electronic music studio of the University of Toronto,' *J of Music Theory*, vol 8, Spring 1963

– 'The space age and electronic music,' *PfAC*, vol 2, Winter 1963

– 'A simple method for control of multi-signal recording,' Audio Engineering Soc reprint no. 299 (1963)

– 'Synthesis and manipulation of natural sounds in electronic music for films,' *J of the Soc of Motion Picture and Television Engineers*, vol 73, Feb 1964

– 'An extension of tone-row techniques through electronic pitch control,' *J of the International Folk Music Council*, vol 16, 1964

Ivey, Jean Eichelberger. 'Electronic music in Toronto,' *Kansas Music R*, vol 26, Oct–Nov 1964

Pedersen, Paul. 'The mel scale,' *J of Music Theory*, vol 9, Winter 1965

'Electronic-music courses offered at the University of Toronto,' *J of the Acoustical Soc of America*, vol 39, Apr 1966

Gabura, A.J., and Ciamaga, Gustav. 'Digital computer control of sound generating apparatus for the production of electronic music,' *Electronic Music R*, vol 1, Jan 1967

'Musical plotter knows the score at University of Toronto,' *Digital Plotting Newsletter*, May–Jun 1967

Cross, Lowell. *A Bibliography of Electronic Music* (Toronto 1967)

– 'Electronic music 1948–1953,' unpubl MA thesis, Toronto 1968

– 'The stirrer,' *Source: Music of the Avant-garde*, 4, Jun 1968

Gotlieb, C.C. and Gabura, A.J. 'A system for keypunching music,' *Q Bulletin of the Computer Soc of Canada*, vol 8, Winter 1967–8

Cross, Lowell. 'Audio/video/laser,' *Source: Music of the Avant-garde*, 8, Jul 1970

Hickman, James. 'David McLey: a new synthesizer composer,' *CanComp*, 72, Sep 1972

'Musiques électroacoustiques,' *Musique en jeu*, 8, Sep 1972

Strange, Allen. *Electronic Music* (n.p. 1972)

Howe, Hubert S. *Electronic Music Synthesis* (New York 1975)

Chion, Michel and Reibel, Guy. *Les Musiques Electroacoustiques* (Paris 1976)

Kieser, Karen. 'Electronic sound: music's youngest offspring,' 'The excitement of that plug-in music,' *Fugue*, Sep 1977

Schulman, Michael. 'David Keane is a composer who's not in a hurry,' *CanComp*, 137, Jan 1979

Prince, Ann. 'A low-key composer manages the U of T's electronic music studio,' *CanComp*, 138, Feb 1979

Freeman, Brian. 'Birth of a performance art: music by computer,' *Maclean's*, 5 Feb 1979

Lake, Larry. 'Electronic music: a Canadian art,' *Mcan*, 40, Sep 1979

Dictionary of Contemporary Music

See also Writings for Gustav Ciamaga; Hugh LeCaine.

FILMOGRAPHY

The Music Machine (Canadian Film Institute 1971)

DP

The Elgar Choir of British Columbia on its Asian tour, 1964

The Elgar Choir of British Columbia. A Vancouver-based young people's choir, mostly girls, numbering between 25 and 40. It was founded in 1924 and conducted until 1974 by Charles *Findlater. First known as the Wesley Methodist Church Junior Choir, in 1935 it was renamed the Elgar Choir with the permission of the composer's daughter. Many of the choristers were students at Findlater's Elgar School of Music, and much of the repertoire was drawn from Elgar and his British contemporaries. The choir performed throughout Canada, in Europe, and in Asia, making 12 trips overseas, visiting 27 countries, and winning awards in international competitions. It made its first appearance abroad at the 1934 Chicago World's Fair. Its 11th overseas tour (1964) was the first around the world by a Canadian choir via the Asian route to Hawaii. It made three recordings, two privately and one for the CBC (RCI 54). The choir ceased operations in July 1975. (TRL)

Elizabethan Singers. Mixed ensemble of 10–12 voices founded in Stratford, Ont, in 1953 and conducted by its founder, Gordon (Delbert) Scott. The first concert, 4 Jul 1954 at the *Stratford Festival's Tent Theatre, was the only musical event of the festival's 1954 season. At the 1955 festival the singers acted as Portia's household in Tyrone Guthrie's production of *The Merchant of Venice*. They also performed independently in public and on CBC radio. Their final concert (8 Apr 1959, a program of Shakespeare and music) was given under Ernesto *Barbini with the National Festival Orchestra. Early members included Lloyd *Bradshaw, Kathryn Root, and two of Gordon Scott's pupils, John *Boyden and Barbara *Collier. Scott (b Eramosa, near Guelph, Ont, 7 Dec 1912) became the organist-choirmaster at St John's United Church in 1942 and began teaching at the *Western Ontario Cons in 1972. (GJ)

ELLARD, Brian (Joseph). Pianist, organist, musicologist, educator, b Ottawa 15 Jan 1940; B MUS (ESM, Rochester) 1966, MA (ESM, Rochester) 1968, PH D (ESM, Rochester) 1973. After studying trade and commerce 1957–9 at the U of Ottawa, he took courses in music 1963–9 at the ESM in Rochester, NY. He was an organist-choirmaster 1953–63 in Ottawa and 1963–9 in Webster, NY, and was accompanist and director 1962–3 of Ottawa's Crawley Choir and 1966–8 of the Rochester Institute of Technology Glee Club. In 1967, for Crawley Films, Ottawa, he composed the music for the film *Holiday Island*, commissioned by the government of Prince Edward Island. Ellard has had extensive experience as a pianist and arranger of pop music and jazz.

Ellard's career as a scholar dates from the period 1967–9 when he studied medieval music and the development of form and tonality from Beethoven to Mahler and Debussy. He served 1970–8 as chairman of the Dept of Music and 1977–8 as vice-dean of the Faculty of Arts at the *U of Moncton and in 1979 was named director of the U of Sherbrooke's new School of Music, scheduled to open in the fall of 1981. He was vice-president 1973–5 and president 1975–7 of *CAUSM and began editing the CAUSM Directory in 1974.

WRITINGS

'Quam pulchri sunt: the Motet and the Mass by Tomas Luis de Victoria,' unpubl MA thesis, ESM, Rochester, 1968

'Edmond Costère's Lois et styles des harmonies musicales,' unpubl PH D thesis, ESM, Rochester, 1973 YC

ELLEFSON, Art (Arthur Albert). Saxophonist, b Moose Jaw, Sask, 17 Apr 1932. A trumpet and euphonium player as a boy, he took up the tenor saxophone at 16 and began his career in Toronto with Bobby *Gimby and others before moving to London in 1952. He played saxophones (soprano, alto, tenor, baritone) and clarinets in British bands, including the Vic Lewis Orchestra 1953–7, and was soloist with the Ronnie Ross–Allan Ganley Jazzmakers (with whom he toured North America in 1959) and 1950–5 with the John Dankworth Orchestra. (Ellefson's recordings with Dankworth are listed in the discography for Kenny *Wheeler.) He was a member of touring bands led in England by Woody Herman and Maynard *Ferguson. In 1974 he returned to Canada, working as a salesman in Barrie, north of Toronto, but playing tenor saxophone with *Nimmons 'N' Nine plus Six until 1977. He has appeared occasionally with his own groups in Toronto and Barrie and has recorded in Canada as a soloist with Nimmons and Wheeler. Jack Batten (Toronto *Globe and Mail* 29 Sep 1976) wrote, 'his sound seems a direct extension of the old masters ... [Coleman] Hawkins and [Ben] Webster and Lucky Thompson, and so is his sing-song lyricism, but the drive and naked passion of his playing comes from later, more beboppy tenor men.'

BIBLIOGRAPHY

Bavin, Pam. 'Canadians in London 2. Art Ellefson,' *Coda*, vol 4, Nov 1961 MM

ELLIOTT, Carleton (Weir). Theorist, composer, choir conductor, b Welland, Ont, 15 Mar 1928; B MUS (Mount Allison) 1951, M MUS (Redlands, Cal) 1959; further studies in theory and choral conducting at Indiana U. He joined the faculty of *Mount Allison U in 1951 and became the founder-director of the Mount Allison Conservatory Chorale in 1953 and the supervisor for Mount Allison Local Centre Examinations in Music in 1967, as well as an adjudicator at music festivals in the Atlantic region. He has written some choral works, but most of his compositions are for young pianists, introducing them to various 20th-century techniques. His publishers are *Leeds, Frederick *Harris, and *Waterloo. He is married to the pianist Patricia Grant Lewis (b Regina 1931), who was a pupil of Lubka *Kolessa in the late 1940s and was appointed to the staff of Mount Allison in 1957.

WRITINGS

'Music in New Brunswick,' *The Arts in New Brunswick* (Fredericton 1967) NV

ELLIS, Vernon (Austin). Educator, pianist, adjudicator, b Port Maitland, NS, 20 Jun 1930; B MUS (Acadia) 1952, M MUS (ESM, Rochester) 1960. After specializing in music education in his post-graduate studies, he taught 1952–8 at Middleton (NS) Regional High School, was music adviser 1958–9 to the Nova Scotia Dept of Education, and taught 1962–6 at Nova Scotia Teachers' College and 1966–74 at *Dalhousie U. He became dean of music at *Acadia U in 1974. He has served as president 1962–3 of the *NSMEA and 1969–71 of the *CMEA. He served 1970–4 on the board of ISME and 1972–4 as chairman of its Canadian committee.

See also School music. WL

ELLOWAY, Kenneth (Albert). Conductor, teacher, b Weymouth, England, 17 Jan 1916, d Halifax 22 Sep 1980; ARCM 1943. He first played cornet and later took up the trombone and string bass. He graduated in 1945 from the RMSM (Kneller Hall). In 1950 he passed the school's advanced examination for military bandmasters. Following a career with British military orchestras and bands, he moved to Halifax in 1955 as music director of the Royal Canadian Artillery band and became inspector of bands for the Canadian Army Eastern Command. He frequently guest-conducted the *Halifax SO, adjudicated at music festivals across Canada, and lectured at *Mount Saint Vincent U, Halifax. Retiring from the army in 1965, he moved to Toronto as head of music at Emery Collegiate Institute. He returned to Halifax in 1966 as conductor of the CBC Halifax Chamber Orchestra (formerly the CBC Halifax Strings). He was acting director 1959–65 and director 1966–70 of the *Maritime Cons of Music and was associate conductor 1967–8 of the *Halifax SO. He guest-conducted the Halifax Wind Ensemble, the *Atlantic SO, and the *Edmonton SO. Elloway became co-ordinator of instrumental music for Dartmouth schools in 1969, music director of the Dartmouth Choral Society in 1971, and the founding conductor of the Chebucto Orchestra in 1975. He taught at *Dalhousie U from 1974 until his death. (JK)

Emigration. Emigration of the talented has constituted a pattern of loss established in the early years of the rise of the music profession in Canada. In the 1850s H.A. *Clarke moved to Philadelphia, Calixa *Lavallée sought his fortune in New Orleans, and Joseph Sharland began a career in Boston. Not surprisingly the USA, with its kindred culture but earlier development, its wider choice of employment, and its geographical proximity, has continued to be the main beneficiary of Canadian emigration. The list includes, among dozens of others, the instrumental virtuosos Alfred *De Sève, Raymond *Dudley, Lynnwood *Farnam, Arthur Gold, Gwendolyn Williams *Koldofsky, Waugh *Lauder, Salomon *Mazurette, Kathleen *Parlow, and Samuel P. *Warren; the singers Eva *Gauthier, Jeanne *Gordon, and Edward *Johnson; and the composers Henry *Brant, Nathaniel *Dett, Sydney *Hodkinson, Charles Jones, Cedric Lemont, Colin *McPhee, and Gerald Strang. But Europe – in particular England and France – also has drawn on the Canadian resource. Opera singers in particular – from Emma *Albani, Pauline *Donalda, Raoul *Jobin, and Rodolphe *Plamondon to Victor *Braun, Joseph *Rouleau, and André *Turp – have made Europe their home.

The emigration pattern also has extended to stars in popular music and jazz, eg, Paul *Anka, Dorothy Collins, Deanna Durbin, Maynard *Ferguson, Robert *Goulet, Beatrice *Lillie, Guy *Lombardo, Libby Morris, Hank *Snow, and Neil *Young; the conductor-arrangers Percy *Faith and Robert *Farnon; the outstanding orchestral players David *Martin, Lorne *Munroe, Joseph Shadwick, and Paul *Scherman; the conductor Arthur *Davison; and the pianist-teacher Russell Chester.

The loss of musicians undeniably has been large in quantity as well as quality, but its seriousness has been exaggerated by well-meaning editorialists and lobbyists. Careers in Canada and immigration have been larger factors in the development of the profession. Besides, it must be remembered that opera singers, concert virtuosos, and conductors of all Western countries tend to have international careers and even at the rank-and-file level a change of residence is far more common among musicians than among accountants or lawyers. The particularly high mobility of Canadian musicians has had much to do with the lack of outlets for opera singers and virtuosos in a developing country and with the need, on the other hand, for teachers, conductors, and instrumentalists steeped in the traditions of more advanced countries. Furthermore the emigration of Canadian musicians sometimes was based on opportunities encountered while studying abroad, as in the case of Frederick *Grinke or Harry M. *Field, or on marriage to a non-Canadian, as happened to Gena *Branscombe, Nora *Clench, and Ethel Codd *Luening. And not only did many Canadians return to their native land to have 'retirement careers' as teachers or organizers – Pauline

Donalda, Sarah *Fischer, Raoul Jobin, Edward Johnson, Kathleen Parlow and Rodolphe Plamondon are prime examples – but in many cases the line between emigration and temporary absence or extended touring is hard to draw.

The editors of *EMC* have had to face few decisions more difficult than whether to treat certain musicians in separate articles or to document their careers briefly under the entry for their country of main activity. The choice has been influenced by the number of adult years spent in Canada and by the strength of Canadian contacts maintained while abroad, but it has been impossible to impose a set of rigid rules and to avoid inconsistencies. Although they spent most of their professional lives abroad, Albani, Branscombe, Johnson, Lavallée, Parlow, and *Vickers have been given separate entries, while such singers as Marie Dressler, Christie MacDonald, and the piano teachers Kate Chittenden and Jeannette Durno are mentioned in the entry on the United States in a section devoted to Canadian contributions made to that country.

See also articles on individual countries: eg, England, France, United States of America, etc; Conductors; Profession of music. HK

Empire Music Publishers Ltd. Educational and popular-music publishing firm founded in 1948 in New Westminster BC, by the teacher-arranger Karle Hodsin. It is affiliated with *PRO Canada. Empire's first best seller (1948) was Elizabeth Clarke's *'Bluebird on Your Windowsill.' Further successes followed in the country music field, including songs by Stu *Davis, Keray Regan, and Scotty *Stevenson. Empire began issuing educational materials (mainly recorder, accordion, guitar, and ukulele methods) in 1955, and these occupied about two-thirds of its catalogue by the mid-1970s. One of the earliest music publishers in British Columbia, it established its own offset printing facility on the premises. Plate numbers are used. Branches were established in the 1960s in London, Ont, Seattle, Wash, and Port Huron, Mich. An affiliate, Empire Music Co Ltd, is an instrument retailer.

BIBLIOGRAPHY
Cluderay, Lawrence. 'Empire Music,' *MSc*, 243, Sep–Oct 1968 (MWI)

ENGEN, Sid (Hanson). Violin maker, b near Oslo, Norway, 9 Nov 1902, d Dauphin, Man, 23 Jun 1976. His family arrived in Winnipeg in 1905, then moved to Saskatchewan before settling in Dauphin in 1919. Entirely self-taught, Engen built 85 instruments (77 violins, 7 violas, and 1 cello) between 1921 and 1975. Of these, 69 were made between 1954 and 1975, after his retirement from his trade as a house builder and cabinet maker. Engen entered his instruments in an international competition, the Annual Violin and Guitar Makers' Contest sponsored by the Violin and Guitar Makers' Assn of Arizona (Globe, Ariz) and won many prizes, including grand awards for his 1966 and 1968 copies of the 'Le messie' Stradivarius and his 1969 copy of a Guarnarius. The 1966 instrument was acquired by Frances Port Watson, a conductor, violinist and teacher in Winnipeg and Dauphin. Most of his other instruments have remained in Manitoba and Saskatchewan, but some 25 per cent have gone to purchasers in British Columbia, Ontario, Alberta, and the USA. Terence Helmer of the *Orford String Quartet acquired an Engen copy (1959) of a Gasparo da Salo viola. Most Engen instruments have European or British Columbia maple backs and Manitoba, US, or European spruce tops, but on rare occasions he used walnut, myrtle, redwood, cherry, or cedar. KW

England. Ruler for more than 100 years of the lands that became Canada and, with France, their foremost colonizer. In the heterogeneous population of Canada in 1980 the largest group was of British extraction, and within that group it remained the assumption that the English predominated: in 1961 they accounted for 23 per cent of the population. (Later figures were unavailable as the 1971 census did not provide specific information. See also Ireland; Scotland; Wales.)

The English presence in Canada dates from John Cabot's voyage of 1497, undertaken in the service of Henry VII. Soon thereafter, the area of what became St John's, Nfld, was used as a stopover by English fishermen. Other early settlements were Saint John, NB (1631), and Halifax, NS (1749). The settlement at Quebec was under British control 1629–32. By the treaty of Paris (1763) the settlements became part of the British Empire, first as colonies and after Confederation as a self-governing part of the Empire, sharing the British monarch and acting as an ally in peace and war.

Prior to the arrival in Canada of large numbers of immigrants of varied backgrounds during the 19th century, the music of the colonies was that of the British and French peoples: their church music, folksongs, and dances, their tastes and prejudices, their ideas and methods of music education, and their writings on music. Even the prevalence of German bandmasters in early 19th-century Canada reflected the state of music in England, since such men abounded in England and in many cases had moved to Canada from there. The large-scale immigration of English musicians began in the early 19th century and continued ceaselessly though it varied in intensity.

To delineate Canada's complex musical relations with England would entail writing virtually the whole story of music in Canada, impossible in this context; thus, only main influences and traditions will be considered here. (See also Coronations; Sovereigns, statesmen, and other public figures.)

1 Church musicians and educators
2 Orchestra conductors, instrumentalists
3 Publishing, criticism, adjudication
4 Ballad opera, operetta
5 Folksong
6 Composition
7 Bands
8 Pop music
9 English visitors
10 Canadians in England

1 CHURCH MUSICIANS AND EDUCATORS. Among the earliest English musicians to arrive in Canada were the Mr Evans who – judging by his name – may have been Welsh but who installed the organ at St Paul's Anglican Church, Halifax, NS, in 1765 and Viere Warner who became the organist at that church in 1768. (See Anglican church music.)

The first relatively important English musician known to have chosen to live in Canada was John *Bentley who arrived in 1786, stayed briefly in Montreal, and then settled in Quebec where he worked as a church musician, composer, and actor. Others, assumed to be English-born, who lived in Montreal were A. Stevenson, author of *The Vocal Preceptor* (Montreal 1811), and S. Brewer, temporary organist at Notre-Dame Church in 1814. In 1816 Stephen *Codman was appointed organist at the Anglican Cathedral of the Holy Trinity in Quebec.

During the 19th century, and well into the 20th, church positions were the mainstay of the music profession. In English-speaking Canada the Church of England, the Presbyterian, Methodist, and Baptist churches, and the *Salvation Army maintained musical (especially choral) traditions established in the homeland and tended to hire British musicians trained in those traditions. (See also Organ playing and teaching; Protestant church music.)

Such musicians often were pioneers in the stoutest, most versatile sense. Not only did they tend their duties at the church, training the choirs and playing the services (or in the case of Salvation Army musicians, training bandsmen and taking the bands into the community), but they also in most cases performed some or several other useful functions: composing music; founding large choral-orchestral societies and leading them in oratorios and cantatas; teaching voice, the keyboard instruments, and theoretical subjects privately, in conservatories, or in schools and universities; establishing choir schools; giving recitals; adjudicating and examining; writing reviews or essays for newspapers and periodicals; and all usually at a high level of proficiency.

Many of these English musicians had been educated soundly and broadly at one of the Royal Schools, or the Guildhall, or a leading university, and the British methods they represented were those adopted by Canada's developing institutions. The *RCMT and the *WBM have followed the English system of examinations with its emphasis on grading and diplomas. England's *AB of the *RSM and *Trinity College, London, for many years sent examiners annually to Canada and issued licentiate diplomas to Canadian residents. The pervasive Tonic Sol-fa sightsinging system, developed in England by Curwen, was introduced into Canada in the 1880s by Alexander *Cringan (a Scot trained in London) and became as common in the schools as the English sparrow in the landscape.

A perhaps less happy outcome of English predominance in music education was the academic theory courses of 19th-century–English type, with their emphasis on harmony and counterpoint by textbook rule, and their relative indifference to performance, contemporary composition, and historical scholarship. Such courses persisted in some Canadian studios, schools, and universities until the middle of the 20th century (by which time they had been superseded long since in England).

The contribution to the practice and development of music in Canada by protean English musicians in the church, choral, and vocal traditions has been immense, as the ensuing list of 19th- and 20th-century names will attest: Robert S. *Ambrose, W.H. *Anderson, Dalton *Baker, Hugh *Bancroft, Vernon *Barford, John *Bearder, Edgar *Birch, Edward Arthur Bishop, Edward *Broome, C. Allanson *Brown, Giles *Bryant, the *Carter brothers, Frederick *Chubb, Douglas *Clarke, Melville *Cook, Richard Westall *Cooke, Hubert Eisdell (the distinguished tenor, who settled in Canada in 1930 and taught at the TCM 1933–6 and at Lakefield College 1936–48), Maitland *Farmer, Charles *Findlater, H.A. *Fricker, Frederick *Geoghegan, Ronald *Gibson, John *Goss, Albert *Ham, C.L.M. *Harris, J.W.F. *Harrison, Charles A.E. *Harriss, Elliott *Haslam, Derek *Healey, Alfred *Heather, Godfrey *Hewitt, W.H. *Hewlett, Derek *Holman, Filmer *Hubble, Percival *Illsley, the *Kent brothers, Harold Eustace *Key, Brian *Law, Frederic *Lord, Leonard *Mayoh, Bernard *Naylor, Lucien *Needham, Charles *Peaker, Harold *Ramsay, Horace *Reyner, Eric *Rollinson, Hugh Ross, Herbert *Sanders, John *Sidgwick, Frederick *Silvester, F.H. *Torrington, Robert *Watkin-Mills, John *Weatherseed, C.E. *Wheeler, Alfred *Whitehead,

Healey *Willan, Leonard *Wilson, and Eric Woodward.

Names which belong on the list, but with a particular emphasis on teaching and / or education in a broader sense are J.E.P. *Aldous, J. Humfrey *Anger, John *Churchill, Arthur *Collingwood, Edwin *Collins, Gwendda Owen *Davies, Harry *Dean, Peter Fletcher, Leonard *Heaton, F.J. *Horwood, Leonard *Isaacs, George *Lambert, Leonard *Leacock, Frederick *Newnham, H.C. *Perrin, Philip and Joseph Shadwick, Leo *Smith, Alan *Walker, John *Waterhouse, Albert Whitehead, Gladys *Whitehead, Norman *Wilks, and David *Zafer.

Textbooks of music theory by J. Humfrey Anger and Albert Ham (both born and trained in England) and by the Englishmen Charles Herbert Kitson, Stewart Macpherson, and Ebenezer Prout were used by generations of Canadian teachers and students as, later, were those on harmony and counterpoint by R.O. Morris, and on orchestral technique by Gordon Jacob.

2 ORCHESTRA CONDUCTORS, INSTRUMENTALISTS. English career conductors and instrumentalists – as distinct from the versatile organist-choirmasters who turned their hands to those disciplines out of opportunity, necessity, or, in any case, accommodation to circumstance – have been fewer in Canada and later arriving, owing no doubt to the later development of orchestras and of an instrumental culture related to the vocal. Nevertheless, their contribution has been varied and significant, especially in the 35 years after World War II. Donald *Heins introduced symphonies of Mozart and Beethoven to Ottawa in the years 1903–27, and Douglas Clarke made his mark with the *Montreal Orchestra after World War I, but it was the post–1945 period that saw Geoffrey *Waddington's appointment as director of music for the CBC and Boyd *Neel's arrival to serve as dean of the RCMT and establish his *Hart House Orchestra. It was still later in that era that Meredith Davies arrived to conduct the *Vancouver SO, Brian Jackson and then Lawrence Leonard to conduct the *Edmonton SO, Maurice Handford to conduct the *Calgary Philharmonic, Leonard Atherton to conduct the *St Catharines SO, and, in particular, in the 1970s, Andrew Davis to take over the directorship of Canada's most active orchestra, the *TS.

The outstanding concert organist Quentin *Maclean settled in Canada in 1939. In the years spanning the two world wars Leo Smith was one of Toronto's leading cellists and Rex *Battle was active as pianist and conductor. Clifford *Poole, another pianist-conductor, continued his career in 1980. David Gray, who had been first horn in the London Symphony Orchestra, moved to Canada around 1970, studied conducting, and led the International SO of Sarnia and Port Huron before becoming the conductor of the Newfoundland SO.

In the instrumental field, Reginald *Godden has made a singular mark as pianist, contemporary-music champion, and Bach scholar, George *Brough as a leading coach-accompanist, George *Zukerman as a foremost bassoonist and impresario, Liona *Boyd as a concert guitarist, Gerald Jarvis as concertmaster of the Vancouver SO, Christopher *Weait as associate principal bassoon of the TS, Simon *Streatfeild as principal viola of the Vancouver SO and later a member of the Faculty of Music at the *U of Western Ontario, and Cardo *Smalley as concertmaster of the *CBC Vancouver Chamber Orchestra. Another Englishman, John Eliot Gardiner, was appointed conductor of the last-named orchestra in 1980.

3 PUBLISHING, CRITICISM, ADJUDICATION. The English have maintained a wide general presence in Canadian musical life through music publications (branch offices of *Oxford, *Chappell, *Boosey & Hawkes, and many agencies; see also Anglo-Canadian Music Co; Ashdown; and AB of the RSM), authoritative reference books (*Grove's Dictionary* and the standard-setting works of Colles, Scholes, Tovey, etc), and periodicals (eg. *The Gramophone, Music and Letters, The Musical Times*). In 1967 the British government presented the *NL of C with a large gift which contained many English music publications.

English-born music critics and essayists have flourished in Canada, among them *A.A.A. (Alexander Alldrick), Thomas *Archer, H. Poynter *Bell, Augustus *Bridle, Lawrence *Cluderay, Graham *George, Ronald Gibson, John *Norris, Edwin *Parkhurst, Robert *Sunter, and Max *Wyman.

In broadcasting, the BBC served as a model for the CBC, in both programming and formats. It also supplied transcriptions of many of its programs and continued to do so in 1980.

English musicians at one time enjoyed a near monopoly as adjudicators at Canadian competition festivals. Among those respectfully remembered are Sir Thomas Armstrong, Edgar Bainton, Sir Edward Bairstow, Sir Granville Bantock, Ronald Biggs, Thomas Dunhill, Sir William Glock, Harry Plunkett Greene, Percy Hull, Leonard Isaacs, Maurice Jacobson, Alec Redshaw, Harold Samuel, Gordon Slater, Frederic Staton, and Jan van der Gucht.

After World War II the gradual lessening of dependence on British performance models created some conflict between those who remained loyal and those who preferred US or continental European concepts. But as the English archetypes showed a phoenixian tendency to re-create themselves and as Canadian musical life matured and settled, many avenues were reopened for contact between the older and younger cultures.

4 BALLAD OPERA, OPERETTA. The operatic performances given in Halifax, Quebec, and Montreal during the late 18th and early 19th centuries were largely of English ballad operas by Dibdin, Linley, Shields, and their contemporaries.

A century later Gilbert & Sullivan operettas could be heard all over Canada. *H.M.S. Pinafore* was so swift a hit that its ink was scarcely dry before a popular political parody, **H.M.S. Parliament*, using Sullivan's music and words by William H. Fuller, was entertaining Canadian audiences. Gilbert & Sullivan have remained almost a cult, their operettas produced repeatedly by both amateur and professional groups.

During the early part of the 20th century the operettas of Edward German and Sidney Jones were performed by the *Eaton Operatic Society, the *Savoyards, and others. The 20th-century ballad operas of Canada's expatriate Englishman Healey Willan were performed at *CPR Festivals at Quebec and Banff.

5 FOLKSONG. A large part of Canada's folksong literature is of English origin (see Folk music, Anglo-Canadian), and actual English folksongs (as distinct from Anglo-Canadian mutants and variants) have been taught in the schools as part of the English heritage and as material for sight-singing systems such as those that are English-language adaptations of the Kodály principles.

Canada's own folk music research owes much to the movement that arose in England at the turn of the century. Marius *Barbeau studied ethnology at Oxford U, and the work of the English collectors Ralph Vaughan Williams and Cecil Sharp gave stimulus to Helen *Creighton, Edith *Fowke, and others.

The Englishwoman Maud Karpeles, who visited the USA as Cecil Sharp's assistant on a collecting trip, returned alone to North America after his death to fulfil his intention of collecting folksongs in Newfoundland. The result of this 1929 trip was two volumes of Newfoundland songs, published in London in 1934, and a further volume, with annotations and accompaniments, published in London in 1971. Karpeles' work was much respected, and she received honorary degrees from *Laval U and *Memorial U.

6 COMPOSITION. By the latter half of the 20th century the English influence on Canadian composition had lessened considerably. Some Canadians or Canadians-by-adoption composed music recognizably in the tradition – notably Anderson, *Bales, Douglas Clarke, *Fleming, *MacMillan, Naylor, *Ridout, Smith, Whitehead, and Willan. But as more Canadian, US, continental-European, and, increasingly, Oriental music came to be broadcast and recorded, and as key positions in conservatories, universities, and symphony orchestras were occupied more often by musicians of non-English background, English music was heard less frequently (except in the church, where at least Parry and Stanford survived) and its effect on Canadian music declined accordingly.

*Morawetz in word and *Bissell in deed showed that they were affected specifically by Britten. But *Charpentier, *Freedman, *Garant, *Mather, *Morel, *Papineau-Couture, *Pentland, *Prévost, *Schafer, *Somers, *Tremblay, and *Weinzweig – to name only 12 – showed not the slightest influence of their English counterparts (though Schafer wrote a book about them); and when *Anhalt, in his *EMC* article on *Beckwith, calls him 'the most characteristically English-Canadian voice in composition,' it is English Canada, not England, that he is invoking. Beckwith, like the majority of his colleagues, has had his 'creative receivers' tuned to an international wavelength in which England has played a relatively small part.

This virtual indifference was not one-sided, however. It would not be incorrect to say that English composers have tended to regard Canada as an export market, if anything, and have shown little interest in that market's own creative product. By 1980 such reciprocity as there was existed more in courtesy than in mutual fascination, and response to a major presentation of concerts of works by 32 Canadian composers, given in London in 1977 under the name *Musicanada, was rather formal.

The CBC from the 1940s to the 1970s broadcast a good deal of Britten (eg, the North American radio premiere of *Peter Grimes*) and documentaries and program series on Britten, Holst, Tippett, and Vaughan Williams; but even on the CBC there was little attempt to stay abreast of the broad spectrum of post-war developments in England. A handful of pre-war works did survive in the repertoire – eg, Holst's *The Planets* and *St Paul's Suite* and Vaughan Williams' *On Wenlock Edge* – supplemented occasionally by performances of the Elgar and Walton concertos; and by the 1970s Britten and Tippett were not only English but international figures and as such were impossible to ignore. In 1980 in Toronto the CBC produced a five-concert festival devoted to Tippett and his contemporaries, and the TS gave the North American premiere of Tippett's *Triple Concerto*.

7 BANDS. From the late 18th century to the late 19th, British regimental bands were stationed in garrisons across Canada. Besides performing on military occasions they provided players for local

orchestras and also set performance and instrumentation standards which were followed by the increasing number of Canadian bands.

Many English bandmasters settled in Canada in the 19th and 20th centuries, eg, William *Atkins, Martin *Boundy, Richard *Coates (who also was one of Canada's first organ builders), Leonard *Camplin, Arthur *Delamont, Kenneth *Elloway, Richard *Hayward, Arthur, Henry, and John *Slatter, Derek *Stannard, and Alfred *Zealley.

A few Canadians were trained at the RMSM (Kneller Hall) in England, among them Armand *Ferland and James *Gayfer. Several English bandmasters have been active in the Canadian Salvation Army. (See also Bands.)

8 POP MUSIC. In popular music the English music hall tradition was perpetuated in Canada in the early 20th century by such entertainers as Jules *Brazil, Jimmie Fax, and Will J. White. English rock music, in its many styles from the Beatles in the mid-1960s to Supertramp in the late 1970s, has rivalled its US counterpart in its popularity with Canadian youth and its influence on Canadian performers. (See Rock.)

9 ENGLISH VISITORS. Among the earliest English musical visitors to Canada were the tenor John Braham in 1841, the baritone Henry Phillips 1844–5, and the soprano Anna Bishop in 1848 and 1851. Among later, more famous visitors were Sir Alexander C. Mackenzie, who conducted the famous *Cycle of Musical Festivals in 1903, and Sir Edward Elgar, who conducted the Sheffield Choir in his *The Dream of Gerontius* in 1911 (see Charles A.E. Harriss).

A long list of notable visiting composers, conductors, instrumentalists, and singers has included Dame Janet Baker, Sir John Barbirolli, Sir Thomas Beecham, Richard Rodney Bennett, Sir Adrian Boult, Sir Benjamin Britten, Dame Clara Butt, Sir Henry Coward, Sir Clifford Curzon, Peter Maxwell Davies, Alfred Deller, Jacqueline Du Pré, Kathleen Ferrier, Dame Myra Hess, Gustav Holst, Gerald Moore (who received much of his musical education in Canada), John Ogdon, Sir Peter Pears, Alan Rawsthorne, Sir Malcolm Sargent, Humphrey Searle, Solomon (Solomon Cutner), Sir Arthur Sullivan, Sir Michael Tippett, Ralph Vaughan Williams, and Sir William Walton.

The English-born musical satirist Anna *Russell, in a category by herself, started her career in Canada and became more than a visitor but less than a permanent national: she was a Canadian citizen 1943–52, and then moved to the USA and became naturalized there.

Innumerable English performing ensembles have appeared in Canada. To name only a few: the Thomas Quinlan Opera, 1913–14, with the tenor Charles Hedmont who received his early training in Montreal; the Dan Godfrey British Band which gave some 80 concerts in Canada ca 1898; the D'Oyly Carte Company on several occasions; the Sheffield Choir which gave 16 concerts on its first visit to Canada in 1908; the London SO under Nikisch in 1912; the London String Quartet in 1921 and several times later; the Griller String Quartet in 1940 and often again.

In more recent times Canadians have heard the Amadeus String Quartet (often); the Royal Philharmonic Orchestra (1963); the Bath Festival Orchestra under Menuhin, the English Opera Group, and the Northern Sinfonietta under Boris *Brott (all at the 1967 World Festival, *Expo 67); the English Chamber Orchestra under Vladimir Ashkenazy; and the St Paul's Cathedral Choir (early 1960s and again in 1980).

10 CANADIANS IN ENGLAND. The number of Canadians who studied in England in the 19th century was relatively small. In the early days there were Romain-Octave *Pelletier (1871–2) and William *Reed (1878). In the 20th century there was a considerable increase. To name only a few: Hugh *Davidson, Victor *Feldbrill (during World War II), John Keane, Ingemar *Korjus, Janet *Stubbs, Catherine *Robbin, and many AB of the RSM scholarship winners including Donald *Bell, Carlina Carr, Smyth *Humphreys, Hugh *McLean, Ross *Pratt, Thomas *Rolston, Winifred Scott, and Robin *Wood.

Among Canadians who have settled or worked extensively in England are Emma *Albani, Les *Allen, Ellen *Ballon, John Mais Capel, Russell Chester, Arthur *Davison, Bonnie *Dobson, Louise *Edvina, Art *Ellefson, Robert *Farnon, Harry *Field, Don *Garrard, Fred *Grinke, Al and Bob *Harvey, Ted *Hockridge, Leslie *Holmes, Doreen *Hume, Laura *Lemon, Patti Lewis, Beatrice *Lillie, David *Martin, Lois *McDonall, Libby Morris, Alfie *Noakes, Jackie *Rae, Tommy *Reilly, Joseph Shadwick, Annon Lee *Silver, Russ Titus, Malcolm *Troup, John Warren, and Kenny *Wheeler. (See also Jazz; Rock.)

English opera companies such as Sadlers Wells, Glyndebourne, the English Opera Group, and the Royal Opera (Covent Garden prior to 1947) have employed numerous Canadian artists, including Albani, Milla *Andrew, David *Astor, Lissant Beardmore, Émile *Belcourt, Donald Bell, Mario *Bernardi, Napoléon *Bisson, Jean *Bonhomme, Victor *Braun, Jules *Bruyère, Edmund *Burke, Donna-Faye *Carr, James W. *Craig, Walter Dinoff, France *Dion, Pauline *Donalda, Roger *Doucet, Carl *Duggan, Jeanne *Dusseau, *Edvina, Sarah *Fischer, Odette *de Foras, Don Garrard, Victor *Godfrey, Beatrice *La Palme, Louise *Lebrun, Audrey *Mildmay (who not only sang at Glyndebourne, but was the wife of the founder, John Christie), James *Milligan, Norman *Mittelmann, Louis *Quilico, Joseph *Rouleau, Robert *Savoie, Annon Lee Silver, Léopold *Simoneau, Teresa *Stratas, Paul *Trépanier, André *Turp, Richard *Verreau, and Jon *Vickers.

Among those who have performed at Wigmore Hall in London are the *Ascher Duo, Mona *Bates, *Beckett and McDonald, *Bedford and Eby, Donald Bell, Ray *Dudley, Ada Twohy *Kent and David Martin, Zara *Nelsova, Émiliano *Renaud, and Winifred Scott and Robin Wood.

Glenn *Gould made his London debut in the five Beethoven concertos with the London SO under Joseph Krips. André *Jobin sang in nearly 1000 performances of *Showboat* at the Adelphi Theatre. The TS played in London's Festival Hall under Seiji Ozawa in 1965. The *NACO has played in London and other English cities, and so has the *Orford String Quartet.

Lois *Marshall, Léopold Simoneau, and Jon Vickers all made major recordings with Sir Thomas Beecham and the Royal Philharmonic Orchestra, and Steven *Staryk was a concertmaster of that orchestra. Vickers became the most famous Peter Grimes of his day and recorded the Britten opera with the Royal Opera Orchestra under Colin Davis. Raoul Jobin sang frequently with orchestra on the BBC and recorded *Alceste* with Kirsten Flagstad for London.

These are but a sampling of the Canadian performers and performing organizations who have performed in England. Canada House in London has arranged many concerts and recitals by young Canadian artists over the years. Hugh Davidson was cultural councillor to the Canadian High Commission in London 1978–81. HK, KW

England. A setting by Ernest *MacMillan for soprano, baritone, eight-part chorus, and orchestra of Swinburne's ode 'England.' Composed 1917–18 in a German prison camp, *England* was accepted by Oxford U as MacMillan's exercise for a D MUS, awarded in 1918 in absentia. MacMillan's largest work (approximately 40 minutes), it was published in 1920 by Novello and first performed 17 Mar 1921 by the Sheffield Musical Union under Sir Henry Coward. Its Canadian premiere followed 12 Apr 1921 with the *Toronto Mendelssohn Choir, led by H.A. *Fricker, and the Philadelphia Orchestra. Excerpts were performed 2 Mar 1964 at the opening of the Edward Johnson Building, *U of Toronto.

ENGLE, (Judith) Marilyn. Pianist, b Calgary 27 Jul 1946; B MUS (Juilliard) 1969, M SC MUS (Juilliard) 1970, MA (New York) 1975. Her piano studies in Calgary with Gladys *Egbert and in New York with Ilona Kabos led to first prizes in the 1966 *CBC Talent Festival and the 1969 J.S. Bach International Competition in Washington, DC. She continued her training with *Canada Council support in Geneva in 1970 with Nikita Magaloff and in New York 1970–5 with Adele Marcus and Jeaneane Dowis. She recorded three works by Bach (1970, CBC SM 140) and has given concerts and broadcasts in Canada and the USA and several recitals 1975–6 for the New York Friends of Mozart Society. In 1975 she joined the Dept of Music of the *U of Calgary. SW

An English Lesson. Ten-minute chamber opera, with music and text by Gabriel *Charpentier. Subtitled an 'opera happening,' it is scored for actress, four male voices, and a chamber orchestra in two sections. The music employs short speech graphs, musical quotations, and occasional serialism, while the text consists entirely of French words and phrases in common English usage. Commissioned by the *Stratford Festival, the work was premiered 3 Aug 1968 by Marilyn Gardner and the singers David Smith, Daniel Tait, Peter Milne, and Oskar Raulfs with the Festival Orchestra under Lawrence Smith. The performance was later broadcast by the CBC. *An English Lesson*, which was produced again in 1971 at the *U of Toronto, is one of a projected group of 10 mini-operas by Charpentier to be called *A Night at the Opera*.

BIBLIOGRAPHY

'Un petit opéra from Stratford,' *CBC Times*, 3–9 Aug 1968

(BJE)

Ensemble cantabile de Montréal. Vocal chamber ensemble formed by Bruno *Laplante, and composed of Céline *Dussault (soprano), Gabrielle *Lavigne (mezzo-soprano, succeeded by Paule Verschelden in 1976), Paul *Trépanier (tenor), and Laplante himself (baritone). The ensemble gave its inaugural concert 11 Aug 1974 at the *JMC Orford Arts Centre. Its repertoire represents all eras and includes duos, trios, art songs, and excerpts from seldom-heard oratorios, operas, and cantatas. It has performed Bizet's one-act comic opera *Le Docteur Miracle* on several occasions in Montreal and on CBC radio and TV. Besides some 60 performances of chamber operas, including (at the Théâtre de la *Poudrière) Debussy's *L'Enfant prodigue* (in a staged adaptation), Donizetti's *Rita*, and Barber's *A Hand of Bridge*, it has given many educational concerts. Accompanied by Janine *Lachance it has recorded music of Bach, Fauré, Hahn, Rossini, Saint-Saëns, and Schumann (1976, RCI 446). The musical and histrionic talents of its members have ensured a high level of performance. (DA)

Ensemble Claude-Gervaise

Ensemble Claude-Gervaise. Early-music group of flexible dimensions and instrumentation, formed in Montreal in 1967 by the flutists Francois Barre, Jean Gagné, Joseph Guilmette, and Gilles Plante, director. Known at first as the Ensemble Pierre-Attaingnant, the group renamed itself in honour of the French musician Claude Gervaise (fl Paris 1541–55), whose spirited songs and 'danceries' roused the enthusiasm of its members. The personnel has ranged from 4 to 20 singers and instrumentalists (according to the program at hand) with a core of 8 or 9 regular members, most of them members or students of the Faculty of Music and the Institute of Medieval Studies at the *U of Montreal. The ensemble has acquired some 150 early string, wind, and percussion instruments (some of them rare originals, a collection considered one of the most important in Canada; see Instrument collections) and in order to achieve the authenticity in interpretation which has been its aim, its members have studied the writings of the major renaissance theorists, including Arbeau and Mersenne.

The ensemble has given educational concerts in many Canadian cities, in the USA (New York, Rochester, Binghamton, Harvard U, etc), and in Europe in 1978, and has performed on CBC radio and TV. Though its repertoire is drawn mainly from the 16th century, it staged the 12th-century drama *Jeu de Saint Nicholas* in 1969 and Adam de la Halle's *Jeu de Robin et Marion* in 1972. The ensemble published a quarterly review, *Carnet musical*, 1971–5. Michel Desroches was publisher and Jean-Pierre Pinson editor. The Éditions de l'Ensemble Claude-Gervaise have published a duo for recorders – a fragmentary manuscript held at Saint-Gall, Switzerland. The ensemble's first LP, *Tout l'monde est malheureux* (1976, Solo SO 25503), comprises songs of the chansonnier Gilles *Vigneault arranged by Pierre *Brault in the style of early music and performed on early instruments. Brault also arranged early Quebec melodies for a second record, *L'Ensemble Claude-Gervaise chante d'amour et la guerre* (1977, Solo SO 25510). (YC)

Ensemble instrumental du Québec. Founded in Quebec City in 1970 by Jacques *Simard. It consisted initially of Simard (oboe) and six other instrumentalists: Chantal *Masson, viola; Zeyda *Suzuki, piano; Barbara Todd, flute; Hermel Bruneau, harpsichord; Rénald St-Pierre, double-bass; and Hidetaro *Suzuki, violin. In 1974 the ensemble was reduced to oboe, flute, double-bass, and harpsichord and incorporated in Quebec as a non-profit-making organization. It began performing under the aegis of the *Institut canadien in Quebec City, where it gave two concerts a season for two years. It filled engagements for the CBC, the *Grand Théâtre in Quebec City, the *Concerts Couperin, the *JMC, the *U of Quebec, and *Laval U, performing in Quebec City, Montreal, Toronto, and Halifax. The *Canada Council subsidized tours in 1972 and 1973 in the Abitibi region and in 1976 in western Canada. The ensemble gave four concerts at the 1976 Festival du printemps at Notre-Dame-des-Victoires in Quebec City. It premiered Alain *Gagnon's *Septuor* and *Les Oies sauvages* in 1973 (both works commissioned by the Canada Council) and Rénald St-Pierre's *Temsurtem* in 1975.

DISCOGRAPHY

J.S. Bach – J.C. Bach – Mozart – Prévost. 1972. RCI 297
Bach – Quantz – Telemann – Lotti. 1978. BSST 5
Telemann – Vivaldi – Bach – Quantz. 1975. BSST 4

BIBLIOGRAPHY

'Ensemble Instrumental du Québec tells its story ...' *Adagio*, vol 1, Jun 1976 MB-L

Ensemble vocal Chantal-Masson. Thirty-voice choir founded in 1965 at *Laval U by Chantal *Masson. It performed for seven years in public and on radio and TV in Canada and abroad. Singing mostly unaccompanied, it gave performances at the *Institut canadien of Quebec, the *Concerts Couperin, the Société de musique de chambre de Québec, the Société des concerts de l'Île d'Orléans, the *JMC Orford Art Centre, and the St-Jean-des-Piles summer festivals (Villa Musica camp, near Trois-Rivières). It premiered works by many Canadians, including Maurice *Dela, Alain *Gagnon, Jacques *Hétu, Roger *Matton, and André *Prévost, while maintaining a wide repertoire of madrigals, motets, and cantatas by Bach, Monteverdi, and Purcell, romantic part songs, contemporary music, and folk music of many countries. During the Canadian centenary the choir toured Ontario, Alberta, and Saskatchewan and was hailed as 'one of the best Canadian choirs' (*Winnipeg Free Press*, 10 Nov 1967). That same year it was invited to participate in Europe Cantat III (in Namur, Belgium) and the Choralies internationales canadiennes in Trois-Rivières, and to perform at the Canadian Pavilion at *Expo 67. In 1968 the ensemble placed fifth (folklore category) at the Concorso Polifonico Internazionale Guido d'Arezzo in Italy. In 1970 it participated in Europe Cantat IV (in Graz, Austria) and toured eastern USA and various cultural centres in Quebec. In 1972, when Chantal Masson was unable to continue as leader, the choir disbanded. Throughout its existence it was financed by its members, concert receipts, and grants from Laval U and the * MACQ. (MB-L)

ENSHER, Phyllis (Lillian) (m Peters). Harpist, b Brockton, Mass, 10 Sep 1931; Performance Diploma harp (Curtis) 1957. She studied with Carlos Salzedo at the Curtis Institute and in 1958 joined the Halifax (now *Atlantic) SO. She has performed widely in the Maritimes, appearing on the CBC TV series 'Kingfisher Cove' and 'Reflections,' at *Confederation Centre in Charlottetown, PEI, and (1974–8) in *NOVA MUSIC concerts. She composed background music for the CBC series *Indian Legends*, and her arrangements of Nova Scotia folksongs for voice and harp (unpublished) have been performed frequently. In 1978 she returned to the USA. BJE

ERICKSON, Lloyd (Reinhold). Choir conductor, administrator, b Tompkins, near Swift Current, Sask, 11 Aug 1921; ARCT 1952, LTCL 1957, B ED fine arts (Alberta) 1958, MA (Columbia) 1963. He studied piano with Jean Cotton and voice with Odette *de Foras in Calgary. He began teaching music in Calgary schools in 1947 and became supervisor of music in 1972. Erickson has been choirmaster at Pleasant Heights United Church 1952–60, music director for the Calgary Exhibition and Stampede 1964–73, and founder and director of Calgary's Young Canadians 1967–73 and the Lloyd Erickson Singers 1964–74. He became minister of music at Central United Church in 1960 and conductor of the Calgary Philharmonic Chorus in 1970. In 1973 he trained and conducted an RCMP chorus from Regina which toured 40 Canadian cities as part of the *RCMP Revue*. He founded the Alberta Choral Directors' Assn and served 1971–5 as president. RDM

Ermitage. Theatre and concert hall located in a Collège de Montréal building at the corner of Côte-des-Neiges and McGregor Ave. Built in 1914 it was used first for student productions. The interior was refurbished 1941–2 by the Messieurs de St-Sulpice, the owners of the building, and about 600 permanent seats were installed in the orchestra and semicircular balcony. The stage was enlarged and the building named 'l'Ermitage' (the hermitage) because of its rather isolated location.

The hall with its remarkable acoustics was the home of the *Little Symphony of Montreal 1942–52. The *McGill String Quartet and an orchestra conducted by Alexander *Brott performed there, the latter group presenting Handel's *Concerti grossi* and Bach's *Brandenburg Concertos*. Wilfrid *Pelletier conducted unusual staged Easter-season performances of the *St Matthew Passion* in 1943 and 1944, and Elisabeth Schumann gave a memorable recital there in 1949. The hall was used by other groups including the *Society of Canadian Music in 1955, 1957, 1958, and 1960 and the *Montreal String Quartet 1959–60.

The CBC began using the hall for live-audience programs, in particular 1944–53 'Radio-Carabin,' a weekly variety show which featured each week a famous artist, from Charles Trenet to Walter Gieseking, and 1947–55 the talent competition *'Nos Futures Étoiles.' Public use of the hall declined and eventually ceased after the CBC obtained a contract (1947–67) guaranteeing priority for its orchestral program *'Little Symphonies' (produced there 1958–65) and other musical broadcasts.

In the early 1970s the hall and adjoining gymnasium reverted to the use of students at the Collège de Montréal. During the 1940s, 1950s, and 1960s, however, l'Ermitage was an important centre for music as well as a venue for plays, conventions, lectures, and exhibitions. ST

Eskimo music. See Inuit.

Estonia. Immigration to Canada from this Baltic nation (which has been under the control of a succession of countries – Sweden 1561–1710, Russia 1710–1918, 1940, 1944, Germany 1941–4 – and was independent 1918–40) began about 1900, when Estonians from the Crimea settled in Alberta. By 1939 some 1000 Estonians lived in Canada; by 1971 the Canadian census recorded some 19,000, two-thirds of these in Ontario.

In Estonian music in Canada the strongest tradition is in choral singing. In 1969 some 45 Estonian choirs were active. Singing festivals began in 1957, and eight had taken place by 1977. At one (at Varsity Stadium, Toronto, in 1969, commemorating the centenary of Estonian Singing Festivals) the massed choir numbered 2000 voices. Notable among Estonian choir conductors in Canada have been the composers Lembit Avesson and Roman *Toi (director of the Estonian Male Choir for over 25 years beginning in 1952 and of the Estonian Mixed Choir 1957–72), as well as Asta Ballstadt,

Charles Kipper, Erich Kokker, Uno Kook, Olaf Kopvillem (director in the 1960s of the Estonian Ladies' Choir of Montreal and 1971–3 of the Toronto Estonian Girl Guides Choir), Eugen Ruus, and Harry Toi. The composer and polemicist Udo *Kasemets, a native of Estonia and, in the 1960s and 1970s, Canada's foremost representative of the 'New York Action School' of avant-garde musicians, conducted the Estonian Ladies' Choir in the mid-1950s.

Among other Estonian-Canadian musicians in Canada are the pianists Stella Kerson, Dagmar Kokker, Hillar Liitoja (a pupil of Anton *Kuerti), Armas *Maiste, Inga Tammsalu-Toi, and Aino Waldin; the soprano Helmi Betlem; the baritone Avo Kittask, who studied with Ernesto *Vinci and Louis *Quilico at the *U of Toronto, began performing with the *COC in 1971, and has sung for the *Guelph Spring Festival and the *Southern Alberta Opera Assn; the baritone Arno Niitof; the bass-baritone Ingemar *Korjus; the cellist-composer Kaljo Raid; the jazz bassist Baron Wilhelm Ernst von Schilling (whose aristocratic lineage was revealed only after his death at 29, 11 Nov 1956 in New York); and the composers Kristi Allik and Peeter Tammearu. The mezzo-soprano Irene Loosberg, who moved to Canada in 1951, gave recitals and appeared with choirs and orchestras in Toronto and other Ontario centres in the 1950s and early 1960s, was a member of the *Royal Cons Opera and the *CBC Opera, was a soloist in the CBC's annual broadcast of *Messiah* in 1956, and was heard on the CBC's 'Songs of My People.' The Estonian Arts Centre, founded in 1975 with Stella Kerson as president, has given scholarships to Ingemar Korjus and Hillar Liitoja for study in Europe. The Estonian Concert Management, also under Kerson's direction, has sponsored series in Toronto by Estonian performers. (RT)

Ethnomusicology. Broadly, the study of the music of a given country, region, city, or age, in its social and cultural context. As the term 'musicology' had been applied to the study of western art music, the newer term 'ethnomusicology' has been associated specifically with investigations of non-western music and folk music. In relation to Canada, 'ethnomusicology' refers to the scholarly investigation of native Indian and Inuit music and the folk music of all ethnic groups. The activities of ethnomusicologists and of the pioneers of their discipline in Canada and the development of that discipline in an academic context will be considered under these headings:

1 Further delineation
2 European observers, 1600–1860
3 Canadian and foreign collectors, 1860–1900
4 Scholarship after 1900, Indian and Inuit
5 Scholarship after 1900, Franco-Canadian
6 Scholarship after 1900, Anglo-Canadian
7 Scholarship after 1900, instrumental folk music
8 Scholarship after 1900, ethnic groups
9 Ethnomusicology as a university discipline

See also Folk music; Folk music, Anglo-Canadian; Folk music, Franco-Canadian; Indians; Inuit. For the folk music of ethnic minorities, see *EMC* entries for the countries of their origin. For the musics of religious groups, see also Religions and music.

1 FURTHER DELINEATION. A number of scholars working in Canada have contributed to the discussion of the definition and scope of ethnomusicology as well as to the development of analytical procedures and research methodology. Among the earliest to publish on these subjects was Mieczyslaw *Kolinski, who, prior to and after his arrival at the *U of Toronto, evolved a series of analytical procedures applicable cross-culturally for the study of tonal and melodic structures, tempo, and melodic contour. Another scholar concerned with methodology has been Jean-Jacques Nattiez at the *U of Montreal, who has developed a semiology of music based on a modification of the work of his French colleague Nicolas Ruwet.

Marius Barbeau and the folksinger Jean-Baptiste Dupuis at Sainte-Anne-des-Monts, Que

Often related to the development of analytical method is the concern of scholars with the history of philosophies and approaches in their discipline. In Canada, Charles Boilès and Jean-Jacques Nattiez have published a history of the discipline which takes into account the developments of the 1970s, 'Petite histoire critique de l'ethnomusicologie' (*Musique en jeu*, September 1977). Ida *Halpern wrote 'Aural history and ethnomusicology' (*Canadian Folk Music Journal*, vol 4, 1976, previously published in *Sound Heritage*, vol 4, no. 1, 1975).

Canadian scholars generally have contributed more to the development of analytical methods in the laboratory than to field techniques. An exception is Kenneth *Peacock, who published *A Practical Guide for Folk Music Collectors* (Ottawa 1966). Needless to say, a diversity of implied or stated philosophies and methods is represented in the work of other Canadian scholars.

2 EUROPEAN OBSERVERS, 1600–1860. As in other countries, ethnomusicology has evolved from the haphazard and amateurish efforts of curious Europeans through the work of trained practical musicians to the labours of highly skilled specialists. The earliest known printed record of Indian songs is Lescarbot's *Histoire de la Nouvelle-France* (Paris 1609), which includes transcriptions of the words and melodies (in letter notation) of four Micmac songs and data about the various functions of Micmac dances. These songs form the basis for several later publications, among them Gabriel Sagard-Théodat's *Histoire du Canada* (Paris 1636). (See Missionaries in the 17th century.) That Canadian indigenous music was of interest to Europeans during the period of colonization is evident also from the publication of an Indian melody, purportedly obtained from a sea captain, in Marin Mersenne's *Harmonie universelle* (Paris 1637) and the melody's somewhat altered reprinting in Jean-Jacques Rousseau's *Dictionnaire de la musique* (Geneva 1767). An Illinois 'calumet' song, possibly transcribed by Louis *Jolliet, appeared in the manuscript 'Récit des voyages et découvertes du Père Jacques Marquette de la Compagnie de Jésus en l'année 1673' and was printed in modified form in Claude Bacqueville de la Potherie's *Histoire de l'Amérique septentrionale* (Paris 1722).

Details about the context of music-making among native groups abound in reports and travel accounts of the 17th to mid-19th centuries. These observers were concerned not with scientific documentation but rather with describing musical customs which they witnessed, unaware of or unconcerned about their ethnocentric biases. In the *Jesuit Relations* Paul Le Jeune and others (see Missionaries in the 17th century) include references to Indian and European oral traditions. Travel accounts with more than passing reference include Louis-Armand de Lahontan's *Nouveaux Voyages dans l'Amérique septentrionale* (The Hague 1703); Pehr Kalm's *Travels into North America* (English translation, London 1770–1), with an extensive account of Indian dancing at St-Jean, on the Richelieu River; Isaac Weld's *Travels through the States of North America* (London 1799, 1800), describing Indian dances and instruments at Malden, opposite Detroit; and Johann Georg Kohl's *Kitchi-Gami* (London 1860), with observations on Ojibwa and voyageur music of the Lake Superior region. There are no extant reports of collections of European-language folk music prior to the 19th century. The earliest publication is *Canadian Airs* (London 1823), based on melodies collected by Lieut George Back. However, the long piano introductions and extensive expressive indications, as well as the replacement of the original texts, demonstrate that the compilers were not concerned with authentic representations of the folk repertoire. Of greater authenticity is Edward Ermatinger's collection (ca 1830) of voyageur songs published by the *Journal of American Folklore* (vol 67, Apr–Jun 1954). L.F.R. Masson, in *Les Bourgeois de la Compagnie du Nord-Ouest*, vol 1 (Quebec 1889–90), recalled a Norwegian, Ferdinand Wentzel, who had collected voyageur songs in the early decades of the 19th century. The collection, in Masson's possession, was considered 'obscene and unfit for publication.'

3 CANADIAN AND FOREIGN COLLECTORS, 1860–1900. This period was characterized by an emphasis on collecting, often with the objective of preserving material before its disappearance and of discovering the national heritage. The collectors usually were practical musicians who trained themselves to notate music in the field. Canada was in the 1890s one of the first countries in which the phonograph was used to record indigenous music. Documentation of song functions, performers, composers, and musical customs was scant, however. Studies more often focused on the origins and diffusion of specific songs in Europe and North America. The Indian and French-Canadian repertoires were the focus of attention.

Ernest *Gagnon's *Chansons populaires du Canada* (Quebec 1865), more fully discussed under Folk music, Franco-Canadian, is cited frequently as the first scholarly study of this repertoire. It contains transcriptions of texts and melodies and notes about origins and variants. Gagnon cautioned the reader against imposing modern attitudes and habits on this repertoire and argued for the rationality, expressiveness, and dignity of the musical system. This marked a decisive change from the attitude expressed in earlier collections. F.-A.-H. LaRue's essay 'Les chansons populaires et historiques du Canada' (*Le Foyer canadien*, Quebec 1863 and 1865) compared French and Canadian variants of song texts. Other late-19th-century sources include Philippe Aubert de Gaspé's novel *Les Anciens Canadiens* (Quebec 1863) and *Mémoires* (Ottawa 1866) and Ernest *Myrand's *Noëls anciens de la Nouvelle-France* (Quebec 1899). A noteworthy unpublished manuscript is Mgr Thomas Hamel's 'Annales musicales du Petit-Cap,' compiled 1865–1908, and preserved in the archives of the

Séminaire de Québec. François *Brassard in *Ethnomusicology* (September 1972) comments on the wide sphere of influence of these publications as demonstrated by the large number of personal and family anthologies, many still extant, which were compiled from them. Ernest Gagnon was one of the earliest collectors of Indian songs. Others were Father Lionel de Saint-Georges Lindsay, whose historical study 'Notre-Dame de Lorette en la Nouvelle France' appeared in *La Revue canadienne* (Montreal, November 1889–March 1902) and John Reade, the literary editor of the Montreal *Gazette* and author of 'Some Wabanaki Songs ...' in the *Transactions of the Royal Society of Canada* (vol 5, 1887).

Investigators of Indian music were less interested in collecting than in defining musical style. Two studies of Canadian interest often are credited as the earliest in the discipline of ethnomusicology: Theodore Baker's *Über die Musik der nordamerikanischen Wilden* (Leipzig 1882), which includes transcriptions of Iroquois songs and references to other Canadian tribes, and Carl Stumpf's 'Lieder der Bellakula Indianer' (*Vierteljahresschrift für Musikwissenschaft*, 1886), a musicological study with nine transcriptions of songs performed by a group of Bella Coola Indians who visited Germany in 1885.

The German-US anthropologist Franz Boas conducted research on Cumberland Sound and Baffin Island and among the Kwakiutl on the Pacific coast. His publications – eg, *The Central Eskimo* (sixth annual *Report* of the Bureau of American Ethnology, Washington 1888) – are noteworthy for their detailed ethnographic descriptions and transcriptions. Boas was associated with James A. Teit, a member of the team of the Geological Survey of Canada. Teit first collected tales among the Salish of the Thompson River area in British Columbia in the 1890s, and in subsequent years recorded songs among various British Columbia tribes. A number of these recordings were submitted by Boas to Otto Abraham and Erich von Hornbostel in Berlin, two of the founders of ethnomusicology, who published their transcriptions and analysis as 'Phonographierte Indianermelodien aus Britisch-Columbia' in *Boas Anniversary Volume* (New York 1906). Walter Fewkes, on field work among US Indians ca 1890, was the first to use a phonograph for the purpose. Boas and Teit were the first to record in Canada; the next was A.T. *Cringan, who transcribed and discussed his wax cylinder recordings (preserved at the *National Museum of Canada) of Iroquois songs in various publications (1898–1913; see Writings for Cringan).

4 SCHOLARSHIP AFTER 1900, INDIAN AND INUIT. Twentieth-century scholarship has reflected the diversity of approach which developed in ethnomusicology. Although scholars such as Marius *Barbeau, Helen *Creighton, and Kenneth Peacock have investigated both folk song and native music, it is possible to make some generalizations distinguishing the work done in the two repertoires. Native music has attracted anthropologists and musical scholars rather than folklorists, and despite an emphasis on documenting and salvaging dying traditions, most research has concentrated on music ethnology and the definition of the musical style of a particular repertoire. While folk music studies have concentrated on the history, diffusion, and variants of individual songs, native music research has focused on the common characteristics of song groups or whole musical cultures. However, attention to the study of song texts and native conceptualization of music remained insufficient in 1980, and virtually no research had been done by natives on their own music. The majority of native music studies have focused on the Inuit, the Pacific Coast tribes, and such agricultural tribes of the Eastern Woodlands as the Iroquois. Several comparative studies of North American Indian musical styles have been attempted: Helen Roberts' *Musical Areas of Aboriginal North America* (New Haven, Conn, 1936), Bruno Nettl's 'North American Indian musical styles' (*Journal of American Folklore*, vol 67, 1954), and Margaret *Sargent's 'The native and primitive music of Canada' (B MUS essay, Toronto 1942; see also Writings for Sargent). All are rather undependable with regard to the Canadian repertoire since so little basic field research on tribal music in Canada had been conducted at the time of their publication.

In the Eastern Woodlands area, after Cringan's pioneering work, W.H. Mechling transcribed Malecite and Micmac songs at St Mary's Bay, NB, in 1911 for the National Museum of Canada. In the same year, Julien Tiersot, having visited the Caughnawaga and Lorette reserves in 1905–6 published some of his observations in 'La musique chez les peuples indigènes de l'Amérique du Nord (États Unis et Canada),' printed in *Notes d'ethnographie musicale*, series 2 (Paris, October 1911). Marius Barbeau recorded Huron and Wyandot songs soon after beginning to work for the National Museum of Canada in 1911, and his 'Seven Songs from Lorette' were published by Margaret Sargent (*Journal of American Folklore*, vol 63, April–June 1950). The US anthropologist Frank Speck recorded Delaware and Tutelo songs at the Six Nations Reserve in Ontario. The largest collection of Iroquois music up to 1980 was that of Gertrude Kurath, a US dancer and anthropologist, who based her publications on research at various Longhouse settlements in New York State and Ontario. Kurath's invention of a system of dance notation provided the first record of the social and ritual dances.

Further recordings were made at the Six Nations Reserve by Douglas *Riley and Mieczyslaw Kolinski in the 1960s. The latter published an analysis of variants of an Apache Rabbit Dance song cycle recorded there (*Ethnomusicology*, September 1972). Jack Frisch recorded Mohawk music and studied midwinter rites at the St Regis Reservation near Cornwall, Ont, in 1968 and 1970, but the results remained unpublished in 1980. Michael K. Foster's anthropological study of the structure and significance of Iroquois speech events, *From the Earth to beyond the Sky* (Ottawa 1974), clarifies the relationship of such musical events as the Great Feather Dance to Iroquois cosmology and to the important skill of oratory. Those Eastern Woodland tribes which were traditionally migratory have received relatively little attention. Ray and Alika Webber have recorded a few songs from Montagnais and Naskapi Indians in Quebec and Labrador (1962), and Richard Preston researched Eastern Cree music at Fort George, Que, in 1968. The Ontario and Manitoba Ojibway have been the subject of several musical studies. Frances Densmore, whose books on a wide variety of North American Indian music are early landmarks, used some Canadian material in *Chippewa Music* (Washington 1910, 1913), and Frederick R. Burton's *American Primitive Music* (New York 1909, reprint Port Washington, NY, 1969) also focused on the Ojibway. More recently, Ghislaine Lecours compiled a manuscript of folklore in Gull Bay, Lake Nipigon, Ont, and Shirley Daniels researched *Ojibway Songs, Narratives and Other Traditions from the Lake of the Woods* (Ottawa 1968). Among the Plains Indians, collecting has concentrated on Blackfoot communities. Clark Wissler 1903–4, Donald Hartle in 1949, and Bruno Nettl in 1952 have collected Blackfoot songs within Canadian borders. Nettl's four-part 'Studies in Blackfoot Indian musical culture' (*Ethnomusicology*, vols 11 and 12, 1967, 1968) examines both the musical structure and the social functions of songs. Ted Brasser, ethnologist with the National Museum of Man, Ottawa, included music in his 1971–3 study of the Blackfoot, and Roma Standefer's manuscript on 'The function of dances in Blackfoot Indian society' (nd) further discusses the subject from an anthropological perspective. Although the literature on the Plains Sun Dance is extensive, only a few studies have been based on events occurring in Canada. These include Wilson Wallis' research on the Canadian Dakota (1947), the Glenbow Foundation film of a Blackfoot Sun Dance (1966), and Pliny Goddard's notes on the Sun Dance of the Alberta Cree (1919). Other collections among western Cree were made in the mid-20th century by Kenneth Peacock and Richard *Johnston. Ken Goodwill collected and transcribed Sioux songs 1958–68. While most studies have focused on traditional musical events, Robert *Witmer has investigated both traditional and 'white' music among Blood Indians in his ' "White" music among the Blood Indians of Alberta' (*Canadian Folk Music Journal*, vol 2, 1974).

Material on the Athapaskan and Plateau tribal musics is not copious. Between 1905 and 1944 Pliny E. Goddard collected Sarcee songs and studied dancing societies of this tribe. From 1912 to 1922, James Teit continued recording music of the Sikani, Tahltan, Tlingit, Carrier, Okanagan, and Thompson Indians in the interior of British Columbia. Alden J. Mason collected Sikani songs in Fort Rae in 1913, incorporating this material in *Notes on the Indians of the Great Slave Lake Area* (New Haven, Conn, 1946) and depositing his recordings at the National Museum of Canada. Associates of the British Columbia Language Project have contributed song collections to the sound archives of the National Museum of Man, as have independent collectors. Studies by trained ethnomusicologists include Michael Asch's work on various aspects of Slavey musical culture using linguistic models in attempts to formulate a transformational grammar of this style. Short studies have been published on the Interior Salish by Graham *George (*Journal of the International Folk Music Council*, vol 14, 1962, based on Barbeau's collection) and on the Dogrib hand game and its music (by June Holm and Nancy Lurie, 1966). (Other literature is cited in the entry on *Indians: 2 / Athapaskan.) Boas' studies of North Pacific Coast tribes in 1895 are at least partly responsible for the greater interest generated and the more intensive research conducted in this area than in any other. As noted earlier, the studies by Stumpf, Abraham, and von Hornbostel are considered the world pioneer products of the new discipline of ethnomusicology. Investigation was continued by Henri Tate, who collected texts 1906–9. In the 1920s Marius Barbeau studied the Tsimshian; among his collaborators, in 1927, was Ernest *MacMillan. In the same decade Edward Sapir collected among the Nootka, Thomas McIlwraith among the Bella Coola and Carrier, and James A. Teit among several tribes. More recently, collections have been made by Elizabeth Cass (Kutchin, 1959), Bill Folan and George August (Nootka, Kwakiutl, 1966–7), Eugen Arima (Haida, Kwakiutl, 1963–5), Suki Anderson (Bella Coola, 1972), Wendy Stuart (Coast Salish, 1972–3), Phil Davis (Bella Coola, 1966–7), and Marie-Françoise Guédon (Tsimshian and Nebesna, beginning in 1969). One of the most extensive and valuable collections is that of Ida Halpern, who began to record Nootka and Haida chiefs in 1949.

The varied approaches have included analyses of isolated musical parameters (George Herzog, Helen Roberts) or more holistic views of music in society with little musical analysis (Guédon, Boas). Anthropological studies such as Homer Barnett's *The Coast Salish of British Columbia* (Eugene, Ore, 1955) and Philip Drucker's *Indians of the Northwest Coast* (New York 1963), though not limited to music, contain the most complete investigations of such important events as the midwinter ceremonials. (See also the Bibliography for Indians: 4 / Pacific Northwest Coast.)

Research on Inuit (Eskimo) music has passed through several phases. In the first quarter of the century, before extensive contact with southern whites had begun, large exploratory parties such as the Canadian Arctic Expedition (1914–18) and the fifth Thule Expedition (1921–4) and independent investigators such as Boas, whose investigations had begun in the 1880s, and Christian Leden (mid-1920s) produced large and important collections of tapes, texts, transcriptions, and detailed ethnographic descriptions of the traditional way of life of the Inuit. Rasmussen's contribution to the *Report of the Fifth Thule Expedition* (vols 7, 8, and 9, 1929, 1931, 1932) and Diamond Jenness and Helen Roberts' *Copper Eskimo Music* (Ottawa 1925) are monuments in the field. In the 1930s and 1940s the chief collectors included Jean Gabus and Helge Ingstad. Gabus's 1938–9 collection of some 200 recordings of Caribou music provided the basis for a series of important studies by the Swiss ethnomusicologist Zygmunt Estreicher, who explored such widely varying subjects as polyphony, melodic structure, and musical evolution. Another pioneer was Laura Boulton, who recorded music on the west coast of Hudson Bay in the 1940s. Asen Balikci made extensive field recordings of Inuit songs, games, and legends from Povungnituq, Que, and Pelly Bay, NWT, during the 1960s for the National Museum of Man, while Guy Mary Rousselière explored the Canadian eastern Arctic.

A renaissance of interest in Inuit music occurred in the 1970s, when scholars in several centres independently undertook in-depth studies of specific areas: Maija Lutz in Pangnirtung, Baffin Island, and Nain, Labrador; Beverley *Cavanagh in Gjoa Haven, King William Island, and Pelly Bay on the Gulf of Boothia; Doreen *Binnington at Coppermine, NWT; members of the Groupe de recherche en sémiologie musicale from the U of Montreal in communities in northern Quebec, at Cape Dorset and Pond Inlet, Baffin Island, and at Iglulik in the Melville Peninsula; and Ramón Pelinski in Rankin Inlet and Eskimo Point on the west shore of Hudson Bay. At the same time, Thomas Johnston was supervising a major study of Alaskan musical styles from the U of Fairbanks, and Poul R. Olsen and Michael Hauser continued to investigate Greenland Inuit music. Johnston's *Eskimo Music by Region: A Comparative Circumpolar Study* (Ottawa 1976) was the first attempt at a comparative survey of Inuit styles. A unique project has been the work of Jean-Jacques Nattiez and the Groupe de recherche en sémiologie musicale. Another has been the independent work of scholars at *Laval U on the throat games of eastern Arctic women. Both Lutz and Cavanagh examined aspects of acculturation, while Pelinski has developed a system for the computer analysis of melodic patterns.

5 SCHOLARSHIP AFTER 1900, FRANCO-CANADIAN. Inspired by the outstanding collections of Gagnon and LaRue, research continued to have a folkloristic orientation. After 1950 the National Museum of Man, Laval U, the U of Sudbury, and the *U of Moncton have played major roles in this work. Both French-speaking and English-speaking scholars have participated.

Turn-of-the-century studies include Cyrus MacMillan's thesis, 'The folk songs of Canada' (PH D, Harvard 1909), and Julien Tiersot's *Forty-Four French Folk-songs and Variants from Canada, Normandy and Brittany* (G. Schirmer 1910). In 1919 E.-Z. *Massicotte's collection of 46 songs compiled since 1883 were prepared by Marius Barbeau for publication (*Journal of American Folklore*, vol 32, January–March 1919).

In 1910 the anthropological linguist Edward Sapir came to Canada to head the anthropology division of the museum branch of the Geological Survey of Canada. A year later he hired Marius Barbeau as staff ethnologist and thereby took a decisive step for ethnomusicological study in Canada. Barbeau was unquestionably the central figure in the study of both native and folk music during the next 40 years. His research and writings are reported in the *EMC* entry and are discussed in the entries on Folk music, Franco-Canadian, and Indians. His work yielded over a dozen published collections of songs in addition to articles exploring many aspects of folklore. Furthermore, Barbeau had a great influence on several generations of younger collectors and scholars, through both his practical and his theoretical work. Songs from his collection were arranged by Ernest MacMillan, Oscar *O'Brien, Healey *Willan, and others, and his collaboration with colleagues laid the foundation for future folklore and folk music studies in Canada.

After Barbeau, Carmen Roy, the first chief (1966–77) of what in 1970 was to be named the Canadian Centre for Folk Culture Studies, investigated folklore in the Gaspé and on Saint-Pierre and Miquelon. Her first monograph, *La Littérature orale en Gaspésie* (Ottawa 1955), includes 23 transcriptions and comments on the oral transmission of songs. Songs from her collection were investigated by George *Proctor during his tenure, 1959–61, as musicologist at the National Museum.

Decisive steps in French-Canadian folk music studies were the founding, in 1944, of the *Archives de folklore at Laval U under the directorship of Luc *Lacourcière and the publishing, begun two years later, of a journal with the same name. The Archives de folklore also published Conrad *Laforte's *Catalogue de la chanson folklorique française* (1958). Laforte's work as cataloguer of the huge collection at Laval U prompted him to tackle the enormous problem of classifying French-language folksong. The 1958 edition includes an alphabetical listing of songs with cross references to variants, other titles, and first lines. Laforte's classification system, which uses structure rather than subject matter as its primary element, was described in *Poétiques de la chanson traditionelle française* (Quebec 1976) and demonstrated in vols 1 and 4 of the revised catalogue (*Chansons en laisse*, 1977, and *Chansons énumératives*, 1979). The scheme has been adopted by the National Museum of Man and the universities at Moncton and Sudbury.

After collecting Franco-Ontarian folklore independently 1948–58 Father Germain *Lemieux was appointed director of the new Institut de folklore (later Centre franco-ontarien de folklore) at the U of Sudbury in 1959. Franco-Ontarian song has been documented in Lemieux's own publications, listed under his *EMC* entry, and in Mary Ann Griggs' *La Chanson folklorique dans le milieu canadien-français traditionnel / The Folk Song in the Traditional Society of French Canada* (Sudbury 1969).

Father Anselme Chiasson collected Acadian music in Cheticamp and Arichat, NS, and with Brother Daniel Boudreau he published five volumes of *Chansons d'Acadie* (Les Éditions de la Réparation 1942, 1945, 1948, 1972, 1979). Previously a series of songs had been compiled by Joseph-Thomas Leblanc for the Moncton newspaper *La Voix d'Évangéline* (1938–41). Geneviève Massignon's dissertation, 'La chanson populaire française en Acadie' (U of Paris, 1955), continued research in this area. Charlotte Cormier, supervisor of the folklore program at the U of Moncton, has reported on the 'Situation de la recherche en folklore acadien' in the *Canadian Folk Music Journal* and has published transcriptions of songs from southeastern New Brunswick, *Écoutez tous, petits et grands* (Moncton 1978). By 1980 the Centre for Acadian Studies had accumulated over 5000 songs and 700 instrumental pieces. Limited work has been done in other provinces. Kenneth Peacock collected French songs in Newfoundland in the 1960s, and Gerald Thomas compiled a catalogue of *Songs Sung by French Newfoundlanders* (St John's 1978). Both Barbara *Cass-Beggs (*Seven Métis Songs*, BMI Canada 1967) and Margaret *MacLeod (*Songs of Old Manitoba*, Ryerson 1959) investigated Métis songs in Manitoba, publishing selections from their collections.

6 SCHOLARSHIP AFTER 1900, ANGLO-CANADIAN. As in French Canada, the majority of researchers in English Canada have concentrated on collecting, and folklore studies to a large extent have outnumbered musicological and anthropological investigations. Furthermore, the geographic distribution of the studies has favoured the Atlantic provinces with their older histories of settlement.

Probably the earliest collection of English-language folksong texts in Canada was James Murphy's *Songs and Ballads of Newfoundland, Ancient and Modern* (St John's 1902; Murphy published other collections in 1904, 1905, 1912, 1923, and 1925). An important early-20th-century collector was W. Roy Mackenzie, who worked along the north shores of Nova Scotia, publishing a major part of his collection in *Ballads and Sea Songs from Nova Scotia* (Cambridge, Mass, 1928, with annotations about origins and variants) and an autobiography, *The Quest of the Ballad* (Princeton, NJ, 1919), describing his activities and informants. Another early collection, excluding songs with texts of British origin and designed for popular rather than scholarly consumption, was the first edition of the St John's merchant Gerald S. *Doyle's *The Old-Time Songs and Poetry of Newfoundland* (St John's 1927; subsequent editions, with musical notation, 1940, 1955, 1966, 1978). In the early 1920s Elisabeth B. Greenleaf had noted some songs around Sally's Cove, and in 1928 she returned with her Vassar colleague Grace Y. Mansfield to continue collecting.

The year 1929 was significant in the history of English language folksong study in Canada for several reasons. Helen Creighton began the field work which was to yield over 4000 songs and numerous publications of the Nova Scotia and New Brunswick repertoires over the next 40 years. Creighton has described her career in an autobiography (*A Life in Folklore*, Toronto 1975), which, like that of Mackenzie, constitutes an important source of information about the social context of folk music in the Maritimes.

Also during 1929 the British folklorist Maud Karpeles visited Newfoundland to search out Canadian variants of old British ballads, and the New England folklorist Phillips Barry published his first collection, *British Ballads from Maine*, which included 39 songs from New Brunswick. More songs from New Brunswick appeared in a series of short articles in the *Bulletin of the Folksong Society of the Northeast* (vols 10–12, 1935–7). The most intensive collecting in New Brunswick itself was done by Louise *Manny at the instigation of Lord Beaverbrook in 1947. In collaboration with James Reginald Wilson, she published *Songs of Miramichi* (Fredericton, NB, 1968). The 1920s saw the appearance of further collections for popular use, such as J.M. *Gibbon's *Canadian Folk Songs, Old and New* (London and Toronto 1927). A parallel to the French-Canadian 'chansonniers' (song albums) of the 19th century were the 'come-all-ye's' (eg, Stuart McCawley's *Cape Breton Come-All-Ye*, Glace Bay, NS, 1929), which generally included texts only.

In the 1950s and 1960s a broadening of the geographic field of activity and of the scope of research could be observed. Many collectors and scholars continued to work in the tradition-rich Maritimes. Margaret Sargent visited Newfoundland for the National Museum in 1950. The museum also sponsored work by MacEdward Leach, from the U of Pennsylvania, on the lower Labrador coast in 1960 (*Folk Ballads and Songs of the Lower Labrador Coast*, Ottawa 1965). The most extensive collection of Newfoundland songs, however, was made by Kenneth Peacock during summer expeditions 1951–61. His three-volume *Songs of the Newfoundland Outports* (Ottawa 1965) includes detailed transcriptions, texts, and short comments about textual ambiguities, stylistic features, and sources. During the same period the New England folklorist Edward D. Ives collected in New Brunswick and Prince Edward Island, investigating the lumbercamp singing tradition in particular. A distinguishing trait of Ives' research is his concentration on folk composers. His studies of Larry Gorman, Joe Scott, and Lawrence Doyle have added an important dimension to our understanding of the processes of oral creation and transmission.

The Folklore Dept of *Memorial U in St John's, under the direction 1968–73 of Herbert Halpert, became established as the main centre for studies in Newfoundland folk music. Neil V. *Rosenberg was appointed director of the university's Folklore and Language Archive in 1976. A large proportion of research there involves Newfoundland material collected and analysed by Memorial U students and faculty. In addition to the study of traditional music, several projects on pop and country music have been completed: Paul Mercer's *The Ballads of Johnny Burke: A Short Anthology* (St John's 1974), Neil Rosenberg's *Country Music in the Maritimes: Two Studies* (St John's 1976) and *Bill Monroe and His Blue Grass Boys: An Illustrated Discography* (Nashville 1974), and Michael Taft's *A Regional Discography of Newfoundland and Labrador* (St John's 1975).

A major achievement of the 1960s and 1970s has been the investigation of musical traditions west of Quebec. Although Eileen Bleakney in the Ottawa area and Ivan Walton in the Great Lakes region had done some collecting in Ontario, Edith *Fowke was a pioneer in the province when she began her work in 1957. In the ensuing years she has amassed over 1000 songs, some published in *Traditional Singers and Songs from Ontario* (Hatboro, Pa, 1965) and *Lumbering Songs from the Northern Woods* (Austin, Texas, 1970). Fowke has made a dual contribution to the field. As a meticulous folklorist she has uncovered much new information about the origins and diffusion of songs. At the same time, she has been active in making folk music available to the general public through her work as both radio commentator and editor of songbooks. In the Prairie provinces less research had been done by 1980. Fowke collected some songs from a Manitoba family in 1975, and Barbara Cass-Beggs recorded some Saskatchewan songs in 1963. Like Fowke, Cass-Beggs has made a considerable contribution through her selection and editing of songs for children (eg, *Canadian Folk Songs for the Young*, Douglas 1975).

Fern Pickering and Kenneth Petersen collected 1966–7 in the western provinces, but the most substantial study to date is the unpublished 'Survey of English language music of the Canadian Prairies and foothills' (1975) by the U of Calgary psychology professor Tim Rogers. Rogers' own interest in both the traditional repertoire and the contemporary popular idioms of Wilf *Carter and others to some extent parallels the work at Memorial U and demonstrates a slowly emerging concern with popular tradition.

In British Columbia a thriving folk music tradition has been maintained by the Vancouver Folk Song Society, which published *Come All Ye* 1972–7 and began issuing the *Canada Folk Bulletin* in 1978. The major collector Philip *Thomas published *Songs of the Pacific Northwest* in 1979.

7 SCHOLARSHIP AFTER 1900, INSTRUMENTAL FOLK MUSIC. Relatively little research had been done by 1980 on the many instrumental traditions of Canada. Old-time fiddling has received some attention in an article by George Proctor (*Contributions to Anthropology*, vol 2, Ottawa 1960) and more recently in a valuable bibliography compiled by Dorothy and Homer Hogan ('Canadian fiddle culture' in *Communique: Canadian Studies*, 1977). Carmelle Begin at the National Museum of Man began investigating fiddle music in the late 1970s. (See also Fiddling.)

8 SCHOLARSHIP AFTER 1900, OTHER ETHNIC GROUPS. Although the earliest collection of material in a language other than in French, English, or Inuit or Indian dialects – Alexander Fraser's 'The Gaelic folk songs of Canada' – was published in 1903 (*Transactions of the Royal Society of Canada*, series 2, vol 9, section 2), the recognition of Canada's ethnic multiplicity was not widespread among the research community in the first half of the century. Marius Barbeau was one of the few whose scholarly interests extended to other ethnic groups (as witness an unpublished study of 'Slavonic cultural influences on the North Pacific Coast,' nd). Another pioneer was the publicity director of the CPR, J.M. Gibbon, who, in collaboration with Barbeau, encouraged public awareness of the diverse ethnic traditions in Canada through the organization of a series of folksong and handicraft festivals beginning in 1927 and including one in Winnipeg in 1928 devoted to the music of 19 different national groups (see CPR Festivals).

The expansion of the scope of the activities of the National Museum was achieved under the direction of Carmen Roy. Kenneth Peacock was at the forefront of this development and presented a paper surveying ethnic folk music across western Canada in 1965. Peacock also published studies of Doukhobor and Lithuanian music. The adoption of the federal government's Multicultural Policy in October 1971 provided support for ethnic groups other than the French-speaking, the English-speaking, the Indian and the Inuit. By 1975 the Canadian Centre for Folk Culture Studies of the National Museum of Man had collected materials from over 60 ethnocultural groups. An inventory at that time was provided by Renée Landry (see Bibliography below). Both a survey of research compiled at the same time by Ramón Pelinski for the *Canada Music Book* and *EMC* entries on individual countries refer to folk music research that has been done in Canada.

9 ETHNOMUSICOLOGY AS A UNIVERSITY DISCIPLINE. The earliest courses in which folk music occupied a prominent place probably were those offered at Laval U in the summer of 1939 with the participation of Marius Barbeau, Luc Lacourcière, and Félix-Antoine Savard. Five years later Laval established a chair of folklore, occupied 1944–77 by Lacourcière. It would appear that the first steps towards specialized instruction in ethnomusicology were the courses given by Ida Halpern at the *U of British Columbia 1964–5 and the program begun by Mieczyslaw Kolinski at the U of Toronto in 1966. In her survey of 'The current ethnomusicology curriculum in Canadian universities' (*Ethnomusicology*, vol 16, September 1972), Roxane C. Carlisle noted major programs at 6 universities – British Columbia, *Ottawa, Sir George Williams (now *Concordia), Toronto, *Windsor, and *York – and minor programs (many of them courses on Canadian concert music with only passing reference to folk music) at 12 others. Subsequently the development of integrated university programs in ethnomusicology has occurred slowly, gradually incorporating relevant methods and approaches from anthropology, linguistics, and other disciplines. In general, by 1980 more emphasis was placed on a holistic study of ethno-music, including both practical and theoretical training and recognizing both musicological and sociological factors.

In the late 1970s undergraduate courses were offered at British Columbia, *Carleton, Concordia, Guelph, McGill, Memorial, Montreal, Ottawa, *Queen's, *Saskatchewan, Toronto, Victoria, Windsor, and York. Some of these universities – eg, British Columbia, Windsor, and York – have given special emphasis to non-western traditions, involving applied study. The U of British Columbia and York U have been foremost in this regard, although a small program in Indian music (involving practical vina study) was initiated at Queen's U in 1977. Attention to east European folk music has highlighted the broad range of ethnomusicological offerings at the U of Toronto, beginning in the mid-1970s. The scholarly study of popular idioms has been cultivated at Memorial and York. In 1980, at the graduate level, York offered an MA in ethnomusicology and Laval an MA and D ès L in Arts et traditions populaires. Major concentration on graduate work in the subject was possible also in various musicology, folklore, and anthropology programs. Opportunities for the study of Canadian oral traditions were available at that time at a majority of universities with music departments, in particular at Laval, Memorial, and Montreal.

Folk music archives and research centres have been maintained at Laval, Moncton, and Sudbury universities for French-language materials, at *St Francis Xavier for Scots-Gaelic music, and at Memorial U for Newfoundland folklore.

BIBLIOGRAPHY

Barbeau, Marius. 'The Ermatinger Collection of voyageur songs (ca 1830),' *JAF*, vol 67, Apr–Jun 1954

– 'Canadian folk songs,' *J of the IFMC*, vol 13, Jan 1961

Lacourcière, Luc. 'The present state of French-Canadian folklore studies,' *JAF*, vol 74, Oct–Dec 1961

Cass-Beggs, Barbara, and Fowke, Edith. *A Reference List on Canadian Folk Music* (Ottawa 1966); rev enl *CFMJ*, vol 1, 1973; ibid, vol 6, 1978

Ethnomusicology, Canadian issue includes articles by Peacock, Fowke, Brassard, Qureshi, Creighton, Guédon, Cavanagh, Carlisle and Landry, vol 16, Sep 1972

Landry, Renée. 'Archival sources,' *Canadian Ethnic Studies / Études ethniques du Canada*, vol 7, no. 2, 1975

Pelinski, Ramón. 'The music of Canada's ethnic minorities,' *CMB*, 10, Spring–Summer 1975

Cormier, Charlotte. 'Situation de la recherche en folklore acadien,' *CFMJ*, vol 3, 1974

Fowke, Edith, and Henderson, Carole. 'A bibliography of Canadian folklore in English,' *Communique: Canadian Studies: Canadian Folk Culture Issue*, vol 3, Aug 1977

Hogan, Dorothy and Homer. 'Canadian fiddle culture,' ibid

The *Journal of American Folklore* has published several issues devoted to Canadian topics: vol 32, Jan–Mar 1919; vol 33, Oct–Dec 1920; vol 63, Apr–Jun 1950; and vol 67, Jan–Mar 1954. (BAC)

Evangeline. Narrative poem (1847) by Henry Wadsworth Longfellow inspired by the expulsion of the Acadians in 1755. Pamphile Lemay made a French translation in 1865. The poem tells of the love and wanderings of two young Acadians, Évangéline Bellefontaine and Gabriel Lajeunesse, who, the day after their betrothal, were deported from Grand Pré, NS, on different Louisiana-bound ships. The pair are reunited years later in a Philadelphia almshouse where she, now a Sister of Mercy, finds him destitute and dying. Several composers – Canadian, US, and French – have written works based on the story. *Evangeline*, the opera by Graham *George, has a libretto based both on Longfellow and on Acadian historical sources, by Paul Roddick and Donald Warren, and was premiered 1 Dec 1948 by the *Queen's U Glee Club and SO, conducted by the composer, in the ballroom of Kingston's La Salle Hotel. Arnold Edinborough was the stage director, the composer's wife, Tjot George, was Evangeline, and Eric Barton was Gabriel. Other operas on the same theme have been written by the French composer Xavier Leroux (1863–1919), whose four-act *Évangéline*, 'légende acadienne,' was premiered in Brussels in 1895 by the Théâtre de la Monnaie, and by the US composer Otto Luening, whose three-act *Evangeline* was performed first at Brander Matthews Hall, Columbia U, New York, in May 1948, antedating George's by seven months. George *Carter composed a cantata *Evangeline* in 1873. Thomas Hahn's dramatic cantata *Evangeline* (1967) for soprano, five male voices, choir, and orchestra, used a text adapted by Joan Fontaine from the Longfellow poem. Robert *Talbot also wrote an oratorio on the subject.

BIBLIOGRAPHY

Willan, Healey. 'Canadian theme in a Queen's opera,' *SatN*, 18 Dec 1948 GP

EVANGELISTA, José. Composer, teacher, b Valencia, Spain, 5 Aug 1943; premier prix composition (Valencia Cons) 1967, L SC physics (Valencia) 1967, M MUS composition (Montreal) 1973. As a student 1961–7 at the U of Valencia he distinguished himself through his work in computer science. At the same time he studied harmony, composition, and orchestration at the Valencia Cons with Vicente Ascencio. After his arrival in Canada in 1969 he studied 1970–3 at the *U of Montreal with André *Prévost. In 1974 he took a course in contemporary music at Darmstadt, and that same year he won first prize in the Confederación Española de Cajas de Ahorros contest (Madrid) for his *En guise de fête* (CBS-LSP-13224, with Pauline *Vaillancourt, soprano). He is interested in problems of texture, especially in dense polyphonic contexts. His main works include *Arabesco* (1975, CBS-LSP-13224, Vaillancourt), *Miroir fugace* for string orchestra (1975), *Coros tejiendo, voces alternando* for choir (1975), *Va-et-vient* for four performers (1976), *Immobilis in mobili* for nine instruments (1977), and *Consort* for voice, harps, and strings (1977). He received grants from the *Canada Council and the Quebec Ministry of Education in 1976. He began teaching musical analysis at the U of Montreal in 1972. Evangelista is a member of the *CLComp and the Sociedad general de autores de España and an associate of the *CMCentre.

WRITINGS

'Une analyse de Madrigal III de Bruce Mather,' *CMB*, 6, Spring–Summer 1973 (ADV)

Evans Brothers Piano and Manufacturing Co, Ltd. Established in London, Ont, in 1871 or 1872 under the name E.B. Litler or Littler. The brothers John and William Evans appear to have formed a partnership with Litler ca 1885. The firm had moved to nearby Ingersoll by 1887 (at which time Litler was no longer a partner) and was purchased by William Watterworth in 1894. According to *Industrial Canada* (February 1904), some 50 workers made about 400 pianos a year; Evans instruments were of average price and quality. Player pianos were introduced before 1912, and a retail store existed in Toronto for some years after 1914. The firm ceased operations before 1935. FH

EVENS, Clifford. Conductor, violinist, b Vancouver 19 Oct 1921, d Toronto 11 Aug 1980. He studied violin with Josef Gingold in Detroit and Cleveland and conducting with Sir John Barbirolli in Manchester and Hideo Saito at the Toho Gakuen, Tokyo. After 10 years as concertmaster and associate conductor of the *Victoria SO, Evens joined the *TSO in 1961 and became principal second violin in 1966. While in Toronto he founded in 1963 and conducted the Canadian Brass Ensemble (not to be confused with *Canadian Brass). The ensemble presented educational concerts in schools. In 1969 he moved to London, Ont, as the first full-time music director and conductor of the *London SO, which under his direction became in 1975 Canada's 11th major orchestra. Evens was a member 1971–5 of the faculty of music at the *U of Western Ontario, where he conducted the university orchestra and opera. He resigned as music director of the London SO in 1979. His wife, Mary Evens (b Bucklin), a pupil of Robert Maas, Kurt Reher, and Leonard Rose, was assistant principal cello of the TSO 1961–70 and principal cello of the London SO 1970–9. PGD

Expo 67. The popular and semi-official title of the Universal and International Exhibition of 1967, initiated by Montreal mayor Jean Drapeau and presented by the City of Montreal with participation by the federal and provincial governments of Canada, foreign governments, private industry, and numerous organizations. It was the largest single manifestation of a year of celebrations marking Canada's centenary. It was created and administered by the Canadian Corporation for the 1967 World Exhibition, under Commissioner General Pierre Dupuy, as a General Exhibition of the First Category sanctioned by the Bureau of International Exhibitions (the first such world exposition was held in London in 1851). It ran from 28 April to 27 October 1967, and its theme was 'Man and His World.' The exposition was located on 400 hectares of man-made islands in the St Lawrence River adjacent to Montreal, and comprised 6 'theme' pavilions, 48 national pavilions, 4 provincial pavilions, 27 private-industry and institutional pavilions, a 54-hectare entertainment complex of theatres, midway attractions, bars, and restaurants called La Ronde, and numerous bandshells, open-air stages, plazas, and small theatres scattered throughout the site.

Associated and concurrent with Expo, and organized by a division of the corporation under an artistic director, Gordon *Hilker, an associate artistic director, Gilles *Lefebvre, and an administrative director, Jean Coté, was the World Festival of Entertainment, featuring several of the world's leading opera, ballet, and theatre companies, orchestras, chamber ensembles, jazz groups, singers, solo instrumentalists, dance bands, and popular and folk singers. The corporation's advisory committee on the performing arts comprised Peter Dwyer, Jean Gascon, John Hirsch, Jean-C. *Lallemand, and Jean *Vallerand.

1 On-site music
2 The World Festival

1 ON-SITE MUSIC. During the six months of the exposition, about 6000 free concerts were presented on the Expo grounds by professional and amateur ensembles from all parts of the world, some being sponsored and paid by their governments and others contributing their services and paying their own expenses. Concerts were presented at scheduled times on bandshells and plazas, strolling groups wandered the site serenading the crowds, groups were imported to play in national pavilions, musical comedies and operettas were presented in the Expo Theatre, cabaret and pop-music performers found employment at La Ronde – in short, music was continuous and pervasive. Composers were commissioned to write works for concerts and scores for films and for the aural environments of some pavilions; among them were R. Murray *Schafer (for the Chemical Industries pavilion, Kaleidoscope), Eldon *Rathburn (for the *NFB pavilion, Labyrinth), Serge *Garant (for the pavilion Man and the Polar Regions), and André *Prévost, Alexander *Brott, Robert *Fleming, and Otto *Joachim (for the Canadian Pavilion). The Man and Music Pavilion was devoted to the work of the *JMC and featured displays, facilities for listening to recorded music, exhibits of major teaching systems such as *Orff and *Kodály, and studios in which master classes in teaching were held each day, observed by the public. The prefabricated concrete building which housed this activity was moved later to become part of the JMC music camp at Mount Orford, Que. Between 16 July and 22 July, on the Expo site and in Montreal, the JMC was host to the 21st World Congress of the Jeunesses musicales International Federation and also held the finals of major national performing competitions and an international composition competition. Winners of the former were Andrew *Dawes (strings), Annon Lee *Silver (voice), and Robert *Silverman (piano), and of the latter Josef Maria Horvath (Austria), Sydney *Hodkinson (Canada), Zsolt Durko (Hungary), Martin Boykan (USA), and Michael Finnissy (England).

The main location for musical performance by Canadians, however, was the Canadian Government Pavilion, named Katimavik (an Inuit word for 'gathering place'). It contained a 500-seat theatre and a 1200-seat open-air bandshell, where 58 shows each week were presented during the run of the fair by all kinds of groups and individual artists. Hugh *Davidson was music consultant to the pavilion's administration, and the federal government contributed about $800,000 to the cost of the entertainment presented there. Four concerts were given each day (except Mondays) in the bandshell: amateur choirs and ensembles at noon, a concert band at 2:30 and 5:00 pm, and chansonniers and folksingers at 3:45 pm. In the theatre (also closed on Mondays) there were organ recitals at noon (on an instrument donated by *Casavant Frères), chamber music and jazz groups at 2:30, two performances each afternoon by Les Feux-Follets (dance troupe), and a musical-comedy revue at 6:15; on Saturdays and Sundays the 2:30 performance featured recitals, the official accompanist for which was John *Newmark.

Week-end recitalists were Pierrette *Alarie, Donald *Bell, John *Boyden, Victor *Braun, Hyman *Bress, Maureen *Forrester, Richard *Gresko, Elizabeth Benson *Guy, Ida *Haendel, Betty-Jean

*Hagen, Walter *Joachim, Lois *Marshall, Zara *Nelsova, Louis *Quilico, Joseph *Rouleau, Robert *Savoie, Steven *Staryk, Bernard *Turgeon, Ronald *Turini, André *Turp, Richard *Verreau, the duo-pianists Victor *Bouchard and Renée *Morisset, and the singers Shirley *Harmer, Pauline *Julien, and Monique *Leyrac.

Weekday 2:30 concerts were given by the *Baroque Trio of Montreal, the *Cassenti Players, the *Duo Pach, the Ensemble Couperin-le-Grand, the *Ensemble vocal Chantal Masson, the *Festival Singers, the Gabora String Quartet, the *Hart House Orchestra, the *Halifax Trio, the *Hidy Trio, the Lance *Harrison Dixieland Band, the Lee *Gagnon Jazz Ensemble, the *McGill Chamber Orchestra, the *Manitoba University Consort, the Moe *Koffman Quartet, the *Orford String Quartet, *Nimmons 'n' Nine, Phyllis *Mailing, the Montreal Brass Quintet, the *Petit Ensemble vocal, the *Quebec Woodwind Quintet, the Ron *Collier Jazz Group, the *Toronto Woodwind Quintet, the Trio Pierre *Leduc, the Tommy *Banks Quartet, the Yvan *Landry Jazz Quartet, and groups organized by the *SMCQ and by *Ten Centuries Concerts. Each group played for four consecutive days, usually in a variety of programs.

Organ recitals in the theatre were given by Françoise *Aubut, Hugh *Bancroft, Douglas *Bodle, Antoine *Bouchard, Barry *Cabena, Raymond *Daveluy, Maitland *Farmer, Frederick *Geoghegan, Kenneth *Gilbert, Conrad Grimes, Gordon *Jeffery, Mireille *Lagacé, Claude *Lavoie, Jean *Leduc, Lucienne *L'Heureux-Arel, Hugh *McLean, Kenneth *Meek, Charles *Peaker, and Gerald *Wheeler.

Bandshell concerts featured Oscar *Brand, Hélène *Baillargeon, Dinah *Christie, Bobby *Curtola, Tommy *Common, Pierre Calvé, Michel Conte and Micheline (Bardin), Bonnie *Dobson, Louise *Forestier, the Maynard *Ferguson Sextet, Tom *Kines, Penny Lang, Gordon *Lightfoot, Raymond *Lévesque, *Malka and Joso, Bruce McKay, Alan *Mills, Jean-Guy Moreau, Ginette *Ravel, La Famille *Soucy, The *Travellers, and Alexandre *Zelkine.

Many of these concerts were recorded by the CBC for subsequent broadcast, and transcription discs in a 'CBC Expo' series were made of over 40 of them.

2 THE WORLD FESTIVAL. The main location for the World Festival events was the *PDA, in mid-town Montreal, which Expo rented for the duration of the fair. Events were held in its three theatres, in the 2000-seat Expo Theatre built for Expo 67 and located just outside the grounds, and in St-Jacques Roman Catholic Church. The corporation announced that 4.3 million tickets were printed for 672 events featuring 110 groups numbering nearly 25,000 performers from 25 countries (the figures included large-scale spectacles like the Armed Forces Tattoo, held in the Autostade adjacent to Expo). Attendance for opera was 87 per cent of capacity and for music 72 per cent. A gala opening on 29 April featured the premiere of André Prévost's choral-orchestral work *Terre des hommes* by the *MSO and the World Festival Chorus (the latter prepared by Marcel *Laurencelle) with Albert Millaire and Michelle Rossignol as narrators and Pierre *Hétu conducting. Wilfrid *Pelletier also conducted the MSO and the Rutgers U Chorus in Beethoven's *Ode to Joy* with Pierrette Alarie, Maureen Forrester, Léopold *Simoneau, and Joseph Rouleau as soloists.

The full companies of La Scala, the Vienna State Opera, the Bolshoi Opera, the Hamburg State Opera, and the Royal Swedish Opera, all making their North American debuts, each gave a number of fully staged performances. The cost of transporting foreign performers and their sets and costumes to and from Montreal was borne by their home governments, while Expo provided theatres, audiences, living expenses, and accommodation. The opera series consisted of the Swedish Opera, conducted by Silvio Varviso and Sixten Ehrling, in Verdi's *Un Ballo in Maschera*, Karl Birger Blomdahl's 'space opera' *Aniara*, Stravinsky's *The Rake's Progress* in the Ingmar Bergman production, and Wagner's *Tristan und Isolde* with Birgit Nilsson and Ken Neate; the Hamburg State Opera, conducted by Hans Schmidt-Isserstedt and Leopold Ludwig, in Hindemith's *Mathis der Maler*, Berg's *Lulu*, Janáček's *Jenufa*, and a concert version of Weber's *Der Freischütz*; the Vienna State Opera, conducted by Karl Boehm, Heinrich Hollreiser, Berislav Klobucar, and Josef Krips in Mozart's *Don Giovanni* and *The Marriage of Figaro*, Strauss' *Elektra* and *Der Rosenkavalier*, and Berg's *Wozzeck*; the Bolshoi Opera of Moscow in Borodin's *Prince Igor*, Mussorgsky's *Boris Godunov*, Tchaikovsky's *The Queen of Spades*, Prokofiev's *War and Peace*, and Rimsky-Korsakov's *The Invisible City of Kitezh*; La Scala of Milan in Verdi's *Il Trovatore* and *Nabucco*, Puccini's *La Bohème*, and Bellini's *I Capuleti e i Montecchi*, and also in a performance of Verdi's *Requiem* conducted by Herbert von Karajan; the English Opera Group, conducted by Benjamin Britten, Rudolph Schwarz, James Lockhart, and Steuart Bedford, in Britten's *Curlew River, The Burning Fiery Furnace*, and *A Midsummer Night's Dream*, Walton's *The Bear*, Handel's *Acis and Galatea*, and John Gay's *The Beggar's Opera* (realized by Britten); the *COC, conducted by Victor *Feldbrill and Otto-Werner *Mueller, in Harry *Somers' *Louis Riel* and Offenbach's *Tales of Hoffmann*, with Bernard Turgeon, Cornelis *Opthof, Joseph Rouleau, Patricia *Rideout, Roxolana *Roslak, Mary *Morrison, André Turp, Colette *Boky, Eleanor *Calbes, Heather *Thomson, Phil *Stark, Jan *Rubeš, Norman *Mittelmann, and Alan *Crofoot; and a two-opera season given by the MSO comprising Verdi's *Otello* conducted by Zubin Mehta, with Jon *Vickers, Teresa *Stratas, and Louis Quilico, and Gounod's *Faust* conducted by Wilfrid Pelletier, with Joseph Rouleau, Richard Verreau, Robert Savoie, and Heather Thomson. The Canadian government contributed $50,000 towards the *Otello* production.

Orchestral concerts were given by the Vienna Philharmonic under Boehm, l'Orchestre de la Suisse romande under Ernest Ansermet and Paul Kletzki, the Concertgebouw Orchestra of Amsterdam under Bernard Haitink, the ORTF Orchestra, the Czech Philharmonic, the Buffalo Philharmonic, the *NYO, the Melbourne (Australia) SO under Willem van Otterloo with the soprano Marie Collier, the Hamburg SO, the New York Philharmonic, the *TS, the Los Angeles Philharmonic, the San Francisco SO, the MSO, the JM International Orchestra, and the Northern Sinfonia of England.

Chamber orchestras and ensembles included the Collegium Musicum of Zurich under Paul Sacher, the Prague Soloists, the Berlin Philharmonic Octet, the Slovak Quartet, the Scarlatti Orchestra of Naples under Mario Rossi and Massimo Pradella, the Solistes de Liège, Belgium, the Bath Festival Orchestra under Yehudi Menuhin, the Danzi Quintet of the Netherlands, and the Stern-Rose-Istomin Trio. Solo recitals were given by Henryk Szeryng, Christoph Eschenbach, and Arturo Benedetti Michelangeli.

Choirs included the Red Army Chorus and the Piatnitsky Choir of the USSR, the Munich Bach Choir and Orchestra, the Copenhagen University Choir, the Lado Folkloric Ensemble of Yugoslavia, and the Swiss Folkloric Ensemble.

Dance and folkdance companies were Belgium's Ballet du vingtième siècle, the Bolshoi Ballet, the Paris Opera Ballet, the Royal Ballet of Britain, the Australian Ballet, the National Ballet of Canada, the Royal Winnipeg Ballet, Les Grands Ballets Canadiens, the New York City Ballet, the Martha Graham Dance Company, the National Dance Theatre of Jamaica, the Troupe nationale folklorique tunisienne, the Japanese Folkloric Art Dance Company, Music and Dance of India, and Fiesta Cubana.

Other events included a gala concert by JMC competition winners, a one-week run of **Anne of Green Gables*, and several performances by Duke Ellington and his Orchestra with Sarah Vaughan. Altogether, the World Festival of Entertainment constituted one of the greatest assemblages of musical talent ever brought together in one city, and certainly the greatest ever convened in Canada.

The official theme-song of Expo 67, selected by a jury after open competition, was 'Hey Friend, Say Friend' (French version 'Un Jour, Un Jour') by Stéphane *Venne. It was recorded and widely played on radio stations in Montreal but did not meet with enthusiasm from Montreal mayor Jean Drapeau, one of the chief proponents of Expo 67, because its lyrics made no mention of the host city.

Man and his World was retained as the name of a summer festival held in following years (continuing in 1980) on the Expo site.

BIBLIOGRAPHY

Rudel-Tessier, J. 'Plans for Expo vague but promising,' *CanComp*, 7, Mar 1966

Green, Robin. 'Opera at the World Festival,' *OpCan*, vol 7, Sep 1966

Rudel-Tessier, J. 'Stéphane Venne wins Expo song contest,' *CanComp*, 14, Jan 1967

'Canadian music at Expo,' ibid

Green, Robin. 'The Expo 67 scene,' *OpCan*, vol 7, Feb 1967

Evans, Ron. 'Expo 67: "Katimavik" the meeting place,' *PfAC*, Spring 1967

'Three Canadian composers set puppet fantasies to music,' *CanComp*, 17, Apr 1967

'Opera at Expo 67,' *OpCan*, vol 8, May 1967

Davidson, Hugh. 'Festival Katimavik,' *Mcan*, Jun 1967

Canadian Composer, 20, Jul–Aug 1967. Issue devoted to music at Expo 67 including articles on jazz, popular entertainment, the JMC pavilion

Kraglund, John. 'Review: Expo's World Festival,' *OpCan*, vol 8, Sep 1967

Canadian Government Pavilion: Expo 67: Theatre and Bandshell Performances (Ottawa 1967)

Expo 67: Official Guide (Montreal 1967)

General Report on the 1967 World Exhibition, 5 vols (Ottawa 1969). Vols 4 and 5 report on the World Festival.

Reviews of performances carried in Montreal in the *Gazette*, the *Montreal Star*, *Le Devoir*, *La Presse*; in Quebec City in *Le Soleil*; and in Toronto in the *Globe and Mail*, *Toronto Daily Star*, and *Telegram* TCB

F

FAIRCLOUGH, W.E. (William Erving). Organist, choirmaster, teacher, b Barrie, Upper Canada (Ontario), 29 Aug 1859, d ?; FRCO 1888. His parents settled in Hamilton, Ont, in 1865, and he sang as an alto in Christ Church choir and studied piano with G.F. De Vine and organ with D.J. O'Brien. Fairclough was organist 1876–83 at Christ Church Cathedral and accompanied various Hamilton choirs. He went to England for studies 1883–5 at the RCM. His teachers were Walter Parratt (organ), Alfred Caldicott (piano), Sir Frederick Bridge (harmony and counterpoint), and Edward Wharton (voice). In England he held appointments 1883–7 as organist-choirmaster in London and Folkestone and also played the organ at the orchestral services conducted at St Paul's Cathedral, London, by Caldicott and George Clement Martin. He formed a choral society in Folkestone, conducted choral-orchestral concerts, and appeared frequently as a solo pianist. He returned to Canada to serve 1887–90 as organist-choirmaster at St George's Church, Montreal, then moved to Toronto to take a similar post at All Saints' (Anglican) Church. Fairclough was active in the Toronto Church Choir Assn and was its conductor for one year. He also gave annual series of organ recitals in Toronto and performed widely in Canada and the USA, notably at the 1901 Pan-American Exposition in Buffalo. By 1893 he was an examiner in harmony, counterpoint, and history for the *U of Toronto. He also taught organ, piano, and theory for many years at the *Toronto College of Music.

Fairclough's younger brother, George (Herbert) Fairclough (b Hamilton 30 Jan 1869, d Saratoga, Cal, 27 Mar 1954), studied with his brother and with D.J. O'Brien and was a church organist in Hamilton, Toronto, and Brantford before studying at the Hochschule für Musik, Berlin, in the 1890s. Moving to the USA, he held several church and synagogue positions and was dean of the American Guild of Organists 1910–13 and head of the School of Music at the U of Minnesota 1920–37. He composed songs, keyboard pieces, and several choral pieces, including a *Te Deum and Jubilate in A* and a *Mass*. His *Varsity Vocal Lancers* was published by *Suckling in 1889. Ashdown, Gray, and Presser also published his works.

BIBLIOGRPAHY

'W.E. Fairclough,' *MCan*, vol 2, Dec 1907

Fairclough, Harry Rushton. *Warming Both Hands* (Palo Alto, Cal, 1941)

(HL, PMW)

FAIRFAX, Joan (b Pickup, m Higgins). Singer, accordionist, arranger, b Blackburn, Lancashire, England, 24 Jun 1926, naturalized US. She was taken at two to Oakville, Ont, but returned to England for a year at seven and there began piano study. She later studied accordion in Toronto with Dixie *Dean. After Canadian tours, singing with the Lifebuoy Follies and in a solo act for the armed forces and Red Cross, she trained as a coloratura soprano for two years at the *RCMT. Subsequently coached by Art *Hallman she sang briefly with Frank Bogart's dance band and 1951–2 with Hallman's orchestra. She made her radio debut in 1951 on CBC radio's 'Latin American Serenade.' A regular performer throughout the 1950s on CBC Toronto TV programs, notably 'Music Hall' 1953–5 and 'The Denny *Vaughan Show' 1955–7, she also starred 1959–60 on 'The Joan Fairfax Show' before moving to the USA. There she appeared in 1961 on the Jack Parr, Ed Sullivan, and Lawrence Welk TV shows and toured 1963–4 with her all-girl orchestra as 'Canada's Blonde Bombshell, The New Ina Ray Hutton.' She settled in Florida, where she has performed in hotels and at conventions, returning to Toronto for occasional TV appearances. (HM)

FAITH, Percy. Conductor, arranger, composer, pianist, b Toronto 7 Apr 1908, naturalized US 1945, d Los Angeles 9 Feb 1976. He began playing violin at 7 and piano at 10 and performed 1920–7 as a silent-film accompanist in Toronto movie houses. He studied at the Canadian Academy and then, at 14, with Frank *Welsman at the *TCM. He made his *Massey Hall debut in 1923 in Liszt's *Hungarian Fantasy* at a TCM annual concert. After an accident at 18 which severely burned his hands and ended the possibility of a concert career, he studied composition with Louis *Waizman and began arranging for the hotel orchestras of Luigi *Romanelli and Rex *Battle. He also wrote arrangements 1929–32 for the CKNC radio orchestra of Geoffrey *Waddington. His own radio career began at CKCL, where he was arranger-conductor for 'Simpsons' Opera Hour' in 1927 and other such programs. On CKCL in 1928 he was heard with the singer Joe Allabough in a duo known as Faith and Hope. He joined the CRBC (*CBC) in Toronto in 1933 and was arranger-conductor 1935–8 of 'Gaiety and Romance,' 'Mardi Gras,' 'Cosmopolitans,' 'Streamline,' 'Bands across the Sea,' and 1938–40 of 'Music by Faith,' which also was broadcast in the USA on MBS. As a result of the program's US popularity, he moved to Chicago as music director 1940–7 of 'The Carnation Contented Hour' on NBC radio. Rising quickly to the front ranks of US popular-music arrangers, he was employed variously as music director 1946–9 of Coca-Cola's 'The Pause That Refreshes' (CBS) and 1955–7 of 'The Woolworth Hour' (CBS) and as arranger-conductor for Columbia Records in New York 1950–9 and Los Angeles 1960–76. He returned to Canada often, directing Victory Bond Drive shows during World War II and later conducting concerts and CBC TV specials. In 1974 he established the Percy Faith Award for music students at the *U of Toronto and similar awards at the U of Jerusalem and the U of Southern California.

Faith composed piano, choral, and orchestra works during the 1940s and won a $1000 prize in 1943 in Chicago for his operetta *The Gandy Dancer*. His publishers include Harms, Mutual Music, and Presser. (See *Catalogue of Canadian Composers* for works prior to 1950.) He enjoyed success 1950–76 with pop-song collaborations and with the film scores *Tammy Tell Me True* (Universal 1961), *I'd Rather Be Rich* (Universal 1964), *The Love Goddesses* (Continental 1964), *The Third Day* (Paramount 1965), *The Oscar* (Universal 1966), and *Love Me or Leave Me* (MGM 1955), the last of which was written with Georgie Stoll and nominated in 1955 for an Academy Award. He worked with many popular singers for Columbia Records, adapting a French folksong in collaboration with Carl Sigman for Guy Mitchell's first success, 'My Heart Cries For You' (1950), and arranging 'Because of You' (1951), 'Cold, Cold Heart' (1951), and 'Rags to Riches' (1953) for Tony Bennett. With his own orchestra and chorus Faith recorded the hit singles 'Delicado' (1952) and 'Song from *Moulin Rouge*' (1953) and the Grammy Award winners 'Theme from *A Summer Place*' (Record of the Year 1960) and 'Love Theme from *Romeo and Juliet*' (Best Performance by a Chorus 1969). His 45 albums include many of his film scores, interpretations of major musicals, and the gold records *Viva* (1957, reissued as 2-Col CG-33606), *Bouquet* (1959, Col CS-8124), and *Themes for Young Lovers* (1963, Col CS-8823). MM

FALCON, Pierre. Chansonnier, poet, bard, b Elbow Fort, Swan River, Rupert's Land (Manitoba), 4 Jun 1793, d St François Xavier, Man, 26 Oct 1876. A Métis, he was educated 1797–? in La Prairie, Lower Canada, and returned in 1808 to his native village. He was an employee of the North-West Company 1808–21, and of the Hudson's Bay Company 1821–5, following the merger of those two firms. In 1825 he retired to Grantown, now St François Xavier, Man, to farm; he was appointed a magistrate there in 1855.

Dubbed Pierriche or Pierre the Rhymer, Falcon had a talent for putting into song local happenings, such as the adventures of voyageurs and hunters. Among those of his songs that have survived are 'La Bataille des sept chênes' / 'The Battle of Seven Oaks' or 'La Chanson de la Grenouillère' (Winnipeg 1816), 'La Danse des bois-brûlés' / 'Lord Selkirk at Fort William' (1816; this song is attributed to Falcon although he has not been positively identified as the author), 'Le Général Dickson' / 'The Dickson Song' (1837; Dickson was an adventurer who left Grantown that year to found an Indian kingdom in California), and 'Les Tribulations d'un roi malheureux' / 'Misfortunes of an Unlucky King' (1869, to the tune of 'Le Juif errant'). It is reported that his ballads were sung on the Prairies by the Métis to the accompaniment of the violin (crincrin). They were carried throughout Canada, from the St Lawrence to the Mackenzie River. *Songs of Old Manitoba* by Margaret Arnett *MacLeod (Toronto 1960) contains all of Falcon's known songs. Lake Falcon in Manitoba was probably named after him.

BIBLIOGRAPHY

Complin, Margaret. 'Chanson de la Grenouillère,' Royal Society of Canada *Transactions*, 3rd series, vol 33 (Ottawa 1939)

MacLeod, Margaret Arnett. 'Bard of the Prairies,' *Beaver* 286, Spring 1956

– 'Dickson the liberator' and 'Songs of the insurrection,' ibid, 287 Spring 1957

DCB, vol 10

(DM)

FALLIS, Mary Lou (m Madgett). Soprano, teacher, b Toronto 22 Apr 1948; B MUS (Toronto) 1970, M MUS (Toronto) 1972. She made her operatic debut at 15 as a Spirit in a CBC-TV production of *The Magic Flute*. She studied with Helen Simmie 1962–6 at the *RCMT, Irene *Jessner 1966–70 and Maureen *Forrester 1970–2 at the *U of Toronto, and Bernard *Diamant privately, beginning in 1971. She won the *CBC Talent Festival in 1973 and the *Metropolitan Opera Regional Auditions in 1974. She has been a member of the *COC 1964–7 and in 1969 and of the *Festival Singers in 1968 and 1971–2. She has sung with the *TS and other orchestras and has performed in recital, as a founding member of the Arioso Trio, and with *Camerata. Her major roles, mainly lyric-coloratura, have included Gabrielle in *La Vie parisienne* and Zerbinetta in *Ariadne auf Naxos* at the 1974 and 1975 *Stratford Festivals respectively and Flora in *The Turn of the Screw* and Papagena in *The Magic Flute* at the *NAC in 1975. She sang in the first complete performance of *Schafer's *Loving* in 1978. In 1979 she sang Mlle Jeunesse in Mozart's *The Impresario*, a joint production of the *Nova Scotia Festival of the Arts and CBC radio. Fallis has taught privately and at *York U, Toronto, in 1972, and the *RHCM 1973–4. She began to teach at *Queen's U in 1978.

FAMEQ (Fédération des associations de musiciens éducateurs du Québec). Founded 12 Mar 1966 in Drummondville during a conference organized by Georges *Little. The federation received a provincial charter in 1968. Its objectives have been to coordinate the work of regional professional associations of French-language music educators, to promote meetings between music teachers, to safeguard professional ethics, to democratize musical education in Quebec, and to contribute to the intellectual, social, and emotional development of the Quebec child.

The member associations are grouped in 10 regions: Quebec, Saguenay–Lac-St-Jean–North Shore, Eastern Townships, Montreal, Chambly-Laval, Hull-Mont-Laurier, North-West, Mauricie, South Shore, and Rimouski. Presidents have been Gilles Fortin (Drummondville), Roger Mongeon (Montreal), Jean Patenaude (Chambly), Normand Laprise (Lac St-Jean), Constance Mainville (Hull), and Roger Mongeon, succeeded by Louise Cloutier in 1979.

FAMEQ has held congresses annually, and among the invited speakers have been Marcel Corneloup, Maurice Martenot (see Martenot Method), and Jacques Chailley, all of France; Erzsébet Szönyi of Hungary (see Kodály Method); and Marcel Rioux (see *Rapport de la Commission royale d'enquête sur l'enseignement des arts dans la province de Québec*). FAMEQ published the magazine *Le Musicien Éducateur* 1967–74 and began issuing a newsletter in 1971.

FAMEQ has defended the interests of the music-teaching profession, has occupied itself with long-term projects, and has sponsored the FAMEQ Band, selected from among the best young players from bands in the 10 regions. Michel *Perrault was appointed director of the band in 1973. FAMEQ is affiliated with ISME and is a member of the *CCA and of the Conseil pédagogique interdisciplinaire du Québec. It collaborates with the *CMEA, the *JMC, the *QMEA, the *CMCentre and the Centrale de l'enseignement du Québec. It is represented on the Quebec Ministry of Education's two consultative committees for the teaching of the arts.

BIBLIOGRAPHY

Corneille, Sister Marcelle. 'F.A.M.E.Q.,' *Mcan*, 8, Jan–Feb 1968 (MB-L)

FARMER, Ernest (Jones). Composer, pianist, teacher, b Woodstock, Ont, 18 Mar 1883, d Toronto 25 Sep 1975; ATCM 1903, BA (McMaster) 1903. After studies at the TCM 1897–1905 with Lena M. Hayes and A.S. *Vogt, in Leipzig 1905–8 with Max Reger and others, and at the *Hambourg Cons 1911–13 with Michael *Hambourg, he taught at the *TCM – where his pupils included Ida *Krehm, Colin *McPhee, and Gerald Moore – and at the Hambourg Cons and gave occasional piano recitals. He was regarded by Luigi von *Kunits as 'a theory teacher of rare originality.' He wrote articles on music (for *The Etude*) and economics and had some piano pieces published (1909) by *Nordheimer. His *Fantasia* for cello and piano, which won a prize at the Hambourg Concert Society Competition in 1912, was performed by Boris Hambourg in London and other cities 'with pronounced success' (von Kunits).

A brother, Broadus (Baxter) Farmer (b Louisville, Ky, 1890, d Toronto 24 Apr 1959), was a violinist and teacher. He studied in Toronto with Lena Hayes, Jan Hambourg, and Henri Czaplinski and taught 1911–23 at the Hambourg Cons and 1923–32 at the TCM. In 1932 he opened the Broadus B. Farmer Studio on Bloor Street in Toronto. In later years he taught at the Bedford Studio in Hamilton. His pupils included Hyman *Goodman, John Moskalyk, Albert *Pratz, Ivan *Romanoff, Bill *Richards, Albert *Steinberg, and Carl *Tapscott.

BIBLIOGRAPHY

Von Kunits, Luigi. 'Ernest J. Farmer,' *CanJM*, vol 2, Feb 1916 (MHI)

FARMER, Maitland. Organist, choirmaster, teacher, pianist, harpsichordist, b London 24 Feb 1904; LRAM 1921, FRCO 19?, B MUS (Toronto) 1947, hon LL D (King's College, Halifax) 1963. A pupil of Reginald Goss-Custard and George Cunningham at the RAM, Farmer took his first appointment as organist-choirmaster at St-André Church in Pau, France, followed by positions in London at Holy Trinity, Cloudesley Square; the Chelsea Old Church; and St Luke's, South Kensington. Ca 1923 he gave his first series of recitals. He also worked for the Aeolian Company of New York, producing and editing Duo Art piano rolls with Percy Scholes.

Farmer moved to Canada and served 1929–31 as organist-choirmaster at the Cathedral of the Holy Trinity, Quebec City, and 1932–44 at St Paul's Anglican Church in Toronto. He moved to Montreal in 1944 to teach piano and organ at *McGill U and organist-choirmaster at St George's Anglican Church and to Halifax in 1946 as organist-choirmaster at All Saints Cathedral, retaining that position until 1972. He was acting head 1948–9 of the piano, organ, and theory department of the Halifax Cons (*Maritime Cons of Music) and also taught privately. His pupils have included Donald Forbes, Alexander *Gray, John Grew, and Michael Gormley. During his term (1951) as chairman of the Halifax Centre of the *RCCO, a fund was established from which organ students could borrow for study abroad. He became organist-choirmaster at St James Anglican Church, Halifax, in 1972.

Farmer's career as one of Canada's leading organ recitalists began with radio broadcasts in 1930. He gave a command performance in 1934 for the governor-general, Lord Bessborough, and played for the *Casavant societies of Toronto (1938 and 1943) and Montreal (1945) and for CCO conventions in Toronto in 1942 and Montreal in 1951. Besides giving over 100 recitals on CBC radio from Toronto and Halifax, he performed daily for a week at the Canadian Pavilion of *Expo 67. He has been harpsichord soloist on several occasions with a CBC string orchestra. (SAB)

FARNAM, (Walter) Lynnwood. Organist, teacher, b Sutton, southeast of Montreal, 13 Jan 1885, d New York 23 Nov 1930. He studied piano in Dunham, Que, and in 1900 was awarded the Lord *Strathcona Scholarship, which paid three years' tuition at the RCM, London. The college granted him an additional year's tuition for excellence. His teachers there were Franklin Taylor (piano) and Sir Walter Parratt and W.S. Hoyte (organ). Farnam returned to Montreal in 1904 as organist at St James' Methodist Church. He was the organist 1905–8 at the Church of St James the Apostle (Anglican) and organist-choirmaster 1908–13 at Christ Church Cathedral. During these years he gave many recitals in Montreal and paid a visit to Boston, where he met and played for several established colleagues. In 1913 as a result of the impression he made he was invited to audition for Emmanuel Church, Boston, and, when asked what he would play, handed the committee his notebook, saying 'Any of these.' The book listed 200 pieces which he had memorized. The post was immediately his, and he retained it till 1918. During his tenure the Canadian organ builders *Casavant Frères installed a 140-stop organ in the church. Farnam was invited to be organist-choirmaster at New York's Fifth Ave Presbyterian Church in 1918, but enlistment for overseas service in the Canadian infantry postponed his acceptance. Illness prevented his going on to the front in France, however, and he remained in England, returning to the USA in 1919 and assuming the New York post that year. He became the organist at the Church of the Holy Communion in 1920 and gave there a notable series of recitals. A dazzling recital that year for the American Guild of Organists consolidated his reputation among his colleagues. In 1925 he made organ rolls of 23 works for the player-organs of the Welte-Mignon Corp, New York, and five more for the Austin player-organ. All these later were transferred to records. He gained fame as a teacher in New York

Lynnwood Farnam

and in 1927 was asked to head the organ department at the Curtis Institute of Music, Philadelphia. He taught there weekly until his death at 45.

Farnam has become a legend in the organ world. He did no improvising, and his only composition, a French-style *Toccata* on the Easter Hymn 'O filii et filiae,' was published posthumously (by Theodore Presser at the instigation of Farnam's pupil Ernest *White; it was recorded by Hugh *McLean). But he was counted among the great interpreters, attracting to his performances not only organists but other leading musicians and a wide listening public. He introduced his audiences to organ music of his day – particularly French and American – as well as to the forerunners of Bach. He championed *Willan's *Introduction, Passacaglia, and Fugue*, thus helping it to fame. His programs also offered the complete works of Brahms, Franck, and other romantics, and in one notable season, 1928–9, he played all of Bach's organ music in 20 recitals, repeating each program once and some twice to meet the public demand. Farnam's success was international, and he gave numerous recitals in England and France on the greatest organs. He played his last recital – at the Church of the Holy Communion 12 Oct 1930 – in great distress. He was taken to hospital immediately afterwards, and terminal cancer of the liver was diagnosed. He died a month later.

The New York critics recognized Farnam's worth. Lawrence Gilman of the *Herald Tribune* wrote that he was truly self-effacing and had whole-hearted dedication kindled by genius, intensity of vision, sincerity, and excelling craft. Richard Aldrich of the *Times* wrote that Farnam had executive power, artistic sense, and a comprehensive knowledge of organ literature. His Canadian pupils included Ernest White, H.W. Hawke, Frederick *Silvester, and Harold *Ramsay. Notable among his pupils in the USA were Ruth Barrett Phelps in California, Alfred Greenfield in North Carolina, Alex McCurdy in Maine, Paul Robinson in North Carolina, and Carl Weinrich in New Jersey.

WRITINGS

'Rambling remarks of an organist's sojourn in England,' *Diapason*, 4 instalments, Sep, Oct, Nov, Dec 1927

'How the organ chose a disciple,' *Overtones*, Apr 1930

DISCOGRAPHY

Bach – Karg-Elert – Sowerby – Vierne. Classic 1040

A Pipe Organ Concert by Lynwood Farnam. 3-Ultra Fidelity.

- UF-1: Farnam – Stebbins – Widor – Stoughton – Rheinberger – Vierne
- UF-2: Widor – Yon – Saint-Saëns – Malling – Faulkes – Merkel
- UF-3: Vierne – Karg-Elert – Yon – Guilmant – D'Every

BIBLIOGRAPHY
'A noted Canadian organist's views on organ playing and repertoire,' *CQR*, vol 1, Nov 1918
'A chat with Lynnwood Farnam,' *MT*, 1 Aug 1923
Worcester, Elwodd. 'Lynnwood Farnam, the modest genius,' *Diapason*, Feb 1931
Hawke, W.H. 'Some Farnam registrations,' *American Organist*, 2 articles, Jul, Sep 1956
'Lynnwood Farnam; his life,' *American Organist*, Jul 1964
Rizzo, Jeanne. 'Lynnwood Farnam – master organist of the century,' *Diapason*, 2 instalments, Dec 1974, Jan 1975
RCCO papers. Hawke, W.H. 'Lynnwood Farnam: 1885–1930,' ms
The Curtis Institute of Music. Farnam collection HWH

FARNELL, Audrey (Bernice) (m Chapple). Soprano, teacher, b Amherst, NS, 28 Jul 1921. She studied 1937–40 at the Mount Allison Cons with Ethel Peake and 1942–5 at the *TCM with George *Lambert and was a winner in the 1945–6 *'Singing Stars of Tomorrow.' She continued her training 1946–8 with Lotte Leonard in New York and 1957–8 with Roy Henderson at the RAM. She sang 1949–51 with the *Nova Scotia Opera Assn and starred on CBC Halifax radio's 'Songs by Audrey Farnell' (1951) and, with Leonard *Mayoh, on 'Sketches of Songs' (1952). She has been a soloist with the *Toronto Mendelssohn Choir, the*Ottawa Choral Union, the *Montreal Elgar Choir, the *Halifax Choral Society, the Hamilton Bach Choir, and the *Vancouver SO (Poulenc's *Gloria* under Charles Munch at the *Vancouver International Festival, 1 Jul 1964). As a recitalist she has toured frequently in the Maritimes and performed in many other Canadian centres and on CBC radio's 'Distinguished Artists' and 'CBC Wednesday Night.' She is heard as Lilla on the *CBC Vancouver Chamber Orchestra recording of Martin y Soler's opera, *Una Cosa Rara* (CBC SM-217). In many years of teaching in Halifax, Farnell's pupils have included Gaelyne *Gabora and others active in the profession. (RSm)

FARNON, Robert (Joseph). Composer, arranger, conductor, trumpeter, b Toronto 24 Jul 1917. He began to study piano with his mother at seven and with Jack Gray at nine. In 1930 he began playing drums in the dance band of his brother Brian; he also studied percussion with Duncan Snider. By 1934, however, he had turned exclusively to the trumpet, and played in the Toronto dance bands of Bus Browne, Stanley *St John, Bob Shuttleworth, and others and in the CRBC (CBC) orchestras of Percy *Faith and Geoffrey *Waddington. He was a member 1937–43 of the *Happy Gang. He was a composition pupil of Louis *Waizman in the 1930s and arranged music for Faith's choral groups and for the orchestras of André Kostelanetz and Paul Whiteman. He completed his first symphony in 1940. Premiered 7 Jan 1941 as *Symphonic Suite* by the *TSO, it also was performed on several occasions by the Philadelphia Orchestra – once in *Massey Hall. After that concert, Augustus *Bridle (*Toronto Daily Star*, 13 May 1942) praised 'its extremely modern design without a single ugly dissonance; its infallible beauty of tone-painting and its continuous enchantment in both themes and harmonic invention; [and] its sagacious instrumentations.' The only scores of this work and of *Cascades to the Sea* (premiered under Jean-Marie *Beaudet 31 Aug 1944) were lost at sea in 1944 along with a shipment of Army Show music and equipment. A second symphony, the *Ottawa*, followed in 1942 and was premiered by the TSO in 1943 on the CBC radio program 'Concert Hour.'

Farnon went overseas during World War II as music director for *The *Army Show* and also conducted the Canadian band of the Allied Expeditionary Forces on the BBC. He arranged music for the English dance bands of Ambrose, Geraldo, and Ted Heath and by 1950 had his own BBC radio programs (eg, 'Journey into Melody'), for which he composed, arranged, and conducted music for a large orchestra. In the late 1940s he began recording commercially for Decca under his own name and as choral arranger for Vera Lynn and others and also made several LPs with the Queen's Hall Light Orchestra for Chappell & Co Mood Music, a library intended for use by the radio, TV, and film industries. His arrangements for Chappell, some conceived for the Canadian army orchestra, are acknowledged generally as having exerted a decisive influence on European and North American composers and arrangers of music for films. Farnon himself has composed the scores for *William Comes to Town* and *Spring in Park Lane* (1947), *Just William's Luck* (1948), *Elizabeth of Ladymead* (1949), *Captain Horatio Hornblower* and *Circle of Danger* (1951), *Maytime in Mayfair* (1952), *His Majesty O'Keefe* (1953), *Gentlemen Marry Brunettes* and *Let's Make Up* (1955), *The Little Hut* (1957), *The Sheriff of Fractured Jaw* (1958), *The Road to Hong Kong* (1962), *The Truth About Spring* (1965), and *Shalako* (1968).

Robert Farnon

Farnon made his home on Guernsey in the Channel Islands in 1958 but continued to work in London studios. He conducted orchestras for the BBC radio series 'Music All the Way' and 'Farnon in Concert' in the mid-1960s and arranged and conducted music for recordings by many performers, including the pop singers Tony Bennett (several LPs), Lena Horne, Peggy Lee, Frank Sinatra, and Sarah Vaughan, the choral groups Singers Unlimited and the Swingle Singers, and the jazz musicians George Shearing, Ben Webster, and Phil Woods. Under his own name Farnon has made many LPs for Decca and Philips, some devoted to the works of an individual songwriter or songwriting team (eg, *Stephen Foster Melodies*, Decca LF 1034, and *Music of Vincent Youmans*, Decca LF 1052) or to songs popularized by a particular performer (eg, *The Hits of Frank Sinantra*). LPs of some of his film scores also have been released.

The most popular of Farnon's compositions have been his orchestral setting of *'À la claire fontaine,' his suite *Canadian Impressions*, his theme for the BBC-TV series 'Colditz' (for which he won a 1972 Novello Award), and his shorter pieces *How Beautiful Is Night*, *Jumping Bean*, *Manhattan Playboy*, *On the Sea Shore* (Novello Award 1960), *Peanut Polka*, *Portrait of a Flirt*, *A Star Is Born*, and *Westminster Waltz* (Novello Award 1956). Some of his melodies have been given lyrics by Milton Raskin. Farnon composed *Pleasure of Your Company* for Oscar *Peterson, *Scherzo* for trumpet and orchestra (recorded by the *CBC Winnipeg Orchestra), *Rhapsody* for violin and orchestra (recorded by Steven *Staryk), *Prelude and Dance* for harmonica and orchestra (written for and recorded by Tommy *Reilly), and *Saxophone Triparti* (premiered by the Canadian-born saxophonist Bob Burns with the London Philharmonic Orchestra). Much of his music has been published by Chappell. Farnon is a member of CAPAC.

Farnon has returned to Canada for CBC appearances in 1961 (the TV program 'Music Makers') and 1969 (the TV special 'The Music of Robert Farnon' shown first in 1970 and again in 1975 and 1976) and for a concert in 1969 shared with Vera Lynn at *Maple Leaf Gardens in Toronto. The Robert Farnon Appreciation Society, founded in England in 1956 to 'further the interests of all good light music in general, and the work of Robert Farnon in particular,' publishes the journal *Journey into Melody* and in 1977 issued a 66-page Farnon discography.

Farnon's brothers Dennis and Brian also have had careers in film composing. Dennis moved to Hollywood in 1951, wrote music for such cartoon characters as 'Mr Magoo' and 'Bullwinkle,' and made several LPs for RCA Victor. He later worked in London and by 1964 had moved to Portugal, where he still lived in the late 1970s. Brian (Bryan) also worked in Hollywood for TV shows before taking a position as music director at Harrah's Club in Lake Tahoe, Nev.

BIBLIOGRAPHY
'Aims to glorify beauty of Canada in his music,' Toronto *Evening Telegram*, 2 May 1942
Graham, June. 'From Happy Gang to Guernsey,' *CanComp*, 44, Nov 1969
Heward, Burt. 'Home for a visit, Robert Farnon talks of patriotism,' *CanComp*, 63, Oct 1971
McCullough, Colin. 'Mood music man Robert Farnon plays serious stuff too these days,' Toronto *Globe and Mail*, 2 Jun 1973
Lees, Gene. 'Canada's forgotten musician,' *Stereo Guide*, vol 3, Fall 1974 (BJE)

FASSIO, Angelo. Violinist, conductor, publisher, composer, b St-Étienne, France, 14 Jan 1888, d Lachute, Que, 1 Aug 1956. He studied violin in Paris with Georges Latour and in Berlin with Heinrich Voss and theory in Barcelona with Nicola de Castro. He was a member of the Cirque d'hiver orchestre in Paris and a conductor in Spain before going to New York with a German opera troupe. In New York he was conductor at the Academy of Music and an instrumentalist at the Capital Theater.

By 1918 some of Fassio's compositions had been published in *Le Passe-Temps* as had his articles on violin technique, but he does not appear to have settled in Canada before the early 1930s. He published the *Musical Review of Canada* October 1933–July 1934 in Lachute and about this time founded two publishing houses, Parnasse musical and Éditions A. Fassio. In 1936 he became director of the Rex cinema band and the 2nd Artillery Regiment Band of Montreal.

Fassio's compositions encompass works for concert band, pieces for violin and piano, and some songs, including 'Le Fort de Chambly' with lyrics by Benjamin Sulte. Several were published in *Le Passe-Temps*.

Éditions A. Fassio published works by *Champagne (*Danse villageoise*) and Alfred (Hilaire-Marie) *Tardif (*Triptyque marial*) as well as others by Maurice Boivin and Dantès Belleau. Parnasse musical published works by Giuseppe *Agostini, Louis Bédard, Félix-R. *Bertrand, Eugène Caron, J.-J. *Gagnier, André *Mathieu, Séverin *Moisse, and others. Fassio also published some anthologies, including *French Folk Songs* (1932), *Germania Album* (1934), *Hungaria Album*

(1936), and *Neapolitan Memories* (1938), which were listed in the catalogue of Edward B. Marks, New York. Parnasse musical also published *Chansons de noces* in the mid-1940s.

After Fassio's death, the assets of these two publishing houses were acquired by BMI Canada. *Berandol then took over the rights for serious music, and Quality Music of Toronto those for light music. GP

Fédération des associations des musiciens éducateurs du Québec. See FAMEQ.

Fédération des associations musicales du Québec (FAMQ). Organization established 1972 and comprising the Quebec associations of bugle, drum, and trumpet bands as well as of majorettes of Quebec. It is subsidized by the Quebec High Commission for Youth, Recreation and Sports. In 1950 a number of schools set up bugle bands patterned on those in the army and thus spearheaded a popular movement. Next, bands began to be formed in the Patronages or 'Patro' (drop-in centres for adolescents) run by the religious community of St-Vincent-de-Paul and soon spread throughout the province. In 1951 a drum and bugle band from Preston (later Cambridge), Ont, the Scouts, created a sensation at a concert in Shawinigan featuring 52 brass bands. The Laval Patro's Clique Alouette, established in 1952, became the first drum and bugle band of this type in Quebec. Others followed and ca 1956–8 the first association of Quebec drum and bugle bands, with Gérard Filion as president, was established in Shawinigan. The Quebec section of the CBA was formed at another competition and lasted several years; among its members were The Emperors, The Gladiators, and the Verdun Olympics. Subsequently an all-girls section was formed in Drummondville. In 1968 the mixed bands, the girls section, and the Assn of Trumpet Bands merged to form the Assn musicale du Québec, which was active until 1972.

The FAMQ, with which eight regional associations were affiliated by 1978, represented about a hundred bands. Adolescents (boys and girls between 9 and 21) at that time made up about 65 per cent of the 12,000 members, recruited through variety concerts presented in the municipalities and schools as well as through the efforts of local newspapers. A monthly review, *Marche et Manoeuvres*, has been distributed throughout Quebec with a circulation in the thousands beginning in 1975. Each year during July and August competitions are held between the different bands of Quebec, as well as those of Ontario and the USA. Among the mixed bands are the Offensive Lion de Jonquière, the Alliance Bois-des-Filion-Terrebonne, and the Troubadours de Victoriaville, who won the 1978 provincial championship in Rimouski. Also that year the Châtelaines de Laval won the girls' world bugle band championship in Denver, Col. ST

Fédération des harmonies du Québec. The name adopted in 1979 by the Confédération des harmonies-fanfares du Québec which encompassed after 1968 both the Association and the Fédération des fanfares amateurs du Québec. Lorenzo Perron of Arvida (Chicoutimi) was the first president after the 1968 merger and was succeeded by John Courtemanche of Marieville. In 1978 the number of amateur musicians playing in the federation's 43 concert bands was estimated at 6000 and included both secondary school bands and semi-professional adult bands. The federation became affiliated to the Confédération des loisirs du Québec and established an office in Montreal.

Little is known of the Fédération des fanfares amateurs du Québec except that it was an independent provincial organization of bands of the province's rural communities.

The Association des fanfares amateurs de la province de Québec grew out of the 50th anniversary of the Union musicale de Trois-Rivières in 1927. Many Quebec concert bands attended the festivities, and a few months later delegates from several bands founded the association. Bands from Trois-Rivières, St-Jean, St-Hyacinthe, Joliette, Drummondville, and Sherbrooke took part in a festival first held in Sherbrooke in 1929. Festivals were held annually thereafter, except during the first three years of World War II. After that hiatus municipalities encouraged their brass bands to resume participation in important local events. Competitions for school bands began in Thetford Mines in 1953 with five groups entered. The student competitions later expanded, adding wind ensembles (three to nine performers, junior and senior groups) and small dance orchestras (10 to 15 musicians) to the solo performer and brass band classifications.

The 1973 Festival scolaire brought to Sorel some 20 concert bands from all over Quebec. Trophies were awarded to the winners in all categories and bursaries were granted for studies at the *JMC Orford Art Centre and the summer camp of the Asbestos Concert Band. Two of the federation's member-bands won eight bursaries at the *CNE, Toronto, in 1978. ST

Federation of Canadian Music Festivals. Winnipeg-based umbrella organization designed to develop the competition festival movement in Canada. Established by George S. *Mathieson, the federation first convened 2 Jan 1926 when representatives of festivals of the four western provinces met in Calgary. Meetings continued annually with only occasional representation from Quebec and northwestern Ontario until 1945. In 1946 eastern Canadian festivals were invited to join.

Initially an informal organization, the FCMF was constituted in 1949. Member festivals (19 in 1950, 39 in 1970) belonged as individuals to the federation until 1971, when provincial chapters were created. By 1980 225 festivals were represented. Annual conferences are held in different cities across Canada, and the resulting discussions and decisions are published in the annual *Digest Report* (Winnipeg 1953–). From its inception the federation has provided its affiliated festivals with adjudicators, thereby ensuring a consistent standard across Canada. In addition it has supervised the awarding of the George S. Mathieson and City of Lincoln trophies and has been the organizing body for the *National Competitive Festial of Music.

Mathieson served as secretary until 1949. His duties were assumed at that time by Richard W. *Cooke (secretary-treasurer) and Reg *Hugo, the first (1949–64) of a succession of presidents which included E.G. Pridham 1964–8, Gordon *Hancock 1968–70, D. Crawford Smyth 1970–2, W.D. Goodfellow 1972–4, Mrs. George Crittall 1974–7, Lieut.-Col Clifford *Hunt 1977–8, and Fred English 1978–80, succeeded by Robert R. Publow in 1980. The federation is affiliated with the British Federation of Music Festivals and the*CMCouncil. (RC)

FELDBRILL, Victor. Conductor, violinist, b Toronto 4 Apr 1924; Artist Diploma (Toronto) 1949, hon FRHCM 1978. The son of Polish-Jewish immigrants, he studied violin privately 1936–43 with Sigmund Steinberg, theory in 1939 with John *Weinzweig, and conducting 1942–3 with Ettore *Mazzoleni at the*TCM. He was conductor 1942–3 of the U of Toronto SO and made his *TSO conducting debut 30 Mar 1943 in a performance of Strauss' waltz *Artist's Life*. While serving with the RCN (1943–5, as a violinist in *'Meet the Navy*), he was stationed in London, where he studied harmony and composition with Herbert Howells at the RCM and conducting with Ernest Read at the RAM. Upon his return to Canada he held the positions of concertmaster and assistant conductor 1945–9 of the RCMT SO and Opera Company and studied violin 1946–9 with Kathleen *Parlow. During these years he also continued conducting studies, at Tanglewood (summer 1947) and with Pierre Monteux in Maine (summers 1949 and 1950). He was a first violin 1949–56 with the TSO and 1952–6 with the *CBC SO, which he also guest-conducted 19 times. He founded the Canadian Chamber Players in 1952 and conducted them for several seasons in *Hart House Sunday concerts and elsewhere. During the 1950s he also conducted for Ontario School Broadcasts ('Music for Young Folk' ca 1952–7) and National School Broadcasts ('Music in the Making' 1953) and freelanced as a violinist and as a conductor for many other CBC radio and TV programs.

Victor Feldbrill

Feldbrill studied conducting with Willem van Otterloo in Hilversum and with Meinhard von Zallinger in Salzburg during the summer of 1956 and was assistant conductor of the TSO 1956–7. In 1958 he conducted the *Hart House Orchestra at the Brussels World's Fair and became the conductor of the *Winnipeg SO, a position he retained until 1968. During his years with this orchestra he expanded its series to include pop and youth concerts and initiated visits to Manitoba communities such as Brandon, Dauphin, and Vernon and to northern US border towns. In 1964 the orchestra and its conductor received an award from the Concert Artists Guild of the USA for their support and guidance of young musicians.

Feldbrill conducted at the *International Conference of Composers at Stratford in 1960 and at the *Vancouver International Festival in 1961. He has been the resident conductor for sessions of the *NYO in 1960, 1961, 1962, 1964, 1969, and 1975. He visited the USSR in 1963 as part of an exchange program and led orchestras in Ukraine – Lvov, Kiev, Odessa, and Zaparozhye. Invited to return during the 1966–7 season he conducted in the Soviet cities of Baku, Minsk, and Tbilisi. After 1960 he has appeared often as guest conductor for the BBC. He spent three months in 1979 as the first Canadian guest conductor at the Tokyo University of the Arts.

In 1968 Feldbrill joined the staff ot the *U of Toronto, assuming duties as conductor of the U of Toronto SO in 1968, special lecturer in 1969, and conductor-in-residence in 1972, also instituting the conductors' workshop there in 1969. He was the TS's director of youth programming 1968–78, that orchestra's resident conductor 1973–7, and the conductor and music director of the TS Youth Orchestra 1974–8. He also began working with youth orchestras at the *Banff SFA in 1975, conducting the Canadian Chamber Orchestra and two sessions of the Canadian Festival of Youth Orchestras. He was appointed acting music director of the *London (Ont) SO for the 1979–80 season.

Feldbrill has guest-conducted CBC orchestras in Vancouver, Edmonton, Winnipeg, and Montreal, and for CBC TV opera productions such as Pergolesi's *La Serva Padrona*, Walton's *The Bear*, and *Ridout's *The Lost Child*. He has appeared with the *Atlantic SO, the *Calgary Philharmonic, the *Edmonton, *Montreal, *Quebec, *Regina, and *Saskatoon SOs, and the *NACO. He has conducted many times for the *COC, notable assignments being the premieres of *Somers' **Louis Riel* in 1967 (and each subsequent performance of the opera to the time of this writing) and *Wilson's *Heloise and Abelard* in 1973. He conducted the *Royal Cons Opera School production of Humphrey Searle's *Hamlet* in 1969.

Recognized as a champion of Canadian music, throughout his career Feldbrill has made a point of including at least one Canadian work in every concert he has conducted. William *Littler, in the *Toronto Star*, 12 Mar 1973, wrote: 'If Victor Feldbrill didn't exist, it is entirely possible that Toronto's musical community would have to invent him...He has made himself an indispensable cog in the city's musical machinery, and it's time we recognized that without him, the machine would run much less efficiently.' In 1967 the *CLComp awarded him the first *Canada Music Citation, and in 1978 the City of Tokyo presented him with a medal in recognition of his services to music and to youth.

The following list gives composers, titles, and years of premiere of Canadian works first conducted by Victor Feldbrill:

Adaskin *Grant, Warden of the Plains* 1967
Archer *Concerto No. 1* for piano and orchestra 1958
Bales *Concerto* for organ and orchestra 1959
Beckwith *Music for Dancing* (orchestral version) 1950
– *All the Bees and All the Keys* 1973
Davies *Variations* 1967
– *From Harmony* 1968
Dolin *Drakkar* 1973
– *Concerto* for piano and orchestra 1975
Eckhardt-Gramatté *Concerto for Orchestra* 1961
Fiala *Eulogy* 1966
Freedman *5 Pieces for String Quartet* 1949 (Feldbrill 2nd vn)
– *Divertimento* for oboe and strings 1949
– *Tableau* 1952 (English premiere 1960)
– *5 Pieces for String Orchestra* 1953
– *Chaconne* 1964
– *March?* 1971
– *Preludes for Orchestra* 1971
Greenberg, Lionel *Prelude and Fugue* 1965
Henninger *Catena* (1st Canadian performance) 1971
Karam *Poem for Strings* 1949
Klein *Fanfares for Orchestra* 1978
Morawetz *Concerto* for brass quintet and orchestra 1968
– *A Child's Garden of Verses* 1973
Naylor *Variations for Small Orchestra* 1961
Pentland *Concerto* for piano and orchestra 1958
– *Symphony No. 4* 1960
– *Ciné-Scene I* 1974
Pépin *Nombres* for two pianos and orchestra 1963
Prévost *Chorégraphie I* 1975
Ridout *The Ascension (Cantiones mysticae No. 2)* 1962
– *In Memoriam Anne Frank* 1965
– *Suite* from *La Prima Ballerina* 1971
– *The Lost Child* 1975
Schafer *Canzoni for Prisoners* 1963
– *No Longer than 10 Minutes* 1971
– *Divan i Shams i Tabriz* 1972
Sherman, Norman *Sinfonia Concertante* for bassoon and strings 1961
Somers *Symphony No. 1* 1953
– *The Homeless Ones* 1956
– *Second Piano Concerto* 1956 (also first concert performance 1978)
– *Faces of Canada* 1956
– *The Fool* 1956
– *Symphony* for woodwinds, brass, and percussion 1967
– *Louis Riel* 1967
– *Improvisation* 1968
– *Enkidu* 1977
– *The Garden and the Cage* 1979
Surdin *Eine kleine Hammer-Klapper-Musik* 1976
Symonds *Concerto Grosso* for jazz quintet and symphony orchestra 1957
– *Nameless Hour* 1966
– *Democratic Concerto* 1967
Weinzweig *Rhapsody for Orchestra* 1957
– *Concerto* for piano and orchestra 1966
– *Dummiyah / Silence* 1969
Wilson *Heloise and Abelard* 1973

WRITINGS

The Widow's irresistable [sic] appeal,' OpCan, Fall 1973

DISCOGRAPHY

Heritage: Canadian Folk-Inspired Compositions: Jones – Champagne – Chotem – Weinzweig – MacMillan – Cable – Adaskin. Toronto Philharmonia. 1967. Dom S-1372

Somers *Symphony* for winds, brass, and percussion. CBC Wind Symphony. 1967. CBC SM-134

Spohr *Overture to 'Faust'* – Bruch *Concerto, Op 58*. Pratz vn, CBC Festival O. 1976. CBC SM-329

Straughan *Enfilony*. Luxembourg Radio O. 1977. Sun-Owl Productions SN-001

See also Discographies for CBC SO; *The Fool*; TS; Winnipeg SO.

BIBLIOGRAPHY

'Bow or baton – Feldbrill now has the final answer,' *CBC Times*, 4–10 May 1958
'The Winnipeg Symphony Orchestra and conductor Victor Feldbrill,' *Sharps and Flats*, vol 5, Apr 1965
'More Canadian works than all others together,' *CanComp*, 5 Jan 1966
Littler, William. 'He's a conductor without an orchestra but still Victor Feldbrill's a happy man,' *Toronto Daily Star*, 25 Apr 1970
Samson, Marc. 'Deux priorités: la musique contemporaine et les jeunes,' Quebec City *Le Soleil*, 3 Apr 1971
Fraser, John. 'Feldbrill: another fade-out in store for the TS's prophet without honor?' Toronto *Globe and Mail*, 3 May 1975 (FH, PW)

FENWICK. 1 / G. Roy and 2 / John, his son, both musicians.

1 **G.** (George) **Roy**. Educator, writer, adjudicator, broadcaster, b Hamilton, Ont, 11 May 1889, d Ottawa 8 Jul 1970; LTCM 1911, B MUS (Toronto) 1927, D MUS (Montreal) 1950. His mother was Maggie Barr, a Scottish soprano. After studies at the Hamilton Cons he became supervisor of music for Hamilton public schools in 1922 and was supervisor and later director of music 1935–59 for the Ontario Dept of Education. Leslie *Bell said of him, 'His greatest achievement has been the musical development of the rural school' (*Toronto Daily Star*, 25 Jul 1959). Fenwick's school broadcasts, 'Music for Young Folk,' were popular for 18 years – 1946–64 – and his competition adjudications were considered kind and fair. He served 1934–5 as president of the music section of the Ontario Educational Assn (see OMEA), 1959–60 as first president of the *CMEA, and 1960–1 as first president of the *Canadian Music Festival Adjudicators' Assn. He represented music graduates 1948–60 on the Senate of the U of Toronto. After retirement he served 1964–70 on a committee for the revision of the Presbyterian *Book of Praise*. His memoirs, *Singers upon Earth*, were published in Toronto in 1961.

See also School music; School music broadcasts.

WRITINGS

– ed. *Hymns for Schools* (Toronto 1935, 1942)
– et al. *High Road of Song*, 3 vols (Toronto 1943)
– and Gibbon, J.M. *Songs of the Commonwealth* (Toronto 1945)
– ed. *Carols of Christmas* (Toronto 1946)
– *The Function of Music in Education: incorporating a History of School Music in Ontario* (Toronto 1951)
– ed *The New High Road Music Series*, 8 vols (Toronto 1954–60)
– et al. *Let's Explore Music*, 13 vols (Toronto 1954–63)
'Music in the Schools,' *Music in Canada*
'The luxury of looking back,' *CME*, vol 8, Jan–Feb 1966
– ed. *Music for Young Canada*, vols 3–8 (Toronto 1967, 1968)

2 (Edward) **John**. Conductor, composer, arranger, b Hamilton, Ont, 1 Aug 1932; B MUS (Toronto) 1954, M MUS (Toronto) 1956. His teachers at the *U of Toronto included Oskar *Morawetz and John *Weinzweig (composition), Boyd *Neel (conducting), and Weldon *Kilburn (piano, organ). While teaching 1956–9 at the U of Toronto he was a CBC TV arranger 1956–8 and music director 1958–61 for Music Fair in Toronto and Melody Fair in Buffalo, two summer theatres-in-the-round. He also served 1959, 1961–5 and 1967 as music director for **Spring Thaw*. Living in Halifax in the mid-1960s he founded and conducted the Atlantic Chamber Orchestra and conducted the *Halifax SO 1964–7 and the CBC Halifax Orchestra 1965–7. He conducted *COC touring productions 1967–74 of *Don Pasquale*, *The Barber of Seville*, *Orpheus in the Underworld*, and *Così fan tutte*. In 1964 he became music co-ordinator for the *Charlottetown Festival, and later he was named music director. In addition to his festival duties he has been music production consultant to Les Feux-Follets, the Royal Winnipeg Ballet, and other companies. As music director and composer 1958–64 for the Crest Theatre Foundation, Toronto, and 1963–7 for the Neptune Theatre, Halifax, he has written incidental music for over 30 stage plays. He also has been an orchestrator for CBC TV productions by Norman *Campbell and others. In addition to the musical play **Johnny Belinda* he has composed a symphony (1955) and various short orchestral and choral pieces.

BIBLIOGRAPHY

Champagne, Jane. 'John Fenwick, master of music,' *CanComp*, 125, Nov 1977 1 / (WL), 2 / (SS)

FENYVES, Lorand. Violinist, teacher, b Budapest 20 Feb 1918, naturalized Canadian 1971. He studied at the Franz Liszt Academy in Budapest, where his teachers included Oscar Studer, Jenö Hubay, Leo Weiner, Imre Waldbauer, and Zoltán Kodály. In 1934 he earned the artist's and teacher's diploma, won the Hubay Prize, and began his career with a tour of Europe and the premiere of Felix Weingartner's *Concerto* in Budapest and Vienna, with the composer conducting. At the suggestion of Bronislaw Huberman, Fenyves emigrated to Palestine in 1936 and became concertmaster of the new Palestine SO (later the Israel philharmonic). There he also helped found the Israel Cons and Academy of Music in 1940. In

Tel Aviv he founded the Fenyves Quartet (1940–56) and helped found the Israel String Quartet in 1948. He moved to Geneva in 1957 as concertmaster of the Orchestre de la Suisse romande and teacher at the Geneva Cons. He came to Canada in 1965 as string coach at the *JMC Orford Art Centre. It was there that he coached a student group destined to become the *Orford String Quartet (the violins of which – Andrew *Dawes and Kenneth Perkins – had been pupils of his in Geneva). In 1966 he joined the Faculty of Music, *U of Toronto, where he continued coaching the Orford Quartet. He also became teacher and coach with the JM World Orchestra, the *NYO, and the *Banff SFA. Fenyves has performed extensively in Europe and North America, as soloist with major orchestras and with such recital partners as Béla Siki, György Sebök, Menahem Pressler, Anton *Kuerti, and Pierre *Souvairan. His pupils have included Adele *Armin, Otto *Armin, and Victor Martin. Many others play in major Canadian orchestras.

DISCOGRAPHY

Adaskin – Bartók – Stravinsky. Souvairan pf. 1973. CBC SM-211

Bartók *Contrasts*. Gugulz cl, Rev pf. Guilde internationale du disque SMS 2491

– *44 Duos for Two Violins*. Martin vn. Ensayo ENY-26/(1973) MHS 1722

– *Deux Portraits*. O de la Suisse romande, Ansermet cond. Lon CS-6407

– *Rhapsody No. 2; Sonata No. 1*. Kuerti pf. 1969. CBC SM-116

– *Sonata No. 2; Rumanian Folk Dances*. Siki pf. 1967. CBC SM-44

– *Sonata* for unaccompanied vn. CBC SM-26

Beethoven *Sonatas No. 6, 9*. Kuerti pf. Victor LSC-3146

Glick *Suite hébraïque No. 2*. Orloff vc, N. Glick cl, D.S. Glick pf, Helmer va. 1972. RCI 389

Rimsky-Korsakov *Scheherazade*. O de la Suisse romande, Ansermet cond. Lon CS-6212/M67076 /M10076

– *Scheherazade*. Vienna Festival O, Van Otterloo cond. (1972). Guilde internationale du disque SMS 5202

The Violin and Piano Sonatas: Schumann. Kuerti pf. 1971. CBC SM-169/Select CC-15.074

The Virtuoso Oboe: Bach *Concerto in C Minor*. Holliger ob, Geneva Baroque O. 1966. Monitor MCS-2088

BIBLIOGRAPHY

Jacobsen, J.B. 'Bird's eye view,' *Music and Musicians*, Nov 1963 (WS)

FERGUSON, Maynard. Trumpeter, flugelhornist, valve trombonist, bandleader, b Verdun (part of Montreal) 4 May 1928. As a child he studied piano and violin (he appeared in a Fox-Movietone short film playing the violin). Taking up the trumpet at nine, he played with the Black Watch Regimental Band. In his teens he played in dance bands led by Stan Wood and Johnny *Holmes (his brother Percy, a baritone saxophonist, also played for Holmes) and studied 1943–8 at the *CMM with Bernard Baker. Ferguson was heard frequently on CBC radio and on one occasion played a *Serenade for Trumpet in Jazz* written for him by Morris *Davis. While leading his own band in the Montreal area during the mid-1940s Ferguson came to the attention of US bandleaders. As Paul *Bley recalled (Montreal *Gazette*, 28 Oct 1978), 'Maynard would always open the show, and he played three octaves higher on trumpet than anyone else, and you ought to have seen the jaws drop on the visiting musicians.' Ferguson went to the USA in 1948 and worked in the big bands of Boyd Raeburn, Jimmy Dorsey, and Charlie Barnet until 1950. It was during his term 1950-3 with Stan Kenton that he first received public acclaim, winning the *Down Beat* readers' polls for trumpet in 1950, 1951, and 1952. He made his first records in 1950, for Capitol, leading the Kenton band of the day. After playing 1953–6 in Hollywood studio orchestras under contract to Paramount and recording with small groups (his own and others), he formed the Birdland Dreamland Band to perform at the New York jazz club Birdland. This was the first of several 'small' big bands (12 or 13 musicians) with which Ferguson toured until 1965, appearing at festivals and in clubs and concerts. He then turned to a smaller ensemble – though he performed and recorded at *Expo 67 with a big band and a sextet, both comprising Montreal musicians. After a year in India studying meditation and lecturing on music, he settled in 1968 in England. It was with a 17-piece English band, which combined the orchestral conventions of jazz and the rhythmic vigour of rock, that he regained and even surpassed his former popularity. The band made its North American debut in 1971. With New York as his home base after 1973, Ferguson gradually replaced the English musicians with young US players, reducing the band again to 13. His recording of 'Gonna Fly Now,' the theme from the film *Rocky*, was a major hit single 1977–8; it was followed by a second lesser hit in 1978, the theme from the movie *Battlestar Galactica*.

Frequent appearances in Canada have been a part of Ferguson's extensive touring activities. He performed on such CBC TV shows as 'Parade' and 'In the Mood' and, with his band, has played at the *Stratford Festival (1958), in many concert halls (*Massey Hall, *PDA, etc), and at the *Canadian Stage Band Festival. He also played solo trumpet in the opening ceremonies of the 1976 Olympics in Montreal. Several Canadians have been members of Ferguson's bands, eg, the singer Anne Marie *Moss, the tenor saxophonist Georgie Auld, and the trombonists Rob *McConnell and Phil Gray; and Kenny*Wheeler composed and arranged for his English band.

While Ferguson's virtuosity in the extreme upper registers of the trumpet (extending with ease to double-high 'C') and the au courant style his band has adopted have taken his popularity beyond the jazz world, they have brought him a certain amount of criticism. His tendency towards exhibitionism – his grandstanding high notes and his frequent choice of an operatic aria as an encore – has led some critics to dismiss him as a mere showman. However, much of his work in the small-group context reveals a mature improviser whose high-note facility becomes a well-integrated aspect of an expressive and lyrical style. A natural leader, Ferguson has the ability to form and mould an ensemble of young musicians, as he has proven several times, and to infuse it with his own considerable energy and enthusiasm.

Ferguson has played trumpet, flugelhorn, valve trombone, bass trombone, baritone horn, french horn, and two hybrid brass instruments – the Firebird (a combination slide and valve trumpet) and the Superbone (a combination slide and valve trombone) – which he designed for the US company Holton-Leblanc.

DISCOGRAPHY

Jam Session. 1954. EmArcy MG36009/Trip TLP-5525

Hollywood Party. 1954. EmArcy MG36046

Dimensions. 1954, 1955. EmArcy MG36044/Trip TLP-5507

Octet. Includes Auld ten sax. 1955. EmArcy MG36021

Around the Horn. 1955, 1956. EmArcy MG36076/Trip TLP-5558

Birdland Dreamband. 1956. Vik LX-1070

Birdland Dreamband, vol 2. 1956. Vik LX-1077

Boy with Lots of Brass. 1957. EmArcy MG36114

Message from Newport. 1958. Rou S52012

Swingin' My Way through College. 1958. Rou S2508

Message from Birdland. 1959. Rou S52027

Maynard Ferguson Plays Jazz for Dancing. Includes Moss v. 1959, 1960. Rou S52038

Newport Suite. 1960. Rou S52047. Reissued with *Message from Newport* on 2-Rou RE-116

Let's Face the Music and Dance. 1960. Rou S52055

Maynard '61. 1960 or 1961. Rou S52064

'Straightaway' Jazz Themes. 1961. Rou S52076

Maynard '62. 1962. Rou S52083

Si! Si! M.F. 1962. Rou S52084. Reissued with *Maynard '61* on 2-Rou RE-112

Maynard '63. 1963. Rou S52090

Message from Maynard. 1963. Rou S52101

Maynard '64. 1963. Rou S52107

The New Sounds of Maynard Ferguson. 1963. Cameo S-1046

Come Blow Your Horn. 1963. Cameo S-1066

Colour Him Wild. Includes McConnell trb. 1964. Mainstream M56031. Reissued as *Dues*. Mainstream MRL 359

Blues Roar. 1965. Mainstream M56045. Reissued as *Screamin' Blues*. Mainstream MRL 316

The Maynard Ferguson Sextet. 1965. Mainstream M56060. Reissued as *Six by Six*. Mainstream MRL 372

Ridin' High. 1967. Enterprise S13-101. Also released as *Freaky*. Atlantic 264 4008

Maynard Ferguson Sextet. With John Christie alto sax, *Barley ten sax, *Maiste pf, Fasano db, Page drums. 1967. RCI 264

Maynard Ferguson and His Orchestra. Includes Danovitch alto sax, Barley and *Ayoub ten sax, *Landry vib, *Romandini guit, Maiste pf. 1967. RCI 265

Maynard and Gustav (Brom). 1968. Supraphon 115 0716

Maynard '69. 1969. Prestige 7636. Also released as *Trumpet Rhapsody*. BASF MB 20662

The Ballad Style of Maynard Ferguson. 1968. CBS 63514

M.F. Horn. 1970. Col SC 30466

Maynard Ferguson. 1971. Col SC 31117

M.F. Horn II. 1972. Col KC 31709. Reissued with *M.F. Horn on 2-Col CG-33660*

M.F. Horn III. 1973. Col KC 32403

M.F. Horn IV and V: Live at Jimmy's. 1973. Col KG 32732

Chameleon. 1974. Col KC 33007

Primal Scream. 1975. Col PC 33953

Conquistador. 1976. Col PC 34457

New Vintage. 1977. Col JC 34971

Carnival. 1978. Col JC 35480

In addition to giving specific details about LPs listed above (titles, personnel, exact date and place of recording, reissues), Edwin Harkins' *Maynard Ferguson: A Discography* (self-published, San Diego 1976) lists Ferguson's recordings with Georgie Auld, the Axidentals, Charlie Barnet (some 60 titles issued over 16 LPs), Louis Bellson, Milt Bernhart, Elmer Bernstein, Buddy Bregman, Sascha Burland, Ike Carpenter, June Christy, Chris Conner, Jimmy Dorsey, Francis Faye, Russ Garcia, Bob Keene, Stan Kenton (some 140 titles 1950–6, about 100 later issued over 18 LPs by the Creative World of Stan Stan Kenton), Sal Salvador, Bud Shank, Leith Stevens, Dinah Washington, and Ben Webster. Also listed are the titles of 46 Paramount film soundtracks on which Ferguson played 1953–6.

BIBLIOGRAPHY

Feather, Leonard. 'Lots of brass,' *Down Beat*, vol 25, 6 Feb 1958

Hoefer, G., and Lees, Gene. 'The man who broke the band barrier,' *Down Beat*, vol 26, 1 Oct 1959

Gitler, Ira. 'Maynard Ferguson: a new appraisal,' *Down Beat*, vol 27, 29 Sep 1960

Wong, Herb. 'Maynard Ferguson: "out of the exosphere and back on the scene",' *Down Beat*, vol 40, 8 Nov 1973

Smith, Arnold Jay. 'Maynard Ferguson: conquistador of double high C,' *Down Beat*, vol 44, 6 Oct 1977

Yanow, Scott. 'Record Review Interview: Maynard Ferguson,' *Record Review Magazine*, Aug 1979 MM

FERLAND, (Joseph Pierre) Armand. Conductor, clarinetist, teacher, adjudicator, b St Boniface, Man, 31 Mar 1926; BA (Manitoba) 1947, LRAM 1953, LGSM 1954, B MUS (Laval) 1965, L MUS (Laval) 1968. He began violin lessons at nine with John *Waterhouse in Winnipeg and later took up clarinet. He studied 1947–51 at the *CMM and 1951–4 in London at the RMSM (Kneller Hall), graduating in 1954. He was music director 1955–67 for the Canadian army, with appointments in Winnipeg and Quebec City. As music director 1961–5 of the famous *Royal 22nd Regiment Band (Van Doos) in Quebec City, he organized and co-directed a successful series of concerts in 1961 at the Citadel and another in 1963 at the *PDA in Montreal and conducted the recordings *The Van Doos – Band of the Royal 22nd Regiment / Je me souviens* (1964, RCA PCS 1007 / 1006), which include his march *Geneviève*. He was inspector of military bands, eastern region, 1965–8, and music director in 1967 of the Canadian Armed Forces Tattoo which toured Canada. He founded, and 1963–8 performed with, the *Quebec Woodwind Quintet on CBC radio and at *Expo 67. He began teaching clarinet and saxophone at *Laval U in 1968 and also conducted the Laval band and orchestra 1968–76. He has played in the CBC Montreal orchestra and performed as a clarinet soloist with the *Quebec SO. He became president of *CAUSM in 1979. His brother is Marcien *Ferland.

BIBLIOGRAPHY

Falardeau, Victor. *La Musique du Royal 22e Régiment: 50 ans d'histoire 1922–72* (Quebec 1976) (JK)

FERLAND, Jean-Pierre. Singer, songwriter, b Montreal 24 Jun 1934. He was a clerk at CBC Montreal 1954–8, and his colleagues encouraged him to develop his singing talent. After leaving the CBC he soon became known for his work with the Bozos, a group he founded in 1959 with Raymond *Lévesque, Hervé Brousseau, Claude *Léveillée and Clémence *Desrochers. Members of this ad hoc society were all newcomers to the world of Quebec song. That same year Ferland made his TV debut as a singer on 'Music Hall' and then starred with Lise Roy in 'Du Côté de la lune.' With Clémence Desrochers he gave a show that ran for a year at the Anjou Theatre.

In 1962 Ferland's song 'Feuilles de gui' (music by Pierre *Brabant) won the CBC competition 'Chansons sur mesure' and the grand prize at the Gala internationale de la chanson in Brussels. He sang it on an LP (Variétés V-9000) made up of the 12 best Canadian songs from the CBC competition. The song was recorded by the *Alliance chorale canadienne as well as by Fernand Gignac, Margot Lefebvre, and (on the organ) Lucien *Hétu.

Ferland sang in 1962 at the cabaret La Tête de l'art in Paris and was co-host for 'L'Été des Bozos' for CBC. The following year he taped two TV programs for Eurovision and gave a show with Colette Rénard at the Bobino in Paris. He represented Canada in Poland at the third International Song Festival at Sopot and won the prize as best singer at Cracow. He starred in 'Jeunesse oblige' on CBC and toured Quebec in 1964. His career abated somewhat in 1965 even though he won the grand prize in the Festival du disque de Montréal that year.

In 1966 Ferland co-starred with Les Feux-Follets in a gala performance at the *PDA. In 1967 he completed another successful Quebec tour, performed in Ontario, Prince Edward Island, New Brunswick, and Nova Scotia, and sang for a month in Paris (Salle de l'Alliance française) where his reputation was growing. Returning to Montreal in 1968, he was heard at the Comédie-Canadienne and at Man and His World. That year he received several prizes, among them the grand prize of the Festival du disque and the Grand Prix du disque de l'Académie Charles-Cros in Paris for *Jean-Pierre Ferland* (Barclay B 800006). He sang in the MacMillan Theatre, *U of Toronto, at a CBC festival in 1969. His career in Paris continued that year when he performed with Marie Laforêt at the Olympia and at La Tête de l'art. He sang in 1970 at the International Exposition at Osaka and at the PDA in Montreal; on a return appearance the following year at the PDA, he was accompanied by the *MSO. In 1974 he gained considerable success with 'T'es mon amour, t'es ma maîtresse,' recorded with Ginette *Reno.

Another facet of Ferland's talent was revealed in 1976 when he became writer, actor, and musician for the film *Chanson pour Julie*. In the same period he co-starred in 'Show des cinq grands' with Claude Léveillée, Gilles *Vigneault, Robert *Charlebois, and Yvon Deschamps in Quebec City as part of the province's Heritage Week (Semain du patrimoine) and in Montreal for the *St-Jean-Baptiste celebrations. In 1978 he was seen nationally on a CBC TV 'Superspecial' entitled 'Between Chopin and William Tell,' taped four programs for the CBC series 'Faut voir ça,' and toured again in Quebec.

Notable among Ferland's hits have been 'Fleurs de macadam,' 'Le Petit roi,' 'Ste-Adèle P.Q.,' 'Un peu plus haut, un peu plus loin,' 'Je reviens cheznous,' 'Marie-Claire,' and 'Quand on aime on a toujours 20 ans.' Claude Danjean, Franck Dervieux, Gilbert Lacombe, Paul *de Margerie, and Lucien Merer have been among his musical directors.

Ferland's songs, as described by Claude Lacombe in *Ici Radio Canada* (25–31 Mar 1978), 'talk of love and women but also memories, anguish, hopes and dreams, always with the familiar irresistible warmth. He surrenders himself to his audience in a musical show of great quality, charged with emotions that range from tender to tempestuous.'

Ferland has published *Chansons* (Montreal 1969), a volume which includes the texts of 75 of his songs. He is a member of CAPAC.

DISCOGRAPHY

Jean-Pierre chante ses compositions. 1959. Music Hall 33-106
J'estime, j'aime, j'amoure. 1962. Sel SSP-24.090
Rendez-vous à la coda. 1962. Sel SSP 24.085
Jean-Pierre Ferland à Bobino. 1963. Sel M-298.05
M'aimeras-tu ou ne m'aimeras-tu pas. 1964. Sel SSP-24.106
Jean-Pierre Ferland, vol 4. 1965. Sel SSP-24.132
Avant de m'assagir / Les noces d'or / Les journalistes ... 1966. Barclay 45511
Jean-Pierre Ferland, vol 5. 1967. Sel SSP 24.149
Le Disque d'or. Sel S 398.149
Jean-Pierre Ferland. 1968. Barclay B 800006
Un peu plus loin. 1969. Barclay 80050
Jaune. 1970. Barclay 80090
Jean-Pierre Ferland. 1971. 2-Barclay 80114–80115
Les Vierges du Québec. 1973. Jaune JF 7300
Le Showbusiness. 1974. Barclay 80208
Quand on aime on a toujours 20 ans. 1975. 2-Barclay 80228
Les Grands Succès Barclay, vol 5. Barclay 75005
La Pleine Lune. 1977. Telson AE 1510
See also Discography for Chansonniers.

BIBLIOGRAPHY

Rudel-Tessier, J. 'Jean-Pierre Ferland: great Canadian success story,' *CanComp*, 13, Dec 1966
Boucher, Jacqueline. *Jean Pierre Ferland jaune ou...* (Ottawa 1971)
Jasmin, Hélène. 'Interview! Jean-Pierre Ferland,' *CanComp*, 109, Mar 1976 HP

FERLAND, Marcien. Choir conductor, composer, b St Boniface, Man; BA (Manitoba) 1964, MA (Manitoba) 1965, B SC (Manitoba) 1968. Younger brother of Armand, he at first began to learn the violin but at 14 turned to the trumpet, which he studied for three years with Albert Simoens. Self-taught in harmony, orchestration, and piano, he studied instrumentation with Marius *Benoist and singing with Georges Paquin. During this time he was choirmaster in nearby parishes (at the churches of Ste-Famille, La Broquerie, St-Norbert and at St Paul's College, Stony Mountain federal penitentiary, and St Boniface Cathedral.

Ferland conducted various choirs including the Chorale des intrépides of St Boniface, a mixed choir which he founded in 1960 with about 30 members of the Association d'éducation des Canadiens français (later Société franco-manitobaine), and which soon grew to more than 60 singers. It presented on tour (Edmonton, Ottawa, Regina, and Vancouver) a repertoire drawn largely from French-Canadian folklore. It has issued two LPs, *Les Intrépides chantent* (1970, private recording) and *Les Intrépides au Festival du voyageur* (1975, FDV-601). It took part in the 1977 performance in St Boniface of Ferland's *La Basilique de St-Boniface* (1977), a cantata for two choirs, dramatic soprano, and orchestra. Ronald *Gibson reviewed it in the *Winnipeg Free Press* (22 Nov 1977): 'The writing for orchestra is effective, and the whole work shows much imagination.' The same year Ferland conducted the premiere of Benoist's *Onadéga ou la tragédie du lac des bois*.

In 1970 Ferland was a co-founder of Mélo-Mani, a federation of the French choirs of Manitoba. He taught French 1966–73 at the U of Winnipeg and solfège in various institutions. On a 1977 *Canada Council grant, he instigated music activities in French-speaking communities in the Winnipeg area. His research into Manitoba folk music resulted in the publication of 130 *Chansons à répondre du Manitoba* (Winnipeg 1979).

An active composer, Ferland has written mostly choral and vocal works. In addition to his cantata, there are two motets for mixed choir (with or without accompaniment), some religious pieces, and *Canon des tonalités* (1974). He has assembled several of his songs for voice and piano in *Les Batteux*, a historical operetta (1976). His song 'Oui, je me souviens' (1973) won a prize in a CBC competition for composers. He has written various works for piano, a *Marche triomphale* (1974) for brass quartet, an *Adagio* (1976) for cello and piano, and a *Thrénodie* (1978) for soprano and instrumental ensemble. His *Rhapsodie espagnole* (1975) was performed in 1977 by the *Winnipeg SO under his direction. AP

FERRARI-FONTANA, Edoardo. Tenor, teacher, b Rome 8 Jul 1878, d Toronto 4 Jul 1936. The son of a surgeon, he studied medicine before taking up a consular post in Montevideo. While there, he drifted into singing, winning great success as an operetta baritone 1902–6 in South America and 1906–10 in Italy. His grand opera debut (in Turin, 2 Mar 1910, as Tristan) was followed by appearances in the major houses of France (including the Paris Opéra), Italy (including La Scala), Spain, and South America, singing under the batons of such conductors as Mascagni, Nikisch, Saint-Saëns, Serafin, Toscanini, and Weingartner. A star 1912–14 of Henry Russell's Boston Opera Company, he was heard 1913–15 at the *Metropolitan Opera only as Avito in Montemezzi's *L'Amore dei tre Re*, a role he had sung in the premiere, 10 Apr 1913, at La Scala. Owing to failing health, his post-World War I appearances were few. In his prime, his mellifluous tenor was especially admired in Latin countries in the Italian versions of *Tristan*, *Tannhäuser*, *Die Walküre*, and other Wagner operas. Early in 1926, Ferrari-Fontana and his second wife (his 1912 marriage to the contralto Margarete Matzenauer having ended in divorce in 1917) came to Toronto at the invitation of the *Hambourg Cons. Soon afterwards he opened a voice studio where he taught until shortly before his death. None of his pupils attained international recognition but several – notably Alice *Strong Rourke, Daphne Walker, Randolph Crowe, and William Sheldon – were prominent in the city's musical life during the 1930s and 1940s. Ferrari-Fontana founded the Music and Arts League of Toronto, which flourished ca 1927–36, and presented operatic concerts annually at *Eaton Auditorium or *Hart House. The tenor's recordings are few: six sides for US Columbia in 1915, two for Italian Odeon ca 1915, and two for Edison 1916–19.

BIBLIOGRAPHY
Reade, Robert. 'Ferrari-Fontana – cosmopolite,' *Toronto Star Weekly* (18 Oct 1930)
Music and Arts League of Toronto Year Book, 3 vols held at NL of C (Toronto 1931, 1933, 1935) JBM

Festival Concert Society. A non-profit organization which began sponsoring tours by professional musicians, dancers, and actors in British Columbia in 1961. Founded as the British Columbia branch of the *JMC by J.J. (Joseph Jean) *Johannesen, the society was renamed in 1972. It revived its original affiliation in 1974 but retained its new name and its autonomy. It has been funded publicly and privately and has sponsored more than 600 concerts and workshops annually for young and adult audiences. Johannesen continued as executive director in 1980. George C. Bradley, president 1967–75, was succeeded by Kenneth Gardner in 1975, and Gardner by Roger J. Duncan in 1978.

Festival Ottawa. Known at first (1971–7) as Festival Canada. It became Festival Ottawa in 1978. It was created, under the artistic direction of the *NACO conductor Mario *Bernardi, as the main summer occupant of the *NAC, and as a tourist-season showcase for the NACO and for leading Canadian singers, instrumental musicians, chamber groups, actors, and entertainers. It was also to be a vehicle for acquainting Canadians and visitors to Canada with the country's ability to produce musical and theatrical fare of international standard, in particular opera but also orchestral and chamber concerts, jazz concerts, films, plays, and variety shows. The program annually has contained some 40 such events. The idea for a summer festival in Ottawa is attributed to Vincent *Massey, who in 1952, during his term as governor general, advocated an event international in character yet emphasizing Canada's own cultural achievements. The concept could not be realized, however, until artistic conditions, performance facilities, and economic conditions permitted. The achievement of this happy circumstance was signalled by the opening of the NAC in 1969. Bernardi (still artistic director in 1980 with Andrée Gingras, appointed 1974, as festival administrator) has conducted most of the operas and in choosing them has tried to maintain a balance between repertoire staples and less familiar works. He has included at least one Mozart opera each season (except in 1978): *The Marriage of Figaro* (1971, 1972, 1976), *Così fan tutte* (1972, 1973, 1979), *Don Giovanni* (1973, 1974), *The Abduction from the Seraglio* (1974), and *The Magic Flute* (1975, 1977). The Festival has presented Offenbach's *La Belle Hélène* (1973, 1975, conducted by Pierre *Hétu), Rossini's *Le Comte Ory* (1974, 1976) and *The Barber of Seville* (1978), Verdi's *La Traviata* (1975, 1978), Tchaikovsky's *The Queen of Spades* (1976, 1979), Strauss' *Ariadne auf Naxos* (1977), Donizetti's *Don Pasquale* (1977, conducted by Piero Bellugi), Britten's *A Midsummer Night's Dream* (1978), and Massenet's *Cendrillon* (1979).

Directors have included Anthony Besch, Paul Buissonneau, Jean Gascon, Václav Kašlík, Brian Macdonald, Carlo Maestrini, and Leon Major. Among the singers have been Donald *Bell, Napoléon *Bisson, Colette *Boky, Pierre Charbonneau, Barbara *Collier, Claude *Corbeil, Pierre *Duval, Maureen *Forrester, Judith *Forst, Don *Garrard, Teresa Kubiak, Gabrielle *Lavigne, Louise *Lebrun, Gwenlynn *Little, André *Lortie, Lois *McDonall, Allan *Monk, Cornelis *Opthof, Louis *Quilico, Patricia *Rideout, Joseph *Rouleau, Robert *Savoie, Heather *Thomson, Jon *Vickers, Frederica von Stade, and Delia Wallis. Robert Prévost and Josef Svoboda are among those who have designed sets for the productions.

For chamber music devotees the festival has provided concerts by Canadian and foreign ensembles, including the *Orford String Quartet (which in 1972 premiered Jacques *Hétu's *String Quartet Op 19*, a CBC commission), the *Pierre Bourque Saxophone Quartet, the Fine Arts and Vermeer quartets, the Beaux-Arts Trio, the *SMCQ Ensemble, the *Lyric Arts Trio, and *Canadian Brass. Recitals have been given in 1971 by Pauline *Julien and by Monique *Leyrac, in 1972 by Renée *Claude and by Oscar *Peterson, in 1973 by Van Cliburn and by Galt *MacDermot, in 1976 by Bruno *Laplante, Ronald *Turini, and the duo-pianists Victor *Bouchard and Renée *Morisset, and in 1978 by Donald Bell and Ingrid Haebler. The festival's reputation grew quickly and by the late 1970s Festival Ottawa was attracting thousands of music lovers from Canada and the USA each summer and was stimulating numerous parallel events in the national capital.

BIBLIOGRAPHY
'World Roundup: Canada: Ottawa,' *OpCan*, Summer 1972
Edinborough, Arnold. 'High quality in Ottawa,' *OpCan*, Summer 1974
Woodward, Anthony. 'A short-lived feast of operatic delicacies,' *PfAC*, Fall 1978 DM, KW, PW

Festivals. '[A festival is] first of all a festivity, a celebration, something very special, which emerges from the routine of winter programs and which must create a particular atmosphere, to which will contribute not only the quality of the works performed but also the landscape, the environment of a city, and the musical tradition of a region' (Denis de Rougemont, *Association européenne des festivals de musique*, 1959).

In Canadian musical parlance in the 20th century the term festival has been used to describe two distinct types of event: the opera or concert (classics, jazz, folk, ethnic, or other) festival which aims to provide a feast of performances usually, though not necessarily, by established artists; and the competition and non-competition festivals. In the latter, orchestras, choirs, bands, small ensembles and solos performers – mostly students, amateurs, or school children – assemble either to compete with others of their kind at their level, in graded classes, for adjudications, marks, and trophies, or simply to perform for each other and work together in clinics and workshops under professional guidance. It is the first type (opera or concert) which is treated here. For the other type (competition and non-competition) see Competition festivals; see also Competitions, a guide to *EMC* articles that treat the various aspects of the topic.

1 Pre-1900
2 1900–30
3 1930–50
4 1950–80

1 PRE-1900. The idea of a festival celebrating a season, a composer or group of composers or type of music, or the musical resources of a city or region gained popularity in Canada during the latter half of the 19th century. What may have been the first such festival, however, occured at Quebec in June 1834, when 64 instrumentalists and 111 singers gave 'A Grand Performance of Sacred Music' under the direction of Stephen *Codman. In 1859 the same city witnessed a Handel Festival which included a performance of *Judas Maccabaeus* and was directed by William *Carter. In 1865 in Ottawa Herbert R. Fripp directed a Sacred Music Festival. In May 1877 a three-day Montreal Music Festival featured the first public performance by the *Montreal Philharmonic Society. In 1883 Quebec City was the site of a festival organized by Arthur *Lavigne, a Quebec musician who had participated in Boston musical jubilees in 1869 and 1872. The event's significance went beyond music: at it, for the first time, Quebec citizens witnessed the lighting of a large hall by electricity.

The *St-Jean-Baptiste societies held large and festive musical celebrations in Montreal in 1874 (the 40th anniversary of the society) and in Quebec City in 1880 (when *'O Canada' had its first public performance).

A three-day, five-concert Wagner Festival by the visiting Theodore Thomas Orchestra in Montreal in June 1884 featured excerpts from *Die Walküre, Tannhäuser, Lohengrin*, and *Tristan und Isolde*. The festival, conducted by Thomas and starring Emma Juch, Christine Nilsson, and the noted Bayreuth singers Amalie Materna, Hermann Winkelmann, and Emil Scaria, was a succès d'estime (described in the Montreal *Gazette* as 'the most important event of its kind the country has known up to this time') but a financial disaster.

F.H. *Torrington in 1886 organized the first Toronto Music Festival and was responsible as well for the three-day festival which opened Toronto's *Massey Hall in June 1894. Hamilton, Ont, mounted a Queen's Jubilee Music Festival in 1887 to celebrate Victoria's 50-year reign. A May Festival of concerts by Toronto school choirs and performing groups was initiated in 1886 and became an annual tradition still observed in 1980. (Though a school festival, this also is a true concert festival, neither 'competition' nor 'non-competition' in type.)

Berlin (see Kitchener and Waterloo), Ont, was the site of a Sängerfest as early as 1862, and other Canadian towns and cities with German-Canadian populations also have held *Sängerfeste over the years. During the 1950s these were revived as 'Big Sings.'

2 1900–30. One of Canada's first and most ambitious festivals in the 20th century was the *Cycle of Music Festivals of the Dominion of Canada. Offering mainly British choral and orchestral music, the festival was held from March to May 1903, in most major Canadian centres. It was directed by Sir Alexander Mackenzie and initiated and organized by C.A.E. *Harriss. Harriss was responsible for a Canadian Music Festival in London in 1906; for the Festival of English Cathedral Music, which took place in eastern Canada in 1908 and featured the English organist Sir Frederick Bridge; and for the Musical Festival of the Empire, which toured the world (including Canada) in 1911.

In 1908 Quebec City celebrated its 300th anniversary with a number of festivities, the musical parts of which were directed by Joseph *Vézina. During the same year the *Winnipeg Oratorio Society was founded; it organized, and participated in, Western Canada Musical Festival 1908–24.

In October 1912 the opening of the Mutual Street Arena provided the occasion for the week-long Toronto Musical Festival, featuring Nahan Franko and his orchestra, along with the sopranos Johanna Gadski and Alice Nielsen and the baritone Giuseppe Campanari (all of the *Metropolitan Opera), the coloratura soprano

Marcella Sembrich, the tenor Orville Harrold, and the violinists Albert Spalding and Arturo Tibaldi.

Montreal's annual Music Weeks began ca 1923. The Halifax Philharmonic Society (under Harry *Dean) sponsored spring festivals 1925–31. In 1927 the first of a series of *CPR Festivals was held at Quebec; others took place during the next three years in Banff, Calgary, Regina, Toronto, Vancouver, Victoria, and Winnipeg, and most were devoted to highlighting the ethnic diversity and local cultures of their regions or provinces.

3 1930–50. In 1931 a Bach Festival in Saskatoon featured the organist Lynnwood *Farnam. In 1934 Music Week was an important part of the celebrations marking Toronto's centenary, in which the *Toronto Mendelssohn Choir took part. The 1930s also saw the initiation of the *Montreal Festivals which recurred annually 1936–65. In Ontario the *Waterloo Band Festival (1932–40 and 1946–58) was host to the 1937 Festival of the Empire, which marked the coronation of George VI. In 1938 a Dominion Folk Festival was held at Toronto's *CNE grounds. During the early 1940s the CSM (*MSO) 'Spring Galas' offered Beethoven's nine symphonies, a concert version of *Boris Godunov*, Berlioz' *The Damnation of Faust*, and other such imposing works. London, Ont, held Bach Festivals in 1948 and 1949. In April 1950 Sir Ernest *MacMillan, the Toronto Mendelssohn Choir, and guest artists presented a Bach Festival to mark the bicentenary of the composer's death.

4 1950–80. In the second half of the 20th century Canada experienced an enormous growth in the number and variety of its festivals. The appended chronological list cites many of these but does not claim to be comprehensive.

'Musical May.' Montreal, early 1950s. Organized by *Canadian Concerts & Artists and held at the Montreal *Forum; guests included the Boston SO, London's Festival Ballet, and the Metropolitan Opera.
*Stratford Festival. Begun 1953
*Vancouver International Festival. 1955–68
*Nova Scotia Festival of the Arts. Tatamagouche, later Halifax. Begun 1956
*Miramichi Folk Song Festival. Newcastle, NB. Begun 1958
Saskatoon Summer Festival of Music. 1959. It was organized by Murray *Adaskin and commissioned works by ten Canadian composers (see U of Saskatchewan).
*International Week of Today's Music / La Semaine internationale de musique actuelle. Montreal, 1961
*Mariposa Folk Festival. Orillia, Ont; later Toronto. Begun 1961
Dawson City Gold Rush Festival. 1962. The festival featured Eskimo drum dancing and a musical based on Ben Jonson's *Volpone* by Ring Lardner Jr and Ian McLellan Hunter.
*Shaw Festival. Niagara-on-the-Lake, Ont. Begun 1962
*CBC Summer Festivals. In many Canadian cities. Begun 1962 in Winnipeg
Mosaic, Regina. Begun 1964. Annual multicultural festival featuring performances by ethnic groups
*Charlottetown Festival. Begun 1965
*University of New Brunswick Chamber Music and Jazz Festival. Fredericton. Begun 1966
*Centennial celebrations. Various locations, 1967
World Festival, *Expo 67. Montreal, 1967
*Guelph Spring Festival. Begun 1968
Festival d'été de Québec. Begun 1968. In 1978 the festival celebrated the 370th anniversary of the founding of Quebec City, presenting the premiere of Claude *Léveillée's *Concerto pour Hélène*.
Victoria Fair. Victoria, BC. Begun 1968. Initiated by the *U of Victoria. Workshops, concerts, chamber music
Regina Folk Arts Festival. Begun 1969. Annual festival featuring Saskatchewan performers. Held in 1978 at the *U of Regina
Festival Canada 1971–7; later *Festival Ottawa. Opera and concerts
Peterborough (Ont) Arts and Water Festival. Begun 1971. Programs of jazz, pop, folk, and ethnic music
Northern Lights Festival Boréal, Sudbury, Ont. Begun 1972. Emphasis on Canadian performers from northern Ontario
*Algoma Fall Festival, Sault Ste Marie, Ont. Begun 1973
Winnipeg Folk Festival. Begun 1973. Canadian and international folksingers and groups
Superfrancofête, Quebec City, 1974. Festival of French-speaking youth, featuring Gilles *Vigneault, Félix *Leclerc, Robert *Charlebois, and participants from several other countries
Sheridan Music Festival, Sheridan College, Oakville, Ont. Begun 1974. It has featured opera, musical theatre, concerts, a folk festival, and a commercial composers' symposium.
Festival des Cantons. Sherbrooke and vicinity. Begun 1974. Annual summer festival of folk and traditional music
Atlantic Folk Festival. Locations in the Halifax area. Begun 1975. It features folk music of various styles, including traditional music of the Atlantic region.
Music for a Midsummer's Day, St Raphael West, near Cornwall, Ont. Begun 1975. Guests have included *Canadian Brass, Paul Horn, the *NACO, the New Chamber Orchestra of Toronto, and *Nexus.
North Bay (Ont) Arts Festival. Begun 1975
Spectrum: Festival of the Arts, Sudbury, Ont. Begun 1975
*World Music Week. Various cities, 1975. Held in conjunction with the 16th General Assembly of the International Music Council
Chant'Août. Quebec City, 1975. Festival of Quebec chansonniers
Arts and Culture Festival. Kingston, Ont, 1976. Held in conjunction with the 1976 Summer Olympics
Heritage Festival, Vancouver. Begun in 1976 as the Habitat Festival, in conjunction with the International Habitat Conference. Renamed in 1977 and co-sponsored by the CBC. A performing arts section with the *Vancouver SO has featured Beethoven (1977), Brahms (1978), a festival of BC choirs, a Folk Arts Festival, and performances by the *Vancouver New Music Society, Janina *Fialkowska, Arthur *Ozolins, and Robert *Silverman.
Northstars Festivals. Toronto. Begun 1976. Sponsored and broadcast by CBC radio and organized by Anton *Kuerti. There have been Bach, Mozart, and Schubert festivals. Robert *Aitken, Vladimir Ashkenazy, James *Campbell, Anna *Chornodolska, Andrew Davis, Lorand *Fenyves, Mieczyslaw Horszowski, the Elmer *Iseler Singers, Greta *Kraus, Lois *Marshall, and the Cleveland, Guarneri, *Orford, and Vermeer quartets have been among the participants.
Summerfolk Music and Crafts Festival. Owen Sound, Ont. Begun 1976
Toronto Spring Festival, 'Primavera.' 1977 and 1978. Organized by the counter-tenor Theodore Gentry. In 1978 the festival offered the Canadian premiere performance of Vivaldi's *Juditha Triumphans*.
Festival of the Arts, Edmonton. 1978. In conjunction with the 11th Commonwealth Games
*Alberta Composers' Association. Begun 1979. Festival of Alberta composers
Spring Festival of Baroque Music, Toronto. Begun 1979, an annual festival sponsored by the performing group Tafelmusik
International Gathering of the Clans, Cape Breton, NS. 1979. Festivals of fiddling, piping, dancing, highland games
Alberta. Celebration of the province's 75th anniversary in 1980. Province-wide tours by performing groups; Jazz City – a festival in Edmonton; the Edmonton Folk Music Festival; the *Calgary Philharmonic in residence at the *Banff SFA
Festival '80. Province-wide celebration of Saskatchewan's 75th anniversary. Tours and performances by artists and groups
Festival of the Sound, Parry Sound, Ont. Begun 1980. Two weeks of concerts, master classes, initiated by Anton Kuerti

Many summer schools and camps have presented festivals of concerts and recitals by guests and resident instructors. The Banff SFA (Banff, Alta), *CAMMAC (Lac Macdonald, Que), the *JMC Orford Art Centre (Mount Orford, Que), and the Victoria International Festival (presented by a committee of the *Shawnigan Summer School of the Arts at various locations in Victoria) are among them.

Organizations offering co-ordination, support, and financial assistance to local festivals in Canada have included Festival Ontario, founded by the government of Ontario in 1973 to make the cultural resources of the province available to its communities, and the Société des Festivals populaires du Québec, established in 1978. Annual events under the auspices of members of the society have included the Festival d'été de Lanaudière, the Festival de folklore inter-ethnique de St-Octave-de-l'Avenir, the Festival de la Grange à Claude (St-Frédéric, Beauce-Nord), the Festival international de folklore de Rawdon and the Festival western de St-Tite.

Other folk and ethnic festivals have included Bavaria Days (Biggar, Sask), the Vancouver Folk Music Festival, *Caravan (Toronto), Highland gatherings and games (various locations), All-Newfoundland Folk Festival (St John's), 'Homelands' (Ottawa), Icelandic Festival (Gimli, Man), the International Folk Festival (Red Deer, Alta), Klondike Days (Edmonton), the National Ukrainian Festival (Dauphin, Man), and Winnipeg's Folklorama.

See also Chautauqua; Musicanada.

BIBLIOGRAPHY

'The Toronto musical festival,' *MT*, vol 1, Aug 1877
MacMillan, Sir Ernest. 'Why not Canadian festivals?,' *Sat N*, 4 Oct 1952
Kallmann, Helmut. 'Music festivals in Canada,' *Stratford Festival Program* (Stratford 1955)
Goldschmidt, Nicholas. 'A Salzburg for Canada?' *Food for Thought*, Jan 1957
Kasemets, Udo. 'The Saskatoon summer festival of music, 1959,' *CMJ*, vol 4, Autumn 1959
MacMillan, Sir Ernest. 'Canada's flirtation with festivals,' *OpCan*, May–Jun 1962
Patterson, Tom. 'Dawson City deserves a joyful celebration,' ibid
'Canadian summer festivals,' ibid
'Festival Canada highlights,' *OpCan*, Feb 1967
Meredith, Joan. 'CBC Festival features works by many Canadian composers,' *CanComp*, 61, Jun 1971
Garvie, Peter. 'The virtue of limits,' *CanComp*, 65, Dec 1971
'Summer festivals Canada 1975,' *PfAC*, Summer 1975
Pedneault, Hélène. 'Chant'Août,' *MSc*, 286, Nov–Dec 1975
Littler, William. 'Once a feast, a festival is now fast food to go,' *Toronto Star*, 28 May 1977

Huot, Guy. 'Summer festivals in Canada,' *Mcan*, 32, May 1977
'Heritage Festival – a year of definition,' *VSO*, vol 1, Mar 1978
Huot, Guy. 'The musical delights of summer,' *Mcan*, 35, Apr 1978
Bailey, Bruce. 'Festivals provide refreshing cultural oasis,' Montreal *Gazette*, 5 May 1979
Callingham, Dale. 'Summer of celebration for visitors in four western provinces,' Regina *Leader-Post*, 16 Jun 1979
Dunlop, Marilyn. 'Festival fever grips Ontario small towns,' *Toronto Star*, 19 Jul 1980
Johnston, Nola. 'On festivals,' *Canada Folk Bulletin*, vol 3, Sep–Dec 1980
Levitch, Gerald. 'A little summer music,' Imperial Oil *Review*, vol 64, no. 4, 1980

The Festival Singers of Canada (until 1968 The Festival Singers of Toronto). The first Canadian choir to develop professional status. Founded in 1954 by Elmer *Iseler (with encouragement from the singers Tom Brown, Joanne Eaton, and Gordon *Wry), the 25-voice choir was heard first on CBC radio in a 1955 Good Friday broadcast of Bach's *Christ lag in Todesbanden*. Shortly thereafter, billed as the Festival Chorus, the choir gave three concerts at the 1955 *Stratford Festival, two of them with the *Hart House Orchestra under Boyd *Neel. The first of these, 9 July, offered the premiere of *Willan's *A Song of Welcome*, B58 (commissioned by the festival and with Lois *Marshall as soloist), and Britten's *Hymn to St Cecilia*. The Festival Singers' first Toronto seasons, held in various halls and churches, won them swift recognition as one of the outstanding choirs of the day. Their concerts, unaccompanied or with a small ensemble, began to be broadcast often by the CBC. Expanding to 32 voices, the singers attracted international attention for their work in the early 1960s with Igor Stravinsky. They had been engaged by the CBC to perform with the *CBC SO in the network's tribute to the composer on his 80th birthday (1962; the program included the North American premiere of *A Sermon, a Narrative and a Prayer* and the broadcast premiere of *The Dove Descending Breaks the Air*). Impressed with their high competence and fine sound Stravinsky and Robert Craft invited them to participate in recordings of Stravinsky's choral music then being undertaken by Columbia. Their recording of *Symphony of Psalms*, conducted by Stravinsky, was nominated in 1965 for a Grammy Award. The choir made its US debut in December 1967 at the White House, Washington, DC

Assuming professional status in 1968 (the choristers receiving contracts which required first call on their services) the Festival Singers became at the same time the core of the *Toronto Mendelssohn Choir. Stabilized at 36 voices, they toured Europe in 1971, appearing in England, Wales, France, Germany, Austria, and Yugoslavia. They toured Europe again in 1972 with the Toronto Mendelssohn Choir. Further US appearances included concerts at Lincoln Center, New York, 26 Jun 1972, Kennedy Center, Washington, 25 Oct 1976, and the Basilica of Saints Peter and Paul, Philadelphia, 4 Aug 1977. In November 1977 the singers toured in England, West Germany, and the USSR. In Canada they toured the west in 1974 and 1977 and the east in 1975 and appeared at the Stratford Festival during the summers of 1955, 1956, 1958, 1963–7 and 1974, the *Guelph Spring, Festival 1968, 1973, and 1975–7, the winter seasons of the *Shaw Festival at Niagara-on-the-Lake 1973–6, and the Olympics in Montreal in 1976. At Guelph they sang two sections of Penderecki's *St Luke Passion* under the composer's direction in May 1976. Annual concert series were given in Toronto, and at the height of their fame the singers gave about 25 concerts each year on the CBC.

The Festival Singers of Canada under Elmer Iseler

English and Canadian critics agreed in their estimations: 'The Festival Singers of Canada made a stunning impression ... The unanimity of attack was astonishing, the intonation flawless and the tonal balance well-nigh perfect' (London *Daily Telegraph*, 2 Jun 1971); 'one could not fault the Singers on tonal beauty, ensemble precision or dignity...the Singers swung effortlessly from subtle pianissimos to lusty fortissimos and maintained a delicate balance in even the most complex interweaving of melodic lines' (Toronto *Globe and Mail*, 1 Jul 1974).

Reflecting Iseler's dedication to Canadian music, the Festival singers commissioned and premiered works by John *Beckwith (*Jonah* 1963), Robert *Fleming (*Heirs through Hope* 1968), Clifford *Ford (*Mass* 1977), Harry *Freedman (*The Tokaido* 1962, *Totem and Taboo* 1965), the choir's accompanist, 1968–79, Ruth Watson *Henderson (*Missa brevis* 1975), Oskar *Morawetz (*Two Contrasting Moods* 1967), Jean *Papineau-Couture (*Viole d'amour* 1967), Harry *Somers (the motet *The Crucifixion* 1966, *Three Songs of New France* 1976), Claude *Vivier (*Journal* 1978), Charles *Wilson (*The Lonely Land* 1976), and John *Wyre (*Utau Kane NoWa* 1975, *Bernie* 1977). The Festival Singers of Canada Choral Series, begun in 1968, edited by Iseler and published by G.V. *Thompson, includes several of these commissions. The choir also gave the premieres of Talivaldis *Kenins' *Lagalaî* (1970), Thomas Baker's *Chinese Love Lyrics*, Wilson's *Images Out of Season* (1973), Derek *Healey's arrangements of *Six Canadian Folk Songs* (1973), Somers' *Kyrie* (1974), Norman *Symonds' *At the Shore* (1976), Alexander *Brott's *Time's Trials Triumph* (1977 in Bonn, Germany), David Fanshawe's *African Sanctus* (revised version, 1978), and several of John Reeves' *Motets* (1978).

Excepting a period of about a year and a half (late 1960 to early 1962) when ill health forced his temporary resignation, Iseler was the Festival Singers' regular conductor until 1978. In Iseler's first absence, Lloyd *Bradshaw conducted several concerts, and Walter *Susskind and Rowland *Pack each conducted one. Iseler himself – as a guest – conducted the final concert in the 1961–2 series prior to returning as artistic director in August 1962, and he retained the position for the ensuing 16 years. Giles *Bryant was named music director in June 1978, and Peter McCoppin, Jon *Washburn, Brian *Law, and John Barnum appeared as guest conductors during the 1978–9 season.

Many solo performers of note, including Mary Lou *Fallis, Albert *Greer, Ingemar *Korjus, Phyllis *Mailing, John *Martens, Mary *Morrison, Patricia *Rideout, Jan *Simons, Lillian Smith Weichel, Margaret Stilwell, Eric *Tredwell, Alan Woodrow, and Gordon Wry were members of the Festival Singers at some time during their careers. The Festival Singers' first governing board came into being in 1968, the year the choir assumed professional status. Board members were enlisted from the music and business communities. Presidents were James Singleton 1968–9, John *Bird 1969–71, Gordon Marshall 1971–2, Mrs Thomas H. Thomson 1972–4, Max Holling 1974–6, Ian Woolley 1976–7 Mrs W.D. Heintzman 1977–8, and Charles Tisdall 1978–9. The Festival Singers announced suspension of activities in April 1979 and filed an assignment of bankruptcy 30 Jul 1979.

DISCOGRAPHY

A Festival of Christmas Music. Iseler cond. 1956. Hallmark ChS-4
Beckwith *The Trumpets of Summer; Three Blessings*. Morrison sop, Rideout alto, Bartle ten, A. Gray bar, Iseler cond. 1969. RCI340/CBC SM-81/Cap ST 6323
Canadian Landscapes, vol 1: Healey – T. Baker – Schafer – Archer. 1974. CBC SM-274
Choral Music of Healey Willan. Iseler cond. 1968. RCI 207/Cap ST 6248
Freedman *The Flame Within; The Tokaido*. Iseler cond, Tor WW Quin (*Tokaido*). 1970. RCI 341/CBC SM-142/ Decca DL 75244
Joyful Sounds: Schütz – Paynter – Praetorius – Dennis Riley – M. Miller – Hartmann. Canadian Brass, Iseler cond. 1973. CBC SM-203
Kent *Mass No. 1* – Willan *Missae breves* IV, X, XI. Iseler cond. 1976. CBC SM-314
Make We Joy: Holman – Applebaum – Charpentier – Wilson – Kent – Anderson – Ridout – Paul – Mather – K. Jones – Freedman – Beecroft. Iseler cond. 1973. Poly Medium Stereo 2917 009
Make We Merry: Willan – Bach – Paynter – Kirkpatrick – Pearsall – Iseler. Iseler cond. 1970. CBC SM-80/RCA LSC 3174
Mundy – Byrd – Gibbons – Lassus – Willan. Iseler cond. 1955. Hallmark ChS-3
Palestrina – Somers – MacMillan – K. Jones – W. K. Rogers – Kenins – Ridout – et al. Iseler cond. 1965. CBC SM-19
Poulenc – Somers – Russell – Beckwith. Iseler cond. 1967. Cap ST 6258
Schoenberg *Kol Nidre; Dreimal Tausend Jahre*. CBC SO, Craft cond. 1969. 2-Col M2S-709
– *Modern Psalm; De profundis*. CBC SO, Craft cond. 1964. 2-Col M2S-780
– *Prelude to the Genesis Suite*. CBC SO, Craft cond. 1962. 2-Col M2S-694
– *Survivor from Warsaw*. CBC SO, Craft cond. 1962. 2-Col M2S-679
Somers *Five Songs of the Newfoundland Outports*. Iseler cond. 1969. RCI 339/CBC SM-105/RCA LSC-3154
Stravinsky *A Sermon, a Narrative and a Prayer; Anthem; Babel; Zvezdoliki* – Bach-Stravinsky *Choral Variations on 'Vom Himmel hoch da komm' Ich her.'* CBC SO, Stravinsky cond. 1962–3. Col MS-6647
– *Recent Stravinsky Conducted by the Composer*. Verrett mezzo, Driscoll ten, CBC SO. (1967). Col MS 7054
– *Stravinsky Conducts Stravinsky*: choral selections. 1963. Col M-31124
– *Symphony of Psalms*. CBC SO, Stravinsky cond. 1963. Col MS-6548
We Magnify Thee: Willan – Byrd – Hindemith – Vaughan Williams – Josquin des Prés. Iseler cond. 1970. CBC SM-179
See also Discography for *Toronto Mendelssohn Choir.

BIBLIOGRAPHY

Kraglund, John. 'Is there a pro choir waiting in wings,' Toronto *Globe and Mail*, 25 Nov 1967
'Festival Singers of Canada,' *CanComp*, 49, Apr 1970
'Festival Singers tour Europe – critics call tour "amazing",' *CanComp*, 62, Sep 1971
Roberts, John. 'Stravinsky and the CBC,' *CMB*, 4, Spring – Summer 1972
Ashworth-Gam, Jean. 'Elmer Iseler and the Festival Singers of Canada: a classic success story,' *Recorder*, vol 19, Mar 1977
Littler, William. 'Why did Elmer Iseler get the old heave-ho?' *Toronto Star*, 25 May 1978
Kraglund, John. 'Festival Singers in bankruptcy,' Toronto *Globe and Mail*, 2 Aug 1979

Hambleton, Ronald. 'Problems that destroyed a choir come to light,' *Toronto Star*, 8 Aug 1979

FIALA, George (Joseph). Composer, pianist, organist, producer, b Kiev, Ukraine, 31 Mar 1922, naturalized Canadian 1955; D MUS musicology (Akademische Hochschule für Musik, Berlin) 1945. Both his parents were pianists, and he began studying the piano at seven. In 1934 he took piano lessons from K. Mikhailoff and began learning theory and composition. A mazurka he composed was selected in 1935 for a collection of pieces by children published in Moscow. At the Tchaikovsky Cons in Kiev he studied 1939–41 under the Ukrainian composers Groudine, Lev Revutsky, Boris Liatoshynsky, and Andrew Olkhovsky. He was able to exchange ideas with Prokofiev, Shostakovitch, and Khatchaturian when they conducted their works in Kiev, and these meetings influenced his artistic development.

Fiala's activities were interrupted by the German occupation during World War II. He went to Berlin where under difficult circumstances he continued his studies in composition with Hansmaria Dombrowski, a pupil of Pfitzner, and took courses in conducting with Wilhelm Furtwängler. His doctoral thesis dealt with the problems of symphonic composition in Soviet Russia.

When the war ended Fiala settled in Belgium and studied with the composer Léon Jongen, director of the Brussels Cons. A scholarship from the Vatican in 1946 enabled him to concentrate exclusively on composition for three years. He produced about 40 works, including his *Symphony No. 2* and his *Piano Concerto No. 3*. During his years in Belgium he took part as a composer, pianist, and conductor in the Séminaire des arts directed by André Souris in Brussels and thus came into contact with the new Parisian school represented mainly by Boulez, Nigg, and Leibowitz.

Fiala emigrated to Canada in 1949 and settled in Montreal where he remained except for 1959–60 which he spent in Sydney, Australia. In addition to his activities as composer, pianist, organist, and teacher, he began in 1967 to produce programs for the Russian section of RCI. The Ukrainian Committee of Canada awarded him the Shevchenko medal in 1974.

Fiala has composed some 200 works of which about 15 have been published. His numerous commissions have been from, among others, the *MACQ (*Montreal*), the *Guelph Spring Festival (*Sinfonietta concertata*, premiered by Joseph *Macerollo with Kelsey *Jones and the *McGill Chamber Orchestra in 1972), the *Canada Council and the Ukrainian Committee of Canada (*Concerto* for violin, premiered by Steven *Staryk and the *Winnipeg SO in 1974), the CBC (*Symphony No. 4*, the 'Ukrainian'), and the *Montreal International Competition (*Musique concertante*). His *Divertimento concertante* was premiered by Eugène *Husaruk and the *MSO in 1968.

Fiala has been attracted to the large forms – the symphony, the concerto, the sonata. Trained primarily in the traditional school, he adhered to the tonal system until the early 1960s. By his own admission he succeeded at that time in 'reconciling his method of composition with the principles of serialism.' This double allegiance was to characterize his subsequent output. His works have a logical structure, and the more recent use a language that is often dissonant. The melodic line, although frequently angular, is lyrical and expressive, and the rhythms are always interesting. The instrumental writing is colourful, with rich contrasts. But on the aesthetic plane Fiala's work follows a traditional pattern. Above all he seeks to be himself, which may explain in part his refusal to commit himself to the more adventurous paths of contemporary writing.

Fiala is a member of the *CLComp, an associate of the *CMCentre, and an affiliate of PRO Canada.

SELECTED COMPOSITIONS

ORCHESTRA

Concertino. 1950. Pf, tpt, tim, str. Ber (rental). RCI 184 (*Goldblatt)
Symphony in E Minor. 1950. Ms
Suite concertante. 1956. Ob, str. Ber (rental)
Capriccio. 1962. Pf, orch. CMCentre
Shadows of Our Forgotten Ancestors. 1962. CMCentre
Divertimento concertante. 1965. Vn, orch. CMCentre
Eulogy 'In memory of President J.F. Kennedy.' 1965. Ber (rental)
Canadian Credo (W.S. Johnson). 1966. SATB, orch. CMCentre
Montreal. 1967. BMIC 1969. RCI 291 (B. *Brott)
Musique concertante. 1968. Pf, orch. CMCentre
Sérénade concertante. 1968. Vc, str. CMCentre
Ouverture burlesque. 1972. CMCentre
Sinfonietta Concertata. 1972. Acc, hpd, str. CMCentre. RCI 385 (*Macerollo)
Concerto. 1973. Vn, orch. CMCentre
Symphony No. 4 'Ukrainian.' 1973. CMCentre
Ukrainian Triptych. 1975. CMCentre

CHAMBER

Chamber Music for Five Wind Instruments. 1948. Fl, ob, cl, hn, bn. CMCentre. CBC SM-22/SM-186 (*Tor WW Quin)
Quartet No. 1. 1955 (rev 1962). 4 sax. CMCentre
Quartet No. 2. 1961. 4 sax. Ber 1970. RCI 279/RCA LSC-3141 (*Pierre Bourque Sax Quar)
Cantilena and Rondo. 1963. Sop, rec, pf. BMIC 1963
Pastorale and Allegretto. 1963. 4 rec. BMIC 1963
Wallaby's Lullaby. 1960–4. Vn, pf. BMIC 1966
Sonatas: vc, pf (1969); vn, pf (1969); sax, pf (1970); vc, pf (1971). All CMCentre
Sonata for Two. 1971. Sop sax, acc. CMCentre
Concertino Canadese. 1972. 4 hp. CMCentre
Sonata Breve. 1972. Cl, hp. CMCentre
Partita da Camera. 1977. 2 vn. CMCentre

PIANO

Children's Suite. 1941 (rev 1975). Wat 1974
Ten Postludes. 1947 (rev 1968). Wat 1969. CMC-2 (*Cavalho)
Australian Suite. 1963. BMIC 1963. CCM-2 (*Cavalho)
Piano Music No. 1. 1976. CMCentre
Concerto da Camera. 1978. pf, 4 hands. CMCentre
Ukrainian Dance. 1979. 2 pf, 4 hands. Ms
Other works, including 8 sonatas for solo pf, 1 sonata for 2 pf, and educational works
Also *Four Russian Poems* (1968, Wat 1972) and 'Psalm' (1974) for v and keyboard

BIBLIOGRAPHY

BMI Canada Ltd. 'George Fiala,' pamphlets (1971, 1976)
Contemporary Canadian Composers / Compositeurs canadiens contemporains

GP

FIALKOWSKA, Janina. Pianist, b Montreal 7 May 1951; B MUS (Montreal) 1968, M MUS (Montreal) 1968. Born of a Polish father and an English mother, she began studying the piano at five with the latter. Later, she studied with Yvonne *Hubert at the *École Vincent-d'Indy and won first prize in the 1966 CBC TV competition 'Jeunesse oblige' (classical music section) and in the 1967 Quebec Music Festivals (*Canadian Music Competition). After a year's study in 1968 in Paris with Yvonne Lefébure, she was a winner in the 1969 *CBC Talent Festival. She went to New York in 1969 on a *Canada Council grant, to study at the Juilliard School under Sascha Gorodnitzki, with whom she has continued to work periodically.

Fialkowska was a finalist in the 1971 *Montreal International Competition and was one of the third-prize winners in the first Artur Rubinstein international piano competition, in September 1974 in Israel. Rubinstein was quoted in *Le Figaro* as saying 'One of the jurors cried with emotion on hearing the Liszt *Sonata*, played beautifully by a 23-year-old Canadian: Janina Fialkowska.' The celebrated pianist advised and supported her in the development of her career.

After 1975 Fialkowska gave recitals throughout Europe and North America. She performed concertos of Liszt, Prokofiev, and Rachmaninoff as a guest with the Los Angeles (Hollywood Bowl) Philharmonic, the Israel Philharmonic (in a tour of Israel), the New Philharmonia Orchestra in London, the Royal Philharmonic (in Birmingham and Liverpool), the Scottish National Orchestra (in Edinburgh and Glasgow), the Little Orchestra of New York, the *NACO, the *TS, and the orchestras of Cleveland, Detroit, Philadelphia, *Quebec, San Diego, and *Vancouver.

On 5 Dec 1976 Fialkowska performed Liszt's *Concerto No. 1* with the *MSO conducted by Hiroyuki Iwaki; the next day Gilles *Potvin wrote in *Le Devoir*: 'She has a magnificent technique and a real pianistic sense...fire and accuracy that remind one of the greatest pianists.' In May 1977 she played for an audience of 7000 at the closing of the Festival Cervantino in Guanajuato, Mexico.

DISCOGRAPHY

Chopin *Sonata in B Flat Minor* Op 35; *Étude in A Minor Op 25, no. 11* – Papineau-Couture *Étude in B Flat*. 1969. CBC SM-114
Chopin 5 *Études*; et al. 1978. RCA RL 37071
Liszt *Sonata in B Minor; Transcendantal Études, No. 5 and 12; Mephisto Waltz*. 1977. RCA FRL 10142

BIBLIOGRAPHY

Pope, Charles. 'An end to justify the means,' *Maclean's*, 8 Mar 1976
Maskoulis, Julia. 'A last chance pushed pianist to success,' Montreal *Gazette*, 4 Mar 1978
Petrovski, Nathalie. 'Le gang des pianos à queue,' *L'Actualité*, Apr 1979

HP

Fiddling (also known as country fiddling, or oldtime or old-time fiddling). The principal instrumental folk music activity of Canada. Fiddling existed in the earliest days of European settlement in Canada, when the violin and bagpipes were the instruments commonly used to make music for dancing, the most popular form of entertainment. Many of the instruments were home-made. Scottish settlements invariably had a bagpiper but 'at their dances within doors, they...generally prefer the old Highland fiddler, or the young one who has learnt the same music, which is at all times played with the spirit and rapidity of which the Scotch reels and strathspeys are so eminently susceptible' (John M'Gregor, *British America*, London 1833).

Scottish fiddling, along with Irish, is at the heart of the Canadian styles. Each, however, has undergone degrees of change under other influences – eg, the western style common in the USA and the styles brought to Canada by continental European immigrants. In Quebec, Irish jigs and reels in particular have been preserved, but through natural transmutation these have become an unmistakably French-Canadian genre. A national or 'nation-wide' style – disseminated by radio and TV – has been attributed by the fiddler Graham *Townsend to Don *Messer, a style 'clean, straight-ahead and neat as a well-tended farm,' and characterized by 'clarity and down-to-earth simplicity' that have made it 'a common language for all Canadian fiddlers, whatever their different dialects' (Dorothy and Homer Hogan, liner notes to Townsend's LP *The Great Canadian Fiddle*); Townsend's study of Canadian fiddle traditions has provided the basis for a number of his recordings.

The fiddling repertoire is founded on such dance pieces as the reel (fast 2/4 or 4/4), the strathspey (slow 4/4), the jig (moderate-to-quick 6/8),

Fishermen on a gillnetter, Rivers Inlet, BC, 1930s

and the waltz. Fiddle compositions are passed on aurally for the most part, their origins largely European, although after the mid-1950s many fiddle tunes have been composed locally. Traditionally played without accompaniment (a tradition not observed rigidly in the 20th century) these pieces usually have, nevertheless, an implied harmonic structure of two or three chords (tonic, dominant, and supertonic or subdominant). As an accompaniment to square dance they often are grouped into sets of three or four to sustain a performance long enough to accommodate dancers. Among the most famous fiddle tunes of Canadian origin are the traditional *Reel du pendu* (*Hangman's Reel*) from Quebec and Ward *Allen's *Maple Sugar* (first recorded in 1957). The repertoire of dance pieces employed by fiddlers is shared with other folk instrumentalists (see also Accordion; Harmonica).

Fiddle styles in Canada may be broken down most conveniently by region and, within those regions, by substyles varying according to type and degree of embellishment. Perhaps the purest style (ie, truest to its European origins) is that of the Acadian fiddler. The strongest tradition, and the most unified stylistically, is that of the Quebec fiddler, the violoneux. His roots are mainly in Irish and, to a lesser degree, Scottish music; his style is characterized by a high degree of ornamentation, an infectious rhythmic buoyancy, and daring speed. Unique to Quebec fiddling is 'clogging,' an ostinato of rhythmic patterns created by the fiddler's feet, alternating heel and toe to provide rhythmic counterpoint for otherwise – and traditionally – unaccompanied performance.

*LeVasseur, in the Quebec City periodical *La Musique* (April 1919), listed the notable violoneux who flourished 1825–70: Jacques Beaumont, Jacques Bezeau, Omer Bouchard, Antoine Bussière, Pierre Déry, Ferdinand Descarreaux, Napoléon Giroux, David Parent, Joseph Roussin, Narcisse Simard (father and son), Élie Siouï, and others identified only by surname – Bertrand, Courtnay [sic], Desjardins, Lajeunesse, Langlois, Savard, and Vachon.

The style and repertoire of these men were passed on to a generation of musicians born in the late 19th century; and recordings made by that generation in the 1920s froze the tradition before it was subjected, as a folk expression, to the deleterious effects of the mass media of the later 20th century. The violoneux recorded at this time included Joseph *Allard, Arthur-Joseph Boulay, Albert and J.O. *LaMadeleine, Joseph Larocque, Fortunat Malouin, Wellie *Ringuette, J.B. Roy, the first to record (ca 1918) for HMV, and Isidore *Soucy.

Still younger musicians who have perpetuated the tradition include Paul Bossé, Joe *Bouchard, Louis *Boudreault, Jean *Carignan, Philippe Gagnon, Paul-Émile Gosselin, Jean-Louis Labbé, and Jules Verret – some with only regional reputations and others, especially Carignan, of international significance. Adrien Avon, Omer *Dumas, and many others have adapted this music for popular ensemble.

Outside influences – among them a slow, swinging, slightly sentimental style from Nashville, Tenn, and novelty styles incorporating acrobatics, tricks, and unlikely implements, eg, baseball bats used as bows to comic effect – have been apparent in the playing of Monsieur *Pointu, Ti-Blanc *Richard, Fernand Thibault, and others.

The novelty style has had its exponents elsewhere in Canada (see Al Cherny), and a novelty category has been a standard part of the many fiddle contests in Canada, including the *Canadian Open Old Time Fiddlers' Contest begun in 1951 at Shelburne, Ont. (There were, by 1980, some 50 other such annual contests in Ontario and numerous contests and jamborees from British Columbia to Newfoundland.)

A significant pocket of fiddling in the Scottish tradition developed on Cape Breton Island in the playing of Dan R. MacDonald and Winston 'Scotty' *Fitzgerald, and the younger John Donald Cameron, Joe Cormier, and Lee Cremo. These players have brought to the style the reedy sound, the use of the drone, and the greater degree of embellishment characteristic of bagpipe music. The tunes show the influence of the bagpipe scale which falls between the Aeolian and Mixolydian church modes. The resulting style is slower and more delicate than the French-Canadian and is closely linked with the playing of Scottish fiddlers such as Niel Gow (1727–1807) and J.-Scott Skinner (1843–1927). The Celtic label has issued many LPs of music in this style.

The Irish influence is evident in the playing of fiddlers from the Ottawa Valley (Reg Hill, Graham Townsend, etc). The US (western) style has been heard in many areas of the country in the playing of 'western-swing' bands led by King *Ganam, Sid Plamondor, and others. A Slavic influence is part of the style of such prairie fiddlers as Victor Pasowisty, and Métis fiddlers have introduced elements of their own, unrestrained by strict metre or standard tuning.

Other fiddlers of note in Canada include Emile Benoit and Rufus Guinchard (Newfoundland); Bill Guest, Johnny Mooring, and Cye Steele (Nova Scotia); Ned *Landry and Eddy Poirier (New Brunswick); Ward Allen, June *Eikhard, Ed Gyurki, Rudy Meeks, Joe, Pat, and Paul Ménard, and Eleanor Townsend (Ontario); and Reg Boutette and Andy *DeJarlis (Manitoba).

The rhythms and tunes of fiddle music have captivated a number of Canadian composers and have appeared either as actual materials or as strong influences in many theatrical and concert works. The 'Fête villageoise' from *Miro's *Vox populi* and *Champagne's much played *Danse villageoise*, both of 1928, are among early 20th-century instances. Later came *Beckwith's *Quartet* (based on actual fiddle tunes); *Blackburn's *Fantaisie en mocassins*; the first section ('Rattle on the Stovepipe' – in the style of a square dance tune) of Donald Coakley's *Directions North*; François *Dompierre's *Concerto* for piano and orchestra and *Les Diableries* for violin and orchestra; the Friends and Neighbours Dance in *Fleming's ballet *Shadow on the Prairie*, and the same composer's *Maritime suite*; the central scene of *Freedman's ballet **Rose Latulippe*; André *Gagnon's *Petit Concerto pour Carignan*; *Gratton's *Cinq Danses canadiennes*; Pierick *Houdy's *Messe québécoise*; Kelsey *Jones' *Miramichi Ballad*; *Ridout's *Fall Fair*; and the Barn Dance from *Weinzweig's **Red Ear of Corn*.

The large collection of recorded and written fiddle music of Don Messer has been deposited at the Public Archives of Nova Scotia. It provides a fine cross-section of the Canadian repertoire. The Allen Ash manuscript book at the *NL of C includes some fiddle tunes current in Ontario in the mid-19th century.

See also Country music; Folk music; Folk music, Anglo-Canadian; Folk music, Franco-Canadian; Dancing, pre-Confederation; Scotland: 2 / Traditional Scottish instrumental music.

BIBLIOGRAPHY

Proctor, George A. *Old-Time Fiddling in Ontario*, National Museum of Canada Bulletin no. 190 (Ottawa 1963)

Fisher, W. Allen. 'Fiddling in retrospect,' *CME*, vol 16, Winter 1974

Beaulieu, Michel. 'Le rétour des violoneux,' *Maclean*, Feb 1975)

Newlove, Harold J. *Fiddlers of the Canadian West* (Swift Current, Sask 1976)

Labbé, Gabriel. *Les Pionniers du disque folklorique québécois 1920–1950* (Montreal 1977)

Hogan, Dorothy, and Hogan, Homer. 'Canadian fiddle culture,' *Communique: Canadian Studies; Canadian Folk Culture Issue*, vol 3, Aug 1977

Begin, Carmelle. 'La musique traditionnelle pour violon: Jean Carignan,' unpubl D MUS thesis, U of Montreal 1979

Rosenberg, Neil J. 'A preliminary bibliography of Canadian old time instrumental music books, *CFMJ*, vol 8, 1980

FILMOGRAPHY

The Country Fiddle (Folkways Records and Services Corp 1958)

The Fiddlers of James Bay (NFB 1980) (GAP, MM)

FIELD, Harry (Marshall). Pianist, teacher; b Aurora, Canada West (Ontario), 14 Dec 1862, d Hampstead, London, 1945? He was educated at Upper Canada College, Toronto, and studied the piano, first with his mother, a skilled pianist descended from the family of the playwright Richard Brinsley Sheridan, and then with Theodore *Martens and Waugh *Lauder. He continued his studies 1884–7 in Frankfurt under Hans von Bülow and at the Leipzig Cons under Carl Reinecke, the Liszt pupil Martin Krause, and others. In 1887 he made his piano debut in Leipzig, in 1888 he became a teacher at the *Toronto College of Music, and later he taught at several girls' schools. In 1896 he went to Leipzig as Krause's assistant. He returned to Canada in 1900, opening a teaching studio in Toronto and heading the piano department at the Peterborough Cons. Moving to Dresden in 1906, Field appeared as soloist with orchestras in Germany and Scandinavia and gave recitals in Dresden, Leipzig, and elsewhere.

During World War I Field was interned at Ruhleben near Berlin (along with Ernest *MacMillan), but in 1916 he was able to leave for England, where he became the head of the piano department of the Hampstead School of Music, retaining the post until his death. He specialized in the music of Chopin and Liszt and wrote a group of six *Klavierstücke* (Jost, Leipzig), said to be Chopinesque. His Canadian pupils included Gladys Seward of Peterborough and Alice Roger Collins.

BIBLIOGRAPHY

Collins, Alice Roger. *Real People*, vol 5 (London, Ont [1936]) HK

FILIATRAULT, Roger. Baritone, teacher, choir conductor, b Montreal 5 Feb 1905, d Lesage, near Montreal, 27 Apr 1973; premier prix voice (Brussels Royal Cons) 1928. He studied piano and violin before taking voice lessons from Salvator *Issaurel. At the Brussels Royal Cons, he worked

1926–8 under Désiré Demest (voice) and Désiré Defauw and Joseph Jongen (choral conducting). He also studied the physiology of the voice with Dr Alexis Wicart in Paris. He returned to Canada in 1930 and with André Trottier founded the *Alouette Vocal Quartet, with which he performed widely in Canada and abroad for some 30 years, becoming its artistic director in 1945.

Filiatrault taught privately and in many institutions including the *CMM and the *École Vincent-d'Indy. Among his pupils were Réjane *Cardinal, Marie-José Forgues, Claire *Gagnier, Jacques *Labrecque, Micheline *Tessier, and Cécile *Vallée. He was the founder, and the director 1948–50, of the Société Euphonia vocal ensemble, a 45-voice mixed choir which gave several concerts. Its repertoire consisted of polyphonic and classical works as well as harmonizations of Canadian folksongs.

Filiatrault was president 1949–51 of the *QMTA. In 1956 the School of Music at the *U of Ottawa awarded him a diploma 'bene merenti.' GP

Films. Films about Canadian music, musicians, and music-making, and Canadian films with music as a significant component, had become fairly numerous by 1980.

In the filmography below – a selection representing some 40 years of film-making – the second section is devoted to films made for television (a genre distinct from video tape, which is excluded).

The first section of the filmography is devoted to films intended for viewing in movie houses, and it is to these that most of the introductory remarks apply. Of the 125 films in this section, 81 are by the *NFB. Of the 81, 19 are under 10 minutes in length. Seven of the 125 films are feature-length (*The Navy Show, A Child Like Any Other, Don Messer: His Land and His Music, Across This Land with Stompin' Tom Connors, The Hard Part Begins, Jean Carignan violoneux*, and *Fidelio*), 12 are in the hour-long category (*Children's Concert, Stravinsky, Conversations with Glenn Gould, Jablonski, Les Philharmonistes, Lookback: A Musical Fantasy, Reel du Pendu, Why I Sing...Words and Music of Gilles Vigneault, Je chante a cheval...avec Willie Lamothe, Rock-a-Bye, Annie North of 60*, and *Musicanada*), and a large number are half-hour films.

By 1980 there still was no cinematic record of Lois *Marshall, Léopold *Simoneau, or Don *Garrard – to name only three of Canada's leading singers – and Canadian composers, conductors, and instrumentalists have been filmed no more thoroughly.

Nevertheless, some exceptions may be cited. Jon *Vickers is Florestan in *Fidelio*, Beethoven's opera, filmed in France. Maureen *Forrester and Eugene *Kash may be seen in the NFB's *Festival in Puerto Rico*, a film on the Casals festival. Another NFB film, *Lonely Boy*, is a revealing 27-minute documentary on the young Paul *Anka. Glenn *Gould is *On the Record* and *Off the Record* in two 30-minute NFB films (usually shown together) in which he talks of composition and plays Bach. *Don Messer, His Land and His Music*, his musicians and his fans, are treated in multi-screen techniques in the 70-minute NFB production. *Toronto Jazz* (NFB, 27 minutes) captures performances by the Lenny *Breau Trio, the Don *Thompson Quintet, and the Alf Jones Quartet. In *Bing, Bang, Boom* (NFB, 25 minutes) R. Murray *Schafer shows children how to assemble sounds into musical patterns. In *Jablonski* (NFB, 50 minutes, filmed in Spain, Poland, and Montreal), Marek *Jablonski talks about his life and plays Chopin.

The NFB lists a series of two- and three-minute animated films under the general title *Contemporary Songs of French Canada*, in which Claude *Dubois, Jean-Pierre *Ferland, Christian Larsen, Claude *Gauthier, and Claude *Léveillée are heard (but not seen) singing their own songs. Stompin' Tom *Connors stomps *Across this Land* to enthusiastic audiences in a feature film by John Saxton. Quebec's most famous fiddler is the subject of the NFB feature film *Jean Carignan violoneux*. The excellent NFB short on Healey *Willan, *Man of Music*, regrettably is withdrawn from circulation, as are many of the early films listed.

One of the few non-NFB movies in the music genre (and shown with success in commercial cinemas) is Maurice *Solway's *The Violin*, a half-hour story film in which Solway tutors a young boy and in so doing performs 18 of his own compositions. The accompaniments are by Leo *Barkin. The sound-track is available as a recording (RCA KXL1-0029). The non-NFB feature film *The Hard Part Begins* (Cinépix) is a portrait of an ageing country singer by the actor Donnelly Rhodes. The music is by Cliff Carroll.

The unique sound techniques developed for film by Norman *McLaren and his use of Canadian music and musicians are described in his entry, and a list of his films is given there.

FILMOGRAPHY

FILMS THAT TREAT MUSIC AND/OR MUSICIANS IN CANADA

1939

Music from the Stars. 12 min. Associated Screen News. Horace *Lapp's orchestra at the Royal York Hotel in Toronto

1944–5

Let's All Sing Together. 8–10 min each NFB. 6-part series (1 and 2, 1944; 3–6, 1945) The Four Gentlemen sing the old favourites illustrated by animated silhouettes.

1945

A City Sings. 11 min. NFB. The annual *Manitoba Music Competition Festival. Shortened version of the film *Listen to the Prairies* (21 min). Mary *Morrison appears in the festival.

Meet the Navy on Tour. NFB. Tour documentary of, and scenes from, the RCN revue *Meet the Navy*

Music in the Wind / Le Vent qui chante. 9 min. NFB. A visit to the *Casavant organ factory, with *Piché and *Willan providing background music. Shortened version of the film *Singing Pipes* (21 min)

The Navy Show. England. Feature film of the RCN show, made in England at the end of World War II

The Toronto Symphony Orchestra I. 12 min. NFB. Sir Ernest *MacMillan conducting the *TSO in *Jamaican Rhumba, À St-Malo*, and Overture to *Colas Breugnon*

The Toronto Symphony Orchestra II. 9 min. NFB. Sir Ernest MacMillan conducting the third movement of Tchaikovsky's *Symphony No. 6*

1947

Christmas Carols. 11 min. NFB. Cartoon presentation of carols sung by the *Leslie Bell Singers

Story of a Violin. 22 min. NFB. George *Heinl builds a violin for a young boy. (Eugene *Kash performs on the sound-track.)

1948

It's Fun to Sing. 11 min. NFB. The Leslie Bell Singers in performance

1949

Children's Concert. 42 min. NFB. Eugene Kash introduces the four sections of an orchestra (*Ottawa Philharmonic) and explains some of the elements of music to a young audience.

Choral Concert. 10 min. NFB. By the Leslie Bell Singers

1951

Dances of the Kwakiutl. 10 min. Orbit Films (USA). The dances of the ancient winter ceremonial rites of the Kwakiutl families, with music recorded on location

Longhouse people. 23 min. NFB. Rain-dance, healing ceremony and celebration of the Iroquois

The Man in the Peace Tower. NFB. The music of the Dominion carillonneur Robert *Donnell

Meet Gisèle. 10 min. NFB. The popular singer performing three songs

The Opera Class. 36 min. NFB. The training of a young opera singer (Marguerite *Gignac) at the *Royal Cons Opera School and her performance as Susanna in *The Marriage of Figaro*

1952

Singing Champions. 10 min. NFB. The *Chorale de l'Université St-Joseph, New Brunswick, in rehearsal and concert

Legende des Caribous. 20 min. J.P. Michéa & Poulenc frères. Songs and singing as a part of *Inuit life are treated in this film.

Music Master. 10 min. NFB. Neil *Chotem performs Chopin, and he and his trio perform instrumental versions of popular songs.

1953

Musician in the Family. 17 min. NFB. The story of a prairie farmer's son who achieves a musical education despite family opposition. Score by Robert *Fleming

Music Professor. 6 min. NFB. One of the Faces of Canada series documenting the work of a piano teacher with his young pupils

The Newcomers. NFB. Includes rehearsal, in Halifax, of *Nova Scotia Opera Assn's *The Marriage of Figaro* with Latvian musicians Alfred *Strombergs and Mariss Vetra

Rehearsal. 12 min. NFB. Paul *Scherman conducts a movement of *Somers' *Suite for Harp* with Marie *Iösch-Lorcini as soloist.

1955

The Musical Ride. 19 min. NFB. The famous RCMP Musical Ride, performed to the accompaniment of band music

1958

The Country Fiddle. 18 min. Marlin Motion Pictures. Includes violoneux demonstrating the different techniques of tuning and fiddling

Music for Children. 13 min. NFB. Demonstration by Doreen *Hall of the *Orff method of teaching music to children

Songs of Nova Scotia. 11 min. NFB. Helen *Creighton collecting folk songs in her native Nova Scotia

Youth and Music / Jeunesses Musicales du Canada. 27 min. NFB. The activities at the annual summer camp of the *JMC

1959

Glenn Gould – Off the Record. 30 min. NFB. Glenn *Gould at his cottage and talking to Franz *Kraemer

Glenn Gould – On the Record. 30 min. NFB. Glenn Gould recording Bach's *Italian Concerto* at the Columbia studios, New York

Man of Music. 17 min. NFB. A portrait of Healey Willan, composer, organist-choirmaster, teacher

1961

Boy Meets Band. 12 min. NFB. Cliff Bryson directs the young members of the community-sponsored West Vancouver Boys' Band.

Circle of the Sun. 29 min. NFB. A gathering of the Blood Indians of Alberta that includes authentic songs

Festival in Puerto Rico. NFB. Maureen *Forrester rehearsing and performing at the Casals Festival

Lonely Boy. 26 min. NFB. An account of the rise of pop singer Paul *Anka

Wilfrid Pelletier, chef d'orchestre et éducateur. 30 min. NFB. The career of conductor Wilfrid *Pelletier

1962

Music from Montreal. 29 min. NFB. The role of Georges *Little as conductor of the *Montreal Bach Choir

1963

Attiuk. 29 min. NFB. The drum dance of the nomadic Montagnais Indians who live near the Strait of Belle Isle

Pipers and A'. 9 min. NFB. A mass march-past of pipes and drums in Maxville, Ont, site of the annual Glengarry Highland Games

I Know an Old Lady Who Swallowed a Fly. 6 min. NFB. Animated film of Alan *Mills' song

Selections from the Christmas Oratorio. 14 min. NFB. The Montreal Bach Choir and soloists, conducted by Georges Little, perform Bach.

Toronto Jazz. 27 min. NFB. A look at three Toronto jazz groups: the Lenny *Breau Trio, the Don *Thompson Quintet, and the Alf Jones Quartet

1965

Stravinsky. 49 min. NFB. An informal study of Igor Stravinsky conducting the *CBC SO in his *Symphony of Psalms*

1966

Campus in the Clouds. 30 min. NFB. A visit to the *Banff School of Fine Arts

Precision. 10 min. NFB. The RCMP Musical Ride, a blend of music, colour, and precise movement

1967

Tattoo 67. 19 min. NFB. Highlights of the 1967 Canadian Armed Forces Tattoo, including parade, tableaux, and massed bands

Twenty Million People. 25 min. NFB. A musical illustraton of the diverse cultures comprising the Canadian mosaic
1968
Ce Soir-là. Arthur Lamothe. Arthur Lamothe's film about the chansonnier Gilles *Vigneault
Marius Barbeau et le Folklore canadien-français. 30 min. NFB. French-language film about the folklorist Marius *Barbeau
The Songs of Chris Cobb. 8 min. NFB. The Newfoundland singer-songwriter performs his songs and poems.
1969
Bing, Bang, Boom. 25 min. NFB. R. Murray *Schafer opens the ears and eyes of Grade 7 Scarborough students to their environment.
Contemporary Songs of French Canada / Chansons contemporains. NFB. Series of six short animated films based on songs sung by popular composer-performers: *Cerveau gelé / Love*, Claude *Dubois; *Les fleurs de macadam / The Asphalt Flowers*, Jean-Pierre *Ferland; *Notre jeunesse en auto-sport / Our Sports Car Days*, Christian Larsen and Claude *Gauthier; *Taxi*, Claude *Léveillée; *Tête en fleurs / Marie*, Claude Gauthier; and *La Ville / Big City*, Jean-Pierre Ferland and Franck Dervieux (1970)
A Rosewood Daydream. 14 min. NFB. A Newfoundland rock group sings in a home for the elderly in St John's
1971
Country Music, Montreal. 38 min. Frank Vitale. A look at the country music scene in Montreal
Jablonski. 50 min. NFB. The Edmonton concert pianist reminiscing and playing Chopin
Pierre Mercure. 34 min. Charles Gagnon. A film dedicated to the Quebec composer
Don Messer: His Land and His Music. 69 min. NFB. Feature film of *Messer and the entire 'Jubilee' cast
The Music Machine. 11 min. National Research Council, Canada. New music created with computer, cathode ray oscilloscope, and piano keyboard at Ottawa's National Research Council
Les Philharmonistes. 59 min. NFB. An encounter with the members of the band, the Société philharmonique of *St-Hyacinthe, Québec
Vaghy. Quarry Film Production. The contribution of the *Vaghy String Quartet to life in Kingston, Ont, and Queen's University
1972
The Big Key. 8 min. Jim Anderson. A slapstick comedy that centres on the antics of a stumbling and frustrated pianist
Je Chante à Cheval...avec Willie Lamothe. 58 min. NFB. A portrait of thh Quebec country singer-songwriter Willie *Lamothe
A Little Summermusik. 8 min. NFB. Two sisters play the piano and flute for their friends.
Lookback: a Musical Fantasy. 54 min. Jack Mlynek. Five friends agree that their music made their high school days bearable.
The Oboe Reed. 21 min. Software Productions. Melvin *Berman illustrates the art of reed-making.
Playing the Viol. York University Production. Peggie *Sampson gives a class in the viola da gamba.
Reel du Pendu. 57 min. NFB. Versions of the traditional reel, played by groups of musicians from Quebec, Acadia, and Louisiana, reflect the varying attitudes of the musicians and their ways of life.
A Child like Any Other. Bellevue Pathé Ltée. Feature film on the career of the young Quebec singer René *Simard
Street Musique. 9 min. NFB. Animated interpretation of the music of Ryan Larkin
This is Stompin' Tom. 22 min. Marlin Motion Pictures. Visual record of the easygoing style of the popular country singer Tom *Connors
Tout écartillé. 6 min. NFB. Animated film illustrating a song composed and sung by Robert *Charlebois
Why I sing...The Words and Music of Gilles Vigneault. 57 min. NFB. The ideas, attitudes, and performance of the renowned chansonnier
1973
Across This Land with Stompin' Tom Connors. John Saxton. Feature film on the personality and music of the popular country singer
Alegria. 28 min. NFB. A study of a craftsman fashioning a guitar
Cavendish Country. 27 min. NFB. The daily life and the songs of Calgary's country singer-songwriter Cal Cavendish
Every Saturday Night. 27 min. NFB. The story of the music and members of the Badlanders – a country band of the Drumheller area in Alberta
Goodbye Sousa. 17 min. NFB. A look at the community contribution of the century-old Newmarket (Ont) Citizen's Band
The Hard Part Begins. Cinepix. Feature film. A profile of an aging country singer, played by Donnelly Rhodes. Music by Cliff Carroll
L'Infonie inachevée. Roger Frappier. Feature film on the Quebec ensemble *l'Infonie
Not Just Any Song. 15 min. York U. Study of singer Debby Dunleavy
Original Sin. 4 min. NFB. Audience reaction to the song 'Original Sin'
Rock-a-Bye. 49 min. NFB. A behind-the-scenes look at the business of pop music, including interviews with some of the stars
The Violin. 30 min. Marlin Motion Pictures. An elderly man (Maurice *Solway) opens the ears of two small boys to the joyous world of music.
1974
Alberta Girls. NFB. Precision marching and music by the Alberta Girls' Band from Edmonton, performing in Munich, Germany
Annie North of 60. 51 min. MPI Productions. Anne *Murray on tour in the Northwest Territories
Don Breaks Out. 10 min. NFB. Profile of Don Fletcher, Maritime violin maker and fiddler
Entropiscape. 11 min. York University Television Productions. An artist, dancers, and musicians present a synthesis of art forms.
'Envoyez de l'avant nos gens.' See 1976: *Le Son des Français d'Amérique*.
Jug Band Music: A Film about the Original Sloth Band. 22 min. Patrick Lee. The Toronto group The Original Sloth Band, rehearsing and performing
Poltava: A Heritage of Dance. 27 min. West Wind Film Group. The music and dance of a Ukrainian folk group
The Stampeders: Short Visit to Planet Earth. 24 min. Mel Shaw Productions. The Calgary rock group – The *Stampeders – in concert
Terry's Lute. Douglas Canton. Terry Philpot, a young craftsman, makes reproductions of medieval instruments.
Le Violon de Gaston. 22 min. NFB. To play his violin in recital or to play hockey in an important game? How a young boy deals with a conflict in his interests and activities.
1975
Halifax Music I and II. 19 min; 18 min. NFB. A two-part documentary on the teaching methods of the Music Dept of the Halifax School Board
Harpsichord Builder. Bernard Sauerman. Wolfgang *Kater, harpsichord builder of Quebec, is the subject.
Monsieur Pointu. 13 min. NFB. A combination animated-film and photographic treatment of the famed violoneux Paul Cormier, Monsieur *Pointu
Musicanada. 58 min. NFB. Cross-section of music-making in Canada, with appearances by Edith *Butler, Maureen Forrester, the *NYO, and Cape Dorset mouth musicians, and many others
Pitou Boudreault, violoneux. See 1976: *Le Son des Français d'Amérique*.
Les Ruine-Babines. See 1976: *Le Son des Français d'Amérique*.
Jean Carignan violoneux. 87 min. NFB. Feature film of the life of Quebec's best-known fiddler
1976
Le Son des Français d'Amérique. Faroun Films (Canada) Ltée. Series of 13 documentary films (1974–6, 27 min each) on the traditional music of francophones in North America. Films with Canadian subjects include:
– *'La Révolution du Dansage.'* Arthur Rouleau, violoneux, and Mme Audet of Île d'Orléans collaborate to preserve the traditional music and dance of their region.
– *'Envoyez de l'avant nos gens.'* Antonio Bazinet, farmer of Lanthier, Que, interprets the old songs.
– *L'en premier*. Traditional music of Acadia as it reflects the effects of the historic deportation
– *Il'allont-y-disparaître*. Members of an Acadian community in northwest Cape Breton sing 'complaintes.'
– *Johnny à Dennis à Alfred*. A look at three generations of Acadian fiddlers in Baie Ste-Marie, NS
– *'Faut pas l'dire!'* How Acadian traditional song and dance have been preserved. Narrated by Charlotte Cormier
– *Pitou Boudreault, violoneux*. Saguenay fiddler Louis Pitou *Boudreault plays music for dancing.
– *Les Ruine-Babines*. Six young Montreal musicians rehearse the music of the Gaspé.
Wingy Manone and the Climax Jazz Band – 1976. 17 min. Joe Showler. Toronto's Climax Jazz Band performs with US trumpeter Wingy Manone.
1977
Crash 'n' Burn. 27 min. Ross McLaren. A look at punk rock in Toronto, featuring the Diodes, the Deadboys, and Teenage Head
Désirs Mouvements. 5 min. Barry Goodwin. Percussion, dance, and abstract art in a collage of sound and movement
Festival of Friends – Live. 45 min. James Aquila. A documentary of the three-day folk art and music festival in Hamilton, Ont
Fidelio. Sunchild Productions. Beethoven opera filmed in Orange, France, with Jon *Vickers, Gundula Janowitz, and William Wildermann. Producer, Pierre Jourdain
Good Luck Boy. 24 min. Patrick Malone. The Canadian folk music scene, featuring Toronto singer-songwriter Raffi
Harmonie. 19 min. NFB. Summer music at *CAMMAC
1978
Bells and Brass. NFB. *Canadian Brass and the carillonneur Gordon *Slater recording 'O Canada'
Celtic Spirits. 57 min. NFB. John Allan *Cameron and Winston 'Scotty' *Fitzgerald trace the Celtic roots of the Canadian folk music of piper, fiddler, and folk singer at the *Mariposa Folk Festival, and on Prince Edward Island.
1979
Al Neil – A Portrait. 40 min. Dave Rimmer. A look at the Vancouver jazz pianist
Harmonium in California. NFB. 1979 tour of the Quebec group as it breaks into the US market
1980
The Fiddlers of James Bay. 29 min. NFB. Cree fiddlers Bob McCleod and Ray Spencers trace the musical link between their ancestors and Scots from the Orkney Islands who came to Canada two centuries ago.
Music for Wilderness Lake. 30 min. Fichman-Sweete Productions. A performance of R. Murray Schafer's composition for 12 trombones and O'Grady Lake

A SELECTION OF FILM DOCUMENTARIES PREPARED FOR TELEVISION (PROGRAMS ON VIDEO TAPE ARE NOT INCLUDED)

For the CBC
1959
'Cantate Domino.' 30 min. A boy's enrolment and training at St Michael's Cathedral Choir School
1961
The Lively Arts series. Programs included Helmut *Blume interviewing Zubin Mehta of the *MSO, Harry *Freedman and Harry *Somers discussing Canadian composers, and a talk with Marek Jablonski.
1962
13 by Saltzman series. Program interview of 84-year-old music teacher William Miles
'Songs of Miramichi.' A visit to the New Brunswick folk festival and an interview with Louise *Manny
'Electronic Music.' Arnold *Walter, Myron Schaeffer, Harvey Olnick, and Helmut Blume discuss the nature and potential of this form of making music.
'Improvisational Classical Music.' Harry Somers, Lukas Foss, and six musicians improvise in a 'classical jam session.'
'The Physics of Music.' Lister Sinclair and Harvey Olnick explore the science of musical sound.
1963
'And Places Where They Sing.' Leonard *Wilson's role as organist-choirmaster at St James Anglican Church in Vancouver
'This Time, This Place.' Quebec's self-discovery through its chansonniers – Lucille *Dumont, *Leclerc, Vigneault, Léveillée, and Claude *Gauthier
1964
'Short Sweet Summer.' Norman *Campbell's coverage of the 1963 NYO session and tour
'Concerti for Four Wednesdays.' Glenn Gould with the *CBC SO, conducted by Heinz *Unger
'This Side of Heaven.' The London, Ont, *Lombardo family
1965
'Diary of a Jewish Cantor.' Cantor Rev Nathan Mendelson of Montreal
'Diary of a Musical Child.' Orff teacher Gabor Bartha's Montreal children's orchestra
Heritage series. Composers of early Canadian church music and performances of works by W.H. *Anderson and Willan

'The Blood is Strong, The Heart is Highland.' A visit with Wishart *Campbell, Canada's 'golden voice of the air'
1966
'The Ecstasy is Sometimes Fantastic.' The Toronto rock group Jon and Lee and the Checkmates
'Alanis.' Profile of Indian folksinger Alanis *Obomsawin
Telescope series:
– 'Lisa Ferance.' Profile of the Alberta blind singer-teacher
– 'Charlie Chamberlain.' The popular singer with Don Messer
– '86 and Not Out: Healey Willan.' Interview
1967
Telescope series:
– 'Lady of the Legends.' Helen Creighton in NS
– '3's a Crowd.' Pop group members discuss their careers.
– 'Oscar Peterson.' Interview
– 'Maureen the Magnificent.' Interview with Maureen Forrester
'Teresa Stratas.' Special film documentary includes interviews with the Canadian soprano who sings opera excerpts, some with *Quilico and *Rideout.
1968
Telescope series:
– 'Guitar by Lister.' Guitar-builder Pat Lister
– 'Travelling Man.' Tommy *Hunter
– 'Mrs Cavazzi.' *Juliette filmed in Toronto and Vancouver
1969
'The Troubadour.' Jean-Pierre *Ferland in Paris
1970
'Music by *McPeek.' The composer of incidental music demonstrates his work.
'*Charlebois.' Interview with the Quebec pop singer
1971
'Annie on the Move.' Career of Anne Murray
'The Brott Baton.' Conductor Boris *Brott
'The Perth County Conspiracy'
'The Huggett Family Players'
'Songs for a Vanishing Friend.' Folksinger Bob Ruzicka on tour in the Arctic
'The Sound of August.' Glenn Sarty's documentary on the 1971 NYO summer
1972
'The Jazz Film Collector.' Toronto collector Joe Showler
'His Name is Paul Anka.' A visit to the Canadian-born singer
1973
'Sights and Sounds at the Conservatory.' The *RCMT
'A Song at Twilight.' Members of a senior citizens' choir discuss the role of music in their lives.
'Sarah Davidson.' Profile of a young Toronto harpist and her musical family
1975
'Sounds of the Rock.' Newfoundland's musical life. Performers include folksingers, fiddlers, choirs, and the pianist Karen Quinton.
1976
'Jon Vickers – A Man and His Music.' Canadian tenor performing and discussing his philosophy of music and of life in a film special
1978
'Music East / Music West.' Norman Campbell's film of the TS tour to the People's Republic of China
1979
'Chip and His Dog: How to Make an Opera.' The *Canadian Children's Opera Chorus performance of Menotti work
1979–80
Spectrum series:
– 'Mad Shadows.' Ann Ditchburn's ballet with score by André *Gagnon
– 'The Bands.' Tribute to brass bands; Central Band of the Canadian Armed Forces, *48th Highlanders Band, and the RCMP Band
– 'Harry and Frances Adaskin.'
– 'Louis Quilico.' A musical biography

Other TV films
1966
Conversations with Glenn Gould. BBC-TV. The Canadian pianist discusses four composers in four 40-minute films: 1 / Bach; 2 / Beethoven; 3 / Schoenberg; 4 / Richard Strauss
1970
'The Eye Hears The Ear Sees.' 58 min. BBC-TV. Tribute to Norman *McLaren's unique contribution to film
1975
'A Man and His Music.' CFQC-TV. Portrait of Saskatoon musician Lyell *Gustin, made for CFQC-TV in Saskatoon PW (GPr)

Film scores. Musical works composed especially for films. The films may be of any duration or type (full-length feature, short, fiction, publicity, documentary, animated cartoon, etc), but those intended for television are excluded unless also shown in halls or movie theatres for commercial purposes.

See also Films; Incidental music.

1 General
2 Work methods
3 Composers and film music
4 Music in the silent-film era
5 Animated films: Norman McLaren
6 Specialized composers
7 Feature-length films

1 GENERAL. Some composers consider film music a poor relation in the music world. In their view the film score, imprinted optically on film, is fixed for all time and only in exceptional circumstances will be honoured with a concert performance. But while it is true that the writing of film music follows very strict rules which may curb the composer's inspiration, it also is true that the dissemination of a cinematographic work sometimes occurs on a very large scale. Thus Maurice *Blackburn may take satisfaction in knowing that on many occasions film enthusiasts in Tokyo have been able to hear the music he wrote for *Blinkity Blank* (produced by Norman McLaren, 1954) while only rarely has that same public had the opportunity to hear a concert work by one or other of his Canadian colleagues.

Music written for the cinema is different in many ways from that intended for concert halls, as the composer Eldon *Rathburn points out: 'It is often constructed of short, telescoped phrases, climaxes reached with little preparation, violent colour and textural changes; of particular note is the absence of long transitional passages. Oddly enough, some of the present-day concert music has many of the above characteristics' (*Musique et Cinéma*). Moreover, music is just one of the elements of a film's sound-track. Speaking of the documentary film (a genre in which he has been particularly active), Maurice Blackburn describes how he conceives his work: 'The dialogue of a film may be compared to a recitative. This is why I attend whenever possible the recording of the scripts, so as to watch over the speaker's intonation and rhythm. It's the same with sound effects: their tone, their rhythm, their emotional value are what have an impact on me, not their realism. You have to beware of imitative music and descriptive commentary; and the sounds must summon up the unknown world of our subconscious' (*Musique et Cinéma*).

2 WORK METHODS. Since a film is the result of a collective effort, the composer working on a film is not free to create in isolation, as he is when composing a concert work. He must submit to such demands as budget, number of performers, timing (occasionally calculated in fractions of a second), the mood of each sequence, the producer's tastes, and the pressures exerted by production schedules.

The ideal work method consists of a collaboration between director and composer from the moment the project is developed (in other words before any shooting), such as that between McLaren and the jazz musician Oscar *Peterson for *Begone Dull Care* in 1949. Unfortunately, this kind of exchange is not always possible. In the majority of cases, the composer is called in after the shooting is over, that is, when the picture strip has been synchronized with the dialogue and sound effects. The musician then screens the film with the director, and together they determine what scenes will contain music, the exact length of each musical insert, and the type of music required by the particular mood of each sequence. For his part, the composer Harry *Freedman is more in favour of 'musical economy': 'Music can wreck a scene or save it. If the scene is well done, well acted and well directed, there may be no need for any underlying music. In that instance the intrusion of music could destroy the beauty of what is already there. However, in other instances, music can provide the mood or momentum that a given scene is lacking in its dramatic presentation ... Music is overused in films today, partly because audiences have grown used to having their reaction dictated to them by the music. And very often music is added for commercial reasons rather than artistic ones. Any half-way decent song that is used in a movie becomes a big hit so that theme and title-songs have become over-used as well' ('Silence really is golden,' James McLarty, *Motion*).

3 COMPOSERS AND FILM MUSIC. In the Canadian feature film industry by 1980 there had been very little recourse to the services of composers of serious music. Why is this so? Are they demanding fees that are too high or, like Stravinsky, do they look down on this field of musical creation? In this regard the prolific composer William *McCauley states: 'There used to be, and to a lesser degree still is, a stigma attached to writing commercial music. It's put down by people who don't write it – sometimes I think it's because they can't write it. Commercialism is almost a dirty word for them. I've spoken to several of these musicians who had very strong views about writing commercial music, and you ask them if they would like to write a score and all of a sudden their attitudes change because they've never been asked before. This negative attitude is changing however. People are realizing that if your music is liked enough to have people pay for it, then there must be some merit in it.' ('A kind of awareness,' Brian Charent, *Motion*).

Maurice Blackburn wrote in 1965 of the difficulties experienced by a composer of serious music in adapting to the very strict demands of this type of composition: 'In the twenty years that I've been writing for film, I've never been able to create the form in which I would have wished, on occasion, to express my ideas. In every instance it is the image that has imposed its structure on my film music' (*Musique et Cinéma*). And Eldon Rathburn expressed similar views: 'It is important that the film composer recognize the fact that his job is not to impose his will on the film but to let the film "speak" to him and in "listening" to the film the composer should be in a receptive mood to enable him to determine its musical needs' (*Musique et Cinéma*).

It also happens that serious music composers are cut off from the production of feature-length films by producers or directors who prefer a more 'popular' sound and call upon rock groups to write the music for their films. Moreover, this occurs not only in Canada but throughout the western world, and usually there is a financial reason. As with themes and title-songs, the music track frequently is sold in disc or cassette form, on a label whose economic ties with the film company are obvious. If the rock group composer and/or performer of the score is known, his participation in the film is highly publicized, thus attracting a public already familiar with the group in question.

Whatever the reasons, only a few composers of serious music have written for Canadian films. Among those who have composed for short films are Robert *Fleming, Serge *Garant, Michel *Longtin, Bruce *Mather, Pierre *Mercure, Barbara *Pentland, Clermont *Pépin, Micheline Coulombe *Saint-Marcoux, Harry *Somers, Gilles *Tremblay, Jean *Vallerand, and John *Weinzweig. Those who have written scores for feature films include Lucio *Agostini, Maurice Blackburn, Walter *Boudreau, Jean-Marie *Cloutier, Larry *Crossley, Harry Freedman, Michel *Gonneville, Hector *Gratton, William McCauley, and Oskar *Morawetz.

4 MUSIC IN THE SILENT-FILM ERA. The origins of music in the Canadian cinema do not coincide with the advent of talking pictures as may be supposed. As a matter of fact, the phrase 'silent film' is a half-truth, since the films of that period, while containing no dialogue or sound effects, were presented with music. The difference was that the music was not recorded on the filmstrip itself, as it came to be after 1927, but was performed 'live' at each performance by one or several musicians located before the screen on which the film was being projected. In this Canada was merely imitating what was happening elsewhere: musicians were employed by the Lumière brothers, Louis and Auguste, and Georges Méliès in France and Thomas Edison in the USA. In some film studios producers even hired musicians during the actual shooting of the film, so as to create the right atmosphere for filming and to 'inspire' the actors and crew.

Among the silent-film accompanists active in Toronto were Reginald *Stewart, Kathleen Stokes, Roland Todd, and Horace *Lapp. Around 1924 Lapp began creating suitable mood music on the organ in the Allen Theatre in Toronto. Leo *Barkin's first employment on his arrival in Canada in 1926 was as a film accompanist at the Rialto Theatre in Toronto. Percy *Faith worked 1920–7 as a film accompanist in Toronto, Reginald *Godden played for the silents in Barrie, Ont, and Lorne Carey accompanied the first movies in Hamilton, Ont. Charles Hofmann, a US silent-film pianist who moved to Canada in 1972, called himself an 'instant composer,' since he never played the piano with a score in front of him. He would sit down in front of the screen and improvise the musical commentary. In the 1960s Lapp and in the 1970s Hoffmann began practising their art once more with the showing of silent films in film-clubs, festivals, and schools.

In Montreal Billy *Eckstein began accompanying silent films at the Lyric Hall in 1906. Six years later he became the regular pianist at the Strand. He was billed as 'The World's Foremost Motion Picture Interpreter.' His reputation went beyond the borders of Canada, and such virtuosi as Sergei Rachmaninoff, Josef Hofmann, and Vladimir de Pachmann visited the Strand to hear him. Eckstein often worked with another pianist, Vera *Guilaroff. While in his teens, Wilfrid *Pelletier was a percussionist in the ensemble at the Windsor Star cinema. In 1926 the 15-year-old Mack White began a brilliant career in Montreal as a silent-film accompanist. Equally skilled as percussionist and pianist, the young White was able to create a vareity of sound effects (gun shots, moving trains, explosions, whistles, bells, etc) on these instruments.

For the more important films the producer would supply a written score. The fashionable cinema had an orchestra of about 15 musicians; the average employed an ensemble of 7; the more humble had 1 or 2.

See also Organ playing and teaching 6 / Theatre organists.

5 ANIMATED FILMS: NORMAN *MC LAREN. The animated film (created either by animated drawings, the shooting of one image at a time, the optical printer, or by any other technique) is a medium which has proven particularly congenial for the composer. Most animated films have no dialogue or spoken commentary; the sound-track consists simply of sound effects and music. Generally, they are very short but allow for an unbroken musical continuity, the creation of which understandably is more interesting for a composer than the fragments written to be interspersed at random throughout other types of film.

One Canadian film producer for whom music and image have been inseparable is Norman McLaren. Even in his films without dialogue, synchronization between the sound-track and the visual element is so complete that it is difficult to imagine viewing one with no sound. McLaren created some 60 films between 1934 and 1980 (see list in McLaren entry). For some he chose the music before drawing the pictures; in others, the music was selected after the drawing was completed. Furthermore – and it is this that places him in the front rank of film composers – McLaren himself 'wrote' the music for a dozen of his films without using a single sheet of music. His method, regarded as a significant innovation, was to 'sketch' sounds by hand directly onto the film, in the space reserved for the optical sound-track. McLaren thus became a complete film artist, creating an imaginary world wherein his brilliant imagination produced a perfectly synchronized interplay of sound and image.

Certain composers specialize in animated films while continuing to write for other kinds. Among the composers most frequently associated with animated films, in addition to McLaren, are Maurice Blackburn, Pierre *Brault, Denis Larochelle, Karl du Plessis, and Normand Roger. It should be observed that the animation films of the *NFB enjoy a high international reputation. The prizes obtained by NFB entries in European and US festivals attest to their quality.

6 SPECIALIZED COMPOSERS. An examination of the filmography of more than 200 Canadian cinema composers reveals that some of them have written large numbers of scores.

Eldon Rathburn has created, mostly for the NFB, some 185 sound environments for animated films (*The Romance of Transportation, Short and Suite, Canon*), documentaries (*Corral, City of Gold, Sky, Morning on the Lievre, Circle of the Sun, A is for Architecture, L'Homme et le froid*) and feature-length films (*Le Grand Rock, Nobody Waved Goodbye*). In 1964 he was awarded the annual prize of the Society of Film Makers. Maurice Blackburn, another who has worked chiefly for the NFB, has over 100 films to his credit, including *A Phantasy, Blinkity Blank, Je, Normétal, Lines-Vertical*, and *Percé on the Rocks*, as well as the feature films *Le Gros Bill, Ti-Coq, Le Festin des morts, Cordélia, Mourir à tue-tête*, etc.

Louis *Applebaum has written several scores for the NFB: *A Little Phantasy, Dollar Dance, Around is Around, Varley, The Jolifou Inn*, and theme music for the series of war films 'World in Action.' During the 1940s and 1950s the prolific composer Robert Fleming wrote numerous scores for NFB shorts, including *Les Aboiteaux, City out of Time, Les Maîtres-sondeurs* and *Phoebe*.

William McCauley has worked mostly in private industry, in particular with Crawley Films in Ottawa. He has written some 125 scores, including the feature film *Between Friends*. He collaborated on the documentary *Upper Canada Village*, produced by Moreland-Latchford Productions for the Ontario Ministry of Tourism and Information, a film which has received many awards.

7 FEATURE-LENGTH FILMS. By 1980 a detailed and analytical history of Canadian music for feature films had yet to be written, and no retrospective production record existed. This report will confine itself therefore to a brief survey, based on incomplete documentation, taking into account the fact that because production companies often have a short and tenuous existence, there are seldom archives that can be studied.

The first original feature film score by a Canadian composer is often said to be that of Ernest *Dainty for *Carry on Sergeant*, presented in Toronto in 1928. According to the periodical *Motion*, however, the film was released as a silent film, and in her husband's biography Gertrude Dainty states that the music was performed by the theatre orchestra during the projection. Therefore the music of Howard *Fogg for *Rhapsody in Two Languages* (1934) may be considered the first original Canadian score for a film with a synchronized sound-track.

The years 1944–54, sometimes termed the heroic days of the Canadian film score, were but a modest prelude to a development that would reach its full potential in the early 1960s. Among the pioneers, mention should be made of Morris C. *Davis, who composed the music for a film produced simultaneously in French (*La Forteresse*) and English (*Whispering City*) but with different actors. One sequence from the film featured a concert in which Neil *Chotem played the *Quebec Concerto*, an arrangement of André *Mathieu's *Concerto No. 3*. Other films of this period were *Le Curé de village* (Davis with Lucio Agostini), *Un Homme et son péché* (Hector Gratton), *Le Gros Bill* and *Ti-Coq* (Maurice Blackburn), *Les Lumières de ma ville* (Pierre Pétel), *Le Rossignol et les cloches* (Allan *McIver), and *La Petite Aurore, l'enfant martyre* and *Coeur de maman* (Germaine Janelle). An English-language film of this period – *Forbidden Journey* – had music by Oskar *Morawetz.

After 1960 production in Quebec grew steadily, and producers called upon both composers and chansonniers. Certain names recur frequently, but the following list may not give an entirely fair representation because it is necessarily incomplete:

Maurice Blackburn. *Le Fastin des morts; Le Temps de l'avant; Mourir à tue-tête; Cordélia; J.A. Martin, photographe*

Pierre Brault. *Le Viol d'une jeune fille douce; Red; Le Temps d'une chasse; La Vraie Nature de Bernadette; Kings and Desperate Men* (with Michel Robidoux); and others, at least a dozen titles in all. Brault also worked with the animation department of the NFB.

Walter Boudreau. *La Chambre blanche; Ultimatum; Les Maudits Sauvages; Une Nuit en Amérique* (the score of which was adapted for concert performance under the title *Variations I*); *Réjeanne Padovani; L'Infonie inachevée* (which employed sterophonic sound)

Bernard Buisson. *Les Bons Débarras; Une Amie d'enfance*

Robert *Charlebois. *Jusqu'au Coeur; Tout l'temps, tout l'temps; À soir on fait peur au monde; Deux Femmes en or*

Alain Clavier. *L'Arrache-coeur*

Jean Cloutier. *Thetford au milieu de notre vie*

Jean-Marie *Cloutier. *Le Règne du jour*

François Cousineau. *L'Initiation*; etc
Jean *Cousineau. *Pour la suite du monde* (with Jean Meunier); *À tout prendre* (with Maurice Blackburn and Serge Garant); *Mon Oncle Antoine; Taureau; Dream Speaker; Ada*
François *Dompierre. *IXE-13; O.K. ... Laliberté* (with Céline Prévost); *La Gammick* (with Alain Clavier); *Partis pour la gloire; YUL 871* (with Stéphane *Venne); *Tiens-toi bien après les oreilles à papa; Bernie pis la gang; Ti-Mine; Aimez-vous les chiens?; St-Denis dans le temps*
Claude *Dubois. *Cerveaux gelés*
Jean-Pierre *Ferland. *Fleur de macadam*
Lewis *Furey. *L'Ange et la femme; La Tête de Normande St-Onge; Jacob Two Two Meets the Hooded Fang; Fantastica*
André *Gagnon. *L'Évasion des carrousels; Les Jeux de la XXIe Olympiade; Night Flight; Running*
Lee *Gagnon, *Chantal en vrac; Seizure; Pousse mais pousse égal*
Claude *Gauthier. *Tête en fleurs; Entre la mer et l'eau douce*
Michel Gonneville. *Tu brûles, tu brûles*
Richard *Grégoire. *Éclaire au chocolat*
Pierick *Houdy. *Comme les six doigts de la main*
Claude *Léveillée. *Patinoire; Taxi; Les Beaux Dimanches*
Andrée Paul. *Patricia et Jean-Baptiste* (with Raoul *Duguay); *Il ne faut pas mourir pour ça; Q-Bec My Love; Les Dernières Fiançailles*
Jacques Perron. *Le P'tit vient vite; Il était une fois dans l'Est; Le Martien de Noël; Les Smattes*
Jean Sauvageau. *Mistashipu* (Wilderness Award 1975)
Louis Spritzer. *Ciné-boum*
Stéphane Venne. *Où êtes-vous donc?; Les Mâles; Seul ou avec d'autres; Jusqu'au cou*
Gilles *Vigneault. *Poussière sur la ville; Ce soir-là; Gilles Vigneault...*

It was in the early 1960s also that the production of feature-length films in English began in earnest. Toronto was the production centre, but some films, especially co-productions, were produced elsewhere in Canada, notably in Montreal. To the customary composers were added jazz and pop musicians. Producers also engaged composers from Quebec, such as Pierre Brault and André Gagnon.

Lucio Agostini. *Inside Out; Ragtime Summer; The Little Brown Burro; Ichabod Crane*
Milton *Barnes. *Blood and Guts*
Bill and Ben Bogaardt. *Time of the Tarsands* (prize, Alberta Film Festival)
Howard *Cable. *Canada Carries On; Small Fry; Ski Skill*; also about 10 scores for the NFB
Neil Chotem. *The Butler's Night Off; U-Turn*
Ron *Collier. *Face Off; A Fan's Notes; Paperback Hero*
Clarence J. Crilley. *Rivers of Romance*
Larry Crossley. *The Johari Window; Wolf Pack; Cry of the Wolf; The Man Who Skied Down Everest*
Gordon *Fleming and others. *Catuor*
Harry Freedman. *Act of the Heart (Acte du coeur)* including the cantata *The Flame Within* (Canadian Film Award 1970); *Isobel; The Pyx*
Hagood *Hardy. *Tukik and His Search for a Merry Christmas; Second Wind; Rituals; Klondike Fever; American Christmas Carol*
Paul *Hoffert. *Outrageous* (Etrog Award 1977); *Circle of Two; Midnight Matinee; Double Negative; The Groanstar Conspiracy; Third Walker; Winter Kept Us Warm*
Paul Horn. *Even Cowgirls Get the Blues*
Milan *Kymlicka. *The Last Act of Martin Weston; The Reincarnate; Wedding in White*
Matthew McCauley. *Between Friends*
William McCauley. *The Neptune Factor; Sunday in the Country; It Seemed like a Good Idea at the Time*
Bob *McMullin. *On the Edge of Ice Pack; Race Home to Die; The Shadow of the Hawk*
Ben *McPeek. *The Rowdyman; Only God Knows; Catch the Sun*
John *Mills-Cockell. *The Clown Murders; Deadly Harvest*
Oscar Peterson. *The Silent Partner* (Etrog Award 1978)
Art Phillips. *The Dionne Quintuplets*
Tibor *Polgar. *In Praise of Older Women*
Morris *Surdin. *Hospital*
Paul Zaza. *Murder by Decree* (with Carl Zittrer); *Stone Cold Dead; Title Shop*

It frequently happens that a director will use the same composer film after film: eg, Jean-Pierre Lefebvre with Andrée Paul, Denis Héroux with François Cousineau, and Paul Almond with Harry Freedman. Besides Norman McLaren, a few directors, eg, John Howe, Pierre Marcoux, Jim Kraemer, and Anne Wheeler, have composed their own music.

When a film has been produced in Canada as a co-production, the music usually has been composed by a musician from the other participating country. This was the case for *Kamouraska* (Maurice Le Roux), *Two Solitudes* (Maurice Jarre), and *Angela* (Henry Mancini).

The Guild of Canadian Film Composers was founded in 1979, with Ben McPeek as interim president. The aims of the guild are to establish a standard contract that will define clearly the rights of composers called upon to write for films and to seek to provide its members with all pertinent information and to represent their interests in dealing with deparments and government agencies.

Anxious to have its members acquire the basic principles of film composition, *PRO Canada in March 1980 organized five workshops for the benefit of its members.

BIBLIOGRAPHY
Morrissette, François. 'Des images en musique,' *CRMA*, vol 6, Feb–Mar 1974
Rooke, Peggy. 'Film music,' ibid
Partley, Gerald. 'Canada's film musicians,' *SatN*, 9 Aug 1952
Fleming, Robert. 'Music for films,' *Jmc*, Jan 1963
Morgan, Kit. 'Original music...the difference between an excellent film and an outstanding film,' *CanComp*, 3, Oct 1965
'Animated sound: a Canadian composer's unique contribution to the advance of the cinema,' ibid
'Canadian "filmography",' ibid, 5, Jan 1966
'Larry Crosley composes original film music,' ibid, 10, Sep 1966
Beattie, Eleanor. *A Handbook of Canadian Cinema* (Toronto, Montreal 1973, 1976)
Motion, 6 articles, vol 4, no. 2, 1975
Pratley, Gerald. 'The ups and downs of creating music for Canadian feature films,' *CanComp*, 104, Oct 1975
Schulman, Michael. 'Two films, two music scores, and two less-than-happy composers,' ibid, 138, Feb 1979
Landry, Jacques. 'More film-scoring jobs available when conditions change,' *MSc*, 312, Mar–Apr 1980
MacMillan, Rick. 'Lively Canadian film scene here to stay – composers,' ibid
Vallerand, François. 'François Dompierre,' *Séquences*, 100, Feb 1980
Applebaum, Louis. 'Film music,' *Music in Canada*
Musique et Cinéma JLm (GP)

FINDLATER, Charles (Edward). Choir director, teacher, adjudicator, b London 2 Jul 1893, d Vancouver 7 Aug 1975; ATCM 1930, LTCL 1933, Associate (Tonic Sol-Fa College, London) 1933. He arrived in Canada in 1914 and settled in Vancouver in 1918. He founded the *Elgar Choir of British Columbia in 1924 and was music supervisor for Vancouver schools ca 1928–31. His Elgar School of Music (ca 1935–ca 1972) offered instruction in singing, piano, and theory (mostly taught by Findlater, who was head of the school until it closed). He taught piano and theory ca 1940–65 at Crofton House School (where he also directed the choirs) and was choirmaster ca 1937–44 at Knox United Church in Vancouver and ca 1944–9 at St Mary's (Kerrisdale). Findlater's choirs were heard from the 1940s to the 1960s over CBC radio. He adjudicated many times at the Coquitlam and Williams Lake festivals and was on the Vancouver auditioning board of the CBC in the 1950s. Findlater was president 1946–55 of the *BCRMTA. His pupils included Betty-Ann Busch, Len Chapple, Gordon Gibson, and Gordon Hunt.

FINE, Allan. Bass, teacher, b Siauliai, Lithuania, 13 Aug 1926, naturalized Canadian 1956; L MUS (McGill) 1967. He studied at the U of Munich 1947–9 and then at *McGill Cons with Ria *Lenssens and Luciano *Della Pergola. He also worked with Boris Goldovsky at the Oglebay Opera Institute in 1963. The following year he premiered in Montreal songs by the Canadian composers *Morawetz, *Applebaum, and *Weinzweig. He performed in recital and as soloist with the *MSO and the Hartford SO in Connecticut and also participated in several radio and TV programs. He took supporting roles with the *Opera Guild of Montreal (*Madama Butterfly*, 1969) and with the *Opéra du Québec (*Salome*, 1972). Though he remained a resident of Montreal, in 1963 he began commuting to Hartford to conduct the Beth Israel Temple Choir and he also performed there in Léon Algazi's *Sacred Service* and other works. In 1964 he made the first of several trips to Israel, where he has participated in broadcasts and recitals with Kol Israel, the state radio. Fine premiered his own arrangements of three Inuit songs in 1974 at the Gardner Museum of Boston and repeated them at the Lennoxville Festival in Lennoxville, Que, in 1976. With the pianist Charles *Reiner, he recorded 'Cry of the Prophet' by Applebaum and 'Dance of Masada' by Weinzweig in 1969 for the LP *Mélodies hébraïques* (RCA LSC-3092). His repertoire comprises works in 12 languages. He taught at McGill U 1968–72. (NT)

Finland. The first Finnish immigrants to Canada arrived via the USA and Alaska during the mid-19th century. Many worked in construction, on such projects as the Welland Canal and the CPR. More substantial waves of immigration occurred during the 1920s (following the establishment of a Finnish republic in 1917) and the 1950s. In 1977 there were more than 70,000 people of Finnish descent in Canada and more than half were Finnish-speaking. The majority lived in Sault Ste Marie, Sudbury, Thunder Bay, Toronto, and Vancouver. Among Finnish-Canadians Lutheran is the most common religious denomination. Finnish newspapers were established in Sudbury in 1917, Thunder Bay in 1915, and Toronto in 1931, and schools were set up to teach the Finnish language.

Until the late 19th century Finnish folksongs usually were performed to the accompaniment of the violin, the clarinet, or the kantele, the last of which resembles an autoharp and is considered the national instrument of Finland. By this time, however, choirs and brass bands had superseded earlier traditions in popularity.

In Canada, Finnish cultural associations have sponsored visits by Finnish groups and provided support for performances by local choirs. A Finnish-Canadian choir of 24 appeared 1 Jul 1938 at the *CNE, Toronto, in a folk festival sponsored by the Native Sons and Daughters of Canada. Finnish-Canadian choirs of the 1970s included the Sault Finnish Choir, the Kaleva Men's Choir of Sault Ste Marie, the Sudbury Finnish Male Chorus, the Otava Male Choir of Thunder Bay, and the Toronto Finnish Male Chorus. While male choirs have predominated in the Finnish tradition, female and mixed choirs were becoming more common in the 1970s.

Frequently performed repertoire included the choral arrangement of the chorale from Sibelius' *Finlandia*, 'Terre Suomeni Maa' (a patriotic song), and 'Poika Ajo Punaruunilla' (a folksong). Central to Finnish vocal and choral music, and an inspiration for instrumental composition, is the national epic poem *Kalevala*, a 19th-century compilation of ancient folk lyrics which has been translated into 30 languages.

Works by Finland's most famous composer, Sibelius, were played in Canada as early as 1909 when the *Welsman TSO performed *Finlandia*. That work soon became a staple of the orchestra's repertoire. Under *MacMillan, the *TSO gave the Canadian premiere of *Symphony No. 2* in 1932 and presented an all-Sibelius program in 1935. The *Montreal Orchestra (1930–41) gave the Montreal premieres of four major works of Sibelius: *Symphony No. 1*, *En Saga*, *Tapiola*, and *Pohjola's Daughter*. By the 1970s most major Canadian orchestras had performed at least *Symphony No. 2* and the *Violin Concerto; Valse Triste* and *The Swan of Tuonela* were pop-concert items and community-orchestra favourites; and the other symphonies had occasional performances. In 1977 Franz-Paul *Decker conducted the complete *Four Legends from the Kalevala* for the 'Grands Concerts' of the CBC French network. Monuments to Sibelius have been erected on St Helen's Island, Montreal, and in Jean Sibelius Park on Kendal Avenue in Toronto. In December 1965, at a concert sponsored by the Toronto Finnish Advancement Society to celebrate the 100th anniversary of the composer's birth, the Finnish ambassador to Canada presented the scores of 230 Sibelius compositions to the *U of Toronto music library on behalf of Canadians of Finnish origin.

Finnish-born musicians who have been active in Canada include Matti Holli (1916–77), the founder and until his death the conductor of the *Windsor SO, and Whitey Pentii Glann, one-time drummer with the rock group *Mandala. Finnish visitors to Canada have included Tauno Hannikainen (who appeared as guest conductor of the *Promenade Symphony Concerts in 1952), the soprano Anita Valkki (who sang with the *MSO in 1963 and again at an *Expo 67 Scandinavian Gala, where she was heard in Sibelius' rarely performed *Luonnotar*, Op 70), the baritone Kalle Ruusunen, and the Helsinki University Chorus, which was heard in Toronto in 1938 and 1953. In 1960 Olavi Pesonen represented Finland at the *International Conference of Composers at Stratford, Ont; in 1975 Pekka Gronow presented a paper at *World Music Week, held in Canada under the auspices of the International Music Council.

Canadians who have visited Finland include the soprano Bertha *Crawford, who sang in Helsinki in 1917, and the pianist Jacinthe *Couture, who taught at Helsinki's Sibelius Academy in 1976. In July 1977 the 38th annual Finnish Canadian Grand Festival took place in Sudbury, Ont. Events included dances, sports activities, gymnastics, a play, and performances by several choirs.

By 1975 the archives of the *National Museum of Man held 138 Finnish songs and 150 instrumental works, collected by Helen *Creighton in New Brunswick, Kenneth *Peacock in Ontario, and Burt Feintuch in British Columbia.

BIBLIOGRAPHY

Feintuch, Burt. 'Sointula, British Columbia: aspects of a folk music tradition as a social phenomenon,' *CFMJ*, vol 1, 1973

Finnish-Canadian Historical Society of Copper Cliff, Ont. Microfilms of archives. Laurentian U Library. (LRH)

FIORE, Nicholas. Flutist, b Port Coquitlam, near Vancouver, 14 Feb 1918, d London, Ont, 18 Mar 1979. He studied first with his father, Pasquale Fiore, an amateur musician who also taught violin and piano. With his sisters he formed the Fiore Quintet, which performed during the mid-1930s in Vancouver churches and on radio. He became principal flute of the *Vancouver SO in 1939 and also played in the *CBC Vancouver Chamber Orchestra. At this time he studied for four summers in Maine with William Kincaid. Later (1966, 1967) he studied and performed for two seasons at the Marlboro Festival, coached by Marcel Moyse, and attended Moyse's classes for two more seasons. In 1952 he became principal flute with the *TSO, and in 1953 he began teaching at the *U of Toronto. He retired from both positions in 1978 to teach at the *U of Western Ontario. He began teaching summers at the Courtenay Youth Music Centre in 1972. His pupils have included Robert *Aitken, Suzanne *Shulman, and two *CBC Talent Festival winners, Douglas Stewart and Jadwiga Michalska. In addition to first performances 1962–75 while he was a member of the *Toronto Woodwind Quintet (later Toronto Winds), Fiore premiered *Weinzweig's *Divertimento No. 1* with the CBC Vancouver Chamber Orchestra in 1946 and *Somers' *12 Miniatures* 2 Feb 1964. He made broadcast recordings of Jean *Coulthard's *Music on a Quiet Song* (RCI 35), Kent Kennan's *Night Soliloquy* with the CBC Vancouver Concert Orchestra (RCI 52), and Lucio *Agostini's *Suite for Flute and Orchestra* (RCI 174). He is soloist on the TS recording of Norma Beecroft's *Improvvisazioni Concertanti No. 1* (Audat 447-4001). See also Discography for Mary *Morrison.

BIBLIOGRAPHY

Creech, Gwenlyn. 'Nicholas Fiore: flutist and farmer,' *Fugue*, Jun–Jul 1978

Kirby, Blaik. 'Fiore creeps into limelight after 26 years,' Toronto *Globe and Mail*, 22 Jul 1978 (WS)

First Symposium of Canadian Contemporary Music. Held in Vancouver 12–15 Mar 1950 at the Hotel Vancouver and the Denman Auditorium under the sponsorship of the Vancouver Symphony Society and the *Community Arts Council of Vancouver. The purposes were 'to play, listen to, discuss, discover and stimulate greater interest in Canadian composers and their music' (Jacques Singer in program brochure). Singer was the initiator and music director of the symposium. Alex Walton, chairman of the symposium, moderated a panel discussion in which Harry *Adaskin, Barbara *Pentland, Singer, and John *Weinzweig participated. Four programs (one each for symphony orchestra, chamber orchestra, small chamber ensemble, and choir) presented works of 33 composers in the largest festival of Canadian music prior to that at *Expo 67. These had been chosen from 155 submissions. The *Vancouver SO performed the symphonic works. The festival featured music from all regions of Canada and from all ranks of composers, from the established (*Willan and *Whitehead) to the very young (*Pépin and *Somers), from the conservative (Edwin A. *Collins, Charles *O'Neill) to those who then were considered avant-garde (Pentland, Weinzweig). The symposium ushered in a decade marked by many special concerts devoted to Canadian music.

BIBLIOGRPAHY

Adaskin, Harry. 'Symposium,' *SatN*, 11 Apr 1950 HK

FISCHER, Sarah (Eugénie, 'Nini'). Soprano, teacher, administrator, b Paris 23 Feb 1896, naturalized Canadian 1912, d Montreal 3 May 1975. She came to Montreal at the age of 12 with her parents, who were of Polish-Jewish origin. While working as a telephone operator, she studied solfège with J.-J. *Goulet, voice with Céline *Marier, and stage skills with Jeanne *Maubourg. In 1917 she competed successfully for a three-year *Strathcona Scholarship to the RCM, but because of World War I she did not go to London till later. She made her stage debut 19 Nov 1918 in Montreal as Micaela in *Carmen* at the *Monument national, singing with Cédia *Brault, Victor Desautels, and Ulysse *Paquin under the direction of Albert *Roberval. C.-O. *Lamontagne described her as 'a stunning Micaela, full of grace and the bloom of youth. Ideally suited to the role, she performs with sincerity, giving an accurate portrayal of the loyal and innocent character of the country girl' (*Canada musical*, 7 Dec 1918). Other roles followed in Montreal and Quebec City: Colette in Messager's *La Basoche*, Philine in *Mignon*, and the title role in *Lakmé* (1919).

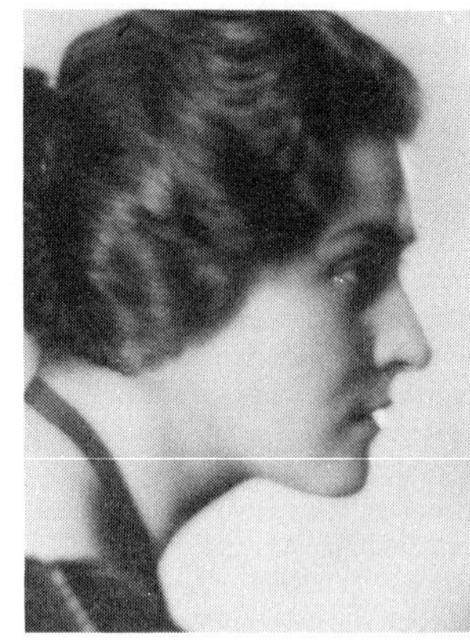

Sarah Fischer (*Le Canada musical*, Feb 1918)

After a leave-taking recital, Fischer left for London to complete her training at the RCM 1919–22 with Cecilia M. Hutchinson. Fischer was a member 1922–3 of the British National Opera Company and sang the roles of Eva (*Meistersinger*), Pamina (*The Magic Flute*), the Countess (*The Marriage of Figaro*), and Marguerite (*Faust*), at Covent Garden and on tour. After a period in Rome, ca 1923–4, when she studied with Vincenzo Lombardi, she sang for the Grand Opera Syndicate at Covent Garden, performing the role of Olga in Giordano's *Fedora* (1925).

Soon after her arrival in London, Fischer became Emma *Albani's protégée. In May 1925 she participated in the benefit gala at Covent Garden arranged by Melba for Albani, in which Sir Edward Elgar and Sir Henry Wood took part. She returned there in 1936 to create the leading role in *Pickwick*, an opera by Albert Coates. In Great Britain the name of Sarah Fischer is forever associated with two events in the history of opera. On 8 Jan 1923, in the first opera broadcast from Covent Garden – *The Magic Flute* – she was heard as Pamina; and on 6 Jul 1934, in the BBC's first opera telecast – 30 minutes of excerpts from *Carmen* – she sang the title role, with the tenor Heddle Nash as Don José, assisted by the dancer Elsa Brunelleschi.

Joining the Opéra-Comique in Paris, Fischer made her debut 20 Nov 1925 as Mélisande in *Pelléas et Mélisande*. (She later was much sought after for that role, which she learned in 10 days.) At the same theatre in 1927 she sang the title role in the 1600th performance of *Mignon*. She sang in various theatres in Monte Carlo and Algiers, and at Liverpool and Bradford in England. In May 1928 she was engaged by Bruno Walter for a series of Mozart operas at the Odéon theatre in Paris. She enjoyed a marked success in the roles of Pamina, the Countess (*The Marriage of Figaro*), and Fiordiligi (*Così fan tutte*). She was acclaimed in recital and performed frequently at Wigmore Hall, London.

In Montreal Fischer sang 1927, 1930, and 1936 for the *Ladies' Morning Musical Club at the Ritz-Carlton Hotel. In December 1930 she repeated the role of Colette (*La Basoche*) at the Monument national for the *Société canadienne d'opérette. Her father's illness and World War II took her again to Montreal in 1940. She opened a studio there, and among her pupils were Roger *Doucet, Yolande *Dulude, Jean-Pierre *Hurteau, and Jeannine Perron.

On 1 Feb 1941 in Montreal Fischer presented the first of the Sarah Fischer Concerts 'for the benefit of Canadian musicians.' She directed this venture until her death, assisted by many she had inspired. Held first at the Art Association of Montreal (later Musée des beaux-arts), then at the Ritz-Carlton Hotel, the annual series of four concerts helped establish numerous Canadian musicians, particularly newcomers. In the course of 145 concerts (the last one in January 1975), debuts were made by many young artists, including Pierrette *Alarie, Violet *Archer, Réjane *Cardinal, Clarice *Carson, Fernande *Chiocchio, Yolande Dulude, Marie-José Forgues, Maureen *Forrester, Hélène *Gagné, Claire *Gagnier, Denis *Harbour, Mary *Henderson, Jacques *Labrecque, Mariana *Paunova, André *Prévost, Jacqueline *Richard, Claude *Savard, Robert *Silverman, and Micheline *Tessier. In 1946 Fischer instituted the Sarah Fischer Concerts scholarships 'in memory of Dame Emma Albani.' Fischer herself sang excerpts from *Pelléas et Mélisande* at the ninth concert, 25 Feb 1942, with José *Delaquerrière and Roger *Filiatrault. It was her last public performance. Subsequently she devoted her life to her pupils and to social and musical organizations such as the *MSO.

In 1919 in New York Sarah Fischer recorded eight titles for Pathé. In London, between 1922 and 1925, she recorded four Elizabethan love songs with string quartet for HMV. A list appears in *Roll Back the Years*. In 1939, again in London, she recorded six songs in English (Haydn, Bunten, Dunhill, Edwards, and Mana-Zucca). These, along with the titles from Pathé and HMV, were reissued on a private LP, *Sarah Fischer*, released in Canada in 1967.

In 1928 Sarah Fischer was made an honorary member of the RCM. In 1968 she was awarded the prize of the Concert Society of Jewish Peoples' Schools and the Peretz Schools; the award was given annually to a personality from the artistic world. She left her personal papers to the PAC.

BIBLIOGRAPHY
Charbonneau, Hélène. *L'Albani: sa carrière artistique et triomphale* (Montreal 1938)
Beker, Marilyn. 'A life bound up with beauty,' Montreal *Gazette*, 4 Mar 1971
Siskind, Jacob. 'Sarah Fischer was a "grande dame" of music,' ibid, 5 May 1975
Potvin, Gilles. 'Une artiste exemplaire: Sarah Fischer,' Montreal *Le Devoir*, 6 May 1975
Ouellette, Louise and Goddard, Diane. 'Sarah Fischer, mezzo-soprano 1896–1975,' *L'Archiviste*, vol 6, Jan–Apr 1979
Musiciennes de chez nous

GP

FISHER, Alfred (Joel). Composer, pianist, teacher, b Boston 30 Jun 1942, naturalized Canadian 1974; B MUS (Boston) 1968, M MUS (Michigan State) 1967, PH D (Michigan State) 1976. He studied piano with Alfred Kanwischer and Pierre Luboshutz, composition with George Crumb, Douglas Moore, John Pozdro, and H. Owen Reed, and musicology with Hans Nathan. He taught 1965–8 at Michigan State U, 1969–72 at the *U of Western Ontario, 1972–3 at the *U of Saskatchewan, and 1973–8 at *Acadia U. In 1978 he became chairman of the theory and composition division at the *U of Alberta. Fisher has written works for the Radio Telefis Eireann Symphony (*Elegaic Variations*, 1976) and *NOVA MUSIC (*The Owl at Dusk*, 1979). His compositions include a *Piano Sonata* (1965), *Six Aphorisms* for piano (1967), *Refrain from Ape and Essence* for choir and orchestra (1968), *Ariel's Whisper* for violin and piano (1973), *Behind the Ranges* for soprano and flute (1974), *Night Elegy* for soprano and chamber ensemble (1974), *Sonata breve* for trumpet and trombone (1975), *To a Gentile Poet* for two cellos (1977, revised for chamber ensemble 1978), *Four Movements for Unaccompanied Clarinet* (1979), and *Two Sacred Motets* for mixed choir (1979). Several of his works have been published by Seesaw Music. He is an associate of the *CMCentre and an affiliate of CAPAC.

BIBLIOGRAPHY
Edwards, Barry. 'The teaching of composition: an extraordinarily complex matter,' *CanComp*, 136, Dec 1978

FISHER, (William) Allen. Teacher, bandmaster, b Cobourg, Ont, 29 Jun 1905; BA English, history (Queen's) 1930, hon LL D (Queen's) 1972. He obtained a specialist certificate in school music teaching. He taught English and history and pioneered instrumental training 1931–6 in several Ontario schools. While head 1937–71 of the history and music departments of Barrie Collegiate Institute, he founded in 1939 and conducted until his retirement in 1972 the *Barrie Central Collegiate Band, which won fame in competition festivals in Canada and abroad. He received in 1972 the Fred L. Bartlett Memorial Award for outstanding work in public school education in Ontario. Al Stanwyk, a big-band trumpeter in Canada and the USA, was a pupil of Fisher. Fisher was invested as a Member of the *Order of Canada in 1974. He is a specialist in the history of the Huronia area of Ontario and has contributed articles to the *Canadian Music Educator*. CF

FISHER, Arthur Elwell. Educator, composer, organist, violist, b England 29 May 1848, d probably in the USA after 1912; B MUS (Trinity, Toronto) ca 1887, ATCL 1889, ACO (Associate, College of Organists) 1889. He studied violin at the Paris Cons and with Henry Holmes in London and was an organist in Liverpool before emigrating to Canada. He lived first in Montreal, where he was the organist 1879–82 at St George's Church. In 1882 or 1886 he moved to Toronto, where he taught piano, violin, voice, and theory 1887–93 at the *TCM and the *Toronto College of Music, played viola in the *Toronto String Quartette, and held church positions. He advocated the holding of local examinations in Ontario and the West and in 1887 became the TCM's first travelling examiner. He founded the St Cecilia Choral Society of Toronto to encourage unaccompanied singing and contributed many editorials and compositions to the *Musical Journal* (Toronto 1887–90). In 1894 Fisher became a music examiner for the *U of Toronto; in 1896 he was music director of the Ladies' College in Kingston. He later taught at the Chicago Cons.

Fisher wrote about 100 songs and piano, violin, and choral pieces, published in Canada by *Suckling, in England by Ashdown, Curwen, and Novello, and in the USA by Century, Ditson, G. Schirmer, and Summy. His larger works include a *String Trio in G, Op 54*, a *Rhapsody* for violin and orchestra, a *Thanksgiving* (or Harvest) *Cantata* intended as a doctoral exercise, and *The Wreck of the Hesperus*, a cantata for female choir and piano, premiered in 1893 and rescored for mixed choir and orchestra for the opening festival of Massey Music Hall (*Massey Hall) in 1894. A song – 'Life,' with words by E. Pauline Johnson – was published in the *Musical Journal* 15 Jul 1887. Hector *Charlesworth considered Fisher 'a man of profound learning, though still under the shadow of the cathedral, like most English musicians of the eighties.' He also found him 'most progressive' but 'extremely tactless.'

BIBLIOGRAPHY
Pazdirek, B. 'Arthur E. Fischer' (sic), *Universal-Handbuch der Musikliteratur* (Vienna 1904–10)
Charlesworth, Hector. *Candid Chronicles* (Toronto 1925)
Collins, Alice Roger. 'Preface,' *Real People*, vol 5 (London, Ont [1936])
Metropolitan Toronto Library. A.E. Fisher scrapbook

HK

FISHER, Constance (m Craig). Stage director, soprano, b Hamilton, Ont, 3 Oct 1928; ARCT piano 1950, ARCT voice 1951. After studies with Alberto *Guerrero (piano) and Weldon *Kilburn and Irene *Jessner (voice) at the *RCMT and with Herman *Geiger-Torel at the *Royal Cons Opera School, she made her debut in 1957 with the Opera Festival of Toronto (later *COC) as the Mother in *Hansel and Gretel*. A member of the COC until 1966, she sang Frasquita in *Carmen* (1961), Gerhilde in *Die Walküre* (1962), Musetta in *La Bohème* (1963), and, in touring productions, Fiordiligi in *Così fan tutte* (1963), Rosalinda in *Die Fledermaus* (1964, 1965), and again Frasquita (1966). She also sang Hebe in *Orpheus in the Underworld* at the 1959 *Stratford Festival. After making her professional debut as a stage director (1968) with a production of *La Bohème* for the COC, she worked 1968–70 as a staff producer at Sadler's Wells, where she rehearsed revivals of *Hansel and Gretel, The Rake's Progress, Count Ory, Così fan tutte*, and *The Queen of Spades* and assisted with productions of *Die Meistersinger* and *Die Walküre*. She also directed productions of *Madama Butterfly, Così fan tutte*, and *Hansel and Gretel* at the *Banff SFA and, later, *The Barber of Seville* (1973), *L'Heure espagnole* (1974), and *Il Trovatore* (1975) for the COC. In 1972 she became stage director and instructor and in 1978 divisional co-ordinator and resident stage director at the *U of Toronto Opera Dept, for which she has directed several productions, including the Canadian premieres of Robert Ward's *The Crucible* (1976) and Janáček's *Katya Kabanova* (1977), both conducted by her husband, W. James *Craig. She also has directed for the *Edmonton, *Southern Alberta, and *Manitoba opera associations and for the Cincinnati Summer Opera – *Don Giovanni*, her US debut, 1977. MM

FISHER, Edward. Administrator, organist, conductor, teacher, b Jamaica, Vt, 11 Jan 1848, d Toronto 31 May 1913; hon D MUS (Toronto) 1898. In 1867, after musical training in Worcester, Mass, Fisher entered the New England Cons, Boston, where he studied with Julius Eichberg (counterpoint and harmony), the Canadian J.B. Sharland (piano), and Eugene Thayer (organ). Fisher at different times was organist at Second Unitarian Church and Phillip's Church, Boston, and Elliot Church, Newton, and was the pianist for the Boston Choral Union and the Newton Musical Assn. In 1874 he studied in Berlin with C.A. Haupt (organ) and Albert Loeschhorn (piano) and in 1875 he moved to Canada as music director of the Ottawa Ladies' College. In Ottawa he gave several

Edward Fisher

organ recitals and conducted the *Ottawa Choral Society.

Moving to Toronto, where he served 1879–99 as organist at St Andrew's Church, Fisher expanded the St Andrew's Choral Society into the 250 to 400-member Toronto Choral Society. Under his direction 1879–91 the society presented such works as Handel's *Samson, Messiah,* and *Israel in Egypt*; Haydn's *The Creation* and *The Seasons* (first part); Mendelssohn's *St Paul, Lauda Sion,* and *Psalm 95*; Rossini's *Stabat mater*; Gounod's *Gallia*; Hiller's *Song of Victory*; Costa's *The Dream*; Gade's *Psyche*; and Schumann's *Paradise and the Peri*. Fisher was music director for several years of the Ontario Ladies' College, Whitby, but his greatest achievement was the founding of the TCM (now *RCMT), which he directed from 1887 to 1913. His pupils included Mona *Bates, Sara Dallas, Eleanor Dallas, Rena Chadwicke, W.O. *Forsyth, and J.D.A. *Tripp. Only two of his compositions are known to be extant: 'Night Hymn at Sea' (Nordheimer 1876) and a *Rondo Caprice, Op 6*, for piano. Fisher was a co-founder (1885) of the Ontario Music Teachers' Assn (later *Canadian Society of Musicians) and was president 1889–90. He was Ontario vice-president (1887) of the Music Teachers' National assn.

BIBLIOGRAPHY
'Music in Canada,' *MCour*, vol 37, 2 Nov 1898
Harrison, Mrs J.W.F. 'An educationalist in music,' *Canadian Magazine*, Jun 1909
'The late Edward Fisher, MUS.D.,' *MCan*, vol 8, Jul 1913

EK

The Fisherman and His Soul. Ballet by Harry *Somers (music) and Grant Strate (choreography). It was premiered in Hamilton, Ont, 5 Nov 1956, by the National Ballet of Canada; George *Crum conducted the orchestra. The plot is based on a story by Oscar Wilde about a fisherman who gives up his soul to win the love of a mermaid. The music, scored for small orchestra, is partly serial, partly tonal. The ballet, about a half-hour in duration, remained in the repertoire of the National Ballet until 1960 and was performed widely in Canada and the USA.

FITZGERALD, Winston 'Scotty'. Fiddler, b White Point, Cape Breton, NS, 16 Feb 1915. Taking up the violin at eight, he learned the traditional repertoire from other Cape Breton fiddlers. Though a carpenter by profession, he has performed on radio stations in Nova Scotia and at many folk and fiddling festivals in Canada. In 1975 he began playing with the fiddle group the Cape Breton Symphony (see John Allan *Cameron). Fitzgerald has made over a dozen LPs for *Rodeo and its Banff, Celtic, and Canadian Cavalcade labels. His recording of *McNabb's Hornpipe* and *Farmer's Daughter* (heard on the LP *Winston 'Scotty' Fitzgerald and his Radio Entertainers*, Celtic CX 34) is regarded as a Canadian fiddling classic. Fitzgerald has been described as 'an excellent fiddler in the Scots Cape Breton style, strong and gutsy, especially at lower and medium tempo, with his own style of phrasing and ornamentation. His versions of dance tunes are both polished and emotional' (Larry Sandberg and Dick Weissman, *The Folk Music Source Book*, New York 1976). The fiddler Joseph Cormier is a Fitzgerald protégé. (RGn)

Five Man Electrical Band (1969–75; the Staccatos 1963–9). Rock band formed in Ottawa as The Staccatos. It performed extensively in Ontario and Quebec, and in 1965, after an early effort for Allied, began recording for *Capitol, which, by 1968, had released nine singles by the group, including 'Small Town Girl,' 'Move to California,' 'Let's Run Away,' and 'Half-Past Midnight,' the last a substantial hit in Canada. With the *Guess Who, The Staccatos shared the LP *A Wild Pair*, made in 1968 as a sales premium for Coca-Cola. In 1969 in Los Angeles they made the LP *Five Man Electrical Band* (Cap ST-165), the title taken from an original song in their repertoire. Adopting the new name, the band regrouped in Ottawa and in 1970 returned to Los Angeles. There it recorded 11 singles (released 1970–5 in Canada by Polydor), including the million-seller 'Signs' and the lesser hit 'Absolutely Right,' both popular internationally in 1971. Other singles included 'I'm a Stranger Here' and 'Werewolf.' The band's later LPs were *Goodbyes and Butterflies* (1970, Poly 2424-020), *Coming of Age* (1971, Poly 2424-047), and *Sweet Paradise* (1973, Lion LN 1009). At this time the band was giving concerts throughout North America and comprised Les Emmerson (guitar), Ted Gerow (keyboards), Brian Rading (bass guitar), Rick Bell (drums), and Mike Bell (percussion). All five sang, and their vocal harmonies characterized the band's sound at its most popular. As songwriter and lead singer Emmerson (b Ottawa? 17 Sep 1943) was the band's figurehead. He also recorded 1972–5 as a soloist for Lion; his biggest hit was 'Control of Me.' After the band broke up in California in 1975, Emmerson pursued a solo career. In 1978 he returned to Ottawa, appearing with the Emmerson Electrical Band in local clubs.

BIBLIOGRAPHY
LeBlanc, Larry. 'Dues are paid ... bus fare now no problem,' *MSc*, 265, May–Jun 1972
Stambler, Irwin. *Encyclopedia of Pop, Rock and Soul* (New York 1974)

MM

Flag songs. The flags of Canada have been the Union Jack (1801) (common to all British Colonies); the Red Ensign (adopted by Canadian ships in 1892 and used abroad after 1923 and domestically after 1945), featuring the Union Jack and the arms of Canada on a red background; and the red and white maple leaf flag adopted 15 Feb 1965. Canada is not known to have had a distinct flag under the French régime. The provinces have individual flags, most of them adopted after 1960.

Of over 40 flag songs known to have been written in Canada, G.W. *Sabatier's *'Le Drapeau de Carillon,' published in 1860, is the oldest found. Alexander *Muir celebrated 'The Old Union Jack,' while J.D. *Kerrison prophesied 'The Flag That Bears the Maple Leaf' as early as 1889, and Alexis *Contant 'Le Drapeau fleur delisé' (with words by François Lapointe) in 1905. The South African War and World War I produced spates of flag songs, among them Charles F. *Harrison's 'The Best Old Flag on Earth' (1914), Gordon V.

*Thompson's 'Heroes of the Flag' (1917) and 'For the Glory of the Grand Old Flag' (1918), and, probably the best-known, M. F. Kelly's *'We'll Never Let the Old Flag Fall' (1915). Later examples are fewer, but Hector *Gratton's 'Le Croix et le drapeau' (Archambault ca 1940), for choir, may be mentioned. Flags decorate many Canadian sheet music covers. (HK)

FLEMING, Gordon (Charles James). Organist, pianist, composer, arranger, b Goderich, Ont, 27 May 1903, d Windsor, Ont, 30 Apr 1959. Much of his early life was spent in Galt (renamed Cambridge), Ont. He started his music studies in 1916 and began playing professionally in 1918 in theatres and churches, in concert, and on radio, in both Canada and the USA. He studied piano with Paul *de Marky in London, Ont, and with Alberto *Guerrero in Toronto and piano and composition with Mischa Kottler in Detroit. He moved to Windsor in 1929 and in 1932 started working as staff organist for the radio station CKLW in that city. He also wrote arrangements for Detroit radio stations. He composed music for the CBC (including Len Peterson's series of radio portraits *Men at Work* in 1947), the *NFB, and other Canadian film producers. Some of his symphonic pieces were played by the Detroit SO and the Chicago Philharmonic. His works for orchestra include a *Symphony*, a *Piano Concerto*, and *Louis des Jardins and the Devil*. He also wrote a *Nocturne* for piano, another for organ, an *Allegro* for string quartet, and a *Communion Service* and *Two Motets* for choir. He should not be confused with the jazz accordionist Gordie Fleming. SW

FLEMING, Robert (James Berkeley). Composer, pianist, organist, choirmaster, teacher, b Prince Albert, Sask, 12 Nov 1921, d Ottawa 28 Nov 1976; LRSM 1941. His family settled in Saskatoon in 1928 and he studied first with his mother, then in England 1937–9 at the RCM with Arthur *Benjamin (piano) and Herbert Howells (composition). Returning to Saskatoon he taught piano, made his formal debut in 1940 at *Darke Hall, Regina, and toured Saskatchewan as a recitalist. While continuing piano study 1941–2 with Lyell *Gustin he was assistant organist at the Church of St Alban the Martyr, Saskatoon. He attended the *TCM in 1941 and 1945 on CPRS (later CAPAC) scholarships. His teachers at the TCM included Healey *Willan (composition), Norman *Wilks (piano), Ettore

Robert Fleming

*Mazzoleni (conducting), and Frederick *Silvester and John *Weatherseed (organ). After teaching piano 1945–6 at Upper Canada College he joined the *NFB, working in Ottawa and later Montreal as staff composer 1946–58 and music director 1958–70. He was music director in 1953 for the Ottawa Ballet Festival and organist-choirmaster 1954–6 at Glebe United Church and 1959–70 at St George's Anglican Church at Ste-Anne-de-Bellevue, Que. In 1970 he returned to Ottawa to teach and lecture at *Carleton U on 20th-century music and Canadian composers. In 1972 he became organist-choirmaster at St Matthias' Church, Ottawa.

Though his music is recognizably of the 20th century, among his contemporaries Fleming was a moderate. His compositions are basically tonal and use traditional techniques, forms, and media in a personal way. His ballets, film scores (over 250), works for orchestra and band (over 50), chamber works (over 25), piano and organ pieces (over 40), choral pieces (over 30), hymns (50), carols (30), and songs (over 50) concern themselves more with usefulness and direct expression than with daring. He has written eight or more settings of the Anglican eucharist, including a *Mass of St Thomas* (Waterloo 1974), and his last composition (November 1976) was a setting for the St Matthias congregation of the new Canadian rite. His music has been performed in North and South America, Europe (including the USSR), Australia, and New Zealand. Individual works like the neo-classical *Sonatina* for piano (1941), the ballet *Shadow on the Prairie* (1952, commissioned by the Royal Winnipeg Ballet), and the song cycle *The Confession Stone* (1966, commissioned for Maureen *Forrester) have enjoyed great currency. A list of his NFB scores (1946–64) may be found in 'Filmographie des compositions canadiens,' the index he compiled for *Musique et Cinéma*.

Ross *Pratt, Maureen Forrester, and John *Newmark, the Central Alumni Choir of Ottawa, and various members of the *NACO gave a memorial concert of Fleming's music (planned prior to his death as a 'Fleming Retrospective') at the *NAC 11 Dec 1976. A co-operative venture by the Ottawa Centre of the *RCCO and 11 other organizations including the CBC, the concert was taped for national broadcast. As a memorial to Fleming, an endowment fund was raised in support of the Robert Fleming Award, administered by the *CMCouncil and given annually to the outstanding graduating student in composition in any Canadian university music faculty, department, school, or recognized conservatory. André Lamarche in 1979 was the first recipient. Denys Bouliane won the award in 1980. In addition, the music department at Carleton U has established the (Robert) Fleming (Memorial) Room to house special collections of scores and books. A second Robert Fleming Award has been established in his memory by the Ottawa Music Festival Assn. Fleming was a member of CAPAC, the *CLComp, and RCCO and an associate of the *CMCentre. His papers have been deposited at the *NL of C.

See also Film scores.

SELECTED COMPOSITIONS

STAGE AND FILM

Chapter 13, ballet. 1948. Ms

Shadow on the Prairie, ballet. 1952. Ms. (*Suite*) RCI 129 (*TSO)

Romance (arr), ballet. 1954. 2 pf. Ms

Music for 3 puppet plays and for over 250 films for NFB and others

ORCHESTRA

Six Variations on a Liturgical Theme. 1946. Str orch. CMCentre

Red River Country and *Seaboard Sketches* (1953). Med orch. Ms

Ballet Introduction. 1960. Full orch. CMCentre. 1967. Col MS-6763 (Tor Philharmonia O, Susskind cond)

Concerto 64. 1964. Pf, orch. Ms

'You Name It' Suite. 1964. Str orch. CMCentre

Prairie Sailor, folk cantata (Kines). 1970. V, orch. Ms

Hexad. 1972. Med orch. CMCentre

Our Mind Was the Singer, song cycle (Finch). 1972. Bar, orch. CMCentre

Of a Timeless Land (M. Fleming). 1974. Alto, orch. CMCentre

Also 5 *Suites* for orchestra (1942–63) and some 10 works for band (1964–74). All ms

CHAMBER

The Wealden Trio 'Song of the Women' (Hardy). 1940. SSA, str quar. Ms

A Musician in the Family. 1952. Trb, pf. CMCentre

A Two Piece Suite. 1958. 2 cl, b cl. Leeds 1970. Dom S-69004 (*Galper)

Colours of the Rainbow and *Maritime Suite*. 1962. Ww quar, str quar, hp. Ms

'Go for Baroque.' 1963. Fl, ob, hpd. Ms

Three Dialogues for Flute or Oboe Solo. 1964. Fl (ob), pf (hpd). Ms. CBC SM-268 (*Berman).

Brass Quintet (1965) and *String Quartet* (1969). Both CMCentre

Almost Waltz. 1970. Fl, pf. Jay 1971. Dom S-69006 (*Aitken).

Divertimento. 1970. Org, 2 ob, 2 vn, va, vc, db. Ms

Explorations. 1970. Accord. Wat 1970

Threo. 1972. Sop sax, pf. Ms

PIANO

Over 40 works including *Sonatina* (1941), OUP 1943, GVT 1974; *Five Modernistics* (1946), FH 1955; *Study No. 4* (1960), FH 1966; and 4 educational works, publ by GVT, FH, and Wat, and recorded in 1970 on Dom S-69002 (*Mould)

VOICE (songs recorded)

Coulter Songs. (1946–54). Ms. RCI 248 (*Boyden)

The Confession Stone. (1966). Leeds 1968. RCI 246 (*Forrester)

Folk Songs from Prince Edward Island. (1973). Ms. CBC SM-259 (*Bell)

Songs on texts by Paul Hiebert (1952–3). All CMCentre

Choral works publ by OUP, Wat, Leeds

Other compositions and film scores are listed in *Contemporary Canadian Composers; Musique et Cinéma*..

WRITINGS

'Biographical notes of a Canadian composer featured on "Canadian Music in Wartime" programme,' *CRMA*, vol 3, Jun–Jul 1944

'Music for films;' *JMC Musical Chronicle*, Jan 1963

'Music and the cinema,' and the index of films in *Musique et Cinéma*

BIBLIOGRAPHY

'Robert Fleming,' *Composers of the Americas*, vol 12 (1966)

'The composer who commutes ...' *CanComp*, 39, Apr 1969

'A film composer's life takes new directions,' *CanComp*, 72, Sep 1972

Thistle, Lauretta. 'Robert Fleming: a tribute to one of Canada's best-loved composers,' *CanComp*, 118, Feb 1977

(EK)

Fletcher Music Method. A 'musical kindergarten' for young children. It was devised by Evelyn Ashton Fletcher (b Woodstock, Ont, 1872, d New York City 31 Dec 1944), who studied music in Canada and for five years in France, Germany, and England, taught in Canada ca 1894–7, and joined the staff of the New England Cons in 1897. Her system grew out of her own needs as a teacher of a class in Bishop Strachan School, Toronto. Designed to teach young children the basics of music in a way they could enjoy, the method covered ear training, knowledge of rhythm and time, sight reading, the piano keyboard, major and minor scales, chords and intervals, finger and wrist control, and a knowledge of famous performers and composers. It employed toys (ie, wooden objects introduced as 'Miss Treble Clef' and 'Mrs Whole Note,' etc, and a wooden 'staff-house' where these objects 'lived'), puzzles (a portable wooden keyboard with detachable keys), games (including rhythmic hand-clapping and wrist and finger exercises), songs, and stories taken from music history. Once assimilated, Fletcher techniques enabled children to read and play simple piano pieces.

By 1901 approximately 250 music teachers were using the method and it had been adopted at several schools and conservatories in the USA and Canada. During the early 1900s a Fletcher Music Method and Piano School was established in Montreal, offering both classes for beginners and instruction in the method for teachers. It remained open for more than 30 years. The method's inventor described her system in a book entitled *What is the Fletcher Method?* (Brookline, Mass, 1915). The system flourished widely for many years and in 1979 still was used by some teachers.

BIBLIOGRAPHY

Dante, Anne. 'The Fletcher Musical Kindergarten System,' *New England Conservatory Q*, vol 4, Feb 1899

(NM)

FODI, John. Composer, b Nagyteval, Hungary, 22 Mar 1944, naturalized Canadian 1961; B MUS (Toronto) 1970, M MUS (Toronto) 1972. The family emigrated to Canada in 1951. Fodi studied in Hamilton in 1964 with Lorne *Betts (theory), at the *U of Toronto 1966–70 with John *Beckwith and John *Weinzweig (composition) and Gustav *Ciamaga (electronic music), and at *McGill U 1970–1 with István *Anhalt (composition). He was a founder and director 1967–70 of the Contemporary Music Group at the U of Toronto and a founder in 1971 of *ARRAY, under whose auspices many of his works have been performed. At McGill U he was co-founder with Mickey Cohen of the New Music Society. After composing during his teens over 40 works reflecting the influence in turn of Johann Strauss, Mozart, and the baroque tradition, Fodi began his current body of work in 1963, reaching Op 48 by 1977. These works, for orchestra, chamber ensemble, keyboard, voice, and tape, include a *Symphony* (1964–6, revised 1975), *Symparanekromenoi* (1969–71, premiered 25 Jul 1974 by the *TS under Alexander *Brott), *Concerto for Viola and Two Wind Ensembles* (1971–2, which represented Canada at the 1973 meeting of the ISCM), *Dragon Days* (1976, performed by the *CBC Vancouver Chamber Orchestra), *Concerto a Quattro for String Quartet* (1973, dedicated to the *Orford String Quartet and performed by the *Purcell Quartet at the 1976 meeting of the ISCM in Boston), *Trio, Op 49* (1977), and *Variations III, Op 52* (1978). Fodi has made serialism the basis of most of his post-1963 compositions, and his work prior to 1972 reflects a particular interest in texture. In the late 1970s he began drawing on ethnic sources; in the mid-1970s he had employed a form of parody, incorporating in his compositions subtle references to pre-existing works or styles. Fodi is a member of CAPAC and an associate of the *CMCentre.

BIBLIOGRAPHY
Schulman, Michael. 'John Fodi: new music to challenge his audience,' *CanComp*, Feb 1977 (PPrn)

FOGG, Howard (Frank). Violinist, conductor, composer, b Lewiston, Me, 27 Apr 1892, d 1953. After studying music in Lewiston, notably with Gustav Haanka, he moved to Montreal in 1913. He was wounded in the right arm during World War I, but was able to resume his activities as a musician, continuing his studies in harmony, composition, and conducting with Gaston Borsch. He conducted and toured in Canada and the USA 1925–30 with the *Dumbells and was music director of the 17th Duke of York's Royal Canadian Hussars.

Fogg prepared and directed a number of musical broadcasts on CNRM radio and later on the CBC. He was arranger and conductor for the Canadian Victor Talking Machine Co. He worked for Associated Screen News and was a pioneer in the composition and synchronization of sound-tracks. In 1934, for George Sparling, one of the company's film directors, he wrote the music for the documentary *Rhapsody in Two Languages*, considered the first original composition for a Canadian film.

Among Fogg's symphonic suites, *Remembrance Day* was published by North American Music; *Land of Beautiful Waters*, *Laurentian Suite*, and *Symphonic Suite* were never published. He also composed works for small orchestra and for band, a *Sonata in D* for violin and piano, piano pieces such as *Thought at Eventide* (G. Schirmer), *Wanatea* 'Indian Intermezzo' (W. Rolfe), *Valse Sybil* (Turcot), and art songs published by *Thompson, Sprague-Coleman, and Turcot. He was an affiliate of BMI Canada. AP

FOLI, Lea. Violinist, teacher, b Kelowna, BC, 8 Sep 1933. He began violin lessons at five in Kelowna, continuing elsewhere in Canada and the USA with Clifford *Evens, Esther Glazer, Oscar Shumsky, and Ivan Galamian. He played 1954–60 in the *Vancouver SO, the *Cassenti Players, and the *CBC Vancouver Chamber Orchestra. In Winnipeg 1960–6 he was concertmaster of the *Winnipeg SO and the violin of the Corydon Trio (1959–62, with Gerald *Stanick, viola, and Claude *Kenneson, cello, the latter succeeded by Peggie *Sampson). He became assistant concertmaster in 1966 and concertmaster in 1968 of the Minneapolis SO (later Minnesota Orchestra) and has appeared annually as soloist with the orchestra in concertos of Beethoven, Tchaikovsky, Mendelssohn, Brahms, Mozart, Prokofiev, Hindemith, Barber, and (1976) William Schuman. He became the leader of the U of Minnesota String Quartet, and was a teacher each summer 1966–76 at the Aspen Festival.

In Canada Foli has appeared as concerto soloist with the *NACO, the *TS, the Winnipeg SO, the *Edmonton SO, and the Vancouver *SO. In 1976 he adjudicated the provincial finals of competition festivals in Winnipeg and Calgary, and in 1977 and 1979 he taught at the George Brown College Summer School of the Arts in Toronto. KMr

Folk music. Few countries possess a folk music as rich and culturally varied as Canada's. Traditional folk music came with the first British and French settlers in the 16th and 17th centuries (see Folk Music, Anglo-Canadian; Folk music, Franco-Canadian). They fished the coastal waters and farmed the shores of what became Newfoundland, Nova Scotia, New Brunswick, Prince Edward Island, and the St Lawrence River valley of Quebec. Men of the fur trade (and, later, the lumbering operations) brought much of this music further west and north into the forested areas of central Canada. The mingling of some of these men with the various native tribes produced a mixed-blood population of non-Treaty Indians known as Métis (see Indians: 3 / Plains; Pierre Falcon).

Four prominent exponents of Canadian folk music: (left to right) Buck Lacombe, Hélène Baillargeon, Alan Mills, (seated) Jean Carignan

Agrarian settlement in eastern and southern Ontario and western Quebec in the early 19th century established a milieu for the survival of many Anglo-Canadian folksongs and broadside ballads from Great Britain and the USA. Despite massive industrialization, folk music traditions persisted in many rural areas into the 1970s. A large Franco-Ontarian population in the north of the province provided similar conditions for the survival of French folk music. Populous Acadian communities in the Atlantic provinces contributed their song variants to the huge corpus of French-Canadian folk music centred in the province of Quebec. The richest source of Anglo-Canadian folk music up to the 1970s was the Atlantic region, especially Newfoundland. Completing this early musical mosaic is the Gaelic music of Scottish settlements, particularly in Cape Breton, and the hundreds of Irish songs that blanketed eastern Canada after the Irish famine of the 1840s forced the large migrations to North America.

In 1874–5 Mennonite and Icelandic settlements in Manitoba heralded the new era of mass immigration to western Canada of peoples from eastern and western Europe and Asia. Ukrainians, Poles, Hungarians, Doukhobors, English, French, and other peoples broke the prairie sod for agricultural use in the late 19th and early 20th centuries. During the same period in British Columbia, Chinese, Japanese, Sikhs, and, again, Doukhobors and other European minorities arrived in increasing numbers to complement the established Anglo-Canadian colonial population. A group of Okinawan-Japanese farmers even settled in the Lethbridge area of Alberta, bringing with them a musical tradition quite different from that of Japan. Many European groups, especially the Finns, joined the new mining, pulp-and-paper, and agrarian communities of northern Ontario and the urban centres in the south.

After World War II a new wave of immigration to urban centres occurred, especially from southern Italy, the Baltic states, Hungary, Portugal, and the Caribbean. Jewish communities long had been a feature of urban and, occasionally, rural life. At least 40 cultures brought their unique musical traditions, adding immensely to Canada's long-established heritage of English, French, Gaelic, and Irish folk music.

Whatever its cultural origin, traditional folk music has its roots in the common people, although there is evidence in certain genres that cross-fertilization between artsong and folksong occurred at various periods in the mother countries. In Canadian fishing villages, rural hamlets, and pioneer farming communities this folk music provided the principal source of entertainment and a sense of continuity with the past. In some regions and cultures folksongs of purely Canadian orientation evolved. Newfoundland – the oldest European settlement in North America – has the highest percentage of indigenous folksongs. In other cultures (eg, Lithuanian and Ukrainian) links with an archaic tribal past are discernible in both melodies and texts, especially in calendric ritual songs the pagan origins of which are not quite obscured by the superficial overlay of Christian content. Christmas carols and New Year's and Easter songs are obvious examples. Others are concerned with the elaborate wedding cycles of many European cultures. English and French songs have lost most of this archaic ritual aspect, rarely showing origins before medieval times. Gaelic tunes have preserved more of the archaic flavour of the Celtic musical past. Most cultures have narrative genres such as ballads; less commonly, epics. Ballad genres cover an immense time span from the medieval period to the 20th century. Topics are manifold: love, war, heroic exploits, revenge, murder, disasters, and so on.

Shorter lyric songs are most often concerned with love in its various aspects: unrequited, betrayed, occasionally fulfilled. Often they equal or surpass artsongs in melodic and poetic beauty. A surprisingly large percentage of the song corpus of a folk culture, whether European or Asiatic, consists of love songs, also dating from early times to the 20th century.

A host of songs about the sea, sailors, fishermen, sea disasters, sealing, whaling, lumbering, mining, railroading, cowboys, and so on, is of predominantly Anglo-Canadian origin, although there are many French examples.

Other genres include lullabies, children's game songs, drinking songs, mouth music (nonsense syllables, often used for dancing), and macaronic songs (French-English, Ukrainian-English, etc). Immigrant songs and patriotic songs are found mostly among cultures of Scandinavian and other European origin, possibly indicating nostalgia for the old countries.

With the exception of fundamentalist Christian sects (Doukhobor, Mennonite, Hutterite), all cultures have folk instruments, played solo or in concert for entertainment or to accompany dancing and, occasionally, singing. In Anglo-Canadian, Franco-Canadian, and Gaelic music, the fiddle is the principal instrument, and it is common in other cultures as well. The most beautifully decorated is the eight-stringed Norwegian Hardinger fiddle, made in Norway Valley, Alta, until ca 1930. Fiddle-makers still were at work in English and French Canada in the 1970s. Other instruments in popular use in Franco- and Anglo-Canadian folk music include the guitar, button accordion, mouth-organ, whistle, jew's-harp, 'bones,' and spoons. Bagpipes, long associated with the Scots and Irish, have been found in more primitive folk versions among the Poles, Czechoslovaks, and other eastern European groups.

A partial listing follows of other instruments transplanted to Canada: zithers: Finnish (kantele), Lithuanian (kankles), Latvian (kokle), Estonian (kannel), Japanese (koto), Chinese (cheng or ch'in), Icelandic (langspil); dulcimers: Ukrainian (cymbaly), Hungarian (cimbalom), Chinese (yang-ch'in); bowed instruments: Chinese (er-hu, gau-hu), Yugoslavian (gusle), Polish (gesle); lutes, etc: Chinese (p'i'pa), Ukrainian (kobza, bandura), Sikh (sitar), Japanese (biwa); unfretted instruments: Japanese (shamisen), Okinawan (shamisen, snake-skin head), Chinese (san-hsien, forerunner of shamisen); flutes: Chinese (side-blown, and end-blown), Japanese (shakuhachi), Ukrainian (sopilka), Yugoslavian (frula); pipes: Lithuanian (skuduciai, single-toned, several lengths); drums and other percussion: Sikh, Chinese, Japanese.

Although much Franco- and Anglo-Canadian folk music has survived in its traditional rural environment in many areas of Quebec, Ontario, and the Atlantic provinces, the music of the later minority cultures has become confined largely to urban centres, large and small. Here, numerous ethnic associations, choirs, instrumental ensembles, and folk-dance societies have transformed much of the simple folksong repertoire into more sophisticated musical presentations, often available on commercial recordings. A similar reprocessing of traditional English and French folksong through the electronic media by professional folksingers began in the 1940s. In the early 1960s a new generation of composer-lyricist-singers from French and English Canada began producing a body of quasi-folksongs solely for concert and electronic presentation.

See also *EMC* articles on individual collectors, ethnomusicologists, folksingers; articles on individual countries (eg, Ireland, Lithuania, Scotland, Ukraine, etc). For a guide to articles on religious groups (eg, Doukhobors, Mennonites) see Religions and music.

See also Accordion; Bagpipes, Great Highland; Ballads; Boîtes à chansons; Canadian Folk Music Society; Chanson in Quebec; Chansonniers; Children's songs, traditional; Christmas; Coffeehouses; Country music; CPR Festivals; Disaster songs; Easter, Lent, the Passion; Ethnomusicology; Fiddling; Folk-music-inspired composition; Guitar; Harmonica; Indians; Inuit; Klondike; Lakes; Lullabies; Occupational songs; String instrument building. Many of these articles include bibliographies and discographies.

The recordings and publications listed below represent more than one ethnic group.

DISCOGRAPHY

Canada's Favourite Folksongs for Kids. 1978. Ber 9031

Canada's Story in Song. A. Mills. 1960. 2-Folk FW 3000

Canadian Folk Songs. Columbia World Library of Folk and Primitive Music, vol 8. 1954. Col SL 211

Canadian Folk Songs: A Centennial Collection. Y. Albert, H. Baillargeon, L. Forestier, C. Jordan, T. Kines, J. Labrecque, A. Mills, D. Oxner, J. Price, R. Roy, J. Sullivan. 1967; 9-RCI and RCA CS 100

Far Canadian Fields: Companion to the Penguin Book of Canadian Folk Songs. 1975. Leader LEE 4057

Folk Songs of Canada. J. Sullivan, C. Jordan. 1955. Hallmark CS3/Wat CS3

Folk Songs of Canada. T. Kines. (1965). RCA Victor PCS 1014

Maple Sugar: Songs of Early Canada. T. Connors, H. Hibbs, E. Moorehead, U of Guelph Folk Choir. 1973. 2-Springwater S1, S2

Songs, Fiddle Tunes and a Folk-Tale from Canada. A. Mills, J. Carignan. 1961. Folk FG 3532

BIBLIOGRAPHY

See also Writings for Marius Barbeau; Barbara Cass-Beggs; Helen Creighton; Edith Fowke; Ernest Gagnon; John Murray Gibbon; Robert Klymasz; Conrad Laforte; Alan Mills; Kenneth Peacock.

Barbeau, Marius. 'Folk-songs,' *JAF*, vol 31, Apr–Jun 1918

– 'Canadian folk songs as a national asset,' Canadian Club of Toronto *Addresses* (1927–8)

Tait, J.A. 'In the realm of folk-song,' *MCan*, vol 7, Nov 1928

Barbeau, Marius. 'Folk songs,' *U of Toronto Q*, vol 16, Jan 1947

Sargent, Margaret. 'Folk and primitive music in Canada,' National Museum of Canada Bulletin no. 123 (Ottawa 1951); repr *J of the International Folk Music Council*, vol 4, Jan 1952

Barbeau, Marius. 'Folk-song,' *Music in Canada*

George, Graham. 'Seven Canadian folk-music records,' *CMJ*, vol 2, Winter 1958

Barbeau, Marius. 'Canadian folk songs,' *J of the International Folk Music Council*, vol 13, Jan 1961

Duncan, Chester. 'Folk song as history,' *Canadian Literature*, Spring 1961

Peacock, Kenneth. 'A Practical Guide for Folk Music Collectors,' CFMS mimeographed (Ottawa 1966)

– 'Folk and aboriginal music,' *Aspects of Music in Canada* / 'La musique folklorique et aborigène,' *Aspects de la musique au Canada*

'Centennial collection of Canadian folk songs issued,' *CanComp*, 23, Nov 1967

Barbeau, Marius, and Creighton, Helen. 'The rediscovery of folk music,' *Canadian Geographical J*, vol 84, Mar 1972

Fowke, Edith. 'Anglo-Canadian folksong: a survey,' *Ethnomusicology*, vol 16, Sep 1972

Kallmann, Helmut. 'Towards a bibliography of Canadian folk music,' ibid

Cass-Beggs, Barbara, and Fowke, Edith. 'A reference list on Canadian folk music,' *CFMJ*, vol 1, 1973; rev, enl, *CFMJ*, vol 6, 1978

'Folklore Canada,' 10th Conference of the CMCouncil: a report, *CMB*, 9, Autumn–Winter 1974

Pelinski, Ramón. 'The music of Canada's ethnic minorities,' *CMB*, 10, Spring–Summer 1975

Hogan, Dorothy. 'Canadian folk music: a foundation for cultural identity,' *Recorder*, vol 18, Sep 1975

Posen, Shelley. 'Explorations in Canadian folklore,' *Quill and Quire*, Jul 1976

'A bibliography of Canadian folklore in English,' compiled by Edith Fowke and Carole Henderson, *Communique: Canadian Studies: Canadian Folk Culture Issue*, vol 3, Aug 1977

Fowke, Edith. 'In the past ... earlier Canadian folk magazines,' *Canada Folk Bulletin*, vol 2, Mar–Apr 1979

Bartlett, Jon, and Ruebsaat, Rika. 'The state of the art: the folk revival in Canada,' *Canada Folk Bulletin*, vol 3, Sep–Dec 1980

PERIODICALS

Singalong, Vancouver Feb 1957–Jul 1958

Sing and String, Toronto, 9 issues, 1959–Fall 1965

CFMS *Newsletter / Bulletin*, twice a year, Jul 1965–

Hoot, Aug 1963–Feb–Mar 1967

Chansons populaires, 7 issues, ca 1970

Canadian Folk Music Journal, annual 1973–

Pourquoi chanter, ca 1977–ca 1978

Canada Folk Bulletin, Vancouver, 6 issues a year, Jan–Feb 1978–80

FOLKSONG COLLECTIONS

Gibbon, John Murray. *Canada in Song* (Toronto 1941)

Barbeau, Marius. *Come A Singing! Canadian Folk-Songs*, National Museum of Canada Bulletin no. 107 (Ottawa 1947, 1973)

Fowke, Edith, and Johnston, Richard. *Folk Songs of Canada* (Wat 1954)

Fowke, Edith et al. *Canada's Story in Song* (Toronto 1960)

Fowke, Edith, and Johnston, Richard. *More Folk Songs of Canada* (Wat 1967)

Fowke, Edith. *Penguin Book of Canadian Folk Songs* (Harmondsworth, England 1973) KP

Folk music, Anglo-Canadian

1 Newfoundland
2 Nova Scotia and New Brunswick
3 Prince Edward Island
4 Ontario and the Prairies
5 British Columbia

1 NEWFOUNDLAND. The folk music of Newfoundland reflects a rich cultural heritage from the British Isles, nurtured in the New World into a unique tradition. The relative isolation of the outports and the extensive travels of seafaring Newfoundlanders are the basic factors behind a body of music which is at once firmly local and broadly eclectic.

Singing styles. The four major published collections of Newfoundland folk music have dealt almost entirely with the province's vocal (rather than instrumental) traditions. Newfoundland folksinging is unaccompanied and is characterized by a straightforward undramatic solo performance with little dynamic variation from stanza to stanza. Personal styles may include vibrato (generally only on lingering notes) and melismatic ornamentation. Tone production usually is clear rather than raspy but may be relaxed or tense depending upon whether the upper or lower portions of the singer's natural range are used. Often the final words of a song are spoken. Emphasis within the tradition is upon words rather than tune (or 'air').

Categories of song. Two very broad categories of song are used by most Newfoundland singers. The 'ditty' is a non-serious song with satirical, derogatory, bawdy, or children's lyrics. The 'story-song,' often simply called a 'song,' is a serious narrative folksong of the type usually called 'ballad' by scholars. The latter is the more important of the two categories, both numerically and in terms of local values.

Newfoundland ballad traditions. The stylistically heterogeneous body of ballads traditional in Newfoundland includes the old English and Scottish popular ballads (see Child ballads in Ballads), British and North American broadsides of the 17th to 19th centuries, 19th- and 20th-century sentimental ballads from British music hall and US popular music traditions, songs from the flourishing 19th-century-Maritime and lumberwoods traditions, sentimental ballads from 20th-century 'cowboy' traditions, and locally composed ballads.

Most of these songs describe a single incident. Stories of disasters such as shipwrecks are popular. Other common motifs include lovers separated and adventures in foreign lands. Settings include sealing, fishing, war at sea or on land, lumbering, and local communities. Such content reflects the environment and daily concerns of the singers and their audiences.

Most of Newfoundland's folk music has been preserved and passed on by oral / aural means, but print has played an important role in the introduction of new material. Principal printed sources have been Irish and US 'songsters,' the 'Old Favourites' page of the Montreal weekly the *Family Herald*, the broadsides and songsters of St John's ballad poets like James Murphy and Johnny Burke, and the five editions of *Old-Time Songs and Poetry of Newfoundland* published by Gerald *Doyle.

Phonograph recordings from England, mainland Canada, and the USA of music hall, popular, and cowboy songs also have influenced the folksong traditions of the province. After confederation with Canada in 1949 and especially after the mid-1960s, Newfoundlanders in their recordings have reintroduced the older traditional songs as well as new material from indigenous sources. Another important influence upon recent song traditions has been the music of immigrant Irish pop groups.

Song performance contexts. Folk singing in Newfoundland occurs most frequently at informal parties called 'times.' Held in outport kitchens or fish stores, 'times' typically involve solo performances by one or several singers. The song commands the attention of all present; words of encouragement are spoken to the singer between verses or during pauses within the song. The end of the song is observed with similar comments and may precipitate a discussion of its contents. Generally there is drinking, the usual fare being dark rum. 'Times' occur almost always at night on weekends, and most frequently in the winter when there is more leisure. There is a 'time' every night somewhere in the outport community during the 12 days of Christmas.

Other occasions for singing include work situations, such as those on shipboard or in the lumberwoods, and formal community 'concerts' held in local church or school halls on religious and national holidays. Usually organized by the teacher or clergyman, concerts involve dramatic skits, dancing, recitations, and other kinds of stage performance by members of the community. Often local singers compose songs for specific concerts. These deal humorously with recent local events and local personalities, and some are sufficiently memorable to become part of local folksong traditions.

Instrumental music. While after 1949 the guitar increased in popularity as an accompanying instrument for young singers, instrumental and vocal traditions generally have been quite separate in Newfoundland. Instrumental music was dance music, and the most popular instrument was the button accordion. Among other instruments used were the harmonica, the tin whistle, and the violin. When no instruments were available for a dance, the tunes would be sung – a practice known variously as 'gob music,' 'mouth music,' or 'chin music.' A great many Newfoundland dance tunes appear to be from Irish traditions, and those in 6/8 and 9/8 meters are as popular as those in 2/4 and 4/4. Dances were held in community halls, kitchens, and fish stores and in the summer on wharves and bridges. A dance had from three to six segments, each of which had its particular rhythm. A good instrumentalist had to know the appropriate tunes for each section and also might be called upon to provide music for solo 'step dancers' between segments of the dance. Occasionally singers would perform between dances; usually a 'mug up' or tea was served afterwards.

Recent trends in Newfoundland's folk music. With the introduction of paved roads, electricity, and TV many of these musical traditions have been altered or become moribund. Younger musicians and singers are apt to perform rock, Irish, or country-western music rather than perpetuate the traditions of their fathers. Dances rarely involve the intricate patterns of earlier times, although step dancing still is quite popular. Increasing emphasis on instrumental virtuosity in playing traditional dance music has replaced the older concern with the ability to accompany dancing properly. Song-writing and local composition still are relatively common, reflecting the fact that Newfoundland's musical culture still is flexible enough to cope with and adopt from mainland influences.

See also 'The Anti-Confederation Song'; Ballads; 'The Banks of Newfoundland'; 'The Blooming Bright Star of Belle Isle'; Disaster songs; 'Hard, Hard Times'; 'Jack Was Every Inch a Sailor'; 'Lukey's Boat'; Occupational songs; 'She's Like the Swallow'; 'Squid-jiggin' Ground'; 'We'll Rant and We'll Roar like True Newfoundlanders'.

DISCOGRAPHY

Folk Songs of Newfoundland. A. Mills. 1953. Folk FW 6831

Folk Songs of Newfoundland. Mills. 1958. Folk FW 8771

Newfoundlanders Sing Songs of Their Homeland. St John's Extension Choir of Memorial U. 1966. RCA Victor CC 1024

Songs and Ballads of Newfoundland. K. Peacock. 1956. Folk FG 3505

Songs from the Newfoundland Outports. 1966. Folk FE 4075

See also Omar Blondahl; Harry Hibbs; Ed McCurdy; Alan Mills; Dick Nolan; Arthur Scammell.

BIBLIOGRAPHY

West, Paul. 'The unwitting elegiac: Newfoundland folk song,' *Canadian Literature*, 7, Spring 1961

Peacock, Kenneth. 'The native songs of Newfoundland,' *Contributions to Anthropology, 1960, Part II*, National Museum of Canada (Ottawa 1963)

Szwed, John F. 'Paul E. Hall: a Newfoundland song-maker and his community of song,' *Folksongs and Their Makers* (Bowling Green, O, 1970)

Casey, George J., Rosenberg, Neil V., and Wareham, Wilfred W. 'Repertoire categorization and performance-audience relationships: some Newfoundland examples,' *Ethnomusicology*, vol 16, Sep 1972

Mercer, Paul. *The Ballads of Johnny Burke* (St John's, Nfld, 1974)

Taft, Michael. ' "That's two more dollars": Jimmy Linegar's success with country music in Newfoundland,' *Folklore Forum*, vol 7, pp. 99–121, 1974

A Regional Discography of Newfoundland and Labrador 1904–1972 (St John's, Nfld, 1975)

'A reference list on Canadian folk music,' compiled by Barbara Cass-Beggs and Edith Fowke, *CFMJ*, vol 1, 1973; rev enl vol 6, 1978

Mercer, Paul. *Newfoundland Songs and Ballads in Print 1842–1974: A Title and First Line Index* (St John's, Nfld, 1979)

'Interview: Jim Payne,' *Canada Folk Bulletin*, vol 3, Jan–Feb 1980

FOLKSONG COLLECTIONS

Greenleaf, Elisabeth Bristol, and Mansfield, Grace Yarrow. *Ballads and Sea Songs of Newfoundland* (Cambridge, Mass, 1933; repr Hatboro, Pa, 1968)

Karpeles, Maud. *Folk Songs from Newfoundland* (Oxford 1934. New version (London 1971)

Doyle, Gerald S. *Old-Time Songs and Poetry of Newfoundland* (St John's, Nfld, 1940, 1978)

Leach, MacEdward. *Folk Ballads and Songs of the Lower Labrador Coast*, National Museum of Man (Ottawa 1965)

Peacock, Kenneth. *Songs of the Newfoundland Outports*, 3 vols, National Museum of Man (Ottawa 1965)

Ryan, Shannon, and Small, Larry. *Haulin' Rope and Gaft* (St John's, Nfld, 1978)

2 NOVA SCOTIA AND NEW BRUNSWICK. Folk music in Nova Scotia and New Brunswick has come largely from five ethnic sources: British, Acadian-French, Gaelic, Micmac Indian, and black. The largest proportion is in the British group. W. Roy Mackenzie has published 162 songs with 42 tunes, Helen *Creighton 689 with tunes for all, and Louise *Manny 101, also with tunes. Folkways have published two ethnic records from the Creighton collection, *Folk Music From Nova Scotia* (1956, Folk FM 4006) with 25 songs and *Maritime Folk Songs* (1962, Folk FE 4307) with 19 songs. There are four flexi-discs in the pocket of her *Folksongs From Southern New Brunswick*, 1971, which contain 17 songs in the voices of the traditional singers. From Manny's New Brunswick collection Folkways issued a record (1962, FM 4053) with 10 songs entitled *Folksongs of the Miramichi*, and Folk Legacy issued a recording by one of her Folk Song Festival singers, Marie *Hare (1962, Legacy FSC-9), with 11 songs.

Traditional Anglo-Canadian songs tell mostly of love and adventure, and many have a sea motif. Of the ancient dramatic songs known as Child ballads (named after the collector Francis James Child, whose five-volume work *The English and Scottish Popular Ballads* was published 1882–98), 49 have been found in Canada, many with variants. Songs of local origin throw light upon life at sea, in the lumber woods, and in the mines where most of the men worked, and many were inspired by tragedy. Those in lighter vein satirize persons or events and whether sad or gay are largely personal in expression. For beauty of words and music the traditional songs are far superior, although many indigenous songs have borrowed tunes from the older imported songs.

Songs in English are usually narratives involving action, unlike Gaelic songs, which often tell about the beauty of a maiden or the charm of the singer's home countryside. The singers perform unaccompanied, and it is characteristic of the 'old timers' to embroider their melodies, the extent of ornamentation depending upon the inspiration of the moment. A singer speaks or shouts (rather than sings) the last word of a song to indicate it has ended. Many singers adopt individual styles and when a song has been introduced by one singer others will not sing it in his presence. In the old days songs seldom were performed in public but were used to pass the time away in the home, at sea, and in the lumber woods. Many went to great length, prolonging a good story to as many as 78 verses. If a line was forgotten a singer would omit it rather than improvise and break with tradition.

Collecting began in 1909, when W. Roy Mackenzie (b River John, NS, February 1883, d there September 1957) discovered that the type of ballad he was studying at Harvard U was still sung near his birthplace on Nova Scotia's Northumberland Strait. With a horse and carriage for transportation and without a mechanical device for recording, he and his young wife spent many summers writing down the songs he discovered. The informants usually were of Scottish descent, but many of their songs had come to them from Acadian-French sources. The Scots' church at one time had frowned upon the singing of secular songs, but not before their French neighbours had committed them to memory. *The Quest of the Ballad* (Princeton 1919) tells the story of the Mackenzies' collecting and gives examples. The book was followed in 1928 by *Ballads and Sea Songs From Nova Scotia* (Cambridge, Mass), a scholarly book with copious commentary. This work became the pattern used by subsequent folksong scholars on this continent for many years, and it has remained on the curriculum of many universities. It contains 162 songs. Mackenzie memorized many of the tunes and sang them later to a friend, who wrote down 42 of them. At that period words were considered more important than music, and the book did not make the widespread impact on performers that had been hoped, but as a textbook it has been invaluable.

In 1928, inspired by the Mackenzie books, Helen Creighton explored near her home in Dartmouth and thus began a career in folklore that continued for nearly 40 years, 19 of them without sponsorship. For 20 years she was employed by the *National Museum, Ottawa, to collect and record folklore in the Maritime provinces. Eventually she collected approximately 4000 songs, of which at least 3000 were in English. Realizing the importance of music, she preserved the tunes of all her songs, at first using a portable melodeon, then a dictaphone. For a few summers an English musician, Doreen H. Senior, accompanied her in the field and transcribed directly from the singers. Later Creighton used a Presto recording machine lent to her by the Library of Congress, Washington, DC, for which she recorded during 1943–4. In 1948 she recorded again, this time sponsored jointly by the Library of Congress and the National Museum. In 1949 the museum acquired its own tape recorders and gradually amassed 2227 of her songs in English in its archives. Other transcriptions were done from these tapes by Kenneth *Peacock and are to be found in Creighton's later books and in manuscript in Ottawa and Halifax. Her research was extended to include the three Maritime provinces and other ethnic groups mentioned at the beginning of this article.

From 1958 to 1970 Louise Manny conducted the annual *Miramichi Folk Song Festival in Newcastle, NB. The festival survived, and singers from lumbering and fishing communities continued to compete in performing traditional and indigenous songs. The festival not only has made known songs which otherwise would be lost, but also has encouraged singers to replenish their own stocks from those of friends in more remote areas and has given scholars an opportunity to study singing styles. Other collectors, notably Edward Ives (collector and singer, b White Plains, NY, 4 Sep 1925; author of several books on Maritime songs) and Helen Creighton, made tape recordings later deposited at the U of Maine, Orono, and the National Museum of Man. Other Manny recordings in English are in the New Brunswick Museum in Saint John. With James Reginald Wilson, who transcribed the music, Manny published *Songs of Miramichi* (Fredericton 1968), 101 songs with extensive notes on the history of lumbering and the value and use of the songs. In Barry, Eckstorm, and Smyth's *British Ballads From Maine* (New Haven, Conn, 1929) 195 texts are from southwestern New Brunswick near the border. Ives also has collected there. Throughout the Saint John River valley songs in English seem to have been neglected.

The fiddle has been the chief instrument for country dancing. Many tunes, traditional and local, have been recorded, principally by Don *Messer's orchestra. (See also Fiddling.) Drums, mouth organ, piano, and chin music often have accompanied the fiddle. The guitar and banjo as popular instruments came later.

The style of folk singing has changed with the times, and there are many songs composed in the folk idiom. Nevertheless the traditional songs so long beloved continue to be heard, although seldom unaccompanied in the old way.

See also Ballads; Disaster songs; 'The Ghost of Bras D'Or'; 'I'll Give My Love an Apple'; 'The Jones Boys'; 'The Nova Scotia Song'; Occupational songs; 'Peter Emberley'; Trade union songs. For information on the Gaelic Language and Folklore Project see St Francis Xavier U; for Gaelic music see also Scotland.

DISCOGRAPHY

Gaelic Folklore of Cape Breton Island. Rodeo RLP 60
Maritime Folk Songs. 1962. Folk FE 4307
The Music of Cape Breton. 1978. 2-Topic 12T353, 12T354
Nova Scotia Folk Music from Cape Breton. 1955. Elektra EKL 23
Orain Cheap Breatain (songs of Cape Breton). Celtic CX 38
Salute to Cape Breton Island: fiddle tunes and mouth music. Celtic CX 18
Songs from Cape Breton Island. Recorded by Sidney Cowell. 1955. Folk FE 4450
Songs of the Maritimes. A. Mills. 1959. Folk FW 8744
Traditional Folk Songs of Nova Scotia. D. Oxner. 1973. Rodeo RBS 1142

BIBLIOGRAPHY

In addition to articles by Creighton listed below, see also Writings for Helen Creighton; Louise Manny.
Mackenzie, W. Roy. 'Ballad-singing in Nova Scotia,' *JAF*, vol 22, Jul-Sep 1909
– 'Three ballads from Nova Scotia,' ibid, vol 23, Jul–Sep 1910
– 'Ballads from Nova Scotia (continued),' ibid, vol 25 Apr–Jun 1912
MacOdrum, Maxwell M. *Nova Scotia Ballads* (Halifax 1922)
McCawley, Stuart. *Cape Breton Come-All-Ye* (Glace Bay, NS, 1935, 1966)
Creighton, Helen. 'Ballads from Devil's Island,' *Dalhousie R*, vol 12, pp. 505–10, 1933
MacDonald, Alphonse. *Cape Breton Songster* (Sydney, NS, 1935)
Barry, Phillips. 'Songs and traditions of the Miramichi,' *Bulletin of the Folksong Society of the Northeast*, 3 articles, vol 10, 1935, vol 11, 1936, vol 12, 1937
Creighton, Helen. 'Nova Scotia folk songs,' *Nova Scotia J of Education*, vol 8, no. 2, 1937
Doerflinger, William. 'Cruising for ballads in Nova Scotia,' *Canadian Geographical J*, vol 16, Feb 1938
Fahs, Lois Sophia. *Swing Your Partner: Old Time Dances of New Brunswick and Nova Scotia* (Truro, NS, 1949)
Senior, Doreen, and Creighton, Helen. 'Songs collected in the province of Nova Scotia, Canada,' *J of the English Folk Dance and Song Society*, vol 6, pp. 83–91, 1951
Creighton, Helen. 'Folk singers of Nova Scotia,' *Canadian Forum*, vol 32, Jul 1952
– 'The songs of Nathan Hatt,' *Dalhousie R*, vol 32, Winter 1953
– 'Folk songs in Nova Scotia,' *Canon*, vol 10, Nov 1956
– 'Songs from Nova Scotia,' *J of the International Folk Music Council*, vol 12, Jan 1960
Ives, Edward D. 'Satirical songs in Maine and the Maritime provinces of Canada,' ibid, vol 14, Jan 1962
Creighton, Helen. 'Nathan Hatt of Nova Scotia,' *Sing Out*, vol 13, no. 1, 1963
'A reference list on Canadian folk music,' compiled by Barbara Cass-Beggs and Edith Fowke, *CFMJ*, vol 1, 1973; rev enl vol 6, 1978
Songs and Stories from Deep Cove, Cape Breton as remembered by Amby Thomas, ed Ron MacEachern (Sydney, NS, 1979)
Lobban, Chris. 'Collecting songs in Saint John NB,' *Canada Folk Bulletin*, vol 3, Jan–Feb 1980
Ruebsaat, Rika. 'Rambles through the Maritimes,' ibid

3 PRINCE EDWARD ISLAND. The Anglo-Canadian folksong tradition of Prince Edward Island differs very little from the traditions of the rest of the Maritimes. Most collections made in Nova Scotia or New Brunswick (or, for that matter, Newfoundland) could represent the Island. In fact, in the 1970s such collections are almost all an Island singer would find for his use, since relatively little field work has been done in this smallest of the provinces. Helen *Creighton has published a few songs in *Maritimes Folk Songs* (Toronto 1962, 1972). The Dibblees published a collection in 1973 that makes no claim to scholarly editing but serves the song lover well. Edward Ives' book, though scholarly, is limited to 21 songs from one tiny section of the Island (West Prince County). Christopher *Gledhill's volume is another practical rather than scholarly compilation. Yet even these few samples provide some surprises, two in particular worth remarking.

First, one would expect that the traditions of such a small area, and an island at that, would be homogeneous. In fact, however, the traditions of Prince County turn out to have more in common with those of Miramichi and the communities of the nearby eastern shore of New Brunswick than with those of Kings County, which in turn have much in common with those of Nova Scotia. It is as if Charlottetown and the Hillsborough River and Bay have divided the island into two. The difference is apparent when the same songs are sung to different tunes in the two areas, and when eastern Kings County songs are not known at all in western Prince County.

Second, local tradition remained strong on Prince Edward Island long after it was weakening in Maine, USA, and the rest of the Maritimes. Two manifestations support this statement. During the silver age of lumbering the thousands of Island boys who went to Maine to work in the woods usually were acknowledged to be the best singers, the ones who sang the most, and the ones who knew the most songs; and around the turn of the century there still were local songmakers on Prince Edward Island composing songs on the old models – men like Lawrence Doyle, Hugh Lauchlan MacDonald, and Larry Gorman, 'the man who made the songs.' Representative titles in the 'come-all-ye' tradition are 'The Flying Cloud,' 'John Ladner,' 'Mantle So Green,' and 'Susan, the Pride of Kildare.'

Although the English-language folksong tradition on Prince Edward Island never has been collected in any depth, the collecting that has been done demonstrates a strong and vital tradition in which the sub-traditions of the two ends of the island had less in common with each other than with neighbouring mainland traditions. See also Don Messer and His Islanders; Occupational songs.

DISCOGRAPHY

'When Johnny Went Ploughin' for Kearon' and Other Tradtional P.E.I. Folksongs. T. Banks, J. Cousins. 1976. PEI Heritage Foundation

BIBLIOGRAPHY

Ives, Edward D. 'Twenty-one folksongs from Prince Edward Island,' *Northeast Folklore*, vol 5, 1963
– *Larry Gorman: The Man Who Made the Songs* (Bloomington, Ind, 1964)
– *Lawrence Doyle: Farmer Poet of Prince Edward Island* (Orono, Me, 1971)
Dibblee, Randall and Dorothy. *Folksongs from Prince Edward Island* (Summerside, PEI, 1973)
Gledhill, Christopher. *Folk Songs of Prince Edward Island* (Charlottetown 1973)

4 ONTARIO AND THE PRAIRIES. Folksongs in English sung in Ontario include a great many that the early settlers brought over from Great Britain. Among these are some old English, Scottish, and Irish popular ballads, many later broadside ballads (songs printed on one side of a single sheet and sold for a penny), and a variety of love songs, laments, comic ditties, drinking songs, lullabies, and children's singing games.

Most native Ontario songs stem from the lumbercamps. Men who farmed in the summer and worked in the woods in the winter came home each spring with a new batch of songs they had learned from men from other districts, as well as some composed in the woods. Thus the camps not only fostered new songs but also preserved and spread older ones. Another important group of Ontario songs featured the ships and sailors of the Great Lakes, some of which also were sung by the shantyboys (lumbercamp workers; see Occupational songs).

Historical and local events inspired other Ontario songs. Two ballads about General Wolfe circulated, 'Come All You Bold Canadians' celebrated General Brock's victory over General Hull at the Battle of Detroit, both a 'Fenian Song' and an 'Anti-Fenian Song' recalled the raids of 1866, and other ballads described the burning of 'The *Sir Robert Peel*' and 'The Battle of the Windmill' in 1838. 'The Poor Little Girls of Ontario' lamented for the boys who headed westward about 1900. Still other songs described jails – 'The Banks of the Don,' 'Johnston's Hotel,' 'The Soo Ste Mary's Jail' – and murders – Birchall killing Benwell, Michael Lee killing Maggie Howie.

Collecting in Ontario came later than in eastern Canada. F.W. Waugh and F. Eileen Bleakney had reported a few songs in a Canadian issue of the *Journal of American Folklore* in 1918, and Maud Karpeles printed five British ballads from a Peterborough woman in the *Journal of the Folk Song Society* in 1930. Franz Rickaby's *Ballads and Songs of the Shanty-Boy* (Cambridge, Mass, 1926) and W.M. Doerflinger's *Shantymen and Shantyboys* (New York 1951) both included some lumbering songs from Ontario singers. Extensive collecting began only in 1957, when Edith *Fowke started recording singers in the Peterborough area. There descendants of the colonists Peter Robinson brought over in 1825 had preserved many old Irish songs and also many lumbering ballads. Over the next few years Fowke located other singers in the Ottawa valley, the Haliburton region, Glengarry county, and scattered pockets throughout the province. She found that people of Irish ancestry had preserved more traditional songs than those from England or Scotland, although singers in

Glengarry county remembered some old Scottish songs. The 300 singing games and rhymes in her *Sally Go Round the Sun* were collected mostly from Ontario children.

Reviewing *Folk Songs of Ontario* (1958, Folkways 4005) in *Midwest Folklore* in 1959, Kenneth Goldstein wrote: 'Mrs. Fowke's informants are among the best traditional singers to be heard anywhere on this continent. In addition to voices of excellent quality and intonation, these singers have some of the best-shaped tunes and texts found any place in the English-speaking world.' The finest of these informants, 85-year-old O.J. *Abbott of Hull, Que, knew well over 100 songs. Reviewing his *Irish and British Songs from the Ottawa Valley* (1961, Folkways 4051) in the *Journal of American Folklore* in 1962, D.K. Wilgus noted: 'Abbott is a great singer, in quantity and in quality. He sings in a beautiful old Irish style, often with declamando endings.'

Traditional singers sang unaccompanied, but fiddle music was used commonly for step dancing and square dancing. George *Proctor described 'Old-Time Fiddling in Ontario' in National Museum Bulletin 190 in 1963, and the Shelburne *Canadian Open Old Time Fiddlers' Contest draws well over 100 participants each summer.

By 1980 few Anglo-Canadian songs had been collected in the three prairie provinces. Most prairie songs came west from eastern Canada or north from the USA. Some cowboy ballads made their way up from Texas, and a few homesteader ditties were borrowed from US sodbusters (see Occupational songs). However, *'The Red River Valley,' long thought to be of US descent, probably originated in the Canadian west.

Margaret *MacLeod's *Songs of Old Manitoba* (Toronto 1960) contains interesting Métis songs, but the few in English are of doubtful value. Barbara *Cass-Beggs produced a pamphlet, *Eight Songs of Saskatchewan* (Canadian Music Sales 1963), and a record, *Folksongs of Saskatchewan* (1963, Folkways 4312). A US folklore student, Michael Weiss, noted a few 'Songs from Western Canada' in the *Canadian Folk Music Journal* in 1973, and Robert C. Cosbey has collected children's skipping songs in Saskatchewan.

See also Ballads; 'The Black Fly Song'; Tom Brandon; LaRena Clark; Disaster songs; Fiddling; Wade Hemsworth; Tom Kines; Lakes; Rivers; 'Saskatchewan'; Trade union songs; Wars, rebellions, and uprisings.

DISCOGRAPHY

Far Canadian Fields: Companion to the Penguin Book of Canadian Folk Songs. 1975. Leader LEE 4057

LaRena Clark: Canadian Garland. 1965. Topic 12T140

Ontario Ballads and Folksongs. 1962. Prestige/International INT 25014

Songs of the Canadian North Woods. W. Hemsworth. 1955. Folk FW 6871

Tom Brandon of Peterborough, Ontario. 1963. Folk-Legacy FSC-10

See also Discography for Occupational songs.

BIBLIOGRAPHY

See also Writings of Edith Fowke; Bibliography for Occupational songs.

Ross, Mary Lowrey. 'Our Ontario folk song,' *SatN*, 27 Aug 1932

Fowke, Edith. 'Folk songs of Ontario,' *Sing and String*, vol 2, Winter 1960

– 'American cowboy and western pioneer songs in Canada,' *Western Folklore*, vol 21, Oct 1962

– 'Folk songs in Ontario,' *Canadian Literature*, vol 16, Spring 1963

– 'British ballads in Ontario,' *Midwest Folklore*, vol 13, Fall 1963

Cass-Beggs, Barbara. 'Folk song collecting in Saskatchewan,' *Sing and String*, vol 3, Winter 1964

Fowke, Edith. *Traditional Singers and Songs From Ontario* (Hatboro, Pa, 1965)

– 'A sampling of bawdy ballads from Ontario,' *Folklore and Society*, ed Bruce Jackson (Hatboro, Pa, 1966)

– 'Ontario songs,' *Hoot*, vol 3, Feb–Mar 1967

Archer, Violet. 'Alberta and its folksongs,' CFMS *Newsletter*, vol 2, Jul 1967

Cass-Beggs, Barbara. 'Saskatchewan and its folksongs,' ibid

Fowke, Edith. 'Ontario and its folksongs,' ibid

– 'Folk songs of the county,' *Peterborough: Land of Shining Waters: An Anthology* (Toronto 1967)

Heath, T.G. 'Protest songs of Saskatchewan,' *Saskatchewan History*, vol 25, no. 3, 1972

Fowke, Edith. 'Songs of a Manitoba family,' *CFMJ*, vol 3, 1975

Rogers, T.B. 'A survey of English language music of the Canadian prairies and foothills,' mimeographed (U of Calgary 1975)

Sarjeant, William A.S. 'Folk music in the Canadian prairies,' *Folk R*, vol. 5, May 1976

Rogers, T.B. 'Is there an Alberta folk music?' *CFMJ*, vol 6, 1978

Canada Folk Bulletin, issue devoted to folk music in Alberta, vol 1, May–Jun 1978

5 BRITISH COLUMBIA. Settlement in British Columbia did not favour the transplanting of regional folkways from the British Isles as in some parts of eastern and central Canada. Nevertheless, traditions and attitudes rooted in the folk song and dance of England, Ireland, and Scotland have played a part in British Columbia's life from the colonial period, 1849–71, to the present.

The tradition is traced most easily in the social dance music in areas where fiddlers and other musicians kept alive the tunes and rhythms of jigs, reels, and other country dances as they became part of the 'old time' and western square-dance music. In addition to fiddling, folk musicians in rural communities made dance music with mouth organ, jew's harp, banjo, mandolin, concertina, piano accordion, and piano. The dominant style of fiddling in British Columbia is akin to that in Ontario and the Maritimes and still can be heard at the fiddling contests held annually at some half-dozen centres throughout the province and at the British Columbia championships each August in Prince George. Old-time dances, including western square dances, were common in rural British Columbia until the 1940s, but for a number of reasons they declined after World War II and have all but disappeared. The tradition continues in some form in modern urban square-dance clubs, but about 1960 these groups began to use commercially recorded music from the USA.

Folksongs in the English language in British Columbia fall into two groups: first, traditional songs and ballads brought by migrants mainly from other parts of Canada and the USA and, second, locally made songs.

The first group includes ballads found in the Child collection ('Lady Isabel and the Elf Knight'), broadside ballads ('The Lady Leroy'), songs of the eastern lumberjacks ('The Jam on Gary's Rocks'), cowboy songs ('The Dying Cowboy'), sea songs and shanties ('The Sailor's Alphabet'), humorous songs ('Braking on the Trains'), and children's songs ('Will You Come Along, John?'). Although these songs form part of British-North American lore, in their distinctive versions they are geographically and to some extent culturally British Columbian. In this group may be included a few traditional songs which were adapted to western settings. For example, 'The Wexford Girl' became 'The Lethbridge Girl' and 'The Lake of the Pontchartrain' became 'The Banks of the Similkameen.' Some 50 traditional songs have been collected as sung in British Columbia prior to 1920. Some singers learned their songs orally in the province, but others brought theirs with them. It appears that after 1920 very few songs of this type were passed on to the following generation.

The second group, the locally made songs, are the most distinctively British Columbian. Most reflect life in the logging, mining, fishing, construction, and transportation industries. They often are topical, arising from specific incidents or situations, but a number mirror general conditions of life and work. A common theme is the acceptance of one's destiny as a miner, fisherman, or other labourer, despite the hardships. Minor trials often are made a grim joke in songs of place: the cold winters of the east Kootenays, the incessant rains of Ocean Falls or Holberg on the west coast. The bitter struggle of miners fighting for the right to have their own unions produced several songs, one of which was recorded 50 years after the events which sparked its creation. The tunes and forms of the songs sometimes are parodies, eg, 'Bring Back My Gillnets to Me.' Generally they use known tunes, such as 'Villikens and His Dinah' (best known on this continent as 'Sweet Betsy from Pike') and 'The Strawberry Roan.' Other tunes, such as 'Climbing up the Golden Stairs' ('Teaming up the Cariboo Road') and 'Are You from Dixie?' ('Are You from Bevan?'), originated in Tin Pan Alley. In all there are some 200 of these songs, some preserved only in manuscript, but many still sung in 1980.

With the revival of interest in the roots of society and a redefining of racial and cultural identities, increasing numbers of these songs are being included in school curricula. The Philip *Thomas collection of some 500 songs recorded in British Columbia has been deposited at the British Columbia Archives.

See also Ballads; Fiddling; Klondike; Occupational songs.

DISCOGRAPHY

Bunkhouse and Forecastle Songs of the Northwest. S. Triggs. 1961. Folk FG 3569

Where the Fraser River Flows – and Other Songs of the Pacific Northwest. Skookumchuk Records (no number), Vancouver.

BIBLIOGRAPHY

Thomas, Philip J. 'B.C. songs,' *B.C. Library Q*, vol 26, Jul 1962

– 'The Caribou wagon road 1858–1968: the opening of a frontier, documents in song,' booklet accompanying tapes of song in a teaching unit on the Caribou Gold Rush (Jul 1964)

McTaggart, Margaret Sargent. 'A preliminary survey of folkmusic in B.C.,' CFMS *Newsletter*, vol 2, Jul 1967

Thomas, Philip J. 'British Canadian folk music in B.C..' *British Columbia Music Educator*, vol 18, Spring 1975

– 'Where the rivers flow,' *CFMJ*, vol 3, 1975

– *Songs of the Pacific Northwest* (North Vancouver 1979)

Canada Folk Bulletin, issue devoted to folk music in BC, vol 2, Nov–Dec 1979 1 / NR, 2 / HC, 3 / EDI, 4 / EF, 5 / PJT

Folk music, Franco-Canadian. Written literature tends to be the work of a relatively affluent intellectual elite. This is the reason why literature made its appearance in Canada only when the historical circumstances became favourable. The literature of the oral tradition, however, is a body of verbal and musical material transmitted and continually recreated by the people, combining enduring traditional elements with recent local variants, and sometimes wedding new texts to existing tunes. Thus, there can be no question of iconoclastic breaks with the past, as there may be in written literature. The first generation of French-Canadians perpetuated the traditional culture which had been part of their intellectual heritage, whether European or American. Furthermore, the forefathers of these settlers had lived in France when the songs of the oral tradition originated. Indeed, some of them may even have been the original composers and authors, and their descendants may still live in Canada. For there are songs in Canada, eg, *'Bal chez Boulé,' *'Les Raftsmen,' and *'Vive la Canadienne,' which are in the purest medieval tradition. Such songs represent a cultural heritage which French-Canadians share with all French-speaking countries.

However, a traditional song is not necessarily the exclusive property of one ethnic group: one finds parallel versions of numerous songs not only in French, but also in English, German, Spanish, and other languages. Such songs have had a larger circulation than was believed by the first folklorists of the 19th century, who attributed to them a local or at least national origin. One can understand that researchers working in a given region may have been inclined to make a special case for their own regions in publishing provincial collections which contributed to a regionalist ideal. In the 20th century, however, we know that all francophone countries have a repertory of songs in common. The fallacy of the regionalist approach has been publicized to such a degree that it no longer is permissible to divide these poetic-lyrical materials geographically. Instead they must be classified according to more logical principles. Consequently, a better idea of French folk-song in Canada has been obtained through the study, within a historical perspective, of early evidence and through the results of investigations and recent studies carried out in research centres.

In the same way that they preserved their language, the first French settlers in America continued to sing folk and art songs as they were sung in France, perpetuating the francophone repertoire, and at once conserving it and enriching it. This was done so naturally that it went unnoticed for a long time. Foreign visitors who heard the singing of the voyageurs – the canoeists, the coureurs de bois, the fur traders of the north – were the first to draw attention to it. The voyageurs sang to set the rhythm of their paddles and to give themselves courage. Their songs excited the admiration of 18th- and 19th-century travellers.

The Irish poet Thomas Moore, who sailed from Kingston to Montreal in August 1804, marvelled at the sight of these men rowing together and singing in chorus against the magnificent panorama of the St Lawrence river. So enthralled was he that he memorized several of their songs in order to teach them to his sister. It was during this journey that he composed his *'Canadian Boat Song.' In 1817 John Bradbury mentioned that in the course of his journey he had heard canoeists sing 'Trois Beaux Canards' (*Travels in the Interior of America, in the Year 1809, 1810 and 1811*, London 1817; 2nd edn 1819, pp 20–1). During Captain John Franklin's expedition to the Arctic Lieut George Back collected voyageur songs and sent them to Edward Knight Jr in March of 1823. Knight provided piano accompaniment for the melodies, and George Soane and J.B. Planche wrote English texts which departed considerably from the original lyrics; the results were published in London with the title *Canadian Airs* (1823). John Mactaggart discovered a 12-verse version of the 'Fille au cresson' (*Three Years in Canada*, London 1829, vol 2, pp 255–6). Before 1830 Edward Ermatinger, an English emigrant of Swiss and Italian descent, collected the melodies and complete texts of 11 canoeists' songs. The Royal Ontario Museum (Toronto) owns a manuscript, signed by Edward M. Hopkins (1861), containing nine songs which appear to have been copied from Ermatinger. The New York weekly *The Albion*, 19 Nov 1836, published an unattributed version of *'À la claire fontaine' under the title 'Original Canadian Boat Song'; the words were in French and the music included a piano accompaniment.

Many other people have noted down songs in their travel diaries, among them Mrs Jameson (*Winter Studies and Summer Rambles in Canada*, London 1838, vol 3, pp 111–13), James H. Lanman ('The American fur trade,' *Merchant's Magazine and Commercial Review*, New York September 1840, p 189), R.M. Ballantyne (*Hudson's Bay*, Edinburgh 1848), John Jeremiah Bigsby (*The Shoe and Canoe* ... , London 1850, vol 2, pp 81, 321–2), and Johann Georg Kohl (*Kitchi-Gami*, London 1860). Kohl recounts the legend of Cadieux (*'Petit Rocher de la haute montagne') and quotes several lines from the lament. Among other foreigners who observed this folkloric survival in Quebec were several from France, including Alexis de Tocqueville, Alphonse de Puisbusque, Xavier Marmier, who published *Chant populaires du Nord* ... (Paris 1842), and Jean-Jacques Ampère.

Canadian writers, like their French contemporaries, had developed the habit of quoting songs for the sake of local colour. Whereas European writers used the songs to evoke the peasantry in their stories, Canadians did so to depict the coureurs de bois and the voyageurs of the north. Philippe Aubert de Gaspé (both father and son), Patrice Lacombe, and several other novelists employed this literary device. Popular song collections devoted considerable space to voyageur songs, whose rhythms and tunes conveyed so well the movement of the canoe paddles.

In England, Germany, Italy, and Spain, major collections of songs and patriotic or popular ballads had been compiled since the early 19th century. It was only in 1853, however, that in France the minister of worship and public education, Hippolyte Fortoul, asked the philology section of the country's Committee on Language, History, and the Arts to undertake a broad survey aimed at collecting all French folksongs. Jean-Jacques Ampère was assigned to draft the *Instructions relatives aux poésies populaires de la France* which appeared in August of 1853 in Paris. The *Journal de Québec* published parts of this document 27, 29, and 31 Dec 1853 and 10 Jan 1854. An immediate response was the publication in 1854 in Quebec City of a 104-page supplement to the *Chansonnier des collèges* which consisted mostly of folksongs. Ca 1856 J. & O. *Crémazie published a collection of seven *Chants canadiens*, with piano accompaniments thought possibly to be by Antoine *Dessane. In 1856, after Fortoul's death, the committee abandoned its work and the survey was cancelled. Thus frustrated, researchers in all of the French provinces published regional collections, and in Paris, Champfleury, with the help of J.-B. Weckerlin, published *Chansons populaires des provinces de France* (1860), a collection which, divided into sections by province, seemed to be a sample of the work left incomplete by the government committee. Since Canada was not represented, a Canadian, François-Alexandre-Hubert LaRue, was moved to publish the article 'Les chansons populaires et historiques du Canada' in *Le Foyer canadien* (1863). The article showed that songs considered characteristic of a particular province were commonly sung with variants in French Canada. A significant repertoire was listed, but without the music. The canny Champfleury was quick to reply: he sent a letter insisting on the necessity of including the tunes. LaRue conveyed this to Ernest *Gagnon, who thereupon set about the publication of his collection *Chansons populaires du Canada* (Quebec City 1865).

A musician and occasional polemicist, Gagnon had just taken an active part in the campaign for the restoration of Gregorian chant, prompted in Quebec by the 1860 Paris publication of Father Pierre *Lagacé's work *Les Chants d'Église, harmonisés pour l'orgue suivant les principes de la tonalité grégorienne*. In the 'General Remarks' prefacing Gagnon's collection, one finds the continuation and conclusion to this debate. The entire work serves to demonstrate that the songs of Canada's country people are not vestiges of barbarism and ignorance but a perpetuation of one of the noblest genres of musical art, Gregorian tonality, with its modal scales and particular rhythm. *Chansons populaires du Canada* was not, therefore, merely the work of a folklorist intent on assembling all the popular songs of a given region, but rather that of a musician prepared to uphold a thesis on folk music compared to Gregorian chant. Gagnon thus alerts his readers: 'The number of our folk songs is without limit. This volume contains only one hundred which I have chosen from among the best known and from those which present a particular type.' From a musical point of view, Gagnon was an innovator. In France, musicians such as Weckerlin published folk tunes with overblown piano accompaniments. Latterly these musicians have been criticized for this very unscientific practice. Ernest Gagnon was one of the first to oppose it, presenting folk melodies without accompaniment. He writes that harmony 'must be added to folk songs only with much discretion and taste'; that, very often, 'it lessens the charm and hinders the rhythm, even if it does not completely destroy the modality'; and that 'in the present climate of scholarship it often is considered much preferable that harmony not appear at all.' Out of regard for authenticity, Gagnon even notated appoggiaturas. But as some singers and voice teachers complained, he removed these embellishments for the second edition (1880). Gagnon's work, containing 104 songs and 122 tunes, was offered as a gift to the subscribers of *Foyer canadien*. The collection was published over six issues, February 1865 to February 1867. The delay which affected the last two sections allowed the author to make additions; to draw parallels with French collections by Bujeaud (1863–4), Durieux and Bruyelle (1864), Damase Arbaud (1862–4), and H. Murger (*Les Vacances de Camille*, nd); and to add variants provided by last-minute contributors and informants.

Musicians and folksong specialists immediately hailed the collection as a model and a French classic in the genre. Canadian writers and men of letters proudly praised it. Over the years it grew in favour among musicians and received similar acclaim among folklorists. As early as 1884, Anatole Loquin grouped it without reservation among French collections ('Notes et notules sur nos mélodies populaires,' *Mélusine*). Even in the 20th century, in his appreciation of Ernest Gagnon, Patrice Coirault wrote: 'Along with the works of Bujeaud, Smith, and several others, this excellent artistic collection compiled by a musician-folklorist is one of the original solid pillars on which the monument of our poetic-musical treasure of oral tradition was built' (*Notre Chanson folklorique*, Paris 1941). On this point Coirault is in agreement with French folklorists. No subsequent serious work on popular song has been written in France without mentioning Gagnon's collection. Summing up the praise and appreciation emanating from both France and Canada, Thomas Chapais declared: 'Everything has been said of his book *Chansons populaires du Canada*, which one can call, in its genre, a national monument, and which revealed to France, perhaps more than any other undertaking, the marvellous fact of French cultural survival in Canada' ('Ernest Gagnon,' *Proceedings and Transactions of the Royal Society of Canada*, Ottawa 1916).

At that time there were many other song collectors in Quebec. Among at least 17 extant manuscript collections (a listing of which is found in *La Chanson folklorique et les écrivains du XIXe siècle* by Conrad *Laforte, 1973), may be mentioned Benjamin Sulte's 'Chansons populaires' (1858) and, the most important, 'Annales musicales du Petit Cap' compiled after 1865 by Mgr Thomas Hamel. About 30 small printed song-books share the same period, but most have no music and mix literary songs with folksongs; among them are *La Lyre canadienne* (Quebec City 1847), *Le Chansonnier des collèges* (Quebec City 1850, 1854), and *Recueil de chansons canadiennes et françaises* (Lovell 1859). Gagnon's collection was, without doubt, the greatest. Indeed, the intellectual élite of Canada thought that it comprised the total of the songs in the country. It was 72 years before another folksong collection of this importance was published.

Several study projects were carried out, however. In the newspaper *Le Français* (Paris 1874), Edme-Jacques-Benoît Rathery published 'Chants populaires des Canadiens Français.' In 1896 William Wood, an English Canadian, undertook a survey of French song in Canada for the Royal Society of Canada. There was also a study by Ernest *Myrand on the *Noëls anciens de la Nouvelle-France* (1899). In 1909, at Harvard U (Cambridge, Mass), Cyrus MacMillan wrote 'The Folk Songs of Canada,' an 1109-page dissertation which deals exclusively with French songs in Canada.

Marius *Barbeau, who in 1911 had been engaged as an anthropologist by the Canadian government, had been put in charge of North American Indian studies. At a convention Franz Boas, a US colleague who was investigating European influences among American Indians, roused Barbeau's interest in the French folklore perpetuated in Canada by asking whether the French Canadians had preserved their formal oral traditions and whether Canada still had old songs and legends. In response Barbeau began collecting popular tales in Quebec as early as 1914. It was in 1916 that he made his first folksong recordings. A few preliminary investigations persuaded him that there were songs not only unpublished but not collected by Gagnon. He first surveyed Charlevoix county, travelling there by boat and bicycling through the countryside with an Edison gramophone and wax cylinders securely tied to the luggage-rack. The invention of sound recording brought a scientific accuracy to the preservation of sound documents, making them relatively permanent and renewable. The Edison invention permitted the making of recordings on wax cylinders, although they could accommodate only very brief items.

Consequently, Barbeau recorded only one verse of a song and set down the others in a notation of his own devising. He continued his research in Charlevoix and the Gaspé during the summers 1916–20 and succeeded in making an extraordinary 3000 sound recordings.

On his return, Barbeau informed newspapers and journals of his findings and imparted his enthusiasm to other researchers. In 1917 he met the archivist of the Montreal Court House, E.-Z. *Massicotte, who formerly had been interested in folksong collecting. Barbeau took along a gramophone and left it behind following a fruitful meeting. Thus encouraged, Massicotte returned to the field and between 1917 and 1921 made about 1400 wax cylinder folksong recordings for the *National Museum. One of Massicotte's informants, Vincent Ferrier de Repentigny, eventually produced an unprecedented 10 recordings more than Barbeau's most prodigious informant, François Saint-Laurent. Another collector inspired by Barbeau was the Franciscan Father Archange Godbout, who recorded 215 songs in the Sorel, Bagot, Dorchester, and Portneuf counties between 1917 and 1919. Still another was Adélard Lambert (b St-Cuthbert, near Sorel, Que, in 1867, and raised in the USA). During frequent visits 1919–28 to his birthplace he recorded 367 songs.

In 1924, through the courtesy of Senator Pascal Poirier, Barbeau's collections grew richer by 110 sung pieces hand-notated on Prince Edward Island by Father P. Arsenault, the parish priest of Mont-Carmel, assisted in the music by Father Théodore Gallant, the parish priest of Sturgeon. Among other occasional contributors who transmitted songs to Barbeau were Jean-M. Lemieux, Georges Mercure, J.-E.-A. Cloutier, Mme C. Cyr, Charles *Marchand, Gustave Lanctot, and Philippe Angers. More than 5000 folksongs and variants in wax-cylinder recordings were assembled by Barbeau at the National Museum in addition to nearly 5000 in manuscript (not recorded), a total of some 10,000 versions of traditional songs.

Barbeau and his contributors sent some of these to newspapers and journals. A group of songs collected by Massicotte was published in the *Journal of American Folklore* in 1919; Massicotte also published several songs (with annotations) in the *Bulletin des recherches historiques*.

Massicotte and Barbeau organized the 'Soirées du bon vieux temps,' devoted to folksongs, folktales, and folkdances; these took place in Montreal in 1919 at the Bibliothèque St-Sulpice (renamed BN du Q) and met with great success. For the *CPR Festivals in Quebec City in 1927 and 1928, Barbeau organized several concerts featuring some of his and Massicotte's musical informants, who competed for the audiences' attention alongside famous artists. The performances gave Barbeau and his contributors the opportunity to introduce the results of their research to the public at large and above all to composers, who soon saw the attraction of arranging them for choir or for voice with piano accompaniment. The songs even were assembled into ballad operas by Louvigny de Montigny (*Le Bouquet de Mélusine*, 1928, Montreal, New York 1928) and Healey *Willan (*L'Ordre de Bon Temps*). In 1929 and 1930 for the CPR Barbeau and Graham Spry arranged concerts of Canadian music in which professional artists, among them Rodolphe *Plamondon, popularized folksongs throughout Canada.

At the same time Barbeau was preparing a collection, *Romancero du Canada*, which came out in 1937 and represented 21 years of investigation and research. The title of the work surprised his contemporaries, who, sharing Frédéric *Pelletier's view, would have preferred *Florilège* to *Romancero*; but Barbeau wanted to underline the scientific method he had borrowed from his French model, Georges Doncieux's *Romancero populaire de la France* (Paris 1904). However, instead of making a strict application of the method employed by Romance language experts, which at that time consisted of restoring original forms through the construction of a critical text obtained from all the known versions, Barbeau composed his text exclusively from Canadian versions. This approach responded to the work's objective of providing a text aesthetically appealing to both the general public and the performing artists. Tunes were chosen not from among the earliest known (as in the French model) but from among the most beautiful. Barbeau's approach and Doncieux's concurred, however, in the notion that no attempt should be made to assemble 'approved' composites from the existing melodic variants. Barbeau concluded his book with rhythmic formulae and musical analyses prepared in collaboration with the noted French musicologist Marguerite Béclard d'Harcourt, who also provided the preface. The collection was greeted with pride by French Canadians. Frédéric Pelletier set the tone with these words: 'Let us salute the man who has made us aware of the true nature of the treasure inherited from France – a treasure the French have forgotten they possess, and one which we have transformed in accordance with our own genius' ('Un livre que nous devrions tous nous procurer,' Montreal *Le Devoir*, 8 May 1937).

After this first volume Barbeau continued to accumulate collections for the National Museum and to organize researchers, offering them encouragement, advice, and help. He never gave up the idea of publishing the complete repertoire of French folksongs in Canada. New collections were added: *Alouette* in 1946 and *Le Rossignol y chante* in 1962. Some 1100 songs from Barbeau's collections were transferred from the wax cylinders to glass recordings for the Library of Congress in Washington. From these recordings, Marguerite and Raoul d'Harcourt derived *Chansons folkloriques françaises du Canada* (1956). Barbeau also took Laura Boulton throughout the province of Quebec so that she might establish a source collection of French sound recordings for the museum of Columbia U, New York. Barbeau's collections, and those of his colleagues and disciples, have been maintained and expanded by the Canadian Centre for Folk Culture Studies, an organization affiliated with the National Museum of Man and set up by Carmen Roy. In *Littérature orale en Gaspésie* (1955) Roy published many songs taken from her collection of several thousand pieces.

In Quebec City, studies have been carried out at the *Archives de folklore of *Laval U under the leadership of Luc *Lacourcière, who received encouragement from Bishop F.-A. Savard and Marius Barbeau. Lacourcière, who in turn trained numerous disciples, elevated the study of folklore to the level of post-graduate research and teaching. Following the example of Barbeau he recorded over 2000 folksongs in Charlevoix and New Brunswick. He then introduced a new method of analysis and presentation of critical texts. This method consists of composing an aesthetically pleasing version from Canadian versions only. But Lacourcière's improvement on Doncieux's technique consists of giving within a scientific framework all the variants and all the melodic versions, thus permitting a complete restoration of each original version. The best examples of the application of this method are Lacourcière's in 1946 of 'Les Écoliers de Pontoise' and Barbeau's in 1947 of 'Trois Beaux Canards' (92 Canadian versions).

Subsequently, studies of the utmost diversity have proliferated. Jeannine Bélanger in 1946 demonstrated the archaic character of versification in folksongs. At Laval U Alfred Pouinard wrote a doctoral thesis entitled 'Recherches sur la musique d'origine française en Amérique du Nord, Canada et Louisiane' (1950). Claude Prey conducted a textual and musical analysis of 'Trois Beaux Canards' in 'Formation et métamorphoses d'une chanson: le canard blanc' (1959), a master's thesis presented at Laval U. In 'Civilisation traditionnelle des Lavalois' (1951), Sister Marie-Ursule published 115 songs, of which about 20 of the tunes were collected by Alfred Pouinard and the remainder by François *Brassard. Brassard is the author of numerous articles, including 'Refrains canadiens de chansons de France' (1946), in which he shows how a song is renewed through its refrains. Elizabeth Brandon's doctoral thesis,

'Moeurs et langue de la paroisse Vermillon en Louisiane' (Laval U 1955), is devoted largely to songs. Russell Scott Young, a US student at Laval, in his 'Vieilles chansons de Nouvelle-France' (1956), presented a sample of 50 songs, chosen from his collection of 727 pieces compiled in the province of Quebec. In this work, Young deals with the problem of rhythm in musical transcriptions. In Charlevoix and Acadia (New Brunswick), with Luc Lacourcière and Bishop Savard, Roger *Matton conducted research for the recording *Acadie et Québec*. He then notated the melodies of the songs from Shippagan collected by Dominique Gauthier and presented them in *Chansons de Shippagan* (1975). In the introduction Matton provides a musical analysis of the 70 songs in this collection.

In 1953 Conrad Laforte undertook an inventory of folksongs with a view to setting up an index-card catalogue of all the French songs in North America; he later added songs from French-speaking Europe (France, Belgium, Switzerland). He derived from this *Le Catalogue de la chanson folklorique française* (partial edition, 1958) in which songs are classified in alphabetical order by title. By 1980 the catalogue exceeded 80,000 entry cards. The critical study of so many songs, in itself an unprecedented undertaking, has allowed Laforte to develop the global perspective essential in establishing a methodical classification of folksongs, something he has accomplished in *Poétiques de la chanson folklorique française* (1976). The word 'poétique' is used here not in the philosophical sense or to connote versification, but in its meaning of compositional technique and literary movement. These 'poétiques' serve as an introduction to the complete edition of the *Catalogue de la chanson folklorique française*, begun in 1977 and planned in six volumes, one each for 'chansons en laisse,' strophic songs, dialogue songs, enumerative songs, short songs, and 'chansons sur les timbres.'

The main characteristic of the 'chansons en laisse' is that they contain a 'laisse' (an old French epic verse) ordinarily obtained by suppressing temporarily the refrain and the repeats. These songs, sung in unison, were used to accompany walking, round dances, and group work. Themes and motives are often medieval, several possessing a religious content or an epic character. Others are heroic-comical songs, those about wedding nights and unhappily married women ('maumariées'), about jealous husbands and cuckolds, and about the joys of marriage. The most archaic among them include the themes and motives of the bouquet (laurel wreath), the harvest, birds, shepherds and shepherdesses, amorous advances, feminine misadventures, marriageable daughters and weddings, suitors, erotic fantasies or lampoons, feast days and tricks.

Strophic songs, which do not contain 'laisses' but are made up of an indeterminate number of fixed-form strophes, are mainly narrative; they may have an epic character or religious themes, or may be simply romantic or comical. One also finds in this group songs that are more or less narrative and deal with idyllic or bucolic love, seasonal songs (hunting, New Year's day, mardi-gras), the travelling cycle (departures, homecomings, deserters, sea voyages, 'coureurs de bois,' lumber-yards, logging, military life, boredom, and messages), songs on civilian life and social conditions, songs for special occasion (weddings, etc), and songs of drunkards and drinking.

Songs in the form of dialogue are sung by two people answering each other: the beautiful maiden and her lover, the shepherdess and her gallant, mother and daughter, mother (or father or priest) and son, father-confessor and maiden, husband and wife, historical and legendary figures, personifications, and finally an individual and a group.

In enumerative songs, the enumeration provides the complete structure. Enumerated items may be numbers in decreasing order (songs of ten, of nine), in increasing order (hours, days, weeks, months, seasons, years, and ages; letters, vowels, and the alphabet; clothes; members and parts of the body and remedies; the members or dismembering of animals, birds, or fish; professions and labours; the qualities of men and women; lists of animals and birds, containers, or contents). Enumerations may be based on verbs, actions, and many other subjects of all kinds such as whimsical elements and cock-and-bull stories, telling lies, proper names, houses, families, places, villages, cities, countries, foods, colours, maps, trees, musical instruments and, lastly, ambiguities.

Short songs are by nature of restricted dimensions: lullabies, nursery rhymes, sung stories, sung-game formulas for skipping or playing fives, children's rounds, mnemonic songs for dancing melodies ('timbres'), the sound of hunting horns and the language of bells, short parlour songs, canons, trick songs, songs from popular tales, isolated song fragments, medleys, cries of pedlars and of marketplaces and fairs, rallying cries, bird songs, and animal cries.

'Chansons sur les timbres' are songs in which new words are adapted to pre-existing melodies. Among them are parodies, farcical songs, historical songs, neighbourhood stories such as fires, drownings (laments), and murders, political and electoral songs, anthems, and Christmas carols.

All the songs in the *Catalogue* have been classified according to their poetical characteristics; for each song, the author has provided a substantial bibliography (for both North America and Europe) and all details pertinent to the music.

By 1980 the Archives de folklore had become part of the CELAT of Laval U. CELAT is the acronym for Centre d'études sur la langue, les arts et les traditions populaires des francophones en Amérique du Nord (Research Centre on the language, arts, and popular traditions of francophones in North America), an organization which employs a group of young researchers. Other Canadian universities also have opened folk-music research centres. In Acadia the collection of the journalist Joseph-Thomas Leblanc, compiled with the help of the newspaper *La Voix d'Évangéline* (1938–41), was added to the collection of Fathers Arsenault and Gallant of Prince Edward Island. The year 1942 saw the publication of the first volume of *Chansons d'Acadie*, consisting of songs collected at Cheticamp (Cape Breton) by Father Anselme Chiasson, with musical transcriptions by Brother Daniel Boudreau. Father Anselme subsequently set up at the *U of Moncton an ethnographic museum and archive department which were the predecessors of the Centre for Acadian Studies. In 1946 Geneviève Massignon, while conducting research to document her work on Acadian speech, recorded 240 songs; the recordings were deposited at the Phonothèque nationale in Paris. Numerous songs have been collected and published by Luc Lacourcière, Bishop Savard, Roger Matton, and Dominique Gauthier. Also worthy of mention are Helen *Creighton in Nova Scotia and Kenneth *Peacock in Newfoundland. In their search for English folksongs, both collected several French ones. At *Memorial U a Franco-Newfoundland Research Centre, headed by Gerald Thomas, has collected an impressive number of folksongs among the French population of Port-au-Port and has published the catalogue *Songs Sung by French Newfoundlanders* (1978). In Ontario Germain *Lemieux, the director of the Centre franco-ontarien de folklore of the U of Sudbury, collected among the French population of northern Ontario over 3000 songs, some of which he published in the two-volume study *Chansonnier franco-ontarien* (1974, 1975). As a matter of interest, Sudbury is located near the old route followed by the voyageurs of Canada, the employees of the Grand Portage fur trading post on Lake Superior, and the coureurs de bois. This water route originated in Montreal, continued upstream along the Ottawa River to Mattawa and through Lake Nipissing and the French River, reached the north of Lake Huron by way of Sault Ste Marie, emerged near Grand Portage to the west of Lake Superior, and from there reached the Red River. Hence, along this route and in Manitoba there are descendants of these former voyageurs of the 'upland country' who were so famous for their songs. A collection entitled *Chansons à répondre du Manitoba* (1979) testifies to the continuing vitality of this tradition. All the above-mentioned research centres are active in both research and teaching, thus ensuring not only the maintenance of the repertoire but also an opportunity for scholarly study.

Brief mention must be made of the concert performers who have succeeded in the artistic use of folksongs, notably Charles Marchand and the Bytown Troubadours, the phenomenal 'personnage' La *Bolduc, the *Alouette Vocal Quartet, Eugène *Daigneault, Ovila *Légaré, Jacques *Labrecque, Hélène *Baillargeon, Alan *Mills, Pierre *Daigneault, Raoul *Roy, Edith *Butler, and many others. See Folk-music-inspired composition for a list of the numerous musicians who, like Oscar *O'Brien and Victor *Bouchard, have composed piano accompaniments or, like François Brassard, have made arrangements for choir. Among the most famous of many orchestrations of traditional melodies are Claude *Champagne's *Suite canadienne*, François Brassard's *Suite villageoise*, and Roger Matton's *L'Escaouette*. It would be of interest likewise to examine the originals used in the composition of these major works. Each song may be looked upon as a document, both a work of man to be admired on its own account and, a marvellous source of inspiration.

See also the entries for the songs 'Ah! Si mon moine voulait danser,' 'À la claire fontaine,' 'Alouette!' 'À St-Malo, beau port de mer,' 'Bal chez Boulé,' 'Bonhomme! Bonhomme!' 'Un Canadien errant,' 'C'est la belle Françoise,' 'C'est l'aviron,' 'Dans les prisons de Nantes,' 'Dans Paris y a-t-un brune,' 'D'où viens-tu bergère?' 'La Guignolée,' 'Isabeau s'y promène,' 'J'ai cueilli la belle rose,' 'Malbrough s'en va-t-en guerre,' 'Marianne s'en va-t-au moulin,' 'Papillon, tu es volage,' 'Petit Rocher de la haute montagne,' 'Les Raftsmen,' 'Le Rossignol y chante,' 'Vive la Canadienne,' 'V'là l'bon vent!,' 'Youpe! Youpe! Sur la rivière!'

See also Fiddling.

DISCOGRAPHY

Songs and Dances of Quebec. Collected by Sam Gesser. 1956. Folk FW 6951

Songs of French Canada. Collected by Laura Boulton, Sam Gesser, and Carmen Roy. 1957. Folk FE 4482

Acadie et Québec. Songs collected by Roger Matton. 1959. RCA LCP 1020/RCA CGP 139

C'est dans la Nouvelle-France. Songs collected by Marc Gagné. (1979). Tamanoir TAMX-27005

See also *Pionniers du disque folklorique*; Raoul Roy; Discographies for Jacques Labrecque, Alan Mills.

COLLECTIONS

Chants canadiens (Crémazie 1856)

Gagnon, Ernest. *Chansons populaires du Canada* (Quebec 1865–7, 1880, 1894, 1900; Montreal 1908; followed by a

number of edns based on the 1880 edn, the last of which appeared in 1968)
Robertson, William Graham. *French Songs of Old Canada* (London 1904)
Prévost, Paul-Émile. *Chansons canadiennes* (Montreal 1907)
Tiersot, Julien. *Forty-Four French Folk-Songs and Variants from Canada, Normandy and Brittany* (G. Schirmer 1910)
Barbeau, Marius, and Massicotte, E.-Z. 'Chants populaires du Canada,' *JAF*, vol 32, Jan–Mar 1919
– and Sapir, Edward. *Folk Songs of French Canada* (New Haven, Conn, 1925)
Barbeau, Marius. *Chansons populaires du vieux Québec / Folk Songs of Old Quebec*, National Museum Bulletin No. 75 (Ottawa 1935)
– *Romancero du Canada* (Montreal, Toronto 1937)
Leblanc, Joseph-Thomas. 'Nos vieilles chansons acadiennes,' *La Voix d'Évangéline* (Moncton 1938–41)
Chiasson, Anselme, and Boudreau, Daniel. *Chansons d'Acadie*, 5 vols (1–3 Montreal 1942–8; 4, 5 Moncton 1972, 1979).
Barbeau, Marius. *Les Enfants disent* (Montreal 1943)
– *Alouette* (Montreal 1946)
– et al. *Come A Singing!* National Museum Bulletin No. 107 (Ottawa 1947, 1973)
Lemieux, Germain. *Folklore franco-ontarien, Chansons*, 2 vols (Sudbury 1949, 1950)
Marie-Ursule, Sister. 'Civilisation traditionnelle des Lavalois,' *Archives de folklore*, vols 5–6 (Quebec 1951)
D'Harcourt, Marguerite and Raoul. *Chansons folkloriques françaises au Canada* (Quebec, Paris 1956)
Young, Russell Scott. 'Vieilles chansons de Nouvelle-France,' *Archives de folklore*, vol 7 (Quebec 1956)
Barbeau, Marius, et al. *Roundelays – Dansons à la ronde*, National Museum Bulletin No. 151 (Ottawa 1958)
Barbeau, Marius. *Jongleur Songs of Old Quebec* (Toronto 1962)
– *Le Rossignol y chante*, National Museum Bulletin No. 175 (Ottawa 1962, 1979)
Lemieux, Germain. *Chansonnier franco-ontarien*, 2 vols (Sudbury 1974, 1975)
Gauthier, Dominique, and Matton, Roger. *Chansons de Shippigan, Archives de folklore*, vol 16 (Quebec 1975)
Cormier, Charlotte. *Écoutez tous, petits et grands: Chansons de Pré-d'en-Haut* (Moncton 1978)
Ferland, Marcien. *Chansons à répondre du Manitoba* (Winnipeg 1979)

BIBLIOGRAPHY
LaRue, F.-A.-H. 'Les chansons populaires et historiques du Canada,' *Le Foyer canadien*, vol 1, Quebec 1863
– 'Les chansons historiques du Canada,' ibid, vol 3, Quebec 1865.
Rathery, Edme-Jacques-Benoît. 'Chants populaires des Canadiens français,' Paris *Le Français*, 3 instalments (19 Feb, 5, 9 Mar 1874); 1st article reprt in Quebec *Courier du Canada*, 23 Mar 1874
Wood, William. 'Footnotes to Canadian folksongs,' *Proceedings and Transactions of the Royal Society of Canada*, vol 2 (Ottawa 1896)
Myrand, Ernest. *Noëls anciens de la Nouvelle-France* (Quebec 1899, 1907; Montreal 1913, 1926)
Seranus [Susie Frances Harrison]. 'On French-Canadian folksong,' *MCan*, Jan 1908
Barbeau, Marius. 'Contes populaires canadiens,' *JAF*, vols 29, 30, Jan–Mar 1916, Jan–Mar 1917
– 'Ballades populaires françaises au Canada,' *R canadienne*, vol 20, Aug 1917
– 'Ballades françaises recueillies au Canada,' ibid, vol 20, Dec 1917
– 'Folksong in Quebec,' London *Times*, 1 Jul 1927
– 'Folk-songs of French Canada,' *Music and Letters*, vol 13, Apr 1932
Rabinovitch, Israël. 'Les anciens éléments dans la chansons populaire des Canadiens-français,' Montreal *Jewish Daily Eagle* souvenir edn, 8 Jul 1932
Barbeau, Marius. 'How folk-songs travelled,' *Music and Letters*, vol 15, Oct 1934
– 'Berceuses et chansonnettes,' *JAF*, vol 53, Apr–Sep 1940
– 'Voyageur songs,' *The Beaver*, outfit 273, Jun 1942
– 'French-Canadian folk-songs,' *MQ*, vol 29, Jan 1943
– 'Modalité dans nos mélodies populaires,' *Proceedings and Transactions of the Royal Society of Canada*, vol 38 (Ottawa 1944)
– and Bélanger, Jeannine. 'La césure épique dans nos chansons populaires,' *Archives de folklore*, vol 1 (Montreal 1946)
Brassard, François. 'Refrains canadiens de chansons de France,' ibid
Lacourcière, Luc. 'Les écoliers de Pontoise,' ibid
Barbeau, Marius. 'Canadian folk-songs,' *U of Toronto Q*, vol 16, Jan 1947
– 'Trois beaux canards (92 versions canadiennes),' *Archives de folklore*, vol 2 (Montreal 1947)
Collection Phonothèque nationale (Paris), Catalogue established by the Commission internationale des arts et traditions populaires (Paris 1952)
Barbeau, Marius. 'La complainte de Cadieux, coureur de bois (ca. 1709),' *JAF*, vol 67, Apr–Jun 1954
– 'The Ermatinger collection of voyageur songs (ca. 1830),' ibid
Roy, Carmen. *Littérature orale en Gaspésie*, National Museum Bulletin No. 134 (Ottawa 1955)
Barbeau, Marius. ' "Rondes" from French Canada,' *J of the IFMC*, vol 8, Jan 1956
– 'La chanson populaire française en Amérique du Nord,' *R de l'U Laval*, May 1956
– 'Folk songs of French Louisiana,' *CMJ*, vol 1, Winter 1957
Laforte, Conrad. *Le Catalogue de la chanson folklorique française*, partial edn (Quebec 1958)
'The Hopkins book of canoe songs,' *The Beaver*, outfit 302, August 1971
Laforte, Conrad. *La Chanson folklorique et les écrivains du XIXe siècle (en France et au Québec)* (Montreal 1973)
– *Poétiques de la chanson traditionnelle française, Archives de folklore*, vol 17 (Quebec 1976)
Rahn, Jay. 'Text underlay in Gagnon's collection of French Canadian folk songs,' *CFMJ*, vol 4, 1976
Laforte, Conrad. *Le Catalogue de la chanson folklorique française*, 6 vols, *Archives de folklore*, vol 18– (Quebec 1977–): vol 1 *Chansons en laisse* (1977); vol 2 *Chansons strophiques* (in preparation); vol 3 *Chansons en dialogue* (in preparation); vol 4 *Chansons énumératives* (1979); vol 5 *Chansons brèves* (in preparation); vol 6 *Chansons sur les timbres* (in preparation)
Thomas, Gerald. *Songs Sung by French Newfoundlanders: A Catalogue of the Holdings of the Memorial University of Newfoundland Folklore and Language Archive* (St John's, Nfld, 1978)
Collard, Edgar Andrew. 'Songs of the voyageurs,' 'The indoor canoes,' Montreal *Gazette*, 26 Jul, 2 Aug 1980

CL

Folk-music-inspired composition. The music of the native peoples and the folksongs of the settlers have prompted composers to produce a large literature of arrangements and new compositions. This literature ranges from chordal harmonizations and figurational accompaniments of the tunes to extended works employing folk motives, authentic or newly invented, as thematic material. The most frequently employed medium, the setting for voice and piano, is followed in popularity by the three-part or four-part choral arrangement. Medleys, suites, rhapsodies, themes and variations, and overtures have been favoured forms for longer compositions. Examples of music from a variety of cultural traditions treated in different ways will be provided in the following columns. (Dates of composition and names of publishers are given only when the composer does not have an entry in *EMC* or if the composition has not been listed in a composer's entry.)

The occasional attempts of European composers in the 18th century to imitate North American Indian music are hardly germane to the present discussion since they were based on fancy rather than on authentic models. (See references to Rameau and Grétry in the article on Canada in European and US music 1 / Stage works.) Probably the earliest piece of music inspired by listening to Canadian folk music was Thomas Moore's *'Canadian Boat Song' (1804). Many editors and commentators have failed to realize that Moore's song is not a harmonization or a new version of a voyageur song but a new tune using the opening motive of such a song merely as a point of departure. The first published volume of *Canadian Airs* (London 1823), collected by Lieut George Back during his travels on the Coppermine River, NWT, shows little respect for the French-Canadian songs: the text is replaced by new English words, and the keyboard accompaniments, written by musicians who had never visited Canada, freely adapted the tunes into the mould of current harmonic fashion. (For further notes on this book see Ethnomusicology; Folk music, Franco-Canadian.)

Folk tunes began to appear ca 1840 in Canadian periodicals. Examples are 'C'est la belle Française' (January 1840) and 'Le Fils du roi' (March 1840) in the *Literary Garland*, and *'À la claire fontaine' (June 1846) in the *Album littéraire et musical de la Revue canadienne*, both of Montreal. They were arranged to suit the modestly skilled pianist, as were several medleys and sets of dances. Among the tunes most frequently included in these medleys were 'À la claire fontaine,' 'En roulant ma boule,' *'Vive la Canadienne,' and *'V'la l'bon vent.' Typical are Antoine *Dessane's *Quadrille canadien* (1855) and Ernest *Gagnon's *Le Carnaval de Québec*, 'quadrille sur des airs populaires et nationaux' (1862).

Perhaps the first piece imitating native music was Gagnon's genre piece *Stadaconé*, a 'danse sauvage' for piano (1858). Gagnon's love of folk music bore fruit in his famous collection of over 100 songs, *Chansons populaires du Canada* (Quebec 1865). The book provided only unaccompanied tunes, but Gagnon's choral arrangements of numerous folksongs appeared in the collections *Les Soirées de Québec* (1887) for three voices and piano, *Cantiques populaires du Canada français* (1897) for SATB and organ, and *Chants canadiens* (no date) for SATB and piano ad lib. After 1865, whether inspired by Gagnon or drawing on personal familiarity with folksong, more and more musicians adapted such material. Oscar *Martel, for instance, wrote *Airs canadiens variés, Op 2* for his violin recitals, Alexis *Contant composed a set of *Variations sur 'Un Canadien errant'* for the piano, and Jules *Hone contributed two violin-and-piano pieces, *La Canadienne* and *Souvenir d'Arthabeska* (sic). Achille *Fortier in his *20 Chansons populaires du Canada* (1893) provided piano parts that are moderately difficult and display harmonic resourcefulness. Probably the first of many Anglo-Canadians to utilize the French folk idiom was Susie Frances *Harrison ('Seranus') in her *Trois Esquisses canadiennes* (1887) for piano and her opera *Pipandor* (late 1880s). The French organist Eugène Gigout wrote a *Rhapsodie sur des airs canadiens* for his instrument (Durand, before 1898). A list of turn-of-the-century band and orchestra works is given in approximate chronological order:

*Lavallée. *Pas redoublé sur des airs canadiens*, band (probably 1870s; first page reproduced in *La Presse*, 9 Nov 1912)
*Vézina. *Mosaïque sur des airs populaires canadiens*, band, 1880
Paul Gilson. *Rhapsodie canadienne*, orchestra (Breitkopf, before 1898)
Contant. *Fantaisie sur des airs canadiens* (1900)
Sir A. Mackenzie. *Canadian Rhapsody, Op 67*, orchestra (Breitkopf ca 1905)
L.-P. *Laurendeau. *Laurentian Echoes*, medley for band or orchestra. *The Shores of the St. Lawrence*, medley for band

The collecting of English-language folk music did not begin in earnest until the early 20th century. Since most of the songs were in the Maritimes and Newfoundland and most of the composers in central Canada, little fertilization took place. However, James Paton *Clarke's *Lays of the Maple Leaf, or Songs of Canada* (1853) deserves recognition as an effort to write songs in the folk idiom to words dealing with the realities of Canadian life.

The 1920s, in some ways a bleak decade in Canadian musical life, were of extraordinary importance in relation to the topic under discussion. They brought about an intimate contact between collectors, composers, performers, and promoters, between folksong and composition. Canada now had a number of well-trained, gifted, and sophisticated young composers who responded enthusiastically to the discoveries of collectors such as Marius *Barbeau, E.-Z. *Massicotte, W. Roy Mackenzie, and others. Barbeau and Massicotte in 1919 published a new collection of tunes and organized the 'Soirées du bon vieux temps' in Montreal. The folksong recitals begun there by Charles *Marchand the following year and continued by his male quartets, Le Carillon canadien (1922) and the Bytown Troubadours (1927), created a practical need for arrangements. Pierre *Gautier and Oscar *O'Brien became his principal arrangers, and O'Brien in turn implanted an interest in folk-music-based composition in his pupils Hector *Gratton and Lionel *Daunais. Furthermore, along with Geoffrey *O'Hara, O'Brien wrote the accompaniments for John Murray *Gibbon's *Canadian Folk Songs, Old and New* (1927), a book of French-Canadian songs, with French and English words, that achieved wide circulation.

While Barbeau deserves first place among the collectors of this decade and Marchand among the performers, nobody surpassed Gibbon as a publicist and organizer. A literary scholar and archaeologist by background, Gibbon became publicity agent for the CPR in 1907. Twenty years later he began to organize a series of festivals (see CPR Festivals) that combined the promotion of CPR hotels and travel with displays of Canadian folk music, handicrafts, dancing, and other arts. At least 17 festivals are known to have taken place between 1927 and 1931, in cities from Victoria to Quebec and in the town of Banff. In 1928 the Quebec festival included the announcement, and sometimes the performance, of the winning works in the E.W. Beatty competition for compositions based on French-Canadian folksongs. Prize-winning works included George Bowles' *Suite for String Quartet*, *Champagne's *Suite canadienne*, and an orchestral suite by Arthur Cleland Lloyd. Compositions and publications of the highly productive years 1927–9, many a result of Gibbon's initiative, include Ernest *MacMillan's *Two Sketches for Strings*, based on French-Canadian airs, *Six Bergerettes du bas Canada* for voices and small chamber ensemble, and *Three Indian Songs of the West Coast* (the fruit of a visit to the Nass River Indians of British Columbia with Barbeau); *Willan's ballad operas *L'Ordre de Bon Temps / The Order of Good Cheer* and *Prince Charlie and Flora* (to words by Gibbon, and using Scottish melodies) and two volumes of *Chansons canadiennes* for voice and piano (from the Barbeau collections); O'Brien's folk operas *Scène des voyageurs* and *Une Noce canadienne-française en 1830* and his *Sonata* for cello and piano on the theme *'Dans les prisons de Nantes'; the first two of Gratton's four *Danses canadiennes*, for violin and piano; Champagne's *Danse villageoise*; Henri *Miro's **Vox populi* for soli, choir, and orchestra; and settings by Alfred *Laliberté, Léo-Pol *Morin, Leo *Smith, and Alfred *Whitehead. An important collective effort was the 1928 volume *Twenty-one Folk-Songs of French Canada / Vingt-et-un Chansons canadiennes* (F. Harris), edited by Ernest MacMillan with arrangements by MacMillan, O'Brien, Achille Fortier, Laliberté, and Leo Smith. The list amounts to a who's who of the prominent Canadian composers of the time. Nor should one overlook a number of compositions written earlier in the decade: Benoît *Poirier's *Rhapsodie d'airs canadiens* (1922) for piano, and arranged for band by Joseph Vézina, G.A. *Grant-Schafer's French-Canadian folksong settings published in 1921 and 1925, Laliberté's *Recueil de chants populaires du Canada* (1925), and settings of songs from a variety of cultural traditions by W.H. *Anderson, Gabriel *Cusson, Léo *Roy, and many others. One should add, as well, four works by foreign composers: Arthur Somervell's *12 Ancient French-Canadian Folk-Songs* (Boosey 1927), Maud Wyatt Pargeter's *String Quartet on Canadian Themes* (Ditson 1929), H. Maurice Jacquet's *Suite canadienne* for violin (or cello) and piano (Birchard 1927), and Louis Victor Saar's *A Cycle of Canadian Folk Songs* (C. Fischer 1928).

The folksong movement – as much of a musical 'movement' as Canada ever had – was Canada's phase of musical nationalism, that phenomenon which had swept 19th-century Bohemia and Norway and early-20th-century Spain and Hungary. Some composers, O'Brien, Gratton, and Lapierre among them, thought that in folk idioms lay the true potential basis of a distinct Canadian music. If this prophecy has not been fulfilled (largely owing to the poly-racial mix of Canadian society, and also because a distinct national idiom presupposes a degree of cultural isolation impossible to maintain in any developed country in the later 20th century), it remains true, nevertheless, that many of the folk-influenced compositions of the 1920s have survived to become a permanent and valuable part of the Canadian concert repertoire, and folksong as the basis of composition has remained an important element in the work of many Canadian composers, even those whose outlook is primarily international.

A few works of the 1930s deserve mention. MacMillan's *Three French Canadian Sea Songs* for voice and string quartet, O'Brien's stage works *À Saint Malo*, *Dix Danses limousines*, and *Pastorale*, and Colin *McPhee's *Sea Shanty Suite* (Kalmus 1930; based on British Columbia sailors' songs) all date from 1930. Gratton wrote two more *Danses canadiennes*. Léo-Pol Morin made an important contribution to piano literature with his *Three Eskimos* and also made numerous adaptations of French, Indian, and Inuit songs, among them 'Trois Chants de sacrifice' (Inuit, for choir and two pianos) (see list in *Catalogue of Canadian Composers* 1952). Anderson, Alfred *Bernier, François *Brassard, Gabriel *Cusson, J.-J. *Gagnier, Gratton, Laliberté, Roy, J.-Antonio *Thompson, Whitehead, and many others went on making arrangements (most of which remained unpublished in 1980). Among foreign composers' contributions Vaughan Williams' piano accompaniments to some of the songs in Maud Karpeles' collection *Folk Songs from Newfoundland* (1934) are worth special note.

The decades between 1940 and 1980 have yielded such a rich harvest of Canadian compositions that only a selection of works based on folk music may be offered here. Those on music stemming from the European traditions will be surveyed first; those on Indian and Inuit music will be outlined next.

As before, settings for voice and piano and for accompanied or unaccompanied choir are the most frequent. Treatments of the tunes vary considerably, from the simple but often unconventional accompaniments by Richard *Johnston in *Folk Songs of Canada*, *Folk Songs of Quebec*, and *More Folk Songs of Canada* and Helmut *Blume's in *Canada's Story in Song* to settings employing artful compositional devices such as John *Beckwith's *Four Love Songs* and *Five Songs*, Keith *Bissell's *Six Folk Songs from Eastern Canada* and *Ten Folk Songs of Canada*, Derek *Healey's *Six Canadian Folk Songs*, and Harry *Somers' *Five Songs of the Newfoundland Outports*. In the Somers work, for example, after a first statement of the melody with relatively traditional harmonies, the composer varies rhythm, melody, and harmony separately or together to create an original work which at times appears to owe little to the folklore which inspired it. Other composers who have made vocal and choral settings include W.H. Anderson, Louis *Applebaum, Violet *Archer, Michael *Baker, Leslie *Bell, Maurice *Blackburn, Howard *Cable, Champagne, Donald Cook, George *Coutts, Lionel Daunais, Raymond *Daveluy, Richard *Eaton, Robert *Fleming, Harry *Freedman, Hector Gratton, Jacques *Hétu, Leonard *Isaacs, Kelsey *Jones, Talivaldis *Kenins, Alfred *Kunz, William *McCauley, Michel *Perrault, Godfrey *Ridout, Jean-François *Sénart, and Robert *Turner. Trevor Jones has written several folk operas, and John *Fenwick has used folktunes in his musical play **Johnny Belinda*. Significant settings by non-Canadians include Émile Vuillermoz' *Chansons populaires françaises et canadiennes* (Salabert 1946), Paul Creston's *French Canadian Folk Songs* (Colombo 1968) for voice and piano, and Cecil Armstrong Gibbs' *Five Canadian Folk-Songs* (OUP 1960) for unison voices and piano.

Many an instrumental work of the mid-20th century extends a folk melody by applying to it a variety of the techniques available to a composer trained in the western tradition. For instance, in Gratton's *Dansons le carcaillou* and *Variations libres sur 'Isabeau s'y promène'* orchestration and harmonization transform the song to such an extent that there can be no doubt the creation is the composer's. Other works, eg, Champagne's *Symphonie gaspésienne*, use folk-like themes which are purely the invention of the composer.

Folk-music-inspired works of the period 1940–80 include:

Murray *Adaskin *Algonquin Symphony* for orchestra; *Saskatchewan Legend* for orchestra
Violet Archer *Habitant Sketches* for piano, 1945; *Ten Folk Songs* for piano four hands
Lorne *Betts *Fantasia Canadiana* for orchestra, 1955
Keith Bissell *A Folk Song Suite* for woodwinds; *Variations on a Folk Song* for piano
Alexander *Brott *From Sea to Sea* for orchestra
Howard Cable *Newfoundland Rhapsody* for band; *Quebec Folk Fantasy* for band, Chappell
Morley Calvert *Suite from the Monteregian Hills* for brass quintet
Claude Champagne *Paysanna* for orchestra; *Symphonie gaspésienne* for orchestra
Neil *Chotem *Songs of the Maritime Provinces* for voice and orchestra, 1973
Jean *Coulthard *Canadian Fantasy* for orchestra, Berandol
Maurice *DeCelles *Six works on French Canadian tunes* for band
Maurice *Dela *Triptyque* for orchestra
Anne *Eggleston *On Citadel Hill* for string orchestra
Walter *Eiger *Overture on Canadian Folk Tunes* for orchestra
Robert *Farnon *À la claire fontaine* for orchestra; *Canadian Impressions* for orchestra
Robert Fleming *Four Fantasias on Canadian Folk Themes* for orchestra or band, 1966; *Maritime Suite* for chamber ensemble; *Shadow on the Prairie* (ballet) for orchestra
Hector Gratton *Fantaisie sur 'V'la l'bon vent'* for orchestra
Frank *Haworth *Songs of Canada* for recorders, Whaley Royce 1964
Eugene *Hill *Serenade québécoise* for string orchestra
Kelsey Jones *Miramichi Ballad* for orchestra
William McCauley *Canadian Folk Song Fantasy* for band; *Kaleidoscope québécois* for chamber ensemble; *Newfoundland Scene* for orchestra; *Quebec Lumber Camp* for orchestra, 1953
Ben *McPeek *Five Pictorial Sketches* for mandolin and orchestra; *Piano Concerto*

Roger *Matton *L'Escaouette* for solo voices, choir, and orchestra; *Concerto* for two pianos and percussion
Léo-Pol Morin *Suite canadienne* for piano
Kenneth *Peacock *Essay on Newfoundland Themes* for small orchestra
Michel Perrault *Sea Gallows* (ballet) for orchestra
Eldon *Rathburn *Steelhenge* for steel band and orchestra
Harry Somers *Little Suite for String Orchestra on Canadian Folk Songs*
John *Weinzweig 'Barn Dance' from **Red Ear of Corn* (ballet) for orchestra

Several immigrant composers, among them S.C. *Eckhardt-Gramatté, George *Fiala, Talivaldis *Kenins, and Tibor *Polgar, have used folksongs of their homelands in works written before or after their arrival in Canada. Works based by foreign composers on Canadian folksongs include Benjamin Britten's *Canadian Carnival* (1939) for orchestra, the Brazilian composer Francesco Mignone's *Tres Preludios sobra temas canadenses* for piano, the US composer George Frederick McKay's *Rocky Harbour and Sandy Cove* for string orchestra (Birchard 1950), the US composer Alan Shulman's *A Laurentian Overture* (Chappell 1952), and Vaughan Williams' music for the film *The 49th Parallel* (1941).

In addition, composers of film and incidental music have drawn extensively on folk material whenever appropriate.

*Indian and *Inuit music also have attracted composers' interest after World War II, although the number of published collections of tunes on which to draw remains small. The most frequent use of such material has been in extended works.

Examples of music inspired by Indian music include:

Murray Adaskin *Nootka Ritual* for orchestra
Jean Coulthard *Love Song of the Haida Indians* (orchestrated by W.M. Miles) for soprano and orchestra, 1944
Malcolm *Forsyth *Three Métis Songs from Saskatchewan* for voice and orchestra or piano
J.-J. Gagnier *Journey* for english horn and strings
Graham *George *Songs of the Salish* for orchestra
Theo *Goldberg *Songs of the Loon and the Raven* for orchestra and tape
Derek Healey *Three Quiet Pieces* for organ (one based on an Ojibway song)
Talivaldis Kenins *Sawan-Oong* for narrators, choir, orchestra
Colin McPhee *Four Iroquois Dances* for orchestra
Séverin *Moisse *Variations sur un thème huron* for piano
Léo Roy *Chant de joie* for piano
John Weinzweig *The Great Flood* for chior and percussion; 'Tribal Dance' and 'Ceremonial Dance' from *Red Ear of Corn* (ballet) for orchestra

An Indian opera, *Tzinquaw*, a musical dramatization of the Salish Indian legend of Tzinquaw the thunderbird and Quannis the killer whale, was performed in 1951 by the Cowichan Indian Players in New Westminster, BC. A large cast of dancers and singers performed to a piano transcription by Frank Morrison.

Inuit music has been used or imitated in a number of compositions:

Murray Adaskin *Qalala and Nilaula of the North* for orchestra
Violet Archer *Three Sketches for Orchestra*
Udo *Kasemets *Recitative and Rondino* for string orchestra
Talivaldis Kenins *Fantasy Variations on an Eskimo Lullaby* for flute and viola, CMCentre 1967
Paul *McIntyre *Fantasy on an Eskimo Song* for woodwind quintet
John Weinzweig *Edge of the World* for orchestra; *To the Lands over Yonder* for choir

Mention should be made also of Morris Eisenstadt's *Suite of Three Canadian Dances* (1952), which includes one movement of Indian- and one of Inuit-based music.

In addition to its first role of preserving for history what the populace sang, the notated folksong has found another function, as a focus for the evolution of a music which, to the degree that the folksong's essence and singularity are maintained, could be described as peculiarly Canadian. The majority of composers, however, even those charmed by folk material, have been inclined to use it more for its incidental and intrinsic appeal than for any self-conscious desire either to champion or to capitalize on its 'Canadianness.'

DISCOGRAPHY

Heritage. K. Jones, Chotem, Weinzweig, MacMillan, Cable, Adaskin, Champagne. Toronto Philharmonia, Feldbrill cond. 1967. Dom S-1372

BIBLIOGRAPHY

Pincoe, Ruth, compiler. 'Compositions based on folk songs,' in Fowke's 'A reference list on Canadian folk music,' *CFMJ*, vol 6, 1978
List of Canadian Music Inspired by the Music, Poetry, Art and Folklore of Native Peoples (CMCentre 1979) (HK, SW)

FONTAINE, L.J. Oscar. Composer, organist, teacher, b St-Hyacinthe, Que, 4 Jul 1878, d New Bedford, Mass, 3 Mar 1950. The son of a superior-court judge in Richelieu County, Fontaine studied in Nicolet, Que, with Léon *Ringuet and Octave *Chatillon (piano) and in Montreal with R.-O. *Pelletier (piano and organ) and Guillaume *Couture (theory). He was assistant organist at St-Hyacinthe Cathedral and organist 1904–10 at Notre Dame Church in Fall River, Mass. He devoted his later years to private teaching. He wrote many pieces for piano or piano duet (reaching Op 155 by 1926), published in Boston by Thompson, in London by Leonard, in Montreal in the journal *La Lyre*, and in Philadelphia in the internationally circulated magazine *The Etude* (Presser). Fontaine also wrote several masses, motets, other choral pieces, and songs. Few Canadian-born composers of piano music have had as wide an exposure.

HK

The Fool. Two-scene chamber opera composed in 1953 by Harry *Somers to a libretto by Michael Fram. It was premiered 17 Nov 1956 in Toronto under the auspices of the *CLComp, with Ernest *Adams (as the Fool), Mary *Morrison, Andrew *MacMillan, and Phyllis *Mailing. Victor *Feldbrill conducted, and Herman *Geiger-Torel directed. The Montreal premiere, 15 Mar 1959, was sponsored by the CLComp and the *Society of Canadian Music. André *Turp was the Fool, John *Boyden, Fernande *Chiocchio, and Yolande *Dulude completed the cast, and Jean-Marie *Beaudet conducted. Set in a medieval court, *The Fool* allegorizes the tragic interplay interplay of four characters, King, Queen, Lady-in-waiting, and Fool. Somers has juxtaposed tonal and atonal material to heighten dramatic and emotional impact. Vocal styles, varied by speech intensity and pitch inflection, range from sung speech to traditional full sung line. A chamber ensemble of 10 accompanies the singers. Subsequent performances of *The Fool* include three in 1962 for the *Montreal Festivals Society, a CBC broadcast in 1965, a CBC Montreal Summer Festival concert performance in 1968 (later broadcast and released as a recording), six performances at the 1975 *Stratford Festival, and a student production in 1976 at the *U of Montreal.

DISCOGRAPHY

The Fool. Feldbrill cond, Roslak sop, Rideout alto, Astor ten, M. Brown bass. 1968. RCI 272/Mel SMLP 4029 FH

FORAND, (Marie Josée) Louise (m Samson). Pianist, coach, b Granby, Que, 12 Aug 1941; B MUS (Montreal) 1962, M MUS (Montreal) 1964. She studied piano 1959–64 at the *École Vincent-d'Indy with Yvonne *Hubert and Lucille Brassard. On a Quebec government grant she spent 1964–5 in Paris studying piano with Vlado Perlemuter and musicology at the Conservatoire with Norbert Dufourcq. Between 1965 and 1968 she took further training in New York with the pianist Nadia Reisenberg; she also participated in *JMC tours with Jean *Laurendeau, crossing Canada several times 1965–9 and performing in Yugoslavia in 1970. During the summers of 1966 and 1968 she worked, respectively, in Siena with Guido Agosti and Arturo Benedetti Michelangeli and in Barcelona with Alicia de Larrocha. She became coach and accompanist at the *CMQ in 1967 and has appeared frequently as the accompanist of Jacques *Simard, particularly on tours in France and Belgium. Louise Forand played Beethoven's *Concerto No. 5* at a concert of the *MSO's Matinées symphoniques in 1961 and has given several recitals on CBC radio and TV. She is married to the music critic Marc *Samson.

WRITINGS

'Quinze ans de vie musicale,' *VM*, 8, May 1968 AP

FORD, Clifford (Robert). Composer, teacher, writer, b Toronto 30 May 1947; B MUS (Toronto) 1970. After lessons in piano, organ, and voice 1957–62 with Eric Lewis in Toronto, and in theory and composition 1960–4 with John *Beckwith at the *RCMT, he studied at the *U of Toronto with Beckwith and *Weinzweig. On a CAPAC Sir Ernest MacMillan Fellowship he studied 1970–1 at *McGill U with István *Anhalt. Further studies were undertaken in 1973 with G. Michael Koenig at the Institute of Sonology in Utrecht, the Netherlands. Ford was a founding member of *ARRAY in 1971. He was a staff researcher and writer for *Contemporary Canadian Composers* and *EMC*; he lectured on theory at *McMaster U 1974–6 and was a member of the Dept of Music of *Dalhousie U 1976–80. Ford has composed in several idioms, his work reflecting a variety of influences. His early pieces employ a Webernian 12-tone technique which evolved into a more refined and delicate (though at times dramatic) polyphonic approach. Among his instrumental works are five string quartets (1965–70); two woodwind quintets (1968, 1975); several chamber works, including *Atman-Source* (1969) for clarinet, viola and piano, *Thorybopoioumenoi* (1972) for soprano, flute, viola and electronic tape, and *Metamorphoses* (1977) for piano trio; and solo pieces for guitar (1971), saxophone (1971), piano (1972), and organ (1972–3). His *Suite for Orchestra* (1973) was premiered in 1974 by the *TS. His choral works include *Cantata* (1972), *Mass* (1976, a commission from the *Festival Singers, premiered by them in 1977 in Toronto and performed that same year at *Musicanada), *Songs of the Sea* (1978), and *Day of Wrath* (1979, commissioned by the *Toronto Mendelssohn Choir). The opera *Hypnos* (1972) was a commission from the Young Canada Opera Theatre. *Valley of the Moon* (NFB 1972) is one of several film scores. Ford is a member of the *CLComp and CAPAC and an associate of the *CMCentre.

WRITINGS

'Array visits the Gaudeamus Festival,' *ARRAY Newsletter*, vol 1, Winter 1973–4
Canada's Music: An Historical Survey (Toronto 1981)

BIBLIOGRAPHY
Schulman, Michael. 'A change of scene helps a composer,' *CanComp*, 143, Sep 1979 FH

FORESTIER, Louise. Singer, songwriter, actress, b Shawinigan, Que, 10 Aug 1943. Though she graduated from the National Theatre School in Montreal, it was as a singer that she came to public notice in 1966 when she received the Renée Claude Trophy from Le *Patriote and was named discovery of the year on the CBC TV program 'Jeunesse oblige.' She contributed to the success of the revues *L'Osstidcho* (1968) and *L'Osstidchomeurt* (1969) along with Robert *Charlebois, Yvon Deschamps, and Mouffe. She and Charlebois recorded 'Lindberg' and took part in a whirlwind tour of France in 1969. She then worked briefly with the pianist Jacques Perron before curtailing her performing career. Several years of inactivity followed, save for an appearance with Charlebois at an *MSO concert in 1971, a few recitals, and a role in the NFB film *IXE-13* in 1972.

With the guitarist Claude Lafrance, and again with Perron, Forestier reappeared in 1973 and took her place among the top Quebec stars with the single 'La Prison de Londres.' Forestier then turned from the hard rock of her early years to a more personal style and a repertoire largely inspired by Quebec folk music. Preferring to present new songs – several (including 'Le reel à ti-Guy') her own – rather than tunes of proven popularity, she has performed regularly on TV and has presented her shows ('On est bien chez vous,' 'Ben sûr que chu folle,' etc) throughout Quebec and in France.

After the first of two 1976 tours of France, Forestier won the 'Manteau d'Arlequin' prize, awarded by the critics of that country for the best presentation of French song. In 1978 she began to assemble a group of young musicians led by the pianist Charlot (Charles Barbeau). That year she took part in the Festival de la chanson francophone in Bourges, France, and in the International Song Festival at Sopot, Poland.

Forestier's 12 LPs, released 1969–78 by *Gamma, include *Louise Forestier avec enzymes* (1970, GS 139) and *Les Grands Succès de Louise Forestier* (1972, 2-Gamma 1004).

BIBLIOGRAPHY
Pontaut, Alain. 'Louise Forestier, dix chanteuses en une,' *Maclean*, vol 10, Feb 1970
Kroll, Stephen. 'The return of a Quebec superstar,' *CanComp*, 87, Jan 1974
Dostie, Bruno. 'Louise Forestier returns to start another new adventure,' *CanComp*, 129, Mar 1978

FORGET, Marthe. Soprano, stage director, teacher, b Ste-Agathe-des-Monts, north of Montreal, 25 Feb 1935; premier prix art lyrique (CMM) 1955, M MUS (Montreal) 1974, D MUS (Paris) 1979. Her first music lessons were given by her mother, also a singer. She was educated at St-Jérôme, Que, and at the same time began her musical training. She studied 1953–5 at the *CMM with Yvonne *Hubert, Gilberte *Martin, Jean *Papineau-Couture, and Martial Singher and in 1955 she received an award from Les *Amis de l'art. During a long stay in Europe on a *Canada Council grant she was a soloist in Bach's *St John Passion* in Beirut in August 1960 and gave recitals at Canada House and Berlioz Hall in Paris. She sang 1961–8 with the Opéra de chambre de l'Île-de-France. After her return to Canada she performed in the premieres of Papineau-Couture's *Chanson de Rahit* (U of Montreal's late evening concerts, the Nocturnales; also on CBC radio) and *Saint-Marcoux's *Ishuma* (performed and also recorded, RCI 422, with the *SMCQ Ensemble). In 1970 she began teaching at the *U of Montreal where she directed a workshop in stage

Louise Forestier

technique which produced Monteverdi's *Il combattimento di Tancredi e Clorinda* in 1975 and *Somers' **The Fool* in 1976. During a sabbatical 1976–8 she wrote her doctoral thesis, 'L'Esthétique du récitatif à l'époque contemporaine.' IP-C

FORGET, Rosario. Violin maker, b Montreal 10 Jan 1893. During the summer of 1905 he worked as a messenger boy for Télesphore-Octave *Dionne, a Montreal violin maker. Three years later, having completed his primary education, he joined the firm as an apprentice. Dionne thought him a serious and gifted worker and decided to train him to take over the business. In 1920, after his employer's death, Forget acquired the workshop. Skilfully constructed, Forget's violins are based on the Stradivarius model and use European woods known to be reliable in the production of fine sound. He made about 30 which he sold to students and to accomplished violinists.

Forget also made a cello from Canadian wood. The cello belongs to his son Raymond, a cellist, bass player, and violin maker, who for many years was a member of the instrumental ensemble of the popular CBC radio program 'Les *Joyeux Troubadours'; Raymond also sang folksongs on the program. Jean-Marc Forget, son of Raymond, also became a violin maker, carrying on the family tradition. CH

FORRESTER, Maureen (Katherine Stewart) (m Kash). Contralto, teacher, b Montreal 25 Jul 1930; hon LL D (Sir George Williams) 1967, hon D LITT (York) 1972, hon D LITT (St Mary's) 1972, hon D MUS (Western) 1974, hon D MUS (Mt Allison) 1975, hon LL D (Wilfrid Laurier) 1975, hon D MUS (Toronto) 1977, hon LL D (McMaster) 1978, hon LL D (Victoria) 1978, hon LL D (Carleton) 1979. Youngest of a family of four children raised in a French-speaking neighbourhood of Montreal, she studied piano as a child. Encouraged by her mother she joined Montreal church choirs, where two organists, Warner Norman at St James United and Doris Killam at Stanley Presbyterian, provided a background in music theory and literature. After she left high school at 15 her studies were financed by her earnings as a secretary supplemented by assistance from the Montreal Social Club. She sang as a soprano until she was 17. She had begun voice studies at 16 in Montreal with Mrs Sally Martin, who soon recognized the potential of her lower voice, and she continued at 19 with Frank *Rowe, a retired English oratorio and opera tenor. Forrester's studies with Bernard *Diamant, whom she has acknowledged as her most important teacher, began in 1950 and continued on a casual basis into the 1960s. She was first runner-up in *'Opportunity Knocks' of spring

Maureen Forrester

1951 and also competed in *'Singing Stars of Tomorrow' and *'Nos Futures Étoiles.'

Forrester made her professional debut with the *Montreal Elgar Choir in Elgar's *The Music Makers* 8 Dec 1951 at the Salvation Army Citadel. With the *Opera Guild of Montreal she was a sewing girl in Charpentier's *Louise* 9–10 Jan 1953 and the Innkeeper in *Boris Godunov* 8–9 Jan 1954. Although she had sung as a church soloist and in contests, Forrester did not make her recital debut until 29 Mar 1953 at the Montreal YWCA. She was then engaged to give a recital for the *Ladies' Morning Musical Club, which subsequently awarded her a scholarship. The expenses of launching a career which many predicted (accurately, as it turned out) would be among the greatest in Canadian annals were assumed by the publisher J.W. McConnell.

After Forrester's *MSO debut 8–9 Dec 1953 in Beethoven's *Ninth Symphony* under Otto Klemperer she appeared on CBC radio and TV, toured Quebec and Ontario 1953–4 for the *JMC, and made her *TSO debut 29 Dec 1954 in Handel's *Messiah*. That same year she married the violinist Eugene *Kash. They have five children. She made her European debut 14 Feb 1955 in Paris at the Salle Gaveau accompanied by John *Newmark, who was to be her regular collaborator. The European tour which followed, planned by the JM of France to last two months, was so successful that they continued to perform in recital and oratorio, and on the BBC and the Westdeutscher Rundfunk until January 1956. A subsequent Canadian tour included the premiere, 11 Aug 1956 at the *Stratford Festival, of Harry *Somers' *Five Songs for Dark Voice*, a work commissioned for her by the festival.

Forrester made her New York debut 12 Nov 1956 at Town Hall and shortly afterwards, at the request of Bruno Walter, she sang in Mahler's *Second Symphony* (the 'Resurrection') in Walter's farewell performances (17–19 Feb 1957) with the New York Philharmonic at Carnegie Hall. (By 1960 she had performed some 23 times with that orchestra under various conductors including André Cluytens and Leonard Bernstein.) In addition to a demanding schedule of recitals, oratorio appearances, and broadcasts in Canada in 1957, she appeared with the Royal Philharmonic in London (under Beecham) and the Berlin Philharmonic in its home city. At the 1958 *Vancouver International Festival she sang Brahms' *Alto Rhapsody* with the *Vancouver Bach Choir under Bruno Walter (repeating it three days later in the presence of HRH Princess Margaret) and premiered Jean *Coulthard's *Spring Rhapsody*. She sang in 1960, 1961, and 1963 at the Casals Festival, and her 1960 performances there of the *Alto Rhapsody* and Scarlatti's recently rediscovered *Salve regina* were filmed by the *NFB (*Festival in Puerto Rico*). In 1961 she gave the Canadian premiere (July 30) of the *Salve regina* at Stratford and the premiere (August 26) of Milhaud's *Bar Mitzvah Israel* at the First Israel Music Festival in Jerusalem. In November she began an eight-concert tour of the USSR, and late in 1962 she toured Australia. Her European and US appearances continued. In 1963 she sang in the NBC TV production of Bach's *St Matthew Passion*. In 1965 she and Lois *Marshall joined the US-based Bach Aria Group (founded in 1946 by William Scheide), bringing the number of Canadians in the group's quartet of singers to three (with Norman Farrow, bass-baritone, an original member). Forrester sang with the group until 1974.

Although she had coached singers previously, Forrester gave her first master classes in the summers of 1965 and 1966 at the *RCMT. In 1966 she became chairman of the voice department at the Philadelphia Music Academy, beginning her second sojourn in the USA. (She had lived for two years in Connecticut preceding her move in 1963 to Toronto.) She returned in 1971 to Toronto and taught 1971–2 part-time at the *U of Toronto, where her pupils included Mary Lou *Fallis.

Often described as one of the world's leading contraltos, Forrester has remained loyal to her Canadian origins and to Canadian music. She has premiered Gabriel *Charpentier's *Trois Poèmes de St-Jean de la Croix* (1955), Jean *Papineau-Couture's *Mort* (1956), Robert *Fleming's *The Confession Stone* (Stratford, 16 Jul 1967), Harry *Freedman's *Poems of Young People*, and Srul I. *Glick's ... *i never saw another butterfly* ... (Toronto, 6 Sep 1969), four of Keith *Bissell's *Six Folk Songs of Eastern Canada* (at a CBC Festival, 12 Jul 1971), Oskar *Morawetz' *A Child's Garden of Verses* (under the title *From the World of a Child*, at a CBC Festival, 10 Feb 1973), Murray *Schafer's *Adieu Robert Schumann* (with the *NACO, 14 Mar 1978), and Jean Coulthard's *Three Sonnets of Shakespeare* (Vancouver, 2 Apr 1978).

Forrester has given as many as 120 performances a year in at least 6 countries (averaging above 30 each year in Canada alone) and has performed with leading orchestras and choirs in Europe and North America under Beecham, Bernstein, Casals, von Karajan, Klemperer, Krips, *MacMillan, Ozawa, Sargent, Szell, Walter, and many other conductors. She has appeared frequently with the MSO and TS and was soloist with the latter on its 1978 tour of Japan and China. Although she sang very little opera until the 1970s, she was Cornelia in a concert performance 18 Nov 1958 of Handel's *Julius Caesar* with the American Opera Society and made her Toronto stage debut 28 May 1962 as Orpheus in *Orpheus and Eurydice* under Nicholas *Goldschmidt at *O'Keefe Centre. Other assignments have included Brangäne in *Tristan und Isolde* in Buenos Aires (1963); Cornelia in Handel's *Julius Caesar* (Forrester's US opera debut, 27 Sep 1966, with the New York Opera); the Witch in Norman *Campbell's CBC TV production (1970) of *Hansel and Gretel* (a role she repeated at the 1979 *Guelph Spring Festival); Ulrica in *The Masked Ball* with the *Edmonton Opera (1971); Fricka in the *COC's *Die Walküre* (1971); *Carmen* in a concert performance (1972) with the *Kitchener-Waterloo SO; Madame Flora in Menotti's *The Medium* (1974 at the Stratford Festival and again in 1977 for the Comus Music Theatre Production in Toronto which also was telecast by CBC in November 1978); Mistress Ford in *Falstaff* for *Opéra du Québec (1974); Erda in *Das Rheingold* for her *Metropolitan Opera debut (10 Feb 1975); Brangäne in *Tristan und Isolde* for Opéra du Québec (May 1975); the Countess in *The Queen of Spades* opposite Jon *Vickers at Festival Canada (*Festival *Ottawa) in 1976 and again in 1979; Herodias in *Salome* with the Edmonton Opera in 1977; and the Marquise in the COC's *Daughter of the Regiment* in 1977 and Festival Ottawa's in 1980.

Forrester's voice, originally a dark mezzo of trumpet clarity and power and at maturity a duskily sumptuous, extraordinarily responsive contralto at ease in the mezzo range, commands virtually the entire repertoire within that range. It is most effective, perhaps, in Lieder, especially Brahms, Schumann, Mahler, and Strauss, in oratorio, and in such orchestral works with voice as Mahler's *Das Lied von der Erde*. From the outset of her career, Forrester's singing has been marked by a reliable and sophisticated musicianship of which impeccable pitch is only one facet. This quality, abetted by stamina and poise in the face of a hectic travel schedule and heavy advance bookings, has made her popular with conductors and managements at home and abroad. In the early years a few critics felt she used the same sound to meet the varied demands of song, with results interpretively placid. However, as her experience deepened and her vocal control became more refined, her communicative powers increased. In the *Globe and Mail*, 5 May 1977, John *Kraglund wrote, 'it seemed to me that a well-ordered musical world would require that all vocal artists – if they could not study with Miss Forrester the art of using the voice as an instrument to interpret meaning as well as notes – should attend as many as possible of her concert performances.'

Forrester has been named a Companion of the *Order of Canada (1967) and has received the U of Alberta National Award in Music (1967), the Council's Prize of the Harriet Cohen International Music Award (1968), and the *Molson Prize (1971) awarded by the Canada Council for outstanding cultural achievement. In 1977 she was made an honorary member of the International Music Council. She was national president of the JMC 1972–5 and a member of the board of the NAC 1973–9. She became a director of the Comus Music Theatre Foundation of Canada in 1975.

WRITINGS

'This is our music: putting words to our musical history,' Imperial Oil *Review*, no. 5, 1980

DISCOGRAPHY

Arne *Songs to Shakespeare's Plays*. Young ten, Vienna Academy Chamb Choir, Vienna Radio O, Priestman cond. 1964. West 17075

Bach *Arias*. Bach Aria Group, Priestman cond. 1972. 2-Desto DC 7139, 7140

– *Cantatas No. 35 and 42*. Stich-Randall sop, Young ten, Boyden bass, Vienna Academy Chamb Choir, Vienna Radio O, Scherchen cond. 1964. West WST 17080/West 8303

– *Cantatas No. 53, 54, and 169*. Vienna Chamb Choir, I Solisti di Zagreb, Janigro cond. (1965). Bach Guild BG 670

– *Cantata No. 170* – D. Scarlatti *Salve regina*. Wiener Solisten, Heiller cond. (1966). Bach Guild BG 683

– *Easter Oratorio*. Raskin sop, R. Lewis ten, Beattie bass, Temple U Cons Choir, Philadelphia O, Ormandy cond. 1963. Col MS 6539

– *St John Passion*. Raskin sop, R. Lewis ten, Shirley ten, Treigle bass-bar, Paul bass, Singing City Chorale, Philadelphia O, Ormandy cond. 1963. Col MS 6539

C.P.E. Bach – J.W. Franck – Schumann – Loewe. Newmark pf. (1958). RCI 149

Beethoven *Missa solemnis*. Arroyo sop, R. Lewis ten, Siepi bass-bar, Singing City Choirs, Philadelphia O, Ormandy cond. (1970). Col M 230083

– *Symphony No. 9*. Seefried sop, Haefliger ten, Fischer-Dieskau bar, St Hedwig's Cathedral Choir-Berlin, Berlin Phil O, Fricsay cond. (1959). 2-Decca 7157/Helio HS 25077-2

– *Symphony No. 9*. Price sop, Poleri ten, Tozzi bass, New England Conservatory Chor, Boston Symphony O, Munch cond. 1958. 2-RCA Victor LSC 6066/2-RCA VICS-6003

– 'Ode to Joy' from *Symphony No. 9*. Chor of Rutgers U, MSO, Pelletier cond. 1967. CBC Expo 1

Brahms *Four Serious Songs* – Wagner *Wesendonck Lieder*. Newmark pf. 1968. CBC SM-100/RCI 330/Lon CCL 6003/Lon STS 15113

– *Two Songs, Op 91*, for contralto, viola, and piano. W. Trampler va, C. Wadsworth pf. (1975). Classics Record Library SMQ 805731

A Brahms-Schumann Recital: Schumann *Frauenliebe und -leben* – Brahms *Zigeunerlieder; Two Songs, Op 91*, for contralto, viola, and piano. O. Joachim va, Newmark pf. 1958. RCA LSC 2275

Casals *El Pesebre*. Iglesias sop, Saharrea ten, Serrano bar, Elvira bass-bar, Puerto Rico Cons Chor, Festival Casals O, Casals cond. (1974). Col M2 32966

A Charm of Lullabies: Britten – Brahms – de Falla – Dela – et al. Newmark pf. 1967. West 17137/West Gold W6S 8124

Cherubini *Missa solemnis in D Minor*. Wells sop, Shirley ten, Diaz bass, Clarion Concerts O and Chor, Jenkins cond. (1972). 2-Vanguard VCS 10110, 10111

Custer *Comments on This World*. Phoenix Quartet. Serenus Ser 12031

Delius *Songs of Sunset* – Vidal *Zino-Zina; Gavotte* – German *Gipsy Suite*. Cameron bar, Beecham Chor Soc, Royal Phil O, Beecham cond. 1957. HMV-Odeon PALP 1983

Famous Contralto Arias. Vienna Academy Chamb Choir, Vienna State Opera O, Zeller cond. (1964). HMV Concert Classics HMV SXLP 20096

Glick ... *i never saw another butterfly* ... – Freedman *Poems of Young People* – Beckwith *Five Songs*. Newmark pf. 1970. CBC SM-77/Sel CC-15.073

Gluck *Orfeo ed Euridice*. Vienna State Opera O and Akademie Choir, Mackerras cond. 1966. 2-Bach Guild BG 686, 687

Handel *Hercules*. Vienna Academy Chor, Vienna Radio O, Priestman cond. 1966. 2-RCA Victor LSC-6181

– *Jephtha*. Amor Artis Chorale, English Chamb O, Somary cond, Forrester alto (Hamor). 1969. 3-Vanguard VCS 10077-10079

– *Julius Caesar*. New York City Opera Chor and O, Rudel cond. (1967). 3-RCA Victor LSC-6182/(excerpts) RCA LSC-3116

– *Rodelinda*. Vienna Radio O, Priestman cond, Forrester alto (Bertarido). 1964. 3-West WST 320/3-West 8205/(excerpts) West WST 17102

– *Serse*. Vienna Academy Chamb Choir, Vienna Radio O, Priestman cond. 1964. 3-West WST 321/3 West 8202/(excerpts) West 17115

– *Theodora*. Amor Artis Chorale, English Chamber O, Somary cond, Forrester alto (Didimus). 1968. 3-Vanguard VCS 10050–10052

Handel – Purcell – Mahler – Duparc – Paladilhe – Debussy – Fleming. Newmark pf. 1967. RCI 246

Haydn *Ariadne auf Naxos* – Coulthard *Spring Rhapsody* – K. Jones *To Music*. Newmark pf. Ca 1961. RCI 203

Le Lied: Schubert – Beethoven – Schumann – Brahms – Wolf – Strauss – Dvorak. Ladhuie va, Newmark pf. 1955. Éditions du Club national du disque CND 7. Also issued as *The Artistry of Maureen Forrester*. Everest SDBR 3247

Mahler *Des Knaben Wunderhorn*. Rehfuss bass-bar, Vienna Festival O, Prohaska cond. (1963). Vanguard VRS 1113/Vanguard SRV 285SD

– *Kindertotenlieder; Songs of a Wayfarer*. Boston SO, Munch cond. 1958. RCA LSC 2371

– *Das Lied von der Erde*. R. Lewis ten, Chicago SO, Reiner cond. (1960). RCA Victor LSC 6087/RCA VICS-1390

– *Symphony No. 2*. Cundari sop, Westminster Choir, New York Phil O, Walter cond. 1958. 2-Col M2S 601/2-Col Y2 30848

– *Symphony No. 3*. Netherlands Radio Women's Chor, Boys' Chor of St Wilibrord's Church-Amsterdam, Concertgebouw O, Haitink cond. (1967). 2-Philips 802711, 802712

– *Symphony No. 3*. Los Angeles Phil, Mehta cond. 1978. 2-Lon 2249

Mozart after Hours. Vienna Academy Choir, Vienna State Opera O members, jazz rhythm group, Kingsley cond and hpd. (1964). Vanguard VRS 9165

Mozart *Ombra Felice* – Somers *Five Songs for Dark Voice*. NACO, Bernardi cond. 1970. RCI 286/RCA LSC-3172

Maureen Forrester Sings Famous Arias of Bach and Handel. I Solisti di Zagreb, Janigro cond. (1964). Bach Guild BG 669

Maureen Forrester Sings Handel: Arias from Rodelinda / Xerxes. Isepp hpd, Vienna Radio O, Priestman cond. 1966. West WST 17114

Maureen Forrester Sings Mahler and Brahms: Brahms *Alto Rhapsody* – Mahler *Five Rückert Songs*. Berlin Radio SO, Fricsay cond. 1957. DGG LPE 17199
Maureen Forrester Sings Operatic Arias and Songs: Handel – Gluck – Mozart – Purcell. Vienna Academy Choir, Vienna State Opera O, Zeller cond. 1964. West 17074
Papineau-Couture *Eglogues*. Duschenes fl, Newmark pf. 1954. Hallmark RS-6
Purcell *Songs*. Young ten, Vienna Radio O, Priestman cond, Isepp hpd. 1968. West WST 17113
Ravel *3 Mallarmé Poems* – Wolf *2 Sacred Songs*. Stratford Ens, Armenian cond. 1978. Cantabile CSPS 1349
Verdi *Requiem*. Amara sop, Tucker ten, London bar, Westminster Choir, Philadelphia O, Ormandy cond. (1964). 2-Col M2S 707
Willan *Songs and Folk Songs* – Fleming *Folk Lullabies* – Bissell *From Six Folk Songs*. Newmark pf. 1971. CBC SM-144
Wagner *Wesendonck Lieder* – Archer *4 Songs*. Newmark pf. 1954. RCI 108

BIBLIOGRAPHY

Harrison, Jay S. 'On stage: Maureen Forrester,' *Horizon*, Mar 1962
'For the first time in my life,' *OpCan*, May–Jun 1962
Gilmour, Clyde. 'Everything always comes up roses for Maureen,' *Maclean's*, 23 Jan 1965
Peyser, Joan. 'She waited for the right moment,' *New York Times*, 25 Sep 1966
Gingras, Claude. 'Je suis émotive; il faut que je croie à ce que je chante,' Montreal *La Presse*, 8 Feb 1969
Mould, Warren. 'Bewitching world Lieder,' *Sound*, vol 2, Mar 1971
Edmonds, Alan. 'Big Mo,' *The Canadian*, 29 Jan 1977
Colgrass, Ulla. 'The battle for excellence – Forrester style,' *Music*, vol 1, Jan–Feb 1978
Harris, Marjorie. 'Travels with Maureen,' *The Canadian*, 6 Jan 1979 (MFr)

FORST, Judith (b Lumb). Mezzo-soprano, b New Westminster, near Vancouver, 7 Nov 1943; B MUS (British Columbia) 1966. She studied piano as a child and voice later with French Tickner of the *U of British Columbia. A participant 1966–8 in the *Vancouver Opera Assn training program, Forst won the 1967 western finals of the San Francisco Opera auditions and the 1968 *CBC Talent Festival. A 1968 audition for the *Metropolitan Opera led to a three-year contract and a 1969 debut as Hansel in *Hansel and Gretel*. Her studies continued in New York with Hans Joachim Heinz. She sang Lola in the Metropolitan's 1971 Zeffirelli production of *Cavalleria Rusticana* and Siebel in its 1968–9 and 1976 presentations of *Faust*. In Canada she sang Hansel in the CBC's 1970 TV production of *Hansel and Gretel* and made her *COC debut in 1972 as Olga in *Eugene Onegin*. Other assignments have included Maddalena in *Rigoletto* (1973), Octavian in *Der Rosenkavalier* (1978), and the title roles in *Carmen* and Rossini's *Cinderella* (1979) for the COC; the Secretary in *The Consul* (1973) and Polly Peachum in *The Beggar's Opera* (1976) at the *Guelph Spring Festival; and a San Francisco Opera debut in 1974 as Suzuki in *Madama Butterfly*. Forst has appeared with the Edmonton, Fort Worth, Manitoba, New Orleans, Seattle, Southern Alberta, and Vancouver operas and in the operatic productions of *Festival Ottawa. She has given duet recitals with the soprano Riki *Turofsky in 1974 in Toronto and at the 1976 CBC Vancouver Festival and has sung in oratorio and with the Seattle, Toronto, and Vancouver SOs. She has recorded music by Carissimi, Rossini, Berlioz, Archer, and Bissell, with the pianist Leo *Barkin (1969, CBC SM-79). (MCv)

FORSYTH, Malcolm (Denis). Composer, teacher, trombonist, conductor, b Pietermaritzburg, South Africa, 8 Dec 1936, naturalized Canadian 1974; B MUS (Cape Town) 1963, M MUS (Cape Town) 1966, D MUS (Cape Town) 1972. After teaching privately and at the U of Cape Town in 1967, playing trombone 1960–8 with the Cape Town SO, and writing orchestrations for the South African Broadcasting Corp, he moved to Canada in 1968. He played in CBC Toronto studio orchestras and that same year joined the *U of Alberta, Edmonton, to teach theory, composition, and trombone. In 1973 he became principal trombone with the *Edmonton SO and began teaching the instrument at the *Banff SFA. A member 1970–4 of the Goliard Brass Quintet, he formed the Malcolm Forsyth Trombone Ensemble in 1974. In 1977 he became music director of the university's St Cecilia Orchestra. His compositions range from works for large orchestra (some performed by the Cape Town SO) to chamber and choral pieces and songs. His style owes more to intuition than to methodology ('Technique must be the servant of the spirit, it *must* be'; *Canadian Composer*, March 1975), has its roots in tonality, and arrives at atonality by ear rather than by 12-tone theory or serial processes. Certain works – notably *Sketches from Natal* (1970, a CBC commission) and *Symphony No. 1* (1972) – show strongly the influence of black South African music, especially Zulu. In Canada his works have been performed by *Canadian Brass (who recorded his *Golyards Grounde* and premiered and recorded *Sagittarius* with the *NACO), the Alberta Chamber Players (*Sketches from Natal*), the Edmonton SO (*Symphony No. 2 ' ... a host of nomads ... '*, premiere 1977), and Maureen *Forrester (for whom the CBC commissioned *Three Métis Songs from Saskatchewan*). He is a member of CAPAC and an associate of the *CMCentre.

BIBLIOGRAPHY

Champagne, Jane. 'Malcolm Forsyth: how to get high on your own music,' *CanComp*, 99, Mar 1975
Dawson, Eric. 'Edmonton composer not afraid to fight for his musical rights,' *Calgary Herald*, 14 Apr 1979
Compositeurs canadiens contemporains (RSt)

FORSYTH, W.O. (Wesley Octavius). Composer, teacher, writer, b Markham Township, near Toronto, 26 Jan 1859, d Toronto 7 May 1937. While a youth, he studied in Toronto with Edward *Fisher, but as a young man he enrolled at the Leipzig Cons, where his teachers 1886–8 included Salomon Jadassohn (composition, harmony, counterpoint, canon, and fugue), Martin Krause (piano), Gustav Schreck and Paul Klengel (composition), Richard Hofmann (orchestration), Robert Papperitz (organ), and Bruno Zwintscher and Adolf Ruthardt (piano). In Leipzig Forsyth heard the Romanza from his *Suite in E Minor* played 5 Dec 1888 by a military orchestra under Alfred Jahrow. Owing to overwork, Forsyth was unable to make a success of his solo debut in Vienna, ca 1888, and thereafter he avoided performing in public. He did perform occasionally, however – eg, in a Toronto recital of his own compositions 3 Oct 1889 with Harry Marshall *Field and A.S. *Vogt. Forsyth went again to Europe, in 1892 (to study in Vienna and Ischl with Julius Epstein and to hear *Parsifal* at Bayreuth), in 1905 (to hear *Tristan und Isolde* in Munich), and in 1912. However, he spent most of his life in Toronto, where he taught piano and theory 1889–92 at the *Toronto College of Music and 1893–4 and 1924–37 at the *TCM. He was the director 1895–1912 of the *Metropolitan School of Music (which had opened in 1894 as the Metropolitan College of Music). He taught 1912–19 privately, as well, and 1919–24 at the *Canadian Academy of Music. At the turn of the century he was an instructor at Upper Canada College and several ladies' colleges in the Toronto area and at the Hamilton College of Music. In 1923 his pupils formed the Forsyth Club for study and discussion. In over 45 years of teaching his pupils included N. Fraser *Allan, Sara *Barkin (Sandler), Elsie Bennett, Hilda Capp, Phyllis Leith, Bruce Metcalfe, Charles E. *Wheeler, and Valborg Zollner-Kinghorn. Forsyth wrote for publications in London, New York, and Philadelphia and was the regular critic 1894–5 for *The Week* in Toronto. Cyril Scott, Arthur Friedheim, A.S. Vogt, and Clarence *Lucas were among his musical friends.

W.O. Forsyth

Though his student compositions included orchestral pieces and keyboard preludes and fugues, Forsyth's later works were mainly short, lyrical piano pieces and songs. The piano works were useful as teaching material and as salon pieces of moderate difficulty. Some of the songs were published under the pseudonym Carl Krueger. Of Canadian composers who spent their careers in their homeland, Forsyth was the first to have most of his output published. A collection of his manuscripts and papers has been deposited at the *NL of C. The W.O. *Forsyth Memorial Scholarship was established in 1968 at the *U of Toronto.

COMPOSITIONS

ORCHESTRA

Abendlied. 1888. Str orch. Ms
Suite, Op 17. 1888. Ms
Legende. 1890s. Str orch. Ms?

CHAMBER

String Quartet. Nd. Ms?
Melodie, Op 37. Nd. Vn, pf. Ms
Romance, Op 69. Vn, pf. FH 1934

PIANO

Floating Echoes 'Idylle,' *Op 4*. Ditson 1882
Impromptu, Op 8. Nordheimer 1885
Summer Hours, Op 14, no. 1–3. Edwin Ashdown 1890
Prelude and Fugue, Op 25. Ang-Can 1897
Two Picturesque Valses, Op 29. Nordheimer 1907
In the Twilight 'Reverie' and *Poeme d'Amour, Op 31, no. 1 and 2*. Nordheimer 1907 (*no. 1*), 1908 (*no. 2*)
Moto Appassionato and *A Night in June, Op 32, no. 1 and 2*. Nordheimer 1910
A Summer Afternoon and *The Lonely Pine, Op 33, no 1 and 2*. John Church Co 1912
Through the Fields and *Song of the Silver Night, Op 34, no. 1 and 2*. WR 1914
On the Highway, Op 40. Nordheimer 1917, rev edn 1924
A Starry Night, Op 44, no. 1. Presser 1917, *The Etude*, vol 35, May 1917
Southern Love Song and *In the Vale of Shadowland, Op 50, no. 1 and 2*. Elkin and Co 1922
Through Enchanting Meadows, Op 54. John Church Co 1921
Bells at Midnight, Op 56, no. 1. Wat 1931, *Musical Canada*, vol 12, Jan 1931
Valse Romantique, Op 62. Ang-Can 1929
The Stream in the Hills, Op 66. FH 1934
Summertime Sketches, Op 68, no. 1–4. Nd. Ms
The Girl with the Wistful Eyes, Op 71, no. 2. GVT 1934

VOICE

'Slipping Away,' Op 5. Suckling 1883
'The Merry, Merry Lark' and 'Fruehlingsabend,' Op 16, no. 1 and 2. Jost and Sander nd
'Whip-Poor-Will,' 'The Valley of Silence,' 'Trust,' Op 20, no. 1, 2, 3. Nordheimer 1889

'The Little Old Red Schoolhouse' and 'Love Took Me Softly by the Hand,' Op 30, no. 1 and 2. Nordheimer 1907, (no. 1) *Home Journal*
'Love's Tribute,' Op 35. Nordheimer 1914
'O Little Wee Girl of Mine' and 'A Crimson Rose,' Op 36, no. 1 and 2. Empire Music and Travel Club 1915, (no. 1) *Canadian Journal of Music* Jan 1916
'Once in a Purple Twilight' and 'Summer Showers Are Falling,' Op 39, no. 1 and 2. Fischer 1915 (no. 2), Fischer 1920 (no. 1)
'The Little Blue Ghost,' Op 60, no. 1. Nordheimer 1927
'The Homelight,' Op 60, no. 2. Wat 1930, *MCan*, vol 11, Dec 1930
Also a work for org, *Prelude and Fugue, Op 18*. Nordheimer 1918

WRITINGS
'Toronto letter,' *New York Musical Courier*, vol 25, Apr 1892
Column 'Music and drama,' *The Week*, vols 11–12, 29 Apr 1894–22 Nov 1895
'Flagrant evils of musical life in Germany,' *The Violin*, Mar 1906
'The winsome, wonderful west,' *CanJM*, vol 1, Sep 1914
'Canadian composers,' ibid, vol 2, Jun 1915
'Cyril Scott,' ibid, vol 2, Mar 1916
'Modernism in music,' *CQR*, vol 8, Autumn 1925
'The newer paths in modern music,' ibid, vol 12, Spring 1930
'The road to pianism,' ibid, vol 17, Mar 1935

BIBLIOGRAPHY
'Story of life and art of W.O. Forsyth,' *Toronto Daily News*, 2 Nov 1912
Hamilton, H.C. 'W.O. Forsyth,' *MCan*, vol 10, Jun 1929
Mason, Lawrence. 'Classified summary of principal works by Allard de Ridder and W.O. Forsyth,' Toronto *Globe*, 18 Jul 1936
Keillor, Elaine. 'Wesley Octavius Forsyth 1859–1937,' *CMB*, 7, Autumn–Winter 1973 EK

W.O. Forsyth Memorial Scholarship. Established in 1968 by the estate of Marjorie Forsyth Barlow in memory of her father. A scholarship 'in the higher art of piano playing' (a phrase coined and copyrighted by W.O. *Forsyth), it is given to outstanding graduating students of the Faculty of Music, *U of Toronto, to pursue their studies. Winners have been Kathryn Root 1970, Jane *Coop 1971, Bonnie Silver 1973, Constance Stewart, Philip Thompson, and Robin Crow 1974, Zenovia Kushpeta 1975, John Hess, Kerry McShane, and Jane Solose 1976, Brenda Baranga, Hillar Liitoja, and Robert Linzon 1977, Walter Delahurt and Valerie Weeks 1978, and Jane Hayes and Mark Widner 1979. No award was made in 1980. Individual awards have varied from $2400 to $6500.

FORTIER, Achille. Composer, teacher, b St-Clet, near Montreal, 23 Oct 1864, d Viauville, Montreal, 19 Aug 1939. He began his musical studies with Father Sauvé at the petit séminaire de Ste-Thérèse, near Montreal, and continued them in Montreal with Guillaume *Couture and Dominique *Ducharme. In 1885 he became the first Canadian to attend regular composition classes at the Paris Cons, studying harmony with Théodore Dubois, composition with Ernest Guiraud, and voice with Romain Bussine. Returning to Montreal in 1890, he taught voice and composition at the Dames du Sacré-Coeur Convent and at the *Institut Nazareth. Jean-Noël *Charbonneau, Gabriel *Cusson, and Édouard *LeBel were among his pupils. He later worked as a translator for the federal government in Ottawa.

Devoting his spare time to composition, Fortier wrote, among other works, a *Mass* for four male voices, organ, and orchestra, performed 22 Dec 1896 at the Notre-Dame Church; a *Marche solennelle* and a *Valse* for orchestra; a *Méditation* for cello and piano; several songs including 'Mon Bouquet,' to a poem by Louis Fréchette; and some motets. Léo-Pol *Morin, in his *Papiers de musique*,

Achille Fortier, a drawing in *Le Samedi*, 6 Apr 1895

praised Fortier's 'happy and fresh inspiration' and the modern romanticism, akin to Fauré's, of his 'supple and elegant harmony.' In 1893 Fortier presented his own works at a vocal and instrumental concert conducted by Couture.

Fortier's published works include *20 Chansons populaires du Canada* (Hardy 1893), the tune 'Canadian Queen's Jubilee Song,' for which William Little wrote the words and was the publisher (1897), and 'Land of All That I Love' for voice and piano (Leo Feist 1928). Although some of his manuscripts were destroyed by fire, more than 30 original scores, including church music, folksong arrangements, and 13 secular songs and choral works, were deposited at the Archives nationales du Québec (Claude *Champagne collection).

BIBLIOGRAPHY
Morin, Léo-Pol. *Papiers de musique* (Montreal 1930) (CG)

FORTIER, Marc. Composer, arranger, conductor, administrator, b Jonquière, Que, 7 Dec 1940; BA (Laval) 1961. He began studies in theory with François *Brassard in 1958. He attended the *CMQ in 1961 and the *CMM 1962–6, studying cello with Walter *Joachim and theory with Sylvio *Lacharité, Gilberte *Martin, Clermont *Pépin, and Gilles *Tremblay. He also studied conducting with Franz-Paul *Decker and Vladimir Golschmann. Fortier was music director 1968–72 of the Chambly Regional School Board and taught 1971–2 at *UQAM. In 1973 he began working for the CBC and other radio stations as arranger and conductor, and with pop singers such as Renée *Claude. His symphonic overture *Un Doigt de la lune*, based on a Hindu legend, was awarded the Ferdinando Ballo Prize in the Ente Pomeriggi musicali di Milano, and was premiered 3 May 1969 at the Teatro Nuovo, Milan, under the direction of Nino Sanzogno. His other orchestral works include *Salambo* (1963), *Bessarah* (1964), and *Quand l'été revient* (1967). He also composed *19 Printemps* (1962, brass quintet) and *Pirouettes* (1966, piano, Jaymar). The majority of his works have been published by Emmef, his own publishing company. He is a director of *CAPAC and in 1974 became president of the Société des auteurs-compositeurs du Québec.

Fortier is married to Céline Prévost – pianist, composer, arranger, conductor, record producer, b Valleyfield, Que, 22 Apr 1948; B MUS (Sherbrooke) 1968, BES (Montreal) 1970. Following studies at the *École Vincent-d'Indy 1965–70, she worked with François *Dompierre, then Fortier, composing musical comedies (*Demain matin Montréal m'attend*) and film scores (*IXE-13*). In 1974 she began composing the music for several CBC TV children's programs – 'Du soleil à 5 cents,' 'La Boîte à lettres,' 'Une Fenêtre dans ma tête,' 'Pop Citrouille,' and 'Don Quichotte.' She is the pianist-conductor for Louise *Forestier, André *Gagnon, and Serge Laprade and has produced a number of records. She has composed more than 150 songs and many jingles and commercials. Prévost is a member of CAPAC.

BIBLIOGRAPHY
Vincent, Pierre. 'A teacher talks about listening,' *CanComp*, 69, Apr 1972
Champagne, Jane, et al. 'Interview! Marc Fortier,' *CanComp*, 99, Mar 1975 GP

48th Highlanders of Canada. Toronto militia regiment formed in 1891, and with a distinguished record of active service in both world wars. The original roster included a small bugle band and several pipers; but the pipe band (under Robert Ireland) and the military band (under John Griffin) both date from 1892. Pipe-Major Ireland, remembered for his tune 'Lieut.-Colonel John I. Davidson,' was succeeded in 1895 by Norman MacSwayed, and MacSwayed in 1898 by Farquhar Beaton, known for his tunes 'The Midlothian Amateur Pipe Band' and 'Colonel D.M. Robertson.' Pipe-Major Beaton led the band until 1913 and experimented with part-playing on Highland bagpipes. In wartime, when the band accompanied the regiment to Europe, it was considerably augmented and sometimes had more than one pipe-major; but the principal pipe-major between 1913 and 1952 was James R. Fraser. He and his successor Archie Dewar, who served until 1965, confirmed the band's musical reputation and led it to victory in many competitions. Subsequent pipe-majors have been J. Ross Stewart 1965–75 and Reay Mackay. In 1980, still the largest military pipe band in the Commonwealth, the Pipes and Drums of the 48th Highlanders of Canada continued to perform both on military occasions and for many concerts, dances, and other engagements; and to tour in the USA and Scotland as well as Canada.

Under Capt John *Slatter, bandmaster 1896–1944, the military band became the foremost unit of its kind in Canada and toured widely in Canada and the USA. It was the first kilted brass band in Canada. In 1980 it continued to perform on numerous occasions, both with the Pipes and Drums and in its own right. Subsequent bandmasters have been Warrant Officer Albert Dobney 1944–54, and Capt (later Major) Donald Keeling 1954–77, succeeded by Capt Tom Whiteside. Notable events in Toronto involving performances by both bands have been Trooping the Colour in 1967, the 48th Highlanders Tattoo in 1969, and the Scottish World Festival, annually at the *CNE beginning in 1972.

DISCOGRAPHY
Pipes and Drums of the 48th Highlanders of Canada. Pipe-Major Archie Dewar. Col CL 972
Here Comes the Famous 48th. Pipe-Major Archie Dewar. Col CS 8338
Scottish Heritage: The Pipes and Drums of the 48th Highlanders of Canada. Pipe-Major Archie Dewar. Col CL 2407
See also *Roll Back the Years*.

BIBLIOGRAPHY
Fraser, Alexander. *The 48th Highlanders of Toronto, Canadian Militia. The Origin and History of This Regiment, and a Short Account of the Highland Regiments from Time to Time Stationed in Canada* (Toronto 1900)
Beattie, Kim. *48th Highlanders of Canada. 1891–1928* (Toronto 1932)
– *Dileas: A History of the 48th Highlanders of Canada, 1929–1956* (Toronto 1957) DW

Forum. Montreal amphitheatre, home of the famous hockey team the Canadiens, and the site of

The Montreal Symphony Orchestra at the Forum

many sporting, musical, and stage events. Situated at the corner of Atwater and Ste-Catherine streets, it is the property of the Canadian Arena Co. The first building was opened 29 Nov 1924 and had a seating capacity of 9000; this was enlarged to 12,500 in 1949 and to 16,500 in 1968, when the architect Ken Sedleigh and his consultants David and Boulva transformed it into a modern building, inaugurated 2 November of that year.

Over the years, both on its own and through impresarios who have rented it, the Forum has presented an imposing array of soloists, opera productions, orchestras, dance companies, and folk productions. Notable were Chaliapin in *The Barber of Seville* in 1924; the Boston SO under Koussevitzky in 1926; the *San Carlo Opera in 1936 and 1940; Beniamino Gigli; Lily Pons and André Kostelanetz in 1943; John McCormack; Erna Sack; the *CSM under Sir Thomas Beecham in 1943 and under Eugene Ormandy that same year in Shostakovitch's *Symphony No. 7*, the 'Leningrad'; the Ballets russes de Monte-Carlo in 1948 and 1950; the *Metropolitan Opera in 1952, 1953, 1955, 1957, and 1958; the Israel Philharmonic Orchestra under Koussevitzky in 1951; the Berlin (1955) and Vienna (1959) philharmonic orchestras, both under Herbert von Karajan; the chorus and dancers of the Red Army and the Paris Garde républicaine Band in 1953; the Boston SO under Pierre Monteux in 1953; the Moisseiev Dancers in 1958; Maria Callas in 1958; Lauritz Melchior and Renata Tebaldi in 1959; and the Bolshoi Ballet in 1959 and 1962.

Popular music has been represented by musical comedies, singers (Frank Sinatra 1944), variety shows, jazz (*Peterson, Ellington, etc), the bands of Sousa and Creatore in the 1920s, the Beatles in 1964, and other important rock groups such as Emerson Lake and Palmer in 1968. The *MSO concerts sponsored by the *Montreal Star* (four annually, 1959–75) were held at the Forum, as was one unsponsored series 1975–6. ST

Foundations. As defined by F. Emerson Andrews, president emeritus of the Foundation Center in New York, a foundation is 'a non-governmental, non-profit organization with funds and program managed by its own trustees or directors and established to maintain or aid social, educational, charitable, religious or other activities serving the common welfare.' Of some 1400 such philanthropic foundations in Canada, most have been established by individuals or families, the remainder by companies, communities-at-large, or other entities. They range from very large to very small. Most have limited their granting to certain well-defined areas. Probably less than 5 per cent of that granting has served music. Only those foundations which to some extent have supported the creation, performance, teaching, housing, or other essential functions of the broad cause of music are mentioned in this article. In grants to music, giving practices have varied. Some foundations have avoided gifts to 'brick and mortar.' Some have stressed education (scholarships, bursaries, etc; though to maintain tax-exempt status they have not made grants to individuals directly but have channelled such monies through colleges and other established organizations that are tax-exempt). In general, requests for aid with individual, terminable projects have been more welcome than those for long-term, ongoing, or repeated funding. In some instances foundations have delegated the administration of their funds to government agencies.

See also entries for Alberta Culture; Amis de l'art; British Columbia Cultural Services Branch; Canada Council; Floyd S. Chalmers Foundation; the Community Arts Council of Vancouver; du Maurier Council for the Performing Arts; the Leon and Thea Koerner Foundation; Lapitsky Foundation; Manitoba Arts Council; Massey family; Ministère des Affaires culturelles du Québec; New Brunswick Cultural Development Branch; Newfoundland Division of Cultural Affairs; Nova Scotia Dept of Culture, Recreation, and Fitness; Nova Scotia Talent Trust; Ontario Arts Council; Maurice Pollack Foundation; Saskatchewan Arts Board; Yukon Arts Council.

The appended alphabetical list cites both private and community foundations.

Atkinson Charitable Foundation, Toronto. Established 1942. Restricted to Ontario. Grants and bursaries. Recipients have included the *COC, the *Hamilton Philharmonic Orchestra, and the Kelso Music Centre (Oakville).

R.A. Beamish Foundation, Ottawa. Established 1947. Restricted to Ontario

Beaverbrook Canadian Foundation, Toronto. Established 1960. Assistance within the provinces of Nova Scotia, New Brunswick, and Prince Edward Island

J.P. Bickell Foundation, Toronto. Established 1951. Scholarships and bursaries, restricted to Ontario. It has made grants to the *RCMT, the *TS, and the Toronto Youth SO

E.W. Bickle Foundation, Toronto. Established 1959. Grants, some annual, to both Ontario and national organizations. It has assisted the COC, the *Chamber Players of Toronto, the *Toronto Mendelssohn Choir, and the TS.

Brandon Area Foundation, Brandon, Man. Established 1965. A community foundation with a limited interest in music and the performing arts. Restricted to western Manitoba

Samuel and Saidye Bronfman Family Foundation, Montreal. Reorganized 1972. Grants to all parts of Canada, including a number to help the technical and managerial staffs of arts and cultural organizations to improve their professional qualifications. A grant has been made towards the publication of the works of André *Mathieu.

Calgary and District Foundation (originally Calgary Community Foundation). Established 1955. Assistance for capital needs, research, initiating costs, and emergencies

Canada Foundation, Ottawa. 1945–ca 1961. Established with Walter B. Herbert as director. The foundation encouraged individual artists through exchange programs with other countries; it acted as the administrative arm of the Canada Council in its early years.

Gordon Cockshutt Foundation, Brantford, Ont. Established 1962. Restricted to organizations in the city of Brantford and Brant county. Those who have received assistance include the Brantford SO and the St John's Girls' Drum Corps.

Eaton Foundation, Toronto. Established 1958. Grants nationwide. Beneficiaries have included the COC, the Chamber Players of Toronto, the *Canadian Music Competitions, the *Festival Singers, the Toronto Mendelssohn Choir, the *Atlantic SO, the *Edmonton SO, the Hamilton Philharmonic Orchestra, the *MSO, the *NYO, the Oshawa SO, the *Vancouver SO, and the *Winnipeg SO. The TS has received annual grants. The foundation also has provided scholarships through the *U of Toronto's Faculty of Music (the Eaton Graduating Scholarship, see Awards).

Sir Joseph Flavelle Foundation, Toronto. Established 1945. Restricted to Ontario. It has contributed to the COC, *Contemporary Showcase, the Edward *Johnson Music Foundation, the Festival Singers, the Healey *Willan Memorial Fund, the NYO, the *Ontario Choral Federation, the RCMT, the Kelso Music Centre, the TS, the Toronto Mendelssohn Choir, and the Toronto Youth Choir.

Hamilton Foundation, Ancaster, Ont. Established 1954. Assistance in the Hamilton area only. Organizations which have received grants include the *Bach-Elgar Choir of Hamilton, the *RHCM, and the music department of *McMaster U.

Charles H. Ivey Foundation, Toronto. Established 1957. Support to Ontario and national projects

Richard and Jean Ivey Fund, London, Ont. Established 1965. Response to requests from within the London and southwestern Ontario areas. It has made funds available to the *London SO for specific projects and to the *Western Ontario Cons.

Edward Johnson Music Foundation, Guelph, Ont. Established 1958. It has sponsored the *Guelph Spring Festival, co-sponsored the National Vocal Competition in 1967 and 1977, and established a scholarship endowment fund.

Laidlaw Foundation, Toronto. Established 1949. Awards on a national basis. Publications, fellowships, research. Recipients of Laidlaw funds have included the TS.

Clifford E. Lee Foundation, Edmonton. Established 1969. Restricted to western Canada. Grants to the Edmonton and *Victoria SOs

J.W. McConnell Foundation, Montreal. Established 1937. Restricted mainly to the province of Quebec. One of the 25 wealthiest foundations in the world, it has preferred to fund short-term innovative projects rather than on-going maintenance costs. It has given support to music and related activities.

J.S. McLean Foundation, Toronto. Established 1945. Except in the area of education, funds restricted to Ontario. Recipients have included the COC, Contemporary Showcase, the Festival Singers, the Hamilton Philharmonic, the Kelso Music Centre, the NYO, the TS, the Toronto Mendelssohn Choir, and U of Toronto opera productions.

Molson Foundation, Montreal. Established 1958. Funds go mainly to projects in the province of Quebec.

Chris Spencer Foundation, Vancouver. Established 1949. Response to requests for scholarships and grants from the Greater Vancouver and Lower Fraser Valley areas. It has given to the *Community Music School of Greater Vancouver, the *Vancouver Opera Assn, and the Vancouver Junior Symphony Society.

Johann Strauss Foundation, Edmonton. Established 1975, by Edmontonians of Austrian origin. Scholarships to Albertans for advanced music studies in Austria. It has presented recipients in recital.

Vancouver Foundation. Established 1943. Grants to area organizations such as the Community Music School of Greater Vancouver, the Kiwanis Music Festival, the Nanaimo Concert Band, the *Vancouver Chamber Choir, the *Vancouver New Music Society, the Vancouver Opera Assn, the Vancouver Philharmonic Society, the *Vancouver Society for Early Music, the Vancouver Symphony Society, the *Victoria Cons, and the Victoria SO

Windsor Foundation, Montreal. Established 1967. Top priority to grants and scholarships in the Maritime provinces

Winnipeg Foundation. Established 1921. The oldest community foundation in Canada. Restricted to grants and scholarships for use within the city of Winnipeg. Support to the Winnipeg SO and music students at the *U of Manitoba

Winspear Foundation, Edmonton. Established 1961. Priority to projects within the Edmonton area. It has given awards to some individuals and to the *Edmonton Opera Assn, the Edmonton SO, the Victoria SO, and the Victoria Summer School of Music.

Other organizations which have made contributions to music in Canada are the J. Barney Goldhar Family Foundation (Toronto, established 1962), the B & B Hamilton Foundation (Toronto, established 1966), the Ontario Paper Co Foundation (Thorold, Ont, established 1958), the Fondation J.A. De Sève, and the Lady Davis Foundation. The last-named brought several artists and scholars (including István *Anhalt) to Canada during the late 1940s. US foundations which have contributed to Canadian music interests include the S. Kresge Foundation (Michigan, established 1924), which gave a substantial grant to the Community Music School of Greater Vancouver, and the Amoco Foundation (Chicago, established 1952, originally the Standard Oil Foundation), which has provided financial assistance to both the *Calgary Philharmonic and the COC.

Corporations which have supported music in ways similar to those undertaken by foundations include Imperial Oil, Labatt's, Molson's, and Seagram Distillers.

BIBLIOGRAPHY

Arlett, Allan. *A Canadian Directory to Foundations* (Ottawa 1973)
Alderman, Tom. 'Money for the asking,' *The Canadian*, 16 Jun 1973
'Giving away money is no easy task: an inside look at the prestigious Vancouver Foundation,' *VSO*, vol 3, Mar 1980

The Four Lads. Popular vocal quartet of the 1950s. First known as the Four Dukes, the group was formed in 1947 in Toronto by Jimmy Arnold (lead tenor), Bernie Toorish (tenor and arranger), Frank Busseri (baritone), and Connie Codarnini (bass). All had attended St Michael's Cathedral Choir School, where they studied with Mgr John *Ronan. After their CBC radio debut in 1949 on Elwood Glover's 'Canadian Cavalcade,' they appeared for some 30 weeks at a New York nightclub, Le Ruban Bleu, and began recording for Columbia as background voices on such hits as Johnnie Ray's 'Cry' (1951) and 'Little White Cloud' (1951) and Frankie Laine's 'Rain, Rain, Rain' (1954), all arranged by Toorish. Remaining with Columbia, the Four Lads had their first independent success with 'The Mocking Bird' (1952) and their second with 'Istanbul' (1953). Of about 20 singles released by 1959, all characterized by the group's expert and closely harmonized singing, hits included 'Skokiaan' (1954), 'Standing on the Corner' (1956), 'Who Needs You' (1957), and the million-sellers 'Moments to Remember' (1955) and 'No, Not Much' (1956). The group also made many LPs for Columbia, Kapp, and Dot. In 1975 the Four Lads were listed by *Billboard* magazine as 167th of the top 200 recording acts of the previous 30 years. Though performing mainly in the USA they continued to appear in Canada. With St Michael's Boys Choir they sang 1 Feb 1960 on CBC TV's 'Music 60 Presents the Jack *Kane Hour.' Codarnini was replaced in 1962 by Johnny D'Arc, and Toorish in the early 1970s by Sid Edwards, both of the USA. Although the group's popularity of the 1950s had long passed, the Four Lads still were touring US and Canadian clubs in the mid-1970s.

BIBLIOGRAPHY

Hutton, Eric. 'Four Lads on a little white cloud,' *Maclean's*, 15 May 1952
Gardner, Paul A. 'Four famous lads,' *Weekend Magazine*, 8 May 1954 MM

'Four Strong Winds.' Song by Ian *Tyson. Inspired by the seasonal movement of workers around the country, from one harvest to the next, and the effect of such transiency on a love affair, it was written ca 1961 and recorded by Ian and Sylvia as the title song of their second LP, and later was included in their *Greatest Hits, Volume I*. The song quickly became a part of the standard folk and country repertoire; some 50 versions had been recorded by 1966. The most popular, 1964–5, was a single (RCA 8443) by the US country singer Bobby Bare. Other versions have been included on LPs by Bonnie *Dobson, Stu *Phillips, and Hank *Snow. It became popular again in 1979 as a single (Rep RPS-1396) by Neil *Young. 'Four Strong Winds' was published in 1963 by Witmark Music and appears in the songbooks *Ian & Sylvia* (Witmark 1965?), *Song to a Seagull* (Toronto 1970), and *Canadian Vibrations* (Toronto 1972), among others.

FOWKE, Edith (Margaret) (b Fulton). Folklorist, collector, writer, teacher, b Lumsden, near Regina, 30 Apr 1913; BA (Saskatchewan) 1933, MA (Saskatchewan) 1937, hon LL D (Brock) 1974, hon D LITT (Trent) 1975. After studies in English literature and history at the U of Saskatchewan and in teaching methods at the Saskatchewan College of Education, she moved in 1938 to Toronto. Her interest in folksong and her disappointment in the small quantity of Canadian song published and recorded led her to begin her own researches in the mid-1940s. She prepared CBC radio's weekly 'Folk Song Time' (1950–63), supplementing available material with music from her several field trips around Ontario in the mid-1950s. The first collector to concentrate on that province's folklore, she found the Guelph, Ottawa Valley, and, especially, Peterborough areas to be rich in folksongs. Among the folksingers she discovered and recorded were O.J. *Abbott, Tom *Brandon, and LaRena *Clark. Also for CBC radio Fowke prepared 'Folk Sounds' (weekly 1963–74), 'Folklore and Folk Music' (42 programs broadcast in 1965 on 'The Learning Stage'), and 'The Travelling Folk of the British Isles' (seven programs for 'Ideas' in 1967). A founding member of the *CFMS in 1956, she became the editor of its publication, the *Canadian Folk Music Journal*, in 1973. In 1971 she began teaching folklore at *York U. She has contributed articles to the *Journal of American Folklore, Midwest Folklore, Western Folklore, Ethnomusicology, Sing Out!*, and the *Canadian Forum* and to such reference books as *EMC* and *Literary History of Canada*. Her field recordings have been deposited at the *National Museum of Man, Ottawa, and at the York U library. Some have been released commercially in LP form. She was made a Member of the *Order of Canada in 1978.

Edith Fowke

WRITINGS

'Canadian folk songs,' *Canadian Forum*, vol 29, Nov, Dec 1949
– and Johnston, R. *Folk Songs of Canada* (Waterloo Music 1954)
'A guide to Canadian folksong records,' *Canadian Forum*, vol 37, Sep 1957
'Canadian folk song records,' *Food for Thought*, Nov 1957
– and Mills, A, Blume, H. eds. *Canada's Story in Song* (Toronto 1960)
– and Glazer, Joe. *Songs of Work and Freedom* (Chicago 1960)
'Folktales and folk songs,' *Literary History of Canada*, ed Carl F. Klinck (Toronto 1967, 1976)
– and Johnston, R. *More Folk Songs of Canada* (Waterloo Music 1967)
Sally Go Round the Sun: 100 Songs, Rhymes and Games of Canadian Children (Toronto 1969)
'Canadian folk songs for children,' *In Review*, Winter 1970
Canadian Vibrations Canadiennes (Toronto 1972)
– and Cass-Beggs, Barbara. 'A reference list on Canadian folk music,' *CFMJ*, vol 1, 1973, rev *CFMJ*, vol 2, 1978
The Penguin Book of Canadian Folk Songs (Harmondsworth, Eng, 1973)
'Folk music in Canada,' *CMB*, 10, Spring–Summer 1975
Folklore of Canada (Toronto 1976)
Ring around the Moon (Toronto 1977)
– and Henderson, Carole. 'A bibliography of Canadian folklore in English,' *Communique: Canadian Studies*, vol 3, Aug 1977
See also Bibliographies for Folk music, Anglo-Canadian 4/ Ontario and the Prairies; Occupational songs; Political songs.

DISCOGRAPHY (recordings made by Edith Fowke)

Far Canadian Fields (companion to *The Penguin Book of Canadian Folk Songs*). 1975. Leader LEE 4057
Jigs and Reels: Square Dances without Calls. Folk FW 8826
Old Time Couple Dances. Folk FW 8827
Sally Go Round the Sun (companion to *Sally Go Round the Sun*). 1970. T 46494-95
Square Dances with Calls. Folk FW 8825
See also Discographies for Folk music, Anglo-Canadian 4 / Ontario and the Prairies; Tom Brandon; LaRena Clark; Lakes; Occupational songs.

BIBLIOGRAPHY

Foster, Ann. 'She tracks down Canada's folk songs,' Toronto *Star Weekly*, 31 May 1958
'Edith Fowke,' *CBC Times*, 11–17 Aug 1962
'How Edith Fowke dug up 2000 songs in – of all places – Ontario,' *Maclean's*, 2 Dec 1964
Harrington, Lyn. 'She merits *her* medal,' *Canadian Author and Bookman*, Fall 1970
Fulford, Robert. 'The pleasures of the folksong collector,' *Toronto Star*, 1 Jun 1974
Donald, Betty. 'Edith Fulton Fowke,' *Profiles*, ed Irma McDonough (Ottawa 1975)
McFadden, David. 'Twenty years of folk song collecting,' *Quill and Quire*, May 1977 (RPn)

FOWLER, Joseph-A. Organist, choirmaster, pianist, composer, teacher, b Montreal 1845, d there 4 Jan 1917. Born of an Irish father and a French-Canadian mother, he was one of the first piano pupils of Paul *Letondal. He began teaching at the Collège Ste-Marie when he was 16 and continued ca 1868–90 at the Sacré-Coeur Convent at Sault-au-Récollet, near Montreal, where Rose MacMillan was his pupil. He was organist-choirmaster 1868–1908 at St Patrick's Church and retired with the title of organist emeritus. In 1915 he donated an organ to the adjoining Lady chapel. Active as pianist and accompanist, he played Beethoven's *Variations on 'God Save the Queen'* at a concert organized by A.J. *Boucher in 1870 to mark the centenary of the composer's birth.

Fowler's *Mass of the Blessed Virgin Mary* (I. Suckling and Sons 1893) and *Mass of the Sacred Heart* (Whaley Royce 1898) were written for mixed choir and orchestra. He composed some songs for voice and piano, including three settings of 'Ave Maria' (I. Sucking and Sons 1890, 1892, Whaley Royce 1895) and some piano pieces including *Jour de bonheur* (1899) published by Whaley Royce.

On occasion Fowler acted as an impresario, and he brought to Montreal the Irish baritone William Ludwig, among others. Alexis *Contant and the pianist and organist Arthur Pépin were among his pupils. Fowler visited Europe on three occasions.

BIBLIOGRAPHY

'Late Prof. Fowler long at St. Patrick's,' Montreal *Gazette*, 5 Jul 1917

GP

FOX, George (Augustus) (b Fuchs). Violinist, pianist, b Galt, Ont, 25 Jul 1870, d Toronto 15 Mar 1913. A child prodigy, Fox accompanied his father, an amateur violinist, in *Carnival of Venice* at a concert in May 1874 in his hometown, Walkerton, Ont. He also performed as a pianist at the Berlin (Kitchener), Ont, *Sängerfest in 1875 and in Detroit in 1878. He learned to read music only after he studied violin at 9 with J.W. *Baumann in Hamilton. Remarkably, at 10 he was able to play Wieniawski's *Légende* and de Bériot's *Air varié No. 5*, and drew the notice of the famous violinist Eduard Remenyi, who, in a letter of 1880 to a Chicago colleague, compared Fox to the child Mozart. As an adult, Fox appeared as a violinist in Canada, the southern USA, and Mexico but made Toronto his home. His playing reputedly had an emotional warmth and a large, rich tone, but his repertoire seems to have been limited. Though he began formal study late for a prodigy, he developed quickly and came to be considered one of Canada's best violinists. A photocopy of a scrapbook documenting his career is held at the *NL of C. HK

FRANCE, William (Edward). Organist, composer, pianist, teacher, writer, b Milberta, Ont, 21 Apr 1912; FCCO 1937, B MUS (Toronto) 1941. He had piano lessons with his mother and later with Catherine Gibson. At 14 he took his first church appointment but carried out the attendant duties at the piano. He did not begin to study organ until he was 17. His later teachers included Thomas Martin and Gertrude *Huntley Green (piano), Charles *Peaker (organ), Frederick *Horwood (theory), and Eugene *Hill and Healey *Willan (composition). In the early years of his career France held positions in churches in a succession of Ontario towns – Tillsonburg, Sarnia, Sault Ste Marie (Central United), Guelph, and Stratford (Knox Presbyterian). He was appointed organist choirmaster at Dominion-Chalmers United Church, Ottawa, in 1950 and held that post until his retirement in 1980. He taught harmony and counterpoint 1973–6 at the *U of Ottawa.

Most of France's choral compositions are for the church, but he also has written songs, piano pieces, organ music, and works for small ensembles (eg, *Miniature Suite* for organ and brass quintet, premiered at Knox Presbyterian Church, Ottawa, 25 Aug 1970). Publishers of his works include BMI Canada, *Berandol, *Harris, Presser, Ditson, Galaxy, *Oxford, *Thompson, and Lorenz. France is a member of PRO Canada. CWt

France. Of all countries, with the possible exception of United Kingdom, France has had the chief and most persistent influence on music in Canada. The French, arriving at the beginning of the 17th century, were the first to colonize the country. They brought with them their songs, a large number of which are known and sung by their descendants after more than three and a half centuries, and also their church music. Among the missionaries who came from France to convert the Indians were men and women who were able to read music and who possessed other musical skills.

It was the French also who brought into Canada the first instruments, including the organ, and the first collections of sheet music. Martin *Boutet and Mother *Marie de Saint-Joseph, an Ursuline sister, were the first to teach music, though they also taught other subjects. In the mid-17th century Louis *Jolliet went to France to pursue his studies, music among them, thus becoming the first Canadian-born resident to travel to the land of his forebears to complete his education.

It is true, however, that under the French regime (1608–1760), music does not appear to have been encouraged and developed systematically despite many interesting individual efforts on its behalf.

Relations between France and its erstwhile colony were interrupted by England's conquest of New France in 1760 but were resumed in the mid-19th century, and the French influence continued to be felt, chiefly in those areas – Quebec, New Brunswick (Acadia), and parts of Manitoba and Ontario – where there were concentrations of Canadians of French origin who perpetuated the French language. In this article the influence of France will be described in relation to those spheres of activity in which it has been most marked.

1 Under the French regime
2 Visitors
3 Opera and operetta
4 Immigration
5 Canadians in France
6 Popular song and chansonniers

1 UNDER THE FRENCH REGIME. Considering the predominant role the Roman Catholic church was to play during the French regime, it is not surprising that the earliest musicians of record in Canada were missionaries or laymen in the employ of the church. Annals of the times, such as the *Jesuit Relations* and *Le Journal des Jésuites*, show that the rudiments of music were taught to children, both French and Indian. The first bishop of Quebec City, Mgr de Laval, was the patron of four 'music officers.' In Quebec City in 1684 he created the post of *Grand Chantre (Precentor), held successively by several French musician-priests. A Jesuit, René *Ménard, apparently wrote some motets around 1640. Jean-Baptiste *Poitiers du Buisson was the first organist of Notre-Dame Church, Montreal, and Paul *Jourdain dit Labrosse signed a contract in 1721 to build an organ for the cathedral in Quebec City. Pierre *DuMesnil described himself as a 'musician and craftsman' in the Quebec City census of 1716. Other names are mentioned in passing in the records, but few details are given concerning their activities.

After the conquest church music gradually was taken over by Canadian-born musicians or by immigrants from Germany or England. However, some French priests, such as Lazare-Arsène *Barbarin, Louis *Bouhier, and Henri *Garrouteigt, subsequently played significant roles.

Little of the available information concerns musical life outside the church. It is possible that some seigneurs owned and even played flutes and violins. These instruments were used at balls and popular festivities and even on occasion in church, as is corroborated by a document from 1645. French regiments, eg, the Carignan-Salières, which arrived in 1665, undoubtedly possessed fife and drum ensembles. Whatever may have existed, few traces have been left. It is known that copies of works by Campra, Charpentier, and Jean-Baptiste Morin found their way to Quebec City in the 18th century, but it is not known that they were performed.

See also Missionaries in the 17th century; Quebec City; Roman Catholic church music.

2 VISITORS. No French musicians seem to have toured in Canada before the middle of the 19th century. In 1841 Quebec welcomed the soprano Euphrasie Borghèse, the tenor Étienne Voizel, and the cellist Henri Billet. The tenor Auguste Nourrit performed in 1842. A musician by the name of Bley served 1845–7 as concertmaster of the *Toronto Philharmonic Society. Two young violin prodigies, Camilla Urso and Paul Julien, visited Canada at about the same time to give concerts. The pianist-composer Henri Kowalski gave several recitals in 1870. In 1893 the organist-composer Alexandre Guilmant performed in Montreal.

The first French instrumental ensemble of any size to appear in Canada was the Band of the Garde républicaine de Paris in 1904. In 1919 the Orchestre de la Société des concerts du Cons de Paris, conducted by André Messager, gave two concerts. The Orchestre national de France visited Canada in 1948, and the Orchestre de Paris in 1964.

The first choral group to come to Canada probably was the Montagnards in 1856. This Basque ensemble achieved considerable success and inspired the formation of many similar ensembles in Quebec (see Montagnards). In 1931 the choir from the school of the Petits Chanteurs à la Croix de Bois of Paris made its first tour in Quebec and it, too, stimulated the formation of a number of like groups.

In the 20th century numerous French artists have performed in Canada, among them Emma Calvé, Robert Casadesus, Alfred Cortot, Marcel Dupré, Marcel Hubert, Pol Plançon, Raoul Pugno, Édouard Risler, E. Robert Schmitz, Jacques Thibaud, Louis Vierne, and Charles-Marie Widor. Among those who have visited after World War II are the trumpeter Maurice André, the violinist Christian Ferras, the pianists Philippe Entremont and Samson François, and the flutist Jean-Pierre Rampal. Among ensembles which performed in Canada before and after the war are the Société des instruments anciens, which came in 1933, and numerous chamber groups (eg, the Pascal and Loewenguth Quartets and the Trio Pasquier). Among the more distinguished French composers to have visited Canada have been Vincent d'Indy, Olivier Messiaen, Darius Milhaud, Francis Poulenc, Maurice Ravel, and Iannis Xenakis (born in Rumania of Greek parents but for many years a citizen of France). Some of the leading French conductors who have appeared in Canada are Serge Baudo, Pierre Boulez, Jean Martinon, Pierre Monteux, and Charles Munch.

3 OPERA AND OPERETTA. It was a Frenchman from Brittany, Joseph *Quesnel, who in 1789 composed the first Canadian comic opera, **Colas et Colinette*. From 1840 on, companies from France and New Orleans visited Canada to perform such staples of the French repertoire as Adam's *Le Chalet*, Auber's *Les Diamants de la couronne*, and, later, Gounod's *Faust* and Bizet's *Carmen*. Gounod's *Jeanne d'Arc* and Boieldieu's *La Dame blanche* were performed respectively in 1877 and 1878 by Canadian theatre companies. In 1940 in Montreal Debussy's *Pelléas et Mélisande* was presented for the first time in Canada. Honegger's *Jeanne d'Arc au Bûcher* received its Canadian premiere in 1953. In 1960 CBC TV presented Poulenc's *Dialogues des Carmélites*, and in 1965 Gilbert Bécaud's *L'Opéra d'Aran* had its North American premiere at the *Montreal Festivals.

French operas and operettas have constituted a large part of the repertoire perpetuated by such Montreal and Quebec City companies as the *Opéra français, the *Montreal Opera Company, the *National Opera Company of Canada, the *Société canadienne d'opérette, the *Variétés lyriques, the *Théâtre lyrique de Nouvelle-France, the *Opéra du Québec, and the aforementioned Montreal Festivals.

4 IMMIGRATION. The conquest of 1760 was followed by the return to France of many seigneurs, administrators, and settlers. Emigration to Canada did not resume until the mid-19th century, though individuals – eg, Jean-Denis *Daulé, Louis *Dulongpré, the organ builder Jean-Baptiste Jacotel, and Joseph Quesnel – continued to arrive. Later many expertly French-trained musicians immigrated: eg, the pianist and composer Charles W. *Sabatier ca 1848, the organist and composer Antoine *Dessane in 1849, the pianist and cellist Paul *Letondal in 1852, the pianist and teacher Gustave *Smith in 1856, the poet and chansonnier Emmanuel *Blain de Saint-Aubin in 1857, the singer and teacher Madame Petipas in 1868, and the tenor and teacher Paul Wiallard ca 1870. It was these musicians, with their solid background, who were to strengthen the foundations of musical life in Montreal and Quebec City. They performed in concert and trained many in the traditions of their country of origin.

Other Frenchmen arrived in the ensuing decades: Raoul *Vennat in 1903, Victor *Occellier ca 1907, Charles *Tanguy in 1907, Henri *Delcellier and Salvator *Issaurel in 1911, Albert *Roberval in 1916, Jean *Riddez in 1920, Jean *Belland and Yvonne *Hubert in 1926, José *Delaquerrière in 1938, Louis *Bailly and Joseph *Bonnet in 1943, Paul *Loyonnet in 1954, Marie-Aimée *Varro in 1955, Antoine *Reboulot in 1967, and Pierick *Houdy in 1970. Without settling in Montreal some distinguished French musicians, including the harpist Marcel Grandjany, the pianist Isidor Philipp, and the baritone Martial Singher, taught there extensively for several years.

5 CANADIANS IN FRANCE. The pedagogical activity of the musicians from France who began to arrive in Quebec in the mid-19th century produced in their best pupils a desire to complete their training in France. Thus began the continuing back-and-forth movement of young Canadian musicians who have undertaken extensive periods of study in France, chiefly in Paris, either in official institutions or with private teachers. The considerable list grows longer each year. Mention here will be restricted to principal instances.

Paris remained a strong attraction for the young musicians, who continued their steady migration even during conflicts like those of 1870–1, 1914–18, and 1939–45. Among the first to go there were Ernest *Gagnon ca 1858, J.-B. *Labelle in the 1850s, Dominique *Ducharme in 1863, Moïse *Saucier and C.-M. *Panneton in 1865, Salomon *Mazurette in 1866, Emma *Albani in 1868, R.-O. *Pelletier ca 1870, Calixa *Lavallée and Guillaume *Couture in 1873, Gustave *Gagnon ca 1873, Oscar *Martel in 1875. Alfred *De Sève in 1876, Alcibiade *Béique in 1877, Charles *Labelle in 1880, Achille *Fortier (the first Canadian to study composition as a regular student at the Cons de Paris) in 1885, François-Xavier *Mercier and Rodolphe *Plamondon in 1895, Victoria *Cartier, Alphonse *Lavallée-Smith, and Céline *Marier in 1896, and Joseph *Saucier in 1897.

Among the first English Canadians to go to France to study were Clarence *Lucas in 1886, Marie *Toulinguet in 1890, and Hope *Morgan in 1892. Elliott *Haslam taught singing in Paris 1901–14, and Elizabeth Campbell did the same from 1920 to the late 1950s.

The trend towards studying in France became more widespread in the 20th century with the departure of Pauline *Donalda in 1902, Louise *Edvina and Éva *Gauthier in 1904, and Arthur *Plamondon in 1905. The creation of the *Prix d'Europe increased it further, making study in France possible for Clotilde Coulombe in 1911, Léo-Pol *Morin in 1912, Jean *Dansereau in 1914, Wilfrid *Pelletier in 1915, Graziella *Dumaine in 1916, Germaine *Malépart in 1917, Auguste *Descarries in 1921, Conrad *Bernier in 1923, Gabriel *Cusson in 1924, Paul *Doyon in 1925, Lionel *Daunais in 1926, Jean-Marie *Beaudet in 1929, Gilberte *Martin in 1930 (also, in 1932, the first Canadian woman admitted to the Cons de Paris), Lucien *Martin in 1931, Bernard *Piché in 1932, Georges *Lindsay in 1934, Georges *Savaria in 1937, Jeanne *Landry in 1946, Clermont *Pépin in 1949, and Josephte *Dufresne in 1950.

Several went to Paris in a private capacity or on scholarships from the *Canada Council or the Quebec government. Among these were Harry *Adaskin, Rosario *Bayeur, François *Brassard, Victor *Brault, Gilles Carpentier, Claude *Champagne, Albert *Cornellier, Andrée *Desautels, Roger *Gosselin, Jean-Pierre *Hurteau, Jean-Paul *Jeannotte, Raoul *Jobin, Bernard *Lagacé, Yvette *Lamontagne, Annette *Lasalle-Leduc, Gilles *Lefebvre, Rafael and Alfred *Masella, Rodolphe and André *Mathieu, Barbara *Pentland, and Georges-Émile *Tanguay.

Canadians studying abroad had the advantage of working with many outstanding teachers, but particular mention must be made of the extraordinary procession to the renowned pedagogue Nadia Boulanger, who, from 1920 until her death in 1979, taught more Canadians than any other teacher in a foreign country. Among her countless pupils were Françoise *Aubut, Pierre *Beaudet, John *Beckwith, Maurice *Blackburn, Richard Boulanger, Walter *Buczynski, Gabriel *Charpentier, Frank *Churchley, Gabriel Cusson, Gwendda Owen *Davies, Isabelle *Delorme, Andrée Desautels, Nathaniel *Dett, Paul Doyon, Elzéar Fortier, Kenneth *Gilbert, Kelsey *Jones, Jeanne Landry, Claude *Lavoie, Roger *Matton, Boyd McDonald (see Beckett and McDonald), Pierre *Mercure, Arthur *Ozolins, Jean *Papineau-Couture, Marguerite Pâquet, Michel *Perrault, Rosette *Renshaw, William Keith *Rogers, John *Ronan, Paul *Scherman, Winifred Scott, Calvin *Sieb, Reginald *Stewart, Yehuda Vineberg, Kenneth *Winters, and Robin *Wood. Among US or European Boulanger pupils who subsequently settled in Canada are István *Anhalt, Sterling *Beckwith, Irving *Heller, Richard *Johnston, Maryvonne *Kendergi, Peter Paul *Koprowski, Pierre *Mollet, Boris *Roubakine, and Peggie *Sampson.

Rodolphe Mathieu and Roy *Royal were pupils of Vincent d'Indy, Claude Champagne studied with André Gedalge and Raoul Laparra, and Bruce *Mather, Boyd McDonald, and Harry *Somers studied with Darius Milhaud.

Another distinguished French teacher of many Canadians is Olivier Messiaen. His classes in analysis and aesthetics at the Cons de Paris have been attended by Françoise Aubut, Serge *Garant, Steven *Gellman, Jacques *Hétu, Talivaldis *Kenins, Sylvio *Lacharité, Roger Matton, Clermont Pépin, André *Prévost, Gilles *Tremblay, and several more.

See also Organ, playing and teaching; Piano, playing and teaching.

Most of the students eventually returned to Canada, but some embarked on international careers in France, chiefly in the field of opera. Such was the case with Emma Albani, Jean Dansereau, Pauline Donalda, Louise Edvina, Éva Gauthier, Raoul Jobin, André Mathieu, François-Xavier Mercier, and Rodolphe Plamondon, as well as Béatrice *La Palme and Sarah *Fischer both of whom, though they did not study in France, did enjoy brilliant careers there, especially at the Opéra-Comique of Paris. Among other Canadians who have performed successfully in France in opera, Pierrette *Alarie, Victor *Braun, Jean-Pierre Hurteau, Louis *Quilico, Joseph *Rouleau, Léopold *Simoneau, Teresa *Stratas, André *Turp, and Jon *Vickers deserve special mention. The conductor Jacques *Beaudry has conducted productions at the Opéra de Paris. Certain Canadian composers, notably Lavallée and Couture, had works performed in France in the 19th century. Later, numerous others had performances, notably Claude Champagne, Rodolphe Mathieu, Roger Matton, Jean Papineau-Couture, André Prévost, and Gilles Tremblay. Several Canadian works were performed in Paris in 1977 at *Musicanada. The Canadians *Aglaé, Roger Gosselin, André *Jobin, and Thérèse *Laporte became stars of French operetta. Numerous Canadians have given recitals in France, among them Paul *Bley, Maureen *Forrester, and Oscar *Peterson. Among ensembles which have appeared in Paris and the provinces are *Canadian Brass, the *Disciples de Massenet, the *Festival Singers, the *Montreal Bach Choir, the *MSO, the *NACO, the *Orford String Quartet, the *Studio de musique ancienne de Montréal, and the *TS. At the invitation of Pierre Boulez, Robert *Aitken appeared in recital during the opening of the Institut de recherche et de coordination acoustique-musique (IRCAM) in the Centre Georges-Pompidou in Paris in 1977.

6 POPULAR SONG AND CHANSONNIERS. If there is one genre in which the influence of France has been predominant it is popular song. For more than two centuries, the French folksong has remained perhaps the strongest musical link between Canada and France. It often has been observed that French folksongs in Canada have been preserved in their purest form, partly because industrialization occurred there considerably later, and also because in Canada they were less exposed to outside influences.

If folksongs were the strongest link, they were not the only one, however. During the 19th century the drawing-room ballad was all the rage, and the works of Nadaud, Boissière, Panseron, and Loïsa Puget were as popular in Canada as they were in France, judging at least from the many editions and collections devoted to this repertoire.

Quebec remained indifferent to the vogue of the Montmartre songs of Aristide Bruant, but the famous entertainer Yvette Guilbert was given a warm reception on her visit in 1906. Later the bard from Brittany, Théodore Botrel, and the chansonnier Albert Larrieu made numerous tours in Quebec promoting what was to become known as 'la bonne chanson.' It was not until 1930 that French popular-song artists and music hall stars regularly visited Quebec, where their repertoire became known through records and films.

Among the stars who have enjoyed a marked success in Quebec and other French-speaking centres in Canada are Charles Aznavour, Gilbert Bécaud, Bourvil, Lucienne Boyer, Georges Brassens, Maurice Chevalier, Philippe Clay, Les Compagnons de la chanson, Annie Cordy, André Dassary, Fernandel, Léo Ferré, Jacqueline François, the Frères Jacques, Juliette Greco, Georges Guétary, Johnny Halliday, Rudi Hirigoyen, Jacques Jansen, Zizi Jeanmaire, Luis Mariano, Marjane, Yves Montand, Patachou, Tino Rossi, Suzi Solidor, and Charles Trenet.

In return, several Canadian writer-composer-performers, beginning with Félix *Leclerc in 1951, carved out important careers in France. Following Leclerc in seeking the Parisian seal of approval were Robert *Charlebois, Diane *Dufresne, Jean-Pierre *Ferland, Pauline *Julien, Jacques *Labrecque, Claude *Léveillée, Raymond *Lévesque, Monique *Leyrac, Gilles *Vigneault, and several others.

See also Chanson in Quebec; Folk music, Franco-Canadian.

Paris was a haven for some expatriate jazz musicians, among them the Canadian-born trumpeter Arthur Briggs, who began living and working there in the mid-1930s; Milt Sealey, a Montreal-born jazz pianist who moved to Paris in the 1950s; and the jazz pianist Wray *Downes, who studied and worked there during the same decade.

Official cultural ties between France and Canada were established in 1882, when the Canadian government sent a representative to Paris. Later the Canadian Embassy acquired a cultural attaché. In the ensuing years several Canadian and Quebec facilities were established in Paris. In the late 1920s the Maison canadienne was established in the Cité universitaire to provide lodging and practice facilities for Canadian music students. In 1970 the Ministry of External Affairs inaugurated the *Canadian Cultural Centre, whose first director was Guy Viau. The province of Quebec in 1961 opened a Délégation générale, in which Raoul Jobin and Jean *Vallerand served as cultural advisers.

At the Cité internationale des Arts three studios are made available each year to young Canadian artists in all disciplines through a program administered by the Dept of External Affairs and the Canada Council. Two of the studios are allocated to music students. GP (HK)

FRANCKS, Don. Singer, actor, b Vancouver 28 Feb 1932. An actor as a child and later a dixieland trombonist, Francks began his CBC career in Vancouver singing on Lorraine McAllister's radio show 'Sing for Your Supper' and starred 1954–5 with McAllister on 'The Burns Chuckwagon Show.' At *TUTS he played leads in *Oklahoma* (1954) and *Anything Goes* (1955). Moving to Toronto in 1957 he sang with Patti Lewis on CBC radio's 'Country Club.' Concurrent with his career in music Francks has played leading roles in many CBC TV dramas and in 1961 starred in *The Drylanders*, the NFB's first feature-length dramatic film. He was in the cast for productions of *The Fantasticks*, and of **Spring Thaw* and other revues, and was co-producer of the Toronto production of the controversial play about drugs, *The Connection*, staged 1960–1 at the House of Hambourg with Francks (as Leach), other actors, and the musicians Maury *Kaye (piano), P.J. *Perry (saxophone), Ian Henstridge (bass), and Archie Alleyne (drums). In 1962 he formed a jazz trio with Henstridge and the guitarist Lenny *Breau, appearing in nightclubs in Toronto and New York (eg, at the Village Vanguard, where they made the LP *Jackie Gleason Says No One in This World Is Like Don Francks*, Kapp KRL 4501, in 1963). Remaining in New York, Francks appeared on Broadway in the musicals *Kelly* (1965) and *Flipside* (1968), both unsuccessful productions, and off Broadway (1965) in a program of theatre songs by Leonard Bernstein. Also in 1965 he made the LP *Lost ... and Alone* (Kapp 3417) with orchestras under Pat Williams' direction. In 1967 he played Woody in the Hollywood film of *Finian's Rainbow*. Largely inactive as a performer after 1969 while he lived on the Red Pheasant Reserve in western Saskatchewan, Francks resumed his career in the mid-1970s, appearing in several Canadian cities in jazz clubs and theatres. In 1975 in Saskatoon he staged *The Insanity of One Man*, using musicians from the reservation. Returning to live in Toronto he played Lugerio in the musical adaptation (1977, for CBC radio) of *Mandragola* by Alan Gordon and Doug *Riley and may be heard in that role on the cast recording (CBC LM-448). In 1978 he operated the nightclub A Nice Place (above *George's Spaghetti House) for four months. Of Francks' varied career, Bob Blackburn (Toronto *Telegram*, 22 Aug 1963) wrote: 'He's furiously driven to communicate with people. He is full of things he wants to say, but so diversely gifted in means of expression that he can't settle on one way to communicate. He keeps trying them all.' Francks wrote the libretto for Ron *Collier's *Hear Me Talkin' to Ya* (1964), basing his text on quotations from jazz musicians and writers. His *Growing Up*, a jazz waltz, has been recorded by Paul *Hoffert and Moe *Koffman. He also has written many songs. He is a member of CAPAC.

BIBLIOGRAPHY

Franklin, Stephen. 'Don Francks: snarling on top of the world,' *Weekend Magazine*, 30 Jan 1965

Coxson, Mona. 'Don Francks is moving in many different ways,' *CanComp*, 143, Sep 1979 MM

FRANKLIN, Barbara (m Perkins). Soprano, actress, b Regina 14 Jun 1929; LRCT 1954, Artist Diploma (Toronto) 1954. A winner in 1950 of the CBC radio contest *'Opportunity Knocks' and a student (summer 1954) of Elisabeth Schwarzkopf at the *Stratford Festival, she first sang with the *Royal Cons Opera as Marguerite in *Faust* (1951) and Papagena in *The Magic Flute* (1952). In 1952 she premiered Lorne *Betts' *Five Songs* and gave the Canadian premiere of Schoenberg's *Ode to Napoleon* with Glenn *Gould's New Music Associates. In 1953 she was a soloist at the first *CLComp concert at Stratford. After appearances with the *CBC Opera in *Turandot, Gianni Schicchi, Rigoletto*, and Arthur *Benjamin's *A Tale of Two Cities*, she worked on CBC TV in 'Summer Show Time' (1956) and her own program, 'Country Style' (1960). She starred in *Salad Days* in Toronto 1955–6 and New York 1956–7, appeared in **Spring Thaw* in 1958 and 1959, and toured Canada 1960–6 in productions of *Mr. Scrooge, Carousel, South Pacific*, and others. Thereafter she continued her performing career as an actress, on stage and in TV, appearing on CBC TV's 'Wayne and Shuster Hour' and as Jenny in the 1974 Theatre Calgary productions of *Threepenny Opera*. (VW)

Frank Marino and Mahogany Rush. See Marino.

FRASER, Ralph. Pianist, organist, vibraphonist, composer, b New Glasgow, NS, 3 Jul 1925; ATCM 1948. He studied piano 1935–42 with Marguerite Fraser and 1946–8 at the *RCMT, where his teachers were Gordon *Hallett and Henry Atack. In 1951 he studied orchestration with John *Weinzweig. Fraser played in Toronto dance bands in the late 1940s and began his radio career in 1950 on the CBC's 'Jazz Unlimited.' He was heard on many CBC radio and TV shows, including 'Holiday Ranch,' 1954–8, and others with *Juliette, Jack *Kane, and Billy *O'Connor. He has led small groups for more than 25 years in the lounges of Toronto hotels, including the Park Plaza (the location of his CBC radio series in 1954), and in such nightclubs as Dooley's. In 1973 he became the organist for Toronto Maple Leaf hockey games at *Maple Leaf Gardens, stopping in 1975 but resuming in 1977. He served similarly 1974–5 at Exhibition Stadium for Toronto Argonaut football games and, beginning in 1978, for Toronto Blue Jay baseball games. His recordings include *Ralph Fraser Plays Variations of Popular Themes* (1964, CTL 1046) with guitarist Al Harris and LPs of pop songs and light-classical pieces, arranged for two pianos, with Carol Hughes (1965, CTLS 5062) and Pat L'Heureux (1967, RCA CTLS 5091/GRT 9207). A member of CAPAC, Fraser has composed several songs and instrumental pieces. MM

Fredericton. New Brunswick's capital city, located on the Saint John River on the site of a 1732 Acadian, and later Loyalist English, settlement at St Anne's Point. The name Fredericton was adopted in 1785. Incorporation as a city was accomplished in 1848. In 1978 Fredericton's population had reached 25,000, and among its main industries were pulp, paper, and metal production. Educational institutions and the provincial government were other major employers.

Music flourished in Fredericton in the early part of the 19th century. There were several civil and regimental bands. In 1832 E.T. Cooke wrote of 'the excellent band of the 34th regiment [which] attracted a crowd of auditors during fine evenings of September' (*A Subaltern's Furlough*, New York 1833). In August 1844 a noteworthy concert was presented by the 33rd Regiment Band under Mr Ricks. It featured the overtures to Mozart's *La Clemenza di Tito* and Romberg's *Die Grossmuth des Scipio* and one of Beethoven's *Leonora* overtures. Included on the program were violin solos by Mr Keyser and glees performed by local singers.

A strong church music tradition originated in the 1840s under the leadership of Bishop John *Medley, a founder of Christ Church Cathedral and conductor of its excellent choir for over 40 years. He was assisted 1867–9 by Lieut-Col Alexander Ewing (b Old Machar, near Aberdeen, Scotland 3 Jan 1830, d Taunton, near Exeter, England 11 Jul 1895), a chorister and supplementary organist who was appointed conductor of the Choral Society. Ewing is remembered as the composer of the hymn 'Jerusalem the Golden.' Another noteworthy musical figure was Rev John Black (d 1871), a rector of King's Clear, whose *Cantate Domino: A Hymnal for Public Worship* (Toronto 1874) was published posthumously.

The City Hall, built in 1876, was used later as the Opera House. Performers who appeared in Fredericton during the late 19th and early 20th centuries included the singers Emma *Albani and Clara Butt, the pianist Mark *Hambourg, and the violinist Marie Hall.

A citizens' band, a chamber orchestra, a civic orchestra (led for many years by Janis *Kalnins), the Cecilian Singers, the York Singers, and the Art Centre Singers all were established after World War II. Fredericton High School's Madrigal

Singers, founded in 1965, performed at *Expo 67 and on the CBC. The Fredericton Music (competition) Festival was founded in 1948. The *U of New Brunswick employed a succession of musicians-in-residence beginning in 1962 (Paul *Helmer, the *Duo Pach, the *Brunswick String Quartet) and established the annual *U of New Brunswick Chamber Music and Jazz Festival under the direction of Arlene Nimmons Pach in 1966. During the 1970s the Community Concerts Assn, the Creative Arts Committee (at UNB), and the *JMC sponsored some 20 concerts a year, and the *Atlantic SO, the rock group Blood, Sweat & Tears, Liona *Boyd, Edith *Butler, Anne *Murray, the *TS, and William *Tritt are among those who have appeared. Most concerts in Fredericton have been given at the U of New Brunswick or at the Playhouse.

The composers Robert C. *Bayley and Janis Kalnins have made Fredericton their home. Among noted natives of the city are Bayley, the composers Winifred *Lugrin Fahey and Cedric Lemont, and the singer-guitarist Fred *McKenna. The composer and music educator Edwin Barnes was born near Fredericton. Ada Dowling (Mrs J.R. Costigan), who was organist at St Dunstan's Church, moved to Calgary in 1887, providing that city with its first piano and first music teacher. The Zildjian Company, a cymbal factory, was built at Meductic, northwest of Fredericton on the Saint John River.

BIBLIOGRAPHY

York and Sunbury Hist. Soc., Papers of Mrs F.A. Good. 'Some random notes on the musical history of Fredericton,' (1933)

Kallmann *History of Music in Canada* (NM, JMn)

FREDETTE, Paul. Bass, b St Jean Baptiste, near Winnipeg, 17 Mar 1928. He studied in Winnipeg with Herbert *Sadler, Doris Mills *Lewis, and Max Kaplick. He has appeared with the *COC, the *Manitoba Opera, Golden Voices Opera Manitoba, and the St Paul Civic Opera for which he sang the Herald in Stuart Robb's English version of *Lohengrin*. For *'L'Heure du concert' 24 Nov 1960 on CBC TV he sang Arkel in *Pelléas et Mélisande*. He has been a soloist with the *Montreal Bach Choir and the *Winnipeg SO and has sung various roles in Winnipeg productions of musicals. He was cast in the leading bass role for the RCA Victor-CBC recording (RCA LSC-2981) of *Lavallée's **The Widow*. His voice is a solid, easily produced dark bass.

MB

FREEDMAN, Harry. Composer, english hornist, educator; b Łodz, Poland, 5 Apr 1922. Raised from the age of three in Medicine Hat, Alta, where his father was engaged in the fur trade, Freedman moved with his parents to Winnipeg in 1931. He enrolled at the Winnipeg School of Art at 13 to train as a painter. Attracted also to big band jazz, he began clarinet lessons at 18. His teacher – Arthur Hart, the leading local orchestral clarinetist, later principal of the *Winnipeg SO – introduced him to symphonic music. Painting and jazz remained influences in Freedman's composition. After serving in the RCAF in World War II Freedman settled in Toronto, where he studied composition 1945–51 with *Weinzweig at the *RCMT and oboe with Perry *Bauman. He also took summer classes with Messiaen in 1949 at Tanglewood. He joined the *TSO in 1946 as english horn and remained with the orchestra for 25 years, serving during his last year as the orchestra's first composer-in-residence. In that capacity, he produced orchestral arrangements of 'O Canada' and 'God Save the Queen,' short pieces for small ensembles to play in the schools, and the large work

Harry Freedman

Graphic I ('Out of Silence ... '), which he composed in 1971 for the orchestra's 50th-anniversary celebrations. After 1971 Freedman devoted himself almost entirely to composing though he also, in 1972, taught and served as composer-in-residence at the Courtenay Youth Music Centre, which commissioned his *Graphic II* for the *Purcell String Quartet and *Encounter* for the violinist Steven *Staryk.

Freedman's earliest work, the *Divertimento for Oboe and Strings*, showed the influence of Weinzweig, whose own *Divertimento No. 1* for flute and strings had been completed the previous year. With *Tableau*, for chamber orchestra, Freedman came into his own, though the use of the 12-tone row (his first) also was founded in the Weinzweig approach, in which the row was regarded as a self-contained melodic unit and a source from which motivic material could be extracted. Freedman's predilections, however, were manifest in the strongly visual connotation. Suggested by a painting of the Canadian Arctic, *Tableau* was the first of several compositions – notably *Images* and *Klee Wyck* – inspired by Canadian paintings. Written in 1958 for the *McGill Chamber Orchestra on a commission from the *Lapitsky Foundation and orchestrated the following year (in their best-known form), the three contrasting *Images* are Freedman's musical impressions of Lawren Harris' *Blue Mountain*, Kazuo Nakamura's *Structure at Dusk*, and Jean-Paul Riopelle's *Landscape*.

Freedman turned away completely from the 12-tone technique in his *Symphony No. 1*, begun in the summer of 1953 while studying with Ernst Krenek at the RCMT and completed in 1960. For symphonic purposes, at that time, Freedman found the technique inhibiting, focused as it was on the strict manipulation of the 12-tone pattern while his instinct dictated expansive melodies and expressive orchestral discourse. The *Symphony* was premiered in 1961 by the *CBC SO under Geoffrey *Waddington at the Inter-American Festival, Washington, DC.

Freedman's return to 12-tone technique – and his only strict use of it – came in 1964. Commissioned to write a work for the *Festival Singers, he chose to set 19 of the 53 classical Japanese poems (in the haiku, tanka, and senryu forms) which accompany the prints in the Tuttle edition of the 19th-century woodblock printer Ichiryusai Hiroshige's *53 Stations of the Tokaido* – the Tokaido being the road that runs east from Kyoto to Tokyo. At the time of the commission Freedman was studying sumi painting, a ritualistic Japanese skill which aims at a high degree of expression achieved with a strict economy of brushwork. The paradox of free aesthetic expression attained through formalized conventions of craft – a premise in all oriental art – suggested to Freedman that the strictures of serial technique (which at one time had seemed merely onerous) would be helpful in forging a light but strong musical support for the delicate and passionate but ritualistic oriental verse he had chosen to set. Once he had accepted the suitability of the technique, he found that the permissible 12-tone manipulations could be made to serve the verses' nature images as aptly as Debussy's expanded tonality served impressionism a generation earlier. Thus, *The Tokaido* became a cornerstone of Freedman's language. Though he wrote no more strict serial works in the next 15 years, he did use elements of serialism – at will, easily and purposefully – in most of his music.

In the early 1960s Freedman became interested in writing music for films, TV, and theatre, and by the mid-1970s he had provided background music for some 15 films and TV productions, including *Pale Horse, Pale Rider, The Pyx, Lies My Father Told Me*, and Paul Almond's *Act of the Heart*. (His cantata *The Flame Within*, which shares an LP with *The Tokaido*, was a focal point for the Almond film and won a Canadian Film Award in 1970.) As a member of the Toronto Film Co-op in the 1970s he has continued to investigate the relation of film and music. (See also Film scores.) He also has written incidental music for *Stratford Festival productions (*Much Ado about Nothing, As You Like It, Twelfth Night*), for Toronto Arts Productions (an earlier *Twelfth Night*), and for Festival Lennoxville (George Ryga's *Sunlight on Sarah*). He has written three scores on commission for the Royal Winnipeg Ballet. The first of these – and the company's first evening-long ballet – was composed for Brian Macdonald's **Rose Latulippe*, premiered at the 1966 Stratford Festival. For small orchestra with harp and percussion, the Hindemithian score reaches its apex in the 'gripping and eerie' (Toronto *Telegram*, 13 Apr 1967) 12-tone fiddle dance that accompanies the central action of the drama. The ballet was produced for CBC TV by Franz *Kraemer and Pierre Morin in 1967. The other Royal Winnipeg Ballet commissions – *Five over Thirteen*, premiered in 1969 at the *NAC, Ottawa, and **The Shining People of Leonard Cohen*, premiered in 1970 in Paris – also were collaborations with Macdonald. The latter ballet combines, on electronic tape, excerpts from Cohen's verse, natural sounds, and the soprano voice of Freedman's wife, Mary *Morrison. Freedman's concert works of the 1970s show the effects of his theatrical writing. In *Pan*, for instance, written for the *Lyric Arts Trio, he requires the three performers to stamp their feet, whisper, cluck, and shout into the piano strings and to act out a comic episode, besides performing their accustomed functions as soprano, flute, and piano.

Freedman's orchestration has won him much praise. After his *Symphony* was premiered (28 Apr 1961) the *Washington Post* critic Paul Hume wrote, 'The influence of Bartók is strong in the symphony, both in orchestral sound and in the powerful employment of melodic lines moving in contrary motion.' Freedman, he continued, 'has an unusual gift for expressive melodic contours.' Reviewing his *Tableau* and *Images*, the composer and critic Udo *Kasemets wrote: 'Freedman's style – frugal and forthright – and his well-trained ear and cultured taste for orchestration serve him well in a work of this nature. He is a symphony player and knows his orchestra, in the true sense, "inside out".' Freedman, he said, succeeded in 'capturing in his music much of the spiritual atmosphere of this country' (*Canadian Music Journal*, Winter 1961). In his painting-inspired works, Freedman himself claims to be concerned more with design than content. 'The most important part of composing,' he says, 'is deciding what the piece is about – what's the mood, texture, orchestration, movement – almost everything else but the notes. The notes are the least important thing' (*Canadian Composer*, December 1974). This is not to say that Freedman is careless or even casual in his choice of notes. On the contrary. In his *Graphic I ('Out of Silence ... ')*, inspired on the one hand by the visual textures in contemporary graphics and on the other by silence as discussed in Max Picard's book *The World of Silence*, Freedman incorporates silence in a fragile web of instrumental and electronic sounds interrelated with a precision which leaves no doubt as to the care he has exercised. And in *Encounter*, fresh sonic relationships between piano and violin are explored with extraordinary delicacy and assurance.

Active in musical causes, Freedman has been a lobbyist on behalf of the *CLComp, an organization he helped found in 1952 and of which he was the first secretary and, 1975–8, president. He has served, as a musician, on the advisory board of Pollution Probe. Except for the years 1960–5, when he was an affiliate of BMI Canada, he has been a member of CAPAC. He is an associate of the *CMCentre. He was the subject of a CBC radio documentary prepared by Norma *Beecroft and broadcast 13 Sep 1977. In 1980 the CMCouncil named him Composer of the Year.

SELECTED COMPOSITIONS

STAGE

Five over Thirteen, ballet. 1969 (Ott 1970). Sm orch. Ms

Romeo and Juliet (original title *Star Cross'd*), ballet. 1973, rev 1975 (Ott 1973). Renaissance consort. Ms

Several sets of incidental music for plays at Stratford, Lennoxville, St Lawrence Centre (Tor)

See also *Rose Latulippe*; *The Shining People of Leonard Cohen*.

FILMS

Act of the Heart / Acte du coeur (cantata *The Flame Within* – Bible, St Augustine, arr P. Almond). 1968. SATB, org. Leeds 1970. RCI 341/CBC SM-142/Decca DL 75244 (*Festival Singers)

Also *Bells of Hell* (1973); *China 'The Roots of Madness'* (1969); *The Dark Did Not Conquer* (CBC TV, 1963); *Friendship* (1975); *Isobel* (1968); *Let Me Count the Ways* (1965); *Lies My Father Told Me* (1974); *November* (1970); *Pale Horse, Pale Rider* (CBC TV, 1963); *The Pyx* (1973); *Romeo and Jeannette* (CBC TV, 1965); *Seven Hundred Million* (CBC TV, 1964); *Spring Song* (1965); *Twenty Million Shoes, Where Will They Go?*; for *NFB, CBC, and other film makers.

ORCHESTRA

Symphonic Suite. 1948. Full orch. Ms. RCI 19 (*TSO)

Five Pieces for String Orchestra. 1949 (Tor 1953). Str orch (str quar). CMCentre. (Str quar version) RCI 43 (*Parlow Str Quar)

Nocturne I. 1949 (Tor 1952). Med orch. CMCentre. RCI 71 (*TSO)

Tableau. 1952 (Tor 1952). Str orch. Ricordi 1960

Images. 1958 (Tor 1960). Orch (str orch). BMIC 1960. RCI 187 (*McGill Chamb O)/Col M2L-356 (*TS)

Symphony No. 1. 1961 (Washington 1961). Orch. BMIC 1961

Fantasy and Allegro. 1962 (Brantford 1962). Str orch. CMCentre. RCI 238 (*Hart House O)

Chaconne. 1964, rev 1977 (CBC Tor 1964). Orch. CMCentre

A Little Symphony. 1966 (Saskatoon 1967). Orch. Leeds 1974

Armana. 1967 (Tor 1967). Orch. CMCentre

Tangents. 1967 (Mtl 1967). Orch. Leeds 1969. Audat 477-4001 (*TS)

Klee Wyck. 1970 (Victoria 1971). Orch. CMCentre

Graphic I. 1971 (Tor 1971). Orch, tape. CMCentre

Tapestry. 1973 (Ott 1973). Orch. CMCentre

Nocturne II. 1975 (Calgary 1977). Orch. CMCentre

SOLOIST(S) WITH ORCHESTRA

Divertimento for Oboe and Strings. 1947 (Tor 1949). CMCentre

Fantasia and Dance. 1955, rev 1959 (Tor 1956). Vn, orch. CMCentre

Trois Poèmes de Jacques Prévert. 1962. Sop, str. CMCentre

Scenario. 1970 (Tor 1970). Alto sax, elec bass guit, orch. CMCentre

Concerto for saxophone and orchestra. 1977 (Hamilton 1977). Ms

CHAMBER

Trio. 1948. 2 ob, hn. Ms

Two Vocalises (no text). 1954. Sop, cl, pf. CMCentre

Quintet. 1962. Ww quin. Kerby 1972. RCI 208 (*Tor WW Quin)

The Tokaido (Japanese poetry, transl T. Tuttle). 1964. SATB, ww quin. CMCentre. RCI 341/CBC SM-142/Decca DL 75244 (*Tor WW Quin, *Festival Singers)

Variations. 1965. Ob, fl, hpd. CMCentre. RCI 219/RCA CCS 1013 (*Baroque Trio of Mtl)

Toccata (syllables). 1968. Sop, fl. Kerby 1972. CBC SM-96 (*Lyric Arts Trio)

Soliloquy. 1970. Fl, pf. Leeds 1971. Dom S-69005/6 (*Aitken fl)

Tikki Tikki Tembo (Mosel). 1971. Narr, ww quin. CMCentre. 1973. RCI 388 (Lorien WW Quin, R. Coneybeare narr)

Graphic II. 1972. Str quar. CMCentre. RCI 394 (*Purcell Str Quar)

Pan (vocal sounds, Indian place names in Ontario). 1972. Fl, sop, pf. CMCentre. RCI 404 (*Lyric Arts Trio)

Lines. 1973. Cl solo. CMCentre. RCI 484 (*Campbell)

Encounter. 1974. Vn, pf. CMCentre

Love and Age (Prévert). 1975. Sop, bar, ww quin, brass quin. CMCentre

Vignette. 1975. Cl, pf. CMCentre

Five Rings. 1976. Brass quin. CMCentre

Fragments of Alice (L. Carroll). 1976 (Sweden 1976). Sop, alto, bar, various instr. CMCentre

The Explainer. 1976. Fl, ob (hn), vc, pf, perc, narr/cond. CMCentre

Tsolem Summer. 1976. Fl, 3 vn, 2 va, vc, db, perc. CMCentre

Mono. 1977. Solo hn. CMCentre

Epitaph for Igor Stravinsky (J. Reeves). 1978. Ten, 4 trb, str quar. CMCentre

CHOIR AND VOICE

Three Vocalises (vowel sounds, syllables, humming). 1964. SATB. Leeds 1965

Anerca (Eskimo poetry, transl K. Rasmussen). 1966. Sop, pf. CMCentre

Poems of Young People (various). 1968. Low v. CMCentre. CBC SM-77/Sel CC-15.073 (*Forrester)

Keewaydin (Ontario place names in Ojibway). 1971. SSA, optional tape. GVT 1972. Poly 2917 009 (*Festival Singers)

Pastorale (phonic sounds). 1977. SATB (divisi), hn. CMCentre

Green ... Blue ... White ... (songs of the eastern provinces). 1978. SATB. CMCentre

Other works for voice and choir; also a *Suite for Piano* (1951), FH 1955 ('Scherzo')

WRITINGS

Letter to the *CBC Times*, 1 Nov 1958

'Parodies and Paraphrases,' CBC radio script, 12 Dec 1962

'Working with Stravinsky,' *Music Across Canada*, vol 1, Feb 1963

'Music and the businessman,' *Music Across Canada*, vol 1, Jun 1963

'? ? ?' CFMTA *Newsletter*, Aug 1978

BIBLIOGRAPHY

Beckwith, John. 'Composers in Toronto and Montreal,' *U of Toronto Q*, vol 26, Oct 1956

Composers of the Americas, Guillermo Espinosa ed (Washington, DC, 1959–)

Winters, Kenneth. 'Harmony in 2 parts: his and hers,' Toronto *Telegram*, 16 Jul 1966

Wilkinson, Bryan. 'Harry Freedman: an exciting composer,' *CanComp*, 17, Apr 1967

'Harry Freedman: a portrait,' *Mcan*, 18, Jan–Feb 1968

'Canadian Film "Isabel" smash hit in New York,' *CanComp*, 33, Oct 1968

Desautels, Andrée. 'The history of Canadian composition 1610–1967,' *Aspects of Music*

Kennedy, Janet, and Holland, Pat. 'Harry Freedman – Canada's first composer-in-residence,' *TS News*, Dec 1970

Hepner, Lee. 'An analytical study of selected Canadian orchestral compositions of the mid-20th century,' unpubl PH D thesis, New York U, 1972

Schulman, Michael. 'Harry Freedman,' *CanComp*, 96, Dec 1974

CAPAC. 'Harry Freedman,' pamphlet and recording (1975)

Thirty-Four Biographies

Contemporary Canadian Composers (LL)

Herbert A. Fricker

FRICKER, Herbert A. (Austin). Choir conductor, organist, teacher, composer, b Canterbury, England, 12 Feb 1868, d Toronto 11 Nov 1943; FRCO 1888, B MUS (Durham) 1893, hon MA (Leeds) 1917, hon D MUS (Toronto) 1923. He had lessons with the Canterbury Cathedral organist William H. Longhurst and was a chorister 1877–83 and assistant organist 1884–90 at the cathedral. He studied further in London with Frederick Bridge and Edwin Henry Lemare. After a time 1891–8 at Trinity Church, Folkstone, he moved to Leeds as city organist. There he founded and was the conductor 1900–17 of the Leeds Philharmonic and 1902–17 of the Leeds SO, was chorusmaster 1904–13 for the Leeds Festivals, and was organist at a succession of churches and schools. He also conducted choral societies in Bradford, Halifax, Dewsbury, and Morley.

Chosen by A.S. *Vogt to be his successor as conductor of the *Toronto Mendelssohn Choir, Fricker emigrated to Canada in August 1917. His first appearance with the choir, 18 Feb 1918 with the Philadelphia Orchestra under Leopold Stokowski, initiated an association, 1918–25, which took both organizations across the US-Canadian border many times. Under Fricker's leadership the choir gave the Canadian premieres of Beethoven's *Missa solemnis* in 1927, Walton's *Belshazzar's Feast* in 1936, and Berlioz' *Requiem* in 1938. Besides his Mendelssohn Choir duties, Fricker was organist-choirmaster 1917–43 at Metropolitan United Church, teacher of organ 1918–32 at the *TCM, on staff at the *U of Toronto, conductor 1922–34 of the *Canadian National Exhibition Chorus, an active organ recitalist, an adjudicator at many competition festivals, and president 1925–6 of the CCO. He retired from the Mendelssohn Choir in 1942, conducting his favourite choral work, Bach's *Mass in B Minor*, at his farewell concert (23 February).

Contemporary comparisons of Vogt and Fricker as choir conductors are discreet and reveal little about either. The manner of Fricker's succession shows that the two men respected one another, and both seem to have been thought extraordinary leaders. Vogt's results perhaps had the edge in precision and clarity, Fricker's in breadth and warmth. This may reflect their repertoires as much as their dispositions, Vogt having founded the choir to perform the unaccompanied music of Mendelssohn and others and Fricker concerning himself from the outset with large choral-orchestral works. Fricker composed several organ works (*Concert Overture, Fantasie Overture, Scherzo Symphonique, Cantilène Nuptiale*, etc), edited others, and made many arrangements for organ. Publishers of these were Novello, Beal, Stuttard, Broadbent, Chester, and Houghton, all of London. His choral music, though mainly for church, included secular pieces and arrangements for the Mendelssohn Choir and the Exhibition Chorus. His choral publishers were *Anglo-Canadian, Novello, and *Whaley Royce. His *Song of Thanksgiving*, published by the Mendelssohn Choir, was performed by Albert Ham's *National Chorus. Fricker's extensive library of books and music (including manuscripts of his own works) was given, after his death, to the Toronto Public Library and became part of the holdings of the Metropolitan Toronto Music Library.

WRITINGS

'Some recollections,' *Mendelssohnian*, 13 instalments, Oct–Nov 1937 to Aug–Sep 1939

BIBLIOGRAPHY

'Exhibition chorus gives musical inaugural at fair,' *Toronto Daily Star*, 31 Aug 1925

Campion-Smith, C. 'Dr. Herbert Austin Fricker,' *MCan*, vol 9, Sep 1928

Young, Scott. 'Conducted by Fricker,' *Maclean's*, 15 Jun 1942

Smith, Ocean G., compiler. *The Toronto Mendelssohn Choir: A History, 1894–1948* (Toronto 1948)

[McLean, Maud]. *A Responsive Chord: The Story of the Toronto Mendelssohn Choir 1894–1969* (Toronto 1969) RPn

Fridolinons! Revue begun in 1938 by the actor and author Gratien Gélinas (b St-Tite, near Trois-Rivières, Que, 8 Dec 1909). In 1937 Gélinas created the character Fridolin on radio station CKAC, Montreal, in a series of variety programs, sketches, and songs entitled 'Le Carrousel de la gaieté,' which he wrote and in which Lionel *Daunais was a regular participant. The following year at the *Monument national Gélinas put Fridolin onto the stage; the 24 performances of *Fridolinons!* constituted a run unprecedented in Montreal at that time. The radio program remained on the air 1938–40 under the title 'Le Train de plaisir.' The revue *Fridolinons!* was presented annually 1939–46 in Montreal (Monument national) and Quebec City (*Palais Montcalm, Capitol theatre); 82 performances were given in 1946. It was revived in Montreal in 1956 at the *Orpheum Theatre as *Fridolinades '56* and in 1964 at the Comédie-Canadienne as *Le Diable à quatre*.

Fridolin was a young boy of about 13, dressed in a cap, knickerbockers, suspenders, and a Canadiens' hockey sweater, and holding a sling. The revue, in a mixture of sketches, music, and dance, dealt with the topics of the day and involved 20 actors, 12 dancers, 15 musicians, and about 15 technicians.

Gélinas wrote the sketches, was director and producer, and acted the role of Fridolin; the choreographer was Elvira Gomez. Maurice Meerte was music director of the radio broadcasts and for the duration of the revue wrote arrangements often inspired by Canadian folk music and current popular French songs.

Among the artists who took part in the revue were Amanda Alarie, Fred Barry, Juliette Béliveau, Juliette Huot, Clément Latour, Julien Lippé, Gisèle Schmidt, and Olivette Thibault.

BIBLIOGRAPHY

Whitaker [sic], Herbert. 'Fridolin – our star,' *Canadian Review*, vol 5, Feb 1946 CV

FRIEDLANDER, Ernst (Peter). Cellist, composer, teacher, b Vienna 6 Oct 1906, naturalized Canadian 1963, d North Vancouver 28 Oct 1966. He studied 1928–30 in Vienna with Anton Walter (cello) and Heinrich Schenker (theory), among others. After an active concert career in Europe he moved in 1937 to the USA, where he was principal cellist with the Pittsburgh, Indianapolis, New Orleans, Kansas City, and Chicago symphony orchestras, was a member 1943–55 of the Pro Arte Quartet, and taught at the universities of Wisconsin and Oklahoma. He made his US solo debut at Town Hall, New York, 19 Nov 1943. In 1958 he moved to Vancouver, where he served as principal cellist 1958–66 with the *CBC Vancouver Chamber Orchestra and the *Vancouver SO. He was cellist 1960–6 with the Vancouver String Quartet and taught 1958–66 at the *U of British Columbia. With his wife, the pianist Marie (Elisabeth) Werbner (b 6 Sep 1917), he performed on *CBC Radio, premiered Milhaud's *Sonata for Cello* at the 1959 *Vancouver International Festival, and recorded works by Malipiero, Cowell, and *Coulthard and his own *Sonata for Cello* (1963) on *Contemporary Music for Cello* (1964, Col MS-6542 / Odyssey XLP-75842). His other compositions include a *Cello Concerto* (1959), *Minnelied* for cello and piano (1964, Emp 1972), a *Rhapsody* for cello or bassoon and orchestra (1964), and works for string quartet, brass sextet, and chamber orchestra.

BIBLIOGRAPHY

Creative Canada, vol 1 (DD)

The Friends of Chamber Music. Vancouver music club formed in 1948 to promote chamber music. Ida *Halpern was the founding president. The first presentation was a concert prepared by the *Vancouver SO concertmaster, Albert *Steinberg. The Friends have increased their program from 4 concerts a year to 10 and have presented major international chamber ensembles. Membership, by subscription, is limited by the size of the *Queen Elizabeth Playhouse, which seats 650.

BIBLIOGRAPHY

Giese, Rochel. *Friends of Chamber Music: A History of 25 Years 1948–1973* (Vancouver 1973)

FULLER, Jerry (Lynn). Drummer, b Calgary 5 Apr 1939. His father, (James) Jerry Fuller (saxophonist, clarinetist, arranger, b Banff, Alta, 17 Jul 1911), who formed a swing band in Calgary in the late 1930s, took the family in 1944 to Vancouver, where he led the house band at the Cave until 1947 and later was an arranger for Ricky *Hyslop, George *Calangis, and other CBC conductors. Jerry Fuller Jr played drums as a child in Calgary and studied 1957–8 with Jim *Blackley in Vancouver. He attended the Westlake College of Modern Music in Los Angeles 1958–9, then worked in Vancouver jazz clubs (eg, the Cellar) and with the bands of Ralph *Grierson and Paul *Perry at resort hotels in western Canada. He also led his own jazz quintet in Vancouver. After playing 1962–3 in Montreal with Maury *Kaye, Fuller settled in Toronto, where he worked in nightclub groups, hotel orchestras, jazz bands, and, eventually, studio orchestras. He has played in the jazz groups of Art Ayre, Ron *Collier, Sonny *Greenwich, Moe *Koffman, and others and was a member 1969–72 of the *Boss Brass. In 1974 he began performing regularly at the Toronto club Bourbon Street, accompanying many leading US jazzmen, among them Pepper Adams, Ruby Braff, Paul Desmond, Lee Konitz, and Zoot Sims. He has recorded with Desmond (see Discography for Ed Bickert), Peter *Appleyard, Collier, Koffman, Don (W.) *Thompson, and others and has accompanied Oscar *Peterson in concert, on TV, and in recordings. MM

FUREY, Albert (Cornelius). Conductor, composer, arranger, b Dublin 26 Feb 1930. He studied in Dublin and, after service with the Irish army, joined the Radio Eireann Light Orchestra as trumpet player and staff arranger. He moved in 1956 to a similar position in Canada, with the Central Band of the RCAF, Ottawa. He graduated in 1965 from the *Canadian Forces School of Music with a fellowship from the *CBA. In 1965 he became assistant music director of the North American Air Defense Band, Colorado Springs, which toured the USA and abroad. He was music director 1969–71 of the Training Command Band, Winnipeg and associate director 1971–5 of the Central Band of the Canadian Forces, Ottawa, and in 1975 was appointed music director of the Naden Band, Victoria, BC. His compositions and arrangements exploit the broadened instrumentation of the modern concert band. He has composed two marches for Canadian Forces units: *Golden Hawks* (1967) and *Mercury March* (1974). He holds the military rank of captain and is a member of CAPAC. JK

FUREY, Lewis (b Greenblatt). Composer, singer, pianist, violinist, actor, b Montreal, of French-US parents, 7 Jun 1949. After studying the violin privately, he made an *MSO debut at 11 as soloist in a young people's concert, then studied 1961–5 at the *CMM with Calvin *Sieb and others and 1964–7 at the Juilliard School in New York, where his violin teacher was Ivan Galamian. By 1974 he had turned to pop music, writing and singing (in English) the music heard on three LPs: *Lewis Furey* (1974, A & M 4522), *The Humours of Lewis Furey* (1976, A & M 4594), and *The Sky Is Falling* (1978, Aquarius AQR 521). According to Christian Gros, his music is characterized by 'a voice that is at the same time cold and passionate, acid humour, sumptuous arrangements, [and an] atmosphere mid-way between Kurt Weill and Lou Reed.'

Furey's well-publicized relationship – personal and professional – with the actress-singer Carole Laure began in 1976, when they appeared together in Gille Carle's film *L'Ange et la femme*. Laure made her singing debut 11 Dec 1976 at a Furey concert in Toronto. They subsequently performed together – he playing violin or piano, she singing – in an untitled revue by Furey staged first in 1978 in Paris at Le Palace to great acclaim and then in Montreal at the Théâtre du Nouveau-Monde. A second show was mounted in Paris in 1979. Furey produced Laure's first LP, *Alibis* (1978, RCA KKL1-0290), which included several of his songs previously recorded in English, among them 'Lullabye,' which, as 'J'ai une chanson,' was a hit in 1978 for Laure in Quebec. In 1979 Furey wrote music for, and appeared with Laure in, Carle's movie musical *Fantastica*. Furey also has composed music for several other feature films; his score for Carle's *La Tête de Normande St-Onge* won a Canadian Film Award in 1976. Furey is an affiliate of PRO Canada.

BIBLIOGRAPHY

Rodriguez, Juan. 'Lewis Furey album invites listener to another stratus,' *MSc*, 284, Jul–Aug 1975

Lanken, Dane. 'He left concert sound for Furey of rock,' Montreal *Gazette*, 9 Jul 1977

Gros, Christian. 'Lewis Furey: échange ananas contre petites filles,' *Le Monde de la musique*, 10, Apr 1979

CGa, MM

FYFE, Beverly (Couper). Choir conductor, tenor, b Neepawa, near Winnipeg, of Scottish parents, 13 Oct 1909. His father was a choirmaster in Saskatoon and conducted the *Arion Male Voice Choir in Victoria. Fyfe attended the *Hambourg Cons in Toronto on a voice scholarship and also studied in Washington State and California. His voice teachers were Mme Varty Roberts, Clement Q. Williams, and John *Goss. After touring in the USA as a conductor of musical comedy Fyfe joined *TUTS as a leading tenor in 1941 and became music director in 1945. He was the tenor soloist in the premiere, 3 Mar 1954, of *Pentland's *The Lake* with the *CBC Vancouver Chamber Orchestra. In 1961 he became chorusmaster and a music director of the *Vancouver Opera. In 1962 in Victoria he directed the Starlight Theatre and conducted Haydn's *The Creation*. For the 1964 *Vancouver International Festival he prepared the choruses in *The Damnation of Faust* for the visiting conductor Charles Munch and also prepared *West Side Story*. As chorusmaster 1965–8 of the *Vancouver Bach Choir he prepared the *War Requiem* and *Belshazzar's Feast* for Meredith Davies and the *Vancouver SO.

BIBLIOGRAPHY

Mertens, Susan. 'Meet Mr. Music,' *Vancouver Sun*, 22 Sep 1978 TRL

G

GABORA, Gaelyne (b Craig). Soprano, b Regina 1931. She studied at Notre Dame Academy in Charlottetown, at the GSM, England, 1953–6, and at the Vienna Academy 1956–9. Her teachers have included Audrey *Farnell in Halifax, Erik Werba in Vienna, Bernard *Diamant in Montreal 1961–8, and Pierre Bernac in Canada and France 1971–3. Her operatic debut, in 1966, was at the Mozartsaal in Vienna. In Canada she has appeared with the *MSO, the *NACO, the *TS, the Groupe baroque de Montréal and *Musica Camerata Montreal, and has sung on CBC radio from Montreal and Winnipeg and for CBC TV from Montreal. In 1965 on CBC radio she premiered Kelsey *Jones' *Songs of Innocence*, which were composed for her. In 1972 she gave the first Canadian performance of Shostakovich's *Vocal Instrumental Suite*. With her husband, the violinist Taras *Gabora, and the pianist John *Newmark, she has recorded music of Villa Lobos, Hovhaness, Joseph Marx, Murray *Adaskin, and Brahms. She has recorded (ca 1967, CBC SM-6) Alexander *Brott's *Songs of Contemplation* with the *McGill Chamber Orchestra. In 1975 she toured Europe and the USSR and, in 1978, Italy. NT

GABORA, Taras (Daniel). Violinist, teacher, b Yellow Creek, Sask, 23 Apr 1932; AMM 1952, Reifeprüfung (Vienna Music Academy) 1956. He studied at the *U of Manitoba with Richard Seaborn, at the Paris Cons 1952–3 with René Benedetti, in Vienna 1953–7 with Ernst Morawec, and in Amsterdam 1957–8 with Szymon Goldberg. (He worked later – 1969 – with Yuri Jankelevich in Salzburg.) In 1956, on graduating from the Vienna Academy, he received the Austrian Grand Prize.

After settling in Montreal in 1962 Gabora played in various orchestras and founded the Gabora String Quartet (1964–8), which performed works of François *Morel, Clermont *Pépin, Michel *Perrault, and others. In 1968 with Gaston *Germain he founded the Groupe baroque de Montréal, an ensemble which varied in size in relation to the works performed.

In 1977 Gabora established Les Jeunes Solistes de Montréal, a group of 16, drawn mainly from his pupils at the *CMM, where he began teaching in 1964; a 1978 Austrian tour by the ensemble was the subject of a CBC TV documentary. Gabora also taught 1962–4 at *McGill U and 1972–4 at the *JMC Orford Art Centre. Among his pupils are Martin Foster, Françoise Morin, and Anne and Lucie Robert.

Gabora has performed frequently on CBC radio and TV and in concerts in Canada, the USA, and Europe. Between 1977 and 1980 he made several tours, notably in Greece and Italy. In 1974 he made an LP with his wife, the soprano Gaelyne *Gabora.

See also Discography for George Zukerman.

NT

GADBOIS, Charles-Émile. Publisher, instrumentalist, composer, b St-Barnabé-Sud, near St-Hyacinthe, Que, 1 Jun 1906, d Montreal 24 May 1981. He studied piano with Télesphore Urbain (organist at St-Hyacinthe Cathedral), violin with Maurice *Onderet, and harp with Juliette Drouin. After his ordination as a priest in 1930 Father Gadbois began teaching, and for five years was director of the band at the St-Hyacinthe Seminary. In 1937, influenced by the Congrès de la langue française held in Quebec City, Gadbois established *La Bonne Chanson to assemble and publish the best French and French-Canadian songs. A tireless promoter of 'la bonne chanson,' he organized festivals, contests, and congresses, including those at the Montreal *Forum (1942) and the Quebec Coliseum (1943) and in Lewiston, Me (1944). He composed some 60 songs and written about 20 folksong arrangements. In collaboration with Conrad *Letendre, he launched *Musique et Musiciens*, a review which appeared monthly 1952–4. He received the golden cross of St-Jean-de-Latran in May 1943 for his dedication to 'la bonne chanson.'

BIBLIOGRAPHY

'Quinzième anniversaire de la Bonne Chanson,' *Musique et Musiciens*, vol 1, Feb 1953 (CH)

Gaelic. The 'Goidelic' sub-branch of Celtic; a Celtic language that includes the speech of ancient Ireland and the dialects that have developed from it, especially those usually known as Irish, Manx, and Scots Gaelic. The term Gaelic pertains to both the language and the peoples who speak it. For treatment of Gaelic music see the *EMC* articles on Fiddling; Folk Music, Anglo-Canadian: 2 / Nova Scotia and New Brunswick; Ireland; Saint Francis Xavier U; Scotland. See also Rodeo Records Ltd.

GAGE, Chris (b Giesinger, Christian). Pianist, b Regina 12 Dec 1927, d North Vancouver 27 Dec 1964 (dates verified, contradicting others published). At seven he was featured at the piano in a dance band led by his brother Jerry, a tenor saxophonist. He was heard in the early 1940s on CKCK radio, Regina, and was leading his own band by 1944 in engagements throughout midwestern Canada. He moved to Vancouver in 1949 and quickly became that city's leading jazz pianist. Declining offers to tour with Louis Armstrong, Gerry Mulligan, and Peggy Lee, Gage remained in Vancouver until his death by suicide. He led the houseband 1961–3 at the nightclub the Cave, was featured on CBC radio in 'Jazz Workshop' and in his own show 'Blues and a Ballad' (1960), and appeared on CBC TV in 'Meet Lorraine' (1958, with Lorraine McAllister) and in 'Quintet' and 'Eleanor' (1962 and 1964, both with Eleanor *Collins).

Although Gage did not record commercially, private tapes made with his usual trio (Stan Johnson, bass, b Calgary 23 May 1931, and Jim Wightman, drummer, b Regina 5 Jul 1930) reveal a master jazz pianist whose percussive, rhythmically and harmonically advanced style was 20 years in advance of its time. He is remembered especially for his abilities as an accompanist. Gage is considered the only pianist in Canada to have rivalled Oscar *Peterson in technical proficiency, something Peterson has acknowledged publicly. Don (W.) *Thompson who, with Terry *Clarke, was appearing with Gage at the Quadra Club at the time of the pianist's death, later wrote *For Chris Gage* in his honour. BSm, (MM)

GAGNÉ. Montreal family of musicians: 1 / Marcelle and 2 / Hélène, her daughter.

1 **Marcelle** (b Duquette). Mezzo-soprano, administrator, b Montreal 27 Oct 1908. Granddaughter of Ellsworth *Duquette and niece of Émile *Taranto, she received her voice training from several teachers, including Céline *Marier, Sarah *Fischer, Pauline *Donalda, and Victor *Brault. She gave numerous public recitals, primarily of art song, and was heard frequently in recitals, opera, and oratorio on CBC radio. In Tudor Hall, in a performance of Gluck's *Orphée et Eurydice*, she sang the role of Orphée 'without ever having to force her voice, while entreating the infernal deities with pathos in the well-known aria' (Montreal *La Presse*, 12 Nov 1941). She was a soloist in 1945 with the *Little Symphony of Montreal in a performance of Mozart's *Coronation Mass* at the *Montreal Festivals. Active on numerous committees, she was president 1965–7, 1969–71, and 1973–5 of the *Ladies' Morning Musical Club and 1976–8 of the *Tudor Singers of Montreal.

2 **Hélène** (Marie Gisèle Marcelle). Cellist, teacher, b Montreal 30 Jan 1950; performance diploma cello (Lausanne Cons) 1968. A pupil of Walter *Joachim 1963–6 at the *CMM, she also studied 1963–8 with Paul Tortelier and Guy Fallot at the *JMC Orford Art Centre. She was soloist with the *MSO in 1963 and the Sarah *Fischer Concerts in 1964 and a member of the *NYO in 1964 and 1965. She won first prize in the string category at the 1966 *CBC Talent Festival. Admitted to the Lausanne Cons, she studied with Fallot 1966–8 and won first prize at the 1967 Concours artistique international in Paris.

After 1965 Gagné made numerous recital tours and performed with the *TSO in 1966, the Lausanne Chamber Orchestra (Haydn's *Concerto in D*) in 1968, the Atlantic SO in 1970, the Belgrade Philharmonic (the Lalo *Concerto*) in 1975, and the Skovran Chamber Orchestra (Boccherini's *Concerto in B Flat*) in 1975. She toured Canada 1970–1 and 1975–7 for the *JMC, Tunisia 1977–8, Yugoslavia 1975–8, and France in 1978.

A US tour took Gagné to New York and to Washington, DC, where she enjoyed a marked success. The critic for the *Washington Post* (24 Oct 1974) wrote, 'Miss Gagné has formidable technique,' adding that the assurance with which she moved 'from the rhapsodic nature of Debussy through the warmth and tenderness of Chopin and Fauré, into the striking modernity of Shostakovich was proof of that. Her tone is well focussed and particularly mellow.'

After 1974 Hélène Gagné taught at the Music Camp in Lanaudière, near Joliette, Que, as well as in that city's cultural centre. After 1977 she taught at *Concordia U, Montreal. During the summer of 1978 she taught cello and chamber music and coached the cellos and basses at the International Festival of Youth Orchestras and Performing Arts in Aberdeen, Scotland.

With the pianist John *Newmark Gagné recorded the Shostakovich *Sonata, Op 40* (1966, CBC SM-10).

BIBLIOGRAPHY

Flanagan, Marie. 'Heard first cello at 3, she's almost pro at 14,' *Toronto Daily Star*, 8 Jul 1964 GP

GAGNIER. Montreal family of musicians. Three generations are represented here, the first by 1 / Joseph Gagnier, who married Elisa Caron and

J.-J. Gagnier

sired 27 children; the second by the seven of those children who pursued musical careers: 2 / J.-J. (Jean-Josaphat), 3 / Guillaume, 4 / René, 5 / Armand, 6 / Ernest, 7 / Lucien, and 8 / Réal; and the third by 9 / Roland, son of J.-J., and by 10 / Claire, 11 / Gérald, and 12 / Ève, children of René.

1 **Joseph**. Clarinetist, b Ancienne-Lorette, near Quebec, 5 Apr 1854, d Montreal 19 Apr 1919. Having decided to make a career in music, he moved in 1874 to Montreal, where he studied theory with Ernest *Lavigne and Joseph Geai and clarinet with Oscar Arnold and Jacques Vanpoucke. He played in several theatres in Montreal and was clarinetist 1890–1919 at *Sohmer Park. During the 1905–6 season he and his son J.-J. agreed to play bassoon in the *Goulet MSO, after the orchestra had tried unsuccessfully to find two bassoonists among the city's other musicians. Joseph Gagnier taught music and a variety of instruments to each of his 27 children, thus forming the Gagnier Orchestra.

2 **J.-J.** (Jean-Josaphat). Conductor, composer, clarinetist, bassoonist, pianist, administrator, teacher, b Montreal 2 Dec 1885, d 16 Sep 1949; D MUS (Montreal) 1934. He studied clarinet with his father and then with Jacques Vanpoucke, L. van Loocke, L. Ménard, and Oscar Arnold, and bassoon with E. Barbot and C. Westermeier. He took lessons in piano with Alexis *Contant and Romain-Octave *Pelletier and theory with Romain *Pelletier, Contant, Charles *Tanguy, and Orpha *Deveaux. At 14 he played in theatres and at *Sohmer Park. At 18 he was conducting bands and choirs, and not much later he was a bassoonist in the *Goulet MSO and in the opera. In 1910 he organized and directed the Montreal Concert Band (also called the Concordia). Impressed by his work at the *Montreal Opera Company, F.S. *Meighen in 1913 placed him in charge of the *Canadian Grenadier Guards Band, a position (with the rank of captain) that he held until 1947. He was music director of the Sohmer Park Concert Band 1916–19, and his reputation as a conductor went beyond the Canadian border; he frequently visited the USA to conduct, for instance, the famous Goldman Band. In 1921 he conducted operas at the St-Denis and Français theatres. He founded, and directed 1920–31, the Montreal Little Symphony Orchestra and in December 1927 reorganized the *MSO, which he kept going after a fashion until 1929. He taught 1925–30 at Mont-St-Louis College and the Collège de Montréal and also gave lessons at the *Cons national, the *McGill Cons, and the *Dominion College of Music. He was interested in radio, and in 1931 he conducted 26 concerts of the Canadian Grenadier Guards Band which were relayed to the USA by the CBS. In 1934 he joined the CRBC and became regional director of music at the CBC, a post he held until his death, directing numerous concerts and operas.

J.-J. Gagnier began the compilation of the first catalogue of works by Canadian composers, issued in mimeographed form by the CBC in 1947 as *Catalogue of Canadian Composers*. According to Réal Gagnier, and contradicting what is said in *Le Passe-Temps* (Aug–Sep 1947), it was in 1942 that he founded the Gagnier Woodwind Quintet. He directed this quintet – which was exceptional in that all its members (J.-J.'s brothers and his son Roland) were professional musicians from one family – until 1949, when bad health obliged him to curtail his activities.

J.-J. Gagnier's activity as a composer was equally intense; he wrote in styles ranging from romanticism to impressionism and exploited orchestral timbres with skill and taste. Gagnier located several of Calixa *Lavallée's compositions and organized their presentation at a public concert in the Lafontaine Gardens in the summer of 1933, when Lavallée's remains were moved from Boston to Montreal. He gave numerous lectures and published critical articles, essays, poems, and memoirs, notably in *Le Passe-Temps*. He was a member of the CBA and of the American Conductor's Assn. The musical rights of his estate are administered by CAPAC. Montreal gave his name to a park in 1959 and to a street in the north of the city in 1963. J.-J. Gagnier's papers were deposited in the BN du Q.

SELECTED COMPOSITIONS

ORCHESTRA AND BAND

Here's to Tommy. Ca 1915. Band. Ms. HMV 216007 (*Canadian Grenadier Guards)

Toronto Bay. 1921. Orch (band). Fischer 1937 (band)

Le Vent dans l'érable effeuillé / The Wind in the Leafless Maple. 1927. Orch (band). Ms. RCI 1 (J.-M. *Beaudet)

Têtes d'enfants. 1930. Str orch. Parnasse 1947

Pan aux pieds de chèvre / The Goatfooted Pan. 1931. Orch (band). Ms

La Dame de coeur / Queen of Hearts. 1934. Orch (band). Fischer (band)

Hands across the Border. Ca 1935. Band. Remick Music Corp 1938

Skip Along. Ca 1935. Band. Fischer 1937

Pyrame et Thisbé (J.-J. Gagnier). 1942. Soloists, choir, orch. Parnasse

Journey. 1944. Orch. Ms. RCI 233/Cap ST 6261 (*CBC Wpg O)

Suite. 1945. Hp, orch. Sam Fox 1945

Reflets. 1946. Orch (strs). Parnasse 1947

Also other works for orch, band, strs, choir and orch, or choir, soloists, and orch. Most in ms

CHOIR OR VOICE

'Hymne à la patrie' (A. Lozeau). V. *P-T*, Jun 1905

'Le Canada' (O. Crémazie). 1915. V. Arch 1935

'Le Chant de l'A.C.J.C.' (H. Lalande). Soloists, SATB. Assn catholique de la jeunesse canadienne 1925

'Quicumque.' V. Frères des Écoles chrétiennes 1925

'Kyrie.' V. Frères des Écoles chrétiennes 1941

'Hamac dans les voiles' (J.-J. Gagnier). SSAA. Parnasse

'As-Ke-Non-Don' (chant iroquois). SATB. Parnasse

'Ressemblances' (Sully-Prudhomme). V. Parnasse

Several other unpublished works

KEYBOARD

Ten Studies in Concert Form. Ca 1939. Pf. Arch 1939

Prélude (arr of *Trois préludes à l'Éternelle Comédie* for sm orch). Ca 1945. Org. Parnasse 1947

Also 3 works for piano and 2 for organ, all unpublished; incidental music; and a work for harp in ms; many arrangements

WRITINGS

'Peintres, sculpteurs, comédiens et musiciens: parents pauvres de chez nous,' *Action universitaire*, vol 15, Oct 1948

BIBLIOGRAPHY

Jackson, Capt T.E. 'Famous bandmaster Capt. J.J. Gagnier retires,' *CanB*, vol 5, Jun 1947

'Un ensemble unique au monde: le Quintette Gagnier d'instruments à vent,' *P-T*, Aug–Sep 1947

Lapierre, Eugène. 'Feu J.-J. Gagnier,' *Radiomonde*, Sep 1949

Laurendeau, Arthur. 'Mort d'un artiste,' *Action nationale*, vol 34, Oct 1949

3 **Guillaume**. French hornist, bassist, b Montreal 9 Dec 1890, d 22 Aug 1962. He began theory lessons with his father and then studied french horn with Charles *Tanguy and a Mr Debleye. In the 1920s he had lessons on the double-bass from Léon Wathieu of the Chicago SO. He was the principal french horn of the *Canadian Grenadier Guards Band in 1913 and the CSM Orchestra 1935–50 and was a member of the Gagnier Woodwind Quintet 1942–9. Guillaume Gagnier appeared in numerous CBC radio and TV concerts and played double-bass in several Montreal theatre orchestras.

4 **René**. Violinist, conductor, composer, euphonium player, b Montreal 30 May 1892, d Trois-Rivières 25 May 1951. He began his studies with his father and then worked with Albert *Chamberland, Saul *Brant, and Alfred *De Sève. He was assistant conductor 1918–29 at Loew's Theatre and played in the *Montreal Orchestra, the Montreal Little Symphony, the CSM Orchestra, and several theatre orchestras. He was second violin 1936–7 of the *Dubois String Quartet, and was assistant conductor and euphonium soloist of the *Canadian Grenadier Guards Band for more than 25 years. He settled in Trois-Rivières in 1939 and there directed the Union musicale for 11 years. He taught at the *CMQ, the Séminaire de Nicolet, and the Académie de Trois-Rivières. He wrote a number of marches, waltzes, and other unpublished pieces.

5 **Armand**. Clarinetist, b Montreal 21 Aug 1895, d there 27 Aug 1952. After studying with his father he continued lessons with Oscar Arnold, Jacques Vanpoucke, and F. Versmissen. He played at *Sohmer Park 1916–19 as well as at Dominion Square Park, often appearing as soloist. In 1923 he became assistant conductor of the orchestra accompanying Sir Harry Lauder's troupe on its US and European tour. He was clarinet soloist 1937–52 in the CSM Orchestra and until 1947 in the *Canadian Grenadier Guards Band, and he was a member 1942–9 of the Gagnier Woodwind Quintet.

6 **Ernest**. Cellist, oboist, b Montreal 12 May 1898, d there 2 May 1931. After some initial work with his father, he studied the cello with Raoul *Duquette and Napoléon Dansereau and the oboe with Léon Kaster. He was oboe soloist 1913–31 with the *Canadian Grenadier Guards Band and cellist in several theatre orchestras in Montreal, with the Hotel Windsor Trio 1916–21, and with the *Montreal Orchestra 1930–1.

7 **Lucien**. Flutist, b Montreal 26 Dec 1900, d there 26 Oct 1956. He began studying the flute at 8 with Pascal Deremouchamps and continued with Francis Boucher while learning theory from his father. At 15 he made his debut with the orchestra of *His Majesty's Theatre. He performed in different theatres in Montreal, was flute in several orchestras, and played obbligatos for the singers Jean Dickenson, Lily Pons, and Erna Sack. He was second flute 1934–56 in the CSM Orchestra. He appeared in numerous CBC radio and TV concerts and was a member 1942–9 of the Gagnier Woodwind Quintet.

8 **Réal**. Oboist, teacher, b Montreal 24 Mar 1905. Like his brothers, he had his initial training from his father; he then studied successively with his brother Ernest for six years, with Alexandre *Laurendeau 1926–32, and with Fernand Gillet 1947–53. He played in several theatre orchestras in Montreal, especially the Capitol, and was principal oboe in the *Canadian Grenadier Guards Band, in the *Montreal Orchestra, and in the *CSM Orchestra 1935–55. He was a member of the Gagnier Woodwind Quintet 1942–9. He taught 1938–63 at *McGill U, 1942–52 at the *CMM, and 1942–72 at the *CMQ, and in 1955 he gave up performing to concentrate entirely on teaching. In 1958 he was invited to the Prades Festival by Casals, but poor health prevented his participation. Armand *Ferland, Bernard *Jean, and Jacques *Simard were among his pupils.

WRITINGS

'Jouez hautbois, résonnez musettes,' *P-T*, 905, Dec 1946

'Réflexions d'un sourcier,' *Bulletin de la BN du Q*, Mar 1977

9 **Roland**. Bassoonist, teacher, b Montreal 17 May 1905, d there 24 Jul 1975. He did all his studies under the direction of his father. He was principal bassoon 1925–47 in the *Canadian Grenadier Guards Band, 1940–53 in the CSM Orchestra, 1953–7 in the *MSO, and 1968–70 in the *Atlantic SO. He was a member 1942–9 of the Gagnier Woodwind Quintet. He taught 1945–50 at the *CMM and took part in several CBC radio and TV broadcasts.

10 **Claire** (m Dionne). Soprano, b Montreal 28 Mar 1924. She studied violin with her father and at 14 began voice lessons with Roger *Filiatrault. She sang in public and on the radio and won first prize in the CBC's *'Singing Stars of Tomorrow' in 1944. On a grant from the Quebec government she went to the Juilliard School, New York, to study with Mme Jean *Dansereau (Muriel Tannahill). On 31 May 1945 she made her stage debut at *His Majesty's Theatre, Montreal, as Susanna in *The Marriage of Figaro* with artists from the *Metropolitan Opera. On 2 June she sang Micaela in *Carmen* at the *Montreal Festivals. In Canada and the USA she took part in many concerts with such artists as Grace Moore, Witold Malcuzynski, André Kostelanetz, and Percy *Faith. She appeared on numerous CBC radio and TV opera presentations, notably *La Bohème* (1955, 1961), *Così fan tutte* and *L'Enfant et les sortilèges* (1956), Benjamin's *Prima Donna* (1957) and *Madama Butterfly* (1958). She repeated Susanna (1956) for the Montreal Festivals and sang Zerlina in *Don Giovanni* (1957) at the St-Denis Theatre. For her CBC programs 'Sérénade' (radio and TV) and 'À la claire fontaine' (TV) she performed operetta, musical comedy, and song – to all of which her voice and personality were particularly well suited. In 1967 she took the role of Resi in a series of performances of *Valses de Vienne* at the Salle Wilfrid-Pelletier of the *PDA. The St-Jean-Baptiste Society of Montreal awarded her its 1972 *Prix de musique Calixa-Lavallée. In 1974 she again sang the role of Zerlina in Montreal and Quebec with the *Opéra du Québec. Claire Gagnier's voice is distinguished by a clear and luminous timbre, effortless elevation, and a range that allows her to take on coloratura as well as lyric roles. To these qualities are added a presence and personal charm which have helped make her one of the best loved singers in Quebec.

DISCOGRAPHY

12 Meilleures Chansons canadiennes du concours 'Chansons sur mesure.' 1962. Variétés V-9000

Puccini 'Musetta's Waltz' – Chopin *Tristesse éternelle*. J.-P. Morel O. Ca 1948. RCA 10-1304 (78)

O. Straus 'Mon Héros' – *Rêve de valse*. J.-P. Morel O. Ca 1948. RCA 10-1305 (78)

11 **Gérald** ('Ray D'Ièse'). Bandmaster, composer, trumpeter, b Montreal 14 Oct 1926, d there 14 Jan 1961; graduate RMSM (Kneller Hall) 1954. His first trumpet, piano, and theory lessons were with his father. He took his general schooling 1939–45 at the Séminaire de Trois-Rivières. In Montreal, he was a student 1945–51 at the *CMM and also studied with Pierre Monteux for three summers. He was a trumpeter in the *Canadian Grenadier Guards Band and taught 1946–9 at the Studio Labelle and 1951 at Mont-St-Louis College, Montreal. With the rank of lieutenant, he directed several bands, including the Fusiliers du Mont-Royal after 1950 and the Royal Canadian Ordnance Corps Band in Montreal 1956–61. He also was assistant director of the *Opéra national du Québec 1951. Among his works are the symphonic poem *Polyphème*, *Prélude* for piano, *Suite romantique* for strings, and *Rolandineries* for piano.

12 **Ève** (m Charbonneau). Soprano, actress, b Montreal 12 Nov 1930. She studied at the *CMM with Martial Singher (voice), August *Descarries (piano), and Marcel Grandjany (harp). She has distinguished herself in numerous operetta and musical comedy roles on the stage and on CBC radio and TV. GG, CH, GP, (CV)

GAGNON. Quebec City family three of whose members – 1 / Ernest, 2 / Gustave, brother of Ernest, and 3 / Henri, son of Gustave – successively occupied the position of organist at the Quebec Basilica, their combined tenures spanning nearly 100 years (1864–1961). Ernest's daughter Blanche and Henri's son Denys also are mentioned herein.

1 (Frédéric) **Ernest** (Amédée). Organist, folklorist, teacher, historian, writer, administrator, b Rivière-du-Loup (renamed Louiseville), near Trois-Rivières, Que, 7 Nov 1834, d Quebec City 15 Sep 1915; D LITT (Laval). Fascinated by the arrival of a piano in the family home, he was given lessons as a young child by his sister Bernardine. He later studied with a certain Beaudoin at Joliette College, with John G. Seebold in Montreal ca 1850, and with Antoine *Dessane in Quebec City. While still pursuing his education, he was organist 1853–64 at St-Jean-Baptiste Church in Quebec City. He studied in Paris 1857–8 with Henri Herz and Alexandre-Édouard Goria (piano) and with Auguste Durand (harmony and composition). He also met Auber, Marmontel, Niedermeyer, Francis Planté, Rossini, Thomas, and Verdi and was in Italy for a short time.

Returning to Quebec City, Gagnon taught 1858–77 at the École normale Laval (where he had taught briefly in 1857), at the Petit Séminaire de Québec, and for the Ursulines, wrote articles – notably in the *Courrier du Canada* – and entered into heated newspaper debates with Antoine Dessane, first on the subject of Adam's *Noël* and then on plainchant accompaniment. He was organist 1864–76 at the Quebec Basilica, and in 1866 became the founder and first director of the *Union musicale de Québec. He was one of the founders in 1868 and president 1868–71, 1874–6, 1887–8 and 1889–90 of the *AMQ. In 1873, as correspondent for the *Courrier du soir*, he made a second trip to Europe. After 1875 he gradually gave up his activities as organist and teacher in favour of a career as a provincial civil servant. He was secretary in that year to Premier Sir Charles-Eugène Boucher de Boucherville and 1876–ca 1905 to the minister of public works. During this period he contributed to *La Revue canadienne* (ca 1888–ca 1909) and published several historical works. The seventh chapter of his *Louis Jolliet* is an often-quoted description of musical life in 17th-century New France, and his *La Nouvelle-France* contains a chapter on Quebec music at the time of Bishop Laval. He gave an address, entitled 'Les sauvages de l'Amérique et l'art musical,' to the 15th Congrès international des américanistes in Quebec City in 1906, which was later published. Other works appeared posthumously, notably *Pages choisies*, of which the chapter 'La musique et les noëls populaires' appeared first in 1891 in *La Revue canadienne*.

Ernest Gagnon

Gagnon is remembered best for *Chansons populaires du Canada*, a compilation of folksongs ('collected and published with annotations') which first appeared 1865–7 in six issues of *La Foyer canadien* and which rescued French-Canadian folklore from oblivion. The work reveals Gagnon's thorough knowledge of traditional song. He took care over the texts and although he fitted words to music in the manner customary at that time he clearly understood verse forms; moreover he respected the modal inflections of the tunes in his transcriptions. (See Folk music, Franco-Canadian).

Gagnon was an organist in the virtuoso tradition and a fluent improviser. In 1902 he became a member of the Royal Society of Canada. He was a corresponding member of the Société des compositeurs de musique of Paris and an officer of the Instruction public de France. He was described by Arthur *Letondal as a 'personality richly endowed with artistic talents, a man of rare discrimination and high ideals, guided by a deep love for the spirit and the characteristics of his country.'

Gagnon's sister Élisabeth (b 1838, d 1897) married Paul *Letondal in 1860. His daughter Blanche published *Musique, Musique religieuse* (1903), and *Musique sacrée* (1915), collections of music composed by her father, and several of his individual works such as 'Ave verum' (1915) for three-part choir and 'Cantique pour la communion' and 'Tantum ergo,' both arranged alternatively for two or three equal voices. She also published several monographs 1921–48 in Quebec City under the pseudonyms Bibliophile, Manrésien, or Amicus. Her father's works *Pages choisies* and *Nouvelles Pages choisies* were published through her efforts. She wrote a column, 'Causerie musicale,' and various articles, 1919–20, for *La Musique*. Her article 'Notre chant national,' which appeared in *Le Soleil*, 29 Jun 1907, under the pseudonym Frimaire, gave her version of the genesis of the national anthem *'O Canada'; in it Ernest Gagnon has a much more active role than in the account of Nazaire *LeVasseur in *La Musique* (June 1920). She presented her version again and with additional details in her *Réminiscences et actualités* (Quebec City 1939).

COMPOSITIONS
KEYBOARD
Stadaconé 'danse sauvage pour piano.' Lovell 1858
Un Soir à bord, quadrille. Pf. Lovell 1859
Souvenir de Venise, grand nocturne. Pf. Lovell 1860
Le Carnaval de Québec 'quadrille sur des airs populaires et nationaux pour piano.' St-Laurent 1862
À la claire fontaine 'transcription de salon.' Pf. ?1894
Accompagnement d'orgue des chants liturgiques 'en usage dans la province ecclesiastique de Québec.' Boucher 1903?, 1912, 1917–18
An accompaniment (ca 1860) to 'O Canada, mon pays, mes amours.' *P-T*, 21 Jun 1913
VOICE OR CHOIR
'Ave Maria,' no. 1 of *Échos du sanctuaire*. V, SATB. Lovell 1859
'Je me voyais au milieu de ma course.' SATB, pf. *Écho du cabinet de lecture paroissial*, Oct 1862
'Ça bergers, assemblons-nous.' SATB, pf. *Écho du cabinet de lecture paroissial*, Dec 1862. RCA Victor 56-5231-A (*Petits Chanteurs de Granby)
'Tantum ergo in D.' 3 female vs, org. *Foyer domestique*, Mar 1879
Les Soirées de Québec. 3 vs, pf. Langlais 1887, Boucher ca 1887. Bluebird B-1265 (Imperial Grenadiers)
Cantiques populaires du Canada français. SATB, org (pf). Brousseau 1897
Petite Maîtrise des collèges. 3 or 4 vs; Book I, Book II 1907, 1908
Cantiques populaires pour la fête de Noël. SATB, org. Boucher 1922, 1938
'Silence ciel! Silence terre!' V solo, choir, pf. Boucher 1951
Chants canadiens. SATB, pf. A. Lavigne, Boucher
Other works, including 'Le Chant de l'Iroquois' for v; and a harmonization of the *Messe des anges* by Henry Dumont for 4 vs and org, published by Boucher
Also *L'Incarnation de la jongleuse*. Vn, pf. Lovell 1862? *Echo du cabinet de lecture paroissial*, Mar 1862

WRITINGS
Chansons populaires du Canada (Quebec City 1865, 1880, 1894, 1900; Montreal 1908, followed by many repr – of which the last appeared in 1968 – conforming to the 1880 edn)
Lettres de voyage (Quebec City 1876)
Louis Jolliet (Quebec City 1902, Montreal 1913, 1926, 1946)
Choses d'autrefois, feuilles éparses (Quebec City 1905)
Chansons des soldats de Montcalm (Quebec City 1907)
Les Sauvages de l'Amérique et l'art musical (Quebec City 1907)
La Nouvelle-France (Quebec City 1908)
Drapeau de Carillon (Quebec City 1910)
Feuilles volantes et pages d'histoire (Quebec City 1910)
Hommes et choses d'autrefois (Quebec City 1917)
Pages choisies (Quebec City 1917)
Nouvelles Pages choisies (Quebec City 1925)
8 other books on biography, genealogy, archeology, or history, all published 1889–1908 in Quebec City

BIBLIOGRAPHY
'Le regretté Ernest Gagnon – l'un de nos musiciens les plus distingués,' *P-T*, 536, 9 Oct 1915
Harmonia. 'M. Ernest Gagnon,' *La Musique*, vol 1, Jan 1919
Gagnon, Blanche. 'L'organiste de S. Antoine,' ibid, vol 2, Dec 1920
LeVasseur, Nazaire. 'Musique et musiciens à Québec,' ibid, vol 3, Aug, Sep 1921
Letondal, Arthur. 'Les Musiciens du passé, Ernest Gagnon 1834–1915,' *Entre-Nous*, vol 1, Feb 1930
– 'Ernest Gagnon, organiste et historien – 1834–1915,' *P-T*, 890, Sep 1945
– 'Ernest Gagnon, écrivain et folkloriste,' *Qui?*, vol 2, Mar 1951
Catalogue de la chanson folklorique française

2 **Gustave** (Adolphe Mathurin). Organist, teacher, composer, b Rivière-du-Loup (now Louiseville), near Trois-Rivières, Que, 6 Nov 1842, d Quebec City 19 Nov 1930; hon D MUS (Laval) 1922. He took piano lessons 1860–4 in Montreal with his brother-in-law Paul *Letondal and then succeeded his brother Ernest as organist 1864–76 at St-Jean-Baptiste Church in Quebec City. In 1870 he went to Europe, where he studied in Paris with Alexis Chauvet (organ), Antoine Marmontel (piano), and Auguste Durand (harmony) and then in Liège with Étienne Ledent (piano) and Jean-Théodore Radoux (harmony). In the summers of 1871 and 1872 he went to Dresden and to Leipzig, where he worked with Robert Papperitz (organ) and Louis Plaidy (piano); he also visited Italy. During his travels he met several famous musicians, including Liszt and Saint-Saëns. Returning to Quebec City in 1872, he became organist at the Basilica in 1876, again in succession to his brother, and retained the position until 1915. He taught 1877–1917 at the École normale Laval and the Petit Séminaire, and also privately. His pupils included his son Henri, J.-Arthur *Bernier, Joseph-Daniel *Dussault, Juliette Rodrigue, and Léo-Pol *Morin. Morin said of him, 'Those who were taught by him, and I am proud to have been one, never saw the limits of his kindness, of his heart, of his devotion, of his wit, and of his intelligence' (*La Lyre*, December 1930). Gustave Gagnon was one of the founders in 1866 of the *Union musicale de Québec and in 1868 of the *AMQ, of which he was president 1878–9, 1881–2, 1883–4, 1885–7, 1893–4, 1895–6, 1897–8, 1899–1900 and 1901–2. He helped found the *Dominion College of Music in Quebec City and served 1922–5 as the first director of the school of music of *Laval U, where he also taught 1922–30. He took up composition and made a harmonization for 4-part mixed choir of the plainchant *Messe royale* by Henry Du Mont (1610–84), which was performed by a 600-voice choir on the Plains of Abraham for the St-Jean-Baptiste celebrations in 1880. His *Marche pontificale pour orgue* was orchestrated by Joseph *Vézina.

COMPOSITIONS
Reflets du passé 'valse de salon.' Pf. Brainard 1869
Marche pontificale. Pf (org). Lavigne 1871, Lavigueur and Hutchison ca 1912
Marche nocturne. Pf. Lavigne 1873
Souvenir de Leipzig. 1874? Pf
Marche pontificale pour orgue. 1886
Gavotte in F. 1890. Pf. Lavigne
Deuxième Marche pontificale avec choeurs. Lavigueur and Hutchison 1896

BIBLIOGRAPHY
'M. Gustave Gagnon,' *La Musique*, vol 1, 1919
LeVasseur, Nazaire. 'Musique et musiciens à Québec,' ibid, vol 3, Aug, Oct 1921
'M. Gustave Gagnon,' ibid, vol 4, Dec 1922
Morin, Léo-Pol. 'Hommage à Gustave Gagnon,' *La Lyre*, 76, Dec 1930

3 (Charles Édouard Gustave) **Henri**. Organist, teacher, composer, b Quebec City 6 Mar 1887, d there 17 May 1961. He studied solfège and piano 1895–1900 with his father Gustave, solfège and harmony 1900–3 with Joseph *Vézina and organ 1900–3 with William *Reed. His success began in 1901 with a concert before a huge audience in the Music Temple at the Pan-American Exposition in Buffalo; the *Buffalo Courrier* (2 Sep 1901) described him as 'a true prodigy.' He then gave recitals in Quebec City and in Cliff Haven, near Plattsburgh, NY. He studied 1903–7 in Montreal with Arthur *Letondal (piano), Romain-Octave and Romain *Pelletier (organ), Guillaume *Couture (harmony and counterpoint), and Father Charles-Hugues *Lefebvre (church music) and was chapel organist 1903–6 at Gesù College and 1906–7 at Loyola College. Having received a certificate in 1906 from the *Dominion College of Music, he left in 1907 for Paris, where he studied plainchant with Amédée Gastoué, organ, plainchant, improvisation, and harmony with Eugène Gigout, piano with Isidor Philipp, and organ with Charles-Marie Widor. He was a soloist in 1908 and 1909 in the Concerts Touche and sometimes deputized for Gigout as organist at St-Augustin Church. In the summers of 1911, 1912, 1914, and 1924 he visited Paris to study with Joseph *Bonnet and Widor.

After he returned to Canada he was assistant organist 1910–15 and organist 1915–61 at the Quebec Basilica, preferring the life of a church musician to a career as a virtuoso. Though he inaugurated many organs in Quebec and Ontario, he devoted himself primarily to the organ-loft of the Basilica, earning for it a prestige similar to that of the famous organs of Europe. He also taught 1917–33 at the École normale Laval and at the Petit Séminaire of Quebec City. In 1923 he began teaching piano and organ at *Laval U and was one of the *CMQ's first teachers and its director 1946–61. His pupils included Jean-Marie *Beaudet, Marius *Cayouette, Father Léon *Destroismaisons, Lucille Dompierre (*Prix d'Europe 1919), Alice Duchesnay, Claude *Lagacé, and Joseph Turgeon. Gagnon possessed the qualities of a born teacher: integrity, a sense of detail, and love of his work. He was president 1929–32 of the *AMQ.

One of Gagnon's most popular compositions was 'Rondel de Thibaut de Champagne,' which Edward *Johnson and Rodolphe *Plamondon included in their repertoires. His *Mazurka* (1907) and *Deux Antiennes*, orchestrated by Maurice *Blackburn and J.-J. *Gagnier respectively, were recorded by a CBC Montreal orchestra under J.-M. Beaudet. A recording – *Hommage à Henri Gagnon* (Alpec A-75008) – was made in 1974 by the Quebec organists Antoine *Bouchard, Sylvain Doyon, Claude Lagacé, and Antoine *Reboulot, all of whom play their own *Variations sur le nom d'Henri Gagnon*.

Henri's son Denys (b Quebec City 27 Sep 1922) studied piano and theory with him 1927–42. In 1953 for the CBC in Montreal he became a producer of dramatic and musical programs, notably 'Divertissement' (TV) and 'Jeux d'orgues' (radio).

COMPOSITIONS
PIANO
Deux Pièces de genre: *Chanson d'été* 'barcarolle'; *Badinage*. 1903, 1904. Lavigueur and Hutchison 1904
Airs canadiens. 1904. Pf-4 hands
Mazurka. 1907.
Mazurka. 1909. Pf-4 hands
Petite Mazurka
ORGAN
Deux Antiennes. *P-T*, Feb 1945
Prélude à l'Introit du IXe dimanche après la Pentecôte. *Revue St-Grégoire* 1950
Prélude sur L'Alléluia de la fête de saint Michel. *Revue St-Grégoire* 1950
Also *Interludes, antiennes d'orgue No. 1*; *Musique d'orgue*; *Quelques Principes d'accompagnement du chant grégorien*. Ms
VOICE
'Cantique au Sacré-Coeur'; 'Ave Maria.' Org. *Manuel de morceaux religieux* by Father Rancourt
'Rondel de Thibaut de Champagne.' 1916
Other works, instrumentation unknown: *Elégie, Op 1*, 1903; *Mazurka*; *Sur le pont d'Avignon*

BIBLIOGRAPHY
'M. Henri Gagnon,' *La Musique*, vol 1, Nov 1919
Morin, Léo-Pol. 'Henri Gagnon,' *Papiers de musique* (Montreal 1930)
A.D. 'Henri Gagnon,' *La Lyre*, 79, Mar 1931 FB (DM)

GAGNON, Alain. Composer, teacher, b Trois-Pistoles, near Rimouski, Que, 22 May 1938; B MUS (Laval) 1963, L Mus composition (Laval) 1964. He began teaching himself the piano but continued under supervision 1949–50 at the Collège Jésus-Marie in Trois-Pistoles and 1951–8 with Father Philippe-Antoine Lavoie at the Rimouski Seminary. In 1960 he enrolled at the CMQ for organ tuition with Henri *Gagnon. He also studied composition with Roger *Matton at *Laval U and in 1963 received the Governor-General's Medal, and in 1964 an award from the French government. He studied composition 1964–5 with Jocelyne *Binet, and in 1965 he received the *Prix d'Europe and scholarships from the *Canada Council and the Quebec Ministry of Education. In Paris he studied 1965–6 with Henri Dutilleux at the École normale and Olivier Alain at the École César-Franck. He also studied briefly at the electronic music studio, U of Utrecht, in 1966 and with André-Francois Marescotti at the Geneva Cons in 1967. In 1967 he began teaching counterpoint, analysis, and composition at Laval U. His *Prélude*, commissioned by the *Quebec SO with the help of a grant from the Canada Council, was premiered by the orchestra in 1969 under Pierre Dervaux. A fervent admirer of Debussy, Gagnon believes that composition is a matter alike of technique and of humanism. Expressing his feelings through essentially melodic music, he aspires to a direct communication with his listener. He is a member of CAPAC and the *CLComp and an associate of the *CMCentre.

SELECTED COMPOSITIONS

ORCHESTRA

Esquisse. 1965. CMCentre
Prélude. 1969. CMCentre

CHAMBER

3 *String Quartets* (1964, 1966, 1970). Ms. (*No. 2*) RCI 363 (*Classical Quar of Mtl)
Prélude. 1968. Guit. Ms
Les Oies sauvages (Maupassant). 1973. Sop, 7 instr. CMCentre
Septet. 1973. Chamb ens. CMCentre
Largo. 1974. 3 guit. Ms
Interlude. 1975. 3 guit. Ms

PIANO

5 *Préludes*. 1964. CMCentre
4 *Sonatas* (1964, 1964, 1966, 1967). Ms. (*No. 3*) CBC SM-52/RCI 274/Sel CC 15.007 / (C. *Savard) / (*No. 4*) Madrigal MAS-416 (A.-S. *Savoie)
Aquarelles. 1966. CMCentre
Mirages. 1966. CMCentre. RCI 252 (J. *Dufresne)
Les Grottes de Castellana. 1967. CMCentre

CHOIR AND VOICE

'Le Cytharède' (Alain Gagnon). 1964. Med v (bar), pf. CMCentre
Illusions d'antan (Alain Gagnon). 1965. Med v (bar), pf. CMCentre. ('Tristesse') RCI 393 (B. *Laplante)
Rumeurs et visions (A. Rimbaud). 1966. 3 sop, SATB. CMCentre
'Que je t'accueille' (St-Denys Garneau). 1968. Med v, pf. CMCentre. RCI 393 (B. *Laplante)

WRITINGS

'Autour d'une sonate,' *VM*, 9, Oct 1968 (MB-L)

GAGNON, André. Pianist, composer, conductor, arranger, b St-Pacôme-de-Kamouraska, Que, 1 Aug 1942?; premier prix harmony (CMM) 1961. He played the piano as a child and began writing short pieces at six. He took theory lessons 1952–3 and 1957 with Léon *Destroismaisons in Ste-Anne-de-la-Pocatière and studied 1957–61 at the *CMM with Germaine *Malépart (piano), Clermont *Pépin (composition), and Gilbert Martin (solfège). At the same time he developed an interest in popular music. In 1961, on a grant from the Quebec government, he studied in Paris with Yvonne Loriod and took courses in accompanying and conducting.

On his return to Canada in 1962 Gagnon became the accompanist for Claude *Léveillée, and he was to serve as music director, arranger, and pianist for most of Léveillée's recordings until 1969. He has accompanied Jacques Blanchet, Pierre Calvé, Renée *Claude, Claude *Gauthier, Pauline *Julien, Pierre Létourneau, and Monique *Leyrac, among others. For Leyrac he arranged several songs. In 1967 he was the soloist in a Mozart concert conducted by Raymond *Dessaints at

André Gagnon

the *PDA. In 1968 he made the LPs *Don't Ask Why* (Col ELS 331), *Pour les amants* (Col FS 680), *Notre Amour* (Col FS 694), and *Encore* (Harmonie KHF 90083).

In 1969 Gagnon gave up accompanying to devote himself to a career as soloist, composer, and arranger, and went to London to record, with the London Baroque Orchestra, his four concertos in the style of Vivaldi, *Mes Quatre Saisons* (Col FS 712), based on themes drawn from the songs of *Ferland, *Leclerc, Léveillée, and *Vigneault. Gagnon was among the artists chosen to represent Canada at Expo 70 in Osaka and in the same year he toured Quebec with the *Quebec SO. In 1971 he made two LPs, *Let It Be Me* (Col FS 90084) and *Projection* (Col FS 90159), and a package of his greatest hits (Col GFS 90006) was released.

With the Hamburg Philharmonic Orchestra in 1972 Gagnon recorded *Les Turluteries* (Col FS 90096), a set of baroque-style suites inspired by the songs of La *Bolduc. He gave a concert of his works at the PDA with the *McGill Chamber Orchestra. The LPs *Saga* (Lon SP 44219) and *Neiges* (Lon SP 44252) were released in 1974 and 1975 respectively. He won a 1976 *Juno Award for the best-selling LP with *Neiges*, from which the instrumental piece *Wow* became a minor international hit. As a result he performed in France in 1975 and 1976 and Mexico in 1976, and his name appeared on many hit charts. He received another Juno as instrumental artist of 1977.

Gagnon wrote the music for Anne Ditchburn's ballet *Mad Shadows* (based on *La Belle Bête*, a novel by Marie-Claire Blais), which was premiered by the National Ballet of Canada at the *O'Keefe Centre in Toronto on 16 Feb 1977. He composed the music for a pas de deux, *Nelligan*, and for the ballet *Adage*, performed in 1977 at the PDA by the Compagnie de Danse Eddy Toussaint. His LP *Le Saint-Laurent* (Lon SP 44301) was selected instrumental record of the year at the 1979 ADISQ recording and showbusiness awards in Montreal. Gagnon wrote the music for the NFB film *Games of the XXI Olympiad*, the CBS TV movie *Night Fright*, and the feature film *Running*. In 1978 he performed in concert at *Massey Hall and at the PDA and the following year he toured Canada and appeared in 10 cities in the USA.

On CBC TV Gagnon was host and accompanist 1962–4 for the program 'Cri-Cri' and music director 1966–70 for 'Moi et l'autre'; he composed the music for several series, including 'Vivre en ce pays' 1967–71, 'Les Forges du St-Maurice' 1972–5, and 'Techno-Flash' 1973–7. He wrote and played the music 1967–76 for a children's program, 'La Souris verte.' As a guest he has appeared on several TV variety programs, including 'Zoom,' 'Vedettes en direct,' and 'Dimanshowsoir.'

In *La Presse* of 11 Oct 1976, Pierre Beaulieu wrote of Gagnon's show at the PDA: 'Whether we like his music a little, a lot, or intensely, he makes sure that we enjoy ourselves: he is a very good pianist – we knew that already – but he's also an excellent "entertainer" in the American sense of the word ... Gagnon has a lot of presence at the piano ... He captivates, he fills the stage. He is at ease and amusing, and he exploits fully (unconsciously perhaps) the unsophisticated image he has always projected.'

André Gagnon's music is less easy to classify than individual works might lead the listener to assume. It ranges widely and makes audacious combinations of elements from both sides of the barrier between the classics and pop music. The baroque pastiches *Les Turluteries* and *Mes Quatre Saisons* borrow forms and styles from Vivaldi and Bach but are given fresh significance for Quebec listeners, and for many outside the province, by their incorporation of melodic materials from the popular cultures of the province. And *Petit Concerto pour Carignan et orchestre* (1976; performed by Jean *Carignan and Yehudi Menuhin in 1978 on CBC TV's 'The Music of Man') draws a witty analogy between the violin writing of the baroque masters and the fiddling style of the famous violoneux for whom it was written. Other Gagnon works visit composers of other eras – Mozart in *Cher Amadeus*, Chopin in *Pour endormir ma mère*. With a light hand, a tidy craft, an apparently warm heart (the pastiches are not satires), and no undue pretension, Gagnon in these works has created entertainments based on the reconciliation of musical idioms which too often, through no fault of their own, have been frozen into postures of mutual exclusion. At the same time, such compositions as *Neiges*, *Smash*, *Chevauchée*, *Surprise*, *Donna*, and *Mouvements* have established Gagnon in the disco and pop fields.

In 1979 Gagnon was made an Officer of the *Order of Canada. He is a member of CAPAC.

BIBLIOGRAPHY

Champagne, Jane. 'André Gagnon: writing with a baroque flavour,' *CanComp*, 64, Nov 1971
Rowcliffe, Katherine. 'A choreographer gambles with a composer,' *Fugue*, Feb 1977
Champagne, Jane. 'Musical discipline: writing for the ballet,' *CanComp*, 120, Apr 1977
Beaulieu, Pierre. 'André Gagnon: un spectacle qu'on écoute,' Montreal *La Presse*, 14 Oct 1978
Rozon, Lucie. *André Gagnon* (Montreal 1978) (BLH)

GAGNON, Lee. Tenor and alto saxophonist, flutist, arranger, composer, b Amqui, on the Gaspé Peninsula south of Matane, Que, of US parents, 2 Sep 1934. His teachers were Joseph Moretti (clarinet, CMM 1952–6), Arthur *Romano (saxophone, CMM 1954–60), Rafael *Masella (clarinet, CMM 1956–9), and Jeanne Baxtresser (flute 1962–6). He also studied composition 1956–61 with Conrad *Letendre at the *U of Montreal and with Michel *Perrault. After playing saxophone and clarinet 1956–9 with the Royal Canadian Ordnance Band, he began working in Montreal cabaret and nightclub orchestras in 1959. In 1960 he formed a 10-piece rehearsal band of Montreal studio and jazz musicians. In its five years, the band performed at the Montreal Jazz Festival in 1962 and in Montreal jazz clubs. Gagnon's quartet (later quintet), in the late 1960s the most popular jazz group in the province, also performed in nightclubs including Gagnon's own Le Jazztek (La Bohème), at *Expo 67, on CBC radio and TV (eg, 'Jazz en liberté'), and with the *MSO. In 1968 the group toured Quebec universities, schools, and Cegeps under the auspices of the MACQ, offering a history of jazz as part of its concert program. Its repertoire included standard jazz works and pieces by Gagnon, the trumpeter Ron Proby, and other Montreal musicians. Gagnon was music director 1969–72 for the singer Charles Aznavour's North American appearances. In 1972 he disbanded his jazz group to work as a studio arranger and composer. Besides his jazz works, he has written music for a ballet (based on Marcel Dubé's *Jérémie* and premiered in 1973 by Les Ballets-Jazz), many jingles, and scores for several movies, including the features *Chantal en vrac* (1968), *Seizure* (1973), and *Pousse mais pousse égal* (1975), and some NFB and industrial documentaries. Collaborating with the lyricists Jean Robitaille and Luc Plamondon he has written songs recorded by France Castel, Emmanuelle, and Ginette *Reno. Gagnon is an affiliate of PRO Canada.

DISCOGRAPHY

La Jazztek. Roberts pf, Donato db, Ranger drums. 1967. Cap ST 6226

Je Jazze. Proby tpt, Leduc pf, Haynes db, Ranger drums. 1968. RCA ST 6253

Jazzzz. Proby tpt, Greenwich guit, Donato db, Provençal drums. 1969. RCI 288/Barclay 80086

Jérémie. Orch, Gagnon cond. 1973. Opus OP 509

Vive la Canadienne!: French-Canadian folk songs. Orch, Gagnon cond and arr. (1976). RCI 430

BIBLIOGRAPHY

Goodwill, Michel. 'The performer and composer in Lee Gagnon vie for supremacy,' *MSc*, 268, Nov–Dec 1972

(EFr, MM)

GALE, Nina (Hungerford Maud). Soprano, teacher, adjudicator, b Elora, near Guelph, Ont, 6 Oct 1884, d Toronto 29 Aug 1964. She studied at the *TCM as a scholarship pupil of Ethel Shepherd, in London with Albert Visetti and Sir Henry Wood, and in Milan with Madame Norri-Baj and Teresa Arkel. Nina Gale made her debut 25 Apr 1914 as Norma at Alba, Italy, and soon added to her repertoire the soprano roles in *Il Trovatore, Tannhäuser*, and *Cavalleria Rusticana*. Leaving Italy for London at the outbreak of World War I, she joined the Carl Rosa Opera Company as leading soprano. She made many concert appearances at this time and also taught, while in London, at a studio in Aeolian Hall. Returning to Canada she joined the staff of the TCM in 1925, became soprano soloist at St Andrew's Church, Toronto, and gave many recitals throughout Ontario. She was noted for her great personal charm and gracious manner, and her name is perpetuated by a scholarship awarded annually to a vocal student at the *RCMT. MMI

Galipeau Musique Inc. Chain of stores and music schools established in Quebec and Ontario by Roméo Galipeau (b Montreal 9 Jun 1929; teaching certificate, U of Montreal, 1947). Galipeau studied at the *Cons national of Montreal with Eugène *Lapierre (organ and piano) and Marcel *Saucier (violin), privately with Claude *Champagne (composition), Georges-Emile *Tanguay (harmony), and in Paris with Léon Algazi (composition).

Galipeau founded the firm Galipeau Musique in 1958 as a combined store and school located on Fleury St East in Ahuntsic, Montreal. In 1963 he opened a downtown branch which he later transferred to a franchisee with the stipulations that the name be preserved and that Galipeau Musique, in Boisbriand, be the exclusive supplier. The formula brought rapid growth, and by 1978 there were 28 branches in Quebec, in Cowansville, Joliette, Lachute, Lac St-Jean, Montreal and 12 outlying municipalities, Sorel, St-Hyacinthe, St-Jérôme, and Trois-Rivières, as well as two in Ontario (Cornwall and Hawkesbury).

In each instance the store offered a selection of instruments and sheet music, and the adjoining school gave music courses (theory, jazz-ballet, guitar, piano, organ, saxophone, violin, etc). The courses are recognized by the Quebec Ministry of Education, which issues certificates of study.

Roméo Galipeau in 1975 became president of Eastern Musical Distributors Ltd, a publishing house which also handles material of other publishers, in particular of Publications Chant de mon pays, which have specialized in songs by Quebec chansonniers and pop composers. In 1978 Galipeau obtained the franchise for Bösendorfer pianos in Quebec.

BIBLIOGRAPHY

De Vincy, Christian. 'Je vous présente M. Romain [sic] Galipeau,' *Progrès de Villeray*, 13 Nov 1958 AP

The Gallery Singers. Vancouver choir, initially of 12 voices and latterly of 22, founded in 1968 by Frederick Carter. The singers have given about five concerts each year in Vancouver (some at the Vancouver Art Gallery, although there is no connection between the two organizations) and other British Columbia centres. Winners in 1969, 1970, and 1971 of the City of Lincoln Trophy awarded by the *FCMF, the singers divided themselves into two groups for the 1972 Tees-side International Festival in England and took first and second places in the small ensembles class. In addition they were semi-finalists that year in the BBC's amateur choral competition, 'Let The Peoples Sing.' They sang again in Great Britain in 1978. Though they possess a wide repertoire, the Gallery Singers have made a specialty of unaccompanied Tudor and 20th-century works. They have released privately four LPs of music by Byrd, Messiaen, Palestrina, Passereau, Stanford, and Vaughan Williams and various folk songs. The singers' founder and conductor, Frederick (George) Carter (b Enfield, England, 5 Mar 1913), became organist-choirmaster at St John's Anglican Church, Vancouver, in 1966 after training in London with Harold Darke and serving as organist-choirmaster 1951–66 at Armagh Cathedral in Northern Ireland. (MW)

GALLOWAY, Jim (James Braidie). Soprano, tenor, and baritone saxophonist, clarinetist, b Kilwinning, Ayrshire, Scotland, 28 Jul 1936. While studying 1954–8 at the Glasgow School of Fine Arts he began playing clarinet, then alto and baritone saxophone. He worked with Alex Dulgleish's Scottish All Stars, then led his own Jazz Makers 1961–4. Moving to Toronto in 1964 he joined the Metro Stompers in 1966 and succeeded Jim *McHarg as leader in 1968. Galloway was the agent and host-musician for several Toronto jazz clubs in the 1970s, and during that time he played often with the journalist-drummer Paul Rimstead, accompanying such noted jazzmen as Wild Bill Davison, Bobby Hackett, Jay McShann, and Buddy Tate. Galloway travelled twice to New Orleans, once on his own in 1971, playing with leading traditional bands there, and once in 1972 with the Stompers. He also appeared at the 1976 Montreux and Nice jazz festivals with his 'All Star Sextet' (the trumpeter Buck Clayton, the tenor saxophonist Tate, the pianist McShann, the bassist Dan Mastri, and Rimstead), and returned there each summer to perform as a soloist. He has performed frequently at other festivals and in jazz clubs in several European countries. In 1978 in Toronto he became the leader of the 17-piece Wee Big Band which has taken as its repertoire the classics of jazz and swing of the 1930s and 1940s. An eloquent soprano saxophonist, well-versed in both dixieland and mainstream traditions, Galloway has been described as 'a friendly player' who makes 'the tiny curved soprano sing in a succession of warm and completely logical solos' (Mark Miller, *Globe and Mail*, 28 Nov 1977).

Under Galloway's leadership, the Stompers continued as a touring band in Canada and the USA until 1970. Thereafter this popular dixieland band appeared regularly only in the Toronto area and with a variable personnel including the cornetists Charlie Gall or Ken Dean, the trombonists Jim Abercrombie or Peter Sagermann, and the pianist Ron Sorley. Galloway is married to the bassist Rosemary Sidgwick. Among his recordings are his own compositions *Blues Alley Bump, Walking on Air, U.F.O.*, and *Sandy*. He is an affiliate of PRO Canada.

DISCOGRAPHY

Three's Company. Wellstood pf, Magadini drums. 1973. Sack 2007

Jim Galloway and the Metro Stompers. Dean cornet, Sagermann trb, Sorley pf, Mastri db, Fearon drums. 1977. Sack 4002

Walking on Air. Wellstood pf and elec pno, Thompson db, Vickery drums. 1978. Bittersweet BC 831

BIBLIOGRAPHY

Rimstead, Paul. Columns, Toronto *Telegram*, 30 Aug–3 Sep 1971

Rimstead, Paul. 'Galloway's first solo album coming out on Sackville,' *MSc*, 287, Jan–Feb 1976

Jones, Max. 'Galloway heading the soprano "invasion," ' *Melody Maker*, 8 Apr 1978

Miller, Mark. 'Jim Galloway,' *Down Beat*, 13 Jul 1978

MM

GALPER, Avrahm (Abraham). Clarinetist, teacher, writer, b Edmonton, 16 Aug 1921. He lived in Palestine until 1946, studying clarinet there at 17 with Tzvi Tzipine and later in New York with Simeon Bellison and in London at the RAM with Frederick Thurston. He became a member of the *TSO in 1947, serving 1952–6 and 1958–73 as principal and 1973–9 as co-principal. (He retired in 1979.) He also played with the *CBC SO (principal, 1951–64) and the *COC. He has appeared in chamber and solo recitals, performed on CBC radio, and recorded Andrew *Twa's *Serenade* for clarinet and strings (1952, RCI 86), short standard pieces with the *Hart House Orchestra (1965, for the *CTL), *Weinzweig's *Quartet for Four Clarinets* and other works for the series *New for Now II, Clarinet* (1971, Dom S69004), and Bartók's *Contrasts* (1974, CBC SM-240).

Galper has written a two-volume instruction book, *Clarinet for Beginners* (Boosey & Hawkes 1970, 1976), led clinics in Canada and the USA, and contributed articles to *The Clarinet*. He began teaching at the *RCMT in 1951 and at the *U of Toronto in 1962. His students have included James *Campbell and members of the Vancouver SO, the National Ballet Orchestra, the Edmonton SO, and the Winnipeg SO. (MFr)

Gamma Records Ltd† / **Disques Gamma Ltée.** Record company founded in 1965 in Montreal by Jack Lazare (president) and his brother Daniel (artistic director). Gamma has devoted itself particularly to Quebec performers and chansonniers, among them Christine Charbonneau, Robert *Charlebois, Clémence *Desrochers, Georges *Dor, Louise *Forestier, Claude *Gauthier, Pauline *Julien, Georges Langford, Tex *Lecor, Raymond *Lévesque, Monique *Miville-Deschênes, Claire Syril, and, later, Francoeur, Claude Légaré, Francine McGee, Ovila, and Nathalie Suzanne. In 1969 Gamma established itself in Paris, thus giving several of its artists exposure in France and in other European countries. Its recordings, distributed in Europe until that time by Barclay, appeared on a new Gamma International label. In 1978 the Société SFPP took over the distribution under the Gamma France label. Following an agreement, certain recordings by the Europeans Mike Brant, Eric Charden, Marie Laforêt, Francis Lai, and St-Preux were released in Quebec through Gamma, whose productions in Canada are handled by Alta Musique Distribution, Ltd. By 1979, Gamma had produced nearly 150 LPs.

BIBLIOGRAPHY

Larsen, Christian. 'Une compagnie de disques québécoise vient de s'installer à Paris,' Montreal *Petit Journal*, 13 Apr 1969 (ST)

GANAM, King (Ameen Sied). Fiddler, composer, b Swift Current, Sask, of Syrian-English parents, 9 Aug 1914. Taught by oldtime fiddlers in his hometown, Ganam played for dances at 9 and on CHWC radio, Regina, at 13. His formal teachers were W. Knight *Wilson and Gregori *Garbovitsky. With his Sons of the West, a country band formed in 1942 in Edmonton, he performed on CBC radio's 'Alberta Ranch House,' won the 1950 World Open Western Band Competition (held in Vancouver), and toured Canada. After moving in 1952 to Toronto, he became a regular performer on CBC TV's 'Holiday Ranch' and starred 1954–5 on his own CBC radio show, 1956–9 on CBC TV's 'Country Hoedown' with a studio version of the Sons of the West, and in 1961 on CTV's 'The King Ganam Show.' Though Ganam moved to California in 1962, he returned frequently throughout the 1960s to perform in Canada. His first recordings, made in the early 1950s for Victor, were issued on the Bluebird label. Four LPs bore the RCA Camden label. Many of his own western-swing tunes, reels, and polkas were among these Victor recordings. Some were printed in *King Ganam's Jigs and Reels* (BMI Canada 1956).

WRITINGS

Ganam, King. 'Our Canadian toe-tapping, knee-slapping "Country Hoedown,"' *Liberty*, Dec 1956 MD

GARAMI, Arthur. Violinist, teacher, b Derecske, Hungary, 20 Nov 1921, naturalized Canadian 1955, d north of Montreal, 12 Jan 1979; performance diploma (Franz-Liszt Academy, Budapest) 1942. In Budapest he studied violin 1935–42 with Geza *de Kresz, chamber music 1937–42 with Imre Waldbauer and Leo Weiner, and Hungarian folk music 1940–1 with Zoltán Kodály. In 1940 he won second prize at the Hubay National Competition. He taught at the National Cons of Hungary and was assistant concertmaster of the Hungarian radio orchestra 1945–6. Garami lived in Paris 1946–9, frequently played in recital or as soloist on French radio, and gave the Paris premiere of William Walton's *Violin Concerto*. He was a prize winner in the 1946 Jacques-Thibaud Competition and the 1947 Geneva International Competition for Musical Performers and appeared in concert in London and on the BBC.

Moving to Canada at the invitation of the Hamilton Cons of Music, (*RHCM) Garami directed the conservatory's string department 1949–54. He broadcast frequently for the CBC ('CBC Wednesday Night,' 'Distinguished Artists,' and 'Sunday Morning Recital' on radio and 'Musicale' on TV) and made his Canadian concert debut 7 Mar 1951 with the *TSO in Hamilton in Tchaikovsky's *Violin Concerto*. He appeared with the major Canadian orchestras and made numerous recital and concert tours 1951–4 in the USA.

Garami moved in 1954 to Montreal where he was a soloist and member 1954–65 of the CBC *'Little Symphonies' Orchestra, concertmaster 1956–9 of the *McGill Chamber Orchestra, and assistant concertmaster 1960–5 of the *MSO. He taught 1955–64 at *McGill U, 1958–64 at the *École Vincent-d'Indy, and 1962–79 at the *CMM.

A *Canada Council fellowship enabled Garami to write the treatise 'The spontaneous performance in the art of violin playing' (unpublished). In May 1964, with his regular accompanist Charles *Reiner, he presented Beethoven's 10 sonatas for violin and piano at Carnegie Recital Hall. After a recital at the *Salle Claude-Champagne, Jean *Vallerand hailed Garami one of the 'best Canadian violinists' (Montreal *La Presse*, 24 Nov 1965). Garami was a founding member, and first violin 1968–76, of the *Classical Quartet of Montreal.

In Paris in 1947 Garami made several 78s for the Pacific label, playing Bartók's *Rumanian Dances*, Dinicu-Heifetz' *Hora staccato*, Dohnanyi's *Ruralia Hungarica*, and several other virtuoso pieces. With Reiner he recorded sonatas by Henry Barraud and Udo *Kasemets (ca 1955, RCI 137). Garami owned a Guarnerius made in Mantua in 1714. (NT)

GARANT, (Albert Antonio) **Serge**. Composer, conductor, pianist, teacher, critic, b Quebec City 22 Sep 1929. He was 11 when his family settled in the Montreal suburb of Verdun. Shortly afterwards he moved with his family to Sherbrooke, where he took up the clarinet and saxophone, becoming especially attracted to jazz. While playing clarinet in the *Sherbrooke SO and saxophone in various jazz groups, he studied piano with Sylvio *Lacharité and harmony with Paul-Marcel Robidoux 1946–50. A hearing of the *Rite of Spring* prompted him to turn to composition, and he commuted to Montreal to study 1948–50 with Yvonne *Hubert (piano) and Claude *Champagne (composition). He composed works for piano, voice and piano, concert band, and string orchestra, some of which were performed, notably at a youth festival in 1950. His *Fantaisie* for clarinet and piano earned him a prize from the Assn of Amateur Bands which enabled him to spend six weeks at New York's Juilliard School.

By this time, Garant was a champion of 20th-century music. In Sherbrooke in 1950 he played Schoenberg on the piano to the astonishment of his fellow citizens. A stay in Paris, where he attended Messiaen's classes in analysis 1951–2, was a decisive step. He also studied counterpoint with Andrée Vaurabourg-Honegger. As his knowledge of serial music deepened he became convinced that Webern was the greatest composer since Debussy. His meetings with Stockhausen and Boulez also opened up new horizons. Some works from this period, such as *Concerts sur terre* and 'Et je prierai ta grâce' show Messiaen's influence, but that influence was short-lived. In succeeding works – *Caprices, Pièce pour piano No. 1*, and *Musique pour la mort d'un poète* – the writing is unreservedly atonal, and pointillistic Webern-like passages may be observed. Even in these, however, more than a trace of Garant's own personality is apparent.

On his return to Sherbrooke, Garant worked as a jazz pianist but soon moved to Montreal, where he briefly continued his studies in counterpoint with Jocelyne *Binet. Anxious to make contemporary music more widely known, he joined forces with François *Morel and Gilles *Tremblay in 1954 to present a concert featuring works of Boulez, Messiaen, and Webern. The following year a second concert was presented to mark the 10th anniversary of Webern's death. In it Garant presented *Nucléogame* 'In memoriam Anton Webern,' recognized as the first Canadian work to combine magnetic tape and instruments. In 1956 these two ventures resulted in the formation of the group Musique de notre temps, which presented two seasons of concerts. To ensure its financial support Garant worked as a rehearsal pianist for ballet and as an arranger, accompanist, and conductor for variety programs on CBC radio and TV. He also did some broadcast work as a critic ('Revue des arts et des lettres') and wrote articles 1954–5 for the weekly *L'Autorité*. He castigated the public, critics, and performers alike for their indifference and hostility towards modern music and the contemporary creative musician.

Serge Garant

His compositional output became increasingly bold and innovative. In 1958 he employed aleatory techniques in *Trois Pièces* for string quartet. He was probably the first to make use of these procedures in Canada. Even though performers often recoiled from the difficulties in Garant's scores, some of his works were premiered by the CBC on radio ('Premières' and 'CBC Wednesday Night') and TV ('L'*Heure du concert'). His **Anerca*, premiered in Montreal in 1961 under the direction of Mauricio Kagel during the *International Week of Today's Music, established him as one of the leading figures in Canadian music.

Two subsequent commissions provided him with the opportunity to write for large orchestra: *Ouranos* for the *Quebec SO and *Ennéade* for the Sherbrooke SO. In 1965 the pianist Claude Helffer played his *Asymétries No. 1* in Paris at one of the concerts of the Domaine musical. The following year Pierre *Mercure engaged him to conduct R. Murray *Schafer's **Loving* on CBC TV, a premiere which established him as a conductor of contemporary music (see list of premieres he has conducted). When the *SMCQ was founded in the autumn of 1966 he was appointed its music director. He has conducted this ensemble in regular concerts in Montreal and on tour in Canada and in Europe. Among appearances of particular note were those at the 9th Festival d'art contemporain in Royan in 1972, and at *Musicanada, the 1977 festival of Canadian music in London and Paris.

In 1967 Garant began teaching analysis and composition at the *U of Montreal, where he gained an eager following. By 1980 his pupils had included Ginette *Bellavance, Walter *Boudreau, Marcelle *Deschênes-Harvey, Richard *Grégoire, Michel *Longtin, and Pierre *Trochu.

Under his first *Canada Council grant (1969), Garant took summer courses in conducting with Boulez in Basel; a second grant (1972) enabled him to spend some time in Bali. The 1973–4 season was spent in Italy on a scholarship from the Canadian Cultural Institute in Rome. Garant has conducted the *MSO on several occasions. In 1968 he led it in the premiere of his work *Phrases II*, sharing the podium with Franz-Paul *Decker. This work, which calls for two conductors, was repeated with the orchestra in 1979 under Garant and Charles Dutoit. Also with the MSO, in 1977, Garant conducted the premiere of Gilles Tremblay's *Fleuves*.

Garant has conducted in Toronto, Vancouver, Quebec City, and other Canadian cities. He was in charge of the orchestra class at the music camp at Lanaudière, near Joliette, Que, in the summers of 1977 and 1978 and conducted the Quebec Youth Orchestra in 1979 and the U of Montreal orchestra 1978–9. In 1971 he became the host for CBC radio's 'Musique de notre siècle.' In 1979 the CBC telecast the half-hour program 'Portrait de Serge Garant' on the series 'Les Beaux Dimanches.'

Garant's output spans three decades and has been remarkably steady. Early influences, in particular Messiaen and Webern, quickly faded, giving way to what Raoul *Duguay calls an 'open structuralism' (*Musique du Kébèk*, Montreal 1971), which displays a remarkably personal writing technique stemming from the establishment of a series of proportions or ratios which govern durations, tempi, registers, and timbres. Notwithstanding the rigour of the writing, in which Garant demonstrates his concern for questions of structure and for organizing each work on its own terms, his music allows the performer freedom to participate creatively, on the one hand offering the possibility of improvising within a relatively defined framework, and on the other allowing a choice in the order of performance of the various sequences of a work.

As for Garant's musical language, it has evolved into a style which, in certain respects, approaches that of Boulez in its serial rigour combined with a penchant for lyricism. Particularly noteworthy in this regard are such works as ... *chant d'amours* and *Rivages*. Beginning with *Anerca*, Garant displayed an astonishing virtuosity in his instrumental writing and a marked originality in his handling of timbres. Far from becoming exhausted along the way, these qualities have reasserted themselves ever more strongly, and they may be found as much in the small ensemble works as in those for large orchestra.

Garant's work as a whole displays elements of proportion, harmony, sensitivity, and precision rarely found to such a degree in one composer. There is in it a balanced mixture of intellectualism and expression, which together produce an art always vital and full-bodied. To those who would accuse him of being primarily cerebral, he replies: 'Fundamentally, I have always thought – and still do – that no technique in itself can explain anything whatsoever. Technique explains nothing. The music is always behind it; it is always a kind of miracle, a kind of wondrous encounter which exists perhaps between certain ways of constructing and certain ways of feeling, with the result that the construction of a work ends up being not very important, yet in spite of it all, that way of feeling would not be there if the construction was not there also' (*Canada Music Book* 9, p 25).

Serge Garant received an Etrog for *Vertiges* at the Canadian Film Festival in 1969, the *CMCouncil Medal in 1971, PRO Canada's Wm Harold Moon Award in 1978 for his contribution to the promotion of Canadian music abroad, the 1979 *Prix de musique Calixa-Lavallée, and the 1980 Jules Leger Prize for *Quintet*. In 1980 Garant was made a Member of the *Order of Canada. He is an affiliate of PRO Canada and an associate of the *CMCentre. He became a member of the *CLComp in 1961.

Garant conducted the premieres of the following Canadian compositions:

Aitken, Robert *Shadows II: Lalita*, SMCQ 1973
Beecroft, Norma *Rasas I*, SMCQ 1968
Charpentier, Gabriel *Orphée I*, NAC 1969
Cherney, Brian *Chamber Concerto for Viola and Ten Players*, SMCQ 1975
Daoust, Yves *Trois fois quatre*, SMCQ 1978
Deschênes-Harvey, Marcelle *Talilalilalilalarequiem*, SMCQ 1974; *Moll, opéra lilliput pour six roches molles*, SMCQ 1976
Evangelista, José *Consort*, SMCQ 1978
Garant, Serge *Phrases I*, Expo 67 1967; *Amuya*, CBC Summer Festival 1968; *Jeu à quatre*, Stratford Festival 1968; *Phrases II* (with Franz-Paul Decker), MSO 1968; *Offrande I*, SMCQ CBC TV 1970; *Offrande III*, SMCQ CBC radio 1971; *Circuit II*, SMCQ 1972; *Circuit III*, CBC Summer Festival 1973; *... chant d'amours* , CBC TV 1975; *Rivages*, Vancouver New Music Soc, 1976
Gonneville, Michel *Variations 'auras,'* SMCQ 1979
Gouin, Jacques *Distorsions*, SMCQ 1977
Hartwell, Hugh *Kâmê'a*, SMCQ 1971
Hawkins, John *Two Pieces for Orchestra*, 7th annual symposium for student composers 1971
Hétu, Jacques *Cycle, Op 16*, SMCQ 1970
Hunt, Richard *Nimbus I*, CMM 1972
Joachim, Otto *Illuminations II*, SMCQ 1969; *Uraufführung*, SMCQ 1977
Lapointe, Rémi *Écarts*, SMCQ 1977
Longtin, Michel *Deux Rubans noirs III*, SMCQ 1979
Mather, Bruce *Madrigal V*, SMCQ 1973
Morel, François *Radiance* (4 mvts), CBC Vancouver 1971; *IIKKII (Froidure)*, SMCQ 1972
Papineau-Couture, Jean *Nocturnes*, U of Montreal 1969; *Obsession*, SMCQ 1973
Pépin, Clermont *Interactions*, SMCQ 1977
Saint-Marcoux, Micheline *Ishuma*, SMCQ 1974
Schafer, R. Murray *Loving*, CBC TV 1966; *Patria II*, Stratford Festival 1972
Steven, Donald *Images (Refractions of Time and Space)*, SMCQ 1977
Tremblay, Gilles *Souffles (Champs II)*, SMCQ 1968; *Fleuves*, MSO 1977
Trochu, Pierre *Miracrose*, SMCQ 1977
Vinet, Michel *Acousmie*, 7th annual symposium for student composers 1971
Vivier, Claude *Lettura di Dante*, SMCQ 1974; *Liebesgedichte*, SMCQ 1975

COMPOSITIONS

EARLY WORKS

Adagio et allegro. 1948. Pf, band. Ms
Musique pour saxophone alto et fanfare. 1948 (rev orch 1950). Ms
Pièces pour quatuor de saxophones. 1948. Ms
Sonatine. 1948. Pf. Ms
Fantaisie. 1949. Cl, pf. Ms
Un grand sommeil noir (Verlaine). 1949. V, pf. Ms
Ode (Ta forme monte comme la blessure du sang) (A. Grandbois). 1950. Str orch. Ms

ORCHESTRA

Ouranos. 1963 (Quebec 1963). Full orch. Ms
Ennéade. 1964 (Sherbrooke 1964). Full orch. Ms
Phrases II (Che Guevara). 1968 (Mtl 1968). 2 orch. Ms
Offrande II. 1970 (Tor 1970). Full orch. Quebec CMCentre 1978

CHAMBER MUSIC

Musique pour la mort d'un poète. 1954. Pf, str. Ms
Nucléogame. 1955. Septet, tape. Ms
Canon VI. 1957. 10 perf. Ms
Pièces pour quatuor à cordes / Study on chance. 1958. Ms
Asymétries No. 2. 1959. Cl, pf. CMCentre
Phrases I (P. Bourgault). 1967. Mezzo, pf, cel. BMIC 1969. RCI 240/RCI Anthology of Canadian Music ACM 2. See Discography.
Amuya. 1968. 20 perf. CMCentre
Jeu à quatre. 1968. 4 instr ens (16 perf). CMCentre. RCI 300/RCI ACM 2 (*SMCQ)
Offrande I (originally titled *Cérémonial du corps*). 1969. 18 perf, pre-recorded sop. CMCentre. RCI 368/RCI AMC 2 (*SMCQ)
Offrande III. 1971. 3 vc, 2 hp, pf, 2 perc. Sala 1973. RCI 368/RCI AMC 2 (*SMCQ)
Circuits I. 1972. 6 perc. CMCentre. McGill U Records 77003 (*Béluse)
Circuits II. 1972. 14 perf. Ms. RCI 368/RCI AMC 2 (*SMCQ)
Circuits III. 1973. 18 perf. CMCentre
... chant d'amours (Salomon, Shakespeare, et al). 1975. 16 perf. CMCentre. RCI 422/RCI AMC 2 (*SMCQ)
Rivages (A. Grandbois). 1976. Bar, chamb ens. CMCentre
Quintette. 1978 (Van 1978). Fl, ob, vc, pf, perc. CMCentre
See also *Anerca*.

SOPRANO AND PIANO

Concerts sur terre (P. de la Tour du Pin). 1951. CMCentre. RCI 201/RCI AMC 2 (*Jeannotte)
'Et je prierai ta grâce' (Saint-Denys-Garneau). 1952. Ms. RCI 201/RCI AMC 2 (Jeannotte)
Caprices (G. Lorca, transl P. Demangeat). 1954. CMCentre. RCI 201/RCI AMC 2 (Jeannotte)
'Cage d'oiseau' (Saint-Denys-Garneau). 1962. BMIC 1968. RCI AMC 2 (P. *Vaillancourt)

PIANO

Pièce No. 1. 1953. CMCentre. RCI 465/RCI AMC 2 (L.-P. *Pelletier)
Musique rituelle. 1954. Ms
Variations. 1954. CMCentre. RCI 135/RCI AMC 2 (J. *Dufresne)
Asymétries No. 1. 1958. CMCentre. RCI 465/RCI AMC 2 (L.-P. *Pelletier)
Pièce No. 2 (Cage d'oiseau). 1962. BMIC 1969. RCI 252 (J. Dufresne)/RCI 465 and RCI AMC 2 (L.-P. Pelletier)
Also music for the films *L'Homme et les régions polaires* (1967, ms) and *Vertiges* (1969, ms)

WRITINGS

'Le compositeur moderne: paria de la musique,' *Le Québec libre*, Jean Depocas ed (Montreal 1959)
'Dire une musique d'ici,' *Cahier pour un paysage à inventer*, 1, 1959
'Un esprit de genèse,' *Liberté 59*, 1, Sep–Oct 1959
'Chronique musicale,' *Cahiers d'essai*, 3, Jan 1961
'Musique 1961,' *Liberté*, vol 3, Mar–Apr 1961
'Music in Montreal 1961–62,' *Canadian Art*, Jul–Aug 1962
'Un mal nécessaire,' Montreal *La Presse*, 30 Dec 1967
'Anerca,' *Document d'information à l'intention des professeurs de musique*, Ministry of Education (Quebec 1968)
'Phrases I,' *Parti pris*, vol 5, Apr 1968
'Notes sur Anerca,' *Musiques du Kébèk*, Raoul Duguay ed (Montreal 1971)
'Une lettre de Rome,' *CMB*, 9, Autumn–Winter 1974
'Serge Garant Offrande II (1970),' *Variations*, vol 3, Sep–Oct 1979
Also several reviews and reports in *Jmc* (1955–68) and in *CMJ* (1956–62).

DISCOGRAPHY

Garant *Phrases I*. Chiocchio mezzo, Lachapelle perc, Garant pf and cel. 1967. RCI 240/RCI AMC 2
Music of Today / Musique d'aujourd'hui, vol 3: Hodkinson *Interplay*. J.-P. Major fl and picc, G. Moisan sax and cl, R. Desjardins db, Lachapelle perc, Garant cond. 1969. RCI 300
Music of Today / Musique d'aujourd'hui, vol 4: Gellman *Mythos II*: Aitken fl, Husaruk vn, Goodman vn, Kudlak va, J.-L. Morin vc, Garant cond. Grégoire *Cantate*: MacKinnon sop, L.-P. Pelletier org, Romandini guit, Lachapelle perc, 12 singers, Garant cond. 1970. RCI 301

BIBLIOGRAPHY

Gingras, Claude. 'Ils diront ce qu'ils voudront, mais c'est nous qui faisons la musique,' Montreal *La Presse*, 4 Jan 1964
Germain, Jean-Claude. 'Les Musiciens québecois pardonnent tout, sauf le péché de compositeur,' Montreal *Petit Journal*, 15 Sep 1968
Gingras, Claude. 'Serge Garant: la musique qui se fait,' Montreal *La Presse*, 25 Apr 1970
Kendergi, Maryvonne. 'Entrevue avec Serge Garant sur "Phrases II",' *Musiques du Kébèk*, Raoul Duguay ed (Montreal 1971)
'Rencontre avec Serge Garant,' interview with Maurice Fleuret, *CMB*, 9, Autumn–Winter 1974
Morel, François. 'Serge Garant, structuralist and lyrical musician,' *Variations II*, Dec–Jan 1978–9
PRO Canada Ltd. 'Serge Garant,' pamphlet (1980)
Kasemets, Udo. 'Serge Garant,' *Contemporary Canadian Composers / Compositeurs canadiens contemporains*
Mather, Bruce. 'Serge Garant,' *Dictionary of Contemporary Music*

GP, HP

GARBOVITSKY, Gregori. Violinist, conductor, teacher, b Kreavri, near Dniepropetrovsk, Russia, 1892, d New York October 1954. He studied violin at the St Petersburg Cons with Leopold Auer (at the same time as Kathleen *Parlow and Jascha Heifetz) and composition with Alexander Glazunov. Upon graduating he became conductor of the Rostov SO, and after the 1917 revolution he went to Berlin, where he became known as a soloist and conductor and led the Berlin SO several times in 1922. Emigrating to Canada in the mid-1920s he continued his career in Winnipeg. It is said that he gave up solo playing after losing his Guarnerius violin in a fire in Winnipeg. About 1927 he moved to Calgary, where he directed the Palace Theatre Orchestra for a year, then reorganized the *Calgary SO and conducted it 1928-39. He also conducted the Ladies' String Orchestra and taught extensively. After guest-conducting in Vancouver (summer concerts in Stanley Park and appearances in 1939 with the *Vancouver SO) he served 1940-6 as director of the Vancouver Junior Symphony. Later he formed the Vancouver Orchestra and Chamber Music Society and conducted the New Westminster SO 1949-53. His pupils during his Vancouver years included Sydney *Humphries. Garbovitsky died in New York while undergoing treatment for cancer. BNSG

GARDNER, Stanley. Pianist, teacher, b Sherbrooke, Que, 13 Dec 1890, d Montreal 17 Aug 1945. He moved to Montreal as a boy and studied piano with Stratford Dawson. About 1912 he went to Berlin, where he spent a few years studying with Ferruccio Busoni and also with Egon Petri. Returning to Montreal, he opened a studio and taught until his death. Samuel *Dolin, Rose *Goldblatt and Dorothy *Morton were among his pupils. Besides giving numerous recitals on his own in Montreal and elsewhere in Canada, he and Goldblatt formed a piano duo which appeared frequently 1936-45 in public recitals and broadcasts. He was one of the early exponents in Canada of the piano music of Debussy and Ravel, and his programs also featured works by North American composers. NT

GARNIER, Rolande (b Rozière). Mezzo-soprano, b Notre Dame de Lourdes, near Winnipeg, 11 Jun 1926. She studied voice at the *CMM and privately 1953-4 with Martial Singher and was the winner (1952-3, with Louis *Quilico) of the CBC French-network radio competition *'Nos Futures Étoiles.' She toured 1953-4, 1958-9 for the *JMC, gave recitals on radio and TV, and appeared as soloist with orchestras, including the *Winnipeg SO, and with the *Winnipeg Philharmonic Choir. She has sung in Winnipeg for Golden Voices Opera (Madame Flora in Menotti's *The Medium*, 1972), Opera Manitoba (Berta in *The Barber of Seville*, 1972) and the *Manitoba Opera Assn (Suzuki in *Madama Butterfly*, 1973; Mercédès in *Carmen* and Annina in *La Traviata*, 1974) and has starred at *Rainbow Stage. She is recognized as a first-rate musician and a gifted actress. (MB)

GARRARD, Don (Donald). Bass, b Vancouver 31 Jul 1929. He was a voice pupil of Glyndwr Jones in Vancouver and a semi-finalist in the CBC's *'Singing Stars of Tomorrow' when his interest in a career as a singer was strongly encouraged at a 1951 summer workshop with Lotte Lehman and John Charles Thomas in Santa Barbara, Cal. The following year (February 22) he made his *COC debut as the Speaker in *The Magic Flute* and won a leading role in the premiere of Dolores *Claman's **Timber!!* at Vancouver's *TUTS. He undertook a sustained course of study 1952-7 at the *Royal Conservatory Opera School with George *Lambert, Nicholas *Goldschmidt, and others. (He later studied abroad with Luigi Borgonovo and George Canelli.) In 1953 for the CBC he sang the title role in the first full-length TV production of *Don Giovanni* (this also was the first production of any complete opera on TV in North America). He won the 'Singing Stars of Tomorrow' in 1953 and *'Nos Futures Étoiles' in 1954 and continued to appear with the COC, as Don Giovanni (1956, 1963), Billy Bigelow in *Carousel* (1957), The King of Nowhere in *The Love of Three Oranges* (1959), Ramfis in *Aida* (1963, 1972), Padre Guardiano in *La Forza del Destino* (1969), Méphisto in *Faust* (1970), Hunding in *Die Walküre* (1971), and Boris Godunov (1974). He also sang the title role in Handel's *Solomon* in a 1972 performance by the *Toronto Mendelssohn Choir and the *NACO at *Massey Hall, Toronto.

Don Garrard

Garrard joined Sadler's Wells as principal bass in 1961, enjoying great personal success in Pizzetti's *Murder in the Cathedral* (1962), as Sarastro in *The Magic Flute*, as Ferrando in *The Thieving Magpie*, as Sparafucile in *Rigoletto*, and as Méphisto in *Faust*. He made his debut at the Royal Opera, Covent Garden, in 1970 as Ferrando in *Il Trovatore*. He has appeared also at the Aldeburgh Festival (as the Abbot in the premiere of Britten's *Curlew River* in 1964), at the Glyndebourne Festival (in 1965 as Rochefort in *Anna Bolena* and in 1966 in Handel's *Jephtha*), at the Hamburg State Opera (1968), the Scottish Opera (*Boris Godunov* 1968), and the Welsh National Opera (*Aida* 1970), and in Washington as Wotan in *Die Walküre* (1975). He was Sarastro at the *NAC in Festival Canada's production of *The Magic Flute* in 1977 (see Festival Ottawa).

With his commanding presence, his keen theatrical sense, and a voice both substantial and flexible Garrard has become respected on both sides of the Atlantic for his effectiveness in the whole range of operatic roles for bass and bass-baritone. He became a resident of England after 1961 but has continued to appear in Canada with the COC, in recital, and on CBC radio and TV. He sang Trulove for the premiere recording (1964) of Stravinsky's *The Rake's Progress*, under the direction of the composer.

WRITINGS

'Working with Britten,' *OpCan*, vol 5, Sep 1964
'Festival in the fields,' *OpCan*, vol 7, Feb 1966

DISCOGRAPHY

Bruckner *Te Deum in C* – Bach *Magnificat*. New Phil O, Barenboim cond. 1970. Angel S 36615
Donizetti *Roberto d'Evereux*. Ambrosian Chorus, Royal Phil O, Mackerras cond, Garrard (Raleigh). Ca 1970. 3 West 323/ABC ATS-20003/(excerpts) ABC ATS 20008/8109 -20008H/5109-20009H
Mozart *Don Giovanni* (excerpts). Scottish Chamb O, Gibson cond. (1976). Classics for Pleasure CFP 40246
Stravinsky *The Rake's Progress*. Sadler's Wells Opera Chor, Royal Phil O, Stravinsky cond. (1964). 3 Col M3S-710

BIBLIOGRAPHY

McPherson, Jim. ' "We're big fish in a small pond",' Toronto *Telegram*, 20 Sep 1969
Littler, William. 'Canadian finds fulfilment in U.K.,' *Toronto Daily Star*, 31 Jul 1970
Fischer-Williams, Barbara. 'Don Garrard,' *OpCan*, Dec 1970
Fraser, John. 'Garrard doesn't convict Boris but opera does,' Toronto *Globe and Mail*, 21 Sep 1974
Mercer, Ruby. 'Credit where credit is due: noted Canadian bass Don Garrard,' *OpCan*, Spring 1980

GARROUTEIGT, (Jean-Joseph) **Henri.** Gregorianist, b Paris 28 or 29 Oct 1875, d Montreal 28 Aug 1965. He joined the Sulpicians in 1893 in Issy and was ordained a priest in 1898 in Paris. He held a degree in philosophy and a doctorate in theology.

From 1903 to 1917 Garrouteigt was a teacher and choirmaster at the Grand Séminaire of Montreal. He introduced Gregorian chant at the seminary in 1903, the year of the *Motu Proprio* by Pius X, and promoted it among the parish clergy and the religious communities. He was appointed head of the board of studies of the *Schola cantorum of Montreal and was director of the school of liturgical singing at the Congregation of Notre-Dame's Institut pédagogique, founded in the late 1920s. Guillaume *Dupuis was one of his pupils.

Garrouteigt was a contributor to the *Revue grégorienne* edited by Dom Mocquereau in Tournai, Belgium, and to the one edited by Dom Pothier in Grenoble. He also wrote 'Le chant grégorien: sa nature, ses différents genres, réponse aux objections' (*Extrait de la Revue canadienne*, Montreal 1909)

GARSON, Alfred (Henrik). Violinist, teacher, composer, b Berthier-en-Haut, now Berthierville, Que, 22 Oct 1924; B MUS (Cape Town) 1950, FTCL 1953, M MUS (Cape Town) 1954, PH D (Montreal) 1970. Two scholarships, a Rhodes in 1945 and a Beit in 1947, enabled him to attend university in South Africa 1946-54. He studied there with Albert Coates (conducting), Maria Neuss (violin), and Lily Kraus (chamber music), among others, and took courses in anthropology and African languages. He won the 1948 and 1950 South African Broadcasting Corporation composition prizes for, respectively, his *Suite* for orchestra and his *Song and Dance for Orchestra* and the Myer Levinssohn prize in 1949 for *The Witch*, a ballet for marionettes, narrator, and chamber orchestra. He was orchestrator and arranger for the Cape Town orchestra 1949-55 and wrote music for the films *Atlantic Express*, *Black Gold*, *Safari Holiday*, *Vineyards of the Cape*, *Mogambo*, and others.

Garson studied composition with Matyas Seiber during an assignment in London 1956-60 as director of the Dept of Cultural Affairs at the South African embassy. He received a Gabriel d'-Honot scholarship in 1958-9 and was able in 1962 to pursue his research in medieval music and literature at the monastery of Montserrat, Spain.

Garson studied 1966-72 with Shinichi Suzuki at the ESM, Rochester, NY, when the Japanese educator was introducing to North America his method of violin teaching. Garson began teaching the method in Canada and England in 1972 and in South America in 1979. He was co-ordinator of the *Suzuki program at *McGill U after 1969 and taught during the summers at the U of Wisconsin and Ithaca College, Ithaca, NY, after 1967.

Garson was president 1965-7 of the Éducateurs de musique du Québec (later the *QMEA), assistant director 1968–9 and director 1969–73 of the *Canadian Music Educator* (for which he wrote about 50 articles, including several on the Suzuki method), and president 1973–4 of the *Canadian String Teachers' Association. He has been a guest lecturer or visiting professor at universities in Canada, the USA, and Europe and has spoken on radio and TV (CBC, NBC, BBC).

Garson's doctoral thesis, *From Creation to Appreciation: An Approach to the Appreciation of Contemporary Music by Young Children through a Creative Method*, was published in Montreal in 1970. He is the author of many published articles and of *The Suzuki Teaching Method* (London 1971).

Garson's compositions include two ballets (1949), *From Morn till Midnight* and *Norskajana* (in collaboration with the choreographer John Cranko); a *Mass* for four soloists, mixed choir, and orchestra (1950); chamber music works, songs, and motets; and choral and instrumental works for children of school age.

In 1975 the South African Eisteddfod instituted the Alfred Garson scholarship. (WL)

GATI, Laszlo. Conductor, violinist, violist, b Timisoara, Rumania, 25 Sep 1925. He studied first in Rumania but moved in 1946 to Budapest, where he attended the Franz Liszt Academy and the National Cons and played in the Hungarian State Orchestra. His teachers were Dezsö Rados (violin), János Ferencsik (conducting), and Zoltán Kodály, Sándor Veress, and Pál Jardanyi (composition). Gati also, in 1950, conducted the U of Economics Chorus and Orchestra and the Hungarian State Philharmonic Orchestra. He taught violin 1953–6 at the Budapest Cons and worked 1954–6 with the Hungarian Radio. He emigrated to Canada in 1957 and was a violist with the *MSO under Igor Markevitch (with whom he studied) and Zubin Mehta. While in Montreal he conducted the Montreal Philharmonia in 1958 and founded the Montreal Chamber Orchestra in 1959. He studied with Hans Swarowsky in Nice in 1964 on a *Canada Council grant. He was conductor of the *Victoria SO 1967–78. He conducted in Columbia and Venezuela in 1978 and became music director of the *Windsor SO in 1979. Gati is a gifted exponent of the romantic composers and of 20th-century Hungarian music, notably Bartók and Kodály, but he is at ease in most styles and includes Canadian works in his repertoire. DBW

GAULTIER DE LA VERENDRYE, Juliette (b Gauthier). Mezzo-soprano, ethnomusicologist, violinist, b Ottawa 7 Aug 1888, d there 21 Aug 1972. She was a younger sister of Eva *Gauthier, and her professional name was derived from that of her supposed forebears. She attended *McGill U and won a four-year scholarship to Europe, where she studied violin with Jenö Hubay at the Royal Academy in Budapest and voice with Vincenzo Lombardi in Florence. She made a debut with the Boston Opera, but her career (ca 1910–30) was confined mainly to recitals of Acadian, Inuit, and Indian folk music, much of which she herself collected and arranged. She learned the language of the Inuit and dialects of the Pacific Coast Indians to sing the songs of the Nootka, Carrier, and Kootenay. She was known to have taught singing at Greenwich House Music School in New York 1922–5. At the 1927 Canadian Folk Song and Handicraft Festival (*CPR Festivals) in Quebec, she sang songs from the Ernest *Gagnon and Marius *Barbeau collections, some arranged by Marion Bauer with viola accompaniment, and at the 1928 festival she added pastourelles of the 15th century. In the late 1920s she sang in Town Hall, New York, and elsewhere in the USA and England. A member of the Author's Club of Canada, she served 1949–53 as director of Gatineau Museum in Kingsmere. Her clear voice is preserved on a few Canadian Victor Black label records made about 1921.

FILMOGRAPHY
Totem Land (Screen News 1921) JBM

GAUTHIER. Montreal family of singers: 1 / Conrad and 2 / Paul-Marcel, Conrad's son.

1 **Conrad**. Folklorist, singer, actor, b Montreal 8 Aug 1885, d there 14 Feb 1964. After some commercial training he worked in theatre, founding in 1902 the Cercle du Drapeau and later the Cercle Lapierre. He was a member of the Assn dramatique de Montréal and the Anciens du Gesù company. In turn printer, editor, cartoonist, director of silent movies, journalist, accountant, and municipal officer, he made his name in Canada and the USA as an actor and amateur singer. He played Gaspard in Planquette's *Les Cloches de Corneville* with the *Société canadienne d'opérette.

In the early 1920s Gauthier was a pioneer in radio and in the recording of Quebec folk music, making 78s, for Victor and Columbia, of more than 100 songs and monologues, often with Elzéar Hamel. The list of his discs appears in *Roll Back the Years* and *Pionniers du disque folklorique*.

Gauthier's great achievement as a folklorist remains the successful concert presentations Veillées du bon vieux temps, which he founded in 1921 and produced until 1941 at the *Monument national. With great verve Gauthier performed French-Canadian folksongs which at the time were enjoying a surge of popularity.

Gauthier's *40 Chansons d'autrefois* (Thérien Frères 1930, 1932) and *40 Autres Chansons d'autrefois* (Archambault 1947) were combined in the collection *Dans tous les cantons* (Archambault 1963). In the preface to *40 Chansons d'autrefois* Gauthier was described by Gustave *Comte as a 'fanatical re-creator of our old customs' and an 'irresistible dispenser of good old-fashioned happiness.'

BIBLIOGRAPHY
Rousseau, Alfred. 'Conrad Gauthier,' *P-T*, 890, Sep 1945

2 **Paul-Marcel**. Chansonnier, songwriter, b Montreal 23 Jan 1910. Father Gauthier, concurrently with his ministry, continued his father's work, performing his songs in 1964 on four LPs entitled *Les Veillées du bon vieux temps* (Dom LPs 48001, 48002, 48010, and 48011). Under the humourous pseudonym Jean-Baptiste Purlenne, he composed 'wholesome' little songs ('nettes'), almost 50 of which were recorded on 45-rpm singles for RCA, including 'La Chanson des p'tits poissons' and 'La Chanson du petit voilier,' performed by Marc *Gélinas and Paolo Noël respectively.

BIBLIOGRAPHY
'A priest-singer keeps his musical memories alive,' *CanComp*, 58, Mar 1971 (PL)

GAUTHIER, (Joseph Pierre) **Claude**. Singer, songwriter, actor, b Lac-Saguay, Que, 31 Jan 1939. His career began in 1959 when he won first prize in 'Étoiles de demain' on radio station CKVL (Verdun). During the summer of 1960 he performed with Pierre Calvé and Marthe Choquette at La Pioukе, a boîte à chansons on Île Bonaventure, Que. He made his first LP that year; *Claude Gauthier* (Col FS-531) contained, among other songs, 'Le Soleil brillera demain,' 'Ton Nom,' and 'Le Grand Six Pieds.' The last song earned him the 1961 Grand prix du disque canadien awarded by Montreal radio station CKAC. He took part in the 1962 *Mariposa Folk Festival and in 1964 he sang at Carnegie Hall, New York, also making TV appearances in that city.

Gauthier subsequently toured Canada, and in 1967 he appeared with Monique *Leyrac, Les Jérolas, and Les Feux-Follets at the Olympia in Paris, where he had performed the previous year with Gilles *Vigneault, Pauline *Julien, and Clémence *Desrochers. In 1968 he performed at Man and His World, Montreal, and in 1969 he won a Festival du disque award for his LP *Cerfs volants*. Another tour took him to New Brunswick and into Quebec Cegeps in 1970. He made several appearances on CBC TV, notably in 'Zoom' (1969, 1970) and 'Témoignages' (1973).

Funded by the MACQ and the Ontario government Gauthier gave many shows in 1971 in Ontario French-language secondary schools. He represented Canada at Spa, Belgium, in the Festival international de la francophonie (1972) and recorded *Le Plus Beau Voyage* (Gamma GS 158) in France. A book of the same title containing the lyrics of 71 of his songs was published in Montreal in 1975.

Gauthier abandoned live shows for two years, 1973–4, to work in motion pictures. He had parts in three films during this period: *Les Ordres*, *Partis pour la gloire*, and *La Piasse*. For the last-mentioned he also composed the theme 'Les Beaux Instants,' which is included on the LP of that name (1975, Presqu'Île PE 7500). In 1966 he had written the music 'Geneviève' and held the leading role opposite Geneviève Bujold in *Entre la mer et l'eau douce*. He had acted in CBC TV's 'Septième Nord' in 1967.

In October 1975 Gauthier made his official return to singing, performing to a full house in the Outremont cinema in Montreal. After a show he gave at *Le Patriote, Johanne Mercier wrote that he still possessed 'the facility, the poetry that consists in singing of his attachments, his wife, his childhood, his land, his life' (*Montréal-Matin*, 21 Apr 1976). During 1977 he sang in Strasbourg at a festival of French song for teachers and made the LP *Ça prend des racines* (Presqu'Île PE 7506).

Gauthier has composed more than 100 songs, many of them performed by Renée *Claude, Louise *Forestier, Pauline Julien, Pierre *Lalonde, Monique Leyrac, and Michelle *Richard. Among his greatest hits have been 'Marie-Noël,' 'Sur la rue du Palais,' 'T'es pas une autre,' 'Parlez-moi de vous,' and 'La Tête en fleurs.' *Gamma released a selection, *Les Grands Succès de Claude Gauthier* (G2 1006) and some other LPs.

'Whether it's a question of funny songs, anti-war songs, ballads, rollicking songs of nationalism or catchy refrains about love, there is in all of Gauthier's written work and in his personal presentations as well – songs, films, theatre and cinema – this theme of friendship which seems to well up from somewhere deep inside him' (*Canadian Composer*, Jun 1969).

Gauthier founded Éditions du jour de l'An in 1974 to publish his songs. He is a member of CAPAC.

BIBLIOGRAPHY
'Claude Gauthier,' *CanComp*, 41, Jun 1969
'In this article, couched in the form of a conversation-plus-narration, Jacques Larue-Langlois writes about Claude Gauthier,' ibid, 48, Mar 1970
Vincent, Pierre. 'A Quebec star's newly changing life-style,' ibid, 70, May 1972
Jasmin, Hélène. 'A Quebec singer makes a comeback,' ibid, 110, Apr 1976
Chansonniers du Québec (HP)

Eva Gauthier

GAUTHIER, (Ida Joséphine Phoebe) **Eva**. Mezzo-soprano, teacher, b Ottawa 20 Sep 1885, d New York 26 Dec 1958. She studied piano and harmony before taking voice lessons with Frank Buels at the age of 13. She was soloist at St Patrick Church in Ottawa and made her professional debut in 1901 in the presence of the governor-general of Canada in Charles A.E. *Harriss' *Coronation Mass for Edward VII*. With the assistance of Sir Wilfrid and Lady Laurier she left for Europe in July 1902. In London she heard *Faust* with Jean de Reszke and Nellie Melba and immediately went to Paris with the intention of studying with Melba's teacher, Mathilde Marchesi, who, however, appears to have offended the young singer by warning her, 'People who have no money do not come here.' In any case, the lessons did not materialize. At the Paris Cons Gauthier studied singing with Auguste-Jean Dubulle and declamation with Sarah Bernhardt. Her studies were interrupted by a serious operation for nodules on the vocal cords.

After months of recuperation Gauthier gradually resumed her studies, this time with Jacques Bouhy, creator of the role of Escamillo in *Carmen*. She later said that Bouhy had been her only teacher. In 1905, in London, her compatriot Emma *Albani engaged her for a tour of the British Isles and for the 50 concerts of her farewell tour of Canada in 1906. Gauthier studied with William Shakespeare in London and with Carigiani and Oxilia in Italy. In Milan, Rina Giachetti, Caruso's sister-in-law, prepared her for her stage debut, at Pavia in 1909, in the role of Micaela in *Carmen*. The critics were favourable, but the four performances left her feeling that perhaps the stage was not for her. She gave a concert with Caruso in Ostend and went back to Paris.

In 1910 Covent Garden invited Gauthier to sing the role of Yniold in the English premiere of *Pelléas and Mélisande* and asked her to meet Debussy. After hearing her the composer recommended her for the role of Geneviève, but it had already been assigned. For technical reasons *Pelléas* was postponed, and she was cast instead as Mallika in *Lakmé* (18 Jun 1910) with Luisa Tetrazzini and John McCormack. However, she was replaced by another singer just at curtain time because Tetrazzini found her voice too powerful. In spite of being offered attractive compensating roles, she thereupon gave up the stage to devote herself to the more intimate art of recital and concert.

Gauthier undertook an extensive trip to the Orient, which fascinated her, and stayed for long periods in Java, where her husband, Frans Knoote (whom she married in 1911 and divorced in 1917), owned plantations. She studied the music of the Orient and gave recitals in Java, in Australia and New Zealand with Mischa Elman, and in Hawaii with Harold Bauer. New occidental music also continued to interest her, and when she made her New York recital debut in May 1915 she showed herself to be something other than a conventional recitalist. A large portion of her programs was dedicated to Ravel, Bartók, Hindemith, Schoenberg, and Stravinsky. She gave the North American premieres of Stravinsky's *Trois Poésies de la lyrique japonaise* in 1917 and of *Pribaoutki* the following year. Her programs showed a rare eclecticism, offering music of lesser-known early masters, songs which she brought from the Orient, and new music such as that by members of France's Les Six, whom she met in 1920. Established in New York, she presented (1 Nov 1923 at the Aeolian Hall) a recital now considered historical. In the second part she sang music of Jerome Kern, Irving Berlin, and George Gershwin with Gershwin at the piano. The press protested against the inclusion of light music in a concert, but it is said that the orchestra conductor Paul Whiteman heard the recital, was impressed by the talent of Gershwin, and commissioned him to write a work for piano and orchestra. The result was to be the famous *Rhapsody in Blue*. Each Gauthier recital contained premieres, and it is estimated that she gave no fewer than 700 during her career.

Gauthier sang in Ottawa in 1927 for the 60th anniversary of Canada's Confederation. In 1936 she gave three retrospective recitals at Gotham Hotel, including highlights from the programs of some 50 New York recitals. The same year she spoke the title role in the New York and Boston premieres of Stravinsky's *Persephone*. Later she devoted herself mainly to teaching (at the American Theater Wing, a professional training school), giving master classes, and serving on juries for important competitions. Honoured by the governments of Denmark and Canada she also, in 1949, received a citation from the Campion Society of San Francisco for her contribution as an interpreter and teacher 'to the study, performance and teaching of the best in song literature in all its phases.' After her death her library and her personal documents were acquired by the New York Public Library.

Eva Gauthier was the sister of Juliette *Gaultier (sic) de la Vérendrye, the violinist and folksinger. Eva Gauthier's voice, whose range extended from contralto to coloratura, was celebrated not only for its technical security but also for an expressive intensity which gave to each song a particular colour. During her farewell tour of Canada in 1906 Emma Albani declared, 'As an artistic legacy to my country, I leave you Eva Gauthier.'

It is thought that Gauthier recorded as early as 1915 for Columbia. In 1917, for Victor, she recorded several French Canadian folksongs, sometimes assisted by a vocal quartet. She also recorded songs of Duparc ('Chanson triste'), Debussy ('Romance' and 'Fantoches'), Février ('La Lettre') and Dessauer ('Le Retour des promis'). Her only incursions into opera are 'Viens avec nous, petit' from *La Vivandière* (Godard) 'Souvenirs du jeune âge' from *Le Pré aux clercs* (Hérold) 'Les Larmes' from *Werther*, and, with the tenor Orville Harrold, the duet 'Depuis longtemps' from *Louise*. In 1938 the label Musicraft undertook a retrospective of Gauthier's art with the assistance of the pianist of her later years, Celius Dougherty, but most of the recordings never were released. However, a few songs ('Seguidilla' by de Falla, 'Mein Bett ruft' by Bartók, and 'La Chevelure' by Debussy) electronically recorded, may be heard on *Eva Gauthier* (New York 1966, Town Hall TH 003), along with other titles, acoustically recorded before 1920. In the USA the International Record Club revived on a 78 disc (IRCC 127) 'Nina Boboh,' a Malayan and Javanese lullaby, and Dessauer's 'Le Retour des promis.' Gauthier's recordings for Victor and Columbia are listed in *Roll Back the Years*.

WRITINGS

'"Were my songs with wings provided,"' *Repertoire*, Nov 1951

'On the edge of opera,' *Opera News*, vol 19, 31 Jan 1955

BIBLIOGRAPHY

Greville, Ursula. 'The art of Eva Gauthier,' *The Sackbut*, vol 3, 1922–3

Robert, Lucette. 'Eva Gauthier,' *Revue Populaire*, Oct 1953

Beaudry, Yvonne. 'She sang with the Sultan's wives,' 'The Canadian who discovered Gershwin,' *Mayfair*, 2 instalments, Apr, May 1959

Miller, Philip L. Biographical note on record jacket (Town Hall TH 003)

Kolodin, Irving. 'The art of Eva Gauthier,' *Saturday Review*, 28 May 1966

Potvin, Gilles. 'Il y a 50 ans, elle fit découvrir Gershwin aux Américains,' *Perspectives*, vol 15, 27 Oct 1973 GP

GAUTIER, Pierre. Organist, teacher, composer, b Argenton-sur-Creuse, Berry, France, 29 Oct 1863, d Eastview (renamed Vanier), near Ottawa, 15 Dec 1940. He studied piano, organ, and harmony in his native city, then worked under Héry in Paris at the Institut national des jeunes aveugles while also performing as an organist. In 1883 he settled in Le Mans where he became organist at Notre-Dame-de-la-Couture Church and taught piano and harmony. He moved to Ottawa in 1920, succeeding Amédée *Tremblay as the organist, 1920–2, at Notre-Dame Basilica. He later performed the same duties at St Charles' Church while continuing to teach music. Gautier harmonized and/or arranged (mostly for choir) more than 125 folksongs of French and Canadian origin, and, to mark Ottawa's centenary in 1927, songs from the repertoire of Charles *Marchand for the Bytown Troubadours. The following year, in the E.W. Beatty Competition organized as part of the second *CPR Festival in Quebec City, he was awarded a special prize of $100 for his arrangement of four songs. He also composed religious works, of which some were performed successfully at international competitions (1912, 1922) set up by the Procure générale de musique religieuse in Paris. He wrote several masses, including a Christmas mass often performed in French-Canadian churches, and in 1930 set to music 'La Patrie,' a poem by Georges Boileau. He also contributed articles to several French journals of religious music.

BIBLIOGRAPHY

'Pierre Gautier,' *La Lyre*, vol 5, Jun–Jul 1927

'Prominent French composer passes in Pierre Gautier,' Ottawa *Citizen*, 16 Dec 1940

'Passing of Pierre Gautier,' *Canadian Music*, vol 1, Mar 1941 (DM)

GAY, Frank (François). String instrument builder, guitarist, lutenist, composer, b Marcelin, north of Saskatoon, of French parents, 23 Apr 1920. His background as a guitarist – he studied in the late 1930s at the New York School of Music – and his qualifications as a watch maker preceded his interest in guitar building. In Toronto he continued to study guitar with Norman Chapman and was his partner in a duo. He also apprenticed in guitar building for two years at R.S. *Williams & Co. In 1953 he established a studio in Edmonton. His first guitars, steel-string acoustics, were popular with country musicians. The US stars Johnny Cash, Don Gibson, Hank *Snow, and others have owned Gay guitars. Three – those owned by Johnny Horton, Webb Pierce, and Faron Young – have been placed in the Country Music Hall of Fame, Nashville. Gay began building classical guitars in the 1960s, using as models a Ramirez flamenco guitar (a gift from Carlos Montoya) and an Esteco classical guitar. He has made guitars for Montoya and Alirio Diaz. He has built folk guitars, the smaller 10-string renaissance guitar, lutes, mandolins, and banjos. An innovative craftsman, he has experimented with construction materials and design and is noted for the fine quality of his inlay work.

Himself a versatile performer, fluent in classical, flamenco, jazz, country, and folk styles, Gay appeared 1958–63 on his own CKUA radio show, was heard often as accompanist and soloist on the CBC, participated in pop music recordings, and performed in concert and in coffee houses. He was the founder in 1959 of a classical guitar society, possibly the first in western Canada, which presented in recital Diaz and Montoya, among others.

BIBLIOGRAPHY
Davies, Mansel. 'Alberta luthier: Frank Gay,' *Canada Folk Bulletin*, vol 1, Mar–Apr 1978 (MM)

GAYFER, James (McDonald). Bandmaster, organist-choirmaster, composer, adjudicator, b Toronto 26 Mar 1916; B MUS (Toronto) 1941, ARCM 1946, LRAM 1947, D MUS (Toronto) 1950. His teachers included Reginald *Godden (piano), Maitland *Farmer (organ), and, at the U of Toronto, Ettore *Mazzoleni (orchestration), Arthur H. Middleton, and S. Drummond Wolff. He also studied 1945–7 at the RMSM (Kneller Hall). He joined the Canadian army in 1940 and served successively as bandsman (clarinet, Royal Canadian Signals Corps, Europe 1943–5), command bandmaster and command inspector of bands (Oakville, Ont, 1947–51), director of music (Canadian Guards Band, Camp Borden, Ont; Korea and Japan; and Camp Petawawa, Ont, 1954–61), and training officer (*Canadian Forces School of Music, Esquimault, BC, 1961–8). During his military career he was organist-choirmaster in various Ontario centres, associate conductor and conductor 1949–54 of the Harmony SO, Toronto, conductor 1962–6 for opera and operetta productions (*Gianni Schicchi, The Mikado, H.M.S. Pinafore*, and others) in Victoria, BC, and guest conductor in 1962, 1963, and 1964 and associate conductor 1963–4 of the *Victoria SO.

After his retirement from the Canadian army Gayfer taught music 1966–72 at Southwood Secondary School in Galt (Cambridge), Ont (where he also was founder, and conductor 1967–70, of the Galt Community Choir and Orchestra) and 1972–4 at *Dalhousie U. He has adjudicated throughout Canada. Gayfer's compositions (listed in part in *Contemporary Canadian Composers*) include two symphonies (1947, 1949); several works for string orchestra; a string quartet (winner of a CPRS award in 1944); *Six Translations from the Chinese* for tenor and small orchestra (winner of a CAPAC award in 1947); a *Suite* for woodwind quintet (Boosey & Hawkes 1950); *Saxophone Concertante* for five saxophones (1972, commissioned by Paul *Brodie); many works for band, some published by Waterloo or Boosey & Hawkes, and including *The Wells of Marah* commissioned by the *Barrie Central Collegiate Band; and many piano pieces (1936–75), songs, hymns, and choral works, all unpublished. Gayfer is a member of CAPAC and an associate of the *CMCentre.

BIBLIOGRAPHY
Meredith, Joan. 'James Gayfer: bandmaster in the classroom,' *CanComp*, 58, Mar 1971 MM

GAYLORD, Monica (m Daellenbach). Pianist, harpsichordist, b New York, of Jamaican parents, 6 Feb 1948; B MUS (ESM, Rochester) 1968, M MUS (ESM) 1969. A pupil of Jane Carlson 1959–63 at the Juilliard School, she made her Town Hall (New York) debut in 1964 and continued her studies 1964–70 at the ESM, Rochester, with Cécile Genhart. In 1970 she moved to Canada, where she worked as an orchestral pianist 1972–3 for the *TS and later for the *NACO and appeared with *NMC in Toronto and on its 1977 European tour. As soloist she has played the Schumann *Concerto* with the *Hamilton Philharmonic 21 Apr 1973 and the TS 13 Jul 1973 and other works (Rachmaninoff's *Concerto No. 2*, Gershwin's *Rhapsody in Blue*, Beethoven's *Concerto No. 4*, etc) with various Ontario community orchestras. She has appeared on CBC TV (eg, 'Music to See' 1974) and CBC radio, and has given many recitals for adult audiences and school children. Some of her programs have been devoted to music by black composers (*Dett, Ellington, Joplin, and others) or Canadian women composers (*Archer, *Coulthard, *Eckhardt-Gramatté, *Pentland, *Saint-Marcoux, and *Southam). In 1977 she premiered William *McCauley's *Piano Concerto No. 1* with the North York SO and, in a CBC public taping for later broadcast, John *Weinzweig's song cycle *Private Collection* with Mary Lou *Fallis. She also has accompanied Melvin *Berman, Walter *Prystawski, David *Zafer, and others. Besides a 'direct-to-disc' LP, *Monica Gaylord Plays Ben McPeek* (1975, Boot BMC 3007), she has recorded with Berman, Christopher *Weait, and (as harpsichordist) the Toronto Baroque Ensemble. MM

GEE, Fred M. (Melsom Edward). Impresario, organist, pianist, b Cardiff 21 Jul 1882, d Winnipeg 8 Jun 1947. His early musical studies were in his native Wales. In 1902 he emigrated to Canada, settling in Winnipeg, where he established himself as organist, accompanist, and teacher. He joined the staff of the Winnipeg College of Music in 1903. That same year he became organist-choirmaster at Westminster United Church, entering the first of a succession of such positions (at Christ Church, All Saints Anglican, Augustine United, St Luke's Anglican) which, with his teaching, were to provide his livelihood until the mid-1920s. He also served as organist for the Winnipeg Oratorio Society throughout its existence, 1908–28. In 1911, with Joseph Tees, he undertook to present a concert by the violinist Mischa Elman. The venture was successful, and Gee continued to present artists, but only occasionally until 1926, when a recital by Amelita Galli-Curci drew an audience of 7200 and persuaded him to give up teaching and become a full-time impresario.

Gee's first Celebrity Concert Series, in 1927, offered seven concerts at Central Congregational Church; his second, in 1928, nine. The 1930 series moved to the Playhouse, and the 1932 series to the *Winnipeg Auditorium, where the opening concert, by the baritone Lawrence Tibbett, drew 4000. Two years later the Winnipeg series was repeated in Calgary, Edmonton, Saskatoon, and Regina. In 1938 his Winnipeg season, with a subscription of 3500, was described as the largest concert series on the North American continent. By 1944, 391 concerts had been given in Winnipeg, Brandon, Regina, Saskatoon, Calgary, and Edmonton. By the time of Gee's death in 1947, a 12-concert season was offered in Winnipeg and a second company – Celebrity Concerts Canada, Ltd – had been founded under the direction of his eldest son, A. (Arthur) K. Gee, to present concerts in Ontario, Manitoba, Saskatchewan, and Alberta cities from Port Arthur to Edmonton. In 1950 the younger Gee, who had succeeded to full control of the Gee concert enterprises, formed with Gordon *Hilker the Western Concert Agency and expanded his circuit to include many towns in northern areas of Alberta, Saskatchewan, and Manitoba.

Fred M. Gee

For some 10 years the new enterprise expanded, but the founder's absence was felt sorely. Fred M. Gee had known personally many of the artists who performed for him, and there always was the feeling, as with the *Hambourgs in Toronto, that he was promoting music and his colleagues in music. Four months before his death, at the 106th performance given in Winnipeg under his management by the Minneapolis SO, Gee himself was the soloist in the *Piano Concerto No. 2* of Edward MacDowell, with Dimitri Mitropoulos conducting.

In Gee's 36 years as an impresario some hundreds of performers appeared in Canadian cities under his aegis. Among these were the sopranos Pierrette *Alarie, Rose Bampton, Eileen Farrell, Kirsten Flagstad, Amelita Galli-Curci, Lotte Lehmann, Lily Pons, Elisabeth Rethberg, Bidu Sayao, Maggie Teyte, and Helen Traubel; the contraltos Marian Anderson, Sophie Braslau, Ernestine Schumann-Heink, Ebe Stignani, and Gladys Swarthout; the tenors Jussi Bjoerling, Richard Crooks, Roland Hayes, Edward *Johnson, Giovanni Martinelli, Lauritz Melchior, John McCormack, Jan Peerce, Tito Schipa, and Richard Tauber; the baritones and basses Feodor Chaliapin, Nelson Eddy, John *Goss, Alexander Kipnis, Ezio Pinza, Paul Robeson, Martial Singher, John Charles Thomas, and Lawrence Tibbett (whom Gee accompanied at short notice in 1933); the pianists Claudio Arrau, Gina Bachauer, Simon Barere, Robert Casadesus, Ignaz Friedman, Ossip Gabrilowitsch, Percy Grainger, Josef Hofmann, Vladimir Horowitz, Josef Lhévinne, Benno Moiseiwitsch, Guiomar Novaes, Ross *Pratt, Sergei Rachmaninoff, Artur Rubinstein, Harold Samuel, Reginald *Stewart, Rosalyn Tureck, and Alexander Uninsky; the organists Joseph Bonnet and Marcel Dupré; the violinists Jascha Heifetz, Fritz Kreisler, Yehudi Menuhin, Nathan Milstein, Kathleen *Parlow, Ruggiero Ricci, Albert Spalding, Isaac Stern, Jacques Thibaud, and Efrem Zimbalist; the violist William Primrose; the cellists Gaspar Cassado, Raya Garbousova, Boris Hambourg, and Gregor Piatigorsky; the *Hart House String Quartet; and the Minneapolis SO under the successive regimes of Mitropoulos, Dorati, and Skrowaczewski.

This by no means exhaustive list could not be matched by the artists presented after Fred M. Gee's death. Steep increases in fees for major artists led inevitably to an increasing admixture of minor ones and a tendency to accept 'package deals' from the New York concert agencies; and improvements in the sound of recorded music left the public critical of live performances in acoustically poor halls. These trends depressed ticket sales, and in 1968 the Celebrity Concert Series, as such, ceased. Celebrity Concerts Canada (1972) Ltd carried on only as a box office for a miscellany of entertainments and as head office for A.K. Gee's World Adventure Tours. A.K. Gee died in 1975, and his wife, Margaret W., succeeded him as president.

BIBLIOGRAPHY
Lepkin, Ben. 'Fred Gee pioneered noted artists' concerts,' *Winnipeg Free Press Magazine Section*, 14 May 1938
Maley, S. Roy. 'Death of Fred M. Gee great loss to the community,' Winnipeg *Tribune*, 15 Jun 1947 (CC,KW)

GEEN, Reginald (Gordon). Organist-choirmaster, teacher, examiner, adjudicator, b Belleville, Ont, 18 Mar 1889, d Oshawa, Ont, 19 Jan 1973; LTCM, hon FRCCO 1958. After training with C.A.R. Wilkinson in Toronto, he studied in Chicago, London, and (reputedly with Vladimir de Pachmann) Paris. While organist-choirmaster 1907–26 at St George's Anglican Church, Owen Sound, Ont, he founded and conducted the Owen Sound Patriotic Chorus and Philharmonic Society. He also in 1914 assisted J.L. Yule in founding the Owen Sound Registered Music Teachers' Assn, the first such organization in Ontario. In 1920 Geen began to adjudicate at festivals and examine for the *TCM, activities he continued for more than 45 years. He moved in 1926 to Guelph, Ont, where at St George's Anglican Church he founded the 100-voice Guelph Vogt Choir (which appeared at the first *Guelph Spring Festival in 1968). He moved to Oshawa in 1931 and was organist-choirmaster until 1972 at Simcoe St United Church. From the mid-1930s until 1958 he also conducted the General Motors Choir of Oshawa (later the Motor City Choir). He was president 1946–8 and 1953–4 of the *ORMTA and a founder (and president 1961–8) of the *Canadian Music Festival Adjudicators' Assn; he also served 1951–3 as president of the CCO and was the *RCCO representative 1955–70 on the *CMCouncil. MG

GEIGER-TOREL, Herman (b Geiger, Hermann). Opera director and administrator, teacher, b Frankfurt-am-Main, 13 Jul 1907, d Toronto, 6 Oct 1976; hon LLD (Prince of Wales, PEI) 1967. His mother was the pianist and composer Rosy Geiger-Kullmann (1886–1964). After private lessons in Frankfurt he entered the Hoch Cons to study opera directing with Lothar Wallerstein. Though concurrently at Goethe U, he soon gave up academic studies in favour of a career in the theatre.

Geiger became an instructor at the conservatory and served 1928–30 as assistant stage director of the Frankfurt Opera and in 1930 as Wallerstein's assistant at the Salzburg Festival. Posts as stage director followed in Aussig, Czechoslovakia, 1930–1, Bremerhaven, Germany, 1931–2, and Troppau, Czechoslovakia, 1934–7. In 1934, when a contract with a German opera house was cancelled because he was Jewish, Geiger began a long association with Latin America by staging six operas (including *La Traviata* and *Manon Lescaut* with Claudia Muzio) for Teatro Colón, Buenos Aires. During a season (1937–8) with the Société du Cinéma du Panthéon in Paris he added Torel to his

Herman Geiger-Torel

surname. Geiger-Torel returned in 1938 to Teatro Colon to direct a production of *Siegfried* with the tenor Max Lorenz and the baritone Herbert Janssen, conducted by Erich Kleiber, and also that year anglicized his given name. He remained in Buenos Aires as stage director and actor with the Free German Theatre until he moved in 1943 to Montevideo, Uruguay, as chief stage director for opera at the SODRE (the national opera). In 1945 he became chief stage director of the Teatro Municipal, Rio de Janeiro. Though he settled in Canada in 1948, he continued to visit Latin America until 1954, directing opera in Cuba, Guatemala, El Salvador, Costa Rica, Venezuela, and Uruguay.

In 1947 Geiger-Torel was invited by Nicholas *Goldschmidt (a colleague in Troppau now living in Toronto) to visit the recently established *Royal Cons Opera School as a guest teacher. He was first in Toronto from January to April 1948, then returned in October as stage director for the school. Though never head of the school, he was a major influence in its development. In 1949 he conceived 'Opera Backstage,' a touring party (singers Mary *Morrison, Patricia Snell, Joanne Ivey, Ernest *Adams, and Andrew *MacMillan; pianist-conductor George *Crum; promoter-manager Walter *Homburger) which took operatic excerpts to western Canada, predating the COC touring company by several years. When in 1950 the Opera Festival Assn of Toronto began as a professional outgrowth of the school he became principal stage director. In 1956 he became artistic director and in 1959 general director, prior to the 1960 official renaming of the company as the Canadian Opera Assn (known popularly, however, after 1958 and still after 1960, as the *Canadian Opera Company.) Geiger-Torel retained the general directorship until 1976 but also preserved his ties with the opera school at the RCMT and later at the U of Toronto.

Geiger-Torel combined musicality with a thorough understanding of the stage, whether dealing with action or with technology. Though an adherent, for practical purposes, of the traditional repertoire, he produced with the COC the Canadian operas *Deirdre*, **Louis Riel*, *The Luck of Ginger Coffey*, and **Heloise and Abelard*. In his years with the COC he staged more than 30 operas, many in several productions, and 1953–9 he directed 13 operas for CBC TV. He was artistic adviser 1948–56 for the *CBC Opera Company (radio). Outside Toronto he staged productions for the *Montreal Festivals, *Théâtre lyrique de Nouvelle-France, the *Guelph Spring Festival, the *Manitoba Opera (Winnipeg), the *Southern Alberta Opera (Calgary), the *Edmonton Opera, the *Vancouver International Festival, and the *Vancouver Opera. In the USA he directed at the New York City Opera and in Portland, Ore, and Cincinnati. As teacher, director, and administrator he was profoundly influential in Canada, where few associated with opera did not experience at some time his wit, temper, kindness, and fierce capacity for work. He was made an Officer of the *Order of Canada in 1969 and received the National Award in Music from the *U of Alberta in 1970. 'Wagner and Valedictory,' a complete taped performance of Geiger-Torel's last COC production of *Die Walküre*, with spoken tributes to Geiger-Torel during the intermission, was broadcast in his memory by the CBC 14 Nov 1976.

BIBLIOGRAPHY
'Opera's happy rebel,' *Maclean's*, 11 Oct 1958
Mercer, Ruby. 'A visit with Herman Geiger-Torel,' *OpCan*, Sep 1967
'I still think opera's a bit funny, but I love it,' *Weekend*, 15 Dec 1973
Ashley, Audrey M. 'Who is the man behind all those operas?' *Ottawa Citizen*, 27 Sep 1975
Peglar, Kenneth. 'Herman Geiger-Torel,' *Remembered Moments of the Canadian Opera Company 1950–1975* (Toronto 1976)
Littler, William. 'Geiger-Torel: he could always get the show on,' *Toronto Star*, 9 Oct 1976
COC Archives

GÉLINAS. Montreal singers: 1 / Gérard and 2 / Marc, son of Gérard.

1 (Joseph Albert Cléophas) **Gérard**. Bass, b Montreal 11 Apr 1907, d there 2 Mar 1965. He studied 1928–30 with Victor *Brault, took supporting roles with the *Société canadienne d'opérette and the *Variétés lyriques, and on occasion sang in the quartets of Charles *Marchand and the Imperial Grenadiers. In 1937 he placed second among 300 competitors in the *'Metropolitan Opera Auditions of the Air.' That year he was a soloist in a performance of Verdi's *Requiem* presented on CBC radio on the death of Marconi and rebroadcast in Italy.

Gélinas went to New York on a grant from the Quebec government and studied 1938–40 with Rose Bampton at the Juilliard School. At the invitation of the composer and organist Pietro Yon he became a soloist at St Patrick's Cathedral. He toured New England and Louisiana with a troupe from the Metropolitan Opera, and though he joined an entertainment unit of the Canadian armed forces in 1942 he continued to perform in opera on occasion, notably in 1943 when he sang Lovitzky in a Montreal performance of *Boris Godunov* with members of the Metropolitan. During a US tour by another (unidentified) troupe he sang the title role in that opera. Gélinas later devoted himself to horticulture but continued to sing as a soloist at the churches of St-Sacrement in Montreal and Ste-Madeleine d'Outrement, and in 1949 he appeared as Méphistophélès in *Faust* with the *Opéra national du Québec.

2 (Joseph Edouard Yves André) **Marc**. Songwriter, singer, actor, b Montreal 28 Nov 1937. He began writing songs at 14 but at first sang those of Francis Lemarque and Joseph Kosma. He made his first single, 'Le Bossu,' a few years later for RCA Victor. He studied singing 1954–5 at the *CMM with Roger *Filiatrault and Martial Singher. On CBC TV 1955–8 he performed the role of a student chansonnier accompanying himself on the guitar in the series 'Beau temps, mauvais temps'; this allowed him to introduce his songs 'Aide-toi et le ciel t'aidera,' 'Boucles blondes,' 'Le Bossu,' 'La Route,' and 'Je ne veux pas.' After acting in several TV programs, he began performing in boîtes à chansons. He also was the host of the CBC TV se-

ries 'En quête de chansons' and 'Sur deux notes' in 1961.

After a virtual absence of four years from the entertainment world, Marc Gélinas returned in 1965 with the songs 'Moïra' and 'De vie à éternité,' which earned him the Festival du disque award for best chansonnier. He founded the firm Editions Marco to publish his own songs and also recorded the young singers Danka, Daniel Malfara, and Normand Séguin. In 1966 Gélinas was awarded the Prix Léo-Le Sieur for the best Canadian pop song ('Tu te souviendras de moi') and the Festival du disque prize for best male singer. He won prizes for songs written to mark *Expo 67: 'La Ronde,' 'Rendez-vous à Montréal,' and 'Lorsque le rideau tombe.'

In 1969 Gélinas was selected by the CBC to perform at the Festival international de la chanson d'expression française ('Chansons sur mesure') in Brussels. The following year, with 'Un Amour,' he won the silver key award in the CBC national competition 'La Clé de la chanson'; he also received a Méritas trophy at the Gala des artistes. He was host of the program 'Le Rideau s'ouvre' on CFTM TV 1970–1 and opened a school for singers which continued until 1974. His TV involvement included being a jury member of CBC auditions and for the CFTM TV program 'Découvertes,' devoted to new singing talent, and writing the music for 'Du feu s'il vous plaît,' 'Bye bye '73,' and 'Rosa' for CBC. He also wrote several theme songs, including those for the Montreal Expos baseball team, the Quebec Games, and the Festival de St-Tite. He was a consultant for the recording and variety section of the UDA 1975–6.

From sadness to humour, tenderness to passion, Marc Gélinas has explored the varieties of love, and to express it he has used syncopated rhythms as readily as the more straightforward means of the sentimental ballad. His songs have been performed by Daniel Guérard, Michel *Louvain, and Ginette *Ravel. Lucien *Hétu recorded organ arrangements of several Gélinas hits. Among Gélinas's songs 'Le Bateau de minuit,' 'Tu te souviendras de moi,' 'T'en vas pas,' and 'Les Nouveaux Amants' stand out in particular for the quality of the lyrics and the simplicity of the music. He is a member of CAPAC.

DISCOGRAPHY

Marc Gélinas chante pour toi. Ca 1957. RCA LCP-1015
Une Soirée au Cochon borgne. 1960. Libération (no number)
Ça c'est du Gélinas. 1965. Jupiter JDY 7003
Trois Fois bravo Marc Gélinas. 1966. Jupiter JDY 7006
Lorsque le rideau tombe. 1967. Jupiter JDY 7013
J'ai du bon feu. 1969. Jupiter JPL 11018
Mes Premières Chansons. 1969? RCA Victor gala CGPS 300
Les Grands Succès de Marc Gélinas. (1973). Col FS 90013

BIBLIOGRAPHY

'Marc Gélinas: he has devoted one-third of his 30 years to his profession,' *MSc*, 238, Nov–Dec 1967
Basil, Lydia. 'My friend Marc Gélinas,' *CanComp*, 53, Oct 1970
'Marc Gélinas: un chansonnier qui ne l'était pas,' *Chansons populaires*, vol 1, Feb 1971 (BLH, ST)

GELLMAN, Steven. Composer, pianist, b Toronto 16 Sep 1947. He studied composition with Samuel *Dolin at the *RCMT and performed his own piano concerto with the *CBC SO for the opening ceremonies of the *U of Toronto's Edward Johnson Building in 1964. That same year he received a BMI Award for Student Composers. He studied 1965–8 with Berio, Persichetti, and Sessions at the Juilliard School; summers 1965 and 1966 with Milhaud at Aspen, Col, where he won first prize in composition in 1966; and 1974–6 with Messiaen in Paris, where he revised his orchestral work *Chori* and composed another – *Animus-Anima* – which was performed 28 Apr 1976 at Salle Gaveau. He has composed on commissions from the Stratford Music Festival (*Stratford Festival) (*Mythos II*, 1968, RCI-301), from the CBC (*Symphony in Two Movements*, 1971, Ric 1972; *Symphony II*, 1972; and *Chori*, 1974), from the *Hamilton Philharmonic Orchestra (*Odyssey*, 1971, Ric 1973), from the *NACO (*Overture for Ottawa*, 1972), and from the Besançon Festival (*Deux Tapisseries*, 1978, in honour of Messiaen's 70th birthday). He also has written *Encore: Mythos I Revisited* (1972, for orchestra), *Quartets: Poems of G.M. Hopkins* (1966–7), five piano works (1962–74), and *Soliloquy* (1966, for solo cello). His works are listed in *Contemporary Canadian Composers*.

Generally loosely constructed, Gellman's music is particularly effective in describing mood. In *Symphony in Two Movements* recorded in 1975 by the Hamilton Philharmonic Virtuosi (CBC SM-295), the first movement is dark and brooding, its tensions derived from the reiteration of two- and three-note figures. The second movement, a scherzo, is sparse, with fragmentary ideas and transitory moods. In *Odyssey*, he teams a rock group and a symphony orchestra in a concerto-like work which attempts a synthesis of material and performance style. In 1976 he began teaching at the *U of Ottawa. He is an affiliate of PRO Canada and an associate of the *CMCentre.

BIBLIOGRAPHY

BMI Canada Ltd. 'Steven Gellman,' pamphlet, 1976 CF

'Les Gens de mon pays.' Song, written by Gilles *Vigneault in 1965. Under a banner of friendship, fidelity, and a spirit of shared adventure, it portrays the honesty, wisdom, and humour of the Quebec people. The melody, almost a recitative, moves along swiftly and presents simple contours, building up gradually to the high point of the text: 'I hear you pass like the river at ice-break, I hear you speak of freedom for tomorrow.'

The song has been recorded by its author (*Gilles Vigneault à la Comédie-Canadienne, Récital à la Comédie-Canadienne, Musicorama*, and *Les Gens de mon pays*), the Cabestans, the *Choeur V'la l'bon vent, Renée *Claude (Sel SSP-24146), Pauline *Julien (Gamma G2 11001 and Zodiaque ZOX 6014), and Louise Poulin. In France it has been performed by Catherine Sauvage, among others.

The text is printed in Lucien Rioux's *Gilles Vigneault* (Paris 1969) and Claude Pruhlière's *Québec ou Presqu'-Amérique* (Paris 1974). The song is published by the Éditions du Vent qui vire. It should not be confused with *'Gens du pays,' also by Vigneault.

Les Gens de mon pays is also the title of a collection of Vigneault's poems, short stories, and songs published in Quebec in 1967. (BR)

'Gens du pays.' Song written by Gilles *Vigneault for the 1975 *St-Jean-Baptiste celebrations on Mount Royal, Montreal. Its popularity has made it almost a national anthem in Quebec, where it is sung frequently by crowds at rallies or on festive occasions. The refrain, in triple time, has a waltz tempo and invites all 'countrymen' to 'let themselves speak of love.' It is used widely at birthdays, the opening word of the phrase 'countrymen, it's your turn' replaced by the name of the person whose birthday it is.

Vigneault has performed the song for the LPs *1 fois 5* (2-Kébec-Disc KD 923-924) and *Gilles Vigneault à Bobino* (Le Nordet GVN-1008-1009). 'Gens du pays' is published by Éditions du Vent qui vire. It should not be confused with *'Les Gens de mon pays,' also by Vigneault. ST

GEOGHEGAN, Frederick (Vladimir Lawrence). Organist, teacher, b Lichfield, England, 23 Jul 1921, naturalized Canadian 1960. Piano studies were begun with his mother and continued at 14 with Wilkinson Urqhart and Tobias Matthay in London. He made his recital debut at 18. He also studied organ with Stanley Curtis and became assistant organist at St Paul's Church, Portman Square, London. Further studies with Sir William McKie at the RAM led to a teaching position there and preceded occasional recitals at Westminster Abbey and in continental Europe. He moved in 1953 to Toronto, where he held positions in various churches until 1975 and taught privately. His pupils included Giles *Bryant, Douglas *Haas, and Derek *Holman. He toured extensively in North America, played on CBC radio ('Distinguished Artists' and 'Organists in Recital'), premiered Charles *Camilleri's *Battalja* in 1965 and Barrie *Cabena's *Homage* in 1967, and gave the first US performance of *Willan's *Passacaglia and Fugue No. 2* in 1959. His CJRT-FM (Toronto) program 'Speaking of Organists,' syndicated in the USA, won a Major Armstrong Award for excellence in 1973. In 1975 Geoghegan joined the faculty at the *U of British Columbia and became organist at St Helen's Anglican Church in Vancouver.

DISCOGRAPHY

Willan *Chorale Prelude No. 3* – Elgar – Schumann – Bach – Vierne – Franck. Ca 1971. Organarts STK 1045
Willan *Chorale Preludes No. 3 and 4; Fantasia; Passacaglia and Fugue No. 2* – Messiaen – Dupré. 1972. CBC SM-202 (BNSG)

GEORGE, Graham. Composer, teacher, theorist, organist-choirmaster, conductor, b Norwich, England, 11 Apr 1912; ARCO 1935, FCCO 1936, B MUS (Toronto) 1936, D MUS (Toronto) 1939. After moving to Canada in 1928 he studied composition in Montreal with Alfred *Whitehead and 1952–3 at Yale U with Paul Hindemith. He studied conducting in 1956 with Willem van Otterloo in Holland. An organist-choirmaster and teacher in Montreal 1932–7 and in Sherbrooke, Que, 1937–41, he moved in 1946 to Kingston, Ont, as resident musician and teacher at *Queen's U. He held church positions in Kingston 1946–61 and 1968–75 and in nearby Gananoque 1961–6, and continued to teach at Queen's U, where he was acting head of the music department from its inception in 1968 until 1971. George founded the *Kingston Choral Society in 1953 and the New SO of Kingston (renamed *Kingston SO in 1963) the next year and conducted both until 1957. He won his first composition award, the Prix Jean-*Lallemand, in 1938 for *Variations on an Original Theme* (1937) and received CPRS awards in 1943 and 1947 for *Variations for Strings* (1942) and the ballet *Jabberwocky* (1947). He has composed extensively for choir, mainly in the 20th-century English idiom, and has completed many concert works on commission, three ballets, and three operas, including **Evangeline* (1948). He has been president of the *CFMS 1965–8 and the *RCCO 1972–4, and was elected secretary-general of the International Folk Music Council in 1969. George has received a research award (1970–3) from Queen's U and an exchange grant (1972) from the *Canada Council and the Ministère des Affaires Culturelles of France. His book *Tonality and Musical Structure* takes a new look at the concept of form as an outcome of key relationships. George is an affiliate of PRO Canada and an associate of the *CMCentre.

SELECTED COMPOSITIONS

DRAMATIC WORKS

Jabberwocky, ballet. 1947 (Kingston 1947). Ms
Peter Pan (1948) and *The King, the Pigeon and the Hawk* (1949), ballets. Both ms

Way Out, opera (George). 1960 (Kingston 1960). Ms
King Theodore, opera (George). 1975. CMCentre
A King for Corsica, opera (George). 1980. Ms
Also incidental music for plays, 5 stock pieces for NFB, and incidental music for radio drama *Love Is the Crooked Thing* (1955). All ms
See also *Evangeline*.

ORCHESTRA AND BAND

Dorian Fugue. 1942 (rev 1957). Str. CMCentre
A Hymn for Christmas Day (J. Taylor). 1954 (Wpg 1969). SATB, orch. CMCentre
Experiences of a Self-made Theme. 1956 (Wpg 1970). CMCentre
Songs of the Salish. 1961 (Quebec 1961). CMCentre
Concerto for Flute and Strings. 1963 (Montreal 1963). CMCentre
Red River of the North (T. Saunders). 1970. SATB, orch. CMCentre
Plus others
3 works for band. 1958–60

CHAMBER

String Trio. 1951 (London 1953). CMCentre
4 *String Quartets* (1936–51). Ms
Quintet. 1967 (Kingston 1967). Pf quin. CMCentre
Quartet for Saxophones. 1972. CMCentre
Figures in a Landscape (Helwig). 1973 (Kingston 1973). Sop, str quar. CMCentre
Sonata. 1974. Fl, cl, pf. CMCentre
Fuguing Music for String Quartet. 1976. CMCentre

ORGAN

Publ by Gray: *Two Preludes on 'The King's Majesty,' Elegy, Passacaglia on 'Lobe den Herren'*
Also *Three Fugues* (Ber 1970), *Suite on 'Grace Church, Gananoque'* (Abingdon 1972), *Wedding Music: Prelude and Fugue* (Gray 1974)
Also 5 works for pf in ms

CHOIR

Publ by Gray: 'Lord of All Power and Might'; 'Benedictus es, Domine'; 'Ride On, Ride On in Majesty'; 'New Prince, New Pomp'; 'Now Glad of Heart'; 'In God's Command'
Publ by others: 'Unto Us a Son is Given' (OUP); *Office of Holy Communion* (BMIC); *Junior Choir Anthems for the Church Year* (Aug); 'Stir Up, We Beseech Thee' (Harris); 'Fight the Good Fight' (Abingdon)
Also several arr of sacred and trad melodies for SATB, some 17 anthems in ms, 3 communion services, 11 hymn tunes, and 8 part-songs
8 works for v, pf (1935–78)

WRITINGS

'Canada's music – 1955: an attempt to assess the quality of contemporary Canadian composition,' *Culture*, vol 16, Mar 1955
'Three Canadian concert halls,' *CMJ*, vol 4, Winter 1960
'Vernon Barford,' *CMJ*, vol 5, Winter 1961
'Music where the wind blows free,' *CMJ*, vol 6, Spring 1962
'Songs of the Salish Indians of British Columbia,' *J of the International Folk Music Council*, vol 14, 1962
'Hymn tunes reconsidered,' *J of Church Music*, vol 5, Dec 1962, Jan 1963
'Towards a definition of romanticism in music,' *Queen's Q*, vol 72, Summer 1965
'Folk music in opera,' *OpCan*, Sep 1965
'The structure of dramatic music 1607–1909,' *MQ*, vol 52, Oct 1966
'"Work-of-artness" of a work of art,' *Queen's Q*, vol 74, Spring 1967
'Hymn tunes – the old vexed question,' *J of Church Music*, vol 12, Oct–Nov 1970
Tonality and Musical Structure (London 1970)
'Tonality and the narrative in "Tristan",' *CAUSM J*, vol 4, Fall 1974
Twelve-note Tonal Counterpoint (Oakville 1976)
Articles and reviews for *SatN*, *CMJ*, AGO / RCCO *Music*

BIBLIOGRAPHY

Smith, Leo. 'Winner of 1943 award,' *CRMA*, vol 3, Jun–Jul 1944
Hepner, Lee. 'Graham George: *Tonality and Musical Structure*,' *CMB*, 3, Autumn–Winter 1971
Contemporary Canadian Composers (CF)

George's Spaghetti House. Restaurant and longest-running jazz club in Canada. Located in downtown Toronto, it was opened by Doug Cole in the summer of 1956, at first offering jazz on weekends 'after hours,' then, beginning 5 Sep 1960, six evenings a week. Except for a period in the mid-1960s when US musicians appeared, usually accompanied by the organist Art Ayre's trio, the restaurant always has presented established Toronto jazz and studio players. The bands of Moe *Koffman, the club's booking agent, have performed there regularly. George's has been the site of many CBC broadcasts and, in the mid-1970s, of recording sessions by Ed *Bickert, Koffman, and Doug *Riley. A second downtown Toronto club, Bourbon Street, was opened in 1971 by Cole. Under the successive direction of agents Jim *Galloway and Paul Grosney it has presented US mainstream and modern jazz musicians with local rhythm sections often led by pianist Carol Britto. It has been the site of recording sessions by Paul Desmond and Jim Hall. Clubs upstairs at both locations, Castle George (later A Nice Place or the King of Hearts) and Basin Street respectively, have been operated intermittently.

BIBLIOGRAPHY

Harris, Marjorie. 'George's and all that jazz,' (*Toronto Star*) *The City*, 22 Jan 1978 MM

George Wade and His Cornhuskers. See Wade.

GÉRARD, Jacques (b Poisson, Gerard). Tenor, b Arthabaska, near Drummondville, Que, 26 Jul 1899, d Old Orchard, Maine, 12 Aug 1957. He studied with Salvatore *Issaurel in Montreal and with Désiré Demest in Brussels. After his debut in Liège in 1927 as Faust, he appeared in several other Belgian cities. He sang leading roles for two seasons, 1929–31, with the Trianon-Lyrique, Paris, and for three seasons, 1931–4, with the Opéra-Comique, where his repertoire included Raoul Laparra's *La Habanera* under the composer's direction. In 1934 he made a concert tour of Quebec. In Montreal he sang several roles with Les *Variétés lyriques at the *Monument national, including Werther (1938), Des Grieux in *Manon* (1939), Gérald in *Lakmé* (1941), Hoffmann (1942), and Alfredo in *La Traviata* (1943). Brought to the attention of Arturo Toscanini by Wilfrid *Pelletier, Gérard made his New York debut in the maestro's October 1942 performances of Berlioz' *Roméo et Juliette*, with Jennie Tourel. He made his *Metropolitan Opera debut 2 Dec 1942 in *Lakmé*. He stayed with the Metropolitan until the 1945–6 season, during which time he shared the French repertoire with his countryman Raoul *Jobin. His younger brother, Roland Poisson (b 1903), studied violin in Montreal, Paris, and Brussels, earning his premier prix in 1926 at Brussels' Cons royal. For many years, he was a member of the *Montreal Orchestra and the *MSO.

BIBLIOGRAPHY

Gour, Romain. *La Palme-Issaurel* (Montreal 1948) JBM

GERMAIN, Gaston. Bass, teacher, administrator, b Quebec City 1 Mar 1933; lauréat (AMQ) 1960, premier prix voice (CMQ) 1961. An accountant 1951–7, he studied voice 1957–61 at the *CMQ with Raoul *Jobin and Ria *Lenssens. He won various competitions, received a grant in 1961 from the Quebec government, and continued his training that year with Rachele Maragliano-Mori in Turin (vocal technique). In 1962 he worked with Erik Werba at the Salzburg Mozarteum (German repertoire) and in 1963 with Pierre Bernac in Paris (French repertoire). He participated in 1963 in the *Quebec SO's Beethoven Festival, performing in the *Ninth Symphony*. The following year he took courses in stage skills at the École normale de Paris and received the Prix d'excellence at the Concours international d'interpretation de la mélodie française. He was soloist in Lully's *Te Deum*, presented by the orchestra of the Paris Cons Société des Concerts.

Germain made his professional Canadian debut 22 Jun 1964 at the *PDA as Antipas in the oratorio **Jean le Précurseur* and toured Canada 1964–5 with an opera trio for the *JMC. In the Brahmssaal of the Musikverein in Vienna during the 1965 World Congress of the JM International Federation he gave a recital which earned him the Vienna Press Prize. He was a soloist in 1966 with the Quebec SO in Mozart's *Requiem* conducted by Sergiu Celibidache. He took further training in the interpretation of German Lieder with John *Newmark and in 1967 toured Europe for JM. In Montreal he appeared at the World Festival of *Expo 67 as Lodovico in *Otello* with the *MSO and as a soloist in the premiere of *Matton's *Te Deum* with the Quebec SO under Françoys *Bernier. The same year he gave a joint recital with Micheline *Tessier at Carnegie Hall.

Germain taught 1968–72 at the Cons de Hull, was general manager 1972–6 of the JMC, and in 1976 was appointed director of the *JMC Orford Art Centre. He was president of the Quebec Youth Orchestra 1977–8 and its administrator 1978–80. These duties have curtailed his vocal career. Nevertheless, he is well versed in Lieder and oratorio and is known through appearances on CBC radio and TV and engagements with Canadian orchestras. He began teaching singing at the *U of Montreal in 1981. He was a founding member of the Groupe baroque de Montréal and the Lanaudière Music Camp. He received the 1973 *Prix de musique Calixa-Lavallée. He is married to Andrée Gauthier, a teacher at the CMM. SW

Germany. In 1979 Canadians of German descent formed the fifth largest ethnic group in Canada – after French, English, Scottish, and Irish. In 1971 the figure was approximately 1,300,000. The arrival of Germans began about 1750 in Nova Scotia and rarely has halted for long. They have settled in every province and have assimilated quickly. Except in certain areas of concentrated German settlement, such as Waterloo County, Ont, folk traditions have not been perpetuated by the second or third generation born in Canada.

There have been three streams of German immigration: from Germany itself (to Nova Scotia and Quebec in the 18th century, to the area west of Lake Ontario after about 1790, and to almost all regions later); from the USA (Loyalists in the 18th century and Mennonites or 'Pennsylvania Dutch'); and from German-speaking pockets of eastern Europe, usually sharing a religious identity (*Mennonites, *Amish, *Hutterites).

1 Musicians of German origin
2 Traditions
3 Visitors from Germany
4 German music in Canada
5 Canadian students in Germany
6 Canadian performers in Germany

1 MUSICIANS OF GERMAN ORIGIN. The period of Canada's growth into a modern nation has coincided with the era in which Austrian and German composers and musical institutions held a position of world prestige. Like Italy in the earlier part of this period and eastern Europe in the later, Germany supplied professional musicians to the international market. Thus it is easy to understand the disproportionately large number of German musicians in Canada throughout the 19th century. It is not easy however to identify this contribution in precise detail, since German-sounding family names are borne by Austrians, and by many eastern European Jews, many Flemish, and many

Swiss. Further, many German immigrants gallicized or anglicized their names or lost them through intermarriage.

The 30,000 mercenary troops from Anhalt, Brunswick, Hanau, and Hesse lent by the Duke of Brunswick to the British government to fight in the American War of Independence 1776–7 included many who eventually settled in what is now the province of Quebec. The 4000 Brunswick soldiers in 1777 included as many as 102 'tambours and oboists' – the latter a generic designation for military musicians (Georges Monarque, *Un Général allemand au Canada*, Montreal 1927). The children of the commander, Baron von Riedesel (1738–1800), were taught music by Frederic Henri *Glackemeyer (apparently not one of the mercenaries), who remained in Quebec to become the prototype of the pioneering all-round musical craftsman. Until about 1860 German names are in the forefront of musical activity in Quebec, Montreal, and Halifax. In Quebec Glackemeyer had a German competitor in Francis *Vogeler and a son-in-law in T.F. *Molt. J.-C. *Brauneis, père, occupies a place in the early history of Canadian bands, Louis Sigismond Pfeiffer (1831–78) was a violinist and organist in the city after 1846, while J.M. Pfeiffer, perhaps a relative (fl 1849), built pianos. Édouard *Glackemeyer, the only native Canadian mentioned so far, became an impassioned amateur of the flute and organizer of musical societies.

Active in both Quebec and Montreal were Molt and J.-C. *Brauneis, fils, also Frederick Hund (fl 1816–24), a music dealer and printer. Hund's associate in Quebec in 1824 (in the former capacity) was Gottlieb Seebold, who later operated a music business in Montreal with his brother John G. Seebold, a teacher of Ernest *Gagnon. Another early piano builder was Isaac Reinhardt (1808?–46) of Montreal; another music teacher and piano dealer, Leonard *Eglaugh.

Among British regimental bandmasters of German origin serving in Canada were Adam Joseph *Schott and the two James Zieglers, father (d 1833) and son. Bandmaster Kästner led a musical society in Antigonish, NS, in the mid-1840s, Professor Weisbecker a Sacred Music Society in Saint John, NB, in 1842, and Theodoric Wichtendahl a Harmonic Society in the same city in the mid-1850s. Peiler & Sichel operated a music store in Halifax for many years.

While native musicians and French immigrants supplied the needs of Quebec City after the middle of the century, Toronto experienced an 'invasion' of German musicians: the *Nordheimers (1844) and the *Heintzmans (1860), who became household names throughout Canada, and, of more temporary importance, the violinist Ferdinand *Griebel, the brothers *Schallehn, and the voice teacher Jules *Hecht. In Hamilton Peter Grossman became a leading bandmaster and music dealer; in Preston, Ont, Hager & Vogt (the latter partner the father of A.S. *Vogt) were an established organ-building firm, and Limbrecht was another.

A fugitive from his creditors, the musicologist Gustav Schilling (b Schwiegershausen, Germany, 1805, d Nebraska 1880) spent some years as a teacher in Montreal in the 1860s; the *Bohrer family contributed to musical life for some 80 years. The Leipzig-trained brothers Carl and Theodore *Martens participated in many facets of Toronto's musical life in the 1880s. The violinist Heinrich *Klingenfeld was active in Halifax and later in Toronto. Charles Reichling (1854-1922) was 12 when his family settled in Montreal. He studied violin with Jules *Hone and became an orchestral and chamber musician with the Montreal String Quartette, played in the *McGill Orchestra, and was appointed violinist to the governors-general Lord Lansdowne and Lord Stanley. Ernst Doering (cellist, b Oldenburg 25 Mar 1868) was engaged to teach cello at the Halifax Cons, stayed to found the Doering-Brauer Cons and (1890) the Leipzig Trio, and also, in the 1890s, taught at the Halifax Ladies' College.

It is possible that two pioneers of music in Winnipeg, Joseph Hecker (fl 1880) and Gustav Stephan (fl 1916), were of German origin. Like many other European musicians active for a while in Canada, they eventually left for the greener pastures of the USA. The *Berliner Gramophone Company was established in Montreal by German-born Emile Berliner.

Those who stayed in Canada included Ferdinand O. *Telgmann, a musical leader for some 50 years in Kingston, Ont, Hans A. *Zoellner and his son Theodor in Berlin (*Kitchener), Paul *Hahn and Otto *Higel in Toronto, and Eugene Schneider, a Stuttgart violinist and violist who was a member of the *Dubois String Quartet of Montreal.

The first famous Canadian-born musician of German (and Swiss) origin was A.S. Vogt, founder of the *Toronto Mendelssohn Choir. Other noted early figures of German descent were Noah *Zeller, George *Fox, and Joseph *Baumann. Because of World War I, the shift of musical gravity to France, the USA, and other countries, and the increasing need for church musicians brought up in British traditions, as well as the growing supply of Canadian musicians, immigration of German musicians dwindled. It was only as a result of political oppression under Hitler that another wave of musicians or music students arrived in Canada. One group, internees transferred from Great Britain to Canada, included Helmut *Blume, Freddie *Grant, Walter *Homburger, Helmut *Kallmann, the violinist Gerhard Kander (who gave recitals in Montreal and appeared with the *TSO in the 1940s but later abandoned his musical career), and John *Newmark. Others included Lotte *Brott, Ulrich *Leupold, Jan *Simons, and Ernesto *Vinci. Victims of Nazi persecution who settled in Canada after World War II included Andreas *Barban, Mario *Duschenes, Herman *Geiger-Torel, Otto and Walter *Joachim, Herbert *Ruff, and Heinz *Unger.

A new wave of German immigrants began about 1950, largely made up of persons who for professional or moral reasons wished to leave their homeland. They have included Wolfgang *Bottenberg, Helmut *Brauss, Franz-Paul *Decker, Gisela *Depkat, Herbie Helbig (pianist and composer of film and TV scores and of jingles), Friedemann Fischer (teacher of woodwinds and ensemble repertoire at *Laval U), Theo *Goldberg, Lothar *Klein, Gabriel *Kney, Jury Krytiuk, Otto-Werner *Mueller, Helmut Seemann (flutist and composer in Montreal and Ottawa, no longer active in music), the country singer Hank Smith, and Phil *Stark. The composer S.C. *Eckhardt-Gramatté spent most of her professional life in Berlin prior to settling in Canada in 1954.

Outstanding 20th-century Canadian-born musicians of German or part-German ancestry include Victor *Braun, Joyce Redekop-Fink, Elmer *Iseler, Alfred *Kunz, John *Martens, Victor *Martens, and George *Ziegler. As recorded-sound archivist and music publisher respectively, the cousins Edward B. and Fred *Moogk (*Waterloo Music Co) have made their mark.

2 TRADITIONS. Research into German folk music traditions in Canada has not been extensive. In her study *Folklore of Lunenburg County, Nova Scotia* (Ottawa 1950) Helen *Creighton found that few German songs had survived. Surveying the field of ethnic music study in 1975, Ramon Pelinski ('The music of Canada's ethnic minorities,' *CMB*, 10, Spring–Summer 1975) noted that the *National Museum of Man had collected 195 songs and 40 instrumental pieces of German origin. The five *manuscript books at the Jordan Historical Museum – the survivors of 20 written by pupils of Clinton Township School (Niagara Peninsula) 1798–1834 – have not yet been investigated at the time of this writing (1979) but are likely to reveal religious and pedagogical rather than folk traditions. It is probable that the majority of German immigrants knew 'songs in the popular tone' (by Reichardt, Silcher, Zelter, etc, taught from books and sung in groups) to a greater extent than true 'folk' songs. The popularity of brass bands (Waterloo from the 1830s) and singing societies (Victoria, BC, 1861; Waterloo ca 1865), resulting in the *Sängerfeste of the late 19th century, supports this premise.

After a period of relative inactivity 1914–50 singing societies sprang up again, reviving some of the old names: Concordia in Kitchener, Germania in Hamilton, Harmonie (instead of the former Harmonia) in Toronto, and Liederkranz in Edmonton. Choirs are associated with many of the German-Canadian clubs and community organizations. A German-Canadian Choir Assn, formed in 1958 in Kitchener, moved its headquarters to Ottawa in 1976. By 1978 the association included 20 choirs from cities in Ontario and Quebec. The traditional German Oktoberfest, in which music plays an important role, has been transplanted to Canada and flourishes in such cities as Kitchener-Waterloo, Regina, Vancouver, Winnipeg, Calgary, and Edmonton.

3 VISITORS FROM GERMANY. Perhaps the first German troupe to visit Canada was Hermann and Co of the Royal Cons of Munich, entertaining the citizens of Halifax and Saint John, NB, in 1832. Of greater significance were the three visits to Canada (including Kingston, Montreal, Quebec, and Toronto) 1850–2 by the Germanians, an orchestra of Berliners who had gone to the USA in 1848. This was probably the first professional orchestra to play in Canada, and its reception was enthusiastic. Individual visiting German artists included Henriette Sontag (soprano, 1854), Hans von Bülow (pianist, 1876), August Wilhelmj (violinist, 1880), Lilli Lehmann (soprano, 1886), and Xaver Scharwenka (pianist, 1890s). There is no need to list the many 20th-century visitors, from Elena Gerhardt and Walter Gieseking to Lotte Lehmann (who gave Lieder recitals in the 1930s in Montreal and in the 1940s in Toronto and master classes at *Mount Allison U in 1962) and Dietrich Fischer-Dieskau. Orchestras have included the Leipzig Philharmonic Orchestra (ca 1901), the Berlin Philharmonic under Herbert von Karajan (1955, 1956), the Bavarian Radio Symphony Orchestra (1968), and the Stuttgart Kammerorchester. During *Expo 67 the Munich Bach Choir and Orchestra and the Hamburg State Opera performed. The latter, conducted by Hans Schmidt-Isserstedt, gave the Canadian premiere of Hindemith's opera *Mathis der Maler*. German conductors who visited Canada include Bruno Walter (Montreal, Vancouver), Otto Klemperer (see MSO), Eugen Jochum, Ferdinand Leitner, Karl Munchinger (*NACO, *Guelph Spring Festival), Klaus Tennstedt (TS 1974 and often thereafter), and Herbert von Karajan (*Vancouver International Festival 1959). The Obernkirchen Children's Choir sang in Toronto in 1955, 1961, and 1962 and in Barrie and Kitchener in 1964. It also appeared in several other Canadian cities. Goethe House, with branches in

Montreal, Ottawa, and Toronto, which is primarily concerned with teaching the German language and literature, also sponsors many and diverse public events featuring the music and performers of Germany. Some of those it has presented are Albert Mangelsdorff, the jazz trombonist, with his quintet in 1967 and as a soloist in 1978; the Westfälische Kantorei, conducted by Wilhelm Ehmann in 1970; the Berlin Philharmonic Octet in 1972; and the duo pianists Alfons and Aloys Kontarsky in 1979. German artists who have toured in Canada under the auspices of the *JMC include pianist Herbert Drechsel (1954–5), the Pfeiffer Quartet (1966–7), and the Stuttgart Trio (1971–2, 1973–4).

4 GERMAN MUSIC IN CANADA. The prime contribution of Germany to Canadian musical life undoubtedly has been the staples of the concert repertoire from Bach and Gluck to Richard Strauss and Carl Orff, overlapping as they do with those from Austria (Beethoven, Brahms, Schoenberg). It would be beyond *EMC*'s scope to provide a list of Canadian premieres of even the main German masterpieces (see Concerts), but one should note that the more popular works of Beethoven were performed long before Bach gained a foothold. (For instance, in 1870, a memorial concert in Montreal was devoted to works of Beethoven.) F.H. *Torrington and R.-O. *Pelletier played Bach's organ music in the 1860s, but it remained for Healey *Willan, Ernest *MacMillan, Herbert *Fricker, and Douglas *Clarke in the 1920s to make the large choral-orchestral works known to Canadians. Wagner's operas had been heard in Montreal (*The Flying Dutchman* in 1871, the *Ring* in 1915, *Parsifal* in 1905), and the *Welsman TSO played some Strauss tone poems, but Germany's national operatic favourite, Weber's *Der Freischütz*, has had few performances. The Toronto Mendelssohn Choir was formed to sing choral music of Mendelssohn and presented several of the composer's motets in 1895 and his setting of Goethe's *Walpurgisnacht* in 1906. Other Canadian choral organizations named after German composers include the Bach Choir of Hamilton, the *Toronto Bach Choir, the *Vancouver Bach Choir, the *Handel Society of Music of New Westminster, and the *Mendelssohn Choir of Montreal. Instrumental ensembles have used the names of Beethoven (trios in both Montreal and Toronto) and of Mendelssohn (trio in Montreal).

German composers who have visited Canada include Wolfgang Fortner, Paul Hindemith, Carl Orff, and Karlheinz Stockhausen. Werner Egk wrote his concert arias *Chanson* and *Romance* for Pierrette *Alarie, who premiered them in 1953. Karl Hoeller and Hermann Reutter were German representatives at the 1960 *International Conference of Composers in Stratford, Ont.

5 CANADIAN STUDENTS IN GERMANY. The first young Canadian to complete his studies abroad – J.-C. Brauneis, fils – included Germany in his trip 1830–3; so did Tom Haliburton (1821–47), son of the creator of *Sam Slick*. Later on, the Leipzig Cons, established in 1843 by Mendelssohn, gained a world reputation and rivalled Paris as a magnet for North American music students. L.-A. *Dumouchel, Gustave *Gagnon, and Joseph Baumann went there about 1870; Nora *Clench, Harry *Field, W.O. *Forsyth, Annie Lampman *Jenkins, Waugh *Lauder, and A.S. Vogt in the 1880s; Frank *Blachford, Harry *Puddicombe, Frank Welsman, and Ernest *Whyte in the 1890s. Those who studied in Berlin included S.P. *Warren 1861–4, Émiliano *Renaud 1898–9, Alfred *Laliberté ca 1900–05, Ernest *Seitz 1910–14, Harold *Sumberg 1922–7, and George *Fiala 1942–5. Canadians who studied in Germany after 1950 include Donald *Bell, Keith *Bissell, Victor Braun, Brian *Cherney, Douglas *Haas, Alan *Heard, Davis *Joachim, Alfred Kunz, Rachel *Martel, John Martens, Victor Martens, Alvin Reimer, Nigel Rogers, and Claude *Vivier. Berlin, Munich, Detmold, and Hamburg appear to hold the greatest attraction for students, while the summer courses at the Kranichstein Institut in Darmstadt have been visited by Gilles *Tremblay, Norma *Beecroft, Bruce *Mather, and other composers. Still others have gained experience as young singers through engagements in provincial opera houses before launching international careers. After studies with Orff, Doreen *Hall introduced the *Orff-Schulwerk method to North America.

6 CANADIAN PERFORMERS IN GERMANY. The first Canadian to receive ovations in Germany was Waugh Lauder, in Leipzig in 1880, for his performance in Beethoven's *Emperor Concerto*. Emma *Albani made her German debut in 1882 and sang Elsa in *Lohengrin* in the presence of the emperor in 1887. Like Albani, Alfred Laliberté played before German royalty. Kathleen *Parlow made her recital debut in Berlin in 1907 to critical acclaim.

Canadians who have appeared on the German lyric stage or concert platform after 1950 include Robert *Aitken, Pierrette Alarie, Kenneth Asch, Donald Bell, Colette *Boky, Victor Braun, Maurice *Brown, Marie *Daveluy, Janina *Fialkowska, Maureen *Forrester, Kenneth *Gilbert, Glenn *Gould, Ida *Haendel, Gladys *Kriese-Caporale, Anton *Kuerti, Bruno *Laplante, Louise *Lebrun, Diane Loeb, Norman *Mittelmann, Geneviève *Perrault, Henriette Platford, Dodi *Protero, Irene *Salemka, Léopold *Simoneau, Steven *Staryk, Lilian *Sukis, Micheline *Tessier, Jon *Vickers, and Jeannette *Zarou. In 1953 the *Royal 22nd Regiment Band played in Germany. The TS (1974) and the NACO (1978) have toured in Germany, and the *SMCQ, the *Festival Singers, and the *Canadian Brass took part in Rendezvous with Canada, a series of concerts in Bonn (17–24 Nov 1977) which featured Canadian composers and performers. The NFB made a film of the successful visit of the Alberta All-Girls Band to Munich in 1974. In 1979 the *Salvation Army Canadian Staff Band included Germany in its European tour and also played at the Canadian Armed Forces Base in Lahr, West Germany. A branch of the *RCMT at this base is visited annually by examiners. Oscar *Peterson has performed and recorded in Germany, the Montreal composer John Warren has led his British jazz band in concert and on radio in 1973 and 1975, and the *CCMC played in Bremen, Munich, and Cologne in 1978.

BIBLIOGRAPHY

LeVasseur, Nazaire. 'Musique et musiciens à Québec,' *La Musique*, 1919–22

Gibbon, John Murray. 'Contribution of Austro-German music to the Canadian culture,' *Proceedings and Transactions of the Royal Society of Canada*, vol 43, (1949)

Johnson, H. Earle. 'The Germania Musical Society,' *MQ*, vol 39, Jan 1953

Milnes, Humphrey. 'German folklore in Ontario,' *JAF*, vol 67, 1954

Leibbrandt, Gottlieb. '100 Jahre Concordia,' *German-Canadian Yearbook*, vol 1 (1973)

Kallmann, Helmut. 'The German contribution of music in Canada,' ibid, vol 2 (1975) (HK)

GESSER, Samuel (Sam). Producer, impresario, record distributor, b Montreal 7 Jan 1930. He worked 1949–59 as a publicity agent. During those years he also wrote more than 300 scripts of various kinds for CBC radio and TV.

In the 1950s, as the Canadian representative of the US Folkways label and under his own label, Allied, *Gesser produced about 100 LPs, recording such artists as Hyman *Bress, Jean *Carignan, Pierrette Champoux, Jacques *Labrecque, Alan *Mills, and Louise Myette. He founded The Record Centre / Le Centre du disque of Montreal, the first record lending library in the metropolis. He gave up the recording field in the early 1960s.

During that same period, with Alan Mills, he founded Gesser & Mills Concerts, and later he founded Samuel Gesser Productions. Among the artists and groups these two companies presented, in Montreal or on tour in Canada, were Joan Baez, Harry Belafonte, Van Cliburn, Dietrich Fischer-Dieskau, Maureen *Forrester, Glenn *Gould, Janis Joplin, Danny Kaye, Monique *Leyrac, Liberace, Nana Mouskouri, the trio Peter, Paul and Mary, Pete Seeger, Isaac Stern, the American Ballet Theatre, Les Feux-Follets, the Salzburg Marionnettes, the New York Philharmonic, the orchestras of Houston and The Hague, Japan's Noh Theatre, and the Peking Opera Theatre.

Gesser collaborated 1954–65 with the *Montreal Festivals and in 1968 founded the Montreal International Summer Festival. He was artistic consultant for the Canadian government's participation in the entertainment sector of *Expo 67. With the music consultant Hugh *Davidson and the theatre manager André Dufresne, he was responsible for the programming at the theatre and bandshell of the Canadian Pavilion, as well as at the Garden of Stars at La Ronde amusement park. The Canadian government also entrusted him with the programming for its pavilion at Expo 70 in Osaka. Thus he was responsible for some 1400 performances of all kinds, including those of the RCMP Musical Ride. He later founded Gesser Enterprises, concerned chiefly with Montreal performances of *Stratford and *Shaw Festival productions.

BIBLIOGRAPHY

Fitzgerald, John. 'A tribute to Sam Gesser,' Montreal *Gazette*, 2 Jan 1980 ST

GHAN, Esther (b Cohen, m Firestone). Soprano, cantor, choral conductor, b Winnipeg 9 Apr 1925. After training as a pianist in Winnipeg with Gwendda Owen *Davies and giving several recitals in western Canada, she began voice studies in 1944 in Toronto with Nina de Gedeonoff and Emmy *Heim. In 1948 she won second prize in an international scholarship contest sponsored by Carnegie Hall. She made her CBC radio debut on 'Canadian Cavalcade,' sang 1949–51 on 'Starlight Moods' and other CBC series, and starred 1957–60 on CBC radio's 'Stardust.' She gave her first recital in 1950 at *Eaton Auditorium, accompanied by her uncle Sherman Ghan (1910–1952; the blind Russian-born violinist and accordionist), who had composed some of the songs on the program. She made her operatic debut as Musetta in *La Bohème* (1951) with the *CBC Opera. Her extensive concert career has included performances with the *TSO (1950, 1951) and the Buffalo Philharmonic (1969, 1970). The only woman cantor known to be active in Canada 1950–80, she has held positions in Toronto at Beth-El Synagogue (mid-1950s to mid-1960s) and at Temple Emanu-El (1977). She also has conducted the YMHA Choral Group and 1967–74 the Toronto Hadassah Women's Choir. In 1971 and 1973, with three of her children, she recorded *Let's Sing English Songs*, a collection of 52 songs for distribution in Japan by the Tokyo Kodomo Club.

BIBLIOGRAPHY.

Flanagan, Marie. 'Music and baby food mix beautifully for her,' *Toronto Daily Star*, 30 Mar 1962

'The Ghost of Bras d'Or.' Cape Breton ballad, with music by Charlie MacKinnon and lyrics by Lillian Crewe Walsh. It tells of the death, in Europe during World War II, of Major (former Piper) Donald John MacPherson from the Bras d'Or area of Cape Breton. The song was recorded first in 1958 by MacKinnon for *Rodeo and was published by Bay Music. Popular with country artists, it has been recorded by the Canadians Stompin' Tom *Connors and Dick *Nolan and the US singers George Hamilton IV, Claude King, and Mac Wiseman, among others.

MacKinnon (b Sydney, Cape Breton, NS, 25 Nov 1919), a railwayman on the Island, is a country singer-songwriter in the Wilf *Carter tradition. He has made several LPs and singles for Rodeo, *Arc, and Marathon and, with Lillian Crewe Walsh, a poet from Neil Harbour, Cape Breton, has written other narrative songs.

GIBBON, John Murray. Writer, publicist, translator, b Udeweller, Ceylon, 12 Aug 1875, d Ste-Anne-de-Bellevue, (Montreal) 2 Jul 1952; BA literature (Oxford) ca 1900, LL D (Montreal) 1946. He received some musical training in London and studied at Oxford U and the U of Göttingen, Germany. Employed by the CPR 1907–13 as European publicity agent and in Canada 1913–45 as general publicity agent, he initiated the sponsorship of literary, artistic, and musical presentations for publicity purposes. During the 1920s and 1930s he organized for the CPR a number of festivals and celebrations, all involving Canadian musicians (see CPR Festivals). He was a prolific author, and much of his writing was done for the CPR. Of his musical writings, concerned mainly with song, *Melody and the Lyric* won a Prix David in 1931 from the Quebec government. He published some lyric poems on Canadian lore, well-intentioned but of questionable merit, and set to traditional tunes or melodies of Schubert and Brahms. He also provided English translations for French-Canadian folksongs. He wrote the libretto for the ballad opera *Prince Charlie and Flora* (1928) and translated *Le Jeu de Robin et Marion* and *L'Ordre de Bon Temps* for the Canadian Folksong and Handicraft Festivals in Quebec (1927, 1928). He was a member of the *CMCouncil.

See also Folk-music-inspired composition.

WRITINGS

- transl. *Canadian Folk Songs, Old and New* (London 1927, rev enl 1949)
- transl. *Le Jeu de Robin et Marion* (Birchard 1928)
- transl. *Vingt-et-un Chansons canadiennes* (Oakville 1928)

'The music of the people,' Empire Club *Addresses* (Toronto 1929)

Prince Charlie and Flora (Dent 1929)

- transl. *The Order of Good Cheer* (Toronto 1929)

Melody and the Lyric (London 1930)

Magic of Melody (London 1933)

The coureur de bois and his birthright (Ottawa 1936)

- lyricist. *Northland Songs*, 2 vols (Toronto 1936, 1938)

Canadian Mosaic (Toronto 1938)

- lyricist. *New World Ballads* (Toronto 1939)
- lyricist. *Pioneer Songs of Canada* (Toronto 1941)
- lyricist. *Canada in Song* (Toronto 1941)

'Folksongs of the French Canadians,' *Think*, vol 7, 1941

'Your theme is your author,' *CRMA*, vol 1, Feb 1942

'Women as folk-song authors,' *Proceedings and Transactions of the Royal Society of Canada*, vol 41, 1947

'Folk-song and feudalism,' ibid, vol 42, 1948

'Contribution of Austro-German music to the Canadian culture,' ibid, vol 43, 1949

BIBLIOGRAPHY

CAPAC. *Tribute to a Nation-builder: An Appreciation of Dr. J.M. Gibbon* (Toronto 1946) (RPn)

GIBBS, Terence. Producer, b London 10 Jan 1921, d Toronto 10 Mar 1973. After service in World War II with the British army in India, he studied piano, composition, and theory at the GSM, London, then joined Decca Records as assistant artist manager. Assigned to the development of Decca's classical-music catalogue, he engaged and recorded several leading European orchestras. He moved to Canada in 1948 as a music producer for CBC Toronto. He helped to develop the CBC's major radio series and was instrumental in the formation of the *CBC Opera Company in 1948, the *CBC SO in 1952, and the *CBC Talent Festival (1959–). He produced over 40 opera broadcasts (including the North American radio premiere of Britten's *Peter Grimes*) and was responsible for the CBC SO's weekly concerts and the recital series 'Distinguished Artists' until 1959, when he became assistant director of music. He returned to production in 1962, assuming responsibility for 'Audio' (heard on CJBC, Toronto), 'Continental Holiday' and 'Anthology.' Gibbs' talents, of which a vivid imagination and a boundless enthusiasm were not the least, found fertile soil in the CBC's increased activities on behalf of cultural development in the postwar years. He was instrumental, particularly, in introducing radio audiences to new works of English and Canadian composers.

GIBSON, Reg (Reginald Milton). Singer, composer, b Carman, south of Winnipeg, 13 Jan 1932. He made his debut at five as 'The Little Yodelling Cowboy' at the Beacon Theatre, Winnipeg, and continued to appear in vaudeville until 1942. After entertaining troups stationed in western Canada during World War II, he sang on radio with Andy *DeJarlis and began a CBC career in 1950 on CBW, Winnipeg, with the program 'Rhythm on the Range,' also appearing 1951–4 on 'Here Comes the Band' (radio) and in a duo with the guitarist Jim Pirie on such shows as 'Shenandoah' (radio 1961) and 'Ballads and Bards' (TV 1962–3). Gibson was 'The Ramblin' Man' (radio 1960–3) and the host for 'Red River Jamboree' (TV 1965) and 'The Group' (TV, summers 1968–70). He also travelled in 1966, 1967, and 1968 to Canadian armed forces bases in Germany and on the Gaza Strip.

Gibson composed and performed theme music for the CBC TV films *Once upon a Marsh* (1966, for which he won a CBC Wilderness Award), *Death of a Nobody* (1968), *Whistling Wings* (1970), *Nis'ku* (1970, for which he won a second Wilderness Award) and *Seaton's* (1974). His recordings include the LP *That Country Feeling* (1970, CBC LM 76). A member 1959–72 of the national executive of ACTRA, he was president of that organization in 1971. He is an affiliate of PRO Canada. MM

GIBSON, Ronald (Wilson). Organist-choirmaster, conductor, teacher, critic, violist, b Maidstone, Kent, England, 28 May 1903; ACCO 1927, B MUS (Manchester) 1949, ARMCM 1949, hon LL D (Winnipeg) 1972. Gibson's family settled in Morden, Man, when he was 10. He began piano lessons there and taught himself to play the violin. He was organist at Morden Presbyterian Church until his family moved in 1918 to Winnipeg, where he studied organ with Arnold Dann at Wesley College, continuing with Arthur *Egerton. Gibson was a violist and assistant conductor 1924–ca 1934 in John *Waterhouse's Winnipeg String Orchestra and in the *Winnipeg SO under Hugh Ross. He held church positions at Young United 1920–5, Broadway Baptist 1925–9, and St John's United 1930–4. In 1934 he became organist at Holy Trinity Anglican Church. He also conducted several organizations including, 1927–9, the Winnipeg Choral and Orchestral Society (with which he had made his concert debut as a pianist in 1925 in Mendelssohn's *Concerto in G Minor*) and, 1935–40, the Manitoba Schools Orchestra. After RCAF service overseas he conducted 24 concerts with the CBC String Orchestra in Winnipeg, then returned to England for studies 1946–9 at Manchester U with Humphrey Procter-Gregg and others and at the Royal Manchester College with Iso Elinson (piano) and Evelyn Rothwell (oboe). Gibson served 1949–63 as director of the School of Music, *U of Manitoba, and continued to teach at the school until his retirement in 1968. He then began writing music criticism for the *Winnipeg Free Press*. He was a regular contributor 1970–7 to **The Canada Music Book*. In 1968 he began composing works for voice, organ, and choir, most of them for church use. *Waterloo published five of his anthems in 1978. He was made an honorary life member of the *RCCO, the *CFMTA, and the *MMEA. He is a contributor to *EMC*. JA

GIDLEY, Muriel (Emily) (m Stafford). Organist, choir director, teacher, accompanist, b Adrian, Mich, 1 Apr 1906; ATCM 1926, LTCM 1927, hon FRCCO 1959. She settled in Leamington, Ont, with her British parents in 1907. In 1921, after only six lessons from a local teacher, she became organist of St John's Anglican Church, Leamington. She studied 1925–7 with *MacMillan, *Willan, G.D. *Atkinson, and Ernest *Seitz at the *TCM and won the gold medal for organ in 1926. She became the first organist-choirmaster of the new (1927) Park Rd Baptist Church and remained there 31 years.

Gidley made her recital debut at the 1933 *CCO convention and in 1948 became the first woman chairman of the Toronto chapter. She also served 1957–9 as the first woman national president of the *RCCO. The annual carol festival under her direction at Park Rd Baptist Church became a model of unhackneyed programming, featuring little-known carols and such longer but intimate works as Willan's *Mystery of Bethlehem*, Martin Shaw's *The Crib*, and Britten's *A Ceremony of Carols*. Muriel Gidley gave many organ recitals 1934–52 in Toronto and was a member 1927–52 of the staff and examiners' board of the TCM (*RCMT), teaching organ and piano. MWM

GIGNAC, Marguerite (Marie) (m Hedges). Soprano, teacher, b Windsor, Ont, 17 Jul 1928; Artist Diploma (RCMT) 1951. She studied 1939–48 at the Music School of the Ursulines in Windsor and then enrolled at the *RCMT, where she worked with Ernesto *Vinci; during the summers 1950–2 she was a pupil of Edith Piper at the Juilliard School in New York. She was organist 1943–7 at Sacré-Coeur Church in LaSalle, Ont.

Gignac made her debut in 1948 at *Eaton Auditorium as Susanna in the *Royal Cons Opera School production of *The Marriage of Figaro*. With the Opera Festival (*COC) she sang Zerlina in *Don Giovanni* (1950), Susanna again (1951), the title role of *Manon* (1952), and Olympia, Giulietta, and Antonia in *The Tales of Hoffmann* (1958). In 1952 she won first prize in the radio competition *'Singing Stars of Tomorrow.'

Assisted by a grant from Myron Taylor, a US patron of the arts, Gignac studied 1952–4 with Roberto Lupi at the Villa Schifanoia in Florence and worked during the summer of 1953 with Ernest Reichert in Salzburg and the following summer at the Accademia Chigiana in Siena. In Italy she toured with Lupi and the Teatro Nuovo orchestra.

Returning to Toronto in 1956, Gignac performed in 1957 at the *CNE and made her CBC TV debut in Gounod's *Faust* on 'L'*Heure du concert.'

In 1958 she sang Rosina in *The Barber of Seville* with the Grand Opéra de Montréal and was soloist with the *MSO in Mozart's *Coronation Mass*. During the 1959–60 season she toured Quebec, the Maritimes, and France for the *JMC and toured in the USA with the Goldovsky Grand Opera Theater, taking part in performances of *Roméo et Juliette*, *Rigoletto*, and *Don Giovanni*. The *Canada Council gave her a grant to study 1960–1 with Pierre Bernac in Paris and Lina Pagliughi in Milan.

Gignac had been a finalist in the 'Metropolitan Opera Auditions of the Air' and was engaged for the festival of Central City, Col, to perform the title role in *Lucia di Lammermoor* (1960) and that of Adina in *L'Elisir d'amore* (1961). At the *Montreal Festivals she sang the role of Blonda in *The Abduction from the Seraglio* (1960), Serpina in *La Serva Padrona* (1961), and Despina in *Così fan tutte* (1962). In 1961 another tour took her to France and Italy. She was Marguerite in the *Opera Guild of Montreal's 1963 production of *Faust* and Musetta in its 1966 *La Bohème* at the *PDA. Also in 1966 she sang Philine in *Mignon* with the *Théâtre lyrique de Nouvelle-France.

After a concert at the Mont-Royal Chalet, Jean Paré wrote 'Marguerite Gignac is an exceptional coloratura who combines technical mastery with a voice that has a rare mellow quality throughout its entire register' (*La Presse*, Montreal, 11 Aug 1960).

In 1961 Gignac married the US flutist William Hedges and settled in St Paul, Minn. After 1967 she appeared often as soloist with the St Paul Chamber Orchestra, on one occasion (1973) in Aaron Copland's *Eight Poems of Emily Dickinson* under the composer's direction. With the Minnesota Orchestra Gignac sang the role of the child in Ravel's *L'Enfant et les sortilèges*. She gave a number of recitals on St Paul's educational TV between 1963 and 1971.

Gignac began teaching singing and opera at St Catherine's College, St Paul, in 1963, and subsequently has taught at the U of Minnesota and occasionally at the Aspen Festival. She has recorded four oratorios by Carissimi (Angelicum LPA 971, 972, 973 and Pastorale et musique PM 30002M) and some folksongs (RCA LCP-1035).

FILMOGRAPHY

The Opera Class NFB 1951

HP

GILBERT, (Joseph) **J.-Alexandre**. Violinist, teacher, b Quebec City 8 Sep 1867, d there January 1950; hon D MUS (Laval) 1922. He began his musical studies at the Collège de Lévis and with A.E. Courchesne (violin) and continued them 1888–94 at the Liège Cons, Belgium, with César Thomson, acquiring, in the words of his pupil J.-Robert *Talbot, 'a classical education ... strict and solid' (*La Musique*, August 1919). Returning to Canada in 1894 he began an active career as a violinist and teacher. One of the founders (1902) of the *Quebec SO, he served it as concertmaster until 1931 and was president 1903–5 and 1912–13. For more than 30 years he was the first violin of the Quatuor à cordes Gilbert, which he founded in 1911.

Gilbert taught at the Académie commerciale de Québec, the Collège de Lévis, Jésus-Marie de Sillery Convent, the Congregation of Notre-Dame boarding school in Bellevue, and the *Séminaire de Québec. He joined the teaching staff of the *Laval U Music School when the school opened in 1922. Besides Talbot, his pupils included Edwin *Bélanger, Maurice *Bernier, and Arthur *LeBlanc.

Gilbert served 1918–20 and 1941–4 as president of the *AMQ, which made him an honorary member in 1948.

BIBLIOGRAPHY

Magnan, Odile. 'Joseph-Alexandre Gilbert,' *Le Lutrin*, vol 2, Oct 1980

CH

GILBERT, Kenneth. Harpsichordist, organist, musicologist, teacher, b Montreal 16 Dec 1931. He studied with Conrad *Letendre (organ) and, at the *CMM, with Yvonne *Hubert (piano) and Gabriel *Cusson (harmony and counterpoint). Gilbert won the 1953 *Prix d'Europe for organ and studied for two years in Europe with Nadia Boulanger (theory), Gaston Litaize (organ), and Gustav Leonhardt and Ruggero Gerlin (harpsichord). Though he was on leave 1953–5 for these studies, he remained officially the organist and music director 1952–67 at Queen Mary Rd United Church, Montreal. In 1955 he gave a recital of Canadian organ music for the RTF (Radio France). Back in Canada he designed and in 1959 supervised the installation at Queen Mary Rd of the first major modern tracker organ in Canada. This instrument (built by R. von Beckerath of Hamburg) and Gilbert's performances on it strongly influenced subsequent organ building practice in Canada. The society *Ars Organi, in the formation of which Gilbert played a leading role, also influenced organ performance standards in eastern Canada.

While in Paris (1965) on a Quebec government grant, doing research on Couperin in preparation for a CBC series (and subsequent RCI recording, released on Harmonia Mundi in France, RCA in England, Music Heritage in the USA, and other labels in Italy and Japan) of the composer's complete works for harpsichord, Gilbert suggested that a new edition would be appropriate to honour the Couperin tercentenary (1968). Heugel agreed to publish Gilbert's edition as part of its early-music series, Le Pupitre. This edition excited much admiration for its scholarly approach, posited on a scrupulous re-examination of the original engraved scores. Following the international success of the Couperin edition, Gilbert began the monumental task of preparing a new edition (with reference to existing editions) of the sonatas (some 550) of Domenico Scarlatti. By 1978 9 of the 11 volumes had been published. The research was subsidized in part by the Gulbenkian Foundation in Lisbon and the *Canada Council. Gilbert also has edited the complete harpsichord works of d'Anglebert. Under way by 1978 were new editions of Bach's *Goldberg Variations*, Frescobaldi's *First Book of Toccatas* and Rameau's complete harpsichord works.

Reflecting his editorial interests, Gilbert's performance after 1965 has been devoted entirely to harpsichord playing, and he has become widely admired for his concerts, broadcasts, and recordings. Stephen Plaistow in *Gramophone* (May 1973) said: 'Kenneth Gilbert's achievement ... is to rescue the music from a small circle of connoisseurs and to make it ... universally enjoyable. He does so by harnessing the discipline of scholarship to his flair for performing the music ... Not since Thurston Dart ... has there been such a fruitful coincidence of the scholar's mind and the performer's fingers in this field.' He has been a soloist several times with the Chicago SO and has performed with the *MSO, the *Quebec SO, the *TSO, the *NACO, and the *Vancouver SO. In 1967, with Robert Koff in Montreal, he played all the Bach violin and harpsichord sonatas. A resident of France in the 1970s, he has given recitals there (and in Germany, England, and Switzerland) and a series of joint recitals with the violinist Robert Kohnen for Radio France.

Gilbert has taught 1957–74 at the *CMM, 1964–72 at *McGill U, 1969–76 at *Laval U, and, as guest professor, 1971–4 at the Royal Flemish Cons in Antwerp. He was artist-in-residence 1969–70 at

Kenneth Gilbert

the *U of Ottawa and also has taught summer courses in Haarlem, Holland. His pupils have included Hubert *Bédard, Martha Brickman, Hélène Dugal, John Grew, Martha Hagen, Jos van Immerseel, Hwaeja Lee, Lucien *Poirier, Réjean *Poirier, Wayne *Riddell, Scott Ross, and John Whitelaw. Gilbert was a judge in 1975 for the Concours international de clavecin, Paris, and in 1978 for the *CBC Talent Festival, Ottawa. The *CMCouncil named him Artist of the Year in 1978.

WRITINGS

'Les livres de clavecin de François Couperin,' *Revue de musicologie*, 2, 1972

'Le clavecin français et la registration,' *L'Interprétation de la musique française au XVIIe et XVIIIe siècles* (Paris 1974)

– ed. *François Couperin* complete harpsichord works, 4 vols (Heugel 1969–72)

– ed. *Domenico Scarlatti* complete works, 11 vols (Heugel 1971–)

– ed. *François Couperin* complete harpsichord works, facsim edn (Broude 1973)

– ed. *d'Anglebert* complete keyboard works (Heugel 1975)

DISCOGRAPHY

d'Anglebert *Suites*. 1973. Harmonia Mundi HMU 941

The Art of Jean-Pierre Rampal. Rampal fl, Duschenes fl. (1971). Orion ORS 7149/Harmonia Mundi HMU 439

Bach *Concerto in D Minor; Italian Concerto*. 1962. Orion ORS 7275

– *French Suites*. 1975. Harmonia Mundi HMU 438

– *Six Concertos* for harpsichord. 1963. Bar BC 2828

– *Sonatas* for viola da gamba and harpsichord. Hsu v da gamba. 1971. Mus H Soc MHS 1362/Da Camera Magna 92905

– *4 Sonatas* BWV1020–1023. Staryk vn. 1965. Bar BCS 2858

Baroque Organ Masters: Buxtehude – Boehm – Walther. 1964. Orion ORS 74155/Saga 5407

Bull – Daveluy – O. Joachim. 1966. RCI 225/RCA CCS-1019

Chambonnières *Livre premier de clavecin*. (1979). Argo ZK 80

Clérambault *Suite du 1er ton, Suite du 2e ton*. 1965. Oryx 1737/Harmonia Mundi HMU 964

Couperin *Complete Works for Harpsichord*. 1970–1. RCI 311-326/Harmonia Mundi HMU 351-366/RCA LHL1 5048-5051/Col Nippon OS-2962-5-HA /Mus H Soc MHS 3128-3131, 3181-3184, 3656-3659

French Masters of the Clavier, vol 1: Rameau – Chambonnières – Dumont – d'Anglebert – Couperin. 1969. Harmonia Mundi HMU 334

French Masters of the Clavier, vol 2: Marchand – Forqueray – Duphly. 1971. Harmonia Mundi HMU 940

Froberger *Suites*. (1979). Archiv ARC 2533419

The Golden Sound of Jean-Pierre Rampal. Rampal fl, Duschenes fl. 1965. Orion ORS 73114

Handel *Suites*. 1976. Harmonia Mundi HMU 447

Purcell *Suites*. (1978). Argo ZK 56

Rameau *Complete Harpsichord Works*. 1976. Archiv 2710 020

– *Suites*. 1965. Bar BC 2853

– *Pièces de clavecin en concert*. Simard ob, Carpenter vc. 1964. Bar BC 2856

Soler 6 *Concertos for Two Keyboards*. Gilbert, Pinnock, hpd and forte-piano. (1980). Archiv ARC 2533445

Sonatas for flute and harpsichord. Rampal fl. 1965. Bar BUS 2878

See also Yaëla Hertz; Discographies for Jean-Paul Jeannotte, Steven Staryk.

BIBLIOGRAPHY

'Cool sound,' Can edn *Time*, 9 Jun 1967

Laliberté, Serge. 'Entretien avec Kenneth Gilbert,' *VM*, 16, Jun 1970

Hawkins, Peter. 'For the next five years two sonatas a week – among other things,' *Montreal Star*, 29 Aug 1970

Maheu, Renée. 'Kenneth Gilbert,' *Mcan*, 31, Feb 1977

Gingras, Claude. 'Two major international events,' *Mcan*, 34, Jan 78

Deacon, Tom. 'Gilbert on big time label at last,' *Fugue*, Feb 1978 MK

GILKISON, Margaret (b Geddes, m Gilkison, m Derry). Organist, pianist, b Aberdeen, d Ontario. She moved to Canada in 1834 and married David Gilkison the following year. The Gilkison and Geddes families, early settlers in Elora, Upper Canada (Ontario), 'brought from Scotland not only means, but education and talents of a very high order ... they have left a mark of refinement in every place they lived' (Connon, p 123). One of Canada's first woman organists, Mrs Gilkison played at St James' Cathedral in Toronto as early as April 1842. During her tenure a new organ was acquired, but her salary, £100 in 1846, was reduced twice until it was £50 in 1848, at which time she resigned. She also appeared in Toronto concerts as piano accompanist. 'She was a good musician but a lady of such an extremely nervous temperament that it was no unusual thing for her to faint and have to be carried out when her portion of the service was concluded' (F.E. Dixon, 'Music in Toronto,' *Daily Mail and Empire*, 7 Nov 1896).

BIBLIOGRAPHY

Connon, J. *Elora* (Fergus, Ont 1930)

St James' Cathedral, Toronto. *Churchwardens Register and Minute Book, 1842–1908* HK

GILLMOR, Alan (Murray). Musicologist, administrator, b Fort Frances, west of Thunder Bay, Ont, 10 Oct 1938; B MUS (Michigan) 1963, MA (Michigan) 1964, PH D (Toronto) 1972. He studied piano 1946–58 and clarinet 1949–53. He has taught 1967–9 at the U of Houston, 1970–1 at *McGill U, and 1971–6 at *Carleton U, Ottawa. He became head of the music department at Carleton in 1976. In addition to his PH D thesis, 'Erik Satie and the concept of the avant-garde,' he has written criticism for the *Michigan Daily* 1961–3 and the Ottawa *Citizen* 1971–4 and contributed articles on Canadian music to the *Encyclopedia International* (New York 1975), *Contact* (Birmingham U, 1974, 1975), the **Canadian Composer*, and *EMC*. He has been a commentator-writer for CBC radio. CF

GILMOUR, Clyde. Critic, broadcaster, b Calgary 8 Jun 1912; hon LL D (McMaster) 1976. He worked on various newspapers in western Canada before contributing film reviews to CBC Vancouver 1947–54 and record columns to *Mayfair* 1947–52. He was movie critic for the *Vancouver Sun* 1949–54, *Maclean's* 1950–4, CBC radio ('Critically Speaking') 1954–64 and the Toronto *Telegram* 1954–71. He joined the *Toronto Star* as movie critic in 1971. During his years with the *Sun* and the *Telegram* he also was a record columnist for each of those newspapers, and in 1973 he began writing record reviews for the magazine *Sound*. In 1956 he initiated CBC radio's popular 'Gilmour's Albums,' a weekly one-hour program of records drawn from his own wide-ranging collection. The program reached its 1000th broadcast in June 1976. For his journalistic work and particularly for this 'program of recorded music ... heard with delight by a national audience,' Gilmour was named a Member of the *Order of Canada in 1975.

BIBLIOGRAPHY

McIver, Jack. 'What makes Clyde Gilmour so special?' *Toronto Star*, 20 Sep 1980 AHC

GIMBY, Bobby (Robert Stead). Trumpeter, songwriter, b Cabri, west of Moose Jaw, Sask, 25 Oct 1918. He played in the Cabri Boys' Band and other western Canadian boys' bands and dance orchestras and was lead trumpet 1941–3, in Toronto, of Mart *Kenney's Western Gentlemen. He formed his own orchestra in Toronto in the mid-1940s and led the Rodeo Rascals in 1949 on CBC radio's 'Bobby Gimby Show,' a program of western music. He was a featured soloist and raconteur 1945–59 with *'The Happy Gang' on CBC radio, and music director 1956–60 for *'Juliette' on CBC TV. He went to Singapore in 1962 and, while there, wrote (and recorded with a girls' choir) 'Malaysia Forever,' dedicated to the idea of a Malaysian federation and sometimes wrongly identified as the Malaysian national anthem. His nickname, 'The Pied Piper of Canada,' originated at this time.

Gimby returned to Canada in 1963 and for the next 15 years led Toronto hotel orchestras and, occasionally, a dixieland jazz band. In 1967 he composed *'CA-NA-DA,' the most popular song of Canada's centennial celebrations. He toured the country – and in later years the USA, Germany, and Japan – leading groups of school children in performances of this and other songs. In 1975 he was the host for CTV's musical-variety show 'Sing a Song.' Gimby's compositions include centennial songs for Manitoba ('Manitoba Hundred') and British Columbia ('Go British Col-umbia'), and 'Little People,' a song written in Malaysia in aid of the United Nations' Freedom-From-Hunger campaign, and many jingles. With the comedian Johnny Wayne he wrote several songs, of which the most popular is 'The Cricket Song' (1956), recorded by Ray Bolger and others. Gimby is a member of CAPAC. G.V. *Thompson has published several of his songs. His recordings include 78s with Kenney and LPs under his own name for the *Quality and *CTL labels. He received the 'Broadcaster of the Year' award from the Central Canada Broadcasters' Assn in 1967 and was made an Officer of the *Order of Canada in 1968.

BIBLIOGRAPHY

Frayne, Trent. 'Bob Gimby,' *Liberty*, Jan 1947

Kenyon, Ron. 'Four lives of Bobby Gimby,' *Star Weekly*, 26 Sep 1959

Rasky, Frank. 'All together now – everybody sing,' *The Canadian*, 10 Jan 1967

'Bobby Gimby's "Canada" a phenomenal success story,' *CanComp*, 20, Jul–Aug 1967 (HM)

GIMEL (Groupe d'interprétation de musique électroacoustique de Laval). Founded at *Laval U in December 1973 by Nil *Parent, with Marco Navratil, keyboard; Michel Breton, cello (replaced in 1975 by Russell Gagnon); Réjean Marois, trombone; and Marcelle *Deschênes-Harvey, Gisèle Ricard, Robert Charbonneau, and Yvan Laberge, electronic instruments. Other players have been added for certain sessions. All the founding members came from traditional music backgrounds.

Parent's research influenced the group's orientation towards the creation of a new type of musical expression, an electro-acoustic music described as 'mixed and in real time': mixed, because conventional instruments converse with electronic instruments; in real time, because the music is produced without prerecorded tape – the actual sounds captured by the microphone are conveyed to the synthesizer where they are modified. Workshop-meetings have explained and demonstrated live electro-acoustic music, permitting participants to familiarize themselves with the new instruments and to learn the basic terminology.

Through subsidies from the *Canada Council in 1974 and 1975 and the Dept of External Affairs in 1976 GIMEL gave numerous concerts in Canada (Montreal, Quebec City, Chicoutimi, Toronto, and Ottawa) and Europe (Belgium, France, Germany, and Holland).

In March 1976, M. de Wonk wrote in *La Libre Belgique*: 'One can hardly remain insensitive to the broad and sustained sound that characterizes this group's varied performances ... GIMEL understands, moreover, how to view music as an intellectual undertaking.'

BIBLIOGRAPHY

Schulman, Michael. 'Nil Parent: getting ahead with electro-acoustic music,' *CanComp*, 116, Dec 1976 MB-L

GINGRAS, Claude. Critic, author, b Sherbrooke, Que, 1 Jul 1931. He studied music with Sylvio *Lacharité and began his career as a journalist in 1952 with the Sherbrooke daily newspaper *La Tribune*. He subsequently contributed to the *Quartier latin*, then to the Montreal newspaper *La Presse*, where, near the end of the 1950s, he became music critic and record reviewer. The author of *Musiciennes de chez nous* (Montreal 1955), a collection of short biographies, he also has been editor-in-chief of *Dictionnaire de vos vedettes* (Montreal 1958) and a contributor to *High Fidelity*, the **Canada Music Book*, **Musicanada*, and other publications. In Claude Gingras's view, the role of the critic is 'essentially to act as an intermediary between the one who gives and the one who receives ... he should love passionately the field in which he works ... should have a complete knowledge of his subject, reliable taste, and sound judgment independent of friendships or enmities. In sum, he should possess the evaluative powers inevitably lacking in those on one side of the footlights or the other' (*Guide du spectacle et du disque*, Quebec 1978). GP

GINGRAS, Rolland-G. (Georges). Organist, teacher, critic, composer, b Quebec City 21 Apr 1899, d there 14 Dec 1964; D MUS (Montreal) 1945. He began lessons in piano and organ with Omer *Létourneau at 12 and continued with J.-Arthur *Bernier, Henri *Gagnon, and Berthe *Roy. He studied harmony with Robert *Talbot and Edmond *Trudel and had tuition in singing, Gregorian chant, composition, conducting, and the performance techniques of various instruments.

Gingras was organist in the Quebec City area at the churches of Notre-Dame-de-Lourdes in 1914, St-Raymond-de-Portneuf in 1917, St-Sauveur 1919–20, Notre-Dame-de-Jacques-Cartier in 1921, St-François d'Assise 1925–50, and St-Albert-le-Grand 1950–64. He conducted the Chanteurs de Saint-François and the Société chorale Saint-Gérard, gave organ and piano recitals, and in 1937 conducted for radio station CKCV.

Gingras was the director in 1925 of the St-Malo Music School. He taught solfège from 1926 to sometime after 1950 at the École des arts et métiers and music in 1929 at the Clerics of Saint-Viateur College in Lauzon. He taught solfège later in Loretteville and in 1964 in Ancienne-Lorette. François *Brassard and Françoise Fiset were among his pupils.

As an impresario Gingras presented the organist Marguerite Lesage and the pianists Yvonne

*Hubert, Gilberte *Martin, and André *Mathieu in Quebec City. He was in demand as a lecturer.

Gingras was a music reporter or critic for various publications, including *L'Action catholique, L'Événement, Mégantic,* and *La Quinzaine musicale,* and was correspondent ca 1935 for the Paris periodicals *Courrier musical, théâtral et cinématographique* and *Le Ménestrel.* In 1933 he drafted a report for the French government on the influences of French music in Canada. In Quebec City he published *Les Hymnes nationaux* (1934) and *Questionnaire de théorie musicale.*

Gingras did some composing, and the critic of *L'Action catholique,* 17 Mar 1925, praised his *L'Appel du missionnaire:* 'The music is perfectly adapted to the words of the librettist [J.-Eugène Corriveau] ... the audience especially enjoyed the operetta's graceful vocal ensembles.' Among Gingras's published works are *Douze Chansons de France* and 'Le Cantique officiel de la Ligue catholique féminine.' Among his compositions in manuscript are *Quatre Chansons populaires,* for soloists, choir, and orchestra, and numerous religious pieces and songs, including 'Le Vieux Missel' with string quartet accompaniment.

Gingras was a juror for the *Prix d'Europe and a founding member and director of the Association des chanteurs de Québec. He was named Commander of the Order 'Honneur et Mérite' of Haiti in 1943 and Chevalier de l'Ordre latin of France in 1949. AP

GIRARD, Jean. Organist, teacher, b Bourges?, France, 8 Aug 1696, d Montreal 23 Feb 1765. He entered the Company of St-Sulpice in 1720 but was not ordained a priest. In 1724 he left Bourges and sailed to Montreal, where for the rest of his life he taught various subjects, probably including music, at the school run by the Sulpicians. Throughout his life in Canada he was active as a musician, playing the organ at Notre-Dame Church (although others are known to have occupied this position until 1734, in 1739, and 1741). Henri Gauthier has described him also as a 'modérateur du chant.'

BIBLIOGRAPHY

Lapalice, Ovide. 'Les organistes et maîtres de musique à Notre-Dame de Montréal,' *BRH,* vol 25, Aug 1919

Gauthier, Henri. *Sulpitiana* (Montreal 1926)

GISÈLE. See MacKenzie, Gisèle.

'Give a Man a Horse He Can Ride.' Concert ballad which was a staple in the North American baritone repertoire from the 1920s to the 1950s. Its music, to verses by James Thomson, was written by Geoffrey *O'Hara during a visit to Kingston, Ont, and was dedicated to J. Arthur Craig of that city. The song was published in 1917 by Huntzinger & Dilworth, New York. Usually a solo but also arranged for male quartet or chorus, it was performed first in the USA – Lambert Murphy was the singer – and by 1931 it had been recorded by John Barclay, Royal Dadmun, Albert Downing (tenor), and Arthur Middleton. (See *Roll Back the Years.*) An unsuccessful attempt was made to revive the song in the mid-1960s. FH

GLACKEMEYER. 1 / Frédéric-Henri and 2 / Louis-Édouard, his son.

1 **Frédéric(k)-Henri** (Friedrich Heinrich). Band conductor, string-instrument player, music dealer, teacher, organist, b Hanover 1751 d Quebec City 12 Jan 1836. His father, Wilhelm Glackemeyer, played the fife in a military band in Hanover. All that is known of Frédéric's youth was related a century and a half later by Nazaire *LeVasseur; it is anecdotal and suggests romanticized fiction. At five he began to learn the viol, and his rapid progress and precocious virtuosity soon drew him to the attention of princes and nobles, who invited him to play at their court. Despite the prospect of a brilliant future in his native Germany, the young Glackemeyer, lured by a spirit of adventure, embarked with his instruments on a sailing ship bound for Canada. After several weeks in Trois-Rivières, the ship's destination, he set out for Quebec City.

Quebec then was the seat of government and the cultural capital of Canada. On arrival there Glackemeyer immediately began teaching viol, bass-viol, violin, and piano. It has been documented that he was band conductor of one of the Brunswick mercenary regiments which arrived in 1776 under the command of Baron von Riedesel and that he gave lessons to the baron's daughter during the winter of 1783 on one of Quebec City's few pianos. (It is also possible that the lessons took place in *Sorel, Que.) Advertisements which appeared 1784–1819 illustrate his activity as an importer and dealer in musical instruments and sheet music, a repairer of instruments, a piano tuner, and a music teacher.

Glackemeyer evidently wanted not only to earn a living but also to foster the development of music in the area. There were subscription concerts in Quebec City at that time, and Glackemeyer, with Francis *Vogeler, is known to have taken part in them in 1790 and 1791. LeVasseur relates that Prince Edward, later duke of Kent, who lived in Quebec City 1791–4 and was a music lover, held the German musician in high esteeem and put him in charge of the regimental band. In 1820, in his old age, Glackemeyer founded (according to LeVasseur) the *Quebec Harmonic Society, for which he apparently imported numerous chamber music and orchestral parts (preserved in the Séminaire de Québec).

A Lutheran who converted to Roman Catholicism, Glackemeyer was organist 1816–18 in the Quebec Basilica. He is believed to have left several unpublished compositions. One of them, the march *Châteauguay,* was played 24 Sep 1818 at a dinner given by the citizens of Quebec City in honour of Lieut-Col de Salaberry, hero of the battle of Châteauguay (1813).

Frédéric Glackemeyer is remembered best as a pioneer; his great influence was due to his competence and the far-reaching effects of his teaching. He can be regarded as one of the fathers of Quebec musical life. One of his daughters, Henriette-Angèlique, married Théodore Frédéric *Molt, and a grandson married a daughter of *Brauneis père.

BIBLIOGRAPHY

Roy, Pierre-Georges. 'La famille Glackemeyer,' *BRH,* Jul 1916

LeVasseur, Nazaire. 'Musique et musiciens à Québec,' *La Musique,* May, Jun, Jul 1919

2 **Louis-Édouard**. Notary, flutist, b Quebec City 7 Dec 1793, d there 10 Feb 1881. Because of a general prejudice against teaching music to men, he was self-taught. He studied the flute without his father's knowledge while working towards a career as a notary. But the latter, hearing him on one occasion play a duo for flute and violin, discovered his son's talent and presented him with a silver flute which he had brought over from Europe.

Édouard's skilful playing in a Pleyel quartet led to the formation of a group comprising Judge Jonathan *Sewell (first violin), Archibald Campbell (second violin), J. Harvicker (cello), and himself. The quartet met every Saturday during the fall and winter and gave subscription concerts.

In addition to a brilliant professional career (he was several times president of the Quebec Chamber of Notaries and was a city councillor), Édouard Glackemeyer played the flute in the 1847 concerts of the *Quebec Harmonic Society and in 1870 became the society's honorary president. He was senior officer and honorary president of the *Septuor Haydn, to which he gave his music library, including several scores that had belonged to his father.

BIBLIOGRAPHY

LeVasseur, Nazaire. 'Musique et musiciens à Québec,' *La Musique,* Jun, Jul 1919 CH, HK

GLEDHILL, Christopher. Educator, organist, composer, b Borden, Kent, England, 21 Mar 1912; BA (Oxford) 1934, B MUS (Oxford) 1936, MA (Oxford) 1946. He is a grandnephew of Edwin *Gledhill. He attended Marlborough College and later the RCM, and was an organ scholar at Oriel College, Oxford. After some years in the army (captain in the Royal Signals, serving in France and Madagascar) he returned to Oxford to receive an MA. He emigrated to Canada in 1946 to become music master at Lakefield School, near Peterborough, Ont. He moved to Montreal in 1954 as organist-choirmaster at the Church of St James the Apostle and remained in that city until 1961, when he became music director of the Prince Edward Island Dept of Education, Charlottetown. He continued in that position until 1977 except for two years (1966–8) spent on the island of Mauritius as music specialist for the Canadian International Development Agency. He was organist-choirmaster and music director of Charlottetown's Kirk of St James 1961–78. He is a linguist and traveller as well as a musician. He has written scripts for the CBC, has given organ and piano recitals, and has appeared on TV as performer, conductor, and panel member. Compositions and arrangements by him include *Two Folksongs* (BMI Canada 1952), *Fiddle Tune* for piano (Harris 1954), and *Folksongs of Prince Edward Island* (Square Deal Press 1973). *Abegweit,* an orchestral suite (manuscript, CMCentre), was commissioned for the Prince Edward Island centenary (1973). WL

GLEDHILL, Edwin. Composer, teacher, b London 3 Jul 1830, d California Feb 1919. He arrived in New York in 1851 with his father, Robert L. Gledhill, who under the name Signor Salvi appeared as tenor soloist on Jenny Lind's North-American tours of 1851–2. After his father's death in 1853 Gledhill went to Philadelphia, moving later to Toronto, where he remained except for two sojourns (1902–8, 1917–19) in California. He was for five years the organist at Bond St Congregational Church but seems to have held no other office. He did teach privately, and his pupils included John Eaton, Henry Pellatt, and other children of well-to-do families. Gledhill's published music, some 30 works, appeared in the 20 years after Confederation. He was the most successful Anglo-Canadian composer of parlour ballads of his time. Such titles as 'Falling Leaves' (Nordheimer 1868), 'I Am Waiting for Thee' (ibid 1867), or 'Stay, Angry Tide' (self-publ 1874) are characteristic. Other works relate to the contemporary scene, eg, the songs 'For Canada Fight' (Nordheimer 1886) and 'The Death of Gordon' (ibid 1886) or *The Hanlan Galop* (ibid 1878) in honour of the champion oarsman from Toronto. Gledhill's distinction as purportedly the first Canadian composer to have had a street named after him was not in fact a musical honour; Gledhill Ave commemorates his ownership of a large tract of land in Toronto's Danforth district. Christopher *Gledhill in his grandnephew. HK

GLEN BRODER, Annie (b Glen, m Broder). Pianist, teacher, critic, b Agra, India, 18?? d Calgary 18 Aug 1937. Educated in England, she was a pupil of Sir Arthur Sullivan and Sir John Stainer at the RCM. She performed widely as an accompanist in England, wrote the manual *How to Accompany* (London 1893), and lectured on the art at the RAM, Dublin U (with Ebenezer Prout), and Oxford U. She was music critic for British periodicals and newspapers before emigrating to Canada, settling in Regina ca 1902. In 1903 she moved to Calgary, where she taught piano and voice. Though she said she had come to Calgary neither 'early enough to be an old-timer nor recently enough to be a novelty,' as music critic for the Calgary *News-Telegram* and later the Calgary *Herald* she was considered the 'grande dame' of music in the city. She also was a contributor to the Toronto *Globe*, the Winnipeg *Free Press*, and the British periodicals *World*, *Pall Mall Gazette*, and *Musical Standard*. Her composition *The Ride of the North West Mounted Police*, attributed to A. Glen Broder (possibly to forestall prejudice against a woman composer) and arranged for band by John Waldron, was printed in 1906 – unattributed to a publisher or place – and was used for many years by RCMP bands. She represented Canada at the Anglo-American Music Conference (1934) in Lausanne. Her pupils included the Covent Garden soprano Odette *de Foras.

BIBLIOGRAPHY

Morgan, H.J. *Canadian Men and Women of the Time* (Toronto 1912)

Kennedy, Norman John. 'The growth and development of music in Calgary, 1875–1920,' unpubl MA thesis, U of Alberta 1952 (RDM)

GLICK, Srul Irving. Composer, radio producer, conductor, teacher, b Toronto 18 Sep 1934; B MUS (Toronto) 1955, M MUS (Toronto) 1958. His father David (b Kishinev, Russia, 15 Apr 1898), emigrated to Canada and settled in Toronto in 1924 and was a cantor in several of that city's synagogues. The younger Glick studied composition with *Weinzweig in Toronto, for two summers in the 1950s with Milhaud in Aspen, and 1959–60 with Louis Saguer and Max Deutsch in Paris. In 1963 he joined the CBC as a music producer, in which capacity he has been responsible for the premieres of many Canadian compositions on such programs as 'Music Alive,' 'Themes and Variations,' 'CBC Tuesday Night,' and 'Music Toronto.' He also taught theory and composition 1963–9 at the *RCMT. In 1968 he became conductor of the choir at Beth Tikvah Synagogue, Toronto (which recorded the privately distributed LP *Music from the Jewish Liturgy*). He also conducted the *Chamber Players of Toronto for a recording of his *Suite Hebraïque No. 2* and *Gathering In*.

Glick's commissioned works include *Pan* for the *Atlantic SO, *Symphony No. 2* for the Toronto Chamber Orchestra, and *Lamentations* for the *Kingston SO. In his works of the 1960s Glick unites lyricism with thick, polytonal textures, at times employing jazz idioms. Several of his works incorporate Jewish subjects and folk materials. The song cycle *... i never saw another butterfly ...*, a commission from the CBC for Maureen *Forrester, sets poems by Jewish children, many of whom died in the Terezin concentration camp during World War II. *Heritage*, commissioned by the New Dance Group of Canada in Toronto, is a ballet about the hardships of a Jewish immigrant family. With *Gathering In* Glick began a series of experiments using a more contemporary language, employing note clusters, for example, but without completely discarding the emotional lyricism of his earlier works. He was president 1966–9 of the *CLComp and is an associate of the *CMCentre and a member of CAPAC.

Srul Irving Glick

Glick's wife is the pianist Dorothy Sandler (b Toronto 4 Jun 1937), a pupil of Boris *Berlin, Albert Jaffy, and Alberto *Guerrero in Toronto and of Giselle Couteau in Paris. She has been a recitalist and concerto soloist in the Toronto area, has performed on the CBC, and has recorded two Mozart *Sonatas*, K330 and K333, for the CBC (1971; CBC SM-221).

SELECTED COMPOSITIONS

BALLET

Heritage. 1967. Chamb orch. CMCentre

ORCHESTRA

Sinfonia Concertante. 1961. Str orch. Summit 1973. RCA LSC-3128 (*McGill Chamb O)

Suite Hebraïque. 1961; arr cl (sop sax) and pf 1963; str quar 1964; str orch 1965. Orch or cl (sop sax), pf or str quar or str orch. B&H 1968 (cl, pf). (Cl, pf) Dom S-69004 (*Galper cl)/(sop sax, pf) Golden Crest RE-7049 (*Brodie sax)

Dance Concertante No. 1 1963. Sm orch. CMCentre

Pan. 1966. Orch. CMCentre

Symphonies No. 1 and 2. 1966, 1967. CMCentre

... i never saw another butterfly ... (children's poems). 1968. Alto, chamb orch (pf). CMCentre, MCA 1972 (alto, pf version only). (Alto, pf version) CBC SM-77/ Sel CC 15.073 (*Forrester)

Gathering In. 1970. Str orch. Summit 1972. RCI 389 (*Chamber Players of Toronto)

Psalm for Orchestra. 1971. CMCentre

Lamentations 'Sinfonia Concertante No. 2.' 1972. Str quar, orch. CMCentre

Four Songs for Tenor and Orchestra (Patchen). 1972. CMCentre

Concerto for violin and orchestra. 1976. CMCentre

Symphonic Elegy, with Line Drawing and Funeral March. 1975. Str orch. Ms

CHAMBER

Petite Suite pour flûte. 1960. GVT 1972. Dom S-69006 (*Aitken fl)

Dance Concertante No. 2. 1964. Fl, cl, tpt, vc, pf. CMCentre

Sonata for Jazz Quintet; Sonatina for Jazz Sextet. 1964, 1965. Ms. CMCentre

Suite Hebraïque No. 2. 1969. Cl, str trio, pf. CMCentre. RCI-389 (*Fenyves vn)

Suite Hebraïque No. 3. 1974. Str quar. CMCentre

Prayer and Dance. 1975. Vc, pf. CMCentre. CBC SM-348 (*Henig pf)

PIANO

Four Preludes. 1958. GVT 1968. Lon CTLS-5107 (*Henig pf)

Song and Caprice. 1960. GVT 1968. (*Caprice*) Dom S-69002 (*Mould pf)

Seven Preludes and *Ballade* (1959). Both ms

VOICE AND CHOIR

Music for Passover (Passover 'Haggadah'). 1975. SATB, str orch. Ms

Two Landscapes (K. Patchen). 1973. Ten, pf. CBC SM-180 (*Vickers)

Also over 30 pieces for SATB for use in the Synagogue (1964–75). Ms. Some works recorded by Beth Tikvah Choir (Tor)

WRITINGS

'Sydney Hodkinson: *Caricatures*,' *CMB*, 1, Spring–Summer 1970

BIBLIOGRAPHY

'Srul Irving Glick: a Canadian who came home,' *CanComp*, 23, Nov 1967

'Srul Irving Glick: a portrait,' *Mcan*, 5, Oct 1967

Champagne, Jane. 'A composer's contribution: being able to say something "peculiar",' *CanComp*, 103, Sep 1975 (CF)

GLOBENSKI, Anna-Marie. Pianist, teacher, b St-Barthélémi, near Sorel, Que, 2 Jul 1929; B MUS (Montreal) 1949, M MUS piano (Montreal) 1951, M MUS (Indiana) 1967. She is a member of one of the first families of Polish origin to settle in Canada. She studied 1946–51 at the *École Vincent-d'Indy with Jean *Dansereau (piano) and Claude *Champagne (theory). Winner in 1951 of the *Prix d'Europe, she studied 1951–2 at the Paris Cons in the foreigners' class with Marcel Ciampi and 1952–6 at the Vienna Academy with Bruno Seidlhofer. In 1954 she received an honourable mention at the International Competition for Musical Performers in Geneva and was heard on Viennese radio. The following year she became the first Canadian to participate in the Frederic Chopin International Competition in Warsaw.

Returning to Canada, Globenski toured 1956–7 for the *JMC, and appeared on CBC radio as a soloist and chamber musician, especially on 'Récital.' She taught 1960–2 at the École Vincent-d'Indy and worked 1960–3 as an accompanist at the *CMM. She continued her studies, taking summer courses 1963–7 at Indiana U, Bloomington, and in 1963 began teaching at *Laval U. Jacinthe *Couture was one of her pupils. She recorded music of Bartók, Beethoven, Debussy, Kreisler, Paganini, Ravel, and Wieniawski with the violinist Liliane Garnier-Lesage (Victor LM LSC 2646).

BIBLIOGRAPHY

Musiciennes de chez nous (SPI)

GLYNNE, Howell. Bass, b Swansea, Wales, 24 Jan 1904, d Toronto 24 Nov 1969. After studying in Swansea and later in London and Vienna, he sang minor roles with the Carl Rosa Opera, making his debut in a major role – Sparafucile in *Rigoletto* – in 1931. He was leading bass at Sadler's Wells 1946–51 and 1956–61 and at Covent Garden 1951–6. Glynne visited Canada in 1961 to sing the Sergeant Major in the *Stratford Festival production of *The Pirates of Penzance* and returned for Stratford's Gilbert & Sullivan productions in 1962 and 1963. He made his *COC debut in 1963 as the Baron Ochs in *Der Rosenkavalier*, settled in Toronto in 1964, joined the teaching staff of the *RCMT, and remained with the COC until 1969, when he died in a car accident. Among his roles for the COC was that of William McDougall in the premiere production of *Somers' **Louis Riel* (1967). He repeated the portrayal in the subsequent CBC TV production of the opera. Glynne's pupils at the RCMT included Peter *Barcza, Gary *Relyea, and Roxolana *Roslak.

BIBLIOGRAPHY

B.M. 'Howell Glynne,' *OpCan*, Dec 1964

Kareda, Urjo, 'Glynne: Stratford's veteran basso buffo,' *Toronto Daily Star*, 1 Aug 1968 GK

GMEINER, Eugen (Friedrich). Organist, teacher, b Bucharest, of Austrian parents, 26 Aug 1927, naturalized Canadian 1962, d Halifax 17 May 1977; M MUS (Michigan) 1967. He studied with

Karl Walter at the Vienna Academy of Music and graduated in 1949. He was an organist-choirmaster 1951–6 in Vienna and often gave organ recitals on Austrian radio. In 1956 he emigrated to Canada, becoming music director at the Wolfville, NS, Baptist Church. He subsequently studied with Marilyn Mason at the U of Michigan. He taught 1956–77 at *Acadia U, where he also was university organist. The winner of the 1962 National (USA) Organ Competition, Gmeiner performed extensively in Canada, the USA, and Europe and was recognized as an outstanding Bach interpreter. He recorded organ works of Bach – *Bach, A Memorial Programme* – for Fantasy Sound. (1973–6, FS23462). AF

GODDEN, Reginald. Pianist, teacher, b Tunbridge Wells, England, 18 Sep 1905; LTCM 1929. His family emigrated to Canada in 1906 and settled in Allendale (now Barrie), Ont; he began piano lessons at 13 and became the silent-movie pianist at the Barrie Opera House at 14, retaining the job until 1928. He commuted to Toronto for organ lessons 1925–9 with Healey *Willan and began advanced piano study in 1928 with Ernest *Seitz. That same year he began 21 years of teaching at the *TCM. In the 1930s he and Scott Malcolm formed a piano duo which played frequently in Toronto, toured North America, and appeared in New York and London. In 1940 he began five years' study with the noted French pedagogue and Debussy pupil E. Robert Schmitz, at the same time embarking on a solo career. During those years he gave Canadian premieres of works by Prokofiev (*Seventh Piano Sonata*, 1944; *Third Piano Concerto*, with the *TSO, 1945), Shostakovich, and Copland. He also premiered the works of several Canadians, notably *Somers (*Strangeness of Heart*, 1943; *Etude, Dark and Light, Flights of Fancy, Arrangement, Moon Haze*, 1945; *Testament of Youth: Sonata No. 1*, 1946; *Solitudes*, 1947) and *Weinzweig (*Piano Sonata*, on 'CBC Wednesday Night,' 1951). During the 1940s he performed with the Baltimore SO and the Budapest String Quartet.

Godden served 1948–53 as principal of the Hamilton Cons (*RHCM), and during 10 years in Hamilton helped found the *Hamilton Chamber Music Society and gave the first integral performance (1956) in Canada of the 32 piano sonatas of Beethoven. Also in 1956, with the *CBC SO under Victor *Feldbrill, he gave the premiere of Somers' *Second Piano Concerto*. Moving to San Francisco, he devoted himself 1958–66 to an intensive study of the music of J.S. Bach, performed Beethoven's *'Appassionata' Sonata* and Bach's *Goldberg Variations* on NET telecasts, and gave many lecture recitals.

Godden returned to Toronto in 1966 and prepared the piano reduction of Somers' *Louis Riel* for rehearsals prior to the opera's premiere. He resumed teaching at the *RCMT in 1969 and joined the faculty at *York U in 1973. In 1975 he was script-writer and commentator for the first two records in the series of 13, called *Music Canada*, produced jointly by the CBC (RCI) and CAPAC. After the first of 13 public lecture recitals on Bach's keyboard music at the RCMT in the fall of 1968, John *Kraglund wrote, 'This will be a series to prompt Bach students and fans to delve more deeply into the musical and emotional content of Bach's music and to awaken the interest of the less devoted and even relatively untutored listener' (Toronto *Globe and Mail*, 23 Sep 1968), and Kenneth *Winters wrote, '[Godden] can cut straight through the sclerotic pomposities and prim pedantries of common highnosed opinion to give you a welcome inkling of the real matter and scope of a music such as Sebastian Bach's' (Toronto *Telegram*, 23 Sep 1968). Godden's pupils include Alfred *Kunz, Walter *MacNutt, Phyllis *Mailing, Earle *Moss, Kenneth *Peacock, Eldon *Rathburn, and Harry Somers. In 1977 he performed the 12 *Études* of Debussy and in 1978 the *Ludus tonalis* of Hindemith.

Reginald Godden

WRITINGS

'The piano études of Claude Debussy,' *Fugue*, Aug–Sep 1978

DISCOGRAPHY

Pentland *Studies in Line* – Peacock *Bridal Suite*. 1949. Lon T.5697 (78)

Somers *Testament of Youth: Sonata No. 1*. 1976. RCI 450

BIBLIOGRAPHY

Dempsey, Lotta. 'He takes Bach with mushrooms,' *Toronto Daily Star*, 11 Dec 1969 KW

GODFREY, (Harold) Graham. Conductor, organist, composer, b Birmingham 1890, d Barton-on-Sea, Hampshire, England, 23 Dec 1955; B MUS (Birmingham), D MUS (Toronto) 1932. He studied in England, at the Midland Institute and with Granville Bantock in Birmingham. He was assistant conductor (to Sir Adrian Boult) of the Birmingham Festival Choral Society and music director of Carr's Lane Congregational Church. He moved to Hamilton, Ont, in 1930 as organist of Melrose United Church and remained there until his return to England in 1950. He founded the Hamilton SO in 1930 and conducted its first concert 27 Jan 1931. He established and was the sole conductor of the Bach Choir of Hamilton, which made its debut 14 Mar 1932 in the *St Matthew Passion* at the First United Church. The choir disbanded during World War II but was reorganized by Charles *Peaker in 1946 as the *Bach-Elgar Choir. Together, the Hamilton SO and the Bach Choir introduced many oratorios to Hamilton audiences. Godfrey's compositions include the cantatas *The Forsaken Merman* and *Pioneers* and several anthems and songs.

BIBLIOGRAPHY

'Graham Godfrey and Hamilton, Ontario, and a new symphony orchestra,' *British Musician*, vol 6, Aug 1930

FAH

GODFREY, Henry Herbert. Songwriter, business executive, b Plymouth, England, 1858, d Westmount (Montreal) 18 Jan 1908. His musical education was informal. After his arrival in Canada in 1874 he worked in a Montreal piano factory, served as a church organist, and led a vaudeville band. About 1883 he became a piano salesman for the *Nordheimer Co in Ottawa, moving to Toronto in 1888. Later he was manager for *Mason & Risch, then for *Gourlay, Winter, & Leeming Piano Co, and in 1903 he returned to Montreal as managing director of C.W. *Lindsay & Co. Nordheimer published some 15 of Godfrey's dances and marches for student pianists. However, it was for his patriotic songs (mostly to his own words) that he was best known. After publication by Mason & Risch, Nordheimer, *Orme, *Whaley Royce, and others, 18 songs were reissued in an album called *Canadian Patriotic Songs and Melodies* (Canadian-American Music 1902). Godfrey's 'The Land of the Maple' and its French version, 'Le Pays de l'érable,' (1897) sold over 100,000 copies, 'The Men of the North' (1897) over 60,000. 'Toronto, or the Pride of the North' (1898) won the prize in a University of Toronto Song Book Committee competition. 'Johnny Canuck's the Lad,' 'Soldiers of Canada,' and 'When Johnny Canuck Comes Home' were written in 1900 during the South African War. Other titles include 'The Story of the Flag,' 'Hark! The Drum' (1897), and 'Canada's Hymn of Empire' (1899). None appears to have been recorded. Godfrey compiled *A Souvenir of Musical Toronto* (Toronto 1897, 1898–9), a useful survey of music and musicians active at the time (see Dictionaries). HK

GODFREY, Victor (John). Bass-baritone, b Deloraine, south of Brandon, Man, 10 Sep 1934. His Covent Garden debut in 1960 followed studies with Gladys *Whitehead in Winnipeg, Jan van der Gucht at London's National School of Opera 1957–9, and Hans Hotter in Munich 1959–60, and his winning of the Kathleen Ferrier Memorial Scholarship in 1959. He sang Orestes in the CBC TV production 23 Jan 1961 of Strauss' *Elektra*. He made his Covent Garden debut in 1960 as the Doctor in *Macbeth* and created Hector in Tippett's *King Priam* in 1962.

During the years 1960–8, as a principal bass at Covent Garden, Godfrey gave some 450 performances in 45 roles. With the English Opera Group he created Abednego in Britten's *The Burning Fiery Furnace* (Aldeburgh 1962), and with the same company he sang Azarias in that opera and Polyphemus in Handel's *Acis and Galatea* in Montreal at the World Festival (*Expo 67). He joined the Deutsche Oper am Rhein, Düsseldorf, as a Heldenbariton in 1968 and at the same time sang with the Landestheater in Hanover. In 1971 he began freelancing, specializing in Wagner and Strauss.

GBr

GOLDBERG, Theo. Composer, teacher, b Chemnitz (now Karl-Marx-Stadt), Germany, 29 Sep 1921, naturalized Canadian 1973; MA (Washington State) 1969, D MUS (Toronto) 1972. He studied composition 1945–50 with Boris Blacher at the Hochschule für Musik, Berlin, and subsequently wrote surrealist and mixed-media works for cabaret and scores for over 350 radio broadcasts and 30 stage productions. His radio opera *Robinson und Freitag* was performed in 1951 over RIAS, Berlin, his studio opera *Engel-Etüde* in 1952 by the International Festival for Theatre and Arts, Berlin, and his ballet *Nacht mit Kleopatra* in 1952 at Karlsruhe.* After emigrating to Canada in 1954 he was associated with the *Vancouver International Festival and wrote the score for John Hirsch's stage production of *Peter Pan*. He taught school in Vancouver and in 1970 began to teach music education at the *U of British Columbia. His later works (eg, *Orion / Changes*, 1978) have moved increasingly into mixed media, pre-recorded tape, and computer participation. He is a member of the *CLComp, an associate of the *CMCentre, and an affiliate of GEMA, the German performing rights organization.

SELECTED COMPOSITIONS

STAGE AND MIXED MEDIA

Nacht mit Kleopatra, opera/ballet (Goldberg). 1950 (Karlsruhe State Opera). Ms

Robinson und Freitag, radio opera (von Cramer). 1951 (RIAS, Berlin). Ms

Engel-Etüde, chamb opera (von Cramer). 1952 (Berlin 1952). Ms

Galatea Elettronica, opera (Goldberg, da Vinci). 1969 (Washington 1969). CMCentre

Jeanne des Anges, chamb opera (Goldberg). 1972. Ms

Variations of a Mandala, mixed media. 1973 (Washington 1973). Tape, sound-related images. Ms

Orphée aux enfers, 'opéra son et lumières.' 1975 (Vancouver 1975). Tape, sound-related images. Ms

ORCHESTRA

Divertissement No. 3 in G. 1957. CMCentre

Sinfonia Concertante. 1967. Fl, cl, tpt, vn, vc, orch. Ms

Songs of the Loon and the Raven (Chief Billy Assu). 1975. Orch, tape. Ms

CHAMBER

Samogonski-Trio (Bergengruen). 1951. Bar, cl, vc, pf. B&B 1952

Clarinet Quintet. 1952. B&B 1952

Divertissement No. 1. 1953. Vn, pf. Ms

Divertissement No. 2. Ca 1955. Ww, vn, pf. Lost

Three Movements for Bassoon and Buchla. 1971. Bn, tape. Ms

Antithesis. 1974. Sax, tape. Ms

St Francis' Sermon to the Birds. 1975. Bn, tape. Ms

See also *Contemporary Canadian Composers*. MW

GOLDBLATT, Rose (m Finkel). Pianist, teacher, b Montreal 28 Aug 1913. She began piano studies with Stanley *Gardner and gave her first public recital at six. Awarded the five-year *Strathcona scholarship of the RCM, she studied with Kendall Taylor and Harold Craxton 1930–5, making her London debut in 1935. Subsequently she worked with Egon Petri in New York. Returning to Montreal, she performed on radio and as soloist with the *Little Symphony of Montreal, the *CBC SO, the *Montreal Women's SO, and the *McGill Chamber Orchestra and gave two-piano recitals with Stanley Gardner. She also toured the USA, playing at New York's Town Hall, Chicago's Kimball Hall, and elsewhere. She introduced much Canadian music to North American audiences and many works (eg, by Violet *Archer, Maurice *Dela, Marvin *Duchow, George *Fiala, and Hector *Gratton) were dedicated to her. During 1955–6 she was the host of 'Piano Party,' a weekly CBC radio program for teenagers. She joined the Faculty of Music, *McGill U, in 1956 and has been co-ordinator of local centres for the Preparatory School of the faculty. She appears on two CBC recordings, playing music by *Kaufmann, *Joachim, and *Morawetz (RCI 133) and Fiala's *Concertino*, with a CBC Montreal string orchestra, with Roland *Leduc conducting (RCI 184). NT

GOLDEN, Ann (Frances) (m Fisher). Contralto, teacher, b Ottawa; L MUS (McGill) 1958, B MUS (McGill) 1968. Among her singing teachers at the *École Vincent-d'Indy and *McGill U were Bernard *Diamant and Jan *Simons. In 1964 on a grant from the *Canada Council she studied with Phyllis Curtin and Jennie Tourel at the Aspen Festival in Colorado. In 1957 in Montreal she created the role of Princess Aurora Borealis in the McGill U production of **My Fur Lady*. She subsequently performed the role some 120 times in several Canadian cities. Also in 1957 she sang the Sorceress in *Dido and Aeneas*, the first production of the *McGill Opera Studio.

Later, Golden concentrated primarily on recital work and was engaged as an oratorio singer by the *Montreal Elgar Choir, the Tudor Singers of Toronto, the *Ottawa Choral Society, the Pro Musica Society of Boston, the Worcester, Mass, Festival, and other organizations. She sang the role of the Nun in the Canadian premiere (Montreal 1964) of Menotti's *The Death of the Bishop of Brindisi*. The following year she was soloist with the *McGill Chamber Orchestra in Christian Ritter's cantata *O amantissime sponse Jesu*. At the *SMCQ she premiered Bruce *Mather's *Madrigal V* in 1973. She has given numerous recitals on the CBC, presenting both classical and contemporary works.

Golden was head of music at St George's School, Westmount (Montreal), in the mid-1960s and began teaching voice at the *Mount Royal College Cons of Calgary in 1979. GP

GOLDSCHMIDT, Nicholas. Conductor, administrator, teacher, baritone, pianist, b Tavikovice, Moravia (Czechoslovakia) 6 Dec 1908, naturalized Canadian 1951; hon FRHCM 1978. A grand-nephew of the Austrian composer Adalbert von Goldschmidt, he studied at the Vienna State Academy with Josef Marx (composition), Paul Weingarten (piano), and Corneille de Kuyper (voice). After conducting in various cities in Czechoslovakia and Belgium he emigrated in 1937 to the USA, where he was director of opera 1938–42 at both the San Francisco Cons and Stanford U and director of the opera department 1942–4 at Columbia U. At the invitation of Arnold *Walter he moved to Toronto, where he served 1946–57 as the first music director of the *Royal Cons Opera School, 1949–57 as the first music director of the *CBC Opera, and 1950–7 as music director of the Opera Festival Assn, conducting productions of 13 operas, including *Rigoletto* (1950, 1954), *The Marriage of Figaro* (1951, 1955), and *Hansel and Gretel* (1957). His position as music director 1950–8 of the *U of British Columbia summer school preceded his appointment as artistic and managing director 1957–62 of the *Vancouver International Festival. While occupied 1964–8 as chief of the performing arts division of the Centennial Commission, responsible for organizing the nationwide celebrations and events of Festival Canada (1967), he also founded (and conducted until 1972) the Centennial Choir in Ottawa.

Goldschmidt became artistic director of the Edward Johnson Music Foundation in 1967 and served 1968–75 as music director of the *U of Guelph, initiating and co-ordinating the *Guelph Spring Festival in 1968 at the university under the foundation's sponsorship. Continuing as the festival's artistic director, he conducted its productions of Britten's *The Prodigal Son* (1969, the North American premiere), *The Burning Fiery Furnace* (1971), *Noye's Fludde* (1972), and *The Rape of Lucretia* (1974), Handel's *Acis and Galatea* (1975), Britten's realization of John Gay's *The Beggar's Opera* (1976), Derek *Healey's **Seabird Island* (1977, the premiere), and a dramatization of Berlioz' oratorio *L'Enfance du Christ* (1980). He also organized and prepared the concert of works by Krzysztof Penderecki conducted at Guelph by the composer 8 May 1976. In 1975 Goldschmidt added to his Guelph duties those of consultant to the *Algoma Fall Festival, Sault Ste Marie, Ont, also conducting productions and organizing the Algoma Festival Choir. In 1980 he served as chairman of the national committee set up to organize celebrations of the Healey *Willan centenary.

Occasionally a soloist in oratorio or a recitalist in Lieder, Goldschmidt has made a specialty of Schubert's song cycle *Winterreise*, accompanying himself at the piano, and he has given many master classes in Lieder. He accompanies himself in Schubert songs on the recording *Emmy Heim – A Self Portrait* (Hallmark SS-2).

Goldschmidt's infectious enthusiasm for music combined with a resilient optimism, an instinct for the ripeness of an opportunity, and an ability to calculate a risk have made him Canada's most active festival entrepreneur in the years following his pioneer work with the Royal Cons Opera. In 1976 he received the *CMCouncil Medal and in 1978 he was made an Officer of the *Order of Canada.

Nicholas Goldschmidt

BIBLIOGRAPHY

Hambleton, Ronald. 'A builder of Canadian opera,' *Fugue*, Apr 1978

Maheu, Renée. 'Nicholas Goldschmidt – chef d'orchestre,' *L'Information médicale et paramédicale*, 20 Nov 1979

(MCv)

GONNEVILLE, Michel. Composer, b Montreal 31 Jul 1950; B MUS (Sherbrooke) 1972. A student at the *École Vincent-d'Indy, he also studied in 1969 at the *CMM with Françoise *Aubut, Gaston *Arel, Irving *Heller, and Gilles *Tremblay. In 1973 a *Canada Council grant made possible a study tour of European electro-acoustic music studios, and in 1975 further grants, from the Canada Council and the Quebec Ministry of Education, allowed him to attend Stockhausen's seminars in Cologne and to take part in an experiment in collective composition at Rolf Gelhaar's composition studio in Darmstadt. His marked interest in Stockhausen was reflected in the early works *Trio*, premiered in 1971 in Montreal at a symposium of young composers; *Ouverture*, premiered in 1972 in New York at the annual symposium of student composers; and *Rôle*, which won an award in the 1975 *CBC National Radio Competition for Young Composers. In 1972 Gonneville composed the sound track for Jean-Guy Noël's film *Tu brûles, tu brûles*. He also wrote the incidental music and arranged some songs for a show for children and composed songs for a theatrical show. He has made orchestral arrangements of pop tunes and classical material. He is a member of CAPAC.

SELECTED COMPOSITIONS

Trio (A. Lamarre). 1971. Vn, trb, pf, perc, spkr. Ms

Ouverture. 1972. Db, pf, 3 perc. Ms

Inclusions. 1973. 4 sax, pf, guit, b guit, perc. Ms

Trois Poèmes d'Alain Fournier. 1974. Fl, cl, sop. CMCentre

Rôle. 1975. Rec, vn, guit, elec hpd. Ms

Guide. 1976. 5 instr. Ms

Contribution à l'étude de certains phénomènes musicaux ... 1977. Pf. Ms

Variations 'auras.' 1978. Fl (picc), eng hn, cl, tpt, hn, trb, vn, va, vc. CMCentre

BIBLIOGRAPHY

Gingras, Claude. 'Gonneville et Longtin: deux créations à la SMCQ,' Montreal *La Presse*, 17 Feb 1979

Petrowski, Nathalie. 'Deux jeunes compositeurs à la SMCQ,' Montreal *Le Devoir*, 19 Feb 1979

'A contemporary composer in Quebec,' *CanComp*, 142, Jun 1979

GOOCH, Bryan N.S. (Niel Shirley). Teacher of English, writer, pianist, conductor, harpsichordist, b Vancouver 31 Dec 1937; ARCT 1957, BA (British Columbia) 1959, LTCL 1959, FTCL 1961, MA (British Columbia) 1962, PH D English (London) 1968. In Vancouver he studied with Ira *Swartz (piano), John *Avison, Nicholas *Goldschmidt and George Schick (conducting), and Allard de *Ridder (composition, arranging). He made his debut as a pianist in 1956 at the Vancouver Art Gallery. While studying 1962–4 in London he conducted the St Thomas Chamber Orchestra and the U of London's opera group and Gilbert & Sullivan Society. He was music director and conductor of the Nanaimo SO 1968–71 and assumed the same position with the New Westminster SO in 1975. He has guest-conducted the *CBC Vancouver Chamber Orchestra and the *Victoria Symphony Chamber Orchestra. Gooch has accompanied Robert *Creech, Gloria Doubleday, Heather *Thomson, and others in recital, and has performed in various chamber groups and in two-piano teams with Hugh *McLean and Robert *Rogers. He taught English literature 1959–60 at the U of British Columbia and in 1964 joined the department of English at the U of Victoria. He also taught piano 1967–70 at the *Victoria Cons. A prolific writer on English literature, Gooch has been interested especially in the relationship between poetry and music. He was co-author with Tory I. Westermark of *Poetry Is For People* (Toronto 1973). He is a contributor to *EMC*.

WRITINGS

'Henry Cart de Lafontaine's *The King's Musick*: The Purcell Family index,' *Notes and Queries*, ns vol 13, Jul 1960

'Ernest Dowson and Frederick Delius: On *Songs of Sunset* as mentioned in Arthur Hutchings' *Delius*,' *Delius Society Newsletter* (1974), reprt in *Music R*, vol 36, May 1975

– and Thatcher, David S. *Musical Settings of Late Victorian and Modern British Literature: A Catalogue* (New York 1976)

– and Thatcher, David S. *Index of Titles and First Lines to Musical Settings of Late Victorian and Modern British Literature: A Catalogue* [Victoria, BC 1977]

– and Thatcher, David S. *Musical Settings of Early and Mid-Victorian Literature: A Catalogue* (New York 1978)

GOODERHAM, Col Albert (Edward). Financier, patron, soldier, b Toronto 2 Jun 1861, d there 25 Apr 1935; hon LL D (Toronto) 1924, appointed Knight Commander of the Order of St Michael and St George (KCMG) 1935 (but not invested). Gooderham was 'a financier by inheritance and a philanthropist by instinct' (*Standard Dictionary of Canadian Biography*, Toronto 1938). Music and education were two of the many areas of social welfare and culture to which he and his wife devoted their active interest and financial support. He was the founder of the *Canadian Academy of Music, and was its president 1911–24. At the time of the academy's merger with the *TCM he became chairman of the Board of Governors, a position he held until his death. He was president 1923–31 and honorary president 1932–5 of the New SO (later *TSO), and his financial support and personal encouragement ensured the survival of that orchestra during its early years. He was a warden and director of musical activities at St James' Cathedral.

BIBLIOGRAPHY

'Sir Albert Edward Gooderham,' Toronto *Globe* (26 Apr 1935) PW

'Good Luck to the Boys of the Allies.' Patriotic song of World War I by the Toronto composer Morris Manley. Published privately by Manley in 1915 ('as sung by Little Miss Mildred Manley, Canada's Greatest Child Vocalist'), it was recorded by Lewis J. Howell (Victor) and Herbert Stuart (Columbia). An arrangement was recorded by the Victor Military Band, and another appeared on piano rolls. The song was revived in 1939 in the folio *Soldier's Songs of Canada* published by G.V. *Thompson. Manley, of whom little is known save that he lived in New York after 1930, wrote other songs, including 'I Love You, Canada' (1915, with Kenneth McInnis), 'Goodbye Mother Dear' (1916, recorded by Henry *Burr), and several which were adapted for piano rolls.

BIBLIOGRAPHY

Roll Back the Years FH

GOODMAN. Toronto musicians: 1 / Hyman and 2 / Erica, his daughter.

1 **Hyman**. Violinist, teacher, b Toronto 28 Jan 1913. He began his violin studies in 1920 with Broadus *Farmer in Toronto and continued 1926–9 with Vladimir Graffman in New York. Returning to Toronto in 1929 he played in the General Electric Hour Orchestra and in Alexander *Chuhaldin's string orchestras on CFRB and CRBC radio, and studied with Chuhaldin. He began to play in the *TSO in 1931. Goodman took further training in the late 1930s with William Primrose and in the early 1940s with Kathleen *Parlow. A flight-sergeant bandsman 1942–6 in the RCAF, he played to servicemen throughout Canada and Europe and performed often on the BBC and Radio Hilversum (Holland). In 1946 he studied briefly with D.C. Dounis in New York. Returning to Toronto he rejoined the TSO and soon was appointed concertmaster, serving 1948–67 in that capacity. He was concertmaster, and occasionally a soloist, 1946–56 with the Toronto Philharmonic Orchestra (*Promenade Symphony Concerts) and performed often during those years on CBC radio. During the 1960s he taught at AF of M String Congresses, and 1968–70 he was on staff at the U of California at Los Angeles. Following a brief return to Canada in the early 1970s Goodman settled permanently in Los Angeles, where he continued to play as a freelance performer.

BIBLIOGRAPHY

Lee, Betty. 'He simply wants to remain top fiddle,' *Globe Magazine*, 20 Dec 1958

Lanken, Dane. 'Finding the last chord in California,' Toronto *Globe and Mail*, 18 Mar 1978

2 **Erica** (m Kamin, m Stanford). Harpist, b Toronto 19 Jan 1948. She studied piano 1958–62 with Myrtle *Guerrero; her harp studies were undertaken with Charles Kleinsteuber 1959–65 at Interlochen, Mich, and at the U of Michigan; 1958–65 with Judy *Loman in Toronto; 1966–7 with Carol Baum at the U of California at Los Angeles; and 1967–9 with Marilyn Costello at the Curtis Institute. In 1960 she performed as soloist with the *NYO and made her CBC TV debut as accompanist to Teresa *Stratas. Goodman was second harp 1962–6 and 1969–73 with the *TSO and made her professional solo debut 5 Feb 1969 playing the Mozart *Concerto* for flute and harp with the Philadelphia Orchestra. She has played for *Ontario Place film soundtracks and has performed several times on CBC radio and TV. She has appeared in concert and recital with the *Festival Singers, Hyman Goodman, Suzanne *Shulman, and Riki *Turofsky and has appeared often with *NMC. With Robert *Aitken in 1970 she formed the Aitken-Goodman Duo, which gave many recitals and in 1976 toured with the US group Tashi. She was a member 1977–8 of the Galliard Ensemble. She gave the New York premiere of *Somers' *Suite for Harp and Chamber Orchestra* with the *NACO 24 Feb 1972 and the premieres of *Morawetz' *Harp Concerto* 23 Apr 1976 in Guelph, Ont, and *Applebaum's *Algoma Central* 19 Sep 1976 at Sault Ste Marie, Ont. She was the winner of the Mona *Bates Award in 1978. In 1979, with the flutist Virginia Markson-Miller and the cellist David Miller she formed Trio Toronto.

DISCOGRAPHY

Krumpholtz – Lasala – Lauber – Inghelbrecht. Aitken fl. 1971. CBC SM-156

Mozart *Concerto* K299. Cram fl, NACO, Bernardi cond. 1974. CBC SM-262

BIBLIOGRAPHY

Bowser, Sara. 'A girl's best friend is a harp,' *Canadian Weekly*, 11 Sep 1965 NM

GOODMAN, Mildred (m Marcus, m Pépin). Violinist, b Montreal 13 Nov 1922. She studied 1936–8 with Sascha Jacobsen at the Institute of Musical Art (Juilliard School) and 1938–40 with Maurice *Onderet at the *McGill Cons and took courses 1943–5 with Jacques Gordon at the ESM, Rochester, NY. She won a Sarah *Fischer Concerts scholarship in the early 1940s and subsequently appeared as a soloist for several Montreal organizations, including the *Ladies' Morning Musical Club, the *CSM Orchestra, and the *Pro Musica Society. Concertmaster 1940–61 of the *Montreal Women's SO, she was second violin 1942–4 in the *McGill String Quartet and 1955–63 in the *Montreal String Quartet. She also played in *Musica Antica e Nuova 1951–5, the Montreal Trio, and various CBC orchestras in Montreal. During the summers 1960–3 she played with the *Stratford Festival orchestra and attended Oscar Shumsky's master classes. She became a member of the *MSO in 1950 and a teacher at McGill U in 1963. She married the composer Clermont *Pépin.

DISCOGRAPHY

Archer *Sonata No. 1*. Newmark pf. 1956. RCI 196

See also Musica Antica e Nuova; and Discographies for Garant (RCI 301, in Gellman *Mythos 11*); Newmark; and Montreal String Quartet. NT

GORDON, Jeanne (b Gordon, Ruby, m Trix). Contralto, b Wallaceburg, near Windsor, Ont, 1884, d Macon, Mo, 22 Feb 1952; ATCM. [The corrected birthdate is a result of recent research by J.B. McPherson.] Her only teacher was Albert *Ham, with whom she studied while attending Toronto's Havergal College. Her father, John Gordon, was a member of Parliament, and as a girl she often sang before Sir Wilfrid Laurier. Married unhappily (1908) to Ralph K. Trix of Detroit, she nevertheless followed him, settling in New York when he joined the US navy and was stationed in Hoboken.

In New York Gordon appeared at the Rialto Theatre, singing operatic 'interludes' as part of a variety program. These appearances led to a contract with the Creatore Grand Opera, and she made her debut 11 Dec 1918 in Brooklyn as Amneris in *Aida*. She toured with the Scotti Grand Opera the following spring and made a highly successful *Metropolitan Opera debut 22 Nov 1919 as Azucena in *Il Trovatore*. She remained a principal contralto with that company for nine consecutive seasons, her repertoire consisting of two dozen roles (in French, Italian, German, and English), including Carmen, Dalila, Eboli in *Don Carlo*, Marina in *Boris Godunov*, Brangäne in *Tristan und Isolde*, and several novelties. She also sang in the premieres of Albert Wolff's *L'Oiseau bleu* and Henry Hadley's *Cleopatra's Night*. For virtually all of her opera roles she was coached by Wilfrid *Pelletier. Maintaining an active concert schedule she sang in Montreal 11 Mar 1926 on an all-Canadian program under Pelletier with Edmund *Burke, Florence *Easton, and Edward *Johnson and in Toronto 27 Jan 1927 with the *National Chorus under Albert Ham. After guest appearances with the Monte Carlo Opera in 1928 in Europe, with the TSO during its 1929–30 season under Luigi von *Kunits, and with the Toronto Promenade Orchestra in 1930 under Reginald *Stewart (her last appearance), she suffered a mental collapse and was admitted to a Missouri sanatorium, where she remained until her death of a heart attack.

A tall and handsome woman with a magnetic personality and a true contralto voice of extraordinary range and richness, Gordon never quite fulfilled the promise evident in such notices as that published by *Musical America* after her 1921 Metropolitan appearance as Brangäne: 'The most satisfactory all-round individual contribution to the performance was made by Jeanne Gordon whose lovely contralto and fine sense of pictorial and dramatic values received thrilling expression.' She recorded nine single-sided 78s for Columbia (1920–2) and two in 1925 for Victor. All are listed in *Roll Back the Years*. In 1927 she appeared in a few Warner Brothers-Vitaphone shorts, singing operatic excerpts with Martinelli, Gigli, and others. She shares with Edward Johnson and Marie Louise *Edvina a Rococo recording (No. 5254) of operatic arias.

BIBLIOGRAPHY

Bell, Dorothy G. 'Jeanne Gordon wins her laurels,' *Maclean's*, 3 instalments, 15 Nov, 1 Dec, 15 Dec 1925

Thompson, Oscar. *The American Singer* (New York 1937)

Manning, E.B. 'Roll Back the Years, Part 2,' *OpCan* Dec 1964

JBM

Gospel songs. See Hymn singing.

GOSS, John. Baritone, teacher, b London 10 May 1894, d Birmingham 13 Feb 1953. A pupil of Victor Beigel and Reinhold von Warlich in London, Goss first performed in Canada at the Vancouver Sea Festival (*CPR Festivals) during a North American tour in 1929. He was the dedicatee of four songs written by Healey *Willan early that same year. Several Canadian appearances followed in the 1930s, including a CPR-sponsored concert in Toronto 6 Feb 1930 of British and Canadian music, tours 1931–7 as leader of the London Singers (a quintet which included Alan *Mills during its final two years), and a performance 5 Feb 1935 of Delius' *Sea Drift* with the *TSO and the TCM Choir. He was soloist with the *Winnipeg Male Voice Choir in its 1934 concert at Town Hall, New York. After two years, 1938–9, in London, where he joined the Communist Party and formed the Unity Male Voice Choir, he returned to Canada to adjudicate at musical competition festivals. Impressed by the quantity of young Canadian talent he took up residence in Vancouver, where 1940–50 he gave concerts and radio recitals, participated in the BCMTA, taught privately, and was a director 1948–9 of the *Friends of Chamber Music. His Canadian pupils included Beverly *Fyfe, May *Lawson, Mary *Morrison, and Sherwood *Robson. In 1949 Goss went to New York but was arrested because of his political sympathies and sent back to Canada. He returned to England in 1950. Goss' publications include *An Anthology of Song* (London 1929) and *Ballads of Britain* (London 1937). (FH)

GOSSELIN, Roger. Bass, director, administrator, b Drummondville, Que, 4 Mar 1919. At St-Frédéric College, Drummondville, he studied violin, trumpet, and french horn 1924–34. He played french horn in the local concert band 1933–8, was violinist in the Drummondville SO, and soloist in the parish choir 1936–40. Moving to Montreal, he studied voice 1940–3 and was a navigator with the RCAF 1942–5. In Paris in 1946 he continued his singing lessons with Mme Louis Fourestier and took stage techniques with Georges Wague.

In 1947 Gosselin made his debut at the Grand Théâtre of Cherbourg as Mephisto in *Faust*. His European career spanned the years 1948–58 and included some 1500 performances of operas and operettas in France, Italy, and North Africa. In 1952 at the Gaîté-Lyrique in Paris he sang in Francis Lopez' *Andalousie* opposite Gise Mey. He taught voice technique and stage techniques 1954–8 in Paris. Jacques *Labrecque was one of his pupils.

Gosselin returned to Montreal in 1958 and served 1958–61 as director general of the Ville d'-Anjou Arts Council. He was artistic consultant 1961–2 for Quebec City's Winter Carnival. A founder, along with the soprano Nelly Mathot, of the *Théâtre lyrique de Nouvelle-France, he was artistic director 1961–7, supervising the production of numerous works over the years and singing supporting roles. He held an administrative position at the *Grand Théâtre in Quebec City until 1978. In 1976 he sang Kromsky in a production of *The Merry Widow* presented by the *Quebec SO in Quebec City and at the *PDA during the 1976 Olympics in Montreal. In 1978 he staged *Faust* for the *Société lyrique d'Aubigny.

Gosselin's wife, Jeanne Guihard (b France, d Quebec City 1966), worked for a few seasons ca 1952–8 at the Paris Opera and sang the roles of Mallika (*Lakmé*, 1962) and Charlotte (*Werther*, 1963) in Quebec City.

WRITINGS

'L'Opéra du Québec ... six pieds sous terre?,' *Musicien québécois*, vol 1 (Aug–Sep 1974, Dec–Jan 1974–5) GP

GOSSELIN, Roland. Bass, teacher, b Quebec City 1 Aug 1926; BES (Quebec Ministry of Education) 1970, M MUS (Sherbrooke) 1970, performance diploma (Sherbrooke) 1971. He was a member of the Petite Maîtrise Notre-Dame de Québec, where he took lessons in Gregorian chant 1936–40 with Father Joseph De Smet. He studied opera repertoire 1946–51 with Isa Jeynevald-Mercier at the Institut d'art vocal.

Gosselin spent 1952–5 in France, where he sang in more than 300 performances at the Opéra de Lyon, appearing with Régine Crespin, Jacques Jansen, Raoul *Jobin, Mady Mesplé, and Mado Robin. His roles included Sparafucile in *Rigoletto*, Mephisto in *Faust*, the Commendatore in *Don Giovanni*, Des Grieux in *Manon*, and Nourabad in *Les Pêcheurs de perles*. He toured France in 1958 for the JM as a member of a vocal quartet.

Returning to Canada in 1955, Gosselin sang in recitals and concerts on radio and TV. He performed 1967–9 in productions of *La Bohème* (Colline), *The Barber of Seville* (Don Basilio), *Tosca* (Angelotti), and *Werther* (le Bailli) by the Théâtre lyrique du Québec. At the *École Vincent-d'Indy he studied voice 1969–71 with Louise *André and Bernard *Diamant. He sang in Stravinsky's *Renard* in 1970 at the *NAC and made his debut at the *Opéra du Québec as Marco in *Gianni Schicchi* (1971), later singing Montano in *Otello* (1973), the Imperial Commissioner in *Madama Butterfly* (1974), and Alcindoro in *La Bohème* (1975). With the *Quebec SO he was a soloist in *Messiah*.

Gosselin taught introductory music courses 1970–7 at the Louis-Philippe Paré polytechnical school in Châteauguay, near Montreal, and after 1977 he gave voice lessons and organized concerts at the cultural centre there. ST

GOULD, Evelyn (m Reiter). Soprano, b Toronto 9 Mar 1925. She sang in several high school productions of Gilbert & Sullivan and studied privately 1940–4 with Nina de Gedeonoff. She made her professional debut in 1943 in a *TSO Secondary School concert – the first of several appearances with the orchestra – and began her radio career on CBC programs with Lou *Snider and Stanley *St John. In 1944 she received a fellowship to attend the Juilliard School, where her teachers were Florence Page Kimball and Queena Mario. She later commuted to New York for private study with Rosalie Miller and Sidney Dietch. In 1945 she was awarded first prize in *'Singing Stars of Tomorrow,' and that same year (and again in 1946) she received the LaFlèche Trophy for her 'contribution to Canadian radio as a classical singer,' largely through her work 1944–6 on CBC radio's 'Music for Canadians.' Later CBC assignments ranged from the starring role 1953–4 in the musical-variety radio series 'Let's Make Music' to leading parts 1953–6, including Zerlina in *Don Giovanni* – the first full-length opera produced for TV in Canada – Adele in *Die Fledermaus* and Musetta in *La Bohème* (also for TV). She sang in CBC radio productions of *Chu Chin Chow*, *The Telephone*, and *La Serva Padrona*. For the *COC she sang Lucinda in Wolf-Ferrari's *School for Fathers* in 1954, Adele in 1955, and Zerlina in 1956. She retired from public performance in 1956.

GOULD, Glenn (Herbert). Pianist, recording artist (piano, harpsichord, organ, spoken word), author and producer of radio documentaries, composer, essayist, commentator, b Toronto 25 Sep 1932; ATCM 1945, hon LL D (Toronto) 1964. At 3 Gould was able to read music and showed that he possessed absolute pitch. His father was an amateur violinist. His mother, one of whose ancestors was a cousin of Edvard Grieg, taught him music, and at 5 he was writing piano pieces and playing them for friends in the east-Toronto neighbourhood where he was raised. He was at no time under pressure, however, to display or exploit his musical abilities. At the *TCM he studied piano 1943–52 with Alberto *Guerrero, obtaining an ATCM at 12 with the highest marks in Canada. He also studied organ 1942–9 with Frederick C. *Silvester and theory 1940–7 with Leo *Smith.

Gould made his debut as an organist, not as a pianist, in a *Casavant Society recital at *Eaton Auditorium, Toronto, 12 Dec 1945. Reviewing the performance Edward W. Wodson of the *Evening Telegram* wrote, 'Not only astonishing technique but interpretive intuition is his in full maturity.' Gould first appeared as a pianist with orchestra 8 May 1946, playing the first movement of Beethoven's *Concerto No. 4* with the TCM Orchestra conducted by Ettore *Mazzoleni. Of this performance Wodson wrote: 'He showed the music lover that scale passages and arpeggios on the humble piano may have spiritual as well as technical beauty and character. His phrasing was eloquent as poetry chanted by the poet himself.' On 14 Jan 1947 Gould performed the entire concerto with the *TSO conducted by Bernard Heinze in a concert for secondary school pupils. Pearl McCarthy wrote in the *Globe and Mail*: 'The boy played it exquisitely. His is not a heavy tone, but delicacy of phrasing and timing give it clear carrying power.'

Gould's network broadcast debut was a CBC 'Sunday Morning Recital' 24 Dec 1950. For Gould this is a significant date because it marks the beginning of what he refers to as his love affair with the microphone. He played Mozart's *Sonata* K281 and Hindemith's *Third Sonata* on a studio piano

Glenn Gould

with heavy, dark bass. When he played a recording of the broadcast he found that by suppressing the bass and boosting the treble he could make the piano sound the way he had tried but failed to do in the studio and that in this way he had overcome the piano's limitations and improved upon his original contribution as performer. His approach to performing and recording was to be dominated thereafter by this discovery and by his awareness of its implications.

By the age of 20 Gould's performing experiences had included tours of western (1951) and eastern Canada, nine appearances as piano soloist with orchestras (Hamilton, Toronto, Vancouver), several public recitals – including his Montreal debut 6 Nov 1952, for the *Ladies' Morning Musical Club at the Ritz-Carlton Hotel, in music of Gibbons, Bach, Beethoven, Brahms, and Berg – and, for the CBC, four or five studio recitals. His interest in modern music was well established; his repertoire included the complete piano works of Schoenberg, Berg, and Webern. But it was not his intention to become a concert pianist. Composition was at that time for him a livelier concern, and already he was demonstrating remarkable abilities as a musical analyst and commentator.

However, in 1954 he gave a recital with Jean-Paul *Jeannotte for the *Pro Musica Society of Montreal, on 3 Jan 1955 he played in the Phillips Gallery in Washington, and eight days later he played in Town Hall, New York. His programs included works by Bach, Berg, Beethoven, Gibbons, Sweelinck, and Webern. The enthusiastic critical response launched Gould on nine years of concert and recital tours. In 1955 he played Beethoven's *Concerto No. 4* with the *CBC SO under Jean-Marie *Beaudet during the only visit of that orchestra to Montreal. In 1956 at the *Stratford Festival he heard the premiere of his *String Quartet*, performed as a solo pianist, and conducted Schoenberg's *Ode to Napoleon*. In 1957 he made his European debut with the Moscow Philharmonic, gave recitals of music by Bach, Beethoven, and Berg in Moscow, Leningrad, and Vienna, played with the Berlin Philharmonic under von Karajan, was the pianist in Brahms' *Quintet, Op 34* with the *Montreal String Quartet at the *Montreal Festival, and gave a recital at Carnegie Hall. He appeared in 1958 with the Concertgebouw Orchestra under Dimitri Mitropoulos at the Salzburg Festival and with the *Hart House Orchestra under Boyd *Neel at the Brussels World's Fair. He also gave 11 performances in 18 days that year in Israel. He appeared on the 1959–60 series of the *MSO and the TSO, giving with the latter the first Canadian performance of Schoenberg's *Piano Concerto*. (He repeated that work in 1961 with the CBC SO under Robert Craft and recorded it for Columbia.) He also made his London debut in 1959, playing the five Beethoven concertos with the London Symphony Orchestra under Joseph Krips.

After his first public performance (1959) of Brahms' *Concerto No. 1* with the *Winnipeg SO under Victor *Feldbrill, Peggie *Sampson wrote to Kenneth *Winters in Paris: 'Gould played the Brahms D minor ... It was marvellous – no, more than that: it was *so clear!*' He repeated the work at the 1961 *Vancouver International Festival under Zubin Mehta, apparently without alarming anyone, but by 1962 his ideas about it had changed. When he played it on 14 April of that year with the New York Philharmonic, Leonard Bernstein, in an announcement prior to the performance, which he was to conduct, disassociated himself from Gould's radical ideas on the music (exemplified by an extraordinarily slow tempo in the first movement), going ahead with the performance only because he felt Gould's thoughts on the subject should be demonstrated in fairness to his remarkable mental powers. The performance embodied perhaps the most notorious example of Gould's penchant for upsetting, or stretching, or simply flouting conventionally held attitudes on music which interests him.

In the 1950s and 1960s, Gould played frequently on CBC radio, alone, and in chamber music with Leonard Rose and Oscar Shumsky, with whom he was co-director of music 1961–4 at the Stratford Festival. His career as a concert artist ended by his own decision in 1964. After that time he occupied himself increasingly with recording for Columbia, broadcasting and telecasting for the CBC, and writing for various journals. His concert-giving days are hardly less well remembered for his eccentric costumes and stage mannerisms than for his repertoire and the quality of his playing. Gould has never understood why people were so interested in the visual aspects of performance, why they did not devote their attention (as he did) to the auditory (ie, the musical) aspects. One reason for his preference for recordings over concerts is that the visual aspects count for nothing in the former.

Gould's famous recording in June 1955 of Bach's *Goldberg Variations* marked the beginning of his exclusive association with Columbia. A glance at the discography will show that this has been a productive and adventurous relationship. Gould insists that a recording is not a souvenir or a reconstruction of a concert. A studio performer need not concern himself with projecting musical effects into an auditorium for the purpose of catching and holding the attention of people sitting there; rather he can subject the music to minute inspection of detail at every structural level, making use of technical devices, including types and placements of microphones, tape-editing, and ultimately control by listeners at the playback stage, of loudness, balance, tempo, tone-colour, and other parameters, most of them formerly under the control only of performers. Outside popular music probably no artist has done more to stretch the technological possibilities of recorded music than Glenn Gould.

His experimentation extends to extremes of tempo and articulation in many of his performances of music from the standard repertoire, and critics have objected to these extremes. But Gould justifies them in terms of the new freedom invested in the listener through technological change: if a recorded performance is too fast, it can be slowed in playback with no effect on pitch; if a performance is too detached and choppy, reverberation can be added, and so on. Moreover, he argues, there is no point in making yet another recording of, say, the *Emperor Concerto* unless one is prepared to offer significant departures from the established, mean-line versions already available on disc. One thing he does not attempt to defend is the vocal noise he makes while playing, which no technical device is able to remove and which apparently he is powerless to prevent.

Gould has not been productive as a composer. Two pieces written when he was a student at the RCMT were performed there in January 1951, but these were not published. His three published works show his preference for highly organized, contrapuntal, diatonic music and his considerable skill with it. His piano transcriptions of Wagner's orchestral music (*The Siegfried Idyll*, the *Prelude to Die Meistersinger*, and Dawn and Siegfried's Rhine Journey from *Die Götterdämmerung*) are subtle reconceptions of the music in pianistic terms rather than literal score reductions. It is difficult to estimate the number of Gould's transcriptions; by 1980 they had not been collected and published. He is known to have unusual facility in reducing orchestral scores to keyboard harmony at sight, but of actual transcriptions we can only count those he has recorded and those he has performed in public circumstances, such as Ravel's *La Valse*, on CBC TV in 1975.

Gould's compositional interests have been rerouted to the production of radio documentaries. In these he combines spoken word and other kinds of soundtrack materials, 'composing' with them in forms similar to such conventional musical forms as sonata-allegro and passacaglia. In 'The Idea of North,' for instance, he displays his ability to control several channels of information simultaneously, an ability also revealed in his extremely lucid playing of contrapuntal music on the piano. Gould had published by 1979 over 45 articles on musical subjects and about as many liner notes for his own record releases. Of several long published interviews with him, some are essentially self-interviews. Gould's writings explain the music he plays, justify his more extravagant peculiarities in repertoire and in interpretation, and comment on culture and life generally. For his many CBC studio recitals he has prepared interviews and commentaries of various kinds.

No levelling off of Gould's creative powers is in sight; for this reason it is too soon to attempt an evaluation of his achievement. His rank among contemporary pianists (achieved and maintained apparently effortlessly and at a high international level despite his lengthening truancy from the concert platform and the absence from his repertoire of such mainstream composers as Schubert, Schumann, Mendelssohn, Chopin, Liszt, Debussy, Bartók, and Stravinsky) is suggested by the following two quotations. 'This young Canadian stands out above all other pianists young and old. The playing style, with its powerful note-to-note continuity of shape and tension, is like no other. So is what it produces – the object in sound completely formed and completely achieved to the exact sonority of the last note ... one's mind is seized by the very first sounds, with their electrifying authority and force, and is held fascinated by the continuous coming into existence of the remainder of the musical object' (Haggin, p 218). '[Gould's] best is undoubtedly to be set alongside the very best that the great pianists of our time can do. Gould sometimes commands an elegance and a transparency unattained by any other living pianist, even Rubinstein' (Kaiser, p 140).

These two evaluations were based upon Gould's concert performances and his earlier recordings. But it is in radio and TV that he now seems most active and innovative, particularly in radio documentaries. Thus far it cannot be said that his radio documentaries succeed entirely as communications. It is true that we do not make as much use as we should of the human mind's ability to handle many lines of communication at one time, but Gould confronts his listeners with what seem to be jumbles of voices and sound effects, too dense and too intricate to be comprehensible except to someone who is familiar with Gould's works in this genre and is prepared to give careful and repeated study to them, which the medium of radio normally does not permit. His early prose writings were similarly opaque; but his recent ones, particularly his radio scripts, contain some of the clearest prose to be found anywhere in 'foreground' broadcasting, and his radio documentaries appear to be developing in the same way, towards increasing clarity.

Among honours received by Gould are the Harriet Cohen Bach Medal (1959), the Canada Council's $15,000 *Molson Prize (1968), and the *CCA's Diplôme d'honneur (1976).

COMPOSITIONS

Twelve-Tone Piano Pieces. 1948. Ms
String Quartet, Op 1. 1953–5. Bar & Bar 1956. RCI 142 (*Mtl Str Quar)/1960. Col ML 5578 (Symphonia Quar)
Cadenzas to the Concerto No. 1, in C for Piano and Orchestra, Op 15, by Beethoven. 1954. Bar & Bar 1958
So You Want to Write a Fugue. 1964. 4-part chorus, pf, (str quar). G. Schirmer 1964. 1968. Stereo Review bonus record GG-101

WRITINGS

'The dodecacophonist's [sic] dilemma,' *CMJ*, vol 1, Autumn 1956
'Let's ban applause,' *Musical America*, vol 82, Feb 1962
'Arnold Schoenberg, a perspective,' U of Cincinnati occasional papers no. 3 (Cincinnati 1964)
'Strauss and the electronic future,' *Saturday R*, 30 May 1964
'The prospects of recording,' *High Fidelity*, Apr 1966
'The search for Petula Clark,' *High Fidelity*, Apr 1968
'Radio as music,' *CMB*, 2, Spring–Summer 1971
'Glenn Gould interviews himself about Beethoven,' *Piano Q*, Feb 1972
'Glenn Gould interviews Glenn Gould about Glenn Gould,' *High Fidelity*, Feb 1974
'The grass is always greener in the outtakes,' ibid, Aug 1975
'Back to Bach (and belly to belly),' Toronto *Globe and Mail*, 29 May 1976
'Streisand as Schwarzkopf,' *High Fidelity*, May 1976
'Portrait of a cantankerous composer,' Toronto *Globe and Mail*, 18 Mar 1978
'In praise of maestro Stokowski,' *NY Times Magazine*, 14 May 1978
Review of *Glenn Gould: Music and Mind* by Geoffrey Payzant, Toronto *Globe and Mail*, 29 May 1978

DISCOGRAPHY

Anhalt *Fantasia* – Hétu *Variations* – Morawetz *Fantasy in D Minor*. 1966–7. Col Masterworks 32110046
Bach *The Art of Fugue: Fugues 1–9*. Gould organ. 1962. Col MS-6338
– *Concertos*
No. 1, in D Minor – Beethoven *No. 2, in B Flat*. Columbia SO, Bernstein cond. 1957. Col ML-5211
No. 2, in E; No. 4, in A. Columbia SO, Golschmann cond. 1969. Col MS-7294
No. 3, in D; No. 7, in G Minor. Columbia SO, Golschmann cond. 1967. Col MS-7001
No. 5, in F Minor – Beethoven *No. 1, in C*. Columbia SO, Golschmann cond. 1958. Col MS-6017
– *English Suites 1–6*. 1971, 1973–6. Col M2-34578
– *French Suites 1–4*. 1972–3. Col M-32347
– *French Suites 5 and 6; Overture in the French Style*. 1971–3. Col M-32853
– *Fugue in E* (WTC II); *Fugue in F Sharp Minor* (WTC II); *Partitas No. 5 and 6*. 1957. Col ML-5186
– *Goldberg Variations*. 1955. Col ML-5060
– *Inventions and Sinfonias*. 1963–4. Col MS-6622
– *Italian Concerto; Partitas No. 1 and 2*. 1959. Col MS-6141
– *Partitas No. 3 and 4; Toccata No. 7 in E Minor*. 1962–3. Col MS-6498
– *Partita No. 5* – Morawetz *Fantasy*. 1954. RCI 120
– 3 *Sonatas* for viola da gamba and harpsichord. Rose vc. 1973–4. Col M-32934
– 6 *Sonatas* for violin and harpsichord. Laredo vn. 1975–6. Col M2-34226
– 7 *Toccatas*. 1976 (1979); Col Vol 1: M-35144. Vol 2: (1980); Col M-35831
– *Well-Tempered Clavier I: Preludes and Fugues 1–8*. 1962. Col MS-6408
– *Preludes and Fugues 9–16*. 1963. Col MS-6538
– *Preludes and Fugues 17–24*. 1965. Col MS-6776
– *Well-Tempered Clavier II: Preludes and Fugues 1–8*. 1966–7. Col MS-7099
– *Preludes and Fugues 9–16*. 1969. Col MS-7409
– *Preludes and Fugues 17–24*. 1971. Col M- 30537
Beethoven *Bagatelles, Op 33, Op 126*. 1974. Col M-33265
– *Concertos* (see also '*Concertos*' under Bach)
No. 3, in C Minor. Columbia SO, Bernstein cond. 1959. Col MS-6096
No. 4, in G. New York Phil, Bernstein cond. 1961. Col MS-6262
No. 5, in E Flat. American SO, Stokowski cond. 1966. Col MS-6888
– *Sonatas*
Op 10, no. 1, 2, 3. 1964. Col MS-6686
Op 13; Op 14, no. 1 and 2. 1966. Col MS-6945
Op 27, no. 2 'Moonlight'; *Op 57* 'Appassionata.' 1967. Col MS-7413
Op 31, no. 1, 2, 3. 1967–73. Col M-32349
Op 109; Op 110; Op 111. 1956. Col ML-5130
– *Symphony No. 5* (transcribed Liszt). 1967–8. Col MS-7095
– *32 Variations in C Minor; 6 Variations, Op 34; 15 Variations and Fugue, Op 35*. 1966–70. Col M-30080
Berg *Sonata* – Krenek *Sonata No. 3* – Schoenberg 3 *Piano Pieces, Op 11*. 1958. Col ML-5336
Berg *Sonata Op 1* – Prokofiev 'The Winter Fairy' from *Cinderella* – Shostakovitch 3 *Fantastic Dances* – Taneyev *The Birth of the Harp*. Pratz vn. 1953. Hallmark RS-3
Bizet *Nocturne in F; Variations chromatiques* – Grieg *Sonata, Op 7*. 1971–2. Col M-32040
Brahms 10 *Intermezzos*. 1960. MS-6237
– *Quintet in F Minor*. Mtl Str Quar. 1957. RCI 140
Byrd – Gibbons: *Selections*. 1967–71. Col M-30825
Handel *Suites 1–4*. Gould hpd. 1972. Col M-31512
Haydn *Sonata No. 3* (Hoboken XVI:49) – Mozart *Fantasia and Fugue* K394 – *Sonata* K330. 1958. Col ML-5274
Hindemith *Das Marienleben*. Roslak sop. 1976. Col M2-34597
– 3 *Piano Sonatas*. 1966–73. Col M-32350
– 4 *Sonatas* for brass and piano. Johnston tpt, Jones hn, Smith trb, Torchinsky tuba. 1975–6. Col M2-33971
Mozart *Concerto* K491 –Schoenberg *Concerto, Op 42*. CBC SO, Susskind cond (Mozart), Craft cond (Schoenberg). 1961. Col MS-6339
Mozart *Sonatas*
No. 1 K279; *No. 2* K280; *No. 3* K281; *No. 4* K282; *No. 5* K283. 1967. Col MS-7097
No. 6 K284; *No. 7* K309; *No. 9* K311. 1968. Col MS-7274
No. 8 K310; *No. 10* K330; *No. 12* K332; *No. 13* K333. 1965–70. Col M-31073
No. 11 K331; *No. 15* K545; *Sonata with Rondo* K533/K494; *Fantasia* K397. 1965–73. Col M-32348
No. 16 K570; *No. 17* K576; *Fantasia and Sonata* K475/K457. 1966–74. Col M-33515
Prokofiev *Sonata, Op 83* – Scriabin *Sonata No. 3*. 1967–8. Col MS-7173
Schoenberg *Fantasy* for violin and piano, *Op. 47*. Baker vn. 1964. Col MS-7036
– 5 *Piano Pieces, Op 23; Piano Pieces, Op 33a and b; 6 Little Piano Pieces, Op 19; Suite for Piano, Op 25*. 1964–5. Col MS-6817
– *Ode to Napoleon, Op 41*. Juilliard Quar, John Horton spkr. 1965. Col MS-7037
– *Songs, Op 1, 2, 15*. Gramm Bass-bar, Faull sop, Vanni mezzo. 1964–5. Col MS-6816
– *Songs, Op 3, 6, 12, 14, 48*. Op posthumous. Gramm bass-bar, Opthof bar, Vanni mezzo. 1964–71. Col M-31312
R. Schumann *Quartet in E Flat* for piano and strings. Juilliard Quar. 1968. Col MS-7325
Sibelius *Kyllikki: 3 Lyric Pieces for Piano; 3 Sonatines, Op 67*. 1977. Col M-34555
R. Strauss *Enoch Arden*. Claude Rains spkr. 1961. MS-6341
Wagner-Gould *Die Meistersinger Prelude; Siegfried Idyll*; Dawn and Siegfried's Rhine Journey from *Die Götterdämmerung*. 1973. Col M-32351

TAPE

Glenn Gould on the Moog Synthesizer. 1968. CBC Learning Systems no. 326L

SELECTED CBC RADIO PROGRAMS

'Arnold Schoenberg – The Man Who Changed Music' (deviser, producer). 8 Aug 1962
'Dialogues on the Prospects of Recordings' (compiler, narrator). 10 Jan 1965
'The Idea of North' (writer, producer). 28 Dec 1967; Rebroadcast 26 Mar 1968. CBC Publication Disc PR-8
'Anti-Alea' (producer). 1968
'The Latecomers' (producer). 1969. CBC Publication Disc PR-9
'Stokowski: a Portrait for Radio.' 2 Feb 1971
'CBC Tuesday Night': Gould recital. Premiere Gould transcription of Wagner *Siegfried Idyll*. 27 Feb 1973
'Casals: A Portrait for Radio' (producer). 15 Jan 1974
'Music of To-Day': 10-week series on Schoenberg (writer, narrator). 1974. CBC FM
'Schoenberg: The First Hundred Years: A Documentary Fantasy.' 19 Nov 1974. CBC AM
'The Quiet in the Land' (writer, producer). Mar 1977
'Richard Strauss: The Bourgeois Hero' (producer). 2, 9 Apr 1979

SELECTED CBC TV APPEARANCES

'The Subject is Beethoven.' 6 Feb 1961
'Glenn Gould and the Music of the USSR.' 14 Jan 1962
'Glenn Gould on Bach.' 8 Apr 1962
'Glenn Gould on Strauss.' 15 Oct 1962
'The Art of Fugue: A Conversation Concert.' 4 Mar 1963
'Concerti for Four Wednesdays.' 4 TV specials. Jun 1964–
'Duo – Glenn Gould and Menuhin.' 18 May 1966
'Conversations with Glenn Gould.' 4 BBC TV programs, with Humphrey Burton. 15, 22, 29 Sep, 4 Oct 1966
'To Every Man His Own Bach.' CBC presentation of BBC series no. 1. 8 Mar 1967
'The Idea of North.' CBC with NET. 5 Aug 1970
Beethoven *Emperor Concerto*. TS, Ancerl cond. 9 Dec 1970
'Stokowski: The Legendary Conductor.' (interviewer). 3 Feb 1971
'Music in Our Time,' 2-part series: 'Ecstasy,' 'The Flight from Order' (host). Feb 1974
4-part series on Gould produced for French TV by Bruno Monsaingeon. 30 Nov, 7, 14, 21 Dec 1974

BIBLIOGRAPHY

Roddy, Joseph. 'Profiles: Apollonian,' *New Yorker*, 14 May 1960
Asbell, Bernard. 'Glenn Gould,' *Horizon*, vol 4, Jan 1962
Haggin, B.H. *Music Observed* (New York 1964)
Kostelanetz, Richard. 'The Glenn Gould variations,' *Esquire*, Nov 1967
Kaiser, Joachim. *Great Pianists of Our Time*, transl D. Wooldridge and G. Unwin (London 1971)
Jessop, John. 'Interview,' *CMB*, 2, Spring–Summer 1971
Goddard, Peter. 'Glenn Gould is a conjurer,' *CanComp*, 68, Mar 1972
Cott, Jonathan. 'The Rolling Stone interview: Glenn Gould,' *Rolling Stone*, 15, 29 Aug 1974
Roberts, John. 'Glenn Gould,' CCA *Arts Bulletin*, May–Jun 1976
Payzant, Geoffrey. *Glenn Gould: Music and Mind* (Toronto 1978)
– 'Glenn Gould and opera: a unique attitude,' *OpCan*, Spring 1978
Snider, Norman. 'Glenn Gould at 45,' *Toronto Life*, May 1978
Drillon, Jacques. 'Glenn Gould, le piano dans la tête,' *Le Monde de la musique*, vol 8, Feb 1979
Aikin, Jim. 'Glenn Gould,' *Contemporary Keyboard*, Aug 1980

RECORDED INTERVIEWS

'At home with Glenn Gould.' Vincent Tovell. 1959. RCI Transcription E-156
'Glenn Gould: Concert dropout.' John McClure. 1968. Bonus disc BS-15 released with Col MS-7095

FILMOGRAPHY

Glenn Gould – Off the Record (NFB 1959)
Glenn Gould – On the Record (NFB 1959)
Glenn Gould (NFB, French language 1960)
Spheres (NFB 1969), performer on soundtrack
Slaughterhouse Five (Universal 1972), performer, arranger, composer
The Terminal Man (Warner Bros 1974), performer on soundtrack

GPz

GOULD, Joseph. Businessman, choir director, editor, composer, b Penn Yan, NY, 28 Jan 1833, d

J.-J. Goulet

Jean Goulet

Charles Goulet in 1950

Montreal 27 Mar 1913. He moved with his family to Montreal in 1848. About 1864, with Freedom Hill (previously associated with the Montreal branch of A. & S. *Nordheimer), he formed the firm Gould & Hill, which succeeded Nordheimer and operated a music and piano store until about 1870 and also published some sheet music. A.J. *Boucher took over the publishing in 1867. Gould subsequently, until 1881, maintained an organ and piano warehouse under his own name. He founded (and managed and conducted 1864–94) the *Mendelssohn Choir of Montreal and for several years was the vice-president of the *Montreal Philharmonic Society. He also edited and published 1892–3 the semi-monthly journal *Arcadia*, devoted to music, art, and literature, and gave lectures on music to Montreal organizations. In 1892 he was approached by some of Montreal's leading musicians to head a new conservatory, but he declined. Gould composed several vocal pieces, two published in 1908 by J.W. Shaw, Montreal, and others 1912–13 by William Maxwell, New York. A few manuscripts are held at the *NL of C. (NT)

GOULDEN, Flora (Henderson) (b Matheson). Violinist, teacher, b Winnipeg 25 May 1905; ATCM 1923. At 8 she was a soloist with the *Winnipeg SO. She continued studies in her home city and at 17 left to study with Leon Sametini in Chicago 1922–4, Geza *de Kresz in Toronto 1924–7, Rezsö Kemény in Budapest in 1927, Eugène Ysaÿe in Brussels 1927–8, and Marcel Chailley in Paris in 1931. She gave recitals in Canada and Europe and performed as soloist with the Winnipeg SO in 1913, 1927, and 1930, the Vienna Philharmonic (under Weingartner) in 1927, and the Budapest SO in 1927. Returning to Canada she was assistant concertmaster of the pre-war Winnipeg SO and the *CBC Winnipeg Orchestra. She moved in 1948 to Ottawa, where she taught privately and served 1955–60 as assistant concertmaster and 1961–3 as concertmaster of the *Ottawa Philharmonic Orchestra, 1958–60 as second violin of the Carleton String Quartet, and 1965–9 as concertmaster of the CBC Ottawa Chamber Orchestra. She was president of the *ORMTA 1961–2 and of the *CFMTA 1967–71. She was named in 1963 to the Board of Studies and Board of Examiners of the *RCMT, for which she compiled several books on violin pedagogy (Oakville 1970, 1971), partly in collaboration with Jack Montague. (CF)

GOULET. Montreal family of musicians of Belgian origin: 1 / J.-J., 2 / Jean, his brother, and 3 / Charles, Jean's son.

1 **J.-J.** (Joseph-Jean). Violinist, conductor, bandmaster, teacher, b Liège 22 Feb 1870, naturalized Canadian 1938, d Montreal 8 Jul 1951; premier prix solfège, theory, harmony (Liège Cons) 1884, premier prix violin, chamber music (Liège Cons) 1889. In Liège, he studied theory with Sylvain Dupuis and Théodore Radoux and violin with Ovide Musin and Désiré Heynberg.

Goulet moved to Canada in 1891 and, at the invitation of Ernest *Lavigne, became concertmaster of the *Sohmer Park orchestra in Montreal. He was the conductor 1893–5 of the *Opéra français. He played a key role in the organization of the *Couture MSO, which he served as concertmaster 1894–6 and which became the Goulet MSO when he became artistic director in January 1898. He was choirmaster of several churches, including St-Joseph 1895–8, St-Sacrement 1898–1913, Notre-Dame 1914–18, and St-Eusèbe-de-Verceil 1918–21. It was at St-Joseph's that he conducted the choral society, the Orphéon Goulet.

In 1900 Goulet was first violin in the Goulet String Quartet with Isaac Silverstone (second violin), Otto Zimmerman (viola), and Louis *Charbonneau (cello). He was a member of the Haydn Trio with Émery *Lavigne (piano) and J.-B. *Dubois (cello).

After a visit to Europe, ca 1920, Goulet devoted himself primarily to teaching, especially at Mont-St-Louis College (where he had begun to teach violin and other instruments in 1904). He conducted the college concert band after 1926. After 1907 he taught free public courses in solfège at the *Monument national and gave lectures on Grétry, Massenet, and Bizet for the *Société canadienne d'opérette, of which he was conductor and music director. He conducted 1910–50 the Temperance Band of the parish of St-Pierre-Apôtre, which later became the Alliance musicale and finally the Fusiliers Mont-Royal Band. In 1926 he was a member of the Montreal board of the *AMQ. He was president 1933–4 of the CBA and three years later he founded the Montreal orchestral club Les Disciples de Mozart. Belgium awarded Goulet the title chevalier de l'Ordre de Léopole II in 1930, and France made him an Officier d'Académie soon afterwards. He received a Canadian military decoration for 'good service' in 1938 and an award from the CBA in 1951.

J.-J. Goulet must be considered a pioneer of instrumental music in Montreal. He wrote numerous works for military bands, including a march called *Wilfrid Pelletier*, which was premiered in 1935 under Goulet's direction.

BIBLIOGRAPHY

Un demi-siècle au Mont-Saint-Louis (Montreal 1939)

2 **Jean** (Antoine Joseph). Violinist, conductor, teacher, b Liège 17 Apr 1877, naturalized Canadian 1919, d Montreal 23 Sep 1965. He studied violin at the Liège Cons. and, while working as a printer, was a member of that city's opera orchestra. He moved to Montreal in 1893 at the encouragement of his brother and became a second violin in the Couture MSO. He played also at *Sohmer Park under Ernest *Lavigne. After living 1897–1906 in Belgium, he returned to Montreal, again at his brother's suggestion. At Sohmer Park he played clarinet and conducted a small orchestra. During these years (1907–14) he played and conducted at several theatres, including the National (where the young Wilfrid *Pelletier was pianist) and the Amherst, as well as at the Bijou and Moulin-Rouge cinemas. He taught 1914–62 at Laval College in St-Vincent-de-Paul, near Montreal, and founded and conducted 1912–24 the Cercle symphonique St-Pierre. He was choirmaster 1921–30 at St-Eusèbe-de-Verceil Church, 1930–6 at St-Stanislas-de-Kostka, and 1936–? at St-Lambert, on the outskirts of Montreal.

In 1920 Jean Goulet became president and music director of the *Assn des chanteurs de Montréal, which he conducted until 1935 in oratorios including, in 1923, Couture's *Jean le Précurseur*. Beginning in 1921, he taught violin and orchestral instruments, and conducted the chamber ensemble, at the Collège de Montréal and at Notre-Dame College. He conducted 1922–6 for the *Société canadienne d'opérette and 1936–55 for the *Variétés lyriques; indeed, he led most of the latter's performances – 895 – including operas and operettas. In 1926 France made him an Officier d'Académie and the following year Belgium named him chevalier de l'Ordre de la Couronne.

3 **Charles** (Émile Jean Julien). Baritone, choir conductor, teacher, impresario, administrator, b Liège 4 Apr 1902, naturalized Canadian 1921, d Montreal 12 Mar 1976; D MUS (Montreal) 1937. He arrived in Montreal with his parents in 1906 and at 6 began studying the violin with his uncle and solfège and theory with his father. At 10 he started lessons in piano with Armand Bluteau and organ with Marie-Louise Laurier and later he studied piano again with Arthur *Letondal. He played the violin in several ensembles including the Cercle symphonique St-Pierre. In 1922 he began teaching violin at Laval College, St-Vincent-de-Paul, and conducted a choir at St-Pierre Church as well as singing there. In November 1921 he had sung in public for the first time and because of his success his father had him take voice lessons from Salvator *Issaurel. He played the piano in hotels and restaurants and was chorus master of the *Assn des chanteurs de Montréal and in the spring of 1923 he conducted an orchestra for the first time.

Goulet decided to continue his musical education in Belgium and studied voice with Jules Massart and harmony and piano with Fernand Mawet in Liège. He was chorus master of La Legia, a male choir of 300 voices, and conducted it to a first prize in a competition at Le Havre. He was engaged by the Liège Théâtre royal, where he made his debut 9 Dec 1923 as Bustamente in Massenet's *La Navarraise*. In two seasons there he sang various roles including Silvio in *I Pagliacci* and Brétigny in *Manon* and took part in several premieres such as Tiarko Richepin's *L'Atlantide*. He was heard in Lille, Roubaix, Spa, and Louvain, as well as in Holland and Luxembourg. His performance in *The Tales of Hoffmann* brought praise: 'M. Goulet was perfect as Spalanzani...This intelligent young artist has first-rate qualities' (Liège *Express*, 1 Mar 1925).

Returning to Montreal, Goulet continued to develop his choral skills as choirmaster 1925–37 of St-Henri Church. In 1928 he founded the *Disciples de Massenet, a mixed choir which he was to conduct for 35 years in many concerts and several recordings. At the same time he was the leading baritone 1927–34 of the *Société canadienne d'opérette, making his debut in Joseph Szulc's *Flup*. He was choirmaster 1937–68 of St-Louis-de-France Church, succeeding Joseph *Saucier, and he also conducted the *Assn chorale St-Louis-de-France.

With Antonio Pager in 1930 Goulet founded the Concerts Goulet-Pager, which presented Montreal appearances by Gigli, the Don Cossacks, Nino Martini, Conchita Supervia, Ruth Slenczynska, the Kurt Joos and Serge Lifar ballets, Chaliapin, the French stars Lys Gauty and Guy Berry, and, in 1937, Igor Stravinsky and Samuel Dushkin. During that time, Goulet also founded the artists' agency Les Concerts canadiens, which he managed for three years.

Along with Les Disciples de Massenet, the great accomplishment of Goulet's career was the *Variétés lyriques; with Lionel *Daunais he was its co-founder and co-director 1936–55. When Les Disciples de Massenet won first prize in 1951 at the Chicagoland Music Festival, Charles Goulet was awarded first prize for choir conducting. He was secretary 1957–76 for the Council of Arts of Greater Montreal and a member in 1974 of the Commission Jeannotte, a MACQ group entrusted with studying the state of music and opera in Quebec. Several of his articles appeared in *Le Guide Mont-Royal* and *L'Illustration* (1939). His doctoral thesis bore the title 'L'art du chant Choral.' At his death, he had completed his autobiography, *Sur la scène et dans la coulisse* (Quebec City 1981). M-CL

GOULET, Robert (Gerard). Baritone, actor, b Lawrence, Mass, 26 Nov 1933. In his early teens he moved with his mother to Edmonton, where he studied voice with Herbert G. *Turner and Jean *Létourneau and in 1950 became a radio announcer on CKUA. He continued his voice training 1952–4 on an *RCMT scholarship with George *Lambert and Ernesto *Vinci. A semi-finalist on CBC TV's 'Pick the Stars' in 1952, Goulet also competed in CBC radio's *'Opportunity Knocks' and *'Singing Stars of Tomorrow.' While singing small roles in 1954 with the *COC and appearing in the chorus of the *Melody Fair series of Broadway musicals produced in Toronto, he made his TV debut in a walk-on role in the CBC production of *The Consul*. Appearances followed in CBC TV's *Sunshine Town* (1954), *The Lady and the Logger*, and *Take to the Woods* (1955). In 1956 he appeared in *Spring Thaw* and sang in *Gentlemen Prefer Blondes*, *Finian's Rainbow*, and *South Pacific* at *TUTS. He co-starred 1957–9 on CBC TV's 'Showtime,' sang Macheath in the *Stratford Festival's 1958 production

Robert Goulet

of *The Beggar's Opera*, and appeared in 1958 in summer-stock musical comedy in Ohio.

Goulet's creation of Sir Lancelot in Lerner and Loewe's *Camelot*, opposite Julie Andrews and Richard Burton, in the premiere at *O'Keefe Centre 1 Oct 1960 and in the New York premiere 1 Dec 1960, brought him particular acclaim. Thereafter he enjoyed a successful US career in Broadway and summer-stock productions, TV, movies, and nightclubs, his popularity attributed to a 'virile attractiveness, stunning showmanship and magnificently rich voice which combine to produce an impact on audiences that can be likened only to the matinee idols of the 1920s' (*Song Hits*, Summer 1967). In 1962 he received a Grammy Award as 'Best New Artist of the Year,' and in 1970 he was given a Tony Award for his performance as Jacques in the Broadway production of *The Happy Time*. With Judy Garland he recorded the voices for the animated film *Gay Purr-ee* (1962). He also appeared in such movies as *I'd Rather Be Rich* (1964) and *Honeymoon Hotel* (1966), in the TV adventure series 'Blue Light' (1966), and in the TV productions of *Carousel* (1967), *Kiss Me Kate* (1968), and the Emmy Award winning *Brigadoon* (1966).

Goulet's recordings include the hit singles 'What Kind of Fool Am I?' (1962) and 'My Love Forgive Me' (1964) and over 30 LPs of popular songs for Columbia or Harmony, as well as the original-cast versions of *Camelot* (Col KOL 5620) and *The Happy Time* (RCA LSO 1144) and the soundtrack of *Gay Purr-ee* (Warner B 1479). Goulet has returned occasionally to Canada, appearing at the *CNE (1963), at *O'Keefe Centre (1966) with his second wife, the singer Carol Lawrence, on CBC TV's 'Show of the Week' (1969), and in various nightclub engagements. In the 1970s his career was confined largely to nightclubs and included frequent engagements in Las Vegas.

BIBLIOGRAPHY

Locke, Jeannine. 'Canada's first matinee idol,' *Chatelaine*, Dec 1956

Carroll, Jock. 'He's ready for the big break,' *Weekend Magazine*, 26 Jul 1958

Gale, Jack. 'From Timber Tom to Sir Lancelot,' *Star Weekly*, 20 Feb 1960

Callwood, June. 'Bob Goulet goes to Broadway,' *Chatelaine*, Oct 1960

Krantz, Judith. 'Life and times of a hot property,' *Maclean's*, 27 Jan 1962 (MH)

GOUR. Two Quebec singers: 1 / Émile, and 2 / Romain, his nephew.

1 **Émile**. Tenor, choirmaster, b L'Assomption, near Montreal, 21 Apr 1893, d Montreal 24 Sep 1970. He studied piano and harmony with Alphonse *Lavallée-Smith and voice with Salvator *Issaurel 1915–22. While pursuing a career as a singer he remained in the employ of the Canadian postal service. He was a soloist at St-Louis-de-France and St-Jean-Baptiste churches and for 10 years at Notre-Dame. From 1940 until his death he was choirmaster at Notre-Dame-de-Grâce and St-Antonin churches. During the era of silent pictures, he was very active, performing songs and excerpts from operas before the films were shown. He participated in concerts given by the organist Joseph *Bonnet in Toronto, Guelph, London, Ont, and elsewhere. After hearing him in the role of Jesus in Massenet's *Marie-Magdeleine* Adrien Arcand wrote, 'M. Emile Gour was the best performer, a powerful voice, admirably controlled and projected with ease' (Montreal *La Presse*, 1 Dec 1922.) He came to be known as 'The Canadian Caruso.' In 1923 he was Samson in a presentation of Saint-Saens' *Samson et Dalila* in Worcester, Mass, and in 1928 he sang in Honegger's *Le Roi David* in Montreal. Gour was a member of the Montreal Quartet along with Armand Gauthier, Charles-Émile Brodeur, and Hercule Lavoie. He was also a member of the first Issaurel Vocal Quartet and the Issaurel Mixed Quartet. In New York, for Columbia, he made several recordings which are listed in *Roll Back the Years*.

2 (Joseph Ferréol) **Romain**. Baritone, writer, b L'Assomption 19 Aug 1899, d Montreal 22 Jul 1968. He studied with Romain *Pelletier and Raoul *Paquet and took singing lessons from Salvator *Issaurel ca 1921–4. In Montreal he was soloist at St-Léon de Westmount, Notre-Dame, and St-Thomas d'Aquin churches. On 18 Nov 1920 at the *St-Denis Theatre he appeared in Massenet's *Thaïs* and on 25 Mar 1926 at the Gesù Church he sang the role of Jesus in Marc-Antoine Charpentier's oratorio *Le Reniement de saint Pierre*. With Jacques *Gérard, Gaston Favreau, and René Tourangeau, he became a member of the Pro Arte Ensemble, and he sang with the third Issaurel Quartet along with Jeanne *Desjardins, Rhéa Labrosse, and Louis La Rue. However his career was short; in 1928 he gave up singing for a career in insurance.

Romain Gour founded, and directed for its entire existence, the quarterly review *Qui?* (1949–54) in which he wrote biographical essays on Francis Archambault, Alexis *Contant, Guillaume *Couture, Emma Lajeunesse (*Albani), Rodolphe *Plamondon, and the sculptor Philippe Hébert. Some were reprinted in *Courtes Biographies canadiennes* (Montreal, 1949–ca 52). He was the author of the critical biography *La Palme-Issaurel* (Montreal 1948) and of a genealogical study, *Pierre Gour 1652–1732, Alexis Gour 1814–1892 et ses descendants* (Montreal 1936). HP

Gourlay, Winter & Leeming, Ltd. Toronto retailer of pianos, player pianos, organs, music boxes, and phonographs, and manufacturer of pianos. The firm was established in 1890 by Robert S. Gourlay (b New York 21 Sep 1852, d Toronto 28 Nov 1932), Francis William Winter, and Thomas Leeming. Formerly the general manager of *Mason & Risch, Gourlay assumed the same position with the new company. The firm was incorporated, with Gourlay as president, in 1915, when Winter and Leeming retired and Gourlay's sons David and Albert became sales manager and manufacturing supervisor respectively. Gourlay himself was active in civic affairs and served terms as president of the Toronto Board of Trade and the Canadian Manufacturers' Assn. After his retirement in 1923 the firm was forced into receivership. In 1924 *Sherlock-Manning purchased its name, stock, patterns, and scales.

Throughout its history the company had a retail store on downtown Yonge St. It began by selling *Heintzman pianos and imported Steinway pianos and Estey reed organs. By 1904 it had begun the production of its own pianos, and by 1911 the factory employed 225 persons. By 1915 8000 Gourlay pianos had been built. The Gourlay company also sold the Gourlay-Angelus line of player piano. FH

The Governor General's Foot Guards Band, Ottawa. Volunteer militia band formed soon after the establishment of the regiment in 1872. Based on the personnel of the Ottawa Brigade Artillery Band, the ensemble made its debut 15 Jun 1872 under its first director, John C. Bonner. One of the most distinguished of Bonner's successors was Arthur A. *Clappé, who led the band for several years, developing a strong complement of 35 men. Joseph Miller Brown, a noted cornetist, was one of Clappé's successors. Brown took the band to New York City in 1906 and again in 1909 on the occasion of the Champlain tercentenary. His son (and successor in 1923) Joseph T. Brown led the band at the opening of Madison Square Gardens in New York in 1925 and at the opening of the International Peace Bridge between Buffalo and Fort Erie in 1937. The band made several appearances during the visit of George VI in 1939.

Later directors have included Maj F.W. Coleman, Capt Alex McCurrdie, the former RCMP band director Edwin Joseph Lydall, and Capt George Aubrey. After World War II the band regained much of its popularity in the Ottawa region. Its summer concerts were broadcast on local radio, and it participated in many massed band displays and tattoos on Parliament Hill. Its conductor in 1979 was Capt W.J. Milne.

Graduel romain. A collection containing all the chants for the Proper of the mass: introit, gradual, tract or alleluia, offertory, and communion, as well as those for the Feasts of Our Lord (the Proper of the Time) and of the Saints (the Common of the Saints). Accompanied by a text, the square notation is printed in movable type on a four-line staff. The name *Graduel* comes from the response sung after the first reading from the bible which, until the papacy (590–604) of Gregory the Great, was read by the deacon on the gradus (steps) of the ambo (oblong elevated pulpit reserved for the proclamation of the Gospel).

The model for the first Canadian edition of the *Graduel romain*, published in Quebec City in 1800, was the Graduel from the diocese of Vannes in Brittany. The first musical notation to be printed in Canada, the Quebec edition came into being through the initiative of John *Neilson, who also published the *Processional romain* [sic] (1801) and the *Vespéral romain* (1802). The three volumes later went through many editions by various publishers. Neilson put a notice in *La Gazette* in Quebec City (23 Nov 1797): 'As it appears that numerous people from different parishes want to obtain portable editions of the Graduel and Vesperal Romain, the Printer informs the public, and particularly the parish priests and other ecclesiastics, that he intends to print and publish the said graduel and Antiphonaire Romain in octavo size following the model of the Vannes edition, adding to both the offices appropriate to the Diocese of Quebec.' In the preface to the *Graduel* the publisher wrote: 'We present to the public a portable edition of the Livres de Chant printed in Quebec City, and conforming to the full-size Lyon edition, the most correct and most recent edition known to exist. It is the first endeavour of its kind in Canada.'

BIBLIOGRAPHY
Tremaine, Marie. *A Bibliography of Canadian Imprints, 1751–1800* (Toronto 1952) (CMr)

GRAHAM, George F. Organist, teacher, writer, fl 1854–66. He was organist at the American Presbyterian Church in Montreal and wrote *The Vocal Tutor* (Montreal 1854), a textbook of musical rudiments. He moved in 1855 to Toronto, where he became organist-choirmaster at St George's Anglican Church. In 1856 he initiated the *Canadian Musical Review*, Canada's first English-language music journal. A copy of the first issue is held at the *NL of C. He participated in Toronto concerts as an organist and a pianist until at least 1866. His *Quintet in F* for piano and string quartet, one of the earliest instances of a chamber music composition in Canada, was performed at a concert in 1858. HK

Granby Song Festival† / Festival de la chanson de Granby. Annual competition begun in 1969 in Granby, Que, by Yves Gagnon and Yves Steinmetz (president 1969–74), to stimulate the writing of original Quebec songs, provide amateurs with a permanent workshop, and encourage international exchange. It is sponsored by Les Loisirs de Granby Inc, with organizational support from the *MACQ and the federal secretary of state.

The festival was conceived as a focus for the talents of French-speaking singer-songwriters and singers 16 years old or over, Canadian or landed immigrants, with 64 to be chosen at annual preliminary auditions throughout Canada and 4 semi-finalists to appear at a gala concert in December at the boîte à chansons L'Escale in Granby. The first-prize winners each have received $1000, and a watch valued at $300, through the financial support of the city of Granby, *CAPAC, *PRO Canada, and local sponsors.

Winners have included Priscilla Lapointe (1969), Jean-Marc Perron (1970), Denise Guénette (1971), Fabienne Thibeault and Calixte Duguay (1974), Madeleine Boucher (1975), and Diane Pichette and Micheline Scott (1977). The singer-songwriter Robert Paquette was among the finalists in 1972 and 1973. Two winners have represented Canada at the Festival international de la chanson française in Spa, Belgium: Jean-Marc Perron (1971) and Madeleine Boucher (1976). The latter won first prize in performance at Spa.

In 1976 the Granby Song Festival added a song competition, Chanson primée, open to any singer-songwriter, for an unpublished song with original lyrics in French, to be sung by the author or by an amateur. That year Yvon Pépin won the $500 prize with 'Berceuse au soleil.' Other prize-winning songs were Robert Garceau's 'Dans un coin d'escalier,' performed by Denis Losier, (1977) and Jean Racine's 'L'Oiseau Jean-Baptiste' (1978).

The development of the regional operations across Canada was such that by 1978 local song festivals could be established. In addition a four-day training program was instituted and the eight semi-finalists of the 1979 festival benefited from the advice of such professionals of the chanson as Daniel Deschesnes, Jacques Michel, and Jean Robitaille, with regard to arrangements, staging, and lyrics. Special lecturers were engaged to discuss all aspects of the songwriting business. The CBC has collaborated actively in the festival.

In 1979 Alain Lecours was president and Pierre Lacouture was co-ordinator. For the 1979 finals the judges were Paul Buissonneau, Neil *Chotem, Richard Fortin, Thérèse Lacombe, and Luc Plamondon.

BIBLIOGRAPHY
Vincent, Pierre. 'Granby Festival helps start careers in Quebec,' *CanComp*, 43, Oct 1972 BLH (ST)

Grand Chantre (Precentor). In the 15th century this term was used to refer to a church dignitary in charge of the singing of the choir in cathedrals and collegiate churches. On special holidays he donned the cope and bore the cantor's rod as symbols of his authority.

Monseigneur de Laval, the first bishop of Quebec, introduced the position to Canada when he formed the chapter of the bishopric of Quebec in 1684. The Grand Chantre's function was to assume 'the overall responsibility for the ceremonies and everything relating to the external form of worship' (Edmond Langevin, *Notice biographique sur François de Laval de Montmorency ...*, Montreal 1874). The first incumbent was Jean Dudouyt or Dudoyt (ca 1628–88), who was appointed by Mgr de Laval in 1684. As he went back to France and never returned to Quebec City, he did not in fact occupy the position. Charles Glandelet was temporary Grand Chantre in 1688. André-Louis de Merlac, a priest who came from France in 1688, held the post from 1690 to 1694. Louis-Ango de Maizerets (1636–1721) was de Merlac's successor and occupied the position from 1698 until his death. Another French priest, Joseph de la Colombière (1651–1723), was appointed in 1722. Father Pierre Hazeur de l'Orme also appears to have served for an indefinite period after 1710. In *La Musique au Québec*, Willy *Amtmann describes Father Charles-Amador *Martin as Grand Chantre, but without disclosing his authority for the claim.

The function of Grand Chantre is similar to that of precentor in England and cantor in Germany. It later merged with that of choirmaster or conductor of choirs in monastic churches. (HK)

GRANDMAISON, Pierre. Organist, teacher, b Montreal 27 Jul 1949; B MUS (Montreal) 1970. He studied piano with Jeanne Gascon and 1966–70 with Marie Roby and Yvonne *Hubert at the *École Vincent-d'Indy. He also studied organ with Eugène *Lapierre 1968–9 and with Françoise *Aubut. Awarded a grant by the Quebec government, he studied 1970–1 in Paris with Maurice and Marie-Madeleine Duruflé.

On his return from France Grandmaison gave organ recitals at the Music Pavilion of Man and His World, on CBC radio, and elsewhere. Assistant organist at the churches of St-Thomas-Apôtre, Notre-Dame-du-Rosaire, and St-Alphonse-d'Youville, in 1973 he became the regular organist at Notre-Dame in Montreal and inaugurated that church's Concerts du midi. In May 1977 he performed with an orchestra at a musical evening offered by the City of Montreal to delegates from 60 countries to an international transportation congress, and the same year he inaugurated the restored *Casavant organ at Mont St-Hilaire, one of the first instruments by that builder.

Grandmaison began teaching sacred music at the Grand Séminaire in Montreal in 1977 and giving courses in organ registration for the diocese of St-Jean in 1978. In 1974 he accompanied Aimé Major on a record in which the latter recites poems (*Jésus et Marie avec Aimé Major*, Sel S-398228), and in 1975 he made the LP *Pierre Grandmaison joue / plays J.S. Bach* (Sel CC-15-111). Pierre *Rolland, reviewing the latter, wrote: 'Pierre Grandmaison plays Bach with sincerity and conviction. He makes admirable use of the reverberation in the church and thus controls the duration of the sound, with the result that the rhythmic pulse is particularly effective' (Montreal *Le Devoir*, 19 Feb 1977). HP

Grand Theatre, Kingston, Ont. Originally the Grand Opera House, built in 1902 on the site of Martin's Opera House (1879), which was destroyed by fire in 1898. The Grand was bought in 1905 by Ambrose J. Small, a theatre-chain owner who had been influential in its original planning. Bernhardt, Melba, and Jolson performed there. In 1936 it was bought by Famous Players, and it reopened as a movie house 19 May 1938. The Kingston Arts Council campaigned for its restoration as a civic theatre, and as the Grand Theatre it opened 20 May 1966 with a performance of **Spring Thaw*. Its new mandate was to accommodate touring and local groups and serve as the home of the *Kingston SO. It has 832 seats, a proscenium stage, and an orchestra pit. PB

Grand Théâtre de Québec. A building complex devoted to the performing arts, located in Quebec City at the corner of Claire-Fontaine St and St-Cyrille Blvd E. Built at a cost of $14 million it consists of three main components – a large hall (Salle Louis-Fréchette), a smaller auditorium (Salle Octave-Crémazie), and a conservatory (the *CMQ) – as well as dressing rooms, workshops, rehearsal rooms, costume storage rooms and display areas, stores, a restaurant, and offices. The project was initiated by Premier Jean Lesage of Quebec, who in 1963 proposed to the prime minister of Canada, Lester B. Pearson, a pooling of federal and provincial resources to build a monument to commemorate Canada's centenary in Quebec City. Following a national competition in 1964, the plans of the Montreal architect Victor Prus were selected. Work began on the main structure in 1967 and on the small theatre in 1970. The inauguration took place 16 Jan 1971, and the opening festival 17–27 January included four concerts by the *Quebec SO conducted by Pierre Dervaux and Wilfrid *Pelletier, a performance by Les Grands Ballets Canadiens, a recital by the *Choeur V'là l'bon vent, and a concert by the *Royal 22nd Regiment Band.

The corporation of the Grand Théâtre de Québec, set up in May 1969 as the administrative body, was dissolved 17 Jul 1970 and replaced by a nine-member board. The president of the Grand Théâtre 1970–6, Jean-Marie Poitras, was succeeded by Charles Cimon in 1977. The managing directors were Guy Beaulne and Michel Rousseau (interim).

The Salle Louis-Fréchette is built of reinforced concrete; an assembly of acrylic rods 2 m in length, each with a light on the end, hangs from its ceiling. It seats between 1571 and 1767 spectators, depending on the use made of the orchestra pit (which can accommodate 120 musicians). The apron measures 8.53 x 33 m and the stage floor 17.68 x 26.98 m. The foyers are located on four

Grand Théâtre de Québec

levels and surround the hall on three sides. A relief sculpture by Jordi Bonet is mounted on the concrete foyer wall, which has a surface area of 3600 square m.

The Salle Octave-Crémazie, a small theatre 33 x 33 m, located one floor below ground level, affords several possible stage layouts: the Italian (allowing 507 seats), the Elizabethan (661 seats), and theatre-in-the-round (871 seats). The CMQ occupies the two floors of the building below ground. It has 75 studios (some of which look onto the landscaped courtyard garden 8 m below street level), a record library, a library, and offices.

The Grand Théâtre has presented many Canadian and foreign artists of international repute, as well as theatre, dance, and opera companies. In 1980 it continued to serve as the home of the Quebec SO, the *Orchestre de chambre Pierre-Morin, the Croque-musique (in collaboration with the *JMC), the Matinées symphoniques, and the Théâtre du Trident. After 1975 ticket sales were controlled by an electronic system linking eight terminals, located in the city and its outlying areas, to the Grand Théâtre's mini-computer.

BIBLIOGRAPHY

Culture vivante, 17, May 1970

Mercer, Ruby. 'Le Grand Théâtre: vieux Québec goes 20th century,' *OpCan*, Winter 1971

Robert, Guy. *Le Grand Théâtre de Québec* (Ste-Adèle, Que, 1971)

L'Allier, Jean-Paul. *Pour l'évolution de la politique culturelle* (Quebec 1976)

Régie du Grand Théâtre de Québec. Annual reports 1971–9 LPr

GRANT, Freddy or **Freddie** (b Grundland, Fritz). Songwriter, pianist, b Berlin 17 Oct 1913, naturalized Canadian 1947. He studied piano, theory, and harmony in Germany, then moved in 1934 to London, where he enrolled at the London School of Music. In England several of his songs were performed by Gracie Fields, Jessie Matthews, Ray Noble, and others. In the USA 'How Can You Buy Killarney?' (1937) was recorded by Bing Crosby and Dennis Day. While interned May–July 1940 in a camp for German and Austrian nationals who were refugees in England at the outbreak of World War II, he wrote his greatest hit, *'You'll Get Used to It,' about life in the camp. After his release in 1942 from a similar camp in Canada (Farnham, Que), he settled in Toronto. There he studied at various times with Ettore *Mazzoleni, Gordon *Delamont, and Oscar *Peterson, and led small groups in nightclubs and, for 25 years at the Toronto restaurant Lichee Garden. Grant also composed 'They Call It Canada (But I Call It Home)' (GVT 1952), sung in schools across Canada and (as 'They Call It America' – Robbins 1952) in the USA. A folio of his patriotic songs, *This is Canada*, was published by *Thompson in 1967. (CF)

GRANT, Sylvia (b Shapiro). Soprano, b Calgary 25 Aug 1928; BA sociology (Toronto) 1950. She appeared regularly 1952–63 with the *Royal Cons Opera and the *COC, singing lyric and dramatic roles including Donna Anna (1956) and Donna Elvira (1963) in *Don Giovanni*, Nedda in Leoncavallo's *I Pagliacci* (1961), and Ortlinde in *Die Walküre* (1962). She sang leading roles in 1960 with the Calgary Opera. She also appeared 1966–8 with the New York City Opera, where her roles were Lucille in the North American premiere of Von Einem's *Danton's Death* (1966), Fata Morgana in Prokofiev's *The Love of Three Oranges*, and Musetta in *La Bohème*. She retired in 1968. Her performances were marked by dramatic force and a voice of brilliant timbre. VW

GRANT-SCHAEFER, George Alfred. Composer, organist, teacher, b Williamstown, near Cornwall, Ont, 4 Jul 1872, d Chicago 11 May 1939. He studied with Dominique *Ducharme (piano) and Guillaume *Couture (voice) in Montreal and with Victor Garwood (piano) and Adolf Weidig (theory) in Chicago. C.A.E. *Harriss was his organ teacher in London. Grant-Schaefer was organist-choirmaster 1896–1908 at Centenary Church, Chicago, and served 1908–20 as head of the vocal department at Northwestern School of Music, Evanston, Ill. His compositions included over 100 piano pieces for pedagogical use and some 90 songs, as well as anthems and the operettas *Derry Down Derry* (Schmidt 1928) and *Rip Van Winkle* (R.A. Hoffman 1925). His piano pieces enjoyed a high reputation among teachers. He maintained a summer home in Quebec, and his music was affected by his sojourns there. Among his earlier publications were *Scènes canadiennes*, seven pieces for piano (Schmidt 1907). He re-harmonized and adapted the music of *'O Canada' for the first edition (1908) of Weir's English text. His arrangements of French-Canadian folk songs, published by Schmidt in 1921 and 1925, achieved popularity. Other publishers included Birchard (*Thirty-six Songs for Children* 1909), Ditson, and Summy International. EK

GRATON, Fernand. Orchestra conductor, choir conductor, teacher, b Montreal 2 Feb 1921. He received his early musical training from his mother and later studied violin, piano, and organ with Auguste *Descarries. He also took courses in theory 1933–40. Interested in conducting, he founded the Montreal Youth SO and was its artistic director 1945–51. With a grant from the Quebec government he studied conducting 1949–51 in New York with Léon Barzin. During the summer of 1950 he worked under Serge Koussevitzky, Hugh Ross, and Jacques Ibert at the Berkshire Music Center, Tanglewood, Mass. The following year he conducted a concert with choir and orchestra at the Tanglewood Festival.

Graton began teaching in 1950 at the *U of Montreal and continued to do so for about 15 years. From 1950 to 1965 he conducted the Choeur bleu et or (renamed Choeur des étudiants de l'U de Montréal in 1962), which performed at Tanglewood in 1961 and 1962 and with the *MSO on several occasions. In 1957 he conducted the Philharmonia, an amateur orchestra founded that year. Under his direction, the Chanteurs du Québec participated in the 1964 triennial Zimrya International Choir Festival in Israel.

He was choirmaster 1958–65 at St-Viateur d'Outremont Church. Graton taught at the Collège St-Laurent and the Ste-Thérèse Seminary and in 1960 gave the instrumental ensemble classes at the *École Vincent-d'Indy. He was appointed secretary general of the *Cons de musique du Québec in December 1964 and became assistant director of the *CMM that year. Director 1967–78 of the Cons de Hull, Graton after 1978 acted as a management consultant for the Cons de musique du Québec with the MACQ. He married the organist Marcelle *Martin. CB

GRATTON, (Joseph Thomas) **Hector**. Composer, conductor, arranger, pianist, teacher, b Hull, Que, 13 Aug 1900, d Montreal 16 Jul 1970. He studied piano in Montreal with Alphonse *Martin and Alfred *Laliberté. The latter introduced him to the works and aesthetics of Scriabin and Medtner. Gratton then studied theory with Oscar *O'Brien, Alfred *Whitehead, and Albertine *Morin-Labrecque. Around 1920 O'Brien harmonized folk songs for the folksinger Charles *Marchand (whom he also accompanied on tours). Gratton, who was enthusiastic about these songs, was employed by Marchand as pianist and arranger, particularly 1927–30 in Quebec City during the Canadian Folk Song and Handicrafts festivals (*CPR Festivals). His first two vigorous *Danses canadiennes*, in which echoes of the violoneux can be heard, were composed at this time. After the difficult years which followed the Depression national radio was established, and Gratton was one of its pioneers. He worked on one of the first major radio series, 'Je me souviens,' which featured scripts by a young writer, Félix *Leclerc. Gratton composed and conducted the incidental music, which contributed greatly to the series' success. In 1937 his symphonic poem *Légende* won the Jean *Lallemand prize in the second annual *CSM composition competition. For the purposes of the competition Gratton used a pseudonym, and *Légende* by 'Ben Marcato' was performed 19 March for jury and public and was repeated 23 April at a subscription concert conducted by Wilfrid *Pelletier and at a *TSO concert the next year under Sir Ernest *MacMillan. Also notable among Gratton's works is the incidental music for Cécile Chabot's Christmas story *L'Imagerie*, heard in 1945 on CBC radio. In his compositions Gratton kept faith with his basic material, which was essentially folkloric and popular. For this reason he avoided harmonic sophistication. His orchestrations, both simple and subtle, contributed substantially to the charm of his works. Most of his manuscripts have been deposited at the *NL of C. He was an affiliate of BMI Canada. The *CMCentre has granted him the associate status reserved for deceased composers whose works the centre holds.

COMPOSITIONS

STAGE

4 ballets: *Les Feux follets* (1952); *La Légende de l'arbre sec; Le Pommier; Marie Madeleine*. All ms

L'Imagerie 'Pastorale de Noël,' radio play (C. Chabot). 1945. Ms

ORCHESTRA

Légende. 1937. CMCentre

Coucher de soleil. 1947. Str orch, pf. CMCentre. RCI 6 (J.-M. *Beaudet)

Fantasia on Two French Canadian Folk Songs (1950); *Fantasia sur 'V'là l'bon vent'* (1952); *Variations libres sur 'Isabeau s'y promène'* (1954). All CMCentre

Dansons le Carcaillou. 1952. CMCentre

3 works (in ms) for v and orch on texts by Marcel Gagnon; several other works for orch, including folksong arr. Most ms

CHAMBER MUSIC

Première Danse canadienne. 1927. Vn, pf. FH 1930

Deuxième Danse canadienne. 1928. Vn, pf or str. FH 1930

Réminiscence. 1928. Vn, pf. FH 1930

Troisième Danse canadienne. Ca 1930. Vn, pf or orch. Ms

Quatrième Danse canadienne. 1935. Vn, pf or str. BMIC 1952 (vn, pf). RCI 136 (*LeBlanc)/(arr str) RCI 186 (*Deslauriers)

Hector Gratton

Chanson écossaise. 1940. Vn, pf. BMIC 1957

Other works, including a *Sonata* for vn, pf

PIANO

La Joie de vivre. Ca 1940. *P-T*, Sep 1945

Tendresse. Ca 1940. *P-T*, May 1946

Crépuscule. 1952. BMIC 1956. RCI 132 (R. *Pratt)

Conte. 1954. BMIC 1958

Also 4 choral works, 2 works for v and pf, 1 arr of 'O Canada,' and many arr of Canadian folksongs

BIBLIOGRAPHY

'Hector Gratton, eminent Canadian composer,' *CRMA*, vol 1, Jan 1943

'Hector Gratton,' *P-T*, 890, Sep 1945 GP

GRAVEL, Louis. Baritone, teacher, b Ste-Anne-de-Beaupré, near Quebec City, 30 Mar 1895. He received his first solfège and singing lessons from his father Joseph, a member of the choir at the Basilica of Ste-Anne. He studied at the École normale in Quebec City with J.-Arthur *Bernier and 1916–18 at the New York Institute of Musical Art with Frank Damrosch and Adrian Freni. He was choirmaster at St John the Baptist Church in Pawtucket, RI, and sang the roles of Valentin (*Faust*) and Laërte (*Mignon*) with the Woonsocket Opera. Returning to Quebec, he was choirmaster 1920–70 at Notre-Dame-de-Jacques-Cartier Church. In 1924 a Quebec government scholarship allowed him to study in Paris with Édouard Rouard of the Opéra and with Mme Garnier. When Rouard left Paris, Gravel accompanied him to Nice, where they gave several concerts. He travelled throughout Canada with the pianist Berthe *Roy. As a private teacher, he taught Léonard *Bilodeau, Rolande *Dion, Raoul *Jobin, Guy Lepage, Fernand *Martel, and Richard *Verreau. CH

GRAY, Alexander (Reid). Baritone, teacher, b Lachine, near Montreal, Que, 31 Mar 1929. He made his stage debut at 17 as Silas Simkins in *Merrie England*. He studied with Merlin Davies (voice) and Maitland *Farmer and Mary Bennett (piano) at the *McGill Cons 1947–8, with Ernesto *Vinci at the *RCMT 1950–5, and with Boris Goldovsky in New York. He appeared with the *COC for 20 years (1955–75) in a wide variety of roles, including Ford in *The Merry Wives of Windsor* in 1960, Sharpless in *Madama Butterfly* 1962, 1964, and 1971, Guglielmo in *Così fan tutte* in 1963, Beauchemin in *The Luck of Ginger Coffey* in 1967, and Lescaut in *Manon Lescaut* in 1975. He has performed in *Banff SFA touring productions 1957–8, in *Stratford Festival productions 1959–62, with the Goldovsky Opera Theatre 1962–7, with the *Edmonton Opera Assn in 1968 (Escamillo in *Carmen*), and, as leading baritone, with the Kiel (Germany) Opera 1969–71.

Gray's performances in a wide range of roles include some 250 as Figaro in *The Barber of Seville* and over 200 as Marcello in *La Bohème*. He has sung on CBC radio and has appeared in CBC TV productions of *H.M.S. Pinafore* (1960), *Elektra* (1961), *Otello* (1962), *The Gondoliers* (1962), and *Rigoletto* (1965). He was Ernesto Vinci's teaching assistant 1965–6 at the *U of Toronto and began teaching at the *U of Calgary in 1971. He became head of the musical theatre division of the Banff SFA in 1975. He founded and was artistic director 1972–5 of the *Southern Alberta Opera. He was the Jailer in the 1976 *Guelph Spring Festival production of Britten's *The Beggar's Opera*.

BIBLIOGRAPHY

'Southern Alberta Opera Association,' *OpCan*, Dec 1975

Creative Canada, vol 1 (RDM)

GRAY, Theresa (Jane) (m Gasparini). Soprano, b Toronto 30 Apr 1921. She began voice studies in 1940 with Helen Plaxton and continued them 1944–6 at the TCM with Albert Kennedy and 1946–8 at the Juilliard School with Florence Page Kimball (voice production), Emanuel Balaban (songs), and Frederick and Elsa Cohen (opera). She was coached privately 1948–54 by Arpad Sandor while studying voice with Mario Pagano. Though maintaining a New York residence she made her radio debut 29 Dec 1947 on the CBC and her Toronto recital debut 22 May 1951 at the Heliconian Club, and appeared 7 May 1952 at *Eaton Auditorium. In 1953 she was acclaimed as Magda Sorel in Menotti's *The Consul* for the Opera Festival Assn of Toronto (later the *COC) and appeared in the *Promenade Symphony Concerts and with the *TSO. She repeated Magda for the festival in 1954 and for the North American TV premiere (17 Jan 1954) of *The Consul* on the CBC. Also for CBC TV she sang Donna Anna in *Don Giovanni* (1953) and the Governess in Britten's *The Turn of the Screw* (TV premiere, 1958). She was the soloist in a broadcast (1955) of Lukas Foss' *Song of Songs* with the *CBC Vancouver Chamber Orchestra.

In the USA Gray appeared in musical comedy and was a member 1954–6 of the New York Co-Opera Group, with which she sang the Countess in *The Marriage of Figaro*, Nedda in *I Pagliacci*, the title role in *Tosca*, and other roles. After her marriage in the late 1950s she lived in Yemen, in Jordan (where she was a recitalist and church soloist), and in Malta. With the Malta Chorale and orchestra, she sang in *Messiah* in 1973. Writing in the *Globe and Mail*, 31 Jul 1953, John Watson said: 'In everything she sings Miss Gray adds to line and colour the third dimension of genuine emotion ... Her voice is gorgeously vibrant and splendidly flexible. Not without her faults of technique, she is capable of imbuing her singing with a kind of sensuous warmth and passion that is completely overwhelming.'

GREALIS, Walt (Walter). Editor, b Toronto 18 Feb 1929. Following service with the RCMP 1947–52 and the Toronto Police Force 1952–6, Grealis entered the recording industry with Apex (now MCA) Records in 1960 and was Ontario promotion manager 1961–3 for *London Records of Canada. In 1964 he founded the trade magazine **RPM*. As its editor and publisher and the guiding force behind its many industry-service projects – including the RPM Gold Leaf Awards (later also known as the *Juno Awards) – he has been a catalyst in the development of a Canadian music industry. At the 1976 Juno Awards ceremony he was presented with a 'people's award.'

BIBLIOGRAPHY

Batten, Jack. 'One man's crusade to Canadianize rock 'n roll,' *Maclean's*, 8 Aug 1964

Yorke, Ritchie. 'In the beginning,' *Axes, Chops & Hot Licks* (Edmonton 1971) MM

Great Britain. See England; Ireland; Scotland; Wales.

Greece. The first Greek immigrants to Canada arrived in 1891. By 1961 there were 56,000 people of Greek origin in Canada; by 1971 124,000. The largest group originated from Peloponnesus, but *Macedonia, Crete, and other regions also are represented. Some 70 per cent profess Greek Orthodoxy; 11 per cent Anglicanism; 7 per cent Roman Catholicism. In the mid-1970s nearly half of all Greek-Canadians lived in Toronto, and another large group lived in Montreal. Many have entered business, especially as restaurateurs (some of whose establishments have become important centres of Greek popular culture in Canada).

Folk music is perpetuated at picnics, weddings, and private parties; regional associations have maintained the traditions of Pontus, Macedonia, and Crete. Many nightclubs (eg, The Odyssey in Toronto and L'Acropole in Montreal) present bouzouki music played by Canadian or touring Greek musicians. (The bouzouki is a round-backed, long-necked instrument of the lute family, with three or four sets of strings.) In Toronto, notable bouzouki players in the 1970s included Harry Kanellos, Louis Kottaras, Ken Nitsotolis, Cleanthis Papaeliou, and Elias Tsatsos. Greek churches and community centres support liturgical and secular music and often sponsor dance ensembles. Orpheus, a Greek-Canadian art association established in 1965 in Toronto, has sponsored a church choir and also a male-voice concert choir, conducted by James Vagalatis and Willis Noble, which has performed at *Expo 67, the *CNE, and *Ontario Place and has broadcast on CBC radio. Records imported from Greece have sold well in Canada. Some Greek bands play rock music, and a few non-Greeks perform Greek songs and dances or play the bouzouki.

Greek-born musicians in Canada include Dimitri Conomos (b 26 Sep 1947, a medieval-music historian who joined the *U of British Columbia in 1975), Angela Florou (a piano pupil of Gina Bachauer and a teacher at the *RCMT after 1964), Stephen *Kondaks, and Kenneth *Sakos. Canadian musicians of Greek descent include the *Calangis family, Rika *Maniates, Gregory *Millar, and Teresa *Stratas.

Among Greek musicians who have performed in Canada are the singers Vikki Leandros, Nana Mouskouri, and Mikos Theodorakis, the conductor Dimitri Mitropoulos (who visitied Canada, especially Winnipeg, many times with the Minneapolis SO), the pianist Gina Bachauer (who appeared with the *TS and the *MSO and gave recitals in several Canadian cities), the Greek-US soprano Maria Callas (who sang in Montreal and in Toronto in 1958 and 1974), and the Rumanian-born (of Greek parents), French-naturalized composer Iannis Xenakis (who was commissioned by the National Ballet of Canada to compose the music for *Kraanerg*, the Roland Petit ballet which opened the *NAC in 1969; Xenakis was present at an *NMC concert of his music in 1976 in Toronto and wrote *Epei* on commission from the *SMCQ, attending its premiere by that group in 1976 in Montreal). Leonard *Cohen and Joni *Mitchell have made the Greek islands of Hydra and Crete their respective homes for brief periods.

BIBLIOGRAPHY

Signell, Karl. 'Greek music in Toronto,' unpubl report, National Museum of Man (Ottawa)

Clery, Val. 'And the beat goes on,' *Weekend*, 7 Dec 1974

(KSg)

Greek Orthodox church music. The musical tradition of the Greek Orthodox Church is perpetuated by many groups in Canada: Ukrainians, Greeks, Rumanians, Serbians, Syrians, Bulgarians, Russians, Estonians, and possibly others (see *EMC* entries on individual countries).

By far the most numerous are the Ukrainians. The Ukrainian Greek Orthodox Church of Canada has about 300 parishes distributed throughout the country. The other groups combined have about 110. It should be noted that about 145,000 Ukrainian Catholics (Greek Catholic) belong to the Eastern Church musical tradition. The first Ukrainian Orthodox church building in Canada was erected in Manitoba just before the beginning of the 20th century although the Ukrainian Greek Orthodox Church of Canada was not constituted officially until 1918. (The first Ukrainian Greek Catholic church building also was built in Manitoba before the turn of the century, and there is controversy as to which was the earlier.)

Traditionally choirs and deacons share the singing duties of the service, and the priest intones his parts in recitative fashion. If there is no choir the congregation sings. Some congregations sing in two-, three-, or four-part harmony.

The prototype for Ukrainian church music is the Znamenny Chant originating in 10th-century Kiev. Thought is divided as to where it originated, but Ukrainian scholars theroize that it came through the Graeco-Syrian branch of the Byzantine tradition and developed its own characteristics through a strong local melodic admixture. By the 16th century Znamenny Chant had evolved into the Kievan Chant which served as the musical foundation for the next 400 years of Ukrainian church music.

The foremost composers in 17th- and 18th-century Ukraine were M. Dyletskyj, Dimitri Bortnianskyj, Maximus Berezovskyj, Artem Vedel, and Piotr Turchaninov. This period is often thought of as the golden age of Ukrainian religious music. As Ukraine became enveloped by her neighbours, musical life became stagnant. It revived only at the beginning of the 20th century, when a host of new composers emerged: K. Stetsenko, Oleksander Koshetz, J. Jatsynevych, P. Honcharov, M. Leontovych, P. Kozytzkyj, and others whose music has come to be sung regularly in Canadian Ukrainian churches. In Canada, Paul (Paolo) Macenko, Serhij Yaremenko, B. Malovanyj, J. Holovko, Sister Juvenalia, and the late Bishop Michael Choroshy all have written music for the church.

The Consistory of the Ukrainian Greek Orthodox Church of Canada stocks liturgical music by Leontovych and Stetsenko and a great many collections of pieces by a variety of composers, including two comprehensive anthologies by Zavitnevich of music for Easter and Christmas. There is also an extensive library at the Consistory and St Andrew's College. The private collection of Oleksander Koshetz, held at the Ukrainian Cultural and Educational Centre of Winnipeg, contains some rare specimens of Ukrainian church music.

Unfortunately, Canadian scholars have tended to neglect Ukrainian religious music. The notable exception is Paolo Macenko of Winnipeg, whose *Konspekt istorii ukrains Koi tserkovnoi muzyky*, a synopsis of the history of Ukrainian church music (Winnipeg 1973), *Narysy do istorii ukrains'Koi tserkovnoi musyky*, a history of Ukrainian church music (Roblin, Man, 1968), and numerous articles reflect substantial research.

St Andrew's College, Winnipeg, offers courses leading to a licentiate in theology and a bachelor of divinity and serves as a training centre for church musicians. St Vladimir's College in Roblin, Man, is a minor seminary for the Ukrainian Catholic Church of Canada.

The choral tradition of Greek Orthodoxy and Greek Catholicism is perpetuated in Canada by church choirs in Vancouver, Edmonton, Saskatoon, Winnipeg, Toronto, Montreal, Windsor, Hamilton, and many smaller centres.

See also Religions and music for a directory of *EMC* articles related to this entry; and Ukraine.

BIBLIOGRAPHY

Liturgical Voices of the Ukrainian Greek Orthodox Church (Saskatoon 1925)

Koshetz, Al. *Genetic Relationship and Classification of Ukrainian Ritual Songs* (Winnipeg 1945)

Høeg, Carsten. 'The oldest Slavonic tradition of Byzantine music,' *Proceedings* of the British Academy, Jan 1953

Echoes from the Past, letters of O. Koshetz to P. Macenko (Winnipeg 1954)

Velimirovic, Milos M. *Byzantine Elements in Early Slavic Chant: The Hirmologion* (Copenhagen 1960)

Macenko, Paolo. *Liturgical Songs of the Ukrainian Greek Orthodox Church of Canada* (Winnipeg 1962)

Trosky, Odarka S. *The Ukrainian Greek Orthodox Church in Canada* (Winnipeg 1968)

Macenko, Paolo. *Synopsis of the History of Ukrainian Church Music* (Winnipeg 1973)

(WK)

GREEN, (James) **Paul**. Educator, conductor, arranger, b Sydney, NS, 15 Apr 1929; ARCT euphonium 1957, B MUS (Toronto) 1954, M MUS (ESM Rochester) 1959, PH D (ESM Rochester) 1974. Following graduation from the *U of Toronto he was head of the music department and conductor of the concert band 1955–65 at T.L. Kennedy Secondary School in Mississauga, Ont. He served 1963–5 as conductor of the *Salvation Army's Dovercourt Citadel Band in Toronto. He taught 1964–5 at the Ontario College of Education and 1964–6 at the Ontario Ministry of Education's Summer School of Music.

In 1965 Green joined the faculty of music at the *U of Western Ontario, where he has taught brass and woodwind techniques and conducting, has given graduate courses in the psychology of music and the philosophy of music education, and served 1969–79 as chairman of the music education department. He conducted the university's Symphonic Band 1969–70 and its Faculty of Music Brass Choir 1965–70.

Green was chairman 1963–5 of the Instrumental Music Curriculum Revision Committee which produced the report *Intermediate and Senior Divisions Instrumental Music* (Ontario Ministry of Education, 1967), president 1964–5 of the *OMEA, and Ontario representative to the *CAUSM Committee of Curricular Standards, whose work resulted in *Standards* (CAUSM, 1969). In 1978 he was named chairman of the Music Discipline Group of the Committee on Academic Planning of the Ontario Council on Graduate Studies. He began examining for the *Western Ontario Cons in 1965 and has adjudicated at many competition festivals.

Green is the composer of *Stephanos* for band (Salvationist Publishing, 1978) and co-author and arranger, with Kenneth *Bray, of the series of wind instrument instruction books *Solos for Schools* (GVT 1978–). Green has written articles for many educational publications and is a contributor to *EMC*.

WRITINGS

'The need for a philosophy of music education,' *Recorder*, vol 8, Sep–Oct 1965

'Music in higher education: programs or politics?' *Recorder*, vol 19, Dec 1976

'Doctoral programs in music: reform or rhetoric,' *CME*, vol 20, Winter 1979

GREEN, Russell (Harry Colman). Composer, organist, choir conductor, b Norwich, England, 10 Apr 1908, naturalized Canadian 1972, d Saskatoon 6 Feb 1975; FRCO, ARCM, FRCCO. He studied at the Birmingham School of Music and privately with G.D. Cunningham and Herbert Howells. In England, besides occupying various church and school positions, he conducted the Olton Orchestra 1926–47, the Birmingham Festival Choral Society 1949–55, and the Russell Green Choir 1949–58. In Canada – after an introductory visit in 1950 as a festival adjudicator and a first post 1959–63 as organist-choirmaster of the First Baptist Church, Ottawa – he was dean of music 1963–5 at *Acadia U, then settled in Saskatoon, where he taught at the *U of Saskatchewan, served 1965–9 as organist-choirmaster at Knox United Church, and was the founder-director of the Russell Green Singers. He was organist-choirmaster at Christ Church, Saskatoon, from 1969 till his death. His compositions include over 350 songs, about 50 keyboard works, 50 sacred and secular choral pieces, *Paean* for orchestra, and a cantata, *Christus mediator* (1962). He designed the organ for the First Baptist Church, Ottawa. He was a member of CAPAC. (SLH)

GREENE, Gordon (Kay). Musicologist, teacher, b Cardston, Alta, 27 Dec 1927; BA (Alberta) 1954, B MUS ED (Alberta) 1954, MA philosophy (Alberta) 1962, PH D musicology (Indiana) 1971. He taught 1955–63 at the *U of Alberta, then studied musicology 1963–6 with Willi Apel at Indiana U. He joined the *U of Western Ontario in 1966 as chairman of the Music History Dept and moved to *Wilfrid Laurier U in 1979 as dean of the Faculty of Music. He has received, among other awards, an Alberta government scholarship (1966), two *Canada Council grants for research in Europe during the summers of 1969 and 1970, and a Canada Council fellowship to study secular music of the 14th century in France 1972–3. He has lectured on aesthetics and music history at Canadian and US universities.

WRITINGS

'Fit for treasons,' *Pleasures of Learning*, vol 9, Dec 1962

'The work of art as a symbol,' unpubl MA thesis, U of Alberta 1962

'Musical homesteading in Alberta,' *PfAC*, vol 2, Winter 1963

'From maid to mistress: the origins of polyphonic music as a visible language,' *Visible Language*, vol 6, Spring 1972

'For whom and why does the composer prepare a score,' *J of Aesthetics and Art Criticism*, vol 32, Summer 1974 CF

GREENWICH, Sonny (b Greenidge, Herbert Lawrence). Guitarist, composer, b Hamilton, Ont, 1 Jan 1936. His father, Herb Greenidge, was a jazz pianist in Hamilton until the early 1940s, then took his family to Toronto, where he retired from music. Greenwich began playing guitar in his late teens, and at about 22 joined a rhythm 'n' blues band led by the pianist Connie (Conrad) Maynard. Influenced by the tenor saxophonist Sonny Rollins, Greenwich developed a unique style – linear rather than harmonic in conception and saxophone-like in tone. The saxophonist John Coltrane and the trumpeter Miles Davis were other influences. The guitarist continued to play both rhythm 'n' blues and jazz in the early 1960s, then turned exclusively to jazz, performing with the US drummer Ed Thigpen (Toronto 1965), the saxophonist Don *Thompson, and others, and appearing at such Toronto venues as The Cellar, The First Floor Club, and The Bohemian Embassy

Sonny Greenwich

with his own bands. After playing 1966–7 with the US saxophonist John Handy in Seattle, San Francisco, and New York, he settled in Boucherville, near Montreal. He appeared at the Village Vanguard in New York for a week in 1968, leading a quartet completed by US musicians, and also worked (late 1960s, early 1970s) in Montreal with Lee *Gagnon, Ron Proby, and others, and in Toronto with Miles Davis and Fred *Stone.

Greenwich has performed only sporadically in the 1970s, retiring for long periods to pursue a personal religion similar to pantheism. Poor health also has restricted his performing and recording career. However he has given some concerts, or appeared in jazz clubs, in Montreal, Quebec City, Ottawa, and Toronto. Greenwich's limited exposure outside Canada has made him something of a legend in jazz circles – known internationally by name, but not by music. Undoubtedly it also has cost him his rightful place in the history of the jazz guitar. Elements of his style, which had few precedents in the early 1960s, had been paralleled by many other guitarists in the 1970s, but in most cases independently, with the result that his originality has been obscured. The strength of his performances, however – that element which has distinguished him from all other Canadian jazz musicians – has not been diminished.

Greenwich's compositions include *Loving* (revised as *New Love*), *Sun Song, Parting, Starlight, Lily (Lotus)*, and *Cross Currents*. Later works, such as *Heaven on Earth* (1975) and *Armageddon* (1978), employ layered chords to create a tonal ambiguity, leaving him with increased improvisational freedom. His songs 'New World Coming' and 'Time-Space,' which his band and the singer Ernie Nelson premiered in 1978, reflect his spiritual interests. Greenwich's bands have included the pianists Maynard, Bob Angus 1964–6, Don *Thompson 1969– , and Doug *Riley 1974–5; the tenor saxophonists Doug Richardson, Ron *Park 1964–5, and Michael Stuart 1974–5; the bassists Michel *Donato, Richard *Homme 1970–5, and Gene Perla in 1978; and the drummers Gerry Fuller 1964–6, Clayton Johnston, Terry *Clarke 1970–4, and Claude *Ranger 1974– . For some concerts in 1979 he added violin, viola, and cello to his quartet. He is an affiliate of PRO Canada.

DISCOGRAPHY

The Old Man and the Child. Thompson pf, Donato db, Houston db, Johnston drums. 1970. RCI 302/Sack 2002

Sun Song. Thompson keybds, Homme db and b guit, Clarke drums, Johnston perc. 1974. RCI 399

Evol-ution, Love's Reverse. Thompson keybds, Perla db and b guit, Ranger drums. 1978. PMR-016

Others with Jimmy *Dale, Gagnon, Moe *Koffman, (D.W.) Thompson, and Handy (see Thompson)

BIBLIOGRAPHY

Norris, John. 'Sonny Greenwich,' *Coda*, Nov–Dec 1965

Gallagher, Greg and Barnes, Lilly. 'Love of jazz dispels contrasts between musicians-composers,'' *MSc*, 263, May–Jun 1975

Waxman, Ken. 'Sonny Greenwich keeps his secrets,' *SatN*, Nov 1978

Miller, Mark. 'Sonny Greenwich,' *Down Beat*, 19 Apr 1979 (EFr, MM)

GREER, Albert. Tenor, choir conductor, teacher, b Toronto 23 Feb 1937; BA (Toronto) 1960, ARCT Gold Medal 1964. He studied with Aksel *Schiøtz at the *U of Toronto and was a member 1956–60 and 1964–7 of the *Festival Singers. He has appeared throughout Ontario and in Quebec as the Evangelist in the Bach *Passions*, in the title role of Britten's *Saint Nicholas*, and in several first performances, including *Heirs Through Hope* by Robert *Fleming (1968), *Lustro* by R. Murray *Schafer (1973), and *La Tourangelle* by Istvan *Anhalt (1975). He was conductor in 1974 of the *Ontario Youth Choir and of the Ontario Youth Choir Octet, which, during the 1974–5 season, visited Ontario towns under the auspices of the *Ontario Choral Federation giving concerts and workshops. With 16 alumni of the 1974 youth choir he founded the Toronto Youth Singers in 1975. After serving 1965–76 as the head of music in two successive North York (Toronto) secondary schools, he left the school system to devote himself to performing, conducting, and private teaching. AHC

GRÉGOIRE, Richard. Composer, arranger, b Montreal 18 May 1944; L MUS (Montreal) 1968. He studied composition at the *U of Montreal with Serge *Garant. In 1969 the *Pro Musica Society and the *SMCQ premiered and recorded (RCI 301, see Discography for Garant) Grégoire's *Cantate* for soprano solo, 12 voices, electric organ, guitar, and percussion. A winner of scholarships from the *Canada Council and the Quebec and French governments, he attended 1969–70 a study session in Paris with the Groupe de Recherches musicales and worked under the direction of Pierre Schaeffer. He also studied analysis and composition with Gilbert Amy and in 1969 participated in the preparation of a collective electro-acoustic work performed at the Avignon Festival. His piece for one or several saxophones, *Trajet*, was played in 1974 at the U of Montreal, where he had begun teaching in 1971. Grégoire has worked extensively in pop music as an arranger for Edith *Butler, Jim and Bertrand, Pauline *Julien, Diane *Juster, Jacques *Michel, les *Séguin, Fabienne Thibeault, and others, as well as for the CBC. He has composed music for the Office du film du Québec, and for the CBC TV drama (telecast November 1977) 'Le Deuxième Coup de feu,' for which his work won him in 1978 the *CMCouncil prize for the best original music for a dramatic or documentary broadcast. He is an affiliate of PRO Canada. (PR)

Grenadier Guards Band. See Canadian Grenadier Guards Band.

GRENIER, (Joseph Jacques) **Albert**. Pianist, teacher, administrator, b Shawinigan, Que, 31 Aug 1939; BA (Montreal) 1957, M MUS (Karlsruhe) 1964, L MUS (Montreal) 1971. He took private piano lessons with Georges *Savaria and studied with him 1954–6 at the *CMM. He then attended the Paris Cons as an auditor and worked with Jean Doyen and Vlado Perlemuter. In 1960 he obtained honourable mention at the Maria Canals Competition in Barcelona. He worked with Yvonne Loriod 1962–4 at the Badische Hochschule für Musik in Karlsruhe, Germany.

During his career as a performer 1962–73, Grenier participated in concerts with the Karlsruhe SO, the *CBC Quebec Chamber Orchestra, and the *Quebec SO and gave recitals in Karlsruhe, Paris, Quebec City, Shawinigan, Trois-Rivières, and Montreal. He premiered, among other works, *1½* by Marcelle *Deschênes-Harvey in Montreal in 1968, and with the flutist Mario *Duschenes he took part in the first Montreal performance of Boulez' *Sonatine* in 1969.

Grenier taught acoustics 1968–70 and piano 1968–73 at the St-Laurent Cegep and lectured on the piano and piano literature 1968–74 at the *U of Montreal. His dissertation for his licentiate was entitled 'Sonate pour deux pianos de Bruce Mather.' He joined the *Canada Council in 1974 and served as comptroller and program organizer until 1979, when he was appointed director of the CMM. LO

GRENIER, (Anne Marie) **Hélène**. Writer, librarian, b Quebec City 25 Jul 1900; MA (Montreal) 1944. She studied at *McGill U as well as the *U of Montreal, where her master's thesis was entitled 'Les précurseurs de la musique symboliste.' A librarian for many years with the Montreal Catholic School Commission, she was associated with the foundation and early years of the CSM orchestra and was secretary and program editor 1935–48 for the children's matinee concerts. She published *La Musique symphonique de Monteverdi à Beethoven* (Montreal 1947).

Her niece Monique Grenier (b 15 Jun 1935) studied voice with Lucie de Vienne Blanc 1950–7 and Anna *Malenfant 1957–60. She joined the CBC in 1954, becoming production assistant with CBC IS in 1956 and a producer in 1968. Recordings produced by her obtained the *CMCouncil's Grand Prix du disque in 1978 and 1979. GP

GRENIER, (Marie Berthe) **Monik**. Pianist, coach-accompanist, teacher, b Montreal 24 Aug 1931; B MUS (Montreal) 1951, M MUS (Montreal) 1953. She had piano lessons 1939–40 in Stratford, Ont, and 1940–2 in Guelph. She studied in Montreal 1948–53 at the *École Vincent-d'Indy with Jean-Marie *Beaudet and Jean *Dansereau (piano), Claude *Champagne (theory, composition), and Louis *Bailly (chamber music). In 1954 she won first prize in the radio competition *'Nos Futures Étoiles' (instrumental category) and obtained the *Prix d'Europe. She continued her training 1954–7 at the Paris Cons with Yves Nat, Marguerite Long, and Yvonne Loriod (piano), as well as Nadia Boulanger (keyboard harmony and accompaniment).

Grenier performed in public recitals and on CBC radio and TV and was accompanist and coach 1960–4 at the *JMC Orford Art Centre. With a grant from the Canada Council she continued her training 1964–5 at several European opera houses while studying the French and Italian repertoires in Paris and Milan and the Mozart operas in Salzburg. She became a rehearsal pianist for the *MSO and the CBC (in particular for the TV programs 'L'*Heure du concert,' 'Son et images,' and 'Les Beaux Dimanches') in 1949 and served in the same capacity at the *CMM 1957–63 and 1971–2, at *Expo 67, and for Les Grands Ballets Canadiens.

After 1972 Grenier taught at *McGill U and was in charge of opera class concerts 1975–7. During the summer of 1975 she was music director for the intermediate levels at the *Banff SFA. She accompanied the instrumentalists and singers at the Cons de Trois-Rivières 1976–8 and began teaching keyboard harmony and improvisation to the classes in accompaniment at UQAM in 1978. ST

GRENON-MASELLA, Claire (b Grenon, m Masella). Soprano, teacher, b Sault Ste Marie, Ont, 14 Sept 1932; B MUS (Montreal) 1954, M MUS (Montreal) 1957. She obtained a teaching diploma in piano from the *École Vincent-d'Indy, where her teachers were Paul *Loyonnet and Sister Rachel-Yvonne. She studied singing with Louise *André and in 1956 won the *Prix Archambault. In 1961, during the *International Week of Today's Music, she premiered Serge *Garant's **Anerca* under the baton of Mauricio Kagel. She was heard in CBC radio performances of Rossini's *Petite Messe solennelle* in 1961 and Debussy's *Le Martyre de saint Sébastien* and Boris Blacher's *The Tide* (*Die Flut*) (the latter on 'CBC Wednesday Night') in 1962. She also sang on the radio program 'Récital' and in several of CBC TV's *'Heure du concert' opera productions, including Poulenc's *Dialogues des Carmélites* in 1960 and (as Judith) Bartók's *Le Château de Barbe-Bleue* in 1962. She was a soloist with the *MSO in Mahler's *Symphony No. 2* in 1965 and in pop concerts in 1966 and 1967. In 1967 she participated in a concert of the *Society of Canadian Music (works of *Anhalt, *Contant, *Freedman, and *Pépin), and appeared as guest artist with the *McGill Chamber Orchestra. She has recorded with the *Montreal Bach Choir and the *Petite Ensemble vocal, groups with which she became associated in 1956. She began teaching theory in 1970 and voice in 1977 at the *Cons de Hull. Her husband is the french-horn player Paul *Masella. ST

GRESCOE, Donna (m Gullichsen). Violinist, b Winnipeg 17 Nov 1927. She began playing the violin at five and appeared in vaudeville at Winnipeg's Beacon Theatre at eight. Studies followed with George *Bornoff in Winnipeg and in 1938 at the American Cons of Music in Chicago on a $5000 scholarship. Assisted by a trust fund established by Winnipeg citizens after her formal debut, 1 Oct 1946, at the Civic Auditorium, she studied in New York with Michel Piastro. She made her New York debut 3 Feb 1947 at Town Hall and performed 30 Jan 1948 at Carnegie Hall. Though based in New York, she toured Canada, accompanied by Leopold Mittman, and performed with the *Winnipeg SO, the *TSO (16 Dec 1949), the CSM (*MSO) and the *Promenade Symphony (7 Jun 1951). Frustrated by the lack of opportunities for a concert violinist, she began nightclub work in 1953. She also performed at the 1955 *CNE, on Ed Sullivan's TV show 'Toast of the Town' (from New York, 4 Sep 1955), and on CBC TV's 'Showtime' (1956). She gave her last solo performance in 1959 and returned in 1962 to Winnipeg, where later she joined the Winnipeg SO. In the late 1970s she moved to Boston as the administrative assistant to George Bornoff in a string-teaching establishment.

BIBLIOGRAPHY

Cook, Lyn. *The Little Magic Fiddler* (Toronto 1951) (SRM)

GRESKO, Richard. Pianist, piano tuner, b Montreal 15 May 1942; premier prix piano (CMM) 1958. His father, a violinist of Ukrainian origin, was a member of the *MSO. Richard began to take piano lessons at five with Marie-Thérèse *Paquin and studied 1952–60 with Lubka *Kolessa at the *CMM. In 1959 he made His debut with the *Quebec SO and in 1960 represented Canada at the Pan-American Union Concert Series in Washington. He toured 1960–1 for the *JMC. The *Canada Council, the *Amis de l'art, and International Nickel awarded him grants, as did the Juilliard School, New York, where he studied 1961–2 with Rosina Lhévinne. He was coached by Jeaneane Dowis. After lessons in the summer of 1963 from Wilhelm Kempff in Positano, Italy, he worked 1963–5 with Irving *Heller in Montreal. A frequent guest on radio and TV, he played Tchaikovsky's *Concerto No. 1* in 1976 with the CBC Montreal orchestra. He appeared with orchestras in Halifax, Edmonton, Victoria, and Quebec City and performed Prokofiev's *Concerto No. 3* with the MSO. He gave numerous recitals in the USA (including New York appearances at Town Hall in 1965 and Carnegie Hall in 1973) and in western Europe. In the *New York Times* on 27 Nov 1973 Donald Henahan wrote: 'The 31-year-old Canadian's performance left no question but that his talent and his level of artistic achievement are considerably above ordinary. He has excellent hands independent and flawlessly accurate at any tempo; a feeling for differing styles linked to an ability to define differences sharply, and a poetic imagination.' In 1967 Gresko became a piano tuner and technician, a craft he learned from Gilles Losier.

DISCOGRAPHY

Prokofiev – Kabalevsky *Miniatures*: music for children. 1977. Lon CCL-60 06

Rachmaninoff *Preludes, Op 32 and 23; Etudes; Moment musical*. 1974. RCI 395

Also as accompanist to harmonica player Claude Garden for a recording of works by Lavallée, Champagne, and others, all arranged by Garden (1976, RCI 443)

BIBLIOGRAPHY

'Début,' Toronto *The Canadian*, 22 Jan 1966 ST

GRIEBEL, Ferdinand. Violinist, b Berlin 1818, d Toronto 18 Feb 1858. He came from a family of musicians and studied violin with Charles-Auguste de Bériot and Wilhelm Ernst. In 1842 he gave concerts in Sweden, Denmark, and England, and later he settled in New York. He is said to have visited Toronto with the Jenny Lind concert troupe in 1851; by 1853 he had become a resident of the city. From then until his death he appeared in many concerts, playing solos of his own composition and concertos by de Bériot. He was concertmaster in the Toronto premiere of *Messiah* in 1857. As late as 1878 he was considered the greatest violinist ever to have resided in Toronto. 'He was equally skilful in playing a solo, in leading the orchestra, or in interpreting chamber music, and had a remarkable talent for directing amateurs in their performance' ('Music in Toronto,' Toronto *Mail*, 21 Dec 1878). HK

GRIERSON, Ralph (Edwin). Pianist, harpsichordist, b New Westminster, BC, 23 Jun 1942; B MUS (Southern California) 1966, M MUS (Southern California) 1968. His teachers 1948–62 in New Westminster, BC, and in Vancouver were Priscilla Eastman, Glenn Nelson, and Glenn Geary. By 1958 Grierson had appeared in 12 children's concerts with the *Vancouver SO. Before and during studies 1962–8 at the U of Southern California with John Crown and Ingolf Dahl he played in Vancouver nightclubs with Fraser *MacPherson, Dal *Richards, Dave *Robbins, and others, and on such CBC programs as 'Sound of the 60s' (radio, 1964–5) and 'Chorus Gentlemen' (TV, 1965, 1966). In 1968 he settled in Los Angeles, establishing parallel careers as a studio musician (playing all the electronic keyboard instruments as well as piano, organ, and harpsichord) and as an interpreter of contemporary music. With Michael Tilson Thomas he made the first recording of Stravinsky's own four-hand piano reduction of *The Rite of Spring*. Grierson frequently has been a soloist with the Los Angeles Philharmonic, playing in Pierre Boulez' *Éclat multiple* (under the composer's baton), Messiaen's *Turangalîla-Symphonie*, and works by Bach, Gershwin, and Gottschalk. He has performed in chamber music series in Los Angeles, often with Tilson Thomas, in programs which have included music by Bartók, Cage, Copland, Gailliard, Kraft, Lanza, Mozart, and Subotnick. He has performed Subotnick's *Liquid Strata* in several US cities. In 1974 he visited Vancouver to give a concert and lecture on ragtime for the CBC.

DISCOGRAPHY

For Ralph Grierson: Kraft – Loseman – Subotnick. 1978. Town Hall S-24

Gershwin 'S Wonderful. A. Kane pf. 1975. Angel S-36083

Magnetic Rag: Joplin. Southland Stingers, Sponhaltz cond. 1975. Angel S-36078

Palm Leaf Rag: Joplin. Southland Stingers, Sponhaltz cond. 1974. Angel S-36074

Stravinsky *The Rite of Spring; Scherzo à la russe*. Thomas pf. 1968. Angel S-36024

Three Dances and Four Organs: Cage – Reich. Grierson and others pf, org, and perc. Ca 1972. Angel S-36059 MM

GRIFF, Ray. Songwriter, singer, pianist, b Vancouver 22 Apr 1942. He was raised in Winfield, Alta, where he took up the piano and played drums with the Winfield Amateurs (a dance group) as a boy, and in Calgary, where he formed and led the Blue Echoes in his teens. One of his first songs, 'Mr Moonlight,' was recorded in 1959 by the US country singer Johnny Horton, with whom Griff subsequently toured. Griff's 'Where Do I Go from Here?' was recorded by Jim Reeves. In 1964 Griff moved to Nashville, where he made a reputation as a songwriter. By the late 1970s he had written over 1500 songs, some 450 of them recorded. 'Baby' and 'Lost in the Shuffle' were hits in 1965, for Wilma Burgess and Stonewall Jackson respectively, and were followed by 'Something Special' (for Mel Tillis, 1968), 'Canadian Pacific' (for George Hamilton IV, 1969), 'Step Aside' (for Faron Young, 1971), 'Better Move It On Home' (for Porter Wagoner and Dolly Parton, 1971), 'Who's Gonna Play This Old Piano?' (for Jerry Lee Lewis, 1972), 'Where Love Begins' (for Gene Watson, 1975), and others. His songs have been recorded by the country stars Bill Anderson, Eddy Arnold, Chet Atkins, George Jones, Loretta Lynn, Marty Robbins, and Hank *Snow and by the pop singers Pat Boone, Wayne Newton, and Roger Whittaker. Griff's songs are published by Blue Echo Music. He is an affiliate of PRO Canada.

Griff began recording his own and others' songs in 1965, first for RCA and then in turn for MGM, Dot, Royal American, Capitol, and *Boot. He has made over 10 LPs and such hit singles as 'The Morning after Baby Let Me Down' and 'Darlin'.' Though he has retained his Nashville base, he has performed often in Canada, leading the New Winfield Amateurs, and in 1975 he was host for Global TV's 'Good Time Country.' In 1978 he recorded *Canada*, an LP of patriotic songs for Boot. MM

GRINKE, Frederick. Violinist, teacher, b Winnipeg 8 Aug 1911; FRAM 1945. After studies with John *Waterhouse and others in Winnipeg, Grinke won a Dominion of Canada scholarship to the RAM in 1927. He studied there with Rowsby Woof and later in Switzerland with Adolf Busch and in Belgium and London with Carl Flesch. He was a member ca 1930–6 of the Kutcher String Quartet and served 1937–47 as concertmaster of the Boyd *Neel Orchestra. In a long and distinguished career as a soloist he has performed in Europe, the USA, Australia, and New Zealand, and at the festivals in Edinburgh, Salzburg, and elsewhere. In 1935 in London, with the pianist Dorothy Manley, he gave the premiere of *Gratton's *Quatrième Danse canadienne*. He has been a soloist at the London Promenade Concerts. In Canada Grinke gave a recital for the *Women's Musical Club of Winnipeg in 1960, was soloist with the *Winnipeg SO in the Elgar *Concerto* in 1967, performed on CBC radio's 'Distinguished Artists,' and was a string coach for the *NYO in 1965 and 1969. Known especially for his performances of 20th-century English music, Grinke is the dedicatee of Vaughan Williams' *Sonata in A Minor* (1952). For English Decca he has recorded that work, along with others by Benjamin, Berkeley, Ireland, Purcell, Rubbra, and Vaughan Williams. Other Grinke recordings include music of Bach, Bartók, Beethoven, Dvorák, Handel, Mozart, Rachmaninoff, and Smetana. A detailed discography is published in *Discopaedia*. Grinke began teaching at the RAM in 1935, and many of Great Britain's leading performers are among his pupils. He also taught 1963–6 at the Yehudi Menuhin School in Stoke D'Abernon, Surrey, and he frequently has served on juries for international competitions. By Vaughan Williams' wish, Grinke and another native Canadian, David *Martin, were invited to perform the Bach *Double Concerto* at the composer's funeral in 1958. Grinke was named a Commander of the Order of the British Empire in 1979. (GBr)

GROOB, Jacob or 'Jack' (b Grobdruk). Violinist, conductor, b Ostropol, near Kiev, 21 Jan 1920. He was brought to Canada as an infant. He studied 1935–8 with Maurice *Solway at the *TCM, then for a year with Mischa Mischakoff in New York. After service in Europe with *The Army Show, he played 1946–9 and 1953–9 in the *TSO and was second violin after 1947 in the Solway Quartet. He was a soloist on CBC radio's 'Bod's Scrapbook,' orchestra leader in 1952 for 'Souvenir of Sometime,' and a member of the *CBC SO and other radio and TV orchestras. He resumed his violin studies with Oscar Back in Amsterdam (summer 1956) and took courses in conducting in Salzburg (summer 1957) and with Jean Morel at the Juilliard School. The Jack Groob Trio (Donald Whitton or George Horvath, cello, and Earle *Moss, piano) and the Jack Groob String Quartet (David *Zafer, second violin, Walter *Babiak or Ross Lechow, viola, and Whitton, cello) were formed in 1956 and 1957 respectively. The trio, which made its debut 30 Jan 1957 and was heard on CBC radio, gave the Canadian premiere (1958) of Villa-Lobos' *Third Trio*.

Groob moved in 1959 to Israel, where he became concertmaster of the Haifa SO and in 1960 formed the Jerusalem String Quartet. He founded the Toronto Chamber Orchestra (1962–9) and rejoined the TSO in 1964. He was conductor 1967–72 of the Oshawa SO and the Toronto Youth Orchestra, leading the latter to a first prize in the 1969 International Symphony Festival in St Moritz, Switzerland. A proponent of Canadian music, Groob premiered Harry *Somers' *Sonata No. 2* (11 Jun 1955 with the composer at the piano) and Harry *Freedman's *Fantasia and Dance* (1956, with the RCMT Orchestra) and conducted the London Philharmonic Orchestra Strings in a performance, 10 Sep 1961 at Wigmore Hall, of Somers' *North Country*, *Weinzweig's *Divertimento No. 1*, and other works.

GROSSMITH, Leslie. Pianist, conductor, violinist, composer, teacher, b Birmingham, England, 19 May 1870, d Victoria, BC, 27 Aug 1957. He received his training in Australia from Henri Kowalski and Max Vogrich and became a violinst in the Municipal Orchestra in Melbourne. Later he played for a Milan opera company, then returned to England to serve as chorusmaster for an English opera company and conductor of various theatre orchestras in London. After 1910 he moved to Victoria, BC, where for a time he was a pianist at the Empress Hotel. He also performed in other Vancouver Island communities. With the opening of Victoria's Capitol Theatre in 1921 he became, for a year, music director of the Capitol Opera Company. He also arranged music for silent films. In the 1920s he was active in Vancouver, but in the 1930s he taught in Victoria.

Grossmith toured as a pianist and entertainer in Canada (twice from coast to coast), Britain, the Middle East, and Asia. His compositions, listed in the *Catalogue of Canadian Composers*, include *Air de ballet*, which won first prize in the *Musical Canada* Pianoforte Composition Contest (*MCan*, Jun 1929); the three-act opera *The Immortal Slave*; the musical play *Zip Van Twinkle of the Canadian Rockies*; the opera *Uncle Tom's Cabin* (1928); and *Jubilee Symphony in D* (1951, written for the Australian Jubilee Symphony Competition). Other pieces for piano have been published by *Musical Canada*, Francis Day & Hunter, and Derek.

BIBLIOGRAPHY

'Leslie Grossmith,' *MCan*, vol 10, Jun 1929 (BNSG)

GRT of Canada, Ltd. Record company established in 1969 in London, Ont, as a subsidiary of General Recorded Tape, California. At first only a distributor for the Canadian tape market, GRT of Canada later in 1969 moved to Toronto and entered into record distribution, representing foreign labels and recording Canadian pop artists for its own GRT label (renamed Magnum in 1979). By 1976 GRT had acquired catalogues of popular music (ABC, Dunhill, Island, and other labels), classical music (Festival, Richesse Classique, and Westminster), blues (Chess), and jazz (America, Impulse, and Musidisc). It also distributed the Canadian labels Axe (including recordings by 'Canada's Polka King' Walter Ostanek and the Shamrock Singers) and Daffodil (*Crowbar, Klaatu, A Foot in Cold Water, and others). Canadian artists recorded by the company included the singers Beverly Glenn-Copeland, Dan *Hill, R. Harlan Smith, and Ian *Thomas, the reggae group Ishan People, *Downchild Blues Band, Moe *Koffman, *Lighthouse, Prism, and Doug *Riley's Dr Music. GRT also operated two publishing houses, Corinth Music (a PRO Canada affiliate) and Tarana Music (a CAPAC affiliate). The company's first president, Ross Reynolds, was president 1973–4 of the *CRIA and a leading member of *CARAS. He was succeeded 1978–9 by Gordon Edwards. In October 1979 GRT went into receivership.

BIBLIOGRAPHY

'GRT emerging as a major label,' *RPM*, vol 25, 11 Sep 1976

Gallo, Nancy. 'Magum records – a new force,' *RPM*, vol 31, 12 May 1979 (RGn)

GRUDEFF, Marian (b Grudeff, Marion, m McDonald). Pianist, composer, teacher, b Toronto, of Bulgarian parents, 18 Apr 1927. She began piano studies with her mother, continued with Mona *Bates at 8, made her first appearance in Liszt's *Hungarian Fantasy* with the *TSO at 11, and shortly after gave a recital at *Eaton Auditorium. After establishing a reputation in Canada she appeared in New York with the New York Philharmonic in 1946 and at Town Hall in 1950. She taught 1948–52 at the *RCMT, continued to give concerts, and toured British Columbia in 1951. Later she studied piano with Eduard Steuermann in New York and composition with Nadia Boulanger in Paris, and performed in Europe. Throughout the 1950s and the early 1960s she was connected with the Toronto revue **Spring Thaw*, beginning in 1950 as a rehearsal pianist, continuing as an arranger, serving 1956–62 as music director, and collaborating 1957–63 with Ray Jessel on lyrics and music.

Grudeff and Jessel subsequently were engaged by the producer Alexander H. Cohen to write songs for the musical *Baker Street* (book, New York 1966; vocal selections, E.B. Marks 1964), based on the story of Sherlock Holmes. The show opened first, 28 Dec 1964, at the Shubert Theatre in Boston, then was revised for Broadway and, after two weeks 'out-of-town' at Toronto's O'Keefe Centre, opened 16 Feb 1965 in New York. Called 'one of the best musicals in the 1960s' (Emory Lewis, *Cue*, 23 Feb 1965), it was recorded (1965, MGM S-4293). Grudeff and Jessel also collaborated on the musical *Life Can Be–Like Wow*, produced 1969 by the *Charlottetown Festival. In 1972 Grudeff resumed teaching at the RCMT and in 1976 she took up her performing career again in a series of concerts (1976–7) with the Royal Conservatory Trio and a solo recital (May 1977) at Town Hall, St Lawrence Centre, Toronto.

BIBLIOGRAPHY

Kritzwiser, Kay. 'Musical about master showman adds a link in Toronto pair's jigsaw,' Toronto *Globe and Mail*, 4 Aug 1962

Gehman, Richard. 'The case of the tortured tunesmiths (or quick, Watson–the music!),' *Maclean's*, 3 Apr 1965

'At times I felt like an oddity...' *Fugue*, Nov 1977 EK

Guelph. Founded 1827 by John Galt in the heart of agricultural Ontario and incorporated in 1879. In 1846 there were 1240 people living in Guelph. By 1974 the population had reached 65,000, in a mixture roughly two-thirds Anglo-Saxon, the remainder mainly Northern European and Italian. Though the *U of Guelph (1964) began to offer a BA with a major in music only in 1967, music in Guelph goes back well over 100 years. Historical records mention Sunley's (brass) Band, which gave public concerts and is reported as playing during a visit (1849) of Lord Elgin, then governor of the Province of Canada. Dyson's Cornet Band (1856), the 30th Battalion Band (1860), and the City Band (1880, becoming the Guelph Musical Society Band in 1898) provided musical entertainment well into the 20th century. William Philp (b Cobourg 1848, d Guelph 30 Jun 1925) conducted the latter as well as bands in Waterloo and Elmira.

Nineteenth-century church musicians played an enterprising role in the growth of Guelph. John Hockin (b St. Trudy, Cornwall, England, 28 Aug 1815, d Guelph 24 Jan 1888), who was music director at the Primitive Methodist Church, carved a cello out of maple and pine to enrich the church's five-or-six-piece orchestra, fashioned a flute to keep his choristers in pitch, and from indigenous black walnut and other available materials built Guelph's first organ ca 1850. William Bell, who came to Guelph in the 1860s to found the *Bell Piano and Organ Company (1864–1928), was awed by Hockin's knowledge and persuaded him to take apart and reassemble his organ to show how it was done. In the 1880s the Jesuit Father Theodorus Fleck (b Niederbronn, Alsace, 8 Nov 1827, d Metz, Belgium, 30 Oct 1897) was said to have the best choir in town. He arrived in Guelph in 1877 to teach Latin and direct the choir at the Church of St Bartholomew, which changed its name in 1878 to the Church of Our Lady. Father Fleck adapted Haydn, Mozart, and Gounod masses for the choir's use and prepared Rossini's *Stabat mater* and Haydn's *Third Mass* for performances conducted by F.H. *Torrington to open the majestic new Church of Our Lady in 1886. Father Fleck left Guelph in 1888 for the Maison Sault-au-Recollet, near Montreal. Mrs Gardiner Harvey (b Anne Catherine Roberta Geddes, Guelph 25 Dec 1849, d there 22 Apr 1930) was organist-choirmaster at St George's Anglican Church for more than 50 years after 1876 and made a mark as a composer. Her opera *La Terre Bonne* was sung in 1910 at Griffin's Opera House, and her oratorio *Salvator*, to her own text, had a premiere at St George's in 1912 followed by performances in Toronto (at Chalmers St Presbyterian Church), Kingston, and elsewhere.

In 1898 the Presto Music Club was formed to present concerts by members and guests. It gave its first concert in 1899, formed its own choral group in 1906, and remained active till 1959. Other noteworthy organizations were the Guelph May Music Festival (1930–1), the Guelph Kiwanis Competition Festival (1946–57), the Guelph Civic SO and Chorale (1955–9), the Community Concerts Association (1963–73), the Guelph Opera and Concert Singers (founded in 1958, successor to the Guelph Light Opera Company, 1955–8), the Guelph Music Club (1973 and the Edward Johnson Music Foundation (founded in 1958). The foundation has sponsored the *Guelph Spring Festival (founded in 1968), and commemorates Guelph's most famous musical son, Edward *Johnson (1878–1959), the *Metropolitan Opera tenor and general manager. A gift of $25,000 from Johnson in the 1920s helped establish music classes in Guelph schools, and at an early product of these–Guelph's first music festival, 7–8 May 1929–Johnson himself sang on the final evening assisted by the Vogt Choir of Guelph and the *TSO.

Other notable natives of Guelph are the jazz saxophonist Jane Fair, Nina *Gale, Laura *Lemon, Joseph *Macerollo, Edith *Miller, David *Ouchterlony, Bill *Phillips, and Tommy *Reilly. The best-known Guelph instrument makers were the Bell Piano and Organ Company and Joseph F. Rainer, who made square pianos 1870–85. A modern firm, Guelph Pipe Organ Builders, opened in 1973.

BIBLIOGRAPHY

Mason, Lawrence. 'Backgrounds and horizons in Ontario's music and drama: XI – Guelph, 'Toronto *Globe*, 12 Sep 1925

Coulman, Donald E. *Take a Look at Us* (Cheltenham, Ont, 1977) KW, (EKd, PW)

Guelph Spring Festival. Founded in 1968 under the sponsorship of the Edward *Johnson Music Foundation, with Nicholas *Goldschmidt as artistic director. The festival habitually occupies the first two weeks of May with concerts, opera, and displays by local, national, and international talent.

A chamber opera became an annual feature beginning in 1969 (Britten's *The Prodigal Son*, 1969; Johann Schenk's *The Village Barber*, 1970; Britten's *The Burning Fiery Furnace*, 1971, and *Noye's Fludde*, 1972; Menotti's *The Consul*, 1973; Britten's *The Rape of Lucretia*, 1974; Handel's *Acis and Galatea*, 1975; Britten's *The Beggar's Opera*, 1976; Derek *Healey's *Seabird Island*, 1977; Charles *Wilson's *Psycho Red*, 1978; Humperdinck's *Hansel and Gretel*, Gian Carlo Menotti's *Chip and His Dog*, and Richard Rodney Bennett's *All the King's Men*, 1979; and a dramatization with giant puppets of Berlioz' *L'Enfance du Christ*, 1980).

Another emphasis has been on the commissioning of new works by Canadians (Wilson's *En guise d'Orphée*, 1968; Lorne *Betts' *Festival Psalm*, 1969; Talivaldis *Kenins' *Chants of Glory and Mercy*, Wilson's *String Quartet No. 2*, and Gerhard *Wuensch's *Music Without Pretensions*, 1970; André *Prévost's *Psalm 148*, 1971; Godfrey *Ridout's *Cantiones mysticae No. 3* and George *Fiala's

Roxolana Roslak and Garnet Brooks in the world premiere of *Seabird Island* by Derek Healey at the 1977 Guelph Spring Festival

Sinfonietta Concertata, 1972; Charles Wilson's *Image out of Season*, Derek Healey's *Six Canadian Folk Songs* and Clermont *Pépin's *Chroma*, 1973; Harry *Somers' *Music for Solo Violin*, 1974; *Norma *Beecroft's 11 and 7 for 5*, Gary Hayes' *Convolution* and James Montgomery's *Reconnaissance for Amplified String Quartet*, 1975; Oskar *Morawetz's *Concerto for Harp and Orchestra*, 1976). In 1977, in celebration of the 10th anniversary of the festival and the sesquicentenary of Guelph, the festival commissioned Wilson's *Song for St Cecilia's Day*, Healey's *Seabird Island*, and David Archibald's musical *The Return of the Tiger*. It also mounted the Second National Vocal Competition that year, with Rose Bampton, Lord Harewood, and Léopold *Simoneau as judges. In 1978 it commissioned *Psycho Red* and Pat *Patterson's musical *The Cabbagetown Kids*. In 1980 it celebrated the Healey *Willan centenary with the premiere of Harry Somers' *Limericks* (dedicated to Willan and performed by Lois *Marshall, the Elmer Iseler Singers, and the Stratford Ensemble), the National Organ Competition finals (at which the winner was awarded the PRO Canada Healey Willan prize), and several performances of Willan's music, including the *Violin Sonata No 1* played by Lorand *Fenyves and Patricia *Parr.

Though major foreign artists such as Marilyn Horne and Jan Peerce have given individual recitals at the festival, Canadian performers (*Bouchard and *Morisset, *Canadian Brass, the *Canadian Children's Opera Chorus, Anna *Chornodolska, the *Festival Singers, Maureen *Forrester, Ingemar *Korjus, André *Laplante, Lois Marshall, the *Orford String Quartet, Oscar *Peterson, Catherine *Robbin, Steven *Staryk, Jon *Vickers, and others) and Canadian orchestras (the *Hamilton Philharmonic, the *MSO, the *NACO, the *Quebec SO, the *TS) have played a sustained role in the evolution of this major small festival, which grew from 6 presentations and a budget of $24,000 in 1968 to 14 with a budget of $154,000 in 1976. The festival is funded by the Edward Johnson Music Foundation with additional support from its members, patrons, the City of *Guelph, the *U of Guelph, the *CBC, the *OAC, and the *Canada Council. As in such European festivals as those at Gstaad (Switzerland) and Bath, the attractions are tailored to the city's accommodations: churches, the War Memorial Hall, the university campus. The charm of these accommodations, abetted by the hospitality of Guelph, has been a factor in the festival's success.

BIBLIOGRAPHY

Benson, Eugene. 'The Guelph Spring Festival: a retrospective view,' *Guelph Spring Festival* souvenir program (1972)

Edinborough, Arnold. 'Why the all-Canadian Guelph Music Festival is becoming our best,' *Financial Post*, 3 Jun 1972
Clapp, Gail. 'Five orchestras to play at the Guelph Spring Festival,' *OCan*, vol 4, Mar 1977
Rowcliffe, Katherine. 'Guelph Spring Festival: small festival earns big reputation,' *Fugue*, Apr 1977 EKd

GUÉRARD, Yoland. Bass, TV host and producer, b Joliette, Que, 11 Oct 1923. He was a bassoonist in the Joliette College ensemble and continued study of the bassoon at the CMM; however, after placing second as a singer in the radio contest 'Les Boursiers de CKAC,' he turned his attention to voice, studying with Albert *Cornellier. His first singing engagement was for CHLP radio, and he subsequently sang on the CBC's 'Soirées de chez nous.' He made his debut at the *Variétés lyriques in 1948 as Wagner in *Faust* and sang Sparafucile in *Rigoletto* (1949) and the Colonel in Posford and Grun's *Balalaika* (1950) for the same company. In 1950 he went to Europe with the *Disciples de Massenet and, with the help of a Quebec government grant, studied with Robert Salvat, Ninon Vailin, and Vanni-Marcoux in Paris. He made his debut at the Lyons Opera as Méphistophélès in *Faust* in 1951, and his success led to a subsequent engagement in Maurice Yvain's operetta *Chanson gitane*.

Guérard's return to Montreal in 1952 coincided with the beginning of Canadian TV, and he participated in numerous opera telecasts, also singing Capulet in *Romeo and Juliet* at the *Montreal Festivals and Jim Bullit in the operetta *Colorado* at the Variétés lyriques, where he was stage director in 1953. In 1954 he sang Pimen in *Boris Godunov* with the *Opera Guild, then left for a two-year US tour, replacing Ezio Pinza in the role of Emile de Becque (*South Pacific*).

Guérard was the founding vice-president of the Grand Opéra de Montréal, for which he sang the title roles of *Don Giovanni* (1957, Montreal Festivals) and *The Barber of Seville* (1958). For the CBC he sang Antonin in *Une Mesure de silence* (*Silent Measures) in 1956, Zuniga in *Carmen* (1961), the title role in *The Barber of Seville* (1965), and Doctor Grenvil in *La Traviata* (1966). At the 1965 *Stratford Festival he sang Trinity Moses in Brecht and Weill's *Mahagonny*. He staged the operettas *Les Mousquetaires au couvent* and *La Vie parisienne* at the *PDA in 1968 and 1969 and sang with the *MSO in concert performances of *Aida*, *La Traviata*, and *Rigoletto*. With the Opéra du Québec he interpreted the role of Sulpice in *La Fille du régiment* in 1972 and the title role of *Don Giovanni* in 1974. During that same period he sang in France with the Marseilles Opera in *Viva Napoli* (1972) and at the Sébastopol theatre in Lille, in *Gipsy* by Lopez (1974). After 1962 he was host and producer at Télé-Métropole for numerous opera broadcasts and variety shows, such as 'Découvertes' (until 1975), 'L'Âme des poètes,' 'Québec sait chanter,' 'L'Univers de Yoland Guérard,' and 'À la bonn'-heure.'

DISCOGRAPHY
Larue-Panzeri *Come prima*–Broussolle-Giraud *Mélodie perdue*. Larose cond. 1958. Music Hall 125 (78)
Noël. Larose cond. Ca 1970. Sel S-398062
Rouzaud-Monnot *Gloria*–Chabrier-Moutet *Toi je t'aimerai*. 1950. Music Hall 118 (78)
Sérénade. Larose. cond. ca 1976. Sel S-398238
Yoland Guérard. Brouillette cond. 1970. Cocorico CV-2002
Yoland Guérard: Peux-tu songer Symphonie vocale de la Fraternité des policiers de Mtl, Larose cond. Ca 1969. Alouette ALP-38
Yoland Guerard: Sur demande. Larose cond. Ca 1969. Alouette ALP-77 (CH)

Alberto Guerrero, ca 1930

GUERRERO, Alberto (b de Garcia y Guerrero, Alberto Antonio). Teacher, pianist, composer, critic, b La Serena, Chile, 6 Feb 1886, d Toronto 7 Nov 1959. A leading figure in Chilean music prior to his first visit (1914) to New York, Guerrero founded and conducted Santiago's first symphony orchestra, was one of the city's most prominent critics, taught the Chilean composers Domingo Santa Cruz Wilson and Alfonso Leng, and introduced to Chile the music of Ravel, Debussy, and their contemporaries on frequent concert tours. Leaving Chile in 1914 he worked until 1919 principally in New York as a pianist and vocal coach.

At the invitation of Boris *Hambourg he moved to Toronto in 1919 as a teacher at the *Hambourg Cons. He joined the *TCM in 1922 and remained there until his death, becoming recognized as one of Canada's leading teachers. His pupils included William *Aide, John *Beckwith, Helmut *Blume, Ray *Dudley, Dorothy Sandler *Glick, Glenn *Gould, his second wife Myrtle Rose *Guerrero, Stuart *Hamilton, Paul *Helmer, Ruth Watson *Henderson, Horace *Lapp, Edward *Laufer, Gordana *Lazarevich, Pierrette *LePage, Ursula *Malkin, Bruce *Mather, Gordon *McLean, Gerald Moore, Oskar *Morawetz, Arthur *Ozolins, George Ross, R. Murray *Schafer, Oleg Telizyn, Malcolm *Troup, and Neil Van Allen.

Concurrently Guerrero pursued a concert career, performing as a solo recitalist, as a soloist with orchestra, and as a member of trios with Frank *Blachford and Leo *Smith, Harold *Sumberg and Cornelius Ysselstyn, and of the Five Piano Ensemble. A former pupil, the scholar and poet Robert Finch, wrote: '[Guerrero's] style of playing was noteworthy for its reasoned sensitiveness. It could be enjoyed for the feeling it conveyed, for the logic of its interpretation, or for both...He left no musical detail, however minute, no musical structure, however extensive, a victim to whimsical or inspirational treatment.'

Several early compositions, apparently of an experimental nature, were destroyed by Guerrero. However, his zarzuela, *El Copihue*, was popular in Chile, and the later *Tango* (Harris 1937) and *Southern Seas* (Harris 1957) have been used in the RCMT syllabus for many years. He completed a textbook on modern harmony, published in Chile; contributed the article 'The discrepancy between performance and technique' to the RCMT *Monthly Bulletin* (Oct 1950); and, with Myrtle Rose Guerrero, wrote the two-volume *The New Approach to Piano* (Oakville ca 1950). The Alberto Guerrero Memorial Prize, a $2000 annual award for an original composition for piano, was initiated in 1978 by Guerrero's daughter Melisande Irvine.

BIBLIOGRAPHY
Beckwith, John. 'Alberto Guerrero, 1886–1959,' *CMJ*, vol 4, Winter 1960 (MWM)

GUERRERO, Myrtle (b Rose, m Guerrero, m Knox-Leet). Educator, b North Battleford, Sask, 5 Aug 1906; ATCM 1939. After private studies 1917–28 in Lethbridge, Alta, she continued her training 1928–32 at the TCM, where her piano teachers were Peter Kennedy and Alberto *Guerrero. She also studied harpsichord with Wanda Landowska and piano with Alfred Cortot 1936–7 in France and piano 1961–2 with Guido Agosti in Siena. An examiner 1940–68 for the TCM (*RCMT), she began teaching piano at the *U of Toronto in 1950 and at *McMaster U in 1977. Her pupils have included Tony Collacott (who, as a teenager in the early 1960s, had a sensational career in Toronto jazz clubs), Angela *Hewitt, and Kathleen Solose (who later studied in Italy and won first prize in the 1973 Alessandro Casagrande International Piano Competition in Terni). Myrtle Guerrero has given many teachers' workshops and lectures in Canada, the USA, and England, and in 1969 she established the Piano Teachers' Workshop, a two-week residential course held each summer at Geneva Park, near Orillia, Ont. With her first husband, Alberto Guerrero, she wrote *The New Approach to Piano* (2 vols, Oakville ca 1950). (ML, MM, PW)

Guess Who. Leading Canadian rock band of the late 1960s and early 1970s. It evolved in 1965 from Chad Allan and the Expressions, a band which had begun in Winnipeg in 1958 as Al and the Silvertones (later Chad Allan and the Reflections). The Expressions were the guitarist Randy Bachman, the bass guitarist Jim Kale, and the drummer Garry Peterson. The name 'Guess Who' was invented to promote the single 'Shakin' All Over' (1965, Quality). The singer-pianist Burton Cummings joined the band in 1965, shortly before the departure of Allan. After the international success of 'Shakin' All Over' the Guess Who appeared in England and the USA. The band recorded many other singles for Quality and performed on the weekly CBC TV rock shows 'Let's Go' (1967–8) and 'Where It's At' (1968–9) from Winnipeg. Its association with producer Jack *Richardson (and through Richardson with *Nimbus 9 Productions) began in 1968 with an LP, *A Wild Pair*, recorded as a sales premium for Coca-Cola (and shared with the Staccatos – later the *Five Man Electrical Band). From the Guess Who's first commercial LP produced by Richardson – *Wheatfield Soul* – came Bachman and Cummings' ballad 'These Eyes,' a million-selling single in 1969. Of over 20 singles released 1969–76, the following also were million sellers: 'Laughing' (Bachman, Cummings) and 'Undun' (Bachman), 'American Woman' (Bachman, Cummings, 'Share the Land' (Cummings), and 'Clap Hands for the Wolfman' (Cummings, Bill Wallace, Kurt Winter). Other substantial hits included 'No Time,' 'No Sugar Tonight,' 'Hand Me Down World,' 'Albert Flasher,' 'Rain Dance,' 'Star Baby,' and 'Dancin' Fool.' Three LPs, *American Woman*, *Share the Land*, and *Best of the Guess Who*, also received awards certifying sales in excess of $1 million. The band won *Juno Awards as the best vocal-instrumental group in 1965 and annually 1967–70.

In its heyday, during which Cummings emerged as the central onstage personality and major songwriter, the Guess Who underwent several personnel changes: Bachman (later to form Brave Belt with Chad Allan, and then *BTO) was replaced in 1970 by the guitarists Kurt Winter and Greg Leskiw, Leskiw in 1972 by Don McDougall, Kale in 1972 by Bill Wallace, and Winter and

Guess Who

McDougall in 1974 by Dom *Troiano. The band toured extensively 1969–75 throughout North America and appeared in New Zealand and Australia in 1973. It performed at the White House in Washington, DC, in 1970 and gave a royal command performance in London in 1973. Canadian appearances included annual concerts 1971–5 before audiences of up to 20,000 at the *CNE. The band, led by Cummings, gave its final concert 13 Sep 1975 at the Montreal *Forum. (A reconstituted group – Kale, McDougall, Winter, and the drummer Vance Masters – began touring and recording in 1978.)

Cummings (b Winnipeg 31 Dec 1947) began a solo career with a concert 8 Nov 1976 at the *Manitoba Centennial Concert Hall. After the international success of the singles 'Stand Tall' and 'I'm Scared' (his own songs), he won the 1977 Juno Awards as best new vocalist and top male vocalist. He received the latter again for 1979. Continuing to perform some of the Guess Who repertoire in concert, Cummings also had made three LPs for Portrait by 1978. He was reunited with Bachman in 1977 on the second LP, and the team performed at the CNE (2 Sep 1977) and on CBC and PBS (USA) TV.

DISCOGRAPHY

Shakin' All Over. (1965). Qual V1756
Hey Ho (What You Do to Me). (1966). Qual V1764
It's Time. Qual V1988
Wheatfield Soul. 1968. RCA LSP 4141
Super Golden Goodies. (1969). Qual SV1827
Canned Wheat Packed by the Guess Who. 1969. RCA LSP 4157
American Woman. 1969. RCA LSP 4266
Share the Land. 1970. RCA LSP 4359
Best of the Guess Who, vol 1. (1971). RCA LSPX 1004
So Long, Bannatyne. 1971. RCA LSP 4574
Rockin'. 1971. RCA LSP 4602
Live at the Paramount. 1972. RCA LSPX 4779
Artificial Paradise. 1972. RCA LSP 4830
Number Ten. 1973. RCA APL1 0130
Best of the Guess Who. (1973). RCA APL1 0269
Road Food. 1974. RCA APL1 0405
Flavours. 1974. RCA APL1 0636
Power in the Music. 1975. RCA APL1 0995
Guess Who's Back. 1978. Aquarius AQ 5072
All This for a Song. 1978. Aquarius AQR 522
Burton Cummings *Burton Cummings*. 1976. Portrait PR 34621
– *My Own Way to Rock*. 1977. Portrait PR 34698
– *Dream of a Child*. 1978. Portrait PR 35481

BIBLIOGRAPHY

Quig, James. 'The beat pounds on,' *Weekend Magazine*, 17 Aug 1968
Allan, Chad. 'Randy Bachman,' *MSc*, 245, Jan–Feb 1969
Batten, Jack. 'Here it is, the big noise in bubblegum music, Canada's richest and raunchiest band, The Guess Who,' *Maclean's*, Jun 1971
Yorke, Ritchie. 'The giant's awakening,' *Axes, Chops & Hot Licks* (Edmonton 1971)
McRae, Earl. 'Coming home is great,' *Canadian Magazine*, 3 Jun 1972
Stambler, Irwin. *Encyclopedia of Pop, Rock and Soul* (New York 1973)
Melhuish, Martin. 'Rock and roll band,' *Bachman-Turner Overdrive* (Toronto 1976)
McRae, Earl. 'Burton's back,' *The Canadian*, 25 Jun 1977
MM

'La Guignolée.' 'A refrain, possibly the only vestige of the Druidic era,' wrote the French historian Jean-Jacques Ampère in describing this song in 1854. In fact, 'la guignolée,' (in France ignolée, guillonée, guillona, or aguilanleu, depending on the region) is a derivation of 'au gui l'an neuf' (words said by the Druids at the mistletoe harvest).

In *Chansons populaires du Canada* (Quebec City 1865), Ernest *Gagnon gave three versions of the song found in the province of Quebec and described the different customs that surround it. At the beginning of each year, people go from door to door collecting clothing and food for the poor–'la guignolée.' The custom has survived especially in small towns and in the country.

Monique *Miville-Deschênes recorded the song (Gamma GS 135), as did Hélène *Baillargeon with the Bouttes en train (Folk FC 7229).

BIBLIOGRAPHY

Ampère, Jean-Jacques. 'Poésies populaires de la France,' *Journal de Québec*, 10 Jan 1854
HP

GUILAROFF, Vera (m Raginsky). Pianist, b London 26 Oct 1902, d Montreal 23 Oct 1976. Taken as a child to Montreal, she studied piano with her sister Olga, a renowned piano teacher in the 1920s, and played at 14 for silent films at the Regent Theatre. Briefly a pupil of Walter Hungerford at the *McGill Cons, she also was a protégé of Willie *Eckstein, with whom she collaborated in radio performances in Montreal and whose exhibitionistic ragtime style she adopted. Little is known of her career except that she toured in the USA with her husband, Harry Raginsky, a drummer, that she performed in England for the BBC, and that she played to raise funds for the armed forces during World War II. She made several piano rolls and, for Apex in the late 1920s, three 78s (listed in *Roll Back the Years*). Her 1926 recording of *Maple Leaf Rag* was reissued on the LP *Black and White Ragtime* (BLP 102047). CGa, MM

Guild of Carillonneurs in North America (GCNA). Formed 3 Sep 1936 in Ottawa with a charter membership of 24 (8 Canadian) to foster the art of the carillon. Percival *Price, at that time dominion carillonneur in Ottawa, was a co-founder; Edward Gammons (USA) was president until 1938 Though intended to operate in two US regions and one Canadian, the GCNA was active only in Canada until 1945. Each summer members combined in recitals on one or more carillons in Ontario, thus giving the first multiple-artist carillon concerts heard outside Europe. With the abolition of the GCNA's regional structure in 1945, annual continent-wide congresses were initiated. Among the guild's significant achievements have been its successful efforts to ensure minimum standards of bell tuning and to establish standard dimensions for carillon claviers. In 1978 membership stood at 133, of whom 12 were Canadians. Among the presidents, several have been Canadian: Percival Price 1947–9, Robert *Donnell 1950–2, Sydney Giles 1956–8 and James B. Slater 1969–71. The GCNA has published a *Bulletin* (usually twice a year), a newsletter, and carillon music. Archives are held (1980) at the U of Michigan. At the second World Congress of Carillonneurs, in 1975 at Douai, France, the GCNA and the several European guilds formed the World Federation of Guilds of Carillonneurs and elected Percival Price honorary president.

Guitar. A plucked-string instrument with a fretted fingerboard. In 16th-century Spain the four-course guitar was a popular instrument and by the early 17th century, with a fifth course added, it gained more serious attention, gradually replacing the vihuela. The modern guitar has metal frets and six single or doubled strings. Classical guitar strings are made of gut or nylon; folk guitar strings generally are steel. The electric guitar, an invention of the early 20th century, has either a hollow body (a variant on the folk guitar) or a solid body (ie, with no resonating chamber); in either case, 'pickups' or microphones sensitive to string vibration are positioned in the body above the bridge and wired through any number of tone-colouring devices to an amplifier.

Canadian craftsmen of acoustic guitars include Michael Dunn, Frank *Gay, George Gray, Jean *Larrivée, Grit Laskin, Charles-Lévis Laterreur, Pat Lister, Linda Manzer, and David Wren. The largest Canadian manufacturer is Norman Guitars Inc (founded in 1972 in La Patrie, Que, by Normand Boucher); its annual production reached 6000 instruments by 1979. Unisonic Inc, another firm in La Patrie, produces the Kamouraska model.

Early references to guitars in Canada are rare. However a letter of 4 Oct 1658 (*Lettres de la Reverende Mère Marie de l'Incarnation*, Tournai 1876) cited in Kallmann's *A History of Music in Canada* describes the use of a guitar to lull Iroquois to sleep, allowing a group of French to escape certain death. Guitars were advertised for sale as early as 1752 in Halifax, and guitar strings in 1788 in Montreal. Instruction was offered in the 19th century by J.-C. *Brauneis II of Montreal, and later as part of the curriculum of some ladies' colleges and at the TCM. Guitars are seldom mentioned in travellers' accounts from the 19th century. It was not until the 20th century, and particularly after World War II, that the instrument's popularity in Canada began to grow, and then only in conjunction with a world-wide resurgence of interest.

1 Classical
2 Jazz
3 Rock and folk

1 CLASSICAL. In 1959 guitar was reintroduced into the syllabus of the RCMT (taught by Eli *Kassner), and in the years following it was recognized by most of the country's major universities. Besides Kassner (who subsequently opened his own school in Toronto and became responsible for the

training of many of Canada's younger concert guitarists of the 1960s and 1970s), important teachers of guitar have included Antonin Bartos and Stephen Fentok in Montreal and Robert Christopher *Jordan in Vancouver. Canadian guitarists have been assisted by the master classes held by Julian Bream (*Stratford Festival), Alirio Diaz (*Banff SFA), and Pierre Augé, the duo Ako Ito and Henri Dorigny, and Alexandre Lagoya (*JMC Orford Art Centre), among others.

Carl Van Fegellen, a teacher at *Dalhousie U, has amassed one of the finest collections of guitars in North America, and Abel Nagytothy-Toth of Montreal, an authority on the literature and music of the instrument, has assembled a library containing many important early editions.

By the 1970s guitarists were on the increase, and Liona *Boyd was among the most popular. Other notable performers included Bartholemew-James Crago (a teacher at the *U of Montreal), Lynne Gangbar (as a soloist and in a duo with the English guitarist John Mills), Paul Gerrits (as soloist, and with Jacques Chandonnet and Claude Gagnon in the *Laval Guitar Trio), Davis *Joachim, Norbert Kraft (grand winner of the 1979 *CBC Talent Festival), Michael Laucke, Robert *Lemieux, Peter *McCutcheon, Martin and Marie Prével, Douglas Reach, Alan Rinehart, Michael *Strutt, Alan Torok, and the duo Don Wilson and Peter McAllister.

Among Canadian composers who have written music for guitar are Milton *Barnes, Robert *Bauer, Walter *Buczynski, Rolland Coté, Robert Daignault, Samuel *Dolin, Robert Feuerstein, Alain *Gagnon, Claude Gagnon, Gary *Hayes, Douglas Jamieson, Otto *Joachim, Denis *Lorrain, Bruce *Mather, François *Morel, Harry *Somers, and John *Weinzweig.

Guitar societies have been established in Edmonton, Ottawa, and Toronto. Each promotes concerts; the Ottawa society published a *Quarterly* 1970–4, and the *Guitar Society of Toronto sponsored the forums Guitar '75 and Guitar '78 in which many leading players performed and a competition for guitar compositions.

See also Spain.

2 JAZZ. With few exceptions, the jazz guitarist plays electric instruments, and his function in a group closely parallels the supportive and solo role of the pianist. Prominent jazz guitarists in Canada have included Ernie Blunt, Oliver Gannon (*Pacific Salt), Ray Norris, and Felix Smalley (Vancouver); Gordie *Brandt (Saskatoon); Lenny *Breau (Winnipeg-Toronto); Georgie Arthur, Ed *Bickert, Art DeVilliers, Sonny *Greenwich, Andy Krehm, Peter Leitch, Lorne Lofsky, Rob Piltch, and Stan Wilson (Toronto); Roddy Ellias (Ottawa); and Greenwich, Ben Johnson, Gilbert 'Buck' Lacombe, Leitch, Tony *Romandini, Nelson *Symonds, and Bill White (Montreal). Studio orchestras usually employ jazz guitarists, among them Bickert, Bobby Edwards, and Bob Mann in Toronto and Lacombe, Richard Ring, and Romandini in Montreal. Tony *Bradan has been an important teacher in the jazz field. The guitarists Eugene Chadbourne and Lloyd Garber explored free improvisation in the 1970s and introduced many new techniques.

The Canadians Arnold 'Red' McGarvey and Danny Perri had careers in the USA, the former briefly with Red Norvo in the 1930s, and the latter with Jack Hylton and for many years as accompanist to Perry Como. The Belgian guitarist René Thomas lived 1958–63 in Montreal; the influential US musician Lonnie *Johnson, 1965–70 in Toronto.

See also Jazz.

3 ROCK AND FOLK. The largest number of guitarists in Canada play in these styles and are essentially self-taught musicians. The level of competence required to play folk or rock music or the music of the chansonniers consists, at its most basic, of a knowledge of a small number of chords, and many singers in these genres accompany themselves, eg, Edith *Butler, Félix *Leclerc (who introduced to Quebec song the self-accompanied singer), Gordon *Lightfoot, and Murray *McLauchlan. Nevertheless many highly accomplished players have developed in both styles, the folk players usually working as accompanists, and the rock players enjoying considerable adulation as part of the cult that has grown around the lead (ie, solo) guitarist.

Among the folk guitarists are Bruce *Cockburn, Amos Garrett, David Rea, and Laurice Milton 'Red' Shea, who were accompanists in the 1960s to Gordon Lightfoot, Ian and Sylvia *Tyson, and others.

Among the rock guitarists, who use electric instruments almost exclusively, are 'Red' Armstrong (Montreal studio musician), David Bendeth, Terry Bush (Toronto studio musician), Randy Bachman (*BTO), Rik Emmett (Triumph), Bill Hill (J.B. and the Playboys), Roger Law (Mother Tucker's Yellow Duck), Alex Lifeson (*Rush), Frank *Marino, Moe Marshall (Jury), Eugene Martynec (*Kensington Market), Michael McKenna (the Apostles, Mainline), Walter *Rossi, Gilles *Valiquette, and David Wilcox. Stacey Heydon, Jamie Robbie Robertson (*The Band), Pat Travers, Dom *Troiano, and Zal Yanovsky have had significant careers in rock outside of Canada. See also Rock.

Of the variants of the guitar, the Hawaiian guitar was popular in North America in the 1920s and 1930s when the singer-guitarist Ben Hokea lived (in turn) in Toronto and Montreal and recorded for Compo and HMV; and the pedal steel guitar, prevalent in country music, has had among its leading Canadian exponents Ernie Hagar, Bob Lucier, and Steve Smith.

See also Blues; Folk music.

BIBLIOGRAPHY

Bauer, Robert. 'Guitar music in Canada,' *Array Newsletter*, vol 1, Spring 1974

Schulman, Michael. 'Toronto celebrates art of classical guitar,' *PfAC*, Summer 1975

Bauer, Robert. 'Guitar 75,' U of T Faculty of Music *News* Summer 1975

Hutchinson, Peter. 'The sound of music making money,' *Maclean's*, 23 Apr 1979

Littler, William. 'Rock ages, classics don't,' *Toronto Star Street Talk*, 21 Jun 1979

(MM, MSt)

Guitar Society of Toronto. Formed in 1956 to 'foster understanding, appreciation and the study of the guitar.' The society has met privately on a monthly basis and also has sponsored public recitals by leading guitarists, beginning with an appearance by Rex de la Torre 8 Jan 1958 at *Eaton Auditorium. Later concerts included the Toronto debuts of Julian Bream, Alirio Diaz, Oscar Ghiglia, Alexander Lagoya, Turibio Santos, and others. Jazz concerts have been given under the society's auspices by Lenny *Breau and Charlie Byrd, folk and flamenco artists also have performed, and student concerts have been given by Dan Beckerman, the young Liona *Boyd, Lynne Gangbar, and others. The society has been host for two international congresses at the *U of Toronto, Guitar '75 and Guitar '78, which brought together over 500 performers and students from various parts of the world for concerts, workshops, master classes, and competitions. A 'Quest for New Music' was held in conjunction with the second congress, drawing 75 entries in a composition competition. Canadian award winners were Charles *Camilleri, Thomas Dusatko, and Douglas Jamieson. Previously the society had commissioned *Somers' *Sonata for Guitar*, premiered by Peter Acker in 1964. The society offers a scholarship named in memory of one of its founders, Ken Young. A *Bulletin* has been published monthly September–May. The society was given the Bertram Atkins Library, collected by the Toronto banker and classical guitarist of that name, and has expanded it to include tapes of performances as well as guitar, lute, and related music. The library is held at the Eli *Kassner Guitar Academy. Presidents of the society have been, successively, Kassner, John Bonfield, Joan York, Harold Smith, Ted Lebar, and Ron Butler. In 1974 20 members of the society formed the Assn of Guitar Teachers of Toronto. (MM, DS)

GUREVICH, Ruben. Conductor, violinist, b Montevideo, Uruguay, 27 Aug 1944, naturalized Canadian 1976. The son of a violinist, he began his own violin and theory studies at 6 with Guido Santorsola in Montevideo and joined the National SO of Uruguay at 17. He continued his studies in the USA, 1966–7 at Antioch College, Ohio, 1967–8 at Indiana U and 1968–9 at the Cleveland Institute of Music, also attending the Yale U and Northwestern U summer schools. His teachers in the USA included Rafael Druian and Josef Gingold (violin) and Jascha Horenstein, Otto-Werner *Mueller, and Hermann Scherchen (conducting). Gurevich then moved to Winnipeg, where he served 1969–73 as assistant concertmaster and 1973–4 as principal second violin of the *Winnipeg SO and 1971–2 as principal second violin of the *CBC Winnipeg Orchestra. He founded the *Manitoba Chamber Orchestra in 1972 and in 1979 remained its sole director. He gave up playing in 1974 to become assistant conductor of the Winnipeg SO, adding to his duties in 1976 the position of music director and conductor of the *Saskatoon SO. In 1977 he became principal guest conductor of the Winnipeg SO. In 1979 he appeared as a guest conductor with the *COC (eight performances of *Carmen*), the *TS (at Ontario Place), and the *CBC Vancouver Chamber Orchestra. (LI)

GUSSET, Monique (Rachel Luce) (b Pariseau). Pianist, harpsichordist, b Montreal 6 Jan 1928. She studied 1944–50 and 1954–6 at the *CMM with Auguste *Descarries (piano), Isabelle *Delorme and Jean *Papineau-Couture (solfège), and Charles *Houdret (chamber music). She was rehearsal pianist for the *Montreal Festivals 1955–6 and accompanist 1955–7 for Le Choeur de Montréal under Lionel Renaud. She has been heard on CBC radio and TV as accompanist to Edward and Norma Lee *Bisha, Francis *Chaplin, Phyllis *Mailing, Ronald Murdock, and Ifan *Williams and as a member of Le Trio acadien (with the soprano Gloria *Richard and the clarinetist Alban Gallant). She moved to Halifax in the late 1950s, when her husband, Georges Gusset, a violinist, joined the *Halifax SO (*Atlantic SO). She herself joined that orchestra as pianist and harpsichordist in 1960. She has been the pianist and sometime music director for children's plays, drama productions at *Dalhousie U and St Mary's U, and musicals at the Neptune Theatre. She toured the USA with Gary *Karr in 1971 and, under the auspices of the Canada Council Touring Office, performed in British Columbia with the percussionist Craig Reiner in 1975. She has appeared regularly with the contemporary music group *NOVA MUSIC. NM

GUSTAFSON, Ralph (Barker). Poet, critic, b Lime Ridge, near Sherbrooke, Que, 16 Aug 1909; MA (Bishop's U) 1930, BA (Oxford) 1933, MA (Oxford) 1963, D LITT (Mount Allison) 1973. He was music master 1929–30 at Bishop's College School. In 1960 he became poet-in-residence and a teacher of English at *Bishop's U. A literary critic, a short story writer, and a widely published poet, he also has shown a sustained interest in the musical experience, and many of his poems reflect this. He is a collector of rare and historic piano recordings (going back to 1903) by Gabrilowitsch, Levitzki, de Pachmann, Godowsky, Samaroff, Grünfeld, Friedman, etc. Assisted by the pianist Howard *Brown, he has transferred many of these to tape and has made copies (the Gustafson Piano Library tape series, beginning with GPL 101) available commercially. In 1960, Gustafson began reviewing new recordings of piano music for the CBC, concentrating on the romantic era from Liszt to Rachmaninoff.

BIBLIOGRAPHY

Reubart, Dale. 'Toward a history of musical performance: tapes of the Gustafson collection,' *CAUSM J*, vol 3, Fall 1973

GUSTIN, Lyell (Adams Raphael). Pianist, teacher, b Fitch Bay, near Sherbrooke, Que, 31 May 1895; hon LL D (Saskatchewan) 1969, hon FTCL 1978. After studies at Stanstead Wesleyan College, Stanstead, Que, he moved to Saskatoon in 1912. He studied there with Blanche St John-Baker (a pupil of Godowsky), in Chicago with Jeannette Durno (a pupil of Leschetizky), and in New York and London with Madeley Richardson. Returning in 1920 to Saskatoon, Gustin opened a piano studio. In over 50 years of teaching, his hundreds of pupils have included Edmund *Assaly, (Garth) *Beckett and (Boyd) *McDonald, Reginald and Evelyn *Bedford, Dorothy *Bee, Alma Harrington *Brock-Smith, Anne *Campbell, Neil *Chotem, Robert *Fleming, Gordon *Hancock, Audrey *Johannesen, Paul *de Margerie, Thelma Johannes *O'Neill, Marguerite *Spencer, Walter Thiessen, and Gordon Wallis.

Gustin directed his own summer school program for over 30 years and served 1944–70 as an examiner for the TCM (*RCMT). He also lectured 1936–42 at the *U of Regina, 1950–1 at the *U of Saskatchewan, and summers 1950 and 1968 at the RCMT. He was the founder in 1924 of the *Musical Art Club, Saskatoon, and a founding member of the *SRMTA; he also served 1941–6 as president of the *CFMTA and 1952–64 as chairman of the music committee of the *Saskatchewan Arts Board. In 1955 he received the U of Alberta National Award in music, in 1967 he was one of six recipients of the CFMTA Centennial Citations for outstanding teaching, and in 1973 he was given the *CMCouncil Medal. In 1975 he was honoured by a CBC radio documentary on his life and work. The Lyell Gustin Piano Studios began publishing the *Studio Bulletin* in 1941; it appeared biennially until 1966 and annually thereafter. Gustin himself began work on his memoirs, *My Life in Music*, in the late 1960s.

BIBLIOGRAPHY

Brandhagen, W.L. 'One man conservatory,' *PfAC*, vol 4, Spring–Summer 1962
Leeper, Muriel. 'A challenging life of cultivating the prairies,' *Music*, Mar–Apr 1980 (IMM)

GUTTMAN, Irving (Allen). Opera director, b Chatham, Ont, 27 Oct 1928. After studies 1941–6 at Strathcona Academy in Montreal he attended the *RCMT (1947–52; his teachers were Oskar *Morawetz and John *Weinzweig) and was an assistant to Herman *Geiger-Torel 1949–54 at the

Lyell Gustin

Opera Festival (*COC). He made his directing debut in May of 1953 in Cornwall, Ont, with Menotti's *The Consul*, for which his cast included the young Maureen *Forrester. That same year he directed a complete *Faust*, the first of some 65 operatic programs for CBC TV over the next six years, including many complete operas for 'L'*Heure du concert.' In 1956 he directed *The Marriage of Figaro* at the *Montreal Festivals and in 1958 he made his US debut directing the Sante Fe Opera's world premiere of Carlisle Floyd's *Wuthering Heights*. After working as a guest director with the New Orleans, Baltimore Civic, Fort Worth, and Houston Grand operas in 1959 and 1960, Guttman became the first artistic director (1960–74) of the *Vancouver Opera. For the *Opera Guild of Montreal at *Her Majesty's Theatre and at *PDA he produced seven productions of six operas between 1963 and 1969. His COC debut, *La Traviata* in 1964, led to seven productions of five operas for that company by 1975. In 1966 Guttman became artistic director of the *Edmonton Opera, and in 1974 he established the opera school at the Courtenay Youth Music Centre. He produced *Faust* for *Expo 67. He has been a guest director with the San Francisco Spring and Philadelphia Lyric operas; in Barcelona, Spain (1969, 1971, 1973); and at the Motnreal Festivals (*La Serva Padrona* and *L'Heure espagnol*, 1961).

WRITINGS

'Pauline Donalda: a memorial tribute,' *OpCan*, vol 11, Dec 1970

BIBLIOGRAPHY

Watmough, David. 'An interview with Irving Guttman,' *OpCan*, vol 9, Feb 1968
Littler, William. 'The young man who went west and made his name in opera,' *Toronto Star*, 11 Nov 1972
Wyman, Max. 'Irving Guttman: a Canadian success story,' *OpCan*, vol 17, May 1976
Aberbach, Alan D. 'Backstage magic: the unique talent of Canadian stage director Irving Guttman,' *OpCan*, Summer 1980 (MW)

GUY, Elizabeth Benson (m Dentay). Soprano, b Halifax, NS, 7 Dec 1925. Raised in Bridgewater, NS, she studied first with her mother, Sarah Louise Anderson, a European-trained singer, and 1942–5 with Ernesto *Vinci in Halifax. She continued with Vinci at the TCM. Later she studied with Lotte Leonard at the Juilliard School. She gave a recital tour of the Maritimes in the early 1940s and was heard also on radio in Halifax. She made her opera debut in 1947 as Marie in the *Royal Cons Opera School's *The Bartered Bride*. She won the 1947–8 CBC's *'Singing Stars of Tomorrow,' and subsequently sang several roles with the *CBC Opera Company, including Violetta in *La Traviata* and Donna Elvira in *Don Giovanni* (1949), Princess

Elizabeth Benson Guy

Turandot in *Turandot* (1950), and Fiordiligi in *Così fan tutte* (1953). She has appeared in other CBC radio productions of opera, including *Don Giovanni* in 1949, *Gianni Schicchi* and *Falstaff* in 1953, *Eugene Onegin* in 1954, *Otello* in 1955, *Jenufa* and *Hippolyte et Aricie* (as Phèdre) in 1957, *Dido and Aeneas* in 1963, and *Sam Slick* in 1967. Also for CBC radio she has given many song recitals, some devoted to works of one composer: Schubert (1949), *Morawetz (1949), Brahms (1965), and Berlioz (*Les Nuits d'été*, 1965).

For the Opera Festival Assn of Toronto, Guy sang Donna Elvira in *Don Giovanni* (1950), Marie in *The Bartered Bride* (1952), and the First Lady in *The Magic Flute* (1952). She was a soloist in *Messiah* with the *Toronto Mendelssohn Choir in 1965 and has appeared frequently with the *Festival Singers. Also enjoying a career as a concert artist she has made debuts at Carnegie Hall, New York, 10 May 1959, and at Wigmore Hall, London, 31 Oct 1967, and has given several major recitals in Toronto. Besides the standard French and German repertoire, she has sung works by Robert *Fleming, Oskar Morawetz, Jean *Papineau-Couture, and Clermont *Pépin. After an *Eaton Auditorium recital, Frank Haworth wrote, 'Her voice was rich, free and colourful, the latter quality being manifest not only in her variety of tonal tint but in her ability to adapt her vocal quality, as it were, to the atmosphere and emotional situation of each item' (*Globe and Mail*, 17 Feb 1964). Guy retired from public performance around 1974. A teacher 1969–79 at the *RCMT and the Faculty of Music, *U of Toronto, she numbered Mark DuBois, John Keane, and Shauna Farrell among her pupils and coached Sheila *Henig prior to Henig's New York debut as a singer-pianist.

DISCOGRAPHY

Fauré *Cinq Mélodies*–Purcell *Songs*. Hamilton pf. ca 1968. CBC SM-32
M. McIntyre–Dela–Hamer. CBC Tor orch, Waddington cond. 1951. RCI 35
Morley–Dowland–Rosseter–Brahms–Debussy: *Songs*. Newmark pf. 1962. RCI 205
Purcell *Duets*–Dvoràk *Strains from Moravia*. J. Simons bar, Newmark pf. RCI 199
Schutz –Hassler –Vivaldi–et al: *Songs*. Kraus hpd. 1969. CBC SM-92
See also Discography for Orford String Quartet (LH)

GUY, Guylaine (b Chailler, m Libman). Singer, painter, b Montreal 6 Apr 1929. She owed her early musical training to her mother, Lise Bonheur (actress, singer, b Leontine Laurendeau, m Chailler, m Lebrun; a niece of Alexandre *Laurendeau), who ran a theatre and dance school. Guylaine made her debut in Montreal in August 1950 at the club Au Faisan doré and enjoyed a swift success. In 1952, after two years of touring and radio work, she was voted Miss

Radio-Television at the Gala des artistes organized in Montreal by the periodical *Radiomonde*. She made some 78s for RCA Victor. On Broadway she was understudy to the famous Lilo in Cole Porter's musical comedy *Can-Can*. *Radiomonde et Télémonde* reported (26 Jun 1954) that the New York press had been 'literally bowled over. The seventeen times that she stood in for Lilo, the critics were unanimous in finding her not only as good, but even better, especially as a singer.'

In 1955 Charles Trenet took Guy to Paris as his protégée, wrote some songs for her, and arranged her debut at the Olympia opposite him. The same year she shared billing with Louis Armstrong. She took up permanent residence in Paris and recorded several of Trenet's songs for Pathé-Marconi. She performed in 1956 at the Bobino theatre and at the cabaret La Villa d'Este, and shared top billing at the Olympia in 1957 with the actors Roger Pierre and Jean-Marc Thibault. During the 1950s she made several tours that included North Africa, the Middle East, Spain, Holland, and Switzerland. In Canada she sang in 1958 at the opening of the Queen Elizabeth Hotel, Montreal, made two series of TV programs in 1961, and played the title role in *Irma la douce* (libretto by Alexandre Breffort, music by Marguerite Monnot) with the Théâtre du Nouveau-Monde at Montreal's *Orpheum Theatre in 1963.

Shortly afterwards, Guy abandoned her singing career to devote herself to painting, which she studied with Jean Picard-Ledoux. She has exhibited her paintings in various Paris galleries. As a singer she attempted a come-back around 1970 with moderate success. In Montreal she took part in a show commemorating the first 20 years of TV and telecast by CBC in 1972.

A sister, Monique (Marie Hélène) Chailler (soprano, actress, m Dumont-Frenette; b Montreal 28 Aug 1922), performed chiefly on CBC radio 1943–65, taking part in such programs as 'Concert intime,' 'Sunday Morning Recital,' and 'Crépuscule' (1962). After 1963, she gave numerous recitals in Canada and abroad. She began teaching teaching singing in Montreal in 1966. Some of her poems, written in French, English, and Spanish, have been set to music by Herbert *Ruff.

Another sister, Colette Bonheur (singer, b Chailler, m Robinson; b Montreal 20 Sep 1927, d Freeport, Bahamas, 15 Oct 1966), made her debut in Montreal at the club Au Faisan doré in 1951. She appeared 1952–4 in the CBC TV program 'Mes Jeunes Années' and starred 1954–7 in 'Porte ouverte' with Jacques Normand and Gilles Pellerin. In November 1961 she moved to the Bahamas with her family. Several of her hit songs are on the LP *Colette Bonheur chante pour vous* (EPIC LF-2007). CV

Guy Lombardo and His Royal Canadians. See Lombardo.

H

HAAS, Douglas. Organist, b Kitchener, Ont, 25 Dec 1936. He studied piano with Earl *Moss at the *RCMT and organ privately with Frederick *Geoghegan until 1958. He continued organ training with Fernando Germani at the Academy of St Cecilia in Rome, and served 1959–60 as organist at All Saints Anglican Church in Rome. Studies followed at the Akademie für Musik in Stuttgart (where he was organist at the Johanneskirche) and with Anton Heiller at the Haarlem Academy in Holland. He returned to Canada in 1967 as music director at St Andrew's Presbyterian Church in Kitchener, where he also founded in 1968, and conducted until 1972, the Kitchener Bach Choir. In 1975 he began performing occasionally with *Canadian Brass.

DISCOGRAPHY

Bach *Cantatas No. 29, 135*. Deutsche Bach Solisten, Stuttgart Madrigal Choir, W. Goennewein cond. 1963. Cantate Bach-Studio 651 216

– *Cantata No. 80; Mass in A*. Württemberg Chamb O, Rilling cond. 1963. Vox DL-1100

Baroque Organ Music. 1967. Vox Turnabout 34135

Handel *Belshazzar*. Choir and orch of the Stuttgart Memorial Church, Rilling cond. 1963. 3-Vox SVBX-5209

Monteverdi *Il Ritorno di Ulisse in patria*. Santini Chamb O, Ewerhart cond. 1964. 3-Vox SVBX 5211

The World of the Organ. 1973. Decca SPA-262 AHC

HAAS, Gaby (Gabriel). Accordionist, composer, b Františkovy Lázně, Czechoslovakia, 7 Nov 1920, naturalized Canadian 1943. He moved to Saskatoon at 18 and began playing accordion at local dances and broadcasting on CFQC. His broadcasts from Edmonton 1940–58 on CFRN and after 1944 on CKUA were carried 1946–55 on the CBC's national networks, establishing him as a popular oldtime and country music performer. He has been host for such ethnic-music programs, unique in western Canada, as CKUA's 'Continental Musicale,' 'German Show,' and 'European Music Shop,' and he has starred on CFRN-TV shows – 1955–69 on 'Chuckwagon,' 1956–71 on 'Noon Show' (later known as 'Eye-Opener), and 1969–74 on 'Country Music.' In 1974 he became host for QCTV's 'QC on Country Music.' Until the early 1970s Haas was the owner of an Edmonton record store, the European Music Shop; he also owns and performs at several of the city's restaurants. Once proclaimed 'Canada's Mr. Polka,' Haas began recording in 1950 with his band, The Barndance Gang; by 1977 he had made over 45 albums and 60 singles, mostly of polkas and waltzes, for the Apex, Point, London, Quality, and Royalty companies. Several folios of his oldtime compositions are published by *Empire and *Canadian Music Sales. He is an affiliate of PRO Canada. (CF)

HADDAD, George (Richard). Pianist, b Eastend, near Swift Current, Sask, 11 May 1918; ATCM 1931, B MUS (Toronto) 1940, MA (Ohio State) 1953. After studies with Mme DeSerres and Margaret Graham, and at the *TCM with Hayunga *Carman, he continued 1940–3 at the Juilliard School with Olga Samaroff. He made his Toronto debut at the *Promenade Symphony Concerts 31 May 1945 and his New York debut at Town Hall 18 Oct 1947. He also appeared with the Detroit SO and in Mexico and Central America in 1947 before touring in Europe and studying 1950–2 with Marguerite Long in Paris. In 1950 he presented a broadcast series of Canadian works on Radiodiffusion Française. In Europe Haddad frequently played works of *Somers, *Pentland, *Dela, *Papineau-Couture, and others. In 1953 he became artist-in-residence at Ohio State U, but he has continued to appear in Canada, performing with the Montreal, Toronto, Regina, Calgary, Vancouver and Victoria SOs and in recital. (FM)

HADFIELD, Donald (James Fletcher). Organist-choirmaster, b Winnipeg 23 Oct 1931; ARCM 1950 BA (St John's College) 1957, B PED (Manitoba) 1958. He studied organ 1946–53 with Douglas *Bodle. He has been organist-choirmaster at a succession of Winnipeg churches: St James Anglican 1946–51, St Aidan's Anglican 1951–3, St John's Cathedral 1953–8, and All Saints' Anglican 1958–65. He returned to All Saints' after a sojourn 1965–7 at St Matthias, Westmount (Montreal). He has given many recitals in public and on the CBC, and with his All Saints' choir he has recorded a collection of anthems and hymns, *Through the Church Year with All Saints' Winnipeg* (1970, Century 21). SLH

HAENDEL, Ida. Violinist, b Chelm, Poland, 15 Dec 1924? (*Grove's* 1954), naturalized British 1940. A child prodigy, she was taken at four to study with Mieczyslaw Michalowicz at the Chopin School in Warsaw; she attracted attention as winner of the Polish prize in the first Wieniawski Competition (1935), a contest in which Ginette Neveu won first prize and David Oistrakh second in the international category. As a child Haendel studied in Paris and London with Carl Flesch and Georges Enesco. Moving with her parents to London prior to the outbreak of World War II, she soon became active in the British musical scene and during the war gave many recitals for the troops. Specializing in the concerto repertoire, she performed with Beecham, Boult, Sargent, Goossens, and Hamilton Harty, and such continental conductors as Munch, Klemperer, Dobrowen, Solti, Markevitch, and Kletzki. Her recording career began in 1943 with Decca, for which company she recorded the Mendelssohn, Tchaikovsky, and Dvořák concertos, among others.

Haendel moved to Canada in 1952, settling in Montreal. However, the orientation of her career remained European. She has continued touring there annually, and has made frequent tours also in South America and Asia. It was not until she had lived five years in Montreal that she made her debut there at the Ritz-Carlton Hotel in a recital sponsored by the Canadian Jewish Congress. The recital was followed by a CBC broadcast. Her first appearance with the *MSO, 7 Apr 1959, was in the Beethoven *Concerto* under Igor Markevitch. Eric *McLean in the following day's *Montreal Star* wrote: 'Her playing ... was the high point of last night's concert. Although the first thing about her performance which attracted the listeners' attention was her full and beautifully controlled tone (surprising from such a tiny person) and her fluent technique, it was not long before they realized that this technical equipment was being put to a particularly musical use ... It takes a real musician – as distinct from a technician – to tie the work together as Miss Haendel did last night.' Haendel's second performance with the MSO – nine years later – was in Lalo's *Symphonie espagnole* under Franz-Paul *Decker. She repeated the Lalo in 1969, played Saint-Saëns' *Concerto No. 3* in 1971 and 1980, repeated the Beethoven in 1973, and performed the Brahms *Concerto* in 1973 and Bruch's *Concerto in G Minor* in 1977. In 1977, with a CBC orchestra under Decker, she gave the Canadian premiere of the Britten *Concerto*, repeating it with the MSO in the 1978–9 season. She also repeated the Beethoven in 1975 under Frühbeck de Burgos.

It was not until 21 Jul 1969 that Haendel made her Toronto debut, with pianist Leo *Barkin, in 'one of the most dazzling recitals of the year' (Kenneth *Winters, Toronto *Telegram*, 22 Jul 1969). The same review noted her 'passionately structural account of the Bach *Chaconne*,' adding that 'Szymanowski's *Nocturne and Tarantella* benefited just as much from her sense of when to open the floodgates and drown us with sheer playing.' Some years before, when Haendel was in Prague to record Lalo's *Symphonie espagnole* with the Czech Philharmonic under Karel Ančerl, she had become friendly with Ančerl. In 1969, when Ančerl moved to Canada as conductor of the *TS he invited her to appear with that orchestra in 1970. She chose the Brahms for that occasion, re-

Ida Haendel

turned in 1973 to play the Sibelius (which she also played on tour in Europe with the TS in 1974), and returned again in 1975 to play the Shostakovitch (No. 1) and in 1978 for an integral performance (including the seldom-played 'Intermezzo') of Lalo's *Symphonie espagnole*.

In 1972 Haendel undertook a highly successful series of sonata recitals with the pianist Ronald *Turini, playing in Canada, Czechoslovakia, and Great Britain. With the London Philharmonic Orchestra under John Pritchard she played in China in the spring of 1973, the first western soloist to be invited to perform there after the revolution. In Canada, in the 1973–4 season, she also appeared with the Quebec and Victoria SOs, and in June 1978 she was soloist with the *Vancouver SO.

Haendel has been admired widely for her interpretations of the major concertos from Bach to Bartók and the solo suites and partitas of Bach, in which flawless intonation and high virtuosity remain at the service of a selfless musical approach.

WRITINGS
Woman With Violin (London 1970)

DISCOGRAPHY
Achron *Hebrew Melody* – Wieniawski *Scherzo-Tarantelle, Op 16*. A. Haendel pf, A. Kotowska pf. Decca K 1047
Albéniz *España, Op 165, no. 3* – Falla 'Danza española' from *La Vida Breve*. N. Mewton-Wood pf, Kotowska pf. Decca K 1073
Bach – Champagne – Beethoven. Newmark pf. 1967. CBC Expo 12
Bach 'Chaconne' from *Partita No. 2* – Handel-Flesch 'Am klaren Bach im stillen Tal' from *Solomon*. V. Yampolsky pf. Mezhdunarodnaya Kniga D 07287
Bartók *Rumanian Folk Dances*. I. Newton pf. Decca K 1873
Bartók – Bloch – et al. G. Moore pf. HMC CLP 1021
Bartók – Corelli – et al. Yampolsky pf. Mezhdunarodnaya Kniga D 07288
Bazzini *La Ronde des Lutins* –Massenet 'Méditation' from *Thaïs*. Kotowska pf. Decca F 7659
Beethoven *Concerto*. Philharmonia O, Kubelík cond. 1955. Victor LBC 1003
– *Sonata, Op 30, no. 3*. Mewton-Wood pf. Decca K 959/60
Bloch *Abodah* – Dinicu *Hora Staccato*. Kotowska pf. Decca K1076
Brahms *Concerto*. London SO, Celibidache cond. HMV CLP 1032
Brahms *Hungarian Dance No. 17* – Wieniawski *Polonaise brillante, Op 4, no. 1*. Moore pf. HMV 3818
Brahms – Bruch *Concerto in G Minor* – et al. Philharmonia O, Kubelík cond (Bruch), Moore pf (others). Victor LBC 1013
Brahms – Kreisler – et al. A. Holeček pf. Supraphon SUAST 50465
Brahms *Waltz, Op 39, no. 15* – Dvořák *Slavonic Dance, Op 72, no. 2*. Kotowska pf. Decca M 495
Copland 'Hoe-down' from *Rodeo* – Kreisler *Sicilienne and Rigaudon*. Moore pf. HMV B 9994
Dvořák *Concerto*. National SO, Rankl cond. Decca K 1744/7
Dvořák *Humoresque, Op 101, no. 7* – Kreisler *Caprice viennois, Op 2*. Kotowska pf. Decca M 521
Elgar *Concerto*. London Phil O, Boult cond. (1978). HMV ASD 3598
Falla 'Danza del Molinaro' from *El Sombrero de Tres Picos* – Ibert *Le Petit Âne blanc*. Kotowska pf. Decca M 603
Falla *Danza española* – Szymanowski 'Chant de Roxane' from *King Roger*. Kotowska pf. Decca K 1214
Glazunov *Concero, Op 82* – Wieniawski *Concerto, Op 22*. Prague SO, Smetacek cond. SUAST 50867
Grieg *Moods, Op 73, no. 2* – Ravel *Pièce en forme d'Habanera*. Moore pf. HMV B 10135
Kreisler *Schön Rosmarin; Tambourin chinois*. Kotowska pf. Decca M 520
Lalo *Symphonie espagnole*. National SO, Jordá cond. Decca K 1275/7
Lalo *Symphonie espagnole* – Ravel *Tzigane*. Czech Phil O, Ančerl cond. (1967). Supraphon SUAST 50615
Leclair *Sonata, Op 9, no. 3* (1st and 3rd mvts) – Sarasate *Danza española, Op 23, no. 2*. Kotowska pf. Decca F 7727
Mendelssohn *Concerto in E Minor*. National SO, Sargent cond. Decca K 1377/80
Nardini – Tartini – Corelli – Vitali. Parsons pf. (1977). HMV ASD 3352
Ravel *Tzigane*. Newton pf. Decca K 1013
Saint-Saëns *Introduction and Rondo Capriccioso, Op 28*. National SO, Cameron cond. Decca K 1171
Sarasate *Carmen Fantasia*. Kotowska pf. Decca M 501/2
– *Zigeunerweisen, Op 20*. Kotowska pf. Decca K 940
– *Zigeunerweisen, Op 20*. Newton pf. Decca K 1842
Sibelius *Concerto; Two Serenades for Violin and Orchestra, Op 69*. Bournemouth SO, Berglund cond. Ca 1975. HMV ASD 3199
Stravinsky 'Danse russe' from *Pétrouchka*. Newton pf. Decca K 1932
Szymanowski *Notturno e Tarantella, Op 28*. Kotowska pf. Decca K 1651
Tchaikovsky *Concerto*. National SO, Cameron cond. Decca K 1444/7
– *Concerto*. Royal Phil O, Goossens cond. HMV DLP 1190
Walton *Concerto* – Britten *Concerto*. Bournemouth SO, Berglund cond. (1978). HMV ASD 3483
Wieniawski *Polonaise brillante, Op 21, no. 2*. Kotowska pf. Decca K 1213

BIBLIOGRAPHY
Schulman, Michael. 'Ida Haendel: a much sought-after yet neglected artist,' *PfAC*, vol 13, Fall 1976
'Ida Haendel – a prodigy grows up,' *Vancouver Symphony Orchestra*, vol 1, Mar 1978
Gingras, Claude. 'Ida Haendel, une violoniste à la première personne,' Montreal *La Presse*, 2 Sep 1978
– 'Ida Haendel on the art of the violin,' *Variations*, vol 2, Nov 1978 JS

HAGEN, Betty-Jean (m Greicius). Violinist, b Edmonton 17 Oct 1930; Artist's Diploma (Toronto) 1951. She began violin lessons at seven with Alexander Nicol in Edmonton and won Alberta Music Festival awards in 1937 and 1938. Studies continued 1938–9 at the Chicago Cons, mainly with Ludwig Becker. She was a member of the Edmonton Philharmonic in the early 1940s, then moved to Calgary in 1946 to study with Clayton *Hare and play in the *Calgary SO. Studies followed 1949–51 at the *RCMT on scholarship with Geza *de Kresz. In 1950 she won the coveted Naumburg Award, which included a recital debut 15 Nov 1950 at Town Hall, New York. After winning the 1951 Eaton Graduating Scholarship (Toronto) she studied in New York with Ivan Galamian and at the Juilliard School. Also in 1951 she won the Pathé-Marconi Prize in Paris and gave recitals in France, Holland, Britain, and Switzerland. Her accompanist was Boris *Roubakine. She was a member 1950–1 of the Columbia Canadian Trio – Joan Rowland (piano), William Hossack (cello) – which toured Ontario, Quebec, and the USA. In 1952 she made her London debut and received the Harriet Cohen Commonwealth Medal as the outstanding woman musician of the British Commonwealth. The Canadian Press named her 'Woman of the Year' in Canadian music in 1953. She also won the 1953 Carl Flesch Medal from the GSM and the 1955 Leventritt Foundation Award.

Betty-Jean Hagen

For her debut 4 Nov 1956 with the New York Philharmonic under Dimitri Mitropoulos Hagen performed Lalo's *Symphonic espagnole*. Appearances followed with the Cleveland Orchestra, the Pittsburgh SO, the (Amsterdam) Concergebouw Orchestra, the London Philharmonic, and the Orchestre de la Suisse romande. Though living in New York (she married Vincent Greicius, a violinist in the *Metropolitan Opera orchestra, in 1954), she had made seven concert and recital tours in Europe by 1960 and performed in Canada on the CBC, in recital, with the *CBC SO under Thomas Mayer at the *Stratford Festival (21 Aug 1957), and with the *Vancouver International Festival Orchestra under Herbert von Karajan (13 Jul 1959). She was a finalist (seventh place) in the 1962 International Tchaikovsky Competition in Moscow. In 1964 she toured western Canada for the JMC.

Though she performed less often after the mid-1960s, Hagan appeared at *Expo 67 and in 1974 gave the 400th concert in the history of *Hart House, U of Toronto (she had given the 300th in 1960). Of her performance in Mozart's *Concerto in D*, K218, at a concert in *Eaton Auditorium in honour of Geza de Kresz, Kenneth *Winters wrote: 'Miss Hagen's immaculate classical style produced music of marmoreal firmness, smoothness and elegance, with again that wonderful level, nourished tone in the slow movement and phrasing of rare cogency' (Toronto *Telegram*, 21 Nov 1969). In the 1970s she devoted herself mainly to private teaching and coaching chamber ensembles in New York, specializing in teenage students.

DISCOGRAPHY
Beethoven – Papineau-Couture – Brahms (arr Joachim) – Szymanowsky. Newmark pf. 1967. CBC Expo 29/RCI 245
Brahms *Sonata* No. 3 – Mozart *Serenade No. 7* 'Haffner' (4th mvt, arr Kreisler). Barkin pf. 1959. RCI 195
Schubert – Schumann – Brahms. Barkin pf. 1969 CBC SM-82/AofD SDD 2157

BIBLIOGRAPHY
Ness, Margaret. 'Singing fingers,' *SatN*, 23 Feb 1952
Thomson, Hugh. 'Saddle-bag to satins,' *Toronto Daily Star*, 10 Aug 1957 (RDM)

HAHN, Bob (Robert Henry). Composer, arranger, administrator, singer, b Kindersley, near Saskatoon, 1920. In the mid-1930s he, his brother Lloyd, and his sisters Kay and Joyce were organized by their father into a musical troupe, The Harmony Kids, which performed throughout Saskatchewan, Montana, and New Jersey, and in New York City. By 1940 the family had settled in Montreal. After RCAF service in World War II Hahn joined the Toronto dance band of Neil Golden, which moved to Hamilton, Ont. There Hahn studied orchestration and composition 1946–8 with Reginald *Bedford. Returning to Montreal in 1948, he formed a vocal quintet which included Joyce Hahn and which performed 1951–6 with the Art *Morrow Orchestra on the CBC radio shows 'Sunshine Society,' 'A Trip to the Moon,' 'Cue for Fun,' and 'A Date with Fred Hill.' Between the early 1950s and the mid-1960s Hahn wrote over 1500 jingles, establishing a high reputation in the field. Some of his many songs employ lyrics by his daughters Cathie and Luckie (singers in the early 1970s with Quebec pop groups). Over 60 of his songs are recorded by Joyce Hahn, the Billy Van Singers, Norrie Paramour, Mitchell Ayres, and others. Several of his orchestral pieces (eg, *Evening in Paris*) have been performed on CBC radio. Hahn established his publishing company, Laurentian Music, in Montreal and became general manager of the music division of Multiple Access Ltd in 1974. In 1978 he established Bob Hahn Productions in Toronto. He is an affiliate of PRO Canada. Hahn's sister Joyce (b Eatonia, near Saskatoon, 1930) sang in Montreal cabarets, first in a duo with Kay Hahn and 1947–50 with Peter Barry's Rhumba Band. A soloist 1948–56 on various CBC Montreal radio shows, including some with her brother's group, she was co-star 1955–60 with Wally *Koster on CBC TV's 'Cross-Canada Hit Parade.' In the 1950s she made several recordings for the Spartan label, and 'Gonna Find Me a Bluebird' (a minor US hit in 1957) for Cadence. She returned to nightclub work in the early 1960s but was making only occasional club and TV appearances by the late 1960s. Her second husband was the pianist Armas *Maiste.

BIBLIOGRAPHY

Benoit, Frank. 'Trailer to the stars,' *Weekend Picture Magazine*, 6 Oct 1951

Frayne, Trent. 'Joyce Hahn's trailer trek to the stars,' *Chatelaine*, Mar 1957

Kirk, Helen. 'Joyce Hahn: waif in wonderland,' *Canadian Home Journal*, Aug 1957 (MM)

HAHN, Paul. Cellist, businessman, b Reutlingen, south of Stuttgart, 11 May 1875, d Balsam Lake, Ont, 20 Jul 1962. He arrived in Canada in 1888 and settled in Toronto. His cello teachers included Rudolph Ruth in Toronto and Alwin Schroeder in Boston. He was a member of the College Trio with Heinrich *Klingenfeld and J. Lewis Browne during the 1890s, of the Klingenfeld String Quartette 1901–3, and of the *Hambourg Trio ca 1910–12. He also gave solo recitals. He taught at the *Toronto College of Music.

Hahn worked 1892–1913 for the A. & S. *Nordheimer Co. and formed his own business in 1913. The Paul Hahn Co. sold sheet music and several makes of piano including Steinway 1928–43. Hahn retired in 1955, and the business continued in the 1970s under the management of his son Paul. The company began acting as agent for the Baldwin piano in 1963. Hahn was a member of the *Arts and Letters Club of Toronto and an authority on extinct and vanishing birds. He was the brother of Gustav Hahn, the painter, and Emmanuel Hahn, the sculptor.

BIBLIOGRAPHY

'Mr. Paul Hahn,' *MCan*, vol 5, Aug 1910

Hair. 'The American Tribal Love-Rock Musical,' book by the US writers Gerome Ragni and James Rado, music by Galt *MacDermot. Establishing a new style for musicals and spawning several imitators, *Hair* reflected the concerns of the hippie culture in North America during the mid-1960s. Some of its initial notoriety came from a nude scene. An off-Broadway production opened 29 Oct 1967 at the New York Shakespearean Festival Public Theatre. After some revision, which virtually eliminated the plotline, *Hair* opened 28 Apr 1968 at the Biltmore Theatre on Broadway and closed 1 Jul 1972, 1729 performances later. The stage director was Tom O'Horgan, the music director MacDermot. A Toronto production at the *Royal Alexandra Theatre ran just over a year (from 29 Dec 1969 to 3 Jan 1971). The Toronto cast included Terrence Black, Gale Garnett, Tobi Lark, Mary Ann MacDonald, and Colleen Peterson. In Montreal *Hair* was translated into French by Gratien Gélinas and Gil Courtemanche for a production which starred François Guy, Marie-Louise Dion, and Sebastien. It opened 22 Sep 1970 at the Comédie-Canadienne; the brief run alternated French and English-language performances. By late 1970 there were eight other productions of *Hair* in North America and 19 overseas.

The most popular songs from *Hair* included the title song, 'Aquarius,' 'Let the Sunshine In,' and 'Easy to be Hard.' The score is published in Canada by G.V. *Thompson. Recordings for RCA by the original casts of the Broadway and off-Broadway productions sold several million copies. *Hair* received a Grammy composer's award in 1968 for best score from an original-cast show album. Productions in England, Germany, France, Sweden, Japan, Israel, Holland, and Australia were recorded, as were over 1000 performances of individual songs from *Hair*. The topicality of the book inevitably dated it, and a revival in 1977 at the Biltmore Theatre, New York, was only moderately successful. However, a feature-length movie was released in 1979, and a cast recording was issued by United Artists. MM

HAKIM, Sadik (b Argonne Dense Thornton), the Muslim name adoped in 1947. Pianist, composer, b Duluth, Minn, 15 Jul 1919, naturalized Canadian 1972. The legendary bebop pianist, who played in New York with Ben Webster 1944–6 and Lester Young 1946–8 and recorded with Charlie Parker in 1945, first worked in Montreal with Louis Metcalf's International Band 1949–50. After associations in the USA with James Moody 1951–4, Buddy Tate 1956–60, and others, and after making the recording *East and West of Jazz* (1962, Charlie Parker Records PLP-805), Hakim returned in 1966 to Montreal. He performed there and 1973–4 in Toronto in clubs, concerts, and CBC broadcasts with his own groups and with Nelson *Symonds and Herbie *Spanier. He toured Europe in 1972 – his *London Suite* was inspired by the trip. In 1976 he returned to New York.

DISCOGRAPHY

London Suite. Hakim pf and elec pno, Abdul Al Khabyyr alto sax and fl, Robinson ten sax, Leitch guit, Angelillo db, McKendry drums. 1973. RCI 378

Hakim Plays Duke Ellington. Hakim pf, Hillary alto sax and fl, Stuart ten sax and fl, Lydell tpt, Boucher db, Johnston drums. 1974. RCI 379

BIBLIOGRAPHY

Gardner, Mark. 'Sadik Hakim,' *Coda*, vol 10, Nov–Dec 1971

Barnes, Lilly, and Gallagher, Greg. 'Sadik Hakim made jazz history but lives for the future,' *MSc*, 288, Mar–Apr 1976

Encyclopedia of Jazz 1960, 1966, 1976 EFr

HALES, Bobby (Robert Arthur). Trumpeter, conductor, arranger, composer, b Avonlea, near Regina, 9 Aug 1934. He studied trumpet briefly in Regina before moving to Chilliwack, BC, in 1947. He attended Westlake College of Modern Music in Los Angeles 1956–7; his teachers were Ollie Mitchell and Dick Groves. Based in Vancouver thereafter, he played and arranged music for Dave *Robbins' big band and led bands in various supper clubs. He was music director in 1963 for CBC TV's 'Music Hop' and 1976–7 for CTV's 'Rolf Harris Show,' and he composed theme music for the CBC series 'The Manipulators' and 'The Beachcombers' and the CBC TV movie 'The Overlanders.'

The Bobby Hales Big Band, a 15-piece (20 by 1975) jazz orchestra, was formed in 1965. The band has been heard often on the CBC's 'Jazz Canadiana' and 'Jazz Radio-Canada,' has performed nightly during the Pacific National Exhibition for several years, and in 1977 gave concerts and workshops in British Columbia and Alberta. The Leading jazz orchestra in British Columbia in the 1970s, the band has included among its soloists the trumpeters Stew Barnett, Don Clark, and Hales himself, the saxophonists Fraser *MacPherson, Dave Quarin, Wally Snider, and Jack Stafford, the guitarist Oliver Gannon, the pianist Bob Doyle, and the drummer George Ursan, all heard on the LP *One of My Bags* (1975, Centreline 0975). Hales' compositions for the band include the popular *Funklicity* and *Formula #1*. He is a member of PRO Canada. MM (JR)

Halifax. Capital of Nova Scotia and major seaport established in 1749 as a British settlement (population 2500) and military base. The influx of Loyalists resulting from the American Revolution caused the population to rise to about 9000 by 1800. By 1841, when Halifax was incorporated as a town, its population had more than doubled, and by 1900 it had reached 40,000. In 1978 the Halifax-Dartmouth metropolitan area had a population of approximately 184,000 and had become the industrial, commercial, and cultural centre of the province.

Halifax's original status as a military base, with monied officers in search of leisure pursuits, ensured an active musical life (see Richard Bulkeley). Guitars and violins were among goods imported from London, according to an advertisement in Canada's first newspaper, the *Halifax Gazette* (23 Mar 1752). In 1765, a Mr Evans installed Halifax's first organ in St Paul's Anglican Church, where, in April 1769, an oratorio was presented by a Philharmonic Society (probably Canada's first) augmented by army and navy officers, and where also, 20 May 1789, the final chorus of *Messiah* and a 'Coronation Anthem' (Handel?) were performed.

As a garrison town, Halifax benefited not only from officers' willingness to pay for and participate in the city's musical life but also from the presence of the regimental bands, whose trained musicians served as teachers and performers, and undoubtedly took part in a concert at the Golden Ball Inn in March 1785. At the British Coffee House in 1797 a band played a 'Simphonie' by Leopold Kotželuch and a 'Concertante for Violin, Hautboy, and Violoncello' by Ignaz Pleyel. The larger forces required for opera were present at the Theatre Royal 14 Feb 1798 when Grétry's *Richard Coeur de Lion* was performed. Ballad operas seem to have been performed almost every year. In 1798 there were at least four: *No Song, No Supper*, Dibdin's *The City Romp* and *The Waterman*, and Linley's *Robinson Crusoe*. Coleman's *The Surrender of Calais* was performed in 1805 and Arnold's *The Review* in 1806.

Singing societies provided much opportunity for the music-making of Haligonians. Among such groups were the New Union Singing Society (1809), St Paul's Singing Society (1819), and the Amateur Glee Club (1836), the last of which was organized by young tradesmen and mechanics. The *Halifax Harmonic Society, founded in 1842, presented Haydn's *The Creation* as its initial work. After ceasing its activity for several years the soci-

The bandstand in the Public Gardens, Halifax, at the turn of the century

ety reorganized to give three concerts at Temperance Hall in the winter of 1858. From 1840 to 1867 Cunard steamers called at Halifax on their voyages between Europe and Boston, and a railway to Montreal was completed in 1876. These conditions ensured that Halifax was not culturally isolated and that performing artists could be brought in from other centres.

On 1 Mar 1869 the Halifax Philharmonic Society performed *Messiah* to a capacity audience in Temperance Hall. Every winter during the 1870s the society presented an oratorio, usually *Messiah, The Creation*, or Mendelssohn's *St Paul*. Another vocal ensemble was the Arion Club, a male choir founded in 1877 by Arthur Bird (1856–1923, a US conductor and composer trained in Germany and active in Halifax as a piano teacher, organist, and chamber musician 1877–81). The Philharmonic Society was succeeded by the *Orpheus Club, a male choir conducted 1882–1906 by Charles H. *Porter and 1907–17 by Harry *Dean and noted for its light-operatic productions.

Performance of orchestral music also developed after 1885, when the Haydn Quintette Club, augmented by bandsmen, gave orchestral concerts. In 1897 Max *Weil founded the first *Halifax SO. Charles Porter formed the Leipzig Trio with Heinrich *Klingenfeld and the cellist Ernst Doering in the early 1890s.

With the 19th-century rise in the popularity of the piano, Henry and John Philips, originally of Hamburg, manufactured pianos in Halifax 1845–59. Thomas and Alfred W. Brockley, who learned the trade at Broadwood and Sons, London, also built pianos 1857–97, as did W. Fraser & Sons 1856–90, Williams & Leverman 1871–89, and P.W. Leverman & Co. 1889–97.

The Academy of Music, a splendid auditorium which served as the centre of Nova Scotia's theatre and concert life for over 50 years, opened in 1877. Built with the financial support of prominent citizens, it had a capacity of 1500. The opening concert was given by the Philharmonic Union under C.H. Porter, with solo artists from Boston. In the academy, local and visiting artists (eg, the Boston SO, the Westminster Choir, Emma *Albani) appeared in concerts and in light operas – *The Mikado* in 1887, *Martha* in 1896, and others. In the days following the great harbour explosion of 1917 the academy functioned as a centre for relief organization, meal distribution, and morale boosting.

The Orpheus Club, which opened the first *Cycle of Musical Festivals in 1903, was reorganized in 1919 as the Halifax Philharmonic Society and was conducted until 1954 by Harry Dean. This mixed choir performed oratorios in Halifax, Truro, and New Glasgow and sponsored spring festivals 1925–31 with soloists from the USA. In 1922 Ifan *Williams founded the Halifax Choral Union (later *Halifax Choral Society). In 1923 the Halifax Madrigal Society visited England and won admiring comment for its precise attack, gradua-tion in volume, and pleasing tone colour.

Halifax musical life received a setback in 1929 when the Academy of Music, renamed the Majestic in 1918, was demolished to make way for the Capitol movie theatre. Thenceforth until the 1950s concerts had to be given in church halls, hotel ballrooms, and the gymnasium of Dalhousie U. Musical life recovered, however, after the hiatus caused by World War II. At that time useful auditoriums were built in connection with the School for the Blind and Queen Elizabeth High School. The 1949 Bicentennial of Halifax was celebrated with Mariss Vetra's successful production of *Don Giovanni*. Out of this endeavour grew the *Nova Scotia Opera Assn, which until the mid-1950s staged operas annually at the Capitol.

When Vetra left Halifax, public interest shifted from opera to symphony. In 1951 the 13-member Halifax Symphonette had been organized under the direction of Alfred *Strombergs. With provincial and municipal support the Symphonette was enlarged in 1955 to form the Halifax SO under Thomas Mayer. The orchestra held a Mozart Festival in 1956 and a Beethoven Festival in 1957. By 1966 it was a 35-piece full-time orchestra giving 70 performances annually in the four Atlantic provinces. In 1967, as part of Canada's centennial celebrations, the Halifax SO gave the premiere of Edward *Laufer's *Variations*. However, the orchestra, along with the *New Brunswick SO, was supplanted in 1968 by the *Atlantic SO, a full-time ensemble based in Halifax but with a board drawn from the Atlantic provinces and a touring program designed to serve them.

The *Halifax Ladies' Musical Club, founded in 1905, promoted music by means of lectures, study, and demonstrations; it tried to encourage the training of young musicians and to give Canadians opportunities for performing. The Halifax Community Concerts Assn, founded in 1931 by the Halifax Philharmonic Society, was active for about 30 years. Among those it brought to Halifax were Van Cliburn, Nelson Eddy, Maureeen *Forrester, Mario Lanza, Witold Malcuzynski, Lois *Marshall, Leontyne Price, William Primrose, Teresa *Stratas, Gladys Swarthout, and the Trapp Family Singers. Among other famous musicians who have appeared in Halifax are Marian Anderson, Louis Armstrong, Leonard Bernstein, Edward *Johnson, Robert Merrill, and Isaac Stern. *Dalhousie U also has presented concert series, especially after the 1971 opening of the 1100-seat *Rebecca Cohn Auditorium in the Dalhousie Arts Centre. With an auditorium comparable to the old Academy, Halifax again was able to play host to such visitors as the *COC, the *Festival Singers, the *NACO, the *TS, the Royal Winnipeg Ballet, and the *NYO, as well as providing a handsome platform for its own major groups and soloists and a regular venue for the Atlantic SO. The Cultural Activities Committee of Dalhousie U has presented chamber music concerts by the Dalart Trio *Canadian Brass, the *Brunswick String Quartet, *Nexus, and *Quartet Canada, and appearances by Liona *Boyd, John Allan *Cameron, Anne *Murray, Anna *Russell, and Buffy *Sainte-Marie. In 1977 it began emphasizing jazz in its concerts. The *NOVA MUSIC series, initiated in 1971, has offered contemporary and electronic music performances. In addition, weekly faculty recitals are given.

Music instruction was introduced into the public schools in 1867. In 1870 the first School Music Festival was held. The Halifax Cons (*Maritime Cons), founded in 1887, exerted a wide influence on musical development and taste. Until the 1960s music education generally followed Anglo-Canadian norms and was notable mainly for the innovative and effectual *school music broadcasts introduced in 1942 by Irene McQuillan, music director for Halifax schools. A significant change occurred in 1966, when Shirley Blakeley introduced the *Kodály method into elementary schools. J. Chalmers *Doane was appointed school music director in 1967, at which time four full-time music teachers travelled to 26 schools teaching 14,000 students. At the end of Doane's five-year plan (1967–72) for upgrading the program, there were 50 full- and part-time music teachers serving 55 schools and 26,000 students. The quality of teaching was improved and courses were extended to include adults. Music history courses first were offered at Dalhousie U in 1961, and the music department was established in 1968.

In May 1935 the Halifax Cons sponsored a competition festival at the Dalhousie U gymnasium. Contestants from all over Nova Scotia, one of them Portia *White, competed to initiate a successful annual event. Although suspended during World War II, the festival was revived in 1947 as part of the *Federation of Canadian Music Festivals, which brought in British adjudicators and attracted competitors from the whole Maritime region. The competition reached its zenith in 1957, when 15,000 musicians competed in 347 classes. The organ classes gained renown throughout Canada. In 1953 the English Singers, directed by F. Harold Wright, won the City of Lincoln Trophy given annually to the Canadian choral group chosen by adjudicators who have judged choirs all across the country that year.

Musicians born in or near Halifax include John *Arab, Helen *Creighton, Denny *Doherty, Elizabeth Benson *Guy, Alan *Heard, Christopher *Jackson, the soprano Marjorie MacGibbon, James *Milligan, Marjorie A. *Payne, Geoffrey *Payzant, Sheila *Piercey, the bandmaster and danceband leader Peter Power, the pianist-conductor Joseph B. Sharland, and Ivan and Nelson *Symonds. Other musicians who have contributed significantly to Halifax life include the jazz saxophonist Bucky Adams, the baritone-teacher Teodor Brilts, Francis *Chaplin, Kenneth *Elloway, Phyllis *Ensher, Maitland *Farmer, Audrey *Farnell, John *Fenwick, Monique *Gusset, Harold *Hamer, Leonard *Mayoh, Gordon *Macpherson, the bluesman Dutch Mason, Don *Messer, Klaro *Mizerit, W.A. *Montgomery, the pop singer Karen Oxley, Diane *Oxner, the organist-choirmaster Samuel Porter, the teacher Charles Underwood, the pianist Neil Van Allen, Ernesto *Vinci, and the trumpeter Don Warner.

Among other significant musical organizations and groups which have flourished in Halifax are the CBC Halifax Chamber Orchestra, the CBC Halifax Strings, the *Armdale Chorus, and the Halifax Trio (see Brandon U Trio). The *Nova Scotia Choral Federation, the *Nova Scotia Talent Trust, and the *Nova Scotia Festival of the Arts are centred in Halifax. The popular TV program 'Singalong Jubilee' originated in the city.

See also Black music.

BIBLIOGRAPHY

'Halifax,' *MCour*, 10–17 May 1899

Talbot, Hugo. *Musical Halifax 1903–4* (Halifax 1904)

Blakeley, Phyllis R. 'The theatre and music in Halifax,' *Dalhousie R*, vol 29, Apr 1949

– 'Music in Nova Scotia 1605–1867' (2 instalments), ibid, vol 31, Summer, Autumn 1951

Fulton, William E. 'Music for everyone–in Halifax,' *MSc*, 274 Nov–Dec 1973

(PRB)

Halifax Choral Society. Choir founded in 1922 as the Halifax Choral Union by Ifan *Williams in association with the Halifax Cons (*Maritime Cons of Music). Williams was succeeded as conductor by Leonard *Mayoh in 1951 (when the later name was adopted), and Mayoh by Charles Underwood in 1959. The society ceased activity in 1960. Originally 150, later between 80 and 100 voices, the choir gave two or three concerts each year, singing unaccompanied or with the *Halifax SO. The society performed *Messiah* nearly every year in Halifax, and on several occasions in nearby towns. Other works included *The Christmas Oratorio, Judas Maccabeus, The Creation, Elijah,* the Fauré *Requiem*, Edward German's *Tom Jones*, and, at the final concert, the Mozart *Requiem*. Guest soloists included Gordon Clinton, Audrey *Farnell, Sheila *Piercey (a former member of the HCS), Jan *Rubeš, Jan *Simons, and Margaret Stilwell. (HWr)

Halifax Conservatory. See Maritime Conservatory of Music.

Halifax Harmonic Society. Choir and instrumental ensemble founded in Halifax 26 Oct 1842 by 38 players and singers. It rehearsed weekly under the direction of John St Luke, a former ballet master at the Theatre Royal, Bristol, England. Devoted to 'the improvement of its Members in the higher departments of Sacred Music,' the society specialized in oratorios by Haydn, Handel, and Mozart, performing *The Creation* at its first public appearance 31 Jan 1843. After thriving for about six years and performing in its own auditorium, the Harmonic Hall, the society declined. It was revived, however, by 7 singers who had been charter members. In 1858 there were 40 members–14 instrumentalists and 18 male and 8 female singers–who gave three public concerts conducted by E. Jeans at Temperance Hall. The society was the first Halifax organization to tackle major choral-orchestral works and to continue performing for a number of years.

BIBLIOGRAPHY

Blakeley, Phyllis R. 'Music in Nova Scotia 1605–1925,' unpubl ms
PRB

Halifax Ladies' Musical Club. Founded in Halifax in 1905 and incorporated in 1909. It was formed by Mrs Charles Archibald (first president), Elizabeth and Margaret White, and Kate Mackintosh. According to the 1906 constitution, 'the objective of the club shall be a more perfect knowledge and understanding of vocal and instrumental music and of musical literature.' As a member of the (US) National Federation of Music Clubs, the Halifax club followed a preordained study program–eg, 'Christmas as illustrated by Bach,' 'An evening with women composers,' and 'The child in Music.' However, the club withdrew from the federation in 1913 and instituted programming more directly suited to the interests of its membership. A meeting usually consisted of a lecture or a paper by a member, with musical examples performed by other members. At first meetings were held weekly in private homes; later they were held monthly from October to May in public locations, including the Hotel Nova Scotian, 1933–46 (when the membership exceeded 300); and the *Dalhousie U gymnasium, 1946–ca 1971 (when membership reached a peak of 700, including students). In the 1970s the club began holding its meetings in the Elsie MacAloney Room of the Dalhousie Arts Centre.

In the early years of the club members were encouraged to compose and prizes were offered. In 1906 a choir was formed under the direction of Frances (Daisy) Foster, an orchestra under Agnes Crawford. About 1913 there were opera performances, and in 1914 two concerts were organized at the Orpheus Theatre for the Belgian relief fund. In 1914 the club began promoting music in the public schools, giving scholarships, donating books, giving monthly concerts (performed by its members), and using its influence to have specialists hired by the school board. From 1951 to 1955 the club sponsored Tops 'n Pops, a junior club designed to 'present music approved by teenagers to young Halifax.' The junior club organized performances by its members in programs combining classical and pop music, and provided $50 scholarships annually for two *Kiwanis Festival winners, a boy and a girl. The senior club for many years has donated awards to the Kiwanis festival, the Maritime Cons, and the County Music Festival; it helped to launch the career of Portia *White.

Prominent among Halifax performers presented in concert by the club have been the *Armdale Chorus, Teodor Brilts, Howard *Brown, Frances *Chaplin, Audrey *Farnell, Elizabeth Benson *Guy, Jean *Macdonald, and Leonard *Mayoh. The club also has presented other Canadian musicians, among them Harry and Frances *Adaskin, Norah and Geza *de Kresz, the *Hambourg Trio, the *Hart House String Quartet, Margaret Ann *Ireland, Frances *James, Kathleen *Parlow, the *Parlow Quartet, Clifford *Poole, and Jan *Rubes. Helen *Creighton, Kay *Dimock, and Gordon *Macpherson are among the many who have presented lectures. In 1980 the club continued in the mainstream of musical life, both in Halifax and the rest of the province, with representation on the boards of the Halifax Kiwanis Music Festival, Dalhousie U, the Tatamagouche Festival of the Arts, the Committee for the Performing Arts in Nova Scotia, the Nova Scotia Arts Council, the *Nova Scotia Talent Trust, the National Council of Education, and the *Maritime Cons.

BIBLIOGRAPHY

Dawson, Dr Vega. *Historial Sketch of the Halifax Ladies' Musical Club 1905–1976* (Halifax 1976)
(VGD)

Halifax Symphony Orchestras. Two distinct eras of symphony orchestra activity in Halifax, 40 years apart, preceded the incorporation in 1968 of the second Halifax SO into the newly formed *Atlantic SO.

1 HALIFAX SYMPHONY ORCHESTRA (1897–1908). Formed by its conductor, Max *Weil, the first HSO gave its inaugural concert 24 Apr 1897 at the Academy of Music. Sponsored by the Local Council of Women, the program, a Schubert Memorial, included the *Unfinished Symphony*. Works by Weil also were performed. The 18 strings (11 women), 8 woodwinds, 8 brass, and 2 percussion in 1897 included 8 bandsmen from British regiments stationed in Halifax. In 1900 the orchestra had 39 members, including 22 string-players. On 26 Feb 1901 it was joined by an 85-voice choir to present a 'Grand Wagner Concert.' The HSO gave four or five concerts each season with important soloists (on one occasion, Leopold Godowsky), and in 1906, 1907, and 1908 it presented series of four pop concerts at a season-ticket price of $1.50. Weil emphasized the classical repertoire and achieved a good standard of performance. The orchestra disbanded with Weil's departure.

2 HALIFAX SYMPHONY ORCHESTRA (1949–68). Initially formed in 1949 by Alfred *Strombergs under the auspices of the *Nova Scotia Opera Assn to accompany opera and ballet presentations, the unnamed orchestra also performed in 1950 for CBC radio prior to reorganization in 1951 as the Halifax Symphonette. The 13 professional musicians continued under Strombergs' direction until 1955, with Julius Silverman as concertmaster. In 1955 the group became the Halifax SO with Thomas Mayer as music director and Francis *Chaplin as concertmaster, and made its TV debut 28 October. Employing 17 full-time musicians, it was augmented by local music teachers and bandsmen from the Royal Canadian Artillery Band and the Stadacona Navy Band. With these forces it was able to give a performance of Beethoven's *Symphony No. 9* on 4 Mar 1957. By 1966 the orchestra had 35 full-time members. Other conductors were Jonathan Sternberg 1957–8, Leo Mueller (a native Viennese, b 19 Sep 1906, who had conducted at the Baltimore Opera, the *NBC TV Opera Theater, and the Metropolitan and San Francisco Operas) 1958–64, John *Fenwick 1964–7, and various guests 1967–8, with Kenneth *Elloway as associate conductor.

Presenting about 70 concerts annually, the orchestra performed in high schools, toured the Atlantic provinces, and gave many CBC broadcasts. It accompanied the *COC's 1966 eastern Canadian tour of *Carmen*. In the 1960s conductors Mueller and Fenwick introduced many modern works into a previously traditional repertoire. Besides performances of works by Murray *Adaskin, John *Beckwith, Sir Ernest *MacMillan, François *Morel, Harry *Somers, and John *Weinzweig, premieres were given of Eldon *Rathburn's *Gray City* (5 Jan 1961, commissioned by the orchestra) and of Edward *Laufer's *Variations* (12 Mar 1967). After army bands in Halifax and Fredericton were abolished by federal government decree and bandsmen prevented from supplementing local orchestras, the Halifax SO and the *New Brunswick SO were supplanted by the Atlantic SO.

BIBLIOGRAPHY

Blakeley, Phyllis R. 'The theatre and music in Halifax,' *Dalhousie R*, vol 29, Apr 1949
Public Archives of NS. MG20 no. 188, Halifax Symphony programs and notes
Blakeley, Phyllis R. 'History of music teaching in Nova Scotia,' unpubl ms (1966)
(PRB)

Halifax Trio. See Brandon University Trio.

HALL, Doreen (Foy). Educator, violinist, b Warrenpoint, County Down, Ireland, 24 May 1921; ARCM, LRCM 1954. Raised in Listowel, near Kitchener, Ont, she took her training in violin with Elie *Spivak at the TCM and served as head of violin studies 1942–5 at Alma College in St Thomas, Ont, and 1945–51 at *Mount Allison U. She performed during the 1940s in concert and on CBC broadcasts. After further studies 1951–4 at the *RCMT and 1954–5 on scholarship with Carl Orff and Gunild Keetman in Salzburg, she began teaching at the RCMT. There she introduced the *Orff-Schulwerk teaching method to North America. In 1956 she joined the faculty of music at the *U of Toronto, lecturing on elementary music education and in 1957 devising and subsequently directing, the university's Orff-based summer course, 'Music for Children.' She has given similar courses at other Canadian and US centres and in 1962 at the Mozarteum in Salzburg, and has lectured widely. With Arnold *Walter she prepared an English-language adaptation of the Carl Orff-Gunild Keetman 5-volume *Music for Children* (Mainz 1956–61). Her other works are *'Music for Children' Orff-Schulwerk Teachers' Manual* (Mainz

1960), *Nursery Rhymes and Songs* (Mainz 1961), and *Singing Games and Songs* (Mainz 1963).

BIBLIOGRAPHY
Brown, Bill. 'Children make music for Doreen,' *Weekend Magazine*, 27 Sep 1958

FILMOGRAPHY
Music for Children (NFB 1958) MH

HALL, Joan (Reid) (m Melsness). Mezzo-soprano, b Winnipeg 22 Sep 1928. She had voice lessons in Winnipeg with her mother and with Doris Mills *Lewis, and in 1944 she won the Tudor Bowl at the *Manitoba Music Competition Festival. While studying with Ernesto *Vinci and Emmy *Heim at the *U of Toronto she won second (1952) and first (1953) prizes for female singers in CBC radio's *'Singing Stars of Tomorrow.' She made her CBC recital debut in 1954. She was a member of the *COC 1950–6, singing in *Rigoletto* (Maddalena), *Madama Butterfly* (Suzuki), and *The Magic Flute*, and of the *CBC Opera Company, appearing in *Il Trovatore* (Azucena) and *Gianni Schicchi*. A recitalist and a soloist with various Canadian orchestras until 1963, she retired to teach privately in Toronto.

HALLETT, Gordon (Arnold). Pianist, teacher, b Nanton, near Calgary, 28 Nov 1905; LTCM 1925. After lessons as a child in Nanton he studied 1922–5 at the *TCM with Paul *Wells and Norah Drewett *de Kresz. He joined the piano faculty there in 1925. He resumed study in 1934 with Mona *Bates and, while performing 1936–42 as a duo-pianist with another Bates pupil, Clifford *Poole, played 1941–2 in her Ten-Piano Ensemble. He took advanced studies in 1946 in New York with Mieczyslaw Horszowski, made his solo debut 4 Nov 1948 at *Eaton Auditorium, Toronto, and continued to perform until 1955. After that he concentrated on teaching. He also has examined for the RCMT and conducted workshops for piano teachers across Canada. His pupils include Norma *Beecroft, Cora Sumberg, Ralph *Fraser, Leon Major, and Mari-Elizabeth *Morgen. He was president of the *ORMTA 1962–3.

See also Piano duos. SLO

HALLMAN, Art (Arthur Garfield). Singer, arranger, saxophonist, pianist, b Kitchener, Ont, 11 Jan 1910. Raised in Vancouver, Hallman began studying piano at 10 and saxophone at 18, and played on CNR steamship cruises to Alaska, then on radio station CJOR. He was pianist, arranger, saxophonist, and featured vocalist 1932–44 with Mart *Kenney and His Western Gentlemen, and formed the Art Hallman Orchestra in 1945 in Toronto, appearing at Casa Loma, the Royal York Hotel, the Palais Royale, and conventions, and touring Ontario. His dance band was featured for many years on CBC radio and was heard in the 1950s and 1960s on CFRB's 'Sunday Night Sing-A-Long.' Its theme song was Hallman's own 'Just A Moment More with You' (Thompson 1945). One of Canada's most popular tenors in the 1940s, Hallman also coached many of his vocalists, including Terry *Dale, Joan *Fairfax, Shirley *Harmer, and Lorraine McAllister. He became music director of American Motors' automobile industry exhibitions in 1962 and was choral director 1963–6 for CBC TV's *'Juliette,' which featured the Art Hallman Singers. He made several 78s with Kenney 1938–44 and others for Musicana, and the LP *Turn Back the Pages of Time* (1973, Audat 477-4014).

BIBLIOGRAPHY
Sturman, Jack. 'Just a moment more with you,' *Canadian High News*, 13 May 1949 (MM)

Hallman organs. Product of a division of J.C. Hallman Manufacturing Co of Kitchener, Ont, makers of farm equipment. Coincidental with the founding of the firm in 1941, Jacob C. Hallman received a patent for his electronic organ, which featured a unique tone generator consisting of an amplified reed picked up electronically. By the late 1960s Hallman had manufactured some 3000 organs in 24 different models, intended mainly for church use. He also built several two- and three-manual custom models. From ca 1964 to 1976, 59 pipe organs were produced, most of them two- or three-manual, small four-rank units with either tracker or direct electric action. In addition to these the company built some single-manual tracker organs, one of which was installed at Acadia U. The largest Hallman organ was built for St John's Church, Shaughnessy, Vancouver, and was a four-manual, 69-rank (including pedal) unit with a separate yet integral single-manual console. The company was sold in 1977 and ceased to make organs. FH

Hallmark Recordings Ltd. One of the earliest companies to concentrate on the recording of Canadian concert artists. It was established in 1952 in Toronto by Keith *MacMillan, Bill Woods, John Gallagher, D'Alton Jolly, and John Mitchell to develop an experimental recording method devised by Woods. Presidents were MacMillan 1952–4, Woods 1954–6, and Douglas Sanderson 1956–ca 1968. During seven years of record production, 1952–9, Hallmark released the first LPs by the *Festival Singers and Glenn *Gould, and others by Greta *Kraus, Charles *Jordan and Joyce *Sullivan, Lois *Marshall (her first solo record), John *Newmark, Albert *Pratz (accompanied by Gould), Pierre *Souvairan, Mike White's Imperial Jazz Band, the *Bishop Strachan School Chapel Choir, *Musica Antica e Nuova, and the *TSO. Two secondary labels, Spiral and Songs of My People, released some 78s of popular and ethnic music respectively. In 1958, a year before the Hallmark label was discontinued, the company founded a subsidiary, Hallmark Studios. Considered the finest of its kind in Canada, it was a leading recording studio in Toronto until about 1968.

BIBLIOGRAPHY
Johnston, Richard. 'Hallmark,' *CMJ*, vol 1, Spring 1957 (EBM)

HALPERN, Ida (b Ruhdörfer). Musicologist, b Vienna 17 Jul 1910, naturalized Canadian 1944; PH D musicology (Vienna) 1938, hon LL D (Simon Fraser) 1978. On completion of her university studies she lectured on music 1938–9 at the U of Shanghai and in 1939 moved to Vancouver. She gave the first courses in music appreciation at the *U of British Columbia 1940–61. She also gave radio talks, participated in TV panel discussions, and was music critic 1952–61 for the *Vancouver Province*. She was a co-founder, the first president (1948–52, thereafter honorary president), and the program chairman 1951–8 of *The Friends of Chamber Music; she is honorary life president of the Women's Auxiliary of the New Artists Assn; and she served 1960–2 as president of the *Vancouver Woman's Musical Club. In 1958 she became the director of *Metropolitan Opera auditions for western Canada. In this connection she has assisted in furthering the careers of several young singers, notably Judith *Forst, Ermanno *Mauro, and Perry Price. She was vice-chairman 1968–72 of the *Community Music School of Greater Vancouver and chairman 1968–72 of the research committee of the *CFMS. Several of her pupils have achieved distinction either as scholars or as performers (eg, Colin Slim, chairman of historical musicology at the U of California; Marion *Barnum, head of piano studies at Iowa U; and Robert *Creech).

Ida Halpern

Halpern's most important work, however, has been in the documentation and preservation of the vanishing music of the Kwakiutl, Nootka, Haida, Bella Coola, and Coast Salish Indians of northern coastal British Columbia. She has recorded and catalogued some 350 of their songs. The collection is held by the *National Museum of Man, Ottawa. Four LPs drawn from this collection, together with booklets containing Halpern's notes and analyses, were released in sets of two (1967 and 1974) by the Folkways Ethnic Library (2-Folk FE 4523 and 2-Folk 4524). Some of the songs were arranged and prepared by Halpern for Lister Sinclair's *World of the Wonderful Dark*, produced at the 1957 *Vancouver International Festival. Halpern's 1964–5 course in ethnomusicology was the first of its kind offered by the U of British Columbia. She was the Canadian delegate to the International Folk Music Council in Ghana in 1966, and she has been a guest lecturer at a number of universities in Canada and the USA. She received research grants from the province of British Columbia in 1977 and the Social Science and Humanities Research Council of Canada in 1979.

As honorary associate of the Centre for Communication and the Arts at *Simon Fraser U she conceived and helped organize the Centennial Workshop on Ethnomusicology in June 1967 at the U of British Columbia. She was interviewed by CBC and foreign radio in 1975 and 1976 on the subject of her ethnomusicological researches. She was a consultant in 1976 to the United Nations' Habitat Conference, and is a contributor to EMC. In 1978 she was named a Member of the *Order of Canada.

WRITINGS
'Franz Schubert in der zeitgenössischen Kritik,' unpubl PH D thesis, U of Vienna 1938
'What is modern music?' *Pacific Northwest Library Assn Q*, vol 2, 1947
'Kwa-Kiutl Indian music,' *J of the International Folk Music Council*, vol 14, 1962
'Music of the BC Northwest Coast Indians,' *Proceedings of the Centennial Workshop on Ethnomusicology*, ed Peter Crossley-Holland (Victoria, BC, 1968)
'On the interpretation of "meaningless-nonsensical syllables" in the music of the Pacific Northwest Indians,' *Ethnomusicology*, vol 20, May 1976

BIBLIOGRAPHY
Cameron, Silver Donald. 'The collector,' *Weekend Magazine*, 6 Dec 1975 (CEB)

Albert Ham

HAM, Albert. Choir conductor, teacher, composer, textbook author, organist, b Bath, 7 Jun 1858, d Brighton, 4 Feb 1940; FRCO 1883, D MUS (Dublin) 1894, hon D MUS (Toronto) 1906, hon DCL (Bishop's) 1933. In Bath he began his studies with Joseph Hewitt and James K. Pyne and was a chorister and later organist at All Saints' Church. Further studies were with James Higgs and Varley Roberts in London and Julius Stockhausen in Frankfurt. He was organist 1880–93 at Ilminster and 1893–6 at Taunton. He moved to Toronto and served 1897–1933 as organist-choirmaster at St James' Anglican Cathedral. He also taught voice, organ, and composition 1897–1919 at the *TCM, 1919–24 at the *Canadian Academy, and again until 1932, at the TCM. After 1908 he lectured and examined at the *U of Toronto. Jeanne *Gordon, W.H. *Hewlett, Leslie *Holmes, and Helen Davies *Sherry were among his pupils. He was the founder and the only conductor 1903–28 of the *National Chorus, and a founder and the first president 1909–21 of the Canadian Guild of Organists (*RCCO). He was an examiner 1923–36 for *Bishop's U. His greatest distinction was, perhaps, his work as a choir trainer and perpetuator of the British choral tradition. In 1936 he retired to England.

Ham's most substantial work is the cantata *The Solitudes of the Passion*, performed in Toronto in April 1925. His compositions were published by *Anglo-Canadian, Ditson, Gray, Hawkes & Harris, *Nordheimer, Novello, and *Whaley Royce.

SELECTED COMPOSITIONS

3 marches
- *Canada*. Whaley Royce 1908
- *The Queen's Own*. (pre-1915)
- *Heroes of Canada*. 1925

Imperium et unitas. 1909. Orch

Hear, O Ye Kings. 1910. SSAATTBB, orch

Hope of the Ages. Pre-1903. Choir, orch. Nordheimer 1903

The Solitudes of the Passion, cantata. Nov 1917

Suite. Pre-1926. Orch (Minuet and Trio arr for org, Novello 1926)

Advent Cantata. Soli, choir, orch

Also a *Berceuse* for vn, pf (pre 1915), anthems, songs, etc, composed mostly before 1914

WRITINGS

A Manual on the Boy's Voice and Its Culture (London 1902)

Canadian Music Text-Book series (London): vol 1 *Musical Ornaments and Graces* (1914); vol 2 *The Rudiments of Music and Elementary Harmony* (1919); vol 3 *Outlines of Musical Form* (1924)

'The boy's voice and its training,' *CQR*, vol 1, Nov 1918

'The study of singing,' *CQR*, vol 1, Aug 1919

'The A.T.C.M. teachers' diploma in singing,' *CQR*, vol 11, Winter 1928

BIBLIOGRAPHY

'Distinguished Canadian organist, Dr. Albert Ham,' *MT*, vol 50, Sep 1909

Hamilton, H.C. 'Albert Ham,' *MCan*, vol 10, Apr 1929

'Albert Ham,' Toronto *Telegram*, 30 Jun 1933 (RPn)

HAMBOURG. A family of Russian musicians several of whom settled in Toronto in 1910, enriching the musical life of that city through their varied activities and through the visits of their many friends in the international musical community. The article treats individually, the following: 1 / Michael, Michael's sons 2 / Jan, 3 / Boris, and 4 / Clement, and, briefly, Michael's eldest son Mark, Mark's daughter Michal, and Clement's son Klemi.

BIBLIOGRAPHY

Hausman, Ed. 'Who remembers 194 Wellesley,' *Toronto Daily Star*, 6 Jan 1968

Metropolitan Toronto Library. Music division. Vertical files

NL of C. Vertical files

1 / **Michael**. Piano teacher, b Yaroslav, Russia, 12 (Julian Calendar, 24) Jul 1855, naturalized Canadian 1910, d Toronto 18 Jun 1916. A pupil of Nicholas Rubinstein, he studied in Moscow and St Petersburg, graduated in 1879 from the St Petersburg Cons, and taught piano in Voronezh 1879–ca 1888, and subsequently, until 1890 at the Moscow Philharmonic Cons. He settled with his family in London after the 1890 debut there of his 11-year-old son Mark (b Boguchar, Russia, 31 May [Julian Calendar, 12 Jun] 1879, d Cambridge 26 Aug 1960). Michael taught at the London Academy, at the GSM, and privately. In 1910 he moved to Toronto. The following year, with his sons Boris and Jan, he established the *Hambourg Cons, of which he was director until his death. Mark, who was to be his most famous son, remained in England, but his international success as a concert pianist brought him occasionally to Canada. (Mark's daughter Michal, also a pianist, b London 9 Jun 1919, made her London debut in 1936.) Michael himself was a pianist of some repute but is remembered chiefly as a teacher and the head of a remarkable family. His pupils included George E. Boyce, Evelyn Chelew-Kemp, Caroline Danard, his sons Clement and Mark, Gerald Moore, Norman *Wilks, Madge Williamson, and Gilbert *Watson.

BIBLIOGRAPHY

Armstrong, William. 'Prof Michael Hambourg on the modern pianist and his art,' *Etude*, vol 22, Dec 1904

'Michael Hambourg dies very suddenly,' Toronto *Globe*, 20 Jun 1916

2 / **Jan**. Violinist, b Voronezh, Russia, 27 Aug (Julian Calendar, 8 Sep) 1882, d Tours, France, 29 Sep 1947. He studied with Émile Sauret and August Wilhelmj in London, Hugo Heermann in Frankfurt, Otakar Ševčik in Prague, and Eugène Ysaÿe in Belgium. His Berlin debut in 1905 initiated a notable career as a soloist, chamber musician, and teacher. He moved with his parents to Toronto and was head 1910–20 of the violin department at the *Hambourg Cons, where his pupils included Jack *Arthur, Ethel Evans, Broadus *Farmer, Samuel *Hersenhoren, and Luigi *Romanelli. He left Canada to pursue a solo career, living thereafter in New York, London, Paris, and, 1936–9, Sorrento, Italy. After his wife's death he returned to England. His last Canadian performance was given in 1935, when he toured with the original *Hambourg Trio. A scholar of Bach, he published an edition of the sonatas and partitas for solo violin (Oxford University Press 1934) and violin arrangements of other music of Bach and Chopin.

3 / **Boris**. Cellist, administrator, b Voronezh, Russia, 27 Dec 1884 (Julian Calendar, 8 Jan 1885), naturalized Canadian 1910, d Toronto 24 Nov 1954. The family moved to England when he was five, and he had cello lessons in London from Herbert Walenn. He studied 1898–1903 with Hugo Becker (cello) and Ivan Knorr (composition) at the Hoch Konservatorium in Frankfurt, and Eugène Ysaÿe coached him in chamber music at Godinne-sur-Meuse, Belgium. His 1903 debut, at Bad Pyrmont, Germany, was followed by appearances in Europe, South Africa, New Zealand, and Australia, alone or with the *Hambourg Trio (Mark, Jan, and Boris) or the Hambourg String Quartet (Jan, John Robinson, Eric Coates, and Boris).

After performances in the USA in 1910 Boris settled with the family in Toronto, where he helped establish the *Hambourg Cons and the Hambourg Concert Society, which presented chamber music. He also taught at the conservatory, and his pupils included Marcus *Adeney and Glen *Morley. After his father's death Boris directed the conservatory, with some assistance from Jan, until it closed in 1951. He continued to perform in Canada, the USA, and, almost annually, Europe and organized a succession of Hambourg Trios.

In 1923 Boris married Maria ('Borina') Bauchope (b Dunedin, New Zealand, d Toronto 1965), a pianist who had studied in London, who taught in Toronto, and whose keen social skills helped establish the Hambourg position in the arts community. That same year Boris became a founding member of the *Hart House String Quartet and remained with it throughout its existence (1923–46). While on tour in England in 1934 he became the first Canadian instrumentalist to play on television (BBC). In 1945 he founded the Toronto Music Lovers' Club, which offered a series of concerts by the *Pirani Trio, the *de Kresz-Hambourg Trio, and the Pro Musica Trio, assisted on occasion by individual artists. Boris also gave cello recitals, often in cycles covering the repertoire from the renaissance to the present. He wrote cello pieces (including six *Preludes* and six *Russian Dances*), and songs, and with Alfred Moffat co-edited cello pieces by 18th-century Italian composers. He recorded as a soloist and as a member of the Hart House String Quartet. He was an active member of the *Arts and Letters Club, Toronto. His main contribution to music was his activity in, and on behalf of, chamber music. New works and classics had first Toronto performances under his guidance, and he gave encouragement and opportunities to his own and a younger generation of musicians.

DISCOGRAPHY (78s)

From the Land of the Sky Blue Water. HMV E142

Harty *Butterflies*–Ireland *The Holy Boy*. G. Moore pf. HMV 120831

Popper *Papillon*. Grace Smith pf. Victor 60064

Schumann *Träumerei*. Grace Smith pf. Victor 60065

Walford Davies *Solemn Melody*. HMV D344

See also Discography for Hart House String Quartet.

BIBLIOGRAPHY

Brewester, Musiel. 'Hand of fate formed the Hart House Quartet,' Toronto *Star Weekly*, 29 Nov 1924

Adaskin, Harry. *A Fiddler's World* (Vancouver 1977)

4 / **Clement**. Pianist, promoter, b London 31 Jul 1900, d Toronto 3 Feb 1973. Trained in London as a pianist by his father, he settled with the family in Toronto and made his concert debut there in 1925. The following years were spent playing in the *Hambourg Trio, giving solo recitals, teaching at the *Hambourg Cons, and operating a recording studio. In 1946 he and his wife, Ruth, opened The House of Hambourg, one of the first after-

hours jazz clubs in Toronto. The musical home of many Toronto musicians who later achieved prominence in the jazz or studio worlds, the club had five successive locations before it closed in 1963. After that Hambourg played the piano in Toronto nightclubs, offering a mixture of classics, jazz, pop tunes, and improvisation. He also appeared in TV commercials. His career was marked by optimistic determination and a benign and catholic musical taste. He wrote arrangements and made several records. His recording with Norm *Amadio of parts of Gershwin's *Rhapsody in Blue* was distributed privately.

Clement's son Klemi, a violinist and teacher (b Ottawa 10 Jul 1928, ATCM 1946, FTCL 1965), taught strings in the Peterborough school system and in 1967 was the founding conductor of the Peterborough SO (see Orchestras 7). He joined the music department of the U of Oregon in 1969.

BIBLIOGRAPHY

Petlock, Bert, and Curtin, Walter. 'House that jazz built,' *Weekend Magazine*, 16 Nov 1957

Ruddy, Jon. 'The ninth life of the ninth cat,' Toronto *Telegram*, 24 Jul 1965

McNamara, Helen. 'Clem Hambourg; the old man and the keys,' *That's Show Business*, vol 1, 18 Oct 1972 (RPn)

Hambourg Conservatory of Music. Toronto private school operated 1911–51 by members of the *Hambourg family. Michael, who had directed the Hambourg Conservatoire in London, began teaching with his sons Jan and Boris at the Heintzman studios in Toronto in 1910. They opened the Hambroug Cons on Gloucester St on the occasion of a visit to Toronto by Mark Hambourg. In 1913 they moved to 194 Wellesley St E at the corner of Sherbourne St. The new conservatory's attic was converted into a student recital hall. After Michael's death in 1916 Jan and Boris served as co-directors until Jan's return to Europe in the early 1920s. Boris was sole director thereafter. His wife, Maria Bauchope, served as business manager and also, with intuitive awareness of Toronto's growing social and cultural needs, developed the conservatory as a centre for the arts with an international flavour. The *Hart House String Quartet and the *Hambourg Trio prepared their concerts there. Many visual artists and writers (eg, the painters Arthur Lismer and John Russell and the poets E.J. Pratt, Charles G.D. Roberts, and Arthur Stringer) dropped by habitually for the pleasure of cosmopolitan company and conversation about the arts.

The Hambourgs brought to Toronto many fine teachers from Europe and also recruited local instructors. The faculty was a large one. In 1914 it comprised 30 teachers of piano, 11 of voice, 8 of violin, 4 of theory, 2 each of cello, organ, flute, mandolin/banjo, and composition, and 1 each of drama, French, German, and dancing. Among notable faculty members, over the school's 40 years of activity, were Marcus *Adeney, Boris *Berlin, Helmut *Blume, Giuseppe *Carboni, Rachel *Cavalho, Ernest J. *Farmer, Eduardo *Ferrari-Fontana, Emil Gartner, Alberto *Guerrero, Clement Hambourg, Redfern *Hollinshead, Eustache Horodyski, Gerald Moore, Elie *Spivak, and Reginald *Stewart. Branches of the conservatory, operated by associated teachers, flourished throughout the city from 1918 to the 1940s, the longest-lived (1919–43) located at 481 Roncesvalles and on Queen St E. During the 1930s some of the teachers travelled to their pupils' homes.

BIBLIOGRAPHY

Hausmann, E.H. 'Who remembers 194 Wellesley?' *Toronto Daily Star*, 6 Jan 1968

Adaskin, Harry. *A Fiddler's World* (Vancouver 1977) (LH)

The Hambourg Trio. Name of a succession of piano-violin-cello ensembles involving one or more of the *Hambourg family. The original group–Mark, Jan, and Boris Hambourg–appeared in England and toured in Europe as early as 1905. After the family moved to Toronto, Jan gave a number of concerts 1910–12 with the pianist Richard *Tattersall and the cellist Paul *Hahn as the Jan Hambourg Trio, but Jan, Boris, and their father Michael also performed together. Mark, Jan, and Boris performed in a Tchaikovsky concert 18 Mar 1915 at *Massey Hall, their only appearance together until 29 Apr 1935 when they played the Beethoven *Triple Concerto* with the *TSO. (They toured briefly that same season.) After 1915 the constant member of the trio was Boris, with the pianists Alberto *Guerrero 1918–22 and Reginald *Stewart 1922–8, and the violinists Jan Hambourg 1918–24, Harry *Adaskin 1925–6 and 1928–9, Elie *Spivak 1926–8, and Vino Harisay in 1930. Geza *de Kresz and Clement Hambourg also performed with Boris. Many of the Hambourg Trios' appearances were for the Hambourg Concert Society, in conjunction with other artists. During some seasons the trio of the day would give concerts in other Ontario towns. RPn

HAMBRAEUS, Bengt. Composer, teacher, organist, administrator, b Stockholm 29 Jan 1928; BA (Uppsala) 1950, PH D (Uppsala) 1956. He studied organ 1944–8 with Alf Linder, musicology 1947–56 with Carl-Allan Moberg at Uppsala U, and composition in the summers 1951–5 with Wolfgang Fortner, Ernst Krenek, Olivier Messiaen, and others in Darmstadt. In 1957 he joined the music department of the Swedish Broadcasting Corp, where he was a program producer 1957–64, head of the chamber music department 1964–8, and thereafter head of production until 1972. After a two-month tour in 1971 in Canada and the USA during which he lectured on the history of Swedish music, he joined the faculty of music at *McGill U in 1972, becoming a full professor in 1975 and a member of the university senate in 1976. He became a member of the Society of Swedish Composers in 1957 and of the *CLComp in 1977.

Hambraeus has composed a large number of works (listed in *Compositeurs canadiens contemporains*) for instrumental ensembles. He has produced several electronic scores in studios in Cologne (1955), Milan (1959), Munich (1963), and, after 1972, at McGill U. His works have been performed at ISCM festivals in Cologne (1960), Amsterdam (1963), Stockholm (1966), London (1971), and Reykjavik (1973), and at other contemporary-music festivals in Japan, Finland, Sweden, and Germany. In Canada his works have been performed by the *Lyric Arts Trio (*Récit de deux*), Hugh *McLean (*Icons*, premiere; and also the recording, RCI 481), the *NACO (*Pianissimo*), the SMCQ (*Notazioni*), and the *York Winds (*Jeu de cinq*, premiere). His compositions *Intrada-Calls, Tornado*, and *Tides* are included on the recording *Concrète and Synthesizer Music* (McGill U Records 76001). *Carillon*, written for the duo pianists Bruce *Mather and Pierrette *LePage, has been recorded by them (McGill U Records 77002).

A concert organist and organ scholar, Hambraeus has given frequent lecture-recitals covering the literature of the instrument from its origins to the 20th century, with emphasis on recent music. He has published numerous essays and articles, and is a member of the editorial board of several Swedish music publications. He is an associate of the *CMCentre.

BIBLIOGRAPHY

Dictionary of Contemporary Music SW

HAMEL, Adolphe (Théophile). Organist, pianist, choirmaster, businessman, b Quebec City 15 May 1842, d there November 1887. He studied violin, then piano and organ with Paul *Letondal as part of the academic studies he began in Montreal and completed in Quebec City. He was organist at the churches of St-Jean-Baptiste in 1864 and St-Patrice 1865–72 and again 1880–6, when he succeeded Calixa *Lavallée who was departing for the USA. At St-Patrice masses by Haydn, Mozart, Gounod, and others were sung under his direction. Hamel was an accomplished choir conductor and is said to have possessed considerable skill as an improviser. He wrote an 'Ave Maria' for two voices.

BIBLIOGRAPHY

LeVasseur, Nazaire. 'Musique et musiciens à Québec,' *La Musique*, vol 3 Nov 1921

Musiciens canadiens

HAMER, Harold (Spensley). Educator, organist, composer, b Leeds 9 Mar 1900, d Halifax, NS, 11 Sep 1980; FRCO 1926, hon D MUS (Mt Allison) 1969. His early musical training was at Durham Cathedral Choristers' School. Hamer moved to Canada in 1927 to teach organ and theory and conduct the choirs at *Mount Allison Cons, which became the university's Dept of Music under his direction in 1937. He formed a large choral society in 1927 and produced Gilbert & Sullivan operas. In 1949 Hamer began lecturing at *Dalhousie U and teaching organ and theory at the Halifax Cons (*Maritime Cons of Music). He was organist-choirmaster at St David's Presbyterian Church and 1961–9 at St Paul's Anglican Church. Among his pupils were Kelsey *Jones, Carleton *Elliott, Allison Patterson, and Paul *Murray.

Hamer initiated music-appreciation programs for CBC school broadcasts, first in New Brunswick and later in Nova Scotia. He also gave numerous organ recitals on CBC radio. Four of his anthems were published by Boston Music (1949, 1950), and a fifth, 'All Hail the Power of Jesus' Name,' with additional accompaniment for band, was published by G.V. *Thompson (1968).

See also School music broadcasts; Competition festivals.

BIBLIOGRAPHY

'Professor Harold Hamer retires as organist,' Halifax *Mail-Star*, 4 May 1961 SAB

HAMILTON, H.C. (Henry Cooke). Composer, writer, organist-choirmaster, b England 24 Jan 1881, d Sudbury, Ont, 23 Mar 1975. Raised in Ireland and in the USA, Hamilton was taken to Mimico (Toronto) as a youth and later studied at the TCM with A.S. *Vogt and J.D.A. *Tripp. He was organist-choirmaster during the 1920s at churches in Lindsay and North Bay, Ont, and subsequently at various Toronto churches, before serving 1963–74 at Queen St United, Toronto. He also taught at the *Hambourg Cons. He wrote many hymns, including four published (1931, 1948) by *Waterloo. His *Familiar Melodies*, a folio of arrangements for organ, was published in 1937 by *Harris. Other compositions listed in the *Catalogue of Canadian Composers* include *Variations on 'O Canada'* and *Variations on 'The Maple Leaf For Ever.'* Hamilton contributed articles to *The Etude, Choir Herald, Musical Courier*, and *Musical Canada*. For the latter publication 1928–31 he wrote a series of biographies of Canadian musicians – including Mona *Bates, J. W. *Bearder, T.J. *Crawford, Ernest *Dainty, W.O. *Forsyth, Albert *Ham, Boris *Hambourg, F.J. *Horwood, Luigi von *Kunits, Ernest *MacMillan, Percival *Price, Harvey Robb,

Léo *Roy, Herbert *Sanders, Bertha *Tamblyn, F.H. *Torrington, A.S. Vogt, Charles *Wheeler, Alfred *Whitehead, and Healey *Willan. MM

HAMILTON, J.P. or **'Doc'** (John Potter). Bassist, tuba player, teacher, b Solsgirth, northwest of Brandon, Man, 17 Jun 1913. He began performing at 17 with dancebands and ethnic ensembles in Alberta and studied bass 1937–42 with Edgar Ghirlanda in New York. Establishing himself as a bassist in Vancouver, he was a member 1939–46 and 1949–52 of Jean *de Rimanoczy's CBC orchestra and was respectively associate principal bass and principal bass 1946–69 with the *Vancouver SO. He played intermittently 1952–66 in the *CBC Vancouver Chamber Orchestra. He also played in the *TUTS orchestra 1950–63, the *Vancouver Opera Assn orchestra 1958–69 (as principal until 1965), the various *Vancouver International Festival orchestras, and groups which accompanied in nightclubs and on CBC radio and TV. He played in the jazz bands of Ray Norris (1940s) and Lance *Harrison and 1955–63 in the Bruno Dalla Porta Continental Ensemble. He also played tuba with Harrison and 1951–9 in the Pacific National Exhibition Band. Hamilton taught 1949–69 privately and 1960–9 at the *U of British Columbia. His pupils include Errol Gay, Brian Hoover, and Robert *Witmer. MM

HAMILTON, (Robert) **Stuart**. Pianist, coach, b Regina 28 Sep 1929; ARCT 1950. He studied piano in Regina with Martha Summerville Allen and at the *RCMT with Alberto *Guerrero and Weldon *Kilburn, making a New York debut at Town Hall in 1967. He performed in 1968 in major Canadian centres and again at Town Hall before concluding his solo career with a concert in 1971 at London's Wigmore Hall. Thereafter he accompanied and coached many singers, including Carrol Anne *Curry, Maureen *Forrester, Lois *Marshall, Roxolana *Roslak, and Mary *Simmons. On occasion he has accompanied Louis *Quilico and Riki *Turofsky. In 1974 he began the annual series Opera in Concert at *St Lawrence Centre in Toronto, presenting concert versions with piano of such rarely heard works as Thomas's *Hamlet* (1974, 1977), Poulenc's *La Voix humaine* and Montemezzi's *L'Amore dei Tre Re* (1976), Bizet's *Djamileh* and Massenet's *Thérèse* (1977), Franz Schmidt's *Notre Dame* (1978), Weinberger's *Schwanda the Bagpiper* (1979), and Peter Cornelius' *The Barber of Baghdad* (1980).

BIBLIOGRAPHY
Kirby, Blaik. 'Stuart Hamilton: opera impresario in a minor key,' Toronto *Globe and Mail*, 12 Oct 1974
Enright, Jane. 'Stuart Hamilton: unsung opera hero,' *Fugue*, Aug–Sep 1978 (JBl)

Hamilton, Ontario. City on Lake Ontario with a natural bay as harbour. Taking its name from George H. Hamilton (1787–1835), who laid it out in 1813, the town was incorporated as a city in 1846 when, with a population of 10,000, it was the second-largest city in Upper Canada. The population of greater Hamilton had passed 400,000 by 1978. Hamilton's major industry is steel.

The first known documented musical activity in Hamilton is that of an amateur band which in 1837 received permission from the Police Board to rehearse weekly. The Sons of Temperance Band, founded in 1851, was reorganized ca 1856 and became attached to the Artillery Militia under the direction of Peter Grossman (b Karlsruhe, Germany, d Hamilton 1901). A music and instrument dealer who also published music, Grossman had settled in Hamilton in the middle of the 19th century. He formed the 13th Regiment Band in 1866 (see Royal Hamilton Light Infantry Band), but soon was succeeded by George Robinson who conducted the band for 40 years. During the 1880s the Independent Band also was active.

Concerts were held 1850–80 in the second-floor auditorium of the Mechanics Hall, which could accommodate some 1000 people, and in several of the larger churches. Sigismund Thalberg played in Hamilton in 1857 and Haydn's *The Creation* was given its first complete Canadian performance 26 May 1858, as was the same composer's *The Seasons* in 1860, by the 90 choristers and 25 orchestral musicians of the Hamilton Philharmonic Society under Edward Hilton. This group, which continued to give oratorio performances throughout the 1870s, relied heavily on bandsmen to complete its wind section. During the same years the Mendelssohn Society, the Handel Society, and the Sacred Harmonic Society performed Handel's *Judas Maccabaeus*, Barnby's *Rebekah*, Rossini's *Stabat mater*, and other works. The Cecilian Glee Club was active 1860–6. G.W. Johnson's lyrics for *'When You and I Were Young, Maggie' were written in Hamilton ca 1864, and Robert *Ambrose's song 'One Sweetly Solemn Thought' was composed there in 1867.

According to the Canadian census, there were 36 musicians in Hamilton in 1851 but only 18 in 1861. By 1856 Hamilton had five music teachers, two music-store proprietors, four piano dealers, and one organ builder. According to the *Hamilton and Wentworth Directory 1868–9*, four businesses offered musical supplies. A. & S. *Nordheimer operated a branch store for the sale of pianos, and three factories produced instruments. The first of these, founded by Thomas W. White in 1853, employed 30 workers and in 1868 and 1869 made 400 cabinet organs and melodeons. 'The organ in the Centenary Methodist Church lately completed was built by Mr. White and cost about 4000 dollars,' reported the *Directory*. The Western Pianoforte Manufactory, established in 1856 by Charles L. Thomas (see Thomas), employed 30 men in 1869 and turned out 75 pianos annually. Thornton & Green, which had commenced business in 1867, had nine employees and produced keys, reed boards, and other parts required in the construction of melodeons and cabinet organs. A 1902 business directory lists one organ builder, eight instrument and sheet music dealers, and the piano builders Ennis & Co and Charles Knott.

The Grand Opera House on James St North, which seated 1100 and opened 29 Nov 1880, provided the city with a proper auditorium for theatrical and musical presentations and attracted North American touring companies. In December 1880 the Boston Ideal Opera Co brought to Hamilton Planquette's *Chimes of Normandy* and von Suppé's *Fatinitza*. Around 1890 this same company reappeared with several operettas, including Offenbach's *The Brigands*.

After 1880 not only touring activity but also local choral, orchestral, and operatic music-making increased in Hamilton. In 1883 the Hamilton Choral Society, later known as the Hamilton Philharmonic Society, was formed. Under F.H. *Torrington, the society's conductor for four years, it became one of the city's most successful ensembles, performing Romberg's *Lay of the Bell*, Mendelssohn's *Elijah*, Michael Costa's *Naaman*, Handel's *Samson*, and the Canadian premiere of A.C. Mackenzie's *The Rose of Sharon*. Clarence *Lucas revived and conducted the society 1889–90. In 1885 J.E.P. *Aldous organized an orchestra, and in 1887, the year of the Queen's Jubilee Music Festival in Hamilton, C.L.M. *Harris founded the Harris Orchestral Club, which he directed until 1901. A 43-piece ensemble, the club performed in the Grand Opera House and in churches.

Despite the increasing number of instrumentalists in Hamilton, major choral concerts of this period still depended for wind players on such groups as the Argyll and Sutherland Band, formed in 1903 under Harry Stares as the band of the 91st Highlanders (later 91st Regiment Canadian Highlanders), and the Royal Hamilton Light Infantry Band, successor to the 13th Regiment Band. In 1905 Bruce *Carey founded the Elgar Choir, which at first presented programs of unaccompanied works and short choral pieces with piano accompaniment. By 1910, however, it was performing works as large as Verdi's *Requiem*, and in the 1920s it presented Mendelssohn's *Elijah* and a concert version of *Aida*. W.H. *Hewlett, the conductor 1922–35, brought in the Cleveland and Detroit SOs for appearances with the choir. Graham *Godfrey's Bach Choir, formed in 1932 for the performance of large choral works with orchestra, disbanded during the early years of the war. The Stelco Male Chorus was formed in 1941 by Cyril *Hampshire, who conducted it until 1948 when he was succeeded by Rod Shepherd. Every spring the choir, some 25–45 Stelco employees, gave a concert in Centenary United Church and travelled to nearby towns. The director and accompanist, though paid by Stelco, were not employees in the steel works. The choir gave its last concert 7 Dec 1953. The *Dofasco Male Chorus, another steel company protégé, was established in 1945. Charles *Peaker became conductor in 1946 of the *Bach-Elgar Choir, an amalgamation of the former Bach and Elgar choirs.

New orchestras appeared after 1900. One such was the Ladies' String Orchestra formed in 1908 and conducted until 1926 by Jean Hunter. The addition of woodwinds swelled its ranks to 35. In 1915 F.J. Domville founded the Hamilton Orchestral Club. At its first concert, at the Odd Fellows Temple, the orchestra gave a program of short pieces and Beethoven's *Fifth Symphony*. Percy Waddington, then I.W. Lomas, conducted a Hamilton SO for several seasons in the mid-1920s. Graham Godfrey reorganized it in 1930 with a membership of 73, and the orchestra made its debut in January of 1931 in Dvořák's *'New World' Symphony* and Wagner overtures. This orchestra was succeeded in 1949 by the *Hamilton Philharmonic Orchestra, which played in high school auditoriums and then at the Palace Theatre before gaining a permanent home when *Hamilton Place opened in 1973. The *Hamilton Chamber Music Society was founded in 1951, and by the late 1970s had presented more than 90 concerts by local and visiting groups.

For opera Hamilton depended in the early days upon visiting companies and its own amateurs. Nevertheless, on 15 Feb 1895 J.E.P. Aldous' patriotic allegorical opera *Ptarmigan* was premiered there. The Hamilton Opera Company was founded in 1898, and the Hamilton Operatic Society in 1926, but little is known of their repertoires or their histories. Many travelling productions visited Hamilton, eg, Massenet's *Salomé* (an adaptation of *Hérodiade*?) in 1913, and several Victor Herbert operettas and Balfe's *The Bohemian Girl* in 1916. In the space of seven days at the Grand Opera House in 1922 the De Feo Opera Company presented *Aida*, *Carmen*, and *Madama Butterfly*. The Russian Grand Opera Company brought Mussorgsky's *Boris Godunov*, Rimsky-Korsakov's *The Snow Maiden*, and Tchaikovsky's *Eugene Onegin* during the 1922–3 season. Another *Hamilton Opera Company (see June Kowalchuk), active 1961–72, merged with the Mohawk College Opera Workshop (which began in 1970) and became the Mohawk College Theatre in 1976. The theatre presented *Quesnel's **Colas et Colinette*, *Lavallée's **The Widow*, and Verdi's *Rigoletto* that year.

In 1889 Ellen *Ambrose, intending to improve her students' sight reading through performance of duet arrangements of Haydn symphonies, formed the *Duet Club. Gradually the club grew into a society which encouraged promising students through scholarships and sponsored solo and chamber recitals by local and visiting artists. Among notable singers and instrumentalists who have performed in Hamilton in the 20th century are Edward *Johnson, Clara Butt, Jeanne *Dusseau, Amelita Galli-Curci, Nellie Melba, Robert Merrill, Marcel Dupré, Mischa Elman, Isaac Stern, Healey *Willan, Murray Perahia, Vladimir Horowitz, Philippe Entremont, and Alexis Weissenberg. The Hamilton Community Concerts Assn, formed in 1932, was still active in 1979, sponsoring four concerts annually. In 1977 it had a membership of over 1900.

Richard Birney Smith (b Detroit 29 Jan 1941, naturalized Canadian 1971, organist-choirmaster in Dundas, Ont, until 1978 when he returned to the USA) established the Te Deum Concert Series in 1968 and presented performances of baroque music for 10 years.

Musical education in Hamilton goes back to the 1840s when the Burlington Academy offered to ladies instruction in piano, harp, guitar, and voice. In the 1860s musical tuition was provided by 10 independent teachers and a few private schools, one of which was the Wesleyan Ladies College, established in December 1863 to offer courses in arts, music, and sciences. Robert Ambrose was music director 1864–89. Music also was taught at Loretto College, founded in 1866 (Norah *Clench studied there). As early as 1869 Hamilton public schools offered some instruction in music, usually voice training. The first school orchestra was formed in 1887.

In 1888 D.J. O'Brien founded the Hamilton Musical Institute (Hamilton College of Music 1889–98). The Hamilton School of Music, under the direction of J.E.P. Aldous, flourished 1889–1908. C.L.M. Harris in 1897 founded the Hamilton Cons of Music, which in 1965 became the *Royal Hamilton College of Music. Music courses at *McMaster U were begun in 1953 and the Music Dept was established in 1965. Hamilton's Cathedral of Christ the King possesses one of the 11 *carillons in Canada. Its 23 bells were installed in 1933.

Among noted musicians born in or near Hamilton have been 'Puff' *Addison, the Ambrose, *Carey, and Littlehales families, Mona *Bates, Mabel *Beddoe, Hector *Charlesworth, the noted pianist and teacher Kate Sara Chittenden, Ralph Cruickshank (see Berandol), W.E. and G.H. *Fairclough, Roy and John *Fenwick, Constance *Fisher, Sonny *Greenwich, Cyril Hampshire, C.F. *Harrison, Hugh *Hartwell, Gary *Hayes, Clifford *Hunt, *King Biscuit Boy (Richard Newell), Gene *Lees, Clarence Lucas, Harry *MacDonough, Thelma Johannes *O'Neill, Arthur *Poynter, Ernest *Seitz, Adrienne *Shannon, T.R. *Sloan, Ian *Thomas, and Rick *Wilkins.

Some noted musicians and groups who have been active in the Hamilton area are the Bartmann family, J.W. *Baumann, Reginald *Bedford and Evelyn Eby, Lorne *Betts, Boris *Brott, *Canadian Brass, the *Czech Quartet, Reginald *Godden, Lee *Hepner, Marta *Hidy, Harold Jerome, Udo *Kasemets, Ada Twohy *Kent, Jean *Macleod, Frank *Thorolfson, Alan *Walker, Gladys *Whitehead, and Jan Wolanek.

Despite the proximity and lure of Toronto with its many and tempting alternatives for Hamilton music lovers, Hamilton has maintained and developed over the years a rich and independent musical life, typified in the 1970s by the established position of the Hamilton Philharmonic Orchestra as one of Canada's major orchestras.

BIBLIOGRAPHY

Reynold, Ella Julia. 'Days before yesterday, music, art, drama and literature,' *Hamilton Centennial 1846–1946* (Hamilton 1946)

'One hundred years of Hamilton music,' *Hamilton Spectator*, 11, 18 Jun 1946

Hall, Fred A. 'Hamilton: 1846–1946: a century of music,' *CAUSM J*, vol 4, Autumn 1974 (FAH)

The Hamilton Chamber Music Society. Founded in 1951 by Delia Calapai of Buffalo and Reginald *Godden, with the support of *McMaster U. The *Spivak Quartet gave the opening concert 19 Jan 1952. The society engaged mainly Canadian performers and emphasized unusual repertoire (eg, music of Scheidt, Henry VIII, Malcolm Arnold, and Victor Ewald, played by *Canadian Brass, 27 Nov 1971; music of George Crumb, Luciano Berio, Harry *Freedman, John *Hawkins, Mario Davidovsky, and György Ligeti, presented by *New Music Concerts of Toronto, 10 Feb 1973). Foreign groups have appeared occasionally, as 14 Feb 1953, when the society presented the Amadeus String Quartet for the first time in Hamilton. The society continued to give between three and five concerts each season until 1972. Its final (91st) presentation was an appearance of the Beaux Arts Trio 23 April 1972. (LB)

Hamilton Conservatory of Music. See Royal Hamilton College of Music.

The Hamilton Opera Company. Founded in 1961 by the soprano June *Kowalchuk and the former D'Oyly Carte singer Clifford Fox. Its first production was *The Gypsy Baron* at Hill Park High School. In nine years of activity productions of works by Johann Strauss, Romberg, Smetana, Puccini, Mascagni, and Bizet were conducted by George *Crum, Lee *Hepner, and William Santor. Beset by the lack of a suitable theatre, of local musicians experienced in opera, and of funds to correct such deficiencies, the company tried to survive through collaboration with the Mohawk College Opera Workshop, mounting at the college productions of *Die Fledermaus* (1970–1) and *The Bartered Bride* (1971–2). After 1972 the company disbanded, and its supporting body, the Hamilton Opera Corporation, transferred its help to Mohawk College's opera productions. (LB)

Hamilton Philharmonic Orchestra. Canada's 10th major orchestra by 1970. It was established in 1949 as a mainly amateur organization with a membership of 60, including a few professional musicians. Several prior orchestras had flourished in the city (see Hamilton).

The philharmonic made its debut 16 Jan 1950 at Hamilton's Memorial School Auditorium. It was conducted 1949–58 by Jan Wolanek (b 25 Jan ca 1895, a pupil of Franz Kneisel, Artur Rodzinski, Joseph Rosenstock, and Otakar Ševčik; a one-time violinist with the Tonkünstler and Vienna Opera orchestras and founder-conductor of groups such as the St Catharines Civic Orchestra and the Hollywood, Fla, Philharmonic Orchestra). Later conductors were Leonard Pearlman and Bryden Thomson 1958–9, Victor *di Bello 1958–62, and Lee *Hepner 1962–9. Boris *Brott succeeded Hepner in 1969. Concertmasters have included Arthur *Garami, Hyman *Goodman, Marta *Hidy, Otto *Armin, and Lance Elbeck.

Following nine seasons at the Memorial Auditorium the orchestra performed at the Westdale Auditorium 1958–62, the Palace Theatre 1962–71, and the Mohawk Theatre 1971–3. It moved into the splendid modern auditorium *Hamilton Place in 1973.

Recognition and support for the orchestra came slowly at first; in 1952 the City of Hamilton awarded it a $500 grant. As a semi-professional ensemble in 1961 it received a *Canada Council grant of $1000 to assist in the presentation of a youth concert. By 1975 it was receiving $115,000 in operational grants and $12,500 for special projects from the Canada Council, and during the remainder of the 1970s these organizations, along with the *OAC and numerous private and corporate donors, provided continual financial support for the orchestra.

The activities of the orchestra expanded greatly under the artistic directorship of Boris Brott, who, with Betty Webster (b Toronto 2 Feb 1925; BA Victoria College, Toronto, 1946), the orchestra's first full-time executive director 1967–75, and with co-operation from the OAC, raised the orchestra by stages to major status by expanding and diversifying the market for its services and reconceiving the contractual arrangements with the players to accommodate the diversification. The OAC helped subsidize an increased number of professional musicians-in-residence in return for a commensurate increase in the orchestra's regional and provincial services and its in-school program. This was made possible by the unusual (at that time) expedient of hiring players not as a contracted indivisible orchestra but as individuals and chamber groups who could come together as an orchestra or disperse into versatile modules for performances and workshops in a wide variety of situations under Hamilton Philharmonic management. The most noted single group to emerge (and later to claim independence) from the orchestra was *Canadian Brass; but other Hamilton Philharmonic groups – the *Czech Quartet, the Sentiri Wind Quintet, H.P.O. Bach (a chamber orchestra), the Lorcini-Elliott Duo (flute and harp), the Lorien Woodwind Quintet, and three more string quartets (the New Arte, the Orpheus, and the Rittenhouse) – performed particularly in the Hamilton area, but some within a much wider Ontario radius, in schools, libraries, churches, and community halls. Players from the orchestra also served as part of the professional nucleus of the *Thunder Bay SO while it was conducted by Brott, 1967–72.

The resourcefulness shown in developing the orchestra was reflected in the colourful approach taken to publicizing all aspects of its, and its conductor's, achievements. Strong promotion of philharmonic players' availability for all manner of small and large concerts, whether in schools, supermarkets, neighbouring town squares, or local steel mills and vivid advertisements featuring Brott as a motorcyclist, or Don Juan, or Santa Claus carried an image of the Hamilton Philharmonic Orchestra as a hustling, insouciant, and youthful enterprise into thousands of homes.

The Hamilton Philharmonic Youth Orchestra, formed in 1965 under the direction of Glenn Mallory and sponsored by the senior orchestra, continued to provide orchestral experience for students in the Hamilton area. In addition, and at a higher level, the Hamilton Philharmonic Institute was created in 1974 to provide tuition and orchestral training for a limited number of fledgling professional musicians, salaried apprentices who would play in the senior orchestra as part of their schooling. This was the first program of its kind to be undertaken by a Canadian orchestra.

In the 1978–9 season the Hamilton Philharmonic Orchestra offered eight pairs of main-series concerts, five pairs of pop concerts, three young people's concerts, two concerts by the youth orchestra, and one special Sunday concert with Isaac Stern as soloist. The many concerts and workshops by the orchestra's chamber groups continued. During the 1970s numerous series were sponsored by corporations, notably Dofasco, *du Maurier, and Stelco. The orchestra has played frequently outside Hamilton. In the late 1970s it appeared annually at *Ontario Place, Toronto. It has appeared at the *Algoma Fall Festival, the *Guelph Spring Festival, and the *Shaw Festival. At the opening of Hamilton Place 24 Sep 1973 it participated with the *Ontario Youth Choir and soloists in the premiere of Galt *MacDermot's *A Mass in Our Time*, commissioned for the occasion and conducted by Thomas Pierson. It played in Montreal in 1974 in an exchange with the *MSO, and in 1976 as part of the cultural program of the Olympics. It has performed frequently on CBC and CHCH TV.

The philharmonic in its early years featured only Canadian solo performers, and 1950–4 six of these were Hamiltonians. As the orchestra expanded, this policy could be adhered to no longer. Nevertheless, a high proportion of Canadian artists have continued to appear with the orchestra. Among these have been Jean *Bonhomme, Anna *Chornodolska, Janina *Fialkowska, Maureen *Forrester, Ida *Haendel, Anton *Kuerti, André *Laplante, Malcolm Lowe, Phyllis *Mailing, Mari-Elizabeth *Morgen, Zara *Nelsova, Arthur *Ozolins, Louis *Quilico, Joseph *Rouleau, Steven *Staryk, Ronald *Turini, Riki *Turofsky, the *Bach-Elgar Choir of Hamilton, the *Dofasco Male Chorus, the *Festival Singers, the Moe *Koffman jazz group, and the *Toronto Mendelssohn Choir. Among noted foreign guests have been Larry Adler, Philippe Entremont, Dizzy Gillespie, Lili Kraus, Chuck Mangione, Ethel Merman, Itzhak Perlman, Leonard Rose, Janos Starker, Richard Tucker, and Barry Tuckwell. Guest conductors have included Kazuyoshi Akiyama, Aaron Copland, Arthur Fiedler, Piero Gamba, and André Kostelanetz. Ella Fitzgerald was the guest artist at a 25th-anniversary benefit concert 10 May 1975.

The orchestra has commissioned works by Lorne *Betts (*Kandario*), Alexander *Brott (*Thunder and Lightning*), *Glick (*Psalm for Orchestra*), *Rathburn (*Three Ironies*), *Symonds (*Three Atmospheres*), and William Wallace (*Canticle for Orchestra*). It has premiered these and also works of *Applebaum (*Place Setting*), Betts (*Music for Orchestra, Variants for Orchestra*), Brott (*H.B.S., B 22*), *Gellman (*Odyssey*), *McCauley (*Concerto Grosso*), and Wallace (*Ceremonies*), and has performed numerous other Canadian works.

Jacques Druelle succeeded Betty Webster in 1975 with the new title of general manager. Mark Warren succeeded Druelle in 1979.

DISCOGRAPHY

Bizet – Gellman *Symphony in Two Movements* – Fauré – Delius. Brott cond. 1975. CBC SM-295

Ravel – Sibelius – Stravinsky. Hamilton Phil Virtuosi, Brott cond. 1972–3. CBC SM-200

Christmas Brott to You: Christmas songs and carols arranged by Bob McMullin. Brott cond. (1971?). CTL 477-5153

McCauley *Concerto Grosso* – Poulenc *Sinfonietta*. Canadian Brass, Brott cond. 1974. CBC SM-264

The HPO also accompanied composer-conductor-flugelhornist Chuck Mangione on *Land of Make Believe*, Mer SRMI-684, recorded in Massey Hall, 1973.

BIBLIOGRAPHY

'Hamilton Philharmonic Orchestra,' *CanComp*, 24, Dec 1967

Graham, June. 'Boris Brott,' *CanComp*, 51, Jun 1970

Montagnes, Ann. 'HPI's students really know the score,' *PfAC*, vol 13, Spring 1976

Dale, Stephen. 'Meet the man who keeps the HPO in business,' Hamilton *Random Scan*, Apr 1979

'Boris Brott,' interview with Michael Schulman, *CanComp*, 142, Jun 1979 (SS)

Hamilton Place. Multi-purpose arts centre, situated on Main St West in downtown Hamilton, Ont. It has two halls and rehearsal facilities, and was opened officially 22 Sep 1973. It was financed by the city of Hamilton and its citizens. The architect was Trevor P. Garwood-Jones and the acoustics were planned by Russell Johnson Associates of New York. It is Hamilton's main performance centre. The Great Hall has a stage 37.35 m wide and 11.4 to 16.2 m in adjustable depth, and an auditorium which seats from 1959 to 2183. The Studio Theatre has no permanent stage and seats from 300 to 400. Hamilton Place is owned and subsidized by the city of Hamilton and administered by an independent board, the Hamilton Performing Arts Corporation. George MacPherson was succeeded as general manager in 1979 by Thomas Burrows. Management serves as both impresario and rental agent. (LB)

HAMPSHIRE, Cyril. Pianist, organist, choir conductor, adjudicator, b Wakefield, England, 12 Oct 1900, d Hamilton, Ont, 18 Nov 1963; ATCM organ 1925, FTCL 1920s. He was assistant organist at 14 at Wakefield Cathedral, and his studies at Leeds College of Music led to other church positions in England. He came to Canada in 1921, settling in Moose Jaw, Sask, where he was a church organist and choirmaster. He served 1928–34 as principal of the Regina College Cons of Music (*Cons of Music, U of Regina) and 1934–8 as music director for the Regina Board of Education. In 1939 he moved to Ontario to take an appointment as principal of the Hamilton Cons of Music (*RHCM). He left that position in 1945 to become director of music for the Hamilton public schools. He served 1942–4 as president of the *ORMTA and 1947–8 as president of the Ontario Educational Assn (see *OMEA). Hampshire wrote or arranged several songs for school children and an *Introduction to Practical Sight Singing* (1951), all published by *Jarman. He conducted the *Bach-Elgar Choir 1948–55, examined for the *RCMT, adjudicated competitions, and directed the Stelco Male Chorus 1941–8. (WL)

Hamilton Place

HANCOCK, Gordon. Administrator, pianist, organist-choirmaster, teacher, b Stoke-on-Trent, Staffordshire, England, 20 Mar 1912, d Regina 22 Jan 1978; ATCM 1930, LTCL 1947, FTCL 1947. His family moved to Canada in 1913. A pupil of Arthur *Bates and Lyell *Gustin, he was an organist-choirmaster in Saskatoon 1928–43, in North Battleford 1943–8, and in Regina 1948–58. He also taught privately until 1948, then at the *Regina Cons until 1958. He and his wife, Mossie McCree Hancock (b Mervin, near Lloydminster, Sask; LRSM 1938, LTCL 1941; a pupil of Lyell Gustin in Canada and Iso Elinson in England), formed a piano duo, their performances including Mozart's *Concerto in E Flat* with the *Regina SO in 1958 and many public and CBC recitals. They were co-hosts 1959–74 for the music appreciation programs 'As You Like It' and 'The Music of Man' on CKCK radio, Regina. Mossie Hancock has written for the *Canada Music Book* and *Musicanada*. In 1958 Gordon Hancock became executive director of the *Saskatchewan Music Festival Assn. During his tenure the festival movement grew substantially. On his retirement in 1976 a scholarship was established in his name. He was Saskatchewan's representative 1958–76 on the *FCMF and served 1969–70 as president of that organization. WLB

The Handel Society of Music. Choir founded in 1966 in New Westminster, BC, and directed by Karel *ten Hoope. It performs in New Westminster at Vincent Massey Auditorium, and in Vancouver at the Holy Rosary Cathedral. Its choral style is continental-European rather than English, and its programs differ from those of many other Canadian choirs in the inclusion of 19th-century music (Mendelssohn, Dvořák) in addition to works from the 18th- and 20th-century repertoire, such as Alessandro Scarlatti's *Messa di Santa Cecilia* (in its first BC performance, 13 May 1972) and Honegger's *Cantate de Noël* (3 Nov 1972, performed with the participation of the British Columbia Boys' Choir). TRL

HANSON, Frank (Franklin Keith). Lecturer, composer, b Lynn, Mass, 8 Aug 1899, d Montreal 16 Jan 1975, naturalized Canadian late 1920s; B MUS (McGill) 1931, D MUS (McGill) 1947. Raised in Lynn, and in Cincinnati where he studied piano, he moved in 1914 with his family to Toronto. There he took organ lessons at the *TCM with Harvey Robb. Studies followed at the Sherwood School of Music (Chicago), the ESM (Rochester), the American Institute of Normal Methods (Auburndale), the Juilliard School and Columbia U (New York), and *McGill U with Douglas *Clarke (composition) and Alfred *Whitehead (organ). He joined the extension department at McGill U in 1923, and taught keyboard harmony and pedagogy there 1935–40. Among his pupils were Rafael *Masella and Ronald *Turini. He became instructor at West Hill High School (Montreal) in 1937 and taught at McGill's MacDonald College 1940–54. He was a music adviser and examiner for the Quebec Dept of Education. By 1963, when he retired, he was chairman of general education, institute of education, MacDonald College. Hanson wrote elementary school textbooks and articles for journals and newspapers. During his teaching career, composition remained a secondary activity. He composed little between 1947 (*Symphony of Canada*, his doctoral thesis) and 1963 except arrangements for choir or organ. His works include *Hornpipe* (1934, performed by the *Montreal Orchestra under Douglas Clarke), a string quartet, and pieces for violin, for piano, and for flute. BNSG

HANSON, Jens. Composer, educator, b Raton, N Mex, 29 Nov 1936; B SC (MIT) 1958, MA (Denver) 1963, PH D (Yale) 1969. He studied composition 1961–3 with Normand Lockwood and in the summer of 1964 with Darius Milhaud; viola in 1961 with Fred Ruhof, in the summer of 1964 with John Garvey, and 1965–8 with David Schwartz; and theory 1965–8 with Allen Forte. In 1968 he joined the staff of the *U of Windsor as a teacher of theory and composition. After being interested in electronic and aleatroic composition Hanson more recently has blended the influences of Forte, Babbitt, and *Schafer. With the exception of *Symphony in Four Movements* (1963) and *Keys* (1974) for concert band, Hanson's output has consisted mainly of chamber works. His compositions include three string quartets (1963, 1975, 1977), *Trio for Flute, Clarinet and Bassoon* (1963), *Psalm 46* (1963) and *Discipline* (1964) for unaccompanied choir, *Festival Sonata* (1965) for organ, and *Mainspring* (1975) for choir, tape, and piano (all mss). In 1974 he wrote the theme music for the movie *The Effect of Gamma Rays on Man-in-the-Moon Marigolds*. He is a contributor to *EMC*. FAH

The Happy Gang. Troupe of musical entertainers heard 1937–59, weekdays at lunchtime, in a variety show of the same name on CBC radio. The show began 14 Jun 1937 on station CRCT (a CBC affiliate in Toronto), moved to the CBC network four months later, and ran for 22 years, nearly 4900 broadcasts. It was heard in its prime years by some two million Canadians daily and also was carried for a time in the USA by the MBS network. It was the model for the CBC French network show 'Les *Joyeux Troubadours,' formed in Montreal in 1941.

The Happy Gang was organized by the singer-pianist Bert Pearl (b Winnipeg 2 Feb 1913), who had played in CBC orchestras under Jack *Arthur, Percy *Faith, and Geoffrey *Waddington. For the first broadcasts Pearl brought together the trumpeter Robert *Farnon, the violinist Blain *Mathé, the theatre organist Kathleen Stokes (b Thorold, Ont, 22 Mar 1894, d Toronto 14 Dec 1979), and the announcer Herb May. In 1938 the singer-accordionist Eddie Allen (b Toronto 1920) was added. While Mathé, Stokes, and Allen remained with the troupe throughout its history, Farnon left in 1943 and Pearl retired to California in 1955. Other instrumentalists were members for varying periods: the trumpeter Bobby *Gimby 1943–April 1959; the saxophonist-clarinetist Cliff *McKay 1943–52, returning in April 1959 to replace Gimby; the keyboardist Jimmy *Namaro 1943–59; the bassist Joe Niosi 1945–59; the organist Lou *Snider 1948–57; the pianist Lloyd Edwards 1950–9; the saxophonist-clarinetist Bert *Niosi 1952–9, replacing McKay; and the accordionist Les Foster 1955–9, added when Allen succeeded Pearl as the show's host. Announcers were May until 1938, Hugh Bartlett 1938–52, and Barry Wood 1952–9; producers were George Temple 1937–56 and Ken Dalziel 1956–9.

The show adhered to a rigid formula, beginning with the sound of knocking on a door, followed by Pearl's question 'Who's there?,' the collective response 'It's the Happy Gang!' and Pearl's invitation 'Well, come on in!' The group then sang the theme 'Keep Happy with the Happy Gang,' written by Pearl. The format included skits, comedy routines, and a variety of musical items, from violin arrangements of classical and traditional melodies played by Mathé, to gems from the theatre-organ repertoire played by Stokes, to ballads or light songs sung by Allen or Pearl and patriotic or farcical songs performed by the troupe. The prevailing temper was a kind of hectic, zany cheerfulness, powered by zest, unpretentious to a fault, seldom solemn except occasionally during the classical solo or a particularly earnest and fervent patriotic song. Among the songs most familiar to Happy Gang audiences were 'Shut the Door' (the refrain, 'Shut the door!' 'They're coming in the window!' 'Well, shut the window!' 'They're coming in the door!' – with ever-changing verses) and *'You'll Get Used to It.' 'There'll Always Be an England' was sung daily during World War II. Pearl, introduced routinely as 'five-foot two-and-a-half of sunshine' (though in fact five-foot seven), was the main generator of the nervous energy, hilarity, and cheek which, allied to the down-to-earth, professional reliability of the performances, probably explain the program's longevity and wide appeal. It received awards from a number of magazines including *Liberty* and *Radio World*. The Happy Gang performed mostly before studio audiences in Toronto but toured Canada in 1947 and 1951. It made a TV debut 9 May 1956 on the CBC's 'Cross-Canada Hit Parade' but did not continue in that medium. RCA Victor released several recordings by the troupe, and Gordon V. *Thompson published two folios, one of war songs, the other of comic songs. Sixteen years after the last regular broadcast, 5 Jun 1959, Billy *O'Connor reunited the Happy Gang for two concerts, 28 Aug 1975, at the *CNE. Each concert drew an estimated 15,000 people and was broadcast by the CBC. O'Connor reunited the troupe a second time for a short tour of western Canada in the summer of 1978.

BIBLIOGRAPHY

Frayne, Trent. 'Liberty profile: Bert Pearl,' *Liberty*, 13 Oct 1945

Brown, Bill. 'The Happy Gang steps out,' Montreal *Standard*, Sep 1949

Callwood, June. 'The not-so-Happy Gang,' *Maclean's*, 1 Feb 1950

'The Happy Gang: will its first reunion become an annual event?' *CanComp*, 104, Oct 1975 (MM)

HARBOUR, Denis. Bass, radio producer, b Oka, near Montreal, 3 Aug 1917. He took voice lessons from Arthur *Laurendeau while studying law. Deciding on a career in music, he worked 1945–53 in New York with Paul Althouse, Léon Rothier, Herbert Graf, and Alfredo Valenti. He took part in numerous concerts, radio programs, and tours, travelling to 46 US states with the Charles Wagner Opera Company. He was engaged by the *Metropolitan Opera for the 1949–50 season after winning the 'Metropolitan Opera Auditions of the Air' in March 1949. He made his debut 26 November as the Jailer in *Tosca*. In New York and on tour he sang 7 roles in 26 performances, including the Helmsman in *Tristan und Isolde*, the Imperial Commissioner in *Madama Butterfly*, Ceprano in *Rigoletto*, Wagner in *Faust*, and one of the three Streltsy in *Khovanshchina*. Toscanini engaged him to sing the King of Egypt in a 1949 NBC broadcast of a concert performance of *Aida*, later released as a recording (VICS 6113) by RCA.

Over the next few years Harbour gave several recitals in the USA and Canada and appeared as a soloist with a number of orchestras. For the *Montreal Festivals he sang Mephistopheles in *Faust* in 1950 at the Delorimier stadium and Frère Laurent in *Roméo et Juliette* in 1952 at the chalet on Mount Royal. During the 1952–3 season he performed in England, Holland, Switzerland, and Scandinavia. He sang 7 Mar 1954 with the Boston SO under Charles Munch in a performance of *Messiah*. With Claire *Gagnier he starred 1953–7 in the weekly CBC radio – later TV – program 'Sérénade.' He was soloist with the *MSO in Verdi's *Requiem* in April 1951, Beethoven's *Ninth Symphony* in December 1953, and Mozart's *Requiem* in April 1956. He sang the prologue of Boito's *Mefistofele* in 1957 with the *Quebec SO. He gave up his singing career and was a radio producer 1959–72 with CBC, subsequently heading the record department of Dupuis Frères, Montreal, until it closed in 1977. A skilful actor, Denis Harbour was noted throughout his career for his warm and powerful voice. GG

'Hard, Hard Times.' William James Emberley of Bay de Verde, Nfld, adapted an older song to describe the plight of Newfoundland fishermen during the great Depression of the 1930s. The collapse of international markets made it difficult to sell fish at any price, and for years many Newfoundlanders lived on the government dole of six cents a day. Emberley's verses – which passed quickly into tradition – are a local application of a pattern established by an 18th-century English broadside which ridiculed certain trades and later was adapted often to describe hard times. The Emberley version has been recorded (*Folksongs of Newfoundland*, Folk FW 8771, and also by Dick *Nolan) and published (Edith *Fowke's *The Penguin Book of Canadian Folk Songs*, by Harmondsworth, England 1973). EF

HARDY, Edmond. Bandmaster, administrator, importer, publisher, teacher, b Montreal 23 Nov 1854, d Montréal-Sud (Longueuil) 18 Sep 1943. He studied music with his father, Guillaume, founder and director of the Hardy Band, and succeeded him when he died 16 Mar 1879 in Montreal. In 1874 Edmond had founded the Montreal Concert Band with about 15 young instrumentalists. In 1878 this number was raised to 35, and in 1880 the group absorbed the Ville-Marie Concert Band to make up an ensemble of 55 musicians. Hardy directed it until 1934 and made it famous in Canada and the USA. It gave a notable performance at the 1883 Foreign Exhibition in Boston. Over the years several regiments – the 3rd Battalion Victoria Rifles, the 85th Battalion of Infantry, the Garrison Artillery, the 6th Battalion Fusiliers, the 5th Battalion Royal Scots of Canada, the Irish Canadian Rangers, and the 65th Regiment Carabiniers Mont-Royal – employed this band. In 1886 Hardy brought together representatives of all the bands in Quebec, and the meeting led to the founding in 1887 of the Assn des corps de musique de la province de Québec. Hardy was the first president, 1887–90. He conducted numerous concerts in Canadian and US cities and was a member of juries for competitions in Guelph, Ont, and in Montpelier, Vt. He was general director 1894–5 of the *Opéra français of Montreal and director 1896–1901 of the Cons of the *Canadian Artistic

Society. For 40 years, 1885–1925, Hardy ran a business importing music and instruments, either alone or in partnership (ca 1887) with George Violetti. He was founder and director of *L'Écho musical*, a monthly magazine of which at least nine issues were published in 1887–8. He also published works by the composers Alexis *Contant, Guillaume *Couture, Arthur *Letondal, and Achille *Fortier, and in 1893 he published Fortier's *20 Chansons populaires du Canada*. In 1898 he was elected first president of the Musicians' Protective Union of Montreal (which became the Montreal Musicians' Guild) and the following year was a member of the committee which set up the Musicians' Benevolent Society, a self-help organization. Appointed in 1904, he taught and directed the Mont-St-Louis Concert Band for thirty years.

Hardy took part in many musical performances, but of particular note were the two 1903 *Monument national concerts at which he conducted works of Contant including the *Mass No. 3* for choir and orchestra, in its premiere. A contemporary of Calixa *Lavallée, he conducted the band assembled 13 Jul 1933 on the occasion of the transfer of Lavallée's remains from Boston to Montreal. He was named an Officier d'Académie in 1911 by the French government and was mayor of the municipality of Montréal-Sud for eight years. At the time of his death at 88 he was considered the dean of North American bandmasters. Place Edmond-Hardy in Rivière-des-Prairies was named in his honour in 1978.

Hardy's brother Alphonse (clarinetist, b Montreal ca 1865, d there 30 Dec 1938), played at the Académie de musique before settling in Quebec City as bandmaster and conductor. The bass, teacher, and writer on music Arthur *Laurendeau was Edmond Hardy's son-in-law, and the ondist Jean *Laurendeau is his great-grandson.

BIBLIOGRAPHY

'Hardy et Violetti,' *Le Commerce de Montréal et de Québec et leurs industries en 1889* (Montreal 1889)

'M. Edmond Hardy,' *P-T*, vol 1, 2 Mar 1895

'M. Edmond Hardy,' *P-T*, vol 4, 5 Mar 1898

'Le décès du doyen de nos musiciens,' Montreal *La Presse*, 20 Sep 1943

GP

HARDY, Hagood. Composer, arranger, vibraphonist, pianist, percussionist, b Angola, Ind, of a Canadian father and a US mother, 26 Feb 1937; BA (Toronto) 1958. Taken to Canada as an infant, he was raised in Oakville, Ont, where he studied piano with Edna Lawrence and Ellen Scott. In the mid-1950s he began playing the vibraphone and, while studying political science and economics at the U of Toronto, performed in local jazz clubs and on CBC TV, leading his own group 1957–61. In 1961 he went to the USA, where he played vibraphone for Gigi Gryce (New York 1961), Herbie Mann (on tour 1961–2), Martin Denny (Hawaii and Las Vegas 1962–4), and George Shearing (on tour 1964–7). Returning to Toronto, Hardy led a jazz trio (Ian Henstridge, bass, and Ricky Marcus, then Dave Lewis, drums) which, with the addition in 1969 of the singers Stephanie Taylor and Carrie Romano, became the Montage, a pop group with jazz and Latin-American leanings. With a personnel which varied in the group's five-year history the Montage appeared infrequently in Canada but was successful in US nightclubs and also toured Europe.

With the group's demise in 1974 Hardy concentrated on the composition and recording of music for jingles, TV, radio, and films, an activity he had begun in the early 1970s. He returned to prominence when he revised and recorded *The Homecoming*, originally composed in 1972 as the jingle for a Salada Tea commercial. Released by Attic Records as a single in 1975, it became an international hit. Its success brought Hardy *Juno Awards as the best composer and the best instrumental artist of 1975; he also was named instrumental artist of the year (1976) by *Billboard* magazine. Hardy received a Juno as instrumental artist of 1976, and was given the Wm Harold Moon Award from BMI Canada (PRO Canada) in 1977. *The Homecoming* was followed by *Love Theme from 'Missouri Breaks,'* a moderate hit in Canada.

Hardy returned to live performance in 1976, appearing with symphony orchestras in several Ontario cities. Playing piano and vibraphone with a rhythm section of jazz musicians, he has featured programs of his best-known jingles and film scores. He starred 23 Apr 1976 on a CBC TV special. Hardy's compositions include scores for a Malcolm Muggeridge program about Feodor Dostoevsky (1975), for 'Bethune' (1977), and for two programs in the 'Newcomers' series (1977), all on CBC TV; and scores for the feature films *Second Wind* (1975), *Rituals* (1976), *Klondike Fever* (1979), and *American Christmas Carol* (1979), as well as several US TV movies. He is an affiliate of PRO Canada.

DISCOGRAPHY

Stop 33. 1967. CTLS 1096/GRT 9211

Hagood Hardy and the Montage. 1970. CBC LM-81

Hagood Hardy and the Montage. 1972. CTLS 0155/GRT 9230-1012

The Homecoming. 1975. CTLS 0191/Attic LAT 1003

Maybe Tomorrow. 1976. Attic LAT 1011

Others as sideman to Cliff *McKay, Herbie Mann (*At the Village Gate*, Atlantic SD 1380; *Right Now*, Atlantic SD 1384; *Returns to the Village Gate*, Atlantic SD 1407; *Brazil Bossa Nova and Blues*, U Artists UAJ 14009), Martin Denny, and George Shearing (*Here and Now*, Cap T-2372)

BIBLIOGRAPHY

Batten, Jack. 'Hagood's homecoming,' *The Canadian*, 13 Mar 1976

– 'Hagood Hardy's next step is stab at U.S. market,' *MSc*, 294, Mar–Apr 1977

(HM, MM)

HARE, Clayton. Violinist, teacher, conductor, b St Catharines, Ont, 13 Jul 1909. Following studies in Buffalo, in Toronto 1928–30 with Geza *de Kresz at the *Hambourg Cons, in London 1932–4 with Henri Temianka, and at the RAM 1934–9 with Rowsby Woof, he joined the faculty of *Mount Allison U in 1939. In 1945 he moved to *Mount Royal College in Calgary, teaching violin and conducting the College SO, which in 1949 was absorbed into the newly re-formed *Calgary SO under Hare's direction. He was dean of music 1955–65 at the U of Portland, Ore, and taught 1965–7 at Boston U and 1967–70 at the U of Maine. He conducted the *New Brunswick Youth Orchestra 1969–70. With his wife, Dorothy *Swetnam, he gave duo recitals publicly and on CBC radio and in 1963 co-founded the Victoria Summer School of Music. In 1970 he returned to Calgary to teach privately. His students have included Francis *Chaplin, Andrew *Dawes, and Betty-Jean *Hagen. (JWS)

HARE, Marie (b Whitney). Folksinger, b Strathadam, on Nor'-West Miramichi River, NB, ca 1913. Her grandfather cleared a sizable farm at Strathadam, her father worked in the lumber woods all his life, and her mother was a member of the family celebrated in the song *'The Jones Boys.' From her parents she learned many traditional songs of Anglo-Canadian origin. Discovered by Louise *Manny, she appeared at several *Miramichi Folk Festivals and recorded *Marie Hare of Strathadam, New Brunswick* (1962, Folk Legacy FSC-9), an LP of 11 songs. An accompanying booklet by Louise Manny and Edward Ives discusses her style and gives notes and texts for her songs. EF

HARMER, Shirley (m Murray, m Bertram). Singer, actress, b Thornton's Corners (now Oshawa), Ont, 25 Mar 1932. At 15 she sang with the Oshawa dance band of Boyd Valleau, her first voice coach. She performed on CBL radio, Toronto, with the 'Microphone Moppets,' and with Johnny *Burt, Cal Jackson, and others, and was coached by Art *Hallman. In 1951 she began singing on CFRB with George *Murray (who in 1954 became her first husband). She made her TV debut on the CBC's 'The Big Revue' in 1953 and won the S.P. Caldwell award as the most promising TV performer of that year. Appearances 1953–4 in the USA on Dave Garroway's NBC TV show, and with Paul Whiteman's orchestra in concert and on ABC radio, were followed by star billing 1954–7 in Canada on Canadian General Electric's 'C.G.E. Showtime' on CBC TV. She was a regular performer 1957–8 in Hollywood on George Gobel's NBC TV show, and she signed a contract in 1958 with Paramount Films but appeared in only one movie *The Hangman*.

On her return to Canada in 1959 Harmer began a nightclub career. She starred on CBC TV's 'A Summer Night' in 1962 and was a guest on several other CBC shows. In 1968 she moved to Italy where she performed until 1973 under the name Vida Durinzi. After a brief return to Toronto she moved in the mid-1970s to Florida and continued performing there in clubs and in concert. In addition to her first recordings (1957) in New York for MGM and others in Milan for Miura, she made the LP *Shirley Harmer Sings* (1964, CTLS 5052).

WRITINGS

'Why I flopped in Hollywood,' *Star Weekly*, 17 Mar 1960

BIBLIOGRAPHY

Rasky, Harry. 'Everybody's young sister,' *SatN*, 26 May 1956

Allen, Joan. 'Back on top again,' *Star Weekly*, 8 Jun 1963

Harmonica (mouth organ, mouth harp, blues harp, musique à bouche, ruine-babines). Fixed-pitch reed instrument invented in the 1820s, probably in Germany (though *Grove's*, vol 5, claims England, 1829). The factors which ensured the instrument's early importation to Canada – its small size, modest cost, and relative ease of mastery – have made it practical for children and popular for informal music making. The painting *L'Enfant au pain* (1890s) by Ozias Leduc shows a small boy playing a harmonica at the supper table. In Canada the harmonica has been an important instrument in two musical genres and a peripheral instrument in several others.

In Quebec the harmonica (popularly known as the 'musique à bouche' or 'ruine-babines') shares with the violin and the button accordion a wide repertoire of folkdances – reels, quadrilles, jigs, and waltzes. Accompanied by piano or by the player's own 'clogging,' the instrument's bright, often harsh (and thus easily heard) sound makes it ideal for dances. Though harmonica music dates from earlier centuries and has developed chiefly through an aural tradition, it was recorded in relatively pure form by several players during the 1920s. The most prolific of these was Henri Lacroix (fl 1921–38) who made many 78s as a solo performer for *Starr, *Victor, *Columbia, and *Brunswick, and others as an accompanist to Conrad *Gauthier, Ovila *Légaré, and Isidore *Soucy. He is known to have accompanied La *Bolduc on occasion, participated in Gauthier's Veillées du bon vieux temps, and led the Trio d'Henri and the Quatuor Lacroix.

Among other Quebec harmonica players who recorded were La Bolduc herself; Joseph Lalonde (1860–1946), a shopkeeper in Côteau-du-Lac, who also appeared in Gauthier's presentations and recorded for Victor and Starr; and Louis Blanchette (1905–69), who recorded many reels in the 1930s for Starr (some re-issued on the LP *Vingt grands succès d'hier*, MCA Coral 37008). Gabriel Labbé, whose bio-discography *Les Pionniers du disque folklorique québécois* (Montreal 1977) includes lists of recordings by Lacroix, Lalonde, and Blanchette, cited Ludger Foucault, Oscar and Aldor Morin (Oscar was once a member of Omer *Dumas's Ménestrels and of the Famille Soucy), and Gaston Tessier, all of Montreal, as the leading harmonica players of the mid-1970s. The younger Alain Lamontagne (b Verdun 14 Jul 1952) has perpetuated the tradition as part of a larger repertoire. The harmonica has not had the same prominence in English Canada, although it has been heard in the bands of Don *Messer and George *Wade in the 1920s and 1930s, and in performances by Mac *Beattie.

Many Canadian bands born of the blues revival in the mid-1960s included (mouth) 'harpists' styled after the Chicago players Sonny Boy Williamson (Rice Miller) from the 1940s and Little Walter (Jacobs) from the 1950s. The best known of these musicians is *King Biscuit Boy. Others include, in Toronto, Luke Gibson (Luke and the Apostles and *Kensington Market), John Kay (*Sparrow), Joe Mendelson (Mainline), Michael Pickett (Whiskey Howl, Wooden Teeth), Rick Walsh (*Downchild), and Chris Whiteley (Original Sloth Band); in Halifax, Rick Jeffreys of the Dutch Mason Blues Band; in Vancouver, Hans Staymer; and in Montreal, Jim Zeller (who has been a sideman to many musicians, eg, Michel *Pagliaro, and has made the LP *Cartes sur table*, Kébec-Disc KDL-966) and Butch Coulter of West End. Lee Oskar, 'harpist' with the San Francisco band War, lived briefly in Toronto but was not active in music.

Following the example of Bob Dylan, various Canadian folk and rock singer-songwriters of the 1960s and 1970s, including Willie P. Bennett, Murray *McLauchlan, and Neil *Young, took up the harmonica. The evocative qualities of the instrument's sound have led to its use in TV, film, and radio scores and in jingles. Bernie Bray of Toronto is one of the leading harmonica players in this context.

While the harmonica has been associated with popular music, the virtuoso Tommy *Reilly has worked in the tradition of Larry Adler and John Sebastian to maintain its place on the international concert platform. (Reilly's father, James, during the early 1930s in Guelph, Ont, led the Elmdale Harmonica Band, one of many such amateur groups active in Canada at that time.) The harmonica as a concert instrument is represented within Canada by Claude Garden (b Claude Jardin, in Verneuil dans l'Eure, France, 27 Feb 1937), who settled in Montreal in 1971, developed a large class of pupils, recorded for RCI (LP 443) in 1976, and toured for *JMC 1978–9. Garden was the soloist with the *MSO in François *Dompierre's *Harmonica Flash*, commissioned by the CBC and recorded by Deutsche Grammophon in 1979. The Ottawa harmonica and guitar player Kevin Gillis, who has played for Peter, Paul and Mary, among others, received a *Canada Council grant in the mid-1970s to research the uses of the harmonica.

(MM)

Harmonium. Montreal rock group consisting of Serge Fiori (composer, guitar, flute), Michel Normandeau (vocals, guitar), and Louis Valois (bass, keyboards). The group made its debut in 1973 at La *Patriote. Its first LP, *Harmonium* (Célébration CEL 1893), was released in 1974. In August of that year Pierre A. Daigneault (brass) and Serge Locat (keyboards) joined the group. In 1975 Harmonium released the LP *Les Cinq Saisons* (Célébration CEL 1900) and took part in the *St-Jean-Baptiste celebrations on Mount Royal. In 1976 Normandeau and Daigneault left, and Denis Farmer (drums, percussion), Monique Fauteux (vocals), Robert Stanley (guitar), and Libert Subirana (saxophone, flute, clarinet) were added. After several months of intensive work the new group recorded *L'Heptade* (2-CBS PFG 90348) in close collaboration with Neil *Chotem and musicians from the *MSO. The lyrics were provided by Normandeau, and the voices of Pierre Bertrand, Estelle Sainte-Croix, and Richard Séguin were featured. *L'Heptade* consists of seven songs ('Comme un fou,' 'Chanson noire,' 'Le Premier Ciel,' 'L'Exil,' 'Le Corridor,' 'Lumières de vies,' and 'Comme un sage'), separated by orchestral sequences by Chotem; it is considered to be Harmonium's most significant production. In *La Presse* (11 Dec 1976) Pierre Beaulieu described the group's music as 'elaborate, refined without being pedantic, subtle, with studied lyrics full of beautiful flashes.'

Harmonium gave many concerts in 1977, particularly in Montreal at the Outremont Cinema and at the Centre sportif of the *U of Montreal, in Toronto at Convocation Hall and *Massey Hall, and in Vancouver. After a concert in London in July 1977 the group toured Europe, appearing with the British group Supertramp. In the autumn of 1978 Harmonium performed in Los Angeles and at the U of Southern California at Berkeley, as well as in the Ontario cities Kingston, Kitchener, London, and Hamilton. The US appearances are documented in the film *Harmonium in California* (NFB 1979). Harmonium's popularity was confirmed by the sales of its three LPs: all received gold record awards. Its music, an aesthetically conceived blend of several elements – classical, Latin American, rock, and jazz – has kept its distance from abstraction and intellectualism.

Fiori (b Montreal 3 Apr 1952) is Harmonium's leader in the areas of conception and composition. All the musicians, save Fauteux, are members of CAPAC.

BIBLIOGRAPHY

Turcot, George A. 'Harmonium. Tout part du ventre,' *Mainmise*, Mar 1976

Bergeron, Raymonde. 'Harmonium. Plus qu'un groupe: un lieu musical,' *Perspectives*, vol 19, 9 Apr 1977

Freeston, David. 'For Harmonium it's music not politics,' *Montreal Star*, 7 May 1977

(ST)

Harmoniums. See Reed organs.

Harp. The date of the harp's arrival in Canada is not known, but one was used in Quebec City 21 Feb 1792 at a 'vocal and instrumental benefit concert on behalf of sieur Jouve, musician to His Royal Highness.' Jouve had come to Quebec City in 1791 with the Duke of Kent and gave harp lessons. The program describes a 'scene and arietta of Atis with harp accompaniment' and 'The sleep of Atis with harp, sung by Messrs. *Bentley, *Glackemeyer, and Jouve.' About this time the harp was one of the instruments being taught at the Ursuline convent.

Over 40 years later a concert by an Irish harpist was reviewed in *Le Journal de Québec* (17 Jun 1843): 'On Wednesday Mr. Wall gave a single recital, as he had announced. The harp is an ungrateful instrument by nature, since despite all the artist's skill, it nevertheless emitted some hard metallic sounds.' Joseph *Lajeunesse, father of the singer Emma *Albani, played the harp and taught it to his daughter. In her concerts in Montreal in 1862 and Albany, NY, in 1864, the future Albani performed her own variations of ' 'Tis the Last Rose of Summer' and thus probably was the first Canadian to write for harp. Her first harp is preserved in the town of Chambly, and another instrument, thought to have belonged to her, is in the Château de Ramezay in Montreal. The harpist Josephine Chatterton, the wife of Henri *Bohrer, performed in Montreal in the 1880s. In 1890 the Montreal violin maker George Violetti advertised harps for sale, and in 1898 a Dame Parratt offered her services as a teacher. Two harpists from New York, the Rasina sisters, performed with great success at *His Majesty's Theatre in March 1901, and one of them played Hasselmans' *Ballade* with the *Goulet *MSO in 1904. Nicolas Eichorn was that orchestra's harpist for the 1905–6 season.

The first recital entirely devoted to the harp in Montreal was probably given by the Italian Alberto Salvi in 1922. In the 1930s Juliette Drouin was the most sought-after harpist, if not the only one, in Montreal. She gave her first recital 9 Feb 1930 at the Ritz-Carlton. Marcel Grandjany, who had been giving recitals since 1926, was invited by Wilfrid *Pelletier in 1943 to start a harp class at the *CMM. He taught there regularly for 20 years, and his many pupils included Gloria *Agostini, Claude Hill (*Metropolitan Opera), Marie *Iösch-Lorcini (*MSO and *London SO), Lise Nadeau (*Quebec SO and assistant to Grandjany in New York), Cécile Préfontaine, and Dorothy *Weldon. A member of the MSO, Weldon taught Manon LeComte and Margot Morris. The Montreal harpist Carla Strauss was for some time a member of the Honolulu SO.

In the mid-19th century the harp was taught in several girls' colleges in Ontario. In Toronto a Mr Ransome advertised as a teacher of flute and harp in 1841–2. The French harpist and composer Nicolas Bochsa performed in Bytown (Ottawa) in 1853, and probably also in Montreal and Quebec City. In 1851 Alfred Toulmin performed at *St Lawrence Hall, Toronto. Fabiani was the harpist of the orchestra of Heinrich *Klingenfeld in 1895.

The first harp teacher at the TCM (*RCMT), Joseph Quintile 1918–23, was followed by John *Duncan 1930–41, Muriel Farrell Donnellan 1932–43, and Nora Phelan Rogers 1943–52. Heloise Macklem, a *TSO member 1923–5 and 1930–1, played the concerto *Lavender and Old Lace* by her husband Francis Paget Macklem, 1 Feb 1927 with that orchestra. Other harpists with the TSO were Donnellan, Rogers, and Maude Watterworth Craig, who also played with the Ottawa Civic Symphony. Carla Emerson (b St John's, Nfld, 4 Mar 1922) studied with Muriel Donnellan at the TCM and then with Grandjany at the Juilliard School, from which she graduated in 1948. She was in London 1950–5, and during part of that time was a member of the Royal Philharmonic under Sir Thomas Beecham. Returning to Toronto, she taught 1955–62 at the RCMT and commuted to play in the *Ottawa Philharmonic Orchestra. She also was second harp 1957–8 for the TSO. Judy *Loman became principal of the TSO in 1959, succeeding Donna Hossack. (Hossack was harpist with the *Vancouver SO during the 1960s, and Lanalee de Kant was principal with that city's orchestra in the late 1970s.) In addition to orchestral work and a solo performing career, Loman has taught, and her pupils include Sarah Davidson, Janice Lindskoog, and Erica *Goodman. The last-named has performed as a soloist, as a duoist with Robert *Aitken, and as a member of chamber groups.

In the *Quebec SO in 1980 the post of principal harp was held by Lucille T. Baby. Janice Lindskoog and Dorothy White have performed as members of the *NACO and the TS. Phyllis *Ensher joined the *Halifax SO in 1958 and for 20 years was that city's leading harpist. A violin pupil of Ysaÿe, the Belgian Frank J. Simons arrived in Winnipeg in 1921, and was that city's only harpist 1949–61. A member of the *Winnipeg SO, he had one pupil, Antoinette Corbeil. Susan George, Barbara Kraichy, and Richard Milton Turner have been harpists with the orchestra. Eva Bohmbach was a soloist with the *Calgary SO in 1913 as well as a member of that orchestra. Other harpists in the city have included Jean Farquharson and Barbara Keenan. The principal chair in Edmonton in the 1970s was held by Regina Watson.

After 1940 Canadian composers began to show a new interest in the harp. J.-J. *Gagnier wrote a five-movement *Suite* with orchestra (1945). Harry *Somers' *Suite* with chamber orchestra (1949) was recorded by the *CBC SO under Geoffrey *Waddington (RCI 86) and, with Judy Loman as soloist, by the same ensemble conducted by Walter *Susskind (Col MS 6285). Michel *Perrault composed *Margoton* (1954) and *Jeux de Quartes* (1961), two works with orchestra. John *Weinzweig's *Concerto* for harp and chamber orchestra (1967, recorded by Loman for the CBC) is among his most important works and has been played in Canada and in Europe. Robert *Turner composed *Little Suite* (1957) and *Fantasy and Festivity* (1970), two works for solo harp. In 1972 George *Fiala wrote a *Concertino Canadese* for four harps, dedicated to the Soviet quartet Chitari Arpi. R. Murray *Schafer's *The Crown of Ariadne* for harp and percussion was commissioned and premiered 5 Mar 1979 by Judy Loman. Her recording of the work (1979, Aquitaine MS 90570) subsequently won a *Juno Award.

See also Instruments: medieval, renaissance, baroque: 1 / Building. (GP)

Harpsichord building. Though harpsichords were produced in Boston and Philadelphia in the 18th century, no such activity seems to have taken place in Canada. The instruments advertised by F.H. *Glackemeyer and others in late-18th-century Quebec almost certainly were imports, including a single-manual instrument built by Kirkman & Sons of London. When the harpsichord revival started ca 1910 with Arnold Dolmetsch's work at the Chickering Piano Co in Boston, again there was no parallel activity in Canada. In the 1950s the extraordinary increase in popularity of baroque and pre-baroque music, however, and a growing interest in hearing such music on the instrument for which it was written, inevitably suggested a need and pointed to a market. At about the same time harpsichord building was spurred by the availability of US 'kits' for assembly, by the arrival of European builders, and finally by the return of a few young Canadian craftsmen, most of whom had been apprenticed to US builders. Builders and designers active in Canada in the 1970s included Jan *Albarda, Wolfgang *Kater, Gaston Ouellet of Île-Perrot (near Montreal), *Sabathil and Son Ltd (builders of the first known double-ended harpsichord), and John Hanaby and Matthew Redsell, both of Toronto. Others were John Bright of London, Ont, who has built some instruments and in 1971 began assembling Zuckermann (New York) kits; and Edward *Turner, a builder of exact replicas of earlier instruments. Hubert *Bédard, who produces kit harpsichords but is best known as a restorer, moved to Europe in 1967.

BIBLIOGRAPHY
'Gaston Ouellet est passé maître dans l'art de construire des clavecins,' *Musique periodique*, vol 1, Dec 1976
Conlogue, Ray. '18th-century craft alive on Queen Street,' Toronto *Globe and Mail*, 31 May 1977
Ainslie, Barry. 'The rebirth of a delicate sound,' *Fugue*, Jan 1978 (MK)

Harpsichord composition. In Canada, as in Europe, the piano had eclipsed the harpsichord by the beginning of the 19th century. If there were any early keyboard compositions written by Canadians with the harpsichord in mind, they have not survived.

In the 20th century, the harpsichord regained some of its former popularity, and Canadian musicians slowly rediscovered it. By the 1950s its use was accepted in Canada, especially in the larger centres, as preferable to the piano for the performance of music originally written for the instrument – though eloquent piano performances of Bach's harpsichord music by Glenn *Gould and by Rosalyn Tureck kept many from closing their minds on the subject. However, as every important musical organization or university music department moved to procure a harpsichord (if it had not one already), original Canadian compositions for the instrument began to appear. Of 'pioneer' works of the 1950s, Gilles *Tremblay's *Trois-huit* (1950) and Clermont *Pépin's *Trois Pièces pour 'La Légende dorée'* (1956) were designated 'harpsichord or piano,' though R. Murray *Schafer's *Concerto for Harpsichord and 8 Wind Instruments* (1954) and Kelsey *Jones' *Sonata da Camera* (1957, for flute, oboe, and harpsichord) were unequivocal. Jones, the harpsichord in the *Baroque Trio of Montreal, later wrote a *Prelude, Fughetta, and Finale* (1963) for strings and harpsichord and a *Sonata da Chiesa* (1967) for his trio. Among other notable pieces of the 1960s and 1970s are Barbara *Pentland's *Canzona* (1961, for flute, oboe and harpsichord) and *Ostinato and Dance for Harpsichord* (1962); Gabriel *Charpentier's *Suite* (from his incidental music for Molière's *Le Bourgeois Gentilhomme*, 1964), *Trois Ricercars* (1966, for oboe and harpsichord), and *Grande Chaconne* (1971, from his music for Brecht's *Galileo Galilei*); John *Beckwith's *Circle, with Tangents* (1967, for harpsichord and 13 strings); John *Fodi's *Sonata* and *Toccata* (both 1968) and *Divisions II* (1972, for piano and harpsichord); Jean *Papineau-Couture's *Nocturnes* (1969, for flute, clarinet, violin, cello, harpsichord, guitar, and percussion) and *Dyarchie* (1971); Bernard *Naylor's *On Mrs. Arabella Hunt Singing* (1970, for soprano, viola da gamba, and harpsichord); and Rudolf *Komorous' *At Your Memory the Transparent Tears Fall Like Molten Lead* (1976, for viola da gamba and harpsichord).

No attempt has been made in these works to compose on archaistic lines. Rather, the composers have attempted to exploit the textures and sonorities of harpsichord sound in the various 20th-century idioms in which they work. Of all those composers mentioned, Charpentier probably has been the most persistent user of the harpsichord. Besides the works mentioned, his *Quand nous serons heureux* (1968–76), *Trois Oraisons* (1971), and *Processional* (1974) and much of his incidental music, contain important harpsichord parts.

Though the list of Canadian works for harpsichord had not reached great proportions by 1979, the surge of instrument makers in the 1970s and the increasing currency of harpsichord playing, combined with the presence of outstanding harpsichordists in avant-garde performing groups (eg, Patrick *Wedd in Vancouver's *Days Months and Years to Come) was expected to swell it.

See also Harpsichord playing and teaching.

SW

Greta Kraus and Arnold Walter performing harpsichord music

Harpsichord playing and teaching. Louis *Jolliet, during his studies in France 1667–8 may have been the first Canadian to learn to play keyboard instruments. It is unlikely however that there was a harpsichord in Quebec on which he could play. Possibly Pierre de Rigaud, Marquis de Vaudreuil, the last governor of New France, owned a harpsichord, and it is certain that such instruments existed in Quebec in the 1780s when a Mr Davis, a Mr Hartog, 'heretofore Music Master at Montreal,' Signor Gaetano Franceschini, and Guillaume *Mechtler advertised as teachers. In 1780 Davis offered to teach in his home, so as to accommodate those who did not own instruments. In 1788 Woolsey & O'Hara advertised 'an elegant Harpsicord [sic] Piano Forte on a new construction,' and Frédéric *Glackemeyer offered to sell harpsichord strings and to repair and tune instruments. In 1791 a single-manual harpsichord built by Kirkman of London was auctioned at Quebec and two years later Glackemeyer advertised a used instrument. It may be assumed that the supply of harpsichords in Montreal, Halifax, and other cities was similar.

With the rise in popularity of the pianoforte during the 19th century the harpsichord fell into disuse. It began to make a comeback in the 1880s when Érard, Pleyel and Gaveau in Paris, Chickering in Boston, and Dolmetsch in England (and in Boston and Paris as consultant to Chickering and Gaveau) gradually improved its design for modern use. In Canada in 1912 a harpsichordist named Laura Walker won a scholarship (for studies in Berlin) from the *Ladies' Morning Musical Club of Montreal. On 21 Jan 1926 the world-renowned Wanda Landowska made what appears to have been her Canadian debut in a concert sponsored by the *Women's Musical Club of Toronto. Landowska returned to Toronto during the spring of 1943 to perform, for CBC broadcast, the modern premieres of five C.P.E. Bach keyboard concertos which had been discovered in Toronto and were authenticated by Adolph *Koldofsky. Among other harpsichordists of note who have played in Canada are Huguette Dreyfus, Albert Fuller, Igor Kipnis, Gustav Leonhardt, Françoise Petit, Daniel Pinkham, Colin Tilney, Fernando Valenti, and Robert Veyron-Lacroix.

In the autumn of 1931 the T. Eaton Co bought a two-manual, seven-pedal Pleyel harpsichord for *Eaton Auditorium in Toronto. The instrument was inaugurated 2 Feb 1932 in a Canadian debut performance by Frances Duncan Barwick (b Kalamazoo, Mich, 30 Jan 1909, a pupil of Marguerite Delcourt in Paris and the Dolmetsches in England). Barwick purchased the Eaton Pleyel during the early 1940s and used it to introduce the harpsichord to audiences in Ottawa and Montreal. On 30 Jan 1945 she played Bach's *Concerto in D Minor* and *Brandenburg Concerto No. 5* with the *Little Symphony of Montreal. She continued to be active in chamber music in Ottawa, her residence after 1939.

In 1938 Greta *Kraus (a pupil of Hans Weisse and Heinrich Schenker in Vienna) arrived in Toronto and soon established a reputation as a soloist, chamber musician, accompanist, and teacher. The first to play harpsichord (rather than piano) continuo for the *Toronto Mendelssohn Choir's Bach performances during the 1940s, Kraus was for many years Canada's best-known and most active harpsichordist.

Kenneth *Gilbert, a pupil of Ruggero Gerlin and Gustav Leonhardt, is a Canadian-born player and scholar of international reputation who has recorded the complete harpsichord works of Rameau and Couperin, and edited the complete harpsichord works of Couperin for the French publisher Heugel, as well as works by other composers.

During the second half of the 20th century the number of Canadian harpsichordists grew noticeably. Denis Bédard, Hubert *Bédard, Douglas *Bodle, George *Brough, Hermel Bruneau, Glenn *Gould (on occasion), John Grew, Martha Hagen, Kelsey and Rosabelle *Jones, Michael Kearns, André *Laberge, Bernard, Geneviève, and Mireille *Lagacé, Hugh *McLean, Kenneth *Meek, Lucien and Réjean *Poirier, Denis *Regnaud, Donald Thomson, Arnold *Walter, Patrick *Wedd, and Gerald *Wheeler have been heard as soloists and in chamber groups. Bodle and Wedd both studied with Kraus. (In 1959 Bodle and Kraus performed a Bach *Concerto* for two harpsichords with the *CBC SO.) Regnaud and Bernard Lagacé were pupils of Isolde Ahlgrimm in Vienna. Bruneau (b St-Félix-de-Valois 23 Apr 1940) studied and later taught at the CMQ and toured 1972–3 and 1973–4 for JMC.

Many younger players have become noteworthy. Martha Brickman (b Montreal 23 Dec 1949), a pupil of Vignanelli in Rome and Gilbert in Montreal, has won awards, has performed in Canada, Europe, and the USA, and has taught harpsichord at the *CMM and *Laval U. Joyce Redekop-Fink (b Winkler, Man, 13 Feb 1941) was a pupil of Irmgard Lechner at Detmold and Ralph Kirkpatrick at Yale, and a member 1963–70 of the *Manitoba University Consort. The English-born Edward Norman came to Canada in 1967 and has been active in Halifax and Vancouver. Bradford Tracey (b Sydney, NS, 7 Jul 1951), a pupil of Rolf Junghanns, has recorded, given recitals in Canada, Europe, and the USA, and performed on CBC radio. Valerie Weeks (b Toronto 6 Dec 1954), a pupil of Gustav Leonhardt and Jean-Claude Zehnder in Europe and Greta Kraus in Toronto, was the grand-prize winner in the *CBC Talent Festival in 1978 (the first year in which harpsichordists were admitted to that competition) and has performed with the Toronto early-music group Tafelmusik. The US-born John Whitelaw (b 1943, a pupil of Kenneth Gilbert) resided in Canada 1967–71 and won the *Prix d'Europe in 1970.

See also Harpsichord building; Harpsichord composition; Instrument collections; Instruments: medieval, renaissance, and baroque: 2 / Playing and teaching.

HARRIS, C.L.M. (Charles Lewis Matthew). Conductor, organist, educator, composer, b Staningly, Yorkshire, England, 1863, d Port Huron, Mich, January 1925; B MUS (Trinity College, Toronto) 1891, D MUS (Trinity College, Toronto) 1898. Taken to Toronto in 1869, Harris began organ study with a Dr Clark in 1870 and took his first organ post at the age of eight at Parliament Street Methodist Church. While organist-choirmaster 1885–1905 at St Paul's Presbyterian Church in Hamilton, Ont, Harris studied at the *U of Trinity College with Arthur E. *Fisher and Frederick J. Karn. He went on to be organist-choirmaster 1905–13 at Erskine Presbyterian Church, Hamilton, and 1915–25 at St George's Episcopal Church, Port Huron, Mich. Founder and conductor 1887–1901 of the Harris Orchestral Club (a 43-piece ensemble which in 1915 became the Hamilton Orchestral Club), he conducted some 35 concerts, many with US or European soloists, during 14 successful seasons. The repertoire included music of Wagner, Beethoven, Haydn, Saint-Saëns, and Schubert. Between 1890 and 1908 Harris also conducted various Hamilton choral and operatic societies. He was director 1892–6 of the Wesleyan Ladies College in Hamilton and also founded, and directed 1897–1907, the Hamilton Cons of Music (*RHCM). He composed songs and an aid to keyboard practice, *Scales, Chords and Arpeggios* (Hamilton 1914). (FAH)

HARRIS, Neil (Foster). Composer, arranger, conductor, b Young, southeast of Saskatoon, 21 Apr 1925; BA (Saskatchewan) 1947, B ARCHITECT (Manitoba) 1968. His studies in piano with Josephine Stableford and in composition with Murray *Adaskin, both in Saskatoon, were separated by a period of employment 1947–50 in Toronto and Ottawa dance bands. He worked during the 1950s for CKCK TV, Regina, and produced musical variety programs 1958–61 for CBC TV in Winnipeg. In 1960 he formed the Neil Harris Singers, a 6-to-12-voice ensemble heard 1965–9 on 'Songs of Faith' and other CBC programs, and on the recordings *Songs of Faith* (1969, CBC LM 63/Cap SN 8001) and *Love in a Cold Climate* (1974, EmmCee EC-107). Freelancing after 1961, Harris conducted and wrote incidental music for productions at the Manitoba Theatre Centre and conducted musicals at *Rainbow Stage. In 1973 he was a guest conductor of the *Winnipeg SO.

Harris' compositions include *Prairie Cantata* (1949); *If You Please* (1950, U of Saskatchewan student revue); *Portrait of a City* (1952, a pageant written for Saskatoon's 70th anniversary); *Suite of Dances* for woodwinds (1953); *Saskatchewan, HA!* (1955, written while Harris was director of musical production for the province's 50th anniversary); *Conversations* (1967, commissioned for an Anglican Church conference in Brandon and later heard on CBC TV); *Rhapsody for the Disgusted* for woodwinds (1973); *Holiday String Quartet* (1975); *Fantasy on a Sentimental Theme* for concert band (1976); and *Meaningful Conversations and Other Illusions* (ca 1979, a series of songs). Though he graduated in architecture in 1968 he continued his musical activities. He began teaching at Red River Community College (Winnipeg) in 1970, and became head of the college's Dept of Creative Communications in 1976. He is an affiliate of PRO Canada.

BIBLIOGRAPHY

Varley, Christopher. 'Neil Harris,' *MSc*, 239, Jan–Feb 1968 (CC)

Frederick Harris Music Co Ltd. Publishing firm founded in London ca 1900, established in Canada in 1910, and controlled after 1944 by the *U of Toronto. Frederick Harris (ca 1866–1945) founded his catalogue on copyrights purchased from C.J. Roeder, Leipzig. He also acquired the British Empire rights to many popular instrumental pieces and songs by composers as disparate as Sibelius and Carrie Jacobs-Bond (whose 'A Perfect Day' sold 11 million copies). Among his lucrative copyrights were Dvořák's *Humoreske*, Leoncavallo's *I Pagliacci*, and Elgar's *Salut d'amour*. Harris first opened a Toronto office to protect his copyrights in Canada, and then entered into a Canadian partnership with (Oliver) Hawkes & Son of London. Hawkes & Harris represented the parent English companies in Canada until Hawkes' death in 1923. The store, which also sold violins and music of other publishers, was considered one of the largest in the Commonwealth and had a staff of over 30. The firm's imprint usually appears on Frederick Harris copyrights, but there was a plate-number series (H & H) of some 50 publications, including an edition of *'The Maple Leaf For Ever' and several songs by D.D. *Slater. On Hawkes' death Harris acquired his partner's shares, and then moved (as the Frederick Harris Co) to Oakville, near Toronto. He discontinued the sale of instruments and made the English office a branch of the Oakville headquarters.

Harris' interest in music education led to an association with the TCM (*RCMT) when he published the conservatory's introductory piano books in 1916 and vocal studies in 1924. By 1944 he had become the TCM's exclusive publisher. Also in 1944 he turned over to the TCM his shares in the firm (which had become a limited company in 1941), stipulating that the profits be used for music scholarships and bursaries. (Though most of the awards have gone to RCMT students, some have been given to *Western Ontario Cons students.) By the mid-1970s RCMT publications (including an LP series of piano examination pieces issued in 1972) constituted 25 per cent of the company's business, while other Harris publications made up 40 per cent and foreign catalogues 35 per cent. Harris publications include much choral music (most of it suitable for small, non-professional choirs) and piano music. W.O. *Forsyth, Sir Ernest *MacMillan, Adelmo *Melecci, David *Ouchterlony, Godfrey *Ridout, John *Weinzweig, and Healey *Willan are represented in the catalogue. In 1971 the London office was reduced to subpublishing status under the control of Alfred Lengnick, as part of a 10-year agreement which established Harris as the North American agent for Lengnick's publications. The Harris firm also distributes Berklee Press and Crescendo Books (both of Boston) and Cambiata Press (Conway, Arizona). During the 1960s it represented Novello (London) and Bärenreiter (Kassel, Germany). A publisher affiliate of PRO Canada, the Harris company established Harmuse (a publisher member of CAPAC) in 1973.

Though untrained in music, Frederick Harris did compose the melody of the waltz *Sunset on the St. Lawrence* (1910), which he whistled to an arranger. The result was published under the pseudonym Maxine Heller.

An expert in copyright law, Harris successfully fought the importation of pirated editions from the USA. He was equally successful, however, in publishing British copyright material which the original publishers, unfamiliar with Canadian law, had thought were protected in Canada. General manager of the company until his death, Harris was succeeeded by R.C.F. (Reginald) Collier, and Collier (who died in 1970) by W. Ray Stephens. Stephens, who became the managing director in 1975 and president in 1979, had joined the company in 1960 as sales manager after serving 1947–60 as manager of the music department of Boosey & Hawkes. He was president 1972–3 of the *CMPA.

BIBLIOGRAPHY

'The Frederick Harris Music Co. Limited,' *Recorder*, vol 7, Nov–Dec 1964

'Frederick Harris lists largest inventory,' *CanComp*, 7, Mar 1966 (MWl)

HARRISON, Charles (Franklin). Lyricist, songwriter, publisher, b Hamilton, Ont, 24 Aug 1883, naturalized US 1927, d Hamilton 11 Nov 1955. He was the son of a prima donna (known alternatively as Mme Yulisse and Marie Harrison) in the Carl Rosa Opera Company. Harrison began writing songs while he was a banker in Vancouver and published his first efforts through his own C.F. Harrison and Co, Vancouver and Toronto. These included 'The Best Old Flag on Earth' (1914) and 'My Own Dear Canada' (1917). The latter sold over 10,000 copies in the Vancouver area alone. A collaboration with Fred R. Weaver, 'Keep on Smiling' (1919), was published by Weaver and Harrison, Vancouver. In 1919, with Fred Brownhold in Chicago, Harrison formed the Ted Browne Music Co. In 1939 the company was bought by Plymouth Music. By 1945 Harrison had collaborated with various US composers on over 100 published songs, including the popular 'I'm Drifting Back to Dreamland' (Mayfair Music 1922), 'How Do You Do' (George Simon/Shawnee Press 1924), theme-song of the Happiness Boys, and the widely recorded 'When Summer Is Gone' (Harms 1928). (HK, EBM)

HARRISON, (Gilbert) **Glen**. Educator, choir conductor, tenor, b Winnipeg 3 Jun 1921; BA (Manitoba) 1950, AMM (Manitoba) 1960, M ED (Manitoba) 1973. His main teachers were Nina *Dempsey and Ruby Moir. He taught school music until 1961 when he became co-ordinator of music in the Seven Oaks school district of West Kildonan, Winnipeg. In 1973, for the Manitoba Dept of Education, he began supervising radio and TV school broadcasts heard in western Canada. In 1978 he became music consultant for Winnipeg School Division No. 1. With Beth *Douglas and Colin Walley he was co-author of the junior high school textbooks *Fanfare Acts I and II* (Toronto 1969). He was the tenor soloist 1951–3 at Young United Church, and became choirmaster in 1956 at Westminster United Church, where, in addition to services, he has presented Haydn's *Nelson Mass*, Vivaldi's *Gloria*, and the Brahms *Requiem*. Harrison began a long association with *Rainbow Stage in 1954 as a member of the chorus. He continued 1955–63 as chorusmaster and 1963–72 as music director. He was named musical co-ordinator in 1973. (RG)

HARRISON, John W.F. Organist, conductor, b Bristol 1847, d Toronto 29 May 1935. He began his training in piano, organ, and voice under George Riseley, the organist of Bristol Cathedral, then studied organ in London and singing in Naples. He arrived in Canada in 1874, living at first in Montreal where he was organist at St George's Anglican Church. He moved in 1879 to Ottawa, where he became the organist-choirmaster of Christ Church Cathedral and music director of the Ladies' College. He reorganized the Ottawa Philharmonic Society (disbanded in the previous decade) in 1880 and conducted it in a number of major oratorio performances. He is credited with the first Canadian performances of Mendelssohn's incidental music to the Sophocles dramas *Antigone* and *Oedipus at Colonos*. In 1886 Harrison became organist at Jarvis St Baptist Church, Toronto. At the Church of St Simon-the-Apostle 1888–1916 he conducted a widely admired choir of 40 boys and men. He also conducted the Whitby Choral Society and the *Musical Union of Toronto. For three years, 1892–4 he directed the annual festivals of the Church Choir Assn, an organization of Anglican clergy and choirmasters (over 700 singers from 25 Toronto churches) of which he was president. In addition he was president (1893) of the *Canadian Society of Musicians. He taught organ and piano at the Ontario Ladies' College in Whitby and was an examiner for the TCM and the U of Toronto. His wife was the composer and writer Susie Francis *Harrison ('Seranus'). He himself was an amateur painter. Little is known of Harrison's later years.

BIBLIOGRAPHY

'J.W.F. Harrison,' *MJ*, 20, Sep–Oct 1888 (WLk)

HARRISON, Lance (Easton). Saxophonist, clarinetist, banjoist, singer, entertainer, b Vancouver 23 Jun ca 1920. At first a banjoist and guitarist, Harrison switched to saxophone in his teens and played in the Vancouver dance bands of Trevor Page, Sandy DeSantis, and Dal *Richards. After service during World War II in RCAF dance and show bands, he was a sideman for over 20 years in Vancouver pit or dance bands and subsequently was the leader of a trio at the Attic. In 1950 he also began leading his own dixieland band, heard on the CBC's 'Hotel Downbeat' (radio), 'The Twenties Roar' (radio), 'Some of These Days' (TV, summers 1961–6), and various jazz radio programs. It also performed in clubs (eg, Pillar and Post) and on the Vancouver Island ferries. Members of the band have included the trumpeters Stew Barnett or Don Clark, the trombonist Jack Fulton, the pianist Bud Henderson, and the bassist Stan Johnson. The band is heard on the LPs *The Vancouver Scene* (1965, RCA PCS-1043), *The Lance Harrison Dixieland Band* (1967, RCI 263, recorded in concert at Expo 67), and *Happy Jazz* (1972, Water St 1636). Harrison is a convincing proponent of the dixieland idiom; his tenor saxophone style reflects the influence of Eddie Miller. Harrison was featured in the CBC TV special 'A Visit to New Orleans,' filmed during a trip to the birthplace of jazz in 1971.

BIBLIOGRAPHY

Norris, John. 'Lance Harrison,' *Canadian Stereo Guide*, Summer 1972 (MM, BSm)

HARRISON, Robin (Keith). Pianist, teacher, b London 28 Jul 1932. He studied 1952–5 with Harold Craxton at the RAM and 1955–6 with Carlo Zecchi in Rome and Ilona Kabos in Salzburg. He performed in the Sir Henry Wood Promenade Concerts and on British, Dutch, and South American radio before moving to Canada in 1970 to teach piano and piano literature at the *U of Saskatchewan, Saskatoon. In Canada Harrison was a member of the *Canadian Arts Trio 1971–4, has given solo recitals throughout Alberta, Manitoba, and Ontario, and toured 1976–7 for the *JMC. He has broadcast as soloist with the chamber orchestras of CBC Calgary and CBC Montreal. A recital he gave at *Eaton Auditorium, Toronto, also was broadcast on the CBC in 1979, the same year that the U of Saskatchewan sponsored his first recording, *Robin Harrison Plays Chopin*, produced in Saskatoon by Studio West. Describing a Harrison performance, Murray *Adaskin noted his 'formidable technique which permits him to sing with the greatest ease and beauty' (*Canada Music Book*, Spring–Summer 1971). Harrison's compositions include a *Bagatelle for piano*.

BIBLIOGRAPHY

Burt, Eric O. 'Saskatoon classical pianist cuts record,' Saskatoon *Star-Phoenix*, 9 Mar 1979 (GW)

HARRISON, Susie (Susan) Frances (b Riley). Composer, writer, pianist, b Toronto 24 Feb 1859, d there 5 May 1935. Wife of J.W.F. *Harrison. She was educated in Toronto and Montreal, studied piano with Frederic Boscovitz in Toronto, and performed as an accompanist and soloist. The author of at least six volumes of poetry and three novels, she also wrote a number of songs and keyboard works published in England and the *USA under the name Seranus. Other songs were published in England under the name Gilbert King. Her compositions include 'Address of Welcome to Lord Landsowne' (1883), written while she lived in Ottawa; 'An Old-Fashioned Love Song' (ca 1885); and *Trois Esquisses canadiennes*: 'Dialogue,' 'Nocturne,' and 'Chant du voyage' (Nordheimer 1887), piano arrangements of French-Canadian airs. Her three-act opera *Pipandor*, with libretto by F.A. Dixon of Ottawa, also incorporated French-Canadian folk songs. Harrison was considered an authority on French-Canadian folk materials and often gave illustrated lectures on the subject. She was the music critic of Toronto's *The Week* from December 1886 to June 1887 under her pen-name, Seranus; she also was editor in the 1900s of the TCM's *Conservatory Monthly* and contributed to the later *Conservatory Quarterly Review*.

WRITINGS

'Historical sketch of music in Canada,' *Canada: An Encyclopedia of the Country*, vol 4, ed J.C. Hopkins (Toronto 1898)

'On French-Canadian folksong,' *MCan*, vol 2, Jan 1908

'Canada,' *The Imperial History and Encyclopedia of Music*, vol 3: *History of Foreign Music*, ed W.L. Hubbard (New York ca 1909)

BIBLIOGRAPHY

Wetherald, A. Ethelwyn. 'Some Canadian literary women – I Seranus,' *The Week*, vol 5, Mar 1888 EK

HARRISS, Charles A.E. (Albert Edwin). Composer, impresario, educator, organist-choirmaster, conductor, b London, midnight 16–17 Dec 1862, d Ottawa 31 Jul 1929; B MUS (Toronto) 1900, hon FRAM 1905, hon D MUS (Cantuar) 1905. Son of Edwin Harriss, an English musician who served 1883–6 as organist-choirmaster at St James the Apostle Church in Montreal, Charles was educated 1873–5 in the English cathedral tradition under Sir Frederick Ouseley at St Michael's College, Tenbury, and subsequently held posts as organist and choir director in Reading and Welshpool. On Ouseley's recommendation Harriss was appointed organist at St Alban the Martyr, Ottawa, in 1882. He did not stay long in Ottawa, however, but moved to Montreal in 1883 as organist-choirmaster at Christ Church Cathedral. He succeeded his father as organist-choirmaster 1886–94 at St James the Apostle. With the elder Harriss he gave joint recitals in Montreal in the 1880s, founded a glee and madrigal society, and taught privately. His marriage in 1897 to a woman of wealth enabled Harriss to indulge his talent for organizing grandiose musical schemes and festivals, his propensity for extensive travel, and his desire to have his compositions published. In 1900 Mrs Harriss purchased Earnscliffe, the Ottawa home of Sir John A. MacDonald, which became the Harriss' permanent residence and the location of lavish entertaining. Appointed honorary director of examinations of the AB of the RSM in 1903, Harriss also served 1904–7 as the first director of the *McGill Cons, a non-salaried position.

An ambitious and indefatigable musician whose lifelong purpose was the promotion of musical reciprocity within the British Empire (according to Percy Scholes, 'a veritable musical Napoleon – always engaged in a tonal campaign somewhere'), Harriss organized concerts in many

Charles A.E. Harriss

Canadian communities where music still was a luxury. He arranged Emma *Albani's 1896 cross-Canada tour, brought Dan Godfrey's Band from England to tour Canada (80 concerts) and the US in 1899, and brought many British artists to North America. He initiated, and planned for two years, the extensive 1903 *Cycle of Musical Festivals. He formed a Montreal choir, the Philharmonic Union, that was active in 1906 and 1907 and performed his 'choric idyll,' *Pan*, with the Pittsburgh Orchestra. Harriss also organized the 1906 British Canadian Music Festival in London which featured a performance of *Pan* with Pauline *Donalda, the Canadian tour of Sir Frederick Bridge in conjunction with the Festival of English Cathedral Music in May 1908, the tour of the Sheffield Choir under Henry Coward later that year, and the tour of His Majesty's Scots Guard Band in 1922. In London he instigated the Empire Day Concerts in 1907. In 1909 he founded the 4500-voice Imperial Choir, made up of several large London choirs, which formed the nucleus of the 10,000-voice choir heard in those concerts in 1911 and again on the occasion of the Peace celebrations in 1919. He also took 2000 members of the Imperial Choir to perform at the 1913 Ghent Exhibition. Harriss travelled extensively 1909–10 in Australia and South Africa, lecturing, conducting, and organizing the Musical Festival of the Empire, a world music tour of Australia, New Zealand, South Africa, Canada, and the USA that took place in 1911. The Sheffield Choir and Henry Coward played a prominent role in this festival, and performed in Canada. (Edward Elgar toured with the choir in the USA and Toronto. He conducted the *Dream of Gerontius* in *Massey Hall on 4 Apr 1911.) Harriss' last major appearance came in 1924 on his appointment as music director of the British Empire Exhibition in Wembley (London).

Harriss enjoyed the rare privilege of having his compositions performed not only in his adopted country but also throughout the British Empire during his lifetime. His first major work, the cantata *Daniel before the King* (1884), was performed 18 Apr 1890 in Canada and published that same year by Schirmer. Other works, all of which show a solid English foundation supporting traditional and contemporary continental influences, include the opera **Torquil* (1894), *Festival Mass* (Boosey 1901), *Coronation Mass for Edward VII* (Boosey 1903), *Pan* (Novello 1904), the ballad *The Sands of Dee* (Novello 1906), and the ode *The Crowning of the King* (Novello 1911). His comic opera *The Admiral* was performed in 1902, his *Canadian Fantasie* for orchestra in 1904. Over 50 songs, anthems, and keyboard works were published. Some manuscripts are held by the McGill U Archives and other papers are held at the NL of C and the PAC.

BIBLIOGRAPHY
Trudel, Tancrède. 'Charles A.E. Harriss,' *Canada Artistique*, vol 1, Dec 1890
'The great musical organizer,' *MCan*, vol 3, Nov 1908
'Dr. Charles Harriss,' *MT*, vol 50, 1 Apr 1909
Mackenzie, Sir Alexander. *A Musician's Narrative* (London 1927)
Turbide, Nadia. 'Charles A.E. Harriss: the McGill years,' unpubl MMA thesis (McGill 1976)
McGill U Archives. RG 39
NL of C. Papers, published works. 13 vols (1882–1927)
PAC. MG 30 (D16)
Musical Red Book (NT)

Hart House. Conceived by Vincent *Massey as a university social, cultural, and recreational centre whose members 'may discover within its walls the true education that is to be found in good fellowship, in friendly disputation and debate, in the conversation of wise and earnest men, in music, pictures and the play, in the casual book' (excerpt from The Founders' Prayer). Designed by the Toronto architects Henry Sproatt and Ernest Rolph, and located in downtown Toronto on the *U of Toronto's St George campus, this gift to the university from the Massey Foundation opened 11 Nov 1919 after eight years in construction. It was named for Hart Massey, grandfather of Vincent. Membership was limited to male students, graduates, and faculty members until 1972, when women were admitted. Hart House's facilities include a music room, rooms for listening to records, a theatre, and the Great Hall, which serves as both dining and concert hall. Upright pianos are provided for use by Hart House members generally, Steinway grands for use by those with advanced training (at least RCMT Grade 10). Activities at Hart House have been co-ordinated by a number of standing committees (including a music committee), and by various clubs, all of which report to the Board of Stewards chaired by the warden of Hart House. The committees are made up of students, graduates, and faculty, with the students in the majority.

Most music events (over 125 recitals and concerts in 1979–80) are arranged by the music committee (though the house committee organizes dances, including the annual New Year's Eve Ball). The relationships of the *Hart House Glee Club, the *Hart House Orchestra, and the *Hart House String Quartet to Hart House itself are described in separate articles. Series of recitals, and of Sunday evening concerts in the Great Hall, long-standing traditions at Hart House, were initiated by the second warden, Burgon Bickersteth, and by J. Campbell *McInnes. The first Sunday evening concert, 12 Nov 1922, featured the pianists Reginald *Stewart and Colin *McPhee, a 30-voice choir, and a six-piece instrumental group conducted by McInnes. Other performers over the years at these concerts have included the *Festival Singers, Maureen *Forrester, Glenn *Gould, Alberto *Guerrero, Elizabeth Benson *Guy, Betty-Jean *Hagen, Viggo *Kihl, Lois *Marshall, Zara *Nelsova, Kathleen *Parlow, Jan *Rubeš, Leo *Smith, and Elie *Spivak. In 1975 in a special Sunday afternoon concert series Anton *Kuerti presented the complete cycle of Beethoven piano sonatas. Student and professional musicians have given informal noon-hour and afternoon recitals in the music room and the east common room. The *Conservatory String Quartet gave performances on the Hart House viols, a chest of six viols purchased ca 1930 by the Massey Foundation and the *Arts and Letters Club. The viols became the sole property of Hart House in 1935 (see Instrument collections). Their use is restricted to experienced 'string musicians for rendering music appropriate to them.' They have been used by the Toronto Renaissance Quintet, led by Wolfgang Grunsky, and by the Hart House Consort, led by Peggie *Sampson.

While there was an early reluctance to include jazz in the music programs at Hart House, by the late 1950s regular jazz concerts had been initiated, and among the noted artists who subsequently appeared were Moe *Koffman and Oscar *Peterson.

In 1958 the CBC began to tape concerts in the Great Hall for broadcast under the title 'University Celebrity Series'; these featured such performers as Rudolf Firkusny, Benno Moiseiwitsch, Andrés Segovia, Janos Starker, and Joan Sutherland. The series was successful and the CBC continued to use the hall. In the autumn of 1979 the music committee and CBC Toronto marked the 60th anniversary of Hart House with a series of four concerts featuring the *Hidy-*Ozolins-*Tsutsumi Trio, Lois Marshall and Greta *Kraus, Adrienne *Shannon, and the Elmer *Iseler Singers with the Toronto Brass.

The 459-seat Hart House Theatre, independent and under a separate administration, has been used by a number of college and faculty groups, including the early *Royal Cons Opera School, for operas, musicals, and plays. As music director for the theatre 1919–25 Healey *Willan composed the incidental music for fourteen productions, beginning 22 Dec 1919 with the premiere of *The Chester Mysteries* and including *Love's Labour's Lost* (1920), *Cymbeline* (1921), *The Tempest* (1922), and *The Winter's Tale* (1925). The *Women's Musical Club of Toronto concert series was given 1929–42 in the theatre.

The Soldiers' Tower of Hart House was dedicated in 1924 and a carillon installed in 1927 (see Carillons).

BIBLIOGRAPHY
Montagnes, Ian. *An Uncommon Fellowship: The Story of Hart House* (Toronto 1969) NM (KW, PW)

Hart House Glee Club. Male student choir formed in 1933 at the *U of Toronto by its first conductor Allan Sly. Most of its members came from faculties other than music. Initially known as the Glee Club, it gave its first concert 8 Feb 1934. Subsequent conductors included Charles *Peaker 1934–43, 1945–50, Ward McAdam 1950–8, Rowland *Pack 1958–62, Walter *Kemp 1962–3, and Walter Barnes 1963–72. The club's repertoire encompassed works from the 16th century to the 20th – notable works from the 19th being Brahms' *Alto Rhapsody* and Schubert's *Song of the Spirits over the Water*. Folksongs and spirituals were also a specialty. In 1935 the choir adopted the name Hart House Glee Club and gave the first of its annual concerts in the Hart House Sunday evening series. Thereafter, until 1970, it gave the final concert in that series each season. It also participated 1938–61 in annual Christmas concerts broadcast by the CBC. For two years (November 1943 to October 1945) the club suspended activities. Revived after the war, it made many tours in Ontario and was a regular host to, and participated in, tri-university concerts with Cornell, Colgate, Buffalo State, Princeton, McMaster, and Guelph universities. It also made recordings for *Hallmark, *Columbia, Arc, and other labels. It appeared at *Expo 67. While the number of singers had fluctuated (from 30 to 130), by 1970 a declining membership signalled the end, and in 1972 the club was disbanded. (NM)

Hart House Orchestra. Chamber orchestra founded in July 1954 by Boyd *Neel – then dean of the *RCMT – along the lines of his famous English group the Boyd Neel Orchestra. The 18 strings and 4 woodwinds of the new group were reduced ca 1957 to 13 strings, with supplementary players for specific works. In turn, John *Dembeck, Albert *Pratz, Andrew Benac, Clifford *Evens, and David *Zafer served as concertmasters. The repertoire ranged the 17th, 18th, and 20th centuries and included commissioned works from Maurice *Blackburn (*Suite for Strings*, 1960), Keith *Bissell (*Three Pieces*, 1961), Harry *Freedman (*Fantasy and Allegro*, 1962), and Morris *Surdin (*Concerto for Accordion and Strings*, 1966, premiered by Joseph *Macerollo); premieres also included Norman *Symonds' *Pastel Blue* in 1963.

The orchestra gave its first concert at Tillsonburg, Ont, 14 Oct 1954, its CBC radio debut 27 October, and its Toronto debut at *Eaton Auditorium 25 November. Concert series followed at *Hart House, and individual programs were presented in other Toronto halls and in various Ontario centres. In 1955 the orchestra played an important role in the *Stratford Festival's first large-scale music program, staying in residence for a month to give the premieres of *Willan's *A Song of Welcome* with Lois *Marshall as soloist and *Morawetz' *Divertimento for Strings*, to perform orchestral programs which included the six *Brandenburg Concertos* of Bach and Godfrey *Ridout's *Two Études*, and to accompany the *Festival Singers and several solo artists including Glenn *Gould and Isaac Stern. In 1958 the orchestra represented the country on Canada Day (25 August) at the Brussels World's Fair, where it appeared with Glenn Gould and Marguerite *Lavergne; its program offered works by Ridout and Morawetz. It also played that year in Montreal. On a tour of Canada in 1960 the orchestra gave 32 concerts, mostly in smaller centres. In 1962 it revisited Montreal. In 1966 it toured in England, Belgium, and Scandinavia, making its London debut 7 June at the Commonwealth Institute and appearing at the invitation of Benjamin Britten at the Aldeburgh Festival. At *Expo 67 the orchestra gave daily concerts of Canadian music for a week, documented in part on the LP RCI 238. On Neel's retirement from the U of Toronto in 1971 the orchestra ceased to give public concerts, although it was not officially disbanded.

The New Hart House Chamber Orchestra, not a successor, founded in 1973 by Bill *Phillips, soon was renamed the New Chamber Orchestra.

DISCOGRAPHY

Blackburn – MacMillan – Surdin – Somers. Neel cond. 1967. CBC Expo 15

Boyd Neel Conducts Handel, Elgar and Holst. 1970. DG 2530 015

The Boyd Neel Touch: Wolf-Ferrari – Collins – Bizet – Dela – et al. 1970. CTL 477-5137/Citadel CT 6013 (released as *A Concert for Strings*) Vox Turnabout CTC 32007

Champagne – MacMillan – Symonds – Fauré – et al. Neel cond. 1963. CTL S 5030

Freedman – MacMillan – Surdin – Somers. Neel cond, Macerollo acc. 1967. RCI 238

Kreisler – Rimsky-Korsakov – Tchaikovsky – Dvořák – et al. Evens cond, Galper cl. 1965. CTL 5058

BIBLIOGRAPHY

'The Hart House Orchestra: continuing two noble traditions,' *CBC Times*, 24–30 Oct 1954

Neel, Boyd. 'Hart House remembered,' *AudioScene Canada*, 4, Apr 1976

(BJE)

Hart House String Quartet. Canada's most famous chamber ensemble of the first half of the 20th century, and the first to be subsidized fully. Not one of the original players was Canadian-born. The quartet's history began early in 1923 when Geza *de Kresz, newly arrived in Toronto, began to practise informally with the violist Milton Blackstone and the cellist Boris *Hambourg (with whom he had played in a student quartet in Belgium, under Ysaÿe, ca 1905–8). On de Kresz's initiative a second violinist was sought, and Harry *Adaskin was chosen to fill this role. After a year of rehearsals the group received permission from Vincent Massey to give its first concert in the *Hart House Theatre (a part of the building given to the *U of Toronto by the Massey Foundation). The program, before an invited audience 27 Apr 1924, comprised Haydn's *Op 76, no 2*, Beethoven's *Op 95*, and the slow movement of Beethoven's *Op 74*. Augustus *Bridle described the playing as 'highly finished and beautiful' (Toronto *Star*, 28 Apr 1924), while the critic for *Saturday Night* (3 May 1924) praised the group as 'the most promising organization of its kind that Toronto has yet produced.' The concert's success prompted the Massey Foundation to establish the quartet on a permanent basis, guaranteeing salaries for the players while allowing them to keep any surplus from box office receipts. It was at this point that the group adopted the name Hart House String Quartet.

Hart House String Quartet: (left to right) de Kresz, Blackstone, Hambourg, Adaskin

Blackstone (b New York 1894, d Toronto 1974), who came to Toronto in 1911, studied with Luigi von *Kunits, played in the *Welsman *TSO and *Academy String Quartet, and was the quartet's business manager until ill health forced his retirement in 1941. The original members stayed together until 1935, when de Kresz (whose schedule had been crowded by duo-recitals with his wife, the pianist Norah Drewett) left, and James Levey (1887–1955, a concertmaster of the Royal Albert Hall Orchestra and first violin, 1917–27, of the London String Quartet) took his place. Adaskin resigned in 1938 and was succeeded by Adolph *Koldofsky, who was followed in 1942 by Henry Milligan. Blackstone was replaced by Allard de *Ridder in 1941. Cyril Glyde replaced de Ridder in 1944. Hambourg was cellist throughout the group's history. Occasionally the quartet appeared with a pianist or singer: Sir Ernest *MacMillan, Campbell *McInnes, Maurice Ravel, or Ernest *Seitz.

In its early years the quartet presented 10 recitals annually at Hart House and 10 more at Convocation Hall, U of Toronto. By 1938 it had undertaken 12 Canadian tours and had given some 30 concerts in New York and over 100 others throughout the USA. A European tour in 1929 included more than 45 engagements in Belgium, England (including BBC broadcasts), France, and Holland, while another trip, in 1937, took the group to Austria, England, France, Holland, Italy, Scandinavia, and Scotland. In 1925 the quartet signed a broadcast contract with the CNR and in 1927 it made a trans-Canada CNR broadcasting tour. It gave many individual radio recitals and took part in CBC broadcast series in 1938, 1939, 1940, and 1942.

The quartet's repertoire was wide-ranging, encompassing music of the classic and romantic eras and works of 20th-century composers, including John Beach, Debussy, Delius, and Dohnányi. With the London, Kilbourn, and Flonzaley quartets the quartet took part in Toronto in a Beethoven Centenary String Quartet Festival (13 Oct 1926–3 Feb 1927) and during the 1934–5 season it performed the late Beethoven quartets in Toronto and Buffalo. It gave the first Canadian performance (25 Oct 1925) of Bartók's *Quartet No. 1* and performed the Ravel *Quartet* in New York, 15 Jan 1928, at the concert in which Ravel made his US debut as a pianist. Later it appeared at concerts featuring Ravel in Albany, NY, and Toronto. It performed several Canadian works as well and premiered Ernest MacMillan's *String Quartet in C Minor* ca 1924 and his *Two Sketches for String Quartet* in 1927, Leo *Smith's arrangements of *Dans Paris ya-t-une brune* and *Joli Coeur de rose* in 1927, and George Bowles' *String Quartet* in 1928. The quartet's last regular concerts took place at Hart House, 12, 13, and 15 Jun 1945. The following year three special farewell concerts were given before invited audiences and were broadcast by the CBC. The last of these, at Hart House 26 Apr 1946, with Koldofsky (substituting for Levey who was ill) and Milligan as first and second violins, featured music by Vaughan Williams and Sir John McEwen and a short address by Boris Hambourg.

From the outset the quality of the quartet's playing was acknowledged to be high. In 1925, a critic for the New York *Herald Tribune* (29 Nov 1925) wrote that 'the four players seemed to have attained a thorough unity in spirit as well as execution and their playing was sensitive and expressive as well as skilled.' The group became one of the dozen or so best on the international scene. Despite personnel changes, it maintained the standards of its early years. A *Globe and Mail* review of 24 Oct 1938 discussed its 'almost absolute perfection in blend, balance, precision, style, jewelled workmanship, masterly interpretation ... silken texture and ravishing beauty of tone' and as late as 1944 the members were described as 'great artists, individual and collective' (Toronto *Telegram*, 27 Nov 1944).

DISCOGRAPHY

Records listed are 10" double-sided discs.

Boccherini *Menuet célèbre* – anon, arr Pochon *Drink to Me Only with Thine Eyes*. 1926. Victor 24001

Haydn *Quartet in F Minor*. 1930. Victor 24009-24011 (Album CMM-1)

MacMillan (arr) *À St-Malo*; *Notre Seigneur en pauvre*. 1927. Victor 24004

Mozart-Beethoven, arr de Kresz 'Variations on "La ci darem"' from *Don Giovanni*. 1927. Victor 24003

Foster, arr Pochon *Old Black Joe; Angel Gabriel*. 1926. Victor 24002

BIBLIOGRAPHY
Mullens, A. Raymond. 'The Hart House Quartet,' *Maclean's*, 1 Mar 1931
– 'Salesman of music,' *Maclean's*, 1 Jun 1933
Dell, Dudley. 'The end of an era,' *Mayfair*, Jun 1946
de Kresz, Geza. 'The Hart House Quartet,' *ConsB*, Mar 1954
Adaskin, Harry. *A Fiddler's World* (Vancouver 1977)
U of Toronto Archives. Hart House String Quartet scrapbooks (1924–41) (HK)

HARTWELL, Hugh (Kenneth). Composer, teacher, b Hamilton, Ont, 18 Jan 1945; B MUS (McGill) 1967, M MUS (Pennsylvania) 1971, PH D (Pennsylvania) 1975. After study with István *Anhalt at *McGill U and with George Rochberg and George Crumb at the U of Pennsylvania Hartwell taught 1971–6 at Kirkland College, Clinton, NY. In 1976 he joined the faculty at *McMaster U. Hartwell's early works, such as the 12-tone *Septet* (1969), employ rhythmic counterpoint in a dense continuity. Later works fragment the continuity, giving a sparse, pointillistic effect, but still are founded on a juxtaposition of rhythmic patterns. Hartwell is an affiliate of PRO Canada and an associate of the *CMCentre.

SELECTED COMPOSITIONS
Matinée d'ivresse. 1966. Cl, vn, vc, pf, perc. Jay 1971
ALBA from 'Langue d'Oc' (Pound). 1967. SATB. CMCentre
Soul-Piece for 6 or 7 Players. 1967; rev 1969. Chamb ens. Ber 1969
Piece for Piano. 1968. CMCentre
'How to Play Winning Bridge' (Hartwell). 1969. Alto, fl, va, perc. CMCentre
Septet. 1969. 3cl, hn, str trio. Jay 1971
Kāmē'a. 1971. Chamb ens. CMCentre
'Resta de dormi noia ...' (Gesualdo, Eng-Hartwell). 1974. CMCentre
Sonata for Orchestra. 1975. Ms

Al and Bob Harvey (A & B Battery Boys in the late 1920s). Song and comedy duo popular in the 1920s and 1930s. Sons of Bert Harvey (d ca 1946), also a singing comedian, Robert (b Toronto 17 Oct 1894, d ?) and Albert (b Toronto 17 Jun 1907, d ?) first broadcast together as the A & B Battery Boys on radio station CKNC, Toronto. Presenting musical skits, novelty songs, and in later years some country music, they appeared in concert, made a few 78s for Apex and Domino (listed in *Roll Back the Years*), and sang 1930–3 on CKNC's 'The Wrigley Hour.' In England 1933–40 they toured the music hall circuit, performed on such BBC radio shows as 'Music Hall' and 'Horner's Corners,' and recorded as the Rocky Mountaineers. In 1939 they appeared on BBC TV's 'Western Cabaret.' After their return to Toronto they sang 1941–4 on CBC radio's 'The Maple Leaf Milling Show.' They performed together as late as 1960. After 1945 Al Harvey also appeared as a singer or compère on CBC radio and TV shows including 'Guest House' (1951–2) and 'Now's Your Chance' (1952–3). He then worked as a department manager for Gordon V. *Thompson. Each brother composed many songs, several published by Thompson or Irwin Dash, London. MM

HARVEY, Christine (b Christina). Soprano, b Montreal 28 May 1939; B MUS (Montreal) 1967, premier prix (École Vincent-d'Indy) 1967. While studying in Montreal with Bernard *Diamant, Louise *André, and Ruzena *Herlinger she was soloist with oratorio societies and, on radio and TV, with the Renaissance Singers. Further studies (1967–9) were in Geneva with Maria Carpi and in Munich at the Gernot-Heindl Opera Studio. In Geneva she performed cantatas of Bach and Handel with the JM World Orchestra; in Salzburg she sang in *Messiah* with the Munich Bach Choir and Orchestra. She sang 1971–2 for the Opera Forum in Enschede, the Netherlands (Papagena in *The Magic Flute*, Mia in *Land of Smiles*, and Marie in Egk's *Der Revisor*), and 1973–6 for the Netherlands Opera (eg, Clarina in *La Cambiale di Matrimonio* and Lesbina in Caluppi's *Il Filosofo di Campagna*). Thereafter she pursued a concert career, singing with orchestras in the Netherlands, Germany, France, and Canada. A specialist in baroque ornamentation, she became a member of the early music group Quatre en Concert (see Peggie Sampson), which toured Ontario universities in 1976, Canada in 1977, and Holland in 1978. Harvey's other Canadian activities have included performances at the *NAC (Alice in Rossini's *Le Comte Ory* 1974; *Messiah* 1978) and a concert (1976) with the *St Catharines SO. For the Mirasound company in Holland she has participated in recordings of large choral works, including Bach's *Magnificat* and *St John Passion* (with the Residentie Bach Choir and Orchestra) and of short choral pieces and opera. FH

Haskell Opera House / Opéra Haskell. A 500-seat theatre which has the distinction of being partly in Canada and partly in the USA. Located in Rock Island, south of Magog on the Quebec-Vermont border, the theatre was built early in the 20th century at a cost of $100,000, the gift of the US philanthropists Martha and Stewart Haskell. The entrance to the hall and an adjoining public library are in the USA; the stage and most of the orchestra pit and balcony are in Canada. Inaugurated in grand style 7 Jun 1904 by the Columbia Minstrels, the tenor Eugene Cowles, and an orchestra from Sherbrooke, the theatre subsequently housed operatic and dramatic productions, recitals, and lectures. Its use declined later in the century but it continued in service, administered by a non-profit-making foundation. Because of its unique location, during World War II the US government declared the opera house a neutral area in order to avoid any complications for performers and audiences who must cross the international boundary line that divides the auditorium.

BIBLIOGRAPHY
Mercer, Ruby. 'A unique little theatre,' *OpCan*, Feb 1966
Coulon, Jacques. 'Rock Island, 2000 habitants, un opéra ...,' *Perspectives*, vol 18, 7 Feb 1976
Blampied, Phil. 'Partly in Vermont: a borderline case,' *Time*, 13 Aug 1979
Coulon, Jacques. 'Un opéra, c'est lourd à la fin,' Montreal *Le Devoir*, 28 Oct 1980 GP

HASLAM, (William) **Elliott.** Voice teacher, choir conductor, b England, 1851?, d Toronto 23 Nov 1915. A son of the concert singer John Haslam, Elliott Haslam was educated in Italy, studied music at London's RAM, and appears to have begun his career as a violinist at the Paris Opera. He is known also to have been associated with The Carl Rosa Opera Company ca 1876. In England he taught music at Brighton High School and Manchester's Britannia College before emigrating to Canada, where he founded the Toronto Vocal Society in 1885 and served 1886–93 as choirmaster at St James' Cathedral. The *Musical Journal* (1 Jan 1887) reported that 'Mr. W. Elliott Haslam was brought to New York at the special request of Chevalier Auguste Vianesi, director of the Royal Italian Opera, London, and the Imperial Opera, St. Petersburg.' The stay, however, was brief, and Haslam, back in Toronto, continued his previous work. In 1888 or 1889 he undertook some writing and editing for the *Musical Journal* and its successor the *Canadian Musical Herald*. In 1890 he resigned from the Toronto Vocal Society and formed the Haslam Vocal Society. In 1891 he became music director at Upper Canada College. In 1892 he left his three posts for health reasons and spent some time in Michigan recuperating, but he remained on contract with the cathedral until 1893. His other activities during his first Toronto sojourn included leading the Harmony Club and teaching at the *Toronto College of Music, where Bessie *Bonsall and Florence *Brimson were among his pupils. In 1894 Haslam went to New York to teach at the National Cons of Music, then under the direction of Antonin Dvořák. When it closed in 1895, he returned to Toronto and resumed teaching. In 1901 he left Canada again and opened a studio in Paris where he continued to teach until World War I. His best-known pupil there was Florence *Easton. Early in 1915 he returned to Toronto, where he taught until his death (by his own hand) several months later.

BIBLIOGRAPHY
'Toronto notes,' *MCour*, vol 15, 9 Nov 1887
'Elliott Haslam has untimely end,' Toronto *Globe*, 25 Nov 1915 (JBM)

Les Hauts et les bas dla vie d'une diva: Sarah Ménard par eux-mêmes. Musical comedy, more precisely a 'monologuerie bouffe' by Jean-Claude Germain, music and songs by Jacques Perron. Staged by Germain with Nicole Leblanc as Sarah Ménard and the pianist Gaston *Brisson as Tony Panneton, it was premiered 6 Nov 1974 at Montreal's Théâtre d'Aujourd'hui. There are only two roles, Panneton also providing the piano accompaniment and musical transitions. Germain describes his work as 'a gigantic permanent short circuit between opera, rock'n'roll, gypsy music, men, the convent, amorous relationships, the city, the countryside and Europe.' In this allegory Sarah Ménard, a 'prima donna, diva new look,' relives her memories at the twilight of an international career. The songs mix high fantasy with satire and bear such evocative titles as 'L'aria d'Eurydice au téléphone' and 'La chanson du bottin de l'opéra italien.' The work is 'humbly dedicated to a great Quebec composer, born in Montreal in 1848, Salomon *Mazurette.' It enjoyed an extraordinary success, completing 200 performances by the end of 1977, playing not only in Montreal but in other parts of Quebec, Ontario, and New Brunswick. The text and the songs are published in one volume (VLB Éditeur 1976). GP

HAWKIN, Edna Marie (b Steele). Pianist, teacher, b Chesterfield, England, 6 Nov 1896, naturalized Canadian 1925; ARCM, LRAM. Following her musical education in England, where she studied with Frederic Lamond, she came to Canada in 1920, living first in Prince Albert, Sask, then in Regina. She taught 1925–32 at Regina College, where Jean *Reti Forbes was among her pupils. After a two-year sojourn in England, which included BBC broadcasts, she settled in Montreal, where she became known as pianist, accompanist, teacher, and adjudicator. She gave classes in pedagogy, accompaniment, and piano ensemble 1956–62 at the *McGill Cons and then taught privately. Her pupils include Gian Lyman, Joan Glithero, and Irene Husaruk. Several have performed as soloists in the *MSO Young People's Concerts. Particularly interested in Bach and Beethoven, she has been heard often on the CBC in works of these and other composers and has accompanied artists for Community Concerts in various centres. She was the first president of the *QMTA 1942–5, president 1946–51 of the *CFMTA, and president 1949–59 of the McGill Chamber

Music Society, with which she also appeared as soloist. In 1967 she was one of six recipients of a *CFMTA Centennial Citation for outstanding teaching LF

HAWKINS, John. Pianist, composer, teacher, b Montreal 26 Jul 1944; premier prix (CMM) 1967, B MUS (McGill) 1967, Concert Diploma (McGill) 1968, MMA (McGill) 1970. He studied piano at the *CMM with Lubka *Kolessa and at *McGill U. He also studied composition with István *Anhalt at McGill U on a Woodrow Wilson Fellowship and in 1969 attended Boulez' conducting class in Basel. He became a lecturer in theory and composition at the *U of Toronto in 1970. Hawkins won the Second-Century Week Composition Competition (jointly with Hugh *Hartwell) for his *Eight Movements for Flute and Clarinet* (1967), and has received other distinctions as both composer and performer. *Waves* (1967) was commissioned by the *SMCQ. He has performed for both the SMCQ in Montreal and *NMC in Toronto. Hawkins' compositions are few, possibly because of his desire to make each work different from the last. *Remembrances*, at the time of this writing his most successful work, quotes Beethoven, Brahms, and Mahler, using figures, chords, or melodic fragments as distant memories. While change is more to Hawkins' taste than consistency, an introspective lyricism pervades most of his works, and the delicate polyphony of Webern has been an influence. He is a member of the *CLComp, an associate of the *CMCentre, and a member of CAPAC.

COMPOSITIONS

Eight Movements; 1966. Fl, cl. CMCentre
Five Short Pieces for Piano. 1967. Jay 1972
Three Cavatinas (Whitman, Yeats, Burroughs). 1967. Sop, chamb ens. BMIC 1969
Sequences. 1968 (Tor 1972). Sm orch. CMCentre
Remembrances. 1969. Chamb ens. Jay 1971. RCI 300 (*SMCQ)
Two Pieces for Orchestra. 1970 (Mtl 1971, movt 2). Full orch. CMCentre
Waves (Hawkins). 1971. Sop, pf. CMCentre. RCI 300 (*MacKinnon)
Spring Song (anon). 1974. SATB. CMCentre
Études for Two Pianos. 1974. CMCentre
Trio. 1975. Fl, vc, xyl. CMCentre
Quintet for Winds. 1977. Ww quin. CMCentre

BIBLIOGRAPHY

Mather, Bruce. 'Le collage musical; "Remembrances" de John Hawkins,' *CMB*, 3, Autumn–Winter 1971
Schulman, Michael. 'For John Hawkins composing isn't easy,' *CanComp*, 83, Sep 1973
Plawutsky, Eugene. 'The music of John Hawkins,' *CAUSM J*, vol 8, Spring 1979
Contemporary Canadian Composers / Compositeurs canadiens contemporains CF

HAWKINS, Ronnie (Ronald). Singer, entrepreneur, b Huntsville, Ark, 10 Jan 1935. A pioneer of rock in Canada, and a father figure to many of the country's leading musicians, Hawkins began touring the Ontario nightclub circuit in 1958 with his US band the Hawks, calling himself 'The King of Rockabilly' and later 'Rompin' Ronnie Hawkins' or 'The Hawk.' Despite some success in the USA with the records 'Mary Lou' and '40 Days' in 1959, he remained in Canada and by 1961 had settled in Toronto. Most of the original Hawks had been replaced by Ontario musicians (see The Band) in the first of several groups formed by Hawkins in Canada. While continuing to tour he operated clubs in the mid-1960s in Toronto and London, Ont, (the Hawk's Nest and Campbell's Tavern respectively) and established Hawk Records, a label devoted to Canadian rock artists. Capitalizing on the international success of The Band, Hawkins enjoyed a well-publicized though only mildly successful US comeback in 1969. He was less active in the 1970s, his appearances largely restricted to Toronto clubs, but he appeared 23 Nov 1976 at The Band's farewell concert in San Francisco and in 1977 toured western Canada. In 1979 he was signed to record for the US United Artists label.

Hawkins is one of rock's most colourful personalities. He is the subject of Gordon *Lightfoot's 'Silver Cloud Rolls Royce' and of many stories. Writing in the Toronto *Globe and Mail* (7 Jul 1977) Paul McGrath commented: 'He's not known for anything he's done in the past decade, but for his sharp ear for young talent ... His fame also rests in his still-clear rock voice, which he can also coax into a smooth country croon with the slightest tightening of his Arkansas accent.'

Many of Hawkins' bands have had successful careers on their own, including And Many Others (as *Crowbar); The Band; Robbie Lane and the Disciples; and (Jim) Atkinson, (Terry) Danko, and (Duane) Ford. The same can be said of Hawkins' sidemen – the guitarists Terry Bush, John Till, Pat Travers, and Dom *Troiano; the pianists Scott Cushnie and Ricky Bell; and the singers *King Biscuit Boy, Beverly D'Angelo, Jackie Gabriel, Tobi Lark, Jay Smith, and David *Clayton-Thomas. Hawkins' later singles included: 'Who Do You Love?' (1963, with The Band), considered the classic version of the Bo Diddley song; 'Bluebird over the Mountain' (1965) and Lightfoot's 'Home from the Forest' (1967), both representing a shift in style to country-folk; and 'Down in the Alley' (1970), a return to the flamboyant and rather lurid rock and roll of his early days.

DISCOGRAPHY

Ronnie Hawkins. 1959. Rou R 25078
Mr. Dynamo. 1960. Rou R 25102
The Best of Ronnie Hawkins Featuring His Band. 1959–62. Rou 42045 (anthology drawn from *The Best of Ronnie Hawkins* and *Mojo Man*, both recorded with The Band for Canadian Roulette)
Ronnie Hawkins. With And Many Others, including the King Biscuit Boy. 1969. Hawk 9019
The Hawk. 1970. GRT 9205-9039

BIBLIOGRAPHY

Batten, Jack. 'The rockin' raucous life of Rompin' Ronnie Hawkins,' *The Canadian*, 11 Dec 1965
Bagnell, Kenneth. 'The simple inner graces of Ronnie Hawkins,' Toronto *Globe Magazine*, 20 Mar 1971
McRae, Earl. 'Last boogie in Sturgeon Falls,' *Canadian Magazine*, 27 Mar 1976
Johnson, B. Derek. 'The Hawk survives – but can he conquer?' Toronto *Globe and Mail*, 25 Oct 1978
Blackadar, Bruce. 'Flying high: the rock 'n' roll comeback of Rompin' Ronnie Hawkins,' (*Toronto Star*) *The City*, 24 Jun 1979 MM

HAWORTH, Frank (Francis). Composer, educator, writer, b Liverpool 13 Jan 1905; LTCM 1927. A self-educated musician, Haworth taught music in Lancashire schools 1925–40 and, after military service in the early years of World War II, was appointed by the British Council in 1943 the first music officer to the West Indies. In Bermuda 1946–56 he was a radio programming director, journalist, and music critic. In 1956 he moved to Toronto, where he wrote occasional music, drama, and art criticism for the *Globe and Mail* and articles for *Saturday Night* and the *CBC Times*. He composed music for the CBC TV children's series 'Mr. O' (1956) and 'Old Testament Tales' (1957) and contributed scripts and commentary to various CBC music and public affairs programs. For the Ontario Dept of Education he was a travelling organizer and instructor 1963–7, offering music courses, seminars, and workshops. Haworth considers himself a 'mainstreamer' who follows traditions but adopts new elements when they seem appropriate. He sums up his music as 'community music,' meant for the amateur rather than the virtuoso. He is a member of CAPAC and an associate of the *CMCentre.

SELECTED COMPOSITIONS

STAGE, RADIO, TV

The Hopeless Dawn 'A Fairly Grand Opera' (Haworth). 1943. Soli, chorus, pf
The Seven Ages of Man, mixed media. 1968. Vn, fl, hn, tpt, wordless chorus. CMCentre
Many other works, including incidental and ballet music

ORCHESTRA

3 suites for str: *Rus in urbe* (early 1930s), *Dalegarth* (1958), *Calday Grange Suite* (1959). All ms
2 suites for hn and str: *Pastoral Suite* (1956), *Cornucopia* (1972). Both CMCentre
Several other works for orch, including *Edenvale Suite* (1969) and *Lomyra* (1975), and many works for band

CHAMBER

Glenrose Suite. 1960. Wind quin. FH 1972
Kernwood Suite. 1972. Sax quin. CMCentre
Others, including a pf quar (early 1930s), 2 str quar (1932, 1940s–1958), a str trio (1964); many short pieces for various combinations

CHOIR AND VOICE

'Dream Pedlary' and 'Reeds of Innocence.' (1956). V, pf. CMCentre
Canada Onward, a miniature cantata (Haworth). 1967. solo, SAT/B, fl, cl, vn, vc, pf
Several other works for choir and v, including mamy early settings of the Latin Mass and other sacred texts, arr of folk songs, Christmas carols, etc
Numerous works for recorder and recorder ens; some other works in miscellaneous categories

WRITINGS

'Healey Willan,' *Composers of the Americas*, vol 6 (Washington 1961)
Leader's Handbook: Instructions for Class Singing, Ont Dept of Education pamphlet (Toronto ca 1963–7)
The Choir Master, Ont Dept of Education pamphlet (Toronto ca 1963–7)
'Music in the parish church,' *Brief to the Bishops* (Toronto 1965)
'*Colas et Colinette*: a character larger than life,' *CanComp*, 31, Jul–Aug 1968
'Music – mirror of the mind, *CanComp*, 32, Sep 1968
'The composer's voice,' *CanComp*, 33, Oct 1968

BIBLIOGRAPHY

'Frank Haworth: a traditionalist without being old-fashioned,' *CanComp*, 31, Aug 1968
'Teaching composing in a Lakehead classroom,' *CanComp*, 53, Oct 1970 (MMI)

HAYES, Gary J. (James). Composer, producer, b Hamilton, Ont, 14 Dec 1948; B MUS (Toronto) 1972. He studied violin with David Mankowitz, percussion with Vair Capper, John *Wyre, and Robin Engelman, and composition with John *Beckwith and John *Weinzweig at the *U of Toronto. He was a founding member 1971–6 of *ARRAY, taught 1973–4 for the York County School Board in the 'Artist-in-the-classroom' project, worked briefly 1974–5 as a folk singer, and joined CBC Ottawa in 1975 as a radio producer. His compositions, mostly for chamber ensemble, reflect an interest in sound colour; *Dementia I* and *II* (1974), *Mists and the Dreams of Mists* (1974), and particularly *Convolutions* (1975, a commission for *Canadian Brass) explore effects obtainable through the dispersement of instruments to separate positions in a hall or playing area. Among Hayes' other works of this period, his *Pythian I* (1974) won one of the four first prizes awarded that year in the *CBC National Radio Competition for Young Composers, and *Soring* [sic] (1975) was written for the *Guitar Society of Toronto. He is a member of the *CLComp, an associate of the *CMCentre, and an affiliate of PRO Canada.

BIBLIOGRAPHY
'Gary J. Hayes,' *Array Newsletter*, vol 1, Spring 1974
PRO Canada Ltd. 'Gary J. Hayes,' pamphlet (1980)
Compositeurs canadiens contemporains (CF)

HAYWARD, Richard (Benjamin). Bandmaster, composer, b London 16 Dec 1874, d Toronto 2 Jan 1961. He enlisted in the British Army as a band boy in 1887, studied cornet, and graduated from the RMSM (Kneller Hall) in 1904. He was bandmaster 1905–14 of the Royal Irish Rifles and became the only serving bandmaster in the British Army to be promoted to a combatant commission. Retiring in 1919 with the rank of captain, he moved in 1921 to Toronto, where he served as music director 1921–8 of the *Queen's Own Rifles of Canada and teacher of wind instruments at the *TCM. He founded the Toronto Police Band in 1926, conducted the Toronto Concert Band 1925–39, and at the outbreak of World War II once again led the Queen's Own Rifles. A charter member (1929) of the American Bandmasters Assn, he was its president in 1940. He also served as dean of bands 1941–5 for the Southern Music Camp, Texas. In 1956 he was made a life member of the *CBA. Hayward's compositions for band (listed in *Cataloque of Canadian Composers*) include overtures, rhapsodies, and suites published by C. Fischer, G. Schirmer, and Boosey & Hawkes. He won the Composer's Competition in 1949. Many of his manuscript scores have been deposited at the *NL of C. He also wrote articles about music for the *Globe* (Toronto), *Metronome*, and the *School Musician*.

BIBLIOGRAPHY
'Captain Richard B. Hayward passes on,' *CanB*, Spring 1960 HK

HEALEY, Derek. Composer, organist, b Wargrave, England, 2 May 1936; B MUS (Durham) 1961, D MUS (Toronto) 1974. He studied at Durham U with Herbert Howells (composition), Harold Darke (organ), and Harry Stubbs (piano). He also studied composition in Italy with Petrassi, Boris Porena, and Berio, before moving to Canada, where he lived for nine years. He taught 1969–71 at the *U of Victoria, 1971–2 at the *U of Toronto and the *U of Waterloo, and 1972–8 at the *U of Guelph. In 1978 he joined the Music Dept at the U of Oregon. He has composed substantial works for organ (eg, *Partita '65*), for orchestra (*Arctic Images*), and for chamber ensembles (*Stinging*, a work notable for the instruments' imitation of the synthetic sounds on the tape). His opera **Seabird Island* was commissioned by the *Guelph Spring Festival and premiered there 7 May 1977. Pre-Canadian works were published by Novello, Chappell, and Boosey & Hawkes. Healey is an affiliate of PRO Canada and an associate of the *CMCentre.

COMPOSITIONS (completed in Canada)
ORCHESTRA AND CHAMBER
Butterflies, Op 36 (Matsuo Basho, Buson, Mortake, Shiki, Shusen). 1970. Sop, orch. CMCentre
Arctic Images, Op 40. 1971. Orch. Ric 1978. CBC SM-265 (*CBC Van Chamb O)
The Raven, Op 37. 1971. Str orch. CMCentre
Stinging, Op 38. 1971. Alto recorder, vc, hpd, tape. CMCentre
Triple Concerto 'Noh,' *Op 42*. 1974. Fl, pf, synth, orch. CMCentre
Primrose in Paradise, Op 45. 1975. Orch. Merion (Presser) 1975. CBC SM-331 (*CBC Van Chamb O)
Concerto for Organ, Strings and Timpani, Op 8. CMCentre. 1970. CBC SM-143 (*CBC Van Chamb O)
Sweet Prospect. 1977. Orch. CMCentre
Desert Landscape with Figures, Op 49. 1978. Orch. CMCentre

CHOIR
Discendi, Amor Santo, Op 28a (Bianco da Siena). 1967. SATB, org. Ms
'Clouds,' Op 41 (Matsuo Basho). 1972. SATB. Wat 1973
'There is One Body' (Ephesians). 1972. SATB, 2 synth (tape). GVT 1975
Six Canadian Folk Songs (trad). 1973. SATB GVT 1973. 1974. CBC SM-274 (*Festival Singers)
'In Flanders Fields' (John McCrae). 1974. Sop, SATB, alto recorder. GVT 1976
The Brown Season. 1978. Fl, perc, SATB. CMCentre
KEYBOARD
Cookham Notebook, Op 30. 1967. Org. Ms. RCI 481 (*McLean)
The Lost Traveller's Dream, Op 35. 1970. Org. Jay 1972
Three Quiet Pieces for Organ. 1974. CMCentre
Lieber Robert, Op 43. 1975. Pf, tape. Ms
Paraphrase – 'Discendi, Amor Santo,' Op 26b. 1975. Org. CMCentre
Summer '73 / Ontario, Op 44. 1975. Org, tape. CMCentre
Also a work for tape, *Incidental Music to Night Thoughts, Op 39* (1972)

BIBLIOGRAPHY
Schulman, Michael. 'Country of residence an influence on Healey's music,' *MSc*, 274, Nov–Dec 1973
BMI Canada / PRO Canada Ltd. 'Derek Healey,' pamphlets (1976, 1980)
Kieser, Karen. 'Derek Healey's new opera based on Indian legend,' *Fugue*, Apr 1977
Contemporary Canadian Composers CF

HEARD, Alan. Composer, teacher, b Halifax, NS, 7 Feb 1942; B MUS (McGill) 1962, MFA (Princeton) 1964. He studied composition with *Anhalt at *McGill U, Sessions and Earl Kim at Princeton U, and Blacher at the Hochschule für Musik in Berlin. He taught at McGill U 1967–71 and at Kirkland College, Clinton, NY, before joining the faculty of music at the *U of Western Ontario in 1976. In his compositions – not numerous but some of them large in scale – Heard has used both serial techniques and aleatory procedures, but in the late 1970s he began writing tonally, his *Sinfonia nello Stile Antico* being the prime instance. Of the earlier works, *Voices* (1969), a Canadian entry in the 1972 ISCM competition, was performed and recorded by the *SMCQ. A setting of Japanese poetry for soprano and five instruments, the work reconceives the moods of the verse in terms of instrumental colour. Heard is an associate of the *CMCentre and a member of CAPAC.

COMPOSITIONS
ORCHESTRA
Symphonic Variations. 1964. Ms
Concerto for clarinet and orchestra. 1966. Ms
Sinfonia nello Stile Antico. 1977. Ms
CHAMBER
String Quartet. 1963. Ms
String Trio. 1965. Ms
Three Comings, song cycle (e.e. cummings). 1965. Sop, fl, ob, cl, tpt, va, pf. Ms
Rondos. 1967. Fl, hp. Ms
Voices (Japanese, transl K Rexroth). 1969. Sop, picc (fl), pf, vc, perc. Ms. RCI 358 (*SMCQ)
Timai 'A Cosmic March for Ten Instrumentalists.' 1973. Chamb ens. Ms
Prelude. 1974 (rev 1978). Str quar. Ms
Double. 1976. Hp, str quar. Ms
Also a piano sonata (1966) and a choral work, *Old Seawoman* (1959, rev 1978). Both ms

HEATHER, Alfred. Tenor, teacher, b London 21 Mar 1876, d Toronto 8 Aug 1932. He studied with T.A. Wallworth, Alessandro Romilly, and Sir Charles Santley, was a lay-vicar (adult chorister) 1905–15 at Westminster Abbey, sang at festivals throughout Britain, toured with the Beecham and Quinlan opera companies, and made many records for HMV and, 1906–11, Pathé. He taught for some years at the GSM, London, and after World War I joined a company which had been assembled to stage a 1920 revival of *The Beggar's Opera* at the Lyric Theatre, Hammersmith. The company toured Canada in 1921 and was disbanded abruptly in the mid-West. Nothing daunted, Heather gave a recital in Regina which prompted Regina College to engage him as a teacher. He left Regina in 1923 to sing in Toronto, and taught 1924–5 at the *TCM. As a singer he was best known in Canada in the role of the Evangelist in the early performances of the *St Matthew Passion* under Sir Ernest *MacMillan. When he sang the role in 1926 a Toronto critic called him 'an artist of very rare distinction.' His was the standard by which other performances in the work were judged for many years. While he did not sing in public after 1926, he directed the *CPR Festivals' opera productions at Banff (1929), and the Toronto production of *Hugh the Drover* (15 and 18 Nov 1929). MWM

HEATON, Leonard (Dunstan). Pianist, teacher, b Hinckley, Leicestershire, England, 1889, d Winnipeg 15 Aug 1963. He studied with Leopold Godowsky in London, with Rudolph Ganz in Europe, and with Alberto Jonas in Berlin before 1909 or in New York after 1914. He moved to Canada in 1909 and settled in Winnipeg, where he taught piano for over 50 years. Also active as pianist, organist, examiner, and adjudicator, he was president 1923–5 of the *Men's Musical Club of Winnipeg and 1944–8 of the *MRMTA. His pupils included Jean *Broadfoot, John Kuchmy, Edward *Lincoln, Helen *Martens, Gordon *McLean, Ross *Pratt, Joyce Redekop-Fink, and Russell *Standing. At the *U of Manitoba School of Music there is a Leonard Heaton Room (a practice room), and there also are two Leonard Heaton Memorial Scholarships, awarded annually.

HECHT, Julius or **Jules.** Baritone, teacher, composer. He came from Frankfurt-am-Main and may have been a student or teacher at the Brussels Cons (a claim which that institution cannot confirm) before coming to Toronto about 1846. He taught vocal music at the Adelaide Ladies' Academy and sang opera and oratorio selections and songs in many Toronto concerts between 1846 and 1857. A. & S. *Nordheimer published at least five of his works, including a *St. Lawrence Polka* and a setting of Longfellow's 'The Light of Stars.' HK

HEIM, Emmy (Emilie) (m Rheinhardt, m Singer). Soprano, teacher, b Vienna 10 Sep 1885, naturalized Canadian 1951, d Toronto 13 Oct 1954. Her first music lessons were from her mother, and by seven she was singing Schubert songs. She studied voice with Frances Mütter in Vienna for 13 years before making her debut as a Lieder singer in that city in 1911. She toured Germany, the Austro-Hungarian Empire, and Poland, and sang for the soldiers during World War I. Her first husband, whom she married in 1915, was the writer Rheinhardt, and through him she became acquainted with some of the greatest European poets of her day, including Rilke and Hofmannsthal. Oskar Kokoschka did a portrait of her in lithograph, dated 11 Apr 1916. In 1917 she married the architect Franz Singer. Besides the songs of Schubert, Schumann, and Wolf, she sang many contemporary works, and she counted among her acquaintances Alban Berg, Arnold Schoenberg, and Igor Stravinsky. On 8 Jun 1919 she sang Stravinsky's *Berceuses du chat* and *Pribaoutki* at a concert of the Schoenberg Verein organized by Schoenberg.

By 1930 Heim had taken up residence in England, where she had made her debut in 1929. She maintained a studio in Salzburg for the summers until the Nazi occupation of Austria. From 1934 until 1939 she spent at least four months of each year in Canada. While in Canada for the first time (1934), visiting her brother Jules in Montreal, she met Sir Ernest *MacMillan in Toronto and sang for him and some friends. Her reception was so warm that she made her Canadian debut in Toronto's *Hart House Theatre 16 Oct 1934. Arrangements for subsequent visits were made by her friend Joy Denton Kennedy. Heim gave lecture-recitals and taught at the TCM (*RCMT) each winter and gave recitals in Cambridge, Mass, and Montreal.

During World War II, which she spent in England, Heim sang at Red Cross hospitals and military camps and was a guest lecturer at Oxford and Cambridge. She moved to Canada in 1946 and taught at the RCMT in Toronto until her death. She was a severe but understanding teacher and viewed music from the standpoint of all the arts and their place in the whole of civilization, insisting that her students acquire cultural awareness, a sense of nature, and a knowledge of history. She expressed her philosophy of art and of teaching in a remarkable 15-minute interview taped by Ronald Hambleton two weeks before her death and broadcast 26 Mar 1955 on CBC radio's 'Experience of Life' series. The tape is held in the CBC Program Archives. Some of her pupils were Joan *Hall, Frances *James, Eileen *Law, Margo *MacKinnon, Lois *Marshall, Joan *Maxwell, James *Milligan, Mary *Morrison, Jan *Simons, and Joyce *Sullivan.

DISCOGRAPHY

Emmy Heim – a Self-Portrait. 1949–54. Hallmark SS-2

BIBLIOGRAPHY

MacMillan, Ernest. 'Emmy Heim,' *ConsB*, Nov 1954 (SW)

HEINL, George. Violin maker, b Schnecken, Austria, 8 Feb 1891, d Toronto 6 Dec 1980. He studied violin making with his father, Joseph, with an uncle, Johann, and in Vienna, where he was apprenticed in various shops and received a violin maker's diploma in 1911. At the request of W.E. Hill & Sons in London he moved to Toronto, where he served 1912–20 as head of the violin department of Hill's Canadian representative, R.S. *Williams & Co. He went to Ottawa in 1920 to establish his own firm but returned to Toronto in 1926 and opened Geo. Heinl & Co, which has remained a major supplier of string instruments (Heinl's own and others') and accessories. In 1944 Heinl passed control of the company to his sons George (b Ottawa 1923) and Frank (b Toronto 1928). Both had been apprenticed as violin makers, but only Frank made instruments (six or seven) professionally. In later years two grandsons, Russell and Richard, joined the business. George Heinl Sr made over 130 instruments, patterned after the Stradivarius, Guarnerius, and Guadagnini models. His violins have been owned by Jacob *Groob and Steven *Staryk. Heinl appeared in the NFB film *Story of a Violin* (1947).

BIBLIOGRAPHY

Burrows, Margaret. 'The man to whom each violin is a new love,' Toronto *Telegram*, 17 May 1969

HEINS, (Francis) Donald (Donaldson). Violinist, violist, conductor, organist, composer, teacher, b Hereford, England, 19 Feb 1878, d Toronto 1 Jan 1949. He studied 1892–7 at the Leipzig Cons with Gustav Schreck (harmony), Richard Hoffmann (orchestration), and Hans Sitt (violin), and continued his training in London with August Wilhemj, also playing in the first violins of orchestras conducted by Elgar, Parry, and others. Heins settled in Ottawa in 1902 and lived there until 1927, teaching at the Canadian Cons of Music (established by his brother-in-law Harry *Puddicombe) and founding, and directing 1903–27, that institution's orchestra, with which he presented the Ottawa premieres of symphonies by Mozart, Beethoven, Dvořák, Tchaikovsky, and others. In 1910 this orchestra became the Ottawa SO. Over a period of 23 years Heins was organist successively in three Presbyterian churches and for three years conducted the Royal Artillery Band of the 43rd Regiment. In 1918, assisted by 14 teachers whom he had trained, he set up a program for teaching violin in Ottawa public schools and then organized and conducted a student orchestra which performed approximately four times a year. Sometime after 1918 he studied with Leopold Auer in New York.

After moving to Toronto in 1927 Heins was concertmaster of the *TSO until 1931, then principal violist until 1938. He remained a member of the viola section thereafter until his death and also was asst conductor 1931–42. He taught at the *TCM 1927–48, was violist of the *Conservatory String Quartet 1929–34, and conductor of the TCM SO 1930–4. Heins also was organist at St Mary the Virgin Anglican Church. He is supposed to have performed his *Concertino in D Minor* for violin and orchestra at the Chicago Musical College and to have played with the Chicago SO, but corroboration and dates have not been found.

Heins composed two short operettas for the CBC, *An Old Tortugas* (1936) and *Yellow Back* (1939), as well as several motets, various pieces for string instruments, and a *Messe de Sainte Ursule* for female choir and small orchestra. *The Awakening*, a symphonic poem, was performed in 1910 in Ottawa.

BIBLIOGRAPHY

'Donald Heins of T.S.O., musician, 70, is dead,' *Toronto Daily Star*, 3 Jan 1949
Catalogue of Canadian Composers
Kallmann *History of Music* (L-GA)

Heintzman & Co Ltd. Piano manufacturing and retailing business based in Toronto 1866–1978 and relocated in Hanover, Ont, in 1978 under the amended name Heintzman Ltd. Among Canadian firms it is the oldest of its kind and one of the oldest music firms of any kind. It was founded by Theodore August Heintzman (b Theodor August Heintzmann, Berlin, 19 May 1817, naturalized Canadian 1886, d Toronto 25 Jul 1899) who had been apprenticed to the piano-building trade about 1831. It is not likely that Heintzman spent all his Berlin years in the piano trade, for various biographical sketches refer to him as a machinist, an instrument-maker, and a cabinet-maker, and one source even claims that he drew the patterns for the first locomotive built in his native city. All these skills must have been of benefit to the future piano builder.

As a result of the political troubles of 1848 the family of Heintzman's wife went to New York, and the young couple followed in 1850. For some time Heintzman worked for the piano makers Lighte & Newton. The story that he worked in the same factory as Henry E. Steinway is not confirmed, but it is true that the two Germans who were to establish the most famous piano firms in Canada and the USA respectively both arrived in North America in the same year. From New York Heintzman in 1852 went to Buffalo, where he worked for the Keogh Piano Co. He then entered the partnership of Drew, Heintzman & Annowski. A square piano built by this firm ca 1854 was still in the possession of Heintzman Ltd in 1980. In Buffalo Heintzman was associated with the

The Heintzman piano factory in Toronto's Junction district in the late 19th century

Western Piano Co, which may have been an alternative name for Drew, Heintzman & Annowski and which failed in 1857.

Heintzman stayed in Buffalo until the political unrest preceding the Civil War and an invitation from the Canadian piano builder John *Thomas caused him to move to Toronto in 1860. He is said to have built his first Canadian piano that year in a Toronto kitchen, to have sold it immediately, and to have continued and enlarged his business with the proceeds. However, the city directories for 1862–5 list Heintzman as working for the Thomas Piano Co at 86 York St. The year often given as the official founding date of the company – 1860 – appears to be justified as the starting point of Heintzman's private piano building in Toronto (probably at his home at 73 Queen St W), but the company was incorporated only in May 1866, with the financial and managerial help of Heintzman's son-in-law, Charles Bender, a prosperous tobacconist. (In 1873 the firm advertised that it had 'commenced business 12 years ago.') Heintzman's first factory – as distinct from workshops at his residence – was opened at 23 Duke St, but by May 1868 it had been relocated at 105 King St W (where it soon employed 12 hands and began turning out more than 60 pianos a year), and by 1873 it had moved down the street to 115–17 where there was space for factory, offices, and sales rooms. That year the company offered eight models of square pianos and one upright or 'cabinet' grand, its most expensive piano. Bender retired in 1875 and died two years later, but the enterprise continued to grow. (A grandson of Bender and a great-grandson of Heintzman, Charles Bender, b 1899, was to be general manager of the company until the mid-1950s.)

In 1876 the young company won awards at the Philadelphia Centennial Exhibition, and by 1879 it had built nearly 1000 instruments. In that year, too, Heintzman exhibited for the first time at the Toronto Industrial Exhibition (*CNE). By 1884 nearly 2000 pianos had been manufactured, and in 1888 a new factory was built in the Junction district of Toronto. The King St premises were retained as sales rooms and warehouse. As a result, production was able to rise from an annual 500 pianos during the 1880s to about 1000 in the 1890s and 2140 in 1906. The trade mark 'Heintzman & Co.' was acquired in 1888.

Unlike some of his competitors Heintzman aimed at high-quality rather than low-cost instruments. He was able to establish and maintain a high reputation from the beginning. Grand pianos were introduced about 1886, and two years later one was demonstrated before Queen Victoria at Albert Hall in London, winning the monarch's praise and thus helping to pave the way for an export trade. As early as 1867 Heintzman advertised its instruments as 'full Agraffe Bar Pianos,' referring to a transverse metal bridge across the cast-iron frame which helps to keep the strings from slipping and makes the tone more even. The agraffe had been introduced in 1809 by Sebastien Erard in Paris, but Heintzman effected some improvements, obtaining Canadian patents in 1873, 1882, and 1896.

After the founder's death in 1899 his son George C. Heintzman (1860–1944), who had been superintendent and general manager since 1885, became president, although other sons – Herman (1852–?), William F. (1856–?), and Charles Theodore (1864–97) – all joined the family business. Early in the years of George C. Heintzman's presidency the first branches were opened, and a 'quarter-grand' piano (1.7 m) was introduced in 1905. The sales and office headquarters at 195 Yonge St, Toronto, which were to remain the nerve centre of the firm until 1971, were occupied in January 1911, at which time the staff, including office personnel and travelling salesmen, numbered about 400. Besides its main lines, Heintzman manufactured player-pianos (grand and upright, manual and electric) until the 1920s. After the temporary drop in business during World War I demand returned sharply in the 1920s. At the beginning of that decade about 3000 Heintzman pianos were sold annually. There were 18 branch stores and 13 distributors, from coast to coast, and the export trade was significant. Two competing companies were acquired when their heads retired in 1927: that of Theodore August's nephew Gerhard *Heintzman, and the *Nordheimer Piano & Music Co.

The effects of the Depression on piano sales, however, were severe; only 200 Heintzman pianos were built in 1934. To broaden the base of its operations the company introduced the sale of sheet music, phonographs and records, Hammond organs, and other instruments – and eventually non-musical household appliances – in all its branches. Under the presidency 1942–56 of George C. Heintzman's son George Bradford (1892–1961) there were 7 branches and 40 agencies, but pianos accounted for less than half of the sales, averaging about 900 annually at the beginning of the 1950s.

In 1956 Edward L. Baker, a former comptroller of Canadian Breweries Ltd, was appointed president, the first not to be a member of the family. However, Herman Heintzman (b Toronto 1922, d 1969), a great-grandson of Theodore, owned a controlling interest in the company and was a vice-president, and other family members continued to occupy key positions: Bradford Craig Heintzman was sales manager until 1968, and William D. Heintzman was factory manager until 1964. In the latter half of the 1950s the annual production of pianos was about 1000. Baker dropped the side lines (such as sheet music and hi-fi equipment) and restored the operations to their original scope, emphasizing the manufacture and sales of pianos, although the sale of electronic organs was continued. Baker increased the number of branches from 9 to 16 and introduced more aggressive sales methods. In 1960 production was about 1450 upright and 50 grand pianos.

In 1962 an up-to-date factory (supposed to be the first built in Canada in the 20th century, but more likely the first after World War I) was built in Hanover, replacing the Toronto Junction plant, although the building of grand pianos continued until 1977 at a Don Mills (Toronto) location, and was moved only in 1978 to Hanover. The Hanover plant was enlarged in 1967, giving it a potential capacity for an annual production of 5000 pianos. Heintzman acquired D.M. Best and Co Ltd in 1973 and continued to operate it as a subsidiary in 1980.

Baker remained president until 1969; after a period of litigation Ann Heintzman (widow of the former vice-president, Herman, who had died in 1969) became president. Meanwhile, another great-grandson of the company's founder, William D. Heintzman, had become president of the *Sherlock-Manning Piano Co and in 1978 a merger of Heintzman and Sherlock-Manning under William's presidency was announced, the name Heintzman Limited was adopted, and headquarters were moved to Hanover, Ont. (The Don Mills plant, which had become the company's head office in 1971, was sold in 1976, although the head office continued to be located in Don Mills until 1978.) The new company continued to produce instruments under both names, with the Heintzman grand piano the top line. All branch stores were sold in 1976, but some dealerships retained the name as agents of the company.

Music publishing has been a marginal activity of the company, based on copyrights taken over from Nordheimer (eg, the Canadian edition of Paderewski's *Minuet*, some TCM graded examination books, and a few pieces by W.O. *Forsyth). A *Heintzman & Co. Waltz* was written under a pseudonym by J.B. Glionna in 1899; there is also a *Heintzman & Co. March* (nd) by H. Zickel, and another (nd) by S. Minnes.

A Heintzman Piano Company Band was active in the 1880s and 1890s. Under the direction of Herbert L. *Clarke until 1892, it had 40 to 45 players, played at Hanlan's Point (one of the Toronto Islands) during summer evenings, and visited the Montreal Exposition in September 1891.

It is reasonable to assume that the serial numbers of Heintzman pianos began at 1000. A few benchmark numbers follow:

1867	1150	1910	35,600
1870	1400	1920	61,700
1880	2310	1930	83,200
1890	7510	1940	86,300
1900	15,700	1950	93,060

In 1980 Heintzman grand pianos were numbered in the 200,000 series, uprights in the 165,700 series.

Apart from the Drew-Heintzman & Annowski instrument and an 1874 specimen owned by the company, early Heintzmans may be seen at the Glenbow-Alberta Institute in Calgary and at the Western Development Museum, Yorkton, Sask. Members of the Heintzman family (whose fifth generation continued to be involved directly in the company until 1981) have been continuously active in the encouragement and support of musical organizations and activities in Toronto as well as in business-related organizations. In May 1979 the Historical Sites and Monuments Board of Canada erected a memorial plaque to Theodore Heintzman at the First Lutheran Church, Bond St, Toronto. In January 1981 Heintzman Ltd was sold by the family to Sklar Manufacturing Company. The new owner announced that it would continue to build pianos in Hanover, Ont.

BIBLIOGRAPHY

The Commemorative Biographical Record of the County of York (Toronto 1907)

Porter, McKenzie. 'The piano with the all-Canadian tone,' *Maclean's*, 11 May 1957

Harbron, John D. 'At Heintzman hustle replaces history,' *Executive*, May 1961

Gibson, Paul. 'Soon play Yankee Doodle on Heintzman & Co. pianos,' *Financial Post*, 19 Sep 1964

Jones, Donald. 'Heintzman's old house enduring as his pianos,' *Toronto Star*, 10 Apr 1976

Harper, Tim. 'The Heintzman family: 110,000 pianos later,' *Fugue*, Sep 1977

Swimmings, Betty. 'Piano firm remains a family affair,' Ottawa *Citizen*, 6 Oct 1979

Dewey, Martin. 'Heintzman piano firm has played its part for 120 good and bad years,' Toronto *Globe and Mail*, 14 Apr 1980

Finlayson, Ann. 'They shoot piano-makers, don't they?' *Maclean's*, 3 Nov 1980 HK, PW

Gerhard Heintzman Co. Toronto piano manufacturers. Gerhard Heintzman (b Hanover 6 Oct 1845, d Toronto 8 Oct 1926), a nephew of Theodore *Heintzman, moved in 1860 to the USA and in 1867 to Toronto. He established the Heintzman Piano Manufacturing Co in 1877 on Little Richmond St and built 10 pianos by himself. In 1879 he moved to 365 Queen St. He began making pianos – almost a third of his output – for A. & S. *Nordheimer in 1881, and by 1885 he was employing 50 to 60 people who produced eight pianos a week. The two companies merged ca 1886 as the Lansdowne Piano Co. After Heintzman withdrew from that partnership in 1890, he established the Gerhard Heintzman Co. The factory was located at 63–75 Sherbourne St in Toronto, and in 1892 it produced a dozen upright pianos each week from seven different designs. A grand piano was introduced in the 1890s. The factory was enlarged in 1900 and a recital hall was added. Showrooms were opened at 97 Yonge in 1905 and at 41–3 Queen St in 1909. After Gerhard's death the business was purchased by Heintzman & Co. The Gerhard Heintzman Co produced over 39,900 instruments.

Gerhard Heintzman's daughter was the composer and pianist Cornelia Heintzman Richardson. EK

HELLER, Irving. Pianist, teacher, b Providence, RI, 18 Nov 19??, landed immigrant in Canada 1960; diploma (Juilliard) 1942. He studied 1940–3 at the Juilliard School with Carl Friedberg (piano) and Vittorio Giannini (composition), and obtained the Harry Rosenberg Memorial Prize in 1942 as best pianist among the graduating students. After working with Eduard Steuermann in New York City and California, he studied 1948–9 in Paris at the École normale de musique with Yves Nat (piano) and at the Paris Cons with Nadia Boulanger (composition). He returned to New York in 1956 and then moved to Montreal, where he taught piano 1960–78 at the *CMM. He also taught at the *JMC Orford Art Centre and at *McGill U. Michel *Gonneville, Richard *Gresko, and Claude *Savard are among his pupils. After 1968 he and Monique Marcil shared the artistic direction of the *Montreal International Competition. He has been a member of the juries of several international piano competitions, including those at Moscow (Tchaikovsky Competition, 1970 and 1974), Lisbon (1972), Munich (1977), and Warsaw (International Chopin Competition 1980). Heller has given recitals in Canada, the USA, South America, and Europe. Zelda *Heller is his wife. NT

HELLER, Zelda (b Cohen). Administrator, music and drama critic, b New Brunswick, NJ, 2 Dec 19??, naturalized Canadian 1972; B SC (Juilliard) 1945, MA (Columbia) 1948. She was an editor in 1948 for the firm Edition Musicus New York Inc and subsequently a representative of Acme Lithography in Brazil. She settled in Montreal in 1960. She was music critic 1965–8 for *The Gazette* and wrote dance and theatre criticism 1968–72 for the *Montreal Star*. She was director of performing arts 1972–4 for the federal Secretary of State and consultant 1974–6 to the drama department and the program 'The National News' for CBC TV in

Toronto. She served 1976–80 as music officer of the *OAC. She married the pianist Irving *Heller.
NT

HELMER, Paul. Pianist, b Kirkland Lake, Ont, 18 Oct 1938; Artist Diploma (Toronto) 1958, BA (Toronto) 1966, MA (Columbia) 1968, PH D (Columbia) 1975. He studied piano with Alberto *Guerrero and Bela Böszörmeny-Nagy in Toronto, and made his debut with the *TSO at 15. Winning the Eaton Graduating Scholarship (1958) from the *U of Toronto and the Ravel Medal (1958) from the French government, he took advanced piano studies 1958–61 in Stuttgart, Berlin, and Vienna, and placed second in the 1959 International Competition for Musical Performers in Geneva. He was resident musician 1962–4 at the *U of New Brunswick before returning to studies at the U of Toronto and Columbia U, New York, where he later completed a PH D thesis, 'European pastoral calls and their possible influence on western liturgical chant.' In 1972 he joined the faculty of music at *McGill U. During an extensive solo career he appeared with major Canadian orchestras and on radio and TV, performing in the Canadian premieres of Messiaen's *Turangalîla-Symphonie* (1964), Boulez' *Structures for Piano*, Book II (1966, with Bruce *Mather), and *Weinzweig's *Piano Concerto* (1966). In the 1970s Helmer appeared frequently as accompanist to such artists as Cathy Berberian, Victor *Braun, and Margarita Schack.

Paul Helmer is the brother of Terence Helmer, the viola of the *Orford String Quartet.

DISCOGRAPHY

Beethoven *Seven Bagatelles; Alla Ungharese Quasi Un Capriccio; 11 Bagatelles*. 1970. CBC SM-120
– *The Diabelli Variations*. 1968. CBC SM-49
Brahms *Piano Pieces, Op. 76; Variations and Fugue on a Theme by Handel*. 1971. CBC SM-183
Charles – Lambert – Whyte – R. Strauss – Debussy (songs). Lynne Cantlon sop, Helmer pf. 1972. CBC SM-184
Romantic Flute Music: Schubert – Franck. Baxtresser fl, Helmer pf. (1977). McGill U Records 77005
Somers Sonata No. 2. 1976. RCI 450
Weinzweig *Piano Concerto*. TS, Feldbrill cond. 1969. CBC SM-104
See also Discographies for Donald Bell; John Boyden; Victor Braun; Patricia Rideout; Bernard Turgeon.

BIBLIOGRAPHY

Mulliette, Maida. 'Paul Helmer, commuting pianist,' Toronto *Glove and Mail*, 8 Mar 1958 SW

Heloise and Abelard. Opera in 3 acts, 16 scenes, by Charles *Wilson, with a libretto taken by Eugene Benson from his own 1953–4 radio play on the tragic love of the 12th-century theologian Peter Abelard and his pupil Heloise, niece of Canon Fulbert. Commissioned by the *COC to mark its 25th anniversary, the opera had its premiere 8 Sep 1973 and two subsequent performances at Toronto's *O'Keefe Centre. The production travelled to Ottawa the following month for two performances at the *NAC. Leon Major was stage director, Victor *Feldbrill conductor, Murray Laufer designer. Heather *Thomson was Heloise, Allan *Monk Abelard, Don *McManus Fulbert. Also in the cast were John *Arab, Peter *Barcza, Émile *Belcourt, Garnet *Brooks, Alan *Crofoot, Patricia *Rideout, and Phil *Stark. The press praised the polish of the score, the libretto, and the production but found the music wanting in strong character delineation.
KW

HEMSWORTH, (Albert) **Wade**. Draftsman, singer-songwriter, guitarist, b Brantford, Ont, 23 Oct 1916. Though he was introduced to folk music as a boy in Brantford, his interest was stimulated by exposure to the folksongs of Newfoundland, where he was stationed during World War II. As a draftsman for Ontario Hydro and 1952–78 for the CNR (Montreal), he travelled widely with survey parties in the northern wilds of Quebec, Ontario, and Labrador. His experiences inspired *'The Black Fly Song,' 'The Log Jam Song' (sung by the composer for the 1959 NFB production *Log Drive*), and 'The Log Driver's Waltz' (sung by Kate and Anna *McGarrigle for the 1978 NFB animation film of the same title). Hemsworth also is known for 'The Wild Goose,' 'Foolish You,' and 'The Story of the *I'm Alone*,' among others. His songs have been published in anthologies of Canadian songs and recorded by Omar *Blondahl, the Couriers, Tom *Kines, the McGarrigles, Chris Rawlings, the *Travellers, and others. According to Dane Lanken, 'Hemsworth creates beautiful music, music that celebrates life lived fully, the fine old values of hard work and its rewards, the wilderness and its myriad wonders. It is ... intensely Canadian music, created with a rawness and vitality that matches the wilderness it describes, captures it like a Tom Thompson [sic] painting.' Though he seldom has appeared in public, Hemsworth sang at the 1963 *Mariposa Folk Festival and has performed for the McGill (U) Folk Song Society and, with the Mountain City Four or alone, at *Bishop's U. He has made many radio and TV appearances. His lone LP, *Folk Songs of the Canadian North Woods* (1955, Folk FP 821), includes his 'The Black Fly Song' and 'The Shining Birch Tree.' Hemsworth is a member of CAPAC.

BIBLIOGRAPHY

Lanken, Dane. 'Hemsworth – songs that are very, very Canadian,' Montreal *Gazette*, 23 Oct 1971 MM

HENDERSON, Mary (m Buckley). Soprano, teacher, b Longueuil (near Montreal) 17 Dec 1912. A study of the violin, begun at 10, led to a licentiate from McGill U. Her vocal studies, begun with Henri *Pontbriand and Pauline *Donalda in Montreal, were pursued in New York with C. Waldemar Alves and Paul Althouse. Returning to Montreal she made her recital debut in a Sarah *Fischer Concert in March 1942. Two months later she sang in the inaugural presentation of Pauline Donalda's *Opera Guild of Montreal. By autumn she was a member of New York's New Opera Company; her roles included Lisa in *The Queen of Spades* and Parassia in Moussorgsky's *The Fair at Sorochintsy*. For two seasons, 1943–5, she toured the USA and Canada as a leading soprano with Fortune Gallo's *San Carlo Opera Company, singing almost 400 performances in such roles as Aida, Marguerite, Micaela, Nedda, Violetta, Mimi, and Butterfly. She made her *Metropolitan Opera debut 30 Mar 1946 as Micaela and remained for two seasons with the company. Subsequently she sang with various orchestras, on radio, and with such touring troupes as the Wagner Opera and the Nine O'Clock Opera. After 1950 she and her husband, the conductor Emerson Buckley, taught at the Manhattan School of Music. She began to teach voice at the U of Miami in Coral Gables, Fla, in 1963. In the early 1950s she recorded an operatic recital (Allegro-Royale 1637).
JBM

HENDRICKSON, John (Henry). Pianist, b Montreal 11 Apr 1956; AMA 1973, LMA 1973. A pupil of Susan Howard, Robert *Pounder, and Alexandra *Munn in Edmonton, he also studied with Irwin Freundlich in New York. He made his debut with the Edmonton Youth Symphony in the fall of 1969. He was co-winner in the 1972 Young Pianists' International Competition at Buffalo, NY, was the highest-ranked North American in the 1973 Van Cliburn Competition, and won the Warsaw Critics' Prize at the 1975 International Chopin Competition. He placed third in the 1976 *Montreal International Competition, in which he won a special award for his performance of the set piece (Jacques *Hétu's *Fantaisie*). Hendrickson has given solo recitals, has appeared with the *Edmonton SO and with the Krakow, Lublin, and Warsaw Philharmonics in Poland, and has been heard over CBC radio (with the *CBC Vancouver Chamber Orchestra) and Radio Poland. His repertoire includes concertos by Bartók, Beethoven, Chopin, Gershwin, Mozart, Prokofiev, Rachmaninoff, Ravel, Schumann, and Tchaikovsky. He has recorded for the Polish label Muza. After a recital at Canada House in London, David Murray described Hendrickson's style as 'individual ... chunky, masculine and yet permitting any amount of sensitive detail' and noted that his performance 'was enough to prove that his great technical security answers to a rigorous musical intelligence' (*Financial Times*, 26 Mar 1980).
(RDM)

HENIG, Sheila (m Sidney). Pianist, soprano, b Winnipeg 19 Feb 1934, d Toronto 15 May 1979; ARCT piano, voice, 1952, Artist Diploma (Toronto) 1955. She studied piano with Jean *Broadfoot and Gordon *Kushner in Winnipeg and with Margaret Miller *Brown at the RCMT. Her voice teachers were Lillian Smith Weichel and Dorothy *Allan Park. In 1955 she was awarded the Eaton Graduating Scholarship by the U of Toronto. A laureate in piano at the International Competition for Musical Performers in Geneva in 1961, she also made her European debut that year in Amsterdam. She returned to Europe in 1964 and played in London at Wigmore Hall and in Greece, Spain, and Austria. In 1976 she performed in Vienna, Salzburg, Brussels, and Rotterdam.

During her career Henig appeared in Canada with the *Victoria SO, the *CBC Vancouver Chamber Orchestra, the *NACO, the *TS, the *Halifax SO, and the CBC Winnipeg and Toronto orchestras. She made her US debut in 1960 with the Houston SO. She also participated in chamber music performances at the *Stratford and *Charlottetown festivals. Returning to singing in 1977, she was coached by Elizabeth Benson *Guy.

At Carnegie Recital Hall, 2 Mar 1978, Henig made her New York debut in the triple role of self-accompanied singer, solo pianist, and piano partner to the expatriate Soviet oboist Senia Trubashnik. Joseph Horowitz, reviewing the recital in the *New York Times* (5 Mar 1978), wrote: 'It was no stunt. Miss Henig left no doubt that she was a richly satisfying artist in all three capacities ... [her playing] distinguished by unusually lucid textures, as well as the necessary impetuosity and wit ... [and] the sweet quivery timbre of her soprano ... most appealing.'

DISCOGRAPHY

Grieg – Glick *Prayer and Dance* – Ginestera – Falla. D. Domb vc. 1978. CBC SM-348
Morawetz – Prokofiev – Liszt. 1970. CBC SM-118
Piano Portraits: Brahms – Schubert – Mendelssohn – Chopin – et al. 1975. Attic LAT 1002
Ravel *Sonatine* – Debussy *Prélude No. 2; Estampes*. 1966. CBC SM-1
Sheila Henig Plays Brahms, Chopin, Debussy, Glick, Philippe, Rachmaninoff. 1968. London CTLS 5107
Willan *Piano Concerto*. CBC Vancouver Chamb O, Avison cond. 1973. CBC SM-205

BIBLIOGRAPHY

Kirby, Blaik. 'Henig's reincarnation in a triple-threat act,' Toronto *Globe and Mail*, 14 Mar 1978 (WS)

HENNINGER, Richard (Jr). Composer, writer, teacher, b Pasadena, Cal, 8 Dec 1944; BA (Pomona) 1966, M MUS (Toronto) 1968, D MUS (Stanford) 1976. He studied composition at Pomona College in Claremont, Cal, and at Indiana U 1966–7, and with John *Weinzweig and Gustav *Ciamaga at the *U of Toronto. He lectured 1968–74 at the U of Toronto and concurrently taught electronic music at the Ontario College of Education. His *Catena* (1969) won the City of Birmingham Orchestra's 50th-anniversary international competition in 1970. His compositions for tape include *Visions from Outer Space* (1969) commissioned for Toronto's McLaughlin Planetarium. He also has composed for chamber ensembles. With his wife Polly he prepared the John Weinzweig dossier for the *CMB* (Spring–Summer 1973). He has written articles for *Contemporary Canadian Composers*. A list of his compositions 1966–72 can be found in *Compositeurs canadiens contemporains*. In 1975 he returned to the USA. He is a member of CAPAC and an associate of the *CMCentre. CF

HEPNER, Lee (Alfred). Conductor, teacher, b Edmonton 24 Nov 1920; ARCT 1950, B MUS (Toronto) 1951, BA (Washington) 1957, MA (Columbia) 1961, PH D (New York) 1972. He organized the Edmonton Pops Orchestra in 1947 before moving to Toronto to study at the RCMT. His doctoral thesis was 'An analytical study of selected Canadian orchestral compositions of the mid-20th century,' based on works of *Freedman, *Somers, and *Weinzweig. He conducted the U of Toronto SO 1949–50 and studied conducting in New York 1950–1, in Hilversum and Los Angeles in 1954, and at the Pierre Monteux school, Maine, during the summer of 1956. He was the founding conductor of the *Edmonton SO in 1952 and directed it for eight years. Moving to Hamilton, he served as music director of the McMaster Operatic Society 1961–7, the *Hamilton Philharmonic Orchestra 1962–9, and the *Hamilton Opera Company 1966–72. He has guest-conducted orchestras in Canada, the USA, and Europe, and has taught in 1959 at the Jeunesses musicales, Weikersheim, West Germany, while on a *Canada Council scholarship in Europe, and 1960–1 and 1970 at Queen's College of the City U of New York. He began teaching at *McMaster U, Hamilton, Ont, in 1961. In 1976, at Dundurn Castle, Hamilton, Hepner conducted the Mohawk College Opera Theatre in the first staged, orchestrally accompanied performance of *Quesnel's **Colas et Colinette* since the 1807 revival. (CF)

HÉRALY, François J.A. Clarinetist, bandmaster, teacher, b Flavin, near Namur, Belgium, 1856, d Montreal 22 Jul 1920. In 1867 he began music study in Brussels, and in 1873 he attended the conservatory at Namur, where he joined a regimental band. He enrolled in 1877 at the Liège Cons and later directed bands in Belgium, France, Switzerland, and Algeria before moving to Quebec to lead the Sherbrooke Band. In Montreal ca 1903 he became music director of *Sohmer Park and of the St-Pierre-Apôtre parish Temperance Band. The young Wilfrid *Pelletier was a drummer in the latter. Héraly also taught most wind instruments.

Héraly's wife (b Ida Campbell in Sherbrooke ca 1860, d Montreal after 1939) studied piano with Mrs Holland (who had studied at the Paris Cons) and received a diploma from the Canadian College of Music. For 54 years she taught piano, solfège, and harmony in Montreal. She was the first teacher (1904–14) of Wilfrid Pelletier.

BIBLIOGRAPHY

Prévost, Arthur. 'C'etait un génie musical,' Montreal *La Patrie*, 5 Aug 1939
Pelletier, Wilfrid. *Une symphonie inachevée* ... (Montreal 1972) GP

J.W. Herbert & Co. Montreal publishing, retailing, and instrument-building firm, active from the mid-1830s to 1861. It built and repaired pianos and organs as early as 1837, when *La Minerve* (1 Jun 1837) printed testimonial letters on behalf of one of the partners, William Dennis. By 1842 the company was established as a dealer in both instruments and music, with wide connections in Europe and the USA. The firm's publications probably began to appear in the late 1840s. The Herbert imprint often is in a secondary position on sheet-music covers, and in all known cases but one a US firm is the primary publisher. Moreover, those publications issued solely by Herbert often bear US plate numbers. Only 3 of the 13 known ones were printed in Canada, and those by John *Lovell. Nevertheless the majority of Herbert publications were by Canadian composers, and on Canadian themes, eg, *Les Bords du St-Laurent* by Patrick O'Leary and *Maple Leaf Polka Mazurka* and *Snow Shoe Tramp* by Harold F. Palmer. The most 'Canadian' compositions of all, Joseph *Maffré's *Original Canadian Quadrilles* (1847) based on traditional Canadian airs, were published in New York by Firth & Hall in collaboration with Herbert. The cover of the collection depicts a beaver and maple leaves, Canadian emblems appearing perhaps for the first time on sheet music. Indeed, Herbert publications are among the first in Canada to have been issued with illustrated covers. Of particular interest for content, design, colour, and execution is the cover of Charles d'Albert's *Grand Trunk Waltzes*, featuring the Victoria Bridge (completed in 1859, officially opened in 1860).

BIBLIOGRAPHY

Calderisi, Maria. 'Music publishing in Canada: 1800–1867,' unpubl MMA thesis, McGill 1976 MC

HERLINGER, Ruzena (b Schwartz). Soprano, teacher, b Tabor, Czechoslovakia, 8 Feb 1890, naturalized Canadian 1954, d Montreal 19 Feb 1978. She began piano lessons at nine and voice study in 1916 in Vienna, continuing later in Berlin with Mme Tömlich. In 1922 she was a member of the newly formed ISCM in Vienna. A music patron in Austria, she gave recitals herself in the major European cities and received at her home the composers Berg, Hindemith, Honegger, Krenek, Ravel, Roussel, Webern, and Wellesz, several of whose works she performed. She gained a hearing for Webern's Lieder, particularly in London. When she commissioned a work from Alban Berg in 1929, he interrupted the composing of *Lulu* to write *Der Wein*, a concert air which he dedicated to her ('Der ersten Interpretin Frau Ruzena Herlinger in herzlicher Ergebenheit'). She gave the premiere 5 Jun 1930 in Koenigsberg under Hermann Scherchen and the Vienna premiere 21 Jun 1932 under Webern. After living in England during World War II she returned to Czechoslovakia in 1946 to conduct the Prague Radio Choir. She arrived in Montreal in August 1949, and taught there, at first privately and then 1957–62 at the *CMM and 1963–ca 1970 at *McGill U. Among her pupils were Josèphe *Colle, Claude *Corbeil, Claire *Gagnier, Christine *Harvey, Joseph *Rouleau, Huguette *Tourangeau, and André *Turp.

BIBLIOGRAPHY

Reich, Willi. *Alban Berg* (London, New York 1965) JCl

Her (His) Majesty's Theatre. Montreal theatre located on Guy St and seating 1750 on a main floor and two balconies. It opened 7 Nov 1898 with *The Ballet Girl*, a musical comedy; and numerous concerts, recitals, and presentations of opera and ballet occupied its stage over the ensuing 65 years. In January 1899 Mr and Mrs Frank Murphy, the owner-managers, welcomed the singers Marcella Sembrich, Thomas Salignac, Giuseppe Campanari, and Pol Plançon. On 2 October that year Victor Herbert's operetta *The Singing Girl* was given its world premiere with Alice Nielsen in the title role and the Canadian-born tenor Eugene Cowles singing Duke Rodolphe. The Charley Opera of New Orleans gave 20 performances of operas and operettas in 1899, followed by the *Metropolitan Opera in 1899 and 1911, the Savage Grand Opera (*Otello* in 1904, four performances of *Parsifal* in 1905), the *Montreal Opera Company 1910–13, the *National Opera Company of Canada 1913–14, the Quinlan English Opera (nine operas by Wagner in 1914, including the complete *Ring of the Nibelungen*), the *Montreal Festivals 1940–6, and the *Opera Guild of Montreal 1942–63, not to mention numerous touring companies such as the *San Carlo, the Columbia, and the Salmaggi.

During the 1900–1 season and the first half of 1901–2 chamber music concerts, with local artists and guests, were held on Sundays, with matinee and evening performances. The J.-J. *Goulet and Alfred *De Sève string quartets were among the performing ensembles. The series was interrupted when the organizer was sentenced to one hour's imprisonment for violating the municipal by-law concerning the Lord's Day Observance Act. Among the orchestras that played there were the *Goulet *MSO 1907–10, the *Canadian Grenadier Guards Band 1920–3, and the *Montreal Orchestra 1931–41. The theatre also presented Marian Anderson, Ferruccio Busoni, Walter Gieseking, Sergei Rachmaninoff, Paul Robeson, and numerous other musical celebrities. It was taken over in 1906 by the J.B. Sparrow Theatrical and Amusement Co, and in 1924 by Theatrical Enterprises. Consolidated Theatres and United Theatres were the owners when it was demolished in 1963.

BIBLIOGRAPHY

'The opening of Her Majesty's Theatre,' *Montreal Daily Star*, 8 Nov 1898
Maskoulis, Julia. 'Her Majesty's Theatre: a royal touch,' Montreal *Gazette*, 3 Jun 1978 GP

HERSENHOREN, Samuel (David). Conductor, violinist, b Toronto 2 Jul 1908. After studies in Toronto with Samuel Barshtz and with Mrs S.R. McCully at the *Hambourg Cons, he made his debut at *Massey Hall at 11. He then studied 1920–5 in Toronto and in several European centres with Jan *Hambourg. On his return to Toronto Hersenhoren made his radio debut in 1925 on CKNC (where he later played in Geoffrey *Waddington's orchestra). He played 1925–7 in the New SO and 1927–44 in the *TSO. He also played in various local theatre orchestras and, in the early 1960s, in the *CBC SO. He was founder (and conductor 1932–40) of the New World Chamber Orchestra – six strings and piano – which toured Ontario, gave school concerts for the Toronto Board of Education, and in 1934 performed with the *Toronto Mendelssohn Choir.

In 1933 Hersenhoren began conducting the orchestras for such CRBC (later, CBC) programs as 'Lullabye Lagoon,' 'Fugitive Melodies,' 'Dancing Strings,' and, during World War II, 'Carry on

Canada,' 'Comrades in Arms,' and the 'Johnny Home Show' 1945–6. In 1943 he conducted CBC radio orchestras in the premieres of *Weinzweig's *Our Canada* and *Willan's *Hymn for Those in the Air*. From 1941 to 1945 he conducted 25 Victory Loan Shows, starring Raymond Massey, Beatrice Lillie, Ronald Coleman, Charles Boyer, and others. In 1945 he began a long association with the comedians Wayne and Shuster, conducting for their CBC radio and TV shows. (The latter began in 1954.) For his radio work Hersenhoren received LaFlèche Trophies in 1945, 1946, and 1947. In 1947 he re-formed and enlarged the New World Chamber Orchestra for a CBC summer series on which he conducted radio premieres or Canadian premieres of Samuel Barber's *Capricorn Concerto*, Gerald *Bales' *Essay for Strings*, Oskar *Morawetz' *Serenade*, Barbara *Pentland's *Colony Music*, Stravinsky's *L'Histoire du soldat*, and Walter Piston's *Divertimento*. The orchestra was active until 1951. Hersenhoren was music director 1952–4 of 'The Big Revue,' the first CBC TV variety show. He was a guest conductor of the *Promenade Symphony Concerts, the TSO, and, for summer series in 1946 and 1947, the Buffalo Philharmonic. He was second violin 1942–51 of the *Parlow String Quartet and in 1945 founded the Canadian Artists Trio with Cornelius Ysselstyn, cello, and Leo *Barkin, piano. In 1950 at the *Royal Alexandra Theatre, Toronto, he conducted the orchestra for the first Canadian ballet festival, at which the Volkoff Ballet gave the premiere of Weinzweig's **Red Ear of Corn*. Active in later years as a freelance violinist in various orchestras, Hersenhoren has continued his association with Wayne and Shuster and was the conductor 1967–9 of the Etobicoke Philharmonic Orchestra.

BIBLIOGRAPHY

'Samuel Hersenhoren starts his 25th year in radio,' *CBC Times*, 11 Sep 1949

'Samuel Hersenhoren: a "radio conductor" *par excellence*,' *CBC Times*, 30 Mar–5 Apr 1952

HERTZ, Yaëla (m Berkson). Violinist, teacher, b Tel Aviv, Palestine (Israel), April 1930. She began studying the violin with her mother, who was concertmaster at the Palestine Opera, and then studied with Oedoen Partos and Avdor. At the Juilliard School, New York, she studied with Mischa Mischakoff, and at 19 she won the Prague Competition. Wearing an Israeli army uniform, she gave recitals and concerts with orchestra in her native country, and then continued her career in Europe and in North America. Settling in Montreal, she became concertmaster of the *McGill Chamber Orchestra in 1959. She appeared frequently as its soloist, notably in 1972 when she played the double concertos of Bach and Vivaldi with David Oistrakh at the *Salle Claude-Champagne. As a member and soloist of this orchestra she performed in the Soviet Union in 1966 and in Mexico in 1974. With the same orchestra she recorded some works by Boyce and the Chevalier de Saint-Georges with the violinist Morry Kernerman (1973, CBC SM-258) and Haydn's *Concerto in F* with the harpsichordist Kenneth *Gilbert (ca 1967, CBC SM-18). She has taught at the *CMQ, the Cons de Hull, the *École Vincent-d'Indy, and 1965–7 at *McGill U. She also performed in recital on CBC radio and TV. With her brother Talmon, cello, and Dale *Bartlett, piano, she formed the Hertz Trio in 1977. In 1976 she premiered Alexander *Brott's *Cupid's Quandary*, a concerto for violin and orchestra.

Talmon Herz – cellist, b Tel Aviv 19 Feb 1933; M MUS (Manhattan School of Music) 1960 – is Yaëla's brother, though he uses a different spelling of their surname. He was educated 1952–6 at the Music Training Teachers' College, Tel Aviv, 1956–7 at the Academy of Music of Israel, and at the Manhattan School of Music. Among his teachers were Bernard Greenhouse, Janos Starker, Joachim Stutchevsky, and Paul Tortelier. After playing 1955–7 with the Ramat-Gan Chamber Orchestra and 1960–1 with the Pittsburgh SO, he was principal cello of the *Calgary Philharmonic Orchestra 1962–4 and 1965–6 and resumed that post in 1969. He has appeared in recital at Carnegie Recital Hall in 1960 and 1965, at Wigmore Hall in London in 1965, and on CBC and European radio and TV, as well as performing as a member of various chamber music ensembles. In 1976 he premiered Alexander Brott's *Evocative Provocations*. Herz began teaching at the *U of Calgary in 1962.

(RDM, SPl)

HESSELBERG, Edouard (Gregory). Pianist, composer, b Riga 3 May 1870, d Los Angeles 12 Jun 1935. He studied at the Cons of the Moscow Philharmonic Society and privately with Anton Rubinstein. After living in Germany and France he came to the USA in 1892 and directed conservatories in various cities. In 1912 he was appointed piano teacher and examiner at the *TCM and at several ladies' colleges. He also taught at the Hamilton Cons and the London Cons. He stayed in Toronto until 1918, and his pupils included Marie Tavery Gresham, Lucy MacDonald, and Hazel Skinner. The composer of over 100 piano pieces and songs (John Church, Whaley Royce, etc), he also compiled 'A review of music in Canada' for a 1913 supplement of the set of volumes *Modern Music and Musicians* (New York, Toronto 1912), which remains a valuable source of information for the period. Hesselberg also used the name D'Essenelli. He was the father of movie actor Melvyn Douglas. HK

HÉTU. Quebec City instrumentalists and singers: 1 / Lucien and 2 / Daniel, his son.

1 **Lucien**. Organist, songwriter, singer, b Ancienne Lorette, near Quebec City, 8 Apr 1928. He first studied organ 1949–51 with Georges *Lindsay. In 1952 as a singer he won the grand prize of the CBC radio competition 'Les Talents de chez-nous.' He studied voice 1952–3 with Paul Dubois and organ 1954–5 with Germaine Janelle. In 1953 he sang and was co-host on the CKAC radio program 'Sans tambour ni trompette.' As a songwriter he took part in the CBC French network's *'Concours de la chanson canadienne.' His 'Parc Lafontaine' placed fourth among the 12 winning songs announced in a gala TV presentation in 1957. Another of his songs, 'Compagnon de route,' came second the following year. 'La Madone,' 'Pourtant je l'aime,' and 'Vague à l'âme' also made an impression at this competition. He then became known chiefly as an organist and in this capacity he directed the opening of CFTM-TV in 1961. During *Expo 67 he gave organ recitals in the US Pavilion on St Helen's Island. Some of the songs from his 1968 recital with his son Daniel at the Comédie-Canadienne were released on an RCA LP (Gala CGPS 295). Father and son also toured Canada that year as singer and pianist, and in 1969 they appeared at the *PDA.

The Montreal Festival du disque awarded Lucien Hétu two trophies in 1968, one as a performer and another for successful sales of his records. In 1970 he received a gold record for the highest sales of the year. He appeared in Paris in 1965, Switzerland in 1968, and Japan in 1970. He has made some 30 LPs for *RCA Victor, as well as some for Visa. Most of his recordings are of dance music or music for festive occasions. In 1978 for Reader's Digest he produced a set of six LPs entitled *Les Mille Visages de l'orgue* (RCA), in which he performed 72 old and new hit tunes. He also recorded several of Marc *Gélinas's hits for the LPs *La Ronde* (Harmonie HF 90140) and *Marc Gélinas: ses chansons interprétées à l'orgue* (Jupiter JPL 11009). He is a member of CAPAC.

2 **Daniel**. Pianist, organist, accompanist, arranger, conductor, singer-songwriter, b Montreal 1 Dec 1950; B MUS (Montreal) 1971. He began studying piano at four with André *Mathieu. His first single, an organ arrangement of 'La Parade des soldats de bois' (1962, for RCA) received the Grand Prix du disque canadien CKAC (children's section). He studied at the *École Vincent-d'Indy 1967–71 and also worked for three years with Neil *Chotem (orchestration and arranging). In 1971 he distinguished himself at the Yamaha International Organ Competition in Nemuno Sato, Japan. The LP *Daniel Hétu joue les grands succès de Roger Whittaker* (RCA Gala CGPSX-392) was released the following year. He was arranger, accompanist, and conductor for René *Simard in 1972 and Ginette *Reno in 1977. He also worked in this capacity on several of his father's recordings and for such artists as Edith *Butler, Renée *Claude, Nicole Cloutier, Patsy Gallant, Aimé Major, and Renée *Martel. He was music director of the CBC TV programs 'Les Coqueluches' in 1976 and 'Faut voir ça' in 1978 and became music director of 'Les Tannants' on CFTM-TV in 1978. In 1979 he made the LP *Je t'attendais* (Célébrité CEL 2001), in which he performed his own songs and instrumental works. He is a member of CAPAC. (DA, DM, ST)

HÉTU, Jacques (Joseph Robert). Composer, teacher, b Trois-Rivières, Que, 8 Aug 1938; premier prix composition (CMM) 1961. After studying piano, harmony, and Gregorian chant 1955–6 at the *U of Ottawa he attended the *CMM 1956–61 and worked with Clermont *Pépin (composition and counterpoint), Isabelle *Delorme (harmony), and Jean *Papineau-Couture (fugue). A *Toccata* for piano, some chamber music, and two symphonies were written during his apprenticeship years. He also studied piano with Georges *Savaria and oboe with Melvin *Berman. In the summer of 1959 he studied composition with Lukas Foss at the Berkshire Music Center in Tanglewood, Mass. He went to Paris in 1961, the year in which he won the *Prix d'Europe (the first time this award was given to a composer since Henri Mercure in 1927) and the prize of the Quebec Music Festivals (*Canadian Music Competitions). Awarded a *Canada Council grant in 1961, he studied composition 1961–3 with Henri Dutilleux at the École normale, obtaining a diploma of excellence, and analysis 1962–3 with Olivier Messiaen at the Cons national. At the same time he sketched an oratorio which emerged in 1967 as the symphonic fresco *L'Apocalypse*.

In 1965 Hétu took part in 'Cours universitaires' on CBC TV, presenting 13 lectures on the history of instrumental music. His *Variations for Piano* – a work frequently played by Glenn *Gould, Robert *Silverman, and Ronald *Turini – was presented at the International Rostrum of Composers in 1968. He also undertook research into music therapy 1970–1 at Ste-Anne's Hospital in Baie St-Paul, Que. He taught 1963–77 at *Laval U, giving classes at first in music literature and analysis, and later in composition, analysis, and orchestration; he also taught composition 1972–3 at the *U of Montreal. Ginette Bertrand, Antoine Padilla, and Jean-Claude Paquet were among his pupils.

After 1977 Hétu devoted himself exclusively to composition. A series of his folksong arrange-

Jacques Hétu

ments was published that year by the *Alliance chorale canadienne in the collection *Turlurette*. Three of his works (*Concerto, Op 15, Quintette, Op 13*, and *Symphony No. 3*) were performed in London and Paris as part of the *Musicanada tour. On that occasion the critic for the London *Daily Telegraph* (5 Nov 1977) stressed the concerto's dazzling virtuoso solo part (played by Silverman) and described it as 'an epic, post-Bergian work.' Hétu was awarded the Victor Lynch-Staunton prize by the Canada Council in 1979. He is a member of the *CLComp, an affiliate of PRO Canada, and an associate of the *CMCentre.

With a solid background in classical forms, as the titles and the often traditional stamp of his works suggest, Hétu likes to contrast movements of considerable energy with adagios steeped in chromatic expressiveness. His early compositions, influenced by Bartók, Hindemith, and various leading French composers, display a marked polytonality and are rich in percussive rhythms and harmonic tension. A pronounced penchant for generative motivic units led him in 1962, with the *Petite Suite*, to adopt a serial style which, in its subtlety and conciseness recalls the techniques of Webern. With *L'Apocalypse* in 1967 he returned to developmental ideas (*Passacaille, Symphonie No. 3*) emphasizing polyphony and melodic profusion. Because of his numerous and varied commissions (eg, *Antinomie*, written for the *NACO and premiered 4 Oct 1977 in Ottawa), the composer continually adjusts his palette; this is seen particularly in the independent qualities of *Cycle* (1972), premiered by the *SMCQ, and the imposing vision of *Les Djinns* (1975), which is based on a poem by Victor Hugo. Although not one of the avant garde, Jacques Hétu possesses without question an imagination and sensitivity which make him one of Quebec's most appreciated composers both in Canada and abroad.

SELECTED COMPOSITIONS

ORCHESTRA

Symphony, Op 2. 1959. Str orch. Ber 1973. RCI 293 (*Beaudry)
Symphony No. 2, Op 4. 1961. Orch. CMCentre
Double concerto, Op 12. 1967. Vn, pf, chamb orch. CMCentre
L'Apocalypse 'Fresque symphonique d'après saint Jean,' *Op 14*. 1967 (version with spkr 1973). Orch. CMCentre
Concerto, Op 15. 1969. Pf, orch. Ber 1976. RCI 477 (*Silverman)
Passacaglia, Op 17. 1970. Orch. CMCentre
Symphony No. 3, Op 18. 1971. Med orch. Ber 1977. RCI 436 (P. *Hétu)
Fantasy, Op 21. 1973. Pf, orch. CMCentre
Antinomie, Op 23. 1977. Chamb orch. Ms

CHAMBER MUSIC

Four Pieces, Op 10. 1965. Fl, pf. Edn Billaudot 1969. Madrigal MAS-402 (A.-S. *Savoie)
Quintet, Op 13. 1967. Ww. CMCentre. RCI 364 (*Ayorama ww Quin)
Cycle, Op 16. 1969. Pf, ww quin, brass quin. CMCentre. RCI 301 (*SMCQ)
String Quartet, Op 19. 1972. CMCentre
Aria, Op 27. 1977. Fl, pf. CMCentre

PIANO

Sonata, Op 6. 1962. 2 pf. CMCentre. RCI 227/RCA CCS 1021 (V. *Bouchard)
Petite suite, Op 7. 1962. CMCentre. RCI 252 (J. *Dufresne)
Variations, Op 8. 1964. Ber 1970. RCI 251 (A.-S. *Savoie)/Col 32 11 0046 (*Gould)/JMC 4 (*Bartlett)/Concert Hall SMS-2937 (*Tritt)
Prélude et danse, Op 24. 1977. Ms

CHOIR OR VOICE

Les Clartés de la nuit, Op 20 (Nelligan). 1972. Sop, pf. CMCentre. RCI 483 (*Chornodolska)
Les Djinns, Op 22 (Hugo). 1975. 2 SATB, perc, pf. CMCentre

WRITINGS

'Pour un style composite,' *VM*, 11, Mar 1969
'Le compositeur est là pour composer ...,' *CMB*, 11–12, Autumn–Winter 1975, Spring–Summer 1976

BIBLIOGRAPHY

'Jacques Hétu – a portrait,' *Mcan*, 27, Mar 1970
Samson, Marc. 'Hétu airs his opinions on composing in Canada,' *MSc*, 262, Nov–Dec 1971
Kieser, Karen. 'Canadian composers you'll be hearing from ...,' *Toronto Symphony News*, Jan–Feb 1977
PRO Canada Ltd. 'Jacques Hétu,' pamphlets (1976, 1979)
CMCentre. *Compositeurs au Québec: Jacques Hétu* (Montreal 1978)
Contemporary Canadian Composers/Compositeurs canadiens contemporains (IB)

HÉTU, Pierre. Conductor, pianist, b Montreal 22 Apr 1936. He studied piano with Germaine *Malépart, privately in 1954 and at the *CMM 1955–7. At the same time he took courses at the *U of Montreal with Jean *Papineau-Couture (acoustics) and Gabriel *Cusson and Conrad *Letendre (harmony and counterpoint). Awarded a Quebec government grant, he studied in Paris 1958–60 with Marcel Ciampi (piano) and Édouard Lindenberg (conducting) and 1960–2 at the Paris Cons with Louis Fourestier. In 1961 he placed first over 34 candidates in the 'professional graduate' category of the International Competition for Young Conductors in Besançon. He continued his training in conducting, notably under Sergiu Celibidache and Alceo Galliera in Siena, under Charles Munch in Tanglewood in the summer of 1962, and under Hans Swarowsky in Vienna and Jean Martinon in Düsseldorf 1964–5. In 1960 in Paris, with Gail Grimstead (flute) and Jacques *Simard (oboe), he founded the Trio canadien; it toured 1962–3 for the *JMC, giving the premiere of André *Prévost's *Triptyque*.

Hétu made his Canadian debut in 1963, conducting the *MSO in a concert organized by the JMC. Claude *Gingras described this debut in Montreal's *La Presse* (6 Mar 1963): 'Pierre Hétu already displays astonishing command. He knows how to keep his orchestra together and what he does is highly professional. You do not become a conductor, you are born one, and I think it can be said that Pierre Hétu is a born conductor.' Appointed assistant to Zubin Mehta, the MSO's artistic director, Hétu was responsible for conducting the Matinées symphoniques; he held the position until 1968. He premiered André Prévost's *Fantasmes* in November 1963 with the MSO and Maurice *Dela's *Projection* in 1967. He also conducted Prévost's *Terre des hommes* for the opening of the World Festival of *Expo 67. He was music director 1968–72 of the Kalamazoo SO in Michigan, combining that responsibility with the job of associate conductor 1970–3 of the Detroit SO. He was artistic director 1973–9 of the *Edmonton SO.

Hétu has conducted many operas: *Mireille* (1965) and *Manon* (1968) with the *Théâtre lyrique

Pierre Hétu

de Nouvelle-France, *Rigoletto* with the MSO (1966), *Faust* with the *COC (1966), *Macbeth* for the CBC (1973), *La Belle Hélène* at the *NAC for the 1973 Festival Canada (*Festival Ottawa) and in Washington (1975), *The Barber of Seville* with the *Opéra du Québec as part of the Arts and Culture program of the 1976 Olympics, and *Turandot* (1973–74), *Carmen* (1974), *The Merry Widow, Manon Lescaut*, and *Die Fledermaus* (1975), *Madama Butterfly* (1976), *Salome* (1977), and *Macbeth* (1978) with the *Edmonton Opera.

For the JMC's 25th anniversary in 1974 Hétu conducted the orchestra of the *JMC Orford Art Centre in Bach's *Mass in B Minor* at St-Patrice Church, Magog. He also conducted the MSO in 1976 in Handel's *Messiah* at Notre-Dame Church, Montreal, and the Nouvelle Orchestre philharmonique de Paris in 1977 in a Paris concert (see *Musicanada) of works by Jacques *Hétu, *Matton, and Prévost. He appeared as a guest with orchestras in Belgium and Switzerland. Commenting on a performance of Shostakovitch's *Symphony No. 10*, a work which 'can only be sustained by a conductor possessing authority, panache, and an intuitive feel for the music,' Gilles *Potvin wrote: 'Hétu literally propelled the MSO to a grandiose and spacious performance, with an inspirational sweep that did not let up for a single moment and called to mind a [Kiril] Kondrashin or a [Eugen] Mravinsky' (*La Presse*, 30 Jan 1975).

DISCOGRAPHY

J. Hétu *Symphony No. 3* – Borodin *Symphony No. 2*. CBC Mtl orch. 1976. RCI 436
Moussorgsky *Pictures at an Exibition* – R. Stauss *Till Eulenspiegal* – Dvořák *Slavonic Dances, Op 46, no. 8*. JM World orch. 1976. 2-Musicus MS2-45101
Prévost *Fantasmes* – Somers *Fantasia* for orchestra. MSO. 1967. RCI 230/RCA LSC-2980
See also *Colas et Colinette*; Discography for Edmonton SO.

BIBLIOGRAPHY

Gingras, Claude. 'Pierre Hétu: un métier exigeant,' Montreal *La Presse*, 17 Jan 1976 (PR)

'L'Heure du concert' / 'The Concert Hour.' A series of CBC TV music programs devoted to the performance of operas, operettas, and ballets as well as symphonic works and concertos, either in their entirety or as excerpts, coupled on occasion with solo recitals of varying length. The first program was presented 14 Jan 1954 and the last 31 Mar 1966. The series did not run during the summer. At first it was scheduled only on the French network, but in subsequent years a considerable number of programs appeared on the English network schedule, either simultaneously with the French network telecast or, after the introduction of recording on videotape, at a convenient alternative time. In exchange, certain major music productions of the English network were scheduled on 'L'Heure du concert.'

In 1953 in Montreal Pierre *Mercure, Gabriel *Charpentier, and Noël Gauvin formed a CBC-TV musical production team whose main activity was 'L'Heure du concert.' They were joined by François *Bernier at the end of 1954. From 1954 to 1966 the CBC presented 207 programs in this series, for which a grand total of 13,957 contracts were drawn up, 533 for foreign artists and 13,424 for Canadians. Over a period of 13 seasons, 133 complete operas or programs of opera excerpts and 133 ballets were presented. The number and frequency of productions varied from one season to another. From 1954 to 1957 the program was broadcast weekly; the 1957-8, 1963-4, and 1964-5 seasons offered one program every two weeks, including one complete opera (occasionally an operatic scene) each month; from 1958 to 1963 one large production, opera or ballet, was scheduled each month; the 1965-6 season saw a return to a rate of one program a week. Whether operas or operatic excerpts, new or classical ballets, concertante works, recitals, or orchestral music, the majority of productions were in black and white and were produced live. It was only towards the end of the series that pre-recording on videotape was employed.

The chief architect of this distinctive CBC-TV French network series was Pierre Mercure, a dynamic producer who was acutely aware of the demands of TV production. Mercure engaged as artistic consultant Gabriel Charpentier, whose multi-disciplinary knowledge and qualities of imagination and invention also contributed largely to the success of the series. Mercure ultimately gathered around him such talented producers as Jean-Yves *Landry, Pierre Morin, and Guy Parent; the scenic artists Claude Jasmin, Robert Prévost, and Jean-Claude Rinfret; the costume designers Solange Legendre, Richard Lorain, Claudette Picard, and André Vaillancourt; and a graphic artist, Frédérick Back – all regular CBC staff members. Mercure and his colleagues also called on the services of stage producers, notably Paul Buissonneau, Jan Doat, Jean Gascon, Irving *Guttman, and Maurice Sarrazin; the choreographers Ludmilla Chiriaeff, Eric Hyrst, Jeanne Renaud and Françoise Riopelle; and the conductors Ernesto *Barbini, Jean-Marie *Beaudet, François Bernier, Alexander *Brott, Jean *Deslauriers, Pierre *Hétu, Roland *Leduc, Igor Markevitch, Ettore *Mazzoleni, Otto-Werner *Mueller, Wilfrid *Pelletier, Heinz *Unger, and Geoffrey *Waddington.

The program policy pursued by 'L'Heure du concert' was a rare combination of daring and compromise. The series was educative in that it presented to a very wide public masterpieces from the broad repertoire of classical music that were rarely produced in Canada and thus little known to viewers. A few titles will suffice to show the range of works presented: Mozart's *Così fan tutte* (26 Jan and 2 Feb 1956); de Falla's *Il Retablo de Maese Pedro* (22 Nov 1956); Honegger's *Jeanne d'Arc au bûcher* (20 Nov 1958); *L'Histoire de Daniel*, an anonymous 13th-century mystery play (24 Dec 1959); Massenet's *Manon* (11 Feb 1960); Gluck's *Orphée et Eurydice* (9 Mar 1961); Bartók's *Bluebeard's Castle* (1 Feb 1962); Offenbach's *La Vie parisienne* (6 Jan 1963); Rameau's *Les Fêtes d'Hébé* (20 Sep 1964); and Rossini's *The Barber of Seville* (7 Mar 1965), a program that earned the producer Pierre Morin and his team an Emmy Award for exceptional quality in a TV program produced outside the USA.

Mercure's personality focused both on multi-disciplinary presentations and on the avant garde, and thus 'L'Heure du concert' accorded significant television exposure to 20th-century art in the widest sense – music, dance, painting, sculpture, and poetry. In 1960 he began engaging noted guest choreographers, such as Alwin Nikolais and Merce Cunningham. George Balanchine and the New York City Ballet appeared on the program in 1956 and returned several times later. Among other programs worthy of mention are excerpts from Berg's *Wozzeck* (21 Feb 1956); Stravinsky's *Les Noces* (8 Mar 1956) and *Oedipus Rex* (29 Nov 1956); Debussy's *Pelléas et Mélisande* (24 Nov 1960); the Pro Musica Antiqua ensemble from Brussels (9 Nov 1961); Webern's *Four Pieces, Op 7* and the *Quartet, Op 22*, and Stockhausen's *Refrain* (6 Feb 1964); and a recital by the pianist Claudio Arrau (5 Nov 1964). In 1963 Pierre Boulez made his Canadian debut, conducting Stravinsky's *Rite of Spring* and his own *Deuxième Improvisation sur Mallarmé: Une dentelle s'abolit*.

As early as 1954 Mercure had engaged two young Canadian musicians recently graduated from the *RCMT: Glenn *Gould and Jon *Vickers. 'L'Heure du concert' thus began its policy of providing a showcase for the greatest possible number of talented Canadians (singers, instrumentalists, dancers, actors, etc.). Some productions had entirely Canadian casts, eg, Ravel's *L'Enfant et les sortilèges* (27 Dec 1956), 'Opera on television' (1957, a special program presented in Salzburg at a meeting of the International Music Council and notable for its live production and its simultaneous transmission of sound and picture), Offenbach's *La Grande-Duchesse de Gérolstein* (9 Oct 1958), and Poulenc's *Les Dialogues de Carmélites* (15 Apr 1960, the cast Canadian except for the great Greek mezzo-soprano Elena Nikolaidi).

Canadian music, well represented during the first two seasons, was heard more and more in the ensuing years, occasionally taking the form of special programs: 'Hommage à Claude *Champagne' (16 Jan 1964); 'Un Compositeur canadien: Roger *Matton' (21 Feb 1965); and the opera **Loving*, with English text and music by R. Murray *Schafer and French words by Gabriel Charpentier. *Loving*, Pierre Mercure's last production before his accidental death, was presented posthumously on 3 Feb 1966. This audio-visual poem, especially conceived for television, with choreography by Françoise Riopelle, was presented under the direction of Serge *Garant and marks an important date in the history of Canadian television. It was, in a sense, the culmination of this remarkable series, all of whose productions were distinguished by high artistic standards and aimed for the highest level of fusion of sound and image. 'L'Heure du concert' in fact created an ideal climate for aural and visual creation in all forms.

In the months following Mercure's death the program underwent various changes in both presentation and content. Beginning on 18 Sep 1966, 'L'Heure du concert' became integrated with the series 'Les Beaux Dimanches.'

BIBLIOGRAPHY

Bernier, François. 'Le visuel au service de la musique,' *Compositeurs au Québec: Pierre Mercure*, CMCentre (Montreal 1976)

Roberts, John. 'Communications media,' *Aspects of Music in Canada*

CBC Times

La Semaine à Radio-Canada (FM-G)

HEWITT. Ottawa musicians: 1 / Godfrey and 2 / Angela, his daughter.

1 (John Lemuel) **Godfrey**. Organist, choirmaster, teacher, b Cudworth, Yorkshire, England, 4 Jul 1909; FRCO 1930, hon ARSCM 1969, D MUS (Cantuar) 1973. After lessons in Leeds with A.C. Tysoe, he studied 1929-31 at the College of St Nicholas in Chislehurst, where he won the Lafontaine Prize (1930) and, as archbishop's scholar, was organist 1930-1 at Lambeth Palace. He declined an appointment as assistant organist at Westminster Abbey to accept one as organist-choirmaster at Christ Church Cathedral, Ottawa, where he served from September 1931 until his retirement in the fall of 1980. Hewitt maintained a high musical standard at the cathedral, in his teaching, and in his appearances as recitalist (in the 1970s often with his daughter) and accompanist (for the *Canadian Centennial Choir, among other groups and soloists). In 1973 Hewitt received the Lambeth Degree (D MUS) from the archbishop of Canterbury. He was named a Member of the *Order of Canada in 1976.

2 **Angela**. Pianist, b Ottawa 26 Jul 1958; ARCT 1972, B MUS (Ottawa) 1977. Her first piano teacher was her mother, Marion Hewitt – b 15 Oct 1922, BA (Toronto) 1944 – a high-school teacher of English and music. Angela's later teachers have included Earle *Moss and Myrtle Rose *Guerrero (piano, 1964-72 at the RCMT), Walter *Prystawski (violin, privately 1970-4), and Jean-Paul *Sévilla (piano, summers 1973-5 in Aix-en-Provence, main terms 1974-7 at the U of Ottawa, and privately). Angela Hewitt has performed with distinction in several competitions, winning the Chopin Young Pianists' Competition (Buffalo 1975) and the piano category in the 1978 *CBC Talent Festival and placing in the top six in competitions in Washington, DC, Quebec City, Leipzig, and Zwickau, East Germany. She has performed with the *NACO, the *MSO, the Ottawa SO, and the *TS, and has given recitals in Paris in 1977 and Washington, DC in 1978, and on CBC radio and TV. She has a particular affinity for the music of Schumann and Ravel and also has programmed works by Barbara *Pentland and Oskar *Morawetz. Steven *Gellman and Gary *Hayes have written pieces for her. 1 / (JSw), 2 / (FH)

HEWLETT, William (Henry). Teacher, organist, choir conductor, composer, b Batheaston, England, 16 Jan 1873, d Bronte, Ont, 13 Jun 1940; B MUS (Toronto) 1902, hon D MUS (Toronto) 1936. He was a choirboy at Bath Cathedral before emigrating to Canada with his family in 1884. He enrolled at the *TCM and studied piano and organ with A.S. *Vogt, theory with Arthur *Fisher and Albert *Ham, and orchestration with Francesco *D'Auria, graduating in 1893 with the gold medal for organ playing and extemporization. At 17 he went to Carlton St Methodist Church as organist-choirmaster. This was his only Toronto post before he moved in 1895 to London, Ont, where he was organist-choirmaster at Dundas Centre Methodist Church and conducted the London Vocal Society 1896-1902; later he went to Hamilton, where he was in charge of the music at Centenary Methodist Church 1902-38. As an advanced student he worked with the pianist Ernst Jedliczka and the composer Hans Pfitzner in Berlin, and with the pianist Vladimir Cernikoff in London.

With A.S. Vogt he was one of the founders of the *Toronto Mendelssohn Choir and served 1895-7 as its first accompanist. He also accompanied Ernestine Schumann-Heink and Dame Clara Butt when they visited Canada. In 1907 Hewlett and two fellow faculty members became co-directors of the Hamilton Cons (*RHCM). Hewlett succeeded the triumvirate and was sole principal 1918-39. During those years he travelled widely in Canada as adjudicator and examiner. He was conductor 1922-35 of the Elgar Choir (see Bach-Elgar Choir), which flourished under his direction and frequently was joined by the Cleveland Or-

William Hewlett

chestra. In 1927 he conducted a 1000-voice choir in a celebration of Confederation.

Hewlett was an able composer but prolific only in the smaller forms. A musical play, *Jappy Chappy*, was published by Novello, and short piano, vocal, and choral pieces were issued by Ashdown, G. Schirmer, F. *Harris, Metzler, and *Anglo-Canadian. The 1917 *Methodist Hymn and Tune Book*, to which Hewlett was a contributing editor, contains five of his hymn tunes. He also was on the committee which compiled the *United Church Hymnary* (1930). His setting of *'In Flanders Fields' (Toronto 1934) has been widely used in schools and at Remembrance Day ceremonies.

Hewlett was a practising musician of broad capabilities, generous with his time and energy. He was one of the most respected Canadian organists of his day and an expert on church-organ installation. He served on the first (1920) Hamilton committee of the CCO and was national president 1928–9. The *Toronto Daily Star*'s Augustus *Bridle described him as 'a wizard player of rickety wheezetrap organs' who later revelled in his great modern *Casavant at Centenary Methodist Church. His Twilight Recitals there, on Saturday afternoons for some 25 years, were a staple of music in Hamilton. The Hamilton Cons Faculty Club established a scholarship in his name in 1947.

BIBLIOGRAPHY
Hamilton Conservatory of Music. *Yearbooks*
A.E. Mullin private collection. William Henry Hewlett diary 1905–39 (EMn)

HEYWOOD, Earl. Singer-songwriter, guitarist, b near Exeter, north of London, Ont, 12 Mar 1917. In his teens he played euphonium in the Exeter Brass Band. Known as 'Canada's No. 1 Cowboy Singer,' and one of the leading country musicians in Canadian radio, Heywood began his career in 1941 singing his own 'Living in the Army' as the theme of a radio show on CFCO, Chatham, Ont. He joined CKNX, Wingham, Ont, in 1942 and has remained with that station as a singer and announcer for over 35 years. He appeared for almost 20 years on the weekly *'CKNX Barn Dance' and was host 1946–53 for 'Serenade Ranch.' In later years 'The Earl Heywood Show' has been heard on CKNX-FM. Heywood began recording for RCA Victor in 1948, completing with his Serenade Ranch Gang 18 78s (reissued on the LP *Earl Heywood Sings*, RCA Camden CAL 2249), including the national hit 'Alberta Waltz.' He also recorded LPs for Rodeo and Banff with the Heywood Family (his wife, Martha, and their children Patricia and Grant), which performed in the early 1960s; Heywood and his wife began appearing as a duo in the Wingham area in 1965. Of Heywood's three LPs for Dominion, the most popular has been *Tales of the Donnelly Feud* (1969, Dom LPS 21013). A corresponding song folio was published by *Canadian Music Sales in 1971. (Two earlier ones were published by the same company in 1948 and 1951.) Of Heywood's over 300 songs some 60 have been recorded by the composer – including 'Moonlight on the Manitoulin Island,' a hit in the recording by the Moms and Dads. Heywood is a member of CAPAC. MM

HIBBS, Harry (Henry Joseph). Singer-songwriter, accordionist, b Bell Island, Nfld, ca 1944. His father, who worked in the Bell Island iron mines, was a fiddler. The younger Hibbs played button accordion as a boy. He moved to Toronto in 1961 and worked in various factories. In 1968 he began singing and playing the accordion as 'His Nibs, Harry Hibbs, Newfie's Favourite Son' at the Caribou Club, a social centre for Newfoundlanders in Toronto. He starred 1968–74 on 'At the Caribou' and then on 'The Harry Hibbs Show,' both on CHCH-TV, Hamilton. With his Caribou Show Band (later called the Sea Forest Plantation) he has performed throughout the Maritimes and Ontario. In the early 1970s he toured the British Isles. Though his career had waned by the late 1970s, he had made over 10 LPs for *Arc, Caribou, and Marathon (those released by 1972 are listed in detail in Michael Taft's *A Regional Discography of Newfoundland and Labrador 1904–1972*, St John's 1975). Sales of his early LPs made him a leading Canadian recording artist of the day and brought several gold-record awards.

Hibbs' repertoire includes jigs, reels, and other dance pieces, as well as his own ballads – most of them tributes to Newfoundland. He has used *'We'll Rant and We'll Roar Like True Newfoundlanders' as his theme. His music was described by Richard Flohil (*Canadian Composer*) as 'down home music from the Island – part Scottish, part Irish, part country-and-western and all Newfoundland,' and his popularity has been attributed by Blaik Kirby (Toronto *Globe and Mail*, 15 Aug 1970) to 'the undemanding music he plays – melodic and tuneful – and his own old-fashioned simplicity, honesty, modesty.' Hibbs is a member of CAPAC.

BIBLIOGRAPHY
Conn Hughes, Barry. 'Harry, you're saying "agin" again,' *Canadian Magazine*, 26 Sep 1970
Flohil, Richard. 'Harry Hibbs: un gout de Terre-Neuve,' *CanComp*, 57, Feb 1971
Rasky, Frank. 'The minstrels who entertain our Newfies,' *Toronto Star*, 27 Jul 1974

HICKS, Gideon. Bass-baritone, teacher, conductor, b Stoke-Climsland, Cornwall, England, 24 Jun 1868, d Victoria, BC, 23 Nov 1958. A pupil of C.C. Bethune in London, where he sang in concert and oratorio, Hicks moved to Vancouver in 1889. Though at first a carpenter, he played flute in Vancouver's first orchestra, sang locally, and tuned pianos on Vancouver Island and in the Fraser Valley. He also established the short-lived piano firm Hicks and Lovick. He moved in 1898 to Victoria, where he was choirmaster 1898–1909 at Metropolitan Church and conductor of the Victoria Choral Society. With an augmented church choir and orchestra he conducted *Messiah* and *The Creation* with such soloists as Emma *Albani and Robert *Watkin-Mills. Until 1922 he was manager for Vancouver Island of *Heintzman & Co.

Frequently a soloist with the Vancouver Musical Society, Hicks also sang in duo recitals with Gertrude *Huntley Green. In about 1921 he made his radio debut in Seattle, accompanied by Leopold Godowsky. Though *Elijah* was his favorite work, he also sang annually in *Messiah* in various contexts for 40 years. Encouraged by Otto *Morando, with whom he studied in the summers 1920–2 during the tenor's visits to Victoria, Hicks opened his own studio in Victoria in 1920 and began teaching part-time in Vancouver in 1925. He moved to Vancouver in 1932 and was president 1939–40 of the Vancouver Music Teachers' Assn. He retired to Victoria in 1949 but continued to teach. His pupils included Bernie Braden, Brian Hanson, Gordon Heron, Derek MacDermot, Satoshi Nakamura, Karl Norman, Eric *Tredwell, and Alan Watson.

Hicks' brothers George and William also were active musically, George as conductor of the Vancouver Choral Society and first supervisor of music 1904–19 in Vancouver schools, William as a choirmaster in New Westminster, BC. BNSG

HIDY, Marta (Iren). Violinist, teacher, conductor, b Budapest 11 Jan 1927, naturalized Canadian 1963; Performance Diploma (Franz Liszt Academy) 1946, hon FRHCM 1978. She studied 1935–46 with Ferenc Gabriel and Ede Zathureczky (violin), Leo Weiner (chamber music), and Zoltán Kodály (folklore) at the Franz Liszt Academy in Budapest, and in 1943 won the Reményi Competition for the academy's outstanding violin student. She subsequently played 1946–51 in the Hungarian Radio SO, led a prize-winning string quartet in the 1950 Prague International Chamber Music Competition, was a winner in the 1952 International Wieniawski Violin Competition in Poland, and was a Hungarian State Soloist 1953–7, during which time she appeared with orchestras in Hungary, Czechoslovakia, Poland, and Rumania.

Hidy emigrated to Canada in 1957, settling in Winnipeg, where she established the Hidy String Quartet and served 1957–65 as concertmaster of the *CBC Winnipeg Orchestra and assistant concertmaster of the *Winnipeg SO. The quartet languished when, with its cellist Klara Benjamin Belkin and the pianist Chester *Duncan, she formed the *Hidy Trio (1961–8). She left Winnipeg to serve 1964–74 as concertmaster and 1969–74 as assistant conductor of the *Hamilton Philharmonic Orchestra. She began teaching violin and chamber music at *McMaster U in 1965. She also served 1967–77 as artistic director of the Philharmonic Children's School. In 1973, with the pianist Arthur *Ozolins and the cellist Tsuyoshi *Tsutsumi, she formed the Hidy-Ozolins-Tsutsumi Trio, which has performed throughout Ontario and on the CBC. In 1974 with 11 strings (from the Hamilton Philharmonic) and harpsichord she formed the Ensemble Sir Ernest MacMillan. The latter was discontinued in 1977 when she became the conductor of the *Chamber Players of Toronto – a position she held until 1979.

Despite a busy regimen of teaching, orchestral playing, chamber music performance, and conducting, Hidy has maintained a significant solo career. With the pianists Ada *Bronstein and Chester Duncan in Winnipeg and Leo *Barkin and Antonin *Kubalek in Toronto she has given many recitals in public and for CBC radio and TV. She gave the premieres of S.C. *Eckhardt-Gramatté's *Suite for Violin Solo No. 4, Pacific* (8 Feb 1970 at the inaugural concert in Town Hall, *St Lawrence Centre, Toronto) and Hugh *Hartwell's *Waltz Inventions* (January 1978 in Hamilton). The work by Eckhardt-Gramatté was commissioned for Hidy by the CBC. Hidy made her Toronto debut 11 Apr 1962, and for the next day's *Globe and Mail* John *Kraglund wrote: 'the greatest technical demands were never allowed to interfere with the musicality of the interpretation.' After her London debut at Wigmore Hall, with the pianist Geoffrey Parsons, the *Times* critic wrote (4 Oct 1972), 'Their performance of the Debussy *Sonata* was one of the most distinguished I have heard.' Hidy has appeared as concerto soloist with the *TSO, the Winnipeg SO, the Hamilton Philharmonic, and the *Regina SO.

DISCOGRAPHY

Franck *Sonata* for piano and violin – Weinzweig *Sonata* for violin and piano. Ozolins pf. 1974. CBC SM-276

Grieg *Sonata No. 3, Op 45* – Debussy *Sonata* for violin and piano. Barkin pf. 1968. CBC SM-54

Morawetz – Bloch – Bartók – Prokofiev – Kodály. Barkin pf. 1966. CBC SM-28/CBC SM-135 (does not include the Prokofiev)

Ravel – Bartók – Prokofiev. Taussig pf. 1971. CBC SM-161

Somers *Sonata No. 1* – Adaskin *Canzona and Rondo*. Duncan pf. 1965. RCI 221/RCA CCS-1015

HIDY-OZOLINS-TSUTSUMI TRIO

Smetana *Trio, Op 15* – Shostakovich *Trio, Op 67*. Ozolins pf. Tsutsumi vc. 1975. CBC SM-288 KW

Hidy Trio. Founded in Winnipeg in 1961 by the violinist Marta *Hidy, with the cellist Klara Benjamin Belkin and the pianist Chester *Duncan; disbanded in 1968 when the leader moved to Hamilton, Ont. It achieved a national reputation through CBC broadcasts and public concerts at the CBC Winnipeg Spring Festivals. Four performances at *Expo 67 resulted in the recording *Music at the Canadian Pavilion* (1967, CBC Expo 24), featuring works of Michel *Perrault and Shostakovich. S.C. *Eckhardt-Gramatté and the Hungarian composer Erzsébet Szönyi composed works for the trio. LI

Otto Higel Co Ltd. Toronto manufacturer of piano and organ supplies. The company was founded in 1896 by Otto Higel (b Silesia, Germany, 1869, d Toronto 2 Jul 1930), who had bought the Toronto piano action and key manufacturing business of F. Koth, for whom he had worked since moving to Canada in 1889. Higel amalgamated in 1901 with Augustus Newell & Co (founded in 1878 as the Newell Organ Reed Co), and the resulting firm – Newell & Higel Co Ltd – manufactured piano actions, keys and hammers, and organ keys, reeds, and reedboards. Higel purchased the firm's assets in 1904 and restored the name Otto Higel Co Ltd, but also used Canada Piano Action and Key Co Ltd. He achieved his greatest success with the manufacture of player-piano actions, begun in 1906. By 1911 he had added a department for the cutting of perforated piano rolls. The company, located at Bathurst and King streets, employed 450 workers in 1912. Player pianos with Higel actions were in use around the world and were in such demand that a second plant was opened in Buffalo, NY, ca 1914, and a third in New York City in 1916. On Higel's death his son Ralph O. Higel assumed direction of the company, which gradually began making other products, such as cabinets and wooden toys. By 1938 control had passed out of the Higel family, though the name was retained. After 1938 the firm apparently made only kitchen cabinets and appliances, and in 1944 business ceased. FH

HILKER, (John) Gordon. Impresario, producer, b Vancouver 19 Sep 1913; B COM (British Columbia) 1934. His mother was a music teacher and he studied piano for some 12 years. In 1937 he initiated the Greater Artists Series, and in the late 1930s he incorporated Hilker Attractions, which presented leading artists in Vancouver and in the later 1940s throughout western Canada, continuing to operate until 1950. He negotiated with the Vancouver Parks Board for the use of *Malkin Bowl for a special paid-admission summer concert in 1938 which established a precedent, paving the way for *TUTS. In fact, when TUTS was ready to open in 1940, Hilker's advice was enlisted and he subsequently produced its shows and tours until 1949. In the 1950s he was occupied mainly as an organizer of centennial celebrations, first in Ontario for Kitchener and St Thomas, and 1956–8 in British Columbia for the province. He was publicity director in 1957 and general manager 1958–64 for the *Vancouver International Festival, artistic director 1964–7 of the World Festival at *Expo 67, and artistic director in 1968 of the Vancouver International Festival. He left Canada to serve 1968–72 as director of the School of Performing Arts in San Diego. BNSG

HILL, Dan (Daniel). Singer-songwriter, guitarist, b Toronto, of US parents, 3 Jun 1954. Self-taught, he began his career playing and singing at the *Riverboat and, on the strength of the success of his first LP, *Dan Hill* (GRT 9230-1061), and the single 'You Make Me Want to Be,' received the 1975 *Juno Award as best new male singer. The LPs *Hold On* (1976, GRT 9230-1065) and *Longer Fuse* (1977, GRT 9230-1073) followed, along with such singles as 'Growing Up,' 'Hold On,' and 'Sometimes When We Touch.' The last-named, written with Barry Mann, was an international hit 1977–8, selling over a million copies. As a result, Hill received the 1977 Junos for best composer, best male singer, and best-selling LP. In 1978 he was named new male vocalist of the year by the US trade papers *Cashbox* and *Record World*. The LP *Frozen in the Night* (GRT 9230-1079), released in 1978, included 'All I See Is Your Face,' a minor hit in Canada. *If Dreams had wings* (Col FC 3644) followed in 1980. Though the accompaniments on his recordings have been heavily orchestrated by Matthew *McCauley and Fred Molin, in concert Hill usually performs alone (accompanying himself on the guitar) or with a pianist. He has performed widely in Canada and made his first US tour in 1978, opening concerts for Art Garfunkel. Despite his popularity, Hill has been criticized for the naïvety of his music and the adolescent sentimentality of his lyrics. A songbook was issued in conjunction with *Longer Fuse* by McCauley Music in 1977. Hill is a member of CAPAC.

BIBLIOGRAPHY

Bennett, Rob. 'Dan Hill: the realities of adulthood, the idealism of youth,' *CanComp*, 107, Jan 1976

Snider, Norman. Dan Hill and the politics of empathy,' Toronto *Globe and Mail*, 29 Mar 1978 MM

HILL, (Lewis) Eugene. Organist-choirmaster, composer, teacher, b Toronto 8 Apr 1909, d Oxford, O, 15 Mar 1976; LAB 1928, FCCO 1930s, B MUS (Toronto) 1937, ARCO 1938, D MUS (Toronto) 1946. After early studies in Winnipeg he enrolled at the *TCM for organ lessons with Charles *Peaker. He also studied 1936–7 at the RAM with G.D. Cunningham (organ) and Eric Thiman (composition) and in 1940, again at the TCM, with Healey *Willan (composition). Hill taught organ and theory 1947–50 at the *RCMT while he was music director at the Church of St Alban-the-Martyr. From 1950 until his retirement in 1975 he was chairman of the dept of theory and composition at Miami U in Ohio. Of his many works for orchestra, piano, organ, choir, and voice (some listed in the *Catalogue of Canadian Composers*), several were published by *Waterloo, Carl Fischer, *BMI Canada, *Oxford, and *Harris, including *Sonatine* for organ (BMI Canada 1949) and *Prelude and Fugue* for piano (BMI Canada 1957). His *Two Sketches* ('Legend' and 'Scherzetto') were premiered in 1941 by the *TSO and performed later by the *CBC Vancouver Chamber Orchestra. His music has been described as romantic and mildly, not markedly, dissonant. (RM)

HILL, Harry (Henry). Educator, choir conductor, composer, b Burnley, Lancashire, England, 21 Aug 1893, d Ottawa 24 Apr 1972; B MUS ED (Sherwood Music School) 1931. He was taken to Peterborough, Ont, at 12. His teachers included Clifford Higgin in Brantford, Ont, and he studied at the U of Toronto, the ESM (Rochester), the American Institute of Normal Methods (Boston), and the Sherwood Music School (Chicago). After teaching school music and serving as an organist-choirmaster 1918–21 in Paris, Ont, and 1921–8 in Kingston, Hill lived 1928–41 in Kitchener-Waterloo as supervisor of school music and conductor of the *Kitchener-Waterloo Philharmonic Choir and 1941–53 in Ottawa, again as public school music supervisor and as organist-choirmaster in several churches. He organized and conducted a 1000-voice choir for the 25th anniversary of the United Church of Canada in 1952, and a 500-voice choir for the Ottawa celebrations of the coronation of Elizabeth II. He was elected in 1953 for the first of three terms with the Ottawa school board, served 1961–2 as chairman, and resigned in 1966. Hill was the editor 1928–32 of the school-music page of *Musical Canada* and was president 1929–31 of the music section of the Ontario Educational Assn (see OMEA). For his school choirs he composed many short pieces, some published by *Waterloo.

WRITINGS

School Music; Its Practice in the Classroom (Waterloo, Ont, 1934)

The Singing Period, 8 vols (Waterloo 1933–8)

A Study of the Voice of the Boy (Waterloo, Ont, 1943)

– ed. *The Singing Period Book of Carols* (Waterloo 1946)

FH, MM

HINCHEY, E. (Edward) **Reginald.** Bandmaster, composer, b Belleville, Ont, 18 Feb 1886, d there 5 Oct 1952. His teachers included Edward Barrett, Albert Cooke, and J.M. Denmark. He toured 21 countries 1908–10 as a member of the Canadian Kilties Band and during World War I was bandmaster of the 21st Battalion and later the 155th Battalion. After the war and until his death he directed a succession of bands in Belleville, including the Argyll Light Infantry Band, the Belleville Municipal Band, and bands of the Independent Order of Odd-Fellows and the Great War Veterans. He was president of the CBA (*CBDA) 1948–9 and a founder (1946) and dean of the CBA's Composers' Guild. Hinchey wrote or arranged several pieces, mostly for concert band; among them are *Athene* (Waterloo 1942, the regimental march of the Canadian Women's Army Corps) and *With Sword and Key* (1943, the official march of the US Quartermaster Corps, written while the composer was attached to that corps). Hinchey also designed military uniforms and during World War II was adviser on cold-weather and aerial clothing for the US Army and the National Research Council of Canada. He was an affiliate of BMI Canada.

FH (NM)

HIRVY, Michel (Mischa) (b Hirschowitz). Pianist, teacher, b Warsaw, October 1900?, d Montreal 31 Dec 1966. He studied piano with Paul Lutzenko and graduated from the Stern Cons in Berlin. After further studies in Austria he lived 1928–39 in Paris, then in Portugal, and settled in Montreal in 1941. He produced a series of silent films 1928–34 in Paris with Louta Nouneberg and 1951–7 in Montreal, showing in slow motion keyboard performances by Backhaus, Cortot, *Gould, Horowitz, Rubinstein, Serkin, Tureck, and others. These films are deposited in the National Film Archives. Hirvy's Canadian pupils included Edmund *Assaly, Albertine *Caron-Legris, Neil

*Chotem, Kenneth *Peacock, Nina Townsend, Vic *Vogel, and Irene Woodburn. HK

His Majesty's Canadian Grenadier Guards Band. See Canadian Grenadier Guards Band.

His Majesty's Theatre. See Her Majesty's Theatre.

History of Canada in music. A consideration of music which, in retrospect, deals with episodes and personages of Canadian history. The association is established usually through a libretto or song text; rarely through musical content, as in a symphonic poem or a piece of program music; and sometimes superficially through a title alone, more likely than not recalling an anniversary. Music more immediately reflecting historical events is dealt with under Battle music; Confederation and music; Coronations; Disaster songs; Patriotic songs; Political songs; Sovereigns, statesmen, and other public figures; Wars, rebellions, and uprisings.

Probably the first historical figure to furnish inspiration for musicians was Jacques Cartier, whose historic landing on the Gaspé coast in 1534 to take possession of the new land for the King of France prompted a symphonic ode, *La Découverte du Canada*, 'written by a teacher and performed 1 May 1905 at Mont-Saint-Louis Hall in Montreal' (*L'Annuaire théâtral*, 1905) and an *Ode à Jacques Cartier* for soloists, chorus, and organ composed in 1935 by Joseph *Vermandere to words of Louis *Bouhier. The members of the Ordre de bon temps, the society founded by Champlain at Port Royal in 1609, provided the title, theme, and characters (Champlain, Poutrincourt, and Lescarbot) of *Willan's ballad-opera *L'Ordre de Bon Temps / The Order of Good Cheer*, first performed in 1928 at the *CPR Festivals. The Jesuit missionary Jean de Brébeuf (1593–1649) is the subject of Willan's cantata **Brébeuf* (1943) to a text of E.J. Pratt, of R. Murray *Schafer's *Brébeuf* (1961, for baritone and orchestra) to Schafer's own text, and of Paul *McIntyre's dramatic symphony *Jean de Brébeuf* (1962). Marie de l'Incarnation (1599–1672), the Ursuline nun and mystic who left a solid middle-class life in France to establish a Roman Catholic order in New France, was the inspiration for *Anhalt's *La Tourangelle* (1975). Marguerite Bourgeoys, who was the founder of the Sisters of the Congregation of Notre Dame in 1658 and was beatified in 1950, was the subject of a 1950 cantata by Omer *Létourneau. Mère d'Youville (1701–71), the founder of yet another order, the Grey Nuns, inspired Marius *Benoist's oratorio *Mère d'Youville*.

Norman *Symonds' *The Spirit of Fundy* (1972) resurrects the story of the rivalry and feud between two 17th-century Acadians – Charles de la Tour and a Monsieur Charnisay. Among 18th-century subjects of 20th-century works are François Bigot (1703–77), the last intendant of New France; the legendary Évangéline (against the background of the 1755 expulsion of the Acadians from Grand Pré, NS); and the United Empire Loyalists who moved to Canada after the US revolution of 1776. *L'Intendant Bigot* is a three-act opera by J. Ulric Voyer to a libretto by Alfred Rousseau; it was performed in Montreal in 1929. **Evangeline* is the title of an opera by Graham *George (1948), of an oratorio by Robert *Talbot, and of works by several other composers. *The Loyalists* is an opera by the Saint John, NB, composer Douglas Major to words by Patricia Collins; it was performed in 1967. A legend with its roots in the life of New France ca 1740 furnished the story for two ballets, both with the title **Rose Latulippe*. The earlier was composed for TV by Maurice *Blackburn in 1953, the later for the Royal Winnipeg Ballet by Harry *Freedman in 1966. Eugène *Lapierre wrote comic operas based on the lives of two composers, Joseph *Quesnel (*Le Père des amours*, 1942) and Calixa *Lavallée (*Le Vagabond de la gloire*, 1947).

Western Canada supplied historical subject matter for four operas, three of them premiered during Canada's centennial celebrations in 1967. Murray *Adaskin's *Grant, Warden of the Plains* (premiered on CBC radio) dramatizes the conflict between Cuthbert Grant of the Hudson's Bay Company and Alexander Macdonnell. Robert *Turner's *The Brideship* (also premiered on CBC radio) is set in British Columbia in the days of the Gold Rush. Harry *Somers' **Louis Riel* (1967) recounts episodes from the life of the tragic hero of the North West Rebellions. Of all musical evocations of Canadian history, Somers' work remained in 1980 the largest in scale and the most striking. Norman Symonds' *Episode at Big Quill* (1979) tells of the tragic deaths by influenza of eight children in a northern-Saskatchewan settlement at the turn of the century.

The *Klondike area of the Yukon, famous during the turn-of-the-century gold rush, has inspired several musicals, among them Gabriel *Charpentier's *Klondyke* (1965), Dolores *Claman's *In the Klondike* (1967), and Tommy *Banks' *Klondike Kate* (1968). John Gray and Eric Peterson's musical *Billy Bishop Goes to War* (1978) is based on the exploits of the Canadian World War I pilot.

Apart from those mentioned relatively few composers have turned to Canadian history for inspiration. This may be due in equal measure to the international orientation of most Canadian composers and to the lacklustre quality of much teaching and writing about the country's past.

There have been numerous shorter compositions of an occasional nature recalling an earlier Canada. A few random examples are Ernest *MacMillan's 'Hail to Toronto' for the 1934 centennial of the incorporation of the city; *Vézina's *Frontenac* (1879) and *Vive Champlain* (1898); H.V. Roy's *Marche Jacques Cartier* (1904), dedicated to the premier of Quebec, Simon Napoléon Parent; Edwin *Gledhill's 'For Canada Fight: A song of 1812' (1886); and C.A. Garratt's 'Brant Memorial Hymn' for choir, written on the occasion of the 1886 unveiling of a statue in honour of the Indian chief Joseph Brant (1742–1807). C.W. *Sabatier's patriotic song *'Le Drapeau de Carillon' (1858) recalled Montcalm's 1758 victory over the British at Fort Carillon (Ticonderoga, NY). It goes without saying that incidental music has been written for countless films, stage plays, and broadcast dramas and documentaries dealing with historical themes.

See also Librettos: 4 / Canadian legend and history. HK (GP)

H.M.S. Parliament, or the Lady who Loved a Government Clerk. Text by William Henry Fuller (published Ottawa 1880), adapted to Sullivan's music for *H.M.S. Pinafore* (1878). Fuller, an Englishman who emigrated to Canada ca 1870, also was the librettist for the operetta *The Unspecific Scandal* (Ottawa 1874). A satire on Canadian politics and personalities in government, *H.M.S. Parliament* was commissioned by the McDowell Comedy Co (led by Eugene A. McDowell, an American who toured in Canada 1875–90). McDowell premiered it in Montreal 16 Feb 1880, then performed it in Ottawa, Toronto, and some 30 other towns and cities in Manitoba and eastern Canada. Drawing on the overwhelming success of *H.M.S. Pinafore*, which had opened in Montreal in January 1879, *Parliament* enjoyed a widespread if brief popularity in Canada during 1880. Highly topical, it concluded with 'a very telling scene between Britannia and Canada on the annexation question' (Toronto *Globe*, 20 Jan 1880). The book and lyrics of *H.M.S. Parliament* were published in *Canada's Lost Plays* (vol 1, Toronto 1978).

BIBLIOGRAPHY

Hambleton, Ronald. 'A Fuller version of Pinafore which this month marks its 100th birthday,' *Fugue*, May 1978

Lawrence, Robert G. 'Dramatic history: H.M.S. Parliament,' *Canadian Theatre R*, 19, Summer 1978

HMV. See RCA Ltd.

HOBAN, Stanley (John). Baritone, teacher, b Dunoon, Scotland, 6 Sep 1900. At 20 he moved to Winnipeg and began studies with Burton *Kurth. Other teachers were Herbert Witherspoon in New York and Harry Plunkett Greene in London. A pioneer of radio in Canada, he gave his first broadcast 22 Jul 1922 in Winnipeg and was heard 1931–43 on various CBC programs, including 'Geoffrey Waddington Conducts' 1938–43 and twice-weekly national recitals 1942–3. He sang with the *Winnipeg SO, the *Regina SO, a CBC Toronto orchestra, and the *CBC Vancouver Chamber Orchestra, and he was a soloist in Handel's *Messiah* (1938), Coleridge-Taylor's *Hiawatha's Wedding Feast* (1939), Dyson's *Canterbury Pilgrims* (1940), Brahms' *A German Requiem* (1943), and other works with the *Winnipeg Philharmonic Choir. He began teaching voice in Winnipeg in 1925 and joined the faculty of the *TCM in 1943. His Canadian pupils included Morley *Meredith. In 1946 he moved to Seattle, where he continued to teach and where he became director of workshops 1968–76 for the National Assn of Teachers of Singing. (CC)

HOCKRIDGE, Edmund 'Ted' (James). Baritone, b Vancouver 9 Aug 1919. He studied piano and voice in Vancouver and was encouraged by the visiting Metropolitan Opera baritone John Charles Thomas, who heard him sing a solo in church. In London during World War II Hockridge studied with George Baker and won an amateur contest at the Canadian Forces' Beaver Club in 1941. This led to engagements on the CBC-BBC programs 'Maple Leaf Matinee' in 1942 and 'Johnny Canuck's Revue' 1942–5, which established his popularity. He also performed on the BBC with fellow Canadians Robert *Farnon (the Canadian Army Orchestra) and organist Sandy Macpherson and with the Queen's Hall Light Orchestra and the Melachrino Strings. After his return to Canada in 1946 he had his own CBC radio shows (heard also in the USA on the MBS) and sang leading roles in CBC productions of 13 Gilbert & Sullivan operas 1948–9 and of *Don Giovanni* and *Peter Grimes* 1949–50. He also sang with the *TSO several times 1946–50, at the *Promenade Symphony Concerts in 1947, and in the title role of *Don Giovanni* with the Toronto Opera Festival in 1950.

Returning to London in 1950, Hockridge appeared in leading roles in West End productions of *Carousel* 1950–3, *Guys and Dolls* 1953–4, *Can-Can* in 1954, and the *Pajama Game* 1955–6, and on many BBC radio and TV series. As a cabaret performer Hockridge has sung in European cities, Nairobi, and Hong Kong. In 1974 in England he devised and presented a one-man show, drawing on his wide repertoire of popular and concert songs, opera, musical comedy, and spirituals. He began to record in 1950 and had made over 15 LPs and some 20 singles for Marble Arch, HMV, Decca, and others by the mid-1970s. 'Hey There,' 'Young and Foolish,' and 'Fountains of Rome' were especially successful. (GBr)

HODGINS, John (Marshall). Choir conductor, organist, teacher, b Toronto 4 Jan 1916, d Oshawa, Ont, 23 Apr 1979; ATCM 1935, LTCL 1940. His teachers were Peter C. Kennedy (piano), Charles *Peaker and Frederick *Silvester (organ), and Healey *Willan (theory). He was organist-choirmaster 1938–42 at Brampton Presbyterian Church, 1942–6 at Eglinton United Church, Toronto, and 1946–64 at Grace Church on-the-Hill, Toronto. He taught 1941–60 and again 1972–9 at the TCM (*RCMT). Under his direction (1949–64) the *Bishop Strachan School Chapel Choir became one of Canada's best-known girls' choirs. In 1964 he moved to Albany, NY, where for four years he was organist-choirmaster of St Peter's Episcopalian Church. In 1968 he moved to Vancouver and in 1972 he returned to Toronto, where for a short time he served as executive secretary of the *Ontario Choral Federation. Taking up again the direction of the BSS choir, he also formed the Bishop Strachan Alumnae Choir (known subsequently as the John Hodgins Singers), a 25-voice female choir which gave concerts in Toronto and performed at the Nassau Cathedral (Bahamas) at Easter 1973 and participated in the Festival of the Arts in Spokane, Wash, in 1974. In a 1976 concert at Walter Hall, U of Toronto, the John Hodgins Singers performed Debussy's seldom-heard work *The Blessed Damozel*, the premiere of Milton *Barnes' *Madrigals*, and pieces by Palestrina, Scarlatti, Ridout, and others. The choir was renamed the Oriana Singers in 1977 when its direction was assumed by John Ford. Hodgins later was conductor of the Brampton Oratorio Society. At the time of his death he was in Oshawa, Ont, to adjudicate at a festival.

W.H. Hodgins & Co. Turn-of-the-century music store and publishing firm in Toronto's Yonge St Arcade. Over 100 copyright and non-copyright sheet music titles are extant, the earliest (1897–1900) published by Amey & Hodgins, and the remainder (1900–7) by W.H. Hodgins & Co. All are in the dance, march, and popular-song fields. Several are composed by W.H. Hodgins, including *Olive Waltz* (1897), *A Rag Time Spasm* (1899), *The Union Jack Forever* (a march), and *The Elmore* (1907, a polka two-step.)

See also Ragtime. HK

HODKINSON, Sydney (Phillip). Composer, conductor, clarinetist, teacher, b Winnipeg 17 Jan 1934; M MUS (ESM, Rochester) 1958, DMA (Michigan) 1968. At the ESM he studied with Louis Mennini and Bernard Rogers. While teaching theory at the U of Virginia 1958–63 he studied composition (1960) at Princeton U with Carter, Sessions, and Babbitt. His doctoral studies were taken with Ross Lee Finney, George Balch Wilson, and Niccolo Castiglioni. He taught theory at Ohio State U 1963–8, directed the Rockefeller New Music Project at the U of Michigan 1968–73, spent 1971 as composer-in-residence in St Paul and Minneapolis as part of the Ford Foundation's Contemporary Music Program, and appeared occasionally 1966–71 as guest conductor of the St Paul Chamber Orchestra, the Minnesota Orchestra, and the Contemporary Directions Ensemble at Ann Arbor. In 1973 he began to teach conducting at the ESM.

Hodkinson has received many awards for composition, including the Prix de composition Prince Pierre de Monaco (1967) for *Caricatures*, and first prize (1966) for the National and second prize (1967) for the World congress of Jeunesses Musicales for *Interplay*. *Arc*, commissioned by the CBC for the *Lyric Arts Trio, was premiered in 1970 in Toronto and repeated at the World Exposition in Osaka. Although his style is couched in highly dissonant, fragmented language (eg, *Taula*), he often has employed elements of jazz to create conflict or, as in *Dissolution of the Serial* and *... another Man's Poison*, humour. He is a member of PRO Canada.

SELECTED COMPOSITIONS

STAGE AND MIXED MEDIA

Lament for Guitar and Two Lovers (Lee Devin). 1962. Actors, dancers, musicians. Presser (rental)
Armistice. 1966. Dancers, musicians. BMIC 1967
Taiwa. 1966. Actors, dancers, musicians. Ms
The Swinish Cult, opera (Lee Devin). 1976. Ms

ORCHESTRA

Caricatures. 1966. Full orch. Ric 1969
Fresco. 1968. Full orch. Job 1971
Drawings, Sets No. 7 and 8. 1970. Str orch. Presser 1974
Stabile. 1970. Youth orch. Job 1971
Valence. 1970. Chamb orch. Job 1971. CRI S-292
Epigrams. 1971. Full orch. Presser (rental)
Daydream. 1974. SATB, narr, orch. Merion/Presser 1974

BAND

Blocks. 1972. Merion/Presser 1974
Contemporary Primer (3 vols). 1972. Merion/Presser 1972
Tower, Stone Images, Pillar. 1974. Merion/Presser 1974

CHAMBER

Drawings, Sets 1–6 1960–5. Publ by Mus for Perc and Merion/Presser
Interplay. 1966. Alto fl (picc), cl (sax), perc, db. Presser (rental). RCI 300 (*SMCQ)
Dissolution of the Serial. 1967. Pf, 1 instr. Ms. CRI S-292
Imagind Quarter. 1967. 4 perc. BMIC 1969
String Quartet, for Five Players. 1967. 2 guit, hp, elec bass, perc. Ms
Arc. 1969. Sop, fl (picc), pf, 2 perc. CMCentre. CBC SM-148 (*Lyric Arts Trio)
Funks and *The Edge of the Old One*. 1969, 1976. Jazz ens. Ms
One Man's Meat ... 1970. Live and taped db. Merion/Presser
... another Man's Poison. 1970. Brass quin. Presser (rental)
Taula. 1974. Ww quin, brass quin. Presser (rental)
Symphony II. 1976. Org, brass, perc. Ms

ORGAN

Megalith Trilogy. 1973. Org, tape. Merion/Presser 1975. 1976. CRI S363 (Albright org)

CHOIR

Vox Populos, chamb oratorio (Devin). 1972. Presser (rental)
4 early pieces in ms; *Menagerie Set No. 1* and *Sea Chanteys* (Merion/Presser)
Also works for v and accompaniment

BIBLIOGRAPHY

Glick, Irving. 'Sydney Hodkinson: *Caricatures*: five paintings for Symphony Orchestra,' *CMB*, 1, Spring-Summer 1970
Schulman, Michael. 'Syd Hodkinson – not of the ivory-tower ilk,' *MSc*, 277, May–Jun 1974
Contemporary Canadian Composers (CF)

HOFFERT, Paul (Matthew). Composer, arranger, keyboardist, b Brooklyn, NY, 22 Sep 1943, naturalized Canadian 1961; B SC (Toronto) 1966. After moving in 1956 to Toronto he studied composition 1957–63 with Gordon *Delamont and vibraphone briefly with Hagood *Hardy and began playing piano and vibraphone in 1960 at jazz clubs. Accompanied by saxophonist Bernie *Piltch, bassist Carne Bray, and drummer Archie Alleyne he recorded *The Jazz Roots of Paul Hoffert* (1961, Chateau CLP 1002). While studying sciences at the U of Toronto he was music director 1963–5 of CBC TV's 'Time of Your Life.' He was co-founder (1968) with Skip Prokop of *Lighthouse and played piano, organ, and vibraphone with that popular rock orchestra until 1974. Thereafter a composer, arranger, and record producer in Toronto, he also was director of contemporary music (1975) at the Blue Mountain School of Music, Collingwood, Ont, and associate director of music (1976) at George Brown College, Toronto.

Hoffert's compositions include several works for jazz group; the musical play *Get Thee to Canterbury* (1968, co-written with Mark Shekter), which was produced off-Broadway in New York; many songs for Lighthouse; jingles; scores for such films as *Winter Kept Us Warm* (1965), *The Groundstar Conspiracy* (1971), *It Seemed Like a Good Idea at the Time* (1974), *Outrageous* (1977), and *Third Walker* (1978); incidental music for stage productions in Toronto; *Ballet High* (1970, for the Royal Winnipeg Ballet and Lighthouse) and *Sweet Summersaults* (1976, for the Toronto Dance Theatre); *Concerto for Contemporary Flute* (1975, premiered by Moe *Koffman); *Violin Concerto* (1976, premiered and recorded by Steven *Staryk under the composer's direction); a work for the *Armin Electric String Quartet; and *Israel*, premiered 4 Jun 1978 by the *Hamilton Philharmonic Orchestra. His score for *Outrageous*, a collaboration with his wife, Brenda, a lyricist, won a Canadian Film Award in 1977 and was released on an LP of the same title (GRT 9230-1074). Hoffert is an affiliate of PRO Canada.

BIBLIOGRAPHY

Waxman, Ken. 'Paul Hoffert's versatility keeps boredom away,' *MSc*, 300, Mar–Apr 1978 (HM)

HOLDER, Bruce (Edward). Violinist, conductor, composer, b Saint John, NB, 8 Jan 1905. His father, Fred Holder, was a trumpeter in local theatre orchestras. Bruce studied violin with Morton L. Harrison and William C. Bowden and began his career in 1919 as a theatre musician in Saint John. He later studied conducting with Pierre Monteux. He was concertmaster 1920–9 of the Imperial Theatre Orchestra; he also conducted a small concert orchestra at the Admiral Beatty Hotel for several years and led a dance band. He began working in radio on a Moncton, NB, station in 1926 and for 15 years was music director and soloist for CRBC and CBC radio shows from Saint John, including 'Holiday for Strings' and 'Fanfare.' He was a founder, and 1954–ca 1958 the conductor, of the Saint John SO and also served 1962–8 as concertmaster of the *New Brunswick SO. He began playing in the *Charlottetown Festival orchestra in 1970; in 1978 he played for the festival's production, *The Dumbells*, having been a member, over 50 years earlier, of the original *Dumbells pit orchestra. In a distinguished career which earned him the nickname 'Mr Music of Saint John,' Holder also served as director for 14 years of the Third Field Artillery Band (a position his son Bruce E. Holder Jr assumed in 1964), music director 1956–71 at Saint John Vocational High School, and string instructor 1966–74 for the *New Brunswick Youth Orchestra and, until his retirement in 1977, for the District 20 school board. He played during the 1977–8 (winter) season with the Clearwater (Florida) SO. (MM)

Holland. See The Netherlands.

HOLLINSHEAD, (Percy) **Redferne**. Tenor, b Eye, Suffolk, England, 1885, d New York 6 Oct 1937. His father, a Baptist minister, moved the family to Canada when Redferne was six. After a few years in Ontario the Hollinsheads settled in Hartney, Man. Redferne first sang solos in Winnipeg's Central Congregational Church and on provincial tours with the Winnipeg Citizens' Band. In 1906 the young tenor was engaged as soloist by Bloor St Presbyterian Church, Toronto. After a sojourn in London for study with Giovanni Clerici he returned to Toronto to teach at the *Hambourg Cons and sing at Timothy Eaton Memorial Church. He also studied with Giuseppe *Carboni, his colleague at the *Hambourg Cons after 1915. He was a member of the first *Adanac Quartet. Hollinshead settled in New York in 1917 and succeeded the renowned Dan Beddoe as tenor soloist at Broadway's Grace Church in 1922. He retained the position until his death. In later years he sang frequently on radio, both in the USA and Canada. In 1927 he toured Canada. Hollinshead made a few cylinders for Edison ca 1912 and also recorded after 1926 as first tenor of the American Singers, a male quartet (see *Roll Back the Years*).

WRITING
'Vox et machina,' *CJM*, vol 1, Jul–Aug 1914 JBM

HOLMAN, Derek. Organist, choir conductor, composer, teacher, b Illogan, near Camborne, Cornwall, England, 16 May 1931; FRCO 1950, ARAM 1958, FRAM 1965, D MUS (London) 1967, Fellow RSCM 1972. He studied 1948–52 at the RAM with Sir William McKie, Eric Thiman, and York Bowen. For two years, 1952–4, he was an instructor in the Royal Army Educational Corps with the British Army of the Rhine, but he returned to music as master 1954–6 at Westminster Abbey Choir School and went on to become assistant organist 1956–8 at St Paul's Cathedral. He was organist 1958–65 at Croydon Parish Church and founder in 1960 of the Croydon Bach Society. From 1956 to 1965 he was tutor, then subwarden, and finally warden of the RSCM. He moved to Canada in 1965 and served as organist-choirmaster at Toronto's Grace Church on-the-Hill 1965–79 and choirmaster (until 1970) at *Bishop Strachan School. In 1967 he joined the staff of the *U of Toronto. He directed the Concord Singers of Toronto 1973–5 and assumed the directorship of the *Canadian Children's Opera Chorus in 1975.

Several of Holman's tunes and harmonizations appear in *The Hymn Book* (1971) of the Anglican and United churches of Canada, for which he was a consultant. A number of his motets, anthems, school songs, and other vocal works have been published by Novello, Schirmer, RSCM, and Gordon V. *Thompson. Two of his *Three Carols* (Novello 1964) were recorded in 1973 (Polydor 2917009) by the *Festival Singers. *Eight Carols for Choir, Soloists, Orchestra and Audience*, commissioned by the *NACO, were premiered in 1972. *Weatherscapes* was commissioned by the *Ontario Choral Federation and premiered in 1973 in Kingston by the *Toronto Mendelssohn Choir and *Canadian Brass. Holman completed a *Symphony in D* in 1967. A *Mass of St. Thomas* (Waterloo 1974) won the St Thomas Church, Toronto, Centennial Competition. 'The North Wind' and 'Weathers,' commissioned by the Keith *Bissell trust fund, were published by *Waterloo in 1978. Holman composed the score for Robertson Davies' play-with-music *Pontiac and the Green Man*, written for the 150th anniversary of the U of Toronto in 1977. Holman belongs, stylistically, to the post-Britten school of English church composers. His writing is vocally oriented and practical in performance. He is an associate of the *CMCentre, a member of the *CLComp, and a member of CAPAC.

BIBLIOGRAPHY
Schulman, Michael. 'Derek Holman calls himself an all-round church musician,' *CanComp*, 147, Jan 1980
Compositeurs canadiens contemporains (MMI)

Holman English Opera Troupe. Probably the first organization to present opera on a regular basis in Canada. It was founded in the USA by George Holman (b New York 1814, d London, Ont, 1888) as the Holman Juvenile Opera Troupe. In 1858, on its first appearance in Toronto, it included Holman, his wife Harriet, and their children Sallie, Julia, and Alfred. They returned in 1864 and 1866 as the Holman National Opera Troupe. In 1867 Holman became lessee and manager of Toronto's Royal Lyceum Theatre and his troupe was the theatre's resident company until 1873, presenting regular seasons of both plays and opera. The troupe also played in Montreal in 1861 and made frequent visits to that city 1871–81. Holman served in 1873 and 1876–8 as manager of the *Theatre Royal in Montreal. In 1873 the family settled in London, Ont, and converted the Music Hall into the Holman Opera House. The troupe toured Ontario, Quebec, and the USA into the 1880s, presenting a repertoire of some 35 operas, including *La Sonnambula*, *Il Trovatore*, *Orpheus in the Underworld*, and *Der Freischütz*. In 1879 it gave the Canadian premiere of *H.M.S. Pinafore*. Singers included the then renowned W.H. Crane and Brookhouse Bowler. Sallie Holman (1852–1888) was the troupe's most celebrated star, and in the 1870s her appearance guaranteed a full house.

BIBLIOGRAPHY
Langton, W.A. 'The Holmans in the 70s,' *SatN*, 22 Jan 1938
Morey, Carl. 'Canada's first opera ensemble,' *OpCan*, Sep 1970 (CM)

HOLMES, Johnny (John). Trumpeter, bandleader, arranger, composer, b Montreal 8 Jun 1916. He began playing trumpet at 10 and studied 1938–40 with C. Van Camp of the *Montreal Orchestra and the CSM (*MSO). After playing 1940–1 in a co-operative band, the Escorts, Holmes took over its leadership in 1941. As the Johnny Holmes Orchestra the band played on Saturday nights 1941–51 at Victoria Hall in Montreal and toured in Quebec and Ontario. It also was heard on CBC radio. One of the city's leading dance bands of the day, it numbered among its members, at various times, Nick *Ayoub, Al *Baculis, Percy and Maynard *Ferguson, (pianist) Bud Hayward, Art *Morrow, and Oscar *Peterson. Lorraine McAllister and Sheila Graham, in turn, sang with the band. Holmes retired from music 1951–9, but returned and was heard 1959–69 on CBC radio in 'The Johnny Holmes Show,' in 'Broadway Holiday with the Johnny Holmes Orchestra' (1963–4), and (with a vocal sextet and jazz quintet) in 'What's New, Part I' and 'What's New, Part II.' The big band, which he has continued to lead periodically, performed in 1978 as Brass Therapy for the CBC's 'Jazz Radio-Canada.' Holmes has written many arrangements for his orchestra and his radio shows, over 40 songs, and such extended works as *The Fair City*, a jazz suite dedicated to *Expo 67. He is an affiliate of PRO Canada. The Johnny Holmes Agency was established in Montreal in 1972. (CGa, HM, MM)

HOLMES, Leslie. Baritone, teacher, b Lesser Slave Lake, Alta, 30 Apr 1901. His father was the bishop of Moosonee. Holmes studied singing in Toronto with Albert *Ham at the *Canadian Academy of Music and in London with Harry Plunkett Greene at the RCM. He also went to France and Germany, where he studied with Claire Croiza, Pierre Bernac, and Reinhold von Warlich. He made his reputation as an oratorio and recital singer in England and was renowned for his interpretation of the Christus in the *St Matthew Passion*. On visits to Canada Holmes gave recitals in 1930, 1931, and 1933 in Halifax, Charlottetown, Saint John, St Stephen, NB, and Montreal and was a soloist with the *Montreal Orchestra and the *TSO. After World War II Holmes returned to Canada to teach at the *TCM. He gave two recitals in Toronto in the spring of 1946 and on 11 Jun 1946 sang the Christus in a performance of the *St Matthew Passion* conducted by Sir Ernest *MacMillan for the *Montreal Festivals. He went back to England, taught 1947–54 at the RAM, and was made an honorary member of that institution. Holmes moved to Canada in 1954 to teach again at the *RCMT and gave recitals in Toronto in 1954, 1955, and 1958.

In addition to oratorio roles Holmes' repertoire included the song cycles of Schubert, Schumann, and Brahms, and a large selection of French, English, and Italian songs. Augustus *Bridle, in a review (*Toronto Daily Star*, 17 Jun 1946) of a recital which featured Schumann's *Dichterliebe, Op 48*, remarked that 'no Canadian quite ever equalled this sincere exposition of a song cycle'; and after a later recital John *Kraglund (Toronto *Globe and Mail*, 22 Oct 1954) noted his 'easy presentation, his air of relaxation and considerable, intelligent artistry.' Prominent among Holmes' Canadian pupils were James *Milligan, Jan *Simons, and Harry *Mossfield. Holmes retired from the RCMT in 1959 and returned to England. (DS)

HOLTBY, Phyllis (Margaret). Pianist, harpsichordist, teacher, b Winnipeg 10 Dec 1906; ATCM 1930, LRSM 1932, LMM 1941. She studied in the 1930s with Winnifred Walker, Mrs E.B. Patterson (Myrtle Ruttan), Russell White, Bernard *Naylor, and Eva *Clare in Winnipeg, Sigismond Stojowski and Ernest Hutcheson in New York, Jacques Jolas at Cornell College, Ia, and Frank Mannheimer in Duluth, Minn. She also had lessons with Harold Samuel and Percy Grainger on their visits to Winnipeg and studied harpsichord with Father Clayton Barclay in Winnipeg. She appeared as soloist with the *CBC Winnipeg Orchestra, the Duluth SO, and the Grand Forks (ND) SO and in 1958 performed Mendelssohn's *Concerto in G Minor* for a performance of Arnold Spohr's *Ballet Premiere* by the Royal Winnipeg Ballet. She has given piano and, occasionally, harpsichord recitals in Winnipeg for the *Women's Musical Club and the *Wednesday Morning Musicale and has performed on CBC radio. She has been a guest lecturer on pedagogy at the U of North Dakota, for many years an examiner for the *U of Manitoba, and in 1978 gave a series of piano workshops in Saskatchewan communities. She is a past president of the Wednesday Morning Musicale. Her pupils have included Scott Baker, Gerald Death, Thelma Harper, Peggy Kennedy, Kevin Kowal, Arlene Powell, Margaret Randell, Rupert Ross, Tom Stevenson (the first Canadian Indian to receive the ARCT), and June Stinson. (RG)

HOMBURGER, Walter. Administrator, impresario, b Karlsruhe, Germany, 22 Jan 1924. He was born into a musical family but did not study music. He left Germany for England before World War II and in 1940 arrived in Canada, where he became interested in managing artists and presenting concerts. As head of International Artists Concert Agency, which he founded by bringing Lotte Lehmann to Toronto for a recital in 1947, he has presented in Toronto in an annual series of concerts and recitals many of the world's outstanding singers and instrumentalists, including Louis Armstrong, Vladimir Ashkenazy, Paul Badura-Skoda (his North American debut), Teresa Berganza, Erna Berger, Victor Borge, Victoria De Los Angeles, Duke Ellington, Kathleen Ferrier, Friedrich Gulda, Emil Gilels, Vladimir Horowitz, Mary Martin, David Oistrakh, Itzhak Perlman, Leontyne Price, Andrés Segovia, Rudolf Serkin, Isaac Stern, Joan Sutherland, Van Cliburn, and Pinchas Zukerman. In addition, he has presented such groups as I Musici, the Netherlands Chamber Orchestra, the Vienna Boys Choir, and many of the great symphony orchestras of Europe and the USA. In 1949 he promoted

Walter Homburger

and managed Opera Backstage, Herman *Geiger-Torel's first attempt at touring opera in Canada. He was the first manager of Donald *Bell, Victor *Braun, Glenn *Gould, Louis *Lortie, Jan *Rubeš, and 1951–5 the National Ballet of Canada.

Homburger became managing director of the *TSO in February 1962, and in this capacity has become known as one of Canada's leading arts administrators, guiding the orchestra's affairs with a decisive blend of shrewdness and caution which has attracted criticism from the musical avant garde but has kept growth constant and attendance strong through years of great economic challenge. In 1974, on Homburger's 50th birthday, a group of friends established the Walter Homburger Scholarship, available each year to a first-year student at the *U of Toronto for outstanding achievement in the completion of the year's work towards a performance degree or diploma. Among events designed to increase the fund was a recital 6 Jun 1977 for which the pianist Rudolph Serkin donated his services.

BIBLIOGRAPHY

Gilmour, Clyde. 'Walter Homburger: the modest merchant of music,' *Maclean's*, 14 Dec 1964

Littler, William. 'Toronto's version of Sol Hurok pulls variety of musical strings,' *Toronto Daily Star*, 9 Oct 1971

HOMME, Richard (Mandt). Bassist, bass guitarist, b Madison, Wis, 4 Dec 1949. Taken to Toronto at 8, he began playing bass there at 13 and studied informally with Ron Carter in Connecticut during the summers of 1964 and 1965. Homme began his career in 1965 with Pete Scofield's dance band, the Young Canadians, and by the early 1970s was a prominent member of the Toronto studio and jazz worlds. He played regularly in the jazz bands of Sonny *Greenwich 1969–76, Ted *Moses 1971–6, and Moe *Koffman 1974–8, recording with each. He has performed on a more casual basis with Peter *Appleyard, Ed *Bickert, Kathryn *Moses, Sam Noto, Don (W.) *Thompson, and such visiting US jazzmen as Dexter Gordon, James Moody, and Eddie 'Cleanhead' Vinson. He has appeared on LPs by Moses, Thompson, Alvinn Pall, and various pop performers. Writing in *Coda* of Homme's work with Greenwich, Barry Tepperman referred to the technical extravagance of his playing (Jan 1975) and called him 'without doubt one of Canada's two finest contemporary bassists' (March 1976). MM

HONE, Jules. Violinist, teacher, composer, conductor, b Liège, Belgium, 7 Apr 1833, d Montreal 15 Sep 1913; shared deuxième prix Liège 1851. He studied violin 1846–54 at the Liège Cons royal with Joseph Dupont, and 1854–6 at the Brussels Cons royal with Hubert Léonard. He emigrated to the USA in 1856 and settled in New York, where he served 1856–65 as conductor of Niblo's Garden Theatre orchestra, which gave concerts and operatic performances. Moving ca 1865 to Montreal, Hone devoted himself primarily to teaching in convents: in Sault-au-Récollet for the Sisters of the Sacred Heart, in Lachine for the Sisters of Ste-Anne, and in Montreal for the Sisters of the Holy Names of Jesus and Mary. He also taught 1881–4 at the Collège Ste-Marie and privately. Among his pupils were François *Boucher, Oscar *Martel, Charles Reichling, Jean *Duquette, and his son Émile Hone, who died at sea in 1883.

Hone also formed an amateur orchestra and gave public concerts in Montreal. It was at his invitation that his compatriot the Belgian violinist Frantz *Jehin-Prume sojourned in Montreal in 1865 for the first time. This social visit was followed by a number of concerts and Jehin-Prume settled in Montreal a few years later. Among Hone's works (several published in Brussels by Schott Frères) are the opera *The Grandee*, sung in 1899 at *His Majesty's Theatre; a *Mass* presented at Notre-Dame Church; *La Canadienne*, fantasy for violin and piano (Boucher, 3rd edn nd); *Souvenir d'Arthabeska* (sic), 'rondc canadienne' for violin and piano (Schott Frères); and a *Marche militaire nationale chinoise* (Durdilly, Hayet 1913), dedicated to Dr Sun Yat Sen. Hone also wrote arrangements and harmonizations of Canadian and Irish folksongs and prepared a *Méthode de violon* (Schott Frères). In 1892 he became a member of France's Société des auteurs, compositeurs et éditeurs de musique (SACEM). At Hone's death Paul-G. *Ouimet in *Le Devoir* described him as 'the first conservatory graduate from Europe to come to Montreal. On his arrival he opened a studio and was for several years the guiding spirit of our artistic movement.'

Hone's eldest daughter, Cécile (Mme Arthur Léger; b New York 1860, d Montreal April 1948), was president 1915–18, 1921–4, and 1929–32 of the *Ladies' Morning Musical Club of Montreal. She wrote a small book *Fifty Years of Musical Recollections* (Montreal 1942). In 1949 the Cécile-Léger Scholarship was established in her memory by the Ladies' Morning Musical Club.

BIBLIOGRAPHY

Huot, Cécile. 'Musiciens belges au Québec,' *CMB*, 8, Spring–Summer 1974

Hone, François. *Un Siècle et demi de documents historiques*, privately publ (Montreal 1976)

Catalogue of Canadian Composers

Kallmann *History of Music*

Musiciens canadiens (CH)

HOOD, Thomas D. Piano manufacturer, fl Montreal 1848–77. A foreman before 1852 for *Mead Brothers piano manufacturers, he took over that operation in 1852 and began building pianos at 29 Notre Dame St, Montreal. In 1857 he built a factory on the Champ-de-Mars, and in 1860 he opened a showroom at 37 Great St James St (moving later to 183 St James). After 1877 Hood is listed in city directories only at his residence; there is no evidence as to the state of his company. A Hood piano is owned by the Royal Ontario Museum, Toronto. FH

HOOPER, Lou (Louis Stanley). Pianist, composer, teacher, of African, Cree, and Irish descent, b North Buxton, near Windsor, Ont, 18 May 1894, d Charlottetown 17 Sep 1977; B MUS (Detroit Cons) 1920. His father, a violinist in Canada for some 20 years, took him at three to Ypsilanti, Mich, where he sang solos in church and at 12 played the trombone in the Hooper Brothers' Orchestra with his older brothers Fred, a trumpeter, and Arnold, a violinist. While he was studying piano 1911–21 at the Detroit Cons with LaVerne Brown, Minor White, and F.L. York, he played in various local dance and theatre orchestras. His studies were interrupted in 1918 by service in Europe with a US Army concert party. In 1921 he moved to New York, where he studied 1923–4 at Columbia U and taught piano at the Martin-Smith Music School (a subsidiary of the Damrosch Institute – later the Juilliard School). In Harlem he worked with the banjoist Elmer Snowden and the clarinetist Bob Fuller under such names as the Three Jolly Miners and the Three Monkey Chasers, making records for Vocalion, Columbia, and other labels (see *Roll Back the Years*). During the 1920s Hooper accompanied, on recordings, many leading New York jazz musicians of the day, including the trumpeters Johnny Dunn and Louis Metcalf and the singers Ethel Waters, Ma Rainey, and Mamie Smith. He accompanied Paul Robeson in 1926 and toured as a member of Lew Leslie's *Blackbirds of 1928*, a revue which closed in 1929 in *His Majesty's Theatre in Montreal. After working in Detroit Hooper returned to Canada to perform at the 1932 *CNE. In 1933 he joined Myron Sutton's Canadian Ambassadors, an all-black dance band active throughout Ontario and Quebec. By 1935 he had settled in Montreal where he formed and conducted a male choir, the Hooper Southern Singers, in concerts and on CKAC radio. He also played in local dance and jazz bands (accompanying the young Billie Holiday during a brief 1939 engagement in Montreal) and taught piano. Oscar *Peterson was one of his pupils. After a term in Europe during World War II with the Royal Canadian Artillery in which he served mainly as a pianist and entertainer in charge of Canadian concert parties, Hooper returned to work in the relative obscurity of Laurentian resort hotels.

Lou Hooper

In 1962 Hooper was rediscovered by Montreal jazz enthusiasts. In 1973 he recorded the LP *Lou Hooper* (RCI 380), a collection of ragtime pieces, including his own *The Cakewalk*, *Black Cat Blues*, *South Sea Strut*, and *Uncle Remus Stomp*. According to Tex Wyndam in *Coda* (March 1976): 'Although slightly on the academic and restrained side, the solos have a firm, bright rhythm, are cleanly executed, and generate a mood of confidence and good cheer.' Hooper's other compositions include the oratorio *Ruth* (1920, written for his B MUS; see Oratorios, Canadian: 8) and several ragtime pieces, three of which were completed as late as 1975. That year he joined the faculty of the *U of Prince Edward Island. During the summer of 1977 he was a regular performer on the CBC TV show 'The Old-Fashioned New-Fangled Vaudeville Show' from Halifax. Hooper was honoured by the International Assn of Record Collectors in 1973 and by the Canadian Congress of Collectors in 1977.

WRITINGS

'The Afro-American folk song; its origin and evolution,' unpubl B MUS thesis, Detroit Cons 1920

'That Happy Road,' unpubl autobiography

BIBLIOGRAPHY

Kidd, Jim. 'Lou Hooper,' *Record Research*, Jun 1966

Batten, Jack. 'Harlem Cakewalk,' *The Canadian*, 23 Jul 1977 (EBM)

HORCH, Benjamin. Conductor, teacher, administrator, broadcaster, b Russia, of German parents, 19 Nov 1907; hon LL D (Winnipeg) 1974. His family moved to Canada in 1909, and in his youth Horch sang in the *Winnipeg Male Voice Choir. After some years of private music study he served 1932–8 as choir director and theory teacher at the Winnipeg Bible Institute. He studied for four years in Los Angeles and returned to serve 1943–55 as music director of the *Mennonite Brethren Bible College and founder-conductor of the Mennonite SO of Winnipeg. During the summers 1943–50 he conducted Mennonite community choirs across Canada. Horch was one of the music editors of the *Gesangbuch* (1952) of the Mennonite Brethren Churches and a contributor to *EMC*. He joined the CBC in 1959 as a producer of serious music for radio and after his retirement in 1973 worked as a freelance broadcaster.

See also Mennonites. (DF)

HORNER, Ralph (Joseph). Conductor, composer, teacher, b Newport, Monmouthshire (now in Gwent, Wales), 28 Apr 1848, d Winnipeg 7 Apr 1926; B MUS (Durham) 1893, D MUS (Durham) 1898. He studied 1864–7 at the Leipzig Cons and returned ca 1868 to London, where he conducted choirs and operatic productions. He also lectured for a time at Nottingham U. He moved in 1906 to New York and in 1909 to Winnipeg, where he was director of the Imperial Academy of Music and Arts ca 1909–11 and music editor of the weekly *Winnipeg Town Topics*. Conductor 1909–12 of the *Winnipeg Oratorio Society, he also directed an opera troupe, which in 1911 presented his comic opera *The Belles of Barcelona*. He was a bandmaster in the Canadian army 1916–17 and later continued to teach music in Winnipeg. Horner's compositions include two oratorios, *David's First Victory* and *St Peter*; the opera *Amy Rosbart*; six operettas; a suite (performed by the Victor Herbert Orchestra in 1909) and *Torch Dance* for orchestra (1911, winner of an Earl Grey Prize); cantatas, including the dramatic cantata *Confucius* (1888); anthems; piano pieces; and approximately 100 songs, some of which were published by Reeder, Weekes, and Ashdown. In Walter McRaye's *Pioneers and Prominent People of Manitoba* (1925), Horner was referred to as a 'grand old man of music' in Winnipeg.

L'Horoscope. 'Suite chorégraphique' for orchestra by Roger *Matton, based on an Acadian legend. Commissioned in 1957 by the CBC, it was premiered 12 Oct 1958 by the *CBC SO under Geoffrey *Waddington on a CBC radio broadcast and was recorded (RCI 185) the same year. It was presented as a ballet by Les Grands Ballets Canadiens, with choreography by Ludmilla Chiriaeff, 6 Nov 1958 on CBC TV's *'L'Heure du concert.' *L'Horoscope* has had numerous subsequent performances, notably by the Symphony of the Air (New York, 1960), the CBC SO (1963), the *NYO (1964), and the *TS (1973).

HORWOOD, Frederick (James). Educator, clergyman, writer, b London 12 Dec 1888, d Toronto 10 Jun 1976; ATCM 1920, BA (Toronto) 1920, B MUS (Toronto) 1921, D MUS (Toronto) 1926, LTCL 1930. He improvised at the piano even as a child, and at his school played for the visiting Queen Victoria. At 12 he left school an expert in shorthand and at 16 he moved to Canada, where he worked on a farm near Lindsay, Ont. While serving as a clergyman he studied for his D MUS at the *U of Toronto, and in 1926 he began to teach music appreciation at the *TCM. From 1934 to 1948 he represented the music graduates on the U of Toronto Senate. He also gave music talks on the CBC. He wrote the column 'Music Makers' 1946–65 for the *United Church Observer*, and the books *Listening to Music* (Toronto 1939), *The Basis of Music* (Toronto 1944), *The Basis of Harmony* (Toronto 1948), and *Elementary Counterpoint* (Toronto 1958). In 1977 the *CFMTA established a composition scholarship in his name. (MHI)

HOUDRET, Charles. Conductor, cellist, composer, b Liège 6 Jul 1905. He studied cello with André Hekking in Paris and composition with Sylvain Dupuis at the Liège Cons, from which he received a diploma. He continued his studies in Brussels with Eugène Ysaÿe (chamber music) and in Vienna with Felix Weingartner (conducting). Ysaÿe presented him to King Albert and Queen Elisabeth of Belgium, who put him in charge of the orchestra of the royal chapel. He conducted numerous concerts in Europe before coming to Canada in 1952 at the invitation of the *Montreal Festivals to conduct the incidental music to Fauchois's drama *Beethoven*.

Houdret stayed in Canada to become music director for the Montreal radio station CKVL. In April 1954, at the Palais du Commerce, he directed five performances of *Parsifal*, the first given in Canada since 1905. In 1959 he was engaged to conduct the Canadian premiere of Humphrey Searle's *The Diary of a Madman* on CBC radio. In 1955 he had conducted the *CMM Orchestra in a recording (RCI 127) of Handel's *Concerto Grosso No. 10* and an arrangement for string orchestra of Corelli's *Trio Sonata, Op 1*, and in 1960 he was put in charge of the CMM's orchestra classes. That same year, with the CMM orchestra at *Plateau Hall, he gave the premiere of *Prévost's *Poème de l'infini*. In Toronto in 1960 Houdret conducted the *CBC SO in the premiere of *Champagne's *Altitude* and in *Turner's *Opening Night*; both performances were preserved on the LP RCI 179. He conducted the CBC SO 10 times between 1954 and 1964. As a cellist, Houdret recorded the six Boccherini sonatas with the pianist Monique Marcil (1963, Bar BC 1815-2815). In August 1963 he helped found and organize the *Montreal International Competition. Nothing is known of Houdret's activities after 1964. GP

HOUDY, Pierick. Composer, organist, pianist, choirmaster, teacher, b Rennes, France, 18 Jan 1929, naturalized Canadian 1976; premier prix composition (Paris Cons) 1954. He began his musical education at seven at the Rennes Cons. In 1939 he was admitted to the Paris Cons, where he studied with Marguerite Long, Lazare Lévy, Noël Gallon, Maurice Duruflé, Messiaen, Milhaud, and Nadia Boulanger. He won the Grand Prix de Rome in 1953 and the Grand Prix de la ville de Paris in 1954. He was appointed director in 1955 of the Tours Cons, teacher in 1963 at the Schola cantorum, choirmaster in 1965 of St-Séverin Church in Paris, and choir conductor in 1966 of the Maîtrise d'enfants of the ORTF. He became known widely in Europe through his numerous recitals. Invited to Quebec in 1970 by *Laval U, he was appointed teacher of composition and theory in 1971 at the *CMQ.

Of Houdy's many compositions the first, *À mes petits amis*, a set of piano pieces, was published by Lemoine in Paris in 1938. He also wrote 16 art songs 1949–57, about 100 short choral pieces 1949–72, 6 cantatas and oratorios, including the *Cantate à saint Michel* (1967) and *La Nuit de Pâques* (1970), the opera *La Petite Hutte* (1963), some film music, about 30 chamber works 1936–74 (8 commissioned by the *Canada Council in 1974), and 6 orchestral works, notably *Les Aveugles de Breughel* (1967). Most of his compositions were published by Leduc. In those works inspired by the Quebec environment he has paid homage to the violoneux with his *Messe québécoise* (1973) for mixed voices, violin, double-bass, and percussion (Éditions Pierick Houdy 1976, London LOS 26604, *CMCouncil award for best Canadian choral recording in 1979) and to Indians on reserves with *Kastchentamoun* (1974) for saxophone, piano, and tape. He also wrote the electronic pieces *Putréfaction* (1972), *La Mort de Dieu* (1973), *Litanies* (1973), and *Contemplation* (1974), as well as a work for choir and orchestra (1975–6) about St Jean-Baptiste and a saxophone quartet *Chemins* (1977). Since he has written often on commission his constant concern with communicating a human view of perceived reality has been brought to bear on a wide range of assignments. He is an associate of the *CMCentre.

Houdy's wife, (Marie Geneviève) Ghislaine de Winter (harpist, teacher, b Paris 9 May 1934, naturalized Canadian 1976; premier prix harp, Paris Cons, 1955) studied in 1950 with Pierre Jamet at the Paris Cons and for several years was a member of Marie-Claire Jamet's French quartet. Settling in Quebec City in 1970, she established the harp class at Laval U. She also introduced the Celtic harp to Quebec. (IB)

Cammie Howard and his Western Five. Country band organized for the CBC in Ottawa by the announcer Byng Whitteker. It made its debut in December 1940 on CBO radio, broadcasting from the Chateau Laurier. Though formed to accompany Oral Scheer, 'The Smilin' Balladeer,' who had sung on CBO previously, the group took its name from its leader, Cammie (Cameron William) Howard (b Montreal 1910), a clarinetist who played 1929–39 in Montreal theatre and radio orchestras. Heard twice weekly until 1953 on the CBC's Trans-Canada network, the group included at various times the guitarist Elwood 'Woody' Hill, the bassist Paul Hebert, the trumpeters George Appleby and Howard 'Red' Calloway, and the guitarist-bassist George Clements. Scheer and the fiddler Gene Cloutier were members of the Western Five throughout their 13 years. Besides broadcasting, the band appeared in eastern Canadian centres and in 1952 toured Korea. Howard was a member of the *Ottawa Philharmonic, an orchestra leader in the city, and a contractor for the *NFB. He retired from music in the mid-1950s. MM

HOWARD, Kathleen. Contralto, b Clifton (Niagara Falls), Ont, 17 Jul 1880, d Hollywood 15 Aug 1956. She was a child when her English parents emigrated to Buffalo, but she returned to Canada in 1903 to tour as soloist with the Coldstream Guards. In 1903–4 she supported Adelina Patti in that diva's farewell North American concerts, one of which was given at the *Montreal Arena 12 Nov 1903. Following study in New York with Oscar Saenger, Paris with Jacques Bouhy and Jean de Reszke, and Berlin with Anna Schoen-René, she made her operatic debut in 1907 at Metz, France, as Azucena in *Il Trovatore*. Three seasons, 1909–12, in Darmstadt were followed by a sum-

Kathleen Howard

mer, 1913, at Covent Garden and two winters, 1913–15, with New York's Century Opera. Following her *Metropolitan Opera debut 20 Nov 1916 as Third Lady in *The Magic Flute*, she became that company's most popular character contralto. Her 12 seasons included appearances as Zita in the world premiere of *Gianni Schicchi* (1918, with Florence *Easton) and Geneviève in the Metropolitan premiere of *Pelléas et Mélisande* (1925, with Edward *Johnson). After her retirement in 1928, Kathleen Howard was active as a journalist and a motion picture character actress. Apart from a single Edison Diamond Disc of 1916, she recorded exclusively 1917–19 for Pathé, her 30-odd discs including duets with Claudia Muzio and Paul Althouse. A list of her recordings appears in *Roll Back the Years*.

WRITINGS

Howard, Kathleen. *Confessions of an Opera Singer* (New York 1918) JBM

HUBBLE, Filmer (Edwin). Organist, choir conductor, teacher, adjudicator, b Dulwich, England, 12 Jan 1904, d Winnipeg 25 Nov 1969; hon LL D (Manitoba) 1967. He moved to Winnipeg in 1921 and studied music with Hugh Ross, becoming his assistant organist at Holy Trinity Anglican Church. He subsequently was organist-choirmaster at various Winnipeg churches, including, from about 1943 until his death, St Stephen's Broadway United. His choir there twice won the City of Lincoln Trophy, highest national award for adult choirs who have won local awards in Canadian competition festivals. He also conducted the Winnipeg Ladies Choir, the Kelvin Grads Choir, the University Glee Club, the United College Chapel Choir, the Manitoba Schools Orchestra 1941–53, and during World War II the *Winnipeg Philharmonic Choir. He was music director for many productions at *Rainbow Stage. Organist for the popular CBC radio program 'Sunday Chorale,' he succeeded W.H. *Anderson as conductor in 1955. He lectured at the *U of Manitoba 1950–1 and 1956–7, and at the *Banff SFA 1958–64, and he was in constant demand as an adjudicator throughout western Canada. Like Anderson, Hubble was something of a father-figure to young Winnipeg musicians in the 1940s and 1950s. A benign and generous spirit, he was never idle, yet never too busy to help, and fees often were brushed aside. (RG)

HUBERT, Yvonne. Pianist, teacher, b Mouscron, Belgium, 28 May 1895; premier prix piano (Lille Cons) 1906, premier prix piano (Paris Cons) 1911. She first took lessons at the Lille Cons. After her exceptional gifts were noticed by Alfred Cortot, Gabriel Fauré, and André Gedalge, she enrolled

Filmer Hubble directing The Choristers of Winnipeg

at the Paris Cons in 1906 and studied piano with Marguerite Long and in 1908 with Cortot. She also studied theory with Maurice Emmanuel and chamber music with Camille Chevillard. Under the guidance of Fauré, who entrusted her with the performance of several of his works, she undertook a career in France, Belgium, Canada, and the USA as soloist, chamber player, and accompanist to her brother Marcel, the cellist.

She settled in Montreal in 1926 and founded the Alfred-Cortot Piano School in 1929 to promulgate the French tradition generally, as well as Cortot's method in particular. She taught 1946–71 at the *CMM, where her students included Suzanne Blondin, Michel *Dussault, Serge *Garant, Gilles *Manny, William *Stevens, and Ronald *Turini. Beginning in 1953 she also worked at the *École Vincent-d'Indy and other institutions; several of the pianists she trained won national and international competitions: Henri *Brassard, Janina *Fialkowska, André *Laplante, Louis *Lortie, William *Tritt, and others. Considered one of the most distinguished teachers in Canada, Hubert has exerted a decisive influence on several generations of pianists. In 1979 she was awarded the *CMCouncil Medal and a Diplôme d'honneur by the *CCA.

BIBLIOGRAPHY

Musiciennes de chez nous HPl

Huggett Family. Ottawa-based vocal and instrumental ensemble devoted chiefly to medieval, renaissance, baroque, folk and pseudo-folk music: Leslie Huggett, his wife, Margaret, and their children Andrew, Jennifer, Ian, and Fiona.

Leslie (b London 1 Jun 1929, a one-time french hornist with the Royal Philharmonic Orchestra in London, who moved to Ottawa in 1954 to direct a chamber music program at the RCAF base and later played in the *Ottawa Philharmonic) is music director and plays bass viol. Margaret (b London 18 Nov 1931) plays virginal, spinet, and harpsichord. Andrew (b Ottawa 22 Jul 1955) plays oboe, baroque violin, lute, and guitar and arranges the repertoire of traditional and contemporary songs. Jennifer (b Ottawa 15 Nov 1957) plays cello and viola da gamba. Ian (b Ottawa 26 Sep 1959) plays viola and treble viol. Fiona (b Ottawa 28 Apr 1961) plays violin and tenor viol. The family performs in costume. All the members sing, and each plays instruments from the woodwind family – recorders, krumhorns, etc.

The family began giving private concerts in 1966 – the children playing only recorders at the time – while Leslie and Margaret were teaching the Orff method in Westchester County (New York) schools. After preparatory work in Greece and England, the family made its formal debut in 1969 at a self-promoted concert at the *NAC. Further study, with *Canada Council support, has taken the Huggetts for several winters to England, where they have studied renaissance music with Edgar Hunt and baroque music with Trevor Pinnock. The children have had extensive training in Ottawa and London as string players. The family has performed frequently at the NAC, across Canada on tour, in London (Wigmore Hall) and Paris (*Canadian Cultural Centre), in Germany and Greece, and on CBC and BBC radio and TV.

In 1975, on tour with Les Grands Ballets Canadiens, the Huggetts performed Harry *Freedman's score for Brian Macdonald's ballet *Romeo and Juliet*. The LPs *The Huggett Family* (1973, Daffodil DAF 10044) and *A Renaissance Delight* (1975, Daffodil DAF 10053) were made in England, and another LP called *The Huggett Family* was made for the CBC (SM-280) in 1977. The family also may be heard in the NFB productions *Aucassin et Nicolette* and *A Christmas Story*. Huggett Family programs, often built around specific themes, include *At the Field of the Cloth of Gold and Beyond* and *King Henry VIII and His Women*, featured at the *Shaw Festival in July 1978. The family made a tour of Canada for the *JMC in 1978–9. Reviewing a performance by the Huggetts at the 1975 *RCCO Convention in Toronto, Kenneth *Winters wrote (in AGO & RCCO *Music*, October 1975): 'Their Renaissance repertory is by far their best... The music was sweetly chosen, the dancing decorous, the singing soft and pure, and all of it radiantly human.'

BIBLIOGRAPHY

Champagne, Jane. 'The Huggett family,' *CanComp*, 107, Jan 1976 DM, MM, PW

HUGHES, Andrew. Musicologist, b London 3 Aug 1937; MA (Oxford) 1962, PH D (Oxford) 1962. An authority on early music, Hughes has taught at Queen's U, Belfast, 1962–4, the U of Illinois 1964–7, and the U of North Carolina 1967–9. He began teaching at the *U of Toronto 1969. At the U of Toronto he organized in 1971 a Medieval Music Group which has performed 12th- and 14th-century liturgical music and which staged the 13th-century musical drama *Samson and Delilah* in 1976. In 1973 he received a Guggenheim Fellowship to investigate and photograph medieval manuscripts in Europe. He has contributed articles to *Music and Letters*, *Acta musicologica*, *Notes*, *The New Grove Dictionary*, *MGG*, and other publications.

WRITINGS

– ed. *Fifteenth Century Liturgical Music: Antiphons and Music for Holy Week and Easter* (London 1968)

– and Bent, Margaret, eds. *The Old Hall Manuscript*, 4 vols (American Institute of Musicology 1969, 1973)

'Ugolino: the monochord and *musica ficta*,' *Musica disciplina*, vol 23, 1969

'The *Ludus super Anticlaudianum* of Adam de la Bassée,' *J of the American Musicological Soc*, vol 23, 1970

Manuscript Accidentals: Ficta in Focus (American Institute of Musicology 1972)

A Bibliography of Medieval Music: The Sixth Liberal Art (Toronto 1974)

'Liturgical manuscripts at Arouca and in other Portuguese libraries,' *Traditio*, vol 31, 1975

Medieval Manuscripts for Mass and Office: A Guide to Their Organization and Terminology in press (CF)

HUGHES, Arthur Wellesley. Composer, band arranger, instrumentalist, b eastern Ontario ca 1870, d New York? ca 1945. Little is known about Hughes' musical background except that he played the piano and a brass instrument, at one time operated the steam calliope for Barnum's Circus, and was a teacher of L.F. *Addison. At the turn of the century he began editing and arranging for a succession of music publishers, including *Whaley Royce in Toronto, *Waterloo in Waterloo, Ont, and Cundy-Bettoney in Boston. Hughes was one of Canada's most prolific writers of marches and dance music, producing ca 1890–1930 some 50 published works and numerous arrangements. Typical are *United Empire March, In Old Quebec, The Rosedale Three-Step, Hail Edward VII*, and *March of the Allies*. He frequently used the pseudonyms Arthur Wellesley and H.W. Arthurs. His publishers included *Anglo-Canadian, W.H. *Billing, Cundy-Bettoney, A.H. Goetting, W.H. *Hodgins, W.F. Shaw, H.H. *Sparks, Gordon V. *Thompson, Waterloo, and Whaley Royce. Recordings of his compositions for band were issued on the Columbia, Pathé, Victor, and other labels (see *Roll Back the Years*). HK

HUGO, Reginald. Engineer, organizer, tenor, b East Molesley, London, 18 Apr 1897, d Winnipeg 14 Aug 1974. He came to Canada in 1906, graduated as a civil engineer (Manitoba 1917), and became a bridge engineer for the CNR. He studied singing with W.H. *Anderson and was a member of the *Choristers. He also sang in the *Winnipeg Male Voice Choir and was tenor soloist successively in three Winnipeg churches, notably St Andrew's, River Heights. His main contribution to music, however, was as an influential member 1923–74 of the *Men's Music Club. Hugo was the club's president in the 1950s and for several years headed the syllabus and program committee of its main project, the *Manitoba Music Competition Festival. He served 1949–64 as president of the *FCMF and remained co-ordinator of the Manitoba festival until the year of his death. RG

Hull. See Ottawa.

HULTBERG, Cortland. Conductor, teacher, composer, b Chicago 5 Sep 1931; B SC music education (Northern Illinois) 1953, M SC music education (Illinois) 1954, M MUS (Arizona) 1958. He made his conducting debut in Chicago in 1948 and conducted army choirs during the mid-1950s. He studied pedagogy in 1953–4 at the U of Northern Illinois and composition 1956–8 with Robert McBride and Andrew Buchhauser at the U of Arizona, where he also taught. In 1959 he emigrated to Canada and taught at the *U of British Columbia. He was made director of the university's Electronic Music Studio in 1965 and professor of theory and composition in 1970. He is the founder and conductor of the *University of British Columbia Chamber Singers. Hultberg's compositions include *Fog* and *3 Songs* for choir, and a *Concerto Grosso* for flute, oboe, two horns, bassoon, and orchestra. He has recorded on CRI and Angel with the chamber singers and the Little Mountain Singers. His pupils include Lloyd *Burritt, Errol Gay, Peter *Huse, David Keeble, Claire *Lawrence, and Barry *Truax.

WRITINGS

'Music education in British Columbia,' *Music Education and the Canadians of Tomorrow* (CMCouncil 1968)

'The role of the electronic music studio in university music programs,' *CAUSM J*, vol 1, Spring 1971 NM

HUMBERT, Stephen. Hymnodist, church musician, ship builder, baker, b New Jersey 1767, d Saint John, NB, 16 Jan 1849. A Loyalist, Humbert arrived in New Brunswick in 1783. He was granted a plot of land in Saint John in 1785 and lived on it until his death. A baker by trade, he later established himself as a ship builder. He also, by turns, was a captain of the local militia, a city alderman, a member of the House of Assembly (1809, 1816, 1819, 1830), and head of a commission to seize by force US vessels engaged in offshore smuggling. But it was, perhaps, as a musical churchman that he made a lasting mark. In 1791 he organized Saint John's first Methodist congregation, and in 1796 he opened a sacred vocal music school. He compiled the first English-language collection of vocal music, **Union Harmony: British America's Sacred Vocal Musick* (printed in New England 1801, with later editions 1816, 1831?, 1840). He also wrote *The Rise and Progress of Methodism in the Province of New Brunswick from Its Commencement until about the Year 1805* (Saint John 1836).

See also Singing schools.

BIBLIOGRAPHY

McMillan, Barclay. 'Tune-book imprints in Canada to 1867: a descriptive bibliography,' *Papers of the Bibliographical Society of Canada*, vol 16, 1977 DJR

HUME, (Edith) **Doreen** (b Hulme, m Mulhinch). Soprano, b Sault Ste Marie, Ont, 14 Jul 1926. She studied voice with John Blackburn in Sault Ste Marie and 1945–53 with George *Lambert at the *RCMT, and was soloist 1946–53 at Grace Church on-the-Hill in Toronto. After winning an *'Opportunity Knocks' award in 1948 she performed on CBC radio (beginning with a 13-week series of her own) and sang in Gilbert & Sullivan operettas with the CBC Light Opera Company. As a member of the *CBC Opera Company she took part in the North American radio premiere of *Peter Grimes* 12 Oct 1949, and in the 1952 repeat broadcast. As a concert soloist she appeared in 1950 with the *Toronto Mendelssohn Choir in Beethoven's *Missa solemnis* and in 1949, 1956, 1957, and 1959 with the *TSO in pop concerts. She also participated in performances of *The Creation* in Halifax and Ottawa.

In 1954 Hume moved to England, where she served 1955–70 as principal soprano soloist of the BBC Light Music department, giving over 1500 radio and TV performances under the direction of Robert *Farnon, Sidney Torch, Carmen Dragon, and others. She was the soprano soloist in London performances of Fauré's *Requiem* (16 Nov 1957) and Handel's *Messiah* (4 Jan 1958), the latter with Maureen *Forrester and Jon *Vickers, and both conducted by Sir Malcolm Sargent. Hume represented England at the Venice Festival of Light Music in 1957, toured in Europe in 1958 with the BBC Concert Orchestra, and represented Canada at a special liberation anniversary concert in May 1965 in Holland. She made over 10 LPs (the first in 1958) of light music and musical comedy for the Philips Fontana label. In 1970 she returned to Toronto. PW

Humphrey and the Dumptrucks. Country-folk band. It was organized in 1967 in Saskatoon as a jugband by the banjoist and dobro guitarist Gary 'Humphrey Dumptruck' Walsh, along with the 12-string guitarist, bassist, and jug player Michael 'Bear' Millar, the guitarist and autoharpist Michael 'Ernie' Taylor, and the guitarist and mandolinist Graeme Card. Each member is also a singer and songwriter. (In 1973 Card left to pursue a solo career, and in 1976 he made a well-received debut LP for Truly Fine Records.) A fulltime and professional band by 1969, Humphrey and the Dumptrucks performed throughout western Canada in clubs, on the CBC, and at festivals, schools (where they gave workshops), and universities. They have appeared often in small Saskatchewan communities, and many of their songs reflect rural prairie life. Collaborators with the Regina playwright Ken Mitchell on the country musical **Cruel Tears*, they also appeared as a Greek-style chorus in its 1975, 1976, and 1977 productions. For the 1977 national tour 'Humphrey' was replaced by the banjoist and dobro guitarist Bob 'Cat' Evans, who in turn was succeeded by the singer Anne Wright. In 1977 Evans, Millar, and Taylor completed the ballet *Goose* (based on Mother Goose rhymes) for the Regina Modern Dance Company. In addition to some transcriptions for the CBC, the band made two LPs for *Boot Records and four (by 1979) for its own mail-order company, Sunflower Records, including one of the music from *Goose*. Humphrey and the Dumptrucks are members of CAPAC and own the publishing company Shoehorn Music. Taylor has described their music as 'prairie music...It's not country and western; that is, it's not a conventional Nashville sound. It's not rock 'n' roll. It's not folk – though it incorporates all three' (*Toronto Star*, 12 Nov 1977).

BIBLIOGRAPHY

Garr, Allen. 'The boys from Blackstrap Mountain,' *The Canadian*, 8 Jan 1977 (MD, MM)

HUMPHREYS, James Dodsley. Tenor, teacher, b Mansfield, Nottinghamshire, England, ca 1811, d Toronto 23 or 24 Feb 1877. Humphreys' claim (*Toronto Patriot*, 26 Apr 1844) to have been 'formerly of the Royal Academy of Music' is not substantiated. His public appearances in Toronto in opera, oratorio, and recital span the years from at least 1835 to 1873. He was conductor or president of several short-lived choral societies and taught singing at Upper Canada College, at ladies' schools, and privately. Four of his waltzes and several ballads were published by J.T. Nunns (New York) in 1843. A song, 'The Junior Warden's Toast,' was dedicated to the members of St Andrew's (Masonic) Lodge No. 1 and was printed in Toronto. Humphreys was described as Toronto's 'favourite tenor' and 'not only a good teacher but perhaps the best performer in our midst.' He appeared in public more often and over a longer period than any other Toronto artist of the mid-19th century.

BIBLIOGRAPHY

Sale, D.J. 'Toronto's pre-confederation music societies.'

Kallmann, Helmut. 'Humphreys, James Dodsley,' *DCB*, vol 10 HK

HUMPHREYS, (Andrew) **Smyth**. Violist, b Liverpool 27 Sep 1910; ARCM 1932. Taken to Canada at one, Humphreys was raised in Chilliwack, BC, where he studied violin with his father, John (Percival), and piano with his mother, Nellie. Both parents were representatives of the *AB of the RSM, and his mother in particular was instrumental in the development of music in the Fraser Valley. He studied with Maurice Sons at the RCM, winning the 1928 gold medal. His association there with Lionel Tertis stimulated his interest in viola. Humphreys returned in 1932 to British Columbia, where he trained school orchestras and conducted chamber concerts in Victoria before serving 1934–7 in the *Vancouver SO as a violinist. He switched to viola in 1937 and was principal 1949–69 and 1973–6 and deputy principal 1969–73. He was principal viola 1942–73 of the *CBC Vancouver Chamber Orchestra and a member of other CBC orchestras. He was the viola 1947–56 of the *de Rimanoczy Quartet, guest second viola with the Hungarian Quartet in a Mozart quintet series at the 1958 *Vancouver International Festival, and a collaborator with Oscar Shumsky in chamber-music concerts at the *Stratford Festival. With the pianist Hugh *McLean he recorded Barbara *Pentland's *Duo*, William Keith *Rogers' *Sonatina*, and Britten's *Lachrymae* (1967, RCI

223/RCA CCS 1017). Humphreys taught privately in Vancouver until the mid-1950s. He also adjudicated in Vancouver and for the *WBM. (MW)

HUMPHREYS, Sydney (Ernest). Violinist, teacher, b Chilliwack, near Vancouver, 26 Sep 1926; FRAM 1960, MA (Newcastle) 1969. He studied violin with Gregori *Garbovitsky in Vancouver, Kathleen *Parlow in Toronto, Thomas Matthews and Frederick *Grinke at the RAM, London, and Georges Enesco in Paris. He was the leader 1952–70 of the Aeolian String Quartet of London, which toured internationally, recorded, and broadcast on the BBC and the CBC. He was a member 1954–65 of the St Cecilia Trio, concertmaster of the Bath Festival Orchestra under Menuhin, and a soloist with several BBC orchestras. He was concertmaster 1972–4 of the BBC Scottish Orchestra and 1974–5 of the Bournemouth Sinfonietta, and he joined the *Victoria SO in that capacity in 1975. He was head of the string department 1970–2 at the *Victoria Cons of Music and resumed that position in 1975. He is a member of *Trio Victoria. FEC

Hungary. In 1971 over 131,000 people of Hungarian origin were living in Canada. The first Hungarians arrived via the USA ca 1886 and settled in Manitoba and Saskatchewan. Other groups immigrated between 1901 and 1911 and several established communities in Alberta. The folk culture of the early settlements has been researched by Kenneth *Peacock, who collected over 150 songs.

After the stiffening of US immigration laws in the 1920s, many Hungarians preferred to enter Canada. A number of farmers and tradesmen settled in the Niagara district, in the grape- and tobacco-growing areas of southwestern Ontario, and in urban centres such as Brantford, Hamilton, and Toronto. In the 1930s very large numbers (perhaps as many as 80 per cent) from the western-Canadian Hungarian communities migrated to eastern Canada.

During the 1920s and 1930s Hungarian cultural activities in urban areas were co-ordinated by local churches. Records deposited with the Multicultural History Society of Ontario show that the Toronto Hungarian Presbyterian Church, the St Elizabeth of Hungary Roman Catholic Church, and the Hungarian Baptist Church in Toronto sponsored choirs, string ensembles, and silver bands. Community organizations – eg, the Kossuth Sick Benefit Society and the Brantford Mutual Benefit Society – also organized choirs and folkdance classes.

Probably the first distinguished Hungarian musician to live in Canada was Clara *Lichtenstein, who claimed to have studied with Liszt and who settled in Montreal in 1899. The violinist Geza *de Kresz lived in Toronto 1923–35 and 1947–59, the violinist Jean *de Rimanoczy settled in Winnipeg in 1925, and the pianist Paul *de Marky took up residence in Montreal in the late 1920s. A central non-sectarian community organization, Hungarian House Inc (later Hungarian Canadian Cultural Centre), was founded in Toronto in 1947 to promote sports and cultural activities, including Hungarian music.

As immigration to Canada increased after World War II a number of Hungarian musicians arrived, among them the cellist George Horváth in 1948 and the composer István *Anhalt in 1949. A major wave of immigration – some 35,000 individuals, mostly urban business and professional people, including many musicians, music teachers, and university students – followed the 1956 Hungarian uprising. The majority settled in Toronto, Hamilton, Montreal, Winnipeg, and Vancouver. By 1960 they had begun to establish additional means of maintaining their musical traditions.

Among Hungarian-Canadian performing groups active in the 1970s was the Hungarian Kapisztrán Folk Ensemble of Winnipeg, a mixed choir, orchestra, and folkdance group founded in 1960 by its conductor, Gertrud Edenhoffer. Affiliated with St Anthony of Padua Hungarian Roman Catholic Church, the ensemble, dressed in regional folk costumes, has appeared on TV and in multicultural and Hungarian folk festivals in a repertoire of church music, folksongs, and works by Bartók, Kodály, and others. The Kodály Ensemble of Toronto was founded in 1960 by George Zadubán, as the Kodály Male Voice Choir. By 1963 a mixed-voice choir, an orchestra, and a dance group had been added. The mixed choir supplemented the *Toronto Mendelssohn Choir in *COC productions of *Aida* (1964) and *Turandot* (1965). In 1979 the ensemble comprised an orchestra, a mixed choir, a chamber choir, and a dance group and was described as the largest and best-known Hungarian group of its kind outside Hungary. Its orchestra, choir, and dance group also have performed separately. The entire ensemble has appeared at festivals in Ontario and has filled engagements in Buffalo, Cleveland, Detroit, and Winnipeg. The Vancouver Hungarian Choir was founded in 1967 by Josef Sallos and was conducted later by Thomas Schadl. It has participated in folk festivals, and in 1969 and 1970 it competed successfully at the Kiwanis Festival. It has made private recordings of Hungarian choral works and Christmas carols.

In 1974 the House of Remenyi (for some years spelled Remeny), a Budapest musical firm which had relocated in Toronto, revived the Reményi Award Competition, a contest initiated in 1902 at the Franz Liszt Academy and suspended in 1950. In its revival of the competition the company was assisted by Lorand *Fenyves and the *U of Toronto (see Awards).

The principles of musical education developed by Zoltán Kodály (see Kodály Method) were introduced to Canada in 1965 through courses at the *RCMT and at Montreal's *École normale de musique. Kodály visited Canada in 1964 and again in 1966, when he gave the MacMillan Lectures at the U of Toronto and received an honorary doctorate from that university. In 1973 the CAPAC-MacMillan Lectures were given by another Hungarian composer, György Ligeti. Among other Hungarians who have appeared in Canada are the pianist Ernst von Dohnányi, who gave a piano recital for the *Ladies' Morning Musical Club of Montreal in 1900 and returned to Montreal during the 1930s to perform with *Clarke's *Montreal Orchestra in the Canadian premiere of his *Variations on a Nursery Rhyme*. The violinist Joseph Szigeti appeared at a Montreal Ladies' Morning Musical Club concert in 1927 and played in Toronto, Winnipeg, and other cities, and the Roth Quartet appeared in Montreal in 1929. Béla Bartók, whose Canadian pupils included Violet *Archer, Agnes *Butcher, and Jean *Coulthard, was to have played in Montreal in the 1930s but was forced to cancel owing to illness. The pianist György Cziffra made his North American debut at the 1957 *Montreal Festivals. The Hungarian String Quartet premiered Harry *Somers' *Third String Quartet* at the *Vancouver International Festival in 1959. The pianists Georges Solchany and Tamás Văsăry, the cellist Janos Starker, the Nouveau Trio hongrois, the Vegh Quartet, and the West German orchestra of refugee Hungarians the Philharmonia Hungarica (formed in the late 1950s) have appeared in Canada, Starker frequently. The pianist Lili Kraus has performed with the *McGill Chamber Orchestra, the *NACO, and the *TSO and has given numerous recitals in Canada.

Emma *Albani sang in the English premiere of Liszt's *St Elizabeth*, with the composer in the audience; Waugh *Lauder was one of Liszt's pupils. Canadians who have performed in Hungary include Mona *Bates, who studied with Kodály, and Alexander *Brott, who conducted there. The pianist David Swan made a recital tour in Hungary in 1978.

Hungarian-born musicians and those of Hungarian origin who have lived in Canada include the cellists Klara Benjamin Belkin, Kristine Bogyó (m *Kuerti), Dezsö *Mahalek, and Ivan Tóth; the clarinetists Lajos Bornyi and Imre Rozsnyai; the composers John *Fodi, Thomas *Legrady, and Tibor *Polgar; the guitarists Antonin Bartos, Frank Nagy, and Abel Nagytothy-Toth; the organists and choirmasters Oscar Buchbinder, Izabella Dedinsky, and Miklos Takacs; the pianists Ernest Bánky, Béla Böszörmenyi-Nagy, Peter Frankl, Endre Gaál, Lajos Ivánfay-Gondos, Eva Hidassy-Hajos (m Jahn), Moshe Hammer, Charles *Reiner, and Ilonka Seder-Szabolcsi; the piano teachers Margaret Hajdu, Judit Kenedy, and Idilkó Vadas; the singers Aurelie Revy Chapman, Veronica d'Eclesis (b Kalfman), Rózsa Erdélyi, Ferenc Korodini, and Margaret Zydron (b Pirositz); the violinists Ilona Adorján, Béla Bucz, Kornelia Dvorzsák, Arthur *Garami, Marta *Hidy, Lajos Molnar, Charles Szilády, Janos Tóth, Elizabeth Tömösváry, Dezsö *Vághy and Árpád Verseghy; the violists Janos Csaba, Ernest Kiss, Tibor Vághy, and Robert Verebes; and the bassist Leslie Obercian, the conductor Laszlo *Gati, the french horn player Eugene *Rittich, the educator Gábor Bartha, the harpist Susanah Remeny, the saxophonist-composer Jerry *Toth, the trombonist Antal Dvorak, and the trumpeter Steven Pettes. The violin and viola builder Otto Erdész settled in Toronto in 1974.

BIBLIOGRAPHY

Peacock, Kenneth. *A Survey of Ethnic Folkmusic across Western Canada*, National Museum Anthropology Paper no. 5 (Ottawa 1963)

– *Twenty Ethnic Songs from Western Canada*, National Museum Bulletin no. 211 (Ottawa 1966) (GZ)

HUNT, Clifford (Onufry). Administrator, trumpeter, band conductor, b Hamilton, Ont, 20 Jul 1917. He began trumpet lessons at seven and later played in *Salvation Army bands. He toured North America, Great Britain, and continental Europe as a solo trumpeter and was a soloist 1940–2 with the RCAF Band. He was music director 1942–3 for the Camp Borden Band and was sent overseas in 1944 with that organization, which then became the Canadian Bomber Group Band, travelling from quarters at Harrogate to give concerts and assist at ceremonies in England. He was music director of the regular Air Force Band 1946–60 and supervisor of music for all Canadian air force bands 1960–4. From 1964, when the headquarters and commands of the Canadian armed forces were integrated, until 1968, when the unification of the three services was completed, Hunt supervised 220 bands, comprising 1000 full-time musicians and some 5000 reserve-force volunteers. He was made a lieutenant-colonel in 1966.

See also Bands: 3 / Regular armed forces.

On his retirement from the armed forces in 1968 Hunt became manager of the music department of the *CNE and music director of the senior program (adult recreation) for the city of Burlington. In 1969 he became director of grandstand shows at the CNE and managing director of the *Canadian Bureau for the Advancement of Music. He was executive director 1973–8 of the *Kiwanis

Music Festival. He served 1954–5 and 1959–61 as president of the *CBA, 1971–2 as president of the American Bandmasters Assn, and in 1973 as vice-president and 1977–8 as president of the *FCMF.

(CF)

HUNTER, Tommy (Thomas James). Singer, guitarist, b London, Ont, 10 Mar 1937. After appearing regularly 1953–4 on Gordie Tapp's 'Main Street Jamboree' on CHML radio, Hamilton, he sang with the Golden Prairie Cowboys from Wingham, Ont, and in 1956 joined CBC (Toronto) TV's 'Country Hoedown' as rhythm guitarist with King *Ganam's Sons of the West. 'The Tommy Hunter Show,' heard weekdays 1960–5 on CBC radio, succeeded 'Country Hoedown' as a CBC TV weekly program in 1965 and was renamed 'Tommy Hunter Country' in 1977. One of the most popular Canadian TV variety shows, it has presented over the years such regular performers as the Allen Sisters, Maurice *Bolyer, Al *Cherny, guitarist-arranger Jim Pirie, the *Rhythm Pals, and others. The trumpeter Dave Woods succeeded Bert *Niosi as the show's music director in 1976; Woods was followed later by Eric Robertson. Hunter, who uses 'Travellin' Man' as his TV theme song, has toured widely in Canada and in the 1960s was the leader of several concert parties to Europe for the Dept of National Defence. For several summers 1963–70 he appeared at the Academy Theatre in Lindsay, Ont, in a concert series broadcast by CBC radio as 'Country Holiday.'

Known as 'Canada's Country Gentleman,' Hunter won the 1967, 1968, and 1969 *Juno Awards as best male country singer. His TV show won a Big Country Award in 1978. In 1974 he received a citation for 'continuous and outstanding contribution to country music' from the Country Music Hall of Fame in Nashville. Despite his popularity Hunter has not been a prolific recording artist. He recorded first with Ganam in 1958, and has completed LPs on the *CTL, Harmony (*CBS Records), and *RCA labels. In an interview with Ralph Thomas (who described Hunter's voice as 'soft and simple, his smooth baritone unmarred by country twang') the singer explained that he attempts 'a middle-of-the-road approach ... something that's just as much pop music as it is country and western' (*Toronto Daily Star*, 3 Dec 1966).

BIBLIOGRAPHY

Collins, Bob. 'Canadian teenagers find a home-grown idol,' *Star Weekly*, 7 May 1960

Rasky, Frank. 'Tommy the troubled troubadour,' *Canadian Magazine*, 5 Aug 1967

Wigmore, Donnalu. 'Why success won't spoil Tommy Hunter,' *Chatelaine*, Mar 1969

Beard, Michael. 'Tommy Hunter – a Canadian television phenomenon,' *RPM*, vol 30, 24 Feb 1979 (MD)

Tommy Hunter

HUNTLEY GREEN, Gertrude (b Huntley, m Green, m Durand). Pianist, teacher, b St Thomas, Ont, July 1889. She studied with W. Caven Barron at the London (Ont) Cons of Music, winning the Barron gold medal and the Heintzman scholarship in 1901. She continued violin and piano studies in Detroit and in Paris, where she made her piano debut 5 Mar 1908 at the Salle Erard in a joint program with her instructors, the pianist Moritz Moszkowski (who ended an 11-year retirement to perform) and the violinist Albert Geloso. She subsequently gave recitals and joint programs in France and England with Joseph Hollman, Marguerite Sylva, and Kitty Cheatham, and in Canada and the USA with Blanche Marchesi, Leopold Godowsky, Charles Marie Courboin, Marcel Grandjany, and Yolanda Mérö. Huntley Green also studied in the late 1920s with Nicolai Medtner in Germany and recorded his *Fairy Tale* and *Danza Festiva* for Ampico Piano Rolls in the 1920s. Godowsky declared her to be 'the future woman champion pianist,' and in 1920 she assisted him in his master classes. Paderewski deemed her a 'great artist'; and after Ernest Newman heard her in 1927 in recital in London, he considered her 'in the foremost ranks of present day world pianists.' She settled in Victoria, BC, ca 1914, and was active there as a teacher of advanced piano students and as a performer. She also conducted an orchestra that assisted in wartime fund-raising projects. She made a number of Canadian tours and was admired for her work with the *Hart House Quartet. Returning to British Columbia in the 1940s, she continued to perform until 1960.

BIBLIOGRAPHY

Lomas, Shira. 'Gertrude Huntley's story,' *Chatelaine*, Mar, Apr 1928 EK

HUOT, Guy. Administrator, editor, b Ottawa 21 Mar 1943; BA (Ottawa) 1962. He was organist 1960–8 at St Joseph's and St Charles' churches in Ottawa. After 1963 he has been a guest organist for special ceremonies at the Ottawa Roman Catholic Cathedral. In the early 1960s he was a freelance music critic for the Ottawa daily *Le Droit* and served 1960–2 as Ottawa president and Ontario representative to the National Council of the *JMC. Huot was head of music 1966–73 for the *Canada Council and music adminstrator 1973–5 of the *NAC. He also has been a member of several boards, including that of the *CMCouncil 1973–5. During his term with the Canada Council he served as an ex-officio advisory board member for such national service organizations as the *ACO. In 1976 he became secretary general of the CMCouncil and editor of its quarterly **Musicanada*. RM

'La Huronne.' Romance for voice and piano, words by Pierre-Gabriel Huot and music by Célestin *Lavigueur composed ca 1861 and a popular patriotic song for several decades. Its inspiration is said to have come from a visit by the authors to the village of Lorette, near Quebec. Nazaire *LeVasseur reports that 'Lavigueur requested Huot to write poetry on the Huron tribe, adding that he would write the music for it' in order to pay the boarding fee for their visit to the Huron colony. The work was published (nd) by Léger Brousseau Frères; on 3 Jan 1862 in *L'Écho du Cabinet de lecture paroissial*; and in 1864 by Lavigueur & Hutchison.

BIBLIOGRAPHY

'La Huronne,' *L'Écho du Cabinet de lecture paroissial*, vol 4, 3 Jan 1862

LeVasseur, Nazaire. 'Musique et musiciens à Québec,' *La Musique*, vol 3, Jul 1921 DM

HURRLE, Norman (William). Organist, choirmaster, teacher, b Peterborough, Ont, 1 May 1927; ARCT 1949; ARCM, ARCO 1959; FTCL 1960. He studied 1946–9 at the U of Toronto and concurrently was organist-choirmaster at Wycliffe College. He held positions 1947–65 as organist-choirmaster in Toronto, Brockville, Newmarket, and Peterborough, Ont, and at St Matthias' Church in Montreal. He also was organist-choirmaster 1965–9 at St James' Cathedral, Toronto, and 1970–3 at Christ Church Cathedral, Vancouver. He taught 1966–70 at the *U of Toronto and in 1974 became music director at St Michael's School, Victoria, BC. During the Second International Congress of Organists (1967) Hurrle's choir at St James' Cathedral became the first in Canada to sing daily cathedral services for a week (16 in eight days, including the Canadian premiere of Walton's *The Twelve*). Hurrle has appeared as soloist with the *TSO and has supervised the rebuilding of the organs in All Saints' Church, Peterborough, St James' Cathedral, Toronto, and Christ Church Cathedral, Vancouver. His pupils include Brian *Cherney, Robert Kennedy, and Patrick *Wedd. PFB

HURTEAU, (Joseph Armand) **Jean-Pierre**. Bass, b Montreal 5 Dec 1924; premier prix (CMM) 1955. He took voice lessons 1947–9 with Sarah *Fischer, and a Sarah Fischer Concerts scholarship in 1949 enabled him to make his recital debut at the Ritz-Carlton Hotel. He studied 1949–51 with Albert Cornellier and 1952–5 with Martial Singher at the CMM. His operatic debut was with the *Minute Opera (the Sailor's father in Milhaud's *Le Pauvre Matelot*, 1952), and until 1955 he sang supporting roles in *Montreal Festivals productions, at the *Opera Guild, and at the *Variétés lyriques. He was Titurel in *Parsifal* with Rose Bampton and Ramon Vinay at Montreal's Show Mart in 1955. Awarded a scholarship by the Quebec government, he studied 1955–8 in Rome with Rachele Maragliano-Mori. At the Capitole theatre in Toulouse he sang Balthazar in Menotti's *Amahl and the Night Visitors* (1957) and Pimen in *Boris Godunov*. Engaged by the Opéra and the Opéra-Comique in Paris, he made his debut in March 1958 in *The Magic Flute*. He remained attached to these theatres until 1970, singing the Commendatore in *Don Giovanni* (1960), Mephisto in *Faust* (1961), La Roche in *Capriccio* (1962), Don Alfonso in *Così fan tutte* (1963), the title role in *The Marriage of Figaro* (1964), Mephisto in *The Damnation of Faust* (1964), and Panthée in *The Trojans* (1969), not to mention a host of roles in productions with Maria Callas, Elisabeth Schwarzkopf, Tito Gobbi, Montserrat Caballé, and others and performances in Lyons, Marseilles, Toulouse, Bordeaux, Grenoble, Monte Carlo, and Orange, and at the Ancient Theatre of Epidaurus in Greece. In Paris he sang regularly with orchestras and on radio, appearing in Verdi's *Requiem* (1958), Handel's *Acis and Galatea* (1966), Prokofiev's *War and Peace* (1967), and other works.

More recently Hurteau sang in Penderecki's *The Devils of Loudun* (Marseilles 1972), Renzo Rosselini's *La Reine morte* (Rome 1974), and Harry *Somers' *Louis Riel* (the role of Mgr Taché in the 1975 *COC production, in Toronto, Ottawa, and Washington). Following his performance in *Capriccio*, the critic Jacques Bourgeois wrote, 'Jean-Pierre Hurteau possesses not only a splendid voice, which will make him a Wotan and a Sachs in a few years, but a remarkable presence and authority as well' (*Arts*, February 1962). René Dumesnil called him 'a perfect Alfonso' (*Le Monde*, 12 Feb 1963). In Canada Hurteau has been heard in recital and on CBC TV, for which he sang

Inigo Gomez in Ravel's *L'Heure espagnole* (1955) and the Comte des Grieux in *Manon* (1959).

DISCOGRAPHY

Berlioz *The Trojans* excerpts. Paris Opera O, Prêtre cond, Hurteau (Narbal). 1964. EMI Angel S-3670

Puccini *Tosca*. Paris Opera O, Rosenthal cond, Hurteau (Sciarrone). 1959. 3-Vega 8001-8003

Saint-Saëns *Samson et Dalila*. Paris Opera O, Prêtre cond, Hurteau (Second Philistine). 1963. Angel S-3639

BIBLIOGRAPHY

Vaillancourt, Benoît. 'Un autre des nôtres a l'Opéra de Paris,' Montreal *Patrie du dimanche*, 23 Nov 1958

Saint-Germain, Pierre. 'Profile: Pierre Hurteau,' *OpCan*, Feb 1967

Rich, Maria F. *Who's Who in Opera* (New York 1976) GP

HUSARUK, Eugène. Violinist, b Warsaw 2 Mar 1932, naturalized Canadian 1954. Born to Ukrainian parents, he immigrated to Canada in 1949 and studied 1950–3 at the *McGill Cons with Alexander *Brott. He continued his violin training at the Vienna Academy with Vaša Přihoda and Ricardo Odnoposoff, studied orchestra conducting with Hans Swarowsky, and took summer courses from Yvonne Astruc at the Accademia Chigiana of Siena. During this period he received two scholarships from the *Ladies' Morning Musical Club. He joined the *MSO in 1957 and deputized as concertmaster during the 1977–8 and 1979–80 seasons. In 1960 he studied with Ivan Galamian at Meadowmount Summer School, NY, and later he worked with Lorand *Fenyves at the *JMC Orford Art Centre. In 1968, as soloist with the MSO, he premiered *Fiala's *Divertimento Concertante*. He participated in *SMCQ concerts after 1969 and with that society's ensemble gave the Canadian premiere (1973) of Betsy Jolas's *États* for violin and six percussionists. He also played this work on CBC TV, which telecast the program in Europe. Husaruk is principal violin in the recording of *Gellman's *Mythos II* conducted by Serge *Garant. He is concertmaster in several CBC radio and TV orchestras and has taken part in performances by the *McGill Chamber Orchestra, the Ensemble Couperin-le-Grand, the Pierre-Rolland Quintet, and Les Grands Ballets Canadiens. He has appeared in recital with the pianists Anna-Marie *Globenski, John *Newmark, Charles *Reiner, and Herbert *Ruff.

Husaruk's wife, Yolande (soprano, b Montreal 14 Jun 1935, daughter of Jean *Deslauriers), won the *Prix Archambault in 1962. On Quebec government grants in 1965 and 1966 she studied Lieder with Erik Werba in Salzburg and Vienna, and then continued her voice training at the *CMM 1966–73 with Lina Narducci. She sang in *Il Trittico* (1971) and *Rigoletto* (1972) with the *Opéra du Québec, gave recitals with various ensembles, including the *Orford String Quartet, the McGill Chamber Orchestra, the MSO, and the *Edmonton SO, and participated in several CBC programs. AP

HUSE, Peter (Franklin). Composer, poet, b Gadsby, Alta, 12 Mar 1938; B MUS (British Columbia) 1963, MFA (Princeton) 1965. After taking courses in architecture during the 1950s he studied composition 1960–3 with Cortland *Hultberg and Barbara *Pentland at the *U of British Columbia and 1963–5 with Roger Sessions and Milton Babbitt at Princeton U. In 1964 he won one of the BMI Awards to Student Composers for three of his compositions: *String Quartet* (1961), *Vanity of Vanities* (1962), and *Sonata* for two pianos (1962). He was associate composer 1967–9 at the Centre for Communication and the Arts at *Simon Fraser U, a lecturer 1969–72 in Montreal at the National Theatre School and *McGill U, and assistant director 1972–5 of the *World Soundscape Project at Simon Fraser U, where he taught courses 1975–6 in renaissance music. In 1977 he became director of the music program for Selkirk College, located at the David Thompson University Centre in Nelson, BC. Huse's music and poetry reflect a feeling for structure developed by his training as an architect. He is a member of PRO Canada.

SELECTED COMPOSITIONS

String Quartet. 1961. Ms

Vanity of Vanities, song cycle (Koheleth). 1962. Ms

Sonata. 1962. 2 pf. Ms

Quintet. 1966. Picc (fl), ob, cl, hn, bn. Ms

Improvisations for Mary's Ism. 1968. V, perc, synthesized sound (on 4-track tape), 12 dancers, lights. Tape

Space Play. 1968. 8-track tape. Tape. RCI 373/Mel SMLP 4027

Music for the Birth of God, film score (L. Kearns). 1973. 3 vs. Ms

World Radio. 1974. Any no. of performers. World Soundscape Project limited edn 1974

Directions (Canadian dialects). 1974. 4-track tape collage. Tape

Happy Birthday, Maurice Ravel. 1978. Jazz ens. Ms

WRITINGS

'Barbara Pentland,' *MSc*, 242, Jul–Aug 1968

'Cross-Canada soundscape tour 1973,' *Sound Heritage*, vol 3, no. 4, 1974 (JDn)

HUSTON, Margaret (b Houghston, m Carrington, m Jones). Mezzo-soprano, teacher, b Toronto ca 1878, d near Greenwich, Conn, 1 Aug 1942. She was an elder sister of the actor Walter Huston. She studied in Europe and in 1903 began a career as a recitalist, gaining particular esteem in England and America as an interpreter of Wolf and Debussy. She gave a 'homecoming concert' in Toronto 26 Nov 1903, appeared at *Massey Hall 6 Nov 1907 and 8 Dec 1910, and sang at the TCM 30 Oct 1912. After her New York debut in 1911 the *Musical Courier* reported: 'Her art is diversified and multiform. It is an admixture of magnetism, science, knowledge, skill, observation, and that indefinable something called personality.' In 1915 she married and retired from singing. In later years she lectured, coached (John Barrymore was a diction pupil), and supported philanthropies. After her first husband's death in 1931 she married the famed scenic designer Robert Edmond Jones.

BIBLIOGRAPHY

'Margaret Huston's unusual art,' *MCour*, 13 Dec 1911

JBM

The Hutterites. Named after Jakob Hutter, they were Anabaptists from Austria and south Germany who began to live communally in Moravia in 1529. After much persecution they emigrated to Russia in 1770 and thence to the USA ca 1870. After 1918 some 50 families emigrated to Canada, settling first in Alberta and Manitoba, then in Saskatchewan. In the 1970s Canadian Hutterites numbered about 15,000.

The Hutterites have preserved their Tyrolean dialect. In their Sunday and daily worship services they use a hymn book entitled *Die Lieder der Hutterischen Brüder* (Songs of the Hutterian Brethren). Most of the hymns, written by Anabaptists and 16th-century Hutterites, have both devotional and historical content. The melodies mainly are those of 16th-century sacred and secular German folksongs, but some are derived from art songs, Meistersinger songs, Gregorian chant, and Reformation hymns; one may have been written by a Hutterite. These melodies are learned by ear. The children copy the texts of the songs and learn to sing them from memory on Saturdays and Sundays. In addition to the songs from *Die Lieder der Hutterischen Brüder*, families sing gospel songs and other hymns in their homes during the evenings. All singing is in unison and octaves except in a few colonies where it is in parallel fourths; often it is led by women.

The Hutterites live in closed communities which they leave only for business, hospitalization, or visiting other Hutterites; they are forbidden to own musical instruments, radios, television sets, record players, and tape recorders and to go to public places of entertainment. Thus, they have almost no exposure to music other than their own singing. Their theology of music, to sing to the glory of God and not for 'carnal pleasure,' is based on the New Testament and the writings of the 16th-century Hutterite, Peter Rideman; the Hutterites sing no secular songs.

See also Mennonites.

BIBLIOGRAPHY

Zieglschmid, A.J.F. 'A song of persecution of Hutterites in Velke-Levary,' *Mennonite Q R*, vol 17, Jul 1943

Die Lieder der Hutterischen Brüder (Calgary 1962)

Peters, Victor. *All Things Common: The Hutterite Way of Life* (Minneapolis 1965)

Martens, Helen. 'Hutterite songs: the origins and aural transmission of their melodies from the sixteenth century,' unpubl PH D thesis, Columbia 1968

– 'The music of some religious minorities in Canada,' *Ethnomusicology*, vol 16, sep 1972 HMr

HUTTON, Charles (Warrington). Organist, music dealer, conductor, b St John's, Nfld, 20 Aug 1861, d there 1 Feb 1949. He was educated in Charlottetown and at the French college, St Pierre, and in 1880 became organist-choirmaster at St John the Baptist Roman Catholic Cathedral in St John's. He held this position for 63 years, but at the turn of the century he spent three years in England furthering his musical education with Oscar Beringer (piano) and others. It was during this sojourn that he deputized on short notice for the absentee accompanist of Emma *Albani at a recital by the great soprano for the Lords Cricket Club. The recital was a great success and the club, in appreciation , made Hutton an honorary member. In 1883 he opened a music store which later was taken over by his sons and which still was operative in 1978. Hutton was a leading figure in Newfoundland musical activities. With his wife, a trained singer, he presented virtually all the Gilbert & Sullivan operettas and many others, whenever sufficient performing talent could be gathered. Ignatius *Rumboldt was a pupil and protégé. In 1924 Pope Pius XI made Hutton a Knight of St Gregory, and in 1938 King George VI appointed him to the Order of the British Empire. A profile of Hutton was broadcast 6 May 1978 on CBC radio's 'Between Ourselves.'

Hymnbooks, protestant. The history of Canadian printed collections, with music, of the hymns and metrical psalms that are traditionally a part of most protestant forms of worship starts with Stephen *Humbert's **Union Harmony* (Saint John, NB, 1801; later editions, 1816, 1831, 1840). This is a substantial oblong-octavo volume modelled after publications of US composers of the Revolutionary era such as Swan, Read, Belknap, and Billings, each of whom in fact is represented in it by several tunes. Also in it are 12 original tunes by the compiler, Humbert, who often approximates the angular harmonies of his New England contemporaries and sometimes adopts their 'fuguing' format (whereby a crudely imitative texture is applied to the final phrase or two of a verse, as a contrast to chordal treatment of the earlier lines). In a 'Concise introduction' to the book Humbert defends this style.

A considerably slimmer volume entitled *A Selection from the Psalms of David* (Montreal, 1821) followed English rather than US models, with its upright format and its placement of the principal melody in the treble (rather than in the tenor, as in the US books and in Humbert). The compiler, Rev George Jenkins, was attached to the Anglican Cathedral in Montreal. The book, one of the most elegant in appearance of early Canadian publications, is acknowledged by Jenkins to be based on a specific English work, Miller and Drummond's *The Psalms of David*.

These two early examples establish the two main influences found in succeeding hymnbooks. The US oblong format, with melody in the tenor part, predominates in the first part of the 19th century. Only very gradually does the British upright reintroduce itself after 1860. US tunes from the popular 'Yankee tunesmiths' were familiar throughout much of the 19th century in Canada, to judge from the continual reappearances of 'China' by Timothy Swan, 'Russia' by Daniel Read, and 'Lenox' by Lewis Edson, even though by the end of the century the latter two are reharmonized and divested of their original 'fuging' character. The newer and more musically 'literate' style of hymn, associated in the USA with Lowell Mason, infiltrates from the 1840s on. After the mid-century, Canadian collections reflect the new appeal of the 'gospel song' style (see Hymn singing), though some do so only in separate appendices devoted to music for evangelical occasions. The Moody-Sankey and Crossley-Hunter evangelical-hymn publications, known internationally in the 1880s and 1890s, sometimes appeared in Canadian reprints and certainly had Canadian imitators and borrowers.

Adaptations from classical music were prevalent. This is an English trait which the Canadian compilers evidently followed both by copying the Handel and Beethoven tunes of their homeland models and by making their own imitations from Mozart, Weber, or, again, Beethoven. For example, a sacred text is fitted to an arrangement from Mozart's *The Marriage of Figaro* (the duet of the two flower girls from Act 3) in Alexander Davidson's *Sacred Harmony* (Toronto, 1838; later editions, 1845, 1848, 1858, 1860). English 18th-century tunes such as Croft's 'St Ann's' ('O God Our Help in Ages Past') recur fairly frequently, but almost no collection is without those traditional standbys 'Old Hundred' and 'Martyrs,' the former from the Huguenot Psalter of the 16th century and the latter from the Scottish Psalter of the early 17th – though both undergo many variations of metrical arrangement and harmonization. The Canadian editors reflect their environment by using local place-names for many tunes ('Goderich,' 'Port Hope,' 'Toronto' three times, 'Montreal,' 'Brockville,' 'Niagara,' and 'Hamilton'; as well as 'Canada' three times and 'Ontario,' whose derivation is given curiously as 'American melody'). Many of these tunes no doubt were original, though attributions often are missing or dubious (one of the 'Toronto' tunes is credited to Arthur Sullivan, and one of the 'Canada' tunes to Lowell Mason!).

The books often were produced for a particular denomination, but throughout the middle and late 19th century the contents vary little from Anglican to Presbyterian to Methodist to Wesleyan. Some exceptions exist: Canadian Baptists and Lutherans, by reason of their different traditions for the use of music, often imported their hymnbooks. The 'Amen,' customarily sung in protestant services at the end of the last verse of a hymn, appears in print only at the very end of the 19th century.

The books provided, besides texts and tunes, virtually the only available contact of Canadians in small communities or rural areas with the principles of musical notation and sight-singing – except for those infrequent occasions when singing masters visited to hold classes. (See Singing schools.) Like their US prototypes, Canadian hymnbooks usually started with a section (often 20 pages or more in length) called 'Introductory lessons and exercises,' 'Elements of music,' or 'Introduction to the science of music.'

Some of the early Canadian hymnbooks contain original tunes and characteristic harmonizations that deserve revival. Such sources are Mark Burnham's *The Colonial Harmonist* (Port Hope, Ont, 1832 – the preface says 'no musical treatise has hitherto been published in this Colony'), the large and anonymously edited *Harmonicon* (Pictou, NS, 1836 or 1837, later editions 1841, 1855), J.P. *Clarke's *Canadian Church Psalmody* (Toronto 1845), Davidson's *Sacred Harmony* already noted, and George Linton's *The Vocalist* (Toronto 1865?). Though the US collections in this period, especially in the midwestern and southern states, cultivate the 'shape-note' notation style (whereby a different shape of note-head corresponds to each sol-fa syllable for greater ease in sight-singing), this does not seem to have caught on extensively in Canada. The 1848 edition of Davidson is advertised as being the first Canadian shape-note publication, but the later editions of this book revert to standard notation. *Chants évangéliques*, a hymnbook for French-speaking Canadians, was published first in 1862 by *Lovell of Montreal; it continued in use in 1980.

Not all publications contained music. Two subtypes surprisingly prevalent in the mid-19th century sometimes included tunes but more often consisted of texts only: these are hymn collections for children or for Sunday school use and hymnbooks employing languages of the various native peoples (Cree, Iroquois, etc). An example of the former (with tunes) is L.C. Everett's *The Canadian Warbler* (Toronto and Montreal 1863); an example of the latter (without) is *A Collection of Ojibway and English Hymns* (ed and transl Peter Jones, Boston ca 1830, later reprinted Toronto). The increasing prevalence and popularity of the catchy evangelical songs in the later 19th century brought a reaction under which the hymnals came to be prepared by advisory committees within the various sects rather than by individual editors, and gradually a more scholarly, more historically correct, and more 'elevating' publication results, although sometimes creative and indigenous expressions are lost in the process.

Rev Alexander *MacMillan's long career as an adviser on Presbyterian and later United Church of Canada hymn-editing policies began with the production of the *Presbyterian Book of Praise* (Oxford and London 1904, revised 1918, preface dated 'Toronto, 1897'). In this book historical perspective of choice, scholarly attributions, and a rather severe style of musical arrangement set a new standard for Canadian compilers.

The *Methodist Hymn and Tune Book* (Toronto 1917), includes an unusually large number (49) of originally composed tunes, by W.H. *Hewlett, Alfred *Whitehead, A.S. *Vogt, G.D. *Atkinson, H.C. *Perrin, and others. The chairman of the musical editorial committee, Herbert *Sanders, wrote nearly half of them himself. Hewlett's tunes are harmonically and melodically the most adventurous. Notably in the first *Hymnary* of the newly formed United Church of Canada (Toronto 1930), a more 'universal' approach (in effect both more scholarly and more European) is in evidence, the original tunes disappear, and newly composed tunes are de-emphasized, though there are seven by Ernest *MacMillan, two by Healey *Willan, and one by Whitehead. The chief editorial adviser was Alexander MacMillan. Willan was largely responsible for choosing and editing music for the Anglican Church of Canada's 1938 revision of its *Book of Common Praise*.

In 1971 precedent was created in a jointly issued and handsomely designed volume, *The Hymn Book* of the Anglican Church of Canada and the United Church of Canada. Godfrey *Ridout, Derek *Holman, and others contributed new melodies to this collection, which however did not attempt to encourage revival of indigenous tunes from older Canadian hymnals, by now quite extensive in number.

Indigenous hymn texts are found throughout the period covered by the above summary. David Willson, patriarch of the *Children of Peace sect in mid-19th century Sharon, Ont, wrote over 1000 hymn verses, which were published in two volumes, without tunes. They have a clarity, sincerity, and found-poetry charm comparable to the naive painted banners of the sect. Joseph Scriven (b County Down, Ireland, 10 Sep 1819, d Rice Lake, Ont, 1886) wrote the text of the much-loved 'What a Friend We Have in Jesus.' Rev Robert Murray (b Earltown, NS, 25 Dec 1832, d Halifax 12 Dec 1910) wrote the words for the well-known 'From Ocean unto Ocean.' Gena *Branscombe wrote both words and music for 'Arms That Have Sheltered Us,' adopted by the RCN in 1960.

See also Anglican church music; Hymnology; Protestant church music; Religions and music.

BIBLIOGRAPHY

Mahon, A.W. *Canadian Hymns and Hymn Writers* (1908)

McMillan, Barclay. 'Tune-book imprints in Canada to 1867: a descriptive bibliography,' *Papers of the Bibliographical Society of Canada / Cahiers de la Société Bibliographique du Canada*, vol 16, 1977 (JB)

Hymnology. The historical and analytic examination of hymns. Until the middle of the 20th century the contribution of Canadians to the hymn repertoire was relatively small, and hymnologists were few, although there has been greater activity subsequently.

Canada is not, however, without any heritage in hymns. Excluding *'Jesous Ahatonhia,' which ought to be understood as a carol, hymn writing in Canada goes back at least as far as 1827, when William Bullock, an ordained clergyman of the Church of England, wrote 'We Love the Place, O God' and had it sung from manuscript for the consecration of his church at Trinity Bay in Newfoundland. It had to wait 27 years before it was published. That hymn appeared 40 years prior to Confederation; and once Rev Robert Murray's 'From Ocean unto Ocean' and Canon F.G. Scott's 'We Hail Thee Now, O Jesu' are acknowledged, there remains little that is significant in Canadian hymn writing before the 20th century. Nearly everything else written in the 19th century is so afflicted with sentimentalism, escapism, subjectivism, fulsomeness, or juvenility of expression as to be unsuitable for common worship or too introspective for personal devotional use. As one scans the church papers of the 19th century for contributions of hymns to the devotional columns, one gets the impression that most authors thought the only requisite for a hymn was rhymed couplets in regular rhythm.

There were reasons for this lack of critical evaluation. The writers did not possess the literary skill to match their vision. Moreover, the popularity of gospel songs (see Hymn singing), which came into Canada from the USA like a flood before the turn of the century, was eroding the belief that a hymn is, first and foremost, praise and response to God. Besides, the hymn had not commended itself at that time to the front rank of Canadian poets and writers.

As the 20th century advanced the importance of the hymn, both text and tune, slowly began to assert itself. *The Book of Common Praise* (Anglican, 1908), with nearly 800 hymns, had 20 texts and nearly twice as many tunes by Canadian authors and composers. In *The Hymn Book* (1971) the proportion of Canadian content rose to approximately 10 per cent. An interesting fact is that composers appear to have been more active than authors.

One of the first practitioners of hymnology in Canada was James Edmund Jones (1866–1939), convenor of the Hymnal Compilation Committee for *The Book of Common Praise* (1908) and secretary of the committee that prepared its revision, *The Hymn Book* (1938; the title 'The Book of Common Praise' is retained on the title page but not on the cover). A magistrate of the city of Toronto and a gifted layman of the Church of England in Canada, Jones published at his own expense an annotated edition (Toronto 1909) of the 1908 book with information about authors and composers. It was revised to complement the 1938 edition. Jones' venture undoubtedly did much to draw attention to the hymn by showing that it was a living form with a real history. (Jones also was the editor of *French-Canadian Songs*, published by *Harris in 1920.)

More important, however, is the work of Alexander *MacMillan, who lectured in hymnology and church music and served as secretary of the committee that prepared *The Hymnary* (1931), the first book of hymns compiled for the United Church. Four years later there appeared his *Hymns of the Church*, a historical treatment of the development of hymnody in the Christian church, with particular reference to the hymns in *The Hymnary*. It established MacMillan as one of the leading hymnologists of his day.

Ulrich S. *Leupold, who directed church music studies at Waterloo Lutheran Seminary 1945–70, was the foremost church musician and hymnologist among Canadian Lutherans in his day. Leupold's administrative and professional duties, however, left him little time for research in the hymnody of Canadian Lutherans, although he was well informed about its roots in the mother church in Germany, as his *Die liturgischen Gesänge der evangelischen Kirche*...(Kassel 1933) makes very clear.

During the 1960s and 1970s the focus rests upon the work of Stanley L. *Osborne, a minister of the United Church of Canada. Inspired by the work of Alexander MacMillan, he began to explore the sources of the texts and tunes in *The Hymnary*. His first book, *The Strain of Praise* (Toronto 1957), maintains that the hymn is primarily an act of praise and prayer to God, and as such is the key to the congregation's response in worship. In 1976 appeared his second volume, *If Such Holy Song*, a commentary on the hymns in *The Hymn Book* (1971). It treats each hymn in its historical setting and also offers an appreciation and critical analysis of the text and the tune. Osborne's library of English hymnals published after 1900 is one of the important North American collections.

In 1980 the movement for liturgical renewal which began in the 1930s showed no sign of losing either its vitality or its momentum. In the 1970s there was a veritable explosion in the writing of hymns. Stylistic changes in music and literature affected the boundaries of the hymn as well as its quality. In the face of such activity and change it became more than ever important to be sure what was essential in a hymn in order to preserve it. It was in this area of challenged tradition that the researches of the hymnologists took on renewed significance.

See also Hymnbooks, protestant.

BIBLIOGRAPHY

Osborne, Stanley. 'Recent Canadian hymnody,' *The Hymn*, vol 29, Jul 1978 (SLO)

Hymn singing. The singing of hymns in Canada goes back to the 17th century when Récollet and Jesuit missionaries (see Missionaries) arrived from France to plant the Christian gospel in the new land. They employed the hymn not only as a vehicle of worship but also as an evangelical tool, a means of spreading the faith. According to *The Jesuit Relations* their training must have been considerable, for they not only led the singing at worship but they also instructed their converts on the best mode of singing. 'All the savages,' it states, 'have much aptitude and inclination for singing the hymns of the Church, which have been rendered into their language' (vol 60, p 145). Antiphonal singing between men and women was employed frequently. Native melodies with a minimum of alteration supplemented French songs. Four-part singing at Quebec in 1646 is documented. Accompaniment was provided by viols or violins brought from France and probably also by flutes and recorders. After the middle of the 17th century an organ was in use in Quebec City to support the singing. Up to the time of the British era in Canada the singing of hymns was confined to religious instruction. Hymns were sung at Mass, but not by the congregation, whose participation was limited to certain liturgical responses.

1 The protestants
2 Gospel songs
3 Denominations
4 Accompaniment

1 THE PROTESTANTS. With the arrival of the protestant settlers in the Maritimes and Upper Canada and the building of their first churches came considerable diversity. Presbyterians brought with them the psalms. Only the Methodists and the Lutherans, and to a limited extent the Baptists and Congregationalists, promoted the singing of hymns. US hymn collections were known and copied widely, the Methodists brought with them the new praise by Watts and the Wesleys, and the Lutherans had their beloved chorales. But of highly trained musicians there were few: amateurs were in charge.

The first settlers had only the hymnals they brought with them. Psalters came without music and the Methodists and Presbyterians, at least in the larger centres, employed precentors, or tune-strikers, to start the singing. Yet there is no evidence that the precentors had any serious training. Only an exceptional one knew more than four or five tunes. Since few people had copies of the psalter, the precentor also had to read out the lines, usually two at a time. The singing was laggard more often than not, if we may judge by the number of times the Methodist superintendents warned their people against 'slowness' and 'dullness.'

By mid-century, melodeons and organs were being introduced into the churches, displacing the flutes and the bass viols, and choirs were being formed to lead the singing. The role of the precentor declined as that of the organist and choir leader expanded. Hymnbooks brought order and uniformity into the singing.

In *Old-Time Primitive Methodism in Canada 1829–84* (Toronto 1894) Mrs F.R. Hopper described the singing in Bay Street Methodist Church in Toronto: 'George McCluskey played the bass viol ...while Henry Harrison played the flute and Robert Walker the melodeon. George McCluskey was never so happy as when praising God on "strings and pipes", accompanied by the "loud-sounding" cymbals'; and commenting upon the singing in Carlton Street Church ca 1890 she remarked that it 'is considered equal to that of any church in Toronto, and while sweet and artistic, is devotional.'

During the last half of the 19th century several factors combined to lend a stimulus to hymn singing. Most important were the arrival of trained musicians from England, Scotland, and the USA and the formation of music schools. Nearly all churches in the cities and towns had organs; melodeons and pianos were to be found in country churches. In devout homes families would often gather around the melodeon or follow the lead of a flute or another instrument to sing hymns. Mrs Hopper refers to her own home: 'My father loved singing: he had a flute and played by note; so we generally spent all Sunday afternoon in sacred song...Mother never could sing. She said herself, the only tune she knew was *Balerma*, and she sang it to "Oh, for that tenderness of heart". She thought she sang *Balerma*, but I do not know even now whether it was the words or the music, that stood for *Balerma* in her mind. It was like no tune on earth.'

Although the Presbyterians were not permitted to sing anything except the metrical psalter until the century was well advanced, the Methodists and Lutherans were not hampered by any such proscription. Indeed they were adjured to promote singing vigorously. In *The Doctrines and Disciplines of the Methodist Church* (Toronto 1884) directions are clear and unequivocal:

> i Choose such hymns as are proper for the occasion, and do not sing too much at once; seldom more than five or six verses.
> ii Let the tune be suited to the words, and do not suffer the people to sing too slowly. Exhort every person in the congregation to sing.
> iii Frequently remind the people of the importance of this part of religious worship, and exhort them to 'sing with the spirit and with the understanding also'.
> iv Recommend our tune book, and appoint some suitable person to conduct the singing.

Singing occured at least three times in every service 'on the Lord's Day' (it was the duty of the superintendent to exercise control in these matters throughout his circuit) and a good deal oftener than that in the Methodist's daily life. Not everyone was charmed by the ubiquity of Methodist singing. In *It Blows, It Snows* (Dublin 1845) a traveller through Canada who identifies himself as C.H.C. complains that

> The inconsiderate habit...of singing hymns and psalms on almost every occasion...is practised among almost every religious persuasion; though I find by the methodistical part of the community its observance is appropriated to a larger share...than by any other. The stranger...must not take it for granted that...such is practised either for the express purpose of communing with the spiritual Author of all consolation, or sounding the depth of His praises on high, for such is not in anywise the case; the music appertains solely to...the lessening of bodily inconveniences...compelling the resources of the mind to take share in the burthen of the operations. The furrowed frill that binds the neck of the lady cannot be laid across the symmetrical restrictions of the Italian iron without an hymn. The gesticulations of the churn-dash are ineffectual without an incantation. And the querulous sigh of the bellows resigns its claim upon ignition bereft of doxology.

But whether C.H.C. enjoyed the custom or not, if hymn singing was as broadly integrated in the day-to-day affairs of Canadians as he suggests, one can see the important role it must have played in the development of the church in the new country; and for warm, fervent singing of hymns it is fair to say the Methodists led the way.

See also Hymnbooks, protestant; Protestant church music; Salvation Army.

2 GOSPEL SONGS. By the end of the 19th century the influence of the gospel song had made itself felt. The phenomenon arose in the USA and came into Canada on the wings of revivalism. The songs of Dwight L. Moody and Ira D. Sankey were typical of the diet in pentecostal circles and overflowed, in varying degrees, into other churches as well. Henry J. Knight, a noted tenor soloist and choirmaster in Bowmanville, Ont, at the end of the last century, more than once attended Canadian meetings which Moody and Sankey conducted. Sankey usually led the singing. Nearly every song had a refrain, otherwise known as a chorus, which the people were taught first if they did not already know it. Then Sankey would sing the stanzas, sometimes asking the choir to join him, sometimes adding new words or new music which he composed on the spot. At the end of each stanza came the chorus, and each time the people were urged to sing it with greater verve. Often antiphonal singing would find men responding to ladies, children to their parents, or the choir to the congregation. Frequently shouts of 'Praise the Lord,' 'Hallelujah,' and 'Amen' would punctuate the singing. Occasionally people were known to 'swoon with the Spirit.' Finally, after the people had been lifted through their singing to a pitch of excitement, Moody would preach 'a thunderous sermon.'

To some, such singing exerted an enormous appeal. Others found it disturbing – short on truth and long on emotion, and tilted dangerously between objectivity and subjectivity. With the adoption of *The Methodist Hymn Book* (1917) and *The Book of Praise* (1918), it was clear that the gospel song had not displaced everything else. *The Billy Graham Song Book*, and two or three collections like it, kept the type alive throughout the mid-century; varieties, including evangelistic pop, had their innings too.

Still, a comparison of the hymn singing heard in the 1920s and 1930s with that in the 1970s brings a realization of immense improvement. Then, good singing was confined largely to the cities; in the 1970s, by contrast, no centre was too small to have an excellent choir, for the number of trained choirmasters had multiplied greatly. Hymn festivals, formerly a rarity, had become a regular feature in many communities. More people were able to read music, more made music, and more attended concerts than ever before.

The CBC broadcasts of W.H. *Anderson's *Choristers in the 1930s, 1940s, and 1950s, and of Sunday services from leading Canadian churches with good choirs, disseminated high standards in hymn singing, and these were carried forward – though in programs with an increasing pop admixture – into the TV era by Eric *Wild's (later Winnifred *Sim's) 'CBC Hymn Sing' which began in October 1965. In the 1970s the *Toronto Mendelssohn Choir under Elmer *Iseler gave several successful concerts devoted entirely to hymns. Church music courses in denominational universities and colleges, and choral workshops organized by such institutions and by the provincial choral federations (see also Choral singing) which sprang up in the 1960s and 1970s concerned themselves with the hymn literature, as did special church congresses for organists and choirmasters, and some competition-festival syllabi offered hymn classes. The secularization of public education made hymn singing in schools a rarity, but rising school-music standards had a good indirect effect on hymn singing in other situations.

The effect of these developments was obvious. An emphasis upon technique invaded the church choir practice: choirs began to sing hymns so as to reveal their dramatic structure. There was a notable increase in the use of hymnals in a full music edition: people found they sang better when words and music were side by side. There was a discriminating demand for a kind of hymn of which *The Hymn Book* (1971) offered a richer selection than did Canadian hymnals that preceded it.

3 DENOMINATIONS. Among Canadian Lutherans and Anglicans, who follow a prescribed order of worship within which hymn singing occurs only at designated points, the hymn has been protected from many of the aberrations that have afflicted it in churches that do not subscribe to the liturgical principle of action-response in quite the same way. Churches with an eye to liturgical fitness do maintain the link with the past and encourage a brisk sense of direction in hymn singing. (See also Anglican church music.)

Like Anglicans, Lutherans lay an emphasis upon plainsong and the English chant, but unlike Anglicans they accord first place to the German chorale. In the 1970s Lutherans were exploring the rich treasure of church song in all churches within the Christian fellowship and appeared to be leading the way in reaching out for new hymn structures and new patterns of singing. (See also Lutherans.)

In the Roman Catholic church hymn singing in the vernacular used to be encouraged only for private devotions and extraliturgical functions, although it was heard in mission churches on the frontier and in the churches of the new Canadians, especially the Ukrainian Catholics and other followers of the Eastern rite. But a notable change occurred at Vatican II: hymn singing officially became the privilege of the congregation. Subsequently the participation of the people in the church's song came to be promoted actively, and Mass to be sung in the vernacular. No celebration was regarded as complete without singing. The full effect of these proclamations cannot be assessed at the time of this writing for new traditions have not yet been established.

In the English-speaking sector the chief hymnal used after Vatican II was the *Catholic Book of Worship* (Toronto 1972). Among several hymnals used in the French communities, *Livret des fidèles* (Montreal 1966) probably was the most common. Home-made hymnals also could be found. In the setting of standards for hymn singing, the importance of the Choir School at St Michael's Cathedral in Toronto cannot be overestimated. In the 1970s approximately 300 boys were enrolled annually. All received instruction in singing, many in piano and organ as well, and their annual concert was one of the outstanding musical events in the Toronto season. Every year the graduates fanned out into parishes across Canada, some to lend support to the singing in small congregations, some to pursue their training until they become choirmasters and organists themselves. This school continued in the 1980s. (See also Choir schools.)

Living with Christ, an aid to personal and family devotions, edited by Father Stephen Somerville and published six times a year by Novalis in Ottawa, has offered much encouragement to hymn singing. Not only does it provide hymns, both new and old, for use in the home, but it also presents new music responses for the liturgy.

In the French-Canadian churches, however, singing, by these standards, retrogressed in the 1970s. The liturgical music of former days was replaced in most instances by Gelineau psalms or by 'new wave' songs. Many people lost contact with a glorious heritage of church music. In a few parishes, however, the traditions were still observed. (See also Roman Catholic church music.)

4 ACCOMPANIMENT. After the advent of the organ the accompaniment to the hymn became the prerogative of the organist. In nearly all protestant churches the organist played the tune over once, after which the people would rise and sing – it was exceptional for a congregation to remain seated – while the organist repeated the same music for all the stanzas. Once in a while a brave organist would dispense with the mandatory 'once through' and improvise a brief phrase in the style of the tune, claiming that to be enough to set the tempo and the pitch for singing.

The more flexible and resourceful organists in Canadian churches often have varied their accompaniments by the use of descants, fauxbourdons, and harmonizations which depart freely from those in the hymnbook in use. Occasionally they have provided alternative settings for voices. Orchestral instruments, especially the brass, have been summoned now and then to supplement the organ or even substitute for it, investing the singing with a majesty that befits the noblest moments in church worship. (See also Organ playing and teaching.)

In the 1980s, as in the past, the choirmaster-organist continued to be the prime mover of vigorous hymn singing. If his or her lead was strong and confident and had the support of responsive, enthusiastic worshipers, it mattered not whether the church was large or small: the singing radiated joy and vigour. Only a congregation of saints could overcome the handicap of a dawdling, faint-hearted organist and they would not need him anyway! As the organist, therefore, so the singing.

See also Religions and music for a directory of *EMC* articles related to hymn singing.

DISCOGRAPHY

Come, Let Us Sing: The United Church Hymn Heritage in Sound. Saskatoon choir, I. Mills cond. 1975. Colly CLS 963

A Companion to the Book of Praise. St Andrew's Presbyterian Church Choir, Toronto. Private J-13162

Devotional Favourites. Danforth Songsters, Salvation Army, Toronto. Private recording

Eric Wild Hymn Sing Chorus: *Come Along and Sing Praises*. Wat CSPS 883

– *Eric Wild's Chorus*. Wat CSPS 632

– *He's a Big God*. Wat CSPS 1218

– *How Great Thou Art*. Wat CSPS 827

450 Voices Sing to the Lord with Cheerful Voice. Christian Reformed Churches Massed Choir, Vancouver, W.J. Bourns cond. KVP records KVP 702F

Great Hymns. Toronto Mendelssohn Choir, Iseler cond. CBC SM-302

How Great Thou Art. Messiah Lutheran Church Choir, Assiniboia, Sask. CS 7308

How Great Thou Art. Nelson Ladies Doukhobor Choir. Private RR 166330

Hymns for the Seasons of the Church. Church of St Simon the Apostle Choir, Toronto. Canterbury CHL-601

The Hymns of Herbert O'Driscoll. Christ Church Cathedral Choir, Vancouver, Wedd cond. KVP records KVP 601

The Lord Is a Mighty God. Wpg Bible College Chapel Choir. HIS HLP-712

Sacred Songs. Gower Street United Church Choir, St John's, Nfld, D. Osmond cond. Rodeo RLP 95

Seek Ye the Lord. St John's United Church Choir. Banff RBS-1029

La Voix des plus petits. A. de Vaulchier cond. Radio-Marie NDC 455902

The choirs of the American Presbyterian Church and of Christ Church Cathedral in Montreal made 78s of hymns for the Apex Radia-Tone and Electrophonic labels.

See also Discography for Christmas; St Mary Magdalene Singers. (SLO)

HYSLOP, Ricky (John Richmond). Violinist, conductor, composer, arranger, b Vancouver 26 Apr 1915. A pupil of Allard de *Ridder and of Jean *de Rimanoczy, Hyslop in his teens was a soloist on CNRV radio, and later was a member, or the concertmaster, of a number of CRBC and CBC Vancouver orchestras. He was music director 1941–53 for CBC Vancouver's 'Harmony House' (heard in western Canada and featuring the singers Pat Morgan and Suzanne, and the pianist Bud Henderson) and conducted for other radio variety shows, including 'Here's *Juliette,' 'String Along,' and 'Scored by Hyslop.' In 1959 he moved to Toronto, where until 1960 he was music director of CBC TV's 'Talent Caravan.' Later he was music director for '1967 and All That' and 'CBC Song Market,' among other CBC radio series, and wrote the incidental music for many CBC TV drama series (including 'The Serial,' 'Opening of the West,' 'Gold – the Fabulous Years,' 'A Place for Everything,' and 'A Gift to Last') and for such CTV series as 'The Human Journey' and 'Being Human.' He also composed scores for the feature film *Why Shoot the Teacher* (1977) and several TV specials. His commissioned works include the symphonic tone poems *Toronto 1830* and *Mizu Uni* (for the Buffalo Philharmonic, premiered in 1966), *Peanut Suite* for solo clarinet (for Avrahm *Galper), *Ballet for 12 Strings* for two guitars, and *Barca* for guitar and soprano (for Gregory Alliston). He conducted a Vancouver orchestra for recordings with singers Juliette and Ernie Prentice (1951, RCI 59 and 60), and a Toronto orchestra for the LPs *The Ricky Hyslop Orchestra* (ca 1966, RCI 261) and *The Art of Stradivarius*, the latter with Albert *Pratz as soloist. Hyslop is a member of CAPAC.

BIBLIOGRAPHY

'Writing background music,' *CanComp*, 23, Nov 1967

Quill, Greg. 'Ricky Hyslop's gift to last: writing music for Canadian TV,' ibid, 151, May 1980 MD, MM

I

Ian and Sylvia. See (Tyson) Ian and Sylvia.

Iceland. The first large group of Icelanders arrived in Canada in 1873 and by 1875 had settled on the western shore of Lake Winnipeg. Their colony (which included present-day Gimli and Riverton, Man), was known as New Iceland, was self-governing, and had its own constitution. When the province of Manitoba was enlarged to include the District of Keewatin, the New Icelanders voted to join the province. Other groups of Icelanders later established settlements across the prairies and in British Columbia. Many moved to Winnipeg to enter trades and professions. The 1971 census listed 27,905 Icelanders living in Canada. Gimli has remained the focal point of Icelandic culture in Canada and is the site of annual Icelandic festivals, which began in 1889.

The Icelanders were among the most literate of Canada's early minority immigrants. Even the poorest families had libraries, however modest. The recitation and composition of poetry was an esteemed avocation, and at least two Icelandic-Canadian poets, Guttormur J. Guttormsson and Stephan G. Stephansson, achieved fame in Iceland.

Several folk poets have perpetuated in Canada the four-line philosophic or nature poems developed to a high level by the 'husgangar' – an Icelandic custom which takes versifiers from house to house in a kind of competition to see whose poems are the best. The quatrains often were chanted to simple tunes. Several other folksong genres have survived in Canada. A few examples of the ancient rimur were collected (recorded) in the 1960s from an elderly male informant – Valdimar Jonsen – in Gimli. These long narratives sometimes comprise 50 to 60 quatrains, their stories describing the exploits of such Icelandic folk heroes as Fertram, Jónsvikinga, and Hjálmar. Again the quatrains are chanted to a simple, archaic tune. The texts are often couched in archaic language. Later folksong genres are more developed musically and much shorter. These include love songs, drinking songs, shepherding songs, fishing songs, religious songs (sometimes satirical), and a host of casual ditties on a variety of topics. (Another Icelandic folk tale was the basis of Jack *Behrens' opera *The Lay of Thrym*.) Few ballads have survived.

Many songs are of literary origin, so the usual distinction between 'folksong' and 'art song' is difficult to maintain. Piano and violin accompaniments add a further dimension of sophistication to folksong presentation. Accompaniment is almost a prerequisite for such locally composed songs as *The Gimli Waltz*. Arrangements of some Icelandic songs have been made by W.H. *Anderson.

A 1962 survey by Kenneth *Peacock of Icelandic settlement in Manitoba noted only one traditional instrument, the langspil, a narrow rectangular box about a metre long, fitted with two metal strings and frets. This instrument was made shortly after 1900 by a farmer south of Gimli. It is housed in the *National Museum of Man folk instrument collection, which also holds more than 270 Icelandic folksongs collected by Peacock in Yorkton, Winnipeg, Gimli, Arnes, and Arborg, Man, and by Magnus Einarson-Mullarky in Manitoba and Saskatchewan.

Musicians of Icelandic origin or descent who have pursued careers in Canada include Omar *Blondahl, Snjolaug *Sigurdson, Frank *Thorolfson (whose father Halldor was conductor of the Winnipeg Icelandic Choral Society), and Thelma Guttormson *Wilson. Sveinbjörn Sveinbjörnsson (1847–1927), a composer of chamber and orchestral music and of the Icelandic national hymn, spent some years in Canada. His son, Thordur John William Swinburne (b Edinburgh 1891, d ?), was a medical doctor and amateur composer in Canada after 1919.

Gunnsteinn Eyjolfsson (b Iceland 1866, d Riverton, Man, 1910), best known in the Icelandic community as a writer and essayist, also composed, learning through correspondence with various US musicians after he settled in New Iceland in 1876. He had 15 songs or choral works published in *Sönglög* (Winnipeg 1936). Jón Fridfinnsson (1865–1936) studied with Eyjolfsson and wrote many songs, and a cantata (text by the Icelandic poet David Stefansson) that was performed in Winnipeg by the Icelandic Male Voice Choir and Choral Society.

Steingrimur Kristjan Hall (b New Iceland 1877, d 1969?) settled in Winnipeg with his wife, the soprano Sigridur Hordal, and was organist at the First Icelandic Lutheran Church until ca 1936. He published three books (1924, 1949, and 1954) of Icelandic songs. Hjörtur Larusson (b Iceland 1874, d ?), a cornetist who moved to Canada in 1890, formed the Jubilee Band, a 19-member wind ensemble (15 members being Icelandic immigrants).

Bjorgvin Gudmundsson (b Iceland 1891, d there 1961) studied with Jonas Palsson (1875–1941) in Winnipeg, where he wrote the cantata *Aveniat regnum tuum* (1924–5). Sponsored by the Icelandic-Canadian community he studied at the RAM and wrote a second cantata in Winnipeg in 1931 before returning to Iceland. The musicologist-composer Hallgrimur Helgason (b Eyrarbakki, Iceland, 3 Nov 1914) lived 1966–74 in Regina, where he taught at the *U of Regina and was deputy concertmaster of the *Regina SO and conductor of the Folksong Harmony Choir.

The violinist Palmi Palmason (b Winnipeg 22 Feb 1909, d Toronto 13 Aug 1974) studied first with the violin builder and teacher Olafur Thorsteinsson in Husavick, Man, and then John *Waterhouse in Winnipeg and was a member of the *Winnipeg SO. He taught his sister, the violinist Pearl Palmason (b Winnipeg 2 Oct 1915), who studied as well with Elie *Spivak and Kathleen *Parlow at the *TCM. She became a member of the *TSO in 1941, played principal second violin 1960–2, and was still a member of the orchestra in 1980. She was a member of the *Hart House Orchestra and has performed as soloist in recital and in concert. Other musicians of Icelandic origin in Canada include the Vancouver soprano and teacher Thora Thorsteinsson Smith, the Toronto teacher Alda Palsson, the choral conductor Ragnar H. Ragnar, the teacher Anna Sveinson Lowe, and the jazz pianist Bob Erlendson.

The Icelandic soprano Gudrun Simonar visited Canada and gave a recital in Winnipeg in the late 1950s. The Icelandic Singers, who first visited Canada in 1946, sang at *Expo 67, where the *MSO performed Jón Leifs' *Iceland Overture, Op 9* at the Scandinavian Gala.

The *Lyric Arts Trio appeared at the 1973 *ISCM festival in Reykjavik, and *NMC performed in 1976 at the Nordic Music Days Festival in that city.

BIBLIOGRAPHY

Einarson-Mullarky, Magnus. *A Selection of Icelandic-Canadian Folklore*, National Museum of Man report (Ottawa 1966–7) KP (FH)

Iconography. The technique and process of preparing lists or catalogues of pictures and other forms of visual representation in order to assemble items sharing a given artist, country, medium, owner, period, etc, or a combination of such criteria, eg, an iconography of oil portraits of 19th-century Canadian musicians. A well-made iconography should provide access to all these criteria through supplementary indexes, and each entry should provide information also on date of creation, physical measurements, provenance, published reproductions, etc. In this sense the aims of iconography are somewhat parallel to those of bibliography, discography, and archival inventories, and might be defined as the description *of* visual art. In a wider sense, however, the term is applied to the description of a given subject, such as music, *through* visual art. Iconography thus is a means as well as an end. A well-indexed iconography on a musical subject may guide the music historian towards knowledge about the use of instruments at concerts, at dances, or in domestic life, at various times and in various places and social strata. Conversely, when such practices are known from musical sources, the information can help to date a painting or identify its locale.

By 1980 research in the iconography of music in Canada was still in its infancy. A National Inventory Programme of the *National Museums of Canada was begun in the 1970s, but *EMC*'s selective list of art inspired by music and musicians (see Art, visual) may be the first attempt of its kind. *EMC* itself provides the first retrospective and contemporary pictorial documentation of Canadian music, though Willy *Amtmann's *La Musi-*

que au Québec 1600–1875 serves the early period well. For the later period, however, photography provides the main element in the visual documentation of music in Canada. Many photographers, particularly those specializing in publicity stills of performers, have photographed Canadian musicians. However, a few – notably Walter Curtin and Tony Hauser – have undertaken special projects, photographing musicians from the historian's and artist's viewpoint. Karsh and Cavouk have made notable individual portraits. Canadian collections of still photography include those of the Public Archives of Canada, the Notman Archives of the McCord Museum at *McGill U, the Musée du Québec, the *NFB, the *CBC, and various other archival institutions, but a simple approach by subject rarely is possible. Separate picture files on music, mainly of photos and reproductions, and often combining Canadian and non-Canadian subject matter, have been established at the BN du Q, the *NL of C, the Vancouver Public Library, the Metropolitan Toronto Library, and elsewhere. The NL of C has indexed pictures of Canadian musicians in periodicals. It also acquired, more than 1000 picture files compiled by the noted English music scholar Percy Scholes; these contain, for the most part, reproductions from journals and countless references to reproductions in separate publications, thus forming an important index to international iconography.

With the aim of documenting representations of music in the visual arts throughout the world, RIdIM (Répertoire International d'Iconographie Musicale) was founded in 1971 under the joint sponsorship of the International Musicological Society, the International Assn of Music Libraries, and the International Council of Museums. Its Canadian work, encompassing not only Canadian subject matter but also works of art from other countries displayed in Canadian museums, has been carried out by a committee of *CAML with the Music Division of the NL of C as headquarters. The Research Center for Musical Iconography at the City U of New York is the world headquarters for RIdIM.

See also Bibliography; Discography. (MC, HK)

'If You Could Read My Mind.' Words and music by Gordon *Lightfoot, his most popular song to date (1979). Written in 1969, the song 'catches the cadences of a hurt lover unused to words that cut too close' (Tom Hopkins, *Maclean's*, 1 May 1978). It had been recorded some 100 times by 1979, first in 1969 by the composer for his LP *Sit Down Young Stranger*. Released as a single, the song was an international hit in 1970. The same recording was used as the theme song of the Canadian feature film *Paperback Hero* (1975). Other recordings include those by Carroll *Baker, Glen Campbell, Skeeter Davis, Johnny Mathis, Barbra Streisand, and Andy Williams. Instrumental arrangements have been recorded by Herb Alpert, John *Arpin, the *Boss Brass, James Last, Sounds Orchestral, and others. 'If You Could Read My Mind' was copyrighted in 1969 and 1970 by Lightfoot's own Early Morning Music and has been included in the folios *Gord's Gold* (Warner) and *Gordon Lightfoot Anthology Volume II* (Warner). MM

'I'll Give My Love an Apple.' A fine Nova Scotia version of an ancient riddle song that dates back to the 15th century. An early form, 'My Sister Sent Me from over the Sea,' seems to have been a dancing song, and similar riddles formed part of the old British ballad 'Captain Wedderburn's Courtship' (Child Ballads no. 46). In 1937 Helen *Creighton collected the Canadian version from Denis Smith, a retired sea captain living in Chezzetcook, and included it in *Traditional Songs from Nova Scotia* (Toronto 1950). A recording by Charles *Jordan and Joyce *Sullivan is included in RCA Victor's nine-LP set *Canadian Folk Songs: A Centennial Collection* (CS-100-1). EF

'I'll Never Smile Again.' Song by Ruth *Lowe. Written in Toronto in June 1939 following the death of her first husband, Harold Cohen, it was introduced by Percy *Faith's orchestra on CBC radio. Tommy Dorsey, who was appearing at the 1939 *CNE, heard a recording of Faith's performance and arranged for the song's publication by Sun Music. Though introduced in the USA by Glenn Miller on radio, the song was a Dorsey hit on a Victor recording featuring Frank Sinatra. Further recordings were made by Miller, the Ink Spots, Tony Martin, and others.

ILLSLEY, Percival (John). Organist, choir conductor, teacher, b Cheddleton, Staffordshire, England, 1865, d Montreal 13 Oct 1924; ARCO 1887, B MUS (Trinity, Toronto) 1893, B MUS (Bishop's) 1894, D MUS (Bishop's) 1913, FRCO 1901, hon D MUS (Cantuar) 1912. He was a pupil and then the assistant of J.B. Lott, organist at the cathedral of Lichfield, England. He was organist at Grendon, Warwickshire, for the Marchioness of Hastings, and then organist at Holy Trinity Church, Queensbury, near Bradford, Yorkshire; he also directed the Queensbury Vocal Union and the Arion Glee Club of Bradford. He excluded women from his church choirs.

In Canada, Illsley was organist-choirmaster 1891–1924 at St George's Anglican Church, Montreal, and he presented there the Canadian premiere of Stainer's cantata *The Crucifixion* and organized several series of organ recitals 1899–1904 and 1906–7. He directed the Montreal Zingari Club 1898–1900 and the Montreal Athletic Assn Glee Club in 1906. He was secretary and examiner 1895–9 at the *Dominion College of Music, was responsible in 1903 for music courses at the Montreal Diocesan College, and was teacher of organ, piano, and theory 1904–8 at the *McGill Cons. Among his pupils were George M. *Brewer, Orpha-F. *Deveaux, and Arthur *Egerton.

Illsley received the Lambeth Degree (hon D MUS) from the Archbishop of Canterbury in 1912. He served 1920–2 as president of the CCO (*RCCO).

Illsley's most important composition, the cantata *Ruth* (1894, text by Archbishop Carmichael) was published in 1894 by *Whaley Royce and was performed successfully twice in 1896 at St George's Church by a 62-voice choir with Ella Walker, Ada Moylan, and James Johnson as soloists. Illsley also wrote hymns and anthems ('There is Joy,' G. Schirmer, before 1910; 'Angels from the Realms of Glory'), part songs ('Ye Mariners of England,' Whaley Royce 1895), and works for organ. He set to music some of William H. Drummond's poems, including 'The Grand Seigneur' (Whaley Royce 1896; sung by Emma *Albani) and 'The Last Portage.' Several of his manuscripts have been deposited with the *NL of C.

BIBLIOGRAPHY

S.M.P. 'Death of Dr. P.J. Illsley,' *MCan*, Nov 1924
Musical Red Book (NT)

'I'm Movin' On.' Country song by Hank *Snow, written in the style of Jimmie Rodgers' 'train songs,' about a transient's life riding the railroads. Composed during Snow's last years in Canada, it was recorded by him in 1950 for RCA Victor (0328) and was his first and most substantial hit. It remained on the *Billboard* country music charts for 44 weeks, 1950–1, making it one of the most successful singles in the first 50 years of recorded country music.

The song has been recorded by many other country performers, among them Don Gibson, Donna Fargo, Mel Tillis, and Doc Watson. Gibson's version (RCA 7629) was a minor hit in 1959. A pop version recorded for Dunhill (4309) by John Kay (see Sparrow) was a minor hit in 1972. Other pop versions were made in the late 1970s by Loggins and Messina and by Tina Turner.

'I'm Movin' On' was copyrighted in 1950 by Hill and Range Music, New York, and was included in that company's folio *Hank Snow, The Singing Ranger* (1951). The song's rights later were taken over by Unichappell Music Inc, New York. MM

Impressionism. Name applied to the work of a group of French painters active in the late 1800s, and most aptly to that of Renoir, Monet, Pissarro, and Sisley, who attempted to capture certain elusive essences of their subjects – usually landscapes, interiors, or figures – by reproducing the transitory effulgences and shadows caused by the refractions of changing light. (Their efforts were distinct from those of the cubists, who abstracted the same material in terms of corporeal outlines and hard structures, and of the expressionists, who tried to translate its emotional impact into vivid, harshly communicative images, often of psychological or sociological import.)

'Impressionism' was used first in music to describe those works of Claude Debussy which attempt to create the fleeting pictures, sounds, and moods of nature through a colouristic – as distinct from an expository or structural – use of melody and harmony and through a subtle exploitation of instrumental and vocal timbres. In Debussy's piano music this involved new applications of touch and of pedal technique. The attendant notion that Debussy's harmonies were vague or indeterminate is dispelled by familiarity with his music, which was sophisticated harmonically for its day but is perfectly cogent to modern ears. Nevertheless, its effect is informal and atmospheric and justifies its classification as impressionism.

Jean Blake Robinson (Mrs Walter *Coulthard) was among the first to introduce the music of Debussy to Canada. She is known to have played several of his piano pieces ca 1908 and drew favourable press notice for her performance in 1910 of *Jardins sous la pluie* (1903). The *Toronto String Quartette and the *Dubois String Quartet of Montreal both had played the Debussy *Quartet* in their respective cities by 1912. Alberto *Guerrero, who arrived in Toronto in 1919, also was a Debussy interpreter of distinction. The *Prelude to the Afternoon of a Faun* was played in Montreal in 1919 by the visiting orchestra of the Société des Concerts du Conservatoire de Paris under Messager, and *Nuages* and *Fêtes* were performed there in 1921 by the Boston SO under Monteux. The *Toronto Mendelssohn Choir sang *La Damoiselle élue* in 1921. Harry *Adaskin and Frances Marr made a specialty of the Debussy *Sonata* (and of Delius' *Third Sonata* in the 1930s). The pianist Léo-Pol *Morin, with the mezzo-soprano Cédia *Brault and the violinist Robert Imandt, presented the first Canadian festival of Debussy's music in 1927 in Montreal, but Morin had begun playing Debussy there as early as 1918. Stanley *Gardner was another early exponent of the piano music of Debussy.

The influence of Debussy on Canadian composers was fairly wide even in English Canada – though perhaps (in pieces of the early 1900s by *Forsyth and *Anger) indirectly through England's Delius and Cyril Scott. In French Canada, signs of impressionism appeared after 1910 in Rodolphe *Mathieu's *Trois Préludes* and *Chevauchée* for piano, and later, to a degree, in the works of *Champagne, *Gagnier, and *Gratton. Mathieu and Champagne studied in Paris; Mathieu with Roussel, d'Indy, and Aubert; and Champagne –

the more influential – with André Gedalge, who had been a student, along with Debussy, in Massenet's class. Gedalge went on to become the teacher of Ravel, Milhaud, and Honegger, and taught Champagne counterpoint and fugue. In such works as *Suite canadienne* (1922), *Images du Canada français* (1943), and *Symphonie gaspésienne* (1945) Champagne integrated the modal character of the folk music of his homeland, the academicism of traditional polyphony, and the sensuous subtlety of impressionism.

Among Champagne's pupils François *Morel, in *Esquisse* (1947) and *Antiphonie* (1953), revealed himself as a neo-impressionist, and even his later works show an impressionist's concern with fine shadings of timbre and colour. In the works of another Champagne pupil, Gilles *Tremblay – particularly those of the 1970s: *Solstices, Oralléluiants, Compostelle I* – the preoccupation with the cultivation of overtone sonics and the devising of sounds which are an ethereal by-product rather than a simple product of instrumental activity lead to a kind of abstract impressionism founded in the mysteries and ephemera of sound itself.

The early works of Leslie *Mann and most of the output of Jean *Coulthard (and of several of her pupils, such as Michael *Baker) derive much from impressionism. Norma *Beecroft has acknowledge Debussy as an early and continuing influence; and even in her 'concerto grosso,' the *Improvvisazioni Concertanti No. 2*, the effect is not so much of structure as of an impression of structure; of structure reflected in a wayward eye and delicately sketched. This 'de-stabilized' effect is enchanced by the soloists' extemporizations.

A brief reference also should be made to the new impressionism which originated in Europe in the late 1950s with Krzysztof Penderecki, and György Ligeti, and others. This style, which shows a predilection for low dynamic levels and chromatic clusters of varying widths within a static framework, was not influential in Canada until the late 1960s, and then primarily in the works of Harry *Freedman (*Graphic I, Graphic II*), R. Murray *Schafer (*Epitaph for Moonlight*), André *Prévost (*Évanescence*), Derek *Healey (*The Lost Traveller's Dream*), and John *Wyre (*Utau Kane NoWa*), to name a few. RM, KW

Imrie & Graham. Toronto firm of book, job, and music printers and music publishers active 1884–ca 1909.

John Imrie, a printer and poet (b Glasgow 1846, d Toronto 1902), moved to Toronto in 1871. He was a subscription salesman for the *Canada Presbyterian* and a foreman at *Strange & Co before he established his own company in partnership with D.L. Graham. After Imrie's death the company was known as Imrie, Graham & Harrap, and – in 1905 when his son John Mills Imrie became managing director – as the Imrie Printing Co Ltd.

More than 50 Imrie & Graham copyright and non-copyright publications have been traced. The former date from the period 1884–94; none have plate numbers. Many are by Toronto composers, including Herbert L. *Clarke, Edwin *Gledhill, J.F. *Johnstone, H.F. *Sefton, G.W. *Strathy, and F.H. *Torrington. Most are patriotic songs (frequently to Imrie's texts) or early 'singing commercials.' Respective examples are the small album *Toronto's 'Welcome Home' to Her Brave Defenders, from the North-West Rebellion! July 1885* and 'We Dye to Live!' (to the tune of 'Tramp! Tramp! Tramp!') issued for R. Parker's Dye Works in 1890. Music and advertising were issued together in Imrie & Graham's Musical Handbills – single sheets with music on one side and an advertisement on the other, of which 71 were issued (ca 1890) in book form.

Imrie founded the weekly *Scottish Canadian* in

1890 and included some music in it. He published *Scottish Songs* too, but the collection of his verse, *Scared Songs, Sonnets, and Miscellaneous Poems* (1886; and several later editions as *Songs and Miscellaneous Poems*) does not include music. HK

Incidental music. Music used to enhance plays and dramatizations, on stage, radio, TV, or film. It encompasses overtures, entr'actes, and interludes; musical occurrences within the action (eg, dances, songs, processions); and musical backgrounds to speech and action, composed to create atmosphere and heighten emotional impact.

During the 19th century and occasionally in the 20th, the first two types often yielded complete sets of pieces which could be performed as concert suites, independently of the plays for which they were composed. Mendelssohn's music for Shakespeare's *A Midsummer Night's Dream* and Grieg's for Ibsen's *Peer Gynt* were typical. The third type of incidental music described above has been used primarily for radio plays, films, and TV rather than for stage dramas. (See also Film scores).

By the middle of the 20th century, when incidental music came into demand in Canada (especially for strictly timed radio and TV dramas, but also for live theatre), Canadian composers showed little interest in producing formal pieces of the traditional kind; overtures were short, and 'bridge' music, used to connect scenes, often was measured in seconds rather than minutes.

In the more leisurely early years of the 20th century a few composers wrote more substantial incidental scores, notably J.-J. *Gagnier; Claude *Champagne, who in 1917 wrote music for Frère Marie-Victorin's *Ils sont un peuple sans histoire*; Healey *Willan, who collaborated on 14 *Hart House Theatre productions in Toronto during the 1920s; George M. *Brewer, who worked with the Montreal Repertory Theatre in the 1930s; and Clarence *Lucas, who did not write complete sets of incidental music but did write overtures to *As You Like It*, *Macbeth*, and *Othello*. Further along in the century many composers wrote music for plays by Shakespeare. During the 1940s Graham *George provided scores for the productions of the Shakespeare Society of Montreal, and Fraser *Macdonald wrote music for Earle Grey's Shakespeare productions at Trinity College, Toronto.

Ontario's *Stratford Festival probably has commissioned more original music (for its productions of plays of Shakespeare and others) than any theatre in Canada – over 100 scores between its inaugural year, 1953, and 1980. In its first 15 years most of the incidental music was supplied by Louis *Applebaum and John Cook. After 1960 an increasing number of other composers, among them Berthold Carriere, Gabriel *Charpentier (many scores), Harry *Freedman, Raymond *Pannell, Godfrey *Ridout, Harry *Somers, and Morris *Surdin received Stratford commissions.

In Montreal the Théâtre du Nouveau-Monde has commissioned scores from *Blackburn (*Célimare le bien-aimé*, 1952; *Le Temps des lilas*, 1958), Charpentier (*Les Choéphores*, 1962; *Richard II*, 1962; *Klondike*, 1965; *Le Soulier de satin*, 1967), Neil *Chotem (*Klondike*, 1967), Rolland *D'Amour (*Philippe et Jonas*, 1953), Andrée *Desautels (*Dom Juan*, 1954), Laurent Jodoin (*Le Corsaire*, 1952), and Clermont *Pépin (*Le Malade imaginaire*, 1956).

Pépin also has written music for productions of Montreal's Compagnie du Théâtre Club (*La Nuit des rois*, 1957; *L'Heure éblouissante*, 1961; *Le Marchand de Venise*, 1964). Charpentier, one of Canada's most prolific composers of music for theatre, had composed more than 50 such scores by 1977, writing for many different theatre groups. As music director for the Crest Theatre in Toronto, then the Neptune Theatre in Halifax, John *Fenwick wrote incidental music for over 30 productions. In 1964 Victor *Davies was music director and composer for Winnipeg's Manitoba Theatre Centre. Neil *Harris and others also have provided music for that company over the years. In Toronto Milton *Barnes received commissions 1964–6 from the Crest Theatre. Allan *Rae has provided music for Theatre Calgary, the Vancouver Theatre Playhouse, and the Theatre Passe Muraille in Toronto. Don *Druick has composed, arranged and conducted music for several Vancouver theatres.

Others who have written music for plays include John *Beckwith (*The Killdeer*, 1959), Ginette *Bellavance (*Le Timide au palais*, 1971; *Dom Juan*, 1972; *Julien, Julien*, 1973; *Cyrano de Bergerac*, 1974), Keith *Bissell (*Incidental Music to 'The Centennial Play,'* 1967), J.-M. *Cloutier (*Visite de la vieille dame*, 1969; *Les Troyens*, 1971), Ron *Collier (*The Mechanic*, 1965), Andrée Desautels (*La Fille du soleil*, 1946), Hector *Gratton (*Légendes aux étoiles*, 1952), Derek *Holman (*Pontiac and the Green Man*, 1977), Laurent Jodoin (*Tessa*, ca 1950), Lothar *Klein (several for Shakespeare plays as well as *Twin Menaechmi*, 1951; *The Bluebird*, 1952; *Marco Millions*, 1953; and *The Bacchae*, 1965), Alfred *Kunz (*Let's Make a Carol*, 1965), Roger *Matton, John *Mills-Cockell (*Memories of My Brother* and *Effect of Gamma Rays on Man-in-the-Moon Marigolds*, both 1972), André *Prévost (*Électre*, 1959), Manus Sasonkin (*The Duenna*, 1978), Jean Sauvageau, and Charles *Wilson (*John Fibber*, 1970). Norma *Beecroft, Robert *Fleming, Harry Freedman, William *McCauley, and Jean *Papineau-Couture have written scores for puppet plays. Harry Somers provided the music for *Vibrations* (1978), presented by the Canadian Mime Theatre at the *Shaw Festival, Niagara-on-the-Lake.

The CBC has commissioned an enormous quantity of incidental music for radio and TV, not only for plays and serials but for documentaries and variety and quiz shows. John *Weinzweig was a pioneer, beginning in 1941 and providing the music for over 100 radio plays. Other contributors to the genre during the 1940s were Ernest Dainty, Gordon *Fleming, Hector Gratton, Quentin *Maclean, Barbara *Pentland, Michel *Perrault, Morris Surdin, and Arnold *Walter. Gratton wrote the music for the series 'Je me souviens,' with text by Félix *Leclerc, and provided the score for a radio production of *Maria Chapdelaine*. Surdin, one of the most active of radio composers, wrote over 150 scores 1950–72 for the series 'Jake and the Kid' and many for the series 'CBC Stage,'

'CBC Playhouse,' and 'Adventure Theatre.' Jean *Vallerand has written music for some 100 CBC radio plays, including those heard in the series 'Radio-Collège' and 'Sur toutes les scènes du monde.' Lucio *Agostini composed for 'CBC Stage,' 'CBC Wednesday Night,' and 'Ford Theatre,' and has been the sole composer for the TV series 'Front Page Challenge.' Alexander *Brott wrote scores for radio's 'Playhouse Theatre.' Neil Chotem provided the music for several of Rupert Caplan's CBC radio presentations – *The Dybbuk, The World's Illusion, The Trial, A Tribute to Eugene O'Neill* – and the series 'The Iliad' and 'The Odyssey,' 1948–50.

Besides being a composer of incidental music for the stage, Applebaum has been a major contributor to both radio and TV productions. For TV, Frank *Haworth composed for the series 'Mr. O' and 'Old Testament Tales' and Claude *Léveillée for the programs *Des souris et des hommes, L'Échéance du vendredi, Millionnaire à froid,* and *Le Pélican*. William McCauley composed and conducted the music for the 1972 series 'The Whiteoaks of Jalna,' and Harry Somers provided the scores for the series 'Images of Canada' (1972–5). Others who have composed for CBC TV include André *Gagnon, François *Morel (*L'Heureux Stratagème*), Antoine Padilla (*Un Mois à la campagne*), and Georges *Savaria (*Yerma* and *La Maison de Bernarda*). Ron Collier, Victor Davies, Samuel *Dolin, Phil *Nimmons, Robert *Turner, and Elliot *Weisgarber have written incidental music for both radio and TV.

Though the cost of commissioning, rehearsing, and performing incidental music has always been high, no inexpensive and equally effective replacement has been found; music's powers of enhancement have remained unrivalled. Electronic scores, it is true, can eliminate certain expenses of performance, but they entail costs of their own and in any case must be considered an extension, not a replacement, of the genre. It is clear that the genre will survive while theatre survives. Of all the arts, theatre is the most immediately susceptible to its audiences' reactions. If they like it, it flourishes; if they do not, it disappears; and in Canada – at Stratford, at the Théâtre du Nouveau-Monde, and at other flourishing theatrical centres – the key role of incidental music in successful theatre has been recognized. By 1980, with theatre – live, broadcast, telecast or filmed – an integral part of Canadian life, the writing of incidental and background music had become an important facet of the Canadian composer's activity – indeed, for some, it is their bread and butter.

BIBLIOGRAPHY

Champagne, Jane. 'The role of music for the theatre,' *CanComp*, 75, Dec 1972

Morley, Glenn. 'Composing for the theatre: contemporary directions,' *Canadian Theatre Review*, Summer 1977

Timmerman, Nicola. 'Music for film is Ron Harrison's job,' *CanComp*, 147, Jan 1980

KW, PW, (SW)

India. In 1975 in Canada there were approximately 60,000 people of Asian Indian origin, more than half of whom had arrived after 1968. Earlier immigrants from India were mostly Sikh labourers who arrived ca 1905–8 from the Punjab. The Sikhs have remained a sizeable group within the Indian community, though most later immigrants have been Hindus from many different regions of India. Asian Indians have settled throughout Canada, but the largest areas of concentration have been in British Columbia and southern Ontario.

Canadians were introduced to Indian music through the visits of dance companies and touring musicians. Probably the first such visit was paid by Uday Shankar and his Hindu dancers and musicians, who toured North America during the 1930s. In 1960 Dancers and Musicians from India, a company directed by Indrani Rahman, appeared in Montreal. A few years later musicians visited to perform at the Indian pavilion at *Expo 67; some settled in Montreal. Among these were Rahul Sariputra (sitar) and Swami Anand Veetarag (tabla), who together formed the Naveen Gallery Company, which has performed at Canadian colleges and universities and which toured for the *JMC in 1977–8. Other Indian artists who have appeared in Canada include the mridangist T. K. Murthy, the sarodists Ali Akbar Khan, Ashish Khan, and Ustad Amjad Ali Khan, the sitarist Ravi Shankar, the tabla player Pranesh Khan, the singer T.V. Sankaranarayanan, and the dancers Sujata and Asoka. The conductor Zubin Mehta made his North American debut with the *CBC SO 26 Apr 1959 and served 1961–7 as music director of the *MSO. The son of Mehli Mehta (a guest conductor with the MSO), he once was married to the Canadian soprano Carmen Lasky.

During the 1970s programs of Indian classical, folk, and popular music, often combined with dance, were presented in many cities by professional and amateur groups, some based in Canada, some visiting from India. Such presentations often have been sponsored by universities and religious or cultural community organizations, generally to celebrate Indian festivals. Examples of the cultural organizations are the numerous branches of the India Canada Assn (found across Canada); the Toronto-based Bharathi Kala Manram (which stresses South Indian culture); the Raga Mala Society of Calgary (founded in 1974 to encourage the presentation and performance of Indian classical music); Hindu Societies in Vancouver, Winnipeg, and other centres; the Friends of India; and the Chinmaya Mission in St. John's, Nfld. In Montreal Rashmi Sharma, who was commissioner of the India pavilion at Expo 67, remained in Montreal, where she has become an impresario for Indian dance, handicraft, and musical events. In Toronto the dancer Menaka Thakkar's Canadian Academy of Indian Dance (Nrtya Kala) has offered instruction in, and concerts of, music and dance.

Traditional songs have been performed at Sikh and Hindu temples in Toronto and Vancouver and also in private homes, where folksongs (including wedding songs) have been perpetuated for use on certain occasions. Courses in Indian music theory and history and in vocal and instrumental performance techniques have been offered at the *U of Windsor and at *York U, Toronto. The latter institution has organized and sponsored many concerts of Indian music and dance. Those who have taught in the program at York include the mridangist Trichy Sankaran, the tabla player Robert Becker (a founding member of *Nexus), and the US-born Jon B. Higgins, who was head of the York program until 1979. Higgins became known internationally as a performer of South Indian classical songs; in 1974 he delivered a paper entitled 'East Indian music in Ontario' to the International Congress of Americanists in Mexico City. Research into the music of Indian communities in Canada has been limited, and in 1980 much remained to be explored.

Canadian musicians who have spent time in India include Welford *Russell, a missionary doctor there 1925–41; Harry *Somers, who visited in 1971; and Gilles *Tremblay, who went there in 1972. The call to prayer of a muezzin in Kashmir provided inspiration for Somers' *Music for Solo Violin* (1973, premiered by Yehudi Menuhin at the *Guelph Spring Festival in 1974). Bailey and John *Bird and Charles and George *Sippi were born in India, as was the baritone Bernard *Johnson. The Czechoslovakian-born Walter *Kaufmann, who lived in Canada 1947–59, was music director 1938–46 for All India Radio in Bombay, became an authority on Indian music, and wrote several books on the subject. Among the Kaufmann compositions performed in Canada some had Indian themes (*Madras Express, Six Indian Miniatures, Three Dances to an Indian Play*). His article 'The forms of the Dhrupad and Kyal in Indian art music' was published in the *Canadian Music Journal* (Winter 1959).

BIBLIOGRAPHY

Qureshi, Regula. 'Ethnomusicological research among Canadian communities of Arab and East Indian origin,' *Ethnomusicology*, vol 16, Sep 1972

Higgins, Jon B. 'East Indian music in Ontario,' Paper presented at the International Congress of Americanists, Museum of Anthropology, Mexico City (Sep 1974)

Sentesy, Helen. 'Music of the East Indians in Toronto,' unpubl ms, National Museum of Man, Ottawa

(NJ, NM)

Indians. Canada's first human inhabitants, the Indians and Inuit (Eskimos), often referred to as 'the native peoples,' have been on the North American continent for many thousands of years. The approximately 303,000 Indians and 22,000 Inuit on Canadian soil in 1980 exhibited a great diversity of habitat, language, and culture. It is agreed that they arrived in North America originally in small groups, and over a long period, across the Bering Strait from various regions of Asia. This theory has been confirmed by studies which provided evidence of relationships, anthropological, genetic, cultural, and even musical, with certain peoples of eastern Asia.

The Indian's original culture has been threatened with extinction as his traditional mode of living – hunting or fishing – has been threatened by western civilization. This trend began with the French traders and missionaries and has produced a large number of Indians, living on 'reserves,' who have forgotten, or almost forgotten, the great skills and arts of their ancestors. White scholars such as *Barbeau, Sapir, *Halpern, *Peacock, *Kolinski, and Guédon have attempted, through collection and study, to help with a restoration of Indian culture, in particular music; they have acknowledged the beauty and intricacy of this Indian art and thus have contributed to a revival of the Indian's pride in his traditions.

The great numbers of tribes and languages have been grouped into four major geographical-cultural units for *EMC*'s purposes. Each is treated by a specialist. Because each specialist has approached the field differently from his colleagues and has a special field of interest, the editors have thought it wise not to suppress duplications of subject matter (eg, several speak about the songs being 'personal property') or conflicts of methodology.

1 Pacific Northwest coast
2 Athapaskan
3 Plains
4 Eastern woodlands

The four articles deal with traditional Indian music in its purest surviving form. The influences of European music, church music in particular, are briefly examined in the entry on Missionaries.

See also Bands 6 / Civilian; Bridge music; Dancing, pre-Confederation; Ethnomusicology; Inuit; Powwow singers; National Museums of Canada; Os-Ke-Non-Ton.

BIBLIOGRAPHY

Jenness, Diamond. *Indians of Canada*, National Museum of Canada Bulletin No. 65 (Ottawa 1932)

Barbeau, Marius. 'Asiatic survivals in Indian songs,' *MQ*, vol 20, Jan 1934
Roberts, Helen. *Musical Areas in Aboriginal North America* (New Haven, Conn, 1936, 1970)
Nettl, Bruno. 'North American Indian musical styles,' *JAF*, vol 67, 1954
Powers, William K. *Indian Dancing and Costumes* (New York 1966)
Lomax, Alan. *Folk Song Style and Culture*, American Assn for the Advancement of Science Publication No. 88 (Washington 1968)
Nettl, Bruno. 'Musical areas reconsidered: a critique of North American Indian research,' *Essays in Musicology*, ed Gustave Reese and Robert Snow (Pittsburgh 1969)
Guédon, Marie-Françoise. 'Canadian Indian ethnomusicology: selected bibliography and discography,' *Ethnomusicology*, vol 16, Sep 1972
Bradley, Ian L. *Indian Culture in Canada: A Basic Bibliography of Resources for Curriculum Development* (Victoria, BC, 1975)
Guédon, Marie-Françoise. 'The first Canadian musicians,' *Mcan*, 37, Nov 1978

1 PACIFIC NORTHWEST COAST. The cultures of the Indians of the Pacific Northwest coast are among the most interesting to be found north of Mexico. The tribes include the Kwakiutl (Kwaguleth), Nootka, Tlingit, Haida, Tsimshian, Bella Coola, and Coast Salish. Cultural development is at its highest in the northern tribes, gradually diminishing as one moves south. The Kwakiutl and Haida are the most important artistically, followed by the Tsimshians.

The music of these tribes was studied first by Franz Boas in the 1890s and later by Marius *Barbeau, Edward Sapir, Thomas McIlwraith, and others. However, much remained to be achieved in the field of research and analysis of the music of the Pacific Northwest Indians by 1950, when Ida *Halpern began an intensive investigation of the music of the Kwakiutl, Nootka, and Salish. This work has revealed a sophistication in dramatic quality rare in the music of indigenous cultures. Her study resulted from the collection of 352 songs, 61 of which have been published, and from unpublished transcriptions and explanatory material. All information in this article comes to the author directly from the Indians themselves.

General remarks on music as it relates to social culture. The music of the Pacific Northwest is based on strict rules which pertain especially to the performance and ownership of songs. For this reason the music has always presented a problem to the collector. The Indians have been reluctant to reveal songs which are part of their heredity, along with emblems and possessions. So strong is this feeling of possession that no chief or member of his family is willing to sing a song belonging to another; if he does so, he will be treated as a thief, shamed and scorned by his own people. On the other hand, a chief might inherit a song or commission it for some important occasion in order to give himself and his proud clan added prestige.

The songs originated with the song-makers of the tribes and were conceived in a state of spiritual trance, in visions and in dreams. The Indian has derived great strength from his songs, turning to them for supernatural help whenever he felt the limitations of his own power.

Originally the power of songs was bestowed only upon chosen people. Indian mythology tells of many heroes who were given songs by guardian spirits in dreams and visions as a special reward, indicating that the song-maker and the medicine man, whose acquisition of supernatural power established direct contact with the spiritual world, were important and highly esteemed individuals. For this reason, also, they were reluctant to allow outsiders to hear their songs.

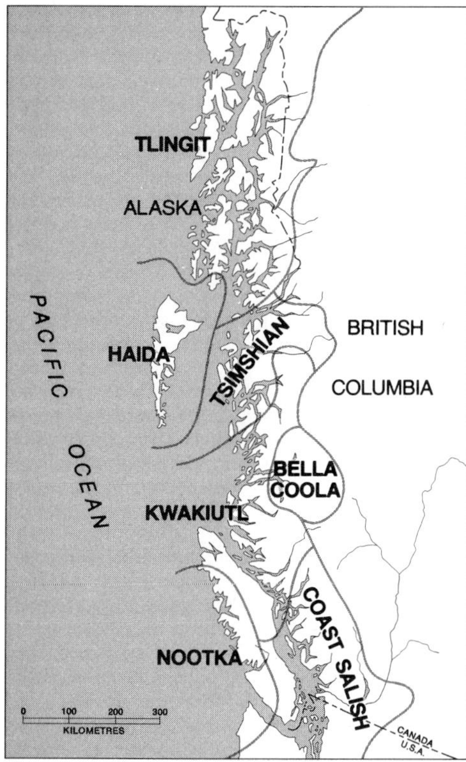

The locations of the main tribes of Pacific Northwest coast Indians

Certain songs were used in the treatment of the sick, while others were believed to ensure success in war, in hunting, and for any purpose requiring supernatural force. The Indian believed that supernatural power resided in man as well as in nature, and that to be one with nature meant a fusion of power into one being, resulting in the creation of the song.

The Hamatsa, a secret society whose members had come under the protection of the cannibal spirits after a rigorous and lengthy initiation, might also be interpreted as a fusion of nature's supernatural power with man. Initiation into this society was a great honour, and compulsory for chiefs. Hamatsa songs, the so-called Cannibal Songs, were sung during the ceremony celebrating the momentous return of the Hamatsa (Cannibal Man) after from four months to four years (depending on the tribe) of solitude in the woods. The Hamatsa society originated with the Kwakiutl and later spread to the Haida and Nootka tribes. (For detailed information on Hamatsa songs, see the notes by Halpern accompanying Folkways recording FE 4523).

Totem poles are an art form characteristic of the tribes of the Northwest coast. The totem was the ancestral tree, with figures and emblems of dozens of clans, telling the story of personal accomplishment and historic events, comparable to the coats-of-arms in European civilization. Each figure on a totem pole had its own song, and each new crest added to the family tradition required a new song. Whenever a chief acquired a new distinction through war or marriage it was recorded on his totem pole and in new songs. The most significant totems of the west coast are the wolf, the raven, the grizzly bear, the eagle, and the whale (Halpern notes, Folk FE 4523).

A strict tradition was kept in the teaching of songs. If a singer were to make a mistake, the consequences would be very serious for him. Kwakiutl chief Mungo Martin said he 'would have to pay very much for one mistake. At times cannot speak any more, only sing – great responsibility' (Halpern notes, ibid).

The nucleus for the Indians' musical activities was the celebrated potlatch, the tribal ceremony which kept all facets of life functioning in high gear. The potlatch, the cultural artery of Indian life, was outlawed 1884–1951 by the Canadian government. During this suppression, the Indian's culture all but disappeared. When the author discussed with the Indians the cultural necessity to preserve their ceremonial songs, passed on by strict oral tradition, Kwakiutl chief Billy Assu was the first to understand the importance of such recordings, admitting that when he died his songs would die with him.

Characteristics of Kwakiutl, Nootka, and Coast Salish music. The Kwakiutl and Nootka songs have several characteristics in common. They are monodic and essentially an amalgamation of words, syllables, and melody, with a minimum use of instruments. The melody consists mostly of microntonic intonations and embellishments. The accompaniment is provided by handclapping, drum-beating, beating with sticks, and beating on planks, rattles, and shells. Purely instrumental accompaniments to the dances also have been collected (eg, Hummingbird songs played on drums, rattles, and shells).

Most of the songs are interwoven with dancing, and some have profound religious meaning. Certain songs are considered fitting only for specific occasions. Indians would not sing a winter dance song in summer, or a ghost song except at the time of death. Love songs, crest songs, and some Hamatsa songs are of a hauntingly beautiful quality, while potlatch songs are declamatory. The style changes programmatically and also melodically within totem songs (animal crest songs such as wolf, raven, or bear). All reveal great dramatic impact and an impeccable sense of timing. Indians are masters of make-believe and showmanship; both are intrinsic in their traumatic ceremonies.

In their songs one can always feel a certain tonic, or predominant, note around which the melodic pattern is built. Tonality seems to exist but in no direct relation to any specific existing system. There are primitive patterns. A few are pentatonic. Some scale formations are quite similar to the pelog system, as understood by comparative musicology. There is the same clinging to the third, sometimes a major, mostly, however, a minor. A tetrachord can be established with a major or minor third above, and a semitone below.

In West Coast songs one finds a strong feeling for the mediant (the third up or sixth down) falling into the octave. Different combinations of this device, in different rhythmic patterns, are prevalent. Semitones are used profusely in the melodic patterns, followed by a jump into the third above or sixth below, resulting in the range of a full octave. Some patterns show advance by a semitone, a jump into a third, a playing with the pattern in variation technique. Sometimes the jump is approximately a fourth, fifth, or octave. An extensive use of seconds prevails in the pattern of the melodies. These 'clusters of seconds' occur with such frequency that they could be considered a main characteristic. Some melodies display triad formations. The range of the scale varies from a fourth to an octave or in some cases a tenth.

The melody and the accompaniment have two definite rhythms. Each rhythm, fairly regular in itself, is independent of the other. Parallel occurrence of the two rhythms results in incidental combinations which can be understood as polyrhythm, *not* as syncopation. According to Mungo Martin, the clapping never comes together with the voice. It comes before the voice sets in or after. Beating can be quite regular, even if the voice has different timing. The possibilities include: 1 / voice out, beat after; 2 / voice out, beat regular; 3 / beat first, voice after. (There is, however, a closer relationship in Nootkan music between the rhythm of the beats and melody than in other coast tribes, eg, the Kwakiutl. The reason might be that the Nootkans were the first Indians to be in contact with the white man, since Captain Cook was greeted by the Nootka in 1778.)

The rhythmic beats of the accompaniment fall into pattern when expressed in meter form used in modal notation of the middle ages, with stressed and unstressed beats, and in poetry: iambus, dactyl, trochee, and anapaest. The Kwakiutl 'would be using a stick hitting a stick. The Nootkans would be hitting a skin drum. It would be the same rhythm but the stress would be changed, onto the fourth beat ᴗᴗᴗ´. That's what they called *cheech chica*.' (For rhythmic features, see descriptions in Halpern's notes for Folk FE 4523, and Folk FE 4524.)

The Nootka, like the Kwakiutl and Tsimshian, have four as their ritual number. Most ceremonial dances and songs are performed four times. Four is an important number in a wolf dance; eg, it takes four songs to call the wolves together. The Hamatsa (member of the secret society) dances four times around the house and climbs the pole four times.

Nootkan songs consist of: *topahti* – an inherited ceremonial song sung only by the owner; *tama* – a social, non-danced song; a *coastal song* – allowed to be sung along the coast.

Whereas plateau dances were 'jumpy,' in a dancer's words, a 'coast dance shows great control – it floats. Women dancers only show rhythm – man dancer provides excitement.' A tradition in Nootkan group performances is the 'leader and follower' pattern. The leader (soloist) starts singing alone, introducing the song, and then his followers join in. Leader and follower are hereditarily defined. Nootkan songs usually begin with syllables only, then words follow accompanied by beats.

A characteristic of much native music is the use of syllables as well as words. These syllables have been referred to as meaningless or nonsensical. However, during research on Kwakiutl and Nootka music, Halpern concluded that the syllables do represent part of the meaning and content of the song. (Examples are given in the notes for Folk FE 4523 and FE 4524.)

Pacific Northwest Coast Indian music may be considered melogenic (melody-dominated). Sometimes it is logogenic (word-bound), as when a chief sings his potlatch songs and recites some parts. Sometimes it can be pathogenic (emotion-induced), as in a medicine-man's song. Often, however, it passes these two primitive stages, blending into the melogenic style which is the style of western culture. In Kwakiutl and Nootka music there is evidence of a distinct variation principle different from the European one. For example, after the first melody has been sung, the repetitions show microtonal changes of pitch, usually in a persistent upward direction. Eg, the melodic statement is repeated four or five times, with the entire gradual pitch rise amounting to approximately one tone. (Western musical notation cannot indicate such microtonal changes. The songs are therefore transcribed with the help of special notational devices; eg, in transcription, + or + + above a note shows a microtonal rise, while – or – – above a note shows a microtonal lowering.)

Most of the songs have a definite structure with well-defined phrases. The melodic material is worked out, enlarged, and diminished in variation and by pitch rises. Songs typically consist of recitative and melody. Four types of recitative can be distinguished: excited high tone recitative, natural speaking voice on medium tone, fast recitatives, and singing recitatives.

It is in Nootka music that the first attempts at polyphony occur among the Northwest Coast Indians in a very significant way. (See Victory Song, L8, Folk FE 4524.) The individual songs are characterized also by specific performance properties; the manner of singing with special voice production, emphasis on single tones, glissandi, tremolos, forceful accents on sustained tones, separation of sustained tones by pulsation, ornamentation, microtonic intonations and embellishments, and unusual simultaneous sounds, as though the singer were producing two tones at once. (For a detailed description of styles and characteristics, see Folk FE 4524.)

Music of other Pacific Northwest coast tribes. The Tlingit are clans-people. Everything belongs to the clan and not to the individual. Crests, songs, and dances are guarded most vigorously by the clan. Most interesting is the peace dance which follows after a murder is compensated by the death of another man of the same rank. The man chosen as such compensation is highly regarded, and before execution he dresses in his ceremonial robes displaying all crests and honours. He then steps forward courageously with his spear and sings a girl's puberty song (see Oberg, 'Crime and punishment in Tlingit society'). The Haida also are clans-people in their social organization. Formerly they had house chiefs and war chiefs. When at war, the wife of the war chief was given the honour of leading the dances in which the wives of the warriors participated until the return of their men.

The Haida adapted and modified the secret society ceremony and Hamatsa songs of the Kwakiutl. Like the Kwakiutl, they were masters in make-believe; eg, whistles were worked with bellows and concealed under a blanket, or a small rattle was hidden under a bracelet. Their medicine men had excessive special power through songs which they received from the supernatural world. Dances were allowed mainly at potlatches. The ceremonial life of the Haida closely resembled the Tlingit's pattern.

The Tsimshian, situated near the Haida, have a wider melodic range than tribes of the more southern coastal regions. Their themes are colourful and rich. Rhythmically they are quite complex. It is noteworthy that the texts of the songs consist more of words than of syllables and are therefore of considerable literary interest. The Tsimshian are similar to the Haida in belief and tradition, having medicine-man songs, feast songs, and potlatch songs.

Bella Coola Indians are noted for their mystery dances and songs demonstrating the regeneration of nature in spring, enacting shrubs, trees, and mother nature. Their music is melodically quite advanced, with a great variety in melodic progression similar to the Tsimshian. The Bella Coola stipulate wearing specific masks for dances. Traditionally they have been subordinate in rank to the Haida and Tsimshian. (See Jenness, *Indians of Canada*, p 202–4.)

Coast Salish music has absorbed many characteristics and customs from the musics of the northern coastal tribes but is lacking in their complexity and richness; eg, the Salish have no Hamatsa ceremonies. Their tonal range is limited and the melodic movement mostly level. Whenever the tonal range is wider, a 'pendulum' movement is noticeable. (See George Herzog, *Salish Music*, Bloomington, Ind, 1961, for further material on melodic development.)

The most important musical activities of the Salish are:

a / The 'Masked Dance' – Swexwe – which is sacred and hereditary. It is danced four times around the fire in the longhouse, the dancer costumed in a white tunic with feathers. Only through initiation is the power received. The dancers are men, and the singers and drummers are women. Of importance are the rattles made out of pectin shells on the legs of the dancers.

b / The 'Spirit Dance' – Seeyowan – is danced without a mask, with only a belt around the waist, a woollen headdress, deer hoof anklets, and wooden paddles on breast and arms. This shorter dance, danced only once around the house by a man or a woman, is not hereditary but the result of a power received by experience with nature, through clean life, and by initiation. This power can be lost if not respected. Only the initiated dancer possesses a deer hoof dance stick. It represents the power of the individual. Such songs and dances can be performed only in winter; otherwise it is believed that sickness may befall. In the spirit dance, the rhythmic beats are fast drum beats, then even, steady beats until the final jumping of the dancer.

The Salish Spirit Song takes place in the longhouse, with dancing around the fire. When the power hits the initiated man, he exclaims 'Hoo Woo' and begins to sing. Then he dances, without singing, with a long deer hoof stick in his hand, only with drumming. He keeps on dancing and begins singing, then he throws his song to the crowd, 'Yunai.' The crowd takes over the song. The dancer keeps on dancing, faster and faster. Nobody else can claim his song. It belongs to the dancer, who received it as a vision or a dream. The moment the dancer sits down, the spirits having finally left him, the crowd stops singing.

The Seeyowan power can come from different animals; eg, the wolf or the bear. The wolf Skeia is sacred to these Indians, and its dance is characterized by steady beats. Louie Maranda, a Squamish singer, and his wife, a hereditary dancer, gave the author three representative beats and explained their complicated dance technique supported by the singers. In 1980 detailed research by Halpern on Snohomish and Squamish, two Salish coastal subtribes, was in preparation for publication.

The Plateau Indians are made up of the following tribes: Interior Salish, Lilloet, West Shushwap, Chilcotin, Kootenay, Thompson, and West Carrier. There has been very little ethnomusicological research on Plateau Indian music.

Although the music of the Interior Salish has many similarities to coast Indian music, it also has differences. Ceremonies and rites are much fewer; the song structures are looser, not as clearly defined; and the variations of rhythm are different. The drum of the interior is the dressed skin of a moose or beaver stretched on a round wooden frame and beaten with a drumstick. The old coastal drum is square, made of red cedar suspended from the roof of the house, and played with a leather-ended stick. However, the newer round coastal drum is made of deerskin. The one is open, the other is closed.

The clans of the Lilloet and West Shushwap have adapted much from the coastal Salish, especially the masked dances during winter and some of the songs of the secret societies. The potlatch with its songs was celebrated in the 19th century, but fell into oblivion. The most frequent festivity was the circle dance or ghost dance. Both tribes felt close kinship with and reverence for the dead.

The Chilcotin have kept strictly to their own language, but have been influenced nevertheless, mostly by the Bella Coola and to a lesser degree by the Kwakiutl and Salish. They have pursued strongly the coastal custom of the potlatch.

The farthest west of the Kootenay Indians have retained a few characteristics of the Salish but have no clan crests, secret societies, or masked dances.

DISCOGRAPHY

Songs of the Nootka and Quileute. Recorded by Frances Densmore. 1953. Library of Congress AAFS L 32

Indian Music of the Pacific Northwest Coast. Collected, recorded, and annotated by Ida Halpern. (1967). 2-Folk FE 4523

Nootka: Indian Music of the Pacific Northwest Coast. Collected, recorded, and annotated by Ida Halpern. (1974). 2-Folk FE 4524

World Library of Folk and Primitive Music, vol 8. Bella Bella and Kwakiutl songs. Recorded by Ida Halpern. 1953. Col SL 211

BIBLIOGRAPHY

Stumpf, Carl Friedrich. 'Lieder der Bella-Kula Indianer,' *Vierteljahresschrift für Musikwissenschaft*, vol 2, 1886

Deans, James. 'A weird mourning song of the Haidas,' *The American Antiquarian*, vol 13, 1891

Fillmore, John C. 'A woman's song of the Kwakiutl Indians,' *JAF*, vol 6, no. 20, 1893

Boas, Franz. 'The dances and songs of the winter ceremonial,' *The Social Organization and the Secret Societies of the Kwakiutl Indians* (New York 1895; repr 1970)

– 'Songs of the Kwakiutl Indians,' *Internationales Archiv für Ethnographie*, vol 9 (Leiden 1896)

Abraham, Otto, and Hornbostel, Erich M. von. 'Phonographierte Indianermelodien aus Britisch Columbia,' *Boas Anniversary Volume* (New York 1906)

Swanton, John R. 'Haida songs,' *American Ethnological Society Publications*, vol 3, ed Franz Boas (Leiden 1912)

Barbeau, Marius. 'Asiatic survivals in Indian songs,' *MQ*, vol 20, Jan 1934

Oberg, Kalervo. 'Crime and punishment in Tlingit society,' *American Anthropologist*, vol 36, Apr–Jun 1934

Ravenhill, Alice. 'Songs, dances and musical instruments,' *The Native Tribes of British Columbia* (Victoria, BC, 1938)

Gellatly, Marjorie G. 'Fourteen Northwest Coast Indian songs transcribed into musical notation,' unpubl MA thesis, U of Washington 1940

Herzog, George. 'Salish music,' *Contributions to Anthropology*, no. 36, 1949

Barbeau, Marius. 'Tsimshian songs,' *The Tsimshian, Their Arts and Music* by V. Garfield, P. Wingert and Barbeau (New York 1951)

– 'The Tsimshian,' *Publications of the American Ethnological Society*, vol 18 (New York 1952)

Roberts, Helen H, and Swadesh, Morris. *Songs of the Nootka Indians of Western Vancouver Island* (Philadelphia 1955)

Drucker, Phillip. *The Northern and Central Nootkan Tribes*, Smithsonian Institution, Bureau of American Ethnology Bulletin 144 (Washington, DC, 1957)

Barbeau, Marius. 'Buddhist dirges of the North Pacific coast,' *J of the International Folk Music Council*, vol 14, Jan 1962

George, Graham. 'Songs of the Salish Indians of British Columbia,' ibid

Halpern, Ida. 'Kwakiutl music,' ibid

Drucker, Phillip. *Indians of the Northwest Coast* (New York 1963)

– 'Musical instruments,' *Cultures of the North Pacific Coast* (San Francisco 1965)

Gunther, Erna. 'Musical instruments,' *Art in the Life of the Northwest Coast Indians* (Portland, Ore, 1966)

Davis, Philip. 'Bella Coola Songs and Tales,' National Museum of Man archives, ms, 1966

Proceedings of the Centennial Workshop of Ethnomusicology, ed Peter Crossley-Holland (Victoria, BC, 1968)

Halpern, Ida. 'Music of the B.C. Northwest Coast Indians,' *Proceedings of the Centennial Workshop on Ethnomusicology*, ibid

Clutesi, George. *Potlatch* (Sidney, BC, 1969)

Densmore, Frances. *Nootka and Quileute Music* (New York 1972)

Meek, Jack. 'Primitive musical instruments of the Northwest coast,' *The Midden*, vol 4, no. 3, 1972

Stuart, Wendy B. *Gambling Music of the Coast Salish Indians*, National Museum Mercury Series No. 3 (Ottawa 1972)

– 'Coast Salish gambling music,' *CFMJ*, vol 2, 1974

MacNair, Peter L. 'Kwakiutl winter dances,' *Artscanada*, Dec 1973–Jan 1974

Bradley, Ian L. *Indian Music of the Pacific Northwest: An Annotated Bibliography of Research* (Victoria, BC, 1975)

Halpern, Ida. 'On the interpretation of "meaningless-nonsensical syllables" in the music of the Pacific Northwest Indians,' *Ethnomusicology*, vol 20, May 1976

Amoss, Pamela. *Coast Salish Spirit Dancing* (Seattle, Wash, 1978)

Halpern, Ida. ' "... a very agreeable harmony." Impressions of Nootkan music,' *Sound Heritage*, vol 7, no. 1, 1978

FILMOGRAPHY

Dances of the Kwakiutl (Orbit Films 1951)

Indians at Banff National Park

2 ATHAPASKAN. Athapaskan refers to a family of languages, branches of which are spoken in western Canada (20,000 speakers), the Alaskan Interior (8000 speakers), and southwestern USA (15,000 Apache and 150,000 Navajo). However, the southwestern group became culturally differentiated many centuries ago, and here we refer only to those Athapaskan who inhabit the harsh environment of the northernmost treeline (northern Manitoba, Saskatchewan, Alberta, and non-coastal British Columbia, and the inner parts of the Northwest Territories, the Yukon, and Alaska), hunt caribou and moose, trap small fur-bearing animals, and fish for salmon. There are about 25 tribal groups in Canada.

For the Athapaskan, song composition is facilitated by supernatural forces through visions and dreams, usually experienced on water and in situations of extreme duress, such as those immediately following the loss of a companion in the rapids or the freezing to death of a father or brother after a snowmobile breakdown. Song ownership is an important part of clan symbolism. Almost every song is someone's property, and the singing of it serves to demonstrate one's special relationship to the deceased, to a guest, or to the host. At significant social events, series of songs are sung by someone, to someone, or for someone, defining and affirming social structure. At weddings and funerals, particularly, musical formality and ritual hold sway. Such feasts are called potlatches.

Songs often gather verses as they gather age, becoming personal historical mementos of fact and family. The songs of one's forefathers are thought to embody the personal strengths of their former owners; they are inherited and greatly prized. This is true particularly in those remote rural communities where the Athapaskan still follows traditional hunting practices, living off the land.

The natives themselves recognize two main classes of Athapaskan song: the 'happy' songs, which are dance songs sung by all at a brisk pace to the accompaniment of a regular duple-meter drumbeat; and the 'sorry' songs, which are slow, unaccompanied, and sung solo by a person or sequence of persons who are kin to the honoured or deceased.

The 'happy' songs are sung by a group of 10–30 men and women standing in a circle with their feet immobile, swaying their trunks from side to side and waving their clenched fists up and down rhythmically in time to the drum, which is held high and beaten by the song-leader. The melodies generally are based upon a five-tone scale, but with the additional use of microtones, ascending and descending glissandi, and slurred appoggiaturas. The use of all these varies according to context, so that there is a subtle relationship between phrase, song structure, word meaning, and pitch. It is partly this relationship which, to an Athapaskan, identifies a song as being truly indigenous. The melodic range is usually about one octave, with a midway reference tone marked by constant reiteration. Intervals of the fourth and fifth are prominent. Song syllables are strongly on the beat, usually in a one-to-one relationship, with almost no syncopation. In this they differ strikingly from the neighbouring Inuit to the north and Tlingit to the south. A common pattern is the matching of alternate syllables with one of the regular drumbeats. Where a syllable lasts for more than one pulse, it is treated by the singers with glottal pulsation, a deliberate jerking of the glottis and diaphragm, in time with the drum and hence the dance movements. For many Athapaskans, this pulsation has become a kind of ethnic trade mark, a badge of group identity affirming otherness.

Apart from the obvious difference in tempo, there are other features which distinguish 'happy' songs from 'sorry' songs.

'Happy' songs utilize mainly vocables such as *he-hani-he-ho*, using only an occasional real word, and then it is often in English, such as 'New Year!' or 'Fire-fighting!' A 'happy' song is composed by and belongs to an individual within a rural community, but at the same time may be sung by any group of residents within that community. It is carried to other communities via inter-village potlatches, learned there (quite legally) by others, and from that point on is sung everywhere and is reputed to advertize the musical skills and prowess of the community of origin. 'Happy' songs are fairly short, are repeated over and over at the loudest possible volume level, and require the singer to employ a piercing, shrill, nasal vocal quality. 'Happy' songs are thought to dispel the gloom and misery of the bereaved by livening up the proceedings.

'Sorry' songs are composed in memory of a loved one, are sung by a near relative at times of remembrance, produce many tears during performance, are rather long and intricate in construction, and carry several stanzas of real words in the Athapaskan language. They are regarded with reverence, may be sung only by those with the ancient right to do so, are rarely borrowed or diffused, and in performance require the singer to adopt a 'pure' soprano-like head voice. They are sung mostly by women because the mortality rate among male hunters is high. 'Sorry' songs are thought to open the way through the thick undergrowth and facilitate the passage of the spirit of the deceased. At funeral potlatches, during the singing of 'sorry' songs, the assembled villagers sit huddled on the floor around the singer, filling the hall, and listening attentively, with great respect. The composer and the reason for each song are announced quietly to the assembly by the singer (who is usually the bereaved).

Among one group of Athapaskans, the Koyukon of Alaska, a large commemorative potlatch is given at great expense every two or three years in mid-March by the widows of hunters who have died recently. Although their village numbers only 300, at least 1500 guests arrive for the week-long event, which is called *hi'o*. *Hi'o* is the name of the tall, stripped, decorated spruce pole around which the participants dance, carrying the gifts which are to be given to a select group of men who, at the ceremony, symbolically represent the deceased, even to the extent of being served delicacies favoured by the deceased. *Hi'o* serves four main goals: it lays to rest the wandering spirit of the deceased; it repays the obligation to those who dressed the body and carried the coffin; it reduces the sense of loss by mystically enabling the pallbearers to assume (temporarily) the identity of the deceased; and it provides emotional release for the community after the height of the winter, reuniting relatives and cementing ties in surrounding villages from which trading partners and others come, like pilgrims.

Athapaskan dancers wear colourful dance tunics of beaded caribou skin, bearing ornamental fringes and tassles which bunch and gather rhythmically during the dance. Feathered headdresses, beaded dance mittens, and fur moccasins complete the costume.

Certain of the dances feature animal mimicry. In the Crow Dance, for instance, a 'cawing' dancer will perform amusingly accurate crow waddles and pecking, within the circle, as the others sing.

All dances are accompanied by a solitary hand-held drum, round and shallow, covered on one side only with a heavy caribou hide. The beater is unusual in that its beating end consists of a small circle, the whole resembling a musical note. Athapaskan singing and dancing may be observed in the north on any of several calendric occasions such as the Inuvik Northern Games, the Eskimo Olympics, the Native Arts Festival, or on major Canadian holidays.

DISCOGRAPHY

Music of the Kutchin (Athapaskan) Indians of Alaska. Folk FE 4070

BIBLIOGRAPHY

De Laguna, Frederica. 'Indian masks from the lower Yukon,' *American Anthropologist*, vol 38, Oct 1936

Sullivan, Robert J. *The Ten'a Food Quest*, Catholic U of America Anthropological Series No. 11 (1942)

Barbeau, Marius. 'Indian songs of the Northwest,' *CMJ*, vol 2, Autumn 1957

Osgood, Cornelius. *Ingalik Social Culture*, Yale U Publications in Anthropology No. 35 (1958)

Loyens, William J. 'The Koyukon feast for the dead,' *Arctic Anthropology*, vol 2, no. 2, 1964

Boyer, L. Bryce et al. 'The Alaskan Athapaskan potlatch ceremony,' *International J of Psychoanalytic Psychotherapy*, vol 3, no. 3, 1974

Guédon, Marie-Françoise. *People of Tetlin, Why Are You Singing?*, National Museum Paper No. 9 (Ottawa 1974)

Johnston, Thomas F. 'The *hi'o* ceremony,' *Beaver*, Spring 1976

3 PLAINS. The ancestral home of the Plains Indians is the vast area occupied by southern and central Manitoba, Saskatchewan, and Alberta (the northern reaches of which are Athapaskan territory). Principal plains tribes are Cree, Blackfoot (including Blood and Peigan), Sarsi, Plains Cree, Stony, Assiniboine, and Saulteaux (Plains Ojibway). Despite their various languages, the musics of these

Blackfoot singers playing bass drum at the Calgary Stampede Indian camp, 1953

tribes are remarkably similar, differing only in localized variants of genre, both religious and secular. A few rites (eg, the Cree Bear Ceremony and the Blackfoot Tobacco Dance Ritual) are unique to each culture.

The most important rite is the annual Sun Dance, a religious and social celebration occurring during the first full moon after the summer solstice in late June or early July. It may last from two or three days to two weeks, depending on the spiritual commitment of the sponsor(s) and the wealth of the reserve. The sacred ceremonies and music are performed in a large circular lodge constructed each year of upright and ridge poles covered with branches. The sacred focal point is the tall central pole, symbolically joining earth and heaven. Here the opening prayers are intoned to the Spirits of the four cardinal directions as well as down (Earth, Mother) and up (Heaven, Father). The songs accompanying these archaic rituals are intoned slowly within a narrow pitch range to asymmetric texts. When the Sun Dance proper begins a large buffalo-hide drum and eagle-bone whistles accompany the numerous fast, rhythmic songs sung by participants in the lodge and by the large group of people seated at the wide eastern entrance. The songs and dancing continue for hours at a stretch. During breaks the people rest, perform social dance songs or visit friends in the large circle of teepees surrounding the central lodge. Late at night young men on horses wend their way through the encampment singing Serenades (Midnight Riders' Songs, Around-the-Camp Songs). These secular songs are very slow, rhythmic, unaccompanied, and of extreme vocal range, beginning high and ending low.

Other sacred songs are connected with the Sweat Lodge Ceremony, a purification rite which often precedes a young man's vision quest alone in the wilderness. This often results in a 'rebirth' through a dream or spirit song. Medicine-Pipe songs, shield songs, honouring songs, famous War Chief songs, healing songs, various songs connected with sacred artifacts in the medicine bundle, and a host of miscellaneous 'personal songs' inherited from ancestors are all considered sacrosanct. They are sung unaccompanied or to the quiet, unpulsed accompaniment of a rattle or hand drum, depending on the type of song.

In direct contrast to this sacred music are the spectacular vocalizations of the social dance songs with their wide range and rhythmic hand-drum or large group-drum accompaniment. Steady or duple pulse genres include the Grass Dance, Prairie Chicken Dance, Hoop Dance, Crazy Dog Dance, and various types of War Dance songs. Scores of fast Hand-Game (Stick-Game) songs accompany this popular gambling game. All the above are male genres.

The most popular triple-time genre is the Owl Dance, in which linked couples (mixed or of the same sex) dance a simple shuffling two-step as part of a large slowly revolving circle. The song is accompanied by the hand drum, and during the 'silent' middle beat the player flicks his middle finger on the underside of the vibrating drum skin to produce a soft buzzing sound, which is terminated by the third beat of the drum stick. Similar triple-time songs accompany women's circle dances and also various types of Powwow ('party') dance songs, which often have verses in addition to the usual vocables, especially among the Cree. The verses are sometimes in English, although the music remains strictly Indian. In Souvenir Dances the couples exchange gifts after each dance. In virtually all these social dance songs the melodic line traces a slowly descending graph, often after an initial leap of an octave to the opening high tone. Pronounced vibrato on anticipatory tones is characteristic. The strains imposed on the vocal apparatus make these virtuoso songs primarily the province of younger men.

Examples of many genres may be heard on the recording *Indian Music of the Canadian Plains* (Folkways FE 4464), selected from Kenneth *Peacock's extensive 1953–4 collection at the National Museum of Man, Ottawa. See also Bruno Nettl's four-part series 'Studies in Blackfoot Indian Musical Culture' published in *Ethnomusicology* (vols 11 and 12, 1967 and 1968). Valuable insight into the cosmogony and psychodynamics of Plains culture is to be found in Black Elk's *The Sacred Pipe* edited by J.E. Brown (Norman, Okla, 1953, Penguin 1971).

DISCOGRAPHY

Dance Songs. Old Agency Singers of the Blood Reserve, Alta. 1972. India House IH 4051-4052

BIBLIOGRAPHY

Potvin, Annette. 'The sun dance liturgy of the Blackfeet Indians,' unpubl MA thesis, U of Ottawa 1966

Dempsey, Hugh A. *Indian Tribes of Alberta* (Calgary 1978)

FILMOGRAPHY

Circle of the Sun (NFB 1961)

4 EASTERN WOODLANDS. Some of the Indian culture areas ignore political boundaries. This is the case with the area of the Eastern Woodlands – from the Great Lakes to the Atlantic – which encompasses Indian tribes living in Canada and in the USA. Therefore, a comprehensive investigation of Canadian-Indian music of the Eastern Woodlands should deal at least marginally with such US tribes as the Algonkian-speaking Menomini of Wisconsin, whose music was explored extensively by Frances Densmore (see Bibliography below). In a few instances even groups belonging to the same tribe are scattered in regions located on both sides of the border. Typical examples are the Ojibwa (also called Chippewa) and the Iroquois. There are a few Iroquois reserves in New York State and in Ontario, including the Six Nations Reserve near Brantford, Ont, which represents not only the most important group but also the most thoroughly investigated culture among the Canadian Indians of the Eastern Woodlands; their music and dance have been thoroughly researched, largely by the Chicago-born dance ethnologist, musicologist, and dancer Gertrude Prokosch Kurath.

The Iroquois were a confederation formed about 1570, of five Iroquoian-speaking Indian tribes: the Cayuga, Mohawk, Oneida, Onondaga, and Seneca. When in 1722 the Tuscarora joined the league, it came to be called the Six Nations. A

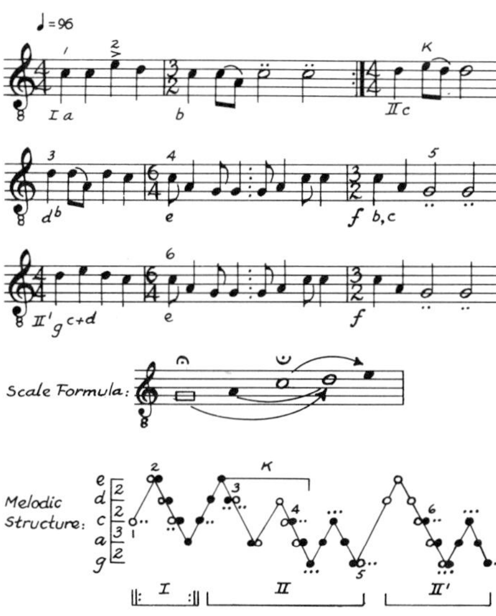

Iroquoian song performed during a Dance for the Dead

considerable portion of the inhabitants of the aforementioned Six Nations Reserve lives in large communal houses, called longhouses, which serve as centres for elaborate ceremonies in which music and dance are interwoven intimately. An annual cycle includes eight seasonal ceremonies: 1 / Midwinter Ceremonies; 2 / Planting Ceremony; 3–5 / Strawberry, Raspberry, and Green Bean Harvest; 6–7 / Green Corn Ceremonies; 8 / Harvest Festival. These ceremonies comprise about 40 dance suites, each composed of a series of songs. The large ceremonies are followed by evenings of social dances, divisible, according to the basic step, into Stomp-type and Fish-type dances. The Stomp-type dances include Robin, Alligator, Cherokee, and Shaking-a-Bush dances; the Fish-type include Raccoon, Chicken, Sharpening-a-Stick, and Choose-a-Partner dances. In addition, there are such occasional events as private medicine dances, drum dances for the Sun and Moon spirits, or war dances to supplicate rain.

Although the Iroquois do not use melody instruments, percussive accompaniment fulfils an important function, because it provides a metric pulsation which co-ordinates dance and music. Most dances are accompanied by water drums and steer-horn rattles.

The illustrated song, performed during a Dance for the Dead, may illustrate some characteristic features of Iroquoian vocal music. It was transcribed by G.P. Kurath (1968, Fig 225), but its notation and evaluation have been modified by this writer. (The methods of analysis employed are given in Kolinski's 1961 and 1965 articles cited below.)

The major-6th scale G–a–c–d–e denotes the pentatonic penta-G mode, with C and D functioning as secondary points of attraction (melodic dominants). Both phrase I and the first two motives of II move in the upper quintal area A–C–D–E, but the strong emphasis on C in I shifts to an equally strong stress on D in II, followed by a descent to the lower quartal area G–A–C with an emphasis on the finalis G. Two-, three-, and four-tone reiterations underline G, C, and D. All notes adjacent in the scale, and the 4th A–D, are employed as steps in both directions, while the 3rd C–E and the 5th G–D occur only upward. The level formula 56°: 0° indicates a moderately descending trend. The song is composed exclusively of recurrent movements, ie, of melodic progressions including two or more members of alternate direction and similar size. An up-flexure in the upper major 3rd area C–D–E (1) opens the song, while another up-flexure, comprising the entire tone material, (5) links phrases II and II′. The remaining recurrent movements are progressing down-pendulums in the quintal area A–C–D–E (2) and in the quartal areas A–C–D (3) and G–A–C (4,6). These movements merge into the following types of complexes: widening-hanging (1+2), narrowing-standing (2+3), falling-overlapping (3+4), and wide-centred standing (4–6). The basic formal structure of the song is I I II II′. Phrase I comprises two metro-rhythmically contrasting motives, from which most of the subsequent rhythmic patterns are derived: the first motive is in 4/4 and consists of a row of quarter notes, similarly to the initial motive of II′; the second includes the three durational values employed in the song. The initial figure combining one quarter and two slurred eighth notes reappears at the start of the two following motives c and d, while the subsequent pulsating reiterations of two half notes (on the same pitch) terminate each of the four phrases. In marked opposition to the otherwise strictly commetric rhythm of the song, motive e, inserted in phrases II and II′, is conspicuously contrametric (syncopated). At the same time, its 6/4 metre creates a clear-cut hemiolic relation to the 3/2 metre of the adjacent terminal motive f. Phrase II′ represents a shortening of phrase II through the condensation of motives c+d into motive g. This modification streamlines the indirect two-trend descent K into a direct descent including all notes of the scale. It exemplifies the principle of incomplete repeat, widely applied in Indian music. The song is preponderantly syllabic and the vocal technique moderately tense.

The preceding analysis attempts to shed some light on the process of composing an Indian melody; moreover, it seems to this writer that in addition to continuous research of the type offered by scholars such as Kurath, large-scale descriptive and comparative musical analyses, using advanced methods, are needed in order to achieve a meaningful stylistic identification of the music of the Eastern Woodland Indians. In the meantime, the interested reader is referred to the section titled 'Eastern Woodlands and Great Lakes Indians' of Marie-Françoise Guédon's 'Canadian Indian ethnomusicology: selected bibliography and discography' in *Ethnomusicology*, which lists numerous studies and recordings of the music of Canadian Indians of the Eastern Woodlands.

See also Writings for A.T. Cringan; Missionaries.

DISCOGRAPHY

Songs and Dances of the Great Lakes Indians. Recorded by Gertrude Kurath. 1956. Folk FM 4003

Six Nations Singers Iroquois Social Music. (1979). Music Gallery Editions MGE 16

BIBLIOGRAPHY

Gagnon, Ernest. 'Les sauvages de l'Amérique et l'art musical,' *Rapport de la 15ième session du Congrès international des Américanistes, Québec 1906*, vol 1 (Quebec 1907)

Densmore, Frances. *Menominee Music*, Bureau of American Ethnology Bulletin 102 (Washington 1932)

Barbeau, Marius. 'Dragon myths and ritual songs of the Iroquoians,' *J International Folk Music Council*, vol 3, 1951

Kolinski, Mieczyslaw. 'Classification of tonal structure,' *Studies in Ethnomusicology*, vol 1, 1961

– 'The structure of melodic movement; a new method of analysis,' ibid, vol 2, 1965

– 'The general direction of melodic movement,' *Ethnomusicology*, vol 9, Sep 1965

Kurath, Gertrude P. *Dance and Song Rituals of Six Nations Reserve*, National Museum Bulletin No. 220 (Ottawa 1968)

FILMOGRAPHY

Longhouse People (NFB 1951)

1 / IH, 2 / TJ, 3 / KP, 4 / MKl

'In Flanders Fields.' Poem which, in various musical settings, has become a traditional part of Remembrance Day services commemorating the armistices of World War I, 11 Nov 1918, and World War II, 8 May 1945. It was written in 1915 (after the second battle at Ypres, France) by a Canadian medical officer, Lieut-Col John McCrae, 'to pass away the time between the arrivals of batches of wounded, and partly as an experiment with several varieties of poetic metre' (a letter from McCrae to Sir Andrew Macphail). The poem was published first in the English magazine *Punch* (8 Dec 1915).

Musical settings of the poem include those by J. Deane Wells (Harris 1917), John Philip Sousa (G. Schirmer 1918, recorded by Joseph Phillips, Okeh 4013), Frank E. Tours (M. Witmark 1918), W. H. Leib (Summy 1918), Harold Eustace *Key (*McGill Song Book* 1921), Charles Ives (G. Schirmer 1921, recorded in 1969 by Thomas Stewart, Col M 30229), Joseph *Roff (unpublished 1948), William Ramsey Spence (Ditson, nd), and Derek *Healey (a commission for the *Festival Singers; Chantecléir 1976). Among the best-known settings are those of J. Deane Wells and W.H. *Hewlett. The latter's was published in the *New Canadian Song Series IV* (Canada Publishing 1934) and is used during Remembrance Day ceremonies in Ottawa.

John McCrae (b Guelph, Ont, 30 Nov 1872, d Boulogne, France, 28 Jan 1918) studied medicine at the U of Toronto, served 1899–1900 in the Boer War, and then became a pathologist at Montreal General Hospital. He died of pneumonia at Boulogne, where he was serving as consulting physician to the British armies in France.

BIBLIOGRAPHY

McCrae, John. *In Flanders Fields and Other Poems*, ed Sir Andrew Macphail (Toronto 1919)

(FC)

Infonie. Montreal mixed-media ensemble devoted to classical, contemporary, and avant-garde concert music adapted for presentation as pop music. Its genesis dates from *Expo 67, where its founders, the saxophonist Walter *Boudreau and the poet-singer Raoul *Duguay, met. They subsequently performed together at the Théâtre Port-Royal (*PDA). With members of the *Quatuor de jazz libre du Québec and other musicians, they formed the Infonie in 1969, making the LP *L'Infonie vol 3* (Poly 542–507) and publishing a *Manifeste de l'Infonie* (1970). A second LP, *Mantra l'Infonie vol 33* (1970, Poly 2424–018), was an adaptation of Terry Riley's *In C* for 20 musicians.

The group dispersed in 1971 but formed again in 1972 after Boudreau's return from studies in Europe. That year the ensemble, now of 10 musicians (among them Sayyd *Abdul Al Khabyyr and Pierre Daigneault, reeds; Michel *Gonneville, piano) made the two-record set *L'Infonie vol 333* (2-Kot'ai KOT 501–502), one record of which was devoted to Boudreau's *Paix*, the other to arrangements of Bach and to other works. The Infonie disbanded again in 1973 but Boudreau continued to lead a saxophone quartet under its name.

Besides its recordings, the Infonie presented mixed-media performances at PDA, in several Cegeps, and in other venues in the province of Quebec. The film *L'Infonie inachevée* was made about the group by Roger Frappier in 1973.

BIBLIOGRAPHY
Rodriguez, Juan. 'Hear to eternity,' *Montreal Star*, 20 Jan 1973
'Interpretation by Infonie makes for musical adventure,' *MSc*, 271, May–Jun 1973 MM

INGLIS, Phylis (Elizabeth) (b Dilworth). Pianist, voice teacher, b Victoria, BC, 23 Nov 1916; LRSM 1936, BA (British Columbia) 1940. A niece of Ira *Dilworth, she studied piano with Gladys Hewlings in Victoria and 1934–44 with Isabel Campbell in Vancouver. In 1936 she won the Gold Medal (for Canada) in the RSM piano examinations. She studied accompanying and singing with Avis *Phillips. In 1942 she began to teach singing. Her pupils include Heather *Thomson, Milla *Andrew, and Shirley Chapman, whom she accompanied many times 1940–67 on CBC radio and TV. Another pupil is Betty *Phillips. In 1959 she formed the Phylis Inglis Singers, at first eight, later 16 voices, which performed on CBC radio and TV and were active until 1967. Inglis has served on various boards and was president 1966–8 of the *Vancouver Woman's Musical Club. She has been an adjudicator in Alberta and British Columbia and has examined voice for the universities of Alberta, Calgary, and Lethbridge. BNSG

inNOVAtions in MUSIC. See NOVA MUSIC.

Institut canadien, Quebec City. Cultural society founded 2 Dec 1847 by a group of young intellectuals, including the future judge Marc-Aurèle Plamondon, the poets Octave *Crémazie and Louis Fiset, the painter Théophile Hamel, and the historian François-Xavier Garneau, to create a francophone literary and scientific milieu through the development of a library, conferences, and publications.

The Quebec association was a branch of the Institut canadien founded in Montreal in 1844, but concerned itself more with history than did its politically oriented parent, and also more with music. The institute's archives reveal that occasional concerts were offered as early as 1860; and that the *Septuor Haydn, the Quatuor vocal de Québec, and some local amateurs performed at ceremonies with which the institute was involved, including the centenary (1875) of the siege of Quebec City and the quatricentenary (1892) of the discovery of America.

After six relocations, the society found an ideal home in 1944, acquiring, with the financial help of Senator Lorne C. Webster and his heirs, the Wesleyan Temple on Ste-Angèle St in Old Quebec City. This renovated temple became one of the city's most popular halls. The frequency of concerts increased gradually, and in 1966, owing to the enthusiasm of Dr Gustave Lachance, several activities were being offered each week.

During the 1970s, the 'stronghold of culture in Quebec City' offered, to a membership which had reached 1650, a choice of fine recitals each season. Performers included the Borodin Quartet, Victor *Bouchard and Renée *Morisset, Maureen *Forrester, Bruno *Laplante, Monique *Leyrac, and the *Pierre Bourque Saxophone Quartet.

Membership privileges include participation in some 60 activities (concerts, lectures, and travelogues). Mondays at the institute are reserved for members, but on other evenings the hall is open to all with the price of admission. A non-profit organization, the institute receives grants from Quebec City and from the *MACQ.

BIBLIOGRAPHY
Institut canadien archives. Minutes 1848–1975; financial records 1850
Bruchési, Jean. 'L'Institut canadien,' *Cahier des Dix*, 12, 1947
Désilets, Alphonse. *Les cent ans de l'Institut canadien de Québec, 1848–1948* (Quebec City 1949) IB

Institut canadien de musique. See Canadian Institute of Music.

Institut Nazareth. Co-educational school for blind children, founded in 1861 in Montreal by Benjamin-Victor Rousselot and the Gray Nuns. Music was a part of the general curriculum from the outset. Rosalie Euvrard (b Châtellerault, France, 1851, d Nancy, France, 1920) arrived from France in 1876 and collaborated with Paul *Letondal to develop a school of music within the institution. She served as both organizer and teacher until 1881, when she returned to France and taught in Nancy.

The newspapers of the time reveal the influence of the school on the cultural life of the area, describing annual concerts which introduced both first-rate performing talents and important new works to the Montreal public and a choir whose reputation led to tours of the province. Many considered the school the earliest conservatory in Montreal. For more than 100 years it offered instruction by leading Quebec musicians, including Françoise *Aubut, Camille *Couture, Achille *Fortier, Gustave *Labelle, François *Morel, and R.-O. *Pelletier; and trained others including Gabriel *Cusson, Paul *Doyon, Alfred *Lamoureux, Conrad *Letendre, Armand Pellerin, and Jeannine *Vanier. The school organized the first workshops in piano tuning in French Canada. In 1917 *Laval U conferred affiliate status upon the school, thus recognizing the high standard of its teaching; and in 1920 the *U of Montreal made the Institut Nazareth one of its first annexed music schools. It was through this connection that the organist Armand Pellerin in 1921 received the first B MUS granted by the U of Montreal. The affiliation was terminated in 1967 by the terms of the new university charter.

The Institut Nazareth changed location in 1932 and again in 1940, and in 1956 an organ was installed. A letter dated 28 Feb 1975, from the director, Sister Thérèse Parent, announced to the staff the 'cessation of all general activities of the Institut Nazareth.' It merged with the Institut Louis-Braille in June 1975, continuing thereafter as the Institut Nazareth et Louis-Braille. Relocated in Longueuil, the two were incorporated under the administration of the Chambly Regional School Board.

Founded 1953 in Montreal as a school for blind boys, and administered by the Order of St-Viateur, the Institut Louis-Braille became noted for its piano-tuning classes. These apprenticeship workshops were established in 1954 by Raphaël Brilotti. Their study program is registered as part of the secondary professional training course of the Ministry of Education of Quebec and remained in 1980 the only courses of their kind in the province.

See also The blind.

BIBLIOGRAPHY
Journal de l'Institut Nazareth [publ in braille] (Montreal 1877–1936)
1861–1961 – Les Trois âges d'une oeuvre séculaire (Montreal 1961)
Institut Louis-Braille. Archives (NTr)

Instrument building. See the following:
Accordion
Bagpipe, Great Highland
Bells
Brass
Guitar
Harpsichord building
Instruments: medieval, renaissance, baroque: 2 / Building
Lute
Organ building
Piano building
Player pianos and nickelodeons
Reed organs
String instrument building

See also Carillon; Dinner horn; Inventions and devices; Mechanical instruments

Instrument collections (private and public). The following list of major Canadian collections is arranged west to east by province and, therein, alphabetically by city.

BRITISH COLUMBIA

Prince George

The Ted Eames Collection. Approximately 150 items (1974), mostly 19th- and 20th-century European woodwind and brass instruments; also a small number of non-European (African, Asian, West Indian) items and some reproductions by Eames, including copies of an Incan slit drum and a pre-historic Danish lur. A selection was displayed at the Vancouver Centennial Museum in 1971. Part of this collection has been acquired by the National Museum of Man.

BIBLIOGRAPHY
Cumming, Duncan. 'Ted, his girls, and his moose shinbone make beautiful music,' *Canadian Panorama*, 4 Apr 1970

Vancouver

U of British Columbia Museum of Anthropology. Houses some 340 instruments (1979), over 220 of them Inuit and Indian, the remainder African, Australian, Chinese, Egyptian, Indonesian, Japanese, Melanesian, and South American.

Vancouver Centennial Museum. The ethnology division had acquired over 200 instruments by 1979, 107 of them Canadian and other North American Indian, 3 Canadian Inuit, 8 South American, 43 Asian, 42 African and 9 Oceanian. In addition there are a few archeological examples such as bone bird whistles. By 1979 the modern history division had acquired 23 instruments, most imported in the 19th century, including a pair of bagpipes, and a concertina from the latter half of the century.

Victoria

Provincial Museum of British Columbia. 322 items by 1978 – rattles, drums, recorders, whistles, clappers, batons, one bull roarer, and five 'objects' of unknown cultural classification – all of British Columbia Indian origin (Bella Coola, Coast Salish, Haida, Kwakiutl, Nootka, Tlingit, and Tsimshian).

Manitoba University Consort Collection, U of Victoria. Sold to the U of Victoria ca 1970; one of the largest collections of historical instruments (all replicas) in Canada.

Phillip T. Young Collection. Initiated by Young in 1958. By 1978, a few brass instruments and a dozen woodwinds (most by early American builders), including a four-keyed bassoon (ca 1760) by John Blockley and formerly in the collection of Anthony Barnes, Oxford, England. The instruments may be viewed by appointment.

ALBERTA

Calgary

Glenbow-Alberta Institute. Instrument collection established ca 1956 and housed in the ethnology and cultural history departments. In 1978, some 730 non-western instruments (including drums, fiddles, flutes, gongs, pan pipes, rat-

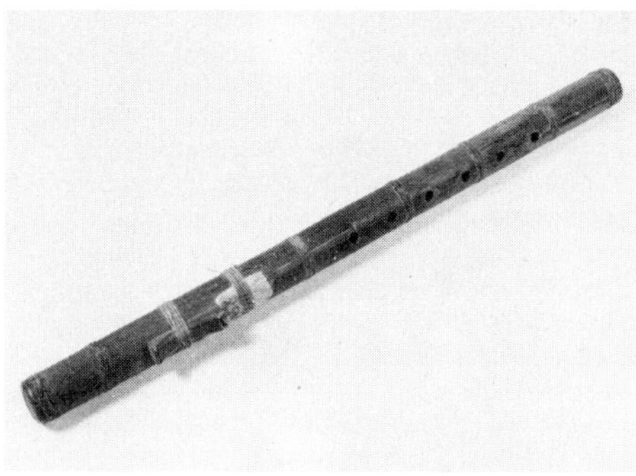

An Iroquois flute

A Northwest Coast rattle

tles, whistles, and a didjeridu, an Australian aboriginal pipe), and approximately 100 western instruments (eg, autoharps, violins, zithers, trombones, coach horns, a psaltery, piano, organs, music boxes, musical glasses, spoons and a violano virtuoso).

SASKATCHEWAN

Regina

The Robertson Conservation Collection of Musical Instruments. Established by Gary Robertson in 1964. By 1978 over 250 ethnic instruments from around the world, predominantly folk flutes, shawms, fiddles, lutes, and original mouth organs. Of special interest: a pi-morn and pi-chawar (shawms) from Thailand, a Rubob lute from Tadzik, USSR, and a Vietnamese kom-boat mouth organ. May be viewed upon request. Typed catalogue available at cost.

Saskatoon

The Stephen Kolbinson Collection. Established 1940 by Stephen Kolbinson (b Brandon, Man, 4 Apr 1888, of Icelandic origin, and a string player in the *Saskatoon SO for some years). Rare string instruments and bows, including cellos by Gennaro Gagliano and Albani, a viola by Antonio (?) Mariani, and violins by Giuseppe (?) Baldantoni, M.A. Bergonzi, F. Gobetti, Giuseppe Guarneri del Gesù, C.G. Testore, and J. Tononi. Kolbinson also owned a quartet of Amati instruments, which he sold to the *U of Saskatchewan in 1959 (see below). Collection may be viewed upon request.

BIBLIOGRAPHY

Moss, Bruce. 'Farmer with a fortune in fiddles,' *Weekend Magazine*, 29 Sep 1962

The U of Saskatchewan Collection. A quartet of Amati string instruments acquired in 1959. The violin (ca 1627) and viola (ca 1606) were built by the brothers Antonio and Girolamo Amati; the second violin (once owned by the Australian violinist Daisy Kennedy) was built by Niccolo Amati in 1637. Niccolo's son, Girolamo, built the cello ca 1690. The collection may be viewed upon request. (See also Amati String Quartet and Canadian Arts Trio.)

BIBLIOGRAPHY

Jalovec, Karel. *Beautiful Italian Violins* (London 1963)

MANITOBA

Winnipeg

Sounds of Yesteryear Museum. Collection of automatic musical instruments that was initiated by Terry and Alice Smythe in 1973. Music boxes, nickelodeons (including a 1905 violano virtuoso), orchestrions (a 1927 Seeburg KT among them), player pianos, and other mechanical instruments. May be viewed upon request. See also Mechanical instruments; Player pianos and nickelodeons.

BIBLIOGRAPHY

Carson, Susan. 'The collecting compulsion,' Toronto Globe and Mail *Weekend Magazine*, 18 Dec 1976

Pasta, Victor. 'Those magnificent men and their music machines,' *Manitoba Moods* (Autumn 1976)

ONTARIO

Guelph

Coleman Collection of Musical Instruments, U of Guelph. Donated to the university by Mrs. Barbara Coleman in 1971. Eight string instruments from North America, Europe, and the Orient, including a Swedish Nykelharpa, an 18th-century French hurdy-gurdy, and a Chinese viol and beggar's fiddle. May be viewed upon request.

BIBLIOGRAPHY

Coleman, Barbara. 'Musical heirlooms of Canadian pioneers,' Dolmetsch Foundation *Bulletin*, Sep 1973; repr in *Early Canadian Life*, Mar 1980

London

The Henry Meredith Collection. Begun in 1975 by the trumpeter and *U of Western Ontario professor Henry Meredith. In 1980 over 350 19th- and early-20th-century instruments, mainly brass, including several natural trumpets, an English slide trumpet, cornopeans by F. Pace (London), Robinson & Bussell (Dublin) and T. *Claxton (Toronto), keyed bugles, double-belled euphoniums, helicons, an 18th-century hunting horn, a Vienna-valved trumpet, and numerous cornets and low brass instruments. Many of the instruments have been used by Meredith in performance and for lecture-recitals. Catalogue on request.

BIBLIOGRAPHY

Newman, Richard. 'Brass on brass,' *London Free Press*, 19 Oct 1978

Meredith, Henry. '76 Ophicleides, 110 cornopeans (or how to start a brass instrument collection),' *Ensemble*, Spring 1978

Ottawa

National Museum of Man. Instruments are housed in the museum's Canadian Centre for Folk Culture Studies and its History Division and Canadian Ethnology Service. The centre in 1979 held 448 instruments representing more than 40 ethnic groups from Africa, Britain, Canada, Europe, the Mediterranean, the Orient, the Slavic countries, and South America. The History Division in 1979 held some 35 instruments, including harps, reed organs, pianos, violins, and zithers and a number of more exotic instruments presented by several countries to a former Canadian governor-general. In the Ethnology Service in 1979 were approximately 1368 instruments, mostly North American Indian and Inuit (whistles, rattles, drums, deer-callers, etc) but also including specimens from other cultures and countries – India, New Guinea, Ceylon, Africa, Mexico, and South America.

Southampton

The Bruce County Museum. Collection established 1953. Over 50 instruments (by 1979), mainly music boxes, pianos, and reed organs, but also some bagpipes and a dulcimer. Most items date from 1880–1900 and some are of Canadian origin.

Toronto

Hart House Viols, U of Toronto. Six viols in a 17th-century chest, purchased by the *Massey Foundation ca 1930. Until 1935 owned jointly by the *Arts and Letters Club of Toronto and *Hart House, but thereafter the sole property of the latter. Two Pardessus de viole (Louis Guersan, Paris 1760, and Nicolas Bertrand, Paris ca 1725), a small English viol (ca 1680), a treble viol (probably Flemish, ca 1700), an alto viol, tuned as a tenor (English ca 1700), and a bass viol (Joachim Tielke, Hamburg ca 1695). The instruments have been heard at many concerts at the university and have been played by groups such as the *Conservatory String Quartet and the Hart House Consort of Viols, led by Peggie *Sampson.

Royal Ontario Museum. Established in 1912, by 1980 the ROM collection was the largest in Canada, with instruments in its Far Eastern, Ethnology, and European departments. In 1980 the Far Eastern collection included Chinese instruments of the Shang and Chou dynasties and 103 instruments manufactured in the 19th and 20th centuries, about one-half of which were displayed. The Ethnology Dept had 707 instruments: 303 North American Indian, including 144 rattles and 43 drums; 11 Inuit, including 4 drums and 4 string instruments; and the remainder from Mexico, South America, Africa, and Oceania. The European Dept collection comprised 230 instruments in 1980. Among the most important were the Johannes Celestini harpsichord, made in Venice in 1596, and the so-called 'Dragonetti' double-bass attributed to Gasparo Bertolotti da Salò, dated 1600. The excellent representation of early English instruments included a viola da gamba bearing the label of Henry Jay, 1610. Another, by Barak Norman, is dated 1697. There also was a 17th-century kit-violin by Cuthbert and 18th-century kits by Henry Jay and W. Taylor, as well as English guitars of the 17th and 18th centuries. Among the 18th- and early 19th-century keyboard instruments were examples of the spinet, harpsichord, and piano by such famous makers as Baker, Harris, Kirckman, Zumpe, and Broadwood. Woodwinds were represented by instruments of Bainbridge, Ellard, and Wood, brasses by works of Mathew Pace and Henri Distin. There also was a British harp lute, the work of Edward Light. In 1980 over 100 instruments were on permanent display. The R.S. *Williams collection formed the basis of the present ROM collection.

BIBLIOGRAPHY

Cselenyi, Ladislav. *Musical Instruments in the Royal Ontario Museum* (Toronto 1971)

Littler, William. 'ROM's musical treasures,' *Toronto Star*, 29 Mar 1980

Music Library, Edward Johnson Building, U of Toronto. Collection established by Sidney Fisher; 21 English, French, and German transverse flutes made between 1760 and 1905. Seven one- to eight-key boxwood flutes (1760–1850); others of locustwood, blackwood, rosewood, sterling silver, and silver-plated brass. One, a Nicholson flute (1825), considerably influenced Boehm in his work.

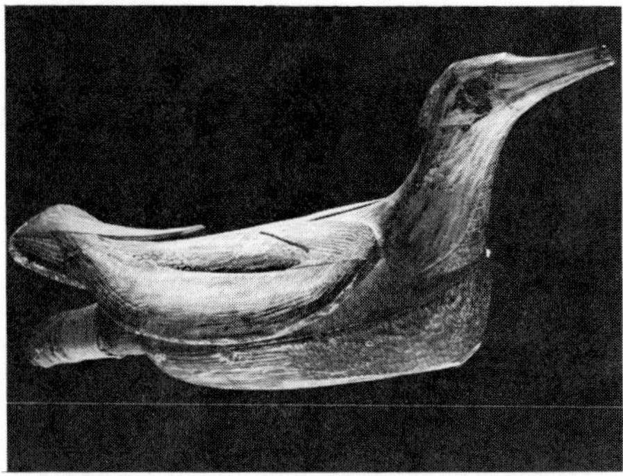

A Nootkan bird rattle

QUEBEC
Montreal

Ensemble Claude-Gervaise Collection. Started in 1968 by Jean Gagné, a member of the ensemble. About 250 instruments in 1978, including both authentic items and reproductions. Of particular interest: a musette and an hautbois de Poitou (both 18th-century), a sculpted Chinese oboe set with moonstones, and a collection of African drums. The collection has been used in performance by the *Ensemble Claude-Gervaise, and viewing may be arranged through the Centre de la flûte à bec, Montreal.

BIBLIOGRAPHY
Catalogue de la collection de l'Ensemble Claude-Gervaise (Montreal 1975)

NEW BRUNSWICK
Saint John

The New Brunswick Museum. A collection of some 35 instruments (1979), most of them owned originally by New Brunswick settlers. A barrel organ, drums, three flutes, a lute, a music box, bagpipes, several pianos, trumpets, violins, and a xylophone. More exotic items are a Nubian harp and two boxes of miniature Japanese instruments.

NOVA SCOTIA
North East Margaree, Cape Breton Island

The Murphy Collection. Almost 100 string and wind instruments (1978). Initiated in 1942 by John and Hilda Murphy, later in the possession of Michael J. Murphy. Items of special interest: an alpine horn, a ukeline, and an African thumb-piano. May be viewed upon request.

BIBLIOGRAPHY
MacDonald, C.A. (Sandy). 'He plays the zan zez,' *Atlantic Advocate*, vol 69, 2 Oct 1978

Halifax

Carl van Feggelen Collection. Private collection begun in 1960. By 1978, some 250 antique keyboard, string, and wind instruments, including accordions, grand pianos, hurdy-gurdies, an Arabian oud, and over 100 rare guitars. Accessible to researchers by appointment.

BIBLIOGRAPHY
Pierce, Gretchen. 'Music professor has 100 guitars,' Halifax *Mail Star*, 24 Dec 1974

Truro

Jan van der Leest Collection. Established in 1975, a private collection – the Organery – of over 60 antique organs, harmoniums, and melodeons by 1980. The oldest item at that time was a melodeon thought to have been built ca 1846 by George Prince of Buffalo. Part of the collection was displayed in Halifax and Truro in 1976. May be viewed by appointment.

BIBLIOGRAPHY
van der Leest, Jan. 'Reed organs: the experiences of a collector,' *The Occasional*, Winter–Spring 1976–7

In addition to all of the above, many local museums, pioneer villages, and restored fortresses display reed organs, square pianos, homebuilt fiddles, and other 18th- and 19th-century instruments, usually acquired as accoutrements of households and churches rather than for their own sakes. Such collections have been assembled at Battleford National Historic Park (Battleford, Sask), Brant Historical Society (Brantford, Ont), Brome County Historical Society Museum (Knowlton, Que), the Bytown Museum (Ottawa), the Château de Ramezay Museum (Montreal), the Doon Pioneer Village (Kitchener, Ont), the Sharon Temple (Sharon, Ont), Upper Canada Village (Morrisburg, Ont), and the Western Development Museum (Yorkton, Sask). Exhibitions of instruments, apart from permanent museum displays, have been rare. Examples include the exhibit of R.S. Williams' collection at the Toronto Mechanics' Institute in 1861, 'Marvellous Music Machines' (shown in Cobourg, Kingston, Kitchener, and Oshawa in 1977), and an international exhibit, 'The Look of Music,' presented at the Vancouver Centennial Museum 1980–1. In 1980 the harpsichordist Kenneth *Gilbert maintained a 'working collection' of 12 harpsichords, early and modern, in Montreal, Paris, and London. Indeed, many performers (string players, pianists, wind and brass players, and percussionists) have acquired for their professional use virtual collections, often containing rare specimens.

BIBLIOGRAPHY
Kallmann, Helmut. *Canadian-built 19th Century Musical Instruments, a Check List* (Toronto 1965, rev Ottawa 1966)
Lichtenwanger, William, et al. *A Survey of Musical Instrument Collections in the United States and Canada* (Ann Arbor, Mich, 1974)
Jenkins, Jean, ed. *International Directory of Musical Instrument Collections* (Buren, Netherlands, 1977)
Barclay, R.L. *Care of Musical Instruments in Canadian Collections*, Canadian Conservation Institute Technical Bulletin 4 (Ottawa 1978)
Young, Phillip T., compiler. *The Look of Music* (Vancouver 1980)
Hopkins, Thomas. 'Tracing the family tree of instruments,' *Maclean's*, 17 Nov 1980
Reif, Rita. 'The siren song of old instruments,' *New York Times*, 4 Jan 1981
Littler, William. 'World's musical treasures are celebrated in silence,' *Toronto Star*, 10 Jan 1981 HK (ML, NM)

Instruments: medieval, renaissance, baroque

1 Building
2 Playing and teaching
3 Some ensembles in Canadian universities
4 Some professional ensembles

See also Guitar; Harpsichord building; Harpsichord playing and teaching; Instrument collections; Lute; String instrument building.

1 BUILDING. In the late 1950s in Canada there was a renewal of interest in performing medieval, renaissance and early baroque music. As musicologists bring to light an increasing amount of information on early instruments, music, and performance practices, performers have attempted to recreate the music authentically.

From this revival has emerged a small number of craftsmen who, through detailed study of specimens surviving in museums and of illuminated manuscripts, treatises, and contemporary pictorial representations, have tried to copy accurately the instruments originally used. In Canada many capable amateurs but only a few professional builders were constructing instruments in the 1970s, mainly lutes, viols, neo-Celtic harps, and hurdy-gurdies, but also reed instruments – krumhorns, dulcians, shawms, racketts, recorders, etc.

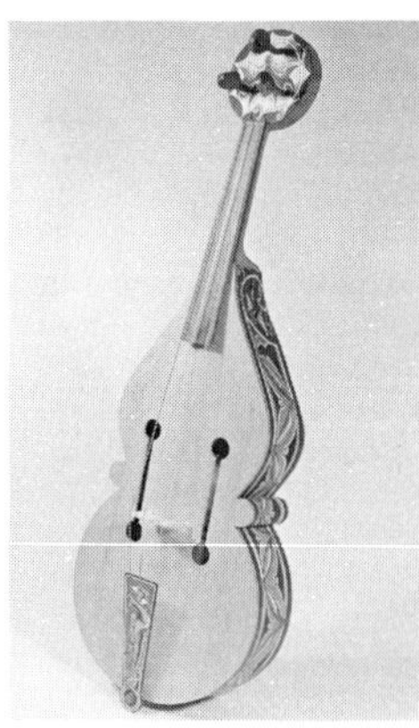

A medieval viol made by Christopher Allworth

Many of the Canadian builders began as, and continued to be, makers of harpsichords, and/or popular instruments like the guitar, the banjo, and the dulcimer. British Columbia has been the scene of most of the activity. A co-operative workshop, the Instrument Shop, was organized in 1971 by nine craftsmen. Among those involved in the venture have been Ray *Nurse, Michael Dunn, Edward (Ted) *Turner, Tim Hobrough, and Allan McNaught.

Dunn (b Sherbrooke, Que, 7 Mar 1943) played guitar from childhood and began repairing instruments in Vancouver in 1965 for George Bowden. He apprenticed 1966–7 with Jose Orti and Jose Ferrer in Bowden's workshop in Palma de Mallorca, Spain. Returning to Vancouver he studied lute making with Nurse. In 1972 he worked with Ted Turner, building harpsichords for the *Vancouver Society for Early Music. He was artist-in-residence at the BC pavilion at the 1974 World's Fair in Spokane, Wash, and a representative craftsman at Artisinage for the 1976 Olympic Games in Montreal.

Hobrough (b Wingham, Ont, 11 Oct 1947) began guitar repair work in 1970 and studied the building of dulcimers and guitars with Dunn 1970–4. Influenced by Vancouver's early music groups he began building harps, first from modern designs and later according to the original Irish and European construction techniques. In 1974 he demonstrated the art of harp building at the World Craft Exhibition in Toronto and appeared at the Spokane World's Fair. He has done research in Great Britain and Europe on Canada Council grants. He has built both baroque and renaissance harps but will build 'one-of-a-kind' instruments when he feels there is enough historical information to make the construction practical.

McNaught (b Listowel, Ont, 18 Aug 1941) began making dulcimers in 1968, when he moved to Galiano Island, BC. He formed ca 1969 an organization of instrument builders called Seedpod, whose membership included Dan Perysko, Craig Peterson, Gray McPhedran, Je Titus, Bob Palumbo, and Steve Fletcher. While the group built folk instruments, notably the dulcimer, they also produced some neo-Celtic (Irish) harps and an instrument called the 'Magic Twanger,' which has a small cittern-like body with guitar scale neck and three to six strings. After Seedpod dissolved in 1972 McNaught worked in Vancouver and later on Desolation Sound, BC, and in 1974 he settled on Hornby Island, BC.

Christopher *Allworth established a workshop in Yarmouth, NS, in 1972 and has produced such medieval instruments as the harp, gittern, fythele (fiddle), viol, and hurdy-gurdy. Allworth also has performed on some of his instruments.

Another east-coast builder is the luthier Thomas Dorward (b Denver, Col, 29 Jul 1946), owner of the Halifax Folklore Centre. Dennis Waring of Winnipeg has built psalteries and dulcimers. Terry Philpot is a luthier working in Bethany, Ont. *Terry's Lute*, a Viking film made in 1974, shows Philpot constructing a lute later displayed at the National Gallery of Canada. Colin Everett of Ottawa built over 50 lutes and racketts between 1968 and 1978. Michael Schreiner of Toronto has made lutes and viols, and in 1978 he constructed a viola da gamba from a 1713 design by Claude Pierray of Paris. Denis Cormier, active in Montreal, studied baroque violin making with Willem Bouman in The Hague.

The craftsmen named have built their instruments individually by hand. Imported materials such as rosewood and ebony are often difficult to obtain and very costly, but many of the other woods used (cedar, maple, and spruce) are available in Canada – most readily to the west-coast builders.

A 1974 exhibit called 'Instrument Makers' at the Burnaby, BC, Art Gallery included Canadian-built instruments.

BIBLIOGRAPHY

Instrument Makers, exhibition catalogue, Burnaby Art Gallery (Burnaby, BC, 1974)

'The instrument makers,' *Craftsman / L'Artisan*, vol 6, no. 1, 1976

2 PLAYING AND TEACHING. The renewed interest in the music of the medieval, renaissance, and baroque periods (approximately 800–1750) stems mainly from the activities and studies of Arnold Dolmetsch in England at the beginning of the 20th century. Although much of the music was known to historians and even had been issued in scholarly editions, little of it was performed at all and, until the revival stimulated by Dolmetsch, none of it was performed on historical instruments or in the style of the time in which it was written. As a result of the revival, it has come to be performed more often and more authentically throughout the western world. In Canada the interest in early music and the teaching of historical instruments began around the middle of the 20th century, with study by individuals and the introduction of university classes. Performing groups began to emerge, and by the 1970s instruments such as the cornemuse, cornetto, gemshorn, krumhorn, lute, portative organ, rackett, rebec, recorder, sackbut, and shawm were no longer mere museum curiosities. Modern replicas were in wide use, some made in Canada, audiences were increasingly familiar with their sounds, and collections (both of working replicas and of museum originals) were held by the performing groups listed below, by universities, and by museums (see Instrument collections). In 1980 the largest single collection of original instruments in Canada was held at the Royal Ontario Museum. Among the pioneers of the performance of early music in Canada were Arnold *Walter, who played the recorder and encouraged such performances in Toronto; Rj *Staples, who used recorders in school music programs as early as 1938; Mario *Duschenes, who began playing and teaching recorders in Montreal in 1948; and Celia *Bizony, who founded the McGill Schola Cantorum and the group *Musica Antica e Nuova in 1949 and 1951 respectively. The Hart House Viols, purchased ca 1930 by the Massey Foundation, were heard in Toronto during the 1930s in performances given by the *Conservatory String Quartet. Wolfgang Grunsky, who began to teach recorder and viol in Toronto in 1951, was the founder in 1953 of the Hart House Viols, a group which as the Hart House Consort of Viols was led later by Peggie *Sampson. The latter also was the co-founder (with Christine *Mather) of the *Manitoba University Consort (an ensemble active 1964–70, giving concerts in Canada and touring in Europe) and in 1978 was the founder of Quatre en Concert (three versatile wind and string instrumentalists and a singer who have explored the renaissance and baroque repertoires). Rowland *Pack established the first of his early music groups in 1955 with his wife, Carol, and Hugh *Orr.

In Montreal, the composer Otto *Joachim founded, and directed 1958–68, the Montreal Consort of Ancient Instruments, for which he built replicas of instruments of the middle ages and the renaissance. During the early 1960s CBC radio and TV began to carry early-music performances by amateur and professional groups from Canada and abroad. Hans-Karl Piltz of British Columbia has been heard in numerous CBC broadcasts as baroque violinist and as lecture-recitalist on the viola d'amore. In most Canadian cities instruction has become available in recorder and harpsichord, and in the large centres, especially those with active university early-music departments, instruction may be given in viols, lute, and the main historical wind instruments as well. In the major centres performance on recorders has been encouraged by organizations such as *CAMMAC. On the West Coast the *Vancouver Society for Early Music has sponsored and promoted early-music concerts, and in Toronto James Matthew Redsell initiated his series of Early Music Concerts in 1978, and the group Tafelmusik initiated a Spring Festival of Baroque Music in 1979. By 1980 probably as many as 15 Canadian universities were offering instruction in early music itself, and several have offered courses in historical performance practice. For students at all levels, summer workshops in early music performance have been held at the *U of British Columbia and at Scarborough College, U of Toronto. In 1978 the *JMC Orford Art Centre established an Académie de musique baroque which in 1979 featured renowned teachers, master classes, and performances. In 1978 the teacher-performer Mary Cyr, who in 1976 formed a duo with the harpsichordist John Grew, uncovered in Paris Rameau's long-lost *Cantate pour le jour de la Saint Louis*, which she dates ca 1735–45.

Other professional and university groups founded to perform medieval, renaissance, and baroque music are cited in the following lists.

3 SOME ENSEMBLES IN CANADIAN UNIVERSITIES

institution / founder(s)

Alberta / Arthur *Crighton
Brandon / James Mendenhall
British Columbia / John Chappell and Eugene Wilson
Calgary
Concordia / Wolfgang *Bottenberg
Guelph / Derek *Healey
Laval / Friedemann Fischer and Paul Gerrits
McGill / John Grew
Montreal / Gerrit Tetenburg
Mount Allison / George *Proctor
Ottawa / John Grew
Toronto / Harvey Olnick and Rika *Maniates
UQAM / Jean-Pierre Pinson
Victoria / Christine Mather
Western Ontario / Gordon *Greene and Tim Aarsett
York / David Mercer and Peggie Sampson

4 SOME PROFESSIONAL ENSEMBLES

name / founder(s) / date founded

Ars Antiqua de Québec, Quebec City / Paul Gerrits and Friedemann Fischer / 1971
Cecilian Ensemble, Vancouver / David *Skulski / 1972
Collegium Ferialis, Montreal / Wolfgang Bottenberg / 1974
Duo Geminiani, Vancouver / Stanley Ritchie and Elizabeth Wright / 1974
*Ensemble Claude-Gervaise, Montreal / François Barre, Jean Gagné, Joseph Quimatte, and Gilles Plante / 1967
Hortulani Musicae, Vancouver / Ray Nurse, David Skulski, and Jon *Washburn / 1972
*Huggett Family, Ottawa / Leslie Huggett / 1966
La Ménestrandise, Montreal / Jean-Pierre Brunet and Guy Marchand / 1978
Le Petit Ensemble baroque de Montréal / Rafael and Margaret de Castro and Anthony King / 1979
Sanz Cuer Ensemble, Montreal / Judy Cohen, Ariane Dind, Susan Palmer, and Michèle Sauvé / 1976
*Studio de musique ancienne de Montréal / Hélène Dugal, Christopher *Jackson, and Réjean *Poirier / 1974
Tafelmusik, Toronto / Kenneth Solway, Susan Graves, and Dan Armstrong / 1977
*Toronto Consort / Timothy McGee / 1972
The Towne Waytes, Vancouver / David Skulski / 1974
Vancouver Waits / David Skulski / 1972

BIBLIOGRAPHY

Sedgwick, Don. 'The lively renaissance of early music: peculiar sounds and shapes of early music conquer Canada,' *Music*, Jul–Aug 1978

Littler, William. 'Going for baroque,' *Toronto Star*, 23 Mar 1979

'The Scarborough workshop,' *Continuo*, Oct 1979

'McGill's musical detective,' *McGill News*, Fall 1979

Pearce, John. 'Medieval strains, Renaissance rhythms,' *Maclean's*, 26 Nov 1979

April issues of *Continuo* list summer workshops.

PERIODICALS

Continuo, monthly, Toronto, Oct 1977– . First 6 issues titled *The Toronto Early Music Directory*

The Rackett, quarterly, Vancouver, Spring 1978–

Musik, quarterly journal of the Vancouver Society for Early Music, Summer 1979–

Le tic-toc-choc, journal of the Studio de musique ancienne de Montréal, Nov 1979– 1 / (BNSG, FH), 2 / (TM)

The International Conference of Composers. Held 7–14 Aug 1960 at Stratford, Ont, under the direction of Louis *Applebaum, and the cosponsorship of the *CLComp, the *CBC, the *Canada Council, the *Stratford Festival, *CAPAC, *BMI Canada, BMI, ASCAP, the AF of M, and the International Music Council. It afforded composers and others closely associated with contemporary music an opportunity to exchange ideas, and presented Canadian points of view and Canadian music to an international group.

Composers from 20 countries participated, among them Henk Badings (Holland), Karl-Birger Blomdahl (Sweden), Klaus Egge (Norway), Iain Hamilton (Scotland), Roy Harris (USA), Vagn Holmboe (Denmark), Ernst Krenek (USA), Otto Luening (USA), Elizabeth Maconchy (England), Zygmunt Mycielski (Poland), Hermann Reutter (Germany), Gunther Schuller (USA), Josef Tal (Israel), and Edgard Varèse (USA). Canadian participants included *Adaskin, *Anhalt, Applebaum, *Archer, *Beckwith, *Champagne, *Charpentier, *Dolin, *Duchow, *Eckhardt-Gramatté, *Fleming, *Freedman, *Joachim, *Kasemets, *Kenins, *Morawetz, *Papineau-Couture, *Peacock, *Rathburn, *Somers, *Twa, and *Weinzweig. Canadians whose works were performed at the five concerts were Anhalt, Freedman, Joachim, Papineau-Couture, *Ridout and Weinzweig.

The ten panels at the conference discussed composers' concerns: serialism, electronic music, form, composer-training, aesthetics, sociology, and composer-performer-audience relations. Papers were given by Luciano Berio (Italy), Henri Dutilleux (France), Luigi Nono (Italy), George Rochberg (USA), and Vladimir Ussachevsky (USA), and by the San Francisco critic Alfred Frankenstein. The book *The Modern Composer and His World* (Toronto 1961), edited by John Beckwith and Udo Kasemets, gives an account of the proceedings and excerpts from the discussions.

BIBLIOGRAPHY
Duchow, Marvin. 'International Conference of Composers at Stratford,' *CMJ*, vol 5, Autumn 1960 (CF)

International Music Store Ltd. Establishment specializing in printed music and located on Ste-Catherine St West in Montreal. A store was opened in 1913 on Drummond St as the International Music Shop, under the management of Martin Hufnagel. The name was changed to International Music Store in 1916. After the Irishman Frank Ramsperger acquired it in 1922, the store began selling radios, phonographs, and musical instruments. With the help of his sons Leo and Fred, Ramsperger expanded the printed music section (which included teaching material), managed by Leo, and the record section, managed by Fred. (The latter closed his section in April 1977 and moved to Toronto.) In the 1940s and 1950s there were studios with pianos for rent. The store was thus a meeting place for musicians, including Billy *Eckstein and Arthur *LeBlanc. The business was managed in 1980 by Leo Ramsperger. It was proud to be able to name among its former employees Norma Shearer, the actress; Yvan Dufresne, director of the record company Discotel; and Terence McEwen, the former artistic director of the classical section of London records, a regular panelist on the intermissions of the *Metropolitan Opera radio broadcasts, and appointed in 1979 to succeed Kurt Herbert Adler in 1982 as general director of the San Francisco Opera. The printed music department, which in 1978 had over a million scores of classical works in stock, was described at that time as one of the largest in Canada.

BIBLIOGRAPHY
Rodriguez, Juan. 'Goodbye to International's record half,' Montreal *Gazette*, 30 Apr 1977
Finlay, Dennis. 'This store knows the score,' *Montreal Scene*, Oct 1977 GP

International Week of Today's Music / La Semaine internationale de musique actuelle. Organized within the framework of the *Montreal Festivals and held 3-8 Aug 1961 in Montreal at the Théâtre de la Comédie-Canadienne (later Théâtre du Nouveau-Monde) and at Redpath Hall, *McGill U.

Pierre *Mercure was its guiding spirit and animating force. An extended visit to the Centre de recherches audio-visuelles of the RTF, Paris, frequent contacts with Pierre Schaeffer, Luc Ferrari, Michel P. Philippot, and Iannis Xenakis, and the impact of the spirit which then enlivened New York's music and dance scene encouraged Mercure to organize a festival based on three principles: the music heard was to be of the present, to link itself closely with the visual arts, and to represent faithfully experimental trends throughout the world.

John Cage was asked to write a work, and the result, his *Atlas Eclipticalis*, was premiered 3 Aug 1961 under Cage's direction. Serge *Garant's **Anerca* also had its premiere, with the soprano Claire *Grenon-Masella as soloist.

In the program, the names of *Anhalt and Mercure were found alongside those of such foreign composers as Babbitt, Behram, Kotónski, Ligeti, Maxfield, Nono, Penderecki, Schaeffer, Stockhausen, Varèse, and Wolff, in addition to those present as speakers (Brown, Feldman, Nikolais), conductors (Cage, Kagel), or performers (Ichiyanagi, Yoko Ono). The pianist David Tudor also was a participant.

Disoriented at having to modify drastically their concept of musical sound, neither the audience nor the press welcomed the festival warmly. Nevertheless the event brought to Canada some new sounds, little-known composers, and challenging interpretive artists. Although it had no immediate sequel, it nevertheless paved the way and created a favourable climate for the foundation of the *SMCQ five years later.

In *La Presse* (8 Aug 1961) Claude *Gingras wrote: 'In all this "music" heard in five concerts there is surely both some value and some deliberate mystification. It is too early to separate the two. It is too easy to laugh and it would be ridiculous to want to make a firm judgment. Only time will be the judge. Perhaps it will be necessary to find new definitions to the words "art," "music," "dance," "beauty," "balance," "taste".'

BIBLIOGRAPHY
Richer-Lortie, Lyse. 'La Semaine internationale de musique actuelle,' *Compositeurs au Quebec: Pierre Mercure*, CMCentre (Montreal 1976) LR-L

Inuit. The music of the Inuit (or Eskimo as other peoples have called them) of Alaska, Arctic Canada, and Greenland falls into two broad categories: songs and dances which formed a traditional and integral part of the nomadic life of this hunting society and modern European- or North-American-influenced songs and dances which, in some central-Canadian areas, began only in the 1960s or 1970s. Contact between outsiders and natives has varied in duration from the approximately 200 years of interaction between Moravians and Inuit in Labrador communities, such as Nain, to the relatively new relationships created by the establishment of government administrations in certain Netsilik settlements in the 1960s. By the 1970s most Inuit lived in settlements during part or all of the year; however, they continued to rely on land and sea animals for food and, occasionally, for clothing and tools. The degree of retention, or in some cases revival, of traditional music has varied considerably from one area to another.

1 Style areas
2 Dance songs and rituals
3 Other traditional musical genres
4 Acculturation

1 STYLE AREAS. A blossoming of scholarly interest in Inuit music took place during the 1970s, and, although much remained to be done before definitive statements about style areas and their relationships could be made, knowledge of the subject increased immeasurably. One thing which became apparent was the diversity of customs, terminology, and styles, not only in different culture groups, but from one community to the next. Nevertheless, several broad culture areas have been identified, from west to east: the Inupiaq-speaking Inuit of north Alaska; the Yupik-speaking people of south Alaska; the Yukon and Mackenzie Delta Inuit; the Copper, Netsilik, Caribou, and Iglulik Inuit of the central Arctic; and the Inuit of Baffinland, northern Quebec, and Labra-

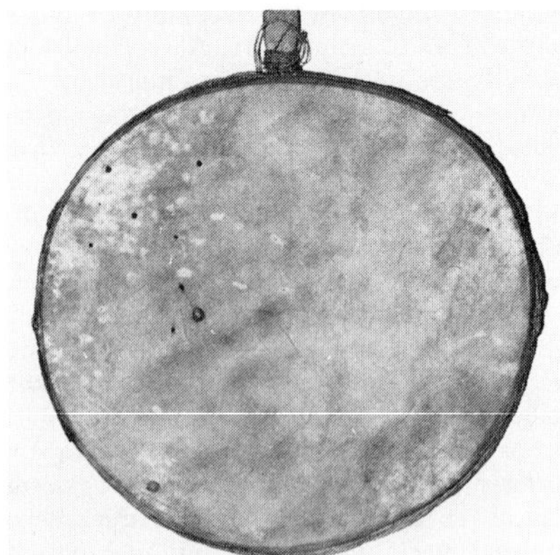

An Inuit drum

dor. In Greenland are the Polar Inuit of the Thule district and the west and east Greenlanders. Although *EMC* limits itself to consideration of music in Canada, this article will contain references to Inuit in Alaska and Greenland for comparison and because style and language often cross official borders. It should be borne in mind that of the 90,000 Inuit known to exist in 1980, only 22,000 were on Canadian territory.

2 DANCE SONGS AND RITUALS. Almost every culture group held periodic celebrations which featured dancing to the accompaniment of monophonic chanting and the beating of a single-headed frame drum. The practice of drum dancing has ceased in northern Quebec and Labrador, but 19th-century ethnographers (eg, Lucien M. Turner, *Indians and Eskimos in the Quebec-Labrador Peninsula*, Quebec 1979 [1894], p 160-2) report the use of drums in an earlier period in those areas, and it has survived in other areas.

Two basic types of drum are used. West of the Mackenzie Delta a narrow (ca 4 cm) wooden frame is covered, usually with a whale-liver covering or walrus-stomach membrane; the drum is held by a notched wooden handle and beaten with a long slender stick. Two distinct timbres can be produced, one by a light stroke which touches only the drum frame, and the second by a harder action which hits both frame and drum simultaneously. In the central and eastern regions a larger frame drum (often up to 40 cm in diameter) is used. This instrument, called the kilaut, has a heavier wooden frame, approximately 8 cm in width, and a caribou-skin cover.

In western regions drums usually are played in groups of two or more, each by a man who sits, with straight back and outstretched legs, to the side of the dance area. Drum rhythms can be quite complex, eg, in 5/8 meters or heterometric configurations (examples of the former may be seen in transcriptions in Johnston *Eskimo Music by Region*, p 196-215).

Groups of dancers, often wearing loonskin head-dresses or special dance mittens and in some areas using dance-fans, perform mimetic actions depicting hunting scenes, animal behaviour, or mythical episodes. A special women's dance (*taliq*) in northwest Alaska imitates paddling. In northwest Alaska, the dances are classified as either *atuutipiaq* (using improvised motions) or *sayuun* (using fixed motions), and these terms also apply to the songs composed for each dance type. Both types are performed at an 'inviting-in,' when visitors travel to other communities for several days of feasting and dance competition. Other Alaskan ceremonial dance songs, many of them associated with local whaling feasts and some regarded as secret, include whalers' spinning-top

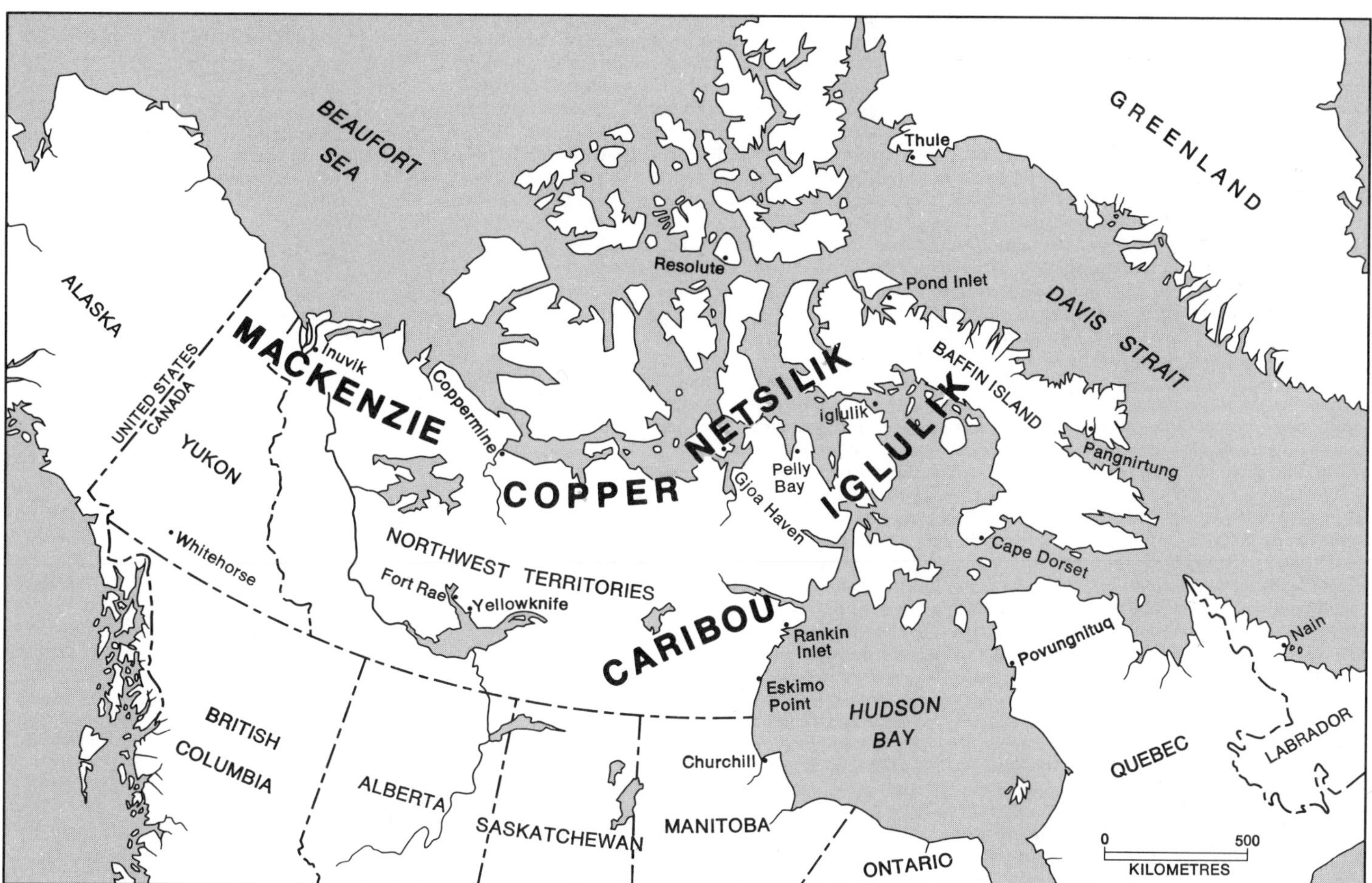

The main Inuit cultural groups and settlements

dance songs (*kiapsaq*), puppet ceremony dance songs (*tohoyaqhuuqaun*), whalers' masquerade dance songs (*uingarung*), Northern Lights dance songs (*kigugiyataun*), box-drum dance songs (*kalukhaq*), and the commonly recorded whalers' skin-toss dance songs (*nalukataun*). The last-named type comprises humorous pieces which accompany the tossing of a contestant into the air using a skin blanket. (All the types are described in Johnston, p 69–76.)

The Mackenzie Delta and Coppermine River Delta peoples share many of the customs of the Alaskans. However, the solo drum dance of the central Arctic is found also among the Copper Inuit. This dance uses the large frame drum or *kilaut* (described previously), played by a solo dancer who strikes it alternately on each side of the frame with a club-like stick (*katuk*) while turning the drum from side to side. The drum-dancer flexes his/her knees and rotates the head and shoulders. In some communities both men and women drum dance, but in others the activity is restricted to men. The drum rhythm is a constant, although somewhat uneven, pulse, often at a slightly different tempo from the accompanying song. Various community members (often exclusively women) constitute a chorus which chants a lyric or narrative song (*pisiq*) composed by the dancer or a relative or friend.

In former times the drum dance occurred when large numbers of people came together (to celebrate the arrival of visitors, for example, or at the time of the annual winter sea-ice camp among the Netsilik people). A dancer might have an *idluriit* or song cousin, often a person from another community, with whom he would carry on a friendly rivalry by an exchange of mocking songs. Such song contests were sometimes followed by fisticuffs or other competitive games. Events were less structured than in the western areas. In the 1970s drum dances were social celebrations, held periodically throughout the year in some communities (eg, Eskimo Point, Pelly Bay) but most frequently at Christmas and Easter. Shamanistic associations with drum dancing (see the illustration in Pelinski, *Inuit Songs from Eskimo Point*, p 9, for example) were no longer maintained, although the vocabulary of song texts included ancient words and phrases associated with the shaman (*angakuq*).

In Greenland drum dance songs have been collected from both north and east Greenlanders, each group using a small membrane-covered frame drum as an accompaniment. Songs are performed for entertainment, for shamanistic ritual, and for 'drum-fights.' The latter, bearing similarities to the central Canadian song contests, were performed by two antagonists who would face each other in a somewhat aggressive posture and, in turn, sing mocking songs about each other. In north Greenland a small stick would be rotated in front of the dancer's face to mark the end of a drum song. The east Greenlanders perform comic drum songs (*uvajernaq*) in which a stick is held in the mouth, stretching the cheeks out and thus changing the vocal quality.

In traditional Inuit society the location for drum dance celebrations varied from one area to the next. Photographs of Greenland drum fights (Thuren, 'On the Eskimo music in Greenland,' figures 4 and 5) depict outdoor settings; on the other hand, taboos on outdoor performances were in force in some central Canadian areas. In many regions a special dance house called a *qaggi* or *kashim* was erected. In Alaska it was a large storage house with an entrance that was tunnelled under the floor (M. Lantis, 'The social culture of the Nunivak Eskimo,' *Transactions of the American Philosophical Society*, 1946, p 35). In the central region it was a large snow house capable of accommodating 50 or 60 people; in the Netsilik region, family igloos were appended to the large dome. Food from the hunt was apportioned here; games and acrobatics took place as well as dancing activities. After prefabricated buildings replaced traditional snow or canvas structures, dances came to be held in schools, community halls, or private homes.

The textual and musical style of drum dance songs is variable from one region to another. Polar Inuit song texts consist almost exclusively of vocables (see transcriptions in Leden, 1952, and Hauser, 'Former structure in Polar Eskimo drum-songs,' *Ethnomusicology*, 1977, p 34), while Caribou Inuit texts have short, meaningful stanzas (see transcriptions in Pelinski) and Netsilik songs are long narrations, most often about hunting adventures (see Cavanagh, 1979, vol 2). Most songs are strophic, each strophe containing a texted stanza (except for untexted Polar songs) and a refrain on vocables such as 'ajaijai ...' Because of these refrains, a drum dance song often is called an *ajaijai* instead of a *pisiq*.

Most melodies are anhemitonic (without semitones) pentatonic, although divergent tonal structures are found within this category. In most areas the melodies contain a common body of formula-like motives which are used in various combinations. Actual intervallic patterns are regionally variable; in the Netsilik region, for example, ascending large intervals and descending major seconds and minor thirds within the range of a minor seventh are common, while in Alaska, wider ranges and interval leaps up to a ninth have been noted by Johnston (p 11). Analytical data about specific tonal types and melodic material have been used by Hauser to trace migration patterns from south Baffin Island to northern Greenland. Most repertoires involve some microtonal ornamentation and flexible intonation areas.

The songs have pulse but very little accentuation or repetition of rhythmic patterns. In the western area the drum beats coincide with song pulses and hence provide a metric organization, while in the eastern Arctic and Greenland the drum tempo is often independent of the song tempo.

While the drum dance repertoire is basically monophonic, polyphony (often in parallel but variable intervals) is common (see Estreicher, 1950, and Pelinski) in the Caribou Inuit region.

3 OTHER TRADITIONAL MUSICAL GENRES. Among the unique sonic creations of Inuit culture are the throat games (*katajjait* in northern Quebec, *pigusiraqtut* in the Iglulik area) performed by pairs of women in the central and eastern Arctic. The partners stand or squat, facing one another at a close distance (from a few centimeters to about 15), and enter into a rapid interchange of rhythmicized noises, both voiced and unvoiced, combined with audible breathing. In some areas (eg, Netsilik), a text underlies each game, while in other regions (eg, northern Quebec) the sounds are non-referential and the delight is in their timbre. Some games imitate animal calls; some outline the pitches of familiar songs, although precise pitch is unimportant in the majority. A kettle, bread pan, parka hood, or other object may be used to reflect or channel the sound towards the partner. A competitive spirit often is evident between teams (see Beaudry). Excellent examples of *katajjait* may be heard on the Philips Unesco recording *Inuit games and songs*.

Other games are accompanied by special songs. The most widely known are the juggling songs (*iglukisaak* in northwest Alaska, *iglukitarut* in central Arctic Canada). Fragments from myths, obscene references, children's rhymes, and vocables are juxtaposed in these texts without regard for continuity of thought. The melodies consist of a concatenation of two- or three-note motives, each usually repeated several times: aaa... bbb... ccc... etc. In some areas (the Iglulik region, Baffin Island, and Alaska, for example) songs are used to accompany cat's cradle or string games. Most communities also have a small repertoire of songs to accompany indigenous variations of hide-and-seek, hopping, or chasing games.

Another traditional genre are songs which form part of stories. These include descriptions of the adventures of legendary figures such as Kiviuq or Kautjajuq and short (usually only one stanza) songs attributed to humanized animals and birds. Some of the latter mock the appearance or activities of other creatures in a manner similar to the contest songs at the drum dance. A unique feature is the incorporation of words and musical motives which represent the cries of the various animals or birds. Story songs may be performed partially or completely in rhythmicized speech, although relative pitch usually is present. Where precise pitches are used, the ranges are relatively limited, and many tone reiterations are a feature. Scales of only two or three pitches are not uncommon.

As in all cultures, stories and story songs are used at children's bedtime. Some areas have specific lullabies (*aqausit* or *maksatuq*). In addition there are in east Greenland short, affectionate songs known as petting songs. A woman will frequently dedicate a petting song to each child in the family; this is not unlike the central Canadian tradition of composing a drum dance song for one's family members.

Although, as stated above, the links between music and shamanism are not readily accessible in present-day Christian settlements, there are many factors which point to the use of music in almost forgotten rituals. Magic songs have been collected in Greenland and in the Iglulik area. Entire shamanistic rituals have been recorded in east Greenland.

4 ACCULTURATION. Where traditional music has endured, the style of the traditional genres has undergone very little change as a result of contact with European and North American cultures, although the location and events with which specific songs and dances are associated have changed. It is not surprising that traditional music is remembered mostly by the elderly. A renaissance of interest has occurred throughout the Arctic in the 1970s, however, as part of the quest for an Inuit identity and in conjunction with Land Claims negotiations. Pan-Arctic meetings such as the annual Arctic Games, of which competitive dancing forms a part, have stimulated a revival of traditions. Areas such as western Greenland and Labrador, which have had the longest contact with European-based society, have perpetuated little traditional music.

The most marked results of culture contact, however, may be seen in the adoption of new instruments, dance, and song styles. Hymns translated into Inuktitut (the Inuit language) probably are the most widely known of the foreign musics. More adaptation of style has occurred in the secular domain. The jigs and reels of 19th-century whalers and explorers, for example, have been modified into forms called 'Eskimo dance' in many communities, and the accordion music used to accompany these may be known as 'Eskimo music' (see Lutz, p 119). Fiddles (*agiarut* or *tautirut*) inspired homemade imitations in northern Quebec; these generally were simple boxes with three strings. In the same area, some Inuit have become skilful jew's harp players; a similar technique of vibrating the quill against the teeth is used to play a feather in Povungnituq. The Labrador community of Nain has maintained a band which was established by Moravian missionaries before the middle of the 19th century. (See Moravian missions in Labrador.)

Certain secular genres directly imitate their southern models. Popular with the younger members of the community are country and western or folk-style songs for voice and guitar, composed in Inuktitut by increasingly numerous groups of Inuit musicians. In Canada the best known of the 'folk' composers is Charlie Panagoniaq of Eskimo Point. Local dance bands (examples of the Pangnirtung band are recorded on the disc which accompanies Lutz' 1978 study) have become common in many communities.

DISCOGRAPHY

The Eskimos of Hudson Bay and Alaska. Recorded by Laura Boulton. 1954. Folk FE 4444

Innuit Throat Singing from Cape Dorset. North West Territories. (1980). Music Gallery Editions MGE 28

Recordings are included in the Lutz and Pelinski publications listed below.

GENERAL BIBLIOGRAPHY

Boas, Franz. *The Central Eskimo*, 6th annual *Report* of the Bureau of American Ethnology (Washington, DC, 1888), repr (Lincoln, Neb, 1964)

Thalbitzer, William, and Thuren, Hjalmar. 'Melodies from East Greenland,' *Meddelelser om Grønland*, vol 40, no. 2, 1911

Thuren, Hjalmar. 'On the Eskimo music in Greenland,' ibid

Roberts, Helen, and Jenness, Diamond. 'Songs of the Copper Eskimos,' *Report of the Canadian Arctic Expedition, 1913–16*, vol 14 (Ottawa 1925)

Rasmussen, Knud. *Report of the Fifth Thule Expedition, 1921–1924*, vols 7–9 (Copenhagen 1927–45)

Lantis, Margaret. *Alaskan Eskimo Ceremonialism* (New York 1947)

Estreicher, Zygmunt. 'Die Musik der Eskimos: Eine vergleichende Studie,' *Anthropos*, vol 45, p 659–720, 1950

Leden, Christian. 'Über die Musik der Smith Sund Eskimo,' 'Über die Musik der Ostgrönlander,' *Meddelelser om Grønland*, vol 152, parts 3 and 4, 1952

Estreicher, Zygmunt. 'Eskimo-Musik,' *MGG*, vol 3

Groven, Eivind. *Eskimo melodies fra Alaska* (Oslo 1956)

Okpik, Abraham, and Spalding, Alex. 'Eskimo drum dance ceremony to be a feature at Dawson Festival,' *OpCan*, May–Jun 1962

Olsen, Poul Rovsing. 'Intervals and rhythm in the music of the Eskimos of East Greenland,' *Proceedings of the Centennial Workshop in Ethnomusicology*, ed Peter Crossley-Holland (Vancouver 1968)

Cavanagh, Beverley. 'Annotated bibliography: Eskimo music,' *Ethnomusicology*, vol 16, Sep 1972

– 'Imagery and structure in Eskimo song texts,' *CFMJ*, vol 1, 1973

– 'Some throat games of Netsilik Eskimo women,' ibid, vol 4, 1976

Estreicher, Zygmunt. 'Esquimaux,' *Science de la musique*, vol 1, ed Marc Honegger (Paris 1976)

Johnston, Thomas. *Eskimo Music by Region: A Comparative Circumpolar Study* (Ottawa 1976)

Beaudry, Nicole. 'Le Katajjaq, un jeu inuit traditionnel,' *Inuit Studies*, vol 2, no. 1, 1978

Hauser, Michael. 'Inuit songs from Southwest Baffin Island in cross-cultural context,' ibid, 2 parts, vol 2, no. 1 and 2, 1978

Lutz, Maija. *The Effects of Acculturation on Eskimo Music of Cumberland Peninsula* (Ottawa 1978). Includes a recording

Cavanagh, Beverley. 'The music of the Netsilik Eskimo: a study of stability and change,' unpubl PH D thesis, U of Toronto 1979

Pelinski, Ramón et al. *Inuit Songs from Eskimo Point* (Ottawa 1979). Includes a recording

Beaudry, Nicole. 'Arctic throat-games: a contest of song,' *PfAC*, Fall 1980

BAC

Inventions and devices

1 Instruments, invented and improved
2 Teaching devices and curiosities

See also Carillons; Electronic music; Harpsichord building; Mechanical instruments; Organ building; Piano building. See also Heintzman & Co and entries for individual instrument manufacturers.

1 INSTRUMENTS, INVENTED AND IMPROVED. Among 19th-century Canadian inventors were James P. *Clarke (ca 1807–77), said to have built an organ with glass tubes which he claimed afforded greater possibilities for tonal variations, and Roch *Lyonnais (1849–1921), who experimented with instruments between 1865 and 1880. Salluste Duval (ca 1857–1917), a chemist, medical doctor, and organist, invented an adjustable organ pedal which began to be used in *Casavant organs in 1884. In 1892 the Casavants built their first electropneumatic organs. One of these was installed in the Ottawa Basilica and another in the Parish Church of Notre-Dame-du-Rosaire at St-Hyacinthe, Que. Morse *Robb of Belleville, Ont, invented an electronic 'wave organ' in 1927, several years before such builders as Hammond produced similar instruments. During the mid-1930s, Oswald *Michaud, a piano technician and acoustics specialist in Montreal, invented and patented an electric piano which he called the Sonobel. In place of a sounding board the Sonobel had near the strings electro-magnets which passed vibra-

tions through an amplifier to a loudspeaker. Though well received the Sonobel was overshadowed by the electronic organ. The two Sonobel prototypes were retained by Michaud's granddaughter. A more recent keyboard invention is the Shaw Concept Organ. Built by Neil Shaw of Burlington, Ont, it features 54 stops and 285 audio channels. Valued at over $100,000, it has been heard in concert and has been rented out on occasion. Also of interest is the monophonic (that is, capable of producing only one note at a time) electronic 'sackbut' invented by the noted physicist Hugh *Le Caine in 1945. Le Caine later invented an instrument which he called the Pauliphone and which was capable of playing two or more notes at once.

2 TEACHING DEVICES AND CURIOSITIES. One of the first music-teaching devices to be patented in Canada was T.F. *Molt's Chromatometer (1832), a box with a sounding board, strings, a movable bridge, and a damper which, with the turn of a knob, produced sounds, chromatically measured. Later in the century William *Bohrer advertised an automatic hand guide for the piano and Pierre-Minier *Lagacé developed a system of musical shorthand – 'Méthode de sténographie musicale,' now deposited at the *Séminaire de Québec. Hugh A. *Clarke tried unsuccessfully for many years to perfect a musical typewriter. On 31 Oct 1900 the *Musical Courier* reported that Laura McLaren of Ottawa had patented a music teacher's device, 'one of the objects of which is to represent to the mind of the pupil a visual embodiment of the construction of scales and their tones and semi-tones.' This was typical of many visual aids devised by teachers: the Cournoyer Musical Ruler, devised by Georges Cournoyer, which won a gold medal at the Salon Mondial des inventions, Brussels, 1976; the Melecci Scales and Chords Builder (mid-1940s), a slide rule invented by Adelmo *Melecci (then principal of the Willowdale Branch of the RCMT); and the several inventions of the Saskatchewan music educator Rj *Staples, including a scale and chord pattern ruler, a chord indicator, and a record indicator, the last of which could locate and isolate any particular selection on a recording (78 rpm). To encourage children's interest in string music, Staples also designed a simplified cello. The Musicographe Liessens, invented by Auguste *Liessens and perfected in 1946, is an instrument which allows the blind to write down music for the use of people who have sight. It has been distributed in many countries.

The Magnetic Board, a magnetic blackboard with painted staves holding movable notational units, was invented by Meier Podolak (b Poland 1904) soon after his arrival in Toronto ca 1952. The device, which made possible the photographing of page after page of perfectly designed musical notation, was much employed by Canadian and US music publishers. After Podolak's retirement in 1974, the blackboard was used for a short time by a firm in London, Ont, then fell into disuse.

Valuable devices for keyboard teaching include Hervé Lemay's 'tableau électronique' (ca 1964) and David *Ouchterlony's Multiple Student Keyboard (early 1960s). Responding to a request by the Baldwin Piano Co for a display board which could be used in conjunction with its electropiano (ie, teaching piano), Lemay, a member of the Frères du Sacré-Coeur in Bromptonville, Que, designed a display screen with visible staves and notes which lit up when played. Though never patented, five of these devices were built, the second and third with consoles for the programming of scales. They found purchasers in Sherbrooke (the *Écoles Sacré-Coeur and Mitchell), Gaspé, and Quebec City.

Ouchterlony's Multiple Student Keyboard (used at the Timothy Eaton Memorial Choir School in Toronto and at the RCMT) comprises several individual electronic keyboards, all of which feed into a central control board equipped with tiny lights representing hundreds of notes, and a sound system which can be turned on or off. By means of lights, the teacher can remain stationary and even without hearing can detect students' errors. Four of these systems, which can be used for teaching elementary composition as well as theory, were built by the Allen Organ Co of Allentown, Penn.

Records of patented inventions and devices may be checked through the Patents Office in Ottawa; unfortunately no subject index of patents had been published by 1980.

BIBLIOGRAPHY

Major, Henriette. 'La musique rendue facile par ... la règle à calcul,' *Perspectives*, 24 Apr 1976

IÖSCH-LORCINI, Marie (Emma) (b Iösch, m Lorcini). Harpist, teacher, b Montreal 1 Jan 1930; premier prix harp (CMM) 1951. She is the daughter of the cellist Marthe *Delcellier and the violinist Pierre Iösch, who were members of the *Montreal Orchestra, the *MSO, and the *Little Symphony of Montreal. She studied piano 1940–3 at the École supérieure de musique in Outremont (*École Vincent-d'Indy) with Sister Rita de la Croix, obtaining her diploma with high distinction. She then turned to the harp, which she studied 1943–51 at the *CMM under Marcel Grandjany. A regular harpist with the MSO 1946–69, she made her debut as soloist with that orchestra in Ravel's *Introduction et Allegro* (1954). In 1952 in Toronto she premiered Harry *Somers' *Suite* for harp and chamber orchestra, a work she repeated in the 1953 NFB film *Rehearsal* and at the 1955 *Stratford Festival. She took part in the premieres of Jean *Papineau-Couture's *Pièce concertante no. 3* in 1959 with the MSO and Michel *Perrault's *Jeux de quartes* in 1961 on the CBC. In 1961 she appeared at the *International Week of Today's Music which was presented as part of the *Montreal Festivals. While continuing to perform in numerous CBC broadcasts ('Divertissement,' 'L'*Heure du concert,' *'The Little Symphonies,' etc), she taught harp 1960–9 at the École Vincent-d'Indy. Moving to London, Ont, in 1969, she became principal harp in the *Hamilton Philharmonic Orchestra and of the *London SO and Sinfonia. She has given recitals throughout Ontario, has played in the orchestras of the *Guelph and *Stratford festivals, has performed for *NMC in Toronto, and has taught at the *U of Western Ontario. In 1978, with the flutist Paula Elliott, she premiered Jean Anderson's *Six Country Sketches* in Guelph, Ont.

See Discographies for the Montreal Bach Choir, MSO, and Geoffrey Waddington.

BIBLIOGRAPHY

Musiciennes de chez nous AP

IRELAND, Margaret Ann (m Carter, m Nagel). Pianist, producer, b Winnipeg 23 Mar 1928. Her teachers included Hayunga *Carman at the TCM 1939–45, Mieczyslaw Horszowski in New York 1945–50, Friedrich Wuehrer in Salzburg and Vienna in 1951, and Marguerite Long in Paris in 1952. After her debut 5 Dec 1944 with the *TSO she gave lecture recitals 1949–52 for CBC radio and toured as a recitalist and broadcaster several times in Europe and twice (1960 and 1962) in the USSR. She made her New York debut at Town Hall in 1963. Her repertoire included works by Robert *Fleming, Oskar *Morawetz (who dedicated his *Fantasy in D Minor* to her), and Arnold *Walter. She withdrew from performance in 1967 and joined CBC Toronto in 1969 as a producer. Under the name of Margaret Ireland she prepared such radio programs as 'Afternoon Concert' and 'Music Heritage.' Her series 'Musicscope' (1971–2) received a Major Armstrong Award (Chicago, 1972). In 1972 she moved to New York as a freelance broadcaster. Her documentaries on Marian Anderson and Artur Rubinstein in 1973 and on Jascha Heifetz in 1974, and her 13-week series 'The Life and Times of Igor Stravinsky' in 1976, have been broadcast on CBC radio. In 1976 she became a production consultant to the Broadcasting Foundation of America.

DISCOGRAPHY

Chopin *Sonata, Op 35* – Tansman *Suite dans le style ancien* – Szymanowski 4 *Mazurkas*. 1964. Cap SW 6065

Schubert *Impromptus, Op 90* – Rachmaninoff 6 *Preludes* from *Op 23*. 1963. Cap SW 6058

Villa-Lobos 'Ciclo Brasileiro' from *Bachianas Brasileiras* – Granados 'Suite' from *Goyescas*. 1963. Cap SW 6057

BIBLIOGRAPHY

Crandall, Ev. 'Margaret Ireland: musician-producer,' *Sound*, vol 2, Nov 1971 MMI

Ireland. The Irish component in the population of Canada is the fourth largest (after French, English, and Scottish) and one of the oldest. Irish fishermen settled in Newfoundland in the early 17th century. By the mid-18th century that island had some 5000 Roman Catholic Irish inhabitants – about one-third of its population. There were Irish among those who founded Halifax in 1749. The United Empire Loyalists who moved to Nova Scotia and New Brunswick after 1776 included many of Irish descent. The famine in Ireland during the early 19th century sent thousands of Irish farmers to Upper Canada (Ontario). By 1871 the Irish were the second largest ethnic group in Canada (after the French); in 1950 there were 1,500,000 Irish, catholic and protestant.

Music of Irish composers has not been performed widely in Canada save for the songs of Dowland, the choral music and songs of C.V. Stanford and Charles Wood, a few of the piano pieces of John Field, and occasional performances of the light operas (notably *The Bohemian Girl*) of Michael Balfe. Huguette *Tourangeau has recorded some arias of Balfe, Lois *Marshall some of Thomas Moore's Irish melodies. The main musical contribution of the Irish to Canada, however, has been to folk music, and predominantly as an influence on Anglo-Canadian songs, though its effect on the repertoire of French-Canada's violoneux will be discussed also.

1 Folk music
2 Traditions
3 Musicians

1 FOLK MUSIC. The Irish influence is notable especially in Newfoundland, where the Irish pronunciation is obvious in such songs as 'I'se the B'y That Builds the Boat.' As Elisabeth Greenleaf noted: 'Folk-song in Newfoundland owes a great debt to the people of Irish descent. They have a genius for music and learn not only the Irish songs but any other lovely airs they hear and they render them most sweetly. I am inclined to credit the Irish with a large share in keeping the Newfoundland folk music so melodious' (*Ballads and Sea Songs of Newfoundland*, Cambridge 1933). The influence is almost equally important in Ontario, where the areas around Peterborough and the Ottawa Valley, settled by Irish, have provided the

province's richest sources of folksong. In New Brunswick, James Reginald Wilson noted, 'Most of the Miramichi tunes are in the Irish folk tradition though many of our singers are of Scottish and English descent' (*Songs of Miramichi*, Fredericton 1968).

The Irish influence shows itself in the large percentage of Irish ballads and songs in the repertoire of Canadian traditional singers, and in the fact that the words of most native Anglo-Canadian folksongs are set to Irish tunes and follow Irish verse patterns. Moreover, persons of Irish descent are persistent in the preservation and circulation of their traditional songs.

Remarkable numbers of Irish ballads turn up in all Anglo-Canadian collections, proclaiming their origin with titles such as 'Patrick Sheehan,' 'The Croppy Boy,' 'The True Paddy's Song,' 'Old Erin Far Away,' 'Erin's Lovely Home,' 'Erin's Green Shore,' 'Groyle Machree,' 'Pat O'Brien,' 'The Lovely Banks of the Boyne,' 'Erin's Flowery Vale,' and 'The Bonny Young Irish Boy.' Quite a few describe the adventures of young men named Riley ('Riley's Farewell,' 'William Riley's Courtship,' 'Riley's Trial,' 'John Riley,' and 'Young Riley'); others reflect the Irish sympathy for Napoleon ('The Plains of Waterloo,' The Bonnie Bunch of Roses,' 'The Green Linnet,' and 'Napoleon's Farewell to Paris'); still others tell humorous tales first aired in Irish music halls ('Finnegan's Wake,' 'Doran's Ass,' 'Courting in the Kitchen,' and 'The Irish Wake').

Among the native Canadian ballads, nearly all of those about sea voyages and shipwrecks, life in the lumbercamps, and tragic accidents in the woods or on the rivers are cast in the typical Irish 'come-all-ye' pattern. This stereotyped form, simple to compose and easy to remember, was well established in Irish song by the end of the 18th century and soon spread through the English-speaking world. It consists of four-line stanzas with seven stresses to each line – sometimes referred to as double stanzas in that they are twice the length of the common ballad stanza used in the older Child ballads (see Ballads). The tunes are usually in 6/8 time and the structure is usually ABBA. As the name suggests, the texts normally begin with some such invocation as 'Come all ye young sailors and listen to me,' or 'Come all you jolly shanty boys wherever you may be.' The rhyme pattern usually is AABB but can vary, especially when it makes use of the characteristic Irish internal rhyme:

> Oh it's by the hush me *boys*, I'm sure that's to hold your *noise*
> And listen to poor Paddy's narration.
> I was by hunger *pressed* and by poverty *distressed*
> So I took a thought I'd leave the Irish nation.

It also was common for traditional singers in Canada to speak the last word or phrase of a song – a pattern borrowed from Ireland. The practice is so characteristic of lumbercamp singers (eg, in Ontario) that some folklorists have assumed it originated with them, but actually it turns up wherever Irish traditions predominate. Elisabeth Greenleaf (ibid) noted, 'It was a perfectly familiar convention to a Newfoundland audience.'

Canadian instrumental folk music is in debt to Ireland, especially for that most important of genres, oldtime fiddling (see Fiddling). Many traditional fiddle tunes popular in Canada are of Irish origin. The Ottawa Valley fiddling style, with its Irish roots, has had a wide influence through the playing of Graham *Townsend and others. Irish tunes and styles are popular also in Quebec; Jean *Carignan took as one of his models the great Irish fiddler Michael Coleman, and has been recognized as the world's leading exponent of Coleman's unique 'Sligo' style. The Irish-born fiddlers Manus and Seamus McGuire of Hamilton, Ont, also play in the Sligo style.

Irish folksongs and dances form a part (directly or indirectly) of the repertoire of the 1970s pop groups Barde, Garolou, and Le Rêve du diable (all of Quebec) and Figgy Duff (of Newfoundland), and of many singers. Carol Brothers, in the 1960s a star on the CBC St John's TV show 'All Around the Circle,' and Charlie Chamberlain of Don *Messer's Islanders made LPs of Irish songs, and Harry *Hibbs, John White, and other Newfoundland singers have popularized Irish traditional material.

2 TRADITIONS. Much Irish music is played in Canada on St Patrick's Day (17 March), and in 1866 and 1867 the Irish community of Montreal built a St Patrick's Hall on Victoria Square. It was the site of many musical occasions, Irish and other, including an appearance in 1872 by Rosa d'Erina, the 'Queen of Irish song.' The hall was destroyed by fire in 1872.

The Irish Choral Society of Toronto, an adult choir of 55–70 voices, was formed in 1960 by Father Peter Fleming (its director until 1970). It performed at *Expo 67 and toured Ireland in 1968. In 1970 some members broke away to form the Irish Gaelic Singers conducted by Richard Scanlon. Comhaltas ceoltoiri Eireann, a society established in Ireland to preserve traditional music, has branches in Ottawa, Montreal, Toronto and Vancouver. The Ottawa group holds a monthly gathering, known as celidhe, for informal music making. 'Celidhe' also was the name of a CBC TV variety show (summers 1974 and 1975; winter 1975–6) devoted to Irish music.

3 MUSICIANS. Though there do not appear to have been great numbers of Irish-born or Irish-descended professional musicians in Canada, it is difficult to trace such persons because of the name changes resulting from intermarriage, or because of the similarity between Irish and Anglo-Saxon surnames. Oscar *O'Brien and Paul-Émile *McCaughan, for instance, were French-Canadian, while Claude *Champagne was of Irish descent on his mother's side. (Healey *Willan, who claimed an Irish 'streak,' had no Irish ancestry discernible in his family tree.)

Among those musicians identifiable as Irish are Richard *Bulkeley (who arrived in 1749); Arthur Corry, who established a musical academy in 1822 in Saint John, NB; John *McCaul (1839); a number of Irish nuns from upper-class families in Dublin and Cork, who went in the 1840s to teach in Newfoundland and included music in their classes; Alexander O'Donovan (1843), a one-time teacher at Carlow College, Ireland, who settled in Carbonear, Nfld, where he organized a band of some 40 players and was said to have composed sonatas; Henry Francis *Sefton (1858); Thomas *Persse (1862); the brothers C.A. and G.B. *Sippi (1865 and 1870 respectively), who, though of Italian descent and Indian birth, were raised in Ireland; Arthur A. *Clappé (1877); Doreen *Hall (1921); Eileen *Law and Jim *Magill (1930s); Sydney Bryans, conductor 1960–6 of the *Winnipeg Philharmonic Choir; Norman *Nelson (1965) and members of such pop groups as Barde, Barley Bree, the *Carlton Showband, the *Irish Rovers, Larry McKee and the Shandonairs, and Ryan's Fancy. The last-named group, formed ca 1970 by Denis Ryan, Dermot O'Reilly, and Fergus O'Bryne in Toronto, but based in the Maritimes, had made LPs for Audat, Harmony, and RCA by 1978 and starred on CBC (St John's) and CHCH (Hamilton, Ont) TV series.

Two 19th-century Canadian music publishers – John *Lovell and William *Briggs – were born in Ireland. The libretto of Willan's opera **Deirdre*, written by Irish-born John Coulter, was based on an Irish saga; and Eugene Benson, born in Belfast, wrote the librettos for **Heloise and Abelard*, *Everyman*, and *Psycho Red*, all by Charles *Wilson.

Among Canadian-born musicians of Irish descent are the folksinger Tom *Brandon, the contralto Maureen *Forrester, the organist Joseph *Fowler, the pop singers Kate and Anna *McGarrigle, the songwriter Geoffrey *O'Hara, the choirmaster Mgr *Ronan, and the conductor Jerry *Shea. David Willson, founder of the *Children of Peace, was of Irish descent. Jimmie *Shields and George *Murray made their names as 'Irish' tenors.

Canadian musicians who have performed in Ireland include Emma *Albani (who often appeared in Dublin); various singers (among them Joseph *Rouleau) who have sung at the Wexford Festival; Jean Carignan, who has played at fiddling festivals; and the folksinger Edith *Butler, who in 1970 undertook a promotional tour in Ireland for the Canadian Government Travel Bureau. Clarence *Lucas composed and conducted an 'Irish musical,' *Peggy Machree*, in 1904. The song 'Sing Irishman Sing,' by the Newfoundland singer Roy Payne, has been popular with the drinking Irish. Alfred *Fisher's *Elegiac Variations* (1976, for cello and orchestra) were commissioned by Radio Telefis Eireann.

Among Irish musicians who have performed in Canada are John McCormack, the leading Irish tenor of his day, who made many appearances in North America; the Irish Guards Band, under C. H. Hassell, which gave three concerts at the Montreal Arena in 1905; the singers Catherine Hayes and Mary O'Hara; the composer-conductor Brian Boydell, who led the *CBC SO in an Irish program 23 May 1955; the flutist James Galway with the New Irish Chamber Orchestra (1978); the pop groups Horselips and the Chieftains; the folksingers Tommy Makem and Liam Clancy; and the rock singer-guitarist Rory Gallagher. Many traditional performers from Ireland have appeared at the *Mariposa Folk Festival.

See also Fiddling; Folk music, Anglo-Canadian.

1 / EF

Irish Rovers. Irish-Canadian pop group formed in Calgary in 1964 by the brothers Will Millar (leader, singer, banjoist, guitarist) and George Millar (guitarist), a cousin, Joe Millar (accordionist), and Jimmy Ferguson (singer). Joe Millar was replaced in 1967 by Wilcil McDowell but returned in 1969, this time playing bass guitar. All members were born in Northern Ireland between 1938 and 1947. The fiddler Bob Donovan was a member 1976–7.

The Rovers began their career at the Depression in Calgary and appeared at other coffeehouses throughout North America (notably the Purple Onion in San Francisco and the Ice House in Los Angeles). The success in 1968 of their Decca recording of Shel Silverstein's children's song 'The Unicorn' took them into leading concert halls and nightclubs. The recording of 'The Unicorn' eventually sold some 8 million copies world-wide. The Rovers' other, and lesser, hits in Canada and the USA were 'Whiskey on a Sunday' and 'The Biplane Evermore,' both for Decca in 1968. The Rovers toured Australia in 1969 (and again in 1974) and appeared at the Canadian pavilion at Expo 70 in Osaka, Japan.

Having taken musical-dramatic roles in the 1968 US TV western 'The Virginian,' the Rovers began their own TV series in Vancouver for the CBC in the spring of 1971. It continued until 1975 as one of the most popular variety shows of the day and was followed by several CBC specials. Though the group did not have as high a profile in later years, it performed for audiences in many parts of the world and in 1979 received the Wm Harold Moon Award from *PRO Canada for its contribution to Canadian music at an international level.

Over the years the Rovers balanced their traditional Irish repertoire with songs by Will Millar, Gordon *Lightfoot, Joni *Mitchell, and others. In 1966 Peter Goddard wrote that they 'whistle, hoot and sing their way through songs with the subtlety of a shillelagh' (*Globe and Mail*, 16 December) but in 1978 noted that they 'are only Irish in passing these days and we're to think of them, now, as singers of international songs' (*Toronto Star*, 20 January).

DISCOGRAPHY
The First of the Irish Rovers. (1967). Decca DL 74835
The Unicorn. 1967. Decca DL 74951
All Hung Up. 1968. Decca DL 75037
Tales to Warm Your Mind. (1969). Decca DL 75081
The Life of the Rover. 1969. Decca DL 75157
On the Shores of Americay. 1971. Decca DL 75302
The Best of the Irish Rovers. (1972). Decca DL7-5386
The Irish Rovers Special. 1972. K-Tel NC420
The Irish Rovers – Live! 1972. Potato POT 3201/Attic LAT 1028
Emigrate! Emigrate! 1973. Potato POT 3203/Attic LAT 1029
Irish Rovers in Australia. (1976). Attic LAT 1038
Children of the Unicorn. 1976. K-Tel NC445

BIBLIOGRAPHY
Millar, Will. *Children of the Unicorn* (Toronto 1974) MM

IRONS, Diedre (Allison) (m Gold). Pianist, b Winnipeg 9 Mar 1945; LRSM 1965, B MUS (Manitoba) 1965, Artist Diploma (Curtis) 1968. After early training with Megan Howes, she began studies at 11 with S.C. *Eckhardt-Gramatté in Winnipeg and subsequently worked with Bernard Weiser in Minneapolis and with Rudolf Serkin and Mieczyslaw Horszowski at the Curtis Institute, graduating from the latter in 1968. She made her debut on the CBC at 8, her debuts with the *Winnipeg SO (Stravinsky's *Concerto for Piano and Winds*) and the *TSO (Schumann's *Concerto in A Minor*) in 1964 and her New York debut at Town Hall in a trio with Donald Peck and Wayne Rapier in 1969. In 1971 she was the soloist with the *NACO in its first Toronto appearance (*Massey Hall 29 March, playing Mozart's *Concerto in C Minor* and the piano part in Frank Martin's *Petite Symphonie Concertante*) and for that orchestra's tour of eastern Canada. Her repertoire includes other concertos of Mozart, and those of Bartók, Beethoven, and Ravel.

Reviewing Irons' performance of the Stravinsky concerto with the WSO (*Winnipeg Free Press*, 28 Feb 1964) Kenneth *Winters admired 'the grandeur of the return to the Largo in the first movement, the conviction of the massive rolled chords and the authority of the cadenzas in the second ... [and] the wonderful marshalling of detail ... in the finale ... She is a player of brain, of executive and organizational power far more than of romantic grace and easy sentiment.'

Irons taught 1968–77 at the Curtis Institute as assistant to Serkin, appeared at the Marlboro Festival, and became resident pianist in 1968 at the Grand Teton Music Festival, Wyoming. In 1976 she was the featured guest at the first S.C. Eckhardt-Gramatté Competition in Brandon, Man, playing a program of her former teacher's works. The recital was broadcast on CBC radio 18 May. In 1977 she moved to New Zealand. She married the US bassist Dale Gold.

DISCOGRAPHY
Eckhardt-Gramatté *Duo Concertante; Suite No. 6 (Drei Klavierstücke)* – Tovey *Elegiac Variations*. Sampson vc. (1967). RCA Victor CCS 1018 (LW)

IRVINE, (Helen) Daryl (m Condie). Pianist, teacher, b Toronto 25 Aug 1932. She studied at the *RCMT with Earle *Moss 1948–51 and Eric *Rollinson 1949–53, graduating in 1951. She won a scholarship from the *AB of the RSM, and studied in London (RCM, 1954–7) with Norman Greenward and Herbert Howells. She appeared in recitals in Europe, winning praise in London and Berlin. Irvine has performed chamber music in Casals' master classes in Switzerland in 1958 and 1959. On *Canada Council scholarships, 1958–60, she studied in England and in Germany with Karl Engel. At the RCM she won the Dannreuther Concerto Prize and the Marie Curtis Prize 'for performance of a Brahms piano piece.' In 1960 she entered a competition in Hamburg and won both first and second prizes for chamber music. In 1960 Irvine began teaching at the RCMT. She includes Canadian music in all her programs. Walter *Buczynski composed his *Sonata* (1967) for her. She has appeared with the Boyd *Neel Orchestra and the *TS and has performed for the CBC with orchestras conducted by Gary Bertini and Lukas Foss. MWM

Irving's Canadian Series of Five Cent Music. An early mass-merchandising enterprise offering cheap, octavo-sized music 'for sale by all newsdealers in the dominion.' The publications were distributed by (and the later ones bore the imprint of) the Toronto News Company Ltd, of Toronto and Clifton (Niagara Falls), Ont, and the Montreal News Company Ltd, both established, ca 1880, for this and other purposes.

The manager and president of both agencies, Andrew S. Irving, was a news agent at a Hamilton, Ont, railway station before he moved to Toronto in 1862 and established himself as a newsdealer, bookseller, and stationer. About 1870 he published two pocket-sized volumes of song texts, *The Canadian Maple Leaf Song Book* and *The Canadian Rosebud Song Book*.

With a few exceptions, the nearly 700 numbered items (mostly dated from 1880 to 1885) of Irving's Canadian Series were vocal music by non-Canadian composers and lacked a copyright notice. Well represented are US songwriters of the 1850s and 1860s such as Stephen Foster, Will S. Hays, George F. Root, and Henry C. Work and their British counterparts Michael W. Balfe, Claribel (Mrs Barnard), and Stephen Glover. The few Canadian items include F.J. Hatton's 'Canada' (no. 114), which had first appeared in *Belford's Magazine* in 1878, and Muir's *'The Maple Leaf For Ever' (no. 269).

Although the series was discontinued in the mid-1880s, the news companies remained active until after World War I. Irving's later music publications, songs by the evangelist John M. *Whyte, were independent of the series. HK

ISAACS, Leonard. Administrator, teacher, pianist, conductor, arranger, b Manchester 3 Jan 1909, naturalized Canadian 1973; ARCM 1928, B MUS (London) 1934. His father was Edward Isaacs, the English pianist-composer and pupil of Busoni. Leonard Isaacs studied 1925–9 at the RCM with Herbert Fryer (piano), Gordon Jacob (composition), Frank Prolyn (harmony), and Malcolm Sargent (conducting). He later studied piano in Paris with Alfred Cortot at the École normale de musique (receiving a diplôme d'exécution in 1930) and privately in Berlin with Egon Petri. First visiting Canada 1931–2 as pianist, coach, and deputy-conductor of the English Light Opera, he returned in 1953, 1957, 1960, and 1963 as an adjudicator for the *FCMF while holding various producing and senior administrative positions 1936–63 with the BBC, notably head of music 1950–4 for the 'Third Programme' and 1954–63 for the 'Home Service.'

Isaacs moved to Canada to serve 1963–74 as director of the School of Music, *U of Manitoba, and after his retirement he was visiting professor 1974–5 at the *U of Calgary and gave courses at *Carleton U and at the *Banff SFA. In the 1970s he was heard frequently on CBC radio programs, as commentator on 'Canadian Concert Hall,' 'New Records,' and 'In Concert,' as host for the CBC Winnipeg Festival (1975, 1976 and 1977), and as writer-commentator for the special series 'Chamber Music' (1976) and 'The Human Bach' (1977).

Isaacs' published works include *Four French Canadian Folk Songs* (Schott 1959) for soprano and harp or piano, piano duets and trios for festival use issued 1954–5 by Curwen, and an arrangement of Bach's *The Art of Fugue* for chamber orchestra (Augener 1952). The latter has been recorded by George Malcolm and the Philomusica of London (Argo SDD-356–7), by the CBC String and Woodwind Ensemble under Alexander *Brott (RCI 126), and by a string and woodwind group under Isaacs (RCI 157).

BIBLIOGRAPHY
Litwack, Linda. 'Winnipeg musician looks back over fifty years,' *Fugue*, vol 2, Feb 1978 (JA)

'Isabeau s'y promène.' Preserved sometimes in song form, sometimes in dance form, this song probably originated in Normandy. Ernest *Gagnon, who gives the best-known song form in his *Chansons populaires du Canada* (Quebec City 1865), notes that it was sung in Champagne to a different tune but one with rhythmic similarities to that known in Canada. In dance form, it was collected in 1916 in Charlevoix County, Quebec, by Marius *Barbeau and published in his *Alouette* (Montreal 1946).

There are two principal versions of the text. In one, the beautiful girl, who has boarded a ship to learn a song from the youngest of 30 sailors she has met, begins to cry because her ring has fallen into the water; the sailor dives for it and drowns. In the other, moved by the young man's song, she cries because of the inconstancy of her heart, which she keeps losing. The sailor tells her not to worry, and that if she will just sing someone will return it to her.

Among Canadian composers inspired by the song form have been Violet *Archer (*Variations on a Canadian Folk Tune, 'Isabeau s'y promène,'* 1941, for piano), Hector *Gratton (*Variations libres sur 'Isabeau s'y promène,'* 1954, for strings, piano, celeste, and harp), and Keith *Bissell (*Variations on a Canadian Folk Song*, 1973, for strings, recorded by the *Chamber Players of Toronto). Arrangements of the tune were made by Healey *Willan for violin and piano (B743, 1929), and by Claude *Champagne for four equal voices (Waterloo 1960). Besides the 78s by Éva *Gauthier, Édouard *LeBel, and Joseph *Saucier, LPs containing the song have been made by Pierre *Boutet (Victor PC 1149, Victor LCP 1021) and by the *Chorale de l'U St-Joseph (Col FL 234).

BIBLIOGRAPHY
D'Harcourt, Marguerite and Raoul. *Chansons folkloriques françaises au Canada* (Quebec City 1956) HP

ISELER, Elmer (Walter). Choir conductor, choral editor, b Port Colborne, near Niagara Falls, Ont,

Elmer Iseler

14 Oct 1927; B MUS (Toronto) 1950; hon LLD (Dalhousie) 1971, hon LLD (Brock) 1972. He studied piano and organ as a youth and organ and church music with Ulrich *Leupold while a freshman at Waterloo Lutheran (now Wilfrid Laurier) U. He continued at the *U of Toronto and in 1950 and 1951, while attending the Ontario College of Education, conducted the U of Toronto SO and the All-Varsity Mixed Chorus. He apprenticed 1951–2 as assistant rehearsal conductor of the *Toronto Mendelssohn Choir and taught orchestral and choral music 1952–64 in Toronto high schools.

In 1954 Iseler helped found the Toronto Festival Singers (see Festival Singers) and during 24 years as their conductor was credited with developing and maintaining a choir of rare excellence. In 1964 he became also the conductor of the Toronto Mendelssohn Choir. He taught choral music 1965–8 at U of Toronto and in 1968 began to edit the *Festival Singers of Canada Choral Series* (Thompson), which includes four of his own hymn arrangements.

Iseler often is described as the outstanding Canadian choir conductor of his generation. He brought to the Festival Singers and the Mendelssohn Choir fresh discipline and versatility, eliciting stylistic resilience, fine tuning, and a healthy sound adaptable to music of all periods, though best in Tudor and 20th-century works. A one-time member of Healey *Willan's St Mary Magdalene Church choir, he is an authoritative interpreter of Willan's choral music.

Iseler received the City of Toronto gold Civic Award of Merit and the Société d'Encouragement et d'Éducation de Paris silver medal in 1973. He received the *CMCouncil Medal and was named an Officer of the *Order of Canada in 1975. In 1978 he formed the Elmer Iseler Singers.

DISCOGRAPHY

See Festival Singers; Toronto Mendelssohn Choir.

BIBLIOGRAPHY

Kraglund, John. 'Elmer Iseler: the man who built a choir that can challenge North America's finest,' Toronto *Globe and Mail*, 1 Dec 1962

'Interview,' *CanComp*, 90, Apr 1974 (MMI)

Islanders. See Don Messer.

'The Island Hymn.' Patriotic song of Prince Edward Island, with music by Lawrence W. Watson to words by Lucy Maud Montgomery. Montgomery wrote the words in 1907, the year before her famous novel *Anne of Green Gables* appeared. The song was performed first on Arbor Day, in early May 1907, at the Charlottetown Public School, to the tune of 'God Save the King.' Watson, a druggist and the organist at St Peter's Cathedral in the city, later wrote a new tune, keeping, however, the rhythm of 'God Save the King.'

The manuscript music, dated Charlottetown, 27 Oct 1908, and correspondence relating to it are displayed at Green Gables House, Cavendish, PEI. An edition for mixed-voice choir was printed by *Leslie Music Supply for the Prince Edward Island 1973 Centennial Committee. HK

Israel. A state formed out of Palestine in 1948. It is inhabited by Oriental Jews and Arabs, as well as Jews whose families fled to Palestine from eastern Europe in the late 19th century, and those – including many musicians – who arrived from various countries after the rise of the Nazis.

By 1980 there had been little emigration from Israel to Canada, and that was mostly to Montreal and Toronto, with smaller numbers settling in Hamilton, Ottawa, and Vancouver. Groups such as the YMHA and YWHA, the Canada-Israel Cultural Foundation (established 1963), and various local organizations have worked to perpetuate and disseminate Israeli culture through classes, demonstrations, concerts, and lectures. In June 1978, in honour of Israel's 30th anniversary, Toronto's *Ontario Place staged the first of what became annual Israeli Day celebrations. Israeli groups which visited Canada to mark this occasion in 1978 included the Israel Philharmonic Orchestra (which had performed in Canada in 1951, 1967, and 1976) and folk artists such as the Yitzhak Argaman Trio.

Among other Israeli artists who have appeared in Canada are the composer Tzvi Avni, the pianist-conductor Daniel Barenboim, the conductors Gary Bertini, Eliahu Inbal, and Uri Segal, the pianists David Bar-Illan, Yefim Bronfman, Varda Nishri, and Menahem Pressler, the violinists Miriam Fried, Shlomo Mintz, Itzhak Perlman, and Pinchas Zukerman, the clarinetist Yona Etlinger, the duo-pianists Bracha Eden and Alexander Tamir, the Ramat-Gan Chamber Orchestra, the Tel Aviv Quartet, the Israel Trio, the Yuval Trio, and the pop singer Shoshana Damari. Gadna, the national youth orchestra of Israel, performed at Montreal's *PDA in the late 1960s.

Israelis who have settled in Canada include Daniel Domb, the principal cello of the *TS, Uri Mayer, the principal viola and assistant conductor of the *MSO, the concert violist Rivka Golani-Erdesz, the violinists Moshe Hammer of *One Third Ninth and Joseph Peleg of the *Purcell String Quartet (both born in Europe but raised and trained in Israel), the violinist Yaëla *Hertz and her brother, the cellist Talmon Herz (sic), Malka Cohen of the folk duo *Malka and Joso, the pianist Elyakim *Taussig, and the conductor Eli *Rubinstein. Moshe Murvitz, the Israeli violinist and assistant concertmaster of the Israel Philharmonic Orchestra, was concertmaster of the TS 1979–80.

A number of Canadians have visited Israel. Among them are the singers Victor *Braun, Allan *Fine, Maureen *Forrester, George *London, and Joseph *Rouleau, the conductors Alexander *Brott, Fernand *Graton, and Ethel *Stark, the pianist Glenn *Gould, and the country singer Tommy *Common. The pianist-conductor Aaron Charloff, raised in Winnipeg, settled in Israel. The clarinetist Avrahm *Galper was trained in Palestine. Lorand *Fenyves, Thomas *Monohan, and George *Zukerman all were members of the Israel Philharmonic Orchestra, Fenyves as concertmaster. Elie *Spivak in 1950 was the first Canadian invited to play in Israel. In 1952 under Ethel Stark and in 1964 under Fernand Graton the Chanteurs du Québec took part in the choir festival at Zimria; among the music they performed was *Weinzweig's 'Am Israel Chai.' Weinzweig's *Cello Sonata: 'Israel'* (1949) was dedicated to the new state.

In 1961 Hugh *Le Caine developed equipment for use in the electronic studio at Hebrew University in Jerusalem. In the summer of 1973 the JM World Orchestra convened in Israel under Zubin Mehta, with Walter *Joachim coaching lower strings and Louis *Charbonneau coaching percussion. Among several young Canadians in the orchestra were the clarinetist James *Campbell and the cellist Guy Fouquet. In 1974 Janina *Fialkowska shared third prize in the first Artur Rubinstein International Competition, in Jerusalem. In 1980 Gilles *Tremblay's *Oralléluiants* was performed at World Music Days, the ISCM festival, held in Tel Aviv.

ISSAUREL, Salvator (Guillaume). Tenor, teacher, b Marseilles 23 Jan 1871, d Montreal 4 Dec 1944. He studied voice in his hometown and later, until 1898, with Masson at the Paris Cons. He made his Opéra-Comique debut 1 Apr 1898 in Paul Lacôme's *La Nuit de St-Jean*, and took part 10 May in the premiere of Vincent d'Indy's lyric drama *Fervaal*, conducted by the composer. He was engaged by the Durieu-Nicosias company as a light tenor, and went to Montreal in October 1899, singing at the *Monument national and then at the *Academy of Music in Quebec City. Under the name of Salvator, he sang the lead roles in *Faust, Mireille, Mignon, Roméo et Juliette, Lakmé*, and *La Juive*. He went with the company to the USA and to Cuba, where it was dispersed following a financial disaster in January 1900. After singing in *Faust* at the French Opera House in New Orleans, he returned to Europe and performed in Belgium and Holland. He was back in France in 1903, and sang in Marseilles and Royan the following year with the Canadian soprano Béatrice *La Palme, whom he married in Paris in 1908.

Several years before his marriage, however, Issaurel had given up performing to study with Jean-Baptiste Faure and Jean de Reszke. He also consulted Dr Marage, a renowned voice specialist. He made a distinguished reappearance in 1907 at the Théâtre de la Gaité in Paris, singing with his financée in a series of performances of Godard's *La Vivandière*. Persistent stage-fright led Issaurel to give up an active career, and in 1909 he and his wife went to London, where he opened a studio. In July 1911 they moved to Montreal; Issaurel taught 1911–14 at the Columbian Cons and then briefly at the *Canadian Academy of Music.

At the end of 1914, Béatrice La Palme also gave up her career, and she and Issaurel opened a vocal arts studio which was in operation until his death. Many of his pupils have become famous in Canada and abroad: Pierrette *Alarie, Camille *Bernard, Germaine *Bruyère, Louis *Chartier, Paul-Émile *Corbeil, Albert *Cornellier, Jeanne *Desjardins, Graziella *Dumaine, Roger *Filiatrault, Marie-José Forgues, Jacques *Gérard, Blanche Gonthier, Charles *Goulet, Émile and Romain *Gour, Jules *Jacob, Jean-Paul *Jeannotte, Joseph-Victor *Laderoute, Marthe *Létourneau, Anna *Malenfant, Ulysse *Paquin, Gérard *Paradis, Jacqueline Plouffe, Léopold *Simoneau, Honoré *Vaillancourt, and Édouard *Woolley.

Issaurel wrote several articles on the voice for *La Lyre* between 1923 and 1929. In the early 1920s for HMV he made two 78s which are listed in *Roll Back the Years*. By the quality of his teaching over 33 years, Salvator Issaurel had a marked influence on the evolution of the art of singing in Quebec. He was a member of the Union professionnelle des maîtres du chant français.

BIBLIOGRAPHY

Gour, Romain. *La Palme-Issaurel* (Montreal 1948) GP

Italy. Though a few Italians were associated with early European exploration in Canada (eg, John Cabot, b Giovanni Caboto), immigration did not begin in earnest until ca 1880, increasing dramatically in the early 20th century. The 1971 census counted 730,820 Canadians of Italian ancestry, over half of them in Ontario. Emigrants from rural areas of Italy have settled in the large urban communities of Canada where the need for unskilled labour has been the greatest.
1 Musicians of Italian origin
2 Traditions
3 Italian Music in Canada
4 Canadians in Italy
5 Italian visitors

1 MUSICIANS OF ITALIAN ORIGIN. Some emigrants have come from the cities of Italy and have had trades or professions, and among these have been musicians who taught and performed. As early as 1783, one Gaetano Franceschini, a violinist and teacher of violin and harpsichord, was active in Quebec City. By 1825 travelling Italian musicians appeared from time to time in Canada, giving concerts and lessons. Vincenzo Mazzocchi, a 'professeur de musique pour le chant d'Église des Récollets' in Montreal and a teacher at the *Séminaire de Québec, is known to have composed *Welcome to Canada* in 1839 in honour of the arrival of Lord Sydenham as governor. Allessandro Liberati (b Frascati, Italy, 1847, d ?, after 1890) was cornet soloist to the governor-general and was a bandmaster 1868–71 in Ottawa. In the late 19th and early 20th centuries Francesco *D'Auria, Giuseppe *Carboni, Giuseppe A. Dinelli, and Eduardo *Ferrari-Fontana played important roles in music education in Ontario. Camillo d'Alessio (b Naples 1869), a violinist and mandolinist who settled in Montreal in 1904, was a member of the *Goulet MSO and founded Estudiantina – the first Canadian mandolin orchestra.

Several Italian families – the *Agostinis, the *Masellas, and the *Mastrocolas – came into the forefront of Montreal musical life in the second decade of the 20th century. Italian musical families in Ontario include the *Lombardos, the *Niosis, and the *Romanellis, and among other Italian-born musicians who have been active in Canada are Michael Angelo (trumpet and cornet teacher, fl 1930s in Toronto), Anthony Antonacci (who began playing flute and piccolo in the *TSO in 1958), Ernesto *Barbini, Enrico Farina (the pop singer, 1970s in Toronto), Ermanno Florio (the violinist and TS apprentice conductor 1978–9), Piero Gamba (conductor of the *Winnipeg SO 1971–80), Giuseppe *Macina, Ermanno *Mauro, Adelmo *Melecci, the Montreal voice teachers Antonio and Lina Narducci, and Dina Maria Narici, Maria *Pellegrini, J. Pompilio (the oboist, who also conducted the Italian Band in Calgary 1928–32), Joseph *Roff, Walter *Rossi, and Dom *Troiano. Among Canadian-born musicians of Italian extraction are Norm *Amadio, Violet *Archer, Guido *Basso, Mario *Bernardi, the music librarian Maria Calderisi, Fernande *Chiocchio, the soprano Emilia Cundari, Bobby *Curtola, Rosita *del Vecchio (granddaughter of one of the earliest Italian immigrants), Victor *Di Bello, the pop singer Lisa Dal Bello, the soprano Barbara Ianni, Joseph *Macerollo, Frank *Marino, Michel *Pagliaro, Louis *Quilico, his wife, Lina Pizzolongo, and son Gino, John *Rea, Tony Roman, Emile *Taranto, Ronald *Turini, and Gino *Vannelli. Many Italian names appear in the personnel lists of Canadian symphony and chamber orchestras: the flutists N.J. Fontana and Nicholas *Fiore, the violinist Frank Fusco and the trumpeter Joseph Umbrico of the TSO; the clarinetist Giulio *Romano and his sons Arthur (clarinet) and Pietro (french horn), and the violinists Agostino and Florent Salvetti of the *MSO; the violinists Clelio Ritagliati and Emile Mignacca of the Winnipeg SO, and Don Dorazio of the *Vancouver SO. Italians also own or operate music shops, selling and repairing instruments and offering instruction.

2 TRADITIONS. The guitar and the piano accordion are the two most popular instruments among amateur musicians in the Italian-Canadian community and are used to accompany singing and dancing at family festivities. Carla Bianco has collected 246 Italian songs for the Canadian Centre for Folk Culture Studies in Ottawa, but folk music plays a decidely minor role among Italian Canadians. However, a few groups – notably the Fogolar Furlan and the Club Abruzzi, which have chapters in several cities – have tried to perpetuate regional songs and dances. The Santa Cecilia Chorus, a 45-voice Toronto male choir established in 1961, includes folk songs in its varied repertoire. Many ballads, such as the Neapolitan songs, have become deeply ingrained in the musical heritage of all Italians. Together with some of the well-loved operatic arias, these have become a sort of folk music.

3 ITALIAN MUSIC IN CANADA. Italian music was heard in Canada long before the Italians began their immigration. Works of Corelli were performed in Quebec City in 1792, and those of Cherubini in 1811. Bellini, Donizetti, and Rossini were mainstays of the mid-19th-century repertoire in the home and at concerts. Some works of Verdi and Puccini were popular shortly after they appeared in Italy. *Madama Butterfly* was performed in Winnipeg and Toronto in 1907, only three years after its premiere at La Scala in Milan. A concert of the *Women's Musical Club of Toronto, 26 Nov 1908, offered 'Italian music, ancient and modern' – consisting of Scarlatti sonatas at the piano, songs by Tosti, and arias by Scarlatti and Leoncavallo. Italian opera – particularly as represented by the main works of Verdi and Puccini – has remained the unchallenged staple of the operatic repertoire in Canada, as a glance at the seasons of the *COC, the *Edmonton Opera, the *Manitoba Opera, the *Montreal Opera, and the *Vancouver Opera will confirm. Indeed, 19th-century opera was virtually all that was heard of Italian music in Canada, apart from a few works by the baroque masters and some classical songs and violin pieces, until the mid-1950s. However, with the establishment by *Ricordi, Italy's foremost publisher, of a sales and rental office in Toronto under the direction of Bruno Apollonio, Canadians began to hear more often the works of Casella, Respighi, Malipiero, and others; and with the rise of groups, in several parts of Canada, devoted to the presentation of contemporary music, the works of more radical composers – Nono, Berio, etc – have had markedly increased exposure.

4 CANADIANS IN ITALY. Many Canadian musicians, particularly singers, have studied in Italy: Emma *Albani (who made her operatic debut in Messina in 1870) and Rosita del Vecchio with Francesco Lamperti; Carlo Boehmer (of Kitchener, Ont, a tenor who sang 1906–14 in Italy under the name Charles Nardi) with Antonio Magini-Coletti; Jean *Bonhomme and W. James *Craig with Luigi Ricci; Richard *Verreau with Beniamino Gigli; Constance *Channon and Myrtle *Guerrero with Guido Agosti; Eva *Gauthier (who made her debut in Pavia in 1909) with Carigiana; Redferne *Hollinshead with Giovanni Clerici; Arthur *Blight, Sarah *Fischer, Juliette *Gaultier de la Verendrye, Edward *Johnson (who made his operatic debut in Padua using the name Edoardo Di Giovanni), and Harold *Meek with Vincenzo Lombardi; Marguerite *Gignac with Roberto Lupi and Lina Pagliughi, Edmund *Burke, Bruce *Carey, Nina *Gale, and W. Davidson *Thompson studied in London with Albert Visetti, Gérard *Caron and André *Mérineau with Fernando Germani; and Norma *Beecroft studied composition with Goffredo Petrassi and flute with Severino Gazzeloni. Among Canadian performers, Ann *Pomer James and the pop singer Shirley *Harmer (using the name Vida Durinzi) lived and worked in Rome following their marriages to Italians. Harvey Sachs who has written a biography of Toscanini (London 1979, Paris 1980), worked 1975–6 as a pianist and coach for Milan's Orchestra dei Pomeriggi Musicali and conducted excerpts from **Colas et Colinette* at the Milan Cons in 1977. Sonja Frisell joined the staff at La Scala in 1964 as a stage director. Paul *Bley, Ray Dudley, Oscar *Peterson, and Steven *Staryk (with the NACO) have performed in Italy. Louis Quilico has sung at the Spoleto Festival, at the Teatro Massimo in Palermo, and at the Rome Opera. Nicholas *Massue, Léopold *Simoneau, and Jon *Vickers have sung at La Scala. Pierre *Mercure, Oskar *Morawetz, and Harry *Somers have won prizes in the Concorso Internazionale di Musica Ritmo-Sinfonica at Cava dei Tirreni; Marc *Fortier the Ferdinando Ballo prize in the 1968 Ente Pomeriggi musicali di Milano; Thomas *Schudel the first prize in the 1972 Premio Città di Triesta for composition; and Kathleen Solose the first prize in the Alessandro Casagrande International Piano Competition in Terni in 1973. Somers and Serge *Garant each spent a year in Italy as recipients of Italian cultural fellowships awarded through the Canadian Cultural Institute in Rome.

5 ITALIAN VISITORS. Visits to Canada by distinguished Italian musicians began as early as 1853, when Luigi Arditi conducted performances of *Norma* with the Artists' Assn Italian Opera Company in Montreal and Toronto. In 1897 the Banda Rossa under Maestro Eugenio Sorrentino played at *Massey Hall. The composer Pietro Mascagni conducted his productions of *Zanetto*, *Cavalleria Rusticana*, and *Iris* in Montreal and *Cavalleria* in Toronto in 1902. Concerts and recordings by Giuseppe Creatore's Band were popular in Canada during the 1920s (the band played at the *CNE 10 times between 1914 and 1926). George J. *Dyke brought the Da Capo Italian Band to Vancouver in the 1930s. The Orchestra of La Scala under Toscanini performed in Montreal in 1921 and 1926, and the entire company made its North American debut at the World Festival, *Expo 67, with *Nabucco*, *La Bohème*, and *I Capuleti e i Montecchi*. Also at Expo 67 the Alessandro Scarlatti Orchestra of Naples gave concerts under Mario Rossi and Massimo Pradella. In 1960 the composer Luciano Berio represented Italy at the *International Conference of Composers, in 1968 he conducted two concerts in Montreal for the *SMCQ, and in 1972 he conducted a program of his own works for the inaugural presentation of *NMC in Toronto. Luigi Dallapiccola has visited Montreal, as has Bruno Maderna. The Virtuosi di Roma first played in Toronto and Montreal in 1950 and returned often thereafter to Canada. The illustrious ensemble I Musici also has visited Canada frequently. The Trio di Milano played at Toronto's *St Lawrence Centre in 1979. The Women's Musical Club of Toronto and the *Pro Musica Society of Montreal have presented several Italian chamber groups to

their audiences over the years. The Italian Cultural Institute, with offices in Montreal, Toronto, and Vancouver, has sponsored visits by Italian artists and groups. Under its auspices the Trio Chitarristico Italiano (classical guitars) performed in Quebec City, Ottawa, Toronto, Kingston, Sudbury, and Vancouver in 1976 and I Musici gave a Toronto concert in 1978. Among solo instrumentalists of international reputation, the pianist Arturo Benedetto Michelangeli played in Montreal, Toronto, and Winnipeg in 1948 and returned to Montreal for the World Festival during Expo 67 and to Toronto in 1970; and the pianist Maurizio Pollini performed in Montreal in 1978. Young Italian musicians also have appeared in Canada. The *JMC have sponsored tours by the pianist Mario Delli Ponti 1961–2, 1966–7, and 1967–8 and by the duo-pianists Mario and Lydia Conter 1966–7.

Needless to say a great many Italian singers have visited Canada, among them Enrico Caruso (1908 and 1920, Toronto and Montreal), Luisa Tetrazzini (1912 Toronto), Amelita Galli-Curci (1918 and 1919 tours that included Toronto, Winnipeg, and Calgary), the Scotti Grand Opera (1921 Montreal and Toronto), Gina Cigna (1937 Toronto), and Luciano Pavarotti (1976 and 1979 Montreal and Toronto). Ferruccio Tagliavini sang at *Eaton Auditorium in 1947, Cesare Siepi gave a recital for the Women's Musical Club of Toronto in 1953. Winnipeg audiences heard Nino Martini, Giovanni Martinelli, Ezio Pinza, Tito Schipa, Ebe Stignani, and Cesare Valetti as well as the pianist Carlo Zecchi, who also performed in Montreal in 1931. Renata Tebaldi sang in Toronto with the TSO in 1956 and returned for a CBC TV special with Louis Quilico in 1965. Renata Scotto and Carlo Bergonzi were soloists at the *COC's tribute to La Scala in 1978 at *O'Keefe Centre.

Many leading Italian pop singers have appeared in Toronto at festivals of song begun in 1955 and at concerts at Massey Hall, *Maple Leaf Gardens, and O'Keefe Centre by Johnny (Giovanni Barbalinardo) Lombardi (b Toronto 4 Dec 1915), the 'mayor of [Toronto's] Little Italy.' Lombardi was host for Italian-language radio shows in the 1940s and 1950s on CHUM and CKFH before purchasing CHIN radio in 1965 and coverting it into a multi-ethnic station.

BIBLIOGRAPHY

Goggio, Emilio. 'The Italian contribution to the development of music in Ontario,' *CRMA*, vol 4, Oct–Nov 1945, Dec–Jan 1945–6

Over 100 Italian Songs / Piu'di 100 Canzone Italiane (Toronto 1974) (MC)

J

JABLONSKI, Marek. Pianist, teacher, b Krakow, Poland, 5 Nov 1939. He studied at the Krakow Cons when he was six. His family settled in Edmonton in 1949, but it was in Calgary and in Banff during the summers that he continued his piano studies with Gladys *Egbert. After winning the Dimitri Mitropoulos scholarship in 1957, he worked at the Aspen School in Denver, Col, and then with Rosina Lhévinne at the Juilliard School. In 1961 he won the grand prize in the *JMC national competition, and that November he played Chopin's *Concerto No. 1* with the *MSO conducted by Zubin Mehta. He performed this work with several groups including the *TSO in 1962 and the American Symphony Orchestra during his Carnegie Hall debut 15 Feb 1963.

Jablonski toured during the 1961–2, 1962–3, 1964–5, 1969–70, and 1971–2 seasons for the JMC and in 1963 in the USA under the auspices of the

Marek Jablonski

Carnegie Hall Corporation. He studied in London with Ilona Kabos on a *Canada Council grant and made his Paris debut at the Salle Gaveau. The critic Clarendon called his interpretation of Chopin's *Sonata No. 3* 'masterful' (*Le Figaro*, 6 Mar 1963). In 1965 he toured in France, Italy, Austria, Yugoslavia, and Poland. He made his London debut 2 Feb 1969 at Wigmore Hall in a recital devoted to Chopin and returned there in November 1969 and February 1971. After a recital given in the *Salle Claude-Champagne, Gilles *Potvin described his interpretation of Brahms' *Sonata No. 3*: 'Jablonski's performance was distinguished by the clear picture he drew of its structure, controlling the entry of each episode and giving each of the five movements a distinct character ... Jablonski also revealed remarkable technique and great power. With this performance, Jablonski again asserts himself as one of Canada's most talented pianists. Here is an artist of breadth, worthy of the world's great concert halls' (*La Presse*, 31 Mar 1969).

Jablonski performed in the USSR four times between 1969 and 1975. A major 1971 tour of Europe took him to Amsterdam, Berlin, Brussels, London, Madrid, Stockholm, and Zurich; he later became well known in South America. In 1971 the *NFB presented the full-length film *Jablonski*. He returned to Spain in 1973 and in 1974 in Brussels gave three recitals and appeared in concert with the Belgian National Orchestra. He was soloist with the *NACO and the *Edmonton SO in 1973, the *Quebec SO in 1974, the *Calgary Philharmonic in 1975, and the *Kitchener-Waterloo SO in 1978. In 1975, 1977, and 1979, he gave recitals at the *PDA. He gave master classes in 1973 in Venezuela and in 1974 in Belgium. In 1975 he began teaching summers at the *Banff SFA, and in 1979 he became a member of the *U of Manitoba School of Music.

DISCOGRAPHY

Brahms *Sonata, Op 5; Intermezzo, Op 117 no. 1*. 1969. CBC SM-106

Chopin *Polonaise, Op 44; 5 Mazurkas; Sonata, Op 58*. 1963. Club du Disque JMC-5

– *Waltz, Op 34 no. 2*; et al. 1967. Aviston Records CLAR 13005

Haydn – Beethoven – Liszt – Chopin. 1971. CBC SM-154

Marek Jablonski: Mozart – Brahms – Chopin. 1961. Club du Disque JMC-2

BIBLIOGRAPHY

McLean, Eric. 'The loneliness of the long-distance piano player,' *Montreal Star*, 13 Dec 1969 (PR)

JACKS, Terry. Singer, songwriter, record producer, b Winnipeg 29 Mar 1944. Raised in Vancouver, he sang and played guitar with the Chessmen in the mid-1960s on CBC TV's 'Music Hop,' where he met his wife, Susan Pesklevits (b Saskatoon 19 Aug 1948). Together, they performed with the Vancouver rock bands Powerline and Winkin', Blinkin' and Nob and in 1968 formed the Poppy Family. Essentially a duo with accompanying musicians, the Poppy Family made three LPs for London and several hit singles: 'Which Way You Goin' Billy' (which sold 2 million copies 1969–70 and won two *Juno Awards for 1969), 'That's Where I Went Wrong' (1970), 'Where Evil Grows' (1971), and 'No Good to Cry.' The group appeared at Expo 70 in Osaka.

In 1973, with the dissolution of the Poppy Family – due to Jacks' reluctance to tour – and after the breakup of the marriage, Jacks began a solo recording career. He formed his own record company, Goldfish, which released several singles. An English version of Jacques Brel's 'Seasons in the Sun' (1973) sold over 10 million copies worldwide and brought Jacks three Junos for 1973. Among his other hits in Canada were 'Rock and Roll (I Gave the Best Years of My Life)' (1974) and 'Christina' (1975). Goldfish also released his LPs *Seasons in the Sun* (1973, GFLP 1001) and *Y'Don't Fight the Sea* (1975, GOLP 1) as well as LPs and singles by Susan Jacks (including the Canadian hits 'You Don't Know What Love Is' and 'I Thought of You Again'), *Chilliwack, and others.

Jacks has attributed the success of 'Which Way You Goin' Billy,' for example, to 'simple music, simple lyrics, and a melody people could remember, a simple performance, a lot of sincerity – sincerity is the main thing – but spontaneity is also very important' (*Axes, Chops & Hot Licks*). Most of his songs are published by Gone Fishin' Music, an affiliate of PRO Canada.

BIBLIOGRAPHY

Yorke, Ritchie. 'The Poppy Family,' *Axes, Chops & Hot Licks* (Edmonton 1971)

LeBlanc, Larry. 'Terry Jacks' one commitment is his music,' *MSc*, 264, Mar–Apr 1972

Read, Jeani. 'Terry Jacks' success attributed to total control,' *MSc*, 280, Nov–Dec 1974

Alderman, Tom. ' "Seasons in the Sun?" Oh yes, you're an American, aren't you?' *Canadian Magazine*, 8 Mar 1975 (FH, MM, JR)

JACKSON, Christopher (Donald). Organist, choirmaster, b Halifax, NS, 27 Jul 1948; premier prix organ (CMM) 1974. He studied 1966–9 at the *École Vincent-d'Indy with Françoise *Aubut (organ) and Jean-François *Sénart (choral conducting) and 1970–4 at the CMM with Bernard *Lagacé (organ) and Gilles *Tremblay (analysis). He continued to study musicology, conducting, and organ 1972–4 at summer schools in the USA and Europe. His education was rounded out by practical experience in organ building. Besides making a systematic study of the historical organs of France and Quebec, he worked as a technician 1969–70 for *Casavant Frères and in 1972 for *Providence Organ. He taught piano and organ 1973–5 at *Concordia U and theory in 1976 at *McGill U. In the summer of 1977 he taught harpsichord, organ, and choral music at *CAMMAC. He was organist-choirmaster of several Protestant churches in Montreal before moving to St George's Anglican Church in 1976. Jackson has been heard often on CBC radio, and has given organ recitals and conducted choirs in several countries. He was a founding member (1974) of the Société des Concerts d'orgue de Montréal and of the *Studio de musique ancienne de Montréal and was co-director of the latter with Réjean *Poirier and president 1976–7.

Jackson's wife, the organist Hélène Dugal (b Verdun, near Montreal, 2 Nov 1949; premier prix organ, CMM, 1972) studied at the CMM with Bernard Lagacé (organ) and Kenneth *Gilbert (harpsichord) and 1972–3 at the Geneva Cons with the aid of a Quebec government scholarship. She has participated in international competitions and has won prizes at Bruges, Geneva, St Albans, Bologna, and Innsbruck. She is a founding member of the Société des Concerts d'orgue de Montréal and of the Studio de musique ancienne de Montréal. In 1975 she became the organist at Marie-Reine-du-Monde Cathedral, Montreal, and in 1976 she established a summer festival at the cathedral.

HPn

'Jack Was Every Inch a Sailor.' A retelling of the Jonah story with a Newfoundland fisherman as the hero. It seems to have been adapted from a New York music-hall song 'Every Inch a Sailor.' The US folklorist Phillips Barry noted that it is a localized version of the words (but not the tune) of 'the original burlesque of "Pinafore," as sung by Miss Venie Clancy and printed in White's *Complete Music Album*, Boston, 1884,' and that ballad singer 'Frank Crumit made a gramophone record of it which was popular' (1928, Victor 21668). It was published by Greenleaf and Mansfield in *Ballads and Sea Songs of Newfoundland* (Cambridge, Mass, 1933) and recorded on *Folk Songs of Newfoundland* (Folkways FW 6931). (EF)

JACOB, Jules. Tenor, record dealer, b St-Prosper-de-Champlain, near Trois-Rivières, Que, 1906, d Town of Mount Royal, Montreal, 16 Jan 1969. In 1930, while studying voice in Montreal with Salvator *Issaurel, he became a member of the *Alouette Vocal Quartet. He sang with the group until 1956 and also, in the late 1930s, succeeded Ludovic Huot as tenor with the *Trio lyrique. He made recordings with both these ensembles.

Jacob made his debut as a soloist in 1938 at a concert performance of Xavier Leroux's opera *Évangéline*. Writing in *La Presse*, Marcel *Valois described the performance: 'Jules Jacob's debut delighted everyone. He has a fine voice, particularly in the upper register, intelligent delivery and precise diction' (15 Sep 1938).

Jacob's theatre debut was made the following year with the *Variétés lyriques in *The Student Prince*. He was a soloist in 1941, 1944, and 1947 in Beethoven's *Ninth Symphony* with the *CSM Orchestra. At the *Montreal Festivals he was a soloist in 1943 and 1944 in the *St Matthew Passion* and sang the role of the Pilot in 1944 in *Tristan und Isolde*. At the *Opera Guild he took part in productions of *Fidelio* (Jaquino, 1946), *Madama Butterfly* (Goro, 1947), *Rigoletto* (Borsa, 1948), *Il Trovatore* (Ruiz, 1949), *Otello* (Roderigo, 1949), and *La Bohème* (Parpignol, 1950). He gave recitals and performed in operetta and opera on CBC radio between 1936 and 1949. His radio career also included such programs as 'Northern Electric Hour' in 1948 and 'Morgantime' 1948–9.

In the mid-1950s Jacob retired from performing to manage a record store. With Albert *Viau, he recorded two items for the series La Bonne Chanson (Bluebird 55-5218). GP

'J'ai cueilli la belle rose.' A 16th-century manuscript in France provides the oldest likely origin of this dance song, introduced to Canada in the 17th century. In the text published by Ernest *Gagnon in *Chansons populaires du Canada* (Quebec City 1865) a beautiful girl picks a rose to take to her father 'between Paris and Rouen.' (The name of the towns varied depending on where the song was sung.) At the end of her journey, however, the young girl finds only a nightingale who advises her to marry. A suitor then offers her 600 pounds a year. In *Romancero du Canada* (Toronto 1937). Marius *Barbeu notes two additional verses which explain this generous offer: 'Et vous n'aurez rien à faire, que mon petit lit de camp; À le faire et le défaire, vous et moi couch'rons dedans' ('And you will have nothing to do, but to make my little campbed; to make it and undo it, you and I will sleep in it'). In his *Catalogue de la chanson folklorique française* Conrad *Laforte refers to two other titles, 'J'ai cueilli la rose rose' and 'Épousez-moi d'abord.' The tune exists in several versions. Maurice *Blackburn made an arrangement for voices in 1949, and the song has been recorded for LPs by Pierre *Boutet (Victor LCP 1021, Victor PC 1149) and by the Joyeux copains de Hawkesbury (Lon MLP 10010).

BIBLIOGRAPHY

Bélanger, Jeannine, and Barbeau, Marius. 'La césure épique dans nos chansons populaires,' *Archives de folklore*, vol 1, Montreal 1946 (HP)

JAMES, (Mary) Frances (m Adaskin). Soprano, teacher, b Saint John, NB, 3 Feb 1903. She spent her childhood in Halifax and Montreal and took her main formative studies on a four-year scholarship at the *McGill Cons with Walter Clapperton. While in Montreal she was soloist 1925–9 at St James' United Church and sang on radio station CKAC. She moved to Toronto to pursue her radio career and ca 1930 continued voice studies with Lisette Patterson. She was the first pupil of the Lieder specialist Emmy *Heim at the *TCM in 1935 and was coached in New York by Enrico Rosati, Maria Kurenko, and Jeanne *Dusseau and in Boston by Roland Hayes.

James participated in the *CPR Festivals in the late 1920s and was a recitalist 1931–41 for the CPR hotel chain, singing in Quebec City, Winnipeg, Regina, Calgary, Banff, Lake Louise, Vancouver, and Victoria. In Banff in 1931 she sang in the premiere of *Willan's ballad opera *Prince Charlie and Flora* and met and married Murray *Adaskin; and also in Banff, in 1939, she sang with Adaskin's Toronto Trio before King George VI and Queen Elizabeth. In Toronto she performed with the *Toronto Bach Choir under Reginald *Stewart in 1934 and was a soloist with the *Toronto Mendelssohn Choir, 11 Feb 1936, in Beethoven's *Missa solemnis*. She had sung in Toronto in 1929 in a CPR-sponsored joint recital with the tenor Stanley Maxted; but the recital she regards as her debut in that city, with Gwendolyn Williams *Koldofsky at the piano, was given at *Hart House in 1935.

James became familiar to a national audience through her performances for many CBC radio series, including 'Friendly Music,' 'Canadian Mosaic,' 'Footlights,' 'Midweek Recital,' 'Distinguished Artists,' and, in 1945, a 22-program contemporary-music series of her own. For the CBC she sang in Sir Ernest *MacMillan's broadcasts of six Handel oratorios in 1942; in the premieres of Willan's *Transit through Fire* (1942) and *Deirdre* (1946) and Bernard *Naylor's *King Solomon's Prayer* (1953); and in the Canadian premieres of Hindemith's *Das Marienleben* (1945), Britten's *Les Illuminations* (1946) and *Peter Grimes* (1949, as Ellen Orford), and Stravinsky's *The Rake's Progress* (1953, as Anne Trulove).

In concert James premiered *Somers' *Three Songs* (Toronto 1946), *Pentland's *Song Cycle* (Toronto 1947), and *Weinzweig's *Of Time, Rain and the World* (Toronto 1949), and participated in the first Canadian performance (Montreal 1946) of Finzi's *Dies natalis*. She and Murray Adaskin participated in Milhaud's summer classes 1949–50 at the Music Academy of the West, near Santa Barbara, Cal. She made cross-Canada tours until the early 1950s, and also performed in the USA, making her debut (1940) as the first Canadian to appear there in an exchange program between the two countries.

Frances James in Banff, ca 1930

Frances James was a pioneer in the presentation of 20th-century music in Canada. As Éva *Gauthier and Cédia *Brault had done in the 1920s and Mary *Morrison, Patricia *Rideout, and Phyllis *Mailing in the 1960s and 1970s, James became a sophisticated medium for the vocal music of the 1930s, 1940s, and 1950s. For student musicians growing to maturity in those years, her CBC recitals were a main source for acquaintance with the songs of Debussy, Hindemith, Milhaud, and Britten, as well as the contemporary Canadians. The voice, though handsome, was not particularly sensuous. It was, however, a firm implement for the conveyance of intelligence, a seriously researched understanding of the musical material in hand, and a broad sense of the culture represented. So pleased was Hindemith with her 1945 broadcast of *Das Marienleben* that he arranged for her to give the first performance of his 1948 revision of the work at King's College, Annapolis, Maryland, and to make the first recording in 1950.

Murray Adaskin became head of the music department at the *U of Saskatchewan in 1952, and Frances James taught voice there from that time until 1967. When Adaskin retired in 1973, the couple moved to Victoria, where both continued to teach, privately and at the *U of Victoria. Among James' pupils, in Saskatchewan and Victoria, several have continued in the profession, including Sheila Osborne, a choir director in Saskatchewan; Audrey Shore Dowler, a soprano and school music supervisor in Manitoba; and the singers Catherine Lewis, Jane MacKenzie, and Karen Smith, all active in British Columbia.

DISCOGRAPHY

Betts – Adaskin – Coulthard – McIntyre: *Songs*. Bernardi pf. 1952. RCI 74

Coulthard – Weinzweig – Pentland: *Songs*. Moss pf. 1950. RCI 20/(Weinzweig) RCI ACM 1

Hindemith *Das Marienleben*. Brough pf. 1950. 2-Lyrichord 6

BIBLIOGRAPHY

A.A.A. 'Frances James develops into thrilling artist,' *Winnipeg Free Press*, 24 Dec 1948

'Frances James – songs by Weinzweig,' *CBC Times*, 4 Sep 1949

Creative Canada, vol 1 (SWI)

Japan. The first Japanese immigrant to Canada arrived in 1877, but it was not until ca 1885 that his countrymen followed his example in any numbers – in the form of a colony of fishermen who worked off the west coast. By 1900, however, more thant 4000 farmers, fishermen, and labourers had settled in British Columbia; by 1961 there were some 30,000 Japanese or Japanese-Canadians in Canada.

Most of the many forms of Japanese traditional music cannot exist outside Japan; they are too

A koto player in Toronto, 1962

much a part of a homogeneous culture. The small amount of Japanese music perpetuated in Canada (and elsewhere outside the home country) has survived due to the zeal of a few ardent practitioners. Prior to World War II musical activities in the Japanese communities along the west coast were few, save for the efforts of the *Utai* and *Shigin* societies, the former concerned with the singing of Noh drama music, the latter with the chanting of poetry in the classical Chinese style. The existence of such societies depended on the presence of teachers well versed in the art and able to pass it along to others in the traditional aural way.

The removal of the Japanese from their west-coast homes in 1941 and their internment during World War II dealt their musical culture, along with many other survivals of homeland custom, a grievous blow. The inland re-settlements after the war, however, augmented by post-war immigration, resulted in important Japanese communities in Alberta, Manitoba, and Ontario; and those families who returned to the Vancouver area have shown particular interest in a revival of musical traditions.

The Koto Ensemble of Greater Vancouver (formerly the Vancouver-Steveston Koto-no-kai), an association of 30 women, was established in the late 1950s under the direction of Miyoko Kobayashi, who also taught koto (a 13-string oriental zither) 1967–8 at the *U of British Columbia. The Koto Ensemble toured eastern Canada in 1975, and has performed regularly in the western provinces. Courses in Japanese music have continued at the university. Also active in Vancouver during the 1970s were Teresa Kobayashi and Wendy Stuart (koto) and Takeo Yamashiro and Elliot *Weisgarber (shakuhachi, a reed flute).

By the 1970s Toronto boasted the largest Japanese community in Canada; and a Japanese Canadian Cultural Centre, which served as a focus for the activities of *nisei* (second-generation Japanese-Canadians), sponsored the Sansei Choir formed in 1964 by Harry Kumano and presented concerts by visiting Japanese artists (eg, the Ensemble Nipponia, under the composer-performer Ninoru Miki, in 1976 and 1978). The centre also has supported a local dance troupe and, from time to time, teachers of the koto and the shakuhachi. There is a Japanese Cultural Centre in Hamilton, Ont.

At the *U of Toronto, David B. Waterhouse began teaching courses in the history of Japanese music in 1968. Kenneth L. Richard of the university and Steven Otto of *York U are accomplished performers on the koto. A Montreal Japanese Choir of 32 mixed voices, founded in 1977 and directed by Takashi Imaizumi, has given several concerts at the Japanese Cultural Centre and in Montreal churches.

Other prominent Japanese musicians in Canada have included: Kazuyoshi Akiyama, who became conductor of the *Vancouver SO in 1972; Seiji Ozawa, the Manchurian-born Japanese who was conductor 1965–9 of the *TSO; the violinist Hidetaro *Suzuki; and the cellist Tsuyoshi *Tsutsumi. Yoko Wong, though born in Manchuria, was raised in Japan, where she was trained by Shinichi Suzuki (himself a visitor to Canada more than once); she became an important exponent of the *Suzuki teaching method in Canada after her arrival in 1965. Canadian-born musicians include the saxophonist Nobuo Kubota and the trombonist Jiro 'Butch' Watanabe.

The Japanese composer Toru Takemitsu has enjoyed a special relationship with the TS, through Seiji Ozawa, and several of his works were recorded by the orchestra. The flutist Robert *Aitken, principal flute of the TS during those years, was influenced by the playing of the shakuhachi player Katsuya Yokoyama, who played as a soloist at TS concerts. Aitken's playing developed a subtler inflection and wider tonal range as a result. He has recorded flute solos by the Japanese composer Kazuo Fukushima. The TS percussionist John *Wyre made his solo debut with the Japan Philharmonic under Ozawa, performing his own *Bells*, dedicated to the conductor and to Takemitsu.

The TS itself toured Japan under Ozawa in 1969 and under Andrew Davis in 1978 with Maureen *Forrester and Louis *Lortie as soloists. Ethel *Stark visited Japan in 1960 and is said to be the first woman to conduct the Tokyo Asahi SO and the Nippon Hoso Kyokai. The *Montreal Bach Choir under George *Little gave six concerts in Japan in 1961. The cast of **Anne of Green Gables*, Edith *Butler, *Chilliwack, and the *MSO with Maureen Forrester and Ronald *Turini all performed at Expo 70 in Osaka.

Among other Canadians who have performed in Japan are Paul *Bley, Bruce *Cockburn and Murray *McLauchlan, Hugh *McLean, Anne *Murray, Oscar *Peterson, René *Simard, Don (W.) *Thompson and Terry *Clarke accompanying the US guitarist Jim Hall, and the Windsor, Ont, rock band Teaze. The Canadian-born jazz saxophonist Georgie Auld had toured there eight times by 1973. The Vancouver SO toured in Japan in 1974. Dorothy *Swetnam Hare taught piano 1934–8 and in 1940 at the Canadian Academy in Kobe.

Arnold *Walter gave lectures in Japan in 1961, and Victor *Feldbrill (who had been awarded the City of Tokyo medal in 1978 for his work with youth) conducted and lectured in Tokyo in 1979. Roy Cox, Clifford *Evens, and Wilson Swift are among the Canadian conductors who have studied with Ozawa's and Akiyama's teacher, Hideo Saito. *Freedman's *Tokaido* (1964), which uses Japanese poems as its text, was inspired by a visit to Japan.

Japanese musicians and groups who have performed in Canada include Tamaki Miura (said to be the first Japanese to sing Cio-Cio-San in *Madama Butterfly*), who sang with the *San Carlo Opera in Montreal in 1922; Viscount Hidemaro Konoye, founder-conductor of the Tokyo SO and a guest conductor of the *CSM in 1937; the Fujiwara Opera (Toronto, Montreal 1956); the avant-garde composer and pianist Toshi Ichiyanagi (Montreal *International Week of Today's Music, 1961); the koto player Kimio Eto (Toronto 1961, 1962, 1966); the Little Singers of Tokyo (1964, 1978); the Japan Philharmonic conducted by Akeo Watanabe (*PDA 1964; Watanabe also was guest conductor of the *Calgary Philharmonic in 1975); the Kwansei Gakuin Symphony Band (Toronto 1964); and the pianist Kyoko Edo-Ozawa (TSO 1964).

The shakuhachi player Katsuya Yokoyama and the biwa player Kinshi Tsuruta performed and recorded with the TS in 1968 and played with the Vancouver SO in 1978; the composer-pianist Yuji Takahashi played with the TS (1969) and performed his composition *Chrom amorphe II* with the *SMCQ in 1969; and the violinist Masuko Ushioda performed in Toronto in 1969 and 1972, in Vancouver in 1971, 1975, 1976, and 1978, and with the pianist Minoru Nojima in Toronto in 1977. Nojima also played with the Vancouver SO in 1974, as did the violinists Teiko Maehashi (1972, 1973, 1974, 1977) and Tsugio Tokunaga (1972).

Hiroyuki Iwaki has conducted the TS in 1973 and 1979 and the MSO in 1976; the pianist Takashi Hironake and the violinist Yasushi Abe were soloists with the Vancouver SO (1975); and the Tokyo Quartet has performed in Toronto (1976, 1977, 1978) and Vancouver (1977). The cellist Ko Iwasaki played with the Vancouver SO in 1973, the pianist Etsuko Tazaki with the TS in 1976, and the violinist Hamao Fujiwara with the TS in 1977 and 1978, and the Vancouver SO in 1977. Makoto Shinohara was a visiting composer at the *U of Montreal in 1977. The Tokyo SO and the Vancouver SO were televised by the CBC in a massed concert in 1978. The trumpeter Toshinori Kondo performed and recorded in Toronto in 1979.

BIBLIOGRAPHY

Walter, Arnold. 'A musical journey to Japan,' *CMJ*, vol 6, Autum 1961

Littler, William. 'Ozawa's farewell present to the Symphony was Ozawa,' *Toronto Star*, 26 Apr 1969

'Music in Japan: a brief outline with Expo 70 in mind,' *CanComp*, 48, Mar 1970

Potvin, Gilles. 'Le Toronto Symphony au Japon: un franc succès,' Montreal *Le Devoir*, 9 Feb 1978

'Can a "nice guy" build a great orchestra?' *VSO*, vol 1, Mar 1978

(DW, EW)

JAQUE, Rhené (b Cartier, Marguerite Marie Alice). Composer, violinist, cellist, teacher, b Beauharnois, near Montreal, 4 Feb 1918; B MUS (Montreal) 1949, L MUS (Montreal) 1955. She joined the sisters of the Holy Names of Jesus and Mary and took her vows in 1938 as Sister Jacques-René (sic). During this time she continued her studies at the École supérieure de musique in Outremont (*École Vincent-d'Indy). Her teacher were Claude *Champagne, Marvin *Duchow, and François *Morel for theory and composition, Jean *Vallerand for orchestration and instrumentation, Louis *Bailly, Camille *Couture, Aurelio Didio, Arthur *Garami, and Maurice *Onderet for violin, and Yvette *Lamontagne for cello. In 1972 she took courses in composition with Tony Aubin at the Académie internationale d'été in Nice. She joined the École supérieure in 1943 as a teacher of violin, cello, and theory.

Rhené Jaque has composed numerous atonal teaching pieces, most of them bearing such fitting titles as *Le Petit Pâtre*, *L'Âne gris*, and *Le Lutin*, intended for young pianists and violinists. In addition to two pieces for organ (1956) and two *Fantaisies* for solo cello (1970), she has written a *Symphonie* for large orchestra and a *Suite* for strings (1967) and some chamber music, songs, and choral pieces. Some of her works have been published by *Berandol, *Thompson, and the Éditions de l'École Vincent-d'Indy. *Rustic Dance / Fête champêtre* and *Deux Inventions à deux voix* were recorded by pianist Rachel *Cavalho (CCM-1), and *Deuxième Suite* for piano, by Antonín *Kubálek (Mel SMLP 4031). Rhené Jaque is an affiliate of PRO Canada.

BIBLIOGRAPHY
Thériault, Jacques. 'Composer's works reveal devotion to young musicians,' *MSc*, Jan–Feb 1972 MT

Jarman Publications Ltd. Established in Toronto in 1947 by Harry E. Jarman (b London 28 Jun 1902), who settled in Canada in 1924. Jarman was editor and advertising manager ca 1926–9 for **Musical Canada* and program director during the 1930s for radio station CKGW. He worked as a producer and arranger for radio station CRCT, for a short time was general manager of Dominion Music Supply in Toronto, and in the last years of the decade operated the Harry E. Jarman Music Co. While associated 1939–47 with *Boosey & Hawkes (Canada) Ltd, he was responsible for the establishment of that company's music and instrument departments and for the Boosey & Hawkes Artists' Bureau. He then established Jarman Publications Ltd in Toronto, publishing Canadian material only and specializing in piano, choral, and square-dance music. The square-dance books, edited by Jarman, have appeared in the Cornhuskers Series and have been among the company's most profitable and popular items. In June 1979 Harry Jarman retired and his son John assumed responsibility for the business.

Among the firm's educational publications are *Olive Bentley's Piano Course* (1961) and *The Zdenka H. Picha Piano Method* (1973). Jarman has published compositions and arrangements, mostly for young musicians, by Boris *Berlin, G. Roy *Fenwick, William *France, Cyril *Hampshire, Charles *Peaker, and others. The firm has been an agent for Belwin, Inc, and other foreign publishers. Harry Jarman was chairman of the *CMPA 1952–3. Jarman Publications Ltd established affiliation with PRO Canada.

JARVIS, Harold (Augustus). Tenor, b Toronto 27 Dec 1864, d Detroit 1 Apr 1924. He was a son of a singer known professionally as Annie McLear. As a child, Harold, in highland costume, became a public favourite singing Scottish songs. In 1878 he entered the merchant marine service operating between Montreal and England. He studied singing, and won a gold medal, at the RAM in London. He subsequently sang widely in Great Britain, Canada, and the USA before settling in Detroit in 1891 as tenor soloist at the First Presbyterian Church. In 1892 he married the singer Laura Geikie of Toronto and continued his concert activity. In 1908 he recorded for RCA Victor, in 1912 for Columbia, and in 1914 for Edison. His most popular record was 'Beautiful Isle of Somewhere' (1914), Vitaphone 10026. *Roll Back the Years* lists his recordings. EBM

Jaymar Music Ltd. Publishing company active 1967–75 in London, Ont, under the direction of Peter J. Martin. The catalogue consisted primarily of organ and sacred choral music by Violet *Archer, Gerald *Bales, Barrie *Cabena, Jean *Coulthard, Derek *Healey, and others, but also included piano and chamber music by Brian *Cherney, Robert *Fleming, and Hugh *Hartwell. Jaymar operated two subsidiaries, Huron Press (CAPAC) and Iroquois Press (BMI Canada). Its US agent was Oxford U Press. After Jaymar closed, its publications were taken over by *Berandol Music.

Jazz. Afro-American music of the 20th century, commonly characterized by its improvised content and its rhythmic vitality. Because jazz antedates its earliest documented evidence (recordings), much controversy surrounds its origins. The least disputed theory (see Marshall Stearn's *The Story of Jazz*, New York 1956) traces these to the socio-musical environment of New Orleans at the turn of the century. The music's commercial beginnings, of greater relevance to its history in Canada, usually are dated from 1917, from the recordings (including one of Shelton Brooks' *'Darktown Strutters' Ball') by the Original Dixieland Jazz Band, a white New Orleans quintet. In the ensuing 60 years jazz has undergone constant and often dramatic change, at times the result of influences from other musical idioms (eg, classical in the 'third stream' of the 1950s and rock in the 'jazz rock' of the 1970s) but more often evolving out of jazz itself through its musicians' innovations.

Although by the 1970s jazz had found its place in the curricula of many Canadian universities and colleges, its tradition is essentially aural, assimilated most often by imitation of admired performers, selective refinement of what has been imitated, and, finally, transmutation of the result into stylistic self-expression. Few Canadians have progressed far enough past the imitative stage to influence the music's main line of development. Paul *Bley and Oscar *Peterson are among the few; others, among them Sonny *Greenwich, have not had the exposure to bring their innovations to other musicians' attention.

Moreover, because opportunities to perform are infrequent and generally unrewarding financially, jazz can be a full-time occupation for only a very few. By far the majority of Canadian jazz musicians must pursue it as a sideline, supported by work in studio, hotel, or dance orchestras, in lounge groups, or, latterly, in rock bands. There has been much transiency among jazz musicians in Canada (see, for example, the careers of Ron *Park and P.J. *Perry) as they look primarily for employment in jazz and secondarily for some security outside the immediate jazz field.

As late as 1978 the critic Barry Tepperman was able to comment: 'There is no "Canadian jazz" at present – there is only jazz in Canada. In Canada's current state as the closest and most easily dominated outpost of the American empire, any thought of independent voices in jazz is premature when the country is unable to support any improvising artists solely by the product of their artistry' (*Jazz Forum*, 53, 1978).

1 Early history in Canada
2 Traditional (or dixieland) jazz
3 Bebop
4 Big bands
5 Third stream
6 Contemporary
7 Avant garde
8 Canadians in the USA and Europe; US and European musicians in Canada
9 Venues and media

1 EARLY HISTORY IN CANADA. The earliest jazz bands heard in Canada were most often of US origin – a quartet led by the saxophonist Bobby Brown and including the pianist Bingie Madison is known to have played in Canada in 1920, and the self-proclaimed 'inventor of jazz,' pianist Jelly Roll Morton, performed ca 1922 at two Vancouver venues, one the Regent Hotel. Hollis Peavey's Jazz Bandits from New York played at Winnipeg's Roseland Ballroom as the Roseland Dance Orchestra in the winter of 1923.

A claim has been made by Tommy *Reilly that his father, Capt James Reilly, led the first Canadian jazz band ca 1920–5 in Guelph, Ont. In 1925 Jimmy (later Trump) *Davidson, with members of his family, formed the Melody Five, styled after Red Nichols and his Five Pennies.

The introduction of jazz into other musical genres, in Canada, came in the mid-to-late 1920s in the form of the 'hot' solos heard in hotel and dance bands in the larger cities. The Gilbert *Watson Orchestra of Toronto, for example, recorded 'St Louis Blues' in 1926 with the trumpeter Kurt Little (from Buffalo, NY) as soloist; this may be the earliest jazz recording by a Canadian band. Other 'hot' soloists of this era included the cornetist Davidson and the trombonist Seymour 'Red' Ginzler of the Luigi *Romanelli Orchestra in Toronto and the fiddlers Bus Totten of Lafe Cassidy's Hotel Vancouver Orchestra and Ben Corber of Montreal. Improvised solos by the alto saxophonist Carmen *Lombardo were heard on the first recordings (1924) of Guy *Lombardo and His Royal Canadians.

In Toronto in the early 1930s, the pianist Harry Lucas formed the Harlem Aces, an all-black sextet which played Jimmy Lunceford and Duke Ellington tunes and arrangements for black audiences. Other black groups and orchestras (see Black musicians) were active in Canada in this period and presumably included some jazz in their repertoires.

Jazz remained an incidental part of Canadian pop music throughout the 1930s and 1940s, with such musicians as Davidson, Bobby *Gimby, Cliff *McKay, Bert *Niosi, and Pat *Riccio in Toronto; Peterson, the fiddler Willy Girard, the US trumpeter Louis Metcalf (at the Café St-Michel), and the saxophonist Stan Wood in Montreal; and the guitarist Ray Norris, the tenor saxophonist Carl DeSantis, and the pianists Bud Henderson and Wilf Wylie in Vancouver responsible for what sporadic activity there was.

Visiting US bands, however, appeared frequently in Canadian dance halls, and jazz recordings were heard as early as 1937 in Vancouver on CJOR radio (Bob Smith, the host) and by 1941 in Toronto on the CBC's '1010 Swing Club' (Byng Whitteker and Elwood Glover, co-hosts).

The late 1940s saw the coincident revival of traditional jazz and the rise of bebop. These unrelated developments served as the foundation of jazz in Canada.

2 TRADITIONAL. 'When traditional jazz moved up the river from New Orleans in the twenties, it didn't stop in Chicago, as history has mistakenly recorded, but merely lingered there for a few decades of rest before it travelled on, via the Great Lakes and the Humber River, to its true and flourishing home in Toronto' (Jack Batten, Toronto *Globe and Mail*, 30 Nov 1976). Behind that intentional exaggeration of fact lies one point of truth: dixieland or 'trad' (traditional) jazz has had a remarkable durability with Toronto audiences.

Though Trump Davidson in the mid-1930s began playing a commercial brand of dixieland, a style patterned after that of the white musicians of Chicago, the international 'trad' revival of the original style of black New Orleans musicians was taken up in the late 1940s by the Toronto musicians Clyde Clarke (pianist and leader of the Queen City Jazz Band, and also a scriptwriter for CJBC's '1010 Swing Club'), Ken Dean (cornetist and leader of the Hot Seven), and others.

In the 1950s and early 1960s the leading Toronto band was (the cornetist) Mike White's Imperial Jazz Band, which often presented US players as guest soloists. Other popular bands were led by Jimmy Scott and the trombonist Bud Hill. The Metro Stompers (led in turn by Jim *McHarg and Jim *Galloway) were the most successful band of the mid-1960s (rivalled by Larry *Dubin's Big Muddys) and survived throughout the 1970s (when the Climax Jazz Band was very popular). In 1979 Jim McHarg organized a festival at Harbourfront, Toronto, at which 12 local bands performed, among them the Stompers, (clarinetist)

Al Lawrie's Jazz Corporation, and the Climax, Excelsior, Maple Leaf, and Silver Leaf jazz bands.

Other cities also have had bands or musicians who have championed dixieland or 'trad': Lance *Harrison in Vancouver, beginning in 1950; the cornetist Peter Power in Halifax during the 1950s; (the pianist) Gordon Bennett's Capital City Jazz Band, formed in Ottawa in the 1950s and still active in 1980, rivalled by the Apex Jazz Band; the Limestone City Jazz Band, 1957–ca 1962, of Kingston, Ont; and the Mountain City Jazz Band (1950s and early 1960s) and the Al Peters Jazz Band (1970s) of Montreal.

With very few exceptions these bands could be described as semi-professional in the sense that many of the musicians also work outside music. Many musicians are of British or European origin, and there is a large contingent of Scottish players: McHarg, Galloway, Lawrie, the cornetist Charlie Gall (leader of Dr McJazz), the trombonist Jim Abercrombie (leader of the Vintage Jazz Band), the pianist Ian Bargh, the trumpeter Malcolm Higgins, the clarinetist Jim Purdie, and the drummer Gordon Urquhart among them.

3 BEBOP. Developed in New York during the early-to-mid-1940s, this harmonically advanced and rhythmically freer style of jazz had made its way to Canada by the late 1940s, as recordings by Moe *Koffman and Oscar Peterson attest. Other early 'boppers' in Canada were Willy Girard, the pianist Argonne Thornton (Sadik *Hakim), the tenor saxophonist Benny Winestone, the pianist 'Steep' Wade, the trombonist 'Butch' Watanabe, and the drummer Mark 'Wilkie' Wilkinson in Montreal during the 1940s; Al *Neil and Ray Norris in Vancouver; and Norm *Amadio, Herbie *Spanier, and the tenor saxophonists Bill Goddard and Dave Hammer, the alto saxophonists Bernie *Piltch and Jerry *Toth, and the pianist Fred Webster in Toronto in the 1950s. Later notable players in the bebop tradition include the pianists Wray *Downes and Maury *Kaye, the saxophonists Sayyd *Abdul Al-Khabyyr, Dale Hillary, Alvinn Pall, Leo Perron, and P.J. Perry, and the US trumpeter Sam Noto (a resident of Toronto after 1975).

Bebop remained fundamental to the styles of most of Canada's popular jazz musicians for the next 25 years, and then was rivalled only by the modal style developed in the 1960s (see section 6). The so-called (US) 'west coast cool' style, which postdates bebop by about five years but attracted some of its players, has been perpetuated in Canada by bands led in the mid-1950s by Ron *Collier and Fraser *MacPherson and especially in the arrangements of Phil *Nimmons and other big band writers.

4 BIG BANDS. The first Canadian 'big band' – some 12 to 21 musicians divided into brass, reed, and rhythm sections – known to have had an extensive jazz repertoire was the Rex *Battle band of Toronto. The band worked in the summer of 1935 at Bob-Lo Island, near Detroit, and was patterned after Bob Crosby's US band. Bert Niosi 1932–50, Trump Davidson 1936–42 and 1944–61, Cy McLean ca 1937–40, and Johnny *Holmes 1941–51 led dance bands with some jazz leanings, but it was not until the 1950s and the formation of bands by Cal Jackson and Phil Nimmons (Toronto), Steve Garrick and 'Butch' Watanabe (Montreal), and Dave *Robbins (Vancouver) that the big band tradition was established firmly in Canadian music. Other bands followed in the 1960s, among them those led by the trombonist Ray Sikora (Vancouver), by Ron Collier, Pat Riccio, and Don *Thompson (Toronto), and by Lee *Gagnon and Vic *Vogel (Montreal).

The rise of the stage-band movement in Canadian schools in the early 1970s led to a growing audience for big bands (with which stage bands share the same instrumentation and repertoire). The *Canadian Stage Band Festival has been the focus for this activity, and Humber College in Toronto its academic centre; three Humber bands – the 'A' and 'B' bands and Ron Collier's Humber Extension – though essentially student ensembles, were among the leading big bands in Canada of the late 1970s. Other important bands have been led by Doug Parker in Vancouver; Tommy *Banks in Edmonton; Shelly Berger, Jim Galloway, Rob *McConnell (*Boss Brass), Ted *Moses, and Fred *Stone in Toronto; and Ron Paley in Winnipeg. Big band recordings won the first three *Juno Awards given in the jazz category: Nimmons' *Atlantic Suite* (1976), the Boss Brass' *Big Band Jazz* (1977), and Tommy Banks' *Jazz Canada Montreux* (1978).

See also Dance bands.

5 THIRD STREAM. This term, invented in the mid-1950s by the US composer-conductor Gunther Schuller, describes a music combining elements of classical music (usually form) with those of jazz (improvisation, rhythmic character, and tonal colour). The third-stream movement flourished in Canada concurrently with activity elsewhere, largely through the efforts of Norman *Symonds, Ron Collier, and other pupils of Gordon *Delamont who employed fugue, sonata, concerto grosso, and other forms as frameworks for improvisation by jazz groups.

Writing of Symonds' *Concerto Grosso* for jazz quintet and symphony orchestra (1957), John *Beckwith described the work as 'more natural than such parallel European works as those of Rolf Liebermann, in which the jazz element is more superficially imitated and more crudely contrasted with the concert-symphonic vocabulary' (*Dictionary of Contemporary Music*). Symonds continued to work in the idiom throughout the 1960s and completed several works for orchestra and jazz soloist or jazz group.

Also in the 1960s the Dave Robbins big band and the *Vancouver SO joined for performances of works in this idiom, among them several by Robbins' bassist, Paul Ruhland. Ruhland, Doug *Riley, and Don (W.) *Thompson have employed the 12-tone row in themes for jazz group. Such jazz soloists as the saxophonist Bernie Piltch and the flugelhorn player Fred Stone (who himself has written pieces in the third stream) have been central figures in the movement, participating in several premieres and later performances of Canadian works.

On a more superficial level, works from the classical repertoire adapted for jazz group by Moe Koffman and Doug Riley enjoyed substantial commercial success in the 1970s; and both Ted Moses and Kathryn *Moses have written or adapted music for jazz group and chamber ensemble. The influence of jazz in turn is evident in composed works by Neil *Chotem, Harry *Freedman, François *Morel, Michel *Perrault, and John *Weinzweig.

6 CONTEMPORARY. In the 1950s and 1960s bebop underwent various subtle changes, resulting in 'hard bop' and 'post bop,' distinguished by their increased assertiveness and virtuosity of execution. These styles were evident in Canada during the 1960s in the work of Nick *Ayoub, Lee Gagnon (and his frequent colleague, the trumpeter Ron Proby), Nelson *Symonds, and Don (W.) Thompson. In the 1960s the dominant influences in jazz were the Miles Davis Quintet and the John Coltrane Quartet. The leaders and their sidemen originated styles adopted at varying rates by Canadian musicians. Saxophonist Coltrane's modal improvisations and emotionally expressive performances, for example, found little immediate support in Canada save in tandem with other influences through the playing (in relative obscurity) of the saxophonists Brian *Barley and Ron Park and indirectly in the guitar style of Sonny Greenwich.

Even in the late 1970s, when the saxophonists Ron Allen, Ayoub, Alvinn Pall, Michael Stuart, and John Tank had adopted Coltrane's style in whole or in part, the music's aggressive nature left it unpalatable to a large part of the jazz audience in Canada. The styles of Coltrane's pianist, McCoy Tyner, and drummer, Elvin Jones, like those of Davis' pianist, Herbie Hancock, and drummer, Tony Williams, were apparent more immediately in the playing of Canadian musicians.

Other Canadian musicians who have led groups which play in the contemporary idiom include the pianists Frank Falco, Pierre *Leduc, George McFetridge, Art Roberts, Bernie *Senensky, and Don Thompson; the saxophonists Eugene Amaro, Bob Brough, Jane Fair, Glen Hall, Jerry LaBelle, and Rick *Wilkins; the drummers Cisco Normand and Claude *Ranger; and the guitaritsts Lenny *Breau and Peter Leitch.

Following Miles Davis' lead, many musicians turned in the 1970s to a 'fusion' music in which the improvisatory principles of jazz were wedded to the technology (amplified instruments and synthesizers) and rhythms of rock, creating a style notable, musically, for its energy and, commercially, for its wide popularity. Proponents of fusion music in Canada have included the bands *Maneige and Aquarelle (Montreal), Zdenka (Winnipeg), Cobra (led by the keyboardist and record producer Dale Jacobs) and *Pacific Salt (Vancouver); and the individual musicians David Bendeth (guitar, Toronto), Moe Koffman, Hugh Marsh (violin, Ottawa), Ted Moses, Ron Paley (bass, Winnipeg), and Doug Riley.

Late in the decade elements of disco were introduced to jazz in much the same way those of rock had been; and in Canada, recordings in the style were made by Koffman.

7 AVANT GARDE (Free Jazz, New Music, etc). Characterized by a variable reliance on composition and/or adherence to predetermined factors governing improvisation, the avant garde in jazz of the 1960s and 1970s may be dated from the innovations of the saxophonist and composer Ornette Coleman and the pianist and composer Cecil Taylor in the late 1950s and from the subsequent stylistic advances introduced by the saxophonists John Coltrane, Eric Dolphy, and Albert Ayler, among other instrumentalists. Coleman's compositions were played as early as 1960 by Canadians – the saxophonist himself had performed in Vancouver in the late 1950s. The earliest free jazz in Canada was that of the *Artists' Jazz Band, formed in Toronto in 1962. Stuart *Broomer led his first bands in 1966 in Toronto, Al Neil turned from bebop to the new music around 1966, and the *Quatuor de jazz libre du Québec was founded in 1967.

After a period of relative inactivity, free jazz in Canada expanded on several fronts: Montreal (the Atelier de musique expérimentale 1973–5 and the Ensemble de musique improvisée de Montréal, formed in 1978), Toronto (the *CCMC, the All Time Sound Effects Orchestra formed in 1975, the Avant Garde Jazz Revival Band 1975–6, Air Raid formed in 1978, and the New Art Music Ensemble formed in 1979), London, Ont (the Nihilist Spasm

Band and Eric Stach), Calgary (Western Music Improvisation Co, fl mid-1970s), and Vancouver (the New Orchestra Quintet formed in 1978).

Individual musicians active in free jazz have included the pianists Broomer, Paul Plimley, Michael *Snow, and Casey Sokol; the saxophonists Maury Coles, Paul Cram, Glen Hall, Nobuo Kubota, Robert Leriche, and Bill *Smith; the guitarists Eugene Chadbourne (a US musician active ca 1973–6 in Calgary, where he also wrote music criticism for the *Herald*), Lloyd Garber, and Randy Hutton; the bassists L.S. Lansall-Ellis and Claude Simard; and the percussionists Larry Dubin and Gregg Simpson. The trumpeter Kenny *Wheeler has been an important player internationally in this style.

8 CANADIANS IN THE USA AND EUROPE; US AND EUROPEAN MUSICIANS IN CANADA. The most distinguished Canadian-born musicians in jazz are Oscar Peterson and the arranger-composer Gil Evans. The latter (b Ian Ernest Gilmore Green in Toronto, 13 May 1912) earned his standing through his innovative writing 1941–2 and 1946–8 for the Claude Thornhill orchestra and his collaborations with the soloists Miles Davis (resulting in the classic jazz LPs *Miles Ahead*, 1957; *Porgy and Bess*, 1958; and *Sketches of Spain*, 1959) and Cannonball Adderley (*Pacific Standard Time* 1958–9).

Other notable Canadian-born musicians with careers in the USA (many of whom, like Evans, left Canada while very young and are not treated individually in *EMC*) include Alvin 'Abe' Aarons (b Toronto 1920), a saxophonist (1950s) with Les Brown; Alfred 'Chico' Alvarez (b Montreal 1920), a trumpeter 1941–51 with Stan Kenton; Georgie Auld (b George Altwerger, in Toronto, 19 May 1919), a prominent swing-era (1930s and 1940s) tenor saxophonist; the pianists Paul Bley and Dave *Bowman; the vibraphonist Warren *Chiasson; the trumpeter Maynard *Ferguson; Hal Gaylor (b Montreal 1929; emigrated to the USA ca 1956), bassist with Chico Hamilton, Kai Winding, Paul Bley, Benny Goodman, and others; the vibraphonist Hagood *Hardy; the pianist Lou *Hooper; Vernon Isaac (b British Columbia), a saxophonist in the 1930s, briefly with Louis Armstrong and Duke Ellington – he retired to Ottawa in the mid-1970s; Kenny Kersey (b Harrow, Ont, 1916), 'one of [the] most advanced swing pianists of his day in early 40s' (Leonard Feather, *Encyclopedia of Jazz* 1960), who played for Red Allen, Andy Kirk, and 1946–9 for the Jazz at the Philharmonic concerts; Al Lucas (b Windsor, Ont, 1916), bassist with Eddie Heywood 1943–6 and in the 1950s, in 1946 with Duke Ellington, and 1947–53 with Illinois Jacquet; Stuart MacKay (b Montreal 1909), a saxophonist with the big bands of Isham Jones, Les Brown, Red Norvo, and others in the 1930s and 1940s; Arnold 'Red' McGarvey and Danny Perri (see Guitar); the singer Anne Marie *Moss; Roy Reynolds (b Ottawa), a tenor and baritone saxophonist with Stan Kenton in the 1970s; Bob Rudd (b Toronto 1920, d Ottawa 1971), bassist during the 1940s in Los Angeles with Noble Sissle, Lucky Thompson, and others and active after 1950 in Montreal; the trumpeters Herb Spanier and Fred Stone; and the saxophonist John Tank in the 1970s in New York.

Canadian-born musicians active in British jazz include Bob Burns of Toronto, a saxophonist in big bands and studio orchestras after the 1950s; Art *Ellefson; Wally Fawkes (b Vancouver 1924), a clarinetist after World War II with British 'trad' bands; Max Goldberg of Toronto, the 'hot' trumpet soloist in British dance and jazz bands of the 1930s; John Warren of Montreal, the composer and saxophonist whose big band toured widely in continental Europe in the 1970s and recorded his suite *Tales of the Algonquin* (1971, Deram SML 1094); and Kenny Wheeler. In Europe the trumpeter Arthur Briggs (b St George, Ont, 9 Apr 1901) began leading bands in France as early as 1919; and the pianists Wray Downes and Milt Sealey and the bassist Lloyd Thompson played in Paris jazz clubs in the mid-1950s.

Most of the major (US) jazzmen have performed in Canada as part of their usual touring regimens. US-born players prominent in Canada have included the trumpeter Sam Noto; the saxophonists Sayyd Abdul Al-Khabyyr and Lee Gagnon (Montreal) and Pat LaBarbera and Steve Lederer (Toronto 1970s); the clarinetist Henry Cuesta (Toronto 1963–72); the flutists Paul Horn (Victoria, BC, 1970s) and Kathryn Moses; the pianists Gene DiNovi (heard in the 1970s at the Charles One nightclub in Toronto, and on CBC radio), Linton Garner (Montreal and Vancouver), Elmer Gill (Vancouver), Paul *Hoffert, Cal Jackson (popular in Toronto clubs and on the CBC 1950–6), Joey Masters (Toronto 1950s), and Sadik Hakim; the guitarists Lenny Breau, Lonnie *Johnson, and Bob Mann (Toronto studio musician 1970s); the bassists Charles Biddle (a frequent partner of Nelson Symonds in Montreal), Richard *Homme, and Wyatt Ruther (Ottawa and Vancouver); the singers Salome *Bey, Dianne Brooks, Jodie Drake of Toronto, and Clarence 'Big' Miller of Edmonton; and the composers and bandleaders Ted Moses and Dave Robbins.

Several European musicians also have spent time in Canada: members of the Climax Jazz Band in Toronto – Bruce Bakewell (clarinet), Chris Daniels (bass), and Geoff Holmes (trombone) of England, Jurgen Hesse (banjo) of Germany, and Bob Erwig (trumpet) of Holland; Peter *Appleyard and the drummer Barry 'Kid' Martyn (the latter a member of Montreal 'trad' bands, ca 1960) of England; the drumming teacher Jim *Blackley and his son Keith, the pianist Joel Shulman (who moved from New York to Toronto in 1972, opening and performing at a small restaurant, the Garden Party) and the saxophonist Benny Winestone (an itinerant dance and jazz band musician in Toronto and Montreal after 1939) of Scotland (see also section 2); the bassist Torben Oxbol (Vancouver 1970s), of Denmark; the composer-bassist Paul Ruhland (Vancouver ca 1952–64, see Dave Robbins) from Austria; the Belgian (gypsy) guitarist René Thomas (Montreal 1958–63, often working with his countryman, saxophonist Bobby Jaspar); the Estonian bassist Bob (Baron Wilhelm Ernst von) Schilling who worked 1952–6 in Toronto and died in 1956 in New York during an engagement with Norm Amadio's quartet; and the singer Aura (Rully) from Rumania.

9 VENUES AND MEDIA. Caught between the worlds of classical and pop music, jazz has lived much of its life in the nightclub environment. The major cities in Canada have had one or more clubs with varying policies. Some, like the Colonial Tavern (Toronto) and the Rising Sun (Montreal), have presented complete US groups; others (eg, the Town Tavern and Bourbon Street in Toronto, the Cellar in Vancouver, and several clubs in Montreal) have presented US soloists with local accompanists; and still others (eg, *George's Spaghetti House and the House of Hambourg in Toronto, Rockhead's Paradise in Montreal) present Canadian-based musicians more or less exclusively.

Concert halls have been the sites of some jazz presentations, eg, the famous Quintet of the Year (Charlie Parker, Dizzy Gillespie, Bud Powell, Charles Mingus, and Max Roach) concert 15 May 1953 at *Massey Hall. Musicians also perform under the auspices of jazz societies, among them those in Vancouver, Edmonton, Calgary, Winnipeg, Toronto, and Ottawa, whose corollary activities have included the publication of newsletters and the preparation of educational presentations.

Though jazz has had relatively little TV exposure – save for the Timex-sponsored specials on the CBC in the late 1950s, other CBC specials (including those devoted to Mingus and Ellington), CTV's 'Oscar Peterson Presents' in 1974, and the syndicated 'Peter Appleyard Presents' of the late 1970s – it has been popularized through many radio programs, of both CBC and private-station origin. The CBC programs, many of which have featured specially recorded performances by Canadian musicians (that is, instead of recordings of US players) include: '1010 Swing Club' 1941–8, and its successor 'Jazz Unlimited' 1948–65 (with Dick MacDougal as host until his death in 1957, and then with Phil MacKellar); 'Jazz at Its Best,' nationally and locally 1950–76 with Ted Miller as host and produced by Henry Whiston in Montreal; 'Jazz Workshop,' featuring bands from various cities 1954–65; 'Jazz Canadiana,' 1965–71; 'That Midnight Jazz,' a record show which began in 1969 and in 1980 still was heard weeknights from different cities; and 'Jazz Radio-Canada,' begun in 1974 from CBC Winnipeg with Mary Nelson and Lee Major as hosts. 'Jazz en liberté,' produced at the *Ermitage in Montreal, in 1965 began weekly half-hour concerts by the city's leading musicians. In the private sector, Ted O'Reilly (CJRT, Toronto), Phil MacKellar (CKFM, Toronto), and Len Dobbin (CJFM, Montreal) have had long-running programs. O'Reilly's 'The Jazz Scene,' begun ca 1965, was heard 24 hours a week by the late 1970s.

Books by Canadians about jazz include *Eric Dolphy, a Bio-Discography* (Washington 1974) by the Toronto medical doctor Barry Tepperman in collaboration with Vladimir Skomioski and *Coming through Slaughter* (Toronto 1976), a dramatized account of Buddy Bolden's life by the Toronto poet-author Michael Ondaatje. Tepperman also wrote extensively 1969–77 for *Coda*. Other jazz journalists include: in Montreal, Len Dobbin (*Coda, The Gazette*), Nighthawk – pen-name of Claude Rachou – (*The Gazette*), and Gilles Archambault (*Le Devoir*); in Toronto, Jack Batten (*Globe and Mail, Toronto Star*, etc), Helen McNamara (*Toronto Telegram*), Mark Miller (*Down Beat, Jazz Forum, Globe and Mail*), John *Norris, Patrick Scott (*Globe and Mail*), Bill Smith, and Ken Waxman; and in Vancouver, Bob Smith (*The Sun*).

Publications devoted to jazz have been *Jazz Panorama* (Toronto ca 1947, edited by Helen McNamara and Marion Madghett and briefly by Patrick Scott) and *Coda*. Canadian columns have appeared sporadically in several non-Canadian jazz publications, among them *Down Beat* (Chicago) and *Jazz Forum* (Warsaw).

Canadian musicians who have remained in their home country have not been recorded extensively. Only Sackville (see *Coda*) and the affiliated Onari label (see Bill Smith) have concentrated on jazz, and Sackville's roster is largely of US musicians. However, small companies and a few major ones have recorded some Canadian players: *Arc (Pat Riccio), Attic (Boss Brass, Joel Shulman), *Capitol (Lee Gagnon, Yvan Landry), Chateau (Trump Davidson), *CTL (Norm Amadio, Ron Collier, and others), *GRT (Moe Koffman, Doug Riley's Dr. Music), *Hallmark (Mike White's Imperial Jazz Band), *London (Milt Sealey), and Umbrella (Boss Brass and Humber College). The New Jersey jazz label, PM, released seven LPs by Canadians 1975–9. Many other LPs, in the late 1970s, were financed and produced by the musicians themselves. The largest collection of recorded Canadian jazz is that of RCI whose approximately 500 albums (by 1980) included some 45 by jazz musicians. The CBC's LM recorded sound series also includes jazz albums.

Discographies of Canadian jazz have been prepared by Jack Litchfield, Lois Moody, and Mary Nelson (see Discography). Other jazz-related entries in *EMC* include Al Baculis; Guido Basso; Ed Bickert; Gordie Brandt; Brass; Terry Clarke; Eleanor Collins; Jimmy Dale; Michel Donato; Double-bass; Don Francks; Jerry Fuller; Yvan Landry; Russ Little; Phyllis Marshall; Ian McDougall; Tony Romandini; and Woodwinds.

BIBLIOGRAPHY

Norris, John, Dobbin, Len, et al. *Coda*, columns, 1958–
Norris, John. 'Jazz in Canada,' *International Musician*, annual review, Jan, 1962–75
'Jazz in Canada,' *CanComp*, 67, Feb 1972
Offstein, Alan. 'The Canadian Broadcasting Corporation Transcription jazz story ... a conversation with Ted Farrant,' *Coda*, vol 10, Aug 1972
Norris, John. '2. CBC,' ibid
Danson, Peter. 'Mr. Bebop recalls,' *Montreal Review*, Spring–Summer 1979. An interview with Len Dobbin
Rodriguez, Juan. 'Jazz lives: the hot spots in town,' Montreal *Gazette*, 26 Jan 1980
Burton, Dennis. 'Toronto jazz,' *Musicworks*, vol 2, Spring 1980
Miller, Mark. 'Canada's do-it-yourself track to recording all that jazz,' *PfAC*, Spring 1980
– 'Canadian jazz musicians in search of a better climate,' ibid, Summer 1980
Golets, N. 'All that Montreal jazz,' *Blow Up*, vol 5, Jun 1980 MM

Jazz libre. See Quatuor de jazz libre du Québec.

JEAN, (Joseph Christian) **Bernard.** Oboist, teacher, b Kénogami (now Jonquière), Que, 21 Sep 1948; premier prix oboe (CMQ) 1968, premier prix oboe (Paris Cons) 1970, premier prix chamber music (Paris Cons) 1971. At the *CMQ, he studied piano 1962–3 with Hélène *Landry and oboe 1962–6 with Réal *Gagnier and 1966–8 with Jacques *Simard. He was a prize winner in 1966 in the *JMC's competition and the *Canadian Music Competitions. He played english horn 1966–8 in the *Quebec SO and toured 1967–8 for the JMC. On a *Canada Council scholarship he continued his studies 1968–71 with Étienne Baudo at the Paris Cons, gave recitals in Paris, and played in 1969 in Nice. In 1971 he studied at the international music camp in Pécs, Hungary, and joined the French Chamber Music Quartet for concerts at the Festival Loewenguth. Returning to Quebec that year, he was the principal oboe 1972–3 of the Quebec SO and taught oboe 1972–5 at *Laval U and at the Cons de Trois-Rivières. He was a founding member (1972) of the *Quebec Woodwind Quintet. He toured Germany 1972–3 with the pianist Colombe *Pelletier for the JMC and in 1973 taught at the *JMC Orford Art Centre's summer camp, recorded a series of recitals on CBC radio, played as a soloist with the *NACO, and was the principal oboe in the CBC Montreal orchestra. In 1975 his performance of Martinů's *Concerto* with a CBC orchestra at the *Salle Claude-Champagne, for the radio program 'Les Grands Concerts,' prompted Gilles *Potvin to describe him as 'a virtuoso and a musician without equal in this exacting work' (*Le Devoir*, 3 Feb 1975). Jean began teaching at the *CMM in 1975. His pupils have included Louise Pellerin, Pierre-M. Plante, and Pierre-V. Plante.

BIBLIOGRAPHY

'Bernard Jean, hautboïste, avec l'Orchestre de la Suisse romande,' *Ici Radio-Canada*, 12–18 Aug 1978 AP

Jean le Précurseur. 'Religious lyric poem' in three parts, the text a free-verse adaptation by Albert Lozeau of the prose of Father Antonio LeBel, the music by Guillaume *Couture. Composed at the request of Mgr Paul Bruchési, archbishop of Montreal (to whom it was dedicated), the oratorio was written over a period of three years, beginning in 1907. Its three sections are The Nativity, The Sermon, and The Martyrdom. The work was inspired by the biblical story of John the Baptist. The score calls for 12 solo voices, a mixed choir, and orchestra.

Though a vocal score was published in Paris in 1914 by C. Joubert, the oratorio was not performed until 6 Feb 1923 at the *St-Denis Theatre in Montreal under the aegis of the *St-Jean-Baptiste Society. Jean *Goulet conducted the *Assn des chanteurs de Montréal with the famous French bass Léon Rothier in the role of John and the tenor Henri *Prieur in that of the Narrator. 'Undoubtedly the best that has been written in its genre in Canada,' wrote Gustave *Comte in *La Patrie*, the day after the performance.

Owing to its success, the work was presented again in the same theatre 5 April, with the same performers except for Rothier, who was replaced by Louis *Verschelden. A third performance was given 29 Apr 1924 at the St-Denis Theatre, again with Goulet, Prieur, and Verschelden. The work was given another performance, this time in the open air at the Montreal Stadium 23 Jun 1928 by the same performers and an orchestra of 100.

According to Léo-Pol *Morin (*Papiers de musique*, Montreal 1930), 'a work like *Jean le Précurseur* teems with fine harmonic achievements, [and] one finds beautifully balanced choral sections, particularly the one which concludes the first part and which is in the form of a fugue. The second part is fairly successful with its themes borrowed from the liturgy, but it is in the third part, the so-called secular part, that the author falls down. The Banquet, the Dances of Salomé and the aria of Antipas: Délices! Voluptés! – these are failures. No, Couture was not in his element here. He was more at ease in the earlier parts, with their religious nature. He was at his best, perhaps, in his religious music, especially the Requiem.'

On 22 Jun 1964 the St-Jean-Baptiste Society's Commission for the Festivities of French Canada presented another performance of the work at the Salle Wilfrid-Pelletier (*PDA) with the *MSO and the choirs of the *JMC and the *U of Montreal under the direction of Wilfrid *Pelletier, with Robert *Savoie as John and Léopold *Simoneau as the Narrator.

See also Oratorios, Canadian (composition and performance) 6.

BIBLIOGRAPHY

Lamontagne, C.-O. 'Événement canadien,' *MCan*, 20, 17 Feb 1923
– 'L'oeuvre grandiose de Guillaume Couture,' *P-T*, 910, May 1947 GP

JEANNOTTE, Jean-Paul. Tenor, teacher, administrator, b Rawdon, north of Montreal, 9 Mar 1926. He studied voice in Montreal in 1944 with Salvator *Issaurel and 1945–6 with Émile *Gour. He continued his studies in Paris in 1947 with Mme d'Estainville Rousset and 1951–3 with Pierre Bernac. In 1947 he made his debut in Cherbourg as Vincent in *Mireille* and Piféar in Adam's *Si j'étais roi*. His Montreal debut came the following year with the *Variétés lyriques as Fritellini in Audran's *La Mascotte*, and he performed often with this company until 1955. With the *Minute Opera in 1949 he sang Bastien in Mozart's *Bastien et Bastienne* and the Narrator in Monteverdi's *Il Combattimento di Tancredi e Clorinda*. In 1950 he toured in France as a soloist with the *Disciples de Massenet.

During the ensuing years Jeannotte made many appearances on stage, in concert, and on radio and TV. He made a series of tours 1952–3 for the *JMC and took part 1955–8 in the weekly CBC radio program 'L'Âme des poètes.' His artistry was particularly apparent in recital, and he excelled in the performance of French, German, and Italian songs during many tours of Canada and a 1961 tour of Europe and the USSR with the pianist Jeanne *Landry. A distinguished Pelléas in Debussy's opera *Pelléas et Mélisande*, Jeannotte sang the role opposite Suzanne Danco in a 1955 CBC concert performance of the opera, and in another, broadcast by the ORTF the same year, with Gérard Souzay as Golaud. Equally noteworthy were his portrayals of Gonzalve in Ravel's *L'Heure espagnole* (CBC 1955), Basilio in *The Marriage of Figaro* (*Montreal Festivals 1956), and Bobino in *Blackburn's **Silent Measures*. He sang Bobino in the 1956 premiere on CBC TV, on stage in Toronto and Montreal, and more than 100 times on a 1960–1 JMC tour and in other productions. He performed with several orchestras and chamber music groups including the Ensemble Jean-Philippe-Rameau which he helped found in 1954.

Jeannotte began teaching at *Laval U in 1964 and conducting the Laval Vocal Quartet in 1973. He began teaching at the *École Vincent-d'Indy in 1973. He was vice president 1964–6 and president 1966–72 of the UDA and a member 1969–76 of the board of directors of the *SMCQ, 1973–7 of the board of the *PDA, and 1976–80 of the administrative council of the *Opéra du Québec. In 1974 he was head of a task force set up by the *MACQ to enquire into the state of lyric art, dance, and symphonic music. Early in 1980 he was appointed artistic director of the Opéra de Montréal and of the Opéra de chambre du Québec.

Jeannotte is the composer of *Propos intimes*, four songs for voice and piano on poems by Éloi de Grandmont (Musica 1948; also recorded, by André *Turp and Paul *Trépanier), and of a *Pater* for choir which was performed in 1950 at Notre-Dame in Paris. Of his performance as Pelléas, the critic René Leibowitz wrote in *L'Express*: 'The choice of the young French-Canadian tenor seemed to me particularly felicitous. I found his intelligent and dramatic interpretation of the role most moving.'

DISCOGRAPHY

Bergerettes, brunettes. Gilbert hpd. Sel M.298.089
Garant 'Et je prierai ta grâce'; *Concerts sur terre*; *Caprices* – Morel *Les Rivages perdus* – Mercure *Dissidence*. Garant pf, Landry pf. 1962. RCI 201
Gounod – Hahn. Landry pf. 1961. Sel M.298.012
Scarlatti *Pastorale cantata* – Rameau *Diane et Actéon*. Landry pf, Baillargeon vn, Mignault vc. 1954. RCI 110/Parrenin Quar, M. Charbonnier hpd. 1956. LUMEN LD-2-120
Schubert – Fauré. Landry pf. 1963. Sel M.298.046
See also Musica Antica e Nuova; Discography for the Montreal Bach Choir. GP

JEDIG, Helly H. (m Sapinski). Soprano, b Neuendorf, Ukraine (later Czechoslovakia), ca 1935. She moved to Germany as a child and studied music and drama at the Hanover Theatre School. In 1955 she emigrated to Canada and settled in Winnipeg, where her teachers included Sara Udow and Nina *Dempsey (voice) and Frans *Niermeier (piano and theory). She won numerous awards, including the Rose Bowl of the *Manitoba Music Competition Festival and the *MRMTA Scholarship (1959). In 1961 she received honourable mention in the *Metropolitan Opera's mid-west regional auditions. Moving to Toronto in the early 1960s she studied 1962–5 with Irene *Jessner. She made her *COC debut in 1964 as Flora in *La Traviata*. Other COC roles have included Liù in *Turandot* (1965), Santuzza in *Cavalleria Rusticana* (1966), Leonora in *Il Trovatore* (1967), Sieglinde in *Die Walküre* (1971), and Leonore in *Fidelio* (1973). She has performed extensively in Germany, singing leading roles with companies at Düsseldorf (*Madama Butterfly*), Essen (*Così fan tutte, The Fairy Queen, La Forza del Destino, Madama Butterfly*, and *Tannhäuser*), Kassel (*Così fan tutte*), and Münster (*The Bartered Bride, The Marriage of Figaro*, and *Tannhäuser*). She has appeared in concert and in oratorio performances. SW

JEFFERY, Gordon (Dumaresq). Lawyer, organist, conductor, b London, Ont, 15 Jul 1919; ATCM organ 1942, FRCO 1957, FTCL 1957, hon FRCCO 1973. While studying law at Osgoode Hall, Toronto, Jeffery took lessons from Charles *Peaker and Healey *Willan. On admission to the bar in 1942 he joined his family's law firm, Jeffery & Jeffery, in London, Ont, and began a long association with St Peter's Cathedral, serving as occasional organist. He studied organ intermittently 1943–6 in New York with the former Londoner Ernest *White and in 1948 arranged for White's return as organist-choirmaster at two London churches and as instructor 1948–51 at the Music Teachers' College.

In 1947 Jeffery purchased the abandoned 65-year-old Beecher United Church, renaming it Aeolian Hall. With assistance from the Silverwood Foundation, the *U of Western Ontario bought the hall in 1949 and spent $50,000 on renovations. Teaching studios and classrooms were installed in the downstairs area. A main hall, seating 500, featured an Aeolian-Skinner organ built to White's design for the New York church St Mary the Virgin. The organ's transfer to London was supervised by White. In 1951 Jeffery bought the hall back and commissioned Gabriel *Kney to effect further renovations of the organ. Aeolian Hall was the home of several Jeffery projects, including concerts by the London Chamber Orchestra (founded in 1945 and conducted by Jeffery) and the Aeolian Choral Society (founded 1949) and sessions of the London School of Church Music (begun in 1950). In 1968 the hall was destroyed by an arsonist. Shortly thereafter Jeffery purchased the former London Town Hall and renovated it in the style of a baroque church. A recital organ was installed (completed, 1972) by Gabriel Kney.

Jeffery was appointed registrar of the (*RCCO) *(CCO) in 1942 and served 1956–8 as president. An avid student of baroque and classical performance practices, Jeffery has displayed stylistic integrity in his orchestral programs, performances of oratorios and operas (which continued at the new Aeolian Hall throughout the 1970s), and organ recitals, both in London, Ont, and in Toronto. He helped plan, and gave a recital at, the International Congress of Organists in London, England, in 1957. He appeared frequently as a recitalist in Europe during the 1950s and recorded two Mozart organ sonatas and a concerto by Handel (with string orchestra conducted by Geoffrey *Waddington) on the Westminster Abbey organ during the International Congress (Mirrosonic DRE 1008). GKG

JEFFREY, Herbert Arthur. Educator, trombonist, conductor, b Kitchener, Ont, 1 Jun 1920; ARCM 1955, LGSM 1955. He played trombone at 10 in Waterloo bands and, after studies 1938–9 at the TCM with Harry Hawe (trombone) and Ettore *Mazzoleni (theory), was principal trombone 1940–5 and assistant conductor 1943–5 and 1946–52 of the RCN Band, Halifax. He studied 1952–5 in England at the RMSM (Kneller Hall), the RCM, and the GSM, returning to Canada to serve 1955–64 as director of *Princess Patricia's Canadian Light Infantry Band, which performed in Europe on several occasions 1957–9. Jeffrey was music director 1963–5 of the Edmonton Civic Opera. He was band consultant 1967–73 to the Saskatchewan Dept of Education and became program consultant to the department in 1973. He has composed a number of works for concert and brass band. CF

JEHIN-PRUME, Frantz (Henry) (b Jehin). Violinist, composer, teacher, b Spa, Belgium, 18 Apr 1839, d Montreal 29 May 1899; premier prix (Cons royal, Brussels) 1852. He began studying the violin at four with Nicholas Servais and was admitted the following year to the class of François Prume, his mother's brother, at the Liège Cons. (After the latter's death in 1849 Jehin added Prume to his own name.) He then enrolled at the Brussels Cons in the class of Hubert Léonard and studied harmony under Fétis. While taking courses in science he continued violin studies with such notable teachers as de Bériot, Wieniawski, and Vieuxtemps. After making his debut as a soloist in Brussels and Spa in 1855, Jehin-Prume embarked upon his first European tour, 1855–7, playing in Germany, Poland, Austria, and Russia. His success brought him many honours as well as another tour in Germany and Russia, where he stayed from 1857 to 1858, performing in Moscow and St Petersburg at concerts in which such celebrities as the Rubinstein brothers, Annette Essipov, and Jenny Lind also participated. He returned to Belgium in 1858, resumed his studies in harmony, and devoted himself to composition. He gave numerous concerts 1860–2 in Holland, France, and Belgium and in 1862 was appointed concertmaster at the Théâtre royal in Liège, but retained the position for only a few months. That same year he made another tour in Germany (Meyerbeer accompanied him at the piano in his Potsdam recital), followed by concerts in Scandinavia and Holland. On his return to Brussels in 1863 he was appointed by Leopold I 'violinist of the king's own music,' succeeding Charles de Bériot. In 1864 Jehin-Prume accepted an invitation to Mexico from the Emperor Maximilian, who had married Princess Charlotte, the daughter of Leopold I. He gave several concerts at the Imperial theatre and for four months continued to perform in the country despite the constant political strife. After a short stay in Brazil and a visit to Havana he arrived in New York early in May 1865.

Shortly afterwards he visited Canada to fish and hunt, at the invitation of his fellow countryman, the violinist Jules *Hone. At the request of the Jesuits, he donated his services for a charity concert in the Salle du Gesù in Montreal. His piano partner for the occasion was R.-O. *Pelletier. Subsequently, D.H. Sénécal and Gustave *Smith, representatives of the musicians of Montreal, visited the artist and drew from him a promise not to leave the country without performing at another concert. This took place 1 June in the Nordheimer Hall with the participation of several Montreal musicians, including A.J. *Boucher and Calixa *Lavallée. Such was his success that, by popular demand, he gave a third concert 8 June at the *Mechanics' Hall. A few days later, at a reception by the mayor, J.-Louis Beaudry, he met the singer Rosita *del Vecchio, whom he was to marry 17 Jul 1866. In the summer of 1865 he performed in several Canadian cities as well as in Detroit and New York on three occasions and later gave other concerts in Quebec and the Maritime provinces. In New York City he was soloist 16 Dec 1865 in the 101st concert of the Philharmonic Orchestra.

Frantz Jehin-Prume

Jehin-Prume and his wife gave numerous concerts in Canada and the USA, including one at the White House in January 1867, and later they appeared in Cuba and Belgium. With the singer Carlotta Patti and the pianist Theodore Ritter they toured Canada and the USA 1869–70, giving 111 concerts in 59 cities. With the fall of the Mexican Empire and the death of Maximilian (1867), and in view of his own marriage, Jehin-Prume decided to settle in Montreal and become a Canadian citizen. He and his wife were to play a leading role in the development of musical life in Montreal.

In the early months of 1871 he gave 'six classical chamber concerts' at the Mechanics' Hall. With colleagues he performed quartets by Haydn, Mozart, Beethoven, and Mendelssohn, some overtures, and, on two occasions, Beethoven's *Pastoral Symphony*. He himself played concertos by Viotti, Mendelssohn, Beethoven, and Vieuxtemps. He became the friend and collaborator of Calixa Lavallée after 1875 and prepared the choir and served as concertmaster of a 58-piece orchestra for some memorable performances of Gounod's *Jeanne d'Arc* in 1877 under Lavallée. He was president of the *AMQ 1877–8.

The untimely death of his wife in 1881 dealt the artist a heavy blow. He went back to Belgium and France in 1885 for a final tour and then returned to Montreal for good, to devote himself mainly to teaching. With several Montreal musicians, however, including his brother Erasme (also a violinist, b Spa 2 Jun 1845, d ?), who had arrived in Canada in 1888, the violinist Robert Gruenwald, the cellist Jean-Baptiste *Dubois, and the pianist Maria Heynberg, he founded in 1891 the Assn artistique de Montréal, the first professional chamber music society in Quebec. By its last concert, in May 1896, the association had presented a total of 31 events.

In addition to his many concerts in Quebec with Lavallée, Jehin-Prume in 1877 had participated as concertmaster of the orchestra in the first concert of the *Montreal Philharmonic Society and in 1887 had been soloist in the Mendelssohn *Concerto* with the same society. At the height of the Assn artistique's success, Jehin-Prume's health began to fail, and he was forced to reduce his activities. He gave his last public concert 16 May 1896 with Victoria *Cartier. He nonetheless continued teaching until the end. Among his pupils were Alfred *De Sève, Béatrice *La Palme, and Émile *Taranto.

Jehin-Prume devoted himself zealously to composition. According to *Une Vie d'artiste*, whose author is presumed to be his only son, Jules, the list of his 'major' works comprises 88 opus numbers, stretching from 1857 to the year of his death. Many of his works are for violin, including two concertos (Op 14 and 31), fantasias, polonaises, mazurkas, caprices, studies, a sonata with piano

(Op 64), and cadenzas for concertos by Viotti, Beethoven, and de Bériot. He also wrote songs and ballads for voice and piano, various isolated pieces and transcriptions, some choral works, and an *Oratorio dédié à Léon XIII*, composed in Nicolet in 1885. Some works were published by Schott, but most remained in manuscript and have not survived. The *NL of C in 1977 acquired five manuscript compositions, four in his own hand.

The dictionaries of Baker, Riemann, and Thompson state that Jehin-Prume was one of the teachers of Eugène Ysaÿe, but the latter's son, Antoine, who was the director of Les Éditions and La Fondation Eugène-Ysaÿe in Brussels, vigorously denied this claim in a letter to Gilles *Potvin dated 28 Jan 1971.

Frantz Jehin-Prume was the first musician of international reputation to choose Canada as his country of adoption, and he remains one of the most accomplished artists in the annals of Canadian music. Along with such men as Calixa Lavallée, Dominique *Ducharme, R.-O. Pelletier, Guillaume *Couture, and Paul Wiallard, he was one of the leaders of Quebec's artistic life.

Endowed with a prodigious technique, he also was a musician of solid and refined taste. 'The one possible reproach,' wrote Frédéric *Pelletier, 'is that he made concessions to the fashions of the day ... But those who knew him intimately – and I am honoured to have been among them – recall how deeply artistic was the soul of this musician and how well he understood the glorious masters of his art.' In *An Encyclopedia of the Violin* (New York, London 1925; New York 1966), Alberto Bachmann wrote: 'He was endowed with a superb technique and a sweet, pure tone.'

Jehin-Prume's son, Jules (b Montreal 17 Jun 1870, d New York, after 1930), studied elocution and singing in Europe and then pursued a career in medicine. He was a throat specialist and oculist in Paris and in Montreal. He is the author of a comedy, *Si bémol*, performed in 1901 at the *Monument national, and a drama, *Vitrix*, premiered in 1902 at the Théâtre national.

BIBLIOGARPHY

Sénécal, D.H. 'Quelques mots sur l'album de F. Jehin-Prume,' *Revue canadienne*, Sep 1865

– 'M. F. Jehin-Prume,' ibid, Oct 1865

Marmette, Joseph. 'Prume et Lavallée,' *Opinion publique*, vol 6, 18 Nov 1875

[Jehin-Prume, Jules]. *Une Vie d'artiste* (Montreal ca 1900)

Pelletier, Frédéric. 'Frantz Jehin-Prume,' *Entre-nous*, vol 1, Apr 1930

Kallmann, Helmut. 'Beethoven and Canada: A miscellany,' *CMB*, 2, Spring–Summer 1971

Catalogue of Canadian Composers

History of Music in Canada

Musical Red Book

Musiciens canadiens (CH)

JELÍNEK, Vladimír. Conductor, composer, b Nove Strašeci, Czechoslovakia, 16 Aug 1923, naturalized Canadian 1975; diploma in orchestra conducting (Prague Academy of Music) 1951. After brief studies in architecture he enrolled at the Prague Cons and spent 1947–51 at the Prague Academy of Music. He was music director 1950–65 of the orchestra of the National Ballet of Czechoslovakia.

Jelínek settled in Montreal in 1965 and was hired by Les Grands Ballets Canadiens as its regular conductor. With this company he toured the USA in 1969 and visited London, Paris, Brussels, and Lisbon in 1970. He conducted the company's ballet version of the Carl Orff trilogy *Carmina burana, Catulli Carmina*, and *Trionfo di Afrodite* in many performances 1966–70, including those at Expo 67 and on the 1969 European tour. Jelínek directed the orchestra for the troupe's 'Hommage à Pierre Mercure' in 1976.

The critic Claude *Gingras wrote in *La Presse* (Montreal, 21 Dec 1966), 'Vladimír Jelínek is an authentic ballet conductor, a competent accompanist who follows the dancers step by step and gives them priority.'

Jelínek has conducted the *MSO frequently, notably on CBC TV in *Le Secret de Suzanne* (1971) and *L'Heure espagnole* (1975) and in concerts in 1978 in Plattsburgh, NY, and at the Maurice Richard Arena, Montreal. He wrote several arrangements of Czech folksongs for choir and orchestra 1955–65, the folk ballet *Une Journée comme une autre* in 1961, and a *Suite québécoise* for orchestra in 1965.

In 1957 Jelínek married Sonia Jelínková – b Pečmanová, violinist, teacher, b Hamburg 15 Sep 1923, naturalized Canadian 1975; L MUS (McGill) 1943. She began her violin studies at five, in Lille, France, and continued them 1939–43 with Rachel Gilbert at *McGill U in Montreal and 1944–8 with Ivan Galamian at the Curtis Institute in Philadelphia. She made several concert tours of Czechoslovakia 1948–65. She was a member of the *McGill Chamber Orchestra and, after 1966, of the MSO. A teacher of violin at the *CMM 1971–3 and 1977–8, she also taught at McGill U after 1965. (DA)

JENKINS, Annie (Margaret) (b Lampman). Pianist, organist, choir director, teacher, b Morpeth, near Chatham, Upper Canada (Ontario), 14 May 1866, d Ottawa 12 Jul 1952. A sister of the poet Archibald Lampman, she studied piano with J.D. *Kerrison and Waugh *Lauder, organ with Edgar Doward in Toronto, and piano 1887–9 with Martin Krause in Leipzig. In 1889 the Leipzig critics praised the clear and delicate performance of the Grieg *Concerto* by the 'American' pianist. Krause considered her Bach playing a very model. In Ottawa, where she had settled in 1885, she appeared in recital as early as 1886, playing Schumann's *Fantasy, Op 17*, the piano part in the same composer's *Quintet, Op 44*, and other music. She became a teacher at Ottawa's Krause School of Pianoforte Playing and Singing (named for the Leipzig teacher and propounding his methods) and later at the Canadian Cons, teaching voice and piano.

For more than 20 years Lampman was organist-choirmaster at St George's Church. She was a charter member of the *Morning Music Club of Ottawa and its president 1920–8. In 1921 she founded the Palestrina Choir, which emphasized unaccompanied singing, and until late in life she remained active as accompanist and teacher. She was Canada's first outstanding woman pianist, but the life of an Ottawa woman of her day inhibited the development of her gifts to the full.

In 1892 Lampman married Frank Maurice Stinson Jenkins (b Kingston, Upper Canada, 6 Jul 1859, d Ottawa 5 Dec 1930), founder and conductor of the Ottawa Amateur Orchestral Society (1894–1900), the *Ottawa Choral Society and the Schubert Club (1894), and organist at several Ottawa churches. Their daughter Dorothy Jenkins McCurry (b Ottawa 6 Nov 1899, d there 29 Aug 1973) was a noted music teacher, choir director (Studio Singers), and musical organizer in Ottawa. Papers documenting the careers of all three are held by the *NL of C. HK

'Jesous Ahatonhia' ('Jesus Is Born') or **'Noël Huron.'** First Canadian Christmas carol. Though widely believed to have been written by the Jesuit missionary Jean de Brébeuf (1593–1649), who taught the song to the Huron Indians near Georgian Bay ca 1642, it is not known whether the verses of 'Jesous Ahatonhia' were written to fit the melody (apparently derived from the 16th-century French song 'Une Jeune Pucelle') with which they have come to be associated. Unrecorded for 100 years, the carol was collected from the Hurons by Father de Villeneuve, a Jesuit stationed 1747–94 at Lorette, Que, and the words were translated from the original Huron into French by Paul Picard, an Indian notary at Quebec City. This version was published in Ernest *Myrand's *Noëls anciens de la Nouvelle-France* (Quebec 1907). An English-language version by Jesse Edgar Middleton was adapted for voice and piano by Healey *Willan (B424, Harris ca 1927) as part of the pageant **Brébeuf* (B29) and later was expanded for choir (B439, Harris ca 1954). The version in *Songs for Worship* (Religious Education Council of Canada 1930) was also Willan's. A third version, composed by Barrie *Cabena, was published in the *Hymn Book* (Anglican Church and United Church 1971). There is also an arrangement (1929) by *Champagne – 'Estenniaton de tsouvé' – for SATB and piano or orchestra (ms CMCentre). The 1977 Canadian postage stamp Christmas series illustrated the theme of the carol.

DISCOGRAPHY

For recordings see Christmas music.

BIBLIOGRAPHY

Oliver, Robert E. *A Canadian Christmas Carol / Un Chant de Noël canadien* (Abitibi Paper Co [1966]). Also publ by the Huronia Historical Development Council and the Dept of Tourism and Information, Province of Ontario, nd

Steckley, John. 'Huron carol told the Christmas story to Canadian Indians,' *Toronto Star*, 24 Dec 1977

FILMOGRAPHY

Huron Indian Christmas Carol, NFB filmstrip, 37 frames

JESSNER, Irene (m de Norby). Soprano, teacher, b Vienna 28 Aug 1908. Although she studied piano at the Vienna Cons, she made her debut (Teplice, 1930) as Elsa in *Lohengrin* and toured Europe in operas and musicals, enjoying particular success in Czechoslovakia as Aida. Invited by Edward *Johnson to join the *Metropolitan Opera in New York, she made her US debut in 1936 in *Hansel and Gretel*. She remained with that company until 1952, singing such roles as Desdemona in *Otello* and the Marschallin in *Der Rosenkavalier*. Again on an invitation from Johnson, she joined the Faculty of Music, *U of Toronto, in 1952. Her Canadian pupils have included Léonard *Bilodeau, Maurice *Brown, Lois *McDonall, Roxolana *Roslak, Teresa *Stratas, Lilian *Sukis, Heather *Thomson, Riki *Turofsky, Portia *White, and Jeannette *Zarou.

Jessner recorded a Rimsky-Korsakov song and a Tchaikovsky arioso for Victor (Vic 17569) and is heard in a complete *Die Meistersinger* (Celebrity EJS 224), pirated from a Metropolitan Opera broadcast 2 Dec 1939, and on a 78 recording of the third act of *Die Walküre* in which she sings both Sieglinde and Ortlinde (8-Col CM-581).

BIBLIOGARPHY

Schill, Florence. 'Soprano finds teaching as exciting as singing,' Toronto *Globe and Mail*, 27 Oct 1955 (GK)

Les Jeunes Chanteurs d'Acadie. Mixed choir of 50 young people, aged between 11 and 22, from the area of Moncton, NB. The choir was founded in 1969 by Sister Lorette Gallant (b Shediac, NB, 16 Jan 1932), who previously had conducted a choir of 66 girls, the Chorale Beauséjour (1957–68). Initially known as the Chorale d'Aberdeen, it took the name Jeunes Chanteurs d'Acadie in 1972.

The choir won three first prizes at the 1974 International Music Eisteddfod in Middlesbrough,

England. In 1976 it sang for Queen Elizabeth II in Fredericton and represented New Brunswick in Montreal at the music festival held in connection with the 1976 Olympics. The same year, it won second prize in the CBC / Canada Council National Radio Competition for Amateur Choirs and received the George S. Mathieson trophy, awarded annually by the *FCMF to the best choir competing in Canadian festivals.

The choir, which sings in English, French, German, Latin, and Welsh, has been heard frequently on CBC radio, notably on the program 'A Cappella,' and has appeared on TV. In July 1978 it took part in the international music festivals in Llangollen, Wales, and in Middlesbrough. It gave two concerts in August 1978 at the 13th conference of ISME in London, Ont. It has made several LPs: *Les Jeunes Chanteurs d'Acadie* (1974, Son Excellence Sound 102), *Revivre nos Noëls / Christmas Reflections* (1976, Inter Media Services WRC 203), and *Jeunes Chanteurs d'Acadie* (1977, Inter Media Services WRC 263). (GA)

Jeunesses musicales of Canada / du Canada (JMC). A non-profit-making organization created to encourage the pursuit of music among Canada's young people and to help talented performers and composers develop their careers in Canada and abroad.

1 Historical review
2 Activities

1 HISTORICAL REVIEW. The JMC was born on 23 Aug 1949 following a meeting between Father J.H. Lemieux, Anaïs Allard-Rousseau, and Alice Desruisseaux-Boisvert, who were brought together in St-Hyacinthe, Que, on the initiative of Gilles *Lefebvre. The latter suggested linking all the existing societies devoted to cultural activities among young people and submitted a plan of action calling for concert tours, new lines of administrative co-operation, scholarships, a summer camp, a permanent home, and exchanges between young performers. An association called Hélicon was founded, comprising the musical clubs of the Quebec towns of Grand-Mère, Mont-Laurier, St-Hyacinthe, Shawinigan, Sherbrooke, and Trois-Rivières. The committee of the Compagnons de l'Art of St-Hyacinthe organized the first tour for the 1949–50 season while Gilles Lefebvre took advantage of a study period in Europe to make contacts, notably with the JM. As proposed by Lefebvre, while a member of the French delegation at the Vienna congress of the JM (1950), the new Canadian organization became a member of the International Federation of the JM, succeeding the *Amis de l'art, which had represented Canada for a short time in 1949–50. The first national JMC congress was held in Trois-Rivières in 1950. On that occasion Gilles Lefebvre accepted the national presidency of the movement, becoming in 1953 its director general, a position he held until 1972. He was succeeded by Gaston *Germain 1972–6 and Germain by Jean-Claude Picard in 1976. The national presidents have been Gaston *Arel 1949–50, Gilles Lefebvre 1950–4, Anaïs Allard-Rousseau 1954–6, Sylvio *Lacharité 1956–8, Victor *Bouchard 1958–60, Raoul *Jobin 1960–2, Sir Ernest *MacMillan 1962–4, Léopold *Simoneau 1964–7, Wilfrid *Pelletier 1967–9, Clermont *Pépin 1969–72, Maureen *Forrester 1972–6, and Gilles *Potvin 1976–80. Potvin was succeeded by John *Roberts. The JMC is administered by a national council made up of representatives of the provincial councils.

The first three tours by Canadian artists 1949–52 occurred under the joint auspices of the JMC and Hélicon. The violinist Noël *Brunet, accompanied at the piano by Suzette Pratte, the soprano

The JM World Orchestra in rehearsal under Pierre Hétu at the JMC Orford Art Centre

Marthe *Létourneau with the pianist Géraldine Lavallée, and the pianist Gilles Breton performed in the six founding centres during that first season. The first exchange of artists with France occurred during the 1951–2 season between the Canadian violinist Noël Brunet and the French pianist Pierre Sancan. In 1954 Gilles Lefebvre was elected for the first of three terms as president of the International Federation of the JM, which by 1980 included 37 member countries. The first world congress of the organization to be held in Canada took place in Montreal in 1955. A major expansion of the JMC outside Quebec, towards the eastern and western provinces, began in 1958. Twenty years later the JMC was active in more than 140 communities, and centres and sections had been established in New Brunswick, Nova Scotia, Ontario, Manitoba, Saskatchewan, and Newfoundland (from which province a representative group joined the JMC in the 1960s). In 1980 the movement had nearly 50,000 members outside British Columbia, and in that province the *Festival Concert Society established an affiliation with the JMC and has sponsored tours by JMC-selected artists.

Of the four founding members of the JMC, one who had a particular influence on the movement was Anaïs Allard-Rousseau (b Allard, m Rousseau). An administrator and teacher (b Ste-Monique-de-Nicolet, Que, 31 Oct 1904, d Fort-de-France, Martinique, 15 Feb 1971), she had studied music and pedagogy. She settled in Trois-Rivières at the time of her marriage in 1926 and in 1942 founded there a concert society, Les Rendez-vous artistiques, and a series of daytime concerts for young people under the name of Club André-Mathieu. She was vice-president of the International Federation of the JM (1952–5) and JMC delegate to the conventions of Geneva (1952), Hanover (1954), Brussels (1958), Palma de Majorca (1963), Paris (1966), Budapest (1969), and Copenhagen (1970). In Trois-Rivières she taught introductory courses in music and the fine arts at the École normale du Christ-Roi (1956–64), the Centre d'études universitaires (1963), and the École normale Maurice-Duplessis (1967). She was made an Officer of the *Order of Canada in 1969. The concert hall of the Centre culturel in Trois-Rivières bears her name.

2 ACTIVITIES. Two major projects came to fruition in 1951: a summer music camp at Mount Orford (see JMC Orford Art Centre) and the *Journal des Jeunesses musicales du Canada* (variously titled, see general list of abbreviations for *Jmc*), whose editor 1951–61 was Andrée *Desautels. Wilfrid Sauvé was responsible for producing the paper from 1961 to its discontinuance in 1971. Subsequently, there appeared, a *Bulletin* 1974–6 and, beginning in 1976, a *Communiqué*, both of them in separate English and French editions.

In 1961 the JMC launched a national competition open to pianists under 30 years. String and voice competitions were alternated with piano in subsequent years. The competition was open to musicians who were taking advanced studies abroad or had completed their studies in Canada in the 12 months preceding the competition. Each participant was required to play an unpublished Canadian work in his/her program. The Canada Council arranged concert appearances with as many as 10 Canadian orchestras for the winners, and the JMC also offered each of them a recital tour in about 40 centres, a recording, and a tour in France under the aegis of the JM of that country. Winners were Marek *Jablonski (piano, 1961), Andrew *Dawes (violin, second prize 1962), Gloria *Richard (singing, second prize 1963), and Dale *Bartlett (piano, 1964). There was no competition in 1965 and 1966. Besides assuming direction of the Man and Music pavilion at *Expo 67, the JMC also organized three national competitions for performers, as well as an international contest in composition. Robert *Silverman, Andrew Dawes, and Annon Lee *Silver were the winners respectively in the categories of piano, violin, and voice. The Austrian Josef Maria Horvath obtained the first prize for composition with *Redundanz II* for string quartet, and the Canadian Sydney *Hodkinson received second prize for *Interplay*. Subsequently JMC competitions were continued only at the regional level.

The Club musical canadien du disque was founded by the JMC in 1956, but it was under the name of Club de disques JMC (CD-JMC) that LPs were produced, notably with the performers Dale Bartlett, Josephte Clément (CD-JMC-3), Marek Jablonski, Gloria Richard, Sylvia *Saurette, and Robert Silverman. Three excerpts from *Pirouette* and *Silent Measures* by *Blackburn were also recorded on this label. In 1954 the JM of France had started the Club national du disque, which recorded on the labels JMF (Pathé-Marconi) and CND; Maureen Forrester and the duo-pianists Victor Bouchard and Renée *Morisset are among Canadian artists who have recorded on CND. To mark the 20th anniversary of the JMC in 1969 RCI and RCA Victor co-produced a set of 10 LPs, *Jeunesses musicales 20 Canada* (RCI 275–84), with the assistance of artists who had taken part in JMC concerts and the Orford Festival: Andrew Dawes, Karl Engel, Guy Fallot, Lorand *Fenyves, Kenneth *Gilbert, Claude Helffer, Anton *Kuerti, Alexander Lagoya, the *Orford String Quartet, the *Pierre Bourque Saxophone Quartet, Hansheinz Schneeberger, and Ronald *Turini.

A JMC season generally consists of four concerts, whose local organization is handled by a voluntary committee. Local organizers receive instructional material containing the necessary information about the instruments or the musical forms. The performance of each work is preceded by a historical and analytical commentary, often supplied by the performer himself. The JMC towns are geographically arranged in regions (12 in 1980), within which the selected artists pursue their tours. The list of these artists is considerable and at various periods has included such outstanding Canadians as Gaston Arel, Adele *Armin, Napoléon *Bisson, Victor Bouchard and Renée Morisset, Lise *Boucher, Hyman *Bress, Michel *Dussault, Maureen Forrester, Kenneth Gilbert, Richard *Gresko, Marek Jablonski, Jean-Paul *Jeannotte, Bernard *Lagacé, Arthur *LeBlanc, Joan *Maxwell, John *Newmark, the Orford String Quartet, Louis *Quilico, Charles *Reiner, Joseph *Rouleau, Claude *Savard, William *Stevens, and Ronald Turini. Among the foreign artists have been Karl Engel, Philippe Entremont, Guy Fallot, François Glorieux, Claude Helffer, John Lill, the Paul Kuentz Chamber Orchestra, Ida Presti and Alexander Lagoya, Henryk Szeryng, Paul Tortelier, the Stuttgart Trio, and Jean-Claude Vanden Eynden. Opera troupes like the Opéra de poche of Paris or dance troupes such as Entre-Six have also made tours. The JMC also has organized operatic productions, including *Silent Measures* and *Pirouette* by Blackburn (1960–1), *Le Magicien* by *Vallerand (1961–2), and *The Barber of Seville* (1975–6). *Pirouette* and *Le Magicien* were commissioned by the JMC

The second congress of the International Federation of the JM to be held in Canada took place in Montreal during Expo 67. An international orchestra comprising some 100 young instrumentalists from many countries was conducted by Zubin Mehta and played Beethoven's *Ninth Symphony* at the *PDA. Three years later the JM World Orchestra was created on the initiative of Gilles Lefebvre and the JMC, with financial support from the cultural arm of the Dept of External Affairs of Canada. Made up of young instrumentalists selected from each member country of the international federation, the JM World Orchestra has been reassembled annually (except for 1979) during a general assembly (annual) or the congress (biennial).

In 1975 the JMC introduced a new pedagogical approach: workshops devoted to various instruments – flute, oboe, english horn, trumpet, brass trio, cello, guitar, accordion, ondes Martenot, harp, and percussion – and to mime. On request, professional artists visit the schools and work with groups of students from primary to senior-secondary levels, with a maximum attendance of 100 for each workshop. Before the presentations, the schools receive instructional material from the national secretariat to prepare the pupils for the workshops, and afterwards the performers themselves answer the young people's questions. By 1980 more than 700 workshops were being presented in this manner each year in Quebec and reached an estimated public of 70,000 children and adolescents.

BIBLIOGRAPHY

Lefebvre, Gilles. 'La Fédération internationale des Jeunesses musicales,' *Jmc*, 5, Mar 1959

Wilson, Elizabeth. 'Les Jeunesses musicales,' *OpCan*, May 1963

Fink, Laure. 'Trio D'Opéra, on tour in Quebec,' *OpCan*, Feb 1966

'Centennial year plans of the Jeunesses musicales,' *CanComp*, 10, Sep 1966

Kemp, Agathe. 'Les Jeunesses musicales marches on,' *MSc*, 238, Nov–Dec 1967

Potvin, Gilles. 'Jeunesses musicales du Canada,' *Art and Culture* (Montreal 1976)

JMC Souvenir Program, for the 30th anniversary (Montreal 1980)

FILMOGRAPHY

Les Jeunesses musicales du Canada 1950–1980 (Ciné-Mundo 1980)

CVI (ST)

Jewish cantors. After the destruction of the second Temple in Jerusalem in the year 70, synagogues were established wherever Jews lived, and in these it was the duty of the chazzan (cantor) to chant a different portion of the Torah (the Five Books of Moses) each sabbath, completing the entire cycle by the end of each year. At first the cantor was merely a beadle whose chanting of the ritual was done in addition to other tasks like teaching children or ritually (ie, humanely) slaughtering animals for community food. Eventually, fine voices and an expanded repertoire of beautiful melodies assured cantors more important places in their communities. Indeed, from the late middle ages until the 19th century synagogue music was almost exclusively the domain of the virtuoso cantor, whose melodic improvisations and renditions of traditional cantillation often represented the cultural pinnacle of the Jewish communities of Europe. Even by 1980, with much choral, and in some cases organ, music incorporated in Jewish worship, the musical role of chazzanut (cantorial chant) remained central and continued to provide synagogue music with its most recognizable characteristic.

Until the time of the Nazi holocaust, the main energy and creativity of the cantorial art was provided by cantors and synagogue musicians from Europe. After World War II leadership in Jewish cultural matters moved to North America. Canadian cantors, perhaps because of their tenacity in holding to tradition, have played a greater role in the preservation of their musical heritage than in innovation. Cantorial music has flourished most vigorously in Canada's three main centres of Jewish population – Montreal, Toronto, and Winnipeg.

Prominent among Montreal cantors are or have been Aaron Rosemarin (b Lutsk, Volhynia, ca 1865, d Montreal 1932), Joseph Dlin (b Bessarabia 1907), Otto Staeren (b Vienna 1907), Nathan Mendelson (b Glasgow ca 1902), Samuel Taube (b ca 1912), and Solomon Gisser (b Warsaw 1917).

Toronto synagogues have been enriched by the contributions of Abraham *Barkin (b 1882, d Toronto 1939), Akiva Bernstein (b Jesiorna, Poland, 1893, d Toronto 1968), Boris Charloff (b Tiktin, Poland, 1896, d Toronto 1972), Alexander Steinberg (b Zhtomer, Russia, 1893, d Toronto 1960), Nathan Stolnitz (b 1893, d Toronto 1969), Bernard Wladowski (b Smila, near Kiev, 1871, d Toronto 1963), and Chaim Meyer Zimmerman (b 1884, d Toronto 1954).

In Winnipeg, the cantors Moshe Jacob (b 1884, d Winnipeg ca 1960) and Benjamin Brownstone (b Bessarabia ca 1888, d Winnipeg 1972) were renowned in their community.

The following two biographical sketches are offered as examples of the careers of Canadian cantors.

Cantor Bernard Wladowski was one of many renowned cantors born in or near Kiev, and he took his early training and first cantorial post in Kiev. He later became successively town chazzan of Bakhmut and Sevastopol, the first cantor of the new synagogue of Constantinople, and chief cantor in the great synagogue of Bucharest, Rumania, where he worked alongside the gifted composer Leo Low. After three years in a major position in Chicago, he moved to Toronto and served as cantor at the McCaul Street Synagogue for over 25 years, until his retirement. A noted choir conductor and composer of synagogue music, he gave many concerts during his career and recorded cantorial music about 1910, one of the first to do so. He died in Toronto at the age of 92.

Cantor Benjamin Brownstone settled in Winnipeg in 1921 and became known as a composer of synagogue music, the author of many scholarly articles on Jewish music, and a dynamic conductor of choral music for adults and children. As director of Winnipeg's Jewish Community Choir he gave many concerts and in 1960 was honoured by Winnipeg's Jewish Community for his achievements. He also received an honorary degree from the Hebrew Union College of New York. One of his greatest contributions was undoubtedly his teaching of the cantorial art. Some of the outstanding cantors of North America received their training and inspiration from Cantor Brownstone.

The three North American schools providing cantorial training in 1980 were all in the USA. Although several graduates from these schools have assumed positions in Canada, many practising Canadian cantors received their training in the time-honoured system of private study with older cantors acknowledged as masters. This is true, for example, of Cantors Joseph Cooper, Tibor Kellen, and Severin Weingort of Toronto (all were born in Europe) and of Cantor J. Smolack of Winnipeg. All completed their studies in Canada and became engaged successfully in synagogue work in their communities. In the 1970s Esther *Ghan was the only woman cantor in Canada.

See also Jewish religious music; The Jews.

BIBLIOGRAPHY

Stolnitz, Nathan. *On Wings of Song* (Toronto 1968)

See also Bibliography for Jewish religious music.

BSt

Jewish Music Month. Annual international celebration established in 1944 in the USA to foster knowledge and stimulate appreciation of Jewish liturgical and traditional secular music and of works by Jewish composers. It was inaugurated in Canada by the Canadian Jewish Congress with a concert by the Canadian Little Symphony under Harold *Sumberg 3 May 1948 at Toronto's Holy Blossom Temple. Because it lasts from six to eight weeks (beginning on Sabbath Shira or in mid-January) it is known in some parts of Canada as the Jewish Music Festival. There have been choral concerts and competitions, radio and TV programs, dance festivals, exhibits, and lectures in concert halls and synagogues in Montreal, Toronto, Winnipeg, and Vancouver. In Montreal annual concerts by the Jewish Music Forum (founded in 1948 by Samuel *Levitan and others) became a feature of the festival.

Among the works commissioned for Jewish Music Month have been Morris *Surdin's *Credo* (1950), Louis *Applebaum's 'Cry of the Prophet' (1952), Alexander *Brott's *Invocation and Dance* (1952), John *Weinzweig's 'Dance of the Massadah' (1952) and 'Am Yisrael Chai!' (1953), Ray Jessel's *Israeli Dances* (1956), *Wedding Suite* (1959), and 'Praise Him in the Heights,' and Ben *Steinberg's *Y'rushalayim* (1973). (RRs)

Jewish religious music. The styles of the religious music of Judaism have changed through the centuries under the influence of the various countries in which Jews have lived. Yet the music rarely has departed from its three fundamental vocabularies: the cantillation, chanted in the synagogue on the sabbath; the Jewish modes, a kind of musical organization for the prayers sung on the holy days; and the relatively recent 'Scarbove' (sacred) melodies developed through the centuries, each of which acts as a sort of 'leitmotif' to delineate musically and to identify the main prayers of these holy days.

Canadian Jews are one or two generations closer to their forebears, who were generally European, than are US Jews. Perhaps because of this, they maintain many more traditional links. While contemporary US synagogue composers have 'modernized' syngogue music both effectively and awkwardly, Canadian synagogue music has reflected more closely its eastern and central European origins and, as a consequence, its semitic-oriental characteristics. Eastern Europe has continued to influence Canadian synagogue music both with its folk music and with its older, more florid, oriental treatment of prayer texts. Its chants tend to be melismatic and, within the framework of specified modes, improvisational. Central Europe, in contrast, has contributed mainly melodies and fragments of melodies (for instance, tunes by the Austrian Salomon Sulzer, 1804–90, and the German Lazarus Lewandowski, 1821–94). These were written in a consciously 'anti-oriental' style which attempted to wed synagogue song to 19th-century rules of art in the same way as Salomone Rossi did during the 17th century. The result in both centuries was what Rabinovitch called 'occidental inhibition and fastidious restraint.'

These influences are not separated in different synagogues but take part equally in most services. Thus, the same congregation which is accustomed to free, melismatic cantorial chant will accept without comment the markedly Germanic 'Sh'ma Yisrael' (Hear O Israel) written by Sulzer in frank imitation of the 19th-century German church music style which he knew and admired.

The three 'divisions' of Judaism represented in Canada are Orthodox, Conservative, and Reform.

Canadian Orthodox Jewry has maintained traditional chant and has permitted few musical innovations. The Orthodox cantor essentially has retained the musical practices of his European predecessors. He chants the prayers with his congregants in responsorial style, sometimes pausing to embellish with music certain important texts (eg, the K'dushah, or Sanctification). No instrument may be played on the sabbath, but a large Orthodox synagogue will maintain a choir of men and boys to lead congregational singing, perform compositions, and accompany the cantor by singing responses or by humming organ-like chordal backgrounds for the cantor's modal improvisations or solos.

The Conservative synagogue in Canada is very close to the Orthodox in its musical style. Unlike its US counterpart, which often permits use of the organ in services, it retains the unaccompanied style of old and, except for a more abbreviated prayer book, is 'Orthodox' in its musical approach. Mixed choirs are allowed, however, and new musical settings may be introduced more easily.

In Reform Judaism the standard combination of mixed choir, organ, and cantor permits ordered musical expansion. The inherent danger of 'westernizing' what is essentially an eastern style has not always been avoided. In recent years, however, composers have shown a greater sensitivity in keeping to the ancient chants while dressing them in 'new garb,' and, indeed, many new musical settings have been created specifically for the Reform prayer book. European examples are Ernest Bloch's *Avodath Hakodesh* and Milhaud's *Service sacré pour le samedi*. Most new works are written for the Reform prayer book. Yet even these are more traditional in Canada than they are in the USA and show a tendency to build on, rather than depart from, the old styles.

Most synagogue compositions by Canadians remained in manuscript in 1980; among the few exceptions are the works of Ben *Steinberg, which have been published in the USA and Israel. Other Canadian composers and conductors of synagogue music have included Benjamin Brownstone (cantor, conductor, composer, b Bessarabia ca 1888, d Winnipeg 1972), Boris Charloff (cantor, composer, b Tiktin, Poland, 1896, d Toronto 1972), Emil Gartner (see Toronto Jewish Folk Choir), Srul Irving *Glick, Yekutiel Kronick (educator, conductor, composer, d Montreal ca 1964), Abraham Krashinsky (conductor, b 1893?, active in Montreal), Gordon *Kushner, Samuel *Levitan, Aaron Rosemarin (cantor, composer, b Lutsk, Volhynia, ca 1865, d Montreal 1932), Jacob Rosemarin (composer, conductor, b Sidilkov, Russia, 1892), Mordecai Sandberg (composer, b Rumania 1897, d Toronto 1973), Sara Udow (choir conductor, soprano, b Winnipeg 1921, d there 1971), Yehuda Vineberg (conductor, b ca 1925, active in Montreal), and Bernard Wladowski (cantor, composer, b Smila, near Kiev, 1871, d Toronto 1963).

See also Jewish cantors; Jewish Music Month; The Jews.

BIBLIOGRAPHY

Idelsohn, A.Z. *Jewish Music in Its Historical Development* (New York 1929)
Stolnitz, Nathan. *Music in Jewish Life* (Toronto 1957)
See also Bibliography for Jewish cantors. BSt

The Jews. The 300,000 Canadians of Jewish extraction represent a great variety of ancestral languages and cultural traditions, only some of which are specifically Jewish in content. Their religious outlooks similarly vary from orthodoxy to non-observance; indeed, apart from the name, they have in common only the ancient history of the Bible and a modern history of persecution. Therefore no purpose would be served by providing a roll call of Jewish musicians. The present article will deal only with:

1 Patterns of immigration
2 Folk traditions
3 Community activities
4 Secular compositions based on Jewish traditions

Separate *EMC* entries deal with Jewish cantors, Jewish Music Month, and Jewish religious music.

1 PATTERNS OF IMMIGRATION. Although British Jews, often of Iberian descent, came to Nova Scotia and Quebec in 1759, the Jewish component in the population remained small until after 1880. One prominent Jewish musical family to arrive before that time, the *Nordheimers (from Germany), soon embraced Christianity. The Tsarist pogroms of 1881–2 precipitated large-scale immigration to Canada not only of Jews but also of *Doukhobors and *Mennonites. Several of the children of Jewish immigrants developed into distinguished performers. All were women, all were born or raised in the province of Quebec, and all retired there after international careers: the singers Pauline *Donalda (b 1882), Irene *Pavloska (b 1889), and Sarah *Fischer (b 1896 in Paris but in Canada from girlhood), and the pianist Ellen *Ballon (b 1898).

Large numbers of Jews began to arrive in Canada at the turn of the century, and this continued until World War I. Most of these, Eastern Europeans deeply rooted in religious traditions and Yiddish culture, settled in Montreal, Toronto, and Winnipeg. It is interesting to note that most Jewish music students born in the first decade of the 20th century took up string instruments. Among them were the *Adaskin brothers, Percy *Faith (who later switched to piano and composition), Louis Gesensway, Samuel *Hersenhoren, Adolph *Koldofsky, Isaac *Mamott, Paul *Scherman, Maurice *Solway, Berul *Sugarman, and Harold *Sumberg.

Peretz School orchestra, Calgary, 1929

While those born in the second decade include such string players as Alexander *Brott, Hyman *Goodman, Eugene *Kash, Zara *Nelsova, Albert *Pratz, and Ethel *Stark, many turned to other specializations. Louis *Applebaum, Henry D. Brant, Samuel *Dolin, Marvin *Duchow, Morris *Surdin, and John *Weinzweig (as well as Brott) became composers, and Minuetta *Kessler, Ida *Krehm, Gordon *Kushner, Samuel *Levitan, and Freda *Trepel, pianists. Eventually Jewish musicians were active in all areas of the musical profession.

Between the two wars, Jewish immigration was small but for the first time included not only cantors but trained secular musicians such as Leo and Sara *Barkin, Boris *Berlin, Jan *Cherniavsky, and Elie *Spivak. In the 1930s the increasing persecutions in Nazi Germany forced many musicians of Jewish or partly-Jewish descent to emigrate. Few had backgrounds in Jewish music; their contributions to Canada have been essentially Austrian, Czech, German, or Hungarian. Because of the Dominion's restrictive immigration policy during the Depression era, only a few during that time (eg, Lotte *Brott, who arrived in 1939 by way of Switzerland, and Emil Gartner, who fled from Vienna in 1938) gained entry into Canada. Some, who had emigrated to England, entered Canada as internees in 1940 – Freddie *Grant, Franz *Kraemer, John *Newmark, and the teenagers Walter *Homburger and Helmut *Kallmann among them. Others arrived by detours made during the war (eg, Oskar *Morawetz via France) or after the war: the *Joachim brothers, Andreas *Barban, Erwin *Marcus, and Herbert *Ruff via Shanghai; Walter *Kaufmann via India; István *Anhalt, Lazlo *Gati, Emmy *Heim, Charles *Reiner, and Heinz *Unger from various European countries.

Post-war Jewish immigration has related less to persecution than to professional appointments or opportunities (eg, Karel Ančerl, Lorand *Fenyves, Ida *Haendel, Paul *Hoffert, Mieczyslaw *Kolinski, Ezra *Schabas, and George *Zukerman). However, in the late 1960s, and increasingly throughout the 1970s, numerous musicians came to Canada to escape anti-Zionist feelings in the USSR. Many Soviet instrumentalists, especially string players, became members of Canadian orchestras; others joined university music faculties, and a few continued their solo careers.

2 FOLK TRADITIONS. At the community level, Jewish traditions have been cultivated by choirs and

mandolin or string orchestras. One of the first groups was the Winnipeg Jewish Folk Choir, founded in 1910 by Cantor Moshe Jacob. Others have included the Toronto Hebrew Male Chorus founded in 1929 by Ernest *Dainty, a non-Jew; the *Toronto Jewish Folk Choir; the Montreal Jewish Folk Choir; the Workmen's Circle Choir of Montreal (fl 1956); and the Sara Sommer Chai Folk Ensemble of Winnipeg founded in 1967.

There has been extensive research into and collection of Yiddish folksongs from eastern Europe. Israel Rabinovitch, whose article 'Les anciens éléments dans la chanson populaire des Canadians français' appeared in the *Jewish Daily Eagle* 8 Jul 1932, drew certain parallels between Jewish songs and the songs in Ernest *Gagnon's collection. Ruth *Rubin's study 'Yiddish folk songs current in French Canada' appeared in the *Journal* of the IFMC (January 1960). Her collection (1948–69) of over 2200 songs from Montreal, Toronto, and New York has been deposited at the National Museum of Man in Ottawa, as have Barbara Kirshenblatt-Gimblett's tape recordings and report 'Yiddish folkore in Toronto' (1968–9) and Dov Noy's research on Ontario Yiddish songs and folklore. Geoffrey Clarfield investigated 'Music in the Moroccan Jewish Community of Toronto' (*CFMJ*, vol 4, 1976). Ramón Pelinski recorded the Sephardic traditions of Spanish-Canadian Jews in 1974 (see *CMB*, 10, Spring–Summer 1975).

3 COMMUNITY ACTIVITIES. The Jewish Music Council was formed in Montreal in 1954 by Israel Rabinovitch under the sponsorship of the Canadian Jewish Congress. The first of many concerts organized by the council took place in 1955. The annual observance of *Jewish Music Month began in Toronto in 1948, in Montreal in 1949, and later in other cities. In the YMHAs, maintained in several large cities, music has been an important activity. Victor *Feldbrill, Gordon Kushner, and Harold Sumberg have been active in Toronto in such organizations as the YMHA Community Music School, established in 1964. Samuel Levitan was active in the Montreal YMHA and also in the Jewish Music Council.

4 SECULAR COMPOSITIONS BASED ON JEWISH TRADITIONS. Secular works by Jewish composers frequently reflect the influence of the music of Jewish liturgy or incorporate the folk melodies of eastern European Jewry. However, many works composed after the years of Nazi persecution are based on expressions, in prose and poetry, of deep grief for Jews who suffered humiliation and death or are joyous celebrations of the re-establishment of Israel, even though overtones of sadness and anxiety remain. Oskar Morawetz' *From the Diary of Anne Frank* received a special award in 1971 from the Segal Foundation of Montreal as the most important Canadian contribution to Jewish music to that time.

Many works have been composed through the efforts of the Music Committee of the Canadian Jewish Congress, an important example being Anhalt's *Symphony No. 1*, which was commissioned in 1958 to celebrate the bicentenary of the settlement of Jews in Canada. While no attempt can be made here to list all the works of Jewish composers, the following selection provides a representative sampling of works inspired by Jewish liturgical or folk music, or by elements of Jewish history. More comprehensive lists of works by many of these composers accompany their entries in *EMC*.

Louis Applebaum 'Cry of the Prophet' 1952
Alexander Brott *Invocation and Dance* 1952; *Israel* 1952
Benjamin Brownstone *Shehecheyanu* 1952
Samuel Dolin *The Hills of Hebron* 1954
Marvin Duchow *Three Songs of the Holocaust* 1978
Harry *Freedman *Psalm 26* 1950
Srul Irving *Glick *Suite Hebraïque No. 1* 1961; *Heritage* 1967; *... i never saw another butterfly ...* 1968; *Suite Hebraïque No. 2* 1969; *Psalm for Orchestra* 1971; *Lamentations (Sinfonia Concertante No. 2)* 1972; *Concerto* for violin and orchestra (*Shir Hamaalot*) 1976
Raymond Jessel *Israeli Dances* 1956; *Psalm 148* 1960
Jack *Kane *Die Zun Fargeht* 1952
Minuetta Kessler *Victory Hora* 1973
Oskar Morawetz *Fantasy on a Hebrew Theme* 1952; *Variations on 'Artzah Alinu'* 1952; *From the Diary of Anne Frank* 1970
Philip Podoliak *Courage, My People* 1950
Leo Spellman *Mood* 1955
Ben *Steinberg *Y'rushalayim* 1973
Morris Surdin *Credo* 1950; *Brasheet (In the Beginning)* 1974
John Weinzweig *Cello Sonata 'Israel'* 1949; 'Dance of the Massadah' 1951; 'Am Ysrael Chai!' 1952
Peter *Zvankin *Congratulations* 1949

BIBLIOGRAPHY
Blackstone, Milton. 'The Jew in the cultural arts,' *The Jew in Canada*, ed Arthur Daniel Hart (Montreal 1926)
Rabinovitch, Israel. *Jewish Music and Other Essays on Musical Topics* (Montreal 1940) (in Yiddish)
– *Of Jewish Music, Ancient and Modern* (Montreal 1952) (in English)
Gottesman, Eli, compiler. *Who's Who in Canadian Jewry* (Ottawa 1965)
Stein, Norman. 'Adventures in Jewish music,' Winnipeg *Jewish Post*, 3 Mar 1966
Rosenberg, Stuart E. *The Jewish Community in Canada*, vol 2 (Toronto 1971)
Jones, Gaynor. 'Anne Frank's diary: the epilogue,' *Maclean's*, 29 Sep 1980 1, 2, 3 / (HK), 4 / (ML)

Jingles. Music for commercials on TV and radio. They are rarely more than 30 seconds in duration, sometimes consist of only a few notes, and are usually settings of catch-phrases devised by advertising agency writers. They have antecedents in the cries of urban street vendors, and like those cries (and like the operatic Leitmotiv) they depend on frequent repetition to promote familiarity in the hearer's mind. A less direct line of descent might be traced through sheet music of the 19th century which carried advertising and often was distributed free by sponsoring merchants. Sometimes the pieces had texts mentioning the firm's activities, as in the unforgettable 'We Dye to Live' issued by Parker's Dye Works of Toronto in 1890.

In the early days of radio the tunes of jingles often were borrowed from traditional or popular songs, preferably those in the public domain. But some original melodies by unknown composers gained a permanent place in listeners' memories: 'Rinso white, happy little wash-day song,' 'Ajax, the foaming cleanser,' 'Floods more suds from Super Suds,' 'That's what Campbell's Soups are, Mm Mm Good' are phrases which, to fairly large numbers of the population, immediately summon up tunes from the memory. The importance of such tunes in the conscious or subconscious musical experience of Canadians hardly can be overestimated, for they might be said to form the staple musical diet of those radio and TV listeners who are not music lovers.

The writing of successful jingles requires the ability to make brief and distinct statements in music, employing materials that will establish an association with the product in the hearer's consciousness. Some have proved so attractive that they have been converted into popular songs, eg, Hagood *Hardy's tune 'The Homecoming,' which began life as a Red Rose Tea jingle. For a *TSO Christmas Box concert some years ago Howard *Cable made a novel symphonic pastiche of current jingle tunes.

Jingle recording is a lucrative employment for musicians (partly because the jingle's short lifespan demands its constant replenishment) and more than a few orchestral players have given up concert work in favour of studio work. Toronto, Montreal, and Vancouver have excellent studio facilities which attract producers from across Canada and from other countries.

Among Canadian composers who have found success in the field are Tommy *Ambrose, Sam Berry, Howard Cable, François *Dompierre, Morris 'Rusty' *Davis, Bob *Hahn, Hagood Hardy, Laurent Jodoin, Yves *Lapierre, Sid Kessler, William *McCauley, Ben *McPeek, Billy *O'Connor, Doug *Riley, Rudy and Jerry *Toth, Larry Trudel, and the teams of *Claman and Morris and Griffiths and Gibson.

Signature tunes or 'theme songs' share some of the characteristics of jingles but, whereas jingles generally have an ephemeral life, signature tunes are nurtured as long as possible. The dance bands which flourished in the period from the 1920s to the 1950s had individual theme songs, and radio and TV programs have continued to have them.

Most European and Asian broadcasting networks have identified their transmissions with individual musical phrases (though the NBC was the only US network that adopted the practice), and the CBC emulated their example for its domestic service in the mid-1970s, commissioning a phrase from François *Morel. The CBC's daily National TV newscast for some years used a theme by Louis *Applebaum and later employed an electronic composition by Terry Rusling. RCI has identified its short-wave broadcasts with the first four notes of *Lavallée's *'O Canada.'

BIBLIOGRAPHY
Reynolds, John Lawrence. 'Don't call them jingles,' *Canadian Motorist*, Sep 1977
Bot, Ellen. 'Jingles hath [sic] charms,' (*Toronto Star*) *Street Talk*, 13 Sep 1979 TCB, HK

JMC. See Jeunesses musicales of Canada.

JMC Orford Art Centre / Centre d'art d'Orford JMC. Summer music camp and cultural centre established in 1951 by the *Jeunesses musicales du Canada in Mount Orford Provincial Park near Magog, 112 km from Montreal. Covering 88.8 hectares, it stands on land leased to it in 1964 for 50 years. It owes its existence to Gilles *Lefebvre, Anaïs Allard-Rousseau and Alice Desruisseaux-Boisvert, and Father J.H. Lemieux, who conceived the idea in 1949. The Quebec government placed two abandoned chalets at the JMC's disposal and the first JMC Music Camp took place in these in August 1951, with 10 campers and two teachers. In 1967, because of the increasing diversity of the camp's activities, it was renamed JMC Orford Art Centre.

The centre gradually acquired new buildings, including a concert hall and some pavilions designed by the architect Paul-Marie Côté. The concert hall was inaugurated 21 Aug 1960 with a premiere of the first work commissioned by the JMC, Clermont *Pépin's *Hymne au vent du nord*. The performance was by Raoul *Jobin and an orchestra conducted by Sir Ernest *MacMillan. (The hall was named Salle Gilles-Lefebvre in 1974.) The 500-seat amphitheatre with its excellent acoustics was built to accommodate concerts and theatre as well as meetings and lectures. Jean-Paul Mousseau designed special modules to light the foyer and an adjoining art gallery. The central pavilion

JMC Orford Art Centre

was added in 1968 to house the administration, a cafeteria, a dining room, and a record library, in addition to a lounge which could be used for meetings. The JMC Pavilion at *Expo 67, 'Man and his Music,' was moved to the centre in 1972, contributing rooms for classes, meetings, and exhibitions, and offices for the director. Two residences with modern, comfortable quarters were built in 1970, and more than 40 chalet-studios were scattered through the neighbouring woods to allow the trainees to work privately.

Throughout the 1970s more than 300 students aged 14 to 30, including some from abroad, enrolled each summer for courses in instruments and voice, pantomime, or theatre and to take part in chamber music ensembles, choirs, and orchestras. Instruction has been provided by a distinguished faculty of guest teachers including, at different times, Pierre Bernac, Victor *Bouchard and Renée *Morisset, Maurice Bourgue, Frans *Brouw, Edgard Davignon, Norbert Dufourcq, Karl Engel, Guy Fallot, Lorand *Fenyves, Claude Helffer, Walter *Joachim, Raoul Jobin, Sylvio *Lacharité, Alexandre Lagoya and Ida Presti, Marcel *Laurencelle, John *Newmark, Vlado Perlemuter, Jacqueline *Richard, Marcel Saint-Jacques, Claude *Savard, Jean-Paul *Sévilla, Gérard Souzay, and Paul Tortelier.

A string quartet formed at the centre in 1965 by four students became the *Orford String Quartet, and its members subsequently taught there on several occasions. The Orford Festival has welcomed the public at concerts, lectures, public courses, and exhibitions, some of these held on Saturdays at St-Benoît-du-Lac Abbey about 20 km away. The centre was host in 1970 and 1976 to the working sessions of the JM World Orchestra, in 1976 to the general assembly of the International Federation of the Jeunesses musicales, and in 1977 and 1978 to the Quebec Youth Orchestra. It began to be open year round in 1972, thus providing accommodation to groups or organizations wishing to hold conventions or seminars outside the summer season.

Gilles Lefebvre directed the centre until 1972, when he was succeeded by Gaston *Germain. That same year the overall responsibility was vested in a corporation independent of the JMC. A joint committee of representatives of the JMC and the corporation was set up to maintain liaison. Subsidized mainly by the *MACQ, the centre has been assisted by the *Canada Council, by corporations and companies, and by private individuals.

BIBLIOGRAPHY

Papineau-Couture, Jean. 'Salle de concert du camp JMC,' *CMJ*, vol 5, Autumn 1960

'La terre des jeunes du monde Orford,' interview with Gilles Lefebvre by Claude Chuteau, *Musica disques*, 134, May 1965

Siskind, Jacob. 'Young musicians blossoming at Orford,' Montreal *Gazette*, 16 Jul 1977

Van Vlasselaer, J.J. 'Musical islands in the summer landscape,' *Mcan*, 34, Summer 1980 CVl

JOACHIM. Montreal family of musicians of German origin who settled in Canada towards the end of the 1940s: 1 / Otto, 2 / Walter, brother of Otto, and 3 / Davis, son of Otto.

1 **Otto**. Composer, teacher, violinist, b Düsseldorf 13 Oct 1910, naturalized Canadian 1957. His father, Emil Joachimsthal, was an opera singer. Otto studied the violin 1916–28 at the Buths-Neitzel Cons. In 1928 he entered the Rheinische Musikschule at Cologne for coaching by Hermann Zitzmann preparatory to a career as a violinist and violist. During his final term, 1930–1, he served as Zitzmann's assistant. In 1934, a year after Hitler came to power, he left Germany for the Far East, where he remained for 15 years, performing and teaching first in Singapore and later in Shanghai. In 1949 he obtained an immigrant's visa to Brazil, which allowed him a month's stay in Canada.

Joachim subsequently decided to settle in Montreal, where he became a member and later principal viola of the *MSO and of the *McGill Chamber Orchestra. With his brother Walter, cello, and Hyman *Bress and Mildred *Goodman, violins, he founded the *Montreal String Quartet. In 1956 he began teaching at the *McGill Cons and at the *CMM. He was in charge of chamber music classes at the latter until 1977. After leaving McGill in 1966 he performed less often in order to devote himself to teaching and composing. His interest in old instruments, however, led to the founding in 1958 of the Montreal Consort of Ancient Instruments, which he directed until 1968, and for which he built replicas of instruments of the middle ages and the renaissance. The consort has made recordings with the *Montreal Bach Choir and the *Petit Ensemble vocal.

Though he was trained in Germany, Joachim the composer developed almost entirely in Canada (the works composed in Germany – the symphonic poem *Asia* and the *Trois Bagatelles* for piano – were not completed there), and the convergence of two cultures in his work lends it a marked singularity. It is as if his will to compose found its nutrients and stimuli wholly in the new country while the techniques brought into play were a legacy of the old country. Thus, works such as *L'Éclosion* and *Concertante No. 1* exude a certain 'Canadianism' which nonetheless is difficult to define. The fact that he began composing rather late in life can be explained by his earlier devotion to performing and teaching.

Almost all of Joachim's works use serial tech-

Manuscript opening page from *Dialogue* by Otto Joachim for viola and piano, 1964

nique. According to Udo *Kasemets (*Contemporary Canadian Composers*), 'Joachim's treatment of the tone-row is at once quite conventional and undogmatic ... his rows are easily recognizable and tuneful.' Without excluding the tonal implications of doubled octaves and literal repetition, his results nevertheless are very advanced and original. Even in earlier works such as *Music* for violin and viola composed in 1953 (RCI 459), *March* for voice and piano (1954), and the *Sonata* for cello and piano, the composer went beyond classic serialism to the point of experimenting with numerical systems applied to the rhythmic parameter. If such methods recall Webern and Boulez, Joachim's way of creating unusual sounds from traditional instruments also shows the influence of Varèse.

In the mid-1950s Joachim set up his own electronic music studio (the third in Canada) and, after several years of study and experimentation, created *Katimavik*, a work on four-track tape commissioned by the Canadian Pavilion at *Expo 67. In 1971 he produced two other wholly electronic compositions, *6 ½* and *5.9*, the titles being the durations (in minutes) of the works.

Joachim's long and significant association with aleatoric music began with *Nonet* (1960) for strings, winds, and piano, perhaps the first piece of chance music to be written in Canada. Subsequently he wrote *Contrastes*, commissioned by the *TS for Canada's Centennial, and *Illumination I*, *Illumination II*, and *Mankind*, three works, commissioned by the CBC, which explore the various relationships between the properties of sound and of light. The players only begin to play when the light above them, controlled by the conductor, is switched on. Thus, certain parameters of each performance become dependent on what the performer sees on the page, with what intensity, and for what duration. For *Illumination II*, the composer received in 1969 the Grand Prix Paul-Gilson from the Communauté radiophonique des programmes de langue française. In *Stimulus à Goad*, for guitar and live electronic sound, the guitarist controls the quality of the electronic sound, so that the instrument elicits certain replies from the synthesizer. On commission from the *SMCQ, Joachim in 1977 composed *Uraufführung* for 13 instruments and live electronic sound. In the summer of 1977 he went to Seoul, Korea, as string coach for the JM World Orchestra. A member of the

*CLComp, he is an affiliate of PRO Canada and is an associate of the*CMCentre.

See also Aleatoric music; Electronic music

SELECTED COMPOSITIONS

ORCHESTRA

Asia, symphonic poem. 1928–39. Full orch. Ber (rental)
Concertante No. 1. 1955. Vn, str orch, perc. BMIC 1960. RCI 293 (*Bress)
Concertante No. 2. 1961. Str quar, str orch. Ber (rental)
Contrastes. 1967. Full orch. Ric 1968

CHAMBER

Sonata for cello and piano. 1954. BMIC 1963. RCI 139 (W. *Joachim)/CBC SM-113 (*Depkat)
String Quartet. 1956. AMP 1959; BMIC 1960. RCI 190 (*Mtl Str Quar)
Interlude 'Quartet for four saxophones.' 1960. CMCentre
Divertimento. 1962. Ww quin. Ber (rental)
Expansion. 1962. Fl, pf. BMIC 1967
Illumination I (A. Purdy). 1965. spkr, chamb ens. BMIC 1968
Kinderspiel, aleatoric music for children (*Le Petit Prince*). 1969. Narr, vn, vc, pf. Privately publ by the composer 1970
Twelve 12-Tone Pieces for the Young. 1970. Vn, pf. Ms
Six Guitar Pieces. 1971. Preissler 1977. RCI 392/Mel SMLP 4025 (D. *Joachim)
Requiem. 1977. Vn (va or vc). Ms
4 *Intermezzi*. 1978. Fl, guit. Ms. (3 *Intermezzi*) RCI 482 (D. *Joachim)
Night Music. 1978. Fl, guit. CMCentre. RCI 482 (D. *Joachim)

KEYBOARD

Bagatelles. 1939. Pf. Ms
L'Éclosion. 1954. Pf. BMIC 1968. RCI 133 (*Goldblatt)/Mel SMLP 4023 (*Kubalek)
Fantasia. 1961. Org. BMIC 1967. RCI 225/RCA CCS-1019 (*Gilbert)
Twelve 12-Tone Pieces for Children. 1961. Pf. BMIC 1961. (No. 1, 3, 4, 5, 7, 8, 9, 10) CCM-2 (*Cavalho)

ELECTRONIC AND MIXED MEDIA

Katimavik. 1967. Tape
Illumination II. 1969. Various instr, 4-track tape, projectors. Ber 1976. (Ca. 1972). RCI 298 (ens of Mtl musicians, O. Joachim cond)
5.9. 1971. 4-track tape. RCI 373
6 ½. 1971. 4-track tape
Mankind (Hebrew literature, the Koran, Catholic and Buddhist liturgy). 1972. 4 spkr, 4 synth, org, timp, incense, slides. Ms
Stimulus à Goad. 1973. Guit, synth. Preissler 1977. RCI 392/Mel SMLP 4025 (D. *Joachim guit)
Uraufführung. 1977. Guit, 14 instr, electronic music. Ms
Other works, including *Psalm* for choir (1960), BMIC 1961, RCI 206 (*Mtl Bach Choir)

DISCOGRAPHY

See Musica Antica e Nuova.

BIBLIOGRAPHY

'Otto Joachim, a portrait,' *Mcan*, 20, Jun 1969
Campbell, Francean. 'Otto Joachim's mastery influences son,' *MSc*, 255, Sep–Oct 1970
BMI Canada Ltd/PRO Canada Ltd. 'Otto Joachim,' pamphlets, 1974, 1978
Richer-Lortie, Lyse. 'Otto Joachim, composer, performer, inventor,' *Variations*, vol 2, Feb 1979
CMCentre. *Compositeurs au Québec: Otto Joachim* (Montreal 1980)
Gingras, Claude. 'Otto Joachim, musicien complet,' Montreal *La Presse*, 26 Apr 1980
Kasemets, Udo. 'Otto Joachim,' *Contemporary Canadian Composers / Compositeurs canadiens contemporains*
Creative Canada, vol 1

2 **Walter**. Cellist, teacher, b Düsseldorf 5 May 1912, naturalized Canadian 1957. At 4 he began studying the violin; at 5, the cello. Studies followed at the conservatory in his home town. At 15, he entered the Staatliche Hochschule für Musik in Cologne, where he was taught 1927–30 by Karl-Maria Schwamberger. During this time he became principal cellist of the Cologne Chamber Orchestra. A series of concerts and recitals in Germany established him as a performer, and from then on he divided his time between touring and teaching. With the Quartetto d'Italia 1930–3 he made two tours across Europe and Asia, as far as Calcutta. He then worked 1934–8 in Prague as a free-lance soloist, chamber musician, and orchestral player. During and after World War II he pursued his career in Malaya and China, teaching and giving concerts 1938–40 in Kuala Lumpur and serving 1940–51 as head of the cello department at the Shanghai Cons and principal cellist of the Shanghai SO.

Joachim settled in Canada in 1952 and joined the *MSO in 1953, soon advancing to the chair of principal cello and retaining that position until 1979, and also playing in the *McGill Chamber Orchestra. Besides giving a number of recitals on CBC radio and TV, he was a co-founder and member of the *Montreal String Quartet. His teaching activity has produced a number of talented young cellists, including Denis *Brott, Guy Fouquet (who succeeded Joachim as principal cellist of the MSO in 1979), Hélène *Gagne, and Marcel St Cyr (*Orford String Quartet). He began teaching at the *CMM in 1952 and also taught 1952–63 at *McGill U, 1953–62 at the *JMC Orford Arts Centre, 1960–72 for the *NYO, and three summers for the JM World O. With the pianist John *Newmark he premiered his brother Otto's *Sonata* in 1954 and Violet *Archer's *Sonata* in 1957 and recorded both (RCI 139). Also with Newmark, he has recorded the *Weinzweig *Sonata* (RCI 209/RCI ACM 1) and works by Bloch, Dvořák, Hindemith, and Martinu (RCI 209). (See also Allan Fine; Musica Antica e Nuova; Discographies for Melvin Berman, Hyman Bress, Montreal String Quartet, John Newmark.)

BIBLIOGRAPHY

Kraglund, John. 'His pupils approach Bach through period costumes' Toronto *Globe and Mail*, 25 Aug 1966
'Meet the orchestra: Walter Joachim: a full life,' *Variations*, vol 1, Apr 1978
Peterson, Maureen. 'First cellist retiring – to a life of more work,' Montreal *Gazette*, 5 May 1979

3 **Davis**. Guitarist, teacher, editor, composer, b Shanghai 20 Jul 1949, naturalized Canadian 1955; B MUS (UQAM) 1975. He began his guitar studies with Antonin Bartos at the *École normale in Montreal. Later he undertook advanced studies with Eli *Kassner in Toronto and John Mills in London. Besides performing regularly, notably for the *SMCQ, he has taught at the *UQAM and at *Concordia U. In 1970 he was awarded a scholarship by *Electron* magazine for his electronic work *Quasar*. He attended the master classes of Siegfried Behrend in Riedenburg, Germany, in the summers of 1974 and 1976. In 1976 the *Canada Council awarded him a grant for the composition of three works. In May and June of the same year he accompanied Jacques *Labrecque on a Canadian tour. He performs his own *Étude* and works by Samuel *Dolin, Rolland Côté, and Otto Joachim on the LP *Canadian Music for Classical Guitar* (Melbourne SMLP 4025), and works by Bach, Giuliani, Villa-Lobos, Brindle-Borsi, and Otto Joachim on RCI 392. With the flutist Eric Wilner in 1977 he formed the Classical Duo of Montreal which in 1978 recorded works by Vinci, Carulli, Margola, and Otto Joachim (RCI 482). He is an affiliate of PRO Canada.

WRITINGS

Guitar music in Canada,' *MSc*, 281 Jan – Feb 1975

1 / RM, 2, 3 / CLE

JOBIN. Quebec tenors: 1 / Raoul and 2 / André, his son.

Raoul Jobin as Don José in *Carmen*

1 **Raoul** (b Joseph Roméo). Tenor, teacher, administrator, senior civil servant, b Quebec City 8 Apr 1906, d there 13 Jan 1974; hon D MUS (Laval) 1952. He came from the working-class district of St-Sauveur, where his father owned a tavern, and was a member of the parish choir and a soloist there for about 10 years. He first took voice lessons from Louis *Gravel and then studied 1924–8 with Émile *Larochelle at *Laval U. He performed in concert using the name Roméo, and after a farewell recital in Quebec City went to Paris, where he continued his studies with Mme d'Estainville-Rousset (singing) and Pierre Chéreau (stage skills). At a 1929 pupils' recital, his exceptional voice captured the attention of the Paris Opéra management, who offered him a contract for the following year. Jobin returned to Quebec to give some concerts early in 1930 and chiefly to marry the soprano Thérèse Drouin. (Later they gave recitals together, and she appeared with him in operatic productions, including a *Carmen* in Montreal in 1946, in which she sang Micaela and he Don José.)

On Jobin's return to Paris, he made his professional debut 28 May 1930 in Liszt's oratorio *Christus* at the Théâtre des Champs-Élysées. His debut at the Paris Opera took place 3 June in *Roméo et Juliette* (the role of Tybalt). During the 1930–1 season he sang many roles, including Nicias (*Thaïs*), the Italian singer (*Der Rosenkavalier*), Iopas (Berlioz' *Les Troyans*), and most notably the Duke in *Rigoletto* (20 Dec 1930), the first major role of his career. In 15 months he sang in 111 performances of various operas. Soon he was in demand with the Parisian orchestras, including that of the Concerts Colonne, with which he performed Beethoven's *Ninth Symphony* and *Missa solemnis* and Berlioz' *Requiem* (1931).

His mother's illness brought Jobin back to Quebec City in the autumn of 1931, and he did not return to Paris till 1934. He gave concerts in Quebec City, Ottawa, and Montreal. In Quebec City he sang Roméo in *Roméo et Juliette* with the De Feo troupe, and in Montreal he participated in many performances of the *Société canadienne d'opérette in Lehar's *Gypsy Love*, Hervé's *Mamz'elle Nitouche*, and Fourdrain's *Secret de polichinelle* (1932). In the spring of 1933 Jobin was engaged by the *San Carlo Opera Company for its Montreal and Quebec City productions, and he enjoyed considerable success in *Faust*, *Rigoletto*, *I Pagliacci*, and *Roméo et Juliette*. The following year he gave eight performances of *The Barber of Seville* in Montreal at the Imperial Theatre, with Caro *Lamoureux, Lionel *Daunais, and Charles *Goulet, and as many again of Bazin's *Voyage en Chine*.

Back in Paris in May 1934, he returned to the Paris Opera on 16 July in *Rigoletto*. At this time he began using the first name Raoul. From then on, his career made rapid progress. As principal tenor at the Opéra-Comique, he was sought after in the provinces, performing successfully in Lyons, Bordeaux, Toulouse, Vichy, Arles, Marseilles, Montpellier, and other cities. Until 1939 the name of Raoul Jobin topped the bill in the opera houses of France, and he sang the French repertoire in particular, with occasional excursions into the Italian and German repertoires. His major roles were Faust, Don José, Werther, Samson, Wilhelm Meister (*Mignon*), Des Grieux (*Manon*), Gérald (*Lakmé*), Hoffmann, Roméo, and Julien (*Louise*); he performed numerous premieres, the most important being Fabrice in Sauguet's *La Chartreuse de Parme* on 20 Mar 1939. He also appeared in Holland, Spain, and Italy. His engagements with orchestras, in concert, and on the radio continued to multiply.

In the fall of 1938 Jobin returned to Quebec and performed with Anna *Malenfant in *Carmen* at the *Variétés lyriques. The next summer he sang in the Municipal Theatre of Rio de Janeiro. Rumours of war persuaded him not to return to Europe, and he went instead to Montreal and then to New York, where, at the suggestion of Wilfrid *Pelletier, he entered the 'Metropolitan Opera Auditions of the Air.' The *Metropolitan soon placed him under contract, and he made his debut there 19 Feb 1940 in *Manon*. He remained with this company until 1950, singing many roles alongside such stars as Lily Pons, Bidú Sayão, Martial Singher, and Ezio Pinza. On 20 Feb 1942 he sang Luca in the premiere of Menotti's *The Island God*. Jobin's North American career extended from the Atlantic to the Pacific, and he performed many seasons in San Francisco, Chicago, Los Angeles, Cincinnati, Philadelphia, Cleveland, Boston, New Orleans, and other cities, as a guest artist with orchestras, on Metropolitan tours, or as a member 1945–6 of the Metropolitan Opera Quartet. Wherever he appeared, his mastery of the French style, the brilliance of his upper register, and the richness of his timbre earned him an enthusiastic reception and praise from the critics. Certain performances stand out, eg, his singing of the title role in Stravinsky's *Oedipus Rex* in Boston in 1940 under the composer's direction and his portrayal of Pelléas in Debussy's *Pelléas et Mélisande*, which he first sang at *His Majesty's Theatre, Montreal, 14 Jun 1940, under Wilfrid Pelletier, with Marcelle Denya as his partner. During the summer Jobin regularly returned to South America for seasons in Rio de Janeiro and at the Teatro Colón in Buenos Aires, as well as to Mexico City. His Renaud in Gluck's *Armide*, in 1943 at the Teatro Colón, deserves special mention.

The Canadian tenor returned to the Opéra-Comique in Paris on 2 May 1947 in *Carmen*; he also sang Don José 12 June in the 2500th performance of this work in that theatre. He was acclaimed at the Paris Opera in the title role of *Lohengrin*, his first major Wagnerian role, and in 1952 in Paris and Vichy he sang Walther in *Die Meistersinger*. Subsequently, Jobin divided his time largely between Europe and America but performing also in North Africa. He maintained his high standard in his accustomed roles and continued to add new ones. In a 1951 performance of *Aida* in Paris he sang his first Radames, repeating the role in Bordeaux and Liège. In 1952 he sang Damon in Rameau's *Les Indes galantes*. In 1955 he performed in two premieres: Mirouze' *Geneviève de Paris* at the Théâtre Romain in Fourvières and Tomasi's *L'Atlantide* in Enghien, near Paris, and then in Vichy, Marseilles, and Lyons. The Opéra-Comique invited him to sing in the 1000th performance of *Louise* in 1956, and he gave his farewell performance with that company in the spring of 1957 in Richard Strauss' *Capriccio*. In 1957 he also sang Ulysse in Fauré's *Pénélope* in several French cities; his performance of the role 24 Jun 1958 in Vichy was his final appearance on the operatic stage.

In Canada Jobin was frequently invited to sing with the principal orchestras of Montreal, Toronto, Quebec City, and other cities. He also performed frequently on the radio, and on CBC TV he sang Canio in *I Pagliacci* 11 Mar 1958. He often appeared with the New York Philharmonic Orchestra (eg, in *Ninth Symphony*, 1949) and with the Cleveland and Chicago orchestras. His numerous recitals were praised but he was less at ease in recital than in opera. In the ensuing years, Jobin reduced his activities considerably. In one of his last public appearances – at the *JMC Orford Art Centre in the summer of 1960 – he premiered Clermont *Pépin's *Hymne au vent du nord* under the baton of Sir Ernest *MacMillan.

In 1957 he began teaching at the *CMM and the *CMQ, and he was director 1961–70 of the CMQ succeeding Henri *Gagnon. He helped train many young singers, including Colette *Boky, Jean *Bonhomme, Gaston *Germain, Louise Gosselin, Jacqueline *Martel, Joan *Patenaude, Jean-Louis Pellerin, and Guy Plamondon. He was a member of the *Canada Council 1961–64. He was cultural consultant 1970–3 to the Quebec government's general delegation in Paris. In 1951 he had been created Chevalier de la Légion d'honneur by France, and in 1967 he was made a Companion of the *Order of Canada.

Although rightly considered the successor to Georges Thill as the greatest 'French' tenor of his time, Raoul Jobin was unable to escape specialization. Yet it was the really substantial roles – whether French (Hoffmann, Samson, and especially Don José), Italian (Cavaradossi, Canio), or German (Lohengrin) – that best lent themselves to the heroic nature of his powerful voice with its triumphant highs, to his dramatic instinct, and to his temperament. Upon his death the French critic Jean Goury said of him: 'Raoul Jobin was undoubtedly one of the most celebrated tenors in the French tradition in recent decades. His voice, with its highly personalized timbre – neither Italianized nor Nordic but permeated with the warm fragrance of the Canadian soil – was capable of surprising variations in dynamics ... Raoul Jobin was a singer in the grand tradition, never sacrificing musicianship to sentiment and maintaining at all times a restraint of the highest order' (Paris *Guide musical opéra*, 9 Feb 1974).

DISCOGRAPHY

Beethoven *Ninth Symphony*. New York Philharmonic, Walter cond. Odyssey 32160322

Berlioz *La Damnation de Faust* (excerpts). London SO, Fistoulari cond. 1954. Decca LW 5319

– *The Damnation of Faust* (excerpts). London SO, Fistoulari cond. 1954. Lon LL 1154

Bizet *Carmen*. Opéra-Comique de Paris O, Cluytens cond. (1951). 3-Col SL-109/3-Col FCX 101-103

– *Carmen* (excerpts). Metropolitan Opera O and Chorus, Sebastian cond. 1945. Col LP-ML 4013/(1973) Odyssey Y 32102

– *Carmen* (excerpts). Peebles contralto, Warren bar, Jobin (Don José), W. Pelletier cond. 1940. RCA Camden CAL-221

Cantiques de Noël. Disciples de Massenet, R. Roy org. 1945. RCA Red Seal LSC-2503/RCA Victor LM-2503/(7 carols) Victor LM-7014

Gluck *Alceste*. Geraint Jones O and chorus, Jones cond. Lon XLL.1543/Richmond SRS-63512

Gounod *Roméo et Juliette*. Paris Opera O and Chorus, Erede cond. Lon LLA 18/Lon A-4310

– *Roméo et Juliette Highlights*. Paris Opera O and Chorus, Erede cond. Lon LL 1111/Lon OS 26270

Massenet *Werther* (excerpts). London SO, Fistoulari cond. Lon LL 1154

– *Werther* 'J'aurais sur ma poitrine' – Bizet *Carmen* 'La Fleur que tu m'avais jetée.' Between 1947 and 1952. Col LFX 827 (78)

A Night at Carnegie Hall: Bizet *Carmen* (excerpts, act I). Metropolitan Opera O, Sebastian cond. Col ML 2113/Col LP 2337

Offenbach *Les Contes d'Hoffmann*. Opéra-Comique O, Cluytens cond. 1948. 16-Col LFX 794-809 (78)

– *The Tales of Hoffmann*. Opéra-Comique O, Cluytens cond. 1948. 3-Col SL-106

Puccini *Tosca* 'Le Ciel luisait d'étoiles' (French and Italian). Between 1947 and 1952. Col LF 270 (78)

Romantic Arias from French Operas – Raoul Jobin. W. Pelletier cond. Col set D-190

Wagner *Siegfried* 'Air de la forge,' *Lohengrin* 'Récit du Graal.' Paris Opera O, Fourestier cond. Between 1947 and 1952. Col LFX 844 (78)

BIBLIOGRAPHY

'Personality of the week, Raoul Jobin,' *Opera News*, vol 7, 15 Feb 1943

Maître, Manuel. 'La vie d'un grand ténor canadien,' Montreal *Patrie du dimanche*, 18 Sep 1960

Rivard, Yolande. 'Raoul Jobin voudrait que les Québécois n'aient pas à s'expatrier pour apprendre leur métier sur une scène lyrique,' *VM*, 4, 1966

Gingras, Claude. 'Raoul Jobin: 30 ans de carrière,' Montreal *La Presse*, 15 Jan 1974

Potvin, Gilles. 'Un illustre chanteur québécois,' Montreal *Le Devoir*, 19 Jan 1974

2 **André**. Tenor, actor, b Quebec City 20 Jan 1933. After 10 years in New York, he went to Paris, where his family had settled, and began studying drama. In 1952 he performed as a member of the Compagnie Jean-Louis Barrault-Madeleine Renaud in Europe, the USA and Canada. During this time he also studied singing, first with his father and later with Janine Micheau. As a singer he made his debut in 1958 at the Théâtre de l'Étoile in *Nouvelle-Orléans*, a musical comedy by Pascal Bastia and Sydney Bechet, who starred in it. His aptitude for playing juvenile leads in operetta subsequently was demonstrated in Joseph Kosma's *Bilitis et l'amour* (the role of Cynésias) and in Georges Van Parys's *Le Jeu des dames* (1960). The following year he tackled classical operetta, particularly the Viennese, where the leading roles gave him ample opportunity to display his talents as a singer and actor.

André Jobin turned to opera in 1963, performing the title roles in Gluck's *Orphée*, Haydn's *The Apothecary*, and *Pelléas et Mélisande*. He became one of the most sought-after interpreters of Pelléas, first singing the role in 1963 at the Opéra-Comique in Paris and repeating it in the famous houses of Berlin, Brussels, Madrid, and San Francisco, where a reviewer declared: 'Vocally brilliant was the new young tenor, André Jobin, who made a thoroughly believable and princely Pelléas' (*San Francisco Chronicle*, 5 Nov 1965). He repeated Pelléas at the New York City Opera in 1970.

André Jobin pursued his career successfully in premieres and in standard repertoire in France and in many other countries. He went to Australia in 1968 to perform *Valses de Vienne* and made his CBC TV debut as Ange Pitou in Lecocq's *La Fille de Madame Angot*. He then played the role of Guy Florès in Benatzky's *L'Auberge du cheval blanc* at the Théâtre du Châtelet in Paris (1968–9). His participation in the recording of Lecocq's operetta *Le Petit Duc* earned him a 1968 Grand prix du disque. In 1970 he sang in *Die Fledermaus* in Geneva and *The Merry Widow* on CBC TV. His career took a new direction in mid-1971, when he accepted the producer Harold Fielding's invitation to sing the role of Gaylord Ravenal in a London production of Jerome Kern's *Showboat* at the Adelphi Theatre. His success in the starring role was so great that he remained in London for almost three years, performing it 935 times. He returned to Paris in 1974 in Jacques Debronkart's *Les Aventures de Tom Jones* and then embarked on a series of performances of *Il était une fois l'opérette* at the Théâtre Bobino, a show that had a successful run in Paris before touring Canada in 1975. André Jobin again distinguished himself on the immense stage of Le Châtelet in 1978 singing Michel Andrassy in the revival of Lehar's *Christmas Rose* and Boris in Francis Lopez' *Volga* at the same theatre. The daily *L'Aurore* described his performance in *Christmas Rose*: 'André Jobin is the house tenor par excellence. He has youth, vitality, and charm and is one of those singers who are no more afraid of high Cs than of soft notes' (17 Nov 1978). In 1979 he sang the role of Sou-Chong in seven performances of the operetta *Land of Smiles* at the *Grand Théâtre in Quebec City in a producion by the *Société lyrique d'Aubigny.

DISCOGRAPHY

Benatzky *L'Auberge du cheval blanc*. Châtelet Theatre O, Bonneau cond. 1968. Philips 844 896 BY

Il était une fois l'opérette. R. Valentino mus dir. 1974. Festival 172

Kern *Showboat*. Ray Cook cond. 1971. Col SCX 6480/Stanyan Records 10048

Lecocq *Le Petit Duc*. Châtelet Theatre O, Grassi cond. 1968. 2-RCA Decca SSL 40.219-220

Lehar *Rose de Noël*. Châtelet Theatre O, Bonneau cond. 1978. IBACH 60529

Lopez *Volga*. Châtelet Theatre O. 1978. IBACH 607092 (MS)

JOHANNESEN, Audrey (b Johnston). Pianist, teacher, b Regina 12 Sep 1930; ATCM 1944, LRAM 1950, premier prix Brussels 1953. She studied with Frances England and Lyell *Gustin in Regina and with Max *Pirani at Banff. Moving to London she resumed her work with Pirani at the RAM, winning the Macfarren Gold Prize. She studied further, 1952-3, with Eduardo del Pueyo at the Cons royal in Brussels and received the Prix Van Cutsem. She returned to Canada in 1959 and subsequently has performed with orchestra, in recital, and on CBC radio. She has toured both Canada (for the *JMC 1963 and 1964) and Europe (1966). A resident of Vancouver, she has given master classes at the *Shawnigan Summer School of the Arts founded by her husband J.J. *Johannesen in 1971. Lyell Gustin has described her as 'a dramatic player' and the critic of the London *Daily Telegraph* commended her 'massive technique [and] ... splendid sound.' WLB

JOHANNESEN, J.J. (Joseph Jean). Administrator, businessman, b Vitry, France, 23 Mar 1928, naturalized Canadian 1976. Educated in Belgium, where he helped establish the JM movement, Johannesen was interested in composing but pursued a career in business. He was a banker 1956-9 in the Belgian Congo, where he met and married the Canadian pianist Audrey Johnston *Johannesen and initiated the Congo's first concert series. He then moved to Vancouver and established an import-export business there. In the early 1960s he was a director of the Vancouver Philharmonic Society and the *Vancouver Bach Choir and in 1961 he introduced to British Columbia the JM concerts (after 1972 known as the *Festival Concert Society). Johannesen served as a director and 1968-71 as vice-president of the *JMC, and in 1980 he was still the executive director of the Festival Concert Society and also of the *Shawnigan Summer School of the Arts, which he founded in 1971.

BIBLIOGRAPHY

'Le plan quinquennal de J.J. Johannesen,' *Jmc*, vol 15, Apr 1969 BNSG

John Adaskin Project. A plan for introducing Canadian composers into schools as creative teachers and teaching creators. In 1961 a 'Graded Educational Music Plan' was conceived and initiated by John *Adaskin, executive secretary of the *CMCentre. The initial aim was to promote increased use of Canadian music in schools. The grading and evaluating of repertoire in terms of its suitablility for student performers began in 1962.

To promote the composition of additional Canadian school music, a Seminar for Graded Educational Music was held in Toronto 11-16 Nov 1963. As part of this seminar, 15 Canadian composers visited schools in the Toronto area, observing student performers with the idea of writing music for their use. 'Seminar II' (Toronto, March 1965), at which the project was renamed in Adaskin's memory, featured concert demonstrations of music by 10 of the 15 'Seminar I' composers and planning for the future of the project.

At a policy conference in Toronto 23-25 Nov 1967, composers, educators, and publishers considered further the development of Canadian music for schools and the need for creativity in education. Enthusiasm at this conference ran high, but action was delayed until 1973, when the *CMEA joined the CMCentre to animate the plan, with the amended name 'The John Adaskin Project (Canadian Music for Schools),' under the direction of Patricia Shand. The aims of the joint project were: to acquaint educators with published Canadian music suitable for student vocal and instrumental ensembles, to promote publication of additional music for student performers, and to encourage Canadian composers to add to the repertoire.

Realization of these aims was well under way by 1977. A published list, *Canadian Music: A Selective Guidelist for Teachers* (Toronto 1978), recommended and described Canadian music available for student bands, orchestras, string orchestras, choirs, and chamber ensembles. Unpublished Canadian music was being collected and evaluated systematically, commissioning had continued, and publishing had advanced. The following are works commissioned by the project and later published:

*Bissell *Two Songs from Shakespeare* (BMIC 1965)
*Fleming, R. 'Madrigal' (Waterloo 1965); '*You Name It' Suite* (GVT 1965)
*Freedman *Three Vocalises* (Leeds 1965)
*Kenins *Nocturne* from *Nocturne and Dance* (B & H 1969)
*Kunz 'A Clear Midnight' and 'Slow, Slow Fresh Fount' (Waterloo 1965); 'To Hear an Oriole Sing' (Waterloo 1965)
*Pépin *Three Miniatures for Strings* (Oxford U Press 1966, then C. Pépin 1966)
*Schafer *Statement in Blue* (BMIC 1966, UE 1971)
*Somers 'The Wonder Song' (BMIC 1964); *Theme for Variations* (BMIC 1966)
*Weinzweig *Clarinet Quartet* (Leeds 1970)

Housed in Toronto at the CMCentre, the project has been funded by the CMEA, the CMCentre, the *Canada Council, the *OAC, the Ontario Ministry of Education, and private foundations.

BIBLIOGRAPHY

'The John Adaskin Project: towards new music in education,' *CanComp*, 23, Nov 1967

CMCentre. *Report on the John Adaskin Project Policy Conference* (Toronto 1968)

Shand, Patricia. 'In search of our own music,' *CME*, vol 17, Winter 1976

Orr, Colleen. 'John Adaskin Project: a history and evaluation,' unpubl M MUS thesis, U of Western Ontario 1977

Shand, Patricia. *Canadian Music: A Selective Guidelist for Teachers* (Toronto 1978) (PS)

Johnny Belinda. Musical play by Mavor *Moore (book) and John *Fenwick (music). It is based on the play of the same name by the US author Elmer Harris, and tells a story of love, murder, and a deaf girl in Souris, PEI, in 1894. Dramatizations of the novel included a Broadway play (1940), a Hollywood movie (1948), a radio play on the CBC (1950), and TV productions on NBC (1958) and ABC (1967). The Moore-Fenwick musical was premiered 1 Jul 1968 at the *Charlottetown Festival, with Fenwick conducting, and was staged there again in 1969 (with performances also in Montreal, Ottawa, and Toronto), in 1974 (with performances also in Toronto, at *O'Keefe Centre), and in 1975. After its Toronto debut at the *Royal Alexandre Theatre, Nathan Cohen wrote, 'what gives the musical its dynamic is its grass roots quality, conveyed first of all in John Fenwick's score, which draws liberally and pertinently on the bountiful folktune heritage of the Maritimes' (*Toronto Daily Star*, 4 Jun 1969). The title role, limited to sign language and dance, was played by Diane Nyland in the first two productions and by Amanda Hancox in 1974 and 1975. Don *McManus was Black John MacDonald in every production mentioned. A TV adaptation, called *Belinda* (with Hancox, and directed by Norman *Campbell), was telecast 9 Mar 1977 by the CBC. (MM)

JOHNSON, Audrey St Denys. Music and drama critic and columnist, b Toronto 21 Dec 1915; piano teachers' LRSM. She went in 1920 to Victoria, BC, where she studied piano (with Stanley Shale), singing, and violin. In 1944 she joined the *Victoria Daily Times* as a columnist, and in 1956 she became a full-time member of staff. She has contributed to the *Christian Science Monitor*, **Opera Canada*, and *Weekend Magazine*. In 1959 she directed Johann Strauss' operetta *Die Fledermaus* for the Victoria Operatic Society and a performance in Christ Church Cathedral, Victoria, of Menotti's *Amahl and the Night Visitors*.

JOHNSON, Bernard. Baritone, announcer, b Rhani Ket, India, of English parents, 18 Jun 1918; FTCL 1950. Taken to England at two and to Canada at five, Johnson was raised in Hamilton, Ont. He studied voice with his mother, Winnifred Johnson, a concert and operetta singer (London, early 1900s) who had studied with John Kennedy, Sir Granville Bantock, and Moston Bell and who taught speech and singing in Hamilton and was the local *TCL representative. Johnson made his radio debut in 1937 on CHML, Hamilton, and, after service in World War II, sang in 1946 with the CKOC Concert Orchestra. Johnson was the winner in 1947 of the first *'Opportunity Knocks' series and was heard that year on his own show, 'The Night and the Music,' and subsequently on other such programs. With the *CBC Opera he sang Schaunard in *La Bohème* (1948), Masetto in *Don Giovanni* (1949), Sharpless in *Madama Butterfly* (1950), and Guglielmo in *Così fan tutte* (1951).

Johnson made his *TSO debut 23 Dec 1949 in a pop concert and returned 14 Mar 1952 as a last-minute replacement for Thomas L. Thomas. Johnson sang in the 1956 TV performance of the ballad opera **The Broken Ring* and in the radio premiere of *Beckwith's **Night Blooming Cereus* in 1959 and the stage version in 1960. Though he continued to sing on radio and TV and in concert and recital, in 1959 he became the announcer-host for CBC radio's record program 'Much Ado about Music.'

After a Johnson recital, Frank *Haworth wrote, 'his voice is of baritone range, but of somewhat tenor-like quality ... and in his use of it he displayed a fine appreciation of the niceties of tonal gradation, rhythm, phrase and nuance' (Toronto *Globe and Mail*, 19 Nov 1956). Johnson sang on the 1954 recording of **Timber!!* MM

JOHNSON, Edward. Tenor, administrator, patron, b Guelph, Ont, 22 Aug 1878, naturalized US 1922, d Guelph 20 Apr 1959; LLD (Western Ontario) 1929, hon D MUS (Toronto) 1934, hon D LITT (Union College, New York) 1943. The son of James Johnson and the former Margaret Jane Brown, he sang as a child in a local church choir. At 20 he was soloist at Guelph's Chalmers Church and already had appeared at amateur functions, including a concert in Stratford in 1897 with the contralto Edith *Miller, who encouraged him to pursue a professional career. Going to New York soon afterwards he studied with a Mme von Feilitsch and filled numerous minor engagements in churches and at YMCA entertainments and the like. By the turn of the century he was established as a young 'assisting artist,' sharing programs with such celebrities as Lillian Nordica, Louise Homer, Vladimir de Pachmann, and Ernestine Schumann-Heink. Most of these engagements were in the northeastern USA, with occasional forays into Canada, where he was heard as soloist in Coleridge-Taylor's *Hiawatha* (Montreal, 27 Jan 1904) and Liszt's *Psalm 13* (Toronto, 16 Feb 1905, with the *Toronto Mendelssohn Choir).

In 1907 Johnson reluctantly agreed to sing the leading role in the North American premiere of Oscar Straus' *A Waltz Dream*. After performances in Philadelphia and Baltimore the operetta opened at New York's Broadway Theater, 27 Jan 1908, and ran 14 weeks. The young tenor found himself an 'overnight star.' More important, the engagement furnished him with the means to study abroad. He sailed for Paris in 1908 and commenced work with Richard Barthélemy. In Paris he met Beatrice d'Arneiro, daughter of the Portuguese viscount José d'Arneiro, and in London, 2 Aug 1909, he married her. The couple settled in Florence, where he studied with Vincenzo Lombardi and where his only child, Fiorenza, was born 21 Dec 1910.

Johnson made his opera debut 10 Jan 1912 as Andrea Chenier at Padua's Teatro Verdi. He called himself Edoardo Di Giovanni (Johnson's own spelling and capitalization, contrary to other references) and under that name achieved his first successes. These included a season 1912-13 at Rome's Teatro Costanzi in such operas as Mascagni's *Isabeau* and Puccini's *La Fanciulla del West* and an important engagement 9 Jan 1914 at La Scala, Milan, where he had a triumph in the title role of *Parsifal* in the first fully staged production of that opera in Italy. In the five years that followed, Johnson was heard at most of the important Italian houses as well as at Buenos Aires' Teatro Colón in 1916 and Madrid's Teatro Real in 1917.

Apart from *Don Carlo* and *Aida* he eschewed the usual 19th-century repertoire, finding that his robust voice and passionate temperament were best suited to the *verismo* school, some of whose leading exponents – Alfano, Montemezzi, Pizzetti – invited him to participate in world premieres during this period. The 'Edoardo Di Giovanni' phase of Johnson's career ended with his wife's death 24 May 1919.

Johnson made his North American opera debut 20 Nov 1919 as Loris in Giordano's *Fedora* with the Chicago Opera and remained with that company for three seasons, performing his customary repertoire as well as the title role in *Lohengrin* and such oddities as Erlanger's *Aphrodite* (with Mary

Edward Johnson

Garden). Johnson made his *Metropolitan Opera debut 16 Nov 1922, as Avito in Montemezzi's *L'Amore dei tre Re*. Thereafter, for 13 consecutive seasons, he was among the most admired artists on that company's roster, bringing to bear his unexceptional but shrewdly managed voice and faultless instinct for romantic portraiture on a wide variety of roles, notably Pelléas in *Pelléas et Mélisande* (which he first sang in the Metropolitan premiere of Debussy's opera, 21 Mar 1925), Canio in *I Pagliacci*, Roméo in *Roméo et Juliette* and Don José in *Carmen*. He sang in the first performances of two operas by Deems Taylor: *The King's Henchman*, 17 Feb 1927; and *Peter Ibbetson*, 7 Feb 1931.

In May 1935 Johnson succeeded Herbert Witherspoon as general manager of the Metropolitan. His regime of 15 years coincided with many unprecedented problems, among them increasing labour union demands, rising taxes, and the advent of World War II. The successes and failures of his tenure are chronicled fully in Irving Kolodin's monumental history of the Metropolitan; but no assessment, however brief, should overlook the fact that it was Johnson who introduced to the company such esteemed artists as Licia Albanese, Jussi Björling, Raoul *Jobin, Robert Merrill, Zinka Milanov, Jan Peerce, Bidú Sayão, Eleanor Steber, Giuseppe di Stefano, Risë Stevens, Richard Tucker, Leonard Warren, and Ljuba Welitsch. During the Johnson years, too, Metropolitan Opera subscribers heard for the first time such masterworks as Gluck's *Alceste*, Mozart's *The Abduction from the Seraglio*, Britten's *Peter Grimes*, and Mussorgsky's *Khovanschina*.

After his retirement from the Metropolitan in 1950 Johnson returned to Canada. He had become a US citizen in 1922 but his ties with Canada had remained strong, as evident in his appointment in 1947 as chairman of the board of the *RCMT, a position he retained until 1959. It was he who induced Gina Cigna, Irene *Jessner, and Boyd *Neel to join the faculty. He helped set up the Edward Johnson Music Foundation, which sponsors the annual *Guelph Spring Festival. Following Johnson's death the *U of Toronto's new Faculty of Music Building and its library were named in his honour and house his memorabilia.

Edward Johnson's recordings are few. The first 10 (which include excerpts from *Andrea Chenier* and *Parsifal*) were European Columbias generally supposed to have been made in Italy about 1915. He made many 1919-28 for American Victor, mostly of trivial ballads of the moment, but also arias from *Carmen, I Pagliacci, La Bohème*, and *Fedora* and (among his very best) 'If, with all your hearts' from Mendelssohn's *Elijah*, recorded in 1920. (A discography can be found in *The Tenor of His Time*.) In recent years, off-the-air transcriptions of complete performances of *Pelléas, Peter Ibbetson*, and Hanson's *Merry Mount* have received limited circulation.

BIBLIOGRAPHY

'Great Canadian tenor gives home-coming recital in Guelph,' *CMTJ*, vol 20, Apr 1920
'Edward Johnson and his musical task,' *MCan*, vol 16, Oct 1920
'The career of Edward Johnson,' *MCan*, ns, vol 1, Dec 1920
Armstrong, Isabel C. 'A chat with Edward Johnson,' *MCan*, ns vol 4, May 1923
Nelson, John. 'Canadian star shines for the world,' *Maclean's*, 15 Oct 1925
Thompson, Oscar. 'Two singers who became managers,' *The American Singer* (New York 1937)
'Edward Johnson: Johnson-Di Giovanni-Johnson: the three-fold career of a Canadian tenor,' *Record News*, vol 2, Feb 1958
Benson, Nathaniel A. 'Edward Johnson,' *CMJ*, vol 2, Spring 1958
Walter, Arnold. 'In memoriam,' *CMJ*, vol 3, Summer 1959
Benson, Eugene. 'Edward Johnson,' *OpCan*, vol 9, May 1968
Mercer, Ruby. *The Tenor of His Time* (Toronto 1976) JBM

JOHNSON, Lonnie (Alonzo). Singer, guitarist, b New Orleans 8 Feb 1899, d Toronto 16 Jun 1970. The guitarist on historic recordings with Eddie Lang, Louis Armstrong, and Duke Ellington in the 1920s and a popular urban blues singer, Johnson visited Toronto in the early 1960s during a comeback in his long and distinguished career. Returning in 1965 to stay, he performed alone and with Jim *McHarg in local clubs, including The Penny Farthing and George's Kibitzeria, and recorded *Stompin' at the Penny with Jim McHarg's Metro Stompers* (1965, Col ELS 310). In 1969 he received a special BMI Canada award for his contribution to Canadian music. He made his last appearance 23 Feb 1970 in a 'Blue Monday' concert at *Massey Hall.

BIBLIOGRAPHY

McHarg, Jim. 'Lonnie Johnson,' *Coda*, vol 7, Dec-Jan 1965
Norris, John. 'Lonnie Johnson,' *MSc*, 244 Nov-Dec 1968
Rust, Brian. *Jazz Records 1897-1942* (London 1970)
Encyclopedia of Jazz 1960, 1966

JOHNSTON, (Albert) Richard. Teacher, administrator, composer, editor, critic, b Chicago, 7 May 1917, naturalized Canadian 1957; B MUS (Northwestern) 1942, M MUS (ESM, Rochester) 1945, PH D (ESM, Rochester) 1951. He studied 1934-5 at Augustana College in Rock Island, Ill, 1942 at Northwestern U, 1944-7 at ESM, and 1943 and 1944 with Nadia Boulanger in Madison, Wis. He taught theory 1947-68 at the *U of Toronto and composed, arranged, conducted, and commented for the CBC, notably on the CBC Wednesday night program, 'Vienna, the Glorious Age' (1951) and the radio series 'Folk Music, A Living Canadian Art' (1958). With Edith *Fowke, he selected, arranged, and edited *Folk Songs of Canada* (Waterloo 1954), *Folk Songs of Quebec* (Waterloo 1957), *Chansons canadiennes françaises* (Waterloo 1964), and *More Folk Songs of Canada* (Waterloo 1967). In 1957, under the sponsorship of the National Museum of Human History, he pioneered in collecting folksongs (over 200) and Métis fiddle music in Saskatchewan.

Johnston was a founding member (1956) of the *CFMS and (1959) of the *CMEA and president 1958-9 of the *OMEA. He has made extensive studies of music education in eastern Europe, and as director 1962-8 of the RCMT Summer School he initiated courses in the *Orff and *Kodály teaching methods and established the *CAPAC-MacMillan lectures. Dean of Fine Arts 1968-73 and professor of music 1973- at the *U of Calgary, he also was a founding member, and president 1971-3, of the

Alberta Music Conference. He was editor-in-chief of *Songs for Today* (Waterloo, nine vols, 1954–70) for schools and of the *WBM piano series *Horizons* (Waterloo 1973). A vice-president 1971–4 of the *CMCouncil, he was appointed to the council's publications committee in 1977. That same year he became the first president of the *Alberta Composers' Assn.

Johnston's exuberant *Symphony No. 1* (1950) has been performed in Canada, the USA, and England; *Portraits: Variations for Orchestra* (1972) was commissioned and performed (1973) by the *Calgary Philharmonic Orchestra; and *Trio* was commissioned and premiered (1979) by *One Third Ninth. Rachel *Cavalho has recorded his *Second Suite for Piano* (CCM-1), Christopher *Weait his *Suite for Bassoon and Piano* (Mel SMLP 4032). His works include piano and orchestral suites, choral works, and the set of songs *The Irish Book* (Waterloo 1971), written for Lois *Marshall. (An extended list of compositions may be found in *Contemporary Canadian Composers*.) His style is marked by elements of romanticism tempered by a certain astringency resulting from a disciplined use of 20th-century compositional devices. Johnston is a PRO Canada affiliate and an associate of the *CMCentre. President of the Alberta Foundation of the Centre, he was instrumental in the establishment in Calgary of the prairie region branch in 1980.

WRITINGS

'New records: Hallmark,' *CMJ*, vol 1, Spring 1957
'Summer schools in transition,' *CanComp*, 2, Aug 1965
'Zoltan Kodaly: a true citizen of the world,' *PfAC*, vol 5, Spring 1967
'Canadian String Quartet,' *Music Across Canada*, Feb 1968
'Music education today in Ontario,' *Music Education and the Canadians of Tomorrow*, CMCouncil report (Montreal 1968
'Tribute to Sir Ernest MacMillan,' *CMB*, 7, Autumn–Winter 1973
'Towards a definition of folk music in a polyglot society,' and 'Tribute to Helen Creighton,' *CMB*, 9, Autumn–Winter 1974

BIBLIOGRAPHY

'Folk Songs of Canada,' *CBC Times*, 30 May–5 Jun 1954
'The spotlight,' *Recorder*, vol 1, Mar 1959
Du Wors, Luella. 'Inner self exposed through composing: Richard Johnston,' *MSc*, 271, May–Jun 1973
PRO Canada Ltd. 'Richard Johnston,' pamphlet, 1979

(KB)

JOHNSTONE, John Francis. Teacher, organist, b Lancashire, England, 1831, d Toronto 24 Feb 1913. A printer by training, and the organist at Edinburgh Cathedral, he emigrated to Canada in 1880 and devoted himself entirely to music after his arrival in Toronto. He was associated with the *CNE, taught privately, and was organist at Broadway Tabernacle and, later, at Christ Church, Lippincott and College streets. *Imrie & Graham published ca 1886–90 a dozen of his songs, some to words by John Imrie. They include 'The Young Musician,' 'The Humber Fairy,' and 'Dear Canada, to Thee.'

Johnstone's granddaughter Lillian, a cellist and pianist, was married to Oliver Eugene Woods, an oboist and french horn player who had played with the John Philip Sousa band and in New York with Damrosch and was an oboe 1923–6 and principal oboe 1925–6 and 1931–2 in the *TSO.

Lillian and Oliver Woods' daughter (and Johnstone's great-granddaughter) Maxine Woods (m Shimer) was born and raised in Toronto and began bassoon studies at 14 with Frank Dennis at the *TCM. In the early 1930s with her father, William Greenwood (english horn), Robert T. Higginson (heckelphone), Frank Dennis (bassoon), and James Milne (contrabassoon), she was a member of the Canadian Double Reed Sextet. At Juilliard on scholarship 1934–7, she was the school's first woman bassoon student. She was the first woman woodwind player (1934–6) in the TSO and was the soloist in its performance 26 Mar 1935 of the Mozart *Bassoon Concerto*. She also appeared as a soloist in the *Promenade Symphony Concerts. After graduating from Juilliard she played in the New York Women's Symphony and other orchestras. She taught bassoon and piano at Montclair State College, New Jersey, and at the Westfield Studio as a representative and instructor for the TCL.

BIBLIOGRAPHY

MacLean, Louise, and Weait, Christopher. 'The first lady of the bassoon,' *TS News*, Jan 1978

HK, PW

JOLLIET, Louis. Explorer, hydrographer, fur trader, organist, teacher, b in or near Quebec City, baptized Quebec 21 Sep 1645, d on a St Lawrence island, probably one of the Mingan Islands, between 4 May and 18 Oct 1700. Though more famous as an explorer and hydrographer, Louis Jolliet was also one of the earliest practising Canadian musicians. He studied philosophy, theology, and some music at the Jesuit College in Quebec City, and his fellow students were Germain Morin, Charles-Amador *Martin, and Pierre de Repentigny de Francheville. At 17 Jolliet received the minor orders preparatory to becoming a priest.

Evidence of Jolliet's musical talent was reported first by Father Jérôme Lalemant, who wrote that on 1 Jan 1665 'Monseigneur the Bishop dined with us, and so did Monsieur Meseré [Maizerets]; and in the evenings we invited the Sieurs Morin and Joliet, our musicians, to supper' (*Jesuit Relations*, vol 49). That Jolliet performed on the organ purchased for Quebec in 1663 by Mgr de Laval is possible but not documented. At any rate he soon abandoned the idea of the priesthood and sailed for France, the first Canadian to broaden his studies in Europe. He remained 1667–8 in Paris and La Rochelle for studies in philosophy and possibly in music.

Jolliet's explorations, mostly at the request of Governor Frontenac, began in 1670 and led him to the Mississippi River and the Lake Superior regions, into the area between the Saguenay River and Hudson Bay, and eventually, as late as 1689 or 1690, to part of the Labrador coast. As a reward, Jolliet was granted the seigniory of Anticosti Island in 1680 and settled there that same year with his family and household. He was appointed hydrographer to the king of France in 1680 and teacher of the subject in Quebec in 1697.

Jolliet is said to have played both the harpsichord and the organ. At a memorial service in 1700, recognition was given to his 'having played the organ in the Cathedral and parish for many years. Done without pay' (quoted in *Gagnon's *Louis Jolliet*, p 145). A document dating from 1720 also recognizes 'the fact that he played the organ and had taught several people from the seminary to play' (ibid).

Jolliet's interest in music is obvious also from a 'chant illinois,' notated on a journey in 1673, either by Jolliet or by Father Jacques Marquette, but probably by Jolliet. In his book, *Amtmann reproduces the notation of this 'calumet song' in its manuscript form (French edn only, p 252) as it appeared in Bacqueville de la Potherie's *Histoire de l'Amérique septentrionale* (Paris 1722) and refers to a long-standing 20th-century debate on whether Jolliet or Marquette transcribed the song, adding his own reasoning in favour of Jolliet. Amtmann also provides a musical analysis.

BIBLIOGRAPHY

Gagnon, Ernest. *Louis Jolliet* (Quebec 1902 and later edn)
– 'La musique à Québec au temps de Monseigneur de Laval,' *La Nouvelle-France*, May 1908; repr in *Pages choisies*, Quebec 1917
Delanglez, Jean. *Life and Voyages of Louis Jolliet* (Chicago 1948); French edn *Louis Jolliet, Vie et Voyages* (Montreal 1950)
Frégault, Guy. 'Louis Jolliet,' *Encyclopédie Grolier*, vol 6 (Montreal 1954)
Amtmann *Musique au Québec*
DCB, vol 1. (See also the entry for Marquette.)

HK, GP

JONES, Cliff (Clifford Ernest Barnett). Composer, lyricist, writer, b Toronto 26 Jun 1943; BA psychology (Toronto) 1965, MA psychology (Calgary) 1967. He studied piano 1948–61 at the *RCMT and arranging 1972–5 with Gordon *Delamont. Beginning as a scriptwriter for such CBC TV programs as 'Music Album' 1970–1 and 'The Tommy Hunter Show' 1971–3, he broadened his experience working as music director and writer for TV Ontario's 'Monkey Bars' 1974–5 and CTV's 'Kidstuff' 1975–6, both children's shows, and for Julie Amato's CTV series 'Julie' in 1976. In 1972 for CBC radio Jones began to write satirical songs heard on the series 'Inside from the Outside' and the special 'Gloria Sent Free.' In 1973 he composed **Kronberg: 1582*, a CBC-commissioned rock musical based on Shakespeare's *Hamlet*. A second CBC commission, *Hey, Marilyn!*, based on the life of Marilyn Monroe, was premiered 16 Feb 1975 on CBC radio's 'The Entertainers.' Jones' *The Rowdyman*, based on the story from the film (later novel) by Gordon Pinsent, was staged in 1976 at the *Charlottetown Festival. Recordings of Jones' songs include *Cliff Jones Six People* (Birchmount BM 549), *Kidstuff* (Rising RILP 101), and *Rockabye Hamlet* (Rising RILP 103), sung by various artists. He is an associate of PRO Canada.

BIBLIOGRAPHY

MacDonald, Dawn. 'Squeaky clean on Broadway,' *The Canadian*, 7 Feb 1976
Cohen, Susan, and Gault, John. 'The kid who didn't conquer Broadway,' *Maclean's*, 8 Mar 1976

(MCv)

JONES, (Herbert) Kelsey. Composer, harpsichordist, organist, pianist, teacher, b South Norwalk, Conn, 17 Jun 1922, naturalized Canadian 1956; B MUS (Mount Allison) 1945, B MUS (Toronto) 1946, D MUS (Toronto) 1951. He moved to New Brunswick in 1939 and studied with Harold *Hamer at *Mount Allison U. He later took classes with Sir Ernest *MacMillan, Healey *Willan, and Leo *Smith at the *U of Toronto and 1949–50 with Nadia Boulanger in Paris. Founder (and conductor 1950–4) of the Saint John SO, he also taught theory 1948–9 and conducted the student orchestra at Mount Allison U. Moving to Montreal, he began teaching counterpoint and fugue at *McGill U in 1954. He has been harpsichordist with the *McGill Chamber Orchestra and the *MSO and in 1957 he co-founded the *Baroque Trio of Montreal, which has recorded his *Sonata da Camera* and *Sonata da Chiesa*. He has also composed for the *Montreal Bach Choir and the Montreal Recorder Group and has composed on commission from the CBC (notably his opera **Sam Slick*), the *JMC, and the *Tudor Singers of Montreal.

Though much of Jones' music reaches back to archaic forms and the contrapuntal devices of earlier eras (*Songs of Experience*), he has taken pleasure in folksong (*Miramichi Ballad*) and has made effective use of polytonality (*Sam Slick*). Believing that music should reach directly the aural understanding and emotions of performer and listener, Jones has shown little interest in the avant garde or even in established tenets of serialism. He has experimented, however, with electronic sounds.

He is a member of the *CLComp and of CAPAC, and an associate of the *CMCentre.

Jones' wife Rosabelle (b Smith) – b Truro, NS, 26 Jul 1922; Licentiate (Mount Allison Cons) 1942, B MUS (Mount Allison) 1946 – is a pianist, harpsichordist, teacher, and librettist who has provided the texts for many of his works. A pupil of Max *Pirani in Toronto in 1947 and Yvonne Lefebure in Paris in 1949, she has performed with Jones as duo-pianist and duo-harpsichordist, in public recital and on CBC radio. She taught privately in Montreal 1954–ca 1970.

SELECTED COMPOSITIONS

STAGE

See *Sam Slick*

ORCHESTRA

Miramichi Ballad. 1954. Full orch. BH 1972. ('Peter Emberly') RCI 152 (*Chotem)/RCI 291 (A. *Brott)/('The Jones Boys') Dom S 1372 (*Feldbrill)

Jack and the Beanstalk (R. Jones). 1954. Full orch (child's v), SATB, pf 4-hands. Ms

A Suite for Flute and Strings. 1954. Fl, str orch. CMCentre. RCI 191 (*Mtl Str Quar)

Songs of Innocence (Blake). 1961. Sop, chamb orch. CMCentre

Prophecy of Micah (adap R. Jones). 1963. SATB, orch. Ms. RCI 355 (*Tudor Singers of Mtl)

Adagio, Presto and Fugue. 1973. Str quar, str orch. CMCentre

Fantasy on a Theme. 1976. Full orch. Ms

CHAMBER

Four Pieces for Recorder Quartet. 1955. CMCentre. Bar BC-1857 (*Duschenes Recorder Quar)

Sonata da Camera. 1957. Fl, ob, hpd. Peters 1972. RCI 192 (*Baroque Trio of Mtl)

Introduction and Fugue. 1959. Vn, pf. CMCentre. RCI 244 (*Duo Pach)/RCI 220/RCA CCS-1014 (*Bress vn)

Rondo for Solo Flute. 1963. Wat 1972. RCI 219/RCA CCS-1013/Sel CC 15.066 (*Duschenes)

Sonata da Chiesa. 1967. Fl, ob, hpd. CMCentre. CBC SM-56/RCA LSC-3091 (*Baroque Trio of Mtl)

Quintet for Winds. 1968. Ww quin. Peters 1972. 1971. RCI 355 (Pro Arte WW Quin)

Passacaglia and Fugue. 1975. Brass quin. CMCentre. 1978. McGill U Records -77004 (Mount Royal Brass Quin)

CHOIR AND VOICE

Nonsense Songs (Lear). 1955. SATB. Leeds 1961. ('Five Limericks') CBC SM-19/Poly 2917 009 (*Festival Singers)

Songs of Time (R. Herrick, T. Jordan, F. Quarles, J. Webster). 1955. SATB, pf 4-hands. CMCentre. RCI 144 (George *Little Singers)

To Music, song cycle (Herrick). 1957. Alto, pf. CMCentre. RCI 203 (*Forrester)

Songs of Experience (Blake). 1958. SATB. CMCentre. RCI 189 (*Mtl Bach Choir)

Songs of Winter (early Canadian poets, adap R. Jones). 1973. Sop, alto, pf. CMCentre

Da Musica, con Amore (R. Jones). 1977. Mixed choir, brass quin. CMCentre

Other works for choir and voice

Also some works for pf, and a work for jazz band, *Jazzum Opus Unum* (1977). CMCentre

DISCOGRAPHY

Schafer *Concerto for Harpsichord and Eight Wind Instruments*. Jones hpd, Mtl CBC ww ens, Jones cond. Ca 1958. RCI 193

See also Discographies for Baroque Trio of Montreal; Melvin Berman; Mario Duschenes.

BIBLIOGRAPHY

'Sam Slick,' *CBC Times*, 2–8 Sep 1967

Bisbrouck, Noël. 'Kelsey Jones, a sincere musician,' *CanComp*, 26, Feb 1968

Contemporary Canadian Composers

Creative Canada, vol 1

(CF)

'The Jones Boys.' The story of the futile efforts of the Jones boys to make their 'goshdarn sawmill pay.' The song is well known in New Brunswick, partly because it was the favourite of the late newspaper baron Lord Beaverbrook, who grew up in the lumbering district of Miramichi. When he gave a set of quarter-hour chimes to the *U of New Brunswick, he had them programmed to play 'The Jones Boys.' According to the US musicologist Norman Cazden the traditional tune possibly is related to the second half of 'Turkey in the Straw.' The tune is used in the first movement of Kelsey *Jones' *Miramichi Ballad* (1954). It is published in *Fowke's *Penguin Book of Canadian Folksongs* (Harmondsworth, England, 1973) and recorded by Folkways (*Songs of the Maritimes*, FW 8744). EF

JORDAN, Albert David. Organist, conductor, administrator, b Seaforth, near Stratford, Ont, 28 Jul 1877, d Magnetawan, northeast of Parry Sound, Ont, 7 Sep 1932. He was the brother of Henri Kew *Jordan and a pupil of F.H. *Torrington at the *Toronto College of Music. He was organist in the 1890s at St Clement's Anglican Church and a guest performer at several other Toronto churches and then moved to Brantford, where he served 1897–1902 as organist-choirmaster at Brant Ave Methodist Church. He founded (1902) and directed the Brantford Male Choir. He went to London, Ont, and was organist-choirmaster 1903–24 at the First Methodist Church and a teacher 1903–19 at the London Cons. He also conducted various choirs, including the London Oratorio Society ca 1905, and gave organ recitals at his church and throughout southern Ontario. He represented Canada at the Pan-American Exposition (1901) in Buffalo and the Pacific Panama Exposition (1915) in San Francisco and gave solo recitals in Pittsburgh and New York. In 1916 Jordan initiated the London Musical Art Society, which engaged and presented well-known artists and orchestras. He founded in 1919, and until his death directed, the London Institute of Musical Art. Moving to Toronto, he was organist-choirmaster 1925–32 at Timothy Eaton Memorial Church and in 1931 founded the Toronto Chamber Music Society. FH

JORDAN (b Wiseman), **Charles** (b Jack). Baritone, teacher, b Montreal 3 Apr 1915. His father George Wiseman was an amateur tenor soloist with choirs in Russia. The younger Wiseman made his radio debut in 1937 as Charles Jourdan, singing French songs under that name for a year on CKAC, Montreal. While performing 1937–40 on that station and with the CBC radio orchestras of Lucio *Agostini and Allan *McIver, he studied voice with Adrienne Bourassa. After he moved to Toronto in 1940 he sang on CBC and CFRB radio and continued his studies with Albert Whitehead (voice, at the TCM 1941–3) and Louis *Waizman (theory, privately, 1942–3). About this time, for CBC radio, he participated in broadcasts of several oratorios and operas, mainly of Purcell and Handel (including the latter's *Acis and Galatea*). He moved to New York in 1944 and sang there on the radio programs 'Sweetwood Serenade' (NBC) and 'Sunday Night Serenade' (MBS) and on the ABC and CBS networks.

Jordan began commuting to Toronto (prior to settling there in 1950) and was a regular performer 1948–53 with the *Leslie Bell Singers on CBC radio's 'C.G.E. Showtime' and sang (1949) in *Messiah* with the *Toronto Mendelssohn Choir. In 1947 Jordan began teaching voice in New York and Toronto. In more than 30 years of teaching in the latter city his pupils have included Susan Clark, Lorne Greene, and William Shatner.

Jordan himself has been active in drama, especially on CBC radio's 'Stage' series and on TV. For the CBC TV production of *The Dybbuk*, he acted and conducted religious chants which he had composed. In 1967 he became second cantor at Holy Blossom Temple in Toronto.

Noted for the adroitness with which he can adapt his singing to different styles of music, Jordan has recorded songs by John *Beckwith and Maurice *Blackburn (1951, RCI 36, with Leo *Barkin, piano) and *Folk Songs of Canada* (1956, Hallmark S-3, with Joyce *Sullivan, pianist Gordon *Kushner, and guitarist Stan Wilson). He participated in *Canadian Folk Songs: A Centennial Collection* (RCA CS 100).

Jordan's sons Marc (b New York 6 Mar 1948) and Myles (b Bowmanville, Ont, 3 Oct 1954) have pursued careers in music. Marc is a singer-songwriter and guitarist who has recorded for CBS and Warner Brothers. Myles is a cello pupil of Marcus *Adeney and a member of the Algoma Quartet at the U of Toronto.

JORDAN, Henri K. (Kew). Choir conductor, organist, manufacturer, b Seaforth, near Stratford, Ont, 30 Mar 1880, d Brantford, Ont, 27 Oct 1949; hon D MUS (Toronto) 1938. He studied piano and organ at the *Toronto College of Music under F.H. *Torrington and Frank *Welsman and was cornet soloist in the *48th Highlanders Regimental Band. He gained experience as a church organist in Toronto, Winnipeg, and Goderich, Ont.

In 1903 Jordan trained the Brantford Festival Chorus, which had been formed for participation in the *Cycle of Musical Festivals, and took over the Brantford Male Choir, which his brother Albert D. *Jordan had conducted in its first season, 1902–3. In 1903 and 1904 the choir was joined in its annual concerts by the Pittsburgh Orchestra under Victor Herbert. In 1906, adding women to the choir, Jordan converted it into the *Schubert Choir, an ensemble that brought fame to Jordan and to Brantford. He also was organist-choirmaster at Brant Ave Methodist (later United) Church, where, early in the century, he presented *The Creation* and *Messiah* and where a memorial plaque was dedicated to him in 1950. Jordan composed songs, anthems, and other choral pieces and led several bands. The Schubert Choir disbanded after his retirement in 1941. His last appearance as conductor probably was in a presentation of Gounod's *Redemption* at an *RCCO meeting in 1948. On an inscribed photograph in 1933 Percy Grainger called him 'one of the greatest musicians and most original and inspired choral conductors I have ever seen.'

During World War I Jordan achieved the rank of major and won the Military Cross. In later years he was president of the Canadian Valve and Hydrant Co of Brantford. HK

JORDAN, Robert (Christopher). Guitarist, teacher, b Oxford 22 Jul 1933, naturalized Canadian 1957. Though he began his career as an orchestral violinist shortly after his arrival in Canada in 1952, he taught himself to play guitar in 1954 and took lessons in 1964 and 1966–7 in Spain with Eduardo Sainz de la Maza. He also studied 1965–7 at the *U of British Columbia and in the summer of 1967 with Julian Bream at Stratford, Ont. In Edmonton, Jordan appeared on CBC radio and TV. In Vancouver in 1969 he opened the Classical Guitar Centre (where Michael Dunn and Michael *Strutt were instructors). In 1976 he joined the faculty of the *Community Music School of Greater Vancouver.

As soloist, accompanist, and arranger Jordan has performed on CBC radio's 'Prairie Chamber Music,' 'Distinguished Artists,' 'Vancouver Recital,' and 'CBC Tuesday Night' and on CBC TV's 'Music to See.' He premiered Stephen Pedersen's *Duet for Guitar and Sunflower* 16 Jan 1974 and Arthur Lewis' *Short Piece for Guitar* 27 Feb 1974. He has appeared at Canadian and US festivals.

Jordan's initial interest in contemporary music had shifted by 1977 to a concern for large-form guitar compositions and works by South American composers. Jordan has recorded as an accompanist to Phyllis *Mailing. BNSG

JOSEPH, A. (Alfred) **Hugh**. Recording director, b Quebec City 25 May 1896; B SC (McGill) 1920. A pioneer in the recording of Canadian musicians, Joseph began his career in 1923 as a chemist with the *Berliner Gram-O-Phone Co, which became the Victor Talking Machine Co of Canada in 1924 and *RCA Victor in 1929. In 1927 he was named general manager of Victor's record depatment, and in 1941 he was put in charge of what became the company's A&R department. Responsible for the selection of artists and for promotion and sales of their recordings, Joseph built the company's roster of the 1930s and 1940s on a wide representation of leading Canadian performers (see RCA Victor) from the Quebec folk, country, dance band, pop song, choral, recital, and symphonic fields. He retired in 1961. EBM, MM

JOURDAIN dit LABROSSE, Paul (Raymond). Wood-carver, organ-builder, master carpenter, baptized Montreal 20 Sep 1697, d there 8 Jun 1769. Though apprenticed as a wood-carver, it was as an organ-builder that he signed a contract 31 Jul 1721 in Montreal with the Quebec City Cathedral Chapter requiring him 'to build an organ with seven stops, including the vox humana' in return for 'the sum of 800 livres' payable upon delivery.

A second contract, signed 1 Aug 1721 by the same parties, stipulated that Jourdain 'is obliged to restore and repair the old organ, in which he will install three complete stops and render the said organ good and valuable and well in tune.' He was to receive the sum of 250 livres once the work was completed. The organ probably was the one brought from France in 1663 by Mgr de Laval and inaugurated the next year. In his *Coup d'oeil* (1941), Morisset states that Jourdain 'made a more-or-less ornate cabinet which contained the existing pipes; he cut tongues and connected levers; he assembled wind-chests which, as far as possible, didn't leak air; he built bellows and polished ivory stops; then he bravely signed: "Paul Jourdain, organ-builder".'

Mgr Henri Têtu, after consulting the Quebec City Chapter archives, mentioned the existence of two invoices from Jourdain, one for work done 1721–2 and amounting to 250 francs 'for the restoration of the small organ'; the other, dated 9 Mar 1723, 'for costs and labour on the organ 800 livres; for installation 90 livres'. Also extant is his bill for trips from Montreal to Quebec City for a total of 1165 livres including '25 livres for the organ-case.'

Jourdain eventually became a renowned cabinet-maker. The organs in the Quebec City cathedral were demolished following Mgr de Pontbriand's decision to rebuild the chapel. The prelate, no doubt like Morrisset two centuries later, felt that Jourdain was a better cabinet-maker than organ-builder.

BIBLIOGRAPHY

Têtu, Mgr Henri. 'Le Chapitre de la cathédrale de Québec et ses délégués en France,' *BRH*, vol 14, Dec 1908

'Paul Jourdain Labrosse facteur d'orgues 1721,' ibid, vol 55, 1949

Brault, Lucien. 'Les instruments de musique dans les églises de la Nouvelle-France,' report of the Société canadienne d'histoire de l'Église catholique (1956–7).

Coup d'oeil

DBC, vol 3

HK (GP)

'Les Joyeux Troubadours.' Popular half-hour CBC radio program broadcast from Montreal at noon five times a week, Monday to Friday, with a cast of singers, instrumentalists, and a host. The program was devoted to humorous or sentimental songs, violin or accordion solos, and comic skits. Broadcasts began on 13 Oct 1941 and continued without interruption until 2 Sep 1977, achieving what generally is regarded as a record of longevity for a Canadian radio program of this kind.

Les Joyeux Troubadours

The program was more-or-less a French-language replica of 'The *Happy Gang,' a program on the CBC English network which had begun in 1937. The original cast of 'Les Joyeux Troubadours' consisted of the host, Henri *Letondal, who also served as scriptwriter, the singers Lucille Laporte and Paul Charpentier, and the instrumentalists André *Durieux (violin), Raymond Denhez (trumpet), Eddy Tremblay (saxophone), Émilia Heyman (accordion), Georges Vincent (guitar), and Séverin *Moisse (piano). Raymond Forget took part 1945–77 as bassist and folksinger.

There were numerous changes in the cast over the years. Lucien *Martin succeeded Durieux in 1942 and was replaced by Lionel Renaud in 1949. Lucille Laporte was succeeded by Marie-José Forgues and Lise Roy, followed by Rolande *Désormeaux in 1944, Marie-Thérèse Alarie in 1950, and Estelle Caron in 1951. Robert *L'Herbier replaced Charpentier in 1942; André Rancourt followed in 1950, and Gérard *Paradis in 1951. Saturno Gentiletti replaced Émilia Heyman on the accordion, and Margot Prud'homme took over at the piano when Moisse left. After Letondal, the hosts were Clément Latour and Jean-Maurice Bailly. André Audet was one of the scriptwriters with Letondal. André Rufiange, who began writing the scripts in 1952, also wrote a book of reminiscences and impressions of the show. The producers were Paul-Émile *Corbeil 1941–53 and François Brunet 1953–7, followed by Simon and Gabriel L'Anglais, and then by Pauline Goyette-Whiting.

The show's format varied only slightly over the years. After a knock, knock, knock on the door, a voice asked 'Qui est là?' and the whole cast replied 'Les Joyeux Troubadours.' Then the voice said 'Mais voyons, entrez, entrez donc!' and the cast struck up the theme song '... never believe all those stories, you are happier that way. Love life and its follies ...' Because of the program's great popularity, the cast was asked to travel outside the city, and thus broadcasts were heard from Quebec City, Sherbrooke, Drummondville, Ottawa, Joliette, St-Jean, and l'Assomption. GP

JULIEN, Pauline. Singer, actress, songwriter, b Trois-Rivières, Que, 23 May 1928. In her teens she acted in Quebec City with the Comédiens de la Nef and in Montreal with the Compagnie du Masque. In 1952 she went to Paris, where she studied dramatic arts with Bernard Bimont, Michel Vitold, Marcel Marceau, Tania Balachova, and Georges Vitaly. She sang first (ca 1957) in a Paris production of Pirandello's play *La Fable de l'enfant échangé* and then, with a repertoire of Weill-Brecht, Léo Ferré, and Boris Vian, in left-bank Parisian boîtes (Café des Anglais, Chez Moineau, Port-Salut, and others) and on French radio and TV. Her career 1957–60 was divided between Montreal (where she made her debut at the Cabaret Au St-Germain-des-Prés) and Paris. She was Jenny 1961–2 in Weill and Brecht's *L'Opéra de Quat'sous* at Montreal's Théâtre du Nouveau-Monde. To her repertoire of Weill-Brecht songs (she introduced these to Quebec) she added material by Raymond *Lévesque and Gilles *Vigneault. Her first LP, *Enfin ... Pauline Julien*, was made in 1962, and her second, *Pauline Julien*, in 1963; these, coupled with performances in the company of Claude *Gauthier and Claude *Léveillée and several TV appearances in 1963 established her as a popular and affecting chanteuse. In 1964 she was the CBC's representative at the International Festival of Song in Sopot, Poland. She won second prize (singing Vigneault's 'Jack Monoloy') and then embarked on a tour of the country. She was hostess 1965–6 for CBC TV's 'Mon Pays, mes chansons.'

Pauline Julien

Julien's success has come equally in Quebec and in Europe. She has made regular appearances on the province's leading stages (the Comédie-Canadienne, *PDA, Le *Patriote, Quebec City's *Grand Théâtre, etc) and in Europe's major cities, in particular Paris (at the Théâtre de l'Est Parisien, the Bobino, the Olympia, the Théâtre de la Ville, the Théâtre de la Renaissance, etc). In 1967 she toured the USSR (she returned there in 1975) and represented Quebec at the Primera Festival de la Cancion Popular in Cuba. In Canada she has performed in Toronto (1964, 1968, 1975; the last-mentioned date for the taping of a CBC TV program, 'Three Women,' with Maureen *Forrester and Sylvia *Tyson), at the 1971 *Mariposa Folk Festival, on tour in Ontario (1972), at Camp Fortune (near Ottawa, 1973), at the *NAC (1974), in Edmonton, Calgary, and Vancouver (1976), at the 1977 *Guelph Spring Festival, and at the Festival of Nations at Glendon College in Toronto (1978).

As an actress Julien has appeared in the Quebec films *La Terre à boire* and *Fabienne sans son Jules* (1964), *The Trial of the Swordfish* (1969), *Bulldozer* (1971), *Pleure donc pas Germaine* (1972), and *La Mort d'un bûcheron* (1973).

In the late 1960s and early 1970s Julien's repertoire consisted exclusively of songs by Quebec writers, reflecting her dedication to French-Canadian culture. In 1968 she began to write the words for some of her songs; her composers over the next 10 years included Jacques Crevier, François *Dompierre, Claude *Dubois, Jacques Perron, Michel Robidoux, Stéphane *Venne, Gaston *Brisson, François Cousineau, and Jacques Marchand; each of the last three served at one time or another as her music director. She also composed songs to words by Michel Tremblay. Without lessening her commitment to political independence for Quebec (in which cause she declined an invitation to sing before Queen Elizabeth II at Charlottetown in 1964 and was arrested and detained during the Quebec crisis of 1970), she took up the feminist cause in the mid-1970s. She introduced the song 'La Moitié du monde est une femme' (written with Marchand) in 1975 and presented the show 'Femmes de paroles' 1977–8 in Quebec and in Europe to great acclaim. In the mid-1970s she restored Weill-Brecht to her repertoire, and in 1978, for Fernand Nault's ballet to Weill's *Les Sept Péchés capitaux* (The Seven Deadly Sins), she sang the role of Anna (danced by Sylvie Kinal-Chevalier), both for the premiere that year at the NAC and for an LP (Kébec-Disc KD-977) along with the tenors Paul *Trépanier and René *Lacourse, the baritone Roland Richard, and the bass Pierre Charbonneau. (The recording also contains the Prologue and Eiplogue in a revised instrumentation by Jacques Marchand, who conducts the performance.)

Julien is a singer known for her expressive power, a quality drawn equally from music and theatre. Jean Gascon, in *La Patrie* (8 Jul 1964) observed: 'Pauline Julien is a curious mixture of strength and fragility, assurance and insecurity, youth and maturity, knowledge and instinct, waif and woman. This bi-polarity makes her at once elusive and extremely engaging. If I had to describe her talent with just one adjective, it would be the word entrancing that I would use.' Among the awards Julien has received are a Grand Prix du disque from the Académie Charles-Cros in Paris for her LP *Suite québécoise* (1970) and the 1974 *Prix de musique Calixa-Lavallée. She is a member of CAPAC.

DISCOGRAPHY

Enfin ... Pauline Julien. 1962. Col FL 290
Pauline Julien. 1963. Col FL 296
Pauline Julien à la Comédie-Canadienne. 1964. Col FL 317
Solidad et Barbarie, pour enfants. V. 1964. ? HFL 8002
Pauline Julien chante Raymond Lévesque. Gamma GM 103
Pauline Julien chante Boris Vian. Gamma GM 107
Suite québécoise. 1970. Gamma GS 112
'Comme je crie, comme je chante ... Pauline Julien chante Gilbert Langevin.' Ca 1970. Gamma GS 125
Album souvenir Pauline Julien. 1971. ? LT 809
Fragile. 1971. Zodiaque ZO 6900
Les Grands Succès de Pauline Julien. 1971. Gamma G2 11001
Au milieu de ma vie, peut-être à la veille de ... 1972. Zodiaque ZOX 6002
Allez voir, vous avez des ailes. 1973. Zodiaque ZOX 6007
Pour mon plaisir ... Gilles Vigneault. 1973. Zodiaque ZOX 6014
Licence complète. 1974. Zodiaque ZOX 6018
Pauline Julien en scène. 1975. Deram XDEF 124
Pauline Julien: Tout ou rien. 1976. Telson AE 1502
Femmes de paroles. 1977. Kébec-Disc KD 935
Mes Amies d'filles. 1978. Kébec-Disc KD 949
Les Sept Péchés capitaux. 1979. Kébec-Disc KD 977
See also Discography for Chansonniers.

BIBLIOGRAPHY

Clavet, Louis-Jean. *Pauline Julien* (Paris 1974)
Bergeron, Raymond. 'Agressive, moi? Grrr ... Jamais!' *Perspectives*, 24 Jul 1974
Guilbert, Alain. 'Quebec's first lady of song writes her own,' *CanComp*, 94, Oct 1974
Bergeron, Raymond. 'Pauline,' *Perspectives*, 6–12 Jan 1980
Rowan, Renée. 'Pauline Julien à fleur de peau,' Montreal *Le Devoir*, 20 Sep 1980

JULIETTE (b Juliette Augustina Sysak, m Cavazzi). Singer, entertainer, b St Vital (Winnipeg), of Polish-Ukrainian parents, 26 Aug 1927. She was taken to Vancouver at 10, sang with Dal *Richards' Hotel Vancouver orchestra at 13, and made her CBC network debut on George *Calangis' 'Sophisticated Strings' at 15. After a year (1943–4) in Toronto on Alan Young's CBC radio show and with Lucio *Agostini's orchestra, she sang on many CBC Vancouver radio programs, including 'Burns Chuckwagon,' a country music show with the *Rhythm Pals, and 'Here's Juliette.' She also appeared at *TUTS. She returned to Toronto in 1954 and co-starred with Gino *Silvi on CBC radio's 'Gino and Juliette.' As 'Our Pet, Juliette' she was a regular performer 1954–6 on CBC TV with Billy *O'Connor's 'The Late Show.'

Juliette succeeded O'Connor with her own program 'Juliette' (1956–66), one of the CBC's most popular shows. On it, Juliette was joined regularly by a singer (George *Murray in 1956, Roy Roberts 1957–8, and Ken Steele 1958–9) and by Silvi's male vocal quartet the Romeos 1959–60 and 1962 and the female vocal group the Four Mice in 1961. The show's music directors were, successively, Bobby *Gimby, Bill Isbister, and Lucio Agostini. After several seasons of TV specials, Juliette returned to regular performance on the CBC TV talk shows 'After Noon' (1969–71) and 'Juliette and Friends' (1973–5).

Juliette recorded a few 78s for RCA's 'X' label and others for Aragon with the Rhythm Pals in the early 1950s and later made three LPs for RCA Camden (*Juliette* CAS 2223, *Christmas World* CAS 2279, and *Country World* CAS 2341). She also was heard on a recording of **Timber!!*

Discussing Juliette's popularity, Antony Ferry commented: 'Her speciality is being "just folks" ... In a pop medium bedecked with tinsel and phoney charm, Juliette retains at least the illusion of old home-body simplicity' (*Toronto Daily Star*, 7 Oct 1961). She was made a member of the *Order of Canada in 1975.

BIBLIOGRAPHY

Moon, Barbara. 'Why should Juliette knock them dead?' *Maclean's*, 26 Apr 1958 (AM)

The Junior Musical Club of Winnipeg. Youth group affiliated with the *Women's Musical Club of Winnipeg and founded in 1900 by Mrs A.R. Wade to promote young talent and the appreciation of music through performances, lectures, and awards. Initially the young members formed the audience but latterly they themselves have performed annually in 14 recitals and a spring concert. The club has presented radio broadcasts, performances for the *Wednesday Morning Musicale, and series of workshops and lectures. In the 1970s the club served some 250 members. Five scholarships and a Rose Bowl are offered yearly.

An exectuive of 22 is made up of teachers and parents. Support has been received from the *U of Manitoba School of Music and from local business firms.

Many former club members, including Emanuel Ax, Diedre *Irons, Alisa Lawson, Erica Schultz, Victor Schultz, Gwen *Thompson, and Eric *Wilson, have become professional musicians. BCl

Juno Awards. Introduced in 1964; the annual awards of the Canadian recording industry. They were known officially as the RPM Gold Leaf Awards and popularly, after 1970, as 'the Junos.' They were established by Walt *Grealis, editor-publisher of **RPM* magazine, and organized each year by Stan Klees, to develop a 'star system' in Canada.

Nominees in performance, production, and composition qualify on the basis of record sales over a 14-month period. Specific categories and their descriptions have varied from year to year. In 1964 there were 16 categories; in 1978, 23. Winners were selected by *RPM* readers until 1975, when the newly formed *CARAS became the co-governing body of the awards. Thereafter only CARAS members participated in the voting process, and CARAS became the sole governing body after 1977. Categories for classical and jazz recordings – judged by a committee of critics and broadcasters rather than by the CARAS membership – began with awards for the year 1976.

Awards are given annually in March for activities of the previous year; reference in *EMC* to the Junos dates the year of activity, not the year in which the award was given. Public presentations of the Juno trophies began in 1970 in Toronto, and CBC TV coverage of the event began in 1974. Past winners have been listed in *RPM's Canadian Music Industry Directory* (Toronto 1965–80).

In 1974 the music industry supplemented the Junos with the Canadian Music Hall of Fame and the Big Country Awards and in 1976 with the Canadian Music Industry Awards.

Performers from Quebec rarely have been represented in the Juno competition and in 1979 the Assn du disque et de l'industrie du spectacle québecois (ADISQ) introduced a similar awards system in their honour. MM

JUSTER, Diane (b Rivet). Singer-songwriter, pianist, b Montreal 15 Mar 1946; BA (Montreal) 1966. She studied piano with Marie-Thérèse *Paquin and Mme Legoff; encouraged by Stéphane *Venne, she began composing in 1971. Julie Arel made Juster's name known by performing her 'Soleil, soleil,' 'Quand tu partiras,' and other songs. Juster herself began performing in May 1974, making a single for the Fleur label of her 'Ce Matin' and 'Vive les roses,' for which she obtained a special prize (in the songwriter category) at the Olympiad of Quebec Song. The LP *Mélancolie* (Fleur FLP 202) followed a few months later.

In the summer of 1975 Justa represented Canada at the Festival international de la chanson française at Spa, Belgium. The same year she made the LP *M'aimeras-tu demain*? (Fleur FLP 205) in Paris and appeared on stage for the first time at the boîte à chansons *Le Patriote in Montreal. Georges-Hébert Germain (*La Presse*, 25 Sep 1975) likened her to the French singer Barbara and continued: 'But she has a style that sets her free from all professional constraints. It is herself that she is expressing, it is her life she performs ... You enter her world, with its interplay of soft lights and subtle hues, her music with its beautiful contours, rich in suggestion. There is grace and a lot of class in each word, gesture, and movement.'

Subsequently Juster made the LP *Regarde en moi* (Kébec-Disc KD 917). *Mes Plus Belles Chansons* (Fleur FLP 217), an LP comprising a selection of previously released material, appeared in 1976. She took part in several CBC TV variety programs; her recital at Camp Fortune, Ottawa, was presented on 'Les Beaux Dimanches' in 1977. At the *PDA she gave a recital in May 1976 and a show entitled 'À coeur ouvert' in November 1977, followed by a tour of 20 Quebec towns and an appearance in January 1978 at the *NAC.

Juster has written several songs for Ginette *Reno, including 'À ma manière,' and she composed the music for the sound-track of the Jean-Claude Lord film *Éclair au chocolat* (1978). Her songs are published by Intermède Musique. She is a member of CAPAC.

BIBLIOGRAPHY

Champagne, Jane. 'Diane Juster: a Quebec star sets her own pace,' *CanComp*, 97, Jan 1975
Mercier, Johanne. 'Diane Juster ou la sensibilité faite femme,' *Sono*, vol 4, Feb 1977 (BR)

K

KALEJS, Felicita (Vilma) (b Maizite). Pianist, teacher, b Riga, Latvia, 20 Oct 1911, naturalized Canadian 1955. A private pupil of Anna Aschmann and a graduate of the State Cons in Riga, she taught at that school 1940–2 and later was an accompanist and coach at the Latvian State Opera. She came to Canada in 1949 with her husband, Janis *Kalejs, to teach piano at the School of Music, *Acadia U. Upon her husband's death she served 1973–4 as acting dean. She appeared in numerous recitals with her husband and has accompanied many artists on CBC radio, among them Teresa *Stratas, Jan *Rubeš, and Audrey *Farnell. HK

KALEJS, Janis (Voldemars). Violinist, teacher, composer, b Riga, Latvia, 7 Jan 1912, d Wolfville, NS, 7 Nov 1973, naturalized Canadian 1955. He graduated in violin from the State Cons in Riga in 1934 and received advanced training in Berlin under Georg Kulenkampff. He was a violinist in the Latvian National Radio Orchestra and, later, in the National Opera orchestra, performed as a concerto soloist, and taught at the State Cons. Upon his arrival in Canada in 1949 he became head of the string department of the School of Music, *Acadia U. He became acting dean in 1965 and dean in 1966. He fostered the growth of the Acadia instrumental music summer camp and was heard in many recitals in eastern Canada and the USA and on many CBC broadcasts. He was married to Felicita *Kalejs. His cantata *The Long Night* is recorded (Kaibala 30C01). HK

KALLMANN, Helmut (Max). Music librarian, historian, archivist, b Berlin 7 Aug 1922, naturalized Canadian 1946; B MUS (Toronto) 1949, hon LL D (Toronto) 1971. With Gilles *Potvin and Kenneth *Winters he is one of the three editors of *EMC*, responsible in particular for content. He received informal piano lessons from his father, an amateur musician, until he emigrated to England in 1939. After a brief period of study in London with Margery Moore (piano) and the Canadian Russell E. Chester (theory) he was interned as a German citizen in 1940 in England and 1940–3 in Canada. After being released to Toronto he had piano lessons from Naomi *Adaskin in 1944, Greta *Kraus 1944–5, and Florence Steinhauer 1947–8. His main teachers 1946–9 in the school music course at the *U of Toronto were Richard *Johnston, Robert *Rosevear, and Arnold *Walter.

Kallmann worked 1950–70 in the CBC Toronto Music Library and in 1962 became its supervisor. In 1970 he was appointed chief of the newly created Music Division at the *NL of C, where his special responsibility has been the building of an all-embracing collection of musical Canadiana.

The lack of Canadian subject matter in the university's music history courses led Kallmann, late in 1948, to search for traces of Canada's musical past. His historical and bibliographical notes continued to expand and have formed a major source of information for *EMC*. His first broad overview, based largely on printed sources, enabled him to add a historical dimension to the CBC's *Catalogue of Canadian Composers* (1952) which he revised and edited 1950–1 and at the same time to begin writing a historical account, published in 1960 as *A History of Music in Canada 1534–1914*, the first on its subject in book form. His research proceeded gradually to more specialized areas, such as the history of Canadian music periodicals and music publishing, the biographies of Joseph *Quesnel, Theodore F. *Molt, and James P. *Clarke, and the inventories of pre-1950 printed music and of surviving Canadian-built 19th-century instruments. This work contributed to the modern revivals of **Colas et Colinette, Siege of Quebec* (see Battle music), and **The Widow*. During the 1960s he became increasingly occupied with exploring primary sources and developed a plan for the collection and preservation of musical Canadiana which found an application at the NL of C.

Kallmann was a co-founder of the *CMLA and its chairman 1957–8 and 1967–8. He initiated Canadian participation in the International Assn of Music Libraries (Canadian delegate 1959–71) and in 1953 became responsible (and was still in 1980) for the Canadian work for its Répertoire international des sources musicales (see Libraries: 8/Training, organization, projects) and, for some years, for other projects. Certain CMLA and *CAML projects grew from his private efforts, including the *Bio-Bibliographical Finding List of Canadian Musicians* (1961) and *Musical Canadiana, a Subject Index* (1967).

Kallmann assisted a number of international music dictionaries to include or correct Canadian entries. He served on the editorial boards of the **CMJ* and the **CMB*. With James Bannerman he wrote a CBC historical radio series, 'Music in Canada' (13 broadcasts in 1965; French adaptation by Andrée *Desautels). His editorial responsibilities have included the *CLComp's *Catalogue of Orchestral Music* (Toronto 1957) and Giles *Bryant's *Healey Willan Catalogue* (Ottawa 1972). Kallmann occasionally has given seminars and lectures at universities and spoken at conferences. His private and job-related work has helped to facilitate the establishment of Canadian music courses at universities and has encouraged others to continue historical research and to perform older Canadian music. He was a director 1970–1 and a vice president 1971–6 of the *CMCouncil, honorary historian of the CLComp, and honorary adjunct professor (1975) at *Carleton U. He was awarded the *CMCouncil Medal in 1977.

WRITINGS

'Canadian music as a field for research,' *ConsB*, Mar 1950

Catalogue of Canadian Composers, rev, enl ed (Toronto 1952)

'Historical background,' *Music in Canada* (Toronto 1955); rev in *Aspects of Music in Canada* (Toronto 1969)

'Audio-visual aids to music education in Canada,' ISME series *Technical Media in Music Education* (1957)

'Kanada,' *MGG* (Kassel 1958)

'From the archives,' *CMJ*, Summer 1958

'From the archives: organs and organ players in Canada,' *CMJ*, Spring 1959

– ed. *Directory of Degree Graduates*, U of Toronto Music Alumni Assn (Toronto 1964)

A History of Music in Canada 1534–1914 (Toronto 1960, 1969)

'Music in Canada,' *CBC Times*, 15–21 May 1965; abridged repr as 'Themes in Canadian history,' *Cons B*, Winter 1966

'Composition in Canada: 1867–1967,' Toronto *Telegram*, special advertising section, 28 Jan 1967

'Music in Canada, 1867, a long glance backward' / 'Musique au Canada en 1867,' *Mcan*, 3, Jul–Aug 1967

'Music,' *Canadian Annual Review*, ed John Saywell (Toronto 1968, 1969, 1970)

'Beethoven and Canada,' *CMB*, 2, Spring–Summer 1971

Articles for the *DCB*, *Dictionary of Contemporary Music*, *Encyclopedia Canadiana*, *Harvard Dictionary*, *MGG*, *The New Grove Dictionary*

Reviews in *The Varsity* (U of Toronto), *CMJ*, *Canadian Library Journal*

Program note essays for *Ten Centuries Concerts

Record album notes for Joseph Quesnel's *Colas et Colinette* and Lavallée's *The Widow*

See also Bibliography; Libraries; Musicology.

See also Bibliographies for CLComp; J.P. Clarke; Criticism; Dictionaries; Germany; National Library of Canada; 'O Canada'; Opera performance; Periodicals; Piano building; Publishing; and Joseph Quesnel.

KALNINS, Janis. Conductor, composer, organist-choirmaster, b Pärnu, Estonia, of Latvian parents, 3 Nov 1904, naturalized Canadian 1954. After training in composition and conducting at the Latvian State Cons in Riga, Kalnins studied with Erich Kleiber in Salzburg and with Hermann Abendroth and Leo Blech in Berlin. He conducted 1923–33 at the Latvian National Theatre and 1933–44 at the Latvian National Opera and was a guest conductor in Sweden (Royal Opera House, Stockholm), Germany, and Poland. He moved to Canada in 1948 to become organist-choirmaster at St Paul's United Church in Fredericton, NB, and retained the position for over 30 years. In 1951 he was appointed conductor of the Fredericton Civic Orchestra and instructor in music education at the provincial teachers' college. He was the sole conductor of the *New Brunswick SO (1962–8) and also has conducted orchestras in Latvian festivals throughout North America. In 1978 he conducted the *Windsor SO in his own *Third Symphony* and *New Brunswick Rhapsody*. Kalnins writes with facility in all the principal forms, and his style blends romantic and modern elements.

SELECTED COMPOSITIONS

ORCHESTRA

Two Latvian Peasant Dances. 1936. UE 1937

4 Symphonies (1939–44, 1953, 1973, 1977). All ms

Concerto in F-Sharp Minor. 1946. Vn, orch. Ms

Music for String Orchestra. 1965. CMCentre

New Brunswick Rhapsody. 1967. CMCentre

The Long Night (Velta Toma). Nd. SATB, orch. Ms.

CHAMBER

Sonata for Oboe and Piano. 1963. Ms

Two Shepherd Songs for voice, oboe, and piano (trad). 1963. Ms

String Quartet in G-Sharp Minor. Nd. Ms

Some works for vn and pf, including *Klusa Stunda* (1968), *Larghetto Serioso* (1975), and *Sonata* (1975). All ms

CHOIR

'The Bird's Lullaby' (E. Pauline Johnson). 1950. FH 1951

'The Lord's Prayer' and 'When Jesus Came to Birmingham.' Ca 1954. FH 1954

The Potter's Field (Bible), cantata. SATB, org. Ms

Latvijai (E. Raisters). 1976. Women's vs, str quin. Ms

Also 4 operas: *Unguni* and *Lolita's Magic Bird* (1933); *In the Fire* (1934); *Hamlet* (1935). All ms. ('Christina's Song' from *Unguni*) DVRV 6621191 (L. Petersone mezzo, N. Zalite pf). A few works for org and several for pf

BIBLIOGRAPHY

'Janis Kalnins,' *Atlantic Advocate*, vol 48, May 1958

'Orchestra-conductor,' ibid, vol 52, Aug 1962

Phillips, Fred H. 'Eminent conductor, Janis Kalnins, leads New Brunswick Symphony Orchestra,' *PfAC*, Winter 1963 (RCB)

KANE, Jack (b John). Arranger, conductor, clarinetist, composer, b London 29 Nov 1924, d Toronto 27 Mar 1961; B MUS (Toronto) 1950. His father was the British music-hall entertainer Barry Kane. Jack was brought to Toronto as a child and by nine was singing with his father in local vaudeville. He studied clarinet 1939–42 with Herbert Pye at the TCM and made his radio debut in 1941 as a member of the High Timers. After serving in the Royal Canadian Signal Corps Band 1942–5 and leading the Khaki Kollegians in the *Army Show 1945–6 he studied composition 1946–8 with John *Weinzweig. At this time he composed a number of concert works, including two interludes for woodwinds (1947), a string quartet (1948–9), *Suite for Orchestra* (1950), and *Concerto for Saxophone* (1951). Later he began a symphony which was never completed. He performed in CBC orchestras after 1946 and became assistant arranger-conductor to Howard *Cable in 1949 and chief arranger for 'Startime' in 1950. He won the 1951 Maurice Rosenfeld Prize as a 'promising newcomer to Canadian radio,' became music director for the CBC TV shows 'On Stage' (1954), 'The Jackie *Rae Show' (1955), and 'Summertime '57,' and was featured on 'Music Makers '58,' 'Music Makers '59,' and 'Music '60 Presents the Jack Kane Hour.' He was music director in the USA for the Steve Lawrence and Eydie Gorme 1958 NBC TV series, Andy Williams' 1959 CBS series, and an Ethel Merman 1959 NBC special. Kane was one of Canada's leading arrangers at the time of his death from cancer. He later was honoured by a special recording of his big band arrangements under the direction of Bert *Niosi.

DISCOGRAPHY

Kane is Able. (1958). Coral CRL 757219

Jack Kane Salutes the Comics. (1959). Dot DLP 25143

Jack Kane Salutes the Women of Show Business. (1960). Hamilton 12105

The Jack Kane Band Conducted by Bert Niosi. 1963. CTLS 036

Other recordings also made in the USA during the late 1950s with Steve Allen and Dorothy Collins

BIBLIOGRAPHY

Trent, John. 'Jack Kane composer, arranger and Music Maker '58,' *Music World*, Nov 1957

Kritzwiser, Kay. 'Jack Kane: he hit the top with a downbeat,' *Globe Magazine*, 17 Oct 1959

Dunwoody, Derm. 'The last days of Jack Kane,' *Star Weekly*, 22 Jul 1961 (HM)

KANTARJIAN, Gerard. Violinist, teacher, b Cairo, of Armenian parents, 1 Oct 1931, naturalized US 1964. A pupil of Adolph Menashes in Cairo and Váša Příhoda in Italy, he toured at 17 in Italy and Switzerland. After studies 1953–8 on scholarship at the Curtis Institute with Ivan Galamian, he placed 11th in the Queen Elisabeth of Belgium Competition in 1959. He performed as soloist with some 20 US orchestras, was concertmaster for a season in Leopold Stokowski's American SO, played in chamber groups, and participated 1960–7 in the Casals Festival, Puerto Rico. At the invitation of Seiji Ozawa he served 1967–70 as concertmaster of the *TS and has held similar positions with the New Chamber Orchestra 1973–5, the North York SO 1974–5, and the Stratford Festival Ensemble (summer 1974). He became concertmaster of the *COC orchestra on its formation in 1977 and has been a member of many Toronto studio orchestras. He was the violinist 1973–6 in the Ararat Trio with the pianist Raffi *Armenian and the cellist Gisela *Depkat, and in 1976 he formed the Gadar Trio with the violist Rivka Golani-Erdész and the cellist David Miller. He has performed as a soloist in recital and with Ontario orchestras, has taught privately, and in 1977 was on staff at the Toronto Summer School of Music (held at Upper Canada College) and the Blue Mountain School of Music, Collingwood, Ont. (MFr)

KAPLAN, David. Administrator, conductor, clarinetist, b Chicago 12 Dec 1923; B MUS (Roosevelt) 1948, M MUS (Oberlin) 1950, PH D (Indiana) 1974. He taught at West Texas State U 1955–9 before moving to Canada in 1960 as chairman of the music department of the *U of Saskatchewan. He was conductor 1963–9 and 1970–1 of the *Saskatoon SO and has performed as clarinetist on CBC radio. He was the founding chairman of the *Saskatchewan Music Council in 1967. Kaplan has arranged or composed pieces for woodwinds, some published by Jack Spratt, New York, and has written about the clarinet and music education. He prepared the *WBM woodwind syllabus (1972) and edited the school-music magazines *Clarinet Corner* and *Band Lab* in the 1950s and early 1960s. His PH D thesis was 'Stylistic trends in small woodwind ensembles, 1750–1825.'

KARAM, Frederick. Composer, organist, choir conductor, trombonist, singer, teacher, b Ottawa, to Lebanese parents, 26 Mar 1926; d there 27 Mar 1978; B MUS (Toronto) 1950, ARCT (1950), D MUS (Toronto) 1953. He went to school in Ottawa, then studied at the *U of Toronto and at the *TCM with Gerald *Bales, S. Drummond Wolff, and Healey *Willan. For his doctorate he submitted his cantata for choir and orchestra, *Lazarus*. He was organist-choirmaster 1950–78 at St Elijah Syrian Orthodox Church in Ottawa, and conducted 1955–65 the *Ottawa Choral Society and, for eight years, an Ottawa CBC orchestra. He also directed the Toronto Opera Lovers' Group and gave theory and voice lessons. He taught harmony/counterpoint, composition, and voice 1962–78 at the *U of Ottawa, and when the Music Dept was established there in 1969 he took on the position of academic secretary. His compositions include *Modal Trumpet* (BMI Canada 1949), *Poem for Strings* (Associated Music 1952), *Scherzo* for piano (BMI Canada 1953), and, for organ, *Gigue* (BMI Canada 1957) and *Divertimento* (BMI Canada 1959). He also wrote a ballet for children and the sound tracks for three films. The musical rights of his estate are administered by PRO Canada.

His brother Ed (Edward Michael) Karam (b Ottawa 28 Aug 1929) played baritone saxophone in the 1950s in CBC Toronto orchestras and in jazz groups led by Moe *Koffman and Phil *Nimmons. He was music director for several CBC TV variety shows and studied 1960–4 with Gordon *Delamont before leaving Canada to work as music director for Paul *Anka. Ed Karam settled in Hollywood, where he has been a studio composer-arranger for recordings and TV shows by US singers (eg, Rod McKuen, Barbra Streisand, and Andy Williams). He also has written TV and film scores. (L-GA)

Karn Piano Co, Ltd. Piano and organ manufacturing firm founded in Woodstock, Ont, by Dennis W. Karn (b North Oxford County, Canada West, 6 Feb 1843, d Toronto 19 Sep 1916). A farmer and amateur musician, Karn taught at *singing schools and built violins as a hobby. About 1867 he joined John M. Miller, who was building one cabinet organ a week. In 1870 Karn bought out Miller. He retained the name Miller & Karn for some years, however, before he adopted the name D.W. Karn Co; in the 1870s the name Woodstock Organ Factory also was used. Production increased rapidly, and Karn's factory on Dundas St was expanded several times and rebuilt after three fires.

The company began to make pianos in the late 1880s. In 1896 it bought out the S.R. *Warren & Son organ company of Toronto, and in 1897 it began to make Karn-Warren pipe organs (tracker, tubular pneumatic, and electro-pneumatic), though reed organs remained in production for some time. The first Karn player piano was built in 1901. During the first decade of the 20th century, branch warerooms existed in London, Ont, Ottawa, Winnipeg, and Montreal (including a 750-seat Karn Hall on St Catherine St West), and branches in London and Hamburg.

Besides operating his company, Karn was active in municipal affairs. He was elected mayor of Woodstock in 1889 and stood twice for election to Parliament. He retired in 1909, at which time the company amalgamated with the *Morris piano makers of Listowel (north of Woodstock). The new firm, Karn Morris Piano & Organ Co, Ltd, with E.C. Thornton as general manager, maintained a head office in Woodstock, but both Karn and Morris retained their original factories and produced their own lines of pianos and player pianos. Only the pipe organs, made at this time under the supervision of C.S. Warren, were known by the name Karn Morris. When the Karn and Morris partnership dissolved in 1920, the Karn assets were purchased by a Toronto concern headed by John E. Hoare (the president of the Cecilian Piano Co) and A.A. Barthelmes (the founder of Sterling Action & Keys, Ltd). However, the new concern went into receivership and was bought in 1924 by *Sherlock-Manning, which continued to make the Karn line. Some 25,000 pianos were made by Karn 1870–1924. Serial numbers provide evidence for the manufacture of 12,000 Karn pianos from 1936 to 1957. (FH)

KARR, Gary (Michael). Bassist, teacher, writer, b Los Angeles 20 Nov 1941. He began playing at nine, and his teachers included Herman Reinshagen, Gabor Rejto (U of Southern California), and Stuart Sankey (the Juilliard School). In 1970 he settled in Halifax, where he taught in elementary schools for two years. He and the pianist-harpsichordist Harmon Lewis formed the Karr-Lewis Duo in 1972 and were artists-in-residence 1972–4 at *Dalhousie U. Karr joined the teaching staff in 1974. As recitalist and orchestra soloist he has performed in Canada, the USA, Mexico and Europe, has made recordings, and has been heard on radio. He has appeared in three CBC TV programs ('Gary Karr and his Friends') and three CBS TV documentaries. He plays jazz, rock, and folk music in addition to the classics. Karr has made transcriptions and has encouraged composers to write for string bass, premiering works by the Canadians Michael *Baker, Alexander *Brott, Dennis Farrell, and Steve Tittle. He has held master classes, workshops, and seminars in Europe, the USA, and Canada. In 1967 he founded and directed the International Institute for the String Bass at the U of Wisconsin, continuing it at North Plainfield, NJ, and in Halifax. He edited the institute's journal, *Bass Sound Post*, renamed (1972) *Probas*. In his writings he advocates changes and improvements in bass design and playing techniques. His article 'Inevitably Canadian bass-ed' (*CBM*, 7, Autumn–Winter 1973) expresses his educational points of view. In 1977 he became artist-in-residence at Hartt College in Hartford, Conn.

DISCOGRAPHY

A. Brott *Profundum praedictum*. McGill Chamb Orch, A. Brott cond. RCA LSC-3128/Sel CC-15.088

Clinician Series: Gary Karr Double Bass. (1973). Golden Crest CR 1011

Eccles – Koussevitzky – Bloch – Lorenziti – Ravel – Paganini. Siegel pf. (1962). Golden Crest RE-7012

Gary Karr Bass Virtuoso: Wilder *Suite and Sonata for Double Bass and Piano – Suite for Double Bass and Guitar*. B. Leighton pf, F. Hand guit. Golden Crest RE-7031

Handel – Tittle – Bruch – Farrell. Lewis hpd and org. 1974. CBC SM-269

Henze *Concerto for Double Bass and Orchestra*. English Chamb O, Henze cond. (1970). DG 2740-150

Jennie Tourel at Alice Tully Hall: Stradella – Monsigny – Beethoven – et al. James Levine pf. (1970). Desto DC 7118/9

Koussevitzky *Concerto for Double Bass*. Oslo Phil, Antonini cond. CRI S-248

BIBLIOGRAPHY

Cameron, Donald. 'The world's greatest bass player lives in Halifax,' *SatN*, Jun 1974

Schulman, Michael. 'Getting the bass on the right track,' *PfAC*, vol 11, Summer 1974 (PS)

KASEMETS, Udo. Composer, pianist, organist, teacher, writer, b Tallinn, Estonia, 16 Nov 1919,

Udo Kasemets

naturalized Canadian 1957. Kasemets studied composition, conducting, and piano at the State Cons in Tallinn and subsequently attended the Staatliche Hochschule in Stuttgart and, in 1950, the Kranichstein Institut in Darmstadt. His principal teachers in Germany were Ernst Krenek (composition) and Hermann Scherchen (conducting). He taught school music in Estonia and Germany and conducted several choral and orchestral societies before emigrating in 1951 to Canada, where he taught piano, theory, composition, and conducting at the Hamilton Cons (*RHCM) until 1957. He served also, 1952–7, as conductor of the Hamilton Conservatory Chorus and the Collegium Musicum of Hamilton. He was music critic for the *Toronto Daily Star* 1959–63 and taught at the Brodie School of Music and Modern Dance 1963–7.

Kasemets was the founder-director 1957–8 of the Toronto Bach Society; 1958–9 of Musica Viva, an organization devoted to the performance of new compositions and seldom-heard early music; 1962–3 of Men, Minds and Music, a series of avant-garde concerts produced under the aegis of the Brodie school; and 1965–7 of the Isaacs Gallery Mixed Media Ensemble, which brought together musicians, visual artists, film-makers, poets, and technicians in nine events featuring works by US and Canadian artists of radical tendencies. In 1968 Kasemets planned and directed Sightsoundsystems, a controversial festival which marked the inception of the Toronto branch of the New York-based Experiments in Art and Technology. In 1970 he joined the Ontario College of Art as a lecturer on music and mixed media.

Kasemets is at once a traditionally trained musician who has exercised his craft in traditional ways and a musical explorer whose experiments in sound have shared the concerns of the international avant garde. In the early 1960s he became a leading Canadian representative of the New York Action School centred around John Cage and his disciples, and although he has retained an interest only in the works he composed after that time (when, in his own words, he came into contact with 'the existing international trends in composition'), the pre-1960 compositions reveal tendencies which have remained close to the surface of his aesthetic outlook. The settings of Estonian folksongs of the late 1940s and early 1950s, for example, have their parallel in the series of works of the mid-1960s and early 1970s entitled *1 + 1*, teaching pieces for young recorder players, pianists, and percussionists, based in the main on familiar folksongs and nursery tunes. Even the mixed-media works and 'game' pieces of the 1970s can be regarded as extensions of this Gebrauchsmusik aesthetic, for behind them one senses an urge on the composer's part to involve his audience in the creative process on a primary level.

Kasemets' compositions of the 1950s are in a traditional vein, with strong melodic lines and classical formal boundaries. The titles alone – *Toccatina, Arietta e Fughetta* (1952), *Sonata da Camera* (1955), *Passacaglia* (1959) – suggest the neo-classicism fashionable in the period, with an emphasis on linear textures, refined sonorities, and strong, bracing rhythms.

After 1960 Kasemets made use of chance operations and unusual performance methods in an attempt to approach a Cageian fusion of art and technology. The preoccupation with Cage's philosophy and cultural heroes is indicated by the titles and the performance media of many of Kasemets' more recent works. T^t (T to the power of t, subtitled 'Tribute to Buckminster Fuller, Marshall McLuhan, John Cage,' 1968), is 'composed' by members of an audience, who fill out computer cards – indicating their choices of frequency, amplitude, colour, and intensity – which then are analysed and developed into graphs to be projected for the audience and used by performers. Another audience-activated piece is *Music for Nothing* (1971, for four readers, four tape recorders, and pendulum-pushers) in which pendulum sounds are fed into a cybernetic sound-system where they are allowed to interact with words on 'nothing' by Samuel Beckett, Norman O. Brown, and John Cage.

It is clear that Kasemets expects his audiences to participate creatively, to respond imaginatively to the infinite variety of sounds in the environment, and thus to achieve a more intense awareness of the contemporary soundscape. With this existential goal in mind he has channelled a great deal of his energy into ingenious 'perception exercises.' *Musicgames* (1971) is conceived as a series of seven sound-perception and sound-conception group exercises; *Songbirdsong* (1971) is a tape-recorded birdsong cognition exercise; *Colourwalk* (1971) involves colour perception; and *Senslalom* (1972) is intended to instruct all five senses.

Kasemets is an artist-prophet whose goal is not chaos but the artistic search for new forms. He sees art as a ritualistic and symbolic expression of the fullness of life here-and-now, the creative act assuming precedence over the art work itself, transmuting artistic practice into celebratory activity.

He is an affiliate of PRO Canada and an associate of the *CMCentre.

SELECTED COMPOSITIONS

PRE-1960

Estonian Suite, Op 20. 1950. Sm orch. BMIC 1959
Six Preludes, Op 30. 1952. Pf. FH 1955 (no. 2)
String Trio, Op 33. 1953. Vn, va, vc. CMCentre
Visions, Op 31 (K. Rumor). 1953. Dancer, narr, sm orch. CMCentre
Poetic Suite, Op 37 (K. Raine). 1954. Sop, pf, str orch. BMIC 1955(?)
Recitative and Rondino, Op 36. 1954. Str orch. BMIC 1954
Sonata da camera, Op 40. 1955. Vc. CMCentre
Concerto, Op 41. 1956. Vn, orch. BMIC 1967
Two Symphonic Songs, Op 43 (Dylan Thomas). 1956. Orch, bar (mezzo). CMCentre
Sonata Concertante, Op 50. 1957. Vn, va, vc, pf. CMCentre
Passacaglia. 1959. Fl, vn, orch. BMIC 1960
Sinfonietta. 1959. Sm orch. BMIC 1959
Also a *String Quartet* (1957) and *Songs from the Atlantic Provinces*, for high or med v and pf (1959). Both ms

POST-1960: 'OPEN FORMS'

1 fixed no. of performers, fixed scores
Logos. 1960. Fl, pf. Ms
19NooN61 (W. Hickling). 1961. V, pf. Ms
Haiku (Japanese, transl H.G. Henderson). 1961. v, fl, vc, pf. BMIC 1963
Squares. 1962. Pf 4-hands. BMIC 1969

2 indeterminate instrumentation, 'multi-purpose scores'
Trigon. 1963. 1, 3, 9, or 27 perf. BMIC 1969
Cumulus. 1964. Any solo instr or instr ens, 2 tape recorders. Ms
Timepiece. 1964. Any solo instr or instr ens. BMIC 1967
Cascando (S. Beckett). 1965. 1–128 perf. Publ in *Focus on Musicecology*, Ber 1970
Calceolaria. 1966. Any no. of perf. BMIC 1967
Octode – a Calceolaria Variation. 1967. Mono tape
OO – Octagonal Oratory with Octode and Ode (Kasemets). 1967. Lecturer, singer, tape, projections
TEA – Technological Experiments and Art: Octagonal Ode/Cumulus (Kasemets). 1968. Lecturer, 3-track tape, 8 radios, Maxfeed, projections
TT – Trigonic Tributes to Buckminster Fuller, Marshall McLuhan, John Cage: Cumulus Realization with *Trigon* and T^t (Fuller, McLuhan, Cage). 1968. 2 vs, 2-track tape
WWWW #1 – A Workable World without War: Octagonal Ode realization (various quotations). 1969. Spkr, 8-track tape, projections, candles
DDD – Deadly Deafening Decibels (various quotations). 1970. 4 spkr, instr. Ms
J.C. – Without Saying Anything about John Cage that Hasn't Been Said by John Cage Himself (Cage). 1972. Reader, tape recorder, record player, doors. Ms
In Memoriam Alan Watts (A. Watts). 1973. Reader, tape recorder, record player, incense. Ms
SSENERAWA (A. Watts). 1976. Reader, transparencies, gong, incense. Ms

3 theatre, 'participation pieces,' 'learningmusic'
5PP – Five Performance Pieces. 1966. Ms
Contactics – A Choreography for Musicians and Audiences. 1966. BMIC 1967
T^t *– Tribute to Buckminster Fuller, Marshall McLuhan, John Cage* (Fuller, McLuhan, Cage). 1968. Readers, synths, projections, audience-controlled cybernetic systems. Ms
Bookmusic (any books by any eight authors or on any eight subjects). 1971. 8 readers, audience-controlled cybernetic sound system
Songbirdsong. 1971. Tape-recorded bird sound-cognition exercises
Time/Place Interface, 1971: *i Trans-Canada* version (sound-collectors/recorders at points across Canada, coast-to-coast radio/tv network). *ii All-Ontario* version (sound-collectors/recorders at points across Ontario, sound reproduction media)
Time/Space Interface: *i OCA* version 'In Search of Stillness' (1971; any no. of participants, any media, a multi-roomed enclosed space); *ii Outdoor* version 'In Search of Oneness' (1973; any no. of participants, cassette recorders, videocorders, polaroid cameras, open space, etc)
Elaborations of Erratum Musical of Marcel Duchamp. 1972. Any no. of participants, any sound-producing media
Quartet of Quartets, 1972: *i Music for Nothing* (text S. Beckett, Cage, N.O. Brown; 4 readers, 4 tape recorder operators, pendulum pushers; ms). *ii Music for Anything* 'Wordmusic' (text any dictionary; 4 or more readers, 4 or more tape recorders, calibrators; ms). *iii Music for Something* 'Windmusic' (windbells, windchimes, etc, windgenerators, 2 opaque projectors, 4 or more tape recorders, pendulart calibrators; ms). *iv Music for Everything* (1 or 4 or 16 or 64 performers, any sound-producing media; ms)
Son of Vexations. 1972. Tape-loop, abacus. Ms
Whole Earth Music. 1972–7. 92 tracks of tape
Mikemusic: *I* (1973–5; 2 or more perc with assts, 2 or more tape recorders). *II* (1976; 1, 2, or 4 pianists, assts, 2 or 4 tape recorders, optional polaroid cameras). *III* (1976; any no. of operators of microphones/tape recorders/mixers). *IV* (1976; any no. of vs and tape recorders)
Wordmusic/Interface (any dictionary). 1973. Readers, tape recorders, mixers, mail, air express courier, radio or telecommunication
Wordsong (traditional). 1973. 1, 2, or 4 readers, live or on tape. Ms
64 Provocations for John Cage with 64 Responses. 1974. Tape-mix
Silencesong 'Litany for Lily' (Kasemets). 1974. Reader, live or on tape (any no. of readers). Ms
In Memoriam Nelson Small Legs Jr. 'Rites of Rights #1' (North American Indian proverbs). 1976. 1–10 readers, any no. of beaters, visual elements
In Support of Justice Thomas Berger 'Rites of Rights #2' (quotations from Martin O'Malley's 'Past and Future Land'). 1976. Any no. of participants playing perc instr of wood, stone, bone, leather, loud-speaker system

Music of the Eighth Moon of the Year of the Dragon 'Watearthundair I' (Thoreau, Joyce, McLuhan, Book of Genesis, Lao-tzu, North American Indian texts). 1976. recordings, tapes, mixers, reader, transparencies
Music of the Tenth Moon of the Year of the Dragon 'Watearthundair II' (Thoreau, F.S. Mathews, Joyce, Book of Genesis, Lao-tzu, Chuang-tzu, Kuang-tzu, North American Indian texts). 1976. Tapes, recordings on magnetoscope, transparencies, mixers, 4 stories, 16 transparency projectors, 8 magnetoscope monitors. Ms
Biographics (Music of the Third Moon of the World of the Serpent). 1977. 8-channel pre-recorded tapes
C(ag)elebration/Messagemix. 1977. Global radiotelephonic sound mixing process
David and David and Larry and James. 1977. 4 perf: vs, acoustic instr, microphones, mixers, synth, amplifiers, quadraphonic loudspeakers
Minutemusics. 1977. Any no. of perf: vs and/or acoustic and/or elec instr and/or pre-recorded tapes
W(h)/y/en/ere/ence/ether/at/(O/W)? (Kasemets). 1977. Readers with biolators
T[H(e)UND(E)Red][let(W)t(O)eR]eD (Joyce, N. Morriseau, Thoreau, D. Godfrey, dictionaries). 1978. Live and prerecorded vocal and thundersounds for 2 readers and quadraphonic tape playback system
M(on)ART: C'EST LA VIE. 1979. 4 pre-recorded cassette tapes
Chronologue (8-track musicollage); *Monologue* (spkr with recording/playback system); *Nonologue* (asking/answering cassette-taperecording/playback and recycling process); *Sonologue* (wave generators, vs, pulse and breath monitors, pickup and mixing systems). All 1979

WRITINGS

'The Saskatoon Summer Festival of Music, 1959' *CMJ*, vol 4, Autumn 1959
'John Weinzweig,' *CMJ*, vol 4, Summer 1960
– and Beckwith, John eds. *The Modern Composer and His World* (Toronto 1961)
'Current chronicle: Ann Arbor,' *MQ*, vol 50, Oct 1964
– ed. *Canavangard* (Don Mills, Ont 1968)
'Nine notes on notation,' *Artscanada*, vol 25, Jun 1968
'Eight edicts on education with eighteen elaborations,' *Source: Music of the Avant Garde*, vol 2, Jul 1968
'Pierre Mercure,' *MSc*, 246, Mar–Apr 1969
– ed. *Focus on Musicecology* (Toronto 1970)
'Prologue to an interlude and an epilogue,' 'Threnody,' *CMB*, 5, Autumn–Winter 1972
Reviews of music in *CMJ*, vols 3–6, Autumn 1958, Summer 1959, Winter, Autumn 1960, Winter, Spring, Autumn 1961, Spring, Summer 1962

BIBLIOGRAPHY

Gregory, Carol. 'When is a happening not a happening?' *Maclean's*, 16 Apr 1966
'Udo Kasemets – a portrait,' *Mcan*, 22, Sep 1969
Beckwith, John. 'Kasemets – torrents of reaction,' *MSc*, 251, Jan–Feb 1970
BMI Canada Ltd. 'Udo Kasemets,' pamphlet (1972)
Dictionary of Contemporary Music
Contemporary Canadian Composers / Compositeurs canadiens contemporains AMG

KASH, Eugene 'Jack.' Violinist, conductor, teacher, b Toronto 1 May 1912. He studied violin 1918–28 with Luigi von *Kunits, 1928–31 at the Curtis Institute with Arthur Meieff and 1931–5 in Czechoslovakia with Otakar Ševčik and at the Vienna State Academy with Bronislaw Hubermann. He was a member of the Neues Wiener Konzertorchester under Scherchen, Klemperer, and Monteux and attended master classes in violin ca 1935 with William Primrose in London. Returning to Canada he studied 1940–1 with Kathleen *Parlow and in 1947 with D.C. Dounis in New York. He also studied conducting during the 1950s with William Steinberg in the USA and with Igor Markevitch in Germany and Mexico. He played 1934–42 in the *TSO and in CBC orchestras and was acting concertmaster 1941–2 for the Toronto Philharmonic Orchestra's *Promenade Symphony Concerts. He joined the *NFB in 1942 and was music director 1948–50. He was concertmaster 1944–50 and conductor 1950–7 of the *Ottawa Philharmonic Orchestra. In 1946 he founded a popular series of children's concerts with that orchestra; one of these was the subject of a 1949 NFB film entitled *Children's Concert*. During the 1940s and 1950s he performed in recitals with Greta *Kraus and Pearl Palmason. In 1952 he premiered Murray *Adaskin's *Sonatine baroque* (a work he had commissioned) and in 1955 he was a featured performer at the *Stratford Festival. A segment of his CBC TV children's series 'The Magic of Music' (1955–8) won an Ohio State Award in 1956. Continuing to perform in Canada and abroad Kash participated annually 1961–75 in the Casals Festival in Puerto Rico and broadcast for the BBC in London and ORTF in Paris. He was assistant conductor and director of youth concerts 1961–3 with the Fairfield County SO in Connecticut, academic administrator of the *NYO in 1963, and conductor 1964–5 of *MSO youth concerts. In 1971 he was host for CBC radio's 'Musicscope.' He taught 1967–71 at the Philadelphia Musical Academy and 1971–3 at *York U, Toronto, where he also conducted the York U Chamber Ensemble. In 1975 he became the conductor of Toronto's Etobicoke Philharmonic Orchestra and the North York Teachers' Orchestra and joined the staff of the *RCMT. He married the contralto Maureen *Forrester in 1954.

DISCOGRAPHY

Handel *Sonata, Op 2, no. 8* – Reger *Trio, Op 2*. Kondaks va, Newmark pf. 1951. RCI 45
Morawetz *Rondo*. Newmark pf. 1949. RCI 9

BIBLIOGRAPHY

Dugan, James. 'Big music for small people,' *Maclean's*, 15 Feb 1951 (IG)

KASSNER, Eli. Teacher, guitarist, b Vienna 27 May 1924, naturalized Canadian 1956. After studies in Vienna and Palestine he moved to Canada in 1951. He studied with Segovia in Spain in 1959 and in Winston-Salem, Mass, in 1966. He performed until 1967, playing on Toronto radio and TV, and in theatrical productions at the *Stratford Festival in 1961 and 1962. He also accompanied the singers *Malka and Joso on three LPs for Capitol Records. He was a co-founder in 1959 and president 1960–6 of the *Guitar Society of Toronto. He began teaching at the *RCMT and the *U of Toronto in 1959. In 1967, when he established the Eli Kassner Guitar Academy, he resigned from the RCMT but continued to teach part-time at the U of Toronto and 1974–6 at the *École normale de musique in Montreal, and in 1976 he began teaching at *Queen's U, Kingston. Kassner's pupils have included Robert *Bauer, Liona *Boyd, Davis *Joachim, and the jazz guitarists Andy Krehm, and Rob Piltch. Dividing his time in the 1970s between music and microphotography, Kassner was a photographer and composer and performer of guitar music for the CBC TV series 'The Nature of Things,' winning the 1975 Bell-Northern Prize and the Monaco Award ($2,000) for the film *The First Inch*.

KATER, Wolfgang. Instrument builder and designer; b Drangstedt, West Germany, 5 Jun 1946; B MUS (McGill) 1972. He came to Canada in 1953 and lived in Toronto until 1959, when he moved to Montreal. Self-taught, he began building instruments at 11, at first producing guitars and later designing and building lutes. By the late 1960s he was constructing clavichords, virginals, and violas da gamba, and in the early 1970s he was commissioned to build his first harpsichord. He taught instrument making 1972–6 at *Concordia U. In the 1970s he studied and exhibited harpsichords in Europe with the help of three grants from the *Canada Council. Working at his studio in Ormstown, Que, Kater has built four to six instruments a year, mostly harpsichords but also spinets, virginals, clavichords, and occasionally guitars, lutes, and violas da gamba. He has built on commission only, and each of his instruments has followed traditional designs adapted to the needs of the individual musician. Those in Canada who have owned and/or played Kater's harpsichords include Wolfgang *Bottenberg, Martha Hagen, Christopher *Jackson, André *Laberge, Mireille and Bernard *Lagacé, and Valerie Weeks. Martin Lucker (Germany) and Edmund Shay (USA) also acquired Kater instruments. Kater was the subject of the 1975 film 'Harpsichord Builder' by Bernard Sauerman. NM

KAUFMANN, Walter. Conductor, ethnomusicologist, composer, teacher, b Karlsbad, Bohemia (now Karlovy-Vary, Czechoslovakia), 1 Apr 1907; hon D MUS (Spokane) 1956, naturalized US 1960. After studies at Prague U (music and philosophy) and with Franz Schreker and Curt Sachs at the Hochschule für Musik, Berlin, he conducted various minor European opera and symphony orchestras. Forced to leave Europe by the political events of the early 1930s, he went to India in 1934 and was music director 1938–46 for All-India Radio in Bombay. He was a guest conductor 1946–7 for the BBC in London and assistant music director for J. Arthur Rank films. He moved to Canada in 1947, living first in Halifax, where he was head of the piano department at the Halifax Cons (*Maritime Cons of Music), and 1948–56 in Winnipeg. There he became conductor of the newly formed *Winnipeg SO, was director 1949–53 of the *Winnipeg Philharmonic Choir, and in 1950 revived the *Winnipeg Male Voice Choir. He conducted the premiere of his opera *Bashmachkin* (composed 1950, not as usually stated) on CBC radio in 1952 with George *Kent in the title role and was guest conductor of the *CBC SO twice in 1953 and once in 1954. His opera *Sganarelle* had its premiere at the *U of British Columbia summer opera school in 1958 under the baton of George Schick. In 1957 he joined the U of Indiana, where he taught musicology until his retirement in 1977.

An authority on music of the East, Kaufmann has written several books on the subject and articles published in US and Canadian periodicals and US and European dictionaries. His two ballet scores, *Visages* (1948) and *The Rose and the Ring* (1949), were commissioned by the Royal Winnipeg Ballet, and several symphonic pieces were written 1949–53 for performance by the Winnipeg SO. His *Coronation Cantata* (1953, to words by the Canadian poet James Reaney) had its premiere that same year on CBC radio. He is a member of CAPAC. He married the pianist Freda *Trepel in 1950.

SELECTED COMPOSITIONS

OPERA

Bashmachkin (Kaufmann, after Gogol). 1950. Ms
A Parfait for Irene (Kaufmann). 1952. Ms
Sganarelle (Kaufmann, after Molière). 1958. Ms
The Scarlet Letter (Kaufmann, after Hawthorne). 1960. Ms
A Hoosier Tale (Kaufmann). Ca 1968. Ms

ORCHESTRA

6 Symphonies (1930–50). Ms
Concerto for piano and orchestra. Pre-1937. Arcadia
2 *Violin Concertos*. Pre-1939. Ms?
Variations for Strings. 1947. CMCentre
Faces in the Dark; Sinfonietta No. 1; Strange Town at Night; Madras Express. All 1948. All CMCentre
Swanee River Variations; Divertimento for strings. 1949. CMCentre
Fantasy. 1949. Pf, orch. Ms
Caprice; Chivaree. 1950. CMCentre
Vaudeville Overture (1951); *Nocturne for Orchestra* (1953); *Short Suite* (1953). CMCentre

Three Dances to an Indian Play. 1954. CMCentre
Concertino for timpani and orchestra. Ca 1960. Ms
Also a *Suite* for str quar; *Partita for Wind Quintet* (ca 1966) and *Passacaglia and Capriccio for Brass Sextet* (1967); *First Sonatina* (1948) and *Sonata* (1950) for pf

WRITINGS

'The forms of *Dhrupad* and *Khyal* in Indian art music,' *CMJ*, vol 3, Winter 1959
Musical Notations of the Orient (Indiana 1967)
The Ragas of North India (Indiana 1967)
Musical References in the Chinese Classics (Detroit 1976)
The Ragas of South India (Indiana 1976)
Tibetan Buddhist Chant (Indiana 1976) (SRM)

KAYE, Maury (Morris) (b Kronick). Pianist, composer, b Montreal 29 Mar 1932. While studying 1945–9 at the *CMM, where Arthur *Letondal was his piano teacher, he began playing for social functions and in nightclubs. As the bandleader 1953–9 at the El Morocco nightclub he accompanied many visiting singers, including Josèphine Baker, Tony Bennett, Sammy Davis Jr, Édith Piaf, and Mel Torme. Based 1960–9 and 1970–4 in Toronto, Kaye played piano with Ron *Collier on radio, and piano, french horn, and valve trombone in Collier's jazz bands, working also in studio and theatre orchestras and composing jingles and music for TV. A fiery stylist in the bebop tradition, Kaye led his own jazz trios and quartets in Toronto clubs and accompanied several US players ca 1968 at Bourbon Street. He returned on many occasions to Montreal in this period – for instance, in 1962, with Al Doctor (alto saxophone), Charles Biddle (bass), and Charlie Duncan (drums) he accompanied the US trumpeter Ted Curson for the LP *Trumpet on the Way Up* (Trans World TWJ-7000); and at other times he played in Montreal jazz clubs with his own group. He formed a jazz quartet in Montreal in 1975 and led other jazz groups with the singer Barbara Reney in Toronto 1977–8 and thereafter again in Montreal. In the late 1970s he also began teaching piano technique and improvisation. During his career Kaye has accompanied many other jazz singers, including Jodie Drake, Carmen McRae, Aura *Rully, and Sarah Vaughan.

BIBLIOGRAPHY

Marion, Claude. 'Maury Kaye,' *Virus Montréal*, vol 2, Mar 1979 CGa, MM

Keates Organ Company, Ltd. Established in 1945 in London, Ont, by Bert Keates (b 1909) to manufacture custom-built pipe organs. The company moved to Lucan, Ont, in 1950, became incorporated in 1951, and relocated in Acton, Ont, in 1961. Upon Keates' retirement, 31 Dec 1971, Dieter Geissler became president. A small firm with about 20 employees in 1980, Keates has built about eight organs a year with electropneumatic action. A few tracker-action instruments also have been made. Aside from the metal pipes, keyboards, and other standard parts, the instruments have been built completely in the company's Acton shop. Keates organs have been installed in churches in Barrie, Brantford, Guelph, Hamilton, and Toronto, Ont. The firm has rebuilt the organs of Hillhurst United Church, Calgary, and Grace Anglican Church, Brantford. FH

Kébec-Disc Inc. Recording company founded in Montreal and incorporated in 1974. Guy Latraverse, its first president was succeeded in 1976 by Gilles Talbot. Besides the Kébec-Disc label, the firm in 1980 owned the Solution, Gatsby, and Le Nordet labels. For a time it also held the Tréma, Flèche, and Frog labels. Among the artists who have recorded for Kébec-Disc are Robert *Charlebois, Neil *Chotem, Yvon Deschamps, Diane *Dufresne, Jim et Bertrand, Diane *Juster, Jean Lapointe, Claude *Léveillée, Ginette *Ravel, Zachary Richard, Fabienne Thibeault, and the group *Offenbach. At the beginning of 1979 its catalogue contained about 100 LPs. In Quebec Trans-Canada Musique Service Inc has distributed the Kébec-Disc catalogue – except for the LP *Starmania*, which was handled by Solo distribution; in Paris the catalogue has been represented by RCA, which looks after most releases in France, Switzerland, and Belgium.

In 1979 Kébec-Disc handled the commercial release of the six LPs entitled *Musique du Québec* (Kébec-Disc KDM 967-972). Containing 108 songs by Quebec composers (adapted for orchestra by nine arrangers, including Marc *Bélanger, Michel Brouillette, and Gaston Rochon) these recordings of background music are a creation of the official publisher of the province of Quebec and were produced by Stéphane *Venne. They also are distributed by RCI to broadcasting organizations abroad. Kébec-Disc was chosen best record producer at the 1979 ADISQ gala recording and show-business awards in Montreal. HP

KEEFER, G. Herald. Organist, organ builder, composer, b Vancouver 12 Apr 1919. He received his early choir training in Vancouver under Frederick Robinson. During World War II, while serving as a radio instructor in the RCAF in Montreal, he studied organ and choir directing with John *Weatherseed. After the war Keefer returned to Vancouver as organist of St Philip's Anglican Church and director of its boys' choir. He continued his organ studies under Richard T. Bevan and later with Leonard *Wilson, who in 1957 commissioned him to build (for Wilson's studio) the first baroque organ in western Canada. While he was serving as secretary of the Vancouver Centre of the *RCCO, his contacts with visiting organists (eg, E. Power Biggs) led to a serious interest in organ building. In 1957, at the International Congress of Organ Builders in Holland, he gathered important ideas from such builders as Dirk Flentrop and Henry Willis. Largely self-taught, Keefer, with his associate Dennis Connorton, began building and rebuilding organs under the company name of G. Herald Keefer and Associate. Between 1959 and 1979 the two have built over 20 pipe organs for customers on the west coast of the USA and Canada. These include instruments for the First Church of Christ Scientist, Seattle (1959), School of Music, U of Washington, Seattle (1961), St Andrew's Wesley Church, Vancouver (1967), Holy Trinity Cathedral, New Westminster (1969), and St Helen's Church, Vancouver (1978). The St Andrew's Wesley organ, their largest, has 6000 pipes in 93 ranks, 120 stops, and four manuals. Keefer also determines the scale of pipes to be used, designing them so as to ensure a distinctive tone. Almost all of his organs are of the electropneumatic type.

Keefer became organist-choirmaster at Holy Trinity Cathedral, New Westminster, in 1969, and taught organ 1972–8 at the Vancouver Bible College, Surrey. He was chairman of the Vancouver Centre, RCCO, in 1962 and also has been a chairman of the music division of the *Community Arts Council of Vancouver. He has given organ recitals at Holy Trinity Cathedral and has written over 30 sacred compositions (unpublished) for the cathedral. JBk

KEETBAAS, Dirk Jr. Flutist, record producer, b Scheveningen, Holland, 20 Jun 1921, naturalized Canadian 1930. He is the son of Dirk Keetbaas Senior, an Ottawa violist and conductor. The younger Keetbaas played in Ottawa 1940–5 with the RCAF Central Band, in Toronto 1946–53 in chamber groups and with the *TSO and the *CBC SO, and in Winnipeg 1953–68 as principal flute with the *Winnipeg SO and the *CBC Winnipeg Orchestra. As a soloist in Winnipeg he premiered S.C. *Eckhardt-Gramatté's *Duo Concertante* with the composer as violinist and Leslie *Mann's *Suite for Flute Solo*. He founded, and directed 1956–66, the Dirk Keetbaas Players – Keetbaas (flute), Alan Williams (oboe), Leslie Mann (clarinet), Norman Sherman, succeeded by Thomas Elliott (bassoon), John Scecina (french horn) – including on their programs the Canadian premieres of many works for woodwind quintet. Keetbaas can be heard both as flutist (in Leslie Mann's *Five Improvisations*, with the pianist Ada *Bronstein) and as composer (*Three Miniatures for Solo Flute*, 1963) on the recording *Music and Musicians of Canada* III (1966; RCI 215/RCA CCS 1009) and as conductor on *Music of Mannheim* (1967, CBC SM 41). He has composed a *Quintet for Winds* (1961). In 1968 he became a producer and co-ordinator for CBC SM recordings in Toronto. (CF)

KEILLOR, (Frances) Elaine. Pianist, musicologist, b London, Ont, 2 Sep 1939; ARCT piano 1951, BA honour music (Toronto) 1970, MA musicology (Toronto) 1971, PH D musicology (Toronto) 1976. Her piano teachers included her mother, Lenore Stevens Keillor, Reginald *Bedford (intermittently 1947–65), and, for brief periods, Claudio Arrau (master classes in Stratford, Ont, 1956) and Harold Craxton (in London, 1959 and 1961). At 11 she became the youngest ARCT graduate in the history of the *RCMT and that same year she began her professional career as a recital and concerto pianist.

Keillor has performed with orchestras in southern Ontario, in Buffalo, and elsewhere, playing concertos by Bach, Schumann, Saint-Saëns, Rachmaninoff, Tchaikovsky, and others. She appeared in the USSR in 1962 and has been heard elsewhere in Europe. She has performed on CBC and NBC radio and TV. She has played much contemporary music and has premiered works by Clifford *Ford, Peter Paul *Koprowski, David Thériault, and other Canadians. In 1958 she won the Chappell medal, awarded by the music publishing house to an outstanding young pianist in the Commonwealth.

Keillor was a teaching assistant 1972–4 at the *U of Toronto and taught 1975–6 at *York U and 1976–7 at *Queen's U. In 1977 she joined the teaching complement at *Carleton U, specializing in musicology and ethnomusicology. She has engaged in biographical and bibliographical research relating to Canadian musical life in the late 19th and early 20th centuries. She has written program notes for the *NAC, assisted in the preparation of *Compositeurs canadiens contemporains*, and has written for *EMC*.

WRITINGS

'Wesley Octavius Forsyth, 1859–1937,' *CMB*, 7, Autumn–Winter 1973
'Leontzi Honauer (1737–ca 1790) and the development of solo and ensemble keyboard music,' unpubl PH D thesis, Toronto 1976 HK

Kelly Kirby Kindergarten Method. System of teaching piano, musical rudiments, and theory to young beginners. It was developed in Toronto in the early 1930s by May and John Kirby. Weekly lessons, employing pictures, stories, games, and movement and designed to develop musical interest and knowledge, are given in a two-year course to small groups of children (usually classes of four). Public performance, discipline, and deportment are part of the method. Teachers' courses are given by correspondence and/or at the *RCMT summer school and by Eleanor Patch in Vancouver. The method is used widely not only in Canada but also in the USA (by more than 500 teachers in 1980) and in Africa, Australia, and England.

May Kelly Kirby (b Mary Beatrice Kelly, Milton, Ont, 5 Feb 1886, d Toronto 26 Mar 1981) studied piano with her mother, then with F.H. *Torrington at the *Toronto College of Music. She began her teaching career in 1900, joining the TCM in 1910. Her husband, John Kirby (piano tuner, b England 1 Sep 1896, d Toronto 21 Apr 1979), assisted her in the development of the workbooks essential to the group approach to piano teaching. He hand-drew the first 1500 books, and the couple tested and refined the system by teaching neighbourhood children. On the recommendation of Sir Ernest *MacMillan, the Frederick *Harris Music Co published the first Kelly Kirby Kindergarten Method in 1936. Included in the series are the *Kelly Kirby Workbooks* (six levels of theory), *Kelly Kirby Sightreading* (grades 1 and 2), *Key to Music Teaching* (teachers' manual), and several sets of flashcards. The Kirbys travelled widely, conducting seminars and demonstrations for teachers. In 1979 May Kirby continued to teach at the Kelly Kirby Kindergarten at the RCMT.

BIBLIOGRAPHY

Kelly Kirby, May B. 'Kindergarten in music,' *Curtain Call*, Apr 1941

Warren, Isobel. 'Octavegenarian [sic]: 79 years of the sound of music,' *Toronto Life*, Jun 1979 PW (JBk)

KEMP, Walter (Herbert). Musicologist, organist, choir director, composer, b Montreal, 16 Nov 1938; ARCT 1955, FRCCO 1959, B MUS (Toronto) 1959, M MUS (Toronto) 1961, MA (Harvard) 1963, PH D (Oxford) 1972. His early organ training was with Viola Benson. At the *U of Toronto he studied composition with John *Weinzweig, Oskar *Morawetz, and John *Beckwith, conducting with Boyd *Neel, musicology with Harvey Olnick, and organ with Eric *Rollinson. He conducted the U of Toronto Chorus 1959–61 and the *Hart House Glee Club 1962–3. He also studied with Leon Kirchner (composition), Nino Pirotta, and A. Tillman Merritt (musicology) at Harvard and, on a *Canada Council fellowship, with Frank L. Harrison at Oxford. His PH D thesis treated Burgundian chanson in the 15th century. He was conductor 1966–72 of the *Kitchener-Waterloo Philharmonic Choir. He won the *RCCO's Golden Jubilee Prize in 1969, became RCCO historian and archivist in 1973, and served 1974–6 as president. He joined the staff at *Wilfrid Laurier U in 1965 and in 1974 became chairman of the music department. In 1977 he was appointed head of the music department at *Dalhousie U. Kemp has composed for orchestra (*Masterless Men* 1961), chamber combinations, chorus, voice, and keyboard. His *Five Poems of William Blake* (1958) are distinctive examples of unaccompanied choral writing, and the pedagogical works for piano *Five Latvian Folk Pieces* (Waterloo 1971) use folk material in an original way. He has written for *AGO/RCCO Music*, the *CMJ*, and *EMC*.

WRITINGS

'A chanson for two voices by Cesaris, *Mon seul voloir*,' *Musica Disciplina*, vol 11, 1966

'University choral music with the University choir,' *CME*, vol 10, Nov–Dec 1968

'Dietrich Bonhoeffer's "Polyphony of Life",' *Church Music*, 1, 1970

'The "Polyphony of Life": references to music in Bonhoeffer's letters and papers from prison,' *Vita Laudanda*, ed Erich Schultz (Waterloo 1976)

'Some notes on music in Castiglione's *Il libro del cortegiano*,' *Cultural Aspects of the Italian Renaissance*, ed Cecil Clough (Manchester 1976)

'Toward the development of truly contemporary listening,' *CME*, vol 17, Summer 1976

To Listen and to Teach: A Report on the Private Music Teacher in Ontario (Toronto 1976)

'The founding of the Royal Canadian College of Organists: an exercise in musical nationalism,' *RCCO Q*, 16, Jun 1977

The Evolution of Musical Composition from the Middle Ages to Bach and Handel, vol 1 of Study Companions in Music History (Waterloo 1979) EK

KENDERGI, Maryvonne. Teacher, writer on music, pianist, commentator, b Aintab, Cilicie (now Gaziantep), Turkey, 15 Aug 1915, naturalized Canadian 1960; teaching diploma (École normale, Paris) 1940, performance diploma piano (École normale, Paris) 1941, L LITT (Sorbonne) 1942, diplôme supérieur history of art (Institut d'art et d'archéologie, Paris) 1944. Her family, of Armenian descent, was forced to leave Turkey during World War I and sought refuge first in Syria, then in France. At the École normale de musique in Paris, Kendergi worked with Alfred Cortot and Nadia Boulanger. She gave several concerts and gained a reputation as a promoter of French music in scholarly and university circles. In 1945 she became co-ordinator of cultural and musical activities for the Cité universitaire of Paris. She held this position until 1952, the year she arrived in Canada.

Kendergi's first position in Canada was record librarian and producer at radio station CFRG in Gravelbourg, Sask. In 1956 she moved to Montreal and became a *CBC commentator specializing in musical and cultural programs. The most noteworthy of these productions are 'Présences' (1968), a series of 13 interviews with such artists as Ernest Ansermet, Jane Bathori, Jean Lurcat, and Boris de Schloezer, and 'Le Café des arts' (1976–7). She travelled 1957–63 to most of the European festivals and brought back more than 150 interviews with prominent figures in contemporary music. These were heard on CBC's 'Festivals européens.' She was a founding member and organizer of *SMCQ in 1966 and became its president in 1973; she was a member of the editorial board of **The Canada Music Book* 1971–6 and became chairman of the Canadian section of the ISCM in 1973, president of the *CMCouncil in 1977, and vice-president of the *CCA in 1978, to name just a few of her numerous positions and functions. She began teaching at the *U of Montreal in 1967 and established Canadian music as an academic subject there. In 1969 she created 'Les Musialogues' to give exposure to Canadian musicians as well as artists from abroad touring in Quebec. These live encounters usually were held at U of Montreal, and guests included *Garant, *Prévost, *Schafer, *Somers, *Tremblay, Stockhausen, and Xenakis. In 1980 Kendergi was made a Member of the *Order of Canada.

WRITINGS

'Canadian music or Canadian composers?' Paris *Cimaise*, 80–1, Apr–Jul 1967

'Le public canadien: pour ou contre la musique moderne?' *Contemporary Music and Audiences*, CMCouncil conference report (Toronto 1969)

'Notes sur la situation musicale,' Paris *Revue d'esthétique*, vol 22, 1969

– and Potvin, Gilles, eds. *Aspects de la musique au Canada* (Montreal 1970)

Other articles for *Vie des arts*, *Carnet des arts*, and the *CMB*

BIBLIOGRAPHY

'Pour Maryvonne Kendergi l'art de la musique est aussi une belle aventure,' Montreal *Nouveau Journal*, 14 Oct 1961

Duguay, Raoul. 'Maryvonne Kendergi, l'animatrice de la musique contemporaine,' *Musiques du Kébèk* (Montreal 1971) (PR, ST)

KENINS, Talivaldis. Composer, teacher, pianist, b Liepāja, Latvia, 23 Apr 1919, naturalized Canadian 1956; B LITT (Champollion) 1939, premier prix (Paris Cons) 1950. His father was a Latvian diplomat, poet, and translator of Baudelaire and Verlaine, his mother a writer. Kenins began playing piano at five and composing at seven, continuing piano studies in France while preparing at the Lycée Champollion in Grenoble for a diplomatic career. He studied piano and composition 1940–4 at the State Cons at Riga with Joseph Wihtol and, forced from Latvia by the Soviet occupation following World War II, continued 1945–51 at the Paris Cons, where his teachers were Simone Plé-Caussade (counterpoint), Olivier Messiaen (analysis and aesthetics), and Tony Aubin (composition). Kenins' *Sonata* for cello and piano was performed publically (for his premier prix) at the Salle Gaveau in 1950, and his *Septet* (1949) was conducted by Hermann Scherchen at the Darmstadt Ferienkurse für neue Musik that same year.

Kenins emigrated to Canada in 1951 to assume duties as organist-choirmaster for the Latvian congregation of St Andrew's Lutheran Church in Toronto. He also founded the St Andrew's Latvian Choir (one of the important choirs of its type in North America) and conducted it until 1958. He became the founder and president of the Latvian Concert Assn of Toronto in 1959.

Kenins began teaching at the *U of Toronto in 1952 and was co-ordinator of the composition division 1977–9. Walter *Kemp, Edward *Laufer, Bruce *Mather, Ben *McPeek, and Arthur *Ozolins have been among his pupils. Owing largely to the communicative disposition of his musical language and the consistency of his craft, Kenins has become one of Canada's most frequently commissioned composers.

In the 1940s and 1950s Kenins' style strove to reconcile the romanticism of his nature and the neoclassicism of a French training. Chromatic excursions, pitting dissonance against consonance, were subordinated to tonal logic. Agitated passages and the toccata-like elements of his fast movements were severely controlled. The concertante style, dominant in his musical speech, was stabilized by counterpoint. The plethora of notes and the tendency to over-emphasis gave way in the 1960s to greater transparency and leaner outlines. His counterpoint recalled his academic training, but his fugues gradually became more sophisticated. The choral passage 'Still the spirit of the sorceress' in *Lagalai* shows his later success in fugal integration within the general weave of a work. In his compositions of the 1970s Kenins has broken consciously with the conservative image he had defended so assiduously. He has taken an increasing interest in the potential of the 'batterie'; the *Symphony No. 4* is a concertante for percussion and ensemble. Linear counterpoint is replaced by cluster patterns and a greater exploitation of colour and aleatoric opportunities.

Kenins is a member of CAPAC, a member (and president 1973–4) of the *CLComp, and an associate of the *CMCentre.

SELECTED COMPOSITIONS

ORCHESTRA

Piano Concerto. 1946. Pf, med orch. Ms

5 *Symphonies*. (1959–75). CMCentre. (*No. 4*) CBC SM-293 (*CBC Van Chamb O)

Folk Dance, Variations and Fugue. 1964. CMCentre. Ca 1965. Album of the Second Latvian West Coast Song Festival (Portland SO)

Concerto for violin, cello, and string orchestra. 1965. CMCentre

A manuscript page from the finale of *Concertino a cinque* for flute, oboe, viola, cello, and piano (1968) by Talivaldis Kenins

Chants of Glory and Mercy; Gloria (liturgical, various texts). 1970. SATB, soli, orch. CMCentre
Fantaisies concertantes. 1971. Pf, orch. CMCentre
Concerto for violin and orchestra. 1974. CMCentre. CBC SM-293 (*Staryk)
Naacnaaca. 1975. Full orch. CMCentre
Sinfonietta. 1976. CMCentre. Ca 1977. World Records WRC-249 (North Toronto Collegiate O, D. Ford cond)
Beatae voces tenebrae. 1977. CMCentre. RCI 477 (B. *Brott)
Sinfonia ad fugam. 1978. Orch. CMCentre

CHAMBER

Septet. 1949. Cl, bn, hn, vn, va, vc, bass. CMCentre. CBC SM-135 (*Barnes cond)
Sonata for cello and piano. 1950. CMCentre. Ca 1968. Christophorus-Schallplatte SCGLV 75980 (Teichmanis vc, Barth pf)
Sonata for violin and piano. 1955. CMCentre. Masters of the Bow MBS 2002 (*Bress)/ca 1977 Kaibala Stereo 60F03 (Lielmane vn, Balter pf)
Suite Concertante. 1955. Vc, pf. CMCentre. Ca 1957. ALA Series G80H-6093 (Naruns vc, Dambrans pf)
Diversions on a Gypsy Song. 1958. Vc, pf. CMCentre. Ca 1962. Latrec 2783 (Treimanis vc, Naruns pf)
Quartet. 1958. Pf, vn, va, vc. CMCentre. RCI 471 (*Quartet Canada)
Divertimento. 1960. Cl (vn), pf. BH 1970 (vn, pf). Dom S-69004 (*Galper cl)
Concertante for flute and piano. 1966. BH 1972. Dom S-69006 (*Aitken fl)
Concerto-Fantasy. 1976. Org, perc. CMCentre
Ancient Song for Solo Harp. 1976. CMCentre
Sextet for bassoon and strings. 1978. CMCentre
Second Sonata for violin and piano. 1979. CMCentre

KEYBOARD

Concertino for Two Pianos Alone. 1956. CMCentre. Ca 1960. Latvian Heritage Foundation CSRV 2258 (The Gutbergs)
Sonata for piano. 1961. Kalnajs/FH 1964. Ca 1967. Cor 580C-3763 (Dambrans)/ca 1964 Daina T-54067 (Leinvebers)/RCI 366 (*Morgen)/CBC SM-301 (*Ozolins)
Sinfonia Notturna. 1978. Org. CMCentre
7 short pieces for piano: *Horse Rider; Tenderness; Little March; Diversities (No. 9 and 12); The Juggler; The Sad Clown* (1956–69). Various publ. All recorded on Dom S-69002 (*Mould)
3 short pieces for piano: *Little Romance* (GVT 1956); *Dance* (FH 1961); *Dreaming* (FH 1966). All recorded ca 1974 on Latrec 2893 (Naruns)
Other works for pf, some for org, including *Suite in D* (1967; CMCentre; 'Toccata' recorded 1973 by A. Rundans on the Album of the 5th Latvian Song Festival of America)

CHOIR

To a Soldier, cantata (I. Viksna). 1953. Mezzo, bar, SATB, org. Kalnajs 1953. Ca 1955. Daina 1008-A (The Shield of Songs)
'Bonhomme! Bonhomme!' (traditional). Arr 1962. SATB. FH 1964. CBC SM-19 (*Festival Singers)
'Lakstīgala kroni pina,' folksong (Latvian). 1966. SSAA, kokles. Ms. Ca 1966. Monitor MFS 495 (Latvian Ens of New York)
3 songs: 'The Carrion Crow,' 'Land of the Silver Birch,' 'The Maiden's Lament' (arr 1967). GVT 1967. Ca 1968. Arc 260 (*Hart House Glee Club)
Lagalai 'Legend of the Stone,' chamb drama (U. Fogels). 1970. SATB, fl, hn, perc. CMCentre
Cantata Baltica (A. Viirlaid, transl T. Ene Moks). 1974. Bass (alto), SATB, 2 tpt, timp, org. CMCentre
Many other works for choir, a large number with Latvian texts, some recorded at Latvian Song Festivals in Canada and the USA; such recordings distributed by the Latvian Song Festival Assns of Canada and the USA

VOICE

Many works for voice, most with Latvian texts. Several have been recorded for labels such as DC Recordings (New York), DVRV Recordings (Germany), Imantica Productions (Sweden), KRC Sound Recordings (Detroit), and Latvian Music (Kalamazoo, Mich). Vocal works recorded include *Ai zaļāja līdaciņa; Bērns; Burvības vieta; Ej saulīte; Ganiņš gana celmalā; Kas cilvēks ir; Miestiņš; Nem mani līdz; Pieci gadi; Vecais burinieks; Virpuļu jūra.*

WRITINGS

'My most successful work: *Symphony No. 1 for Chamber Orchestra*,' *CanComp*, 3, Jul–Aug 1968

BIBLIOGRAPHY

'Professor Talivaldis Kenins: from diplomat to composer,' *CanComp*, 22, Oct 1967
'Talivaldis Kenins: a portrait,' *Mcan*, 18, Apr 1969
Berzkalns, Valentins. 'Talivaldis Kenins,' *Latvju Mūzika*, 3, 1970
CAPAC. 'Talivaldis Kenins,' pamphlet and recording (1975)
Levitch, Gerald. 'Talivaldis Kenins: one of Canada's best-known composers talks about his musical life,' *CanComp*, 107, Jan 1976
Rundans, Anita. 'The organ works of Talivaldis Kenins,' *RCCO Q*, Jun 1977
Kemp, W.H. 'Sacred choral music of Talivaldis Kenins,' ibid.
Hepner, Lee. 'Talivaldis Kenins,' *Contemporary Canadian Composers* (WHK)

KENNESON, Claude (Emile). Cellist, writer, teacher, b Port Arthur, Texas, 11 Apr 1935, naturalized Canadian 1973; B MUS (Texas) 1957, M MUS (Texas) 1959. He began cello studies at six with Leon Woska and continued at the U of Texas with Horace Britt, at the Berkshire Music Centre in 1957, and with Pablo Casals in California in 1960. Moving to Canada in 1959, he was the original cello, 1962–5, of the Corydon Trio (with Lea *Foli, violin, and Gerald *Stanick, viola) and music director 1962–5 of the Royal Winnipeg Ballet. In 1965 he began teaching at the *U of Alberta and, seasonally, at the Havas Summer School, Dorset, England, and the *Banff SFA. He was a founding member of the *U of Alberta String Quartet in 1969. Often performing on an 18th-century Brescian cello once owned by David Popper, Kenneson has given recitals and played in chamber groups and with orchestras in Canada, the USA, Europe, and Mexico. He has composed for ballet, voice, and instrumental ensemble, has written *A Cellist's Guide to the New Approach* (New York 1974) and *Bibliography of Cello Ensemble Music* (Detroit 1974), and has contributed articles to the *American String Teacher* (1960), *The Strad* (1969), and the *Canadian Music Teacher* (1971). He has been an adjudicator and lecturer in North America and Great Britain. Eric *Wilson was one of his pupils. (RSt)

Mart Kenney and His Western Gentlemen. Canada's leading dance band in the 1930s and 1940s, formed in 1931 for an engagement at Vancouver's Alexandra Ballroom by Mart (Herbert Martin)

Mart Kenney and his orchestra at the Brant Inn, 1942

Kenney (b Toronto 7 Mar 1910, an alto and baritone saxophonist and clarinetist who played during the late 1920s in the CJOR radio orchestra and with Len Chamberlain's Hotel Vancouver orchestra). The founding five – Kenney, the trumpeter-pianist Glen Griffiths, the trumpeter Jack Hemming, the saxophonist Bert Lister, and the bassist Hec MacCallum – were joined later in 1931 by the drummer Ed Emel and in 1932 by the vocalist-saxophonist-pianist Art *Hallman. The band made its radio debut in 1934 on CJOR from the Alexandra Ballroom and for three seasons appeared at the Waterton Glacier International Peace Park in Alberta. There, as Mart Kenney and His Western Gentlemen, it made its CRBC debut in 1934 with the program 'Rocky Mountain Melody Time,' taking the 1922 Billy Hill-Larry Yoell waltz 'The West, a Nest and You, Dear' as its theme-song. A succession of engagements followed, 1934–7, at CPR hotels, including the Hotel Vancouver, where the band's most popular CRBC / CBC program, 'Sweet and Low,' began in 1935. The band initiated summer tours of eastern Canada in 1937 and appeared for the first of many seasons at Toronto's Royal York Hotel. In 1938 it began recording for RCA Victor and by 1951 it had made 18 78s for that company, 7 for Bluebird, and 2 for Dominion. Hits included 'The West, a Nest and You, Dear,' 'There's Honey on the Moon Tonight,' and the Kenney song 'We're Proud of Canada.'

Relocating in 1940 in Toronto, the band continued 'Sweet and Low' 1940–2 and was featured until 1949 on other commercially sponsored CBC programs. Its broadcasts were picked up in the USA by CBS or the NBC 'Blue' network and in Britain by the BBC. During four cross-Canada tours 1943–5 the band was heard twice-weekly on 'The Victory Parade with Canada's Spotlight Band,' broadcasting from army camps and war plants. After 1949 Mart Kenney's Ranch, a dance hall near Woodbridge north of Toronto, was the site of the band's CBC broadcasts. Other groups, usually country and western, also appeared there as Kenney continued to tour into the 1960s. With his retirement to Mission, BC, in 1969, the band broke up and the ranch closed. Thereafter Kenney organized bands for special occasions such as CBC TV's 'In the Mood' in 1971 and a *CNE appearance in 1975, and for engagements in the Vancouver area.

Although initially a septet, the Western Gentlemen among them played some 30 instruments and featured the vocal trio 'Three of a Kind' (Kenney, Griffiths, and Hallman). A 12-piece band on its first recordings, it added four violins for 'Sweet and Low' from Vancouver and Toronto and for some of its later Victor recordings in Montreal. Violinists in Vancouver included Ricky *Hyslop and Cardo *Smalley; in Toronto, Hyman *Goodman, Samuel *Hersenhoren, and Albert *Pratz. Featured singers were Hallman 1932–44, Eleanor Bartelle in 1936, Georgia Dey in 1937, Beryl Boden in 1940, Judy Richards 1940–3, Veronica Foster 1943–4, Norma Locke 1944–69, Roy Roberts 1946–9, and Wally *Koster 1949–52. The band's most popular vocalist, Norma Locke (b Montreal 15 Oct 1923, a one-time student at the TCM and singer with the Joe DeCourcy and Howard *Cable dance bands), married Kenney in 1952. The personnel of the Western Gentlemen changed frequently after 1940, and some former members, including the pianist Jack Fowler, Bobby *Gimby, Hallman, and the saxophonist Stan Patton, formed their own bands, which were initially managed by the Kenney booking agency established in the late 1940s. A versatile dance band, neither excessively 'sweet' nor too boldly 'swinging,' Mart Kenney and His Western Gentlemen made a particular impact on the Canadian public with their tours during the war years and achieved some popularity in the USA through their recordings and broadcasts. In 1980 Kenney was made a Member of the *Order of Canada.

DISCOGRAPHY

The West, a Nest, and You, Dear. 1938–49. RCA Camden CAL 776 (anthology)

Mart Kenney and His Orchestra. 1964. CTLS 5053

NL of C. Unpubl detailed discography compiled by Ross Brethour

BIBLIOGRAPHY

'Mart the maestro,' *CBC Times*, 23–9 Mar 1952

'Mart Kenney: his gentlemen and his friends,' *CBC Times*, 18–24 Apr 1954

Morgan, Kit. 'The true story of the real estate salesman and the piano tuner,' *CanComp*, 69, Apr 1972

Bands Canadians Danced To MM

Kensington Market. One of Canada's most distinctive rock bands. Named after a downtown Toronto neighbourhood it was organized in 1967 by Bernie Finkelstein, who became its manager. At first a quartet, with the singer-songwriter-quitarist Keith McKie, the guitarist-pianist Eugene Martynec, the bass guitarist Alex Darou, and the drummer Jimmy Watson, it performed regularly in Yorkville coffeehouses and recorded the singles 'Mr. John' and 'Bobby's Birthday' for Stone Records. Later in 1967 the singer Luke Gibson, leader 1964–8 of Luke and the Apostles, joined the Market, followed in 1969 by the keyboardist John *Mills-Cockell. Although in live performances an exuberant and adventurous band, it recorded two rather subdued and complex LPs, *Avenue Road* (1968, Warner Brothers WS 1754) and *Aardvark* (1969, Warner Brothers WS 1780), and the score for the film *The Ernie Game* (NFB 1968). Other singles were 'I Would Be the One' (1968) and 'Side I Am' (1969).

The band dispersed in 1969 after its second US tour. Its figurehead, McKie (b St Albans, near London, 20 Nov 1947), was largely inactive until 1977, when he began performing alone in Toronto and briefly led The Village. Martynec became a producer-studio musician for *True North Records and later (1976) a member of the Silver Tractors, formed to accompany Murray *McLauchlan. Gibson re-formed the Apostles briefly 1970–1, performed in Paul Almond's film *Journey* (1971), recorded *Another Perfect Day* (1971, TNorth TN6), and sang in Toronto with the band Killaloe 1976–7 and, in McLauchlan's place, with the Silver Tractors in 1978.

BIBLIOGRAPHY

LeBlanc, Larry. 'Kensington Market,' *Hit Parader*, Mar 1969

Flohil, Richard. 'Getting Luke Gibson off from the farm isn't easy,' *CanComp*, 66, Jan 1972 MM

KENT, Ada (Jane Fairlina) (b Twohy). Pianist, organist, composer, b Denver, Colo, of Canadian parents, 8 Feb 1888, d on a visit to London 23 Jul 1969; LAB 1904, B MUS (Toronto) 1906. Taken at 13 by her mother to Hamilton, Ont, she studied piano 1901 with Helen Wildman and piano and organ 1902–5 with J.E.P. *Aldous and 1905–8 in Toronto with A.S. *Vogt. She gave a solo recital 25 Oct 1904 in Toronto. Commuting 1905–8 between Hamilton and Toronto, she served in Hamilton as organist at St Paul's Presbyterian Church and taught at the Hamilton School of Music. In Toronto she taught 1907–16 at the *TCM and the Moulton Ladies' College and served 1909–18 as organist at Trinity Methodist Church and accompanist to the *Toronto Mendelssohn Choir.

Also active 1909–13 as a soloist, Kent toured in southern Ontario (her repertoire included works by Aldous and H.A. *Fricker) and played the first movement of Grieg's *Concerto* with the *Welsman TSO. She was organist 1920–2 at Deer Park United Church, Toronto. Among her works (written after 1933 and listed in *Catalogue of Canadian Composers*) are the vocal pieces 'At Christmastide,' 'Long Ago,' and 'Dominion Hymn' (all Waterloo 1934), the children's song collections *Sing a Song of Canada* (Thomas Nelson 1937), *Let's Pretend* (Gage), and *Tiptoe Tunes for Tiny Tots* (Waterloo 1952), and the widely performed anthem 'No Flower So Fair' (Carl Fischer 1940). Some of her songs were performed in 1938 by Jeanne *Pengelly before the *Vogt Society and by the contralto Mary Jarred, accompanied by the composer, on a BBC broadcast to Canada from London. In a Wigmore Hall recital of her songs and violin pieces 2 Jun 1938, David *Martin played her *Variations on an English Theme*, described in *The Times* of London as 'none the worse for recalling greater achievements' and in the *Daily Telegraph* and *Morning Post* as 'of a type nearer to Corelli than to Brahms or Elgar.' She was a member of CAPAC. MM, PW

KENT, George Edward. Tenor, choir conductor, b Winnipeg 17 Oct 1915. His father, Thomas (1889–1924), and uncles Linton (b 1893) and Albert (b 1897), all originally from Southbank, Yorkshire, England, were tenor soloists in various Winnipeg churches. George sang in the Winnipeg Boys' Choir under Ethel *Kinley and was the tenor soloist 1934–5 at St Luke's Anglican Church before moving to Vancouver for studies with David Ross, William *Dichmont, and Clement Q. Williams. During World War II service in England he sang with George Melachrino's orchestra on BBC radio. On his return to Winnipeg he was soloist, then choirmaster 1948–58, at Knox United Church. He conducted the *Winnipeg Male Voice Choir 1955–7. He is remembered, however, as Winnipeg's reigning tenor of the 1940s and 1950s, excelling equally as a recitalist and as an oratorio soloist. His voice was a resonant and expressive robust-lyric. He was memorable in *Elijah*, the Bach *Passions* and Beethoven's *Ninth Symphony* and in 1961, at the apex of his solo career, was Winnipeg's first Gerontius in the Elgar oratorio *The Dream of Gerontius*. (RG)

E.C. Kerby Ltd. Publishing company established in 1971 in Toronto by Elvira Colombo Kerby, who came to Canada from the USA. She is the wife of Franco Colombo, who for many years was a music publisher in New York. Kerby has published music in all genres, by several Canadians, including Robert *Aitken, Louis *Applebaum, Keith *Bissell, Donald Coakley, Malcolm *Forsyth, Harry *Freedman, Rudolph *Komorous, Norman Sherman, Jack *Sirulnikoff, Harry *Somers, Donald Steven, and Norman *Symonds, as well as by many US composers. The Canadian distributor for the US publishers Consort Music Inc of Connecticut and Philadelphia Corp, and the North American agent for Amphion Éditions musicales of Paris, Kerby also secured the world distribution rights to the catalogue of Colfranc, publisher of the works of Edgard Varèse. Kerby is a CAPAC member. A subsidiary, Caveat Music Publishers, is a PRO Canada affiliate. Printing is done at the *W.R. Draper Co in Weston, Ont, and plate numbers are used. MWI

KERR, Muriel (m Benditsky). Pianist, teacher, b Regina 18 Jan 1911, d Los Angeles 18 Sep 1963. She began her career at seven, performing a Mozart concerto. She studied with Paul *Wells in Toronto, with Alexander Raab in Chicago, and with Percy Grainger. She began lessons with Ernest Hutcheson in 1922 after a Canadian tour and continued with him 1926–31 at the Juilliard Graduate School, making a Carnegie Hall debut in Rachmaninoff's *Concerto No. 2* 5 Dec 1928 with the Philharmonic SO of New York conducted by Mengelberg and a Town Hall recital debut in January 1929. After these successful debuts she undertook numerous tours of Canada and the USA, appearing with orchestras in Philadelphia, Cincinnati, Baltimore, Chicago, Los Angeles, Washington, and Toronto and at various music festivals including that at Worcester, Mass, in 1930. She made her first European tour in 1948. She taught 1942–9 at the Juilliard School and 1955–63 at the U of Southern California. In 1957 she became the director of the Punahou Music School in Honolulu and organized there an annual festival of contemporary music and art. She was honoured in 1958 by the Sigma Alpha Iota for her contribution to the musical development of Hawaii. Muriel Kerr's concert repertoire ranged from Bach to Hindemith, and critics praised her for an art which combined meticulous attention to detail and great freedom of expression. She recorded piano music of Schumann and Hindemith (LM-2891) for RCA Victor. EK

KERRISON, (John) Davenport. Pianist, teacher, composer, editor, b London 1841, d Jacksonville?, Fla, after 1927. He studied in England with John Boardman and Benedict Rolfs and in the USA with J.N. Pattison and Louis Gottschalk. About 1866 he settled in Toronto and became organist at St John's Church. He organized the Choral Union, which first sang at the Music Hall, 21 Jan 1868. Until 1875 Kerrison conducted and played in Toronto, and in July 1872 he toured southern Ontario with the violinist J.W. *Baumann. By 1873 he had become conductor of the Toronto Orchestral Union, which accompanied operas and operettas and gave concerts. He returned to New York to become organist (mid–1874?–October 1878) of St Stephen's Church and to teach at the Grand Cons of Music.

Kerrison was back in Toronto by 1878 and opened a school, staffed by himself and his wife, in rooms at the Grand Opera House. His chosen name for the school (Royal Canadian Cons of Music) was, it would appear, disallowed because of the unauthorized use of the word 'Royal.' He amended the name in 1879 to Toronto College of Music (not to be confused with the *Toronto College of Music founded in 1888). In October 1880 he began *Arion*, a monthly 'Canadian Journal devoted to music, art, literature and the drama' and published it until October 1881. In the Ontario Music Teachers' Assn (*Canadian Society of Musicians) composition competition of 1886 Kerrison was one of five successful entrants. In 1887 he and his wife taught in private studios which they called the Canadian Cons of Music. There is no evidence to indicate that he was a resident of Toronto after 1888. Eventually he obtained a D MUS from the U of New York.

Kerrison's larger works include *Canada*, a symphonic overture in four movements first performed in Toronto 22 Jun 1881 in a four-piano arrangement; a *Concerto in E Minor* and a *Concerto-caprice*, both for piano and orchestra; *The Bells, Op 35* (1908), a four-movement symphonic poem; an operetta, *The Oreads*, performed in Toronto 23, 25, and 26 Feb 1870; two light operas, *The Curfew*, performed in Toronto 30 and 31 Jul 1879, and *The Maid of the Mill*; and a grand opera, *The Last of the Aztecs* (1914). He also composed numerous piano pieces and songs, including 'God Preserve Our Native Land' (1883) and 'The Flag That Bears the Maple Leaf' (1889). Among his publishers were *Nordheimer and *Suckling in Toronto and W.F. Shaw, Presser, and G. Schirmer in the USA.

BIBLIOGRAPHY

Hipsher, Edward Ellsworth. *American Opera and its Composers* (Philadelphia 1927, 1934)

EK

KESSLER, Jack. Violinist, b Swindon, Wiltshire, England, 23 Nov 1906, naturalized Canadian ca 1965. He studied 1916–26 at the Franz Liszt Academy in Budapest, graduating from the master class of Jenö Hubay. In his teens he toured Europe for three years as second violin of the Hungarian String Quartet. He was for ten years concertmaster of the Lucerne Municipal Orchestra, then served 1945–55 as assistant concertmaster of the Philharmonia Orchestra of London and 1947–9 as concertmaster of Britten's English Opera Group Chamber Orchestra. In the early 1950s he taught at the TCL.

Moving to Canada in 1955 Kessler served 1956–67 as concertmaster of the *CBC Vancouver Chamber Orchestra, the *Vancouver Opera, and the *Vancouver International Festival orchestra and was concertmaster 1964–5 of the *Vancouver SO. A founding member (1958) of the Vancouver String Quartet, he also played 1967–70 in *Trio Victoria. In 1966, on Zurich radio, he gave the first European performance of Robert *Turner's *Sonata for Violin and Piano*. Kessler taught 1964–7 at the *U of British Columbia, then at the *U of Victoria. He also was head of the string department at the *Victoria Cons until 1972, when he returned to Vancouver. Several of his students, including Barbara Allen and Denise Phillips, have become professional orchestra players.

WRITINGS

'Is string training at an impasse?' *British Columbia Music Educator*, vol 16, Spring 1973

BNSG

KESSLER, Minuetta (b Schumiatcher, m Borek, m Kessler). Composer, pianist, educator, b Calgary 5 Sep 1914. She first performed her compositions in public at five. Her piano teachers included Gladys *Egbert in Calgary and Ernest Hutcheson and Ania Dorfmann at the Juilliard School, where she also studied composition with Ivan Langstroth. After graduating in 1934 and continuing with post-graduate studies until 1936, she taught at the Juilliard for several years. She made a Town Hall debut in 1945. Her *New York Suite* and *Ballet Sonatina* won CAPAC awards in 1945 and 1946. She premiered her *Alberta Concerto* (20 Nov 1947) on CBC radio and performed the work with orchestras in Montreal, Toronto, Quebec, Calgary, Regina, and Boston. She repeated it for Calgary's centennial celebrations in June 1975, with the Calgary Century SO. As a recitalist Kessler has been heard on CBC radio's 'Distinguished Artists' and 'Masters of the Keyboard' and on WNYC radio, New York. In 1952 she moved to Cambridge, Mass, and in 1953 to Belmont, Mass. She founded the New England Jewish Music Forum in 1958 and was president 1965–7 of the New England Pianoforte Teachers' Assn. Specializing in the teaching of very young children, she has created a music teaching game, *Staftonia* (Belmont 1960), and has published *Piano Is My Name* (Belmont 1975), which employs a simplified notational system, 'Dash-a-Notes.' She contributed articles about music and children to the *Christian Science Monitor* 1964–5.

SELECTED COMPOSITIONS

Baby's Music Box (Kessler). 1944. V, pf. Ms
New York Suite. 1944. Pf, orch (pf solo). Ms
Ballet Sonatina. 1945. Pf. Ms
Alberta Concerto. 1947. Pf, orch. Transcontinental Music 1947
Etude Brilliante. 1948. Pf. Self-publ. 1948. Transcontinental Music 1973
Sonata. 1949. Vn, pf. Ms
Memories of Tevye Ballet. 1954. Pf, cl, vc, perc (pf solo). Ms
Confirmation Prayer. 1956. V, org (pf). Transcontinental Music 1957
Sonata Concertante. 1957. Vn, pf. Ms
Trio No. 1. 1957. Pf, vn, vc. Ms
Peace and Brotherhood through Music, cantata (Kessler). 1960. Soli, SATB, pf (org). Transcontinental Music 1967
Kiddy City, children's operetta (Kessler). 1961. Ms
Thought Is a Bird of Space, cantata (Gibran, *The Prophet*). 1961. Soli, SATB, pf. Ms
Sonata. 1961. Vc, pf. Ms
Trilogy (Gibran, *The Prophet*). 1963. Sop, pf. Ms
Hear My Prayer (Bible). 1967. SATB. Transcontinental Music 1967
Victory Hora (Kessler, transl Hebrew N. Glatzer). 1967. SATB, pf. Transcontinental Music 1973
Bicentennial Sonata. 1975. Pf. Ms
Several other works for pf; some also for v and for choir

(FH, FM)

KEY, Harold Eustace. Organist, choirmaster, conductor, arranger, composer, b London 1881, d ? After studies at the GSM he moved to Canada in 1904, occupying positions as organist-choirmaster in Dunnville, St Thomas, and Brockville, Ont, before settling in Montreal in 1914. There he served until 1916 at St James Church and after 1920 at Emmanuel Church, founded (in 1921) the Elgar Women's Choir, conducted (1921–4) the *McGill University Glee Club, and led (mid–1920s) the *Mendelssohn Choir. He was associated with the CPR's John Murray *Gibbon in a number of ventures – eg, he was music director of *CPR Festivals in Quebec, Winnipeg, Vancouver, and Banff, conducted the premiere, in 1929 at the Banff Highland Gathering, of *Willan's *Prince Charlie and Flora*, and arranged the music for the first volume of Gibbon's *Northland Songs* (Thompson 1936). Key also contributed choral settings and editorial advice to *The McGill University Song Book* (McGill Students' Council 1921) and composed orchestral suites, anthems, part-songs, and songs. Among the latter are *Two Songs* (with words by E.R. Sill and Thomas Moore respectively; Nordheimer 1907). Key's setting of *'In Flanders' Fields' appears in *The McGill University Song Book*.

HK

KIDD, George. Journalist, critic, b Toronto 23 Feb 1912. He joined the Toronto *Evening Telegram* in 1929 and was music critic 1952–69. He served in the Canadian armed forces during World War II and worked on the army newspaper the *Maple Leaf* in France, Belgium, Holland, and Germany. Kidd was the only Canadian critic to cover the New York debuts of Lois *Marshall, Glenn *Gould, Jon *Vickers, and Teresa *Stratas. He is a contributor to *EMC*.

Viggo Kihl

KIHL, (Richard) Viggo. Pianist, teacher, b Copenhagen, 11 Nov 1882, d Toronto 10 Jul 1945. He studied in Copenhagen and 1897–1901 with Robert Teichmüller at the Leipzig Cons. He made his debut in 1901 in Copenhagen and toured Scandinavia. After his London debut in 1903 he taught and performed for 10 years in England. He toured Europe and South Africa in 1912. At the invitation of A.S. *Vogt he moved to Toronto in 1913 to teach at the *TCM and remained there until his death. He toured Canada frequently, performed in many small Ontario communities, and gave annual recitals at Toronto's *Eaton Auditorium. He was a soloist with the New SO and the *TSO and also performed in duos and other chamber groups with Luigi von *Kunits, Boris *Hambourg, Harry *Adaskin, Ferdinand Fillion, and others. He was a member of the Five Piano Ensemble with Norah Drewett *de Kresz, Alberto *Guerrero, Ernest *Seitz, and Reginald *Stewart in 1926. He contributed articles on pianists, piano technique, and musicianship to musical journals in England and Canada. He also published some piano transcriptions. Among his pupils were Cora B. *Ahrens, Mona *Bates, Agnes *Butcher, Arthur Gold, Weldon *Kilburn, Gwendolyn Williams *Koldofsky, Ida *Krehm, Mischa 'Max' Meller, and Florence Steinhauer.

BIBLIOGRAPHY

'The conservatory portrait gallery, no. 5 – Mr. Viggo Kihl,' *CQR*, vol 9, Autumn 1928

RPn

KILBURN. Toronto family of musicians: 1 / Weldon and his sons 2 / Nicholas, 3 / Michael, and 4 / Paul.

BIBLIOGRAPHY

Kirby, Blaik. 'Kilburn's musical dynasty,' *Toronto Daily Star*, 17 Mar 1962

1 (Nicholas) **Weldon**. Teacher, pianist, organist, coach, b Lloydminster, Alta, 9 Sep 1906; ATCM 1925, LAB. He studied piano, organ, cello, and voice in Edmonton before moving to Toronto in 1926; he then studied piano and organ at the *TCM with Viggo *Kihl, Norman *Wilks, and Healey *Willan while serving as organist-choirmaster at St Alban's Church and coaching singers. In 1930 he joined the TCM (*RCMT) as a piano teacher. During the 1930s he gave recitals in Toronto. In 1936 he became the voice teacher and accompanist of Lois *Marshall and continued in that capacity until 1971, also recording with her. During the early 1940s he took master classes with E. Robert Schmitz in Denver and San Francisco. Influenced by Schmitz's application of physiology to piano playing, he advocated major changes in the RCMT piano syllabus. In 1960, after an eight-month tour

with Marshall in western Europe, the USSR, and Australia, he left the RCMT to establish his own studio. His voice pupils have included Bob Bossin, Victor *Braun, Constance *Fisher, Glenn Gardiner, Marie-Lynn Hammond, Ilona Kombrink, Phyllis *Mailing, Kathryn McBain Rose, and Welford *Russell; among his piano pupils were Norma *Beecroft, Samuel *Dolin, John *Fenwick, Stuart *Hamilton, Godfrey *Ridout, and Ben *Steinberg. Udo *Kasemets described Kilburn as 'not only an expert accompanist but also possibly the greatest vocal pedagogue this country has produced' (*Toronto Daily Star* 30 Jan 1961). Kilburn's first wife, the mother of his four sons, was the pianist and teacher Marion Wibby (1907–68, LTCM 1930). Lois Marshall was his second wife.

2 **Nicholas** (Weldon). Bassoonist, teacher, b Toronto 21 Jun 1932. At the *RCMT 1948–51 his teachers were Elver Wahlberg (bassoon), Weldon Kilburn (piano), Samuel *Dolin (theory and harmony), and John *Weinzweig (orchestration). He also studied bassoon with Raymond Allard (New England Cons, 1951) and Sol Schoenbach (Curtis Institute, 1952–5). Kilburn was a member 1955–8 of the National Ballet Orchestra and 1955–9 of the *CBC SO. He joined the *TSO as principal bassoon in 1959, becoming co-principal with Christopher *Weait in 1968. His solo performances include the premiere of Dolin's *Isometric Variables* with the *Hart House Orchestra in 1959, the first complete performance of Weinzweig's *Divertimento No. 3* with the CBC SO in 1961, and appearances with the TS in Mozart's *Bassoon Concerto* in 1965 and Haydn's *Sinfonia Concertante, Op 84* in 1978. He has performed in concert and on recordings as a member 1955–70 of the *Toronto Woodwind Quintet. In 1955 he began teaching at the *U of Toronto where his pupils have included Mitchell Clarke, William *Douglas, James McKay, Gordon *Slater, and Norman Tobias. His first wife was the soprano Ilona Kombrink (b St Louis, Mo, 1932), who sang leading roles in the late 1950s and early 1960s with the *COC and the *Stratford Festival and in CBC TV productions of *Tosca* (1958, title role), *Elektra* (1961, Chrysothemis), and *Otello* (1963, Desdemona). She returned to the USA in 1963 and subsequently taught at the U of Wisconsin.

3 **Michael**. Cellist, b Toronto 4 Aug 1934; Artist Diploma (Toronto) 1953. He was a pupil of Cornelius Ysselstyn 1946–53 and Zara *Nelsova (summer 1952) in Toronto and of Leonard Rose (summers 1954–7) at Meadowmount, NY; he played 1956–64 in the *TSO and was a soloist with that orchestra in a 1962 performance of Tchaikovsky's *Variations on a Rococo Theme*. That same year he participated in the Tchaikovsky competition in Moscow and played during the summer in the London SO. He taught 1965–9 at *McGill U and joined the Cons de Trois-Rivières in 1966. He was a member 1966–8 of the *MSO and rejoined that orchestra in 1976.

4 **Paul**. Pianist, teacher, composer, b Toronto 7 Feb 1936; B MUS (Toronto) 1958. His teachers at the TCM (*RCMT) included his father (piano) and Samuel *Dolin (piano, theory, and composition). At the *U of Toronto he studied composition with John *Beckwith and Oskar *Morawetz. In 1976 he took master classes with Karl Ulrich Schnabel at the RCMT. Kilburn began teaching piano and theory privately in Toronto in 1958. His piano compositions, written 1970–2 in the 12-tone idiom, include *Trio for Piano Solo, Reflections on Ice,* and *Sonata,* all premiered (and the sonata recorded) by Antonin *Kubálek. Kilburn performed his own *Five Pieces* on CBC radio's 'Arts National' in 1978.

HCs, MM, PW

KILBY, Muriel (Laura). Pianist, marimbist, composer, b Toronto 5 Nov 1929. She began playing the piano at 7 and a toy marimba at 10. While studying with Hayunga *Carman (piano) and Oskar *Morawetz (composition) at the TCM, she enjoyed a brief career as a concert marimbist, playing works written originally for violin or piano and making her TSO debut 23 Nov 1945 in the first movement of Chopin's *Concerto in E Minor*. She won *CAPAC prizes in 1949, 1950, and 1951 for her songs and piano pieces. Her compositions from this period are listed in the *Catalogue of Canadian Composers*. On scholarships to the Chautauqua Summer School in 1951 and then to the Juilliard School, she studied piano with James Friskin. She made her US radio debut (1951) on the ABC network, playing the Schumann *Piano Concerto*. Continuing to live in the USA, she was staff pianist at the Chautauqua Music Festival (appearing annually with the festival's symphony orchestra) and in 1962 settled in Detroit, where she taught at Mercy College. While in the USA she played Prokofiev's *Concerto No. 2* in Detroit and Chicago, and in 1963 she repeated the work in Canada with the *CBC SO. Her concerto repertoire also included Saint-Saëns' fifth and the Ravel G major. She appeared frequently as a soloist in TSO pop concerts and gave many CBC radio recitals. After her 10th appearance (17 Jan 1960) with the TSO, John *Kraglund (*Globe and Mail*) called Kilby 'technically well-equipped and musically sound' and complimented her on 'precise execution and nicely-rounded tone.' MM

Kilties. See Bands: 6 / Civilian.

KINDNESS, George. Violin maker, b Edinburgh 11 Apr 1888, d Toronto 24 Aug 1968. He apprenticed in Edinburgh and came to Canada in 1911. He worked as a violin builder for *R.S. Williams & Sons in Toronto, then operated his own Bay Street shop 1921–31. He continued building during the 1930s and 1940s, at the same time working as a wood finisher for the Robert Simpson Co. In 1945 his son Robert (b Toronto 26 Jan 1924) joined the business and together they opened a store on Church Street. During his lifetime Kindness built approximately 150 violins, mostly Stradivarius models. Those who owned Kindness violins included Henri Czaplinski and Fred Tobias (member of the TSO 1925–7). Robert Kindness became the head of the firm in 1968, and his son David also joined the staff. No longer builders, George Kindness & Son in 1980 continued to sell and service violins and all stringed instruments. NM

KINES, Tom (Thomas Alvin). Tenor, folklorist, ballad historian, editor, administrator, b Roblin (Manitoba, near the Saskatchewan border) 3 Aug 1922. He sang in public at the age of five and learned many of the folk tunes that his grandfather had picked up in logging camps. As a teenager Kines played drums in local brass, pipe, and dance bands. World War II interrupted his studies at the U of Manitoba, but his interest in performing and researching folk music was kindled while he was serving in the RCN in Northern Ireland. After the war he settled in Ottawa and built up a repertoire ranging from Elizabethan songs and Lieder to songs of Vaughan Williams and folk ballads. He was a founding member of the Tudor Singers of Ottawa (1949–61, proponents of the Elizabethan repertoire) and appeared as a soloist with the *Ottawa Choral Society, the Toronto Bach Society, and (in Gilbert & Sullivan roles) the *Orpheus Operatic Society of Ottawa.

It was as a folksinger, however, that Kines became best known. The NFB composers Maurice *Blackburn, Robert *Fleming, and Eldon *Rathburn and the organist-composer William *France provided him with voice-and-piano settings of folksongs; in recital Kines usually was accompanied by Lilian Forsyth. He appeared in Montreal and at Stratford, Ont, in concert and on CBC radio and performed five or six times at the *Mariposa Folk Festival. In 1958 he appeared on the two CBC TV children's series 'The Song Shop' and 'Magic in Music.' His CBC radio series, 'The Song Pedlar,' was heard intermittently 1959–ca 1970, his 'Folk Fair' (a mixture of recorded and live music) 1977–9. He has appeared also on CTV and NBC TV. He has toured Canada, and in 1961, as a soloist with the *Montreal Bach Choir, he toured Japan. In 1962 he appeared at New York's Town Hall with Alan *Mills, Hélène *Baillargeon, and other Canadians in a Folkways Records presentation of Canadian singers. In the 1960s he gave 32 recitals for the *Saskatchewan Junior Concert Society; in the 1970s he gave 44 for the Eastern Ontario Library Assn. On both tours he accompanied himself on the guitar, lute, autoharp, mountain dulcimer, recorder, or other instrument. Kines wrote the story line and selected the songs for *Prairie Sailor*, a cantata with musical arrangements by Robert Fleming, commissioned by the CBC and premiered as part of the Ottawa CBC Summer Festival in 1970 at the *NAC.

A *Canada Council travel grant enabled Kines to engage in folk music research at Cecil Sharp House in London and to intensify his search for the authentic tunes of Robert Burns' *Merry Muses*, a collection of ballads. His edition of the ballads – the first to include musical notation – remained unpublished in 1980. Another anthology, *Songs from Shakespeare's Plays and Popular Songs of Shakespeare's Time*, was issued in 1964 by Oak Publications.

In 1966 Kines was appointed national director of CARE Canada.

DISCOGRAPHY

Of Maids and Mistresses. (1957). Elektra 137

Songs from Shakespeare's Plays and Popular Songs of Shakespeare's Time. (1961). Folk FW 8767

An Irishman in Americay (sic). (1962). Folk FG 3522

Folk Songs of Canada. (1965). RCA Victor PC 1014

Canadian Folk Songs: A Centennial Collection. Kines et al. (1967). 9-RCI/RCA CS 100

BIBLIOGRAPHY

Meredith, Joan. 'Tom Kines: a new approach to balladry and folk music,' *CanComp*, 60, May 1971 (MH, HK)

KING, John Reymes. Organist, teacher, composer, conductor, b Hinckley, Leicestershire, England, 2 Jul 1910; ARCM, FRCO, FRCCO, BA, B MUS, MA Cantab, PH D (Toronto) 1950. His doctoral thesis, 'An aesthetic and musical analysis of the madrigals of Thomas Morley,' earned him the first PH D in music granted in Canada. He settled in Canada in 1935 and has taught at the *McGill Cons, the *RCMT, and the *U of Alberta in Edmonton (as first occupant of the chair of music, established in 1945). Prior to his years in Canada he taught at Birmingham U, England; subsequent to them (beginning in 1956) he taught at the U of Massachusetts. He has glven lectures at *Queen's U, Kingston, Ont, at Boston U, and at the summer school in Kingston, Jamaica. He has been organist-choirmaster at St James United Church, Montreal, and Knox Church and Metropolitan United Church, Toronto. He wrote several choral pieces (Boston Music) during his stay in Canada. He has glven organ recitals in North America, Europe, and elsewhere and has broadcast for the CBC 1945–6 and for networks in Europe, Australia, and New Zealand. His recordings (organ, choral-orchestral) are on the Allegro label (ALG 3018, 3021, 3027, 3038). MMl

KING BISCUIT BOY or **SON RICHARD** (b Richard Newell). Harmonica player, singer, guitarist, b Hamilton, Ont, 9 Mar 1944. Introduced to the blues by US radio shows, he began playing the harmonica in 1961 and worked 1961–5 with a series of related blues and rock bands – The Barons (Hamilton), Son Richard and the Chessmen (Hamilton and Michigan), and Son Richard and the Gooduns (Germany) – then joined the Midknights (Toronto 1966–7) and Ronnie *Hawkins (Toronto and the USA 1968–70). It was Hawkins who named him King Biscuit Boy after the popular blues program 'King Biscuit Time' on KFFA radio in Arkansas. King Biscuit Boy made his first LP, *Official Music* (Daffodil SBA-16001), and the single 'Corrina, Corrina' in 1970 with Hawkins' former back-up band, And Many Others (see Crowbar). Besides his other LPs, *Gooduns* (1971, Daffodil SBX-16006) and *King Buscuit Boy* (1974, Epic E-32891), he has appeared on recordings by Hawkins, Crowbar, *April Wine, Laurie *Bower, Gary *Buck, Walter Rossi, the US band the Electric Flag, and many others. A rough-voiced blues shouter and a volatile harpist, he performed 1970–1 as a guest with Crowbar and in 1973 with the Full-Tilt Boogie Band and later appeared in clubs and concerts in Canada and the USA with his own band. His and Hawkins' bands joined forces in 1976 and remained together until late 1978. His 'Biscuit's Boogie' has been particularly popular in live performance.

BIBLIOGRAPHY

Yorke, Ritchie. 'Canada's rock invasion,' *Axes, Chops & Hot Licks* (Edmonton 1971) MM

Kingston. City of over 56,000 (1979) at the eastern end of Lake Ontario, founded by Frontenac as Fort Cataraqui in 1673 and later renamed Fort Frontenac. It was captured by the British in 1758 and named Kingston in 1783 by Loyalists fleeing from New York. The first focal point of music in Kingston was St George's (Anglican) Church, which had received a barrel organ before 1800. The barrels were limited in number, however, a fact which caused the minister to comment that the congregation never found it necessary to complain about new hymns (Anderson, p 15). About 1802 a choir of 30 began to sing at the Sunday services, and in 1818 a keyboard organ was donated by the Kingston Patriotic Society. Cultural life revolved around the officers of the garrison, and as early as 1812 the *Gazette* reported a performance of *The Doctor's Courtship*, 'interspersed with vocal and instrumental music,' by the Theatrical Amateur Society of the Gentlemen of the Army and Navy. The regimental band entertained the citizens at parades and concerts and supplied a quadrille section to provide music for balls, dinners, picnics, and charities.

From 1841 to 1844, when its population was about 8000, Kingston was the seat of the Canadian government; in 1841 *Queen's U was founded. During these years the 'limestone city' experienced a building boom, and musical life blossomed. On 13 Sep 1841 the English tenor John Braham gave a 'Grand Concert'; in 1842 the Kingston Vocal Sacred Music Society was active; in 1843 the Kingston Amateur Band gave concerts. Several merchants advertised pianos and other musical wares; one of them was Abraham *Nordheimer, who arrived in 1842 to teach music and who may have been an organizer of the Kingston Harmonic Society in 1844, the year he moved to Toronto. A Philharmonic Society was founded in 1846. There were two theatres and two public halls, and music was taught at several ladies' schools. The growth period was followed by a brief decline, however, and in 1849 the editor of the *British Whig* was lamenting the demise of the Philharmonic Society and the cancellation of the promised Promenade Concerts by the 20th regimental band. However, the visit in 1850 by the Germanians, an orchestra of Berliners, provided some relief.

KINGSTON HARMONIC SOCIETY.

Third Private Concert,

THURSDAY, 7TH MARCH, 1844.

PROGRAMME.

PART 1ST.

OVERTURE—To the Opera of "Il Seraglio," *Mozart.*
GLEE—The Bark before the Gale,......*Sir J. Stevenson.*
SONG—A Life on the Ocean wave,.......*Russel.*
AIR WITH VARIATIONS—Recollections of Mont Blanc,—(Flute and Piano Forte.)
DUETT—Love and the Sun Dial,.......*Sir J. Stevenson.*
SONG—"Woodman, spare that Tree".....*Russel.*
FANTASIA—Selection from Opera of Norma—Violin and Piano Forte........*Bellini.*
FINALE—"Di Felice"—from "Il Barbiere"—(Duett, Piano Forte,)............*Rossini.*

PART 2ND.

OVERTURE—To Il Barbiere di Seviglia,...*Rossini.*
GLEE—"Come to the Old Oak Tree,"....*Divereaux.*
SONG—"Tu Vedrai" (from Il Pirata,)....*Bellini.*
OVERTURE—to Maçon, (Piano Forte, Flute, and Violoncello,)......................*Auber.*
GLEE—Mynheer Van Dunck,.... ......*Bishop.*
SONG—The Sea,............*Chevalier Neukomm.*
OVERTURE—to Norma, (Piano Forte,)....*Bellini.*
CATCH—Old Chairs to mend,............
SONG—The Little Lady,...............
SONATA—with Air Ecossois,............*Pleyel.*
CHORUS—God save the Queen.

In 1862 John C. Fox, from New York, established a piano factory which soon gained a reputation as the largest in Canada at the time. Fox died in 1868, and in the 1870s Weber & Co (*Weber Piano Co) became the city's main instrument manufacturer. Other companies in the 19th century included J. Reyner (reed organs and melodeons) and Wm Wormwith (pianos).

In 1879, three years after the founding of the Royal Military College, Martin's Opera House opened. It was here, in 1889, that one of 19th-century Canada's most successful light operas, *Leo the Royal Cadet*, a 'Canadian military opera' set in the military college, had its first production. The theatre burned down in 1899, but three years later the Grand Opera House (later *Grand Theatre) was erected on its site and became host to such celebrities as Nellie Melba and Ernestine Schumann-Heink and to the D'Oyly Carte Co.

Oscar *Telgmann, the composer of *Leo*, contributed to musical life in Kingston for over 50 years. He and his wife, Alida Jackson, founded the Kingston Cons of Music and School of Elocution in 1892 and continued teaching until the late 1930s. The Telgmann Concert Party, formed in the early 1880s, developed into the Kingston SO (1912–38) (see Kingston Symphony Association). The orchestra was revived by Graham *George in 1953 and later came under the direction of Alexander *Brott.

St George's, which became a cathedral in 1862, developed a sterling musical reputation. After George *Maybee's appointment as organist-choirmaster in 1942 the Gentlemen and Boys of St George's Cathedral came to be considered one of the best 'English' choirs in the world. During a visit to England in August 1954 the choir was the first non-British group to be invited to sing daily in Westminster Abbey, a signal honour. In 1965 the choir was similarly honoured by St Paul's Cathedral, York Minster, and King's College Chapel, Cambridge. In 1974 John Gallienne succeeded Maybee.

Smaller church choirs active in the 1970s included those of Chalmers United under David Cameron, Sydenham United under F.R.C. *Clarke, and St Mary's under Denise Narcisse-Mair. The 100-voice *Kingston Choral Society was founded in 1953 by Graham George, whose contribution to music in Kingston, begun in 1946, has ranged over many fields – university teaching, church music, conducting, and composition.

Other vocal groups have included the Parr Christie Singers, the Gadabouts, the Sweet Adelines (under Olive Higdon), and the Meistersingers. The Kinsmen's Club has produced an annual succession of Broadway musicals.

Queen's U, which started a music degree program in 1969 and opened a music building in 1974, encouraged instrumental music by appointing the *Vaghy String Quartet as artists-in-residence in 1968. The quartet, like the Canadian Wind Quintet, has occupied first desk positions in the Kingston SO. In 1968 the Kingston Youth Orchestra was founded; its directors have been Edouard Bartlett and the composer Clifford Crawley.

Concurrent with the 1976 Olympics in Montreal, Kingston (the site of the Olympic sailing competitions) held an Arts and Culture Festival the musical portion of which featured the Kingston SO, the Kingston Camerata, the Vaghy String Quartet, the Canadian Wind Quintet, and, as visitors, *Camerata, *Canadian Brass, and the Paul Horn Quintet. The *NYO held summer sessions in Kingston 1977–9. Among composers resident in Kingston in 1980 were István *Anhalt, F.R.C. Clarke, Graham George, and David Keane. Kingston is the birthplace of the teacher Katherine Burrowes, H.A. *Dyde, the baritone George MacFarlane, Walter *Murdoch, and Billy *O'Connor.

BIBLIOGRAPHY

Anderson, Allan J. *The Anglican Churches of Kingston* (Kingston 1963)
Spurr, John W. 'Fortress Kingston 1810–1818,' *Historic Kingston*, 17, 1969
Whittingham, Tony. 'Kingston choirs: it's a long story,' Kingston *Whig-Standard*, 22 Mar 1974
Trent, Bill. 'Happy days: keeping out of the rocking chair,' *Weekend Magazine*, 8 Nov 1975
Finnigan, Joan. *Kingston: Celebrate This City* (Toronto 1976) (PB)

Kingston Choral Society. Amateur choir founded in 1953 by Graham *George. The 100-voice ensemble made its debut in Haydn's *The Creation* 12 Apr 1954. After George, directors have been Lloyd Zurbrigg 1957–8 and F.R.C. *Clarke. Appearing with the *Kingston Symphony at Grant Hall (*Queen's U) and the *Grand Theatre, the choir has performed many major works, including Bach's *Mass in B Minor*, Beethoven's *Ninth Symphony*, Elgar's *The Dream of Gerontius*, Vaughan Williams' *A Sea Symphony* and *Flos Campi*, and Orff's *Carmina burana*. On 11 May 1973 it premiered Clarke's *Festival Te Deum*, commissioned by the Kingston Symphony Assn to mark the tercentenary of Kingston. It also performed in 1974 with the *NACO under Mario *Bernardi on 'CBC Tuesday Night.' AHC

The Kingston Symphony Association. The second symphony orchestra formed in *Kingston, Ont. Organized in 1953 as the New Symphony Association of Kingston, it succeeded several short-lived ensembles and the first Kingston SO directed 1912–38 by Oscar *Telgmann. It became the Kingston Symphony Association in 1963. Under its first conductor, Graham *George, it made its debut 12 Apr 1954 at Grant Hall in Haydn's *The Creation* with the *Kingston Choral Society and a team of soloists that included James *Milligan. There were two concerts a year until 1957, but by 1976 the orchestra was presenting six regular, six children's, and two out-of-town concerts. It was conducted by George 1954–7, William Hill 1957–9, Frédéric Pohl (one concert in 1960), and Edouard Bartlett 1960–5. Alexander *Brott, who succeeded Bartlett, developed the orchestra into an important community orchestra of 65 musicians, amateur and professional, including, in the latter category in first-chair positions beginning in 1968, the *Vaghy String Quartet and, beginning in 1974 the Canadian Wind Quintet. The affiliated Kingston Youth Orchestra was formed in 1968 by Bartlett and was conducted later by Clifford Crawley.

BIBLIOGRAPHY
Whalley, George. 'Growth of an orchestra: the Kingston Symphony Orchestra,' *CanComp*, 37, Feb 1969 (AW)

KINLEY, Ethel A. (Adams). Educator, choir conductor, b Gladstone, near Winnipeg, 3 Jan 1887, d Winnipeg 24 Sep 1967. After teaching in Delta and Killarney, Man, she moved to Winnipeg in 1913, then taught in San Bernardino, Cal, while studying music at the U of Southern California. She returned in 1919 to Winnipeg, where she taught music and conducted the choirs at Earl Grey School and 1925–37 at Daniel McIntyre Collegiate. From 1937 until her retirement in 1947 she was supervisor of music in Winnipeg schools. Throughout her career she continued music study with such teachers as George Dodds in England and Burton *Kurth, Winona Lightcap, Bernard *Naylor, and Hugh Ross. An authority on the voice change in males, she founded (1925) and conducted the Winnipeg Boys' Choir under the aegis of the Winnipeg *Men's Musical Club and also conducted the Junior Men's and Young Women's Musical Club choirs. She compiled the *Manitoba School Song Book* (Toronto 1940), *Sing Hey Ho! A Songbook for Canadian Boys and Girls* (Toronto 1951), and *Fundamentals for Singers* (Toronto 1953). Young musicians who came under her influence and later went on to high accomplishment included Beth *Douglas, Chester *Duncan, Frederick *Grinke, Glen *Harrison, Lola *MacQuarrie, David *Martin, Glen *Pierce, and Ross *Pratt.

See also School music; School music broadcasts.

BIBLIOGRAPHY
Douglas, Beth. 'Miss Ethel Kinley,' *Sharps & Flats*, vol 6, Nov 1965 (RG)

Kitchener and Waterloo. Twin cities in southwestern Ontario. In both, a significant proportion of the population has always been of German and Mennonite stock. Kitchener, the larger of the two cities, was called Ebytown until 1824 and Berlin until 1916. It was settled in 1807 and became a city in 1912; Waterloo was settled is 1806 but became a city only in 1948. The combined populations reached about 178,500 in 1979. Industrial enterprises and insurance companies are major employers, and there are two universities, the *U of Waterloo and *Wilfrid Laurier U (also in Waterloo). Conrad Grebel College is an affiliate of the former and shares its campus.

Choral singing was cultivated in the early days in both communities. *Singing schools were established and choral societies sprang up in their wake. One of the first was the United Male Singing Society of Berlin, Bridgeport, and Waterloo, formed in 1853 under J. Biedermann. An athletic club, the Turnverein of Waterloo, organized twice-weekly singing sessions in 1861. The following year Berlin was host to the first of many subsequent *Sängerfeste (singing festivals; see list in entry) which featured competitions as well as performances by massed choirs and small vocal groups, bands, and instrumental soloists. Another memorable celebration was the Friedensfest (peace festival) at the end of the Franco-Prussian War in 1871. Among the choral groups were three male choirs: the Liedertafel of Waterloo, formed in 1865, the Orpheus Singing Society of Waterloo, formed in 1866, and the Sängerbund of Berlin, organized in 1883. The last two were conducted by Theodor *Zoellner, who had arrived from Germany as a child and who became the leading musical figure in the community. Zoellner also conducted the Harmony, an 1894 amalgamation of the Liedertafel and the Orpheus Society, and the Berlin Philharmonic Society, established in 1883 and dedicated to the presentation of oratorios.

Brass bands had gained popularity in Berlin and Waterloo by the middle of the 19th century. One of the first was the Berlin Band under a Mr Kelk. The Berlin Music Band, organized by Heinrich Glebe in 1859, received a grant of $100 from the town council in 1863. Another band was formed by William Kaiser, but the two merged in the mid-1860s to form the Berlin Musical Society under Kaiser. Reed instruments were added ca 1875, and the band was chosen in 1877 as the band of the 29th Waterloo Battalion of Infantry. According to contemporary records the Berlin Musical Society had at its disposal 22 players and a quadrille band of six. Of its various bandmasters in the course of the years, Noah *Zeller was the most outstanding. Between two terms as leader of the band, Zeller was the founder and conductor 1881–1900 of the *Waterloo Musical Society.

The anti-German sentiment aroused by World War I not only led to the name change from Berlin to Kitchener but also resulted in the eclipse of the German singing societies and the Sängerfeste. A new Orpheus Male Choir emerged ca 1917 and the *Kitchener-Waterloo Philharmonic Choir, formed in 1922 by J.L. Yule, eventually grew into a large oratorio choir. The Schneider Men's Chorus, formed in 1938 of employees of the J.M. Schneider Meat Packing Co, merged with the Orpheus Male Choir in 1947 to become the Schneider Orpheus Male Chorus, later the Schneider Male Chorus. Paul Berg, its director 1942–75, was succeeded by Fred E. Lehman. In 1965 the choir appeared in Hamilton, Bermuda, and in 1972 it performed in Vancouver and other cities on a cross-Canada tour. In 1952, 1954, and 1957 it was host to the Big Sing, a series of international male-choral festivals which revived the tradition of the Sängerfest.

In 1955 as part of Kitchener's centennial celebrations the city organized its first full-fledged Sängerfest in more than 50 years, and in 1969 and 1970 Alfred *Kunz co-ordinated two more. Kunz had organized the Kitchener-Waterloo Chamber Choir in 1959 and had become conductor of the Germania Male Choir in 1962 and the Concordia Male and Mixed Choirs in 1968, and Master-of-all-choirs for the German-Canadian Choir Assn in 1968. Douglas *Haas founded another chamber choir – the Kitchener Bach Choir – in 1968 and conducted it until 1972 when he was succeeded by Howard Dyck. Other choral groups active in the 1970s have included the Menno Singers, founded and directed by Abner Martin and later directed by Jan *Overduin, the Inter-Mennonite Children's Choir, directed by Helen *Martens, and several barbershop groups. The Menno Singers joined other choirs from southwest Ontario in 1975 to form the Mennonite Mass Choir, which has presented several oratorios including Haydn's *The Creation*.

A major influence in the area of bands and music festivals was Charles F. *Thiele, who moved to Waterloo in 1919 and was director 1919–50 of the Waterloo Musical Society's band. He founded the *Waterloo Music Co in 1920, served as the first president of the Ontario Band Assn, in 1931 helped organize the Canadian Bandmasters' Assn (serving also as first president, see CBDA), and in 1932 organized the *Waterloo Band Festival, held annually 1932–40 and 1946–58 in Waterloo Park under the auspices of the Waterloo Musical Society. In 1946 Thiele founded the Waterloo Music Camp for Boys, calling it 'Bandberg.'

George *Ziegler, director 1925–32 of a 94-member Ladies' Band, also contributed to the intensity of band activity in Kitchener. He served 1924–67 as the conductor of the Kitchener Musical Society Band. This band, known in 1980 as the Kitchener Concert Band, was led by a variety of conductors after 1967, including Arthur Freund.

After World War I orchestras gradually attained the continuity and prominence that for years had been the province of bands. During the 1920s James Galloway conducted a small orchestra in Kitchener. In 1944 Glenn Kruspe, C.F. Thiele, and the percussionist Archie Bernhardt founded the *Kitchener-Waterloo SO, whose first concert was given with the Kitchener-Waterloo Philharmonic Choir in April 1945 at Kitchener's Lyric Theatre.

Raffi *Armenian, who became conductor of the Kitchener-Waterloo SO in 1971, formed the full-time, 13-member Stratford Ensemble in 1974 to serve the *Stratford Festival as a theatre orchestra, the Kitchener-Waterloo region as a chamber orchestra, and the Kitchener-Waterloo SO as a regular nucleus. The ensemble also strengthened the Kitchener-Waterloo Chamber Music Society. (Nathaniel Stroh had formed that organization in 1947.) Armenian also served 1976–9 as conductor of the affiliated Kitchener-Waterloo Junior SO led in 1975 by Stuart Knussen. Louis Lavigueur assumed the direction of the Youth orchestra in 1979.

In 1971 the Centre Opera Studio began presenting concert versions and stage productions of operas, conducted either by Armenian or by Jacqueline *Richard, with the Kitchener-Waterloo SO and visiting soloists. The works presented in concert versions were *The Tales of Hoffmann* (1971), *La Traviata* (1972), *Carmen* (1973), *La Bohème* (1974), *Don Giovanni* (1975), *Rigoletto* (1976), and *Hansel and Gretel* (1977). Staged were Monteverdi's *Il Combattimento di Tancredi e Clorinda* (1977), *Gianni Schicchi* (1977), and *The Rape of Lucretia* (1978).

A branch of the Gilbert & Sullivan Society was formed in 1959, and Kitchener Musical Productions staged a major musical each season. Concert life has been enriched by the Kitchener-Waterloo *Community Concerts, the U of Waterloo's Performing Arts Series concerts, the Kitchener Public Library concerts and recitals, the Canadian-German Society recitals, and Wilfrid Laurier U's Dept of Music noon-hour recitals. A multi-purpose hall, The Centre in the Square, opened in Kitchener in September 1980.

Music education in Kitchener-Waterloo extends back to the time of the early choral societies. Theodor Zoellner served 1897–1922 as singing master in the public school system and at St Jerome's College. George Ziegler founded the Ziegler Associated Studios in 1911. These became the Berlin Cons in 1913 and the *Kitchener Cons in 1916, and survived until 1974, when Ziegler retired. J.L. Yule, who in 1922 succeeded Zoellner as supervisor of school music, was succeeded in

1928 by Harry *Hill. The Dept of Music at Wilfrid Laurier U, formed in 1967, became a Faculty of Music in 1975.

Kitchener has been the location of several music businesses. In the late 1890s Frederick Schneider, J.M. Staebler, and others financed the Berlin Piano Co, which during its peak years turned out 20 instruments each week and employed 100 workers. Around 1906 the shareholders sold the firm to the *Nordheimer Piano Co of Toronto, which, as representative of the US firm Foster-Armstrong, turned out pianos bearing this name at the Berlin plant. Other names used were Marshall & Wendell and Haines Bros. The Berlin Piano Co closed in 1929. *Hallman Organs were built in Kitchener 1941–77. The Waterloo Music Co, besides manufacturing music stands, has imported and published music, imported and repaired instruments, and produced recordings.

Musicians born in or near Kitchener-Waterloo have included Joseph W. *Baumann, Carlo Boehmer (see Italy: 4 / Canadians in Italy), Beverley *Cavanagh, Douglas Haas, Art *Hallman, Herbert Arthur *Jeffrey, Mari-Elizabeth *Morgen, A.S. *Vogt, Robert *Witmer, and George Ziegler.

See also Germany; Mennonites.

BIBLIOGRAPHY

Staebler, H.L. 'Random notes on music of nineteenth century Berlin, Ontario,' *37th Annual Report of the Waterloo Historical Society* (Waterloo 1949)

Eby, Ezra, and Snyder, Joseph. *A Biographical History of Early Settlers and Their Descendants in Waterloo Township*, ed Eldon D. Weber (Kitchener 1971) (JCm)

Kitchener Conservatory of Music. Founded in Berlin, Ont, in 1911 by George *Ziegler, as the Ziegler Associated Studios. It became the Berlin Cons in 1913 and, reflecting the new name of the city, the Kitchener Cons in 1916. Instruction was offered in piano, orchestra and band instruments, voice, guitar, theory, and elocution. The conservatory, which had by 1950 a staff of 21 and at one time as many as 700 students, closed when Ziegler retired in 1974. In the early years Ziegler directed the Berlin Cons Chorus of 124 voices and an orchestra of 54 students and teachers. Over the years many concerts were presented, ranging from conventional solo recitals to such rarities as a six-piano–12-player ensemble. JCm

The Kitchener-Waterloo Philharmonic Choir. Conceived by the Kitchener Music Club as part of a plan in which public school music instruction and choral training would lead to participation in a community choir under the same director. It was founded in 1922 and directed 1922–8 by J.L. Yule and 1928–41 by Harry *Hill, both school music supervisors. Besides standard part-songs, the repertoire included such works as Alfred Gaul's *Joan of Arc*, performed in 1927. The choir won regularly at competition festivals and by World War II had grown to 100 voices. It sustained local interest during the war years with its 'Olde Tyme' concerts, which incorporated topical satire and popular ballads. Under the direction 1941–60 of Glenn Kruspe the choir grew, became the principal oratorio ensemble of the region, and in 1944 developed an accompanying orchestra, which was to become the *Kitchener-Waterloo SO. In the 1950s the choir engaged such rising young soloists as Lois *Marshall, Jon *Vickers, and James *Milligan and introduced works by Britten, Schoenberg, and *Schafer. After Kruspe, its directors were Frédéric Pohl 1960–2, Donald Landry 1962–6, and Walter H. *Kemp 1966–72. Howard Dyck succeeded Kemp in 1972. The choir participated in the concert marking the inauguration of the Centre in the Square in September 1980 in Kitchener. WHK

Kitchener-Waterloo Symphony Orchestra. Founded in 1944, to accompany the *Kitchener-Waterloo Philharmonic Choir, by Glenn Kruspe (the choir's conductor 1941–60), Charles *Thiele, and the percussionist Archie Bernhardt. Choir and orchestra first performed together 17 Apr 1945 at Kitchener's Queen Street Auditorium. The first orchestral concert followed 21 Oct 1945 at Kitchener's Lyric Theatre, and the program included the Grieg *Concerto* with Ada B. Eby as soloist. Kruspe – b Tavistock, near Stratford, Ont, 25 Jan 1909; ATCM 1931, ARCM 1935, B MUS (Toronto) 1940, D MUS (Toronto) 1949 – studied at the TCM with George Veary, at the RCM with Percy Buck, Ernest Bullock, and Charles Kitson, and at the U of Toronto with Charles *Peaker and Healey *Willan and was organist-choirmaster 1934–9 at Zion United Church. After 16 years as conductor of the Kitchener-Waterloo SO he was succeeded by Frédéric Pohl (b Strasbourg 17 Mar 1898, d Kitchener 13 Apr 1979), a violinist who moved to Canada in 1958 after playing in and conducting opera orchestras and training opera choirs in Strasbourg and Lyons. During Pohl's term, 1960–70, the 65-piece orchestra performed at the Capitol Theatre and at Kitchener Collegiate. A Kitchener-Waterloo Junior SO (later renamed the Kitchener-Waterloo Youth Orchestra) was formed in 1967 and performed under the senior orchestra conductor.

Raffi *Armenian succeeded Pohl as music director in 1971 after a 'search year' of guest conductors. In 1972 the orchestra moved for its concerts to the Humanities Theatre at the *U of Waterloo. In 1974 Armenian formed the 13-member Stratford Festival Ensemble which, in addition to festival duties, functioned as the professional core of the orchestra. (When the ensemble was dissociated from the festival in 1976, changing its name to the Stratford Ensemble, it continued under 48-week contract as the nucleus and chamber music arm of the Kitchener-Waterloo SO and as a hire-ensemble under the orchestra's management. In 1980 it changed its name again, becoming the Canadian Chamber Ensemble. The ensemble was Maureen *Forrester's accompanist in a 1978 recording of music by Ravel and Wolf.)

During the 1976–7 season the orchestra presented three series of symphony concerts besides a pop series, four Oktoberfest concerts, and many educational concerts. In the early 1970s it began to program music by Canadian composers (eg, *Applebaum, *Beckwith, *Somers, *Schafer) and concert versions of operas (*La Traviata*, 1971; *Carmen* with Maureen Forrester, 1972; *La Bohème*, 1973; *Fidelio*, 1975; *Don Giovanni*, 1976) and to present outstanding Canadian soloists (eg, Gisela *Depkat, Raymond *Dudley, Anton *Kuerti, and Jan *Rubeš). The orchestra also accompanied productions of the Centre Opera Studio (founded Waterloo, 1977). In the 1977–8 season it participated in four such productions: *Hansel and Gretel*, *La Bohème*, *Così fan tutte*, and *The Rape of Lucretia*, of which the last-named was presented as part of the orchestra's regular symphony series. In 1980 the orchestra began performing in its new home, the Centre in the Square.

See also Kitchener and Waterloo.

BIBLIOGRAPHY

'Kitchener-Waterloo Symphony ... ' *CanComp*, 23, Nov 1967

Edds, Jack. 'See what the black walnut produced,' *OCan*, vol 4, Sep 1977 (SS)

Kitsilano Boys' Band. Vancouver concert band founded in 1928 and conducted solely by Arthur W. *Delamont. It held its first rehearsals at General Gordon School and made its debut in 1928 playing 'O Canada' to welcome the Olympic gold medallist Percy Williams to Vancouver. Members ranged in age from about 13 to 18 and numbered from 40 to 70 brass, reeds, and percussion. The repertoire encompassed a wide variety of material, from symphonic overtures arranged for concert band to medleys from Broadway musicals. The band performed in Great Britain, Holland, Germany, and the USA. On several trips to England it was billed as the Vancouver Boys' Band. In 1962 it performed in the USSR. The band gave freely of its time to many causes, especially during World War II, when it raised funds for the Victory Loan campaign and for the Red Cross. It enjoyed considerable critical acclaim and received over 200 awards in competition. In the mid–1930s the band recorded Sousa marches and other music in England for the Bluebird and Regal Zonophone labels. By the late 1970s its activities were reduced to an occasional rehearsal, though concerts in which current members were joined by past members were organized in 1975 and 1978. At the latter over 300 musicians participated. Delamont was responsible for the training of the boys and gave many the grounding for a professional career. Among the KBB alumni are Bob Buckley, Don Clark (*Pacific Salt), Arnie Chycoski, Ron *Collier, Gordon *Delamont, Bobby *Gimby, Ted Lazenby (*Vancouver SO), Marek Norman, Dal *Richards, Bernard Temoin (*TS), and Bill Trussell. The Arthur W. Delamont Concert Band, formed in 1976, has included many former KBB musicians.

BIBLIOGRAPHY

Daniels, Alan. 'At 86, Arthur still loves to face the music,' *Vancouver Sun*, 28 Jan 1978

Dykk, Lloyd. 'Goodbye and welcome back, Arthur Delamont,' ibid, 6 Feb 1978 BNSG

Kiwanis festivals. Competition festivals sponsored by Canadian branches of the international Kiwanis Service Clubs founded in the USA in 1915 and in Canada in 1917. The impetus for involvement in festivals came in 1943, when the Toronto Kiwanian George W. Peacock, inspired by the success of competition festivals in western Canada, suggested that Kiwanis might foster greater public interest in music through the establishment of similar festivals. This sentiment was endorsed by Sir Ernest *MacMillan, who challenged the Kiwanis Clubs to become involved in the musical life of Toronto. An organizational committee was formed in 1943 with Peacock as chairman. Gordon V. *Thompson was among the committee's members.

The first Canadian Kiwanis Festival was held 7–16 Feb 1944 in Toronto's *Eaton Auditorium. Adjudicators included Arthur *Collingwood, Bernard *Naylor, Charles *O'Neill, and Max *Pirani. W.B. Rothwell became the festival's first director. Approximately 7000 competed, and among the winners was the 10-year-old pianist Glenn *Gould.

Kiwanis clubs in other parts of Canada began to organize their own festivals shortly thereafter, or in some instances assumed responsibility for well-established existing festivals (eg, Edmonton, Stratford, Calgary, Vancouver). By 1980 the organization was responsible for 30 annual competitions throughout Canada: 20 in Ontario, 5 in Alberta (including Calgary, Edmonton, and Lethbridge), 2 in Nova Scotia (Halifax and Sydney), 2 in Newfoundland (St John's and Grand Falls), and 1 in British Columbia (Vancouver). All were members of the *FCMF. The Kiwanis Music Festival of Greater Toronto remained the largest in 1979, with 35,000 participants.

Performance categories at festivals include solo voices and instruments, choral and instrumental ensembles, bands and orchestras; many also include speech. The ages of participants may range from 4 or 5 to over 30, mostly students at all levels and amateurs. Most Kiwanis festivals attract local performers only, though some draw competitors from other provinces or even other countries. The choice of adjudicators (chiefly Canadian, US, and British) lies with the individual organizing body but usually has been made in co-ordination with the FCMF. Kiwanis festivals have offered a variety of scholarships and trophies (ie, rosebowls, silver trays, etc), determined by available funds. Some festivals have only one sponsoring Kiwanis club, while others in large centres may have 5, 10, or more branches contributing support. It has been the custom for a festival to present a special concert by a selection of its winners following the conclusion of the competition.

Noted Canadian performers who have been among the winning participants in Kiwanis festivals include Derek Bampton, the *Barrie Central Collegiate Band, Jean *Bonhomme, Maurice *Brown, Lynn Channing, Jane *Coop, Andrew *Dawes, Mary Lou *Fallis, Judith *Forst, Don *Garrard, Angela *Hewitt, Gerald Jarvis, Allan *Monk, Mari-Elizabeth *Morgen, Kenneth Perkins, Karen Quinton, Catherine *Robbin, Guillermo Silva-Marin, Annon Lee *Silver, Lilian *Sukis, Caralyn Tomlin, Sylvia Fricker *Tyson, Alan Woodrow, and Jeannette *Zarou. (NM)

'K-K-K-Katy.' Comic song, with words and music by Geoffrey *O'Hara. It was written in Kingston, Ont, and became one of the most popular songs of the World War I era, especially among the troops. Published 16 Mar 1918 by Leo Feist with the subtitle 'The Stammering Song,' it sold over a million copies and was recorded with great success that same year for Victor (18455) by the US tenor Billy Murray. Several other recordings of 'K-K-K-Katy' from the 1920s are listed in *Roll Back the Years*. In 1940 the song was revived by Jack Oakie in the movie *Tin Pan Alley*.

KLEIN, Lothar. Composer, administrator, b Hanover, Germany, 27 Jan 1932; BA (Minnesota) 1954, PH D (Minnesota) 1961. He studied composition with Paul Fetler at the U of Minnesota, orchestration privately 1956–8 with Antal Dorati, and composition in 1956 with Goffredo Petrassi at Tanglewood and on a Fulbright Fellowship 1958–60 with Josef Rufer and Boris Blacher in Berlin and Luigi Nono in Darmstadt. He taught at the Hochschule für Musik (as assistant to Blacher 1958–60) and at the universities of Minnesota 1962–4 and Texas 1964–8 before joining the Faculty of Music at the *U of Toronto in 1968. He became chairman of the faculty's graduate department in 1971. Klein's compositions, which have won Rockefeller New Music prizes (1965 and 1967) and the Greenwood Choral Prize (1968, for *Three Chinese Laments*), reflect influences as disparate as Varèse (*Symmetries for Orchestra*) and jazz (*Musique à Go-Go*). He has contributed many articles to journals in the US and Canada. He is a member of the *CLComp, an associate of the *CMCentre, and a member of ASCAP.

SELECTED COMPOSITIONS

Symmetries for Orchestra. 1958. Large orch. Presser 1972

Musique à Go-Go. 1966. Orch. Presser 1972

Three Chinese Laments (Chinese Book of Songs, transl Robert Payne). 1968. SATB. Presser 1968

Eroica 'Variations on a Promethean Theme.' 1970. Band. Ms

Passacaglia for the Zodiac. 1971. Str orch. CMCentre

Music for Violin and Orchestra. 1972. Vn, chamb orch. CMCentre

Six Exchanges. 1972. Sax. CMCentre; Tritone-Tenuto Publications 1972. Golden Crest RE 7056 (*Brodie)

Masque of Oriana. 1973. Orch. CMCentre

The Philosopher in the Kitchen (Brillat-Savarin). 1974. V, orch. CMCentre

Invention, Blues and Chase. 1975. Accord, str orch. CMCentre

Musica antiqua. 1975. Consort, orch. CMCentre

Orpheus (classical authors). 1976. Sop, ten, narr, SATB chorus, various instr. CMCentre

Voices of Earth (traditional, A. Lampman, R.L. Stevenson, J. von Eichendorf, R. Herrick). 1976. Sop, children's chorus, orch. CMCentre

Three Reflections (St Teresa, transl Longfellow, R. Herrick, Bhartrihari-Sanskrit). 1977. SATB. CMCentre

Fanfares for Orchestra. 1978. Orch. CMCentre

Numerous other works including 3 early ballets, several works for orch, chamb ens, many for choir, voice. See *Contemporary Canadian Composers*.

WRITINGS

'The ISCM festival at Hamburg,' *CanComp*, 42, Sep 1969

'Stravinsky's poetics: music and life style,' *CAUSM J*, vol 2, Fall 1972

'Stravinsky and opera: parable as ethic,' *CMB*, 4, Spring–Summer 1972 CF

KLINGENFELD, Heinrich. Violinist, conductor, educator, b Nuremberg, 19 May 1856, d 19?. He studied with Ludwig Abel and Benno Walter in Munich and 1882–4 with Adolf Brodsky at the Leipzig Cons. He played in the Gewandhaus and Bayreuth Festival orchestras and made solo tours in Germany, Sweden, and Denmark. He moved to Canada in 1885 and taught at the Halifax Cons (*Maritime Cons of Music). He enlarged the Haydn Quintette Club to present a number of orchestral concerts. With the pianist Charles *Porter and the cellist Ernst Doering he formed the Leipzig Trio ca 1890. Klingenfeld joined the staff of the *Toronto College of Music in 1893, performed as a soloist with the Toronto Orchestra, and began teaching at the Metropolitan Cons in 1894. Ysaÿe endorsed his treatise on violin training published in 1894 in Europe as *Méthode élémentaire* and in 1900 by Breitkopf, New York, as *The Elements of Violin Playing*. Klingenfeld gave recitals alone and with his wife, the US-born singer Marie Klingenfeld, and was a member of the College Trio (with J. Lewis Browne, piano, and Paul *Hahn, cello) and the Beethoven Trio (with H.M. *Field, piano, and Rudolf Ruth, cello). He organized Klingenfeld's Orchestra, which gave its first concert 2 Apr 1895 and remained active for at least two years. He also taught 1895–9 in Toronto, at the *Metropolitan School of Music, St Joseph's Convent, Loretto Abbey, and Havergal College. In 1900 he established the Klingenfeld College (later Cons of Music) in Brooklyn, NY. His wife, who also taught, became principal of this conservatory in 1903. However Klingenfeld appears to have divided his time between Toronto and Brooklyn. He returned to Toronto to teach, first at the Metropolitan School of Music in 1901, then at the *TCM 1902–5. He also organized the Klingenfeld String Quartette (1901–5 with William Beardmore, second violin, J.S. Loudon, viola, and Paul Hahn, cello, by 1903 replaced by Jas O. Close, violin, Frank C. Smith, viola, and H.S. Saunders, cello). Klingenfeld wrote *Violaschule für Violinisten*, published by Breitkopf in Germany and England. EK

Klondike (also spelled Klondyke). The name is derived from a Kutchin Indian word, *thron-duick* (hammer river), and identifies a town, a river, and a range of hills in the Yukon. It also is used colloquially (as 'the Klondike') to describe the 'placer' area around what became Dawson City, where gold could be panned. This was the site of the great 1896 gold rush which inspired literature (see *Oxford Companion to Canadian History and Literature*, Toronto 1967) and, to a lesser extent, music. The gold rush gave rise to such songs as 'Rush to the Klondike' (1897, by W.T. Diefenbaker, father of Canada's 14th prime minister, John G. Diefenbaker), 'I've Got the Klondike Fever' (1898, music by Dr A.L. Shanks and words by Lance Grill), and 'La Chanson du Klondyke' (1920s, by Conrad *Gauthier), and to 'The Klondike Gold Rush' (recorded as a folksong by Charles *Jordan).

In his book *Klondike: The Life and Death of the Last Great Goldrush* (Toronto 1958, rev 1972) Pierre Berton refers to drinking songs about personalities of the day (eg, the 'George Cormack Song') and to a Tin Pan Alley ballad, 'He's Sleeping in a Klondike Vale Tonight' (verses from the *New York Journal*), a Cockney ditty, 'Klondyke' (first published in England's *Daily Chronicle*), and the song 'Ho for the Klondyke, Ho.' Piano pieces include *Klondyke Lancers* (1897) by J. Stanton Gladwin, *The Klondike Waltz* (1898) by Édouard Célestin-Lemieux, *Klondyke* (1897) by O.F. *Telgmann, and *The Klondyke* (1897) by B.J. Winkup.

With the resurgence of Klondike nostalgia spurred by the Berton book, several musicals were written. *Foxy*, a US creation based on *Volpone* but set in the Klondike, with music by the Canadian expatriate Robert Emmett Dolan, was premiered 2 Jul 1962 at the Palace Grand Theatre during the Dawson City Gold Rush Festival and played 16 Feb–18 Apr 1964 at the Ziegfeld Theater on Broadway. *Klondyke*, by Jacques Languirand (book) and Gabriel *Charpentier (music), was premiered 14 Feb 1965 by Le Théâtre du Nouveau-Monde at the *Orpheum Theatre in Montreal and was presented also in 1965 in London at the Commonwealth Festival of the Arts and at the Old Vic Theatre. Other musicals include *In the Klondike*, written by Dolores *Claman, Richard Morris, and Michael Leighton after the works of Robert Service and produced on CBC TV in April 1967; *Paradise Hill* (words and music by Pierre Berton), which opened 3 Jul 1967 for one season at the *Charlottetown Festival; *Klondike Kate*, the story of Kathleen Rockwell, written by Tommy *Banks (music), Al Oster (lyrics), and Colin McLean (book) and heard 6 Oct 1968 on CBC radio; and *Jack of Diamonds* by Phil Schreibman, a 'musical medicine show' set in the Klondike, produced in 1977 at the New Theatre, Toronto.

Al Oster recorded several songs about the Klondike, including *'When the Ice Worms Nest Again' (on the LP *The Yukon Stars*, 1967, RCI 262), and various artists recorded *Yukon and Other Songs of the Klondike* (1973, Stamp ST 3-5). Some songs from earlier gold rushes in Canada are collected in James Anderson's pamphlet *Sawney's Letters and Cariboo Rhymes* (Barkerville, BC, 1869, reprinted 1962). None of these, however, has become traditional. (EF, FH, MM)

KLYMASZ, Robert (Bogden). Folklorist, b Toronto 14 May 1936; BA Russian (Toronto) 1957, MA Slavic Studies (Manitoba) 1960, PH D (Indiana) 1971. A specialist in Ukrainian folk traditions, Klymasz served 1967–76 as head, and later as senior co-ordinator, of the Slavic and Eastern European Program of the Canadian Centre for Folk Culture Studies of the *National Museum of Man in Ottawa. He mounted several exhibits and collaborated on filmed documentaries for the museum. He has taught briefly at Harvard U, the *U of Manitoba, and the *U of Ottawa. In 1976 he became the executive director of the Ukrainian Cultural and Educational Centre in Winnipeg. Between 1959 and 1977 he contributed over 25 articles and more than 20 reviews, many dealing with Ukrainian-Canadian music and customs, to *Folklore and Folk Music Archivist*, *Ethnomusicology*, *Journal of the Folklore Institute*, and *EMC*. In 1975 he was one of the founders of the Folklore Studies Assn of Canada.

WRITINGS

'Field work in the Canadian prairie provinces,' *J of the Soc for Ethnomusicology*, vol 10, 1966

'An introduction to the Folklore Division of the National Museum of Canada, Ottawa,' *Folklore and Folk Music Archivist*, vol 10, 1967

See also Bibliography for Ukraine. (GKG)

KNEY, Gabriel. Pipe organ builder, b Speyer, Germany, ca 1930. After an apprenticeship with Paul Sattel in Speyer and four years as assistant to Franz Nagel, Kney moved to London, Ont, in 1951, working as a builder and voicer for the *Keates Organ Co. In 1955 with John Bright he co-founded the Kney and Bright Organ Co in Acton, Ont, to build tracker-action instruments. Their 'Opus 1,' a five-stop positive organ, spearhead of the tracker revival in Canada, was reviewed favourably in J.E. Blanton's *The Organ in Church Design* (Albany, Texas 1967) but found no purchaser. Opus 2 to Opus 31 were built with electro-pneumatic action, but Opus 32 and subsequent instruments had tracker actions. The company installed organs in Toronto and Brantford churches and, in the early 1960s, rebuilt those in London's Aeolian Hall and Toronto's St Michael's Cathedral. Kney founded Gabriel Kney and Co in 1967 in London, Ont, and by 1976 had built over 50 tracker-action instruments for clients in Ontario and the USA. In 1979 Gabriel Kney and Co were contracted to build the pipe organ for the new *Massey Hall, scheduled for completion in 1982.

AB, MG

Kodály method. Name casually applied to a number of related systems of interval recognition and sight-singing using the folk music of a country, all issuing from the concept developed for schools in Hungary by the composer Zoltán Kodály. In 1964 Richard *Johnston, at the time director of the *RCMT Summer School, became the first representative of a Canadian institution to visit Budapest for first-hand information on the concept. The following year Ann Osborn gave a pilot course for teachers at the summer school. In July 1965 at the invitation of the U of Montreal, Erzsébet Szönyi, assistant to Kodály in Budapest, presented a series of introductory courses at the *École normale de musique. With subsidies from the OISE, Johnston and Harvey *Perrin circulated their observations on the Kodály method following a sojourn in Hungary in 1966. In July of that year Kodály himself visited Toronto to receive an honorary doctorate from the *U of Toronto, to deliver the 1966 CAPAC-MacMillan lectures, and to observe the introduction of the Kodály concept to the RCMT Summer School through choral sight-singing and rhythmic-interpretation courses. Ann Osborn, who supervised the courses that year, subsequently spent three years in Hungary in further study of the Kodály concept and its applications. The summer school continued to offer Kodály courses by a number of guests, including the Hungarian educators Katalin Forrai, who specialized in the teaching of pre-school children, and Ilona Bartalus, who taught for several years at the *U of Western Ontario.

Jacquotte Ribière-Raverlat, a French educator who was responsible for an authorized French adaptation of the Kodály principles, headed an experimental venture in the province of Quebec in 1967. This consisted of training courses for teachers, supervision of student teachers, and later a pilot project at the elementary level at the Villa-Maria Convent in Montreal. The project began in 1970 and consisted of a daily period of music instruction along the Kodály principles but adapted to French and Quebec folklore. In 1973 a specialist from Budapest, Miklos Takacs, continued Ribière-Raverlat's work by adding an integrated choral dimension.

English-speaking training centres at various educational levels developed in Halifax, Vancouver, Toronto, and Ottawa, as well as at *McGill U starting in 1969. The US educator Mary Helen Richards, who has published her own variants of the Kodály procedures, has given workshops in the Windsor, Ont, area. During the 1969–70 season Mary *Syme adapted the Kodály ideas for a series of CBC school broadcasts. The fourth program, 'Rhythm Patterns,' won an Ohio State Award. Thomas *Legrady's French-Canadian adaptation of the Kodály concept, for use by teachers and their pupils, is published in the four-volume *Lisons la musique* (Ottawa 1967, Montreal 1970). Harvey Perrin was general editor and one of the authors of an English-Canadian adaptation, *The New Approach to Music*, published in two volumes (Toronto 1969, 1972).

A bilingual professional association, the Kodály Institute of Canada, was founded in 1973 with Mae Daly as executive director and its head office in Ottawa. This organization, of which Gordon *Kushner was president until 1979, when he was succeeded by Kenneth *Bray, has devoted itself to ensuring the diffusion and promotion of the authentic Kodály concept. To this end the magazine *Notes* began quarterly publication in 1976. In 1973 the first international Kodály symposium, held in Oakland, Cal, was attended by Canadian delegates, including Sister Marcelle *Corneille and Kaye *Dimock. The latter was secretary of the institute 1973–7. Subsequent symposia have been held in Kecskemét, Hungary, in 1975, in Wolfville, NS, in 1977, and in Australia in 1979.

The Kodály concept is founded on the folk music of the country and on a type of movable-doh solmization, the latter consisting of the awareness of a relationship (soh-me, for example) which the ear recognizes because it has heard it in one or several songs without knowing the nature of this relationship. The child learns to read it at the same time, and each time he sees this arrangement of the two notes on the staff, he associates what he hears with it and thus is able to sing it. Kodály advocated starting with the pentatonic scale, considering the diatonic scale too difficult for small children. Teaching on Kodály principles in Quebec schools is based on the 1000 French-language folksongs collected in the two volumes of Jacquotte Ribière-Raverlat, *Un Chemin pédagogique en passant par les chansons* (Paris 1974, 1976). Each of these books includes a teacher's guide and a workbook for the student, *Chant-Musique*. An English version of Erzsébet Szönyi's book (Budapest 1956), including four volumes for the student with teacher's guides, has been published by Boosey & Hawkes under the title *Musical Reading and Writing* (Budapest 1973) and is used widely in Canada.

BIBLIOGRAPHY

Hicks, Wessely. 'Nobody is too great to compose music for our children,' *CanComp*, 12, Nov 1966

Ribière-Raverlat, Jacquotte. *L'Éducation musicale en Hongrie* (Paris 1967)

Rapport de la Commission royale d'enquête sur l'enseignement des arts dans la province de Québec, vol 2 (Quebec 1969)

Daly, Mae. 'Kodály Institute of Canada,' *Recorder*, vol 18, Sep 1975

Szönyi, Erzsébet. *Quelques Aspects de la méthode de Zoltán Kodály* (Budapest 1976) (MCr)

Koerner Foundation (The Leon and and Thea Koerner Foundation). Established 1955 with a capital grant of $1 million by Leon and Thea Koerner. Leon (1892–1972), a Czech refugee, settled in Canada in 1939 with his brothers Theodor, Otto, and Walter and formed a timber company in British Columbia. The objectives of the foundation are to foster higher education and cultural activities and to contribute to the public welfare, particularly in British Columbia, through project grants to individuals or institutions (libraries, universities, and organizations devoted to the fine arts). A board of directors is advised by a committee of experts in the foundation's areas of interest. Of $1.5 million distributed 1955–72, about a third went to music schools and performing groups.

The *Baroque Strings of Vancouver, the *CBC Vancouver Chamber Orchestra, and the *Vancouver Cello Club received single grants in 1970, and Intermedia received a grant in 1972. Annual assistance began to be provided for the *Community Music School of Greater Vancouver, the *Vancouver Opera, and the *Vancouver SO in 1969, the *Victoria SO in 1970, and the Okanagan SO in 1971. CF

KOFFMAN, Moe (Morris). Flutist, alto and saprano saxophonist, clarinetist, bandleader, composer, arranger, b Toronto 28 Dec 1928. He began studying violin at 9 and alto saxophone at 13, and soon afterwards attended the TCM, where his teachers were Herbert Pye (clarinet) and Sam *Dolin (theory). In his mid-teens he began playing in dance bands, working in turn with Horace *Lapp, Leo Romanelli, and Benny Louis. One of the first Canadian jazzmen to adopt the new bebop style born in New York in the early 1940s, Koffman won a (CBC) 'Jazz Unlimited' poll as best alto saxophonist in 1948 and made his first recordings (78s) in Buffalo with US musicians for the Main Stem company that same year. He studied with Gordon *Delamont at this time. In 1950 he moved to the USA, where he played in the big bands of Sonny Dunham, Jimmy Dorsey, and others. Settling in New York, he studied flute with Harold Bennett (of the Metropolitan Opera orchestra) and clarinet with Leon Russianoff (principal of the New York Philharmonic Orchestra). Koffman returned to Toronto in 1955, thereafter dividing his extremely active career between his jazz group and studio work.

Koffman made his first Toronto appearances at the House of Hambourg. He became the booking agent for *George's Spaghetti House in 1956 and remained in this capacity for over 20 years, also appearing there one week each month with his band. The Canadian and US success, in 1958, of his recording of his *'*Swinging Shepherd Blues*' established his reputation as a flutist and at the same time assisted in the wider acceptance of that instrument in jazz. In the 1960s Koffman engaged in various experiments, none necessarily original: eg, playing two saxophones at once, employing electronics to amplify and modify the saxophone's sound, and incorporating elements of rock into jazz. These left Koffman straddling the pop and jazz worlds and brought him unusually wide exposure for a Canadian jazz musician, including appearances in the mid-1960s on NBC TV's 'Tonight Show.' In the 1970s, assisted by the producer-arranger Doug *Riley, he and his jazz group made several popular LPs of arrangements

Moe Koffman

of music by Bach, Berlioz, Debussy, Gluck, Grieg, Mozart, and Vivaldi. Of his 10 LPs in the 1970s only 3 could be considered purely jazz recordings: *Solar Explorations*, *Live at George's*, and *Museum Pieces*. For *Solar Explorations* he commissioned works in honour of the planets from Ron *Collier, Riley, Fred *Stone, Don (W.) *Thompson, and Rick *Wilkins. Koffman himself wrote *Neptune* and *Venus*. *Museum Pieces*, co-produced by *GRT and the Royal Ontario Museum (Toronto), comprises works by Koffman (*Museum Pieces* and *Evolution Blues*), Marty Morell, Riley, Thompson, and Wilkins, inspired by various aspects of museology. Leading perhaps the most popular Canadian small jazz group of the day – a quartet or a quintet in which Ed *Bickert has been the most constant member – Koffman has toured in Canada and has performed at many festivals, among them *Expo 67, the *Shaw Festival (in a Mozart program with *Camerata, 1975), a series of CBC festivals in western Canada in 1978, and the *Ontario Place Jazz Festival in 1979. His band appeared with the *TS in 1975 (when he was the soloist in Lucio *Agostini's *Flute Concerto*) and with the *Hamilton Philharmonic and the Sudbury SO in 1979. After a virtual 20-year absence Koffman returned to perform in the USA in 1979, appearing in Lewiston, NY (Artpark), and at the Monterey Jazz Festival. In 1980 Koffman and the band toured in Australia.

Koffman has been a soloist on many pop recordings and has played in jazz-oriented TV orchestras led by Guido *Basso, Jimmy *Dale, Rob *McConnell, and others. He became a member and featured soloist of the *Boss Brass in 1972 and has played in Canadian orchestras led by Benny Goodman, Woody Herman, and Quincy Jones at the *CNE. He led his own big band as music director for Global TV's 'Everything Goes' in 1974.

The wide range of Koffman's activities has been seen by some as evidence of an inquiring musical mind but criticized by others as merely the exercise of a keen popularist instinct. Peter Goddard (*Toronto Star*, 6 Nov 1977) wrote, 'His ability to absorb new styles and then come back with his own version has made some of his work seem a trifle trendy at times.' Nevertheless, Koffman's standing in the studio world attests to his technical facility and musicianship. As an improviser he has maintained his allegiance to bebop and is one of Canada's best players in that style when he shuns his usually fashionable stance. Of his flute playing, Jack Batten (Toronto *Globe and Mail*, 28 Mar 1973) wrote: 'The sound he gets is remarkably pure and distilled, free of all flaws, imperfections and blemishes. Maybe the improvisations aren't as imaginative as you might ask for, but the crystal quality of the sound is enough to sweep along your interest.'

Koffman's son Herb (b New York 22 Apr 1955), a trumpeter who studied with Don Johnson and Ted *Moses, began leading his own jazz group and playing in other Toronto bands in the late 1970s. Koffman's brother Bernie played trumpet in Toronto dance bands (eg, with Pat *Riccio) in the 1950s before turning to a career as a lawyer.

Moe Koffman is an affiliate of PRO Canada; his compositions are copyrighted by Herblar Music.

DISCOGRAPHY

Hot and Cool Sax. Long tpt, McConnell trb, E. Karam bar sax, Bickert guit, Curry db, Rully drums. 1957. Jubilee 5311

The Shepherd Swings Again. Bickert guit, Curry db, Rully drums. 1958. Jubilee JLP 1074

Moe Koffman the Swinging Shepherd Plays for Teens. 1962. Ascot AS 16001

Tales of Koffman. Amadio pf, Bickert guit, Britto db, Rully drums. 1962. U Artists JS 14209

The Moe Koffman Quartet. Bickert guit, Price db, Rully drums. 1963. CTLS 5029

Moe Koffman Quartet. Ayre org, Binsted db, Cree drums. 1967. CBC Expo 31/RCI 268

Moe Koffman Goes Electric. Ayre org, Pirie guit, Binsted db and sitar, Cree drums. 1967. Jubilee JGS 8009

Turned on Moe Koffman. 1968. Jubilee JGS 8016

Moe's Curried Soul. Riley Keybds, Breau guit, Young db, Lewis drums. 1969. Revolver RLPS 502

Moe Koffman Plays Bach. Riley keybds, Edwards guit, Thompson db, Clarke drums. 1971. GRT 9230-1008

Vivaldi's Four Seasons. Str orch, Riley keybds, Edwards guit, Bush guit, Thompson db, Clarke drums, Craden perc. 1972. 2-GRT 9230-1022

Master Sessions. Riley keybds, Thompson db, Clarke drums. 1973. GRT 9230-1041

Solar Explorations. Orch including soloists Basso tpt, Stone flhn, Riley el pno, Greenwich guit, Thompson pf and db, Homme db and bass guit, Clarke drums, Ranger drums, Craden perc. 1974. 2-GRT 9230-1050

Best of Moe Koffman. (1975). GRT 9230-1053

Live at George's. Thompson elec pno and pf, Riley pf, Bickert guit, Homme db and b guit, Fuller drums. 1975. 2-GRT 9230-1005

Jungle Man. Mallory guit, Mann guit, Riley el pno, Szczesniak b guit, McLaren drums, Leonard perc. 1976. GRT 9230-1066

Museum Pieces. Str orch, Riley keybds, Thompson keybds, Bickert guit, Homme db and b guit, Morell drums. 1977. GRT 9230-1072

Things Are Looking Up. Str orch, Thompson keybds, Mann guit, Bickert guit, Homme db and b guit, Morell drums. 1978. GRT 9230-1078

Back to Bach. Riley keybds, Mann guit, Szczesniak b guit, McLaren drums, Leonard drums. 1979. Anthem ANR-1-1023

BIBLIOGRAPHY

Steward, Hartley. 'Back to Bach with the Swingin' Shepherd,' *Canadian Magazine*, 17 Mar 1973

McNamara, Helen. 'Koffman saw musical opportunities in Canada, returned to stay,' *MSc*, 276, Mar–Apr 1974

MM

KOLDOFSKY, Adolph. Violinist, b London 13 Sep 1905, d Los Angeles 8 Apr 1951. The son of Russian-Jewish parents, Koldofsky came to Canada in 1910 but later returned to Europe for advanced violin studies with Ysaÿe and Ševčik. He also toured Czechoslovakia as leader of the Ševčik String Quartet. He played in the *TSO intermittently from 1923 to 1938, when he became second violin of the *Hart House String Quartet. He gave recitals with his wife, the pianist Gwendolyn Williams *Koldofsky, and appeared as soloist with orchestras. He undertook extensive research to authenticate manuscripts of C.P.E. Bach keyboard concertos that had turned up in the estate of an old Toronto family and in March and April 1943 conducted a series of seven CBC radio broadcasts in which Wanda Landowska gave the modern premieres of five of the concertos. (The manuscripts were deposited later in the library of the U of California at Berkeley.) In 1944 Koldofsky became concertmaster of the *Vancouver SO and conductor of the Junior Symphony. In 1945 he moved to Los Angeles, where he played in the RKO studio and in chamber music recitals and established a local chapter of the ISCM. He premiered Schoenberg's last two instrumental works, the *String Trio, Op 45* and the *Fantasy, Op 47* which was written for him. A scholarship fund was set up in his memory at the U of Southern California. His sister is Eleanor *Sniderman.

DISCOGRAPHY

Schoenberg *String Trio, Op 45*. Koldofsky Trio. Dial 3

Schoenberg *Fantasy, Op 47*. E. Steuermann pf. Dial 14

BIBLIOGRAPHY

CBC. Program brochure for CBC radio broadcasts, Toronto 14 Mar–25 Apr 1943

HK

KOLDOFSKY, Gwendolyn (b Williams). Accompanist, voice coach, b Bowmanville, Ont, 1 Nov 1906. She studied piano in Toronto with Viggo *Kihl, in London with Tobias Matthay and (accompanying) Harold Craxton, and in Paris with Marguerite Hasselmans. Married 26 May 1943 to the violinist Adolph *Koldofsky she lived in Toronto until 1944. She then spent a year in Vancouver before settling in 1945 in Los Angeles, where she was engaged to teach accompanying – a position created for her – at the School of Music of the U of Southern California. She has given master classes for singers and accompanists at other universities and music schools in North America. She has accompanied (in North America, Europe, and the Far East) Rose Bampton, Jeanne *Dusseau, Herta Glaz, Jan Peerce, Hermann Prey, Martial Singher, and her own pupil Marilyn Horne. She assisted Lotte Lehmann on many tours during the latter's last 8 years of performing and for 11 years was Lehmann's accompanist and coach-assistant at the Music Academy of the West in Santa Barbara. A recording of a recital given in 1951 by Lehmann and Koldofsky was released in 1977 by Aquitaine (MS 90420).

HK

KOLESSA, Lubka (m Phillips). Pianist, teacher, b Lvov, Galicia (now USSR), 19 May 1904. She studied with Louis Thern and Emil Sauer in Vienna. In 1920 she undertook the first of several European concert tours. Furtwängler took a keen interest in her career. She was forced to abandon her home in Austria in 1938, moving briefly to the USA and later to Ottawa. She gave her first Canadian recital 21 Dec 1940 at the *Hambourg Cons in Toronto and made her first appearance with the *TSO in 1941, playing Weber's *Konzertstück*. That same year she performed the Chopin *Concerto in E Minor* at the *Promenade Symphony Concerts and joined the staff of the TCM. She taught there until 1949. During this period she undertook a South American tour, a Beethoven Sonata series (1943) for CBC radio, and a Carnegie Hall debut (1948) and built a reputation as one of Canada's foremost pianists. She played a concerto with the New York Philharmonic 26 Feb 1949 and returned to Carnegie Hall 3 Apr 1950 for a second recital. A critic for *Musical America* (April 1950) wrote, 'Her principal assets were a conspicuously fluent technique, exceptional skill in the subtle tinting of tone and an unusual resourcefulness in the use of the pedal.' She taught 1952–73 at the *CMM and 1955–66 at the *École Vincent-d'Indy. Her pupils have included André *Asselin, Mario *Bernardi, Tova Boroditsky, Howard *Brown, Carol (Wright *Pack) Birtch, Paul *Crawford, Patricia Grant Lewis *Elliott, John *Hawkins, Gordon *Kushner, Edward *Laufer, John *McKay, Louis-Philippe *Pelletier, Clermont *Pépin, and Karen Quinton.

DISCOGRAPHY
78s
Beethoven *Concerto No. 3* – Hummel *Rondo in E Flat*. Saxon State O, Böhm cond. Ca 1938. HMV G DB 5506-10
Chopin *Waltz No. 1* – Mozart *Romance in A Flat*. Ca 1938. HMV G DB 4654
Mozart *Variations in G* K 455. Ca 1938. HMV G DB 4621
Scarlatti *Sonata in C; Sonata in B Flat*. HMV G DA 4454
LPS
Brahms *Variations, Op 24; Intermezzi*. Ca 1952. Concert Hall CHS 1108
Schumann *Symphonic Etudes; Toccata*. Ca 1952. Concert Hall CHS 1111 EK

KOLINSKI, Mieczyslaw. Ethnomusicologist, composer, b Warsaw 5 Sep 1901, d Toronto 7 May 1981, naturalized Canadian 1974; PH D (Berlin) 1930. He studied piano and composition 1923–6 with Leonid Kreutzer and Paul Juon at the Hochschule für Musik in Berlin and musicology at Berlin U with Erich von Hornbostel, Hermann Abert, Arnold Schering, and Curt Sachs. As assistant to Hornbostel 1926–33 at the Berlin Staatliches Phonogramm-Archiv, he made several field trips to the Bavarian Alps and the Sudeten. During the mid-1930s he transcribed collections of Surinamese, Dahoman, Togonese, Ashanti, Haitian, and Kwakiutl Indian music for Northwestern U and Columbia U. He lived 1938–51 in Brussels and 1951–66 in New York, where he was a music therapist at Goldwater Memorial and St Albans Naval hospitals, an editor for Hargail Music Press, and a co-founder, and president 1958–9, of the Society for Ethnomusicology. He taught ethnomusicology 1966–76 at the *U of Toronto.

Kolinski's particular contributions to ethnomusicology lie in his development of analytical methods which can be applied cross-culturally and in his insights into perceptual problems and acoustical phenomena (see Writings). As a composer he did not use any single method consistently. His style has elements of modernism without attaching itself to any school or method. His compositions range from concise and simple bagatelles to large works of (in the composer's own words) 'transparent complexity.'

In 1976, on his retirement from the U of Toronto, Kolinski received the title Scholar Emeritus, the first such honour awarded by the university. His pupils include Beverley *Cavanagh, Peter Goddard, Alison Mackay, Jay Rahn, Doug *Riley, George Sawa, Bang-song Song, and Lu-lien Wang. Kolinski was an associate of both the *CMCentre and PRO Canada.

SELECTED COMPOSITIONS
STAGE
3 ballets: *Bu Ru Ru* (1931), *Railroad Fantasy* (1935), and *Man and His Shadows* (1948). All ms
ORCHESTRA
Preludes. 1958. Full orch. CMCentre
Dance Fantasy (based on *Man and His Shadows*). 1968. Str orch. CMCentre
CHAMBER
Lyric Sextet (Rilke, Hesse, Scholz, Lasker-Schüler, Bierbaum). 1929. Sop, fl, str quar. Ber 1978
String Quartet. 1931. Ms
Little Suite. 1933. Vn, pf. Harris 1974
Chamber Sonata. 1937. Pf quar. CMCentre
8 *Preludes*. 1939. Carillon. Ms
3 *Three-Part Inventions* (vocalise). 1950. Sop, va, vc. Ber 1958
Dahomey Suite. 1951 (fl or rec, pf), rev 1953 (fl, str orch), rev 1959 (ob, pf). Har 1952 (fl or rec, pf). 1959. Folk 3855 (Wann ob, Kolinski pf)
Hatikvah Variations. 1960. Str quar. CMCentre
6 settings of *French Folksongs*. 1969. Sop, fl, pf. Ber 1975
Merry-Go-Round. 1970. Acc. Wat 1970
Encounterpoint. 1973. Arr 1974. Org, str quar; arr fl, cl, vn, vc, pf. Ms
Concertino (vocalise). 1974. Sop, cl, pf. Ber 1978
Settings and arr for rec of folksongs and carols, duets and trios for rec, many publ by Har. For sop, fl, pf: 45 settings of German, Dutch, Slovak, US, Canadian, Yiddish, Sephardic, Hebrew folksongs; all 1977, 1978; all CMCentre; some recorded in 1978 on Folkways FTS 31314 (*Shulman fl)
PIANO
4 *Suites*. 1929, 1934, 1936, 1946. Ber 1976
Sonata. 1946, rev 1966. Har 1972 (later version)
Music for Dance Rhythms. 1958. Ms. 1959. Folk FC-7673 (Kolinski)
Many other works, including pf duets, some publ by Fischer, Har, Boston, MCA
VOICE
Numerous songs and song settings, including US, French, German, Yiddish, and Sephardic folksongs, in ms

WRITINGS
'Suriname music,' *Suriname Folk-Lore*, ed Melville and Frances Herskovits (New York 1936)
'The evaluation of tempo,' *Ethnomusicology*, vol 3, May 1959
'A new equidistant 12-tone temperament,' *J of the American Musicological Soc*, vol 12, Summer–Fall 1959
'The origin of the Indian 22-tone system,' *Studies in Ethnomusicology*, vol 1, 1961
'Classification of tonal structures, illustrated by a comparative chart of American Indian, African Negro, Afro-American and English-American structures,' *Studies in Ethnomusicology*, vol 1, 1961
'Consonance and dissonance,' *Ethnomusicology*, vol 6, May 1962
'The general direction of melodic movement,' *Ethnomusicology*, vol 9, Sep 1965
'The structure of melodic movement: a new method of analysis (revised),' *Studies in Ethnomusicology*, vol 2, 1965
'Recent trends in ethnomusicology,' *Ethnomusicology*, vol 11, Jan 1967
'An Apache rabbit dance song cycle as sung by the Iroquois,' *Ethnomusicology*, vol 16, Sep 1972
'A cross-cultural approach to metro-rhythmic patterns,' *Ethnomusicology*, vol 17, Sep 1973
'A study of melodic analysis, as applied to a collection of medieval tunes,' unpubl ms, 1974
'A co-ordinated denomination and notation of pitch,' *CAUSM J*, vol 6, Spring 1976
'Final reply to Herndon,' *Ethnomusicology*, vol 21, Jan 1977
'The structure of music: diversification versus constraint,' *Ethnomusicology*, vol 23, May 1978
'The universe of chords: complete chord classification, based on the cycle of fifths,' unpubl ms, 1978
Many review articles contributed to *Ethnomusicology*, *Journal* of the IFMC, *Yearbook* of the IFMC, *Musical Quarterly*
Transcription and analysis of 117 French-Canadian folksongs and versions, 1972, deposited at the *National Museum of Man, Ottawa

BIBLIOGRAPHY
Kennedy, Raymond. 'A bibliography of the writings of Mieczyslaw Kolinski,' *Current Musicology*, Spring 1966
Schulman, Michael. 'Kolinski's music affected by international travelling,' *MSc*, 276, Mar–Apr 1974
Contemporary Canadian Composers BAC

KOMAR, Ted (Theodore Stanley). Accordionist, arranger, teacher, adjudicator, b Winnipeg, of Ukrainian parents, 6 Jun 1929. He began his career as an accordion soloist 1947–58 on CBC radio's 'Prairie Schooner' and formed the Ted Komar Orchestra in 1952. With a repertoire of oldtime music the orchestra has performed widely in Canada and the USA. It has recorded *Happiness is Resi* (with Resi Dux, 1975, Drum R-1000) and *Reflections* (1975, KSP 75-1). Komar also has conducted studio orchestras on CBC radio's 'George LaFleche Show' 1955–60 and 'Ramblin' Man' 1960–5 and has led the Selkirk Settlers, the house band 1959–65 on CBC TV's 'Red River Jamboree.'

Komar established in Winnipeg two Ted Komar Music Schools (1950 and 1970), which specialize in accordion and guitar instruction. He was president 1967–8 of the Canadian Accordion Teachers' Assn and has adjudicated at many competition festivals; he has published two instruction books, *My Kind of Guitar* (1974) and *My Kind of Accordion* (1974). With the *Winnipeg SO he was accordion soloist 10 May 1975 in his own arrangement of *Three Ukrainian Folk Dances*. Among Komar's many pupils is his brother Ron (b Winnipeg 12 Aug 1940), a free-bass accordionist who has operated his own music school at a third address in Winnipeg and has led a dance band. (CC, FH)

KOMOROUS, Rudolf. Composer, bassoonist, teacher, b Prague 8 Dec 1931, naturalized Canadian 1974. In Prague he studied bassoon 1946–52 at the State Cons and 1952–9 with Karel Pivonka at the Academy of Musical Arts. He also studied composition with Pavel Borkovek at the academy. He was a winner at the 1957 International Competition for Musical Performers in Geneva, taught bassoon 1959–61 at the Peking Cons in China, and, on his return to Prague, became first bassoon of the National Theatre (State Opera House). In 1959 he also took a special course in electronic music in Russia and Poland, and in 1961 he co-founded Musica Viva Pragensis. Although he emigrated to Canada in 1969, he was employed 1969–71 as visiting professor at Macalester College in St Paul, Minn, resuming Canadian residency only when he joined the *U of Victoria as director of the electronic music studio in 1971. At Victoria he also served 1975–6 as acting chairman, and subsequently chairman, of the music department. He has performed frequently on CBC radio. An increasingly prolific composer after his move to Canada, Komorous has received commissions from Paul *Brodie (*Dingy Yellow*), from the Early Music Workship of the U of Victoria (*Preludes*), from Peggie *Sampson (*At Your Memory the Transparent Tears Are like Molten Lead*), from *NMC (*Rossi*), from *Days Months and Years to Come (*The Midnight Narcissus*), and from the *Vancouver New Music Society (*Twenty-Three Poems about Horses*). He is a member of the *CLComp and CAPAC and an associate of the *CMCentre.

SELECTED COMPOSITIONS
ORCHESTRA
The Gloomy Grace. 1968. Sm orch. UE (rental)
Bare and Dainty. 1970. Orch. UE (rental)
Rossi. 1975. Chamb orch. UE (rental)
CHAMBER
The Sweet Queen. 1963. Mouth hmca, bass drum, pf. UE 1965
Olympia. 1964. Flexatone, mouth hmca, nightingale, acolyte bells, sleigh bells, rattle. UE 1966. Supraphon 1-10-0471
Mignon. 1965. Four 4-str instr. UE (rental). Supraphon
Chanson. 1965. Guit, clock spiral, va. UE (rental)
York. 1967. Fl, ob (tpt), bn, triangle, pf, mand, db. UE 1972
Untitled 2. 1973. Tpt solo. Kerby 1977
Untitled 3-5. 1974. Various instr. Ms
Preludes. 1974. 13 early instr. Kerby 1978
At Your Memory the Transparent Tears Are like Molten Lead. 1976. V da gamba, hpd. Ms
The Midnight Narcissus. 1977. Alto fl, picc, hn, ob, vc, pf, triangle. Ms
Twenty-Three Poems about Horses (Li-Ho, transl Dr Frodsehan). 1978. Narr, 2 vn, 2 va, 2 vc, db. Ms
PIANO
The Devil's Trill. 1964. UE (rental)
for piano. 1973. Ms
ELECTRONIC
Untitled 1. 1973. Tape
Anatomy of Melancholy. 1974. Tape and tape jockey
The Tomb of Malevich. 1965. Tape. UE (rental). Supraphon DV 6221
Other works in all categories, including a chamb opera, *Lady Whiterose* (1966), and *An Anna Blume* for choir (1971). Both ms

BIBLIOGRAPHY
Champagne, Jane. 'A composer-teacher makes music on the West Coast,' *CanComp*, 95, Nov 1974
Contemporary Canadian Composers (PFB)

KONDAKS, Stephen. Violist, teacher, b Salonika, Greece, 15 Feb 1919, naturalized Canadian 1920. He studied violin 1930–6 with Harold *Sumberg at the TCM and 1936–8 with Sascha Jacobsen at the New York Institute of Musical Art (Juilliard). He then took up the viola, training 1938–9 with Hans Letz at the Juilliard Graduate School. In Montreal he was a member 1940–2 of the *McGill String Quartet and principal viola in the *McGill Chamber Orchestra. He attended Louis *Bailly's courses 1947–51 at the *CMM. As soloist as well as chamber and orchestral player he has taken part in numerous radio and TV broadcasts. He began teaching and coaching with the *NYO in 1963 and joined the faculty at *McGill U in 1967. GP

KONRAD, John. Violinist, teacher, choir conductor, b Halbstadt, southern Ukraine, 22 Nov 1899, d Winnipeg 24 Nov 1962. He studied violin in Russia and emigrated to Canada ca 1926, settling in Winkler, Man, and moving to Winnipeg in 1931. He was choirmaster 1935–43 at the First Mennonite Church, 1945–50 at Bethel Mission Church, and 1950–5 at Sargent Mennonite Church. In 1937 he joined the staff of the *Bornoff School of Music as a violin instructor and head of the string department. Konrad also, 1947–54, was the first head of the music department at the *Canadian Mennonite Bible College and ca 1959–62 directed the choir of the Canadian German Society. With his wife, Emma, a singer, and his daughter Irma, a pianist, he gave recitals in rural areas of Manitoba and Ontario. He also conducted choral workshops in the predominantly *Mennonite towns of Winkler, Gretna, and Morden, Man. Often criticized by the brethren for an approach to music that was worldly, as distinct from exclusively religious, he nevertheless exerted a significant influence on the development of music among the Mennonites in Manitoba.

In 1949 Konrad assumed ownership and direction of the Bornoff School, changing its name in 1950 to the Konrad Cons of Music. During the late 1950s the conservatory had an enrolment of 350 students, half of them in the string department, which, in its day, was the largest in Canada. Group instruction was emphasized, along with private lessons and tri-weekly ensemble practices. Students gained national recognition and won numerous scholarships from the *RCMT, the *U of Manitoba, and Eaton's Good Deed Club. The school closed shortly after Konrad's death. His pupils included Sergei Bekorvany (*Atlantic SO), Taras *Gabora, Eugene Kowalski (*Winnipeg SO), Victoria Polley Richards (*TS), Gerald *Stanick, Vera Tarnowsky (TS), and George Turnlund (London SO, England). (JTs)

KOPROWSKI, Peter Paul. Composer, pianist, teacher, b Łodz, Poland, 24 Aug 1947, naturalized Canadian 1976; Artist Diploma (State Music College, Łodz) 1966, MA (Higher School of Music, Krakow) 1969, D MUS (Toronto) 1977. He studied 1966–9 with Boleslaw Woytowicz in Krakow (where he also was music director for the new-music group Ars Nova) and 1969–71 with Nadia Boulanger in Paris, while living in London. He emigrated to Canada in 1971 and studied 1971–7 with John *Weinzweig at the *U of Toronto. Koprowski has taught theory and composition virtually all of his years in Canada – 1971–3 at the U of Toronto, 1973–4 at *McGill U, and thereafter at the *U of Western Ontario, where he became coordinator of new music at campus concerts and conductor of the New Music Ensemble. In Montreal he was artistic director 1973–4 for the Troupe de Junction and composer-in-residence 1974–5 for the Contemporary Dance Theatre.

A prolific composer, Koprowski has written over 50 works for stage, orchestra, chamber ensemble, solo instruments, and electronic media. In Canada he has written a *Canzona for 13 Soloists* (1972), a *Sonata* for cello solo (1975), a *Nocturne* for mezzo-soprano and chamber orchestra (1976, commissioned by the Canadian Federation of University Women and premiered by the U of Western Ontario Chamber Ensemble in 1977), and *Peripeteia* for orchestra (1977). In his works, especially those of the 1970s, Koprowski has sought the 'continuous motion and independence of voices and the avoidance of cadences' found in the music of two renaissance polyphonists he particularly admires – Ockeghem and Josquin. From the same models he has absorbed 'the avoidance of strong beats, even of pulse ... I constantly avoid stating the downbeat' (*Musicanada*, Oct 1977). Among Polish composers Szymanowski has been an influence because of his interest in the restoration of traditions and his employment of old principles in new contexts. Koprowski's music thus may be described as neo-renaissance. Koprowski is a member of CAPAC and the *CLComp and an associate of the *CMCentre.

SELECTED COMPOSITIONS (pre-1971)

Symphony Grotesque. 1966. Children's choir, orch. Ms

String Quartet No. 1. 1967. Ms

Psalm 42. Chamber cantata. 1968. Bar, chamb ens. Ms

The Workshop. 1968. 7 perf, 2 fl, various wind instr, vc bow, perc, tape, live vocal sounds. Ms

Concerto Grosso. 1969. Str quar, str orch. Ms

Symphony. 1969. Ms

BIBLIOGRAPHY

'Karen Kieser talks with Peter Paul Koprowski,' *Mcan*, 33, Oct 1977

Schulman, Michael. 'The composer as perfectionist: continual revision and polishing,' *CanComp*, 152, Jun 1980

Compositeurs canadiens contemporains NM

Korea. In 1972 over 6000 Koreans were living in Canada. The majority had arrived after the mid-1960s from Seoul, South Korea, and had settled in the Metropolitan Toronto area. More than half possessed professional skills. Korean community organizations (the largest of which, in the late 1970s, was the Korean-Canadian Assn of Metropolitan Toronto) have presented in Toronto annual events such as a Korea Festival in the fall and a Miss Korea Contest in the spring, which sometimes feature Korean music.

The most important aspect of Korean musical tradition is learned folk music, vocal and instrumental. The traditions and instruments are described in Bang-song Song's 1973 study, which includes transcriptions of 21 Korean folksongs and nine instrumental works. Altogether, by 1979, Song (at that time director of the National Classical Music Institute of Seoul) had collected 34 songs and 22 instrumental pieces.

Korean musicians living and performing western music in Canada in the late 1970s included the pianist In-Sung Chun, a former child prodigy; the violinists Young-Dae Park, Yoon-Im Chang, and Bok-Soo Kim, the last of whom was named concertmaster of the *Saskatoon SO in 1978; and the tenor Jae-Yu Paeng, who has recorded *Korean Art Songs* for RCA Victor. Among Korean pop performers who have appeared in Canada are the Comet Sisters and the Korean Seoul Kittens. The Little Angels of Korea, a children's choir, has toured in Canada, and the violinist Kyung-Wha Chung has performed with the *MSO.

In 1977 the JM World orchestra held its annual session in Seoul, and Otto *Joachim and Paul Duplessis were instructors for strings and percussion respectively. The soprano Joan *Patenaude gave a recital in Seoul in 1979, as did the organist Raymond *Daveluy. The Korean composer Isang Yun devised the title role of his opera *Sim Tjong* for the Canadian soprano Lilian *Sukis, who participated in the work's premiere at the Munich Olympic Festival in 1972.

BIBLIOGRAPHY

Song, Bang-song. *The Korean-Canadian Folk Song: An Ethnomusicological Study* (Ottawa 1974) (B-SS)

KORJUS, Ingemar. Bass-baritone, b Stockholm, of Estonian parents, 8 Apr 1950, naturalized Canadian 1960; ARCT performance 1970, ARCT teaching 1971. His parents emigrated to Canada in 1952 and settled in Toronto, where he studied voice 1966–72 and intermittently thereafter with Megan Rutledge. He also studied 1972–5 with Erik Werba in Vienna and Hans Hotter in Munich and in 1976 with Pierrette *Alarie and Léopold *Simoneau in San Francisco. He made his professional debut in 1971 in a performance of *Messiah* with the *Atlantic SO. He won the top male prize in the 1973 International Hugo Wolf Lieder Competition and first prize (voice) and a special outstanding performer award in the 1974 *CBC Talent Festival. In 1977 he placed second in the National Vocal Competition sponsored by the Edward Johnson Foundation. In 1978 he won first prize in the baritone and bass category at the International Competition for Singers at 's-Hertogenbosch, Holland, and second prize at the International Music Competition in Munich.

Korjus' repertoire encompasses songs, oratorio, opera, and operetta, standard and contemporary. He has appeared in recital and concert in Canada, the USA, and Europe and has been heard many times over CBC radio. He made his *COC debut in 1977 as the Monk in *Don Carlos* and the Speaker in *The Magic Flute*. He has sung with the *NACO, the *TS, and the *Vancouver and *Thunder Bay SOs, as well as the Mozarteum Orchestra in Austria and the Haydn Orchestra in Italy. He has participated in the *Algoma Fall Festival and the Brattleboro Bach Festival in Vermont (1976, *Mass in B Minor*). At the *Guelph Spring Festival in 1977 he sang in the premiere of *Healey's **Seabird Island* and the Canadian premiere (1978) of Schubert's oratorio *Lazarus*. In 1978 Korjus signed a two-year contract (effective 1979) with the Düsseldorf Opera; he was to sing leading baritone roles such as Masetto in *Don Giovanni* and Gremin in *Eugene Onegin*. He appeared as Gremin at the 1979 Aldeburgh Festival. In 1980 he returned to Canada to sing Schubert's song cycle *Die schöne Müllerin* at the St Lawrence Centre, Toronto. NM

KOSLOWSKY, Peter. Tenor, b near Sargeov, Ukraine, 15 May 1919, naturalized Canadian 1946. He was brought to Canada in 1926 by his Mennonite parents, who settled near Niverville, south of Winnipeg, on a farm which Koslowsky has continued to operate. He was the first of a succession of outstanding singers who emerged from the *Mennonite community into Manitoba's music scene in the 1950s. Although he studied music for two years at the *Mennonite Brethren Bible College and voice privately with Winona Lightcap, Nina *Dempsey, and, 1953–8, Gladys *Whitehead, his singing remained a highly developed avocation, seriously but not ambitiously and never exclusively pursued. Koslowsky's supple, easily produced lyric tenor nevertheless made him the natural successor to George *Kent as Winnipeg's foremost oratorio tenor in the 1950s and 1960s. He also sang the significant Lieder cycles of Schubert, Schumann, and Beethoven (*An die ferne Geliebte* was a specialty) and gave memorable performances of Vaughan Williams' *On Wenlock Edge*, in public and on CBC radio. With the *TSO and the *Vancouver SO he sang both the roles of the Evangelist and the reflective arias in the *St Matthew Passion* and the *St John Passion*. He has recorded as Gaspard Minard in **The Widow* and in recital (Schumann's *Liederkreis*, Berg's 'Nachtigall,' and Schubert's 'Der Wegweiser' and 'Wohin') with the pianist Ada *Bronstein (1966, CBC SM 40). (RG)

KOSTER, Wally (Walter Serge). Singer, trombonist, actor, b Winnipeg, of Polish-Russian parents, 14 Feb 1923, d Toronto 11 Dec 1975. Though a promising athlete, Koster decided to devote himself to music after singing in 1939 with Joe DeCourcy's dance band in Winnipeg and at Jasper Park, Alta. Possessing a vigorous baritone voice, he performed on CJRC radio, Winnipeg, and made his CBC network debut replacing George *Murray on the Woodhouse and Hawkins comedy show. After serving as a bandsman in World War II he sang with Ellis *McLintock's dance band in Toronto and became a trombonist and featured vocalist 1949–52 with Mart *Kenney. In 1952 Koster appeared on the CBC's first TV show. He starred in 1954 on CBC radios 'Trans-Canada Hit Parade,' co-starred with Joyce *Hahn 1955–60 on CBC TV's 'Cross-Canada Hit Parade,' and was host in 1960 for CBC TV's 'The World of Music.' Entering live musical comedy in 1959 as Sky Masterson in *Guys and Dolls* at *Rainbow Stage he also sang there in 1960 as Billy Bigelow in *Carousel*. He appeared in 1962 in *Most Happy Fella* at *O'Keefe Centre and in 1967 in *Paradise Hill* at the *Charlottetown Festival. In the mid-1960s Koster began singing and playing trombone in nightclubs with his band, the Music Men. In the years following he acted in several CBC TV dramas. Koster recorded in 1949 with Kenney and made a single in 1954 for Sapphire. He also made LPs for *Capitol (*Broadway Hit Parade* SN 6301), RCI (173 with Albert *Pratz' orchestra), *CTL, and the CBC LM series.

BIBLIOGRAPHY
Callwood, June. 'How to be a singing star ... the hard way,' *Maclean's*, 18 Aug 1956 (AM)

KOUDRIAVTZEFF, Nicolas (de). Impresario, b Nikolayev, near Odessa, 7 Feb 1896, naturalized Canadian 1960, d Montreal 31 Aug 1980. He studied violin, then piano, while attending university in Odessa and St Petersburg. In 1919 he left Russia for Paris, where he became a journalist, a publicist, and a writer/editor of concert and theatre programs – notably for Russian opera and ballet productions during the 1920s. When Colonel Wassili de Basil organized the Ballets de Monte Carlo he asked Koudriavtzeff to arrange the international tours of the group, and the arrangements took him to Canada for the first time in 1934. In 1943 he founded and became president and director-general of both *Canadian Concerts & Artists Inc. in Montreal and American-Canadian Concerts & Artists in New York. Koudriavtzeff's efforts in promoting artistic exchanges between Canada and the USSR resulted in 1960 in an official agreement between the two countries. In 1973 he was made a Member of the *Order of Canada. When Canadian Concerts & Artists declared bankruptcy in 1976, he founded and became president of Concerts & Artistes canadiens, Inc. He received the *CMCouncil Medal in 1980.

BIBLIOGRAPHY
Béraud, Jean. 'Le métier d'impresario,' Montreal *La Presse*, 2 Dec 1961
Gingras, Claude. 'Les 35 ans d'enthousiasme d'un grand impresario,' ibid, 24 May 1980
McLean, Eric. 'An era ends with the death of a great impresario,' Montreal *Gazette*, 6 Sep 1980 GP

KOWALCHUK, June (Marie Hollis Ann) (m Eggleton). Soprano, administrator, b Regina 20 Jun 1929. A pupil of Alicia *Birkett at the *Regina Cons and Ernesto *Vinci at the *RCMT, she was a winner in the CBC competitions *'Nos Futures Étoiles' (1950) and *'Singing Stars of Tomorrow' (1951). Her 1948 professional debut in operetta in Regina was followed by her 1950 *COC debut as Gilda in *Rigoletto* and a second COC role, Cio-Cio-San in *Madama Butterfly* in 1951. She sang often 1949–50 on radio and TV and appeared as soloist with several Canadian orchestras before ill health affected her career in 1952. She was co-founder in 1961 with Clifford Fox and president 1961–5 of the *Hamilton Opera Company. In 1961 she taught at the Hamilton Cons (*RHCM) and later she directed the opera workshop at Mohawk College in Hamilton, where she became artist-in-residence in 1971. She has studied and performed at the Accademia Musicale Chigiana in Siena (summers 1972, 1974, 1976) and has worked with coaches in Italy and the USA.

BIBLIOGRAPHY
Frayne, Trent. 'Singing Cinderella,' *Chatelaine*, Oct 1951 (JBl)

KRAEMER, Franz. TV and radio producer, administrator, b Vienna 1 Jun 1914, naturalized Canadian 1947. His musical training included private studies in composition with Berg 1932–5 and orchestration under Hermann Scherchen in 1938. He emigrated to Canada in 1940 and studied composition and conducting briefly at the TCM (*RCMT) under Arnold *Walter and Ettore *Mazzoleni. Kraemer joined the CBC IS in 1946 as a producer, then moved to the English network of CBC TV, working first as a producer and 1952–70 as an executive producer. He was a pioneer of opera on TV, and among his notable productions were Britten's *The Turn of the Screw* (1958, TV premiere) and *Peter Grimes* (1959, TV premiere), Strauss' *Elektra* (1961, North American TV premiere), Verdi's *Otello* (1963), Mozart's *The Magic Flute* (1966), and, with Leon Major, *Somers' **Louis Riel* (1969, TV premiere). Kraemer also produced documentaries marking the 80th and 85th birthdays of Igor Stravinsky and the *TS's 1970 tour of Japan and recitals by Rostropovich, *Gould, *Quilico, and *Stratas.

In 1971 Kraemer was appointed music director of the Toronto Arts Foundation (later Toronto Arts Productions), responsible for co-ordinating music programs at the *St Lawrence Centre, which under his guidance became known particularly for the breadth and variety of its chamber music programs and for its revival of solo recitals in Toronto. His interest in promoting new talent led in 1971 to the establishment of the centre's annual recital series Young Canadian Performers. In May 1976 he produced Canadian Sound, a retrospective of the work of Canadian composers and poets over the past 30 years. The 16-program series offered performances of more than 25 Canadian works. Phil *Nimmons, Harry Somers, and Gilles *Tremblay were among the many composers represented, and Harry *Freedman's *Alice in Wonderland* was given its premiere. In 1979 Kraemer was named head of the music section of the *Canada Council.

BIBLIOGRAPHY
Winters, Kenneth. 'Franz Kraemer to the rescue,' Toronto *Telegram*, 13 Apr 1971
O'Toole, Lawrence. 'The rebel at St. Lawrence Centre scorns the safe approach to music,' Toronto *Globe and Mail*, 17 Jan 1976 MSh

KRAGLUND, (Börge) John. Critic, b Hjørring, Denmark, 27 Apr 1922, naturalized Canadian 1949; BA (Toronto) 1948. His parents emigrated to Canada in 1929, settling on a farm in Prince Edward County, Ont. After university he studied theory and criticism with Leo *Smith and in 1952 succeeded Smith as music critic for the Toronto *Globe and Mail*. His drily sardonic, usually brief reviews, pragmatic in the face of a midnight deadline, became a hallmark of Toronto scepticism, and it has been said that a measured enthusiasm from Kraglund was the equivalent of a panegyric from a colleague. Among Toronto critics of the second half of the century Kraglund was the most attentive to local and provincial endeavours, often sending a deputy to visiting attractions in order to review himself recitals by local musicians, programs of new works by young composers, concert ventures by Toronto organizations, and musical events at the Stratford, Guelph, and Shaw (Niagara-on-the-Lake) festivals. In addition to his daily reviews, he has written for the *Canadian Music Journal*, *Opera Canada*, *Musicanada*, the *Canada Music Book*, *International Musician*, *Musical America*, *Musical Courier*, *Mayfair*, and other publications. AHC

KRAMER, Alex (Charles). Songwriter, pianist, b Montreal 30 May 1903. He studied at the *McGill Cons, played piano in Montreal movie houses, and conducted orchestras on CFCF and CKAC radio before moving in 1938 to New York. There he coached singers and worked in vaudeville as a pianist and orchestra leader. In 1940 he became a staff composer for a New York publishing company. With the ban on broadcasting the music of ASCAP composers in 1941 (see Dance bands), Kramer and his wife, Joan Whitney, were among the first songwriters to join BMI, and they enjoyed considerable radio exposure as a result. They often collaborated with Hy Zaret and others, and many of their songs were hits, including 'High on a Windy Hill' (Gower 1940), 'It All Comes Back to Me Now' (Gower 1940), 'My Sister and I' (Gower 1941), 'It's Love, Love, Love!' (Joy 1943), 'Candy' (Leo Feist 1944), 'Ain't Nobody Here But Us Chickens' (Pickwick 1947), 'Love Somebody' (Kramer-Whitney 1947), 'Far Away Places' (Laurel 1948), and 'No Other Arms, No Other Lips' (Whitney-Kramer-Zaret 1952). Their English version of 'Comme ci, comme ça', a popular French song, was a hit in the late 1940s. Recordings of some of their songs were made by Perry Como, Bing Crosby, Vic Damone, Jimmy Dorsey, Tony Martin, Dinah Shore, Frank Sinatra, Margaret Whiting, and others. (EBM)

KRAUS, Greta (m Dentay). Harpsichordist, pianist, teacher, b Vienna 3 Aug 1907, naturalized Canadian 1944. She entered the Vienna Academy in 1923 and received a Music Teacher's Diploma in 1930. Her teachers were Hans Weisse 1924–31 and Heinrich Schenker 1931–4. First a pianist, she made her harpsichord debut in 1936 in a version for eight instruments of Bach's *Musical Offering* conducted by Hermann Scherchen. In 1937 she appeared in London with the Boyd *Neel Orchestra and performed over the BBC. In 1938 she gave a lecture-recital for the Vienna Bach Society and performed for several other Viennese societies. That same year she moved to Canada and quickly made a name as a harpsichordist, appearing as soloist, chamber musician, and accompanist in concert and over the CBC.

In 1965 with the flutist Robert *Aitken she formed the Aitken-Kraus Duo, which was still active in 1980. After a concert by Kraus and Aitken at the *St Lawrence Centre, Toronto, the critic John *Kraglund wrote: 'She is still Canada's outstanding harpsichordist ... Anyone accustomed to most of today's harpsichordists, in or out of Cana-

Greta Kraus

da, is likely to wonder what could be special about a particular one, as most of them sound exceedingly sober, lacking in imagination and equipped with tin instruments. That, essentially, is where Miss Kraus differs. The tin has apparently been omitted from her harpsichord, which projects a resonant warmth and tone ... not associated with harpsichords. No less important, when she is performing, all Baroque compositions do not sound as if they came out of the same school' (Toronto *Globe and Mail*, 11 Dec 1976).

Kraus has appeared as a pianist as well, performing with many distinguished musicians, including the violinists David and Igor Oistrakh on their Canadian visits. In 1979 she was the partner of the soprano Lois *Marshall in a memorable performance of Schubert's song cycle *Die schöne Müllerin* at *Hart House, Toronto. She coached Lieder and chamber music and taught piano and harpsichord at the *RCMT 1943–69 and at the *U of Toronto 1943–76. Among her pupils are Douglas *Bodle, Austin *Clarkson, Elizabeth Keenan, R. Murray *Schafer, Patrick *Wedd, and Valerie Weeks. Singers she has coached include Elizabeth Benson *Guy, Ingemar *Korjus, Andrew *MacMillan, Mary *Morrison, Gary *Relyea, and Roxolana *Roslak. She succeeded Ernesto *Barbini as director, 1963–76, of the Collegium Musicum for the schooling of advanced faculty students in the performance style of the baroque. She founded the Toronto Baroque Ensemble (1958–63), whose members were Elizabeth Benson Guy, soprano, Nicholas *Fiore, flute, Donald Whitton, cello, and Corol McCartney, violin. In 1973 she received a citation from the Ontario Confederation of University Faculty Associations for 'an outstanding contribution to university teaching.'

DISCOGRAPHY

Mozart *Variations in D* – Scarlatti *Four Sonatas*. 1952. Hallmark RS-2

Bach *Chromatic Fantasia and Fugue*; *Aria variata*. 1954. Hallmark RS-5

– *Partita in B Minor*. Ca 1960. RCI 210

See also Discographies for Aitken; Guy; Toronto Mendelssohn Choir.

BIBLIOGRAPHY

Milne, Dorothy. 'Greta Kraus, Canada's eminent harpsichordist,' *CRMA*, vol 5, Oct–Nov 1946 (WS)

KREHM, Ida (m Pick). Pianist, teacher, conductor, b Toronto 24 Feb 1912 of Russian parents, naturalized US 1944. In Toronto she studied piano with Ernest J. *Farmer, Norah Drewett *de Kresz, and Viggo *Kihl and theory with *Willan. She won many piano awards as a child and was teaching at 13. Her first public appearance (1924) was at Bloor St United Church, Toronto. In 1929 she went to study with Rudolph Ganz in Chicago. In 1936 in Chicago she married Joseph Richard Pick (pianist, composer, textile broker, b Chicago 1901, d there 8 Dec 1955), whose sympathy and support were significant in her career. In 1937, in the course of three weeks, she won the Schubert Memorial Award (three appearances with the Philadelphia Orchestra under Ormandy), the National (US) Federation of Music Clubs cash prize, and the Naumburg Foundation Award (a New York Town Hall debut recital, 14 Dec 1937). For the first time ever the Naumburg award was made without a final hearing, so impressed was the jury with Ida Krehm's performance.

Krehm made her Canadian professional debut 2 Mar 1939 at *Hart House, U of Toronto, for the *Women's Musical Club of Toronto. She soon gained wider recognition as a recitalist and as an orchestral soloist in North America (Chicago, Cleveland, Detroit, St Louis, Toronto), Europe, and South America. She was Ernest Bloch's chosen soloist for the premiere 2 Dec 1950 of his *Scherzo fantasque* with the Chicago Symphony and has introduced works by Jiri Antonin Benda, Norman Dello Joio, M.K. Ciurlionis, Rudolph Ganz, Carlos Surinach, Alexander Tansman, and Alexander Tcherepnin. In 1962 at Hilversum, Holland, she made her debut as pianist-conductor, and she has repeated this dual function in Berlin, London (English Chamber Orchestra, Melos Ensemble), Toronto (CBC), and Trondheim, Norway; at the first Orvieto Festival (1976); and in India and the Phillippines. In 1958 she took up residence in Hampstead, England. On an *OAC grant she commissioned Srul Irving *Glick's *Concertino* (1977), written especially for her to conduct from the keyboard. She has recorded Schumann's *Fantasia, Op 17* (Delyse ECB 3154) and works of Tchaikovsky, Rachmaninoff, Scriabin, and others (*Piano Music from Russia*, CBC SM-247). Her work is characterized by high competence and a questing intelligence. ESn

KRIESE-CAPORALE, Gladys or **Claudia** (m Caporale). Mezzo-soprano, b Winnipeg 11 Jan 1931. While studying 1947–52 with Doris Mills *Lewis in Winnipeg, she sang the alto solo in Vaughan Williams' *O vos omnes* with the *Winnipeg Philharmonic Choir under Bernard *Naylor in 1949 and won the Rose Bowl at the *Manitoba Music Competition Festival in 1950. Further studies were taken 1952–9 in New York with Sidney Dietch. She placed second in the 1953–4 *'Singing Stars of Tomorrow' radio competition and received the Marian Anderson Award, the Liederkranz Award, and the Cincinnati Award in 1961. A member 1961–6 of the *Metropolitan Opera, she made her debut as the Mother's Voice in *Tales of Hoffmann* and sang such roles as Annina in *Der Rosenkavalier*, First Lady in *The Magic Flute*, Marcellina in *The Marriage of Figaro*, and Fricka in *Die Walküre*. Reviewing her performance in the New York Opera Festival production of *Aida* Paul Hume, in the *Washington Post* of 17 Aug 1964, described 'an Amneris that insinuated as often as it threatened, that pled softly as well as soared in assured triumph.' In his review of the same festival's *Il Trovatore*, Hume wrote, 'Miss Kriese sang an Azucena of supple, rich tone, overdoing no dramatics ... but what stirring singing, and how easily she managed all the tough spots.'

Engaged in 1966 by the Deutsche Oper, Berlin, to sing Azucena and other leading roles, Kriese moved to Europe, where in the following 10 years she sang as Claudia Caporale in Hamburg, Frankfurt, Düsseldorf, Vienna, and smaller French and German centres. In 1970 her roles included Eboli in *Don Carlos* with the State Theatre in Leipzig, Amneris in *Aida* with the State Theatre in Stuttgart, and Brangäne in *Tristan und Isolde*, Klytemnestra in *Elektra*, and Herodias in *Salome* with the Deutsche Oper, Berlin. In 1978 she was living in Italy. (TT)

Kronberg: 1582 (Rockabye Hamlet). Rock musical by Cliff *Jones after Shakespeare's *Hamlet*. Commissioned by the CBC, *Kronberg: 1582* was premiered 1 Dec 1973 on CBC radio's 'The Entertainers' with Cal Dodd as Hamlet and Nancy White as Ophelia. It was staged at the *Charlottetown Festival in 1974 and again in 1975 and toured eastern Canada in 1975 with Brent Carver as Hamlet and Beverly D'Angelo as Ophelia. Renamed *Rockabye Hamlet* and substantially revised by Jones under the direction of the producer Gower Champion, it opened 17 Feb 1976 at the Minskoff Theater on Broadway and closed after only seven performances. Though the Broadway cast was largely from the USA, D'Angelo retained her role as Ophelia. Songs from *Rockabye Hamlet* were recorded on the Rising label (RILP 103). A four-part radio documentary about *Kronberg: 1582*, 'A Bite of the Big Apple,' prepared by *Malka (Cohen), was broadcast on the CBC's 'The Entertainers' in 1977.

BIBLIOGRAPHY

MacDonald, Dawn. 'Squeaky clean on Broadway,' *Canadian Magazine*, 7 Feb 1976

Cohen, Susan, and Gault, John. 'The kid who didn't conquer Broadway,' *Maclean's*, 8 Mar 1976 MM

KUBÁLEK, Antonín. Pianist, b Libkovice, Czechoslovakia, 8 Nov 1935, naturalized Canadian 1974. Accidentally blinded at 10, he attended a school for the blind in Prague and began piano study with Otakar Heindl, continuing 1952–7 at the Prague Cons with Oldřich Kredba and 1957–9 at the Academy of Music with Zděnek Jílek and František Maxián. Kubálek regained partial sight in one eye at this time. While teaching 1961–8 at the Prague Cons he performed in public and on radio and recorded for Supraphon. He moved to Canada in 1968 and made his North American debut 24 Oct 1969 at Walter Hall, U of Toronto. Frequent solo recitals and CBC broadcasts followed. He has appeared as soloist with the *TS in 1969, 1972, and 1977 and with other Ontario orchestras and in chamber concerts with Paul *Brodie and the *Vaghy and *Orford string quartets. In the 1974–5 season at St Paul's Centre in Toronto he presented the complete piano sonatas of Mozart. He returned to Europe for a tour in 1974. Noted for his interest in 20th-century Czech and Canadian music, Kubálek has premiered works by Paul *Kilburn (*Reflections on Ice Sonata* and *Trio for Piano Solo*) and Rudolf *Komorous (*for piano*). He has participated in such unusual projects as a recording of Korngold's *Sonata No. 1*, produced by Glenn *Gould, and an LP commemorating the US bicentenary with several of his own arrangements of Sousa's music. Kubálek has taught privately, 1969–75 at the Brodie School of Music in Toronto, and summers 1975, 1976 at the Blue Mountain School of Music, Collingwood, Ont. He began teaching at the *RCMT in 1979. He is an affiliate of PRO Canada.

DISCOGRAPHY

Antonin Kubalek in Recital: Brahms – Schumann. 1977. Citadel CT 6027

Antonin Kubalek Plays Canadian Music:

– *Album I*: Joachim – Papineau-Couture – Kilburn – Somers. 1974. Mel SMLP 4023

– *Album II*: Coulthard – Archer – Jaque – Pentland – Southam. 1976. Mel SMLP 4031

Chausson *'Concert' for Piano, Violin and String Quartet, Op 21.* Dawes vn, Orford Str Quar with O. Armin vn. 1974. CBC SM-246
Franck *Prelude, Chorale and Fugue* – Prokofiev *Romeo and Juliet: Piano Suite No. 2.* 1973. Golden Crest RE 7057
Hindemith *1922 Suite for Piano* – Janáček *In the Mist* – Martinu *Étude in F; Polka in A; Étude in F.* 1972. Golden Crest RE 7050
Korngold *Sonata, Op 2; Fairy Pictures, Op 3.* 1973. Genesis GS 1055
– *The Wunderkind; The Snowman* (selections); *Don Quixote; Sonata No. 1.* 1976. Citadel CT 6001O
Morawetz – Kilburn – Kymlicka – Smetana – Vorisek. 1973. CBC SM-187
Mozart *Rondo in A Minor* – Beethoven *Sonata in F, Op 54* – Janáček *On an Overgrown Path.* 1970. CBC SM-125
Other Side of Sousa. 1975. Antilles AN 7015
Paderewski *Sonata, Op 23; Variations and Fugue, Op 21.* 1978. Citadel CT 7001
Smetana *Czech Dances* (complete). 1975. Genesis GS 1064
– *Memoires of Bohemia; Reveries.* 1976. Citadel CT 6009
Also some recordings for the European label Supraphon (pre-1968)
See also Discography for Paul Brodie. (RM)

KUERTI, Anton (Emil). Pianist, teacher, composer, b Vienna 21 Jul 1938, naturalized US 1944; B MUS (Cleveland Institute) 1955, hon FRHCM 1978. After lessons as a child with Edward Goldman in Boston he made a debut at nine, playing the Grieg *Concerto* with the Boston Pops Orchestra. He studied 1948–52 at the Longy School, Cambridge, Mass, with Erwin Bodky and Gregory Tucker (piano) and Arthur Shepherd (composition); 1952–3 at the Peabody Institute with Erno Balogh (piano) and Henry Cowell (composition); 1953–5 at the Cleveland Institute with Arthur Loesser and Beryl Rubinstein (piano) and Marcel Dick (composition); and 1955–8 at the Curtis Institute with Rudolf Serkin and Mieczyslaw Horszowski. Of his many teachers, he regards Loesser and Serkin as having had the greatest influence on his musical thinking.

During his student years he was a soloist with the Zimbler Sinfonietta (1950) and with the MIT SO (1951) and gave recitals (1953) at the Gardner Museum, Boston, and the Phillips Gallery, Washington. He also performed annually 1953–6 at the Marlboro Festival. His professional concert career began in 1957, when he won the Philadelphia Orchestra Youth Prize, the National Music League Award, and the Leventritt Award (which includes engagements with major US orchestras; he consequently appeared with the Cleveland Orchestra, the Detroit SO, the New York Philharmonic, and the Pittsburgh SO). Over the next 20 years he performed with many other US orchestras, including the Philadelphia and the Minnesota, and, before or after settling in Canada in 1965, with all of the main Canadian orchestras, including the *TSO (the first time in 1961 as a replacement for Myra Hess), the *MSO, the *NACO (in Ottawa and, in 1973, on tour to New York, Washington, Moscow, Leningrad, Warsaw, and Rome), the *Winnipeg SO, and the *Vancouver SO. He also has appeared with major orchestras in Belgium, Czechoslovakia, England, the Federal Republic of Germany, the German Democratic Republic, Holland, Italy, Poland, and the USSR. He has played at the Aspen, Spoleto, Prague, Santa Fe, Grand Teton, and other festivals and performed frequently on radio and TV in Europe and Canada.

As a performer and active concert planner Kuerti has concerned himself with surveys of the piano, voice, and chamber music repertoires of individual composers. In 1972 he broadcast a Scriabin series on CBC radio. His integral performances of the 32 *Sonatas* of Beethoven, 1974–5 in Toronto and Ottawa, led to a CBC broadcast of the cycle (in 19 programs, 1976), a complete recording (Aquitaine), which in 1976 won the first *Juno Award

Anton Kuerti

given to a recording in the classical-music category, and repetitions of the cycle in Hamilton, Ont, Montreal, New York City, and Toronto in the 1978 season. Kuerti also participated as a soloist and chamber musician in the 1977 Brahms concerts at *St Lawrence Centre, Toronto; and, as founder and director of Northstars Concerts, Inc, he presented himself and other leading musicians in Toronto festivals of Schubert (1976–7), Mozart (1977–8), and Bach (1979–80). Highlights of the Schubert and Mozart festivals included Kuerti's appearance with Lois *Marshall in a complete *Winterreise* and with the 85-year-old Mieczyslaw Horszowski in a program of Mozart's four-hand *Sonatas.* As pianist-in-residence 1965–8, associate professor 1968–72, and artist-in-residence thereafter at the *U of Toronto, he has taught several younger pianists of note, including Jane *Coop, Kathryn Root, and Elyakim *Taussig.

In 1971 Kuerti returned to a student enthusiasm, composing, with his *Linden Suite* for piano. He quickly added five more works: *Magog* for cello and piano (1972) *String Quartet No. 2* (1972; his first quartet dates from 1954), *Symphony 'Epomeo'* (1973), a *Violin Sonata* (1973), and *Six Arrows* for piano (1973). Kuerti's compositions (all in manuscript) are rooted in Scriabin, early Berg, and the dissonant post-romantics. He has given the premieres of his own piano works and of several by other Canadian composers, including *Morawetz (*Piano Concerto No. 1,* 1963 with the MSO; *Suite for Piano,* 1969 in Montreal) and *Eckhardt-Gramatté (*Symphony-Concerto,* 1968 with the TS). As one of the two or three top pianists at work in Canada he commands a large and discriminating public. William *Littler, the critic for the *Toronto Star,* wrote (10 May 1977): '[Kuerti] habitually pays his listeners the compliment of assuming that their ears come to him in search of stimulation rather than massage ... You can't just sit back and let the music wash over you. The playing is too intense, too probing. Almost in spite of himself, the listener becomes drawn into the action.' Kuerti is a member of CAPAC.

WRITINGS

'Anton Kuerti's step by step guide for determining if your piano is in good registration,' *Clavier,* May–Jun 1973
'Thoughts about composing,' CFMTA *Newsletter,* Feb 1976
'It's a thrill to create your own universe in music. It also can be drudgery,' Toronto *Globe and Mail,* 20 Nov 1976
Also, detailed notes accompanying his recording of the *Complete Beethoven Sonatas.* See Discography.

DISCOGRAPHY

Beethoven *Sonatas No. 6, 24, 25, 26.* 1965. Monitor MCS 1075
– *Fantasia, Op 77; Sonata, Op 14, no. 1; Andante Favori; Sonata, Op 26.* 1969. RCI 278/RCA LSC 3140
– *The Complete Piano Sonatas; Diabelli Variations.* 1974–5. Aquitaine M3S 90365, 90369, and M4S 90361, 90374
Chopin *Études, Op 25* – Mozart *Fantasia in D Minor* K397. 1971. Monitor MCS 2133
Eckhardt-Gramatté *Symphony-Concerto* for piano and orchestra. CBC Festival O, A. Brott cond. 1968. RCI 328/CBC SM-107/RCA LSC 3175
Liszt *Sonata in B Minor* – Glazunov *Sonata, Op 74.* 1976. Aquitaine XM90414
Mendelssohn *Rondo Capriccioso; Fantasy, Op 28; Preludes and Fugues; Scherzo in B Minor; Scherzo a Capriccio in F Sharp Minor.* 1968. Monitor MCS 2128
Morawetz *Piano Concerto No. 1.* TSO, Susskind cond. 1964? (1975). Cap SW-6123/Pathé SPAM 68023/RCI 212
– *Piano Concerto No. 1.* CBC Mtl orch, J.-M. Beaudet cond. 1965? RCI 213-A
Schubert *Wanderer Fantasy; Sonata, Op 78.* 1966. Monitor MCS 2109
Schumann *Kreisleriana; Sonata No. 2.* 1969. CBC SM-83/A of D SDD 2154
– *Fantasy, Op 17; Toccata, Op 7.* 1971. CBC SM-157
– *8 Novelettes, Op 21.* 1975. VEB Deutsche Schallplatten Berlin/Eterna 8 26 524
– *Quintet* for piano and strings. Orford String Quartet. 1971. CBC SM-213
Scriabin *Sonatas No. 4 and 6; 5 Preludes; 6 Études* – Berg *Sonata, Op 1.* 1971. Monitor MCS 2134

BIBLIOGRAPHY

Bowers, Faubion. 'Anton Kuerti – "a pianistic supernova",' *New York Times,* 27 Feb 1972
Peredo, Sandra. 'A Beethoven freak who works for Stompin' Tom,' *Canadian Magazine,* 8 Feb 1975
Levitch, Gerald. 'The role of the recitalist-composer,' *CanComp,* 97, Jan 1975
Schulman, Michael. 'Anton Kuerti's fight against fame,' *PfAC,* Spring 1975
Harper, Tim. 'The controversy of Kuerti,' *Fugue,* vol 1, Feb 1977
Hathaway, Thomas. 'Kuerti's Schubert,' *Canadian Forum,* vol 56, Mar 1977
Marchant, Janet. 'Passionate rebel of the keyboard,' *Maclean's,* 11 Aug 1980 KW

KUINKA, William. Mandolinist, bassist, guitarist, b Anyox, near Prince Rupert, BC, 28 Jan 1916; ARCT 1951. After service in World War II as a member of an *Army Show unit, he studied at the *RCMT with Charles Rose (string bass), John *Weinzweig (theory), John Moskalyk (violin), and others, at the Advanced School of Contemporary Music, Toronto, with Ray Brown (bass), and in New York with Fred Zimmerman (bass). He has taught himself to play various fretted instruments, specializing in mandolin but attaining proficiency also in guitar. He has played double-bass in several Canadian orchestras (*CBC SO, *TSO, Pro Arte Orchestra, *Hamilton Philharmonic Orchestra) and mandolin solos with the Ivan *Romanoff orchestra on radio, TV, and recordings and in concert. While a member 1963–5 of the Toronto Renaissance Quintet (playing viola da gamba and mandolin), he formed the Toronto Mandolin Chamber Ensemble in 1964 for concerts in libraries, art galleries, and schools. The ensemble continued until 1969.

In 1966 Kuinka received a *Canada Council grant for research in Europe into teaching methods and repertoire for fretted instruments. He began teaching at the *Brodie School of Music, Toronto, in 1965, and for the Etobicoke Board of Education (Toronto) in 1969. He has encouraged Canadian composers to write for the mandolin and has premiered or participated in the premieres of Charles *Camilleri's *Sonata da Camera* (1963), Morris *Surdin's *Concerto for Mandolin and Strings* (1966), Walter *Buczynski's *Trio/67,* Frederick *Karam's *Concerto for Mandolin and Large Orchestra* (1969), Robert *Bauer's *Mao* (1973, recorded with the composer), and Gary T. *Hayes' *Preludes and Dances,* Book 1 (1978). He has also played in *NMC presentations. (MH)

Luigi von Kunits

KUNITS, Luigi von (b Ludwig Paul Maria). Conductor, violinist, teacher, composer, b Vienna 20 Jul 1870, d Toronto 8 Oct 1931; D JURIS (Vienna) ca 1891, hon D MUS (Toronto) 1926. In Vienna he studied violin with Jakob Grün and Otakar Ševčik, composition with Bruckner, and music history with Hanslick. At 11 he was asked by Brahms (who knew his father) to attempt the second violin in one of the composer's quartets. He was acquainted with Goldmark and Johann Strauss. At 21 he performed his own violin concerto with the Vienna Philharmonic. He went to the USA with an Austrian orchestra to perform at the 1893 World's Fair and remained there, teaching violin in Chicago 1893–6 and at the Pittsburgh Cons 1896–1910. It was as concertmaster 1897–1910 and assistant conductor of the Pittsburgh SO that he first visited Toronto for a performance with the *Toronto Mendelssohn Choir.

In 1912, after two years in Europe performing his own *Violin Concerto in E Minor* and concertos by Brahms, Wieniawski, Mendelssohn, and Paganini to excellent reviews, he was invited to become conductor of the Philadelphia Orchestra and at the same time was asked to teach at the *Canadian Academy of Music in Toronto. Because of a heart condition von Kunits decided, on advice, to accept the quieter of the two positions. In Toronto he formed the *Academy String Quartet (1912–23), which was noted for its repertoire of contemporary music. In 1922 at the request of the Toronto musicians Louis Gesensway and Abe Fenbogue he formed the New SO, which in 1927 became the *TSO. The string section contained many of his pupils. The excellence of that section was noted by Stokowski (who had accepted the Philadelphia position declined by von Kunits) when he conducted the orchestra. Two of von Kunits' pupils, Gesensway and Manny Roth, accepted invitations to join the Philadelphia Orchestra. Others of note were Harry *Adaskin, Vera Bairstow, the US composer Charles Wakefield Cadman, Ernest *Dainty, Francesco Fusco, Harvey *Perrin, Albert *Pratz, Paul *Scherman, Stanley *Solomon, Maurice *Solway, Albert *Steinberg, Berul *Sugarman, and Geoffrey *Waddington. Von Kunits shaped a generation of string players, some of whom continued to play with the TS in 1980.

Von Kunits' education went beyond music. He knew Latin and Greek, he founded the *Canadian Journal of Music* (1915–19), he contributed to several periodicals, and he wrote an unpublished book on Beethoven, *The Hero as Musician* (1913). Many of his critical reviews had the byline 'A.L.' ('All Lies'). His compositions (listed in the *Catalogue of Canadian Composers*) include two violin concertos, a string quartet (1890), a *Scotch Lullaby* for violin and orchestra (1916), and a viola sonata (1917). Several works for voice or violin and piano were published by Detmer, C. Fischer, *Harris, and G. Schirmer, and three songs appeared in *Musical Canada* (1931). His string quartet, first performed in 1915 by the Academy String Quartet, was revived in 1975 by the *Orford String Quartet. The *NL of C holds many of his manuscripts.

BIBLIOGRAPHY

Bridle, Augustus. 'Luigi von Kunits, master in music, culture and energy,' *Luigi von Kunits*, brochure (Toronto 1931)

'Musical bibliographies of Canadian composers, no. 5,' Toronto *Globe*, 1 Aug 1936

Campbell, Aglaia. 'He founded the Toronto Symphony,' *Mayfair*, 2 instalments, Oct, Nov 1957

Edinborough, Arnold. *A Personal History of the Toronto Symphony* (Toronto [1971])

Edwards, Aglaia von Kunits. 'Memories of a musician's daughter,' *TS News*, Dec–Jan 1972–3, Jan–Feb 1973

(CF)

KUNZ, Alfred (Leopold). Composer, conductor, administrator, b Neudorf, near Regina, Sask, 26 May 1929. He studied composition and conducting 1949–55 at the *RCMT and for several summers in the 1960s with Stockhausen and others in Europe. In 1965 he completed the state examinations in choral conducting at the Musikhochschule in Mainz and was assistant conductor of the Mainz City Opera Theatre. He returned to Germany in 1968 to direct the German-Canadian Choir on tour and to conduct the premiere of his choral cycle *The Face of Love*. He began teaching in Kitchener, Ont, in 1955, organized the Kitchener-Waterloo Chamber Music Orchestra and Choir in 1959, and was organist-choirmaster 1959–64 at Mount Zion Evangelical Lutheran Church. He became assistant conductor in 1962, and conductor in 1968, of the Concordia Male and Mixed Choirs. He also began conducting the Germania Male Choir in 1962 and was first master-of-all-choirs 1968–79 (after three years as second master) in the German Canadian Choir Assn. He was principal 1965–7 of the Canadian Music Teachers' College, Burlington, Ont, and director of musical activites (eg, Concert Choir, Stage Band, Concert Band, Little SO) 1965–79 at the *U of Waterloo. He coordinated the revival (1969, 1970) of the International *Sängerfest in Kitchener. A prolific composer, emphasizing choral works of medium difficulty, he has extended his interest in Gebrauchsmusik from the amateur choral field to the piano and accordion repertoire. Kunz is eclectic in his use of both traditional tonal idioms and contemporary note-cluster and aleatoric effects. He is an affiliate of CAPAC.

SELECTED COMPOSITIONS

STAGE

The Damask Drum, chamb opera (Hecken). 1961. Ms

Moses, ballet. 1965. Ms

Let's Make a Carol, play with music (J. Reaney). 1965. Wat 1965

Other stage works, including an operetta, *The Watchful Gods* (1962). CMCentre

ORCHESTRA

Several works for orch, including 2 *Sinfoniettas* (1957, 1961), *Five Night Scenes* (1971), *Concerto* for 6 perc and orch (1973), *Piano Concerto* (1975), *Chamber Symphony – 14 players* (1976), *Three Pieces for Clarinet and Strings* (1977), all ms; and *Overture for Fun* (1978), CMCentre

Also some works for chorus and orch, including 2 oratorios: *The Big Land* (1967) and *The Creation* (1972). Both CMCentre. See also Oratorios, Canadian (composition and performance) 9.

CHAMBER

Many works, including *Sonata* (1958, vn, pf), *Emanation No. 1 and 2* (1964, various instr), *Fun for Two* (1964, 2 bn or 2 bass cl), *Love, Death and Full Moonlight* (1964, v, chamb ens), *Quintet* (1964, ww quin), *Three Fanfares* (1964, brass, perc). All CMCentre

KEYBOARD

Five Excursions. 1964. Pf. Ms

Three Excursions. 1964. Org. CMCentre

Music to Do Things by, vols 1 and 2. 1965, 1969. Pf. Wat 1969

Also works for acc solo, and various works for acc orch (1963–7), publ Wat

CHOIR AND VOICE

Several works for choir, with pf or unaccompanied, including *Will You Come?* (1960), *Contrasts* (1966), *Eight Impressions on Japanese Haiku Ideas* (1969), *3 Pieces for Male Chorus* (1972), *Book of Diverse Songs, Sounds and Thoughts* (1976) publ Wat; and *Sketches of Waterloo County* (1974) publ GVT

Also 18 songs for v and pf (1960). Ms

WRITINGS

'Composers' corner: Alfred Kunz,' *CanComp*, 13, Dec 1966

'My most successful work,' *CanComp*, 25, Jan 1968

BIBLIOGRAPHY

Contemporary Canadian Composers (WHK)

KURTH, Burton (Lowell). Singer, educator, b Buffalo, NY, 27 Apr 1890. He studied in Winnipeg with Herbert Witherspoon and, 1920–4, Francis Fisher Powers; in New York with Witherspoon, Joseph Regneas in 1931, and William Brady; and in Chicago, summers, with Theodore Harrison. He moved to Winnipeg in 1909 and married the contralto Olive Quast in 1917. He taught singing in Winnipeg till 1927 and was organist-choirmaster successively at St Andrew's United, Broadway Baptist, and Young United churches. In 1921 he founded the St Cecilia Ladies' Choir, which sang Debussy's *La Damoiselle élue* in 1923 with the Minneapolis SO. He moved to Vancouver in 1927 to be organist-choirmaster at Chown United Church. He later became supervisor of music for Vancouver schools. Kurth has composed many songs, published by *Western Music, for use in schools and has compiled, in collaboration with Mildred McManus and Murray S. Cormack, *Little Songs for Little People* (Clarke, Irwin 1943), *Music Makers* (Western Music 1945), *Sing Me a Song* (Dent 1956), and *We Like to Sing* (ibid 1959). He also wrote *Sensitive Singing* (Oakville 1973), a book of advice for young singers. (RG)

KUSHNER, Gordon (b Kushnir, George Gershon). Teacher, pianist, conductor, b Winnipeg 25 May 1916; LRSM 1938. A pupil in Winnipeg of Myrtle Ruttan Patterson (piano) and Gwendda Owen *Davies (theory), he formed with Neil *Chotem a piano duo which broadcast 1940–2 on CBC radio. After serving as a bandsman in the RCN in World War II he toured Central and South America in 1946 as accompanist to the contralto Portia *White. That same year he resumed his studies at the *RCMT – piano with Lubka *Kolessa and conducting and theory with John *Weinzweig.

In 1948 Kushner became choir director at Beth Tzedec Synagogue in Toronto, and subsequently he composed several choral settings for the sabbath service. He joined the education and cultural committee of the Canadian Jewish Congress in 1950 and became co-chairman of its central-region music committee in 1967. He inaugurated the YMHA Community Music School in Toronto in 1964.

Kushner worked at the CBC as assistant to Jack *Kane and directed the music for several of Norman *Campbell's TV productions and musicals. In 1956 he was accompanist for Charles *Jordan and Joyce *Sullivan on the recording *Folksongs of Canada*. He taught 1963–73 at the *U of Toronto and, after studying European methods of elementary music education on a *Canada Council grant in 1967, was appointed director of the RCMT Summer School in 1969. He became administrative assistant to the principal of the *RCMT in 1973 and served as acting principal in 1978. He served 1973–9 as the first president of the Kodály Institute of Canada. (ESn)

KYMLICKA, Milan. Arranger, composer, conductor, b Louny, Czechoslovakia, 15 May 1936, naturalized Canadian 1974. Prior to his arrival in Toronto in 1968, Kymlicka had studied with Emil

('Lazy Stream') won first prize in a 1968 Czech songwriting competition. By the early 1970s he was established as one of Canada's leading studio arranger-conductors. He has arranged music for the CBC radio shows of Ivan *Romanoff and others and for recordings by such popular artists as Bill Amesbury, Peter *Appleyard, Peter Foldy, the Good Brothers, Ray Materick, Anne *Murray, Suzanne Stevens, Sweet Blindness, and Ian *Thomas. The composer of many radio and TV jingles, Kymlicka also has written scores for the films *The Last Act of Martin Weston* (1970), *The Reincarnate* (1971), and *Wedding in White* (1972), as well as music for student chamber ensembles and a *Sonatina* for piano (Leeds 1975). His *Two Dances* (Leeds 1970) for clarinet and piano were recorded by Avrahm *Galper, and his *Four Pieces for Piano* (Leeds 1974) were recorded by Antonín *Kubálek. Kymlicka conducted his own *Scheherazade – A Journey* for broadcast 12 Dec 1976 on CBC TV's 'Music to See.' He has conducted his own compositions and arrangements on the LPs *In the Evening* (1971, CBC LM 115/Kanata KAN 6/CTLS 6001), *Clockwork Orange ... Music by Milan* (1972, CTL 477-5158), *Collage* (1974, GRT 9230-1047), and *Milan Kymlicka Orchestra* (1975, CBC LM 415). In 1978 he began teaching theory and composition at the *U of Western Ontario. He is a member of CAPAC.

BIBLIOGRAPHY

Meredith, Joan. 'Milan Kymlicka's story: how to start again in a new country,' *CanComp*, 55, Dec 1970

'A Czech with a cancon niche,' *RPM*, 4 Sep 1976 (BJE)

L

LABELLE. Family of musicians: 1 / Charles, 2 / Gustave, son of Charles, and 3 / Adrienne, daughter of Charles.

1 **Charles**. Organist, composer, conductor, teacher, b Champlain, NY, 15 Aug 1849, d Montreal 21 May 1902. He studied at the Collège de Montréal, where, at 12, he was put in charge of the solfège class. Shortly thereafter he became the school organist. He had begun his musical studies with his father and later he took lessons in singing and accompaniment with a Mme Petipas.

In 1874 Labelle replaced Guillaume *Couture as the choirmaster of St-Jacques Church. In 1878 he sang in Boieldieu's *La Dame blanche* under the direction of Calixa *Lavallée. Following a sojourn (1880) in Paris, where he studied singing with Romain Bussine, he was organist-choirmaster 1884–91 at St-Henri and Notre-Dame churches, Montreal. From 1892 until his death, he held the same post at St-Louis-de-France Church.

Labelle taught singing at the Hochelaga Convent, the Collège de Montréal, and the Collège Ste-Marie-de-Monnoir and in 1891 founded the *Association chorale St-Louis-de-France. In 1895, when the conservatory of the *Canadian Artistic Society was established, he was engaged to teach solfège and choral singing. Among his numerous private pupils were his son and daughter, and Céline *Marier.

In 1890 Labelle founded the Société philharmonique canadienne-française which, that year, presented Rossini's *Stabat mater* and choruses from Gounod's *Jeanne d'Arc* at *Queen's Hall. He was the author of a *Petit Traité de solfège* (Montreal 1892), approved by the Conseil de l'Instruction publique du Québec, and of a treatise on instrumentation. Among his compositions were a *Funeral Mass*, a 'Pie Jesu,' a 'Dies Irae,' and an 'O member of the Institut populaire de France ca 1895.

BIBLIOGRAPHY

'La Société artistique canadienne et les professeurs du futur conservatoire,' Montreal *Le Samedi*, 6 Apr 1895

'M. Charles Labelle,' *P-T*, 35, 4 Jul 1896

'Charles Labelle,' *P-T*, 648, 27 Jan 1920

2 **Gustave**. Cellist, teacher, composer, b St-Henri (Montreal) 1 Nov 1878, d Montreal 31 Mar 1929. He began his musical studies with his father and then studied cello with Jean-Baptiste *Dubois. He was a member of various theatre orchestras and of the *Goulet *MSO ca 1907, the *Beethoven Trio 1907–10, and a cello quartet which he had organized.

Labelle taught 1907–22 at the *McGill Cons, 1921–9 at the École de musique de Montréal, and for some years at the *Institut Nazareth. Among his pupils were Gabriel *Cusson, Raoul *Duquette, Suzette Forgues, Yvette *Lamontagne, Henri *Letondal, and Brahm Sand. He composed a few works, including an *Élégie* for cello which he performed at *Windsor Hall 1 Oct 1903, *Je vous salue, Marie* published in *La Lyre* (May 1929), and some orchestral pieces. He wrote articles in periodicals, notably *MusiCanada* 1922–3.

BIBLIOGRAPHY

'M. Gustave Labelle,' *La Lyre*, Apr 1929

3 **Adrienne**. Soprano, teacher, b Montreal, fl 1904–10. She studied voice with her father and Céline *Marier and piano with Alexis *Contant and Émery *Lavigne. She completed her voice studies in 1903 with Auguste-Jean Dubulle in Paris. Following her return to Montreal in 1904 she was a soloist in numerous concerts, including those of the *Goulet *MSO, and specialized in the French repertoire. She also taught singing and opera.

BIBLIOGRAPHY

'Adrienne Labelle,' *P-T*, 223, 10 Oct 1903 (CG)

LABELLE, Jean-Baptiste. Organist, pianist, composer, conductor, b Plattsburgh, NY, of Canadian parents, 8 Sep 1828, d Montreal 9 Sep 1898. He was 15 when he became a church organist in Boucherville, near Montreal. In about 1846 he took a similar post in Chambly, Que. It was at this period that he received lessons from the Austrian pianist Leopold von Meyer, who was touring North America 1845–7. He studied 1847–9 with Sigismund Thalberg in Paris.

On his return Labelle became the organist at Montreal's Notre-Dame Church, remaining in the position for 41 years while teaching at the Collège de Montréal, the Collège Ste-Marie, the Collège Mont-St-Louis, the École normale, and the convents of Villa-Marie, Mont-Ste-Marie, and Ste-Anne in Lachine.

In 1857 Labelle toured the USA and South America, and in November of the same year he organized a 'Grand Operatic Concert' in which he presented; at *Mechanics' Hall, excerpts from works by Bellini, Donizetti, Adam, Schubert, and Meyerbeer. In 1863 he conducted the Société philharmonique canadienne of Montreal.

In 1891 Labelle was succeeded at Notre-Dame by Alcibiade *Béique. In December 1896 he was struck by an illness which left him paralysed.

Labelle left compositions in several genres, from the popular ballad or piano piece to larger concerto, and some 20 film scores. His *Lindy brod* fore 1868) and 'Avant tout je suis Canadien' (*Chansonnier des Collèges* 1860), both to words by Sir George-Étienne Cartier, and 'Chant des Zouaves canadiens' (*L'Album musical*, Dec 1881). His piano pieces included the popular *Marche canadienne*, with cornet cues (*L'Album littéraire*, Aug 1846), and *Quadrille national canadien* (Montreal nd). His *Cantate: La Confédération*, a setting of a text by Auguste Achintre, was premiered in 1868. He also composed *La Croisade canadienne*, a 'Cantate aux Zouaves pontificaux,' in 1886 to words by A. Bellemare. His operetta *La Conversion d'un pêcheur de la Nouvelle-Écosse*, to words by Elzéar Labelle (Boucher ca 1869) was premiered in 1884.

Labelle compiled and edited or composed a number of collections, including *Le Répertoire de l'organiste*, a Gregorian anthology with accompaniments by Labelle (at least 10 editions have been issued, the first in 1851); *Les Chansons les plus populaires*, a compilation of popular songs of the day; and *Échos de Notre-Dame*, a collection of his own choral pieces (published 1887) of which Oscar Comettant wrote 'In these unpretentious pieces, written in an out-and-out polyphonic style, I find a very fine religious sentiment and much melodic charm ... I will just mention *O Gloria Virginum*, which is truly inspired, perfectly developed, skilful in its modulation and piercing in its grace' (Paris *Le Siècle*, 20 Feb 1888).

BIBLIOGRAPHY

'Nos musiciens: M. J.B. Labelle,' 'Feu M. J.B. Labelle,' *Art musical*, Apr, Sep 1898

'Silhouettes musicales: Feu J.B. Labelle,' *P-T*, 92, 1 Oct 1898

Lortie, Jeanne d'Arc. 'Mes rimes,' *Dictionnaire des oeuvres littéraires du Québec*, vol 1, ed Maurice Lemire (Montreal 1978) (CG)

LABERGE, (Joseph Philippe) **André**. Organist, harpsichordist, b Beauharnois, near Montreal, 23 Aug 1940; BA (Montreal) 1960, B TH (Sherbrooke) 1969, premier prix organ, harpsichord, analysis (CMM) 1972, deuxième prix counterpoint (CMM) 1973, premier prix organ (Toulouse Cons) 1978. In 1960 he joined the Benedictines of St-Benoît-du-Lac, the monastery on Lac Memphrémagog, Que, and served there as organist. He was ordained in 1969 and then studied at the *CMM with Bernard *Lagacé (organ), Kenneth *Gilbert (harpsichord), Gilles *Tremblay (analysis), and Françoise *Aubut (counterpoint). In the summer of 1971 he took further organ training with Piet Kee and Luigi Tagliavini at the Haarlem Academy in Holland. He taught organ and harpsichord for *CAMMAC during the summers of 1972 and 1973 and began teaching at the *JMC Orford Art Centre in 1974. With the trumpeter Jean-Louis Chatel he recorded works by Fantini, Schmidt, Viviani, Handel, and Gerhard *Wuensch (1976, RCI 406).

On a *Canada Council grant 1977–9 Laberge studied organ with Xavier Darasse at the Toulouse Cons and took private harpsichord lessons with Gustav Leonhardt in Amsterdam. In France he played at the St-Thomas d'Aquin Church, Paris, and (with musicians from the Capitole) at the Carmelites' chapel in Toulouse. One of his recitals was broadcast by Radio France and rebroadcast by Cologne Radio.

Laberge has given numerous organ and harpsichord recitals in Canada – on the CBC, on Radio-Québec, and at the *Institut canadien, as well as for *Ars Organi, *Pro Organo, and the *Amis de l'orgue de Rimouski.

According to Gilles *Potvin, 'Dom Laberge plays with great musicological accuracy, but without affectation or dryness' (Montreal *Le Devoir*, 9 Aug 1975).

WRITINGS

'Homage to Medtner,' *Nicolas Medtner*, ed and transl Richard Holt (London 1955) (HPn)

LABERGE (La Berge, LaBerge), **Bernard R.** Impresario, organist, pianist, critic, lawyer, b Quebec 11 Oct 1891, naturalized US 1940, d New York 28 Dec 1951. His academic studies were taken with the Fathers of the Sacred Heart in Caraquet, NB, at the Séminaire de Rimouski, and at Laval U. Called to the bar in 1918, he opened a law office in Montreal and at the same time studied organ and piano and wrote music criticism for the newspaper *Le Canada*. After reviewing a concert by the tenor Paul *Dufault he was asked by Dufault to organize (1919) a trans-Canada tour in association with Henry Michaud.

Laberge opened an agency in Montreal afterwards, and by 1926 the Administration Bogue-Laberge also had an office in New York. During his career Laberge brought to North America the composers Goossens, Honegger, Milhaud, Prokofiev, Ravel, Respighi, Schmitt, and Tansman, the conductor Vladimir Golschmann, and the Band of the Royal Belgian Guides.

It was, however, in the field of organ and chamber concerts that Laberge was a true pioneer. He organized tours by the European organists Joseph *Bonnet, Charles Courboin, Marcel Dupré (who played the entire organ works of Bach in 10 Montreal recitals during 1923 and gave some 800 recitals under Laberge's management), Germani, André Marchal, Flor Peeters, Günther Ramin, Louis Vierne, and Carl Weinrich. He also sponsored recitals by North American organists, including the Canadian Bernard *Piché. Among the chamber ensembles which toured North America for Laberge were the Hungarian, Paganini, Pascal, Pro Arte, and Roth quartets, the Nuovo Quartetto Italiano, the Pasquier Trio, the Belgian Piano Quartet, and the Pro Musica Antiqua of Brussels.

Laberge managed the pianists Clara Haskil, Yvonne *Hubert, Léo-Pol *Morin, Ross *Pratt, Édouard Risler, and E. Robert Schmitz; the violinist Mischa Elman; the cellist Marcel Hubert; the harpist Marcel Grandjany; and the singers Jean *Riddez and Vladimir Rosing.

At Laberge's death the business was acquired by the US impresario Henry Colbert, who continued it until 1962 under the name Colbert-LaBerge Concert Management.

Laberge was married to the New York organist Claire Coci. His brother Dominique was music critic for *La Patrie*. Laberge was decorated with the cross of a Knight of the Crown of Belgium.

BIBLIOGRAPHY

Prévost, Roland. 'Un Canadien qui nous fait honneur, Bernard La Berge,' *P-T*, Feb 1947

Dion-Lévesque, Rosaire. *Silhouettes franco-américaines* (Manchester, NH 1957) GP

LABERGE, Rosemonde. Violinist, violist, teacher, b Ottawa 27 May 1928. She studied violin 1938–43 with Albert Tassé at Bruyère College in Ottawa and viola with Otto *Joachim in Montreal. In 1964 in Cornwall she founded the Riverdale Music School to provide tuition in string instruments, piano, and singing. The excellence of her teaching is evinced by her pupils' success in numerous competition festivals.

The Riverdale String Ensemble, established by Laberge in 1969 and made up of young musicians aged 8 to 18 from elementary and secondary schools, distinguished itself in regional and provincial festivals in Ontario and Quebec; its repertoire includes classical works and excerpts from musical comedies.

Three of Laberge's pupils, Joël Derouin (violin), Eileen Rudden (viola), and Thérèse Motard (cello), formed the Riverdale Trio in 1974 under the guidance of Otto Joachim. This trio won the 1975 Rose Bowl at the *National Competition Festival of Music. The group became a piano trio when Marc Durand joined it following Rudden's departure in 1976. Besides giving regular concerts in schools, the trio made a *JMC tour 1976–7 and another in France early in 1980.

Laberge has taught 'introduction to music' classes in Cornwall's elementary schools. ST

LABRECQUE, Jacques. Baritone, folksinger, storyteller, producer, publisher, b St-Benoît, near Montreal, 8 Jun 1917. He developed an interest in singing on his parents' farm. In Montreal he studied voice with Céline *Marier, Henri *Pontbriand, and Roger *Filiatrault, French repertoire with Marie-Thérèse *Paquin, and harmony with Oscar *O'Brien, who imparted to him his enthusiasm for French-Canadian folk music. Labrecque made his debut at 17 as a tenor, performing popular songs with much success on CBC radio programs such as 'Le Réveil rural.' In 1937 he played the role of Rigobert in Varney's *Les Mousquetaires au couvent* at the *Variétés lyriques. He signed a three-year contract with National Concerts and Artists of New York in 1946 and made a tour of Acadia. Three years later he represented Canada at an international folk festival in Venice, and from then on he devoted himself to the performance and dissemination of folk music.

Labrecque spent seven years in Europe, mainly in Paris (1951–6), where he sang with the Robert Dhéry troupe at the Variétés theatre. He made numerous tours for the Alliance française, appeared on ORTF and BBC radio and TV, and sang at the London Hippodrome. With the pianist Jean Guillou he gave 80 concerts for the *JMC in 1955–6 and then settled in Montreal, where he continued to sing while acting as producer and publisher of Musicana records. In addition to French and Canadian folksongs, he performed songs by new composers whose careers he had assisted or whom he had actually introduced to the public, such as Jean-Paul Filion ('La Parenté'), Gilles *Vigneault ('Jos Monferrand'), and Laurence Lepage ('Kino l'Indien'). He enjoyed a marked success at the 1958 *Stratford Festival and the 1961 *Mariposa Folk Festival.

After another JMC tour 1970–2, during which he presented an audio-visual show on folklore, he returned to Paris 1972–5 on a French government grant. He taught French-Canadian folksongs to students in psychomotor re-education at the U de Paris VI, while giving many recitals in France and other countries. He performed at the Canadian Cultural Centre in Brussels, as well as at the JM Camp in Belgium. On one of these occasions *La Cité* (Brussels, 7 Mar 1974) reported that he was 'endowed with naturalness, verve, and a voice magnificent for gentleness, or strength, or irony'; it continued: 'an excellent mimic, a natural actor, undoubtedly the most truly Canadian of Canadian singers, Jacques Labrecque restores to the verses of old Quebec all their dreamlike charm ... He evokes splendidly the eternal soul of Canada.'

Jacques Labrecque

In the summer of 1976 Labrecque presented on CBC radio a series of 14 half-hour programs, 'Chansons voltigeantes ... chansons dolentes,' devoted to different versions of folksongs. He performed at the *Grand Théâtre in Quebec City in December 1979.

Labrecque's supple and expressive voice, jovial temperament, sense of humour, and ability to touch his audience have made him an outstanding personality, bringing comparisons with Burl Ives or the actor Raimu. He is a member of the Société d'ethnographie française of Paris.

DISCOGRAPHY

French Operetta Airs: Lecocq – Adam – Planquette – et al. Legrand cond, Robertson cond. 1950. Lon LS 268/(*Extraits d'opérettes françaises / Music from French Operettas*) Decca LX-4527

Le Canada chante pour vous. Pathé AT 1029

Chansons populaires du Canada. Lon LB 957

Folk Songs of France and French Canada / Chansons populaires de France et du Canada. 1957. Folk FG 3560

Noël et carillons. Lon MB 1

Carnaval à Québec avec Labrecque. Lon MB 17

Jacques Labrecque présente Ti-Jean. Lon MB 52

Jacques Labrecque en France. Lon SMB 40033

On va t'y n'avoir du plaisir. Lon APM 1402

French Folk Songs from Canada. Fentok guit. 1960. RCI 162

La Parenté est arrivée ... 1961?. Lon MLP 100 14

L'Inimitable Jacques Labrecque. 1962. Lon MLP 100 25

Canadian Folk Songs: A Centennial Collection / Chansons folkloriques du Canada: Collection du Centenaire. (1967). 9-RCI and RCA CS 100

BIBLIOGRAPHY

Kiesel, Frédéric. 'Jacques Labrecque raconte et chante le vrai Canada,' Brussels *La Cité*, 28 Nov 1974

Lessard, Denis. 'Jacques Labrecque: le folkloriste du temps des fêtes,' Montreal *La Presse*, 30 Dec 1980

(TC-C, AP)

LACHANCE, Janine (m Munro). Pianist, teacher, b Quebec City 22 Feb 1932; premier prix piano, harmony (CMQ) 1950. She studied piano for two years with Omer *Létourneau and worked 1944–50 at the *CMQ with Hélène *Landry (piano), Françoise *Aubut (harmony), and Ria *Lenssens (solfège). She won the *MSO Concours in 1945 and in 1952 she received the *Prix d'Europe, which enabled her to work in Paris 1952–4 with Yvonne and Monique de la Bruchollerie. She studied voice 1954–5 with Mario Basiola in Milan.

Returning to Canada, Lachance was the accompanist 1955–8 for the instrumental classes at the CMQ. At the *CMM she was the coach-accompanist 1958–63 for Raoul *Jobin's class and the regular pianist 1963–8 for the classes and concerts of Léopold *Simoneau and Pierrette *Alarie. She studied Italian opera 1967–8 with Dick Marzollo and in

1968 became the accompanist for Lina and Antonio Narducci. She accompanied the Dutch baritone Max Van Egmond when he sang in 1970 for the *Ladies' Morning Musical Club and was coach-accompanist for the special courses given by Pierre Bernac and Hans Hotter in Montreal.

Lachance made recordings with Colette *Boky, Claude *Corbeil, the *Ensemble cantabile de Montréal, Bruno *Laplante, Léopold Simoneau, and Paul *Trépanier. With Bruno Laplante she recorded Quebec and French music for Paris radio programs during two European tours in 1976 and 1977. In 1977 she began teaching voice at the CMM. (MP)

LACHAPELLE, Guy. Percussionist, teacher, composer, b Granby, Que, 2 Mar 1931; premier prix (CMM) 1954. He studied at the *CMM 1948–54 with Saul Goodman. In 1954 he joined the *MSO, becoming its principal percussionist in 1958. He gave numerous concerts in Montreal and appeared on several CBC radio and TV programs as a member of an orchestra and sometimes as soloist. He took part in numerous festivals with the *SMCQ and served 1968–78 on its board of directors. In the early 1960s he was active in the jazz field; he belonged to the Montreal Jazz Society 1962–5 and, with Hans Kunst, ran a Montreal nightclub called Tête de Lard. About 1966, however, he abandoned jazz entirely.

Lachapelle's composition *Per-Q-Délic* (1967) for one percussionist was written for the Montreal dance company the Groupe de la Place royale. An abridged version of this work, entitled *Phases*, was recorded (RCI 409) in 1974. In 1972–3 for another Montreal dance troupe, the Groupe Nouvelle Aire, he composed a collective work with Micheline *Saint-Marcoux, Pierre *Béluse, and Robert Leroux: *Épisodies I, II, III* for three percussionists. *Épisodie II* was televised by the CBC and presented in 1973 at the MIDEM; this very successful program was sold to several countries. In 1975 Lachapelle began teaching at the CMM.

DISCOGRAPHY

Saint-Marcoux *Trakadie*. 1976. RCI-CAPAC RM 222, vol 13

See also Discographies for Josephte Dufresne; Serge Garant; SMCQ (RCI 358); and Gilles Tremblay. (LD-B)

LACHARITÉ, Sylvio. Conductor, administrator, composer, b Sherbrooke, Que, 3 Oct 1914; BA (Sherbrooke) 1936. He began his studies with his brother Lonia and Paul-Marcel Robidoux and then took piano lessons from Germaine *Malépart in Montreal. He also took courses in Gregorian chant with Dom Georges Mercure at St-Benoît-du-Lac Abbey.

Lacharité became interested in orchestra conducting and in 1939 with some friends founded the *Sherbrooke SO. He was to remain the regular conductor of that orchestra until 1969. To improve his skills he spent eight summers 1944–9 and 1953–4 at the school run by Pierre Monteux in Hancock, Me. In 1950 the maestro allowed him to consider himself one of his 'disciples,' an honour previously granted to only four young conductors. The same year, Lacharité went to Paris and studied composition and analysis with Olivier Messiaen and Andrée Vaurabourg-Honegger. In the summer of 1959 he attended Igor Markevitch's classes in Salzburg.

Because of Lacharité's talent and perseverance, the Sherbrooke SO, a community orchestra, was able to tackle such works as Beethoven's *Ninth Symphony* and Honegger's *Le Roi David*. Lacharité guest-conducted the CBC orchestras in Montreal and Quebec City, as well as the *CBC SO during the 1954–5 and 1955–6 seasons. In 1958 he conducted the orchestra of the Concerts Pasdeloup in Paris.

Lacharité has shown a keen interest in young people and teaching. He was president in 1950 of the Assn of Canadian musicians in Paris and national president 1955–7 of the *JMC. At the *CMQ he taught the orchestra class in 1952, analysis and aesthetics 1966–7, and pedagogy in 1970 and was appointed assistant director in 1971. He served 1974–7 as director of the Chicoutimi Cons.

Lacharité was appointed principal conductor of the *CBC Quebec Chamber Orchestra in 1964 and was music director 1962–5 of the *Théâtre lyrique de Nouvelle-France. For the latter he conducted performances of *Lakmé* in 1962, *Tosca* and *Werther* in 1963, and *Così fan tutte* in 1964. He was music director of the *Concerts Couperin in Quebec City and on several occasions was director of the orchestra class at the *JMC Orford Art Centre. In 1964 he conducted the premiere of *Ennéade*, a work by his former piano pupil Serge *Garant.

Lacharité himself composed several works for orchestra, including the overture *Vision d'Ézéchiel*, the symphonic poem *Le Vaisseau d'or*, and the suite *Portraits en miniature*. He made numerous arrangements and transcriptions, including those of most of the songs of Marius *Barbeau's *Romancero du Canada*.

WRITINGS

'Souvenirs et réflexions d'un professeur de conservatoire,' *VM*, 10, Dec 1968

BIBLIOGRAPHY

David, Jean. 'Sylvio Lacharité, compositeur, chef d'orchestre,' *Qui?*, vol 1, Mar 1950 (MB-L)

LACOURCIÈRE, Luc. Ethnographer, folklorist, writer, teacher, b St-Victor, Beauce, Que, 18 Oct 1910; BA (Laval) 1932, L LITT (Laval) 1934, hon D LITT (McGill) 1966, hon doctorate in ethnography (Memorial) 1975, hon D LITT (Laurentian) 1977. After classical and university studies in Quebec City, he went to France and also spent 1936–7 as a teacher at the Collège St-Charles in Porrentruy, Switzerland. He taught Latin 1938–9 at the Collège Bourget of Rigaud, Que, and was assistant director of the French summer courses 1938–48 at *Laval U. He received a scholarship from the Royal Society of Canada in 1939 and began studying anthropology in relation to folklore with Marius *Barbeau at the *National Museum in Ottawa; he also visited certain US universities to consult specialists.

Lacourcière taught French literature 1940–63 at Laval U and lectured 1941–2 for the CBC program 'Radio-Collège.' On a grant from the Guggenheim Foundation he spent some time in 1943–4 examining the systems at the Library of Congress, Washington, and the Harvard U Library in Cambridge, Mass. Besides teaching folklore and ethnography 1944–78 at Laval U, he was director of the department of Canadian studies 1963–71. He established the *Archives de folklore in 1944 and was its director until 1975. In addition he initiated and edited the Archives de folklore publication series, and his own numerous articles for the series included a critical study of the popular song 'Les Écoliers de Pontoise' (vol 1, 1946) and writings on Canadian children's rhymes (vol 3, 1948) and burlesque songs (vol 4, 1949). Conrad *Laforte and Roger *Matton were among his collaborators. With a grant from the Rockefeller Foundation in 1956, he began compiling an indexed catalogue, *Bibliographie raisonnée des traditions populaires françaises d'Amérique*. He organized the 14th Congress of the IFMC in Quebec City in 1961.

Lacourcière participated in several congresses and gave numerous lectures in France (including several in 1953 and 1965 at the Institut scientifique franco-canadien), the USA, and Canada. He directed more than a hundred masters' and doctoral theses between 1941 and 1978. He was a member of the *Canada Council 1962–5 and became a member of the Société des Dix in 1966 and was awarded the Prix Duvernay and the medal of the Saint-Jean-Baptiste Society of Montreal in 1969. He was made a Companion of the *Order of Canada in 1971 and Fellow of the American Folklore Society in 1973; he received the *CMCouncil Medal in 1974 and the Order of Merit and medal of the Saint-Jean-Baptiste Society of Quebec City in 1976. He was named honorary president of the Canadian Assn for Studies in Folklore in 1976.

WRITINGS

– and Savard, F.-A. *L'Histoire et le folklore* (Montreal 1945)

'Le Noël des animaux,' *Archives de folklore* (Quebec 1950)

– and Savard, F.-A. 'Canadian folk songs collected at Baie-des-Rochers (Charlevoix),' *Annual Report of the National Museum of Canada for the Fiscal Year 1949–1950*, Bulletin 123 (Ottawa 1951)

'Nos cousins chantent,' *La Chanson du pays* (Paris 1953)

'Bibliographie raisonnée de l'anthropologie canadienne,' *Mémoires de la Société généalogique canadienne-française*, vol 9, Jul–Oct 1958

'Les transformations d'une chanson folklorique: du Moine tremblant au Rapide-Blanc,' *Recherches sociographiques*, vol 1, no. 4, 1960

'The present state of French-Canadian folklore studies,' *JAF*, vol 74, Oct–Dec 1961

– and Savard, F.-A. *Le Folklore acadien* (Toronto 1968)

BIBLIOGRAPHY

Cass-Beggs, Michael. 'Hommage à Luc Lacourcière,' *CMB*, 9, Autumn–Winter 1974

Dupont, Jean-Claude, ed. *Mélanges en l'honneur de Luc Lacourcière* (Montreal 1978)

Dionne, René. 'Hommage à Luc Lacourcière,' *Lettres québécoises*, 13, Feb 1979

'Entrevue: Luc Lacourcière,' interview with Adrien Thério, ibid (DM)

LACOURSE, René. Tenor, choir conductor, b St-Hubert, near Montreal, 13 May 1931. After studies 1950–6 with the baritone Louis *Bourdon he worked with Jacques *Gérard until the latter died in 1957. He also studied conducting 1965–6 with Michel *Perrault. He began his career in 1953 in the chorus at the *Variétés lyriques, began singing in CBC choirs in 1956, and two years later became a member of the *Montreal Bach Choir and the *Petit ensemble vocal. He made his solo debut in the title role of the medieval play *The Play of Daniel* presented on CBC TV in December 1959 by the New York Pro Musica conducted by Noah Greenberg. For the *SMCQ he sang in the Canadian premiere of Lutoslawski's *Paroles tissées* (1969).

Lacourse first worked as a choir conductor in 1965 when he was engaged by the *Montreal Festivals to prepare the chorus of Gilbert Bécaud's *Opéra d'Aran*. Beginning in 1967 he directed the choirs of the *MSO for its performances of opera (eg, *Faust*, 1967) and oratorio (Haydn's *The Creation*, Britten's *War Requiem*, Verdi's *Requiem*, etc). He was appointed music director of the *Disciples de Massenet in 1970 and was chorus master 1971–5 for the *Opéra du Québec and for productions of *Festival Ottawa at the *NAC. GP

LADEROUTE (Ladéroute), **Joseph** (Victor). Tenor, teacher, b Sault Ste Marie, Ont, ca 1913. Born of French-Canadian parents, he sang as a child in the parish choir and at seven began studying singing with Mrs S.L. Pieke. Three years later he entered the Paulists' Seminary in New York and toured in the USA 1927–8 as soloist with the Paulist Choristers. He continued his voice training in Toronto and Cincinnati, and then in New York with Léon Rothier, and studied Lieder with Erno Balogh and choral music with Charles Baker. In about 1942 he studied with Salvator *Issaurel in Montreal.

In 1938 Laderoute was soloist with the *Toronto Mendelssohn Choir in Berlioz' *Requiem*. He was a soloist with the Dessoff Choirs in New York in 1940 and gave a recital at the *Ladies' Morning Musical Club in Montreal the same year. He appeared with the orchestras of Chicago 1939–40, Detroit (*Elijah*) in 1940, and Toronto in 1940 and sang again with the *TSO in the Canadian premiere of Mahler's *Das Lied von der Erde* in 1945. He was Jacquino in the 1944 NBC SO broadcast of *Fidelio* under Arturo Toscanini; the performance was released later as a recording (RCA-Victor, 2-LM-6025).

With the *Opera Guild of Montreal Laderoute sang the Astrologer in *Le Coq d'or* (1944), Florestan in *Fidelio* (1946), and Manrico in *Il Trovatore* (1949). Thomas *Archer described him in *The Gazette* on 4 May 1946 as 'possibly the best choice that could have been made on this continent for the role of Florestan. [His portrayal was] a striking creation in many respects.' In 1948 he sang the title role in *Faust* at the Mount Royal Chalet for the *Montreal Festivals.

Laderoute was a soloist at the Bach festivals in Bethlehem, Pa, and in Cincinnati and sang five roles in the North American premiere (1948) of Honegger's *Jeanne d'Arc au bûcher* with the New York Philharmonic Orchestra. He gave many recitals in Town Hall, New York, and on the NBC, CBS, and MBS networks, as well as on the CBC. He was director of vocal studies 1952–4 at the Jordan College of Music of Butler U, Indianapolis, and later taught at the Kansas City Cons and the Peabody Cons, Baltimore. He eventually abandoned his musical career to become an Oblate at the Benedictine monastery in Belmont, NC. GP

Ladies' colleges and convent schools. Until the late 19th century in Canada, music training was considered more suitable for young women than for young men. At first, even to women, it was available only privately and on a limited basis, but early in the century it was offered in a few ladies' and girls' schools. A prospectus of the Young Ladies' Academy of the Ursuline Convent in Quebec City offered lessons in accordion, guitar, harp, organ, and piano, and the girls at the boarding school of Quebec City's Hôpital général were taught by organists from the Quebec Basilica. Later (1857–68) music instruction was provided by the nuns of the Hôpital général.

1 Ladies' colleges
2 Convent schools

1 LADIES' COLLEGES. By the 1840s the Canadian middle classes had begun to view music as a proper and necessary part of education for young women. As a result, an increasing number of ladies' colleges added it to their curricula. At Cobourg, Ont, Upper Canada Academy (later Victoria U), incorporated by the Conference of the Methodist Episcopal Church of Canada in 1836, had a separate ladies' department, which offered music lessons as early as 1839. A few years later the appendix to William S. Darling's *Sketches of Canadian Life* (London 1849) included advertisements for Toronto boarding schools, such as Mrs Scobie's, where students might study 'Music, French and Drawing, on the most moderate terms,' and for a young ladies' French and English school (run by M and Mme Deslandes) which provided music instruction for boarders and 'German, Italian, Singing and Dancing on the Usual Terms' for day students. Such lessons appear to have been optional and available only for an additional fee.

Other Ontario schools and colleges with music teachers on staff during the 19th century were the Adelaide Ladies' Academy and Miss MacNally's, both in Toronto, the Burlington Academy in Hamilton, the Misses Dunn School for Ladies in Cobourg, the Oakville Ladies' Academy (Oakville), St Mary's Academy in Windsor, Ont (where Salomon *Mazurette was music director 1875–6), the Ottawa Ladies' College (Edward *Fisher, music director ca 1875), and Hellmuth College in London. The last-named of these was founded by the Church of England in 1869 and offered courses in choral singing, voice, harmony, history, organ, piano, theory, and violin. Music directors at Hellmuth included W. Waugh *Lauder, who held the position 1883–5; among those who taught there ca 1884–94 were William Caven Barron (piano and organ), Thomas Martin (piano), Roselle Pococke (violin), and Nelda von Seyfried (voice). Another noteworthy school was the Wesleyan Ladies College, Hamilton, incorporated by the Conference of the Methodist Church of Canada in 1861. Teachers in the music department (initiated in 1870) included Robert Steele *Ambrose (instrumental and vocal music), C.L.M. *Harris and Clarence *Lucas (harmony), Emma Kellogg (voice), and L.H. Parker (organ). The Ontario Ladies' College at Whitby and Alma College at St Thomas both have made significant contributions. Among those who taught at the Whitby college are G.D. *Atkinson, Edward Fisher, Stanley *Osborne, and F.H. *Torrington. Teachers at Alma College, whose music department was established by St John Hyttenrauch, have included Frank *Welsman (also music director 1928–31), Gertrude *Huntley Green (music director during the 1930s), and Doreen *Hall.

In western Canada, a Mrs Mills and her daughters oversaw a girls' school established at the Red River Colony (Winnipeg) ca 1851; music instruction, including piano lessons, was available to its students. In New Westminster, BC, St Ann's Academy (founded in 1865) offered thorough training in piano. St Hilda's College for Girls (established in Calgary during the late 1880s) was another western school which provided music lessons. Among those who taught there were Ada Dowling Costigan, who brought the first baby grand piano to Calgary, and Annie *Glen Broder.

On the east coast an important teaching centre was established in Sackville, NB. By the 1890s *Mount Allison Ladies' College was one of the largest such schools in Canada, with one of the largest music teaching facilities as well.

In Montreal two girls' schools established with financial assistance from Lord *Strathcona offered music instruction. The first of these, founded as the Trafalgar Institute (Trafalgar School for Girls after 1887, and affiliated with *McGill U in 1911), included music appreciation and class singing in its regular curriculum. Among its teaching staff were Frantz *Jehin-Prume and Victor *Brault. The Royal Victoria College for Women, founded in 1896, had a music department established by Clara *Lichtenstein when the school opened in 1899. The department amalgamated in 1904 with the McGill Conservatorium.

2 CONVENT SCHOOLS. Particularly in the province of Quebec, music education has been largely the preserve of the Roman Catholic female religious orders, which have established schools and academies where children (in later years boys as well as girls) can be enrolled for a general education and, in some instances, specifically for music training. While most such schools are in Quebec, the major orders have established similar ones in all the other provinces of Canada. Only a selection of these can be described here.

During the 1870s Lady Dufferin, the wife of the governor-general, visited several Quebec convent schools, including that of Jésus Marie at Sillery, where she viewed a hall with '12 glass boxes, each containing a piano so that the pupils can practise simultaneously; whilst in another glass house sits the mistress, overlooking, but happily for her, not overhearing' (*My Canadian Journal 1872–78*, Toronto 1969, p 24). Lady Dufferin also toured the Sacred Heart Convent in Montreal, at whose school in February 1878 she heard students perform 'an original operetta' (ibid, p 285).

The religious order the Congregation of Notre Dame (founded in Montreal in 1658 by Marguerite Bourgeoys) began to offer piano lessons at its boarding school in 1834. Teachers included Eugénie Kilchen de la Peronnière, W.H. Warren, and J.-C. *Brauneis II. In 1845 the school was presented with a harp by the governor of Lower Canada; Henry Berlyn gave lessons on it. Among the school's directors of music during the 19th century were Henriette Dufresne (Sister St-Michel) 1845–?, and Sister Ste-Berthe 1895–1910. In 1908 the congregation established in Montreal an École d'enseignement supérieur (a teacher training school) affiliated with *Laval U. Romain-Octave *Pelletier was among the first to teach there. In 1926 Sister Ste-Anne-Marie founded the Institut pédagogique (renamed Collège Marguerite-Bourgeoys in 1976) and the *École normale de musique, both also in Montreal.

In order to maintain uniformity in the music programs offered at all of its houses, the Congregation of Notre Dame created the position of director general for music studies in 1936. In 1943 a 10-year course of study, open to all regular students, was initiated. In 1958 137 of the order's houses in Canada and the USA and three of its missions in Japan offered music instruction. Among many others who have taught for the order over the years are J.-Arthur *Bernier, Charlotte *Cadoret, Albert *Chamberland, Guillaume *Couture, J.-B. *Dubois, Henri *Gagnon, Arthur *Laurendeau, Omer *Létourneau, and Berthe *Roy.

Founded in Montreal in 1844 by Sister Marie-Rose, the Institute of the Sisters of the Holy Names of Jesus and Mary began to offer piano lessons in 1845. These were given at first by William Benzinger and 1872–80 by a Mrs Petipas, who was engaged to teach singing and piano. In 1920 Sister *Marie-Stéphane was named the order's director of music studies. During her tenure a nine-year program of music studies was established for regular students, and a system by which senior sisters visited the order's schools in Quebec and Ontario was implemented to assist teachers and to examine students. A certificate was offered for the first six years of tuition successfully completed and a diploma for the last three. In 1932 Sister Marie-Stéphane founded the École supérieure de musique d'Outremont (renamed *École Vincent-d'Indy in 1951). By 1979 14 of the order's schools continued to offer music instruction. Those who have taught music for the order include Lazare-Arsène *Barbarin, Louis *Bouhier, Jean-Noël *Charbonneau, Alexis *Contant, Guillaume Couture, Alfred *De Sève, Arsène Dubuc, Jules *Hone, Alfred *Lamoureux, Émery *Lavigne, Arthur *Letondal, and Romain-Octave Pelletier.

The Sisters of the Holy Cross arrived in Canada in 1847 and began to teach piano at their boarding school at St-Laurent, Montreal, in 1848. Their graduates' diplomas were awarded at first by the *Dominion College of Music and later by the *Cons du Québec. In the 20th century both a school and a college (the École and the Collège de musique Ste-Croix) were established under Sister

Marie de Ste-Jeanne-du-Rosaire, who was appointed the order's music director in 1936. The school provided instruction for youngsters, while the college catered to advanced students, awarding certificates and degrees in performance and teaching. The college was affiliated with the *U of Montreal 1957–67. In 1968 both the school and the college were absorbed by the St-Laurent Cegep. In the province of Quebec, approximately 24 Sisters of the Holy Cross institutions have offered music instruction. In addition, courses in music have been given at the order's Musica School founded in 1962 in Cornwall, Ont, at 11 of its convents in Alberta, and at a number of its convent schools in the USA. Among those who have taught for the order are Françoise *Aubut, Yvonne *Hubert, Czeslaw Kaczynski, Yvette *Lamontagne, Michel *Longtin, Armas *Maiste, Maurice *Onderet, Michel *Perrault, Calvin *Sieb, Georges-Émile *Tanguay, and Jean-Eudes *Vaillancourt.

Music lessons offered by the Sisters of Ste Anne were given at first only by secular instructors. Some of the first students at the order's Lachine (Montreal) boarding school received instruction from J.-B. *Labelle, and after 1869 the program of studies initiated there served as a model for the order's other schools. In 1876 an examining board was established at Lachine for the purpose of awarding certificates; after 1899 many diplomas were issued by the *AMQ. For some years beginning in 1871 Paul *Letondal oversaw the music studies programs. The order's music school in Montreal was affiliated in 1937 with the U of Montreal as the École supérieure de musique; in 1965 it was renamed the École de musique Wilfrid-Pelletier. Principals of the school have included Louisa *Paquin, Diane Villeneuve (Sister Marie-Héloïse), and Rosa Lavallée (Sister Marie du Sénacle), succeeded in 1961 by Geneviève Gauthier (Sister Marie-Thérèse-Eugénie).

There have been approximately 60 Sisters of Ste Anne houses offering music instruction in Quebec. The order also has schools in British Columbia; music training was begun in New Westminster in 1865. In 1900 music programs were initiated at the schools in Kamloops, Vancouver, and Victoria. Among those who have taught for the Sisters of Ste Anne are Lydia *Boucher, Claude *Champagne, Camille *Couture, Gabriel *Cusson, Bernard *Diamant, Pauline *Donalda, Salvator *Issaurel, Charles-Marie *Panneton, Raoul *Paquet, and Antoinette Wilscam. Among noted musicians who have studied at Sisters of Ste Anne schools are Fernande *Chiocchio, Marie *Daveluy, Marguerite *Lavergne, and Louis *Lortie. The order has published the *Dictionnaire biographique des musiciens* (Lachine 1922) and the *Dictionnaire biographique des musiciens canadiens* (Lachine 1935), as well as several books on theory and solfège. 1 / (DRA), 2 / (HP)

The Ladies' Morning Musical Club. Montreal musical institution, one of the oldest in Canada, founded in 1892 by Mary Bell, who wanted to bring together her friends for serious study and appreciation of the classics. She was assisted by Adèle Sise and intended the membership to be both French- and English-speaking. The first administrative committee, of which she was president, decided to hold weekly meetings each Thursday at 11 am, hence the name adopted by the club. The modest fees – $1 for active members, who participated in the early concerts, and $2 for associate members – contributed to the immediate success of the enterprise.

During the 1892–3 season about 20 concerts were organized, with works by Bach, Chopin, Dvořák, Gounod, Grieg, Liszt, Massenet, Mendelssohn, Saint-Saëns, and Wagner, among others, and the occasional participation of a vocal ensemble. Among the first guest artists were Guillaume *Couture, Dominique *Ducharme, J.-J. *Goulet, and R.-O. *Pelletier. Lectures were added to the concerts shortly afterwards to foster appreciation of composers then considered difficult to understand, such as Bach and Wagner.

The club's first concert by an internationally known performer took place at the *Monument national in 1895. The violinist Eugène Ysaÿe made his Canadian debut on this occasion, and the general public was invited to attend. Always at the forefront of musical exploration, the club presented excerpts from Debussy's *Pelléas et Mélisande* in 1917, 23 years before its Canadian premiere. The concerts accorded a special place to contemporary composers: Bloch, Hindemith, Medtner, Reger.

Numerous Canadian and foreign artists who later acquired international reputations were introduced to Montreal or even to Canada by the club, often through the efforts of Mme Cécile Léger (née Hone), an original and active member of the club who took the trouble to inform herself about outstanding new talents through visits to New York and elsewhere. Percy Grainger (1912), Pauline *Donalda (1915), Yvonne *Hubert (1922), Walter Gieseking (1928), Vladimir Horowitz (1930), and, later, Glenn *Gould and Maureen *Forrester performed for the club. Chamber music groups such as the Kneisel String Quartet (1896), the London String Quartet (1921), the Paris Instrumental Quintet (1934), and the Amadeus, Juilliard, and Pro Arte Quartets have appeared on numerous occasions.

While actually presenting in recital a large number of Canadians, the Ladies' Morning Musical Club also has contributed each year, through the Mary Bell Scholarship Fund, established in 1907, to the development of Canadian student musicians. The Cécile Léger Award, established for student members of the club, was granted until 1967. The annual Kerry-Lindsay award of $100, begun in 1928, was created to assist student members of the club.

In 1940, concert time was changed to 2:30 pm; in 1969, males for the first time were invited to attend. The concerts were held successively at the YMCA Hall (Dominion Square), at the Windsor and Ritz-Carlton hotels, at the Comédie-Canadienne, at the Mount Royal Hotel, and, beginning in 1971, at the Maisonneuve theatre in *PDA. While retaining the initials LMMC, the club has adopted the optional name of Les matinées de musique de chambre. In 1977 it had more than 900 members, who enjoyed 12 concerts annually.

BIBLIOGRAPHY

Léger, Cécile. *Fifty Years of Musical Recollection 1892–1942* (Montreal 1942)

Brosseau, Cécile. 'Le Ladies' Morning a déjà accordé pour plus de $40,000 en bourses,' Montreal *La Presse*, 19 Sep 1973

Rowan, Renée. 'Le bénévolat des femmes dans le secteur culturel,' Montreal *Le Devoir*, 4 Oct 1976

Charest, Nicole. '85 ans de problèmes, de travail et de succès,' *Perspectives*, 23 Jul 1977

Ladies' Morning Musical Club. Annual reports 1892–3– CH

LAFERRIÈRE, Marie (Cécile Hélène) (m Doane). Mezzo-soprano, b St-Barthélemy, near Trois-Rivières, Que, 21 May 1949; B MUS (Montreal) 1970, M MUS (Sherbrooke) 1972. At the *École Vincent-d'Indy 1966–72 she studied with Louise *André and Bernard *Diamant, and at the Salzburg Mozarteum in 1971 she was coached by the pianist Erik Werba. She won the *Prix d'Europe in 1972 and resumed study with Werba at the Vienna Academy 1972–3, as well as with Bernard *Turgeon at the *Banff SFA (summers of 1972, 1973). She was a pupil of Léopold *Simoneau in San Francisco 1974–6 and placed first in auditions held by that city's opera company. At the Accademia Chigiana of Siena she worked in 1975 with the coach Giorgio Favaretto. She won a number of prizes, including a bronze medal and a special prize for performance at the 1975 Geneva International Competition for Musical Performers, a second prize that same year at the Competition of 's Hertogenbosch in Holland, and a prize in 1979 from the Concert Artists Guild of New York. The Guild prize entitled her to a performance at Carnegie Recital Hall on 27 November of the same year. Raymond Ericson said of her on that occasion: 'Miss Laferrière's singing was notable for the kind of forward diction common to French artists, which communicates text and music immediately to the audience. This was just as true of the lively Rossini songs and the more sober cycle of Schumann (*Frauenliebe und Leben*) as it was of the French works. The mezzo's direct expressiveness was a constant pleasure, particularly because she understood the nature of the music she was singing, its relationship to the texts and its various stylistic demands. Her voice was attractive, steady, slightly cool in timbre. It moved cleanly and was always on pitch' (*New York Times*, 2 Dec 1979). Marie Laferrière has given numerous recitals in Canada, Europe, and the USA. She has performed frequently on the CBC in recital and she participated in the premiere of *Garant's ... *chant d'amours* (1975). She sang in the San Francisco Opera's 1975 production of Donizetti's *Viva la Mamma*. In 1976 she married the US tenor David Doane.

BIBLIOGRAPHY

'Debut in New York,' *Music*, Mar–Apr 1980 GP

LAFORTE, Conrad. Ethnologist, librarian-archivist, teacher, b Kénogami (Jonquière), Que, 10 Nov 1921; BA (Laval) 1946, BLS (Montreal) 1949, L LITT (Laval) 1968, diplôme d'études supérieures (Laval) 1970, D LITT (Laval) 1977. He was educated at the Petit séminaire in Chicoutimi, at Laval U, and at the U of Montreal. He was librarian-archivist 1951–75 and secretary 1973–5 of the *Archives de folklore of *Laval U.

In 1954 Laforte began an important ethnographic study in Quebec, collecting some 150 hours of recordings of songs, dance tunes, stories, and legends, some of which were published in the *Cahiers* of the Archives de folklore (1970–2, vols 10, 12, and 14) and in the *Cahiers d'histoire* (1970, no. 22). In 1953 he began to compile a *Catalogue de la chanson folklorique française* which grew until it contained more than 80,000 listings. A selection of these was published (Quebec City 1958) and earned him the 1959 Prix Raymond-Casgrain. Upon its appearance the selection was hailed by Roger Lecotté in the *Bulletin folklorique d'Île-de-France* (Oct–Dec 1958) as an 'indispensable catalogue for all researchers'; the introduction, Lecotté said, demonstrated the author's conscientiousness and his scientific abilities: 'It is clear, logical, critical, in a word, authoritative.' *Chansons en laisse*, volume 1 of the projected six-volume complete, descriptive edition of the catalogue (see General bibliography), was published in Quebec City in 1977; and volume 4, *Chansons énumératives*, appeared in 1979. The *Catalogue*'s classification system was adopted by the *National Museums of Canada, the *U of Moncton, and the U of Sudbury.

Laforte in 1956 directed the classification of the songs collected by Édouard-Z. *Massicotte at the Montreal City Library and of those collected

1959–62 by Marius *Barbeau for the National Museum of Canada. He did research 1964–5 in Paris on a *Canada Council grant and took part in numerous ethnological conferences. At Laval U, he was assistant lecturer 1965–73 in the department of Canadian studies and taught after 1973 in the history department.

Two of Laforte's numerous studies are *La Chanson folklorique et les écrivains du XIXe siècle (en France et au Québec)* (Montreal 1973) and *Poétiques de la chanson traditionelle française* (Quebec City 1976). Laforte has contributed to many collections and periodicals in Canada and abroad, notably to the *Dictionnaire des oeuvres littéraires du Québec* (Montreal 1978) and to *EMC*. GP

LAGACÉ. Montreal family of organists and harpsichordists: 1 / Bernard, 2 / Mireille, his wife, and 3 / Geneviève, their daughter.

1 **Bernard**. Organist, harpsichordist, teacher, b St-Hyacinthe, Que, 21 Nov 1930. He began his studies with Yvonne *Hubert (piano), Conrad *Letendre (organ), and Gabriel *Cusson (harmony and counterpoint). He was awarded a grant in 1954 by the Quebec government and studied in Paris 1954–5 with André Marchal (organ). In 1956 he worked in Vienna under Anton Heiller, also learning the harpsichord from Isolde Ahlgrimm and Eta Harich-Schneider. Returning in 1957 to Montreal, he taught 1957–78 at the *CMM and was appointed to the staff of *Concordia U in 1978. He taught during the summers 1962–74 at the *CAMMAC Music Centre, 1974–6 at the *JMC Orford Art Centre, and 1975 and 1977 at the Académie d'été de St-Hubert in Quebec. He also began teaching summers at the Choate Music Seminars in Wallingford, Conn, in 1969. Among his many pupils have been Hélène Dugal, Dom André *Laberge, Lucien and Réjean *Poirier, and William Tiemersma. He became a member of the group *Ars Organi and has been active in the revival of the classical organ in North America. He has served on the juries of international organ competitions held in 1971 in St Albans, England, and in 1973, 1976, and 1979 in Bruges, Belgium. Lagacé has become known internationally as an organ recitalist. He has performed many times in Canada (notably on the CBC) and in the USA and has taken part frequently in important festivals, including those in Avignon, Bruges, London, Paris, and St-Maxim. He became organist at the Sanctuaire Marie-Reine-des-Coeurs in Montreal in 1966.

Although he has played most of the important works of the organ repertoire, Lagacé is considered a specialist of baroque music, and of Bach in particular. He performed the complete organ works of Bach 1975–7 in 12 recitals at the Immaculée-Conception Church in Montreal. In 1978–9 he performed Buxtehude's complete organ works in six recitals with his wife in the same church. After a recital 28 Jun 1978 at St Joseph's Chapel in Montreal, Gilles *Potvin commented on his interpretation of Bach's six *Schübler Chorale Preludes*: 'Bernard Lagacé is an exceptional interpreter who is able to use all the resources of the chapel's superb von Beckerath, giving each piece a variety of individual colours, while keeping the necessary stylistic unity' (*Le Devoir*, 30 Jun 1978). In 1978 Lagacé was awarded the Prix Denise-Pelletier by the Quebec government.

WRITINGS

'François Morel, musicien canadien,' *Liberté*, vol 60, Sep–Oct 1960

DISCOGRAPHY

Bach *The Art of Fugue*; et al. 1977. 3-Arion ARN 3360-13

Brahms 11 *Chorales; Fugue in B Flat Minor*. 1978. Titanic Ti-38

Bernard Lagacé

Chorales for Organ: Scheidt – Buxtehude – Pachelbel – Böhm – Bach. 1965. Madrigal MAS-400

Couperin *Messe pour les couvents*. 1965. Madrigal MAS-403/Oryx ORYX 723

Cycle d'orgues en Avignon: English music of the 16th and 17th centuries. 1975. 3-Arion ARN 3360-07

Frescobaldi *Missa della Madonna* (org); *Aria detta la Frescobalda*; et al (hpd). 1965. Madrigal MAS-401

Pachelbel *Toccata*; et al. 1975. Arion ARN 38273

D. Scarlatti *Stabat mater* – Buxtehude *Cantate Domino* – Schütz *Rorate coeli; Hodie Christus; Veni sancte*. Choeur polyphonique de Mtl, Courville cond. 1966. Madrigal MAS-409

With Mireille Lagacé: The complete organ works of Buxtehude. 1977–8. 8-Calliope CAL 1731–1738 (2 boxed sets). Also available singly on Calliope CAL 1731, 1733, 1735, 1737 (Bernard); 1732, 1734, 1736, 1738 (Mireille)

See also Discography for Micheline *Tessier.

BIBLIOGRAPHY

Gingras, Claude. 'Lagacé: Je suis content qu'on ait pensé à l'orgue,' Montreal *La Presse*, 7 Oct 1978

2 **Mireille** (b Bégin). Organist, harpsichordist, teacher, b St-Jérôme, Que, 8 Jun 1935. She studied in Montreal with Germaine *Malépart (piano), Conrad *Letendre (organ), and Gabriel *Cusson (theory). She went to Austria in 1956 on a Quebec government scholarship and studied organ with Anton Heiller and choir conducting with Hans Gillesberger. Returning to Montreal, she continued her organ and harpsichord studies 1957–62 with her husband and took part in the activities of the group *Ars Organi. Between 1962 and 1965 she won several international prizes (Munich and Geneva, 1962), and in 1964 she founded the Ensemble Couperin-le-Grand. She taught organ and harpsichord at the *U of Montreal 1967–72 and at the *CMM 1973–5 and again in 1977. Mireille Lagacé also began teaching at the New England Cons in Boston in 1970. During the summers she taught baroque music 1964–74 at the CAMMAC music centre and began teaching harpsichord in 1974 at the *JMC Orford Art Centre and in 1970 at the Choate Music Seminars in Wallingford, Conn. She has pursued a busy career as a soloist and an ensemble player in Canada (where she has performed often on CBC TV and radio), the USA (where she has performed under the auspices of the American Guild of Organists), and in western Europe. She has played with the Ensemble baroque de Montréal and with the *Ensemble Claude-Gervaise. Jean *Papineau-Couture dedicated his *Dyarchie* to her, and she premiered it in 1971 in Boston. In 1977 she was chosen for a Victor M. Lynch-Staunton Award by the Canada Council, and in 1978 she began to record Bach's complete works for harpsichord for Calliope in Paris. After the first recital in the series devoted to Buxtehude's complete organ works by Mireille Lagacé and her husband 1978–9, Maureen Peterson wrote, 'Her handling of the various works, the chorales especially, could force a listener to let go, to follow the music into a higher realm' (Montreal *The Gazette*, 3 Oct 1978).

Mireille Lagacé

DISCOGRAPHY

ORGAN

Dietrich Buxtehude, Works for the Organ. 1975. Titanic Ti-11

A. Gabrieli – Merulo: *Ricercari, Toccatas* – (with Geneviève Lagacé) duets by Frescobaldi – Merula. 1978. 2-Titanic Ti-43, 44

Magnificat: Cavazzoni – Frescobaldi – Scheidt – Buxtehude – et al. 1966. Madrigal MAS-410

Organ Music: Scheidt – Cabezon – Merulo – et al. 1978. Titanic Ti-37

HARPSICHORD

Bach *Inventions; Sinfonias*. 1978. Calliope CAL 1651

– *Goldberg Variations*. 1978. Calliope CAL 1652, 1653

Boismortier 4 *Suites*. 1978. Calliope CAL-1865

L'Ensemble baroque de Montréal: Attaingnant – Couperin – Marais – Purcell – et al. Lyman v da gamba, Samuelson rec. 1966. Janus JA 19001

See also Discographies for C. Corbeil; B. Lagacé; Micheline Tessier.

BIBLIOGRAPHY

Stanton, Ginette. 'Mireille Lagacé, femme et musicienne,' Montreal *Le Devoir*, 1 Apr 1978

3 **Geneviève**. Organist, harpsichordist, b Montreal 14 Nov 1957; premier prix organ (CMM) 1976. She studied organ with her father and harpsichord with her mother 1973–7 at the *CMM. In 1975 she won first prize in the John Robb Competition in Montreal, third prize in the Paul Hofhaimer International Competition in Innsbruck, and first prize in the *RCCO competition. With the aid of a *Canada Council grant she studied 1977–8 with Gustav Leonhardt in Amsterdam. She gave recitals on CBC radio, playing both the harpsichord and the organ, and with her mother she made a recording of organ works by Frescobaldi and Merula for the label Titanic. After a recital of works by Buxtehude, Bach, Brahms, and Reger, which she gave on the organ in St-Joseph Chapel in Montreal, Claude *Gingras wrote in *La Presse* (17 Aug 1978): 'She plays with a man's strength ... with the maturity of someone twice her age ... She was exceptional in every respect.' With Hélène Dugal and Jacques Lecavalier she took part in the presentation of Sweelinck's complete works in Montreal during 1979–80.

BIBLIOGRAPHY

Gingras, Claude. 'Geneviève Lagacé: "Là, c'est rendu moi",' Montreal *La Presse*, 19 Aug 1978 (PR)

LAGACÉ, Claude (Pierre Édouard). Organist, choirmaster, educator, b Sorel, Que, 1 May 1917; BA (Laval) 1938, B PH (Laval) 1939, B MUS (Laval) 1954, Associate American Guild of Organists 1957. He received his training in Quebec City from Henri *Gagnon and Germaine *Malépart and in Hartford, Conn, from Clarence Watters. During his stay in the USA (1944–61), he lived 1946–50 in Holyoke, Mass, 1950–4 in Woonsocket, RI, and also in Toledo, O, where he was organist-choirmaster of the cathedral 1954–61 and taught at the Gregorian Institute of America, receiving from the latter a diploma in 1960. His pedagogical treatise *Sixteenth-Century Counterpoint* was published by the institute in 1958. Upon his return to Quebec City in 1961 he became organist at Notre-Dame Basilica, succeeding Henri Gagnon, and joined the staff of *Laval U, becoming assistant director of the music school in 1972. He taught at *CAMMAC in 1973. (RGg, DM)

LAGACÉ, Pierre(-Minier). Priest, educator, b Sainte-Anne-de-la-Pocatière, Lower Canada (Quebec), 17 Oct 1830, d Quebec City 6 Dec 1884. He was ordained a priest in 1854, taught music 1854–63 at the Collège classique de Sainte-Anne-de-la-Pocatière, and was vicar 1863–5 and 1866–71 at the Roman Catholic Cathedral of Quebec City. He was a founder of the *AMQ in 1868 and its president 1872–4. From 1871 until his death he was principal of the École normale Laval.

Lagacé's *Les Chants d'Église, harmonisés pour l'orgue suivant les principes de la tonalité grégorienne* (Paris 1860) embodied Louis Niedermeyer's theories of plainchant accompaniment, studied during a visit in France. The publication called forth a brief polemic between Ernest *Gagnon, siding with Lagacé, and Antoine *Dessane. At this time (1860–2) Lagacé wrote several articles on plainchant for *Le Courrier du Canada*. Lagacé's discourse *De la musique*, delivered on St Cecilia's Day 1866, was published (Quebec 1866), but his 'Théorie de la musique' and 'Méthode de sténographie musicale' (deposited at the *Séminaire de Québec) were not.

Lagacé published some books on elocution: a *Traité de prononciation française* (Montreal nd) and a *Cours de lecture à haute voix* (Quebec 1875). HK

LAJEUNESSE. 1 / Joseph (father of Emma *Albani), and 2 / Cornélia, his second daughter.

BIBLIOGRAPHY

Legendre, Napoléon. *Albani, Emma Lajeunesse* (Quebec 1874)
Massicotte, Édouard-Zotique. 'La famille d'Albani,' *BRH*, vol 37, Nov 1931
Charbonneau, Hélène. *L'Albani* (Montreal 1938)
Albani, Emma. *Forty Years of Song* (London, Toronto 1911)

1 **Joseph** (Marie) **Lajeunesse dit Saint-Louis**. Teacher, organist, harpist, violinist, pianist, b St-Martin (later part of Laval), near Montreal, November 1818, d Chambly, near Montreal, 30 Jul 1904. Although he intended to study medicine, he took up classics instead at the Séminaire de Ste-Thérèse in 1839. Nothing is known of his music studies, but he may have lived 1842–6 in the USA and he was a church organist 1849–53 at Chambly. He married Mélina Mignault 7 Jan 1846 and at that time described himself as 'a musician planning to study medicine.' The marriage produced six children, of whom three died in infancy. His two surviving daughters were Emma, born in 1847, and Cornélia.

Widowed in 1856, Lajeunesse undertook personally the musical education of his daughters, first at home, then at the Sacré-Coeur Convent at Sault-au-Récollet, where he taught from 1858 until the departure of the family for the USA in 1865. Besides working as a musician and itinerant teacher, he tuned pianos and repaired instruments. From 1854 to 1859, he may have resided periodically in Ottawa, teaching and directing the choir at St Andrew's Presbyterian Church.

In 1856 and 1857 he organized tours and concerts for Emma throughout Quebec and later he arranged others for Emma and Cornélia as a duo. He presented a benefit concert in Montreal in September of 1862 with the object 'of helping the Misses Lajeunesse to meet the expenses of their forthcoming trip to Paris, where they intend to study at the Conservatoire.' When the proceeds were not what he had hoped, Lajeunesse and his daughters set off for the USA in 1865, finally settling in Albany, NY. From there Emma left for Paris in 1868.

The two girls and their father met in Europe ca 1870 and Joseph Lajeunesse lived in London or Paris until 1879. On his return to Canada, he lived at first in St-Jean, Que, and then in Chambly, where Emma had bought him a home. He was known by the name of Lajeunesse dit Saint-Louis.

2 (Marie-Lélia) **Cornélia** (Cordélia) **Nelly**. Pianist, teacher, contralto, b Chambly, Que, near Montreal, 31 Mar 1849 or 29 May 1854, d London? ca 1932. Like her sister Emma she received her musical training from her parents and at the Sacré-Coeur Convent at Sault-au-Récollet, near Montreal. As a singer and pianist she participated in her sister's first concerts in Montreal in September 1862 and in the USA after 1864. She often played the second piano, Emma the first, in a '*Grand Duett* for 2 pianos (25 pages) composed by Mlle Emma.' She met her sister in Europe ca 1870 and accompanied her on several of her trips. After three years of study at the Stuttgart Cons she received a diploma in harmony ca 1874. She lived a long while in Spain as music teacher for the children of the royal family. She rejoined her sister in London in the early 1900s. GP

LAJEUNESSE, Emma. See Albani, Emma.

Lakehead University. Non-denominational arts, education, and science institution with master's-level graduate programs. Lakehead U, located at Thunder Bay, Ont, evolved from Lakehead Technical Institute (founded 1946) and Lakehead College of Arts, Science, and Technology (founded 1957). The college gained university status in 1962 and granted its first degrees in 1965, the same year it was officially given the name Lakehead U.

By 1980 Lakehead U's music department had offered no music degrees, though Manuel Suarez, director of music 1972–4, had introduced theory, history, applied music courses, and conducting as electives in the BA programs. Suarez was succeeded in 1974 by Dwight Bennett.

The university and the Thunder Bay SO (which both Suarez and Bennett have served as conductors) have shared the services of resident musicians. A summer festival, conceived as representing a different instrument (including voice) each year, was initiated in 1977. In 1978 a master class in voice, organized by Rita Ubriaco, was given at the festival by Elisabeth Schwarzkopf and Walter Legge.

Lakes. With the exception of the Great Lakes which border Ontario on the south, Canada's lakes no longer play a significant role in the country's development; rather they serve recreation, provide hydro-power, and are valued for their natural beauty.

The Great Lakes, the world's largest chain of inland water bodies, have been the inspiration for several songs and instrumental works – more so than Canada's many other lakes. Probably the earliest of these is R.J. Fowler's *The Lakes Quadrille* (1848). Later 19th-century examples are *Storm on the Lake*, a souvenir of Toronto by W.H. Clarke, *The Blue Ontario Rockaway*, by Carl *Martens; and 'The Wreck of the Algoma,' by (?) Hughes. Folksongs include 'It's Me for the Inland Lakes' and 'On Gravely Bay,' collected by Edith *Fowke and included in her book *Folklore of Canada* (Toronto 1976). The LP *Songs of the Great Lakes* (Folk FM 4018), comprises material, also collected by Fowke, largely about Great Lakes boats. Among pop songs, Gordon *Lightfoot's 'Christian Island' (Georgian Bay) and 'The Wreck of the Edmund Fitzgerald' (Lake Superior) date from the 1970s. The best-known concert work on the subject is John *Beckwith's *The Great Lakes Suite* (1949) to a text by James Reaney. An orchestral work is Lorne *Betts' *Kanadario* (1966), its title the Iroquois word for Lake Ontario.

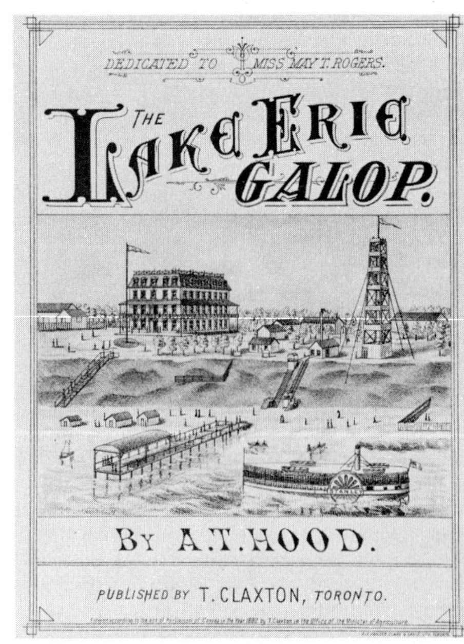

Musical items inspired by other lakes include the folksong 'The Lake of the Caogama' (Quebec); Angus MacPherson's song 'Lake Louise' (Armand-Grieg 1923) and Clifford Higgin's choral-orchestral piece *Lake Minnewanka* (1949), both evocations of lakes in Banff National Park; Paul *Pratt's piano piece *Sur le Lac Champlain*; the French-Canadian folkdances *Galop du Lac St-Charles* (recorded by the fiddler Joe *Bouchard), *Clog du Lac St-Jean* and *Quadrille du Lac St-Jean* (recorded by the accordionist Tommy Duchesne), *La Grande Gigue simple du lac St-Jean* (recorded by the fiddler Louis 'Pitou' *Boudreault), and *Reel de Moose Lake* (recorded by the fiddler J.O. *La Madeleine); and E.B. Sutton's 'Lovely Lake Muskoka' (Whaley Royce 1903), Bessie Maude Kerr's *Lake of Bays Suite* for voice, and Marcus *Adeney's *From the Lake of Bays* for solo cello (1948), all referring to lakes in the Muskoka resort area of southern Ontario.

See also Disaster songs; Rivers.

LALANDE, Germain. Gregorianist, teacher, b Ste-Scholastique (Mirabel), near Montreal, 21 Sep 1903; L LITT (Paris) 1933, diploma in liturgical singing (Institut grégorien, Paris) 1933. After being educated in Ste-Thérèse and at the Grand séminaire de Montréal, where he studied singing with Jean-Noël *Charbonneau and Guillaume *Dupuis, he was ordained a priest in 1929. During a stay in Paris 1930–3, he joined the Company of Saint-Sulpice in 1931 and studied with Auguste Le Guennant (Gregorian technique), Marc de Ranse

(harmony), and Henri Potiron (Gregorian accompaniment).

Lalande returned to Canada and was a teacher and choirmaster 1934–45 at the Collège de Montréal, became bursar in 1945 of the Grand séminaire de Montréal, and was director 1951–67 of its schola. A member of the diocesan committee on sacred music, he was appointed in 1964 to the episcopal commission on liturgical reform.

From 1964 on, Lalande composed for the commission and worked with several women's religious communities on the liturgy. His settings of parts of the Kyriale, along lines suggested by Vatican II, have appeared in the weekly religious booklet *Prions en Église* from time to time. (CMr)

LALIBERTÉ, (Joseph-François) **Alfred**. Composer, pianist, teacher, lecturer, b St-Jean, Que, 10 Feb 1882, d Montreal 7 May 1952. He was no longer a child when he took up the piano, studying with a Miss Malsberg, J.-B. *Denys, R.-O *Pelletier, Dominique *Ducharme, and Émiliano *Renaud. As early as 26 Apr 1902 *Le *Passe-Temps* published his patriotic song 'Le Canada,' on a text by Octave *Crémazie.

In 1902 Laliberté went to Berlin, where he spent four years at the Stern Cons, studying with Paul Lutzenko (piano), Ernst Baeker (harmony), and Wilhelm Klatte (counterpoint and composition). His success in competitions ensured that his grants from the German government were renewed. He played at the ducal court of Cobourg and the imperial court of Berlin in the presence of Wilhelm II. Back in Canada, he gave a highly successful recital 22 Nov 1906 at the *Monument national. Hearing of the arrival in New York of Alexander Scriabin, a composer whose works he admired, Laliberté wrote the Russian musician in February 1907 and at his invitation travelled to New York. On Scriabin's advice he then left for Europe, spending some more time in Berlin, where he worked with Teresa Carreño. He joined Scriabin in Brussels, becoming his pupil and disciple. Laliberté gave recitals in London, under the aegis of Emma *Albani and Lord *Strathcona, and in Germany.

Returning in 1911 to Montreal, Laliberté opened a studio and began promoting the works of Scriabin. Two years later he also opened a studio in New York and gave courses and lectures, but the war put an end to the venture. He taught at the *Cons national of Montreal and the

Alfred Laliberté, ca 1917

Ottawa Cons. In Montreal he taught 1926–35 at the mother house of the Sisters of the Holy Names of Jesus and Mary (*École Vincent-d'Indy). Among his pupils were Hélène *Baillargeon, Morris *Davis, Gérald *Desmarais, Hector *Gratton, Djane *Lavoie-Herz, Antonio *Létourneau, Marie-Thérèse *Paquin, Wilfrid *Pelletier, and Bernard Pinsonneault.

The friendship between Scriabin and his Canadian disciple deepened to the point where the composer entrusted him with the manuscripts of some of his works, including *Poem of Ecstasy* and *Sonata No. 5*. These precious manuscripts remained in Montreal until 1972, the centenary of Scriabin's birth, when the composer's widow herself placed them in the Scriabin museum in Moscow. Laliberté also had a profound admiration for Nicolas Medtner and Marcel Dupré. Medtner dedicated to him his *Sonata minacciosa, Op 53 no. 2* and his song *The Captive, Op 52 no. 7*, and Dupré his *Variations, Op 22* for piano.

Few of Laliberté's major works were finished. The most ambitious, *Soeur Béatrice*, an opera in three acts with text by Maeterlinck, exists only in piano score and has never been staged. Excerpts were performed in concert, in particular by the tenor Rodolphe *Plamondon. Laliberté's *Passacaille et choeur final* for pinao, organ, orchestra, and wordless chorus remained unfinished. A cycle of 15 songs with orchestra or piano on poems from *La Chanson d'Ève* by Charles van Lerberghe is almost complete. Three excerpts, published by Eschig in Paris, had numerous performances in their day. Laliberté also wrote pieces for piano, violin, and string quartet and a number of harmonizations of French-Canadian, Scottish, English, US, Indian, and Inuit folksongs, some published by Eschig under the title *Recueil de chants populaires du Canada* (Paris 1925) and others appearing in *Le Passe-Temps*. He also contributed articles to *Le Passe-Temps*, including one on Scriabin (May 1946).

The *CMCentre has granted Laliberté the associate status reserved for deceased composers whose works it holds. Alfred-Laliberté St, Montreal, is named not in honour of the musician, however, but of his namesake, the sculptor (1878–1953).

WRITINGS

'The spirit of Medtner,' *Nicolas Medtner*, ed and transl Richard Holt (London 1955)

BIBLIOGRAPHY

Albrecht, Otto E. 'Adventures and discoveries of a manuscript hunter,' *MQ*, vol 31, Oct 1945

Raizenne, Gabrielle. 'Dans le studio de M. Alfred Laliberté,' *P-T*, 906, Jan 1947

Scriabine, Marina. 'Alexandre Scriabine 1872–1915,' *CMB*, 3, Autumn–Winter 1971. Includes reprints of three letters from Scriabin to Laliberté. GP

LALLEMAND, Jean (Clovis). Banker, businessman, patron of the arts, b Montreal 19 Dec 1898; BA (Montreal) 1919. His mother, an excellent pianist, was the sister of Arthur *Laurendeau. Though Lallemand never studied music, he was extremely interested in the musical life of his city and was an active patron. His name appeared frequently in printed programs for having assisted young musicians in their studies or debuts or having contributed to the support of musical organizations. In 1936 he established a $500 composition prize bearing his name. Henri *Miro won it with *Scènes mauresques*, as did Hector *Gratton (*Légende*, 1937), and Graham *George (*Variations on an Original Theme*, 1938). Lallemand founded the *Petite Maîtrise de Montréal (1938–44) with Alfred *Bernier.

In 1939 Roland *Leduc, the cellist, organized the Jean Lallemand Quartet. (Maurice *Onderet was first violin, and two members of the recently dissolved *Montreal String Quartet, Annette *Lasalle-Leduc and Lucien *Robert, were second violin and viola). The quartet performed mainly for the CBC but gave a public recital 20 Feb 1940 at the École supérieure de musique in Outremont (*École Vincent-d'Indy) and another 29 April at the Ritz-Carlton Hotel.

Lallemand participated in the founding and development of the *MSO, of which he was made an honorary president for life. He was honorary treasurer 1940–75 of the Sarah *Fischer Concerts, vice-president 1942–69 of the *Opera Guild, and president 1954–69 of the *Society of Canadian Music. Lallemand received the Gold Medal of the Alliance française and in 1968 was made an Officer of the *Order of Canada. He received a *CMCouncil award in 1979.

Lallemand has respected the freedom of those who have benefited from his remarkably varied assistance. (IP-C)

LALONDE. Montreal singers: 1 / Jean, and 2 / Pierre, his son.

1 **Jean** (Gabriel). Singer, host, administrator, b Montreal 4 May 1914. After studying voice with José *Delaquerrière, he began his career in 1933 at radio station CKCO in Ottawa, often singing songs made famous by Bing Crosby, to whom he was compared. In 1934 he returned to Montreal, where station CKAC hired him as a singer and a bilingual host and where he remained for about 20 years. One of his programs, 'Le Don Juan de la chanson' (ca 1936–45), was very popular, and its title became associated with his name. He also participated 1941–3 in the CKAC series 'Café-concert Kraft.' He sang in French, English, and Spanish, sometimes under the pseudonym Jack Forbes, and performed many US and South American hits, which he translated into French. About 1955 he moved to St-Jérôme, north of Montreal, and opened radio station CKJL, which he owned until 1974. On the CBC radio program 'Au temps du 78 tours' (1971) he relived the best moments of his singing career. The French songs 'Petite madame bonsoir,' 'Sous le pont des soupirs,' and 'Vous qui passez sans me voir' were among his biggest hits. Several of his most successful songs were rereleased on an RCA LP. When he gave up his station in St-Jérôme, he left the world of entertainment, except that in 1974 he was co-host with his son for 'Les Don Juan' on radio station CKLM and in 1977 appeared on 'Dimanshowsoir,' part of the 'Beaux Dimanches' series on CBC TV.

2 (Joseph Alphonse Jean) **Pierre**. Singer, actor, announcer, b Montreal 20 Jan 1941. He made his singing debut at the age of four on the CKAC radio program 'Café-concert Kraft' and later acted in radio drama series and on CBC TV in 'Sourire de France.' Mme Jean-Louis Audet, Bernard *Diamant, Roger Larivière, and Simone *Quesnel were among his teachers. In 1954 he moved to the USA to study drama. Returning to Quebec in 1960, he worked first at radio station CKJL and in 1961 at CJMS. He was named 'discovery of the year' with Michèle *Richard in 1963 at the Montreal Gala des artistes. His first single (Apex) was released in 1962 and included the songs 'Chip Chip' and 'Mlle Marianne.' In 1962 he became co-host with Joël Denis of CFTM-TV's 'Jeunesse d'aujourd'hui' (later 'Jeunesse'), a popular program that presented the top pop hits; he soon became the sole host and held the position until 1971, except for a brief period in 1965 when he left it to serve as host for CBC TV's 'Jeunesse oblige'. In 1963 he made his first LP, *En d'autres mots*. In 1966 he formed a record company, Prestige (not to be confused with the US label), and in 1975 he formed another called Youppi. He had some success in New York in 1967 with his own program, 'The Peter Martin Show'; he also made a record under this name. Lalonde was elected Monsieur Radio-Télévision and the Assn des producteurs du disque canadien-français awarded him a trophy in 1970 during a 'Jeunesse' broadcast.

Until the early 1970s Lalonde appealed primarily to the young, who liked his easy, rhythmic songs, with their skilful blending of North American and French styles. A decline in his popularity caused him to undertake an in-depth revision of his style following the advice of Stéphane *Venne. Recitals at the *PDA, in Quebec City, and in Ottawa, as well as the LP *Inouik* resulted from the Venne-Lalonde association and revealed a new side of Lalonde, both in performance and in choice of songs. He also has performed in several cabarets. Besides those programs already mentioned he was the host for 'Pierre, Jean jasent' with the actor Jean Duceppe (1973) and 'Showbizz' (1976–7) on CFTM TV, as well as the quiz show 'Mad Dash' on CTV. As an actor, he appeared in the film *La Maîtresse* (1973) as well as at the Théâtre de Variétés in Montreal in three different productions.

Lalonde composed the music of the songs 'Tout' and 'Montréal,' and Marc *Gélinas and Christian Simard are among those who have written for him. His hits include the gold records 'Caroline,' 'Louise,' 'C'est toujours comme ça,' 'Donne-moi ta bouche,' and 'Attention, la vie est courte.' He performed four songs on each of the LPs *Chansons du Quebec* (Cap. SQ 70.033) and *Les Grands prix du disque: Festival 1965* (Lero L-725).

DISCOGRAPHY

En d'autres mots ... 1963. Apex ALF 1552
Pierre Lalonde chante pour la jeunesse d'aujourd'hui. Apex ALF 1560
Dans le vent. Apex ALF 1565
Jet ... Première classe. Apex ALF 1571
The Young Years. Cap ST 6337
Pierre Lalonde. Cap ST 6367
Pierre Lalonde. Cap SKAO 70.022
Mon ami Pierrot. Cap ST 70.025
Du gazon, de l'air pur, Brandy et moi. Cap ST 70.026
Inouik. Cap ST 70.028
Les Titres d'or de Pierre Lalonde. (1972). Cap 70.030
Caroline. Cap SM 70.061
Louise. Lero L-726
À Montréal. Lero L-748
À toi. Lero LS-762
Revenez à Montréal. Solo SO-21101
Honey Honey. (1973). Victor KPL1-0016
Ça pousse. (1974). Victor KPL1-0072
Entre dans ma vie. (1977). Telson AE 1506
Pierre Lalonde. Prestige PL 100
Petite fille. Prestige PL 101
Hit Songs from Peter's Television Shows. Prestige PLS 103
Pierre Lalonde – Hier et aujourd'hui. K-Tel KF 146

HP

LaMADELEINE. French-Canadian family of folk musicians: 1 / J.O. and 2 / Albert, his son.

1 **J.** (Joseph) **O.** (Ovila). Violoneux, b Valleyfield, Que, 1 May 1880, d Montreal 28 Jan 1973. He took up the violin at 10 and was an accomplished fiddler in 1919 when he moved to Montreal. There he participated in many folk music events and in 1927 made his first records for *Starr. Over the next 15 or more years for that company he made 54 78s (listed in *Pionniers du disque folklorique québécois*), accompanied on some by his son Marcel, a guitarist. On others he performs with the singers Aurore Beaulé (his daughter) and Ovila *Légaré. The discographer Gabriel Labbé notes that *Polka de Donalda, Polka canadienne, Valse des lilas,* and *Valse du bonheur* were LaMadeleine's most popular recordings. LaMadeleine operated a music store at 6674 rue Boyer in Montreal in the late 1920s.

2 (J.O.) **Albert**. Violoneux, b Valleyfield 10 Mar 1905. He studied with his father and at 17 began to play for dances, making his career initially in the northeastern USA. Settling in Montreal he worked for an oil company but continued to perform for dances and festivals and made his first 78s for *RCA Victor in 1929, completing nine (listed in *Roll Back the Years*) for that label. He also recorded with his father for Starr. With a trio that included the harmonica player Henri Lacroix, he was heard in the 1930s on radio station CHLP, Montreal. He was performing still in the 1970s when Bonanza released three LPs under the name J.O. Albert LaMadeleine: *Trois Petits Coups d'archet* (B-29544), *Volume 2* (B-29573), and *Le Reel Mirabel* (B-29656).

MM

LAMARCHE, Gérard. Administrator, producer, b Montreal 27 Sep 1918. He studied voice with Salvator *Issaurel, winning a first prize in the baritone category at the 1938 Festival-concours de musique du Québec. After army service he joined the *CBC, becoming in turn producer of French language educational broadcasts, director of Radio-Collège, director of French network radio programs, director of radio and TV programs, and director general of the Quebec division and of the French network. He was a member of the board of directors 1957–62 and artistic director 1964–5 of the *Montreal Festivals. He became director general of the *PDA in 1964 and administrative director of the *Opéra du Québec in 1971. In 1977 he was made a Member of the *Order of Canada.

BIBLIOGRAPHY

Chartrand, Maurice. 'L'Homme du mois,' *Revue Commerce*, Mar 1979

GP

LAMBERT, Constance. Soprano, b Ste-Ursule, near Trois-Rivières, Que, 17 Jan 1927; Lauréat, voice and piano (Montreal) 1946. After studying piano in Ottawa with her brother Marcel, she took voice lessons there 1946–50 with Adine (Mrs Antonio) Tremblay and in Montreal 1950–3 with Anna *Malenfant. Her CBC radio debut, on 'Radio-concert canadien' (1947), was followed by appearances on 'Radio-Carabin,' 'Théâtre lyrique Molson' (1948), and several other programs. She was the female winner of the 1950–1 *'Nos Futures Étoiles,' and subsequently gave recitals throughout Quebec and starred on CBC radio in operettas such as Kalman's *Countess Maritza* and *La Bayadère* (1952) and on CBC TV in Lehar's *The Land of Smiles*. She made her stage debut with the *Variétés lyriques during the 1952–3 season in Oscar Straus' *The Chocolate Soldier*. A scholarship from the Quebec government enabled her to continue her studies 1953–7 in Milan with Mario Basiola and Antonio Narducci. Upon her return, she was heard in the 1957 CBC TV presentation of Poulenc's *Stabat mater*. In New York she took advanced studies with Victor Trucco in 1957. By this time a well-established artist, she sang Musetta for the Boston Opera under Sarah Caldwell. She appeared subsequently with the Theater under the Stars in Atlanta, at the Empire State Music Festival in Ellenville, NY, and at other festivals. On CBC TV's 'L'*Heure du concert' she appeared in Poulenc's *Dialogues des Carmélites* in 1960 and co-starred with George *London in scenes from Charpentier's *Louise* in 1967. In 1980 Lambert was living in Paramus, NJ.

(SW)

LAMBERT, George (James). Baritone, teacher, b Long Preston, Yorkshire, England, 17 Dec 1900, d Toronto 13 Sep 1971. He was a choir boy in Riblesdale but began adult voice studies after World War I with Frederic *Lord, singing in oratorio and playing soccer professionally. In the mid-1920s he studied in Rome with Alfredo Martino and made his operatic debut there as Germont père in *La Traviata*. Returning to England he was coached by Sir Henry Wood and sang in public and on the BBC. He followed Lord to Brantford, Ont, for further study and moved briefly to New York.

In 1932, after an engagement with a CPR concert party at Banff, Alta, Lambert joined the teaching staff of the *TCM; he taught there until his death, and served 1938–9 as president of the *ORMTA. During the 1930s and early 1940s he continued to sing in public (eg, frequently with the *TSO, and 1938–45 as the Christus in Sir Ernest *MacMillan's annual presentations of Bach's *St Matthew Passion*). His large, flexible voice easily accommodated English, Italian, French, and German opera, as well as song and oratorio. One of his last assignments was the role of Cathva in the premiere (CBC radio, 20 Apr 1946) of *Willan's *Deirdre*.

After 1946 Lambert devoted himself entirely to teaching. His pupils, many of whom have had international careers, include Léonard *Bilodeau, Jean *Bonhomme, Pierre *Boutet, Victor *Braun, John *Doddington, Audrey *Farnell, Don *Garrard, Robert *Goulet, Doreen *Hume, Gwenlynn *Little, Phyllis *Mailing, Ermanno *Mauro, Joan *Maxwell, David *Mills, Peter Milne, Bernard *Turgeon, Jon *Vickers, Alan Woodrow, and Lesia Zubrack *Romanoff.

BIBLIOGRAPHY

Corriveau, Louis de B. 'George Lambert, baritone,' *CRMA*, vol 3, Feb–Mar 1944

GR

LAMONTAGNE. Montreal family of musicians: 1 / Charles-Onésime, baritone and administrator, and his wife, Annette Plamondon, soprano and pianist; and 2 / Yvette, their daughter, cellist and teacher, and Jules their son, pianist.

1 **Charles-Onésime**. Baritone, impresario, administrator, critic, b Montreal 21 Jan 1865, d there 21 Jan 1957. He was a member of the *Montreal Philharmonic Society for about 15 years and belonged 1890–1912 to the choirs of the Gesù Church, St James Cathedral, and Notre-Dame Church. His interest in music led him to set up an importing and publishing business on Notre-Dame St, where he also ran an agency for artists and a copying, transposition, and orchestration service. He was editor-in-chief of the monthly *L'Art musical* (1898) and director 1917–24 and

again in 1930 of the fortnightly *Le* *Canada musical*, which he founded. For several years he was correspondent for New York's *Musical America* and for the Brussels *Guide musical*.

Lamontagne became an impresario in 1895, presenting the violinist Marsick, and later Busoni, Casals, *Albani, Melba, Thibaud, Dufault, Rodolphe *Plamondon (Lamontagne's brother-in-law), the Flonzaley Quartet, and others. Lamontagne was administrator 1895–6 of the *Couture *MSO and 1910–13 of the *Montreal Opera. In 1914 he helped negotiate the publication of the vocal score of Guillaume Couture's **Jean le Précurseur* by Joubert in Paris. However, the work's premiere that year was cancelled because of the war.

Lamontagne's wife, Annette (b Plamondon), appeared frequently as soprano soloist with the Couture MSO and took part in many other concerts.

WRITINGS

'Montreal Opera Company,' Montreal *Gazette*, 3, 10,17 Aug 1947

– and Gour, Romain. 'Frank Stephen Meighen, dilettante et mécène,' *Qui?*, vol 5, Mar 1954

'Notre passé musical,' excerpts *Amerique française*, vol 12, Sep 1954

BIBLIOGRAPHY

Hamelin, Jean. 'C.-O. Lamontagne, témoin de 60 ans de vie musicale à Montréal,' Montreal *Petit Journal*, 6 Feb 1955

2 **Yvette**. Cellist, teacher, b Montreal 26 Dec 1898. She studied for three years on scholarship with Gustave *Labelle at the *McGill Cons. She then went to Paris, where she worked under Francis Touche and Marcel Hubert (brother of the pianist Yvonne *Hubert) and took courses in interpretation with André Hekking and Pablo Casals at the École normale de musique. After returning to Montreal she was a member in 1922 of the Trio de Montréal with Jeanne Labrecque (violin) and Albertine *Morin-Labrecque (piano). She gave numerous recitals in Quebec, Ottawa, and the USA and was a member of the first *Montreal String Quartet. She taught 1922–63 at the McGill Cons, and at the *CMM and the *École Vincent-d'Indy. Among her pupils were Pierre *Morin, principal cello of the *Quebec SO, and Lyse Vézina, a member of the *MSO.

Yvette's brother Jules, a pianist and pupil of Arthur *Letondal, was coach-accompanist for the Montreal Opera. (JMlt)

LAMONTAGNE, Gilles (Joseph Antoine Émilien). Baritone, administrator, b Montreal 21 Mar 1924. He studied in Quebec City with Isa Jeynevald-Mercier, at the *RCMT with Herman *Geiger-Torel (stage skills), in New York with Mario Reichlin-Rubini, and in Milan with Mario Basiola. In 1947–8 he won first prize in the CBC's two radio competitions, *'Singing Stars of Tomorrow' and *'Nos Futures Etoiles.' He went on to sing leading roles in the French and Italian operatic repertoire in Europe, North Africa, and Canada. In the summer of 1950 for the *Montreal Festivals he sang Valentin in *Faust* at the Delorimier Stadium. In Toronto for the Opera Festival (*COC) he performed the title role in *Rigoletto* (1950, 1954), Valentin in *Faust* (1951), Sharpless in *Madama Butterfly* (1951), Lescaut in *Manon* (1952), and Marcello in *La Bohème* (1954). He sang Méphistophélès in *Faust* on the CBC in 1957.

Lamontagne toured twice for the *JMC: in 1959–60 in joint recital with Marguerite *Gignac and in 1960–1 as Antonin in Maurice *Blackburn's **Silent Measures* and the original Michael in the same composer's **Pirouette*. With the *Théâtre lyrique de Nouvelle-France, of which he was assistant general manager 1964–7, he sang Marcello in 1962, Scarpia in *Tosca*, and Albert in *Werther* in 1963, and Zourga in *Les Pêcheurs de perles* and Sharpless in 1964.

Reviewing Lamontagne's Sharpless, Maryvonne *Kendergi wrote that he 'brings to the performance the weight of his physical presence (physique and voice) and of his professional maturity' (Montreal *Le Devoir*, 17 Nov 1964). A gifted actor, Lamontagne excelled in roles such as Rigoletto and Scarpia, in which the dramatic and vocal elements are extremely interdependant. (MS)

LAMOTHE, Willie (William). Singer, songwriter, guitarist, harmonica player, b St-Hyacinthe, Que, 27 Jan 1929. He began his career as a teacher of dance and then turned to singing, his act including imitations of Maurice Chevalier and Charles Trenet. While in the army, he learned to play the guitar and wrote his first songs.

Discovered by *RCA in the mid-1940s, Lamothe recorded his own 'Je suis un cowboy canadien,' 'Allo, allo, petit Michel,' and 'Je chante à cheval,' all of which were hits. Through these and subsequent recordings (some reissued in the collection *Mes Premières Chansons* (RCA Victor Gala CGP 286) he became one of the leading cowboy singers in Quebec. He performed on radio in Sorel (CJSO) and Montreal and appeared throughout the province in concerts during the 1950s headlined by such country stars as Gene Autry and Hank *Snow and in shows and concerts of his own. He has performed also in the country music capital, Nashville, Tenn.

Lamothe was the host 1970–6 in Montreal for CFTM TV's 'Le Ranch à Willie,' and was the subject of the NFB documentary *Je chante à cheval ... avec Willie Lamothe* (1970). He has appeared in dramatic roles in several feature films, including *Death of a Lumberjack* (1974) and *Mustang* (1974). His recordings for RCA and, after 1960, *London, include many of his more than 200 songs and of his translations of some 300 US country hits. He has made more than 100 78s, some 70 45s, and more than 20 LPs. Among his other popular recordings are 'Mon Voyage en Louisiane,' 'Le Long du Mississippi,' and 'Tu n'existes plus pour moi,' included on the LP *30 ans puis ... Nashville* (1975, Lon WL 100); 'Johnny' (from *Mustang*); and 'Les CB à Willie.'

Lamothe is an affiliate of PRO Canada; his music is published by Éditions Maskoutaine. He was made a Member of the *Order of Canada in 1979. His son Willie JR (b Michel) was bass guitarist 1969–77 for *Offenbach.

BIBLIOGRAPHY

Godin, Gérald. 'Ils ont inventé le cowboy québécois,' *Maclean*, Dec 1965

Carle, Gilles. 'Le rêve de Willie,' *Maclean*, May 1973

LeSerge, Diane. *Willie Lamothe, Trente ans de showbusiness* (Montreal 1975)

Jobin, Claude. 'Willie Lamothe marks 30 years as a performer,' *MSc*, 285, Sep–Oct 1975

Moore, Gilbert. 'The lone Willie rides again,' *Montreal Star*, 18 May 1978 (BLH, MM)

LAMOUREUX, Alfred. Composer, organist, pianist, singer, teacher, b Montreal 29 Dec 1876, d there 19 Mar 1954; hon D MUS (Montreal) 1937. At the *Institut Nazareth 1889–97 his teachers included Achille *Fortier (harmony, composition, voice), Romain-Octave *Pelletier (organ), Victoria *Cartier (piano), and Frantz *Jehin-Prume and J.-J. *Goulet (violin). He taught 1897–1940 at several institutions in the Montreal region: St-Laurent College; the Marie-Rose, Mont-Royal, Hochelaga, and St-Lambert boarding schools; the Académie Cherrier; the Victor-Doré School; and the Institut Nazareth. His pupils included Louise *André, Hervé Cloutier, Gabriel *Cusson, Gérald *Desmarais, and Sister *Marie-Stéphane. He was a soloist in numerous Montreal churches.

Lamoureux's activities as a composer lent a particular significance to his work as a teacher. He wrote four masses, of which one, based on Christmas carols, was premiered 25 Dec 1913 in St-Laurent, Que, and was published by J.-R. Gaudin. Among his other works are the oratorios *Tragédie d'Esther* and *La Samaritaine*, numerous motets (some published), and much secular choral music which has remained in manuscript.

This blind musician's erudition was manifest in his lectures *Causeries sur l'art musical* and *Causeries sur différents musiciens* (Montreal 1946), which were transcribed into braille. He was the author of the *Manuel d'histoire de la musique pour les couvents et les collèges* and a summary of the history of the plastic arts and literature as they relate to music (Montreal 1917). His writings were deposited in the library of the Institut Nazareth. NTr

LAMOUREUX, Caro (Marie Julienne Pauline Caroline) (m Beaulieu). Soprano, b Montreal 3 Jan 1904. She studied voice with Céline *Marier and stage technique with Jeanne *Maubourg and Albert *Robertval. She made her debut at 16 in the Salle Montcalm and worked for nine years as a semi-professional, primarily singing supporting roles in operettas presented in Quebec by French troupes.

In 1929 Lamoureux made her debut with the *Société canadienne d'opérette in Victor Massé's *Les Noces de Jeannette*, replacing a colleague at the last minute, and sang Leila in *Les Pêcheurs de perles*. The appearances marked the beginning of a long association with this society and with the *Variétés lyriques, of which she was one of the main attractions until 1946. She performed some 30 leading roles in French and Viennese operetta. In opera her numerous assignments included the title role in *Mireille* (1930), Nedda in *I Pagliacci* (1930), Baucis in Gounod's *Philémon et Baucis* (1931), Néméa in Adam's *Si j'étais roi* (1933), Rosina in *The Barber of Seville* (1934), and Philine in *Mignon* (1943), as well as Gamma in the Canadian composer J.-Ulric Voyer's *L'Intendant Bigot* (1931).

In his review of the 1942–3 season and of Lamoureux's performance of Violetta in *La Traviata*, Marcel *Valois wrote: 'With a voice that is fresh, resonant, and supple, she sang the role with a purity of style and brought to it a feeling and character that will long be remembered' (*La Presse*, 20 Mar 1943).

Lamoureux sang many major roles 1930–43 on CBC radio under the direction of various conductors, including Jean-Marie *Beaudet. In 1936 she was chosen the most popular classical singer in a competition organized by radio station CKAC. During the summer of 1939 she starred with Réda Caire in *The Merry Widow* in a series of performances in Salon, Mîmes, and Sète in the south of France. Towards the mid-1940s she began a new career as a florist in Montreal. GP

Lande Collections. Holdings of Canadiana collected by Lawrence Lande and housed in the McLennan (Redpath) Library of *McGill U.

Lande – a notary, b Ottawa 11 Nov 1906; BA (McGill) 1928, LLB (Montreal) 1931, hon D LITT (McGill) 1969 – is one of the most successful private collectors of Canadian books, a poet and author, and an amateur composer whose works (for piano and for voice) have been recorded on several privately produced LPs.

In June 1976 the Lande Collections held 11,257 items, of which the musical content was small but significant. The core of the collection is described in two bibliographies. *The Lawrence Lande Collection of Canadiana in the Redpath Library of McGill University* (Montreal 1965) lists 2328 items, including 55 of musical interest: sheet music from the late 19th century, hymn and instruction books, and the texts of *Colas et Colinette* and of C.W. *Sabatier's *Cantata*. *Rare and Unusual Canadiana: First Supplement to the Lande Bibliography* (Montreal 1971) lists 2451 items, about 130 of them relating to music, mostly sheet music but also material by T.F. *Molt. Most of the material listed in *A Checklist of Early Music Relating to Canada* (Montreal 1973) was sold to the *NL of C in 1979, including 70 pieces of sheet music, several with reference to General Wolfe; the manuscript of Beethoven's canon 'Freu Dich des Lebens,' inscribed to Molt; and hymn and song-books.

The Lawrence M. Lande Foundation for Canadian Historical Research has published a series of books, including the above *Rare and Unusual Canadiana* (no. 6 in the series); the *Checklist* (no. 8 in the series); *Beethoven & Quebec* (1966, in French and English, no. 2 in the series), which details T.F. Molt's meeting with the master; and *Joseph Quesnel, 1749–1809, Selected Poems* (Montreal 1970, unnumbered in the series) edited by M. Gnarowski.

LANDRY, Hélène (m Labelle). Pianist, teacher, b Ottawa. She studied for several years in Ottawa at the Canadian Cons of Music under its director Henry *Puddicombe and obtained diplomas in teaching and performance. She gave many concerts during the 1920s and went on to study with Alfred Cortot for three years in Paris. After receiving a diploma from the École normale de musique, she worked with Yves Nat (piano) and Nadia Boulanger (harmony). Upon returning to Canada she was named director of studies at the School of Music at the *U of Ottawa (1931). During a second stay in Paris in 1933 she concentrated her studies on the evolution of piano playing. She was at the *CMQ from its inception in 1944 until the late 1960s and taught, among others, Françoys *Bernier, Léon *Bernier, Victor *Bouchard, François *Dompierre, Janine *Lachance, and Lorraine *Vaillancourt. ST

LANDRY, Jeanne. Pianist, accompanist, teacher, b Ottawa 3 May 1922. She began studying piano at nine at the Grey Nuns' Convent in Ottawa and continued 1934–42 under Irene Miller, a pupil of Josef Hofmann. Settling in Montreal in 1942, she studied 1942–4 with Arthur *Letondal and then enrolled at the École supérieure de musique d'Outremont (later *École Vincent-d'Indy), where her teachers were Jean *Dansereau (piano) and Claude *Champagne (theoretical subjects). She won the *Prix Archambault in 1945 and the *Prix d'Europe in 1946 and went to Paris to study piano with Yves Nat and harmony and counterpoint with Nadia Boulanger and Noël Gallon.

Landry returned to Canada in 1948 and gave numerous recitals in public and on CBC radio. She accompanied the tenor Jean-Paul *Jeannotte for 25 years in concert, and on radio and TV, touring with him in Canada, the USA, and, in 1961, France, Austria, and the USSR. She was accompanist 1949–52 for the *Minute Opera. Noted also as a duo-pianist, she performed with Jean-Marie *Beaudet (Montreal premiere of Bartók's *Sonata* with percussion, 1950), Josephte *Dufresne (premiere and recording of *Matton's *Concerto* with percussion, 1955), and Serge *Garant (Canadian premiere of Boulez's *Structures*, Book 1, 1958).

In 1956 with Serge Garant, Otto *Joachim, and François *Morel, Landry founded the organization Musique de notre temps. She toured 1957–8 for the *JMC with the clarinetist Rafael *Masella and has accompanied numerous other singers and instrumentalists, including Fernande *Chiocchio, Joseph *Rouleau, and Jacques *Simard. In 1976 she performed with the French flutist Alain Marion at the *JMC Orford Art Centre. She has performed often with the pianist Robert *Weisz; in 1976 the team appeared with the *Quebec SO in Martinu's *Two-Piano Concerto*.

At *Laval U, Landry began teaching harmony and counterpoint in 1951 and accompanying in 1974. She has composed several piano pieces and some art songs.

See also Jacques Simard; and Discographies for Josephte Dufresne and Jean-Paul Jeannotte.

BIBLIOGRAPHY
'Jeanne Landry ou l'habitude de la maîtrise,' *Musique périodique*, vol 1, Jan-Feb 1977 GP

LANDRY, (Joseph Henri) **Jean-Yves**. Producer, conductor, b Trois-Rivières, Que, 5 Dec 1925; premier prix (Paris Cons) 1951. His early studies, 1933–40, were in his native city with J.-Antonio *Thompson and Brother Hippolyte. He studied 1946–7 at the *CMM with Alfred *Mignault (solfège), Claude *Champagne (composition), and Jean *Vallerand (orchestration) and 1948–50 at the Chicago Musical College with Rudolph Ganz (orchestral conducting), serving at the same time as regular conductor of the Trois-Rivières SO. On a Quebec government scholarship 1950–2 he attended Eugène Bigot's conducting class at the Paris Cons and Arthur Honegger's composition class at the École normale de musique. On his return to Canada he was engaged by the *JMC as a tour commentator.

In 1956 Landry joined CBC TV, for which he produced the series 'Concerts pour la jeunesse,' 'Concerts,' and 'L'*Heure du concert' and the 'specials' (operas, concerts, or documentaries) Bizet's *Carmen* (1960), 'Hommage à Charles Munch' (1963), 'Hommage à Claude Champagne' (1964), Puccini's *Suor Angelica* (1964), Orff's *Carmina burana* (1968), 'Hommage à Wilfrid Pelletier' (1969), Gounod's *Faust* (1970), 'Le Ballet Bolchoi' (1973), Penderecki's *Canticum canticorum Salomonis* under the composer's direction, and others. He won prizes at the Czechoslovakian International Festival 'Prague d'Or' for his TV productions of two works of Igor Stravinsky – *Sacre du printemps* in 1979 and *L'Oiseau de feu* in 1980, both played by the *MSO. *L'Oiseau de feu* won an Emmy award in 1980.

Landry first conducted for the CBC in 1955 and subsequently has led orchestras on radio and TV in Montreal and Toronto and has conducted the *Quebec SO. In the early 1960s he studied conducting with Josef Krips.

In 1956 Landry married the pianist Josephte *Dufresne.

BIBLIOGRAPHY
Boone, Mike. ' "Bird" soars to an Emmy award,' Montreal *Gazette*, 29 Nov 1980 GP

LANDRY, Ned (Frederick Lawrence). Fiddler, composer, b Saint John, NB, 2 Feb 1921. Though as a boy he taught himself to play the violin, Landry first appeared, in 1934 on Don *Messer's CHSJ radio show 'Backwoods Breakdown,' as a mouth organist. In 1939, with the New Brunswick Lumberjacks, he placed second in CBS radio's 'Major Bowes' Amateur Hour' in New York, and then in Boston became the first oldtime fiddler to perform on TV. He began recording for *RCA Victor in the late 1940s, completing eight LPs for that label and others for *Arc, MMC, and Afton. The winner in the open class of the 1956, 1957, and 1962 *Canadian Open Old Time Fiddlers' Contest, Landry appeared in the 1950s on CFBC radio, Saint John, and in the 1960s on 'Don Messer's Jubilee' and other TV shows. He has performed throughout Canada and has recorded many of his more than 40 fiddle tunes, composed in various Canadian styles. Some are published in the folios *Ned Landry Favorite Fiddle Tunes* (Empire 1952) and *Bowing the Strings with Ned Landry* (Thompson 1959).

LANDRY, Rosemarie (Yvonne) (m Doucet). Soprano, b Timmins, Ont, of Acadian parents, 25 Apr 1946; B MUS piano and singing (Montreal) 1969, M MUS singing (Laval) 1971. She studied with Rolande Ouimet 1966–8 at the Wilfrid Pelletier School in Montreal; with Bernard *Diamant 1966–71 in Montreal and 1973–9 in Toronto; with Jean-Paul *Jeannotte 1969–71 at *Laval U; with Pierre Bernac 1971–2, 1975–6, and 1979 in Paris; and with Gérard Souzay and Dalton Baldwin 1975 and 1976 at the *JMC Orford Art Centre and in Europe. She won the voice category of the *CBC Talent Festival in 1976 and in the ensuing four years her career moved ahead swiftly.

Landry appeared as soloist with the *Winnipeg SO, the *TS, and several other Canadian orchestras and with the *Canadian Centennial Choir (Handel's *Samson*, 1978), the *Tudor Singers of Montreal (Haydn's *Lord Nelson Mass*, 1978), the Calgary Festival Chorus (Vaughan Williams' *A Sea Symphony*, 1979), and the *Festival Singers and the *NACO (Beethoven's *Mass in C*, 1979). In 1978 she sang Mrs Gobineau in the CBC telecast of Comus Music Theatre's production of Menotti's *The Medium* and Mélisande in Stuart *Hamilton's concert presentation of *Pelléas et Mélisande* at the *St Lawrence Centre. That same year she sang in the Schubertiads at the *Guelph Spring Festival, toured the Maritimes with the pianist Jane *Coop, and appeared with the pianist Dalton Baldwin at the International Art Song Festival in Princeton, NJ. Baldwin subsequently accompanied her in recitals in Canada and the USA. In 1979 she was the Countess in the *COC's touring production of *The Marriage of Figaro* and sang in the first French performances (Lyons and Paris) of Berio's *Passagio*.

After a recital at *Hart House, Toronto, the critic John *Kraglund wrote that she achieved a 'heartbreaking interpretation of [Gounod's] "Ce que je suis sans toi" and ... soared to fluting heights in his Serenade.' He added that her growing stature as a Lieder singer was revealed in a group of Richard Strauss songs: 'The typically soaring sweep of Strauss phrases, like that closing "Hat Gesang – Bleibt's nicht dabei", might have been composed for Miss Landry's voice' (*Globe and Mail*, 7 Dec 1979). (NM)

LANDRY, Yvan. Vibraphonist, pianist, percussionist, arranger, composer, b Montreal 19 Apr 1931. He was a pupil 1945–50 of Lucien Jolicoeur and made his first professional appearances as a pianist in nightclubs. He taught himself to play the vibraphone and other percussion instruments and made his career with his own jazz group and in Montreal studio orchestras.

Landry's quartet has appeared on CBC radio ('Jazz en liberté') and TV, at *Expo 67, with the *MSO during the 1968 summer season, and in Switzerland at the 1971 Montreux Jazz Festival. The quartet – Landry, Rudy Pontano (piano), Don Habib (bass), and Roger Simard (drums) – recorded *Jazz en liberté!* (1967, Cap ST 6231). With Art *Maiste replacing Pontano it made the LP *Café au lait* (1969, Cap ST 6321). Landry plays vibraphone on LPs by the Canadian All-Stars led by Al

*Baculis and a Canadian big band led by Maynard *Ferguson.

Landry has been pianist, music director, and conductor or vibraphonist for several CBC Montreal radio and TV series, among them 'Café au lait,' (ca 1969) and 'Mon Ami,' 'Les Coqueluches,' 'Boubou,' and 'Les Beaux Dimanches' (mid-1970s). He has written signature tunes for some of these shows and music for *NFB films and other movie productions.

BIBLIOGRAPHY

Campbell, Francean. 'Yvan Landry keeps jazz alive and well in Montreal,' *CanComp*, 67, Feb 1972 (EFr)

LANGELIER, (François) **Denis**. Administrator, agent, b Coaticook, near Sherbrooke, Que, 3 May 1940. Following studies in philosophy and political economy at the U of Montreal he worked as an announcer and reporter for radio station CHEF in Granby. He worked in public relations in Montreal and Toronto 1960–7, then became assistant managing director of the *TS and co-ordinator of its educational programs. He served 1970–3 as general manager of the *MSO. He was a member of the steering committee that established the *ACO and was the association's first vice-president. The *Canada Council appointed him co-ordinator of information and publicity for its Touring Office in 1974 and he was put in charge of Concerts Canada the following year.

In January 1977 in Toronto Langelier established his own agency. known at first as Impresario Canada, then as Denis Langelier Artists' Management. In 1980 the agency represented Anna *Chornodolska, soprano; Bernard *Turgeon, baritone; John *Hendrickson, pianist; James *Campbell, clarinetist; Ida *Haendel, violinist; Eric *Wilson, cellist; and the *Hertz Trio, among others.

LANZA, Alcides (Emigdio). Composer, conductor, pianist, teacher, b Rosario, Argentina, 2 Jun 1929, naturalized Canadian. In Buenos Aires he studied piano with Ruwin Erlich, conducting with Roberto Kinsky, and composition with Julián Bautista and Alberto Ginastera. He was pianist and coach-accompanist at the Teatro Colón 1959–65 and received a scholarship in 1963–4 from the Instituto Torcuato di Tella of Buenos Aires, where he took advanced studies in composition, including electronic music. A Guggenheim fellowship allowed him to live 1965–71 in the USA, and he worked with Vladimir Ussachevsky at the Columbia-Princeton Electronic Music Center, in addition to teaching and composing. During this period he received grants from the Ford Foundation in 1966 and the Pan American Union 1967–9. He studied composition with several teachers, including Olivier Messiaen, Riccardo Malipiero, Aaron Copland, and Bruno Maderna, as well as piano with Yvonne Loriod.

In Latin America, the USA, and Canada, Lanza has striven, both as pianist and conductor, to promote contemporary and avant-garde music. To this end he founded the Composers / Performers Group whose multi-media presentations in several cities, including New York and Montreal, have aroused a great deal of controversy. While continuing to be active on the international scene, he settled in Montreal in 1971 to teach composition at *McGill U and in 1974 became director of its electronic music studio. In 1972 he conducted the *SMCQ Ensemble and presented works by Argentinian composers and his own composition *Eidesis II*.

In 1975, on commission for the SMCQ, Lanza wrote *Plectros IV* for two pianists (one male and one female), electronic tape, and a robot named Eric. It was premiered the same year by Bruce *Mather and Pierrette *LePage, to whom the work was dedicated. Lanza's numerous works make use of traditional instruments, of electronic sounds and extensions, and of lights. Most are listed in the US catalogue of Boosey & Hawkes, which also handles rental of material, tapes, and scores.

Lanza was president of the Agrupación Música Viva of Buenos Aires and was appointed associate director of the Composers' Group for International Performance. He was composer-in-residence 1972–3 at the Deutscher Akademischer Austauschdienst of Berlin and toured Scandinavia and Germany at that time. In 1975 he helped organize the Week of New Music in Montreal, at which his work *Penetrations VII* (for voice, lights, electronic tape, and extensions) was presented with the participation of his wife, the actress and singer Meg Sheppard. Lanza is an associate of the *CMCentre.

BIBLIOGRAPHY

Dictionary of Contemporary Music GP

La PALME, (Marie Alice) **Béatrice** (Béatrix) (m Issaurel). Soprano, violinist, teacher, b Beloeil, near Montreal, 27 Jul 1878, d Montreal 8 Jan 1921; ARCM 1900. She studied violin with Frantz *Jehin-Prume and performed successfully in public in 1894. She left for London in 1895, as first winner of the Lord *Strathcona scholarship to the RCM, and studied there with the Spanish violinist and conductor Fernandez Arbos. Shortly thereafter she began studying voice with Gustave Garcia and sang at an RCM concert in July 1898. In Montreal she appeared as both singer and violinst in the Karn Hall in October 1898 under the patronage of Lord Strathcona.

Returning to London, La Palme followed Emma *Albani's advice to devote herself exclusively to singing, working with Nelly Rowe, a pupil of Mathilde Marchesi. In Paris La Palme sang for Massenet who, according to Romain *Gour, declared: 'It is unbelievable, you move me to tears with my own music!' The day after a concert at the *Windsor Hall in Montreal (17 Oct 1902), *La Presse* wrote: 'One cannot imagine a soprano voice greater in range, clearer, or more admirably beautiful.'

La Palme made her Covent Garden debut 18 Jul 1903, replacing Fritzi Scheff at the last minute as Musetta in *La Bohème* at a gala performance in the presence of Edward VII. The cast included Melba, Bonci, Scotti, Journet, Gilibert, and Dufriche. She sang Mireille and Micaela in Lyons during the 1903–4 season and in Royan during the summer of 1904. She also portrayed Juliette, Mimi, and Lakmé in Royan. One of her singing partners was the French tenor Salvator (*Issaurel), whom she married in Paris in 1908.

La Palme made her Opéra-Comique debut 10 Sep 1905 in *Mireille* and for four years sang numerous roles there, including Sophie (*Werther*), Eurydice (*Orphée et Eurydice*), Marie (*La Fille du régiment*), Bettly (*Le Chalet* by Adam), Rhodis and Myrtho (*Aphrodite* by Erlanger), the title role in *Mignon*, and Madelon in the world premiere, 5 Jun 1907, of Messager's *Fortunio*. During the summer of 1909 La Palme joined the Moody-Manners Company at the Lyric Theatre in London. Singing in English, she interpreted the roles of Marguerite (*Faust*), Elsa (*Lohengrin*), Eva (*Die Meistersinger*), and Leonora (*Il Trovatore*) in London and on tour. The following year she was engaged by Thomas Beecham for the summer season at His Majesty's, where she sang with Maggie Teyte and Zélie de Lussan. La Palme opened the season in *Werther*

Béatrice La Palme as Suzanna

and then sang Suzanna (*The Marriage of Figaro*), Despina (*Così fan tutte*), Miss Silverbell (*The Impresario*), Adele (*Die Fledermaus*), Antonia (*The Tales of Hoffmann*), and Lisa (*Summer Night* by G.H. Clutsam). When Beecham retained her for his autumn season at Covent Garden, she added to her repertoire the roles of Aline in *Le Chemineau* by Leroux and Gretel in *Hansel and Gretel*. She also established herself as a singer of Lieder and French art songs in two recitals at Aeolian Hall during May and June 1911.

In July 1911 La Palme returned to Montreal with her husband. Her homecoming recital, 2 October at the *Monument national, was a resounding success. With the *Montreal Opera Company she made her debut in November in the role of Micaela and then sang Juliette, Marguerite, Mimi, and Rosina and visited Quebec, Toronto, and Ottawa. In November 1912 she undertook a second season with the company, adding to her roles Gilda (*Rigoletto*), Giulietta (*The Tales of Hoffman*), and the title-roles in *Madame Chrysanthème* by Messager and *Cendrillon* by Massenet.

La Palme made her debut at the Century Opera House, New York, at the end of November 1913, as Thaïs. In 14 weeks she sang 56 performances of 15 operas. In addition to her regular roles she sang Manon, Louise, Martha, Nedda, Santuzza, and the newly created roles Nuri (*Tiefland* by Eugène d'Albert), Eunice (*Quo Vadis?*, by Jean Nouguès), and Natoma in the opera of that name by Victor Herbert. From 27 Jul to 6 Sep 1914, La Palme was in Chicago for the season at Ravinia Park. In addition to eight roles from her repertoire, she sang Countess Gil from *The Secret of Suzanne* and Maliella in *The Jewels of the Madonna*, two operas by Wolf-Ferrari. 'Her art is astonishing' wrote the critic for the *Music News* (Sep 1914).

However, physical exhaustion, hearing problems, and the uncertainty created by World War I ended La Palme's career prematurely. When negotiations with the Metropolitan Opera failed, she settled permanently in Montreal at the end of 1914. Only 36 years old, she nevertheless decided to devote herself to teaching and joined her husband in the studio he had opened in 1911. Among her numerous pupils were Camille *Bernard, Marie-Anne Couture, and Graziella *Dumaine. She sang in public for the last time 14 Nov 1919 in a recital with her husband at the Ritz-Carlton Hotel in Montreal.

After Emma Albani, Béatrice La Palme was the first Quebec singer to star in the great opera houses. Her gifts as singer and actress, her personality, and the range of her voice made her an artist much sought after. Remembering her, Sir Thomas Beecham, in a letter written to Romain Gour on 23 Apr 1945, described her as 'a highly accomplished singer and one of the most resourceful and versatile artists of my time.' Unfortunately no recording of this distinguished artist is known to exist.

BIBLIOGRAPHY
Gour, Romain. *La Palme-Issaurel* (Montreal 1948) GP

LAPIERRE, Eugène. Organist, teacher, composer, writer on music, administrator, b Montreal 8 Jun 1899, d there 21 Oct 1970; D MUS (Montreal) 1930. He began his musical training under the choirmaster Lucien Perreault at Ste-Brigide Church, where he was solo soprano. He showed a strong aptitude for the organ, studied with Étienne Guillet, and soon was an accompanist at St-Jean College. He received a degree in 1922 from the École des hautes études commerciales and a diploma from the School of Journalism at the U of Montreal and worked as a journalist for *La Patrie* while continuing his organ studies with Benoît *Poirier. Music took up more and more of his time. After 1920 he was organist in a succession of Montreal churches: Ste-Philomène de Rosemont, St-Denis, St-Jacques 1922–4 and 1928–36, St-Stanislas-de-Kostka 1936–44, and St-Alphonse-d'Youville 1944–70. By 1921 he was secretary of the *Cons national.

Lapierre obtained a Quebec government grant to study 1924–8 in Paris and enrolled at the Institut grégorien of Paris (certificate, 1926) and at the Schola cantorum (diploma, 1928). He studied composition with Vincent d'Indy and Georges Caussade, organ and improvisation with Marcel Dupré, and piano with Simone Plé-Caussade and P. Sylva Hérard. He visited the Benedictine abbey at Solesmes to improve his knowledge of Gregorian chant. In 1927 he had been appointed the incoming director of the Cons national in Montreal. He took the opportunity during his final year in France to acquaint himself with the workings of the Paris Cons. Upon his return to Canada he reorganized the Montreal conservatory; he was to remain its director until his death. His pupils included Gaston *Allaire, Émilien *Allard, Françoise *Aubut, Albertine *Caron-Legris, Alfred *Mignault, and Colombe *Pelletier. The *U of Montreal awarded him its first regular doctorate in music in 1930.

Lapierre's growing reputation as a teacher of Gregorian accompaniment brought him invitations from other countries, and he gave courses in 1935 at the Liturgical School of Music in Burlington, Vt, 1945–ca 1968 at the Gregorian Institute of America in Toledo, O, and in the autumn of 1955 at the Cultural Institute of Lisbon. He was also director 1963–70 of the Academy of Musical Arts of the Detroit Seminary.

Lapierre's activities were indeed many: lecturer in 1935 at the Congrès de la langue française in Quebec City; Quebec delegate in 1946 at the Music Educators National Conference in Cleveland, O; delegate in 1949 to a congress for sacred music in Mexico City; president of the Concerts d'orgue du Québec; vice-president 1958–64 of *CAPAC; vice-president 1962?–9 and president 1969–70 of the Société historique de Montréal; member of the Interdiocesan Commission for Sacred Music and of the Quebec Commission for the Advancement of Music, and so on. He also gave more than 60 recitals and inaugural organ concerts across North America.

Lapierre published numerous works in Montreal: *La Rôle social de la musique* (1930), *Les Vedettes de la musique canadienne* (1931), *La Musique au sanctuaire* (1932), and *Pourquoi la musique?* (1933). He instigated the transfer in 1933 of Calixa *Lavallée's body from Boston to Montreal and published *Calixa Lavallée, musicien national du Canada* (1936, 1950, 1966), an important biography which, in 1937, earned him the Prix David for literature from the Quebec government. *Un Style canadien de musique* (Quebec City 1942) and *Le Mouvement musical dans le Québec* (1948) were among his subsequent writings. He was editor of *La Quinzaine musicale* and wrote articles and reviews for other periodicals and newspapers (Montreal *Le Devoir* 1948–51, *L'Action nationale, Radiomonde, Notre Temps*) and the article 'Canada: musique' for the *Encyclopédie Grolier* (Montreal 1947).

Lapierre composed numerous pieces for organ, piano, choir, and voice, notably masses, motets ('Ave Admirabilis' 1948, 'Qui ad justitiam' 1950, etc), and songs. Some of these were published by *Archambault, *Boucher, *Fassio (Lachute), Hérelle (Paris), Gordon V. *Thompson, *La Bonne Chanson, and Le Parnasse musical.

Lapierre's principal works include *Le Père des amours* (1942), a comic opera based on the life of Joseph *Quesnel and premiered in December 1942 at the *Monument national as part of the Montreal tricentennial celebrations, the musical comedy *Le Vagabond de la gloire* (book by Aimé Plamondon, based on the life of Lavallée) premiered in Montreal in 1947; the cantata *Les Clochers canadiens*; and *Cantique à Saint Jean de Dieu* (Boucher 1935). He also wrote *Le Traversier de Boston*, a dramatic comedy inspired by Lavallée's exile and performed in Montreal in 1933.

Lapierre prepared a new version (Boucher 1945) of Joseph-Julien *Perrault's *Messe de Noël* and published the treatises *Simplified modal accompaniment to the Vatican Kyriale and the Requiem Mass* (Toledo 1946), *Traité sommaire d'accompagnement grégorien* (Montreal 1949), *Gregorian Chant Accompaniment* (Toledo 1949), and *80 Cantiques à Sainte Anne* (1958, English transl 1959). With Émilien Allard, he recorded 12 Christmas carols.

Lapierre's achievements were recognized officially when he was awarded the Jubilee and Coronation medals in 1935 and 1937 by George V and George VI respectively and the Bene Merenti de Patria medal by the *Saint-Jean-Baptiste Society in Montreal. In 1963 he was named Chevalier of the Order of Malta in Toledo, O. He was a member of CAPAC. Yves *Lapierre is his grandnephew.

BIBLIOGRAPHY
Creative Canada, vol 2 (CH)

LAPIERRE, Yves. Composer, arranger, singer, b Montreal 9 Aug 1946. He is a grandnephew of Eugène *Lapierre. He studied at the *École Vincent-d'Indy and took conducting and instrumentation classes 1969–70 with Michel *Perrault. He was the director 1963–8 of the folk group *Les Cailloux and subsequently worked as composer, arranger, and producer for recordings by Julie Arel, Edith *Butler, Renée *Claude, Patsy Gallant, Jean Lapointe, Claude *Léveillée, Suzanne Stevens, and others. He has written such songs as 'Get That Ball,' 'Le Désamour,' and 'Moi, de la tête aux pieds' and has composed and (as singer and instrumentalist) recorded many jingles. The LP *Evidence of Yves* (1974, CTLS 5184/Celebration CEL 1898) presents his arrangements of songs by Quebec composers played by a studio orchestra under his direction. He was music director for CBC French TV variety shows, in particular 'Monsieur B' and 'L'Heure de pointe' (1976–7). He composed the music for Guy Fournier's TV serial 'Jamais deux sans toi' which began in 1977. He has written music for several Quebec feature films, including Marcel Lefebvre's *Mustang* (1975). He is a member of CAPAC.

Samuel Lapitsky Foundation. Established in Montreal in March 1956 by Samuel Lapitsky, a retired businessman, to foster artistic creativity in Canada and provide assistance for cultural and educational endeavours. In the field of music several works for orchestra were commissioned from Canadian composers: *Divertissement* (Pierre *Mercure, 1956), *Images* (Harry *Freedman, 1957), *Three Astral Visions* (Alexander *Brott), *Cordes en mouvement* (Jean *Vallerand, 1959), *Concertante No. 2* (Otto *Joachim, 1961), *Monade I* (Clermont *Pépin, 1963), *Suite Lapitsky* (Jean *Papineau-Couture, 1965), and *Profundum praedictum* (Alexander Brott, 1965). These works were premiered by the *McGill Chamber Orchestra, except for *Images*, which was first performed by the *TSO, and *Suite Lapitsky*, which was first performed by the *MSO. After 1965 the foundation ceased to commission works. In 1980 Murray Lapin continued as its only president and administrator.

LAPLANTE, (Joseph) **André** (Roger). Pianist, b Rimouski, Que, 12 Nov 1949; B MUS (Montreal) 1968, M MUS (Montreal) 1970. He began studying piano at seven and continued after 1964 at the *École Vincent-d'Indy with Sister Nathalie Pépin and Yvonne *Hubert. In 1965 he won the *MSO Matinées prize for young performers, and in 1968 he took first prize at the *MSO Concours and the Quebec Music Festival. He continued his studies 1970–1 in New York at the Juilliard School with Sascha Gorodnitzki and, with the aid of *Canada Council grants, 1971–4 in Paris with Yvonne Lefébure. For three summers he attended music camps in France, Portugal, and Hungary, giving recitals and performing with chamber music ensembles. He worked again 1976–8 at Juilliard with Gorodnitzki. By this time he had performed as soloist with several Canadian orchestras, and in 1974–5 had toured for the *JMC.

Laplante's career accelerated after his success in several international contests; he took third prizes in the Marguerite Long-Jacques Thibaud Competition in Paris (1973) and in a competition in Sydney, Australia (1977), and in 1978 he tied with the French pianist Pascal Devoyon for second prize in the International Tchaikovsky Competition in Moscow. His great popular success in Moscow, with 91 pianists from 23 countries competing, made him known around the world.

After a brief tour in the USSR Laplante returned to Canada and was soloist in Tchaikovsky's *Concerto No. 1* with the *TS at *Ontario Place and with the *MSO in the Joliette Cathedral and 21 Oct 1978 made his recital debut at New York's Carnegie Hall. He played the same program 13 November at the *PDA and 24 November at Toronto's *St Lawrence Centre. He later played Rachmaninoff's *Concerto No. 2* with the MSO, and in October 1979 he repeated it with the *Quebec SO.

Laplante's career continued to grow internationally, and he made an important recital tour (including a second appearance at Carnegie Hall in March 1980) and gave concerts with orchestras in Canada, the USA, and Europe during the 1979–80 season.

Critics generally have praised his virtuosity. 'On the technical level, Laplante worked wonders. At least half his program was very demanding from the standpoint of virtuosity ...' wrote Claude *Gingras (Montreal *La Presse*, 14 Nov 1978). They occasionally have expressed reservations about his interpretation, however. Harriett Johnson described his performance of Prokofiev's *Sonata No. 7* as 'an interpretation which encompassed the notes (no small feat) but communicated little of the ferocity of the first and last movements or the unsettled quiet of the Andante caloroso' (*New York Post*, 23 Oct 1978).

Laplante has recorded the Bach-Busoni *Toccata in C* and Chopin's *Sonata No. 2* (1977, RCI 440). The

André Laplante

LP *André Laplante in Moscow* features his performance of Rachmaninoff's *Concerto No. 3* with the Moscow Philharmonic Orchestra conducted by Alexander Lazarev, recorded during the final round of the Tchaikovsky Competition at the Moscow Cons 4 Jul 1978 (CBC SM-352).

Laplante married the Montreal pianist France de Guise. He moved to New York in 1979. That year the *CMCouncil named him Performer of the Year, and CBC TV presented 'Portrait d'André Laplante,' a documentary produced by Peter *Symcox.

BIBLIOGRAPHY

Petrowski, Nathalie. 'André Laplante – les débuts d'une brilliante carrière,' Montreal *Le Devoir*, 1 Aug 1978

'From Russia with fame (and probably fortune),' *Maclean's*, 21 Aug 1978

Whittingham, Tony. 'André Laplante,' *Fugue*, Feb 1979

Petrovski [sic], Nathalie. 'Le gang des pianos à queue,' *Actualité*, Apr 1979

Dumesnil, Thérèse, 'André Laplante, pianiste,' *Perspectives*, vol 21, 15 Dec 1979

Thompson, Leslie. 'Laplante turns instant fame into a concert career,' *Music*, Jan–Feb 1980 (SW)

LAPLANTE, Bruno. Baritone, b Beauharnois, near Montreal, 1 Aug 1938; premier prix voice (CMM) 1964. He studied 1958–64 with Dina Narici, Raoul *Jobin, Roy *Royal, and Dick Marzollo at the *CMM. With the help of a bursary 1964–5 from the Quebec government, the *Prix d'Europe in 1966, grants 1966–8 from the *Canada Council, and a bursary in 1967 from the Goethe Institute of Munich, he studied in Germany, in Paris with Pierre Bernac, and in Montreal with Lina Narducci. He gave his first Paris recital in 1966 and made his opera debut in Cimarosa's *Il Matrimonio segreto* in Germany in 1968. His European tours established him as a recitalist of international stature. After his return to Canada, he received the special interpretation prize at the 1967 National *JMC competition in Guelph, Ont, for his premieres of Canadian songs.

For the JMC Laplante gave recitals and toured 1969–70 with the actor Jacques Zouvi, 1970–1 with Anna *Chornodolska, 1973–4 in *The Magic Flute*, and 1975–7 in *The Barber of Seville*. He sang Roger in *Ciboulette* (1970) with the Théâtre lyrique du Québec; Morales in *Carmen* (1971) with the *MSO; and Albert in *Werther* (1969), Count Gil in *The Secret of Suzanne* (1971), Mercutio in *Roméo et Juliette* (1972), Ananias in *The Burning Fiery Furnace* (1973), and Ramiro in *L'Heure espagnole* (1975) for the CBC. With the *Opéra du Québec he sang the Notary in *Il Trittico* (1971), M de Brétigny in *Manon* (1973), and Masetto in *Don Giovanni* (1974). He sang the title role in *Vallerand's *Le Magicien* at the Théâtre de la *Poudrière in 1974 and the same year founded the *Ensemble cantabile de Montréal. In 1977 he was Roderick in the premiere, on German TV, of Debussy's unfinished and unpublished opera *The Fall of the House of Usher* and performed Serge *Garant's *Rivages* on the *SMCQ's European tour.

Laplante's supple and expressive voice and his exceptional qualities as an interpreter of romantic song won him (1977) the Grand Prix du disque for the album *Le Livre d'or de la mélodie française*. In 1978 he and the pianist Janine *Lachance made a three-week tour of France, Belgium, and Norway.

DISCOGRAPHY

Chabrier 13 *Mélodies*. Lachance pf. 1978. Calliope CAL 1880

Daunais *Fantaisie dans tous les tons; Sept Épitaphes plaisantes*. L.-P. Pelletier pf. 1971. RCI 294

Liszt – Lavallée – Pépin – Prévost. Lachance pf. 1977. RCI 426

Le Livre d'or de la mélodie française: Massenet – Hahn – Gounod. Lachance pf, Mignault vc, Millaire spkr. 1975–6. 3-Calliope CAL 1830–1850. Available singly as Calliope CAL 1830 (Massenet), 1840 (Hahn), 1850 (Gounod)

Les plus belles mélodies de Chausson. Lachance pf. 1977. Calliope CAL 1860 (DA, AP)

LAPLANTE (Marie Irène) **Louise** (m Courchesne). Administrator, teacher, b Montreal 2 Oct 1943; B MUS (Montreal) 1966, M MUS piano (Montreal) 1967, BES (Quebec Department of Education) 1968, L MUS (Montreal) 1972. She studied 1962–8 at the *École normale de musique with Claude *Champagne (theory) and Jean *Leduc and William *Stevens (piano). In 1971 she took a course in ethnomusicology with Laszlo Vikar at UQAM and a course in Amerindian ethnology at the *U of Montreal, where her regular studies 1968–72 were with Françoise *Aubut (fugue) and André *Prévost and Serge *Garant (analysis). As a pianist she won prizes in 1959, 1961, and 1962 at the Quebec Music Festivals (now the *Canadian Music Competitions) and appeared in several concerts, notably in 1962 at *Plateau Hall with the *MSO.

Laplante taught 1969–73 at the École normale de musique and gave courses 1970–6 in music literature, the history of Canadian music, and ethnomusicology at UQAM. She also taught (French) literature at UQAM 1972–3. She lectured at the U of Quebec at Chicoutimi in 1972 and began teaching at the *École Vincent-d'Indy in 1974. In 1974 and 1975 the Quebec Dept of Education published her teaching guides to three works by, respectively, *Morel, Champagne, and *Schafer. She edited *Compositeurs canadiens contemporains* (Montreal 1977, the French-language edition of *Contemporary Canadian Composers*) and has been responsible for the preparation of the continuing series of *CMCentre brochures *Compositeurs au Québec*, begun in 1974. She served 1973–80 as Quebec regional director of the CMCentre, In 1980 she was appointed general director of the Orchestre des jeunes du Québec.

WRITINGS

'Essai de systématisation de chants amérindiens,' unpubl L MUS thesis, Montreal 1972

'Essai d'analyse d'un chant montagnais,' *Recherches amérindiennes au Québec*, vol 11, Apr 1972

'A portrait of contemporary music in Quebec,' *Numus West*, vol 11, Spring 1975

'Le centre de musique canadienne à Montréal,' *L'Interdit*, 253, Sep–Oct 1976

'Michel Longtin,' *MSc*, 292, Nov–Dec 1976

'En coulisse, le Centre de musique canadienne,' *Variations*, vol 1, Jan 1978 HP

LAPOINTE, Marthe (m Charlebois). Soprano, violinist, b Quebec City 29 Nov 1910; lauréat (AMQ) 1930. At six she began to study voice, solfège, violin, and piano with the Grey Nuns in St-Anselme, near Quebec. In about 1921 she entered Mont-Ste-Marie Convent in Montreal, where she studied violin with Émile *Taranto. In Quebec she studied harmony and voice 1927–51 with Berthe *Roy. She also studied violin, harmony, and ear training for five years privately with Robert *Talbot and for two years at *Laval U.

Though a violinist ca 1929–33 with the Société symphonique de Québec (*Québec SO), Lapointe became increasingly interested in an operatic career. Her gifts in opéra-comique and operetta were conditioned under the guidance of Lucienne Defrenne, whom she approached ca 1932, and in 1935 she made her debut as Marguerite in a presentation of extracts from *Faust* at the Capitol Theatre in Quebec. She was a leading soprano 1936–55 with the *Variétés lyriques in Montreal. She sang on such CBC radio series as 'L'Heure brève' and 'Everybody's Hour' and gave many recitals. Lapointe retired in 1966, having sung in some 10 operas and over 65 operettas, including those of Lehar, Offenbach, Lecocq, and Oscar Straus. After retirement from the stage, she taught music appreciation to children in five primary schools in Ville d'Anjou, Que, until 1970. CV

LAPORTE, Thérèse (m Benoit). Soprano, b Montreal 11 Jun 1932. After taking violin lessons, she studied voice with Albert *Cornellier and 1949–50 with Martial Singher at the *CMM. For the *Variétés lyriques, she sang leading roles in Posford and Grün's *Balalaika* in 1950, Francis Lopez' *La Belle de Cadix* in 1951, and Vincent Scotto's *Violettes impériales* the following year. In 1952 she sang Lucy in Menotti's *The Telephone* at the *Minute Opera.

On a Quebec government grant Laporte studied 1952–5 in Paris with Yvonne Brothier (voice) and Fanély Revoil (operetta). She and the baritone Michel Brothier formed a duo and gave recitals in 1954 at the Maison canadienne and the École normale de musique. That year she also sang Nina in Marcel Delannoy's *Philippine* at the Studio des Champs-Élysées.

In 1955 Laporte sang in Offenbach's *La Vie parisienne* for the Variétés lyriques in Montreal and in Pierre Pételʼs *Un Amour de Cadeau* on CBC TV. She also was engaged by the Théâtre de la Gaîté-Lyrique to sing the leading soprano role opposite Luis Mariano in 70 performances of the Rys and Bourtayre operetta *Chevalier du ciel*. Following her success, that theatre engaged her to sing the role of Calico, with the Compagnons de la chanson, in the premiere 13 Dec 1956 of Georges van Parys' operetta *Minnie Moustache*; it ran for six months and excerpts were recorded by Columbia (LP 25cm, FS 1067).

Early in 1956 the Laporte-Brothier duo toured France, giving 20 recitals of art song and operetta. Epinal's *La Liberté de l'Est* (24 Jan 1956) wrote: 'Thérèse Laporte is graceful and overwhelmingly spontaneous and natural; in turn naive and disarmingly subtle, she blends the evocative gesture with a delightful soprano voice in a completely easy manner.' Laporte sang Hermia in Offenbach's *Barbe-bleue* in 1959 for the *Montreal Festivals, Mi in Lehar's *Le Pays du sourire* (*Land of Smiles*) in 1965 for the *Théâtre lyrique de Nouvelle-France, and Oreste in Offenbach's *La Belle Hélène* in 1966 at the *PDA. She subsequently moved to Quebec City and turned to the chansonnette, taking part in several TV programs and performing in supper clubs and boîtes à chansons.

BIBLIOGRAPHY

Saucier, Pierre. 'Les compagnons de la chanson nous enlèvent une Canadienne,' Montreal *La Patrie*, 19 Aug 1956

Freund, Gisèle. 'Therese gets her big break,' *Montreal Star*, 26 Jan 1957 GP

LAPP, Horace (Gladstone). Pianist, organist, conductor, writer, b Uxbridge, near Toronto, 3 Mar 1904. Lapp was a church organist 1917–20 in Beaverton and 1920–2 in Port Hope, Ont; a pianist with Luigi *Romanelli's orchestra in Toronto; and an accompanist to the *Toronto Mendelssohn Choir on tour (1923). He studied with Alberto *Guerrero (piano, 1922–4) and Healey *Willan (organ, 1923) at the *TCM.

Although Lapp gained some recognition as a composer at this time, composition remained an avocation. In addition to songs and orchestral works listed in *Catalogue of Canadian Composers*, however, he completed a concerto for piano and voices in 1958. As a member 1924–35 of Jack *Arthur's various Toronto theatre orchestras he composed and conducted music for stage shows at Shea's Hippodrome and the Imperial Theatre.

Lapp led a dance band 1934–6 at the Royal Muskoka Hotel and 1936–44 in Toronto at the Royal York Hotel. The band was heard on CBC radio and appeared in a 12-minute Screen News film, *Music from the Stars*, in 1939. Lapp was the organist on Kate Aitken's public affairs programs (1935–54, first on CFRB and then also on CBC radio) and the regular organist at *Maple Leaf Gardens in the early 1950s. He was the pianist, arranger and occasional conductor 1952–9 for the CBC's *'Opportunity Knocks,' the conductor for the *Eaton Operatic Society 1962–5, and a producer of shows at the *CNE Bandshell 1964–7.

One of the last surviving silent-film accompanists in Canada in 1980, Lapp resumed this activity in the late 1960s, performing for screenings of historic movies at the Ontario Film Institute (Toronto) in 1968 and at the Stratford Film Festival (*Stratford Festival) and in Ottawa in 1972. He also recorded sound-tracks for CBC TV's 1969 series of the 37 extant Laurel and Hardy movies. In 1978 for a Film Institute screening of the 1928 Canadian silent movie *Carry On Sergeant*, Lapp played Ernest *Dainty's original accompanying score.

Lapp's writings include a music column 1962–73 for the *Arts and Letters Club monthly letter and an unpublished autobiography. (HM)

LARIVIÈRE, Roméo (Clément). Composer, Gregorianist, b Montreal 21 Nov 1880, d Joliette, Que, 5 Mar 1939. He entered the Institut des Clercs de Saint-Viateur as a teaching brother while very young and was attached mainly to St-Joseph College in Berthierville and the Bourget College in Rigaud, Que. Except for a few piano lessons in Montreal from Jean-Baptiste *Denys, he was largely self-taught as a musician. Nevertheless, he became a teacher of liturgical song and a respected composer.

Larivière collaborated with the *Schola cantorum of Montreal, which in the early 1920s published his *Cantique pour une première messe* and a *Cor Jesu* for choir. These were followed by other religious works: the offertory *Terra tremuit*, a *Regina coeli* (1925), the Christmas offertories *Laetentur coeli* and *Tui sunt coeli* (1927), and two requiem masses (1930), not to mention numerous motets and sacred songs. His patriotic song 'Dollard' was performed first in Carillon, Que, in 1922.

Larivière's *Manuel de chant grégorien* was well received when it was published in 1930; the work is based on the Gregorian principles of Dom Pothier, Amédée Gastoué, and Dom Lucien David. After Larivière's death, Dom David wrote: '[he was] very gifted musically ... [He] played an important role for some 40 years in the reaffirmation of sacred vocal music [ie, Gregorian plainsong] in Canada' (*Revue du chant grégorien*, Paris, May 1939).

Through their simplicity, their honest approach, and, on occasion, their brilliance, the compositions of Brother Larivière have provided for choirmasters a repertoire much needed and well suited to its liturgical purpose. FL

LAROCHELLE, Émile. Tenor, teacher, pianist, organist, b Quebec City 13 Aug 1891, d there 9 Oct 1958. At 10 he sang in various churches and studied piano with Olivier Hudson. He took classical studies at the Séminaire de Québec and at *Laval U, where he was active as pianist, organist, and singer. He served as choirmaster in several parishes in Quebec City before studying voice (1923) in Paris with Mme Charlotte d'Estainville and Louis de Laquerrière. He also took classes at the Schola Cantorum and at the Institut Grégorien, was tenor soloist in Paris churches (including St-Eustache), and sang in the choir of the Concerts Lamoureux.

After his return to Quebec City Larochelle taught voice and performed in concert and on radio. He was soloist in Sunday concerts at the Château Frontenac Hotel for more than four years and principal tenor of the Quatuor laurentien and the Trio harmonique. He initiated free solfège courses in the St-Malo and St-Sauveur districts. He was a committee member (1925) and secretary (1951) of the *AMQ. At Laval U he taught choral conducting and voice and Pierre *Boutet, Violette Delisle, Raoul *Jobin, Léopold *Simoneau, and Richard *Verreau were among his pupils. His four recordings for Victor Orthophonie are listed in *Roll Back the Years*. (CH)

LARRIVÉE, Jean (Jean-Claude). Guitar builder, b Montreal 6 Jun 1944. A mechanic by training and for three years a guitar pupil of Robert Neveu at the *RCMT, Larrivée apprenticed as a guitar builder intermittently for five and a half years (mid-1960s) with Edgar Münch, a German builder then living in Toronto. He also worked in New York with Manuel Valasquez before opening his own studio in Toronto in 1968. His production in the late 1960s reached about 30 instruments a year. In 1970, after guidance from Matty Umanov in New York, he began making steel-string instruments, modifying the Martin design. In 1977 Larrivée moved to Victoria, BC, and established a workshop which by 1979 had 16 workers and an annual production of 1000 guitars, two-thirds of which were steel-string instruments. His guitars are played by many Canadian pop musicians (among them Bruce *Cockburn and Eugene Martynec) and have been distributed in Western Europe, Australia, Japan, and, through a Swiss agency, in Eastern Europe. Among Larrivée's apprentices have been Sergei DeJonge, George Gray, Grit Laskin, Linda Manzer, and David Wren.

BIBLIOGRAPHY
Laskin, Grit. 'An interview with Jean Larrivée,' Mariposa Folk Festival *Newsletter*, Mar 1975 MM

LASALLE-LEDUC, Annette (b Lasalle). Violinist, teacher, writer, b Montreal 9 Jul 1903. As a child she began studies with Émile *Taranto (violin) and J.-Noël *Charbonneau (harmony). In May 1921 she gave her first recital. After a year's study in New York with Alfred Migerlin, she continued at the Paris Cons with Maurice Hayot and Édouard Nadaud (violin) and Noël Gallon (harmony). On her return to Montreal Lasalle gave recitals and broadcasts. With her husband Roland *Leduc (cello) and brother-in-law Jean *Leduc (piano), she played in the Trio Leduc. She was a member 1935–45 of the CSM orchestra and of the CBC *'Little Symphonies' orchestra conducted by her husband. She was second violin with the *Montreal String Quartet and the Quatuor Jean-*Lallemand.

An art and music historian and critic, Lasalle-Leduc has taught, lectured, and written many articles. She was the host for CBC radio's 'Le Musée d'art.' She was a member of the Council of Arts of Greater Montreal 1956–67 and of the *Canada Council 1964–7.

WRITINGS

La Vie musicale au Canada français (Quebec 1964, 2nd printing slightly enl 1964)

'La musique de 1860 à 1930,' *Cahiers de l'Académie canadienne-française*, 10, 1966

'Emma Albani,' *Encyclopaedia universalis*, vol 1 (Paris 1968)

BIBLIOGRAPHY
Musiciennes de chez nous GP

LATOUR, Conrad. Choirmaster, musicologist, teacher, editor, b Montreal 3 Dec 1899, d there 23 Oct 1975. After a secondary education in Ottawa he entered the Oblate Order in 1918 and was choirmaster 1920–30 at the Scolasticat St-Joseph in Ottawa. He was ordained priest in 1925. He took voice lessons with Jean *Riddez and then attended the Schola Cantorum in Paris, where he studied Gregorian chant with Amédée Gastoué and Guy de Lioncourt. He also studied with Dom Lucien David.

Latour was the director of choirs 1930–9 at Sacré-Coeur Church and the *U of Ottawa, and he founded, and directed 1931–9, the school of music and elocution at the university. He was music director 1936–9 of CBC radio's 'L'Heure dominicale.' He was choirmaster at the Oblate Seminary of Chambly, Que, 1939–41; at St-Pierre Church in Montreal 1948–51; and at Rouyn College. He taught various subjects at the college until his retirement in 1973.

Latour's publications include the six editions of *Recueil de cantiques* (Ottawa 1931–60, a total of 70,000 copies printed), *Pie X le musicien* (Ottawa 1929), *Le Cantique liturgique* (Ottawa 1938), *Chants populaires pour les missions et les retraites, heures saintes, ...* (Ottawa 1938), and *Cantuale ad Benedictionem SS Sacrementi* (Rouyn, 1955, 1958). GP

Latvia. Latvians began arriving in Canada at the end of the 19th century, and the number increased after the Russian revolution of 1905. The independence from Russia which Latvia achieved in 1918 (after the 'great' Russian revolution of 1917) was lost again when the country was incorporated into the USSR in 1945. More than 15,000 Latvians-in-exile settled 1946–63 in Canada. By 1975 the number of Latvian-Canadians exceeded 18,000, about 70 per cent residing in Ontario. Most Latvians are Lutherans; some are Baptists or Roman Catholics.

Latvians brought to Canada a rich folklore, the product of a long national memory. Most of their folksongs are dainas, four-line stanzas of two-verse pairs, in falling rhythm without anacrusis. Composed of four icti, 95 per cent of the songs' lines are in trochaic dipodies. Diminution, repetition, and parallelism also are reflected in the music, because the melodies – primarily syllabic and often modal – match the metre and rhythm of the text. This stability of text and tone has been an important factor in the successful oral transmission of the songs over the centuries. Favourite themes include the rituals, mythology, customs, and labours of the farm; the family; the indispensable horse; courtship and abduction; oppression; and, particularly, natural phenomena as a metaphor for the human spirit and condition.

Latvian-Canadian youth have shown a keen interest in the animation and revival of this folklore. Some 189 folksongs of Latvian origin were collected in Toronto for the *National Museum of Man by Aija B. Beldaves, Helen *Creighton, and John Glofcheskie. Young people have been encouraged to perform on the kokle, a 5–12 string (plucked) instrument distantly related to the medieval dulcimer. The kokle is Latvia's national instrument, suitable for accompanying song and dance.

The annual National Song Festivals which began in Latvia in 1873 have been broadened by the many communities of Latvian exiles into an international movement. Concerts of church, orchestral, and chamber music by Latvian composers and performers, as well as folk-dance displays, theatre presentations, and arts and crafts exhibits, serve as a focus for the Latvian cultural identity. Such festivals have been held in Toronto in 1953, 1957, 1961, 1965, 1970, and 1976.

Almost half of Latvia's leading musical figures left the homeland after 1944, several of them settling in Canada: the composer-conductors Janis Cirulis (1897–1962), Janis *Kalnins, and Janis Norvilis (b 1906); the singer-teachers Janis Niedra (1887–1956) and Mariss Vetra (1902–65); and the violinist Janis *Kalejs and his wife, the pianist Felicita *Kalejs. Vetra, the baritone and teacher Teodor Brilts, and the conductor Alfred *Strombergs were active in the *Nova Scotia Opera Assn. The piano teacher Edouard *Hesselberg taught 1912–18 at the *TCM. The composer Talivaldis *Kenins has established himself as one of Canada's most successful composers and has achieved international renown. Musicians of Latvian descent include the German-born pianist Arthur *Ozolins. Several expatriate Latvian musicians living in the USA appeared in Toronto during the 1960s under the auspices of the Latvian Concert Assn.

BIBLIOGRAPHY

Graham, Allen W. 'Latvian artists aid development of Halifax opera,' *Musical America*, Aug 1950

Berzkalns, Valentins. *Latviesu Dziesmu Svetki Trimda* (Draugs 1968). A history of the song festivals, including those held in Canada

Latvju Muzika (Kalamazoo, Mich, 1968–). Magazine devoted to Latvian music in North America (WHK)

LAUBACH, Frank (L.). Bandmaster, composer, b Edinburgh July 1857, d Vancouver 4 Mar 1923. He played in English and Scottish orchestras and was a bandmaster to the King's Bodyguard in Scotland. He moved to *Regina in 1904 and founded the Regina Philharmonic Society in 1905 and the Regina Orchestral Society in 1907. He was in part responsible for the first (1909) music festival held in Saskatchewan. In 1913 he co-wrote and co-produced a musical comedy, *The Mystic Light*, with Charles Shrimpton. Laubach also composed marches, church music, dances, and a *Gaberlunsie Overture*. After service overseas 1915–17 as bandmaster of the 68th Battalion, Canadian Expeditionary Forces, he returned to Regina and in 1919 inaugurated the Regina Choral and Orchestral Society. According to *Who's Who in Western Canada* (1913) he wrote a *Treatise on Musical Instruments* (Edinburgh 1893). Until his retirement in 1922 he was an acknowledged leader of Regina's musical life. WLB

LAUDER, W. (William) **Waugh**. Pianist, lecturer, writer, b Oshawa, Canada West (Ontario), 24 Oct 1858, d after 1911. His mother, Marie Elise Turner, was a gifted writer; his father, Abram W. Lauder, a barrister and, after 1867, a member of the Ontario legislature. As a youth Waugh Lauder sang in the choir of Metropolitan United Church, Toronto, and accompanied the *Toronto Philharmonic Society.

During three visits (1878–82) to Europe Lauder studied in Heidelberg, and at the Leipzig Cons with Robert Papperitz, E.F. Richter, and Oscar Paul (theory) and Carl Reinecke (piano). For his graduation recital he played Beethoven's *Emperor Concerto*, 'surpassing all his fellow contestants by the sureness and correctness of his technique as well as the energy of his touch and the spiritual elevation of his interpretation. He may be considered ready for concert appearance' (*Neue Zeitschrift für Musik*, 30 Apr 1880).

Lauder is considered 'the only Canadian who can justly claim the honour of being a pupil of Liszt' (*MT*, 1 Apr 1885). He spent the summers of 1879 and 1881 with the master at Weimar and the winter of 1880 at the Villa d'Este. Lauder played before the pope and before royalty in Italy and Saxony and in concert halls in Rome, Frankfurt, and other cities. In Venice he played piano arrangements of Wagner's operas to the composer.

On returning to Canada, Lauder served 1883–5 as music director at Hellmuth Ladies' College, London, Ont, before moving to the USA, where he taught at Eureka College, Illinois; 1887–9 at the New England Cons, Boston; 1889–93 at the Cincinnati Wesleyan College and the Ohio College of Music; and subsequently in Kansas City and other US cities.

Lauder has been credited with introducing the lecture-recital to North America as a means of spreading the appreciation of classical music. By 1889 he had given some 350 such recitals in Ontario alone. A champion of Wagner and Liszt, he gave a memorial recital at the *U of Toronto after Wagner's death in 1883 and played Liszt's *Concerto No. 2* and *Sonata* in Boston in 1888. Like Calixa *Lavallée he was an enthusiastic promoter of US composers. As a lecturer he appeared before the *Canadian Society of Musicians and the Music Teachers' National Assn. His essays (publications not traced) and, presumably, his lecture topics included 'The music of the first Christian era,' 'A critical sketch of American music,' 'A year of study with Liszt at Weimar,' and 'Facts about ancient theory.'

Although Lauder was one of 19th-century Canada's finest and best-known pianists, little is known about his later life except that he lived in Chicago after 1911. Annie Lampman *Jenkins and Harry Marshall *Field were among his pupils.

BIBLIOGRAPHY

Mathews, W.S.B. ed. *A Hundred Years of Music in America* (Chicago 1889) HK

LAUFER, Edward. Composer, teacher, b Zurich 25 Nov 1938, naturalized Canadian 1953; M MUS (Toronto) 1960, MFA (Princeton) 1964. He was raised in Halifax, where his family settled in 1939. He studied composition with John *Weinzweig, John *Beckwith, Oskar *Morawetz, and Talivaldis *Kenins at the *U of Toronto, with William Bergsma and Vincent Persichetti at the Juilliard School, and with Milton Babbitt, Earl Kim, and Roger Sessions at Princeton U. He taught at Smith College 1969–71 and the State U of New York at Purchase 1972–3 and was composer-in-residence 1974–5, and then a member of the Faculty of Music, at the U of Toronto. His later works, such as *Variations for Orchestra Part I* (commissioned by the *Halifax SO) and *Nostos* are atonal. He is an associate of the *CMCentre and a member of CAPAC.

SELECTED COMPOSITIONS

ORCHESTRA

Composition. 1964. Ms

Prelude. 1966. Ms

Variations, Part I. 1967. CMCentre

Variations, Part II. 1968. CMCentre

Divertimento for Chamber Orchestra. 1972. Ms

CHAMBER

Sonata. 1961. Fl, pf. Ms

String Quartet. 1962 (rev 1963). Ms

Nostos (Simonides, transl J.W. MacKail). 1965 (rev 1967). Sop, alto fl, b cl, vc, pf. CMCentre

Septet. 1966. Ms

Variations for Seven Instruments. 1967. Fl (picc), cl, bn, tpt, pf, vn, vc. NVMP 1972

VOICE

'Sonnet to Orpheus 19' (Rilke). 1964. Sop, pf. Ms

'Sonnet to Orpheus 22' (Rilke). 1965. Sop, pf. Ms

BIBLIOGRAPHY

'Edward Laufer,' *PfAC*, vol 5, Feb 1967

Contemporary Canadian Composers (CF)

LAURENCELLE, Marcel. Choir conductor, teacher, b Montreal 15 Jan 1914. A soprano in the boys' choir of the Church of the Immaculée-Conception, Montreal, he began music studies at nine with Émile Fontaine, continuing with Alfred *Bernier and Georges-Émile *Tanguay and 1943–8 at the *CMM with Léon Barzin, Claude *Champagne, Jean *Vallerand, and Séverin *Moisse.

Laurencelle was assistant director 1938–44 of the *Petite Maîtrise de Montréal and choirmaster 1941–50 at St-Étienne Church. He also founded the Choeur Berlioz and conducted it 1945–58. He was choir director 1944–65 for the *Montreal Festivals, 1946–69 for the *Opera Guild, and 1957–8 for the Grand Opera de Montreal. In 1950 he began preparing choirs for the *MSO and the CBC. He was assistant director of the *JMC 1954–5 and directed that organization's choir 1958–67. He prepared the choirs 1971–2 for the Opéra du Québec. Laurencelle began teaching theory and choral singing at the CMM in 1949 and the *JMC Orford Art Centre in 1951. He taught 1951–5 at the *U of Montreal. In 1976 he became choirmaster at Montreal's Notre-Dame Church. (PR)

LAURENDEAU. A family of Montreal musicians including 1 / Arthur and 2 / Jean, grandson of Arthur.

1 **Arthur**. Bass, choirmaster, conductor, teacher, writer on music, b St-Gabriel-de-Brandon, near Montreal, 30 Nov 1880, d Montreal 26 Oct 1963. After studying the violin and the double-bass at the Séminaire de Joliette, he went to Montreal to study law and began to take voice lessons from Guillaume *Couture. He was soloist and choirmaster 1901–6 at St James Cathedral. He was called to the bar but decided to devote himself to singing and ca 1909 went to Paris, where he studied with Pierre-Émile Engel and Jacques Isnardon and was advised and encouraged by Vincent d'Indy. On his return he gave recitals and began teaching.

Laurendeau was choirmaster in 1913 at the Gesù Church and succeeded Couture the following year as choirmaster at St James Cathedral; he remained there until 1952. In 1917 he began teaching solfège at the École normale Jacques-Cartier, succeeding Romain-Octave *Pelletier. In a recital with Léo-Pol *Morin that year at the YMCA hall he performed works by Rodolphe *Mathieu and Georges-Émile *Tanguay.

On the advice of his doctor Arthur Laurendeau gave up singing; he devoted himself thereafter to directing opera. With the support of Mme Damien Masson, he staged Massé's *Les Noces de Jeannette* with his pupils Léonide Letourneux and

Honoré *Vaillancourt in the leading roles. The success of this presentation led to the founding in 1917 of the Société nationale d'opéra-comique, whose first production, *La Basoche*, at the *Monument national 24 Jan 1918, marked the resumption of professional opera in Montreal. Laurendeau also directed Thomas's *Mignon* in 1919 and Delibes's *Jean de Nivelle* for the Assn d'art lyrique.

At this point Laurendeau began to concentrate on teaching at the *Cons national de musique in Montreal and the *Schola cantorum. His pupils included Amanda Alarie, Arthur *Blaquière, Albert *Cornellier, Guillaume *Dupuis, Gaston Favreau, Armand Gauthier, Denis *Harbour, Arthur Lapierre, and Alfred Normandin. He founded a male choir, the Orphéon de Montréal (1931–4) which premiered in 1934 Rodolphe Mathieu's 'Lève-toi, Canadien.'

Laurendeau was president 1916–18 and 1926–9 of the *AMQ and 1930–1 of the Société des artistes musiciens and wrote many articles for *L'Action française*, *Le Canada*, and *Le Devoir*.

Laurendeau married Blanche Hardy, a pianist and accompanist, daughter of Edmond *Hardy. In 1917 she founded the César-Franck Trio with the violinist Leon Kofman and the cellist Raoul *Duquette.

WRITINGS

'Musique de chambre et musique d'église en Montréal / Chamber and church music in Montreal,' *The Year Book of Canadian Art*, compiled by The Arts and Letters Club of Toronto (Toronto, London 1913).

'Guillaume Couture,' *Entre-Nous*, vol 1, Jun 1930

'Musiciens d'autrefois: Dominique Ducharme, Alfred Desève [sic], R.-O. Pelletier, Guillaume Couture, Paul Letondal,' *Action nationale*, vols 35 and 36, appeared irregularly, Feb–Dec 1950

BIBLIOGRAPHY

Tancrède, Frère. 'M. Arthur Laurendeau,' *Action musicale, littéraire et artistique*, vol 1, 9 Apr 1932

2 (Marie François) **Jean**. Clarinetist, ondist, teacher, b Montreal 11 Aug 1938; premier prix clarinet (CMM) 1959, premier prix clarinet (Rouen Cons) 1964, premier prix chamber music (Rouen Cons) 1965, licence de concert (École normale, Paris) 1965. After studying clarinet 1950–9 at the *CMM with Joseph Moretti and Rafael *Masella, he worked 1959–60 at the New England Cons, Boston, with Gino Cioffi and then returned to Canada, where he played 1960–2 in the *Quebec SO. He continued his training 1962–3 in Paris with Ulysse Delécluse. Having met Jacques Lancelot at the Académie international de Nice in the summer of 1963 he worked with him 1963–5 at the Rouen Cons. He also studied the ondes Martenot 1962–5 with Jeanne Loriod at the École normale de Paris and 1964–5 with Maurice Martenot at the Paris Cons, where he received a medal in this subject.

Returning to Canada in 1965, Jean Laurendeau began a career as a chamber musician and a soloist on the clarinet and the ondes. He and the pianist Louise *Forand toured Canada several times 1965–9 for the *JMC, and Yugoslavia in 1970 accompanied by the percussionist Vincent *Dionne. This trio premiered *Prolifération*, a work it had commissioned from Claude *Vivier.

Laurendeau has played the ondes Martenot in a number of North American performances of Messiaen's *Turangalîla-Symphonie*, appearing with the Quebec SO, the *MSO, the *TS, and orchestras in Buffalo, Chicago, Cleveland, Los Angeles, Miami, Pittsburgh, and San Francisco. After participating in 1977 in *Musicanada as a member of the *Quebec Woodwind Quintet, he toured Germany, Belgium, and France with the *SMCQ Ensemble. He was a regular performer with that ensemble and also served 1963–72 as a member of the SMCQ board and 1972–5 as an adviser. He has played on CBC radio and TV, at the *U of Montreal's Nocturnales, and for *NMC in Toronto.

Laurendeau taught at the *JMC Orford Art Centre for several summers and in 1970 began teaching clarinet and ondes Martenot at the CMM, thus establishing the first ondes class in the country. He founded a group of ondists which in 1977 premiered Richard-Gaudreault *Boucher's *Begonia Rex* at the SMCQ. His pupils include Nicolas Desjardins (clarinet) and Marie Bernard and Johanne Goyette (ondes).

WRITINGS

'Un instrument au son électronique: l'onde Martenot,' *VM*, 5/6, 1967

DISCOGRAPHY

See Quebec Woodwind Quintet and Discographies for SMCQ; Gilles Tremblay. 1 / GP, 2 / (FM-G, AP)

LAURENDEAU, (J.-) **Alexandre** (Zénon). Oboist, clarinetist, b Lachenaie, near Montreal, 13 Dec 1870, d Montreal 13 Jul 1933. He was clarinetist in the Montreal Concert Band under the direction of Edmond *Hardy and, after 1890, in the *Sohmer Park orchestra. He later studied oboe with a Father Geay.

Laurendeau became principal oboe in 1899 for the summer tours of the John Philip Sousa Band and during the winter ca 1900 he recorded with the band for *Berliner. Around this time he joined the Pittsburgh SO. In 1905 he successfully competed with 105 others for the coveted post of solo oboe of the New York Philharmonic Society, and he remained 12 years with that orchestra. At the same time he recorded concert pieces with Columbia Gramophone studio groups (see *Roll Back the Years*). He was also principal oboe 1910–20 of the New York Symphony Society under the direction of Walter Damrosch.

After losing the use of two fingers Laurendeau returned to Montreal in 1920 and concentrated on teaching and composing. His pupils included Réal *Gagnier after 1926. He was second cousin of the composer Louis-Philippe *Laurendeau and the brother-in-law of George Violetti, a music dealer.

BIBLIOGRAPHY

P-T, 272, 26 Aug 1905 AP

LAURENDEAU, Louis-Philippe. Composer, writer, b St-Hyacinthe, Que, 1861, d Montreal 13 Feb 1916. He was active for many years in Montreal and was bandmaster at the École militaire of Saint-Jean, but later he devoted himself entirely to composition and arranging. Though a resident of Longueuil (near Montreal), he occupied an editorial position with Carl Fischer, the New York publishers.

Some 200 of Laurendeau's compositions and arrangements, mostly for band and published by Fischer and Cundy-Bettoney, are listed in F. Pazdírek's *Universal-Handbuch* (Vienna 1904–10). His intermezzo *Twilight Whispers, Op 202*, won first prize in the 1895 *Metronome* competition. Works of specific Canadian interest include *Shores of the St Lawrence*, a medley for band, and *Land of the Maple, Op 235*, a march.

Laurendeau taught as well, and Fischer published several of his volumes of band instruction and repertoire, including *The New Era Band Book* (Grades 2, 3) and *The Practical Band Arranger*. He used the pseudonym Paul Laurent, but the *NL of C has record of only one publication on which it appears. A Montreal street was named after Laurendeau in 1931.

BIBLIOGRAPHY

'Mort de L.-P. Laurendeau,' *P-T*, 26 Feb 1916
Roll Back the Years (FMB, HK)

Laurent, Laforce & Bourdeau (Laurent et Laforce, 1861–4; Laurent, Laforce & Cie, 1865–88). Montreal music and instrument dealers, publishers, and piano manufacturers. Though first documented in 1861, Laurent et Laforce were established sufficiently by 1862 to survive a fire, to sell a large part of their stock to the newly founded Boucher et Manseau (with whom they began sharing premises), and to expand their piano and harmonium business.

The few examples of sheet music which have been found date the firm's publishing activities to the years before Confederation. The scant output indicates collaboration with US publishers, notably G. Schirmer in New York, whose plate number appears on one of the pieces and whose advertisement decorates the back cover of another. The latter piece, M.F.E. Valois's 'La Mansarde' (ca 1864, arranged by Calixa *Lavallée) is the fifth in the series 'Lyre canadienne,' of which the sixth, 'La Vierge de France' (ca 1864), also has been found.

As Laurent, Laforce & Cie, the firm advertised as piano manufacturers, then continued in retail business until 1901. The firm became Laurent, Laforce & Bourdeau in 1888. MC

LAUTREC, Donald (b Bourgeois). Singer, actor, songwriter, b Jonquière, Que, 13 Jul 1940. He began his career in 1957 as an acrobat, and his singing debut took place at the Central Hotel in St-Martin in 1963. He made two LPs for Apex, the first – *Personne au monde* – of songs by Cécile Coulombe and Marc *Gélinas. Among his early hits were 'Lobby-Ho,' 'Tu dis des bêtises,' 'Le Ska' (written in collaboration with Pierre Nolès), and 'Loin dans ma campagne,' from the film *Pas de vacances pour les idoles* (1964), in which he also acted.

Named male singing discovery of the year at the 1965 Gala des artistes in Montreal, Lautrec was part of the Variétés '65 Quebec tour. In 1966 he went to France and sang for the ORTF on several variety programs, including 'Feux de joie' and 'La Grande Lucarne.' That autumn he toured Quebec again and finished the tour with a recital at the *PDA. He premiered the *Expo 67 theme song 'Un jour, un jour' ('Hey friend, say friend') by Stéphane *Venne and gave a recital at the Expo Theatre.

The CBC sent Lautrec in 1967 to the Festival of Sopot, Poland, where he sang Georges *Dor's 'La Manic,' among other songs. The same year he represented Canada at the Festival of Popular Song in Rio de Janeiro. In 1968 he toured the French provinces with several artists, including Nana Mouskouri, and gave a recital on Warsaw TV. He went to Spain to make the film *Le Diable aime les bijoux* (1969) and sang one of the songs on the recording of the film score (Jupiter JPLS 11020).

In Canada that summer Lautrec was the host for 'Coup de soleil,' a program which became 'Donald Lautrec chaud' on CBC TV (1969–70). When that ended he took part in the 1971 Musicorama tour of Quebec and appeared at the PDA in the 1972 *MSO summer concerts. René Homier-Roy described his performance: 'Self-assured but not aggressive, cool, calm, and somewhat amused, he sang some old songs and almost all [the songs] from his new LP in an amazingly sure voice ... He is, in a word, good, and he finally inspired the orchestra. It all made for an exceedingly attractive show' (*La Presse*, 12 Jul 1972).

In 1974 Lautrec sang at the *St-Denis and other theatres and made some films. For CBC TV he appeared in 1973 in the series 'The Entertainers', was singer and host 1974–6 for 'Tempo,' and in January 1979 acted in 'Faut voir ça'.

Donald Lautrec's LPs (some 15 by 1979) include one of a recital he gave at the Comédie-Canadienne in 1970 (Jupiter YDS 8030) and *Fluffy*, containing several of his compositions (1972, Trans-World TWK-6501). The reissues *Donald Lautrec, ses succès 'chauds'* (Jupiter JPL 11019) and *Donald Lautrec 1960–1970* (Neptune NEPS 6007) were released in 1969 and 1971 respectively.

Among Lautrec's main hits were the songs 'Candy,' 'Heloïse,' 'Hosannah,' 'Le Mur derrière la grange,' 'Kyrie eleison,' 'Toujours le même,' and 'Le Jour du dernier jour' (a French-language version of 'A Whiter Shade of Pale' by Procul Harum). In addition to his own material he has performed songs by Michel Conte, Jean Fortier, Claude *Gauthier, and Stéphane Venne. He is a member of CAPAC.

BIBLIOGRAPHY

Brien, Lucien. 'Donald Lautrec not merely a singer,' *CanComp*, 29, May 1968

Flohil, Richard. 'Donald Lautrec,' *CanComp*, 56, Jan 1971

ST

Laval Guitar Trio† / Trio de guitares Laval. Ensemble founded in 1975 in Quebec City by Paul Gerrits, Jacques Chandonnet, and Claude Gagnon, all teachers at *Laval U. They gave their first concert in October 1975 in Cleveland for the American Guitar Foundation. Since then the trio has appeared at Laval U, *McGill U, and the *U of Montreal, at the *PDA and the *Grand Théâtre in Quebec City, and on the CBC. It has performed as well in many Quebec towns, mainly on *JMC tours (1977–9). The instruments employed in addition to the guitar are the cittern, the lute, the orpharion, the theorbo, and the vihuela – all plucked strings. The trio's repertoire, which has been published in Quebec by Doberman, consists chiefly of renaissance and baroque pieces its members have adapted; it also contains arrangements of Canadian folksongs, and contemporary works such as Claude Gagnon's *Sensations* (1975). The ensemble has made two LPs for Doberman. The first, with Francine Déry (*Musique pour trois et quatre guitares*, 1977, DO-13D) features works by Dowland, Bach, Attaignant, Sermisy, Alain *Gagnon, and Claude Gagnon. The second (DO-17D), made in 1978, contains Alain Gagnon's *Interlude* as well as Claude Gagnon's *Adanac* (1976, theorbo, vihuela, and cittern), *Kaléidoscope* (1977, three guitars), and *Suite folklorique* (1977, guitar, vihuela, and cittern).

Paul Gerrits – b Nijmegen, Netherlands, 7 Nov 1935, naturalized Canadian 1977; performance diploma in lute (Cologne Cons) 1966 – studied the lute in Germany with Walter Gerwig. On moving to Canada in 1966 he settled in Quebec City and began to teach at Laval U the following year. He made two LPs in Europe and wrote a *Méthode de guitar et de luth* (Möseler 1966) and, for the guitar, a *Méthode pour débutants* (Musantiqua 1973). He has edited various collections of guitar pieces, some in collaboration with Chandonnet and published by Doberman. Chandonnet – b Quebec City 2 Apr 1947; B Mus guitar (Laval U) 1972 – studied guitar with Martin Prével and Alexandre Lagoya and lute with Gerrits. He began teaching guitar at Laval U in 1968 and has played as a soloist on CBC radio. Claude Gagnon – b St-Pacôme-de-Kamouraska, Que, 28 Sep 1950; B Mus (Laval U) 1975 – a brother of André, obtained his training as a guitarist from Gerrits and Marie Lévesque at Laval U, where he began teaching in 1971. In addition to pieces for the trio he has written incidental music and works for solo guitar.

AP

LAVALLÉE. Quebec family of musicians: 1 / Augustin 2 / Calixa, his most famous son, and 3 / Charles, Joseph, and Cordélia, his other sons and daughter.

1 (Jean-Baptiste André) **Augustin Pâquet dit Lavallée.** Luthier, bandmaster, teacher, music dealer, b Verchères, Lower Canada (Quebec), 1816, d Montreal 15 Feb 1903. He had been a blacksmith, a logger, and a gunsmith, when he moved with his family to St-Hyacinthe, Que, around 1850 to begin working with the organ manufacturer Joseph *Casavant, who had built his first organ in 1840. Lavallée opened his own string-instrument workshop in St-Hyacinthe in 1852 and also conducted the village band before setting up in business in Montreal in 1869 with his son Charles under the name of Lavallée & Fils. Self-taught as an instrument maker, he is believed to have made close to 200 violins. According to the anonymous author (Jules Jehin-Prume?) of *Une Vie d'artiste*, a biography of Frantz *Jehin-Prume, the latter entrusted Lavallée with his Guarnerius after it had been crushed by a sleigh, and Lavallée restored it to its owner 'as good as new.'

2 **Calixa** (Calixte). Composer, pianist, conductor, teacher, administrator, b Verchères, Lower Canada (Quebec), 28 Dec 1842, d Boston 21 Jan 1891. The first child of Augustin Lavallée and Charlotte-Caroline Valentine, he was born into the eighth Canadian generation of the family Pasquier (also spelt Pasquet or Pâquet) dit Lavallée. His ancestor on the paternal side was Isaac Pasquier dit Lavallée, a native of Poitou who arrived in New France in the summer of 1665, a soldier in the Carignan-Salières regiment. His ancestor on the maternal side was Maj James Fendor Valentine of Melrose, Scotland, who settled in Verchères and married a Quebec woman named Leclerc.

Calixa was born on a concession called 'de la Beauce' (which in 1881 became the parish of Ste-Théodosie and in 1946 the village Calixa-Lavallée), and on the day of his birth he was baptized in the Roman Catholic faith in St-François-Xavier Church in Verchères. While he was quite young he displayed a remarkable aptitude for music and had lessons from his father; he soon played piano, violin, organ, and cornet. At the same time he attended college in St-Hyacinthe, where the family had settled ca 1850. In 1853 he was asked to help out in an emergency by playing the organ for Montreal's Notre-Dame Church choir which was passing through St-Hyacinthe. His talent made a vivid impression on Messire Barbarin, the curé of Notre-Dame. Two years later Lavallée went to Montreal to study piano with Paul *Letondal and Charles Wugk *Sabatier. A wealthy butcher, Léon Derome, became his adoptive father and sponsor. The young Lavallée often accompanied Derome to the *Theatre Royal, and he may have played the piano there.

In 1857 Calixa Lavallée left Canada to seek his fortune in the USA. He won first prize in an instrumental competition in New Orleans and then departed for a tour of South America, the West Indies, and Mexico with a Spanish violinist named Olivera. Nothing more is known about this period of his life. He was reported in Baltimore in 1860 and in Providence in September 1861, when he enlisted as a 'musician, first class' in the Fourth Rhode Island Regiment, soon becoming its principal cornet. He fought in the US Civil War and is supposed to have said later that he was wounded in the leg at the Battle of Antietam in Maryland.

Calixa Lavallée

Discharged in the fall of 1862, he returned to Verchères the following year. On 24 Jan 1864 he gave a concert in Montreal as a pianist, violinist, and cornetist, and for a while he taught and gave concerts. He struck up a friendship with the Belgian violinist-composer Frantz *Jehin-Prume on the latter's arrival in Montreal in 1865.

Back in the USA in 1865–6, Lavallée spent some time in California, taught in Louisiana, and then returned to New England; he married a US woman, Josephine Gentilly or Gently, in Lowell, Mass, in 1867. He settled in Boston, then moved to New York, where ca 1870 he was appointed music director and superintendent of the Grand Opera House, an opera and variety theatre. A production of his comic opera *Loulou* was announced early in 1872 but was cancelled when the owner of the establishment, James Fisk, was murdered.

After this misfortune Lavallée returned to Montreal. A public subscription organized by Derome enabled him to spend 1873–5 in Paris, where he studied piano with Marmontel and harmony and composition with Bazin and Boieldieu fils. Little is known of his stay in Paris, except that he composed a series of studies for piano, including one in E minor, *Le Papillon*, which was placed on the study list of the Paris Cons. This work subsequently went through numerous editions in Europe and America, continued to appear in collections and anthologies, and was recorded several times, eg by Myrtle Eover (Victor 21012, nd) and by Frank La Forge (Victor Red Seal 64083, 1908). In Paris, according to Charles *Labelle (Montreal *L'Écho musical*, 1 Jan 1888), 'a *Suite* for orchestra was performed in July 1874 by an orchestra of 80 musicians under the direction of the celebrated conductor Maton.'

Lavallée returned to Quebec City 25 Jul 1875. In his pocket was a letter from Marmontel dated 5 July: 'I bid you a cordial farewell and wish you all the success you deserve by your continuous and courageous work. I am certain that your friends ... will find your talent transformed from two standpoints: style and controlled virtuosity ... ' In Montreal he opened a studio in conjunction with Jehin-Prume and the latter's wife, the soprano Rosita *del Vecchio. On 9 September he gave a free concert at the Reading Room on Notre-Dame St for those who had helped him during his stay in Europe. He presented some of his works in Quebec City on 1 December and in Montreal at the *Mechanics' Hall eight days later. Guillaume *Couture, writing in Montreal's *La Minerve* 9 and 10 Dec 1875, acclaimed Lavallée as 'one of our national glories,' adding that he had learned how 'to be by turns brilliant, elegant, fiery, tender and impassioned.'

Lavallée served 1875–9 as choirmaster at St James Church and conducted his choristers in 18 stage performances of *Jeanne d'Arc*, a drama by Jules Barbier with music by Gounod, at the *Académie de musique (1877). *La Minerve* on 15 May 1877 described the premiere as a 'resounding success,' adding that 'nothing like it had ever been seen before in this city.' Lavallée was unsuccessful, however, in his efforts to obtain funds from the Quebec government to open a conservatory. He was elected president of the *AMQ (1876–7, 1879–80).

In April and May 1879 Lavallée conducted in Montreal and Quebec City a production of Boieldieu's *La Dame blanche* and then moved to Quebec City, where he hastily wrote a cantata to commemorate the visit of the governor-general of Canada, the Marquis of Lorne, and his wife, Princess Louise, a daughter of Queen Victoria. The work was performed on 11 Jun 1879 with considerable success, but the Quebec government refused to reimburse Lavallée for his expenses and the composer found himself several hundred dollars in debt. After this, Lavallée lived for some time in obscurity, giving lessons and earning a meagre living as choirmaster at St-Patrice Church and conductor of a band. On 2 Dec 1879, however, he took part in a concert presented by Jehin-Prume at the Mechanics' Hall in Montreal.

On the occasion of a national convention of French Canadians to be held in June 1880 Lavallée, who had been named a member of the music planning committee, composed a national song with words by Judge A.-B Routhier. *'O Canada' was performed jointly by three bands 24 Jun 1880 at a convention banquet at the Skaters' Pavilion in Quebec City and was received enthusiastically. But Lavallée's financial position remained precarious, and he began suffering the first attacks of the illness (diagnosed as tubercular laryngitis) that would eventually claim his life. After giving some concerts with Jehin-Prume and del Vecchio, he went with them to Hartford, Conn, for an engagement on 3 Dec 1881. His comic opera **The Widow* was presented during this period in New Orleans and other cities. The chronology of subsequent events is somewhat confused. He accompanied the Hungarian soprano Etelka Gerster on a US tour in the early 1880s but did not appear with her when she performed in Canada. Next he was the pianist on a Colonial Line ferry between Boston and New York. In Boston he opened a studio around 1882 and taught harmony, orchestration, and composition at the Carlyle Petersilea Music Academy while serving as choirmaster at the Roman Catholic Cathedral of the Holy Cross. In 1883 he published a 'melodramatic musical satire' **TIQ* (*The Indian Question Settled At Last*).

Lavallée's reputation spread rapidly in US music circles. He publicly declared himself in favour of annexing Canada to its southern neighbour. As an active member of the Music Teachers' National Assn, he organized and participated in a concert devoted entirely to US composers, the first of its kind, held in Cleveland 3 Jul 1884. A year later, a similar concert was presented at New York's Academy of Music, on which occasion an *Offertoire* by Lavallée was performed. In 1886 he was president of a group of French-Canadian emigrants, the League of Patriots of Fall River, Mass, and was elected president of the Music Teachers' National Assn, which sent him to a convention of the National Society of Professional Musicians in London in January 1888. There Lavallée gave a remarkable speech on the general outlook of US musicians and performed a *Marche américaine* he had composed. He returned to Boston via Montreal and again embarked on an intensive round of activities: lessons, concerts, newspaper articles, and composition. Though permanently settled in the USA, he did not forget Canada: 'My aim in all this,' he wrote Aristide Filiatreault 14 Mar 1890, 'is to try to wake up our dear population, and by occasional small doses we may be able to make them understand that you must learn to walk before you can run.'

In July 1890 Lavallée organized the Music Teachers' National Assn convention in Detroit, where his *Suite* (*Concerto*) for cello and piano was received enthusiastically in a performance by himself and the cellist Charles Heydler. To the teachers present who asked to see the score he had to admit that only the cello part had been written down! Later a noted publisher of band music, Cundy, suggested to him that he could make a lot of money writing music of that kind. Lavallée replied: 'I would rather be remembered for a few artistic compositions than to grow rich in other lines of musical effort' (recounted by Henry F. Miller, a Boston piano manufacturer, in *Freund's Music and Drama*, 31 Jan 1891).

In the autumn of 1890 illness confined Lavallée to bed and forced him to give up his responsibility for organizing the 1892 Chicago convention. The pain in his throat became more acute, and his general condition worsened. Early in January 1891 Léon Derome hastened to his bedside. On 21 January, around midnight, Lavallée breathed his last at his home at 4 Brookford Road in the Dorchester district; he was 48 years and 24 days old. A formal funeral service was held two days later in the Cathedral of the Holy Cross in the presence of Archbishop John Joseph Williams and many US and Canadian colleagues. However, no sermon or eulogy was delivered. The violinist Alfred *De Sève was among the pallbearers. Lavallée was buried in Mount Benedict Cemetery.

Through the initiative of a Montreal committee, including Eugène *Lapierre, the bass Ulysse *Paquin, and the band conductor Joseph-L. Gariépy, Lavallée's body was returned ceremoniously to Montreal on 18 Jul 1933, 42 years after his death; it was interred in the Côte-des-Neiges Cemetery after a funeral service at Notre-Dame Church. On this occasion, an avenue adjoining Lafontaine Park was named after him. More recently, the name of Calixa Lavallée was given to a secondary school in metropolitan Montreal, to streets in Quebec City and St-Hyacinthe, and to the music department building of the *U of Ottawa.

Lavallée is perhaps the most illustrious representative of that generation of pioneers who nourished the growth of music in Canada after the long period of stagnation and false starts which summarized musical life in North America from the years of French and English colonization to the mid-19th century. Although he was exceptionally gifted, Lavallée received his training in Montreal and Paris along traditional lines, and this accounts for the conventional nature of his works and their adherence to the fashions of his day. He was a fervent admirer of Gounod and does not appear to have been sensitive to the innovations of Berlioz or Wagner, for example. Nevertheless, Lavallée's works display great facility and an innate feeling for melody and rhythm. His harmonic vocabulary and his forms rarely depart from tradition. Because he was travelling constantly and was obliged to earn his living in circumstances which seldom afforded him time to contemplate and plan, he found it difficult to write large-scale works or to cultivate a personal style. Composing as the need arose, he was inclined to write technically dazzling piano pieces, fashionable ballads, light operettas, and occasional cantatas in the style of Gounod, Offenbach, or Sullivan. Certain more ambitious works, though unfinished, indicate that he could have become a composer of substance. He was a fine pianist, and the brilliance and clarity of his playing impressed his audiences, especially in his own bravura pieces. However, he evidently could perform such works as Beethoven's *Appassionata* sensitively and perceptively. His natural brio and his facility for composition earned him the immediate recognition of at least a few of his more perceptive countrymen, who declared him a 'national musician' long before he composed the song that became Canada's national anthem and ensured his place in history.

In human terms, Lavallée's devotion to the artistic advancement of his compatriots is undisputed. He contributed, at least partially, to the training of Alexis *Contant, Bernadette Dufresne, the Count of Premio-Real, Philéas *Roy, Joseph *Vézina, and many others. His initiatives in teaching and operatic production were many, but he had to fight continually against the ignorance, indifference, and even hostility of his own people. His voluntary exile in the USA suggests that it was only beyond the borders of his country that he was able to find an atmosphere in which his activities could flourish freely.

Lavallée must be considered one of the first musicians of completely professional calibre born in Canada and one of the musical pioneers of his own country and even of the USA. It seems evident that he gave little thought to the fate of his works: he was concerned with producing for the moment and paid no heed to posterity. Thus, of the many works he composed, more than half have been lost or destroyed. Their discovery undoubtedly would call for a revaluation of his entire output. Although it is difficult to determine its precise extent, Lavallée's influence is beyond doubt. For his contemporaries, for succeeding generations, and even today, Calixa Lavallée remains the embodiment of a talented, honest, and persevering musician, a zealous craftsman devoted to his art. In the words of Lapierre: 'For Lavallée, as for some other great artists, his masterpiece was his life.'

With the exception of 'O Canada,' Lavallée's work has remained largely unknown to the public. Nevertheless, because of the efforts of such musicians and researchers as Lapierre, Joseph Vézina, J.-J. *Gagnier, and Helmut *Kallmann, certain works have been discovered and performed. CBC radio and TV programs have helped bring the musician and his works wider attention. Excerpts from *The Widow* have been recorded, and the work was revived on stage in Hamilton in 1976. The music of the ballet *Pointes sur glace* was assembled and orchestrated by Edmund *Assaly from several Lavallée pieces. Lavallée's life and career are the subject of the play *Le Traversier de Boston* (1933) by Eugène Lapierre and the musical *Le Vagabond de la gloire*, for which Lapierre wrote the music and Aimé Plamondon the book. The *CMCentre has granted Lavallée the associate status reserved for deceased composers whose work the Centre holds.

COMPOSITIONS

STAGE

Loulou, comic opera. Ca 1872. Ms lost

Salomon, opera – 2 fragments: 'Le Jugement,' 'Marche du trône.' Ca 1886. Ms Lost

See also *TIQ* (*The Indian Question Settled at Last*); *The Widow*.

ORCHESTRA OR CONCERT BAND

Marche indienne / Indian March ('Military March,' no. 6 from *TIQ*). Ditson 1891

Pas redoublé sur des airs canadiens. Ca 1872. Montreal *La Presse*, 9 Nov 1912

Rhapsodie sur des airs irlandais. Ms lost

King of Diamonds, overture. Cundy-Bettoney 1888
The Bridal Rose, overture. Cundy-Bettoney 1888. RCI 233/Cap ST-6261 (*CBC Wpg O)
The Golden Fleece, 'companion to Poet and Peasant,' overture. Cundy-Bettoney 1888
2 orchestral suites, including one performed in Paris 1874. Mss lost

CHAMBER MUSIC
Grande Fantaisie, *Op 75*. Cornet, pf. Fischer 1880
Méditation. Cornet, pf. Fischer 1880. (Arr hmca and pf) RCI 443 (*Gresko pf)
Suite or *Concerto*. Premiered in Detroit 1890. Vc, pf. Ms lost
1 *Sonata* for vn and pf, 2 *String Quartets*, 1 *Trio* for pf, vn, vc. All lost

PIANO
Bon Voyage 'galop de concert.' Nd (premiered 1876). Ms
La Couronne de lauriers. Boucher after 1866
The Ellinger 'polka de salon,' *Op 8*. Cluett 1863. CBC SM-204 (L.L. *Thomas)
The First Welcome, polka. Gordon
Fleur de mai / Mayflower 'polka de salon.' Gordon
Grande Marche de concert, *Op 14*. Eveillard & Jacquot. CBC SM-204 (L.L. *Thomas)
Grande Valse de concert, *Op 6*. Gordon
Marche américaine. 1887 (London 1888). Published
Marche funèbre 'Hommage à Pie IX.' Ca 1878. Lamoureux. CBC SM-204 (L.L. *Thomas)
Mouvement à la pavane, *Op 41*. White & Smith 1886
L'Oiseau-mouche / Humming Bird 'bluette de salon,' *Op 11*. Boucher after 1861. CBC SM-204 (L.L. *Thomas)
La Petite Hermine 'galop.' Gordon 1887?
Première Valse de salon, *Op 39*. White & Smith 1886. CBC SM-204 (L.L. *Thomas)
Shake Again Galop. Alexander Barnes 1866
Souvenir de Tolède 'mazurka de salon,' *Op 17*. Eveillard & Jacquot
Vol-au-vent, galop; *La Minerve*
The War Fever 'galop caractéristique,' *Op 4*. Gordon 1861
Also a *Grande Fantaisie* on *Il Trovatore*, an *Impromptu-Caprice*, a transcription of the march from *Faust*, and 30 studies including *Le Papillon / The Butterfly*. Eveillard & Jacquot. RCI 252 (J. *Dufresne)/CBC SM-204 (L.L. *Thomas)

CHORAL
Cantata in honour of the Marquis de Lorne and Princess Louise (N. Legendre). 1879. Ms lost
Hymne à la paix / Hymn of Peace 'dedicated to all the nations of the world. Ms
Symphony 'dedicated to the city of Boston.' Chorus, orch. Ms lost
Tu es Petrus / Glory, Blessing, Praise and Honor 'offertorium.' Before 1883 (New York 1885). Sop, bass, chorus, orch. White & Smith 1883
See also 'O Canada.'

VOICE
'L'Absence' (R. Tremblay). *Album musical*, 1 Dec 1881/*P-T*, Aug 1933. RCI 426 (B. *Laplante)
'Andalouse' 'boléro pour soprano,' Op 38 (Musset, transl L.C. Elsen). White & Smith 1886
'Beautiful Girl of Kildare' (R.A. Warren). Whittemore 1869
'Do I Love You?' (F. Johnson). V, pf. Pond 1863
'Le Facteur' (J.H. Malo). *P-T*, Feb 1909
'Harmonie' (F.-A.-H. LaRue). 1879. V, pf. A. Lavigne 1879
'Leaving Home and Friends' (F. Dumont). Whittemore 1869
'The Lost Love' (F. Dumont). Whittemore 1869
'Nuit d'été'/'Summer Night' (N. Legendre). A. Lavigne 1880. RCI 426 (B. *Laplante)
'Restons Français' (R. Tremblay). *P-T*, 22 Jun 1901 (v only), Aug 1933
Trois Chansons (Mme Duval-Thibault). Ms
'Violette'/'Violet' 'cantilène' (N. Legendre, transl P.J. Curran). A. Lavigne 1879/*P-T*, Aug 1933
2 songs from *The Widow*: 'With Pleasure in Each Glance,' 'The Rocks and Hills.' Curwen

WRITINGS
Speech delivered in London 3 Jan 1888 as delegate of the Music Teachers' National Assn of America to the convention of the National Society of Professional Musicians of Great Britain. Original English text in the *Standard* of London (4 Jan 1888); French translation in appendix of Eugène Lapierre's *Calixa Lavallée* (3rd edition only, Montreal 1966)
'L'E muet,' *Canada artistique*, vol 1, Feb 1890
'L'art musical au Canada,' ibid, Apr 1890

BIBLIOGRAPHY
David, L.O. 'Calixa Lavallée,' *Opinion publique*, vol 4, 13 Mar 1873
Marmette, Joseph. 'Prume et Lavallée,' ibid, vol 6, 18 Nov 1875
– 'L'Art musical au Canada: Lavallée,' Montreal *La Presse*, 23 May 1878
Musical World (24 Jul 1886)
Labelle, Charles. 'Calixa Lavallée,' *Écho musical*, vol 1, 1 Jan 1888
'Conference of the National Society of Professional Musicians,' *MT*, vol 29, Feb 1888
Filiatreault, A. 'Calixa Lavallée,' *Canada-Revue*, vol 2, Jan 1891
'Calixa Lavallée, the career of an eminent musician,' *Freund's Music and Drama*, vol 15, 31 Jan 1891
The Week (13 Feb 1891)
[Jehin-Prume, Jules]. *Une Vie d'artiste* (Montreal ca 1900)
Comte, Gustave. 'Calixa Lavallée – notes biographiques inédites sur le chantre de la nation,' *P-T*, 374, 24 Jul 1909
Logan, John Daniel. 'Canada's first creative composer,' *Canadian Courier*, vol 2, 27 Jan 1912
Comte, Gustave. 'Le Monument Lavallée, comment on réalisera une idée que le "Passe-Temps" a été le premier à lancer,' *P-T*, 460, 9 Nov 1912
Letondal, Arthur. 'Calixa Lavallée,' Montreal *Le Devoir*, 6 Nov 1915
– 'Calixa Lavallée,' *La Musique*, vol 2, Feb 1920
Magnan, Hormisdas. 'Calixa Lavallée,' *BRH*, vol 33, Jul 1927
Hipsher, Edward Ellsworth. *American Opera and Its Composer* (Philadelphia 1927)
Comte, Gustave. 'La première troupe canadienne d'opéra et Calixa Lavallée,' *Quinzaine musicale*, 26 Dec 1931
Salter, Sumner. 'Early encouragements to American composers,' *MQ*, vol 28, Jan 1932
Issue devoted to Lavallée, *P-T*, 864, Aug 1933
Chartier, Ferrier. 'Calixa Lavallée,' *Action nationale*, vol 2, Sep 1933
'The lesson of Calixa Lavallée,' *Musical Review of Canada*, vol 1, Oct 1933
Lapierre, Eugène. *Calixa Lavallée, musicien national du Canada* (Montreal 1936, 1950, 1966)
Desrochers, Félix. 'Calixa Lavallée,' *Conférence du Club musical et littéraire de Montréal*, vol 2, 1941–2
Blanchet, L.-J.-N. *Une vie illustrée de Calixa Lavallée* (Montréal 1951)
Letondal, Arthur. 'Calixa Lavallée 1842–1891,' *Musique et musiciens*, vol 1, Nov 1952
Lapierre, Eugène. 'La belle vie de Calixa Lavallée,' *L'Écrin* (Montreal 1952?)
Daniels, D.S. 'Again the people rescue from oblivion our O Canada composer,' *Canadian Tribune*, 31 Jan 1955
Denechaud, Jean. 'La vie errante de Calixa Lavallée,' Rouyn and Noranda *La Frontière*, 19 Jun 1968

3 **Charles**. Conductor, cornetist, music dealer, b Verchères, Lower Canada (Quebec) 13 Jul 1850, d Montreal 28 Nov 1924. He worked with his father as a violin maker and importer of instruments and ran the business on his own after the latter's death. As a cornetist he travelled throughout America and was conductor of the *Bande de la Cité and the Victoria Rifles Band. He was one of the founders of the Musicians' Protective Union of Montreal (now the Montreal Musicians' Guild, local 406 of the AF of M) and its president 1905–14. His brother Joseph (d 1913) was a trombonist in New York concert bands and orchestras. His sister Cordélia (pianist, singer, b Verchères, ca 1847, d Montreal Oct 1920) was the wife of the violinist Jean-A. *Duquette. Their cousin Marie-Louise Lavallée was the mother of the pianist Jean *Dansereau. GP

LAVALLÉE-SMITH, (Louis) **Alphonse**. Organist, teacher, composer, b Berthierville, near Trois-Rivières, Que, 17 Apr 1873, d Ste-Agathe-des-Monts, near Trois-Rivières, 23 Jul 1912. He was the son of Dr Wenceslas Smith and Zénobie Lavallée (first cousin of Calixa *Lavallée). When his family moved to St-Thomas-de-Pierreville he completed his academic education 1886–93 at the Nicolet Seminary and studied music with Octave Hardy (dit *Chatillon).

Lavallée-Smith served three years as organist at the Nicolet Cathedral. He then settled in Montreal, where he studied with Romain-Octave *Pelletier while making his living as a music salesman. He was assistant organist at St-Jacques Church before assuming the same position in 1896 at Notre-Dame Church. He left that year for Paris, however, where he studied with Théodore Dubois, Eugène Gigout, Alexandre Guilmant, and Charles-Marie Widor. On his return near the end of 1897, he became organist at St-Henri Church and teacher of piano and harmony at the Collège de Montréal.

The great accomplishment of Lavallée-Smith's short life was the *Cons national de musique, which he founded in Montreal in the fall of 1905 and directed until his death. Émile *Gour, Germain Lefebvre, and J.-Élie *Savaria were among his pupils.

Lavallée-Smith's compositions include the *Cantate du Séminaire de Nicolet* (1903, text by Louis Fréchette), written to mark the centenary of the institution; another cantata, *La Nativité*; an operetta in one act, *Gisèle*, premiered in 1924 but extant only in the rehearsal score for voices and piano; some religious music for soloists or choir; and some patriotic songs, art songs, and organ pieces. A few have been published by *Archambault and in **Le Passe-Temps*.

A *Requiem Mass*, dating from the last years of Lavallée-Smith's life, was rehearsed under his direction but was performed for the first time at his funeral at St-Henri Church. In August 1932 a concert of his works was presented on radio station CKAC in Montreal. Several of his manuscripts and published works have been deposited in the BN du Q (Inventory of the Jean Chatillon collection). GP

Laval University† / **Université Laval**. Oldest French-language university in North America. It was founded 8 Dec 1852 by virtue of a charter signed by Queen Victoria granting the *Séminaire de Québec 'the rights and privileges of a university.' In 1876 in Montreal it opened a branch which in 1919 became the *U of Montreal by a writ of Pope Benedict XV. A second charter vesting supreme authority in the Laval U council was proclaimed in 1971. Laval U comprises 12 faculties, 9 affiliated schools, and a department of continuing education. In 1978–9 a total of 1396 teachers (not including numerous part-time lecturers) gave instruction to more than 20,000 students.

The School of Music was created 9 Jun 1922 and attached to the faculty of arts. The names of Arthur *LeBlanc and Henri *Vallières (who was to teach there 1931–66) appeared on the first student registration list of 11 women and 18 men. The curriculum gave priority to religious music and consisted of courses in solfège, harmony, theory, and history. In 1924 instruction in piano, violin, and organ was added. The first students to obtain the B MUS were Charles Lapointe and Sister Thérèse de l'Enfant-Jésus in 1929. A department of sacred music, including organ courses, was established officially in 1932. The *Motu proprio* (1903) of Pius X had aroused the enthusiasm of the Quebec clergy by proposing a return to Gregorian music. Some members of the school, including Marius *Cayouette and later Elzéar Fortier, played an active role in this liturgical revival. In 1923–4 a group of teachers formed the steering committee of the journal *La Musique* in its last year of existence. Some years later, musicians associated with the School of Music helped edit the *Revue Saint-Grégoire*, 1949–63, which was devoted to sacred music.

Gustave *Gagnon, the first dean, held the post 1922–5 and was not officially replaced until 1932; Father Pierre-Chrysologue Desrochers administered the school in the interim. Robert *Talbot, who had been secretary since 1922, was dean 1932–54; under his administration highly successful summer courses were instituted in 1937. The school awarded its first doctorates in 1933 to Antoine Montreuil, Joseph-Romuald Pelletier, and Robert Talbot. In 1936 it established a 'licence' (licentiate) program whose first diplomas were awarded in 1946 to Olga Gosselin and Sisters Jean-du-Sacré-Coeur, Sainte-Cécilia, Rose-de-la-Trinité, and Thérèse-des-Lys. Through the collaboration of the school and the Benedictines of St-Benoît-du-Lac, summer courses in Gregorian chant were instituted in 1944.

The opening of the *CMQ that year created some difficulties for the school. The CMQ was offering free instruction and its varied instrumental courses were given by teachers of renown, with the result that Laval's enrolment dropped and instrumental instruction was cut back to courses in piano, organ, and singing. As early as 1942 the school had decided to discontinue its own extramural degrees, formerly granted through other schools; the result naturally was a further loss of students. Thereafter, only diplomas for the level below the baccalaureat continued to be issued extramurally (25,000 of these were granted in 1977). An agreement was concluded with the CMQ in 1944, however, to enable certain students to obtain their training from both institutions; but this remained in effect for only a year.

Onésime Pouliot took over as director in 1954 and held the post until 1962. Under him the number of highly trained teachers (eg, Jocelyn *Binet and Jeanne *Landry) increased. In part because of its summer courses, the school experienced a period of growth starting in 1959. It offered a training program for teachers in the *Ward method and began to restructure the program of Gregorian chant.

Under Lucien *Brochu, who was director 1962–77, the school took on the dimensions appropriate to a major university; programs were expanded and the number and quality of students increased as a result. From 1963 to 1969, studies required for the undergraduate programs were spread over four years. In 1970 an electronic music studio was founded by Nil *Parent. A laboratory for computer-assisted studies was created in 1973 under the direction of Martin Prével to work in the fields of research and ear training. Teachers and students from various faculties took part in this project. In 1974 the program for the second study level, until then the equivalent of the licentiate curriculum, was restructured and became a master's program. The same year a musicology research team was formed to study and make an inventory of the musical journals in France in the 19th century. Directed by Robert Cohen (until 1979), the team worked with the Paris Cons and encouraged student exchanges. In the area of jazz, a stage band, founded in 1972 by Robert Monette, was conducted in 1979 by Pierre Lessard. A course in improvisation was begun in 1974, and a course in arranging was established the following year. In 1976 a group of teachers working with the university's education department set up a research team in ear training co-ordinated by Gilles Simard.

After the appointment of Antoine *Bouchard as dean in 1977 there was an attempt to restore the balance among the range of the instrumental disciplines. In addition to the contemporary music workshop (under Paul Cadrin) and a small vocal ensemble, several flourishing instrumental groups have been co-ordinated by Chantal *Masson (large ensembles) and Armand *Ferland (chamber music). Jeanne Landry took charge of classes in piano accompaniment, Chantal Masson of the choir, Scott Ross, Michel Ducharme, and Friedemann Fischer of the baroque music ensemble, and Abe Kniaz of the chamber orchestra. The concert band has played under David Bircher and a guitar ensemble under Paul Gerrits. *GIMEL, an electro-acoustic music group directed by Nil Parent, and the Choeur de clarinettes under Armand Ferland were organized by the school as supplements to its academic program. The latter ensemble took part in the 1979 International Clarinet Congress in Libramont, Belgium. In the university at large – ie, beyond the jurisdiction of the School of Music – the Laval U choir developed under the direction of André Martin. The choir was administered by the Dept of Socio-cultural Activities until 1978, when the responsibility was assumed by the choir's members. La Gaillarde, an ensemble also conducted by Martin, was formed under the jurisdiction of the Dept of Socio-cultural Activities as a successor to the Groupe instrumental de l'Université Laval.

In 1980 the music library at Laval (for statistics see Libraries) held a substantial collection of 17th-to 19th-century publications in the fields of musicology, the history of music, and pedagogy. Gisèle Ricard was placed in charge of a documentation centre independent of the library and specializing in musical education and contemporary music. She also has organized the 'Concerts de musique actuelle' in collaboration with the universities of Montreal and McGill.

Over the years the school has occupied numerous locations, but in 1979 it moved to the former Grand Séminaire, renamed the Pavillon Casault in honour of the university's first rector, Father Louis-Jacques Casault.

In the academic year 1978–9, 50 professors and 62 lecturers taught the 361 students in a choice of seven programs at the baccalaureat level – B MUS in performance, composition, education, history and literature, rhythmics, or general, and the BES (baccalauréat en enseignement secondaire) with a major in music; six at the master's (M MUS) level – musicology, analysis and theory, composition, education, performance, and instrumental teaching; and one at the doctorate (D MUS) level – musicology. Among doctorates granted under the new curriculum were those to Monique *Vachon in 1966 and Juliette Bourassa-Trépanier in 1972.

Among the students at different periods were Jean-Marie *Beaudet, Maurice *Blackburn, Jacinthe *Couture, Raoul *Jobin, Marthe *Lapointe, and Jules Payment; among the staff members Yves *Bédard, Antoine Bouchard, Gustave Gagnon, J.-Alexandre *Gilbert, Anna-Marie *Globenski, Jacques *Hétu, Jean-Paul *Jeannotte, Arthur LeBlanc, Marthe *Létourneau, Omer *Létourneau, Roger *Matton, Élise Paré-Tousignant, Lucien *Poirier, Antoine *Reboulot, Hidetaro and Zeyda *Suzuki, and Robert *Weisz. In 1968 the school began to offer courses in music at the Cegep level at the Collège Ste-Foy.

Laval has conferred honorary D Mus degrees on Gustave Gagnon, J.-Alexandre Gilbert, Arthur *Lavigne, and Joseph *Vézina in 1922, Robert Talbot in 1933, Berthe *Roy in 1943, Sir Ernest *MacMillan in 1947, Désiré Defauw, Raoul Jobin, and Wilfrid *Pelletier in 1952, Father Joseph-G. Turcotte in 1960, François *Brassard in 1961, Léopold *Simoneau in 1973, Jon *Vickers in 1978, and the *Quebec SO conductor James De Preist in 1980. While acting as host to the 14th IFMC Congress in 1961 it awarded hon D ès L degrees to Helen *Creighton and Maud Karpeles, as well as to Bertrand Harris Bronson, a professor at the U of California, and to Claude Marcel-Dubois, the director of the department of ethnomusicology at the Musée national des arts et traditions populaires in Paris.

In the music field Les Presses de l'université Laval, founded in 1950, have published volumes 5 to 19 of the *Archives de folklore* (1951–79) and Monique Vachon's study *La Fugue dans la musique religieuse de W.A. Mozart* (1970). See also Archives de folklore. (JB-T)

LAVERGNE, Marguerite (m Ghedin). Soprano, b Montreal 23 Nov 1931; B MUS piano (Montreal) 1951. She studied piano at the École supérieure de musique of the Sisters of Ste-Anne in Lachine and voice with Sister Louis-Raymond. She received the grand prize (1952) in *'Opportunity Knocks,' the Cécile-Léger scholarship (1953), and the 1954 *Prix Archambault and won first place in 1956 in *'Singing Stars of Tomorrow.' On a Quebec government scholarship she studied 1956 in Vienna with Ferdinand Grossmann and Erik Werba. After making her debut (1954) as the first Flower Maiden in a production of *Parsifal* under the direction of Charles *Houdret at the Show Mart in Montreal, Lavergne sang Oscar and Elisabetta, respectively, in the *Opera Guild of Montreal's productions of *The Masked Ball* (1955) and *Don Carlos* (1956). For the *Montreal Festivals she appeared as the Countess in *The Marriage of Figaro*, sang in Bach's *Mass in B Minor* in 1956 and in Brahms' *Requiem* under Erich Leinsdorf in 1958, and was Fiordiligi in *Così fan tutte* (a role she had sung first in 1956 on CBC TV) in 1962.

Lavergne gave many recitals and sang frequently in radio and TV opera productions, notably in the title role of Gluck's *Alceste*. She premiered Pierre *Mercure's *Dissidence* in 1955 and his **Cantate pour une joie* in 1956. In 1958, with the *Hart House Orchestra, she sang Britten's *Les Illuminations* at the Brussels Worlds Fair.

Married to Alfonso Ghedin, a violist with I Musici and later with the Quartetto Beethoven, Lavergne has lived for many years in Italy where, in 1977, she was invited by conductor Pierluigi Urbini to be the soloist in Mahler's *Symphony No. 4* presented in Rome by the Orchestra Sinfonica dell' Accademia Nazionale di Santa Cecilia.

Lavergne's voice, one of great beauty and range, is heard on recordings of *Cantate pour une joie*, of Jean *Papineau-Couture's *Psaume CL* (with the *Montreal Bach Choir), and, with the Pro Musica Orchestra of Vienna under Ferdinand Grossmann, of Mozart's *Exsultate, Jubilate* and the Benedictus sit Deus from the *Offertorium pro omni tempore*, K117 (Turnabout 34029). GP

LAVIGNE (Tessier dit Lavigne), (Jean Moïse) **Arthur**. Violinist, publisher, music dealer, critic, teacher, administrator, b Montreal 8 Feb 1845, d Quebec City 11 Jan 1925; hon D MUS (Laval) 1922. The brother of Ernest and Émery, he began violin studies in 1853 with J. Follenus. He also studied with Octave Hardy dit *Chatillon.

In May 1868 Lavigne opened a music store on St-Jean Street in Quebec City in partnership with A.J. *Boucher; Lavigne became sole owner ca 1872. The store soon became a rendezvous for local musicians – the *Gagnons, the *Dessanes, the *Jehin-Prumes, Calixa *Lavallée – and the business prospered for 50 years.

Having taken part in the Peace Jubilees held in 1869 and 1872 in Boston, Lavigne in 1883 organized a huge, successful music festival in Quebec City. As a concert organizer he engaged Leopold Godowsky, Henri Marteau, Ovide Musin, Léon Rothier, and Eugène Ysaÿe.

Lavigne was a founding member in 1868 and president 1904–5, 1906–7, and 1908–9 of the *AMQ,

Arthur Lavigne, ca 1905

after having been the first candidate at its competitions. Previously a member of the Septett Club, he was a founder in 1871 and principal violin of the *Septuor Haydn. He was president 1905–8 of the Société symphonique de Québec (*Quebec SO), which succeeded the Septuor Haydn. In 1922 he was among the first teachers engaged by the Music School of *Laval U.

In 1880 Lavigne played an important role in the initial recognition of *'O Canada,' taking the manuscript to Lieutenant-Governor Théodore Robitaille and publishing the original edition. He published other works by Quebec composers, including Ernest Gagnon, Frantz Jehin-Prume, Calixa Lavallée, and Joseph *Vézina, as well as the Count of Premio-Real's *Seize Mélodies*, with a preface by Lavallée (1879). He wrote reports and articles for various publications.

BIBLIOGRAPHY
'Arthur Lavigne,' *Le Commerce de Montréal et de Québec et leurs industries en 1889* (Montreal 1889)
P.L. 'M. Arthur Lavigne,' *La Musique*, vol 1, Apr 1919
LeVasseur, L.-N. 'Musique et musiciens à Québec,' ibid, vol 4, Nov, Dec 1922
Massicotte, E.-Z. 'Trois grands artistes,' *BRH*, vol 39, Jan 1933
Magnon, Odile. 'Arthur Lavigne: d'hier à aujourd'hui,' *Le Lutrin*, vol 1, May 1980
Musiciens canadiens GP

LAVIGNE (Tessier dit Lavigne), (Horace) **Émery**. Pianist, organist, teacher, b Montreal 27 Jan 1859, d there 2 Jul 1902. The brother of Arthur and Ernest Lavigne, he studied with Romain-Octave *Pelletier. After a sojourn in Paris in 1877 he served for five years as organist at St John's Church in Oswego, NY. Returning to Montreal, he demonstrated pianos for Lavigne & Lajoie and taught. He was organist 1887–1902 at the Church of the Messiah.

Lavigne was acknowledged as an exceptional sight-reader and participated in the concerts of the *Montreal Philharmonic Society, the *Mendelssohn Choir of Montreal, and *Couture's *MSO, with which he played Saint-Säens' *Rhapsodie d'Auvergne* in 1894. He was the accompanist for numerous touring musicians: the violinists Camilla Urso, Sam Franko, and Ovide Musin, the cellists Anton Hekking, Jean Gérardy, and Joseph Hollman, the baritone Sir Charles Santley, and others.

With J.-J. *Goulet and J.-B. *Dubois, Lavigne founded the Haydn Trio (1896–8). His gavotte for piano, *Les Ondes*, was included in the collection *L'Écrin musical* (1887). He served 1892–3 and 1900–1 as president of the *AMQ and held the distinction of the Palmes académiques, conferred by the French government.

Ernest Lavigne (*Le Canada artistique*, Jan 1890)

BIBLIOGRAPHY
Couture, Guillaume. 'Émery Lavigne,' *Canada artistique*, vol 1, Oct 1890
P-T, vol 7, 19 Jul 1902
Massicotte, E.-Z. 'Trois grands artistes,' *BRH*, vol 39, Jan 1933 GP

LAVIGNE (Tessier dit Lavigne), **Ernest**. Bandmaster, cornetist, composer, publisher, b Montreal 17 Dec 1851, d there 18 Jan 1909. The brother of Arthur and Émery, he studied at the Collège de Terrebonne and in 1868 went to Rome with the 4th detachment of the Papal Zouaves. There he joined the band of the Roman Zouaves, becoming cornet soloist in 1869. After the city's capture by the Italians in September 1870 he spent a year in Naples and travelled through several European countries before going in 1873 to New York. He performed there as a soloist with great success, as he did also in Philadelphia and Boston. He returned to Montreal at the end of 1874. Shortly afterwards he moved to Quebec City and went into business with Arthur, who had opened a music store. Ernest organized and conducted brass bands in the region and even as far away as Rimouski. In 1876 he visited Philadelphia as head of Montreal's *Bande de la Cité, which won first prize at the Centennial Exposition. The same ensemble distinguished itself again at a national competition in May 1878 in Montreal. As a soloist Lavigne won many honours and prizes, including two gold-plated cornets. In 1885 he inaugurated free concerts at the Viger Garden, where his brilliant performances made him a star attraction.

In 1877 Lavigne became involved in the music trade in Montreal, and in 1881 he went into partnership with Louis-Joseph Lajoie as Lavigne & Lajoie. The company published about 50 compositions by Canadians, notably Ernest and Émery Lavigne and Joseph *Vézina, and was the distributor for hundreds of imported pieces. It issued a catalogue, *L'Écrin musical*, in 1887. However, the publishing activities of Lavigne & Lajoie appear to have ceased in 1891. A born organizer, Lavigne encouraged the firm to acquire in 1889 a large piece of land on the St Lawrence River, and there he set up an amusement park known as *Sohmer Park. Until his death Lavigne directed the concerts and shows there, employing as his regular ensemble the Bande de la Cité. He wished to expand the band into an orchestra and to this end engaged many young, highly trained Belgian and Italian instrumentalists. Some remained in Canada and established a valuable tradition of instrumental performance and teaching. Thus Lavigne may be considered one of the pioneers of instrumental music in Canada. As a composer he specialized in songs. Three were published in the Paris *Annales politiques et littéraires* at the beginning of the century. In 1909 *Archambault published *25 mélodies / 25 Songs*, a handsomely produced collection of songs which the composer had published individually in 1901. Lavigne also wrote patriotic songs, of which 'Vive la France' enjoyed great popularity.

Gabrielle Lavigne

BIBLIOGRAPHY
Trudel, Tancrède. 'Ernest Lavigne,' *Canada artistique*, vol 1, Jan 1890
De Montigny, Louvigny. 'Les mélodies d'Ernest Lavigne,' *P-T*, 156, 16 Mar 1901
Pelletier, Frédéric. 'Les musiciens du passé, Ernest Lavigne 1851–1909,' *Entre-Nous*, vol 1, Mar 1930
Massicotte, Édouard-Z. 'Trois grands artistes,' *BRH*, vol 39, Jan 1933
– 'Leur dernier succès,' *BRH*, vol 52, Jan 1946 GP

LAVIGNE, Gabrielle. Mezzo-soprano, b Montreal 16 Mar 1940. She graduated from the Montreal School of Fine Arts in 1961 and pursued her musical studies 1961–9 at *McGill U with Ria *Lenssens (voice) and at the *CMM with Dick Marzollo (repertoire) and Pierre Héral (stage skills). During these years she taught plastic arts for the Montreal Catholic School Board. She was a finalist in the 1967 Concorso internationale de Voci verdiani in Busseto, Italy, a medal winner with distinction at the 1969 International Competition for Musical Performers in Geneva, winner of the first prize in her category in the 1970 *CBC Talent Festival, and a finalist in the 1970 *Metropolitan Opera regional auditions.

Lavigne made her stage debut with the *Vancouver Opera as Azucena in *Il Trovatore*. Sadler's Wells engaged her for the role the following year. In the autumn of 1973 she returned to Vancouver, this time to sing Eboli in *Don Carlo*. In 1974 she was Federica in Verdi's *Luisa Miller* and Maria in Rossini's *Mosè in Egitto* for the Koninklijke Opera, Ghent, and Mistress Page in *Falstaff* for the *Opéra du Québec. That December she sang Marie in *L'Enfance du Christ* with the *NACO in Ottawa and New York City. For *Festival Ottawa she portrayed Ragonde (Rossini's *Le Comte Ory*, 1974, 1976), Berta (*The Barber of Seville*, 1978), and Dorothée (Massenet's *Cendrillon*, 1979). According to Claude *Gingras (Montreal *La Presse*, 23 May 1979), her Marguerite in the *MSO's presentation of *La Damnation de Faust* was 'quite striking in vocal beauty, distinction, and expression.'

Gabrielle Lavigne has performed as soloist with many orchestras, including the *McGill Chamber Orchestra (1971, 1972), the MSO (*L'Enfance du Christ*, 1972; *La Vida Breve*, 1976; Beethoven's *Symphony No. 9*, 1977), the *Quebec SO (Verdi's *Requiem*, 1973), the *TS (*Le Roi David*, 1974;

*Mercure's *Cantate pour une joie*, 1978), the *Victoria SO (1971), the *Hamilton Philharmonic (1971, 1972), and the NACO (1971, 1973). 'An excellent musician, she brings the greatest artistic care to all she touches,' wrote Gilles *Potvin (Montreal *Le Devoir*, 11 May 1978), following her performance with the MSO of Wagner's *Wesendonck Lieder*.

Lavigne has given many recitals on the CBC, and in the series 'Les Grands Concerts' she revealed herself as a sensitive interpreter of French art songs and Lieder. She was a member 1974–6 of the *Ensemble cantabile de Montréal.

BIBLIOGRAPHY

Mercer, Ruby. 'Gabrielle Lavigne: some exciting firsts for a Montreal mezzo,' *OpCan*, Feb 1976
'Gabrielle Lavigne artiste lyrique qui peut chanter tous les Français,' *Musique périodique*, vol 1, Nov 1976
'Gabrielle Lavigne,' *Variations*, vol 1, Feb 1978
'Gabrielle Lavigne,' ibid, vol 2, May 1979 (SW)

LAVIGUEUR, Célestin. Violinist, composer, teacher, b Quebec City 19 Jan 1830, d Lowell, Mass, 11 Dec 1885. Though his early violin training came from an amateur, François Huot, Lavigueur's talent and dedication prompted Nazaire *LeVasseur to write, 'his phrasing and bowing deeply affected his listeners.' He conducted the concert given in 1878 by the *Quebec Harmonic Society.

While teaching 1850–80 at the *Séminaire de Québec Lavigueur composed two works – *La Fiancée des bois*, a three-act operetta with libretto by Pamphile Lemay, and *Un Mariage improvisé*, a comic opera – which may be the first by a native Canadian for the lyric stage. Lavigueur's lesser works include *Fantaisie sur la Fille du régiment*, for violin; 'Le Nom de ma soeur,' a ballad; 'O Canada, beau pays, ma patrie,' a patriotic song (Bernard & Allaire 1880); 'Donnez,' a hymn to charity; 'Soyez la bienvenue,' a song of welcome for Princess Louise; and the popular *'La Huronne' (Léger Brousseau Frères nd).

Lavigueur retired (ca 1880) to live with a son in Lowell, Mass. At his death he left unfinished the opera *Les Enfants du manoir* (to his own libretto). Some of Lavigueur's works appeared in *L'Écho du cabinet de lecture paroissial* (Montreal 1862–3) and *Le Foyer domestique* (Ottawa 1877). CH

LAVOIE, Claude. Organist, teacher, composer, b Rivière-du-Loup, Que, 19 Jul 1918. He began studying piano and organ in 1933 at the Collège de Lévis with Father Alphonse *Tardif. A winner in 1942 of the *Prix d'Europe, he studied 1942–5 at the Longy School in Boston with Nadia Boulanger, E. Power Biggs, and Melville Smith and at the New England Cons in Boston with Francis Findlay. In 1950–1 he worked in Paris under André Marchal, Gaston Litaize, and Simone Plé-Caussade. He was an organist first in Boston and then at Beauport, near Quebec City, and became in 1959 the organist of Saints-Martyrs-Canadiens Church, Quebec City. His virtuoso career includes more than 200 concerts as soloist and with orchestra in Quebec, Ontario, New Brunswick, and the USA, particularly in Boston. Between 1938 and 1969 he inaugurated nearly 30 Canadian organs, including the *Casavant instruments in the Moncton Cathedral in 1956 and the Cathedral of Notre-Dame-du-Cap, Que, in 1965. He taught 1952–69 at the *CMQ and trained such fine organists as Denis *Bédard, Antoine *Bouchard, Sylvain Doyon, Richard Gagné, Gérard Gagnon, Noëlla Genest, Robert Girard, and Jacques Montgrain. By his skilful improvisations, his compositions, and his lively and colourful interpretations, Lavoie has helped to stimulate interest in organ music in Quebec.

DISCOGRAPHY

Claude Lavoie aux grandes orgues des Saints-Martyrs-Canadiens, Québec. 1963. Radio Marie NDC 336311
Greene – Dandrieu – Bach – Balbastre – Vierne – Dupré – Duruflé. 1968. RCA (unnumbered)
See also Les Rhapsodes.

BIBLIOGRAPHY

'Claude Lavoie a redonné vie à l'orgue,' *Musique périodique*, vol 1, Mar 1977 IB

LAVOIE-HERZ, Djane (b Lavoie, m Herz). Pianist, teacher, b Ottawa 1889, d New York? She studied in Montreal with Alfred *Laliberté and, after 1905, in London, Paris, Berlin, and Brussels. In Brussels she had lessons with Laliberté's teacher, Alexander Scriabin. Another teacher, probably in Berlin, was Artur Schnabel. Lavoie's recitals in Ottawa, Montreal, and elsewhere (1908–14) received much praise and were devoted in particular to works by Liszt, Scriabin, and Brahms. In 1911 or 1912 Lavoie married a writer, Siegfried Herz (b Barmen, Germany, 1883), who had come to Canada in 1907, worked for *Nordheimer, and contributed articles to *Musical Canada* and who assumed the name Lavoie-Herz. A recital was planned for October 1914 at Aeolian Hall, New York, followed by a US tour, but it appears to have been postponed a year. (She played in New York 21 Oct and 23 Dec 1915 to favourable notices).

In 1914 the Lavoie-Herzs settled in Toronto, where he worked as a salesman for Nordheimer and she opened a studio and gave recitals. A typical program, at Nordheimer Hall 25 Jan 1916, offered music of Bach, Mozart-Liszt, Liszt, Chopin, and Scriabin. Several of Lavoie-Herz's pupils – Margaret McCallum, Edwin Gray, and Estelle Beder – gave solo recitals in Toronto ca 1916–17.

The couple are listed in the Toronto city directory until 1919, but there is reason to assume they moved to the USA (probably New York) in 1918, since she was a piano teacher 1918–21 of the US composer Ruth Crawford Seeger (stepmother of Pete). Her husband changed his name to Hearst and became a successful manager in New York, associated in the 1940s and 1950s with National Concert and Artists' Corporation. It is known that she was teaching privately at that time. (HK, PW)

LAW, Brian (John Taylor). Conductor, organist, harpsichordist, b Brighton, England, 14 Apr 1943; LRAM 1963, FRCO 1963, ARSCM 1973. After studies with Derek *Holman, Martindale Sidwell, and Gerald Knight 1960–3 at the RSCM, Law moved to Canada in 1965 as organist-choirmaster of St Matthew's Anglican Church, Ottawa, where he developed a men's and boys' choir noted for its recital work. In 1965 he began conducting the Cantata Singers of Ottawa, who became the resident choir at the *NAC. In 1967 he became the director of the *Ottawa Choral Society and in 1971 he trained and conducted the first *Ontario Youth Choir. He was appointed assistant conductor and chorusmaster of Festival Canada (*Festival Ottawa) in 1972 and made his operatic conducting debut in 1976 in the festival production of *The Marriage of Figaro*.

Law has performed regularly as harpsichordist with the *NACO, and he made his concert debut as a solo organist at the NAC in 1974. He became conductor of the Ottawa Civic SO in 1975 and in 1977 began Thirteen Strings, a chamber group drawn from the NACO. Law has contributed greatly to choral standards in Ottawa and has developed three of the city's choirs into regularly performing units. In 1979 he became the conductor of the Ottawa Youth Orchestra. MG

LAW, Eileen (m Marshall). Contralto, teacher, b Belfast 16 Oct 1900, d Toronto 30 Nov 1978; LCAM, ACAM mid-1920s. She studied 1922–6 with Jenny Taggart (voice) and Ernest *MacMillan (piano) at the *Canadian Academy of Music (earning the above-mentioned diplomas) and privately in 1926 and 1936 with Hope *Morgan. She also studied in 1936 with Emmy *Heim in Toronto, in 1940 with Pauline *Donalda in Montreal, and in 1941 with Louis Bachner in New York.

During her career Law sang with the *TSO, the *Promenade Symphony Concerts, and the Detroit and Minneapolis SOs and appeared as soloist with the *Ottawa Choral Union, the *Toronto Mendelssohn Choir, and the Apollo Musical Club Choir of Chicago. In April 1936 she was heard with the Toronto Mendelssohn Junior Choir in the Canadian premiere of Harvey Gaul's cantata *The Singers* at *Eaton Auditorium. In January 1945 she appeared with the TSO in the Canadian premiere of Mahler's *Das Lied von der Erde* and in 1946 she was soloist in Beethoven's *Missa solemnis* at the *Montreal Festivals under Bernard *Naylor.

Law was contralto soloist 1923–36 at Timothy Eaton Memorial Church and 1936–45 at the First Church of Christ Scientist and sang in Toronto performances of Bach's *St Matthew Passion* for 25 years. She was heard many times over the CBC, NBC, and CBS radio networks; during the early 1930s she sang in Canadian Industries Ltd's 'Opera House of the Air' under Reginald *Stewart.

In the late 1930s Law was invited to appear with the Vienna State Opera, a debut which was cancelled because of Hitler's invasion of Austria. In February 1942 she was a soloist in Bach's *Mass in B Minor*, in H.A. *Fricker's farewell appearance as conductor of the Toronto Mendelssohn Choir. In May 1946 she appeared in Verdi's *Manzoni Requiem* with the Mormon Tabernacle Choir in Salt Lake City. Describing her talents, the critic Hector *Charlesworth wrote that she was 'famous not merely for the clarity, breadth and emotional appeal of her tones, but for her mastery of diction and phrasing' (Toronto *Globe and Mail*).

Law was a teacher 1938–77 at the *RCMT and 1952–61 at the Faculty of Music, *U of Toronto and gave summer courses at various centres, including Mount St Vincent Academy in Halifax. James Crackokatt, Millard Williams, Mary Alice Rodgers, Constance Newland, and Donna Small were among her pupils. NM

LAWRENCE, Claire. Saxophonist, flutist, organist, producer, composer, b Elk Point, near Edmonton, 24 Jul 1939. He was raised in Victoria, played trumpet in that city's boys' band, and at 14 was an alto saxophonist in a dance band with his father, an oldtime fiddler.

While studying 1964–7 at the U of British Columbia with Douglas Talney, Elliot *Weisgarber, and Cortland *Hultberg, Lawrence was cofounder (1964) of The Classics, a rock band which became The Collectors, 1966–70, and thereafter *Chilliwack. He played saxophone, flute, organ, bass guitar, and violin until 1972 with the band and collaborated on its music, including the popular 'What Love Suite.' In 1974 he began producing the CBC (Vancouver) rock-music program 'The Great Canadian Goldrush' and in the following years he produced records by *Valdy, Susan Jacks, Bim, and others.

Lawrence continued to play saxophone and flute in Vancouver studios and with the Hometown Band which he formed to accompany Valdy on tours in the USA (1976) and Canada (1977). The Hometown Band, without Valdy, and with singer-violinist Shari Ulrich as its figurehead, continued to tour in Canada and the USA before breaking up in 1979 and made the LPs *Flying* (1976, A & M SP 4605) and *The Hometown Band* (1977, A & M SP 4671). Lawrence performed on and produced each LP. The band won a *Juno Award as 'best new group' of 1977.

Lawrence's other compositions include 'Into the Night' and 'Sweet Emma,' recorded by the Hometown Band, and 'Village in the Green,' heard on his own LP *Leaving You Free* (Haida HL 5103). He is an affiliate of PRO Canada.

BIBLIOGRAPHY

Read, Jeani. 'Performing live is Claire Lawrence's first love,' *MSc*, 294, Mar–Apr 1977

Farrell, David. 'Musical diversity about to click for Hometown Band,' *MSc*, 303, Sep–Oct 1978 MM

LAWSON, May. Contralto, teacher, b West Calder, Scotland, 29 Mar 1901, d Winnipeg 28 Apr 1965. She arrived in Canada in 1914 with her parents and studied singing in Winnipeg with W. Davidson *Thomson, Rhys Thomas, and Bernard *Naylor and in Toronto with J. Campbell *McInnes. She was coached by and studied repertoire with Frank St Leger in New York and with John *Goss during the summer of 1943 at Gimli, Man, and the summer of 1948 on Galiano Island, BC. At the Gimli school she sang Orpheus in Goss' production of Gluck's *Orpheus and Euridice*.

Lawson was a soloist 1923–6 at St Luke's Anglican Church and 1926–46 at Knox United Church in Winnipeg. During those years she was repeatedly a soloist in oratorio with the *Winnipeg Philharmonic Choir and the *Winnipeg SO in such works as Handel's *Judas Maccabaeus* and *Messiah*, Bach's *Mass in B Minor*, and Mendelssohn's *Elijah*. She was the soloist in Brahms' *Alto Rhapsody* with the *Winnipeg Male Voice Choir and appeared in Winnipeg Light Opera Company productions (*The Chocolate Soldier*, 1934, *The Red Mill*, 1935, etc).

With the pianist Marjorie Dillabough Wrightson Lawson gave public recitals, and with John *Avison or Gordon *Kushner she was heard frequently on CBC radio. She was a soloist-member of the *Choristers in the late 1930s and the 1940s. Her recital repertoire consisted mainly of arias and songs of the German composers; of English songs, Elizabethan to early-20th-century; and of Scottish traditional songs, which she sang with sensitivity and affection.

Though she retired from public performance in the late 1940s Lawson came to be recognized as one of Winnipeg's foremost teachers, and her research and correspondence with her brother, the medical doctor and baritone recitalist James Terry Lawson of New Westminster, BC, led to the preparation and writing of the latter's *Full-throated Ease: A Concise Guide to Easy Singing* (Vancouver 1955), a book which came into wide use in the USA and Europe.

May Lawson taught privately throughout her career and at the *Canadian Mennonite Bible College in Winnipeg from 1958 until her death. Among her many pupils were Orville Derraugh, David Falk, Robert Jeffrey, Corinne Kirby, Heather Lindsay, Jean McBride, Elaine Oakley, Noella Poulain, Carol Robson, William Thiessen, and Peggie Anne Truscott. KW (RG)

LAZAREVICH, Gordana. Musicologist, pianist, b Belgrade 28 Feb 1939, naturalized Canadian 1958; Licentiate Diploma (Toronto) 1960, B SC (Juilliard) 1962, M SC (Juilliard) 1964, PH D (Columbia) 1970. She studied 1957–60 with Alberto *Guerrero, won the 1960 *CBC Talent Festival, and twice performed as a pianist with the *TSO. On a succession of scholarships she studied at the Juilliard School 1960–4 and at Columbia U, where she specialized in 18th-century Italian comic musical theatre and completed her doctoral thesis on the Neapolitan intermezzo.

After teaching 1969–74 at Columbia U, Lazarevich joined the *U of Victoria in 1974, and then became director of graduate studies in music. She has appeared there as a pianist in concerto and ensemble performances. Her writings include a critical edition of the 18th-century intermezzo *Larinda e Vanesio* by Adolf Hasse, published in the series Music in the Classic Era (Wisconsin 1978) and the book *The Italian Comic Musical Theater of the Eighteenth Century* (1978). She has contributed articles and reviews to *Current Musicology*, *Musical Quarterly*, *Notes*, *The Schirmer History of Music* (New York 1979), *The New Grove Dictionary*, and *MGG* and has delivered papers, mostly on 18th-century music, at conferences.

LEACOCK, Leonard (Henry). Pianist, teacher, composer, b London, 28 May 1904; ATCM 1924, LRSM 1935. His family moved to Canada in 1908 and settled in Banff, Alta. He spent the years of World War I in Boston and took his first piano lessons there with a Mrs R. Holbrook. He continued his piano studies in Banff with W.E. Round, in Toronto with Thomas *Crawford and Arthur Oliver, and in Calgary with Gladys *Egbert and Jean Cotton. In 1924 he began teaching at *Mount Royal College in Calgary and in 1946 he became a regular examiner for the *WBM.

Leacock has given many recitals at Mount Royal College and for the Aeolian Chamber Music Series and has performed with the *Calgary SO. His compositions include the beginner's pieces *Sea Horses* (Thompson 1954) and *Tic-Toccatina* (Harris 1959), *Partita for Solo Violin*, an orchestral tone poem *The Lonely Lake* (1956), works for violin and piano, and many songs. Several of his piano pieces have been used as competition test pieces.

The Leacock Theatre of Mount Royal College was dedicated in his honour, 18 Nov 1972. In 1973, for service to music, he was presented with an Alberta Achievement Award by the provincial government. He is also a skilled photographer.

BIBLIOGRAPHY

Potter, Carl. 'Musician-mountaineer,' *CanComp*, 48, Mar 1970 (RDM)

Leamington Choral Society. Choir of 50–65 voices founded in 1960 in Leamington, near Windsor, Ont, by Helen (Marguerite) Law. At first composed of graduates from the Mennonite High School, it presented an abridged version of *Hansel and Gretel* for its debut in 1961. The choir was opened to all singers in 1963, and the name Leamington Choral Society was adopted. Christmas and spring concerts, unaccompanied or with orchestra, followed in local churches and school auditoriums.

In 1970 the choir competed at the Llangollen International Musical Eisteddfod in Wales. It placed third – the first Canadian adult choir to win a prize there – and was described in the adjudication of Herbert Howells and Sir Thomas Armstrong as an example of 'the gentler paths of choralism – clear, clean, thoughtful. Technically compact in style, still reticent; but alive in all its quietude.' The choir performed in Bulgaria after winning a first award in one section of the 1979 International Choral Competition at Varna.

For concerts in Windsor and Detroit accompanying ensembles have included the *Windsor SO, beginning in 1970; the Classical Brass in 1973; and chamber orchestras from Wayne State U, Michigan, in 1973 and from the Detroit SO in 1975.

The choir's sole conductor has been Helen Law (b Chatham, Ont, 14 Aug 1915), a piano pupil of Edward Bredshall and a voice pupil of Thelma von Eisenhauer in Detroit and Pauline *Donalda in Montreal. Mrs Law has taught voice and piano privately and has held church positions in Leamington. She was named a Member of the *Order of Canada in 1979. MM

Lebanon. Immigration to Canada from Lebanon (formerly part of the Ottoman district of 'Greater Syria') began in 1882. The first wave of immigration brought mainly small merchants; the second wave (1946 onward; including Palestinians) brought mainly blue-collar workers; the third wave (1962 onward; including Palestinians) brought white- and blue-collar workers in about equal numbers.

Lebanese-Canadians have tended to abandon their native language and culture more completely than have, for example, Syrian-Canadians. Thus, there is marked acculturation among second-generation Lebanese-Canadians, and those of the third generation, apart from occasionally dancing the 'Dabkah,' have assimilated entirely into Canadian culture.

Among first-generation Lebanese-Canadians, structured public performances (see Arabic music) have consisted almost entirely of commercialized classical, folk, and popular Arabic music. While classical Arabic music is not popular among Lebanese-Canadians, Lebanese folkdances (mainly the 'Dabkah') are performed publicly by the Arab Folklore Group with recorded music. In addition, authentic folksongs are sung, with or without instrumental accompaniment, at private gatherings by those from the same region who wish to preserve their heritage. Canadians of Lebanese descent active in music have included John *Arab, Nick *Ayoub, Norman *Brooks, Frederick and Ed *Karam, and Jeannette *Zarou. GDS

LeBEL, Édouard. Tenor, civil servant, b Wotton, near Sherbrooke, Lower Canada (Quebec), 11 Dec 1865, d Montreal 17 Feb 1939. He studied voice with Achille *Fortier and Guillaume *Couture in Montreal. A member ca 1885 of the *Montagnards, he later was a soloist at the Gesù and Notre-Dame churches in Montreal and for 30 years at St James Cathedral (Marie-Reine-du-Monde) and was appointed choirmaster at St James in 1912. He was frequently a soloist with the Couture *MSO and the *Montreal Philharmonic Society, performed supporting roles in *Elijah*, *Samson et Dalila*, *Tannhäuser*, and *Roméo et Juliette*, and sang the role of Abel in the 1905 premiere of Alexis *Contant's **Caïn*. He was secretary of the *AMQ for 24 years and a municipal civil servant 1899–1934.

After LeBel's death, Frédéric *Pelletier recalled having heard him in 1885: 'I have rarely heard since, here or elsewhere, so beautiful a voice so artistically handled. Twenty years later those who remembered it did not hesitate to compare it to Caruso's' (Montreal *Le Devoir*, 25 Feb 1939). For HMV LeBel recorded 16 titles, listed in *Roll Back the Years*.

LeBel's wife was Charles *Labelle's sister. Their daughter Germaine (soprano, b Montreal 22 Mar 1894, d there 14 Jun 1972) studied singing and interpretation with Alfred *Laliberté and often performed his original works (eg, *Chansons d'Ève* with the *CSM, 1935) and his harmonizations of folksongs (*CPR Festivals 1927, 1930). She sang Salomé during the 1923 premiere of Couture's **Jean le Précurseur*. She was described as a soprano 'with an agreeable and light voice' (Montreal *La Patrie*, 14 Apr 1926). She also interpreted the music of

Debussy and Nicolas Medtner and participated in numerous CBC broadcasts. (GB)

LeBLANC, (Joseph) **Arthur**. Violinist, composer, b St-Anselme, near Moncton, NB, 18 Aug 1906. His father, a violin maker and teacher, gave him, at three, his first lessons along with his first violin. The museum of the U of Moncton has two violins made by Joseph LeBlanc for his son. Arthur spent his youth in Moncton except for three years in the Boston area (Cambridge), where his father owned a music store. At five he was acclaimed a prodigy by the critics. He studied 1919–23 at the Séminaire de Québec, his expenses borne by members of the clergy. Father Chrysologue Desrochers (who conducted the orchestra at the seminary) and the violinist J.-Alexandre *Gilbert helped launch his career, and he gave five public concerts early in 1921. A pupil of Gilbert, he was one of the first to enrol at the School of Music at *Laval U in 1922. Rejoining his family in Boston in 1923 he toured New England with the singer Désiré Bourque, and then studied at the New England Cons for two years with Richard Burgin, concertmaster of the Boston SO, and with Felix Winternitz.

On a Quebec government grant in 1930 LeBlanc studied at the École normale de Paris with Georges Enesco, Maurice Hayot, and Jacques Thibaud. While a member of the orchestra there he performed as a soloist under Cortot. In 1934 he passed his performance examination with great distinction, earning an extensive tour during which he played in Liège, Basel, Geneva, Lausanne, and Le Havre. He was a member of the first violins in the Paris SO during the 1935–6 season under Pierre Monteux.

LeBlanc returned to Canada in 1938 and performed the Brahms *Concerto* 3 Feb 1939 with the *CSM. That May he made his debut at Town Hall, New York, and later in the year he appeared twice at Carnegie Hall. 'Mr. LeBlanc possessed the well developed technique expected from any concert performer,' wrote the *New York Times* critic, 'but what made his work quite unusual was the extreme beauty and purity of his tone and the rich fund of expressiveness that helped to give his performances true distinction' (27 Nov 1939).

Accompanied by either Jean-Marie *Beaudet or Ross *Pratt LeBlanc performed in many Canadian towns. Managed 1941–6 by the US agency Columbia Concerts, he appeared in the USA both alone and with such artists as Rose Bampton, Richard Crooks, Gregor Piatigorsky, and Bidú Sayão. He performed 6 Dec 1941 at the White House and in 1944–5 gave 26 concerts in six weeks.

Milhaud composed his *Concerto No. 2* for LeBlanc in 1946, and the violinist gave its premiere in 1948 at the Théâtre des Champs-Elysées with the Concert Society of the Paris Cons under André Cluytens. Its North American premiere, in which he performed with the *MSO under Désiré Dufauw, took place 13 Jan 1953.

LeBlanc also taught, in particular at Laval U and 1943–7 at the *CMM. Poor health obliged him to curtail his travelling after 1953, but he continued his career through radio and TV performances, working with John *Newmark or Charles *Reiner. He played Schumann's *Fantasia* and Saint-Saëns' *Havanaise* 12 Jun 1955 with the CBC *'Little Symphonies' Orchestra. His last public appearance occurred in 1965 at the *JMC Orford Art Centre with Charles Reiner as accompanist. After being hospitalized for several years, he retired in 1971 to Ste-Pétronille on Île d'Orléans. In 1976 he moved to Quebec City.

LeBlanc had been a composition pupil of Paul Dukas and wrote a few works, including the *Petite Suite canadienne* for violin and piano, one movement of which, 'Chant des pins,' often appeared on his programs.

Arthur LeBlanc

In 1938 LeBlanc acquired a Guadagnini, which he broke in an unfortunate accident just before a recital in Quebec City. A public subscription in 1946 allowed him to buy the 1733 Stradivarius called 'Des Rosiers' after the Lyons family who had owned it for more than 100 years. He also acquired the Tourte bow given to Wieniawski by the Austrian emperor.

DISCOGRAPHY

LeBlanc – Fraser – Gratton – Archer. Reiner pf. Ca 1954. RCI 136

7 pieces for vn and pf. Reiner pf. Acadia LL200

9 pieces for vn and pf. Reiner pf. Acadia 3000CB

BIBLIOGRAPHY

Morin, Léo-Pol. 'Arthur LeBlanc, violoniste,' *Le Canada*, vol 36, 27 Mar 1939 JB-T

LEBRUN, Louise. Soprano, b Montreal 9 Jan 1940; Artist Diploma (École Vincent-d'Indy) 1964. She studied 1956–64 at the *École Vincent-d'Indy with Sister Gertrude-des-Anges and Sister Reine *Décarie (voice), Roy *Royal (French art songs), Bernard *Diamant (Lieder), and Pierrette *Alarie (stage techniques). In 1958 she won a scholarship from the Sarah *Fischer Concerts and was a prize winner in the 1965 *CBC Talent Festival.

Engaged for the 1964–5 season by Sadler's Wells in London, Lebrun sang various light soprano roles, including the Fire, the Princess, and the Nightingale in Ravel's *L'Enfant et les sortilèges*. She was attached 1967–9 to the Regensburg Stadttheater, where she sang lyric and coloratura roles in *The Tales of Hoffmann, Fidelio, Falstaff, Der Rosenkavalier, The Marriage of Figaro*, and *The Barber of Seville*. After engagements in Czechoslovakia and Yugoslavia she gave recitals in Canada and made her debut in 1970 at the New York City Opera as Gilda in *Rigoletto*. After her performance Robert Sherman wrote in the *New York Times* (2 Mar 1970): 'There is musicality behind every phrase.' She also sang Constanze in *The Abduction from the Seraglio* and Susanna in *The Marriage of Figaro*.

Lebrun participated in the Glyndebourne (1970), Santa Fe (1971), and Salzburg (1974) festivals, singing one of her best roles, that of the Queen of the Night in *The Magic Flute*. She also sang this role in 1975 in the Festival Canada (*Festival Ottawa) production at the *NAC. For the *Opéra du Québec she sang the title role in Donizetti's *The Daughter of the Regiment* (1971), Gilda in *Rigoletto* (1972), and Nanetta in *Falstaff* (1974). She sang the title role in *Lucia di Lammermoor* (1973) at the Opera Nacional de Mexico, and other leading roles at the Toulouse Théâtre du Capitole (1974, 1975) and the Philadelphia Academy of Music (1975). At the *PDA in July 1976 she was Rosina in *The Barber of Seville*, presented by the Opéra du Québec during the Olympics in Montreal.

Louise Lebrun has appeared as soloist with several Canadian and European orchestras, notably the *MSO and the *Quebec SO, and has given public recitals on CBC radio and TV. During 1976 she sang Isotta in Strauss' *Die schweigsame Frau* and Marguerite de Valois in Meyerbeer's *Les Huguenots* in Radio France opera productions. For Italian radio-TV (RAI) in 1977 she sang the Countess in Rossini's *Le Comte Ory*.

Louise Lebrun's voice is remarkable for its timbre and its control of the coloratura register, and Claude Rostand, in *Figaro littéraire* (2 Mar 1965), rightly emphasized her 'perfect vocal ease.'

DISCOGRAPHY

Airs d'opéras: Mozart – Rossini – Verdi. Norddeutsches Phil O, Richter cond. 1972. Sel CC-15.075

Soirées musicales: Rossini – Bellini. Sévilla pf. 1973. Sel CC-15.100 IP-C (GP)

LEBRUN, Roland (Le soldat Lebrun). Singer, songwriter, b Amqui, Que, 10 Oct 1919, d Quebec City 2 Jan 1980. The considerable vogue enjoyed by this country singer was limited mainly to the years of World War II. He joined the Canadian army in 1939 but spent the war in the military camp at Valcartier, Que. He began to write and sing songs, accompanying himself on the guitar. The songs – simple, even banal, words and music, delivered in Lebrun's monochromatic voice and uninflected style – became widely popular.

Lebrun spoke for simple folk like himself, servicemen separated from family and friends. 'Je suis loin de toi, mignonne,' 'L'Adieu du soldat,' and 'La Complainte d'une mère' are typical of his many hits. Le soldat Lebrun was unique in his unquestionable sincerity and disarming simplicity.

For Benoît L'Herbier, 'Le soldat Lebrun's success was singular because it did not open up a road for others to take. His example was not followed though he created a precedent. He is remembered as a passing and short-lived phenomenon' (*La Chanson québécoise*, Montreal 1974). Some considered him the male counterpart of La *Bolduc. Like her, he reached ordinary folk grappling with the difficulties of everyday life.

Lebrun's records, 45s and 78s, were successful in Quebec in the 1940s. Material from them was reissued on the LPs *Le soldat Lebrun – Grands succès d'hier* (MCA Coral 37001) and *Amour, victoire, liberté* (Carnaval 497). In 1970 Lebrun received a gold record for sales exceeding one million.

Lebrun retired to Beauport, near Quebec City, in 1966, but occasionally made appearances with his wife and five children, especially between 1967 and 1972. He spent the last of his retirement years as a school crossing guard. GP

Le CAINE, Hugh. Physicist, composer, b Port Arthur (Thunder Bay), Ont, 27 May 1914, d Ottawa 3 Jul 1977; M SC (Queen's) 1939, PH D (Birmingham) 1952, hon D MUS (McGill) 1971, LLD (Toronto) 1973. He studied piano, graduated in science from *Queen's U, and worked 1940–74 with the National Research Council. During World War II he assisted in the development of radar components. On an NRC grant he studied nuclear physics 1948–52 in England.

As early as 1937 Le Caine had designed an electronic organ, and in 1952 he began to develop electronic instruments at the NRC. He co-operated in the installation of Canada's first electronic music studio (1959, *U of Toronto) and another (1964) at *McGill U and in 1966 gave the first of many seminars on his subject at these universities. In

1961 he developed equipment for the studio at Hebrew U, Jerusalem.

Among Le Caine's inventions is the electronic sackbut, begun in 1945, notable for its touch-sensitive keyboard. It is employed in several of his compositions, including *Ninety-nine Generators* (1956). Recorded in a 26-foot-diameter radome, the piece achieves timbral variation created by the resulting long reverberation. In *A Noisome Pestilence* (1957) he used white noise and a touch-sensitive organ which controlled an octave filter split into seven distinct frequency ranges.

Le Caine's works represent a duality of art and science: they extend the aesthetic field of electronic music while serving as clear demonstrations of the instruments he invented. Works include *Invocation* (1957), *The Burning Deck* (1958), *Textures* (1959), *Nocturne* (1964), *Dripsody* (1955; Folkways FM-34360, 1967), and *Mobile* (1970; RCI 373, 1971).

The Harrison-Le Caine Hall at Queen's U was named (1973) in his honour. In 1978 members of the *Canadian Electronic Ensemble organized the Hugh Le Caine Project to assemble and disseminate information on Le Caine and to publish a newsletter, which began to appear in June 1979. The ensemble included at least one work by Le Caine in every concert in the 1978–9 season, in Canada, the northern USA, and Europe. On 3 Jun 1979 the CBC broadcast a radio program featuring music by Le Caine, music dedicated to him, and music written for his instruments.

See also Electronic music.

WRITINGS

'Electronic music,' *Physics in Canada*, vol 10, Winter 1954

'Touch-sensitive organ based on an electrostatic coupling device,' *J of the Acoustical Soc of America*, vol 27, Jul 1955

'Electronic music,' *Proceedings of the IRE*, vol 44, 1956

'A touch-sensitive keyboard for the organ,' *CMJ*, Spring 1959

Revised Specifications for a Tape Recorder for Use in Electronic Music Studios Developed by the National Research Council of Canada. Government of Canada report ERB-581 (May 1961)

'A tape recorder for use in electronic music studios and related equipment,' *J of Music Theory*, vol 7, Spring 1963

'Electronic music,' *New Scientist*, 16 Dec 1965

'Some applications of electrical level controls,' *Electronic Music Review*, 4, Oct 1967

– and Ciamaga, Gustav. 'A preliminary report on the serial sound structure generator,' *Perspectives of New Music*, vol 6, Fall-Winter 1967

'Apparatus for generating serial sound structures,' *J of the Audio Engineering Soc*, vol 17, Jun 1969

– and Ciamaga, Gustav. ' "The Sonde" a new appraoch to multiple sine wave generation,' *J of the Audio Engineering Soc*, vol 18, 1970

BIBLIOGRAPHY

Gillmor, Alan. 'Hugh Le Caine: a pioneer in electronic sound generation,' *CanComp*, Feb 1976

Rickerd, J.P. 'Hugh LeCaine – portrait of a scientist/musician,' *Science Dimension*, vol 9, no. 6, 1977

Anhalt, Istvan. 'Hugh Le Caine,' *Mcan*, 33, Oct 1977 (CF)

LECLERC, Félix (Eugène). Singer-songwriter, poet, novelist, playwright, actor, b La Tuque, Que, 2 Aug 1914. He was the 6th of 11 children of a lumber and grain dealer, and the family members all sang and played various instruments. At the age of 8 he was drawn to the music of Mozart and Schubert, which his elder sister learned to play on the piano. At 18 he began his academic studies at the *U of Ottawa, where he wrote his first song, 'Notre Sentier.' Forced to abandon his schooling in 1933 because of the Depression, he went to work as a labourer and farmhand at Ste-Marthe. He was to draw on this experience for several of his songs. After holding various jobs, including that of assistant to an embalmer, he became a radio announcer and scriptwriter 1934–7 at CHRC in Quebec City and later at CHLN in Trois-Rivières. His radio stories attracted attention, and Mgr Albert Tessier, a writer and film producer, encouraged him to publish them.

Félix Leclerc

In 1941 Leclerc joined the CBC in Montreal as a scriptwriter, and several of his series were extremely popular, including 'Je me souviens,' for which Hector *Gratton composed the incidental music, and 'Théâtre dans ma guitare.' At the same time, Leclerc took guitar lessons from Victor Angelillo and acted in the CBC's radio drama series 'Un Homme et son péché' and 'Vie de famille' and on stage 1942–5 with the Compagnons de St-Laurent. He also published collections of his scripts, under the titles *Adagio* (stories), *Allegro* (fables), and *Andante* (poems), which sold well. In 1948 he and two friends, Guy Mauffette and Yves Vien, founded the troupe VLM, which presented his plays *Le P'tit Bonheur* and *La P'tite Misère* in Montreal and elsewhere in Quebec. That year his play *La Caverne des splendeurs* won first prize in a one-act-play competition organized by the *Amis de l'art.

In 1939 Leclerc had made his debut on the CBC as a chansonnier, performing 'Notre Sentier' on the radio program 'Le Restaurant d'en face.' A number of his other songs – 'Le P'tit Bonheur,' 'Le Train du Nord,' 'Bozo' – became popular in Quebec in the late 1940s, especially through his own CBC program, 'Félix Leclerc et ses chansons.' In 1950 Leclerc's career as a chansonnier became international. An influential impresario from Paris, Jacques Canetti, artistic director of Philips records, heard Leclerc perform in Montreal and immediately offered him a five-year recording contract and an engagement in Paris. Thus Leclerc made his debut in 1950 in a large Paris music hall, the ABC, sharing the bill with the Compagnons de la chanson. The success of his debut was followed by his first recordings and by tours of France, Belgium, and Switzerland. Dressed in a checkered lumberjack shirt and accompanying himself on the guitar, he delivered his earthy songs in a robust baritone and soon became a top-ranking star. In 1951 he was awarded the Grand Prix du disque by the Académie Charles-Cros in Paris for his song 'Moi, mes souliers.' Beneath his name, printed in large letters on the billboards, was 'le Canadien.' Leclerc subsequently divided his time between Europe and Canada. In France, his participation in major radio programs, his appearances in the leading variety theatres and boîtes à chansons (eg, the Trois-Baudets and Bobino), and his numerous tours made him a superstar.

Leclerc's singular qualities had a revitalizing effect on the chanson in France and are said to have provided a catalyst for the careers of such personalities as Georges Brassens, Guy Béart, and Jacques Brel. Thus Christian Larsen wrote: 'Félix Leclerc is to the Canadian chanson what Trenet was to the French chanson: a revolutionary, a turning point, and a leader. Because of him, fortune-hunters, poets and shopkeepers set out in search of a new Klondike ... although he did not create the Canadian chanson, Leclerc produced its public and its market and to some extent was responsible for the present generation of young chansonniers' (*Chansonniers du Québec* 1964).

When he returned to Montreal in 1953 to take part in the *Montreal Festivals, Leclerc was given a hero's welcome. His career later obliged him to spend long periods of time in Europe, but he frequently appeared in Canada; of special note were his western tour in 1965 and his appearances at Montreal's Le *Patriote in 1966, 1970, 1972, 1975, and 1976 and at the *NAC in 1971. He made a major tour of France, Belgium, and Switzerland in 1973 and of France again in 1975 and 1977. He had received another Grand Prix du disque in 1958 for *La Drave*, and in 1973 he received the same award again for his work in general. Perhaps his greatest triumph in Quebec was his appearance in 1974 with Gilles *Vigneault and Robert *Charlebois at the Superfrancofête in Quebec City.

Félix Leclerc's art and songs have been analysed by numerous writers and critics. Benoît L'Herbier, in *La Chanson québécoise* (Montreal 1974), wrote: 'From the beginning Félix Leclerc's poetry has existed on a philosophic plane reminiscent of the finest and most illuminating works of La Fontaine. For, whether as writer or composer, Félix Leclerc is a moralist.' In his book *Félix Leclerc* Luc Bériment writes: 'Leclerc's character is rich, complex, beyond grasp. He's a singer, of course, and a composer and performer, but of a kind to which music-hall standards cannot be applied. Félix Leclerc is an exception in a world where the chanson, mass-produced, is purely a commercial matter.' Musically, some of Leclerc's songs, eg, 'Le Chant d'un patriote,' recall traditional songs of France. Certain medieval influences also may be discerned: alternating minor and major modes, binary and ternary rhythms as required, and guitar accompaniment.

The lyrics of the songs, whether narrative or reflective, are written in verses which recall folk forms, and they speak to men of themselves. The naturalistic and mythical aspects of man's origins have been retained. He draws inspiration from the elements – water, earth, sun, fire, and wind – and his themes reflect a love of animals and nature. His songs are embodied in a character who is either happy or sad according to whether or not he has relinquished his childhood. There is much in them of castles, kings, and dancing festivities in a swirling picture of the tribulations and glories of human existence. His poetry, simple and direct, conveys a tragic vision of existence. To him the tragic character of humanity is rooted in nature. Human effort occasionally may lead to death under the yoke ('McPherson'), but at the same time it provides a link with the beyond and adds a spiritual dimension to everyday actions and indeed to life in general. Nature is omnipresent in Leclerc's songs. The seasons provide the backdrop to the recurring themes of escape, death, God, woman, and country.

Since 1970 this eternal 'rough peasant' has turned his forthright qualities towards public comment and protest with caustic irony as his primary weapon. In the song 'L'Alouette en colère' Félix Leclerc presents his vision of a Quebec that has been plundered and dispossessed. But while acknowledging his province's ambiguities, he maintains the sensitive voice of a steady conscience. A great believer in living traditions, he has helped the people of Quebec to lose their complexes. His public spans three generations. He has pointed the way for a dynasty of singer-poets and is their revered ancestor.

Leclerc appeared in the films *Les Brûlés* (1958), *Félix Leclerc, troubadour* (1959), and *La Vie* (1967) and has received many honours over the years. A float was dedicated to him at the 1966 *St-Jean-Baptiste Society parade in Montreal, and in 1971 he was made an Officer of the *Order of Canada. He received the 1976 *CCA Diplôme d'honneur, at the same time as the writer Félix-Antoine Savard, and he won the 1975 *Prix de musique Calixa-Lavallée. In 1977 the Prix Denise-Pelletier for the performing arts, conferred for the first time, was awarded to him by the Quebec government. The *MSO performed a medley of his works at the 1978 St-Jean-Baptiste festivities. A school in La Tuque and another in Pointe-aux-Trembles bear his name, and the Montreal Festival du disque granted a Prix Félix-Leclerc to Gilles Vigneault for *'Mon Pays' in 1965, to Georges *Dor in 1968, and to Robert Charlebois for 'Lindberg' in 1969. Leclerc's songs (words and music) have been published in *Les Chansons de Félix Leclerc – le Canadien* (Paris 1950), *Félix Leclerc, 12 chansons nouvelles* (Archambault 1958), *Les Chansons de Félix Leclerc* (Paris 1969), and *24 Chansons de Félix Leclerc* (Paris nd). His songs have been performed by the *Séguins, Monique *Leyrac, André *Gagnon, and others. He is a member of CAPAC.

DISCOGRAPHY

Mes Premières Chansons. Philips 840.571BY
Moi, mes souliers I. 1950. Philips 844.711/Poly 2424 148
La Drave II. 1957. Philips 844.712/Poly 2424 149. Also released as *Félix Leclerc chante* (Philips Réalités v5) and *Félix Leclerc et sa guitare I* (Epic LF 2001)
Félix Leclerc et sa guitare II. Epic LF 2008
Félix Leclerc et sa guitare III. Epic LF 2012
L'Héritage III. 1959. Philips 844.713/Poly 2424 151
Le Roi heureux IV. 1959. Philips 844.714/Poly 2424 151
Le Jour qui s'appelle aujourd'hui V. 1964. Philips 844.715/Poly 2424 152
Mes Longs Voyages VI. 1966. Philips 844.716/Poly 153
La Vie VII. 1967. Philips 844.717/Poly 2424 154
J'inviterai l'enfance VIII. 1969. Philips 849.491/Poly 2424 155
Pleins feux sur ... Félix Leclerc. (1971). 2-Philips 6499 061-6499 062
Pleins feux sur ... Félix Leclerc. 2-Philips 9286 396-9286 397
L'Alouette en colère. 1973. Philips 6325 022/Poly 2424 145
Le Tour de l'île. 1975. Philips 6325 242/Poly 2424 146
Merci la France. 1976. 2-Philips 6679 011/2-Poly 2675 133
Félix Leclerc / Claude Léveillée: Le Temps d'une saison. 1977. 2-Poly 2675 144
Mon Fils. 1978. Poly 2424 187
See also Discography for Chansonniers.

BIBLIOGRAPHY

Bérimont, Luc. Félix Leclerc (Paris 1964)
Renaud, Benoît. 'Félix Leclerc et ses chansons,' *Incidences*, 6, Oct 1964
Gabriel-de-l'Addolorata, Sister [Colette Bergeron]. 'L'univers poétique de Félix Leclerc,' unpubl MA thesis, U of Montreal 1964
Charland, Roland-M., and Samson, Jean-Noël. *Félix Leclerc*, in the series Dossiers de documentation sur la littérature canadienne-française (Montreal 1967)
Despins, Carmel. 'Les thèmes de Félix Leclerc,' unpubl MA thesis, Laval U 1967
Le Pennec, Jean-Claude. *L'Univers poétique de Félix Leclerc* (Montreal, Paris 1967)
Sylvain, Jean-Paul. *Félix Leclerc tel que raconté par sa femme* (Montreal 1968)
Chauvin, Marie-Josée, and Dufour, Jean. *100 Chansons* (Montreal 1970, 1974)
Champagne, Jane. 'Félix Leclerc: returning home to Canada,' *CanComp*, 86, Dec 1973
'Un pays avec des mots,' interview with Pierre Beaulieu, Montreal *La Presse*, 30 Dec 1978
The New Grove Dictionary (DM, BR)

LeCOMTE, (Joseph Gustave) Jacques. Trumpeter, teacher, b Montreal 15 May 1924; premier prix trumpet (CMM) 1948. He took piano lessons 1931–5 before switching to clarinet and then to trumpet, which he began studying in 1937 with Joseph-Laurent Gariépy. Under Gariépy's direction he became a member of the Victoria Rifles Band. When the *CMM opened, in 1943, he was admitted to Bernard Baker's class.

As principal trumpet 1945–61 with the *MSO, LeComte performed with the orchestra on several occasions as soloist in the standard concertos; he appeared from time to time on CBC radio and TV until 1971. In the early 1950s he performed the *Concerto, Op 27* for trumpet, timpani, and strings by the Austrian composer Kurt Roger with the *Little Symphony of Montreal and in 1953 he premiered Michel *Perrault's *Fête et parade* for trumpet and orchestra.

LeComte began teaching at the CMM in 1948 and many of his pupils, including Guy Archambault, Jean-Louis Chatel, Serge Chevanelle, Léon Deit, and Daniel Doyon, obtained positions in orchestras in Canada and abroad.

LeComte was a member of the jury of the *CBC Talent Festival for four years and, in 1964, a juror for the Paris Cons competition. GP

LECOR, Tex (b Paul Lecorre). Singer-songwriter, painter, b St-Michel-de-Wentworth, near Montreal, 10 Jun 1933. He studied 1957–63 at the Montreal School of Fine Arts and began writing poetry and music for pleasure.

In the late 1950s Lecor opened La Poubelle, a Montreal boîte à chansons, where he made his debut. Between 1963 and 1966 he sang in various Quebec cabarets and boîtes à chansons and made his first LPs for London, *Le Dernier des vrais* (MLP 10060) and *Mes Premières Chansons* (MB 125-126), along with a single, 'Noël au camp.' In 1969, for *Gamma, he made *Je t'amène avec moi* (GS 114), *Le Québécois* (GS 118), and *Chansons interdites à la radio et à la télévision* (GS 127).

Lecor achieved international success in 1970 with the Georges Langford song 'Le Frigidaire,' which he recorded in five languages for different labels. He was host 1970–4 of the CFTM-TV variety program 'Sous mon toit,' the name taken from a Lecor song and also the title of one of his LPs (Gamma GS 141). Other LPs for Gamma included *C'est moi ... et lui aussi* (1972, GS 147), *Quand je rêve ... c'est en couleur* (1973, GS 170), *Tex Lecor* (1974, GS 183), and *Mon Plus Récent Lecor* (1978, GP 248); two reissues *Les Grands Succès de Tex Lecor* (G2 1005 and G2 1011) appeared in 1973 and 1975 respectively. The LP *Il était une fois* (SLP 20084) was made for London in 1974. Musical direction and arrangements have been provided over the years by François *Dompierre, Eric Nico, Paul Baillargeon, and Léon Aronson.

Lecor took part in CBC TV variety programs including 'Mon Pays, mes chansons' and in CKAC radio's 'Tex matinal,' 'Insolences d'un téléphone,' 'Festival d'humour,' and 'Patrick et moi-même.'

Throughout his shows and many tours, Lecor has remained an unpretentious and hard-working person, maintaining his popularity in later songs such as 'Bienvenue chez nous,' 'Le draveur,' 'Quand ça ne tourne pas rond,' 'Rame, rame,' 'Tout le monde est d'bonne humeur,' and 'Lucille.'

Lecor's paintings have been exhibited in Montreal, Quebec City, Toronto, and New York. He is a member of CAPAC.

BIBLIOGRAPHY

Piazza, François. 'Tex Lecorre: hard-working chansonnier,' *CanComp*, 30, Jun 1968
Vincent, Pierre. 'Tex Lecor – "last of the real Quebeckers" – finds success at last,' *CanComp*, 69, Apr 1972 (BLH)

LEDUC, Jean. Pianist, organist, teacher, b Montreal 4 Jun 1910, brother of Roland *Leduc. After piano studies 1922–7 with Victoria *Cartier and Romain-Octave *Pelletier he worked in Paris 1927–30 with Paul *Loyonnet and Marcel Dupré and in Hollywood 1930–2 with the French pianist and noted teacher E. Robert Schmitz. Leduc was official pianist of the *CSM 1935–40 and performed as soloist, accompanist, and chamber musician, frequently playing compositions by *Lavallée, *Contant, *Renaud, *Champagne, and *Mathieu. Returning to California, he performed in competitions and appeared with leading string quartets (Budapest, Pro Arte, San Francisco, etc) and with Darius Milhaud 1940–2. He also was co-director 1940–56 of the E. Robert Schmitz Piano School and taught 1945–52 at San Francisco State College. In 1950 he began to teach at the *École normale de musique, and in 1956 he settled permanently in Montreal. He taught piano 1961–76 at the *CMM and in 1976 began teaching at the *UQAM. He, his brother, and his sister-in-law Annette *Lasalle-Leduc performed for a while as the Trio Leduc. He married Monique Schmitz (pianist, b Paris 11 Aug 1917, daughter of E. Robert Schmitz). In Montreal Monique Leduc taught 1961–5 at the École normale de musique and was co-ordinator of music education 1965–77 for elementary and secondary schools for the Catholic School Commission.

Another Jean Leduc, the organist, *Prix d'Europe 1957, has been active in Canada, in the USA, and in Paris, where he performed the complete organ works of Bach. He recorded organ works by Froberger, Pachelbel, Leduc, Cabezon, and Oxinagas in 1967 (CBC Expo 9/RCI 253). NT

LEDUC, Pierre. Pianist, composer, arranger, b Montreal 27 Jul 1941; B MUS (Montreal) 1977. Leduc was a pupil of Auguste *Descarries and studied 1956–7 at the *CMM and later (mid-1970s) at the *U of Montreal. At 14 he was an accompanist in Montreal cabarets, and at 16 he began playing jazz under the influence of Erroll Garner. By the early 1960s Leduc was a major figure among Montreal jazzmen, an original player whose 'adventurous piano approach reflects an understanding of the values inherent in such diverse pianists as Lennie Tristano, Bud Powell, Thelonious Monk and Cecil Taylor' (John Norris, *Coda*, Aug 1972), though his early training also was apparent. He played in clubs, eg, Jazz Hot 1965, and in concerts, eg, *Expo 67, with his own group of three to five musicians and accompanied such leading US players as Coleman Hawkins (1963, Montreal Jazz Festival), Jimmy Heath, and Sonny Stitt. He also performed with Walter *Boudreau and Lee *Gagnon.

After a 100-concert tour, 1969–70 for *JMC, Leduc gave up jazz performance, working as music director 1970–2 for Claude *Léveillée and 1973–6 for Ginette *Reno and as the accompanist for Angèle *Arsenault, Edith *Butler, François *Dompierre, Diane *Dufresne, and Jean-Pierre *Ferland. Leduc has written several pieces for his jazz group (including *Synchronisation*, recorded also by Boudreau), scores for CBC TV dramas by Marie-Claire Blais, Michel Tremblay, and Paul Dupuis, the music for Pauline *Julien's song 'La Croqueuse de 222,' and arrangements for Léveillée and Reno. Leduc is a member of CAPAC. In 1976 he began to teach arranging and improvisation at *UQAM.

DISCOGRAPHY

Information. Donato db, Normand perc. 1966. Elysée ELS-2003
Pierre Leduc et son quatuor. Barley sax and cl, Haynes db, Wikjord perc. 1967. RCI 267

Pierre Leduc, renaître. Orch and chor, Stanciu pan pipes, J.-M. Benoit guit, Donato db and Provençal drums, Leduc pf, cond, and comp. 1977–8. Martin M16210

Others as soloist with Boudreau, Gagnon, the tenor saxophonist Billy Robinson (*Evolution's Blend*, 1972, RCI 375), and the singer-poetess Marie Savard (*Marie Savard*, 1966, Apex ALF 1574); and as accompanist-arranger-conductor with Léveillée and Reno

BIBLIOGRAPHY

Gallagher, Greg. 'A jazz pianist turns to the classical,' *CanComp*, 111, May 1976 MM, CV

LEDUC, (Joseph Augustin Georges) **Roland**. Cellist, conductor, teacher, administrator, b Longueuil, near Montreal, 25 Jul 1907; premier prix (Brussels Royal Cons) 1929, prix de virtuosité Van Cutsem (Brussels Royal Cons) 1930. He began studying the piano with his mother at 6, switching to cello at 14. He then took private lessons with Jean-Baptiste *Dubois and studied theory with Louis Michiels. On a Quebec government grant he studied 1927–31 with Marix Loevensohn at the Royal Cons of Brussels. At the same time he took private lessons in harmony and counterpoint with Paul Gilson. He was a regular member of the conservatory orchestra and sometimes played with the Brussels Philharmonic Orchestra and at the Defauw Concerts. He also took part in a concert conducted by Ravel, and another conducted by Richard Strauss.

Leduc returned to Montreal in 1931 and gave recitals and performed as a soloist, notably in Boccherini's *Concerto in D* at the CSM orchestra's fifth concert in April 1935. He formed the Trio Leduc ca 1932–4 with his wife, the violinist Annette *Lasalle-Leduc, and his brother, the pianist Jean Leduc. Roland was a member 1934–40 of the *Montreal String Quartet, with which he went to Paris in 1939 to study chamber music with André Tourret. At the same time he took the opportunity to study with Maurice Maréchal. On his return he was principal cello 1940–8 of the CSM orchestra.

Leduc taught 1940–53 at the École superieure de musique d'Outremont (*École Vincent-d'Indy), resuming the position he had held 1937–9. He also taught in Sherbrooke, was among the *CMQ's first teachers, and taught cello and orchestra at the *CMM. His pupils included Dorothy Bégin, Raymonde *Martin, Monique Mercure, and Émile Préfontaine. He was a member of the short-lived CMM Quartet.

Orchestra conducting became a preoccupation for Leduc in the early 1940s, and he conducted for the CBC radio programs 'Les Maîtres de la musique,' 'Images de la Renaissance' (later 'Le Musée d'art'), and 'Radio-Collège.' For the last, he was the producer and conductor of a series of introductions to the orchestra and its instruments. During the summer of 1947 he studied with Pierre Monteux in Hancock, Me. On 11 Jan 1948 he inaugurated the weekly CBC series *'The Little Symphonies' to which his name was attached until 1965. He also conducted for 'L'*Heure du concert,' 'Concerts pour la jeunesse,' and 'Les Grands Concerts,' as well as for televised opera (*Così fan tutte* and *Oedipus Rex* in 1956). He often conducted the *CBC SO, notably in Stravinsky's *Symphony in C* and in the Canadian premiere of Dutilleux's *Symphony No. 1*.

Leduc was a guest conductor with all the principal Canadian orchestras and toured Europe in 1952, 1968, and 1969–70, leading the BBC Manchester orchestra as well as radio orchestras in Brussels, Lausanne, Lugano, Paris, and Turin. In 1952 he conducted the first *Montreal Festivals orchestra concert devoted exclusively to Canadian works. For the same society he conducted productions of *King David* (1954), *The Marriage of Figaro* (1956), *Don Giovanni* (1957), and *The Abduction from the Seraglio* (1960); he was its music director 1960–3. In 1957 he was a founding member of the Grand Opéra of Montreal.

Roland Leduc

Leduc succeeded Wilfrid *Pelletier in 1961 as director of the CMM, and was inspector-general of music 1967–70 at the *MACQ. During his 1968 European tour he became the only Canadian to have conducted the Orchestre national of the ORTF in the series 'Les Grands Chefs d'orchestre.' He was director 1970–5 of the Expo-Théâtre in Montreal and produced 1975–6 a series of introductions to music, 'De concert avec vous,' on Radio-Québec.

Leduc recorded Jean *Coulthard's *Sonata* for cello and piano with John *Newmark (1949, RCI 4). He was made a Member of the *Order of Canada in 1980.

DISCOGRAPHY (as conductor)

Champagne *Concerto in D Minor* – Adaskin *Suite*. CBC Mtl orch, Chotem pf. 1950. RCI 17

Champagne *Images du Canada français*. CBC Mtl orch and choir. Ca 1955. RCI 152

Champagne *Paysanna* – Papineau-Couture *Prélude* – Rogers *A Coronation Tribute*. CBC Mtl orch. 1953. RCI 90

Morel *Cassation*. CBC Mtl chamb orch. 1956. RCI 128

Morel *Rituel de l'espace* – Pépin *Symphony No. 2*. CBC Mtl orch. (1975). RCI 212/RCA CCS 1007

Somers *Sketches* – Cusson *Suite No. 2*. CBC Mtl orch. 1953. RCI 88

See also Rose Goldblatt. (YR)

Leeds Music (Canada), a Division of MCA Canada Ltd. Established in Toronto in 1960 as Leeds Music (Canada) Ltd, a branch of a New York company which had offices in Great Britain and Australia. The branch was set up to promote the publications of the parent firm and to publish Canadian music. Bailey *Bird was appointed vice-president and general manager. In 1967 Leeds was purchased by MCA Inc, and in 1970, following the reorganization of the MCA Canadian holdings, Bird became president of Leeds Music (Canada), a Division of MCA Canada Ltd, and a vice-president of MCA Inc.

The publishing and distribution activities established by Leeds were continued and expanded in Canada. A wide variety of publications emerged, ranging from educational material to concert works by Murray *Adaskin, Louis *Applebaum, Norma *Beecroft, Robert *Fleming, Harry *Freedman, Kelsey *Jones, Oskar *Morawetz, Clermont *Pépin, Norman *Symonds, John *Weinzweig, and others. The W.R. *Draper Co of Weston, Ont, became the printers of music for Leeds. Plate numbers do not appear on Leeds Music (Canada) publications.

Leeds became the Canadian distributor for the publications of Eulenburg, Schott of London, Schott's Söhne of Mainz, Sikorski of Hamburg, Belwin-Mills, Edward B. Marks, and Lawson-Gould of New York, and *Ricordi (Canada), but in 1980 discontinued these services.

BIBLIOGRAPHY

Schrank, Don. 'Leeds Music (Canada) Limited invests in Canadian composers,' *CanComp*, 14, Jan 1967 MWI

LEES, Gene (Frederick Eugene John). Lyricist, writer, singer, composer, b Hamilton, Ont, 2 Aug 1928. After working as a reporter for the Hamilton *Spectator* in 1948, the Toronto *Telegram* in 1949, and the Montreal *Star* 1952–5, he was music and drama critic 1955–9 for the Louisville (Ky) *Times* and editor 1959–62 of the jazz magazine *Down Beat* (Chicago). He studied composition by correspondence with the Berklee College of Music, Boston, in the early 1960s and piano with Tony Aless and guitar with Oscar Castro-Neves in New York. Specializing in pop music and jazz, he was a critic 1962–5 for *Stereo Review* (New York) and in 1965 became a columnist (later also a contributing editor) for *High Fidelity* (Great Barrington, Mass).

Lees' writings include a novel about a musician (*And Sleep Until Noon*, New York 1967) and articles in *Saturday Review*, *Maclean's*, the *New York Times*, the *Los Angeles Times*, the *Globe and Mail*, and other publications. In 1978 he received the ASCAP Deems Taylor Award for a series of articles published in *High Fidelity* about US music.

Lees has written the lyrics for many pop songs, including 'Quiet Nights of Quiet Stars, 'Someone to Light Up My Life,' 'Song of the Jet,' and 'Dreamer,' all with Antonio Carlos Jobim; 'Paris Is at Her Best in May' and 'Venice Blue' with Charles Aznavour; 'Bridges' with Milton Nascimento; 'Yesterday I Heard The Rain' with Armando Manzaneiro; and 'Waltz for Debby' with Bill Evans. The most successful, 'Quiet Nights of Quiet Stars,' had been recorded by some 150 performers by 1980, among them Tony Bennett, Perry Como, Vic Damone, Peggy Lee, Sergio Mendes, Frank Sinatra, Sarah Vaughan, and Andy Williams.

Lees has sung in nightclubs, appeared in three CBC specials (among them 'Words, Words, Words, and Music' in 1972), and recorded several of his songs for a CBC LP, LM-117, released commercially as *Bridges: Gene Lees Sings the Gene Lees Songbook* by Kanata (KAN 2), the Toronto company of which he was president 1971–4. (Kanata also released LPs by Tommy *Ambrose and Bruno Gerussi, Guido *Basso, Peter Foldy, the *Governor General's Foot Guards Band, Milan *Kymlicka, Matt Lucas, Ray Materick, Doug *Randle, and the *Travellers.) Lees is a member of CAPAC.

BIBLIOGRAPHY

'Gene Lees: how to start a record company with Mr Nixon's help,' *CanComp*, 68, Mar 1972 MM

LEFEBVRE. Montreal musicians: 1 / Germain Sr and 2 / Germain Jr.

1 **Germain Sr**. Lyric bass, choirmaster, teacher, b St-Henri, Montreal, 3 Jun 1889, d there 12 May 1946. He studied in Montreal under Alexis *Contant, Salvator *Issaurel, Alphonse *Lavallée-Smith, Rodolphe *Mathieu, and Joseph *Saucier. He was assistant choirmaster at St-Henri 1906–13, solo bass at Notre-Dame 1914–15, and choirmaster at St-Jean-Baptiste 1915–46.

Lefebvre was a founding member of the Orphéon de Montréal and gave many concerts in Canada and the USA as a soloist or member of vocal ensembles, particularly with Émile *Gour and Louis *Verschelden. His repertoire included the roles of Joseph in *L'Enfance du Christ*, Vitellius in Massenet's *Hérodiade*, and the High Priest in

Samson et Dalila. In 1923 he sang the role of Antipas in the premiere of Guillaume *Couture's **Jean le Précurseur*, and two years later he sang the Pharisee and Zacharias in the same oratorio. He was among the first performers to be heard on radio stations CKAC and CFCF, and also on the CBC ('Silhouettes campagnardes'). Lefebvre was a teacher at the *Schola cantorum in 1922 and also taught privately. Henri Éthier and Dollard Lachapelle were among his pupils.

Lefebvre's wife Maria (née Verner), a pianist, frequently accompanied him in his recitals.

BIBLIOGRAPHY
Musiciens canadiens

2 **Germain Jr**. Lyric bass, choir conductor, teacher, b Montreal 10 Jan 1924. After early music training at the school of the Sisters of the Holy Names of Jesus and Mary in Outremont, he took private lessons in Gregorian chant 1936–42 from Clément *Morin. He studied 1942–4 under Salvator *Issaurel and then for 10 years under Pauline *Donalda.

Lefebvre succeeded his father as choirmaster at St-Jean-Baptiste Church in 1946 and remained there until he moved in the same capacity to St-Sylvain de Laval, Que, where he stayed until 1977. As a recitalist or chorister he performed on CBC radio and TV in such programs as 'CBC Wednesday Night,' 'La Terre qui chante,' and 'L'*Heure du concert.' He was a teacher 1960–72 and a teaching consultant thereafter for the Chomedey-Laval school board and set up several school choirs and instrumental ensembles. He was the founding director (1968) of the Choeur Laval. AP

LEFEBVRE, Charles-Hugues. Choirmaster, writer, critic, teacher, b St-Hugues, east of Montreal, 28 Aug 1864, d Montreal 22 Feb 1948. While receiving his education at the St-Hyacinthe Seminary, he studied piano and singing with Father Charles-Édouard Brunault. He entered the Society of Jesus and was ordained a priest in 1901; he completed his musical training through private lessons and a brief stay at the Benedictine Abbey at Solesmes, France, in 1903.

As choirmaster at the Gesù Church in Montreal 1903–15 and 1929–37, at Notre-Dame-du-Chemin Church in Quebec 1923–9, and at the Jesuit College in Quebec 1937–41, Lefebvre contributed to the reform of church singing in conformity with the *Motu proprio* of Pope Pius X (1903). In the same spirit he founded, and directed 1924–9, the Chorale Désy, a Quebec City mixed choir. Guillaume *Dupuis and Henri *Gagnon were among his pupils.

Under various pseudonyms Lefebvre contributed numerous articles to *Le Messager canadien* 1899–1909, to *La Musique* 1919–22, and especially – as L.A. Muzette – to the Quebec City daily *L'Action catholique*, for which he wrote a weekly column 1924–8. In 1908 the *Manuel de prières, de chants liturgiques et de cantiques notés à l'usage de tous fidèles* by R. Vandandaigue, SJ, was published in Montreal. Lefebvre wrote the preface and became generally recognized as the person mainly responsible for the musical part of the work; it went through three subsequent editions (Paris 1924, 1929, 1931) and was used in the schools and colleges of France. He also edited *Documents officiels sur la musique sacrée parus depuis cinquante ans* (Montreal 1934).

Lefebvre composed an offertory of the mass for the dead, 'Domine Jesu Christe,' the psalm words sung by the choir in unison with soloists and quartet ad lib (Schola cantorum of Montreal 1921). He also composed hymns and plainsong harmonizations.

BIBLIOGRAPHY
Bernier, Alfred. 'Nécrologie,' *Lettres du Bas-Canada*, vol 2, Montreal 1948
Litterae annuae Provincial Canadae Inferioris S.J. (Montreal 1951)
Musiciens canadiens RPv

LEFEBVRE, Gilles. Violinist, senior administrator, b Montreal 30 Jun 1922; hon D LITT (Montreal) 1978. He began taking violin lessons at the École supérieure in Outremont (now *École Vincent-d'Indy) while pursuing academic studies at the Collège Ste-Marie. He then studied 1939–42 with Armand Weisbord at the *U of Ottawa, where he founded a string quartet and an instrumental ensemble. While a musician 1942–5 with the RCAF he gave numerous recitals for the troops, and several duo-recitals with the violinist Henryk Szeryng. In Montreal in 1945 he gave the premiere of André *Mathieu's *Sonata* for piano and violin, with the composer. That year he also worked under Arthur *LeBlanc. With his DVA allowance and a scholarship from the French-Canadian Institute in Ottawa he studied 1946–7 in France at the École normale de Paris with Jacques Gentil (violin and chamber music) and Georges Dandelot (harmony and analysis), and took special courses 1948–50 with René Benedetti and Georges Enesco.

Lefebvre and Colombe *Pelletier gave about 50 recitals 1948–9 in Canada, and Lefebvre was struck by the interest of the young in music and by the infrequency of concerts in the small centres. In 1949 with a group of people who shared his ideals he founded the Hélicon, an association which was to become the nucleus of the *JMC. He then left for Europe to explore the means of developing cultural activities for youth in Canada. He met the director of the JM of France, René Nicoly, who invited him to join a delegation to the 1950 Congress of the International Federation of JM in Vienna. Supported by this international body, the JMC expanded rapidly in Quebec and then in the other provinces of Canada. With modest subsidies Gilles Lefebvre in 1951 created the JMC music camp which in 1967 became the *JMC Orford Art Centre, one of the centres of Canadian musical culture. He also in 1951 established the *Journal des Jeunesses musicales du Canada* and in 1961 organized the first JMC National Music Competition in Montreal. In August 1974, during the JMC's 25th-anniversary celebrations, the concert hall which had been inaugurated in 1960 was named after him.

In 1964 Lefebvre was commissioned by Unesco to visit leading musical organizations in the Far East; he also began drawing up the program for the World Festival of *Expo 67, of which he was associate artistic director 1964–7. He was president 1950–4 and general director 1953–72 of the JMC and president 1954–7, 1967, 1970–4 of the International Federation of JM, becoming honorary president in 1974. He represented the latter organization on the International Music Council and Unesco and was president 1970–9 of the board of the JM World Orchestra, which he founded in 1970. In addition he was director 1972–8 of the *Canadian Cultural Centre in Paris and in 1978 was appointed director general of international cultural relations with the Dept of External Affairs of Canada. He received the 1963 *Prix de musique Calixa-Lavallée and in 1967 was made an Officer of the *Order of Canada. The *CCA, of which he was president 1971–2, awarded him the Diplôme d'honneur in April 1978. A musician, an educator, a humanist, and a born organizer, Gilles Lefebvre chose to dedicate his life to the music education of Canada's youth, to the search for new talent, and to the advancement of Canadian artists' careers at home and abroad.

Gilles Lefebvre

WRITINGS
'Musiciens-éducateurs, les Jeunesses musicales ne peuvent rien sans vous,' *Jmc*, Apr 1969
"L'élaboration d'une politique de la musique au Canada,' *CMB*, 5, Autumn-Winter 1972

BIBLIOGRAPHY
Samson, Marc. 'Gilles Lefebvre: une réalité énergique,' Québec *Le Soleil*, 30 Aug 1969
Maheu, Renée. 'Gilles Lefebvre: in the beginning there was music,' *Mcan*, 36, Aug 1978
Brousseau, Jean-Paul. 'Gilles Lefebvre et les échanges culturels,' Montreal *La Presse*, 26 Jul 1980 TC-C (ST)

LÉGARÉ, Ovila. Folklorist, singer, actor, scriptwriter, host, b Montreal 21 Jul 1901, d there 19 Feb 1978. He became deeply interested in Quebec's traditional music and began playing the violin. Having injured his hand while working as a printer he turned to the theatre and to singing. He did some amateur acting in Drummondville, Que, and became known in Montreal as a singer and square dance 'caller.'

Légaré was active as an actor in theatre, radio, and, later, TV, until his death. He wrote and took part in many series, the most famous of which was 'Nazaire et Barnabé,' which began in 1939 on radio station CKAC, Montreal, and in which he played 14 roles. His stature as an actor was confirmed in dramatic works, including the role of César in *Marius* and *Fanny* by Marcel Pagnol, which he played in 1944. In the early 1940s he played leading roles in such Canadian films as *Le Père Chopin*, *Le Curé du village*, *La Forteresse*, and *Un Homme et son péché*. On CBC TV he became a top star as Père Didace in the series 'Le Survenant' by Germaine Guèvremont.

Légaré's career as a folklorist gained momentum when he appeared in the Soirées de famille at the *Monument national, beginning in 1920, and in the evening concerts produced by Conrad *Gauthier. In 1927 Légaré met Charles *Marchand, who helped him to perfect his style. His popularity grew through radio and recordings. On radio he served with extraordinary zest as host for many folk music programs.

Légaré made 19 78s for *Starr Gennett and 9 for Columbia, accompanied in turn by Blanche Gauthier, the Henri Lacroix trio, Juliette Béliveau, and La *Bolduc. La Bolduc made her first recordings with Légaré; she also accompanied him on the violin and jew's harp.

Three of Légaré's songs, 'Dans l'temps du Jour de l'An,' 'La Bastringue,' and 'Chapleau fait son Jour de l'An,' were extremely successful and established his reputation. The economic situation in 1930 inspired him to write 'Faut pas s'faire de bile,' another song that was popular and that Bruno Roy called 'a jewel of originality, true to tradition' (*Panorama de la chanson au Québec*, Montreal 1977). Several of his songs were assembled in *Les Chansons d'Ovila Légaré*, with a preface by Tex *Lecor (Montreal 1972).

The complete list of Légaré's 78s may be found in *Pionniers du disque folklorique*. In addition, he made the LPs *Ovila Légaré et ses chansons* (Lon MB 10) and *Tout l'monde 'swing' avec Ovila Légaré* (Lon MB 27).

BIBLIOGRAPHY

Provost, Gilles. 'Mort d'un titan du spectacle: Ovila Légaré,' Montreal *Le Devoir*, 20 Feb 1978 GP

LEGENDRE, Napoléon. Writer, lawyer, civil servant, b Nicolet, Canada East (Quebec) 13? Feb 1841, d Quebec City 16 Dec 1907; D LITT (Laval) 1888. He was educated at Ste-Marie College in Montreal and in 1865 was called to the bar of Lower Canada. In 1876 he became clerk of the Legislative Council of Quebec and six years later he became a founding member of the Royal Society of Canada.

Legendre published a biography, *Albani – Emma Lajeunesse*, in Quebec in 1874, when the singer was beginning her career. He also published a novel and numerous essays, and contributed to several magazines, including *Le Canada artistique* (1890), for which he wrote the articles 'Le piano' and 'Le chant dans les écoles.'

Legendre was the author of two poems, 'Violette' and 'Nuit d'été,' which were set to music by Calixa *Lavallée. He also wrote the words to Lavallée's *Cantata* (1879), a work presented in Quebec City to mark the visit of the governor general, the Marquis of Lorne, and Princess Louise.

A street in Montreal was named after Legendre in 1912.

BIBLIOGRAPHY

Rivard, Adjutor. 'Napoléon Legendre,' *Transactions and Proceedings of the Royal Society of Canada*, 3rd series, vol 3, 1909

Le Jeune, Louis-Marie. *Dictionnaire général de biographie, histoire, littérature, agriculture, commerce, industrie et des arts, sciences, moeurs, coutumes, institutions politiques et religieuses du Canada*, 2 vols (Ottawa 1931) GP

Franklin Legge Organ Co. Prominent organ builder in the first half of the 20th century. Founded in 1915 in Toronto by Charles Franklin Legge (organist, b St Catharines, Ont, 21 Dec 1891, d Toronto 18 Feb 1948), the firm installed its first instruments in Chapleau in northern Ontario and in Williamsburg near Ottawa.

In 1919 William F. Legge joined the firm, and a factory was built on Dufferin Street in Toronto. There, more than 250 instruments of two to four manuals were designed and built for buyers in North and South America. Almost entirely enclosed, the Legge organs used all-electric action and English-style diapasons and reeds. A self-player employing hand-recorded rolls was offered for use in homes and funeral parlours.

One of the best known Legge instruments, originally built for Casa Loma, was a 15-rank three-manual organ with 100 stops and effects. It was purchased by CKNC (taken over in 1933 by the CBC) and was installed first in the CKNC Davenport Road studios and then in CBC studio 'G' where, until 1966, it was used for various radio programs including 'Nocturne.' The instrument was associated mainly with the organist Quentin *Maclean.

The C. Franklin Legge Organ Co ceased operation in 1947, and its service contracts were assumed by the T. Eaton Co in 1948. At about that time, however, William Legge, briefly in Eaton's employ, formed in Woodstock, Ont, the William F. Legge Organ Co, which was purchased (1963) by C.F. David Legge, son of C. Franklin, and continued as the Legge Organ Co. MG

LEGRADY, Thomas (Theodore). Composer, teacher, b Budapest 22 Mar 1920, naturalized Canadian 1962. He graduated from the Bartók Cons and obtained a PH D in political science at Erzsébet U in Pécs. He emigrated to Canada in 1956, settling in Montreal and teaching solfège and orchestration at Loyola College and music-teaching methods at *McGill U and the *École normale de musique. He moved to Toronto in 1972 as teacher of woodwinds at Étienne Brûlé High School and conductor of the North York Student Orchestra.

Legrady's *Suite* for brass was the winning submission in a 1963 contest sponsored by the Montreal Brass Quintet. Before leaving Hungary, Legrady had written a *Divertimento* for brass quintet and another for flute, oboe, and string trio, besides several film scores. In Canada he has composed the music for the NFB film *Sunrise and Eclipse*, written orchestrations 1956–9 for CBC Montreal variety shows, and prepared the teaching text *Lisons la musique; adaptation canadienne-française de la Méthode Kodaly* (Montreal 1970).

BIBLIOGRAPHY

Robitaille, Pierrette. 'A success in Canada,' *CanComp*, 81, Jun 1973 SLO

LeLACHEUR, Rex (A. de Putron). Composer, baritone, choir conductor, b Guernsey, Channel Islands, 5 Jan 1910. He studied first in Guernsey with his father, F.M. LeLacheur. He moved to Canada in 1927 to enter the United Church ministry but instead continued to study music in Toronto with the English musician John Hughes Howell and with H.A. *Fricker. He sang on several commercial radio stations in Toronto, performed occasionally on the CBC with Ernest *Dainty's trio, and was a finalist in the 1944 "Metropolitan Opera Auditions of the Air.' He moved to Ottawa, where he worked for a time in insurance, but in 1951 he resumed full-time musical activity, teaching, conducting choirs, and composing. The same year he recorded six songs with harp accompaniment for Dominion.

Although mainly a choral composer, preferring religious or patriotic texts, LeLacheur also completed *Sonata da Chiesa* (1957) for the carillonneur Robert *Donnell. Songs and choral pieces, published by *Canadian Music Sales, *Leeds, *Harris, *Chappell, and *Archambault, include 'Forever England' (1940, performed by the *Toronto Mendelssohn Choir) and 'Centennial Hymn' (1967). He wrote two recitations for Anna *Russell, and some of his songs were sung by Ezio Pinza, John Charles Thomas, and Lawrence Tibbett.

His choral works have been performed by the Rex LeLacheur Singers (founded 1956), a 50-voice mixed choir which has recorded parts 3 and 4 of his cantata *The Resurrection and the Ascension* (Q63-1163). LeLacheur is a member of CAPAC.

BIBLIOGRAPHY

Thistle, Lauretta. 'Ottawa composer writes official centennial hymn,' *CanComp*, 15, Feb 1967 (FF)

LEMAY, (Marie Adée) **Jacqueline**. Singer-songwriter, guitarist, b Guérin, Témiscamingue, Que, 23 May 1937; supplementary teaching certificate (École normale Ville-Marie, Témiscamingue) 1954, advanced teaching certificate (École normale de Sherbrooke) 1958. At 17 she was teaching as well as singing rock and roll in English during the evenings in the cabarets of Rouyn-Noranda. She was a member of the religious community the Institut séculier des Oblates 1957–63, and while fulfilling her academic assignments in Sherbrooke she began writing songs that were mainly religious in inspiration and performing them to her own guitar accompaniment. She became known through her singles 'Vive la vie,' 'Route claire,' and 'Si tu vois la mer,' recorded in 1960 (Radio Marie NDC). In Quebec City she studied voice with Patricia Poitras 1961–2 and guitar with Johan Van Veen in 1963. Her first LP, *Compagnon* (Radio Marie NDC 336203), appeared in 1962. She toured in Quebec and the USA and performed on radio and TV.

Lemay's departure from the Oblates in 1963 set her career on a different course, which she pursued both in Quebec and in Europe. In 1967, after a successful recital at Le *Patriote in Montreal, she made the LP *Un Long Voyage* (Col FL 336). With a grant from the *MACQ in 1969 she went to Paris to work with Annie Charlot and Jean Lumière. She also wrote and performed the songs in a French version of George Ryga's play *The Ecstasy of Rita Joe*, presented at the Comédie-Canadienne in 1969. She toured Canada as a singer with Les Feux-Follets in 1973. The following year she founded the recording company SPPS (Société de production et de programmation de spectacles) along with Lise Aubut, Angèle *Arsenault, and Edith *Butler. For International Women's Year in 1975 she composed and performed 'La Moitié du monde est une femme'; the song was also sung by Pauline *Julien in Quebec and Isabelle Aubret in French-speaking Europe. She used its title for an LP (SPPS SP 19902) and for an anthology of her poems and songs (Leméac 1976). In 1977 she made an LP for children, *C'est la récréation* (SPPS EP-990-0), with Angèle Arsenault and Edith Butler, as well as singles of 'Aut' fidélité' and 'Les Jeans.' Jacqueline Lemay has composed more than 300 songs, several of which are published by the Éditions de l'Échelle. 'Je voudrais être' and 'Le Fil de la rivière' are two of those she wrote for Edith Butler. She is the sister of Jérôme Lemay, who was a member of the duo Les Jérolas. She is a member of CAPAC.

BIBLIOGRAPHY

Jasmin, Hélène. 'International Women's Year was a good one for Jacqueline Lemay,' *CanComp*, 107, Jan 1976

(HPn)

LEMIEUX, (Joseph) **Germain**. Folklorist, teacher, b Cap-Chat, near Matane, Que, 5 Jan 1914; MA history (Laval) 1955, PH D history and oral literature (Laval) 1961, hon LL D (York) 1977, hon D LITT (Ottawa) 1978. He entered the Jesuit order in 1935 and was ordained in 1947. He began studying Franco-Ontarian oral folklore in 1948 when he was asked by the Société historique du Nouvel-Ontario to investigate the subject in the Sudbury region. He visited singers and story tellers in Sturgeon Falls, Verner, and Sudbury. Between 1948 and 1958 he accumulated a valuable collection of recorded materials (more than 600 songs, about 30 stories, and many legends) and published two collections of songs, *Folklore franco-ontarien – Chansons*, (2 vols, Sudbury 1949, 1950). Meanwhile he studied 1953–5 at *Laval U.

In 1958 the Société historique du Nouvel-Ontario transferred its recorded collections and the responsibility for folklore research to the U of Sudbury (an affiliate of Laurentian U), which in 1959 appointed Father Lemieux director of its Institut de folklore (renamed the Centre franco-ontarien de folklore in 1975). In the summer of 1959 Father Lemieux undertook a series of investigations in untapped areas of Ontario and Quebec, where he collected more than 300 songs and some 30 tales. He returned to Laval U to study 1959–61 with Luc *Lacourcière; his doctoral thesis, *Placide-Eustache* (Quebec City 1970), dealt with a single popular tale. With grants in 1963, 1964, and 1966 from the *Canada Council, he began transcribing and codifying the institute's recorded collections. At Laval U 1965–9 he gave courses based on the documentation at the U of Sudbury's Institut de folklore. He was responsible for the publication of *Chanteurs franco-ontariens et leurs chansons* (Sudbury 1963–4), *Chansonnier franco-ontarien* (2 vols, Sudbury 1974, 1975), and works on Franco-Ontarian stories. During his field trips, Father Lemieux also collected old implements and musical instruments, several of which had been made by the country people themselves. He wrote the chapter 'La chanson folklorique canadienne-française' in *La Chanson française*. In 1973 the Conseil de la vie française en Amérique awarded him the Prix Champlain. Lemieux researched and prepared the texts for the 1975 CBC-FM series 'Dans le mémoire des hommes.' The nine programs were rebroadcast in 1980.

BIBLIOGRAPHY

Keir, Robert. 'Priest works to save folklore,' Toronto *Globe and Mail*, 4 Jul 1966

'Brief on the Institute of Folklore of the University of Sudbury Ontario,' *CFMS Newsletter*, vol 4, 1969

Hamel, Réginald, et al. *Dictionnaire pratique des auteurs québécois* (Montreal 1976) DM

LEMIEUX, (Edmond) **Robert**. Guitarist, teacher, b Noranda, Que, 1 Aug 1946. He took private guitar lessons in Montreal 1955–6 with Stephen Fentok and 1956–61 with Florence Brown and in New York 1964–5 with Alice Artzt. He also studied with Alexandre Lagoya and Ida Presti 1965–6 in Paris and at the Académie internationale de Nice; Lagoya and Presti had invited him to join their classes when they were in Montreal in 1964. Between 1966 and 1970 he studied in Paris with Karel Harms and then gave recitals in France before returning to Quebec in 1972. He performed that October on CBC TV (English network) and played in various halls, including the Centaur Theatre in Montreal, and at the *UQAM.

In April 1977 Lemieux became the first Quebec guitarist to give a recital at the *PDA. Jacob *Siskind described his performance in *The Gazette*: 'Lemieux does play his instrument with great sensitivity. He phrases with a romantic freedom that is reminiscent of the great performers of the first quarter of the present century' (26 Apr 1977). Lemieux participated in the 1977 summer festival in Quebec City, and in February 1979 he played Rodrigo's *Concierto de Aranjuez* with the *MSO.

Lemieux taught 1972–7 at the *École Vincent-d'Indy, where his pupils included Serge Leboeuf.

BIBLIOGRAPHY

'Robert Lemieux maîtrise un instrument qui échappait à Paganini,' *Musique périodique*, vol 1, Oct 1977 AP

LEMON, Laura (Gertrude) (m Heath). Composer, pianist, b Guelph, Ont, 15 Oct 1866, d Redhill, Surrey, England, 18 Aug 1924. She was of United Empire Loyalist stock and was raised in Guelph and Winnipeg. In 1890 she went to study at the RAM and remained in England. Although she wrote some piano and violin music, she was most successful as a writer of songs, some two dozen of which were published, mostly by Boosey. "'My Ain Folk, a ballad of home,' is one the best-known songs by a Canadian composer. Emma *Albani sang Lemon's 'Slumber Song' for Queen Victoria. Of Canadian interest are 'Canada for Ever!' (Boosey 1907), 'Mighty Dominion' (ibid 1910) and 'Canadian Song Cycle' (4 songs, ibid 1911). Lemon wrote the texts of some of her songs, using the pseudonyms Austin Fleming and Ian Macdonald. *Three Moravian Dances* for violin and piano (Weekes 1910) were dedicated to Kathleen *Parlow. HK

LENSSENS, (Maria Francisca Theresia) **Ria** (m Heyninx). Soprano, teacher, choir conductor, b Antwerp 2 Jun 1903, naturalized Canadian 1954; premier prix voice (Brussels Cons) 1924. She taught singing and solfège 1931–48 at the Brussels Cons royal, where she had studied, and gave lessons at the École de musique de St-Josse-Schaerbeek. During the same period she gave recitals and concerts with orchestras, notably for the Société philharmonique de Bruxelles, and performed on radio across Europe, singing the premieres of several Belgian compositions. She moved to Montreal in 1948 and taught 1948–71 at the *CMM, 1948–57 at the *CMQ, 1948–67 at *McGill U, 1954–60 at the *École normale de musique (where she also directed the Petit Ensemble vocal), and 1955–67 at the *U of Montreal. Gaston *Germain, Gabrielle *Lavigne, and Jacqueline *Martel were among her pupils. She conducted the choir of the Villa-Marie convent 1955–63. At the request of the *MACQ in 1974 she created on tape an ear-training program designed for the Cons de musique du Québec; in 1980 it had not been implemented. She recorded 16 French and Flemish art songs for Columbia. In 1942 she sang the Virgin in the first recording of Honegger's *Jeanne d'Arc au bûcher* (Gramophone G-W 1546-54; reissued on LP HMV FALP 213-214) with the Orchestre national de Belgique, the Caecilia d'Anvers chorale, and the children's choir of the Institut Notre-Dame de Cureghem, conducted by Louis de Vocht. She took part in a concert conducted by Léon Jongen in 1946 during which the Institut national de radiodiffusion (renamed Radio-Télévision belge) recorded Caplet's *Le Miroir de Jésus* for Columbia. Ria Lenssens has given many lectures, including one to the Assn Belgique-Canada, and has been an examiner in Belgium and Canada. (NT)

Leo, The Royal Cadet. A Canadian 'military' opera in four acts, written ca 1889 in Kingston, Ont, the libretto by George Frederick Cameron and the music, for chorus, 16 solo voices, and orchestra, by Oscar Ferdinand *Telgmann. First performed 11 Jul 1889 at Martin's Opera House in Kingston 'under the patronage of the Commandant and Staff and Gentlemen Cadets' of the nearby Royal Military College, the opera was published in vocal score in 1891 by John Henderson, a local book seller. It was performed again in Kingston in 1893 at the opera house and at the college's armouries.

Incorporating elements of local colour, the opera traces the career of Leo before, during, and after he entered the college; his battle with the Zulus in Africa; his winning of the Victoria Cross; and his reunion with his true love, Nellie, on a village green on the St Lawrence River.

Telgmann directed the work in several Ontario towns, from Ottawa to Woodstock, and in Utica, NY. More than 150 complete performances were given, the last in 1925 under the direction of Telgmann's daughter, Mignon. The performance material was still owned in 1980 by Telgmann's son Jackson, also of Kingston.

BIBLIOGRAPHY

Bourinot, Arthur S. *Five Canadian Poets* (Ottawa 1954)

Waldhauer, Erdmute. 'A chronicle of Kingston's theatrical entertainment 1870–1898,' unpubl ms (Kingston Hist Soc 1976) PB

LePAGE, Pierrette (Marie Ethel Claudette) (m Mather). Pianist, harpsichordist, teacher, b Montreal 25 May 1939; B MUS (Laval) 1952, Artist Diploma (Toronto) 1959, BA (Toronto) 1960. She studied piano with Constantin Klimoff 1951–5 in Quebec City; with Alberto *Guerrero 1955–60 in Toronto, while attending the *RCMT and the *U of Toronto; and with Lazare Lévy 1960–2 in Paris. She has performed with the *TSO and the *CBC SO, and has fulfilled numerous other solo engagements across Canada. In about 1970 she and her husband, Bruce *Mather, began performing as duo-pianists specializing in contemporary music. Pierrette LePage taught 1964–6 at the U of Toronto and 1966–74 at *McGill U.

DISCOGRAPHY

Bolcom *Frescoes*. Mather pf. Nonesuch 71297

Hawkins *Études* – Hunt *Merkabah*. Mather pf. 1978. RCI 464

Wyschnedgradsky – Mather – Hambraeus. Mather pf. 1977. McGill U Records 77002 WS

LEROUGE LeSAUNIER, Jenny (Marie Chantille Augustine). Pianist, teacher, b Brussels 25 Aug 1886, d Edmonton 11 Mar 1971; hon LLD (Alberta) 1966. She took her studies at the Lille Cons, at the Paris Cons (with Isidor Philipp), and in Berlin. She moved with her parents to Ottawa after the death of her sister, Sidonie, a violinist. In Ottawa she played by invitation before Sir Wilfrid Laurier, then prime minister of Canada, and before Earl Grey, then governor-general. In late 1907 she moved with her family to Red Deer, Alta. She married Charles LeSaunier in 1909 and began teaching in Red Deer.

Lerouge LeSaunier was persuaded by Ernest *MacMillan to move to Edmonton, and she opened a studio there in 1922. She remained in Edmonton until her death, playing concerts and establishing herself as a prominent teacher. Her pupils included Donna Fraser, Eleanor Kerr, Fraser *Macdonald, Geraldine Mason, and Doreen Stanton. On 30 Jun 1950 she was decorated by the French government with the Palmes Académiques and the title Officier d'Académie and in 1967 she received a *CFMTA Centennial Citation recognizing her as one of Canada's outstanding piano teachers. RDM

Lesage Pianos Ltd. A piano and organ manufacturing firm established in Ste-Thérèse-de-Blainville (renamed Ste-Thérèse), near Montreal, early in 1891 by Damase Lesage (d Sep 1923 or 1924). In 1892 Lesage went into partnership with Procule Piché and the firm became Lesage & Piché. Adélard Lesage (1879–1954), the son of Damase, later joined his father, and the name Lesage & Fils was adopted. Production rapidly increased, reaching an output of 500 pianos yearly, and Lesage & Fils became the most important supplier of pianos in Quebec. It produced instruments under its own name but also on behalf of the C.W. *Lindsay and *Willis companies. Because Willis & Co wanted to manufacture their own instruments, they acquired a majority of the shares in Lesage & Fils ca 1900. Adélard Lesage eventually sold his interest to the Willis family and in 1911 founded his own company, A. Lesage; he was joined by his sons Jacques-Paul ca 1925 and Gérard in 1929. The new concern flourished, and the factory was enlarged in 1916 and again in 1926. In 1930 Lesage bought the Craig Piano Co, which had been established in Montreal in 1856, in 1934 the *Bell Piano and Organ Co of Guelph, Ont, and in 1939 the *Weber Piano Co of Kingston, Ont. In addition to the pianos bearing his name, Lesage continued to manufacture such brand names as Bell, Mendelssohn, Schumann, and Belmont, all well known in Canada.

In 1942 the business adopted the name Lesage Pianos Ltd / Les Pianos Lesage Ltée, naming Jacques-Paul as president, Gérard as vice-president and the latter's son Jacques as director of marketing. About 1975 Gérard took over as president. The enduring popularity of the pianos made by Lesage, in 1980 the oldest surviving piano manufacturer in Quebec, has been due to their excellent sound as well as to the elegance and variety of their design. Lesaqe has specialized in uprights, although it did make some grand pianos ca 1934–48. In the 1970s distribution was exclusively Canadian, but at one time Lesage exported instruments to Europe, South America, and even to Japan and Australia. The cumulative total production, which was about 2100 in 1900, had risen to over 30,000 in 1950. About 1970 the company introduced an electronic piano, turning out some 280 in one year although only 12 were built in 1978. That year the firm's output of all types of piano was 1800. The Lesage firm has confined itself to manufacturing, leaving retail sales to agents. The firm employed about 60 people in 1979 at its factory on Lesage St, which received this name shortly after the 1911 founding of the firm. (DM)

Le SIEUR, Léo. Organist, pianist, composer, b Lowell, Mass, of French-Canadian parents, 21 May 1897. He studied piano, organ, and theory but began his career as a singer. He lived 1922–4 in Montreal but returned to New England, where he worked as an organist-choirmaster before settling permanently in Montreal in 1928.

Le Sieur recorded for the Apex label and was pianist or organist in various cinemas, including the Capitol. It was reported in *La Lyre* (April 1929) that 'he excels in the art of improvisation' and that his music 'helps the viewer to understand the dramas or comedies projected on the screen.' While studying with Rodolphe *Plamondon Le Sieur taught organ and piano. He conducted a dance band at the cabaret Au Matou botté, played at the Midway cinema, staged variety shows, and was producer, soloist, and accompanist at radio station CFCF.

Le Sieur worked for both the English and French networks of the CBC, directing the Sweet Caporal choir and orchestra 1934–7 and numerous other ensembles over the next 28 years. He coached several young artists, including *Aglaé, Pierrette *Alarie, Estelle Caron, Lucille *Dumont, and Monique *Leyrac. In 1965 he left the CBC but continued his private teaching.

Le Sieur composed songs and light instrumental works, many of which were published by Baron, Feist, and Prima, or in *La Lyre*, of which he was one of the founding directors. Some of his songs ('Pourquoi?,' 'I Went to the Market,' and 'Tou-di-la-di-tou,' sung or recorded by Fernand Gignac, Yoland *Guérard, Fernand Perron, and others) were very successful. A list of his organ recordings for Apex is found in *Roll Back the Years*. A prize bearing his name was awarded to Marc *Gélinas at the 1966 Festival du disque in Montreal. Le Sieur is a member of CAPAC. (HD-G)

The Leslie Bell Singers. The Alumnae Singers, a female choir formed in 1939 from former pupils of Leslie *Bell at Parkdale Collegiate Institute, Toronto, became the Leslie Bell Singers in 1945. They were perhaps the most popular choir in Canada in the late 1940s and early 1950s, partly because of their CBC programs 'Your Host – C.G.E.' on radio and 'C.G.E. Showtime' on TV.

Usually 30 voices but on occasion as many as 100, the singers combined a penchant for varied vocal effects (their staggered breathing in *God Save the Queen* left a generation of Canadians gasping), a healthy, blended sound, and strong showmanship. They toured in Canada and, beginning in 1951, in the USA (where they were heard on MBS radio) and sang for many years at the *CNE Bandshell. The repertoire, mostly unaccompanied, ranged from Palestrina to folk and popular arrangements and transcriptions, many by Bell himself.

Besides appearing in three NFB films – *Christmas Carols* (1947), *It's Fun to Sing* (1948), and *Choral Concert* (1949) – the Leslie Bell Singers recorded Christmas songs for RCI (166) and RCA (*The Story of the Nativity*, LCP 3001), pop songs for Dominion (*Sentimental Journey*, Dom 1203), and folksongs from English Canada for RCI (167).

Lois Ogilvie Blanchette, Marian Antliff Owens, Joyce *Sullivan, and Margaret Zeidman were among the more than 1000 who at one time or another were members of the choir. The singers disbanded after Bell's death in 1962, but were responsible for establishing in 1973 the Leslie Bell Scholarship competition for choral conductors.

BIBLIOGRAPHY
Gough, R.I. 'Leading man to 80 women,' *SatN*, 25 Dec 1948 (AHC)

Leslie Music Supply. Publishing company established in 1970 in Oakville, Ont, by Joan Leslie, who had purchased the stock of the *Western Music Co of Vancouver. In 1980 Leslie continued to publish choral music for church and school and pieces for piano, organ, and recorder (much of it reprinted Western material) by W. H. *Anderson, Hugh *Bancroft, Bernard *Naylor, Alec Rowley, and Healey *Willan. Leslie's printers, the W.R. *Draper Co of Weston, Ont, have not used plate numbers. Leslie became the Canadian distributor for J.B. Cramer, for Leonard, Gould and Bolttler, and for Pitman Hart (all of London), and for Brodt Music Co of Charlotte, NC. The company is a member of CAPAC. MWl

LETENDRE, Conrad. Organist, teacher, musicologist, composer, b St-Zéphyrin-de-Courval, near Trois-Rivières, Que, 9 Jan 1904, d Montreal 20 Nov 1977. As a student 1913–27 at the *Institut Nazareth for blind youth, Montreal, he was taught violin by Camille *Couture, piano and organ by Arthur *Letondal, and theory by Achille *Fortier and Romain *Pelletier. In St-Hyacinthe, Que, he was the organist 1927–33 at Notre-Dame-du-Rosaire Church and a teacher of piano and organ 1927–35 and 1942–52 at the seminary there. He also taught at the convents of the Soeurs de la Présentation and the Soeurs de Saint-Joseph. He served 1942–54 as artistic director of *La Bonne Chanson and 1952–4 as editor-in-chief of the periodical *Musique et musiciens*. He taught harmony 1955–62 and organography for two years at the *U of Montreal, and also organ at the Institut Nazareth.

Letendre taught theory or practical subjects to a number of prominent musicians, including Gaston *Arel, Jean *Chatillon, Raymond *Daveluy, Gilles Fortin, Kenneth *Gilbert, Bernard and Mireille *Lagacé, Lucienne *L'Heureux-Arel, Michel *Perrault, Gertrude Perrault-Mongeau, and Jeannine *Vanier, and to his wife, Aline Letendre (b Chénier).

Aline Letendre studied as well with Gabriel *Cusson, and taught theory 1968–71 at the Cons de Chicoutimi and thereafter at the CMM, where she had been Cusson's assistant 1955–68. She was appointed organist at the Gesù Church in Montreal in 1957.

With the help of an *MACQ bursary, and part of the time at his own expense, Conrad Letendre conducted research in musical science for several years, continuing to teach organ during that period. He left some teaching works which touched on his scientific work, and these (still unpublished in 1980) led two of his followers, Jean Chatillon and Michel Perrault, along with several others, to found in 1970 the Institut de sciences musicales Conrad Letendre, which later became *Pantonal Inc.

Conrad Letendre composed several organ works, including two suites and a *Berceuse modale*. His wife gave a recital of his works on CBC radio on the first anniversary of his death. A prize in his name – including a $500 scholarship – was awarded first in 1979 to the young Brantford, Ont, organist John Vandertuin. A Conrad Letendre Festival of four concerts at St-Hyacinthe took place in the spring of 1979.

BIBLIOGRAPHY
Chatillon, Jean. 'Le Cas Letendre,' *VM*, 14, Dec 1969 JC

Lethbridge. Alberta's third largest city, settled around 1870 and incorporated as a town in 1891 and as a city in 1906. It was named after William Lethbridge (1824–1901), first president of North Western Coal and Navigation Co. The population (approximately 50,000 in 1978) includes a large group of Japanese origin, and the district contains *Mennonite and *Hutterite communities. The main industries of the area are agriculture, coal mining, and farm-implement manufacture.

Documented early musical activities include a production of *The Pirates of Penzance* in the 1880s. In 1907 W.J. Nelson and his wife, Kate Bryce (b Marquis, a pupil of Frank *Welsman), began pioneer work in music. Ernest F. Layton, the organist at Knox Presbyterian Church prior to 1919, and his wife, Stella, a soprano, also were prominent until the 1930s. George and Katherine Brown (violin and piano respectively) accompanied silent movies and in 1935 established the city's first music store, later known as Leister's Music.

In 1933 Jack Patey formed a dance band called the Ambassadors' Orchestra. The military band of the 20th Battery, Royal Canadian Artillery, conducted by Lewis Hurlbutt, flourished in the late 1930s. Also discontinued by the war but revived briefly in the 1950s was the Rotary Club Minstrel Show begun by J. Milton Moffat in 1935. A 16-voice female choir, the Glee Singers, was founded in 1936 and directed by Janet McIlvena McLeod into the 1940s. Another female ensemble, the Youth Choir, formed in 1943 by Anne *Campbell, developed in 1963 into the Teen-Clefs, which in turn in 1968 became the nucleus of the Anne Campbell Singers. These groups won prizes in competitions in Europe and performed at *Expo 67 in Montreal and at Expo 70 in Osaka. The Lethbridge Junior Band (1946–67) was formed by Frank Hosek Sr.

Among touring performers who appeared in or near Lethbridge were Mart *Kenney and His Western Gentlemen, who in the 1930s played several summer engagements at Waterton Lakes Park, and the artists presented by the Lethbridge Women's Music Club (see Lethbridge Music Club). After its introduction to Alberta in 1946, Fred M. *Gee's Celebrity Concert Series, served Lethbridge, sponsored at first by the Lethbridge Junior Chamber of Commerce and later by the Quota Club. The Allied Arts Council of Lethbridge, organized in 1957, and the Lethbridge *Overture Concerts, formed in 1959, also presented touring artists. Harry Belafonte, Liona *Boyd, Clara Butt, the *Calgary Philharmonic Orchestra, *Canadian Brass, the *COC, the Don Cossack Choir, the *Edmonton SO, Mario Escuadero, the Fisk Jubilee Singers, Maureen *Forrester, Fernando Germani, the Glasgow Orpheus Choir, the Hart House String Quartet, the *Hertz Trio, Harry Lauder, Lois *Marshall, the Minneapolis SO, John Ogdon, *One Third Ninth, Lily Pons, Presti and Lagoya, *Quartet Canada, John Charles Thomas, Thomas L. Thomas, Jon *Vickers, the Vienna Boys Choir, and William Warfield are among the noted performers and performing groups who have appeared in Lethbridge.

In 1960 24 amateur musicians conducted by Albert Rodnunsky formed the Lethbridge SO. Kenneth Hicken replaced Rodnunsky for the 1966–7 season, followed by Peter Heyblom 1967–8, Wilf Woolhouse 1968–70, Lucien *Needham 1970–6, and John P. Jackson 1976–8. Stewart Grant succeeded Jackson in 1978. Clifford Palmer, the concertmaster 1961–77, was succeeded by Norbert Boehm. In 1977 the orchestra, with Louise Needham as the solo pianist, premiered Lethbridge composer-teacher Dean Blair's *Lethbridge Concerto*, commissioned by the orchestra with a grant from the *Canada Council. The orchestra – about 50 players in 1978 – also has played in several neighbouring communities (Pincher Creek, Taber, Fort McLeod, Vauxhall, Brooks, Medicine Hat, etc). Some of the orchestra's musicians joined various medical doctors, dentists, teachers, and students in 1963 to form the Big Band, conducted by J.H. Noble. Other offshoots of the Lethbridge SO have been the Symphony Chorus, the Symphony Women's League, and the Southern Showcase, which in 1964 became the Lethbridge Musical Theatre and presented *Finian's Rainbow* and *Oklahoma* under the direction of Rodnunsky.

In order to produce more string players a subcommittee of the symphony association set up the Lethbridge String Instrument Program. With Norbert Boehm as instructor, a school violin program (using the *Suzuki method) began in 1975. Cello classes started in 1978 under David Conroy. Boehm and Conroy were employed to form the beginnings of a professional core for the Lethbridge SO. The String Instrument Program, which they initiated with the support of *Alberta Culture, the Canada Council, School Districts 51 and 9, the Kiwanis Club, the *U of Lethbridge, and Dresser Clark Ltd, was so successful that the Lethbridge school system initiated a string program at the grade 4 level in September 1978.

Musical education in Lethbridge goes back at least to the 1920s, when P.J. Collins taught tonic sol-fa in elementary schools. Janet McIlvena McLeod, as 'Miss McIlvena,' presented on the CBC during the 1940s Alberta's first school broadcast, 'Sing and Play.' She was music supervisor in the city schools. In 1942, Kate B. Nelson and Florence B. Campbell organized the Lethbridge branch of the Alberta Music Teachers' Assn (*ARMTA after 1947). In 1965 Albert Rodnunsky started a school band program at Hamilton Junior High School. The Dept of Music of the U of Lethbridge opened in 1967 and granted its first B MUS in 1975.

The first Lethbridge District Competition Festival took place in 1930 with Healey *Willan as adjudicator. In 1952 the Lethbridge Festival Assn was taken over by the Kiwanis Club.

Among musicians born in or near Lethbridge are Dale *Bartlett (at New Dayton), Joni *Mitchell (at Fort McLeod), and Linda Lee *Thomas (at Cardston). (MN, PMW)

Lethbridge Music Club. Founded 26 Sep 1932 as the Lethbridge Women's Musical Club by Kate Bryce Marquis Nelson (1880–1959, a piano pupil of Frank *Welsman in Toronto and Isidor Philipp in Paris), who taught and performed in Lethbridge after 1907. The club was inactive during World War II but was revived in 1951 by Mrs W.A. Nelson, daughter-in-law of the founder. It was renamed the Lethbridge Music Club in 1958.

During its first years the club offered annually, at the Capitol Theatre, six concerts, including a 'young artist' recital (in conjunction with the *ARMTA and the *CFMTA) and a concert by Kiwanis scholarship winners and top examination students. In the 1970s, the annual number of concerts was reduced to four.

Maureen *Forrester, Carlina Carr, Constance *Channon Douglas, Bernard *Turgeon, the *Hart House Orchestra under Boyd *Neel, and Murray *Adaskin and Frances *James are among the established artists who have been presented. In 1958 the club established two scholarships for Kiwanis Music Festival winners. (MM)

LETONDAL. Family of musicians: 1 / Paul and 2 / Arthur, his son – both leading organists, pianists, and educators in Montreal – and 3 / Paul II and 4 / Henri, sons of Arthur.

1 **Paul**. Pianist, organist, cellist, teacher, composer, b Montbenoît, near Besançon, France, 25 Jan 1831, d Montreal 24 Jul 1894. Having lost his sight in early childhood, he received his training at the Institut des jeunes aveugles in Paris, studying piano with Kalkbrenner or one of his disciples. He moved to Montreal in 1852 and, at the request of the Jesuits, taught at the Collège Ste-Marie and was organist 1852–69 at the Gesù Chapel. The 'inimitable blind cellist' performed 27 Dec 1854 Franchomme's *Souvenir de Norma* and *Fantaisie brillante sur des thèmes russe et écossais* in the Bonsecours hall, along with a *Grande fantaisie concertante sur les airs nationaux, la Canadienne, God Save the Queen et St. Patrick's Day* by an anonymous composer (perhaps Letondal himself). At the piano he performed his own 'grande fantaisie,' *Souvenir de France*, and accompanied his pupil Denise Rapin, a 12-year-old 'Canadian prima donna.' Evidently he was involved in business as well, since Letondal and Co are advertised as importers of French pianos in *La Minerve* of January 1855.

Probably the first blind musician to settle in Canada, Letondal had some noteworthy pupils, eg, Édouard *Clarke, Euphémie Codère, Dominique *Ducharme, Joseph-A. *Fowler, Gustave *Gagnon, Calixa *Lavallée, Clarence *Lucas, Salomon *Mazurette, Charles-Marie *Panneton, Marie Regnault, Moïse and Joseph *Saucier, Marguerite Sym, Eugénie Tessier, and Antoinette Wilscam. He was a founding member and president 1882–3 and 1888–9 of the *AMQ, and also a founding member and director of *La Revue canadienne*. In 1876 he began to collaborate with Rosalie Euvrard in organizing the teaching of music at the *Institut Nazareth. A cultivated man and an outstanding musician, Paul Letondal must be considered one of the pioneers of the profession of music in Canada. In 1860 he married Élisabeth (Élise) Gagnon, sister of Ernest and Gustave Gagnon.

See also The blind.

BIBLIOGRAPHY

Gagnon, Blanche. 'Paul Letondal 1831–1894,' *La Musique*, vol 2, Mar 1920

Laurendeau, Arthur. 'Musiciens d'autrefois: Paul Letondal,' *Action nationale*, vol 36, Dec 1950

2 **Arthur** (Joseph August). Pianist, organist, teacher, writer on music, b Montreal 30 Apr 1869, d there 12 May 1956; lauréat (Brussels Cons) 1893, D MUS (Montreal) 1925. After studying with his father, he obtained his diploma ca 1886 at the *AMQ and taught for a few years at the Collège Ste-Marie. He then followed the advice Paul Letondal gave his most gifted pupils and spent the years 1890–4 in Europe. At the Paris Cons he studied piano with Antoine-François Marmontel and harmony with Antoine-Barthélémy Taudou. Drawn by the reputation of the organist Alphonse Mailly, he worked under his direction at the Brussels Cons, also studying with Édouard Samuel (harmony), Arthur de Greef (piano), and Ferdinand-Hubert Kufferath (counterpoint and fugue). Kufferath and Mailly had a profound influence on Letondal's career as an organist and an accompanist of Gregorian chant.

Arthur Letondal (*Le Samedi*, 6 Apr 1895)

Returning to Montreal Arthur Letondal was organist 1894–1900 at the Pères du St-Sacrament Church, 1900–23 at the Gesù Church (where he succeeded Dominique *Ducharme), and 1923–49 at St-Jacques-le-Majeur Cathedral, following Romain-Octave *Pelletier. Like his father, he was an exceptional teacher; he taught 1895–1900 at the *Canadian Artistic Society Cons, after 1901 at the *Institut Nazareth, 1904–10 at the *McGill Cons, and, most important, in 1943 he was appointed to the teaching staff of the CMM. He trained several winners of the *Prix d'Europe, including Léo-Pol *Morin (1912), Germaine *Malépart (1917), Paul *Doyon (1925), Alice Ste-Marie (1926), Rita Savard (1927), Gilberte *Martin (1930), Marcelle *Martin (1941), and Clermont *Pépin (1949), and he also taught Gabriel *Cusson, Isabelle *Delorme, his cousin Henri *Gagnon, Lucien Jolicoeur, Jules *Lamontagne, Conrad *Letendre, Raoul *Paquet, Éva *Plouffe, Paul *Pratt, Caroline *Racicot, Émiliano *Renaud, Georges-Émile *Tanguay, and others. He was a member of the Société des auteurs et éditeurs de musique (Paris), president 1898–9, 1905–6, 1913–14, and 1920–3 of the AMQ, and honorary president of the *Schola cantorum.

Arthur Letondal wrote works for piano including *Gavotte* (*Le Piano-Canada* 1895), *Trois Pièces de genre* (Hardy 1897), which subsequently were orchestrated by J.-J. *Gagnier, *Mazurka sentimentale* (*L'Art musical* 1899), *Berceuse* (Musica), *Sarabande* (Ditson), and *Danse Moyen Age* (Lavigueur & Hutchison); works for organ such as *Prélude grave* (Édition Belgo-Canadienne 1924), *Offertoire* (ibid 1925), and *Toccata* (J. Fischer); and religious songs.

Letondal gave numerous lectures and wrote articles for several publications. His study of Calixa Lavallée was published in *L'Action française* (Oct 1919) and reprinted in *La Musique* (Feb 1920) and *Musique et musiciens* (Nov 1952). He also wrote 'Considerations générales sur l'éducation musicale au Canada' (*L'Art musical*, Oct 1896), 'Un musicien oublié, Charles Waugh Sabatier' (*L'Action nationale*, Oct 1933), 'Le Gesù ... musical!' (*Album annuel du collège Sainte-Marie*, Montreal 1939), and 'Ernest Gagnon, écrivain et folkloriste' (*Qui?* Mar 1951).

BIBLIOGRAPHY

Tanguay, Yves. 'Nos jeunes artistes trouveront toujours avantage à étudier dans les grands centres d'Europe et d'Amérique,' *P-T*, 882, Jan 1945

3 **Paul** II. Physician, violinist, critic, b Montreal 29 Oct 1898. He took violin lessons with Alfred *De Sève while studying medicine. His articles appeared in various publications including *La Musique* (1919) and the Montreal newspaper *Le Devoir*. He is the father of the actresses Lucienne and Ginette Letondal.

4 **Henri**. Critic, administrator, cellist, playwright, actor, b Montreal 1901, d Hollywood 1955. He studied the cello with Gustave *Labelle. He was a man of wide interests and wrote many sketches and revues, including, on occasion, the music. He began ca 1929 to cover concerts and variety shows for *La Patrie* (Montreal) and served 1926–9 as that paper's Paris correspondent. He also wrote about music for *Le Petit Journal* and was music critic ca 1935 for *Le Canada*. For CKAC radio in Montreal he was artistic director 1929–37 of 'L'Heure provinciale,' which was sponsored by the Quebec government to promote the province's musicians and composers. He founded on St-Denis St, Montreal, and directed 1930–1 the artists' cabaret Le Matou botté, which sometimes featured classical singers, including Germaine *Bruyère, Louis *Chartier, and Georges Bétournay. In 1934 he played a central part in the formation of the *CSM. It has been estimated that Henri Letondal wrote some 160 radio plays 1937–48, producing them himself and occasionally writing the music. He also was director general of the film company France-Film. In the early 1950s he embarked on a Hollywood screen career and took a prominent role in the film *The Razor's Edge*. GP

LÉTOURNEAU. 1 / Antonio and 2 / Marthe, his daughter.

1 **Antonio**. Organist, pianist, teacher, b Quebec City 28 Aug 1885, d Montreal 29 Oct 1948. As a child he was a soloist in Notre-Dame Church in Montreal. He began his musical studies in 1900 with Caroline *Racicot and after 1904 was a pupil of R.-O. *Pelletier (piano and organ) and later of Alfred *Laliberté. He was organist 1917–20 of St-Georges Church and 1920–48 of St-Louis-de-France, where he had been assistant organist 1913–17. He was a teacher of solfège at the *Schola cantorum, taught piano and organ privately and at the *Cons national, and was on the conservatory's board of directors. His pupils included Françoise *Aubut and Colombe *Pelletier. In 1912 he married the singer Marie-Anne Godbout (b Quebec City 8 Oct 1885, d Montreal 5 Mar 1972).

2 **Marthe**. Soprano, teacher, b Quebec City 27 Jun 1916. She took lessons in piano, phonetics, and diction before studying singing 1934–44 with Salvator *Issaurel and Pauline *Donalda. In 1938 she placed first in her competitions in the Quebec Music Festival and won a silver medal. She sang often 1940–50 on Montreal radio stations CKAC and CKVL and on the CBC, gave recitals in the other provinces, and undertook several roles for the *Opéra national du Québec and the *Variétés lyriques. Her roles for the latter included Antonia in *The Tales of Hoffmann* in 1942. The same year, she created Josette in the premiere of Eugène *Lapierre's comic opera *Le Père des Amours*. In 1948 she won CBC radio's *'Opportunity Knocks' and made her debut at the *Opera Guild as Gilda in *Rigoletto*. She sang this role 'with an infinite regard for truth,' according to Jean *Vallerand of Montreal's *Le Devoir*, who also noted the mastery of technique evident in her remarkable vocal shading. With the violinist Noël *Brunet and the pianist Gilles Breton she made one of the first three tours organized 1949–50 by the newly founded *JMC.

In 1950 Létourneau went to Europe as soloist with the *Disciples de Massenet and, on a grant from the Quebec government, stayed in France and Italy. In Paris she worked with Pierre Bernac; in Rome, with Luigi Ricci and Ré Koster. She gave radio recitals in France and took part in concerts conducted by Nadia Boulanger.

Back in Canada Létourneau toured again 1952–3 for the JMC and frequently appeared on the CBC TV programs 'L'*Heure du concert' and 'Concerts pour la jeunesse.' She completed her training at the *CMM 1957–8 with Bernard *Diamant, Dick Marzollo, and Otto-Werner *Mueller. During the 1960–1 season, after a JM tour of 50 concerts in France as member of a vocal quartet, she toured for the JMC in Maurice *Blackburn's **Silent Measures*.

Marthe Létourneau appeared as soloist with the *MSO and the *Quebec SO and taught voice 1940–2 at Sherbrooke's Mont Notre-Dame, 1960–2 at the *École Vincent-d'Indy, 1960–6 at the *Institut Nazareth, 1962–3 at the Institut pédagogique de Montréal, and 1960–6 at the Grey Nuns' School in Hull. She began teaching at *Laval U in September 1966 and was a member of a vocal quartet there 1972–4.

DISCOGRAPHY

Brahms *Berceuse* – Chaminade *L'Anneau d'argent*. Bluebird 55 5222 (78)

Thomas *Connais-tu le pays?* – Godard *La Chanson de Florian* – Beaulieu *L'Alouette du matin*. Bluebird 55 5212 (78)

See also *Silent Measures* / *Une mesure de silence*. GP, IP-C

LÉTOURNEAU. Quebec City family of musicians: 1 / Omer; 2 / Paul, 3 / Jean, and 4 / Claude, sons of Omer; and Coleen (with her father 3 / Jean).

1 (Joseph Hercule) **Omer**. Organist, pianist, composer, music dealer, publisher, and teacher, b Quebec City 13 Mar 1891. His father gave him his first lessons. At 11 he was able to substitute for the school's music teacher for a whole term. In 1904 he began lessons in piano and organ with J.-Arthur *Bernier. In August 1907 he became organist at Notre-Dame-de-Lourdes Chapel, while continuing his studies and working in a commercial establishment. In 1912 he graduated from the *AMQ and the following year he won the *Prix d'Europe for organ.

In 1913 Létourneau settled in Paris and began studying organ with Louis Vierne and harmony and composition with Félix Fourdrain. The war put an abrupt end to his stay, and he returned to Quebec City in 1914. The following year he was appointed orqanist at St-Sauveur Church, succeeding his former teacher J.-Arthur Bernier. Early in 1919 he founded the monthly journal *La *Musique* and managed it with Hector Faber. In November he returned to Europe to claim the second year to which the Prix d'Europe entitled him. He enrolled in the organ class of Abel Decaux at the Schola Cantorum in Paris and took courses in Gregorian chant with Amédée Gastoué, improvisation with Lejealle, and choir conducting with Marc de Ranse.

In June 1920 Létourneau returned to Quebec City, where he resumed his work as organist of St-Sauveur and editor of *La Musique*. He was active as a pianist, performing in recital with Arthur *LeBlanc, Paul *Dufault, Théodore Botrel, and, above all, with the violinist Edwin *Bélanger, who later was to become his son-in-law and his partner in a series of some 125 sonata performances over the radio station CHRC in 1935.

During this time (1925–34) Létourneau taught privately and at *Laval U and gave courses at the Académie commerciale de Québec and at the Ursuline convents in Trois-Rivières and Rimouski. He was president of the AMQ 1935–8. In 1934 he acquired Gauvin & Courchesne, a music firm which he had helped found. As the *Procure générale de musique it became a publishing establishment and music store.

Létourneau's considerable output as a composer includes three operettas – *Vive la canadienne* (1924), *Coup d'soleil* (1930), and *Mam'zelle Bébé* (1933) – all of which were staged successfully at the *Palais Montcalm and performed elsewhere in the province; a cantata, *Dieu te garde, mon Canada* (Procure générale 1934); seven masses; some songs (sung by Paul Dufault and Rodolphe *Plamondon among others); hymns for solo or chorus; and folksong arrangements. His instrumental works, fewer in number, consist of pieces for piano, violin, and organ, mostly published by Procure générale.

In addition Létourneau wrote theoretical works including *École de dictée musicale* (in 2 vols), *Théorie de la musique* (Quebec 1943), and *Questionnaire de la théorie musicale*. In 1978 he completed his memoirs with the assistance of Cécile Huot.

Létourneau's wife's sister, the pianist Clotilde Coulombe, b Quebec City 4 Apr 1892, studied with J.-Arthur Bernier and was the first recipient of the Prix d'Europe in 1911. She studied in Paris with Alfred Cortot and Alfred Casella (piano), Félix Fourdrain (harmony), Lucien Berton (voice), and Camille Chevillard (ensemble). For a year after her return she was active as teacher and concert pianist, but she ended her career to enter a religious order. Returning later to secular life for reasons of health, she subsequently married Dr Gaston Ouellette.

BIBLIOGRAPHY

La Musique (1919–24)

Morisset, Denis. 'Dans un bain de musique perpétuel,' *Culture vivante*, 17, May 1970

'L'Homme extraordinaire de la Procure générale de musique a pris sa retraite,' *Musique périodique*, vol 1, Nov 1976

2 **Paul**. Cellist, administrator, b Quebec City 21 Oct 1916. He studied cello in Quebec with Pierre Marchand and Henri Talbot and in Montreal with Jean *Belland, continuing 1938–40 at the Juilliard School with Willem Willeke and 1942–4 at the *TCM with Leo *Smith and Zara *Nelsova. In the ensuing years he became one of Quebec's most prominent instrumentalists. He began teaching at the *CMQ in 1945, played for 10 years in the *Quebec SO, and gave recitals on CBC radio. He also specialized in the technology of instruments, especially the piano.

3 **Jean**. Tenor, french hornist, teacher, b Quebec City 12 Apr 1921. He studied singing 1944–5 at the TCM. He played french horn for a time, mainly in the *Quebec SO in 1947, but then devoted his energies to singing and performed 1948–51 at Radio City Music Hall in New York. He has sung in opera and oratorio in Montreal and Toronto and has been a soloist with the *TSO and the *Toronto Mendelssohn Choir. He later opened a teaching studio in Edmonton. He was the founder of the Edmonton Professional Opera Assn (*Edmonton Opera Assn) and its first artistic director 1963–6. In 1969 he was appointed soloist at Edmonton's St Joseph's Cathedral. In 1972 he joined the faculty of the *U of Alberta. His wife (m 1946), the pianist

Kathleen Busbee, became attached to the U of Alberta as an accompanist.

Their daughter Colleen (soprano, b New York 27 Sep 1948) began her career as a dancer and was a member of the Alberta Ballet Company for nine years. She studied singing with her father and in 1975 became a pupil of Léopold *Simoneau in San Francisco. She has taken part in productions by the Edmonton Opera (*La Traviata, Carmen, Madama Butterfly*) and by the *Banff SFA (Menotti's *The Telephone*). She also appeared (1968) in the musical comedy *Bye Bye Birdie* at the Civic Musical Theatre in Edmonton.

4 **Claude**. Violinist, educator, b Quebec City 11 Nov 1924. He studied violin with Edwin *Bélanger and Arthur *LeBlanc and entered, in turn, the *CMQ, the *CMM, and the *TCM. Between 1941 and 1947 he took courses in violin, clarinet, and conducting in New York and at the Berkshire Music Center. He was awarded seven bursaries by the Quebec government and obtained the *Prix d'Europe in 1945. In 1948 he became a teacher at the CMQ and the *Seminaire de Québec where he directed the Société Ste-Cécile 1960–ca 1967. While a member of the *Quebec SO 1940–63 and 1973–9, he founded the Létourneau String Quartet which gave concerts in schools throughout the Quebec City region between 1950 and 1960. He founded the *Société musicale Le Mouvement Vivaldi.

JB-T

LÉTOURNEAU, Claude. Baritone, choirmaster, educator, b Montreal 26 May 1923; premier prix singing (CMM) 1954. He held advanced certificates in teaching (École normale Jacques-Cartier 1944) and in Gregorian chant (Laval U 1948) and studied voice with Pauline *Donalda and Victor *Brault and at the CMM with Martial Singher. He was on staff 1946–69 at the École normale Jacques-Cartier, first as teacher of music education and later as director of students. He then became, in turn, coordinator of the arts division and director of audio-visual production for the Quebec ministry of education. He was choirmaster 1953–76 at Notre-Dame Church, Montreal, and in 1954 he began his career as a singer, performing on radio and TV and with the *Opera Guild, the *MSO, the *Montreal Festivals, the *SMCQ, the *Opéra du Québec, and other organizations. As a member of the Montreal Vocal Trio and of the *Petit Ensemble vocal, he has participated in many CBC broadcasts. He sings the role of Monsieur Dolmont in the recording of *Colas et Colinette*. In 1980 he succeeded René *Lacourse as director of *Les Disciples de Massenet.

JCl

LEUPOLD, Ulrich (Siegfried). Musicologist, Lutheran minister, administrator, b Berlin 15 Jan 1909, d Kitchener, Ont, 9 Jun 1970; PH D musicology (Berlin) 1932, hon DD (Knox College) 1969. His father was an organist, his mother a voice teacher. He emigrated in 1938 to the USA, settling briefly in Toledo, O, before moving in 1939 to Kitchener, Ont, where he was ordained. He served as a pastor in Kitchener and Maynooth, Ont, until 1945, when he taught New Testament theology and church music at Waterloo Lutheran Seminary and was music director at Waterloo College (see Wilfrid Laurier U). He became dean, and in 1968 principal, of the seminary.

One of the first trained musicologists to settle in Canada, Leupold was a specialist in Lutheran church music. He contributed to many musical and theological journals and reference books and edited collections and individual pieces of church music. He served on many Lutheran and ecumenical councils, in 1965 was chairman of the committee on music of the Lutheran Church of America Commission on Worship, and in 1966 was president of the Canadian Society of Biblical Studies.

See also Lutherans.

WRITINGS

Die liturgischen Gesange der evangelischen Kirche im Zeitalter der Aufklärung und der Romantik (Kassel 1933)

'Lied, C.,' 'Das Kirchenliede, 11,' 'Nordamerika,' *MGG* (Kassel 1960)

– ed *Luther's Works*, vol 53, *Liturgy and Hymns* (Philadelphia 1967)

The Two-Staff Organ Book, 2 vol (Waterloo Music 1948, 1953)

The Church Choir, 2 vol (Waterloo 1950, 1951)

Liturgical Chorale Book (Augsberg Publishing House 1955)

Organ Book (Chantry Music Press 1962)

A Manual on Intoning (Fortress Press 1967)

Laudamus: Hymnal for the Lutheran World Federation, 4th ed (Geneva 1970)

BIBLIOGRAPHY

Vita Laudanda: Essays in Memory of Ulrich S. Leupold, ed Erich Schultz (Waterloo 1976)

HK

LeVASSEUR, (Louis-Zéphirin) **Nazaire**. Historian, organist, violinist, bassist, composer, b Quebec City 6 Feb 1848, d there 8 Nov 1927. At six he began to study music with Antoine *Dessane. While completing his academic studies at the Petit Séminaire de Québec and taking medical courses at Laval U, he took lessons in piano, organ, and flute and studied violin with Roch *Lyonnais. In 1869 he helped Dessane found the *Société musicale Ste-Cécile, serving as assistant director and 1873–85 as director. In 1878 he conducted Félicien David's *La Perle du Brésil*. LeVasseur was a founder (1871) and the second violin of the *Septuor Haydn and served the group later as secretary and president. He succeeded Dessane in 1873 as organist of St-Roch Church (serving until 1881) and Calixa *Lavallée in 1880 as director of the Quatuor vocal.

In 1880 LeVasseur served as secretary of the music committee which had been established by the St-Jean-Baptiste Society to commission a national anthem. He recounted the origin of *'O Canada' in an article, 'La genèse de l'hymne national "Ô Canada!"' (Montreal *La Presse*, 11 Dec 1920), the essence of which was reproduced in *Vie Musicale* (vol 3, 1966).

LeVasseur was a lieutenant in the 9th Infantry Regiment (Quebec Rifles) and participated in the campaign to put down the North West Rebellion of 1885, rising to the rank of major on his return to Quebec City. He played double bass for the Société symphonique de Québec (*Quebec SO, founded in 1903), and served the orchestra as vice-president. He left several works, including the songs 'Aurora Snow Shoe Club' (Quebec City 1884), 'Le Jour de l'An' and 'On me disait' (Demers & Frère, Quebec City 1887); other songs; a romance for string quintet; and a military march.

LeVasseur wrote a series of historical and geographical articles published 1884–1913 in the report *Société de géographie de Québec*. His name is remembered chiefly, however, for a series of chronicles and reminiscences published 1919–22 in *La Musique* under the title 'Musique et musiciens à Québec' and in the volume *Réminiscences d'antan* (Quebec City 1926). In his writings, anecdotal flavour sometimes prevails over historical accuracy, but they remain important sources of information about musical life in Quebec in the 19th century.

At LeVasseur's death, *La Presse* wrote: 'With him disappears one of Quebec's most colourful characters, and one of her best artists, a lively and talented writer who for fifty years was involved in the political, social and artistic life of Champlain's city.'

GP

LÉVEILLÉE, Claude. Singer-songwriter, actor, b Montreal 16 Oct 1932; BA (Montreal) 1954. He made his debut in 1955 in the revue *Bleu et Or* at the *U of Montreal, where he was studying social sciences. In 1956 he was seen in 'Le Secret de la Rivière perdue' on CBC TV; he also created a character, Clo-Clo, as well as the decor, continuity, scripts, and music for the children's TV program 'Domino' 1957–9 and 1961–2. With other Quebec chansonniers he founded Les Bozos in 1959. Among his first songs were 'Frédéric,' 'L'Hiver,' 'Les Vieux Pianos,' and 'Rendez-vous.' He worked in Paris 1959–60 with Édith Piaf, who in 1963 recorded songs he had written for her: 'Boulevard du crime,' 'Ouragan,' 'La Voix' (ballet), and 'Le Vieux Piano' (a new version of 'Les Vieux Pianos'). In 1964 he became the first Quebec artist to give a solo performance at the *PDA. He collaborated with the pianist and arranger André *Gagnon 1962–9; subsequently his accompanists have been Pierre *Leduc 1970–2, Cyrille Beaulieu 1973–5, Michel Lefrançois 1975–7, and Réjean Émond beginning in 1977.

Léveillée made many tours in Canada, France (appearing in particular in Paris at the Théâtre de Bobino and the Olympia), the USSR (1968, 1972), and Japan (1970), as well as in Belgium, Switzerland, and central Asian countries. In 1972 he represented the Quebec chanson at the Sopot Festival in Poland. He has written the music for several CBC TV plays, including a French version of 'Of Mice and Men,' 'L'Échéance du vendredi,' 'Le Pélican,' and 'Millionnaire à froid,' and has collaborated with the author Marcel Dubé and the producer and director Louis-Georges Carrier in the production of such dramas as *Zone, Au retour des oies blanches*, and *Un Simple Soldat*. He also composed the music for the film *Les Beaux Dimanches* (1973) and wrote seven musical comedies: *Doux Temps des amours* (1964), *Il est une saison* (1965), *Ne ratez pas l'espion* (1966), *Elle tournera la terre* (1967), *On n'aime qu'une fois* (1967), *L'Arche de Noé* (1968), and *Posters* (1968). He composed the sung concerto *Contact* (1972) and also set to music a tale by Gilles *Vigneault, *Le Dict de l'aigle et du castor* (1972); some traditional stories *Salut l'Indien* and *Requiem 1837* (1977); and a tale by Félix *Leclerc, *Le Petit Ours gris de la Mauricie* (1977). A book of Leveillée's poems, *L'Étoile d'Amérique*, was published in Montreal in 1971. Early in 1976 on tour in Quebec he presented an autobiographical stage show entitled 'Ce matin un homme' and wrote the ballet *Fleur de lit*, danced by Les Ballets-Jazz du Québec during the Montreal Olympic Games. He participated in 1976 and 1977 in the *St-Jean Baptiste celebrations in Montreal and appeared in 1977 in several TV specials in Paris, Montreal, and Toronto. He composed the musical drama *Concerto pour Hélène* in honour of Hélène Boulé, the wife of Samuel de Champlain, the founder of Quebec City. The *Quebec SO, Danielle Licari, and the choir of St-Dominique Church premiered the work, 3 Jul 1978, as part of the city's 370th anniversary celebrations.

Julie Arel, Isabelle Aubret, Neil *Chotem, René *Claude, André Gagnon, Daniel Guichard, Pauline *Julien, Georgette Lemaire, Monique *Leyrac, and Roger Williams are among the artists who have sung or played Léveillée's songs. He has won several awards, including the Grand Prix du disque canadien of Montreal radio station CKAC (1962), the Grand Prix of the 1966 Montreal Festival du disque in the singer-songwriter category (Prix La Bolduc), and a prize in 1977 from the Académie Charles-Cros in Paris for the LP *1 fois 5* (see Discography for Chansonniers). Léveillée is a member of CAPAC.

From 'Frédéric' to 'L'Étoile d'Amérique' Léveillée has contributed many outstanding works to

Quebec music; through their intensity of expression and sincerity, his compositions have reached a very high level of attainment. Always deeply felt and often steeped in nostalgia, Léveillée's works appeal to widely diverse social groups. In *La Chanson québécoise* Benoît L'Herbier described him as a 'creator of immediate and moving melodies of indefinable beauty' (Montreal 1974). His lyrics reflect the universal themes of love, solitude, and sometimes even despair.

DISCOGRAPHY

Claude Léveillée (Les Vieux Pianos). 1961. Col FS 535
Claude Léveillée (Frédéric). 1962. Harmony HFS 9084
Léveillée-Gagnon (Poissons). Léveillée pf, Gagnon pf. 1963. Col FS 631
Léveillée + 10 (Encore). 1963. Col FS 646
Claude Léveillée à la PDA. 1964. Harmonie KHF 90209
Claude Léveillée chante Un simple soldat. 1964. Col FS 651
Clo-Clo à la ferme. 1964. Col HFL 8001
1 voix, 2 pianos. Léveillée pf, Gagnon pf. 1964. Col FS 662
Léveillée à Paris (Mon pays). 1965. Col FS 618
Noël avec Clo-Clo. 1965. Col HFL 8003
Léveillée à Paris (Les Coeurs). 1966. Col FS 639
Elle tournera la terre. 1967. Col FS 677
Le Cérémonial de l'amour. 1968. Col FS 726
L'Étoile d'Amérique. 1968. Leko KS 100
Claude Léveillée (Une petite fleur). 1969. Leko KS 101
Clo-Clo et Bibi en vacances. 1969. Barclay 10021
Si jamais / If ever. 1969. Leko KS 102/Leko KS 103
Cheval de bois. 1971. Barclay 80125
Les Grands Succès de Claude Léveillée. (1971?). Col GFS 90012
Claude Léveillée. (1972). Harmonie KHF 90086
La Vie en elle. G. Gondin narr. 1972. Barclay 80140.
Les Amoureux de l'an 2000. 1972. Barclay 80174
Contact. 1973. Barclay 80147
Les Beaux Dimanches. 1973. Barclay 80202
Une Nuit, un moment. Gagnon pf. (1973). Col GFS 90128
Dix Succès pour toi de Claude Léveillée. 1974. Barclay 80206
Pour les amants. (1974?). GFS 90122
On remonte en amour. 1975. Barclay 80216
Léveillée PDA 1976. 2-Kébec-Disc KD-M911-912
Le Temps d'une saison (Leclerc-Léveillée). 1977. Poly 2675 144
Black Sun. 1978. Poly 2424 171

BIBLIOGRAPHY

Bisbrouck, Noel. 'Claude Léveillée: from song to musical comedy,' *CanComp*, 25, Jan 1968
Gingras, Claude. 'Claude Léveillée back from USSR tour,' *CanComp*, 34, Nov 1968
Genest, Jean et al. 'Léveillée,' *Musique: orchestres et analyses d'oeuvres* (Montreal 1972)
Champagne, Jane. 'A Quebec composer on the move again,' *CanComp*, 77, Feb 1973
Chansonniers du Québec (BLH, DM, ST)

LÉVESQUE, Raymond. Singer-songwriter, actor, b Montreal 7 Oct 1928. After studying the piano with Rodolphe *Mathieu and drama with Mme Jean-Louis Audet, he began writing songs in 1943. In 1947 he came to the attention of Fernand Robidoux, who invited him to appear on his CKAC (Montreal) radio program and performed some of his compositions. Lévesque was co-host 1949–51 of the CBC radio program 'Grand'maman Marie' and later was a singer and host in programs on CKAC ('Paulette et Raymond' with Paulette de Courval) and CHLP ('Raymond Lévesque et ses chansons'). After serving as host 1952–4 for the CBC TV variety series 'Mes Jeunes Années' with Colette Bonheur, he left for Paris. He remained there for five years, singing in cabarets in Montmartre (Patachou, Chez ma cousine) and on the Left Bank (L'Échelle de Jacob, L'Écluse). He also made four singles for Barclay, performed on several radio programs, and toured France with the entertainer Annie Cordy. Eddy Constantine recorded Lévesque's song 'Les Trottoirs' in 1954, while Bourvil popularized his 'La Vénus à Mimile.' In 1956 Lévesque wrote *'Quand les hommes vivront d'amour.'

On his return to Montreal Lévesque performed 1959–60 as a member of the Bozos, sang in various clubs (Le Club des Arts, Le P'tit Caporal), and acted on stage and in TV dramas, often appearing in the plays of Marcel Dubé. While working in a succession of his own cabarets (Le Bar du Music-Hall, Parlement, L'Évêché), he staged some 40 revues (summers 1961–74) at the Butte à Mathieu in Val-David, north of Montreal. He has been a featured performer in many variety shows in Montreal (at *Expo 67, Comédie-Canadienne, Le *Patriote, *PDA) and Quebec City (La Résille, *Grand Théâtre) and has been a guest on many TV programs.

In 1980, after a career of more than 30 years, Raymond Lévesque remained as Claude *Gingras once described him in *La Presse* (Montreal 19 Feb 1968): 'a genuine artist, who has something to say, who has wit, who can fine just the right words, and who knows how to write a song.' Through his poems, his monologues, and such songs as 'Le Coeur du Bon Dieu,' 'Rosemont sous la pluie,' and 'Bozo-les-culottes,' he has slowly drawn away from the influence of Charles Trenet. His compositions, at one time so sentimental, have become more and more humorous, incisive, and socially committed. Without really ever achieving stardom himself, Lévesque opened the way for the wave of chansonniers in the 1960s. He published several collections of poetry – *Quand les hommes vivront d'amour* (Quebec 1968), *Au fond du chaos* (Montreal 1971), *Le Malheur a pas des bons yeux* (Montreal 1971), and *On veut rien savoir* (Montreal 1974) – and one play, *Bigaouette* (Montreal 1970).

DISCOGRAPHY

À la Butte à Mathieu. (1966). Gamma GS-102
Après 20 ans ... (1967). Gamma GS-111
Chansons et monologues de Raymond Lévesque. Sel M-298.045
Raymond Lévesque. 1969?. Alouette SAD.519
Raymond Lévesque chante les travailleurs. 1975. Deram DEF.1004
Le P'tit Québec de mon coeur. 1977. Filoson FIL 77101
See also Discography for Chansonniers.

BIBLIOGRAPHY

Léger, Pierre. 'Mon ami Raymond Lévesque,' *Maclean*, Jun 1965
Saint-Jean, Armand. 'Raymond Lévesque 20 ans après,' Montreal *La Presse*, 28 Oct 1967
L'Herbier, Benoît. *La Chanson québécoise* (Montreal 1974)
Thériault, Jacques. 'En poésie comme en chanson ... Raymond Lévesque continue à dénoncer "les misères" de l'humanité actuelle,' Montreal *Le Devoir*, 19 Feb 1975
Corrivault, Martine. ' "Le plus difficile, au Québec, c'est de durer"(Raymond Lévesque),' Quebec *Le Soleil*, 14 Aug 1976 (BLH)

LEVITAN, Samuel. Pianist, conductor, composer, teacher, b Buckingham, near Hull, Que, 24 Sep 1919. His teachers included Paul *de Marky (piano 1933–8), Claude *Champagne (theory and composition, 1937–8 and 1940–3), James Friskin (piano, 1938–40 at the Juilliard School), Auguste *Descarries (piano, 1943–6 at the CMM and 1946–50 privately), and Léon Barzin (conducting, 1943–6 at the CMM).

Levitan made his debut at *Tudor Hall, Montreal, in 1936 and began performing on CBC radio in 1939. He was soloist with the *MSO in 1949 and with the *'Little Symphonies' in 1954 and the *CBC SO in 1960. He toured in Canada as a partner to the violinist Arthur *Garami and the cellist Walter *Joachim in 1955 and to the violinist François D'Albert in 1956 and has appeared in recital in Montreal and Toronto. He premiered Marvin *Duchow's *Prelude* (1947) and *Sonata* (1956), Ernest Bloch's *Piano Sonata* (1950, Canadian premiere), Alexander *Brott's *Vignettes en caricature* (1956), Harry *Somers' *Sonata No. 3* (1958), and Samuel *Dolin's *Queekhoven and A.J.* (1976, commissioned for him by the *OAC).

Levitan was a founder, in 1948, of the Jewish Music Forum in Montreal and was conductor 1945–7 of the YMHA Orchestra and 1964–7 of the annual *Jewish Music Month concerts. He began teaching piano in 1940 and was an instructor 1955–63 at the *McGill Cons. In 1973 he began teaching at the *RCMT.

Levitan's compositions include the ballet suite *And Time Is the Master*, premiered in 1954 on CBC TV under his direction, and *Hebraic Miniatures* for violin and piano, premiered in 1956 on the CBC by François D'Albert and the composer. Levitan's *Four Poems by Carl Sandburg* (1956) and *Psalm 23* (1960) were premiered by his wife, the mezzo-soprano and pianist Fanny Gabinet (b Brussels 5 Jun 1928).

Levitan has contributed reviews to *The *Canada Music Book*.

LEWIS, Doris (b Mills). Teacher, soprano, b Fort William (Thunder Bay), Ont, 1908, d Vancouver 29 Dec 1966. She studied piano in Fort William and voice (with Ruth Morgan) and piano in Brandon, Man, before moving to Winnipeg. There she concentrated on voice, studying with a succession of teachers including Stanley *Hoban, Gladys *Whitehead, and J. Roberto Wood. She also took some lessons with John *Goss. She was never a leading soloist, but she sang in several choirs, including the CBC *Choristers.

Lewis became known as one of Canada's outstanding teachers. Her pupils were noted for warm, natural, well-projected sound, fine enunciation, and a developed sense of musical values. In 28 years in Winnipeg, where she taught 1938–46 at the *Bornoff School and 1946–66 privately, her pupils included Paul *Fredette, Joan *Hall, Norma Harrison, Dorothy Howard Brooks, Gladys *Kriese-Caporale, Joan *Maxwell, Norman *Mittelmann, Mary *Morrison, Kathleen Morrison Brown, Anne Mounce, Elaine Oakley, Henriette Platford (*Ascher Duo), Robert Publow, Sylvia *Saurette, and Phyllis (*Cooke) Thomson. CC

LEYRAC, Monique (b Tremblay, m Dalmain). Singer, actress, b Montreal 26 Feb 1928. She studied drama with Jeanne *Maubourg and in 1943 took the role of Bernadette in Franz Werfel's *Le Chant de Bernadette* on radio station CKAC's 'Radio-théâtre Lux.' After some years as a radio actress she turned to singing and appeared in 1948 at the cabaret Au Faisan doré with Charles Aznavour, Pierre Roche, and Jacques Normand, performing South American songs and drawing on the repertoire of Édith Piaf. She made a few 78s for *RCA Victor, played and sang Pierre Pitel's songs in the film *Lumières de ma ville* at the end of 1949, and made a tour 1950–1 of France, Switzerland, and Belgium, and also performed in Lebanon. On her return to Montreal she sang in the cabarets Le Montmartre and Au St-Germain-des-Prés and met the French actor Jean Dalmain, whom she married in 1952. Following two sojourns in Paris (1952–4, 1955–8), during which she worked in the theatre, she was seen in Montreal in many roles, including Polly Peachum in the Brecht-Weill musical *The Threepenny Opera* (1962). With Pierre Thériault she co-starred 1962–4 in the CBC radio show 'Plein de soleil.'

The growing popularity of Quebec songwriters induced Leyrac to develop a new repertoire that included their work, though she still retained some French songs. She completed her first recording of songs by *Vigneault and *Léveillée in 1963. The following year she was the host and featured singer in CBC TV's 'Pleins feux' and co-star at *PDA with the Swingle Singers. She was chosen by the CBC to sing at the 1965 International Song Festival in Sopot, Poland, and won the Grand Prix of

Monique Leyrac

International Day for her rendition of Vigneault's *'Mon Pays' and that of Polish Day with 'La Petite Mélodie qui revient.' In the same year she won the Grand Prix at the Song Festival in Ostend, Belgium. She then performed at Town Hall, New York; the day after the concert Simone Auger wrote: 'Monique Leyrac is unique. And US audiences know it well, responding with deafening applause after each song and reserving an ovation for the end ... All subjects and all registers suit her. She makes transitions from French to English and from past to present with extraordinary ease ... Besides a voice and an intelligence she has at her command the skills of the actress.' (Montreal *La Presse*, 26 Mar 1966).

Shortly after this Leyrac starred in the variety show 'Pleins feux sur le Canada' at the Olympia in Paris and toured the USSR, appearing in Moscow, Leningrad, Tallinn, and other cities. She taped 39 radio shows for the CBC in Toronto. In 1967 she appeared at *Massey Hall in Toronto, at Carnegie Hall in New York, and before Princess Margaret in London. Accompanied by the pianist André *Gagnon, she also performed at the Expo Theatre and at the Canadian Pavilion at *Expo 67. She was a guest on 'The Rolf Harris Show' (BBC London, 1968) and 'The Ed Sullivan Show' (CBS TV New York, 1969). Parisians heard her once more at the Bobino theatre in February 1970. That year she took a major role in Paul Almond's film *Act of the Heart* and sang at the Place des nations at Man and His World (exhibition on the site of Expo 67) and at Le *Patriote. In 1972 CBC TV presented her portrait-recital 'Une femme comme les autres' on the program 'Les Beaux Dimanches.'

Monique Leyrac has given concerts at the Comédie-Canadienne (1965, 1970), at the PDA (1968, 1971 with the *MSO, 1972), at the Capitol Theatre in Ottawa (1968), and at the *NAC (1969), and has toured Quebec (1965, 1968, 1970) and elsewhere in Canada (1967, 1970). In 1972 she performed at the *Stratford Festival in *The Threepenny Opera*. That same year she went to France, where she stayed until 1975, returning to Montreal to play the title role in Robert Athayde's *Mademoiselle Marguerite* at the Théâtre du Nouveau-Monde. She sang next at the Kennedy Center in Washington and the *Manitoba Centennial Concert Hall in Winnipeg and recited and sang the poetry of Émile Nelligan in a concert she devoted to him at Le Patriote, the Gesù Hall, and on tour in Quebec and Ontario. (The show was revived in Paris in 1977 and 1979.) She sang songs of Félix *Leclerc in a Montreal concert 'of incomparable richness' (Pierre Beaulieu, *La Presse*, 27 Oct 1976), and repeated the success in Quebec City. In the fall of 1978 she performed at the boîte à chansons of the Meridien Hotel and then was featured as the host of four shows in the CBC TV series 'Faut voir ça.' Her comedic gifts were particularly evident in 'Ragtime,' a show she presented at the PDA in April 1979. Leyrac was proclaimed 'best singer of the year' twice and 'woman of the year' twice in the Canadian Press' annual survey of women's editors. After an opening night at the Olympia in Paris, Pierre Kyria wrote: 'Monique Leyrac heightens emotion as she reconstitutes the seasons of the heart with the fullness of a spiritual adventure. Whether she is admirably served by poets like Vigneault and Léveillée or whether she chooses whimsy or tenderness in her surprisingly diverse repertoire, she sings with a sound and a degree of sensibility that are without deception' (*Combat*, 1 Sep 1966). She was named an Officer of the *Order of Canada in 1968 and received the 1978 *Prix de musique Calixa-Lavallée.

DISCOGRAPHY

Monique Leyrac chante Vigneault et Léveillée. 1963. Col FS 601/Harmonie KHF 90084
Pleins feux sur Monique Leyrac. 1964. Col FS 622. Re-recorded as *Mes Premières Chansons*. (1973). Harmonie KHF 90232
Monique Leyrac en concert. Montreal 1965, Paris 1966. Col FS 644
Monique Leyrac (in English). 1967. Col ELS 316
Monique Leyrac à Paris. 1967. Col FS 657
Beautiful Morning. 1968. Col ELS 324
Monique Leyrac. 1969. Col FS 720
Monique Leyrac chante la joie de vivre. 1969. Col FS 695
Les Grands Succès de Monique Leyrac. (1971?). Col GFS 90009
Monique Leyrac (1678–1972). 1972. Zodiaque ZOX 6003
Qui êtes-vous Monique Leyrac? 1972. RCI F-679
Parlez-moi de vous. (1973). Col GFS 90019
Monique Leyrac chante Nelligan. 1975. Barclay 9001
Monique Leyrac chante Félix Leclerc. 1977. Poly 2424-157
See also Discography for Chansonniers.

BIBLIOGRAPHY

Keable, Jacques. 'Une voix comme un vent long et doux, c'est Monique Leyrac,' Montreal *La Presse*, 30 Oct 1965
Trent, Bill. 'Songs of her people,' *Weekend Magazine*, 22 Oct 1966
Cobb, David. 'Monique Leyrac is *the* Canadian star,' Toronto *Telegram*, 18 Feb 1967
'Reluctant chanteuse,' *Time* (Canadian edn), 3 May 1968
Homier-Roy, René. 'Monique Leyrac: reculer pour mieux bondir,' Montreal *La Presse*, 13 Mar 1969
Adam, Marcel. 'Monique Leyrac, un être de contradiction,' ibid, 24 Feb 1970
Heller, Zelda. 'Monique Leyrac,' *Montreal Star*, 5 Sep 1970
McDonald, Marci. 'Leyrac: chanteuse extraordinaire tries her hand at acting again,' *Toronto Star*, 24 Jun 1972
Lemieux, Louis-Guy. 'La rencontre d'une interprète et d'un auteur,' Quebec *Le Soleil*, 29 Jan 1977
Petrowski, Nathalie. 'Interview: Monique Leyrac,' *CanComp*, 140, Apr 1979 (BR)

LEYTON-BROWN, Howard. Violinist, conductor, administrator, teacher, b Melbourne, Australia, 19 Dec 1918, naturalized Canadian 1963; LGSM 1952, FGSM 1955, DMA (Michigan) 1972. After studies in Australia, Germany, and Belgium, and in England with Carl Flesch and Max Rostal at the GSM, he joined the London Philharmonic Orchestra as deputy concertmaster in 1948 and became concertmaster in 1951.

Leyton-Brown had lived briefly in Canada during the early 1940s, and he returned to serve 1952–5 as head of the string department of the *Regina Cons. He was director 1953–76 of the *WBM and in 1955 he became director of the Regina Cons, where he had begun conducting the Conservatory Chamber Orchestra (later *U of Regina Chamber Orchestra) in 1953. His pupils include Brian Boychuk, Gary Kosloski, Malcolm Lowe, and Donald Whyte. He was the conductor 1960–71 of the *Regina SO and has appeared as soloist (beginning in 1953) with the symphony orchestras of *Calgary, Regina, and *Saskatoon and the CBC orchestras of Winnipeg, Vancouver, and Toronto. He served 1967–71 on the *SAB and 1971–4 on the *Canada Council.

WRITINGS

'Regina Symphony Orchestra,' *CanComp*, 28, Apr 1968
'The training of contemporary string players,' *CME*, Feb 1972

BIBLIOGRAPHY

Wilson, Ruth. 'Young man, old violin make magic on air,' *Winnipeg Free Press*, 15 Jul 1950 WLB

L'HERBIER, (Joseph) Robert (Fernand) (b Samson). Singer, administrator, songwriter, b Lévis, near Quebec City, 5 Feb 1921. He studied music for 12 years, and his teachers included Alphonse *Tardif (piano) in Lévis and Mme Jeynevald-Mercier (voice) in Quebec City. He also studied diction with José *Delaquerrière. In 1940 he took L'Herbier as his professional name out of friendship for the French film-maker Marcel L'Herbier. His career as a singer, pianist, arranger, and conductor began in 1941 on radio station CHLT, Sherbrooke. In Montreal he was the star 1942–9 of CBC radio's 'Les *Joyeux Troubadours.' His first hit record, 'Rita,' for *RCA Victor, was one of his own songs, and he was voted most popular artist (1946, 1948) in a competition sponsored by the weekly *Radiomonde*. He and Lucille *Dumont were co-hosts 1948–50 of 'Café-concert Kraft.' He founded the review *Radio '49* with Fernand Robidoux and took the leading role in Henri *Miro's comic opera *Le Roman de Suzon* (1950) in Sherbrooke. In the early 1950s he became a record dealer, founding the firm L'Herbier & Latour in Montreal; in 1979 the business was still in operation with the same name but under different management. L'Herbier also made several tours and often performed in Quebec City at the *Palais Montcalm, the Capitol Theatre, and the cabaret Chez Gérard.

In 1945 L'Herbier had married the singer Rolande *Désormeaux; they sang together in 1947 and 1951 at the Arcade Theatre and the Théâtre national. He made his CBC TV debut in 'Showtime' with his wife in Toronto in 1954; they were then hosts for 'Rolande et Robert' (Montreal 1954–9), a series for which he also wrote the script. In 1954 they participated in an 18-week radio series shared among stations CKVL, CKAC, and the CBC. The CBC TV program *'Concours de la chanson canadienne' was initiated by him in 1956. During the period 1956–7 he founded the Amicale de la chanson and the Comité de la diffusion de la chanson canadienne and was founder and president of the publishing house Société amicale de la chanson. In 1960 he was named assistant program director of the new Montreal TV station CFTM, whereupon he terminated his singing career. Six months after his appointment, he became program director, soon also adding the position of assistant manager. In the 1967 Montreal 'Gala des artistes' he was honoured for his contribution to the expansion of TV. In 1968 he became vice-president in charge of programming and production.

L'Herbier has composed some 30 songs, about a third of which were published in France. His biggest record hits, however, were of other composers' songs, including Francis Lopez' 'Heureux comme un roi' and Charles Trenet's 'Douce France,' which may be found on an RCA LP (Gala CGP 144). L'Herbier is a member of CAPAC. His son Benoît L'Herbier is the author of *La Chanson québécoise* (Montreal 1974) and a contributor to *EMC*. HP

L'HEUREUX-AREL, Lucienne (b L'Heureux, m Arel). Organist, teacher, b St-Jude, near St-Hyacinthe, Que, 6 Jan 1931; lauréat organ (AMQ) 1953. She studied piano 1948–52 with Aline Letendre and organ 1948–52 with Conrad *Letendre and 1952–3 with Raymond *Daveluy. In 1955 she married the organist Gaston *Arel. In 1960 on a *Canada Council scholarship she went with Arel to Hamburg, where she studied with Charles Letestu. In 1964 she made a second trip.

L'Heureux-Arel has given solo recitals on the CBC, at *McGill U, and for Concerts d'orgue du Québec, *Ars Organi, the *JMC, and the Concerts spirituels of St Joseph's Oratory; has given joint recitals with her husband; and has accompanied choirs. She gave the first performance of Jean *Chatillon's *Suite Pantomimes* at *Expo 67.

L'Heureux-Arel has been organist at several churches, notably the Ascension of Our Lord Church in Westmount (Montreal) 1965–72. She began teaching organ in 1966 at the *École normale de musique (renamed Institut Marguerite-Bourgeoys in 1976) and in 1969 at the *UQAM. PD

Libraries

1 Introduction
2 Historical notes
3 Public libraries
4 University libraries
5 Performance libraries
6 Canadiana collections
7 Private resources
8 Training, organizations, projects

1 INTRODUCTION. Music libraries are organized collections of scores, recordings, and literature about music and such materials as clippings, concert programs, posters, or films. Many also own archival materials (see Archives). Music libraries serve such different patrons as performers, scholars, students, broadcast organizers, and the music-loving public at large. Corresponding to the special needs of each group, choral, orchestral, academic, broadcasting, public, and other libraries have assumed specific, though often overlapping, functions.

Surveys conducted by the Canadian Library Assn's Music Libraries Committee in 1956, by the *CMLA in 1965, and by the *NL of C 1978–9 show that resources have increased considerably during the 1960s and 1970s but that distribution across Canada is uneven, corresponding in general to the wealth of each province. Toronto has the largest public and university library music collections; but the city's concentration of resources in five major collections (at the Metropolitan Toronto Library, the *U of Toronto, the CBC, the *CMCentre, and *York U) stands in marked contrast to the multiplicity of collections in Montreal (at the BN du Q, *CAMMAC, the *CBC, the CMCentre, the *CMM, the *École Vincent-d'Indy, *McGill U, the Montreal City Library, the *U of Montreal, and others). Quebec City has the oldest collections. The combination of public and university resources (the latter usually accessible to the general public) provides good services in Calgary, Edmonton, Hamilton, London, Ottawa, Vancouver, and Victoria.

2 HISTORICAL NOTES. A detailed history of music libraries in Canada had not been written by 1980. Such a history would confirm, no doubt, that the first music volumes were part of the collections of religious orders and churches of New France. At *Laval U, imported early-18th-century publications of motets and cantatas by Nicholas Bernier, André Campra, Jean-Baptiste Morin, and their

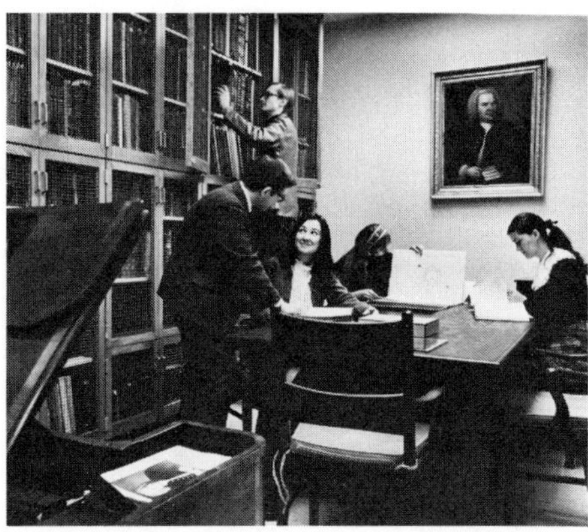

The Rare Book Room, Edward Johnson Music Library, University of Toronto

contemporaries have survived. The Monastère des Ursulines, the Monastère des Augustines de l'Hôpital Général, and the Hôtel-Dieu, all in Quebec, have preserved printed or manuscript church music used by the clergy of New France.

There is some evidence as well of privately owned music volumes in the earliest period of colonization. Jean Nicollet (ca 1598–1642), an explorer, administrator, and interpreter who settled in Trois-Rivières in 1637, is known to have had two music books in his library of 30 volumes. The intendant Claude-Thomas Dupuy, in Canada 1726–8, had a library of some 50 music volumes, including many Lully operas, but that collection returned to France with its owner.

Late-18th-century newspapers occasionally advertised imported sheet music. This trade – from England and the USA – helped music lovers and musicians to build collections, supplemented by their own *manuscript books. Throughout the 19th century private music libraries and the collections of choral and instrumental parts of the many church choirs, bands, and philharmonic societies remained the main repositories of printed music and literature about music. Undoubtedly university and public libraries had some music, but only rarely was it collected systematically. The subscription list to the complete Bach edition (Breitkopf & Härtel 1851–99) has only one Canadian name, Samuel Prowse *Warren, a concert organist who found fame after settling in the USA.

The main 18th- and 19th-century collection to have survived is the body of orchestral and chamber music parts and other sheet music successively added to by Frederic and Édouard *Glackemeyer, Jonathan *Sewell, the *Quebec Harmonic Society of the 1820s, the Desbarats and Sheppard families, the Septett Club, the *Septuor Haydn, and others and preserved at Laval U. The earliest volumes prove through written indications that Mozart quintets and Haydn quartets were performed in Canada in the 1790s.

Alfred *Paré, violinist and a president of the Septuor Haydn, is the first Canadian known to have been a part-time music librarian. The group's minute book reveals in its 11 May 1874 entry that Paré had compiled a catalogue of the library and that it was ready to be printed. As the septuor's librarian, Paré made a public appeal in 1878 for donations for a 'Bibliothèque nationale de musique du Canada,' to add to the $2000-worth of music housed at Laval U.

It is reasonable to assume that other societies had valuable collections; and indeed fragmentary collections, eg, that of the Ottawa Amateur Orchestral Society later deposited at the NL of C, have come to light. But most of the old collections may be assumed to have been scattered or destroyed.

Some of the conservatories that sprang up in the 1880s and 1890s had small libraries to encourage students and staff to explore musical literature and to broaden their sight-reading skills, but more often than not such collections consisted of a bookcase in the director's office, not of an organized unit.

About the turn of the century public libraries began to take music seriously, and those in Toronto, Hamilton, and Ottawa, among others, soon had respectable collections to serve the layman. University collections remained small since courses concentrating on theory rather than musicology required little in the way of library materials and most professors were performers rather than research scholars.

As late as 1956, when the first survey of music libraries was undertaken, holdings of more than 5000 items (combining the figures for scores, books, and recordings) were reported only by the public libraries in Hamilton, Ottawa, Toronto (more than twice as large as any of the others), Windsor, and Winnipeg. (Vancouver, had it reported, probably would have been included.) The largest education institution with a collection of more than 5000 items, the *RCMT, had only about one-third as many items as the Toronto Public Library; the other academic institutions with more than 5000 items were Laval U, McGill U, *Mount Allison U, and Regina College. There were two libraries, however, that surpassed the Toronto Public Library in numbers of scores and recordings, although they had few books and periodicals: the CBC music and record libraries in Montreal and Toronto.

Shortly after the survey was made, music libraries entered a period of dramatic growth, owing mainly to the 'LP explosion' and the vast expansion of academic music programs. By 1979 some 75 music libraries in Canada had holdings of more than 5000 items, and of these some 30 held more than 20,000 items.

3 PUBLIC LIBRARIES. Canadian public libraries generally are well-equipped, provide efficient service, and offer generous loan policies (including interlibrary loan). Free service dates back to the Ontario Free Libraries Act of 1882. Among the earliest music collections was that of the Toronto Public Library (now Metropolitan Toronto Library). In 1915 it issued a list of 828 circulating 'books of music and relating to music,' and until the mid-1950s it remained the largest music library in Canada, to be surpassed eventually by the CBC libraries and by the U of Toronto and several other university libraries.

The following tabulation provides basic statistics for scores, books, and recordings in the largest public music collections. It excludes the combined holdings of library systems, common in metropolitan areas – eg, the North York (Toronto) system, whose 19 branches have a total of more than 75,000 recordings. All figures in this and the following tabulation for university libraries should be considered deliberately approximate, since each library employs its own method of classifying pamphlets, sheet music, individual volumes in publication series, etc, and applies varying units of measurement – volumes, titles, occupied shelf feet – and degrees of precision in counting its holdings, which may or may not include cataloguing backlogs, supplementary sheet music collections, and so on. In the main, figures are based on those reported by the libraries to the NL of C's 1978–9 resources survey and those collected and submitted to the *Directory of Music Research Libraries* in 1978 (to be published in Kassel in

1981); information was supplemented by visits and reference to miscellaneous sources. The list is ordered by the approximate size of the collection.

	books	*scores*	*records*
Metro Toronto Library	13,000	30,000	10,000
Winnipeg	3,000	700	32,000
Edmonton	4,100	4,200	24,000
London, Ont	1,700	7,100	20,500
Vancouver	8,000	8,000	
Ottawa	1,500	1,600	12,000
Calgary	2,500	500	10,500
Saskatoon	1,800	200	12,000
Hamilton	4,500	3,200	3,200
Kitchener	1,200	700	9,500
Windsor	4,700	2,000	3,000
Regina	2,200	150	5,000
Thunder Bay	2,600		7,100
Montreal	4,000	1,000	

The number of recordings outweighs the number of scores in nearly all libraries except those in the largest cities, Montreal, Toronto, and Vancouver. While records can be appreciated by a far larger number of people, only scores can encourage active music-making and promote the survival of musical literacy. Indeed, in the 1970s many public libraries, having built up large record collections, turned to strengthening their holdings of scores. The absence of recordings at the Vancouver Public Library has been compensated for by the public accessibility of the recreational Wilson Collection of about 20,000 recordings at the *U of British Columbia; in Toronto and its suburbs nearly all branch libraries are well-stocked with recordings.

Many of the libraries listed (and others) have extensive vertical files, program collections, and local history documentation. In the late 1970s the Metropolitan Toronto Library was the only one able to support serious research on a wide scale.

4 UNIVERSITY LIBRARIES. Until the 1950s university collections of music were negligible in size and importance, although they held more sets of collected editions and books in foreign languages than did the public libraries. In the 1960s, with the introduction of music history and literature as major subjects of study, with the engagement of musicologists as professors, and with the increasing availability of a vast literature on recordings, in new critical editions or in reprints, music libraries entered a period of spectacular expansion. Once inadequate and neglected, in a few years they became the nerve centres of academic music departments.

The following table is based on the 1978–9 resources cited previously; collections are listed in approximate order of size, a ranking not necessarily related to overall quality. The difficulties in providing measurements are similar to those encountered in public libraries; thus a piece of catalogued 4-page sheet music counts the same as a 40-volume set of one composer's works when the library measures its titles, but not when it reports volumes.

The tabulation is limited to books (which in the classification practice of some libraries includes periodicals and pamphlets), scores, and recordings. An attempt has been made to combine holdings in main libraries, in music department libraries, and in storage, but separate recreational, orchestral, and choral collections, and holdings of affiliated colleges, are not included.

	books	*scores*	*records*
U of Toronto	30,000	65,000	133,000
U of Western Ontario	22,000	37,000	23,000
U of Victoria	25,000	8,000	21,000
Laval U	13,000	18,000	16,000
U of British Columbia	16,000	20,000	9,500
U of Calgary	24,000	16,500	2,500
U of Alberta	11,500	18,500	5,000
McGill U	10,000	12,000	9,500
U of Saskatchewan	8,000	5,500	18,000
U of Montreal	5,000	8,000	18,000
McMaster U	5,500	10,500	8,000
Carleton U	5,000	13,000	6,000
U of Ottawa	9,500	10,500	4,000
York U	8,000	7,000	8,500
Mount Allison U	5,000	8,500	9,500
Queen's U	5,000	10,500	5,500
U of Manitoba	12,500	4,000	4,000
U of Regina	6,000	4,000	3,500
Brandon U	3,500	5,500	4,000
U of Windsor	3,500	5,500	2,500
Dalhousie U	4,000	3,000	4,000
Wilfrid Laurier U	3,000	2,500	5,500

In all the collections the main ingredients are the basic literature of music and those more specialized publications that were available during the years of intensive collection-building. Most libraries have acquired some material on the second-hand market or through bequests from retired staff members or deceased musicians (see section 7).

Special holdings, apart from the archival ones described under Archives, are rare. One might note the almost complete representation of collected editions and monuments, and a fine collection of Brahms first editions, at the U of British Columbia; Wagneriana and books about music in Vienna at the *U of Calgary; and significant collections of 18th-century opera at the *U of Western Ontario, *McMaster U, and the U of Toronto. The last-named is rich in many other areas. It has, for instance, a large collection of 78s and a wealth of flute music. Laval U has notable collections of Catholic church music, of original editions of late-18th- and early-19th-century chamber music and orchestral parts, and of 18th- and 19th-century French music.

5 PERFORMANCE LIBRARIES. No point is served by providing tabulations of the holdings of libraries that have musical performance as their main purpose, so varied are the methods of classifying, filing, and counting.

Without doubt the broadcast libraries have the largest collections of scores and recordings, although they have few books. In 1980 the CBC's Montreal and Toronto libraries each had more than 100,000 printed or manuscript items in musical notation and, respectively, 250,000 and 175,000 recordings. The CBC music and record libraries in Vancouver, Winnipeg, and Halifax were next in size, and record collections served many other stations, CBC and private. The CBC Montreal and Toronto music libraries have covered all genres of music but are particularly strong in printed and manuscript popular music and in original and arranged music written for broadcast. The CBC program archives in the two cities preserve recordings of many live music productions.

Conservatory libraries, emphasizing performance needs rather than scholarship, flourish at the Conservatoires de musique in Montreal, Quebec City, and other centres in the province and at the École Vincent-d'Indy in Montreal.

The most common type of music library, without doubt, is the choral library. There must be more than a thousand in Canada, in schools, churches, and the premises of choral societies. Band and orchestra libraries are next in number. Most of these collections, of course, serve only one ensemble, and the borrowing of rarely used or unique materials is made difficult by the lack of widely distributed catalogues.

In 1980 no public or commercial national lending library of performance materials existed in Canada, though the CAMMAC library, established in 1959, made available to CAMMAC members a large selection of choral music, chamber music, and songs and a smaller one of orchestral music.

Recreational, ethnic, and amateur musicians' organizations and some music federations have maintained music libraries accessible to their members. Examples are the libraries of the *Alliance chorale canadienne and the Jewish Public Library in Montreal, the Ukrainian Cultural and Educational Centre of Winnipeg, and the *Vancouver Cello Club.

6 CANADIANA. The largest holdings of musical Canadiana, folk music excepted, are those of the National Library of Canada in Ottawa, the Canadian Music Centres in Calgary, Montreal, Toronto, and Vancouver, and the CBC. In 1980 the Bibliothèque nationale du Québec in Montreal was building a comprehensive collection of Laurentiana. The music division of the NL of C (with its large printed collection of non-Canadian publications intended mainly as a back-up resource for other libraries) has been developed in such a way that it complements, rather than duplicates, the function of the CMCentre. The CMCentre specializes in contemporary concert music, most of which is unpublished, while the NL of C specializes in contemporary published material and in retrospective material of all types and in all genres of music, as does the BN du Q in its more limited area.

Current Canadiana are acquired by many university and public libraries, but usually according to the same principles of selection applied to the music of other countries. Some libraries pay special attention to the published or recorded music of local area musicians.

Strange though it may seem, comprehensive collections of historical (ie, pre-1950) Canadiana generally are more recent in growth than those of current Canadiana. This is because librarians had little incentive to collect retrospectively as long as universities, private teachers, individual performers, and broadcasters showed little interest in Canada's musical past. Besides, much of the Canadian output of former times was trivial or ephemeral in nature, and contemporary librarians did not fathom the importance such materials might hold for future historians.

It is inexcusable, however, that no Canadian library has acquired the scores of *Lavallée, *Forsyth, *Harriss, or *Lucas or the recordings of *Albani, *Donalda, *Parlow, or the *Hart House String Quartet; that many music journals have been allowed to disappear save for odd copies or volumes; and that no complete run of **Musical Canada*, **Le Passe-Temps*, or the **Canadian Music Trades Journal* has been preserved in any library.

When interest in collecting historical Canadiana began after 1950, libraries had to acquire such material item by item from second-hand dealers, rummage sales, and private donors. The following list includes some of the more significant collections of historical Canadiana (for manuscripts see Archives), with an indication of main specializations. The list is arranged by province from west to east, and alphabetically by city, within each province.

British Columbia

Vancouver

Vancouver Public Library. Sheet music, program files, picture files, information files, indexes

Victoria
Provincial Archives of BC. Published music by British Columbia composers, programs, information files on musicians, musical societies, etc

Alberta
Calgary
Glenbow-Alberta Institute. Sheet music, programs, scrapbooks, primarily of western Canadian origin

Saskatchewan
Regina
Regina Public Library. Sheet music, program files, information files
Saskatoon
Saskatoon Public Library. Sheet music, program files, information files

Ontario
Hamilton
Hamilton Public Library. Volumes of music, sheet music, documentation of local musical life
Kingston
Queen's U. Douglas Library, special collections. Sheet music, program files
Ottawa
National Library of Canada. Books, periodicals, volumes of music, recordings, program files, picture files, information files, indexes
Thunder Bay
Thunder Bay Historical Museum Society. Sheet music
Toronto
Massey College, U of Toronto. Volumes of music, sheet music
Metropolitan Toronto Library. Periodicals, volumes of music, sheet music, program files, picture files, information files, documents of local musical life

Quebec
Montreal
Bibliothèque nationale du Québec. Periodicals, volumes of music, sheet music, recordings, program files, picture files, information files
McGill U. Lande Collection and Music Library. Hymn and instruction books, sheet music
Montreal City Library. Books, periodicals, volumes of music, sheet music
U of Montreal. Periodicals, volumes of music, sheet music, program files, information files
Quebec City
Laval U. Books, periodicals, volumes of music, sheet music, program files
Legislative Library. Periodicals, volumes of music

New Brunswick
Sackville
Mount Allison U. Songbooks, volumes of music, sheet music, program files

USA
Providence, RI
Brown U. Sheet music of art songs
Washington, DC
Library of Congress. Periodicals, volumes of music, sheet music

Significant collections in private hands include those of Edward B. *Moogk, London, Ont, of recordings (bequeathed to the NL of C in 1980) and Alan Suddon, Toronto, of sheet music.

7 PRIVATE RESOURCES. No survey of private music collections has been conducted, but it may be said that the larger or more valuable collections are those of practising musicians rather than of bibliophiles.

Many private collections have been absorbed, after their owners' retirement or death, by public and university libraries. They include those of George B. *Sippi (U of Western Ontario), C.A.E. Harriss (McGill U and Ottawa Public Library), H.A. *Fricker and F.H. *Torrington (Metro Toronto Music Library), Emil Cooper (CMM), Max *Bohrer (Fraser-Hickson Institute, Montreal), Arnold *Walter, Herman *Geiger-Torel, Mateusz Glinski, and Reginald H. *Barrow (U of Toronto), Heinz *Unger (NL of C), Kenneth *Sakos and Carlo Boehmer (Kitchener Public Library), Albert Duquesne (Montreal City Library), Mary Mellish Archibald (Mount Allison U), Claude *Champagne (U of Montreal), J.J. *Goulet and Irene *Pavloska (McGill U), and Lionel *Daunais and José *Delaquerrière (BN du Q).

Collections of bibliophiles transferred to public institutions include those of R.S. *Williams (Royal Ontario Museum, Toronto), Walter Kunstler (McGill U, Montreal), and Philéas Gagnon – musical Canadiana a small but significant component (Montreal City Library).

Private collections accessible to the public include the William Veneer library of literature about organs, in Ottawa, and the Ralph *Gustafson Piano Library of historical piano recordings, tapes of which are available from *Bishop's U, Lennoxville, Que.

Historical sound-recording collections, such as Gustafson's, constitute probably the most significant type of private resource, since very few public institutions have preserved collections of 78-rpm discs and wax cylinders and few collect them retrospectively. The major CBC libraries are private, the U of Toronto and NL of C public collections.

Private individual collectors have been particularly active in such genres as jazz and pop music. Contact with collectors may be gained through several *Record collector clubs and through perusal of *A Preliminary Directory of Sound Recording Collections in the U.S. and Canada.*

8 TRAINING, ORGANIZATIONS, PROJECTS. Until the early 1950s most music librarians were orchestra musicians who had 'drifted' into their jobs (eg, the CBC librarians and those of many orchestras) or general librarians with an interest in music. At that time several library schools began to provide lectures or courses on special libraries in which problems of music collections might be touched upon and musical topics might be assigned for student exercises. No special courses for music librarianship had been established by 1980, though occasional courses had been given at intervals and some were available on (sufficient) demand.

The first Canadian to hold degrees in both music (1952) and library science (1953) was Ogreta *McNeill, then the head of the music collection of the Toronto Public Library and first president 1956–7) of CMLA. By 1980 Canada had about 40 music librarians with specialized degrees, some of them US-trained.

CMLA, a section of the Canadian Library Assn, was replaced in 1971 by *CAML, a national branch of the International Assn of Music Libraries. Many Canadians also have belonged to, and participated in the work of, the (US) Music Library Assn.

Canadian librarians have taken part in projects sponsored or co-sponsored by the international association, including RIdIM (Répertoire International d'Iconographie Musicale; see Iconography), RILM (Répertoire International de Littérature Musicale; see Bibliography), and RISM (Répertoire International des Sources Musicales; Canadian headquarters at the NL of C).

In 1952 RISM initiated a concerted attempt to locate and list each pre-1800 specimen of printed or handwritten music or musical literature held in a library or collection. Considering the lack of a Canadian tradition, it is not surprising that only some 2600 items had been located in Canada by 1980 – many of them mid-20th-century acquisitions – compared to tens of thousands in many European countries and the USA. The largest holdings in Canada in 1980 were the following:

U of Toronto 888
U of Western Ontario 706
McMaster U 376
Laval U 161
U of British Columbia 73
Metropolitan Toronto Library 54
McGill U 50
NL of C 49
BN du Q 33
Mount Allison U 33
Royal Ontario Museum 31

Among the earliest publications found in Canada were Johann Pfeyl's *Missale Bambergense*, 1499 (U of Toronto); *Pontificale* (Giunta), Venice 1520 (NL of C); *Pontificale secundum rituum*, 1542 (Laval U); and Zarlino's *Istitutioni harmoniche*, 1562 (Metro Toronto). In 1980 publication of the *Repertoire International* (Kassel and Paris) had progressed far towards its conclusion.

GENERAL BIBLIOGRAPHY

A List of Books of Music and Relating to Music Which May Be Found in the College Street Circulating Library of the Toronto Public Library System (Toronto 1915)
Desrochers, Félix. 'Bibliothèque et musique,' *Montreal Music Year Book 1931* (Montreal 1931)
Canadian Library Association / Association canadienne des bibliothèques. 'Music collections in libraries,' *Bulletin* vol 8, Sep 1952
– 'Music in libraries,' vol 9 (Mar 1953), vol 12, Apr 1956
'Directory of music collections,' *Canadian Library Directory* (Ottawa 1956)
Duchow, Marvin. 'Canadian music libraries, some observations,' Music Library Assn *Notes*, vol 18, Dec 1960
Dean, Kathryn F. 'Four Canadian music libraries, their history and objectives,' unpubl M SC thesis, Catholic U of America 1961
McNeill, Ogreta, compiler. *A Survey of Music Collections in Public and University Libraries in Canada* (Edmonton 1966)
Benton, Rita, compiler. *Directory of Music Research Libraries, Part 1: Canada and the United States* (Iowa City 1967)
A Preliminary Directory of Sound Recording Collections in the U.S. and Canada (New York 1967)
Dufourcq, Norbert. 'Un manuscrit français du XVIIIe siècle à la Bibliothèque de la faculté de musique de l'Université Laval (Québec),' *Recherches sur la musique française classique*, vol 8, 1968
Dwyer, Melva J. 'Fine arts and music libraries,' *Librarianship in Canada 1946 to 1967* (Ottawa 1968)
Gilpin, Wayne. *Directory of Musical Canada* (Edmonton 1978)
NL of C. *Music Resources in Canadian Collections*, Research Collections in Canadian Libraries no. 7, Ottawa 1980
Both the *CMLA Newsletter* and the *CAML Newsletter* contain many articles describing individual libraries. HK

Librettos. Canada's earliest librettist was Joseph *Quesnel, the poet and playwright who wrote the words and music for *Colas et Colinette*, premiered in 1790. (Frances Brooke, an English woman who lived 1763–8 in Quebec, wrote the libretto of the widely performed *Rosina* in 1782, after her return to Europe; thus Canada cannot claim this lady as one of her librettists.) Canadians have produced texts, original or adapted, for operas, operettas, and musicals on numerous topics, foreign and domestic. This article will mention a selection of those which actually have been set. See also Oratorios, Canadian (composition and performance).

1 19th century
2 Early 20th century
3 Later 20th century
4 Canadian legend and history
5 Composer-librettists

1 19TH CENTURY. Besides *Colas et Colinette*, Quesnel wrote the libretto for his light opera **Lucas et*

Cécile, and some 150 years later (1942) was himself the subject of a light opera with words and music by Eugène *Lapierre – *Le Père des amours*. Calixa *Lavallée used English-language librettos for his light operas **The Widow* (Frank H. Nelson), *Loulou* (Arnold de Thiers), and **TIQ* (Will F. Sage). Elzéar Labelle collaborated with J.B. *Labelle on the texts for several of the latter's operettas, including *La Conversion d'un pêcheur de la Nouvelle-Écosse*. The poet Pamphile Lemay provided the libretto for *La Fiancée des bois* by Célestin *Lavigueur, who had written the libretto for his own opera *Les Enfants du manoir*.

W.H. Fuller used Sullivan's popular music for *H.M.S. Pinafore* as the basis for **H.M.S. Parliament*, in which his libretto lampooned Canadian politics. The *NL of C holds the libretto of the two-act comic opera *Bunthorne Abroad or The Lass that Loved a Pirate* by the Toronto poet-cartoonist John Wilson Bengough (1851–1923). Using 'the best music and characters of Gilbert & Sullivan's *Patience, Pinafore* and *Pirates*,' it was presented in the Toronto Horticultural Gardens Pavilion in 1883. The text of Oscar *Telgmann's four-act 'military' opera, **Leo the Royal Cadet*, was written by the poet-journalist George F. Cameron.

2 EARLY 20TH CENTURY. Joseph *Vézina used texts by a variety of writers for his operettas: Félix-Gabriel Marchand (premier of Quebec) for *Le Lauréat*, the Quebec civil servant Benjamin Michaud for *Le Rajah*, and a team, A. Langlois and A. Plante, for *Le Fétiche*. Marchand also wrote the libretto for *Amour vainqueur*, the music written under the pseudonym 'Cello' and orchestrated by Edmond *Hardy. For the operetta *The Cavaliers*, Herbert *Spencer used a text prepared by the playwright W.A. Tremayne, while Émiliano *Renaud provided his own English-language libretto for his musical farce *Djymko*. Rad and Henri *Letondal wrote the words for Henri *Miro's *Le Roman de Suzon*. In Winnipeg the lawyer Charles S. Blanchard wrote the book and lyrics for William *Dichmont's musical play *Miss Pepple (of New York)*. Amédée *Tremblay's *L'Intransigeant* used a libretto by the journalist-poet Rémi Tremblay; Oscar *O'Brien's *Philippino*, one by the notary Gaétan Valois.

The libretto for one of Omer *Létourneau's operettas – *Coup d'soleil* – was written by the broadcaster Alfred Rousseau (who also provided the text for J. Ulric Voyer's *L'Intendant Bigot*), while the texts for Létourneau's *Vive la canadienne* and *Mam'zelle Bébé* were prepared by the Quebec City notary Aimé Plamondon and the noted writer and lecturer J.-Eugène Corriveau. The latter also collaborated with the composer Rolland *Gingras on the operetta *L'Appel du missionaire*. The first noted French-Canadian woman poet, Blanche Lamontagne-Beauregard, wrote the three-act comic opera *Francine* for the composer Albertine *Morin-Labrecque.

John Murray *Gibbon collaborated with Healey *Willan on several ballad operas, including *Prince Charlie and Flora*, and possibly on two lost works – *Maureen* and *The Indian Christmas Play*. He also provided the English translation of the French-Canadian author Louvigny de Montigny's original libretto for *L'Ordre de Bon Temps / The Order of Good Cheer*. For **Transit through Fire* and **Deirdre*, Willan worked with the playwright John Coulter.

3 LATER 20TH CENTURY. The Halifax writer Donald Wetmore used a historical event – the *Saladin* mutiny of 1844 – as the basis of the text for Trevor Jones' folk opera *The Broken Ring*.

Maurice *Blackburn's wife, Marthe Morisset, supplied the librettos for his **Pirouette* and *Une Mesure de silence* (the English-language version, **Silent Measures*, was prepared by Guy Glover). Another husband-and-wife team, Elaine and Norman *Campbell, collaborated on the book, lyrics, and music for the musicals *The Wonder of It All* (based on the life of the painter Emily Carr), *Private Turvey Goes to War*, and **Anne of Green Gables* (the last-named also with Don Harron and Mavor Moore). Using T.C. Haliburton's early-19th-century satire *The Clockmaker*, Rosabelle Jones wrote **Sam Slick* for her husband, Kelsey *Jones.

Harry *Somers has worked with several librettists: the Toronto lawyer and poet Michael Fram (**The Fool, The Homeless Ones*); Mavor *Moore and the Montreal playwright Jacques Languirand, who provided the two-language text of **Louis Riel*; and the Toronto director and playwright Martin Kinch (*Enkidu*). Languirand also wrote the historical musical comedy *Klondyke* (see Klondike) with the composer Gabriel *Charpentier.

The poet James Reaney has collaborated with John *Beckwith on a variety of works, including two chamber operas – **Night Blooming Cereus* and *The Shivaree*. The Hungarian poet George Jonas, who moved to Toronto in 1956, used a poem by Schiller as the basis of the libretto for Tibor *Polgar's opera *The Glove* and also provided the text for Polgar's earlier opera *A European Lover*. Michel Tremblay fashioned a libretto from Aristophanes' *Lysistrata* for Neil *Chotem.

The Toronto poet and novelist Ronald Hambleton has written librettos for Samuel *Dolin – *Casino (Greed)* – and for Raymond *Pannell – *The Luck of Ginger Coffey* (after the novel by Brian Moore). Pannell also has written operas on texts by his wife, Beverly: *Exiles, Midway*, **Aberfan*, and *N-E-W-S*. The playwright Eugene Benson, a teacher at the U of Guelph, began his collaboration with the composer Charles *Wilson with the grand opera **Heloise and Abelard* followed by the chamber operas *The Summoning of Everyman* and *Psycho Red*. The Toronto writer John Reid based the libretto for Godfrey *Ridout's opera *The Lost Child* on a story by the novelist Morley Callaghan. The Canadian playwright Jack Gray prepared the libretto for the English composer Carey Blyton's opera *The Girl From Nogami*, premiered 7 Mar 1978 at the Guildhall School of Music in London.

4 CANADIAN LEGEND AND HISTORY. Canada's past has provided the subject matter for several Canadian operas. Norman Newton, the Vancouver poet, playwright, and CBC radio producer, used a Tsimshian Indian story as the basis for his libretto for Derek *Healey's **Seabird Island*, and Dorothy Livesay, twice winner of the Governor General's Award for her poetry, drew her text for Barbara *Pentland's *The Lake* from an Okanagan Indian legend. *Tzinquaw*, a musical dramatization of a Salish Indian legend by Frank Morrison, includes Cowichan Indian songs and dances. Murray *Adaskin's chamber opera *Grant, Warden of the Plains*, which deals with the Métis Cuthbert Grant, has a libretto by the Winnipeg poet Mary Elizabeth Bayer.

5 COMPOSER-LIBRETTISTS. The following composers have written or adapted librettos for their own works:

Archer *Sganarelle* (from Samuel Eliot's English adaptation of the Molière text)
Benoist *Onadéga* (on an English drama by Filion Milway)
Betts *Riders to the Sea* (on Synge's play); *The Woodcarver's Wife* (on a poem by Marjorie Pickthall)
Bissell *His Majesty's Pie*
Borré *L'Amour d'Apache*
Buczynski *From the Buczynski Book of the Dead*
Cabena *The Selfish Giant* (after Oscar Wilde)
Charpentier *A Night at the Opera* (10 short operas)
George *Way Out; King Theodore* (on memoirs of Sebastian Costa and letters of Horace Walpole and Sir Horace Mann)
Goldberg *Nacht mit Kleopatra; Galatea Elettronica; Jeanne des anges*
Healey *Mr Punch* (adapted from Collier and Mayhew)
Kalnins *Hamlet* (Shakespeare)
Kaufmann *Bashmachkin* (Gogol); *A Parfait for Irene; Sganarelle* (Molière); *The Research; Ansuya; A Hoosier Tale; The Scarlet Letter* (Hawthorne)
Komorous *Lady Whiterose*
Kunz *The Watchful Gods*
Lavigueur *Les Enfants du manoir*
McIntyre *Death of the Hired Man* (on the poem by Robert Frost)
McPeek *The Bargain*
Pannell *Aria da Capo* (texts by Edna St Vincent Millay); *Go; Push* (on texts by Osip Mandelstam and Ezra Pound)
Poynter *The Birth of Our Lord*
Robitaille *Les Volatiles*
Schafer **Loving* (French: Charpentier)
Symonds *Laura and the Lieutenant; Charnisay versus La Tour* (or *The Spirit of Fundy*)
Vallerand **Le Magicien*
Willan *The Beggar's Opera* (from John Gay)
Wilson *The Selfish Giant* (after Oscar Wilde); *Kamouraska* (from *Kamouraska* by Anne Hébert)

(NM)

LICHTENSTEIN, Clara. Pianist, teacher, b Budapest, ca 1860, d Dorset, England, 3 May 1946. Born into a musical family, she studied at the Charlotte Square Institute in Edinburgh, founded by her uncle, George Lichtenstein. Her first public performance was in piano duets with Sir Charles Hallé in 1880. She spent the following year at the Royal Academy of Music in Vienna and is said to have had lessons with Liszt about this time. After her uncle's death she became principal of the Charlotte Square Institute.

At the invitation of Lord *Strathcona, she moved in 1899 to Montreal to organize the music department of the new Royal Victoria College and quickly established herself as the right person for such a task. *The Ladies' Magazine*, Toronto, reported that 'Miss Lichtenstein's work at the Royal Victoria College is of so high an order as to make the musical course at the College famous in the United States as well as in Canada ... She possesses strong magnetism and an attractive, unassuming manner, which wins her friends wherever she goes.' When the *McGill Conservatorium was founded in 1904, she was appointed vice-director. She remained as head of staff and was responsible for the teaching of piano, voice, history, and theory until 1929. She also frequently performed and lectured in public. Her pupils included the soprano Pauline *Donalda, the pianists Ellen *Ballon and Marguerite *Spencer, and the bass Edmund *Burke.

BIBLIOGRAPHY

'Miss Clara Lichtenstein,' *Ladies' Magazine*, Apr 1901
Morgan, Henry James. *The Canadian Men and Women of the Time* (Toronto 1912)
Vaughan, Susan E. 'Clara Lichtenstein,' *McGill News*, Summer 1946
McLean, Eric. 'Clara brought touch of class to Montreal,' Montreal *Gazette*, 12 Jan 1980
McGill U. Archives. RG39

NT

LIDOV, David. Composer, teacher, b Portland, Ore, 9 Jan 1941; MA (Columbia) 1965. He studied composition with Otto Luening at Columbia and has written a *Symphony* (1965), chamber works in-

Clara Lichtenstein

cluding *Istanpittas* (1968, for cello, saxophone, and trombone), and songs and choral pieces on texts by Yeats, Pratt, Blake, and, for *The Vision of Louis Riel* (1968), John Robert Colombo. Using computers, he has researched the musical applications of mathematical linguistics and the relationships between the logic of phrasing in music and grammar in speech. He was music specialist 1968–70 at Lower Canada College and conductor 1968–70 of the Montreal Jewish Folk Choir. In 1971 he joined the music staff at *York U, Toronto. Christopher *Weait and Monica *Gaylord recorded his *Fantasy* for bassoon and piano (Mel SMLP 4032). He is an associate of the *CMCentre and an affiliate of PRO Canada.

WRITINGS

'Freedom and responsibility in musical interpretation,' *CMB*, 8, Spring–Summer 1974 CF

LIESSENS, Auguste. Organist, composer, bandmaster, choir conductor, teacher, inventor, b Ninove, near Brussels, 17 Aug 1894, naturalized Canadian 1953, d Sorel, Que, 8 Jul 1954. Liessens was blind from infancy. In 1901 he entered the Institut royal pour les aveugles at Woluwe-St-Lambert, Belgium, where he studied various instruments and theory. He was clarinet soloist in the institute's band at 12 and received a diploma from the Brussels Cons royal before he was 20.

At the request of the Frères de la Charité, Liessens went in 1913 to Sorel to teach music at the Collège du Mont-St-Bernard. He played a major role in the musical life of his adopted city and was organist at Notre-Dame Church in 1916 and at St-Pierre Church from 1929 until his death. He was director 1917–42 of the Zouaves Band (later the Sorel Concert Band) and founded, and directed 1924–49, the Société chorale Liessens, for which he wrote many works, including *Les Sept Paroles du Christ*, *À Ste-Cécile*, *Hérodiade*, *À la Patrie*, *L'Érable*, *Ô Vous*, *Héros*, and *Marche au drapeau*, for band or mixed choir. His religious works include a *Messe Lauda Sion*, an *Ave Maria*, and about 40 canticles, the majority for three equal voices. His compositions, all in manuscript, are in the Archives nationales du Québec.

He invented the Liessens Music Writer / Musicographe Liessens, a machine allowing the blind to write music for the sighted. The American Foundation for the Blind, New York, has distributed the machine in several countries.

Liessens was made an honorary citizen of his birthplace in 1953 and was awarded a Diplôme d'honneur by L'Aveugle, a Belgian association. A street in Sorel was named after him in 1975. LV-L

Gordon Lightfoot

LIGHTFOOT, Gordon (Meredith). Singer-songwriter, guitarist, pianist, b Orillia, Ont, 17 Nov 1939; hon LLD (Trent) 1979. As a boy soprano in Orillia he performed on local radio, in oratorio and operetta, and in Kiwanis festivals. He appeared at 13 in a concert of Kiwanis festival winners at *Massey Hall, the site of many of his later triumphs. In his teens he sang in a barbershop quartet, studied piano, and taught himself to play drums. He also studied jazz orchestration 1957–8 at Westlake College of Modern Music in Los Angeles. Returning to Canada, he worked 1958–61 in Toronto with such groups as the Swinging Eight (the choral and dance group on CBC TV's 'Country Hoedown') and the Gino *Silvi Singers. He played drums for Ben *McPeek in the revue *Up Tempo 60* at the King Edward Hotel, then began singing folksongs and playing guitar, appearing with Terry Whalen as the Two Tones in southern Ontario coffeehouses, on the LP *Two Tones Live at the Village Corner* (1962, Chateau CLP 1012), and at the 1962 *Mariposa Folk Festival. His recording of 'Remember Me' (Chateau) was a hit locally at this time.

After a sojourn in Europe, where he was host in the summer of 1963 for BBC TV's 'Country and Western Show,' Lightfoot was drawn to the urban folk music movement led by Bob Dylan and others. He appeared in coffeehouses and bars in Ontario, Quebec, and eastern USA and in 1964 at the Mariposa festival. Despite his personal appearances in the USA, Lightfoot initially was known there more widely as a songwriter. Ian and Sylvia (*Tyson) were the first to sing and record his songs, beginning with 'For Lovin' Me' and *'Early Morning Rain.' The first was a substantial hit in 1965 for Peter, Paul and Mary, and later was recorded by Chad and Jeremy, the Johnny Mann Singers, and others. 'I'm Not Saying,' Lightfoot's first record hit (1965, Compo) in Canada, was popular with US country fans as recorded by Leroy Van Dyke. 'Ribbon of Darkness' was a hit in the same field as recorded by Marty Robbins and brought Lightfoot an ASCAP award in 1965. Lightfoot songs also were introduced to new audiences at this time through recordings by Harry Belafonte, Judy Collins, George Hamilton IV (who later made an LP, *Lightfoot Country*, RCA Cam CAS 2379, exclusively of Lightfoot songs), Richie Havens, and the Kingston Trio.

In the wake of the popularity of his songs, Lightfoot performed in 1965 at the Newport Folk Festival, RI, and at Town Hall, New York, and in 1966 he toured England. Though the urban folk music movement, in which Lightfoot had become a significant figure, eventually waned, he made the transition easily to the larger pop audience, becoming in Canada the most important pop musician of the late 1960s and 1970s. On 31 Mar 1967 he gave one concert at Massey Hall, the first in what was to become an annual series. In 1969 one of his three concerts there was recorded and released as the LP *Sunday Concert*. In 1978 he gave an unprecedented series of nine Massey Hall concerts in as many nights – each one sold out. He made his first cross-Canada tour in 1967, appearing 8–14 May at *Expo 67 and has continued to tour throughout the country. He also has given an average of 70 concerts annually in the USA (with multi-concert series in New York and Los Angeles and, in 1977, a Las Vegas engagement) and has toured each spring in Europe. By 1979 he had toured twice in Australia.

Lightfoot has been accompanied in live performance by one, then two, then four musicians: a guitarist (David Rea in 1965 followed by Laurice Milton 'Red' Shea in 1966 and Terry Clements in 1971), a bass guitarist (Paul Weidman, added in 1966 and followed that year by John Stockfish and in 1969 by Rick Haynes), a steel guitarist (Pee Wee Charles, added in 1975), and a drummer (Barry Keane, added in 1975). Lightfoot himself is a competent six-string and 12-string guitarist in the folk style.

A prolific songwriter, Lightfoot by 1979 had composed over 500 songs, of which he had recorded about 150. His songs are published by M. Witmark, New York, or by his own company, Early Morning Productions, established in Toronto in 1969. Folios have been issued in conjunction with his LPs, and anthologies have been published by Warner Brothers.

Several of his records have been hits in Canada: 'Spin Spin' (1965, U Artists), 'Bitter Green' (1968, U Artists), 'Summer Side of Life' (1971, Reprise), and 'Same Old Obsession' and 'You Are What I Am' (1972, Reprise). Others, released by Reprise, were major hits in Canada and the USA: *'If You Could Read My Mind' (1970), the million seller 'Sundown' (1974), 'Carefree Highway,' (1974), 'Rainy Day People' (1975), and 'The Wreck of the *Edmund Fitzgerald*' (1976, a ballad inspired by the sinking, in Lake Superior, of the ore carrier *Edmund Fitzgerald*). Lightfoot also recorded Dylan's 'Just Like Tom Thumb's Blues' and Kris Kristofferson's 'Me and Bobby McGee,' both hits in Canada.

Other well-known Lightfoot songs include 'Alberta Bound,' 'Did She Mention My Name,' 'Home from the Forest' (recorded by Ronnie *Hawkins), 'I'm Not Supposed to Care,' 'Last Time I Saw Her,' 'Minstrel of the Dawn,' 'Song for a Winter's Night,' 'Steel Rail Blues' (for which he received an ASCAP award in 1966), and 'The Way I Feel.' His 'Canadian Railroad Trilogy,' a favourite in concert, recounts the construction of the CPR across Canada in the 1880s. Commissioned by the CBC for a centennial show, '100 Years Young,' seen New Year's Day 1967, this three-part narrative song was performed by the composer with the Ron *Collier orchestra. Lightfoot has recorded it for the LPs *The Way I Feel* and *Sunday Concert*. Recordings of Lightfoot songs arranged for orchestra have been made by John *Arpin and Neil *Chotem.

Lightfoot's singing has been described as 'almost crooning – a style which understates and redeems the rhetorical and sentimental conventions intrinsic to all formal songwriting' (Stephen Holden, *Rolling Stone*, 14 Mar 1974). Reviewing the LP *Sundown*, Geoffrey Stokes (*Village Voice*, 14 Feb 1974) noted Lightfoot's 'strong, supple voice,' 'insinuating melodies,' and 'extraordinary sensitivity to pain – his own and others – and joy ... Vulnerable and open in a way that he denied in his earlier writing, Lightfoot's is the voice of the romantic. For him (as for Don Quixote, one of his chosen heroes) perfection is always in view and always slipping from his grasp.' Lightfoot's detractors, however, refer to his 'way of presenting nothing new and nothing old at the same time, building on but sticking faithfully to the patterns that served him well 10 years ago' (Paul McGrath, *Globe and Mail*, 25 Jan 1978).

In his *Maclean's* article Tom Hopkins observed: 'He has obliquely managed to fulfill the most honorable role of the folksinger, the role of chronicler. Many of the secrets he keeps are those of the nation. Such songs as 'The Wreck of the *Edmund Fitzgerald*' ... and 'Canadian Railroad Trilogy' ... although no masterpieces of lyricism, nonetheless grasped the smell of the land, captured its textures so that for many he has become a sort of aural Pierre Berton, a codifier, a scribe and in a land of harping factions and endless miles, a link between the tribes.' Paul McGrath (*Globe and Mail*, 22 Mar 1977) added: 'He has been rooted here for so long, and has worked from Canadian geography and Canadian imagery in such an encyclopedic fashion, that any Canadian musician who plays what might be termed folk music has to come to grips with what Lightfoot has already composed.'

Lightfoot received 15 *Juno Awards 1965–78: as best folksinger of 1965, 1966, 1968, 1969, 1974, 1976, and 1977; as best male singer of 1967, 1970, 1971, 1972, and 1975; as composer of the year in 1972 and 1976; and for the folk album of the year (*Old Dan's Records*) in 1973. He was made an Officer in the *Order of Canada in 1971. He is a member of CAPAC.

DISCOGRAPHY

Lightfoot. 1966. U Artists UAS 6487
The Way I Feel. 1967. U Artists UAS 6587
Did She Mention My Name. 1968. U Artists UAS 6649
Back Here on Earth. 1968. U Artists UAS 6672
Sunday Concert. 1969. U Artists UAS 6714
Best of Gordon Lightfoot. U Artists UAS 6754
Sit Down Young Stranger. (1970). Reprise RS 6392
Summer Side of Life. 1970–1. Reprise MS 2037
Classic Lightfoot. (1971). U Artists UAS 5510
Don Quixote. 1971. Reprise MS 2056
Old Dan's Records. 1972. Reprise MS 2116
Sundown. 1973. Reprise MS 2177
Cold on the Shoulder. 1974. Reprise MS 2206
Gord's Gold. (1975). 2-Reprise 2RS 2237 (anthology)
Summertime Dream. (1976). Reprise MS 2246
Endless Wire. 1976. Warner KBS 3149
Dream Street Rose. (1980). Warner XHS 3426

BIBLIOGRAPHY

Batten, Jack. 'I just write songs I think Canadians will dig,' *Canadian Magazine*, 5 Feb 1966
Harris, Marjorie. 'Gordon Lightfoot,' *Maclean's*, Sep 1968
Markle, Robert. 'Early morning afterthoughts,' *Maclean's*, Dec 1971
Ross, Penelope. 'Canada's most successful singer-songwriter talks about his music,' *CanComp*, 99, Mar 1975
Markle, Robert. 'Knowing Lightfoot,' *The Canadian*, 16 Apr 1977
LeBlanc, Larry. 'Lightfoot on the record,' (*Toronto Star*) *The City*, 2 Apr 1978
Hopkins, Tom. 'Gordon's song,' *Maclean's*, 1 May 1978
Gabiou, Alfrieda. *Gordon Lightfoot* (Toronto 1979) MM

Lighthouse. Toronto rock orchestra, formed in 1969 by the drummer-singer Skip (Ronn) Prokop and the keyboardist-vibraphonist Paul *Hoffert. Organized as a 13-piece band, it comprised a rock nucleus (Prokop, Hoffert, the singer Pinky Dauvan, the guitarist Ralph Cole, and the bass guitarist Grant Fullerton) and string and reed/brass 'sections' made up of Toronto studio and jazz players.

Lighthouse made its debut 14 May 1969 at the Rock Pile (Masonic Temple) in Toronto and performed 15 May at the Boston Pop Festival, 25 May at Carnegie Hall (returning in 1972), and later in 1969 at the Newport Jazz Festival. To the high energy of rock Lighthouse added skilfully conceived arrangements (by Hoffert, the saxophonist Howard Shore, and others) for the string and horn sections (previously employed in rock only under studio conditions) and improvised solos by Cole, Hoffert, Prokop, and the jazz-oriented players (at various times the trumpeters Bruce Cassidy and Mike Malone, and the saxophonists Shore, Dale Hillary, and Keith Jollimore, among others).

Initial popularity resulted from the band's live performances, but success in recording soon followed with the singles 'Hats Off (to the Stranger)' (1971), 'One Fine Morning' (1971), 'Take It Slow' (1971), 'Sunny Days' (1972), and 'Pretty Lady' (1973), all made for *GRT. Besides performing widely 1969–74 in North America (and travelling in 1970 to Japan and to the Isle of Wight pop festival), Lighthouse, in 1970, appeared with the *TS (twice), the *MSO, the *Edmonton SO, and the Cincinnati and Philadelphia orchestras and also toured with the Royal Winnipeg Ballet production *Ballet High*, by choreographer Brian Macdonald to Hoffert's music (a paraphrase of Ravel's *Bolero*).

After frequent personnel changes – Prokop and Cole were the only founding members remaining in 1974 – Lighthouse was reduced to 10 musicians by 1972. Bob McBride succeeded Dauvan as the lead singer 1970–3, and others, including Prokop, assumed the role later. Hoffert left in 1972 and was replaced as the keyboardist by in turn Larry Smith (the band's trombonist 1970–2) and Sam See. Lighthouse disbanded after a lengthy Canadian tour in 1974 but was revived twice under Cole's direction, appearing in Toronto and performing as group-in-residence at the Blue Mountain School of Music, Collingwood, Ont, in 1975, and working in Ontario and Quebec 1978–9.

Of the other Lighthouse members, Shore became the music director of NBC TV's 'Saturday Night Live' (New York) in 1975; Fullerton, playing guitar, led Fullerton Dam 1974–7, then formed the Madcats; and McBride and Prokop, who wrote several of the band's most popular songs, pursued solo careers, the former recording for Capitol and MCA, the latter for Quality.

DISCOGRAPHY

Lighthouse. 1969. RCA Victor LSP-4173
Peacing It All Together. (1970). RCA Victor LSP 4325
One Fine Morning. (1971). GRT 9230-1002
Thoughts of Movin' On. 1971. GRT 9230-1010
Lighthouse Live! 1972. GRT 9230-1018
Sunny Days. 1972. GRT 9230-1021
Can You Feel It? 1973. GRT 9230-1039
Good Day. 1974. GRT 9230-1046
The Best of Lighthouse. (1975). GRT 9230-1052

BIBLIOGRAPHY

Kirkland, Bruce. 'Writer combines styles for final Lighthouse sound,' *MSc*, 268, Nov–Dec 1972 MM

LILLIE (Lady Peel), **Beatrice** (Gladys). Comedienne, singer, b Toronto 29 May 1898. The daughter of Lucy Ann Shaw, a concert singer, and John Lillie, a former British army officer who became a Canadian government official, she was educated at Loretto Academy in Toronto and St Agnes' College in Belleville, Ont. Beatrice, her mother, and her sister Muriel performed throughout Ontario as the Lillie Trio before moving to England in 1914. There, in 1914, Beatrice made her stage debut at the Chatham Music Hall and her London debut in *The Daring of Diane*. In 1920 she married Sir Robert Peel (1898–1934) but continued her career, making a New York debut in the English production *Andre Charlot's Revue of 1924*.

Although she became known mainly for her Broadway and London West End successes and for her appearances in films and on radio and TV, Beatrice Lillie began recording quite early – in England for Columbia 1915–19, and in New York for Columbia in 1925, Victor in 1926, the Gramophone Shop in 1934, and Liberty Music Stores in 1939. The early recordings were said not to do justice to her high comedic gifts, but those made in the LP era – *Auntie Bea* (Lon X 5471) and *Beatrice Lillie Souvenir Album* (Decca DL 5453) – captured her qualities with considerable success. Her autobiography, *Every Other Inch a Lady* (Garden City 1972), gives a colourful account of her years in Canada.

BIBLIOGRAPHY

Dugan, G. 'Ungilded Lillie,' *Maclean's*, 15 Jul 1948
Rust, Brian. *The Complete Entertainment Discography* (New Rochelle 1973) (EBM)

LINCOLN, (George) **Edward**. Pianist, administrator, b Teulon, near Winnipeg, 2 Nov 1921; LRSM 1939, ARCT 1940, LMM 1946. He studied 1937–41 and 1945–6 with Leonard *Heaton in Winnipeg (winning the Aikins Memorial Trophy at the *Manitoba Music Competition Festival in 1939), with Harold Craxton 1946–50 in London, and with Alfred Cortot 1950–1 in Paris. Drawing mainly on the romantic repertoire, he has given broadcasts on the BBC (1950), and the CBC and completed a 12-year series (1952–64) for Winnipeg's CJOB. During the 1950s he was coached for a time by John *Melnyk. His concert appearances include chamber music and duo recitals and solo performances with the *'Little Symphonies' Orchestra in Montreal and the Grand Forks (ND), Edmonton, Winnipeg, and CBC Winnipeg orchestras. Lincoln began teaching at the *U of Alberta in 1966, when he also became the Alberta director of the *WBM. In 1974 he became the first director of the board's central administration. RDM

C.W. Lindsay & Co. Retail chain selling pianos, phonographs, and sheet music. The enterprise originated in 1877, when Charles William Lindsay (b Montreal 6 Apr 1856, d there 7 Nov 1939), who had been blind since adolescence, returned from Boston after studying piano tuning and repair at the Perkins Institute for the Blind. He started practising his trade but soon began to sell reconditioned pianos. He became the agent for *Heintzman in 1883 and then obtained contracts with two Boston companies, Miller and, in 1896, Chickering. Lindsay bought the local branch of A. & S. *Nordheimer in 1897, *De Zouche & Atwater of Montreal some time afterwards, and C.A. McNee of Ottawa in 1905. In 1902 the business became a limited liability company, and Lindsay built his own seven-storey building on Ste-Catherine St West. He bought out other enterprises: part of *Orme & Son of Ottawa (1909), Cordingly of Brockville, Ont (1910), Foisy Frères of Montreal (1914), Riggs of Belleville, Ont (1916) and in 1917 J.-A. Hurteau and the Compagnie générale des phonographes de Montréal. In 1928 C.W. Lindsay & Co Ltd was reorganized as a public company with its shares listed on the stock exchange, and the founder sold his shares and withdrew from the business. J.-A. Hébert became president and general manager.

Besides selling player-piano rolls, phonographs, sheet music, and records, the Lindsay Co bought pianos, particularly those manufactured by *Lesage and Craig, and sold them under its own name. The Woodhouse department store in Montreal bought out C.W. Lindsay & Co in 1944 and gradually acquired the different branches by the 1950s. An advertisement dated 1947 mentions three stores in Montreal as well as branches in Kingston and Ottawa, Ont, and in Quebec City, Trois-Rivières, and Verdun, Que.

C.W. Lindsay was made a KBE in 1935. Sir Charles was a philanthropist who generously supported hospitals and charitable organizations. He also created prizes for musical achievement, in particular an annual scholarship of $100 (1928–after 1944) given by the *Ladies' Morning Musical Club. In 1932 a street in Montreal was named in his honour.

BIBLIOGRAPHY
'Sir C. Lindsay, philanthropist, dies aged 83,' *Montreal Star*, 7 Nov 1939 (GP)

LINDSAY, Georges. Organist, teacher, administrator, b L'Isle-Verte, near Rivière-du-Loup, Que, 6 Aug 1909. After taking piano and organ lessons at the Collège de Lévis from Father Alphonse *Tardif, he won two lieutenant-governor's medals for those instruments in 1929 and the *AMQ harmony scholarship in 1932. He studied at *Laval U at first with Henri *Gagnon and then with Jean-Marie *Beaudet (piano and organ), J.-Robert *Talbot (harmony and counterpoint), Alphonse Saint-Hilaire (violin), and Canon Joseph-Romuald Pelletier (Gregorian chant). He won the *Prix d'-Europe in 1934 and went to Paris to continue his training under Louis Vierne and Ferdinand Motte-Lacroix.

Between 1935 and 1969 Lindsay gave organ recitals, live, broadcast, and telecast, in Europe, the USA, and Canada. He began to teach piano, organ, and theory in 1936 and taught the organ class 1950–67 at the *École Vincent-d'Indy. He was an adjudicator for various festivals in Quebec and New Brunswick. He was organist for 25 years at Marie-Reine-du-Monde Cathedral in Montreal and was also organist for the *CSM. He was the founder and the director 1967–74 of the Cons de musique de Chicoutimi and president 1977–9 of the *QMTA. He was a member of the board of the AMQ, as well as its secretary and archivist, and was in charge of its syllabus. He joined the teaching staff of the *CMQ in 1972.

WRITINGS
'La musique religieuse souffre-t-elle de cancer?,' *VM*, 5–6, 1967 LF

Literature set to music
1 Anglo-Canadian
2 Franco-Canadian

See also Anerca; Art song; *Brébeuf*; Chanson in Quebec; *Evangeline*; History of Canada in music; Incidental music; 'In Flanders Fields'; Librettos; Literature with musical content; 'Suzanne.'

1 ANGLO-CANADIAN. Excellent literature can be fit material for the composer in any country. In Canada most of the texts employed by composers have some intrinsic literary merit, and those who have exercised discrimination in selecting suitable words have tended to produce settings that are of equally high quality.

Not surprisingly the works of some well-known writers have been used frequently. Composers often have selected pieces by Earle Birney, Bliss Carman, Marjorie Pickthall, E.J. Pratt, and Duncan Campbell Scott. Works by less famous figures also have been set to music, and certain composers (eg, *Brott, *Cohen, and *Schafer) at times have provided their own texts. Certain curious facts emerge from a study of settings of English Canadian literature, and one of the most curious is that some poets of substantial reputation seem not to have attracted the attention of the musicians, or at least have attracted very little attention. There are, for instance, no settings (to date) of works by Roy Daniells, and only relatively few of pieces by A.M. Klein, Dorothy Livesay, Miriam Waddington, Wilfred Watson, and Phyllis Webb. Some poets, on the other hand, have been set seldom but significantly: Margaret Atwood by John *Beckwith (*The Trumpets of Summer*) and Gustav *Ciamaga (*Solipsism While Dying*); Leonard Cohen by himself, by Norma *Beecroft (*Elegy* and *Two Went to Sleep*), and by Harry *Freedman (**The Shining People of Leonard Cohen*); Eldon Grier by *Anhalt (*Cento*); and Dennis Lee by Beckwith (*Place of Meeting*) and Freedman ('Ookpik'). Notable are certain productive collaborations; for example, the ones between Livesay and Barbara *Pentland, between Anne Marriott and Pentland, and between Eugene Benson and Charles *Wilson. The collaboration between James Reaney and Beckwith resulted in a number of works with specifically Canadian themes, eg, *Canada Dash, Canada Dot* (1965–7 – 'a centennial collage-trilogy'), *Great Lakes Suite* (1949), *A Message to Winnipeg* (1960), and *Twelve Letters to a Small Town* (1961). The Reaney / Beckwith operas **Night Blooming Cereus* (1958) and *The Shivaree* (1979) have Canadian settings. (Reaney's verse, it should be noted, has interested other composers as well, eg, Walter *Kaufmann, Alfred *Kunz, and Kenneth *Winters.)

By far the largest number of treatments of English-Canadian texts has been by Canadian composers and not by musicians of other nationalities – for instance, W.H. *Anderson set verses by a great many minor Canadian poets but also by Sir Charles G.D. Roberts and Duncan Campbell Scott; Beckwith, in addition to his Reaney, Atwood, and Lee settings, has composed to words of David Willson (*Sharon Fragments*) and verse of Colleen Thibaudeau (songs); Robert *Fleming set words of John Coulter, Robert Finch, Paul Hiebert, and Tom *Kines; Ernest *Whyte's songs are to verses of Archibald Lampman, Duncan Campbell Scott, and others; Wilson's song cycle *Image out of Season* uses words of seven Canadian poets – Isabella V. Crawford, F.R. Scott, Miriam Waddington, E.J. Pratt, Jay Macpherson, Irving Layton, and Robert Hogg. A few non-Canadians have treated Canadian verse, however. One should mention the US percussionist-composer Warren Benson's music (performed by *Nexus) to words by Birney, Barney Child's settings of some John Newlove poems, and the English composer Richard Arnell's use of writings by Ralph *Gustafson.

Some ideas prove clearly congenial to composers ('inspirational' is a less accurate and more dangerous word in an overview such as this), and certain poems (eg, Pickthall's 'Quiet') have been set by more than one composer. People and human concerns and feelings serve as the basis of the largest group of textual themes, while nature – the pastoral element in so far as it can be detached from human emotion – lies at the centre of the next largest group. Certain texts within both groups deal with Canadian persons or places, eg, *David* (1949) – Birney / Lorne *Betts and Birney / Lloyd *Burritt; *Christmas in Canada* (1968) – Ernest Buckler / Keith *Bissell; *To the Ottawa River* (1949, pub 1962) – Archibald Lampman / Oskar *Morawetz; **Louis Riel* (1967) – Mavor *Moore and Jacques Languirand / Harry *Somers; *The Brideship* (1967) – George Woodcock / Robert *Turner; and **Brébeuf* (1943–ca 1947, two versions) – Pratt (from *Brébeuf and His Brethren*) / Healey *Willan. Other works are far more universal (or general) in their subject matter, dealing with love, spring, etc. Pieces which take pointedly national themes or which seek to glorify Canada are in the minority, and there are few which take as their theme and motivation a special national occasion.

Nevertheless, the centennial year (1967) provided the opportunity for an increase in the writing of a number of works with clearly Canadian themes, and many of these were written as the result of commissions (*Canada Council, *CBC, and others). It is natural enough that vocal works resulting from such support frequently have had a national or regional flavour. Moreover, many radio and TV plays and adaptations have necessitated the writing of incidental music, eg, works by Birney – *Damnation of Vancouver*, *Queen of Spades* (from Pushkin), etc., (music by John *Avison); W.O. Mitchell – *Jake and the Kid* (music by Morris *Surdin); and Atwood – *The Journals of Susanna Moodie* (music by Beckwith).

Certain Canadian composers have tended to seek out the texts of their fellow countrymen and to have done so as a result of a sense of obligation, of national consciousness. Nevertheless, this tendency has not meant a substantial compromise with respect to the literary merit of the words used, and, as has been implied above, Canadian composers have not said 'Canadian words – at any price.' It is clear also that many Canadian writers have delighted in some of the compositions which have resulted – Livesay stated, 'Violet *Archer's music is "sympathique" to me' – though certain writers lament what they feel is a lack of attention from their country's composers. However, such a lack of attention is not likely to persist for long if the attitudes and interest of, for example, Alexander Brott and Jean *Coulthard continue. And if the quality of the musical writing is as sensitive as that in, say, Coulthard's handling of Birney's *Quebec May* (1948) or Pratt's *Sea Gulls* (1954), Canadian writers have little ground for fear.

Indeed, the only ground for real alarm is the degree to which settings of Canadian writers are unknown and unperformed. Not only was the cataloguing of such works incomplete in 1980 – a number of writers themselves were not aware of settings of their words – but the incidence of performance was far from high. Too often a fine work will have been given one or two hearings only, and such neglect is unfortunate and undeserved.

2 FRANCO-CANADIAN. Quebec has a long tradition of song. The first inhabitants in the 17th century brought with them the traditional songs and instrumental music of their native provinces of France and passed them from generation to generation. The song as a poetic form has a long history in France, and much of the early poetry of Quebec used the rhythmic patterns of this form. So it seemed most natural to sing the poems to the traditional French melodies. In the preface of his *Recueil de cantiques à l'usage des missions, des retraites et des catéchismes* (1795) which gave only words, Father Jean-Baptiste Boucher-Belleville asked 'Is it not possible to substitute these pious verses ... for the indecent ones that corrupt hearts ... ?' Father Jean-Denis *Daulé, for his part, in 1819 published the *Nouveau Recueil de cantiques à l'usage du Diocèse de Québec*, containing not only words but also music for the songs, and some of both were of his own composition.

For the period 1765 to 1867, over 300 songs have been discovered in the periodical press. In most cases, the poem only is printed, the melody being indicated by the title of a traditional song. This outburst of patriotic sentiment in Quebec reached a peak of intensity in the period from 1825 to 1840. Four songs sung to traditional French melodies characterize this period: 'La Chanson patriotique' by Augustin-Norbert Morin (1825); *'Sol canadien, terre chérie' by Isidore Bédard (1829), later set to music by T.F. *Molt; *'O Canada! mon pays! mes amours!' by George-Étienne Cartier (1835); and finally, *'Un Canadien errant' by Antoine Gérin-Lajoie (1840). The last-named gained a new audience in the 1960s when it was performed by Nana Mouskouri.

By the 1840s musicians were becoming interested in French-Canadian poetry. Charles *Sauvageau set François-Magloire Derome's 'Chant national' and F.-R. Angers' 'Chant canadien' for voice and piano. *'Le Drapeau de Carillon' became Octave *Crémazie's most celebrated poem when in 1858 Charles Wugk *Sabatier wrote an accompanying melody for it. Other works by Crémazie were set to music later, including the 'Chant du vieux soldat canadien' and the 'Chant des voyageurs' by Antoine *Dessane, and 'Le Canada' by Alfred *Laliberté in 1902, A.-P. Derome in 1906, Auguste Fontaine in 1909, and J.-J. *Gagnier ca 1935. In 1862 Antoine Dessane had set to music *Blain de Saint-Aubin's poem 'La Mère canadienne.' The period also saw the Canadian blossoming of another popular genre, the drawing room ballad. *Lavallée's 'Nuit d'été' to a poem by Napoléon *Legendre, A.J. *Boucher's 'Que je voudrais avoir des ailes,' and *Jehin-Prume's 'Les Caprices du coeur' and 'Car vous étiez si gentille' are typical. Louis Fréchette's 'Mon Bouquet' was set to music by Achille *Fortier ca 1890 and Albert Lozeau's 'Hymne à la patrie' by J.-J. Gagnier in 1939.

Joseph *Quesnel was the first Quebec composer to attempt the setting of more elaborate texts. He wrote his own librettos for the comic operas **Colas et Colinette* and **Lucas et Cécile*. The *Cantate: La Confédération*, with text by Auguste Achintre and music by J.-B. *Labelle, was composed in 1868. In 1879 Lavallée's *Cantata* (text by Napoléon Legendre) was performed in Quebec City in honour of the visit of the Marquis of Lorne and the Princess Louise. The following year Lavallée wrote the melody for a song destined for particular fame: *'O Canada.' The words, by Adolphe-Basile Routhier, were written after the music. It was around 1880 also that Célestin *Lavigueur composed the operetta *La Fiancée des bois* to a libretto by Pamphile Lemay.

Joseph *Vézina's operetta *Le Lauréat*, to a libretto by the ex-premier of Quebec, Félix-Gabriel Marchand, was completed around the beginning of the 20th century. Of Alexis *Contant's two oratorios **Caïn* was to a text by Brother Symphorien and *Les Deux Âmes* had words by Henri Roullaud, a French poet who had settled in Canada. Guillaume *Couture's oratorio **Jean le Précurseur* was based on a religious poem by Albert Lozeau.

In 1937 the foundation of the publishing firm La *Bonne Chanson coincided with an increased demand for songs with pleasant melodies and lyrics chosen more for their patriotic or religious content than for their literary quality. Nevertheless, this movement contributed to the gradual rediscovery of the Quebec heritage and prepared the way for the birth of a literature that was committed socially and politically.

The appearance on the Quebec scene of the chansonnier Félix *Leclerc in the early 1950s marked a turning point in the evolution of French Canadian literature in its relation to music. Leclerc was the first representative of the generation of *Vigneault, *Léveillée, *Ferland, etc, whose poems are intended to be recited or sung. The chanteuse Monique *Leyrac has revealed to a wide public the poetry of Émile Nelligan both in readings and in settings by André *Gagnon and others. Maurice *Dela has set to music Vigneault's

The first page of 'Chant du vieux soldat canadien' by Antoine Dessane

'Le Paysage.' Robert *Charlebois has collaborated with Claude Péloquin and others.

Poems which, unlike those of the chansonniers, lend themselves to concert treatment have formed the basis of numerous contemporary musical works: Alfred Desrochers's *Hymne au vent du nord* set to music by Clermont *Pépin (1960); from the poetical works of Émile Nelligan, three songs by Maurice *Blackburn (1949), Maurice Dela's 'Le Vaisseau d'or' (1967), and Jacques *Hétu's *Les Clartés de la nuit* (1970); Cécile Chabot's *L'Imagerie* set to music by Hector *Gratton (1945); Félix-Antoine Savard's French-language version of the *Te Deum* set to music by Roger *Matton (1967); and Wilfrid Lemoine's *Les Rivages perdus* set to music by François *Morel (1954). The works of Saint-Denys-Garneau have inspired Serge *Garant ('Et je prierai ta grâce,' 1952; 'Cage d'oiseau,' 1962), Jean *Vallerand (*Quatre Poèmes de Saint-Denys-Garneau*, 1954), Alain *Gagnon ('Que je t'accueille,' 1968), and Jean *Papineau-Couture (*Paysage*, 1968). Papineau-Couture's *Églogues* (1942) are to words of Pierre Baillargeon. José *Evangelista's *En guise de fête* (1974) employs a text by Anne Hébert. Richard-Gaudreault *Boucher's cantata *Anges maudits, veuillez m'aider* (1979) takes its inspiration from a poem by Émile Nelligan. Léo *Roy is believed to have set 62 of Nelligan's poems to music some years ago.

Gabriel *Charpentier, the poet and composer, collaborated on the text for R. Murray *Schafer's **Loving* (1966) and wrote the libretto and music for his own opera *Orphée I*. Other Charpentier texts (*Ils ont détruit la ville, Dissidence*, and **Cantate pour une joie*) were set by Pierre *Mercure. On the 10th anniversary of the latter's death, Charpentier wrote *Artère* for baritone. Among Charpentier's compositions to words of other poets are the vocal trio 'Jamais' and *Quand nous serons heureux*, both with text by Jacques Brault.

Of the younger poets writing in the 1970s, mention should be made of Michèle Lalonde, whose long poem *Terre des hommes* was set to music by André *Prévost for Expo 67. Micheline Coulombe *Saint-Marcoux employed texts by Noël Audet and Gilles Marsolais for *Makazoti* (1971), by Nicole Brossard for *Alchera* (1973), and by Paul Chamberland for *Ishuma* (1973-4). Some composers – eg, Lionel *Daunais (*Sept Épitaphes plaisantes, Fantaisie dans tous les tons*) and Rodolphe *Mathieu – have composed mostly to their own texts, but collaborations between representatives of the literary and musical worlds became quite common in the 1970s and made a distinctive contribution to the development of Canadian music.

1 / BNSG, KW, 2 / JH

Literature with musical content

1 Anglo-Canadian
2 Franco-Canadian
See also Literature set to music.

1 ANGLO-CANADIAN. The first musical references to appear in English-Canadian literature were to boat songs, sea shanties, and Indian chants, drums, and dances. Early literary efforts mention festive balls given in Quebec and elsewhere, though the dance music itself was not described. Descriptions of Indian drums and willow flutes in 19th-century literature gradually gave way to mentions of snare drums and bugles and references to church bells and, later, pipe organs.

In his romance *The Golden Dog: A Legend of Quebec* (Montreal 1877, Toronto 1887), William Kirby wrote 'The boat-songs of the Canadian voyageurs are unique in character and very pleasing when sung by a crew of broad-chested fellows dashing their light birch-bark canoes over the waters ... As might be inferred, the songs of the voyageurs differ widely from the sweet little lyrics sung in soft falsettos to the tinkling of a pianoforte in fashionable drawing-rooms and called "Canadian boat songs"' (Montreal edition, p 274). Kirby described the singing of boat songs with violin accompaniment and also showed how mood changed as the singers went from one song to another, and how the refrains were taken up eagerly by those on shore.

In the Atlantic region of Canada, the feelings of fishermen and sailors often were expressed in sea-shanties. References to shanties appear in stories, novels, poems, and folklore. Thomas Haliburton's *The Old Judge; or, Life in a Colony* (London 1849, Toronto 1968), a travelogue on 19th-century Nova Scotia, includes a glimpse of local musical life. In it, Mr. Nehemial Myers, 'singing-master to the tribe of Levi, as he calls himself,' travels on foot and pays for the hospitality offered him by 'singing or playing on his violin, having a choice collection of psalmody for the sedate families, of fashionable songs for those who are fond of such music, and bacchanalian ditties for bar-rooms of inns' (Toronto, p 206).

A later account of travelling experiences in Canada was Lady Dufferin's *My Canadian Journal 1872-78* (London 1891, Toronto 1969). In it the wife of Canada's governor-general described her visits to various cities, including details of musical events such as costume balls, concerts by Carlotta Patti, Giuseppe Mario, and the Boston Quintette Club, a performance of the operetta *The Maire of St. Brieux* (written especially for her ladyship's entertainment by Frederick W. *Mills), and a phonograph demonstration. See Recorded sound: 2 / Technology.

By the late 19th century pianos were to be found in even the remotest towns. In 'The Shooting of Dan McGrew' from *Songs of a Sourdough* (Toronto 1907), the poet Robert W. Service vividly limned a talented pianist who pours out the story of his defeats and frustrations in a northern mining camp barroom.

Ethel Wilson's *Hetty Dorval* (Toronto 1947, 1967) tells the story of a late-19th-century British Columbia woman who has a small grand piano in her home. The instrument enthrals Frankie, a rancher's daughter, who listens avidly while Hetty plays.

The cottage organ, smaller and easier to transport than the piano, gradually made its way into remoter parts of the country. In Martha Ostenso's *Wild Geese* (New York 1925, Toronto 1971), its music is used to underline the cruelty of Caleb Gore, who commands his daughter Ellen to play the organ to entertain his guest. An uncertain and very shy organist, she misses many notes, yet plays steadily against the murmur of voices and bursts of laughter as her father converses with his friend.

Among other authors who have written novels dealing with music and musicians are Sinclair Ross, Robertson Davies, Adele Wiseman, Leonard *Cohen, and Margaret Laurence. Mrs. Bentley, the narrator in Ross' *As For Me and My House* (New York 1941) is a pianist and organist who has given up her career to marry. The organist Humphrey Cobbler is a character who appears in three of Davies' novels: *Tempest Tost* (Toronto 1951), *Leaven of Malice* (Toronto 1954), and *A Mixture of Frailties* (Toronto 1958), the last of which has for its heroine a singing student named Monica Gall. In Wiseman's *The Sacrifice* (Toronto 1956), the character Moses is a music student. Cohen's *Beautiful Losers* (Toronto 1966) uses the music of Mozart as a device to mirror character. In *The Diviners* (New York, Toronto 1974) Margaret Laurence introduces the reader to Piper Gunn, who had played for a group of Scottish Sutherlanders during their journey to the Red River, to Jules and Billy Joe, both of whom sing and play the guitar, and to Pique, who is a singer and songwriter. She appends an 'album' to the text; included in it are the melody and lyrics of four songs, three of which have music composed by Ian Cameron. Other novels in which music assumes significance are Robert Fontaine's *The Happy Time* (New York 1945), Edward McCourt's *Music at the Close* (Toronto 1947), and Raymond Fraser's *The Bannonbridge Musicians* (St John's, Nfld, 1978). Hugh Hood's novel *Reservoir Ravine* (Ottawa 1979) includes a description of the Romanelli dance band, which was active in Toronto in the 1920s.

Several Canadian poets have referred to music. W.H. Drummond's poem 'When Albani Sang' (*Complete Poems*, Toronto 1926) describes the response of a habitant to the art of the famous soprano. P.K. Page in 'The Bands and the Beautiful Children' (*As Ten, As Twenty*, Toronto 1946) observes the approach of a band:

brasses ascending on the strings of sun
build their own auditorium of light,
windows from cornets
and a dome of drums.

In 'Bega' (*The Complete Poems of Marjorie Pickthall*, Toronto 1967) the poet characterizes the voices of three bells: Tatwin, with a 'golden voice,' Turkful, with its 'rings and rolls,' and Bega, which says

'Still the dreams of music float,
Silver from my silver throat.'

E.J. Pratt's 'The Titanic' (Toronto 1935) describes the tragedy of that boat's sinking and includes a description of a band which played on in the face of death. Archibald Lampman (brother of the pianist Annie Lampman *Jenkins) wrote a number of poems dealing with the powerful effect of music on the listener and the poet – among them, 'The Organist,' 'Music,' 'The Piano,' 'The Minstrel,' and 'The Violinist.' Pianos, violins, and lutes are mentioned in his poems (*The Poems of Archibald Lampman*, Toronto 1974). Duncan Campbell Scott's 'Piper of Arll' presents a piper as a symbol of poetic vision. In his 'Powassan's Drum' he paints a strong picture of an Indian medicine man (Duncan Campbell Scott *Selected Poems*, Toronto 1951). In 'The Wind our Enemy,' Anne Marriott pictures a schoolhouse dance during the drought years on the prairies:

One Hungarian boy
Snapped at a shrill guitar
A Swede from out north of town
Squeezed an accordion dry
And a Scotchwoman from Ontario
Made the piano dance (in *Sandstone and Other Poems*, Toronto 1958).

Anna Donaldson, in 'The Shaping' speaks of influences on her life during the 'hungry, lean years' of the Depression, among them her young brothers and

Their accordion, bought with threshing money,
The five dollar violin,
Both played at lively country dances
Held in the one-room country school house (in *Alberta Writers Speak: Fifth Issue*, Edmonton 1969).

Early short stories on musical themes include John H. Willis' 'A Concert' (1825); later ones include Jack Hodgins' 'The Concert Stages of Europe' (*Saturday Night*, July–August 1978), Jack Richards' *Johann's Gift to Christmas* (Vancouver 1972, about a music-loving mouse who writes the Christmas carol 'Silent Night'), and Ralph Thomas Allan and Maurice *Solway's *The Violin* (Toronto 1976). Chester *Duncan's *Wanna Fight, Kid?* (Winnipeg 1975) contains autobiographical vignettes which capture the hilarities and sadnesses of a young musician's bid for aesthetic awareness in the Prairies in the first half of the 20th century.

There are several literary works which feature musical titles, regardless of their subject matter. Among these are the novels *Singer of the Kootenay* (New York 1911) by R.E. Knowles, *Drummer* (Toronto 1915) by J.P. Buschlen, *Drums Afar* (Toronto 1918) by J.M. Gibbon, and *Swiss Sonata* (London 1938) by Gwethalyn Graham; the play *Drums are Out* (1951) by John Coulter; the short story *The Pied Piper of Dipper Creek* (Edinburgh 1939) by Thomas Raddall; the children's story *The Blind Highland Piper* (London 1818) by Catharine Parr Traill; and several poetry collections, eg, Mary and Sarah Herbert's *The Aeolian Harp* (Halifax 1857), John McPherson's *Harp of Acadia* (Halifax 1862), Bliss Carman's *Music of Earth* (Toronto 1931), Watson Kirkconnell's *Manitoba Symphony* (ca 1937), A.B. Garvin's *The Flute and Other Poems* (Toronto 1950), Goodridge MacDonald's *Beggar Makes Music* (Toronto 1950), Desmond Pacey's *The Cow with the Musical Moo* (Fredericton 1952), Irving Layton's *Music on a Kazoo* (Toronto 1958), and Miriam Waddington's *The Glass Trumpet* (Toronto 1966).

2 FRANCO-CANADIAN. It is not surprising that the first references to music in French-Canadian literature are found in the poetry of Joseph *Quesnel, for besides being one of the earliest poets in Canada he was also the first composer. In his 'Epistle to Mr. Labadie' (1804) Quesnel finds Canadians hospitable enough but despairs of their music ('at table ... some old drinking ditty; in church two or three worn-out old motets') and of their capacity to appreciate a little piece he composed 'for some religious business ... was it or was it not for Christmas Day?' It seems his audience on that occasion criticized his effort, one saying it was theatre music, another, severely, that it made him want to dance. A third thought the composer should be shipped back to France. Among the devouter ladies one said that such music would lead the saints to sin, another that it sounded like a quarrel among all the demons of hell. Quesnel himself – candid in the afterglow of his fine outburst of antic indignation – confides that his piece was not perhaps a masterpiece but asks 'did they want a Handel, a Grétry?' adding that for his part, he felt he deserved something better in the way of an audience.

French-language folksongs, the expression of a people in the process of forging a distinct identity and thus adapted to the purposes of the times and seasoned in use by the mass of 18th- and 19th-century French-Canadians, demonstrate a striking poetic maturity. Their riches are inexhaustible. There are few situations or human relationships they have failed to explore or describe. For two centuries they formed a backdrop to the lives of Canadians while themselves undergoing transformation and increasing in depth. It is to them that French-speaking Canadians may turn for an understanding of the rhythms, melodies, deepest thoughts, and moral conduct of their ancestors. In them poetry and music are indissolubly mingled, and of this fusion was born the reality of the French regime in Canada.

Philippe Aubert de Gaspé (1786–1871) was aware of this and afforded them a place of honour in his novel *Les Anciens Canadiens* (1863), along with the rustic tale. A latecomer to literature, this scion of aristocratic landowners succeeded in recreating the atmosphere of the 18th century in the years preceding the conquest of Canada by the English. Joie de vivre lies at the very heart of the music. Aubert de Gaspé has managed to portray the balancing forces of a society that was both patriarchal and free. His references to music are numerous; but his concern is popular music. Could it be that sophisticated music was unable to come into its own except in an urban situation? Nevertheless, though he invoked only the popular muse, Philippe Aubert de Gaspé remained the sole writer of his time to place music in a social context, where it plays a role, participating in the evolution of custom and adding to its meaning. In his tale *Forestiers et voyageurs* (Quebec 1863), Joseph-Charles Taché (1820–94) seeks to rediscover the picturesque element in Canadian life. On his travels to western Canada he encounters many characteristic songs and dances.

By contrast, neither Louis-Honoré Fréchette (1839–1908) nor his romantic disciples attached much importance to music. In this they faithfully reflected their era, which cared little for it. Poets, like musicians, were looked upon as 'eccentrics and lunatics,' to use Fréchette's phrase. However, *Conteurs canadiens-français* (Montreal 1908) contains a delightful story, 'The Money Musk,' in which Fréchette describes the exploits of one Fifi Labranche or Joe Violon, a musician and storyteller: 'It was like a top spinning, my friends; the bow whirled in Fifi's hands, defying description, like an eel on a hook ... And zing! zing! zing! ... and zing! zang! zong! ... Uncontrollably, our feet made pirouettes in the snow bank. Methinks the fiddler had never played like that in his life ... And the Money Musk went on and on. Fifi sawed away like a demon.' Captivated by the diva Emma *Albani, Fréchette wrote three poems in her honour: 'On the Occasion of Her Visit to Montreal' (1883), 'On the Occasion of Her Charity Concert in Quebec City on 13 May 1890,' and 'At Queen Victoria's Deathbed' (1901). The singer also inspired Gonzalve Desaulniers (1863–1934) to write a sonnet, 'À l'Albani,' published in *Les Soirées du Château de Ramezay* (Montreal 1900).

It was not, however, until the symbolist generation, in particular the École littéraire de Montréal, that music began to appear in literature to any significant degree. By virtue of the strong personality that dominated his milieu and times, the psychological boldness of his verse, and the pathos inherent in his tragic fate, Émile Nelligan (1879–1941) is the most important Quebec literary figure of the late 19th century, as his *Poésies complètes* (Montreal 1952) attest. Born into a middle-class family, Nelligan was acquainted with music from birth, and it affected him deeply. He concerned himself chiefly with salon music, in particular the piano music of Chopin, which at the time of Nelligan's childhood was considered appropriate to the drawing-room. Both Chopin and Schumann provided inspiration for and influenced the rhythms of Nelligan's verse. His poetry was written as if to be set to music and sung. In addition to Chopin and Schumann, Mozart, Paganini, Liszt, and Paderewski are referred to in his poems. Certain titles also allude to music: 'Clavecin céleste,' 'Lied,' 'Musiques funèbres,' 'L'Organiste du Paradis.' Prior to the time of Nelligan French Canadians had lived an aesthetically dependent existence, and their ties with Europe and America rested upon a misunderstanding. It was taken for granted that the intellectual (ie, literary and musical) elite could do no more than focus its attention on trends in Paris; that it feared innovation and was content with pale imitations of European models. In fact, as Nelligan and the poets of the 'Montreal Literary Schools' sensed, it thirsted for more than that; and thus, though they remained disciples of the European masters these young poets shunned academic description and the simple superimposition of Canadian imagery onto French models.

A stronger musical presence was to be found among the writers of the generation called 'La Relève,' after a literary review founded in Montreal in 1934. The dominant personality of this generation was Hector de Saint-Denys-Garneau (1912–43). Saint-Denys-Garneau was obsessed with music and like many of his contemporaries discovered music not in the concert hall but through recordings. His idols were Bach and Mozart; his admiration for them was shared by his friends Jean Le Moyne, Paul Beaulieu, Robert Charbonneau, and Robert Élie. Except in Élie's *La Fin des songes* (Montreal 1950) there is no reference to musicians in any of their works, not even in those of Saint-Denys-Garneau; but music itself frequently is alluded to in terms which recognize its powers as a psychological or literary device. It is certain – and the *Journal* (Montreal 1954) and Saint-Denys-Garneau's correspondence attest to it – that Bach and Mozart were an integral part of the intellectual equipment of these poets, novelists, and essayists; and by 1980 no one in the Quebec literary world since Nelligan had given more thought to music and its presence in Canadians' lives.

Other poets or varying importance have been inspired by music. 'Musique,' a sonnet by Louis-Joseph Doucet (1874–1950) was published in the first edition of the periodical *La Musique* (1919). Blanche Lamontagne-Beauregard (1889–1958) was the author of a poem 'Xavier Mercier,' dedicated to the Quebec tenor. Medjé Vézina (b 1896) wrote 'Musique, pays d'où mon âme est venue' (1934). The enthusiasm of Robert Choquette (b 1905) for the composer of *Tristan und Isolde* is revealed in his poem 'Wagner,' published in *Poésies nouvelles* (1931). Music appears also in the poems of Albert Lozeau (1878–1924), Paul Morin (1889–1963), and Rina Lasnier (b 1915).

Certain poets who are also composers, eg, Gabriel *Charpentier, have attempted to create works in which music and poetry are wholly integrated. Despite the value of these experiments, by 1980 there were no further developments.

The life of Calixa *Lavallée was the subject of two works by Eugène *Lapierre – the comic opera *Le Vagabond de la gloire* (a collaboration with Aimé Plamondon) and the dramatic work *Le Traversier de Boston*.

Music has an important place in the work of the poet, essayist, and novelist Fernand Ouellette. In his *Journal dénoué* (Montreal 1974) he wrote: 'During those endless years, I lived with Mozart, my white god ... With Mozart, we pass all at once from sunlight to the dark abyss that envelops us ... Next to the flame of Francis of Assisi, the light of Mozart was the greatest gift I received from life.' Ouellette also wrote the monograph *Edgard Varèse* (Paris 1966).

Music occurs from time to time in the tales, novels, or short stories of Marie-Claire Blais, Robert Charbonneau, Jean Éthier-Blais, Félix *Leclerc, Jean Le Moyne (*Convergences*, Montreal 1961), Paul *Roussel, and others. In the field of children's literature there is *Le Violon magique* (Ottawa 1968) by Claude Aubry.

However, the influence of music in literature remains to be examined in depth, and there is no doubt that many examples, from both poetry and the novel, could be added to the rather cursory list presented in this article.

Several writers have given their works musical titles, but the connotation does not necessarily extend beyond the title. Such is the case with *La Chanson du passant* by L.-J. Doucet (Montreal 1908), *Un Canadien errant* by Ernest Bilodeau (Quebec 1915), and *Symphonies* by Léo d'Yril (Montreal 1919).

BIBLIOGRAPHY

Desautels, Andrée. 'Saint-Denys-Garneau et la musique,' *Jmc*, Jun 1954

Wyczynski, Paul. *Nelligan et la musique* (Ottawa 1971)

Guay, Marie-Thérèse. 'Saint-Denys-Garneau et Beethoven,' *R de l'Areq*, Sep 1977 1 / (ACN), 2 / (GP)

Lithuania. Immigrants from this Baltic country began arriving in Canada in significant numbers early in the 20th century, the largest wave following the country's reabsorption into the Soviet hegemony in 1940 (after 22 years of independence). About 30,000 Lithuanians lived in Canada in the 1970s; most resided in the larger urban centres.

However, the Lithuanian folk culture is predominantly rural in its orientation. Many dainos (folksongs) are rich in pagan symbolism, especially those in the huge corpus connected with the wedding cycle. Other ancient genres include calendric ritual songs that have become christianized through their association with Advent, Christmas, Easter, and other church observances. A host of male and female occupational songs (grinding, spinning, weaving, harvesting, shepherding, herd-tending, and so on) have survived in Canada through individual singers. (Kenneth *Peacock collected 409 songs and 63 instrumental pieces for the *National Museum of Man in 1962 and 1967–8.) Some of this material has been assimilated into more sophisticated choral and instrumental presentations for concerts, festivals, and banquets.

The melodies of some archaic songs are very short – using only three or four different pitches, some of which are repeated. Others are more developed, possessing a major or minor diatonic orientation, depending on the province of origin in Lithuania. Long narrative genres, such as ballads, are rare. A few songs of 19th-century origin are sentimental and banal when compared with those of the ancient tradition.

The most unusual songs are the sutartinė (from 'sutarti': to sing in accord). These polyphonic songs often are characterized by clashing major and minor seconds and by canonic devices. Sung only by women and children, they draw on the entire range of folksong subjects. A rhythmic word or onomatopoeic vocable is repeated by some voices as the text continues in other voice parts. The sutartinė is unique to Lithuanian music and has been a source of fascination for musicologists. The male counterparts of the sutartinė are played by men and boys on single-toned pipes (skudučiai) of varying lengths. Each player holds two or three pipes and plays the correct tone at the appropriate moment in the piece – rather as in group bell-ringing. A Canadian innovation in the construction of skudučiai is the use of bamboo, with the natural joints forming the closed ends. Other instruments include the popular kanklės (zither), also of various sizes, and the Pentecost horn, a holed reed instrument.

Lithuanian groups in Canada have included the Aušros Vartu Parapijos Choras of Montreal, a 50-voice mixed choir established in 1950 (directed successively by A. Piešina, V. Kerbelis, A. Ambrozaitis, and Madeleine Roch); Varpas (meaning 'bell'), a Toronto mixed choir of 50 voices, conducted by Stasys Gailevicius, which was active in the mid-1950s; and a male choir, also in Toronto, which gave its first concert 6 May 1978 under its founder Vaclovas Verikaitis. A Lithuanian Song Festival was held in *Maple Leaf Gardens in the summer of 1978.

The soprano Lilian *Sukis and the bass Allan *Fine were born in Lithuania. The violinist Dana Pomeranz (who with her husband, the Ukrainian violinist Yuri Mazurkevitch, moved to Canada in 1974) was born in Kaunas, Lithuania, and raised in Austria. The soprano Gina Capkas (Capkauskiene, b Lithuania 1930) studied with Pauline *Donalda and Lina Narducci in Montreal and has performed in opera and concert in Australia, the USA, and Canada.

BIBLIOGRAPHY

Peacock, Kenneth. *A Garland of Rue: Lithuanian Folksongs of Love and Betrothal* (National Museum of Man, Ottawa 1971) KP

Little, Carl (Maurice). Administrator, pianist, organist, radio producer, b Campbellton, NB, 17 Mar 1924; L MUS (Dalhousie) 1945, B SC (Dalhousie) 1945, LRAM performance 1952, ARCM teaching 1952. He studied music history and theory in 1947 with Douglas *Clarke at *McGill U and piano 1946-8 with Isidor Philipp at the *CMM and 1951-2 with Harold Craxton in London. He gave piano recitals on CBC radio from Halifax and Montreal and on tours of eastern Canada and was organist at various Montreal and Toronto churches. With his brother, Georges, he was co-founder in 1953 and a longtime director of the Otter Lake Music Centre (*CAMMAC). In 1952 he joined the CBC in Montreal as a producer. He moved to CBC Toronto in 1959 as a producer and served as program organizer and 1972-5 as supervisor of radio music for the English network. He was manager of the *NACO 1975-8. He is the brother of Georges *Little and of Edna Knock. CF

LITTLE, (Lloyd) **George** or **Georges**. Choir director, organist, educator, administrator, b Sydney, NS, 4 Sep 1920; B MUS (Dalhousie) 1944, B MUS (Toronto) 1949. He obtained provincial teaching certificates from Nova Scotia in 1939 and Quebec in 1945 and 1963 and diplomas in organ and harpsicord from the *CMM in 1944, the École normale de musique de Paris in 1949 and 1951, and the Cons national de Paris in 1951. He taught piano and pedagogy 1942–4 in Halifax and school music 1944–5 at William Dawson College, Montreal. He lectured in 1948 and 1950–5 at *McGill U Summer French School and taught organ and solfège

Georges Little

1951–7 at the CMM and choral singing and conducting 1953–69 at the *CAMMAC Centre and 1955–63 at McGill U. He was music director 1962–4 for French protestant secondary schools and served 1965–9 as chief of the music section of the Quebec Ministry of Education, where he was put in charge of arts teaching at primary and secondary levels in 1969. He was organist-choirmaster 1939–64 at churches in Nova Scotia and Quebec, including Montreal's Erskine and American United Church, where he served 1951–64. He made his debut as a concert organist on a 1950 CBC Wednesday Night broadcast from Montreal's Notre Dame Church and as a choral conductor that same year in Bach's *Christmas Oratorio* at the *Ermitage.

Little attained attained a national reputation as the founder, and conductor 1951–65, of the *Montreal Bach Choir with which he presented the premieres of many Canadian works and performances of major pieces from the renaissance, baroque, classic- and 20th-century repertoires. He also founded and conducted 1957–71, the *Petit Ensemble vocal and, with his brother Carl in 1953, co-founded the Otter Lake Music Centre (CAMMAC), which he co-directed till 1965. In 1966 he was a founder of *FAMEQ. He has been active in many organizations, including the *CMCouncil (vice-president 1975–6), and is a frequent speaker at Canadian and international conferences. A *Canada Council grant enabled him, 1972–3, to research choral singing in Asian and African countries. (See also School music.)

Little's sister, Edna Knock (b Fredericton 29 Feb 1928), studied education and voice at McGill U, piano at the CMQ, and the Orff method at the RCMT. She conducted church and school choirs and directed CBC junior school music broadcasts in the Maritimes and was a member of the Montreal Bach Choir before joining the School of Music and Faculty of Education at *Brandon U in 1969. She has written three educational series, 'Sight Skills,' produced by CBC TV for use in Manitoba and Saskatchewan.

WRITINGS

'Organ and choral aspects and prospects,' *10th Music Book*, ed Max Hinrichsen (London and New York 1958)

'Music education in Quebec,' *MSc*, 241, 242, May–Jun, Jul–Aug 1968

'La formation de l'artiste pour 2001,' *CMB*, 2, Spring–Summer 1971

'Une éducation musicale pour l'homme,' *CMB*, 10 Spring–Summer 1975

DISCOGRAPHY

K. Jones *Songs of Time*. George Little Singers, Little cond, K. and R. Jones pf 4-hands. 1957. RCI 144

See also Montreal Bach Choir; Petit Ensemble vocal.

FILMOGRAPHY

Music From Montreal (NFB 1962)

Québec 4-5-6 (Office du Film du Québec 1969) NT

LITTLE, Gwenlynn (Lois) (m. Davidson). Soprano, b Grand Valley, near Orangeville, Ont, 14 Apr 1937; ARCT piano 1957, ARCT voice 1957. Her teachers at the *RCMT were Margaret Miller *Brown (piano) and George *Lambert (voice). After her debut (1962) as Mimi in a *COC touring production of *La Bohème* she sang Gilda in the COC main company's production of *Rigoletto* (1962), and served 1963–5 as leading soubrette with Boris Goldovsky's New England Opera Company. She sang 1965–8 in the *Stratford Festival's Mozart productions and appeared with the *Montreal Opera Guild and the *Vancouver and *Edmonton operas. Further COC roles included Sara Riel in **Louis Riel* (1968), Adele in *Die Fledermaus* (1969, 1975), Zerlina in *Don Giovanni* (1970), and Concepción in *L'Heure espagnole* (1974).

Little has sung frequently in Festival Canada (*Festival Ottawa) productions (Susanna in *The Marriage of Figaro* in 1971 and 1972, Zerlina in *Don Giovanni* in 1973 and 1974, and Echo in *Ariadne auf Naxos* in 1977) and with the Pittsburgh Opera and the New York City Opera. With the New York company she has sung a variety of roles, including Echo, the Mozart roles, the title role in *Manon*, Gilda in *Rigoletto*, and Nanetta in *Falstaff*. In 1979 her assignments included Susanna to Victoria de los Angeles' Countess and Micaela to her Carmen.

Besides the standard lyric soprano roles of Italian, French, and German opera, Little has sung a wide variety of both opera and concert music by 20th-century composers – Argento, Britten, Menotti, *Somers, and others. In 1979 with the *NACO she premiered Sydney *Hodkinson's *Chansons de jadis*, which was written for her. She has appeared as a soloist with the *TS, the *Winnipeg SO, and the *Vancouver SO.

BIBLIOGRAPHY

Canadians in profile,' *OpCan*, vol 14, Fall 1973 JBl

LITTLE, Russ (Russell Scott Mario). Trombonist, composer, arranger, conductor, b Toronto 13 Dec 1941; B MUS (Toronto) 1967. His teachers were George MacRae (trombone) at Malvern Collegiate, Toronto, and Ward Cole (conducting) and Godfrey *Ridout (composition) at the *U of Toronto. During his studies he played in hotel orchestras and with a rhythm and blues band, the Silhouettes. After graduation he worked in the big bands of Woody Herman (USA and Europe 1967, 1968), Slide Hampton (Belgium 1968), and Ted Heath (England 1968) and was a member 1969–70 of *Lighthouse and 1972–5 of the *Boss Brass. He also has led or played in Toronto studio orchestras and appeared with small bands in the city's jazz clubs. Of Little's jazz style, Peter Goddard wrote: 'Its roots lie somewhere in bop by way of rhythm and blues, with a funky, edgy tone that bites little phrases out. With a small group his solos swarm with notes, looping in and around a melody line.' Little has led groups for CBC LM extended-play recordings and appears on LPs by Lighthouse. He has served as music director for many CBC and CTV Toronto series, among them (late 1970s) 'The Patsy Gallant Show,' 'Canadian Express,' 'Circus,' 'The Gene Taylor Show,' and 'Shake, Rock and Roll.' His compositions include *Black Hallelujah*, a collaboration with Norman *Symonds, telecast by the CBC in 1971; *Cosmic Orpheus*, a commission from the New York City Ballet, performed 1974–5; signature tunes for TV shows; and songs recorded by Salome *Bey, Dusty Springfield, and others. He is an affiliate of PRO Canada.

Little's half brother is the tenor and soprano saxophonist Michael (Willis) Stuart (b Annotto Bay, Jamaica, 2 Dec 1948), who moved to Toronto in 1969. There he began in 1974 to play with drummer Keith Blackley in a duo (later a quartet). Stuart also has performed with Sonny *Greenwich 1974–5 and Ted *Moses' Mother Necessity Big Band 1976–7. He has recorded with Blackley (*Determination*, 1979, Endeavour ST 1001), Sadik *Hakim, the US drummer Elvin Jones (with whom he toured in Europe in 1977 and 1978), Doug *Riley, and Don (W.) *Thompson.

BIBLIOGRAPHY

Goddard, Peter. 'Russ Little, musical Pilgrim's Progress,' Toronto *Telegram*, 5 Feb 1970

'Russ Little in action is a musical dynamo,' *MSc*, 263, Jan–Feb 1972

Miller, Mark. 'Michael Stuart,' *Down Beat*, 23 Feb 1978

Waxman, Ken. 'Michael Stuart a jazz veteran at 30,' *MSc*, 309, Sep–Oct 1979 MM

LITTLER, William. Critic, teacher, b Vancouver 12 Jul 1940; BA (British Columbia) 1963. He began piano lessons at 12 with Dorothea Limpus, a pupil of J.D.A. *Tripp, and studied theory with Limpus, A.B. Hendrickson, and Desmond Burdon-Murphy. Though a general arts student at the U of British Columbia, he attended Harry *Adaskin's classes in the repertoire of music and Leonard *Wilson's in criticism. He wrote his first music reviews for the university paper *Ubyssey* and in 1962 began freelancing for the *Vancouver Sun*. He joined that daily as music and dance critic in 1962 and remained there until 1966, when he was appointed music critic of the *Toronto Daily Star*. In 1971 he added regular dance criticism to his duties at the *Star*, and in that connection took summer courses in dance music, technique, composition, and criticism at Connecticut College in 1971 and 1972.

Littler's concurrent career as a broadcaster began in 1964 in Vancouver and continued in Toronto. His reviews have been heard on the CBC radio series 'Critically Speaking,' 'The Arts in Review,' 'Records in Review,' 'The Dance,' 'Music and Opinion,' 'Sound Reviews,' 'Two New Hours,' 'Arts National,' 'Stereo Morning,' and others. While in Vancouver he was writer and host for the 1965 nine-week CBC TV series 'Summer Concert.' In Toronto he was writer-host for CBC TV specials on the *NACO and the *TS.

Littler began giving courses in music and the theatre, and in dance criticism, at *York U in 1974, and he directed a workshop in interdisciplinary criticism there in 1978. He has been a guest lecturer at the *U of Waterloo, the *U of Calgary, *McMaster U, Kent State U, Connecticut College, Ohio State U, and the Peabody Cons. He has been on juries for the *CBC Talent Festival, the Baldwin National Piano and Organ Competition, the *Metropolitan Opera Auditions, and the Kennedy Center Friedheim Award (1980) for the best US orchestral composition of 1979.

Littler was vice-president 1969–77 of the Music Critics' Assn, and in 1973 he participated in the first US-Canadian exchange organized by that association, trading positions for the summer with the music critic of the *Houston Post*. In 1974 he became the founding chairman of the Dance Critics' Assn of North America. He directed the first Critics' Institute in Canadian Music, held in 1975 in Toronto, Ottawa, and Montreal. At the request of the *Canada Council, he acted as consultant to the firm Urwick, Currie & Partners for the study and report entitled *An Assessment of the Impact of Selected Large Performing Companies upon the Canadian Economy* (Ottawa 1974).

Littler's own occasionally equivocating reviews have become known for their graceful and amusing prose style and balanced argument. As well as regularly in the *Toronto Star*, they have appeared occasionally in the *Edmonton Journal*, the *New York Times, Opera News*, **Opera Canada, The Canadian, Today*, and several dance publications. He has written for *Encyclopedia Americana* and prepared liner notes for CBC, Golden Crest, Moss Music Group, and Sefel recordings.

WRITINGS

'Music and the newspapers of Canada,' *CMB*, 7, Fall–Winter 1973

'The changing critic in a changing press,' *CMB*, 11–12, Fall–Winter 1975, Spring–Summer 1976

'The critic, the community and their orchestra,' *OCan*, vol 4, Jul 1977 KW

'The Little Symphonies' / 'Les Petites Symphonies.' A radio series from CBC Montreal featuring music performed exclusively by the Little Symphonies Orchestra / Orchestre des Petites Symphonies, a large chamber ensemble. The programs were broadcast initially on the French network, later also on the English network, and for a few years on the MBS network in the USA. The orchestra was founded in 1948 by Roland *Leduc, its regular conductor until it disbanded in 1965. The weekly 30-minute broadcasts were produced by Albert *Chamberland, Romain-Octave *Pelletier II, and Jacques *Bertrand successively.

The ensemble (which on occasion numbered close to 50 musicians) at first concentrated on the music of the 17th and 18th centuries, but in 1950 it began to include works by 19th- and 20th-century composers such as Brahms, Britten, Dallapiccola, Debussy, Fauré, Franck, Honegger, Malipiero, Martin, Milhaud, Ravel, Roussel, and Webern. In 1957 it began to commission and/or premiere Canadian works, among them *Pépin's *Symphony No. 2* and *Monologue*, *Morel's *Rituel de l'espace*, and Violet *Archer's *Concerto* for violin, the last with Hyman *Bress as soloist. The orchestra also gave some public concerts at the *Ermitage in Montreal and at the Comédie-Canadienne in 1960 and 1962 as part of the *Montreal Festivals. During a 1950 concert *Champagne's *Piano Concerto* was premiered with Neil *Chotem as soloist. 'The Little Symphonies' welcomed many other Canadian soloists, including Pierrette *Alarie, Hervé and Gilles *Baillargeon, Jean *Belland, Lise *Boucher, Frans *Brouw, Paul *Doyon, Rose *Goldblatt, Glenn *Gould, Ida *Haendel, Jean-Paul *Jeannotte, Walter *Joachim, Wolfgang Kander, Stephen *Kondaks, Jacques *LeComte, Joseph and Raphaël *Masella, Zara *Nelsova, Ross *Pratt, Cécile Préfontaine, André-Sébastien *Savoie, Robert *Savoie, and Léopold *Simoneau. Among the program's foreign guests were René Benedetti, Karl Engel, Leon Goossens, Henri Honegger, Antonio Janigro, Yvonne Loriod, Marcel Mule, Vlado Perlemuter, Jean-Pierre Rampal, Max Rostal, Pierre Sancan, Gérard Souzay, Henryk Szeryng, Blanche Tarjus, Paul Tortelier, and Aline van Barentzen. Alexander *Brott, Sylvio *Lacharité, Maurice Le Roux, Michel *Perrault, and Alberto Pizzini conducted on occasion. Among the concertmasters were D'Arcy *Shea, Arthur *Garami, George Lapenson, and Calvin *Sieb, all of whom also performed as soloists. George H. Lapenson (b Chatham, Kent, England, of Latvian descent, ca 1920) studied with Adolphe Metz at the Riga Cons and as a young man became concertmaster of the UFA film studios SO in Berlin and gave concerts and recitals throughout Europe. Arriving in Montreal in 1949, he was often a soloist on CBC radio and TV programs (eg, 'L'*Heure du concert,' '*Opportunity Knocks,' 'Tzigane'). He also conducted some concerts in the 1954 and 1956 Montreal Festivals.

Because of the painstaking selection of its members and the extreme care with which the broadcasts were prepared, the Little Symphonies Orchestra soon became known for its excellence and polish. Before 1958 the program was honoured twice with the Canadian Radio Award (a competition sponsored by the Canadian Assn for Adult Education). This orchestra should not be confused with the *Gagnier Montreal Little Symphony Orchestra or with the *Little Symphony of Montreal.

See also Discography for Roland Leduc.

BIBLIOGRAPHY

'The Little Symphony Orchestra of Montreal,' *CBC Times*, 30 Nov–6 Dec 1952

'10e anniversaire des "Petites Symphonies",' *SemRC*, vol 8, 1 Feb 1958

'The tenth birthday concert of "Little Symphonies",' *CBC Times*, 2–8 Feb 1958

'Précieux apport à la culture musicale depuis plus de onze ans,' *SemRC*, vol 9, 28 Mar–3 Apr 1959 AP

The Little Symphony of Montreal / La Petite Symphonie de Montréal. The chamber orchestra founded in 1942 by Bernard *Naylor (its first conductor) and Mrs Graham Drinkwater after the demise of the *Montreal Orchestra to complement the large-orchestra repertoire of the *CSM. Its first concert, 8 Dec 1942 at the *Ermitage, featured works by Mozart, Corelli, and Gossec. Before its dissolution in 1952 the orchestra had given 82 concerts comprising some 245 separate works, including those of Mozart (41 – 3 as part of the *Montreal Festivals of 1945 and featuring *Bastien and Bastienne* and the *Coronation Mass*), Haydn (23), Handel (16), Beethoven (12), and Bach (11). The orchestra gave the Canadian premieres of Martinu's *Sinfonia concertante* (13 Feb 1950) and Tcherepnin's *Concerto da camera* for flute, violin, and orchestra (26 May 1952, Hervé *Baillargeon, flute, and Alexander *Brott, violin). Among other composers whose works were performed were Bartók, Britten, Brott, Copland, Elgar, Hindemith, Mica, Poulenc, and Vaughan Williams.

Naylor was followed by Carl Bamberger 1947–8 and 1950–1 and George Schick who conducted 1948–50 and 1951–2. The position of assistant conductor and concertmaster was held successively by Maurice *Onderet, Pierre Iösch, and Alexander Brott. Guest soloists included Maureen *Forrester, Doris Killam, Frances Magnes, Rafael *Masella, Ross *Pratt, Jan *Rubeš, Franz Rupp, George Schick, and André *Turp. Some concerts were broadcast by the CBC. NT

LOMAN, Judy (Judith Ann) (b Leatherman, m Umbrico). Harpist, teacher, b Goshen, Indiana, 3 Nov 1936; Diploma (Curtis) 1956. She studied harp with Carlos Salzedo – at the Salzedo Harp Colony in Camden, Me, 1947–56, and at the Curtis Institute in Philadelphia – and was his assistant in the Salzedo Harp Ensemble in 1957. She moved to Toronto in 1957 and became the principal harp of the *TSO in 1959. Her many appearances as soloist with the TS have included performances of the *Weinzweig *Concerto*, which was written for her, and of *Somers' *Suite for Harp and Chamber Orchestra*, which she played with the orchestra on its European tour in 1965. She also has appeared as soloist with the *Calgary Philharmonic and the *Edmonton SO. She has given many recitals and has performed on CBC radio and TV, with the *Festival Singers, at the *Stratford Festival, and with the *York Winds at the *Shaw Festival. Robert *Turner and John Felice have written works for her, and she premiered *Schafer's *Crown of Ariadne* 5 Mar 1979 for *NMC, playing both percussion and harp; her recording of the work received a *Juno Award as best classical album of 1979. Some of her arrangements, realizations, and transcriptions of music for harp may be heard on her recordings. She became a member of the Faculty of Music, *U of Toronto, in 1966 and established a summer school for harpists near Fenelon Falls, Ont, in 1977. Her pupils have included Rhonda Baker, Nora Bumanis, Sarah Davidson, Erica *Goodman, Janice Lindskoog, Charlotte Moon, Julie Umbrico, and Elizabeth Volpe.

Judy Loman

Loman's husband, Joseph Umbrico (b Thorold, Ont, 26 Apr 1934), a pupil of Samuel Krauss at the Curtis Institute, became principal trumpet of the TSO in 1957 and continued to be so in 1980. He held the same position 1961–4 in the *CBC SO. He has taught privately, and in 1979 he joined the teaching staff of the *RCMT.

DISCOGRAPHY

Britten – Hovhaness – Salzedo – Loman, arr – Dussek – Debussy – Prokofiev. 1971. CBC SM-167

Contemporary Canadian Music: Somers *Suite for Harp and Chamber Orchestra*. CBC SO, Susskind cond. 1963. Col MS 6285

Fauré – Hindemith – Salzedo – Scarlatti – Haydn. 1969. CBC SM-93

Folk Songs of the British Isles. Marshall sop. 1975. CBC SM-248

Loman Sentient: Scarlatti – Handel – C.P.E. Bach – Prokofiev – Tournier – Salzedo. 1978. Aquitaine MS 90505

Make We Merry: carols – Britten 'Interlude' from *Ceremony of Carols*. 1970. RCA LSC-3174

Peschetti *Sonata in C Minor* – Turner *Fantasy and Festivity*. 1971. CBC SM-188

Schafer *The Crown of Ariadne* – Britten – Tailleferre. 1979. Aquitaine MS 90570

Selections. F. Chaplin vn, Johnny Burt orch. 1966. CTLS 5075

Weinzweig *Concerto for Harp and Chamber Orchestra*. Toronto Repertory Ensemble, Barnes cond. 1967. CBC SM-55/RCI ACM 1

BIBLIOGRAPHY

O'Toole, Lawrence. 'A harp and trumpet and a melodic marriage,' Toronto *Globe and Mail*, 29 Jan 1977 (WS)

LOMBARDO, Carmen. Saxophonist, singer, songwriter, b London, Ont, 16 Jul 1903, d Miami 17 Apr 1971. He was a brother of Guy *Lombardo. He studied flute in London and played flute and C-melody saxophone in western Ontario with the Lombardo Brothers' Orchestra and Concert Company before 1920. At 19 he worked in Detroit as an alto saxophonist with the Wolverine Hotel orchestra. A founder and a member 1923–70 of Guy Lombardo and His Royal Canadians, he was the orchestra's music director, lead saxophonist, and, until 1940, a reluctant featured singer. His vocal and saxophone styles, both characterized by a smooth vibrato, were widely imitated and often satirized.

Lombardo was also a prolific songwriter and, in collaboration with various US lyricists and composers, most notably John Jacob Loeb, provided the Royal Canadians with such hits as 'Coquette' (Feist 1928), 'Sweethearts on Parade' (Mayfair / Charles Newman 1928), 'Boo-Hoo' (Ahlert-Burke / Flojan / Frank 1937), 'Sailboat in the Moonlight' (De Sylva, Brown, and Henderson 1937), and 'Get Out Those Old Records' (Lombardo 1950). Many of his songs, introduced by the Royal Canadians, were performed successfully or recorded by other popular artists. Notable were 'Snuggled on Your Shoulder' (Feist / Warock 1931) and 'Ridin' Around in the Rain' (Anne-Rachel 1934) sung by Bing Crosby, 'Seems Like Old Times' (Feist 1946), the theme song for Arthur Godfrey's radio program, 'Powder Your Face with Sunshine' (Lombardo 1948) sung by Evelyn Knight, and 'Return to Me' (Southern 1957) sung by Dean Martin. Also with Loeb, he wrote the words and music for Guy Lombardo's stage productions of *Arabian Nights* (1954, 1955), *Paradise Island* (1961, 1962) and *Mardi Gras* (1965, 1966) at Jones Beach, NY. MM

Guy Lombardo and His Royal Canadians. Dance band formed in London, Ont, named in Cleveland in 1923, and known for 'the sweetest music this side of Heaven,' a description coined by Ashton Stevens of the *Chicago Tribune* in 1928.

Guy (Gaetano Alberto) Lombardo – b London, Ont, 19 Jun 1902, naturalized US 1938, d Houston 5 Nov 1977; hon D MUS (Western Ontario) 1971 – was its leader from its inception, ca 1917 as the Lombardo Brothers' Orchestra and Concert Company, until his death. The 'orchestra' was a quartet: Guy (violinist), his brothers Carmen (flutist, saxophonist, singer; see previous entry) and Lebert (drummer, trumpeter, b London, Ont, 1904), and Freddie Kreitzer (pianist). The 'company' included, variously, the Lombardos' sister Elaine (soprano) and father, Gaetano (tailor, baritone, b Lipari, Italy, ca 1873, d Stamford, Conn, 6 Oct 1954), and occasionally a Scottish comedian and dancers.

The Lombardo quartet fulfilled its first significant engagement at an outdoor dance pavilion at Grand Bend, Ont, during the summer of 1919. With an expanded group, the Lombardos spent the winter season 1922–3 at the Winter Garden in London and the summer of 1923 at Port Stanley. Curtailing its second season at the Winter Garden late in 1923, the Lombardo Brothers' Orchestra – the quartet plus Archie Cunningham (saxophone, later a popular radio entertainer in Toronto), Jim Dillon (trombone), Eddie Mashurette (tuba), Francis 'Muff' Henry (guitar), and George Gowans (drums) – went to Cleveland and remained in the USA thereafter, save for appearances in Canada in later years.

In 1924 the orchestra, now called Guy Lombardo and His Royal Canadians, took a two-year residency at the Claremont Tent (a Cleveland nightclub), where it was coached by the owner, Louis Bleet. Bleet has been credited with slowing the band's tempos and lowering its volume and with introducing the idea of a medley to accommodate the many requests from his patrons. These innovations to the dance band style of the day, together with the developing Lombardo sound, contributed substantially to the Royal Canadians' popularity. Several elements characterized the Lombardo sound: the smooth vibrato of the saxophones, led by Carmen's alto; Carmen's emotive singing, often satirized for its marked tremolo and precise diction; the preponderance of

Guy Lombardo and His Royal Canadians, ca 1927

schottisches in the orchestra's repertoire; the use of the tuba instead of a double-bass, and in a harmonic rather than rhythmic role; and the quiet drumming of Gowans, barely audible to any but the other musicians.

In Cleveland Guy used the fledgling medium of radio to his advantage, arranging to play an unsponsored program on station WTAM and developing a substantial following for the Canadians' appearances in the area. The band made its first recordings 10 Mar 1924 in Richmond, Ind, for Gennett. After performing in and around Cleveland until 1927, it moved to Chicago, where it played at the Granada Cafe and broadcast over station WBBM, eventually attracting several sponsors. In 1929 it began a 33-year residency at the Roosevelt Grill in New York. The broadcast (and later, telecast) by CBS of the Canadians' annual New Year's Eve performance at the Roosevelt Grill (and later at the grand ballroom of the Waldorf Astoria) became a traditional part of festivities throughout North America; its rendition of 'Auld Lang Syne' (part of the band's repertoire since the days when the band played in Scottish communities near London) was heard each year by millions.

The Royal Canadians also took residencies in Los Angeles in the 1930s and long engagements in other New York nightclubs after leaving the Roosevelt Grill in 1962. The orchestra toured extensively in the USA and Canada, performing for dances in small communities and in the nightclubs of major cities. Though heard most often on the CBS network, it also had radio shows on NBC and MBS and a series in the mid-1950s telecast from the Roosevelt Grill on WNBT, New York. It appeared in the movies *Many Happy Returns* (1934), *Stage Door Canteen* (1943), and *No Leave, No Love* (1946). It played at the inaugural balls for every US president from F.D. Roosevelt to Eisenhower and for several World Series at Yankee Stadium, New York. On Guy's death, direction was assumed by another brother, Victor (b London 1912), a saxophonist and clarinetist who first joined the Canadians in 1930 and later led his own band in the Lombardo style, and the orchestra continued its touring regimen.

The personnel, which grew to 16 by the late 1940s, remained remarkably stable over the years. Besides the Lombardo brothers, three other early members passed the 40-year mark: Gowans, Kreitzer, and the saxophonist Fred 'Derf' Higman (who had replaced Cunningham in 1924). Other Lombardos to perform with the Canadians were Rose Marie, a sister (b London 22 Nov 1925), and the orchestra's singer 1941–8, and Lebert's son Bill, who succeeded Gowans in 1971 and by 1979 had taken over direction of the Royal Canadians. The US singer Kenny Gardner, who assumed the role of featured vocalist from Carmen in 1940, married Elaine Lombardo and remained with the Royal Canadians for over 30 years. Among the other Canadians to play in the orchestra were Bernard Davies, replacing Eddie Mashurette ca 1926; and Hugo D'Ippolito, one of several pianists to join Kreitzer in a two-piano team.

Besides two 78s for Gennett, the Royal Canadians made more than 45 78s 1927–31 for Columbia and about 40 1932–4 for Brunswick. In 1934 they began recording for Decca. Their recordings 1924–42 are listed in Brian Rust's *Complete Dance Band Discography 1917–1942* (New Rochelle 1975), and some were re-issued 1961–5 in a series entitled *The Sweetest Music This Side of Heaven*: 1926–32 (Decca 78962), 1932–9 (Decca 74229), 1941–8 (Decca 74328), and 1949–54 (Decca 74329). The Royal Canadians recorded until 1957 for Decca, and thereafter for Capitol. Decca continued to issue previously unreleased material after 1957, while Capitol recorded new performances.

At the time of Guy Lombardo's death, about 100 LPs had been released comprising pop songs of the day (many written by Carmen Lombardo, and many more introduced to the public by the Lombardo orchestra), show tunes, folksongs, Italian and other national songs, and light classical pieces performed individually or arranged in medleys. The recordings of 'Winter Wonderland,' '*The Third Man* Theme,' 'Easter Parade,' and 'Humoresque' were million sellers. By the early 1970s total sales of recordings exceeded 300 million, confirming the status of Guy Lombardo and His Royal Canadians as the most popular dance band of the day.

Independent of the Royal Canadians but with the participation of his brothers, Guy began producing musical extravaganzas at the Jones Beach Marine Theatre (near his home at Freeport, Long Island, NY) and continued for over 20 years. He also competed in hydroplane races 1940–2 and 1946–63, winning many throughout North America.

BIBLIOGRAPHY

Best, Katharine. 'Some like it sweet,' *Stage*, Jan 1939
Israels, Josef, II. 'Corn is always green,' *Maclean's*, 15 Jul 1949
Various 25th-anniversary tributes. *Variety*, 28 Sep 1949
Herndon, Booton. *The Sweetest Music This Side of Heaven* (Toronto 1964)
Carroll, Jock. 'Luck of the Lombardos,' *Weekend Magazine*, 4 and 11 Jul 1964
Miller, John. 'The sweetest music this side of Kilgore,' *Canadian Magazine*, 26 Dec 1970
Wilson, John S. 'Guy Lombardo,' *International Musician*, Sep 1971
Lombardo, Guy, with Altschul, Jack. *Auld Acquaintance* (New York 1975)
Fenwick, Harry. 'Should old acquaintance be forgot,' *Weekend Magazine*, 31 Dec 1977
Cline, Beverly Fink. *The Lombardo Story* (Don Mills, Ont, 1979). EBM, MM

LONDON, George (b Burnstein). Bass-baritone, stage director, b Montreal 30 May 1919, 1920, or 1921, of Russian-Jewish-US parents living in Montreal. He was registered at birth as a US citizen and moved with his parents to California when he was 15. After varied experience, amateur and professional, he went abroad in 1947 for study with Enrico Rosati. He returned to tour 1947–8 in Canada and the USA with the Columbia Bel Canto Trio (the other members of which were Frances Yeend and Mario Lanza). He made his European debut 3 Sep 1949 as Amonasro in *Aida* at the Vienna State Opera. His success was immediate, and he soon was heard in most of the important musical centres, including Edinburgh (1950), Bayreuth (1951), Salzburg (1952), and Milan (La Scala, 1952) and was the first North American to sing the title role in *Boris Godunov* at the Bolshoi Opera, Moscow.

London's *Metropolitan Opera debut, 13 Nov 1951, as Amonasro, was followed by 17 consecutive seasons there in such diverse roles as Boris Godunov, Don Giovanni, Scarpia in *Tosca*, Golaud in *Pelléas et Mélisande*, Deland in *Der fliegende Holländer*, Amfortas in *Parsifal*, Eugene Onegin, and Méphistophélès in *Faust*. He appeared with the Metropolitan Opera in Toronto as Scarpia in *Tosca* (1953, 1957) and as the Count in *The Marriage of Figaro* (1957) and in Montreal as Scarpia in 1953 and also with the *MSO in 1964. During these years, too, his dark voice and penetrating interpretations were much admired on the recital platform.

London was *Don Giovanni* in the memorable performances at the first *Vancouver International Festival in 1958 in a cast that included Joan Sutherland, Léopold *Simoneau, and Pierrette *Alarie and he also sang in that festival's presentation of the Verdi *Requiem* with Lois *Marshall, Jon *Vickers, and Maureen *Forrester. In 1967, for CBC TV in Montreal, he sang the Father in scenes from Charpentier's *Louise*, with the soprano Constance *Lambert.

In 1971 the retired singer made his debut as a stage director, producing *The Magic Flute* for New York's Juilliard School. Subsequently, he was appointed executive director of the National Opera Institute, Washington, DC, and general director of the U of Southern California's Opera Theater.

Beginning in 1949, London recorded copiously for various labels, notably English Decca (London). His long discography of recitals and major roles in complete operas includes two versions (1951 and 1962) of *Parsifal*, recorded during performances at Bayreuth. JBM

London. Namesake of the city in England, situated in southern Ontario halfway between Toronto and Windsor on the namesake of England's Thames river. It was laid out in 1826 and incorporated as a town in 1846, by which time it had a population of 3500. It became a city in 1855. With a population exceeding 250,000 in 1980 it had become a prosperous centre for insurance companies, educational institutions (*U of Western Ontario, Fanshawe College), and diversified agro-industrial activities.

London's first church organ, built for St Paul's Anglican Church in 1846, was destroyed a year later by a fire. In 1850 an organ was installed in the Wesleyan Methodist Church on Queen's Avenue. The North Street Wesleyan Methodist Church choir, conducted by Samuel Screaton ca 1853–70, was said to have achieved a high choral standard.

In the mid-19th century, brass bands attached to fire brigades and the British regiment provided musical entertainment. A Mrs Raymond advertised in 1849 as a teacher of piano and accordion. She remained active into the 1870s as both a teacher and an organizer of amateur concerts. For many years W.T. Erith, an English immigrant (fl 1856) taught singing and piano. An advertisement of 1860 proclaimed the availability of 'E.H. Longman / Organist & Professor of Music / Teacher of the / Organ, Pianoforte, Flute / Violin / AND SINGING / also Harmony, thorough Bass and / Composition.'

In 1851 James Gillean, bookseller, announced in the London *Free Press* that he had commenced stocking all kinds of new music. There was also an expanding trade in instruments. A year later, Coone & Co, as the agent for Gilbert & Co, offered pianos 'at Boston and New York prices, adding freight and duty only, and ... delivered to Toronto, Hamilton, Port Stanley or London.'

W. T. ERITH,
(FROM LONDON, ENGLAND,)
PROFESSOR OF
CLASSICAL MUSIC!
FIFTEEN YEARS
Member of the London Sacred Harmonic Societies,
GENTLEMAN OF HER MAJESTY'S CHAPEL ROYAL, AND
Lecturer on Ancient & Modern Sacred Music,
TEACHER OF
SINGING & PIANO-FORTE.
RESIDENCE:—No. 8, HORTON STREET EAST,
LONDON, C. W.

An advertisement in the *City of London Directory*, 1856

A vital musical pioneer, the Danish pianist, bandmaster, and clarinetist St John Hyttenrauch, settled in London in 1857. In 1863 he organized a choral-orchestral concert in aid of Lancashire spinners suffering from the declining trade caused by the US Civil War. In the mid-1860s Hyttenrauch formed the 7th London Fusiliers Band, which achieved an excellent reputation. He was teaching music in London schools by 1870 and served 1887–8 as president of the *Canadian Society of Musicians.

Two Irish brothers of Italian ancestry made a significant contribution. Charles Augustus *Sippi and George B. *Sippi participated in the musical life of London for over 50 years, as teachers, organists, choirmasters, and instrumental musicians. In 1874, when Hyttenrauch presented the first part of *Messiah* with a 150-voice choir, George played first violin in an orchestra of 25–30 and Charles was the tenor soloist and also played in the orchestra. The success of this concert led to the formation of the London Musical Union (also known as London Music Society) which had some 90 singers and 19 instrumentalists. Its programs included Mozart's *12th Mass* (later deemed misattributed) and, in 1875, the 'Spring' section of Haydn's *The Seasons*. The society flourished until around 1880.

The *Holman English Opera Troupe moved from Toronto to London in 1873 and converted the Music Hall into the Holman Opera House. W. James Birks, who succeeded Ephraim Plummer at the Dundas Centre Methodist Church 1878–92, built an 80-voice choir without equal in the city at the time. He also brought in guests to participate in choral concerts and give recitals and was the conductor of the Arion Club, founded in 1884. In 1888 he arranged a festival in which he directed a choir of several hundred voices, while Patrick S. Gilmore and his famous US touring band furnished instrumental music. Thousands at the Amusement Palace were regaled by choruses from *Tannhäuser* and *Il Trovatore*, the latter 'startlingly enhanced by the discharge of cannon.'

Handel's *Dettingen Te Deum* and Sullivan's oratorio *The Prodigal Son* are believed to have received their first Canadian performances in London in 1884 and 1885. Queen Victoria's diamond jubilee (1897) was celebrated by a performance of Handel's *Samson* with a chorus of 250 and an orchestra of 60. These numbers of participants were surpassed in an *Elijah* presented in 1900 by a chorus of 300 and the Boston Festival Orchestra. This performance was prepared by Roselle Pococke, a violinist and regimental bandmaster who became active in London in the early 1870s. In the 1880s Pococke founded a London SO and London Oratorio Society, amateur groups with which, over the next seven or eight years, he performed Haydn's *'Surprise' Symphony*, Mozart's *39th*, and Beethoven's *First*, the oratorios *Messiah, The Creation*, and *Christ on the Mount of Olives*, and other works. He prepared London's Festival Chorus for the 1903 *Cycle of Musical Festivals. An ardent promoter of chamber music, Pococke organized Sunday afternoon musicales which survived into the 1920s.

The Women's Music Club of London, founded in 1894 with 200 members, engaged in study sessions and discussions and presented six concerts a year, two by noted foreign artists. By 1925 the club had over 600 members. In addition to performances by local musicians, London enjoyed many visits by internationally known performers, eg, Emma *Albani (1889) and Ignace Jan Paderewski (ca 1902 at the Grand Opera House, which had been built in 1901, became a movie house in 1924, and a home for London's Little Theatre in 1945, and was restored and renovated as Theatre London in 1978). At the turn of the century the main choirs were the London Vocal Society under William *Hewlett and the London Oratorio Society under A.D. *Jordan. Orchestras usually were adjuncts to choral groups. Thus E.W.G. Quantz in 1910 assembled a 45-piece orchestra to perform cantatas at Askin St Methodist Church, and Jordan later formed a chorus and orchestra at his London Institute of Musical Art. An impetus for purely orchestral music was provided in 1922 by a visit from the Cleveland Orchestra. As supervisor of school music, Quantz brought the orchestra to London for a special children's matinee, which was followed by a survey and subsequent study of the children's responses. The challenge was taken up by César Borré, a resident of London 1920–37, who formed a Philharmonic Union in the early 1930s.

The Depression, the ascendancy of radio and recordings, and World War II combined to slow the growth of London's musical activity during the 1930s and 1940s. Nonetheless, in 1937 Bruce Sharpe reconstituted a London orchestra from the ensemble formerly conducted by A.D. Jordan.

After the war growth resumed. The *London SO (London Civic SO) prospered 1949–69 under Martin *Boundy. With the completion in 1967 of the *Centennial Hall, the orchestra gained its own home. In 1969, when Boundy became music director of Fanshawe College and conductor of Fanshawe's Four Counties Choir, Clifford *Evens became the London SO's first full-time music director and conductor, serving in that position until 1979. The London Youth SO was established ca 1961 and continued in 1980 as a focus for orchestral training. In 1947 the lawyer, organist, and arts patron Gordon *Jeffery renovated a church to create the Aeolian Hall, which became home to the London Chamber Orchestra (established in 1945) and the Aeolian Choral Society (formed 1949).

The *Salvation Army band of the London Citadel was conducted by Ed Judge 1940–70. In 1947 the Royal Canadian Regiment Band was formed in London, and until it was relocated in 1970 it performed in the city and throughout southern Ontario. The *Don Wright Chorus, founded in 1947, was heard until 1956 in radio broadcasts throughout North America.

Earle *Terry, who became music director for the London Board of Education in 1947, founded (and directed 1948–63) the Earle Terry Singers, a female choir. During the late 1950s and early 1960s the choir that he had formed at the London Cons sang with the Cleveland Orchestra when it visited London.

Educational institutions have played an important part in London music. For example, Hellmuth Ladies' College employed William Caven Barron (b St Mary's, Ont, 1864), the Sippi brothers, W. Waugh *Lauder (music director 1883–5), and the pianist Thomas Martin (b Ireland 1860, a pupil of Carl Reinecke and the college's music director from 1885 to sometime after 1913). Charles E. *Wheeler, a native of London and an organist and conductor, was music director at the Normal School. Caven Barron, organist at First Presbyterian Church, founded the London Cons of Music in 1892. He was succeeded as director ca 1910 by F.L. Willgoose. In 1922 the Institute of Musical Art (founded in 1919 by A.D. Jordan) absorbed the London Cons. The institute, in turn, was absorbed in 1934 into the newly incorporated *Western Ontario Cons of Music, directed first by Frederick *Newnham, then 1938–57 by Harvey Robb. For more than 40 years, Thomas *Chattoe examined for the conservatory. In 1969 the Music Teachers' College, in affiliation with the U of Western Ontario, became the university's Faculty of Music, which by 1978 with almost 700 students became Canada's largest university music school. With such ensembles as the U of Western Ontario SO, the Faculty of Music Chamber Orchestra, and the resident piano quartet *Quartet Canada, the students and staff of the faculty have added much to London's concert life. The International Society for Music Education (ISME) held its 1978 world congress in London.

Music businesses located in London have included the *Evans Bros Piano & Manufacturing Co, the *Sherlock-Manning Piano Co, *GRT of Canada (record company), *Sparton records, *Starr records, *Keates Organ Co, Gabriel *Kney & Co (organs), and *Jaymar Music Ltd (publishing). London has been the home of such distinguished musicians as Max *Pirani and Alfred *Rosé; and the city and its environs have been the birthplace of Reginald *Bedford, Victor *Braun, George M. *Brewer, Garnet *Brooks, Gustav *Ciamaga, William *Douglas, Garth Hudson of The *Band, Tommy *Hunter, Joanne Ivey *Mazzoleni, Gordon Jeffery, the *Lombardo family, Rob *McConnell, the *Niosi brothers, Rowland *Pack, Raymond *Pannell, Harry *Puddicombe, George *Smale, Frank A. Veitch (1871–?, publisher in 1907 of the *Musical Red Book of Montreal* and manager of the *Couture and *Goulet *MSOs), and Ernest *White.

BIBLIOGRAPHY
Mason, Lawrence. 'Ontario vistas: IV – London,' Toronto *Globe*, 18 Jul 1925
'The whole country looks to London, Ontario,' *CBC Times*, 23–9 Mar 1952
Crawford, Lenore. 'City bands, choirs famous,' London Centennial pamphlet (London 1955)
Hines, Frances R. 'Concert life in London Ontario 1870–1880,' unpubl M MUS thesis, U of Western Ontario 1975 (PGD, PMW)

London Conservatory of Music. See Western Ontario Conservatory of Music.

London Institute of Musical Art. See Western Ontario Conservatory of Music.

London Records of Canada (1967) Ltd. Until 1980 the Canadian subsidiary of Decca Records of England. The parent company, founded in 1929, has been responsible for several technical advances in recording, including (1946) 'Full Frequency Range Recording' (or 'ffrr'), the stereo LP in 1958, and the Dolby Noise Reduction System in the 1970s.

Decca established the London Gramophone Corp in North America in 1947 to market its 'ffrr' recordings and founded the London Gramophone Corp of Canada in 1948 with offices in Montreal and Fraser C. Jamieson as chief executive. (Jamieson later became president, and his wife vice-president.) Upon the consolidation in 1967 of Decca's various Canadian holdings, the company became London Records of Canada (1967) Ltd.

The first Canadian to record for London (in Europe) was Jacques *Labrecque; the first record made in Canada for London was by the duo Pierre Roche and Charles Aznavour. Subsequently London included on its Canadian roster the Band of the Royal Canadian Regiment, the Black Watch (R.H.R.) of Canada, Paul *Brunelle, the Central Band of the Canadian Armed Forces, Renée *Claude, Michel Conte, Andy *DeJarlis, André *Gagnon, Reginald *Godden, Gaby *Haas, Willie *Lamothe, Marcel *Martel, the Poppy Family, Ti-Blanc *Richard, the jazz pianist Milt Sealey, René *Simard, and Sweeney Todd.

London has distributed European recordings made for it by Ellen *Ballon, Jules *Bruyère, Pierre *Duval, Raoul *Jobin, George *London, Zara *Nelsova, Louis *Quilico, Joseph *Rouleau, Huguette *Tourangeau, Jon *Vickers, and others.

London's Ace of Diamonds line has included recordings – many originally produced as part of the CBC's SM series – by the *CBC Vancouver Chamber Orchestra, Maureen *Forrester, Betty-Jean *Hagen, Anton *Kuerti, Lois *Marshall, the *McGill Chamber Orchestra, the *Orford String Quartet, and Albert *Pratz.

The company has distributed several independent Canadian labels: Aquarius (until 1978), founded in 1968 by Terry Flood, who enlisted *April Wine, Lewis *Furey, Walter *Rossi, the *Guess Who, and others; Attic, formed in 1974 in Toronto by Alexander Mair and Tom Williams, who have recorded the *Boss Brass, Shirley *Eikhard, Patsy Gallant, Hagood *Hardy, Sheila *Henig, Joel Shulman, Nancy White, and others; *Boot (and Cynda); Gamma (until 1978); Goldfish, founded in 1973 by Terry *Jacks; *Rodeo (including the Banff, Caprice, Celtic, and Melbourne labels); and, until 1976, Select.

London distributed the recordings which Philippe *Bruneau, Jean *Carignan, and others made for Philo, a Vermont-based company founded in 1973 by Phil Hresko; it also handled, in Canada, various European labels. It controlled the publishing-rights companies Burlington Music (CAPAC) and Felsted Music (PRO Canada). When Decca of England became part of PolyGram Inc (see Polydor) in 1980, London Records of Canada (1967) Ltd ceased operations and closed its pressing plant in Montreal. Marketing and distribution of London records and tapes was subsequently taken over by PolyGram Distribution Inc.

BIBLIOGRAPHY
Sherman, David. 'Disc exec: at the top for 30 years,' Montreal *Gazette*, 22 Sep 1978
'Fraser Jamieson and London Records of Canada: a thirty-year relationship,' *RPM*, 30 Sep 1978 (EBM, MM)

London Symphony Orchestra. Founded by Bruce Sharpe at London, Ont, as the London Civic SO (civic charter 1937). It was disbanded during World War II and re-formed in 1945. Postwar conductors were Sharpe 1945–9 and Martin *Boundy 1949–69. Under Boundy the orchestra established itself as one of Ontario's leading community orchestras. Letters patent of 1957 made the shorter name official.

Clifford *Evens, Boundy's successor, served 1969–79 as the orchestra's first full-time conductor and artistic director. Evens' skill and patience in rehearsal and the persistence and adroitness of his tactics in raising the calibre of the player force gained him a reputation as an orchestra builder. In the late 1960s and early 1970s he made the utmost use of the *OAC's Resident Artists' Plan (collaborative financing of player-teachers by the orchestra, the *U of Western Ontario, and the OAC). In 1974 the orchestra appointed its first full-time manager, Mark Warren, who with Evens began the economic conversion necessary to the support of increased community and regional services by the orchestra and an increased number of full-time players.

In 1975 the Richard and Jean Ivey Fund made the orchestra a grant of $100,000 which enabled it to place 30 musicians under annual contract to play as the London Sinfonia and to form the full-time nucleus of the symphony orchestra, thus qualifying it as Canada's 11th major orchestra. In the 1977–8 season the London SO gave a 10-concert main series, 2 5-concert sub-series, 6 pop concerts, 5 children's concerts (in *Centennial Hall, its main performance venue, and thus distinct from the many children's in-school concerts), and 1 oratorio performance (*Messiah*). Among other concerts in London and region was a 3-concert series by the sinfonia in Stratford.

During the 1970s the orchestra commissioned and performed works by Peter Clements (*Suite Grotesque*), Peter Paul *Koprowski (*In Memoriam Karol Szymanowski*), William Miller (*Au bord de la forêt*), André *Prévost (*Corégraphie IV*), Alfred *Rosé (*Adagio* for cello and orchestra), and Jerome Summers (*Images*). In that same period it programmed 25 other works by Canadians, including three by *Symonds (*Impulse, Three Atmospheres,* and *Pastel for Strings*), two by Prévost (*Célébration* and *Évanescence*), two by *Somers (*Fantasia for Orchestra* and *Five Songs for Dark Voice* with Maureen *Forrester), and major pieces by *Champagne (*Symphonie gaspésienne*), *Freedman (*Tangents*), and Jacques *Hétu (*Symphony No. 3*).

Among guest conductors in the 1970s were Kazuyoshi Akiyama, Arthur Fiedler, and Karl Richter. Among some 60 solo performers in that period, of whom about two-thirds were Canadian, were William *Aide, Claudio Arrau, Colette *Boky, Liona *Boyd, Nicholas *Fiore, James Galway, Hagood *Hardy, Eugene Istomin, Anton *Kuerti, Louis *Lortie, Jessye Norman, John Ogdon, Louis *Quilico, Leonard Rose, Anna *Russell, Sylvia *Saurette, Peter Serkin, Gwen *Thompson, Tsuyoshi *Tsutsumi, Ronald *Turini, Riki *Turofsky, Galina Vishnevskaya, and George *Zukerman.

With the resignations of Evens and Warren in 1979 Victor *Feldbrill was engaged as acting music director pending the appointment of a new conductor, and Erling Alfee was appointed orchestra manager. In 1980 the Austrian-born conductor Alexis Hauser was named artistic director, effective the fall of 1981. The London Youth SO, founded in 1961 by the London SO and conducted by James White, continued under the senior orchestra's sponsorship in 1980.

BIBLIOGRAPHY
'The London Symphony Orchestra,' *CanComp*, 22, Oct 1967
'Orchestra Canada salutes London Symphony Orchestra,' *OCan*, vol 2, Nov 1975
Hanson, Gary, 'London Sinfonia on tour,' *OCan*, vol 4, Jul 1977 (PGD, KW)

LONGTIN, Michel. Composer, teacher, b Montreal 20 May 1946; BA (Montreal) 1967, B MUS (Montreal) 1973, M MUS (Montreal) 1975. He studied at the *U of Montreal with André *Prévost (composition), Serge *Garant (analysis), and others and briefly in July 1971 at the *RCMT with Samuel *Dolin. He also worked in the electronic music studio of *McGill U – 1971–2 with Paul

*Pedersen, 1972–3 with Bengt *Hambraeus, and 1974–5 with Alcides *Lanza. He won the 1971–2 BMI Award to Student Composers with *Il était une fois* (1971) for orchestra, choir, and magnetic tape and the 1972 *Alliance chorale canadienne prize for *Pays de neige* (1971). He received a grant from the *Canada Council in 1974 and the *CLComp prize in 1975 for *Le Pèlerin d'Alnéoïl* (1974).

Two of Longtin's works, *Rituel II* (1971) and *Mi e meta* (1971), were performed at the *PDA (June 1972) by the dance group Nouvelle-Aire, which also took part in the premiere, December 1977 at the Centaur Theatre, Montreal, of his *Pour conjurer la montagne* (1977).

In addition to his concert works, Longtin has written sound-tracks for the films *Copies conformes* (1973) and *Sidbec-Dosco* (1974); music for a series of advertisements for Loto-Québec (1975); and the score for the NFB's *Poids lourds* (1976). Two of his works for magnetic tape, both composed in 1972, have been recorded: *La Mort du Pierrot* (RCI 373) and *Fedhibô* (Mel SMLP 4027).

Though he has several instrumental works to his credit, Longtin has become known chiefly for electroacoustic compositions, some of which have been heard in Europe and the USA. Most of his works are unpublished, but some have been deposited with the *CMCentre, of which he is an associate.

Longtin began teaching theory at the U of Montreal in 1973 and music of the 20th century at the *École Vincent-d'Indy and composition at the St-Laurent Cegep in 1975. He is an affiliate of PRO Canada.

BIBLIOGRAPHY

Laplante, Louise. 'Longtin's creativity includes orchestra, film scores,' *MSc*, 292, Nov–Dec 1976

PRO Canada. 'Michel Longtin,' pamphlet (1978)

Gingras, Claude. 'Gonneville et Longtin: deux créations à la SMCQ,' Montreal *La Presse*, 17 Feb 1979

Petrowski, Nathalie. 'Deux jeunes compositeurs à la SMCQ,' Montreal *Le Devoir*, 19 Feb 1979

Contemporary Canadian Composers / Compositeurs canadiens contemporains (PR)

LORANGE, (Marie Thérèse Rolande) **Nicole** (m Grédiaga). Soprano, b Montreal 28 Nov 1942; M MUS (Montreal) 1965. She began her studies privately with Roger *Filiatrault, continuing at the *École Vincent-d'Indy with Pierrette *Alarie, Louise *André, Bernard *Diamant, Filiatrault, and Roy *Royal. In 1967 she worked at the Vienna Academy with Alexandre Kohlau, Wolfgang Steinbruck, and Erik Werba. Her scholarships include one from the *Ladies' Morning Musical Club in 1963 and several from the *Canada Council 1967–70. On 22 Apr 1963 she was a soloist at the 100th Sarah *Fischer Concert, in the summer of 1964 she was a *JMC delegate to the 5th Zimriya Choral Festival in Tel Aviv, and in 1965 she won the *MSO Concours. She sang Desdemona in *Otello* (1968–9) at the Linz Opera, Musetta in *La Bohème* (1972) with the *COC in Toronto, Leonora in *La Forza del Destino* (1975) in Mahon in the Balearic Islands, Giulietta in *The Tales of Hoffmann* (1975) in Dublin, and Nedda in *I Pagliacci* at the Barcelona Gran Teatro del Liceo with Placido Domingo. She was a soloist with the *MSO in 1979 and sang the title role in *Tosca* for the Opéra de Montréal's seven inaugural performances at the *PDA in October 1980.

DISCOGRAPHY

Opera en voces de oro del siglio XX: operatic duets by Verdi and Puccini. Aragall ten, New Philharmonia O, Guadagno cond. 1977. Col SCE 983

Puccini *Tosca*. Aragall ten, Quilico bar, Bisson bar, New Philharmonia O, Guadagno cond. 1977. 2-Zofiro SA Dorado ZOR-1011

Verdi – Puccini – Boito. New Philharmonia O, Guadagno cond. 1977. Col SCE 982 (DA)

LORD, Frederic. Choir director, teacher, organist, composer, b Bingley, Yorks, 15 Nov 1886, d Brantford, Ont, 15 Aug 1945. He performed in recital at 10 and was a church organist at 11 before studying piano in Montreux, Switzerland, with Ladislas Gorski and in England with Eaglefield Hull. He was organist at Barnoldswick, Lancashire, and at Settle, Yorkshire. He moved (1923) to Brantford, Ont, as organist-choirmaster of the First Baptist Church, taught piano and organ there and was music director at the Ontario School for the Blind until his death.

Lord organized and conducted (1928–45) the Canadian Choir of Brantford. The choir, managed by his wife Dorothy, a violinist and teacher, first performed in 1929, won fourth prize at the Blackpool Music Festival (October 1930), sang 3 Nov 1930 at Albert Hall, London, during a tour of Scotland and England, and performed 23 Nov 1931 at *Massey Hall, Toronto, and 1937–8 in New York. The choir won praise at home ('undeniably a virtuoso choir' – Toronto *Globe*) and abroad ('In beauty of tone and perfect precision they are the equals of any choir I have heard anywhere' – London *Evening Standard*).

Lord's compositions include choral works (G. Schirmer, Novello, and Anglo-Canadian); a symphony; two piano concertos; the cantata *The Battle of Morgarten*; a setting of *Psalm 90* for baritone solo, choir, and orchestra; and piano pieces (Chester). He was an inspiring voice and choir teacher. His pupils included George *Lambert.

BIBLIOGRAPHY

'The criticized critic,' *MCan*, vol 12, Jan 1931

'Musical bibliographies of Canadian composers: no. 10,' Toronto *Globe*, 31 Oct 1936 (MFr)

LORRAIN, Denis. Composer, b Ithaca, NY, of Canadian parents, 29 Jul 1948; B MUS (Montreal) 1971, MMA (McGill) 1973. In 1967 he entered the *U of Montreal, where his teachers were Jean-Marie *Cloutier, Jean *Papineau-Couture, and André *Prévost. On graduation he joined the staff at *McGill U, where he taught until 1974 and also continued his studies with Bengt *Hambraeus, Alcides *Lanza, Bruce *Mather, and Paul *Pedersen. At the same time he attended classes given by Serge *Garant and (1973) by Iannis Xenakis at the U of Montreal.

Lorrain's interest in electronic music involved him 1970–2 in the research team Informatique-musique. On a *Canada Council scholarship he attended the Arts and Music Computer Symposium (1971) in Duluth, Minn. In 1972 he studied with Xenakis at the Center of Mathematics and Automated Music in Bloomington, Ind, worked with Jean-Claude Risset at the U of Aix-Marseille in France, and attended a computer science course at the Centre national d'étude des télécommunications in Paris. On scholarships from the Canada Council and the Government of the Netherlands in 1973, he spent some time (1974) at the Institute of Sonology in Utrecht.

Lorrain won a BMI Award to Student Composers (1969–70) and a *CLComp scholarship (1970) for *Arc* (1969, for string orchestra), which was premiered in April 1970 in Boston and performed in 1971 by the *Quebec SO. His others works include *P-A* (1970–1, for talking voices), *L'Angelus* (1971, for clarinet and tape), *Suite* for two guitars (1972, winner of another BMI award), *Séquence* (1972, for organ), *Polyphrase* (1973, for orchestra), *Contra mortem* (1975, for clarinet), *Droite* (1976, for tape), *Le Talon d'Achille* (1976, for flute), and *Extrema* (1977, for organ and one percussionist), which won the 1977 Prométhée special composition prize in Lourdes. *Di mi se mai ...* (1979) was commissioned by the *SMCQ and was premiered in 1980. He is an affiliate of PRO Canada and an associate of the *CMCentre.

BIBLIOGRAPHY

Thériault, Jacques. 'New mathematical approach to music fascinates Lorrain,' *MSc*, 273, Sep–Oct 1973 (PR)

LORRIE, Myrna (Lorraine) (b Petrunka). Singer, songwriter, guitarist, b Cloud Bay, near Thunder Bay, Ont, 1941? She began singing at 12 on CKPR radio (Fort William, now Thunder Bay) and soon was featured on the show 'Harmony Trails.' At 14 she rose to country-music stardom with the record 'Are You Mine?,' released by Abbott Records, sung with Buddy DuVal, and co-written with DuVal and Don Grashey; it was a major hit during 1955 in Canada and the USA, reaching number one on *Billboard* magazine's country and western chart. Lorrie performed throughout the late 1950s in both countries in concerts – touring with Hank *Snow and others – and on TV.

After a period of inactivity, Lorrie resumed her performing career in 1963 and, in 1964, formed the Myrna Lorrie Show, the leading touring troupe in Canadian country music for five years. She was a guest performer on many CBC TV country music shows, including, 1966–8, 'Don *Messer's Jubilee,' was co-host 1970–4 with Don Tremaine for CBC Halifax TV's 'Countrytime,' and in 1974 starred in the summer series 'Country Sunshine.' In 1977 she became co-host with Tom Kelly for 'Nashville Swing,' a syndicated TV series produced in Toronto. In 1978 she appeared as a country singer in the US feature film *High Ballin'*, which was shot in Toronto.

Though her later recordings have not achieved the success of 'Are You Mine?', Lorrie had a hit with 'Changing of the Seasons' in 1968 and made the LPs *Myrna Lorrie* (Harmony HE 90055) and, with the cast of the TV show, *It's Countrytime* (CBC LM 87/MCA 7009). She won the 1970 and 1971 *Juno Awards as the best female country singer and the 1977 Big Country Award for outstanding performance by a female country singer.

Blaik Kirby (*Globe and Mail*, 1 Aug 1974) wrote: 'Her interpretations, by and large, were gentle and feminine, without artificiality. She's not yet an impressive interpreter, but she's a gentle, likeable one.' Margaret Daly (*Toronto Star*, 28 Jun 1976), recounting Lorrie's triumphant appearance at the *Mariposa Folk Festival, referred to her 'fresh, lovely appearance and her modest, unassuming stage presence ... Lorrie earned her bravos without compromising her style or her repertoire.'

Lorrie is an affiliate of PRO Canada.

BIBLIOGRAPHY

Cobb, David. 'There's got to be more to life than talking to dirty old men,' *Canadian Magazine*, 12 Dec 1970

Cameron, Frank. 'Myrna Lorrie rebounds to national TV scene,' *MSc*, 261, Sep–Oct 1971 MM

LORTIE, André. Tenor, b Montreal 11 May 1930. His first singing teacher was Roger Larivière. He later studied at the *CMM and in New York. In 1952 he made his debut with the *Variétés lyriques as Alexius in Oscar Straus' operetta *The Chocolate Soldier*. For the *Montreal Festivals he sang the role of Porcus in *Jeanne d'Arc au bûcher* (1953), Basilio in *The Marriage of Figaro* (1956), and Torquemada in *L'Heure espagnole* (1961). With the *Opera Guild he portrayed Spoletta in *Tosca* (1957), Caius in *Falstaff* (1958), Remendado in *Carmen* (1960), Gastone in *La Traviata* (1962), Goro in *Madama Butterfly* (1965, 1969), Benoît in *La Bohème* (1966), and Basilio in *The Marriage of Figaro* (1967). A grant from the Quebec government enabled him to work in 1960 with the American Opera Society in Philadelphia, Washington, Baltimore, and New York; he took the part of Lalouf in Poulenc's *Les Mamelles de Tirésias* in its US premiere at Carnegie Hall. During the World Festival (*Expo 67) he performed with the *MSO, the *COC, and the *Théâtre lyrique de Nouvelle-France. The same year he participated in the premiere of *Somers' **Louis Riel* (the roles of Ambroise Lépine and Père André) in Toronto, and repeated the roles in Montreal and on CBC TV. He sang at the *NAC in *The Marriage of Figaro* in 1971 and 1972 and *La Belle Hélène* (Ajax II) in 1973 and 1975. With the *Opéra du Québec he sang the roles of Roderigo in *Otello* in 1973, Bardolfo in *Falstaff* and Goro in *Madama Butterfly* the following year and Benoît in *La Bohème* in 1975. In 1973 he also sang in Edmonton and Vancouver in *Tosca* and at Hartford, Conn, in *Carmen*. André Lortie handles tragic roles as easily as comic parts. His performances of Beppe in *I Pagliacci* and Spoletta in *Tosca* have established his reputation in Canada as a singer of character roles. SW

LORTIE, Louis. Pianist, b Montreal 27 Apr 1959. He began to study piano at seven, working successively with Nicole Pontbriand-Beaudoin, Sister Simone Martin at the Wilfrid-Pelletier School and Yvonne *Hubert at the *École normale de musique. He gained recognition at the *Canadian Music Competitions for five successive years (1968–72), at the *MSO Concours in 1972, and in the Czechoslovakian radio's Concertino Praga in 1973 and 1975. After winning the 1975 *CBC Talent Festival and International Stepping Stones of the Canadian Music Competitions the same year, he gave numerous recitals and played on the CBC. He continued his studies 1975–6 in Vienna with Dieter Weber and, after Weber's death, at Indiana U with Menahem Pressler. In 1978 Andrew Davis chose him to be one of the soloists (the other being Maureen *Forrester) for the *TS tour in Japan and China. He made his debut at *Massey Hall with this orchestra in Liszt's *Concerto No. 1* and played it again with great success in Tokyo, Peking, Shanghai, and Canton. On his return he performed the same work with the *MSO; Eric *McLean described him as 'unquestionably one of the most gifted pianists this country has produced in recent years' and continued, 'This kind of facility, with this kind of temperament is what great artists are made of' (*Montreal Star*, 3 Apr 1978). Lortie has performed subsequently in several Canadian cities and has appeared abroad.

BIBLIOGRAPHY

Traynor, Dave. 'Local pianist to tour China,' *Montreal Star*, 16 Jan 1978

Potvin, Gilles. 'Le pianiste Louis Lortie, une jeune carrière qui a démarré en Chine,' Montreal *Le Devoir*, 4 Mar 1978

Thompson, Leslie. 'Short on ambition, endowed with talent,' *Music*, Oct 1978

Petrovski (sic), Nathalie. 'Le gang des pianos à queue,' *L'Actualité*, Apr 1979 GP

LOTH, J. (John) **Ferris**. Teacher, editor, b Milverton, near Kitchener, Ont, 3 Jun 1908, d Kitchener 29 Jan 1972. Born into a musical family, Loth studied piano with George Lethbridge in London, Ont, Ernest Tailby in Doon, Ont, and George *Ziegler in Kitchener and later attended the *Hambourg Cons in Toronto, completing a course in school music teaching. In 1930 he settled in Kitchener, where he taught piano and operated a music kindergarten. His numerous teaching publications remained in print in 1980.

WRITINGS (published by Waterloo Music Co Ltd)

Scales and Chords for Piano, 2 vols, (1944)

Students Selected Sonatinas (1945)

Students Basic Exercises for Piano, 5 vols, (1945–51)

Beginners Scales and Chords for Piano (1946)

Piano Play for Every Day, 5 vols, (1946–7)

Piano Play for Older Child Beginners (1946)

Twenty Lessons on Note Writing (1957)

Twenty Lessons on Counting Time (1958) EBM

Louis Riel. Opera in three acts (18 scenes), by Harry *Somers, to an English-and-French libretto by Mavor *Moore and Jacques Languirand. The opera was commissioned by the Floyd S. *Chalmers Foundation and produced by the *COC with financial assistance from the Canadian Centennial Commission, the *Canada Council, and POCA (*OAC).

Louis Riel had its first performances at the *O'Keefe Centre in Toronto 23 and 28 Sep and 11 Oct 1967 and at the Salle Wilfrid-Pelletier, *PDA, in Montreal 19 and 21 Oct 1967. Victor *Feldbrill conducted, Leon Major directed, and Murray Laufer and Marie Day designed the sets and costumes. The original cast included Bernard *Turgeon as Riel, Cornelis *Opthof as Sir John A. Macdonald, Joseph *Rouleau as Monseigneur Taché, Patricia *Rideout as Riel's mother, Mary *Morrison as his sister, Roxolana *Roslak as his wife, Howell *Glynne as William McDougall, and Ermanno *Mauro as Baptiste Lépine.

The libretto depicts the post-Confederation political events bounded by the Indian and Métis uprising of 1869–70 and 1884–5 and the personal tragedy of the uprisings' leader, the Manitoba schoolteacher and Métis hero Louis Riel. After the premiere, Kenneth *Winters described the opera in the Toronto *Telegram* (25 Sep 1967) as a 'pastiche ... big, efficient, exciting, heterogeneous ... It had no ring of eternity but it was a vigorous harnessing of current and choice; a brash, smart, cool hand on the pulse of a number of fashions, social, dramatic and musical.' The production was repeated in 1968 in Toronto – six performances with the assistance of the Chalmers Foundation – and was adapted by Franz *Kraemer in 1969 for CBC TV.

In 1975 *Louis Riel* was revived by the COC for several performances, including one in Toronto, 27 September, honouring the International Music Council's 16th General Assembly; three (14, 16, and 18 October) at the *NAC, Ottawa; and one (23 October, the US premiere) at the Kennedy Center, Washington, DC, as part of Canada's contribution to the USA's bicentennial celebrations. Wendell Margrave of the *Washington Star* described the opera as 'one of the most imaginative and powerful scores to have been written in this century.'

'Kuyas' – the lullaby sung in Act III by Riel's wife to their child – was used prior to the opera's premiere as the test piece for the *Montreal International Competition in 1967.

BIBLIOGRAPHY

Somers, Harry. 'The score,' *OpCan*, Sep 1967

'The making of an opera,' *Mcan*, 4, Sep 1967

Graham, June. 'Louis Riel,' *CBC Times*, 25–31 Oct 1969

Schafer, R.M. *The Public of the Music Theatre – Louis Riel: a Case Study* (Vienna 1972) KW

LOUNT-TYSON, Adele. Pianist, composer, b ca 1875, d 1901? The daughter of W.L. Tyson of Clarksburg, near Owen Sound, Ont, she studied piano and composition in Germany for five years and became a resident of Philadelphia in 1898. Her performance in January 1900 of Grieg's *Piano Concerto* at a private concert with Paderewski at the second piano was lauded by New York critics. A concert 18 Sep 1900 in Dresden presented Lilli Lehmann singing 2 of Lount-Tyson's 10 songs with original texts in German and a French pianist playing her *Moods* and *Fantasie-Stücke*. Little else has been traced of her career although she is known to have suffered a serious, probably fatal illness early in 1901. EK

LOUVAIN, Michel (b Poulin). Singer, b Thetford Mines, Que, 12 Jul 1937. Taking the name of an older French-Canadian singer (André Louvain) Michel Louvain began his career as master of ceremonies and singer when he replaced his brother (who appeared under the name André Roc) at a cabaret in St-Georges de Beauce. He then sang in Sherbrooke and Quebec City. In 1957 he made his TV debut on the CBC's 'Gala des splendeurs' and began recording for Apex. His first 78, 'Buenas noches mi amor,' was a substantial hit. A hugely successful career followed.

In the next 20 years Louvain was the reigning matinee idol of Quebec, known by his many recordings for Apex and his work as host for a succession of CFTM (Montreal) and CBC TV variety shows. Louvain has been called Quebec's first pop star; his success was comparable in Quebec with that of Presley in the USA; and for many years his performances took his young (largely female) fans to the brink of hysteria. Initially his personal appearances were centred in nightclubs, but later, when his following grew more mature, he turned to concerts, and in the late 1970s he appeared at the *PDA and the *NAC.

Louvain has made more than 25 LPs, the majority for Apex (which has issued *Mes Plus Grands Succès '57–'67*, ALF 71592), and the balance for Lero, Ciné, and others. A collection, *21 Disques d'or Michel Louvain*, has been issued by the Archives du disque québécois (AQ 21006). His most popular recordings include his versions of 'Sayonara,' 'D'aventure en aventure,' 'Lison,' 'Louise,' 'Lynda,' 'Sylvie,' 'La Dame en bleu,' 'Harmonie,' and 'Un Certain Sourire.'

BIBLIOGRAPHY

Beaulieu, Pierre. 'Louvain: 22 ans de cote d'amour,' Montreal *La Presse*, 7 Jul 1979 MM

LOVELL, John. Printer, publisher, b Bandon, County Cork, Ireland, 4 Aug 1810, d Montreal 1 Jul 1893. He arrived in Canada in 1820 and began his career as a printer in Montreal in 1835, concentrating on periodicals and newspapers. Lovell's company – known variously as Lovell & Gibson (1842–50, with a Toronto branch ca 1848–67), John Lovell (1850–75), Lovell Publishing and Printing (1875–9), and John Lovell & Son (1879–) – became known for its schoolbooks, gazetteers, and directories.

Lovell's music publications, all typeset, were consistent with his high standards of workmanship. The earliest examples are found in the monthly *Literary Garland* (1838–51) and contain compositions by the Canadians Joseph *Maffré, Charles *Sauvageau, W.H. Warren, and others. Many of the Canadian books from the 1850s and 1860s known to include musical notation were published by Lovell. Among these are *A Collection of Original Sacred Music* (1848) by F.H. Andrews, *Répertoire de l'organiste* (1851) by J.-B. *Labelle, *Business Guide to the City of Montreal with a Collection of Popular Songs* (1860), and *Tsiatak nihonon8entsiak ... Le livre des sept nations, ou Paroissien iroquois* (1865).

Lovell published, or printed for other publishers, a fair amount of sheet music. His issue of Lehmann's *Merry Bells of England* (1840) is one of the two earliest-known Canadian examples of the genre. Other composers published between 1840

THE

MERRY BELLS OF ENGLAND.

SONG,

BY

J. E. CARPENTER.

Composed, and Respectfully Dedicated

TO

Major Daniel Bolton, R. E., Bytown,

BY

J. P. LEHMANN.

MONTREAL:
Printed by John Lovell, in the Office of the Literary Garland,
SAINT NICHOLAS STREET.

1840.

The earliest known typeset piece of Canadian sheet music

and 1862 include J.-C. *Brauneis fils, Guillaume Fleury d'Eschambault, Ernest *Gagnon, Octave Peltier (*Pelletier), and Charles Wugk *Sabatier. Lovell's music publishing had slowed by 1870 and ceased after 1893.

BIBLIOGRAPHY

Gundy, H. Pearson. *Book Publishing and Publishers in Canada before 1900* (Toronto 1965)

Lochhead, Douglas. 'Introduction,' *Specimen of Printing Types and Ornaments in Use at the Printing Office of Lovell & Gibson, 1846* (Toronto 1975)

Calderisi, Maria. 'Music publishing in Canada: 1800–1867,' unpubl MMA thesis, McGill 1976 MC

Loving (also known to French-speaking audiences as *Toi*). Opera with music and text by R. Murray *Schafer. It was completed in 1965. The first ('Geography of Eros') of its four sections, however, was completed in 1963 and premiered in Toronto by Mary *Morrison. The other sections are titled 'Air d'Ishtar,' 'Modesty,' and 'Vanity.' Portions of the text were intended to be sung in French and were translated for that purpose by Gabriel *Charpentier from Schafer's English.

The work was commissioned by the CBC French network and performed first (in part) as *Toi* on the TV series L'*Heure du concert' 3 Feb 1966. The producer was Pierre *Mercure. The music director was Serge *Garant. It was rebroadcast on the English network as *Loving*, 25 May 1966.

Loving was performed complete for the first time 11 Mar 1978 in Toronto by a cast which included Mary Lou *Fallis, Jean McPhail, Susan Gudgeon, and Kathy Terrell and with a chamber orchestra conducted by Robert *Aitken. It was recorded that year (2-Mel SMLP 4035-4036) by the same performers.

In Schafer's words *Loving* is a 'synaesthetic work' in which 'several arts are employed in extremely close, frequently interpenetrating relationships.' There is no plot in the sense of unfolding action; rather there is a series of comments on and suggestions about love between man and woman. The seven characters sing in French and English.

The work is scored for small ensemble (but requires six percussion players) and lasts about 70 minutes. It was published by *Berandol in 1980 under the single title *Loving*.

BIBLIOGRAPHY

Littler, William. 'Canadian gets his premiere ... only twelve years late,' *Toronto Star*, 4 Mar 1978 (CM)

LOWE, Ruth (m Cohen, m Sandler). Songwriter, pianist, b Toronto, of US-Canadian parents, 12 Aug 1914, naturalized US 1937, naturalized Canadian 1942, d Toronto 4 Jan 1981. After living in her early teens in California she played piano in Toronto music stores at 16, promoting the sale of sheet music. With Sair Lee she performed in a two-piano team in Toronto nightclubs, and under the name Nancy Lee she worked in 1933 with the singer George Taggart on radio station CKNC. She was staff pianist with CKLC; sang with The Shadows, a female vocal trio, on CKNC; and performed with Red Hickey's dance band before joining Ina Ray Hutton's all-girl orchestra 1935–7 in the USA. She was pianist 1937–9 with the publishers Bregman, Vocco and Conn in Chicago.

Lowe returned in 1939 to Toronto, where she was an accompanist on CBL and wrote her first hit song, *'I'll Never Smile Again.' Collaborating on a number of other songs, she wrote the music for 'Too Beautiful to Last' (Feist 1940) and the lyrics for 'Put Your Dreams Away (For Another Day)' (Barton Music 1942), the latter for many years Frank Sinatra's closing theme song. She retired from performance in the early 1940s but continued to compose.

BIBLIOGRAPHY

'Toronto composer wrote Sinatra hit,' Toronto *Globe and Mail*, 5 Jan 1981 MM, PW

LOYONNET, Paul. Pianist, lecturer, writer, teacher, b Paris 13 May 1889. He studied at the Paris Cons with Charles de Bériot, J.-B. Ganaye, C.-M. Widor, and Isidor Philipp. He made his debut at 17 and subsequently appeared in recital and with orchestras throughout Europe, especially after World War I. It is estimated that he had 2000 engagements between 1918 and 1932. Through his association with the violinist Lucien Capet he developed an intense dedication to the piano music of Beethoven, and at the Collège des Sciences sociales he gave a series of recitals, with commentary and courses, to mark the Beethoven centenary (1927). Loyonnet chose to retire in 1932, and he re-emerged only after the outbreak of World War II to play in unoccupied France, Spain, Portugal, North and South Africa, Canada, the USA, and Latin America.

Loyonnet visited Montreal in 1951 to give concerts and lectures and settled there in 1954 to teach piano at the *École Vincent-d'Indy. Some 10 years later he began teaching at *McGill U. His pupils have included Gisèle Daoust (*Prix d'Europe 1960), Albert Dessane (Paris), Claire *Grenon-Masella, Pierre Jasmin, Jean *Leduc, and Boris *Roubakine.

In Paris, Loyonnet published articles in *Le Courrier musical* and *La Revue musicale*. He has made two LPs of Beethoven sonatas for the Janus label (JA 19005 and JA 19006).

WRITINGS

Beethoven 'ce mal connu' (Paris 1967)

Les 32 Sonates pour piano. Journal initime de Beethoven (Paris, Tours 1977)

BIBLIOGRAPHY

Allard, Ghyslaine. 'La technique pianistique de Paul Loyonnet,' unpubl L MUS thesis, Montreal 1962 GP

LUCAS, Clarence (Reynolds). Composer, conductor, writer, b Smithville, near Hamilton, Ont, 19 Oct 1866, d Sèvres, near Paris, 1 Jul 1947; B MUS (Toronto) 1893. The eldest child of Rev D.V. Lucas, a widely travelled Methodist minister, he lived in several small Ontario towns before his parents settled (1878) in Montreal. There he studied piano, organ, and violin and organized a school orchestra. Although offered a scholarship to McGill U to study for the ministry, he preferred to work as conductor of an amateur orchestra, trombonist in a theatre orchestra, organist in various churches, and violinist in the *Montreal Philharmonic Society. In 1885 he gave a piano recital in *Queen's Hall. Shortly thereafter he went to England. On hearing Anton Rubinstein he abandoned his dream of becoming a concert pianist. Lucas then studied privately in Paris with Georges-Eugène Marty, and at the conservatoire with Théodore Dubois, returning (1888) to Toronto to teach harmony and counterpoint at the *Toronto College of Music. Lucas' first wife, the English pianist Clara Asher who had studied with Clara Schumann, made her Toronto debut 7 Dec 1888 at the college. In 1889 Lucas became music director of the Wesleyan Ladies College in Hamilton and revived the Hamilton Philharmonic Society, conducting performances of *Messiah* (December 1889) and Sir Michael Costa's oratorio *Eli* (April 1890).

Clarence Lucas, a drawing by his son, Milton Lucas (*The Etude*, June 1933)

Lucas taught 1890–2 in Utica, NY, before returning (1893) to London, where he read proofs and revised manuscripts for *Chappell and prepared a new vocal score of Gounod's *Faust*. He also taught theory and composition privately (his pupils including Mark and Jan *Hambourg and the famous French woman ballad writer Guy d'Hardelot) and conducted 1902–4 the Westminster Society. In 1903 he became London correspondent for the *Musical Courier* of New York, an association which continued in various forms for 30 years. In 1904 he composed and conducted an Irish musical *Peggy Machree*, starring Denis O'Sullivan, and in 1905 he conducted with George Edwardes Gaiety Productions in London and on tour in the British Isles.

Lucas was engaged by the US actor Richard Mansfield to arrange and conduct Grieg's incidental music for Ibsen's *Peer Gynt* at its US premiere (1906) in New York. He then toured the USA with the production. His second wife, Gertrude Pidd, was a member of the company. Following Mansfield's death (1907), Lucas conducted *Peggy Machree* on a short US tour. In New York (1907–19) he was on the editorial staff of the *Musical Courier*, conducted musicals for George M. Cohan, and composed songs and keyboard pieces, some of a popular nature.

Moving in 1919 to London and in 1923 to Sèvres, Lucas freelanced as a transcriber, arranger, lyricist, and translator. He organized and participated in musicales of the Students' Atelier at the American Church of Paris and remained Paris correspondent to *Musical Courier* until 1933. He also wrote for the US music periodical *Etude*. Returning in 1933 to London he concentrated once again on composition while continuing editorial tasks.

Lucas' songs and piano pieces in popular vein do not reveal the depth of his abilities and tend to create the impression that he composed mostly 'light' music. In fact his major works, of which surviving copies are rare, established his reputation according to London's *Morning Post* as 'an accomplished musician and earnest composer' (21 Sep 1898). Leschetizky is said to have remarked to Mark Hambourg that the *Prelude and Fugue, Op 38* had the best modern fugue for piano. The opera *The Money Spider*, the cantata *The Birth of Christ*, and the overtures to *Othello*, *As You Like It*, and *Macbeth* were performed in several British and North American cities to favourable comment, eg, 'The melodies he writes have vitality and beauty and appeal to musician and layman alike. From this it is not to be concluded he is not a master of all resources of modern harmony and orchestration. He can be as modern as the most rabid anticlassicist could desire' (Chicago *Tribune*, Feb 1901). Like *Lavallée, Lucas in his day was Canada's most versatile composer. His son is the British composer Leighton Lucas (b London 1903).

COMPOSITIONS

STAGE WORKS

Anne Hathaway, opera (?). Written before 1898
The Money Spider, opera. Written ca 1897
Peggy Machree, musical play. 1904. J. Church 1904
At least 2 other operas (?): *Arabia* and *Semiramis*

ORCHESTRA

As You Like It, Op 35, overture. Chap 1899. RCI 233 (*CBC Wpg O)
The Birth of Christ, Op 41, cantata. Chap 1901
Macbeth, Op 39, overture. Chap ca 1900
Others, including *Othello* (overture), a symphony, and 2 symphonic poems

CHAMBER

Ballade, Op 40. Vn, pf (orch). Chap 1901
Ballade, Op 71. Vn, pf. Lucas 1939
Élégie, Op 30. Vn, pf. Breitkopf & Härtel 1895
Five Lyrical Pieces, Op 48. Vn, pf. Schott 1908
Légende, Op 42. Vn, pf. Schott 1903
Three Impromptus, Op 70. Vn. Bevan Music Prod 1938
Other works published by Donajowski in 1892

PIANO

Ariel, Op 55. Chap 1913; G. Schirmer 1914
Deux Mazurkas, Op 13. Nord 1890
Deux Morceaux, Op 2. Suckling 1889
Epithalamium, Op 54. Chap 1913
Holiday Sketches, Op 61. (No. 4) Boosey 1915
Praeludium et fuga, Op 32. Forsyth Brothers 1898
Prelude and Fugue, Op 38. Chap 1900; G. Schirmer 1916
Saga, Ein isländisches Märchen, Op 25. Breitkopf & Härtel nd

ORGAN

Canadian Wedding March, Op 66. Chap 1917
Seven Short Pieces, Op 75. Ascherberg, Hopwood & Crew 1945
Trois Morceaux pour grand orgue, Op 35. Schott 1900
Two Compositions for Organ, Op 73. Ascherberg, Hopwood & Crew 1941
Other works for pf and org publ by Naux, Breitkopf & Härtel, Presser, Augener, Chap, Schott, Michael Reane; many others without op no., some publ

CHOIR

'Battle Ode,' Op 65. Part song. Boosey 1915
'The Bells,' Op 56. Madrigal. Boosey 1913
Others with and without op no., some publ by Leonard, Gould & Bolttler, and Ascherberg, Hopwood & Crew

VOICE

Album of Six Baritone Songs, Op 29. Chap 1894
Five Songs, Op 45. Med v. J. Church 1904
Two Lyrics, Op 8. Ashdown 1889
Several vocal pieces without op no.; also many arr, including Chopin's *Nocturne, Op 15, no. 2* for v, with words by Lucas; vocal scores of Gounod's *Faust*, Monckton's *Country Girl*, etc

Recordings of 'Song of Songs' and 'The Perfect Song' (of which Lucas was lyricist) are listed in *Roll Back the Years*.

WRITINGS

The Story of Musical Form (London 1908, repr Boston 1977)
Many articles and reports for *Etude* and *Musical Courier*

BIBLIOGRAPHY

Logan, J.D. 'Canadian creative composers,' *Canadian Magazine of Politics, Science, Art and Literature*, vol 41, Sep 1913
Forsyth, W.O. 'Clarence Lucas, a Canadian distinguished in musical composition and in letters,' *CanJM*, vol 1, May 1914
MacMillan, Elsie. 'Clarence Lucas,' *MCan*, vol 9, Jul 1914
Forsyth, W.O. 'Canadian composers,' *CanJM*, vol 2, Jun 1915
'Clarence's dream,' *MCan*, vol 16, Jun 1920 SLH

Lucas et Cécile. Comic opera, of which only the vocal parts have survived. Libretto and music are by Joseph *Quesnel. In 1963, the major lines of the plot were reconstructed from the words of the 17 airs, duos, and ensembles. Lucas and Cécile are in love with one another. Cécile's mother, Thérèse, does not approve of the romance, but her husband, Mathurin, does. They consult DuSotin, who suggests that the lovers should be made to study Latin. Since DuSotin is himself the teacher, he plans on using the lessons to court Cécile. But the girl is bored by the teacher's elegant talk and prefers to marry the unpretentious Lucas.

The five roles are in the soprano or tenor registers and one of DuSotin's airs (no. 10) has a melody used by Quesnel in the 'vaudeville' (no. 13) of **Colas et Colinette*. No composition date appears on the manuscript, which is kept in the *Séminaire de Québec's archives (Verreau collection). By 1980 no clear evidence of a performance had been discovered, although the manuscript bears instructions in the composer's hand that no. 8 and no. 10 should be deleted, suggesting that a performance may have taken place, or at least been planned. (HK, DM)

LUENING, Ethel (b Codd). Soprano, teacher, b Regina, Sask, 23 Dec 1905. She studied voice with Yvonne Gagnon in Vancouver and in 1925 won first prize in the *Saskatchewan Music Festival. Following a tour with the Brandon Opera Company she studied on scholarship at the ESM. She made her debut in 1926 in the first opera season ever given at Chautauqua, NY, as Mabel in *The Pirates of Penzance* and Santuzza in *Cavalleria Rusticana*. The following winter she was a member of the admired American Opera.

After her marriage in 1927 to the composer-conductor Otto Luening she became known as an exponent of such contemporary American composers as Ernst Bacon, Henry Cowell, Charles Ives, and, of course, Luening. In 1934 the couple began a long association with Bennington College in Vermont. She retired from public singing in the mid-1940s and was divorced in 1959.

Ethel Luening may be heard on recordings of cantatas by Buxtehude (1937, Musicraft 1008 and 1009) and Handel (1937, Musicraft 1010), and of Luening's *Suite for Soprano and Flute* (New Music Recording 1513). JBM

LUGRIN FAHEY, Winifred (b Lugrin). Soprano, teacher, composer, b Fredericton 22 Sep 1884, d Victoria, BC, 28 Oct 1966. Of United Empire Loyalist stock, she studied with R. Thomas Steele in Vancouver. Her singing career (ca 1912–33) was confined by choice almost exclusively to Canada, although occasional US appearances included a New York recital, 18 Feb 1920, after which the *Times* described 'a voice of more than common capabilities – a voice of excellent natural quality, richness of range, and abundant power at both extremes.' In Toronto 1920–44, she was occupied largely with teaching but also composed several operettas, notably *The Bride Ship*, for performance by her students. A woman of immense enthusiasm and charm, she married John MacDonald Fahey in 1908.

BIBLIOGRAPHY

Pringle, Gertrude. 'Winifred Lugrin Fahey achieved success by brains and diligence,' *Maclean's*, 1 Oct 1924
– 'Her voice is but one of her many gifts,' *Canadian Magazine*, Feb 1927
Forbes, Elizabeth. 'Her voice rang out for victory,' Victoria *Times*, 2 Nov 1966 JBM

'Lukey's Boat.' Comical song widely sung on the east coast of Newfoundland and collected by Elisabeth Greenleaf in 1929 in Twillingate, Nfld. Greenleaf noted that the song was cast in the same metre as the famous shanty 'In Amsterdam There Lived a Maid' and thus may have originated as a shanty. Helen *Creighton, who in Nova Scotia collected a shorter version known as 'Loakie's Boat,' says that her singers told her it was about a man who came from Lunenburg.

The song has many stanzas which vary with the person singing it, but the usual ones describe Lukey's boat and tell of his return from a fishing expedition to discover that his wife is dead, which doesn't seem to grieve him much, for he announces that he'll get another in the spring (or the fall) of the year.

Creighton included it in *Songs and Ballads from Nova Scotia* (Toronto 1932) and it is also in Greenleaf and Mansfield's *Ballads and Sea Songs of Newfoundland* (Cambridge, Mass, 1933). Alan *Mills recorded it (*Folk Songs of Newfoundland*, Folk FW 6931). Harry *Somers used the tune as a theme in the opening movement of his *Little Suite* for string orchestra (1955). EF

Lullabies. Most lullabies sung in Canada came originally from the old world, except for those of the Indians and Inuit. A few Indian lullabies have become fairly well known, including 'Nadu Nadudu,' which Marius *Barbeau collected from a Nass Indian in British Columbia in 1920, the Iroquois 'Ho Ho Watanay,' which Alan *Mills heard in the Caughnawaga reservation in 1955, 'Baba Baby,' which Helen *Creighton noted from a Micmac mother in New Brunswick, and 'Tah Ne Bah,' which Barbara *Cass-Beggs got from a Sioux woman, Dorothy Francis, in Regina. An attractive Inuit lullaby which Rev D.H. Whitbread taped in Cape Dorset has been sung in an English translation beginning 'Still now and hear my singing.' (See also Inuit: 3 / Other traditional musical genres.)

Among English-speaking Canadians the best-known lullaby is probably 'Rockabye Baby,' and Creighton has published several forms of it in *Folksongs from Southern New Brunswick* (National Museum of Man, Publications in Folk Culture, vol 1, 1971). Among French-Canadians the favourite is 'C'est la poulette grise,' and Creighton noted an Acadian one, 'Dors, dors, le p'tit bibi.' Also perpetuated are 'Fais dodo, Colas mon p'tit frère,' and 'Dodo, l'enfant, do.' Icelanders in Manitoba and Saskatchewan sing a much-loved Icelandic lullaby, 'Bi Bi Og Blaka,' and German-Canadians have preserved their traditional Wiegenlieder. Seven of the items mentioned appear in *Folk Lullabies* by Barbara and Michael Cass-Beggs (Oak 1969).

Several Canadian musicians have composed music for lullabies, but most of the texts are from

European sources. The few with Canadian texts include *MacMillan's arrangement of 'Nadu Nadudu,' the 'Kuyas,' based on a traditional Cree lullaby, with which Riel's wife soothes her baby in *Somers' opera *Louis Riel*, and Kenneth *Winters' setting for children's voices of the lullaby in James Reaney's *Names and Nicknames*. Those who have published music for lullabies by European poets, named or anonymous, include *Anderson, *Archer, *Bissell, *Brott, *Coulthard, *Dela, *Eggleston, Robert *Fleming, *Morawetz, and *Willan. Berceuses or cradle songs for instruments – piano, alone or in duo with other instruments – have been written by Brott, *Brabant, *Fiala, *Gratton, von *Kunits, *Mathieu, *Matton, and *Pépin. Brott also has written a berceuse for small orchestra and one for saxophone quartet, and *Champagne and Dela have written berceuses for orchestra. Other compositions exist in manuscript at the *CMCentre.

DISCOGRAPHY (lullabies by Canadian composers)
Archer *Cradle Song*. *Forrester. RCI 108
Brott *Cradle Song* for small orchestra. *Beaudet cond. RCI Canadian Album No. 3
– 'Cradle Song' from *Songs of Contemplation*. *Marshall. RCI 116/*Gabora. CBC SM-6
– 'Lullaby' from *Lullaby and Procession of Toys*. *Beaudet cond. RCI 5
Coulthard, arr *Cradle Song*. H. *McLean cond. RCI 226/RCA CCS-1020/*Forrester. West WST 17137
Dela *Berceuse béarnaise*. *Forrester. West WST 17137
Eggleston 'Armenian Lullaby,' 'Jewish Lullaby,' 'Norse Lullaby' from *Five Lullabies of Eugene Field*. *Patenaude. RCI 247
Fleming, arr *Folk Lullabies*. *Forrester. CBC SM-144
Kalnins *Lullaby*. *Waddington cond. RCI 35
Matton *Berceuse*. J. *Dufresne. RCI 135
Somers 'Lullaby to a Dead Child' from *Three Sonnets*. K. Quinton pf. RCI 450
Weinzweig *Berceuse*. A. Florou pf. 1970. CBC SM-99 (EF)

Lumbering songs. See Occupational songs, Anglo-Canadian: 2 / Lumbering.

Lunenburg. Seaport community founded in 1753 on the south shore of Nova Scotia by German, Swiss, Huguenot, and British settlers at a site known previously as Malagash. In 1971 its population was 3215.

A Harmonic Society was formed 5 Dec 1828 by 24 men who met weekly to sing church music. The society seems to have joined forces with the St John's Singing Society, organized 17 Dec 1830. These were two of the earliest music societies in Canada. As far as is known, musical education of the young began with a singing school established in the 1850s.

Otherwise, music in Lunenburg was centred in the churches during those early years. Congregational singing was led by a church leader or schoolmaster with the aid of a tuning-fork. M.B. DesBrisay's *History of the County of Lunenburg* (Toronto 1895) refers to excellent choirs in the county's churches where descendants of the original Germans gathered.

Band music began in 1837 with a fife and drum band organized by the First Artillery Co of the Lunenburg Militia and remained an important element of life in Lunenburg until the dissolution of the Lunenburg Citizens' Band in 1974.

Choral groups outside the church were slower to develop. The Lunenburg Male Choir was formed in 1929 by Pearl Oxner, and the Lunenburg Glee Club in 1930 under the direction of Doris (Mahoney) Baker. The latter gave many concerts and was heard nationally on the CBC. A girls' choral club was formed in 1937 at the Lunenburg Academy, where, under the direction of Pearl Oxner, students also mounted operettas annually 1938–63. Lunenburg is the birthplace of Diane *Oxner.

BIBLIOGRAPHY
Oxner, Pearl. 'The Progress of Music in Lunenburg,' *Lunenburg's Bicentennial 1753–1953* (Lunenburg 1953)
Creighton, Helen. *Folklore of Lunenburg County, Nova Scotia* (Toronto 1976)
Ullmann, Christiane. 'German folksongs of Lunenburg County, NS,' *The German-Canadian Yearbook*, vol 5 (Toronto 1979)
Silver, B. 'Some music makers in Lunenburg County,' ms, Public Archives of NS (MCa, HK)

Lute. Plucked-string instrument with a body in the shape of a halved pear, a flat finger-board usually with 12 frets, and a pegbox set almost perpendicular to the neck. The 16th-century lute had at least six courses, normally tuned G, C, F, A, D, G.

There are few early instances of lute playing in Canada. It is known that Maisonneuve (1612–76), the founder of Montreal, had studied the instrument while still in Europe; his musical activities, if any, in Canada have not been traced. As the lute is an extremely fragile instrument, its maintenance in the Canadian climate is difficult and would have been almost impossible in an age when temperature and humidity controls were unknown.

In the 1950s the lute experienced a world-wide renaissance, due in part to the rise in popularity of guitars and in part to the increase of interest in early music, evident in Canada in the activities of the *Vancouver Society for Early Music (and its ensemble, Hortulani Musicae, with lutenist Ray *Nurse), the *Toronto Consort (lutenist Garry Crighton), the *Studio de musique ancienne de Montréal (lutenist Guy Marchand), and other such groups.

The increase in Canada of the number of amateur and professional lute players, and of lute makers, has been rapid. Among the players are Miles Dempster, an English-born guitarist; the German-Canadian Hans Kohlund (also a harpsichordist), who has made many CBC appearances, beginning in Toronto ca 1956; the US-born Richard Kolb, who studied guitar with Eli *Kassner and has been a recitalist throughout Ontario and on the CBC; the Hungarian-Canadian Abel Nagytothy-Toth, a guitarist, who has performed throughout Quebec; Alan Rinehart, a guitarist; and Michael *Strutt.

Among the lute builders are Michael Dunn and Ray Nurse of Vancouver, Colin Everett of Ottawa, Edward Rusnac of Montreal, Terry Philpot of Bethany (near Peterborough, Ont), and Michael Shriner of Toronto.

Most lutenists have had experience as guitarists, and so the teaching of the two instruments usually is combined. In the late 1970s lute was taught at the *RCMT by Richard Kolb and Ernest Hills, at the *U of Manitoba by Richard Burleson, at *Laval U by Paul Gerrits, at the *U of Montreal by Bartholemew-James Crago, and at *McGill U and the *U of Ottawa by Michael Strutt.

See also Instruments: medieval, renaissance, baroque. (MSt)

Lutherans. In 1980 Canada's fifth-largest Christian denomination, numbering approximately 716,000 persons, of whom 302,736 were members of congregations. Lutheran congregations appeared in Canada during the mid-18th century, when German immigrants and United Empire Loyalists of German origin settled in Upper Canada and Nova Scotia. Later, successive waves of Lutherans from continental Europe and Scandinavia spread across the country, taking with them a wide variety of hymn repertoires and service orders. Nationalistic, linguistic, and, to a certain extent, theological barriers worked against the formation of a united Lutheran Church of Canada.

By 1980 there had emerged no distinctively Canadian Lutheran hymnal. Well into the 20th century congregations in the new land either used the hymnbooks of the old country or imported those published by the US synods (New York, Ohio, and Pennsylvania) upon which they depended for pastors and mission support. Musical uniformity among congregations could not be afforded by the hymnbooks brought from Germany, as the contents of these collections were diversified by regional practice and tradition; in Germany an authorized body of Stammlieder was agreed upon only in the *Evangelische Kirchengesangbuch* of 1949.

An example of separatism practised through music is that of the German-speaking Lutherans from the lower Volga who settled in western Canada in the 19th century:

> Their church hymns, though sung according to tunes which originally were the same as ours, now strongly deviated from them. But their hymns really lived among them; for their Volga hymnal was used in daily devotions, in their prayer meetings, side by side with gospel hymns, and in their Sunday services either with a preacher or lay reader. And this hymnal was said to contain some really precious hymns. All these things combined to make this book very dear to these people so that they would not easily part from it.
>
> To hear these Volga Lutherans sing was quite an experience. One would hear the first, second, third, fourth and still some more voices sing, each weaving itself into the other with fairly good harmony and with gusto. The women sang their soprano and alto, the men grunted their bass and other men with a high tenor voice supported the soprano, not tenderly but with power. They sang without an organ, and if there was an organ it was played by ear to match the singing. (Wiegner, p 7–8)

North American pressures for cultural assimilation accelerated a movement for English-language liturgies and hymns. This helped in the unification of the various synodical groups. However, Lutherans from the Baltic states and some German-speaking congregations retained services and hymns in their mother tongues. Lutherans of Scandinavian origin preserved into this century a core of their own traditional texts in translation while adopting hymns of other denominations (see Nyholm, p 332–6; Eylands, p 201).

Beginning in the 18th century, however, Lutheran synods of the USA, particularly those under the influence of the patriarch Henry Melchior Muhlenberg, issued a sequence of both German and English hymnals which displayed strong unionist tendencies and included selections of hymns of Anglican and Wesleyan origin. These culminated in the *Common Service Book* (music edition, Philadelphia 1917).

Its successor, the *Service Book and Hymnal* (Minneapolis 1958), has been adopted by some two-thirds of North American Lutherans. The decidedly ecumenical repertoire of this book includes 14 plainsong melodies, 37 Scandinavian chorales, and British tunes that outnumber German chorales two to one (283 vs 145). The three settings of the service are, respectively: 'Anglican Chant,' a chorale plainsong mixture devised primarily from the Swedish *Mässbok*, and an adaptation by Ernest *White of the Gregorian *Missa orbis factor*. Matins and Vespers are in 'Anglican Chant.'

In 1980 Canadian churches belonging to the Lutheran Church–Missouri Synod continued to use *The Lutheran Hymnal* (St Louis 1941). This book represents a tradition closer to the confessional movement within Lutheranism. In it the original rhythmic versions of the German chorales make up half the collection. The choice of texts reflects the theological preference of the Missouri Synod with its stress on doctrine as a factor in hymnody: 'the doctrinal repristination spreading as much by singing as by preaching' (DeLaney, p 113).

Both hymnals maintain the Lutheran practice, dating from the 16th century, of collecting into one volume the hymns, the psalter, and the liturgical orders with propers and lections. What does unite the Lutheran churches in North America is the singular contribution of Reformation Lutheranism to congregational worship: the emphasis upon the role of congregational singing in the corporate worship response and especially upon the crucial place the hymn assumes both in the service and in the home, the hymnal as 'the people's prayer book' (Reed, p 186). Congregations sustain a healthy tradition of volunteer choirs and concern themselves with the acquisition of good quality pipe organs. The major influence of Lutheran musical life in Canada has been its contribution to the development of choralism in the community: in the founding of local choral societies and through participation in Sängerfesten.

The Lutheran musical climate has fostered the incipient musicianship of two of Canada's most distinguished choir conductors, A.S. *Vogt and Elmer *Iseler. The latter's interest in choral music developed at Waterloo College (*Wilfrid Laurier U) under the guidance of Ulrich *Leupold, who was in charge of the church music courses at the college's Waterloo Lutheran Seminary and was the foremost church musician in Canadian Lutheranism. Leupold's influence – pastoral, theological, and musical – was felt in the parishes through his encouragement of amateur music making and proper standards of service performance. He served on many Lutheran and ecumenical councils and was chairman in 1965 of the committee on music of the Lutheran Church of America Commission on Worship.

The spirit of lively musical Gemeinschaft (community) in Canadian Lutheranism has not encouraged significant composition of church music or the cultivation of professionalism in parish musical leadership. The exception lies in those individual congregations (eg, Latvian and Estonian) whose concert choirs serve a nationalistic as well as an ecclesiastical function and whose small but qualitatively substantial repertoire of anthems and cantatas developed after World War II.

In 1980 no Lutheran institution in Canada was devoted exclusively to musical training, and no Lutheran university was musically active, unlike some in the USA. The choir-school movement was non-existent. The English-language congregations depended for service material upon the US Lutheran publishing houses, and there were no Canadian musicians on the inter-Lutheran Commission on Worship responsible for the preparation of a series of new liturgical settings, orders, and hymnals.

BIBLIOGRAPHY

Eylands, Valdimar J. *Lutherans in Canada* (Winnipeg 1945)
Wiegner, Paul E. *The Origin and Development of the Manitoba-Saskatchewan District of The Lutheran Church* (St Louis, Mo [1957])
Reed, Luther D. *The Lutheran Liturgy* (Philadelphia [1959])
Cronmiller, Carl Raymond. *A History of the Lutheran Church in Canada*, vol 1 (Evangelical Lutheran Synod of Canada 1961)
Nyholm, Paul C. *The Americanization of the Danish Lutheran Churches in America* (Minneapolis 1963)
Schalk, Carl. *The Roots of Hymnody in the Lutheran Church* (St Louis, Mo, 1965)
Ryden, Ernest R. 'Hymnbooks (Lutheran),' *The Encyclopedia of the Lutheran Church*, vol 2, ed Julius Bodensieck (Minneapolis 1965)
DeLaney, E. Theo. 'What makes it Lutheran,' *The Musical Heritage of the Church*, vol 7, ed Theodore Hoelty-Nickel (St Louis, Mo, 1970) (WHK)

Lye Organ Company. After the *Casavants, the Lyes in 1979 were the oldest surviving family in the music trade in Canada. The company was founded by Edward Roome Lye, an Englishman (b Somerset ca 1829, d Toronto 1919) who came to Canada during the late 1840s, settled in Toronto, and, after working for a time in a furniture factory, began building organs. By 1873 he had opened a sales outlet at 195 Yonge Street. He established a factory in the neighbourhood of St Nicholas and Wellesley (at that time, St Alban's) streets, and in 1864 he established Edward Lye & Sons (Arthur H., Edward J., Herbert H., and Walter L.).

After the senior Lye's death the sons carried on the business, though by the 1930s only Arthur and Walter remained active in it. The company manufactured organs until 1934, when financial problems forced it to close. Walter and his son William (b Toronto 1911) formed the Lye Organ Co shortly thereafter, and were joined later by William's brothers Norman and Murray. For a time the new company occupied the St Nicholas St premises, but in 1939 it relocated on Stephenson Ave in Toronto's east end.

During World War II the company concerned itself mainly with servicing and repairs. In 1944 it moved to Markham Road in Scarborough, Ont. Owing to the decreased demand for mechanical organs and a shortage of skilled labour it stopped building ca 1952 and became an agent for the Baldwin Piano and Organ Co. In the late 1970s William Lye was still repairing organs.

Most of the 300 to 400 organs built by Edward Lye & Sons and the Lye Organ Co were of the small two-manual tracker variety and were made for churches in western Ontario. However, a few were installed as far away as Campbellton, NB; Dawson, the Yukon; and Fortune, Nfld. Lye built the original organs for Toronto's Little Trinity Anglican Church, St Clement's Anglican Church, Our Lady of Mount Carmel Church, and Cooke's Presbyterian Church, and that in the last-named still was in use in 1979. Of those installed in Haileybury, Meaford, Mitchell, Parry Sound, Port Hope, Stratford, Uxbridge, and other Ontario towns, many still were played in 1979, as was the Collingwood Baptist Church Lye organ rebuilt by William Lye during the 1950s.

The Lye family was known also, in Toronto, for its tradition of bell-ringing at St James' Cathedral, where Edward Sr rang 1867–91, Walter 1888–1958, and Walter's son Murray 1958–9. Altogether the family was associated with the cathedral for 96 years and 'rang in' the New Year annually during that time. (See also Bells.) (FH, NM, PW)

LYONNAIS (Bossu or Bossue, dit Lyonnais). Quebec family of string-instrument makers. Four generations are treated here: 1 / Pierre-Olivier fils; 2 / Joseph fils, nephew of Pierre-Olivier; 3 / Roch and 4 / Léon, sons of Joseph; and 5 / Cyrille-Roch, eldest son of Roch and his second wife.

BIBLIOGRAPHY

Lyonnais, A.G. *Généalogie de la famille Lyonnais* (Ottawa 1901)
LeVasseur, Nazaire. 'Musique et musiciens à Québec,' *La Musique*, vol 1, 2, 1919, 1920
– *Réminiscences d'Antan* (Quebec City 1926)
Massicotte, Édouard-Z. 'Violons et luthiers,' *BRH*, vol 41, Apr 1935
Royer, Henri. 'Lutherie à Québec,' *R Saint-Grégoire*, Mar 1951
– 'Mosaïque québécoise,' *Cahiers d'histoire*, 13, 1961

1 **Pierre-Olivier fils**. String-instrument maker, b Quebec City 12 Jul 1798, d there 8 Sep 1860. A roofer by trade, he suffered a fall ca 1820 which left him disabled. Since he had to support his parents, he made small carvings until ca 1825, when he took up violin making, probably at the instigation of Adam Joseph *Schott, a bandmaster stationed in Quebec City. One of the first makers of string instruments in that city, Lyonnais is said to have built more than 80 violins, violas, and cellos, assisted for some dozen years by his nephew Joseph.

2 **Joseph fils**. Violin maker, instrumentalist, conductor, teacher, b Quebec City 28 Nov 1821, d there 6 Jan 1889. He learned the craft of violin making from his uncle after 1835. In 1842 he opened his own workshop in Quebec City's St-Roch district, specializing in 'the manufacture of violins which he is not afraid to compare with the best imported,' in the repair of 'violins, clarinets, flutes, accordions, etc. etc.' (*L'Événement*, 30 Aug 1844), and in the making of wooden characters for printing. He took over his uncle's workshop and in turn passed it on to his son Roch, who also had become a violin maker. In 1879 father and son put on display a trapezoidal violin made from a design by the French scientist Félix Savart but embodying 'improvements dictated by [Joseph Lyonnais's] great knowledge as a manufacturer.'

Joseph was also a practising musician in Quebec City, having received lessons from Charles *Sauvageau and David Parent. By 1836 he was playing the hunting-horn in the *Musique canadienne conducted by Sauvageau and probably also playing violin in the Sauvageau orchestra and the Orchestre canadien under Parent. He also played the violin, cello, and double-bass 1872–82 in the orchestra founded by Roch Lyonnais. He himself founded and directed a number of small ensembles, the most important of which was that of the Institut catholique. Among his pupils were Jean-Baptiste *Labelle, Séraphin-D. *Vachon, and Nazaire *LeVasseur.

3 **Roch** (also known as Joseph-Roch). Violin maker, musical instrument dealer and repairer, instrumentalist, composer, teacher, conductor, b Quebec City 28 Dec 1849, d there 1 Jan 1921. He owed his craft and musical skills to his father and to his uncle Séraphin-D. *Vachon, who gave him lessons in violin playing. He evidently studied several specialized books on instrument making and was strongly influenced by them. Thus, after giving up manufacturing violins because of competition, he built his first accordion in Canada and a violin based on the Savart model; he also designed and produced 1865–80 a bagarina and various mechanical instruments. His innovative mind was demonstrated in 'The influence of music,' a well-documented lecture which he delivered in Dec 1879 at Biddeford, Me, and in which he exhorted doctors not to neglect the therapeutic nature of music; he supported his case by quoting and identifying evidence going back to ancient times. He translated J.-B. Logier's treatise on harmony, *System der Musikwissenschaft* (Berlin 1827), into French as 'Règle fondamentale de l'harmonie' (apparently unpublished). According to A.G. Lyonnais, he taught the techniques of all kinds of instruments to over 500 pupils.

Roch Lyonnais himself played violin, viola, cello, and occasionally saxophone in Quebec City in the orchestras of Hamel, Lavigueur, Vachon, and Thibault. He founded and conducted the Lyonnais orchestra 1872–82. In 1873 he was appointed conductor for the French theatre company Maugard. In 1881 he became conductor of a band which included some members of the Lyonnais orchestra. In 1891 he founded and directed the Zouaves du Sacré-Coeur Band, which was still active in 1980. These activities were pursued alongside his instrument making, which he practised from 1866 until 1906, when he limited himself to repair work and to operating a theatre-costume rental business. He was also a composer and publisher. A list of his vocal and instrumental works (polkas, waltzes, and quadrilles), both in manuscript and published, was compiled by Nazaire *LeVasseur. According to LeVasseur some of these pieces reflect Lyonnais's studious and reserved nature. Erudition, diversity of talents, skill, and ingenuity seem to have been combined in the personality of Roch Lyonnais, one of the most engaging figures in late-19th-century Quebec City.

BIBLIOGRAPHY
David, L.O. 'Roch Lyonnais,' *Opinion publique*, vol 2, 14 Sep 1871

4 **Léon II**. Amateur musician, singer, b Quebec City 12 Sep 1851, d ?. A printer by trade, he participated in musical activities in Quebec City on at least two occasions, according to 19th-century accounts. He played piccolo in the Lyonnais orchestra and took part 26 Jan 1880 in a charity concert as an actor and a singer of 'comic songs.'

5 **Cyrille-Roch** (also known as Roch fils). String-instrument maker, music dealer, teacher, b Quebec City 13 Jul 1876, d there 10 Nov 1925. He was initiated into the secrets of his craft by his father, operated a workshop 1896–1907 in Notre-Dame-de-Lévis, and then moved to Quebec City. Extreme mental instability led him to change his address every year. Cyrille-Roch claimed on his marriage contract in 1918 that he was a soldier. He was, nevertheless, the last representative of a line of Quebec violin makers who were highly respected by their contemporaries. (LPr)

Lyric Arts Trio. Formed in 1964 by the soprano Mary *Morrison, the flutist Robert *Aitken, and Aitken's wife, the pianist Marion Ross. Though begun for recreation, the trio soon was in public demand, partly because of the established individual reputations of its members and partly because of the freshness of the repertoire for such a combination – a surprising variety of duos and trios, mostly baroque, rococo, and fin-de-siècle French – and a few 20th-century pieces, eg, Frank Martin's *Trois Chansons de Noël* and Albert Roussel's *Deux Poèmes de Ronsard*, with which the trio made its debut 14 Oct 1965 before the Brantford (Ont) Music Club.

In the mid-1960s Canadian composers, perhaps disillusioned by the public neglect into which the Schoenberg revolution had led them, were reaching out again for audiences. While retaining faith in a kind of music to which the public had remained largely indifferent, they saw hope for it in the manipulation of other elements of the concert experience. They were tempted to incorporate theatrics and sonic novelties to shake apathy, disarm hostility, amuse, and even to help explain. This was not new strategy, even in Canada, let alone the larger musical world; but the emergence of a group such as the Lyric Arts Trio – combining, as it did, virtuosity, charisma, and a good-humoured sense of adventure – provided a focus for the trend. Quick to recognize advantage, the composers rallied and by 1974 had produced enough new works, tailored for the trio, to make up four different programs. The list (see below) continued to grow with the trio's reputation.

Besides performing frequently in Toronto the Lyric Arts Trio appeared throughout Canada for music clubs, music schools, and new-music societies and at Ontario's major seasonal events, notably the *Shaw Festival (1970, 1971, 1972), *Festival Ottawa (1973, four appearances), and the *Stratford Festival. It also performed in Montreal at the 1976 Olympics. It was the only Canadian chamber ensemble invited to appear at Expo 70 in Osaka, where it worked in consort with Lukas Foss and with Stockhausen's group; it also gave the premiere of Sydney *Hodkinson's *Arc*, written to exploit both the performers and Osaka's uniquely equipped 1000-speaker theatre.

During 1971–2 Aitken, Morrison, and Ross, with support from the *Koerner Foundation and the *Canada Council, were engaged as artists-in-residence at *Simon Fraser U. While there, they gave concerts and seminars and performed in schools in and near Vancouver. The trio also has performed to great acclaim in US cities and in Europe, appearing at the 1973 ISCM festival at Reykjavik and completing tours that year, and in 1975, which took it to London, Paris, Brussels, Stockholm, Frankfurt, and other major centres. In 1976 it returned to Scandinavia and Great Britain with *NMC; in 1977 it gave three concerts in Tokyo at the invitation of the composer Toru Takemitsu; and in 1978 it performed Canadian works at the Warsaw Autumn International Festival.

The addition to the trio's repertoire of works by many US, European, and Asian composers (eg, Bedford, Boone, Crum, Davidovsky, Eakin, Ezaki, Goyevaerts, Hayashi, Luciuk, Sveinsson, Takemitsu, and Wolff) reflects the expansion of its activity. The trio has captivated listeners on both sides of the Atlantic. In its home city, the critic for the *Telegram* wrote (8 Apr 1968): 'These three by now are more than just a first-rate singer and two first-rate players. They are musicians whose tender and vital concern with the stuff of their art gives their choice of program significance, so that composers can be glad of their favour and the rest of us can be grateful for their selectivity.' In 1980 the trio continued to be among Canada's outstanding advocates of 20th-century music, in regular appearances with NMC in Toronto, the *SMCQ in Montreal, and other such groups at home and abroad.

PREMIERES OF CANADIAN WORKS
*Barnes *Two Poems*, 1966
*Beckwith 'Daisy's Aria' from *The Shivaree*, 1967
*Beecroft *Elegy* and *Two Went to Sleep*, 1967
*Buczynski *Two French Love Poems*, 1967; *Milósc*, 1971; *Zeroing In No. 4*, 1973
*Charpentier *A Tea Symphony*, 1972; *Clarabelle-Clarimage*, 1979
*Cherney *Eclipse*, 1972
*Ciamaga *Solepsism while Dying*, 1973
*Douglas *Three Dances*, 1978
*Freedman *Pan*, 1972
*Hambraeus *Récit de deux pour trois exécutants*, 1973
*Hartwell *Resta di darma noia*, 1974
*Henninger *Three Songs of Winter*, 1972
*Hodkinson *Arc*, 1970
*Kolinski *Six French Folk Songs*, 1967
*Mather *Madrigal IV*, 1973
Pedersen, Paul *An Old Song of the Sun and the Moon and the Fear of Loneliness*, 1973
Pedersen, Stephen *Three Haiku*, 1968
*Somers *Zen, Yeats and Emily Dickinson*, 1975
*Symonds *... deep ground, long waters*, 1972
*Weinzweig *Trialogue*, 1971
PREMIERES OF WORKS BY FOREIGN COMPOSERS
Sveinsson *Bizarreries*, 1971
Tiensuu *Trio*, 1975
Sculthorpe *Eliza Fraser Sings*, 1978

DISCOGRAPHY
Freedman *Toccata; Three Old Dutch Christmas Carols* – F. Martin – et al. 1969. CBC SM-96
Hodkinson *Arc; Aria with Interludes* – Mamangakis – et al. 1970. CBC SM-148
Mather *Madrigal II; Madrigal III; Madrigal IV*. 1972. RCI 369
Pedersen *An Old Song of the Sun and the Moon and the Fear of Loneliness* – Beecroft *Elegy; Two Went to Sleep* – R. Hunt *Four Songs* – Freedman *Pan*. (1975). RCI 404

BIBLIOGRAPHY
Schulman, Michael. 'The Lyric Arts Trio – musical missionaries,' *MSc*, 275, Jan–Feb 1974 KW

M

McCARTNEY, Stanley. Clarinetist, teacher, b Vancouver 15 Mar 1930. He first studied clarinet in Vancouver with Bernard Temoin. He worked in New York in 1953 with Daniel Bonade and later in Cleveland with Robert Marcellus. He was a member of the *Victoria SO 1953–7 and then moved to Toronto, where he joined the *CBC SO. He joined the *TSO in 1964, becoming assistant and later co-principal clarinet and held the latter position until 1980. In addition he performed as principal clarinet in the *Stratford Festival orchestra throughout the 1960s. McCartney joined the *Toronto Woodwind Quintet in 1960 and remained with the group until it ceased its activities in 1978. He has appeared as a soloist with the TS and has been guest artist with the Aeolian String Quartet (England), the *Festival Singers, the *Orford String Quartet, the Voirin Ensemble, and the cellist Lynn Harrell. He gave the premiere of Murray *Adaskin's *Nocturne* for solo clarinet at the 1978 International Clarinet Congress in Toronto. He was a member of the teaching faculty for the *NYO during the summer of 1967 and was an instructor at the *U of Toronto 1972–80. In 1980 his pupils held positions in several Canadian orchestras.

McCartney's wife, Corol (b Dorothy Murray, Vancouver, 23 Mar 1931), studied violin with Gregori *Garbovitsky in Vancouver and Joseph Fuchs in New York and was a member of the Victoria SO 1953–7 and of the TSO 1957–80. (SS, PW)

McCAUGHAN, Paul-Émile. Organist, teacher, composer, b Montreal 18 May 1911, d there 22 Aug 1953; BA (Montreal) 1932, B TH (Montreal) 1935, L TH (Montreal) 1936, B MUS (Montreal) 1938, L MUS (Montreal) 1939, D MUS (Montreal) 1945. He studied with Frédéric Payette, Jean-Julien *Clossey, Étienne Guillet, and Georges-Émile *Tanguay and was organist at the Collège de St-Jean, Que, and 1932–6 at the Grand Séminaire in Montreal. Ordained a priest in 1936, he taught 1936–9 and 1941–50 at the Collège André-Grasset and gave courses at the *Cons national. After obtaining a teaching diploma in Gregorian chant (1933) and in choral conducting (1934) from the *Schola cantorum in Montreal, he published his doctoral thesis, *La Philosophie de la musique* (Montreal 1946). He wrote several works for choir and organ, including two high masses, a *Messe cathédrale*, motets, and songs. About 10 were self-published (Éditions du Blé d'or). Father McCaughan also composed the *Valse du souvenir* and other period pieces 'rendered at the piano' by Mlle Angélique in the CBC radio series adaptation of Claude-Henri Grignon's *Un homme et son péché*. A list of his compositions to 1951 may be found in the *Catalogue of Canadian Composers*. (CMr)

McCAUL, John. Educator, theologian, impresario, b Dublin 7 Mar 1807, d Toronto 16 Apr 1886; BA (Dublin) 1824, MA (Dublin) 1828, LL D (Dublin)

1835. A specialist in classic languages, McCaul moved to Toronto in 1839 as principal of Upper Canada College. He became vice-president in 1842 and president in 1849 of King's College (renamed the *U of Toronto in 1850) and was president 1853–80 of University College, U of Toronto. A keen and skilled amateur musician, McCaul organized in 1845 two concerts of choral and orchestral works by Handel, Haydn, Mozart, Beethoven, Rossini, Schubert, Mendelssohn, and others. He organized the *Toronto Philharmonic Society and was its president 1845–7 and 1854. He was also president 1851–3 of the Toronto Vocal Music Society. The musician most often associated with McCaul in these ventures was James P. *Clarke, with whom McCaul revived the Philharmonic Society in 1872 for a performance of Handel's *Messiah* with a 150-voice choir. Also in collaboration with Clarke he composed *Blessed Be the Man* (Nordheimer), which was performed in Toronto in 1846. Of his own works (which included other anthems and a vocal quartet) the ballads 'Waters of Babylon,' 'Merrie England,' 'Riflemen Form,' and 'In the Springtime of the Year' enjoyed a measure of popularity.

BIBLIOGRAPHY

'Toronto's Pre-Confederation Music Societies'

(FH, MHl)

McCAULEY, William (Alexander). Composer, arranger, conductor, trombonist, pianist, administrator, b Tofield, near Edmonton, 14 Feb 1917; ATCM 1947, B MUS (Toronto) 1947, M MUS (ESM, Rochester) 1959, D MUS (ESM, Rochester) 1961. He studied piano in Tofield and Edmonton and at 16 formed a dance band which worked locally and broadcast on CFRN, Edmonton. He began studies at the *TCM in 1936 and worked 1936–40 as an arranger, pianist, and trombonist with Horace *Lapp. After RCAF service 1940–5 as a bandsman and later as assistant bandmaster of the Toronto Manning Pool Band he returned to the TCM, played in the Harmony SO and worked with Trump *Davidson, Art *Hallman, and Ellis *McLintock. His TCM teachers included Healey *Willan (composition), Leo *Smith (harmony), Margaret *Parsons (piano), and Harry Howe and Rudolph Baumler (trombone). Briefly music director, 1947–9, at Ottawa Technical High School, he was music director 1949–57 at Crawley Films, composing and arranging scores for over 100 films (see also Film scores). He also was principal trombone with the *NFB and *Ottawa Philharmonic orchestras. After further studies in composition at the ESM with Alan Hovhaness, Bernard Rogers, and Howard Hanson (composition) and in conducting in Maine with Pierre Monteux, he was appointed (1960) house music director of *O'Keefe Centre in Toronto. While he was music director 1961–9 at *York U, Toronto, the York U Choir under his direction won the 1967 City of Lincoln Trophy. McCauley became music director at Seneca College in 1970 and conductor of the North York SO in 1973. In 1979 he was founder-conductor of the North York Philharmonic Orchestra.

He composed the score for the CBC TV series *The Whiteoaks of Jalna* (1972) and contributed music to the feature films *The Neptune Factor* (1973), *Sunday in the Country* (1973), and *It Seemed Like a Good Idea at the Time* (1975). His score for CBC TV's historical drama *Riel* (1979) is heard on the original soundtrack recording (GRT 9230-1080).

Early in his career McCauley developed the adaptable and eclectic style so necessary for incidental composition, and he has remained a composer without a school. Folk tunes figure in several of his orchestral works, as do elements of jazz. The *Five Miniatures for Flute and Strings* (1958) and the *Concerto Grosso* (1973), both neoclassical, are lyrical and rhythmic. In his music generally dissonance is counteracted by appealing rhythms, cohesive counterpoint, and an uncomplicated sense of direction. McCauley's students include his son Matthew (b Ottawa 1 Apr 1954), a keyboard player, composer, and arranger, who has written scores for CBC TV and the feature film *Between Friends* (1973) and, through the independent production company, McCauley Music, has produced LPs by Dan *Hill, Ronney Abramson, and others. William McCauley is an associate of the *CMCentre and both McCauleys are members of CAPAC.

SELECTED COMPOSITIONS

ORCHESTRA AND BAND

Five Miniatures for Flute and Strings. 1958. Fl, str orch. Leeds 1961. Mer SR 90277 (Eastman-Rochester O, Mariano fl)/Dom S-69006/CRI SD 317 (*Aitken)

Theme and Deviations. 1960. Orch. Leeds 1961

Canadian Folk Song Fantasy. 1966. Band. Smith 1972

Metropolis. 1967. Band. OUP 1967

Concerto Grosso. 1973. Brass quin, orch. CMCentre. CBC SM-264 (*Hamilton Phil O)

Christmas Carol Fantasia. 1975. Marseg 1975

Concerto No, 1. 1977. Pf, orch. Self-publ. 1977

Also 4 works for orch: *Newfoundland Scene, Quebec Lumber Camp, Saskatchewan Suite, Manitoba Theme* (1952–6). 1964. CTL S5043 (McCauley cond)

CHAMBER

Five Miniatures for Six Percussionists. 1962. Leeds 1970

Five Miniatures for Four Saxophones. 1972. Sop, alto, ten, and bar sax. Ms

Miniature Overture. 1973. Brass quin. CMCentre. Boot BMC 3001 (*Canadian Brass)

Five Miniatures for Brass Quintet. 1974. Marseg 1975. ('Staggering') Boot BMC 3003 (*Canadian Brass)

Kaleidoscope Quebecois. 1974. Fl, cl, vn, vc, 2 pf. 1974. McCauley Music 1974

Five Miniatures for Four Trombones. 1977. CMCentre

CHOIR AND VOICE

'Immanence' (Wilson MacDonald). 1957. SATB. CMCentre. Cap ST 6071 (York U Choir, McCauley cond)

Other works for choir, including arr of French Canadian folk songs. Col FL 226

Over 100 scores for films and TV; a puppet play, *Beauty and the Beast* (1967); educational pieces for piano published by FH and GVT; and the songs 'He's Special' and 'I've Been Waiting for You,' recorded by McCauley (CTLS 5043), and 'Clear the Track, Here Comes Shack' and 'Warming the Bench' (1966, Smith 1966)

DISCOGRAPHY

Noël à Québec. William McCauley Choir. Ca 1955. Col FL 207

The William McCauley Choir Sings Canadian Folk Songs. 1958. Col FL 226

Showstoppers from the O'Keefe Centre. Cap ST 6048

The Music of William McCauley. 1964. CTLS 5043

BIBLIOGRAPHY

'Dr. William McCauley: success in many directions,' *CanComp*, Nov 1966

'Dr. William McCauley: wins Alberta composition contest,' *CanComp*, Dec 1967

'Film-making at a music camp,' *CanComp*, Oct 1969

Champagne, Jane. 'William McCauley helps make Jalna live once more,' *CanComp*, Mar 1972

Guill, Greg. 'Mollins and McCauley: running to keep ahead of a busy schedule,' *CanComp*, 119, Mar 1977

Contemporary Canadian Composers / Compositeurs canadiens contemporains

FMB

McCONNELL, Rob (Robert Murray Gordon). Valve trombonist, composer, arranger, b London, Ont, 14 Feb 1935. Though raised in Toronto, where he played slide trombone in high school, McConnell began his career in Edmonton in 1954 with the band of the saxophonist Don *Thompson. After working for three years with a brokerage firm in Toronto (during which time he began playing the valve trombone), he resumed his career first as a pianist with the drummer Alex Lazaroff's Rhythm Rockets, then (while studying 1958–62 with Gordon *Delamont and playing in Delamont's rehearsal band) as a trombonist with Bobby *Gimby. He also formed his own rehearsal band.

McConnell worked in 1964 in New York with Maynard *Ferguson's big band, then returned to Toronto, becoming one of that city's leading studio players, active also as an arranger and composer. While a member 1965–9 of *Nimmons 'N' Nine Plus Six, he formed the 16-piece (later 22-piece) *Boss Brass in 1968. He has continued, however, to perform in clubs and on CBC radio with smaller groups, including quintets with the saxophonist Rick *Wilkins and the (slide) trombonist Ian *McDougall. During one such engagement David Lancashire (Toronto *Globe and Mail*, 15 Nov 1978) wrote of McConnell's valve trombone style: 'McConnell turns the instrument's mushy response to advantage to produce a mellow, legato delivery that adds to his compelling lyricism.'

Besides his LPs with the Boss Brass, McConnell has recorded with Guido *Basso, Ferguson, Moe *Koffman, Nimmons, and others. The Boss Brass has recorded his compositions *My Man Bill, It's Hard to Find One, That's Right, Tribute to Art Fern, Runaway Hormones*, and *4,389,165th Blues in B Flat*. McConnell has written other works and also arranged the music sung by Singers Unlimited and the Hi-Lo's on their recordings with the Boss Brass. He is a member of CAPAC.

McConnell's brother Dan played drums in the 1950s with the jazz musicians Peter *Appleyard, Dave Hammer, Moe Koffman, and Mike White.

BIBLIOGRAPHY

Dampier, Bill. 'Rob McConnell: meet the boss of the Boss Brass,' *Sound*, vol 2, Aug 1971

'McConnell: jazz is not commercial,' *CanComp*, 67, Feb 1972

Levitch, Gerald. 'Boss Brassman Rob McConnell: musician, arranger, composer, band leader,' *CanComp*, 117, Jan 1977

(HM, MM)

McCOOL, Brian (Samuel). Educator, adminsitrator, conductor, b London, 20 Oct 1901; BA (Toronto) 1923. He became head of the English department at Mimico (near Toronto) High School in 1924. At Harbord Collegiate, Toronto, he was head 1926–8 of the physical training department, taught classical languages, and was head 1928–39 of the music section. From 1939 to 1941 he was officer commanding, B Company, The Royal Regiment of Canada, commanding officer of the Viking Force (first Canadian commandos 1941–2), and principal landing officer at Dieppe in 1942. Following two years as a prisoner of war he was second echelon representative, Pacific Force 1945. In 1945 he received the MBE.

The Ontario Dept of Education appointed McCool assistant director of music in 1945 and he was vice-principal of its Summer Music School 1945–9 and principal 1956–70. From 1959 to 1968 he was music director for Ontario schools. He was music professor 1948–9 at the Ontario College of Education. From 1947 to 1960, through the music branch of the Dept of Education, he organized concerts in 75 Ontario towns, in which more than 300 young performing artists (including Jon *Vickers and Lois *Marshall) gave and received invaluable musical experience.

A man of prodigious energies, McCool has engaged in many community activities. He was conductor 1945–8 of the Harmony SO and assistant conductor of the *Leslie Bell Singers. An ardent Gilbert & Sullivan fan, he has conducted over 100 productions of their works in the years 1932–70. He has also been Ontario chairman of the Citizen's Forum 1945–9 and, since retirement, secretary for both the provincial and the federal Boundaries Commissions. In 1974 he was awarded L'Ordre militaire et hospitalier de St-Lazare de Jerusalem. With Healey *Willan he edited the 1951 edition of the *School and Community Song Book* (Toronto). In 1966 the Toronto *Kiwanis Festival established the Brian S. McCool trophy to be awarded annually to the school accumulating the most points in choral, orchestral, and band classes.

BIBLIOGRAPHY

Woodburn, Dawson. 'The spotlight on Major Brian S. McCool,' *Recorder*, vol 11, Feb – Apr 1967 WL

McCURDY, Ed (Edward Potts). Folksinger, songwriter, b Willow Hill, Pa, 11 Jan 1919. McCurdy developed an interest in folk music while he was a student in Oklahoma and worked in US vaudeville and radio. He moved in 1945 to Vancouver, where his CBC radio program 'Ed McCurdy Sings' (1947–8) was the first on the English network devoted to folksong. The baritone's other CBC shows included 'Singing in the Wilderness' (Toronto, 1949), 'Young People's Radio Magazine' (Vancouver, 1953), and the children's TV program 'Ed's Place' (Toronto, 1953–4). He also sang the role of Mal Tompkins in the 1954 CBC TV production of Mavor *Moore's *The Hero of Mariposa*.

After returning in 1954 to the USA McCurdy continued to appear in Canada and was host for such CBC TV shows as 'Ed and Ross' (Toronto, 1957–9), a children's show with Ross Snetsinger, and 'Folksongs with Ed McCurdy' (Halifax, 1961). He also performed in Canadian coffeehouses and at the 1962 *Mariposa Folk Festival. A popular interpreter of Anglo-Canadian folk songs, McCurdy became one of the most recorded folk artists in North America. His first LP, *Folk Songs of the Canadian Maritimes and Newfoundland* (1955 Whitehall 850), was followed by many others, largely of non-Canadian material, recorded in the USA for Riverside, Elektra, and Tradition. Of his own songs, 'Last Night I Had the Strangest Dream' has been the most popular.

BIBLIOGRAPHY

Brown, Bill. 'CBC's sorrowful troubadour,' Montreal *Standard*, 20 Jul 1949 (LHv)

McCUTCHEON, Peter. Guitarist, teacher, b Montreal 27 Jun 1951; B MUS (Montreal) 1972, premier prix guitar (Paris Cons) 1975. After taking lessons for six years with Florence Brown, he continued 1968–9 at the *CMM with Marie Prével and 1969–72 at the *U of Montreal with Marie and Martin Préval. He studied 1972–5 in Paris with Alexandre Lagoya after taking summer courses with him 1968–72 at the *JMC Orford Art Centre. McCutcheon performed in 1976 on CBC TV's 'Concert populaire' and 'Sons et Images' and in 1977 on CBC radio's 'Jeunes Artistes' and 'Récital.' At the *PDA 3 Oct 1976 he inaugurated the series 'Sons et brioches.' In February 1977 with the *Orchestre de chambre Pierre-Morin at the *Grand Théâtre in Quebec City he played a Vivaldi *Concerto in C* and the Giuliani *Concerto in A*. He gave a recital in April 1978 at the Théâtre Port-Royal (PDA). Following his 1979 New York debut, Peter G. Davis described him as a 'rare type of musician for whom the mechanics of playing the guitar seemed as natural and simple as breathing' (*New York Times*, 15 Apr 1979). He began teaching at the JMC Orford Art Centre in 1974 and was appointed to the faculty of tne U of Montreal the following year. With the guitarist Tony *Romandini and the harmonicist Claude Garden he recorded arrangements of works by Scheidt, Villa-Lobos, Ibert, Chopin, and Garden (1976, RCI 443). ST

MacDERMOT, (Arthur Terence) **Galt**. Composer, pianist, b Montreal 16 Dec 1929; BA English and history (Bishop's) 1950, B MUS (Cape Town) 1953? After living in several Canadian cities – including Toronto, where he studied at Upper Canada College (his father, T.W.L. MacDermot, was the principal and taught history there) – he went to Cape Town in 1950 when his father was appointed Canadian high commissioner to South Africa. He studied organ and composition at the U of Cape Town, and the African music he heard in the urban ghettos influenced his composition, in particular its rhythms.

MacDermot returned to Montreal in 1954, played piano in jazz clubs, and was the organist-choirmaster at Westmount Baptist Church until 1961. During this time he collaborated with James de B. Domville and Harry Garber on the score for the 1957 *McGill U *Red and White Revue*, **My Fur Lady*. (His main contributions were the chorus 'Royal Victoria Rag,' the female chorus 'The So-Glad-You-Could-Pay-For-Me-Dad Waltz,' the Censors' ensemble 'Snip,' and the Princess' song 'I'm for Love.') His *African Waltz*, written in Cape Town, was popularized through recordings by Cannonball Adderley and John Dankworth and won Grammy Awards in 1961 as best jazz and best instrumental composition and a Novello Award (England) in 1961 in a similar category. With Stan Zadak (bass) and Pierre *Béluse (drums) he made the LP *Art Gallery Jazz* (1960, Laurentian CTM 6002), which included *African Waltz*. In 1961 he went to London, where he played with Tony Coe and others.

In 1963 MacDermot settled in New York, playing in studio and rhythm-and-blues groups. He wrote the score for **Hair* in 1967 and, with that rock musical's success, began to devote most of his time to composition, playing piano only for the staging of some of his productions and in rare public appearances (eg, the *CAPAC-MacMillan Lectures at the U of Toronto in 1972). He wrote scores for musical versions of *Hamlet, Troilus and Cressida* (an opera entitled *Cressida*, with country and western influences), and **Two Gentlemen of Verona*, all produced by Joseph Papp and the New York Shakespeare Festival. He also collaborated on two musicals for the London stage, *Isabel's a Jezabel* and *Who the Murderer Was*; these were not successful, perhaps because of their subject matter (abortion and murder, respectively), though of MacDermot's music for the former John Barber wrote: 'He is a composer so strong, both harmonically and rhythmically, that he could set a catalog to music – and here he has done so. His use of counterpoint, of background choruses and recitative passages keeps the air tingling and the limping show on its feet' (London *Daily Telegraph*, quoted in the *Canadian Composer*, Feb 1971). Two subsequent musicals, *Via Galactica* and *Dude*, had short runs on Broadway in 1972.

MacDermot's other compositions include scores for the films *Cotton Comes to Harlem, Fortune and Men's Eyes, Duffer, Woman Is Sweeter*, and *Rhinoceros*; the religious works *Mass in F* and *Take This Bread* (the latter, subtitled 'A Mass in Our Time,' written for and performed at the opening of *Hamilton Place in 1973); the choral piece *Ghetto Suite*, with text taken from poems by black children in New York; the orchestral work *Incident at Turtle Rock*, commissioned by the *NACO and premiered 30 Apr 1975; and scores for the ballets *A Private Circus* (the music taken from his *Mosaic* for wind quintet), *La Novela*, and *The Referee* (or a *Pre-Rock Dance Suite*, premiered in 1975 and also performed by the Ballet Nacional de Cuba in 1977). MacDermot established his own record label, Kilmarnock, in 1972 and released *The English Experience* (1962, 70001), *Hair-Cuts* (1969, 69001), and recordings of *Ghetto Suite, Isabel's a Jezabel, Dude, Fortune and Men's Eyes*, and *Woman Is Sweeter*. His company, Wonish Music (Staten Island, NY), holds the copyright to his music. He is member of CAPAC.

WRITINGS

'Notes from a lecture,' *CanComp*, 73, Oct 1972

BIBLIOGRAPHY

Berkvist, Robert. 'The composer of Hair,' *CanComp*, 41, Jun 1969
McNamara, Helen. 'Galt MacDermot,' Toronto *Telegram*, 10 Jan 1970
Flohil, Richard. 'Galt MacDermot: where the action really is,' *CanComp*, 71, June 1972
Posner, Michael. 'Galt MacDermot: failure doesn't faze the shy man who composed Hair,' *Impetus*, Jun 1974
Shaw, Peter, and Sawchuk, Taunia. 'Our most successful composer,' *Ottawa Journal*, 11 Mar 1978
Brownstein, Bill. 'That's my kind of music,' Montreal *Gazette*, 4 Apr 1979 FH, MM

McDONALD, Boyd. See Beckett and McDonald.

MacDONALD, Fraser (Pringle). Radio producer, writer, composer, b Toronto 3 Apr 1912; BA (Alberta) 1935. He studied piano with Jenny *Lerouge LeSaunier and began composing in Edmonton. In 1941 he studied composition with *Weinzweig at the *TCM and then (1942) joined CBC Toronto, where he worked in the record library and the continuity department, selecting programs and writing scripts and later serving as host for CBC radio's 'Ballet Club.' In 1966 he became producer of the radio programs 'Opera Time' (with Ruby *Mercer as host) and 'Opera Theatre.' He retired in 1977. His compositions (to 1951) are listed in *Catalogue of Canadian Composers*. They include works for piano and orchestra, piano solo and duet, and string quartet. He composed many Shakespearean songs in the late 1940s and early 1950s for Earle Grey's outdoor productions of Shakespeare at Trinity College, U of Toronto. Several of his works have been performed on CBC radio. A letter Macdonald wrote to Deems Taylor, the US critic and composer, emerged as a full chapter in Taylor's book *The Well Tempered Listener* (New York 1940) under the heading 'Guest speaker.' LL

MacDONALD, Jean (Hastings) (m Haddow). Mezzo-soprano, organist, b Strathlorne, Cape Breton, NS, 11 Dec 1895, d Toronto 17 Nov 1979. She studied 1913–14 at the Halifax Cons, (see Maritime Cons) 1915–16 with Lee Pattison (piano) at the New England Cons, and then privately in Boston with Rose Stewart (voice). Alexander Graham Bell took a great interest in her career. She taught 1924–30 at Boston's Academy of Speech and 1928–31 at Wellesley College in Massachusetts. During the 1920s and 1930s she appeared as soloist with the Boston Festival Orchestra, the Boston SO (under Koussevitzky), and the *TSO (in an 'All-Canada Symphony Hour' broadcast 6 Apr 1930 over the CNR network) and also with the Cecilia Society of Boston, the Harvard Glee Club, the McDowell Club Chorus, the Radcliffe Choral Society, and the Wellesley College Choir. In 1922 she sang at the funeral of Alexander Graham Bell at Mrs Bell's request. During the 1920s she often performed with the Ross Scottish Concert Company which toured throughout New England, New York State, and New Jersey, and in 1929 she sang at the Scottish Festival, Annapolis Royal, NS. In 1931 she moved to Toronto, where she appeared in recitals with Alberto *Guerrero. Until the early 1940s she also gave joint recitals in eastern Canada and the USA with her sister Anna – pianist, b Strathlorne, NS, 15 Jul 1894, L MUS (Dalhousie) 1921, LRAM 1933; a pupil of Bruce Symonds and Tobias Matthay, a teacher 1935–42 at the Halifax Cons and frequently during the 1930s a recitalist on CBC radio.

McDONALL, Lois. Soprano, b Larkspur, near Edmonton, 7 Feb 1939. She was a semi-finalist in the 1964 *Metropolitan Opera auditions, studied 1965–8 at the *U of Toronto with Irene *Jessner, and made her *COC debut in 1967 as Kate Pinkerton in *Madama Butterfly*. She sang the title role in *Tosca*, Constanze in *The Abduction from the Seraglio*, and Elsa in *Lohengrin* 1968–9 in Flensburg, Germany, before becoming a resident artist at Sadler's Wells in 1969. She made her debut there on short notice, 21 Oct 1970, in the title role of Handel's *Semele* when Elizabeth Harwood became ill in the first act. McDonall sang all subsequent performances that season, also Nedda in *I Pagliacci* and Constanze in *The Abduction from the Seraglio*. In the 1972–3 season at Sadler's Wells she assumed several new roles: Fiordiligi in *Così fan tutte*, Rosalinda in *Die Fledermaus*, Antonia in *The Tales of Hoffmann*, Freya in *Das Rheingold*, and Hanna in *The Merry Widow*. In following seasons she added, among others, Jenny in *Mines of Sulphur* (1973), *Manon* (1974), the Marschallin in *Der Rosenkavalier* (1975; the critic of *The Times* wrote: 'a beautifully poised reading, distinguished by her properly aristocratic highness of tone and the breadth of her phrasing...her tone for "Hab mir gelobt" was gloriously rich, her phrasing replete with emotion') and Donna Anna in *Don Giovanni* (1976). She has returned to Canada for performances with Festival Canada (the Countess in *The Marriage of Figaro* 1974; see Festival Ottawa), the COC (*Fledermaus*, 1975; John *Kraglund wrote in the *Globe and Mail* that her 'warm, pure voice floated effortlessly and musically...She was surely as convincing and lovely a Rosalinda as we have had here in many seasons'), and the *Edmonton Opera (Donna Anna, 1977). She can be heard in the English National Opera recording of *Das Rheingold* (4-Angel S-3825).

BIBLIOGRAPHY

Mercer, Ruby. 'An interview with Lois McDonall,' *OpCan*, Oct 1975
Wadsworth, Stephen. 'Canada's Lois McDonall,' ibid, Dec 1977
Littler, William. 'Edmonton soprano takes flight in London,' *Toronto Star*, 10 Sep 1979 (RMr)

MacDONOUGH, Harry (John Scantlebury) (b MacDonald). Ballad tenor, b Hamilton, Ont, 30 May 1871, d New York 26 Sep 1931. He was one of the two most popular ballad tenors of his day, the other being his compatriot Henry *Burr. He began his career as a church soloist. In 1898 he made a few recordings for the Michigan Electric Co of Detroit for use in its slot machine phonograph parlours. In 1899 he was invited to record for Edison and became second tenor in the Edison Male Quartet, which later recorded for *Berliner and Victor as the Haydn (corrupted to Hayden) Quartet. Macdonough became a professional recording artist for the Victor Co participating in the Victor Mixed Chorus, Light Opera, and Opera; the Victor Opera Trio, Quartet, and Sextet; the Haydn Quartet; the original Lyric Trio and Quartet; and the Orpheus Quartet. After his retirement from singing he became manager and an assistant recording director of Victor's New York recording laboratories. In 1925 he joined Columbia as director of recording studios. Listings of his recordings both as a soloist and in groups are given in *Roll Back the Years*.

BIBLIOGRAPHY

Walsh, Ulysses. 'Favourite pioneer recording artists,' *Hobbies Magazine*, Nov, Dec 1943 EBM

McDOUGALL, Ian (Walter). Trombonist, composer, b Calgary 14 Jun 1938; B MUS (British Columbia) 1966, M MUS composition (British Columbia) 1970. His father, George McDougall, played banjo and guitar in Calgary dance bands during the 1920s. The younger McDougall took up the trombone at 11 in Victoria, BC, studying with Jack Kraeling, and began playing in bands at 12. In 1960 he went to England, where he was a member 1960–1 of John Dankworth's orchestra (with which he made two LPs; see Discography for Kenny Wheeler) and also played with Ted Heath's orchestra. Returning to Canada in 1961 and settling in Vancouver in 1962, McDougall played 1962–4 in the *Vancouver SO, was a member of the houseband at the Cave under Chris *Gage and Fraser *MacPherson, and attended the U of British Columbia (where his teachers included Cortland *Hultberg). In 1966 he was briefly a member of Woody Herman's orchestra. McDougall led jazz groups of various sizes in Vancouver, including a 12-piece big band and an 18-piece brass band, which often were heard on the CBC. In 1970 he founded *Pacific Salt, remaining its leader until 1973, when he moved to Toronto.

There McDougall has been a studio musician, a member of the *Boss Brass, and the leader of jazz groups. For a 90-minute documentary of his career, broadcast 11 and 12 May 1979 on CBC's 'Jazz Radio-Canada,' McDougall led an 11-piece band. He has made an LP with a big band (1970, CBC LM 93); two with Pacific Salt; one with a trio (Oliver Gannon, guitar, and Ron Johnston, piano) for his own Energy label (*Three*, 1976, E 464); and several as a sideman and soloist with the Boss Brass. His compositions include the CBC commissions *The Jazz Suite* (1967) and *The Vancouver Suite* (1971), both for big band, and *British Columbia Centennial Suite* (1971) for brass band. The Vancouver SO commissioned *Tidelines* (1971) and the RCMP commissioned *Mini-suite for the RCMP* (1979). His *Pellet Suite* (1976) was written for, and recorded (Umbrella UMB-GEN 1-12) by, the Boss Brass. He has written many other works for jazz group or orchestra. He is an affiliate of PRO Canada.

McDougall's wife, Barbara – b Allen, Vancouver 1 May 1946; B MUS (British Columbia) 1966 – studied violin with Esther Glazer (Vancouver), Oscar Shumsky (the Juilliard School, New York), and Lorand *Fenyves (U of Toronto), was a member 1969–72 of the Vancouver SO, and became a freelance musician after 1973 in Toronto chamber, symphony, and studio orchestras.

BIBLIOGRAPHY

Bavin, Pam. 'Canadians in London, 1: Ian McDougall, *Coda*, Sep 1961 MM

MacDOWELL, (John) Lansing. Educator, organist-choirmaster, b Brockville, Ont, 30 Oct 1918; BA (Toronto) 1942. A pupil of Charles *Peaker in Toronto, he taught music and modern languages in high schools there 1943–5 and in Simcoe, Ont, 1945–52 and 1953–6. He conducted 1954–6 the Cockshutt Male Choir of Brantford. He moved to London, Ont, as music master 1956–65 at the London Teachers' College and organist-choirmaster at Bishop Cronyn Memorial Anglican Church. In 1965 he became a music inspector and regional consultant for the Ontario Ministry of Education. In this role and as an adjudicator and examiner he has worked particularly to raise choral standards. He has been president 1950–1 of the *OMEA, 1966–7 of the *ORMTA, and 1976–9 of the *Canadian Music Festival Adjudicators' Assn. With Vera Russell, John Wood, and Charles Winter he wrote volumes 3 to 8 of the graded elementary school text *Songtime* (Holt, Rinehart, Winston 1963–7). He conducted two of the pieces sung and recorded (Gavotte LPG 100, 107) by the Associated Male Choirs of Ontario and America at the 1952 and 1954 Big Sing.

See also School music. (GKG)

McEACHERN, Murray. Trombonist, saxophonist, b Toronto 16 Aug 1915. After violin studies with Geoffrey *Waddington at the *TCM he gave a recital in *Massey Hall at 12. Further studies (clarinet and saxophone) preceded engagements in Montreal with Lucio *Agostini and the dance bands of George Sims and Dick *Todd, and on Toronto radio with Percy *Faith (CRBC) and Johnny *Burt (CFRB). By now proficient on several instruments, including trombone, trumpet, and bass, he made his US debut as a novelty act in 1936 in Chicago, then toured in the USA and Canada with, in turn, Jack Hylton's orchestra, Benny Goodman's big band (as trombone soloist 1936–8), and Glen Gray's Casa Loma Orchestra as trombonist and alto saxophonist 1938–41). His recordings with Goodman and Gray are listed in Brian Rust's *Jazz Records 1897–1942* (London 1972) and have been included in various anthologies of these leaders' work.

McEachern was assistant director in 1941 of Paul Whiteman's orchestra and a member of the US Armed Forces Entertainment Division during World War II; he also led his own band and played with Bob Crosby's radio orchestra in the 1940s. Thereafter a Hollywood studio musician, he played the trombone solos heard in the movies *The Glenn Miller Story* (1953), *The Benny Goodman Story* (1955), and *Paris Blues* (1961), and under his own name made the LPs *Music For Sleepwalkers Only* (Key 711), *Caress* (Cap T-899), and *Warm Trombone* (Dot 25620). In 1972 he toured Europe, playing Billy May's *Concerto for Trombone and Saxophone*, written for him. Briefly a member of Duke Ellington's Orchestra in 1973 and 'ghost leader' of the Tommy Dorsey Orchestra in 1974, he then worked again in various Los Angeles orchestras.

BIBLIOGRAPHY

Tynan, J. 'Where's the melody? asks Mr. McEachern,' *Down Beat*, 20 Feb 1958 HM, MM

Macedonia. Balkan nation conquered and divided by Rome in 168 BC, ruled by various countries in the ensuing centuries but surviving as a region and a culture with a language predominatly Slavic. It was partitioned in 1913 by *Bulgaria, *Greece, and *Serbia (now Serbian *Yugoslavia). The influx to Canada of Macedonians from the villages near Kastoria and Florina in Greece began after 1903; of those from Yugoslavia, after 1945. In 1976 65,000 persons of Macedonian descent lived in Canada, many of them businessmen or restaurateurs in Toronto.

The musical life of the motherland has been maintained in the Macedonian communities in Canada, where some 20 associations have been established by groups from specific villages of Greece and Yugoslavia. Women continued in the 1920s and 1930s to gather each day for coffee, singing, and dancing; and in the 1970s the Kastoria-area women still practised a three-part vocal polyphony similar to that heard in Albania.

Many of the older men play the kaval (flute) and a few play the gajda (bagpipe). A Macedonian Children's Orchestra of 40 instruments (mandolins and violins) performed at the 1938 *CNE.

In the mid-1970s music was heard at dances and picnics sponsored by orthodox churches and by the village associations. It was a necessity at weddings and also was heard at engagements, christenings, and namedays. A dozen bands, consisting of clarinet, accordion, and drums, with the substitution or addition of saxophone, organ, electric guitar, and bouzouki, played a variety of dances: berache, armensko, and bufsko (12/8), na ramo and levoto (6/8), pajdushko (5/8), tsigansko (7/8), and the Greek dances syrto and chamiko. In the mid-1970s Macedonians in Toronto supported three dance and folksong ensembles, the most active of which, the Selyani Macedonian Folklore Group, directed by Olga Sandolowica, has performed for the Society of Ethnomusicology (Toronto 1972), at the Montreal Olympics (1976), at the International Eisteddfod in Wales (1977), and for many years at the *Mariposa Folk Festival. It has made the LP *Village Music of Macedonia* (Selyani Productions 770 489). TR

MACEROLLO, Joseph (Nicholas Anthony). Accordionist, teacher, b Guelph, Ont, 1 Oct 1944; B MUS (Toronto) 1965, MA musicology (Toronto) 1969. He began accordion lessons at seven with Nicholas Antonelli and studied briefly in 1960 with Charles *Camilleri, winning many classes and awards 1957–64 at competition festivals and subsequently playing in nightclubs and for a time (1969) with Phil *Nimmons. He began teaching at the *RCMT in 1969, collaborating on the first free-bass accordion syllabus, and at *Queen's U the same year, adding duties at the *U of Toronto to his teaching activities in 1972. He has performed often on CBC radio and TV. In public appearances with the *Canadian Electronic Ensemble, the *Chamber Players of Toronto, the *Hart House Orchestra, the *NACO, the *Orford String Quartet, and the *Purcell String Quartet, as well as in solo recitals, he has premiered free-bass accordion works by Milton *Barnes, Luciano Berio, Walter *Buczynski, Samuel *Dolin, George *Fiala, James Hiscott, Lothar *Klein, Barbara *Pentland, R. Murray *Schafer, Morris *Surdin, and Gerhard *Wuensch. In 1978 he toured the USSR. He has been president 1970–4 of the Confédération internationale des accordéonistes and 1974–7 of the Canadian Accordion Teachers' Assn. While president 1972–6 of the *Contemporary Showcase he organized the first International Free-Bass Accordion Symposium (1975) as part of his sustained effort to establish the instrument in the concert field. In 1979 he founded and became first president of the Classical Accordion Society of Canada.

WRITINGS

Accordion Reference Manual (Toronto 1979)

DISCOGRAPHY

Interaccodinotesta: Pentland – Krenek – Nordheim – Schafer. Morrison sop, Purcell Str Quart. 1977, 1978. Mel SMLP 4034

Surdin *Concerto* for accordion and strings. Hart House Orchestra, Neel cond. 1967. RCI 238

Surdin – Wuensch – Dolin – Fiala. 1973. McGill Chamb O, Brott cond. RCI 385

BIBLIOGRAPHY

MacMillan, Rick. 'Joseph Macerollo works for acceptance of free-bass accordion,' *MSc*, 286, Nov – Dec 1975 (WS)

McGARRIGLE, Kate and Anna. Folk singers and song-writers. Born of French-Canadian and Irish parents in St-Sauveur-des-Monts, northwest of

Joseph Macerollo

Montreal, the sisters Anna (b 4 Dec 1944) and Kate (b 6 Feb 1946) studied music at the local convent. Both sing in English and French and play piano, guitar, banjo, and button accordion. They sang 1963–7 in Montreal coffeehouses with the Mountain City Four, a folk group completed by Jack Nissenson and Peter Weldon. In the 1970s they attracted international attention as songwriters. Anna's 'Heart Like a Wheel' was recorded in 1972 by McKendree Spring and, as the title song of an LP, in 1975 by Linda Ronstadt; and Anna's 'Work Song' was recorded by Maria Muldaur along with Kate's 'Cool River.' In 1975 they made their first LP, *Kate and Anna McGarrigle* (Warner BS 2862), then appeared at McGill U, in Boston, and at the 1976 Chorley Wakes folk festival in Lancashire, England. After their notable London debut 25 Jul 1976 at Victoria Palace, Michael Watts in *Melody Maker* (31 Jul 1976) called their music 'a holy marriage of strong sentiment and brilliant, pure singing...Anna's, lilting and airy, Kate's, deeper and fiercer – these are amongst the very best voices to be heard in popular music today.'

The McGarrigles' repertoire includes their own songs, which reflect the various influences of a century of North American popular music, and French Canadian folk music. Other McGarrigle songs include 'Kiss and Say Goodbye' and 'Mendocino.' They returned to Europe in 1977 for a 35-concert tour of Ireland, England, Belgium, and Holland. They have performed in Montreal, Toronto, and Ottawa, and in the USA. They usually are accompanied by a small band, which has included Anna's husband Dane Lanken (trumpet), Chaim Tannenbaum (harmonica), and Ken Pearson (organ). In 1976 their first LP was hailed as 'rock album of the year' by *Melody Maker* and also as one of the year's finest by the *New York Times* and the (New York) *Village Voice*. Their second LP, *Dancer with Bruised Knees* (1976, Warner BS 3014), also was well received critically. A third, *Pronto Monto* (Warner BSK-1248), was released in 1978.

BIBLIOGRAPHY

MacGregor, Roy. 'The fluke,' *The Canadian*, 28 May 1977

Bossin, Bob. 'Sweet harmony,' *Weekend*, 2 Sep 1978

Bergeron, Raymonde. 'Les soeurs McGarrigle,' *Madame au foyer*, Oct 1980 MM

McGill Chamber Orchestra / Orchestre de chambre McGill. During the 1945–6 season Alexander *Brott assembled a group of professional instrumentalists and presented Bach's six *Brandenburg Concertos* at the *Ermitage in two concerts (26 October and 15 March) under the auspices of the *Montreal Festivals. Under the same sponsorship the 12 Handel *Concerti grossi* were presented during the 1946–7 season in four concerts. In 1947 the McGill Chamber Music Society / Société de musique de chambre McGill was founded to sponsor the *McGill String Quartet's concerts, and two or three chamber orchestra concerts were included among them. Gradually the orchestra concerts increased in number and the quartet's concerts decreased. When the quartet disbanded in 1953, the name McGill Chamber Orchestra was adopted to identify the new orchestra of some 15 string players. The ensemble's concerts were given 1949–51 in Moyse Hall, 1951–66 at Redpath Hall, 1966–7 at the Mount Royal Hotel, 1967–8 in the Maisonneuve Theatre at *PDA (a double series of six concerts), 1968–9 at the Port-Royal Theatre, and thereafter in the Maisonneuve Theatre. In 1979–80 the season consisted of eight concerts, all conducted – as was customary – by Alexander Brott.

In 1980 the orchestra continued to have a core of 15 string instruments, with added woodwinds, brass, and percussion as required. Yaëla *Hertz became the concertmaster in 1959. Brott has presented programs ranging from baroque to contemporary. The many premieres have included several of Brott's compositions and a number of works commissioned by the Samuel *Lapitsky Foundation. Besides its customary eight Monday evening concerts, the orchestra has given free concerts at the Montreal Museum of Fine Arts, and in 1967 it began presenting gala annual concerts at Notre-Dame Church with noted soloists including Peter Pears, Henryk Szeryng, and Yehudi Menuhin. In 1976 the orchestra presented four special concerts devoted to works of the last two centuries inspired by the Olympic Games; the concerts were based on research by Walter Kunstler. The orchestra has presented numerous Canadian and foreign soloists. These have included Paul Badura-Skoda, Colette *Boky, *Bouchard and *Morisset, John *Boyden, *Canadian Brass, Ida *Haendel, Marek *Jablonski, Gary *Karr, John *Newmark, David and Igor Oistrakh, Jean-Pierre Rampal, Mstislav Rostropovitch, Gérard Souzay, Janos Starker, Barry Tuckwell, and Rosalyn Tureck. Among the major works performed have been Leonard *Isaacs' instrumentation of Bach's *Art of Fugue* (1954, and again in 1979) and Igor Markevitch's of the same composer's *Musical Offering* (1958).

The orchestra has received financial assistance from the *Canada Council, the *MACQ, and the Council of Arts of Greater Montreal. In 1979–80 its operating budget was about $150,000. Foreign tours have been made to the USSR (1966), the USA (1959, 1967), Switzerland and France (1973), Mexico (1974) and Poland, Czechoslovakia, and Hungary (1978). *The News* described a concert the orchestra gave in Mexico City: 'The program containing works by Corelli, Mercure, and Bartok showed Alexander Brott's impeccable stylistic sense. The sixteen men and women are extremely competent and even virtuoso musicians, capable not only of pinpoint precision in ensemble playing, but also of brilliance in solo parts' (18 May 1974). Presidents of the society have been Mrs. H. Mortimer Jaquays 1947–9, Edna Marie *Hawkin 1949–59, and Mrs Lawrence Weir Davis 1959–67. Mrs Robert A. Plaw became president in 1967.

DISCOGRAPHY

J.C. Bach *Sinfonietta No. 1* – Bach *Sinfonia No. 3*; *Concerto in C* for 2 pianos. Morton, Masters pfs. Ca 1975. CBC SM-290

Benda – Bach – Roussel. Rampal fl. Ca 1965. Pirouette S19012

Boyce – Chevalier de Saint-Georges – Rameau. Y. Hertz vn, Kernerman vn. 1973. CBC SM-258

A. Brott *Arabesque* – Freedman *Images*. Nelsova vc. 1963. RCI 187

A. Brott *Circle, Triangle, 4 Squares* – Vallerand *Cordes en mouvement*. (1967). RCI 216/RCA CCS-1010

McGill Chamber Orchestra

A. Brott *Profundum praedictum* – Glick *Sinfonia Concertante* – Pépin *Monade I*. Karr db. Ca 1966. RCA LSC-3128/ (*Profundum praedictum*) Sel CC15.088/(*Monade I*) CRI SD-317
A. Brott *Sept for Seven*. D. McGill narr. Ca 1956. RCI 131
A. Brott *Songs of Contemplation* – Mercure *Divertissement*. G. Gabora sop. Ca 1967. CBC SM-6
A. Brott *Three Astral Visions*. 1963. RCI 188
Corelli *Concerto grosso*, Op 6, no 1 – Mozart *Serenata Notturna* K239; *Adagio et fugue* K546. 1968. CBC SM-58
Haydn *Concerto in F* for violin and harpsichord – Mozart *Divertimento in D* K136. Y. Hertz vn, Gilbert hpd. Ca 1967. CBC SM-18
Haydn *Symphonies No. 44 and 49*. 1969. CBC SM-89/A of D SDD 2160
F.-X. Mozart *Concerto in C* for piano. J. Holtzman pf. (1975). RCI 407
Schubert–Mozart – Beethoven – A. Brott *Seven Minuets, Six Canons*. 1973. CBC SM-236
Telemann *Suite in A* for flute and strings; *Don Quichotte*. Rampal fl. Ca 1965. Pirouette S19016
See also Discography for Jean Carignan; Joseph Macerollo.

BIBLIOGRAPHY

McLean, Eric. 'McGill Chamber Orchestra's twenty-fifth birthday,' *Montreal Star*, 27 Feb 1965
Siskind, Jacob. 'The McGill Chamber Orchestra...after 34 years,' *Placedart*, Sep – Oct 1973
Edds, Jack. 'The McGill Chamber Orchestra: a forty-year romance with the Brotts,' *OCan*, Feb 1980 GP

McGill Conservatorium. See McGill University.

McGill Opera Studio / Atelier d'opéra de McGill. Founded in 1956 by Edith and Luciano *Della Pergola at the Faculty of Music of *McGill U. It was called a Repertory Class 1968–70 and an Opera Workshop 1970–4, before the name McGill Opera Studio was adopted in 1974. The workshop was directed jointly by the two teachers until 1977, when Luciano Della Pergola began to concentrate particularly on staging while his wife directed the musical aspects of the productions. By 1978 more than 25 complete operas and 125 excerpts had been presented, most of them in their original language. The majority of the soloists, chorus, and orchestra are students at McGill U. Both excerpts and operas are offered in costume, but the excerpts are presented in stylized staging and with piano accompaniment. In 1977 Barry Wiesenfeld was succeeded as accompanist by Monik *Grenier and Marie-Thérèse *Paquin. The orchestra has been conducted successively by Alexander *Brott, Eugene Plawutsky, and Michel *Perrault. Uri Mayer succeeded Perrault in 1977. The first program of the 1956–7 season featured Purcell's *Dido and Aeneas* and Pergolesi's *La Serva Padrona*. Among the other complete works presented have been *Beckwith's **Night Blooming Cereus*, Britten's *The Rape of Lucretia*, Cimarosa's *Il Matrimonio Segreto*, Debussy's *Pelléas et Mélisande*, Donizetti's *Don Pasquale*, Haydn's *The Apothecary*, Menotti's *The Consul*, *The Telephone*, and *The Old Maid and the Thief*, Mozart's *Così fan tutte* and *The Marriage of Figaro*, Poulenc's *La Voix humaine*, Puccini's *Suor Angelica*, Ravel's *L'Heure espagnole*, *Vallerand's **Le Magicien*, the Canadian premiere of Malcolm Williamson's *The Growing Castle*, and two Bach cantatas. The programs of operatic scenes are performed for the public free of charge and are held mainly in the Recital Room of McGill U as part of the series 'Concerts of the First of the Month' and 'Sunday at the Opera,' each of which presents three to five concerts a year. A fixed admission price is charged for the complete productions. The latter have been held successively at Moyse Hall (McGill U), Redpath Hall, and Pollack Hall.

BIBLIOGRAPHY

Bailey, Bruce. 'Couple strives to keep opera alive,' Montreal *Gazette*, 26 Jan 1980 (AP, NT)

McGill String Quartet / Quatuor à cordes McGill. The first McGill Quartett (sic) was formed in 1904 by three McGill teachers, Alfred *De Sève (principal violin), J.-J. *Goulet (second violin), and J.-B. *Dubois (cello), and one of De Sève's pupils, Albert *Chamberland (viola). It had a brief existence, as did a second ensemble of the same name formed ca 1930 by four teachers, Maurice *Onderet and Eric Zimmerman (violins), Harry Norris (viola), and Jean *Belland (cello).

In 1939 a third quartet was founded by Alexander *Brott (first violin), with Edwin Sherrard (second violin), Joseph Oriold (viola), and Belland (cello). Stephen *Kondaks replaced Oriold in the autumn of 1940, and in 1942 Mildred *Goodman became second violin, Sherrard viola, and Lotte Goetzel cello. Florence Hood was second violin briefly in 1944. Beginning with the 1944–5 season, the quartet comprised, in addition to Brott, Lionel Renaud (second violin), Lucien *Robert (viola), and Lotte Goetzel *Brott (cello). D'Arcy *Shea was second violin in 1949.

After a debut at the McGill Faculty Club 11 Feb 1940 and a broadcast on radio station CFCF the following 9 March, the quartet presented the first concert in an inaugural series of three at *McGill U's Moyse Hall; for the second and third concerts, 13 March and 24 April, Douglas *Clarke was guest pianist in the Schumann and Brahms quintets respectively. During the summer of 1940 the ensemble spent some time at Lac Manitou in the Laurentians and gave several benefit concerts for the Red Cross at the Red Barn Hotel. The *Montreal Festivals presented it in seven seasons of from six to eight concerts each, 1940–4 in the Prince of Wales room of the Windsor Hotel and 1945–7 at the *Ermitage. The McGill Chamber Music Society / La Société de musique de chambre McGill, founded in 1947 with Mrs H.M. Jaquays as president, sponsored the quartet's concerts in 1947–8 at the Royal Victoria College and later at Moyse Hall. However, the quartet's activities slowly diminished and became part of a season which also included concerts by a chamber music ensemble conducted by Brott and, on occasion, Clarke. The quartet disbanded in the early 1950s but reformed for a single concert in 1954 to mark the 50th anniversary of the McGill Cons. On that occasion it performed works by Violet *Archer, Brott, and Robert *Turner, all former McGill U students. The quartet performed in Toronto in 1943 and in Ottawa in 1945.

Many guests performed with the ensemble, including the pianists Jean-Marie *Beaudet, Arthur *Benjamin, Judith Carinov, Douglas Clarke, Jean *Dansereau, Sir Ernest *MacMillan, Germaine *Malépart, Marie-Thérèse *Paquin, Ross *Pratt, George Schick, Henrietta Schumann, and Reginald *Stewart; the violinist Jacques Gordon; the cellists Orlando Cole, Maurice Eisenberg, and Zara *Nelsova; the double-bassist Charles Hardy; the flutists Hervé *Baillargeon and Mario *Duschenes; the oboists Réal *Gagnier, Léon Goossens, and Robert McBride; the bassoonist Roland *Gagnier; the clarinetists Armand *Gagnier and Rafael *Masella; the french-horn players Guillaume *Gagnier, Joseph *Masella, and Pietro *Romano; and the singers Pierrette *Alarie, Jeanne *Desjardins, Audrey *Mildmay, and William *Morton.

In addition to the regular quartet repertoire it performed such works as the Beethoven *Septet*, the Schubert *Octet*, Chausson's *Concert*, Fauré's *La Bonne Chanson*, and Vaughan Williams' *On Wenlock Edge*. Among the Canadian works on its programs were the *Quartet* (1941), *Lullaby and Procession of the Toys* (1943), *Quartet No. 2* (1946), *Quintet* with recorders, and *Critic's Corner* with percussion (1950), all by Brott. Also in 1950 a *Quartet* by Andrew *Twa received an award in a national competition organized by the ensemble.

BIBLIOGRAPHY

'The McGill String Quartet,' *CRMA*, 9, Jan 1943
Siskind, Jacob. 'The McGill Chamber Orchestra...after 34 years,' *Placedart*, Sep – Oct 1973 GP

McGill University. Founded in Montreal in 1821 as the University of McGill College; in 1980 well established as the chief English-language university in the province of Quebec.

In 1813 James McGill, a prominent Montreal citizen and merchant, bequeathed £10,000 and a 18.4-hectare plot of land to the Royal Institution for the Advancement of Learning (established in 1801 to promote education in Lower Canada) to found a college or university. In 1821 George IV granted a charter establishing the University of McGill College, a non-denominational institution. A reorganization of the college was ratified by an 1852 charter, signed by Queen Victoria, and in 1885 the name was changed to McGill University. Courses began in 1829 in the Faculty of Medicine and in 1843 in the Faculty of Arts, the campus gradually expanding from its original location on the southeast side of Mount Royal. In 1978–9 McGill U comprised 11 faculties at the undergraduate level, a faculty of graduate studies and research (masters and doctorate degrees), 9 schools, and 3 affiliated colleges, and some 2500 professors and lecturers taught close to 20,000 students.

When the teaching of music began in 1884, it was reserved for women, and it remained so until the opening of the McGill Conservatorium of Music. In 1889 at the request of the students a teaching specialist was engaged by means of a gift of

$200 from the university's chancellor, Donald A. Smith (Lord *Strathcona). The latter founded the Royal Victoria College for girls in 1896, and when it opened in September 1899 he brought Clara *Lichtenstein from Europe to be in charge of its music department.

The official establishment of the McGill Conservatorium in 1904 was mainly the result of Lichtenstein's remarkable work at the Royal Victoria College, the financial support of Lord Strathcona, and the moral encouragement of the principal, William Peterson. It was, however, the introduction in 1902 of the examinations of the *AB of the RSM of London, accomplished through the efforts of Charles A.E. *Harriss, that firmly established music's place at McGill U. Harriss was appointed director of the board of examinations as well as director of the conservatorium, which began classes 21 Sep 1904 in Workman House (a gift of Lord Strathcona). Lichtenstein was named vice-director, a position she held until 1929. At the official inauguration 14 Oct 1904, in the presence of the Governor-General, Lord Minto, a recital was given by two young artists, the pianist Ellen *Ballon and the violinist Albert *Chamberland. The first session was attended by 462 students from Quebec, New Brunswick, Newfoundland, and New York State, and 26 instructors were hired on an hourly basis. During these early years the teaching body included Frederick H. *Blair, Albert *Clerk-Jeannotte, Guillaume *Couture, Alfred *De Sève, Jean-Baptiste *Dubois, J.-J. *Goulet, Percival J. *Illsley, Arthur *Letondal, Romain-Octave *Pelletier, and Horace *Reyner, and instruction was offered in composition, theory, and performance. When Harriss resigned in the summer of 1907, he recommended reducing the number of instructors in favour of a chair in music, whose incumbent would enjoy the same status as other professors at the university. This request was granted by the university council, which, through a gift from Lieut-Col Jeffrey H. Burland, engaged as professor and director Harry Crane *Perrin, the organist of Canterbury Cathedral. Lichtenstein filled the post 1907–8 on an interim basis and in 1908 Perrin began a career at McGill U that was to span 21 years. He formed McGill's first university symphonic ensemble and in 1909 set up McGill U's own system of music examinations in 56 centres spread across Canada. By dissociating itself from the AB of the RSM the institution reinforced its autonomy and established the originality of its contribution in teaching and examinations.

A substantial gift from Sir William MacDonald in 1917 to endow the conservatorium permitted the establishment 26 Apr 1920 of a Faculty of Music. For the next 10 years Perrin combined the duties of director of the conservatorium and dean of the faculty. Premises, professors, and budget were shared.

Having laid the foundations for the teaching of music at the university level, Perrin resigned in 1930. He was succeeded as dean of the faculty by Douglas *Clarke, who had been appointed director of the conservatorium in 1929. There followed a marked increase in musical activities of interest to the public. Clarke established a series of concerts (Sunday Evening Series) which featured such renowned musicians as Ernest Ansermet, Georges Enesco, Gustav Holst, Nicolas Medtner, Ignaz Jan Paderewski, Serge Prokofiev, Leopold Stokowski, and the London String Quartet, and such lecturers as Edmund Fellowes, Percy Scholes, and Charles Sanford Terry. On the academic side, the programs began to be revised in 1930. The composer Claude *Champagne was a member of the teaching staff 1932–41. Clarke's main achievement undoubtedly remains the *Montreal Orchestra (1930–41), which included in its ranks the more advanced McGill students.

Growth of the faculty was impeded, however, by the fact that the position of dean still constituted the only full-time job, by meagre financial resources, and by the effects of World War II. In addition the school did not have suitable premises. Between 1948 and 1971 the conservatorium and the faculty moved several times. This did not deter the conservatorium from celebrating its 50th anniversary with a series of concerts (November – December 1954), the last of which was presented on 8 December with the participation of Ellen Ballon and Douglas Clarke. At this time the teaching staff consisted of 34 instructors, most of them part-time.

Following Clarke's retirement in 1955, Marvin *Duchow became acting dean. The conservatorium and the faculty were reorganized, and three departments were created within the faculty: theoretical music (chaired by Duchow), keyboard instruments and voice with Helmut *Blume as chairman, and instrumental music with Alexander *Brott as chairman. The conservatorium was divided into a senior department and a junior department, the courses of the former leading to diplomas and those of the latter confined to basic musical training. Duchow was confirmed as dean in 1957 and remained in the post until 1963 while continuing to direct the theoretical-music department.

Under Helmut Blume (acting dean, 1963–4, dean 1964–76), the faculty underwent considerable expansion. Having grown until it occupied all or part of half-a-dozen different buildings, widely separated on the campus, it finally received adequate and permanent premises, moving in 1971 into Royal Victoria College on Sherbrooke St West, which was renovated and renamed the Strathcona Music Building. Through a bequest from the Maurice *Pollack Foundation in 1966 the ground floor cafeteria was renovated and the Assembly Hall on the floor above was converted into a modern 600-seat concert hall. Through careful planning excellent control of the acoustics was achieved. The stage can be reduced by using movable reflecting wall panels, and for opera performances or certain stage productions the orchestra pit can be concealed from view by extending the stage floor. The Pollack Concert Hall was inaugurated 10 Apr 1975 with a concert including works by Beethoven, Liebermann, Kelsey *Jones (*The Prophesy of Micah*), and Bengt *Hambraeus (*Intrada*). This concert was followed by the McGill Music Month, a festival of 32 events, in which former and present teachers and students participated. That year 75 teachers gave courses to 469 students.

In 1966 the McGill Conservatorium was supplanted by the McGill Preparatory School of Music; the budget and teaching staff of the school initially were shared with the faculty, but the two institutions were separated in 1970. The dean continued to be in charge of the two levels of teaching until 1978, when the Preparatory School became the McGill Conservatory of Music, with Oleg Telizyn as its first director.

The McGill Conservatorium introduced in 1904 the licentiate diploma (L MUS) for instrumentalists who had completed three years of study. The associate diploma after one year was also granted 1939–66. The Faculty of Music began awarding the concert diploma at post-graduate level in 1966, and the Quebec Ministry of Education's Diplôme d'études collégiales (DEC) was awarded 1969–74. The B MUS degree, first offered in 1904, was subdivided into three options in 1956 (composition, performance, music education) and was enriched by the addition of the B MUS in theory (honours) and B MUS in history in 1966. A B MUS (honours) in performance (orchestra conducting) was offered between 1966 and 1976. MMA degrees were offered in composition in 1968, musicology in 1968, theory in 1970, and performance in 1975; in 1976–7 these became respectively the M MUS in composition, the MA in musicology, the MA in theory, and the M MUS in performance. A general B MUS and an MA in music education were introduced in 1978. An M MUS in sound recording was introduced in 1979 (and a modern recording studio opened in January 1980). The D MUS in composition, offered 1904–55, reappeared in 1974; Charles Henry Mills was the first to earn it, in 1911. The most recent programs were realized through the efforts of Paul *Pedersen, who became dean in 1976; he also had the idea for McGill U Records, a series to which composers, soloists, and ensembles of the faculty have contributed.

Honorary degrees have been granted to Sir Thomas Beecham (1949), Pauline *Donalda and Ellen Ballon (1954), Wilfrid *Pelletier (1968), Clément *Morin (1970), Hugh *Le Caine and Violet *Archer (1971), Burt Bacharach (1972), John *Newmark (1975), Jean *Carignan (1977), and John *Beckwith (1978). Distinguished alumni include Burt Bacharach, Ellen Ballon, Henry *Brant, Alexander Brott, Pauline Donalda, Marvin Duchow, Richard *Eaton, Frances Goltman, Frank *Hanson, Rafael *Masella, John *McKay, Eric *McLean, Kenneth *Meek, Charles *O'Neill, Wayne *Riddell, Robert *Silverman, Jacob *Siskind, William *Stevens, Robert *Turner, and Alfred *Whitehead.

The high quality of a McGill training has been maintained through the efforts of such teachers as the conductor-in-residence Alexander Brott (conducting), Marvin Duchow (history, literature, analysis), Bengt Hambraeus and Bruce *Mather (composition, analysis, theory), Kelsey Jones (harmony and counterpoint), Helmut Blume, Dorothy *Morton, and Charles *Reiner (piano), Stephen *Kondaks (violin, viola), John Grew (organ, harpsichord), Jan *Simons (voice), and Gisela *Depkat (cello). The Mount Royal Brass Quintet is composed of members of the teaching staff (James Thompson and Robert Gibson, trumpets; Nona Talamantes, french horn; Richard Lawton, trombone; and Ellis Wean, tuba) and gave its first concert in February 1977 in Pollack Hall. It has recorded Kelsey Jones' *Passacaglia and Fugue* (McGill U Records 77004), among other works. Also made up of staff members, the first *McGill String Quartet was formed in 1904 and a second was set up ca 1930, but both had only a brief existence. Alexander Brott reorganized the quartet in 1939 and gave several series of concerts under various auspices before the McGill Chamber Society took over and served as sponsor until 1947. An independent body unaffiliated with the university, the society later sponsored the concerts of the *McGill Chamber Orchestra, which Brott founded and in 1980 continued to conduct.

At the faculty various instrumental and vocal groups for students have flourished: the baroque chamber ensemble conducted by Mary Cyr beginning in 1976 (in 1977 it presented excerpts from Rameau's *Acante et Céphise* in a modern premiere); two wind ensembles under Donald Hughes (succeeded in 1976 by Robert Gibson) and Richard Lawton; and the McGill Percussion Ensemble founded by Pierre *Béluse in 1969. The McGill Symphony Orchestra was created by Harry Crane Perrin in 1909 and consisted at that time of 45 musicians, most of whom were not connected with the faculty. For a long time it was conducted by Reginald *Tupper. In 1980 it was made up entirely of McGill students. The orchestra was conducted by Eugene Plawutsky until 1976, when Uri Mayer took it over. In addition to its regular concert season, the orchestra has undertaken to accompany the faculty choirs, including the Concert Choir conducted by Wayne Riddell, and performances by the opera workshop. The *McGill Opera Studio, established in 1956 by Luciano and Edith *Della Pergola, has staged some 32 complete operas and numerous excerpts, ranging from Purcell's *Dido and Aeneas* (1956) to Britten's *The Rape of Lucretia* (1977). Gina Fiordaliso, Mariana *Paunova, and Joan *Patenaude are among its alumni. The McGill Jazz Band, set up in 1967 by Gerald Danovitch, had to be divided into three groups to accommodate the numbers of interested pupils. Kelsey Jones wrote his *Jazzum Opus Unum* for it in 1977. During an academic year in the late 1970s close to 200 public concerts would be given including student recitals and concerts with soloists of international reputation presented at the Faculty Fridays or the Celebrity Concerts with the CBC.

One of the first electronic music concerts in Canada was presented at McGill in 1959. The McGill Electronic Music Studio (EMS) was established in 1964 with the help of the National Research Council, which supplied equipment on a long-term loan basis. The studio was fitted out not only with standard items such as recorders, filters, mixers, a Moog synthesizer, and a spectrogram unit, but also with specific instruments (designed by Hugh Le Caine) such as a waveform control, a multitrack recorder, 24 sinewave generators with keyboard control, and a serial structure generator. The studio consists essentially of three voltage-controlled laboratories with provision for quadraphonic recording and playback, a montage studio, and listening facilities. Each year about 30 students, in addition to staff composers from McGill and elsewhere, work in the studio, which is one of the most complete in Canada. Directors have been István *Anhalt 1964–71, Paul Pedersen 1971–4, and Alcides *Lanza. Works have been produced there by Anhalt, Ted Dawson, Bengt Hambraeus, Lanza, Michel *Longtin, Denis *Lorrain, Pierre *Mercure, Pedersen, R. Murray *Schafer, and David Sutherland, among others.

By 1980 the faculty library, housed in the same building, had amassed over 20,000 general works, specialized journals, and scores, and about 10,000 recordings. The Carnegie Foundation, the London Gramophone Corporation, and the British Council donated a substantial number of the recordings. An additional 2000 scores were available to professors for classroom use. In 1980 the library was named in memory of Duchow.

In the area of research the faculty, in collaboration with the English department, had in preparation in 1980 an edition of the correspondence of the music historian Charles Burney (1726–1814). Another project resulted from the experimental course Music Design, introduced in 1975–6 by a visiting professor, Mario Bertoncini. In this course the students apply their knowledge of acoustics to the design of new musical instruments; on occasion they demonstrate them in concert. The ensemble MUD, which grew out of this course, changed its name to Sonde and subsequently became an independent organiztion. The bulletin *Music McGill*, published twice a year, first appeared in the summer of 1976.

In September 1977 the faculty received an anonymous gift of $200,000 for the acquisition of an organ for Redpath Hall. Hellmuth *Wolff was engaged to build the instrument, a French classical model with mechanical action, and completion was expected 1980–1. A positif organ built by Gerhard Brunzema and donated by Mrs. Arthur Henderson was inaugurated in Pollock Hall in 1980. The campus already owned two *Casavant organs of 7 and 10 stops respectively and two Karl *Wilhelm organs of 3 and 4 stops (positifs).

Donations and interest from endowments have provided the source of bursaries awarded each year. Some $23,500 was available for the 1978–9 year. To mark the centenary of Canada's confederation (1967), works by István Anhalt, Alexander Brott, Claude Champagne, Douglas Clarke, Kelsey Jones, and Robert Turner were presented at the *PDA in a special concert entitled 'McGill and its Music.'

See also College Songs.

BIBLIOGRAPHY

Montreal Music Year Book 1931 and *1932* (Montreal 1931, 1932)

Festival of the Conservatorium of Music, McGill University to mark its fiftieth year 1904–1954 (Montreal 1954)

McGill Music Month: April 10 to May 8, 1975 (Montreal 1975)

Frost, Stanley B. 'A short account of the history of the faculty of music,' unpubl paper presented to the James McGill Society (7 Dec 1978); partial report as 'McGill's musical memories,' *McGill Reporter*, 13 Dec 1978

Bailey, Bruce. 'McGill gets into record business – if you qualify,' Montreal *Gazette*, 6 Oct 1979

Archives, McGill U

Aspects of Music in Canada

Musical Red Book

La Vie musicale

NT (CGa, AP)

McHARG, Jim (James). Bassist, composer, b Glasgow in March 1927, naturalized Canadian 1970. In Scotland he played drums with a country dance band, then banjo with the Clyde Valley Stompers, a traditional jazz group. When he first lived in Toronto, 1957–60, he played bass with Ed Brady's Scottish Ramblers. Returning to the city in 1963, he formed a succession of dixieland groups: the Vintage Jazz Band in 1964, the Metro Stompers also in 1964 (taken over in 1968 by Jim *Galloway), a second Vintage Jazz Band in 1970, the Midnight Special (a trio with the guitarists Mike Roberts and Vic Newman) in the 1970s, and the Maple Leaf Jazz Band in 1979.

With the Stompers McHarg performed widely in Canada and the USA and held long-term engagements in Toronto nightclubs. He also appeared at *Expo 67 and at the 1968 *Mariposa Folk Festival. The personnel of the band varied; the best-known grouping comprised Charlie Gall (cornet), Jim Galloway (saxophones, succeeding Eric Neilson, clarinet), Jim Abercrombie (trombone), Ron Simpson or Dave Moody (banjo), and Bernie Nathan or Jim Glenn (drums). The Stompers made LPs for Columbia (*Stompin' at the Penny Farthing with Lonnie Johnson*, 1965, ELS 310), RCA (*Jim McHarg's Metro Stompers*, 1966, CTLS 1083/Camden CAS 2354), and Arc (*Thumbs Up*, 1966, AC 5016; *Stompin' at the Sheraton*, 1968, AS 5023; *Trad Mad*, AS 5028). McHarg also has played in Toronto bands accompanying the US musicians Lil Hardin Armstrong and Muggsy Spanier. Through his performances and his organizational work (in 1976 he became music director of the newly opened Harbourfront Jazz Club – later Molson's Jazz Club – in Toronto's waterfront recreational complex), McHarg has been a major contributor to the popularity of traditional and dixieland jazz in Toronto. He has composed several tunes, of which the most popular has been the pop song 'The Monster of Loch Ness.' He is an affiliate of PRO Canada.

BIBLIOGRAPHY

Scott, Patrick. 'From the Loch Ness Monster to dixieland bonanza,' *Toronto Daily Star*, 4 Aug 1964

Waxman, Ken. 'Jim McHarg's traditional jazz began in U.K.,' *MSc*, 295, May – Jun 1977

PG, MM

MACINA, Giuseppe (Francesco). Tenor, opera director, teacher, conductor, b Bari, Italy, 20 Jun 1938; Artist Diploma voice (Toronto) 1967. He came to Canada in 1954 and settled in Toronto, where his teachers included Gina Cigna and Ernesto *Vinci at the *RCMT and Irene *Jessner at the *U of Toronto. He made his operatic debut as Don Ottavio in *Don Giovanni* in a 1962 *Royal Cons Opera School production and sang supporting roles 1963–9 with the *COC and 1967–8 with the *Vancouver Opera. He has performed in oratorio and concert with the *Orpheus Choir of Toronto and the Brantford and McMaster SOs. A stage director 1969–74 at the U of Toronto's opera department, he also began directing Mohawk College (Hamilton) Opera Theatre productions in 1971. He served 1973–9 as conductor of the Santa Cecilia Chorus of Toronto. His pupils, in voice or operatic stagecraft, have included Barbara Carter, Deborah Jeans, and Marilyn Lightstone. In 1967 Macina became the first artistic director of the newly formed Toronto Opera Repertoire, organized to provide performance opportunities for young singers. Operating under the auspices of the Toronto Board of Education, the company has presented *La Bohème, Cavalleria Rusticana, Carmen, The Impresario, Lucia di Lammermoor, Macbeth, Madama Butterfly, A Masked Ball, Norma, I Pagliacci, Rigoletto, Suor Angelica, Tosca*, and *La Traviata* at Toronto's Central Technical High School. Among former members of the company are Susan Gudgeon, Sister Barbara Ianni, Deborah Jeans, Diane Loeb, Louise *Roy, Guillermo Silva-Marin, and Belva Spiel. NM

McINNES, (James) **Campbell**. Baritone, teacher, b Holcombe Brook, Lancs, England, 23 Jan 1873 or 1874, d Toronto 8 Feb 1945. He studied in London (with William Shakespeare, George Henschel, Charles Santley) and in Paris (with Jacques Bouhy) and, following his debut in 1899, quickly established himself as a favourite concert baritone and a familiar participant in the English festivals, beginning with Leeds in 1910 (where he sang in the premiere of Vaughan Williams' *A Sea Symphony*) and Worcester in 1911 (premiere of the same composer's *Five Mystical Songs*). In 1919 McInnes settled in Toronto, where for the next 25 years he worked tirelessly in the cause of music and diction, founding during the 1924–5 season two choral groups, the Canadian Singers and the Sunday Evening *Hart House Songsters, and a concert series, Tuesday Nine O'Clock (fl 1921–3). He also continued his singing career, appearing 15 times as the Christus in the *St Matthew Passion* with the *TSO. In later years he frequently lectured on musical subjects, and at the time of his death was teaching English and diction at Wycliffe and Trinity Colleges, the U of Toronto. The organ at Wycliffe was installed in his memory. On his passing, Vaughan Williams wrote, 'The death of Campbell McInnes recalls wonderful memories ... of a lovely baritone voice, a fine sense of words and above all the power which few singers possess to make a tune live.' His voice may be heard on the 1915 Gramophone Co record (B581) and on a private recording issued shortly before his death.

WRITINGS

'Music in Canada,' *Yearbook of the Arts in Canada*, ed Bertram Brooker (Toronto 1929)

The Music of Language (Oakville, Ont, 1939)

BIBLIOGRAPHY

McInnes, Graham. *Finding a Father* (London 1967) JBM

McINTOSH, Diana (b Lowes). Pianist, b Calgary; ARCT 1957, LMM 1961, B MUS (Manitoba) 1972. Her teachers were Gladys *Egbert (Calgary), Boris *Roubakine (RCMT, Banff SFA), Adele Marcus (Summer Music School, Aspen, Col, and New York), and Alma *Brock-Smith and Leonard *Isaacs (Winnipeg). Living in Winnipeg after 1959, she has performed works by *Papineau-Couture, Roussel, and Schumann with the *CBC Winnipeg Orchestra in 1971, 1972, and 1973 respectively and has been heard in chamber concerts broadcast on CBC radio's 'Music Manitoba,' 'Music West,' and 'Two New Hours.' In 1972 she also began to give solo and lecture recitals in various Canadian centres.

A champion of 20th-century Canadian music, McIntosh has premiered, or participated in the premieres of, works by Peter Allen (*Logos* 1977), Robert Daigneault (*Corridors, Reminiscences* 1977), Boyd McDonald (*Fantasy* 1974), Ann *Southam (*Four Bagatelles* 1964, *Integruities* 1973, *Inter-views* 1975), Robert *Turner (*Homage to Melville* 1974) and John Winiarz (*Vortices* 1977), and has included in her repertoire works by S.C. *Eckhardt-Gramatté, Robert *Fleming, Jacques *Hétu, and Oskar *Morawetz. In 1976 she established Music Inter Alia, a concert series ('contemporary music for people who don't like contemporary music') presented at the Winnipeg Art Gallery and broadcast in part on CBC radio. Her own recitals often mix media, employing slide projections, mime, and narration. She has explored the influence of painting on music by performing compositions in the presence of their visual inspiration. Among her own compositions, *Paraphrase No. 1* (1976) is based on Lawren Harris' 'Maligne Lake' and *Paraphrase No. 2* (1977) on an abstract painting by Marcel Barbeau. She is a member of PRO Canada.

BIBLIOGRAPHY

Hamilton, Andrew, and Creech, Gwenlyn. 'Where nothing happened they made music thrive,' *Music*, vol 1, Mar – Apr 1978

MacMillan, Rick. 'Pianist introduces new music with the help of paintings,' *MSc*, 300, Mar – Apr 1978

Schulman, Michael. 'Contemporary music groups thriving across Canada,' *MSc*, 303, Sep – Oct 1978 (LI)

McINTYRE, Paul (Poirier). Composer, pianist, conductor, administrator, b Peterborough, Ont, 1 Oct 1931; ARCT 1950, B MUS (Toronto) 1951, Artist Diploma (Toronto) 1952, D MUS (Toronto) 1958. He studied with Eileen MacManamy (piano) and Eric *Rollinson (theory) in Hamilton and with Oskar *Morawetz and Arnold *Walter (composition) and Bela Böszörmenyi-Nagy and Alexander Uninsky (piano) at the *RCMT. He also studied piano with Claudio Arrau at Stratford (summer 1955). On a Canadian Amateur Hockey Assn Scholarship, 1953–4, he attended the Paris Cons, where his teachers were Tony Aubin and Olivier Messiaen (composition), and the Salzburg Mozarteum, where he studied conducting with Igor Markevitch, Sixten Ehrling, and Wolfgang Sawallisch. In 1960 and 1961 (summers) he studied conducting with Pierre Monteux.

McIntyre was assistant conductor of the Opera Festival of Toronto in 1954 and of the Opera Summer School at the *U of British Columbia in 1955. He was conductor of the *Regina SO 1959–60. During the 1950s he was heard as a solo recitalist and accompanist on CBC radio and was accompanist to Jan *Rubeš 1955–9 for *Community Concerts. While head of the music department at the U of Alaska 1961–4 and a Carnegie visiting associate professor, he conducted the Fairbanks SO. He received a resident fellowship from the Huntington Hartford Foundation, Los Angeles, in 1963, taught at the U of Minnesota 1964–7, and was chairman of the music department of the College of Saint Catharine, St Paul, Minn, 1967–70, prior to a term 1970–7 as head of the music department at the *U of Windsor. He then served 1977–80 as director of the School of Music at that university.

McIntyre has employed various styles and techniques in his compositions, many of which are vocal works on dramatic texts. His *Symphonia sacra* was completed for his doctorate. The cantata *Judith*, which won the $1000 prize in the 1958 *Vancouver International Festival Competition, had its premiere at that festival with Lois *Marshall as soloist. In *Out of the Cradle Endlessly Rocking*, among other works, he used a 12-tone row. His orchestral work *Commedia*, an *Edmonton SO commission, was premiered by that orchestra in 1979. He is an associate of the *CMCentre, a member of the *CLComp and CAPAC, and a contributor to *EMC*.

SELECTED COMPOSITIONS

STAGE, TV

The Death of the Hired Hand, chamb opera for TV (Frost). 1961. CMCentre

This Is Not True, comic opera (J. Schevill). 1966. CMCentre

VOICE AND ORCHESTRA

Judith, melodrama-cantata (Bible, Douay Bible, anon). 1957 (rev 1958). Sop, narr, orch. CMCentre

Symphonia sacra (R. Crashaw). 1958. Alto, ten, bass, SATB, orch. CMCentre

Jean de Brébeuf, dramatic symphony (Brébeuf). 1962. Bass, orch. CMCentre

The Little Red Hen, cantata (traditional). 1976. Vs, chamb orch. CMCentre

Several other works for orch or band, incl the *Piano Concerto* (1952), *Song of Autumn* (1955), *Pavan* (1961) and *Commedia* (1978). All ms

CHAMBER

Fantasy on an Eskimo Song. 1962. Ww quin. CMCentre

Abstract 1963. Fl. CMCentre

Out of the Cradle Endlessly Rocking (Whitman). 1966. V, fl, va, vc, hpd. CMCentre

Permutations on a Paganini Caprice. 1966. Str quar. CMCentre

Encounters. 1971. Vn, pf. CMCentre

Sandwich Music 'Motet Bagatelle for String Trio.' 1977. CMCentre

Other chamb works, including *Trio Serenade in E* (1949) and *String Quartet in A Minor* (1951). Both ms

Also a few works for pf, for org, and for choir; several works for v, including arr of European folksongs

WRITINGS

'University of Windsor, music department,' *MSc* Jul – Aug 1973

'Black Pentecostal music in Windsor,' report, Museum of Man (Ottawa 1973–4)

BIBLIOGRAPHY

Contemporary Canadian Composers (EK)

McIVER, (Joseph) Allan. Composer, arranger, pianist, conductor, b Thetford Mines, south of Quebec City, 17 Jan 1904, d Montreal 15 Jun 1969. Raised in Sherbrooke, Que, where he studied violin, flute, and (with Alfred E. *Whitehead) piano, he was a pianist for silent films after moving to Montreal in 1926. He later studied harmony with Oscar *O'Brien. McIver's first radio engagements (ca 1930) were as a singer (baritone) and pianist. He appeared in the early 1930s as a piano soloist with the *CSM and the *Ottawa Philharmonic Orchestra. In 1936 he went to New York as accompanist and arranger for the *Trio lyrique, remaining there for a year as a staff arranger for the CBS network. Back in Montreal, he continued to work with the Trio lyrique, became a leading conductor and/or arranger for CBC radio shows (eg, 'The Play of the Week,' 'Light Up and Listen,' and 'Serenade for Strings') and wrote background music for many radio dramas. He was associated with Peake Radio Productions. During World War II he wrote and conducted music for the Victory Loan shows and radio broadcasts in Montreal. He also conducted for shows given by Jack Benny at army bases across Canada. A participant in the opening telecast on CFTM-TV, Montreal, 5 Sep 1952, he then served as music director for the CBC TV variety shows 'Silhouettes,' 'Paillettes,' 'Northern Electric Concert,' 'Le Trio lyrique,' and 'Sunday Night Shows.' Besides incidental music McIver wrote several pieces for orchestra (one, *Francesca*, published by Southern Music) and the score for the feature film *Le Rossignol et les cloches*. The musical rights of his estate are administered by CAPAC.

BIBLIOGRAPHY

Selinger, Jac. 'Alan [sic] McIver says it with music,' *Radio World*, 17 Mar 1945 (MM)

McKAY, Cliff (Clifford John). Clarinetist, saxophonist, danceband leader, b Seaforth, near Stratford, Ont, 1909. His father, Archie McKay, was a noted fiddler in Guelph, Ont. The younger McKay studied piano there at 10 and began playing saxophone at 15 before moving in 1926 to Toronto to work with Harry Rich's orchestra, the Versatile Canadians. After playing in Joe DeCourcy's dance band in Ottawa and leading his own orchestra at the Seigniory Club, Montebello, Que, and in Bermuda, he returned in 1935 to Toronto, where he worked in radio, theatre, and hotel orchestras under Percy *Faith, Horace *Lapp, Rex *Battle, and others.

A soloist 1941–52 on CBC radio's *'The Happy Gang,' McKay also performed 1948–52 on 'Starlight Moods' and frequently as a soloist on 'Jazz Unlimited' and other shows. He was music director and host musician 1952–8 for CBC TV's 'Holiday Ranch.' With several Toronto jazzmen, including Hagood *Hardy, he made the LP *The Other Side of Cliff McKay* (Sparton SP 208) in 1958. After returning to The Happy Gang for a brief time in 1959, McKay led orchestras and small groups in Toronto nightclubs. In the late 1960s he played Grandpa Schnitzel on the children's show 'Schnitzel-house' (CHCH TV, Hamilton) and also began teaching instrumental music in Toronto separate schools. He made several appearances in the early 1970s with Trump *Davidson's band and again led his own jazz group in 1979.

BIBLIOGRAPHY

McKay, Cliff. 'I ain't no hillbilly on TV's "Holiday Ranch",' *Liberty*, Feb 1956

Sangster, Dorothy. 'The most baffling show on television,' *Maclean's*, 9 Jun 1956

Lancashire, David. 'Happy Cliff McKay: "Comeback? I call it a resurrection",' Toronto *Globe and Mail*, 11 Aug 1979 MM (HM)

McKAY, John. Pianist, teacher, b Montreal 11 Nov 1938, B MUS (McGill) 1961, DMA (ESM, Rochester) 1977. He studied as a youth with Lubka *Kolessa in Montreal and 1961–5 with Bruno Seidlhofer in Vienna and Cologne and Stefan Askenase in Brussels, and won Quebec's *Prix d'Europe in 1962. He taught 1969–72 at the *U of Toronto and the *RCMT, and was head of the piano department 1972–4 at *Dalhousie U. In 1975 he won a *Canada Council fellowship to complete a DMA in performance at the Eastman School of Music. Following his doctoral studies he began teaching in 1976 at Gustavus Adolphus College in St Peter, Minn. He has given recitals and broadcasts in Canada and Europe. His programs have included works of several Canadian composers. In 1962 he premiered Clermont *Pépin's *Toccata No. 3*. McKay recorded *Somers' *Sonata No. 4* (1976, RCI 452) and the Bartók *Sonata for Two Pianos and Percussion* (1976, Mus H Soc 3679), the latter with Joseph Werner and the percussionists John Beck and David Mancini. (AHC)

MacKAY, Ronald R. Bandmaster, conductor, teacher, hornist, composer, b Dunnville, Ont, 26 Sep 1928. He studied conducting with Ifan *Williams at the *Maritime Cons and french horn with Keith Vernon and Reginald *Barrow of the Detroit and Toronto SOs respectively. He graduated as a bandmaster from the *Canadian Forces School of Music in 1959 and taught there 1961–3. While in the Royal Canadian Navy he served as principal horn, then bandmaster of several navy bands. He also held the position of music director at Pt Edward Naval Base, Royal Canadian Sea Cadets. He played principal horn for the *Nova Scotia Opera, the Halifax Symphonette, and the *Halifax and *Victoria SOs and performed with the Alfred Coward Contemporary Jazz Octette. He served 1970–4 as director of *Acadia U's Summer School for Instrumentalists, 1975–9 as director of the Nova Scotia Summer Music Camp, and 1976–9 as director of St Mary's U Concert and Stage bands. MacKay organized the Nova Scotia Provincial Band (non-competition) Festival and Workshop in 1973 and the Atlantic Stage Band Festival in 1975, and co-ordinated the latter again 1978–9. In 1979 he began teaching and directing the bands at the Cobequid Educational Centre, Truro, NS. The centre's symphonic band, formed in 1966, has appeared throughout the Maritimes, in Ontario and Quebec, and in Bermuda, England, and the USA. MacKay has written several marches, including *March 'Nova Scotia'* for former Nova Scotia premier Gerald Regan and *Happy Hundred Song* in honour of Truro's centennial. NM

McKENNA, Fred. Singer, guitarist, songwriter, b Fredericton 17 Feb 1934, d Toronto 18 Nov 1977. Born blind, McKenna was raised in Fredericton but educated at the Halifax School for the Blind. He began playing the guitar at 11, holding the instrument across his lap in the manner of a Hawaiian guitar and chording with three fingers of his left hand. He also played the mandolin and the fiddle in this fashion. In his late teens he began performing throughout the Maritimes, and later he won a talent contest which led to a performance in Wheeling, WV, on WWVA radio's 'Jamboree.' This in turn brought him to the attention of Don *Messer.

McKenna began his TV career on the CBC's 'Don Messer's Jubilee' in 1958 and joined the cast of 'Singalong Jubilee' in 1961. Though he moved to Toronto in 1968 he continued to travel to Halifax for appearances on that show, and on CBC TV's 'Countrytime,' until 1973. He also was a regular performer on Harry *Hibb's 'At the Caribou' and toured extensively as a solo performer in eastern Canada. In 1973 he became music director of the privately syndicated 'George Hamilton IV Show' (from Hamilton, Ont), a position he held at his death. McKenna began recording for the *Rodeo label in the 1950s and later made three LPs for *Arc and one for *RCA, some of which included his own songs. His musical estate is administered by CAPAC.

BIBLIOGRAPHY

Grigsby, Wayne. 'Meet the least-known television star of them all,' *CanComp*, 66, Jan 1972 (RGn)

MacKENZIE, (Marie Marguerite Louise) Gisèle or Gisele (b LaFlèche, m Shuttleworth, m Klein). Singer, violinist, b Winnipeg 10 Jan 1927; naturalized US 1955. Though she studied with Flora Matheson *Goulden (violin) in Winnipeg and with Kathleen *Parlow (violin) and Godfrey *Ridout (theory) on scholarship 1941–7 at the TCM, she turned from a promising career as a concert violinist to one as a pop singer. In 1946 she played the violin and sang with the dance orchestra of Bob Shuttleworth, who arranged a CBC audition for her. She made her CBC debut 8 Oct 1946 on her own program, 'Meet Gisèle,' which continued until 1950. For RCI she recorded 35 songs on seven LPs (RCI 24 to RCI 30) in 1950. She also recorded for Musicana.

Known simply as Gisèle in Canada, she adopted her father's second given name, MacKenzie, as her professional name when she moved in 1950 to the USA. There she sang with Percy *Faith's orchestra on CBS radio in New York, joined Bob Crosby on CBS TV's 'Club 15' in Hollywood in 1951, and began a long association with the comedian Jack Benny in 1953. She often played violin duets with Benny, and the contrast of their playing abilities became the basis of a comedy routine. She was a regular performer 1953–7 on NBC TV's 'Your Hit Parade' (at first sharing the spotlight with the Ontario-born singer Dorothy Collins) and starred 1957–8 on her own NBC TV series. Gisèle also played leading roles in summer stock productions of *South Pacific* (Dallas 1955), *Annie Get Your Gun* (Kansas City 1956), *The King and I* (US tour 1957), and other musicals in the 1960s. Her single recordings included 'Hard to Get' and 'Pepper-Hot Baby' for the 'X' label and 'The Star You Wished upon Last Night' for Vik. Two LPs, both entitled *Gisele*, were released by RCA (1958, Victor LSP-1790; 1959, Camden 532); and two more, *Gisele MacKenzie at the Empire Room of the Waldorf Astoria* and *Gisele MacKenzie Sings Lullaby and Goodnight*, were released in the 1960s by Everest (1069) and Pickwick (SPC 3185) respectively. She performed less frequently after the early 1960s but appeared on special occasions with Jack Benny or Sid Caesar. In 1976 she opened the summer concert season at *Ontario Place in Toronto. In common with such other Canadian singers as her contemporary *Juliette and the younger Anne *Murray, Gisèle MacKenzie achieved fame through a distinctive combination of cool-headed cheerful candour and an easy, pleasant voice of medium range, always in tune and handled with a disarming lack of affectation.

Mackenzie's brother, the bilingual pop singer-composer Georges (Edouard) La Fleche (b La Flèche in Winnipeg 27 Jan 1936), began his career in St Boniface, Man (radio) and Montreal (radio and TV), made his CBC TV debut (Toronto 1957) on 'Club O'Connor' and starred in the 1960s on CBC radio and TV shows from Winnipeg (eg, 'Music Break' 1960), Calgary, Edmonton, and Vancouver and on CTV in Toronto ('Musical Showcase'). He has made two LPs for London and one for Rada. He is a member of CAPAC.

BIBLIOGRAPHY

Helleur, Stan. 'Under the spell of Gisele,' *New Liberty*, Sep 1951

MacKenzie, Gisele. 'Look what's happened to me!' *Liberty*, May 1954

Moore, Jacqueline. 'Gisele MacKenzie,' *Weekend*, 31 Mar 1957

Helleur, Stan. 'Gisele MacKenzie tells her story,' *Maclean's*, 4 instalments, 27 Feb – 9 Apr 1960

FILMOGRAPHY

Meet Gisèle (NFB 1951) MM

McKINNON, Catherine (m Harron). Singer, actress, b Saint John, NB, 14 May 1944. As a child she lived in her native city, in Shiloh and Churchill, Man, in Halifax, NS, and in London, Ont, making her radio debut at 8 in Saint John and her TV debut at 12 in London. She studied music at the Mount Saint Vincent College in Halifax. In the mid-1960s she was a regular performer on the CBC TV shows 'Singalong Jubilee,' 'Don *Messer's Jubilee,' and 'Music Hop,' and starred on CBC radio's 'That McKinnon Girl.' Her recording of Buffy *Sainte-Marie's 'Until It's Time for You to Go' was a hit in Canada in 1966. On moving to Toronto she appeared in the 1967 **Spring Thaw* and starred 1968–9 on CTV's 'River Inn' and 1970–1 on that network's 'Catherine McKinnon Show.' She was co-host in 1974 for Global TV's 'Everything Goes.' She has made TV appearances in England, Scotland, and Ireland. Though she began her career as a folk singer – her first LP and substantially her biggest seller, *Voice of An Angel*, was a collection of folk material – she became a skilled nightclub performer in the 1970s, adding to her repertoire ballads and torch songs and works by Leonard *Cohen, Joni *Mitchell, and others. Her voice was described by Peter Goddard (Toronto *Telegram*, 18 Oct 1969) as 'rich, controlled, completely sure in its sense of pitch' and later drew the recollection from Blaik Kirby that it was 'a sound so ravishingly beautiful you could worship it' (Toronto *Globe and Mail*, 8 Apr 1976). Kirby, reviewing an appearance at the Imperial Room of the Royal York Hotel, regretted McKinnon's change of style but called her 'a thoroughly-schooled pop singer.' McKinnon also has sung in concert with the *Saskatoon and *Winnipeg SOs and the *Hamilton Philharmonic and in musical theatre at the *Charlottetown Festival (**Turvey* 1970) and *Rainbow Stage (*The Wizard of Oz* 1970, *My Fair Lady* 1975). In 1972 she played the artist Emily Carr on the CBC TV musical *The Wonder of It All*, written by her husband, Don Harron, in collaboration with Norman *Campbell. She sings on cast recordings of 'Singalong Jubilee' (Arc A 608; Arc A 659) and *Sea to Sea* (Arc CNE 68, from the 1968 *CNE Grandstand show in which she performed) and has made the LPs *Voice of An Angel* (two vols: Arc AS 628; Arc AS 666), *I'll Be Home for Christmas* (Arc AC 27), *Both Sides Now* (Arc AS 777), *Everybody's Talkin'* (Arc AS 814), and, with the Jimmy *Dale orchestra, *Catherine McKinnon* (RCI 448).

McKinnon's sister Patrician Anne also has had a career on radio and TV as a folk and pop singer.

MacKINNON, Margo (m Baculis). Soprano, teacher, b Windsor, Ont, 21 Apr 1931; ARCT 1948, B MUS (Toronto) 1952. She sang on radio station WJR in Detroit when she was about 14. Later she studied at the *RCMT and at the *U of Toronto with Herman *Geiger-Torel, Dorothy *Allan Park, Emmy *Heim, and Ernesto *Vinci. She obtained several scholarships between 1955 and 1957 and was a Rose Bowl winner at the Toronto *Kiwanis Festival and at the *CNE. During these years she sang with the *TSO at pop concerts and appeared on several CBC TV programs, including 'Big Review' and 'Your Hit Parade.' After taking part in productions of the musicals *Candide* and *Oklahoma!* in 1955 she was seen in the annual revue **Spring Thaw* in 1956, 1957, and 1960. In addition she performed in 1959 on the CBS TV program 'Arthur Godfrey Talent.' In 1963 she married the clarinetist Al *Baculis and moved to Montreal.

In 1966, in the *SMCQ's inaugural concert, she performed Serge *Garant's **Anerca* and Ishtar's aria from R. Murray *Schafer's opera **Loving*. Subsequently she premiered several works with the SMCQ Ensemble, including John *Hawkins' *Waves* (1971), performed again in Paris and Brussels in 1973; Bruce *Mather's *Madrigal V* (1973); Gilbert Amy's *Sonata pian' e forte* (1974); and Jean Barraqué's *Chant après chant* (1979). In Montreal she also sang Alan *Heard's *Voices* in 1970 and Norma *Beecroft's *Rasas III* in 1975. She sang and acted in the Quebec film *Réjane Padovani* and was a soloist on the sound-tracks of the films *Bingo* and *A Star Is Lost*, and of several NFB films. She has recorded more than 300 jingles. On CBC TV she sang with groups in variety programs and was a soloist in other programs, including the 1975 production of Neil *Chotem's ballet *Pythagore 1 à 7*. In 1977 she began to teach singing at the Vanier Cegep in Ville St-Laurent, Montreal.

DISCOGRAPHY

Musique d'aujourd'hui, vol 3: Hawkins *Waves*. Mather pf. 1972. RCI 300

See also Discographies for Garant (RCI 301); and SMCQ (RCI 358). ST

McLAREN, Norman. Film maker, b Stirling, Scotland, 11 Apr 1914; hon LL D (McMaster) 1966, hon D LITT (York, Toronto) 1972. He became interested in cinematic techniques while studying 1932–7 at the Glasgow School of Art and spent his spare time making films and playing the organ. His gifts attracted the attention of John Grierson, who offered him a position in the British General Post Office Film Unit when he left the school. McLaren remained with the unit until 1939. About this time he began to experiment with synthetic sound and developed a considerable range of semi-musical effects, mostly percussive. After working independently 1939–41 in New York, he joined the *National Film Board of Canada (of which Grierson had become the director) and began to develop the innovative animated film techniques that eliminated the camera and required the artist to draw directly on the film. McLaren also created 'animated sound,' a form of 'visible' or synthetic sound made by hand-drawings on the soundtrack of the film. He explains his method in the short film *Pen Point Percussion*. The implications of the method have been of considerable interest to electronic composers and have earned McLaren high regard as a sound pioneer. In addition to his synthetic sound-tracks, he has integrated a wide variety of musical forms into his films. The *Trio lyrique of Montreal sings a folksong in *Le Merle*; Ravi Shankar and Chatur Lal perform in *A Chairy Tale*; Glenn *Gould plays Bach for *Spheres*; a calliope is used in *Hoppity Pop* and panpipes in *Pas de Deux*; jazz by Eldon *Rathburn is featured in *Short and Suite* and jazz by the Oscar *Peterson Trio in *Begone Dull Care*. In *Lines Horizontal* and *Lines Vertical* pure animation, in patterns of straight lines etched directly on the film interprets music by Pete Seeger and Maurice *Blackburn respectively.

McLaren has earned an international reputation for his imaginative and skilled contribution to the art of film. He has received honours from many countries. Those from his own include the first medal of the Royal Canadian Academy of Arts in 1963, the *Canada Council Medal in 1966, the *Molson Prize in 1971, and the Diplôme d'honneur of the *CCA in 1978. In 1973 he was made a Companion of the *Order of Canada. A general list of his films and of his numerous awards (to 1968) is given in *Creative Canada*, vol 1.

FILMS WITH MUSIC

Love on the Wing (General Post Office film unit 1938). Ibert *Divertissement*

Allegro (Guggenheim Museum 1939). Synthetic sound

Rumba (ibid 1939). Synthetic sound

Stars and Stripes (ibid 1939). March tune

Dots (ibid 1940). Synthetic sound

Loops (ibid 1940). Synthetic sound

Boogie-Doodle (ibid 1940). Albert Ammons plays boogie.

Mail Early for Christmas (NFB 1941). Benny Goodman's 'Jingle Bells'

V for Victory (NFB 1941). Sousa march

Five for Four (NFB 1942). Ammons plays 'Pintop's Boogie.'

Hen Hop (NFB 1942). Barn dance music

Dollar Dance (NFB 1943). Music by Applebaum; lyrics by Guy Glover and McLaren

Là-haut sur ces montagnes (NFB 1946). The singing of the folksong from which the film takes its title

A Little Phantasy on a 19th-Century Painting (NFB 1946). Synthetic sound

Hoppity Pop (NFB 1946). Barrel organ music

Fiddle-De-Dee (NFB 1947). Fiddler plays 'Listen to the Mocking Bird.'

La Poulette Grise (NFB 1947). Anna Malenfant sings the folksong.

Begone Dull Care (NFB 1949). Oscar Peterson Trio plays jazz.

Pen Point Percussion (NFB 1950). Synthetic sound

Around Is Around (NFB 1951). Music by Louis Applebaum

Now Is the Time (NFB 1951). Synthetic sound

Neighbours (NFB 1952). Synthetic sound

A Phantasy (NFB 1952). Maurice Blackburn's music for saxophone and synthetic sound

Two Bagatelles (NFB 1952). Synthetic sound

Blinkity Blank (NFB 1954). Synthetic sound and music of Blackburn

Rythmetic (NFB 1956). Synthetic sound

A Chairy Tale (NFB 1957). Music performed by Ravi Shankar and Chatur Lal

Le Merle (NFB 1958). Trio lyrique sings the folksong 'Mon merle.'

Serenal (NFB 1959). Grand Curacaya Orchestra of Trinidad

Short and Suite (NFB 1959). Eldon Rathburn's music for jazz ensemble

Lines Vertical (NFB 1960). Blackburn plays electronic piano.

Lines Horizontal (NFB 1962). Pete Seeger plays winds and strings.

Canon (NFB 1964). How a musical canon is constructed, using music by Rathburn.

Mosaic (NFB 1965). Synthetic sound

Pas de Deux (NFB 1967). Panpipes

Spheres (NFB 1969). Gould plays Bach *Fugue* 24 and *Prelude* 20 (Book I) and *Fugue* 14 (Book II) from *The Well-tempered Clavier*.

Synchromy (NFB 1971). Synthetic sound

Ballet Adagio (NFB 1972). Albinoni *Adagio*

WRITINGS

'Some notes on animated sound: abridged from a paper by Norman MacLaren [sic],' *CanComp*, 44, Nov 1969

BILBIOGRAPHY

'Animated sound: a Canadian composer's unique contribution to the advance of the cinema,' *CanComp*, 3, Oct 1965

'The eye hears and the ear sees...' *CanComp*, 44, Nov 1969

'Filmography,' *The Drawings of / Les Dessins de: Norman McLaren* (Montreal 1975)

FILM

The Eye Hears The Ear Sees (BBC TV 1970) SW (PW)

McLAUCHLAN, Murray (Edward). Singer, songwriter, guitarist, pianist, harmonica player, b Paisley, Renfrewshire, Scotland, 30 Jun 1948. Brought to Canada at 5, McLauchlan learned folk guitar from Jim McCarthy and began his career in Toronto's Yorkville coffeehouses at 17, making his first major appearance at the *Mariposa Folk Festival in 1966. His early 'Child's Song' and 'Old Man's Song' were recorded by the US singer Tom Rush. McLauchlan continued to work in Ontario and Quebec coffeehouses and briefly 1970–1 in New York, until the success of his albums and the popularity of his 'Farmer's Song' resulted in 1973 in the first of annual concert tours across Canada and appearances in the USA with Neil *Young and, beginning in 1974, on his own. With Bruce *Cockburn he toured Japan in 1977. His 1976 Canadian tour included concerts in over 50 cities and was supplemented by CBC TV appearances on Gordon *Lightfoot's 'Olympic Benefit' and in his own special, 'On the Boulevard.' With 'Farmer's Song,' which won a gold record in 1973, McLauchlan won 1973 *Juno Awards for best folk single, best country single, and composer of the year. He also won the 1976, 1977, and 1979 Juno Awards for best male country singer.

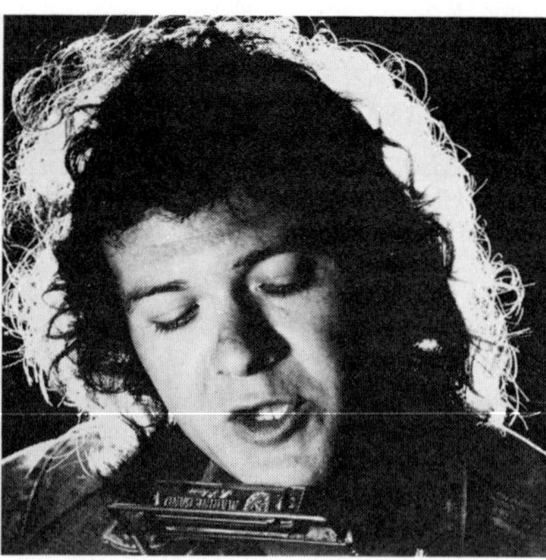

Murray McLauchlan

McLauchlan's songs, published by Oyster Music and Blackwing Music, include the popular 'Down by the Henry Moore,' 'Hurricane of Change,' 'Honky Red,' 'Linda Wontcha Take Me In?', 'Little Dreamer,' and 'Getting Harder to Get Along,' and have been recorded also by *Three's A Crowd, Judy Lander, Renée *Claude, Bob Neuwirth, and David *Wiffen and used in the movies *Rip-Off* (1971) and *Partners* (1976) and in the BBC – TV Ontario co-production *Reflections of Toronto* (1975). Although influenced initially by folk and country styles, McLauchlan turned gradually to rock, touring 1976–7 with The Silver Tractors (comprising his long-time bass guitarist Dennis Pendrith, the guitarist Eugene Martynec, the violinist-mandolinist Ben Mink, and the drummer John Anderson). The LP *Whispering Rain* represented a return to the country style. Of McLauchlan's music, Bryan Johnson wrote: 'As hard-edged of voice and mind as he is, he has the ability to turn that attitude on to the softest of subjects – old men, lonely girls and, above all, love – and make it work. The result is a unique mixture of tenderness and caring without false sentimentality' (Toronto *Globe and Mail*, 3 Aug 1976). McLauchlan is a member of CAPAC.

DISCOGRAPHY

Song from the Street. 1971. TNorth TN 4

Murray McLauchlan. 1972. TNorth TN 9

Day to Day Dust. 1973. TNorth TN 14

Sweeping the Spotlight Away. 1974. TNorth TN 18

Only the Silence Remains. 1975. TNorth GTN 19

Boulevard. 1976. TNorth TN 25

Hard Rock Town. 1977. TNorth TN 29
Murray McLauchlan's Greatest Hits. 1978. TNorth TN 35
Whispering Rain. 1978. TNorth TN 36

BIBLIOGRAPHY

Flohil, Richard. 'Murray McLauchlan: back on the street,' *CanComp*, Jun 1971
Batten, Jack. 'How Murray McLauchlan found inspiration in a dried up creek bed,' *Weekend Magazine*, 13 May 1972
McCracken, Melinda. 'Street Singer,' *Maclean's*, Mar 1973
Flohil, Richard. 'Interview! Murray McLauchlan,' *CanComp*, 91, May 1974
MacGregor, Roy. 'Minstrel Boy,' *Canadian Magazine*, 9 Oct 1976
Kostash, Myrna. 'Macho Murray and me,' *SatN*, vol 92, Apr 1977
Boland, Kevin. 'A child of the streets comes home to roost,' *Toronto Star Street Talk*, 26 Oct 1978 RF (MM)

McLAUGHLIN, D'Alton. Organist-choirmaster, b Plattsville, Ont, 3 Oct 1892, d Toronto 8 Apr 1968; hon FRCCO 1959. He studied in Brantford, Ont, and Toronto, and in Europe with Widor, *Bonnet, and Dupré. For 43 years, 1919–62, he was organist-choirmaster at Toronto's Yorkminster Park (formerly Bloor St, then Yorkminster) Baptist Church; it was his one posting. During his tenure he brought to his church's console such distinguished guests as Tertius Noble, Siegfried Karg-Elert, Marcel Dupré (three times, once with his wife, Marguerite), Clarence Mader, Clarence Dickinson, and Virgil Fox. Noble dedicated a choral work, *Eternal Mysteries*, to McLaughlin. McLaughlin presented the first Toronto Candlelight Carol Concert in 1933 with the Yorkminster Choir. He retired from his post as organist-choirmaster 4 Feb 1962. Besides his work at the church, he taught voice and piano and examined for the *RCMT. In April 1962 he was made organist emeritus of Yorkminster. He also published a pamphlet entitled *These Forty-Three Years* which lists, with dates, the recitals and special choral services at Yorkminster Baptist Church. KC

McLEAN, Eric (Donald). Critic, historian, pianist, b Montreal 25 Sep 1919. He studied piano in Montreal with Alfred *Laliberté and Paul Lafrance and later studied harmony and composition with *Champagne, privately and at the *McGill Cons. During World War II he was a wireless operator for the RAF Transport Command. In 1946 he joined the *Montreal Standard* as assistant editor, becoming its music critic the following year. In 1949 he succeeded H.P. *Bell as music critic of the *Montreal Daily Star* and served in that position until the *Star* closed in 1979. In November of that year he became music critic of the Montreal *Gazette*. One of the first advocates of the preservation of historic Montreal McLean became a member of the Jacques Viger Commission in 1962 and has written *The Living Past of Montreal* (Montreal 1964). He is a fellow of the Royal Society of Arts (England), served on the *Canada Council 1970–7, was appointed to the Council of Arts of Greater Montreal in 1966, and was president of the Music Critics' Assn of America 1965–6. He was awarded the *CMCouncil Medal in 1973 and was made an Officer of the *Order of Canada in 1975. His translation of Jean Palardy's *Meubles anciens du Canada français* was published in 1963 as *The Early Furniture of French Canada*. He has contributed articles to several music and art publications (**Opera Canada*, the **Canada Music Book*, the **Canadian Music Journal*, *The New Grove Dictionary*, and *EMC*) and has broadcast often for CBC radio as a critic or commentator. His reviews are a deft mixture of lucid writing, perceptive judgment, scholarship, and subtle humour.

WRITINGS

'Hanslick had it better,' *The World of Music*, vol 14, no. 3, 1972 GP

McLEAN, Gordon. Pianist, teacher, b Winnipeg, 6 Oct 1909; LAB 1926, LRAM 1938, ARCM 1938. He studied piano with Leonard *Heaton in Winnipeg, Alberto *Guerrero in Toronto, Rudolph Ganz in Chicago, and, following World War II service in **The Army Show*, with Louis Kentner and Claudio Arrau in London. He performed as a soloist and chamber musician on BBC radio. Returning from London he served 1958–75 as head of the piano department of the *Regina Cons. He has examined for the *WBM, adjudicated for the *Saskatchewan Music Festival Assn, and taught 1966–75 at the *U of Saskatchewan. He has given many recitals and, with Howard *Leyton-Brown, performed the complete violin-piano sonatas of Mozart, Beethoven, Schubert, Brahms, and Grieg. In 1975 he retired to Victoria, BC SRM

McLEAN, Hugh (John). Organist, choirmaster, pianist, harpsichordist, administrator, teacher, musicologist, b Winnipeg 5 Jan 1930; AMM (Manitoba) 1947, LRSM organ 1948, LRSM piano 1948; ARCO 1950, ARCM 1951, FRCO 1953, BA (Cambridge) 1954, B MUS (Cambridge) 1956, FRCCO 1957, MA (Cambridge) 1958. A boy chorister at All Saints' Anglican Church in Winnipeg, McLean studied piano in Winnipeg with Russell *Standing and organ there, and in Vancouver 1947–8, with Hugh *Bancroft. He also studied piano in Vancouver with Phyllis *Schuldt. In 1949 on an AB scholarship he entered the RCM, where his teachers were Arthur *Benjamin (piano), Sir William H. Harris (organ), and W.S. Lloyd Webber (composition). While studying 1951–6 on an organ scholarship at King's College, Cambridge U, he won the 1954 Arnold Bax Commonwealth Medal and the 1955 Harriet Cohen Bach Medal.

McLean returned to Vancouver and served 1957–73 as organist-choirmaster at Ryerson United Church. He founded the *Cantata Singers of Vancouver in 1958 and remained their conductor until 1967; he also led the Hugh McLean Consort 1957–67 in musicologically authentic performances of baroque music for Vancouver audiences. He taught 1967–9 at the *U of Victoria and in 1969 and 1972–3 at the *U of British Columbia prior to serving 1974–80 as dean of the Faculty of Music at the *U of Western Ontario. As an organ recitalist McLean has been heard frequently on the CBC and has appeared publicly in every major Canadian centre, in San Francisco, Los Angeles, and Chicago, and at two of Bach's churches, the Blasiuskirche of Mühlhausen and the Thomaskirche of Leipzig. In 1975 he performed on Polish radio as a conductor. He gave the Canadian premiere (16 May 1972) of Hindemith's *Organ Concerto No. 2* with the *CBC Vancouver Chamber Orchestra and has been a soloist with the *TS, his appearances including performances, 3 and 4 Apr 1979, of Saint-Saëns' *Symphony No. 3*. He premiered Bengt *Hambraeus' *Icons* 29 Sep 1975 in Toronto.

As a musicologist specializing in 17th- and 18th-century studies McLean was awarded *Canada Council grants in 1960 and 1965 to investigate the Cummings collection of western manuscripts at the Nanki Music Library in Japan, and a further grant in 1972 to travel to Poland and the German Democratic Republic (East Germany) where he located works by C.P.E. Bach (an unknown symphony), Haydn, Alessandro Scarlatti (a lost opera), and J.H. Schein. He has published editions of the organ works of Purcell (Novello 1968) and J.L. Krebs (Novello 1975) and individual works by Mozart, William Felton (both Oxford U Press 1957), and John Blow (Novello 1971). He also has

Hugh McLean

written some 40 articles for *The New Grove Dictionary* and has had others published in the *Musical Times*, the *AGO/RCCO Music Magazine*, and the **Canada Music Book*. He has presented papers to many learned societies and has given radio talks and reviews. McLean became a director of the *CMCouncil in 1975. In 1977 he was made a fellow of the Royal Society of Canada.

WRITINGS

'Blow and Purcell in Japan,' *MT*, vol 104, Oct 1963
'New Polish sources for the German Baroque,' *CAUSM J*, vol 2, Fall 1972
'Technology in the education of the musician,' *ISME Yearbook*, vol 2, 1974
'Mozart parodies and Haydn perplexities: new sources in Poland,' *Studies in Music from the U of Western Ontario*, vol 1, 1976
'*Caritas domi incipit*: an early 18th-century organ book,' ibid, vol 2, 1977

DISCOGRAPHY

Bach *Das Orgelbüchlein*. 1973. Veriton SXV 767/8
Bach – Holst – Deems Taylor – Vaughan Williams – Stanford. Vancouver Bach Choir. 1971. Ensemble ES 7002
Batten – Stanford – Hadley – et al. King's College Chapel Choir. 1956. ARGO 99
Collected Works for Organ and Solo Instruments by J.L. Krebs. Org with ob, fl, tpt, hn. 1973. 2-Muza SXL 0982-3
Coulthard *Five Part-Songs for Voices and Piano* – Turner *Six Voluntaries for Organ*. CBC Vancouver Choir, McLean org and cond, R. Rogers pf. Ca 1966. RCA CCS 1020
Ein' Feste Burg: Chorales for Organ, Brass and Chorus. Brass quar, Vancouver Motet Choir, John Wiebe cond. 1962. Teldon 9001
Festival of Lessons and Carols: Bach – Cornelius. King's College Chapel Choir. 1954. ARGO R639
Music for Christmas: Shaw – Purvic – Edmunson – Bach – et al. 1972. CBC SM-209
Organ Music for the Festival of Christmas by J.S. Bach. 1973. Veriton SXV 752
Orlando Gibbons: Tudor Church Music I. King's College Chapel Choir. 1956. ARGO R 680
Pentland *Duo for Viola and Piano* – Rogers *Sonatina*. Humphreys va. 1967. RCI 223/RCA CCS-1017
Pierné – Sowerby – Dvořák – Sherard. Hugh McLean Consort. 1967. CBC SM-70
Willan *Two Hymn Preludes* – Cabena *Paean: Resurrection of Christ* – Matton *Suite de Pâques* – L.Farnam *Toccata: O filii et filiae* – Healey *Cookham Notebook* – Hambraeus *Icons*. 1978. RCI 481
Wilson *The Lord's Prayer; Missa brevis No. 2; Meditation: Canzona, Antiphon*. CBC Vancouver Choir, McLean org and cond. Ca 1964. RCI 255
See also Discography for Baroque Strings of Vancouver. (JA)

MACLEAN, Quentin (Stuart Morvaren). Organist, composer, teacher, b London 14 May 1896, d Toronto 9 July 1962. He studied 1904–7 in England under Harold Osmund, F.G. Shuttleworth, and Sir Richard Terry; 1907–9 in Vienna under Hermann Graedener; and 1912–14 in Leipzig under

Karl Straube (organ) and Max Reger (composition). During World War I he was interned at Ruhleben (near Berlin), where he met Ernest *MacMillan. In 1919 he served as assistant organist to Terry at Westminster Cathedral, then toured British theatres with the newsman Lowell Thomas, providing background music for the lecture-film *With Allenby in Palestine*. From 1921 to 1939 he was theatre organist at many English cinemas and in 1925 he began to broadcast regularly on BBC radio, his performances encompassing the British premiere of Hindemith's *Organ Concerto* in 1934, his own *Organ Concerto* in 1935, the inauguration of the BBC theatre organ in 1936, and hundreds of light-music programs and recitals. He emigrated to Canada in 1939 and continued his theatre organ career at Shea's Hippodrome (eight years) and Victoria Theatre (two years) in Toronto. During the years 1940–62 he was organist-choirmaster at Holy Rosary Church and taught at the *TCM and St Michael's College, *U of Toronto. He was heard regularly on CBC radio, giving recitals, and providing background music for plays and poetry readings and music for children's programs. Through his broadcasts he became one of the best-known organists in Canada.

Maclean's works include concertos for organ (two), harpsichord, piano, electric organ (two), harp, and violin; a dozen pieces for orchestra (some published by Keith Prowse); a setting of the *Stabat mater*; 10 masses, a cantata, and numerous choral pieces; about 50 songs; 21 piano pieces; eight organ works; and a string quartet, three trios, and a violin-piano duo. Maclean was notable for the diversity of his musical interests, as well as for his taste, technical skill, and exceptional musical memory. He achieved wide popular success as a theatre organist, while maintaining high standards in the composition and performance of serious music, secular and liturgical. His compositions are traditional in style, often with a modal tonality.

BIBLIOGRAPHY
'"Background music" which can steal the show,' *CBC Times*, Sep 16–22 1951
Creative Canada, vol 2 TCB

MacLELLAN, Gene. Songwriter, singer, guitarist, b Val-d'Or, Que, 1939. Raised in Toronto, he played guitar at 18 with the popular rock band Little Caesar and the Consuls. After working outside music and touring with an evangelist, he settled near Charlottetown, PEI. He appeared on 'Don *Messer's Jubilee' in 1966, then joined Hal Lone Pine (*Breau) for four months. While a regular performer on CBC Halifax TV's 'Singalong Jubilee,' he rose to prominence as the composer of *'Snowbird,' an international hit in 1970 as recorded by Anne *Murray. He then curtailed his performing career and in 1978 was living at Hunter River, PEI. Among MacLellan's other songs are 'Bidin' My Time,' 'The Call,' and 'Put Your Hand in the Hand,' all recorded by Murray; the last-named song also was recorded by the Toronto rock band Ocean, selling over two million copies in 1971. Also popular in the early 1970s were 'Thorn in My Shoe' and 'Shilo Song.' Several of these songs are included on the LP *Gene MacLellan* (1970, Cap ST 6348). MacLellan is an affiliate of PRO Canada; his songs have been published by Beechwood Music of Canada.

BIBLIOGRAPHY
MacDonald, Dick. 'So little snowbird take me with you when you go,' *Weekend Magazine*, 23 Jan 1971
LeBlanc, Larry. 'Country music, country living are Gene MacLellan's life,' *MSc*, 261, Sep – Oct 1971 MM

McLEOD, F.M. or **Ray** (Francis Murray). Bandmaster, b Grand Forks, near Nelson, BC, 27 Nov 1918. After training as a trumpeter with 'Tug' Wilson in Vancouver and playing in dance and radio orchestras, he joined the Canadian armed forces in 1941 and became a bandsman. In 1946 he went to the RMSM (Kneller Hall) for additional training in conducting and composition under Gordon Jacob and Jack Mackintosh and in 1950 he graduated with the highest award in composition. On his return he was appointed inspector of bands for the Western Command (Edmonton) and in 1953 he became commanding officer for the *Princess Patricia's Canadian Light Infantry Band in Calgary. He was senior music director for the Lord Strathcona Horse Band in Calgary from 1957 until his retirement (with the rank of captain) in 1965. With David Peterkin he organized and directed 1958–69 the Alberta provincial summer band workshops. McLeod became director of the Calgary Concert Band in 1962 and has also directed 1968–74 the Calgary Stampede Band. He was music director 1960–5 of the Calgary Musical Theatre and of the Canadian Tattoo at the 1962 Seattle World's Fair. In 1965 he began teaching trumpet, theory, and band techniques at the *U of Calgary. RDM

MACLEOD, Jean (m Betts). Contralto, harpist, b Pio Pio, New Zealand, of Scottish parents, 18 May 1918; naturalized Canadian 1969. Her mother, Jessie Mary MacLennan, was in her day a leading interpreter of Scottish folk songs. Raised after 1923 in Canada, Jean Macleod studied voice with Dorothy *Allan Park and harp with Carla Emerson at the TCM and voice with Roy Henderson in London. Specializing in Scottish, Hebridean, and Celtic folk songs – her repertoire included some 500 – she made her debut 17 Apr 1948 at the (Royal Ontaro) Museum Theatre in Toronto. Accompanying herself on the clarsach (a 31-string harp), she has appeared throughout Canada, in the USA (Town Hall, New York, 5 Mar 1950), and in Great Britain. She has performed for St Andrew's Society meetings in many North American centres and has appeared on CBC radio's 'Trans-Canada Matinee' and other radio and TV variety shows. She was heard also in 1948 and 1964 on the Scottish network of the BBC. With accompaniment by her husband, Lorne *Betts, she made the LPs *Scottish Songs* (1960, Rodeo RLP 79), *Songs of the Hebrides* (1962, Celtic CX 10), and *Beloved Hymns* (1963, Banff RBS 1179). In 1973 she became a *Community Concerts field representative for the Great Lakes region of Canada and the USA. MM

MacLEOD, Margaret (b Arnett). Historian, collector, b Kerwood, west of London, Ont, 1877, d Winnipeg 17 Feb 1966. Educated in Brandon, Man, and Winnipeg, she devoted herself to researching the social history of Manitoba and especially of the Red River Valley. In 1947 she was elected to the Council of the Champlain Society, the first woman to be so honoured. She edited *The Letters of Letitia Hargrave* (published in Toronto, 1947, by the Champlain Society) and wrote five books, 1935–63, on Red River topics. MacLeod was the first to collect indigenous Manitoba songs. All were of known authorship, and many were about the Red River Valley. However, the music originated in Quebec, Ontario, Scotland, or the American frontier. Some were published in *The Beaver* and in her book *Songs of Old Manitoba* (Toronto 1959). Among her discoveries were songs by the Métis poet Pierre *Falcon, including one celebrating the Seven Oaks Massacre. She contributed to *The Beaver* such articles as 'Bard of the prairies' (Spring 1956) and 'Songs of the insurrection' (Spring 1957). MacLeod died in a house fire.

McLINTOCK, Ellis (Lee). Trumpeter, conductor, arranger, b Toronto 18 Nov 1921. His father, Ellis (euphonium soloist, b Denshaw, Lancashire, England, 10 Nov 1889, d Toronto 2 Jan 1955), moved to Toronto in 1912 and was principal of the Imperial Concert Band under Walter *Murdoch. The senior McLintock also was head 1942–55 of the brass department at the TCM (*RCMT), where his pupils included Don Johnson, Eldon Lehman, Gordon Rushworth, and W. Bramwell *Smith. The younger McLintock studied cornet with his father and at 14 was one of the four Canadian representatives in the British Empire Boys' Band in London. He also studied trumpet with A.J. Williams (whom he succeeded as principal 1940–2 of the *TSO) and in New York 1940 and 1941 with Ernest Williams. He toured in 1941 throughout North America as a member of the All-American Youth Orchestra under Stokowski.

After service in the RCAF as soloist with the Central Band in Ottawa McLintock was principal trumpet 1944–5 of the TSO, and between 1944 and 1950 he led a dance orchestra which appeared successively at Casa Loma, Toronto; the Aragon Ballroom, Peterborough; the Palais Royale, Toronto; Bigwin Inn, Muskoka; Belmont Park, Montreal; and the Brant Inn, Burlington. McLintock began to play in CBC radio orchestras in the late 1930s, under Lucio *Agostini, Samuel *Hersenhoren, Jack *Kane, and others, and was principal trumpet 1952–63 of the *CBC SO. In 1960 he formed the 60-piece Ellis McLintock Concert Band. The same year he began to lead a dance orchestra again, continuing for several years at the Old Mill, Toronto. For seven years in the 1960s he was music director for the chorus, orchestra, and dance ensemble of the Community Folk Art Council of Canada (responsible for the annual 'Nationbuilders – Canada' seen at the *CNE Grandstand) and in 1967 he was music director of the Canadian Pavilion Concert Band at *Expo 67. In 1971 he joined the staff at Thornlea Secondary School in Thornhill, Ont. McLintock is conductor and performer on the LPs *At the Old Mill* (1962, RCA Camden CAS-967), *Trumpets-A-Plenty* (1964, CTLS 5054), *Ellis McLintock, His Trumpet and Orchestra* (1965, CTLS 5070), and *Canadian Pavilion Concert Band* (1967, RCI 232/RCA PCS 1179). MM

McMAHON, Edmond. Choirmaster, singer, lawyer, b Ste-Rose (later Laval), near Montreal, 18 Oct 1852, d Westmount, Montreal, 2 Feb 1942. He was called to the bar in Montreal in 1881, becoming coroner in 1892 and justice of the peace in 1894 of the City of Westmount. He was choirmaster at St-Joseph Church, 1888–93 at the Montreal Cathedral, and 1897–1906 at Notre-Dame Church. He was chief editor ca 1880 of the music section of the newspaper *La Minerve* and wrote articles for *L'Art musical* (1896–99). His *Méthode élémentaire de plain-chant romain* (Montreal 1880) was praised by Ernest *Gagnon: 'On every page of your book it is evident that you possess the necessary learning to give your work far larger dimensions, but that you decided quite intentionally to stay within your own prescribed framework. You did the right thing in limiting yourself to an elementary treatise: it is essential to popularize the study and practice of plainsong, and this aim will not be achieved by lengthy studies' (letter to the author, dated 25 Aug 1880 and published in *Le Canada musical*, 1 Apr 1881). GP

McMANUS, Don (Donald Leslie). Bass, actor, b Edmonton 30 Aug 1932. While studying voice 1950–8 in Vancouver with Anna Nicholls and William *Morton, he made his acting debut (1952) at *TUTS. Dramatic and singing engagements followed with such organizations as the Bastion Theatre in Victoria, the *Vancouver Opera Assn, Melodyland in Berkeley, Cal, and the J.C. Williamson Theatre Co in Australia, which invited him to perform in several Gilbert & Sullivan operettas. During three years 1962–5 in Australia he also served as stage director for two Sadler's Wells operetta productions for the Garnett Carrol Theatre Co. He has sung in Canada with the *Calgary Philharmonic and the *Vancouver and *Victoria SOs, and was Black John MacDonald (1968, 1969, 1974, 1975) in *Johnny Belinda* at the *Charlottetown Festival. His performance of 'Dick Dead-Eye' in the 1956 CBC TV production of *H.M.S. Pinafore* caught the attention of Herman *Geiger-Torel and led to several roles with the *COC, including Angelotti in *Tosca* (1957), Rocco in *Fidelio* (1970), Banquo in *Macbeth* (1971), Fulbert in the premiere (1973) of *Heloise and Abelard*, and General Boum in *The Grand Duchess of Gerolstein* (1976). In 1977 he sang with the COC Touring Co: Bartolo in *The Barber of Seville* and the Marquis in *La Traviata*.

McManus married the soprano Marie Gauley (b Toronto 24 Jun 1931), who studied at the *RCMT with Dorothy *Allan Park. She has sung with the COC, in *Stratford and *Guelph Festival opera performances, and in CBC TV productions. (RM)

McMaster University, Hamilton, Ont. Founded in 1887 as the result of the union of Toronto Baptist College and Woodstock College (a Baptist preparatory school), and named after Senator William McMaster. The first degrees were awarded in 1894. Originally situated in Toronto (in the building which in 1980 still housed the *RCMT), the university was relocated in Hamilton in 1930 and became a private non-denominational institution in 1957. McMaster's growth has been characterized by expanding programs in arts, science, engineering, and health sciences, leading to undergraduate and graduate degrees in many fields, and also by major research in nuclear science.

George *Proctor, who served 1954–7 as McMaster's first director of music, organized courses and extra-curricular activities. Frank *Thorolfson, appointed in 1959, pioneered music history courses on TV in the early 1960s and introduced a B MUS program within the Faculty of Humanities. When the Music Dept was founded in 1965, Thorolfson served as its first chairman. He was succeeded in 1971 by Alan *Walker, and Walker in 1980 by Fred Hall.

In 1980 two degrees were offered in music – a B MUS (a four-year honours course) and a BA (a three-year pass course), both established in 1966. In 1977–8 there were 100 undergraduates and 33 teachers (11 full-time, 22 part-time) including Hugh *Hartwell, Lee *Hepner, and Fred Hall. The department has been strengthened by its close association with the chamber groups and individual players of the *Hamilton Philharmonic Orchestra. For example, Marta *Hidy, for some years concertmaster and assistant conductor of the orchestra, joined the department in 1965 as teacher of violin and chamber music; and the *Czech Quartet, of which all four members occupied chairs in the orchestra, was quartet-in-residence at the university 1969–74.

By 1980 the Music Library, a separate unit within Mills Memorial Library, contained a notable collection of contemporary scores and recordings; there were modest electronic music facilities; and the department presented a Celebrity Series and a Thursday Noon Concert Series. Performing groups within the university have included the McMaster U Choir, Concert Band, Symphony Orchestra, and Madrigal Singers. In 1962 an honorary doctorate was conferred upon Healey *Willan.

See also Archives; College songs.

BIBLIOGRAPHY

Hepner, Lee. 'Music at McMaster University,' *Recorder*, vol 7, May – Jun 1965

Wallace, William. 'Hamilton, McMaster music department complement each other,' *MSc*, 263, Jan – Feb 1972

McMaster University. President's Report, 1953–73 JPG

MacMillan. Scottish-Canadian Toronto family whose contribution to music in Canada has been important and varied. Three generations are considered here: 1 / the Rev Alexander MacMillan, 2 / his son Sir Ernest, and 3 / Sir Ernest's son Keith.

1 **Alexander**. Presbyterian minister, hymnologist, b Edinburgh 19 Oct 1864, d Toronto 5 Mar 1961; hon DD (Presbyterian College, Montreal) 1919, hon D MUS (Toronto) 1943. After his graduation in 1887 from the U of Edinburgh and his ordination in the same year by the Presbyterian Church of Scotland he moved to Canada, serving Ontario Presbyterian and United churches in Huron County, Toronto, and nearby Mimico. In 1893 he was appointed a member of the committee which produced *The Presbyterian Book of Praise* (Oxford, London 1904). With W.S. Milner he edited *The University Hymn Book* (Toronto 1912). He became full-time secretary of the Committee on Church Praise in 1914, lecturing on hymnology and church music in theological colleges and editing *The Book of Praise* (Toronto 1918). He was co-editor of *The Ukrainian Book of Praise* (London 1922). On the union in 1925 of the Presbyterian, Methodist, and Congregational churches he became secretary of the Committee on Church Worship and Ritual of the United Church of Canada. He edited *The Hymnary of the United Church of Canada* (Toronto 1931) and wrote *Stories of Our Hymns* (Toronto 1930) and the survey history *Hymns of the Church* (Toronto 1935, 1965). His influence extended to the USA and Great Britain through articles written on hymnody for various periodicals. In *The Presbyterian Record* Charles *Peaker called Alexander MacMillan 'our greatest hymnologist' (January 1973).

See also Hymnbooks; Hymnology.

2 **Sir Ernest** (Alexander Campbell). Conductor, organist, pianist, composer, educator, writer, administrator, b Mimico (Metropolitan Toronto) 18 Aug 1893, d Toronto, 6 May 1973; ARCO 1907, FRCO 1911, B MUS (Oxford) 1911, BA history (Toronto) 1915, D MUS (Oxford) 1918, FRCM 1931, hon LL D (British Columbia) 1936, hon member RAM 1938, hon LL D (Queen's) 1941, hon D MUS (Laval) 1947, hon D LITT (McMaster) 1948, hon LL D (Toronto) 1953, hon LL D (Mount Allison) 1956, hon D MUS (Rochester) 1956, hon LL D (Ottawa) 1959, hon D ED (Sherbrooke) 1962. One of the major figures in Canada's musical history, MacMillan influenced virtually all facets of the country's musical life both by his precocity and brilliance as a performer and by his tireless activities on behalf of education. His service with the many national organizations that benefited from his help often occurred during their founding stages and was marked by shrewdness of vision and adherence to traditional artistic values. At the same time he achieved international recognition through his performances, publications, and wide travels.

One of four children, he showed early an exceptional musical bent, in his attempts to imitate the sounds of the street barrel organ on the piano, in his composition of songs and the score of a children's opera, and especially in his organ playing. He began organ study at 8 with Arthur Blakeley (b Leeds, d USA after 1937), who was organist-choirmaster 1897–1911 at Sherbourne St Methodist Church. Shortly thereafter MacMillan performed in public, and at 10 he appeared at the Festival of the Lilies at *Massey Hall. The surviving photograph of a confident-looking boy wearing a starched collar and flowing tie and seated at the organ is strangely prophetic of the later connection between MacMillan's performing career and the hall in which so much of it took place.

Sir Ernest MacMillan

While his father fulfilled an engagement 1905–8 in his native Edinburgh the younger MacMillan continued organ study there with the noted blind organist Alfred Hollins, occasionally playing services in his teacher's stead. He also received permission to attend music classes at the U of Edinburgh under Friedrich Niecks, W.B. Ross, and others and studied privately with Ross in preparation for his first diploma. In later life MacMillan regarded Edinburgh with a special fondness, and his speech occasionally took on a noticeable burr, sometimes on purpose, sometimes evidently not.

The return to Toronto, nevertheless, was a return home for MacMillan. (For the last 40 years of his life he lived in central Toronto, two miles from Massey Hall and a block from the public school he had attended.) At 15 he took his first appointment, as organist at Knox Presbyterian Church. Church records indicate that the appointment was considered exceptional. An improved instrument had just been installed, and the annual stipend was increased. The young musician responded with strong leadership and aimed seriously for high musical standards, not only in his playing but also in ancillary activities such as reading to the church youth group a paper on 'The Life and Works of Mendelssohn.'

He retained the post at Knox for two years, then spent a year in Edinburgh and London completing the work towards the FRCO and the extramural B MUS from Oxford U, both awarded in 1911 before his 18th birthday. Back in Toronto he studied modern history 1911–14 at the *U of Toronto and served as organist-choirmaster at St Paul's Presbyterian Church in Hamilton, commuting each weekend from Toronto for rehearsals and services. Though not a music major (there was then no resident degree program in music at the university), he quickly related his musical and organizational experience to undergraduate life, playing the organ for convocations and other university functions, helping to form a musical club, and contributing to *The University Hymn Book* (Toronto 1912).

In later years MacMillan said he felt his musical education, which has emphasized mastering the organ before the piano, had been incorrect. The remark typified his frequent belittling of his own largely self-made achievements. Perhaps out of some such self-critical feeling he went to Paris in 1914 to study piano privately with Thérèse Chaigneau. A visitor at the Bayreuth Wagner Festival that summer (and thus in German territory at the outbreak of World War I), he was detained at Nuremberg for over a month. During this period of uncertainty he completed the first version of his *String Quartet in C Minor*. He then became a prisoner of war at Ruhleben, a converted race-track near Berlin, for the remaining war years. (In the circumstances, and taking into consideration the excellent record of his three undergraduate years, Toronto in 1915 conferred on him a BA in absentia.) At Ruhleben he learned German and the basics of such crafts as bookbinding, and formed lasting friendships with, among others, the English composers Benjamin Dale and Quentin *Maclean. MacMillan led the small camp orchestra in concerts and accompaniments for camp musicals (such standards as *The Mikado* and such originals as *Don't Laugh*), gaining what he later felt to be valuable technical experience as a conductor (a capacity in which, characteristically, he had no formal training). He also concentrated diligently on composition and, through the Prisoners-of-War Education Committee, submitted a setting of Swinburne's ode **England* as part of the requirements for his D MUS from Oxford U.

Returning to Canada in 1918, MacMillan embarked on a lecture-recital tour of the west, his program usually consisting of a short organ recital and a talk on his experiences as a prisoner. In 1919 he became organist-choirmaster at Timothy Eaton Memorial Church, Toronto (a position he was to hold until 1925), and 31 Dec 1919 he married Laura Elsie Keith. In 1920 he began teaching organ at the *Canadian Academy of Music. On the amalgamation of the academy with the *TCM MacMillan retained his post, and in 1926 he succeeded A.S. *Vogt as principal. In 1927 he succeeded Vogt again, this time at the U of Toronto as dean of the Faculty Of Music – virtually a titular position then, but one which was to assume greater importance during his lengthy tenure. As a TCM examiner and a festival adjudicator he made annual trips to all parts of Canada, thus giving personal stimulation to musical life in many small centres and directly encouraging more than a generation of Canadian students. In the 1930s he undertook the preparation of texts on sight-reading and ear-training, often collaborating with Boris *Berlin. However, apart from some private teaching in the 1920s and some lecturing, such as the summer courses he gave on *The Well-tempered Clavier* in the 1940s (which developed no pupils but many disciples), MacMillan was an educator, an administrator, and a developer of systems and policies rather than a teacher. Thus, though innumerable young Canadians heard him lecture or met him as an examiner or in other ways felt his influence, that influence tended to be on groups rather than on individuals. There were some actual pupils, however, including the organists Charles *Peaker and Frederick *Silvester.

In 1922 at Sherbourne St United Church G.D. *Atkinson led the first complete Toronto performance of Bach's *St Matthew Passion*. The following year MacMillan amalgamated his TCM choir and those of Richard *Tattersall and Healey *Willan (both of whom assisted in the preparation) and conducted the same work in the first of 30 annual performances under his baton (with the Toronto Conservatory Chorus in later years and with the *Toronto Mendelssohn Choir after 1942).

MacMillan continued to compose new music and arrange old as required. Reviewing *Folk Songs of French Canada* by Edward Sapir and Marius *Barbeau, he noted two melodies that especially attracted him, 'Notre Seigneur en pauvre' and 'À Saint-Malo.' At the request of J.M. *Gibbon, he arranged these for strings as *Two Sketches for Strings* for performance at the 1927 Folksong and Handicraft Festival (*CPR Festivals) in Quebec City. Thus originated his most frequently played work. An attractive sequel, *Six Bergerettes du bas Canada* for voices and small ensemble, was presented at the 1928 CPR Festival. MacMillan had met the ethnologist Marius Barbeau at the first festival, and with characteristic energy he set off with him that summer (1927) to hear, record, and notate music of the native peoples in the Nass River area of northern British Columbia. MacMillan's 70-odd transcriptions were published in *The Tsimshian, Their Arts and Music* (by V. Garfield, P. Wingert, and M. Barbeau, New York 1951). He also arranged some of the songs for concert use, as did Leo *Smith following his example. In 1929 he completed the anthology *A Book of Songs* (reissued in 1937 as *A Canadian Song Book*), often used in Canadian schools.

In 1924, at the invitation of Luigi von *Kunits, MacMillan had conducted the *TSO in his *Overture*, and in 1931, aware of the illness that was to take his life shortly afterwards, von Kunits suggested that MacMillan succeed him as conductor of the TSO. The nomination was accepted by the TSO's board in view of the leadership qualities MacMillan had displayed in so many spheres. Yet MacMillan never actually had led a professional orchestra, and his knowledge of orchestral literature, though extensive, had not been gained on the podium. Nevertheless his eagerness, energy, and enormous talent caught the orchestra at an appropriate moment of early growth. In his youth he had sensed this direction for his career, writing from Ruhleben, 'I can't play for nuts and I've never written anything worthwhile but I *can* conduct,' and in fact MacMillan fulfilled much of his own musical potential in this new enterprise.

In 1935 MacMillan was knighted by King George V for 'services to music in Canada.' Although the practice of granting Canadian titles had been discontinued in 1919, it had been revived by the government of R.B. Bennett. The list for 1935 (the final year of such honours and the last of King George V's reign) included two figures in the arts, Charles G.D. Roberts in literature and MacMillan in music. The investiture was received from the governor-general, Lord Bessborough, who was known to have favoured the award. A knighthood for a 42-year-old Canadian in the 20th century was regarded by some as anachronistic, and MacMillan's acceptance met with a certain amount of criticism. His own view, expressed in a candid chapter ('The knight has a thousand sighs') of his memoirs (ms), was that he had been obliged to accept, out of respect for the Canadian musical groups he had worked with and represented.

In 1936 a Vancouver music teacher, Marjorie Agnew, founded a series of music appreciation groups for young people in British Columbia towns. Known as the *Sir Ernest MacMillan Fine Arts Clubs, they were a precursor of the *JMC movement, with which MacMillan was associated closely later.

By the late 1930s MacMillan also gained fame as a conductor in the USA, appearing in such prominent series as the Hollywood Bowl concerts and with the symphony orchestras of Minneapolis, Philadelphia, and Washington, DC, as well as with the NBC SO and on the 'Ford Sunday Evening Hour.' In 1938 MacMillan sought a conducting position elsewhere but was persuaded to stay in Toronto. He actually tendered his resignation in 1939, withdrawing it only with the entry of Canada into World War II. That the TSO did not disband during the war period, as its forerunner did in World War I, was a tribute to the stability it had attained under MacMillan's leadership. Correspondence shows, however, that for many years he had refunded part of his annual conducting stipend to assist the TSO's solvency. Repeated efforts (in which MacMillan participated) to obtain a civic arts grant finally were rewarded in 1943.

In 1942 MacMillan was honoured by, but (owing to his Canadian obligations) did not accept, an invitation to succeed Donald Francis Tovey (d 1940) in the Reid Chair of Music at the U of Edinburgh. He nevertheless resigned the principalship of the TCM but continued as dean of the Faculty of Music at the U of Toronto until 1952. Also in 1942 he succeeded Herbert A. *Fricker as conductor of the Toronto Mendelssohn Choir. With its well-established traditions and wide reputation the choir was in a more mature phase at his appointment than the TSO had been a decade earlier. Moreover, some participants and observers felt that choral conducting was the musical task which brought out MacMillan's gifts most fully. His annual presentations of the *St Matthew Passion* and *Messiah* had a robust grandeur reminiscent of the English choral style, with touches of dramatic fervour that were his own.

In early 1945 MacMillan filled conducting engagements in Australia and in 1946 he was invited to conduct concerts in Rio de Janeiro. Largely at his initiative the *CMCouncil was established in 1946. MacMillan became its first chairman. He also served 1947–69 as president of *CAPAC, one of his first projects being the organization of a special TSO concert of Canadian music. Though himself unproductive as a composer in later years, MacMillan showed by this venture and by conducting more premieres of Canadian music than anyone else in his time – as well as in talks and articles – his recognition of the central role of creative artists in a country's culture. Though resistant by taste and training to avant-garde trends, he was more liberal than might be supposed in his choice of repertoire.

Combining his improvisational fluency and his natural buoyancy and sense of fun MacMillan made in the 1940s orchestral arrangements, medleys, and parodies for TSO performances on such occasions as the popular 'Christmas Box' benefit concerts. His interest in the piano had returned and, with Kathleen *Parlow and Zara *Nelsova (as the Canadian Trio, 1941– ca 1943), he participated in recitals, CBC broadcasts, and a performance (10 Nov 1942) of the Beethoven *Triple Concerto* with the TSO. He also performed the standard Lieder with Emmy *Heim and Ernesto *Vinci. In 1950 came a peak of his performing life, a week-long festival to celebrate the Bach bicentenary. MacMillan led the Toronto Mendelssohn Choir in the *St Matthew Passion*, the *Magnificat*, and the *Mass in B Minor* and gave a lecture-recital devoted to Book 3 of the *Clavierübung* (the 'organist's catechism'), which he performed in full from memory. It was a special act of devotion to music by the master he had loved above all others since boyhood.

The early 1950s brought the second and third controversies in which MacMillan became embroiled. The first, in 1936, had occurred when MacMillan sought Healey Willan's resignation as vice-principal from the TCM for economic reasons, only to create the new position of 'executive assistant,' which was filled by Norman *Wilks. The second, the 'Symphony Six' affair (1951–2), saw MacMillan stand aloof from the firing by the TSO board of six orchestra members who were unacceptable to US immigration authorities then sensitive to the McCarthy 'witch-hunts' rather than jeopardize the orchestra's first invitations to perform in the USA. The third followed the reorganization in 1952 of music teaching at the U of Toronto. MacMillan had sat for two years on the planning committee which, after its deliberations, recommended a full-time deanship, a position MacMillan could not accept. It was not offered, however, to the candidate he preferred, Ettore *Mazzoleni, then the RCMT principal. The resulting clash between MacMillan and the U of Toronto administration made such headlines as the *Globe and Mail*'s front-page 'Mac retires, Mazz resigns, as discord rocks the Royal Conservatory' (28 Apr 1952). Troubled and overworked, MacMillan took a previously planned extended leave in the fall of 1952, travelling in England, Scotland, and continental Europe.

On his return to Canada he embarked vigorously on new projects, recording *Messiah* and the *St Matthew Passion* with the Toronto Mendelssohn Choir, members of the TSO, and leading Canadian soloists for the specially formed *Beaver Records and editing an anthology of essays, *Music in Canada*. He tendered his resignation as conductor of the TSO at the end of his 25th season (1955–6). Although in effect an early retirement, he acknowledged it to be in both his own and the orchestra's best interests. Tribute was paid publicly to the great strides the TSO had made under his command. The orchestra had lengthened its season, attracted renowned instrumentalists to its ranks, branched out into recording and broadcasting, and altogether solidified its claim to status among major North American orchestras. It had introduced Canadian audiences to a new repertoire (sometimes over objections from board members and subscribers, with whom MacMillan had to deal diplomatically), including works by Bartók, Copland, Roy Harris, Holst, Nielsen, Sibelius, Walton, and others. MacMillan returned as guest conductor on a few occasions and also accepted engagements with the newly formed *CBC SO and other groups. In 1957 he relinquished the conductorship of the Toronto Mendelssohn Choir. He immediately assumed another conducting role, with the various radio orchestras involved in the *CBC Talent Festival. This took him again on regular travels to all parts of Canada and, as in the 1930s, gave him a direct and personal medium through which to encourage younger musicians. As a result of declining health and a serious eye operation he stopped this gruelling work in 1963 but appeared frequently in the mid-1960s as a commentator on CBC radio musical programs. His long radio experience had included a few seasons in the late 1940s as a 'classical disc jockey' for CKEY, Toronto, and, of course, regular CBC network appearances with the TSO and Toronto Mendelssohn Choir.

In these later years, MacMillan became recognized as Canada's musical elder statesman. In addition to his role as a founder of the CMCouncil he served 1957–63 as a founding member of the *Canada Council, his advice being especially valued not only because of the strength of his experience and personality, but because he was one of the few active professional artists among the appointees. MacMillan also became interested in the formation of the *CMCentre and the JMC, and he was president of the former 1959–70 (succeeding Arnold *Walter) and of the latter 1961–3. The experience and wisdom and the sheer energy he devoted to these various activities (the last of which, the chairmanship of the CMCentre board, he gave up in 1970) were recognized by many new honours.

In the new home of the U of Toronto's Faculty of Music (the Edward Johnson Building, occupied 1962, opened officially 1964) the MacMillan Theatre was named after him. In 1963 the U of Toronto at its summer school inaugurated the MacMillan Lectures (later the *CAPAC-MacMillan Lectures), and in 1964 MacMillan himself delivered the three public talks in this annual series, choosing as his topic 'The Canadian musical public.' He received the *Canada Council Medal in 1964. On his 70th and 75th birthdays there were public tributes, special publications, and revivals of his works. His large-scale choral pieces *England* and the *Te Deum* were performed during this period, his *String Quartet* was recorded by the Amadeus Quartet, and his arrangments, such as the masterfully sonorous choral setting of the French-Canadian ballad 'Blanche comme la neige,' became widely known to a new generation of listeners. Also at this time he completed a major portion (14 chapters) of his memoirs, dealing with his career until the late 1940s. In 1970 he was made a Companion of the *Order of Canada, and CAPAC established a fellowship in his name. He suffered a stroke in 1971, and his death followed a second stroke in 1973. In 1973 he was posthumously awarded the *Canadian Music Council Medal, and the Toronto Mendelssohn Choir established a scholarship at the U of Toronto in his memory. A memorial tribute was held in Convocation Hall, U of Toronto, the high point of which was the singing by Lois *Marshall (accompanied by an ensemble of TS players) of an aria from the *St Matthew Passion*.

SELECTED COMPOSITIONS

STAGE

Prince Charming, ballad opera (J.E. Middleton, based on Scottish and French tunes). 1933. 7 soloists, sm orch, chorus. Ms

ORCHESTRA, ORCHESTRA AND CHOIR, BAND

Overture 'Cinderella.' 1915. Med orch. Ms

Two Sketches for Strings 'based on French-Canadian Airs.' 1927. Str orch (str quar). OUP 1928. CBC IS Canadian Album No. 2 (*TSO)/RCI 238 and CTL M1030 (*Hart House O)/Col MS 6962 and Col M2S 276 (*TSO)/('À Saint-Malo') Dom S-3172 (Tor Philharmonia O, *Feldbrill cond)/(str quar) RCI 236 and DG 139900 (Amadeus Quar)

God Save the Queen. Arr ca 1934. Full orch. CMCentre

A Song of Deliverance (Old 124th, Scottish Psalter 1650). Arr 1944. SATB, orch (org). OUP 1945

Christmas Carols. Arr 1945. Full orch. CMCentre

Fantasy on Scottish Melodies. 1946. Full orch. CMCentre

Fanfare for a Festival. 1959. Brass, perc. CMCentre

Fanfare for a Centennial. 1967. Brass, perc. CMCentre

See also *England*; *Te Deum laudamus*.

CHAMBER

String Quartet in C Minor. 1914 (rev 1921). CMCentre. RCI 236/DG 139900 (Amadeus Quar)

2 *Fugues* for string quartet. 1917. Ms

Six Bergerettes du bas Canada (traditional, transl Mrs H. Ross). Arr 1928. Sop, alto, ten, 4 instr. OUP 1935

Three French Canadian Sea Songs (traditional). Arr 1930. Med v, str quar (orch). CMCentre

There Was an Old Woman (traditional nursery rhyme). 1946. Mezzo, str. CMCentre

I Sing of a Maid and *The Storke* (both 1925), and *Two Carols* (1927), all FH 1927. All for v and str trio (pf)

KEYBOARD

Gavotte. Nd. Pf. FH 1931(?)

Cortège académique. 1953. Org. Novello 1957

D'où viens-tu bergère? Arr, nd. Pf 4 hands. GVT 1958

CHOIR AND VOICE

'Du bist wie eine Blume' (H. Heine). 1913. V, pf. Ms

'O Mistress Mine' (Shakespeare). 1917. V, pf. Ms

Three Songs for High Baritone from 'The Countess Cathleen' (Yeats). 1917. V, pf. Ms

Songs from Sappho (B. Carman). 1920. V, pf. Ms

'I Heard a Voice from Heaven' (text from burial service). Ca 1925. SSAA. Ms

'Padded Footsteps' (A. Bourinot). 1925, V, pf. Ms

'That Holy Thing' (George McDonald). 1925. V, pf. Ms

'Recessional' (Kipling). 1928. SATB (v), pf. Ms

'Sonnet' (E.B. Browning). 1928. V, pf. FH 1928

Three Indian Songs of the West Coast. 1928. V, pf. FH 1928

'Last Prayer' (C. Rossetti). 1929. V, pf. Boston 1929

'O Canada' (A. Routhier, transl J.W. Garvin). Arr, nd. SATB, orch (str orch or band or pf). WR 1930

'Hail to Toronto' (C.V. Pilcher). Ca 1934. SATB. GVT 1934

'The King Shall Rejoice in Thy Strength' (Bible, Yattendon Hymnal). Ca 1935. SATB, org. FH 1935

Northland Songs, vol 2 (J.M. Gibbon). Arr 1938. V, pf. GVT 1938

Canada Calls / Debout Canadiens! (A. Plouffe). Nd. V, pf. GVT 1942

'Land of the Maple Leaf' (C.V. Pilcher). Ca 1943. SATB, pf. GVT 1943

Ballads of British Columbia (J.M. Gibbon). Arr 1947. V, pf. GVT 1947

4 arrs for TTBB: 'Au Cabaret / At the Inn,' 'Blanche comme la neige / White as Cometh the Snowflake,' 'C'est la belle Françoise / The Fair Françoise,' 'Dans tous les cantons / In All the Country Round.' All 1928. All Boston 1928. 'Blanche comme la neige' rev for SATB 1958, GVT 1968. RCI 339/CBC SM-105/RCA LSC 3154 (*Tor Mendelssohn Choir)/CBC SM-19 (*Festival Singers)

Also several sacred and secular vocal and instrumental works dating from 1904 (including an early opera, *Snow White*, 1907); others, including over 60 arrs of French-Canadian and Canadian Indian songs

See also Discographies for Emmy Heim; Toronto Mendelssohn Choir; Toronto Symphony.

WRITINGS

- ed. *Vingt-et-un chansons canadiennes / Twenty-one Folk-Songs of French Canada* (F. Harris 1928)
- ed. *A Book of Songs* (Toronto 1929)
- and Berlin, Boris. *The Modern Piano Student* (Oakville 1931)
- and Willan, Healey. *Graded Sight-reading Exercises for Piano*, 2 vols (Oakville 1939)

On the Preparation of Ear Tests (Oakville 1938)

- and Berlin, Boris. *Twenty-One Lessons in Ear-Training* (Oakville 1939)
- ed. *A Canadian Song Book* (Toronto 1937, rev edn 1948; formerly *A Book of Songs*)
- ed. *Music in Canada* (Toronto 1955)

ARTICLES

'Potted music,' *Canadian Forum*, vol 2, Jan 1922

'Tendencies in modern British music,' ibid, vol 3, Jul, Sep 1923

'Our musical public,' ibid, vol 4, Jul 1924

'A few aphorisms,' *CQR*, vol 7, Feb 1925

'The university and music,' *U of Toronto Q*, Mar 1926

'Music at the educational conference,' *CQR*, vol 8, Spring 1926

'The Folk Song Festival at Quebec...some impressions,' *CQR*, vol 9, Summer 1927

'Some notes on Schubert,' *The School*, vol 16, Oct 1927

'The musical season in Toronto,' *Canadian Forum*, vol 8, May 1928

'Hymns and hymn singing,' *Diapason*, 1 Oct 1929

'Choral and church music,' *CQR*, vol 9, Winter 1929

'Impressions of the Lausanne conference,' *CQR*, vol 14, Autumn 1931

'Organ accompaniments in church services,' *CQR*, vol 13, Winter, Spring 1931

'Musical relations between Canada and the U.S.A.,' *Proceedings of the Music Teachers' National Assn* (1931)

'Those music exams!' *Chatelaine*, Nov 1933

'Three notable British composers,' *CQR*, vol 16, Aug 1934

'Problems of music in Canada,' *Yearbook of the Arts in Canada*, ed B. Brooker, vol 2 (Toronto 1936)

'Music in Canada,' *RCO Calendar 1936–7*

'Canadian musical life,' *Canadian Geographical J*, vol 19, Dec 1939

'Hitler and Wagnerism,' *Queen's Q*, vol 48, Summer 1942

'Musical composition in Canada,' *Culture*, vol 5, June 1942

'Music in wartime,' *Music Bulletin*, Oxford U Press no. 10, 15 Oct 1942

'We need music,' *Chatelaine*, Dec 1942

'Orchestral and choral music in Canada,' *Proceedings of the Music Teachers' National Assn* (1946)

'Musical composition in Canada,' *TSO News*, vol 3, Apr 1947

'The outlook for Canadian music,' *International Musician*, Oct 1948

'Music in Canada,' *Royal Commission Studies* (Ottawa 1951)

'Music and the summer: why not Canadian festivals?' *SatN*, 4 Oct 1952

'Festival report – Edinburgh's varied offerings,' *SatN*, 18 Oct 1952

'After Edinburgh – home thoughts from abroad,' *SatN*, 25 Oct 1952

'Emmy Heim,' *ConsB*, Nov 1954

'Some problems of the Canadian composer,' *Dalhousie R*, vol 36, Spring 1956
'In music – progress?' *Mount Allison Record*, vol 39, Fall 1956
'The Canadian Music Council,' *CMJ*, vol 1, Autumn 1956
'Music: concert performance,' *Encyclopedia Canadiana*, vol 7 (Toronto 1958)
'Music in Canadian universities,' *CMJ*, vol 2, Spring 1958
'The organ was my first love,' *CMJ*, vol 3, Spring 1959
'What shall we do with a hundred million?' *Crescendo*, vol 2, Apr 1959
'The music is alive,' *Saturday R*, 24 Oct 1959
'Healey Willan as I have known him,' *American Organist*, Aug 1960
'Canada's voice – the Canadian Music Centre,' *PfAC*, vol 1, Mar 1961
'What is good music?' *NY Herald Tribune Sunday Forum*, 21 May 1961
'Marius Barbeau – his work,' *Canadian Author & Bookman*, vol 38, Winter 1962
'Canada,' *La Musica*, ed Gatti (Turin 1966)
'Reminiscences of Marius Barbeau,' *Mcan*, 18, Apr 1969
Also reviews published in *Canadian Forum*, *U of Toronto Q*, *CMJ*, and *Canadian Author & Bookman*.

BIBLIOGRAPHY

'A new choral writer,' *MT*, 1 Sep 1920
Hamilton, H.C. 'Ernest Campbell MacMillan,' *MCan*, Oct 1928
Barbeau, Marius. 'The Thunder Bird of the mountains,' *U of Toronto Q*, vol 2, Oct 1932
Hollins, Alfred. *A Blind Musician Looks Back: an Autobiography* (Edinburgh, London 1936)
MacKelcan, F.R. 'Sir Ernest MacMillan,' *Queen's Q*, vol 43, Winter 1936–7
McStay, A. 'Prodigy's progress,' *Maclean's*, Oct 1940
Muir, Mary. 'Music – Sir Ernest MacMillan resigns Conservatory principalship,' *U of Toronto Monthly*, Oct 1942
'Sir Ernest and "Maple Leaf",' *SatN*, 11 Jul 1950
Hannon, Leslie. 'The elegant enigma of Sir Ernest,' *Mayfair*, Feb 1953
'MacMillan, Sir Ernest Campbell,' *Current Biography*, vol 16, Mar 1955
McCready, Louise. *Famous Musicians* (Toronto 1957)
'A tribute to Sir Ernest MacMillan,' *Music Across Canada* (special issue), vol 1, Jul – Aug 1963
Ridout, G. 'Sir Ernest MacMillan: an appraisal,' *CME*, vol 6, Nov – Dec 1964
Ketchum, J.D. *Ruhleben* (Toronto 1965)
Winters, Kenneth. 'Sir Ernest at seventy-five,' Toronto *Telegram*, 10 Aug 1968
'A tribute to Sir Ernest MacMillan,' *CBC Times*, 23–9 Nov 1968
Kraglund, J. 'Sir Ernest's 75th: special musical celebration,' *CanComp*, 35, Dec 1968
Bryant, Giles. 'In practically every facet of the most spiritual of the arts we would be weaker in opportunity, tradition and environment, but for this man,' *AGO/RCCO Music*, vol 3, Feb 1969
'Sir Ernest MacMillan,' *CanComp*, 45, Dec 1969
'Sir Ernest MacMillan, 1893–1973,' *CanComp* (special issue), 82, Jul 1973
Beckwith, John. 'Sir Ernest MacMillan,' *Contemporary Canadian Composers*
MacMillan, Keith. 'Unforgettable Sir Ernest MacMillan,' *Reader's Digest*, Feb 1978 / 'Mon chef d'orchestre préféré,' *Sélection du Reader's Digest*, Jun 1979

3 **Keith** (Campbell). Administrator, producer, writer, editor, b Toronto 23 Sep 1920; BA (Toronto) 1949, MA (Toronto) 1951. While attending Upper Canada College 1934–8 he began private studies with Boris *Berlin and Ettore *Mazzoleni (piano and theory) and David *Ouchterlony (organ). He resumed organ study 1946–9 with Charles *Peaker. At the U of Toronto, where his main courses were in biology, MacMillan wrote and produced the musical *What, No Crumpets!* (1947) and the operetta *Saints Alive* (1949) with Ronald Bryden as librettist. He co-founded *Hallmark Recordings with Douglas Sanderson in 1952, serving also as first president (until 1954) and as producer. That same year he became a producer for CBC Radio, preparing programs, mostly musical, for 'CBC Wednesday Night,' 'Folk Song Time' (with Edith *Fowke), 'CBC Concert Hall' and 'Distinguished Artists.' He also served 1961–4 as the broadcast producer of the *CBC SO.

In 1964 Keith MacMillan succeeded John *Adaskin as executive director of the *CMCentre, in which capacity he worked tirelessly to promote the music of Canadian composers through his writings, lectures, and participation on the boards and committees of such organizations as the *CCA, the *CMEA, the *CMCouncil, *EMC*, the *Toronto Mendelssohn Choir, and the *TSO. He was secretary 1964–76 and president 1976–7 of the Music Information Centres Commission of the International Assn of Music Libraries and was president 1974–5 of *CAML. Besides editing the CMCentre's catalogues of Canadian compositions, he edited its *Newsletter / Bulletin de nouvelles* (1964–6) and the magazine **Musicanada* throughout its first phase (1967–70). He lectured 1969–70 on 'Man and His Music,' and in 1974 on Canadian music at *York U. His advocacy of Canadian music proceeded thus on the broadest of bases. His calm persistence and sturdy good nature countered official and public indifference effectively, and his correlative intelligence worked on all fronts to unify the ideals and purposes of Canada's musical agencies. In 1977 he became chairman of the music department at the *U of Ottawa. He was awarded the *CMCouncil Medal in 1978.

Of Keith MacMillan's four children, three have pursued interests in music. His brother Ross, a chemical engineer, married the pianist Gwen Beamish (ARCT 1948, LRCT 1952), a pupil of Boris Berlin and Boris *Roubakine at the RCMT and of Claudio Arrau and Alexander Uninsky in master classes at Stratford, Ont. She began teaching at the *Banff SFA in 1959 and at the *U of Western Ontario in 1970.

WRITINGS

'Making the most of your tape recorder,' *CMJ*, vol 4, Winter 1960
'New sound equipment,' *CMJ*, vol 4, Spring 1960
Review of *Canada's Story in Song*, *CMJ*, vol 5, Winter 1961
'Music,' *Canadian Annual Review*, ed John Saywell (Toronto 1964, 1965, 1966, 1967)
'Canadian Music Centre: developing a new tradition,' *OpCan*, Dec 1964
'Of garbage and modern music,' *CME*, vol 6, Jan–Feb 1965
'The process of discovery,' *PfAC*, vol 4, no. 4, 1966
'National organizations,' *Aspects of Music in Canada* / 'Les organismes nationaux,' *Aspects de la musique au Canada*
'New Canadian music – are we afraid of it?' *CME*, vol 10, Mar–Apr 1969
'Thriving ten-year old,' *OpCan*, vol 10, May 1969
'Report from Victoria,' *CMB*, 2, Spring–Summer 1971
'The changing image of Canada and its new music,' *Music and Artists*, vol 4, Sep–Oct 1971
'Music in Canada today,' *The Musicians' Guide* (New York 1972)
'Tribute to Elmer Iseler,' *CMB*, 10, Spring–Summer 1975
– and Beckwith, John, eds. *Contemporary Canadian Composers / Compositeurs canadiens contemporains*
'Music-lover claims sausage-makers ruining CBC radio,' Toronto *Globe and Mail*, 20 Apr 1976
'Music on the CBC: the English service division of CBC radio,' *Mcan*, 31, Feb 1977
'Canadian composers you'll be hearing ...' *Toronto Symphony News*, Apr–May 1977
'Established and imported, or brash and fresh, arts response growing,' Toronto *Globe and Mail*, 26 Nov 1977
Articles on Canadian music for the *Encyclopedia Americana*, *The International Cyclopedia of Music and Musicians*, *The New Grove Dictionary*, *Rizzoli Editore*

BIBLIOGRAPHY

Littler, William. 'Mr. Canadian music inherits dad's mantle,' *Toronto Star*, 4 Jun 1977

1 / (AHC), 2 / JB, 3 / (FRC)

MacMILLAN, Andrew. Bass-baritone, stage director, b Glasgow 22 Nov 1914, d Toronto 7 Feb 1967. His family moved to Canada ca 1916 and settled in Montreal where, at 17, he studied with Finlay Campbell. In the 1930s he sang in Gilbert & Sullivan productions with the Lyric Operatic Society, performed with the Dominion Opera Guild, and sang in oratorio. He was a member of the Canadian **Army Show* during World War II. After the war he enrolled at the *Royal Cons Opera School, Toronto, where his voice teacher was Ernesto *Vinci. In 1949 he joined the teaching staff as assistant to Herman *Geiger-Torel. In 1950 he joined the *COC as both a singer and the assistant stage director. His roles with the company included Fiorello and Dr Bartolo in *The Barber of Seville*, Colline and Schaunard in *La Bohème*, Zuniga in *Carmen*, the Secret Police Agent in *The Consul*, Don Alfonso in *Così fan tutte*, Leporello in *Don Giovanni*, Frank and Eisenstein in *Die Fledermaus*, Papageno in *The Magic Flute*, Almaviva, Figaro, and Dr Bartolo in *The Marriage of Figaro*, Falstaff in *The Merry Wives of Windsor*, Del'-Aqua in *A Night in Venice*, and Jupiter in *Orpheus in the Underworld*. During the early 1950s he sang with the Opera Assn of Central America, touring in Guatemala, San Salvador, and Costa Rica.

During the 1950s and 1960s MacMillan also was heard in opera and recitals over CBC radio and TV, appeared in **Spring Thaw*, was stage director for the opera department of the *Banff SFA, and continued to coach at the Royal Cons Opera School. For the COC he directed *Madama Butterfly* (1962), *La Bohème* (1963, 1965), and *Die Fledermaus* (1964). After MacMillan's death Herman Geiger-Torel wrote of him (*Opera Canada*, Feb 1967): 'His knowledge of languages, his excellent musicianship, his fabulous acting talent paired with a very fine voice made him prominent in the upcoming world of opera in Canada.' SW

MacMillan Fine Arts Club. See Sir Ernest MacMillan Fine Arts Club

McMULLIN, Robert or **Bob** (Wesley). Composer, arranger, conductor, b Lewiston, Ut, 29 Apr 1921, naturalized Canadian 1946. Taken at 4 to Raymond, near Lethbridge, Alta, he played drums at 11 with his brother's dance band and later with other groups. During World War II he led an RCAF dance band in Europe. After the war he settled in Edmonton and played trumpet and clarinet in CBC radio orchestras. In the early 1950s he was music director for several programs, including 'Linger Awhile' and 'The Bob McMullin Show.' His first major work, *Sketches from the Rocky Mountains*, was completed in 1948 and premiered that year by the *TSO under Sir Ernest *MacMillan. It was performed later by the *MSO and, with the composer conducting, by the *Edmonton SO. The TSO recorded the second sketch, 'Pass River,' in 1950 (RCI 19). In 1952 McMullin wrote *Essay for Orchestra* on commission for the Edmonton SO.

McMullin moved to Winnipeg in 1955, working as music director, arranger, or player for many CBC programs including the TV series 'Music Hop.' He has been music director for productions by *Rainbow Stage and the U of Manitoba Glee Club and has conducted *Winnipeg SO pop concerts and stage shows by Canadian and US pop singers. After 1970 he divided his time between Winnipeg and Toronto, writing music for films and TV programs, including CBC TV's 'House of Pride,' 'The Collaborators,' 'Sidestreet,' and 'King of Kensington' and the feature films *On the Edge of the Ice Pack* (USA 1972), *Race Home to Die* (1973), and *The Shadow of the Hawk* (1976). Among his other concert works are *Prairie Sketches* (1958, Waterloo 1960; a work for school orchestra, commissioned by the *OMEA and premiered in April of 1959 by the *CBC SO), *Concerto for Orchestra* (1974), and

Concerto for trumpet and orchestra (1979) commissioned by the US trumpeter Doc Severinsen. McMullin has arranged music for LPs by the US singer Enzo Stuarti, the Winnipeg pop singer Ray St Germain, and the Metro-Gnomes, and for his own LP, *Bob McMullin and his Orchestra* (1966, CTLS 5078). He is an affiliate of PRO Canada.

BIBLIOGRAPHY
O'Neill, Dennis H. 'Versatility in Winnipeg,' *CanComp*, 4, Dec 1965
Topalovich, Maria. 'Bob McMullin keeps composer's role low-key in film work,' *MSc*, 289, May–Jun 1976
BD, MM

McNEILL, Ogreta (b Ormiston). Librarian, teacher, b Gabarus, Cape Breton Island, NS, 2 Aug 1903; ATCM 1932, B MUS (Toronto) 1952, BLS (Toronto) 1953. She was raised in Victoria, BC, where she studied and taught piano. The young John *Beckwith was one of her pupils. Moving to Toronto in 1932, she worked 1942–68 in the Toronto Public Library's music library, for some 20 of those years as its head. She developed the holdings, began the record collection, and organized concerts at Ferguson House (the music library's home 1959–77). She was a founding member of the *CMLA (renamed *CAML) and served 1956–7 and 1964–5 as its chairman. She was also president 1960–3 of the Pro Arte Orchestra. After her retirement she became music consultant to the Forest Hill Learning Resources Centre.

WRITINGS
'Music in 19th century Toronto: a bibliography,' U of Toronto Library School, 1953
'Basic music collection for a small public library,' *Ont Library R*, vol 39, Aug 1955
'Music collections in Canadian libraries, 1: Public libraries,' *Canadian Library Assn Bulletin*, vol 12, Apr 1956
'Music libraries,' ibid, vol 13, Apr 1959
'Peregrinations of a music library,' *Ont Library R*, vol 42, Aug 1959
'House of Music,' *Toronto Symphony News*, Mar 1960

BIBLIOGRAPHY
Beckwith, John. 'A tribute to Mrs. Ogreta McNeill,' *CMLA Newsletter*, Dec 1968
(FCR)

MacNUTT, Walter (Louis). Composer, organist-choirmaster, b Charlottetown 2 Jun 1910; ATCM 1932. After studies in Prince Edward Island with W.E. Fletcher and Roberta Spencer he attended the TCM 1929–32, winning the *Vogt Memorial and Marion Ferguson scholarships. His teachers included Healey *Willan (organ and composition) and Reginald *Godden (piano). He held posts as organist-choirmaster at Trinity Church, Barrie, Ont 1931–5, Holy Trinity Church, Toronto 1935–42, All Saints' Church, Winnipeg 1946–9, and All Saints' Church, Windsor, Ont 1949–53, where he also conducted the Windsor Singers for two years in CBC broadcasts. His last post prior to retirement was at St Thomas' Church, Toronto 1954–77. MacNutt's early compositions (listed in *Catalogue of Canadian Composers*) include works for choir, voice, and orchestra and a *Piano Suite* (Harris 1939). His later compositions, written mainly for use in the Anglican church, include two *Missae breves* (BMIC 1962, Waterloo 1965), and a *Mass of St James* (Waterloo 1974), as well as choral, vocal, and organ pieces. Of his many songs, his settings of works by William Blake and 'Take Me to a Green Isle' (a poem by H.E. Foster) became popular. MacNutt's publishers include *BMI Canada, Faith, Fischer, *Harris, *Waterloo, and *Western. He is an affiliate of PRO Canada. JA

McPEEK, Ben (Benjamin Dewey). Composer, conductor, arranger, pianist, b Trail, BC, 28 Aug 1934, d Toronto 14 Jan 1981; ARCT 1954, B MUS (Toronto) 1956. Moving to Toronto in 1953, he studied at the *RCMT and also at the *U of Toronto, where his teachers included John *Beckwith, Talivaldis *Kenins, Oskar *Morawetz, Godfrey *Ridout, and John *Weinzweig. He began his career playing the piano in Toronto dance bands and sang on the CBC with the Five Playboys. Entering musical theatre in 1960 as music director of the revue *Up Tempo 60*, produced at the King Edward Hotel, he wrote music 1963–8 for *That Hamilton Woman, Suddenly This Summer, Actually This Autumn*, and the 1968 **Spring Thaw*. His opera bouffe, *The Bargain* (1963, based on the Faust legend), was telecast in 1966 by CBC Montreal and was staged in 1978 by Comus Music Theatre for the Toronto Spring Festival in a revised version with an electronic score. His musical, *Joey*, written with Helen Porter, was produced at the *Charlottetown Festival in 1973.

In 1964 McPeek established Ben McPeek, Ltd, and soon became one of the busiest jingle writers in Canada. In 1966 he was a founder of *Nimbus 9 Productions. By 1979 McPeek had written, and directed recordings of, about 2000 jingles. (His *Commercial Overture*, an orchestral medley of some of his best-known jingles, has been played by the *Hamilton Philharmonic.) He also composed scores for the feature films *The Rowdyman* (1972) and *Only God Knows* (1974) and for the documentary *Catch the Sun* (1973). In 1979, with Harry *Freedman, he formed the Canadian Film Composers Guild. His other compositions include a *Piano Concerto*, six piano sonatas, and many other piano pieces (inventions, waltzes, rags, etc); works for brass and woodwind quintet, including the *Paul Bunyan Suite* (Thompson 1977, recorded by *Canadian Brass); and the orchestral works *Northern 484, Fantasia*, and *Concert Suite*. His *Trillium Suite* (saxophone and chamber ensemble) was commissioned by Paul *Brodie and his *Five Pictorial Sketches for Mandolin and Orchestra*, based on Ukrainian and Canadian folksongs, by the Shevchenko Music Ensemble. He also wrote a collection of novelty items for Canadian Brass, which recorded the music under the pseudonym the Pucker and Valve Society Band. An album of McPeek's piano music has been recorded by Monica *Gaylord. McPeek himself made the LPs *Ben McPeek, His Voices and His Orchestra* (1965, CTLS 5060), *Original Sounds of Ben McPeek* (1966, RCA CTLS 1080/Camden CAS 2351), *Play Me* (1973, RCA KXL 1-0032), *Ben McPeek's Latest Fling at the Record Scene* (RCA CASX 2537), and *Thinking of You* (1975, Attic LAT 1008). McPeek's music is copyrighted by Critique Music Publishers, Toronto. The musical rights of his estate are administered by CAPAC.

BIBLIOGRAPHY
Bennett, Ray. 'Mr. McPeek: the music factory,' Toronto *Globe and Mail*, 20 Jan 1968
'Ben McPeek: "It was time to start doing something",' *CanComp*, 29, May 1968
Kirby, Blaik. 'The prolific composer McPeek,' Toronto *Globe and Mail*, 1 Jan 1970
Flohil, Richard. 'Ben McPeek: a time for new directions,' *CanComp*, 86, Dec 1973
HM, MM

McPHEE, Colin. Composer, pianist, writer, b Montreal 15 Mar 1901, d Los Angeles 7 Jan 1964. He studied composition until 1921 with Gustav Strube at the Peabody Cons in Baltimore, Md, and piano 1921–4 with Arthur Friedheim in Toronto. With the New SO (*TSO) he performed his *Concerto No. 2* 15 Jan 1924 under the direction of Luigi von *Kunits. *Musical Canada* (February 1924) called the work 'interesting, as it depicts very forcibly the modern spirit of youth – headstrong, heedless, at times quite unreasonable.' McPhee studied 1924–6 in Paris with Paul Le Flem (composition) and Isidor Philipp (piano). Also a pupil of Varèse in New York and a winner of two Guggenheim scholarships, he lived 1934–9 in Indonesia, particularly in Bali and Java. His studies of the music, dance, and theatre of these regions gained him international recognition as an authority on the subjects. They also influenced several of his symphonic and choral compositions. The rhythms and resonances of the gamelan orchestra are found particularly in *Tabuh-Tabuhan* (1936), composed at the request of Carlos Chávez for the National Orchestra of Mexico. Frequently performed later, this work was part of the program of Canadian music conducted by Leopold Stokowski 16 Oct 1953 at Carnegie Hall. It won its composer the American Academy of Arts and Letters' Prize in 1954.

Among McPhee's other compositions may be cited *Four Iroquois Dances* for orchestra (1944), *Symphony No. 2* (1957), *Symphony No. 3* (1962), and *Sea Shanty Suite* (1929) for baritone, male choir, two pianos, and two sets of timpani. His *Concerto* for piano and wind octet (1929) was recorded by Grant Johannesen (Columbia ML-5105), and again, with his *Nocturne*, by members of the *CBC Vancouver Chamber Orchestra and Linda Lee *Thomas. *Nocturne* also was recorded by the Hessian Radio SO under David Van Vactor (Composers' Recordings CRI S-219), and the *Symphony No. 2* by the Louisville Orchestra, with Robert Whitney conducting (Louisville 592). McPhee also composed the wartime song 'Arm, Canadians' (Whaley Royce 1917). Several of his works, listed in *Baker's* and *Grove's*, were published by Associated Music, Kalmus, Peters, and G. Schirmer, and his early *Four Piano Sketches, Op 1* were published in Toronto by the Empire Music and Travel Club in 1916.

As a writer, McPhee completed three works dealing with his years in Indonesia: *A House in Bali* (New York 1946), *A Club of Small Men* (New York 1948), and *Music in Bali* (New Haven 1966). He also reviewed compositions 1939–45 for *Modern Music*, the publication of the US League of Composers. He taught 1958–64 in the Institute of Ethnomusicology at the U of California in Los Angeles. He was an affiliate of BMI.

BIBLIOGRAPHY
Bridle, Augustus. 'Who writes our music? A survey of Canadian composers,' *Maclean's*, 15 Dec 1929
Brooker, Bertram, ed. *Year Book of the Arts in Canada 1928–9* (Toronto 1929)
Riegger, Wallingford. 'Adolf Weiss and Colin McPhee,' *American Composers on American Music*, ed Henry Cowell (New York 1962)
Dictionary of Contemporay Music
MGG
GP

MacPHERSON, (John) **Fraser**. Tenor and alto saxophonist, flutist, clarinetist, b Winnipeg 10 Apr 1928. Raised in Victoria, BC, he played clarinet as a youth under the influence of traditional New Orleans jazz, and then took up alto and tenor saxophone and adopted a mainstream style drawn from the playing of Stan Getz, Ben Webster, and Lester Young. Living after 1948 in Vancouver, except for a period 1956–7 when he studied in New York with Vincent James Abato (saxophone) and Henry Zlotnick (flute), MacPherson worked for 20 years in the city's nightclubs, among them the Palomar (1950–4, in turn with the bands of Chuck Barber, Bob Reid, and Lance *Harrison) and the Cave (1961–3 with Chris *Gage, 1964–70 with his own band). In 1951 he began playing saxophone, flute, and clarinet in Vancouver studio orchestras, rising to first-call status. In 1958 he began playing alto saxophone with the *Vancouver SO on a freelance basis.

MacPherson has performed on CBC radio and TV jazz shows, beginning with 'Jazz Workshop' in 1954; in jazz clubs and concerts with his own groups in the dixieland or mainstream style; and as a featured soloist in bands led by Gage, Bobby *Hales, Ian *McDougall, Ray Norris, Doug Parker, Dave *Robbins, and others. He can be heard on LPs by the Hales and McDougall big bands and has made *The Sounds of Fraser MacPherson* (1970, CBC LM-90, with Parker's orchestra), *Fraser / The Shadow* (1970, Pacific North PNR 700), and two extended-play 45s for the CBC's LM series.

In 1975 MacPherson formed a trio with the guitarist Oliver Gannon (see Pacific Salt) and the bassist Wyatt Ruther (b Pittsburg 5 Feb 1923). Known as Fraser and Friends (or, more casually, as the Flat Earth Swing Band), it made the LP *Fraser: Live at the Planetarium* in 1975. Released by MacPherson on his own label, West End, the LP garnered laudatory reviews from leading jazz publications and was taken over by RCA for national distribution and in 1979 by the US label Concord for world distribution. The trio made a second LP for Concord in 1979. Besides touring extensively in western Canada for *Overture Concerts, the trio gave 13 concerts in the USSR in the winter of 1978 and performed under the sponsorship of RCI in Europe in the summer of 1979.

Among the most respected jazz musicians in western Canada, MacPherson was the subject of the CBC TV program 'Diary of a Musician' in 1966 and of a 90-minute radio documentary aired 24 Sep 1976 on the CBC's 'Jazz Radio-Canada.' He was host in the summer of 1977 for a 'Jazz Radio-Canada' series devoted to the history of jazz. He has taught at Douglas College, New Westminster, BC, and at the Vancouver Community College.

BIBLIOGRAPHY

Read, Jeani. 'Blowing your own horn,' *Maclean's*, 18 Apr 1977

Andrews, Marke. 'Soviet admirers delight jazz group,' *MSc*, 308, Jul–Aug 1979

Miller, Mark. 'Fraser MacPherson,' *Down Beat*, May 1980

MM

MACPHERSON, Gordon (Clarke). Pianist, conductor, b Moose Jaw, Sask, 14 Nov 1924; LRCT 1948, Artist Diploma (Toronto) 1953, M MUS (Indiana) 1974. His teachers were Cyril *Hampshire 1942–3 at the Hamilton Cons (*RHCM) and Margaret Miller *Brown and Bela Böszörmenyi-Nagy 1946–53 at the *RCMT, where Macpherson himself taught piano 1948–50. He moved to Halifax in 1953 and founded the Halifax Trio in 1955. He was music adviser to the CBC's Maritime region 1955–66, conducted the CBC Halifax Strings 1958–66 and the CBC Halifax Chamber Orchestra 1963–6, and was conductor for the CBC TV program 'Reflections' 1960–2. From 1953 to 1966 he was head of the piano department at the Halifax (later *Maritime) Cons. He moved with the Halifax Trio (*Brandon University Trio) when the trio became artists-in-residence at *Brandon U in 1966, and he joined the teaching faculty there in 1967. Macpherson took doctoral studies with Menahem Pressler at the U of Indiana in 1975. (KN)

MacQUARRIE, Lola (Frances Lane) (b Smith). Educator, writer, b Winnipeg 30 Dec 1909, d there 24 Jan 1966; B SC (Manitoba) 1931. She was steadily involved in Winnipeg musical life after 1920, notably in the 1940s as choir director at Daniel McIntyre High School. Her choirs, with those of Gladys Anderson Brown at Kelvin Collegiate, set new provincial standards in their field. She became assistant director in 1947 and director in 1955 of music for Winnipeg schools, and in that position she revised the school music curriculum. She wrote and narrated many CBC school music broadcasts (notably 'Music for Juniors'), was co-author with Beth *Douglas of *Melody Makers, Treasure Tunes*, and *Happy Harmonies* (Toronto 1959, 1961, 1965), and was an adjudicator of competition festivals throughout Manitoba. She was a founder (1959) and honorary president of the *MMEA and president 1963–5 of the *CMEA. The MMEA established a trust fund in her memory in 1966.

See also School music; School music broadcasts. (BCn)

McTAGGART, John. Composer, teacher, organist, conductor, b Liverpool, of Scottish parents, ca 1873, d Selkirk, Man, 15 Jul 1953; ARCM, LRAM, LTCL. His teachers included Sir Charles Stanford (composition) and Alberto Visetti (voice) in London. He taught at a conservatory in Sutton, Surrey, then moved to Scotland, where he was organist-choirmaster for several churches and a conductor of choral groups, light opera societies, and orchestras. The year of his arrival in Canada was probably 1930, and it is known that he conducted a choir in Winnipeg for a touring English production of *Merrie England* ca 1932. In Winnipeg McTaggart taught voice at the *Bornoff School, then acquired a studio at the *Shinn Cons. He also lectured at St John's College on public speaking. He conducted choirs for the Winnipeg radio stations CKY and CBW, and the CBC's Zephyr Strings, and was choir director at several churches including Grace Church United. At the request of the city's musicians' union he conducted a 65-piece symphony orchestra for a year and a half in an attempt to establish such an organization permanently. He moved to Selkirk, northeast of Winnipeg, in 1952, but continued to teach twice weekly in Winnipeg. McTaggart's compositions, listed in the *Catalogue of Canadian Composers*, include a Christmas cantata, *A Ruler in Israel* (Curwen); an operetta for school use, *Peridot and Mirami*; choral pieces published by Beal, Stuttard, by Curwen, and by Paterson; piano pieces for students; and songs.

The Madrigal Singers. A 20-voice mixed choir formed in 1970 by Phyllis *Mailing to perform 16th-century music for the World Shakespeare Congress at *Simon Fraser U, Burnaby, BC, in 1971. The choir, still active in 1980, maintained its connection with Simon Fraser, where it has given choral workshops and programs combining readings from English literature and performances of renaissance music under Mailing's direction.

MAFFRÉ, Joseph. Bandmaster, teacher, fl 1840–55. He was a leading musical figure in the Montreal of his time. In 1840 he was bandmaster of the 71st regiment, a position he may have held during the entire stay in Montreal of the 71st Highland Light Infantry, 1838–52. An advertisement in 1841 proclaimed his 'perfect knowledge' of the piano, organ, and string and wind instruments and his ability also to teach the elements of singing, thorough bass, and orchestration. In the same year he proposed the formation of choral and orchestral societies. These hopes were not realized fully, but Maffré is known to have led the orchestra in a Montreal Choral Society concert in 1844. He trained and led the amateur singers at the Récollets Church 1843–6 and at St Patrick's Church 1847–8. He also led a quadrille band (in 1855 jointly with Henry *Prince). The *Literary Garland*, (May, Nov 1840) includes quadrilles composed by Maffré, and his *Original Canadian Quadrilles* (J.W. Herbert 1847) were dedicated to the Countess of Elgin. Some music from his personal library survives at *McGill U.

BIBLIOGRAPHY

Lapalice, Ovide. 'Les organistes et maîtres de musique à Notre-Dame de Montréal,' *BRH*, vol 25, Aug 1919 HK

Le Magicien. One-act opera, with libretto and music by Jean *Vallerand, commissioned by the *JMC to serve as a curtain raiser for Debussy's *L'Enfant prodigue* on one of its tours. The work was inspired by the commedia dell'arte: a magician brings to life the marionettes Colombine and Arlequin, who then refuse to return to their former state. It was premiered 2 Sep 1961 at the *JMC Orford Art Centre by the soprano Louise Gosselin (Colombine), the tenor Claude Gosselin (Arlequin), the baritone Napoléon *Bisson (Magician), and the pianist Colombe *Pelletier, with Raoul *Jobin as director. It was performed more than 100 times during the JMC 1961–2 Canadian tour shared by two casts – the original one and another comprising Cécile *Vallée, Pierre *Boutet, and Jules *Bruyère. The radio premiere, 6 Jun 1962 on the series 'CBC Wednesday Night,' starred Pierrette *Alarie, Léopold *Simoneau, and Napoléon Bisson, with an 18-piece orchestra under Jean-Marie *Beaudet. Beaudet also conducted three performances of the work in August 1962 at the Comédie-Canadienne as part of the *Montreal Festivals. The roles were sung on that occasion by Claire *Gagnier, Jean-Louis Pellerin, and Napoléon Bisson, in a production staged by the composer. *Le Magicien* was recorded in 1967 (CBC SM-42) by Louise *Lebrun, Jean-Louis Pellerin, Gaston *Germain, and a CBC orchestra conducted by Michel *Perrault. GP, SW

MAGILL, Jim (James Creighton). Fiddler, composer, b Northern Ireland 1902, d Toronto 28 Jan 1954. He moved to Toronto in the early 1930s and worked in the CNR's telegraph department for 20 years. A skilful and admired oldtime fiddler, Magill, with his band, the Northern Ramblers, performed for square dances in Toronto and was heard 1946–54 on radio station CFRB. He made many 78s for *London. His most popular pieces were *Saskatoon Breakdown* and *The Crooked Stovepipe*. A folio of his square dance tunes was published by Harry *Jarman in 1952. RGn

---

MAHALEK, Dezsö. Cellist, teacher, b Hungary, ca 1890, d Vancouver 23 Mar 1961. He studied cello in Hungary and was a child prodigy. His teachers included David Popper at the Royal Cons of Budapest, Julius Klengel in Leipzig (where Mahalek became a friend and associate of the celebrated cellist Emanuel Feuermann), and Joseph Malkin. Moving to Canada as a young man, he studied engineering briefly at McGill U, then resumed his musical career. He moved (ca 1912) to Winnipeg, where he played in hotel and theatre orchestras and proved to be a significant teacher. Isaac *Mamott, Lorne *Munroe, Zara *Nelsova, and others were among his pupils. He moved to Vancouver, where he established himself as an ensemble performer and teacher. (Malcolm *Tait was among his Vancouver pupils.) A member 1936–61 (and principal in the 1940s) of the *Vancouver SO, he also played in CBC orchestras and in trios and quartets with Allard de *Ridder, Adolph *Koldofsky, and Arthur *Benjamin.

Mahalek's wife, Caroline Henderson (b Durham, England, ca 1897, d Vancouver 14 Jun 1957), moved to Winnipeg in 1914. She studied voice in Toronto and performed with her husband on early radio broadcasts. She taught singing in Vancouver 1936–57. BNSG

Mahogany Rush. See Frank Marino and Mahogany Rush.

MAILING, Phyllis (Margaret). Mezzo-soprano, b Brantford, Ont, 4 Nov 1929; ARCT voice and piano 1950, hon FRHCM 1978. After studies at the Hamilton Cons (*RHCM) with Bertha *Carey Morrow (voice) and Reginald *Godden (piano) she attended the *RCMT 1952–7, where her teachers were George *Lambert, Weldon *Kilburn, and Aksel *Schiøtz. In 1954 she became a member of the *Toronto Mendelssohn Choir and an original member of the *Festival Singers. In the next three years she sang several small roles with the *COC. She resumed study 1959–60 in Stuttgart, in Vienna with Giselle Rathanser, and in London with Bruce Boyce. Returning to Canada she sang in Toronto 1961–3 and moved to St John's, Nfld, to teach voice and the Orff method 1963–5 privately. She conducted the St John's Madrigal Singers 1964–5 and was heard often in recital on CBC radio from Halifax. In 1965 she was a winner of a Concert Artists Guild Town Hall recital (New York) and sang thereafter throughout North America, France, and accompanied by William *Aide, in the USSR in 1971. She was artist-in-residence 1965–7 and 1970–5 at *Simon Fraser U, where she conducted three choirs. On leave-of-absence 1974–5, she collaborated with Raymond *Pannell in Co-Opera Theatre in Toronto. She began teaching at the *Community Music School of Greater Vancouver in 1975.

Mailing had adjudicated competitions and has served on the boards of *EMC* and the *Vancouver New Music Society (of which she was a founding director and, beginning in 1972, president). Though she does not neglect the standard repertoire, Mailing has specialized in contemporary music, appearing regularly with *NMC, *NOVA MUSIC, the *SMCQ, and the Vancouver New Music Society. She has sung (or sung in) the premieres of many of the works of R. Murray *Schafer (to whom she was married 1960–75), including *Three Contemporaries* (1958), *Kinderlieder* (1963), *Minnelieder* (1965), **Loving* (1966), *Protest and Incarceration* (1967), **Requiems for the Party Girl* (1967), *Dream Passage* (CBC 1969), *Sappho* (1970), *Music for the Morning of the World* (1971), *Patria II* (1972), and *Okeanos* (1972).

Mailing has also sung in premieres of works by *Anhalt (*La Tourangelle*, 1975), *Babiak (*Three Songs of Time*, 1956), *Behrens (*The Lay of Thrym*, 1968), *Coulthard (*The Pines of Emily Carr*, 1969; *Two Songs for Midsummer*, 1970), *Goldberg (*Daedalus*, 1977), *Healey (*Seabird Island*, 1977), *Mather (*Au Château de Pompairain*, 1977), Pannell (*Exiles*, 1973), *Pauk, (*Underneath an Afternoon*, 1977), *Pentland (*News*, 1971; *Sung Songs 4 and 5*, 1972; *Disasters of the Sun*, 1977), *Somers (*The Fool*, 1956), *Traux (*She*, 1974; *Trigon*, 1975), and *Turner (*The Brideship*, 1967).

Mailing has recorded *Requiems for the Party Girl* twice, Somers' *Five Songs for Dark Voice* with the *CBC Vancouver Chamber Orchestra, Schafer's *Minnelieder* with the *Toronto Woodwind Quintet, and works by Ravel, Chausson, and Hindemith with the *Purcell String Quartet. With Christopher *Jordan (guitar) and Derek Bampton (piano) she has recorded songs of Falla and Seiber and Schafer's *Kinderlieder* (1970, CBC SM-141), and with L'Ensemble instrumental de Montréal she has recorded Anhalt's *Foci* (RCI 357). She received the *CMCouncil Medal for outstanding service to Canadian music in 1977.

See also Discography for SMCQ. (BNSG)

MAISTE, Armas or **Art** (b Armas). Pianist, b Tallinn, Estonia, 9 Mar 1929, naturalized Canadian 1965; B MUS (McGill) 1972. After early study at the State Academy of Music in Estonia and six years at the State Academy in Stockholm (where he developed an interest in jazz), Maiste moved to Montreal in 1950. There his career has included nightclub engagements as a soloist and as an accompanist to Sammy Davis Jr, Joyce Hahn (to whom he was married in the mid-1950s), Carmen Miranda, and others and concert, radio, and TV performances in classical, jazz, and variety programs. In 1958 he became the orchestral pianist with the *MSO, a position he has held for over 20 years. Maiste appeared at the 1971 Montreux Jazz Festival, at the 1973 EBU-sponsored festival in Oslo, and as a member of the RCI-sponsored All Star Jazz Sextet at the 1979 Montreux Jazz Festival.

Phyllis Mailing

With bassist Michel *Donato and drummer Keith 'Spike' McKendry he recorded *Pianostyles* (1972, RCI 398), an LP of improvisations in the styles of jazz pianists as diverse as Pete Johnson, Oscar *Peterson, and Bill Evans. Maiste also has accompanied Maynard *Ferguson on records and played for the bebop violinist Willy Girard on the LP *Jazz Violin* (1971, RCI 371). In 1974 he began teaching jazz improvisation at *McGill U, where Steve Holt has been among his pupils. His other recordings include *Bach and the Blues* (1966, Camden CAL 1085) and several collections of pop instrumentals – three LPs on RCA Victor and one each on RCA Camden and CTL. He has performed many contemporary works and has recorded Eldon *Rathburn's *The Metaphoric Ten* as a member of a 10-piece chamber ensemble and Violet *Archer's *Sonata for Horn and Piano* with Pierre Del Vescovo (RCI 412). He is a member of CAPAC.

BIBLIOGRAPHY
Peterson, Maureen. 'Concert pianist is a jazz preacher,' Montreal *Gazette*, 17 Feb 1979 EFr, MM

La Maîtrise du Chapitre de Québec. Quebec City choir school for 50 boys, founded in 1915 at the request of Cardinal Louis-Nazaire Bégin to provide a choir for capitular mass, high mass, and divine services at the Quebec basilica, and to teach boys the art of choral singing. Originally called the Petite Maîtrise Notre-Dame, in 1947 the school became the Petits Chanteurs à la Croix de bois de Québec, following affiliation with the Fédération internationale des manécanteries (International Federation of Choir Schools). The name in use in 1980 was adopted in 1954. The school was directed 1915–19 by Father Placide Gagnon, 1919–53 by Father Joseph Smet, and 1953–4 by Father Fernand Biron. Canon Georges Marchand succeeded Father Biron.

Aged 9 to 12, the boys receive an academic training (according to standards set by the Quebec Catholic School Board) in addition to theory classes, singing classes, and lessons in a choice of piano, violin, or recorder. The school is situated in the old presbytery of St-Patrice Church on St-Stanislas Street. The choir has given numerous concerts and has performed with the *Quebec SO and in stage productions. At the 1962 and 1963 Quebec Music Festivals (renamed *Canadian Music Competitions) it came first in its class. Its repertoire includes polyphonic and Gregorian works, masses, religious and secular songs, Christmas carols, folksongs, and action songs. Radio-Marie has released an LP of religious songs (1965, ND-36521) and a single of songs composed by members of the choir (ND-57203). For several years the Maîtrise has enrolled its members in summer camps in various parts of the province of Quebec (see Summer camps and schools).

See also Choir schools. MB-L

MAJOR, Jean-Paul. Flutist, teacher, b Ville St-Laurent (Montreal) 28 Apr 1929; premiere prix (CMM) 1950. He played in a brass band before entering the *CMM in 1944. There he studied flute with Hervé *Baillargeon, René Le Roy, and Marcel Moyse. Graduating in 1950 he spent another year with Moyse and studied bass with Roger *Charbonneau. He also won an award from Les *Amis de l'art at this time. Some years later (1973) on a bursary from the Quebec government he studied with Jean-Pierre Rampal and Maxence Larrieu at the Académie internationale d'été in Nice.

Major was a member of the *MSO 1950–71 and the *Quebec SO 1955–7, and he has performed often as a soloist at the Nocturnales (late evening concerts) of the *U of Montreal and with the *McGill Chamber Orchestra, the *Masella Woodwind Quintet, the St-Laurent Cegep ensemble, and the *SMCQ Ensemble. For the latter he has performed Berio's *Sequenza I*, Antonio Tauriello's *Serenata II*, and Gerardo Gandini's *Il Concertino*. He taught 1967–70 at the *Cons de Trois-Rivières, 1967–70 at *McGill U and the U of Montreal, 1967–74 at the Vanier and St-Laurent Cegeps, 1970–1 at the Lac-St-Jean Music Camp, and 1973–4 at the *JMC Orford Art Centre. He began teaching in 1970 at the CMM, and by 1978 seven of his pupils had obtained the premier prix, including Marcel St-Jacques and Robert Langevin, both also *Prix d'Europe winners. He participated in the SMCQ's European tour in November 1977.

See also Disographies for Garant and SMCQ (RCI 358). IP-C

'Malbrough s'en va-t-en guerre'. The numerous victories of General John Churchill (1650–1722), Duke of Marlborough, familiarly called 'Malbrough' and a famous figure in English history, inspired this song, which Napoleon liked to hum. It is attributed at times to Mme de Sévigné, at times to unknown soldiers. F.-A.-H. LaRue notes in *Le Foyer canadien*, vol 1, (Quebec City 1863) that it may have been inspired by the 'Chanson du duc de Guise,' which it resembles closely. In French Canada it became one of the most widely sung folksongs. It tells how Malbrough's wife, awaiting his return from battle, is given the news of her husband's death by a page.

In English Canada the melody has been popularized under the title 'For He's a Jolly Good Fellow.' William Parker Greenough reports in *Canadian Folk-Life and Folk-Lore* (New York 1897) that it also is sung to the melody 'We Won't Go Home till Morning'; moreover, he gives a different version, in both text and music, from that which appears in Ernest *Gagnon's *Chansons populaires du Canada* (Quebec 1865). In *Chansons canadiennes* (Montreal 1907, harmonized by P.E.

Prévost, 'words and music by our Canadians') there are two other versions, both different from Gagnon's. In the *Bulletin des recherches historiques* (January 1921) Édouard-Z. *Massicotte mentions the song 'Peper' n'va pas-t-en guerre,' which is sung to the best-known melody, the text alluding to Louis-Joseph Papineau, the mid-19th-century politician. 'Malbrough' has been recorded for LPs by Roger Gravel, Ovila *Légaré, Alan *Mills (Folk FP 708 B), and Les *Cailloux (Cap T 70 000), among others.

BIBLIOGRAPHY

McLennan, William. *Songs of Old Canada* (Montreal 1886)

HP

MALENFANT, Anna. Contralto, teacher, composer (under the name of Marie Lebrun), b Shediac, near Moncton, NB, 16 Oct 1905; hon D MUS (Moncton) 1975. She began her singing career in Moncton in Gilbert & Sullivan's *The Mikado*. A bursary took her in 1924 to Boston to study with Rose Stewart at the New England Cons, thence to Paris to work 1925-6 with Félia Litvinne and to Naples for lessons 1927-9 with Massimiliano Perilli. Returning to North America she sang for a year for radio station WITC, Hartford, Conn, under the name of Louise Malmont. She continued her studies 1930-9 in Montreal with Salvator *Issaurel. She sang at the Windsor Hotel in 1930 and with Ludovic Huot and Lionel *Daunais founded the *Trio lyrique in 1932. Active in public and on radio, she was a soloist 4 Feb 1935 with the *CSM and later appeared with that orchestra in Verdi's *Requiem*, Beethoven's *Ninth Symphony*, Debussy's *La Damoiselle élue*, etc.

With the *Variétés lyriques her first assignment (1937) was the title role in *Carmen*, opposite Raoul *Jobin. The following year she sang Charlotte in *Werther*, with Jacques *Gérard. In 1943 she was Marina in *Boris Godunov*, with Ezio Pinza and artists from the *Metropolitan Opera at the *St-Denis Theatre, and in 1944 she performed at the *Ladies' Morning Musical Club. From then on she devoted her time mainly to recital work and teaching. In 1958 a *Canada Council grant enabled her to go to Rome to perfect her knowledge of vocal technique with Maria Canelli and Tito Schipa. Her voice may be heard in the NFB production *Chantons maintenant*. Among her pupils are Constance *Lambert and Colette Merola. She has composed songs inspired by her native region, some of which were published under a pseudonym (*Huit Chants acadiens de Marie Lebrun*, Archambault 1955) and were recorded by her ca 1958 (RCI 150, with John *Newmark at the piano). She also recorded with the Trio lyrique and with Arthur *Blaquière. The following comment appeared in *La Presse* (31 Oct 1934): 'The vocal authority of this singer, who sings as naturally as others breathe, is generally acknowledged. Her voice, which is of unusual beauty and amplitude, is used with extraordinary accuracy and authority.'

BIBLIOGRAPHY

Tanquay, Yves. 'Anna Malenfant,' *P-T*, Apr 1945
Gingras, Claude. 'Le folklore et la chanson d'Acadie,' Montreal *La Presse*, 24 Jun 1955

GP

MALÉPART, Germaine. Pianist, teacher, b St-Vincent-de-Paul (now Laval), near Montreal, 7 Jul 1898, d Montreal 19 Apr 1963. She began studying piano at 7 with Arthur *Letondal and made her debut at 13 at the *Ladies' Morning Musical Club in Montreal. She won the *Prix d'Europe in 1917 and a scholarship in 1920 from the Ladies' Morning Musical Club, and spent five years in Paris, working at the Paris Cons with Isidor Philipp and Maurice Amour (piano) and Roland Broche (harmony and composition). During that time she gave recitals at Salle Gaveau and Salle Pleyel. Returning to Montreal she performed 21 Nov 1922 at the Ritz-Carlton Hotel. The reviewer for *La Patrie* wrote: 'Mlle Malépart plays with clarity and rhythmic precision and has a beautiful touch, firm phrasing with well-defined contours; in short, she communicates with sincerity and distinction.' She subsequently toured widely in Canada and the USA, gave radio recitals, and was a soloist in 1936 and 1941 with the *CSM. In 1942 she began to concentrate on teaching at the École supérieure de musique in Outremont (now *École Vincent-d'Indy) and at the *CMM, where she gave the first instrumental course. Her many pupils included Lise *Boucher, Pierre *Hétu, Mireille *Lagacé, François *Morel, Renée *Morisset, Claude *Savard, William *Stevens, Gilles *Tremblay, and Ronald *Turini. A hall in the CMM was named for her in 1978.

Germaine Malépart

BIBLIOGRAPHY

Morin, Léo-Pol. 'Mademoiselle Germaine Malépart,' Montreal *La Patrie*, 14 Dec 1926
Gleason-Huguenin, Madeleine. *Portraits de Femmes* (Montreal 1938)
Musiciennes de chez nous

AD

MALEY, S. (Stephen) Roy. Critic, b Brockville, Ont, 10 Mar 1897. He studied piano with his mother, the organist at the Methodist Church in Brockville, then voice with Cyril Rickwood and H. Bramwell Bailey in Ottawa, where he was baritone soloist at St James United Church. He also studied French song in Ottawa with Eugène LeDuc, formerly of the Paris Cons. In 1929 he went to Winnipeg for a thyroid operation which, though medically successful, affected his singing. He began writing for the Winnipeg *Tribune* in 1930, becoming music critic in 1938 and contributing a weekly column after his retirement in 1967. His criticisms were encouraging more often than adjudicative, but their tolerance was valuable in a musical society making the transition from high-level amateurism to the steadily increasing professionalism of the 1950s and 1960s. He is a contributor to *EMC*. Over the years he has collected some 5000 autographs and 500 photographs of famous musicians. JA

Malka and Joso. Folksingers active in the mid-1960s. Malka (b Stein, m Himel, m Cohen; actress-singer, b Kfar-Saba, Israel, 21 Jan 1936) moved to Toronto after her first marriage in 1954. Joso Spralja (b Zadar, Yugoslavia, 23 May 1929), a singer who had studied in Yugoslavia with Antonio Solvaro and Nellie Horvath (later Malka's teacher in Toronto), moved to Toronto in 1961. Malka and Joso met at Yorkville 71, a coffeehouse, where he was singing. After she taught him various songs they made their debut as a team 1 Apr 1963 at the Lord Simcoe Hotel, Toronto. They appeared at the 1963 *Mariposa Folk Festival, continued to sing in Toronto folk and supper clubs and in 1965 toured western Canada and the Yukon for *Overture Concerts. They appeared 26 Nov 1966 at Carnegie Hall, New York, and in 1967 before Princess Margaret in England. Malka and Joso, of whom one writer remarked that their voices were 'as ideally matched as gin and tonic' (Toronto *Telegram*, 'TV Week,' 15-22 Jul 1966), were hosts in 1966 for the CBC TV series 'A Wonderful World of Music.' They made three LPs: *Introducing Malka and Joso* (Cap ST 6108), *Mostly Love Songs* (Cap ST 6129), and *Jewish Songs* (Cap ST 6169). They also appeared on *Folk Songs* (CTL M1049). The LP *Malka et Joso – Autour du monde* (Cap ST 70.007) was compiled from their other Capitol LPs.

After the dissolution of their partnership in 1967 Joso returned as a solo performer to Yorkville 71 (by then known as Act One, Scene One, and later until 1977 as Joso's Coffee House). Malka, usually accompanied by the guitarist Kevin Knelman, also continued to perform in coffeehouses (and briefly, 1968-9, as a nightclub singer) into the early 1970s. Her second career, as a freelance announcer-interviewer, began in 1969, when she was co-host for the CBC radio program 'Holiday.' In the mid-1970s she contributed interviews with Pablo Casals, Leonard *Cohen, Joni *Mitchell, and others to such radio series as 'Concern' and 'The Entertainers.' Her four-part program 'A Bite of the Big Apple' (1977) for 'The Entertainers' documented the performance history of **Kronberg: 1582* on Broadway and won an ACTRA Award in 1978 in the radio documentary category.

BIBLIOGRAPHY

Franklin, Stephen. 'Two at the top,' *Weekend Magazine*, 15 Jan 1966
'The remaking of Malka,' *Star Weekly*, 25 May 1968
Holtz, Patricia. 'Malka's mission,' *The Canadian*, 12 Feb 1977
Livingstone, David. 'The Malka mystique,' *Toronto Star, The City*, 20 May 1979

(LHv)

MALKIN, (Elizabeth) Ursula. Pianist, teacher, b Vancouver, 6 Jun 1908; ATCM 1928, B MUS (British Columbia) 1964. The daughter of Marion Malkin, for whom the *Malkin Bowl is named, she studied piano with Doris Duke, Della Johnston, and Jan *Cherniavsky in Vancouver, with Berta Jahn-Beer in Vienna 1930-2 and Boston in 1940, and with Alberto *Guerrero in Toronto. Her first major performance (1930), Beethoven's *Concerto No. 4* with the *Vancouver SO, was followed by concerts throughout British Columbia and appearances and broadcasts 1937-8 in Australia. In Vancouver she played chamber music with Allard de *Ridder and the visiting *Hart House String Quartet, broadcast for the CBC, and was frequently a soloist (until 1954) with the VSO. She began teaching in 1945, working towards the establishment of a music department at the *U of British Columbia (1959), and helped found the *Community Music School of Greater Vancouver (1969). She has been music committee chairman 1955-8 of Vancouver's *Community Arts Council and president 1956-8 of the Vancouver Junior Symphony. BNSG

The Malkin Bowl (Marion Malkin Memorial Bowl). Outdoor theatre built in 1934 in Stanley Park, Vancouver, as a two-thirds-size replica of the Hollywood Bowl. W.H. Malkin, a former mayor, endowed it in memory of his wife. Designed as a band and orchestra shell, it opened 8 Jul 1934 with a performance by the *Vancouver

SO. It became the home of *TUTS in 1949. In 1952 the stage was modified to its present dimensions, 12.3 m wide at the front, 7.8 m wide at the rear, 13.8 m deep, 6.18 m high at the centre, and 5.1 m high at the sides. The surrounding grounds have accommodated up to 12,000 people. DD

Malta. The majority of Maltese in Canada arrived after World War II, though a few immigrated prior to 1930. Gaetano Francesco Farrugia settled in Halifax and achieved local recognition for his *Agnes Waltzes* during the mid-19th century. Some years later (1870–1) the Canadian-born soprano Emma *Albani spent five months in Malta, singing in productions of *L'Africaine, The Barber of Seville, Lucia di Lammermoor, Robert le Diable*, and a new opera buffa, Carlo Romani's *Il Mantello*, at the Royal Opera House in Valetta. News of Albani's success in Malta led to her Covent Garden engagement in 1871.

In 1979 over 40,000 Maltese were living in Canada, approximately 25,000 of these in Toronto. Smaller communities were established elsewhere in Ontario (Guelph, Hamilton, London, Oshawa, St Thomas, Windsor) and in Montreal, Vancouver and Winnipeg. Because Malta was a British Crown colony until 1962, many Maltese are fluent in English, and this has facilitated their integration into Canadian society. No necessity appears to have been felt for the forming of Maltese national associations, although there are local organizations in some communities. The first Maltese church in Canada was that of St Paul the Apostle (Roman Catholic), founded in Toronto in 1931 with assistance from the Maltese Canadian Society of Toronto, the oldest Maltese organization in North America.

Maltese music is heard at celebrations for Republic Day (13 December), at traditional Imnarja Carnival celebrations, and for the historic national day (8 September). Reflecting the popularity of village bands in the homeland, Malta Band Clubs of 25 or more members have been organized in Maltese-Canadian communities. Toronto's 60-musician Malta Band Club, conducted by Paul Gaucci, celebrated its ninth anniversary in 1980. Several organizations have sponsored visits by Maltese popular singers, as well as entertainment by local groups at concerts and dances. A typical Maltese folk festival, 'Lejla Maltija' (Maltese Evening), held in Toronto in June 1978, featured the folksingers Michael Abela and Michael Cutajar from Malta, the traditional folksinger and improviser Karmnu Xuerab from Detroit, and a folk dance group from Whitby, Ont. Popular Maltese folk dances are 'il-Maltija,' a national country dance, and the 'parata,' which is performed with wooden sticks. Viva Malta, a group of Maltese musicians who play traditional instruments, performed at the Commonwealth games in Edmonton in 1978. The first Maltese radio program in North America originated in Windsor, Ont, in 1954. The Maltese community in Toronto is served by 'Wirt Malta' or 'Maltese Heritage' on CHIN radio and by other community programs on cable TV which feature both Maltese and Maltese-Canadian performers.

The Maltese composer and accordionist Charles *Camilleri lived in Canada 1959–65 and 1977–9. In 1959 George Bonavia (editor of *Kaleidoscope Canada*, published by the Dept of Employment and Immigration) donated to the Windsor Public Library a collection of Maltese books and of recordings of Maltese folksongs and other music. In 1964 Folkways issued the LP *Folk Songs and Music From Malta* (FM 4047) extracted from these recordings, with notes by Bonavia. (LRH)

MAMOTT, Isaac. Cellist, teacher, b Lutzk, Ukraine, 25 Apr 1907, naturalized Canadian 1934, d Toronto 5 Apr 1964. Taken to Winnipeg at six, he had lessons there in violin and piano and at 10 began to study the cello with Dezsö *Mahalek. He made his radio debut in 1922. After playing for a time in a quartet with the violinists Joseph Shadwick and John Sutter and the violist Eugene Hudson, he founded the Tudor String Quartet (Eugene Hudson, then Valberg Leland and Joseph Sera, violins, Michael Barten, viola), which was heard for 10 years on CBC Winnipeg. He also had a solo program on radio. In 1940 he moved to Toronto, where he played 1941–3 and was principal cello 1943–50 with the *TSO and was co-founder and a member 1943–52 of the *Parlow String Quartet (although a heart condition prevented his full participation in the later years). He also served 1952–64 as principal cello of the *CBC SO and was a member (with Albert *Pratz and Glenn *Gould) of the Festival Trio, which performed at the first (1953) *Stratford Festival, and of the Festival Orchestra there. He was a member of Heinz *Unger's York Concert Society Orchestra. He gave the premiere, 15 Oct 1950, of *Weinzweig's sonata *Israel* with Leo *Barkin at the piano.

Mamott taught in Winnipeg and 1942–64 at the *RCMT; his pupils included William Finlay (TS), James Hunter (*Vancouver SO), Ron Laurie (TS), and Rowland *Pack. Mamott died of a heart attack during a performance with the CBC SO of Richard Strauss' *Also sprach Zarathustra*, in which he had played several solos.

Mandala (Five Rogues, Rogues, Bush). Leading Canadian rhythm and blues band of the 1960s. It was formed in 1964 in Toronto by the guitarist Dom *Troiano, the singer George Olliver, the bass guitarist Don Elliott, the organist Josef Chirowski, and the drummer Whitey (Pentii) Glann. The Rogues were the house band 1964–5 at the Toronto rhythm and blues club The Blue Note, where they accompanied Stevie Wonder, the Supremes, and other US stars. For three months in 1965 they worked with David *Clayton-Thomas. Renamed Mandala in 1966, the band played in an aggressive, rough-edged style which, highlighted by Olliver's exaggerated showmanship, often generated hysteria. After the band's first US appearances, in 1966, Olliver and Chirowski were replaced by Roy Kenner (formerly of the Toronto band R.K. and the Associates) and Hugh O'Sullivan. The following year (1967–8) was spent in clubs throughout the USA. Returning to Toronto Mandala gave its last performance 1 Jun 1969 at The Hawk's Nest. The band's recordings included the singles 'Opportunity' (1967) and 'Love-itis' (1968) and the LP *Soul Crusade* (1968, Atlantic SD 8184). In 1970 in Arizona Troiano, Kenner, Glann, and the bass guitarist Prakash John (who had replaced Elliott in Mandala) formed the jazz-influenced rock band Bush. After one critically acclaimed LP (*Bush*, 1970, RCA DS-50086) and some touring in the USA and Canada, the group disbanded. Kenner then sang with the US rock groups The James Gang and Law before rejoining Troiano in 1978, while Glann and Prakash became one of the leading rhythm sections in rock, recording and touring with the US stars Lou Reed and Alice Cooper in the mid-1970s.

BIBLIOGRAPHY

Yorke, Ritchie. 'Bush,' *Axes, Chops & Hot Licks* (Edmonton 1971) MM

Maneige. Pop group formed in Montreal in the fall of 1972 by Alain Bergeron (flute, saxophone, piano), Jérôme Langlois (clarinet, piano, organ), Vincent Langlois (percussion, piano), Yves Léonard (electric bass, double-bass), Paul Picard (percussion), and Gilles Schetagne (drums, percussion), all musicians who studied at the *École Vincent-d'Indy and the *CMM. In 1975 Denis Lapierre (electric and acoustic guitar) joined the group, which took part that year in the *St-Jean-Baptiste celebrations on Mount Royal. The following year Maneige gave concerts at the *PDA, the Outremont Cinema in Montreal, and the Cartier Cinema in Quebec City and appeared in New Brunswick. The group also appeared at the boîte à chansons L'Évêché of the Hotel Nelson in old Montreal in 1975 and 1977, toured in Quebec in 1976, 1978, and 1979, and performed in 20 cities across Canada in 1978. It composed and recorded the theme song of the CBC radio program 'Temps présent' in 1978. The group made the LPs *Maneige* (1974, Harvest St 70035), *Les Porches* (1975, Harvest St 6438), *Maneige. Ni vent ... ni nouvelle* (1976, Poly 2424 143), *Libre Service* (1978, Poly 2424 176), and *Composite* (1980, Poly 2424 206).

Often termed scholarly, classical, and even obscure in its early days, Maneige moved towards a more popular group sound after the departure of Jérôme Langlois in 1976. While keeping its original direction and spirit of musical experiment, the group has achieved a synthesis which involves frequent changes of approach and style. It tackles genres as different as jazz, rock, blues, folk, classical, and electronic music, which makes it difficult to classify. The style has two equally important basic aspects: the sound itself and the image suggested or engendered by the music. All the musicians are composers and members of CAPAC.

BIBLIOGRAPHY

L'Heureux, Christine. 'Magique et savant Maneige,' Montreal *Le Devoir*, 30 Jan 1976

Beaulieu, Pierre. 'Maneige; une nouvelle musique, plus sensible,' Montreal *La Presse*, 16 Mar 1977

'Maneige: an eight-year formula,' *CanComp*, 150, Apr 1980 ST

MANIATES, (Maria) Rika. Musicologist, b Toronto 30 Mar 1937; ARCT 1958, BA (Toronto) 1960, MA (Columbia) 1962, PH D (Columbia) 1965. She studied piano 1940–58 with Margaret Butler and Marian *Grudeff at the *RCMT and musicology subsequently with Harvey Olnick at the *U of Toronto and with Paul Henry Lang, Edward Lippman, and Walter Wiora at Columbia U. During her student years she was the recipient of many scholarships and awards, including the Rockefeller Grant in Musicology for 1964–5. She was organist-choirmaster 1953–7 at St George's Greek Orthodox Church in Toronto. While at Columbia U she sang and played harpsichord and recorder with the Collegium Musicum. She joined the musicology department of the Faculty of Music, U of Toronto, in 1965 and served 1973–8 as chairman of the department of history and literature. She has held cross-appointments to U of Toronto graduate programs in medieval studies, renaissance studies, and drama, and was visiting professor (summers 1967 and 1976) at Columbia U. She was director 1965–9 of the U of Toronto's Hortus Musicus Torontonensis, a student early-music ensemble with which she appeared in the 1969 CBC TV special 'Ars Nova Musica.'

A specialist in the philosophy of music and music of the renaissance, Maniates has contributed numerous articles to *Acta musicologica*, the *Journal of the American Musicological Society, the Musical Quarterly*, and *The New Grove Dictionary* and was associate editor 1963–5 of *Current Musicology* and 1970–2 of the *Toronto Renaissance and Reformation Bulletin*. Maniates has a particular interest in the concept of mannerism in music (see Writings) and has delivered papers on that and other subjects at symposia in Canada and the USA. She edited five of Nicholas Gombert's works for the Waterloo Choral Art Series in 1963. She has been a board member of the American Musicological Society and the International Musicological Society.

WRITINGS

'The sacred music of Nicolas Gombert,' *CMJ*, vol 6, Winter 1962
'Combinative techniques in Franco-Flemish polyphony: a study of mannerism in music 1450–1530,' PH D thesis, Columbia 1965
'Mannerist composition in Franco-Flemish polyphony,' *MQ*, vol 52, Jan 1966
'Quodlibet revisum,' *Acta musicologica*, vol 38, Apr–Dec 1966
'Musical treatises in the renaissance,' *Toronto Renaissance and Reformation Bulletin*, vol 3, Jun 1967
'The D minor symphony of Robert Schumann,' *Festschrift Walter Wiora* (Kassel 1967)
'Musical form: product and process,' *Current Musicology*, vol 6, no. 6, 1968
'*Sonate, que me veux-tu?* The enigma of French musical aesthetics in the 18th century,' *Current Musicology*, vol 9, no. 9, 1970
'Combinative chansons in the Dijon chansonnier,' *J of the American Musicological Soc*, vol 23, Summer 1970
'Musical mannerism: effeteness or virility?' *MQ*, vol 57, Apr 1971
'Vicentino's *Incerta et occulta scientia* reexamined,' *J of the American Musicological Soc*, vol 28, Summer 1975
'Combinative chansons in the Escorial Chansonnier,' *Musica disciplina*, vol 29, 1975
'*Maniera*: the central issue in the 16th-century musical controversy,' *CAUSM J*, vol 7, 1977
Mannerism in Italian Music and Culture 1530–1630 (Chapel Hill, NC 1979)
'Musical symbolism,' *The World of Music*, vol 21, 1979

(FH, NM)

Manitoba Arts Council. Independent agency created by the Manitoba government in 1965 to encourage and promote in the province the study, enjoyment, production, and performance of works in the arts. The council's 12 members, appointed for three-year terms by Manitoba's governor-in-council, serve without pay. While the council reports annually to the minister of cultural affairs and historical resources (Norma L. Price in 1980), it has been free to establish its own policies and programs. The chairman in 1980 was J.D. Benson; the executive director, who was in charge of the council's salaried administrative staff, was E.W. Stigant. From monies allocated annually by the Manitoba government with the approval of Cabinet, and by Western Lottery-Manitoba Distributor Inc, the council has made grants 1 / to non-profit musical organizations to assist with their operations, 2 / for commissioning, publishing, and preparing for performance works by Manitoba composers, and 3 / for a variety of special projects. It also has sponsored artists-in-the-schools and artists-in-the-community programs. The council has been advised on grant applications by its own subcommittees on dance and theatre, music and opera, visual arts and literature, and interdisciplinary arts projects. Organizations which have received the council's support include the Associated Manitoba Festivals, the *CBC National Radio Competition for Young Composers, the International Music Camp, the *Manitoba Chamber Orchestra, the *Manitoba Opera Assn, the *Men's Music Club of Winnipeg, Music Inter Alia, the *NYO, the S.C. *Eckhardt-Gramatté Competition, the Southern Manitoba Concert Assn, the *Western Board of Music, and the *Winnipeg SO.

In the 1977–8 fiscal year the council awarded over $150,000 to musical endeavours in the province. In 1979, in conjunction with the Touring Office of the *Canada Council, it co-sponsored the first Contact Manitoba, a performing arts gathering at Winnipeg featuring workshops, exhibits, and, in particular, a variety of auditions for the benefit of performers, agents, and prospective employers. The council publishes an annual report.

Manitoba Centennial Concert Hall. Located on Main St, Winnipeg, and owned and operated by the province. It was designed as part of the Manitoba Centennial Centre by the architectural firms Green Blankstein Russell Associates, Moody Moore and Partners, and Smith Carter Searle Associates and the acoustical engineers Russell Johnson Associates. It opened 27 Mar 1968 with a performance by the *Winnipeg SO. With a proscenium stage 24 m wide and 12 m deep, a hydraulic orchestra pit, and 2263 seats, it has been acclaimed for its excellent acoustics. It is the home of the Winnipeg SO, the Royal Winnipeg Ballet, and the *Manitoba Opera Association. CC

Manitoba Chamber Orchestra. Founded in 1972 in Winnipeg and conducted by Ruben *Gurevich, the MCO employs 7 to 35 players drawn largely from the *Winnipeg SO. It has given an average of four concerts each season at the Art Gallery, Westminster United Church, or Young United Church. Its repertoire ranges from the baroque to the contemporary. Arthur *Polson's *Concerto* for flute, strings, and percussion (1974) and *Concerto* for oboe, piano and, strings (1978) were commissioned by the orchestra. Guest artists have included the *Festival Singers, Maureen *Forrester, Ivan Moravec, Walter *Prystawski, and Steven *Staryk.

BIBLIOGRAPHY

Zanger, Pat. 'Chamber orchestra has new zest for life,' *Winnipeg Free Press*, 31 Jul 1978

Manitoba Music Competition Festival. Founded in Winnipeg in 1918 by the Men's Musical Club (*Men's Music Club), which has continued to organize and sponsor it annually. The first festival took place 13–16 May 1919 in the Central Congregational Church. Some 2500 individuals took part. In later years the increase in the number of solo performers and of classes open to them necessitated an extension to two weeks, with several halls in simultaneous use for daytime classes and evening finals in the *Winnipeg Auditorium. In 1979 there were 2079 entries representing some 30,000 individuals.

In 1922 the festival became the first Canadian competition to affiliate with the Federation of British Music Festivals. Adjudicators for the first two years had been H.A. *Fricker of Toronto and Tertius Noble of New York. In 1923 Harry Plunket Greene and Granville Bantock were among the judges, initiating what was to become a tradition of employing British adjudicators. Among these were Sir Thomas Armstrong, Sir Edward Bairstow, Ronald Biggs, Sir William Glock, Maurice Jacobson, Sir Hugh Roberton, Gordon Slater, and Frederic Staton. Leonard *Isaacs, who later became the director of the School of Music, *U of Manitoba, was another. In later years Canadians were used as well, among them Martin *Boundy, Lloyd *Bradshaw, Clayton *Hare, Filmer *Hubble, Joseph *Macerollo, Sir Ernest *MacMillan, J. Campbell *McInnes, Donald McKellar, A.S. *Vogt, Frank *Welsman, and Gladys *Whitehead.

The festival syllabus sets out competitions at many levels, for solo voice, duets, trios, and choirs; for solo instruments, chamber groups, bands, and orchestras; and for speech arts. There were 517 categories or classes in the 1979 competition. Numerous trophies are awarded, the major ones being the Rose Bowl, established in 1924 and competed for by winners of senior vocal classes, and the Aikins Memorial Trophy, established in 1930 and competed for by winners of senior instrumental classes. Choral classes have been a particular pride of the festival, and the competition by the leading church, high-school, Mennonite, Ukrainian, and Polish choirs for the Lord Tweedsmuir Memorial Trophy, established in 1930 for winners of adult choir classes, vies annually for public favour with the Rose Bowl and Aikins trophy. Its most persistent winner – 14 times between 1941 and 1962 – was the St Stephen's Broadway Church Choir, conducted for many of those years by Filmer Hubble. Beginning in 1978, financial assistance for study purposes was made available in connection with some festival trophies.

Winners of the Rose Bowl have included Devina Bailey (*Duggan), Myfanwy Evans, Cora Doig James, Helly (Sapinski) *Jedig, Ursula Koons Dahlgren, Gladys *Kriese-Caporale, Wallace Lewis, Nona Mari, Morley Margolis (*Meredith), John *Martens, Maxine Miller, Mary *Morrison, Alvin Reimer, Phyllis *Cooke Thomson, Albert Whiteman, and J. Roberto Wood. Winners of the Aikins trophy have included Marvin Johnson, Ailsa Lawson, Edward *Lincoln, Gilbert *Munroe, Sheila *Munroe, Pearl Palmason, Ross *Pratt, Joyce Redekop-Fink, Victor Schultz, Winifred Scott *Wood, Freda *Trepel (Kaufmann), and Eric *Wilson.

The festival was the subject of a 1945 NFB film, *Listen to the Prairies*. It is an affiliate of the *Associated Manitoba Festivals and the *FCMF.

NM

Manitoba Music Educators Association (MMEA) / **L'Association Manitobaine des Éducateurs de Musique** (AMEM). Founded 10 Oct 1959 in Winnipeg with 36 members drawn from among school and university teachers to provide a liaison among music-education groups in Manitoba and between Manitoba groups and those elsewhere in Canada, and to assist in curriculum revision, teacher training, and music-education research. Presidents have been May McInnes 1959–60, Lorne *Watson 1960–1, Herbert Belyea 1961–2, Colin Walley 1962–3, Frances Wickberg 1963–5, Beth *Douglas 1965–7, Watson 1967–9, Fred Merrett 1969–71, Jake Redekopp 1971–3, Winnifred Voigts 1973–5, Derek Morphy 1975–7, and Judy Kruger 1977–9. Kruger was succeeded by Betty Friesen. *The Manitoba Music Educator Newsletter* was begun in 1959 and appeared annually until 1974. *The Manitoba Music Educator* was begun in 1960 and appeared three times a year until 1974. In 1974 the newsletter ceased, and *The Manitoba Music Educator* became a quarterly.

The MMEA sponsors regular provincial and regional conferences. By 1977 membership had reached about 350, with chapters in Brandon and Winnipeg (River East). Though not affiliated with the CMEA, the MMEA was invited to be host for the 1981 national convention in Winnipeg.

The Manitoba Opera Association. Formed in Winnipeg in 1969 by A. Kerr Twaddle and 13 others to produce grand opera. A membership drive was co-ordinated with an operatic concert (1969) by the *Winnipeg SO featuring Jon *Vickers and Teresa *Stratas. Incorporated in 1970, its first venture was the sponsorship of the Winnipeg performance of the *COC's touring production of *Orpheus in the Underworld*. This was followed by a concert version (1972) of *Il Trovatore* and a staged

A scene from a Manitoba Opera Association production of *Die Fledermaus*

production (1973) of *Madama Butterfly* directed by Irving *Guttman and conducted by Piero Gamba. By 1975 the association was offering three operas a year, with a budget which had leapt from $28,000 in 1972 to $260,000 made up of box office revenue, private donations, and grants from the city of Winnipeg, the *Manitoba Arts Council and the *Canada Council. Productions have included *Rigoletto* (1975), *Manon Lescaut* (1976), *The Masked Ball* (1977), *Lucia di Lammermoor* (1977), *The Flying Dutchman* (1979), and *Nabucco* (1981).

Of 24 operas presented 1972–81, Irving Guttman directed 16, Herman *Geiger-Torel 2, James Lucas 3, and Steven Thomas, Constance *Fisher, and Barbara Karp each one. Ernesto *Barbini (appointed music director in 1974) has conducted 7, Piero Gamba 3, Imre Pallo 5, Alfredo Silipigni and Anton Guadagno 2 each, and Bryan Balkwill, Victor *Feldbrill, Henry Holt, John Mauceri, and Andrew Meltzer each one. Singers in leading roles have included Peter *Barcza, Victor *Braun, Barbara *Collier, Judith *Forst, Alexander *Gray, Marina Krilovici, Ermanno *Mauro, Joan *Patenaude, Louis *Quilico, and Heather *Thomson. Supporting roles and chorus are cast locally. The noted baritone Norman *Mittelmann, a native of Winnipeg, returned to sing the Count di Luna in the 1979 producation of *Il Trovatore*. The Winnipeg SO accompanies performances, and dancers and scholarship students of the Royal Winnipeg Ballet are engaged for ballet scenes. The association is governed by a board of volunteer directors and two permanent professional directors: administrative and artistic.

BIBLIOGRAPHY
Edinborough, Arnold. 'Winnipeg really has something to sing about: its opera,' *Financial Post*, 9 May 1975

Manitoba Registered Music Teachers' Association. Founded in 1919 as the Winnipeg Music Teachers' Assn by some 80 teachers brought together by Eva *Clare and Mrs R.D. Fletcher, who then was the president of the Women's Musical Club of Winnipeg. Rhys Thomas was elected the first president. Among the aims was the introduction of an optional credit for music study in high school – whether the study was taken at the school or, as more often was the case, privately. The plan was adopted by the provincial department of education in 1920, and the association prepared a syllabus and established an examining board. About 125 candidates were examined the first year. The number had increased to 2000 annually by the mid-1970s.

In 1921 the association took the name Manitoba Provincial Music Teachers' Assn, with representation in 16 cities throughout the province. A founding member-body (1935) of the *CFMTA, it changed its own name to the MRMTA in 1939 and had branches in Winnipeg, Brandon, and Portage la Prairie. It was responsible for the institution of licentiate (LMM) and associate (AMM) diplomas at the *U of Manitoba in 1935. The MRMTA has held workshops and master classes to encourage its members in systematic preparation for the professional of teaching. It has sponsored concerts and local competitions. In 1948 the Winnipeg branch established a scholarship contest to assist talented performers and to provide them with the opportunity to play in public. The first winners (1949) were the pianist Sydney *Young (McInnis) and the soprano Sara Udow. Later winners (annually two 1949–58 and four or more thereafter) include: Gladys *Kriese-Caporale (1951), Belva Boroditsky (1952), Phyllis *Cooke Thomson (1956), Victor *Martens (1958), Helly *Jedig Sapinsky (1959), Nona Mari (1960), Carl *Duggan (1960), Diedre *Irons (1962), Heather Ireland (1965), Gwen *Thompson (1965), Karen Redekopp (1968, 1969), Jane Vasey (1969, 1970), and Heather Wilberforce (1971, 1972, 1974).

MRMTA presidents have been Rhys Thomas 1919–20, Eva Clare 1920–1, R. *Watkin Mills 1921–2, Mary L. Robertson 1922–3, Burton *Kurth 1923–4, W. George Rutherford 1924–5, 1941–4, Cecilia *Waterhouse 1925–7, Wilfred Layton 1927–9, Ronald *Gibson 1929–31, Louise McDowell 1931–3, Myrtle N. Ruttan 1933–5, Russell *Standing 1935–6, 1948–50, W.L. Wright 1936–8, Beryl Ferguson 1938–9, Ada Eames 1939–41, Leonard *Heaton 1944–8, Violet Isfeld 1950–2, Lorne *Watson 1952–3, Doris Fox 1953–5, Nina *Dempsey 1955–7, Beth Cooil 1957–9, Frances Wickberg 1959–61, Thelma *Wilson 1961–3, Irene Rowlin 1963–5, Ilene Rogers 1965–7, Edith Motley 1967–9, Helen Weare 1969–71, Phyllis *Holtby 1971–4, Margaret Leese 1974–6, and Shirley McCreedy 1976–8. Jean *Broadfoot succeeded McCreedy.

BIBLIOGRAPHY
Rowlin, Irene. 'Manitoba Registered Music Teachers' Association Inc. historical resumé 1919–1978,' CFMTA *Newsletter*, Fall 1978 (IR)

Manitoba University Consort. Founded as the Christine Mather Consort in Winnipeg in 1963, by Christine *Mather and Peggie *Sampson, to perform music written between 1100 and 1800. In 1964 it presented its first concert and changed its name to the Manitoba University Consort. It also was known as the Manitoba Consort. In addition to Sampson (gamba) and Mather (winds, lute, psaltery), the original members included Victor *Martens (tenor), Phyllis *Cooke Thomson (soprano), Paul Palmer (winds), Harold Vogt (treble viol), and Joyce Redekop-Penner – later Redekop-Fink – (harpsichord). Subsequent members included Douglas *Bodle and Lawrence Ritchie (harpsichord and portative organ), Heather Ireland (mezzo-soprano), and Sylvia McDonald (soprano).

Mather and Sampson were responsible for the collection and transcription of music for the group. Its repertoire included works by Machaut, Dufay, Dowland, Praetorius, Buxtehude, Rameau, Telemann, and Bach. The consort assembled one of the largest and most comprehensive collections of historical instruments in Canada – some 5 viols, 30 wind instruments, lute, portative organ, psaltery, rebec, vielle, bells, and percussion, all replicas. Despite its relatively short existence, the ensemble gained an international reputation through its appearances in western Canada (1965), England (1966, when it appeared by invitation at the 1966 Aldeburgh Festival, and 1968), California (1967), Germany, and Switzerland (1968). It also performed in Montreal in the Canadian government pavilion at *Expo 67 and at the *NAC during the centre's inaugural ceremonies in 1969. The group was heard regularly over CBC radio and, while in Europe, broadcast over the BBC, Radio Suisse romande, and Hessischer Rundfunk. It disbanded in 1970 and most of its instruments were sold to the *U of Victoria.

DISCOGRAPHY
Adam de la Halle – Machaut – Landini – et al. Ca 1966. CBC SM-17
Donato – Praetorius – Buxtehude – et al. 1967. CBC Expo 8
Jenkins – Schütz – Luzzaschi – et al. 1968. CBC SM-66
Telemann – Marais – Praetorius. 1969. CBC SM-130 (LW)

MANLEY, (John) Gordon. Pianist, b Vancouver 1 Aug 1915, d New York, 31 Dec 1957. His early training in Vancouver was followed by study in New York with Sigismund Stojowski, at the Mannes School, and with Egon Petri. In 1944, after the first of three Town Hall appearances, he started a two-year tour of the USA as a soloist and as accompanist for Marjorie Lawrence. From 1943 to 1949 he performed frequently in Toronto and Montreal, in public concert and on the CBC. He was often a guest on Milton Cross's 'Piano Playhouse' on CBS radio and between 1949 and 1951 made two European concert tours and gave two recitals at Carnegie Hall, all to critical acclaim. Failing health forced him to abandon his concert career in the mid-1950s and he managed the Fargo Travel Agency in New York City until his death. His scrapbooks are deposited at the *NL of C. WL

MANN, Leslie (Douglas). Composer, clarinetist, b Edmonton 13 Aug 1923, d Balmoral, Man, 7 Dec 1977. Though he took lessons in clarinet at 13 and in composition at 15, he was largely self-taught. He became principal clarinet of the *CBC Winnipeg Orchestra in 1958 and of the *Winnipeg SO in 1960. He led the Winnipeg Woodwind Quintette and was a member 1956–66 of the Dirk Keetbaas Players. Leaving the WSO in 1971 he devoted increasing time to composition and received a number of CBC commissions. The works he wrote after 1970 show an individual and undoctrinaire mind, a grasp of form, and a predilection for counterpoint. His music thus shows a nearer relationship to Alan Hovhaness, Robert Simpson, Samuel Barber, and, in an earlier generation, Sibelius than to the descendants of Schoenberg and Webern. He was a member of the *CLComp, and an associate of the *CMCentre, and the musical rights of his estate are administered by CAPAC.

SELECTED COMPOSITIONS
Five Improvisations for Flute and Piano. 1954. CMCentre. RCI 215/RCA CCS 1009 (*Keetbaas)
Sonata, Op 17. 1962. Va (cl), pf. CMCentre. RCI 459 (*Reiner pf)

My Master Hath a Garden, cantata (Elizabethan poets). 1963. Sop, orch. CMCentre
The Donkey's Tale, chamb opera (fairy tale). 1971. Sop, mezzo, ten, bar, orch. Ms
Concerto Grosso for Chamber Orchestra. 1972. CMCentre
Meditations on a Chorale. 1972. Str orch. CMCentre
3 *Symphonies*. (1973–4). CMCentre. (No. 1) CBC SM-281 (*CBC Wpg O)
Weep You No More Sad Fountains. (Elizabethan poems). 1974. V, chamb orch. CMCentre
String Quartet, Op 38. 1975. CMCentre
Suite for Saxophone Solo. 1976. CMCentre
Other works for orch, including concerti for cl (1970), bn (1971), and fl (1974). Also sonatas for vc and pf (1953) and solo vn (1974); some suites for solo instr; works for ww quin; 4 works for pf and 4 song cycles. All CMCentre

BIBLIOGRAPHY

Hambleton, Ronald. 'Manitoba composers: a collective voice,' *CanComp*, 52, Sep 1970
Contemporary Canadian Composers / Compositeurs canadiens contemporains (LI)

MANNING, Ed. See Moogk, Edward B.

MANNY, Gilles. Pianist, teacher, administrator, b Montauban, near Trois-Rivières, Que, 6 Aug 1929; premier prix piano (CMM) 1950. He studied at the *CMM with Yvonne *Hubert (piano) and Jean *Papineau-Couture (harmony), receiving the *Prix Archambault in 1948. On a scholarship from the Quebec government, he completed his training 1952–8 in Paris with Antoine *Reboulot. He has been heard in many CBC and ORTF broadcasts and has performed frequently in Montreal, notably at the U of Montreal Nocturnales (late evening concerts) and with the *SMCQ. Though his repertoire spans all periods he is much in demand for performances of 20th-century music. He was the pianist in Messiaen's *Turangalîla Symphonie* with the ORTF Orchestra at *PDA in September 1967 and in the same composer's *Les Oiseaux exotiques* (1969) and Berg's *Kammerkonzert* (1970) for the SMCQ. His recordings of André *Prévost's *Sonata* and Papineau-Couture's *Concerto* won prizes at the Festival du disque in Montreal, in 1965 and 1969 respectively. In 1967 Manny became artist-in-residence and teacher at the *U of Montreal and in 1968 he was appointed vice-dean of music, in which capacity he collaborated on research and inquiries into the teaching of the arts in Quebec. He was Papineau-Couture's successor, 1973–9, as dean. William *Tritt was among his pupils.

DISCOGRAPHY

Papineau-Couture *Concerto* for piano. CBC Mtl orch, A. Brott cond. 1967. RCI 235/RCA CCS-1029
Prévost *Sonata*. Verdon vn. 1964. Bar JAS-19002

BIBLIOGRAPHY

Paul, Andrée. 'L'interprétation de la musique contemporaine,' *Musiques du Kébèk*, ed Raoul Duguay (Montreal 1971) (PR)

MANNY, Louise (Elizabeth). Collector, b Gilead, Me, 1890, d Newcastle, NB, 17 Aug 1970; hon LL D (St Thomas College, Chatham) 1961, hon LL D (New Brunswick) 1961. Taken to New Brunswick at three she lived in Newcastle on the Miramichi River and developed an interest in the local history, on which she wrote and broadcast extensively. She was commissioned in 1947 by Lord Beaverbrook to collect and record the songs of the Miramichi lumbermen. Continuing to collect after the commission had been completed, she presented the songs in weekly broadcasts 1947–68 on CKMR radio, Newcastle. She founded the *Miramichi Folk Festival and directed it 1958–69. Some of the songs she collected may be heard on the LP *Folksongs of the Miramichi* (1962, Folk FM 4053). Others are published in *Songs of Miramichi* (Fredericton 1968, 101 songs compiled, edited, and annotated by Manny and James Reginald Wilson). In 1967 she received the Woman of the Century medal from the National Council of Jewish Women of Canada, and in 1969 her name was given to a mountain – Mount Manny – in New Brunswick's Historians' Range.

WRITINGS

'Larry Gorman – Miramichi balladist,' *Maritime Advocate and Busy East*, vol 40, Oct 1949
'New Brunswick: collecting songs of Canadian lumber woods and ballads,' *International Musician*, vol 52, Dec 1953

BIBLIOGRAPHY

Daye, Vera L. 'Songs for Beaverbrook,' *SatN*, 18 Oct 1949 HC

The *Cobourg Waltz*, on the last page of the Allen Ash manuscript book

Manuscript books (Early 19th century). Until the mid-19th century, when dealers established large stocks of imported music and when music printing gained a foothold in Canada, musicians anxious to build repertoires depended largely on copying by hand from the few available scores and from each other's manuscripts. The few extant manuscript books thus developed are invaluable documents of contemporary taste, for nobody had to copy what he did not like or did not expect to perform. Many fiddlers and all folk singers picked up their material purely by ear from others, but some of the more educated did notate the popular repertoire. Thus Allen Ash (1800–89), a farmer in the district of Newcastle, Ont, filled 28 pages of a manuscript book (*NL of C) with waltzes, reels, galops, hornpipes, and other dances, including a *Cobourg Waltz* probably of his own composition. Other examples are the music notebook of Elisha Styles Lyman inscribed 'Montreal, August 28, 1821' (Carillon Museum, Carillon, Que) and the one of Havilah Jane Thorne of Bridgetown, NS, dated 1839 (Public Archives of Nova Scotia).

A mixture of dances, songs (including the 'Marseillaise'), and more sophisticated music is found in the manuscript music book of Miss Caroline Rachel Frobisher of Montreal, begun in April 1793 when she became a pupil of 'Mr. M.' (possibly Guillaume *Mechtler). The accurate dance-step descriptions written in after the final bars of more than a dozen pieces provide a contemporary account of how the music actually was danced – an important aid to the authentic reconstruction of dances of the period. In 1980 the book was held at the Hôpital général in Quebec City.

Examples of manuscript books compiled by professional musicians are the two (held at the NL of C) of Frederick Andrews (1804–85, the organist at the Anglican cathedral in Quebec City). Begun in 1828, they include sacred music by Handel, Haydn, and Mozart and instrumental pieces by Corelli, Cherubini, and Weber, as well as two of Andrews' own songs. Two manuscript books labelled 'Musique sacrée' and containing T.F. *Molt's repertoire were acquired by the NL of C, and manuscripts in the hand of Louis-Édouard *Glackemeyer, probably for use by his own chamber ensemble and the *Quebec Harmonic Society, became the property of *Laval U.

The use of manuscript notebooks before schoolbooks were available is seen in examples (dated 1804–34, from the pupils of the German school in Clinton Township, Lincoln County, east of Hamilton, Ont) preserved at the Jordan Historical Museum of the Twenty, Jordan, Ont.

Another important type of manuscript book was that devoted to folksongs. The collection of Edward Ermatinger, which dates from ca 1830, belongs to the Public Archives of Canada (see Ethnomusicology). A list of such books is given in Conrad *Laforte's *La Chanson folklorique et les écrivains du XIXe siècle* (Montreal 1973). Most of these, however, contain only words. The original manuscript books are preserved at the *National Museum of Man in Ottawa, the Archives du Séminaire de Québec, and the Montreal City Library.
SW (HK)

Maple leaf. The maple leaf at first was considered an emblem of French Canada, and in 1834 the St-Jean-Baptiste Society adopted it formally. The cover design of Joseph *Maffré's *Original Canadian Quadrilles* (J.W. Herbert 1847) is the first known sheet music publication to use the leaf (and the beaver as well). John *McCaul's literary annual *The Maple-Leaf*, which first appeared in 1847, and James P. *Clarke's setting of 'The Emblem of Canada' (to words taken from the annual, Nordheimer ca 1850) and his *Lays of the Maple Leaf* (Nordheimer 1853) indicate that the emblem had become accepted in Upper Canada as well. More than any other music, however, Alexander *Muir's *'The Maple Leaf For Ever' (1867) popularized the emblem. Other 19th-century examples of 'maple leaf music' are Harold Palmer's *The Maple Leaf Polka Mazurka* (J.W. Herbert ca 185?), Roch *Lyonnais's polka *Feuilles d'érables*, and H.H. *Godfrey's 'The Land of the Maple' (Mason & Risch 1897). J.D. *Kerrison's 'The Flag That Bears the Maple Leaf' (Suckling & Sons 1889) anticipates Canada's official adoption of the maple leaf flag by 76 years. Another popular song was William Westbrook's 'A Handful of Maple Leaves' (H.H. Sparks 1901). Numerous songs of later years – eg, R. Goublier's 'Les Érables' (1909) and Gustave Goublier's 'La Voix des érables' – refer to the leaf in title or text, and even more frequently the leaf is part of the cover design. The fiddler Ward *Allen of 'Maple Leaf Hoedown' fame was the composer of *Maple Leaf Two-Step* and the widely played *Maple Sugar*. Orchestral scores include L.-

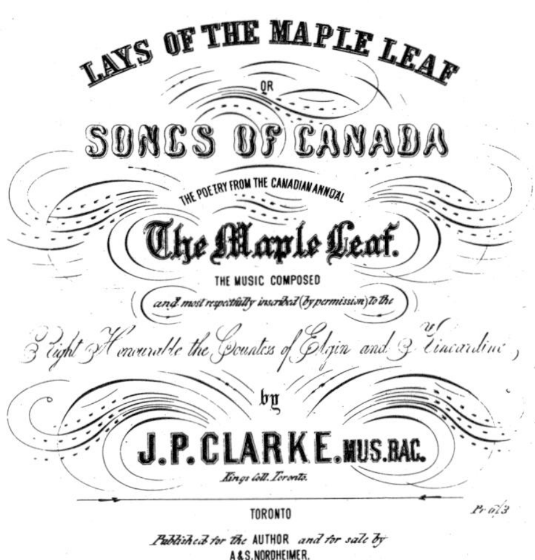

P. *Laurendeau's march *Land of the Maple* (Carl Fischer 1907), J.-J. *Gagnier's *Le Vent dans l'érable effeuillé* (1927), Hector *Gratton's *Sous les érables* (1940), and Charles *O'Neill's *The Land of the Maple and Beaver*. The famous *Maple Leaf Rag* (1899) by the US composer Scott Joplin has only a tenuous connection with the Canadian emblem (see Ragtime). HK

'The Maple Leaf For Ever'. Patriotic song composed by Alexander *Muir in October 1867; both words and music are Muir's. Next to *'O Canada,' which it antedates by 13 years, it has been the most popular patriotic song composed in Canada. However, because Muir's outlook was purely English-Canadian, his song has not become popular among French-Canadians, nor has it remained so even among English-Canadians past the middle of the 20th century.

The poem was written as a last-minute entry in the patriotic poetry contest of the Caledonian Society of Montreal and won the second prize. The topic was suggested while Muir and his friend George Leslie were walking in Toronto near Leslie's Gardens (located near Queen St, east of the Don River, and named after the Leslie family of Leslieville, a former suburb of Toronto) and a falling maple leaf lodged on Leslie's coat sleeve, despite efforts to brush it off. 'There Muir! There's your text! The maple leaf is the emblem of Canada! Build your poem on that,' Leslie is said to have exclaimed. The poem was written and despatched to Montreal a few hours later. Muir's search for a suitable tune in local music stores proved futile, so he wrote his own.

The original edition, supposedly of 1000 copies, bears no date and no copyright notice. It was issued probably early in 1868, 'published for the author,' and printed at the Guardian Office in Toronto, the publishing outlet for the Methodist Book Room. The story that Muir paid $30 to have the song printed and took in less than half that amount is plausible. On the other hand it is hard to believe Leslie's claim that Muir did not receive 'one cent' of royalties from *Nordheimer, who brought out the first copyrighted edition in 1871. This edition advertised on its cover that the song was 'sung with great applause by J.F. Hardy, esq., in his popular entertainments,' thus contradicting another story which purports that the first public performance of 'The Maple Leaf For Ever' took place 24 Jul 1874 when Muir directed school children during the laying of the foundation stone of a church in Newmarket, north of Toronto, in the presence of the Earl of Dufferin.

The text of the song was revised by Muir several times. On a copy of the original edition, pre-

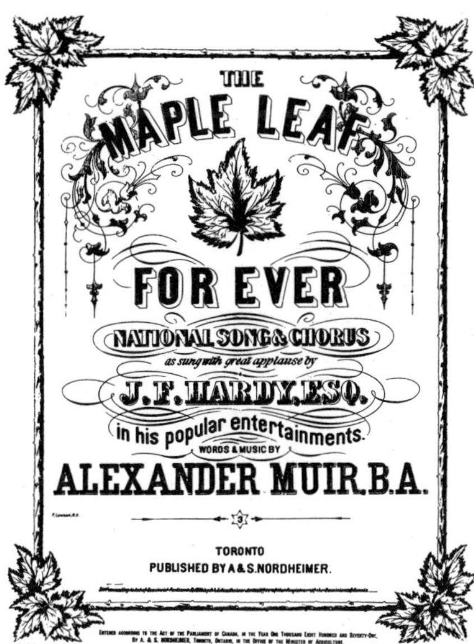

The first Nordheimer edition, 1871

served at the *NL of C, Muir's own hand has corrected the first line of the chorus 'The Maple Leaf, the Maple Leaf, the Maple Leaf for ever!' to read 'The Maple Leaf, our emblem dear, the Maple Leaf for ever!' There were other small revisions and a major one in 1894. On 8 September of that year the Toronto newspaper *The Empire* quoted a letter written by Muir in which he complained that incorrect versions of the words of his song had been circulated and went on to give the correct version. This appears to have been a deliberate mystification, for not only do all known pre-1894 versions conform to the original text and its minor adjustments, but the 'correct' version really was a new one, having five stanzas instead of four. In fact, the two versions share only two stanzas. The 1894 version, with the awkward opening 'In days of yore, the hero Wolfe Britain's glory did maintain,' appeared in several publications at the turn of the century, but the original version has remained the popular one: 'In days of yore, from Britain's shore, Wolfe the dauntless hero came.'

To make good the oversight of the French heritage in Canada, some later editions changed 'The thistle, shamrock, rose entwine' to read 'The lily, thistle, shamrock, rose'' but no French translation of the song has been located. There is however a poem written by Octave *Crémazie before 1862 – 'Salut, ô ma belle patrie!' – paired with Muir's melody in *Choix de chansons* (Montreal 1914).

The music almost always is printed in the key of B flat. The tune is cheerful, but its organization is confusing. Verse and chorus begin with the same eight notes, except that the fourth and fifth are at different pitches of the same chord. The sequence G–B flat–F occurs five times, but in four different melodic contexts. It is no wonder that Alexander *Cringan, in his school edition, marked five notes with asterisks, warning the teacher that these 'are sometimes sung incorrectly.'

In 1964 *Thompson published 'Our Home, Our Land, Our Canada' – Muir's music with lyrics by Victor Cowley, who had won the Canadian Authors Assn Maple Leaf song contest.

DISCOGRAPHY

Canadian Armed Forces Tatto Centennial 1967. Dom LPS 21004

This Is My Country. Mormon Tabernacle Choir. Col MS 6419

See also *Roll Back the Years*.

BIBLIOGRAPHY

'Mr. Muir's new national song,' Toronto *The Empire*, 8 Sep 1894

Robertson, John Ross. 'Alexander Muir's life,' *Landmarks of Toronto*, series 6, Toronto 1914

Belcher, A.E. 'How Alexander Muir wrote "The Maple Leaf",' *CMTJ*, vol 24, Aug 1923; also in Toronto *Globe*, 20 Jul 1923 HK

Maple Leaf Gardens. Downtown Toronto sports arena, home of the Maple Leaf hockey team. Designed by Ross & Macdonald with associates Jack Ryrie and Mackenzie Waters, it was built in 1931 at a cost of about $1.5 million on the northwest corner of Carlton and Church streets. Originally it held 13,000 persons for hockey and 16,000 for other events. Renovations and alterations over the years increased the capacity to over 16,000 for hockey and over 18,000 for concerts. The arena has been the site of opera (the Canadian Grand Opera Company's *Faust* in 1936 and the *Metropolitan Opera's visiting productions 1952–60), programs by Toronto's ethnic minorities (eg, Johnny Lombardi's festivals of song, which present Italian singers), the annual Metropolitan Toronto Police concerts, and, in the 1960s and 1970s, virtually all the large-scale pop concerts (save a few outdoor presentations each summer) by the Beatles, the Rolling Stones, Frank Sinatra, Bruce Springsteen, and others. In the absence of an 8000-to-10,000-seat hall in Toronto, a 'concert bowl' of that size was created inside the Gardens in the mid-1970s by placing a portable stage at 'centre ice' to face one half of the hall (divided lengthwise), and partitioning off the other half with curtains. In 1973 Maple Leaf Gardens, through Concert Productions International (CPI), began producing its own concerts. CPI became an independent company in 1974 but in 1980 continued to enjoy an unwritten agreement with the Gardens which gave it exclusive use of the hall for concerts. MM

MARCHAND, Charles. Baritone, folklorist, b St-Paul-L'Ermite, near Montreal, 10 Jun 1890, d Montreal 1 May 1930. He was educated at L'Assomption and Rigaud colleges prior to settling in Hull in 1910 as a federal civil servant. Captivated by French song, he dreamed of becoming a performer and to that end studied voice in Montreal with Jean *Riddez and Max Pantaleieff. He made an unheralded debut in Ottawa with a song by Théodore Botrel, wearing a sailor's costume he had designed himself. To his surprise the debut was a success and led to several engagements in the Ottawa area, mainly benefit performances. With the same repertoire he made his Montreal debut in March 1919 at the Salle Lafontaine. Shortly afterwards, he was entranced by Lorraine Wyman's performance of French-Canadian folksongs at the Veillées du bon vieux temps. He decided to concentrate on Canadian folk music, and his first recital, in May 1920 at the *Monument national, was a brilliant success.

Abandoning the security of a career in the civil service, Marchand settled in Montreal. He renewed his association with Oscar *O'Brien, who had accompanied him as early as 1915 and who went on to harmonize some 150 songs for him; with the poet Maurice Morisset, O'Brien also wrote for Marchand some original songs in popular style. In 1922 Marchand founded a vocal quartet, Le Carillon canadien, which became the basis of a movement dedicated to promoting Canadian songs. A monthly publication, *Le Carillon* or 'the voice of song,' was launched in 1926 but was absorbed soon by *La Lyre*. During this period Marchand performed throughout Quebec, in Ontario, elsewhere in Canada, in Franco-American centres in New England, and in New York City.

Charles Marchand

When he was put in charge of the music for the celebration of Ottawa's centenary in 1927, Marchand joined the tenor Émile Boucher and the basses Miville Belleau and Fortunat Champagne to form the Bytown Troubadours, a vocal quartet which thereafter enjoyed considerable success. Pierre *Gautier prepared numerous folksong arrangements for the group. In May 1927 Marchand and his group were a hit at the first *CPR Festival in Quebec City. Marchand was responsible for part of the artistic direction of the 1928 and 1930 festivals in Quebec City. In the intervening year he went to Europe. His sudden death caused the 1930 festival to be postponed until October, at which time Lionel *Daunais sang in Marchand's place. Shortly afterwards the quartet ceased to exist.

Charles Marchand's career was short but brilliant. The first important advocate of French-Canadian song, he also was appreciated by English-speaking audiences, for whom he sang in translations by John Murray *Gibbon. A man of high ideals, he had made it his objective, as Frédéric *Pelletier explained (*Entre-Nous*, May 1930), to 'understand and to love the soul of man as revealed in his naive yet profound music ... He could make his naturally harsh voice respond to the slightest nuance of expression and his lively features adapted themselves to the mood of the song, whether it was a gentle ballad, a trapper's simple lament, or a tongue-in-cheek commentary.' *Pionniers du disque folklorique* lists his recordings and those of the Bytown Troubadours on the Columbia, Brunswick, Edison, Diamond, Victor, and Starr labels.

BIBLIOGRAPHY
Morisset, Maurice. 'Après le triomphe,' *La Lyre*, 52, May 1927
Pelletier, Frédéric. 'Charles Marchand,' *Entre-Nous*, vol 1, May 1930
D'Aragon, Alexandre. 'Charles Marchand,' *Action musicale, littéraire et artistique*, vol 1, 14 May 1932 GP

***March 'de Normandie*.'** One of the oldest Canadian compositions to survive in regular performance in the 20th century. It is said to have been written to welcome to Quebec City the Duke of Kent, Queen Victoria's father, the commander of the Royal Fusiliers during the regiment's service in Canada August 1791–1801. Like its companion piece, the fast march *Royal Fusiliers Arrival at Quebec* (1791), it lay in oblivion for more than a century and a quarter, but after a memorial tablet had heen unveiled 1 Jul 1928 in Quebec to commemorate the Royal Fusiliers' service in Canada, a Mrs Elmire C. Pourtier in 1929 presented the manuscripts of both works to the regiment. The regimental band performed the *March 'de Normandie'* during a historical display at the Royal Tournament in 1930, and from then on the march was regarded as the regimental slow march (*The British Grenadiers* being the fast one). As the march is a mere 20 measures long (plus repeats), the bandmaster, Tulip, added a Trio section.

In J.M. *Gibbon's *Canadian Mosaic* (Toronto 1938), and hence in the *Catalogue of Canadian Composers*, F.H. *Glackemeyer was credited as the composer. However, an inquiry at the Regimental Museum of the Royal Fusiliers revealed that after their acquisition both manuscripts were framed and under each was printed – presumably on Mrs Pourtier's advice – 'Composed by Charles Voyer de Poligny D'Argenson, notary of Quebec who died there 1820.' Neither manuscript bears a composer's name, but both appear to have been written in the same handwriting. A note on the *March 'de Normandie'* says 'copied by Jouve, band master to the Duke of Kent.' Both marches are notated as piano arrangements, and the manuscript of the *March 'de Normandie'* also has the beginning of a choral *Stabat mater*.

Both pieces have been recorded by the Central Band of the Canadian Forces (disc 2, 'The British'; London SW 99559) and the *March 'de Normandie'* by the Trio Nouvelle-France of Montreal (Louise Courville, flute, Jocelyne Leduc, cello, and Ariane Dind, harpsichord) on RCI 500. HK

MARCOUX, Joseph-Désiré. Clarinetist, farmer, b Beauport, near Quebec City, 20 May 1850, d St-Prime, Lac St-Jean, Que, 5 Feb 1888. He taught himself music and took part in all the musical soirées in the Beauport region. As a soloist with the Notre-Dame de Beauport Concert Band, founded in 1875 and directed by Joseph *Vézina, he enjoyed great success at the Montreal Band Festival in 1878. In 1885 he settled at St-Prime, in the Lac St-Jean district, and was placed in charge of musical organizations there. He was founder in 1887 and conductor of the Roberval concert band – the Union musicale Sainte-Cécile – and gave free lessons to each of the instrumentalists. He died after an accident at work. His daughter Albertine recounted his life in *Musicien et paysan, fatal destin d'un agriculteur-musicien* (Quebec City 1957). DM

MARCUS, Erwin. Choir director, composer, teacher, b Vienna 1902, d Montreal Apr 1956, naturalized Canadian 1956. He took music lessons privately and studied musicology at the U of Vienna. Between 1920 and 1938 he coached and conducted choirs and operatic groups and accompanied such singers as Leo Slezak and Vera Schwarz. In 1938 he went to Shanghai, where he conducted the Grand Opera and International Choral Society and taught at the National Cons. He moved in 1949 to Montreal, where he taught, coached, accompanied, and, for several years, conducted the Workmen's Circle Choir. In 1955 he joined the staff of *McGill Cons. His compositions include *Die Brücke* (an oratorio for children's choir and small orchestra), instrumental fugues, a string quartet, and several songs. A quartet for clarinet, violin, cello, and piano, a piano sonata, and a piano suite were written in Canada and performed over the CBC. HK

'Marianne s'en va-t-au moulin.' Folksong popular in France and Canada. The text gives a spirited account of the adventures of Marianne, whose donkey, tied up behind a mill, is devoured by a wolf. The miller offers her another animal as compensation, and when she gets home Marianne explains to her father that donkeys change their coats on St Michael's Day. The tune and words are found in Ernest *Gagnon's *Chansons populaires du Canada* (Quebec 1865); the lyrics also appear in *La Lyre canadienne* (Quebec 1886) and other publications. Jean *Papineau-Couture wrote music for celesta and strings for 'Marianne s'en va-t-au moulin,' a puppet show presented on CBC TV in 1952. Hector *Gratton composed a fantasy for soprano, tenor, and orchestra on the tune, and Morley *Calvert employed it in the first movement of his *Suite from the Monteregian Hills* (1962) for brass quintet. Among the harmonizations for voice and piano are those of Alfred *Laliberté (*Le Passe-Temps*, August 1946) and Claude *Champagne (Harris 1959). The song was recorded by Louis *Chartier (Brunswick 3421, a 78), and Marguerite *Gignac (RCA LCP-1035, an LP). HP

Mother MARIE DE ST-JOSEPH (b Marie de Savonnières de la Troche). Ursuline nun, musician, b Château de Saint-Germain in Anjou, France, 7 Sep 1616, d Quebec 4 Apr 1652. She joined the Ursulines at Tours at 14 and sailed to Canada in 1639 in company with Mother Marie de l'Incarnation. She studied native languages, and her good nature won the trust of the Indians. In her task as teacher of both French and native girls at Quebec, music played an important role. Sister Anne de Ste-Claire wrote in a letter on 2 Sep 1640: 'She is the teacher of our little seminarists, whom she loves as a mother loves her children. After catechism she teaches them to sing hymns and to play them on the viol; sometimes, she has them dance in the manner of the Indians' (*Les Ursulines de Québec*, Quebec 1863). After her early death a chronicler remembered that 'she had a beautiful voice and understood Music well, not only did she sing and chant the psalms, but she also led the Choir, for which office she doubtless had aptitude; for she succeeded in it marvelously, notwithstanding her lung troubles' (*Jesuit Relations*, vol 38, p 149)

BIBLIOGRAPHY
Amtmann *Music in Canada* HK

MARIER, Céline (also known as Célina or Célinie). Soprano, teacher, b Montreal ca 1871, d there 4 May 1940. After voice studies with Charles *Labelle she performed in 1894 in Montreal and other towns before going in 1896 to Liège, where her teachers were Duysinx and Sylvain Dupuis, and later to Paris, where she worked with Romain Bussine. On returning to Montreal she participated in numerous concerts, particularly with the first MSO, for which she appeared with the French bass Pol Plançon in 1900 and sang the title role in Massenet's dramatic oratorio *La Vierge* in 1902. She soon became absorbed in teaching, however, first (1905) at the *Cons national and later privately. She staged several operas, including *Carmen* and *Mignon*, with her best pupils. Among her pupils were Louis Bourdon, Cédia *Brault, Lionel *Daunais, Roger *Doucet, Lottie Farrar, Sarah *Fischer, Jacques *Labrecque, Caro *Lamoureux, Simone *Quesnel, and Alice Raymond. Frédéric *Pelletier wrote: 'Here was a singing teacher who never considered her profession as a trade to provide her with an income but rather as a calling to which she responded with all her time, all her thoughts and all her love.'

BIBLIOGRAPHY
Pelletier, Frédéric. 'Mlle Célinie Marier,' *Entre-Nous*, vol 1, Jun 1930
Gleason-Huguenin, Madeleine. *Portraits de femmes* (Montreal 1938) GP

MARIER, John (René). Composer, scientist, b Ottawa 27 Oct 1925. He studied piano, violin, and theory with his parents, both Ottawa musicians. His grandfather C.J. Arthur Marier led dance and theatre orchestras and wrote piano pieces (eg, *Princess Louise Dragoon Guards*, nd), and his great-uncle Eugene had compositions published by *Orme. A scientist with the National Research Council of Canada, John Marier also has been active as a composer and music director for musical theatre productions in the Ottawa area. Among his compositions are over 300 songs (most unpublished); 10 song cycles, including the widely performed *Island of Canada* (1964); and more than 10 musicals, including *gOTTA WAke up* (1964, chosen in competition for performance at the 1966 Festival of the Arts), *The King of the Thousand Islands* (1964), *Adamant Eve* (1968, broadcast over CBC radio in 1969), and *A Land of Dreams* (1968, presented by CBC TV in 1972). Marier has written incidental music and several TV scripts for the CBC. His epic poem *A North-American Indian Looks at the Past 100 Years* was circulated in the Canadian Indian press ca 1967. A few of his songs have been recorded, notably 'Life is a Merry-go-round' (RCA Victor PCS 1175) and the 1968 CBC Song Market Competition winner, 'Colours of the Rainbow' (Winterlea Music 1968), which has been recorded by CBC-LM, CTL, Dominion, PA Record, and RCA. Marier is a member of CAPAC.

BIBLIOGRAPHY

Thistle, Lauretta. 'Ottawa's legendary lumberjack comes alive in musical,' *CanComp*, 19, Jun 1967
– 'Marier's "Colours of the Rainbow" wins CBC Song Market contest,' ibid, 34, Nov 1968

FH

Sister MARIE-STÉPHANE (b Hélène Côté). Teacher, composer, b St-Barthélémi, near Trois-Rivières, Que, 9 Jan 1888; D MUS (Montreal) 1936. She began musical studies at five with her elder sister and continued them in her parish convent. In Montreal she took lessons in piano and organ with Romain-Octave *Pelletier for seven or eight years. After joining the Sisters of the Holy Names of Jesus and Mary she immediately began preparing for a teaching career in music while continuing her training with Alfred *Lamoureux (voice and harmony), Alfred *Laliberté (piano), Claude *Champagne (counterpoint, fugue, composition), Raoul *Paquet (organ), and, in Paris, Guy de Lioncourt (composition and orchestration).

In 1920 Sister Marie-Stéphane was appointed director of musical studies for her congregation, and in 1932 she founded in Outremont the École supérieure de musique, which later became the *École Vincent-d'Indy. In 1935 she went to Europe to acquaint herself with great musical institutions such as the Cons national, the École César-Franck, and the École normale, Paris; the RCM and the RAM, London; the Vienna Academy; and the Brussels Cons. Upon her return, in 1936, her school made new strides and continued to develop and expand. In 1967 age and illness forced her to retire. In 1973 she was awarded the *CMCouncil Medal.

Sister Marie-Stéphane's compositions include two works for female choir (SSA) – *Cantique au Sacré-Coeur* and *Motets au Saint-Sacrement* (Schola cantorum 1920); two works for mixed choir (SATB) – *Je n'ai qu'un seul Ami* (fugue) and *Motets liturgiques* (École Vincent-d'Indy 1965); and an *Andante* for string quartet, unpublished but recorded on tape (1957) by the Loewenguth Quartet of Paris as a tribute to her 50 years of religious life.

WRITINGS

Manuel d'harmonie (Outremont 1926, 3rd edn 1958)
Analyse musicale (Outremont 1927, 4th edn 1972)
Théorie de la musique (Outremont 1929, 7th edn 1975) / *Theory of Music*, transl (Outremont 1946, 1967)
La Musique au point de vue éducatif (Outremont 1948)

BIBLIOGRAPHY

Prévost, Roland. 'Une grande institution canadienne, L'École supérieure de musique d'Outremont,' *P-T*, 913, Oct 1947
Musiciennes de chez nous

(CH)

Frank Marino and Mahogany Rush (Mahogany Rush 1970–6). Rock band formed in 1970 in Montreal by the guitarist-keyboardist-singer-songwriter Frank Marino with the drummer Jimmy *Ayoub and the bass guitarist Paul Harwood. The group patterned itself after contemporary British blues-rock bands, and Marino adopted the exhibitionist style of the guitarist Jimi Hendrix. After its early rehearsals drew many casual listeners, the trio began appearing in Montreal coffeehouses and high schools and performed in 1971 for a pop festival at Man and His World, the annual summer exhibition which survived on the site of *Expo 67. The band made its first three LPs in Canada (*Maxoom*, 1972, Kot'ai KOT 3001; *Child of the Novelty*, 1973, Kot'ai KOT 3302; *Strange Universe*, 1974, Kot'ai KOT 3308). When these became popular in the USA, however, it moved to Detroit. The LPs *Mahogany Rush IV* (1976, Col KC-34190), *World Anthem* (1977, Col PC-34677), *Frank Marino and Mahogany Rush Live* (1977, Col PC-35257), and *What's Next* (1979, Col JC-36204) followed, the second-last-named recorded in various cities during one of several extensive US tours. The band made its British debut in 1977 and has performed occasionally in Canada. It toured Japan late in 1978. Its popularity centres around Marino (b Montreal 20 Nov 1954), 'a rip-roaring, crowd-pleasing rocker whose playing runs from excessive repetition for its own sake to fine solo work that reveals several influences ... of the many aspects of Hendrix's style, the one most successfully interpreted in concert is the rampaging firebreather – stoked with wah-wah, distortion, feedback and bizarre harmonics' (Tom Wheeler, *Guitar Player*, Jun 1978). Marino is an affiliate of PRO Canada. Mahogany Rush should not be confused with the Toronto trio *Rush.

BIBLIOGRAPHY

Gingras, Pyer. 'Mahogany Rush launched from Quebec,' *MSc*, 274, Nov–Dec 1973
Caraway, Steve. 'Frank Marino: reincarnated rock and roll?' *Guitar Player*, Sep 1976

CCr, MM

Mariposa Folk Festival. In 1980, one of the oldest continuing music festivals in Canada; also the country's leading folk festival. It was founded in 1961 in Orillia, Ont, by Ruth Jones, her husband, Dr Crawford Jones, and Pete McGarvey. The name 'Mariposa' was taken from Stephen Leacock's book *Sunshine Sketches of a Little Town*, in which the 'little town,' a thinly disguised Orillia, was called Mariposa. The first festival, held 18 and 19 Aug 1961 out of doors at Oval Park, was produced by Ed Cowan with Ted Schaefer as artistic director. Among the artists presented were O.J. *Abbott, Al *Cherny, Jean *Carignan and Alan *Mills, Jacques *Labrecque, Finvola *Redden-Bower, the *Travellers, and Ian and Sylvia (*Tyson). Some 1500 people attended. The 1962 and 1963 festivals, three-day events (as were all to follow), were produced by Jack Wall. Control of the festival passed through several hands before it was taken over by the Toronto Guild of Canadian Folk Artists in 1969, and by the Mariposa Folk Foundation in 1977. Estelle Klein became artistic director in 1964 and retained that position in 1979. Klein had assistance in programming in 1976 from Ken Whiteley (who also, in Klein's absence due to illness, was artistic director for the 1978 festival) and in 1979 from Jeanine Hollingshead. Banned from the Orillia area in 1964 because of public disturbances by festival-goers in the first three years, Mariposa made its home that year at the Maple Leaf (baseball) Stadium in Toronto and 1965–7 at Innis Lake, northwest of the city. In 1968 it moved to Centre Island, off the Toronto waterfront, its site until 1979. Over the years the festival has been scheduled progressively earlier in the summer; in 1979 it took place 15–17 June. In the late 1970s on Centre Island attendance was limited of necessity to about 8000 people a day. The island festival was discontinued in 1980 in favour of weekly events and a Mariposa Fall Festival at Harbourfront.

In its first 10 years Mariposa presented a mixture of Canadian and US folk and folk-influenced performers in daytime workshops (in which the audience could participate) and evening concerts. In 1962 the performers included Oscar *Brand, Claude *Gauthier, Ed *McCurdy, Finvola Redden-Bower, the Two Tones (Gordon *Lightfoot and Terry Whalen), the Travellers, and the Tysons; in 1963 Al Cromwell, Bonnie *Dobson, Stu *Phillips, and the Tysons; in 1964 Jean Carignan, Rev Gary Davis, Mississippi John Hurt, Lightfoot, and Buffy *Sainte-Marie; in 1965 Joni Anderson (*Mitchell), John Hammond, Jr, and Lightfoot; in 1966 Tom *Brandon, LaRena *Clark, Lightfoot, Mitchell, Pete Seeger, the Staple Singers, and David *Wiffen; in 1967 Leonard *Cohen, Louise *Forestier, Buddy Guy, Alanis *Obomsawin, and David Rea. In 1968, with the move to Centre Island, an area was set aside for crafts displays and workshops. Artists presented that year included Dobson, Jim *McHarg, Mitchell, and Gilles *Vigneault. In 1969 Joan Baez, John Allan *Cameron, Bruce *Cockburn, Dobson, Jesse Fuller, Taj Mahal, and Doc Watson, among others, were heard. In 1970 a native peoples' area was established which, each year until 1978, presented traditional and contemporary performers (eg, Alanis Obomsawin, the area's programmer 1970–6; Willy Dunn; Inuit Throat Singers; Métis performers; and Shingoose).

After disruptions during the evening concerts of Joni Mitchell, James Taylor, and others at the 1970 festival, Mariposa's structure of presentation was changed in 1971. Six stages were set up with simultaneous activities running from late morning to dusk. The festival also turned away from the presentation of 'name' performers (a policy announced as early as 1968, although Baez, Mitchell, and Taylor were heard in the years after). Throughout the 1970s Mariposa was an informal mixture of workshops and concerts, each generally of an hour or less in length. Some 150 individual presentations by 50 or more performers and groups were heard over the festival's three days. Workshops brought together performers of many backgrounds to demonstrate or explore particular themes – for example: in 1977 'Tunes, Stories and Songs of French Canada' with Louis *Boudreault, Denis Coté, Gilles Losier, Robert Paquette, and Métis performers; 'Country Music: Here in Canada' with David Essig, Kenny Jackson, Myrna *Lorrie, Paquette, and Colleen Peterson; 'Jazz Beginnings' with John *Arpin, Ken Bloom, the Original Sloth Band, Bill Usher, Jackie Washington, and David Wilcox; and in 1978 'The Fiddle – Different Styles' with Émile Benoit, Chris Crilly, Seamus and Manus McGuire, Kelly Russell, Graham *Townsend, and Claude Williams, and 'From the Ottawa Valley' with Lennox Gavan, Donegal and Gina Gilchrist, Ian Robb, and Graham Townsend. Among the several hundred performers who have appeared at Mariposa in the 1970s, others of note include David Amram, Pauline *Julien, Murray *McLauchlan, Jay McShann, and Leon Redbone. Every performer is paid the same, a minimal fee plus expenses. Organizational and on-site operations are handled by a largely volunteer staff.

The Mariposa Folk Foundation issued a 2-LP set of performances recorded at the 1975 festival. It also in 1970 initiated the Mariposa in the Schools (MITS) program to provide Toronto area schools with folk presentations for children. The program has involved many Toronto musicians, among them Sharon (Hampson), Lois (Lilienstein) and Bram (Morrison), Raffi, and Chick Roberts. Eighteen performers are heard on the MITS-produced LP *Going Bananas*, released in 1979. A book of stories from Mariposa performers, *For What Time I Am in this World*, edited by Bill Usher and Linda Page-Harpa, was published in Toronto in 1977.

BIBLIOGRAPHY

Lewis, Joe. 'Mariposa Folk Festival seventh season,' Toronto *Telegram*, 10 Aug 1967

McDonald, Marci. 'You don't find Ian and Sylvia, Buffy St. Marie, Gordon Lightfoot or Leonard Cohen at Mariposa '68 ... why?' *Toronto Daily Star*, 10 Aug 1968

'A folk festival sets some new directions,' *CanComp*, 62, Sep 1971

Sharp, Debra. 'Mariposa: how times have changed,' *For What Time I Am in this World* (Toronto 1977) MM

Maritime Academy of Music. See Maritime Conservatory of Music.

Maritime Conservatory of Music. Established in 1954 in Halifax through the amalgamation of the Halifax Cons of Music (1887–1954) and the Maritime Academy of Music (1934–54).

The Halifax Cons was founded by Rev Robert Laing in conjunction with the Halifax Ladies' College and attracted students from the Maritime provinces. C.H. *Porter, an organist and a graduate of the Leipzig Cons, was the first director. Many of his pupils went on post-graduate work in Berlin and Leipzig. By 1890 the Halifax Cons had 240 students; in 1898 it became affiliated with *Dalhousie U and began granting licentiate diplomas and B MUS degrees. In 1900 Porter was succeeded for one year by Felix Heink (brother-in-law of Ernestine Schumann-Heink). Heink's successor, Percy Gordon, another Leipzig graduate, was director until 1906. One of Gordon's pupils, Elsie Taylor, also studied in Germany and taught 1906–43 at the conservatory, becoming head of the piano department in 1934. Harry *Dean was director 1906–34, then left to found the Maritime Academy, taking part of the conservatory staff with him. Ifan *Williams directed the conservatory until 1954; its ties to the Halifax Ladies' College were cut in 1952. In 1947 Mariss Vetra became head of the vocal department and established an opera class, whose activities resulted in the formation of the *Nova Scotia Opera Assn.

Under Dean's direction the Maritime Academy of Music became the largest music school in Halifax, with over 1000 pupils. It offered certificates in accompanying and school music, and (through its affiliation until 1962 with Dalhousie U, where students could undertake the required academic studies) a licentiate diploma (two-year course) and a B MUS (four-year course).

In 1954 the Halifax Cons purchased the assets of the Maritime Academy and became the Maritime Cons. Directors have been Ifan Williams 1954–8 and Kenneth *Elloway 1961–70. There was no official director in the periods 1958–61 and 1970–7. Klaro *Mizerit assumed the directorship in 1977. In 1956 the MCM took over a building on the St Mary's U campus; in 1978 it became associated with that university. Branches have been opened in the Halifax suburb of Fairview and in Bedford. The conservatory grants an associate diploma (performance or teaching) and certificates for successfully completed examinations for grades 1 to 10. Advanced students may participate in a chamber music program. The dance department offered instruction in ballet 1947–76 and other dance programs (ballroom, Highland, tap, jazz) thereafter. (SAB, MSm)

MARQUIS, G. (George) Welton. Musicologist, administrator, b Walla Walla, Wash, 4 Mar 1916; MA music (Whitman) 1942, PH D musicology (Southern California) 1950. He was an arranger-composer-conductor 1937–41 in Hollywood and has been head 1951–4 of the music department of Northern Illinois U, dean 1954–8 of the school of music, Women's College of the U of North Carolina, and a Fulbright Professor 1957–8 at the U of Oslo. He served 1958–71 as head of the Dept of Music of the *U of British Columbia and after that time continued to teach music history and theory there. In 1967 he gave the *CAPAC-MacMillan lecture at the RCMT Summer School. He was a president 1969–71 of *CAUSM.

WRITINGS

'Our musical education – a professional view,' *Community Arts Council News and Calendar*, vol 12, Feb 1961

'Music – a serious school subject,' *CME*, vol 5, Mar–Apr 1964

Twentieth Century Music Idioms (Englewood Cliffs, NJ 1964)

'Canadian music at the University of British Columbia,' *CanComp*, 2, Aug 1965

Yes Sir, That's My Wolfgang: An Irreverent History of Music (Englewood Cliffs, NJ 1967)

'Canadian music education,' *CanComp*, 21, Sep 1967

'Voice from the West,' *CanComp*, 38, Mar 1969

'Introducing CAUSM,' *College Music Symposium*, vol 10, 1970 CF

MARR, Frances. See Adaskin, Harry.

MARSHALL, Lois (Catherine). Soprano, b Toronto 29 Jan 1924; Artist Diploma (Toronto) 1950, hon LL D (Toronto) 1965, hon LL D (Saskatchewan) 1966. One of Canada's leading sopranos in the 1950s and 1960s, she began voice lessons at 12 with Weldon *Kilburn, whom she married in 1968 and who remained her coach and accompanist until the 1970s. She also studied Lieder interpretation 1947–50 with Emmy *Heim.

In 1947 Sir Ernest *MacMillan engaged her for the soprano solos in his annual presentation of Bach's *St Matthew Passion* with the *Toronto Mendelssohn Choir and the *TSO. In an interview (Toronto *Telegram*, 10 Aug 1968) Sir Ernest recalled: 'Lois hadn't sung the St. Matthew before, and she was young for it, really just a child. But we knew of her voice, radiant even then, and were interested to hear her try it. So we sent her off home with the score. Four days later she returned with every note of that taxing role not merely learned but so completely inside her, so deeply and personally understood, that I could only say to her "My child, you have won the engagement".' He re-engaged her for the part for many seasons thereafter and also for the New York performances in 1954 and the recording. With the same forces she also appeared (1950s) in Bach's *Mass in B Minor*, the Verdi *Requiem*, and Handel's *Messiah*.

In 1950 she won the top award in *'Singing Stars of Tomorrow' and the Eaton Graduating Scholarship for the outstanding graduate of the *RCMT's Senior School. The same year she sang with the National SO (in Washington, DC, for that city's sesquiscentennial celebrations, her first of many performances there) and appeared at the Bach (bicentenary) Festival in Toronto.

Marshall won the coveted Naumburg Award in 1952 and made her New York debut 2 December at Town Hall. As a result of this recital Arturo Toscanini chose her to appear 28 Mar 1953 with the NBC SO in a performance of Beethoven's *Missa solemnis* and in the subsequent recording. That same year she premiered Godfrey *Ridout's

Lois Marshall

Cantiones mysticae No. 1 at Carnegie Hall under Leopold Stokowski. Many other important US orchestral engagements followed – with the Chicago, Boston, and Philadelphia SOs, the New York Philharmonic, and many others. In 1955 she sang in Beethoven's *Ninth Symphony* with the Minneapolis SO. In 1956 she made her London debut with the Royal Philharmonic Orchestra under Sir Thomas Beecham in a performance of Mozart's *Exsultate, jubilate*, also singing and recording that season, with the same orchestra, Handel's *Solomon* and Mozart's *The Abduction from the Seraglio*. The following year (1957) she appeared in recital with Weldon Kilburn at the Edinburgh Festival and at the Royal Festival Hall in London. During the fall of 1958 she made the first of several tours of the USSR with Kilburn, and in 1960 she undertook a world tour which included visits to Australia and New Zealand, performing with orchestras, in recital, and over ABC radio. Also in the mid-1960s she gave joint orchestral-concert appearances with the tenor Richard *Verreau in Toronto, Montreal, and Quebec City and with the baritone Peter *van Ginkel in Winnipeg.

Marshall has sung with virtually all the major orchestras in Canada (the *CBC SO, the TSO, the *MSO, the *Winnipeg SO, the *Vancouver SO, the *NACO, etc) and abroad (the Bavarian Radio SO, the Cleveland Orchestra, the Hallé Orchestra, the Victoria (Melbourne) SO, and many others in Australia, England, the Netherlands, New Zealand, and the USA). She appeared in 1958 and 1959 at the *Vancouver International Festival; in 1971, 1972, and 1974 at the *Guelph Spring Festival; in 1957, 1963, 1964, and 1965 with Heinz *Unger's York Concert Society; and many times at the *Stratford Festival. Some of her most interesting assignments were for the latter two. With the York Concert Society she sang arias of Weber and Wagner; the *Four Last Songs* of Strauss (which she also sang at Stratford and in 1967 with the TSO, both in Toronto and in Montreal at the World Festival, *Expo 67); and, at a memorial concert for Heinz Unger 23 Mar 1965, *Les Nuits d'été* of Berlioz. At the Stratford Festival in 1962 she sang Hindemith's *Das Marienleben* with Glenn *Gould at the piano, and in 1965 she appeared there as the Queen of Sheba in the *Festival Singers' performance of Handel's *Solomon*. (She repeated this role with thrilling effect in 1972 with the Toronto Mendelssohn Choir and the NACO in Toronto, 16 years after her recording with Beecham.) Also at Stratford in 1970 with the baritone Louis *Quilico, she gave a memorable recital of operatic arias and duets. She has been a soloist innumerable times with the Toronto Mendelssohn Choir and the Festival Singers (with whom she toured western Canada and the USSR in 1977) and has appeared with other major Canadian choirs (*Winnipeg

Philharmonic, Vancouver Chamber, etc) and concert organizations. In 1965 she became a regular member of the illustrious Bach Aria Group (based in New York) with which, subsequently, she has toured extensively. Her association in that group with her compatriot Maureen *Forrester led in the early 1970s to a number of joint recitals by the two singers – at the *JMC Orford Art Centre; on tour in the Atlantic provinces in 1973 (Halifax, Fredericton, St John's, Nfld, etc); at *Massey Hall, Toronto; and at the 1972 Guelph Spring Festival.

While her career has been mainly that of a recitalist and concert and oratorio soloist, Marshall has sung opera as well. Despite the effects of severe polio at the age of two, which made a full stage career impossible, her dramatic acuity, immaculate musicianship, and extraordinary communicative gifts and vocal powers (at their peak able to meet authoritatively a wide range of soprano challenges, dramatic, lyric, and coloratura) have tempted producers to stage works especially for her. In 1949 and 1950 she sang Donna Anna in *Don Giovanni*, and in 1950 Leonora in *Fidelio*, in radio performances with the *CBC Opera Company. In 1952 she appeared for the first time on stage as the Queen of the Night in *The Magic Flute* for the Opera Festival Assn (*COC) at Toronto's *Royal Alexandra Theatre. She sang in concert performances of *Don Giovanni* ca 1955 with the National SO in Washington, DC, and was Ellen Orford in the TV premiere (CBC, 13 Jan 1959) of Britten's *Peter Grimes*. She has appeared twice with the Boston Opera under Sarah Caldwell – in 1959 as Mimi in *La Bohème* and in 1960 as *Tosca*. She also sang Massenet's *Thérèse* for Stuart Hamilton's 'Opera in Concert' series in 1976 at the St Lawrence Centre, Toronto, and the role of Filipyevna in a concert performance of *Eugene Onegin* with the TS in 1980.

Reviewing a Marshall performance, Kenneth *Winters described her in the Toronto *Telegram* (3 May 1967) as 'one of those rare singers concerned more with the colours, tempers and strengths of the music than with the colours, tempers and strengths of the voice. She subordinates her glorious voice to song, not the reverse. And the result, each time she sings, is not just singing but music itself in the full range of its implication.'

Though not regarded as a protagonist of music of the avant garde, Marshall has sung, or sung in, the premieres of several 20th-century Canadian works – in 1945 in Montreal *Brott's *Songs of Contemplation*; in 1950 in Toronto *Beckwith's *Four Songs to Poems by e.e. cummings* (commissioned by her for her graduating recital) and *Great Lakes Suite*; in 1952 in Toronto Ridout's *Esther*; in 1958 in Vancouver *McIntyre's *Judith*; in 1966 in Montreal *Freedman's **Anerca*; in 1968 in Toronto Ridout's settings of *Folk Songs of Eastern Canada*; in 1970 in Toronto *Morawetz's *From the Diary of Anne Frank*; in 1972 Richard *Johnston's *The Irish Book*; and in 1980 in Guelph, Ont, Harry *Somers' *Limericks*.

In the mid-1970s Marshall began to sing as a mezzo-soprano. Her lower voice always had been unusually strong and resilient, and since her repertoire already contained several works customarily sung by mezzos the change was by no means drastic, excluding high soprano material but on the other hand admitting the French operatic mezzo repertoire and many important Lieder in the original keys. Notable consequences of this have been her Toronto performances of Schubert's *Winterreise* (1976), of Schumann's *Frauenliebe und -leben* and *Dichterliebe* and Brahms' *Vier ernste Gesänge* (1977, with the pianist Anton *Kuerti), and of Schubert's *Die schöne Müllerin* with the pianist Greta *Kraus.

Marshall has done a limited amount of teaching – 1973–4 as artist-in-residence at Ohio State U and after 1976 at the *U of Toronto – but feels that teaching is too great a responsibility for a touring artist who must be away from her pupils for long periods of time. She has received numerous honours, including a *U of Alberta National Award in Music (1962), a Centennial Medal (1967), a *CMCouncil Medal (1972), and a Medal of Excellence from the *OAC (1973). She was awarded the *Molson Prize in 1980 and was made a Companion of the *Order of Canada in 1968. The CBC simultaneously broadcast and telecast an hour-long tribute to Lois Marshall 10 Dec 1980.

DISCOGRAPHY

Bach *Arias*. Bach Aria Group, Priestman cond. 1972. 2-Desto 7139/40

Bach *Cantata No. 51* – Mozart *Exsultate, jubilate*. TSO, MacMillan cond. 1953–4. Hallmark CS-2

Bach *Mass in B Minor*. Bavarian Radio SO, Jochum cond. Ca 1958. 3 Epic BSC-102

– *St Matthew Passion*. Toronto Mendelssohn Choir, MacMillan cond. 1953. Beaver LPS 002

Beecham in Rehearsal: Die Entführung aus dem Serail. Beecham Choral Soc, Royal Phil O, Beecham cond, Marshall (Constanze). 1957. 2-Angel S 3555 B/L

Beethoven *Missa solemnis*. Robert Shaw Chorale, NBC SO, Toscanini cond. 1953. 2-RCA Victor LM-6013

British Folk Songs. W. Kilburn pf. Ca 1958. World Record Club PE-714/HMV ALP 1671

A. Brott *Songs of Contemplation*. CBC Mtl orch, Waddington cond. 1954. RCI 116

Elwell *Pastorale*. TSO, MacMillan cond. 1953. Hallmark CS-1

Falla *Seven Popular Spanish Songs* – Purcell-Britten *Three Divine Hymns*. Kilburn pf. 1952. Hallmark RS-1

Folk Songs of the British Isles [and Elizabethan songs]. Loman hp. 1975. CBC SM-248

Handel *Messiah*. Toronto Mendelssohn Choir, MacMillan cond. 1952. Beaver LPS 001/3-RCA Victor LM-6134/ (excerpts) Beaver LPS 1003/RCA Victor LM-2088

– *Solomon*. Beecham Choral Soc, Royal Phil O, Beecham cond. 1956. 2-Angel S-3546-B

Lois Marshall Sings Folk Songs. Kilburn pf. Ca 1957. Capitol Cap W 6012 (originally released on Angel)

Mozart *Die Entführung aus dem Serail*. Beecham Choral Soc, Royal Phil O, Beecham cond, Marshall (Constanze). 1957. 2-Angel 35433-35434

Operatic Arias: Purcell – Handel – Mozart – Weber – Verdi – Bellini – Puccini. London SO, Pedrazzoli cond. (1959). HMV ALP 1642

Oratorio Arias: Handel – Haydn – Mendelssohn. London SO. Bernard cond. Ca 1957. Angel 35531

Purcell – Debussy – Barber. Kilburn pf. Ca 1968. CBC SM-30

Purcell – Mahler – Strauss – Traditional English and Hebridean songs (anon). Kilburn pf. Ca 1965. CBC SM-12

Respighi *Il Tramonto*. Orford Str Quar. 1971. CBC SM-188

Schubert – Duparc – Russell – four traditional or folk melodies (anon). Kilburn pf. 1969. RCI 333/CBC SM-101/AofD SDD-2155

Schumann *Frauenliebe und -leben*. Kilburn pf. Melody 5904

Frauenliebe und -leben – Falla *Seven Popular Spanish Songs*. Kilburn pf. Ca 1969. CBC SM-31

Schumann *Spanische Liebeslieder*. R. Sarfaty mezzo, Simoneau ten, Warfield bar, Gold and Fizdale pfs. 1961. Col MS 6461

Verdi 'Pace, Pace' from *La Forza del Destino* – Mozart *Exsultate, jubilate*. TSO, MacMillan cond. 1953. Hallmark SS-1

BIBLIOGRAPHY

Callwood, June. 'The launching of Lois Marshall,' *Maclean's*, 1 Feb 1953

Kraglund, John. 'Lois Marshall sings for the maestro in brilliant triumph of her young career,' Toronto *Globe and Mail*, 30 Mar 1953

'Celebrity artist,' *CBC Times*, 12–18 May 1962

Littler, William. 'Lois Marshall's special radiance glows in concert,' *Toronto Star*, 16 Oct 1976

Waller, Adrian. 'Lois Marshall: Canada's queen of song,' Canadian *Reader's Digest*, Nov 1978

Creative Canada, vol 2 (MFr)

MARSHALL, Phyllis (Irene Elizabeth) (m Lee, m McGibbon). Singer, actress, b Barrie, Ont, 4 Nov 1921. She studied piano as a child but made her debut at 15 as a radio singer on CRCT and performed in 1937 with Jack *Arthur and on CBC radio with Percy *Faith. Encouraged by the CBC announcer Byng Whitteker to sing blues and jazz, she performed during the 1940s with various Toronto dance bands, with her own trio, and on tour 1947–8 in the USA with Cab Calloway's orchestra. She appeared 1949–52 on CBC radio's 'Blues for Friday' (later 'Starlight Moods') and starred on CBC TV's 'The Big Revue' 1952–4, 'Cross-Canada Hit Parade' 1956–9, and other shows. She also performed in England on BBC TV in 1959 and again in 1964 in nightclubs. In the company of the US jazz stars Buck Clayton and Buddy Tate she recorded the *Juno award-winning LP *That Girl* (1964, Col FS 614). Her acting career began in 1956 at Toronto's Crest Theatre and included dramatic and musical roles in stage, radio, and TV productions such as the revue *Cindy-Ella* (1964) and CBC radio's *The Amen Corner* (1970).

BIBLIOGRAPHY

'That magic something on *The Big Revue*,' *CBC Times*, 8–14 Nov 1953

Frayne, Trent. 'No bottle tops, no props, now Phyllis wants to act,' *Star Weekly*, 16 Aug 1958

Franklin, Stephen. 'Phyllis Marshall's swinging comeback,' *Weekend Magazine*, 21 Nov 1964 (HM)

MARTEL. Family of pop singers: 1 / Marcel and his wife Noëlla Therrien, and 2 / Renée their daughter.

1 (Joseph Gaston) **Marcel**. Singer-songwriter, quitarist, b Drummondville, Que, of French Canadian-US parents, 1 Feb 1925. Born into modest circumstances, he began to sing and accompany himself on the accordion at 10 and took part in numerous amateur nights. About 1941 he took up the songs of Le soldat *Lebrun, then in vogue, accompanying himself on the guitar. With Ovila *Légaré he toured briefly in connection with the CKAC radio program 'Nazaire et Barnabé.' After his period of military service he made a tour of various Quebec radio stations in 1944. In 1945 he began writing his own songs in the country style, both words and music. The nostalgic character and the simplicity of his material made him very popular. The success in 1947 of his first 78 for *Starr, 'La Chaine de nos coeurs' and 'Souvenir de mon enfance,' resulted in a series of engagements in New England. Martel and his musicians were the stars of the weekly radio program 'L'Heure de Drummondville' 1947–9 on CHLN, Trois-Rivières. Another 78, 'Charme hawaien' and 'Près d'un feu je chante' (1950), was followed by about 100 others for Starr and Apex. With his wife, Noëlla Therrien, and his daughter Renée, he toured 1951–7 in Quebec, Ontario, and New Brunswick. His own TV program, 'Marcel Martel' (1962–5 on CHLT, Sherbrooke, Que) was extremely popular. By 1979 he had made some 130 singles and 40 LPs for Compo, London, and Bonanza. One was recorded with his wife (*Un coeur, un amour, un bonheur*, Bonanza B-29604), and others were made with his friend Paul *Brunelle or with other singers. He has performed as a guest on several programs, among others 'Le ranch à Willie' and in 1978 CFTM-TV's 'Patrick et Renée.' He is a member of CAPAC.

BIBLIOGRAPHY

Godin, Gérald. 'Ils ont inventé le cowboy québecois,' *Maclean*, Dec 1965

2 (Marie) **Renée**. Singer, b Drummondville 26 Jun 1947. As a child she participated in her parents' tours and at six she gave her first cabaret show. She also appeared on radio and TV in Sherbrooke (especially on her father's CHLT program) and sang at dances. Her success took her to Montreal

in 1967. Proclaimed 'Discovery of the Year' at the 1968 Gala des artistes, she increased her TV appearances and took part in a Musicorama tour in Quebec. The sales of her three singles, 'Liverpool,' 'Je vais à Londres,' and 'Viens changer ma vie,' earned her three gold records in 1969; she received another in 1972 for 'J'ai un amour qui ne veut pas mourir.' During the period 1968–73 she studied voice with Roger Larivière. The LP *Renée Martel* (RCA Victor Gala CGPS-316), a reissue of her best known singles, appeared in 1969. Among her LPs for Spectrum are *Mon roman d'amour* (SP-108), *Un amour qui ne veut pas mourir* (SPX-200), the reissue *Mes Plus Grands Succès* (SPS-1600), and *Réflexions* (SPS-1601, devoted to the songs of Marcel Lefebvre and Jean-Guy Chapados). She also made several LPs for Trans-World. Abandoning her early concentration on country repertoire, in 1973 she began to write the lyrics for most of her songs, which are primarily sentimental in nature, such as 'Donne-moi un jour.' In addition to many tours in Quebec, she has appeared in Montreal at the Théâtre des Variétés, at the Maisonneuve Theatre of the *PDA (1974, 1975, 1977), and at the Boîte à chansons in the Meridien Hotel (1977). In Quebec City she performed at the *Grand Théâtre in 1977. In 1978, with René *Simard, she made the LP *Souvenirs de vacances* (Nobel-1801). Songs such as 'Le Bateau de bonheur,' 'Prends ma main,' 'Finalement,' 'À demain my darling,' and 'Cowgirl dorée' (the last written for her by Robert *Charlebois in 1976) are among her greatest successes. With Patrick Zabé, she became co-host of 'Patrick et Renée' on CFTM-TV, Montreal, in 1977.

BIBLIOGRAPHY

Vincent, Pierre. 'Renée Martel refera la paire avec son père,' Montreal *La Presse*, 10 Jul 1969

ST

MARTEL, Fernand. Baritone, organist, pianist, b Quebec City 11 Aug 1919. He studied singing at *Laval U with Louis *Gravel. During World War II he toured as soloist with the Band of the *Royal 22nd Regiment. He studied with Queena Mario and Maggie Teyte 1944–8 on scholarship at the Juilliard School, obtaining his diploma in 1948 and that same year, on 25 March, making his debut with the New York City Opera as Pelléas in *Pelléas et Mélisande* opposite Maggie Teyte. He worked with Pierre Bernac in Paris prior to his Canadian debut in 1949 with Montreal's *Minute Opera in *Le Secret de Suzanne* and *Le Pauvre Matelot*. He took part in productions by the *Opéra national du Québec and sang on CBC radio in Menotti's *The Telephone*, Martinu's *Comedy on the Bridge*, Sauguet's *Les Caprices de Marianne*, Ravel's *L'Heure espagnole*, and numerous works from the repertoire. At Tanglewood in 1950 he took part in the US premiere, in the composer's presence, of Jacques Ibert's opera *Le Roi d'Yvetot*. In 1952 he sang Lescaut in Massenet's *Manon* with the Miami Opera Guild. Shortly afterwards he embarked on a solo career, accompanying himself on the piano, the organ, or the guitar. He has composed several songs. Besides five singles and one LP for London, in the USA he has made the LP *Fernand Martel at the Rodgers 340 Theatre Organ* (Concert Recording CR-CR18). After 1955 he pursued his career in Los Angeles. GP

MARTEL, Jacqueline (m Cistellini). Soprano, b Quebec City 6 Aug 1940. She began piano studies in 1946 at the Mallet convent and continued in 1952 at the *CMQ. In 1955 she began voice lessons there with Ria *Lenssens. She won the *Prix Archambault in 1957 and continued her training 1959–61 at the *CMM with Dina Maria Narici and (on a 1960 *Prix d'Europe) 1961–4 in Rome with Maria-Teresa Pediconi at the Santa Cecilia Cons and with the pianist-accompanist Giorgio Favaretto at the Accademia Santa Cecilia. She also has worked under Luigi Ricci. She has received several first prizes and honours, including a diploma of distinction from the Accademia Chigiana in Siena.

Martel made her debut in Rome in 1963 as Laetitia in Menotti's *The Old Maid and the Thief*. Until 1967 she pursued her career mainly in Italy, France, and Switzerland, but she did visit Montreal, Toronto, and Quebec City, especially, for the *Théâtre lyrique de Nouvelle-France to sing leading roles in *The Barber of Seville* (1963), *Les Pêcheurs de perles* (1964, 69), *Mireille* (1965), and *La Bohème* (1967). In the *Gazette* (19 Feb 1963), Montreal critic Thomas *Archer declared himself seduced by her 'light Latin way' with the role of Rosina and delighted by her brilliant qualities as an actress. In 1965 she premiered in Rome two works by Virgilio Mortari and made several tours, including one with I Musici Antichi and another, in Italy, France, and Switzerland, with Favaretto. She sang the title role in *Manon* for the Théâtre lyrique du Québec in 1967 and toured for the *JMC in 1968 with the harpist Dorothy *Weldon. She instituted the voice class at the Cons de Trois-Rivières in 1974 and has continued to perform on radio and TV and with the *Quebec SO and the *MSO. (MB-L)

MARTEL, Jules. Choir conductor, musicologist, historian, editor, b Acton Vale, near St-Hyacinthe, Que, 23 Feb 1905; hon D MUS (Ottawa) 1974. He entered the order of the Missionary Oblates of Mary Immaculate in 1924 and was admitted to the priesthood in 1929. He taught voice 1930–6 in Montreal and at the *U of Ottawa. Thereafter until 1939 he studied at the Pontifical School of Sacred Music in Rome, the Institut grégorien in Paris, and the École César-Franck, receiving a diploma from each institution. He was director of the school of music 1939–65 and of the Schola Cantorum 1939–43 at the U of Ottawa. He was music director 1939–42 of CBC radio's 'L'Heure dominicale' and the founder, and director 1946–58, of the choir of the Marian Congress in Ottawa – renamed the *Palestina Choir in 1948. He became the president of the Comité interdiocésain de musique sacrée du Québec. Martel has written numerous articles on sacred music and after 1940 published several books of hymns, masses, and psalms, including *Service pour les défunts* (Ottawa 1965), *Refrains liturgiques*, and *Le Livre du psalmiste* (ibid 1967). He contributed the chapters on 'church music' to *Music in Canada* and *Encyclopedia Canadiana*, vol 2. GP

MARTEL, Oscar. Violinist, teacher, b L'Assomption, near Montreal, February 1848, d Chicago 1924; premiers prix violin, string quartet (Liège Royal Cons) 1870. Starting at five he studied violin with his grandfather, Pierre Martel, a violin teacher at the Collège de L'Assomption 1837–42 and a violin maker. Oscar received his first lessons in solfège from an itinerant musician named Lumsden. He left the Collège de L'Assomption in 1865 to continue his violin studies in Montreal with Jules *Hone. While preparing for a concert career he taught violin 1865–9 at the Collège de Montréal where Alfred *De Sève was among his pupils. In 1869 he studied for several months at the Liège Royal Cons with Désiré Heynberg, Ysaÿe's first teacher, as well as with Ovide Musin and César Thomson; in the evenings he played in the orchestra of the Theatre Royal. Returning to Canada in 1870 he gave recitals and resumed his position at the Collège de Montréal. He also taught at the Gesù and Mont-St-Louis colleges.

Oscar Martel

In 1875 Martel again left for Paris and Brussels, where he took lessons from Alard, Vieuxtemps, and Hubert Léonard. Back in Canada in 1876, he married Hortense Leduc-Fortin, a voice teacher at the Villa-Maria Convent in Montreal. He spent three years in Montreal and then returned again to Paris in 1878 as member of the first violins at the Théâtre lyrique. He also performed at the Salle Érard and the Immaculée-Conception Church. After 18 months' study, he went back to Montreal in 1879 and gave numerous concerts; critics compared him to the greatest violinists of the day – Wilhelmj, Camilla Urso, and Kaiser. Declining offers to teach at the conservatories of Liège and Paris, he concentrated instead on writing a series of articles on the art of music which appeared June 1879–May 1880 in *Le Courrier* of Montreal, and he also made a concert tour of Canada and New England. In 1896 Edmond *Hardy organized the Cons of the *Canadian Artistic Society, and Martel joined its staff as a violin teacher; his pupils included Henri Arnoldi and Chambord Giguère. In *Passe-Temps* 19 Dec 1896 Gustave *Comte wrote that Martel especially excelled 'in those broad gestures through which passion, great sorrow or boundless enthusiasm may be conveyed more easily.' He continued, 'Modern music, which has succeeded in probing the deepest feelings of the human heart, gives him the chance to make his violin sing or weep desperately.'

In 1905 Martel took a position at a conservatory in Chicago. He obtained the coveted position of director of violin teaching and spent his last years in that city. He died tragically, asphyxiated by a gas leak in his apartment.

Other information about Martel (some of which, including the year of birth, cannot be verified) was provided by Georges Dorval of Chambly, Que, and published in the *Passe-Temps* of April 1947. According to Dorval, Martel 'was the son of Amédée Martel and the brother of the notary Zébédé Martel, whom I knew. His father was a painter and violin maker who also had made a small organ for the local college. He made good violins which Oscar sold at good prices in Montreal. Oscar Martel was born in 1847; he attended the college for three years. After his studies in Belgium, he became a violin teacher at the New England Conservatory of Boston where his portrait in oils may be seen.'

Martel left several unpublished compositions for violin, including *Hommage à mon pays*, a *Fantaisie de concert*, some *Variations sur 'Vive la Canadienne,'* a *Concerto in A*, a *Berceuse* and a *Mazurka* in memory of Wieniawski, some *Improvisations sur 'Old Folks at Home,'* and a *Fantaisie sur des airs écossais*, as well as several songs. None of these works had been traced in

1980, but the BN du Q holds a copy of his *Airs canadiens variés, Op 2* for violin and piano (Gevaert et fils, Liège, nd).

BIBLIOGRAPHY
'La Société artistique et les professeurs du futur conservatoire,' Montreal *Le Samedi*, 6 Apr 1895
Trépanier, Léon. 'Le violonist Oscar Martel de L'Assomption révélé par de vieux papiers de famille,' Montreal *La Patrie*, 2 Apr 1950
'Oscar Martel, violonist et professeur,' *Qui?*, vol 4, Mar 1953 (CG)

MARTEL, Rachel (m Cantin). Pianist, teacher, b La Tuque, Que, 12 Mar 1939; premier prix piano (CMQ) 1959. She studied 1953–6 at the École supérieure de musique in Nicolet and 1956–9 at the *CMQ with Guy *Bourassa. In 1959 she obtained the *Prix d'Europe and a *Canada Council scholarship. She worked in Paris with Yvonne Loriod and in Karlsruhe, Germany, at the Badische Hochschule für Musik, from which she graduated in 1963. She received the special interpretation prize for her performance of Kelsey *Jones' *Passacaglia*, the Canadian set piece in the first (1961) *JMC National Competition, and toured for the JMC in 1962–3 and 1966–7. With Pierre *Morin she premiered André *Prévost's *Cello Sonata* in Paris in 1962. Appointed coach-accompanist at *Laval U in 1967, she also has accompanied Pierre *Boutet, Chantal *Masson, the violinist Liliane Garnier-Lesage, and the clarinetist John Van Bockern; and with the soprano Ginette Duplessis she premiered Jacques *Hétu's *Les Clartés de la nuit* at Quebec City in 1973. She returned to France in 1968 to study harpsichord with Robert Veyron-Lacroix in Nice. A pianist often praised by critics for the elegance and musicality of her playing, Martel has performed also as a harpsichordist on CBC radio and TV. In 1964 she made the LP *Oeuvres pour flûte et piano* with her husband Roger Cantin (Radio-Marie RM 36503). (MB-L)

Martenot. Method of music education created by the French pedagogue Maurice Martenot (b Paris 1898, d there 1980), the inventor of the *Ondes Martenot. The method's principles were introduced to Quebec in 1954 in the training of kindergarten teachers at the Institut pédagogique of the Congregation of Notre-Dame, Montreal. The method endeavours to make teachers aware of the considerable differences, from the educational point of view, between the elements that give material form to music and music itself. Its purpose is 'to liberate, nurture, and respect the creative essence of life while instilling the necessary techniques.' It is concerned as much with developing the personal qualities of its practitioners as with imparting a teaching method. According to Martenot, the fundamental principles of music education may be applied to art and dance as well as to solfège and piano. Based on the 'three Montessori steps' – imitation, recognition, and reproduction – they are in complete contrast to traditional methods in that they analyse the evolution of learning from sense perception to the acquisition of knowledge.

From 1965 to 1971 Martenot gave instruction in these principles, tailored to the development of musical aptitudes for application in solfège in the classroom, in teacher training sessions at the *École normale de musique in Montreal. The aspect of the method dealing specifically with the piano was taught by his sister Ginette Martenot (b Paris 1902) at the *Laval U summer course five times between 1959 and 1971.

The Martenot method is known mainly in France, Spain, and Portugal, but is taught as well in Quebec and South America. An advanced Martenot diploma is granted in France; in Quebec study certificates were given by the École normale de musique. By 1980, in its music education program, *UQAM was offering courses on several methods of teaching music, including Martenot's. Instructors in the method may obtain the five LPs of the *Jeux musicaux Martenot* (La Pléiade P 3107-11) and a book by the author, *Se relaxer* (Paris 1977), materials published by the Éditions Magnard. Among Maurice Martenot's Canadian pupils are Jean *Laurendeau and Gilles *Tremblay.

BIBLIOGRAPHY
Rapport de la Commission royale d'enquête sur l'enseignement des arts dans la province de Québec, vol 2 (Quebec 1969) (MCr)

MARTENS, Helen. Teacher, choir conductor, ethnomusicologist, b Sagradowska, Ukraine, 21 Feb 1928, naturalized Canadian 1935; LRSM 1952, BA (Minnesota) 1954, MA (Minnesota) 1956, PH D (Columbia) 1968. Her family emigrated to Canada in 1930, settling in Sanford, Man. She studied piano with Leonard *Heaton in Winnipeg and musicology with Paul Henry Lang, Edward Lippman, Denis Stevens, and Walter Wiora at Columbia U. After teaching 1954–6 at H.J. MacDonald High School in Winnipeg, she taught piano 1959–62 at Bluffton College in Ohio and joined the staff at Conrad Grebel College, *U of Waterloo, in 1965, teaching courses in choral music and music history and appreciation. She is the founder (1966) and conductor of the Inter-Mennonite Children's Choir of Waterloo, which in 1978 won top prize in the CBC/Canada Council National Radio Competition for Amateur Choirs. Her pupils have included Doria Lora and Jeremy Constant. She has become an authority on the music of the *Hutterites and *Mennonites and has contributed articles on these to *EMC* and *Ethnomusicology*. (NM)

MARTENS, John (Ernst). Tenor, b Winnipeg 15 Oct 1935; BA (Toronto) 1963, M MUS (Southern Methodist) 1969, DMA (Michigan) 1972. A pupil (but not a relation) of Victor *Martens, he made his professional oratorio debut 5 Dec 1963 in *Messiah* with the *Winnipeg Philharmonic Choir and the *Winnipeg SO and won the Rose Bowl at the 1964 *Manitoba Music Competition Festival. He gave up school teaching in 1967 for a career in music, increasing his qualifications with study 1969–72 on a *Canada Council doctoral fellowship with Thomas Hayward and Lloyd Pfautsch at Southern Methodist U, Dallas. He taught briefly (1972) at the U of Michigan, moved to Toronto as a member of the *Festival Singers 1972–4, and returned in 1974 to Winnipeg to teach music at the *Mennonite Brethren Bible College. Leading Canadian choral conductors (Melville *Cook, Elmer *Iseler, Hugh *McLean, Wayne *Riddell) and several in the USA have chosen him repeatedly as an aria soloist or the Evangelist in the Bach passions, so that by the mid-1970s he came to be regarded as the foremost current Canadian exponent of those roles. He has also sung in numerous *Messiah* performances, including those by the *Toronto Mendelssohn Choir at *Massey Hall in 1973 and *Ontario Place in 1976 and 1977. Other engagements have included Haydn's *The Creation* (1966) with the Winnipeg SO, Honegger's *Jeanne d'Arc au bûcher* (1972) with the Detroit SO under Sixten Ehrling, Bach's *Christmas Oratorio* (1974) with the *Vancouver Bach Choir, the Monteverdi *Magnificat* (1974) with the Toronto Mendelssohn Choir at the *Guelph Spring Festival, Stravinsky's *Pulcinella* (1974) with the *Vancouver SO under Lukas Foss and (1976) with the *TS under Andrew Davis, and Lukas Foss' *Psalms* (1975) with the TS and the Toronto Mendelssohn Choir. In Winnipeg he gave the premiere, 18 Jun 1976, of Leslie *Mann's *Seven Elizabethan Songs*. Excerpts from his performance of Schubert's *Die schöne Müllerin* were captured on a 30-minute videotape released by the U of Michigan TV Studio in 1972. After Martens' Rose Bowl performance Kenneth *Winters, writing in the *Winnipeg Free Press* (20 Apr 1964) praised 'a fine tenor voice, a sensitive musical conscience, a reliable ear and the kind of quiet authority that radiates from honest work well done.' (AHC)

MARTENS, Theodor(e) (Heinrich August). Pianist, teacher, b Hamburg 28 Sep 1845, d after 1914. The son of a musician, he studied in Hamburg and later, 1864–7, at the Leipzig Cons with Moscheles and Reinecke. In 1868 he went to New York and toured the USA with Ole Bull. A year later he became music director at Mount Allison Wesleyan Academy, Sackville, NB, and in the early 1870s was appointed organist at Holy Trinity Church in Saint John, NB. After a visit to Germany he settled in Toronto ca 1879. He edited the *University of Toronto Song Book* (Suckling 1887) and *Canadian National and Patriotic Songs* (Suckling 1890) and was music master (1889–91) at Upper Canada College. Harry Marshall *Field was among his pupils. He is known to have been in California in 1894.

His brother Carl (Johann Christian) Martens, a pianist, composer, and teacher (b Hamburg, 10 Apr 1853, d ?), also studied in Hamburg and with Reinecke in Leipzig 1877–9. He settled about 1880 in Toronto, where he became a partner in the Crossin & Martens Piano Manufacturing Co and a teacher at the *Toronto College of Music. He composed the *Blue Ontario Rockaway, Electric Light Schottische, Toronto's Jubilee 1834–1884*, and other trifles. He participated in chamber music concerts with the *Toronto String Quartette and as accompanist for the soprano Emma Juch in 1885. HK

MARTENS, Victor. Tenor, teacher, conductor, b Yarrow, east of Vancouver, 18 Feb 1931; ARCT 1955, BA (Waterloo Lutheran) 1963. After lessons in Winnipeg with Gladys *Whitehead he studied at the Nordwestdeutsche Musikakademie, Detmold, under Frederick Husler, Theodore Lindenbaum, and Kurt Thomas. A recitalist and oratorio soloist noted for his interpretation of Lieder and of the Evangelist roles in the Bach passions, Martens has sung on radio in London, Frankfurt, Zurich, and Geneva and in concert with orchestras in Germany. He also has performed on CBC radio (eg, the Male Chorus in Britten's *The Rape of Lucretia* in 1963), with the NACO, and with the Winnipeg, Saskatoon, Edmonton, and Vancouver SOs. He was a member 1965–72 of the *Manitoba Consort and has recorded with that group. With the *Kitchener-Waterloo SO he sang the leading tenor roles in concert versions of *La Traviata* in 1972, *Carmen* in 1973, *Fidelio* in 1975, and *Don Giovanni* in 1976.

Martens was music director 1958–69 at Winnipeg's *Mennonite Brethren College and conductor there of the Oratorio Choir and the A Cappella Choir. He moved to Waterloo, Ont, in 1969 to teach voice and direct the Collegium Musicum at Waterloo Lutheran (*Wilfrid Laurier) U. His pupils in Winnipeg and Waterloo have included Paul Frey, John *Martens, Wilmer Neufeld, Alvin Reimer, Elizabeth Strauss, Ingrid Suderman, and Phyllis *Cooke Thomson. Martens' wife, Dorothea Epp (soprano, b Winnipeg 13 Oct 1934), studied with Gladys Whitehead and won the Rose Bowl at the 1966 *Manitoba Music Competition Festival. (WHK)

MARTIN. Quebec family of musicians: 1 / Alphonse and his wife Corinne, and their four daughters, 2 / Gilberte, 3 / Marcelle, 4 / Magdeleine, and 5 / Raymonde, musicians and teachers in Quebec.

1 **Alphonse**. Organist, pianist, teacher, b Trois-Rivières, Que, 18 Feb 1884, d Montreal 6 Jun 1947. A pupil of Lévis Dussault, he taught piano and organ in Montreal, where he was a member of the board of the Cons royal de musique and organist at St Mary's Church. Rodolphe *Mathieu was one of his pupils. He gave a few concerts with his wife, Corinne Boisvert (b St-Stanislas, near Trois-Rivières, Que, 20 Jul 1887, d Montreal 30 Jun 1961). She studied with Arthur *Letondal and was organist at St-Jean-Vianney Church, as well as teaching 1951–61 at St-Laurent and Ste-Thérèse colleges in Montreal.

2 **Gilberte** (m De Bellefeuille). Pianist, teacher, administrator, b Montreal 22 May 1910. She studied 1914–30 with Arthur *Letondal (piano) and Georges-Émile *Tanguay (harmony). She won numerous prizes, grants, and diplomas, including the *Prix d'Europe in 1930. At the École normale de Paris she studied piano with Mme Bascourret de Gueraldi and obtained a Prix de virtuosité. Alfred Cortot, Lazare Lévy, and Maurice Amour also were among her teachers. In 1932 she was the first Canadian woman admitted to the Paris Cons as a regular student; she also enrolled in Georges Caussade's fugue class. She gave numerous recitals before returning to Montreal in 1934. She was a soloist with the *CSM in 1935 in Vincent d'Indy's *Symphonie sur un chant montagnard français* and in 1937 in Giovanni Sgambati's *Concerto*, and she gave public recitals and performed on radio. At the *CMM, she taught piano, solfège, and harmony 1943–69 and was the staff representative to the administration 1969–71 and finally associate director and interim director 1971–4. She also taught 1955–65 at the *Institut Nazareth. Her numerous activities besides teaching have included examining and setting up study programs and examination criteria at the CMM and the *AMQ and for festival competitions. Following one of her recitals in Paris, *Le Monde musical* described her as 'one of the best Canadian pianists' and continued, 'She combines great sensitivity with flawless sober playing.'

WRITINGS

Doigtés pour les gammes en doubles-tierces et en doubles-sixtes et pour les arpèges de trois et quatre sons (Montreal 1943)

3 **Marcelle** (m Graton). Organist, pianist, teacher, b Montreal 19 Aug 1917; lauréat organ (AMQ) 1941. She studied piano with her father, her aunt Marie-Louise Boisvert, her sister Gilberte, and Arthur *Letondal and theory and organ with Georges-Émile *Tanguay. She won the *Prix d'Europe for organ in 1941 and pursued her organ studies 1941–5 with Joseph *Bonnet and Gaston Dethier at the Juilliard School in New York. She received numerous grants and took part in many radio broadcasts. While in New York she participated in the WKR radio program 'School of Ethical Culture' and was organist at St-Vincent-de-Paul Church. After her return to Montreal, the Bureau des concerts canadiens and the impresario G.-A. Robert presented her in public concerts. She performed in the *Casavant Society series and gave a recital at St-Viateur Church, Outremont, where she resumed the post of organist, which she had in 1938 while still a student. In 1953 she became organist at St-Joseph Church in the Town of Mount Royal. She was a soloist with the CBC and performed with the Montreal Youth SO and the *MSO, notably in Saint-Saëns' *Symphony No. 3* conducted by Zubin Mehta. She also played the Poulenc *Concerto* with the *Montreal Women's SO under Ethel *Stark. She taught 1949–54 at St-Laurent and Ste-Thérèse colleges, ca 1967 at the *U of Montreal, 1970–6 at the *CMM, and 1975–6 at the Cons de Rimouski. She married the conductor Fernand *Graton.

4 **Magdeleine**. Pianist, teacher, b Montreal 28 Aug 1921. She studied piano with her sister Gilberte and organ and harmony with Georges-Émile *Tanguay. In 1943 she was admitted to the *CMM; her teachers there were Isidor Philipp (piano) and Joseph *Bonnet (organ). With the help of grants from the French and Quebec governments she studied 1948–53 at the Paris Cons and obtained several diplomas. Her subjects there were analysis with Olivier Messiaen, piano with Mme Bascourret de Gueraldi, theory with Simone Plé-Caussade, and musicology with Alexis Roland-Manuel and Marcel Beaufils. Upon her return she gave recitals on the CBC and on radio station CKAC. She taught history, analysis, and theory 1953–73 at the *CMQ and theory beginning in 1973 at the CMM. Her pupils include Noëlla Genest, Pierre Genest, Nil *Parent, and Paul-Émile *Talbot.

5 **Raymonde**. Cellist, teacher, b Montreal 27 Apr 1923. She enrolled at the *CMM in 1943 and studied solfège and harmony with her sister Gilberte and cello with Jean *Belland and later with Roland *Leduc. At the same time she improved her knowledge of chamber and orchestral music. A member 1940–50 of the *Montreal Women's SO, she performed Boellmann's *Variations symphoniques* at the Matinées symphoniques of the *MSO and Saint-Saëns' *Concerto No. 1* in 1949 with the Montreal Youth SO. During these years she also played on radio and in public recitals. She won the *Prix Archambault in 1947 and a Quebec government grant in 1950 and attended the Paris Cons for four years, studying with Simone Plé-Caussade (theory) and Paul Bazelaire (cello). During the summer of 1953 she again worked with the latter at the American Cons at Fontainebleau, while attending Nadia Boulanger's classes. In 1955 she gave up performing to teach in private schools. She also taught at the *U of Ottawa 1967–71 and at the Cons de Hull beginning in 1967. 1 / IP-C, 2 / NTr, 3, 4, 5 / IP-C

MARTIN, Charles-Amador. Priest, musician, b Quebec City 7 Mar 1648, d Ste-Foy, near Quebec, 19 Jun 1711. He was the son of Abraham Martin (whose name is perpetuated in the Plains of Abraham), was a pupil of Martin *Boutet at the Jesuit College, and studied theology at the Seminaire de Québec. The second Canadian-born priest, he was ordained in 1671 and served as curé in a number of parishes near Quebec City, his longest term, 1698–1711, being that at Notre-Dame-de-Sainte-Foy. He was also a teacher and administrator (ca 1680) at the Seminaire de Québec and a canon 1684–97 and (according to Amtmann) grand chantre after 1698 at the Quebec Cathedral. As early as 1662 the *Jesuit Relations* mention 'Amador' as a church singer.

About 20 years after Martin's death Mother Marie-Andrée Regnard Duplessis de Ste-Hélène (1687–1760), the chronicler of the Hôtel-Dieu in Quebec, reported that Martin, 'a capable singer, composed the chant of the Mass and the Office of the Holy Family in its present form.' Later historians, including Ernest *Gagnon and Auguste-H. Gosselin, accepted only that Martin wrote the

The beginning of Charles-Amador Martin's prose 'Sacrae familiae' in *Graduel romain*, 1854 edition

music for the Prose of the Office, but Eugène *Lapierre even assigned a date, 1670, to the composition ('Canada, Musique,' *Encyclopédie Grolier*, Montreal 1947). The Prose 'Sacrae familiae felix spectaculum' survives in a number of 18th-century manuscripts and was printed first in the *Processionel romain* in 1801. It was chanted at the Quebec cathedral on the Holy Family feastday until the 1950s. Was Martin really the composer of the Prose, and is the latter Canada's oldest preserved composition? Although the Holy Family celebration goes back to 1665, the date 1670 cannot be accepted, since the final text of the Office was written much later and was used for the first time in 1703. This text was commissioned from a French poet, the Abbé Simon Gourdan, and (according to Amtmann, who has examined the problem in great detail) it is possible that the music too was written in France and that Martin's 'composition' was merely an assembling of the different musical components for the celebration. Comparison of an early manuscript with Martin's known handwriting has not settled the matter.

BIBLIOGRAPHY

Marie-Andrée Regnard Duplessis, mère de Ste-Hélène. [De la dévotion à la Sainte-Famille], ms, ca 1730
Gagnon, Ernest. *Louis Jolliet* (Quebec, 3rd edn 1926)
Amtmann. *Music in Canada*
DCB, vol 2 HK

MARTIN, David. Violinist, teacher, b Winnipeg 2 Aug 1911; LRAM 1931, ARCM 1938, FRAM 1949. He took violin lessons 1919–28 in Winnipeg with George Rutherford and in 1928 in Regina with Kathleen *Parlow, then won a scholarship through the *AB of the RSM in 1928 and studied 1929–34 at the RAM with Rowsby Woof. His solo debut in London (Wigmore Hall, 1935) led to a second recital there in 1936, and he was an assisting artist at the 1938 Wigmore Hall recital of music by Ada Twohy *Kent, performing the *16 Variations on an English Theme* with the pianist-composer. In the years following he frequently was a soloist at the Promenade Concerts in Royal Albert Hall and was the leader of the Philharmonic String Trio 1935–40 and the Martin String Quartet 1948–68. He formed the Martin Piano Trio in 1945. With these groups he has recorded chamber music of Beethoven, Dvořák, Françaix, Mozart, and Schubert; the trio's recording (SAGA 5230) of the John Ireland *Piano Trios* was the only one of this music available in the 1970s. He also performed frequently with Frederick *Grinke. In 1943 Martin became a teacher at the RAM, and thereafter he coached at summer schools in England, Austria, and Canada (the *NYO 1967, the *Banff SFA 1968–73). Among his Canadian pupils are Gerald

Jarvis, Sydney Mann, and Thomas *Rolston. Martin is also the teacher of Peter Cropper, Ralph Holmes (who has performed frequently in Canada), Hugh Maguire, Raymond Ovens (see Purcell String Quartet), Kenneth Sillito, John Stein, Peter Thomas, Alan Traverse, and Trevor Williams.

(GBr)

MARTIN, Lucien. Violinist, conductor, composer, b Montreal 30 May 1908, d there 29 Oct 1950; licence de concert (École normale, Paris) 1933. He took his first violin lessons from his father, Cyrice, a violinist and string-instrument maker; at seven, on the recommendation of Claude *Champagne, he was accepted as a student at the *Cons national of Montreal, where his swift progress led to a gold medal. In 1916 he played at the Central Theater in Biddeford, Me. He studied 1917–20 with Albert *Chamberland, 1920–3 with Alfred *De Sève, and 1923–5 with Camille *Couture and took courses in harmony with Georges-Émile *Tanguay. Between 1925 and 1928 he performed in various US cities. When he returned to Montreal he continued his studies with Camille Couture until 1931. Awarded the 1931 *Prix d'Europe he left in September for France to study under Maurice Hayot.

Martin returned to Canada in July 1933 and gave recitals later that year at the Imperial Theatre in Montreal and at the Salle Montcalm in Quebec City. Settling in Montreal, he gave a recital for the *Ladies' Morning Musical Club and was heard on radio. He was a member of the first violins of the CSM orchestra and was soloist at its second concert, 4 Feb 1935, in Bruch's *Concerto No. 1*. The critic for Montreal's *La Presse* the following day praised his 'passionate interpretation and confident technique.' After another period in Paris, working with Georges Enesco, he returned to Montreal and was second violin 1937–8 of the *Dubois String Quartet. In the late 1930s he was a soloist and orchestra member for numerous radio programs, particularly on station CKAC and on CBC's *'Les Joyeux Troubadours.' He conducted CKAC's 'Café-concert Kraft' orchestra in 1949 and other ensembles and also conducted public concerts, including one at *Plateau Hall 22 Sep 1948 and one at the Delorimier stadium, where his program included *Miro's *Scènes mauresques*. His only published composition, the art song 'La Chanson des belles' (Musica Enrg), to words by Tristan Klingsor, was premiered by Jeanne *Desjardins on the CBC program 'Sérénade pour cordes.' DM

Mart Kenney and His Western Gentlemen. See Kenney.

'Mary Ann.' Canadian version of a 19th-century British broadside which has been reprinted and recorded frequently. Marius *Barbeau heard it in 1920 in Tadoussac, Que, from Edouard Hovington, a former Hudson's Bay trapper, then about 90, who had learned it from an Irish sailor ca 1850. Barbeau included it in the National Museum of Canada publication *Come A Singing!* (1947). It is one of the large group of songs in which parting lovers vow to be faithful and is related to such older verses as 'The True Lover's Farewell' and 'The Turtle Dove.' The song was recorded by Charles *Jordan for the RCA Victor / RCI nine-record set *Canadian Folk Songs: A Centennial Collection* (CS 100-4). EF

MASELLA. Montreal family of instrumentalists of Italian origin: 1 / Raffaele, 2 / Frank, his son, and Frank's eight sons, 3 / Rafael, 4 / Pietro, 5 / Joseph, 6 / Rodolfo, 7 / Alfred, 8 / Paul, 9 / Mario, and 10 / Giulio.

The Masella family in 1954

BIBLIOGRAPHY

Johnstone, Ken. 'How Papa Masella made his boys make music,' *Maclean's*, 1 Mar 1954

1 **Raffaele**. Clarinetist, cabinet-maker, wood-carver, b Ischitella, Italy, 12 Mar 1865, naturalized Canadian 1908, d Montreal 31 Dec 1952. He was a clarinetist in 1898 in the Banda Bianca in San Severo, Italy, before coming in 1905 to Montreal, where his family joined him four years later. He was a member of the Montreal Concert Band and the Victoria Rifles Band. A cabinet-maker and wood-carver, he made furniture for the Montreal firm McAndrew, Cerini, and Jenkins.

2 **Frank** (Francesco). Clarinetist, b Ischitella, Italy, 26 Mar 1897, d Montreal 28 Jun 1979. He studied solfège in San Severo and clarinet with Giulio *Romano in Montreal, where he settled in November 1909. Later he was a member of various orchestras, performing at the Family Theatre in 1912, the Théâtre français in 1917 (*Lakmé, Carmen, Mignon*, and *Faust*), and the Passe-Temps Theatre in 1918. Between 1914 and 1919 he also played in *Sohmer Park and at Dominion Square. He belonged in 1915 to the Concordia Concert Band and 1916–46 to the *Canadian Grenadier Guards Band. On 4 Jun 1921 he married Giovanna Leonelli, whom he had met in Montreal; they had eight sons. He led the Banda Rossini 1927–9 and like other Montreal conductors of the day provided music for silent movies and for live performances at the Orpheum, Imperial, and Capitol theatres. He was principal clarinet of the *Variétés lyriques orchestra for 13 years and of the *Quebec SO 1950–2 and a member of the *Montreal Orchestra and the *MSO. He also played with the *Little Symphony of Montreal and gave recitals on the CBC.

3 **Rafael** (Raffaele). Clarinetist, teacher, composer, b Montreal 1 Oct 1922; L MUS (McGill) 1939, premier prix clarinet (Paris Cons) 1948. After taking lessons in theory and solfège from his father and grandfather he studied clarinet with Joseph Moretti 1935–9 at *McGill U and with Jan Williams and Arthur Christman 1939–41 at the Juilliard School, New York. In 1937 he was a member of the *Canadian Grenadier Guards Band. He went back to McGill U for further studies with Claude *Champagne (theory), Henri *Miro, and Frank *Hanson (harmony and composition). He was principal clarinet in the RCAF Band 1943–5, studied at the Paris Cons 1946–8 with Auguste Périer and François Étienne, and obtained second prize at the Geneva International Competition for Musical Performance in 1947, the first Canadian to win an award in this competition. That year he performed Émilien *Allard's *Divertissement* for clarinet and orchestra at a festival of Canadian music in Paris. (In 1975 he performed the work again, along with Weber's *Concerto, Op 64*, on the CBC TV program 'Concerto.') With Colombe *Pelletier and Gilles *Lefebvre he formed the Trio canadien, which performed in 1948 at the Salle Gaveau, Paris, as well as in Belgium, Luxemburg, and Canada. Masella went on *JMC tours in Quebec in 1957–8 and 1960–1. He was principal clarinet with the *MSO 1944–6 and 1948–70 and guest soloist with numerous orchestras, including the *McGill Chamber Orchestra, with which he played Andrew *Twa's *Serenade* (1964) and other works. In 1963 he and the saxophonist Arthur *Romano performed Marius Flothius' *Double Concerto* with the CBC *'Little Symphonies' Orchestra. He has appeared in recitals with his wife, the harpist Dorothy *Weldon. He taught 1955–65 at the McGill Cons and began teaching at the *CMM in 1958; he was instructor in 1976 for the wind section of the JM World Orchestra and in 1978 for the clarinet section of the *NYO at the *Banff SFA. Gilles Carpentier, Jean *Laurendeau, and Victor Sawa were among his pupils.

Masella's *Fantaisie* for piano was premiered in 1940 on the CBC by Fleurette *Beauchamp, his former piano teacher. His other compositions include an *Ave Maria* for soprano and piano (1941), a *Menuet* for piano, *The Nanyon Parade* (1941), a *Valse* for piano and military band (1942), and a *Sonata* for violin and piano premiered in 1949 by Norman Herschorn and Gilbert Hill at *Tudor Hall. Masella also composed two songs, 'L'Entrée de mon amour' and 'Till We Meet Again.'

See also Discography for the Montreal String Quartet.

4 **Pietro** (Ottavio). Oboist, teacher, b Montreal 6 Jan 1924. Giuseppe *Agostini gave him his first oboe lessons in 1935. His first experience as an orchestra player was in the *MSO under the baton of Bruno Walter in 1941. While on military service he took courses 1943–6 at the *CMM with Bruno Labate and Michel Nazzi and studied 1946–50 at the Paris Cons with Pierre Bajeux. Back in Canada he joined the CBC Montreal orchestra and the *McGill Chamber Orchestra and returned to the MSO in 1952. He began teaching at the Cons de Hull in 1970 and at the Vanier Cegep in Ville St-Laurent in 1974.

5 **Joseph** (Giuseppe). French hornist, teacher, b Montreal 28 Jul 1925; premier prix french horn (CMM) 1946. After some instruction from the clarinetist Joseph Moretti, he studied at the *CMM 1943–6 with Harry Berv. He was principal horn with the *MSO and the CBC Montreal orchestra 1943–69 and a member of the CBC *'Little Sympho-

nies' Orchestra for several years. With his brothers Paul and Giulio he premiered Michel *Perrault's *Serenade per tre fratelli* on CBC TV in 1964. He taught at the CMM and the *CMQ 1946–64 and at the Cons de Trois-Rivières after 1965. Paul Marcotte, who attained his premier prix in 1977, was one of his pupils. See also Discography for Noël Brunet.

6 **Rodolfo**. Bassoonist, teacher, b Montreal 7 Oct 1928. His first instrument was the cello, which he studied with Raoul *Duquette and later with Jean *Belland at the *CMM 1943–6. He then began to concentrate on the bassoon, which he studied 1948–52 with Louis Letellier and Simon Kovar and in the summer of 1954 in Philadelphia with Sol Schoenbach. He was appointed bassoonist with the *Variétés lyriques and the *MSO in 1946 and served 1954–68 as the latter's principal bassoon. He and his brother Rafael performed Karl Stamitz' *Double Concerto* with the CBC *'Little Symphonies' Orchestra in 1962. He became a teacher at the CMM in 1958 and vice-president of the Montreal Musicians' Guild in 1970. He became personnel manager of the MSO and musicians' representative for Les Grands Ballets Canadiens and for CBC programs such as 'Les Grands Concerts.'

7 **Alfred** (Alfredo). Violinist, teacher, b Montreal 18 May 1930. He studied at *McGill U 1942–7 with Rachel Gilbert and at the Paris Cons 1947–53 with André Asselin (violin) and Gaston Poulet (chamber music). On his return to Canada he joined the *MSO and the CBC *'Little Symphonies' Orchestra and other ensembles. He moved to Paris in 1969 and became a regular member of the Orchestre de l'Opéra in 1977. He began teaching at several regional conservatories in the Paris suburbs in 1973 and joined both the orchestra of the Concerts Colonne and the Fernand Oubradous Chamber Orchestra.

8 **Paul** (Élie). French hornist, teacher, b Montreal 19 Sep 1931; premier prix french horn, chamber music (CMM) 1956. He studied piano with John *Newmark 1949–51 and Jean-Marie *Beaudet 1951–2. He took french horn lessons 1951–6 from his brother Joseph and Harry Berv at the *CMM and from Milon Yanchich at Saranac Lake, NY. He was principal horn with the *Quebec SO 1952–7 and the *McGill Chamber Orchestra 1966–9 and soloist with the CBC Montreal orchestra. He also performed in chamber and orchestral works in various programs in the CBC radio series 'CBC Tuesday Night' 1968–70 and 'Les Grands Concerts' 1974–7. He was a member of the *MSO 1956–69. On CBC radio he premiered Michel *Perrault's *Concerto* for french horn in 1968. He taught 1957–60 at the CMM and 1965–8 at the *École Vincent-d'Indy. In 1967 he was appointed instructor of the orchestra class and director of the chamber ensembles at the Cons de Hull. Michael Gent and François Trottier were among his pupils. He married the soprano Claire *Grenon.

9 **Mario** (Antonio Giovanni). Violinist, b Montreal 12 Aug 1934. He studied first with George Lapenson and Rachel Gilbert, in Paris 1951–3 with André Asselin, and at the *CMM 1953–7 with John Charuk. He received the *Prix Archambault in 1956. He joined the *MSO in 1958 and has played in various CBC orchestras.

10 **Giulio** (Luigi). French hornist, teacher, b Montreal 8 Dec 1935; premier prix french horn (CMM) 1952. His brother Joseph and Harry Berv taught him at the *CMM 1947–55. He joined the *MSO in 1954 and began to play regularly in CBC orchestras and ensembles in 1965. He also played 1965–75 in the *McGill Chamber Orchestra. He took occasional lessons 1969–70 from the Australian horn player Barry Tuckwell at Dartmouth College, NH, to perfect his skills. He was a founding member of the *SMCQ Ensemble and continued to perform with the group in 1980. In 1974 he founded the Quebec Brass Ensemble, chiefly to give workshops in schools. In 1974 he began teaching at the UQATR and in 1975 at the St-Laurent Cegep.

DISCOGRAPHY

H. Davidson *Divertissement*. Iacurto cl, Moisan b cl. (1963). RCI 192

See also Discography for Gilles Tremblay.

The Masella Wind Trio, consisting of Pietro, Rafael, and Rodolfo, was particularly active in the decade 1950–60. It made a JMC tour of Quebec in 1950–1, gave concerts in Montreal, and took part in the CBC program 'Radio-Collège,' among others. Joseph Masella and the pianist John Newmark joined the trio to record Beethoven's *Quintet, Op 16* in 1951 (RCI 48). The five also performed in Ottawa and at the Montreal Museum of Fine Arts as part of the *Montreal Festivals in August 1960. ST

Mashmakhan. Montreal rock band formed in 1965 as The Triangle to accompany the rhythm and blues singer Trevor Payne. The members, who had worked together in other bands as early as 1960, were the singer-composer-organist-flutist Pierre Sénécal, the guitarist Ray Blake, and the drummer Jerry Mercer. On leaving Payne, they made their debut in February 1969 at the Montreal club the Laugh-In, then gave the first rock concert heard at the *NAC, Ottawa. After the addition of the bass guitarist Brian Edwards they adopted the name Mashmakhan (after an exotic hallucinogen) and released the LP *Mashmakhan* (Col ELS 365), from which the single 'As the Years Go By' (Sénécal) was taken. A substantial hit in Canada, the USA, and Japan in 1970, it led to concerts in those countries, including a Tokyo appearance in 1971 before 40,000 fans. A second LP, *Family* (Epic E30813), was released in 1971. The group, whose music was characterized by a certain complexity of structure, disbanded in 1972, though Sénécal attempted to revive Mashmakhan in 1973 with Brian Greenway (guitar), Steve Lang (bass guitar), and Lorne Nehring (drums).

BIBLIOGRAPHY

Bist, Dave. 'Mashmakhan's success based on people contact,' *MSc*, 258, Mar–Apr 1971 (MM)

MASON, Lawrence. Critic, b Chicago 8 Oct 1882, d Toronto 9 Dec 1939; PH D (Yale) 1916. He studied at Harvard U and Yale U and taught English at the latter for 17 years before his appointment in 1924 as music and drama critic for the Toronto *Globe* (after 1936 the *Globe and Mail*). He also was editor of the *Globe*'s Saturday page 'Music in the Home – Concert – The Drama.' In his writings he staunchly supported the fledgling *TSO. In 1925 he wrote an 11-part survey (4 Jul–26 Sep) of music and drama in communities of southwest Ontario; in 1936 he compiled bibliographies (actually biographies with bibliographic additions, and published 30 May–31 Oct) of 18 Canadian composers. He also contributed some 130 Canadian entries to *Thompson's International Cyclopedia of Music and Musicians* (New York 1938). Mason travelled widely in Canada and visited Great Britain as a lecturer, reporter, and drama adjudicator. On his death John A. Atkinson, director of the *Canadian Bureau for the Advancement of Music, wrote that he was 'a fine, fair, capable music critic, and a friend and strong supporter of every development of the love of music in the mind of the public and especially of children ... He was keenly interested in the development of Canadian talent and a great supporter of music festivals throughout Canada' (*Globe and Mail*, 11 Dec 1939). DS

Mason & Risch. A leading Canadian piano manufacturing firm established in 1871 in Toronto by the former A. & S. *Nordheimer accountant Thomas G. Mason, with Vincent M. Risch and Octavius Newcombe. During its first six years it imported and sold music and instruments. Risch supervised piano tuning and repairs. The first piano was built in 1877. A year later the Mason-Risch-Newcombe partnership was dissolved, and Mason & Risch continued their business association, developing a cross-country retail chain (which later included the distribution of records and talking machines) and making extensive sales abroad. Among the many prizes and endorsements received by Mason & Risch was a tribute from Liszt, who sent them a life-size portrait of himself in 1881. By 1900 the company had built some 20,000 pianos; by 1950, over 65,000. In 1948 it was sold to Winter & Co of the USA but continued to manufacture pianos in Toronto under the Mason & Risch name. The cross-Canada retail network was terminated with the closing in 1949 of the Vancouver outlet, but that same year Mason & Risch (Winter & Co) bought Sterling Action & Keys Co of Brantford, Ont. In 1959 the Winter family purchased the controlling interest in the US Aeolian Corp and set up Aeolian of Canada, a holding company for Mason & Risch. In 1969 Mason & Risch purchased the George Dansereau & Sons Lumber Mill in Grenville, Que. In 1971 the Sterling Action & Keys Co was closed, and in 1968 the Toronto factory was moved to new premises in Scarborough, from which it continued to manufacture Mason & Risch uprights. After 1950, however, all grand and player pianos were manufactured in the USA and exported (to Canada and elsewhere) by Aeolian. (CM)

Masses. In music, 'mass' usually means a setting, monodic or polyphonic, of portions of the congregation's part of the mass – the unchanging Ordinary, as distinct from the varied (according to the day) Proper. Other names in English for settings of the mass are 'the Office of Holy Communion' and 'the Communion Service.' The movements of the sung mass are: Kyrie eleison, Gloria in excelsis Deo, Credo, Sanctus with Benedictus, and Agnus Dei. The monodic Gregorian mass was used widely until the 12th century, when polyphonic masses began to appear, usually for three voices and by composers whose names have not survived. The *Messe de Nostre Dame*, a four-voice setting composed between 1349 and 1363 by Guillaume Machault, was a culmination of this first flowering of the polyphonic mass.

The publication in 1549 of the *Book of Common Prayer* made acceptable the setting of the texts in English, though the Greek (Kyrie) and Latin titles were retained (excepting the Responses to the Commandments, introduced to the English liturgy in 1552). Anglican composers have continued to set both Latin and English texts. That vernacular masses were regarded as unsuitable by the Roman church of the day is borne out by Pius V's *Missale romanum* (1570), which prescribed the exact sequence of the Proper and the Ordinary and decreed the exclusive use of Latin. These dicta remained in force until the 1960s, and consequently the mass cultivated by Quebec's Roman Catholic composers prior to that date was the Latin mass.

Mason & Risch Display Room, Toronto, 1912

Though spoken mass is the custom in many Canadian churches, sung mass has been perpetuated by some Roman Catholic and High Anglican congregations. Even by these, however, it commonly is retained for Sundays, Feast Days, Holy Days, and special occasions, and the settings used vary widely in quality and difficulty, depending on the predilections and ambitions of individual choirmasters and the capabilities of their choirs.

The first mass settings by Anglo-Canadian composers probably were hymn-like or chant-like in nature, for use by local congregations. Examples may be seen in *The Book of Common Praise* (1908, rev 1938). Later, as the sophistication of congregations, choirs, and particularly choirmasters increased, more elaborate settings were written for particular choirs. Charles A.E. *Harriss wrote two ambitious settings with orchestral accompaniment – a *Festival Mass* in 1901 (premiered that year in Buffalo and sung the following year at the Basilica in Ottawa) and a *Coronation Mass Edward VII* in 1902 (written for the *Cycle of Musical Festivals). Clarence *Lucas completed a *Requiem Mass* in 1937 (some 46 years after he had left Canada). The 14 *Missae breves* composed between 1928 and 1963 by Healey *Willan gave an impetus to English-language settings of the mass without Gloria or Credo. No fewer than four titled *Mass of St Thomas* (by *Bancroft, *Betts, Robert *Fleming, and *Holman) emerged in 1974, the 700th anniversary of the death of St Thomas Aquinas, and of these all but Betts' were published in that year by the same house: *Waterloo. Other *Missae breves* have been composed by *Camilleri, F.R.C. *Clarke, Margaret *Drynan, Fleming, Graham *George, *MacNutt (four published), *MacDermot (a rock treatment), Ruth *Watson Henderson (Thompson 1966), Charles *Wilson, and Leonard *Wilson.

Quentin *MacLean wrote several Latin masses, and the Latin texts have been set as well by Keith *Bissell, Clifford *Ford (full text, including Credo), and Bernard *Naylor. However, certainly prior to the Vatican II Council of 1963–6 (which authorized and encouraged the use of the vernacular, to facilitate congregational participation), the Latin mass was cultivated more assiduously in French Canada than in English Canada. The four *Messes* of Antoine *Dessane (dating probably from the 1850s and 1860s), the *Messe des morts* and *Messe de Noël 'Deo infanti'* (the latter published in 1870) of J.-J. *Perrault, and in particular the three *Messes* of Alexis *Contant (the earliest from 1884, the latest performed in 1903) bear witness to the earlier development of the Quebec tradition (both French and Irish) of the Latin mass. J.A. *Fowler's *Mass of the Blessed Virgin* (Suckling 1893) and *Mass of the Sacred Heart* (Whaley Royce 1898) are Latin mass settings written for his choir at St Patrick's Church, Montreal. Guillaume *Couture's *Requiem Mass*, written ca 1900 and performed in Montreal in 1906 and 1915, represents an inheritor of that tradition in his maturity, as do Achille *Fortier's mass of 1902, Charles *Labelle's *Messe funèbre*, and the Belgian-born Jules *Hone's mass, which was sung at Montreal's Notre-Dame Church.

Later, Perrault's *Messe des morts* and Couture's *Requiem Mass* were joined by others in that genre (called, variously, *Messe pour défunts*, *Messe funèbre*, and *Missa pro defunctis*) by Alexandre d'Aragon, Auguste *Descarries, Roméo *Larivière, Joseph-Léopold Lemieux, Oscar *O'Brien, Frédéric *Pelletier, J.-Antonio *Thompson, Amédée *Tremblay, and Benoit *Verdickt. Three *Christmas Masses* followed Perrault's – by Édouard Desjardins, by Alexandre d'Aragon, and by Thompson, who also wrote an *Easter Mass*. Other settings from French Canada for particular purposes or commemorations include those by Édouard Biron (*Messe de Notre-Dame-de-la-Paix*, *Messe au Christ Roi*), Maurice *Blackburn (*Mass*, 1949, for children's voices), Charlotte *Cadoret (*Messe à Notre-Dame*, in addition to one generically named), Claude *Champagne (*Missa brevis*), Donald *Heins (*Messe de Ste-Ursule*), Alfred *Lamoureux (*Messe du Saint-Nom-de-Marie*), and O'Brien (*Messe de St-Joachim*). The three by Paul-Émile *McCaughan (1938, 1943, and 1944) are solemn masses for regular use. Gabriel *Charpentier's eight-minute three-voice setting (1952) of the Latin mass is suitable for church use by sufficiently sophisticated singers. Among 'post-Vatican II' masses Pierick *Houdy's *Messe québécoise* uses French-language texts.

André *Prévost's *Missa de profundis*, like Clifford Ford's *Mass*, is, for practical purposes, a concert piece, though in theory it could be used in the eucharist because of the traditional Greek and Latin text and in spite of the spoken interpolation of the De profundis text. But Clermont *Pépin's *Messe sur le monde, Symphonie No 4* has unconventional texts by Teilhard de Chardin and is essentially a concert piece. Like Prévost's, Walter *Buczynski's setting of the Latin text includes the De profundis (following the Agnus Dei) and also incorporates an Asperges me (before the Kyrie).

The 1970–1 translations of the texts of the liturgies by the International Consultation on English Texts have been set by Godfrey *Ridout (*The Hymn Book*, 1971) and Barrie *Cabena (*Catholic Book of Worship*, 1972). Victor Togni and Father Stephen Somerville have written settings for the Roman Catholic rite, and Cabena has published a *Mass in the Dorian Mode* with multiple texts. The many settings by Canadian composers of sections of the mass have not been treated here, but mention should be made of Harry *Somers' 23-minute *Kyrie* for four solo voices, choir, and instruments. (GBr, GP, KW)

MASSEY. Toronto family, manufacturers of farm equipment and active patrons of the arts. The Massey Manufacturing Co (operated as Massey-Harris 1891–1953 and as Massey-Ferguson after that time) was founded in 1847 at Newcastle, Ont, by Daniel Massey (1798–1856). In 1855 sole ownership of the company was assumed by Daniel's son Hart (1823–96). Hart remained in charge until 1870, when ill health forced him to retire. Responsibility for the business passed thereafter to Hart's children and grandchildren, though after 1926 no Massey has headed the firm.

In 1881 the Massey Manufacturing Co moved to Toronto, where the family was to make its greatest contribution to musical life. Late in the 19th century the Masseys took part in the Methodist *Chautauquas situated near Lake Erie and purchased a number of organs for Methodist chapels in Toronto. Hart's sons Charles (1848–84) and Frederick Victor (1867–90) displayed musical abilities, the former as a church organist, the latter as an amateur flutist. Carrying this interest into the family business, Charles founded the Massey Cornet Band and oversaw the construction of company facilities for an employees' orchestra and glee club. *Massey's Illustrated*, a magazine begun in the early 1880s, published poems, short stories, and music. Charles Massey died in 1884, and in his memory his father built Toronto's Massey Music Hall (*Massey Hall), which opened in June 1894.

Hart Massey died in 1896, and his will decreed that the greater part of his estate be disposed of by 1916 for the benefit of various public institutions and causes. However the trustees (family members) determined to establish the Massey Foundation. Incorporated in 1918, the foundation was first trust of its kind in Canada. It was set up to create projects, not to maintain existing ones. Besides funding the completion of *Hart House (begun in 1911 with Massey estate funds and named for Hart Massey) the foundation financed the Hart House Theatre 1919–46, established and provided the support for the *Hart House String Quartet, made possible the purchase of the Hart House Viols (see Instrument collections), and in 1933 undertook the renovation of Massey Hall. The foundation also built and endowed Massey College at the *U of Toronto in 1962. The trustees of the Massey Foundation were family members, including Hart's son Chester (1850–1926) and Chester's son Vincent (1887–1967); Chester and Vincent also served as trustees of Massey Hall.

Chester Massey presented Metropolitan United Church in Toronto with a carillon in memory of his wife, Anna; it was the first carillon in North America (see Carillon). Hart's daughter Lillian Massey Treble (1854–1915) willed money for a new pipe organ to the same church. Another of Hart's sons, Walter (1864–1901), built an estate known as Dentonia Park in Toronto's east end; during the 1930s both the *TSO and the Hart House String Quartet played there.

Vincent Massey, the first Canadian-born governor-general (1952–9), was president 1920–1 of the *Arts and Letters Club, chairman 1931–4 of the TSO Board, and chairman of the Commission on National Development in the Arts, Letters and Sciences (1949–51), more commonly known as the *Massey Commission. Vincent's younger brother, Raymond Massey, won fame as an actor.

In 1978 the Massey family was the subject of a two-part CBC TV documentary, 'The Masseys: Chronicles of a Canadian Family,' produced by Vincent Tovell (a grandson of Walter Massey), with music by Louis *Applebaum.

BIBLIOGRAPHY

Massey, Vincent. *What's Past Is Prologue* (Toronto 1963)
Gillen, Mollie. *The Masseys: Founding Family* (Toronto 1965)
Collins, Paul. *Hart Massey* (Toronto 1977)
Wolfe, Morris. 'The Masseys: a star-crossed family saga,' *SatN*, Sep 1978
Gray, Charlotte. 'The Massey mystique,' *Weekend Magazine*, 16 Jun 1979 NM (PW)

Massey Commission. Name commonly applied to the Royal Commission on National Development in the Arts, Letters and Sciences, appointed by the federal government by an Order in Council dated 8 Apr 1949. Vincent *Massey, at that time chancellor of the *U of Toronto, was chairman. The commissioners were Arthur Surveyer, a civil engineer of Montreal; Norman A.M. MacKenzie, president of the *U of British Columbia; the Most

Rev Georges-Henri Lévesque, dean of the Faculty of Social Sciences, *Laval U; and Hilda Neatby, professor of history at the *U of Saskatchewan. In the major cities of Canada between August 1949 and July 1950 the commission held public sessions at which most of the 450 submitted briefs were heard, and it invited experts in various fields to prepare special studies. Among these was one on music, written by Sir Ernest *MacMillan. In 1951 the commission issued a report which became known as the 'Massey report' and gained recognition as a document of utmost importance in the cultural history of Canada since it advocated the principle of federal government patronage of a wide range of cultural activities and proposed the establishment of a *Canada Council for the Encouragement of the Arts, Letters, Humanities and Social Sciences.

The first part of the Massey report contains a stocktaking of achievements and shortcomings. Impressed by the 'evidences of vigour and variety of musical life' it noted the phenomenal growth of music in Canada during the previous 25 years, a growth due largely to the new technologies of radio and the phonograph, to the contribution made by CBC music programming, and to the competition festival movement. Orchestras and opera companies had built large and loyal audiences, and performance was fostered in schools and by amateur associations. However, professionalism tended to concentrate in the four largest cities, Montreal, Toronto, Vancouver, and Winnipeg, and smaller centres rarely enjoyed performances by the top Canadian talent. This was due, the commission found, not to lack of talent or of willingness to travel, but to the great cost of touring in a country with vast distances between cities. It was due also to the extensive domination of concert life by US agencies whose roster of artists included few Canadians and few artists with an interest in Canadian music. It was difficult for a young Canadian performer to break into the concert circuit except by emigrating. (The report noted however a countertrend fostered by the *CBC, the *NFB, and by certain Canadian-operated concert series.) The country's deficiency in adequate halls was remarked upon in a section which described (p 191) performances forced to take place 'in inappropriate and incongruous settings, in gymnasiums, churches, hotel rooms, school halls or in motion picture theatres rented for the occasion at ruinous cost.' The most distressing difficulties, however, were those of the composer of concert music. Lack of opportunity for performance of new music was blamed on the high cost of copying orchestral parts and scores but also on the prejudices of audiences and publishers. As a result, composers remained little known despite their being championed by the CBC. The report also pointed out the lack of a first-class music library, of a published history of music in Canada, of an information centre, and of university facilities for graduate training in musical research. Recognizing (p 271) that their task was 'concerned with nothing less than the spiritual foundations of our national life,' the commissioners set about to search for 'what can make our country great, and what can make it one' – the last remark a reference to the duality of French and English heritages.

The report was under no illusion that an appraisal of Canadian intellectual or cultural life justified complacency (p 272). 'If modern nations were marshalled in the order of the importance which they assign to those things with which this inquiry is concerned, Canada would be found far from the vanguard; she would even be near the end of the procession.' Some of the reasons are suggested in an earlier chapter: vast distances, a scattered population, Canada's youth as a nation, 'easy dependence on a huge and generous neighbour.' These factors all pointed towards the need for state patronage – not to supersede but to supplement and enhance volunteer effort – to be administered not by a federal ministry of fine arts and culture but by a separate agency, the Canada Council.

Patronage would take the form of scholarships at the undergraduate and graduate levels and (p 363) of grants for artists, musicians, and men of letters to study in Canada or abroad. The Canada Council also (p 377, 380) would perform the functions of a National Commission for Unesco and give consideration, among other things, to (p 381) 'the encouragement of Canadian music, drama and ballet (through the appropriate voluntary organizations and in co-operation with the Canadian Broadcasting Corporation and the National Film Board) by such means as the underwriting of tours, the commissioning of music for events of national importance, and the establishment of awards to young people of promise whose talents have been revealed in national festivals of music, drama or the ballet.' The Canada Council, the commissioners felt, should promote knowledge of Canada abroad by such means as subsidized foreign tours by Canadian performers. Other specific recommendations relating to music included (p 191) the collecting of folk music from all immigrant groups; the recording of Canadian orchestras and Canadian compositions; the production of films about Canadian music; and the establishment of national associations of music clubs, composers, music schools, and other interest groups.

To appreciate the historical importance of the Massey report it must be remembered that state support of the arts – long since taken for granted in most European countries and already flourishing modestly in the province of Quebec – was an unpopular idea in North America. Many people felt that any enterprise that did not pay for itself did not deserve to exist; others feared that state support would mean state control and maintained that patronage of the arts was the preserve of private munificence. Advocacy of the spending of public funds for artistic endeavours indeed was considered suicidal by elected politicians. The change was brought about partly by the model of the Arts Council of Great Britain, founded in 1945, partly by the government's embarrassment at being a member of Unesco (established 1945) without having an apparatus to provide information and representation, but largely by popular sentiment, a sentiment born of pride in Canada's wartime achievement and expressed in the brief submitted in 1944 by a 'music committee' (forerunner of the *CMCouncil) to the House of Commons Committee on Post-War Reconstruction. The Massey report was not the only cause of the unprecedented expansion of musical creativity and appreciation characteristic of the period after 1950, but it did provide a great stimulus through its recognition of the importance of the arts and letters, its moral support of the intellectual community, and its proposals for practical support, translated into reality in 1957 with the establishment of the Canada Council. The results, after 30 years, may be said to have surpassed the commission's boldest hopes for a flourishing culture.

BIBLIOGRAPHY

Royal Commission on National Development in the Arts, Letters and Sciences, 1949 1951. *Report* (Ottawa 1951)

Royal Commission Studies: A Selection of Essays Prepared for the Royal Commission on National Development in the Arts, Letters and Sciences (Ottawa 1951)

Walter, Arnold. 'A Canadian pattern,' *CMJ*, vol 1, Spring 1957

Ostry, Bernard. *The Cultural Connection* (Toronto 1978)

HK

Massey Hall. Famous Canadian concert hall on Shuter St in downtown Toronto. It was built by Hart A. *Massey as a gift to the city in memory of his son Charles Albert Massey and to foster 'an interest in music, education, temperance, industry, good citizenship, patriotism, philanthropy and religion.' It opened 14 Jun 1894 with a performance of Handel's *Messiah* as part of a three-day festival. Known until 1933 as Massey Music Hall, it then seated 4000 in the orchestra, two balconies, six private boxes, stage boxes, and tiered onstage seating. It was designed by C.R. Badgely (a Canadian architect residing in Cleveland) and constructed of brick at a cost of $150,000 under the supervision of the Toronto architect George M. Miller. Administered by a board of trustees, it has been managed by I.E. *Suckling 1894–1900, Stewart Houston 1900–10, Norman Withrow 1910–32, John P. Carter 1932–3, Wilfred James 1933–43, and Ross Creelman 1943–68. Joseph Cartan succeeded Creelman in 1968.

The first major structural changes were undertaken in 1933 and reduced seating to the present (1980) 2765 by enlarging the lobby and adding the balcony lounge. That year the building was officially recognized by its popular name, Massey Hall. A second renovation, undertaken in 1948, lowered the stage, and replaced the wooden floors of stage, basement, and orchestra with floors of reinforced concrete. Since then the hall's acoustics have been praised by audiences for their warmth and criticized by orchestral musicians for their deceptiveness. (One TS musician has said that players cannot hear each other clearly because of reverberation and that consequently a focused ensemble is difficult to achieve.) In 1976 a site on King St West was approved as the location of a new building to be completed in the 1980s and to take over the main functions of Massey Hall.

For many years the only building in Canada designed expressly for concert use, Massey Hall became the home of the *Toronto Mendelssohn Choir in 1895, served the first *Toronto Symphony Orchestra 1906–18, and began to house the concerts of the TSO in 1923. It provided the facilities for Toronto's growth as a major choral centre and gave the city a window on the world. A random selection from the innumerable events at 'The Old Lady of Shuter Street' (Vincent Massey's nickname for the hall when he visited it in 1953) indicates the range of its use. There were notable appearances by Paderewski (1896), Patti (1903), *Albani (1903, 1906), Caruso (1908), Tetrazzini (1912), Galli-Curci (1917), Heifetz (1918, the year of his teenage New York debut), and Kreisler (1934); speeches by Winston Churchill (1900, 1901), Carrie Nation (1901), and Lloyd George (1919); a concert by the London Symphony Orchestra under Nikisch (1912); the wedding (1908) of the Canadian-Indian athlete Tom Longboat; an exhibition boxing bout (1919) by Jack Dempsey; and a performance (1911) of Elgar's *The Dream of Gerontius* by the Sheffield Choir conducted by the composer. There also have been movies, silent and sound; regular boxing matches; visits by touring opera, ballet, and theatre companies; annual May Festival Concerts (begun in 1894) by Toronto school choirs; countless folk, rock, jazz, choral, and symphonic concerts; and recording sessions by the Toronto Mendelssohn Choir during the 1950s, by the Dizzy Gillespie-Charlie Parker

Massey Hall

Quintet of the Year in 1953, by the *CBC SO and the *Festival Singers conducted by Stravinsky (in the premieres, 1962, of his *A Sermon, a Narrative and a Prayer* and *8 Instrumental Miniatures*), by Gordon *Lightfoot, by *Crowbar, by *Rush and by various performers for the CBC's SM and RCI series. The TS and the Toronto Mendelssohn Choir continued to perform regularly in Massey Hall in 1980.

(GK, PW)

MASSICOTTE, Édouard-Zotique (pseudonyms: Blondel, Cabrette, Mistigri). Folklorist, historian, archivist, poet, dramatist, botanist, b Montreal 24 Dec 1867, d there 8 Nov 1947; LL B (Laval) 1895, hon D ès L (Montreal) 1936. After graduating in law in 1895 he abandoned the legal profession for journalism, which he had attempted first in 1886, and began contributing to several Montreal newspapers, including *Le Monde illustré*. An actor on occasion, he also wrote a play, *Les Cousins du député*, produced in 1896. His interest in folklore began in 1883, when he started collecting songs in the Montreal region. He was a founding member of the École littéraire de Montréal in 1895 and was appointed archivist of the judicial district of Montreal in 1911.

He met Marius *Barbeau in 1917 and collected with him in Montreal and in the Trois-Rivières area. The words and music and some recordings of these songs have been deposited with the *National Museum of Canada as well as with the Montreal City Library. Massicotte collected some 5000 versions of songs and stories. At the same time he published many articles and works on the traditions and customs and the anecdotal history of Quebec. The high regard in which he was held won him election as a fellow of the Royal Society of Canada in 1920; in 1936 he was awarded the society's Tyrrell gold medal. With Barbeau he collaborated in the first Soirées du bon vieux temps in 1919, and the following year he organized the Soirées de famille for which Ovila *Légaré was host at the *Monument national. A street in Montreal was named after him in 1950.

WRITINGS

'Les théâtres et lieux d'amusements à Montréal pendant le XIXe siècle,' *L'Annuaire théâtral*, ed G.H. Robert (Montreal 1908)

'Le premier théâtre de Montréal,' *BRH*, vol 23, Dec 1917

– and Barbeau, Marius. 'Chants populaires du Canada,' *JAF*, vol 32, Jan–Mar 1919

'Une noce populaire il y a cinquante ans,' *Proceedings and Transactions of the Royal Society of Canada*, vol 17 (Ottawa 1923)

'Auberges et cabarets d'autrefois,' ibid, vol 21 (Ottawa 1927)

'Hôtelleries, clubs et cafés à Montréal de 1760 à 1850,' ibid, vol 22 (Ottawa 1928)

'Quelques anciens pianos,' *BRH*, vol 37, Oct 1931

'Recherches historiques sur les spectacles à Montréal de 1760 à 1800,' *Proceedings and Transactions of the Royal Society of Canada*, vol 26 (Ottawa 1932)

'Trois grands artistes,' 'La musique militaire sous le régime français,' *BRH*, vol 39, Jan, Jul 1933

'Violons et luthiers,' ibid, vol 41, Apr 1935

– and Brassard, T.L. 'Les deux musiciens Braunies [sic],' ibid, vol 41 (Nov 1935)

'Brève histoire du Parc Sohmer,' *Cahiers des Dix*, 11, 1946

Also about 50 chansons published in *Le Canard* (1896–7)

A complete list of his published writings is given in *Dictionnaire pratique des auteurs québécois* by Réginald Hamel et al (Montreal 1976).

BIBLIOGRAPHY

Mauranlt, Olivier. 'É.-Z. Massicotte,' *Cahiers des Dix*, 13, 1948

Morin, Victor. 'É.-Z. Massicotte (1867–1947),' *Proceedings and Transactions of the Royal Society of Canada*, vol 42 (Ottawa 1948)

GP

MASSON, Chantal (m Bourque). Violist, choir conductor, teacher, b St-Denis, near Paris, 24 Oct 1937, naturalized Canadian 1977; premier prix viola (Paris Cons) 1958. She studied at the Toulouse Cons and the Paris Cons. Later she worked with Micheline Lemoine (viola) and Georges Dandelot and Marie-Claire Alain (harmony and counterpoint) and was principal viola with the Orchestre de chambre français. She pursued her training in choir conducting 1960–1 within the movement À Coeur Joie, becoming national instructor in 1962. In 1964 she joined the faculty of *Laval U, where in 1980 she continued to teach viola, conducting, aesthetics, choral singing, and chamber music. She has performed as a soloist with the CBC orchestras in Quebec City and Montreal, the *Quebec SO, and the chamber orchestra of the *Concerts Couperin. She conducted the *Ensemble vocal Chantal-Masson 1965–72 and the choir of Laval U 1965–9 and began directing the Choeur symphonique de Québec in 1969. The last-named has become noted for its discipline and fine blend.

CH

MASSUE, Nicholas (Nicolas). Tenor, b Varennes, near Montreal, 31 Jul 1903, d there 1 Jul 1974. From the age of five, he spent long periods in Italy with his parents and was educated in Florence, Rome, and Fribourg, Switzerland. Not until he was 24 did he begin to pursue a singing career. In Florence he studied with the baritone Mario Ancona and then continued his training in Milan. As Giuseppe Massù, he made his debut in 1931 in Lecco singing the Duke in *Rigoletto*; the critics praised his voice and stage presence. He then sang in Catania, Syracuse, Trieste, Palermo, and Legnano, finally making his debut at the Teatro alla Scala in Milan in 1934 as Lorenzo in Auber's *Fra Diavolo*. La Scala soon offered him leading roles in *La Traviata*, *Tosca*, *Madama Butterfly*, *Faust*, *Lohengrin*, *Mefistofele*, *Manon*, and other operas. He took part in the premiere of Casella's *La Favola d'Orfeo* in 1932 in Venice and of Zandonai's *La Farsa amorosa* in 1933 in Rome.

He was engaged by the *Metropolitan Opera and made his debut there 16 May 1936 as the Duke in *Rigoletto*. He remained for the five seasons 1936–41 and performed various roles including Arturo (*Lucia di Lammermoor*), the Astrologer (*Le Coq d'Or*), Cassio (*Otello*), Paris (*Roméo et Juliette*), the Italian Singer (*Der Rosenkavalier*), Narraboth (*Salome*), and Parke (Damrosch's *The Man without a Country*). In Montreal he was a soloist in Bach's *St Matthew Passion* in June 1936 during the first festival of the CSM orchestra and was soloist in January 1938 at one of its regular concerts. He gave a recital in 1937 at *Plateau Hall which Frédéric *Pelletier described in *Le Devoir* (19 October) as a 'fine evening of vocal art.'

In outlook, education and training, Massue had become a true Italian artist. Thus it was an immense disappointment to him when, with the outbreak of World War II, Italy cancelled his contracts because of his Canadian nationality. Massue enlisted in the RCAF but eventually withdrew to the family estate in Varennes. For many, this renunciation of a flourishing career remains inexplicable. Yet his close friends knew that the war years had affected him so deeply that he preferred to live in seclusion near his mother.

His voice, 'with a timbre recalling that of Lauri-Volpi' according to the *New York Herald-Tribune*, may be heard in the 1939 recording *Great Scenes from Verdi's Otello*; he sings the role of Cassio, with Jepson, Martinelli, Tibbett, and the Metropolitan Opera chorus and orchestra, under the direction of Wilfrid *Pelletier.

Massue was a knight of the Papal Order of the Holy Sepulchre.

CH

MASTROCOLA. Montreal musicians, 1 / Joseph and 2 / Roméo, his son, both closely associated with the *MSO for over 40 years.

1 **Joseph**. Violinist, violist, b Campobasso Province, Italy, 19 Dec 1890, d Montreal 11 Oct 1957. He studied violin in Milan and emigrated to the USA at 16, staying in Rhode Island for seven months before settling ca 1908 in Montreal; there he played in theatre orchestras, in particular at the Capitol, where he also was assistant conductor. He was the viola ca 1920–38 in the *Dubois String Quartet and a founder-member in 1930 of the *Montreal Orchestra and of the SCSM (*MSO) in 1934. He was associate principal viola of the MSO at the time of his death.

2 **Roméo**. Violinist, administrator, b Montreal 19 Mar 1914. He began his studies at nine with Émile *Taranto and Eugène *Chartier privately and with Maurice *Onderet at the *McGill Cons. He studied 1928–9 in Milan with Alberto Poltronieri and completed his studies with Onderet. He joined the Montreal Orchestra in 1932 and the SCSM (*MSO) in 1935. He became personnel director of the MSO in 1952 and occupied that position full-time 1958–77.

BIBLIOGRAPHY

'Nos musiciens,' *Variations*, vol 1, Sep–Oct 1977

GP

MATEJCEK, Jan (Vladimir). Administrator, music editor, critic, b Hamburg, of Czech parents, 29 Dec 1926, naturalized Canadian 1974. He studied composition, piano, and musicology in Prague and received a Doctor of Laws degree in 1951 from Prague's Charles U. He was foreign relations secretary 1954–61 for the Guild of Czechoslovak Composers, manager 1961–2 of the Prague SO, head of the music department 1962–4 at DILIA (Divadelň a literarní agentura, the Czech theatrical and literary agency), and general manager 1964–6 and director general 1966–8 of Panton, the guild's music publishing house. After a year with the publishers B. Schott's Söhne in Mainz, Germany, he emigrated to Canada in 1969 and became a consultant to the *CMCentre. In 1970 he served as executive secretary of the *OFSO and of the *Ontario Choral Federation, which he helped organize. In 1971 he was a member of the steering committee and founding board of the *ACO. That same year he joined *CAPAC as executive assistant to the general manager. In June 1977 he was appointed assistant general manager in charge of the international division of *PRO Canada and in 1980 he was promoted to managing director. He has been a lecturer and panelist on contemporary music at numerous congresses and has contributed articles to European music magazines.

WRITINGS

99 Tschechische Komponisten von Heute (Prague 1957)
Music in Czechoslovakia (Prague 1967)
– ed. *Contemporary Czechoslovak Piano Music*, 2 vols (Gerig 1967)
Catalogue of Canadian Music Suitable for Community Orchestras (Toronto 1971)

MSh

MATHÉ. Ottawa family of musicians, maternal-line descendants of Emmanuel *Blain de St-Aubin. Napoléon Magloire Mathé (b Ottawa 1863, d there 1937) was a civil servant, writer, and choir leader for 20 years at Notre-Dame Basilica. His wife, Marie (b Quebec City 1868, d Ottawa 1940, a daughter of Emmanuel Blain de St-Aubin), was a pianist, accompanist, singer, and chamber musician.

Napoleón and Marie Mathé had four sons: Paul, Charles, Blain, and Jean-Marie. Paul (b Ottawa 1896, d there 1941) was a violinist who played in recital and ca 1918–25 in the Chateau Laurier Orchestra, and also a violin teacher. Charles (Eugène) (b Ottawa 1897, d Toronto 17 Jun 1980) was a pupil of J.-B. *Dubois in Montreal, cellist 1920–2 with the Cincinnati SO and 1938–57 with the *TSO, and a member for 25 years of various CBC orchestras. Blain (de St Aubin) (b Ottawa 14 Feb 1907, d Toronto 9 Dec 1967) was a pupil of Donald *Heins, violinist 1932–40, 1959–60 and principal second violin 1962–5 with the TSO, and a member 1937–59 of the *Happy Gang. Jean-Marie (b Ottawa 4 Aug 1913) was the choir leader at Our Lady of Mount Carmel, Ottawa, ca 1960–9 and at Notre-Dame de Lourdes, Vanier, Ont, 1969–75.

(HG)

MATHER, (James) **Bruce**. Composer, pianist, teacher, b Toronto 9 May 1939; B MUS (Toronto) 1959, MA (Stanford) 1964, D MUS (Toronto) 1967. He studied 1952–7 at the *RCMT and 1957–9 at the Faculty of Music, *U of Toronto, where his teachers were Alberto *Guerrero, Earle *Moss, and Alexander Uninsky (piano) and Godfrey *Ridout, Oskar *Morawetz, and John *Weinzweig (theory and composition). On scholarships from the *Women's Musical Club of Toronto and the Beta Sigma Phi International Sorority he spent the summers of 1957 and 1958 at the Aspen Festival, Col. There he was introduced by Uninsky to Darius Milhaud, who was to have a marked influence on his subsequent development. At Aspen in 1958 Mather's *Venice* for soprano and instrumental ensemble was performed, and he played the solo part in the first performance of his *Concerto* for piano and chamber orchestra.

With the help of a grant from the *Canada Council, Mather studied 1959–61 at the Paris Cons. His teachers were Milhaud (composition), Simone Plé-Caussade (counterpoint and fugue), Olivier Messiaen (analysis), and Lazare Lévy (piano). He spent the summer of 1960 in Darmstadt, where he came into contact with Pierre Boulez. A grant from the Norma Copley Foundation of Chicago and another from the French government allowed him to stay an extra year in Paris. His *Cycle Rilke* (1960) was performed on French radio and he then embarked on the writing of a cantata, *The White Goddess*, to a text by Robert Graves. Mather studied composition 1962–4 at Stanford U, Palo

Bruce Mather

Alto, Cal, with Leland Smith and Roy Harris, winning a Kurt Weill Foundation prize in 1963. His *Étude* for solo clarinet (1962) and *Orphée* (1963) were performed there. Returning to Canada in 1964, he taught 1964–6 at the Brodie School of Music and Dance and at the U of Toronto. He joined the teaching staff at *McGill U in 1966. His *Symphonic Ode* was presented in 1965 at the International Rostrum of Composers, followed by his *Madrigal II* in 1969 and his *Sonata* for two pianos in 1971. He studied conducting in the summer of 1969 with Boulez in Basel and was in charge 1970–3 of the contemporary music workshop at the *U of Montreal. On study leave 1975–6 he returned to France for a year. While he was a visiting teacher at the Paris Cons 1978–9, the French composer Claude Ballif was his replacement at McGill.

In addition to being a composer and teacher, Mather is a remarkable pianist and has given many premieres of contemporary works, both as a soloist and as a duo-pianist with his wife, Pierrette *LePage. He was a member 1964–6 of the executive of *Ten Centuries Concerts, Toronto. On moving to Montreal in 1966 he became a member-director of the *SMCQ and also served as treasurer.

Mather began composing while very young. In 1949 (aged 10) he was awarded a *CAPAC prize. After 1956 his output became regular, and works were commissioned by the *CBC, Ten Centuries Concerts, the SMCQ, the French Ministry of Cultural Affairs, the *Lyric Arts Trio, the *MSO, the *U of Manitoba, the U of Toronto, the *Stratford Festival, and other organizations. His works have been performed frequently in Canada and the USA and also by the National Orchestra of Spain, the Rouen Chamber Orchestra in 1971, and the Collectif musical international de Champigny (2e2m).

A polished and highly cultured musician, Mather has displayed a marked preference for works requiring small ensembles. His attraction to poetry, particularly French poetry, may account for the importance of the voice in his output, as well as for the intimate character of much of his work. Especially remarkable in this regard are the five *Madrigals* for one or two voices and instrumental ensemble; in four of them Mather employs poems and fragments of poems by Saint-Denys-Garneau. According to Bengt *Hambraeus, 'the music is increasingly transformed into a spiritual seance, evoking an irrational spirit in infinite space, where sonorities materialize and float, at times ecstatically ... Mather's vocal music is extraordinarily well articulated, the product of a musician-poet who is aware of the innermost values of the poets he has chosen' (CMCentre, *Compositeurs au Québec: Bruce Mather* 1974).

A member of CAPAC and the *CLComp, Mather also is an associate of the *CMCentre. Among his pupils are Walter *Boudreau, John Burke, Paul *Crawford, Richard Hunt, Denis *Lorrain, Donald Steven, and Alexander Tilley. Mather has written for numerous publications, including the *Dictionary of Contemporary Music* for which he prepared articles on Serge *Garant, François *Morel, and Gilles *Tremblay. In 1979 he was awarded the Jules Léger Prize for his *Musique pour Champigny*.

SELECTED COMPOSITIONS

ORCHESTRA

Two Songs for Bass-Baritone and Orchestra (Hardy). 1956. Ms
Concerto. 1958. Pf, wind quin, str quar. CMCentre
Elegy for Saxophone and Strings. 1959. Wat 1965. Golden Crest RE 7037 (*Brodie)
The White Goddess, cantata (R. Graves). 1960–2. 1st part pf; 2nd part bar, perc, hp, pf, str; 3rd part sop, orch; 4th part SATB, orch. CMCentre
Symphonic Ode (Catromjep). 1964. Orch. CMCentre
Music for Vancouver. 1969. Sm orch. CMCentre. CBC SM-143 (*CBC Van Chamb O)
Musique pour Rouen. 1970–1. Str orch. CMCentre. CBC SM-331 (*CBC Van Chamb O)
Au Château de Pompairain. 1975. Mezzo, orch. CMCentre

CHAMBER

Étude. 1962. Cl. CMCentre. CBC SM-184 (J. *Campbell)
Orphée (Valéry). 1963. Sop, pf, perc. CMCentre. RCI 217/RCA CCS-1011 (M. *Morrison sop, Mather pf)
Madrigal II (Saint-Denys-Garneau). 1968. Sop, alto, fl, hp, str trio. Job 1970. RCI 369 (*SMCQ)
Madrigal III (Saint-Denys-Garneau). 1971. Alto, hp, mar, pf. CMCentre. RCI 369 (*Rideout alto, Mather pf)
Madrigal IV (Saint-Denys-Garneau). 1972. Sop, fl, pf. CMCentre. RCI 369 (*Lyric Arts Trio)
Madrigal V. 1972–3. Sop, alto, chamb orch. CMCentre
Eine kleine Bläsermusik. 1975. Wind quin. CMCentre. SNE-501 (*Quebec Woodwind Quintet)
Musique pour Champigny. 1976. Sop, mezzo, alto, cl, hn, hp, pf, perc. CMCentre

PIANO

Fantasy 1964. 1964 (rev 1967). CMCentre. CBC SM-48 (*Troup)/1978. RCI 464 (Mather)
Sonata. 1970. 2 pf. CMCentre. RCI 354 (*Beckett and McDonald)/McGill U Records 77002 (*LePage)
In Memoriam Alexandre Uninsky. 1974. CMCentre. 1978. RCI 464 (Mather)
Also film music, including *Smaragdin* (1960) for pf; works for chor and v, including *La Lune mince ...*, 1965, SATB, CMCentre, RCI 299 (*Tudor Singers of Montreal)/Poly 2917 009 (*Festival Singers)

WRITINGS

'La Société de musique contemporaine du Québec,' *Mcan*, 25, Dec 1969
'Notes sur "Requiems For the Party-Girl" de Schafer,' *CMB*, 1, Spring–Summer 1970
'Le collage musical: "Remembrances" de John Hawkins,' ibid, 3, Autumn–Winter 1971
'Pierre Boulez: "Structures pour deux pianos" (2e livre),' *Musiques du Kébèk*, ed Raoul Duguay (Montreal 1971)

DISCOGRAPHY

See LePage; MacKinnon.

BIBLIOGRAPHY

'Bruce Mather, a portrait,' *Mcan*, 11, May 1968
'Bruce Mather: teacher, pianist, secretary, composer,' *CanComp*, 49, Apr 1970
Duguay, Raoul. 'Bruce Mather,' *Musiques du Kébèk* (Montreal 1971)
Grenier, Albert. 'Sonate pour deux pianos de Bruce Mather,' unpubl L MUS thesis, U of Montreal 1971
Campbell, Francean. 'Bruce Mather: of woodblocks and mobiles,' *CanComp*, 87, Jan 1974
CMCentre. *Compositeurs au Québec: Bruce Mather* (Montreal 1974)
Waltz, Martin J. 'Cinq madrigaux de Bruce Mather, Une analyse formelle et stylistique,' unpubl M MUS thesis, U of Western Ontario 1977
Schulman, Michael. 'Bruce Mather: composing again,' *CanComp*, 124, Oct 1977
Hambraeus, Bengt. 'Bruce Mather,' *Contemporary Canadian Composers / Compositeurs canadiens contemporains*
Schafer, R. Murray. 'Bruce Mather,' *Dictionary of Contemporary Music*

GP

MATHER, Christine (Kyle). Administrator, musicologist, bassoonist, b York 24 May 1929; ARCM 1952, PH D musicology (Michigan) 1971. She studied bassoon 1948–52 at the RCM with Archie Camden and performed 1956–62 as a recitalist, concerto soloist, and chamber musician in Great Britain before emigrating to Canada. She settled in Winnipeg in 1962, continued to perform, and in 1964 began to teach at the *U of Manitoba. A practical as well as a scholarly interest in music of the 12th to the 16th centuries led her to begin a collection of that music and the instruments for which it was written. She also established the *Manitoba University Consort, one of the first successful ensembles of its kind in Canada. On leave 1968–9 from the university she studied musicology under Louise Cuyler at the U of Michigan. After a further year at Manitoba she returned to Michigan to complete her PH D (her thesis was 'The secular vocal works of Heinrich Isaac'), then joined the *U of Victoria as director 1971–5 of the graduate program in musicology. She became dean of the faculty of music at *Wilfrid Laurier U in 1975 and resigned in 1979 to become the director of music administration for the *Victoria Cons.

WRITINGS

'Problems of performance in the lieder of Heinrich Isaac,' *CAUSM J*, vol 2, Spring 1972

'Print 33 of Maximilian I's *Weisskunig*,' *Early Music*, Jan 1975

'Dufay's Missa "Ave Regina Caelorum": a performing edition,' *CAUSM J*, vol 5, Spring 1975

MATHIESON, George S. (Simpson). Organizational pioneer, b Glasgow 16 Dec 1873, d Winnipeg 7 Feb 1951. After an apprenticeship in the grain business in Scotland he joined the Norris Grain Co in Winnipeg and rose to a vice-presidency. He was internationally recognized – especially during World War II – as an expert on grain marketing and was president of the Winnipeg Grain Exchange. To the Winnipeg public, however, he was better known for his vigorous activities on behalf of the city's musical development. He was secretary 1916–44 of the Men's Musical Club (*Men's Music Club) and president in 1944. He was a co-founder in 1918 of the *Manitoba Music Competition Festival and the secretary until 1944, and was the organizer and the secretary 1926–49 of the informal interprovincial association which in 1949 became the *FCMF with Mathieson as honorary president. The George S. Mathieson Trophy, named in his honour, is one of two major choral trophies (the other being the City of Lincoln Trophy) which in 1980 continued to be presented annually by the FCMF. He was a director of the *Winnipeg SO in the 1920s, and in 1935 he published, under the nom de plume G Sharp Minor, *Crescendo: A Business Man's Romance in Music*, a history of 20 years' musical activity in Winnipeg. RG

MATHIEU. Montreal family of musicians: 1 / Rodolphe, and 2 / André, his son.

1 (Joseph) **Rodolphe**. Composer, teacher, writer, pianist, b Grondines, near Quebec City, 10 Jul 1890, d Montreal 29 Jun 1962. Born into a rural family, he moved to Montreal at 16 and studied piano 1906–8 with Alphonse *Martin and voice at the same time with Céline *Marier. He dedicated his first important work, the choral piece 'Le Poème de la mer' (1908), to Marier. She introduced him to Alfred *Laliberté, who acquainted him with the works of Scriabin. The young musician was deeply impressed with these, and some

Rodolphe Mathieu

of his piano compositions, *Chevauchée* (1911) and the *Sonata* (1927), show the influence of the Russian composer.

In 1907 Mathieu was appointed organist at St-Jean-Berchmans Church and began teaching piano, solfège, harmony, and counterpoint. Several of his pupils were winners of the *Prix d'Europe: Jean *Dansereau, Wilfrid *Pelletier, Ruth Pryce, and Auguste *Descarries, among others. His studies ca 1910 with Alexis *Contant led him in the direction of composition. In 1913 he wrote the song 'Un peu d'ombre,' which was sung in 1926 by Marguerite Béritza at the Concerts Lamoureux in Paris and later by Sarah *Fischer in London. The pianist Léo-Pol *Morin included *Chevauchée* and *Trois Préludes* in his repertoire.

With the aid of funds raised by his friends, Mathieu went to Paris in 1920. On the advice of Albert Roussel he enrolled at the Schola Cantorum, where he studied composition with Vincent d'Indy and orchestration with Louis Aubert. He also studied orchestral conducting with Vladimir Golschmann and psychology with Pierre Janet at the Collège de France. At this time he composed the works that may be his most significant: *String Quartet*, *Trio*, *Monologues* for violin, and *Dialogues* for violin and cello. In 1923 a grant from the Quebec government, the first awarded to a composer, enabled him to prolong his stay. On his return to Montreal in 1927 he taught at the Institut pédagogique of the Sisters of the Congregation of Notre-Dame and at the convent of the Sisters of St Anne at Lachine. Among his many pupils were Fleurette *Beauchamp, Lydia *Boucher, Pierre *Brabant, Father Paul Lachapelle, Raymond *Lévesque, and Cécile Préfontaine. In 1927 he wrote his *Sonata* for violin and piano. In 1929 he founded the *Canadian Institute of Music. He also directed the International Society of Music, which in 1934 became the Édition exclusive de musique canadienne, through which he published some of his own works. After 1930 he organized the Soirées Mathieu, monthly concerts held intermittently until 1952. The first took place 28 October and was devoted to his own works. During the years 1930–56 he completed 'Tests d'aptitudes musicales,' in which he extended certain ideas previously expressed in 'Problèmes–Aperceptions,' a treatise on creativity he had begun in 1915.

After 1934 Mathieu devoted most of his time to teaching and to furthering the career of André, the son of his marriage to the violinist Mimi Gagnon. Of the few works he wrote during this time, the *Quintet* for piano and strings probably is the most accomplished. He taught analysis 1955–9 at the *CMM. The *Symphonie pour voix humaines* for six-voice choir with brass accompaniment, begun in 1956, was never finished. It may be viewed as a last attempt by the composer to rediscover the inspiration of the 1920s.

Rodolphe Mathieu's work reflects two currents which dominated the late 19th and early 20th centuries: first, the revolution in aesthetics and musical language achieved by Debussy and, second, the wave of romanticism that came through Wagner and, later, the post-Wagnerianism of Schoenberg and Berg. In his earliest compositions, Mathieu deliberately aligned himself with the music of Debussy. One senses in his compositions the same determination to break boundaries, the same pursuit of sonority for its own sake, and the same occasional use of the whole-tone scale, parallel chords, and cadences built on chords with added notes. Yet Debussy's influence remains partial and is limited to certain technical features. Mathieu is first and foremost a romantic, and his roots are Wagnerian; his language is infused with the Wagnerian spirit and with a desire for display. As evidence of this Wagnerian quality, one observes his use of the chromatic scale, creating temporary tonal resting-points yet continually developing, with progressions marked 'crescendo.' In pushing chromaticism to its limit, he realized that he had to find a new way of organizing the scale. The path he chose was similar to that taken by pre-serial composers and led him to the solution later called complementarity. He may have been influenced in this by Scriabin's theory of the attraction of unstable harmonies by stable ones. Whether this is so or not, the process of resolution by complementarity is evident in the passages which link the various sections of the *Trio* and in most of the compositions of that period. The thematic outline suggests a serial model, and Mathieu takes great pains to eschew tonality and to avoid repetitions. It would be wrong, however, to conclude from this that he accepted the serial system in its entirety, and in fact it is possible that he did not understand it fully. At one point in his writings, he denounced it vigorously: to accept it, according to him, was to free oneself from traditional boundaries only to be subjected to an even more tyrannical discipline, one which is arbitrary and contrary to the elementary laws of aesthetics and expression. There is a duality in Mathieu which on the one hand compels him to a rigorous organization of micro-structures, yet on the other causes him to place lyrical expression in the foreground and to employ expansive and proliferating forms. Although the latter tendency in his work is not surprising, the former may be explained as a need to pursue a path in which form must be invented continually. With Mathieu, the need for freedom was always uppermost; but such freedom meant choosing, on occasion, a rigour that was not customary for his time.

By his determination to invent a new language, his post-romantic tendency advocating continual variation and the use of generative cells, and his strong belief in the necessity of change in artistic expression, Mathieu asserted his position – modestly perhaps but nonetheless spontaneously and at a certain risk – in the general development of contemporary music. His rich imagination and the ease with which he expressed his ideas have helped give his works an intrinsic value as well as an undeniable interest. His music portrays, to some extent, what Baudelaire described as 'the elusive and trembling character of nature.'

At a time when Mathieu would have liked to secure a wider public for his works, neither audiences nor critics – with the notable exception of Léo-Pol Morin – were prepared to perceive or understand his musical language, despite the immediacy of its emotional impact. The novelty of his methods created a barrier. At that time, simply adopting the syntax of Debussy was sufficient to bestow an aura of privacy on the musical language and to classify the composer as a mere aesthete. To have infused this language with an even more contemporary Germanic element could serve only to cut him off from all contact with a milieu firmly entrenched in traditionalism. Rodolphe Mathieu's talent did not gain for him the recognition as a pioneer of the new Canadian music that he would appear to deserve. In any case his music, being rejected, was unable to point the way to creativity for newer (and younger) talents. In the 1960s, when some of his works finally were heard, a new school was gaining prominence, and Mathieu, though of a stature to have done so, could not preside over it.

The *CMCentre has conferred on Rodolphe Mathieu the associate status reserved for deceased composers whose works the centre holds. An avenue in northeast Montreal was named after him in 1965.

COMPOSITIONS

CHAMBER

Lied. 1915. Vn, pf. Hérelle 1921
String Quartet. 1920. Ms
Trio. 1921. Pf, vn, vc. Ms
12 Études modernes 'Monologues.' 1924. Vn. Ms. RCI 243 (*Staryk)
22 Dialogues. Ca 1924. Vn, vc. Incomplete ms
Sonata. 1928. Vn (vc), pf. Ms
Quintette. 1942. Pf, str quar. CMCentre. RCI 123 (*Reiner)/L'Oiseau-Coeur OC S-02 (M. *Dussault)

PIANO

Chevauchée. 1911. International Soc of Music
Three Preludes 'Sur un nom,' 'Vague,' 'Une muse.' 1912–15. Pf (orch version nd). CMCentre (orch), Hérelle 1921 (pf). RCI 135 (*Dufresne)
Sonata. 1927. CMCentre. RCI 123 (*Bourassa)/ L'Oiseau-Coeur OC S-02 (M. *Dussault)

CHOIR OR VOICE

'Le Poème de la mer' (R. Mathieu). 1908. Chorus. Ms
'Les Yeux noirs' (J.-E. Marsoin). 1911. V, pf. Ms. L'Oiseau-Coeur OC S-02 (M. *Daveluy)
'Un peu d'ombre' (P. Newton). 1913. Sop, orch. CMCentre. (Sop, pf) L'Oiseau-Coeur OC S-02 (M. *Daveluy)
'Larmes' (R. Mathieu). 1919. ?
'Harmonie du soir' (Baudelaire). 1924. Sop (ten), vn, orch. CMCentre
Saisons canadiennes (R. Mathieu). Before 1927. Bass, pf. Ms
Symphonie-ballet avec coeurs. 1927. Chor, orch. Incomplete ms
Deux poèmes 'Après ton appel,' 'Quand tu pleures' (R. Mathieu). 1928. Ten, str quar. CMCentre. (Sop, str quar) L'Oiseau-Coeur OC S-02 (M. *Daveluy)
Sanctus et Benedictus. 1931. SATB or 2 parts, org. International Soc of Music 1931
Prière: 'O Jésus vivant en Marie.' 1933. Male vs, org. Ms
'Lève-toi, Canadien' (R. Mathieu, also transl). 1934. SATB, orch (band). Édition exclusive de musique canadienne 1934
'Petite main' (F. Gaudet-Smet). 1955. Sop, pf. Ms. L'Oiseau-Coeur OC S-02 (M. *Daveluy)
Symphonie pour voix humaines. 1960. 12 vs, brass. Incomplete ms

WRITINGS

'Problèmes – Aperceptions,' incomplete ms of 1208 pp, 1915–30
'Perception,' *Le Nigog*, Feb 1918
'Tests d'aptitudes musicales,' ms 1930–56
'Le sujet en musique,' *Opinions*, Jan 1931
'Simplicité et médiocrité,' *La Lyre*, Mar 1931
'L'étatisation de la musique,' Montreal *Le Canada*, 25 Sep 1931
'Le sentiment amoureux en art,' *Opinions*, Apr 1932
Parlons musique (Montreal 1932)
'Le dernier testament ou les idées révélées par les faits,' ms 1944–52

BIBLIOGRAPHY

Morin, Léo-Pol. 'M. Rodolphe Mathieu et le terroir,' *Le Nigog*, 5, May 1918
– 'Les compositeurs canadiens: Monsieur Rodolphe Mathieu,' Montreal *La Patrie*, 1 May 1926
Archer, Thomas. 'Composers hold forth,' Montreal *Gazette*, 26 Apr 1964
Bourassa-Trépanier, Juliette. 'Rodolphe Mathieu (1890–1962),' unpubl D MUS thesis, Laval U 1972
La Vie musicale

2 (René) **André** (Rodolphe). Pianist, composer, b Montreal 18 Feb 1929, d there 2 Jun 1968. As a very young child he revealed an exceptional talent for the piano and for composition, which encouraged his father to give him his first lessons. He composed *Trois Études* for piano at four and gave a recital of his works 25 Feb 1935 at the Ritz-Carlton Hotel, creating a sensation. Early in 1936 he was soloist in his *Concertino No. 1* on CBC radio with an orchestra under J.-J. *Gagnier. He was given a grant by the Quebec government to go to Paris to study piano with Yves Nat and Mme Giraud-Latarse and harmony and composition with Jacques de la Presle. In December 1936 his recital at the Salle Chopin-Pleyel was received enthusiastically by Parisian critics. He again performed his works 26 Mar 1939 at the Salle Gaveau, and the critic Émile Vuillermoz wrote, 'If the word "genius" has a meaning, it is surely here that we will be able to find it.'

Mathieu returned to Montreal the following summer only for a holiday, but the war compelled him to remain in North America. He gave a series of recitals in Canada and made a remarkable debut 3 Feb 1940 at New York's Town Hall. Settling in New York with his family, he continued his studies in composition with Harold Morris, at the same time fulfilling numerous concert and radio engagements. In June 1941 he premiered his *Concertino No. 2* in Montreal under Sir Thomas Beecham. The work that year won first prize ($200) in a young composers' competition organized by the New York Philharmonic to mark its centenary. Mathieu performed it 21 Feb 1942 at Carnegie Hall and again shortly thereafter with the National Orchestra, Washington. He also played his compositions at a concert of the League of Composers.

Mathieu returned to Montreal in 1943 and gave numerous recitals, performing Bach, Beethoven, Chopin, Debussy, Liszt, and Ravel, as well as his own works. On 18 Nov 1945 he presented his most recent compositions, including a *Sonata* for violin and piano, at the Windsor Hotel. The *Quebec Concerto*, an abridged version of his *Concerto No. 3* for piano and orchestra, was played by Neil *Chotem in the Canadian film *La Forteresse* (in English, *Whispering City*). In the autumn of 1946 he returned to Paris for a year to study composition with Arthur Honegger and piano with Jules Gentil.

In the years that followed, André Mathieu's career declined, although he continued to compose – *Piano Trio* (1947) and *Piano Quintet*, among other works. Although he did some teaching, he began in his performances to lapse into musical exhibitionism, taking part in 'pianothons' which received much gaudy publicity but which deeply disappointed those who had seen in him an exceptional talent.

Considering the rich promise of his youth, the fact that his gifts did not develop further can only be deplored. He possessed undeniable qualities as a pianist, to which the Canadian and foreign press almost unanimously attest, as do his few recordings. As a composer he leaned in his maturity to the late-romantic school of Rachmaninoff. The works of his youth, however, revealed a freshness and originality that he did not always recapture later.

In 1976 both the welcoming song and official theme-music of the Montreal Olympics (recorded on Polydor 2424-124; see Petits Chanteurs du Mont-Royal) were arranged from excerpts of works by André Mathieu. The same year the André Mathieu foundation was established to promote his works and to prepare a definitive edition of them. His *Concerto No. 3* ('Romantic'), which he performed in 1948 with a CBC Montreal orchestra under Jean-Marie *Beaudet, was presented in 1977 in Tunisia by the pianist André-Sébastien *Savoie and the Tunis Orchestra conducted by Raymond *Dessaints. The *Quebec Concerto* (an abridged version of the *Concerto No. 3*) was published in 1948 by Southern Music and was recorded in London and released on 78s by Parlophone. Mathieu is said to have written a fourth concerto, of which only a third movement remains. For piano and violin he composed *Fantaisie brésilienne* (Le Parnasse musical), a *Sonata*, a *Berceuse*, and *Complainte*. Among his vocal works, 'Le ciel est si bleu' was published in *Le Passe-Temps* (907, Feb 1947). He also wrote 'Hymne du Bloc Populaire,' 'Les Chères Mains' (1946?), and *Quatre Mélodies* (1948) and made arrangements of a few French-Canadian folksongs.

André Mathieu wrote many works for the piano. Among the compositions of his youth, the *Trois Études* (1933) and *Les Gros Chars* (1934) were published by Southern. *Procession d'éléphants* (1934), *Trois Pièces pittoresques* (1936), *Hommage à Mozart enfant* (1937), and *Les Mouettes* (1938) appeared in Paris (Maurice Sénart) and a few others in Montreal (Institut canadien de musique). In 1939 he wrote *Suite pour deux pianos*, *Les Vagues*, and *Saisons canadiennes* and recorded on 78 his *Trois Études*, *Dans la nuit*, *Les Abeilles piquantes*, and *Danse sauvage* for the French Boîte à musique label (BAM 26). His *Fantaisie* was written in 1945.

The André-Mathieu Club, founded in 1942 at Trois-Rivières by Mme A.J. Rousseau to promote an interest in music among the young, later became part of the *JMC. In 1978 a Salle André-Mathieu was dedicated at the Montmorency Cegep, Laval, Que.

BIBLIOGRAPHY

Vuillermoz, Émile. 'Le Mozart canadien,' Paris *Excelsior*, 27 Mar 1939
Morin, Léo-Pol. 'André Mathieu, créateur d'images musicales,' Montreal *Le Canada*, 27 Nov 1939
Moraude, Jean. 'Mozart parmi nous,' *Action nationale*, vol 14, Dec 1939
Potvin, Gilles. 'André Mathieu: un jeune Mozart à l'heure du COJO,' Montreal *Le Devoir*, 25 Oct 1975
Rudel-Tessier, J. *André Mathieu, un génie* (Montreal 1976)
'Savoie jouera André Mathieu en Tunisie,' *Musique périodique*, vol 1, Mar 1977 1 / JB-T, 2 / GP

MATTON, Roger. Composer, teacher, ethnomusicologist, b Granby, Que, 18 May 1929. After studying piano and theory 1941–3 with Sister Yvette Dufault, he enrolled at the *CMM, where he studied under Claude *Champagne (composition), Gabriel *Cusson (ear training), Isabelle *Delorme (solfège, harmony), and Arthur *Letondal (piano). He continued his studies in Paris with Andrée Vaurabourg-Honegger (piano) privately in 1950 and 1952–3 at the École normale, and with Nadia Boulanger (analysis, counterpoint, and composition) privately 1952–5. He attended Olivier Messiaen's classes in analysis at the Conservatoire in 1950 and again 1953–4. In 1954 he received a scholarship from the Canada Foundation.

On his return to Montreal in 1955 Matton wrote background scores for CBC radio and TV, but he does not list these among his works. At the end of that same year he settled permanently in Quebec City. Already alerted to the potential of folk music through his studies with Champagne, he at-

Roger Matton

tended a 1956 study and apprenticeship program under Marius *Barbeau at the *National Museum of Canada prior to serving 1956–76 as a researcher and ethnomusicologist at the *Archives de folklore of *Laval U. Between 1957 and 1959 he transcribed nearly 300 Acadian songs which had been recorded on tape by Dominique Gauthier; 70 were published in *Chansons de Shippagan* (*Archives de folklore*, vol 16, Quebec 1975) with an introduction by Matton. The recordings *Acadie et Québec* (1959, RCA LCP 1020 and RCA CGP 139) and *Documents d'enquête* (1974, Cible RQA 2) were produced under his direction. Meanwhile he pursued his activity as a composer, and most of his works, in particular the *Concerto* for two pianos and percussion, *L'Escaouette* and *L'*Horoscope* (two CBC commissions), and the *Te Deum*, to some extent show the effect of his long association with folk music. During these same years he was a teacher at Laval U, first in the École de musique, where he taught composition (Alain *Gagnon was one of his pupils) and the history of contemporary music 1960–3, and later in the Dept of Canadian Studies, where he taught ethnomusicology 1964–71. In 1971 he began giving courses in ethnomusicology in the Dept of History, Arts, and Popular Tradition.

Matton's views on contemporary music are precise, as revealed to the critic Marc *Samson: 'I write my music to be listened to, not for the sake of putting it down on paper. To this end I call upon auditory memory, within the broadest limits, and upon acoustics. For I believe in the acoustic virtues of music, not in cerebral data' (Quebec City *Le Soleil*, 19 Dec 1970). Upon hearing the *Concerto* for two pianos and orchestra, dedicated to the duo-pianists *Bouchard and *Morisset, the critic Jean *Vallerand wrote: 'Roger Matton is an "angry" composer, but also a healthy one. Despite a few repetitions and an occasionally irritating use of groups of pedal notes, his *Concerto* for two pianos is the work of someone who has something to say. It is not music conceived in the abstract for manuscript paper or derived from some purely formal designs but is music that first of all has been heard. The most inspired movement, in my view, is the second, in which the piling up of sonorities creates an entrancing effect' (Montreal *La Presse*, 15 Mar 1975).

A skilled and resourceful orchestrator, Matton has written mostly for large instrumental forces. 'His music is characterized by a highly original style, with a vibrant rhythmic capacity, a good sense of symphonic writing, and an idiom which – while entirely modern – retains tonal centres' (*Thirty-four Biographies*). His *Mouvement symphonique II*, commissioned by the *MSO for its European tour in 1962, was premiered in Montreal and later played in Moscow, Leningrad, and Kiev – one of the first symphonic works by a Canadian composer to be performed in the Soviet Union. His monumental *Te Deum*, though written in 1967 for the inauguration of Quebec City's *Grand Théâtre, was performed first at the 65th anniversary of the *Quebec SO. It also was given in Europe in 1969 by the choir and orchestra of the ORTF and in 1977 at the 125th anniversary of Laval U. The *Te Deum* was followed by a seven-year silence, after which the *Mouvement symphonique III* (commissioned by the Grand Théâtre) was premiered in 1974. The *Mouvement symphonique IV* was programmed for the 1980 concert season of the Quebec SO.

Bouchard and Morisset's recording of Matton's *Concerto* for two pianos and orchestra won the Prix Pierre-Mercure at the 1966 Festival du disque, Montreal. Matton himself was awarded the Prix de création musicale canadienne at the 1965 Congrès du spectacle, Montreal, and the *Prix de musique Calixa-Lavallée in 1969. In 1977 he was made an honorary member of the *Montreal Elgar Choir. He is an associate of the *CMCentre, a member of the *CLComp, and an affiliate of PRO Canada.

SELECTED COMPOSITIONS

ORCHESTRA

Danse lente (Gymnopédie). 1947 (Sherbrooke 1947). Chamb orch. Ms

Concerto. 1948 (Mtl 1948). Sax, str orch. Ms

Pax. 1950. Full orch. Ms

L'Escaouette (traditional Acadian themes). 1957 (Mtl 1957). Sop, mezzo, ten, bar, SATB, full orch. CMCentre

Mouvement symphonique I. 1960 (Quebec City 1960). Full orch. Ric 1978

Mouvement symphonique II (Musique pour un drame). 1962 (Mtl 1962). Full orch. Ric 1979. RCI 230/RCA LSC-2980/Vic VICS 1040 (*MSO)

Concerto. 1964 (Quebec City 1964). 2 pf, orch. CMCentre. CRI SD-317/Cap W/SW-6123 (V. *Bouchard)

Te Deum (F.-A. Savard). 1967 (Quebec City 1967). Bar, SATB, orch, tape. CMCentre. RCI 290/Sel SSC-24.188 (R. *Savoie)

Mouvement symphonique III. 1974 (Quebec City 1974). Full orch. CMCentre

Mouvement symphonique IV. 1980 (Quebec City 1980). Full orch. CMCentre

See also *L'Horoscope*.

CHAMBER MUSIC

Étude. 1946. Cl, pf. Ms

Esquisse. 1949. Str quar. Ms

Concerto. 1955. 2 pf, perc. CMCentre. RCI 145 (J. *Dufresne)/RCI 442 (D. *Morton)

KEYBOARD

Berceuse. 1945. Pf. Ms. RCI 135 (J. *Dufresne)

Danse brésilienne. 1946 (rev orch 1971). 2 pf (orch). CMCentre. (2 pf) RCI 145 (J. *Dufresne)/RCI 442 (D. *Morton)

Trois Préludes. 1949. Pf. CMCentre. RCI 135 (J. *Dufresne)

Suite de Pâques. 1952. Org. CMCentre. RCI 481 (H. *McLean)

WRITINGS

'J'étais élève de Claude Champagne,' *Culture vivante*, vol 2, Dec 1968

'Mouvement symphonique no 2 de Roger Matton,' *VM*, 17, Sep 1970

BIBLIOGRAPHY

Bisbrouck, Noël. 'A "L'Heure du concert," un compositeur canadien: Roger Matton,' *SemRC*, vol 15, 20–6 Feb 1965

'Un musicien canadien, Roger Matton,' *Culture information*, 20 Jul–20 Aug 1966

'The creative life of Roger Matton,' interview with Helen Weinzweig, *CanComp*, 33, Oct 1968

Kendergi, Maryvonne. 'Roger Matton: *Te Deum*,' *CMB*, 2, Spring–Summer 1971

Brisson, Irène. 'Matton's music untouched by fashionable trends,' *MSc*, 297, Sep–Oct 1977

Bourassa-Trépanier, Juliette. 'Roger Matton,' *Variations*, vol 2, Sep–Oct 1978

PRO Canada Ltd. 'Roger Matton,' pamphlet (1978)

Brisson, Irène. 'Roger Matton,' *Contemporary Canadian Composers / Compositeurs canadiens contemporains*

Dictionary of Contemporary Music

HP

MAUBOURG, Jeanne (m Roberval). Mezzo-soprano, actress, teacher, b Namur, Belgium, 10 Nov 1875, d Montreal 12 May 1953. She received her musical training in Nancy, Algiers, and Paris. In 1897 she joined the Théâtre de la Monnaie, Brussels, and was assigned numerous roles, including Musetta (*La Bohème*), Hansel, and Carmen. She appeared 1900–4 at London's Covent Garden and was engaged 21 Dec 1909 by the *Metropolitan Opera. She appeared at the Metropolitan until 1914 in an impressive number of supporting roles. After visiting Montreal to sing operetta she settled there permanently in 1917 with her husband, the conductor Albert *Roberval. She took part in numerous productions of operetta before joining the *Société canadienne d'opérette in 1923 and the *Variétés lyriques in 1936, singing chiefly character roles with both companies. She also took up teaching (Pierrette *Alarie, Fleurette *Beauchamp, and Honoré *Vaillancourt were among her pupils) and appeared frequently on radio as both an actress and a singer. In Montreal in 1965 Maubourg Ave was named in her honour. She was a member of the Union professionnelle des maîtres du chant français. The list of her recordings – about 15 titles for *Starr-Gennett and Edison Diamond – appears in *Roll Back the Years*.

GP

MAUL (or Maule), **Adam**. Bandmaster, instrumentalist, teacher, fl 1843–62. One A.D. Maule was a student at King's College, Toronto, in 1843. The musician appeared in Toronto concerts from 1850 on, playing clarinet and violin, and was music master 1850–8 at Upper Canada College. He conducted his own band in a series of promenade concerts (1855, 1856). A. Maul, the organizer and first bandmaster of the *Queen's Own Rifles Band (Dec 1862) is said to have been an Englishman who had served in the imperial army. He held the position only briefly.

MAURO, Ermanno. Tenor, b Trieste 29 Jan 1939, naturalized Canadian 1963. He emigrated to Canada in 1958 and studied with Jean *Létourneau in Edmonton before enrolling in 1964 at the *Royal Cons Opera School, Toronto, where his teachers were George *Lambert, Herman *Geiger-Torel, and Ernesto *Barbini. He created the role of Naisi in *Willan's *Deirdre* in the Royal Cons Opera School production in April 1965. When the Manrico in the *COC's 1967 production of *Il Trovatore* became ill in mid-performance, Mauro was asked to step out of the chorus and sing the remainder of the performance, which he did to critical acclaim. He became house tenor at Covent Garden later in 1967 and remained there until 1972.

Between 1972 and 1980 Mauro performed in Canada with the *Vancouver Opera, the COC, the *Edmonton Opera, the *Southern Alberta Opera, and the *Manitoba Opera, and with such European and US opera companies as the Netherlands State, the Vienna State, and those in Frankfurt, Los Angeles, and San Diego. He made his New York debut 3 Feb 1975 as Calaf in *Turandot* with the New York City Opera. He made an unofficial *Metropolitan Opera debut 6 Jan 1978, when he replaced Jon Vickers in *I Pagliacci*, singing Canio to Louis *Quilico's Tonio, and made his official debut there 25 Jan 1978 as Radames in *Aida*. He made his debut at La Scala in the spring of 1978 and that same year sang Turiddu at the Royal Opera, Covent Garden. During the 1978–9 season he sang at both the Metropolitan Opera and the New

York City Opera, and during the 1978 season he was teamed again with Quilico opposite Renata Scotto in the Metropolitan production of *La Gioconda*.

Mauro appeared frequently 1972–80 in concert, singing with such orchestras as the Scottish National, the Welsh Philharmonic, the London SO, and the *TS and has been heard on the BBC and on CBC radio and TV. His repertoire, largely operatic, encompasses most of the leading tenor roles in Italian and French.

BIBLIOGRAPHY
Pearton, Maurice. 'Artists in profile: Ermanno Mauro,' *OpCan*, Summer 1971
Kirby, Blaik. 'For Ermanno Mauro the opera life is a bunch of jets,' Toronto *Globe and Mail*, 14 Sep 1976

MWM

MAWSON, Elizabeth (Anne) (b Burlington). Mezzo-soprano, actress, b Toronto 14 Feb 1927. While studying voice with Ruth Cross-Vanderpott, 1945–51 at the *Hambourg Cons and 1951–9 privately, she sang soubrette roles in Gilbert & Sullivan and other operetta productions by the Toronto Light Opera Society and the *Eaton Operatic Society and in 1954 became a soloist at St Andrew's United Church, Toronto, a position she continued to hold in 1980. She appeared in 1957 with the Opera Festival Assn of Toronto as Anna in *The Merry Widow* and also that year sang Carrie Pipperidge in *Carousel*. After the association had become the *COC she sang Martha in *Faust* and Flora in *La Traviata* (1966) and was Miss Todd in its *Prologue to the Performing Arts presentations (1968, 1973) of Menotti's *The Old Maid and the Thief*. She also sang in opera and operetta at the *Stratford Festival, her roles including Hebe in *H.M.S. Pinafore* in 1960 and Marzellina in *The Marriage of Figaro* in 1964 and 1965, and appeared with the Gilbert & Sullivan Society of Toronto as Katisha in *The Mikado* in 1968, Angela in *Patience* in 1969, Sophia in *The Grand Duke* in 1970, and Pitti-Sing in *The Mikado* in 1975. In 1968 she joined the *Charlottetown Festival company, with which her roles have included Marilla in annual productions (beginning in 1971) of **Anne of Green Gables* and in 1978 she was Queen Mary in the premiere of David Warrack's *Windsor*. She is married to the baritone Howard *Mawson. MM, PW

MAWSON, Howard. Baritone, actor, b Toronto 23 May 1920. He studied with Ruth Cross-Vanderpott, 1943–51 at the *Hambourg Cons and 1951–8 privately, and with Irene *Jessner at the *RCMT in 1959. He was co-founder (1943) with his father, Frederick Mawson, of the Toronto Light Opera Society, which mounted productions of Gilbert & Sullivan until 1955, and also sang with the *Eaton Operatic Society. Mawson has sung in light opera at the *Stratford Festival (1960–5, his roles including Dick Deadeye in *H.M.S. Pinafore* in 1960) and with the Gilbert & Sullivan Society of Toronto (beginning in 1967) in such character roles as Sir Joseph Porter in *H.M.S. Pinafore*, the Major General in *The Pirates of Penzance*, and Grosvenor in *Patience*. He also sang minor roles in the *COC's *La Traviata* and **Deirdre* in 1966. Mawson became baritone soloist at St Andrew's United Church, Toronto, in 1952. He married the mezzo-soprano Elizabeth Burlington (*Mawson).

MM

MAXWELL, Joan (m Rempel). Mezzo-soprano, b Winnipeg 17 Nov 1930. A pupil of Gladys *Whitehead in Winnipeg, she continued studies at the BC Institute of Music and Drama in 1948 and at the *RCMT in 1950. Other teachers included Emmy *Heim, George *Lambert, and Ernesto *Vinci at the RCMT and in 1963 Otakar Kraus in London. She was first runner-up in *'Opportunity Knocks' (winter 1954) and a winner of the 1955–6 *'Singing Stars of Tomorrow' and made *JMC tours in 1954 and 1959. She also won the 1957 *Metropolitan Opera regional auditions in Minneapolis. That year she sang small roles with the *COC. Based in Winnipeg, she was often a soloist 1956–68 with the *Winnipeg SO and the *Winnipeg Philharmonic Choir and was the star (ca 1958–9) of CBC TV's 'Moods in Music.' She also appeared with the *Vancouver Opera, with the *CBC Opera in productions of *Eugene Onegin*, *Il Matrimonio Segreto*, and Benjamin's *Prima Donna*, and with the COC as Maddalena in *Rigoletto* (1969). In 1969 she also toured as a soloist with the *Festival Singers. Her career was curtailed after 1969 by poor health. Works written for her include Murray *Adaskin's *Of Man and the Universe* (premiered 13 Aug 1967 at *Expo 67) and Bernard *Naylor's *The Nymph Complaining of the Death of Her Faun* (which was premiered, however, by Heather Ireland). She is heard in recordings of *The *Widow* and a recital (1969, CBC SM-103) of songs by Samuel Barber, Michel *Perrault (arr), Richard Strauss, and Brahms, accompanied by Chester *Duncan.

MAYBEE, George (Nelson). Organist, choirmaster, educator, b Madoc, Ont, 13 Mar 1913. d Kingston, Ont, 31 Jul 1973. He studied in Canada with F. Ernest Wheatley and Healey *Willan and in England under Sir Sidney Nicholson at the (then) English School of Church Music, Chislehurst. He had become well established as a choir director in eastern Ontario, particularly during his tenure as organist-choirmaster at Christ Church (Anglican), Belleville, when in 1942 he was appointed organist-choirmaster at St George's Cathedral, Kingston. His training had fostered in him a strong commitment to the music and liturgy of the Church of England and to the training of men-and-boys' choirs, and he soon developed St George's into a major centre of Anglican choral music, maintaining a high standard for nearly three decades. The Gentlemen and Boys of St George's Cathedral Choir visited Great Britain in 1954 and 1965, the first overseas choir to sing the regular services at Westminster Abbey, St Paul's Cathedral, York Minster, and King's College Chapel, Cambridge. The choir also made many North American tours and gave a concert in Washington, DC, in November 1964, dedicated to the late President Kennedy.

Maybee was made a Doctor of Humane Letters at Hobart College, NY, and a Fellow of Westminster Choir College, Princeton, NJ. In 1965 he was invested by Queen Elizabeth II as Fellow and Canadian Commissioner of the Royal School of Church Music. In this capacity he travelled widely and did much to improve standards of choral singing in Canada and the USA. Maybee, whose specialty was 19th- and early 20th-century English church music, was known also for his flamboyant and engaging personality, and was once described by *Time* as 'a genial Simon Legree' (referring to his success as an organizer and promoter). He was also a successful high-school music teacher and became co-ordinator of music and the arts for the Frontenac County Board of Education. He was a visiting lecturer at *Queens U. One of his last appearances was with the St George's choir before Queen Elizabeth II during her Canadian visit in 1973.

BIBLIOGRAPHY
Klyn, Doyle, and Beaver, Bert. 'They'll sing in the Abbey,' *Weekend*, 17 Apr 1954

AW

MAYOH, Leonard. Baritone, choir conductor, b Eagley, England, 8 Jan 1918, d Winnipeg 26 Jul 1978; ARMCM 1947, B MUS (Acadia) 1964. A pupil of Richard Evans and Frank Mullins at the RMCM, and of Roy Henderson in London, he was a recitalist and oratorio soloist in England before moving to Nova Scotia in 1951 as head of the voice department at the Halifax Cons. He continued to teach in Halifax until 1967, holding positions also at the U of King's College (*Dalhousie U), the Halifax School for the Blind, and *Acadia U. Mayoh conducted the *Halifax Choral Society 1951–9 and founded and conducted the Acadia Chapel Choir, which won the Leslie *Bell Trophy in 1965 and City of Lincoln Trophy in 1966. As soloist or guest conductor of the *Halifax SO he participated 1954–60 in performances of *Messiah*, *Elijah*, *The Creation*, *The Christmas Oratorio*, and similar works. He also sang in 1952 with Audrey *Farnell on CBC radio's 'Sketches of Songs' and made the LPs *Songs from the Land o' the Kilt* (1969 Rodeo RLP-22) and *Sea Shanties* (Banff RBS-1096). In 1958 he received the Nova Scotia Centennial Medal for 'distinguished service to music.'

Mayoh began teaching in 1967 at *Brandon U, where he also conducted the Brandon U Chorale. He was conductor 1967–73 of the Western Manitoba Philharmonic Choir, which, with the *Winnipeg SO, presented *Messiah* in 1967 and Mozart's *Requiem* in 1971 under his direction. In 1969 he was a soloist with both organizations. He was active in the festival movement both as an adjudicator and, with his choirs, as a successful competitor. His pupils included Sheila Brand, Nancy DeLong, Nelson Lohnes, Sheila *Piercey, Judith Pringle, and Judith Wright. Brandon U posthumously named him professor emeritus.

BIBLIOGRAPHY
'Leonard Mayoh,' *Winnipeg Free Press*, 12 Aug 1978

(LI)

MAZURETTE, Salomon (or Solomon). Pianist, composer, organist, teacher, baritone, b Montreal 26 Jun 1847, d Detroit 19 Sep 1910. As a child he sang for five years as a soloist in Notre-Dame Church. He took piano lessons for eight years with Paul *Letondal, studied 1865–6 at the *U of Ottawa, and then went to Paris to work with the virtuoso pianist Jacques Herz and the organist Édouard Batiste. In Paris Mazurette apparently gave successful concerts with the violinist Joseph Dawsrahk. After returning to Montreal in 1870 he set out on an extended concert tour which took him through New England, Michigan, and Illinois. Back in Montreal, in November 1873, he gave two recitals at Queen's Hall; an anonymous critic wrote in *L'Opinion publique*: 'M. Mazurette is already a master. He has more than just talent, he has the inspiration of genius. Like Liszt, his illustrious rival, our Canadian artist makes the piano speak and sing.'

Mazurette moved to Detroit in 1873, returning only on rare occasions to give concerts in Canada. In May 1890 he gave two concerts in Montreal at the Victoria rink, one with Emma *Albani. 'Leading critics admit that he has no superior on the American continent,' wrote *La Minerve* on this occasion, adding that 'the sounds he draws from the piano one would believe possible only in flights of ecstatic imagination.' In Detroit he was for many years the organist at St Anne's Church, and in neighbouring Windsor, Ont, he was music director of St Mary's Academy for at least the 1875–6 school year. He was awarded a gold medal in 1876 for his performance at the Centennial Exposition in Philadelphia.

Dubbed the 'King of Canadian pianists,' Mazurette belongs to that generation of 19th-century pianist-composers whose considerable success with the public was due to their spectacular performance style and to compositions in which bravura passages and facile sentimental melodies abound. He was an unusually prolific composer, and his works were much in demand among publishers. The best-known was *Home, Sweet Home, Op 17*, 'a brilliant Romance with variations imitating waves during a storm,' which he composed in August 1870 aboard ship on his return journey from France. Numerous editions were produced by Ditson, Schott, Ashdown, and Sheard. *Old Folks at Home*, 'a grand concert paraphrase' published by Gordon, bears the opus number 275, an indication of the abundance of his output. Mazurette wrote mainly for piano and voice, but he also composed a *Mass in D Minor*, sung in 1875 in Trinity Church, Detroit. He dedicated some sentimental ballads to famous singers such as Emma Albani ('O! Give me back my native hills'), Annie Louise Cary, Clara Louise Kellogg, and Marie Roze.

Despite the active life he appears to have led in Detroit as organist, teacher, and composer, he died destitute and was buried in a pauper's grave. In 1964 a street in north Montreal was named after him. His daughter Hortense (mezzo-soprano, b 1889, d 16 Jan 1927) studied with Fernando Tanara. It is thought that she sang at the *Metropolitan Opera until 1917, when she gave up the stage.

BIBLIOGRAPHY
'Monsieur S. Mazurette,' Montreal *Gazette*, 10 Jan 1873
'M. Salomon Mazurette,' Montreal *L'Opinion publique*, 6 Nov 1873
'Salomon Mazurette,' *La Minerve*, May 1890
'Mazurette is dead; master of music forgotten by the thousands he had thrilled,' *Detroit News*, 20 Sep 1910 GP

MAZZOLENI, Ettore. Conductor, teacher, administrator, b Brusio, Ticino, Switzerland, of Swiss-Italian parentage, 18 Jun 1905, naturalized Canadian 1949, d Oak Ridges, near Toronto, in a traffic accident 1 Jun 1968; BA (Oxford) 1927, B MUS (Oxford) 1927, hon D MUS (Rochester) 1949, hon FRCM 1961. Taken as a child to England he studied mathematics and later music at Oxford U and piano at the RCM. Two years, 1927–9, on the opera staff at the RCM brought him into contact with Sir Adrian Boult and Ralph Vaughan Williams, and when he moved to Toronto in 1929 as a music master at Upper Canada College he became involved immediately in the preparation of the *TCM Opera's production of Vaughan Williams' *Hugh the Drover*. Remaining at Upper Canada College until 1945, latterly as an English instructor, Mazzoleni succeeded Donald *Heins as conductor of the TCM SO in 1934. He became the program annotator of the *TSO in 1932 and served the orchestra 1942–8 as associate conductor. In 1932 he began to teach music history and conducting and to examine for the TCM. He was appointed principal when the conservatory was reorganized in 1945. A further controversial reorganization of the conservatory – by then renamed the *Royal Conservatory of Music of Toronto – left Mazzoleni still the principal and also director 1952–66 of the *Royal Cons Opera School. He was director 1951–3 and general director 1954–7 of the opera school's offspring, the Opera Festival of Toronto (later the *COC) and conducted the COC productions of *Die Fledermaus* (1957, 1964), *The Tales of Hoffmann* (1958), *The Barber of Seville* (1959), *A Night in Venice* (1960), *The Bartered Bride* (1961), *Hansel and Gretel* (1962, 1963), and *Deirdre* (1966). He appeared as a guest conductor with the *CBC SO, the *Halifax SO, the *Hart House Orchestra, the *MSO, the Pro Arte Orchestra, the *Quebec SO, the Toronto Philharmonic Orchestra, the *Vancouver SO, and the *Victoria SO and conducted often for CBC radio, notably in a

Ettore Mazzoleni

1942 series with two harpsichordists (Greta *Kraus and Arnold *Walter) and string orchestra, broadcast from Upper Canada College, and in various programs for 'CBC Wednesday Night,' including the North American premiere (1954) of Arthur *Benjamin's *A Tale of Two Cities*.

Mazzoleni conducted the premieres of *Willan's *Transit through Fire* and *Deirdre* and the *CLComp's first concert, 16 May 1951, a *Weinzweig program. With the TCM SO Mazzoleni introduced to Canada works by Howard Hanson, Holst, Vaughan Williams, George Butterworth, and others. For the CBC he conducted the TV premiere, 13 Jan 1959, of Britten's *Peter Grimes*. Among his pupils at the TCM were Louis *Applebaum, Howard *Cable, Victor *Feldbrill, Robert *Fleming, George Hurst, Franz *Kraemer, and Godfrey *Ridout. Mazzoleni was the author of several transcriptions for orchestra, including Bach's *Passacaglia and Fugue in C Minor* and the Handel and Bononcini overtures to *Muzio Scevola*. Mazzoleni's first wife was the sister of Sir Ernest *MacMillan. His second wife, (Edith) Joanne Ivey (b London, Ont, 27 Oct 1923), a mezzo-soprano and gifted comic, studied with Helen Simmie and Emmy *Heim and at the Royal Cons Opera School and later in New York and Florence, making her debut in 1951 with the RCMT Opera as Dame Marthe in *Faust*. She remained with the company until 1962, singing Orlofsky in *Die Fledermaus* (1955) and *Carmen* in 1956. She also appeared in concert and oratorio.

WRITINGS
'Wartime overture,' *Curtain Call*, vol 11, Sep–Oct 1939
'Music and the Massey report: do handicaps out-weigh hopes?' *SatN*, vol 66, 17 Jul 1951
'Music in Canada,' *Queen's Q*, vol 60, Winter 1954
'Solo Artists,' *Music in Canada*

DISCOGRAPHY
Willan *Coronation Suite*. CBC Orch and Chor, Mazzoleni cond. 1954. RCI 118

BIBLIOGRAPHY
'Ettore Mazzoleni,' *OpCan*, Sep 1964
Geiger-Torel, H. 'In memoriam: Dr. Ettore Mazzoleni,' *OpCan*, Sep 1968
Creative Canada, vol 2 GR

MEAD, George, James, and **John**. Brothers, probably from Boston, who were active 1827–53 in Montreal and 1839–44 in Toronto as piano builders and instrument and sheet-music importers. Several firm names have been traced: Mead, Mott & Co, harp and piano makers (Montreal, fl 1836); Mead and S.R. *Warren (Montreal, partnership formed and dissolved in 1837); Mead, Brothers & Co, music and instrument importers and piano manufacturers (Montreal, fl 1841–52); John Mead (Toronto dealer, fl 1839–40); J(ohn) and J(ames) Mead (Toronto 1840–4?); and Mead and Fowler (Montreal ca 1853). It is known also that the Mead business was established in 1827 and that George, who retired in 1852 and had died by 1854, was succeeded by Thomas D. *Hood. The family relationship between the Montreal and Toronto firms is borne out by a joint advertisement in the Kingston *Chronicle and Gazette* dated 31 Jul 1841. They also had announced in 1840 in a Toronto paper that James Mead had just arrived from London after working for one of that city's principal builders for three years. Mead pianos undoubtedly were among the first to be built in Canada. A specimen by Mead, Mott & Co is exhibited at the Château de Ramezay in Montreal and one by Mead, Brothers & Co at the Archibald Campbell Memorial Museum in Perth, Ont. The Montreal firm also engaged marginally in music publishing, its catalogue including pieces by J.-C. *Brauneis Jr, R.J. Fowler, and Henry *Schallehn, although the Mead, Brothers & Co imprint is secondary to a US imprint on most items. HK

Mechanical instruments (non-electronic). Machines designed to produce music mechanically, sometimes with an operator but without a performer and without the aid of a loudspeaker. Before the end of the 19th century such instruments operated on a 'barrel and pin' system which dated back at least five centuries. Included within this category were instruments which operated by means of clockworks, such as mechanical organs and 18th-century flute clocks, or by crank, such as barrel organs. During the late 19th century a second type of mechanism was perfected. This was the perforated paper roll used in the operation of player and reproducing pianos, phonolas, pianolas, etc.

For entries in *EMC* on mechanical instruments see Barrel organs; Music boxes; Player pianos and nickelodeons. See also Instrument collections.

BIBLIOGRAPHY
Bowers, Q. David. *Encyclopedia of Automatic Instruments* (New York 1973)
Ord-Hume, Arthur W.J.G. *Mechanical Music* (London 1973)

Mechanics' Hall / Salle des artisans, Montreal. An assembly or concert hall built in 1854 at the corner of St-Pierre and St-Jacques streets in Montreal. Emma Lajeunesse (Emma *Albani) made her debut there as singer, pianist, and harpist in 1856 and performed there again in 1862. It was there too that Calixa *Lavallée was billed in 1864 as piano, violin, and cornet virtuoso and performed in 1875 with Frantz *Jehin-Prume and Rosita *del Vecchio shortly after his return from Paris. Jehin-Prume gave six 'classical chamber' concerts at the hall during the early months of 1871. The *Montreal Philharmonic Society presented its programs in this hall 1878–80, as did the *Mendelssohn Choir 1876–80. The shifting of the population northwards and the construction of more spacious halls around Ste-Catherine Street led the Mechanics' Institute to convert the hall into a museum and reading room in 1885.

BIBLIOGRAPHY
Béraud, Jean. *350 ans de théâtre au Canada français* (Montreal 1958) GP

Mechanics' Hall, Toronto. On the ground floor of the Mechanics' Institute Building, at Church and Adelaide streets, it was designed by Cumberland and Stone and completed in 1856, with alterations in 1861. It had a capacity of 500 with raised semicircular seating. The *Musical Union gave regular concerts there in the early 1860s, and the *Toronto Philharmonic *Society performed there for the first time in 1874 under *Torrington. The Mechanics' Institute organized concerts, and the hall was also used for theatrical productions, public meetings, and lectures. After 1883, when the building was sold to the city and became Toronto's first public library, the hall was used as storage space; it was demolished in 1930. RPn

MECHTLER, Guillaume. Organist, teacher, composer, b Brussels ca 1763, d Montreal 15(?) Feb 1833. He advertised in the *Quebec Gazette* (12 Jul 1787) that he had 'quitted entirely the business of the theatre' and would settle in Quebec City as a music teacher. Two years later he had moved to Montreal, where he announced that he would take pupils in 'forte piano, harpsichord and violin,' and became assistant organist at Notre-Dame Church. He was regular organist there 1792–1832 except for a period in 1814–15. An announcement for a concert 14 Sep 1796 lists a 'Concerto on the Piano Forte – Mr. Mechtler.' He was certainly the performer but not necessarily the composer. However, he is known to have received £48 for 'works of his composition' in 1811 and may have been the first Canadian to be paid as a composer. Mechtler also is thought to have been the first of many Belgian musicians to settle in Montreal. One Mrs Mechtler, a singer who appeared 1790–2 in Halifax and later in New York and Boston, was not the wife of Guillaume, who married in Montreal in 1793.

BIBLIOGRAPHY
Lapalice, Ovide. 'Les organistes et maîtres de musique à Notre-Dame de Montréal,' *BRH*, vol 25, Aug 1919
Huot, Cécile. 'Musiciens belges au Québec,' *CMB*, 8, Spring–Summer 1974 HK

MEDLEY, John. Clergyman, choirmaster, composer, b London 19 Dec 1804, d Fredericton 9 Sep 1892. Medley, the Oxford-educated first Anglican bishop (1845) of Fredericton, had studied the writings of the 19th-century musical theorist Adolf Bernhard Marx. For over 40 years Medley directed the choir at his cathedral. 'No choir practice was considered complete until every anthem and introit, every chant and hymn was perfect' (Col George Maunsell, quoted by Ketchum, p 323). 'It would have been difficult to meet with a better [musical] service out of England' (Alexander Ewing, quoted by Ketchum, p 328). 'He ... was a good musician. Church music was beginning to change, from the style of Tate and Brady to that which produced *Hymns Ancient and Modern*; and the Bishop did all he could to promote this improvement in his own diocese' (Mockridge p 116). Medley composed about 20 anthems and many introits, services, and other pieces of church music. In 1855 he edited *Hymns for Public Worship in the Diocese of Fredericton* (Saint John, NB, 1855, 1863, 1870).

BIBLIOGRAPHY
Ketchum, W.Q. *The Life and Work of the Most Reverend John Medley, D.D.* (Saint John 1893)
Mockridge, C.H. *The Bishops of the Church of England in Canada and Newfoundland* (Toronto 1896) HK

MEEK, Harold (after ca 1912 'Edouard Albion'). Baritone, impresario, b Port Stanley, near London, Ont, 24 Mar 1887, d there 27 May 1972. He studied at 18 with Cyril Dwight-Edwards in London, Ont, with Frank King Clark and Oscar Seagle in Paris, and with Vincenzo Lombardi in Florence. Known for most of his career as Edouard Albion, he toured the USA and Canada with Luisa Tetrazzini in 1912 and was a member 1913–14 of the *National Opera Company of Canada, making his debut in Montreal as the Herald in *Lohengrin*. A concert tour of Canada followed in 1916. On failing to interest Ottawa authorities in a new opera house for the city he moved to Washington, DC, and there founded, directed, and performed with the National Opera. In that company's 18 years (1918–36) Meek brought to Washington many outstanding singers of the day, including the Canadians Jeanne *Gordon, Edward *Johnson, and Bertha *Crawford. After appearing as Nilakantha in *Lakmé* in one of the company's last productions, Albion toured the USA and Canada. In later years he taught voice in Philadelphia, Atlanta, Chicago, and, after retirement, in Port Stanley.

BIBLIOGRAPHY
Smith, Patrick F. 'Edouard Albion-Meek,' *OpCan*, May 1968 JBM (FH)

MEEK, Kenneth. Organist, choirmaster, harpsichordist, composer, teacher, b Truro, Cornwall, England, 21 May 1908, d Montreal 18 Aug 1976; L MUS (McGill) 1927, B MUS (Toronto) 1936. A Canadian resident after 1914, he studied in Ottawa 1920–7 with Herbert *Sanders and in Toronto in 1936 with Herbert *Fricker. While teaching organ, piano, and theory in Ottawa 1924–39, in Kingston 1940–4, and at *McGill U (1945–76, his pupils including Mary Blaikie, Gian Lyman, Wayne *Riddell, Gordon White, and Robert Wight), he was organist-choirmaster at churches in those cities, including the First Church of Christ Scientist, Ottawa, 1926–36 and Christ Church Cathedral 1956–65 and the Church of the Messiah, Montreal, 1965–76. Organist at the Church of St Andrew and St Paul in Montreal 1945–56, he presented the complete organ works of J.S. Bach in 12 recitals 1950–1. Meek's compositions include *Trouvères* (E.C. Schirmer 1961) and *Ophelia's Songs* (BMIC 1963) for recorder quartet, *Three Easter Carols* (BMIC 1957) and 'A Carol of Thanks' (Gray) for choir, *Three Christmas Carols* (Western 1951) for choir and organ, and *Three Plainsong Preludes* (Gray 1959), *Three Preludes* (BMIC 1960), and *The Agincourt Song* (BMIC) for organ. Other works are listed in the *Catalogue of Canadian Composers*. His recording *The Romantic Organ* includes works by Bach, Reger, Franck, Widor, and Vierne (Laurentian CTM 6086). The musical rights of his estate are administered by PRO Canada. NT

Meet the Navy. Royal Canadian Navy musical revue produced during World War II under the supervision of Capt Joseph P. Connolly, director of Special Services for the RCN. Rehearsals began in June 1943 at *Hart House in Toronto. The production staff and company were recognized officially – somewhat after the fact – by a government of Canada Treasury Board order-in-council, 13 Aug 1943, as 'an Establishment to be known as "The Navy Show" for the ... Entertainment of Naval, Army and Air Force personnel on Active Service; Promotion of recruiting; [and] Maintenance of public morale and goodwill.'

The show itself, called *Meet the Navy* and directed by Louis Silver (a Hollywood producer) and Larry Ceballos (a Broadway choreographer), was premiered for servicemen 2 September at Toronto's Victoria Theatre and opened to the public 4 September. It opened in Ottawa 15 September at the Capitol Theatre. During a year-long national tour, which covered some 10,000 miles by train, *Meet the Navy* entertained about a half-million Canadians. It travelled in 1944 to Britain, opening 23 October in Glasgow and touring England (11 cities in the provinces), Ireland, and Wales and playing at the Hippodrome in London (1 Feb–7 Apr 1945, including a command performance 28 February). Performances followed in Paris' Théâtre Marigny, the Brussels Music Hall, and Amsterdam's Carré Theatre. *Meet the Navy* closed 12 September in Oldenburg in occupied Germany. In 1945 the NFB produced the film *Meet the Navy on Tour*. Though plans for a Broadway run fell through, the show itself was filmed in November in Britain.

Meet the Navy included skits, dance routines, and several songs: 'In Your Little Chapeau,' 'Rockettes and the Wrens,' 'Brothers-in-Arms,' 'Meet the Navy,' and 'Beauty on Duty,' all by R.W. Harwood (words) and P.E. Quinn (music); 'The Boys in the Bellbottom Trousers' by Quinn; 'Shore Leave' by Noel Langley and Henry Sherman (words) and Quinn; and the showstopper (sung by John Pratt) *'You'll Get Used to It,' with words by Pratt to music by Freddy *Grant. Eric *Wild (who conducted the pit orchestra) and Robert Russell Bennett arranged the music. Leading roles were taken by Pratt, Robert Goodier, Cameron Grant, and Lionel Merton. Other featured performers included Dixie *Dean, Ivan *Romanoff (who conducted the balalaika orchestra and chorus in 'Scena Russki'), Carl *Tapscott (who did choral arrangements), the bass Oscar Natzke, and the dance team Alan and Blanche Lund. Members of the 25-piece orchestra included the violinists Victor *Feldbrill, Bill *Richards, and Joseph Sera, the trombonist Ted Elfstrom, and the saxophonist-clarinetist Howard 'Cokie' Campbell.

After the London debut of *Meet the Navy*, Beverley Baxter wrote in the *London Evening Standard*: 'Why is this piece so exhilarating, so completely satisfying and, since the first class always touches the emotions, why was it so stirring? Perhaps the answer is that quite outside the professional slickness and the terrific pace of the whole thing, we were seeing the story of Canada unconsciously unfolding itself to our eyes.'

In 1980, to celebrate the 70th anniversary of the Canadian navy, the Nova Scotia government revived *Meet the Navy* with several members of the original cast.

BIBLIOGRAPHY
Phillips, Ruth. 'The history of the Royal Canadian Navy's World War II show *Meet the Navy*,' unpubl ms (1973)
MM

MEIGHEN, Frank Stephen. Businessman, patron of the arts, impresario, army officer, b Perth, Ont, 26 Dec 1870, d Montreal Jan 1946; BA (McGill) 1889. He inherited his father's fortune and was an astute businessman involved mainly in railways and the milling trade. Although he studied piano with Paul *Letondal, his passion was opera. Deploring the absence of a regular company in Montreal, he collaborated with Albert *Clerk-Jeannotte in 1910 to found the Montreal Musical Society, which the following year became the *Montreal Opera Company. In three seasons, 1910–13, the company gave close to 300 performances in Montreal and other Canadian and US cities. Meighen personally financed the undertaking, which, at the time of its dissolution, had cost him more than $100,000.

As a lieutenant-colonel, then a general, in the Canadian army, he served at the front during World War I. Upon his return to Canada in 1919, he displayed his generosity again, underwriting the concerts of the *Canadian Grenadier Guards Band at the *Orpheum Theatre 1919–20 and at *His Majesty's Theatre 1920–3. He served 1927–9 as president of *Gagnier's *MSO. From 1936 until his death he was a member of the board of directors of the *Montreal Festivals Society and subsidized several musical concerns, including the

MSO. He published several articles of musical criticism in the Montreal *Gazette*. He was made a Companion of the Order of St Michael and St George in 1915 and an Officer of the Legion of Honour in 1924.

BIBLIOGRAPHY

Lamontagne, Charles-O., and Gour, Romain. 'Frank Stephen Meighen, dilettante et mécène,' *Qui?* vol 5, Mar 1954 GP

MELECCI, Adelmo. Teacher, composer, organist, b Felonica Po, near Venice, 18 May 1908, naturalized Canadian 1928. Leaving Italy in 1920 he studied at the New York School of Music and at the *TCM, where his teachers were Healey *Willan and Ernest *Seitz. Melecci joined the TCM in 1928 as a piano, organ, and theory teacher. He subsequently became principal of the Willowdale branch and organist at the Richmond Hill United Church. He composed a number of choral works, songs, and piano pieces for children. Some of his songs were recorded and published by Walt Disney. 'The Candle' (Harris 1957; dedicated to Perry Como) was sung on CBC TV at Christmas 1963. RRs

MELNYK, John. Teacher, pianist, composer, b Winnipeg, of Ukrainian parents, 17 Jun 1916; LRSM 1935. He studied 1924–38 in Winnipeg with Maria Kekishiwna (a pupil of Anton Rubinstein), Leda Omansky, and Beryl Ferguson. He participated 1930–6 in the Saturday Night concert series sponsored by the *Men's Music Club of Winnipeg. In the late 1930s he toured as accompanist to Frederick *Grinke, Lorne *Munroe, and John *Waterhouse, and in the early 1940s he played for the Viennese soprano Olga Lepkhova and the Ukrainian violinist Roman Prybatkhevytch on their Canadian appearances. Melnyk began teaching privately in 1938, his method influenced by that of Leopold Godowsky. His pupils have included Emanuel Ax, Anne Henderson, Marvin Johnson, Cornelia Gayowsky-Kuchmy, Edward *Lincoln, Nadia March, Gilbert and Sheila *Munroe, Marion Ross, Pearl Snyder, and Kenneth *Winters. He has taught more than 20 winners of the Aikins Memorial Trophy, the senior instrumental award of the *Manitoba Music Competition Festival. Melnyk's compositions, unpublished and all for piano, include three preludes, a sonata, a concerto, and two sets of variations.

Melnyk's son John (Stephen Nicholas) – pianist, b Winnipeg 4 May 1955; BA mathematics (Harvard) 1977 – was a pupil of his father 1963–79 and of Rowland Sturges in Boston 1973–7. He won the Harvard-Radcliffe Concerto Competition in 1977 and was soloist with the Boston Pops Orchestra in Gershwin's *Concerto in F* in 1977 and Rachmaninoff's *Rhapsody on a Theme of Paganini* in 1978. He also played Gershwin's *Rhapsody in Blue* with the *Vancouver SO guest-conducted by Arthur Fiedler 27 and 28 Feb and 2 Mar 1978. JA

Melodeons. See Reed organs.

Melody Fair. Theatre-in-the-round which presented musicals and operettas 1951–4 in Toronto. Sponsored by Music Circus of Canada Ltd (R. Stuart Lampard, president) and directed by Leighton K. Brill (executive producer) and Ben Kamsler (general manager), Melody Fair mounted 10 to 12 productions each summer, first (1951–2) at Dufferin Park, then (1953) at the *CNE grounds, and finally (1954) in the Mutual Street Arena. Leading roles were taken by US performers, and lesser roles were filled by Canadians, many at the beginning of their careers, including Kathryn Albertson, Glenn Gardiner, Robert *Goulet, Sylvia *Grant, Alexander *Gray, and Joan *Maxwell. Among the 43 productions were *Brigadoon, Carousel, The Desert Song, Finian's Rainbow, Rose Marie, Show Boat*, and *Song of Norway* (the 1951 production of which featured Mario *Bernardi playing the Grieg *Piano Concerto* in the last act). (GK)

Memorials and honours. An examination of the ways in which Canadians have honoured their musicians, publicly and permanently, does not reveal – save in Quebec – a significant measure of gratitude; rather it points to neglect and forgetfulness. Few Canadian musicians' names have been given to towns, streets, parks, halls, or buildings or have been honoured in memorials or plaques; postage stamps honouring music and musicians were issued for the first time only in 1980. Portraits and memorial awards and scholarships are encountered more frequently (see Art, visual; Awards), but these usually are initiated from within the profession and tend not to reflect recognition by the political community or the larger public. There are, however, exceptions to these general observations.

Calixa *Lavallée, the composer of *'O Canada,' is perhaps Canada's most commemorated musician, with a town (Calixa-Lavallée, previously Ste-Théodosie, near Verchères), several streets (Montreal, Quebec City, St-Hyacinthe, etc), and the music building of the *U of Ottawa (Pavillon Calixa-Lavallée) named in his honour, a plaque placed on the site of the house (after it was destroyed by fire) in which he was born. The custom of naming streets after noted persons in the arts has been established in a few Canadian cities, notably Montreal, where more than 30 musicians have been honoured, beginning with Rodolphe *Plamondon (1911) and including Napoléon *Legendre (1912), Alfred *De Sève (1931), Alexis *Contant (1962), and Emma *Albani (1969; an earlier 'avenue Albani' disappeared in a realignment of streets). There are both streets and squares in Montreal named for Guillaume *Couture and Joseph *Casavant. Barbara *Pentland is honoured in the Ottawa suburb of Kanata, and Arthur Thomas *Bushby in New Westminster and Victoria. The Alexander *Muir Memorial Gardens in Toronto were dedicated to the composer of *'The Maple Leaf For Ever.' There is a park in Montreal named for J.-J. *Gagnier (1959), and a street was named after Gagnier in 1963. In Toronto there is a *Nordheimer Ravine, though in the latter case the name is popular rather than official. Toronto also has a park named for Jan Sibelius, complete with a monument to the Finnish composer. Another monument to Sibelius may be found on Île Ste-Hélène, Montreal. An island in the North West Territories is named for the Swedish soprano Jenny Lind. Other world figures in music have had streets named in their honour: over a dozen in Montreal and at least three in Toronto.

Mount Manny in New Brunswick commemorates the collector Louise *Manny, Barbeau Peak in the Canadian Arctic the collector Marius *Barbeau, and Waterhouse Bay, Charleswood, Man, the violinist John *Waterhouse. Buildings and halls, if they bear family names, traditionally have been named for donors (eg, the *Malkin Bowl, *Massey Hall, and, in Halifax, the *Rebecca Cohn Auditorium). However, several in recent years have been named for musicians: Brunton Hall, at the Marjorie Young Bell Cons, *Mount Allison U, for James Noel Brunton, head of the conservatory 1919–36 (the conservatory also houses the Alfred *Whitehead Memorial Music Library); Eva *Clare Hall, *U of Manitoba; the Leonard *Leacock Theatre, *Mount Royal College; Harrison-*Le Caine Hall, *Queen's U; *MacMillan Theatre and *Walter Hall in the Edward *Johnson Building, *U of Toronto; the Boris *Roubakine Auditorium, *Banff SFA and the Roubakine Hall, *U of Calgary. In the province of Quebec, halls also have been named in honour of François *Brassard (in Jonquière), Maurice *Dela (in Chambly and, by Dela's name at birth, Albert Phaneuf, in St-Hubert), Gilles *Lefebvre (at the *JMC Orford Art Centre), André *Mathieu (in Laval), and André *Prévost (in St-Jérome). Canadian public schools have been named for Marius *Barbeau, Vernon *Barford, Claude *Champagne, Guillaume Couture, Gladys *Egbert, Calixa Lavallée, Félix *Leclerc, Alexander Muir, Wilfrid *Pelletier, and the Calgary musicologist Dr E.P. Scarlett.

Plaques marking buildings where famous musicians were born or died are rare. No such identification marks the house on rue Couillard in Quebec City where Lavallée lived when he wrote 'O Canada,' or Sir Ernest MacMillan's birthplace or his Park Road residence in Toronto (although the latter was designated a building of historic interest in 1979), or Healey *Willan's residence on Inglewood Drive (Toronto). However, a plaque marks the site of the house on rue Martel in Chambly where Emma Albani was born, and placques in Cobourg and Guelph, Ont, proclaim those cities the birthplaces of, respectively, Marie Dressler and Edward Johnson. In 1979 a plaque also was placed on the First Lutheran Church in Toronto to commemorate Theodore August *Heintzman. Three songs have been commemorated by plaques: one on Nebo Rd near Burlington, Ont, on the grounds of the childhood home of Maggie Clark, whose memory is perpetuated in *'When You and I Were Young, Maggie'; one marking the grave (near Port Hope, Ont) of Joseph Medicott Scriven (1819–86), the author of the poem 'Pray Without Ceasing,' later set to music as 'What a Friend We Have in Jesus'; and one at the grave (Fergus, Ont) of George Clephane, whose death is believed to have moved his sister Elizabeth to write the poem 'The Ninety and Nine,' later set to music by the US evangelist Ira D. Sankey.

The first Canadian stamps honouring Canadian musicians were issued in pairs in 1980. One pair carried a portrait of Emma Albani on one stamp and a portrait of Healey Willan on the other. The other pair marked the 100th anniversary of 'O Canada' with, on one stamp, portraits of Lavallée, Routhier, and Weir and on the other the opening bar of the song.

The memories of revered church musicians have been honoured in various ways: eg, Herbert *Sadler (Westminster United Church, Winnipeg) and Vernon Barford (All Saints Cathedral, Edmonton) by memorial organs, Filmer *Hubble (St Stephen's Broadway United Church, Winnipeg) and A.S. *Vogt (St Paul's Anglican Church, Toronto) by stained glass windows (the Vogt window donated by the *Toronto Mendelssohn Choir, and Henri Kew *Jordan (Brant Avenue United Church, Brantford, Ont) and Cyril F. Musgrove (Holy Trinity Anglican Church, Winnipeg) by plaques.

Among other memorials to Canadian musicians are a headstone set in 1964 at the previously unmarked grave of Marie *Toulinguet in Twillingate, Nfld, and a water fountain, in Stratford, Ont, with a carved inscription to W. Freeland, Stratford's first school music director. In the *PDA subway station in Montreal is a wall-sized, backlighted glass memorial mural representing the major musical figures of Montreal, including Albani, Champagne, *Mercure, and many others.

Memorial University of Newfoundland. Nondenominational university in St John's. It evolved from Memorial U College, founded in 1925 as a memorial to Newfoundlanders killed in World War I. It gained university status in 1949 and moved to a new campus in the city in 1961. With graduate studies offered in several departments (though not music), Memorial U has achieved distinction in the fields of marine science, folklore, medicine, and engineering.

Before 1952 musical activity consisted mostly of non-credit appreciation courses and sporadic attempts at a student choir. In 1952 Ignatius A. *Rumboldt was appointed on a part-time basis to organize and direct a student glee club. In 1960 he was appointed specialist in music with the university and music consultant with the university's extension service. For the latter Rumboldt developed community choirs in Newfoundland and Labrador and orchestras in St John's and Corner Brook. The St John's orchestra detached itself from the university in 1969 to become the St John's SO. R. Murray *Schafer was artist-in-residence at Memorial U 1963–5.

Donald F. Cook (b 1937), a specialist in music in the Faculty of Education, established the first of several credit courses in music in 1969, and soon the teaching staff had to be enlarged to accommodate the demand for these. H. Doreen Coultas (b 1926) was appointed to teach music education in 1972.

The Dept of Music was established in 1975 with D.F. Cook as head and registered its first students in 1976. In 1978–9 it had 55 students and 16 teachers (9 full-time, 7 part-time). Programs offered in that academic year were the four-year B MUS (Applied Major) and the five-year conjoint degree of B MUS and B MUS ED. Neil Van Allen was acting head during Cook's leave in 1979–80.

In 1975 the department established a music preparatory school for students of pre-university age. Responsibility for a summer instrumental camp for young musicians (established in 1972 by the university's Extension Service) was transferred in 1975 to the Dept of Music, under Cook's direction.

The department's musical activities, including a concert series in the 420-seat concert hall, have received strong community support. Performing groups in 1980 included the Memorial U Chamber Orchestra, Chamber Choir, Choral Society, Concert Band, and Stage Band; department facilities included a seven-rank *Casavant tracker organ and a John Broadwood forte-piano (ca 1808), the latter a gift of Roy Mickleburgh, Bristol, England.

Memorial U's important Folklore and Language Archive, established in 1968, was directed until 1976 by Herbert Halpert, then by Neil V. *Rosenberg. The Dept of Folklore was founded by Halpert in 1968 and directed by him until 1973. He was followed by a number of acting heads, then by Kenneth S. Goldstein 1976–8. Goldstein was succeeded by David D. Buchan in 1979. In 1970 the university conferred an honorary degree on the folklorist Maud Karpeles, who had collected in Newfoundland.

At Memorial U's Regional College in Corner Brook, Ignatius Rumboldt established a college choir during his term as director of music 1975–7. When he returned to St John's to become director of glee clubs for Memorial's Extension Service, he was succeeded in Corner Brook by B. Wayne Rogers. The Regional College began a music preparatory school in 1977. It also has sponsored concert and recital series.

See also Archives; Bibliography; Ethnomusicology.

BIBLIOGRAPHY
Rowe, F.W. 'Memorial University of Newfoundland,' *Education and Culture of Newfoundland* (Toronto 1976)
Bartlett, Jon. 'Memorial University publications,' *Canada Folk Bulletin*, vol 3, Sep–Dec 1980 (DFC)

MÉNARD, René. Priest, missionary, composer, b Paris 2 Mar 1605, d Wisconsin, August 1661. He joined the Jesuits in 1624, was ordained, and was sent to Canada in 1640. He went on numerous missionary expeditions to the Nipissings, Algonkins, Iroquois, and Hurons and succeeded in winning their confidence. He was the superior of the Jesuits' residence at Trois-Rivières 1651–6. A letter written by Sister Anne de Ste-Claire from Quebec, 2 Sep 1640, mentions that Ménard had 'composed several motets which we sang after the elevation' (*Les Ursulines de Québec*, vol 1, p 39). Willy *Amtmann has examined the circumstances of this early instance of composition in Canada and speculates that a copy of some of Ménard's music may survive in a manuscript compilation at the Quebec Ursuline convent.

BIBLIOGRAPHY
Les Ursulines de Québec (Quebec 1863)
DCB, vol 1
Amtmann *Music in Canada* HK

Mendelssohn Choir. See Mendelssohn Choir of Montreal; Toronto Mendelssohn Choir.

The Mendelssohn Choir of Montreal. Founded 1864 by Joseph *Gould, it began as a group of eight singers from the American Presbyterian Church who met at Gould's home to sing unaccompanied part-songs of Mendelssohn. During its 30-year history it became one of North America's leading amateur unaccompanied choirs with an average membership of over 100 voices. Some of its early concerts took place in the American Presbyterian Church, but later ones were given 1876–81 at the *Mechanics' Hall, 1881–90 at *Queen's Hall, and 1890–4 *Windsor Hall. The last concert took place there 10 Apr 1894. In addition to the unaccompanied repertoire the choir performed with accompaniment several times each season, often with guest artists such as Calixa *Lavallée and Frantz *Jenin-Prume. The sale of associate memberships ensured the financial security of the organization but reduced the audience. Nevertheless the Mendelssohn Choir with its 19th-century repertoire of unaccompanied choral pieces established a reputation as one of Montreal's most durable and active musical societies. After its final concert the choir donated some 250 volumes of musical literature and history to the Redpath Library of *McGill U. Another Mendelssohn Choir, conducted by H.E. *Key, Saul *Brant, and John *Weatherseed, flourished in the 1920s and early 1930s.

BIBLIOGRAPHY
Gould, Joseph. 'The Mendelssohn Choir.' A handwritten account of the founding of the choir. McGill University Archives. Classified List of Records No. 512
Musical Red Book NT

The Mendelssohn Piano Company. A leading Toronto manufacturer of pianos in the early 1900s. It was formed by Henry Durke (b Liverpool 1863, d Toronto 1929) and David M. Best with assets of an unsuccessful company of the same name purchased in 1892 by Durke. (The earlier company, of which Durke had been an employee, was founded ca 1886 by William Wilson, president, and William Baird, managing director with facilities on King and Duke streets.) By 1897 Durke had become the sole proprietor and manager. His erstwhile partner later (ca 1900) founded D.M. Best & Co, makers of piano strings and hammers. Durke prided himself on producing a moderately priced piano and advertised it in the *Canadian Music Trades Journal* as 'made in Canada, by Canadian workmen, for use in Canadian homes.' The factory and showrooms were located on Adelaide St West. The company had built some 25,000 pianos before its sale in 1919 (on Durke's retirement) to the *Bell Piano and Organ Co of Guelph, Ont. The Mendelssohn Piano Co continued in name until 1928, when Bell began advertising itself as the manufacturer of the Mendelssohn instrument. After Bell's sale in the early 1930s to the *Lesage Co, St-Thérèse-de-Blainville, Que, the latter company continued to use the Mendelssohn name on some of its instruments into the early 1970s. FH

The Mendelssohn Trio / Le Trio Mendelssohn. Montreal piano trio founded by the violinist Émile *Taranto with the pianist Éva *Plouffe and the cellist Rosario *Bourdon. The first concert, 24 Oct 1904 at Karn Hall, offered two movements from Beethoven's *'Ghost' Trio*, Arensky's *Trio in D Minor*, instrumental solos, and some songs sung by Joseph *Saucier. Similar concerts were presented at fairly regular intervals during the three seasons of the trio's existence. At the second concert, in March 1905, Bourdon, who had left Montreal, was replaced by Jean-Baptiste *Dubois, and the reviews continued to be favourable. The trio's second season offered four concerts at the Art Gallery in the period from November 1905 to March 1906. In its third season the trio consisted of the violinist Jules Desterbecq and the pianist Hans Harthan, along with Dubois. Two concerts took place at the end of 1906, and the trio ceased to exist in 1907 when Harthan left Montreal for Philadelphia. IP-C

Mennonite Brethren Bible College and College of Arts. Theological and liberal arts college, founded in Winnipeg in 1944. The arts division became associated in turn with Waterloo Lutheran U (now *Wilfrid Laurier U) in 1961 and the U of Winnipeg in 1970. Music has been a part of the curriculum from the outset under the direction of Benjamin *Horch 1944–55, Henry Voth 1955–8, Victor *Martens 1958–69, and Peter Klassen 1969–72, succeeded by William *Baerg in 1972. The music staff in 1978–9 included three full-time and several part-time teachers. The college offers a Bachelor of Religious Education degree (BRE) with a major in music. Two choirs founded by Horch in the 1940s – the Oratorio Choir and the A Cappella Choir – have continued to flourish. In 1965 the former began giving annual presentations jointly with the *Canadian Mennonite Bible College Choir and members of the *Winnipeg SO, conducted alternately by the heads of the two colleges' music departments. Among the works performed have been the Bach *Passions* and *Christmas Oratorio*, Handel's *Messiah*, Mendelssohn's *Elijah*, Bruckner's *Mass in F Minor*, Honegger's *King David*, and Walton's *Belshazzar's Feast*. By 1978 the A Cappella Choir had represented Canada twice in the BBC competition 'Let the Peoples Sing.' College graduates include William and Irmgard Baerg, Victor Martens, Alvin Reimer, and William *Reimer.

See also Mennonites. (CC)

The Mennonite Children's Choir. A 40-voice Winnipeg choir founded in 1957 and conducted by Helen Litz. Girls and boys aged 8 to 16 from *Mennonite congregations in the city are selected by audition. Drawing its repertoire mainly from German folk songs and from German and British

Mennonite Children's Choir of Winnipeg conducted by Helen Litz

part-songs sung in the original languages, the choir travels to other Canadian and US cities annually and broadcasts frequently on regional and national CBC radio and TV. In 1963 it won the George S. Mathieson Trophy awarded by the *FCMF. It has appeared with the *Winnipeg SO and participated in CBC TV's 1967 production of *Hansel and Gretel*.

One of the first Canadian ethnic choirs to achieve international recognition, the Mennonite Children's Choir has broadcast on the BBC and Radio Hilversum and has competed in various European choral festivals, placing first at the 1970 International Tees-side Eisteddfod in England, in two classes at the 1973 International Choral Festival in Montreux, and in two classes at the 1977 International Music Festival, The Hague. It has been compared to the renowed Obernkirchen Children's Choir (Vancouver *Sun*, 12 Apr 1969), and its members have been praised for 'a range of dynamics that goes with an incredible ability to spin out a tone with the finesse of an adult artist' (London *Free Press*, 31 Mar 1970). The choir represented Canada at the 1980 ISME meeting in Warsaw. Complying with an unwritten tenet of the Mennonite faith which holds that music, as an art, must serve a philanthropic purpose, the Mennonite Children's Choir has sponsored several 'Save the Children' projects with proceeds from its concert tours. The Mennonite Children's Choir can be heard on RCA, CBC SM, and several privately produced LPs. It appears in the 1975 NFB film *Musicanada*.

DISCOGRAPHY

Mennonite Children's Choir. H. Litz cond, L. Ritchey org. 1972. CBC SM-208

The Winnipeg Mennonite Children's Choir. H. Litz cond, B. Anderson org, L. Enns pf. (1973). RCA KCL 1-0028

BIBLIOGRAPHY

Rassok, Noel. 'Mennonite Children spread the musical word,' *PfAC*, Spring 1975 (BHr)

The Mennonites. The term 'Mennonite' can be used to refer both to members of the various Mennonite churches and, on a more general level, to non-practising descendants of Mennonites. Derived from the 16th-century Anabaptist movement, the Mennonite church was named for Menno Simons (1492–1559), one of its early leaders. Mennonites practise adult baptism, refuse to take oaths or go to war, and believe in the separation of church and state.

Mennonites first came to Canada from Pennsylvania during the late 18th century and settled mostly in Ontario, particularly in Essex, Lincoln, Perth, Waterloo, and York counties (though some small groups went as far west as Saskatchewan and Alberta). These so-called eastern or 'Pennsylvania' Mennonites were of German-Swiss and South German origin, and the dialect spoken among them was basically high German, mixed with a considerable amount of English. While today English is used both at home and at church by most Mennonites of this group, conservative Pennsylvania Mennonites (Old Order) still use dialect at home and German almost exclusively at church. Other Mennonites to arrive in Canada emigrated directly from Europe (chiefly from Russia) during the 1870s and 1920s and following World War II, establishing communities in the western provinces and, to a lesser degree, in Ontario – in Waterloo County, on the Niagara Peninsula, and along the shore of Lake Erie. In the 1970s only a small minority continued to use German, and the churches which used it also provided services in English.

Most Mennonites have remained in rural areas, agriculture being their chief occupation. Some, such as the *Amish and the Old Order and Old Colony Mennonites live separately from the rest of society, wear distinctive traditional dress, attend separate schools, and shun technological advances and 'wordly' entertainments. Other groups (the largest branches of the church, including the Old Mennonites, General Conference, and Mennonite Brethren) are less strict and mix in the mainstream of society.

The only music allowed in the Amish, Old Colony, and Old Order churches is unaccompanied unison congregational singing. Old Colony Mennonites (approximately 32,000 baptized members in 1975) use a 19th-century Russian Mennonite hymnal. It was printed first under the title *Geistreiches Gesangbuch* in Prussia (Königsberg 1767 and Marienwerder 1780) but is reprinted in a revised edition as *Gesangbuch: Ein Sammlung Geistlicher Lieder zur Allgemeinen Erbauung und zum Lobe Gottes* (Mennonitisches Verlagshaus 1977). For each hymn this book includes a 'long' melody (lange Weise), which is slow and ornamented, and a short melody (kurze Weise), also referred to as the 'wordly' melody. Despite official disapproval, some Old Colony young people also sing secular songs and engage in square dancing. The Old Order Mennonites (approximately 2200 baptized persons in 1975) use a hymnal entitled *Die Gemeinschaftliche Liedersammlung* (Berlin, Ont, 1836; and later editions). Most of its 205 hymns were taken from a US Mennonite hymnal, *Unpartheyisches Gesang-Buch* (Johann Bärs' Söhne, Lancaster, Pa, 6th edn 1854), which included many from a Reformed Church hymnal, *Neu-Vermehrt und Vollständiges Gesangbuch* (np 1753). Old Order young people sing 'fast' hymns and country and western songs at their Sunday evening 'singings,' and some engage in folk dances to the music of the mouth organ.

In most other Mennonite congregations, singing is in four-part harmony accompanied by the organ. In some, such singing is conducted by a songleader. The (Old) Mennonites, General Conference, and Mennonite Brethren publish their own hymnals. *The Mennonite Hymnary* (General Conference of the Mennonite Church of North America 1940) and *The Mennonite Hymnal* (Faith and Life Press 1969) are examples. Although some of their hymns have been written by Mennonites, the majority are found in hymnbooks of other denominations. Almost all such publications have been prepared by joint committees representing Mennonites in several countries. Ben *Horch participated along with committee members from Canada, the USA, and South America in the preparation of the *Gesangbuch der Mennoniten Bruedergemeinde* (Winnipeg 1952), and George Wiebe – b Winnipeg 25 Dec 1927, AMM 1955, ARCT 1957, M MUS (Southern California) 1962, a pupil of Robert Shaw and John Finlay Williamson – was involved in the compilation of the *Gesangbuch der Mennoniten* (Faith and Life Press 1965) and the above-mentioned *Mennonite Hymnal*. An earlier *Gesangbuch der Mennoniten* (General Conference of North America 1942; edited by D.H. Epp, J.G. Rempel, and David Paetkau) is believed to be the first German hymnal for use in Canada produced solely by a committee of Canadian editors.

The quality of 'Russian' Mennonite choirs in Canada can be attributed to a strong choral tradition and to the frequent Mennonite song festivals or 'Sängerfeste.' Men such as Ben Horch, John *Konrad, Kornelius *Neufeld, and David Paetkau were outstanding early travelling conductors in western Canada. The *Mennonite Children's Choir of Winnipeg, led by Helen Litz, has achieved national recognition. Other choirs include the *Canadian Mennonite Bible College Choir (George Wiebe, conductor), the Inter-Mennonite Children's Choir of Kitchener-Waterloo (Helen *Martens, conductor), the Menno Singers of Kitchener-Waterloo (Abner Martin and, later, Jan *Overduin, conductors), the *Mennonite Brethren Bible College Choir of Winnipeg (William *Baerg, conductor), and the Victor Martens Singers and the *Wilfrid Laurier U Choir of Waterloo (Victor *Martens, conductor). Also noteworthy is the Mennonite SO, founded and conducted 1943–55 in Winnipeg by Ben Horch and revived in 1978 as the Mennonite Community Orchestra. Made up of advanced students from the Canadian Mennonite Bible College and the Mennonite Brethren Bible College and of members of the community at large, this orchestra is concerned particularly with commissioning and recording works for historical and archival purposes by Mennonite composers.

The Canadian Mennonite Bible College and the Mennonite Brethren Bible College, both in Winnipeg, offer degree courses in church music. Music is taught at these and other Canadian institutions by teachers of Mennonite background, such as William Baerg, Doreen Klassen, Peter Klassen, and George Wiebe.

Among many noted musicians of Mennonite persuasion or background are the pianist Irmgard Baerg, who with the *Winnipeg SO premiered Victor *Davies' *Mennonite Piano Concerto* (1975); the harpsichordist and erstwhile member of the *Manitoba University Consort Joyce Redekop-Fink; the tenors Peter *Koslowski, John *Martens, and Victor Martens; the baritones Victor *Braun, Jacob Klassen, and Alvin Reimer; and the soprano Ingrid (Mary) Suderman – b Winkler, Man, 25 Oct 1944, a pupil of Teo Lindenbaum, Donald Brown, Jacob Hamm, and Luigi Wood – a winner in 1971 of the Western Canada District and Northwest Region auditions of the Metropolitan Opera, a semi-finalist in 1972 in the *Montreal International Competition, a member of Vancouver's early music ensemble Hortulani Musicae, and a frequent performer with major Vancouver choirs. Harold (Irwin) Redekopp – b Winnipeg 30 Oct 1942, AMM 1965, ARCT 1966, ARCCO 1968, BA (Manitoba) 1965, MA (Manitoba) 1968, and B ED (Manitoba) 1970 – was a pupil of Filmer *Hubble and Frans *Niermeier, was the organist-choirmaster 1969–73 at St Stephen's Broadway United Church, Winnipeg, and became a Toronto producer of serious music programs for CBC radio in 1973. Mennonite choir conductors include Howard Dyck, Leonard Enns, and Wilbur Maust in the Kitchener-Waterloo area and Henry Engbrecht in Winnipeg.

BIBLIOGRAPHY
Peters, Victor, and Elizabeth. 'Our heritage of music in Manitoba,' *Mennonite Life*, Apr 1948
Mennonite Encyclopedia, 4 vols, ed Cornelius Krahn and Harold S. Bender (Scottdale, Pa, 1955)
Toews, Abraham P. *American Mennonite Worship* (New York 1960)
Wiebe, George D. 'The hymnody of the General Conference Mennonite Church in Canada,' unpubl MA thesis, Southern California 1960
Peacock, Kenneth. *Twenty Ethnic Songs from Western Canada* (Ottawa 1966)
Martens, Helen. 'Music of some religious minorities in Canada,' *Ethnomusicology*, vol 16, Sep 1972
Epp, Frank H. *The Mennonites of Canada* (Toronto 1974)
Loewen, Esko. 'The Mennonite hymnal,' *The Mennonite*, 14 Mar 1978
Baerg, William. 'Mennonite Brethren music-making: where is it going?' *Mennonite Brethren Herald*, 12 Oct 1979 (HMr)

The Men's Music Club (Men's Musical Club of Winnipeg 1915–60; Men's Music Club of Winnipeg 1960–2). Founded 11 Dec 1915 to 'promote, assist and encourage a high standard in the art of music in Manibota.' The founders were Joseph M. Tees and George S. *Mathieson, and Rev Dean Coombes was the first president. There were 120 charter members, of whom some 35 were professional musicians. (In 1978 the membership remained at 120 men, of whom 16 were directors, and 40 women, of whom 3 were directors.) The club sponsored the formation of the *Winnipeg Male Voice Choir in 1916, the *Manitoba Music Competition Festival in 1918, the Winnipeg Orchestral Club in 1923, and the Winnipeg Boys' Choir in 1925.

The boys' choir, led 1925–43 by Ethel *Kinley, achieved through firm discipline a reputation for unforced, natural singing, a tradition perpetuated by Kinley's assistant 1940–3 and successor 1943–62, Beth *Douglas. It was operated 1943–74 as two choirs, a junior and a senior. After Douglas, conductors of the senior group included Sydney Bryans 1962–4 and 1965–6, Keith Tinsley 1964–5, Helga Anderson 1966–74, and Ron Butterfield 1974–5. In 1975 the choirs were merged under Ardyth McMaster.

The Men's Musical Club also sponsored the formation in 1944 of the Winnipeg Civic Music League, a citizens' committee designed to take both advisory and active interest in musical matters of civic importance. The league helped establish the *Winnipeg SO in 1948 and was instrumental in planning the major expansion of the *U of Manitoba School of Music in 1963. Before the formation of the league, the club had promoted the building of the *Winnipeg Auditorium and prepared the inaugural concert, 27 Oct 1932. The club assumed sponsorship of the *Winnipeg Philharmonic Choir in 1929 and continued its support until 1968. Douglas *Clarke, Bernard *Naylor, Hugh Ross, and Peter Temple were among the outstanding musicians the club introduced to Canada as conductors of the Male Voice and Philharmonic choirs. The club supported the establishment of *Rainbow Stage in 1954.

In 1970 the club assumed sponsorship of the Winnipeg Girls' Choir, founded in 1944 by Beth Cruikshank, its conductor until 1970, and Maurine Pottruff, its accompanist during the early years. It later was divided into two choirs, junior and senior. After Cruikshank, conductors of the senior group have included John Standing 1970–6; and Frances Seaton, appointed in 1976.

In the years after World War I, besides presenting its own performing organizations in concert, the Men's Musical Club sponsored recitals by distinguished performers of international standing (eg, in the early 1920s, Sophie Braslau, Alfred Cortot, H.A. *Fricker, Joseph Hislop, and Cyril Scott). It continued, seasonally, to present weekly recitals by visiting and local artists until 1939. Series were held the first year at the Royal Alexandra Hotel and subsequently at the Board of Trade Auditorium and the Winnipeg Auditorium. In 1953 the club established a women's auxiliary and a citizen's advisory council to assist in the reestablishment of the club's enterprises in the postwar period. In 1978 the Winnipeg Girls' Choirs (senior and junior), the Winnipeg Boys' Choir, and the Manitoba Music Competition Festival still were active under club sponsorship. Though the club does not grant annual scholarships it occasionally has given single bursaries, drawing on the interest of invested donations.

BIBLIOGRAPHY
G Sharp Major [George S. Mathieson]. *Crescendo* (Winnipeg [1935])
Leah, Vince. 'Cultural life enhanced by music club,' 'Music club provided city with festival,' Winnipeg *Tribune* (27 Mar, 3 Apr 1976) (RG, SRM)

MERCER, Ruby (m Por). Writer, broadcaster, soprano, b Athens, Ohio, 26 Jul 1906; BA (Ohio) 1927, B MUS (Cincinnati) 1930, hon D MUS (Ohio) 1978. She was a pupil of Ruth Townsend at the Cincinnati Cons and of Marcella Sembrich and Florence Page Kimball at the Juilliard School. She won the Naumburg Award in 1935 and made her New York recital debut in 1936. With the *Metropolitan Opera she sang Nedda in *I Pagliacci* (1936) and Marguerite in *Faust* (1937). She appeared in three Broadway productions and on radio and TV, and was the producer and host of WNYC's 'Mr and Mrs Opera' (1949–57) and of the MBS's 'The Ruby Mercer Show' (1954–6). She first sang in Canada in a 1937 performance of Beethoven's *Symphony No. 9* at *Plateau Hall, Montreal, with the *Disciples de Massenet. She returned in 1944 and 1945 to sing in *TUTS productions in Vancouver. She moved in 1958 to Toronto where she edited **Opera Canada* 1960–76 and became that periodical's publisher in 1976. She served 1962–79 as host of CBC radio's weekly 'Opera Time' and in 1979 continued as host of a revised and expanded version of that show, renamed 'Opera in Stereo.' Mercer is the author of *The Tenor of His Time* (Toronto 1976), a biography of Edward *Johnson. In 1968 she founded the *Canadian Children's Opera Chorus and in 1980 she continued to serve as its first president. She has contributed articles to *EMC*.

The Mercey Brothers. Country trio formed by three brothers from Hanover, south of Owen Sound, Ont. Larry Mercey (b 12 Dec 1939) began singing in 1956 on the *'CKNX Barn Dance' (Wingham, Ont) and was joined in 1958 by Ray (b 21 Nov 1940). Patterning themselves after the close-harmony pop duo, the Everly Brothers, they placed second in 1960 in the CBC's 'Talent Caravan,' appeared on other CBC programs, and recorded for Chateau. They spent a brief, unsuccessful period (ca 1961) in New York under contract to RCA and returned to Canada. In 1965 they were joined by Lloyd Mercey (b 12 Dec 1945) and began one of the most successful careers in Canadian country music.

Within the trio, Larry is the lead singer and guitarist; Ray, a singer and bass guitarist; and Lloyd, a singer and drummer. The trio has appeared frequently on the major Canadian country-music TV shows and has performed in cities in Canada and Europe and at the Grand Ole Opry in Nashville. According to Roy MacGregor the Mercey Brothers 'shy away from the traditional stomping grounds of country and western music – drinking, driving, brawling and adultery – and stick to their own trademarks of simple sentimentality and lasting love.'

Though the group's recording career has not been of major proportions, it has been characterized by shrewd business judgment. The Mercey Brothers retained ownership of their recordings, leasing commercial rights to *Columbia (for three LPs) and to *RCA (for six LPs, including *The Best of the Mercey Brothers*, 1976, RCA KNL1-0109). They established their own label, MBS (Mercey Brothers Sound) in 1978 – having opened a 16-track recording studio in Elmira, near Waterloo, in 1973 – and their first LP, *Comin' On Stronger* (1978, MBS-2000) received a gold record sales award in 1979. Among their most popular singles have been 'Uncle Tom,' 'Hello Mom,' 'Kentucky Turn Your Back,' 'California Lady,' and 'If I Believed in Myself' (all for RCA) and 'Stranger' (for MBS). MBS has recorded Terry Carisse (who, with Bruce Rawlins, has written several of the Mercey Brothers' hits), Marie Bottrell, and Lee Bach, in addition to the Mercy Brothers themselves. The Mercey Brothers have written and recorded many jingles. Their publishing company, established in 1966, is a PRO Canada affiliate.

BIBLIOGRAPHY
Martin, Robert. 'Mercey Brothers run things their way now,' Toronto *Globe and Mail*, 3 Feb 1976
MacGregor, Roy. 'Clean cut country,' *Canadian Magazine*, 1 May 1976
Gallo, Nancy. 'The Mercey Brothers: comin' on stronger than ever,' *RPM*, 15 Apr 1978
Lorimer, Cliff. 'Versatility is key to Mercey Brothers' success,' *MSc*, 311, Jan – Feb 1980 (MD)

MERCIER (Merçay), **François-Xavier**. Tenor, teacher, b Champlain, near Trois-Rivières, Que, 13 Aug 1871, d Quebec City 22 Dec 1932. He sang in Quebec City from his early childhood, especially at the Church of the Congregation of Notre-Dame (now Jacques-Cartier). He performed as a soloist in the hall of the Académie commerciale and thus came to the notice of the school's director, who accepted him as a non-paying student at the institution and in 1891 found a position for him as bookkeeping teacher at the Collège Mont-St-Louis, Montreal. Mercier lived 1892–4 in Toronto, where he studied elocution with J.H. Cameron and solfège with Adèle Lemaître. In Boston he performed the role of the Duke in *Rigoletto* at Castle Square but soon returned to Toronto to open a voice studio.

By means of a subscription and the proceeds of some concerts given at *Massey Hall, Mercier went to Paris and studied voice for five years with Jacques Bouhy and solfège and stage techniques with T. Valdejo. In January 1899 he was chosen from among 18 tenors to sing at the Opéra-Comique; he made his debut in Méhul's *Joseph*. *Le Gaulois* commented: 'Mercier's tone was superb. A powerful voice, perfect diction, expressive features; he is actor and singer rolled into one.' Later he sang in *Carmen*, *Mireille*, and *Manon*.

In 1901 Mercier performed in *Faust*, *Les Huguenots*, *Carmen*, *Roméo et Juliette*, and *Le Roi d'Ys* at Covent Garden, London, in casts which included Calvé, Journet, Melba, Plançon, Scotti, and Tamagno. He returned to Paris for rehearsals of *William Tell* and he later sang in this opera in Bordeaux and in Rouen, where according to *Le Nouvelliste*, he received seven curtain calls for his performance of the aria 'Asile héréditaire.' After singing in *Faust*, *L'Africaine*, *Les Huguenots*, *Sigurd*, and *La Juive* on tour in France, he visited Italy and Switzerland. He repeated his roles in *Les Huguenots* at The Hague and *William Tell* at Spa with Noté. In December 1906, while preparing for a season at the theatre in Lyons, he had to return to Quebec City because of his mother's death. In 1907 he sang in Toronto and in Quebec City, and that November he left once again for Paris. Mercier spent the 1908–9 season in Constantine (Algeria), where he triumphed in *Les Hugenots*, and then in *Werther*, *Carmen*, *La Navarraise*, *I Pagliacci*, *Marie-Magdeleine*, *Sigurd*, and *Hérodiade*. In Algiers and Oran, he sang *William Tell* and *La Juive*. His next undertaking was to participate in 22 opera and oratorio concerts at Queen's Hall, London, under Sir Henry Wood. After another tour of France and Algeria he returned to Quebec City in August 1913 with his wife, the singer Isabelle de Besson (Mlle Jeynevald), whom he had met in Constantine and married in Lyons in 1909.

In 1914 Mercier founded the Institut de l'art vocal. He taught there until his death, training hundreds of pupils, including Arthur *Blaquière and Jean-Marie Lachance. In 1931 he was named honorary president of the newly founded Assn des chanteurs de Québec. He wrote a series of articles, 'Classement et pose de la voix,' that appeared in *La Musique* in 1919, and in 1923 he published *Souvenirs de ma carrière artistique*, reprinted under the title 'Gerbe de souvenirs' in his study *Techniques de musique vocale* (Quebec 1928). He composed numerous songs, including 'Ce que je chante,' Op 65, which was published in 1918, and 'France et Canada,' Op 106, published in 1929.

BIBLIOGRAPHY
Art Musical, Sep 1898
Ristark, A. 'Un ténor canadien,' *P-T*, 220, 29 Aug 1903
Morgan, H.J. *Canadian Men and Women of the Time* (np 1912)
Caouette, J.-B. 'M. F.-X. Mercier,' *La Musique*, 9, Sep 1919 (GB)

MERCURE, Pierre. Composer, TV producer, bassoonist, administrator, b Montreal 21 Feb 1927, d in an accident near Avallon, France, 29 Jan 1966; premier prix harmony, counterpoint, deuxième prix bassoon (CMM) 1949. The integration of the creative media (ie, a combination of theatre, music, dance, painting and sculpture) was the axis around which Pierre Mercure's life and work revolved. He studied 1944–9 at the *CMM with the avowed goal of becoming an orchestra conductor and concentrated on harmony and counterpoint with Marvin *Duchow and Claude *Champagne, as well as on instrumental techniques. His bassoon teachers were Roland *Gagnier and Louis Letellier, and he studied conducting with Léon Barzin. Champagne helped him discover French music and develop the talent for orchestration which was evident even in his first works, *Kaléidoscope* and *Pantomime*. Before going to Paris in 1949 for further eduction, Mercure participated in some modern ballet productions with a group of young poets, musicians, dancers, and painters whose artistic views were much influenced by the painter Paul-Émile Borduas. In May 1949, at the Théâtre des Compagnons, he took part with the choreographer Françoise Sullivan, the poet Claude Gauvreau, and the painter Jean-Paul Mousseau, in realizing three works: *Dualité*, *Femme archaïque* and *Lucrèce Borgia*. This collaboration with the 'automatists,' however, had little immediate influence on Mercure's musical language. Its effects were not measurable until 1961, or perhaps even 1965.

Philosophically disturbed by Paul-Émile Borduas's *Refus global* (1948), a proclamation denouncing the conservatism of society and demanding freedom for the artist, Mercure sought new means of expression. He enrolled in Nadia Boulanger's classes as soon as he arrived in Paris in the autumn of 1949. Increasingly attracted by new music, however, Mercure preferred to work on improvisations, superimpositions of forms,

Pierre Mercure

and collective compositions with his composer friends Gabriel *Charpentier, Jocelyn *Binet, and Clermont *Pépin. His association with Boulanger thus was short-lived, but despite this setback he pursued his studies in orchestration with Arthur Hoérée and Darius Milhaud and in conducting with Jean Fournet. Two short works, *Emprise* for clarinet, cello, bassoon, and piano and *Ils ont détruit la ville* for choir and orchestra, belong to this period. The latter, based on a poem from *Aire* by Charpentier, won him a prize in the CBC competition of 1950. After a year filled with new experiences, Mercure returned to Montreal, still searching for new means of expression. The musical forms of past centuries no longer satisfied him.

On a grant from the Quebec government Mercure spent the summer of 1951 at Tanglewood studying composition with Luigi Dallapiccola, who became both a teacher and a friend. Once he had assimilated the principles of the 12-tone method Mercure was torn between a need for greater creative freedom and a need to organize, to see ahead, to construct. He finally rejected strict 12-tone writing because he saw in it a serious impediment to his flexibility as an artist. His essentially lyrical nature was revealed in *Dissidence*, three songs which with *Ils ont détruit la ville* formed the core of the **Cantate pour une joie* for soprano, choir, and orchestra on poems by Charpentier. *Divertissement*, for string quartet and string orchestra, and *Triptyque*, for full orchestra, marked a point of arrival after a hesitant but extensive search, full of the impulsiveness of youth.

Throughout the period 1948–59 Mercure was looking for new sonorities. Finding his wishes impossible to fulfil, he aligned himself not with tradition as such but with a kind of spontaneous lyric expression realized through traditional forms. Stravinsky, Milhaud, and Honegger were his models. He was not indifferent to US popular music and jazz; several of the themes he used were derived from songs made popular by Glenn Miller and his orchestra; the rhythms are insistent, the orchestration glittering. These elements are found in his numerous background scores of 1950–4 for CBC radio dramas (for example, *Amal* by Tagore and *Le Mystère de la Nativité* by Gréban) and for stage productions by Les Compagnons (eg, Anouilh's *Le Bal des voleurs*). This association with theatre, dance, and even painting was a determining influence on Mercure. In January 1952 he joined the CBC and became its first producer of TV music programs. He produced 41 programs 1954–9 in the series 'L'*Heure du concert' and several 'Concerts pour la jeunesse,' and he also supervised 'Jazz Workshop,' 'Music Hall,' 'Pays et merveilles,' and others. His style became recognizable by its taste and its recurrent ventures into

A page from *Lignes et points* by Pierre Mercure

the visual realm, often with a touch of audacity. Starting in this period his work rose more and more from a need for continual experimentation and a compulsion to grapple with the most up-to-date art-forms. In practical terms, during 1959–62 he sought a new language, exploring the field of electroacoustics. This exploration grew out of his encounters with the Groupe de recherches musicales of the RTF and with Pierre Schaeffer during his second study trip to Europe 1957–8. *Répercussions*, *Structures métalliques I* and *II*, *Incandescence*, and *Improvisation* are works built from concrete sounds transformed by means of electronic equipment. The works were accompanied sometimes by choreographic movement and often by projections.

The composer's intense activity peaked in preparations for an avant-garde music festival, the *International Week of Today's Music, of which he was the guiding force. The festival was held in August 1961, and Mercure invited, among others, John Cage, Serge *Garant, Mauricio Kagel, Karlheinz Stockhausen, Christian Wolff, and Iannis Xenakis. He wanted to show Montreal the latest manifestations of new music, and he looked for new sounds which might build a new audience. This isolated event, which Mercure would have liked to make annual, prepared the way for what in 1966 became the *SMCQ. Mercure's third study trip to Europe – to Paris, Darmstadt, and Dartington during the summer of 1962 – allowed him to gain a closer knowledge of music from electronic sources. *Structures métalliques III*, composed during this period, was presented 16 Sep 1962 at the Fluxus Internationale Festspiele Neuester Musik in Wiesbaden.

In the autumn of 1962 Mercure undertook the composition of a cantata for radio, *Psaume pour abri*, the first of three attempts at a synthesis of electronic and conventional music. This psalm essentially cries out against barbarism, atrocity, and absurdity. It is composed of seven parts, of which the last three are a non-literal recapitulation of the first three. They depart from, and at length return to, a human standpoint. This new avenue continues in **Tétrachromie*. In September 1963, Mercure wrote *Lignes et points* for full orchestra, commissioned by the *MSO. A suite of variations on a single theme, the work shows a compositional similarity to the previous two; the same melodic cells of three, four, or five notes are central features in the organization. Most of the sequences are notated graphically by means of colours; in the first two, Mercure used sine-tones transformed with filters, echo-chamber, etc, and in the third he translated the same processes into orchestral terms. Moreover, he tried with *Lignes et points* to obtain from the orchestra a range of timbres comparable to that achieved through electroacoustic means.

At the time of his death in a traffic accident Mercure had scarcely reached maturity. During the previous summer in Darmstadt, he had written *H_2O per Severino*, for from four to ten solo instruments, a work in open form, with neither beginning nor end, in which chance events of the moment together constitute a formal entity. This work was another step towards realizing his ideal of freedom governed by human thought.

In 1966 the Montreal Festival du disque awarded the Prix Pierre-Mercure for the best recording of a Canadian composition to the duo pianists *Bouchard and Morisset for their performance of *Matton's *Concerto*. Mercure's manuscripts and papers were deposited in the Archives nationales du Québec in 1977. The rights of his musical estate are administered by PRO Canada, and the *CMCentre granted him the associate status reserved for deceased composers whose work the centre holds.

COMPOSITIONS

BALLET, FILM

Dualité, ballet. 1948 (Mtl 1948). Tpt, pf. Ms lost
La Femme archaïque, ballet. 1949 (Mtl 1949). Pf, tim. Ms lost
Lucrèce Borgia, ballet. 1949 (Mtl 1949). Tpt, pf, perc. Ms lost
Emprise, ballet. 1950 (Paris 1950). Cl, bn, vc, pf. Ms lost
Improvisation, ballet. 1961 (Mtl 1961). Prepared pf on tape
Incandescence, ballet. 1961 (Mtl 1961). Tape
Structures métalliques I and *II*, 2 ballets (Mtl 1961). Metallic sculptures by A. Vaillancourt. Tape. Ms
Manipulations, ballet. 1963 (Que City 1964). Tape
Surimpressions, ballet. 1964 (Mtl 1964). Prepared pf on tape. Ms
La Forme des choses, film. 1965. Brass quin, concrete sounds. Ms
Élément 3, film. 1965. Fl, concrete sounds. Ms
See also *Tétrachromie*.

ORCHESTRA, CHOIR AND ORCHESTRA

Kaleidoscope. 1948, rev 1949 (Mtl 1948, rev version Mtl 1949). Full orch, rev med orch. Ric 1960 (med orch). CBC SM-132 (*Atlantic SO)/CBC SM-334 (*Wpg SO)
Ils ont détruit la ville (G. Charpentier). 1950 (Mtl 1950), later rev and included in *Cantate pour une joie*. SATB, 18 instr. Ms lost. RCI 35 (*Waddington)
Divertissement. 1957, rev 1958 (Mtl 1957). Str quar, str orch. Ric 1970. RCI 154 (A. *Brott)/CBC SM-6 (*McGill Chamb O)
Triptyque. 1959 (Van 1959). Full orch. Ric 1963. Col MS 6962/Col Odyssey Y 31993 (*TSO)
Lignes et points. 1964 (Mtl 1965). Full orch. Ric 1970. RCI 230/RCA LSC 2980/Vic VICS 1040 (*MSO)
See also *Cantate pour une joie*.

CHAMBER

Pantomime. 1948. Ww, str, perc. Ms incomplete. 3 revised versions of the above, all 1949: 1 / 14 ww, perc; ms lost; RCI 2 (J.-M. *Beaudet). 2 / Vc, pf; ms incomplete. 3 / 18 ww, perc; Ric 1971; RCI 117 (*Waddington)
H_2O per Severino. 1965. 4–10 instr. Ms

VOICE

'Colloque' (Valéry). 1948. Med v, pf. BMIC 1950, Master MA 275 (D. *Mills)
Dissidence (G. Charpentier). 1955, later rev and included in *Cantate pour une joie*. Sop (ten), pf. CMCentre. RCI 201 (*Jeannotte)/Allied ARCLP-4 (J. *Dufresne pf)

ELECTRONIC (see also BALLET above)

Jeu de hockey. 1961. tape
Répercussions. 1961. Japanese wind chimes on tape
Structures métalliques III. 1962. Tape
Psaume pour abri (F. Ouellette). 1963. Narr, 2 SATB, brass quin, str quar, hpd, pf, hp, perc, tape. Ms incomplete

WRITINGS

'Commentaires,' *Musiques du Kébèk*, ed Raoul Duguay (Montreal 1971)

BIBLIOGRAPHY

Pearce, Pat. 'Mercure's contribution to music on television,' *Montreal Star*, 12 Feb 1966
Kasemets, Udo. 'Pierre Mercure,' *MSc*, 246, Mar–Apr 1969
Bernier, Françoys. 'Pierre Mercure: *Lignes et points* (1964),' *CMB*, 2, Spring–Summer 1971
Maillard, Jean. 'Pierre Mercure (1927–1966): Psaume pour abri (1963),' *Éducation musicale*, 179, Jun 1971
CMCentre. *Compositeurs au Québec: Pierre Mercure* (Montreal 1976)
Kieser, Karen. 'Canadian composers you'll be hearing,' *TS News*, Mar–Apr 1977
Richer-Lortie, Lyse. 'Pierre Mercure 1928–1966 *Lignes et points* (1964),' *Variations*, vol 2, Mar 1979
PRO Canada Ltd. 'Pierre Mercure,' pamphlet (1979)
Richer-Lortie, Lyse. 'Pierre Mercure,' *Contemporary Canadian Composers / Compositeurs canadiens contemporains*
Dictionary of Contemporary Music
Thirty-Four Biographies

FILM

Pierre Mercure (Charles Gagnon 1971) LR-L

MEREDITH, Morley (b Margolis). Baritone, b Winnipeg 8 Feb 1932. He studied singing with W.H. *Anderson and medicine at the U of Manitoba. He was winner, as Morley Margolis, in the CBC's 1948–9 *'Singing Stars of Tomorrow,' and went on to study with Boris Goldovsky at Tanglewood, Mass, with Alfredo Martino at Mannes College of Music in New York, and later (1959–60) with the Metropolitan Opera bass Melchiore Luise.

Meredith's New York City Opera debut in 1957 as Escamillo in *Carmen* was followed in 1958 by an appearance with the *COC in the role of the four villains in Offenbach's *Tales of Hoffmann*. He enjoyed success in the same role in his *Metropolitan Opera debut (1962). He returned often to the Met, singing such roles as Scarpia in *Tosca*, Don Alfonso in *Così fan tutte*, Jochanaan in *Salome*, Pizarro in *Fidelio*, and Klingsor in *Parsifal*.

In 1970 Meredith made his European debut with the Grand Théâtre de Genève, singing Scarpia. He returned the following year to sing Pizarro with that company and repeated the role with the Scottish National Opera. In 1976 he sang Telramund in the Metropolitan Opera's new production of *Lohengrin*.

Meredith has performed with major companies in Chicago, San Francisco, Philadelphia, Fort Worth, and Washington and with orchestras in Toronto, New York, Philadelphia, and Chicago. His roles have included Prince Andrei in Prokofiev's *War and Peace*, Amonasro in *Aida*, Iago in *Otello*, Germont in *La Traviata*, and the title roles in *Eugene Onegin*, *The Flying Dutchman*, and *Wozzeck*.

In concert Meredith has made a specialty of the solo roles in dramatic choral-orchestral works such as Penderecki's *Dies irae* (North American premiere 10 Mar 1978 with the *Winnipeg SO) and Orff's *Carmina burana* which Meredith has sung innumerable times and has recorded (Vanguard 2066). After his performance in that work with the Winnipeg SO, Kenneth *Winters wrote in the *Winnipeg Free Press* (31 Jan 1964) that he 'sang with superb assurance, applying the required variety of voices with skill and point, spinning out a cavernous falsetto here, a sweet lyric baritone there, and a commanding basso when the score called for it.' Also appearing in musicals, he is heard on the original cast recording of *Christine* (ca 1960, Col OL 5520). (HCs)

MÉRINEAU, (Joseph-Henri) André. Organist, teacher, b Montreal 5 Oct 1929; premier prix organ (CMM) 1950, premier prix harmony (CMM) 1952. He took piano lessons from Gilberte *Martin and

Morley Meredith

Alfred *Laliberté and studied the organ at the *CMM with Georges-Émile *Tanguay and Conrad *Bernier. In 1949 he won the *Casavant Society prize and the Joseph-Bonnet medal. Awarded a Quebec government grant in 1953 he entered the Accademia Santa Cecilia in Rome; there he studied with Fernando Germani, organist at St Peter's Basilica, and was his assistant for five years. In 1957 he obtained his diplomas for organ and composition, and the Holy See awarded him the Latran Cross. He was a lecturer, summers 1953–7, at the Accademia Chigiana in Siena. In 1959 he returned to Rome on a *Canada Council grant to study Bach under Germani. While there he taught organ, harmony, and counterpoint at the Accademia Santa Cecilia. He has been the organist at several US and European churches, and at the Gesù Church and St-Vincent Ferrier Church in Montreal. In 1962 he began teaching organ, improvisation, and harmony at the CMM. He has given numerous recitals in Canada and abroad, and he toured the USSR in 1968 and 1973. In the French periodical *Diapason* (Oct 1972), Jean Gallois paid tribute to his solid technique and to the restraint, emotion, and inner sensibility with which he approached the organ pieces of Jehan Alain recorded at St-Eustache Church in Paris.

WRITINGS

'Un organiste du Québec en URSS,' *VM*, 19, Mar 1971

DISCOGRAPHY

J. Alain *Pièce pour orgue*. 1972. Pathé-Marconi EMI C 065-12170
Couperin – Bach – Champagne – B. Pitché. 1967. RCI 254
Tournemire *Chorals-poèmes pour les Sept Paroles du Christ*. 1972. Pathé-Marconi EMI C 065-12169 GP

Don Messer and His Islanders. Old-time music group, the most popular in Canada during the mid-20th century. It was formed in 1939 for CFCY radio in Charlottetown by the fiddler Don (Donald Charles Frederick) Messer (b Tweedside, near Fredericton, 9 May 1909, d Halifax 26 Mar 1973).

Messer, who began playing the violin at five, learned fiddle tunes from local players – his uncle Jim Messer, Bowman Little, Charlie Bell, and others – and Scottish and Irish songs from his mother. At seven he was performing at barn dances, weddings, and other social gatherings in the area. After living for three years in Boston, where from Henry Davis and Edith Hurter he had his only formal instruction in music, he began his radio career in 1929 on CFBO, Saint John, NB. A local merchant subsequently sponsored regular programs by Messer's small band.

In 1934 the band began a radio show for the CRBC, broadcasting from CHSJ (Saint John) under the name the New Brunswick Lumberjacks. Charlie Chamberlain (b Bathurst, NB, 14 Jul 1911, d

Don Messer (left) with Catherine McKinnon, Charlie Chamberlain, and Marg Osburne

there 16 Jul 1972), Messer's long-time vocalist and the only band member who had worked in lumber camps, joined at this time. The studio band had grown to as many as 19 performers (including Chamberlain, Ned *Landry playing harmonica, the bassist-banjoist Julius 'Duke' Nielsen, Maunsell O'Neil providing continuity in the persona of an Acadian lumberjack 'Joe LeBlanc,' and Eldon *Rathburn, piano), but Messer led a smaller group, the Backwoods Breakdown, in his personal appearances throughout the Maritimes and the northeastern USA.

On joining CFCY, Charlottetown, as music director in September 1939, Messer formed the Islanders – Chamberlain, Nielsen, Jackie Doyle (piano), Ray Simmons (clarinet and, later, also announcer, replacing Art MacDonald), and Bill LeBlanc (drums). By 1944 the group was heard nationally thrice weekly on the CBC. In 1942 it began to record for Apex, making more than 35 78s by 1952, including the popular *Rippling Water Jig*, *Woodchoppers Breakdown*, *Cotton Eyed Joe*, *Don Messer's Breakdown*, *Highlevel Hornpipe*, and *Spud Island Breakdown*, most of compositions by Messer. Some 30 LPs have been released by Apex and by MCA and Rodeo and their affiliate labels. Among several reissues, *The Good Old Days* (MCA TVLP 79052), released in 1980 to more than 100,000 advance orders from distributors, was particularly successful.

The personnel of the Islanders changed over the years, but included such long-time members as the drummer Warren MacRae (who joined in 1942), the pianist Waldo Munro (1951), and the guitarist-fiddler Cecil McEachern (1951). Other instrumentalists, including the banjoist Vic *Mullen and the organist Ray Calder, played with the Islanders for shorter periods. The singer Marg Osburne (b Moncton, NB, 1928, d Rocklyn, Ont, 16 Jul 1977) joined in 1947 and became (with Messer and Chamberlain) the artist most commonly identified with the Islanders.

Once the show was established as one of the most popular on Canadian radio, Messer and the Islanders began to appear outside the Maritimes, making their first tour of Ontario in 1949. They had made 18 tours by 1969, including a centennial trip for Festival Canada in 1967 which lasted three months and covered 61 centres. In 1956 the group began to appear regularly on CHBY-TV, Halifax. A nationally broadcast CBC TV summer series 'The Don Messer Show,' begun 7 Aug 1959, continued in the fall as 'Don Messer's Jubilee.' The show won a wide audience, and its cancellation in 1969 brought many complaints from viewers and raised questions in the House of Commons.

However, a syndicated version of 'Don Messer's Jubilee' from CHCH-TV, Hamilton, Ont, began that same year and continued until Messer's death. 'Don Messer's Jubilee,' a half-hour program, was rigidly structured, beginning with 'Goin' to the Barndance Tonight' and including a couple of fiddle tunes by Messer, songs from Osburne, Chamberlain (who favoured Irish material), and a guest performer, a closing hymn sung by Osburne and Chamberlain, and 'Till We Meet Again' played under the final credits.

Regular performers added during the TV era were the Buchta Dancers, led by Gunter and Irma Buchta, and the Scottish accordionist-singer Johnny Forrest who joined in 1966. Frequent guest performers included 'Stompin' Tom' *Connors, Myrna *Lorrie, Catherine *McKinnon, Fred *McKenna, and Graham *Townsend. With the demise of 'Don Messer's Jubilee' Marg Osburne began a nightclub career – enjoying particular success in western Canada – and was hostess (1977) for CBC TV's 'That Maritime Feeling.'

Messer insisted that his music was 'not Western or cowboy music. Our tunes have been around for two or three hundred years. They're folk tunes passed from generation to generation' (*CBC Times* 11–17 Apr 1964). Besides the traditional hornpipes, jigs, and reels, the Islanders played many tunes by Messer. Albums of his pieces were published by *Thompson: *Original Old Tyme Music* (1942), *'Way Down Fiddlin' Tunes* (1948), *Canadian Hoedowns* (1952), and *Barndance Breakdowns* (1954). A fifth was published by *Canadian Music Sales in 1967. Messer's musical rights are administered by CAPAC.

Though capable of playing sophisticated music, Messer had a keen sense of what his audience wanted to hear – quick, recognizable, and danceable tunes. On these he built his enormous popularity. He has been credited (by folklorists Dorothy and Homer Hogan in their liner notes for Graham Townsend's LP *The Great Canadian Fiddle*) with a synthesis of the many and varied fiddle traditions in Canada, influencing other fiddlers with a style 'as clean, straight-ahead and neat as a well-tended farm' and marked by its 'down-to-earth simplicity.' His stature among Canadian fiddlers is attested by the LPs dedicated to him by Townsend, Bill Guest, and Reg Hill. His library and papers were deposited at the Public Archives of Nova Scotia, and one of his fiddles was placed in the Country Music Hall of Fame in Nashville.

BIBLIOGRAPHY

MacDonald, David. 'The breakdown boys from Spud Island,' *Maclean's*, 15 Oct 1953

Russell, Franklin. 'This band won't believe it's famous,' *Star Weekly*, 23 Jan 1960

McCall Newman, Christina. 'What makes the Messer show go?' *Chatelaine*, Jan 1961

Dexter, Susan. 'Everybody here loves Charlie Chamberlain,' *Maclean's*, 18 Sep 1965

MacLeod, Stewart. 'Good grief, it's Charlie Chamberlain,' *Weekend Magazine*, 5 Nov 1966

Hillen, Ernest. 'The death of Don Messer's Jubilee,' *Weekend Magazine*, 21 Jun 1969

Sellick, Lester B. *Canada's Don Messer* (Kentville, NS, 1969)

Brown, Dick. 'Marg Osburne's home on the range,' *Canadian Magazine*, 19 Jul 1975

Guettel, Alan. 'Rookie producer "finds" Messer,' *Toronto Star*, 4 Jan 1980

RGn (MM)

Metropolitan Opera Company. Illustrious and venerable (founded 1883) New York company which has influenced the development of opera in Canada through its tours, broadcasts, and talent-development programs.

After an appearance in Toronto (26 Jan 1892 at the Pavilion, in excerpts from Rossini's *Semiramide*) by Adelina Patti supported by Metropolitan Opera soloists, chorus, and orchestra under Luigi Arditi, and after four concerts in Montreal (1896 at *Windsor Hall) by the Metropolitan orchestra under Anton Seidl, the Metropolitan as a company gave its first season in Canada in 1899 performing *La Traviata*, *Carmen*, *Faust*, *Romeo and Juliet*, and *The Barber of Seville* at the Toronto Grand Opera House and Montreal's *Her Majesty's Theatre. Singers included Marcella Sembrich, Giuseppe Campanari, Emma Calvé, Pol Plançon, and Édouard de Reszke. The Met returned to Toronto and Montreal in 1901 with *Lohengrin*, *Romeo and Juliet*, *Faust*, *Manon*, *Carmen*, and *Tannhäuser*. Singers included Sybil Sanderson, Emma Eames, and Marcel Journet.

Four operas were offered in Montreal in 1911: *Aida* with Louise Homer, Emmy Destinn, and Antonio Scotti under Arturo Toscanini; *Madama Butterfly* with Geraldine Farrar; *Tannhäuser* with Olive Fremstad, Alma Gluck, and Leo Slezak; and *Faust* with Jeanne *Maubourg as Siebel. A 'Metropolitan Opera Artists' Ensemble' comprising Grace Moore, Rose Bampton, Edward *Johnson, and Richard Bonelli performed at *Eaton Auditorium in Toronto in 1934.

In September 1941, the Montreal-based France-Film, leading French film distributor in Canada and owner of the *St-Denis Theatre, joined forces with the *Montreal Festivals to present at that theatre 'Metropolitan Opera au Saint-Denis,' seven performances using singers from the company and a number of Canadians for supporting roles, a chorus of 40, and 16 dancers all from the New York house, with Wilfrid *Pelletier and Jean Morel as conductors, Désiré Defrère as stage director, and Fausto Cleva as chorus master. The Met technical staff and scenery were used but the orchestra was that of the Montreal Festivals. Leading Met singers included Bampton, Martinelli, Warren, and Jennie Tourel. These were Tourel's first performances in Montreal; she sang the title roles in *Mignon* and *Carmen*. Canadians who appeared with the troupe were Rose Comète-Morin, Paul-Émile *Corbeil, Jeanne *Desjardins, Dolorès Drolet, Marcelle Monette, and David Rochette.

A season in September 1942 offered 10 operas including Charpentier's *Louise* and Massenet's *Thaïs*, but was under France-Film's sole sponsorship, with Pelletier as artistic director. Met singers included Moore, Steber, Sayão, Jepson, Martini, Peerce, Tibbett, Thomas, and Pinza. Canadians were included again in 1943 in *Boris Godunov*: Desjardins (The Innkeeper), Anna *Malenfant (Marina), and Gérard *Gélinas (Lovitzky). In 1944 *Pelléas et Mélisande* was one of seven operas offered. In 1945 Desjardins appeared in *Manon*, *Faust*, and *Lakmé*. Jean-Marie *Beaudet was a guest conductor in 1943 and 1944.

In 1945 performances of *Lakmé*, *Manon*, *Carmen*, *Faust*, *La Traviata*, and *La Bohème* were given in Toronto's *Massey Hall and in Quebec City's Capitol Theatre as well as in Montreal under France-Film auspices. Although these performances used the Metropolitan's singers, chorus, and ballet, they were not officially Metropolitan Opera performances. In the same category is a production of Gounod's *Roméo et Juliette* which Pelletier conducted in Montreal, Quebec City, Ottawa, Toronto, and Windsor in May 1943. Jeanette MacDonald (who never sang at the Met) and Armand Tokatyan sang the title roles, Pinza was Frère Laurent, and there were other Met singers in the cast along with three Canadians: Lionel *Daunais (Mercutio), Jeanne Desjardins (Gertrude), and Gérard Gélinas (Gregorio). The orchestra, chorus, and ballet were borrowed from the New York house.

Though the Met as such did not perform again in Canada until 1952, its radio broadcasts from New York, originating in 1931 and sponsored after 1940 by Texaco on a US network (in turn NBC, ABC, CBS, and a private syndication – the Texaco-Metropolitan Opera radio network), were heard for several years over the CRBC and thereafter on the CBC, giving Canadians (who otherwise would have heard little opera during those years) a regular experience of first-class opera performance. The broadcasts continued in 1980.

The Met's 1952 performances in Canada were given at Toronto's *Maple Leaf Gardens (where a production of *Carmen* with Risë Stevens established an attendance record – 11,352 – for opera indoors) and at the Montreal *Forum. Performances continued at the Gardens (annually until 1960) and the Forum 1952, 1953, 1955, 1957, and 1958), and six operas were presented in Toronto at *O'Keefe Centre in 1961. The Toronto visits (1952–61) were sponsored by the Rotary Club. Prohibitive costs prevented Canadian appearances by the full company in the years following. However, the Metropolitan Opera National Company, a youthful troupe under the artistic direction of Risë Stevens, performed at O'Keefe Centre and Montreal's Salle Wilfrid-Pelletier (*PDA) in 1965 (*Cinderella, Madama Butterfly, Carmen*, and Carlisle Floyd's *Susannah*) and 1966 (*La Bohème, La Traviata, The Marriage of Figaro*, and *The Rape of Lucretia*). Canadians in the company included Clarice *Carson, who made her debut with the main company in 1967; Huguette *Tourangeau, who made her debut with the main company in 1973; and Peter *van Ginkel.

To discover and encourage new talent, in 1935 the Met (under the initiative of Wilfrid Pelletier) began the radio program 'Auditions of the Air' which continued annually (except for the seasons 1945–6 and 1946–7) under Pelletier's baton until 1958. By 1958 the Metropolitan Opera National Council Regional Auditions, begun in 1954, had taken over the function of the radio auditions. Pierrette *Alarie won the 'Auditions of the Air' in 1945, Denis *Harbour in 1949, and Louis *Quilico in 1955. The regional auditions, preceded by district competitions, were organized in 16 areas of the USA, and several accommodated Canadian participation.

Ernesto *Vinci, Irene *Jessner, and Frederick *Newnham were among the judges for several years. Ida *Halpern was an organizer of the western region auditions. Among Canadian finalists in the auditions have been Joan *Maxwell (1957), Milla *Andrew (1958), Norman *Mittelmann (1959), Teresa *Stratas (1959), Heather *Thomson (1961), Lois *McDonall (1964), Huguette Tourangeau (1964), Maria *Pellegrini (1965), Judith *Forst (1968), Gabrielle *Lavigne (1970), Ingrid Suderman (1971), Peter *Barcza (1971), Jill Pert (1973), Lynn Blaser (1973), Mary-Lou *Fallis (1974), and Michèle Boucher (1977).

Wilfrid Pelletier began his association with the Met in 1917 as rehearsal pianist and coach. He conducted his first opera there (Deems Taylor's *The King's Henchman*) on 14 Apr 1928 and was appointed conductor in 1929, a position he held until 1950. Edward Johnson was in turn a leading tenor (1922–35) and general manager (1935–50). Irene *Pavloska was a member of the auditioning committee in the 1930s, and Ernesto *Barbini was a member of the conducting staff 1946–52.

Canadians who have performed with the Metropolitan Opera Company (with the years of their first performances there) are listed below:

1891 Emma *Albani
1901 Albert Quesnel
1915 Louise *Edvina
1916 Kathleen *Howard
1917 Florence *Easton
1919 Jeanne *Gordon
1922 Edmund *Burke, Edward Johnson
1929 Edward Ransome
1936 Nicholas *Massue, Jeanne *Pengelly, Joseph Royer
1940 Raoul *Jobin
1941 Mona Paulee
1942 Jacques *Gérard
1945 Pierrette Alarie
1946 Mary *Henderson
1949 Denis Harbour
1951 George *London
1956 Emilia Cundari
1959 Teresa Stratas
1960 Jon *Vickers
1961 Gladys *Kriese-Caporale, Norman Mittelmann
1962 Morley *Meredith
1963 Léopold *Simoneau, Richard *Verreau
1966 Lilian *Sukis
1967 Colette *Boky, Clarice Carson
1968 Judith Forst
1972 Louis Quilico
1973 Phil *Stark, Huguette Tourangeau
1975 Maureen *Forrester
1976 Allan *Monk, Cornelis *Opthof
1978 Alan *Crofoot, Ermanno *Mauro, Mariana *Paunova

Foreign-born artists who have lived or spent time in Canada and have appeared at the Met include Jeanne Maubourg (Met debut 1909), Eduardo *Ferrari-Fontana (1914), Irene Jessner (1936), Ruby *Mercer (1937), and Richard Manning (1944).

BIBLIOGRAPHY

Metropolitan Opera Annals compiled by William H. Seltsam (New York 1947; suppl 1957; suppl 1968)
Pelletier, Wilfrid. *Une Symphonie inachevée* (Montreal 1972)
Mercer, Ruby. 'Long live the Met,' *OpCan*, vol 13, Summer 1972
Rubin, Stephen E. 'Radio opera,' *Stereo Review*, Jan 1973
Mercer, Ruby. 'The Canadian Opera Company: a 150 year history,' *OpCan*, vol 14, Fall 1973
'Metropolitan Opera in Toronto,' *Canadian Opera Company 1950–1977* (Toronto 1977)
Eaton, Quaintance. *Opera Caravan: Adventures of the Metropolitan Opera on Tour 1883–1956* (New York 1978)
Musical Red Book HK, GP, KW

Metropolitan School of Music. Founded in 1893 in Toronto as the Metropolitan College of Music and reorganized in 1895 as the Metropolitan School of Music. W.O. *Forsyth became the director at the time of the reorganization and remained so until 1912, when the school was absorbed by the *Canadian Academy of Music. The school occupied a four-storey building on Queen St West, housing offices, classrooms, studios, and lecture and concert halls. Private lessons and class instruction were offered in theoretical subjects, teacher training, violin, piano, and voice. A musical kindergarten employed the *Fletcher Music Method. The staff included Peter C. Kennedy, Heinrich *Klingenfeld, Walter H. Robinson, and Fred Warrington. For the terms 1902–03 and 1905–06, the syllabi included brief biographies of its instructors – in number, 17 and 21 respectively.

Mexico. See South and Central America, Mexico, and the West Indies.

MICHAUD, Arthur. Tenor, teacher, b Northampton, Mass, of Canadian parents, 1892, d Hollywood, Cal, 25 Feb 1942. After studying commerce 1904–8 at the Collège Mont-St-Louis in Montreal he was a soloist at the basilica of that city. He completed his training in Milan and Paris and with Marie Lehmann in Berlin. Upon his return he gave a recital 11 Oct 1923 in the hall of Mont-St-Louis but left almost at once to take up residence in New York, where he sang and taught until 1936. Michaud visited Montreal to sing the title role in the premiere, 12 Feb 1924, of *La Vision de Dante* by Raoul Brunel and until 1930 he gave concerts regularly in Ottawa, Quebec City, Rimouski, St-Jean, and other Quebec centres. His first role (1925) with the New York Symphony Society was that of Jaquino in *Fidelio* in a performance conducted by Walter Damrosch. He was heard on several occasions over US and Canadian radio stations and in November 1926 gave a recital at Town Hall, New York. On 12 Apr 1930 he gave a gala concert in New York in the presence of Paul Claudel, then French ambassador to the USA, and in the same year he married the soprano Ethel Killion. In 1936 he moved to Hollywood where he taught until his death. Michaud's voice and delivery aroused considerable enthusiasm and many praised a 'timbre, volume and sonority reminiscent of Caruso' (*Le Droit*, May 1929). GB

MICHAUD, Oswald. Acoustician, pianist, inventor, b Verner, near North Bay, Ont, 18 Jul 1891, d Montreal 24 Aug 1966. At 18 he went to work for a piano manufacturer in Ste-Thérèse-de-Blainville, near Montreal, and learned piano technology and tuning; in 1910 he obtained a diploma as a piano tuner/technician in Battle Creek, Mich. At the same time he took private courses in piano, harmony, electonics, and industrial chemistry. He began practising his trade as a tuner at *McGill U in 1911. Sometime later he joined the teaching staff at the *Cons national of Montreal and there taught acoustics and was an examiner for 25 years. He also played the piano for silent movies ca 1911–22. In 1922, in partnership with Euclide and Jérémie David, he founded the piano manufacturing firm David & Michaud and was its secretary-treasurer. He was the regular tuner for the Montreal studios of the CRBC (later the CBC) from its creation until the late 1950s.

In 1937 Michaud developed an electric piano, which he named the Sonobel. Having removed the soundboard from an upright piano, he thought of attaching a small electromagnet to each of the 88 strings, linking these in turn to an amplifier connected to one or several loudspeakers. While the natural timbre of the instrument was preserved, each string could resonate fully. Since a pedal allowed the sound to be increased or diminished, a considerable variety of expression was possible. According to the inventor, 'it gives a whole new colour to the sound texture – powerful bass notes, and crystal clear high notes – and is suitable for the whole range of piano literature, early, classical, or modern' (Montreal *Petit Journal*, 20 May 1951).

In 1939 Paul *de Marky played the Sonobel on the CBC and in Charlottetown at an official reception for King George VI and Queen Elizabeth. Paul *Doyon, Alfred *Laliberté, and the famous pianist

Egon Petri performed on the instrument. In a letter to Michaud dated 16 Jan 1941 Petri praised his 'extraordinary Sonobel piano' and spoke of it as 'a wonderful invention in which pianists will take delight.' Because of the scarcity of materials during World War II the invention could not be exploited commercially. Michaud had to be satisfied with making a second prototype, which he installed in a CBC studio in the early 1950s.

BIBLIOGRAPHY

Morin, Dollard. 'Un expert canadien-français crée un piano électronique,' Montreal *Petit Journal*, 20 May 1951

GP

MICHEL, Jacques (b Rodrigue). Singer-songwriter, b Ste-Agnès-de-Bellecombe, near Rouyn, Que, 27 Jun 1941. At 16 he sang in cabarets in his region, performing songs by Gilbert Bécaud, Charles Aznavour, and Mouloudji to which he gradually added his own compositions. In 1965 he took part in a show starring Muriel *Millard at the Comédie-Canadienne in Montreal, and the same year he won the chanson trophy of the Montreal Festival du disque with 'Je retourne chez moi.' It was the song 'À cause d'une fleur' that brought him wide recognition, winning the special prize of the jury of the 1969 Festival de la chanson québécoise. The following year he won the Grand Prix de la Communauté radiophonique des programmes de langue française in Spa, Belgium, for his song 'Amène-toi chez nous' and a second prize at the Tokyo International Song Festival for 'Un nouveau jour va se lever.' With Richard *Grégoire as his music director he appeared at Le *Patriote annually 1971–7, at the Théâtre du Nouveau-Monde in Montreal in 1973, at the *Grand Théâtre in Quebec City, at the *NAC, and elsewhere. Each of his appearances in 1971, 1973, 1975, 1976, 1978, and 1979 at the *PDA was followed by a Quebec tour. He also toured the Maritimes 1971–2 and Ontario in 1971, 1975, and 1978. In 1972 he sang at the *St Lawrence Centre, Toronto. He has taken part in many CBC TV variety shows, including 'Zoom' (1973), 'Vedette en direct' (1974, 1976, 1978), 'Dimanshowsoir' (1977), and 'Les Beaux Dimanches' (1978). He also appeared in the Télé-Métropole (Montreal) series 'Tête d'affiche' (1977). In 1974 he founded a production management firm, Les Productions Rojamic. Several of his songs have been recorded, notably by Isabelle Aubret in France and by Julie Arel, Pauline *Julien, Ginette *Reno, and René *Simard in Quebec. In language that can be tender or violent, his songs evoke eroticism, friendship, freedom, life, and childhood. It has been said (*Canadian Composer*, February 1975) that 'they last because they are labours of love.' Michel is a member of CAPAC.

DISCOGRAPHY

Jacques Michel et ses chansons. 1965. Fantastique FAN 6405
Jacques Michel, Grand Prix du Festival du disque. 1965. France-Canada SCL 33010
Jacques Michel. 1966. Apex ALF 1594
Jacques Michel. 1967. Jupiter JDY 7017
Jacques Michel. 1969. Jupiter YDS 8029
Citoyen d'Amérique. 1970. Zodiaque ZOS 6906
S.O.S. 1971. Zodiaque ZOX 6000
Pas besoin de frapper pour entrer ... 1972. Zodiaque ZOX 6005
Dieu ne se mange plus. 1973. Zodiaque ZOX 6009
Jacques Michel à la Comédie. 1973. Zodiaque ZOX 6012
C'que j'ai l'goût d'dire. 1974. Zodiaque ZOX 6019
Migration. 1975. Trans-World TI 6026/Disque Total DT 22014
Ma Nouvelle Saison. 1976. Poly 2424 126
Le Temps d'aimer. 1977. Poly 2424 160
Le Coeur plus chaud. 1978. Poly 2424 185

BIBLIOGRAPHY

Chansons populaires, vol 1 (1971)
Trudel, Pierre. 'Jacques Michel: Quebec superstar,' *CanComp*, 55, Feb 1971
Lavoie, Benoît. 'A passionate and patient and determined songwriter,' ibid, 98, Feb 1975
Fecteau, Hélène. 'Jacques Michel depuis qu'il vit seul avec Sophie,' *Châtelaine*, Jun 1976

(HPn)

Mickey and Bunny (Sheppard). Ukrainian-Canadian pop music duo: Mickey (singer, guitarist, accordionist, b Modest William Theodore Sklepowich in Ethelbert, Man, 27 Mar 1932) and his wife Bunny (singer, b Orissia Ewanchuk in Rosa, Man, 13 Feb 1938). They began appearing together in 1964 in concert halls and nightclubs and at fairs, rodeos, and ethnic festivals across Canada and in parts of the USA. They performed Ukrainian, Polish, and German songs and dances, country music, and their own compositions. Their version of 'This Land Is Your Land' was very popular. For four years in the 1960s they were accompanied by the D-Drifters-5, an instrumental group led by the accordionist and bass guitarist Dave Roman and known for its Ukrainian versions of songs by the Beatles and other British pop groups of the 1960s.

For the Winnipeg company V-Records Mickey and Bunny made more than a dozen LPs and many singles, including collections of Ukrainian country music (VLP-3001, VLP-3065), Ukrainian Christmas carols (VLP-3019), Ukrainian and English beer parlour songs (VLP-3064), and *Songs of Inspiration* (VLP-3031). Their concerts at *Massey Hall, Toronto, and at the Ford Auditorium, Detroit, were recorded for release on two LPs (VLP-3026 and VLP-3044). Mickey and Bunny separated in the 1970s and Mickey pursued a solo career, but they continued to appear together occasionally. CC

MIGNAULT. Montreal musicians: 1 / Alfred and 2 / his son André.

1 **Alfred** (Joseph Édouard). Organist, composer, teacher, b St-Augustin-des-Deux-Montagnes, near Montreal, 8 Dec 1895, d Montreal 10 Jul 1961. He took his first lessons with his mother, an organist and a pupil of R.-O. *Pelletier. At the suggestion of his piano teacher Alfred *Laliberté, whom he had met in 1916, he left university to devote himself to music. He continued his studies in piano with Léo-Pol *Morin and in organ with Eugène *Lapierre and Émile Lambert. He was briefly organist at the Montreal churches of St-Alphonse d'Youville, St-Étienne, Ste-Cunégonde, Ste-Catherine, and St-Georges, before serving 1924–57 as organist and 1944–57 as choirmaster at St-Enfant-Jésus Church. In 1937 he began broadcasting as organist and pianist on CBC radio. He was artistic director 1938–40 of 'L'Heure provinciale' on radio station CKAC, succeeding Henri *Letondal. He was teacher of solfège and musical dictation 1943–61 at the *CMM and director 1944–57 of voice and solfège teaching for the Montreal Catholic School Board.

Although he devoted himself mainly to teaching, Mignault composed vocal and instrumental works in his leisure time. He was a self-taught composer, and some of his works were published at his own expense ('Cor Jesu', 'Ecce fidelis' for choir, 'Souvenez-vous, Vierge Marie' for voice), others by *Boucher (*Petite Pastorale en ré* for organ, 'Homo quidam' and 'O salutaris' for choir, 'Ave Maria' for voice) and *Archambault (Je vous salue, Marie'). For cello he wrote a *Suite dans le style ancien, Berceuse, La Fileuse, Pensée musicale*, and *Pastourelle*, the last four dedicated to his son André.

In 1938 several of Mignault's piano compositions were played by Annette Brunet in a recital at the Gesù Church hall, and his *Divertissement sur deux thèmes canadiens* for piano and orchestra was performed with Brunet as soloist and the composer conducting 2 October on the program 'L'Heure provinciale,' along with his *Petite Suite*. Mignault's major work, a *Messe brève de requiem* (1944) for four equal voices and organ, was premiered in 1944. He later orchestrated it. Mignault also wrote numerous songs, piano pieces, and harmonizations of folksongs.

2 **André** (Marcel). Cellist, teacher, b Montreal 22 Dec 1931; premier prix cello (CMM) 1952, premier prix cello (École supérieure de musique, Paris) 1955. After taking theory lessons from his father he studied cello 1946–52 at the *CMM with Jean *Belland and 1952–5 at the École supérieure de musique in Paris with André Navarra. He was a member 1955–7 of the Ensemble Jean-Philippe-Rameau with J.-P. *Jeannotte and others and a member 1958–72 of the *MSO; he played in recitals and on CBC radio and TV. He was appointed to the staff of the Cons de Hull in 1968 and also taught 1970–5 at the *U of Montreal. In 1978 he gave courses at the summer school at the Domaine Forget in Charlevoix, Que. He has made recordings of Scarlatti and Rameau cantatas with Jeannotte, and he and Bruno *Laplante made an LP devoted to Massenet. 1 / (MH-D), 2 / GP

MILDMAY, (Grace) Audrey (Louisa St John) (m Christie). Soprano, b Hurstmonceaux, Sussex, 19 Dec 1900, d Glyndebourne, England, 31 May 1953. She was three months old when her father accepted a post as first vicar of the Church of England parish in Penticton, BC. Her first public appearance was in a children's operetta presented by the *Vancouver Woman's Musical Club. In 1924 she went to London for study with Walter Johnstone-Douglas and in 1927–8 she toured North America in *The Beggar's Opera*. She joined the Royal Carl Rosa Opera Company, and sang Musetta, Gretel, Micaela, Nedda, and other roles.

Mildmay married John Christie in 1931 and subsequently aided him in realizing his dream of establishing an annual opera festival on the family estate near Lewes, Sussex. On 28 May 1934 the first Glyndebourne Festival opened with *Le Nozze di Figaro*, featuring Mildmay as Susanna. Within five years the festival was recognized as one of the world's outstanding artistic events. During the 1930s the soprano was heard in several European centres. She moved to Canada with her two children at the outbreak of World War II, and remained until 1944. Her last operatic appearances were in Montreal (May 1943) as Susanna. On her return to England her health began to fail and, after her efforts (in collaboration with Rudolf Bing) to establish the first Edinburgh Festival (1947), she declined rapidly.

Mildmay's voice was a light lyric soprano employed with much charm. She may be heard on the complete HMV / Glyndebourne recordings of *Le Nozze di Figaro* (1934, Turnabout 4114-4116) and *Don Giovanni* (1936, Turnabout TV 4117-4119) and on a recording of *The Beggar's Opera* (issued 1940, Victor DM 722).

BIBLIOGRAPHY

Blunt, Wilfrid. *John Christie of Glyndebourne* (London 1968)
Bing, Sir Rudolf. *5000 Nights at the Opera* (New York 1972)

JBM

MILETTE, Juliette (Sister Henri-de-la-Croix, Congregation of the Holy Names of Jesus and

Mary; pseudonym Rose de Montroy). Organist, teacher, composer, b Montreal 17 Jun 1900; lauréat (AMQ) 1927, M MUS (Montreal) 1934, L MUS (Montreal) 1939, D MUS (Montreal) 1949. She studied at the École supérieure de musique in Outremont (*École Vincent-d'Indy) with Alfred *Laliberté (piano), Raoul *Paquet (organ), and Claude *Champagne (composition). She received a teaching diploma in 1933 from Montreal's *Cons national and a diploma for Gregorian chant in 1938 from the *U of Montreal. In 1926 she began teaching solfège, harmony, analysis, piano, organ, choral singing, and Gregorian chant at the École Vincent- d'Indy. Under her pseudonym she has composed a work for organ and choir, *Notre-Dame du Canada* (1950, Notre-Dame du Cap 1950, and recorded on the Radio-Marie label); the organ accompaniment to the *Cantuale ad Benedictionem SS. Sacramenti* (1958, Collège de Rouyn 1958); and (unpublished) hymns, organ pieces, and choral works including masses, motets, and an oratorio, *Leur Maison*, written to mark the centenary, in 1944, of her religious order (see Oratorios, Canadian 11/).

WRITINGS

Formation pratique au chant grégorien (Outremont 1942)
Formation pratique à l'harmonisation (Outremont 1944)
La Mission spirituelle de la musique (Montreal 1950)
Principes élémentaires de la musique, transl of *Keys to Music Rudiments* by Boris Berlin (Toronto 1968)
Rythme et son, transl of *Basics of Ear Training* by Boris Berlin (Toronto 1969)

BIBLIOGRAPHY

Catalogue of Canadian Composers (CMr)

MILLAR, Gregory. Conductor, tenor, b Prince Albert, Sask, 9 Jun 1929; of Greek descent; BA (British Columbia) 1949, MA (California) 1951, MA (Mills College, Oakland) 1953. He was a pupil of Dalton *Baker, Ian Barrie, Arthur *Benjamin, William Gratch, and Jean *de Rimanoczy in Canada and of Leonard Bernstein, Darius Milhaud, and Dimitri Mitropoulos in the USA. Millar taught at St Louis U 1949–50, at the U of California 1959–60, and at the Manhattan School of Music 1960–4. He was conductor of the San Francisco Little SO 1951–9, the Monterey County SO 1954–9, the Kalamazoo Symphony 1962–8, the Grand Rapids SO 1968–72, and the Tucson SO 1966–76. He served 1960–2 as assistant conductor of the New York Philharmonic, 1968–73 as director of the Opera Assn of Western Michigan, and 1973–5 as director of the National Opera of Mexico. He was appointed conductor of the *Regina SO in 1978 and also conducted the Saskatchewan Opera performances of *Madama Butterfly* in May 1979. Millar gave voice recitals in San Francisco, sang Siegmund in *Die Walküre* in Austin, Texas, and was tenor soloist in Verdi's *Requiem* with the Dallas SO in May 1978. He has been a guest conductor of the *CBC Vancouver Chamber Orchestra. With the San Francisco Little SO he recorded works by Hindemith (1957, Fantasy 5001), Skalkottas (Fantasy 5002), Handel (1959, Fantasy 5004), and Bartók (1964, Fantasy 8009). He has recorded with the California Symphony, the Manhattan Orchestra, and the Kalamazoo, Grand Rapids, and Tucson symphonies. (IBr)

MILLARD, Muriel. Singer, actress, dancer, b Montreal 1924. She won several first prizes in the 'Catelli Young Talent' competition on radio station CKAC in 1938. Her success with the French song 'Y a pas de cerises en Alaska' brought her wide fame. She toured in Quebec with the impresario Jean Grimaldi's troupe. At that time she generally imitated French singers such as Josephine Baker, Lucienne Boyer, Mireille, and Mistinguett. Between 1943 and 1945 she performed at the Old Europe nightclub in New York. In 1945 she made her debut at the Théâtre national in Montreal and the following year she performed on radio CKAC in 'Le Gala humoristique et musical à la salle paroissiale.' Because of her great popularity on the air she was elected queen of radio in 1950 by the Montreal weekly *Radiomonde*.

In 1952 Millard toured in New England and Quebec and performed for the armed forces in Korea and Japan. During these years she often appeared in clubs in Quebec and as far afield as Florida. On CBC TV she was heard in 1955 in 'Feux de joie,' subsequently in 'Music-Hall' and 'Porte ouverte,' and in 1961 in 'Miss Music-Hall,' the name by which she came to be known best. She appeared in variety shows, at the *PDA, the Montreal *Forum, and elsewhere in 1964, and for the following two years at the Comédie-Canadienne. The show she gave there in 1966, 'Gai Gai la belle province,' included the premiere of a Canadian ballet based on the Gilles *Vigneault song 'Jack Monnoloy' and was repeated at the *Palais Montcalm in Quebec City. Jean Basile wrote: 'We are indebted to Muriel Millard for continuing along a generally neglected path by presenting again this year, at the Comédie-Canadienne, a real music-hall show in which she is the MC. Despite its flaws, some of which are serious, you will have a fine evening of fun, charm ... and feathers' (Montreal *Le Devoir*, 24 Aug 1966). That year she also played in a French musical comedy, Louiguy's *La Quincaillère de Chicago*, at the *St-Denis Theatre in Montreal. Other productions in which she starred include *Vive la Canadienne* at *Expo 67, *Terre des femmes* at the Comédie-Canadienne and at the Latin Quarter in New York the same year, and *Avec la femme* at Man and His World in 1968.

After 1960 Muriel Millard wrote most of her own songs, the most popular of which was undoubtedly 'Les Vieilles maisons.' She made several LPs for Trans-Canada. She began to concentrate on painting in 1969 but returned briefly to the nightclub circuit in 1970 and made an LP, *Faut que jeunesse passe* (Totem 9209) in 1975. She is a member of CAPAC.

Millard's younger sister, the singer Marie King, performed in Quebec for the first time in 1961. Named 'Reine du western,' she received a trophy from the Montreal Festival du disque in 1969. Sales of her records are said to have exceeded a million since her debut. She writes the lyrics of her songs to music provided by her husband, the guitarist Bob King, who has accompanied her on many tours in Quebec, Ontario, New Brunswick, and the USA. 'Allô, mon p'tit Bobby' and 'Quand le soleil dit bonjour aux montagnes' are among her hits. She has made numerous LPs with London and Trans-World, as well as for the Bonanza label (*Qualalinta* 1976, B 29626), and her most popular songs were featured on the LP *Mes Plus Grands Succès* (Bonanza B 29664). Marie and Bob King are both members of CAPAC. ST

MILLER, Edith (Jane) (m Colyer-Fergusson). Contralto, b Rothsay, near Guelph, Ont, 26 Feb 1875?, d Gravesend, Kent, 18 Jun 1936. She was raised in Portage la Prairie, Man, but began vocal studies with Francesco *D'Auria at the *TCM. Later she studied with Alberto Randegger in London and Mathilde Marchesi and Jean de Reszke in Paris. Throughout the 1890s she was active in Ontario music circles and in 1898 she was engaged as soloist at St Bartholomew's Church, New York. After her London debut in 1905 she became one of the most admired concert contraltos in England; her repertoire ranged from classical arias to French-Canadian folksongs. She appeared frequently in oratorio but only rarely in opera. She married Max Colyer-Fergusson in 1913 and retired following the birth of her only child in 1917. Described by the *Toronto Daily Star* in 1909 as 'one of the great concert singers of the day,' her death prompted *The Times* of London to recall: 'Her success was due not only to the sweetness, purity, and power of her voice, but to her sensitive interpretation and phrasing, intelligence and good taste.' JBM

MILLER, Michael (Richard). Composer, pianist, b Lisbon 24 Jul 1932, naturalized Canadian 1972; BA (New York U) 1955, MA (ESM) 1956, PH D (ESM) 1971. He studied composition at the ESM with Bernard Rogers and Wayne Barlow. He taught at New York U 1961–5 and Vassar College 1965–6. He emigrated to Canada in 1967, began teaching piano, composition, and theory at *Mount Allison U, and performed 1967–74 with the Mount Allison Trio. Miller has composed for choir, voice, piano, orchestra, and chamber ensemble. He employs various 20th-century techniques (pandiatonic, serial, aleatoric, etc) though his works usually retain identifiable metre, timbre, and tonality. The Kyrie and Gloria from his *Mass for Peace* (1962, Kalmus 1964) have been recorded (1973) by the *Festival Singers (CBC SM-203). He is a member of CAPAC and an associate of the *CMCentre. NV

MILLIGAN, James. Baritone, b Halifax, NS, 5 Apr 1928, d Basel 28 Nov 1961. He studied 1948–55 with Emmy *Heim and Leslie *Holmes at the *RCMT and made concert and oratorio appearances in Toronto and nearby cities during those years. He was one of two winners of the 1951 *'Nos Futures Étoiles.' In the early 1950s, often in company with two other rising young artists of the day – Lois *Marshall and Jon *Vickers – he was a soloist on many occasions with the *Toronto Mendelssohn Choir. In 1953 he sang the title part in *Elijah* and the Christus in both the performance and the recording of the *St Matthew Passion*; in 1954 he was a soloist in the choir's performances of *Messiah* and the *St Matthew Passion* in Carnegie Hall, New York. That same year he won the radio competition *'Singing Stars of Tomorrow.'

Milligan was making his name as a dramatic baritone during the 1950s, first in the *Royal Cons Opera School productions and later in the Opera Festival productions that grew out of those and that were, in effect, the beginning of the *COC. He sang Marcello in *La Bohème*, Monterone in *Rigoletto*, and Cancian in *School for Fathers* in 1954; Germont père in *La Traviata* in 1955; and Don Carlo in *La Forza del Destino* in 1959. In 1958 he had an outstanding success as Scarpia in the CBC TV production of *Tosca*.

The two last-named roles came after his discovery abroad. In the summer of 1956 he sang Arbace in the Glyndebourne Festival production of *Idomeneo*. In 1957, after winning first prize in the International Competition for Musical Performers in Geneva, he continued his studies in London with Roy Henderson and came to the attention of Sir Malcolm Sargent. He quickly became one of Sargent's favourite baritones and under his baton in 1958 sang in *The Damnation of Faust* and *The Dream of Gerontius* in England and in *Messiah*, the Fauré *Requiem*, and Walton's *Belshazzar's Feast* at the Vienna June Festival. He recorded *Messiah*, *Belshazzar's Feast*, and several Gilbert & Sullivan operettas under Sargent.

Other significant roles in Milligan's meteoric career were Escamillo in *Carmen* at Covent Garden in 1959 and Don Carlo in *La Forza del Destino* with the COC that same year. Prior to his debut at Bayreuth as the Wotan / Wanderer in the 1961 pro-

James Milligan

Alan Mills

duction of *Siegfried* with Birgit Nilsson and Hans Hopf, he had joined the Basel Opera.

In her book *New Bayreuth* (London 1969), Penelope Turing discussed Milligan's performance at the Wagner festival: 'A fine Wanderer does not always become Wotan in toto. Therefore it is dangerous to hail even an outstanding performance of the Wanderer as promise of a world Wotan. Yet there was that in Milligan's singing which made many of us throw caution to the winds and believe that we had heard one of the very great Wagnerians of the future ... He had a glorious voice of ringing quality, power and range, and he used it with real musicianship. As an actor he had that indefinable quality which we call stage presence ... He *was* the Wanderer in a way which I have never seen displayed except by singers who have had years of experience in this part. It was a thrilling occasion.'

Milligan died suddenly and tragically in Basel, four months after that auspicious debut.

DISCOGRAPHY

Gilbert & Sullivan *The Gondoliers*. Pro Arte O, Glyndebourne Festival Chor, Sargent cond, Milligan (Antonio). 1959. 2-Angel 3570
– *HMS Pinafore*. Pro Arte O, Glyndebourne Festival Chor, Sargent cond, Milligan (the Boatswain). (1956). 2-Angel 3589
– *The Pirates of Penzance*. Pro Arte O, Glyndebourne Festival Chor, Sargent cond, Milligan (Pirate King). (1956). 2-Angel 3609
Gounod 'Avant de quitter ces lieux'; 'Bendemeer's Stream.' Agostini cond. 1954. Victor 10-4221 (78 rpm) / Victor 49-4221 (45 rpm)
Handel *Messiah*. Royal Liverpool Phil O, Huddersfield Choral Soc, Sargent cond. 1959. 3-Sera SIC-6056
Morawetz *Songs*. Morawetz pf. 1953. RCI 121
Mozart *Idomeneo*. Glyndebourne Festival Chor and O, Pritchard cond, Milligan (Arbace). 1956. 3-Sera SIC 6070
Walton *Belshazzar's Feast*. Royal Liverpool Phil O, Huddersfield Choral Soc, Sargent cond. 1958. HMV ALP 1628
See also Discography for Toronto Mendelssohn Choir.

JBM, KW

MILLS, Alan (b Albert Miller). Folksinger (baritone), writer, actor, b Lachine, near Montreal, 7 Sep 1913, d Montreal 14 Jun 1977. Interrupting a career as a journalist in Montreal (1929–47, mainly at *The Gazette*), Mills made his singing debut as a bass with John *Goss' London Singers (an English quintet) and toured with them 1935–7 in Canada and the USA. He sang small roles in *The Magic Flute* (1945) and *Madama Butterfly* (1947) for the *Opera Guild of Montreal.

Mills began his successful career as a folksinger on CBC radio in the program 'Folk Songs for Young Folks' (1947–59) and continued in the program 'Songs de Chez Nous' (1952–5) with Hélène *Baillargeon and the Art *Morrow Singers. He was heard abroad 1948–55 through his programs and recordings for the CBC International Service, and later he toured Europe twice. In 1953 he sang the Leader in Weill's folk opera *Down in the Valley* for the *Minute Opera of Montreal. His first concert performance (Ottawa, 1949) was followed by many others in concert and at festivals throughout North America. His performances with Jean *Carignan at the 1960 Newport Folk Festival were preserved on a Vanguard recording (2087). He also appeared with Carignan at several *Mariposa Folk Festivals. His song 'I Know an Old Lady Who Swallowed a Fly' (Southern 1951) became popular among folksingers. A Burl Ives performance of the song served as the soundtrack of a 1964 *NFB film of the same name. Mills appeared in a few NFB productions and also acted in English and French radio dramas and TV commercials in Montreal. His play *Ti-Jean and the Devil*, based on a French-Canadian tale related by Carignan, was premiered 21 Jun 1961 on CBC radio. A leading popularizer of Canadian folklore and a favourite of Canadian children, Mills made over 30 LPs, including several with the guitarist Gilbert 'Buck' Lacombe, who often accompanied him.

In 1967 Mills participated with other leading non-traditional folksingers in the nine-volume *Canadian Folk Songs: A Centennial Collection* (RCA CS-100) and wrote the accompanying English-language booklet. Mills was made a Member of the *Order of Canada in 1974. His library and papers were deposited at the NL of C. He was a member of CAPAC.

SONG BOOKS

Alan Mills' Book of Folk Songs and Ballads (Whitcomb & Gilmour 1949). Republ as *Folk Songs for Young Folk* (BMI Canada 1957)
Favorite Songs of Newfoundland (BMI Canada 1958)
– and Fowke, E., Blume, H. *Canada's Story in Song* (Toronto 1960)
Chantons un peu (BMI Canada 1961)
Favorite French Folk Songs (Oak 1963)
– and Bonne, R. *I Know an Old Lady* (Rand McNally 1961)

DISCOGRAPHY

ON DOMINION
Chantons un peu. H. Baillargeon. Dom 1221
Folk Songs for Young Folk, 2 vols. (1965). Dom 1280, 1281
Also several 45s, seven in French with H. Baillargeon, two in English with G. Lacombe, guit
ON FOLKWAYS
Folk Songs of French Canada. 1952. FW 6929
Folksongs of Newfoundland. 1953. FW 6831
Duets and Songs of French Canada. H. Baillargeon. 1955. FW 6918
Folk Songs of Acadia. H. Baillargeon. 1956. FW 6923
Folk Songs for Young Folk, 2 vols: no. 1 *Animals*, no. 2 *More Animals*. 1956. FC 7021, FC 7022
French Songs for Children. 1957. FC 7018
Favorite Songs of Newfoundland. 1958. FW 8771
Songs of the Maritimes. 1959. FW 8744
Canada's Story in Song. 1960. 2-FW 3000
Songs, Fiddle Tunes and Folk Tales from Canada. J. Carignan vn, G. Lacombe guit. 1961. FG 3532
Raasche and Alan Mills Sing Jewish Folk Songs. 1962. FW 8711
14 Numbers, Letters and Animal Songs for the Very Young. 1972. FC 7545
Also *Chantons en français* (with H. Baillargeon, 4-FC 7719, 7720, 7721, 7722); *Christmas Songs from Many Lands* (FC 7750); *French Folk Songs for Children* (FC 2708); *More Songs to Grow On* (FC 7009); *Songs of the Sea* (FA 2312); and songs on Folkways FW 7545
ON RCA
Canadian Folk Songs: A Centennial Collection. 1967. RCA CS-100
Some 78s: RCA 56-0030, 56-0031, 56-0032, 56-0051, and 56-0058
Chansons à boire. RCA Victor CGP-289
ON RCI
Songs by Alan Mills. 1950. RCI 21
With G. Lacombe, guit. 1952. RCI 81-84
Songs of the Maritimes. Art Morrow, G. Lacombe. 1954. RCI 102
OTHERS
Chansons à boire (with a choir and orch conducted by G. Lacombe; Venus VL 301); *Folkloriquement vôtre* (Totem TO-9208); *Le Noël des Artistes* (London VL-304)
Some 45s for Capri and HMV

BIBLIOGRAPHY

Gallant, Mavis. 'His songs tell a story,' Montreal *Standard*, 10 Feb 1951
McNamara, Helen. 'Alan Mills – Canada's balladeer,' *SatN*, 13 Dec 1952
'Alan Mills celebrating the 10th year of his folk-song show,' *CBC Times*, 5–11 May 1957
Cadoret, Charlotte. 'In memoriam,' CFMS *Newsletter*, vol 12, Fall–Winter 1977

(LHv)

MILLS, David. Bass, b Moose Jaw, Sask, 29 Jan 1929; ARCT 1957, BA (Toronto) 1966. While studying 1947–9 at the *Regina Cons with Alicia *Birkett he sang in churches, on radio (CKRM and CKCK), and in recital. Studies followed at the *RCMT with George *Lambert and D'Alton *McLaughlin. Though mainly a recitalist, Mills made his oratorio debut in 1953 with the Yorkminster Choir (Toronto) under McLaughlin and sang the bass solos (1954) in Beethoven's rarely performed *The Glorious Hour* (*Der Glorreiche Augenblick*, Op 136) with the *Toronto Jewish Folk Choir under Emil Gartner. He sang with the National Opera (Toronto) in 1953, with the Marseilles Opera in 1957 and 1958, and at the 1958 Summer of Musicals in Chicago. Accompanied by his wife, the pianist Marjorie Mutter, Mills has made recital tours of Europe (1960, 1961, 1965, 1970, and 1977) and in Canada (1969) began performing a program of Canadian art songs. He has premiered songs by Welford *Russell ('The Conqueror' and 'Farewell to Arms'), Court Stone, the Polish-Canadian Boleslaw Szczeniowski, and Leon *Zuckert. Szczeniowski and Zuckert have set Mills' own poems to music. Mills gave master classes in 1972 at the Okanagan Summer School of the Arts.

DISCOGRAPHY

David Mills Sings Pop Concert Favourites. Mutter pf. 1969. Quality V1636
David Mills Sings Art Songs by Canadian Composers: Dela – Mercure – Russell – Szczeniowski – Weinzweig – Zuckert. Mutter pf. 1975. Master Recordings MA 275
Cry of the Prophet and Other Canadian Song Classics. Mutter pf. 1977. Master Recordings MA 377

(WLB)

MILLS, Frank (William). Composer, arranger, singer, pianist, b Montreal 27 Jun 1942; associate diploma (McGill) 1965. While studying composition 1961–5 with István *Anhalt and Kelsey *Jones at *McGill U, he wrote two of the university's *Red and White* revues. He was the pianist 1969–71 with the pop group the Bells, for whom he wrote the hits 'Stay Awhile' and 'Fly Little White Dove Fly.' Under his own name he made several LPs of pop instrumentals 1971–4: *Seven of My Songs* (Poly

2424-030), which included 'Love Me Love Me Love,' a hit in Canada and the USA in 1971 as a single with lyrics added and sung by Mills; *Reflections of My Childhood* (Poly 2424-060); *Images d'un Bistro* (Sonogram LSG-72001); and *Frank Mills* (Sonogram LSG-72005). The last, reissued in 1978 as *The Poet and I* (Poly 2424-170), included the instrumental *Music Box Dancer*, a hit single internationally 1978–9; both the namesake LP and the single received gold record awards in Canada and the USA. Versions of *Music Box Dancer* were recorded by Roberto Delgato, James Last, and others. In addition, sheet music sales of *Music Box Dancer* (published by Chappell) reached 900,000 by mid–1979. *Pied Piper* was a second major hit in 1979. Mills made the LP *Look at Me Real* (1976, Attic LAT 1009). He appeared in concert or on TV occasionally in the early 1970s and, after the success of his records, began touring in 1979. He received *Juno Awards as composer and instrumental artist of that year and in 1980 was given the Wm Harold Moon Award by PRO Canada. Peter Goddard has used the words 'romantic,' 'slightly nostalgic,' and 'easy listening' in describing Mills' music. Mills is an affiliate of PRO Canada.

BIBLIOGRAPHY

MacDonald, Dick. 'Frank Mills' music picked up by broadcasters,' *MSc*, 275, Jan–Feb 1974

Linden, J.J. 'Frank Mills: a four year smash success,' *RPM*, 23 Dec 1978

Goddard, Peter. 'Canadian clobbers musical competition,' *Toronto Star*, 5 May 1979

Elliott, Kate. 'Frank Mills' answer is instrumentals,' *MSc*, 307, May–Jun 1979

Lavoie, Denis. 'Frank Mills dans l'ombre d'un succès,' Montreal *La Presse*, 20 Dec 1980 (MM)

MILLS, Frederick (William). Organist, composer, choir conductor, fl 1867–77. He was a co-founder in 1868 and president 1871–2 of the *AMQ. In 1869 with Antoine *Dessane he revived the *Quebec Harmonic Society. He moved to Ottawa ca 1872 as organist at Christ Church and in 1874 he was the conductor of the *Ottawa Choral Union. While in Ottawa he composed the operetta *The Maire of St Brieux* (libretto by Frederick Augustus Dixon) for Lady Dufferin's private theatricals in March 1875 at Government House. An excerpt, 'Only a Daisy,' was published by *Nordheimer. Several of Mills' waltzes and piano pieces were issued by *Orme, and his light opera, *The Witch of Fairy Dell*, written after he had moved (ca 1877) to Philadelphia, was published by C.F. Summy in 1916.

BIBLIOGRAPHY

Lady Dufferin. *My Canadian Journal 1872 78* (London, New York 1891) HK

MILLS, Isabelle (Margaret). Educator, writer, conductor, b Fleming, Sask, near Brandon, Man, 3 Sep 1923; ARCT 1948, BA (Manitoba) 1964, MA (Columbia) 1965, ED D (Columbia) 1971. She studied in Brandon and summers (1947, 1949, and 1950) at the *RCMT. She taught music and music education 1947–67 at Brandon College and in 1967 joined the *U of Saskatchewan at Saskatoon, where, besides teaching, she has done much research on Canadian (including native) music, especially that suitable for young listeners. She has directed church choirs, the U of Saskatchewan Quance Chorus, and a choral group (recruited from Saskatoon churches) which recorded *Come, Let Us Sing: The United Church Hymn Heritage in Sound* (1975; Colly CLS 963). Mills is a contributor to *EMC*.

WRITINGS

'Canadian music: a listening program for intermediate grades with teaching guide,' unpubl ED D thesis, Columbia, 1971

'Canadian music for young listeners,' *CME*, vol 14, Spring 1973

'Doctoral dissertation fills gap in music education,' *MSc*, 272, Jul–Aug 1973 JSn

MILLS-COCKELL, John. Composer, synthesizist, pianist, organist, b Toronto 19 May 1943. His teachers at the *RCMT and the *U of Toronto included John *Coveart (piano), Samuel *Dolin (composition), and Gustav *Ciamaga (electronic music). Mills-Cockell won a BMI Award for Student Composers in 1967 for his *Movements* for orchestra and *Reverberation* for solo trombone and two stereo tapes.

As pianist, organist, and one of the first musicians in Canada to employ the Moog and Arp synthesizers in live performance, Mills-Cockell performed in 1968 with Intersystems (a mixed-media group with sculptor Michael Hayden, architect Dick Zander, and poet Blake Parker), in 1969 with *Kensington Market, in Vancouver 1969–70 with Hydro-Electric Streetcar, and in Toronto 1970–2 with Syrinx. The last-named group, completed by Doug Pringle (saxophones), Allan Wells (percussion), and, later, Malcolm Tomlinson (drums and voice), made the LPs *Syrinx* (TNorth TN 2) and *Long Lost Relatives* (TNorth TN 5). It played the theme music on camera for the CTV series 'Here Come the Seventies' and appeared on the CBC TV show 'Music to See' playing Mills-Cockell's *Stringspace* (1971) with the Toronto Repertory Ensemble under Milton *Barnes.

Concentrating after 1972 on composing and recording, Mills-Cockell has made only occasional live appearances (eg, a tour of Ontario in 1973 and two weeks at the CN Tower's Top of Toronto restaurant in 1977). For most of the period 1972–4 he lived in England. He made three LPs 1973–7: *Heartbeat* (TNorth TN 12), *The Third Testament* (TNorth TN 17, music written in 1973 for a TV series of the same name), and *Gateway: A New Music Adventure* (Anubis ANX-1). Of the last, Peter Goddard (*Toronto Star*, 13 Aug 1977) wrote, 'The sound ... is heavy, ponderous at times, and as Wagnerian in density as anything Phil Spector ever dreamed up' and described the result as 'a musical synthesis of rock, with all its presence and power, and such mainstream compositional techniques as serialism and aleatoric freeform approaches,' referring also to the disparate influences of Kurt Weill and Debussy.

Among Mills-Cockell's other works are scores for the feature films *The Clown Murders* and *Deadly Harvest*; for theatre productions at *St Lawrence Centre; for the National Ballet of Canada (*January Tree* and *For Internal Use Only* 1971), the Toronto Dance Theatre (*Starscape* 1971), and the Anna Wyman Dance Company (*Deflections* 1976); and for many CBC radio and TV shows. He is an affiliate of PRO Canada.

BIBLIOGRAPHY

MacLaurin, Doug. 'Mills-Cockell's music expressed electronically,' *MSc*, 258, Mar–Apr 1971 MM

MILLSON, (George) Douglas. Organist, choirmaster, carillonneur, b Kingsville, near Windsor, Ont, 20 Jun 1908. He was the son of a Methodist minister and played the organ in his father's church at 13. He later studied at the *TCM and the Union Theological Seminary, Ohio. He was organist-choirmaster 1936–52 at churches in Port Hope and Chatham, Ont, before moving to Edmonton, where he served 1952–74 as organist-choirmaster at Robertson (renamed Robertson-Wesley) United Church and was the conductor 1954–7 of the Edmonton Male Chorus. He introduced handbell ringing into the program at the church. He was sent by the Alberta government to study campanology 1966–7 at Riverside Church, New York, and at Princeton U. These studies marked the beginning of his tenure 1966–79 as carillonneur at the Alberta Legislative Buildings, Edmonton. RDM

Mining songs. See Occupational songs, Anglo-Canadian: 4.

Ministère des Affaires culturelles du Québec (MACQ). Before 1960 Quebec government subsidies to artistic societies were controlled by the secretary of the province of Quebec, whose responsibilities included fine arts. This department was responsible for the *Prix d'Europe and the *Cons de musique du Québec, created under its auspices in 1942. Study grants for young musicians, however, came under the Ministry of Youth. When the Quebec Liberal party was brought to power in 1960 the first plank in its platform called for the creation of a ministry of cultural affairs. The organizational structure and operation were established by Georges-Émile Lapalme, and in presenting the bill, 2 Mar 1961, Premier Jean Lesage declared, 'Government does not create culture, neither does it control it ... it merely attempts to create a climate in which the arts may flourish.' The act passed by the National Assembly 24 Mar 1961 provided for the establishment of a ministry and also of a provincial arts council, which in 1980 still existed by virtue of the act but which last met in 1968. The ministers have been Georges-Émile Lapalme 1961–4, Pierre Laporte 1964–6, Jean-Noël Tremblay 1966–70, François Cloutier 1970–2, Denis Hardy 1972–4, Jean-Paul L'Allier 1974–6, Louis O'Neill 1976–8, and Denis Vaugeois, who was succeeded by Clément Richard in 1981. One of the main architects of the policies of the MACQ was Guy Frégault, deputy minister 1962–8 and 1970–5.

After the conservatories that make up the Cons de musique du Québec were placed under the jurisdiction of the MACQ, the responsibility for music instruction was assumed by Wilfrid *Pelletier 1961–7, Victor *Bouchard 1967–71, and Jean *Vallerand 1971–8. Vallerand later also became director of performing arts. Victor Bouchard was director of the music section 1971–5 and a consultant 1975–8; he again became director of conservatories in 1978 after Uriel Luft held the post for a few months that year on an interim basis. Léopold *Simoneau was assistant to the director of music 1968–70 and artistic director in 1971 of the *Opéra du Québec, a creation of the ministry. The administrative structure of the music section has undergone numerous changes and was reorganized in 1978. In 1979 its director was Jacques Langevin, whose immediate superior was Georges Cartier, head of the ministry's arts and letters section.

In 1980, besides subsidizing the principal musical societies of Quebec, the MACQ continued to be responsible for the conservatories and to organize the annual Prix d'Europe competition. (Study grants had become the responsibility of the Ministry of Education.) The MACQ has played a leading role in the establishment of musical societies, which it subsidizes but which enjoy much artistic and administrative autonomy. Particular mention should be made of the *SMCQ (begun in 1966), the Opéra du Québec (1971–5), the Quebec Youth Orchestra (begun in 1977), and the Opéra de chambre du Québec and the Opéra de Montréal (both begun in 1980). In 1977 the MACQ created the Prix Denise-Pelletier for the performing arts; recipients have been Félix *Leclerc in 1977, Bernard *Lagacé in 1978, and the actor Jean Duceppe in 1979.

In 1963–4 the total budget of the MACQ was $5,070,000. By 1978–9 it had increased more than thirteenfold, to $67,318,800, of which $12,553,600 was earmarked for the support of the performing arts and $8,415,300 for the teaching of them. During the same season 57 societies or musical organizations were assisted by the MACQ, the highest subsidies going to the *Quebec SO ($572,400), the *MSO ($486,600), and the Quebec Youth Orchestra ($398,500). The subsidies were distributed across Quebec's nine administrative regions to such diverse organizations as the *JMC ($95,000), the *CMCentre ($58,900), the SMCQ ($41,200), the *Granby Song Festival ($78,000), and the Assn des violoneux ($15,000). The MACQ also allocated $645,820 for private instruction in music. These funds were distributed among 11 music schools, 2 preparatory schools, and 9 music camps. Furthermore, it has contributed to capital investment in buildings at the *JMC Orford Art Centre and the Asbestos Music Camp. The MACQ has provided assistance to performers, composers, and scholars and has subsidized periods of study in other countries. It instituted 'Aspects du Québec,' a multidisciplinary program intended to assist projects reflecting regional culture. Bursaries to assist artists and encourage creativity are allocated at the recommendation of specialized selection committees.

PUBLICATIONS

Lasalle-Leduc, Annette. *La Vie musicale au Canada français* (1964)

Vie musicale, periodical (1965–71)

Culture vivante, quarterly periodical (1966–73)

Cormier, Normand, et al. *La Chanson au Québec 1965–1975* (1975)

Guide de spectacle et du disque (1978)

L'Industrie de la musique Québec 1980, 3 vols (1980): I *Titres et fonctions*; II *Répertoire*; III *Fournisseurs*

BIBLIOGRAPHY

Annual reports of the MACQ, beginning 1961–2

L'Allier, Jean-Paul. *Pour l'évolution de la politique culturelle* (Quebec 1976)

GP

Minute Opera / Opéra Minute. A chamber opera company founded in Montreal in 1949 by Francis *Coleman (music director), Noël Gauvin (director), Jean-Paul *Jeannotte (adviser), and Gilles *Potvin (administrator). Set up as a co-operative, the troupe presented 11 works in four seasons (1949–53) in a total of 31 performances. Its inaugural program at the Théâtre des Compagnons in 1949 consisted of three works: Mozart's *Bastien et Bastienne*, Monteverdi's *Le Combat (Il combattimento di Tancredi e Clorinda)*, and Wolf-Ferrari's *Le Secret de Suzanne*. The second season (spring of 1950) comprised Bach's *Coffee Cantata* under the title *Love in a Coffee Cup*, Pergolesi's *La Serva padrona* and Milhaud's *Le Pauvre Matelot*. The Milhaud was repeated in the fall, along with Menotti's *The Old Maid and the Thief*. In 1952 in the Gesù Church hall the troupe presented the Canadian premieres of Menotti's *The Telephone* and *The Medium*. Its last season (1953) consisted of Offenbach's *Le Mariage aux lanternes* and Weill's *Down in the Valley*. The Bach cantata was presented as part of the radio series 'CBC Wednesday Night' in 1950 and in 1953 CBC TV presented the productions of *The Telephone* and *Down in the Valley*. Some of the operas were given in Quebec City in 1950 and Ste-Adèle, north of Montreal, in 1950, 1952, and 1953.

The conductors were successively Francis Coleman, Jean-Marie *Beaudet, and Michel *Perrault. In addition to Gauvin, the stage directors were William Butler, Allen Waine, and Guy Hoffmann. Pierre *Beaudet and Jeanne *Landry were among the pianists who served as accompanists. The high quality of both staging and performance was praised by Thomas *Archer, for whom the performance of *The Telephone* and *The Medium* was 'an extraordinary evening of theatre' (*Gazette*, 29 Feb 1952), and by Gilles Marcotte, who termed *Le Pauvre Matelot* 'both a dramatic and a musical success' (*Le Devoir*, 2 Jun 1950). Because young professional singers were increasingly in demand by TV, the company disbanded in the summer of 1953.

Among the singers who participated were Adeeb Assaly, Michèle Bonhomme, Claire Duchesneau, Marie-José Forgues, Yoland *Guérard, Jean-Pierre *Hurteau, Jean-Paul Jeannotte, Simone Lamarche, Andrée Lescot, Thérèse *Laporte, Fernand *Martel, Colette Merola, Alan *Mills, Gisèle Phaneuf, Guy Piché, Giselle Poitras, David Rochette, Joseph *Rouleau, and Irene *Salemka.

BIBLIOGRAPHY

Bosco, Monique. 'Opéra Minute,' *Revue moderne*, Mar 1953

GP

Miramichi Folk Song Festival. Founded in 1958 by Louise *Manny and held annually at Newcastle, NB, for three evenings in June at the Town Hall. It has provided a platform for traditional folksingers, story-tellers, and instrumentalists from the area (eg, Frank and Ray Estay, Marie *Hare, and Wilmot MacDonald) and from other parts of Canada and the USA. Only amateurs have been eligible to perform. So great has been the demand to appear that after a few years each performer was allowed to present only one or two items. The festival has served to encourage genuine folk artists to maintain and expand their repertoires. It has contributed thus to the preservation of the folk music tradition and has provided scholars with the opportunity to hear and analyse folk material in its purest form. The festival was directed by Manny until 1969 when it was taken over by Maisy Mitchell, herself a trilingual (English, French, and Arabic) folksinger.

DISCOGRAPHY

Folk Songs of the Miramichi. 1959. Folk 4053

BIBLIOGRAPHY

Ives, Edward D. 'The first Miramichi folksong festival,' *Northeast Folklore*, vol 1, 1958

Scott, John Anthony. 'Miramichi – the sound of tradition,' *Sing Out!*, 15, Jul 1965

Folster, David. 'Pioneer echoes on a river of change,' *Maclean's*, 3 Sep 1979

MM

MIRO, Henri (Enrique). Composer, conductor, arranger, pianist, critic, b Tarrega, Spain, 13 Nov 1879, d Montreal 19 Jul 1950. He studied music at the monastery of Montserrat in Catalonia with Padre Domingo de Guzman and worked in 1895 with Bienvenido Socias at the Barcelona Cons. He went to France in 1898 as leader of an opera troupe and arrived in Montreal in 1902. Two years later his *Messe solennelle* was premiered at the *Monument national. During the next 40 years he was active as composer, conductor, arranger, pianist, and teacher. Lucio *Agostini, Fleurette *Beauchamp, and Rafael *Masella were among his pupils. He was music director 1916–21 of the *Berliner Gramophone Co and later of the *Compo record company. *Le Passe-Temps* (8 May 1915) reported a single Montreal performance of Miro's opera *A Million Dollar Girl*. His operetta *Le Roman de Suzon*, which had been performed in 1914 at the Princess Theatre, was revived in November 1925 by the *Société canadienne d'opérette at the Monument national and in September 1926 in Sherbrooke, Que. He conducted his cantata **Vox populi* 24 Jun 1929 at the Stadium in Montreal and the premiere of his *Symphonie canadienne* 27 Oct 1931. On the CNR's radio station in 1930–1 he conducted a series devoted to operetta and opera, which included some of his own works. In 1936 Miro entered the first competition for composers organized by the SCSM and won the Prix Jean-*Lallemand for *Scènes mauresques*; the work was premiered 3 Apr 1936 at *Plateau Hall under the direction of Wilfrid *Pelletier. A second operetta, *Lolita* (with libretto by Armand Robi), was presented 9 Jan 1944 on the CBC. Miro also composed symphonic suites – including *Luxor*, which was published by the *Édition Belgo-Canadienne – two cello concertos, some pieces for violin, and a considerable number of songs, chansons, and ballads for solo voice and for choir. He was not only an operetta and concert conductor but also a pioneer among radio conductors. His series of CBC programs devoted to Spanish music, 'Sevilliana' and 'Mexicana,' were extremely popular. Several of his works were published in *La Lyre*, to which he also contributed articles and reviews. He conducted for recordings on the HMV, Apex, and Starr labels, and the titles of these are listed in *Roll Back the Years*. He was a member of CAPAC. Miro Avenue, Montreal, was named in his honour in 1962.

WRITINGS

'Instrumentation,' *La Lyre*, 7 instalments, vol 1, Nov, Dec 1922, Feb–Jun 1923

'Cours d'harmonie de "La Lyre",' ibid, 16 instalments, vol 3 (4 articles in 1925, 10 articles in 1926), vol 4 (Jan, Feb 1927)

'De l'étude de l'harmonie,' ibid, vol 3, Jan 1926

GP

Missionaries in the 17th century. The presence of Roman Catholic priests, lay brothers, and nuns among the first settlers in New France was an important factor in the development of the colony. The prime object was to convert the natives but the missionaries also looked after the spiritual needs of the colonists. The first missionaries, who arrived in Quebec City in 1615, belonged to the Récollet order. They were reinforced by Jesuits in 1625, and after the brief period of British rule 1629–32 (during which most of the priests returned to France) the Jesuits became the leading order. Their work was supported in Quebec by the Ursuline nuns, who were active mainly as teachers and nurses after 1640. In Montreal the Sulpician fathers were established in 1657.

The education of a French priest included the rudiments of music, and the missionaries frequently applied their knowledge of these in their work with the Indians. The following paragraphs represent a sampling of the information about music to be gleaned from the *Jesuit Relations* (which cover the years 1632–73 and are the prime documents of Canada's early music history – see General Bibliography), and from other contemporary accounts. The excerpts are grouped under three headings:

1 Descriptions of Indian music
2 Uses of music in missionary work
3 Church music in the parishes

1 DESCRIPTIONS OF INDIAN MUSIC. Although Jacques Cartier had observed musical activity among the Indians, and Marc Lescarbot had notated the pitches of some songs of the Souriquois (Micmacs) at Port-Royal (Nova Scotia) in the first decade of the 17th century, it was the Récollet historian Father Gabriel Sagard-Théodat (fl 1614–36) who first devoted an entire chapter to music and dance: 'Des dances, chansons et autres cérémonies ridicules de nos Hurons' in his *Histoire du Canada* (Paris 1636, new ed, Paris 1866). For the first time, Canadian Indian music appeared in notation, but, as *Amtmann (*Music in Canada*) has

pointed out, the music is based on Lescarbot's earlier examples and is not Huron music, but Souriquois and Brazilian Indian in origin and European in arrangement. It remained to Father Jacques Marquette and Louis *Jolliet, on their journey of 1673, to notate, for the first time in reasonably accurate form, an Indian song – the first, at least, to have survived, in Bacqueville de la Potherie's *Histoire de l'Amérique Septentrionale* (Paris 1722).

Typical impressions of Indian music are to be found in the diary entries of Father Paul Le Jeune (1591–1664) who served 1632–9 as superior of the Canadian missions. In 1632 he relates that the Iroquois 'began to sing, in order to show that they were not at all afraid of death, however cruel it might be. Their singing seemed to me very disagreeable; the cadence always ended with reiterated aspirations, "oh!oh!oh!ah!ah!ah!hem!hem! hem!" etc. After singing for some time, they were made to dance, one after the other' (*JR*, vol 5, p 27; 1632–3).

In 1634 Le Jeune provided a description of the use of music in the healing of the sick: 'They make use of these songs, of this drum, and of this noise or uproar, in their sicknesses ... I have seen so much foolishness, nonsense, absurdity, noise, and din made by this wretched sorcerer in order to cure himself, that I should become weary in writing and would tire your reverence, if I should try to make you read the tenth part of what has often wearied me almost beyond endurance. Occasionally this man would enter as if in a fury, singing, crying and howling, making his drum rattle with all his might; while the others howled as loudly as he, and made a horrible din with their sticks, striking upon whatever was before them; they made the little children dance, then the girls, then the women; he lowered his head and blew upon his drum, then blew toward the fire; he hissed like a serpent, drew his drum under his chin, shaking and turning it about; he struck the ground with it with all his might, then turned it upon his stomach; he closed his mouth with the back of one hand, and then with the other; you would have said that he wanted to break the drum to pieces, he struck it so hard upon the ground; he shook it, he turned it from one side to the other, and, running around the fire several times, he went out of the cabin, continuing to howl and bellow; he struck a thousand attitudes, and all this was done to cure himself. This is the way they treat their sick' (*JR*, vol 6, p 187,189).

A third quotation from Father Le Jeune is in the form of a generalization: 'The Savages are great singers; they sing, as do most of the nations of the earth, for recreation and for devotion, which, with them, means superstition. The tunes which they sing for pleasure are usually grave and heavy. It seems to me that occasionally they sing something gay, especially the girls, but for the most part, their songs are heavy, so to speak, sombre and unpleasant; they do not know what it is to combine chords to compose a sweet harmony. They use few words in singing, varying the tones, and not the words ... They say that we imitate the warbling of birds in our tunes, which they do not disapprove, as they nearly all take pleasure both in singing and in hearing others sing; and although I told them that I did not understand anything about it, they often invited me to sing some song or prayer' (*JR*, vol 6, p 183,185; 1634).

2 USES OF MUSIC IN MISSIONARY WORK. Possibly the earliest account of the successful use of music in the conversion of Indians comes from the lay priest Jessé Fléché and antedates the arrival of the Récollets and Jesuits. At Port-Royal, where he had arrived in 1610, Fléché taught the Micmacs the simpler parts of the church service. Within a year he was able to baptize the chief Membertou and his tribe. At the ensuing ceremony the converts joined in the singing of the Te Deum (*JR*, vol 2, p 137).

About 1623 Father Gabriel Sagard-Théodat embarked on a canoe voyage up the Ottawa River to visit the Hurons. His report includes the following passage: 'One must also train oneself to good humour and present a cheerful appearance of modest satisfaction, and sing hymns and sometimes spiritual songs, both for one's own comfort and relief from toil and for the edification of the savages, who take peculiar delight in hearing sung the praises of God rather than profane ditties, to which I have sometimes seen them show impugnance. O Jesus, who condemnest evil Christians, singers of dissolute and worldly songs!' (*Histoire du Canada*, transl H.H. Langston, ms p 146–7, U of Toronto Library).

The superior of the missions in New France, Father Le Jeune, repeatedly praised the Indians for accepting the music of the church: 'We finish with a *Pater noster* that I have composed, almost in rhyme, in their language, which I have them sing ... It is a pleasure to hear them sing in the words that they have learned. The women sing also, and come occasionally to listen at the window of my class room' (*JR*, vol 5, p 189; 1633). 'The Nuns sang the Exaudiat, to the delight of our Savages; and it gave our French great joy to hear two Choirs of Virgins praising the Greatness of God in this new world' (*JR*, vol 15, p 229; 1639). 'We have two kinds of Christians in these countries: some have been baptized when very ill, after rather slight instruction but sufficient to allow of their receiving that Sacrament in that condition; the others have been baptized in full health, after having been well instructed in the principal and most necessary articles of our creed. Altogether, they number four hundred and fifty or thereabout, including the Hurons, who constitute by far the majority ... it is a blessing deeply felt to see them attending prayers and the instructions that we give them; present at Mass on Festivals and Sundays, and some on working days; coming to Vespers when they are sung in our Chapel at Sillery, chanting the *Pater* and the *Credo*, the Commandments of God and some Hymns composed in their Language' (*JR*, vol 16, p 59, 61; 1639). '[Mme de La Peltrie] often visits them [the 'Savages'] at other seasons, and takes with her some Indian girls from the Ursuline seminary, who have learned to sing very sweetly, both in their own language and in French' (Preface to *JR*, vol 18, p 5; 1640).

The Jesuit priest François-Joseph Le Mercier (1604–90) expressed his satisfaction with the singing of the converted Hurons: 'The beauty of their voices is exceptionally rare, especially those of the girls, for whom there have been composed, and adapted to the airs of the Church hymns, some canticles in Huron language, which they sing in a charming manner. It is a holy consolation, far from being barbaric, to hear the fields and forests resound so melodiously with the praises of God, in the midst of a country which not long ago one called barbaric' (*JR*, vol 41, p 141; 1653–4; Amtmann transl).

In 1670 Father Louis André (1631–1715) reported from a missionary post on Manitoulin Island (Lake Huron) that he had written some spiritual canticles: 'No sooner had I begun to have these sung in the Chapel, accompanied by a sweet-toned flute ... than they all came in crowds, both adults and children; so that, to avoid confusion, I let only the girls enter the Chapel, while the others remained without, and thus we sang in two choruses, those without responding to those within' (*JR*, vol 55, p 147; 1670).

Two years later a report from the mission of Notre-Dame de Foye, near Quebec, confirms once again the success of music as a handmaid of missionary work: 'The example of the French pupils – who every night, on leaving school, go to sing at benediction in the chapel of Notre-Dame de Foye – has had the good effect that the little savages, in order to imitate them, have learned to sing beautiful hymns in their own language; and they sing them even in their houses, in the streets, in the fields, and wherever they happen to be. Thus these little creatures, ignoring all the profane songs of their ancestors, have on their lips only the spiritual motets that the Father teaches them. The result is, that in a short time they learn with pleasure the mysteries of our faith, and all their prayers, which they are made to sing to various airs, changing the words and the music as is done in the church, on the return of the yearly festivals' (*JR*, vol 57, p 61, 63; 1672 or 1673).

In 1676 Father Jean Enjalran reported about the Indians from the Huron seminary west of Quebec: 'One is charmed to hear the various choirs, which the men and women form in order to sing during mass and at vespers. The nuns of France do not sing more agreeably than some savage women here; and, as a class, all the savages have much aptitude and inclination for singing the hymns of the church, which have been rendered into their language' (*JR*, vol 60, p 145; 1676).

Father François Vachon de Belmont (1645–1732), a Montreal Sulpician, translated the Latin texts of ritual music into Iroquois. He taught the natives how to sing these, accompanying the chants on his lute. (See *DCB*, vol 2, and Amtmann *Music in Canada*.)

3 CHURCH MUSIC IN THE PARISHES. The *Jesuit Relations* and other 17th-century documents contain many references to the priests' chanting of the *Te Deum*, the *Salve Regina*, or the *Stabat Mater* and their celebrating the *Mass*. Among these men was Jean Le Sueur (also known as Abbé Saint-Sauveur, ca 1598–1668) who had arrived in Quebec in 1634 and was the first secular priest on the shores of the St Lawrence. As he had 'a beautiful baritone voice and a perfect acquaintance with plainsong he offered his services to help with the town ceremonies; this, one invited him frequently to do' (J.B.A. Allaire, *Dictionnaire biographique du clergé canadien-français*, vol 6, Montreal 1934). To quote some contemporary evidence: 'Monsieur de St. Sauveur excellently sustained the music. At the temporary altars we tried to have two boys sing some clauses of the litany of the name of Jesus – 5 or 6; but Monsieur the prior had to aid them' (*JR*, vol 28, p 197; 1645 or 1646). Another capable singer was Father Jean de Quen (1603–59), the founder of the Saguenay missions and a teacher at Quebec, Sillery, and Tadoussac.

The first native-born Canadians to be ordained as priests, Germain Morin and Charles-Amador *Martin, participated in the church service as musicians. René Chartier (in Canada 1643–7) and Claude Dablon (1618 or 1619–1697) are two other priests whose chanting is documented in the *Jesuit Relations*. Other priests occupied the office of *grand chantre in Quebec, supervising the ceremonial and musical aspects of divine service.

It is difficult to identify with certainty those priests who composed music since the word 'composed,' as it is found in contemporary records, may apply also to selecting the music (ie, to composing the programs of music to be used). The priests who may be considered in this context include René *Ménard (1605–61), Charles-Amador Martin, Louis André (1631–1715), and Jean de

Brébeuf (1593–1649), who has been associated by tradition with the origin of the Huron carol *'Jesous Ahatonhia.'

See also Roman Catholic church music. HK

MITCHELL, Gifford (Jerome). Educator, organist, choir director, b Cobden, Renfrew County, Ont, 29 Apr 1913; BA (McGill) 1934, B MUS (Toronto) 1948. He taught history and languages in Westmount, Que, after graduating from *McGill U. During World War II he spent five years in the RCAF. After studies in music education at the *U of Toronto he served as music supervisor 1948–51 for the Westmount Protestant School Board and 1951–69 for the Protestant School Board of Greater Montreal.

During 21 years in Montreal he conducted the *Montreal Elgar Choir 1951–69, was active in church music, taught 1955–69 at McGill U, and directed the McGill Choral Society. He was president 1960–2 and executive director 1962–6 of the *CMEA. He joined the staff of Sheridan College in Oakville, Ont, in 1969 and there conducted the Whiteoaks Choral Society until 1978.

Mitchell was a collaborator on the three-volume *Songs of Praise for Schools* (Toronto 1956, 1957, and 1958); was co-author with W. Earle *Terry of the teaching text *Music 7* and, with Terry and G.H. Wood, of *Music 8*; and was a contributor to the *Hymn Book of the Anglican Church of Canada and the United Church of Canada* (Toronto 1971). He appears as choir director on three recordings: *National Anthems*, with the Elgar Choir (RCA 56-3287, 1958), *Sing at Christmas* (International IRCM-1204, 1959), and *Spring Song* (Laurentian CTM 2-6003, 1960, 1961) with the McGill Choral Society. (WL)

MITCHELL, Joni (Roberta Joan) (b Anderson). Singer-songwriter, guitarist, pianist, b Fort Macleod, near Lethbridge, Alta, 7 Nov 1943. She was raised in Saskatoon and developed childhood interests in painting, poetry, and music, all of which found expression in her later career. She studied piano briefly as a child, bought a baritone ukulele while in high school, and turned to the guitar in the early 1960s. She studied for a year at the Alberta College of Art in Calgary and sang at a local coffeehouse, the Depression. She moved to Toronto, writing her first songs ('Day by Day,' 'Carnival in Kenora,' 'Play Little David Play' for the guitarist David Rea – and others) and performing in such Yorkville coffeehouses as the Penny Farthing.

Mitchell made her first significant appearance at the *Mariposa Folk Festival in 1965. Of her performance there in 1966, Arthur Zelden wrote 'Miss Mitchell plays guitar tolerably; her voice is an interesting, although not unusual version of Joan Baez's. The songs that she writes and delivers so feelingly, though, are lovely, poetic, even Canadian in their tone' (*Toronto Daily Star*, 6 Aug 1966).

During her marriage 1965–6 to the US folksinger Chuck Mitchell, she lived in Detroit and performed in the northern USA and in Ontario. At this time the US folksinger Tom Rush began singing her songs 'Urge for Going' and 'The Circle Game.' Other artists, including Judy Collins, Ian and Sylvia (*Tyson), and Buffy *Sainte-Marie, also introduced her songs to new audiences. Mitchell moved in 1966 to New York – appearing in Greenwich Village coffeehouses – and settled in 1968 in Los Angeles. In 1971 she had a home built at Half Moon Bay, north of Vancouver, thereafter dividing her time between the USA and Canada.

Mitchell's first two LPs, and the song *'Both Sides Now' as recorded by Collins and others, brought her international fame. With the LP

Joni Mitchell

Clouds she won the 1969 Grammy Award for best folk performance. In 1969 she appeared at the Miami Pop, Newport Folk, Mariposa Folk, and Stratford festivals and toured North America opening concerts for the group Crosby, Stills & Nash. After two years of little activity she resumed her performing career at a less hectic pace. In the period 1970–8, for example, she performed in Toronto at Mariposa in 1970, at *Massey Hall in 1972 and 1974 as part of North American tours which included other Canadian centres, and at *Maple Leaf Gardens in 1975 as a member of Bob Dylan's Rolling Thunder Revue. She has performed in Great Britain (appearing in 1970 at the Isle of Wight pop festival and elsewhere), where readers of the trade paper *Melody Maker* named her best female singer several years in a row. In Canada she received a *Juno Award as best female vocalist of 1975.

Mitchell's LPs have been more successful, commercially, than her singles, all eventually receiving certification for sales of more than a million dollars. Nevertheless, some of her singles (all of her own songs) have been popular: 'Big Yellow Taxi' (1970, re-released in a concert version in 1975), 'Carey' (1971), 'You Turn Me On, I'm a Radio' (1972), 'Help Me' (1974), and 'Free Man in Paris' (1975). Other songs of note from her LPs include 'Chelsea Morning,' 'Woodstock' (a hit in 1970 as recorded by Crosby, Stills, Nash & Young), 'Cactus Tree,' and 'All I Want.' Among other artists who have recorded her songs are Bing Crosby, Bob Dylan, Ian Matthews, Sergio Mendes and Brasil '66, and Frank Sinatra.

Despite the autobiographical nature of Mitchell's songs (many on the subject of love, focusing considerable attention on her personal life), the images in which they are expressed attain universality; the response of many of her listeners is one of identification. Her lyrics have been published on the covers of her LPs (some of which she designed or painted herself) and have appeared in anthologies of poetry. Her songs have been published by Siquomb Music, Crazy Crow Music, or Joni Mitchell Publishing Co. Two volumes of the *Joni Mitchell Songbook* for the periods 1966–70 and 1970–5 were issued by Warner Brothers in 1970 and 1975. Individual folios have been issued in conjunction with several of her LPs.

From the relative simplicity of her early folk-based work, Mitchell's music has grown increasingly complex. She has employed, for example, several unusual guitar tunings. (At a 1969 concert at Carnegie Hall she accompanied herself at the piano.) With the LP *Court and Spark* she introduced a distinct jazz flavour into her music by using the saxophonist-flutist Tom Scott and the LA Express as her accompanists. The influence of jazz increased, as evident in the ensuing LPs with the participation of members of the LA Express, the (Jazz) Crusaders, and Weather Report (particularly the bass guitarist Jaco Pastorius), culminating in *Mingus*, a collaboration with Charles Mingus, just before the bassist's death, in which she wrote lyrics to several of his compositions.

Of Mitchell's lyrics on the earlier *Heijira*, Doug Fetherling wrote in *Saturday Night*: 'She fits them into melodic lines that test her great skill at phrasing ... she bunches, stretches, and condenses phrases in unusual ways, somewhat like a poet whose breath control is as much a part of his writing as the images on the page ... It is as though she were using her voice as another instrument; in fact she is creating an almost contrapuntal relationship between melody line and lyric.' Also of *Heijira*, Perry Meisel observed in the *Village Voice* (24 Jan 1977): 'Mitchell's language also creates the phonemic density and variation that only singers like Ella Fitzgerald and Sarah Vaughan can impart to the relatively simple verbal mannerisms of most pop tunes as they are written.'

DISCOGRAPHY

Song to a Seagull. (1968). Rep RS-6293
Clouds. (1969). Rep RS-6341
Ladies of the Canyon. (1970). Rep RS-6376
Blue. (1971). Rep MS-2038
For the Roses. 1972. Asylum SD 5057
Court and Spark. (1974). Asylum 7ES 1001
Miles of Aisles. 1974. 2-Asylum AB 202
The Hissing of Summer Lawns. 1975. Asylum 7ES 1051
Heijira. 1976. Asylum 7ES 1087
Don Juan's Reckless Daughter. 1977. 2-Asylum BB-101
Mingus. (1979). Asylum X5E-505
Shadows and Light. 1979. Asylum 2XBB-704

BIBLIOGRAPHY

Nagle, Patrick. '... ssshhhhhh ... listen, listen to Joni,' *Weekend Magazine*, 11 Jan 1969
Malka. 'Face to face,' *Maclean's*, Jun 1974
DeVoss, David. 'Rock 'n' roll's leading lady,' *Time*, 16 Dec 1974
Fleischer, Leonore. *Joni Mitchell* (New York 1976)
Fetherling, Doug. 'Joni as the older woman,' *SatN*, Mar 1977
Scanlon, Kevin. 'Joni Mitchell's back in town,' *Toronto Star*, 2 Dec 1980 MM

MITCHELL (Mitchel), **Louis**. Organ builder, b Montreal 1823?, d there 6 May 1902. Little is known of his early training, except that his desire to become an organ builder originated during his stay at the music school run by Father Charles-Joseph *Ducharme at the Collège de Blainville in Ste-Thérèse, Que. Apprenticed 1855–60 to Samuel Russell *Warren – later one of his principal competitors – he opened his own workshop in 1861 in partnership with Charles Forté, who also had trained under Warren and who was to remain with Mitchell until ca 1865. The name of his father, Samuel Mitchell, also appears in articles dealing with organs produced by the firm. Louis Mitchell began building instruments in 1861, and the first three were installed at the Church of Beloeil, the Pied-du-Courant in Montreal, and St-Joseph-de-Bytown Church in Ottawa. Paul *Letondal, in *La Minerve*, 24 Sep 1861, described the Ottawa instrument as 'a real success in both workmanship and effect.'

In the ensuing years Mitchell organs were installed in Ste-Scholastique, Que, at the Hôtel-Dieu in Montreal, and in Lanoraie, Que: instruments 'with no more than fifteen stops ... solid, well-balanced' (*Coup d'oeil*). The excellent reception accorded his first products earned Mitchell in 1864 the contract for the restoration of the great organ of the Basilica in Quebec City. He transformed the 16-stop Elliott organ of 1802 into a handsome 32-stop instrument. From then on his business prospered, as attested by the organ he built in 1870 for the Jesuit Fathers in Chicago, an instrument immediately acknowledged as one of the foremost in North America in both size (63 stops) and quality; and by the organ in St-Boniface Cathedral in Manitoba in 1875.

At first Mitchell imported his pipes from France, but after 1874 he made them himself with the help of a European foreman; he avoided the use of zinc, preferring an alloy of tin and lead which ensured an excellent sound quality. He occasionally used stops of pure tin, imported from the USA. *Le Canada musical* reveals that in 1879 his workshop employed six carpenters, three metalworkers, and two tuners.

Some Mitchell organs were installed in churches in towns outside Quebec, eg, Tignish, PEI (1882, the organ identified as Op 129), Brockville, Ont, and Guelph, Ont. The majority, however, were installed within the province: in St-Jacques Church, Montreal, in 1867; in the Gesù Church, Montreal (though supplanted by a *Casavant in 1901); in the convent of the Dames du Sacré-Coeur, Sault-au-Récollet, in 1877; in St-Patrice Church, Quebec City; in Notre-Dame Church, Lévis (near Quebec City) and in the churches of many Quebec towns: St-Nicholas in 1883, St-Pierre-de-Sorel in 1884, St-Croix-de-Lotbinière in 1887 (rebuilt by Casavant after 1910), L'Ancienne Lorette, St-Augustin-de-Portneuf, St-Janvier, St-Romuald, St-Zotique, Terrebonne, St-André-de-Kamouraska, St-Michel-de-Vaudreuille, St-Roch-sur-Richelieu, and St-Norbert.

Even in 1980 the organs at St-André, St-Michel (1871), St-Roch, and St-Norbert, and the very fine 1870 instrument at Notre-Dame-de-Lévis – in all of which the subsequent adaptations for the most part have respected the original pipe work – remained an eloquent tribute to the workmanship and artistic sense of Louis Mitchell. Their solid construction, the quality of the materials, the overall sense of proportion, the beautiful timbres (particularly the reed-stops), and the graceful lines of the organ-chest (mostly in the Gothic style) explain the high level of popularity enjoyed by this organ manufacturer until the business ceased in 1893.

According to the organist Christopher *Jackson, certain elements of Mitchell's work recall that of the French organ builder Calinet, who was active at the beginning of the 19th century. Nothing indicates that Mitchell ever visited France, but according to Arthur *Laurendeau (*L'Action nationale*, Jun 1950) he did study his craft in London, at an undetermined date.

BIBLIOGRAPHY

'Visite à la Fabrique Nationale d'Orgues de M. Louis Mitchell,' *Canada musical*, vol 2, 1 Feb 1876

'L' orgue de la chapelle du couvent des Dames du Sacré-Coeur, du Sault-au-Récollet,' ibid, vol 4, 1 Sep 1877

'Manufacture d'orgues canadienne-française de M. Louis Mitchell,' ibid, vol 6, 1 May 1879

(AP)

MITTELMANN, Norman. Baritone, b Winnipeg 25 May 1932. He studied with Doris Mills *Lewis in Winnipeg, with Richard Bonelli, Martial Singher, and Vladimir Sokoloff at the Curtis Institute, and with Lotte Lehmann at the Academy of the West in Santa Barbara, Cal. He was coached in Italian opera by Enzo Mascherini.

Mittelmann's first operatic roles were in Lehmann's productions of *The Marriage of Figaro* and *Ariadne auf Naxos*. In 1956 he appeared in the US premiere of Milhaud's *David*. He made his Canadian operatic debut with the *COC in 1958, as Marcello in *La Bohème*, and later sang in Europe with companies in Essen and Düsseldorf, joining the

Norman Mittelmann

Deutsche Oper am Rhein ca 1959. He made his *Metropolitan Opera debut 28 Oct 1961 as the Herald in *Lohengrin*. Returning to Europe he appeared with the Berlin Deutsche Oper, the Munich Staatsoper, the Vienna Staatsoper, and companies in Hamburg and Karlsruhe. In 1965 he joined the Zürich Opera and made his debut with the Royal Opera, Covent Garden, as Germont in *La Traviata*. In 1966 he sang Ruprecht in Prokofiev's *Angel of Fire* with the Chicago Lyric Opera.

In 1967 Mittelmann returned to Canada to sing the four-part role of Lindorf, Coppelius, Dappertutto, and Dr Miracle in a COC production of *The Tales of Hoffmann* in Toronto and at *Expo 67. The critic of the Toronto *Telegram* wrote of this quadruple portrayal (21 Sep 1967): 'Dr. Miracle has his changes rung with superb authority by the baritone Norman Mittelmann ... The portrayal seemed tailored not only to the requirements of the role but also to the propensities of Mittelmann. It is no mean feat bringing an abstract and an ego into such close alignment. Mittelmann of course is first-rate material ... a splendid singer, a decent actor and an experienced operatic performer.'

In 1970 at the Hamburg Staatsoper Mittelmann was Daniel in the premiere of Willy Burkhard's *Ein Stern geht auf aus Jaakob*. He sang with the San Francisco Opera in 1973 and 1974, appeared in Chicago as Shaklovity in Mussorgsky's *Khovantchina* in 1976, and was Amonasro in *Aida* at the San Diego Opera's Verdi Festival in 1978. He has performed with companies in Buenos Aires, Florence, Frankfurt, Marseilles, Paris, and Palermo. Mittelmann sang in opera in his native Winnipeg for the first time in April 1979, as the Count di Luna in the *Manitoba Opera production of *Il Trovatore*. He appeared there later that year as Germont in *La Traviata* and also that season sang the title role in *Rigoletto* with the *Edmonton Opera.

Among the other roles Mittelmann has sung are Achilles in Schoeck's *Penthesilea*, Don Carlos di Vargas in *La Forza del Destino*, Escamillo in *Carmen*, Gerard in *Andrea Chenier*, Gunther in *Götterdämmerung*, Iago in *Otello*, Kurwenal in *Tristan und Isolde*, Jokanaan in *Salome*, Mandryka in *Arabella*, Mephistopheles in both Berlioz' *The Damnation of Faust* and Gounod's *Faust*, Ramiro in *L'Heure espagnole*, Scarpia in *Tosca*, Silvio in *I Pagliacci*, Wolfram in *Tannhäuser*, and the title roles in *Eugene Onegin*, *Falstaff*, *Prince Igor*, and *Simon Boccanegra*. Mittelmann also has appeared in recital and as soloist with orchestra. In 1980 he maintained residences in Zürich and in Escondido, Cal. (JBk, FH)

MIVILLE-DESCHÊNES, Monique. Singer-songwriter, writer, actress, b St-Jean-Port-Joli, Que, 1940. She was discovered through the series of TV competitions 'St-Georges Côté et ses amateurs' in Quebec City, which she won twice in 1956; of special note was her performance of Félix *Leclerc's 'Notre Sentier.' The following year she studied Quebec folk music with Raoul *Roy and began appearing in boîtes à chansons in Quebec. In 1961 her first single, 'Salut la terre,' became the theme song of the semaine des Jeunes ruraux. In 1961–2 she took part in the program 'Au pays de Neuve-France' on CBC TV. Her first LP (Sel SSP 24.092) was issued the next year. In 1964 she gave a recital at *Plateau Hall and was the opening performer for a concert by Félix Leclerc at the National Theatre. She took part in a tour of Leclerc's play *Le Petit Bonheur*, presented in 1964 in Quebec and the following year at the Théâtre des Trois-Baudets in Paris, where she also performed as a singer. In 1965 she made a second LP (Sel SSP 24.127). On 15 Nov 1966 she represented Quebec in Brussels at the gala of the Communauté des programmes radiophoniques de langue française. After a recital during Quebec City's 1968 Summer Festival, Jacqueline Mondy drew attention to the 'unaffectedness of this performer, who wastes no time on empty introductions' as well as to the 'simplicity of the songs in which everyday words take on poetic meaning' (*Journal de Québec*, 8 Jul 1968). For the Gamma label she made two LPs in 1969, one of her own songs (GS 134) and the other, *Jé sous AHATONNIA* (GS 135), of Christmas songs; her LP *Battus des vents* (Gamma GS 195) was released in 1975.

With the actors Yves Massicotte and Louis de Santis she formed in 1965 a troupe called Les Gesteux, for which she wrote several plays, including *La Guerre des saisons* in 1968 and *Le Temps et les sons* and *Les Oiseaux de Bélonie* in 1969. The troupe made tours for the *JMC in 1968–9, 1969–70, and 1970–1, and with a subsidy from the *MACQ in 1971–2 it toured Ontario, Quebec, and New Brunswick with her play *Enfin les poètes sont à vendre*. In April 1971 she performed at Le *Patriote. Her dramatic piece *Une croix de chemin* was presented 1973 and 1974 in the gardens of St Joseph's Oratory in Montreal.

Monique Miville-Deschênes, who accompanies herself on the guitar, has always displayed restraint as well as a strong attachment to her origins. Her early writing, which is descriptive and imbued with rustic poetry, evoked the charm of the country life and the seascapes of her region. Her concern for people is found in more recent songs: 'Si mon père,' 'Dépêchons-nous d'être heureux,' 'Soldat de velours,' 'La Chanson du vieux Henri noyé au large d'Anticosti,' and 'L'Enfant de septembre.'

BIBLIOGRAPHY

Massicotte, Yves. 'Monique Miville-Deschênes – a beautiful name, beautiful talent,' *CanComp*, 43, Oct 1969

(CB, ST)

Mixed media (or multi-media) **music**. Music which incorporates one or more additional modes of expression, eg, speech, action, film, light effects, sculpture, dance. The idea of a 'total art work,' promulgated in the music dramas of Wagner, underwent a transmutation in the anti-romantic climate of the 20th century. Stravinsky's *L'Histoire du soldat* and *Oedipus Rex*, with their purposely startling juxtapositions of singing, narration, and mime, dealt in a kind of theatric polyphony remote indeed from the monolithic euphony of a Wagner opera. Their fundamental intention, 'intensification through mixture,' was not very different, though, and in a sense all staged musical pieces, including opera, are mixed media. This article, however, will concentrate on music which incorporates *uncustomary* extra-musical presences, rather than on those ensconced in tradition.

Rooted in the bizarre refreshments of surrealism and dada (1910–20, Breton, Apollinaire, Duchamp, etc) mixed media flowered in theatre, music, film, and the visual arts after World War II. As the trend became a movement, John Cage emerged as the prime musical mover and his 'happenings' influenced both composers and other creative artists.

In Canada, Norman *McLaren carried out experiments with sound film in the late 1940s and early 1950s. McLaren was the first to draw with coloured inks directly on film and on optical sound tracks to create, in effect, a unification of sound and light (*Begone Dull Care*, NFB 1949; and *Short and Suite*, NFB 1959). However, these were cinematic studies, for the most part using fairly simple images and sound sources. Among more sophisticated and musically oriented works, *Mercure's *Structures métalliques, I, II and III* (1961–2) were pioneer essays, mixing electronically manipulated real sounds with the sounds of metal sculptures struck onstage. Other mixtures of media have occurred in *Beckwith's radio collages *Wednesday's Child* (1962) and *Canada Dash – Canada Dot* (1965–7), *Joachim's *Illuminations I and II* (1965 and 1969), *Somers' *Improvisation* (1968), *Charpentier's *Orphée* (1969), *Weinzweig's *Around the Stage in 25 Minutes during which a Number of Instruments Are Struck* (1970), *Schafer's *Patria II* (1972), Joachim's *Mankind* (1972), *Tremblay's *Oralléluiants* (1975), *Cherney's *Tangents I and II* (1975–6), and *Deschênes-Harvey's *Moll, opéra lilliput pour six roches molles* (1976).

These examples employ elements of theatre (in what otherwise would be concert pieces); or mechanically or technologically produced effects; or – in the case of *Mankind* – slides and incense, four synthesizers, and four readers (ordained priests of four established religions), in addition to piano, timpani, and organ. Few of these would be considered hardcore mixed-media works, but they do represent Canadian composers' substantial, if conservative, response to multi-media possibilities.

The foremost and most refractory exponent of mixed media in Canada probably has been Udo *Kasemets who, in Toronto in the early 1960s, devised improvisational works for various combinations of performers (singers, instrumentalists, and/or dancers). Kasemets was the director of a number of concert series, culminating in the Synergetic Theatre at the Isaacs Gallery where happenings of a duration sometimes exceeding 24 hours took place in the mid-1960s. He began lecturing on music and mixed media at the Ontario College of Art in 1970.

Works by some of Canada's younger composers of the 1960s and 1970s incorporated mixed-media techniques, eg, Don *Druick's sound sculpture *Tennessee-Buffalo Run* (1971); John *Fodi's *Musick Bockxd* (1969) for three actors/dancers and seven music boxes; Clifford *Ford's *Living Space* (1973) for two dancers, lights, and 4-track tape; and Michel *Gonneville's *Guide* (1976) for five performers – voice, flute, clarinet, piano, and mime – whose task is the unification of five works of different eras.

By the mid-1970s the financial difficulties of mounting such happenings and the continuing apathy of the public toward them caused a thinning of the ranks of mixed-media proponents. Nevertheless, occasional if not persistent champions survived the decline, eg, R. Murray Schafer, whose *Apocalypsis* – a two-hour costumed dramatic pageant representing the apocalyptic vision of St John the Divine and employing 500 performers (orchestra, choirs, speech choirs, soloists, dancers, sound poets) and film – was performed 28 Nov 1980 in London, Ont, as part of the city's 125th-anniversary celebrations.

BIBLIOGRAPHY

Gregory, Carol. 'When is a happening not a happening?' *Maclean's*, 16 Apr 1966

Austin, Larry, et al, eds. *Source: Music of the Avant-Garde* (Sacramento, Cal, 1967–)

Kasemets, Udo ed. *Canavangard* (Don Mills, Ont, 1968)

Salzman, Eric. 'Mixed Media,' *Dictionary of Contemporary Music*

KW (JB, CF)

MIZERIT, Klaro (Maria). Conductor, composer, b Monfalcone, Italy, 12 Aug 1914, naturalized Canadian 1973; diplomas in violin (Ljubljana Cons, Yugoslavia) 1941, conducting (Ljubljana Academy) 1947, and conducting and composition (Vienna Academy) 1948. He was the founder and first violin of the Slovenian String Quartet and taught at the Ljubljana Academy. He conducted the Dubrovnik Festival Orchestra 1951–8 and the Rhenish Philharmonic Orchestra in Koblenz, Germany, 1958–68 and was a guest conductor of orchestras in other countries. He moved to Halifax in 1968 as music director of the newly formed *Atlantic SO and also that year founded the Atlantic Choir and the Atlantic Chamber Orchestra, serving as conductor of both. Under his baton until 1977, the Atlantic SO premiered works by several Maritime composers and Mizerit's own *Two Maritime Aquarelles* (1970, based on songs in the Helen *Creighton collection) and *Maritime Suite* (1975). He became co-director of the Pierre Monteux Summer School in Hancock, Me, in 1969 and director of the *Maritime Cons of Music in 1977. Mizerit has made recordings with the Rhenish Philharmonic Orchestra (1966, Garnet 40 139) and the Atlantic SO. JSr

MOISSE, Séverin (Joseph). Pianist, composer, teacher, b Chastre or Walhain-Saint-Paul, Belgium, 8 Jun 1895, naturalized Canadian ca 1931, d ca 1965. He received his training at the Royal Cons of Brussels from Arthur de Greef and Joseph Jongen. After teaching in Charleroi, Gembloux, Brussels, and Thuin and giving numerous concerts in Europe, he moved in 1926 to Montreal. He was orchestral pianist 1930–41 for the *Montreal Orchestra and soloist with the orchestra 25 Feb 1934 in Liszt's *Concerto No. 1*. He taught piano at the *McGill Cons, the *CMM, and the *CMQ and was heard often on radio, particularly as the pianist 1941–5 for CBC's 'Les *Joyeux Troubadours.' His Canadian pupils included Maurice *Dela, Marcel *Laurencelle, and George *Little. He returned to Belgium ca 1951. Several of his works for piano – *Variations on a Theme of Paganini, Étude in C Minor*, and *Six Petites Études symétriques* – and his *Consolation* for voice, as well as some songs, have been published by Le Parnasse musical. The *Menuet dans le style ancien* from his *Sonata in C Minor* for violin and piano (dedicated to Lucien *Martin) appeared in *Le *Passe-Temps* (Feb 1945), and his *Variations sur un thème huron* for piano was published by BMI Canada (1955). GP

MOLENAAR, Piet. Violin-maker, b Indonesia, of Dutch parents, 2 Aug 1903, naturalized Canadian 1957. He was educated in Holland and his prime interest was chemistry, but he also studied violin in The Hague and, ca 1919, with Alfred Indig. He began making violins in 1916 but it was not until 1926 that he entered into a professional apprenticeship with Joseph Vedral of The Hague. He undertook further studies in Paris in 1936 and set himself up as a dealer, luthier, and repairman in Groningen, Holland, the following year. At about that time he began a prolonged study of the techniques and varnishes of the Cremona masters. He moved to Amsterdam in 1946 and emigrated to Canada in 1951, setting up shop in Toronto. His researches, which he continued, persuaded him that Stradivari and Guarneri deliberately gave their instruments a chipped-varnish finish to make them look old. Molenaar has duplicated this finish on his own instruments and in 1979 was preparing a book on Italian varnishes. He has built some 300 violins and about a dozen violas and cellos, all of European maple and spruce and finished with his own colours and varnishes. In 1948 the cellist Paul Tortelier wrote commending him for a cello he had made for Regina Wijnalda, a chamber music partner of Dame Myra Hess. The Indig Quartet, led by the aforementioned Alfred Indig (a member of the Budapest Quartet prior to 1923), performed on a set of instruments made by Molenaar. Molenaar retired in 1976 but continued to build one or two instruments a year.

MOLLET, Pierre. Baritone, teacher, administrator, choir conductor, b Neuchâtel, Switzerland, 23 Mar 1920, naturalized Canadian 1974; premier prix performance (Lausanne Cons) 1946. While directing amateur choirs he studied voice at the Lausanne Cons with Charles Panzéra and obtained a second prize at the 1946 Geneva International Competition for Musical Performers. He moved to Paris in 1947, taking courses in interpretation with Nadia Boulanger, with whom he participated in many concerts. Between 1948 and 1962 he made extensive tours in France and North Africa for the JM in addition to being soloist with Parisian orchestras. He took part in several festivals, including those of Strasbourg and Aix-en-Provence, and made his debut in 1952 at the Opéra-Comique in the role of Pelléas (*Pelléas et Mélisande*). He recorded the role for London the same year under the direction of Ernest Ansermet (LON LLA-11) and later sang the role almost 100 times in major cities of Europe and South America.

Mollet came to Canada in 1967 as a jury member at the *JMC national competition and as soloist with the Orchestre de la Suisse romande at the World Festival of *Expo 67. He settled in Montreal, teaching 1968–78 at the *CMM. Christiane Guénette, Gilbert Patenaude, and Cassandra Robertson were among his pupils. He also taught at the *JMC Orford Art Centre 1967, 1968, and 1974, gave many recitals in Quebec devoted to the Lied and to French art song, and performed on the CBC. In 1975 he became one of the organizers of the *PDA Concerts Midi. The Quebec Ministry of Education asked him in 1978 to devise a plan for stimulating musical endeavours in primary schools in the Montreal area.

In addition to *Pelléas et Mélisande*, Mollet recorded Gluck's *Iphigénie en Tauride* (Oreste) in Europe for Pathé-Marconi. For Decca he recorded *Roméo et Juliette* (Mercutio), Ravel's *L'Enfant et les sortilèges* (the Clock, the Cat), Honegger's oratorio *Le Roi David* (under the composer's direction), Frank Martin's *In terra pax* and *Golgotha*, Berlioz' *The Damnation of Faust* (Brander), and songs by Fauré and Debussy.

In 1979 Mollet married the pianist Suzanne Blondin (b Montreal 16 Mar 1950; premier prix CMM 1970), who studied at the CMM with Germaine *Malépart and Yvonne *Hubert and 1970–3 at the Juilliard School with Sascha Gorodnitzky. Blondin was a concerto soloist in 1969 and 1977 with the *MSO and in 1974 with the *Quebec SO. She has made several tours as Pierre Mollet's accompanist and performed as a soloist on the CBC as well as on radio in Lausanne and Geneva.

WRITINGS

'Du chant,' *VM*, 19, Mar 1971

Musique d'été, photographs by Mia and Klaus (Montreal 1976)

BIBLIOGRAPHY

'Ansermet et Honegger ont admiré le baryton Pierre Mollet,' *Musique périodique*, vol 1, Jan–Feb 1977 GP

Molson Prize. Award of $20,000 created to recognize and encourage outstanding contributors to the arts, humanities, social sciences, or national unity. Established in 1963 and administered by the *Canada Council, it is financed by the interest on a $900,000 gift to the Canada Council from the Molson Foundation. Of some 43 awards given by 1980, 5 had gone to musicians: Glenn *Gould (1968), Maureen *Forrester (1971), Jon *Vickers (1975), the members of the *Orford Quartet (1975), and Lois *Marshall (1980). The film maker Norman *McLaren was a recipient in 1971. The painter-musician Michael *Snow received the prize in 1979 for his work in the visual arts.

MOLT, Theodore Frederic (b Johann Friedrich). Teacher, writer, organist, b Gschwend, near Stuttgart, 13 Feb 1795, d Burlington, Vt, 16 or 19 Nov 1856. The son of a Lutheran organist, he received his first music lessons from his father and an elder brother. Soon after entering university he became a soldier in Napoleon's army and was accountant and assistant paymaster of his regiment. 'They reached Waterloo on the day of the battle [18 Jun 1815], too late to participate in the strife, but not too late to survey that fatal field, strown [sic] with the dead and dying – a scene which ever after lived in vivid remembrance in his mind' (Converse). After leaving the army he studied music and in 1823 he went to Quebec; possibly he had been in Philadelphia before going to Canada since a song, 'Know'st Thou the Land,' and his *Post Horn Waltz with Variations* (piano) were published there.

In Quebec Molt established himself as a music teacher, in 1823 married Henriette, a daughter of F.H. *Glackemeyer, and in 1824 formed a Juvenile Harmonic Society. However, in June 1825 he had his household goods and musical instruments auctioned and left for Europe to further his education. When he returned a year later he announced that he had studied with Beethoven, Czerny (Vienna), and Moscheles (London). Converse adds the name of Schubert.

Only the visit to Beethoven is documented in musical literature. Introducing himself in writing to the deaf composer, he said 'I am a music teacher in Quebec in North America. Your works have delighted me so often that I consider it my duty to pay you my personal gratitude.' A few days later he wrote a letter to Beethoven, including a blank sheet on which he asked the composer to write 'from his great soul' a souvenir 'which shall remain for me in a distance of nearly 3000 hours (whither I am travelling again from here) an eternally precious document' (Thayer, German edn only, ed Riemann, Leipzig 1923; transl H. Kallmann).

Beethoven complied and on 16 Dec 1825 (Beethoven's 55th birthday) presented to Molt the canon 'Freu Dich des Lebens' (works without opus no., Kinsky 195). The manuscript, once in the possession of one of Molt's sons, was acquired in 1933 by the Berlin antiquarian J.A. Stargardt. Some 30 years later it turned up at a New York autograph auction, and in 1966 the Montreal bibliophile Lawrence Lande (see Lande Collections) acquired the manuscript from the purchaser. The *NL of C bought it in 1979. (The canon forms the basis of Alexander *Brott's *Paraphrase in Polyphony*, 1967.)

The canon written for Molt by Beethoven

Molt taught piano, organ, violin, voice, and thorough bass both privately and institutionally 1826–33 and 1840–9 in Quebec City (*Séminaire de Québec and Hôpital Général de Québec), 1833–7 in Burlington, Vt (Burlington Female Seminary), and 1837–40 in Montreal. Like F.H. Glackemeyer he was a convert to Roman Catholicism and an organist-choirmaster (1840–9) at the Quebec Basilica. He was the first of this church's organists to play during the *St-Jean-Baptiste celebrations. In the early 1840s at the Quebec Cathedral he formed an amateur choir which later became the Société philharmonique. The 36-voice choir presented three concerts in 1844.

Molt was a hard-working and respected teacher and wrote several of the earliest musical instruction books to appear in Canada, including the first bilingual one. Molt's song *'Sol canadien, terre chérie' (words 1829 by Isidore Bédard; Sénécal, Daniel 1859) is one of the oldest Canadian patriotic songs. However, of his accompaniment to 'Myrtillo's Lament' from *Il Pastor fido* the London *Harmonicon* (1827) said 'so much bad taste, not to say error, in so short a space, we have rarely seen.' A *Mass* by Molt is preserved in manuscript at the Desrochers Collection of *Laval U, and the Lande Collection includes two notebooks of 'Music sacrée.' Molt obtained a patent in 1832 for his Chromatometer (see Inventions and devices).

Two of Molt's sons became musicians. Theodore E. (ca 1824–63) taught piano at the Burlington Female Seminary, and Hermann (ca 1825–64) taught music in Montreal.

WRITINGS

Elementary Treatise on Music / Traité élémentaire de musique (Quebec 1828)

New and Original Method for the Pianoforte (Burlington 1835)

Remarks on Piano Forte Instruction, pamphlet (Burlington 1836)

Lyre sainte, livraison I and II (Quebec 1844, 1845)

Traité élémentaire de musique vocale (Quebec 1845)

The Pupil's Guide and Young Teacher's Manual, or The Elements of Piano Forte Playing (Burlington 1854)

Elementary Method for the Piano Forte, I: *The Pupil's Guide* (Boston 1855); II: *51 Progressive Lessons* (published, ?); III: *Scales and Chords* (published, ?)

Also *Messe musicale du sixième ton, d'après de la Feillée*, rev and ed (Quebec 1842), and *Recueil de Musique Sacrée* (Quebec? 1843), both reported by W. Antmann in *La Musique au Québec*. Amtmann attributes the *Messe* to Molt.

BIBLIOGRAPHY

Converse, John K. 'Burlington Female Seminary,' *The Vermont Historical Gazetteer*, vol 1 (Burlington 1868)

LeVasseur, L.-Nazaire. 'Musique et musiciens à Quèbec,' *La Musique* (Quebec 1919)

'Le recueil de cantiques de M. Molt,' *BRH*, vol 46, Jun 1940

Thayer, A.W. *The Life of Ludwig van Beethoven* (New York 1921; rev edn Princeton 1964)

Beethoven & Quebec, Foreword by Lawrence Lande. Lawrence Lande Foundation for Canadian Historical Research, No. 2 (Montreal 1966)

Malouin-Gélinas, France. 'La vie musicale à Québec de 1840 à 1845, telle que décrite par les journaux et revues de l'époque,' unpubl M MUS thesis, Montreal 1975 HK

MONCRIEFF. Winnipeg family of musicians: 1 / John (James), 2 / his son John (May), and 3 / his daughter Anna Hovey.

1 **John** (James). Journalist, choirmaster, conductor, bass-baritone, b Scalloway, Shetland Islands, 19 Oct 1865, d Winnipeg 11 Apr 1939. His family settled in the Red River Settlement of St Andrews when he was 10. There he played violin with a small orchestra. Though his professional life was spent as a journalist (he was a co-founder of the Winnipeg *Tribune* in 1890 and associate editor 1920–36) he followed a parallel career in music. He was a pupil of a Signor Montegriffo and a bass soloist at Knox Presbyterian Church. He sang in an 1896 production of *The Daughter of the Regiment* and later appeared as the baritone in Liza Lehmann's song cycle *In a Persian Garden*. He was choirmaster and soloist 1906–25 at Augustine Church to which he invited the organist Lynnwood *Farnam and others. He organized concert series featuring other internationally known artists. A founder in 1908 and a conductor of the *Winnipeg Oratorio Society, he prepared the choir for many performances of *Messiah* and *Elijah* with the visiting Minneapolis SO. In 1915 Moncreiff was a founding member of the *Men's Music Club of Winnipeg.

BIBLIOGRAPHY

'Editor and musician dies: served *Tribune* nearly 50 years,' Winnipeg *Tribune*, 12 Apr 1939

2 **John** (May). Bass, b Winnipeg 10 Mar 1891, d Windsor, Ont, 19 Feb 1966. After studies with Otto *Morando in Toronto and Vladimir Rosing in Rochester and a concert tour of Canada, he made his stage debut in 1926 in the first season of opera presented at Chautauqua, NY. Subsequently he toured 1926–30 with the American Opera, singing 15 roles; the most successful was Mephisto in *Faust*, which he sang some 133 times. He understudied Feodor Chaliapin during the company's 1928 season. In the 1930s he sang on NBC radio in New York. Declining health forced his retirement and in later years he led a reclusive life on Pelee Island in Lake Erie.

3 **Anna** (m Hovey). Pianist, b Winnipeg 1902. A pupil of Mary L. Robertson, J.W. Matthews, and Eva *Clare, she performed on the first radio broadcast on CKY, Winnipeg, and in 1932 participated in the opening concert of the *Winnipeg Auditorium. She became an outstanding accompanist and over the years was invited to appear as the partner of such artists as Betty-Jean *Hagen, Mack Harrell, Bronislaw Huberman, Zara *Nelsova, Kathleen *Parlow, and Thomas L. Thomas in their Winnipeg recitals. A charter member of the *MRMTA, she taught privately in Winnipeg for many years. (JBM, SRM)

Moncton. New Brunswick city originally known as LeCoude and first settled in 1750 by Acadians. The Acadians were dispersed in 1758 but returned in sufficient numbers to constitute a fundamental segment of the Moncton community. Yorkshiremen, Loyalists, Highland Scots, Irishmen, and 'Pennsylvania Dutch' also contributed to the settlement's early population. The settlement was known as The Bend until 1855, when it was incorporated as a town and named 'Monckton.' The later spelling, 'Moncton,' was adopted in 1860. Moncton was incorporated as a city in 1890, when its inhabitants numbered 8700. By 1978 the population was nearing 57,000, about two-thirds English-speaking and one-third French-speaking.

Little is known about the first hundred years of musical life in Moncton. Toward the end of that period the congregation of the Methodist Church (opened 1848) sang its hymns to an accompaniment of violin, flute, and bass viol. Performing groups outside the church appear not to have developed until later in the century. It was after 1875, for example, that Moses White led the Moncton Citizens' Concert Band. Operettas, vaudevilles, plays, and lectures were presented from time to time in the Opera House, an auditorium forming the top floor of the Town Hall, which was completed in 1885. An indication that music had begun to flourish is provided by an 1889 advertisement by Miller Brothers, a music store located at Church and Main streets: 'Pianos and organs from the most popular makers, violins, guitars, piccolos, band instruments, accordions, sheet music, music publications, instruction books, in fact, every article used by the musical profession can be obtained through this firm.'

In 1895 John Philip Sousa and his band gave a matinee concert at the Victoria Rink. Sousa's visit roused great enthusiasm for band music. When the governor-general, Lord Aberdeen, visited in 1897, he was greeted by no fewer than three bands – the Citizens', the Orange (Loyal Protestant after 1907), and the 74th Battalion. After World War I Ferdinand Malenfant revamped the Band of the 165th (Acadian) Battalion to form L'Assomption Band, an organization which continued to play in the 1950s. Fred Cosman and Arthur Burbank organized an Odd Fellows' Band, one of many such civic organizations. The Sousa band, visiting again in 1926, gave two sold-out concerts at the Sunny Brae Rink. In the 1930s a *Salvation Army Band flourished under Arthur Deadman.

String players, however, were in short supply, so orchestras were slower to emerge. The Goulet *MSO accompanied the Festival Chorus trained by George H. Brown for the 1903 *Cycle of Musical Festivals. During the 1920s small orchestras accompanied silent movies. Among the players were Maude and Arthur Burbank, two US vaudeville artists who settled in Moncton in 1920. When the talkies obviated live accompaniment for movies, the Burbanks and others busied themselves with bands, amateur orchestras (eg, the St Bernard's Orchestra, conducted by Mrs Burbank), and the instruction of young musicians.

In 1932, with the support of the Women's Musical Club, a Moncton SO was formed under Percy Belyea, head of the music department of the T. Eaton store. When the orchestra disbanded for financial reasons, some of its musicians formed the Central United Church Orchestra, conducted by Len Barnes and later by Ernest W. Freeborn. Orchestral music received new impetus in the 1960s with the formation of the *New Brunswick SO and visits by the *New Brunswick Youth Orchestra and the *Atlantic SO, performing in the auditorium of the Moncton High School.

Until the 1930s local musical entertainments were supplied by the T. Eaton Co Glee Club, the Moncton Massed Choir, local Gilbert & Sullivan groups, and performers in the Sunday Night Capitol Theatre Concerts. The Women's Musical Club presented recitals and lectures 1930–50 by artists from further afield and in 1934 organized the Moncton *Community Concerts which have presented between three and six concerts annually. Among the Canadian artists who have appeared in this series are Pierrette *Alarie and Léopold *Simoneau, *Canadian Brass, Maureen *Forrester, Arthur *LeBlanc, Lois *Marshall, Louis *Quilico, Teresa *Stratas, and Ronald *Turini.

In 1949 the Moncton Chapter of the *RCCO began sponsoring an annual carol festival featuring participation by local church choirs.

The vitality of singing in the Acadian community was due in part to Léandre Brault, who conducted the *Chorale de l'Université St-Joseph and was succeeded by Roland Soucie and then Neil Michaud. The latter was Brault's successor in the mid-1950s as choral director at the U St-Joseph (later *U of Moncton). Michaud conducted the Chanteurs du Mascaret and the Chorale mixte de l'U de Moncton.

In the 1950s the Chorale Notre-Dame d'Acadie, under Sister Marie-Lucienne, won the City of Lincoln and George S. Mathieson trophies awarded by the *FCMF. Other groups which performed during the 1960s and 1970s include the Chorale Beauséjour (the forerunner of the *Jeunes Chanteurs d'Acadie), the Chorale Alouette, the Chorale La Mi, the Chorale Champlain, and Les Alinos – all members of the Alliance chorale de Nouveau-Brunswick, which established headquarters, under the direction of Aline O'Brien, in the Centre culturel de Moncton. This centre, opened in 1974, became a focus of musical activity in the area.

The city and region are rich in folk music, and Father Arthur Anselme (Anselme Chiasson) has collected Acadian song. Another collector, Charlotte Cormier, became the ethnomusicologist at the U of Moncton, where the Centre for Acadian Studies was established in 1968. Cormier has researched Acadian music and has presented the program 'L'Acadie chante' over CBAF radio.

The Aberdeen School, which opened in 1898, had an orchestra. However, the first regular public music teacher in New Brunswick was Mary McCarthy, who worked 1905–15 for the Moncton School Board. Among private music teachers prominent in the city after World War I was the aforementioned Maude Burbank (b Island Pond, Vt, 1881, d Moncton 1967), who formed a number of bands with her pupils. In 1970 the city established the annual Maritime Band Festival, first named in her honour. Burbank's long and significant contribution to music was recognized in 1958 when the U de St-Joseph conferred an honorary doctorate upon her.

Another recipient of an honorary degree (*Mount Allison U, 1954) was Alice May Harrison (b 1878, d 1980), who supervised music 1924–46 in Moncton schools. She also taught until 1936 at Moncton High School and organized a glee club there, worked with the Women's Musical Club to organize the Junior Piano Festival (1935–7) and the Moncton Music Festival (begun in 1937), and in 1950 was co-founder of the New Brunswick Music Teachers' Assn (later the *NBRMTA).

Harrison's successor 1936–48 at Moncton High School, George Ross (b Scotland 9 Apr 1875, d USA 1 Oct 1967), formed an orchestra at the school and was organist-choirmaster at St John's United Church. Robert C. *Bayley succeeded Harrison as supervisor of school music, serving until 1963. Ernest W. Freeborn served 1948–ca 1973 as Ross' successor at Moncton High School.

Among musicians born in or near Moncton have been Robert C. Bayley, Félix-R. *Bertrand, Charlotte Cormier, Mrs Walter *Coulthard, June *Eikhard, Sister Lorette Gallant, Arthur LeBlanc, Anna *Malenfant, and Margaret Osburne (see Don Messer).

BIBLIOGRAPHY

Robinson, Cyril, and Jaques, Louis. 'Maude makes music wherever she goes,' *Weekend Magazine*, 28 Nov 1959

Elliott, Carleton. 'Music in New Brunswick,' *The Arts in New Brunswick* (Fredericton 1967)

Ayling, Vera. 'Moncton haven for music-makers,' *Atlantic Advocate*, vol 64, May 1974

Vogan, Nancy F. 'Pioneer music educator celebrates hundredth birthday,' *CME*, vol 20, Winter 1979

Moncton Museum Archives. T.H. O'Brien papers

(CAP)

MONK, Allan (James). Baritone, b Mission, near Vancouver, BC, 19 Aug 1942. He moved in 1957 with his family to Calgary, where he began voice studies with Elgar Higgin and became interested in musical theatre. His voice attracted notice in the USA at Boris Goldovsky's summer workshops which he attended in 1963, 1964, and 1966.

Monk was engaged for his first leading roles by San Francisco's Western Opera Theatre in 1967 (Figaro in *The Barber of Seville*) and the San Francisco Opera in 1969 (Figaro in *The Marriage of Figaro*, Capulet in *Roméo et Juliette*, and the Music Master in *Ariadne auf Naxos*). With the latter company in 1973 he sang Enrico in *Lucia di Lammermoor*, Donner in *Das Rheingold*, the High Priest in *L'Africaine*, and the Teacher in von Einem's *The Visit of the Old Lady*. He returned there in 1975 to sing Tomsky in *The Queen of Spades*, Papageno in *The Magic Flute*, and Paolo in *Simon Boccanegra*.

In the 1970s Monk performed frequently in Canada. For Festival Canada (*Festival Ottawa) he sang Figaro in *The Marriage of Figaro* in 1971, Guglielmo in *Così fan tutte* in 1972, 1973, and 1979, the title role in *Don Giovanni* in 1973 and 1974, Tomsky in *The Queen of Spades* in 1976 and 1979, and Dr Malatesta in *Don Pasquale* in 1977. At the *Guelph Spring Festival Monk sang the role of Noye in *Noye's Fludde* in 1972, John Sorel in *The Consul* in 1973, and Tarquinius in *The Rape of Lucretia* in 1974. In 1974 he sang Escamillo in *Carmen* for the *COC, the *Southern Alberta Opera, and the *Edmonton Opera. For the last-named company he sang the role of Lescaut in *Manon Lescaut* in 1975 and 1979.

A notable achievement in 1973 was Monk's creation of the role of Abelard for the *COC in Charles *Wilson's **Heloise and Abelard*. Of his performance Jacob *Siskind, in the Montreal *Gazette* of 10 Sep 1973, wrote 'Allan Monk is probably the member of the cast most successful in combining characterization and musical projection ... his Abelard had dignity and warmth.' Monk sang the role in both the Toronto premiere and the subsequent performances in Ottawa.

In March 1976 Monk made his *Metropolitan Opera debut as Schaunard in *La Bohème* and the following year he sang Schaunard, Kothner in *Die Meistersinger*, Roucher in *Andrea Chenier*, the King's Herald in *Lohengrin*, and Angelotti in *Tosca*, establishing himself as a versatile singer and a resourceful actor in this variety of supporting roles. In 1978 he appeared as the Father in *Hansel and Gretel*, the Speaker in *Die Zauberflöte*, Sharpless in *Madama Butterfly*, and Wolfram in *Tannhäuser*. Also in 1978 he was Silvio in the telecast of *I Pagliacci* and Masetto in *Don Giovanni*. Continuing to perform in Canada, he appeared in the title role in the 1977 COC production of *Wozzeck* and as Tonio in the 1979 *Vancouver Opera production of *I Pagliacci*.

As a concert artist Monk premiered *Ridout's *Cantiones mysticae No. 3* in 1972 and toured as soloist with the *NACO in Europe in 1973. Also in 1973, he performed with the *Vancouver SO in Beethoven's *Ninth Symphony* and with the *Calgary Philharmonic in Vaughan Williams' *A Sea Symphony*. In 1978 he sang Mahler's *Songs of a Wayfarer* with the *Quebec SO.

Monk may be heard in the supporting role of Roucher on the recording (RCA RL 02046) of *Andrea Chenier* by the John Alldis Singers and the National Philharmonic Orchestra under James Levine. Monk was nominated in 1971 by *Musical America* as an Outstanding Young Artist of the Year. In the 1970s he established a residence in Teaneck, NJ.

BIBLIOGRAPHY

Rockwell, John. 'Profile: Allan James Monk,' *OpCan*, vol 9, Feb 1968

Wadsworth, Stephen. 'Allan Monk,' *OpCan*, vol 19, Spring 1978 (RDM)

MONOHAN, Thomas (Shahan). Bassist, teacher, b Louisville, Ky, 30 Jun 1937, naturalized Canadian 1971; Artist Diploma (Curtis) 1958. He studied at the Curtis Institute with Roger Scott and played 1958–65 with the St Louis SO, the Israel Philharmonic, the National (Washington, DC) SO, and the Detroit SO. In 1966 he became principal bass of the *TSO and began to teach at the *U of Toronto. He was a coach 1966–73 for the *NYO. Many of his pupils have joined major Canadian orchestras: Peter Madgett of the *Hamilton Philharmonic and then of the TS; John Gowan of the TS; Joel Quarrington (1975 Eaton Graduating Scholarship and 1976 *CBC Talent Festival winner), principal of the Hamilton Philharmonic; and others with the *NACO, the *MSO, the *Winnipeg SO, and the *Edmonton SO. Monohan has written *Melodic Studies for the Double Bass* (Harris 1973). He has been heard often in CBC recitals and in 1966, with *New Music Concerts, he gave the first Canadian performance of Vittorio Giannini's *Psalm 130* with the TSO. He commissioned Walter *Buczynski's *Duo* (1975) for bass and piano and premiered it 16 May 1976 in Toronto. CF

'Mon Pays.' Song commissioned from Gilles *Vigneault by the *NFB for Arthur Lamothe's 1965 film *La Neige a fondu sur la Manicouagan*. Vigneault wrote both the music and the words and completed the song in 1964. The opening phrase – 'Mon pays, ce n'est pas un pays, c'est l'hiver' ('My country is not a country, it's winter') – provides a good illustration of the character of the song, in which Vigneault speaks above all of winds, cold, snow, and ice. But 'in this land of snowstorms' the author still vows to remain faithful and hospitable like his father before him, who built a home there: 'the guestroom will be such that people from the other seasons will come and build next door to it.' He also evokes in the second verse the solitude of wide open spaces and the ideal of brotherhood. Vigneault then ends with these words: 'My country is not a country, it's the reverse of a country that was neither country nor homeland. My song is not a song, it's my life. It is for you that I want to possess my winters.'

For many people this chanson has assumed a political character. Benoît L'Herbier, for example, describes it as 'a Quebec anthem if there is one at all, hummed with self-respect and pride' (*La Chanson québécoise*, Montreal 1974). However, in an interview with Pierre Nadeau, Vigneault denied having intended to give his song such a meaning or, more generally, to compose national anthems (*L'Actualité*, September 1979).

'Mon Pays' earned its author, among other honours, the Prix Félix-Leclerc, awarded by the Montreal Festival du disque (1965). For her performance of the song, Monique *Leyrac won the grand prize of International Day at the International Song Festival in Sopot, Poland (1965). Patsy Gallant recorded a disco version in French and also a disco version in English under the title 'From New York to L.A.' and with lyrics completely different from those of the original. The latter was extremely popular in Canada and the USA in 1976. Vigneault performs 'Mon Pays' on the LPs *Gilles Vigneault à la Comédie-Canadienne*, *Mon Pays*, and *Les Grands Succès de Gilles Vigneault*, as well as on *Les Chansonniers du Québec* (2-RCI 360-361), *J'ai vu le loup, le renard et le lion* (Les Productions du 13 août enrg. VLC 13), and *Les Chansons d'or du Québec* (Deram DEF-1000). Several other artists have recorded the song, including Salome *Bey, Neil *Chotem (instrumental version), Roger *Doucet, the *Ensemble Claude-Gervaise, Judy Lander ('My Country'), Danielle Licari, Monique Leyrac, Ginette *Reno, Gaston Rochon, Catherine Sauvage, and René *Simard. André *Gagnon used it as the theme for the first movement of the fourth concerto of *Mes Quatre Saisons*. The text alone has appeared in a collection of Vigneault's poems, *Avec Les Vieux Mots* (Quebec 1964). Edith *Fowke gives the words and music in *Canadian Vibrations* (Toronto 1972). The sheet music (harmonization and arrangement by Gaston Rochon) is published by the Éditions du Vent qui vire.

Vigneault composed a sequel, 'Mon Pays II,' originally published by the same firm (again in a harmonization and arrangement by Rochon), but later also by Sibecar (Paris 1969) for France, Switzerland, and the Benelux countries. The lyrics of 'Mon Pays II' at first reduce the country to very small dimensions and then go on to identify it with a town, a province, and finally a planet 'which on a window sill is spun around by a child's finger.' (HP, ST, SW)

'Monsieur Pointu.' See Pointu.

Montagnards. Name adopted by various Montreal and Quebec City choral societies in the wake of a tour across Quebec (August 1856) by the Montagnards basques, a French company directed by Alfred Rolland. This group was enormously successful, particularly in the harmonized songs 'La Chasse aux Isards' and the 'Tyrolienne des Pyrénées' from which the famous refrain 'Halte-là, les montagnards sont là!' remained engraved in people's memories.

On 13 Feb 1861 François Benoît (1824–77), choirmaster at St-Pierre Church, founded the Société musicale des montagnards canadiens in Montreal. By 1863 this choral group numbered 26 members and had presented eight concerts. It seems that Les Orphéonistes de Montréal, a 30-voice choir also directed by Benoît, replaced the Société musicale des montagnards canadiens ca 1864. It is known that the Orphéonistes sang in St-Hyacinthe in September 1866.

On 17 Apr 1876 Benoît re-established the Montagnards group, beginning with 16 voices. The number of members soon rose to 21. In 1875 another group, 12 members of the Notre-Dame Church choir of Montreal, formed the Choeur montagnard under the direction of F.-A. Lavoie. These new Montagnards wore costumes: wide white trousers and dark violet Montagnard caps and vests with white facings. 'They thrilled the crowds who flocked to hear them through the majesty and power of their songs,' reported *Le Canada musical* (1 Nov 1875).

Arthur Renaud (b Montreal 1851, d Verdun, Montreal, 1934; choirmaster at St-Joseph Church in 1878, St-Gabriel Church in 1879, Ste-Anne Church in 1880, and later at Ste-Cunégonde and St-Henri churches) founded the Chorale des montagnards, also known as the Montagnards canadiens, in Montreal ca 1878. This 25-member group adopted as its costume grey stockings, trousers, and jackets, and grey felt hats with red feathers. The repertoire included religious and secular works, individual programs depending on whether the choir was contributing its services to charity events or was appearing in concert. The soprano C. Leblanc, the tenor Édouard *LeBel, and the deep bass Hormisdas Saint-Cyr were soloists with the Montagnards on several occasions. In 1897 the *Guide de Montréal* referred to them as a 'very popular and very well-known institution.'

The name of the Montagnards was adopted also by various choral groups in small localities (eg, in L'Assomption, Que, in 1866). As late as 1881 the Batiscan choir performed the successful works of the Montagnards basques repertoire.

BIBLIOGRAPHY

Massicotte, Édouard-Z. 'Le chant des Montagnards,' *BRH*, vol 34, 1928

'Les Montagnards,' 'Les Montagnards sont là!' ibid, vol 38, 1932

'Encore les montagnards,' ibid, vol 39, 1933 (GB)

MONTGOMERY, William Augustus. Organist-choirmaster, composer, b Hawick, Scotland, 25 Nov 1872, d Halifax 18 Dec 1948; LTCM 1894, B MUS (Durham) 1897, LRAM 1905, FRCO 1910. He studied piano, organ, and theory in Great Britain with Charles Edward Allum, G.H. Haselock, Arthur William Marchant, and A. Eaglefield Hull. After serving as organist-choirmaster of Gainsborough parish church in England, he emigrated to Canada in 1913. He was organist-choirmaster 1913–14 at St Peter's Church, Sherbrooke, Que; 1914–21 at the pro-Cathedral, Calgary; and 1921–42 at All Saints Cathedral, Halifax, becoming organist emeritus there on his retirement. His compositions – of which more than 100 were published and some 20 are listed in the *Catalogue of Canadian Composers* – include works for organ, piano, violin and piano, and choir. His publishers were Novello, *Waterloo, Mozart Allan (Glasgow), Ditson, J. Schirmer, and others.

Montreal. City located on the island of the same name at the junction of the St Lawrence and Ottawa rivers in the province of Quebec. The island is one of a cluster that also includes Île Jésus (which became part of the city of Laval in 1965) and the islands of Bizard and Perrot. Montreal stands at the foot of Mount Royal, from which it took its name, 'réal' being a modification of 'royal.'

The Victoria Rifles Band of Montreal, 1867

The French explorer Jacques Cartier discovered the island in 1535 and found an Indian village there named Hochelaga. He named the mountain Mount Royal in honour of King François I. Seventy-five years later the founder of Quebec City, Samuel de Champlain, arrived and set up a fur trading post which he called Place Royale. Paul de Chomedey, sieur de Maisonneuve, a French soldier born in Champagne, founded on 17 May 1642 a colony to which he gave the name of Ville-Marie. Along with about 50 settlers, he worked on behalf of the Société Notre-Dame de Montréal, an organization founded in Paris by Jérôme le Royer de la Dauversière, a French official primarily concerned with converting the Indians to Christianity. In 1663 the whole island was conceded as a seigniory to the Messieurs de Saint-Sulpice, a society of Catholic priests founded in Paris in 1639. Though threatened by the Iroquois, Montreal began to develop after 1665 and became the embarkation-point for missionaries, explorers, and traders for the whole of North America.

In 1701 the town had a population of 2000, and in 1760, at the time of the conquest by England, there were some 5000 inhabitants, the great majority of French origin. Following immigration by the English and the departure of many French, the two groups gradually became equal. The population numbered 58,000 in 1851 and nearly doubled in the next 10 years. In 1900 it was 370,000.

In 1974 the population of the whole island was 2,100,000, and the neighbouring city of Laval numbered 240,000. After 1945 heavy immigration from Europe and from French-speaking countries changed its character somewhat, but in 1980 Montreal remained the second largest French-speaking city in the world after Paris. In 1969 the island's 29 municipalities were linked to comprise the Montreal Urban Community.

1 1642–1850. In his *Histoire du Montréal* (Montreal 1868) / *A History of Montreal, 1640–1672* (Toronto 1928), Dollier de Casson relates that Maisonneuve, the founder of Montreal, learned the lute to pass the time when he was alone. Little is known, however, concerning such musical activity as may have existed prior to 1750, except that there was choral singing in the church and a certain amount of rudimentary instruction in music dispensed by some of the missionaries. It is possible that the only church had no organ until the end of the 17th century. J.-B. *Poitiers du Buisson, who arrived in Montreal in 1698, is the first organist whose name has come down to us. He played in the parish church from 1705 until around 1718. Among his successors were Guillaume *Mechtler, J.-C. *Brauneis II, Leonard *Eglauch, Henry Berlyn, and J.-B. *Labelle. Since the first newspaper, *The Gazette*, did not appear regularly before 1785, there is almost no information on musical life before that date. In 1786 this publication announced, however, that 'several musicians recently arrived from Europe will give a vocal and instrumental concert,' and a monsieur Duplessy was offering music lessons. The same year *The Enchanters*, a pantomime by John *Bentley, was presented.

The year 1789 was important, for it was then that Louis *Dulongpré, Joseph *Quesnel, and a handful of citizens founded the *Théâtre de Société on Notre-Dame St. Quesnel's comic opera **Colas et Colinette* was performed there early in 1790. Duni's *Les Deux Chasseurs et la laitière* was another French-language production, and touring companies presented such English-language comic operas as Shield's *The Poor Soldier* and Dibdin's *The Padlock*. Charles Watts of London opened a music school in 1789, as did Dulongpré in 1791. At a concert 'at Mr. Cushing's long room' in 1796 George E. Saliment performed his own *Concerto of Flute* (sic) and an *Overture Grand Orchester* (sic) by Pleyel; a *Concerto on the Piano Forte* (sic) by Mechtler shared the program. There were numerous concerts by regimental bands.

Another date of importance was 1825, when the brewer John Molson, with the assistance of numerous shareholders, built the *Theatre Royal, the first institution in Canada devoted exclusively to the performing arts. Messrs Duff and Honey were its music directors. In August 1843 a French comic-opera company directed by Mlle Cavé performed Auber's *Les Diamants de la couronne* and Adam's *Le Chalet* there. In this theatre, as well as in hotel halls, there occurred musical events of variable quality, in which prima donnas and Italian tenors vied with acrobats and other attractions, all supported by concert or regimental bands. Even so, Italian opera had appeared in Montreal as early as 1841, when M and Mme Seguin of Covent Garden and their opera company presented such works as *La Sonnambula, Fra Diavolo, La Cenerentola*, and *L'Elisir d'amore*. Other artists heard during this period were the tenor John Braham at the Rasco Hotel, the pianist Leopold von Meyer, and a blind harpist, M. Wall. The manufacture of organs and pianos was begun around 1820 by Jacotel and continued later by Fay, Samuel R. *Warren, and John M. *Thomas. John *Lovell published music, and J.W. *Herbert was both publisher and merchant.

2 1850–1900. Set in a difficult economic context and preoccupied with political struggles, Montrealers had very little time for leisure and music. There were few professional musicians, and high calibre music teaching was virtually non-existent. In 1852, however, a ship from France brought two men who were to play leading roles. One was A.J. *Boucher, a Canadian by birth who became active as a musician, publisher, and music dealer; the other was the Frenchman Paul *Letondal, a blind pianist and cellist. Another Frenchman, C.W. *Sabatier, had settled in Montreal in 1848.

A musical life gradually began to develop, owing to the initiative of men like J.-B. Labelle, who, for example, conducted a concert of operatic excerpts at the new *Mechanics' Hall in 1857 and six years later founded a short-lived philharmonic society. Future great names began to appear: Calixa *Lavallée, Moïse *Saucier, the three *Lavigne brothers, Dominique *Ducharme, and Romain-Octave *Pelletier, and later Guillaume *Couture and Alexis *Contant. The singer Emma *Albani, née Lajeunesse, the first Canadian diva to receive international acclaim, gave her first concerts in Montreal in 1856 and 1862 but did not return to her homeland until 1883 for the first of several tours. Around 1865 the Belgian violinist Jules *Hone settled in Montreal, to be joined shortly by his compatriot Frantz *Jehin-Prume, the famous violinist who was the first musician of international reputation to take up residence in Canada. Jehin-Prume played a large role in the development of music through his concerts and teaching. He presented 'classical concerts' by a string quartet in 1870 and founded the Assn artistique in 1892. Montreal was host at this time to such renowned artists as Adelina Patti, Henri Vieuxtemps, Auguste Wilhelmj, Eduard Remenyi, Camilla Urso, Louis-Moreau Gottschalk, Sigismond Thalberg, and several others.

Choral singing, heretofore confined mostly to the church, became popular in concert after 1861, with the formation of several ensembles known as the *Montagnards. The *Mendelssohn Choir was founded by Joseph *Gould in 1864 and presented concerts over a period of 30 years. The *Montreal Philharmonic Society (1877–99) acquainted Montrealers with the great oratorios as well as with the operas of Wagner, and in 1897 it presented for the first time in Canada Beethoven's *Ninth Symphony*. The dearth of good local string and wind players, however, often made it necessary to import an orchestra from Boston. Some 20 instrumentalists, who had come from Belgium and France around 1890 at the invitation of Ernest Lavigne to play at *Sohmer Park, comprised the nucleus of the first *MSO, established in 1894 by J.-J. *Goulet.

Opera was largely the prerogative of touring companies until 1877, when Lavallée conducted Gounod's *Jeanne d'Arc* and, the following year, Boieldieu's *La Dame blanche* with the entire cast, as well as the orchestra, recruited locally. The *Opéra français presented a varied repertoire of operas and operettas in its own theatre 1893–6. Emma Albani and her troupe gave performances at the *Académie de musique in 1890 and 1892. In this theatre, Victor Herbert's *Cyrano de Bergerac* was given its world premiere in 1899. Montreal also received theatre companies from France and New Orleans, and in 1899 saw the *Metropolitan Opera at *Her Majesty's Theatre.

Concerts were held at *Windsor Hall, which opened in 1890. The *Monument national was inaugurated in 1893, Her Majesty's Theatre in 1898. In the latter, Herbert's operetta *The Singing Girl* had its premiere in 1899. The *Ladies' Morning Musical Club was founded in 1892 and in 1980 could claim to be one of the oldest active musical societies in Canada.

The increasing growth of musical life during this period found an echo in an astonishingly flourishing and specialized musical press. *L'Artiste* appeared in 1860, followed by the magazine *Les Beaux-Arts (1863–4)*, *Le *Canada musical* (1866–7, 1875–81), *L'Écho musical* (1888), *Le Canada artistique* (1890), *Le *Passe-Temps* (1895–1949), and *L'Art musical* (1896–9). Among the regular contributors were Gustave *Smith, A.J. Boucher, Guillaume Couture, Gustave *Comte, Aristide Filiatreault, Charles *Labelle, and C.-O. *Lamontagne.

Music was taught privately for the most part, although several 'collèges classiques,' post-secondary schools, and convents had acquired the services of specialized staff. A certain standardizing of quality was achieved through organizations commissioned to set examinations, such as the *AMQ, the *Dominion College of Music, and the *AB of the RSM. At the advanced level, instruction remained for a long time in an embryonic stage, despite such initiatives as C.E. Seifert's Montreal Cons, the conservatory of Edmond *Hardy's *Canadian Artistic Society, and the *Institut Nazareth for young blind people. The creation of the *Strathcona Scholarship in 1895 was one initiative that brought swift results: its first recipients were Béatrice *La Palme, Ada Moylan, Lynnwood *Farnam, and Pauline *Donalda. The arrival of Clara *Lichtenstein in 1899 began a whole new chapter in the field of advanced music education. Despite the slowness and uncertainty of this era of growth, several outstanding talents emerged, eg, Alexis Contant, Émiliano *Renaud, François *Boucher, Arthur *Letondal, R.-O. Pelletier, Joseph *Saucier, Alfred *De Sève, and Oscar *Martel. Among instrument makers of note were *Mitchell, Craig, and *Pratte. Boucher, Hardy, *De Zouche, Lavigne, and *Yon were active as publishers.

3 1900–45. The first half of the 20th century was to bring about the consolidation of preceding efforts along with an increasing population, the development of means of transport and communication, and the beginnings of the industrial era. This growth, however, suffered a slowdown during World War I, and the ensuing recovery was dampened by the economic crisis of the 1930s.

The survival of the MSO was due chiefly to the tenacity of J.-J. Goulet, who had taken over its direction in 1897 and retained it until 1919. His participation in the 1903 *Cycle of Musical Festivals of the Dominion of Canada was considerable, not only in Montreal but also in Halifax, Moncton, and Saint John, which the MSO visited for the concerts given in those cities. After 1919 concerts were given through the efforts of such men as Jerry *Shea and Henri *Delcellier, but sporadically. Earlier, the *Montreal Opera Company (1910–13) and the *National Opera Company of Canada (1913–14) had given symphonic concerts as well as operatic performances. J.-J. *Gagnier revived the MSO in 1927, but it was not until the founding of the *Montreal Orchestra in 1930 under Douglas *Clarke and of the orchestra of the *CSM in 1934 that Montreal acquired two established orchestras of professional calibre. The advent of radio in the early 1920s also fostered symphonic activity, and station CKAC had its own orchestra for a while, conducted by such musicians as Henri *Miro, Delcellier, and Edmond *Trudel. The Montreal stations of the CRBC and later the CBC soon had their own ensembles set up by J.-J. Gagnier and J.-M. *Beaudet. Miro was also music director 1916–21 for the *Berliner Gramophone Co and made numerous recordings for the company. One of the first chamber orchestras was formed by Gagnier; it was followed by the *Little Symphony of Montreal and by a radio orchestra formed by the CBC for its program *'Little Symphonies.'

Following the disappearance of the Montreal Philharmonic Society, the *Montreal Oratorio Society, founded by Horace *Reyner, was active 1902–8. Choral music was perpetuated by the *Assn chorale Saint-Louis-de-France, which came into prominence about 1907, and the *Assn des Chanteurs de Montréal, founded in 1918 by Jean *Goulet. Shortly afterwards came the *Assn chorale Brassard (1921), the *Montreal Elgar Choir (1923), led by Berkley E. *Chadwick, and the *Disciples de Massenet (1928) under Charles *Goulet.

The period also saw a tremendous upsurge in interest in opera. The Metropolitan Opera company returned in 1901, performing at the *Montreal Arena, and again, with Toscanini conducting, in 1911, this time at His Majesty's Theatre. Members of troupes that had come from France settled in Montreal as teachers, among them Salvator *Issaurel, Victor *Occellier, and Jean *Riddez. Of particular note is the foundation of the Montreal Opera Company by Albert *Clerk-Jeannotte and Frank *Meighen. The company's three seasons (1910–13) were distinguished as much by the repertoire as by the quality of the performances. This new attempt to create a permanent opera company was followed by another, the National Opera Company of Canada, which also folded for financial reasons after just one season (1913–14). After the war, other driving forces such as Arthur *Laurendeau, Henri Delcellier, Albert Roberval, and Céline *Marier toiled in the same spirit; but a measure of stability was achieved only with the *Société canadienne d'opérette in 1923, followed by the *Variétés lyriques in 1936. These two societies presented operas and operettas, but the *Opera Guild (1942–69) devoted itself solely to opera. Founded in 1936, the Société des Festivals de Montréal (later *Montreal Festivals) presented annual events devoted mainly to oratorio until 1965, but attempted opera in 1940 with the first performance in Canada of *Pelléas et Mélisande*. Wilfrid *Pelletier conducted performances by a group called the Canadian Opera Company (unconnected with the later COC) in 1930 and was the originator of the autumn opera seasons given 1941–5 at the *St-Denis Theatre.

Montrealers had welcomed the Orchestra of the Metropolitan Opera conducted by Anton Seidl in 1896, and in 1902 Pietro Mascagni came to conduct three of his operas in the Arena. The soprano Lillian Nordica and the pianists Raoul Pugno and Edward MacDowell were heard the same year. A concert devoted entirely to Canadian works was presented in Windsor Hall in 1903. Unforgettable for many Montrealers were the numerous concerts of Emma Albani in 1903 and in 1906, the year of her farewell tour.

Post-secondary instruction, which had been somewhat inadequate until that time, now received attention through some remarkable initiatives. At *McGill U, the conservatorium was founded in 1904 by Charles *Harriss; the following year Alphonse *Lavallée-Smith founded the *Cons national de musique. The two institutions' growth was considerable during the decades that followed. The second was affiliated to the *U of Montreal in 1921 and remained so until 1951. (The affiliation was terminated because the university founded its own faculty of music in 1950.) Post-secondary schools for girls, and later mixed schools, were opened, eg, the École normale de musique in 1927 and the École supérieure d'Outremont (later *École Vincent-d'Indy) in 1932. The most original innovation in this field, however, was the *Cons de musique du Québec, inaugurated in Montreal in 1943. Established on European models, particularly that of Paris, it provided from the outset free post-secondary instruction in all disciplines. During this period the composers Rodolphe *Mathieu, Auguste *Descarries, and Alfred *Laliberté, among others, were able to organize performances of their works, and Claude *Champagne emerged as not only a gifted original composer but as a teacher of virtually all the composers of the succeeding generation.

The growth of musical life in all its forms impelled the daily press to secure the services of better informed music critics, such as Thomas *Archer, Philip King, and H.P. *Bell in the English press and Léo-Pol *Morin, Henri *Letondal, Paul-G. Ouimet, Frédéric *Pelletier, Eugène *Lapierre, Marcel *Valois, Jean *Vallerand, and Dominique Laberge in the French press. Specialized periodicals, however, seldom survived for long. *Le Canada musical* reappeared (1917–24 and briefly in 1930); *La Lyre* (1922–31) was one of the last important publications before World War II, although *Le Passe-Temps* continued to publish until 1949.

Although the period 1939–45 was not particularly favourable to new developments, the majority of existing institutions managed to survive despite increasingly serious financial constraints. Alexander *Brott founded the *McGill String Quartet in 1939, succeeding the *Dubois String Quartet, which had presented regular concert seasons from 1910 to 1938. The *Campbell Free Band Concerts, founded in 1924, provided enjoyment for devotees of concert bands (as it continued to do in 1980). After Emma Albani, Montreal artists such as Béatrice La Palme, Pauline Donalda, Ellen *Ballon, Sarah *Fischer, and Rodolphe *Plamondon won acclaim abroad.

Among the patrons who contributed to musical growth during this period were Frank Meighen, Cécile Léger, Jean *Lallemand, and Mme Athanase *David. The recording industry began to develop with Berliner, *Compo, *Starr-Gennett, and other labels such as Baroque, *London, and Madrigal.

4 1945–80. The immediate post-war period brought with it the powerful stimulus of regenerative ambition, and the resumption of musical life parallelled the economic development of the metropolis, aided by greater government participation and by the arrival of numerous accomplished European musicians. As early as 1941 the CSM orchestra had acquired the services of Désiré Defauw as artistic director. Defauw raised the orchestra to the standard of the best on the continent, in part by broadening its repertoire and engaging distinguished soloists. After 1950 the orchestra (which became the MSO in 1953) was directed in succession by Otto Klemperer, Igor Markevitch, Zubin Mehta assisted by Pierre *Hétu, Franz-Paul *Decker, Rafael Frühbeck de Burgos, and – after his appointment in 1978 – Charles Dutoit.

The *McGill Chamber Orchestra grew out of and succeeded the McGill String Quartet and gave regular seasons beginning in 1953, under the direction of Alexander Brott, who had been a pupil of Claude Champagne. A genuine Montreal school of composers came into being: Violet *Archer, Maurice *Blackburn, Brott, Jean *Papineau-Couture, Robert *Turner, and Jean Vallerand. Others followed, among them Gabriel *Charpentier, Serge *Garant, Roger Matton, Pierre *Mercure, François Morel, Micheline Coulombe *Saint-Marcoux, Gilles *Tremblay, and Claude *Vivier.

A significant year was 1963 which saw the opening of the Salle Wilfrid-Pelletier of the *PDA. In the elegant salle, the MSO finally found a worthy home after 30 years in *Plateau Hall, an inadequate auditorium with 1300 seats. The Maisonneuve and Port-Royal halls were added to the PDA in 1967. This auditorium and theatre complex provided the central platforms for the six-month World Festival of *Expo 67, one of the most impressive aggregations of musical events of modern times.

The Montreal Festivals enlarged the scope of their activities after 1950, while continuing to reserve an important place for concert and operatic performances. Under their auspices in 1961 Pierre Mercure organized the *International Week of Today's Music, which caused much controversy and elicited strong reaction from a divided press and a divided audience. There had been few opportunities for the performance of new Canadian music until 1953, when the *Society of Canadian Music was founded to provide or facilitate such opportunities. The society in turn relinquished the main burden of its responsibilities to the *SMCQ, which was founded in 1966 by Serge Garant, Maryvonne *Kendergi, and others. Choral music, which had been championed chiefly by the Disciples de Massenet and the Montreal Elgar Choir, enjoyed a new emphasis with the advent of the *Montreal Bach Choir founded by George *Little in 1951 and the *Tudor Singers founded by Wayne *Riddell in 1962. Chamber music was served especially well by the *Montreal String Quartet (1955–63), which comprised Hyman *Bress, Mildred *Goodman, and Otto and Walter *Joachim, (The Joachims had come from China in the late 1940s.) In 1948 Gertrude Gendreau founded the *Pro Musica Society, which gave Montrealers regular opportunities to hear the best chamber music ensembles. Early music was ignored until Celia *Bizony founded *Musica Antica e Nuova in 1951, a society in which John *Newmark and Mario *Duschenes took part. The latter did much to popularize the recorder, particularly among members of *CAMMAC. The *Baroque Trio of Montreal was active 1955–73, and the *Studio de musique ancienne was founded in 1974.

The organ was always popular in Montreal owing to the presence of a large number of fine instruments, most of them built by *Casavant. Recitals were given regularly in the 1940s by the *Casavant Society. A movement supporting the return to the classical organ, with tracker action, developed in 1960 with the foundation of *Ars Organi by a group of young organists including Gaston *Arel, Raymond *Daveluy, Kenneth *Gilbert, Bernard and Mireille *Lagacé, and Lucienne *L'Heureux-Arel. Montreal acquired many instruments of this type built by Rudolf von Beckerath, Karl *Wilhelm, and Hellmuth *Wolff, among others.

Opera remained in a relatively flourishing state after 1945 with the Variétés lyriques, the Opera Guild, the Montreal Festivals, and the *Minute Opera. These four societies disappeared one after the other between 1953 and 1969. The MSO initiated some productions 1964–8, but it was not until 1971 that a serious attempt was made to form a permanent company, the *Opéra du Québec. It, too, ceased its activities (1975), but a new company, the Opéra de Montréal, presented its first season in 1980–1. Several Montreal artists in the meantime had followed the example of their predecessors and distinguished themselves on the international stage: Pierrette *Alarie, Colette *Boky, Clarice *Carson, Pierre Duval, Maureen *Forrester, Louis *Quilico, Robert *Savoie, Huguette *Tourangeau, and André *Turp.

The daily press began to attach more importance to the arts in general and to music in particular. Among the practising critics were Claude *Gingras (*La Presse*), Eric *McLean (the *Montreal Star* and later the *Gazette*), Gilles *Potvin (*Le Devoir, La Presse, Le Nouveau Journal*), Pierre Prévost (*Le Jour*), Paul *Roussel (*Le Canada, L'Autorité*), Jacob *Siskind (the *Standard*, the *Gazette*), Brian Macdonald (the *Montreal Herald*), and Roy *Royal (*Le Petit Journal*).

To promote the appreciation and study of music among young people, the *Amis de l'art was founded in 1942, followed by the *JMC in 1949. The secretariat of the latter organization was set up in Montreal, as was that of the *Canadian Music Competitions. The *Montreal International Competition, the only one of its level and scope in Canada, was established in 1963. The *CMCentre opened its Montreal office in 1973. The *Alliance chorale canadienne was founded in 1961 and established a secretariat in Montreal. The Council of Arts of Greater Montreal, one of the first of its kind in Canada, was founded in 1957. It was renamed the Conseil des arts de la Communauté urbaine de Montréal in 1980.

Though the Quebec chanson and the chansonniers were not particularly a Montreal phenomenon, it was chiefly in the metropolis that they began their conquest of the francophone world. The first of a long list was Félix *Leclerc in the early 1950s. This was also the time of the first *boîtes à chansons, and the vogue of the chanson spread rapidly, thanks to such writer-composer-performers as Raymond *Lévesque, Jean-Pierre *Ferland, Claude *Léveillée, Jacques Blanchet, and Robert *Charlebois and to such performers as Pauline *Julien and Diane *Dufresne. (See Chansons; Chansonniers.) The city's hotels and cabarets employed *dance bands which provided Montrealers with pleasant evenings. In the *jazz world, individuals and groups gained renown, particularly following World War II. Numerous soloists and groups devoted to *country music, *rock, *blues, and *ragtime continue to flourish.

Montreal differs from other cities, not only in Canada but also in the USA, in that it has a considerable number of streets, avenues, and boulevards bearing the names of musicians. In 1980 there were at least 30. Several schools, parks, and public squares also have been named after musicians (see Memorials and honours).

At the same time as the reforms in education that occurred in Quebec in the 1960s, music departments were opened at *UQAM, and *Concordia U, and in numerous *Cegeps.

Important archival deposits and other documents relating to music may be found at the Montreal City Library, the Archives nationales du Québec, the BN du Q, the Marvin *Duchow Library of McGill U, the Jewish Public Library, the *CMM, the U of Montreal, and private institutions.

5 MUSICIANS BORN IN MONTREAL. Among the musicians born in Montreal or in the region (see individual *EMC* entries or the index) are Pierrette Alarie, Émilien Allard, André Asselin, Gilles and Marcel Baillargeon, Fleurette Beauchamp, Pierre Béique, Pierre Béluse, Alfred Bernier, Félix-R. Bertrand, Jacques Bertrand, Napoléon Bisson, Paul Bley, Max Bohrer, Colette Boky, Colette Bonheur, Lise Boucher, Richard G. Boucher, Louis-H. and Rosario Bourdon, Pierre Brabant, Henry Brant, J.-Arsène Brassard, Cédia and Victor Brault, Pierre Brault, Michel-Georges Brégent, the Brott family members: Alexander, Boris, and Denis, Noël Brunet, Germaine Bruyère, Réjane Cardinal, Albert Chamberland, Claude Champagne, Jean-Noël Charbonneau, Renée Claude, Alexis Contant, Paul-Émile Corbeil, Marcelle Corneille, François, Jean and Luc Cousineau, Guillaume Couture, Lionel Daunais, Reine Décarie, Maurice Dela, Isabelle Delorme, Rosita del Vecchio, Auguste Descarries, Alfred De Sève, Jeanne Desjardins, L.-Édouard Desjardins, Jean Deslauriers, Gérald Desmarais, Rolande Désormeaux, Pauline Donalda, Roger Doucet, Paul Doyon, Claude Dubois, Jules Dubois, Charles-Joseph Ducharme, Dominique Ducharme, Yolande Dulude, Guillaume Dupuis, Pierre Duval, Maynard Ferguson, Jean-Pierre Ferland, Janina Fialkowska, Roger Filiatrault, Rosario Forget, Joseph-A. Fowler, Hélène and Marcelle Gagné, J.-J. Guillaume, the Gagnier family members: René, Armand, Ernest, Lucien, Réal, Roland, and Gérald, Conrad Gauthier, Gérard and Marc Gélinas, Samuel Gesser, Michel Gonneville, Mildred Goodman, Pierre Grandmaison, Fernand Graton, Richard Grégoire, Richard Gresko, Guylaine Guy, Denis Harbour, Edmond Hardy, Pierre Hétu, Jean-Pierre Hurteau, Marie Iösch-Lorcini, Jean-Paul Jeannotte, Paul Jourdain dit Labrosse, Diane Juster, Walter Kemp, Jean Lallemand, Gérard Lamarche, C.-O. and Yvette Lamontagne, Gilles Lamontagne, Alfred Lamoureux, Caro Lamoureux, Eugène Lapierre, Bruno Laplante, Louise, Laplante, Thérèse Laporte, Roméo Larivière, Annette Lasalle-Leduc, Marcel Laurencelle, Jean Laurendeau, Calixa Lavallée, Marguerite Lavergne, Arthur, Émery and Ernest Lavigne, Gabrielle Lavigne, Louise Lebrun, Jacques LeComte, Jean and Roland Leduc, Germain Lefebvre I and II, Gilles Lefebvre, Ovila Légaré, Arthur and Henri Letondal, Claude Léveillée, Monique Leyrac, C.W. Lindsay, Michel Longtin, Nicole Lorange, André Lortie, Louis Lortie, Germaine Malépart, Charles Marchand, Oscar Martel, Gilberte, Magdeleine, Marcelle and Raymonde Martin, Lucien Martin, Rafael, Pietro, Joseph, Rodolfo, Alfredo, Paul, Mario and Giulio Masella, Nicholas Massue, É.-Z. Massicotte, André Mathieu, Salomon Mazurette, Paul-Émile McCaughan, Peter McCuthcheon, Edmond McMahon, Colin McPhee, Pierre Mercure, André Mérineau, Alfred and André Mignault, François Morel, Clément Morin, Jean C. Morin, Pierre Morin, Albertine Morin-Labrecque, Charles-Marie Panneton, Jean Papineau-Couture, Marie-Thérèse Paquin, Gérard Paradis, Hector Pellerin, Colombe Pelletier, Louis-Philippe Pelletier, Romain-Octave I, Frédéric, Romain, and Romain-Octave II Pelletier, Wilfrid Pelletier, Joseph-Julien Perrault, Michel Perrault, Oscar Peterson, Joseph, Eudore and Bernard Piché, Gilles Potvin, Henri Prieur, Albert Quesnel, Caroline Racicot, Ginette Reno, Jacqueline Richard, Lyse Richer-Lortie, Lucien Robert, Tony Romandini, Paul Roussel, Ruth Rubin, Moïse, Joseph and Marcel Saucier, Claude Savard, J.-Élie and Georges Savaria, Robert and André-Sébastien Savoie, Lucien Sicotte, Émile Taranto, J.-Antonio Thompson, Huguette Tourangeau, Amédée Tremblay, William Tritt, Pierre Trochu, Ronald Turini, André Turp, Honoré Vaillancourt, Gilles Valiquette, Jean Vallerand, Marcel Valois, Jeannine Vanier, Stéphane Venne, Louis and Paule Verschelden, Albert Viau, Claude Vivier, Vic Vogel, and Dorothy Weldon.

BIBLIOGRAPHY

Laurendeau, Arthur. 'Chamber and Church music in Montreal' / 'Musique de chambre et musique d'église en Montréal,' *The Year Book of Canadian Art*, compiled by the Arts and Letters Club of Toronto (Toronto, London 1913)

Atherton, William Henry. *Montreal 1535–1914* (Montreal, Vancouver, Chicago 1914)

Lapalice, O. 'Les organistes et maîtres de musique à Notre-Dame de Montréal,' *BRH*, vol 25, Aug 1919

Lamontagne, C.-O. 'La musique à Montréal il y a un demi-siècle,' *Canada musical*, 6 Oct 1923

Montreal Music Year Book 1931, 1932 (Montreal 1931, 1932)

Kallmann, Helmut. 'From the archives: the Montreal Gazette on music from 1786 to 1797,' *CMJ*, vol 6, Spring 1962

Valois, Marcel. *Au carrefour des souvenirs* (Montreal 1965)

Slemon, Peter John. 'Montreal's musical life under the union with an emphasis on the terminal years, 1841 and 1867,' unpubl MMA thesis, McGill 1976

Musical Red Book

See also Writings for É.-Z. Massicotte. GP

Montreal Arena / Aréna de Montréal. Covered amphitheatre, intended mainly for sporting events and horse-shows and erected in 1898 on Ste-Catherine St West at the corner of Wood Avenue. Built at a cost of $75,000 by the Montreal Arena Co, this structure of steel, wood, zinc, and brick seated 7000 people.

Several musical events took place there: the performance of Charles A.E. *Harriss' dramatic legend **Torquil* in 1900; *Metropolitan Opera productions of *Carmen, Faust, Manon*, and *Tannhäuser*, with casts including Emma Calvé, Marcella Sembrich, Sybil Sanderson, Marcel Journet, and Pol Plançon, in 1901; and Mascagni's operas *Cavalleria rusticana, Zanetto,* and *Iris* conducted by the composer in 1902. Patti was heard there (a farewell appearance in 1903), and so were Lilian Nordica and Édouard de Reszke (1903), Calvé (1905), Pauline *Donalda on her return from Europe (1906), and Emma *Albani in her farewell recital of the same year. The arena presented some famous concert bands – Sousa's in 1902, the Coldstream Guards in 1903, the Republican Guard of Paris in 1904, and the Irish Guards (3 concerts) in 1905. In 1906 the Montreal Oratorio Society produced the Canadian premieres of *The Dream of Gerontius* and *Messiah* at the arena. Enrico Caruso performed there in 1908, Luisa Tetrazzini in 1911, Mary Garden in 1912, Eugène Ysaÿe in 1917.

On 2 Jan 1918 the building was destroyed by fire. The damage was an estimated $200,000. GP

The Montreal Bach Choir / La Chorale de Bach de Montréal. A 35-voice ensemble founded in 1951 in Montreal by George *Little to present both unaccompanied and accompanied choral music. The choir offered two Bach works annually, including in various years the *St Matthew Passion, St John Passion, Christmas Oratorio,* and *Mass in B Minor,* but also presented other music, ranging from the renaissance to the 20th century, on radio, TV, and in concert.

The choir's first concert, Bach's *Christmas Oratorio* and *Cantata No. 5,* was held at the *Ermitage 19 Dec 1951. Subsequent concerts were held regularly at Redpath Hall and Erskine and American United Church with such permanent or associate members as Patricia Creighton, Marcelle Dumontet, Maureen *Forrester, Claire *Grenon-Masella, René *Lacourse, Claude *Létourneau, and Jan *Simons performing as soloists. Other guest singers included Pierrette *Alarie, Marguerite *Lavergne, Robert *Savoie, and Léopold *Simoneau.

In 1958 the choir toured four European countries, broadcasting for the BBC and Swiss and French radios and performing with the *Hart House Orchestra at the Brussels World's Fair and with the Orchestre national at the Théâtre des Champs-Elysées in Paris. It was the first Canadian choir to perform at the Edinburgh Festival (1958). The choir toured western Canada (1959, 1961) and Japan (1961), performed with the New York City Ballet and the Montreal Consort of Ancient Instruments, and appeared in the film *Music from Montreal* (NFB 1962). The choir's last performance before disbanding was of Bach's *St John Passion,* 6 Apr 1966 at the *Salle Claude-Champagne.

The choir included in its repertoire works by François *Brassard, Gabriel *Charpentier, Jean *Coulthard, Robert *Fleming, and Michel *Perrault and premiered Violet *Archer's *Proud Horses* (1953) and *Apocalypse* (19 Jan 1959), Jean *Papineau-Couture's *Psaume CL* (1955), Pierre *Mercure's **Cantate pour une joie* (1956), Kelsey *Jones' *Songs of Time* (27 Feb 1957) and *Prophecy of Micah* (5 Feb 1964), Robert *Turner's (commissioned) *Mobile* (9 Mar 1962), and John *Beckwith's *The Trumpets of Summer* (29 Nov 1964).

DISCOGRAPHY

Archer – Bennett – Turner – Des Prez – Issac – Hassler. 1952. RCI 70

Bach – Somers – Turner – Champagne – Vanier – Joachim. (1965). RCI 206

Byrd *Mass for Four Voices; Mass for Five Voices.* (1962). Vox STDL 500.880

de Brumel – Mauduit – Charpentier – Jones – Coulthard – Archer. (1962). RCI 189

Janequin choral works. (1961). Vox STDL 500.710

Mon Canada: Chansons folkloriques. (1960s). Vox STPL 511.860

Music from the Court and Chapel of Henry VIII. Consort of Viols, O. Joachim cond, Lyman org and spinet. (1963). Vox STDL 500.950

Music of the Spanish Renaissance at the Court of Emperor Charles the Fifth. Consort of Viols, O. Joachim cond, Lyman org. (1968). Vox TV 34264

Palestrina *Adoramus te Christe* – Britten *Ceremony of Carols.* Iosch hp. 1953. RCI 89

Papineau-Couture *Psalm CL.* Instr ens, Little cond, Lavergne sop, Jeannotte ten, Aubut org. 1956. RCI 128

Victoria *Missa alma redemptoris: Motets.* (1964). Vox STDL 501.090

BIBLIOGRAPHY

Lee, Betty. 'These amateurs impress the pros,' Toronto *Globe Magazine,* 21 Nov 1959 (NT)

The Montreal Elgar Choir / Chorale Elgar de Montréal. Amateur mixed choir with a membership in 1977 of nearly 200 singers. It was formed in 1923 by the amalgamation of the Elgar Women's Choir (founded in 1921 by Harold E. *Key) and the Apollo Glee Club, conducted by Berkley E. *Chadwick. Chadwick directed the new choir 1923–51. Subsequent conductors have been Gifford *Mitchell 1951–69, Graham Knott 1969–71, Iwan Edwards 1971–2, and Brock McElheran (see USA) 1972–9, succeeded by Louis Lavigueur. The accompanists have been George M. *Brewer 1923–31, Harriet Prutsman 1932–9, Edna Marie *Hawkin 1939–47, Doris Killam 1947–63, Graham Knott 1963–9, and Richard McLaughlin and Frank Armstrong 1969–71, succeeded by Marian Siminski.

Beginning in 1926 the choir was accompanied in public performances by an instrumental ensemble, first by the Montreal Elgar Orchestra (some of whose members formed the Chamber Music Society, later called Montreal String Quartette), and subsequently by members of the *MSO. The choir's members are chosen by audition. Among the soloists who have appeared with the choir are Ann *Golden, Anna *Malenfant, Léopold *Simoneau, and Jan *Simons. In 1951 Maureen *Forrester was the soloist in Elgar's *The Music Makers,* one of her first professional engagements.

The programs for an average of three concerts a year are drawn largely from the standard choral-orchestral works of Bach, Handel, Haydn, Mendelssohn, Elgar, and Fauré. The choir has performed Orff's *Carmina burana,* Stravinsky's *Symphony of Psalms,* and a number of Canadian works including *Willan's **An Apostrophe to the Heavenly Hosts* (presented in 1926), McElheran's *Funeral March on the Death of Heroes* (Montreal premiere in 1973), and *Matton's *L'Escaouette* (1976).

The choir sang at the opening of the Montreal *Forum 22 Apr 1925. The same year it gave its first performance of a complete oratorio, Elgar's *The Dream of Gerontius,* at *His Majesty's Theatre. It took part 1938–46 and in 1949 in the *Montreal Festivals, performing Beethoven's *Missa solemnis,* Bach's *Mass in B Minor* and *St Matthew Passion,* Mozart's *Requiem* and *Coronation Mass,* and Berlioz' *Requiem,* under several different conductors – notably Wilfrid *Pelletier, Eugene Ormandy, Thomas Beecham, and Bernard *Naylor. It participated in the North American premiere (1945, under Emil Cooper) of the Berlioz *Te Deum.* At *Expo 67 it sang Vivaldi's *Gloria* and excerpts from *Messiah.*

The choir has given concerts at St James United Church, at the Victoria and Windsor halls, and, more recently, at the *PDA (where the choir has sung frequently with the MSO) and at the *Salle Claude-Champagne. The Elgar Choir has been subsidized by the Council of Arts of Greater Montreal, the *MACQ, and the *Canada Council. 'God Save the King,' arranged by Elgar, and 'O Canada' were recorded ca 1954 for release on a 45 (RCA Victor 56-3287).

BIBLIOGRAPHY

McLean, Eric. 'Found: a leader; wanted: singers,' *Montreal Star,* 7 Oct 1972

Allen, Francis. 'Choral calisthenics with the Elgar Choir,' *Montreal Scene,* 7 Apr 1973 AP

The Montreal Festivals / Les Festivals de Montréal. Concert and opera festivals founded by the Hon Louis-Athanase *David and his wife and held annually 1939–65. They grew out of the Festival de musique de Montreal, which, under the auspices of the SCSM (*MSO), presented summer seasons of musical events 1936–8 in an attempt to establish in Canada a festival similar to the great annual festivals of Europe. The Festival de musique opened 15 and 17 Jun 1936 with performances of Bach's *St Matthew Passion* and Beethoven's *Symphony No. 9* in the chapel of St-Laurent College on the outskirts of Montreal; Wilfrid *Pelletier conducted, and the choirs were the Cathedral Singers and the *Disciples de Massenet. Bach's *Mass in B Minor* and Verdi's *Requiem* followed in 1937, Beethoven's *Missa solemnis* in 1938, and Mozart's *Requiem* in 1939.

The Montreal Festivals became incorporated as an independent company in 1939 and began to expand and diversify under the direction of Mme David, who served as president until 1951. Notable among the festivals' early presentations was the Canadian premiere, in June 1940, of Debussy's *Pelléas et Mélisande,* with Pelletier as conductor and Marcelle Denya and Raoul *Jobin in the title roles. Because wartime rationing of gasoline made performances around the periphery of Montreal impractical the work was presented at *His Majesty's Theatre.

From 1941 to 1945 Sir Thomas Beecham was associated with the festivals, conducting the Brahms and Fauré requiems, Elgar's *The Dream of Gerontius,* Wagner's *Tristan und Isolde* and Gounod's *Roméo et Juliette,* and a series of popular concerts in the *Forum. The company formed its own orchestra and in subsequent seasons presented open-air productions of *Aida, La Bohème, Madama Butterfly, Carmen, Tosca, Manon, Die Fledermaus,* and other operas, either at the Molson Stadium or at the Chalet atop Mount Royal. During the winter season, it gave concerts of chamber music, mainly by the *McGill String Quartet, as well as a series devoted to French song.

During the presidencies of Paul Gouin, 1952–5, and Robert Letendre, 1956–65, the company ventured into theatre, dance, arts and crafts exhibitions, folk music, operetta, jazz, film, solo recitals, and contemporary music. It continued to operate within the framework of a summer festival, and Canadian content was emphasized increasingly. The responsibility for music was held by Françoys *Bernier 1957–9, Roland *Leduc 1960–3, and Gérard *Lamarche 1964–5. In 1961 Pierre *Mercure organized the *International Week of Today's Music for the company.

The festivals' record of 30 consecutive seasons (1936–65) may be regarded in retrospect as impressive, varied, and dynamic. In addition to the 1940 *Pelléas et Mélisande,* Montreal or Canadian premieres worthy of mention are Strauss' *Ariadne auf Naxos* in 1946; Stravinsky's *L'Histoire du soldat* in 1949; Daudet's play *L'Arlésienne,* with the music of Bizet, in 1950; Honegger's *Jeanne d'Arc au bûcher* in 1953; Racine's *Athalie* with music by Jean-Baptiste Moreau and Clermont *Pépin in 1956; Ildebrando Pizzetti's *Murder in the Cathedral* in 1959; Ravel's *L'Heure espagnole* in 1961; Monteverdi's

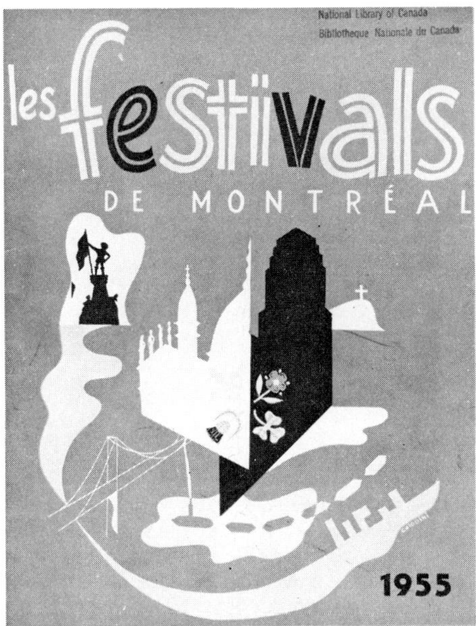

Vespro della Beata Vergine in 1962; and Gilbert Bécaud's *L'Opéra d'Aran* in 1965.

The company's offerings were enriched by a roster of internationally known musicians, such as the conductors Emil Cooper, Laszlo Halasz, Erich Leinsdorf, Charles Munch, Charles O'Connell, and Eugene Ormandy; the pianists Gyorgy Cziffra, José Iturbi, and Wilhelm Kempff; the singers Rose Bampton, Marjorie Lawrence, Grace Moore, Martial Singher, and Eleanor Steber.

Despite steady support from the public and substantial grants from governments, corporations, and individuals, the company accumulated a large deficit over the years. The building of an arts centre, a project it had long championed, was achieved in 1963 with the inauguration of the *PDA. After 1965, preparations for the monumental World Festival held during *Expo 67 were expected to require all its energy, and the company therefore decided to end its activities. On 31 Aug 1965 Pelletier, who had inaugurated the Montreal Festivals 30 years earlier, conducted Haydn's *The Seasons* in the PDA. It was the last presentation by an organization which profoundly affected the artistic life of Montreal.

A souvenir of the era may be found in a recording of Fauré's *Requiem* (1942, RCA Victor DM-844) performed at St-Laurent College under Pelletier by the Disciples du Massenet, the Montreal Festivals Orchestra, and singers Marcelle Denya and Mack Harrell. The recording received world distribution and was reissued on LP (LCT 7003, later withdrawn from the catalogue).

BIBLIOGRAPHY

Pelletier, Wilfrid. *Une Symphonie inachevée ...* (Montreal 1972) (CH)

Montreal International Competition / Concours International de Montréal. Organization founded in 1963 to set up major, regularly recurring international competitions for outstanding young performing musicians, and to place Montreal and Canada in the mainstream of such international activities. It was instigated by the businessman and music lover Florent Marcil, the pianist Monique Marcil, the cellist Charles *Houdret, and the lawyer Micheline Corbeil. It was incorporated in 1963, with Wilfrid *Pelletier as honorary president, Jean-J. Dury as president, Monique Marcil as director general, and with Irving *Heller, joint artistic director, and Isabelle *Delorme, Bernard *Diamant, John *Newmark, and Calvin *Sieb as members of a consulting committee.

The first Montreal International Competition was held in May–June 1965 and was devoted to the piano; the 1966 competition was for the violin and the 1967 one for voice. Until 1974 the competitions ran on a three-year cycle alternating according to the above order; beginning in 1975 and still in effect in 1980 one year of rest followed the third year of the cycle, and the order was changed to violin, piano, and voice. The violin and piano competitions are open to performers 16 to 30 years of age, and the voice competition to those 20 to 35 years of age. Each competition consists of three tests: two preliminary rounds and one final, in which the *MSO has taken part. Because of its rigourous admission standards, the requirements of the program, and the quality of the jury the Montreal International Competition has become one of the most highly regarded. In 1966 it was accepted as a member of the Geneva-based Fédération des concours internationaux de musique.

From 1965 to 1976 the Montreal International Competition was host to nearly 500 participants from 41 countries. The competition winners have shared prizes totalling $22,500 allocated as follows: Grand Prix Florent-Marcil (in memory of the founder and president) $10,000; second prize $5,000, third $2,500, fourth $1,500, fifth $1,000, and four prizes of $500 each. A special prize of $500 is offered to the best interpreter of the unpublished Canadian work commissioned as a set piece ('pièce imposée') in the final test. Composers of set pieces have been *Fiala (1965, 1968), *Prévost (1966), *Somers (1967), *Vallerand (1969), *Papineau-Couture (1970), *Pentland (1971), *Pépin (1972), *Schafer (1973), *Morawetz (1975), J. *Hétu (1976), *Applebaum (1977), and *Dompierre (1978). *Morel was commissioned to write for the 1980 competition. In 1980 the competition continued to be supported by the *Canada Council, the *MACQ, the Council of Arts of Greater Montreal, and several private organizations.

WINNERS

1965 *Piano* 1st Jean-Claude Pennetier, France, and Albert Lotto, USA
1966 *Violin* 1st Vladimir Lancman (Landsman), USSR; 2nd Hidetaro *Suzuki, Japan, and Gueorgui Balev, Bulgaria
1967 *Voice* 1st Marina Krilovici, Rumania, and Yury Mazurok, USSR
1968 *Piano* 1st Garrick Ohlsson, USA; 2nd Peter Rösel, East Germany
1969 *Violin* 1st Vladimir Spivakov, USSR; 2nd Oleg Krissa, USSR, and Ghidon Kremer, USSR
1970 *Voice* 2nd Maurice *Brown, Canada (no 1st awarded)
1971 *Piano* 2nd Peter Basquin, USA (no 1st awarded)
1972 *Violin* 1st Ruben Agaronian, USSR; 2nd Mikhaïl Bezverhny, USSR
1973 *Voice* 1st Gheorgue Emil Crasnaru, Rumania; 2nd Makvala Karashvilli, USSR
1974 No competition
1975 *Violin* 2nd Dong-Suk Kang, Korea, and Yuval Yaron, Israel (no 1st awarded)
1976 *Piano* 1st Eteri Andjaparidze, USSR; 2nd Nicolaï Demidenko, USSR, Naïm Grubert, USSR, and Gerhard Oppitz, West Germany
1977 *Voice* 2nd William Parker, USA, and Louise Wohlafka, USA (no 1st awarded)
1978 No competition
1979 *Violin* 1st Peter Zazofsky, USA; 2nd Mihaela Martin, Rumania
1980 *Piano* 1st Ivo Pogorelic, Yugloslavia; 2nd Christopher O'Riley, USA, and Vladimir Ovchinnikov, USSR

CH

Montreal Opera Company / Compagnie d'opéra de Montréal. Opera company founded in 1910 by Albert *Clerk-Jeannotte, with the financial support of Frank Stephen *Meighen and the assistance of Charles-O. *Lamontagne as business administrator. Clerk-Jeannotte engaged musicians from the New San Carlo Opera along with their conductor, Agide Jacchia (b Lugo, Italy, 5 Jan 1875, d Siena 29 Nov 1932), a pupil of Mascagni. They were joined by singers and instrumentalists from Montreal and New York and, as the Montreal Musical Society, opened 31 Oct 1910 at *His Majesty's Theatre. During the company's eight-week season it gave 48 performances, at first alternating *Tosca* and *Lakmé* and then presenting Giordano's *Fedora*, Massenet's *Manon*, Bizet's *Carmen*, Puccini's *La Bohème*, and *Madama Butterfly*, Verdi's *La Traviata*, Massenet's *Thaïs*, and Mascagni's *L'Amico Fritz*, as well as eight symphony concerts. Frances Alda, Natale Cervi, Edmond Clémont, Ugo Colombini, Louis Deru, Ester Ferrabini, Lydia Lipkowska, Alice Michot, Alice Nielsen, Giuseppe Pimazzini, Simone Rivière, and Eugenio Torre were among the singers. In December of that year the company went to Quebec City for a week at the *Auditorium but on arrival it learned that the Catholic bishop had forbidden all Catholics to attend the performances, considering such attendance a sin. The scores were submitted to him immediately for approval, and with two exceptions, *Manon* and *Thaïs*, the ban was lifted. The company went on to play at the *Russell Theatre in Ottawa, the Lyceum in Rochester, NY, and the Princess Theatre in Toronto. It ended the season with a deficit of over $22,000.

For the 1911–12 season at His Majesty's the name was changed to the Montreal Opera Company (or Compagnie d'opéra de Montréal), and the orchestra increased to 45. Jacchia directed the Italian operas, and Louis Hasselmans (b Paris 25 Jul 1878, d San Juan, Puerto Rico, 27 Dec 1957) came from Paris to take charge of the French repertoire. This was expanded to 12 operas: Gounod's *Faust* and *Roméo et Juliette*, Massenet's *Cendrillon*, *Le Jongleur de Notre-Dame*, *La Navarraise*, and *Werther*, Messager's *Madame Chrysanthème*, Charpentier's *Louise*, Saint-Saëns' *L'Ancêtre*, Leroux's *Le Chemineau*, Godard's *La Vivandière*, and Erlanger's *Noël*. The cast included some Canadians, notably the soprano Béatrice *La Palme (who made her debut in the role of Micaela), the soprano Irene *Pavloska, and the bass Georges Panneton. The French tenor Edmond Clément and the US soprano Beatrice Bowman also appeared. The second season ended with a further deficit of close to $50,000 after 97 opera performances – 69 in Montreal and 28 on tour – and 13 symphony concerts.

The repertoire for the third season was even more ambitious, including Verdi's *Aida*, Massenet's *Hérodiade*, and Leoncavallo's *Zazà*. The sopranos Maria Gay and Carmen Melis, the mezzo-soprano Marie Claessens, the tenors Léon Laffite and Giuseppe Gaudenzi, the baritone Jean *Riddez, and the bass Giovanni Polese were among the soloists. The Canadian Louise *Edvina sang Marguerite in *Faust* as well as the title roles in *Louise* and *Tosca*, which she had sung at Covent Garden. The chorus was directed by Henri *Delcellier, and Wilfrid *Pelletier worked with him as rehearsal pianist. The deficit for this season was about $65,000. It was decided, therefore, that the 1912–13 season would be the last.

In three seasons the Montreal Opera Company gave nearly 300 performances, of which 139 were of French opera and 137 of Italian, as well as numerous symphony concerts. Meighen spent over $100,000 to cover the deficits. After the company collapsed, some of its members established the

*National Opera Company of Canada in the autumn of 1913 under the auspices of Max Rabinoff, a US impresario of Russian origin. The principal conductor was Agide Jacchia, who later moved on to conduct the Century Opera of New York, the Boston National Opera Company, and 1917–26 the Boston Pops Orchestra. Louis Hasselmans was engaged for the 1918–19 season by the Chicago Opera, 1919–22 by the Opéra-Comique of Paris, and 1922–37 by the *Metropolitan Opera.

BIBLIOGRAPHY
Lamontagne, Charles-O. 'Montreal Opera Company,' Montreal *Gazette*, 27 Jul, 3, 10, 17 Aug 1946
Lamontagne, Charles-O., and Gour, Romain. 'Frank Stephen Meighen, dilettante et mécène,' *Oui?*, vol 5, Mar 1954 GP

Montreal Oratorio Society. Mixed choir of more than 200 voices founded by Horace *Reyner in 1902 after the disbandment of the *Montreal Philharmonic Society (1875–99) and the Motet Choir (1897–1901). Conducted by Reyner 1902–6, J.E.F. Martin 1906–7, and Frederick H. *Blair 1907–8, the society generally performed at *Windsor Hall, the *Montreal Arena, or the Dominion Douglas Church. It gave the first complete performances in Canada of Coleridge-Taylor's *Hiawatha* (27 Jan 1904) and Elgar's *The Dream of Gerontius* (12 Apr 1906) and supplied the chorus for such special events of the day as the Duss-Nordica concert, the *Cycle of Musical Festivals' Montreal presentation (24 Apr 1903) under visiting RAM principal Sir Alexander Mackenzie, and the Ottawa performance (1904) of C.A.E. *Harriss' *Pan*. The society performed with the Goulet *MSO, 11 Mar 1908 at the New Lyric Hall. It presented the last of its several performances of *Messiah* 17 Apr 1908 at St James Methodist Church and disbanded that year. NT

The Montreal Orchestra. Seventy-member symphony orchestra founded in 1930 as a co-operative venture by Montreal theatre musicians who banded together under the initiative of clarinetist Giulio *Romano to give concerts when the new sound films put them out of work. Each musician reportedly received $4 after the first concert, 12 Oct 1930 at the *Orpheum Theatre. Payment rose to about $15 in the last years before disbandment in 1941. Though it was the musicians' intention to engage guest conductors, they invited the first, Douglas *Clarke, to take over on a permanent basis. This he did, serving without remuneration during the orchestra's 11 years. Shortly after the beginning of its first season of 25 concerts, the orchestra moved to His (*Her) Majesty's Theatre, where it continued to play on Sunday afternoons, the number of concerts reduced to 20 annually 1931–3, 18 annually 1933–6, and 10 annually 1936–41. The orchestra gave 10 concerts in 1932 on the CPR radio network and alternated 1938–9 with the *CSM on the CBC. It also gave children's concerts 1935–9 in the ballroom of the (Sheraton) Mount Royal Hotel. The notion of a musicians' co-operative soon was abandoned as production costs exceeded box-office receipts. A volunteer committee was formed to attend to the orchestra's business, and several benefactors were enlisted to cover the year-end deficit. Only in its last three years did the orchestra receive an annual subsidy of $1000 from the province.

There had been regular concerts in Montreal prior to those by the Montreal Orchestra, largely through the pioneering efforts of such people as Guillaume *Couture and J.-J. *Goulet in the 1890s and J.-J. *Gagnier in the first three decades of the 20th century. But these men were working with ad hoc ensembles of 30 to 50 musicians, many of them amateurs, and their programs often were a mixture of symphonic extracts and solo pieces. By contrast the Montreal Orchestra employed some 70 professionals and introduced its audiences to full symphonic programs, often of works now regarded as standard repertoire but previously unperformed in Montreal – eg, Berlioz' *Symphonie fantastique* and Brahms' *Violin Concerto*, *Symphony No. 1*, *Symphony No. 4*, and *Piano Concerto No. 2*.

A rehearsal of the Montreal Orchestra, ca 1935

Among those Canadian soloists who appeared with the orchestra were the pianists Ellen *Ballon, Gertrude *Huntley Green, Paul *de Marky, Séverin *Moisse, and Ross *Pratt; the duo-pianists Etta Coles and Naomi Yanova; the violinists Maurice *Onderet (concertmaster of the Montreal Orchestra 1930–41 and soloist in the Brahms concerto), Kathleen *Parlow and Ethel *Stark; the baritones Lionel *Daunais and Leslie *Holmes; the soprano Jeanne *Dusseau; and the mezzo-soprano Cédia *Brault. Canadians who conducted the orchestra included Claude *Champagne in the Canadian premiere (1933) of his *Suite canadienne*, Reginald *Tupper in a 1934 performance of his *Suite of Old English Pieces*, Henri *Miro, who conducted his *Symphonic Praeludium* in 1935, Alexander *Brott in a 1939 performance of his *Oracle*, and Bernard *Naylor, who conducted two concerts in 1941. Clarke conducted the Montreal premiere of *Willan's *Symphony No. 1* in 1937 and the premiere of Violet *Archer's *Scherzo Sinfonico* in 1940. Foreign artists who appeared with the orchestra included Webster Aitken, Harold Bauer, Harriet Cohen, Georges Enesco, Emanuel Feuermann, Ria Ginster, Percy Grainger (who conducted his *Green Bushes* and *Colonial Song* in 1938), Gustav Holst (who conducted 'Jupiter' from his *The Planets* in 1932), Nathan Milstein, William Primrose, Felix Salmond, E. Robert Schmitz, Albert Spalding, Paul Wittgenstein, and Efrem Zimbalist.

The demise of the Montreal Orchestra was the result of a dispute between the English- and French-speaking members of the board. Some of the francophones, led by Mme (Louis) Athanase *David, sought a greater role in the choosing of programs and soloists, which they regarded as excessively English – a charge not substantiated by an examination of the records. More likely the reason for the discord was Clarke's personality; he did not succeed in identifying with Canada, regarding himself instead as an Englishman residing abroad. He refused to abdicate any fraction of his authority in regard to program or the choice of soloists. The matter came to a head in 1934 when Mme David quit the committee and formed another orchestra, the CSM (*MSO). Most of the musicians in the new orchestra had played under Clarke's baton for nearly five years and indeed continued to play in both. Thus in a very real sense the Montreal Orchestra was the father of the CSM and grandfather of the MSO. However, Montreal, which had difficulty supporting one orchestra, now found itself under the embarrassing obligation of supporting two. The contest could not continue for long: one or the other organization would have to withdraw, and Mme David had the singular advantage of political influence at a time when it really counted in Quebec. That the Montreal Orchestra continued for another six years is a measure of its pertinacity and standing. The onset of World War II and Clarke's serious illness led to the orchestra's collapse after the 1940–1 season.

BIBLIOGRAPHY
Dufresne, J. 'L'Orchestre symphonique de Montréal,' *La Lyre*, vol 8, Nov 1930
Alexander, B.M. 'How the orchestra is financed,' *Montreal Music Year Book 1931* (Montreal 1931)
Bell, H.P. 'The Montreal Orchestra,' ibid
Clarke, D. 'The Montreal Orchestra,' *Montreal Music Year Book 1932* (Montreal 1932)
Herbert, C.H. 'History of the Montreal Orchestra,' *Conservatorium of Music Year Book* (Montreal 1935)
Bell, H.P. 'The Montreal Orchestra and Les Concerts symphoniques,' *Curtain Call*, Jan 1940
Bishop, A.E. *The Montreal Orchestra, Retrospect 1930–41*, priv publ (Montreal 1974) EM

The Montreal Philharmonic Society. Choral and orchestral association founded in August 1875 by Arthur M. Perkins. It first performed in public in May 1877, presenting Handel's *Messiah* and other works during a three-day Montreal Music Festival. Its first concert on its own, 17 Dec 1877 at the *Academy of Music, included Mendelssohn's *42nd Psalm*. Conducted 1877–9 by Dr P.R. MacLagan (organist at Christ Church Cathedral and later active in Winnipeg), for one concert, 28 May 1879, by Joseph *Gould, 1879–80 by Fred E. Lucy-Barnes, and 1880–99 by Guillaume *Couture, the society gave 87 concerts before its dissolution in 1899. It performed at the Academy of Music, *Mechanics Hall, the Victoria Skating Rink, 1880–9 at *Queen's Hall, and 1890–9 at *Windsor Hall.

In its early years the society brought together for each concert instrumentalists from Montreal and Quebec, but it was not always able to assemble a full complement and on one occasion it had to import a timpanist from Boston. To ensure that performances would be well rehearsed, Couture created the Société des Symphonistes which, however, did not survive. Subsequently orchestras from the eastern USA or made up of US and Canadian musicians were employed. Among these, the Boston Festival Orchestra came most frequently. The choir grew from 130 voices in 1878 to 275 in 1894.

The Montreal Philharmonic Society achieved particular renown under Couture, who introduced many oratorios and operas (in concert form) and a surprisingly varied symphonic repertoire. Canadian premieres included Schumann's *Paradise and the Peri* (8 Jan 1885), Cherubini's *Requiem in C Minor* (17 Dec 1885), Berlioz' *La Damnation de Faust* (17 Apr 1890), Beethoven's *Ruins of Athens* (19 Mar 1891), Mackenzie's *The Story of Sayid* (25 Mar 1892), Saint-Saëns' *The Deluge* (23 Mar 1892) and *Samson et Dalila* (14 Apr 1895), and G.W. Chadwick's *The Lily Nymph*, dedicated to the society (28 Apr 1896). Receiving their first Montreal performances were Mendelssohn's *Elijah* (15 May 1884), Handel's *Judas Maccabaeus* (17 Mar 1881) and *Samson* (21 Mar 1889), the overture to Weber's *Der Freischütz* (17 Mar 1888), Max Bruch's *Arminius* (18 Mar 1891), and Beethoven's *Mount of Olives* (14 Mar 1893). The society performed Wagner's *The Flying Dutchman* (3 Apr 1895) and *Tannhäuser* (29 Apr 1896), Beethoven's *Symphony No. 9* (8 Apr 1897), and works by Bennet, Dubois, Dvořák, Gounod, Massenet, and Sullivan. C.A.E. *Harriss' cantata *Daniel before the King*, the first published major work by a Canadian resident, was performed 18 Apr 1890.

By 1890 the Montreal Philharmonic Society has presented some 120 large choral-orchestral works, unaccompanied works, or pieces for choir and soloists and had attained a high reputation. Soloists included the singers Emma *Albani, David Ffrangcon-Davies, Emma Juch, and Robert *Watkin-Mills; the violinist Frantz *Jehin-Prume; and the pianist Calixa *Lavallée. Guest conductors included G.W. Chadwick, Emil Mollenhauer, and Henry Schmidt. In 1896 a small journal, *The Philharmonic Bulletin*, was published to promote the interests of the society.

However, growing deficits and a marked change in the size and taste of its audiences led to the society's demise. In its final concert (25 May 1899), assisted by the Paur SO from New York, it performed Beethoven's *Symphony No. 5*, Mendelssohn's *Hymn of Praise*, Liszt's *Grand Solo de concert* (solo-piano-and-orchestra version of the two-piano piece *Concerto pathétique*, with Richard Burmeister as soloist), and Goldmark's concert overture *Sakuntala*.

BIBLIOGRAPHY
Montreal Daily Star, 28 Mar 1890
Musical Red Book

NT

Montreal String Quartet. The name of three string quartets that existed in Montreal between 1925 and 1963.

1 **Montreal String Quartette** (fl ca 1925–8) was composed of Florence Hood and Mary Izard, violins, Robert H. Bryson, viola, and Yvette *Lamontagne, cello, succeeded by Jean *Belland in 1928. Works by Mendelssohn and Schumann were among those performed in 1926 in *Windsor Hall.

2 **The Montreal String Quartet† / Quatuor à cordes de Montreal** (1934–40) consisted of Lucien *Sicotte and Annette *Lasalle-Leduc, violins, Lucien *Robert, viola, and Roland *Leduc, cello. It gave its first concert 24 Nov 1934 in *Tudor Hall and was greeted by the critic Henri *Letondal as a 'young and enthusiastic ensemble [which] made a most favourable impression.' The quartet performed frequently on CBC radio, at the *Ladies' Morning Musical Club, and as the guest of several other concert-giving societies. Sicotte was absent in 1937 and the quartet reduced its activity that year to a single concert, but it performed as usual in 1938, its programs including the premiere of a string-quartet version of *Champagne's *Danse villageoise*. In April 1939, after a farewell concert, the quartet left for Europe for intensive training under André Tourret, subsidized by the Quebec government and the patron Jean-C. *Lallemand. The quartet's stay in France was cut short by the declaration of war; after a hasty return to Canada the ensemble performed at the École supérieure de musique in Outremont (*École Vincent-d'Indy). Not long afterwards internal problems caused the group to disband.

3 **The Montreal String Quartet / Quatuor à cordes de Montréal** (1955–63) was composed of Hyman *Bress and Mildred *Goodman, violins, Otto *Joachim, viola, and Walter *Joachim, cello. Its first performance, 2 Mar 1955 at the *Ermitage under the auspices of the *CLComp, was devoted to works of Canadian composers: *Vallerand, *Papineau-Couture, *Betts, *Morel, *Archer, *Freedman, and *Turner. Over the years the CBC IS and the CBC French and English networks often called upon the ensemble to perform or record Canadian works as well as the classical repertoire. It premiered Glenn *Gould's *Quartet* (1956), Otto Joachim's *Quartet* (1957), and Clermont *Pépin's *Quartet No. 2* (1957) and *Quartet No. 4* (1960). The ensemble frequently performed for the *Pro Musica Society, the Ladies' Morning Musical Club, and the *Montreal Festivals (1957, the Brahms *Quintet* with Glenn Gould, piano), and it also played in Toronto and other Canadian cities. In February 1958 it made its New York debut at the Carnegie Recital Hall; 'Characteristics of [the players'] interpretations were their good rhythmic sense and their obvious love for the music,' reported *Musical America* (Mar 1958). During the 1959–60 season the quartet presented two series of six concerts in the Ermitage Hall sponsored by the *Canada Council. For these concerts, in addition to works of Haydn, Mozart, Beethoven, Schumann, Debussy, Bloch and Bartók, the quartet performed music by Pépin, Joachim, Papineau-Couture, and *Weinzweig. When it disbanded during the 1962–3 season the quartet was considered one of the finest in Canada.

DISCOGRAPHY
Brahms *Quintet, Op 34*. Gould pf. 1957. RCI 140
Champagne *String Quartet*. 1956. RCI 143
Gould *String Quartet No. 1*. 1956. RCI 142
O. Joachim *String Quartet* – Haydn *String Quartet, Op 103*. (1963). RCI 190
K. Jones *Suite* for flute and strings – Tomkins *Fantaisie* – Ferrabosco *Allemande*. Duschenes fl, N. Clair ob. (1963). RCI 191
Pentland *String Quartet No. 1* – Vallerand *String Quartet*. (1958). RCI 141
M. Perrault *Sextet* for strings, clarinet, and harp. Rafael Masella cl, Weldon hp. 1955. RCI 125
Schumann *Quintet, Op 44*. Newmark pf. 1953. RCI 96

IP-C, NT

Montreal Symphony Orchestra (MSO) / Orchestre symphonique de Montréal (OSM). The name of four successive Montreal symphonic ensembles. The first (1894–6) was directed by Guillaume *Couture, the second (1898–1919) by J.-J. *Goulet, and the third (1927–9) by J.-J. *Gagnier. The fourth – in 1980 one of the principal large orchestras in Canada, rivalled only by the *TS – was founded in 1934 as the Société des concerts symphoniques de Montréal (SCSM or CSM) and in 1953 adopted the bilingual name Orchestre symphonique de Montréal (OSM / Montreal Symphony Orchestra (MSO), reverting to the French-only designation in 1979. The four orchestras are discussed hereunder – and referred to throughout *EMC* – as:

1 Couture MSO
2 Goulet MSO
3 Gagnier MSO
4 MSO (or, for historic references, SCSM or CSM).

1 COUTURE MSO (1894–6). As early as 1845 a notice in *Le Spectateur canadien* invited Montreal instrumentalists to join a philharmonic society. However, it was not until 1863 that the Société philharmonique canadienne was born, bringing together about 30 musicians under the direction of J.-B. *Labelle. At its first 'grand concert,' 26 March in Nordheimer Hall, the 'full orchestra' played the overture to Auber's *La Muette de Portici* and accompanied Rossini's *Stabat Mater*. It is not known whether the concert was followed by others. The six classical chamber concerts conducted by Frantz *Jehin-Prume at the *Mechanics' Hall early in 1871 marked another stage. In addition to string quartets the programs included one or more movements of Beethoven's *Pastoral Symphony* and overtures by Mozart, Weber and, Rossini, and the orchestra accompanied the violinist-conductor in concertos by Beethoven and Mendelssohn. For an orchestra to accompany the inaugural concert – a performance 28 May 1877 of *Messiah* – of the *Montreal Philharmonic Society 'Dr. MacLagan was obliged not only to combine all the available talent of Montreal and Quebec, but even to go as far as Boston for a player of the timpani, which instrument, as the programme naively remarks, was unknown in Montreal' (*Musical Red Book*). When Couture became conductor of the society in 1880 he founded the Société des symphonistes in an attempt to provide the choir with a regular accompanying orchestra, but the attempt failed because of the dearth of competent instrumentalists. It was probably J.-Arthur *Boucher who first called an orchestra 'Symphonie de Montréal' (1887) but nothing more than this is known of his endeavour. A decisive year in the progress towards a regular Montreal orchestra was 1890, when Ernest *Lavigne brought over from Europe, especially from Belgium, some 20 qualified young instrumentalists to fill the ranks of the symphony orchestra at *Sohmer Park. The orchestra only played a few seasons, and Lavigne's plans for a conservatory – which had attracted the players – came to naught. However, most of the musicians remained in Montreal, and it was they who formed the nucleus of the first MSO, set up as a co-operative by its concertmaster, J.-J. Goulet. Guillaume Couture fulfilled the duties of conductor for two seasons (1894–6) at *Windsor Hall. The 40-or-so instrumentalists gave 10 concerts in 1894–5 and 8 in 1895–6. At the first of these, Beethoven's *Symphony No. 1* 'was given a masterly rendition' according to the anonymous critic of *La Patrie* (8 November), who added, 'At last we have in Montreal a full symphony orchestra; thanks to that we are going to have our Concerts Colonne and our Orchestre Lamoureux just like Paris.' Couture performed the *Rienzi* and *Tannhäuser* overtures and symphonies by Schubert (No. 8), Mendelssohn (No. 4), and Schumann (No. 1). Among the soloists were Joseph *Saucier, baritone, Émery *Lavigne, pianist, Ellsworth *Duquette, bass, and the orchestra principals Goulet, J.-B. *Dubois (cello), and B. Gerome (bassoon). The two seasons concluded without a deficit, but the orchestra ceased to exist as a result of internal conflicts. During the whole 1896–7 season and the first half of the 1897–8 season Montreal was without a symphony orchestra.

2 GOULET MSO (1898–1919). At the beginning of 1898, J.-J. Goulet again assembled about 30 instrumentalists under the name MSO, and this time he became the conductor, pledging to pay any deficit

from his own pocket. Joseph Saucier was the soloist in the first concert, 14 January at *Queen's Hall. The *William Tell* overture and Haydn's *Military Symphony* were performed. In 1898–9 this well-organized orchestra, with the cellist Victor Pelletier as secretary and Frank A. Veitch as administrator, gave 12 concerts. After the fire at Queen's Hall in 1899, l'Orchestre Goulet, or the Goulet Orchestra as it also was known, moved to Windsor Hall. In 1903 it comprised 45 instrumentalists and moved into a larger hall, the *Académie de musique, subsequently giving six to eight concerts a season. At the end of 1905–6 the treasurer proudly reported a surplus of $70. Soloists from abroad, including the violinists Henri Marteau, Mary Hall, and Otie Chew, were engaged. Also among the soloists were the Canadian bass Edmund *Burke, and the famous pianist Emil von Sauer, who played Beethoven's *Emperor Concerto* in 1908. In 1900 Goulet presented the pianist Émiliano *Renaud, who performed his own *Concertstück*. In 1903 the Goulet MSO went to Halifax, NS, and Moncton and Saint John, NB, to participate in the *Cycle of Musical Festivals of the Dominion of Canada. For several seasons the concertmaster was Émile *Taranto, who also, in 1904, appeared as soloist with the orchestra. The repertoire chosen by Goulet at times was ambitious. It included the symphonies No. 2, 3, and 4 by Beethoven, the No. 7 and 8 by Schubert, the No. 3 and 4 by Mendelssohn, and No. 40 by Mozart.

After the demolition of the Académie de musique in 1910, Goulet took his orchestra to *His Majesty's Theatre. During the war the concerts occurred less frequently, and in 1919 at the Princess Theatre the Goulet MSO gave its last concert. Other symphonic seasons took place in Montreal beginning in 1910; these were usually short, often adjuncts to operatic seasons. For instance, the orchestra of the *Montreal Opera Company presented eight concerts at His Majesty's under the direction of Agide Jacchia during the 1910–11 season and five under Louis Hasselmans during the 1911–12 season. Among the soloists were Jacques Thibaud, Wilhelm Backhaus, and the contralto Jeanne Gerville-Réache. In 1913–14 the *National Opera Company of Canada presented eight concerts at His Majesty's under the direction of Jacchia, Alexander Savine, and Oscar Spirescu. Thibaud, Backhaus, Harold Bauer, and Kathleen *Parlow were among the soloists. In 1914 J.J. *Shea put together an orchestra of 50 which presented just one season at the Imperial Theatre. Florence *Easton was among the soloists, along with the Canadians Albert *Chamberland, Jean *Dansereau, and Gustave *Labelle. The Symphonie royale of Henri *Delcellier gave some concerts at the same location.

3 GAGNIER MSO (1927–9). The foundation of this third MSO was announced in December 1927, with J.-J. Gagnier as the orchestra's artistic director and Frank S. *Meighen as its president, the first concert took place 22 Jan 1928 at the Princess Theatre. On that occasion Haydn's *Oxford Symphony* was played, along with Roussel's *Le Festin de l'araignée* and Elgar's *Caractacus*. Later Gagnier performed major works of Schubert, Beethoven, Wagner, Sibelius, Ravel, and Honegger. The Depression struck the orchestra hard, however, and it ceased its activities. Gagnier also conducted a Petite Symphonie de Montréal, still active in 1930–1, taking part in a performance of Constant Lambert's *Rio Grande*.

Around 1930, Eugène *Chartier formed the Montreal Philharmonic Orchestra (originally the orchestra of the *Cons national de musique) and gave concerts with it at the Mount Royal Hotel. Much later (ca 1943–6) a professional ensemble by the same name presented a few seasons at the *St-Denis Theatre featuring famous guest conductors, including Pierre Monteux, Igor Stravinsky, Jascha Horenstein, Lorin Maazel, and Wilfrid *Pelletier.

4 MSO (SCSM, CSM). At the time of the foundation of the SCSM in the autumn of 1934, the *Montreal Orchestra, which presented weekly Sunday concerts under the direction of Douglas *Clarke, had been in existence for four years. The idea of founding a second orchestra in the middle of the Depression seems to have developed for two reasons. The first in all likelihood was the desire of French Canadians to have an orchestra of their own, since the Montreal Orchestra was much more identified with the English-speaking milieu of the metropolis. The second was a result of the repeated refusal of the management of the Montreal Orchestra to accord a reasonable place to Quebec soloists, conductors, and composers, especially the winners of the *Prix d'Europe and other holders of grants from the Quebec government. To overcome this resistance, the Hon Louis-Athanase David, the provincial secretary at that time and the person responsible for the arts and humanities, had offered a subsidy, which was refused. Others pointed to the inordinately large place afforded to British composers, but a survey of the orchestra's programs proves this allegation to have been unjustified.

The idea of a second orchestra gained ground, nurtured by a campaign in the press, particularly by the critic Henri *Letondal. The latter and a group of citizens were the instigators of the project, for which David obtained a grant of $3000 from the Quebec government. A committee was formed and the first concert set for 14 Jan 1935. The first printed program contains the names of 37 founder-members and those of the executive committee, comprising David, honorary president, Ernest Tétreau, president, and Mme (Louis) Athanase *David, Annette Doré, Ubald Boyer, Victor Doré, Jean C. *Lallemand, and Henri Letondal. On page 2 of the program it was stated that 'the creation of a symphony orchestra in the east end of Montreal fulfils a long standing request by the French population of our city' and that 'two-thirds of its players are French-Canadian.' In fact, the personnel of the two orchestras was appreciably the same.

Wilfrid Pelletier, who was living in New York at that time, was enthusiastic in his support. The first concert, held in *Plateau Hall, was conducted however by Rosario *Bourdon, with the pianist Léo-Pol *Morin as soloist in Mendelssohn's *Capriccio brillant*. Bourdon led the orchestra in two overtures (Beethoven's *Leonora No. 3* and Goldmark's *Sakuntala*), in Tchaikovsky's *Symphony No. 6*, and in his own arrangement of *Lavallée's famous piano piece *Le Papillon*. Edmond *Trudel, Eugène Chartier, and J.-J. Gagnier followed on the podium, with Pelletier finally making his debut 11 Apr 1935. Shortly afterwards Pelletier became the first artistic director, and during his tenure, 1935–40, several new directions were taken: symphonic matinees for young people in 1935, the annual Prix Jean-Lallemand for composition 1936–8, an annual festival 1936–8 in the suburb of St-Laurent, and summer concerts 1938–64 on the promenade at the Chalet on Mount Royal.

The SCSM received its official charter in 1939. Meanwhile, conductors and soloists began coming from abroad: Vladimir Golschmann, Jean Morel, Paul Stassevitch, Fritz Stiedry, Alexandre Brailowsky, Mack Harrell, Zino Francescatti, Artur Rubinstein, Jesús-María Sanromá, Rudolf Serkin, and others. Attempts to merge the two Montreal orchestras proved unsuccessful, but some degree of collaboration was established and maintained until the disappearance of the Montreal Orchestra in 1941. After an internal dispute, the Davids left the MSO, and Mme David took charge of the *Montreal Festivals, which had become autonomous in 1939. Kept increasingly in New York by his work at the *Metropolitan Opera, Pelletier turned over the artistic directorship to the Belgian conductor Desiré Defauw (b Ghent 1885, d Gary, Ind, 1960) who filled the position 1940–52. Defauw's long experience in his native Belgium and elsewhere in Europe and his international reputation were beneficial, though his presence in Montreal became less and less frequent, especially after his appointment to the Chicago SO in 1943. Defauw presented special events such as a festival of Beethoven symphonies (1941) and spring gala performances featuring operas, eg, *Boris Godunov* and *The Damnation of Faust*, with Les *Disciples de Massenet. Besides the French and German repertoire, Defauw performed works by Belgian composers, and within three years of their composition works such as Strauss' *Metamorphosen* and Shostakovitch's *Symphony No. 9* were given under his direction. In the 1944–5 season the Tuesday programs were repeated on Wednesday. During this period, the most distinguished conductors began appearing with the orchestra, among them Sir Thomas Beecham, Leonard Bernstein, Fritz Busch, Georges Enesco, Erich Leinsdorf, Pierre Monteux, Charles Munch, Paul Paray, Victor de Sabata, Georg Solti, Leopold Stokowski, Igor Stravinsky, George Szell, and Bruno Walter. Among soloists of international repute were Claudio Arrau, Eileen Farrell, Emanuel Feuermann, Kirsten Flagstad, Jascha Heifetz, George *London, Yehudi Menuhin, and Gregor Piatigorsky.

Désiré Defauw, artistic director of the Montreal Symphony Orchestra 1940–52

Canadian conductors and soloists, such as Jean-Marie *Beaudet, Noël *Brunet, Jean Dansereau, Lionel *Daunais, Raoul *Jobin, Arthur *LeBlanc, Roland *Leduc, Sir Ernest *MacMillan, Anna *Malenfant, Gilberte *Martin, and Ettore *Mazzoleni also were among those invited to perform. Over the years the MSO has continued to engage illustrious guest soloists and conductors, reserving a special place for Canadian performers, who appeared with the orchestra in increasing numbers during the 1970s.

While disembarking from the airplane that had brought him to inaugurate the 1951–2 season, Otto Klemperer (b Breslau 1885, d Zurich 1973) suffered a severe accident and was hospitalized for several months in Montreal. While convalescing there he resumed his activities little by little (conducting from a chair), and for two seasons he dispensed advice to the orchestra, albeit in an unofficial capacity. Gradually he returned to his international schedule, and the ensemble once again called on the services of a number of guests. Charles Munch, Pierre Monteux, Thomas Schippers, and Josef Krips were frequent visitors at the time. Coming first as a guest, Igor Markevitch (b Kiev 1912) served 1957–8 as artistic consultant and 1958–61 as regular conductor. In more than one respect his term marked a turning point in the MSO's history. In 1957 he took that decisive step represented in the life of an orchestra by performance of *Sacre du printemps*, and he also was one of the architects of the restructuring of the MSO into a permanent body with members on annual contract. Supplementary series were organized at the Plateau Hall, and pop concert series (which were to flourish annually 1958–76) were begun at the *Forum with the support of the *Montreal Star*.

With the assistance of the newly formed Young People's Committee Markevitch instituted the annual commissioning of a work from a Canadian composer. The first to receive this commission was Harry *Somers; his *Fantasia* was premiered by Markevitch in 1958. Subsequent works commissioned and premiered were *Papineau-Couture's *Pièce concertante No. 3* in 1959, *Morel's *Boréal* in 1960, Alexander *Brott's *Spheres in Orbit* in 1961, *Matton's *Mouvement symphonique II* in 1962, *Morawetz' *Concerto No. 1* for piano in 1963, *Prévost's *Fantasmes* in 1963, *Mercure's *Lignes et points* in 1965, Morawetz' *Sinfonietta* in 1966, *Pépin's *Quasars, Symphonie No. 3* in 1967, *Garant's *Phrases II* in 1968, *Schafer's *Son of Heldenleben* in 1968, *Saint-Marcoux's *Hétéromorphie* in 1970, Jacques *Hétu's *Passacaille* in 1971, Pépin's *Prismes et cristaux* in 1974, and *Tremblay's *Fleuves* in 1977. Works premiered in addition to those which won the Prix Jean-Lallemand included *Descarries's *Rhapsodie canadienne* (1936), *Blackburn's *Symphonie en un mouvement* (1942), *Vallerand's *Le Diable dans le beffroi* (1942), *Champagne's *Symphonie gaspésienne* (1945), Brott's *War and Peace* (1945), Pépin's *Variations symphoniques* (1948), Brott's *Delightful Delusions* (1950), Brott's *Analogy in Anagram* (1956), and Morel's *L'Étoile noire* (1962).

After being housed for 28 years in the cramped quarters of the Plateau Hall auditorium (which seated an audience of only 1300), the MSO moved to the Grande Salle of the *PDA in September 1963. When Markevitch was ill he had been replaced at short notice in October 1960 by a young Indian conductor of 24, Zubin Mehta (b Bombay 1936), who was engaged by the administrator, Pierre *Béique. Mehta achieved so outstanding a success that he was invited to succeed Markevitch and did, in fact, serve 1961–7 as the orchestra's artistic director. The MSO could not hope to retain Mehta's exclusive services for long, and he became associate conductor of the Los Angeles Philharmonic Orchestra in 1963 as well as accepting more and more engagements as guest conductor in North America, in Europe, and in particular with the Israel Philharmonic Orchestra. The MSO was enriched by Mehta's personal dynamism and prodigious talent. The orchestra's European tour under his direction in 1962 – which included concerts in Moscow, Leningrad, Paris, and Vienna – was the first undertaken by a Canadian symphony orchestra. On 21 Sep 1963, Mehta shared with Pelletier the honour of conducting the inaugural concert at the PDA. Consisting now of 95 instrumentalists and performing in a 3000-seat auditorium, the MSO had attained the status of a major orchestra. During Mehta's directorship the MSO also undertook operatic productions, Mehta himself conducting *Tosca* and *Carmen* (1964), *La Traviata* and *Aida* (1965), *Tosca* (1966), and *Otello* (1967). With other conductors the MSO presented *Rigoletto* (Hans Swarowsky, 1966), *Faust* (Pelletier,

Igor Markevitch, artistic director of the Montreal Symphony Orchestra 1958–61

Zubin Mehta, artistic director of the Montreal Symphony Orchestra 1961–7

1967), and Puccini's *Manon Lescaut* (Franz-Paul *Decker, 1968). The MSO was the regular orchestra 1971–5 for the *Ópera du Québec, and Mehta returned to conduct memorable productions of *Salomé* in 1972 and *Tristan und Isolde* in 1975.

In 1966 Mehta and the MSO embarked on a second European tour, limited this time to French-speaking countries (France, Belgium, Switzerland). The same year, he inaugurated an exchange program with the TS.

After Mehta's departure the MSO welcomed Franz-Paul Decker, who was to serve 1967–75 as the orchestra's artistic director. It was a difficult transition, but Decker soon made his presence felt through well-ordered and meticulously prepared performances. He further developed the orchestra's sound palette and expressiveness and introduced new works while continuing the Austro-German tradition of his predecessors, Klemperer and Mehta. Under his direction the orchestra gave concerts in Japan in 1970.

The MSO concerts for young people gained particular impetus in 1970, when Mario *Duschenes was appointed to conduct them. Pelletier had conducted them originally, and Defauw followed his precedent 1942–48, but Pelletier resumed their direction 1948–63. His successors were Pierre *Hétu 1963–4 and 1965–8 and Eugene *Kash 1964–5.

The Spaniard Rafael Frübeck de Burgos (b Burgos, Spain, 1933) succeeded Decker at the beginning of the 1975–6 season but did not complete his initial three-year term. Like Defauw and Mehta before him, he had the responsibility of a second orchestra, the National Orchestra of Spain. His Montreal concerts rarely roused much enthusiasm, but he did make better known a number of works by Spanish composers, including Manuel de Falla (*La Vida breve, El Retablo de Maese Pedro*), Granados, and Albeniz. In 1976 the MSO made its US debut in Carnegie Hall under his direction, and then embarked on a third European tour (France, Switzerland, Great Britain, Czechoslovakia). Frühbeck de Burgos also gave remarkable performances on Haydn's *The Creation* and Bach's *St Matthew Passion*.

Frühbeck's hasty departure a few days before a concert (November 1976) and his resignation a few weeks later appear to have been a result of misunderstanding and of inaccurate press interpretation of comments he had made with regard to certain members of the orchestra. The remainder of the 1976–7 season was assigned to guest conductors, including the Swiss Charles Dutoit (b Lausanne 1936), who was engaged to assume the artistic directorship of the orchestra at the beginning of the 1978–9 season.

A considerable part of the MSO's development must be attributed to Pierre Béique, honorary treasurer 1936–9 and administrator 1939–70. Through his dedication, his eagerness to provide Montreal with a first-rate orchestra, and his connections with the musical establishment, he was able to govern the fortunes of the MSO with undisputed success. After acting 1970–5 as special adviser to the president, in 1977 he became music consultant to the executive administrator, and in 1978 special assistant to the artistic director. Another driving force behind the MSO's success, and a generous patron besides, has been Jean C. Lallemand, several times president before his appointment as honorary president for life. After Béique, MSO administrators have been Denis *Langelier 1970–3, Jacques Druelle 1973–4, John C. Goodwin 1975–8, succeeded by Roger Larose in 1979.

The position of concertmaster was held by Albert Chamberland 1935–41, Maurice *Onderet 1941–5, Alexander Brott 1945–58, Hyman *Bress 1958–9, and Calvin *Sieb 1959–79. Eugène *Husaruk was interim concertmaster during the 1977–9 period and again after 1979. The post of assistant conductor has been filled 1939–48 by Chamberland, 1948–61 by Brott, 1963–9 by Pierre Hétu, and 1978–80 by Uri Mayer. Mayer was appointed associate conductor in 1980.

The administration of the MSO is overseen by a board of directors and an executive committee. An advisory committee has among its members all former presidents. A women's committee has been especially active in organizing the symphonic matinees for young people and the *MSO Concours, begun in 1965 and held annually for the purpose of discovering new talent, the winners taking part in concerts with the MSO. The competition was known 1940–62 as the *Prix Archambault.

In the 1978–9 season the MSO engaged its musicians for 46 weeks and offered four subscription series – the Grands concerts, the Concerts gala, the du Maurier Concerts, and the Esso Concerts. It also appeared in Toronto and Ottawa and gave regular concerts in Quebec City, Orford, Sherbrooke, Joliette, Sorel, and other Quebec centres. The orchestra's budget for the 1978–9 season was close to $4 million. Financing was achieved by the customary means: ticket sales, three-level-government subsidies, and annual subscription campaigns aimed at corporations and the public. For that season it received subsidies from the *Canada Council ($745,000), the *MACQ ($486,600), and the Council of Arts of Greater Montreal ($230,000). The MSO has been the recipient of a number of gifts from corporations, some of which have given their names to series of concerts.

Charles Dutoit, artistic director of the Montreal Symphony Orchestra 1978–

An acute financial crisis at the close of the 1973 season was alleviated by a large supplementary subsidy from the MACQ and the generosity of the public. The opening of the 1975–6 season was delayed for several weeks as a result of a work stoppage by the musicians. A second conflict of the same nature disrupted the 1977–8 season for a two-month period.

In 1980 the MSO received a *PRO Canada Award of $3500 for the exceptional quality of its contemporary music programming.

A contract signed in 1980 with the Decca-London company provided for the recording of at least three LPs, including Ravel's *Daphnis et Chloé* (the complete ballet) under Dutoit's direction. From the end of 1977 to the beginning of 1980 the MSO published 16 issues of a periodical, *Variations*.

DISCOGRAPHY

Dompierre *Concerto in A* for piano; *Harmonica Flash*. E. Boivin-Béluse pf, Garden hmca, Dutoit cond. 1979. DG 2531 265

Montreal International Competition (voice) – concert of winners. Mueller cond. 1967. CBC Expo-10

Montreal Symphony Orchestra: Matton *Mouvement symphonique II* – Mercure *Lignes et points* – Prévost *Fantasmes* – Somers *Fantasia*. Mehta cond, P. Hétu cond. 1967. RCI 230/RCA LSC 2980. Also released in 1969 under the title *The New Music*, vol 5. Vic VICS 1040

Pépin *Quasars; Symphony No. 3* – Schafer *Son of Heldenleben*. Decker cond. 1973. RCI 387/ Sel CC-15.101

Place des arts: Papineau-Couture *Pièce concertante No. 5* – Ravel *La Valse* – Mahler *Symphony No. 1*. Pelletier cond, Mehta cond. 1963. Limited ed 2-record set (no label, no number)

Prévost *Terre des hommes* – Beethoven 'Ode to Joy' from *Symphony No. 9*. Alarie sop, Forrester alto, Simoneau ten, Rouleau bass, World Festival Chorus, Rutgers U Choir, P. Hétu cond, Pelletier cond. 1967. CBC Expo-1

BIBLIOGRAPHY

Miro, Henri. 'Montréal peut-il avoir un orchestre symphonique,' *La Lyre*, Jun 1924

Herzberg, Marthe. *Desiré Defauw, portraits et souvenirs* (Brussels 1937)

Bell, H.P. 'The Montreal Orchestra and Les Concerts symphoniques,' *Curtain Call*, Jan 1940

Breslin, Cathie. 'Zubin Mehta, Montreal's musical wonder man,' *Canadian Weekly*, 6–12 Oct 1962

McLean, Eric. 'Montreal Symphony, no more hussars,' *Musical America*, Sep 1963

Graham, Harriet. 'The hottest hand in music,' *Maclean's*, 4 Jul 1964

McLean, Eric. 'The Montreal Symphony opera season,' *OpCan*, May 1965

Thériault, Jacques. 'The SMCQ is ahead of the game, because the MSO cannot change with the changing times,' *CanComp*, 46, Jan 1970

An interview with Mr. Pierre Béique of the Montreal Symphony Orchestra,' ibid, Feb 1970

Verriest, Guy. 'Desiré Defauw,' *Vie musicale belge*, Sep–Oct 1971

Pontaut, Alain. 'L'Orchestre des autres,' *L'Actualité*, Jan 1977

Siskind, Jacob. 'Montreal: will a real conductor please stand up?' *PfAC*, Spring 1977

Robert, Véronique. 'Meeting Charles Dutoit,' *Variations*, vol 1, Sep–Oct 1977

Bookspan, Martin, and Yockey, Ross. *Zubin: The Zubin Mehta Story* (New York 1978)

Rolland, Pierre. 'Charles Dutoit: a man brimming with projects,' *Variations*, vol 1, May 1978

Vaux, Agathe de. 'The MSO through the years,' *Variations*, 16 instalments, vol 1–3, Sep–Oct 1977–Dec–Jan 1979–80

History of Music in Canada

Musical Red Book

Music in Canada

La Vie musicale CH, GP

The Montreal Women's Symphony Orchestra / La Symphonie féminine de Montréal. First women's symphony orchestra in Canada. Founded in 1940 by Madge (Mrs H.B.) Bowen and Ethel *Stark, its only conductor, the orchestra numbered some 75 professional and amateur musicians. (Amateur musicians were not used after 1947.) The orchestra's first concert, 29 July 1940, was followed by four in the 1941–2 season and an average of 10 annually thereafter until dissolution in the late 1960s. Its home auditorium was *Plateau Hall. It was the first Canadian symphony orchestra to perform at Carnegie Hall (22 Oct 1947), and it appeared as well in Toronto, Kingston, and London, Ont. The extent of its repertoire is indicated by such works as Strauss' *Tod und Verklärung*, Schoenberg's *Verklärte Nacht*, Schubert's *Mass in G*, Ravel's *Piano Concerto for Left Hand Alone* (with the dedicatee Paul Wittgenstein as soloist), and *MacMillan's *Two Sketches*. It premiered Violet *Archer's *Sea Drift* and *Leaves of Grass* and introduced to Canada Bloch's *Concerto grosso No. 2*. Soloists included Ellen *Ballon, Percy Grainger, Witold Malcuzynski, Zara *Nelsova, and Joseph *Rouleau. After 1954 the orchestra alternated in concert with its subsidiaries, the Montreal Women's Symphony Strings and the Ethel Stark Symphonietta. (SSI)

Monument national. Four-story building erected 1891–4 in Montreal, on St-Laurent Blvd south of Ste-Catherine St, to serve as a French-Canadian cultural centre and to house the administrative services of the St-Jean-Baptiste Society of Montreal. Its 1620-seat theatre, which boasts an orchestra pit, was inaugurated in 1893 while still uncompleted. In the ensuing years it has welcomed innumerable solo artists, opera companies, and other musical troupes and ensembles, including Emma *Albani, Eugène d'Albert, Pauline *Donalda, Yvette Guilbert, Alfred *Laliberté, Ignace Jan Paderewski, Pol Plançon, Edith Piaf, Elisabeth Schumann-Heink, and Eugène Ysaÿe, the Nicosias-Durieu and Charley opera troupes in 1899 and 1900 respectively, the Veillées du bon vieux temps ca 1919–41, the *Société canadienne d'operette 1923–33, the *Variétés lyriques 1936–55, and the **Fridolinons!* revues 1938–46. Numerous orchestral concerts and oratorios were presented there, including *Miro's *Messe solennelle* in 1904 and Alexis *Contant's **Caïn* in 1905. In 1971 the National Theatre School acquired the building for $350,000. It was declared a historic monument by the *MACQ in 1977.

BIBLIOGRAPHY

Morin, Victor. 'Cent vingt-cinq ans d'oeuvres sociales et économiques,' *Cahier des Dix*, 23, 1958

Bean, Audrey, et al. *Le Monument national*, brochure (Montreal 1976) GP

MOOGK, Edward B. (Balthasar). Recorded-sound archivist, discographer, broadcaster, b Weston (later part of Metropolitan Toronto) 15 Jul 1914, d London, Ont, 18 Dec 1979. He had piano lessons as a child and played drums 1938–43 with the Bob Donelle and Willis Tipping dance bands. Under the professional name Ed Manning he pursued a career 1942–72 in radio and the recording industry. He was assistant manager 1942–50 of radio station CKCR in Kitchener, Ont, and manager of record divisions at Gordon V. *Thompson Ltd 1951–5 and at *Sparton of Canada 1955–9. He was director of public service 1959–72 for CFPL-TV, London, Ont. During his radio years he was host for the CBC record programs 'Audio,' 'Den of Iniquity,' and 'Roll Back the Years.' The last, which began in Kitchener in 1945, was a network feature 1950–70. For Gavotte and Rococo he produced the records *The Big Sing* (two vols: 1952, Gav LPG 100; 1954, Gav LPG 107) and *American Vaude and Variety* (two vols: Rococo 4006, 4009, released in the late 1960s).

A lifelong record collector, Moogk became an authority on Canadian recordings, and in 1967 the Centennial Commission adopted his plan to assemble a Canadian archive which became the nucleus of the *NL of C's recorded-sound collection, of which he was the custodian 1972–9. He organized the exhibits '85 Years of Recorded Sound' (1975) at the NL of C and '100 Years of Recorded Sound' (1977) at the *CNE.

Moogk's book, *Roll Back the Years: History of Canadian Recorded Sound and Its Legacy, Genesis to 1930* (Ottawa 1975), is a pioneer work in the field of Canadian discography. Moogk wrote as well for *Opera Canada*, *Record News*, *Ontario Library Review*, the *London Free Press*, *Electron*, *EMC*, and other publications.

See also Recorded sound. CF, HK

MOORE, (James) Mavor. Producer, director, actor, author, administrator, librettist, composer, b Toronto 8 Mar 1919; BA (Toronto) 1941, hon D LITT (York) 1969. Though known mainly for his work in drama (stage, radio, and TV), Moore has been called 'the man who really has made the greatest contribution to the musical theatre in Canada to date' (Ross Stuart, *Canadian Theatre Review*, Summer 1977).

Moore studied composition with Gladys *Willan and John *Weinzweig and during the 1940s wrote songs, including settings of William Blake. He contributed many songs to **Spring Thaw*, the annual review which he originated in 1948 and produced until 1966. His musical version of Voltaire's *Candide* was broadcast 9 Jan 1952 as *The Best of All Possible Worlds* on CBC radio, staged 13 Sep 1956 as *The Optimist* in Toronto, and revived 17 Jan 1968, with its radio title, on CBC TV.

Moore wrote book, lyrics, and music for an adaptation of Stephen Leacock's *Sunshine Sketches of a Little Town*, presented 31 Mar 1954 on CBC radio as *The Hero of Mariposa* and 19 Dec 1954 on CBC TV as *Sunshine Town*. Probably the most ambitious Canadian musical to that time, *Sunshine Town* had performances by the New Play Society (of Toronto) in 1956 in London, Ont, Toronto, and Montreal. It was revived in 1968 at the *Charlottetown Festival and in 1978 at the *Banff Festival. Selected songs from *Sunshine Town* and *Spring Thaw* have been published by BMI Canada.

In 1967 Moore collaborated with Jacques Languirand on the libretto for *Somers' **Louis Riel* and in 1968 he wrote the book and lyrics for John *Fenwick's **Johnny Belinda*. He was the librettist, with composer Harry *Freedman, for the 60-minute comic opera *Silents!* commissioned for performance at the Courtenay Youth Music Centre in 1978.

For the *COC Moore directed *The Love of Three Oranges* (1959), *A Night in Venice* (1960), *The Bartered Bride* (1961), and *Don Giovanni* (1963). He served 1965–7 as artistic director of the Charlottetown Festival and 1966–70 as general director of the *St Lawrence Centre, Toronto. He joined the faculty of fine arts at *York U in 1970, was made an Officer of the *Order of Canada in 1973, and was appointed chairman of the *Canada Council in 1979.

BIBLIOGRAPHY

Whittaker, Herbert. 'The multi-talented Mavor Moore sets political history to music,' *PfAC*, Winter 1979

Creative Canada, vol 1

(PPrn)

MORANDO, Otto. Tenor, teacher, b Prague 1869?, d Los Angeles 16 Nov 1953. After study in Austria and Italy he sang in opera in various European centres before turning to teaching. During his years in Toronto, teaching privately and at the *Canadian Academy of Music 1913–24 (and also teaching during the summers 1920–2 in Victoria, BC), he developed many young singers, among them Eva Baird, Mary *Bothwell, Douglas Stanbury, Margaret George, Gideon *Hicks, John *Moncrieff, Nellye Gill, and Victor Edmonds (b Edmond Petch). Morando moved to California in 1924 and was active there as a voice coach for film celebrities, notably Franchot Tone, Bebe Daniels, Joan Crawford, Marion Davies, and Charlotte Greenwood. JBM

Moravian Missions in Labrador. The first permanent mission in Labrador was founded in 1771 at Nain, on the northern coast, by the Moravian Brethren, a protestant sect from Saxony. Additional settlements to the north and south soon were established and by the early 19th century the conversion of the local Inuit (Eskimo) was essentially complete.

As in other Moravian missions, music was central to both worship and community life. The Inuit were taught in their own language and instruction included the singing of chorales (of which some 200, in the original German, have been preserved in manuscript at Nain). Chorale texts were used for practice in reading and writing. At weekly 'singing meetings,' an Inuit equivalent of Zinzendorf's *Singstunde*, a Bible lesson was contemplated solely through the singing of related hymn verses. A harmonium was brought to Nain in 1828 and string and brass instruments soon followed.

The Inuit eventually began teaching each other and, with the reduction of missionary influence in the 20th century, have taken control of the musical tradition. In the mid-1970s the musical establishment at Nain consisted of six string players, two organists, a five-piece brass band (which appeared in the 1973 NFB film *Labrador North*), and a mixed choir of 10 to 15 voices. The choir has performed in St John's, Nfld, and in 1971 it issued a recording (Marathon MS 2104) to commemorate the bicentenary of the Moravian missions. A seven-inch LP – *Nain Eskimo Choir* (Condor C 97191) – was inserted in the Winter 1977 issue of the periodical *Inuttituut*.

On important liturgical occasions the band parades outdoors, its instruments wrapped in cotton duffle. At church services the choir leads in the singing of chorales and performs a liturgically prescribed repertoire of anthems drawn from Inuit translations of 18th- and 19th-century German church music, including Mozart's 'Ave verum' and Haydn's 'The Heavens Are Telling.' The string players sit behind the choir, usually doubling the voices but in some anthems playing independent parts. As there is no conductor and no formal rehearsal the organist simply begins and the others join in spontaneously. This unique ritual has been passed orally from one generation to the next and in 1980 continued in Nain and neighbouring Hopedale and Makkovik.

See also Inuit: 4 / Acculturation.

BIBLIOGRAPHY

The Moravians in Labrador (Edinburgh 1833)

History of the Mission of the Church of the United Brethren in Labrador for the Past Hundred Years (London 1871)

Hamilton, J.T., and Hamilton, K.G. *History of the Moravian Church: the Renewed Unitas Fratrum: 1722–1957* (Winston-Salem 1967)

'Eskimoes using 100-year-old manuscripts,' *University Affairs*, May 1974

EKv

MORAWETZ, Oskar. Composer, teacher, b Světlá nad Sázavou, Czechoslovakia, 17 Jan 1917; naturalized Canadian 1946; B MUS (Toronto) 1944, D MUS (Toronto) 1953. His teachers were Karel Hoffmeister (piano) and Jaroslav Kricka (theory) in Prague and, after the Nazi invasion (1938) of Czechoslovakia, Julius Isserlis (piano) in Vienna and Lazare Lévy (piano) in Paris. He developed an ability to sight-read orchestral scores at the piano and at 19 was recommended by George Szell for the assistant conductor's post with the Prague Opera.

In 1940 Morawetz emigrated to Canada and began studies at the *U of Toronto with Alberto *Guerrero (piano) and Leo *Smith (theory). As a composer, however, he is essentially self-taught. He began teaching theory and composition at the *RCMT in 1946 and joined the faculty of music at the U of Toronto in 1951. Austin *Clarkson, Anne *Eggleston, John *Fenwick, Walter *Kemp, Alfred *Kunz, and Edward *Laufer have been among his pupils.

Morawetz first came to notice with his *String Quartet No. 1* and *Sonata Tragica* (1945), which won CPRS (*CAPAC) Awards in 1945 and 1946 respectively. Other honours followed: his *Piano Concerto* won first prize in a 1962 competition sponsored by the *MSO; his *Sinfonietta for Winds and Percussion* won the Critics' Award over 104 other works from 32 countries at the 1966 International Competition for Contemporary Music at Cava dei Tirreni, Italy; and his *From the Diary of Anne Frank* received a special award from the Segal Fund in Montreal in 1971 as the most important contribution to Jewish music in Canada.

Morawetz' music is among the most performed of any by a Canadian composer. His orchestral compositions have been played by more than 100 orchestras on four continents and have been conducted by Ančerl, Boult, Ehrling, Kubelik, *MacMillan, Mehta, Ozawa, Solomon, Steinberg, and *Susskind.

Among Morwetz' many commissioned works are the *Second Symphony* (the first work commissioned for the *TSO's subscription concerts), *Memorial to Martin Luther King* (for the cellist Mstislav Rostropovich), *Concerto for Brass Quintet and Orchestra* (for the New York Brass Quintet), *A Child's Garden of Verses (for Maureen *Forrester), and Concerto for Harp and Chamber Orchestra* (for the *Guelph Spring Festival).

Such early compositions as *Divertimento for Strings* and *Overture to a Fairy Tale* reveal Morawetz' Slavic temperament and youthful optimistic tone and foreshadow later characteristics of his style: rhythmic vitality, colourful orchestration, and mastery in polyphonic writing. Works of a tragic nature, however, have appeared with increasing frequency since World War II. Unlike many composers of his generation, Morawetz rejected serial technique and avant-garde experiments and developed his style by exploring expanded tonality, polytonality, and (occasionally) atonality.

Oskar Morawetz

Morawetz is at once a clear thinker and an emotional man. His music combines a secure sense of proportion, clear outlines, and sophisticated know-how with expressive, even programmatic content. There is no place in his music for technical display or novelty as such. For him, technique is a means of integrating all elements – including the element of strong feeling – into an artistic whole. Morawetz varies his ideas by using motivic transformation or changes of texture or by combining the main themes at the dynamic climaxes of his larger works. Equally characteristic is his polyphonic weaving of two streams of block chords.

Among Morawetz' many piano works the best known are his youthfully exuberant *Scherzo*, the idiomatic *Fantasy Elegy and Toccata* and *Suite for Piano*, and the *Piano Concerto* which, after its premiere in 1963 by Anton *Kuerti and the MSO under Zubin Mehta, was praised by Jean *Vallerand in *La Presse* as 'one of the best Canadian compositions played by our orchestra in many years.' His many songs display a particular sensitivity to the word-tone relationship.

Morawetz' unusual treatment of the harp in the *Concerto for Harp and Chamber Orchestra* and his exploitation of the contrasts between different sections of the orchestra in his *Sinfonietta for Winds and Orchestra* testify to his interest in new sounds. In his *Memorial to Martin Luther King*, responding to Rostropovich's request for an unusual orchestration, Morawetz used the solo cello as the only string instrument against an orchestra of winds, piano, and percussion. The composer creates a sombre, solemn atmosphere by antiphonal orchestration and a polytonal harmonic treatment of King's favorite spiritual, 'Free at Last.'

Morawetz' intensely dramatic *String Quartet No. 2* demonstrates his usual contrapuntal skill and his fondness for extraordinary sound effects. In the second movement, inspired by the tragedies of World War II, the closely spaced trills are suggestive of the sounds of battle drums.

From the Diary of Anne Frank, premiered in 1970 by the TS and the soprano Lois *Marshall, has been performed in many other countries including the USA, Australia, and Israel. Anne Frank's fear and prayer for the survival of her former school friend, Lies, form the poignant text of this work. The music expresses the text with great sensitivity and moves from moods of tenderness and religious fervour to outbursts of suffering and despair. After the US premiere in Carnegie Hall by the TS under Ančerl, Winthrop Sargeant wrote in the *New Yorker*: 'Morawetz' use of atonality is deft indeed ... Morawetz is a master of orchestration and the treatment of the underlying orchestral fabric is highly original' (22 Apr 1972).

Morawetz can be heard as solo pianist and as accompanist to James *Milligan in a recording of his works (RCI 121). He is a member of CAPAC and of the *CLComp and an associate of the *CMCentre.

COMPOSITIONS

ORCHESTRA

Carnival Overture. 1946. Full orch. Leeds 1970. RCI 41 (*TSO)

Serenade for Strings. 1948 (rev 1954 as *Divertimento for Strings*). (*Divertimento*) Summit 1959. (*Serenade*) RCI 5 (J.-M. *Beaudet)

2 *Symphonies* (1953, 1959). CMCentre. (*No. 2*) CBC SM-4 / CBC SM-104 (*TSO)

Overture to a Fairy Tale. 1956. Med orch. B & H 1959. RCI 180 (*CBC SO) / CBC SM-308 (*CBC Van Chamb O)

Sinfonietta for Winds and Percussion. 1965. Leeds 1967. RCI 392 (*Deslauriers cond)

The Railway Station, symphonic poem. 1980. Full orch. Ms

SOLOISTS WITH ORCHESTRA

Elegy 'I Am So Tired' (A. Wilkinson). 1947. V, orch (pf). Leeds 1961 (v, pf). RCI 121 (*Milligan bar) / CBC SM-180 (*Vickers ten)

I Love the Jocund Dance and *Land of Dreams* (both Blake). 1949. V, orch (pf). GVT 1953 (v, pf). CBC SM-8 (*Zarou sop)

Grenadier (Housman). 1950. Bar, orch (pf). Leeds 1962 (v, pf). RCI 121 (*Milligan bar) / CBC SM-42 (Maurice *Brown bar)

Piano Concerto No. 1. 1962. Leeds 1966. RCI 213A / Pathé SPAM 680231 / Cap SW-6123 (*Kuertl)

Concerto for Brass Quintet and Orchestra. 1968. Leeds 1975

Memorial to Martin Luther King. 1968. Vc, orch. CMCentre. RCI 212 (*Nelsova)

From the Diary of Anne Frank (A. Frank). 1970. V, orch. Priv publ 1973

A Child's Garden of Verses (R.L. Stevenson). 1972. Alto (mezzo), orch. CMCentre

Fantasy for Violin and Chamber Orchestra. 1975. Ms

Concerto for Harp and Chamber Orchestra. 1976. CMCentre

CHAMBER

3 *String Quartets* (1944, 1952–5, 1959). Ms.

Rondo for Violin and Piano. 1946 (rev 1947 as *Duo for Violin and Piano*) Summit 1961 (*Duo*). (*Rondo*) RCI 124 (*Pratz vn) / (*Duo*) RCI 244 / CBC Expo-16 (*Duo Pach) / CBC SM-28 / CBC SM-135 (*Hidy vn)

Sonata No. 1. 1956. Vn, pf. CMCentre. RCI 194 (*Pratz vn)

Trio. 1960. Fl, ob, hpd (pf). CMCentre. RCI 219 / RCA CCS-1013 (*Baroque Trio of Mtl)

Two Fantasies for Cello and Piano. 1962 (rev 1970). CMCentre. (no. 1) CBC SM-305 (V. *Orloff)

Two Preludes. 1965 (rev 1972). Vn, pf. CMCentre. Masters of the Bow MBS-2002 (*Bress)

Three Improvisations for Brass Quintet. 1977. Ms

Also sonatas for fl and pf and for hn and pf (both 1978). Ms

PIANO

Scherzo. 1947. B & H 1958. 1953. RCI 121 (Morawetz) / 1968. CBC SM-65 (E. Coop) / CBC SM-118 (*Helmig)

Fantasy in D Minor. 1948. CMCentre. RCI 120 / Col Master 32 11046 (*Gould)

Fantasy on a Hebrew Theme. 1951. CMCentre. RCI 133 (*Goldblatt)

Scherzino. 1953. FH 1955. RCI 121 (Morawetz)/RCI 397 (J. Holtzman)

Ten Preludes for Piano. 1966. FH 1966. (No. 1 and 9). (No. 9) CBC SM-65 (E. Coop)

Suite for Piano. 1968. Leeds 1971. CBC SM-187 (*Kubalek)

Fantasy for Piano 1973. 1973. CMCentre. CBC SM-279 (*Taussig)

CHOIR

Two Contrasting Moods (A. Lampman). 1966. SATB. CMCentre

Crucifixion (Negro spiritual). 1968. SATB. Leeds 1971

Who Has Allowed Us to Suffer? (A. Frank). 1970 (rev 1972). SATB. CMCentre

'The Song My Paddle Sings' (E.P. Johnson). 1975. SATB. CMCentre

VOICE

About 20 songs for v and pf, including:

- 'The Chimney Sweeper' and 'Mad Song' (both Blake). 1947. Leeds 1961, 1962. RCI 121 (*Milligan bar) / CBC Expo-22 (*Quilico bar)
- 'Piping Down the Valleys Wild' (Blake). 1947. GVT 1953. CBC SM-8 (*Zarou sop) / CBC SM-180 (*Vickers ten)
- 'To the Ottawa River' (A. Lampman). 1949. Leeds 1962. RCI 121 (*Milligan bar)
- 'Father William' (Lewis Carroll). 1957. (rev 1973 and 1974). CMCentre. RCI 391 (*Ascher Duo) 'Psalm 22' (Bible). 1978. Ms

BIBLIOGRAPHY

Graham, June. 'Oskar Morawetz,' *CBC Times*, 12–18 Jul 1969

'Oskar Morawetz goes from Guelph to Tel Aviv for 2 musical firsts in a busy composer's career,' *CanComp*, 113, Sep 1976

'Oskar Morawetz celebrates 60th birthday with CBC special in context of Jewish Festival,' *CanComp*, 122, Jun 1977

Creech, Gwenlyn. 'Oskar Morawetz: his music captures epic events,' *Fugue*, vol 2, Jan 1978

'Oskar Morawetz,' *Variations*, vol 2, Sep–Oct 1978

Jones, Gaynor. 'Anne Frank's diary: the epilogue,' *Maclean's*, 29 Sep 1980

Hepner, Lee. 'Oskar Morawetz,' *Contemporary Canadian Composers* (VS)

MOREL, (Joseph Raoul) **François** (d'Assise). Composer, pianist, b Montreal 14 Mar 1926; lauréat piano (AMQ) 1947, piano-teaching diploma (AMQ) 1950, deuxième prix piano (CMM) 1951, premiere prix fugue (CMM) 1953. He studied piano privately 1935–43 and then became one of the first musicians to be educated at the *CMM. He studied there 1944–53 with Claude *Champagne (composition), Jean *Papineau-Couture (acoustics), Isabelle *Delorme (harmony, counterpoint, fugue), and Arthur *Letondal, Germaine *Malépart, and Edmond *Trudel (piano). It was there that his friend Gérald *Gagnier taught him the elements of orchestra conducting. Unlike most of his fellow composers, Morel received all his training in Quebec.

Although *Esquisse* was Morel's first important work, it was *Antiphonie*, premiered 16 Oct 1953 under the direction of Leopold Stokowski at a concert of Canadian music at Carnegie Hall, that marked the start of his career as a composer. The previous year he had won a second prize for composition with *String Quartet No. 1* on the occasion of the centenary of *Laval U. In 1954–5 Morel joined forces with Serge *Garant and Gilles *Tremblay to promote European and Canadian contemporary music; at the CMM they presented two concerts which provoked sharp reactions. In them Morel himself gave the Canadian premieres of Messiaen's piano pieces *Île de feu II* and *Neumes rythmiques*. In 1956 the group reorganized and adopted the name 'Musique de notre temps.' Morel now was associated with Garant, Otto *Joachim, and Jeanne *Landry. He taught analysis and composition 1959–61 at the *Institut Nazareth.

Morel worked 1956–ca 1970 for CBC radio as composer of background music, music consultant, and researcher and 1964–6 as host for the radio program 'Festivals.' He also wrote the station-break theme introduced by CBC radio in 1974 and composed the music for several TV plays ('L'Heureux Stratagème' by Marivaux, 'The Andersonville Trial' by Saul Levitt, and 'Piège pour un homme seul' by Robert Thomas) and dramatic series ('Quelle Famille' and 'Grand-papa'). Several of his works – *Spirale*, *String Quartet No. 2*, *Prismes-Anamorphoses*, *Trajectoire*, and *Radiance* – were written in response to CBC commissions. He composed a number of scores for the *NFB over a period of 15 years.

Morel served 1972–8 as a director of the *AMQ. He returned to teaching in 1976, accepting a position at the Bourgchemin Cegep in Drummondville. In 1979 he began teaching orchestration and composition at both the *U of Montreal and *Laval U, also directing the contemporary music workshop at the latter.

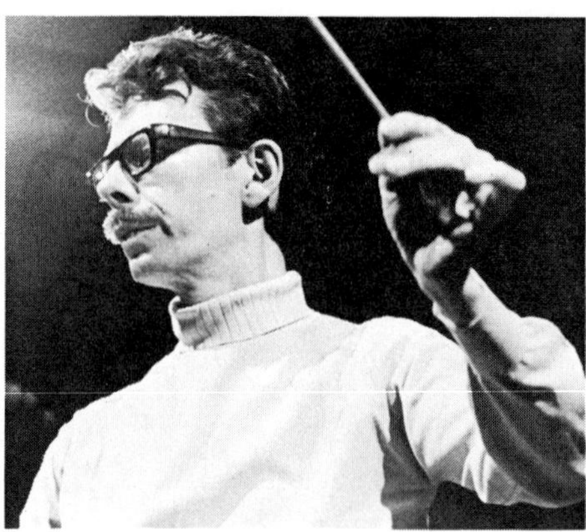

François Morel

In 1960 the *MSO, conducted by Igor Markevitch, premiered *Boréal*, which had been commissioned by the orchestra's Young People's Committee. The work also was performed in 1978 by the *TS on its tour of Japan and China. As in *Rituel de l'espace* and *Nuvattuq*, the language of *Boréal* reveals the influence of Morel's meeting with Varèse during the summer of 1958. In 1962 the MSO, under Thomas Schippers, premiered *L'Étoile noire*, a work inspired by the Quebec artist Paul-Émile Bourduas's painting of the same name. In 1976 the orchestra, conducted by Rafael Frühbeck de Burgos, premiered *Jeux*, commissioned for the inauguration of the 78th session of the International Olympic Committee prior to the opening of the Olympics.

Reflected throughout Morel's work is a concern for rhythmic drive and a search for a richer sound palette. This is particularly evident in *Rythmologue* and *Deux Études de sonorité*. The *Études* are in the repertoires of many Canadian pianists including André *Laplante, Arthur *Ozolins, André-Sébastien *Savoie, and William *Stevens.

The composer himself has divided his output into three broad categories: 'After a period in which my writing was totally preoccupied with modes (*Antiphonie*), I became attracted to total chromaticism, although not elevating it to a system (*Rituel de l'espace*). Finally, I grasped the importance of a coherent system such as the one suggested by Arnold Schoenberg and his school, but I must add, immediately, that I used the twelve-tone "series" with extreme discretion and caution' (*Variations*, Sep–Oct 1978). The third approach is found in *L'Étoile noire, Radiance*, and *IIKKII (Froidure)*.

In the preface to the *CMCentre publication *Compositeurs au Québec: François Morel* (Montreal 1974), Lyse *Richer-Lortie gives a succinct analysis of Morel's development: 'Educated according to French traditions, François Morel underwent a slow interior evolution, each step marked by a sign of exorcism. From an analysis of the form and structure of works by Debussy, Ravel, Stravinsky, Messiaen, and others, his language followed the direction traced by Bartók, finally to embrace decisively the spatial territory associated with Varèse. To accomplish this, winds and percussion were given preferential treatment; a few attempts at electronic music were rejected because of the likelihood of writing a work fixed in time and unable to evolve. A quality of vitality, always so essential for a musical work, has penetrated Morel's thought – and led him to revise, reconstruct, and even rethink certain works which bore evidence of a period that had passed. This compulsion might be interpreted as a need to follow fashion, to identify with the avant garde among Quebec's various musical movements. François Morel vigorously denies this. He remains a composer who uses rich colours and dazzling sonorities. He is also a man whose free and spontaneous sense of wonder gives way readily to the satisfaction afforded by a well-written work which sounds well.'

Morel joined the *CLComp during its first year of existence (1951). He is an affiliate of PRO Canada and an associate of the CMCentre.

SELECTED COMPOSITIONS

ORCHESTRA

Esquisse. 1947. Med orch. BMIC 1964. RCI 129 (*TSO)
Antiphonie. 1953. Full orch. BMIC 1960. RCI 180 (*CBC SO) / (Ca 1965) Lou LS 661 (Louisville Orch, R. Whitney cond)
Boréal. 1959. Full orch. Ber 1976
Rituel de l'espace. 1959. Full orch. CMCentre. RCI 213 RCA CCS-1007 (R. *Leduc)
L'Étoile noire (Tombeau de Bourduas). 1962. Full orch. BMIC 1964. Odyssey Y 31993/Col MS 6962 (*TSO)
Prismes-Anamorphoses. 1967. Orch. Ms. RCI 292 (*Deslauriers)
Radiance. 1972. Small orch. Ric 1974. RCI 367 (*SMCQ)
Melisma. 1980. Pf, orch. Ms

CHAMBER MUSIC

Dyptique (originally *Suite pour petit orchestre*). 1948 (rev 1956). 23 instr. Ms. (1948 version) RCI 7 (J.-M. *Beaudet)
2 *String Quartets*. 1952; 1963. Ms.
Cassation. 1954. Ww septet. Ms. RCI 128 (R. *Leduc)
Rythmologue. 1957 (rev 1970). 6 or 8 perc. Ms. 1970. RCI 298 (Ens de perc de Mtl, Morel cond), McGill U Records 77003 (*Béluse)
Quintette. 1962. Brass. CMCentre. CBC SM-216 (*Canadian Brass)
Nuvattuq. 1967. Fl solo. CMCentre. RCI 409. (J. *Morin)
Départs. 1969. 2 perc. guit, hp, 14 str. CMCentre. RCI 367 (*SMCQ)
IIKKII (Froidure). 1971. 18 instr sol. Ric 1974. RCI 367 (*SMCQ)
Me Duele España. 1975. Guit solo. CMCentre. 1978. RCI 457 (Michael Laucke)

KEYBOARD

Ronde enfantine. 1949. Pf. BMIC 1953. RCI 135 (J. *Dufresne)
Deux Études de sonorité. 1954. Pf. BMIC 1966. RCI 251 (A.-S. *Savoie)/CBC SM-182 (*Savard)/(No. 2) Laur CTM 6036 (*Stevens)
Prière. 1954. Org. BMIC 1965
Alleluia. 1964–8. Org. CMCentre
Other works for orch and for instr ens; 2 works in ms for v and pf: *Quatre Chants japonais* (1949) et *Les Rivages perdus* (1954), recorded on RCI 201 (*Jeannotte)

WRITINGS

'La conscience du son et de l'espace,' *Liberté 59*, vol 1, Sep–Oct 1959
'Faire sonner la musique,' 'Quintette pour cuivres,' *Musiques du Kébèk*, Raoul Duguay ed (Montreal 1971)
'Boréal (1959),' *Variations*, vol 1, Feb 1978
'L'Étoile noire (1961),' ibid, vol 2, Sep–Oct 1978
'Serge Garant, structuralist and lyrical musician,' ibid, Dec–Jan 1978–9

BIBLIOGRAPHY

Lagacé, Bernard. 'François Morel, musicien canadien,' *Liberté*, vol 2, Jan–Feb 1960
'François Morel,' interview with Jacques Thériault, *MSc*, 256, Nov–Dec 1970
Richer-Lortie, Lyse. 'François Morel,' *Contemporary Canadian Composers / Compositeurs canadiens contemporains*
Mather, Bruce. 'François Morel,' *Dictionary of Contemporary Music*

HP

MOREY, Carl (Reginald). Musicologist, teacher, b Toronto 14 Jul 1934; ARCT 1953, B MUS (Toronto) 1957, M MUS (Indiana) 1961, PH D (Indiana) 1965. He studied piano at the *RCMT and music history and literature at *U of Toronto. His post-graduate work was at Indiana U. A *Canada Council doctoral fellowship in 1963 enabled him to work in Italy on his dissertation 'The late operas of Alessandro Scarlatti.' He taught 1962–3 at Wayne State U, Detroit, and 1967–70 as head of the Music Dept at the *U of Windsor and began teaching at the U of Toronto in 1970. He has written articles and reviews for periodicals and has prepared entries for reference works such as *Contemporary Canadian Composers, The New Grove Dictionary*, and *EMC*. In 1967 he researched and wrote the CBC series 'Great Voices of the Past.' His special interests are opera and the musical history of Toronto, and in the mid-1970s he began a musical index of the Toronto *Globe and Mail*.

WRITINGS

'Alexander Gordon, scholar and singer,' *Music and Letters*, vol 46, Dec 1965
'The diatonic, chromatic and enharmonic dances by Martino Pesenti,' *Acta Musicologica*, vol 38, 1966
'Opera and politics,' *OpCan*, vol 7, Sep 1966
'Pre-Confederation opera in Toronto,' *OpCan*, Sep 1969
'Social criticism in the musical theatre,' *OpCan*, Summer 1972
'Misalliance ... the state of music education,' *Canadian Music Teacher*, vol 26, Sep 1972

CF

MORGAN, (Mary) Hope. Soprano, teacher, b Newmarket, near Toronto, 23 Mar 1862, d Toronto 30 Oct 1936. Educated at Toronto's Loretto Abbey, she subsequently studied voice with Mathilde Marchesi in Paris and made her debut in 1895 in a concert marking that lady's 40th anniversary as a teacher. Following a single operatic appearance in Italy she confined her activities to the recital platform, mainly in England. After a coast-to-coast tour of Canada 1905–6 she settled in Toronto where she taught privately until her death, her pupils including the contraltos Eileen *Law and Vera McLean. The possessor of a well-trained lyric soprano, she had a large repertoire in several languages but lacked the physical stamina necessary for the stage. Although she is known to have made one or two trial recordings, none seems to have survived.

BIBLIOGRAPHY

Brewster, Muriel. 'Marchesi of Canada once made great Melba jealous of high note,' Toronto *Star Weekly*, 21 Mar 1925

JBM

Robert Morgan. Music and instrument dealer 1861–84 in Quebec City. In addition to retailing, the firm published sheet music, mostly for piano, by such Canadians as Napoléon *Crépault, Damis *Paul, G. Raineri, Moritz Relle, Octave Tourangeau, and Joseph *Vézina. Some pieces bear plate numbers of US publishers, notably Tolman and Ditson, both of Boston, for whom Morgan probably acted as an agent.

BIBLIOGRAPHY

Calderisi, Maria. 'Music publishing in Canada: 1800–1867,' MMA thesis, McGill 1976

MC

MORGEN, Mari-Elizabeth (m Paratore). Pianist, b Kitchener, Ont, 11 Dec 1944; ARCT 1962, Artist Diploma (Toronto) 1967, B MUS (Juilliard) 1970, M SC (Juilliard) 1971. She was a pupil of Gordon *Hallett at the *RCMT. She won the concerto competition for three consecutive summers at the National Music Camp, Interlochen, Mich. After studies at the *U of Toronto with Jacques Abram and Pierre *Souvairan she won first prize in the 1968 J.S. Bach International Competition in Washington with an unprecedented mark of 100 per cent. She was also the recipient of several *Canada Council bursaries. While studying at the Juilliard School with Ilona Kabos, Rosina Lhévinne, and Rosalyn Tureck she won (1970) the Young Concert Artists Auditions in New York. The award included a Town Hall debut 23 Nov 1970. Subsequently she appeared widely in Canada and the USA in concert and on radio and TV as a recitalist and with orchestras. She moved in 1971 to Cambridge, Mass, with her husband, the pianist Anthony Paratore.

DISCOGRAPHY

Bach *English Suite No. 2; Well-Tempered Clavier* (selections). 1971. CBC SM-158
– *Goldberg Variations*. 1969. CBC SM-84
Bach – Chopin (selections) – Kenins *Sonata*. 1969. RCI 366

WS

MORIN, Clément. Teacher, choir conductor, theologian, b L'Épiphanie, near Joliette, Que, 2 Nov 1907; lauréat teaching of choral conducting (Montreal) 1930, diploma in scriptures (Pontifical Bible Institute, Rome) 1934, D TH (Montreal) 1942, hon D MUS (McGill) 1970. He received his general education 1919–26 at the Séminaire de Joliette, where he took part in musical, literary, and dramatic activities. While studying for the priesthood 1926–30 at the Grand séminaire de Montréal, he was flutist in an orchestra there. He later conducted the orchestra as well as the seminary's choir. He was ordained a priest in 1930, entered the Sulpician Order, and took advanced studies in the scriptures and sacred music 1931–4 in Paris and Rome. On his return to Canada in 1934 he began teaching in the Faculty of Theology of the *U of Montreal and once more conducted the choir of the Grand séminaire. He was appointed professor and a member of the council of the Faculty of Music when it was set up in 1951. That year he returned to Rome, however, to study musical paleography with the Benedictine Dom Cardine at the Pontifical Institute of Sacred Music; he remained there until 1954. Morin was dean and director of studies of the Faculty of Music of the U of Montreal 1955–68 and regularly taught several courses, including performance and aesthetics of Gregorian chant, and history and analysis. He reorganized the *Choeur Pie X in 1955, founded the Choeur Sainte-Cécile (a choir composed of nuns from 20 religious communities) in 1956, and conducted both until 1965. He participated in many CBC radio programs between 1942 and 1958.

Morin became a member of the board of directors of the *Pro Musica Society when it was established in 1948. He also served on the Council of Arts of Greater Montreal 1963–78 and was president of *CAUSM 1967–9. He became a member of the International Assn of Musicology, the Council of International Conventions of Sacred Music, and the Council of the International Federation of the Pueri Cantores. In 1966 he began going to Italy each summer to give courses at the U of Bologna and to conduct concerts. He has published *Genèse de l'hexacorde* (Biblioteca di Quadrivium, Bologna 1971) and 'Motet Christi miles' (from the manuscript of Pluteus of Florence), a contribution to the Festschrift published in honour of Federico Ghisi by the Biblioteca di Quadrivium in 1972. In 1973 the Faculty of Music of the U of Montreal named him professor emeritus. In January 1977 he began conducting seminars there on musical paleography and early notation. He was guest professor 1945–60 at the Gregorian Institute of America in Toledo, O, and in 1979 at California State U and became a guest professor at St Michael's College, Winooski Park, Vt, in 1978. He gave courses in Gregorian chant in 1976 and 1977 at the abbey in Solesmes, France, and began to give similar courses in 1977 both in Ireland and at the Centres culturels français of the Sénanque and Fontevraud abbeys. Clément Morin has mastered about 10 languages (including 3 dead and 2 eastern). His research, publications, and teaching have earned him an international reputation. He has contributed to *EMC*.

BIBLIOGRAPHY
'Enfin, l'opinion de Clément Morin,' *Musique périodique*, vol 1, Dec 1976 PR

MORIN, Jean C. (Charles). Flutist, teacher, b Montreal 26 Aug 1933; BA (Montreal) 1952, B MUS (Oberlin) 1957. He studied 1953–7 with Robert Willoughby at the Oberlin Cons in Ohio and made his debut in 1958 in a recital at the *Ermitage, Montreal, where he returned 5 Apr 1960 to give the premiere of Clermont *Pépin's *Quatre Monodies pour flûte seule*. He took master classes during the summers of 1956 and 1957 with William Kincaid, 1963 with Julius Baker, and 1973 with Jean-Pierre Rampal and Marcel Moyse at the Académie internationale de Nice. He was soloist with several chamber ensembles and orchestras, among them the Gulbenkian Orchestra of Lisbon in October 1966. He was principal flute in the *Quebec SO 1960–4 and also taught at the *CMQ during this period and at the U of Wisconsin during the summers of 1963 and 1964. He was assistant principal flute 1964–9 in the *MSO and taught 1965–71 at *McGill U. He took part 1969–77 in *SMCQ concerts and in 1972 became a member of the *Quebec Woodwind Quintet. He began teaching at the Cons de Chicoutimi in 1969 and was principal flute in the orchestra of Les Grands Ballets Canadiens 1972–4. He is a brother of Pierre *Morin.

DISCOGRAPHY
J. Hétu – Bach – Dutilleux – Poulenc. A.-S. Savoie pf. 1965. Madrigal MAS 402
Morel *Nuvattuq*. (1975). RCI 409
See also Discographies for Micheline Tessier; Gilles Tremblay. ST

MORIN, Léo-Pol (Léopold). Pianist, music critic, teacher, composer (under the name James Callihou), b Cap St-Ignace, near Quebec City, 13 Jul 1892, d in an accident near Lac Marois, north of Montreal, 29 May 1941. In Quebec City he studied with Gustave *Gagnon (solfège, dictation, piano) and Henri *Gagnon (piano, organ), making his debut in 1909 before the Quebec Ladies' Musical Club. In Montreal he studied piano with Arthur *Letondal and harmony with Guillaume *Couture, winning the *Prix d'Europe in 1912.

He studied piano in Paris 1912–14 with Isidor Philipp, Raoul Pugno, and, on the latter's death, Ricardo Viñes, the pianist who premiered many works by Ravel. He was present in 1913 at the premiere of Stravinsky's *Rite of Spring*. He completed his musical education with Jules Mouquet, studying harmony, counterpoint, and fugue.

In Paris Morin gave his first recital (ca 1912) in the salon of Mme Charles de Pamairols, playing works of Franck and Ravel which, according to his friend the poet Marcel Dugas in the preface to Morin's *Musique*, 'he articulated with finesse, communicating all the music's melancholy tenderness. His playing had the fluidity of the play of light in crystal. Rarely has he performed so well.' Returning in 1914 from Europe because of the outbreak of World War I, Morin devoted himself to teaching and concerts. In 1918 he was one of the founders of an audacious arts periodical, *Le Nigog*.

Back in Paris after the war Morin participated 1919–25 in the city's musical life alongside Viñes, Ravel, and Alexis Roland-Manuel. In 1921 at Salle Pleyel he played Rodolphe *Mathieu's *Trois Préludes*, which were dedicated to him. He performed also in England, Belgium, and Holland to raise funds for a monument to Debussy. He toured the same countries with Ravel in 1923. After a Paris recital, 15 Jan 1923 at the Salle Gaveau, in which Morin played music of Bartók, Debussy, Ravel, Roussel, Scriabin, and others, the critic Paul Le Flem (*Comoedia*, 18 Jan 1923) wrote:

Léo-Pol Morin (*Le Canada musical* Sep 1917)

'Much praise is due the initiative of this intelligent musician who in a single evening was able to present so effectively music of such diversity. Evincing the subtlest grasp of idiom this artist passed easily from one composer's music to another's, finding the appropriate expression and the right emphasis for each one's thought. He brought to bear brilliant technical accomplishment as well, yet only to demonstrate how a vibrant touch and a sure instinct for sonority could remain submissive to the control of the spirit of the music.'

Morin returned periodically to give concerts in Canada, but it was not until the autumn of 1925 that he settled again in Montreal. In 1926 he became secretary of the newly formed Montreal chapter of the *Pro Musica Society and through his concerts and writings instigated various movements on behalf of the new French music, which he succeeded in imposing on Quebec, though not always without challenge from his peers.

In December 1927 in Montreal Morin and Victor *Brault organized the first North American festival of music by Debussy, with the participation of the mezzo-soprano Cédia *Brault and the violinist Robert Imandt. Writing in *La Patrie* (12 Dec 1927), Jean Dufresne (Marcel *Valois) called Morin 'always the incomparable interpreter of Debussy, and all who heard, in Montreal or Paris, his performance of the *Cathédrale engloutie*, retain a keepsake of this beautiful work carved in memory.'

In 1927 Morin was heard playing the works of James Callihou (his pseudonym as a composer) for the first time. In 1928 he participated in a concert given by Ravel in Montreal. The following year he began teaching at the *Cons national in Montreal.

Morin wrote on music 1926–9 for *La Patrie* (206 articles). In 1929 he began weekly contributions to *La Presse*, and by 1931 he had written 95 articles. Some of his articles about Canadian music were published (1929) in Paris in *Le Monde nouveau* and *La Revue musicale*. Other articles appeared in *Canadian Forum* (Jul 1928), *Vie canadienne* (Apr, May, Sep 1928), and *Opinions* (Apr 1929). From 1931 until the mid-1930s Morin lived mostly in Paris and wrote for various publications while continuing to give concerts and lectures. He wrote 380 articles, one a week 1933–41, for the newspaper *Le Canada*. (See Criticism.)

In 1933, during a visit to Canada, Morin gave a concert of contemporary French music at the Stella Theatre in Montreal. For the first concert of the SCSM (*MSO), 14 Jan 1935, he played Mendelssohn's *Capriccio brilliant*. He continued his travels – visiting the USA in 1934 and Spain and Morocco in 1936 – and taught 1936–41 at the École supérieure de musique in Outremont (*École Vincent-d'Indy). His last trip to Europe, in the summer of 1939, was interrupted by the outbreak of World War II.

For the CBC Morin gave many concerts and lectures at this time, all the while continuing to teach. He participated regularly on the CBC weekly quiz show 'S.V.P.,' and it was with other regular members of this series that he died in an automobile accident in the Laurentians.

As James Callihou he composed *Suite canadienne* (Archambault 1945) and *Three Eskimos* for piano. He harmonized French-Canadian folksongs for voice and piano and composed *Chants de sacrifice* (inspired by Indian and Inuit folklore) which were transcribed for choir and two pianos by Victor Brault.

Morin's writings reflect both a lively interest in Canadian music and a particular attention to different folkloric sources and their integration in composition.

Morin was one of the principal propagandists of the French music of his time, giving premieres in Canada of works by Ravel, Debussy, Fauré, Satie, Milhaud, Poulenc, Roussel, and others.

Both his writings and his concerts showed Morin to be ahead of his time. A caustic spirit, an original, a personality compounded of intelligence and sensibility, he influenced two generations of musicians in Quebec. His pupils included Paule-Aimée Bailly, François *Brassard, and Jean *Papineau-Couture. Rodolphe Mathieu dedicated to Morin his *Sonata* (1927), a work – along with others by Brassard, *Champagne, Gagnon, *Renaud, Léo *Roy, and *Tanguay – which the pianist performed in France and Canada.

WRITINGS
Papiers de musique (Montreal 1930)
Musique (Montreal 1944)

BIBLIOGRAPHY
Paradis, J.G. 'Léo-Pol Morin,' *La Musique*, vol 1, Feb 1919
Brassard, François. 'Léo-Pol Morin et la composition canadienne,' *Canada français*, Mar 1942
Éthier-Blais, Jean. 'Léo-Pol Morin,' *Jmc*, Feb 1963
Valois, Marcel. 'L'esprit étincelait chez Léo-Pol Morin,' *Au carrefour des souvenirs* (Montreal 1965)
Villeneuve, Claire. 'Léo-Pol Morin, musicographe,' *CAUSM J*, vol 4, Autumn 1974
– 'Léo-Pol Morin (1892–1941), musicographe,' unpubl M MUS thesis, U of Montreal 1975
Catalogue of Canadian Composers
Musiciens canadiens AD

MORIN, Pierre (Paul). Cellist, conductor, teacher, b Montreal 27 Nov 1936; performance diploma cello (École normale, Paris) 1963. He studied 1954–8 at the *CMM with Yvette *Lamontagne and won the *Prix Archambault in 1957. In Paris 1958–63 he worked under André Navarra (cello), Jean Françaix (chamber music), and Yvonne Loriod (piano). He also studied summers with Navarra at the Accademia Chigiana in Siena. In Paris, in March 1962, with the pianist Rachel *Martel, he premiered André *Prévost's *Sonate*, which was dedicated to him. In 1967 he became principal cello with the *Quebec SO and a teacher at the *CMQ. He founded the *Orchestre de chambre Pierre-Morin in 1970 and continued to conduct it in 1980. He is the brother of Jean C. *Morin. His wife, the cellist Huguette Pierre (b Nancy, France, 11 Mar 1936), studied in 1951 at the Nancy Cons with Edmond Dervaux and 1952–61 at the Paris Cons with André Navarra and Maurice Maréchal (cello) and Jacques Février (chamber music). She also took Navarra's courses 1956–61 at the Accademia Chigiana. She was appointed assistant principal cello in the Quebec SO in 1964 and began teaching at *Laval U in 1970. ST

MORIN-LABRECQUE, Albertine (Rosalie Odile) (b Labrecque). Pianist, soprano, educator, composer, b Montreal 8 Jun 1886, d there 25 Sep 1957; hon D MUS (Montreal) 1935. She began studying piano at five, giving her first recital two years later and obtaining at eight the premier prix for theory and the senior class diploma from the *AMQ. She continued her piano training with Romain-Octave *Pelletier and soon mastered the standard repertoire, which she played in numerous recitals in Canada and the USA beginning in 1901. She began studies in harmony and composition at this time and completed them with J. Macaire in Paris. In that city she also studied voice with Arthur *Plamondon. She performed in concert in Paris, Brussels, and New York and on her return to Montreal ca 1920 married a lawyer, Zénon Morin. She taught pedagogy, piano, and analysis at the *Cons national de musique of Montreal and piano and voice 1922–51 (adding analysis and pedagogy after 1930) at the *U of Montreal. Gérard *Caron and Hector *Gratton were among her pupils. In 1922 she founded the Trio de Montréal with her sister Jeanne, violin, and Yvette *Lamontagne, cello, and published *L'Art d'étudier le piano* (Montreal 1922). She also wrote *Recueil de modèles et de dictées musicales* and *Méthode de piano* (2 vols).

Morin-Labrecque composed a 'Chinese opera' *Pas-chu*, two comic operas – one of which, *Francine*, was presented in 1930 in Montreal – four ballets, the symphonic poem *Le Matin*, two concertos for two pianos, and various works for orchestra or band. Several works for instrumental ensemble, piano, piano duet, organ, choir, or voice were published by *Archambault, Leduc, Parnasse musical, and Zimmerman (Cincinnati). The Éditions du conservatoire (Cons national) published her *Pantomime* for violin and piano in 1931. She wrote monographs and short essays on Bach, Beethoven, Chopin, Gounod, Liszt, Massenet, Mendelssohn, Mozart, Schubert, Schumann, Verdi, and Wagner, which were published in Montreal in the 1940s.

BIBLIOGRAPHY

'Albertine Morin,' *Biographies canadiennes-françaises* (Montreal 1923)

Couture, Raymonde. 'Notes bio-bibliographiques de Mme Albertine Morin-Labrecque,' ms 1961, U of Montreal library

CG

MORISSET, Renée (m Bouchard). Pianist, teacher, b St-Damien-de-Bellechasse, near Quebec City, 13 Jun 1928; deuxième prix piano (CMM) 1946, premier prix piano (CMM) 1947. After studying piano 1932–3 at the Notre-Dame-du-Perpétuel-Secours convent she took lessons 1937–44 from Henri *Gagnon in Quebec City. She studied under Germaine *Malépart 1944–5 at the *CMQ and 1945–8 at the *CMM. She also worked at the CMM with Louis *Bailly and John *Newmark (chamber music) and Georges-Émile *Tanguay (theory). She continued her training with Malépart privately until 1950. She gave recitals in public and on radio and in 1950 was a soloist with the *Quebec SO in concertos by Bach and Mozart. That year she married the pianist Victor *Bouchard, and from then on her career was linked professionally with that of her husband. They studied in Paris 1950–3 and formed a two-piano team that soon gained an international reputation. She taught 1955–66 at the *JMC Orford Art Centre and has been a member of juries for the 1968 *Montreal International Competition, for the *Canada Council, and for other competitions and granting bodies.

For the discography and details of the Bouchard and Morisset two-piano team see Victor Bouchard. GP

MORLEY, Glen (Stewart). Conductor, composer, arranger, cellist, b Vancouver 17 Sep 1912; ARAM 1927. He studied cello 1927–8 with Bruno Coletti in Oregon and 1928–39 with Boris *Hambourg and Marcus *Adeney in Toronto. He took conducting lessons in 1937 with Reginald *Stewart in Toronto, in 1943 with Sir Henry Wood and Ernest Read in London, and 1945–7 with Ettore *Mazzoleni in Toronto. He studied composition 1945–7 with John *Weinzweig and 1947–9 with Bernard Rogers at the ESM.

Morley was a cellist 1932–4 on the CPR's *Empress of Japan* and 1934–7 with the *Vancouver SO; the assistant conductor and chorus master, ca 1937, of Cesar Borre's Toronto Opera Co; an arranger 1937–9 for CBC radio; and the conductor and music director 1938–9 of the Barrie (Ont) Civic Band.

During World War II Morley was an arranger and conductor for the Canadian Army Concert Parties and for BBC broadcasts, to Canadian troops in England, of programs such as 'Maple Leaf Matinee' and 'Johnny Canuck's Revue.' He toured 1943–4 with the 'Tin Hats' in North Africa and Italy and, after the war, in Canada with the reformed Tin Hats, part of the Canadian *Army Show*.

Morley was a cellist 1947–52 with the Rochester Philharmonic Orchestra and music director 1952–4 for Eastman Kodak's motion picture division. In 1954 he became a freelance conductor, composer, and arranger, working mainly for CBC radio in Vancouver.

Morley's compositions include *Christmas Overture* (1950, revised 1960, Berandol rental) and *'The Dog Watch' Overture on Nautical Themes* (1977), both for orchestra, the latter written for the Captain Cook Bicentennial. Other works are *Five Preludes* for viola and piano (1946, revised 1951) and *Nocturne* for piano (1946, BMIC 1954). He composed and conducted the music for the British film *Playtime for Workers* (1943). A pop song, 'Alone with My Dreams,' was written in the 1940s and recorded by Leslie Hutchison for HMV.

Morley married the US-born composer Diane Morgan. He is a member of PRO Canada. NM

'Morning Dew' ('Walk Me Out In the Morning Dew'). Song by Bonnie *Dobson. One of her earliest, it was composed in 1961 while she was living in Los Angeles and was popular in the 1960s. Its lyrics reflect the melancholy of disappointed young romantics of that era. It was recorded initially (ca 1964) by the New York folksinger Fred Neil for the LP *Vince Martin and Fred Neil* (Elektra 7248). A second recorded version by the US singer Tim Rose (who added a verse of his own) was a minor hit ca 1967. By late 1968 the Dobson-Rose version had been recorded by, among others, the Jeff Beck Group (with Rod Stewart) and Lulu in England and the Grateful Dead and Lee Hazelwood in the USA. Dobson's own rendition, recorded in 1969, is included on the LP *Bonnie Dobson* (RCI 348 / RCA LSP-4219). Originally published by Nina Music, 'Morning Dew' was taken over by Warner Brothers. MM

Morning Music Club. Founded in Ottawa in 1892 by Louise Carling, its first president, who was a daughter of the brewer Sir John Carling, and by the Countess of Aberdeen, the honorary president, who was the wife of the governor-general. It was originally a social club that presented concerts organized and frequently performed by its members. The meetings were held initially at the Carling residence and later in the principal halls of the city. Under Annie *Jenkins (president 1920–8), the club's social character, based on weekly meetings, gradually disappeared, and evening recitals by foreign artists were occasionally added to the morning concerts. In 1944, under Mrs H.O. McCurry, the season comprised one evening and four afternoon concerts. Beginning in 1946 all concerts took place in the evening, and at least one Canadian artist was presented in recital each season. The club took the name Pro Musica Society of Ottawa in 1962 and became the Concert Society of Ottawa / La Société des Concerts d'Ottawa in 1969. The *NAC gave the society grants and the use of its theatre, but the steeply increasing cost of presenting concerts in the 1970s resulted in the society's demise. The last concert was held 12 May 1974. Throughout its 82 years of existence, the organization maintained a consistently high quality, presenting chamber music ensembles and solo artists of international renown, such as Benjamin Britten with Peter Pears, Pablo Casals, Dietrich Fischer-Dieskau, Glenn *Gould, Lotte Lehmann, Kathleen *Parlow, Francis Poulenc with Pierre Bernac, Andrés Segovia, the Amadeus String Quartet, the *Parlow String Quartet, the Trio Italiano, and the Virtuosi di Roma.

BIBLIOGRAPHY

L.W.H. 'Women's Morning Music Club of Ottawa,' *MCan*, vol 2, Nov 1907

'The new look of an old friend,' *Ottawa Journal*, 6 Sep 1969

DM

MORRISON, Elizabeth (Isabella) (b Milne). Teacher, choirmaster, adjudicator, b Peterhead, Scotland, 27 Dec 1889, d Saskatoon 4 Aug 1965. She studied in Aberdeen with Gordon Ritchie, a pupil of Vaughan Williams. She moved to Canada in 1915 and settled in Saskatoon where she was choirmaster 1923–8 and 1932–57 at the First Baptist Church and 1929–32 at the St Thomas Wesley United Church and conducted the Maids and the Middies, a choir heard nationally 1933–43 on CBC radio, and the Saskatoon Ladies' Choir. She began to adjudicate at Saskatchewan music festivals in 1933. Under the initials 'E.M.' she contributed articles on the local musical scene to the Saskatoon *Star-Phoenix*. One of Saskatoon's leading voice teachers, she numbered Anne *Campbell, Lillian Foster Carpenter, Carmen Lasky Mehta, and Russell H. Marshall among her pupils. On her death the *Women's Music Club of Saskatoon (of which she was a member) established the Mrs F.B. Morrison Scholarship for winners at the Saskatoon Music Festival. WLB

MORRISON, Mary (Louise) (m Freedman). Soprano, b Winnipeg 9 Nov 1926; Artist Diploma voice (RCMT) 1948. She studied in Winnipeg with Doris Mills *Lewis (voice 1942–4) and Mary *Bornoff (piano) and in Vancouver with John *Goss (voice, summer 1942). In her teens she was acclaimed in her native city for her singing (radio debut 1944) in the CBC's 'Sweethearts' and 'Prairie Schooner' and CKY's 'Music for You,' at the *Manitoba Music Competition Festival (where in 1944 she became the only person ever to win, in the same year, the Tudor Bowl and the Rose Bowl, highest awards for grades B and A singers), and in Gladys Anderson Brown's highly regarded Kelvin High School operetta productions.

While Morrison was an *RCMT Senior School student she returned from Toronto to sing in one of the Kelvin productions. In the cast with her was a young local tenor called Jon *Vickers, whom she helped persuade to move east for further voice study and operatic training at the RCMT. She herself studied there 1945–8 with Myrtle Rose *Guerrero (piano), Ernesto *Vinci (voice), and

Mary Morrison

Emmy *Heim (Lieder) and was coached in 1948 by Greta *Kraus and Weldon *Kilburn.

Youthful Toronto debuts with orchestra (*TSO 1947) and in both radio opera (CBC, 1948, as Eurydice in Gluck's *Orfeo*) and live opera (*Royal Cons Opera School in 1949, and Opera Festival in 1950 as Mimi in *La Bohème*) established her quickly. Her success in these roles and the prestige, in 1951, of reaching the finals in the CBC's *'Singing Stars of Tomorrow' and *'Nos Futures Étoiles' presaged a long and busy Toronto-based career as a freelance artist. For the *CBC Opera she was Micaela in *Carmen* (1949), Liu in *Turandot* (1950), Mimi in *La Bohème* (1948, 1951), Lucie in Arthur Benjamin's *A Tale of Two Cities* (1954), the Countess in *The Marriage of Figaro* (radio and TV, 1956), and Fiordiligi in *Così fan tutte* (1958). She also was heard as soloist on the CBC's 'Northern Electric Hour,' 'Startime,' 'Sunday Strings,' and 'Showtime.' For the *COC she was Marguerite in *Faust* (1951), Pamina in *The Magic Flute* (1952), Marie in *The Bartered Bride* (1952), Fiordiligi in *Così fan tutte* (1953), Felice in Wolf-Ferrari's *School for Fathers* (1954), the Countess in *The Marriage of Figaro* (1955, 1960), and Sara Riel in **Louis Riel* (1967).

During those same years Morrison was a soloist in innumerable symphony and oratorio performances, eg, the TSO-*Toronto Mendelssohn Choir Bach Festival of 1950; the CBC's 80th (1962) and 85th Stravinsky birthday celebrations, conducted by the composer, with the *Festival Singers (of which Morrison was an original member and, frequently, a featured soloist); and the TSO-Toronto Mendelssohn Choir performance of Britten's *Cantata academica* and *Spring Symphony* (1967). In Winnipeg, she sang the Verdi *Requiem* (1951) with the *Winnipeg Philharmonic Choir and *Winnipeg SO; in New York, *Jeanne d'Arc au bûcher* (1968) with the New York Philharmonic; and, in San Francisco, the Bach *Magnificat* (1973).

Morrison's particular contribution to Canadian musical life, however, has been her advocacy of 20th-century music. With notable poise and generosity of spirit and with manifest enjoyment of the material, she has contrived successfully to banish its bogies and reveal its not always readily apparent charms. Composers have been quick to appreciate this, and to devise new works for the clear, resilient soprano voice on which it all depends. The list below shows the premieres in which she has sung.

Much of her work in contemporary music has been as a member (with Robert *Aitken and Marion Ross) of the *Lyric Arts Trio, with which she has toured in North America, Scandinavia, Japan, Iceland, France, and England. Both as soloist and as trio member she has performed often with the *SMCQ in Montreal and *Ten Centuries Concerts and *NMC in Toronto, usually in Canadian works or in Canadian premieres of US and European works (Berio, Birtwistle, Crumb, Globokar, Ligeti, Pousseur, etc).

Among the milestones of her career Morrison cites the *CLComp concert of 1953 (works of *Papineau-Couture and *Morawetz), the premiere of *Somers' **The Fool* (1956), the Ten Centuries Concerts presentation of *Schafer's *Geography of Eros* (1964), the Canadian Concert (1968) at the Sigmund Samuel Canadiana Building of the Royal Ontario Museum, and concerts with the Lyric Arts Trio at Expo 70 (Osaka 1970), the ISCM festival (1973) in Reykjavik, and the Musée d'art moderne in Paris (also 1973).

Morrison married the composer Harry *Freedman in 1951 and is the voice heard in his scores for the films *The 700 Million*, *The Roots of Madness*, and *The Pyx* and for the ballet *The *Shining People of Leonard Cohen*.

Morrison was a member 1972–5 of the advisory arts panel of the *Canada Council and artist-in-residence in 1976 at *Simon Fraser U. In 1977 she began teaching singing at the *U of Western Ontario and *McMaster U, and in 1980 she gave an intensive five-week course at the Vocal Academy of the *Banff SFA and began teaching at the Faculty of Music, *U of Toronto. During the 1970s she was in demand as a competition juror, festival adjudicator, and examiner. She received the *Canada Music Citation of the CLComp in 1968.

Morrison's sister, the Winnipeg soprano Kathleen Morrison Brown (b Winnipeg 5 Sep 1928) has enjoyed a durable career in Winnipeg as a soloist in oratorio, operetta, and concert, and has been heard often on the CBC.

PREMIERES OF CANADIAN WORKS IN WHICH MORRISON HAS SUNG

*Anhalt *La Tourangelle*, 1975
*Applebaum *Algoma Central*, 1976
*Barnes *Nocturne* for flute and voice, 1963
*Beckwith *The Trumpets of Summer*, 1964; *Canada Dash – Canada Dot*, 1967
*Beecroft *From Dreams of Brass*, 1966; *Rasas III*, 1974
*Buczynski *How Some Things Look*, 1967
Callon, Gordon *Three Songs*, 1975
*Cherney *Mobile IV*, 1972
*Dolin *Drakkar*, 1973
*Fisher *Behind the Ranges*, 1976
*Freedman *Two Vocalises*, 1954; *Fragments of Alice*, 1976
Grimes, David *Sotto Voce*, 1975
*Heard *Three Comings*, 1971
*Naylor *On Mrs. Arabella Hunt Singing*, 1971
*Ridout *The Ascension*, 1962; *In Memoriam Anne Frank*, 1965
*Schafer *Five Studies on Texts by Prudentius*, 1963; *Geography of Eros*, 1964; *The Enchantress*, 1972; *Arcana*, 1974; *La Testa d'Adriana*, 1978
*Somers *The Fool*, 1956; *Twelve Miniatures*, 1964; *Louis Riel*, 1967; *Kuyas*, 1967
Steven, Donald *The Transient*, 1975
*Symonds *Autumn Nocturne*, 1960; *Opera for Six Voices*, 1961
*Wilson *Angels of the Earth*, 1967

Morrison also has participated in premieres of works by *Garant, *Mather, *Pannell (**Aberfan*), and *Tremblay.

DISCOGRAPHY

Garant *Anerca* – Mather *Orphée* – Somers *Twelve Miniatures*. (*Anerca*) chamb ens of Ten Centuries Concerts; (*Orphée*) Mather pf, Wakefield perc; (*Twelve Miniatures*) Fiore fl, Buczynski spinet, Whitton vc. (1967). RCI 217/RCA CCS-1011/(*Anerca*) RCI ACM-2

Schafer *La Testa d'Adriana*. Macerollo acc. 1978. Mel SMLP 4034 – *Arcana*. Ens of New Music Concerts, Hodkinson cond. (1977). RCI 434

See also Discographies for CBC SO; Festival Singers; Lyric Arts Trio; SMCQ; Toronto Mendelssohn Choir.

BIBLIOGRAPHY

'Canada Music Citation 1968,' *Mcan*, 17, Mar 1969
Morey, Carl. 'An interview with Mary Morrison,' *PfAC*, Fall 1972

KW

Morris Pianos, Ltd. Established in 1892 by three businessmen in Listowel, northwest of Waterloo, Ont, as Morris, Feild, Rogers Co, Ltd. Described in *Industrial Canada*, February 1904, as successor to the Brantford Piano Co, it produced pianos, piano cases, and piano and organ keyboard blanks. The company received a bronze medal at the 1900 Paris Exhibition. By 1907 it was known by Morris' name alone, but in 1909 it amalgamated with the *Karn Piano Co to become the Karn Morris Piano and Organ Co, with its head office at Woodstock. By then it had made over 10,000 pianos. The company separated from Karn and was re-organized as Morris Pianos, Ltd, in 1920, with E.C. Thornton as managing director and J.H. Pettit as president. The head office was located in Toronto; the factory remained in Listowel. The company was not listed in the *Canadian Business Directory* after 1924. FH

MORROW, Art (Arthur). Conductor, arranger, composer, b Westmount (Montreal) 11 Dec 1919. Morrow studied piano 1930–5 with Rose Blackwell in Montreal. He began his career as a saxophonist and arranger with Johnny *Holmes' dance band before (and after, until 1948) service in World War II as leader of one of *The *Army Show*'s Tin Hat Revues. He was an arranger 1946–55 for the CBC conductors John *Adaskin, Giuseppe *Agostini, Neil *Chotem, Jean *Deslauriers, Maurice *Durieux, Henry Matthews, and Allan *McIver.

Morrow was music director and conductor 1951–66 of more than 25 CBC Montreal radio and TV shows – usually produced by Ken Withers. These included 'Sunshine Society' 1951–2, 'Fiddle Joe's Yarns' 1951–4, 'Songs Chez Nous' 1952–5 with Alan *Mills, 'A Date with Fred Hill' 1953–6, 'Cap-aux-Sorciers' (TV) 1955–7, 'Music Hall' (TV) 1955–9, 'Meet Mr. Morrow' 1958–60, 'Variety Showcase' 1960–2, 'Sheila Sings' 1962 with Sheila Graham, and 'Music Scene' 1964–6.

After 1966 Morrow worked with Bob *Hahn, played piano 1967–71 at the Queen Elizabeth and Bonaventure hotels in Montreal, and wrote arrangements for the Nick Martin orchestra and singer Danièle *Dorice. In 1973 he became assistant to the secretary treasurer of the Musicians' Guild of Montreal.

Morrow's compositions include the scores for the film *Séraphin* (1950) and for the jazz ballet *Postscript* (1956, choreography by Brian Macdonald, performed for three seasons by the Montreal Theatre Ballet). He wrote the accompaniments for two folksong anthologies by Alan Mills – *Folk Songs for Young Folk* and *Chantons un Peu*. Morrow is an affiliate of PRO Canada. BH, MM

Morse Code (Les Maîtres 1967–70). Montreal instrumental and vocal rock group whose members included Raymond Roy (drums), Michel Vallée (bass guitar), and Jocelyn Julien (guitar). Christian Simard (keyboards, voice) was added in 1968. The group performed songs by the Beatles, the Bee Gees, *Charlebois, and *Léveillée before turning to its own compositions. It made some singles for RCA as Les Maîtres prior to adopting the new name for its English-language LP *Morse Code Transmission* (1971, RCA LSP-4575). After changing guitarists several times the group added Daniel Lemay (also a flutist) in 1975. Several singles for Capitol were successful: 'Cocktail' and 'Punch' in 1975 and 'Cérémonie de minuit,' 'Sommeil,' and 'Je suis le temps' in 1977. A progressive group with a tendency towards contemporary classical music, Morse Code often appeared at Quebec universities and Cegeps, notably during a tour of more than 40 cities in the fall of 1976. The style of Simard (b Quebec City 29 Apr 1949) dominated after his arrival. He composed most of the group's songs, collaborating with the lyricists Chantal Dussault for the band's LP *La March des hommes* (1975, Cap ST-70038) and with Jean Robitaille for *Procréation* (1976, Cap SKAO 70046) and *Je suis le temps* (1977, Cap ST-70051). Simard also has written for Veronique Béliveau, Jean-Pierre *Ferland, Pierre *Lalonde, Donald *Lautrec, Céline Lomez, Ginette *Reno, and Suzanne Stevens. Morse Code disbanded in November 1977 and its members became freelance accompanists.

BIBLIOGRAPHY

Pedneault, Hélène. 'Morse Code provides inspiration for composer Christian Simard,' *MSc*, 288, Mar–Apr 1978

(CCr)

MORTIFEE, Ann. Composer, singer, b Durban, South Africa, 30 Nov 1947, naturalized Canadian 1961; BA (British Columbia) 1968. While studying English 1964–8 at the U of British Columbia, she began her career as a folk and blues singer-guitarist in local clubs and gained an avid regional following. In 1967, with Willy Dunn, she composed the score for George Ryga's play *The Ecstasy of Rita Joe* and toured as the Musician-Singer in the Vancouver production which appeared in 1969 at the *NAC in Ottawa. In Ottawa she was co-host (1969–70, with David *Wiffen) for 'Both Sides Now' on CJOH-TV and performed in 1969 at the *NAC in a production of the revue *Love and Maple Syrup* which moved to New York for a brief run 1969–70 off-Broadway. Mortifee stayed in New York and appeared in 1971 in *Jacques Brel Is Alive and Well and Living in Paris*. Returning to Vancouver, she revised and performed the music of *The Ecstasy of Rita Joe* for a ballet by Norbert Vesak for the Royal Winnipeg Ballet in 1971.

Mortifee composed scores for *The Grey Goose of Silence* (by Vesak for the North Carolina Dance Theatre), *Klee Wyck* 'a ballet for Emily Carr' (performed by the Anna Wyman Dance Theatre on CBC TV in 1975), and *Variations pour une souvenance / Yesterday's Day* (1975) produced by Les Grands Ballets Canadiens. She has composed film and TV scores and, with lyricist Valerie Hennell King, has written many songs for her own one-woman shows.

After travelling the world for two years Mortifee returned to performance with concerts in Vancouver (*Queen Elizabeth Theatre) and Toronto (Convocation Hall, *U of Toronto). Besides participating in the recording *The Ecstasy of Rita Joe* (1973, Kerygma KRS-1005 UA-LA 126F) she made the solo LP *Baptism* (1975, Cap ST-6437). Her music is published by Jabula Music. She is an affiliate of PRO Canada.

BIBLIOGRAPHY

LeBlanc, Larry. 'Recording is next step for Ann Mortifee,' *MSc*, 270, Mar–Apr 1973

Grescoe, Paul. 'Far from the madding hype,' *The Canadian*, 8 May 1976

(JR)

MORTON, Dorothy (b Breitman). Pianist, teacher, b Montreal 17 Sep 1924. She was a piano pupil of Stanley *Gardner and then entered *McGill U, where she studied theory and composition 1941–9 with Claude *Champagne, Douglas *Clarke, Marvin *Duchow, and Violet *Archer. At the *CMM she studied piano 1943–54 with Germaine *Malépart and Isidor Philipp, then took private tuition with the latter in New York. She won the Delphic Study Club scholarship in 1931 and the Sarah *Fischer Concerts scholarship in 1942 and received numerous other private grants. She has performed extensively on radio and in concert, and in 1955 she became a teacher at McGill U, where her pupils have included Robert *Silverman, Robert Mayerovitch, Paul Berkowitz, and Donald Steven. She was on the faculty at the *JMC Orford Art Centre in 1977 and 1978. Most of her concert activity, however, has been as part of a two-piano team with Esther Master (b Riga, Latvia, 11 Sep 1922, m Berman), whose family settled in Montreal when she was an infant. Master studied piano in Montreal with Rose *Goldblatt and in 1945 in New York with Robert Casadesus. She also studied with Philipp at the CMM, where the Morton-Master Duo was formed and was coached by Louis *Bailly, head of the chamber music department. The Morton-Master Duo made its concert debut at the Ritz-Carlton Hotel in 1955. It has given numerous CBC radio recitals and has recorded works by Chopin, Infante, and Schumann (1973, CBC SM-207), by Saint-Saëns (1973, CBC SM-242), by *Matton and Ravel (1977, RCI 442), and by Bach with the *McGill Chamber Orchestra (CBC SM-290). Master began teaching at McGill U in 1975. (NT)

MORTON, William. Tenor, teacher, b Deloraine, south of Brandon, Man, 27 Sep 1912. First trained as a violinist – he played in a dance orchestra at 13 – Morton studied voice in Regina with Alicia *Birkett and in 1933 made his radio debut on CKCK. Moving in 1935 to Toronto, where he studied with Albert Whitehead and James *Rosselino, he was heard often on CBC radio.

Morton sang the Evangelist 1938–51 in the annual performances (and CBC broadcasts) of the *St Matthew Passion* by the *Toronto Mendelssohn Choir and in 1940, 1946, and 1950 performances of the work in Montreal. After the 1940 performance under Wilfrid *Pelletier, Thomas *Archer, in *The Gazette* 11 Jun 1940, wrote: 'Mr. Morton possesses a lyric tenor, sweet in quality and full of nervous energy. He understands how to convey the extraordinary pathos of the simple melodic line which Bach suspends over a series of mere keyboard chords. In fact, there were times when this young tenor created emotional effects that were almost unbearably touching.'

A regular performer with the CBC Light Opera and the *CBC Opera, Morton sang in the radio premieres of *Willan's **Transit through Fire* (1942, as the Dancing Master) and **Deirdre of the Sorrows* (1946, as Naisi), in 13 Gilbert & Sullivan operettas, in John Gay's *The Beggar's Opera* (Frederick Austin version?), Edward German's *Merrie England*, and the Canadian premieres of Benjamin's *The Devil Take Her* and Britten's *Peter Grimes* (1949, title role).

Concurrently (1942–51) Morton was a founding member (with tenor Jack Reid, baritone Ernest Berry, and bass Ernest Taylor, the latter replaced by John Harcourt) of the Four Gentlemen, a group formed to sing on Samuel *Hersenhoren's CBC radio show 'Carry On Canada.' The quartet was heard weekly on CBC radio for several years, singing 'old songs,' art songs, hymns, and folksongs. (In 1954 the Four Gentlemen, with Alan Sawyer replacing Morton, joined the Commodores as the nucleus of the Carl *Tapscott Singers.)

In 1952 Morton moved to Vancouver where he founded and conducted the Vancouver Opera Theatre and has taught privately for more than 20 years. His pupils have included Wendy Martin, Don *McManus, Harry *Mossfield, Karl Norman, and Maurice Pearson. (SWI)

MOSES, Kathryn (Bethene) (b Taylor). Flutist, singer, saxophonist, composer, b Wynnewood, Okla, 19 Sep 1943; B MUS (Central State, Oklahoma) 1965. Her teachers have included Feodora Stewart (flute) and Coleman Smith (voice) at Central State U and Ted *Moses (composition) in Toronto. She played 1963–7 in the Oklahoma City SO before moving in 1967 to Toronto. There she was a member of Ted Moses' various jazz groups until 1976 and played with I Ching, the *York Winds (1973), and in studio and ballet orchestras. She has been a soloist with the orchestra of US trumpeter Chuck Mangione on North American tours 1974–6 and with *Nexus (Massey Hall, 20 Feb 1977), the *Chamber Players of Toronto (22 Oct 1977, playing *Weinzweig's *Divertimento No. 1*), and various Toronto jazz groups. In 1975 she began leading her own quartet and quintet in Toronto nightclubs, quickly becoming one of the city's most popular jazz artists. Writing in the *Globe and Mail* (8 Sep 1976) Jack Batten described her voice as 'small and firm and beautifully under control' and referred to the 'intimate and seductive quality of the Moses flute.' She has recorded as a soloist for LPs by Bruce Cockburn, Hagood Hardy, Mangione, Murray McLauchlan, Ted Moses, Tom Rush, Fred *Stone, and others. Her LP *Kathryn Moses*, comprising her compositions for jazz sextet and string quartet, won the first *CMCouncil Award (1977) as Canadian jazz recording of 1976. Moses' other compositions include about 30 works for jazz group, songs, ballet music, and some improvised scores for children's theatre and radio presentations. She is an affiliate of PRO Canada.

DISCOGRAPHY

Kathryn Moses. Moses fl and v, *Bickert guit, Williamson pf, *Homme db, *Clarke drums, Morell perc, A. *Armin vn, B. McDougall vn, P. Armin va, R. Armin vc. 1976. CBC LM-437

Music of My Heart. Moses fl, v, and sop sax, R. *Piltch guit, *Riley pf, *Goodman hp, D. Piltch db and b guit, Clarke drums, and others. 1978. PMR-017

BIBLIOGRAPHY

Batten, Jack. 'The magic flute,' *The Canadian*, 22 Jul 1978

MM

MOSES, Ted (Teddy Lavern). Composer, pianist, soprano, alto and tenor saxophonist, trumpeter, teacher, b Tulsa, Okla, 23 Oct 1943; BA (Central State, Oklahoma) 1967. He moved in 1967 to Toronto where he has led and composed for a succession of bands: the Sunnyside Symphonia, a rock band in 1968; the Ted Moses Quintet (formed in 1971), which toured western Canada in 1974; the 11-piece Mother Necessity 1972–4; the 18-piece Mother Necessity Big Band 1976–7; and a 13-piece band in 1978. In 1975 he founded the Canadian Foundation for the Improvised Arts and was music director of its Mother Necessity Jazz Workshop which opened 4 Jan 1976 as a venue for Toronto bands, among them his big band, and closed 27 Feb 1977. Mark Miller (*Globe and Mail*, 29 Nov 1978) described Moses' music as 'fashionable enough, in its electricity and rockish vitality, to sell, but no less valuable for its intelligence and discipline.' Moses also has composed and arranged music for chamber orchestra (including a group presented in 1973 on CBC TV's 'Music to See') and for mime, film, and dance productions. As a teacher of jazz theory and composition he has been a major influence on Toronto musicians, guiding such players as Shelly Berger, Herb Koffman, Michael Malone, Bob McLaren, Kathryn *Moses, David Piltch, Ken Ramm, Howie Silverman, and Michael Stuart. Moses is an affiliate of PRO Canada; the copyrights of his compositions are held by Mother Necessity Music.

DISCOGRAPHY

Sidereal Time. Moses keybds and ten sax, K. Moses fl, Malone tpt, Homme db and b guit, Clarke drums. 1974. RCI 400

More than Ever. Orch with soli (Moses keybds and alto and sop sax, Senensky synth, Malone and Cassidy tpts, Kogan ten sax, R. Piltch guit, D. Piltch b guit). 1978. CBC LM 459

The Farther You Go, the Farther You See. Moses keybds and sop sax, Malone tpt and flhn, R. Piltch guit, D. Piltch b guit, Clarke drums. 1978. Mother Necessity Music MNM-001

BIBLIOGRAPHY

Batten, Jack. 'Moses creates atmosphere for jazz growth in Toronto,' *MSc*, 289, May–Jun 1976 MM

MOSS. Toronto family of musicians: 1 / Cyril and 2 / his son Earle.

1 **Cyril** (Albert). Organist, teacher, composer, b Strood, Kent, England, 3 Jan 1891, d Toronto 6 Jan 1965; LTCM, RCCO ca 1925. He moved to Canada in 1908 and studied at the *TCM with George Knight and Sir Ernest *MacMillan and at the ESM in Rochester, NY, with Harold Gleason. Known throughout Ontario as an organist, he also taught at the TCM and was the composer of many choral and organ pieces.

2 **Earle** (Roderick). Teacher, pianist, b Toronto 11 Apr 1921; LTCM 1944. He studied piano at the *TCM with his father and with Ernest *Seitz and Bela Böszörmenyi-Nagy, and theory with Healey *Willan and Charles *Peaker. He also studied piano with Soulima Stravinsky at the Music Academy of the West (Santa Barbara, 1951) and with Gerald Moore (summers 1958, 1959). A proponent of the principles of Leschetizky (which he learned from G.D. *Atkinson and Ernest Seitz), he began teaching at the TCM in 1946 and has included among his pupils Walter *Buczynski, Arthur *Crighton, Barry Gosse, Douglas *Haas, Angela *Hewitt, Daryl *Irvine, Bruce *Mather, and Brock McElheran. In 1950 he became the co-ordinator of the RCMT graded piano books. He also wrote *Handbook for Technique* (Oakville 1966). With Weldon *Kilburn and Boris *Roubakine he advised on the selection and grading of material for *14 Piano Pieces by Canadian Composers* (Harris 1955). He became music director at Forest Hill United Church in 1957. Active 1948–65 as an accompanist, he has played for the singers Maureen *Forrester, Frances *James, and Jon *Vickers, the string players Eugene *Kash, Mischa Mischakoff, and Elie *Spivak, and other performers. He has given Canadian premieres of works by Bartók (*Improvisations, Op 14*), Dutilleux (*Sonata* for piano), Ravel (*Collage*), and others. He is the dedicatee of Godfrey *Ridout's *Three Preludes on Scottish Themes* for organ and of Eugene *Hill's anthem 'O God of Earth.'

MOSS, Anne Marie (m Paris). Singer, b Toronto 6 Feb 1935. Except for lessons in breath control from Portia *White in 1955, she did not study formally. She began performing as a child and sang jazz first in the early 1950s with the groups of Joey Masters and Cal Jackson, two US pianists living in Toronto. She also sang with the dance bands of Ferde Mowry and Benny Louis and throughout the 1950s appeared on CBC TV variety shows. She performed occasionally with the jazz groups of Norman *Symonds and Ron *Collier and toured 1956–8 in Canada and the USA with the saxophonist Don *Thompson. In 1959 she joined Maynard *Ferguson's big band in the USA, where she also sang with the Count Basie Orchestra and replaced Annie Ross briefly in the jazz vocal trio Lambert, Hendricks & Ross. In 1961 she married, and began singing with, the US singer-guitarist Jackie Paris. The two have appeared together in nightclubs across the USA and made the LP *Live at the Maisonette* (Different Drummer 1004). When they made a rare Canadian appearance in 1976 at the Toronto nightclub Bourbon Street, Jack Batten wrote: 'Miss Moss' voice and attack ... have grown more middle-of-the-road than they were in her earlier Toronto days. She seems to go in less for lofty flights and improvisations and concentrates more on plain old projection and communication. She's got all the equipment for that job – excellent diction, an intelligent awareness of lyrics, and a voice that's pure, professional and very assured' (Toronto *Globe and Mail*, 13 Oct 1976).

BIBLIOGRAPHY

Lazenby, Dick. 'Anne Marie Moss,' *Coda*, vol 2, Oct 1959

MM

MOSSFIELD, Harry. Baritone, b Sydney, Australia, 7 Jul 1919. He was known as a singer in Australia when he emigrated in 1952 to Vancouver. Moving in 1955 to Toronto, he performed 1956–8 with the *COC (his roles including Scarpia in the 1957 *Tosca*); studied at the *Royal Cons Opera School; appeared in 1956, 1960, and 1961 at the *Stratford Festival; and sang with the *TSO, the *Edmonton SO, the *Regina SO, and the Ottawa Civic SO. He studied briefly in Italy and sang 1963–5 at Sadler's Wells and on the BBC. In 1967 he toured Canada presenting 'One Hundred Years of Musical Comedy.' The following year he formed a touring trio called the Western Savoyards with the soprano Christine Anton, the tenor Edward Greenhalgh, and the pianist Eugene Deagle. He settled in Vancouver, teaching privately and touring twice yearly. With his wife, Pearl Kerr, a concert pianist, he has given many CBC broadcasts. He draws his repertoire largely from Gilbert & Sullivan, Puccini, Britten, and Johann Strauss.

(GK)

MOSSOP, Cyril (Stephenson). Organist, choirmaster, teacher, conductor, b Calgary 14 Jun 1910. He studied piano first with his mother and later with a Mrs Titchmarsh, receiving an LTCL and an ATCM. He studied organ 1933–6 with Harold Heeremans.

Mossop has been an organist-choirmaster and taught piano, organ, voice, and theory privately, 1928–44 in Summerland and Kelowna, BC, and 1944–50 and again after 1972 in the Calgary area. He was director 1944–51 of the *Mount Royal College Cons of Music and was supervisor of music 1951–72 in Calgary schools. He has adjudicated at more than 30 festivals in western Canada 1945–74 and at the *CNE music competition in Toronto and has examined 1944–50 and after 1974 for the *WBM.

Mossop has composed choral pieces, mostly for school use (McGraw-Hill, Ryerson, Canadian Music Sales), and three organ works. He has often, in Calgary and Kelowna, conducted large-scale choral-orchestral works and has given many workshops at conventions. He is the father of the violinist Elaine Mossop Sargous. CF

MOTLEY, Phillips (Carey). Organist-choirmaster, conductor, b Montreal 12 Jul 1912; BA (McGill) 1934, LRSM 1935, B MUS (Toronto) 1939, FRCCO 1940. Studies in Montreal with R.F.L. Picard and Alfred *Whitehead preceded appointments there as organist-choirmaster at various churches: St Jude's Anglican in 1934, First Baptist 1935–47, St Andrew's United 1948–56, and St Andrew and St Paul 1956–72; and at the Temple Emmanu-El 1948–56. He moved to the Church of the Ascension in 1972. Since the mid-1930s Motley has given more than 300 organ recitals, his playing marked by clarity, precision, and careful attention to phrasing. He has conducted many choral and hymn festivals in Montreal, usually under the auspices of the *RCCO. He was a member of the committee which produced the Baptist *Hymnal* ([Brantford, Ont] 1973) and has served on the music committee of the Roman Catholic Diocesan Liturgical Commission. SLO

MOULD, Warren. Pianist, teacher, administrator, b Toronto 28 Jun 1933; LTCL 1948, FTCL 1949. He studied at Trinity College of Music in London with James Lyons and Max *Pirani and privately in Toronto with Mona *Bates, making his debut in 1948 at *Eaton Auditorium, Toronto, and his New York debut in 1951 at Carnegie Hall. He has given numerous recitals on CBC radio and has toured in Canada and the USA. He was assistant registrar 1963–6 and registrar 1966–76 at the *RCMT and was a member 1975–6 of the RCMT Trio. With his wife, the soprano Burnetta Day (b Chatham, Ont), he moved to Europe ca 1977.

A specialist in the preparation of piano instruction materials, Mould has composed teaching pieces for piano and was co-author with Boris *Berlin of a teacher's manual, *Basics of Ear Training* (Toronto 1968). He has written articles on Jon *Vickers and Maureen *Forrester for the periodical *Sound* (see Bibliographies for Forrester and Vickers).

Mould has recorded eight graded albums of the RCMT's books of piano studies (1971, RCP-GI to RCP-GVIII) and *New For Now Piano Vol. 1* (1970, Dom S69002). He was president 1963–4 of the *ORMTA.

Mould's mother Nellie (b England ca 1891) taught music in Canada for 60 years and in 1977 was the recipient of an honorary FTCL. She taught both Warren and another son, Neville, the latter a pianist who appeared with the *TSO and whose promising career was cut short by his death from polio at 15. (MH)

Mountains. As an inspiration for Canadian music, mountains have enjoyed limited popularity. Not unexpectedly the mountains most often referred to are the Rockies of Alberta and British Columbia. However the earliest known compositions about mountains, *The Royal Mountain Waltzes* (1866) by Moritz Relle, were inspired by Mount Royal (Montreal), as was J.-Amédée Roy's 'reverie' *Dans les Sentiers du Mont Royal* (ca 1914). French-Canadian folkdance recordings made in the 1920s and 1930s include *Reel des Laurentides* (accordionist Tommy Duchesne), *Reel des montagnes* (fiddler Joseph *Allard and accordionist Tommy Duchesne), *Quadrille Mont-Laurier* (harmonica player Henri Lacroix), *Quadrille des Laurentides* (fiddler Isidore *Soucy), and *March Mont Saint-Louis* (Joseph Latour and Alfred Montmarquette, both accordionists).

Among folksongs is the 'Ballad of Frank Slide' which refers to Turtle Mountain, BC (see Disaster songs). Pop songs include Stu *Davis' 'Black Mountain Rag' and 'When the Snowbirds Cross the Rockies' and Ray Calder's 'Blue Laurentian Moon.' The country song 'Blue Canadian Rockies' (Berandol 1960) was written by the US singer Cindy Walker and has been recorded over 25 times, eg, by Gene Autry, Mac *Beattie, the Canadian Sweethearts (see Lucille Starr), Wilf *Carter, and Scotty *Stevenson.

Concert works include Edmund *Assaly's *Mount Royal Fantasy* (1948, piano and orchestra), Pierre *Brabant's *Caprice Laurentian* (1945, piano), Morley *Calvert's *Suite from the Monteregian Hills* (1962, brass quintet), *Freedman's 'Blue Mountain' (from *Images* for orchestra; the first movement; inspired by the Lawren Harris painting), Clifford Higgin's *Rocky Mountains*, Robert *McMullin's *Sketches from the Rocky Mountains* (1948, for orchestra), and François *Morel's *Le Mythe de la Roche percée* (1961, wind and percussion).

The major concert work is Claude *Champagne's *Altitude* (1959), a three-part orchestral-choral suite ('The Primitive Age,' 'Meditations,' and 'The Modern Age') which depicts an imaginary journey through the Rockies. These same mountains inspired 'Land of the Misty Giants' in Oscar *Peterson's *Canadiana Suite*.

Mount Allison University. United-Church-affiliated, non-sectarian university in Sackville, NB. Prior to its incorporation in 1963 its functions had been carried out by three separate but interrelated institutions: the Mount Allison Wesleyan Academy for Boys (1840–1958), the Ladies' College (1854–1958), and Mount Allison College, which was established with degree-granting powers on behalf of the other two in 1862. Most of Mount Allison U's approximately 1500 students in 1979–80 were undergraduates in the liberal arts, but there was a small component of graduate students working on masters' degrees in the sciences.

Mount Allison Ladies' College instituted a music program at its inception. In 1874 its first music diplomas, both in piano, were awarded to Ravinia Stewart and Alma Hickman.

The Mount Allison Cons (which later would become the music-teaching department of Mount Allison College), founded in 1885 with two teachers, offered diplomas in piano, violin, and voice. It was one of Canada's first conservatories, and in 1980 in its transformed state was probably the oldest surviving in the country. A conservatory building was erected in 1890, and a music library was begun in 1891. In 1892 the conservatory broadened its diploma course to allow students a choice of artist or teacher concentrations. The requirements for each followed European models. Conservatory directors were Albert A. Mack 1885–93, Charles Landon 1893–4, Frederick Lillebridge 1894–6, J.J. Wootton 1896–8, Almon Vincent 1898–1901, George Wilson 1901–9, Harry Horsfall 1909–11, James Noel Brunton – b Stranraer, Wigtonshire, Scotland, 25 Jun 1876; ATCL 1903, artist's diploma (Stern Conservatorium, Berlin) 1906; a pupil of Franz Orosz, Paul Lutzenko and Leopold Godowsky, a teacher in London 1907–11, and head of the piano department at Mount Allison 1936–46 – 1911–14 and 1919–36, Fritz Read 1915–19, and Harold *Hamer 1936–47.

The B MUS degree was introduced in 1912 and was awarded first in 1917 to Mary Elsinore Tait. As diploma courses were more popular, the second B MUS degree was not awarded until 1933. In 1923 Mount Allison's Ladies' College became the first Canadian college to broadcast a program of music.

In 1937 the conservatory was made the Music Dept of Mount Allison College's Faculty of Arts. Heads of the department have been Harold Hamer (first appointed to the conservatory teaching staff in 1927) 1936–47, Alfred *Whitehead (staff member 1913–15) 1947–53, Howard *Brown 1953–67, and George *Proctor 1967–74. James *Stark succeeded Proctor.

During their long history, the degree programs of the Music Dept have undergone many changes which cannot be described here in any detail. In addition to the B MUS, there have been the Musical Leadership Diploma (emphasizing public school music, and begun in 1934), a Licentiate in Music (artist's and teacher's), the AMACM (Associate Mount Allison Cons of Music), and the BA (music major). Degree programs being offered in 1979–80 were B MUS (music education, history, theory, composition, and Special Certificates in performance), BA (concentration in music: honours degree), and B MUS / B ED (five-year integrated program). Mount Allison conferred its first honorary Doctorate of Music (1944) on James Noel Brunton. Honorary doctorates in law were awarded to Alice May Harrison (1954), Alfred Whitehead (1954), Sir Ernest *MacMillan (1956), and Helen *Creighton (1957), and honorary doctorates in music to Arnold *Walter (1966) and to John *Beckwith, Francis *Chaplin, and Maureen *Forrester, the last three on the occasion of the centennial of the first degree conferred at Mount Allison (1974). Student enrolment in the department has been limited to approximately 100. In 1978–9 there were 13 full-time faculty members and 4 part-time. Prominent faculty members have included Carleton *Elliott, Doreen *Hall, Kelsey *Jones, Evran Kinsman, Allison Patterson, and Stanley *Saunders.

In 1959 Saunders, in co-operation with the extension department, initiated a summer instrumental music camp. In 1974 enrolment in this summer session (three weeks each July) exceeded 600. In conjunction with the extension department, groups of music education students have visited schools throughout the Atlantic provinces each May. The Music Dept in 1962 began conducting annual examinations of extramural (privately taught) music students. In the years following as many as 900 candidates have been entered in a single year. In 1966 the department moved into the newly built Marjorie Young Bell Conservatory building, donated to the university by the dedicatee's husband, Ralph Pickard Bell, Chancellor Emeritus, and containing two classrooms, two rehearsal halls, 11 office-studios, 25 practice rooms, the 370-seat Brunton Auditorium, a radio control centre, a practice organ, and a small electronic studio. Two *Casavant organs have been installed as part of the department's facilities. The Bell Conservatory also houses the Alfred Whitehead Memorial Music Library, the largest of its kind in the Atlantic provinces. Another important collection at Mount Allison, the Mary Mellish Archibald Library, is rich in folk music material. The Ralph Pickard Bell Library Publications in Music Series has made several important contributions to musical bibliography, including catalogues of the university's Canadian music holdings, of the folk music holdings in the Archibald Library, and of other special collections. (See entry for Bibliography.)

Recitals, workshops, and collegia musica given by students, faculty members, and visiting musicians have become an integral part of the music program. The Performing Arts Series was established to present guest performers of distinction. Student performing groups in 1980 included the Choral Society (which in 1979 joined forces with the *New Brunswick Youth Orchestra to present Mendelssohn's *Elijah* in Saint John, Fredericton, and Sackville), the Conservatory Chorale, the Symphonic Band, the Chamber Orchestra, and the Jazz Ensemble. Many student and faculty performances have been broadcast over CBC radio.

See also Archives; College songs.

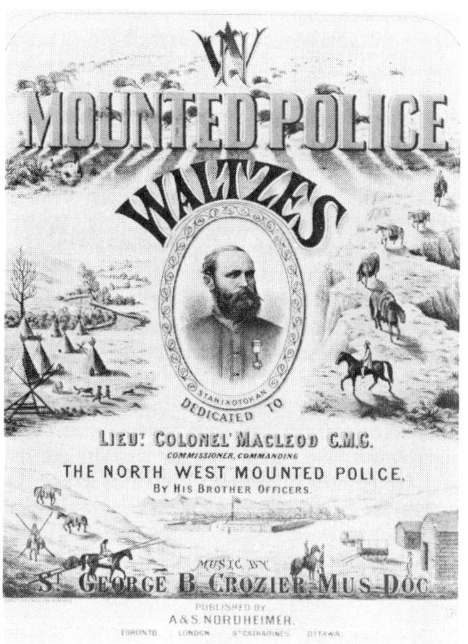

BIBLIOGRAPHY

Allison, L.M. 'Mount Allison summer institute,' *CMJ*, vol 1, Autumn 1956

Proctor, George. 'Department provides music teachers for Atlantic region,' *MSc*, 259, May–Jun 1971

(JCm, PMW)

Mounties. North West Mounted Police (Royal Canadian Mounted Police after 1920), formed in 1873 to police the area from Lake Superior west to the Pacific. The 'Mounties' played a prominent role in the settlement of the West, quelling rebellions and representing such law as there was during the construction of a national railroad and the rush for gold in the Klondike. The Mountie emerged in the late 19th and early 20th centuries as a symbol of peace and order and has been idealized in literature, poetry, and the visual arts, but to a lesser extent in music. He is little mentioned in the 19th-century ballads which might have been expected to tell of particular events in which the force had been involved.

The Mountie first appears in Canadian music in the piano waltzes *North West Mounted Police* (1870s) by St George B. *Crozier. In 1906 Annie *Glen Broder wrote *The Ride of the R.N.W.M.P.*, for band. 'The Mountie' (Thompson 1937), an arrangement by Harold Eustace *Key of an ancient Welsh air, with words by John Murray *Gibbon, portrays the Mountie as a dashing hero: 'Muffled in wind come the cantering hoofbeats, herald of Mountie patrolling the trail ... braving all danger, disdaining bravado, terror to outlaw and tough desperado.' But his most romantic treatment remains that accorded him in the popular US operetta *Rose Marie*. Dolores *Claman's *The Mounties* was published by Severn Music in 1963.

See also Bands 5 / Police bands. FH

Mount Royal College Conservatory of Music and Speech Arts. Music school of Mount Royal College, established in Calgary in 1910 by the Methodist (later United) Church as a residential high school. In 1931 the college became affiliated with the *U of Alberta and began offering two-year undergraduate courses leading to a diploma.

Though the speech arts department was established only in 1945, the music department has been part of the college from the outset. It opened with a faculty of five under the direction of Wilfred Oaten and a student enrolment of less than 100. In 1977, under the newly appointed director Norman Burgess, the faculty numbered about 50 on campus and 20 in branch studios and the enrolment was more than 2,000. Programs are offered in performance and pedagogy.

Other directors of the conservatory have been J.E. Hogson, Frederic Rogers, P.L. Newcombe, Jascha Galperin 1940–4, Cyril *Mossop 1944–51, Harold *Ramsay 1951–62, John Garden 1962–3, Peter Hodgson 1963–4, J.S. Peter *Bach 1964–74, and Leona Flegal Paterson 1974–7. The teaching faculty has included, in addition to the directors, Gladys *Egbert, Clayton *Hare, Leonard *Leacock (for whom the Leacock Music Theatre – opened on campus in 1972 – was named), and Mary *Munn.

The conservatory is known especially for its orchestras. The Mount Royal College SO, organized in 1937 by Jascha Galperin and known then as the Baby SO (made up of children aged four to 12), became the basis of the *Calgary SO under Clayton Hare in 1949. Frank Simpson, music co-ordinator of the college's Community Services dept, founded in 1968 and continued to conduct in 1980 the Calgary Youth Orchestra, under the auspices of the conservatory. In the mid-1970s the conservatory supported three orchestras (junior, youth, and community), three bands (junior, senior, and jazz), and two choirs.

BIBLIOGRAPHY

Steven, Margaret L. 'Heredity's not the biggest factor in making a good musician,' *Calgary Herald*, 17 Jun 1939

'Mount Royal College,' *Music in Alberta*, vol 3, Spring 1974 (FM)

Mount Saint Vincent University. Non-denominational (formerly Roman Catholic) institution founded, owned, and operated in Rockingham (Halifax), NS, by the Sisters of Charity and known familiarly as 'The Mount.' Initially Mount Saint Vincent Academy, it was founded in 1873 as a teachers' college for nuns and was opened to local girls generally in order to promote the higher education of women. From the outset music education was an integral part of the curriculum, and an agreement signed with *Dalhousie U in 1914 enabled the academy to offer the first two years of a bachelor's degree program, the final two years being given by Dalhousie.

In 1925 the academy was chartered as Mount Saint Vincent College, the Commonwealth's only independent degree-granting women's college. Licentiate and degree courses were offered in performance and music education; Sisters Mary Ludovica, Mary Corona, and Margaret Young, successively, headed the music department. The first graduate in music, Mary Montague (Boyd), received a B MUS in 1928. The *Armdale Chorus originated in the college in the 1930s. By 1962, when the college's lack of money and Dalhousie's expansion of music programs had forced the closure of the Mount's music department and degree program, 20 licentiates and degrees had been granted.

In 1966 the college became fully accredited as a university, and in 1972 a friendly association was formed with the Nova Scotia College of Art and Design. Despite the closure of the music department a teacher of music has remained on the faculty, and music history has continued to be taught in the Fine Arts Dept, music methodology for classroom teachers in the Education program, and introduction to art, music, movement, and drama in the Child Study degree program.

Among the university's facilities are the theatre-in-the-round of the Seton Academic Centre and the three-manual *Casavant organ in the chapel. Concerts have included light musicals, and during 1978–9 three public performances were given by the Trio del Mar, artists-in-residence for that year only. A tribute to Helen *Creighton titled 'The Collector' was presented 28–30 Mar 1980. Under the artistic and musical direction of Sister Margaret Young, the 90-minute musical entertainment, which involved a cast of 60 and was based on Creighton's life work, presented with careful attention to authenticity a mosaic of the music of many of Nova Scotia's ethnic groups, from Cape Breton Ceilidh to the Acadian tradition. (ML, MY)

MOUSSART, François du. Drummer, organist, music teacher, b Ennelat, near Clermont, Auvergne, France, ca 1646, d? The *Jesuit Relations* (vol 49) mentions in July 1665 that a drummer of one of the military companies that had arrived that year, a 19-year-old named François du Moussart, 'was given to us by sieur la Tour, his Captain, because he was an excellent musician; but with the design that we should do him the charity of making him study.' The 1666 census lists François du Moussard (sic), 23, maître de musique, as one of the 'hommes de travail' at the Collège de Québec. According to Auguste Gosselin (Amtmann *Music in Canada*), the young man played the organ at the parish church 1666–70, but no documentary evidence was found by *Amtmann to prove this. Nothing is known about du Moussart's later life.

BIBLIOGRAPHY

Sulte, Benjamin. *Histoire des Canadiens-Français 1608–1880*, vol 4, Montreal 1882 HK

Mouvement Vivaldi. See Société musicale Le Mouvement Vivaldi.

MOZETICH, Marjan. Composer, b Gorizia, Italy, of Yugoslav parents, 7 Jan 1948, naturalized Canadian 1957; ARCT piano 1971, B MUS (Toronto) 1972. His family moved to Canada in 1952. He studied in Hamilton 1965–8 with Reginald *Bedford (piano) and at the *U of Toronto 1968–72 with Lothar *Klein and John *Weinzweig (composition) and Margaret *Parsons and Clifford *Poole (piano). While at university he organized concerts of new music by student composers and helped found (1971) *ARRAY, for which he became concert co-ordinator in 1975. He studied composition 1973–5 with Luciano Berio in Rome, Franco Donatoni in Siena, and David Bedford in London and received a fellowship in 1974 from the Instituto Musicale F. Canneti to attend a seminar in Vicenza, Italy.

Mozetich's wind quintet *It's in The Air* (1975) won a second prize at the International Gaudeamus Composers' Competition in Bilthoven, the Netherlands, and his *Nocturne* (1975) for string orchestra was chosen to represent Canada at the adjudication for the 1978 ISCM Festival in Helsinki. In 1977 he won *CAPAC's Sir Ernest MacMillan Award. Mozetich's other compositions include: *Changes* (1971), premiered by the *Orford String Quartet; various chamber works premiered by ARRAY and *Days Months and Years to Come; *Serenata del Nostro Tempo* (string quintet, 1973), premiered by the Forum Players of Rome; and solo pieces for piano (*Maya* 1973) and viola (*Disturbances* 1974).

Mozetich refers to his music as 'post-A-Bomb romanticism,' his works before 1977 reflecting a highly expressive, unusually melodic use of avant-garde devices and retaining a strong sense of tonal centre. In 1977 he began to find inspiration in the music of the Canadian Indian and Inuit. He has invented his own material, however. He is a member of CAPAC and an associate of the *CMCentre.

BIBLIOGRAPHY

Schulman, Michael. 'A composer straightens out the confusions in his life,' *CanComp*, 130, Apr 1978 (FH)

MSO Concours / Concours OSM. Annual competition initiated in 1965 as a successor to the *Prix Archambault which had been discontinued in 1963. Its aim has been to discover talented young Canadians, help them continue their training through scholarships, and provide the opportunity for prize winners to appear as soloists with the *MSO. Until 1973, one (or several) of the following disciplines was represented each year: piano, string instruments, wind instruments, and voice. Beginning in 1973, piano and voice alternated with strings and winds. The age limit is 25 years for instrumentalists (piano and strings subdivided: under 18, and 18–25), 30 for singers. The auditions, open to the public, have been held each autumn. Juries have been recruited from among Canadian, and some foreign, composers, conductors, and performers. The number of participants grew from 30, when the competitions began, to 65 in 1977.

The scholarships have been provided by the Women's Committee of the MSO (which also organizes the competition), the MSO Young People's committee, the *Amis de l'art Foundation (Aline-Hector Perrier Scholarship), and private donors. In 1977, depending on discipline and category, amounts of $1000 to $1500 (1st prize), $500 to $1000 (2nd prize), and $500 (3rd prize) were awarded.

Among the winners have been the soprano Nicole *Lorange (1965); the pianists Henri *Brassard (1965), André *Laplante (1968), William *Tritt (1970), and Louis *Lortie (1972); the cellist Denis *Brott (1967); and the violinists Adele *Armin (1969), Denise Lupien (1974), and Chantal Juillet (1974). In 1975, the winners were the pianists Adrienne *Shannon and Anne-Marie Dubois and the soprano Gina Fiordaliso; in 1976, the cellist Johanne Perron, the violinists Angèle Dubeau and Jean-François Rivest, and the oboists Pierre-M. Plante and Louise Pellerin; in 1977, the pianists Jacques Després and Janice Lin, and the baritone Ronald Costley; in 1978, the cellists Gary Hoffman and Ofra Harnoy, the violinist Céline Leathead, and the flutist Jeffrey Khaner; and in 1979 the pianists Angela Cheng and Lisa Nagatami and the soprano Marie-Danielle Parent. AP

MUELLER, Otto-Werner. Conductor, teacher, pianist, b Bensheim, Germany, 23 Jun 1926. He studied at the Musisches Gymnasium, Frankfurt-am-Main. At 19 he made his debut as music director of Stuttgart Radio, where he founded and conducted a vocal ensemble.

Mueller moved to Montreal in 1951 and worked as a rehearsal pianist, and later as a conductor, for CBC radio and TV, in particular for the programs 'CBC Wednesday Night' and 'L'*Heure du concert.' He took lessons with Igor Markevitch in Mexico and in 1958 won second prize in the Pan-American competition for conducting. His next appointment was as chorus master for the opera class of the *CMM. He was a founder (1963) and the first director (until 1965) of the Victoria (BC) School of Music. He became the conductor of the *Victoria SO in 1963 and spent part of that same year in, Moscow as a guest professor at the Tchaikovsky Cons where Maxim Shostakovich and Rudolph Barshai were among his pupils.

In 1967 Mueller left the Victoria SO to teach at the U of Wisconsin in Madison. In 1968 and 1970 he conducted in Moscow, Leningrad, and Riga. In 1965 he conducted the CBC TV production of *The Barber of Seville* which won an Emmy Award (US) for the best foreign production. He joined the staff of the Yale School of Music in New Haven in 1973. He became the conductor of the Yale Philharmonia and has appeared as a guest conductor in many Canadian and US cities.

During his years in Canada Mueller conducted the premieres of several Canadian works including *Pyknon* (MSO, 1966) and *Diallèle* (TS, 1968) by André *Prévost, the *Symphony-Concerto* (TS, 1968) of S.C. *Eckhardt-Gramatté, and the *Symphony No. 2* (Edmonton SO, 1977) of Malcolm *Forsyth. During the summer of 1978 he conducted the second session of the Orchestre des Jeunes du Québec at the *JMC Orford Art Centre.

See also Discographies for MSO; Zara Nelsova.

GP

MUIR, Alexander. Songwriter, school principal, poet, b Lesmahogow, near Lanark, Scotland, 5 Apr 1830, d Toronto 20 Jan 1906; BA (Queen's) 1851. His parents settled, when he was three, in Scarborough Township, east of Toronto, and he later taught 1853–60 in several Scarborough schools. He was principal 1860–70 at Leslieville School and in the ensuing years was teacher or principal of schools in Newmarket, Beaverton, and Toronto, including Gladstone Avenue School 1888–1906 which was later renamed in his honour.

Although Muir's musical activities were on an amateur level, they were strongly emphasized along with athletics and patriotism during his teaching career. He wrote words and music for several patriotic songs including the famous *'The Maple Leaf For Ever' (1867). Others are 'Canada, Land of the Maple Tree' and 'The Old Union Jack' (both published by Suckling 1890), 'Canada Forever' (Whaley Royce 1894), and 'Young Canada Was Here' (Whaley Royce 1900). Some of his poetry was published in Newmarket and Toronto newspapers.

A park, built in his honour in Toronto in 1933, was re-dedicated to Muir in 1952 when its location was changed (see Memorials).

BIBLIOGRAPHY

Robertson, John Ross. 'Alexander Muir's life,' *Landmarks of Toronto*, series 6 (Toronto 1914)

Caswell, Edward S. ed. *Canadian Singers and Their Songs* (Toronto 1925)

RPn

MULLEN, Vic (Melvin Victor). Banjoist, guitarist, mandolinist, fiddler, record producer, b Woodstock, Yarmouth County, NS, 28 Jan 1933. He began playing guitar at 12 and took up, in turn, mandolin, fiddle, and banjo. He was influenced by Wilf *Carter, but by the late 1940s he had become interested in bluegrass music.

Mullen joined Ned *Landry's band in 1948 and later played with the Birch Mountain Boys, the Rainbow Valley Boys, and other groups, touring in the 1950s in the Maritimes and in Maine. After leading the Bluenose Boys in CTV's 'Cross Country Barndance' (early 1960s) and playing 1962–9 on 'Don *Messer's Jubilee,' he was music director 1970–3 of CBC TV's 'Countrytime.' In 1974 he became co-host for CBC radio's 'Country Road.' In the mid-1970s Mullen was leading two bands: The Hickorys, a contemporary country group which performed on 'Countrytime,' and Meadowgreen, an oldtime and bluegrass group.

As an A & R man (mid-1960s) for the *Rodeo label, Mullen produced several artists' recordings and played on others as a sideman. By 1976, under his own name, he had made three LPs for Rodeo and one each for *RCA and MCA. He has composed in several country styles. He is a member of CAPAC and operates a music store in Dartmouth, NS.

(RGn)

Multi-media music. See Mixed media.

MUNDINGER, Eric. Accordionist, teacher, music engraver, b Offenburg, Germany, 25 Jun 1910, naturalized Canadian 1935. After studies in Germany with Karl Fink and tours in Europe as a concert soloist, Mundinger settled in Toronto in 1929. He continued his studies in the USA with Pietro Deiro and until 1939 performed as a soloist in concert and on radio. He also recorded for RCA and Deutsche Grammophon. His Mundinger School of Music, established in Toronto in 1935, offered only accordion lessons at first but added instruction in other instruments after 1952. The school closed in 1971. Mundinger published piano accordion methods in 1955 and 1959. The 125-member Mundinger Accordion Orchestra, made up of his pupils, performed 1951–6 under his direction in southern Ontario centres including Toronto (*Massey Hall 1951 and 1953). Its repertoire included many of his own transcriptions of symphonic works. Mundinger was founder and president ca 1952–71 of the Mundinger Music Co, which operated several music stores in the Toronto area. He began music engraving as a hobby in 1936 and established the firm Musictype Ltd in Goodwood, northeast of Toronto, in 1968. (AHC)

MUNN, Mary (Elizabeth). Pianist, teacher, b Montreal 28 Jun 1909; LRAM 1928, RAM Certificate of Merit 1929, M MUS (New England Cons) 1967, DMA (Boston) 1973. Born blind, she studied 1920–6 with Catherine Smut in Montreal, 1926–9 at the RAM, where her principal teacher was Percy Waller, and for another two years in London with Tobias Matthay. She also attended the summer classes of Wilhelm Kempff in the summer of 1938. She made debuts in Montreal in 1931, London in 1931, Berlin in 1935, and New York in 1937. Other notable performances were with the *TSO (Liszt's *Hungarian Fantasy*) 14 Dec 1945, the *Vancouver SO in 1947, the London SO (under Sir Malcolm Sargent) in 1948, and the *CBC Vancouver Chamber Orchestra in 1953. She has given recitals in North America and Europe, and she presented a series of commentaries, 'In Town Tonight' (1951–2), over BBC radio. She taught 1953–65 at *Mount Royal College in Calgary and briefly (1956) in Victoria, BC. She resumed her education at 57, purportedly becoming the first blind woman in the world to receive a doctorate in music. She has explained, 'I wanted to see whether, by taking it myself, it would open up the field for other blind people' (*Calgary Herald*, 8 Jun 1973). In 1973 she returned to Calgary as principal of the Calgary Cons.

BIBLIOGRAPHY

Dawson, Eric. 'Blindness didn't shut Mary Munn out of a "glorious" musical life,' *Calgary Herald*, 2 Apr 1979

RDM

MUNN, Sandra (Alexandra Marguerite). Pianist, choir conductor, b Calgary 16 Sep 1934; A MUS (Alberta) 1952, L MUS (Alberta) 1953, LRSM 1953, Diploma (Juilliard) 1955. She studied piano with Gladys *Egbert and theory with Phyllis Chapman Clarke Ford 1946–53 at the U of Alberta and continued on scholarship with Irwin Freundlich 1953–6 at the Juilliard School and, in the summer, in Canada, the USA, and Italy.

Munn's recital debut was before the *Calgary Women's Musical Club in 1956 and her debut with orchestra was with the *Calgary Philharmonic in 1957, in Beethoven's *Concerto No. 3*. She has performed often on CBC radio and has toured for *JMC.

In 1962 Munn was appointed to the *U of Alberta where she has taught piano and conducted the *Richard Eaton Singers 1967–73 and the Da Camera Singers 1968–73. She became director of the *Edmonton Opera Chorus in 1966. Among her pupils have been Beth Coop, Jane *Coop, John *Hendrickson, Albert Krywolt, Michael Massey, and Sylvia Shadick. (CF)

MUNROE. Winnipeg family of musicians: Walter, a painter and amateur violinist; his wife Zoë, a pianist and teacher, b Ekaterinoslav (Dniepro Petrovsk), Russia, 18 Apr 1898; and their children, 1 / Lorne, 2 / Sheila, and 3 / Gilbert.

1 **Lorne**. Cellist, teacher, b Winnipeg 24 Nov 1924. At three he took his first cello lessons on his father's violin, to which his teacher, Dezsö *Mahalek, had attached a 'leg,' and at 10 he won the senior cello class at the *Manitoba Music Competition Festival. Sponsored by Arthur *Benjamin, that year's adjudicator, he attended the RCM, London, 1937–9 on scholarship with Ivor James. In 1939 he gave a joint recital with Benjamin for the Young Men's Musical Club of Winnipeg. The program included Benjamin's *Sonatina*, written for the 14-year-old cellist the previous year. He completed his studies 1939–47 on scholarship at the Curtis Institute, Philadelphia, with Felix Salmond, Orlando Cole, and, before and after service in World War II, as a protégé of Gregor Piatigorsky.

Lorne Munroe won the only Naumburg Award granted in 1949 and as a result made his formal New York recital debut 16 November at Town Hall, playing works of Haydn, Weber, Dvořák, and Fauré. He was a member 1949–50 of the Cleveland Orchestra and principal cello 1950–1 of the Minneapolis SO before joining the Philadelphia Orchestra as principal cello in 1951. While with the last-named he was director of a 15-player ensemble drawn from it, the Amerita String Orchestra, which performed in the USA and Europe under the sponsorship of the American-Italy Society of Philadelphia. Munroe became principal cello of the New York Philharmonic on the invitation of Leonard Bernstein in 1964 and has continued in that position, appearing also as soloist with the orchestra in the concertos of Saint-Saëns, Elgar, Dvořák, Kabalevsky, Britten, etc. He began teaching in 1951, privately, at Temple U, and at the Musical Academy in Philadelphia, where he maintains a home, and in 1964 at the Juilliard School in New York. He has performed as concerto soloist or recitalist in Toronto (Dvořák *Concerto*, *TS, 1 May 1970), Ottawa, Winnipeg (Schumann *Concerto*, 17 Nov 1978), and Vancouver and in major cities of Europe, Israel, and Japan. He owns a 1707 Matteo Gofriller cello.

After Munroe's performance in Strauss' *Don Quixote*, 20 Jan 1951 in Carnegie Hall with the Philadelphia Orchestra conducted by Pierre Monteux, Virgil Thomson wrote in the *Herald Tribune*: 'Lorne Munroe, the cellist, impressed ... with his fine, sombre tone and his extraordinary ability to play in tune. I don't remember ever hearing this work read so enchantingly'; and Olin Downes, in the *New York Times*, wrote: 'Most prominent and commanding, of course, was Mr. Munroe. He has a noble, sonorous tone, with every possible gradation in it, and there was every characterization and sensitivity in his performance.'

DISCOGRAPHY

Corelli *Concerto Grosso, Op 6, no. 8*. Philadelphia O, Ormandy cond. (1959). Col ML 5402

First Chair Encores: Fauré *Élégie, Op 24*. Philadelphia O, Ormandy cond. (1965–7). Col MS 6791

Lorne Munroe

Music from Spain: Casals *Song of the Birds*. M. Niska sop, orch, Kostelanetz cond. (1950s). Col MG 32455
Strauss *Don Quixote*. New York Phil O, Bernstein cond. (1970). Col M30067
– *Don Quixote*. Philadelphia O, Ormandy cond. nd. Col ML 5915
– *Don Quixote*. Philadelphia O, Ormandy cond. (1958). Col ML 5292
Weber-Piatigorsky *Adagio and Rondo*. Philadelphia O, Ormandy cond. nd. Col ML 4629

BIBLIOGRAPHY
Thompson, Leslie. 'First chair takes talent and stamina,' *Music*, Oct 1980

2 **Sheila** (m Rodgers). Pianist, b Winnipeg 3 Aug 1928. She studied piano with her mother and with John *Melnyk, won the Aikins Memorial Trophy (the top instrumental award) at the 1946 *Manitoba Music Competition Festival, and, after a brief concert career, has taught privately in Winnipeg and 1974–5 at the *Victoria (BC) Cons.

3 **Gilbert**. Pianist, teacher, administrator, b Winnipeg 18 Jan 1933; ARCT 1954, LRSM 1954, BA (Manitoba) 1955, B ED (Manitoba) 1961, B MUS (Manitoba) 1970, M MUS (Alberta) 1971. He studied piano with his mother and with John *Melnyk and theory with Frans *Niermeier, won the Aikins Memorial Trophy at the 1949 *Manitoba Music Competition Festival, and continued piano study 1954–6 in London with Harold Craxton and John Simons. He returned to Canada and, after teaching music in Winnipeg schools for several years and performing occasionally, became music director at Medicine Hat College and director of the Medicine Hat Cons of Fine Arts in 1971. He also served 1974–5 as vice-president of the Allied Arts Conference in Alberta. After a sabbatical in England 1977–8 he returned to Winnipeg, where he taught privately for a year. He joined the staff of the *Victoria Cons in 1979. RG, KW

MURDOCH, Walter (Mackenzie). Union administrator, bandmaster, b Kingston, Ont, 1888, d Toronto 11 Apr 1972. As a boy in Hamilton, Ont, he played alto horn, then cornet and trumpet. He began working for the CNR in his mid-teens but moved to the lithography trade in his twenties, and retired in 1940 after 20 years as president of Litho-Print Ltd. Murdoch was co-founder after 1914 of the Imperial Concert Band in Toronto and was bandmaster 1936–58 of the *Royal Regiment of Canada Band, retiring with the rank of captain. The regimental band performed for several years under his direction at hockey games in *Maple Leaf Gardens. He was also conductor 1926–58 of the Toronto Regiment Band. His union career with the Toronto Musicians' Assn (AF of M local 149) began in 1917. An autocratic and often controversial administrator, Murdoch served 1932–57 as president and for many years (1938–65) was the sole Canadian member of the international executive of the AF of M. See also Unions.

BIBLIOGRAPHY
Beattie, Earle. 'Walter Murdoch and the entertainment war,' *Maclean's*, 1 Sep 1954
Nichol, James Y. 'A man of many hassles,' Toronto *Star Weekly*, 20 Sep 1958 MM

MURPHY, Kenneth (Soutar). Administrator, editor, journalist, cellist, b Winnipeg 16 Jun 1930, BA (Manitoba) 1951. He studied cello 1951–4 with Peggie *Sampson in Winnipeg and was a reporter 1951–6 and music editor 1955–6 for the *Winnipeg Free Press*, but took a leave of absence 1954–5 when he won a string scholarship from the *WBM to study at the Peabody Cons in Baltimore. He played in various Winnipeg orchestras 1949–60 and was the first teacher of Eric *Wilson. He was editor 1956–60 of the *CBC Times*, Prairie edition, and information officer, and later a producer of transcription records, 1960–7 for the CBC IS in Montreal. He was appointed assistant director of public relations for the *NAC in 1967 and served 1969–75 as manager of the *NACO and 1975–8 as music administrator of the centre itself. In 1979 he became manager of extension services and placement at the *Banff SFA. He edited *History of Canada*, a compilation of CBC IS broadcast scripts by Canadian historians. CF

MURRAY, (Morna) **Anne** (m Langstroth). Singer, b Springhill, NS, 20 Jun 1945; B PHYS ED (New Brunswick) 1966, hon LL D (New Brunswick) 1978. As a child she studied piano for six years; at 15 she began three years of voice lessons with Karen Mills in Tatamagouche, NS. Though trained as a soprano, Murray sings more naturally in a lower range, in what the *New York Times* critic John Rockwell has called 'a conversationally husky, womanly mezzo soprano' (reprinted, *Globe and Mail*, 14 Feb 1978). She appeared in her teens on CKCW-TV, Moncton, NB, and CHSJ-TV, Saint John, NB, and performed in revues at university. On graduation she taught physical education 1966–7 in Summerside, PEI. In 1966 she became a member of the chorus on CBC Halifax TV's 'Singalong Jubilee,' a folk music summer series which began in 1960. (Bill Langstroth, producer and host of that show until 1971, married Murray in 1975.) She then was seen on CBC Halifax's pop music TV show 'Let's Go' 1967–8 and continued as a featured performer on 'Singalong Jubilee' until 1970, appearing also on other CBC pop music shows during these years.

Murray began recording with Arc in 1968, first with the cast from 'Singalong Jubilee' and then as a soloist. She moved to Capitol Records in 1969, and the success of her recording of *'Snowbird' in 1970 effected a dramatic rise in her career. She sang several times that year on CTV's 'Nashville North' (Toronto) and joined the US country singer Glen Campbell on the CBS TV show 'The Glen Campbell Goodtime Hour,' making her debut 4 Oct 1970 and continuing as a frequent guest until the end of the 1971–2 season. She also starred 23 Oct 1970 in the first of several annual CBC TV specials which continued until 1974 and resumed in 1976.

During the 1970s Murray was the most popular Canadian female singer in Canada. Beginning with 'Snowbird,' she has enjoyed great success with pop and country audiences in North America and Britain. In the 1970s she appeared in several different contexts, from nightclubs (eg, the Imperial Room of the Royal York Hotel, Toronto, in 1970, and regularly in Las Vegas, beginning in

Anne Murray

1971) to concerts for country audiences with Glen Campbell. She has toured extensively in North America and Britain with her own band (led in turn by Skip Beckwith and, after ca 1975, Pat *Riccio Jr), has appeared as a guest on many US TV variety shows and in her own BBC TV specials, and, in 1977, performed in Japan. In 1978 she gave a week of concerts with a 20-piece orchestra at the *Royal Alexandra Theatre, one of several venues at which she has appeared in Toronto, her home after 1971.

Murray's repertoire includes songs by Shirley *Eikhard, Gordon *Lightfoot, and Gene *MacLellan, Robbie MacNeill (an early guitar accompanist), Brent Titcomb, and other Canadians. Among Murray's hit records are 'Sing High, Sing Low' (in Canada only, 1970–1), 'Talk It Over in the Morning' (1971), 'Cotton Jenny' (Canada 1972), 'Robbie's Song for Jesus' (Canada 1972), 'Danny's Song' (1972–3), 'What about Me?' (1973), 'Love Song' (1973–4), 'You Won't See Me' (1974), 'Walk Right Back' (1978), 'You Needed Me' (1978, a million seller), and 'I Just Fall in Love Again' (1979). She has received *Juno Awards as best female vocalist (annually 1970–4 and in 1978 and 1979), as country female artist (1974, 1975, and 1979), for pop LP of the year (1973, *Danny's Song*; 1979, *New Kind of Feeling*) and for children's LP of the year (1978, *There's a Hippo in My Tub*); some of her recordings have won Junos in production categories. She also won an ACTRA award in 1973 as best variety performer on TV and Big Country Awards in 1979 as country artist and female singer of the year. A nominee for Grammy Awards on several occasions, she was the recipient of Grammies as best female singer in the country category (1974) and in the pop category (1978). She has received similar awards from other US and British organizations and gold record sales awards for many of her singles and LPs. In 1975 she was named an Officer of the *Order of Canada.

In his review of her appearance at the Bottom Line in New York, John Rockwell (ibid) also wrote, 'To everything she sings she brings an aptness of phrasing and an intelligence of manner that are very appealing.' Though noting a lack of commitment in her interpretations and the fact that 'Miss Murray doesn't seem very comfortable singing loudly or reaching high; her voice takes on a tense hardness when she does so,' Rockwell closed with the observation that she 'is a fine singer within her range and compared with most country-flavoured middle-of-the-roaders ... she is a veritable princess of taste and style.' While expressing similar reservations about Murray's range and interpretive powers, William *Littler acknowledged: 'And yet she obviously does have something. Call it Doris Dayism if you will, but there is an appealing naturalness about the musical Maritimer, reinforced by the kind of sexuality that manages to be both provocative and clean' (*Toronto Star* 4 Mar 1974).

Murray's brother Bruce (b Springhill 11 Apr 1952) also had formal training at Tatamagouche, NS. He began his career in 1975 with the LP *Bruce Murray* (Qual JV 1920), his initial exposure resulting from his connection with Anne. A second LP, *There's Always a Goodbye* (CBS PC 80015), was released in 1979.

DISCOGRAPHY

What about Me? 1968. Arc AS 782
This Way Is My Way. 1969. Cap ST 6330
Honey, Wheat and Laughter. (1970). Cap ST 6350
Straight, Clean and Simple. 1970. Cap ST 6359
Talk It Over in the Morning. 1971. Cap ST 6366
Anne Murray/Glen Campbell. 1971. Cap SW 869
Annie. (1972). Cap ST 6376
Danny's Song. (1973). Cap ST 6393
A Love Song. (1974). Cap ST 6409
Country. (1974). Cap ST 6425
Highly Prized Possession. 1974. Cap ST 6428
Keeping in Touch. 1976. Cap ST 11559
There's a Hippo in My Tub. (1978). Cap ST 6454
Let's Keep It That Way. 1978. Cap ST 11743
New Kind of Feeling. 1978. Cap SW 11849

BIBLIOGRAPHY

Conn Hughes, Barry. 'Will Anne Murray spoil success?' *Canadian Magazine*, 25 Jul 1970
Howell, Bill. 'Upper Canada romantic,' *Maclean's*, May 1972
Windeler, Robert. 'Introducing Anne Murray,' *Stereo Review*, vol 28, Jun 1972
LeBlanc, Larry. 'The flip side of Anne Murray,' *Maclean's*, Nov 1974
Doig, John. 'The other Murray,' *The Canadian*, 18 Jun 1979
King, Paul. 'Jackpot: Anne Murray is the best bet in Las Vegas,' (*Toronto Star*) *Today*, 26 Apr 1980
Livingstone, David. 'The prime of Ms. Anne Murray,' *Maclean's*, 20 Oct 1980

MM

MURRAY, George (Alexander). Tenor, actor, b Winnipeg 24 Apr 1913. In his youth he studied voice with Charles Ross and sang in Daniel MacIntyre High School productions of *H.M.S. Pinafore* and *The Mikado*. He made his radio debut in 1930 on the Western Broadcasting Bureau and performed 1935–6 on CJRC and CRBC and 1938–9 on the CBC's Woodhouse and Hawkins comedy show. In Toronto, where he played Bill Craig 1939–56 in the CBC radio drama 'The Craigs,' he also sang for many years on his own CFRB radio show and on several CBC radio and TV programs, including 'The Big Revue' 1952–4 and *'Juliette' in 1956. He created Peter Pupkin in the CBC premiere, in 1954, of Mavor *Moore's *The Hero of Mariposa*. During his marriage 1954–8 to Shirley *Harmer he lived 1956–8 in Hollywood and was not active in music. Returning to Toronto he was host in 1959 for CBC TV's 'Talent Caravan.' After a brief nightclub career Murray returned to acting. He appeared in dramatic roles on TV, created Squire Western in the musical *Tom Jones* (1968) on CBC TV, and played small roles at the 1968 and 1969 *Charlottetown Festivals. An 'Irish tenor,' popular for his renditions of folksongs and ballads, Murray made some 78s for RCA in the 1950s.

MURRAY, Paul (Burns). Organist, choir director, educator, broadcaster, b Saint John, NB, 21 Mar 1927; L MUS (Mount Allison) 1949, ATCM 1951, B MUS (Toronto) 1952, FCCO 1952, ARCM 1953, FRCO 1954. Murray was director of school music 1955–61 in Saint John before moving to Toronto as organist-choirmaster 1961–71 at Metropolitan United Church and supervisor of music for Scarborough schools. He was also a school music chairman 1963–7 for the North York Board of Education. In 1967 he returned to the Maritimes as music consultant for the Nova Scotia Dept of Education. He became a board member in 1972 and president in 1977 of the *CMEA and a director of the *CMCouncil in 1976, becoming vice-president in 1978. He is an experienced adjudicator and has been heard on the CBC in talks, on panels, in recital, and as host for the program 'Organists in Recital.' WL

Musgrave. Toronto music dealer and publisher, located in the Yonge St Arcade. The business was opened in 1909 by the brothers Charles E. and George A. Musgrave; about 1914 it was briefly A.L.E. Davies and Musgrave Brothers; after 1926 it was run as Charles E. Musgrave & Son (Edward C.); in the early 1930s it became the Musgrave Music Shoppe. After that closed (probably 1933), George A. Musgrave briefly (ca 1936) operated Musgrave's Music Shop at a different Yonge St location. The brothers continued to be active as musicians in Toronto in the 1940s.

Musgrave's publications, notable for their coloured cover illustrations, include some 50 patriotic and popular pieces. Among the more successful were 'Toronto Town' (1912) by John G. Strathdee, excerpts from the comic opera *The Golden Age* (1911) by Joseph Nevin *Doyle, *Canadian Patrol* (1911) by Arthur L.E. Davies, 'I Love You Canada' (1915) by Kenneth McInnis and Morris Manley, 'The Made in Canada Campaign Song' (1915) by N. Fraser *Allan, and 'Flying' (1918) and 'Take Me Back to Dear Old Canada' (1918) by Will J. White. The last Musgrave copyright traced is 'The Land of Prosperity (Canada)' (1927) by Nelson H. Bell. HK

Musica Antica e Nuova. Society founded in Montreal in 1951 by Célia *Bizony for the purpose of organizing concerts of early and contemporary music. The appeal of the group lay mainly in the fact that, possibly for the first time in Canada, early music was researched intensively and given performances as nearly authentic as possible. During its five years of existence the society enlisted the participation of Bernard *Diamant, Mario *Duschenes, Maureen *Forrester, Mildred *Goodman, Jean-Paul *Jeannotte, Otto and Walter *Joachim, John *Newmark, Jan *Simons, Jon *Vickers, and other outstanding musicians. Sunday recitals and four or five other concerts a year were presented in the auditorium of the YWCA, at Victoria Hall, or at other halls. Five chamber music concerts for the *Montreal Festivals in 1953 and 1954 consisted of little known works by composers ranging from Telemann to Alban Berg. The society ceased to exist in 1955, when Bizony returned to England. In 1954, with the above-mentioned instrumentalists and singers, it made an LP (Hallmark RS-6) containing, among other works, Jean *Papineau-Couture's *Églogues*. HPn

Musica Camerata Montreal. Association of professional musicians offering each year 14 free concerts of chamber music on Saturday afternoons. Founded by Hans Nemenoff, businessman and music enthusiast, his wife, Imy, Robert Verebes, Charles *Reiner, and Larry Combs, it presented its first concert 3 Mar 1971 at the *Ermitage. Financial support has been provided by federal, provincial, and municipal governments, by the Montreal Musicians' Guild, and by individual donors, the last-named thereby designated 'Friends of Musica Camerata.' A continually varied ensemble of up to 10 musicians has been presented in performances of unusual program fare, including several Canadian works each season (*Champagne, *Contant, Kelsey *Jones, *Papineau-Couture, *Somers, etc). The 1973–4 series was presented at Sir George Williams (*Concordia) U, and 1974–8 the concerts were held in Christ Church Cathedral, with summer concerts at the Pointe Claire Cultural Centre in suburban Montreal. Two Beethoven concerts in 1977 and three Schubert concerts in 1978 marked the 150th anniversaries of the composers' deaths. In 1978 the ensemble recorded a *Quartet* for piano and strings by Anne *Eggleston and *Mobiles* by André *Prévost (RCI 472).

BIBLIOGRAPHY

Proulx, Michelle. 'Long road from mouse-ridden hall,' Montreal *Gazette*, 15 Oct 1977 (NT)

Musical Art Club. Founded in 1924 by the teacher Lyell *Gustin to introduce to the public Saskatoon's young male music students. Among the other leading teachers whose students benefited were Florence Hanson (violin), Helen Davies *Sherry (voice), and Frederick *Silvester (organ). Reginald *Bedford and Silvester were among the charter members, and Percy Grainger, one of the club's first performing guests, was honorary president until his death in 1961. He was succeeded in that office by Gustin. Women were admitted to the club in 1931. Besides presenting, every year from October to March, monthly concerts of both emerging and established artists (Garth *Beckett, Neil *Chotem, Lynnwood *Farnam, Boyd McDonald, Margaret Matzenauer, Thelma *O'Neill, Marguerite *Spencer, Toscha Seidel, and others), the club has sponsored a Beethoven centenary (1927, three concerts), a Schubert centenary (1928, three concerts), a Bach festival (1931, three concerts), a Haydn bicentenary (1932, two concerts), and numerous other such anniversary observances. It also has offered performances of the operas *Hansel and Gretel* (1931), *Madama Butterfly* (1932), *Le Coq d'or* (1940), and *Carmen* (1942), of Bach's *Coffee Cantata* (1938) and *Peasant Cantata* (1939), and of Debussy's *The Blessed Damozel* (1941). Young people's clubs were organized by Bedford in 1930 and reorganized by Dorothy Adams in 1946. After 1941 recitals were given entirely by Saskatoon artists and club members. The club gave its 400th program 5 Dec 1976.

Musical Canada. Monthly journal founded in Toronto in 1906 by Edwin *Parkhurst. The original name – *The Violin* – was changed in 1907 to *Musical Canada*. One of the longest-lived Canadian music magazines, it was owned until 1920 by Parkhurst, 1920–8 by A.L. Robertson (with Augustus *Bridle, H. Cecil Fricker, and Robertson as successive editors), 1928–33 by C.F. *Thiele, and briefly by Gordon V. *Thompson. (It fell victim to the Depression in 1933 before Thompson was able to put out his first issue.) Though issues are held by the Toronto Public Library, the *U of Toronto Faculty of Music library, the *NL of C, the Library of Congress, the New York Public Library, Hamilton Public Library, and *Mount Allison U, no library owns a complete set, and certain volumes cannot be found in any. (The volume numbering continued from that of *The Violin*. It began anew in December 1920, after volume 16 no. 6, with the first change of ownership. The final issue, February 1933, was volume 13 no. 9.)

During the Parkhurst era, *Musical Canada* was essentially a 'journal of musical news and comments' devoted to concert reports and news about performers. Later it became increasingly a combination of sections which served special-interest groups. In 1924 Robertson incorporated *The Canadian Bandsman and Orchestra Journal* (which he had edited previously as a house publication of R.S. *Williams & Co) and in 1928 the CCO began to use

Musical Canada as its bulletin, as did the music section of the Ontario Educators Assn. When Thiele acquired the journal he moved its offices to Waterloo, Ont. Enlarging the format he inserted sheet music, much of it copyrighted by his *Waterloo Music Co, into each issue. Composers included Frederick *Egener, Ernest *Dainty, Albert *Ham, Clifford Higgin, A.W. *Hughes, W.O. *Forsyth, Leslie *Grossmith (whose *Air de Ballet* won a *Musical Canada* contest and was printed in the June 1929 issue), Luigi von *Kunits, Louis *Waizman, and other Canadian and foreign composers. Of historical importance is a series (1928–33) of biographical essays by H.C. *Hamilton on Canadian musicians. HK

Musical theatre. Canadian musical theatre composition has taken a long time to arrive at a stage at which it can be described as both plentiful and sophisticated. Foreign works and productions monopolized 19th-century theatres, and Canadian content was present only in short burlesques. In the 20th century, a Canadian style developed in revues before beginning to emerge in musicals in the late 1970s.

Canadian musical theatre pieces will be considered in six approximately chronological categories:

1 Pageants and entertainments (ie, large-scale theatricals)
2 Light operas and operettas (rooted in the operatic tradition but more informal and tuneful)
3 Burlesques (parodies or satires)
4 Revues (programs of songs and skits)
5 Musicals (either plays or comedies, related to popular music)
6 Cabarets (intimate revues).

See also Ballets; Concert halls and opera houses; Incidental music; Librettos; Opera performances; Operas.

1 PAGEANTS AND ENTERTAINMENTS. Canada's first theatrical presentation, Marc Lescarbot's European-style **Theatre of Neptune* (1606), was a masque with music performed aboard ship in the harbour of Port Royal to celebrate the governor's return. *L'Ordre de Bon Temps* (1928), a dramatization of life in the colony by Louvigny de Montigny, was translated in 1928 by John Murray *Gibbon as *The Order of Good Cheer* and utilized French-Canadian folksongs harmonized by Healey *Willan. It was performed at the *CPR Festival in Quebec City in 1928.

F.A. Dixon, who had presented original musical entertainments at Rideau Hall in Ottawa during Lord Dufferin's term, collaborated with the composer Arthur *Clappé on a masque entitled *Canada's Welcome* (1879) in honour of the Marquis of Lorne's installation as governor-general.

In the 20th century the masque has given way to the spectacular pageant, usually historical and commemorating significant events, perhaps best exemplified by the annual Grandstand shows at the *CNE, Toronto, during the 1920s and 1930s, which featured such themes as the settlement of western Canada, incidents in British history, or successions of events in Canadian history.

Father Daniel Lord's mammoth 1949 *Salute to Canada* at the Martyrs' Shrine near Midland, Ont, marked the 300th anniversary of the massacre there. Neil *Harris composed the music for *Portrait of a City*, a pageant celebrating Saskatoon's 50th anniversary in 1952. In 1968 *From Sea to Sea* (by Howard *Cable, Gordon *Lightfoot, and Donald Harron) utilized the entire CNE Stadium in Toronto to tell the story of the building of the CPR. (See also *Brébeuf*.)

A Calgary production, ca 1923, of *The Highwood Trail*, with music by Jack Bullough

2 LIGHT OPERA AND OPERETTA. In 1774 the men of the English garrison in Montreal performed 'a piece in two acts consisting of vocal and instrumental music.' (Discussion of performances of other operas and ballad operas in the remaining decades of the 18th century may be found in the entry on Opera performance.)

Throughout most of the 19th century Canadians enjoyed operettas from abroad. The *Holman English Opera Troupe, built around the George Holman family, was the most important Canadian musical touring company from the 1860s to the 1880s. The Holmans added *H.M.S. Pinafore* to their repertoire of grand and light operas and burlesques in 1879, only a year after its London premiere. *The Mikado* created a sensation in Toronto in 1885, the same year it opened in London. Amateur performances followed throughout English Canada. The *Orpheus Club of Halifax performed it in 1887. In 1898, Calgary and Brandon amateurs were presenting Sidney Jones' *The Geisha*, only three years after its premiere. John Philip Sousa's *The Charlatan* had its premiere in Montreal in 1898, and Victor Herbert's *The Fortune Teller, Cyrano de Bergerac*, and *The Singing Girl* had theirs there in 1898, 1899, and 1899 respectively. Although Frances Brooke, the librettist of the widely performed *Rosina* (1782), resided in Quebec 1763–8, John *Bentley's pantomime music *The Enchanters, or The Triumph of Genius* (Montreal, 1786) may be regarded as the first light stage work to have been written in Canada. Joseph *Quesnel is acknowledged as the first Canadian light opera composer for his 'comedy with ariettas,' **Colas et Colinette*, produced in 1790 by Montreal's *Théâtre de Société. (See also *Lucas et Cécile*.)

Several decades passed before composers in Canada began to write operettas. One who introduced Canadian subject matter into his works was Célestin *Lavigueur, composer of two operas and the operetta *La Fiancée des bois* (words by Pamphile Lemay; mid-19th century). Calixa *Lavallée's operettas, including **The Widow* (1882), were produced in the USA after he left Canada. The same held true for the works of the later expatriates Geoffrey *O'Hara, who wrote 12 operettas, and Clarence *Lucas, whose *Peggy Machree* was performed in England in 1904 and in the USA in 1907.

A few composers did manage to arrange amateur presentations of their operettas in Canada. *Prince Tommy* by William Delaney of Lunenburg, NS, was produced in 1898. Amedée *Tremblay's *L'Intransigeant* was performed in Ottawa in 1906. In 1911 Ralph *Horner's own group in Winnipeg presented his *The Belles of Barcelona*. Montrealer Henri *Miro's *Le Roman du Suzon* and *Lolita* were given for the first time in 1914 and 1922 respectively. *The Golden Age* by Joseph Nevin *Doyle was staged in Ontario in 1915. Performances of Oscar *Telgmann's 'military opera' **Leo, the Royal Cadet* (1889), in Kingston and other Ontario towns, exceeded 150 over the next 40 years, a record for a Canadian stage work probably surpassed, much ater, by that of **Anne of Green Gables*. In 1895 Hamiltonians saw an amateur production of J.E.P. *Aldous' short comic opera *Ptarmigan*.

Despite all these efforts, the best-known 'Canadian' operetta has continued to be **Rose Marie*, by Rudolf Friml, a composer who never visited Canada and who knew very little about it. Healey Willan's version of *The Beggar's Opera*, the first of his ballad operas, was completed in 1927. Sir Ernest *MacMillan's *Prince Charming* (1933) was a ballad opera written on French and Scottish tunes.

Other Canadian composers of operetta and light opera are Violet *Archer (*Sganarelle*, 1973), Marius *Benoist (*Secret des Amati*), Irvin *Cooper (*Full o' the Moon*), Clifford Higgin (*The Queen of Romance*), J.-B. *Labelle (*La Conversion d'un pêcheur de la Nouvelle-Écosse*, Boucher ca 1869), Alphonse *Lavallée-Smith (*Gisèle*), Omer *Létourneau (*Coup de soleil*, 1930), Oscar *O'Brien (*Philippino*, 1931–3 and other works), Percy *Faith (*The Gandy Dancer*, ca 1943), Harry *Somers (*The Homeless Ones*, 1955), Herbert *Spencer (*The Cavaliers*), and Joseph *Vézina (*Le Lauréat*, 1906).

3 BURLESQUES. While the English amateur performer Horton Rhys was touring Ontario and

Quebec im 1859, he concocted a burlesque entitled *A Country Manager's Perplexities*, supplementing existing songs with two of his own. Most of the made-in-Canada burlesques which followed in the next 40 years also were written for specific productions. Often they satirized Canadian politics and society. In 1865 'Sam Scribble' of Montreal wrote two pro-Canada musical satires: *Dolorsolatio*, 'a local political burlesque,' and *The King of the Beavers*. In 1880 Eugene A. McDowell's professional company toured throughout Canada performing William Henry Fuller's political satire **H.M.S. Parliament*, which utilized Sullivan's music for *H.M.S. Pinafore* only two years after its premiere and one after its Canadian premiere.

The Northwest Rebellion provided the stimulus for two other burlesques. Sgt L. Dixon's *'Our Boys' in the Riel Rebellion*, staged in Halifax in 1886, included both borrowed and original melodies. George Broughall used a similar mixture of old and new music in his *90th on Active Service*, presented in Winnipeg in 1885.

4 REVUES. By 1980 revue had been the most successful form of indigenous Canadian musical theatre in the 20th century. Minstrel shows, variety, and vaudeville ante-date revue. The renowned Christy Minstrels (USA) played in Montreal as early as 1861 and countless other troupes performed across Canada in the following decades. Cool Burgess and the celebrated step-dancer George Primrose were Canadians who became burnt-cork stars. When vaudeville was organized, Canadian theatres quickly joined large US circuits. The only route to celebrity for talented Canadians such as Eva Tanguay and May Irwin was emigration to the USA.

Canada's first international success in musical theatre was the *Dumbells, Merton Plunkett and Jack McLaren's World War I all-male soldier troupe. The Dumbells' revues, presenting a mixture of topical songs, entertainment routines, and broad comedy, continued to play for several years after the war, and one (*Biff, Bing, Bang*) enjoyed a triumphant Broadway engagement in 1921. At the beginning of World War II a few of the original Dumbells regrouped to appear in *Chin Up*. After two editions of the all-forces revue *Ritzin' the Blitz* (1941 and 1942), each service developed its own show featuring such young entertainers as Alan and Blanche Lund and Wayne and Shuster (see *The Army Show; Meet the Navy; RCAF Blackouts*).

More intimate satirical musical revues developed from informal club shows dating back to the late 19th century. Toronto and Montreal were early centres for such entertainments. In Toronto the *Arts and Letters Club presented its first revue (*The Old Court Minstrels*) in 1918 and staged the first of Napier Moore's annual *Spring Revues* in April 1930. The latter recurred annually until 1939, sporadically during the 1940s, and annually again beginning in 1954. They also inspired local imitations such as *Town Tonics* (Toronto, 1930s). In Montreal Gratien Gélinas produced his successful **Fridolinons!* annually 1938–46, using music derived from traditional French-Canadian sources and presenting satires on everything from language to Canada's national image.

Canada's most celebrated revue, **Spring Thaw*, lasted 24 years and toured extensively. Its director, Mavor *Moore, set the pattern for its enduring success in the initial 1948 edition, mixing songs and dances, low comedy and high satire, with the emphasis on Canadian topics. Its greatest legacy was a generation of experienced performers which included Dave Broadfoot, Jack Duffy, Robert *Goulet, Barbara Hamilton, Donald Harron, Eric House, Rich Little, Jane Mallett, and Toby Robbins.

Spring Thaw had many rivals. John Pratt starred in two, which toured Canada and some US centres 1949–51. The first, *There Goes Yesterday*, used mostly imported material, with additional words and music by Dorothy Watkins and Jessie MacDonald; the second, *One for the Road*, was more original and featured music by Roy Wolvin. Other imitators of *Spring Thaw* included *Fine Frenzy* (1955), Araby Lockhart's *Clap Hands* (1958–62), and *Our First Affair* (1959), all in Toronto; *Bonfires of 1962*, in Winnipeg; and *Up Tempo*, produced by Jack Greenwald during the 1960s, and *Squeeze*, presented in the early 1970s, both in Montreal. Other Montreal revues during the 1960s were *Vive la difference*, produced by Peter *Symcox, and Gélinas's *Le Diable à quatre*, both in 1964.

The *McGill U spoof **My Fur Lady* (1957), *Spring Thaw*'s best-known heir, gave national exposure to the talents of the choreographer Brian Macdonald and the composer Galt *MacDermot. It began as an edition of McGill's annual *Red and White Revue*. Other university and college revues have included Ryerson Polytechnical Institute's *Riot*, the U of Montreals *Revue bleu et or*, and the U of Western Ontario's *Tachychardia*.

The producer Louis Negin's late-1960s revue *Love and Maple Syrup* ended up in New York as a display of Canadiana compiled from the work of musicians such as Gilles *Vigneault and Gordon Lightfoot and writers ranging from Stephen Leacock to Leonard *Cohen.

5 MUSICALS. From the days of the performance of the prototype musical comedy *The Black Crook* (Montreal, 1875) to the present, Canadians have loved big Broadway shows. One professional theatre, Winnipeg's *Rainbow Stage, has specialized in them and until 1980 had continued to ignore Canadian works. Toronto's *Melody Fair devoted its seasons to Broadway musical hits.

There were some early Canadian musicals, however, including John Ernest Lawrence's *The Western Countess* (1911, described as 'A musical cyclone from the wooly west in two breezes'), Frank *Laubach and Charles Shrimpton's *The Mystic Light* (Regina, 1913), William *Dichmont and C.S. Blanchard's *Miss Pepple of New York* (Winnipeg, 1916), and N. Fraser *Allan's *The Canadian Passing Show* (Toronto, 1917).

Mavor Moore deserves credit as father of the modern Canadian musical theatre. He first tried, unsuccessfully, to establish an indigenous musical theatre in the 1950s with *Sunshine Town*, his tribute to Stephen Leacock, and *The Optimist*, adapted from *Candide*. In 1964 he became the first director of the *Charlottetown Festival, which under his successor Alan Lund dedicated itself to producing original Canadian musicals by composers such as Howard Cable, Marian *Grudeff, Ray Jessel, and Ben *McPeek. Already the festival has had one triumph, *Anne of Green Gables* (music by Norman *Campbell, book and lyrics by Elaine Campbell and Donald Harron), and several noteworthy efforts: **Johnny Belinda* (John *Fenwick / Mavor Moore), *Ballade* (Michel Conte / Arthur Samuels), and **Kronberg: 1582* (Cliff *Jones' rock version of *Hamlet*). Charlottetown, however, had no monopoly on new musicals.

In Victoria Leslie *Grossmith wrote *Zip Van Twinkle of the Canadian Rockies*, and in Toronto Court Stone wrote *Farmer in the Dell* (1951). Together Louis *Applebaum and Jack Grey wrote *Ride a Pink Horse* (1959). Dolores *Claman's **Timber!!* (1952) was performed by Vancouver's *Theatre under the Stars. Later, with her husband, Richard Morris, Claman wrote *Mr. Scrooge*, produced twice by Toronto's Crest Theatre in the 1960s. Milton Carman, Alex Barris, and Allan Manings wrote another Crest musical, *Evelyn* (1964). Lucio *Agostini collaborated with Donald Harron on *Here Lies Sarah Binks* (1968). Bill Solly's *Made in the Mountains* opened the *Banff SFA's musical theatre division in 1965. Morris *Surdin, who in 1962 had provided the score for Len Peterson's *Look Ahead*, worked with W.O. Mitchell to turn a *Jake and the Kid* story into *Wild Rose* (1967) for Canadian centenary celebrations in Calgary. The US composer Stanley Silverman and the Canadian lyricist Tom Hendry produced their controversial *Satyricon* in 1969 at the *Stratford Festival.

In the province of Quebec, others were at work. Jacques Languirand and Gabriel *Charpentier wrote *Klondyke* in 1965. (Languirand also collaborated with the composer Norman *Symonds on the multi-media experiment *Man, Inc*, which opened Toronto's *St Lawrence Centre in 1969.) Neil *Chotem composed the music for Michel Tremblay's modern adaptation of Aristophanes' *Lysistrata* (1969). Pierre *Brault wrote the music for Clémence *Desrochers's *Le Vol rose du flamant* (1968), which was claimed to be the first Quebec musical. Chansonnier Claude *Léveillée's musicals have included *Doux Temps des amours* (1964), *Il est une saison* (1965), and *On n'aime qu'une fois* (1967). Léveillée has collaborated with Marcel Dubé on several musicals for Marjolaine Hébert's Théâtre de Marjolaine in Eastman, Que. Léon *Bernier's *Un Simple Mariage double* (1978) also was produced at the Marjolaine.

In the 1970s Canadian writers began to liberate themselves from Broadway formulas by experimenting with other styles, and their works have been produced in many parts of the country. In Vancouver Ann *Mortifee wrote a folk-oriented score to enhance George Ryga's *The Ecstasy of Rita Joe* (1967). The Vancouver rock band the Collectors helped to turn Ryga's 1969 play *Grass and Wild Strawberries* into a joyous celebration. For Edmonton's Citadel Theatre Richard Ouzanian first created *Scapin!* and in 1976 he and Patrick Rose wrote *Olympiad* about the Olympic Games. Theatre Calgary commissioned Allan *Rae's science-fiction musical *Trip* (1970), and later Rae and Tink Robinson's *Festival*. For Calgary's Alberta Theatre Projects, William Skolnick collaborated with Paddy Campbell on *Hoarse Muse*, about the legendary newspaper editor Bob Edwards.

From Saskatoon, **Cruel Tears* (1975; Ken Mitchell's 20th-century prairie truckers' *Othello* set to evocative bluegrass music by *Humphrey and the Dumptrucks) entertained audiences across Canada in 1977. In 1974 the Manitoba Theatre Centre premiered Patrick Rose and Merv Campone's *Jubalay*, an 'entertainment in song,' seen later in many Canadian cities and in New York, where it appeared under the title *A Bistro Car on the CNR*. Theatre London (Ont) first staged the Peter Colley-Bert Carriere work *The Donnellys* in 1974. George Blackburn's *A Day to Remember*, about a town flooded by the St Lawrence Seaway, opened a summer theatre in Morrisburg, Ont, in 1978.

From the small alternative theatres in Ontario have come such musicals as Stephen Jack and Tom Hendry's *Gravediggers of 1942* (1973, which treats the Dieppe raid as a 1940s show) and *Justine* (1970, by Robert and Elizabeth Swerdlow, founders of Toronto's Global Village musical theatre). Other composers whose work has been nurtured in these intimate theatres are Glenn Morley (*Fresh Disasters*, 1976), Sandy Crawley (*White Noise*, 1977), Phil Schreibman (*Jack of Diamonds*, 1977), and the folksinger Cedric Smith, who provided the effective score for Toronto Workshop Productions' *Ten Lost Years* (1974), which toured Canada.

Montreal's Théâtre du Nouveau-Monde in 1976 presented *Marche, Laura Secord!* by Claude Roussin and James Rouselle, with music by Cyrille

Beaulieu. The Acadian folk entertainer Calixte Duguay wrote music and lyrics for Jules Boudreau's *Louis Mailloux* (1976). In Newfoundland Roy Hynes has provided songs for several Mummers Theatre collective creations.

A genre unto itself is the operetta or musical for children, and specimens range all the way from cut-and-paste makeshifts for school occasions, incorporating existing songs into practical adaptations of children's stories, to polished works in which adroit and sophisticated compositional skills are put to the service of psychologically acute children's theatre. Some of the best pieces, inevitably, have been written by composers who have made their livings as teachers and gained, thereby, practical insights into the needs and fascinations of young minds. But there is no rule about this, and good composers of children's musical theatre, in Canada as elsewhere, come from many departments of the profession.

Early operettas for children include those of Ethel Norbury (b 1872) of Edmonton and A.J. Dyke. Mid- and later-20th-century pieces may be exemplified by those of Keith *Bissell (*Rumpelstiltskin*, 1947; *His Majesty's Pie*, 1966) and Alfred *Kunz (*Jack and Jill*, 1976). Among composers of children's musicals are Victor *Davies (*Reginald the Robot*, 1970), Sandra Jones and Bert Carriere (*Ready Steady Go*, 1974), Pat *Patterson and Dodi Robb (among others *The Dandy Lion*, 1964), Allan Rae (*Beware the Quickly Who*, 1971), Ernie Swartz (*Aladdin and the Magic Lamp*), and Paul Vigna (*Cyclone Jack*).

6 CABARETS. After the 1964 success of *Suddenly This Summer* at Toronto's Theatre in the Dell, light cabaret stressing entertainment rather than satire flourished across Canada on similar intimate, usually liquor-licensed premises. Many cabaret shows have comprised collections of songs by famous composers (ie, Roderick Cook's *Oh Coward*, 1970) or of one kind of music such as *Flicks* (film music, 1978) or *Indigo* (1978, black music). Sneezy Waters used dialogue and songs to recount the story of the great country singer in Maynard Collins' *Hank Williams: The Show He Never Gave* (1977).

However, numerous original Canadian shows have been performed. David Warrack, the writer of *Oops* (1972) and *Tease for Two* (1974), is typical of the new generation trained in cabaret. Warrack also contributed to Sandra O'Neill and Barbara Hamilton's *Sweet Reason*, an affectionate look at women's liberation. Another cabaret success has been Jim Betts, the creator of *I'll Tell You Mine ... If You Tell Me Yours* (1977). Allan Guttman's *Tonight at 8:30 ... 9:00 O'Clock in Newfoundland* completed its second edition in 1979 and was still playing in 1980.

A new cabaret form emerged in the late 1970s: the mini-musical, in which a plot line supplies the frame for the songs. Examples are David Warrack's *Counter Melody* (1976), set aboard an airplane, Jim Betts' *Stagefright* (1978), Jeri Craden's *The Clowns* (1975), and Blaine Parker's *Sweet City Lights*.

Cabaret in Quebec is often more political and satirical than its equivalent elsewhere in Canada. For example, Guy Moreau's *Mon cher René, c'est à ton tour* was a friendly tribute in song sketch to René Levesque, leader of the Parti québécois and elected premier of Quebec in 1976. *Heureux celui qui meurt*, by Jacqueline Barrette, another leading contributor to cabaret in Quebec, ran several months 1976–7. Among Clémence Desrochers's revues, given at her little theatre le Patriote à Clémence, are *La Grosse Tête* (1967), *Les Girls* (1968), *La Belle Amanchure* (1970), and *C'est pas une revue, c't'un show* (1971), with music by Pierre Brault, François Cousineau, Jacques Crevier, and the team Gaston *Brisson and Louis-Philippe *Pelletier respectively.

In English Canada, many talented composers have begun to outgrow the restrictions of cabaret. David Warrack produced his full-length *Praise* (1978) at the Bayview Playhouse in Toronto. The Charlottetown Festival, which has become increasingly aware of new writers, commissioned Warrack's *Windsor* (1978), Joey Miller and Stephen Witkin's *Eight to the Bar* (1978), and Jim Betts' *On a Summer's Night* (1979). In this genre, probably the country's most acclaimed young writer-composer of the late 1970s was John Gray, whose *Eighteen Wheels* and *Billy Bishop Goes to War* (1978), both intimate cabaret-like shows which could be performed in regular theatres, had notable success.

See also *Hair; Les hauts et les bas dla vie d'une diva: Sarah Ménard par eux-mêmes; TIQ (The Indian Question Settled at Last); Turvey; Two Gentleman of Verona*.

BIBLIOGRAPHY

Rudel-Tessier, J. 'The theatre and Canadian composers,' *CanComp*, 12, Nov 1966
Thistle, Lauretta. 'Ottawa's legendary lumberjack comes alive in musical,' ibid, 19, Jun 1967
'Hits from Canadian musicals recorded by chorus and orchestra,' ibid, 21, Sep 1967
Graham, Franklin. *Histrionic Montreal* (New York 1969)
Thompson, Neil. 'David Warrack moves from typewriter to piano to stage with ease,' *MSc*, 273, Sep–Oct 1973
Wachel, Eleanor. 'Pat Rose's marathon,' *UBC Alumni Chronicle*, vol 30, Summer 1976
Ball, John and Plant, Richard. *Bibliography of Canadian Theatre History 1583–1975* (Toronto 1976)
Conlogue, Ray. 'From Futz to ruby red, composer likes it raw,' Toronto *Globe and Mail*, 20 Jun 1977
Stuart, Ross. 'Song in a minor key: Canada's musical theatre,' *Canadian Theatre Review*, Summer 1977
Nickson, Liz. 'Musical theatre in Canada ripe for development,' *MSc*, 298, Nov–Dec 1977
'Pauline Julien and company: a show for and about women,' *CanComp*, 126, Dec 1977
Smith, Rebecca. 'Charlottetown's cabaret gives tired main stage second wind,' *PfAC*, Fall 1978
Canada's Lost Plays, vol 1 (Toronto 1978)
Lacey, Liam. 'Cabaret blossoms in the city,' Toronto *Globe and Mail*, 28 Apr 1979
Kirkland, Bruce. 'Showbiz veterans hit right note,' *Toronto Star*, 12 Jul 1979
Joyce, Linda. 'Come to the cabaret,' *PfAC*, Summer 1979
James, Donald. 'Sneezy Waters scores again with the show Hank never gave,' *PfAC*, Spring 1980
Petrowski, Nathalie. 'The on-again, off-again saga of Quebec's best-known musical,' *CanComp*, 150, Apr 1980

RSr

Musical Union

1 A Toronto choral society which performed intermittently 1862–7 at *Mechanics' Hall. Founded in 1861 by John *Carter it gave its first concert 25 Mar 1862 with a chorus of 80 and an orchestra of 40 drawn mainly from regimental bands. Handel's *Dettingen Te Deum* and Mendelssohn's *Hymn of Praise* were performed. The next season (1863–4) was cancelled due to lack of support but was revived 10 Mar 1864, when 30 performers presented the Upper Canada premiere of Andreas Romberg's *Lay of the Bell* and excerpts from *The Creation*. The final two seasons (1865–7) included concert performances of *Il Trovatore* (21 and 31 May 1866) and *La Sonnambula* (30 Nov 1866).

2 A second Toronto choral society of the same name, conducted by J.W.F. *Harrison, was founded in 1886 with the aim of presenting 'shorter works of the best masters which are rarely heard' (*Musical Journal*, February 1887). It gave a concert, 1 Mar 1887 at the Pavilion, accompanied by two pianos and a cabinet organ. The program included Sullivan's *The Prodigal Son*. No further information has come to light.

BIBLIOGRAPHY

'Toronto's Pre-Confederation Music Societies' RPn

Musicanada. 'A presentation of Canadian contemporary music / Présence de la musique canadienne contemporaine.' The first large-scale festival of Canadian music in Europe, held 4–17 Nov 1977 under the aegis of the Dept of External Affairs and the *Canada Council. A total of 41 works by 32 composers were presented in five Paris concerts (Salle Gaveau) and five London concerts (St John's Church, Smith Square) by Canadian ensembles, and in one concert at St John's Church by the BBC SO and one in the Grand Auditorium of the Maison Radio-France by the Nouvel Orchestre philharmonique of Paris. The BBC SO, conducted by Mario *Bernardi, performed *Aitken's *Spiral*, *Beecroft's *Improvvisazioni Concertanti No. 2*, *Freedman's *Tapestry*, Jacques *Hétu's *Concerto, Op 15*, for piano and orchestra with Robert *Silverman as soloist, and *Schafer's *Son of Heldenleben*. The Nouvel Orchestre philharmonique was conducted by Pierre *Hétu in Jacques Hétu's *Symphonie No. 3*, *Matton's *Concerto* for two pianos and orchestra with the duo-pianists *Bouchard and Morisset, and *Prévost's *Fantasmes* and by Gilles *Tremblay in his own *Jeux de solstices*.

Under Serge *Garant's direction the *SMCQ Ensemble presented *Cherney's *Chamber Concerto* for viola and 10 performers, Garant's *Rivages*, *Mather's *Madrigal IV*, *Steven's *Images*, and Tremblay's *Solstices*. The *Quebec Woodwind Quintet made its European debut in Coulombe *Saint-Marcoux's *Genesis*, Hétu's *Quintette, Op 13*, *Jones' *Quintet*, Mather's *Eine kleine Bläsermusik*, and *Papineau-Couture's *Fantaisie*. Elmer *Iseler conducted the *Festival Singers in works by *Anhalt (*Cento*), *Ford (*Mass*), Mather (*La Lune mince...*), Papineau-Couture (*Viole d'amour*), Prévost (*Soleils couchants*), *Somers (*Five Songs of the Newfoundland Outports*), and *Vivier (*Jesus erbarme dich*). The *Orford String Quartet performed Freedman's *Graphic II* and *Glick's *Suite Hebraïque No. 3* as well as quartets by *Pépin, Schafer, and *Wilson. *Canadian Brass played works by *Beckwith (*Taking a Stand*), *Calvert (*Suite from the Monteregian Hills*), *Crosley (*The Days before Yesterday*), Malcolm D. *Forsyth (*The Golyardes' Grounde*), *Hodkinson (*another ... man's Poison*), *McCauley (*Miniature Overture*), *McPeek (*Ragtime for Brass*), *Morel (*Quintette*), *Rathburn (*The Nomadic Five*), and *Weinzweig (*Pieces of Five*).

'An extensive operation ... original ... and effective' (*Le Nouvel Observateur*, 21–7 Nov 1977), Musicanada contributed significantly to making Canadian music better known in France and England. Audiences that were generally small in number but steadfastly attentive received the many works presented with interest and were particularly appreciative of the high level of performance. It would appear that contemporary Canadian music was perceived mainly as reflecting a creative and liberal artistic milieu, emphasizing individual composers' personalities more markedly than any style or manner of thought which might typify a national school. That, at least, was the reaction of critics such as Maurice Fleuret, who declared (ibid), 'Canada has no sophisticated musical heritage, but it is this very lack which offers its creative artists greater freedom,' and Gérard Condé, who wrote in *Le Monde* (19 Nov 1977), 'Though in reality suggestive neither of the avant garde nor of its uninspired imitators, the music of these quartets [and] symphonies ... affirmed the vitality of a contemporary music activity without always leaving the impression that Canada has a clearly defined school or language.' This opinion was shared by Joan Chissell, who wrote in *The Times* (10 Nov 1977): 'Nationalism in music is out of date ... no specifically Canadian characteristic emerged.'

BIBLIOGRAPHY
McLean, Eric. 'Exporting Canadian music,' *Montreal Star*, 19 Nov 1977
Fleuret, Maurice. 'Des Canadiens à Paris,' *Nouvel Observateur*, 680, 21–7 Nov 1977
Shepherd, John. 'Musicanada,' *Music and Musicians*, Nov 1977
Musicanada: A Presentation of Canadian Contemporary Music program (Ottawa 1977) AP

Musicanada. Periodical issued May 1967 to December 1970 by the *CMCentre and revived November 1976 by the *CMCouncil. In its first phase, edited by Keith *MacMillan and published in Toronto, separately in French and in English, it completed 29 issues of 15–20 pages each. It achieved a consistency and informational density possibly unprecedented in a Canadian musical periodical. A house organ of the centre, its essential concern was composers and their works. Each issue (nos. 7 and 26 excepted) contained a short interview with a leading composer, giving him or her the opportunity to pronounce on fundamental aesthetic and technical matters. Interviewees, listed in order of appearance, were Murray *Adaskin, Clermont *Pépin, Jean *Papineau-Couture, Harry *Somers, Srul Irving *Glick, John *Beckwith, Harry *Freedman, John *Weinzweig, Serge *Garant, Bruce *Mather, Godfrey *Ridout, Violet *Archer, R. Murray *Schafer, István *Anhalt, Roger *Matton, Alexander *Brott, Talivaldis *Kenins, Norma *Beecroft, Otto *Joachim, Barbara *Pentland, Udo *Kasemets, S.C. *Eckhardt-Gramatté, Gilles *Tremblay, Oskar *Morawetz, Jacques *Hétu, Lorne *Betts, and Robert *Turner. Most issues also listed new scores received at the centre and contained a news section ('Here and There'). Some carried up-to-date lists of composition contests. Other special lists included Rachel *Cavalho's 'Canadian piano music for teaching' in issue 12; a survey of recordings of Canadian works in issue 26; and a comprehensive list of works written for the Canadian centenary in issue 7. Contributors to the first phase of *Musicanada* included, in addition to the aforementioned, C. Laughton *Bird, Sister Marcelle *Corneille, Stephen Freygood, Helmut *Kallmann, George *Little, Joseph *Macerollo, and Sir Ernest *MacMillan. *Musicanada* was discontinued in 1970 when the centre committed itself to the publication of a series of monographs on Canadian composers and felt unable to finance both projects.

Musicanada was revived – in title though not in format – with issue 30, published in Ottawa in November 1976 under new aegis: the CMCouncil. Guy *Huot, the council's executive secretary, was appointed editor. This second phase, planned as a quarterly (though it produced only three issues in its first full year of publication), offers its contents in French and English in the same issue and covers Canadian musical life more broadly than did its predecessor. It contains regional reports, festival news, book and record reviews, competition results, and a variety of short features. The list of new compositions received at the CMCentre is a notable carry-over from the previous *Musicanada*. Neither magazine described above should be confused with the *MusiCanada*, which ran to three issues (October and December 1922 and February 1923) in French, or with *Music Canada*, a pop-music journal published monthly in Toronto from September 1970 to December 1971 by J. Cee Productions, and its successor, *Music Canada Quarterly* (1972–6). KW

Music boxes. Both cylinder and disc-type music boxes found in Canada during the 18th, 19th, and early 20th centuries were manufactured, it would appear, in Europe, particularly in Switzerland and Germany. They were at their most popular during the latter half of the 19th century. Main brand names seen in Canada included Polyphon (Leipzig) and its daughter, Regina Music Box (New Jersey). Music boxes were the first mechanical home entertainment devices available and also were used fairly widely in tearooms and other public places. In 1828 a circus visiting Toronto exhibited the 'Androides, or Grand Musical Machine' from Germany, which may have been an elaborate sort of music box. Music boxes were found in areas as remote as the Yukon, where a 1.8-metre, 33.45-kilogram German-built model was delivered ca 1900. Most cylinder specimens were built between 1840 and 1890, using pinned cylinders which contained 8 or 10 tunes. Disc boxes were developed towards the end of the 19th century, and music for these was stamped on interchangeable metal discs. Though music boxes were able to provide their owners with surprisingly varied programs, the advent of sound recording early in the 20th century destroyed their appeal as purveyors of music. Such boxes may be found still in many private and public collections across the country, however, cherished for their quaintness, the cunning of their mechanisms, their beauty, or their age. Collectors include Murray Draper of Clinton, Ont, Franklin Foley of Belleville, Ont, and Terry Smythe of Winnipeg.

Other musical curiosities of the cylinder type include an organ, advertised by F.H. *Glackemeyer, which was 'superior in excellence ... several instruments of Music perform with it, by self-moving machinery, and when in motion form a complete band in perfect concert' (*Quebec Gazette*, 13 Jul 1815). Also popular during the 19th and early 20th centuries were the Orchestrion (a mechanically driven piano, cymbals, and drums) and the Polyphon, a large spring-wound music box. Examples of these are housed in the Sounds of Yesteryear Museum in Winnipeg. See also Barrel organs; Instrument collections; Player pianos and nickelodeons.

BIBLIOGRAPHY
Townsend, Elaine. 'Mechanical music,' *Canadian Collector*, vol 10, Nov–Dec 1975
Taylor, John A. *Marvellous Music Machines* (Cobourg, Ont, 1977)
Lower, Thelma. 'Mechanical memories,' *Music Market Canada*, Dec 1977

Music Council of the Newfoundland Teachers' Association. One of 21 special-interest councils of the NTA. It was formed in 1960 and affiliated with the *CMEA in 1975. The council's activities have included liaison between its five regional divisions and the NTA, co-operative efforts with music festival committees, and the organization of workshops and student and adult concerts. A newsletter – *Opus* – is issued three times a year. Membership is open to anyone with a professional interest in music, though executive posts may be held only by NTA members. Presidents have been Brother G.R. Bellows 1966–7, D.F. Cook 1967–9, James Prowse 1969–72, B. Wayne Rogers 1972–4, S. Paul Maynard 1974–5, Carol E. Harris 1975–7, Gary F. Graham 1977–9, succeeded by Sister Lois Greene. CEH

Music Education Council of the New Brunswick Teachers' Association. Formed 23 May 1959 in Fredericton as the New Brunswick Music Educators' Assn. It became a subject council of the NBTA in 1962, resumed its independent status for two years (1971–3), and then rejoined the NBTA. The council became affiliated with the *CMEA in 1974. Full membership is available only to school music teachers, but associate membership is granted to private and university teachers. In 1977 there were 84 members and 10 associate members. Conferences are held in spring and autumn, and a newsletter, *Accents*, is published thrice yearly. Presidents have been Thomas Morrison 1959–60, 1970–1, Neil *Michaud 1960–1, Douglas *Major 1961–2, Winnifred Ball 1963–5, Margaret Fairweather 1965–7, Lorne Poitras 1967–8, Walter Ball 1968–70, Carolyn Nielsen 1971–4, Joy Broad 1974–6, and Shirley Sutherland 1976–8, succeeded by Brenda Trefford. CN

Music education research. Though to a large extent still in its infancy in Canada, music education research increased in the 1970s. Attendant upon this increase was the formation in 1973 of the *Canadian Music Research Council, whose survey (1974–5, updated 1977) provides the basis of this overview. (The CMRC also has investigated areas of research outside education, including musicology and ethnomusicology.) Most studies in Canada have been undertaken after 1970, though it should be stressed that these are only the visible result of a large body of support data accumulated over many years and by many agencies in Canada and the USA.

Research in the area of curriculum and instruction concerns itself principally with testing new methods and materials in classroom situations. Rigorous experimental techniques are employed. Topics include curriculum and staff evaluation (Duane A. Bates and James Rahn, *Queen's U), aural and visual skills (Ian Bradley, *U of Victoria), group keyboard instruction (Frank *Churchley, U of Victoria), the rating of musical performance (Harold Fiske, *U of Western Ontario), musical improvisation with children (Martin Prével, *Laval U), creative-affective programs (Natalie Kuzmich, *U of Toronto), band instruction (Alan Smith, *U of Alberta), and psychology of creativity (Margery Vaughan, U of Victoria).

Research in the history and literature of musical and/or pedagogical practices in Canada includes work in Canadian music (Ian Bradley; Austin *Clarkson and James Rahn, *York U), Canadian folk music for young children (Barbara *Cass-Beggs, Algonquin College, Ottawa), Canadian doctoral programs (Paul *Green, U of Western Ontario), Canadian music for schools (Isabelle *Mills, *U of Saskatchewan at Saskatoon), French-Canadian folksongs (Lorraine Thibeault, *McGill U), and history of music education (Diana Brault, Ontario; William Bartlett, Prince Edward Island).

Funding for such work has been piecemeal; universities support individual faculty members, and several provincial agencies support educational research directly applicable to instructional practice. Information about Canadian research studies can be obtained from the indexes of the Educational Resources Information Centre (ERIC) in Washington, DC (to which the major universities have access), and the Canadian Music Research Council. In addition to the council's twice-yearly newsletter *Music Research News*, relevant articles are published in the U of Western Ontario's annual *Studies in Music* and in the *CAUSM Journal*. The U of Western Ontario has been the site of symposia of research in music education in 1976, 1977, and 1979, bringing together researchers and teachers in formal and informal presentations and discussions and thereby providing a focal point for this work in Canada.

See also Ethnomusicology; Musicology

BIBLIOGRAPHY
Vaughan, M.M. 'Dimensions of music research in Canada,' *CME*, vol 16, Fall 1974
Cooper, E.A. 'The role of research in the implementation of school music innovations,' *CME*, vol 16, Summer 1975 MMV

Musicology

1 Introduction
2 Canada as subject matter for musicological study
3 Musicological research and teaching in Canada

1 INTRODUCTION. Musicology may be described as the pursuit of musical knowledge and insight by accurate, objective, and critical methods of fact-finding, analysis, and interpretation. While musical scholarship has existed in most highly developed cultures of the past, the principles and techniques used in the 20th century were formulated only in the late 19th and have remained in a process of refinement and transformation. Musicology has two main branches: historical (the history of western art music) and systematic (the study of universal principles underlying the vocabulary of music – scales, rhythms, melodies, etc – and of acoustics, aesthetics, psychology, sociology, and other disciplines in their relationship to music). Musicology is complemented by *ethnomusicology, the study of folk music and non-western art music.

An academic degree or position, though advantageous, is not essential in the accomplishment of musicological work, and many Canadians whose specialty is performance or composition have applied expert skill in the interpretation and editing of scores in obsolete notations or in the study of exotic tonal systems. However, in Canada at least, the label musicologist is often applied too freely to broadcaster-commentators, journalists, and other popularizers, in fact to any well-read musician or music lover. Perhaps the mark of the true musicologist is the possession of the techniques to do original research and the ability to generalize, ie, to place individual facts and observations into larger patterns of relationships and historical dynamics.

2 CANADA AS SUBJECT MATTER FOR MUSICOLOGICAL STUDY. Though the scholarly investigation of music in Canada entered its formative stage only in the third quarter of the 20th century, much of the work previously done by chroniclers, journalists, and general historians deserves recognition. Its importance lies in the fact that it transmits much information, often based on personal observation, that would be lost otherwise; its weakness lies in the lack of access to adequate documentation and the resulting narrow chronological and geographical perspective and frequent inaccuracy of name spellings and dates.

As in Brazil and other new-world countries, the musical curiosity of the earliest European chroniclers in Canada – Marc Lescarbot and several of the 17th-century *missionaries – was captured by the unfamiliar music of the natives rather than the musical life among the colonists, which was so much like that of dozens of small French or English towns. Later European visitors – the baron de Lahontan in his *New Voyages to North-America* (English edn 1703), Pehr Kalm in *Travels in North America* (English edn 1770), or the Duc de La Rochefoucault-Liancourt in his *Travels through the United States of America, the Country of the Iroquois, and Upper Canada* ... (London 1799) – likewise recorded unaccustomed musical impressions, whether the music of the Indians or the singing of the voyageurs.

The earliest known attempts at a historical record of musical life, one in English and one in French, date back only to 1878 and 1881–2 respectively. In the Toronto *Mail* of 21 Dec 1878 an anonymous writer presented 'Music in Toronto: reminiscences of the last half century,' which is rich in factual detail; and in the periodical *L'Album musical* of Montreal, Gustave *Smith wrote a series of 12 articles, 'Du mouvement musical en Canada,' concerned with the quality rather than the facts of musical life in the 25 years of his Canadian experience. At the same time appeared a historical account of one musical society, *Historique de la Société musicale Sainte-Cécile de Québec* (Quebec 1881). These publications set a pattern for many to follow in the next 50 years, among them F.E. Dixon's 'Music in Toronto, as it was in the days that are gone forever' in the *Daily Mail and Empire*, 7 Nov 1896; Mgr Henri Têtu's series of 'Impressions musicales' in *Action Sociale* (13 Mar 1915, etc); Herbert Kent's 'Musical chronicles of early times' in the *Victoria Daily Times* (7, 14, 21, 28 Dec 1918); and Nazaire *LeVasseur's 'Musique et musiciens à Québec,' in monthly instalments in *La Musique* (15 Jan 1919–22 Dec 1922). The last-named is the most important, not only because of its length and its wealth of documentation (largely from the author's own scrapbooks and memorabilia), but also because for the first time a chronicler reached back to the times long before his own childhood. Despite its many inaccuracies, its gaps, and its mixture of anecdote and fact, LeVasseur's account remains a classic in the historiography of Canadian music.

The extraordinary growth of musical life about the turn of the century provided the incentive for a flurry of stock-takings, all of which reflect pride of achievement. Separate publications, with accounts of local concert life, musical worthies, and institutions, were H.H. *Godfrey's *A Souvenir of Musical Toronto* (Toronto 1897, 1898–9), Hugo Talbot's *Musical Halifax 1903–4* ([Halifax 1904]), and B.K. Sandwell's *The Musical Red Book of Montreal* (Montreal 1907). Sandwell, who later was known as a literary critic, provided a detailed account of 13 seasons of concert life, biographical sketches of some 94 musicians, specifications of church organs, and much other documentation. Though to some extent continued in the *Montreal Music Year Book* (Montreal 1931, 1932), Sandwell's compilation remains unsurpassed in the documentation of Canadian musical life.

Surveys that appeared in reference books at least attempted to cover the whole of Canada. Based generally on superficial information-gathering and lacking historical depth, they range in size from F.H. *Torrington's four-page essay 'Musical progress in Canada' in J. Castell Hopkins' *Canada, An Encyclopedia of the Country* (Toronto 1898–1900) and Susie (Mrs J.W.F.) *Harrison's 23-page article 'Canada' in *The Imperial History and Encyclopedia of Music* (New York, Toronto 1909) to the 5 chapters of Edouard *Hesselberg's 'A review of music in Canada' in the international edition of *Modern Music and Musicians* (New York, Toronto 1913) and the 11 chapters, by 9 different authors, in *The Year Book of Canadian Art* (London, Toronto 1913).

All this literature was written in English. In French-speaking Canada meanwhile several historians and archivists began to search 17th- and 18th-century literature and documents for information about musical life. Among the results were Ernest *Myrand's *Noëls anciens de la Nouvelle-France* (Quebec 1899, 1907, Montreal 1913, 1926), the musical references in Ernest *Gagnon's *Louis Jolliet* (Quebec 1902, 1913, 1926, 1946), Gagnon's 'La musique à Québec au temps de Mgr de Laval' in *La Nouvelle-France* (May 1908), Ovide Lapalice's 'Les organistes et maîtres de musique à Notre-Dame de Montréal' in *BRH* (vol 25, August 1919), and É.-Z. *Massicotte's 'La musique militaire sous le régime français' in *BRH* (vol 39, July 1933). *Le Bulletin des recherches historiques* (Lévis, Que, 1895–1956) also featured many short contributions on music by Massicotte, J.-Edmond and Pierre-Georges Roy, Benjamin Sulte, and other historians.

The first person said to have begun writing a history of music in Canada was John Daniel Logan (journalist and professor of English, b Antigonish, NS, 1869, d Milwaukee, Wisc, 1929). No trace of it has been found, although Logan published valuable articles on Calixa *Lavallée, 'Canada's first creative composer' (*Canadian Courier*, vol 2, 27 Jan 1912), on 'Musical composition in Canada' (*The Year Book of Canadian Art*), and on related topics.

The second quarter of the 20th century produced little evidence of a growing awareness of Canada's musical past. However, there appeared three French-language biographies that kindled a pride in past glories: *Calixa Lavallée* (Montreal 1936, 1950, 1966) by Eugène *Lapierre, *L'Albani* (Montreal 1938) by Hélène Charbonneau, and *La Palme-Issaurel* (Montreal 1948) by Romain *Gour. The scholarship revealed in these works is uneven; Lapierre, for example, neglected to consult biographical source material and inspect published scores in US libraries that would have been easy to locate.

Theses on Canadian topics began to be written in the 1930s. J.-R. Pelletier wrote an 'Aperçu historique sur le chant liturgique de l'église, en Europe et dans la province ecclésiastique de Québec' (MUS D, Laval 1932), and Thomas C. *Chattoe submitted 'Music in Canada' for a B MUS (Birmingham 1931). In the next decade Brother Pierre-Alphonse dealt with 'Chant et musique sacrée dans la Nouvelle-France' (MA, Ottawa 1948), and Kathleen M. Hobday compiled a *Survey of the Musical Resources of the Province of Ontario* (MA, Toronto 1946; Toronto 1946), an effort rivalling Sandwell's in thoroughness. At the same time Antonine Bernier of Montreal proposed the chapter structure for a history of music in Canada (four volumes to be devoted to Quebec, Montreal, Ottawa, and Toronto, each volume divided into sections on 'musique profane' and 'musique religieuse'; copy in the files of Marius *Barbeau), but this was not realized. The first broad panorama was unfolded in Marcelle Rousseau's thesis 'The rise of music in Canada' (MA, Columbia 1951).

A broad panorama also was Helmut *Kallmann's aim when he began, in 1948, to collect data on Canada's musical history. He examined and compared the published literature mentioned above and proceeded to scan reference books, periodicals, local histories, travel accounts, and such primary sources as were available, extracting facts and relevant passages for alphabetical filing in much the way *EMC* is organized. Among the first byproducts of Kallmann's research were two outlines of Canadian music history: a chapter, 'Historical background,' in *Music in Canada* (1955) and an entry on Canada in *MGG* (1958). His main effort, however, was the preparation, begun in 1950, of *A History of Music in Canada 1534–1914* (1960). The book for the first time assembled facts and quotations from scattered and often obscure sources to reveal the overall pattern of the transplantation of European music and of colonial development. The dearth of available sources during the 1950s – many published and manuscript compositions, music periodicals, and concert programs and much musicians' correspondence, etc, have come to light only in the 1970s – caused the author to stress musical 'life' rather than 'creativity,' and there is a lack of reference to simultaneous developments in the sister arts. Nonetheless, in demonstrating the diversity and age of musical endeavour in Canada, in identifying some of the shaping forces and establishing a framework of periodization, the book was a pioneer effort. In 1980 it remained the only one of its kind, although Kallmann and others proceeded to investigate certain periods, aspects, and biographical subjects in greater detail.

The most detailed research in any special era has been that of Willy *Amtmann on music under the French régime. Originally written as a doctoral thesis, his 'La vie musicale en Nouvelle-France' (Strasbourg 1956) was expanded later into *Music in Canada 1600–1800* (1975) and further enlarged in its French-language version *La Musique au Québec 1600–1875* (1976). In fact both volumes essentially are limited to the history of the province of Quebec. Amtmann brought an impressive technique of documentation, authentication, and comparison to bear on certain significant episodes, such as the Prose 'Sacrae familiae felix spectaculum' attributed to Charles-Amador *Martin and the installation of the first organs in Quebec. He was concerned particularly with the elucidation of 17th-century musical terminology and was able to correct many errors or question assumptions made by earlier, more superficial, writers. Amtmann could not, however, overcome the sparseness of ascertainable musical facts of 17th- and 18th-century Canada, and he too was forced to make assumptions, albeit better founded ones.

Musicological research into Canadian history, no matter how much hampered by the lack of available documentation, was able to yield practical results during the 1960s in the revival of 18th- and 19th-century compositions (notably *Quesnel's **Colas et Colinette*, under *Ten Centuries Concerts auspices; and Lavallée's **The Widow*, under CBC auspices). It also provided an impetus for the establishment of some of the first university courses on Canadian (or North American) music, including those at the *U of Calgary (*Johnston), *Carleton U (Amtmann), the *U of Montreal (*Kendergi, *Richer-Lortie), the *U of Saskatoon (*Adaskin), and the *U of Toronto (*Beckwith, *Morey).

The dearth of musicological studies – relating both to history and to contemporary composition – was felt keenly when early in the 1970s the editors of *EMC* began planning their work. While international music encyclopedias usually are harvesters of work already done by specialists, *EMC* in the main has been a mobilizer of musicological activity. While many *EMC* entries are written by established experts, by far the greater number are by scholars who became specialists in the course of preparing an entry or a group of entries. A basis for musicological research in Canadian subject areas also was created in the 1970s with the establishment of a music division at the *NL of C in 1970 and the development of a music collection at the BN du Q after 1968. The entries for *Archives and *Libraries provide details about the contents of these and other collections of historical and current Canadiana. The NL of C in particular has become a resource and consultation centre for historical and bibliographical research on music in Canada.

The following summary attempts to show the range of scholarly work done between World War II and 1980. Theses and publications mentioned on the previous pages of this entry are not repeated, nor is work listed which was done especially for *EMC*. It will be noted that most of the work has been in the nature of graduate theses; a fair amount also has been accomplished by journalist-scholars and by archivists, but the contribution by academics remains small.

Overviews. Andrée *Desautels has provided a French-language summary of Canadian music history, 'Les trois âges de la musique au Canada,' in *La Musique* (vol 2, Paris 1965); the three ages are the French régime (17th century and the 18th to 1760), the British colonial period (1763–1918), and the modern period. Gordon Howell's 'The development of music in Canada' (PH D, Rochester 1959) combines a historical outline with a discussion of contemporary music.

Regional history. In this area important work has been done by archivists. Phyllis Blakeley has written on musical life in Halifax and Nova Scotia, J. Russell Harper prepared a manuscript called 'Spring tide: an enquiry into the lives, labours, loves, and manners of early New Brunswickers' (ca 1954) while at the New Brunswick Museum in Saint John, and Dorothy Blakey Smith wrote on 'Music in the furthest west a hundred years ago' (*CMJ*, vol 2, Summer 1958).

Theses include Norman John Kennedy's on musical life in Calgary 1875–1920 (MA, Alberta 1952), David Sale's on concert life in Toronto 1845–67, with a valuable itemization of all known programs (MA, Toronto 1968), William Lock's on Ontario church choirs and choral societies 1819–1918 (DMA, Southern California 1972), France Malouin-Gélinas's on musical life in Quebec City 1840–5 as described in newspapers and magazines of the day (M MUS, U of Montreal 1975), and Peter Slemon's on Montreal in the years 1841–67 (MMA, McGill 1976).

Regional research by university teachers included that of William Bartlett on Prince Edward Island, Juliette Bourassa-Trépanier on Quebec City, Frederick Hall on western Ontario cities, Elaine *Keillor on Ontario at the turn of the century, and Carl Morey on Toronto. J.-Antonio *Thompson's history of musical life in Trois-Rivières was published in that city in 1970, and an account by Norman Draper of bands and band music in Calgary appeared in 1975.

Composition. Theses on specific forms of composition or on groups of composers have included Stephanie Owen's on piano concertos (PH D, Washington 1969), William Lister's on violin sonatas (DMA, Boston 1970), Mary Beaulieu's on keyboard music (M MUS, Indiana 1970), Isabelle *Mills' on music suitable for listening programs (ED D, Columbia 1971), Lee *Hepner's on orchestral music (PH D, New York 1972), and Norman Chapman's on piano music (PH D, Case Western Reserve, 1973). George *Proctor's book *Canadian Music of the 20th Century* was published in Toronto in 1980. Lyse Richer-Lortie has made comparative studies of music in Montreal and Toronto.

Studies of individual composers or some of their works, in addition to the books listed under *Biography, included the following:

Patricia Doyle (M MUS, Western Ont 1977) on W.H. *Anderson

Marie-Paule Provost (MA, Montreal 1970), Louise Bail-Milot (M MUS, Sorbonne 1972), and Anne Walsh (PH D, Catholic U 1972) on Claude *Champagne

Vivienne Rowley (DMA, Boston 1973) on Jean *Coulthard

Elaine Smith (M MUS, Western Ont 1978) on S.C. *Eckhardt-Gramatté

Hubert Tersteeg (M MUS, Western Ont 1978) on Robert *Fleming

Albert *Grenier (L MUS, Montreal 1971) and Martin J. Waltz (M MUS, Western Ont 1977) on Bruce *Mather

Juliette Bourassa-Trépanier (D MUS, Laval 1972) on Rodolphe *Mathieu

Claire Villeneuve (M MUS, Montreal 1975) on Léo-Pol *Morin

Roch Poulin (MA, Montreal 1961) and Clotilde Denis (L MUS, Montreal 1972) on Jean *Papineau-Couture

Sheila Eastman (M MUS, British Columbia 1974) on Barbara *Pentland

Wayne Gilpin (M MUS, Alberta 1978) on Godfrey *Ridout

David Duke (MA, North Carolina 1973), Frances Smith (M MUS, Western Ont 1973), and Edward Gregory Butler (DMA, Rochester 1974) on Harry *Somers

Douglas Webb (PH D, Rochester 1973) and Malcolm Hines (M MUS, Western Ont 1975) on John *Weinzweig

Robert Skelton (D MUS, Indiana 1976) on the string quartets of Weinzweig, *Gould, and *Schafer

Jacob Wagner (PH D, Union Theological Seminary 1957), Robert Massingham (M MUS, North Texas State 1957), Alan Lehl (M MUS, Rochester 1957), Frederick Telschow (PH D, Rochester 1969), William Marwick (PH D, Michigan State 1970), Joylin Campbell Yukl (DMA, Missouri 1976), and Norman Johnson (DMA, Southern Baptist U 1979) on Healey *Willan

Research, largely bibliographical and biographical has been carried out by the following, among others: Marvin *Duchow on Champagne; Helmut Kallmann on J.P. *Clarke and Joseph Quesnel; Elaine Keillor on W.O. *Forsyth; Sharyn Hall on Clarence *Lucas; and Giles *Bryant and F.R.C. *Clarke on Healey Willan.

Biography. In addition to biographical research on composers and to published biographies, theses have been prepared by Nadia Turbide on C.A.E. *Harriss (MMA, McGill 1976) and by Cécile Huot on Wilfrid *Pelletier (doctoral thesis, Toulouse 1973). J.B. McPherson and Ruby *Mercer have written on Canadian singers, and Gilles *Potvin has done extensive research on Emma *Albani and Eva *Gauthier.

Subject studies. By far the largest single subject for Canadian theses is music education. A selection of such theses is found in the bibliography under School music. Several have been written on church music. Among the relatively few other subjects are pre-Confederation music publishing (Maria Calderisi, MMA, McGill 1976), Ukrainian musical culture in Canada (Philip Bassa, MA, Montreal 1955), and the socio-economic status of Canadian composers (Marie Vachon, MA, Carleton 1975).

Organ building has been investigated by Antoine *Bouchard of *Laval U and John S. McIntosh of the *U of Western Ontario. In 1979 Laurent Lapointe published a comprehensive account of the first 100 years of the Quebec organ builders *Casavant Frères 1879–1979* (St-Hyacinthe 1979). Edward B. *Moogk made the history of sound recording a lifelong study. Thelma Reid Lower of Vancouver has written extensively on choral societies. Other subject specialists are mentioned in the entries on Bibliography; Discography; and Hymnology. For a directory of *EMC* articles on church music see Religions and music.

3 MUSICOLOGICAL RESEARCH AND TEACHING IN CANADA. The introduction to Canada of musicology as an academic study dates back only to 1954, when the U of Toronto appointed Harvey J. Olnick (b New York 18 Dec 1917, a graduate of Columbia U) to organize and teach a course leading to the M MUS degree. (Olnick was the first chairman of the history and literature department created in 1968, and in 1980 continued to teach at the university.) Until then music history had been a

stepchild of university teaching, more often than not entrusted to a non-specialist. As late as the 1940s the same history lectures were given to U of Toronto undergraduates and to teenage students at the RCMT. The main point of studying music history, in the view of some of the older England-trained lecturers, was to carry on intelligent conversation on music or to write feuilletons. An elegant turn of phrase counted for more than the examination of facts. Scholarship was not to be an end in itself and 'musicology' suggested a suspect Teutonic learnedness.

It was at least 10 years after Olnick's appointment before professors had the encouragement or the time to engage in musical research. However, the emphasis on 1 / the teaching of history and literature and 2 / the training in research methods increased rapidly in the 1960s and 1970s, and by 1980 most university music departments offered musicology taught by specialists.

There had been individual musicologists in Canada before 1954, of course, but they rarely worked in their own field. The first was Gustav Schilling (b Germany 1805, d Nebraska 1880), author or editor of at least 21 books on music, including a 6-volume *Encyclopädie*. Leaving Germany in 1857 he vainly tried to establish a conservatory in New York, then in Montreal, where he resided for some 10 years as a private teacher and a participant in musical societies. Though Schilling was castigated by Robert Schumann and later German writers for the shallowness and charlatanism of his writing, he was commended by Warren Dwight Allen in *Philosophies of Music History* (New York 1939) as one of the first to relate the history of music to the social and political environment and to the history of ideas. This first bona fide musicologist in Canada has left no known contribution to the field during his Montreal years.

Central Europe remained the centre of musicology for many generations. The exodus of musicologists to the USA as the result of the Hitler régime (Willi Apel, Manfred Bukofzer, Alfred Einstein, Curt Sachs, and many others) had a fainter echo in Canada. Ida *Halpern and Ulrich *Leupold, from Vienna and Berlin respectively, arrived in Canada in 1939, the first with PH D degrees in musicology in the country. Halpern's main research has been in ethnomusicology. A specialist in Lutheran church music, Leupold was engaged in musicology only marginally in Canada. The same was true of Arnold *Walter and Walter *Kaufmann, whose main energies were devoted to administration and conducting respectively. Another two persons from Vienna and Berlin, Willy Amtmann and Helmut Kallmann, who arrived in 1940, developed their musicological interests only in Canada and became the authors of the first books relating Canadian music history.

Among the first Canadian-born musicologists were Robert *Talbot, a specialist in the theory of music who in the early 1930s was the only Canadian member of the International Musicological Society (Société internationale de musicologie), and Alfred *Bernier, whose field was church music. Both held D MUS degrees from Laval or Montreal and devoted their teaching careers to these universities. Other first-generation Canadian musicologists have been Marvin Duchow of Montreal, Michael Winesanker (see USA), Giveon Cornfield (see Canada Baroque Records), and Andrée Desautels (Desautels was probably the first Canadian-born specialist in the teaching of music history; she began in 1949). Like many Canadian-born musicologists of a younger generation, these received an essential part of their training in the USA or another foreign country.

The following summary of musicological activity is organized according to main subject areas. It includes Canadian-born as well as immigrant musicians but, in the absence of means to evaluate each contribution precisely, preference in selection has been given to those whose contribution has been in more than one of the following fields: dissertation, teaching, published writing, and editing. Where applicable, the name of a university and major specialty has been indicated. It may be taken for granted that individuals have worked in other periods or subjects as well.

Medieval and renaissance music

Gaston *Allaire (Moncton; music theory, Claudin de Sermisy)
Terence *Bailey (British Columbia, Western Ontario; plainchant)
Bruce Bellingham (U of Connecticut; renaissance, Georg Rhau)
Yves Chartier (Ottawa)
Dimitri Conomos (British Columbia; Byzantine chant)
Eugene Cramer (Calgary; Polish renaissance)
Robert Falck (Toronto; 13th century)
Jean Gagné
Andrew *Hughes (Toronto; medieval liturgical music)
Walter Kemp (Dalhousie; late medieval English music, Canadian organ history)
H. Bruce Lobaugh (Regina; late 16th century)
Rika *Maniates (Toronto; renaissance)
Christine *Mather (Victoria, Wilfrid Laurier; Heinrich Isaac)
Timothy McGee (Toronto)
Neil K. Moran (Byzantine chant)
Élisabeth Morin (Montreal; early keyboard music)
H. Colin Slim (California; renaissance)
Dujka Smoje (Montreal; middle ages)

17th and 18th centuries

Mary Cyr (McGill; French opera and Rameau)
Marvin Duchow (McGill; late 18th century)
Kenneth *Gilbert (keyboard music)
Warren Kirkendale (Duke; 18th century chamber music)
Gordana *Lazarevich (Victoria; Italian musical theatre)
Ulrich Leupold (Wilfrid Laurier; Lutheran music)
Hugh *McLean (Western Ontario)
Carl Morey (Toronto; Alessandro Scarlatti)
Jaroslav Mráček (Southern California)
Harvey Olnick (Toronto; Italian baroque)
Lucien *Poirier (Laval; baroque keyboard music)
Rudolf Schnitzler (Queen's; baroque)
James *Stark (Toronto; early baroque)

19th century

Marion *Barnum (Iowa State; J.N. Hummel)
H. Robert Cohen (Laval, British Columbia; France)
Gaynor Jones (Toronto; Weber)
Donald McCorkle (British Columbia; Brahms)
Zoltan Roman (Calgary; Mahler)
R. Murray Schafer (E.T.A. Hoffmann)
Alan *Walker (McMaster; Chopin, Liszt, Schumann)
Gerhard *Wuensch (Toronto; Max Reger)

20th century

Kathryn *Bailey (Western Ontario; dodecaphony)
Alan M. *Gillmor (Carleton; Satie)
Lothar *Klein (Toronto; Stravinsky)
R. Murray Schafer (Ezra Pound and music)

Special subjects

Graham *George (Queens; tonality)
Jean-Jacques Nattiez (Montreal; semiology of music)
Geoffrey *Payzant (Toronto; aesthetics, perception)
Paul *Pedersen (McGill; psychology)
Percival *Price (Michigan; campanology)
Eric Regener (Montreal; computer science and music)
Margery Vaughan (Victoria; psychology of creativity)
See also Acoustics research in Canada; Music education research; Psychology of music; Religions and music.

Most of those mentioned above have published articles, and many have written books or prepared scholarly editions of music (more often than not for foreign publishers and publication series). There is no space here to provide a list of such works, but as examples of the tracing of lost or neglected scores (and at the risk of ignoring the discoveries of other scholars) one might cite Mary Cyr's location of Rameau's *Cantate pour la fête de Saint Louis*, Andrée Desautels's of a Marc-Antoine Charpentier manuscript in Quebec, and Hugh McLean's of C.P.E. Bach, Haydn, A. Scarlatti, and J.H. Schein compositions in Poland and East Germany.

Private research also has produced some significant work, although much of it remains unpublished. Walter Kunstler, a Montreal surgeon, did research on the olympic theme in music which shaped the *McGill Chamber Orchestra's programming during the 1976 Montreal Olympics. E.P. Scarlett, a Calgary physician, has investigated the causes of death of certain famous musicians. Thomas Archer's study of Richard Strauss, Francean Campbell's work on Milhaud, and J.B. McPherson's biography of Ernestine Schumann-Heink remain manuscripts, but Fernand Ouellette's book on Edgard Varèse was published. A Toronto professor of English, William Blissett, is an authority on Wagner. Jean-Louis Côté of Ottawa has made an intensive study of Boccherini. Paul Macenko of Winnipeg has written on Ukrainian musicians and edited Ukrainian music. There are other examples of private research.

Individual Canadian musicologists belong to the American Musicological Society and the International Musicological Society. No specific association exists in Canada, but the *Canadian Assn of University Schools of Music (CAUSM), with its annual meetings held as part of the Learned Societies' conferences and its *Journal*, provides an outlet for the reading and publishing of papers and for personal contact. In addition, informal meetings of Canadian musicologists have taken place at the U of Toronto in 1970 ('Canadian Studies Seminar'), at *Queen's U in 1979, and at *York U in 1980. Other outlets for musicological studies have been the **Canadian Music Journal*, the **Canada Music Book*, and *Studies in Music from the University of Western Ontario* (1976, 1977, 1978).

BIBLIOGRAPHY

Chartier, Yves. 'La musicologie à l'université,' *R de l'Université d'Ottawa*, vol 38, Jul–Sep 1968
Kallmann, Helmut. 'Canadian tasks for musicology,' *Report of the First Canadian Studies Seminar*, U of Toronto, 7 Nov 1970 (Toronto, typescript 1970)
Bradley, Ian L. *A Selected Bibliography of Musical Canadiana* (Victoria, BC, rev edn 1976)
Sandvoss, Joachim. 'Canadian graduate theses in music and music education 1897–1978,' ms (1978)
Chartier, Yves. 'Situation de la recherche sur la musique au Canada français,' *Bulletin du Centre de recherche en civilisation canadienne-française de l'Université d'Ottawa*, Dec 1979

HK

The Music Scene / La Scène musicale. Periodical published six times yearly in Toronto by *PRO

Canada (and previously, until July–August 1977 by BMI Canada). Through articles, interviews, and newsbriefs it promotes and publicizes the activities of composers, writers, and music publishers affiliated with the performing rights society. It is published in separate English and French editions and distributed free of charge. The international circulation is 11,000. Editors have been Anthony Hagerty and Nancy Gyokeres (who was introduced as editor in the November–December 1969 issue, though the magazine did not begin printing staff credits until 1971).

The Music Scene succeeded and incorporated the *BMI Canada Newsletter* (1947–66) and *In Tune with the Times* (no dates available); this explains why its first issue, September–October 1967, is numbered 237. Besides articles on PRO Canada members, on musical organizations, conferences, and other activities of interest to professional musicians, it has featured stories on the BMI Canada (PRO Canada) annual awards dinners, a regular column by the managing director, and a 'Welcome to our new affiliate members.' Issues 262 (November–December 1971) to 289 (May–June 1976) provided lists of newly acquired scores in the *CMCentre library. Extended analyses and scholarly discussions of Canadian music are beyond the magazine's scope, though sympathetic reactions from critics to new works by affiliate composers are quoted. Spread among issues 251 (January–February 1970) to 272 (July–August 1973) was a series of brief articles on Canada's university music departments. The magazine also provides a pictorial record of PRO Canada affiliates. FH, HK

Music therapy. The scientific use of music in the rehabilitation and training of patients. Working with a medical team the music therapist participates in the analysis of problems and the projection of treatment before carrying out prescribed music activities to achieve therapeutic goals. Most music therapists function in mental hospitals, rehabilitation centres, training institutions, or special education, and their work has assisted people suffering from cerebral palsy, asthma, mental retardation, physical disabilities (notably blindness and deafness), learning disabilities, and emotional disturbance. It also is used in work with the culturally deprived and the aged. Types of musical therapy vary as widely as the ills they treat.

Forms of musical therapy existed in the ancient world and have occurred in most subsequent cultures. An early instance in 19th-century Canada was described in the *Report of the Commissioners*, Beauport Asylum, Quebec, January 1849: 'In several cases we have found music and dancing of great benefit as remedial agents. In one case they roused a patient from a state of the most abject melancholy, and gave a stimulus to his mental faculties, which resulted in perfect recovery.' This was more than a coincidence, for in his *Hochelaga, or England in the New World* (London 1846), Eliot Warburton said in 1845 (p 176) about the same asylum: 'With very few exceptions, music appears to cause them great pleasure, soothing rather than exciting them.' In 1879 in Biddeford, Me, the Canadian Roch *Lyonnais is known to have read a paper stressing the therapeutic value of music. Its practical introduction to Canada, however, is related directly to developments in Great Britain and the USA.

As early as 1919 Columbia U (New York) offered courses, and in 1941 a National Foundation for Music Therapy was established in the USA. The use of music in rehabilitation programs in military hospitals late in World War II led to the establishment in 1944 of a degree program to train music therapists at Michigan State College, and by 1977 some 28 US colleges offered degree programs. The National Assn for Music Therapy, with headquarters in Lawrence, Kan, was formed in 1950. In England the British Society of Music Therapy, founded in 1958 as the Society for Music Therapy and Remedial Music, collaborated with the GSM to develop a one-year post-graduate program leading to an LGSMT (Licentiate, Guildhall School of Music Therapy).

In Canada Alfred *Rosé initiated one of the first pilot projects (1952–61) at Westminster Hospital in London, Ont. Other programs began in the early 1960s in Weyburn, Sask, (under Dorothy Twente Sommer), at the St Thomas (Ont) Psychiatric Hospital (under Norma Sharpe), and in Kitchener, Ont (under Earl A. Charboneau). By the mid-1970s over 20 centres across Canada had implemented music therapy programs. Among the most prominent therapists in Canada have been Thérèse Pageau of the Louis-Hippolyte Lafontaine Hospital (Montreal), Frances Herman of the Crippled Children's Centre (Toronto), and Norma Sharpe. In 1974, at the first national conference of music therapists in Canada, held at St Thomas Psychiatric Hospital, 63 delegates formed the Canadian Assn for Music Therapy with Norma Sharpe as first president. Other conferences have been held at the *U of Manitoba (1975), the *U of Western Ontario (1976), and *Concordia U (1977). The association's official publication (variously titled) is *The Journal* (established in Kitchener, 1973, as the *Canadian Music Therapy Journal* with Earl A. Charboneau as editor). Until the mid-1970s most accredited music therapists in Canada had taken their training in England at the GSM, or in the USA. However, degree or diploma programs were established at the *UQAM in 1975 and at Capilano College, Vancouver, in 1976, and a course was begun at *McGill in 1978.

BIBLIOGRAPHY

'Music therapy as an approach to patient rehabilitation,' *The Recorder*, vol 17, Sep 1974

Underbakke, Lois. 'The music therapist,' *CFMTA Newsletter*, vol 30, Feb 1977

Pageau, Thérèse. 'La musicothérapie à l'hôpital Louis-Hippolyte Lafontaine,' *L'interdit*, Nov–Dec 1977

Smith, Beverley. 'Music therapy: "a powerful tool to alter moods",' Toronto *Globe and Mail*, 12 Jul 1979

Richer, Anne. 'Musique au thérapie pour soulager le cancer,' Montreal *La Presse*, 6 Dec 1980 (EAC, JPG)

La Musique (1919–24). Quebec City monthly music journal edited and published jointly by Hector Faber and Omer *Létourneau. The first issue, 15 Jan 1919, announced its aims: 'To give musicians a point of contact ... to stimulate their energies, and to interest the public in musical affairs.' Its contributors were drawn from among the best known figures in Quebec City's musical life at the time and included Joseph-Arthur *Bernier, Octave Bourdon, Henri and Blanche *Gagnon, J.-Alexandre *Gilbert, Louis *Gravel, Charles-Hughes *Lefebvre, Arthur *Letondal, Nazaire *LeVasseur, Olivier Maurault, Frédéric *Pelletier, and J.-Robert *Talbot. The usual offerings were biographical sketches, portraits and illustrations, reviews, news, and musical chronicles, of which the most important, 'Musique et musiciens à Québec' (15 Jan 1919–22 Dec 1922), was written by LeVasseur. In January 1923 the journal became a *Laval U publication and the official organ of the School of Music, whose staff members formed its board. Because of its appeal to a general audience, it was a valuable vehicle of musical culture, and its demise with the issue of April 1924 was justly lamented. (CH)

Musique Canadienne. Band organized in Quebec City in 1836 by Charles *Sauvageau. It replaced the Régiment d'Artillerie band (formed in 1831 by Jean-Chrysostome *Brauneis, but disbanded on its leader's death from cholera in 1832). According to Nazaire *LeVasseur Musique Canadienne was composed of three clarinets, a piccolo, a tuba, a bassoon, a trumpet, three hunting horns, two trombones, timpani, 'marmites,' triangle, and bass drum. Under Sauvageau's direction the band participated in several St-Jean-Baptiste parades and in many official ceremonies until its dissolution on the death of Sauvageau in 1849.

BIBLIOGRAPHY

LeVasseur, L.-Nazaire. 'Musique et musiciens à Québec,' *La Musique*, vol 1, Jul 1919

Roy, Pierre-Georges. 'La première fanfare Québécoise,' *BRH*, vol 43, 1937; rep *P-T*, 911, Dec 1948 GP

Muzak. Name of a company formed to record and program a specially prepared music product, bearing the same name as the company, for distribution mainly to public environments in which it is intended to affect its hearers psychologically in specific ways without drawing undue attention to itself or making any demand to be listened to consciously.

In Canada, as in 20-odd other countries, this US brand of programmed background music is ubiquitous. The brand-name has been so successful as to be used generically – like Xerox, Coke, and Kleenex. Its inventors and franchise-owners are quick to point out that not all background music is Muzak; there are several competing companies.

Mention should be made of one untypical rival: Omnison, established in Quebec in 1978 by Stéphane *Venne with the intention of capturing the Quebec market by using Quebec chansons as the base material. While the idea was not original (Muzak added 23 chansons to its repertoire in the late 1970s and planned to add more), Venne's project had the advantage of being totally of Quebec origin at a time when such a regional commitment was important in the province. By 1979 the Omnison repertoire contained about 3500 unimpeachably Quebec items (the eventual aim was 5000), and a by-product had been issued: a six-record album, subsidized by a grant from the Quebec Ministry of Communications and distributed by *Kébec-Disc, containing smooth instrumental versions of 108 tunes by 58 Quebec *chansonniers. (The album was distributed abroad by RCI.)

Muzak Inc started in New York in 1934. Its product was nurtured by the 'music while you work' movement in World War II, and the company began its international growth in the immediate post-war period. Its earliest Canadian franchises date from 1946; by the 1970s, four major franchise-owners covered virtually all of urban Canada.

Distinguishing Muzak from at least some of its competitors ('soothing-sound' radio stations, tape-rental libraries) are its controlled choice and arrangement of musical selections and its special programming approach. Material is chosen from a wide popular-song and show-tune repertoire; ethnic, religious (including gospel), country, and Hawaiian pieces are avoided, as are songs of emotional passion, protest songs, and songs whose catchiness might incite physical responses (for example, rhythmic clapping). Though almost all the melodies used are from songs, arrangements for Muzak are purely instrumental.

These arrangements feature steady tempo, steady solo-tutti relationship, uninterrupted phrase-continuity, smooth joins between sections, absence of dramatic highs or sudden silences, and a definite beginning and end to each item (rather than the expressive or impressionistic fade-out effects of commercial recordings). Muzak describes itself in promotional literature as 'music with the entertainment value removed,' a vaguely pleasurable musical sound that 'does not require conscious listening.'

Muzak moreover regards itself as 'a technique of contemporary management,' and therefore not a medium of art or entertainment. Its programming distinguishes three services respectively available by contract to offices, industrial plants, and public areas (one might term them the white-collar, the blue-collar, and the all-purpose). The office and industrial services arrange songs in 15-minute groups (separated by 15-minute breaks), each showing a general tempo sequence from slow to quick. The intensity and pace of the groups themselves also increase and decrease over a workday cycle corresponding to highs and lows of workers' monotony or other environmental and psychological factors determined by the New York office's 'human engineering department.' In these two services, surveys commissioned by the company demonstrate Muzak's positive effects in combating fatigue and monotony, decreasing error rates and job turnover rates, and increasing productivity (especially, as one promotional pamphlet says, with those of 'lower educational background') – and therefore also profits.

The 'public' service is similar in repertoire but more continuous, since besides its mood function it is intended to 'mask' ambient sounds (conversation, the clatter of dishes, shopping-carts, and cash registers). Public areas infiltrated by Muzak include restaurants, supermarkets, banks, car salesrooms, apartment elevators, school corridors, and funeral homes. It has been installed in many doctors' and dentists' offices and is also used as a supplement to anaesthesia in some hospital operating rooms. When a caller by phone to the Muzak Inc office is placed on 'hold' he or she is treated to Muzak. A separate service by mobile tapes covers planes and trains.

Licensed to convey its product by wireless radio and phone lines in Canada, Muzak Inc thereby has been subject to *CRTC Canadian-content regulations. Thus, since the early 1970s a certain portion of its recording has been done in Canadian studios by Canadian performers. Its repertoire has remained overwhelmingly of US origin, its arrangements entirely so. It has paid performing-rights royalties to Canadian licensing bodies for the use of copyrighted songs.

The Canadian composer and writer R. Murray *Schafer has questioned the validity of Muzak's claim to 'mask' less desirable sounds such as factory machines or supermarket clatter. He has satirized the famous brand-name, calling it 'Moozak' and has described the product, in its growing ubiquity, as an invasion of privacy and a denial of freedom of choice. He also sees in Muzak the seed of a general dulling of aesthetic sensitivity, whereby the inescapable exposure to its quasi-music could make unwary ears gradually less and less receptive to the conscious listening experiences not only of true art- and entertainment-music but also of the natural environment.

BIBLIOGRAPHY

Magner, Brian. 'The cocoon of sound Muzak spins,' Toronto *Globe Magazine*, 25 Dec 1959

Noble, June. 'Rings on her fingers and bells on her toes, she shall have Muzak wherever she goes,' Toronto *Telegram*, 2 Nov 1968

Winters, Kenneth. 'And, says Kenneth Winters, it must stop,' ibid

Hertz, Kenneth. 'Sounds ubiquitous,' *Montreal Scene*, 19 Nov 1977

Lanken, Dane. 'The sweet sound of aural soma,' *Recorder*, vol 20, Jun 1978

Levitch, Gerald. 'Up to our ears,' *(Toronto Star) The City*, 1 Apr 1979

Beaulieu, Pierre. 'Un "Muzak" québécois,' Montreal *La Presse*, 24 Feb 1979

Petrowski, Nathalie. 'Et en avant la Musak!' Montreal *Le Devoir*, 24 Feb 1979 JB

'My Ain Folk.' Song sub-titled 'A ballad of home,' words by Wilfrid Mills and music by Laura *Lemon, written in England and published (1904) by Boosey & Co, New York. The lyrics are in English with mild concessions to Scottish dialect and express an emigrant's longing for the home country. One of the most popular ballads by a Canadian-born composer, 'My Ain Folk' was recorded on 78s by Clara Butt, the Canadian-born tenor Craig Campbell, Louise Homer, Maggie Teyte, and several other singers (listed in *Roll Back the Years*). The melody also was recorded on a piano roll, and a 78 was made by the Harry *Thomas Trio. Sheet-music sales have persisted.

***My Fur Lady*.** The 1957 *McGill U 'Red and White Revue' which proved so popular that it toured Canada 1957–8 giving 402 performances in 82 centres. Its book was by Timothy Porteous and Donald MacSween, its lyrics were by Porteous to music by James de B. Domville, Galt *MacDermot, and Harry Garber, and additional songs were by Roy Wolvin. Orchestrations were by Ed *Assaly and choreography by Brian and Olivia Macdonald. It was premiered 7 Feb 1957 in Montreal by McGill U students. Discontinued briefly while the cast returned to its studies, it was reopened in Montreal 23 May 1957 under the auspices of the McGill U Graduate's Society, then played at the *Stratford Festival as a fringe attraction before beginning a national tour. A satirical look at the Canadian Establishment, *My Fur Lady* recounts the search of Princess Aurora Borealis (the contralto Anne *Golden) of 'Mukluko' ('near' Baffin Island) for a husband, in order to retain her country's independence from Canada. The music combined 1940s sentimentality, 1950s rock, and various elements of jazz, while the lyrics reflected the political events of the times. *My Fur Lady* was recorded 12 Jun 1957 by the original cast (MRS-LPM 5).

BIBLIOGRAPHY

'The triumph of *My Fur Lady*,' *The McGill You Knew: An Anthology of Memories 1920–1960*, ed Edgar Andrew Collard (Don Mills, Ont, 1975)

Fulford, Robert. 'My Fur Lady: the McGill show that grossed a million,' *SatN*, Mar 1977 SW

'My Own Canadian Home.' Patriotic verse known in the late 19th century as 'Canada's National Song.' It was published in 1887 in Saint John, NB, by its author, Edwin G. Nelson, a local bookseller, and was given several musical settings – the first by Nelson and another (1888) by Thomas Morley, the conductor of the Saint John Oratorio Society. Morley McLaughlin's setting was published in 1890 by the Maritime Lithography Co, Halifax and Saint John, and E. Cadwallader's appeared the same year in the Saint John *Daily Telegraph*. McLaughlin's proved the most popular, selling over 1.5 million copies according to an 1896 report. Widely sung in Maritime schools and played in an arrangement for band, it was reprinted several times in Saint John newspapers and was included in *Whaley-Royce Edition of Select Choruses and Part Songs* (Toronto 1912). Though its popularity had faded by World War II, the song was revived and adopted (17 Dec 1967) as the official song of Saint John. Another 'My Own Canadian Home,' with text and music written by the Toronto songwriter Florence M. Benjamin and arranged by Jules *Brazil, was published in 1921 by the composer.

BIBLIOGRAPHY

' "My Own Canadian Home" too fine to be forgotten,' *CanComp*, 23, Nov 1967 MM

MYRAND, Ernest. Historian, publicist, librarian, b Quebec City 29 Jun 1854, d there 31 May 1921. After studying at *Laval U, he joined *Le Canadien* as a journalist under the supervision of that Quebec daily's editor, Israël Tarte. Later, at the Palais de justice in Quebec City, he held a position which enabled him to pursue his historical research. In 1902 he was appointed registrar in the provincial secretary's office and in 1912 he became the librarian of the Quebec Legislative Assembly. He was elected to the Royal Society of Canada in 1909. In addition to his numerous historical works he published *Noëls anciens de la Nouvelle-France* (Quebec City 1899, 1907, Montreal 1913, 1926), the first historical study of a subject related to music in Canada.

BIBLIOGRAPHY

Savard, René. 'Bio-bibliographie d'Ernest Myrand,' unpubl BLS thesis, Montreal 1947

Hamel, Reginald, et al. *Dictionnaire pratique des auteurs québécois* (Montreal 1976)

Bélisle, Louis Alexandre. *Référence biographiques*, vol 4 (Montreal 1978)

Lebel, Maurice. 'Noëls anciens de la Nouvelle-France,' *Dictionnaire des oeuvres littéraires du Québec*, vol 1, ed Maurice Lemire (Montreal 1978) DM

N

NAMARO, Jimmy (James J.). Vibraphonist, marimbist, percussionist, band leader, arranger, composer, painter, b La Rosita, Mexico, 14 Apr 1915 or 1919, naturalized Canadian ca 1945. His family moved in 1921 to Hamilton, Ont, where he studied piano with Sid Walling and Eric Lewis. He made his radio debut as a marimba player on CHML, Hamilton, and was heard in his teens on CFRB, Toronto, and on the CBC.

Namaro pursued dual careers as the leader of pop or light jazz trios and quartets in nightclubs in Toronto (most memorably at the Polo Lounge of the Westover Hotel) and New York and as a popular CBC radio performer. He was a member 1943–59 of the *Happy Gang and bandleader or soloist on several other CBC programs. He conducted orchestras at the *CNE and in Toronto parks.

Namaro's discography includes LPs for *Sparton (*With Mallets A Four Thought*, SP 209), *Quality, Columbia, *RCA Camden (*The Latin Touch of Jimmy Namaro*, CAS-2357, and others), and the *CTL. He has composed music for CBC dramas (eg, the TV series 'Seaway'), for the Broadway production *Andorra*, and for ballet. He has also composed many jingles. He was an affiliate of BMI Canada (PRO Canada) until 1972, when he became a member of CAPAC.

In the late 1970s Namaro was living in San Diego. His paintings, in the primitive style, have had several exhibitions.

BIBLIOGRAPHY
Crandell, Ev. 'Jimmy Namaro,' *MSc*, 242, Jul–Aug 1968

(MM)

NAPIER, Ronald (Richard). Administrator, editor, b London 9 Feb 1921. He studied 1947–8 at the Guildhall School of Music and moved to Toronto in 1948. He joined BMI Canada (*PRO Canada) in 1956 and served 1959–69 as head of publishing and thereafter as manager of Concert Music Administration.

Napier served as chairman of the *CMLA 1965–6 and of the *CMPA 1966–8, president of the *CMCouncil 1973–5, and secretary of the *NYO 1974–6, vice-president of that organization 1976–8, and president 1978–9. He became a member of the advisory board of the International Library of Piano Music in 1973. An amateur musician, Napier studied recorder with Hugh *Orr and has edited Jean-Baptiste Loeillet's *Twelve Sonatas, Op 2* for recorder and continuo (BMIC 1966–7) and the collection *Baroque Arias and Dances* for recorder duet (BMIC 1968).

Through his Avondale Press Napier has published his own *A Guide to Canada's Composers* (Willowdale, Ont, 1973, 1976), Joseph *Macerollo's *Accordion Resource Book* (Willowdale 1980), and his wife's *A Guide to Good Singing* (Willowdale 1975). Napier's wife, Gerda Nielsen (b Breslau 17 Sep 1906, naturalized Canadian 1935, d Toronto 28 Jan 1977) was a dramatic soprano 1925–48 with the Dresden and Wiesbaden state operas and Covent Garden and a teacher 1948–76 in Toronto. CF

National and royal anthems. 'O Canada' and 'God Save the Queen' / 'Dieu sauve la Reine' were approved by Parliament in 1967 as Canada's national and royal anthems. Legislation to this effect was passed only in 1980, however, and applied only to 'O Canada.'

Some European countries had national anthems by the 18th century, but the practice of governmental designation of a particular patriotic song for national use became widespread only in the late 19th century.

The Canadian situation closely parallels the slow political evolution from colony to nation. After the fall of New France in 1760, the British anthem 'God Save the King,' which appeared in print in its modern form in 1744, came to be sung or played on appropriate occasions. The need for specifically Canadian national songs arose with the desire for self-government early in the 19th century, and a list of would-be national anthems, beginning with the year 1836, is provided under Patriotic songs. Many of these gained a fair measure of popularity (especially, though only among English-Canadians, 'The *Maple Leaf For Ever'), but by World War I one of them, Calixa *Lavallée's *'O Canada' (1880), had received acceptance, first among French-Canadians and after 1900 among English-Canadians.

Custom had made 'O Canada' and 'God Save the King (Queen)' the de facto national anthems of Canada, and in 1964 Prime Minister Lester Pearson proposed to take action regarding an *official* national anthem. Three years passed before a Special Joint Committee of the Senate and House of Commons on the National and Royal Anthems was appointed. The committee first met in February 1967; and on 12 Apr 1967 its unanimous recommendation – that 1 / the music of 'God Save the Queen' be designated the official royal anthem, 2 / the music of 'O Canada' be designated the official national anthem, and 3 / the Crown acquire the copyright to the music of 'O Canada'–was approved (but not legislated) by the House of Commons.

Later that year the committee was charged with considering the question of lyrics for the two anthems. With Rex *LeLacheur as music consultant it met 12 times and received more than 1000 proposed lyrics, in English and in French or a combination of the two. One submission, by Jo (Mme Jacques) Ouellet, presented a mixed bilingual verse of 'O Canada.'

In its report, presented in February 1968, the committee unanimously recommended that *one* verse of each anthem, in each of the two official languages, be adopted. For the English text of 'O Canada' the Robert Stanley Weir version of 1908 was recommended, with a few minor changes; for the French text of the royal anthem, the version that had been adopted in 1952 for the coronation of Queen Elizabeth II. The committee recommended also that 'steps be taken to commemorate in some appropriate and permanent form the originators of our National Anthem, i.e. Calixa Lavallée, Adolphe-Basile Routhier and Robert Stanley Weir.'

In October 1969 the offer by the G.V. *Thompson music-publishing firm to sell the copyright of the Weir 'O Canada' text to the Crown for the sum of one dollar was accepted, and the rights were vested formally in the government on 13 Oct 1970. A bill (C-158) to turn the committee's recommendations into law was introduced in the House of Commons in 1972 and in several other sessions. The bill still had not, however, come to debate in 1979. At last, on 27 Jun 1980, three days after the centenary of the song's first performance, the House of Commons passed Bill C-36, 'An act respecting the national anthem of Canada' / 'loi concernant l'hymne national du Canada,' which designates the words and music of 'O Canada' as national anthem and declares both as being in the public domain, allowing, however, for a later review of Weir's English words.

A custom had arisen according to which every concert, theatrical performance, and other public event began with a national song. In Toronto usually this was 'God Save the Queen,' in Montreal 'O Canada,' in Winnipeg 'O Canada' at the opening and 'God Save the Queen' at the end. When the Toronto city bylaw to this effect was abolished in 1967, the custom already was on the wane. Where the tradition persists – at gala openings, major sports events, and certain ceremonies – the two anthems often are performed in combination: the first six bars of 'God Save the Queen' followed by the first four bars and the last four bars of 'O Canada'; this combination is called the Vice-Regal Salute.

BIBLIOGRAPHY
Canada. 27th Parliament, second session. Special Joint Committee of the Senate and House of Commons on the National and Royal Anthems. *Minutes of Proceedings*. No. 1, 2 (1967), No. 3 (1968). Ottawa

(HK)

National Arts Centre / Centre national des arts. Theatre and auditorium complex situated on the west bank of the Rideau Canal in Ottawa and inaugurated in 1969. It is the outcome of a 1963 proposal to the government of Canada by the National Capital Arts Alliance, a citizens' group. In 1964 the government adopted the proposal and turned it into a project to commemorate Canada's centenary (1967), appointing G. Hamilton Southam (b Ottawa 19 Dec 1916) as co-ordinator in the Secretary of State Dept. The NAC Act, passed by Parliament in 1966, established an independent corporation under the jurisdiction of the Secretary of State to 'operate and maintain the centre, to develop the performing arts in the National Capital Region and to assist the *Canada Council in the development of the performing arts elsewhere in Canada.' The corporation's national board of trustees appointed Southam director-general of the centre beginning 1 Apr 1967 for a five-year term (renewed in 1972).

Two advisory committees, one for theatre and one for music, were set up to plan the facilities. The music committee, chaired by Louis *Applebaum, recommended a dual-purpose opera and concert hall; the theatre committee, a 900-seat theatre and a 300-seat studio. The approved design was by the architect Fred Lebensold of Montreal in collaboration with the acousticians Russell Johnson Associates. It encompassed the Theatre, the Studio, and the smaller, hexagonal Salon, all suitable for theatrical presentations, chamber concerts, and recitals; and the Opera for opera and concerts, with 2300 seats, none further than 33 m from a stage 33.6 m wide. The orchestra pit of the Opera can accommodate 110 musicians, and the acoustics may be altered to suit the sound of opera, orchestra, or choir by means of hydraulically controlled sounding boards and curtains in the ceiling and walls. For symphony concerts an acoustic shell can be lowered onto the stage.

The four theatre-auditoria, along with their vast shared lobby and performers' dressing rooms, restaurants, administrative offices, and subterranean parking facilities, are integrated in one large structure occupying 2.6 hectares on the canal bank. The sprawl of the centre draws integrity from the structural recurrence of the hexagon. The decors are more various; indeed many (the Opera curtain; the Salon doors; the chandeliers, tapestries, and hangings; the outdoor sculptures, etc) are individual works of art.

The centre was completed in 1969 at a cost of $46 million, and opened 2 June, in the Opera, with the National Ballet of Canada's performances of two commissioned ballets – *The Queen* by Grant Strate to music of Louis Applebaum, and *Kraanerg* by Roland Petit to music of Iannis Xenakis. Among other groups and solo performers who appeared in the two-week inaugural festival were the *MSO under Franz-Paul *Decker, with Jon *Vickers as soloist; the *TS in its last concert under the directorship of Seiji Ozawa, in a program which included Harry *Freedman's *Tangents*; the *NYO; the *Cassenti Players; the *Duo Pach; the *Manitoba University Consort; the *Orford String Quartet; the contralto Maureen *Forrester; the soprano Sylvia *Saurette; the chanteuse Monique *Leyrac; and the singer Gordon *Lightfoot. Gabriel *Charpentier's one-act opera *Orphée* was commissioned to open the Studio during the second week of the festival.

National Arts Centre, Ottawa

In the course of the next four years two organs were presented to the NAC by the Dutch-Canadian community 'in appreciation of the role played by Canadian troops in liberating the Netherlands in 1945.' Both organs were built by Flentrop Orgelbouw of Zaandam, Holland. The small, six-stop positiv organ was delivered in 1970. The large (8.2 m high, 2.7 tonne in weight) two-manual 21-stop tracker concert organ was delivered in 1973. Both can be stored and moved. They were inaugurated 7 Oct 1973 in a recital by Albert de Klerk, municipal organist of the City of Haarlem, Holland.

To fulfil the mandate set out in the NAC Act, the centre is required to mount productions of opera, ballet, and theatre; to present concerts and recitals; to send its resident orchestra and theatre companies on tour throughout Canada; and to invite other Canadian and foreign companies and performing artists to appear on its platforms. It also, initially, was to provide touring management services for Canadian performing artists and groups, but this function was assumed by a touring office created for the purpose in the Canada Council administration in 1973.

The music program of the centre was singularly successful during its first decade, particularly through the extraordinary distinction and tireless activity of the resident *National Arts Centre Orchestra (which made its debut 7 Oct 1969 under its conductor Mario *Bernardi) and through its summer opera and concert program *Festival Ottawa, begun in 1971 as Festival Canada, with Bernardi as artistic director and conductor and Andrée Gingras as festival administrator.

Performances by the residents, however, were only a part of the centre's larger music program which offered, for example, during the 1969–70 season, 65 orchestral, chamber, and choral concerts; 13 recitals; and 12 performances of opera, 39 of ballet and other dance, and 142 of different kinds of musical show. In the 1977–8 season the number of concerts had increased to 100; of opera performances, to 19.

Many performing organizations and individual artists, Canadian and foreign, appeared at the centre in the 1970s. Among the choirs were the *Festival Singers, the National Choir of Israel, the Ottawa Philharmonic, the *Toronto Mendelssohn Choir, and the *Vancouver Bach Choir; among chamber groups, the Beaux Arts Trio, *Canadian Brass, the Dalart Trio, the Fine Arts Quartet, the *Hertz Trio, the *Huggett Family, Les *Petits violons, the *SMCQ, and the Vermeer Quartet. Jazz and pop performers included the *Carlton Showband, Bruce *Cockburn, Diane *Dufresne, the *Irish Rovers, the Ramsay Lewis Trio, George Shearing, Gino *Vannelli, Gilles *Vigneault, Margaret Whiting, and the orchestras of Count Basie, Bob Crosby, Duke Ellington, Maynard *Ferguson, Guy *Lombardo, Freddy Martin, and Phil *Nimmons. Among visiting symphony orchestras (besides the MSO and the TS in annual visits) were the Chicago Symphony, the Cleveland Orchestra, the Leipzig Gewandhaus Orchestra, the *Hamilton Philharmonic Orchestra, the Scottish Chamber Orchestra, the *Vancouver SO, the *Winnipeg SO, and the Czech, Israel, Moscow, and New York philharmonics; bands included the Central Band of the Canadian Forces and the band of the RCMP. Among solo performers one could cite Geza Anda, Donald *Bell, Lazar Berman, Norman *Brooks, Edith *Butler, Janina *Fialkowska, Louise *Forestier, Marek *Jablonski, Bruno *Laplante, Jaime Laredo, Alicia de Larrocha, Liberace, Michel *Louvain, Mari-Elizabeth *Morgen, Nana Mouskouri, Anne *Murray, Vladimir *Orloff, Arthur *Ozolins, Luciano Pavarotti, Leonard Rose, Frederica von Stade, Elisabeth Schwarzkopf, and Steven *Staryk. The Anna Wyman Dance Theatre, the Ballet Folklorico of Mexico, the *COC, the D'Oyly Carte, Entre-Six, Les Grands Ballets Canadiens, the *Opéra du Québec, the Royal Winnipeg Ballet, the Toronto Dance Theatre, the Peking Opera, and the Shanghai Ballet of the People's Republic of China have all made visits. The centre has been host, also, to productions of Canadian operas (*Louis Riel*, **Seabird Island*) and Canadian musicals and revues (**Kronberg: 1582*, **Les hauts et les bas d'la vie d'une diva: Sarah Ménard par eux-mêmes*, and *The Legend of the Dumbells*).

According to the 1977–8 annual report, more than 800 performances were attended that season by audiences totalling more than 800,000 (nearly double the first year's attendance) and 94.4 per cent of that number were accounted for by subscribers. Production, promotion, and general operation cost the centre $13.65 million during that performing year, $4.6 million of which was recovered in box-office receipts, touring revenues, and CBC broadcast fees, and $8.7 million through an appropriation voted by Parliament. The deficit of more than $700,000 was reduced by about two-fifths the following season. These figures show that though federal government subsidy of the NAC's far-reaching program has been substantial, it has not been unlimited.

Three levels of administration affect or control the centre's musical activities. As general director, Donald MacSween (b Montreal 1935 and general director of the National Theatre School in Montreal 1973–7) succeeded Hamilton Southam at the top level in 1977. In addition to his duties as conductor and artistic director of the NACO and Festival Ottawa, Mario Bernardi succeeded Jean-Marie *Beaudet as music director for the centre in 1969. The music director is assisted by the music administrator – Hugh *Davidson 1971–3, Guy *Huot 1973–5, and Kenneth *Murphy (previously manager of the NACO) 1975–8, succeeded by Michael Aze. Lawrence Freiman, first chairman of the NAC board, was succeeded by François Mercier in 1969. Arthur Gelber became chairman in 1978 and was succeeded by Pauline McGibbon in 1980.

BIBLIOGRAPHY

Mercer, Ruby. 'An inspiration and a challenge,' *OpCan*, Sep 1969

Beckett, Barbara. 'The National Arts Centre ... eight months after,' *CanComp*, 49, Apr 1970

Cowle, Alan H. 'The National Arts Centre organ and attendant reflections,' *RCCO Q*, Jan 1974

Edinborough, Arnold. 'After five years the National Arts Centre has finally made it,' *PfAC*, Summer 1974

'National Arts Centre,' *OpCan*, Oct 1975

Schiff, Marvin. 'Donald MacSween new NAC chief,' Toronto *Globe and Mail*, 27 Oct 1976

'All the culture that money can buy,' *Maclean's*, 16 Oct 1978

Allen, Carroll. 'The National Arts Centre,' *Homemaker's Magazine*, Jul–Aug 1979

MacSween, Donald. 'Canada has the NAC,' *OpCan*, Summer 1980

Annual reports (Ottawa 1968–) KW (CF)

National Arts Centre Orchestra / Orchestre du Centre national des arts. The only orchestra in North America to be virtually state-supported. It was formed in 1969 and is resident at the *National Arts Centre, Ottawa. Mario *Bernardi, its first conductor, and Jean-Marie *Beaudet, then music director of the arts centre, selected the players after auditioning many candidates, especially Canadians, several of whom were pursuing careers abroad. A classical orchestra (44 players, later 46) was deemed practical for the capital city, where visiting Canadian and foreign orchestras could be counted upon to provide programs of heavily scored works. The NACO's repertoire comprises the baroque and the classical, certain 19th-century music, and much contemporary music including, by 1979, 17 works commissioned from Canadian composers. The first of these was Murray *Adaskin's *Diversion for Orchestra*, premiered at the inaugural concert 7 Oct 1969. (See list below.)

The NACO often is enlarged to accommodate specific orchestral works. It also accompanies choral societies, visiting ballet and opera companies, and the NAC's summer series of opera presentations, *Festival Ottawa (founded as Festival Canada in 1971). In Ottawa the NACO annually gives 24 subscription concerts in three evening series, a Family Pops Series of six evening concerts, a morning series of three Young People's Concerts, and many student concerts. It also sponsors Music for a Sunday Afternoon, five or six chamber concerts for which ensembles from the orchestra are coached by established visiting artists and groups.

The NACO fulfils its mandate as Canada's national orchestra through command performances on state occasions and extensive Canadian tours. It has toured western Canada in 1971, 1974, and 1977 and the Atlantic provinces in 1973 and 1975 and also has performed in northern Ontario and Quebec. It appears often in Toronto and Montreal. In 1973 the orchestra toured Europe, performing in London, Versailles, Rome, Venice, Warsaw, Riga, Moscow, Leningrad, and other cities, and was described as 'an already mature and accomplished ensemble ... there was a splendid litheness and buoyancy in the rhythms and suppleness in the shaping of the melodic lines' (London *Daily Telegraph*, 2 Jun 1973). In 1978 it returned to Europe to perform in Germany and Italy. The orchestra made its first US appearance at

National Arts Centre Orchestra under Mario Bernardi

Alice Tully Hall, Lincoln Center, New York, in 1972 and also performed at the Kennedy Center, Washington, in 1973. It made its Carnegie Hall debut in 1974 and toured the USA and Mexico in 1975. The NACO was prominent during Canada Week in the US bicentennial celebrations at the Kennedy Center during 1976. In the same year, it toured the eastern USA, giving 10 concerts, including one in Carnegie Hall and another in Boston.

The orchestra has featured many Canadians as soloists, among them Robert *Aitken, Otto *Armin, Pierrette *Alarie, Donald *Bell, Mario Bernardi himself, Colette *Boky, Pierre *Boutet, Liona *Boyd, Denis *Brott, *Canadian Brass, Claude *Corbeil, Mark DuBois, Raymond *Dudley, Lorand *Fenyves, Janina *Fialkowska, Nicholas *Fiore, Maureen *Forrester, Gaston *Germain, Erica *Goodman, Elizabeth Benson *Guy, Ida *Haendel, Sheila *Henig, Diedre *Irons, Marek *Jablonski, Sharon Krause, Anton *Kuerti, Gabrielle *Lavigne, Bernard *Lagacé, André *Laplante, Gwenlynn *Little, Judy *Loman, Louis *Lortie, Malcolm Lowe, Hugh *McLean, Phyllis *Mailing, Lois *Marshall, Mari-Elizabeth *Morgen, Mary *Morrison, Zara *Nelsova, Vladimir *Orloff, *Duo Pach, Walter *Prystawski (the NACO concertmaster), Louis *Quilico, Karen Quinton, Gary *Relyea, Joseph *Rouleau, Jean-Paul *Sévilla, Robert *Silverman, Léopold *Simoneau, Steven *Staryk, Janet *Stubbs, Janice Taylor, Tsuyoshi *Tsutsumi, and Ronald *Turini. Canadian or resident Canadian guest conductors have included Kazuyoshi Akiyama, Raffi *Armenian, Jean-Marie Beaudet, Boris *Brott, Franz-Paul *Decker, Mario *Duschenes, Victor *Feldbrill, Piero Gamba, Harman Haakman, Pierre *Hétu, and Boyd *Neel.

Many foreign conductors have appeared as guests of the NACO, including Geza Anda, Vladimir Ashkenazy, Rudolf Barshai, Charles Dutoit, Kiril Kondrashin, Raymond Leppard, Karl Münchinger, Karl Richter, Maxim Shostakovitch, Walter *Susskind, and Sir Michael Tippett. Among foreign solo artists to appear as guests have been Elly Ameling, Martha Argerich, Claudio Arrau, Janet Baker, Robert Casadesus, Phyllis Curtin, Pierre Fournier, Kyung-Wha Chung, Jessye Norman, John Ogdon, Leonard Rose, Peter Serkin, Janos Starker, and Frederica von Stade.

Ken *Murphy was orchestra manager 1969–75, followed by Carl *Little, who was succeeded by Andreas Hackh in 1978.

The following works have been commissioned for the NACO, by the NAC unless otherwise indicated (the date is that of the premiere):

*Adaskin *Diversion for Orchestra* 1969
*Beecroft *Improvvisazioni Concertanti No. 2* 1971
*Bissell *Cantate Domino* (commissioned by the NACO Assn) 1977
*Colgrass *Delta* 1979
*Fleming *Hexad* 1972, *Our Mind Was the Singer* 1973
*Freedman *Tapestry* 1973
*Gellman *Overture for Ottawa* 1974
*Hétu *Antinomie* 1977
*MacDermot *Incident at Turtle Rock* 1975
*Mather *Au Château de Pompairain* 1977
*Prévost *Évanescence* 1970
*Ridout *George the Third, His Lament* 1976
*Schafer *East* 1973, *Cortège* 1977
*Somers *Those Silent, Awe-Filled Spaces* 1978
*Tremblay *Jeux de solstices* 1974

DISCOGRAPHY (with Bernardi as conductor)

Beethoven *Symphony No. 1* – Malcolm Forsyth *Sagittarius*. Canadian Brass. 1976. CBC SM-328
– *Symphony No. 2* – Adaskin *Diversion for Orchestra*. 1977. CBC SM-333
– *Symphony No. 4* – Morel *Esquisse*. 1977. CBC SM-332
– *Symphony No. 8* – Weinzweig *Ballet Suite from the Red Ear of Corn*. 1977. CBC SM-345
Brahms *Serenade No. 1*. 1972. CBC SM-197
Italian Arias: Rossini – Monteverdi – Paisiello – Leoncavallo. von Stade mezzo. 1977. Col M35138
Mozart *Flute Concerto No. 2* K314; *Concerto* for flute and harp K299. Cram fl, Goodman hp. 1974. CBC SM-262
– *Violin Concerto No. 3* K216 – Haydn *Symphony No. 83*. Staryk vn. 1971. CBC SM-174
– *Violin Concerto No. 5* K219; *Serenata notturna No. 6* K239 – Beecroft *Improvvisazioni Concertanti No. 2*. Staryk vn. 1972. RCI 382/RCA KRL 1-0007
– *Symphony No. 38* K504 – Eckhardt-Gramatté *Triple Concerto*. Collins tpt, Morton cl, Corey bn. 1974. CBC SM-272
– *Symphony No. 39* K543 – Tchaikovsky *Variations on a Rococo Theme for Cello, Op 33*. Brott vc. 1974, 1976. CBC SM-306
– *Symphony No. 41* K551; *Ombra felice* – Somers *Five Songs for Dark Voice*. Forrester alto. 1969. RCI 286/RCA LSC 3172
Prokofiev *Symphonie classique* – Prévost *Évanescence* – Haydn 4 *Arias*. Alarie sop, Simoneau ten. 1970. RCI 332/RCA VCCS 1640
Schafer *East*. 1977. RCI 434
Schubert *Symphony No. 6* – Wagner *Siegfried Idyll*. 1972. CBC SM-201
Tippett *Fantasia Concertante on a Theme of Corelli; Divertimento on 'Sellinger's Round.'* Prystawski vn, Roy vn, Whitton vc. 1975. CBC SM-287

BIBLIOGRAPHY

Applebaum, Louis. 'A Proposal for the Musical Development of the Capital Region,' unpubl report (Ottawa 1965)
'L'Orchestre du Centre national des arts,' *Jmc*, Apr 1969
Van Vlasselaer, J.J. 'The NAC Orchestra in Germany and Italy,' *Mcan*, 36, Aug 1978
Littler, William. 'Bernardi and his band,' *The Canadian*, 8–9 Sep 1979
Southam, Hamilton. 'Genesis of an orchestra,' *Prelude*, vol 2, Sep–Oct 1979
Ericson, Raymond. 'Music notes: here come the Canadians from Ottawa,' *New York Times*, 14 Oct 1979
Bernardi, Mario. 'The growth of an orchestra – 1969–79,' Toronto *Globe and Mail*, 27 Oct 1979 CF, KW

The National Chorus of Toronto. A 200-voice choir assembled to sing 18 Apr 1903 on 'National Night' in Toronto, one of the events of the *Cycle of Musical Festivals of British music conducted that year in Canada by the president of the RAM, Sir Alexander Mackenzie.

Prepared by Albert *Ham, the choir was so successful on its first appearance that it continued to perform annually until its dissolution on Ham's retirement in 1928. Each concert featured a famous guest (among them Vera Barstow, Maggie Teyte, Efrem Zimbalist, Giovanni Martinelli, and Pablo Casals) who shared the program and often performed with the choir. When required, a boys' choir from St James' Cathedral assisted.

During the early years the chorus was accompanied by the New York SO, the Chicago SO, and other such orchestras. It was the first (1910) choral group to perform with the *Welsman *TSO. However, the choir was known mainly for its repertoire of short unaccompanied British pieces.

BIBLIOGRAPHY

'National Chorus souvenir issue,' *MCan*, vol 3, Jan 1909
'The National Chorus, a short history,' *Sunday World*, 30 Jul 1923
'The National Chorus,' *CQR*, vol 10, Spring 1928 RPn

The National Competitive Festival of Music. Annual competition initiated in 1972 by the *FCMF in co-operation with the *Canadian Bureau for the Advancement of Music and sponsored by the Canadian Imperial Bank of Commerce. The FCMF and the Quebec Music Festivals had organized a national competition of a similar kind in Saint John, NB, in 1967, but it was not repeated.

By 1980 the National Competitive Festival of Music was still being held regularly in August or September at the *CNE, Toronto. To be eligible to perform in the festival competitors must have won city, then provincial competitions in piano, voice, strings, brass, woodwinds, or (beginning in 1975) instrumental ensemble.

Scholarships have been awarded to first-, second-, and third-place winners in each category, and in 1974 the Bank of Commerce Rose Bowl was introduced to reward the most distinguished performer at the final concert of winners. Rose bowl winners have included the cellist Cameron Lowe in 1974, the Riverdale String Trio in 1975, the pianist Douglas Finch in 1976, the pianist Walter Prossnitz in 1977, the oboist Elizabeth Lambert in 1978, the mezzo-soprano Irena Welhasch in 1979, and the violinist Martin Chalifour in 1980.

In 1973 the FCMF established the custom of announcing the winners of the George S. Mathieson and City of Lincoln trophies (administered by the federation and awarded annually to the outstanding junior and senior choirs heard in competition festivals across Canada) at the final concert of the festival.

The National Concert Bureau. A forerunner 1969–74 of the *Canada Council's Touring Office. The bureau was established as a non-profit enterprise with a grant from the Canada Council to provide management for outstanding young Canadian performers. It was directed by Edith Binnie, was housed at the *U of Toronto Faculty of Music, and initially managed the *Orford String Quartet, Garnet *Brooks, Denis *Brott, Arthur *Ozolins, Roxolana *Roslak, Claude *Savard, and the pianist Stephanie Sebastian, all chosen by a national panel of judges. Other artists, added later on the recommendation of the Canada Council, were Adele *Armin, Anna *Chornodolska, Gisela *Depkat, Gabrielle *Lavigne, the violinist Malcolm Lowe, Mari-Elizabeth *Morgen, Gary *Relyea, and William *Tritt.

The bureau's functions were transferred in 1974 to the Touring Office, Ottawa.

National Conservatory Ltd. See Conservatoire national de musique.

National Film Board of Canada (NFB) / **Office national du film du Canada** (ONF). An organization created by the Canadian government following the adoption of a National Film Act in 1939. The NFB's mandate was to produce and distribute films serving the national interest and intended specifically to make Canada better known both to Canadians and to people of other countries. At the invitation of the federal government, the British documentary maker John Grierson came to Canada in 1938 to study the situation of the government's film production, at that time the responsibility of the Canadian Government Motion

Picture Bureau. It was his report that prompted the National Film Act, the effect of which, in the context of the times, was to make the NFB during its first years a wartime propaganda office. In 1942, however, a production and animation department was created around the exceptional skills of Norman *McLaren, who perfected a technique of composing music directly onto film. A revision of the Act in 1950 removed all possibility of direct governmental intervention in the administration of the organization. In 1956 the production centre of the NFB moved its technical installations to Montreal, but the head office remained in Ottawa. After this, production was divided between two autonomous sectors, French and English, and yielded full-length films and short features, documentaries, fiction films, informational films, animated films, etc. The board has continued to report to Parliament through the secretary of state.

By 1980 there had been three official music directors at the NFB: Louis *Applebaum 1942–8, Eugene *Kash 1948–50, and Robert *Fleming 1958–70. From the beginning the NFB included composers – notably Maurice *Blackburn and Eldon *Rathburn – on its permanent staff. Others were hired on contract, among them Howard *Cable, Neil *Chotem, Luc *Cousineau, Larry *Crosley, André *Gagnon, Phyllis Gummer, Yvan *Landry, Michel *Longtin, Oskar *Morawetz, Barbara *Pentland, Godfrey *Ridout, Tony *Romandini, Morris *Surdin, Vic *Vogel, and John *Weinzweig. The board chose music as the subject of several films, including *The Singing Pipes / Le Vent qui chante* (1945, devoted to *Casavant Frères), *Story of a Violin* (1947, with the participation of George *Heinl), and a film on musical notation in Braille (1950, made with Paul *Doyon). Composers, performers, choirs, and orchestras also have been the subjects of films: Paul *Anka, the *Leslie Bell Singers, Jean *Carignan, Glenn *Gould, Marek *Jablonski, Willie *Lamothe, Félix *Leclerc (*Les Brûlés*), Don *Messer, Wilfrid *Pelletier, R. Murray *Schafer, the *TSO under Sir Ernest *MacMillan, Gilles *Vigneault, and Healey *Willan. In 1975 *MusiCanada*, a full-length film on the different facets of Canadian musical life, was produced by Malca Gilson and Tony Ianzelo to mark *World Music Week. Among the best-known artists appearing in the film were *Beau Dommage, *Canadian Brass, Maureen *Forrester, Glenn Gould, Paul Horn, the *Lyric Arts Trio, the *NACO, the *NYO, and Les Grands Ballets Canadiens.

In 1980 the NFB maintained numerous production studios across Canada and offices in New York, Chicago, London, Paris, and Sydney. Some NFB films have been adapted into as many as 60 different languages and distributed for non-commercial use by more than 80 diplomatic missions and commercial agencies in Canada and abroad. Local showings have been assured by 92 viewing centres in Canada's main cities, and films have been lent free of charge to both individuals and groups. Copies of films, and in some cases video tapes, have been purchasable. In 1975 the NFB began producing films for the CBC and, reciprocally, handling showings of some CBC films. By 1980 more than 3000 films had been produced, including a large number presented at international festivals, and the NFB had received over 1800 awards, including six Oscars (Hollywood), three Palmes d'Or (Cannes), and five Robert Flaherty awards (England).

See also Films; Film scores.

BIBLIOGRAPHY

'National Film Board stresses original scores,' *CanComp*, 5, Jan 1966

Grierson, John. Letter to Lou Applebaum. *CanComp*, 38, Mar 1969

Véronneau, Pierre, et al. *Le Cinéma canadien* (Montreal, Paris 1978)

– and Dumesnil, Thérèse. 'L'Office national du film: chasseur d'images depuis 40 ans,' *Perspectives*, vol 21, 25 Aug 1979

Musique et Cinéma

The National Film Board of Canada issues annotated catalogues of films in current distribution. (DM, ST)

National Library of Canada / Bibliothèque nationale du Canada. Created as the Canadian Bibliographic Centre in 1950, it was expanded into the National Library in 1953 and administered jointly with the existing Public Archives of Canada under the direction of W. Kaye Lamb until his retirement in 1968. The two federal government departments have continued to occupy the same building (opened in 1967) in Ottawa but are separate entities. Guy Sylvestre was appointed National Librarian in 1968.

The main tasks of the library include collecting Canadian imprints and literature of Canadian interest; compiling the national bibliography, *Canadiana*; building a comprehensive collection of materials in disciplines supporting Canadian studies and of selected materials in other areas, in order to supplement, through interlibrary loan, the resources of other Canadian libraries; and providing a reference service to patrons in person and by telephone and Telex. Also included in these tasks are liaison with other government libraries and research in library technology and bibliography.

Patrons may consult holdings at the library and, for example, listen to records or play scores on a piano, but items may be borrowed only through other libraries (periodicals are included, but sound recordings, rare and fragile materials, and manuscripts are not available for loan).

The Music Division, part of the Public Services Branch, was established in 1970 under Helmut *Kallmann and consists of a printed collection, a recorded sound collection, and a manuscript collection. In 1979 the division held about 11,000 books, 7500 printed scores, 42,000 pieces of sheet music, 600 titles of music periodicals, 30,000 concert programs, 11,000 information files, 4000 picture files, 35,000 sound recordings, and 150 manuscript and archival collections. (A list of some of the last is provided in the Archives entry.)

Many of the printed materials and most of the programs, recordings, and manuscripts are Canadian in content. In fact, the NL of C is one of the few national libraries striving for comprehensive coverage of its country's musical documentation. In 1980 its collection of musical Canadiana was the largest in existence and unlikely to be superseded in this distinction. Among the first components of the collection were copyright deposit copies of Canadian sheet music from Confederation on (with gaps), scores – Canadian and foreign – that were transferred from the Library of Parliament, the record collection assembled by Edward *Moogk as a Centennial (1967) project, and the papers of Healey *Willan, acquired in 1969. Further growth came through the legal deposit of printed music and musical literature (1951) and sound recordings (1969) and, in the 1970s, largely through the acquisition of the papers and libraries of many Canadian musicians and through the establishment of extensive information, concert-program, pamphlet, and picture files. In 1980, 250 Canadian music periodicals were represented and the division held about 200 pre-Confederation musical imprints.

To encourage and assist research in Canadian music history, the Music Division has developed certain useful finding aids, such as indexes of biographical articles about Canadian musicians, of Canadian instrument manufacturers, of concert-giving organizations, and of music publishers. The division maintains a national Union Catalogue of Canadian Music Publications up to 1950 which lists approximately 12,000 items.

Extensive non-Canadian holdings exist only in the printed collection. These include a general reference collection, the basic books and scores of world literature, and more specialized collections. Among the last are a collection of some 19,000 French song publications of the 19th century (although in many cases only the cover illustration is held) and the information files (about 500,000 items) of the British music lexicographer Percy Scholes, whose library forms the nucleus of the book and score collection. Non-Canadian holdings in other areas are the Dr. Andre and Pearl Ross Collection of some 500 spoken-word recordings by famous actors, statesmen, and monarchs of the early 20th century; sound recordings from about 1890 onwards, including what is possibly the largest collection held anywhere of early Emile *Berliner recordings; and, scattered throughout the archival holdings, letters and other autograph writings by composers such as Clara Schumann, Liszt, Elgar, Vaughan Williams, Hindemith, Milhaud, and Stravinsky.

Besides mounting numerous exhibitions at conferences and at the *CNE in Toronto, the Music Division has provided regular showcase displays in the library and has held a large number of special exhibitions, eg, 'Healey Willan, the Man and His Music' (1972), '85 Years of Recorded Sound' (1975), 'Percy Scholes 1877–1958' (1977), and 'Alexis Contant: the Composer and His Milieu' (1979).

From 1977 to 1979 the NL of C carried out a survey of music library resources in Canada, and the findings were to be published as a report and directory – *Music Resources in Canadian Collections (Research Collections in Canadian Libraries, No. 7) / Ressources musicales de bibliothèques canadiennes (Collections de recherche des bibliothèques canadiennes, No. 7)* (Ottawa 1981). Also among the library's publications are a *Healey Willan Catalogue* (1972, suppl expected 1981) by Giles *Bryant, Edward B. Moogk's *Roll Back the Years* (1975), an *Alexis Contant Catalogue* (expected 1981) by Stephen Willis, and *Music Publishing in the Canadas: 1800–1867 / L'Edition musicale au Canada: 1800–1867* (1981) by Maria Calderisi.

The Music Division is the Canadian headquarters for the RISM and RIdIM projects of the International Association of Music Libraries. It has been a major source for information published in *EMC*.

See also Bibliography; Discography; the Lande Collection; Libraries.

BIBLIOGRAPHY

Kallmann, Helmut. 'The Percy Scholes Collection: nucleus for a National Music Library,' *CMJ*, vol 2, Spring 1958

Lamb, W. Kaye. 'Canadian library of recorded sound,' *CMLA Newsletter*, May 1969

Kallmann, Helmut. 'The Music Division of the National Library: the first five years,' *CMB*, 10, Spring–Summer 1975

Potvin, Gilles. 'Pour musicologues et chercheurs,' Montreal *Le Devoir*, 10 Jan 1976

Wees, Ian. *The National Library of Canada: Twenty-five Years After / La Bibliothèque nationale du Canada: vingt-cinq ans après* (Ottawa 1978)

Reports on the Music Division appear in *Musicanada* in many issues beginning with no. 30, November 1976.

HK

National Museum of Man. See National Museums of Canada.

National Museums of Canada / Musées nationaux du Canada. Crown corporation created in 1967 and comprising the National Gallery of Canada / Galerie nationale du Canada, the National Museum of Man / Musée national de l'Homme, the National Museum of Natural Sciences / Musée national des sciences naturelles, the National Museum of Science and Technology / Musée national des sciences et de la technologie, and the Canadian War Museum / Musée canadien de la guerre. The corporation reports to the Minister of Communications. Only the National Museum of Man is of prime importance to music, though the National Gallery owns paintings of musical interest, some of which are reproduced as illustrations in *EMC* (see also Art, visual), and the National Museum of Science and Technology owns sound reproduction equipment of historical significance.

Formed in 1842, the Museum Branch of the Geological Survey of Canada / Musée de la Commission géologique du Canada moved into the Victoria Memorial Museum building at Metcalfe and McLeod streets in Ottawa in 1911. The name National Museum of Canada was adopted in 1927; a division into museums of Human History and Natural History took place in 1957. Three divisions of the National Museum of Man have contributed to the preservation of musical heritage.

In 1980 the History Division owned some 35 European-type or exotic instruments, some of them built in Canada. The instruments had been acquired on an occasional rather than a systematic basis.

The Canadian Ethnology Service / Service canadien d'Ethnologie and the Canadian Centre for Folk Culture Studies / Centre canadien d'études sur la culture traditionelle, directed respectively by A. McFadyen Clark and Pierre Crépeau, both originated in the Anthropology Division, created in 1910 with the appointment of Edward Sapir (1884–1939), a US-educated social anthropologist and linguist of German birth. Possibly the first work of musical interest done for the new division was W.H. Mechling's transcription of Malecite and Micmac songs in New Brunswick in 1911. That same year marked the appointment of Marius *Barbeau as ethnologist and anthropologist, a fruitful association that continued long past Barbeau's official retirement in 1948 and that did much to enhance the museum's fame. In 1926 Sapir was succeeded as the division's chief by Diamond Jenness (b Wellington, New Zealand, 1886, d Ottawa? 1969). Like Barbeau an Oxford-educated anthropologist, Jenness remained in the position until 1948.

In 1957, when a Folklore Section was created within the division, Carmen Roy (b Bonaventure, Gaspé, Que, 1919) became its head. A specialist in French-Canadian folklore, Roy had been a museum adviser since 1948. In 1966, when the Anthropology Division was divided into an Ethnology Division (renamed Ethnology Service in 1974) and a Folklore Division (renamed Canadian Centre for Folk Culture Studies in 1970), Roy became the chief of the latter, moving to the position of senior scientist in folk culture in 1977.

The responsibilities of the Ethnology Service have included the collecting, analysis, preservation, and dissemination of Indian, Inuit, and Métis music and the housing of a large collection of instruments (see Instrument collections). By 1980 its recordings and transcriptions spanned over 80 years of collecting activities. While not all of the approximately 7000 tapes and wax cylinders were of music, they contained many traditional and new songs and about 5000 pieces of dance music (instrumental). The collectors included Asen Balikci, Marius Barbeau, A.T. *Cringan, Diamond Jenness, Christian Leden, William Mechling, and Edward Sapir and collecting continued. Open to researchers, the collections have made possible the study of ethnic identity, of musical styles, of instruments, and of mutual influences among the indigenous peoples of Canada. In 1980 the manuscript resources included transcriptions of songs in about 90 dialects from 12 linguistic families. Some were translated.

Until the early 1960s the holdings of the Folklore Division were almost exclusively in the French and Anglo-Saxon traditions. In 1962 however the museum decided to expand its research program to include Canadian folk music of other ethnic origins as well. The impressions reported in Kenneth *Peacock's *A Survey of Ethnic Folkmusic across Western Canada* in 1963 were positive and in 1966 the first collection in this cultural area was undertaken. The federal government's multicultural policy, announced in 1971, further encouraged such investigations. An outline of the 5000-odd items of music of ethnic minorities collected under museum auspices prior to 1975 is given in *CMB* no. 10 (1975). At the end of the 1970s French- and English-language materials continued to form the major holdings. In 1979 there were some 200 collections of folksongs and instrumental music on more than 3000 wax cylinders and more than 5000 tape recordings, the majority transcribed into notation. Among the collectors, on staff or on contract, have been Marius Barbeau, Carmelle Begin, Laura Boulton, Emilia Comisel, Helen *Creighton, John Glofcheskie, Richard *Johnston, Robert B. *Klymasz (1967–76, head of the Slavic and East European section and later co-ordinator of the Slavic and East European program), Ivan Macak, É.-Z. *Massicotte, Paul *McIntyre, Kenneth Peacock (field researcher), Carmen Roy, Ruth *Rubin, Helen Sentesy, and many others. The staff has included George *Proctor as musicologist 1959–61 and Roxane Carlisle as ethnomusicologist 1972–6. Carmelle Begin joined the staff as ethnomusicologist in 1975.

See also Ethnomusicology; Folk music; Indians; Inuit.

PUBLICATIONS. The publications of the National Museums have been issued in several numbered series – some no longer active – including the Anthropological Papers / Études anthropologiques; Anthropological Series / Série anthropologique; Miscellaneous Series / Série diverse. Many of these publications also bear a number in the overall bulletin numbering system. More recent series have been the Folklore Series / Série de folklore (late 1960s); Publications in Folk Culture / Publications sur la culture traditionnelle (1971 only); Publications in Anthropology / Publications d'Ethnologie (early 1970s); and Mercury Series / Collection Mercure (begun in 1972). Many publications, especially after 1960, have been bilingual. A guide, *Publications in Folk Culture / Publications sur la culture traditionnelle* (typescript constantly updated, available from the museum) in 1980 listed 131 publications, about one-third of musical interest. They included song collections, surveys, essays, and research reports. Listings of many of these will be found in *EMC* entries for Folk music, Indians, Inuit, and various ethnic minorities and in the entries for individual collectors and ethnomusicologists.

BIBLIOGRAPHY

Alcock, F.J. 'Folklore studies at the National Museum of Canada,' *JAF*, vol 67, Apr–Jun 1954

Peacock, Kenneth. *A Survey of Ethnic Folkmusic across Western Canada*, National Museum of Man Anthropology Papers No. 5 (Ottawa 1963)

– 'Establishing perimeters for ethnomusicological field research in Canada: on-going projects and future possibilities at the Canadian Centre for Folk Culture Studies,' *Ethnomusicology*, vol 16, Sep 1972

Roy, Carmen, ed. *Presentation du Centre canadien d'études sur la culture traditionnelle / An Introduction to the Canadian Centre for Folk Culture Studies*, Mercury Series No. 7 (Ottawa 1973)

Pelinski, Ramón. 'The music of Canada's ethnic minorities,' *CMB*, 10, Spring–Summer 1975

Publications in Folk Culture / Publications sur la culture traditionnelle (Ottawa 1980)

Landry, Renée. 'A descriptive list of selected manuscript collections at the Canadian Centre for Folk Culture Studies, National Museum of Man, Ottawa,' *Canadian Ethnic Studies*, vol 7, 1975 (HK)

The National Opera Company of Canada. Following the collapse of the *Montreal Opera Company (1910–13) an effort was made to establish a successor with some of the same personnel. The resulting National Opera Company of Canada, managed by the Russian-American impresario Max Rabinoff (1879–1966), barely survived one season, 1913–14.

Performances began at *His Majesty's Theatre on 17 November with a well-received production (probably the first in Canada) of Ponchielli's *La Gioconda* with the American soprano Marie Rappold in the title role. The ensuing eight weeks saw several outstanding performances in Montreal; then began a tour including Ottawa, Toronto, Cleveland, Detroit, Kansas City, Houston, and Denver. It was in Denver, 17 Feb 1914, that the financial difficulties which had plagued the troupe culminated in confusion, scandal, and disbandment.

In its three months of existence the ill-fated company managed to present more than 80 performances of 14 operas; in chronological sequence, they were *La Gioconda*, *Madama Butterfly*, *Thaïs*, *Cavalleria Rusticana*, *Il Segreto di Susanna*, *Samson et Dalila*, *Hérodiade*, *Tosca*, *Carmen*, *I Pagliacci*, *Lohengrin*, *La Navarraise*, *La Bohème*, and *Otello*. In addition, throughout the Montreal season, afternoon concerts were given, featuring such celebrated instrumental artists as Kathleen *Parlow and Wilhelm Backhaus. Anna Pavlova and her Ballet Russe appeared briefly 22–5 Dec 1913 under the company's banner.

Leading singers included the sopranos Ester Ferrabini (a former Montreal Opera favourite) and Luisa Villani, the contraltos Jeanne Gerville-Réache and Rosa Olitzka, the tenors Mischa Léon and Leo Slezak, the baritones Max Salzinger and José Segura-Tallien, and the basses Natale Cervi and Giovanni Martino. The only Canadian known to have appeared in solo roles was the baritone Harold *Meek. The conductors were Agide Jacchia, Alexander Savine, and Oscar Spirescu.

BIBLIOGRAPHY

Slezak, Leo. *Song of Motley* (London 1938)

McPherson, Jim. 'The National Opera Company of Canada 1913–1914,' *Record Collector*, vol 21, Jul 1973 JBM

National Research Council. See Acoustics research in Canada; Electronic music; Hugh Le Caine.

The National Youth Orchestra of Canada / L'Orchestre national des jeunes du Canada. Seasonal school established in 1960 to provide Canada's most gifted young instrumentalists with an intensive and controlled experience of orchestral playing. It has been financed by grants from the *Canada Council, the 10 provinces, and private donors.

Members of the National Youth Orchestra

The NYO had its roots in ideas put forward by Walter *Susskind, who in 1956 had carried to Canada the success story of a youth training orchestra in Great Britain. Susskind's ideas had their first realization in a pilot venture in the summer of 1960 – an orchestra workshop organized by James McIntosh and co-directed by Susskind and Harman Haakman at Stratford, Ont. A group of citizens which included Jack Bernstein, Bailey *Bird, John William Herold, Mrs F. Van *Snell, Philip Torno, and Ayala Zachs visited the session and resolved immediately to establish and support an annual training session of the kind. The NYO Assn was chartered in 1960 as a non-profit organization. The first formal training session (in Toronto during Christmas week 1960) led to the NYO's debut 31 Dec 1960 at *Massey Hall in a program consisting of Weber's *Euryanthe* overture, Beethoven's *Fifth Symphony*, Mozart's *Flute Concerto in D* with Robert *Aitken as soloist, *Weinzweig's *'Our Canada' Suite*, and the prelude to Act I of Wagners *Die Meistersinger*. Victor *Feldbrill and Wilfrid *Pelletier shared the podium. A two-week summer session at Stratford and a one-week Christmas session in Montreal followed in 1961.

The NYO has continued to hold annual sessions (which reached a duration of seven weeks by 1974). These often have been in Toronto (1962–7, 1969–72, and 1975), but occasionally have been elsewhere (Quebec City 1968 and 1976, Vancouver 1973, 1974, and 1978, Kingston 1977, 1979, and 1980) and sometimes a session has begun in one city and finished in another. Each year more than 100 players, aged 14 to 24 and chosen through annual nationwide auditions, have participated in full-orchestra and sectional rehearsals and in chamber ensembles and have received private coaching.

Emphasis in the early years was placed on the preparation of works for a two-week concert tour. In the 1970s, however, increasing stress was laid on training and repertoire. Faculty members have been drawn from Canada, the USA, and elsewhere. Conductors have included Feldbrill 1960, 1961, 1962, 1964, 1969, and 1975, Pelletier 1960 and 1961, Haakman 1960 and 1975, Susskind 1961, 1963, and 1966, John *Avison 1964, Franz-Paul *Decker 1965 and 1968, Brian Priestman 1967 and 1970, Georg Tintner 1971, 1974, 1975, 1977, and 1979, Rudolf Schwarz 1972, Kazuyoshi Akiyama 1973 and 1978, Marius Constant 1976 and 1979, Uri Mayer 1978, and John Lubbock 1980.

Guest soloists have appeared in the concerts or have come just to rehearse with the NYO, and Canadian composers have assisted in preparing their own works. Each year at least one Canadian work has been studied and performed, and several have been commissioned for the NYO: Harry *Freedman's *Tangents* (1967), Serge *Garant's *Offrande II* (1970), Robert Aitken's *Shadows – Part I: Nekuia* (1971), and R. Murray *Schafer's *North / White* (1973). Under Haakman's direction, the NYO recorded (RCI 431) the 1975 commission, Norman *Symonds' *Big Lonely*.

The NYO has presented concerts in every major city in Canada and several in the USA. On a 1966 European tour, it appeared in Croydon in England; in Dieppe, Lyon, and Vichy in France; and in Berlin. It also performed at the Edinburgh Festival.

Writing in the Toronto *Globe and Mail*, 4 Aug 1969, John *Kraglund said of the orchestra that 'no matter how high one's expectations, this youthful ensemble somehow manages to surpass them.' Evidence of the NYO's success was the need in 1969 and 1971 to form a supplementary chamber orchestra to accommodate promising young musicians not accepted into the NYO and in 1971 and 1973 to provide pre-season sessions for string players and wind players respectively.

Besides winning critical and public acclaim, the NYO has contributed to the development of a generation of Canadian musicians. Notable alumni are the *Armin family, James *Campbell, Ermanno Florio, Hélène *Gagné, Erica *Goodman, Denise Lupien, Johanne Perron, Joel Quarrington, Suzanne *Shulman, and Gwen *Thompson. Many have become members of leading Canadian orchestras and chamber ensembles or instructors in schools, conservatories, and universities.

Four TV features on the NYO have been seen nationally: 'The Short, Sweet Summer' produced in 1963 by Norman *Campbell for the CBC, 'Youth and Music' filmed in 1968 in Quebec City by the CBC, 'The Sound of August' produced in 1971 by Glenn Sarty for the CBC, and a performance of Rimsky-Korsakov's *Scheherazade* conducted by Haakman, produced in 1975 and telecast several times by TV Ontario.

NYO presidents have included J.W. Herold 1960–1, Jack Bernstein 1962–3, Ayala Zacks 1964–5, J.G. Barrett 1966–7, Bailey Bird 1968–9, Keith *Bissell 1970–1, John Craig Eaton 1972–3, Gordon Sharwood 1974–5, W. Culver Riley 1976–7, and Ron *Napier 1978–9, succeeded by Stanley *Saunders. NYO managers have included Ezra *Schabas 1960–2 and 1965, assisted by Ben *Steinberg and John *Adaskin during 1962; Jay *Armin 1963; Eugene *Kash 1964; Bruce Corder 1966; Jack Elton, assisted by John McDougall, 1967; and John McDougall 1968–70, assisted by Richard Ford during 1969. John Brown was appointed the first full-time manager in October 1970. A dedicated and innovative administrator, Brown has worked assiduously, if autocratically, at broadening and refining the NYO's training concepts, and his ideas have had a significant effect on the development of youth orchestras in Canada.

BIBLIOGRAPHY

'A National Youth Orchestra for Canada,' *Recorder*, Jun 1960

Schabas, Ezra. 'The National Youth Orchestra of Canada,' *CMJ*, vol 5, Spring 1961

Taylor, Patricia. 'A Canadian composers' "first class ticket",' *CanComp*, 3, Oct 1965

'National Youth Orchestra to play Mercure's Triptyque,' *CanComp*, 9, May 1966

Wyman, Max. 'What matures but never grows older? The National Youth Orchestra – that's what,' *PfAC*, vol 10, Fall 1973

National Youth Orchestra of Canada: Who We Are and What We Do ([Toronto 1979]) (PS)

Native music. See Ethnomusicology; Indians; Inuit; Moravian missions in Labrador.

Bernard Naylor

NAYLOR, Bernard (James). Composer, conductor, organist, b Cambridge, England, 22 Nov 1907; B MUS (Oxford) 1930, hon LLD (Manitoba) 1980, hon LLD (Winnipeg) 1980. Grandson of John Naylor (1838–97) and son of Edward (Woodall) Naylor (1867–1934), both English organists and composers of note, he studied with Gustav Holst, John Ireland, and Vaughan Williams at the RCM and was an organ scholar 1927–31 at Exeter College, Oxford U. During his first Canadian sojourn, 1932–5, he was conductor of the *Winnipeg Male Voice Choir, the *Winnipeg Philharmonic Choir, and the *Winnipeg Symphony Orchestra and was organist-choirmaster at Holy Trinity Anglican Church. He took a post in England as organist and musical director 1936–9 at Queen's College, Oxford, but returned to Canada in 1940, founded the *Little Symphony of Montreal in 1942, and conducted that orchestra until 1947. After another short term, 1948–9, with the Winnipeg Philharmonic Choir he left again for England, where he taught 1950–2 at Oxford U and 1952–9 at Reading U. In 1959 he took up permanent residence in Canada, working thereafter almost entirely as a composer, first in Winnipeg and after 1968 in Victoria, BC.

Naylor wrote large-scale, heavily scored orchestral and choral works as a young man but rejected many of these later. There was a period after 1935 when he ceased composing, but he resumed in 1947 and gradually evolved an intensely personal style of choral writing, lean yet passionate, singular yet idiomatic, exemplified by the *Three Latin Motets* and *Nine English Motets*. Commissions have been received from the CBC (*King Solomon's Prayer*, written in honour of the coronation of Elizabeth II), the Winnipeg *Choristers (*Missa da camera*), the *U of Manitoba Chamber Music Group (*The Nymph Complaining ...*), and Peggie *Sampson (*On Mrs. Arabella Hunt Singing*). Though he has composed mainly to liturgical texts, it would be incorrect to label him a church composer. It is poetry itself – often but by no means exclusively poetry of the church – which has attracted him. Naylor is an associate of the *CMCentre and a member of CAPAC.

SELECTED COMPOSITIONS

ORCHESTRA AND VOICE

The Living Fountain (R. Watkyns). 1947–63. High v, str orch. Novello 1966

The Annunciation According to Saint Luke (Bible). 1949. Sop, ten, SATB, chamb orch. Novello 1949

King Solomon's Prayer (Wisdom of Solomon IX). 1953. Sop, SATB, chamb orch. UE 1955

Three Shakespearean Sonnets. 1957. Bar, orch. Ms

Stabat mater (13th-century liturgical). 1961. SSAA, orch. Novello 1964

Three Sacred Pieces (liturgical). 1968–71. SATB, full orch. Ms

Personal Landscapes (P.K. Page). 1971. Sop, chamb orch. Ms

CHAMBER

Sonnets from the Portuguese (E.B. Browning). 1948. Mezzo, str quar. Ms

String Trio. 1960. CMCentre

The Nymph Complaining for the Death of Her Faun (Marvell). 1965. Mezzo, chamb ens. CMCentre

Not So Far as the Forest (E. St-Vincent Millay). 1966. Sop, str quart. Novello (rental)

On Mrs. Arabella Hunt Singing (Congreve). 1970. Sop, v da gamba, hpd. CMCentre

Dejection (Coleridge). 1973. Bar, ww trio, hn, str quar, pf. CMCentre

CHOIR

Three (Latin) Motets (various). 1949. SATB, soli. Western 1950

Nine (English) Motets (Bible, Apocrypha). 1952. SATB, soli. Novello 1960. (1965). Argo ZRG-5426 (John Alldis Choir)

Six Poems from Miserere (D. Gascoyne). 1960. 2 sop, SSAATTBB. Rob 1972

Exultat mundus gaudio (various 16th century, adapted A. Freeland). 1969. Sop, alto, ten, bass, SATB. Rob 1972

Missa sine Credo a 4 (liturgical). 1969. SATB. Rob 1973

The Three Stars / Epode (D. Gascoyne). 1973. Sop, ten, bass, SSAATTBB. Ms

VOICE

Presences (M. Webb). 1947. High v, pf. Ms

Songs of Regret (M. Webb). 1947. Low v, pf. Ms

Four Dreams and a Vision (R. Pitter). 1974. Low v, pf. Ms

Three Feminine Things (R. Pitter). 1974. High v, pf, Ms

Several other works for orch and chamb ens, numerous works for choir; some works for film and stage, including music for the play entitled *The Cloak* (1967). All ms

BIBLIOGRAPHY

Winters, Kenneth. 'The composer speaks,' *Winnipeg Free Press*, 20 Jan 1962

Morgan, Kit. 'A word portrait of Victoria composer Bernard Naylor,' *CanComp*, 57, Feb 1971

Aide, William. 'Bernard Naylor,' *Contemporary Canadian Composers* JA

NEEDHAM, Lucien (Arthur). Conductor, teacher, administrator, pianist, b Kingston-upon-Hull, England, 5 Apr 1929, naturalized Canadian 1965; ARCM 1952, AGSM 1954, hon FGSM 1965. After studies in Hull 1945–52 and at the GSM 1952–6 (his courses including summer sessions in conducting with Sir Adrian Boult, John Hopkins, and Maurice Miles), he held teaching, conducting, and church positions in Hull and London.

Needham emigrated to Canada to serve 1956–60 as conductor of the *Winnipeg Philharmonic *Choir and the *Winnipeg Male Voice Choir. He was the conductor 1965–7 of the Western Manitoba Philharmonic Choir, which he founded, and 1968–74 of the *U of Lethbridge Choir. In 1970 he became conductor of the Lethbridge SO. As a pianist he has been heard on CBC radio, alone and in duo recitals with Francis *Chaplin, Thomas *Rolston, and others. He taught at the *U of Manitoba 1958–60 and *Brandon U 1959–67 before joining the music dept of the U of Lethbridge in 1967 and serving 1969–71 as its chairman. He has examined for the *WBM.

Needham has contributed articles to the *Canadian Music Educator*, the *Music Scene*, and the US periodicals *Piano Quarterly* and the *Bulletin* of the National Assn of Teachers of Singing. He is an affiliate of PRO Canada. He has composed *The Fields Abroad* (1955, BMI Canada) for string quartet, *Christmas Gradual* (1957, BMI Canada), several choral arrangements of Christmas carols, and *Canticle* (1962) for mezzo soprano.

Needham's first wife was the Winnipeg mezzo-soprano Nora McLean.

Needham's second wife is the pianist Louise Chapman (b Brandon, Man, 24 Feb 1938), who studied at Brandon College (BA 1958), with Willi Apel and Frederick Baldwin at Indiana U (M MUS 1962), and with Terence Beckles in Europe. She taught 1958–60 and 1962–7 at Brandon College and joined the teaching staff of the U of Lethbridge in 1968. (CF)

NEEL, (Louis) Boyd. Conductor, administrator, lecturer, writer, b Blackheath (London) 19 Jul 1905, naturalized Canadian 1961; BA (Cambridge) 1926, MA (Cambridge) 1930, hon member RAM 1965, hon D MUS (Toronto) 1979. Destined originally for a career in the British navy, he turned to medicine, studying at Caius College, Cambridge, and specializing in surgery. At that time a pianist and an amateur conductor, he went on to study theory and orchestration at the GSM in 1931, even though he still considered music a hobby.

Boyd Neel

In 1932 Neel formed the Boyd Neel Orchestra, 17 young professional string players, several of them Canadians living in London. (Frederick *Grinke, another Canadian, became concertmaster in 1937.) After a successful debut 22 Jun 1933 at Aeolian Hall, the orchestra made several international tours and premiered Britten's *Variations on a Theme of Frank Bridge* (written at Neel's request) at the 1937 Salzburg Festival. Its concerts frequently offered music of contemporary British composers and it premiered works of Arnold Bax, Gordon Jacob, and others. The orchestra was in the vanguard of the baroque revival and between 1934 and 1952 it committed to disc for Decca much of the chamber-orchestra repertoire, notably (1936–7) the first complete recording ever made of the Handel *Concerti grossi Op 6*.

Neel conducted at the first Glyndebourne Festival (1934), 1945–7 at Sadler's Wells, and 1948–9 for the D'Oyly Carte Company. Before and after World War II he was a guest conductor with many English orchestras including the Royal Philharmonic, the London Philharmonic, the London SO, and the BBC SO. During the war he served as a medical officer but also did a lecture tour of the Mediterranean for the Admiralty and, with the Sadler's Wells orchestra, gave several hundred concerts to troops in England. With his orchestra he visited Canada in the fall of 1952, touring in Quebec, Ontario, and the Maritimes.

In 1953 Neel was appointed dean of the *RCMT (which at the time included the Faculty of Music, *U of Toronto), holding the position until 1971. He was a leader in the campaign to build a new home for the faculty. The campaign was a success and resulted in the Edward Johnson Building.

Neel was the founder in 1954 and the conductor until 1971 of the *Hart House Orchestra (with which he toured and made several recordings), conducted the *CBC SO in some 27 performances 1953–64, and for 'L'*Heure du concert,' 1954–5, conducted several TV programs of opera including *Il Tabarro* with Louis *Quilico. He conducted the *TSO for the first time 15 Feb 1955, after which John *Kraglund (Toronto *Globe and Mail*) wrote 'Neel's conducting is conservative and undemonstrative. Indeed, it has about it the restraint which suits the intimacy of a chamber concert.' In the summer of 1955 Neel conducted the Hart House Orchestra in eight concerts at the *Stratford Festival. Glenn *Gould, Lois *Marshall, and Elisabeth Schwarzkopf were among the solo artists who appeared with the orchestra for that series.

Neel became a regular instructor for the *OAC and U of Toronto Student Conductors' Workshop at its inception in 1969 and continued his connection with it until the late 1970s. In 1971 he became the first conductor of the Mississauga SO, continuing after 1978 as conductor emeritus. In 1977 he conducted a specially formed Toronto Chamber Orchestra in direct-to-disc recordings of Mozart's *Eine kleine Nachtmusik* and *Divertimento No. 11* (Umbrella UM DD6) and of Bach's *Violin Concerto in E* (with Steven *Staryk as soloist) and other works (Umbrella UM DD9). He also led the orchestra in a subsequent digital recording of Britten's *Simple Symphony*, Elgar's *Serenade*, and an *Air and Gigue* by Arne (Ultrafi ULDD10).

A calm and assured after-dinner speaker and radio commentator, Neel has been heard nationally on such CBC programs as 'Sunday Concert,' 'Tuesday Night,' 'Concerts from Two Worlds,' and his own 'Opera with Boyd Neel' (1954). In 1961 he was host for a CBC school broadcast of Britten's *Let's Make an Opera* and in 1972 he was the commentator for a documentary about Vaughan Williams. He contributed a series of essays, 'This Week's Music,' to the *CBC Times* in 1959, and his writings have appeared in *Opera Canada*, the *Journal of Music Education*, and the U of Toronto *Bulletin*. He was the subject of a CBC FM series – 'The Boyd Neel Memoirs' – in 1979.

Neel was made a Commander of the British Empire in 1953 and an Officer of the *Order of Canada in 1973.

WRITINGS

The Story of an Orchestra (London 1950)

'Small orchestras: musical need,' *SatN*, 19 Feb 1955

'Music in Canada,' *Tempo*, 38, Winter 1955–6

'Opera,' *The Arts in Canada* ed Murray Ross (Toronto 1958)

'Laughter and boos at Bayreuth,' *Fugue*, vol 1, May 1977

'Muzak, ha!' *Fugue*, vol 2, Apr 1978

BIBLIOGRAPHY

'Boyd Neel, Dean of the Royal Conservatory,' *RCMT Monthly Bulletin*, May–Jun 1953

Hardly, John. 'The new man at the Con,' *Mayfair*, Sep 1953

McCall, Christina. 'Dr Boyd Neel's prescription for musical success,' *Maclean's*, 29 Aug 1959

Wimbush, Roger. 'Boyd Neel,' *The Gramophone*, Jul 1972

Littler, William. 'Boyd Neel laughs off retirement,' *Toronto Star*, 14 Apr 1973

Fraser, John. 'Boyd Neel strikes back at the vulgar age,' Toronto *Globe and Mail*, 8 Jun 1974 (BJE)

NEIL, Al (Alan Douglas). Pianist, composer, b Vancouver 26 Mar 1924. Essentially self-taught, Neil was drawn to jazz by the music of the bebop players Bud Powell and Lennie Tristano. He began playing in Vancouver clubs in the late 1940s, with his own groups and as a sideman to other musicians, becoming the leading bebop musician in western Canada.

Neil was a central figure ca 1956–64 at the musician-operated Vancouver club the Cellar, where he accompanied such US jazzmen as Carl Fontana, Art Pepper, and Sonny Red. He performed on CBC radio and TV programs and appeared in the NFB's *In Search of Innocence* (1963). An LP, *Kenneth Patchen Reads With Jazz* (Folk 9718), on which Neil's quartet (Dale Hillary alto saxophone, Lionel Chambers bass, Bill Boyle drums) accompanies the poet, is indicative of the pianist's style in this period.

After a period of inactivity, Neil returned in 1966 to performance with a freer and more personal, if not eccentric, style. With a trio completed by bassist Richard Anstey and drummer Gregg Simpson (both much younger musicians and each, like Neil, a visual artist), he presented mixed-media programs at his own venues, the Sound Gallery and the Motion Studio, and at the Vancouver Art Gallery. He gave a one-man show, 'West Coast Locus,' at the Vancouver Art Gallery. A contributor to the art festival Canada Trajectories 73, held at the Paris City Museum of Contemporary Art, he gave solo concerts there and in Amsterdam. In later years he was not very active in music and lived in a beach shack at Deep Cove, Burrard Inlet, near Vancouver. He gave concerts in Toronto in 1979.

In a review of the limited edition LP, *The Al Neil Trio Retrospective: 1965–1968* (Lodestone lr-7001), released in 1976, Richard Baker (*Coda*, Feb 1977) observed that Neil's music from this period 'sounded strange even to ears already accustomed to Ornette [Coleman], Cecil Taylor and Sun Ra. Neil derived as much from John Cage, Alfred Jarry, the I Ching ... as from any trends in free jazz or, for that matter, bop ... developments during the intervening years make it difficult to realize what a departure these performances represented at the time.'

Neil is a member of CAPAC.

BIBLIOGRAPHY

Lemon, Sandy. 'Al Neil: music and life,' *Coda*, vol 7, Dec–Jan 1966–7

Smith, Bill. 'Sacred and profane,' *Coda*, vol 9, Feb 1970

FILMOGRAPHY

Al Neil (David Rimmer 1979) MM, BSm

NEILSON, John. Publisher, politician, b Balmaghie, Kirkcudbrightshire, Scotland, 17 Jul 1776, d Quebec City 1 Feb 1848. Neilson at 14 joined his elder brother Samuel in Lower Canada to work in the printing house of their uncle, William Brown, the first printer in Quebec and founder of the *Quebec Gazette*. John Neilson inherited control of that newspaper in 1793, and under his guidance it became an influential and respected voice in the community.

Neilson published a considerable amount of other material, including music. No earlier example of Canadian musical typography has been discovered than his *Graduel romain* (1800), 645 pages of mass texts and chants in square notation on four-line staves, all printed from moveable type. This was followed by the *Processional* [*sic*] *romain* (1801) and the *Vespéral romain* (1802). An *Extrait du processional* [*sic*] *romain* (1819) is the only other known example of music published by Neilson. Neilson attempted to print Joseph *Quesnel's *Colas et Colinette*. Letters (1807–9) from Quesnel to Neilson reveal the latter's difficulties in preparing the opera for printing and indicate that it was to be engraved rather than typeset – further proof of Neilson's enterprising approach to his trade.

In 1818 Neilson was elected to the provincial assembly and, to avoid a conflict of interest, turned over his publishing activities to his eldest son, Samuel. Samuel Neilson, in partnership with William Cowan, published second editions of the *Processionnal romain* (1825), the *Graduel romain* (1827), and the *Vespéral romain* (1828) and the bilingual *Elementary Treatise on Music / Traité élémentaire de musique* (1828) by T.F. *Molt.

On Samuel Neilson's death in 1837, his younger brother William took over the publishing house and issued third editions of the three books (1841–2) as well as two hymnbooks, one in French, *Recueil de messes, d'hymnes, de proses, de motets* (1843), and the other in Algonkian, *Aiamieu Kushkushkutu mishinaigan* (1847) edited by Frère Flavien Durocher, probably the first in Canada to include music with the native texts.

BIBLIOGRAPHY

Audet, Francis. 'John Neilson,' *Mémoires de la Société Royale du Canada*, vol 22, 1928

Morgan, Henry J. *Sketches of Celebrated Canadians* (Quebec 1862) MC

NELSON, (Richard) Norman. Violinist, b Dublin 1 Aug 1931. He studied 1945–51 at the RCM with George Stratton and Sascha Lasserman, who was a pupil of Leopold Auer. Nelson joined the London Philharmonic Orchestra in 1951 and the Sadler's Wells orchestra in 1952. He was assistant concertmaster of the London SO 1956–7 and 1959–62, the London Philharmonic Orchestra 1957–9, and the BBC SO 1962–5.

Nelson served 1965–73 as concertmaster of the *Vancouver SO and 1966–72 and 1976 as concertmaster-director of the *Baroque Strings of Vancouver. He has appeared often in recital and as soloist with orchestras, in England and Canada. He founded and served 1968–79 as first violin of the *Purcell String Quartet and founded in 1973 and directed until 1979 the Academy Strings, an ensemble for advanced students at the *Community Music School of Greater Vancouver. In 1979 he joined the Dept of Music at the *U of Alberta and became first violin with the *U of Alberta String Quartet.

Nelson has recorded as soloist with the Academy of St Martin-in-the-Fields, of which he was an original member. MW

NELSOVA, Zara (b Nelson, Sarah). Cellist, teacher, b Winnipeg 23 Dec 1918, naturalized US 1953. She received her earliest musical training from her father, a flutist and graduate of the Petrograd Cons. She also studied 1924–8 with Dezsö *Mahalek, 1929–35 with Herbert Walenn, and during the 1940s with Pablo Casals, Emanuel Feuermann, and Gregor Piatigorsky. She first played in Winnipeg as a child of five. She and her sisters Anne, a pianist, and Ida, a violinist, performed together at *Manitoba Music Competition Festivals. Shortly after the family moved to England in 1928 the sisters became known as the Canadian Trio. The trio appeared at Wigmore Hall during the 1928–9 season and continued to perform under that name until 1939. Nelsova made her recital debut in London ca 1930 and her concert debut in the Lalo *Concerto* one year later with the London SO under Sir Malcolm Sargent. With the trio she toured Australia, Northern Africa, and South Africa ca 1934–6.

During the late 1930s Nelsova returned to Canada where she was principal cellist 1940–3 with the *TSO and a member 1941–4 of a second Canadian Trio, this time with Kathleen *Parlow and Sir Ernest *MacMillan. During the early 1940s she taught at the *TCM. She made her New York debut at Town Hall in 1942. In 1949 Ernest Bloch invited her to play *Schelomo* at a festival of his works in London; she later recorded the work under Bloch's baton. In 1954 she spent two months performing in Israel and made a 27-day tour of Alaska and the Canadian Northwest Territories. In 1966 she became the first North American cellist to tour the Soviet Union.

Nelsova has performed extensively in concert and recital throughout North and South America and in Europe and has appeared at several music

Zara Nelsova

festivals (including the Aspen, the Bergen, the Casals, the Prague, the Tanglewood, and the *Vancouver International and *Expo 67). She has appeared as soloist with more than 30 orchestras including the BBC Orchestra, the *Montreal Women's SO, the *MSO, the *NACO, the TSO, the Boston, London, *Vancouver, and *Winnipeg SOs, the London and New York philharmonic orchestras, and the Orchestre de la Suisse romande.

With the BBC Orchestra Nelsova gave the first European performance (1950) of Barber's *Cello Concerto* and later recorded the work with the composer and the New SO. She premiered Hindemith's 'A Frog He Went a-Courting' in London in 1947, Alexander *Brott's *Arabesque* (version for cello and orchestra) in Montreal in 1958, Alexei Haieff's *Cello Sonata* in 1963, and Hugh Wood's *Cello Concerto* (at Tanglewood with the Boston SO under Colin Davis) in 1969. The Haieff was commissioned by Nelsova with a grant from the Ford Foundation. In 1972 she gave the US premiere of Robert Casadesus' *Sonata*. In 1955 in London (Wigmore Hall) and New York (Town Hall) she gave series of recitals of works for cello alone, the programs ranging from Bach to Kodály, Prokofiev, and Reger.

Nelsova has appeared on CBC TV and has been heard over CBC radio many times: in the five Beethoven sonatas with Lubka *Kolessa and Ross *Pratt 1942–3 and in various programs for 'Distinguished Artists' 1945–6, 'L'*Heure du concert' ca 1954–5, 'Recital' 1959–62, 'University Celebrity Recital' (October 1964), 'Centenary Concerts' (July 1967), and 'Music' (July 1968). She was the soloist for the London concert by the NACO during its 1973 European tour.

Nelsova's husband, the US pianist Grant Johannesen, has been her partner in many recitals. During the 1970–1 season the couple appeared at Town Hall in Toronto as part of James *Norcop's Canadian Platform series. In May 1976 they toured Canada as soloists with the Vancouver SO and premiered, as dedicatees, Robert *Turner's *Capriccio concertante*.

Writing in the Toronto *Telegram* (23 Mar 1966) after a performance of Bloch's *Schelomo* by Nelsova and the TS, Kenneth *Winters described Nelsova as 'a player of magnificent presence, grand verve, consummate skill and unflagging strength ... Of [*Schelomo*'s] longueurs she made a rhapsody; of its bombast, she made drama; of its sentiment she made warm, quiet lyricism.'

Nelsova began teaching at the Juilliard School in 1962. Her pupils include Lotte *Brott and Denis *Brott. Among the instruments Nelsova has played are a 1726 Stradivarius and a 1735 Pietro Guarnerius.

DISCOGRAPHY
Bach – Kodály – Reger. Decca LXT 5252
Barber *Concerto, Op 22*. New SO, Barber cond. 1951. Lon LPS 332
Beethoven *Sonata, Op 69; Variations, Op 66*. Balsam pf. Ca 1957. Decca LXT 5268
Beethoven – Debussy – Brahms. Johannesen pf. 1968. CBC SM-51
Bloch *From Jewish Life*. Bloch pf. Lon LPS 298
– *Schelomo*. London Phil, Bloch cond. 1949. Lon LS-138
– *Schelomo*. Utah SO, Abravanel cond. 1967. Van C010007
– *Schelomo; Voice in the Wilderness*. London SO, Ansermet cond. 1956. Lon LL 1232
Brahms *Sonata, Op 99*. Newmark pf. 1952. RCI 72
A. Brott *Arabesque*. McGill Chamb O, A. Brott cond. 1963. RCI 187
Chopin *Sonata, Op 65*. Johannesen pf. 1968. CBC SM-52
Chopin – Franck – Poulenc – Rachmaninoff: *Sonatas*. Johannesen pf. 2-Golden Crest GC 40899
Dvořák *Concerto, Op 104*. London SO, Krips cond. Decca ACL 92
– *Concerto, Op 104; Rondo, Op 94; Waldesruhe, Op 68*. St Louis SO, Susskind cond. 3-Vox QSVBX-5135
Frederick the Great *Sonata* – Schubert *Arpeggione Sonata*. Newmark pf. 1951. RCI 34
Hindemith *Sonata, Op 11*. Newmark pf. RCI 197
Hindemith – Casadesus: *Sonatas for Cello and Piano*. Johannesen pf. Golden Crest CRS 4099
Rachmaninoff *Sonata, Op 19*. Balsam pf. Ca 1956. Decca LXT 5228 (SRM)

Neoclassicism. The 'new classicism' which appeared in the work of European composers in the early 1920s. Prokofiev's *Classical Symphony* (1917) was a possibly unwitting prototype but the trend was established and took on the dimensions of an ethos with Stravinsky's *Pulcinella* (1920), Hindemith's *Kleine Kammermusik* (1922), Holst's *Fugal Overture* (1922), Vaughan Williams' *Concerto Accademico* (1925), and subsequent works by these and other composers, persistently Stravinsky but also Les Six (mostly Milhaud and Poulenc) and, later, Tippett in England, Françaix in France, and Piston in the USA.

Neoclassic works by these 'modern' men revived the principles, as distinct from the fabrics, of classicism. The return was not to 18th-century harmony but, rather, to stylistic essences: the objectivity, balance, clarity, economy, directness, and grace epitomized in the music of Bach and Scarlatti, Haydn and Mozart. It stemmed from reaction against the lush harmony, loose forms, obese orchestra, and extravagant emotionalism of late romantic music (Strauss, Mahler, Elgar, Franck, etc). It gained additional credibility (in at least its more boldly dissonant manifestations) as an alternative to *12-tone music (Schoenberg's repudiation of tonality, first demonstrated in 1921 in some of his *5 Klavierstücke, Op 23*).

The serious neoclassicist, however, is not to be confused with the ubiquitous reactionary, opposed to decadence on the Right and dodecaphony on the Left. The neoclassicist was of necessity a positive, even advanced thinker, for his 'neo'-ness had to compete resourcefully with the news of dodecaphony, his 'classicism' to survive comparison with the real article.

Neoclassicism first attracted Canadians in the late 1930s. Canadian music until then had been, in Murray *Schafer's words, 'run by the pommies' (*CMB* Spring–Summer 1973), those powerful conservatives, represented at the administrative level by Sir Ernest *MacMillan, Healey *Willan, Eugène *Lapierre, and Douglas *Clarke, for whom Schoenberg's ideas were impractical and unappealing and most of what had happened after Strauss and Elgar, Debussy and Ravel, was a strain and a nuisance. However reactionary and suppressive this position may have seemed to the fulminating young talents of the day, an element of sense in it dulled any tendency among those talents to fall into dodecaphonic fanaticism.

John *Weinzweig was rebel enough to leave Canada and study where Schoenberg and Berg were tolerated if not championed. But he stayed aware of the patterns and balances in the work of these great radicals and of the valuable order in the expanded diatonicism of Stravinsky. Barbara *Pentland, though willing to dare, was repelled by the neurosis that seemed to her implicit in the arbitrations of the dodecaphonists and found more to admire in the forthright contrapuntal resilience of Hindemith and Stravinsky. Jean *Papineau-Couture, as a pupil of Nadia Boulanger, was introduced directly to neoclassic Stravinsky and discovered in himself a powerful affinity for the clean textures and acoustic moderation intrinsic to neoclassicism.

So it was that three figures in the vanguard of Canadian composition in 1940 arrived by characteristically different (but similarly fastidious) routes at a neoclassicism which never has been abandoned entirely by any of them and is present as an influence in much Canadian music written between 1940 and 1970.

The unarguable neoclassics of Canadian music emerged, however, mainly in the 1940s and 1950s: Weinzweig's *Suite No. 1* for piano (1939), *Divertimento No. 1* for flute and strings (1946), *Divertimento No. 2* for oboe and strings (1948), *Sonata: Israel* (1949) for cello and piano, *Piano Sonata* (1950), and *Violin Concerto* (1954); Pentland's output in the 1940s and well into the 1950s, notably the *Concerto* for violin and small orchestra and the piano *Variations* (both 1942), but also, in at least an aesthetic sense, much later works such as the *Piano Concerto* (1956) and the *Symphony for Ten Parts* (1957); and the main body of Papineau-Couture's output, but most obviously the works of those two decades – the *Sonata in G* (1944, rev 1953), the *Étude in B-flat Minor* (1945), the *Concerto grosso* (1943, rev 1955), the *Symphony in C* (1948, rev 1956), and the *Psaume CL* (1954).

Neoclassics of the period include also *Archer's *Sonatina No. 2* (1946), *Fanfare and Passacaglia* (1949), *Sonata* for cello and piano (1956), and other works; *Somers *Piano Sonata No. 4* (1950), *Symphony No. 1* (1951), fugues *12 × 12* (1951), *Passacaglia and Fugue* (1954), *Violin Sonata No. 1* (1968), and organizational elements in several of his other works; and *Adaskin's *Serenade Concertante* (1954), along with much of his other music.

*Morawetz, too, has been a proponent of neoclassicism (*Divertimento for Strings* 1948, rev 1954, and *Sinfonietta for Strings*, 1963, rev 1968) and so has *Blackburn (*Concertino*, 1948, for piano and winds). Many other Canadian works (eg, Jacques *Hétu's *Variations* for piano, 1964, and for violin, 1967; his *Passacaille* for orchestra, 1970; and other works) contain elements of neoclassicism, strong or mild, practical or aesthetic.

During the 1960s reaction set in. Abstraction and balance began to look like sterile tidiness, and expressionism seemed the answer to a growing need, among composers and their audiences, for something lustier. By 1970 the neoclassic movement had been overborne by a combination of circumstances: a nostalgia for romanticism; the return, among serious composers, of a desire to entertain (nudged by the challenge and seductions of pop); and the resurgence of the appetite for sheer sound (a dormant inheritance from Debussy, Bartók, Varèse, and Oriental music) whetted by the sound-potential of the new technology (electronics, stereophony, the acoustic revolution in concert-hall architecture). Weinzweig said (*CanComp*, January 1971): 'It's silly to think of writing a sonata today, not because sonatas are silly but because they originally grew out of needs very different from ours. I'm moving away now from abstract works and toward theatrical ones.'

But though the neoclassic movement had languished, the principles that informed it were not shed so easily. The most apparently successful Canadian works of the 1970s continued to attempt objectivity, balance, clarity, economy, directness, and grace, and very little neo-Mahler or neo-Strauss (Schafer's *Son of Heldenleben* and Hétu's *L'Apocalypse* notwithstanding) had come to the fore.

BIBLIOGRAPHY
Duke, David. 'Neo-classical compositional procedures in selected works of Harry Somers, 1949–59,' unpubl MA thesis, U of North Carolina, 1973
Proctor, George A. 'Neo-classicism and neo-romanticism in Canadian music,' *Studies in Music*, vol 1, 1976
– 'The 1950s: neo-classicism at its height,' *Canadian Music of the Twentieth Century* (Toronto 1980) KW (RM)

Netherlands. The first Dutch immigrants to Canada arrived via the USA during the late 18th and early 19th centuries, as part of the United Empire Loyalist contingent. By 1867 there were 29,000 persons of Dutch origin; in 1974, more than 450,000, many of whom arrived soon after World War II.

Most of the Dutch immigrant population assimilated quickly into Canada's cultural and social life. Members of the Dutch Reformed Church, however, have stayed relatively separate, many establishing their own churches and schools in rural communities throughout Canada or settling together in cities in southern Ontario, Alberta, and British Columbia. Dutch Reformed Church choirs have maintained their own repertoire and have perpetuated their folk music through choral arrangements by the Dutch composers Rudolf Mengelberg, Willem Pijper, and Johan Wagenaar. In addition, these churches have sponsored Canadian tours by Dutch choirs and organists.

The Dutch secular music tradition has been kept alive in Canada by credit unions and social clubs which hold evening gatherings and picnics at which Dutch popular and folk music is performed. These organizations, too, have sponsored Canadian tours by Dutch performers. In Toronto and Vancouver private radio stations have broadcast daily programs of recorded music by Dutch artists; in many areas with smaller populations, brief programs have been heard once or twice a week.

Dutch-Canadian folk groups of note have included the Laus Deo Choir, founded in 1953 in Fort William (Thunder Bay), Ont; the Duca Choir of Toronto, founded in 1964 under the auspices of the Dutch-Canadian Toronto Credit Union; and the Dutch-Canadian Choir of Calgary. The last of these, conducted by John Vanderbeld, made the recording *The Dutch Canadian Choir of Calgary Goes Commonwealth* (Westmount WSTM 7812).

Concert works by Andriessen, Flothius, Wagenaar, and other Dutch composers have been performed by the *MSO and *TSO, by CBC orchestras, and by other ensembles.

Among musicians of Dutch origin or extraction who have lived and worked in Canada are the bandmasters Bernardus *Bogisch and Cornelius Godry; the baritones Bernard *Diamant and Cornelis *Opthof, the bass-baritone Peter *van Ginkel, and the tenor Roelof Oostwoud; the carillonneur Herman *Bergink; the cellist Cornelius Ysselstyn; the composers Walter Hekster and Rudi *van Dijk; the conductors Eduard Bayens, Willem Bertsch (founder and conductor 1959–63 of the Okanagan SO), Nick Rooij, Allard de *Ridder (who, besides his work with orchestras, conducted the Holland Choir in Vancouver after 1952), Harman Haakman, and Henry Plukker; the

The Flentrop Organ, National Arts Centre, donated by the Netherlands to Canada

flutists Wolfgang Kander and Dirk *Keetbaas (the latter also a record producer for the CBC, and son of the violist-conductor Dirk Keetbaas senior); the Calgary oboist Peter Heyblom; the bass guitarist Ronnie King of The *Stampeders; the classical guitarist Carl van Feggelen; the harpsichord builder Jan *Albarda; the music librarians John van Vugt (TSO 1946–68) and Henry Mutsaers (*CMCentre, Toronto, beginning in 1963); the organists Frans *Niermeier, Jan *Overduin, and Karel *ten Hoope; and the trumpeter Bob Erwig of the Climax Jazz Band. Some of the many other Dutch instrumentalists who had been contracted after 1945 to augment the personnel in Canadian armed forces bands remained in Canada, and most of these were absorbed into the commercial music field.

Dutch artists who have visited Canada include the soprano Christina Deutekom, who sang the title role in a 1971 *COC production of *Lucia di Lammermoor*; the baritones Max Van Egmond and Bernard Kruysen; the pianists Theo Bruins and Rinus Groot (both of whom appeared under *JMC auspices); the pianist Steven de Groote who played for the Montreal *Ladies' Morning Musical Club in 1979; and the conductors Eduard van Beinum, Hubert Soudant, and Edo de Waart. Among chamber groups and orchestras which have performed in Canada are the Netherlands Wind Ensemble, the Amsterdam Concertgebouw Orchestra under Bernard Haitink, the Hague Residentie Orkest under Willem van Otterloo, and the Netherlands Chamber Orchestra under Szymon Goldberg. The Netherlands Chamber Choir (directed by Felix de Nobel) has given concerts in Canada, as has the Netherlands String Quartet. In 1960 Henk Badings attended the *International Conference of Composers at Stratford, Ont. Dutch students in Canada have included Princess Christina of the Netherlands, who took lessons with Bernard Diamant in Montreal.

Many Canadians have visited Holland, to perform or to study. The first probably was Emma *Albani who sang there in 1884 and 1886. Victor *Feldbrill studied conducting with Willem van Otterloo in Hilversum in 1956. The organist Raymond *Daveluy took part in an improvisation competition in Haarlem in 1959. Ida *Krehm made her debut as pianist-conductor in Hilversum in 1962. Dom André *Laberge studied organ with Piet Kee in Haarlem in 1971, Denis *Bédard and Geneviève *Lagacé with Gustav Leonhardt in Amsterdam in 1976–7 and 1977–8 respectively. Claude *Vivier studied composition with Michael Gottfried Koenig at the Institute of Sonology, Utrecht, in the early 1970s, as did several other young Canadians. Among the numerous Canadian singers who have sung in Holland are Clarice *Carson, Joanne Dorenfeld, Raoul *Jobin, Huguette *Tourangeau, and Riki *Turofsky. The soprano Doreen *Hume sang there in 1965 at a concert commemorating the 20th anniversary of Holland's liberation from German occupation. The *Royal 22nd Regiment Band (Van Doos) toured Holland in 1975.

Canadian winners in s'Hertogenbosch International Competition for Singers have included the soprano Christine *Harvey (1972), the mezzo-soprano Marie *Laferrière (1975), and the bass-baritone Ingemar *Korjus (1978). Harvey, a member 1973–6 of the Netherlands Opera, has appeared as well with the Netherlands Bach Choir, the Netherlands Chamber Orchestra, and the Hague Residentie Orchestra, recording with the latter. She toured Holland in 1978 as a member of Peggie *Sampson's group Quatre en Concert. In 1971 the ladies choir of the *Vancouver Bach Choir won a first in the International Koorfest in Scheveningen.

Other Canadians who have won prizes in Dutch competitions include Jacques *Beaudry, who studied in the Netherlands with Paul van Kempen and Willem van Otterloo and won a Radio-Netherlands conducting competition in 1954; Marjan *Mozetich, who received second prize in the 1976 Gaudeamus Composition Competition (for his wind quintet *It's in the Air*); and the *Barrie Central Collegiate Band and the West Vancouver Boys' Band, both of which won firsts at Kerkrade World Music Festivals. In 1977 the jazz pianist Don *Thompson appeared at the EBU-sponsored International Jazz Festival at Larens.

Franz-Paul *Decker was music director of the Rotterdam Philharmonic, and Alexander *Brott, who studied with the Dutch-American composer Bernard Wagenaar in New York, has guest-conducted in Holland. Brott's composition *Songs of Contemplation* for voice and orchestra was given its Netherlands' premiere by the Dutch soprano Gré Brouwenstijn in 1948. The violinist Steven *Staryk was concertmaster of the Amsterdam Concertgebouw Orchestra 1960–3 and also taught at the Amsterdam Cons.

As an expression of gratitude for Canada's role in the liberation of the Netherlands during World War II, the Dutch-Canadian community in 1970 purchased two Flentrop organs – one large and one small – for the *NAC in Ottawa.

During the late 1960s Dutch-Canadians residing in British Columbia made a gift to the province of a Dutch-built carillon known as the Netherlands Centennial Carillon. Located in Victoria, this carillon was given in honour of Canada's 1967 centennial; it may be heard in a private recording which features both the British Columbia carillonneur Herman Bergink and the Dutch carillonneur Leen 't Hart. (KV)

NEUFELD, Kornelius (Herman). Choir conductor, educator, administrator, composer, b Nikolajewa, south Russia, 10 Dec 1892, d Winkler, Man, 14 Jan 1957; hon D MUS (Saskatchewan) 1953. As a youth he studied voice at the Moscow Cons and with Max Pohl in Berlin and sang in Moscow's Simin Opera Chorus.

Emigrating to Canada in 1923, Neufeld settled in Winkler, a *Mennonite community south of Winnipeg. He organized the Bergthaler Church Choir there in 1928. He subsequently established and conducted choirs and instrumental groups among Mennonite communities from Ontario to British Columbia, and for this work was nicknamed 'the Wandering Conductor.'

Neufeld considered it his mission, among Canadian Mennonites, to 'transform a cultural hinterland into a singing people.' The prevailing tradition of Mennonites in Canada at the time excluded secular forms of musical expression, and Neufeld has been credited with creating an increased tolerance of the secular repertoire. He accomplished this by founding in 1936 the Winkler Musical Festival, which stimulated the establishing of similar events in other Mennonite centres, and by strengthening regional choral workshops in conjunction with the traditional Mennonite 'Sängerfeste.'

Neufeld attempted to establish a western Canadian Mennonite music publishing operation and indeed published his own choral works (see *Catalogue of Canadian Composers*) and two cantatas, *To the Youth* and *Zion, the City of God* (1952). He also imported music published by Swiss companies. In later years, however, the business continued only as a printing company.

BIBLIOGRAPHY

Brown, Frank. *History of the Town of Winkler Manitoba: 1892–1973* (Winkler 1973) BHr

New Brunswick Cultural Development Branch. Established in 1975; a division of the New Brunswick government's Dept of Youth, Recreation and Cultural Resources. The branch has concerned itself with dance, drama, music, and the literary and visual arts. John Saunders, the branch's first director, remained in the position in 1980.

Services to various parts of the province have been administered through a network of regional offices equipped to promote cultural activities in both English-speaking and French-speaking communities and funded by the provincial government. Provision in music includes operational grants for camps and schools; subsidies for orchestras and ensembles within the Atlantic regions, and for New Brunswick-based soloists; bursaries for advanced post-secondary music studies (awarded to candidates selected by a panel of independent experts); and travel grants to groups and individuals to attend conferences, competitions, and festivals held in Canada and abroad. The branch has provided financial assistance to volunteer organizations such as community arts councils, to provincial music federations and festivals, to musical groups for the purpose of recording, to small communities towards the purchase of pianos for public use, and to Canadian performers generally for in-province travel costs. In addition it has sponsored artists-in-the-schools and artists-in-the-community programs. In collaboration with the Touring Office of the *Canada Council and the Nova Scotia Dept of Culture, Recreation and Fitness, it has sponsored the annual workshop and artist showcase Contact East, begun in 1976.

The Dept of Youth, Recreation and Cultural Resources' annual report has summarized the department's activities. The first edition of a handbook entitled *Resources for the Arts*, also published by the department, appeared in 1977.

BIBLIOGRAPHY

Claus, Jo Anne. 'New Brunswick goes to work to spread the cultural word,' *PfAC*, Spring 1977

Maillet, Desmond. 'Review of Contact East 1979,' Touring Office *Bulletin*, Jan 1980

New Brunswick Registered Music Teachers' Association. Organized in 1950 as the New Brunswick Music Teachers' Association by Alice

M. Harrison and other members of existing city groups. The first annual meeting was held 27 Sep 1952 when a constitution was adopted. In 1954 the NBMTA became affiliated with the *CFMTA which paid the cost of its incorporation in March 1961 when the name was changed to New Brunswick Registered Music Teachers' Association. There were 78 members in 1979. A *Newsletter* was begun in 1965 and in 1980 continued to be published several times a year.

The chief aim of the NBRMTA, beyond professional development and fellowship, has been to win recognition for music from the New Brunswick Dept of Education, school boards, and the public. After years of lobbying it succeeded in having music accepted as a high school credit course – first through a written matriculation examination with a practical credit, and then as an in-school subject in those centres where it is taught. In 1977 the NBRMTA was still striving to persuade the department to give credit for practical and theory examinations passed after study under private teachers.

The NBRMTA arranges workshops at its annual and mid-year meetings and promotes Canada Music Week with considerable emphasis on the Music Writing Contest of the CFMTA. Members assist on music festival committees, arrange examination centres for *RCMT and *Mount Allison examiners, and organize student recitals under the auspices of local branches.

Presidents of the NBRMTA have been Robert C. *Bayley 1950–2, Howard *Brown 1952–6 and 1960–1, James Manchip 1956–8 and 1961–4, Ernest Freeborn 1958–60 and 1964–5, Elsa Noble 1965–7, Greta MacKenzie 1967–70, Elizabeth Armour 1970–3, Hester Jackson 1973–4, Kathleen Fensom 1974–6, and Margaret King 1976–8, succeeded by Elizabeth Armour. MCK

New Brunswick Symphony Orchestra. A 55-60 member, provincially oriented orchestra formed in 1962 and based in Saint John. It drew its personnel from the former Fredericton Civic and Saint John Symphony orchestras and the Royal Canadian Dragoons Band from Camp Gagetown near Fredericton.

The orchestra's first concert, 21 Nov 1962 at Saint John High School, included Beethoven's *Symphony No. 4*, Bach's *Two-Piano Concerto in C* (soloists: Rosabelle and Kelsey *Jones), and Jones' *Miramichi Ballad*. Concerts (10 during the first season) followed in Fredericton, Moncton, Sussex, and St Andrews. In subsequent years the orchestra gave fewer concerts and travelled less. During its six-year history Janis *Kalnins was the conductor, Douglas Major the assistant conductor, and Bruce *Holder the concertmaster. Soloists included the singers Diane *Oxner and Gloria *Richard. The orchestra sponsored the formation of the *New Brunswick Youth Orchestra in 1966.

In 1968 the New Brunswick SO, along with the *Halifax SO, was superseded by the newly formed *Atlantic SO.

BIBLIOGRAPHY
Ball, Walter. 'New Brunswick Symphony,' *Music Across Canada*, Mar 1963 SS

New Brunswick Youth Orchestra. Founded as a provincial orchestra in 1965 at the instigation of Philip W. Oland, then president of the *New Brunswick SO. Its members range in age from 12 to 24 years.

The New Brunswick Youth Orchestra gave its first concert 22 Oct 1966 in Woodstock, NB. It performed at *Expo 67 and in the same year won first place at the Dominion Centenary Festival of Music for Senior Orchestras. It has made annual tours of New Brunswick and has appeared on TV. It performed at the *NAC in 1972 and was the only Canadian participant at the Festival of International Youth Orchestras in Great Britain in 1973. In 1974, 1976, and 1978 it performed at the Canadian Festival of Youth Orchestras in Banff, Alta. In 1978 it won a *PRO Canada Orchestra Award for imaginative programming of contemporary music.

When the New Brunswick SO was discontinued in 1968 to make way for the *Atlantic SO the New Brunswick Youth Orchestra became, in effect, the home orchestra of New Brunswick, funded by private, municipal, and provincial grants and with a board of directors drawn from across the province. Rehearsals are held in various locations throughout New Brunswick.

Conductors have been Stanley *Saunders 1965–8 and 1970–4, Kelsey *Jones 1968–9, Clayton *Hare 1969–70, and Kenneth *Elloway 1974–5, succeeded by Rodney McLeod. (NV)

Newcombe Piano Co, Ltd. Founded in Toronto in 1878 by Octavius Newcombe (b Hankford-Barton, Devonshire, England, 19 Nov 1846, d Toronto? ca 1905). Newcombe had been a partner 1871–8 with *Mason & Risch before establishing his own firm, Octavius Newcombe & Co (incorporated as Newcombe Piano Co, Ltd, in 1912). He was joined in business in 1879 by his brother Henry at premises on Church St. A factory built in 1887 on Bellwoods Ave was destroyed by fire in 1926. It was not rebuilt; the firm acted only as a retailer thereafter until about 1934. Newcombe built all kinds of pianos – squares, grands, and uprights. A silver medal and the Jurors' Report of Commendation at the World's Industrial and Cotton Centennial Exposition (New Orleans 1884–5) are credited with helping to open the US market to the company. At the Colonial and Indian Exhibition (London 1886), Newcombe was awarded a medal and a diploma. There, also, Sir Arthur Sullivan selected a Newcombe grand piano for Queen Victoria; it was housed at Windsor Castle in the Audience Chamber. Another medal and diploma were received at the Chicago World's Fair (1893) and a gold medal at the Paris Exposition (1900). After the firm's demise the Newcombe line was carried on by *Willis. FH

Newfoundland Division of Cultural Affairs. A branch of the Newfoundland Dept of Tourism (Dept of Tourism, Culture and Recreation in 1980), created as a full division in 1972. Prior to that date support of culture and the arts within the province had been the responsibility of the Dept of Provincial Affairs, which, before it ceased to exist in 1972, oversaw the establishment of Newfoundland's first *Arts and Culture Centre (opened 1967 in St John's). The position of director of cultural affairs was created in March 1971, prior to the establishment of the Cultural Affairs Division. In 1980 the post was held by John Perlin, who also was director general of arts and culture centres.

The division has functioned solely on funds provided annually by the provincial government. Its responsibilities have included the operation of the province's five arts and culture centres (located in Corner Brook, Gander, Grand Falls, Stephenville, and St John's). In addition, it has administered a modest program of grants and awards and the Newfoundland Arts and Letters Competition, which includes a section for original compositions; winning entries have been published by the division. The Newfoundland Federation of Music Festivals, the Newfoundland SO, and several folk arts groups have received assistance from the division.

The Newfoundland and Labrador Arts Council was created as an agency of the provincial government early in 1980, to foster and promote the arts in the province, advise the government on arts policy, and administer the funds allocated by the government ($180,000 in 1980) for grants to individuals and organizations. The first chairman of the 12-member board (appointed by the Dept of Tourism, Recreation and Culture) was George Story. The executive director in 1980 was Edythe Goodridge.

NEWMARK (Neumark), **John** (Hans Joseph). Pianist, accompanist, chamber musician, b Bremen, Germany, 12 Jun 1904, naturalized Canadian 1946; hon D MUS (McGill) 1975. Born into a family which cultivated music and painting, he studied piano 1912–19 in Bremen with Karl Boerner and 1920–1 in Leipzig with Anni Eisele. At 17 he auditioned in Berlin for Coenraad V. Bos, the noted accompanist, who predicted a brilliant future for him. He was urged to tour in Europe and America, but his father sent him to study drawing in Dresden where, in 1925, he met the violinist Szymon Goldberg with whom he gave recitals. In 1929 he returned to Bremen and soon began to devote himself entirely to music. With the cellist August Wenzinger he founded the Neue Kammermusik Bremen society whose concerts presented many contemporary works. Continuing his activity as a pianist, he was director 1930–3 of music programs on the Bremen radio. He settled in 1933 in Berlin but for political reasons was forbidden to play in public, so he toured 1933–5 in Spain with Goldberg.

Newmark wanted to leave Germany, but it was not until 1939 that he was able to get to London. There he took part in concerts, notably with the soprano Emmy *Heim and the violinist Max Rostal. Because of his status as an alien, however, he was interned in 1940 on the Isle of Man and then in Canada. In 1942 he went to Toronto and studied harmony and conducting with Ettore *Mazzoleni. The soprano Frances *James engaged him in 1943 for a tour that took him as far as Vancouver and Victoria.

In 1944 Newmark settled permanently in Montreal where his services were soon in demand by eminent Canadian and foreign soloists. That year, with the violinist Alexander *Brott and the cellist Roland *Leduc, he was the first to perform the complete Beethoven trios on CBC radio; and in 1945 he and the violinist Noël *Brunet performed 19 Mozart sonatas on the CBC. He also joined Marie-Thérèse *Paquin in 1946 to present for the first time a series devoted to the original repertoire for piano four hands. In 1949 he gave concerts in South America with Goldberg and accompanied the famous contralto Kathleen Ferrier on two extended tours of North America. With her, in 1950, he recorded song cycles of Schumann and Brahms for Decca-London; Brahms' *Vier Ernste Gesänge* in 1952 won a Grand prix du disque de l'Académie Charles-Cros.

Newmark has taken part in thousands of recitals, concerts, and radio and TV broadcasts. He has accompanied more than 80 foreign and at least 160 Canadian artists and has recorded with several of the most prominent. His long collaboration with Maureen *Forrester began in 1953; with her he has toured the world. After a Toronto recital by the team John *Kraglund wrote (*Globe and Mail*, 18 Jan 1960): 'Superb as Miss Forrester was, much of the credit for the exceptionally high quality of the recital must go to Mr. Newmark. Always a reliable accompanist, he gave inspired performances throughout the evening, providing an integral

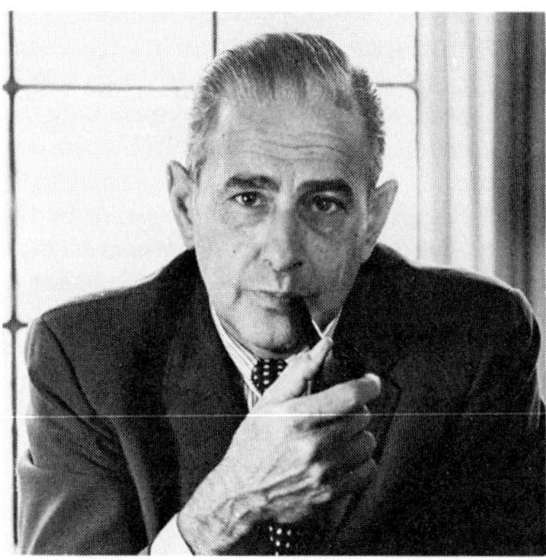

John Newmark

part of each song, without being guilty of either too much or too little.'

In 1950 Newmark acquired a Clementi piano built in London in 1810, and on it he has given recitals and made recordings.

Newmark was one of the artistic advisers 1972–5 to the *Opéra du Québec, has served on many competition juries, and has taken part in the premieres of numerous Canadian works.

Newmark renewed his youthful activities as a painter and exhibited his work in 1962 at the Montreal Museum of Fine Arts, in 1963 at the Mansfield Book Mart in Montreal, and in 1964 at Le Bouquinier, a bookstore in Quebec City. In 1975 he completed his memoirs (still unpublished in 1980) and in 1979 he read selections from them in a CBC radio series, 'An Accompanist's ABC.' He was made an Officer of the *Order of Canada in 1974 and received the *CMCouncil Medal in 1979.

DISCOGRAPHY

AS SOLOIST

The Clementi Piano I: C.P.E. Bach – J.C. Bach – W.F. Bach. 1962. Folk FM 3341

The Clementi Piano II: Clementi *Sonatas, Op 40, no. 1; Op 50, no. 3*. 1964. Folk FM 3342

Duchow – Barclay – Papineau-Couture – Pentland – Brassard – Coulthard – Bartley – Beckwith – Hurst. 1955. RCI 134

Haydn – C.P.E. Bach – Clementi. 1953. Hallmark RS-4

Reger. 1965. 2-AofD ABD-4

WITH FOREIGN ARTISTS

Brahms *Vier Ernste Gesänge*. Ferrier alto. 1950. Ace of Clubs ACL 306

Falla *Siete canciones populares españolas*. C. Torrès sop. 1947. 2-RCA Victor 120336-7

Pièces pour violoncelle. P. Tortelier vc, M. Tortelier vc. 1958. Pathé-Marconi RALP 599

Schumann *Frauenliebe und -Leben; Volksliedchen; Widmung*. Ferrier alto. 1950. Ace of Clubs ACL 307

– *Frauenliebe und -Leben*. U. Graf sop. 1950. Allegro 73

WITH CANADIAN ARTISTS

Beethoven *Trio Op 121a* (Kakadu Variations), *Trio Op 153, Trio Op 44* (14 variations on an original theme). M. Goodman vn, W. Joachim vc. 1970. CBC SM-122

Coulthard *Sonata* for oboe and piano. C. Perrier ob. 1949. RCI 4

Debussy *Première Rhapsodie* for clarinet and piano – Hindemith *Sonata* for clarinet and piano. A. Gallant cl. 1966. CBC SM-11

Haydn *Trio in D* – Mozart *Trio in E* K542. M. Goodman vn, Rosemarin vc. 1951. RCI 44

Hessenberg – Turina – Bloch. M. Goodman vn, W. Joachim vc. 1968. CBC SM-59

Music from Latvia: Medins – Dvarionas – Lapenson – et al. Lapenson vn. 1969. Poly 542-005

For recordings as accompanist with other Canadian artists see Alarie, Ascher Duo, D. Bell, Boyden, Bress, Maurice Brown, Brunet, Daunais, Diamant, Forrester, G. Gabora, H. Gagné, M. Goodman, E.B. Guy, Hagen, W. Joachim, Kash, Kondaks, R. Leduc, Malenfant, Masella family, Nelsova, Montreal String Quartet, Simoneau, Verreau.

BIBLIOGRAPHY

Barré, Geneviève. 'Pianist John Newmark,' *CBC Times*, 21–7 Feb 1954

McLean, Eric. 'Recognition overdue,' *Montreal Star*, 20 Apr 1974

Creative Canada, vol 1

GP

New Music Concerts. Organization established in 1971 in Toronto to present and foster new music and to provide performers with opportunities to master its techniques. By 1979 New Music Concerts was recognized, nationally and abroad, as Ontario's major proponent of contemporary music of all countries and as one of the two or three most effectual organizations of its kind in Canada. The founders were Norma *Beecroft (president), Robert *Aitken (artistic director), John A. Wright, John Brown, John *Beckwith, and C. Laughton *Bird.

Annual series of concerts at the *U of Toronto began in 1972, and concerts have been given at *York U and in several Ontario cities. Tours in 1976, of Europe and of Nova Scotia, Quebec, and Ontario, were followed by an appearance 24 Oct 1976 at the ISCM Festival in Boston.

New Music Concerts has devoted entire programs to the works of Luciano Berio in 1972, George Crumb in 1974, Mauricio Kagel in 1974, Peter Maxwell Davies in 1976, John Cage in 1977, Karlheinz Stockhausen in 1979, Gabriel *Charpentier in 1979, and Witold Lutoslawski in 1980, with the composers present and often conducting or performing. Other composers whose works have been featured include Lukas Foss and Heinz Holliger in 1975; Alcides *Lanza, Toru Takemitsu, and Iannis Xenakis in 1976; Elliott Carter in 1977; R. Murray *Schafer and Sylvano Bussotti in 1978; and Milton Babbitt, Harrison Birtwistle, Lou Harrison, and György Ligeti in 1979.

Works commissioned and premiered by New Music Concerts include Gustav *Ciamaga's *Solipsism while Dying* (1972–3), Alan *Heard's *Timai* (1973), Sydney *Hodkinson's *Taula* (1974), Norma Beecroft's *Rasas III* (1974) and *Collage '76* (1976), Rudolf *Komorous' *Boogie Woogie* (1974), Takemitsu's *Bryce* (1975), John *Hawkins' *Trio* (1975), Donald Steven's *The Transient* (1975), Alcides Lanza's *kron'ikəlz* (1976), Serge *Garant's *Rivages* (1976), and Harry *Freedman's *Fragments of Alice* (1976). In addition to those already mentioned, Canadian composers who have had works premiered by New Music Concerts include Beckwith, *Hambraeus, *Hayes, Jaeger, *Koprowski, *Laufer, *Mather, *Pauk, *Pentland, *Saint-Marcoux, *Somers, *Symonds, Tilley, *Tremblay, *Weinzweig, and *Wyre.

Among the many performers who have appeared in New Music Concerts presentations are Otto *Armin, James *Campbell, Robin Engelman, Monica *Gaylord, Erica *Goodman, the *LePage and Mather Duo, Joseph *Macerollo, Jean MacPhail, Mary *Morrison, Gary *Relyea, and Patricia *Rideout. Groups appearing have included *Canadian Brass, the *Canadian Electronic Ensemble, the *Lyric Arts Trio, *Nexus, the *Orford String Quartet, David *Rosenboom and Associates, the Toronto Winds, and the *York Winds (Canada); the K & K Experimental Studio and Pupo Drom (Austria); the Solistes des choeurs de l'RTF and the Percussions de Strasbourg (France); Aloys and Alfons Kontarsky, and Trio Exvoco (Germany); Musica Elettronica Viva (Italy); the Warsaw Music Workshop (Poland); the Extended Vocal Techniques Ensemble, and Steve Reich (USA); and Vinko Globokar and New Phonic Arts (Yugoslavia).

BIBLIOGRAPHY

Schulman, Michael. 'New Music Concerts successful in attracting young audiences,' *MSc*, 280, Nov–Dec 1974

– 'Contemporary music groups thriving across Canada: New Music Concerts,' *MSc*, 303, Sep–Oct 1978

CF

NEWNHAM, Frederick (Laurence). Baritone, teacher, organist, b Ryde, Isle of Wight, England, 3 Apr 1901; ARCM 1928, LRAM 1929, ARAM 1934, FRAM 1962. He studied voice in England with Thomas Meux 1922–3, Arnold Fulton 1923–5, and Harry Plunkett-Greene in 1928 and in Montreal with Gustav Fewks 1944–5, and organ in England with Reginald Steggall 1922–5.

In 1927 Newnham was appointed head of the voice department and associate professor of organ at *Acadia U, positions which he held until 1933. He was head of the voice departments 1933–4 at the Halifax Cons and 1934–5 at the Maritime Academy of Music. He was music director 1935–8 at the *Western Ontario Cons and the *U of Western Ontario and director of master classes in voice 1936–8 for the Ontario Board of Education Summer School. He lived 1946–50 in Winnipeg as an organist-choirmaster and singing teacher prior to serving 1950–73 as the head of the voice and organ departments at Pacific Lutheran U, Tacoma, Wash. From 1973 to 1977 he lived and worked in Calgary. In 1977 he returned to Tacoma.

Newnham has performed extensively in Canada and abroad and has been heard on many radio networks, including the CBC, BBC, CBS, and NBC. During a stay in Europe prior to World War II he was principal lyric baritone of the Carl Rosa Opera Company. He appeared in 1936 and 1937 as the soloist in Walton's *Belshazzar's Feast* with the *TSO and the *Toronto Mendelssohn Choir. He has conducted several Canadian choirs, and has been organist-choirmaster at churches in Great Britain, Calgary, Winnipeg, and Tacoma.

Newnham was president in 1946 of the Central Alberta Music Festival and in 1948 of the *Alberta Music Festival. During the 1960s and 1970s he was chairman of the adjudicating committee for the northwestern regional auditions of the *Metropolitan Opera.

Newnham has taught throughout his career; his pupils have included Jean Patterson Edwards, Norman Farrow, Jon *Vickers, and Kenneth *Winters.

NEWTON, Gertrude. Soprano, teacher, b Manchester 1895, d Victoria, BC, 30 May 1972. She was a pupil of Rhys Thomas in London and, after moving in 1910 to Winnipeg, of Winona Lightcap. She became a soloist at Fort Rouge United Church in 1916 and at Knox United Church in 1923. With the *Winnipeg Oratorio Society she sang in Beethoven's *Mount of Olives* and Mendelssohn's *Elijah* in 1923 and Debussy's *The Blessed Damosel* in 1924. While studying 1930–2 with a Mme Cappiani in London she sang on BBC radio; in Stockholm, Oslo, and Copenhagen; and in 1932 at Wigmore Hall, London. Returning to Winnipeg she sang Nadina in *The Chocolate Soldier* (1933), Serpolette in *Chimes of Normandy* (1934), and Hanna in *The Merry Widow* (1935) with the Winnipeg Light Opera and during the next 10 years was one of the city's reigning oratorio sopranos, appearing in *Messiah, The Creation*, and other works with the *Winnipeg Philharmonic Choir. She taught and coached voice in Winnipeg and in Kenora, Ont. Her pupils included William Goertzen. After serving 1947–54 as soloist and choir leader at Harstone United Church, she moved to California. She returned to Canada in 1964 and spent her remaining years in Victoria, BC. CC

New Westminster. City east of Vancouver near the mouth of the Fraser River. After its designation (1859, incorporation 1860) as the capital city

New Music Concerts: (left to right, front row) John Hawkins, Monica Gaylord, Robert Aitken, (middle row) Mary Morrison, Robin Engelman, Lawrence Cherney, William Kuinka, James MacDonald, (top row) Russell Hartenberger, Patricia Rideout, Allan Beard, Erica Goodman

of British Columbia it was named New Westminster by Queen Victoria, and hence nicknamed 'The Royal City.' The seat of government was transferred to Victoria in 1866, and a fire destroyed the business section in 1898, but New Westminster grew nevertheless into a thriving industrial and commercial centre with a population of 45,000 in 1975. Although culturally in the shadow of Vancouver, New Westminster has a longer musical history.

An active Bell Ringers' Club performed on the peal of eight bells (the first chime in British Columbia) installed in Holy Trinity Church in 1865. All but one of the bells were destroyed, however, in the 1898 fire.

The New Westminster Choral Union, conducted 1882–93 by Bishop Acton Windeyer Sillitoe (b Australia 1841, d New Westminster 1894), presented *Messiah, Elijah*, Bennett's *May Queen*, Stanford's *Revenge*, and other choral works in its home city and in Granville (Vancouver) and Ladner. By 1893 it had given 37 performances. The Westminster Amateur Operatic Society also flourished in the 1890s, and a mixed choir of more than 100 voices, prepared by A.E. White, sang with orchestra under Sir Alexander Mackenzie in the 1903 *Cycle of Musical Festivals. The Westminster Operatic Club began its productions (usually Gilbert & Sullivan) in 1914.

By 1920 the New Westminster SO had presented 18 concerts; this group lasted another 15 years. A competition festival was initiated after World War I and the New Westminster Oratorio Society and Orchestra ca 1933. In 1944 the Civic Orchestra (New Westminster Symphony – see Orchestras: 7 / Some Canadian community orchestras) was established; it numbered about 50 musicians in 1977 (many from other cities) and though at that time still an amateur group it had undertaken ambitious programs (including Schumann and Brahms symphonies) with some success. The Symphony Society has sponsored the Pacific Evergreen Youth Choir (begun in 1968) and the young-adult Con Brio Singers (1971–6).

The Karellers (1955–63) and the *Handel Society of Music (formed in 1966) have flourished under the direction of Karel *ten Hoope. The pipe organ in Holy Trinity Cathedral was rebuilt by G. Herald *Keefer who became the cathedral's music director and organist in 1969.

Bands have been a notable feature of Royal City music. These include the New Westminster Boy Scout Band (later the New Westminster Junior Band), conducted 1926–46 by C.J. Cornfield; the Royal City Concert Band (fl 1935); and various school bands.

The music department of New Westminster Schools began an annual jazz festival in 1970. Devoted to British Columbia and northwest US school stagebands, the festival was recognized in 1980 as one of the largest in Canada. The New Westminster Secondary Schools Jazz Ensemble, directed by Bob Schaeffer, won a first in its class at the 1978 Reno (Nevada) International Jazz Festival.

Two country music firms established offices in New Westminster – the publisher *Empire Music and Aragon Records – and the *Rhythm Pals began their career on radio station CKNW.

Musicians born in New Westminster include Judith *Forst, Ray *Nurse, Joan *Peebles, and Lyn *Vernon.

BIBLIOGRAPHY

Salisbury, Dorothy E. 'Music in British Columbia outside Vancouver,' *CMJ*, vol 2, Summer 1958

'From the archives,' ibid

BNSG

New Zealand. See Australia and New Zealand.

Nexus. Toronto-based percussion ensemble formed in 1971 by the US-born musicians Robert Becker, William Cahn, Michael Craden, Robin Engelman, Russell Hartenberger, and John *Wyre. In programs encompassing African drumming, ragtime, 20th-century works, and freely improvised music, the group has mastered the many percussion instruments of the world's major music traditions and introduced numerous instruments invented by its players.

Nexus has performed regularly in Ontario and New York state. At the invitation of Toru Takemitsu, who commissioned Jo Kando's *Under the Umbrella* for Nexus, the ensemble toured Japan in 1976. In December 1978, it toured in England, giving performances and workshops. With the *Festival Singers, the group premiered Wyre's *Utau Kane NoWa* (1975), *Bernie* (1976), and *Connexus* (1978). Nexus itself commissioned John *Arpin's *Summer Suite* (1976).

Nexus appeared in the NFB film *Musicanada* (1975) and on CBC TV's 'Music to See' in 1976 and taped programs for the CBC's 'Jazz Radio Canada' in 1976 and (with solo performers David Darling, Kathryn *Moses, and Bernie *Piltch) in 1977. It is heard on the soundtracks of the films *Journey* (1971) and *The Man Who Skied down Everest* (1974, an Academy Award winner), and it made the LPs *Paul Horn + Nexus* (1975, Epic KE 33561) and *Nexus Ragtime Concert* (1976, Umbrella UMB DD2). Nexus has been the resident group at *York U (1973), Wesleyan U in Middleton, Conn (1974), the Courtenay Youth Music Camp (1974), the Chautauqua (NY) Institute (1974), and the *U of Toronto (1976), offering workshops in the percussion musics of the world and in improvisation.

Engelman, a principal percussionist 1968–72 of the *TS, taught at the U of Toronto in 1971 and joined the teaching staff at York U in 1972. Hartenberger joined the Faculty of Music at the U of Toronto in 1974. Craden has performed and recorded with Moe *Koffman, the *Boss Brass, and other Toronto jazz groups; he formed his own percussion-oriented group, Poke-A-Dope, in 1975. In Canada Becker and Cahn have worked only with Nexus. AHC

Niagara Falls, Ontario. City first settled in 1782, adjacent to and named after the seventh wonder of the world, and situated directly across the Canadian- US border from Niagara Falls, NY. Originally composed of three settlements (Drummondville, Clifton, and Elgin) it took the name Niagara Falls in 1861 and was incorporated as a city in 1904. By 1975 it had a population of around 67,000 and was long established as a major tourist centre.

In the 20th century, notable musicians and ensemble directors have included Charles Buff, Gordon Mitchell, Harold Jones, and Donald Gill. In 1929 the 40-member Temple Male Choir, directed by Walter McDowell, was founded under the auspices of the Masons. It gave two regular concerts a year, competed in Ontario music festivals, and ceased operations in 1943 because of the war. *Chautauqua visited the city in the early 1930s. Local groups active before World War II were the Niagara Falls Male Voice Choir and the Niagara Falls Choral Society. The Niagara Falls Kiltie Band, attached to the Canadian Corps, unit 104, presented about 35 concerts annually during the war.

The *Community Concerts organization, active 1949–75 in Niagara Falls, presented many noted artists – eg, Glenn *Gould and Teresa *Stratas. In 1975 a volunteer group called Niagara Concerts assumed that function, presenting such ensembles as the *TS, and the Georgian Trio on its first tour outside the USSR.

For many years the Oratorio Society has given annual performances of *Messiah*, in earlier days with such singers as the young James *Milligan and Jon *Vickers. Other concerts have been given by the Niagara Falls Music Teachers' Assn and by the Gentlemen Songsters, the Fred Willett Concert Band, the Rainbow Tones Barbershop Group, and the Music Theatre Company. The Chopin scholar Mateusz Glinski conducted a Niagara SO in the late 1960s. During the 1970s the *St Catharines SO (renamed Niagara SO in 1977) served the entire Niagara region including Niagara Falls. The Niagara Falls Kiwanis Music Competition Festival, founded in 1926, became one of the largest in Ontario.

Niagara Falls is the birthplace of Nathaniel *Dett, Kathleen *Howard, Alexander 'Ragtime' Read, the pianist Kathleen Solose, and the soprano Penny Speedie. The 55 bells of the Rainbow Tower *carillon (one of 11 in Canada) were installed in 1947. June Hamilton, Robert *Donnell, and Leland *Richardson have served as carillonneurs.

See also Niagara Falls in music. (AS)

Niagara Falls in music. The thundering waterfalls have provoked the imagination of several composers. Of the pieces by European visitors, *Niagara* (violin and piano ca 1845), by the Norwegian violinist Ole Bull, is perhaps the earliest. The British songwriter Henry Russell wrote a vocal scena 'Mighty Niagara' (words by Charles Mackay), the Polish-French pianist Henri Kowalski the piano piece *Aux bords du Niagara* (1872), and the German composer Friedrich Wilhelm Tschirch a concert overture *Am Niagara* (1872). Rimsky-Korsakov visited the falls in 1863 and Offenbach in 1876; Ravel, who saw them in 1928, is said to have exclaimed 'Quel majestueux si bémol!' But none of these famous men was inspired to compose. Works by US composers include Anthony Philip Heinrich's *The War of the Elements and the Thundering of Niagara*, a 'capriccio grande' for orchestra (before 1845); George Bristow's *Niagara* cantata (1898); Harvey Gaul's *The Masque of Niagara* (1934), which includes 'Thunder of Waters' and 'Indian River Song' sections; and Johan Franco's *Rainbow Bridge Nocturne* for the Rainbow Tower carillon.

R. Nathaniel *Dett, a native of Niagara Falls, Ont, wrote a *Cave of the Winds* march (1902). John *Beckwith's *Great Lakes Suite* (words by James Reaney, 1949) pauses briefly at the Falls. Joseph *Roff's suite *Niagara* (1953) is a musical portrait of the Falls and their attendant attractions. Popular music has its share of Niagara polkas, schottisches, and 'souvenirs.' Willie *Eckstein wrote 'Where the Niagara Flows' (1933); two pieces share the title *A Trip to Niagara*, one by train (by Clifford V. Baker, 1905) and one by steamer (by William J. Cornish, ca 1915). HK

Niagara-on-the-Lake (Newark until 1798, Niagara 1798–1906). First capital of Upper Canada (Ontario) and the site of the *Shaw Festival. Situated at the mouth of the Niagara River, on the shore of Lake Ontario, the town was settled in the mid-1780s by Loyalists and was the seat 1792–6 of the Parliament of Upper Canada.

As the capital and a garrison town Newark enjoyed the first documented performance of European music in Upper Canada, that of the regimental band at the fortnightly officers' balls, noted in April 1793 by Mrs John Graves Simcoe in her published diary (Toronto 1911). Another instance is documented for 4 Jan 1797: 'a band of music' led a procession 'playing Masonic airs.' Indeed, in 1980 military bands continued to preside at local functions.

Evidence of the relatively high standard of comfort attained in Niagara by 1830 are the square pianos imported from England by Captain Sibbald of the Royal Scots and by Lieutenant-Governor Colborne and still on display 150 years later in the local museum. It is known that a Band-Major, Joseph Harkness, offered in 1853 to train a choir at St Andrew's Church and to hold two fund-raising concerts for repairs to the church. Prior to the installation of organs in the town's churches, the Presbyterians relied on their precentor, John Crooks, who used a tuning fork (and possibly the three wooden tuning boxes held by the local museum) to lead the singing, while the Methodists were served by a Mr Varey, bass violist. The church of St Vincent de Paul installed a pipe and reed organ ca 1870 and other area churches soon followed suit. When *Chautauqua began in Niagara during the summer of 1887, music courses were part of the program.

Niagara-on-the-Lake became the site of the Shaw Festival with the conversion of its court house into a theatre in 1962. JLF

Niagara Symphony Association. See St Catharine's Symphony Orchestra.

Nickelodeons. See Player pianos and nickelodeons.

NIERMEIER, Frans (Cornelis). Organist, pianist, violinist, teacher, composer, b Deventer, Holland, 19 Mar 1903; FCCO 1934, B MUS (Toronto) 1935, D MUS (Toronto) 1940. In Holland he studied several instruments 1911–18 at the Arnhem Cons. He moved to Canada in 1924 and studied 1926–9 in Winnipeg with Herbert *Sadler (organ) and Gwendda Owen *Davies (theory), 1933–4 privately in Toronto with Charles *Peaker, and 1933–40 at the *U of Toronto with Frederick *Horwood.

Niermeier has been a church organist 1931–3 in Fort Frances, Ont, 1934–5 in Kitchener, Ont, 1936–43 and 1962–9 in Winnipeg, and after 1970 in St Catharines, Ont. During World War II he was an arranger for CBC Winnipeg and a violinist in the *CBC Winnipeg Orchestra. He taught theory privately, piano and organ at the *Bronoff School for several years beginning in 1937, and theory at the *Mennonite Brethren Bible College in Winnipeg 1947–60.

Niermeier's compositions, all unpublished and some listed in the *Catalogue of Canadian Composers*, include a symphony; a string quartet; sonatas for violin and piano, for cello solo, and for piano four-hands; 10 organ preludes and fugues; many pieces for accordion; and some choral works and sacred songs. He is an affiliate of PRO Canada.

Night Blooming Cereus. Hour-long one-act opera for soloists and small orchestra, composed 1953–8 by John *Beckwith to a libretto by James Reaney. It became a CBC commission after its actual completion ensured its radio premiere (4 Mar 1959), for which the cast comprised Ann Stephenson (as Alice), Patricia *Rideout (as Mrs Brown), Phyllis Antognini, Irene *Byatt, Alexander *Gray, Bernard *Johnson, Jean Marie Scott, and Patricia Snell.

The story, a parable of the deep-rooted, miraculous continuity of life, unfolds in a small-town Ontario house. Alice arrives there in search of her grandmother, Mrs Brown, whose daughter, Alice's mother, had broken the family tie years before. The meeting and forgiveness, and the resolution of the problems of various townsfolk, coincide with the mystical blooming of the cereus, a rare plant which flowers once in 100 years. After the broadcast, Kenneth *Winters described Beckwith's music as 'apt, active, serious and witty. It came off handsomely in performance ... taking its comic and dramatic suggestions from the words sensitively and artfully' (*Winnipeg Free Press*, 5 Mar 1959).

The work was repeated on CBC radio the following year and had its first stage production at *Hart House Theatre, Toronto, 5 and 6 Apr 1960, conducted again by *Mazzoleni, directed by Pamela Terry (Beckwith), and designed by Louis de Niverville, with Sheila *Piercey and Ruth Ann Morse replacing Scott and Antognini in the otherwise original complement of singers. Subsequent productions have been mounted by the *McGill U Opera Workshop in 1968 and by Clifford *Evens at the *U of Western Ontario in 1971. The libretto appears in *The Killdeer and Other Plays* (Toronto 1962). KW

Nimbus 9 Productions. First major independent record-production company of the LP era (post-1950) in Canada. Its downtown-Toronto recording studio, Soundstage, has been recognized as one of the world's finest of the mid-1970s.

Established in 1968 by Peter Clayton, Al Macmillan, Ben *McPeek, and Jack *Richardson, it developed its first artists, the *Guess Who, into international stars. Under the supervision of Richardson and, until 1976, Bob Ezrin (both among North America's leading producers) the studio has been the site of recording sessions by the Bay City Rollers, Alice Cooper, Peter Gabriel, and many others.

Canadian artists recorded by Nimbus 9 for various labels include Bonnie *Dobson and the rock groups Cat, Homestead, and Wireless. A 'direct-to-disc' label, Umbrella, introduced by the company in 1976, has released LPs by the *Boss Brass, *Canadian Brass, violinist Philip Frank, the Humber College Big Band, the Greta *Kraus–Robert *Aitken duo, *Nexus, Rough Trade, and the Toronto Chamber Orchestra with Steven *Staryk.

BIBLIOGRAPHY

Lepka, Stan. 'Teamwork, experience add up to Nimbus 9 success,' *MSc*, 256, Nov–Dec 1970 MM

NIMMONS, Arlene. See Duo Pach.

NIMMONS, Phil (Philip Rista). Composer, arranger, bandleader, clarinetist, teacher, b Kamloops, BC, 3 Jun 1923; BA (British Columbia) 1944. He was raised in Vancouver and began playing clarinet in high school. While studying 1940–4 at the U of British Columbia in preparation for a career in medicine, he played in dance bands (Sandy DeSantis, Stan Patton, and Dal *Richards) and joined the jazz quintet of the guitarist Ray Norris, heard on CBC radio's 'Serenade in Rhythm.' Nimmons wrote many arrangements for Norris' group and composed incidental music for the CBC Vancouver radio drama series 'Anthology.' He studied clarinet 1945–7 at the Juilliard School with Arthur Christmann and composition 1948–50 at the *RCMT with Richard *Johnston, Arnold *Walter, and John *Weinzweig.

Nimmons early compositions included *Sonatina* (1948, for flute), *Toccata* (1949), *String Quartet* (1950), and, for orchestra, *Scherzo* (1950) and *Suite for Spring* (1951). In 1950 he began writing incidental music for programs broadcast on 'CBC Wednesday Night' (and that program's successors) and 'Stage' and for the CBC series 'Affectionately Jenny,' 'Dr. Dogbody's Leg,' 'High Adventures,' and 'The Fantastic Emperor.' Nimmons was the orchestrator for several CBC TV programs produced by Norman *Campbell and directed by Norman Jewison and wrote the score for Paul Almond's CBC TV film 'Power by Proxy' (1961).

In 1953 Nimmons formed his own jazz band which, after some CBC broadcasts, made its concert debut in 1956 at the *Stratford Festival. In December of that year it played with the *TSO. In 1957, as 'Nimmons 'N' Nine,' it began a long association with *CBC radio, appearing first on a weekly show of the same name and subsequently for over 20 years as a regular feature on 'Jazz Workshop' (alternating with Dave *Robbins), 'Jazz Canadians,' and 'Jazz Radio-Canada.' The band played Nimmons' music for the films *A Dangerous Age* (1957) and *A Cool Sound from Hell* (1959)

Phil Nimmons

and was seen 1958–9 as the house band on CBC TV's 'The Barris Beat.'

Nimmons enlarged the band to 16 musicians in 1965 – the name 'Nimmons 'N' Nine Plus Six' was coined by the CBC announcer Bruce Marsh. In 1974 Nimmons' musicians' other commitments forced him to re-organize the band with several younger players. (See Discography for details of personnel.) For a short tour in 1978 the band was joined by the singers Clarence 'Big' Miller and Kathryn *Moses. Its recording of Nimmons' four-part *Atlantic Suite* (1974, comprising 'Harbours,' 'Islands,' 'Tides,' and 'Horizons') received, in 1976, the first *Juno Award given in the jazz category.

Nimmons' other major jazz compositions (to 1980) were *Suite PEI* (1973, recorded by a band under the direction of Guido *Basso, with the composer as soloist, CBC LM-300), the five-movement *Transformations* (1975, commissioned by the *OAC and the CBC for *World Music Week), and the three-movement *Invocation* (1976, comprising 'Gold – The Challenger,' 'Silver – The Prayer,' and 'Bronze – The Contest' and commissioned by the *OAC and COJO in honour of the Olympics in Montreal).

The balance of the band's repertoire, recorded and in live performance, is a combination of Nimmons' arrangements of pop songs and jazz tunes and his own compositions. Of his more than 200 short compositions (many listed in *Contemporary Canadian Composers*) his band has recorded *Muggs, Rhumba Pseudo, Humphy, Kicks, Swing Softly, In a Minor Mode, Who Walks, Little Poppy, On the Autobahn, Squeeze Play, Jasper, Steve's Theme, As a Rully, Watch Out for the Little, Room at the Back, Ed's Comp, Gone with the Blues, One More for Baby, The Thirty Blues, Nosey,* and *Dorian Way.*

Nimmons' early writing style was that of the US 'west-coast cool' school popular in the 1950s. The band's four-man reed section, topped by his clarinet (both unusual features in big band instrumentation), gives it a thinner and dryer sound than that of similar organizations. With his later, major works, Nimmons has moved into bolder orchestration; his *Invocations* has been described as being 'full of large, vivid, almost visible chunks of sound, suggesting a prayer at times, then an anthem, then a symphony' (Jack Batten, Toronto *Globe and Mail,* 31 Jul 1976).

Nimmons also has led a quartet (drawn from the big band) in Toronto nightclubs. During one such engagement, Jack Batten wrote 'his basic clarinet style belongs in the jazz mainstream, straight down through Benny Goodman and Buddy DeFranco,' and referred to 'a wonderful warmth ... especially in the lower register, a kind of enveloping round sound' and 'an arranger's sense of construction, everything in its proper place' (*Globe and Mail,* 11 Jun 1975).

Nimmons' interest in the development of educational facilities for jazz and related music took shape first in the Advanced School of Contemporary Music which he operated 1960–3 with Oscar *Peterson and Ray Brown in Toronto. Nimmons became director of jazz study programs at the *U of New Brunswick Chamber Music and Jazz Festival in 1971, at the faculty of music, *U of Toronto, in 1973, and at the *Banff SFA in 1974. The director of the stage band at the U of Toronto, he has adjudicated for the *Canadian Stage Band and *Kiwanis festivals. His band has performed and given clinics in many Canadian schools – the concerts often recorded for broadcast by the CBC. Nimmons was one of the first jazz musicians to find a sympathetic ear in the *Canada Council and the OAC; and both, along with the CBC, have helped to sustain his band and support its tours.

He is a founding member of the *CLComp, an affiliate of PRO Canada, and an associate of the *CMCentre.

DISCOGRAPHY

The Canadian Scene Via Phil Nimmons. Erich Traugott tpt, Ross Culley trb, J. *Toth alto sax, Julian Filianowski ten sax, *Karam bar sax, Centro acc, R. Toth pf, Murray Lauder db, Jack McQuade drums. 1956. Verve MGV-8025

Nimmons 'N' Nine. As on *Canadian Scene,* but Roy Smith for Filianowski, *Bickert guit for R. Toth. 1963. Verve MGV-8376

Take 10. As on *Canadian Scene,* but *Rully for McQuade. 1963. RCA LCPS-1066

Mary Poppins Swings. As on *Canadian Scene,* but Butch Watanabe for Culley, Jack Taylor for Karam. 1964. RCA PCS-1005

Strictly Nimmons. As on *Canadian Scene,* but add *Basso, Julius Piekarz, and *Stone tpt and flhn, *McConnell and *Roderman trb, Ron Hughes b trb. 1965. RCA RCS 1047

Nimmons Now. As on *Canadian Scene,* but Bob Day for Basso, Alvinn Pall for J. Toth, *Wilkins for Smith. 1970. CBC LM-74

The Atlantic Suite. Darryl Eaton, Mike Malone, Bram *Smith III and *Spanier tpt and flhn, Terry Lukiwski, Dave McMurdo, Rick Stepton trb, John Capon b trb and tuba, Keith Jollimore alto sax, *Ellefson ten sax, T. Toth bar sax, Tom Szczesniak el pno and pf, Andy Krehm guit, David Field db and b guit, Stan Perry drums. 1975. Sack 2008

Transformations / Invocation. As on *Atlantic Suite,* but Jerry Johnson for Stepton, Gary Williamson for Szczesniak. 1976. 2-CBC LM 452

See also Oscar Peterson.

BIBLIOGRAPHY

Crandell, Ev. 'Phil Nimmons,' *MSc,* 245, Jan–Feb 1969

Gallagher, Greg. 'Nimmons and big bands thrive for two decades,' *MSc,* 290, Jul–Aug 1976

Flohil, Richard. 'The big band beat of Phil Nimmons,' *PfAC,* vol 15, Fall 1978

Waxman, Ken. 'Phil Nimmons a part of stage band festivals,' *MSc,* 303, Sep–Oct 1978

Batten, Jack. 'Anybody wanta pay attention!' *The Canadian,* 23 Jun 1979

MM

NIOSI, Bert (Bartolo). Bandleader, clarinetist, saxophonist, composer, arranger, b London, Ont, 10 Feb 1909. He began studying flute and saxophone at nine with Pasquale Venuti in London, Ont, and for a time in his teens played with Guy *Lombardo and His Royal Canadians in Cleveland. He then toured on the Loew's vaudeville circuit with his own band, the McPhillips Buescher Boys' Orchestra, which included his brother Joe (bassist, b London, Ont, 26 May 1906, d Toronto 14 May 1977), Tony Briglia (drummer, later a founding member of the Casa Loma Orchestra), and Hugo D'Ippolito (pianist, later a member of the Royal Canadians).

In 1931 Niosi formed a nine-piece band to play at the Embassy Club in Toronto. In 1932 he expanded the band and moved to the Palais Royale dance hall where, in an 18-year residence, he became an institution in Canadian pop music and was known as 'Canada's King of Swing.' The band was heard nationally on CBC broadcasts and toured Canada in 1945 and 1946. It included Niosi's brother Johnnie (drummer, b London, Ont, 26 Sep 1914, d Toronto 21 Nov 1965).

Bert Niosi

Niosi next embarked on a career with the CBC, as a member 1952–9 of the *Happy Gang, and later became music director of the series 'Four for the Show,' 'Cross-Canada Hit Parade,' and, 1965–76, 'The Tommy *Hunter Show.' He continued to lead a dance band on occasion and returned to the Palais Royale for appearances as late as 1979.

A versatile musician, Niosi was proficient on trumpet and trombone as well as with his accustomed alto saxophone and clarinet; accompanied by his brothers he played all four instruments on a CBC TV show ca 1957. On an earlier occasion (1950) he played Mozart's *Clarinet Quintet* with the *Solway String Quartet on CBC radio.

Niosi's recordings include several 78s from the 1940s with a jazz sextet, for *RCA Victor and Musicana, and one with his orchestra for Zephyr; an LP as leader of the Jack *Kane Band (1963, CTLS 5036); and others as a soloist with the Albert *Pratz Orchestra (RCI 173 and 174) and with the Johnny *Burt Strings (1964, CTLS 5044). On another CTL LP his orchestra accompanied the singer Tommy *Common. He has had his compositions recorded by Lucio *Agostini and by the pianist Alexander Read.

Niosi is a member of CAPAC and served 1967–8 on its board of directors. He was honoured at a *CNE Bandshell concert in 1978, and portions of that concert were seen in a CBC TV special devoted to Niosi's career and broadcast in 1979.

Johnnie Niosi played with an RCAF band in Ottawa after he left his brother's orchestra in 1942. Joe Niosi played bass in the 1930s with Luigi *Romanelli, Horace *Lapp, and Trump *Davidson (touring in Britain with the latter's band under Ray Noble) and was a member of the Happy Gang 1945–59 and of CBC orchestras under Cliff *McKay, Chicho *Valle, and others.

BIBLIOGRAPHY

Frayne, Trent. 'Bert Niosi,' *Liberty,* 26 May 1945

'Versatile Bert Niosi: composer, conductor, musician,' *CanComp,* 19, Jun 1967

McNamara, Helen. *Bands Canadians Danced to*

MM (HM)

NOAKES, Alfie (Alfred). Trumpeter, b Toronto 26 Jun 1903. He was a cornetist at 10 with the Riverdale Silver Band in Toronto, subsequently played with the Imperial Concert Band under Walter *Murdoch, and was a trumpeter in the dance bands of Burton Till, Luigi *Romanelli, and Frank Whiteman. He travelled to England with the nine-piece co-operative band which performed and recorded 1924–6 as the New Princes' Toronto Band (see also Les Allen; Dance bands). Thereafter one of the leading dance-band musicians in Britain, Noakes was noted for his fine articulation and pure tone. He was lead trumpet with the orchestras of Alfredo, Ambrose, Jack Harris, Ray Noble, Lew Stone, Jay Wilbur, and others in the 1930s and with Geraldo in the mid-1940s and was on several hundred recordings by these orchestras. He retired from music in the mid-1950s and continued to live in England – at Christchurch in the mid-1970s. EMI

NOLAN, Dick (Richard Francis). Singer-songwriter, guitarist, b Corner Brook, Nfld, 4 Feb 1939. In his early teens he sang on local radio and in 1954 he gave his first CBC broadcast. In 1958 he moved to Toronto, performing in various nightclubs and making 11 LPs for *Arc Sound, some recorded in duet with Marlene Beaudry or with his daughter Bonnie Lou Nolan (see Michael Taft's *A Regional Discography of Newfoundland and Labrador 1904–1972*, St John's 1975). He returned to Corner Brook in 1972, and appeared on TV and at the Bella Vista nightclub and elsewhere.

In 1972 for RCA Nolan recorded 'Aunt Martha's Sheep' (which he wrote with Ellis Cole). Written in the traditional ballad style but with contemporary references in its lyrics, it was Nolan's biggest hit, and was followed 1972–4 by such singles as 'Home Again,' 'Johnny's Moonshine,' 'Happy Newfoundlanders,' 'Me and Brother Bill,' and 'Japanese Gin,' some of which received gold record sales awards. He has made several LPs for RCA or its Pickwick label.

Nolan returned in 1973 to Toronto where he performed in restaurants and nightclubs catering to Newfoundlanders. He has appeared on many CBC TV country music shows and in Nashville at the Grand Ole Opry. His songs have been published by Bay Music and Dunbar Music. He is an affiliate of PRO Canada.

NORCOP, James (Michael). Administrator, baritone, b Oxnard, Cal, 29 Sep 1930; BA (Southern California) 1952. As a child he sang professionally in the Robert Mitchell Boychoir in Hollywood, appearing in concerts and in movies (eg, *Going My Way*). After studies 1948–54 in literature and drama at the U of Southern California and in dance at the American School of Dance, Hollywood, he took music courses 1955–8 at the U of Southern California. He went to Europe for voice lessons 1958–60 with Ria Ginster at the Zurich Cons and 1961–3 with Kurt Rapf privately in Vienna. Returning to the USA he was a Ford Foundation administrative intern and assistant manager 1963–5 of the Seattle SO.

Norcop emigrated to Canada in 1965 to manage the *Vancouver Opera. He established the Vancouver Opera Training Program and the British Columbia Opera Ensemble, both of which helped to develop the careers of such Canadian singers as Lyn *Vernon, Riki *Turofsky, and Judith *Forst. In 1967 he moved to Toronto as music officer for POCA (*OAC) and executive director of *OFSO and served 1968–70 as the founding executive director of *Co-ordinated Arts Services.

Norcop returned to the OAC as special consultant in charge of the council's concerts and artists program, 'a service to professional [Canadian] soloists and concert groups.' In this capacity he developed the OAC's sophisticated and altruistic audition congresses Contact 72, 73, etc, beginning in 1972, which have brought together employers and performers from across Canada. He conceived and published (1972) the musicians' directories (later the OAC's *Ontour* catalogues) which were the prototype for the *Canada Council's massive *Touring Directory*. In 1974 Norcop's responsibilities were expanded to include direction of the OAC's touring program for all the performing arts.

Norcop's wife, Charlotte Holmes, served 1967–78 as dance and theatre officer of the OAC and in 1978 became the council's executive officer in charge of operations. KW

NORDHEIMER. German-Canadian family prominent in Toronto musical circles: 1 / Abraham, 2 / Samuel, his brother and 3 / Albert, his son.

1 **Abraham**. Music dealer, publisher, teacher, b Memmelsdorf, Bavaria, 24 Feb 1816, d Hamburg 18 Jan 1862 while on a visit to Germany. With Samuel he followed his older brother Isaac, an Oriental scholar, to New York in 1839.

Several 20th-century accounts relate that a Canadian officer on a visit to New York induced Abraham to move to Kingston, Canada West (Ontario), as music teacher to the family of Sir Charles Bagot, governor-general of British North America 1841–3. There is proof only that Nordheimer was a newcomer in Kingston in July 1842, when he advertised as a piano, voice, and violin teacher. Soon afterwards he opened a music store. In 1844 tickets for the Kingston Harmonic Society could be obtained at his store – a shred of evidence for another claim, that he founded a musical society.

In the spring of 1844 Abraham moved to Toronto and, with Samuel, opened the A&S *Nordheimer music store and publishing firm. Abraham was on the committee of the *Toronto Philharmonic Society in the late 1840s and played second violin in its orchestra. A successful businessman, he also was prominent in musical circles and active in the Toronto Hebrew Congregation. As the senior partner in A&S Nordheimer, he deserves the chief credit for having established Canada's pioneer music specialty house.

BIBLIOGRAPHY
Kallmann, Helmut. 'Abraham Nordheimer,' *DCB*, vol 9

2 **Samuel**. Music dealer, publisher, financier, b Memmelsdorf, Bavaria, 6 Feb 1824, d Toronto 29 Jun 1912. He was a partner with Abraham in the formation of A&S Nordheimer, and after his brother's death he managed the company alone until he was joined by his nephew Albert in the 1870s. Samuel was president of the Toronto Philharmonic Society for many years, organized the Chamber Music Assn in 1886, and became chairman and chief fund-raiser of the Toronto section of the *Cycle of Musical Festivals in 1903, but apparently was not a practising musician. He also was president of the Federal Bank of Canada, German consul for Ontario, and a member of various company boards. A Toronto ravine came to be known as the Nordheimer ravine.

3 **Albert**. Music dealer, publisher, piano manufacturer, b Toronto ca 1850–5, d there 2 Dec 1938. Educated at Upper Canada College, Toronto, and in Europe, he joined A&S Nordheimer in 1870 and became managing director and later (1912–27) president. For more than 50 years he chaired the music committee of St James' Cathedral, Toronto, and in 1902 he became Dutch consul-general for Canada. He composed at least nine songs and dances which were published 1895–1916 by his firm. Among them was a setting of Bliss Carman's 'Hunting Song (Tarantara)' (1908).

Nordheimer's publication with plate number 1, ca 1845

Albert's son Gerald (b Toronto 2 Jul 1929) was general assistant 1947–57 at *Boosey & Hawkes (Canada) and music librarian 1957–73 at CBC Toronto (responsibilities including the *CBC SO), prior to becoming stage manager and librarian of the *Vancouver SO in 1974 and personnel and stage manager in 1978. HK

A&S Nordheimer Co (after 1890 the Nordheimer Piano & Music Co). Music dealers and publishers, piano dealers and later manufacturers, active in Kingston, Canada West (now Ont), 1842–4 and in Toronto 1844–1927.

The company's publicity has claimed 1840 as the founding date, but the claim cannot be supported. It is certain, however, that Abraham *Nordheimer opened a music store in Kingston in the fall of 1842 and moved to Toronto in 1844 to establish the A&S Nordheimer Co at a King St East location with his younger brother Samuel. (The store moved to Yonge St in 1915.) Abraham remained the senior partner until his death in 1862; Samuel was president 1862–1912 and Albert (Abraham's son) 1912–27, having served previously as managing director.

Branches were opened in Hamilton, London, Ottawa, St Catharines, Montreal, Quebec, and Winnipeg, but most were short-lived and local firms took over as agents. Only the Montreal branch was active over a long period – ca 1848–67 and again ca 1880–1911.

Nordheimer began to publish sheet music after the move to Toronto, and its output soon surpassed that of all other Canadian firms. When the company joined the Board of Music Trade of the USA in 1859 it satisfied the condition of membership – that of having published at least 1000 pages of music. In 1870 it had 272 titles in print. The pre-Confederation output included Canadian and foreign composers in about equal numbers. Among the former were J.P. *Clarke, St George B. *Crozier, Jules *Hecht, Henry *Schallehn, and G.W. *Strathy; among the latter, Balfe, Bellini, and the young Offenbach. Also offered was a piece misattributed to Beethoven. Most publications were for piano or voice and piano, but Clarke's *Lays of the Maple Leaf*, a song cycle or glee (and the longest Canadian publication in sheet music size up to its time, 1853), contained duets and a choral piece. Publication series included The Band, 'a selection of fashionable dances for the piano.'

Plate numbers were used until the early 1850s (reaching about 100) and again after 1890 (beginning where they had left off, and reaching 386 by 1918). The engravers included Ellis of Toronto and Wakelam and Birch of New York. The engraving and paper were of a high quality; cover illustrations were rare and copyright registrations undertaken in the USA. The first copyright known to have been registered by Nordheimer in Canada was Martin Lazare's 'Canadian National Air' of 1859.

Among the Canadians published after Confederation were R.S. *Ambrose, Jennings *Burnett, Francesco *D'Auria, A.E. and Edward *Fisher, W.O. *Forsyth, Edwin *Gledhill, H.H. *Godfrey, Albert *Ham, J.W. and S.F. *Harrison, J.D. *Kerrison, Clarence *Lucas, Albert Nordheimer, C.E. *Wheeler, and Ernest *Whyte. Bestsellers included the first copyright editions of *'The Maple Leaf For Ever' (1871) and R.S. Ambrose's 'One Sweetly Solemn Thought' (1876). Among the series were Nordheimer's Collection of Popular Songs and Ballads (1886), Nordheimer's Octavo Edition, The Ball Room, and For Study and Recreation (First Year Classics). Nordheimer also issued books of *TCM examination pieces.

As early as 1845 the company was an agent for Stodart & Dunham of New York, Chickering of Boston, and other US piano manufacturers. In 1858 Steinway was added. Nordheimer did not establish its own piano factory until about 1890 (having operated the Lansdowne Piano Co jointly with Gerhard *Heintzman ca 1886–90), but then produced upright and grand pianos of a high quality – about 5000 by 1901, 11,000 by 1910, and 21,500 by 1927.

Among those who gained experience with the firm before setting out on their own were Paul *Hahn, T.G. Mason and V.M. Risch (*Mason & Risch), and George E. *Suckling. The senior staff included A.H.S. Van Koughnet, factory manager; W.W. Wakelam, sheet music department manager; and Walter Duffett, secretary treasurer.

In addition to carrying on their commerce, the Nordheimers invited foreign artists to perform in Canada and opened a concert hall in Montreal, 'the handsomest concert hall in Canada' (Horton Rhys, *A Theatrical Trip*, London 1861). Emma Lajeunesse (*Albani) sang there in 1861. A recital hall and studio facilities were later established on Scott St in Toronto.

After Albert Nordheimer's retirement at the end of 1927, *Heintzman & Co took over the business in January 1928, including the factory in the Junction district of Toronto. Heintzman kept the Nordheimer name for certain styles of pianos until 1960 (discontinuing production at 27,846), thus making it the oldest brand name in use in Canadian music. Heintzman continued to use the Nordheimer name on casings for approximately another 10 years.

BIBLIOGRAPHY

The House of Nordheimer 1840–1903 (Toronto 1903)

Calderisi, Maria. 'Music publishing in Canada: 1800–1867,' unpubl MMA thesis, McGill U, 1976

Complete Catalogue of Sheet Music and Musical Works Published by the Board of Music Trade of the United States of America, 1870, reprint edn (New York 1973)

HK

NORMAND, Émile or **'Cisco'** (Roland). Drummer, vibraphonist, composer, painter, b Windsor, Ont, 21 Nov 1936. He studied piano, trumpet, and vibraphone in Windsor and Detroit and played in a dance band led by his mother in the late 1940s and early 1950s. After working in Detroit jazz clubs with Yusef Lateef, Donald Byrd, and others in the late 1950s, he moved to Montreal in 1960 and was a central figure in that city's burgeoning jazz scene during the following decade. He accompanied many musicians (eg, Nick *Ayoub, Pierre *Leduc, Art Roberts, and Sonny Stitt) as a drummer and led his own groups (some combining Latin music and jazz) as a vibraphonist in jazz clubs and concerts in Montreal and elsewhere in Quebec. He has been heard in both capacities on CBC radio's 'Jazz en liberté.' Normand was less active in jazz in the 1970s, working instead with the popular singers Georges *Dor, André *Gagnon, Pauline *Julien, Claude *Léveillée (with whom he toured in the USSR in 1968), and Monique *Leyrac and playing in theatre and ballet orchestras (eg, for the Montreal production of *Hair* in 1970 and for Les Grands Ballets Canadiens on tour in the USA in 1972).

Also a visual artist, Normand has worked as a painter under contract to Eaton's of Canada.

Normand has composed several pieces for his jazz groups (eg, *Rudy and Me, Hustle, Basic Ingredients, Michel's Line*, and *S.T.P.*) and was one of the first musicians in Canada (ca 1960) to play compositions by the innovative US saxophonist Ornette Coleman. Normand is a member of CAPAC.

DISCOGRAPHY

Emile Normand Ensemble. Normand vib and mar, Joe Christie fl, Romandini guit, B. Gagnon b guit, Roberts pf, May perc, Émond drums. 1969. RCI 306

Others as a sideman (drummer) to Ayoub, Leduc, and Pierre Nadeau (*Trio Pierre Nadeau*, 1970, RCI 307)

CGA, MM

NORRIS, John. Critic, editor, broadcaster, promoter, record producer, b West Clandon, Surrey, England, 9 Jun 1934. While a clerk in London, he operated his first jazz club. Moving to Canada, he operated the Montreal Traditional Jazz Society 1956–7. In 1957 he went to Toronto, where he operated the Traditional Jazz Club of Toronto, opened the Galleon jazz club, and promoted concerts. In 1958 he established the magazine *Coda*, serving until 1976 as editor and thereafter (with Bill *Smith) as co-publisher. Norris was the manager 1962–8 of the jazz department of the Sam the Record Man store on Yonge St, Toronto, and developed there one of the most extensive stocks of jazz recordings in the world, rivalled later by the combined retail and mail-order operation of the Jazz and Blues Centre established by Norris and Smith through Coda Publications in 1970.

A leading authority on jazz, Norris has written extensively for *Coda* and has contributed to the magazines *Jazz Journal, Jazz Monthly, Jazz News*, and *Melody Maker* (all of London), *Down Beat* (Chicago), *International Musician* (New York), and the *Music Scene* and the **Canadian Composer* (Toronto). He was jazz critic for the *Globe and Mail* in 1967, contributed to the Toronto *Telegram* and the *Toronto Daily Star*, and was a radio jazz program host and / or writer 1958–61 on CHFI, Toronto, and in the 1960s and early 1970s on the CBC (eg, 'Strictly Jazz' and 'That Midnight Jazz'). He prepared a jazz history series broadcast on the CBC's 'Jazz Radio-Canada' in the summer of 1978.

Norris has produced or co-produced many LPs for Sackville, a label he, Smith, and others established in 1968.

MM

North Bay, Ontario. Railway and tourist centre on Lake Nipissing, incorporated as a town in 1890 and as a city in 1925, and reaching a population of more than 51,000 by 1980. Among the city's early musical organizations were the North Bay Choral Union, organized in 1907 and led for 20 years by F.A. York, the Columbus Band (1913) conducted by E. Virgili, and the North Bay Premier Band which in 1924 won a first prize at the *CNE, Toronto. The 32-member North Bay T&NO (Timiskaming and Northern Ontario) Railway Band, founded in 1925, gave radio broadcasts and concerts in the park. In 1950, it joined the Engineers' Band of the Canadian Armed Forces Eighth Field Squadron (later North Bay Area Band).

The 42-member North Bay Community Orchestra was formed in 1930. The Choral Union performed *The Mikado* with a cast of 50 under H. Shorse in 1931. The Choral and Orchestra Society was formed in 1932. Its directorship was assumed by Dawn Wallis in 1976.

The North Bay *Community Concert Assn, established in 1943, presented series of concerts in the auditorium of the Vocational School and later in the Capitol Theatre. Its first series featured the contralto Jean Watson, the Don Cossacks Chorus, and the Bary Ensemble. The association presented annually three concerts of classical music and one of light classics. Its membership exceeded 1500 by 1976.

In 1977 Robert Ryker, formerly a tuba player in the *MSO , was appointed community musician under a program by the *Canada Council in conjunction with the local Canadore Community College. That same year, Ryker organized the North Bay SO which gave concerts alone and with the North Bay Choral Society. He also took on the direction of the North Bay Area Band and formed the Northern Musical Arts Assn as a coordinating body for musical activities. In July and August 1978 this association, along with the Theatre Circle and Canadore College, presented the first 'Artsperience,' a community festival and workshop.

Notable performers who have visited North Bay include the Trapp Family Singers (1945), Gregor Piatigorsky (1946), Maureen *Forrester, Lois *Marshall, John Sebastian, Ronald *Turini, the Columbus Boy Choir, the Vienna Academy Chorus, the *NACO, and several European orchestras.

Joseph *Beaulieu lived and taught in North Bay 1946–65. A music camp and a concert hall – library centre were named in his honour in 1967 and 1968 respectively. North Bay is the home of the McFarlane family of country musicians. 'Dapper Don' McFarlane, head of the family, was one of the original members of the CBC's 'Holiday Ranch.'

(DSt, PMW)

NORTHCOTT, Tom (Thomas Herbert). Singer-songwriter, b Vancouver 29 Aug 1943. His career as a folk-influenced pop singer began in 1963 at the Vancouver coffeehouse The Inquisition. Appearances followed in San Francisco and on CBC (Vancouver) TV. Though his popularity was confined largely to western Canada, Northcott was the recipient in 1967 of a *Juno Award as 'most promising male vocalist.' His singles 1967–70, 'Sunny Goodge Street' (written by Donovan), 'Girl from the North Country' (Bob Dylan), '1941' and 'The Rainmaker' (Harry Nilsson), and 'Crazy Jane' (Northcott), were minor hits in various areas of Canada and the USA. Most were included on the LP *The Best of Tom Northcott* (New Syndrome WS 1859). A second LP, *Upside Downside* (1970–1, UNI 73108), was released in 1971.

With the *Vancouver SO under Meredith Davies, Northcott premiered (1970) *And God Created Woman*, his own 12-minute 'symphonette.' The work was repeated by the *Hamilton Philharmonic under Boris *Brott with the rock band Tranquility Base. The co-founder (1968) of Stage 3 Productions, one of Vancouver's first major recording facilities, Northcott was no longer performing by 1973. He is an affiliate of PRO Canada.

BIBLIOGRAPHY
LeBlanc, Larry. 'Tom Northcott takes a break from recording, producing to write,' *MSc*, 260, Jul–Aug 1971
Yorke, Ritchie. *Axes, Chops & Hot Licks* (Edmonton 1971)

(JR)

Norway. It is believed that the Norse (Vikings) were the first North American settlers – arriving around the year 1000. However, people from modern Norway, the western kingdom of the Scandinavian peninsula, immigrated to Canada from the USA during the 1890s and moved into the Prairies and particularly to British Columbia, whose coastline so closely resembled that of their homeland. In 1971 there were 180,000 people of Norwegian origin living in Canada.

Probably the first Norwegian musician, and one of the first European players of note, to visit Canada was the violinist Ole Bull, who performed in Montreal in 1844, in Toronto in 1844 and 1857, and in Saint John, NB, in 1853. More recent guests have been the conductor Øivin Fjeldstad, who appeared at the 1959 *Vancouver International Festival; Klaus Egge, who represented Norway at the 1960 *International Conference of Composers at Stratford, Ont; the conductor Sverre Bruland, who appeared with the *CBC Winnipeg Orchestra; and the pianist Robert Riefling, who performed the Grieg *Piano Concerto* at a Scandinavian Gala in Montreal in 1967. Among early Norwegian residents of Canada was Ferdinand Wentzel, a North West Company employee who collected voyageur songs in the Athabasca and Mackenzie regions in the early 19th century and whose musical talent 'brightened the long and dreary hours of his life and contributed to keep all cheerful around him' (Masson's *Les Bourgeois de la Compagnie du Nord-Ouest*, vol 1, part 2, Quebec, 1889, p 71). The accordionist-composer Olaf *Sveen settled in Canada in 1954. The music educator Helen *Dahlstrom has Norwegian ancestors. In November 1902 at Montreal's Windsor Hall Éva *Plouffe gave what may have been the earliest Canadian performance of the Grieg *Piano Concerto*, with an orchestra led by J.-J. *Goulet. In 1906 Clarence *Lucas is said to have conducted the US premiere of Grieg's incidental music to *Peer Gynt*. As a student W.O. *Forsyth met Grieg in Leipzig.

Canadians who have visited Norway include Emma *Albani (1888), Ida *Krehm, Gertrude *Newton, the *Hart House Orchestra, the double-bass and piano team Gary *Karr and Harmon Lewis (1978), and the pianist Paul Bempechat. The last-named premiered *IV Journeys* by Gary *Hayes and *Oneg Shabbath* by Halifax's Tim Jackson at Baerum, Norway, ca 1978. The flutist-composer Robert *Aitken has given master classes at the Bergen Cons. Kathleen *Parlow, who toured Scandinavia many times, received her famous 'Viotti' violin (a 1735 Guarnerius del Gesù) from a wealthy Norwegian family by the name of Björnson. By 1975 26 Norwegian songs and 18 instrumental pieces had been collected in Canada and were deposited at the Canadian Centre for Folk Culture Studies of the National Museum of Man.

'Nos Futures Étoiles.' National singing competition conceived and organized by CBC Montreal. The unsponsored program ran 1947–55 on the French-language radio network and was produced by Berthe Lavoie-Fortin and Marcel Henry. Auditions were held before each season. Each week the orchestra, conducted by Giuseppe *Agostini, accompanied two candidates who performed in a broadcast before an audience at the *Ermitage. In addition to a prize of $500 each ($1000 each by 1954), the two winners – chosen after broadcast final auditions – took part as guests on each of the broadcasts the following year.

The winners were Yolande Lagrenade (soprano) and Gilles *Lamontagne (baritone) 1947–8 (on the basis of a single audition), Louise *Roy (soprano) and Jean-Pierre Comeau (bass) 1948–9, June *Kowalchuk (soprano) and William Blaine Williams (baritone) 1949–50, Constance *Lambert (soprano) and James *Milligan (baritone) 1950–1, Margaret Kerr (mezzo-soprano) and Jon *Vickers (tenor) 1951–2, Rolande *Garnier (mezzo-soprano) and Louis *Quilico (baritone) 1952–3, Joan *Maxwell (mezzo-soprano) and Don *Garrard (bass) 1953–4, and Lesia Zubrack (soprano) and Pierre *Boutet (tenor) 1954–5.

The CBC replaced the program with *'Concours de la chanson canadienne' in 1956. ST

NOVA MUSIC (inNOVAtions in MUSIC). Halifax group of composers and performers dedicated to the presentation of new or seldom-performed music. It was founded in 1971 by the percussionist and teacher James Faraday, the composer Dennis Farrell, the composer-trombonist Adrian Hoffman, the pianist John *McKay, the composer-flutist Stephen Pedersen, the composer-contrabassist Alexander Tilley, and the composer Steve Tittle. By 1979 Tilley and McKay no longer were members.

NOVA MUSIC gave its first concert 9 Apr 1972. Beginning with its 1973–4 season it presented six free concerts a year, all at the Arts Centre of *Dalhousie U, and some broadcast by CBC radio. At first the group adhered to its original policy and performed both new and rarely performed older music, but soon new music had become its mainstay.

Additional performers for most of the concerts have been drawn from the *Atlantic SO, but guest performers have been engaged for special performances. Among the latter have been Robert *Aitken, the *Canadian Electronic Ensemble, Udo *Kasemets, the Kronos String Quartet, the duo-pianists Pierrette *LePage and Bruce *Mather, the clarinetist Robert Marcellus, Mary *Morrison, the pianist Yuji Takahashi, and the Warsaw Music Workshop – Takahashi and the Warsaw group through the assistance of *NMC, Toronto.

NOVA MUSIC has premiered several works by its composer-members, notably Farrell's *Six Sonatas* for harpsichord (1973) and *The Birthday of the Infanta* (1979), Hoffman's *... of shape of sound of shape* (1972) and *Portrait* for tape and percussion (1973), and Tittle's *Moondance* (1972), *This Time That Time* (1973), *Winter's Not Forever* (1974), and *i asked her where and she said right here* (1975). In addition the group has premiered John Felice's *A.E.H. for Solo Trombone* (1973) and Alfred *Fisher's *The Owl at Dusk* (1979) and has performed works by Aitken, *Anhalt, *Beecroft, *Bottenberg, Bruce *Davis, *Ford, *Garant, *Hartwell, *Hawkins, Jacques *Hétu, *Joachim, *Laufer, Mather, Michael *Miller, *Pentland, *Schafer, *Somers, *Tremblay, and *Wilson. Besides introducing much Canadian repertoire to Haligonians, NOVA MUSIC has given the first Halifax performances of works by Bartók, Berio, Cage, Carter, Hindemith, Hovhaness, Ives, Kagel, Messiaen, Penderecki, Schoenberg, Stravinsky, Webern, Xenakis, and others.

The group has received financial assistance from private donors, corporations, the *Canada Council, the province of Nova Scotia, and the music dept of Dalhousie U.

NOVA MUSIC's founders have had careers in performance and teaching outside the group.

Dennis Farrell – b Green Bay, Wisc, 18 Sep 1940; BA (St Norbert College) 1963, M MUS (Wisconsin) 1966, PH D (Wisconsin) 1968 – joined the Music Dept at Dalhousie U.

Adrian Hoffman – b Columbus, Miss, 22 Jul 1943; M MUS (New England Cons) 1967 – joined the Atlantic SO in 1969 and became a radio producer for CBC Halifax.

Stephen Pedersen – b Calgary 8 Dec 1935; BA (Alberta) 1957 – was a pupil of Robert Aitken, Samuel *Dolin, and Joan Pecover and a member of the *Hamilton Philharmonic and the Halifax Woodwind Quintet prior to joining the Atlantic SO.

Alexander Tilley (b Montreal 8 Nov 1944) was a pupil of Thomas Martin, Bruce Mather, and István Anhalt and became a founding member of the Halifax Early Music Quartet and a school teacher.

Steve Tittle – b Willard, O, 20 May 1935; B MUS ED (Kent State) 1962, M MUS (Wisconsin) 1966, DMA (Wisconsin) 1974 – began teaching at Dalhousie U in 1970, founded Murphy's Law, an improvisational and multi-media performing group, and composed *It is all there all the time*, recorded by Gary *Karr. (Karr also recorded Farrell's composition *Suite catholique*.)

BIBLIOGRAPHY
Edwards, Barry, and McGregor, Nancy. 'inNOVAtions in Halifax,' *Fugue*, Nov 1977
Schulman, Michael. 'Contemporary music groups thriving across Canada,' *MSc*, 303, Sep–Oct 1978

Nova Scotia Choral Federation. Umbrella organization for the province's choirs. Formed in 1975 at a choral workshop sponsored by the Nova Scotia Cultural Affairs Division, Dept of Recreation, it was incorporated 2 Jul 1976 with Ruth H. Lawley as president and Janet Hull as executive director. An office was opened in Halifax. Membership, composed of both individuals and choirs, approached 300 in July 1977. The federation established a lending library of choral music and reference books in Halifax and began the bulletin *NSCF News* in 1976.

Prior to 1980 besides sponsoring in various centres the gatherings called Choirs in Concert and workshops for individual choirs, the federation held two week-long choral sessions (Sing Summer '76 at *Acadia U and Sing Summer '77 at the Agricultural College in Truro) and the Canadian Choral Conductors' Seminar (1978, at the Dalhousie Arts Centre, U of King's College).

See also Alliance chorale canadienne; Ontario Choral Federation.

PUBLICATIONS
NSCF Choral Annual (Halifax 1977)
History of Choral Music in Nova Scotia (Halifax 1978)

MM, PW

Nova Scotia Department of Culture, Recreation and Fitness. Provincial government department created in 1973. Included within its structure is the Cultural Affairs Division, which functioned as part of the Dept of Education prior to 1977. The director of the division in 1980 was Allison Bishop.

The department has worked to develop a cultural policy for Nova Scotia, attempting to provide greater opportunities in the arts within the province and, to this end, working closely with arts and cultural organizations. Its activities have included the sponsorship of *Atlantic SO provincial tours, the co-sponsorship of a *NYO training session in Halifax in 1975, the establishment (ca 1975) of a program to assist community bands, assistance to the *Nova Scotia Festival of the Arts, and help in the creation of several provincial federations, including the *Nova Scotia Choral Federation.

In some instances the department has provided such federations with full-time or part-time administrations. It also has co-operated with the *Canada Council Touring Office and the *New Brunswick Cultural Development Branch in sponsoring the annual performing artists' showcase Contact East, begun in 1976. Through its Cultural Affairs Division the department has made grants to individuals, bands, choral groups, music camps, festivals, and musical societies. It has sponsored representatives to national and international competitions and conferences and has provided grants to artists for travel both inside and outside Nova Scotia. Among the responsibilities of the department's music officer (James C. Aulenbach in 1980) have been maintaining a list of community sponsors for touring attractions and bringing together agents, artists, and sponsors.

The Nova Scotia Festival of the Arts. An annual arts and crafts festival organized under the direction of Guy Henson (first president) and inaugurated in August 1956 at Tatamagouche, NS. It moved in 1968 to Wolfville and in 1970 to Halifax where it eventually became a regular feature in the summer activities of the *Dalhousie U Arts Centre.

With a provincial government grant of $2000, the festival began as a platform for professional and amateur Nova Scotia talent. In its early days it featured freelance arts teachers, army bands, the Acadian Male Quartet, and such noted musicians as Francis *Chaplin, Audrey *Farnell, Gordon *Macpherson, Diane *Oxner, and Don Warner, all of whom donated their services. In 1962 the entertainment policy was changed and, with the help of a *Canada Council grant, performers were paid. Subsequent guests have included John Allen *Cameron, Maureen *Forrester, Les Grands Ballets Canadiens, Ed *McCurdy, Catherine *McKinnon, Murray *McLauchlan, Alan *Mills, the *NYO, and Teresa *Stratas.

During the early 1970s the festival was greatly expanded; a Halifax office was opened and efforts were made to take some of the activities to other parts of the province. The government, meanwhile, had repeated its initial grant with slight increases each year until 1973. At that time, the newly created Department of Recreation made a handsome expansion grant of $44,500. The festival responded and in 1975 the program listed more than 270 events during a nine-day period, but incurred a deficit of $17,000. The government thereupon curtailed its support and by 1978 the festival had retrenched to three days of mostly amateur performances.

Festival presidents have included, besides Guy Henson, Isobel MacAuley, Rev Russell Elliott, Phyllis Stott 1969–72, Glen Hancock 1972–4, and John Barteaux 1974–5, succeeded by Dean Naugler. (DWt)

Nova Scotia Music Educators' Association. Formed 22 Oct 1960 after a meeting at East Hants Rural High School (East Hants district, near Truro) of 52 school music teachers. The decision to organize had strong encouragement from the *CMEA, which had been pressing for the establishment of professional associations in all the provinces.

The CMEA convention of 1963, to which the NSMEA played host in Halifax, helped to persuade the Nova Scotia Dept of Education, the province's school boards, and the public at large of the growing importance of music education in the general school program. The NSMEA added its voice to that of Home and School Associations, school inspectors, and others to persuade the Dept of Education to appoint a provincial music director. Peter Hinkley was named to this post in 1963. The title subsequently was changed to music consultant. In 1968 the NSMEA became the first provincial organization of its kind to affiliate with the CMEA.

Through the co-operation of Paul *Murray, appointed provincial music consultant in 1967, the NSMEA annual conference grew from a one-day gathering of local specialists and novice teachers to a three-day meeting featuring clinicians from Canada, the USA, and Britain. By 1980 NSMEA membership had reached 280.

In February 1980 the Nova Scotia Youth Orchestra premiered Terrence Hill's *Variations on an Idea for Orchestra*, commissioned by the NSMEA through a grant from the province's Dept of Recreation and Cultural Affairs. This was the first such commission by the association. NSMEA presidents have been Catherine *Allison 1959–61, Vernon *Ellis 1961–3, Shirley Blakeley 1963–5, Vivian Brand 1965–7, Edith Rowlings 1967–9, Wilf Harvey 1969–70, Chalmers *Doane 1970–2, Don Hill 1972–4, Frances Tyrrell 1974–6, Terrence Hurrell 1976–8, and Sister Rita Clare 1978–80. The Catherine Allison Scholarship, established in 1963 in honour of the first president, is awarded annually to a university student in music education. In 1960 the NSMEA began to publish a quarterly newsletter. (CAl)

Nova Scotia Opera Association. Halifax company born of the marriage of Nova Scotian talent and Latvian artistry and experience, the latter supplied by Mariss Vetra and Alfred *Strombergs, both from Riga. Vetra's successful 1949 presentation of *Don Giovanni*, produced in the Dalhousie gymnasium and aided by a Halifax city bicentennial grant, led to the founding of the Nova Scotia Opera Assn in 1950.

Vetra (b Latvia 1902, d Toronto 24 Dec 1965) had been the director of the Latvian National Opera when he moved to Canada in 1947 to take over the voice department and establish an opera course at the Halifax Cons (see *Maritime Cons of Music). He served as artistic director of the association until 1953. He was succeeded by Teodor Brilts in 1954, Brilts by Thomas Mayer in 1955.

The orchestra (the Halifax Symphonette, formed to accompany the operas and later the basis of the *Halifax SO) was conducted 1949–55 by Strombergs and 1955–6 by Thomas Mayer.

The Tales of Hoffmann and *La Traviata* were presented in 1950, *Madama Butterfly* and *The Marriage of Figaro* in 1951, and *Countess Maritza* in 1952. A commissioned work, Trevor Jones' **The Broken Ring*, was premiered 15 Aug 1953. *Orpheus and Eurydice* (with the young Maureen *Forrester) and *Cavalleria Rusticana* were presented in 1954, *Rigoletto* in 1955, and *Faust* (with Jan *Rubeš) in 1956.

Operas were staged at the Capitol Theatre in 1950, 1951, 1952, 1955, and 1956 and in the Queen Elizabeth Auditorium in 1953 and 1954. Some productions were taken to Antigonish, Glace Bay, Moncton, Sydney, Truro, and Wolfville.

Singers included Ronald Beare, Teodor Brilts, Audrey *Farnell, Karen Kierstead Mills, Diane *Oxner, Diane Parker, Jean Parker, Audrey Ryan, Raymond Simpson, and Corey Smith.

The association's productions ceased in 1956 as the result of financial difficulties, declining interest, and the dispersal of the participants to other centres in Canada. However, the supporting group sponsored appearances by the *COC Touring Company in 1958 and 1960. (GHn)

Nova Scotia Registered Music Teachers' Association. Founded in 1937 and incorporated in 1941 as the Nova Scotia Music Teachers' Assn, with Harry *Dean as first president. It became affiliated with the *CFMTA in 1944 and became the NSRMTA in 1951.

In 1976 there were five chapters – Pictou, Cape Breton, Halifax, Dartmouth, and Antigonish – with 90 active members and 10 associates. (A sixth chapter, The Valley, had been discontinued in 1969 pending reorganization.) The chapters have concerned themselves with their own localities, serving as consultants in music festivals, aiding in the presentation of young performers, and providing leadership and financial support for Canada Music Week activities. The NSRMTA established a $200 scholarship in 1975, to be awarded annually to the winner of a student competition.

In 1980 the NSRMTA, in the absence of a publication of its own, continued to use the *CFMTA Newsletter* as its information outlet. The organization's archives, as well as a brief history of music teaching in Nova Scotia (prepared by Phyllis R. Blakeley and B.C. Silver for the NSRMTA in 1966), are held by the Public Archives of Nova Scotia in Halifax.

NSRMTA presidents have been Harry Dean 1937–8, 1945–6, and 1949–51, Edwin *Collins 1938–9, 1951–3, and 1956–7, Douglas Baker 1939–40, and 1942–3, Alex MacKinnon 1940–1, Cyril O'Brien 1941–2, Rita Morton 1943–4, Langston Miller 1944–5 and 1947–8, Clifford Gates 1946–7, Elsie MacAloney 1948–9, Vernon MacDonald 1953–4, 1968–9, and 1973–5, Harold *Hamer 1954–5, Elsa Stramberg Noble 1955–6, Sister Helene Waddeb 1957–9, David Howatt 1959–60, Vernon Atkinson 1960–2, Elaine Burns Ellis 1962–4, Mae Cameron 1964–6, Martha Russell 1966–8, Sister Rodriguez Steele 1969–71, James Colby 1971–3, Owen Stephens 1975–7, and Jean Fraser 1977–80, succeeded by Matt Hughes. RSl

'Nova Scotia Song.' A sailor's lament sometimes identified as 'Farewell to Nova Scotia.' In the third quarter of the 20th century it became the best known of all Nova Scotia songs, partly because the Halifax CBC TV show 'Singalong Jubilee' (1961–74) used it as a theme and Catherine *McKinnon recorded it (*Something Old, Something New*, Arc 256). It was published by G.V. *Thompson (1964).

Helen *Creighton collected the song in the 1930s from a half-dozen singers in the Petpeswick and Chezzetcook districts, some 40 km east of Halifax; they told her it formerly was sung in the schools. She included it in *Traditional Songs from Nova Scotia* (Toronto 1950). Carrie Grover, who learned the song as a child in Nova Scotia, gives it in *A Heritage of Song* (Norwood, Pa, 1973) as 'Adieu to Nova Scotia,' and Marius *Barbeau found a related song, 'On the Banks of the Jeddore,' in Beauce County, Que, and published it in the National Museum of Man's *Come A Singing!* in 1947. EF

Nova Scotia Talent Trust. Independent non-profit organization, established in 1944 to assist the career of Portia *White. Founders included the mayor of Halifax, the president of the *Halifax Ladies Musical Club, the lieutenant-governor of Nova Scotia, and representatives of the provincial government. Soon allowed to languish, the trust was reactivated in 1949 to assist Nova Scotians in various fields of the arts to study in the major cultural centres of the world. Funds for the trust have been received through government grants, special donations, benefit programs, and public subscription. By 1978–9, when 14 recipients were awarded a total of $13,200, more than 100 artists had benefited directly from the trust. These included, from the field of music, the tenor John

*Arab, the educator J. Chalmers *Doane, the soprano Audrey *Farnell, the soprano Deborah Jeans, the tenor Ronald Murdock, the soprano Diane *Oxner, the folksinger Finvola *Redden-Bower, the soprano Annon Lee *Silver, the pianist Neil Van Allen, and the cellist Ifan *Williams. (RSm)

NURSE, Ray. Lutenist, lute builder, bass, b New Westminster, BC, 1 Feb 1947. His teachers included Diana Poulton (lute playing and building, 1967–8) in Ely, England, French Tickner (voice, 1968–70) at the *U of British Columbia, and Eugène Dombois (lute, 1972) in Switzerland. Nurse began studying voice with Jacob Hamm at the *Community Music School of Greater Vancouver in 1974 and with Luigi Wood privately in Vancouver in 1976. A founder of Hortulani Musicae (1968) and the *Vancouver Society for Early Music (1969), Nurse has performed as lutenist with the former, in recital and on the CBC. He had built more than 30 lutes by 1977. He has taught lute privately and has given seminars in California, at the *U of Victoria Early Music Workshop (summers 1974, 1975), and for the American Lute Society in Rhode Island (summers 1976, 1977). He joined the early music program at the U of British Columbia in 1976 and was acting director in 1977. Co-director 1976–7 of the Collegium Musicum at that university, he began teaching lute there in 1977. A member of the *Vancouver Chamber Choir and a winner of the 1976 Vancouver *Metropolitan Opera auditions, Nurse has sung with the *Vancouver Opera (the Doctor in *La Traviata* and Silvano in *Un Ballo in Maschera* in 1977), the *Edmonton Opera, and in Haydn's *Missa Sancta Nicolai* at the 1977 Vancouver Four Choirs Festival. BNSG

Oakville. Town founded in 1825 on Sixteen Mile Creek at Lake Ontario, between Toronto and Hamilton. A regimental brass band was formed in 1866 by the 20th Halton Battalion Infantry but was supplanted in 1881 by the infantry's Lorne Rifles Pipe Band. The brass players then formed the Oakville Citizens' Band (brass) which performed thereafter at important town functions and continued to do so in 1980. In 1857 music instruction was offered at the Oakville Ladies' Academy, and around that time a pipe organ, built by Oakville resident Richard *Coates, was installed at St Jude's Anglican Church and carried on in use when a new building was erected in 1883. A choir was organized ca 1868 at the Canada Presbyterian Church. In the 19th century balls and stage entertainments were held at Temperance Hall, Town Hall, and Commins' Music Hall (1894–8). Musical activities of an occasional kind continued in the 20th century but – perhaps because Toronto was so near – organizations giving regular concerts did not flourish until later. The Oakville SO, founded in 1967 under the direction of Kenneth Hollier (succeeded in 1973 by David Gray, and Gray in 1976 by Anthony Royse), began giving annual series of concerts, as did the Whiteoaks Choral Society, formed in 1968 under Gifford *Mitchell. Other organizations active in 1980 included the Kelso Music Centre, founded in 1972, the Tempus Youth Choir, formed in 1972, and the Sheridan Music Festival begun in 1974. The 500-seat theatre in the Oakville Centre, opened in 1977, became the venue for both community and touring musical performances. In 1924 the headquarters of The Frederick Harris Co (now the Frederick *Harris Music Co) moved to Oakville from Toronto.

BIBLIOGRAPHY

Mathews, Hazel C. *Oakville and the Sixteen: The History of an Ontario Port* (Toronto 1953) (MWM)

OBOMSAWIN, Alanis. Singer, filmmaker, b Lebanon, NH, 31 Aug 1932. An Abenaki Indian princess raised on the Odanak Reservation on the St Francis River, northeast of Montreal, she has worked to preserve the native peoples' cultures in Canada through her films and other audio-visual productions for the *NFB, and through her concert performances of songs, chants, and stories. Singing songs of her own tribe and those of other tribes (always in the original language), self-accompanied on a hand-drum or rattle, she has performed at the *Guelph Spring Festival, the *NAC, the *PDA, and for many years the *Mariposa Folk Festival (where she was co-ordinator 1970–6 of native peoples' programming). She appeared regularly for several years (1970s) on the NET (US) children's program 'Sesame Street.' In 1978 she was named to the Conseil de la Langue Française by the Quebec government. (WWt)

O'BRIEN, Oscar. Folklorist, composer, pianist, organist, teacher, b Ottawa 7 Sep 1892, d Montreal 20 Sep 1958. He studied piano and organ with Amédée *Tremblay while pursuing his studies at the De La Salle Academy and the *U of Ottawa, and was appointed Tremblay's deputy organist at the Notre-Dame Basilica. In 1915 he began a 15-year collaboration with Charles *Marchand as the latter's accompanist and arranger. Two years later he moved to Montreal as a teacher, orchestral pianist, and accompanist. Because of Marchand's influence folk music remained central to O'Brien's activities. Their collaboration intensified through tours, recordings, and recitals, and in 1927 they performed in Quebec in the first *CPR Festival, O'Brien participating as composer, arranger, and pianist. They also took part in the 1928 Festival. With Marchand's untimely death before the 1930 festival O'Brien became the assistant music director of the festival, the last one held in Quebec. During the ensuing 15 years (1930–45) O'Brien served as the artistic director of the *Alouette Vocal Quartet and wrote many of the group's arrangements. He entered the Benedictine monastery of St-Benoit-du-Lac, Que, in 1945 and took his vows in 1947. He was ordained a priest in 1952, and from then on was known as Dom Oscar O'Brien.

O'Brien's fairly large output comprised original pieces (often inspired by folklore, which he thought could serve as a a base for a national music) as well as some 400 folksong harmonizations and arrangements for various vocal ensembles. Among the compositions are *Philippino* (1931–3, CMCentre), an operetta in three acts performed on CBC radio in 1943; *La Belle du Nord* (1938), a 'Canadian musical comedy'; a *Trio* (manuscript lost) for piano, violin, and cello; a *Sonata* (1927) for cello and piano, on the theme *'Dans les prisons de Nantes'; four *Préludes* (1922–3, CMCentre) for piano; and about 60 songs for voice and piano with French or English texts. He also composed a *Messe de requiem* (1934–5) *and a Messe de Saint Joachim* (1935–6) for unaccompanied equal voices. Works inspired by folk music and written for the theatre include *Scène des voyageurs* (1928), *Une Noce canadienne-française en 1830* (1929), *À Saint-Malo* (1930), *Dix Danses limousines* (1930), *Pastorale* (1930), and *La Passion* (1935). He wrote piano accompaniments for the songs collected in the three-volume *Chansons d'Acadie* by Father Anselme and Brother Daniel (La Réparation 1942–8), and collaborated on *Canadian Folk Songs Old and New* (Dent 1927, 1949) and *Twenty-one Folk Songs of French Canada / Vingt-et-une Chansons canadiennes* (Harris 1928). Several of his works or harmonizations were published 1924–7 in *La Lyre*.

Oscar O'Brien

As arranger or accompanist O'Brien's name may be found on several Starr, Victor, Brunswick, Columbia, and Bluebird recordings. He gave lectures and wrote articles on folklore, eg, 'Le folklore source d'inspiration pour les artistes' (*Le Canada français*, January 1944, reprinted in *Aujourd'hui*, March 1944). In 1978 CBC radio paid tribute to O'Brien in 'Folklore,' a series of six broadcasts devoted to his harmonizations. Among his pupils were Lionel *Daunais, Hector *Gratton, Jacques *Labrecque, and Lucien *Sicotte. The musical rights from his estate are administered by CAPAC.

BIBLIOGRAPHY

Larose, Paul. 'Oscar O'Brien,' Ottawa *Le Droit*, 1 Dec 1934
Horizons, Nov 1939
'A troubadour turns monk,' *Caecilia*, vol 80, Jul–Aug 1953
Catalogue of Canadian Composers
Musiciens canadiens GP

'O Canada.' National anthem, approved by the Parliament of Canada in 1967 (see National and royal anthems) and adopted officially 27 Jun 1980. Originally called 'Chant national,' it was written in Quebec City by Adolphe-Basile Routhier (words in French) and Calixa *Lavallée (music) and first performed there in 1880. It began to be sung widely in French Canada at that time and later spread across Canada in various English-language versions, of which the best known was written by Robert Stanley Weir in 1908.

A national song had long been desired by the French Canadians. One of the first attempts, *'Sol canadien, terre chérie,' with words written in 1829 by Isidore Bédard and music by T.F. *Molt, was short-lived. In 1834, at the founding of the St-Jean-Baptiste Society, George-Étienne Cartier sang his composition *'Ô Canada! mon pays! mes amours!' to an existing French tune. Other songs like Célestin *Lavigueur's *'La Huronne,' *'Le Drapeau de Carillon' by Octave *Crémazie and Charles W. *Sabatier, and 'Ô Canada, mon pays, mes amours' with music by J.-B. *Labelle enjoyed a certain popularity. In *Chansons populaires du Canada* (Quebec 1865) Ernest *Gagnon wrote of *'Vive la Canadienne' that 'the melody of this song and that of *Claire Fontaine* [ie, "À la claire fontaine"] take the place of a national anthem until something better comes along.' In 1878 the St-Jean-Baptiste Society of Montreal officially adopted *'À la claire fontaine' as a national song.

The need for a rallying song was placed on the agenda of the French-Canadian national festival, which was to be held 23–5 Jun 1880 in Quebec City during the Saint-Jean-Baptiste festivities, bringing together delegates from Canada and the USA. A music committee, appointed 15 Mar 1880,

'O Canada,' the first edition

consisted of 23 members, including Calixa Lavallée, Arthur *Lavigne, Gustave *Gagnon, Alfred *Paré, Louis-Nazaire *LeVasseur, and Joseph *Vézina. Ernest Gagnon was president, and Clodomir Delisle was secretary.

In a chapter of the 'official report,' *Fête nationale des Canadiens français* by Honoré-Julien-Jean-Baptiste Chouinard (Quebec 1881), Amédée Robitaille stated: 'The music committee was not satisfied with ensuring that the musical side of the festivities was successful, and wished to be remembered for something more enduring than the enthusiasm and applause of the moment. One subject that has been debated often, in the press and in our public assemblies as well as our popular societies, is the adoption of a national anthem or song acceptable to all French Canadians. Among the many projects suggested to our committees from all sides, the selection of such a song was the one that attracted the attention of the 24 June organizers. It was a letter dated 24 Jan 1880 from the Reverend Napoléon Caron, priest of the diocese of Trois-Rivières, that proposed a competition as a means of choosing a national anthem or song for 24 June. The inevitable difficulties surrounding competitions and the little time remaining before 24 June kept the music committee, to which the matter had been referred, from carrying out the project in its entirety. But Calixa Lavallée, the distinguished artist whose works are highly esteemed by connoisseurs, was invited to compose a national anthem for 24 June. He went to work enthusiastically and, after several attempts, presented the committee with the national anthem which perpetuates his name and increases daily in popularity.'

The circumstances surrounding the composition and first performance of 'Ô Canada' vary depending on who is writing the account. In *La Musique* of June 1920 Blanche Gagnon declared that her father, Ernest, has been 'secretary of the organizing committee' and asserted that he 'invited Calixa Lavallée to compose some music for the national anthem. The artist set to work and shortly after invited the principal musicians of the town to his home in order to submit three manuscripts for their consideration. The day or the hour not being convenient for everyone, Ernest and Gustave Gagnon were the only ones to appear. Their choice coincided with the composer's own preference for one of the three sketches, which was, in fact, much superior to the other two. Mr [Ernest] Gagnon asked the honourable Judge A.-B. Routhier, president of the Congress, to write words to this music; and in order to suggest the rhythm to him, he used as an example: Ô Canada, terre de nos aïeux ... thinking that M Routhier would keep only the beat and little suspecting that he himself had just sung the first line of our national song.'

Six months later, in December 1920, under the heading 'The genesis of the national anthem "Ô Canada!",' Nazaire LeVasseur, who claimed to be 'secretary of the music committee,' published an article in *La Presse* refuting Blanche Gagnon's version: 'One day, Judge A.-B. Routhier took up his pen and wrote *Ô Canada*, which immediately won everyone's approval. At this time, the lieutenant-governor, M. Théodore Robitaille, an intimate friend of all men of letters, was in the habit of inviting them frequently to his residence, Spencer Wood; among his visitors was Calixa Lavallée, an excellent conversationalist and artist. One evening Dr Robitaille, holding M Routhier's poem in his hand, begged him to write some music for it. Caught off guard, M Lavallée consented. The next day he went to Arthur Lavigne's music shop on St-Jean St, showed him the poem, and told him of his promise to the lieutenant-governor. The famous violinist *Jehin-Prume was present. The three agreed to meet that evening at the home of M Lavallée. The composer showed them a rough outline which they all rejected at once. The scene was repeated on eight to ten consecutive evenings. I witnessed one or two of them. Some of the composer's efforts were set aside for later scrutiny, which vexed him considerably while amusing his friends, who purposely exaggerated their criticisms. Finally, however, M Lavallée one evening casually handed them a manuscript in pencil, went to the piano, and played it from memory. He was made to repeat it; he had created the tune of the national anthem.'

LeVasseur's version was long held to be authentic. It was reproduced by Louis LeJeune in his *Dictionnaire général du Canada* (Ottawa 1931) and by Eugène *Lapierre in the biography *Calixa Lavallée* (Montreal 1936). LeVasseur had concluded brusquely: 'Such is the real genesis of the national anthem. Such were the various phases of its creation, gestation, and birth. On stage and surrounding the event there were no other players than those I have designated. There is nothing to add, nothing to be removed. Thus let it be told, today and tomorrow.' Lapierre rejected 'the other accounts,' which 'too obviously aspire to capture a little glory on behalf of a particular family. We discard them.' He added in a footnote: 'We even refrain from quoting them out of respect for the filial sentiments that dictated them.'

A letter from Routhier to Thomas Bedford Richardson, however, dated 12 Feb 1907 and presented to the NL of C by the latter's daughter Mrs Florence Hagerman, appears to contradict LeVasseur's thesis and to support Blanche Gagnon's. In this letter, written in English and brought to light around 1975, Routhier declares: 'M. Ernest Gagnon ... was a great friend of mine and of M. Lavallée and taking with me a great part in the preparation of the festivities. At his suggestion, Lavallée and I agreed to compose a national song. Lavallée insisted to compose the music first and so he did – and then I made the verses, or the stanzas, with the metrical and the rhyme that were suitable to the music.' Another letter to Richardson, from the lawyer and politician Armand Lavergne and dated 8 Jan 1907, contains Ernest Gagnon's own testimony, which agrees with the account later upheld by his daughter. Gagnon in fact declares that he brought Lavallée's music to Judge Routhier and at the same time suggested the first line of the anthem.

Routhier's version of the birth of 'O Canada' is expanded in comments which he supplied to his grandson Adolphe Routhier in May 1920, shortly before his death. The substance of Judge Routhier's story was made public in June 1980 in a statement in Parliament by Senator Arthur Tremblay. Details had been submitted to, but ignored by, Eugène Lapierre when he was revising the 1966 edition of his biography of Lavallée. They were published in full in *Le Droit* (Ottawa, 22 Jul 1980). They reveal that Routhier heard Lavallée perform the 'grand air' or 'marche héroïque' at the latter's residence on Couillard St and that all four verses were written during the following night. The grandson's notes add that, instead of being commissioned by the music committee (as Amédée Robitaille had stated), Lavallée, Ernest Gagnon, and Routhier took the initiative on their own, because time was short. In order not to antagonize the other members of the committee, the three set about persuading the lieutenant-governor, Théodore Robitaille, to commission Lavallée and Routhier 'officially' to write the song.

But to return to the sequence of events as related by LeVasseur: Lavallée himself went to Lavigne's store with a copy of his composition written in ink, 'only he had forgotten to put his signature to it, an omission rectified by Lavigne himself. Arthur Lavigne thereupon sent Lavallée's manuscript posthaste by messenger to the lieutenant-governor. The latter, for his part, did not delay in returning it to Arthur Lavigne through his aide-de-camp, asking Lavigne to become its publisher, a request to which he immediately acceded.'

Another interesting testimony is that of Judge Joseph Kearney Foran (1857–1931), who was at that time a law student at *Laval U. In a lecture in French, 'Souvenirs des temps jadis,' given in Montreal in February 1918 and published in *A Garland* (Montreal 1931), he reported: 'One evening there were six or seven of us in the room; it was around 9 o'clock when we saw Father Pierre Rousselle, secretary of the university, come in, together with Maurice Baillargé and Trudel – the great tenor – and a small man, very nervous and agitated. He was almost bald, with a halo of black hair falling in ringlets behind his ears. He was very excited and kept tapping his hands and saying "I've got it! I've finally found it, I've succeeded; come; listen." They went to the dais and the small man sat down at the piano. For a brief instant his fingers seemed to send an electric current through the keyboard; then, throwing back his head he played us, for the first time, the masterpiece of his genius – it was Calixa Lavallé [sic]; he played *O Canada*. A few minutes later Trudel sang for us Routhier's words accompanied by the composer of the excellent Canadian anthem himself. In my imagination I was transported to the town of Strasbourg to the night when Rouget deLisle [sic] played and sang *La Marseillaise* for the first time in the midst of a small group of privileged friends.'

Notwithstanding the contradictory accounts of the composition of the anthem and the imprecise chronology of events, it is certain that 'O Canada' was completed by early May 1880, since Trois-Rivières's *Le Constitutionnel* published on 12 May an article attributed to the *Journal de Québec*: 'At last we have a truly French Canadian National Song!' adding that Ernest Gagnon, president of the music committee, had approved the song by Lavallée and Routhier. He furthermore declared that there would be 'a run of 6000 copies, of which 5000 will be distributed to the public' and that the concert and brass bands invited to the French-Canadian National Festival 'will also receive a complete score.'

The house in which Lavallée is believed to have composed the anthem still stood in 1980 at 22 Couillard St, occupied by a restaurant. The original manuscript has not been found. The first edition has a portrait of Lieutenant-Governor Théodore Robitaille on the title-page and is decorated with maple leaves; the single copy known to be extant is deposited in the archives of the *Séminaire de Québec. The original version, in G, is for four voices and piano.

Lavallée's work was to be premiered during a high mass held on the Plains of Abraham on the morning of Thursday, 24 June. According to Chouinard this performance, attended by some 40,000 people, did indeed take place. 'The parts of the mass that were sung were: the Kyrie, the Gloria, the Sanctus, the Agnus Dei; the choirs sang a Tantum ergo on a Russian air at the elevation of the Host; after the mass, God Save the Queen; and after the peroration by Mgr Racine, the national anthem of Calixa Lavallée.' *Le Canada musical*, however, stated the opposite on 1 Jul 1880: 'Through a regrettable misunderstanding, the national song of M Lavallée could not be performed after the mass as had been agreed; yet we would much have preferred this song to the Tantum ergo, whose beauty we were not yet able to appreciate sufficiently to approve the choice made in this instance.' Nor did the Quebec City newspapers report a performance of Lavallée's work during the mass.

It is certain that 'O Canada' was performed on the evening of 24 June at a banquet at the skaters' pavilion attended by more than 500 distinguished people, including the Marquis of Lorne, governor-general of Canada. The account given by Robitaille (Chouinard) is explicit: 'The bands of Beauport, the 9th Battalion [Quebec Rifles], and Fall River, Mass, performed our national airs as well as this stirring song composed by Lavallée, with words by the honorable Judge A.-B. Routhier.' It appears that Lavallée's work, played and not sung, served as a finale to a *Mosaique d'airs canadiens* written for the occasion by Joseph Vézina, who also conducted.

'O Canada,' under the title 'National Song,' was repeated the following day at a large reception for 6000 in the gardens of Spencer Wood. Five or six concert bands were present, and the combined force played the song twice. Two subsequent renditions were reported in *Le Canadien* of 30 Jun 1880: 'Yesterday morning, at the mass held in St-Roch Church, the Société Ste-Cécile graciously presented the national anthem composed by M C. Lavallée for our national holiday. This anthem has a masterful character and when sung by a great number of voices creates a most impressive effect. Our Canadian artist has been patriotically and religiously inspired by such a great festive occasion as that of 24 June. Unless we are much mistaken, this national anthem will compel recognition of its own accord and inevitably will join our other national anthems which in all life's circumstances burst instinctively from the hearts of French Canadians at home and abroad. The congregation of the church in the St-Jean suburb, accompanied by a large orchestra, sang it to great effect at Mass last Sunday, after the Agnus Dei.'

Concerning this performance of 27 June at St-Jean Church, *Le Canada musical* commented: 'The magnificent national song was given most effectively after the Dona nobis. This work, in which we can recognize the composer of the Cantata to Princess Louise, is a broad, patriotic song which at the same time has a religious aspect; it seems to embody all the beauty we look for in the national song of a people, and once it spreads to our towns in Canada it undoubtedly will become the chosen song of French Canadians.'

The popularity of 'O Canada' grew rapidly in Quebec, but the anthem was not heard in English Canada until 20 years later. It apparently was sung in Toronto in 1901 for the visit of the Duke of Cornwall and York, the future George V. The English translation of two of the four verses of Routhier's poem, provided by T.B. Richardson and published by *Whaley Royce in 1906, was sung in *Massey Hall in 1907 by the *Toronto Mendelssohn Choir. This literal translation was not well received, and in 1908 the magazine *Collier's Weekly* (Canadian edition) organized a competition to find a translation acceptable in English Canada. The winner was Mrs Mercy E. Powell McCulloch. The English version most widely used, however, is the one by Robert Stanley Weir, published by Delmar in November 1908 with an arrangement of the music by Alfred *Grant-Schafer. The copyright to Weir's text passed to Leo Feist Ltd in 1929 and to Gordon V. *Thompson Ltd in 1932. Thompson and Weir's heirs surrendered their rights to the Canadian government in 1970 for the symbolic sum of one dollar.

'O Canada' is a 28-bar song written as a formal march in 4/4 time and marked 'maestoso è risoluto.' The original key of G is particularly suitable for instrumental performances. A lower key, F, E, or E flat, is preferable when it is sung. The original French publication by Arthur Lavigne was followed by several others, notably by A.J. *Boucher and Edmond *Hardy. The song has appeared in many versions, arrangements and transcriptions: by Richardson (Whaley Royce 1906), Amédée *Tremblay (McKechnie 1909), Edward *Broome (Anglo-Canadian 1910), C.O. *Sénécal (*Le Passe-Temps*, no. 482, 1913), Ernest *MacMillan (Dent 1928, Whaley Royce 1930), *Willan (Harris 1940), *Ridout (Thompson 1965), Kenneth *Bray (Gage 1969), and Rex *LeLacheur (Harris 1978), among others. There have been numerous unpublished orchestrations, in particular by J.-J. *Gagnier, Albert *Chamberland, Léo *Roy, Herbert *Spencer, and Roger *Matton. English translations have been written by Augustus *Bridle, Ewing Buchan, and his brother Lawrence, and Wilfred Campbell. A scrap book containing some 25 translations is found in the Metropolitan Toronto Library.

In his biography of Calixa Lavallée Lapierre devotes an entire chapter to an aesthetic analysis of 'O Canada' and refutes charges of plagiarism against Lavallée. A considerable number of recordings of the anthem have been made, the first 78s early in the century by Joseph *Saucier, Paul *Dufault, Edward *Johnson, Édouard *LeBel, and Percival *Price. Two postage stamps were issued 6 Jun 1980 by the Canadian government to mark the anthem's centenary.

BIBLIOGRAPHY

Chouinard, H.-J.-J.-B. *Fête nationale des canadiens-français célébrée à Québec en 1880*, chapters 1–3 in part 2 deal with 'O Canada' written by Amédée Robitaille (Quebec 1881)
– *Annales de la Société Saint-Jean-Baptiste de Québec*, vol 4: 1902 (Quebec 1903)
Gagnon, Blanche. 'Notre chant national,' *La Musique*, Jun 1920
LeVasseur, Louis-Nazaire. 'La genèse de l'hymne national "Ô Canada!",' Montreal *La Presse*, 11 Dec 1920
Sullivan, Alan. 'O Canada,' *Maclean's*, 1 Jul 1924
Richardson, P.B. (sic). 'O Canada,' *A Dictionary of Modern Music and Musicians*, ed A. Eaglefield-Hull (London, Toronto 1924)
Magnan, Hormisdas. 'Ô Canada terre de nos aïeux, chant national des Canadiens français,' *BRH*, vol 33, Feb 1927
– *Cinquantenaire de notre Hymne national 'O Canada, terre de nos aïeux'* (Quebec 1929)
'Hommage à l'auteur de l'Hymne National du Canada,' *P-T*, 864, Aug 1933, souvenir issue
Buchan, H.P. *'O Canada.' The Story of the Buchan Version* (Vancouver 1947)
Lapierre, Eugène. *Calixa Lavallée* (Montreal 1936, 1950, 1966)
Ouellet, Jo. 'The stormy life of O Canada and the moody man who wrote it,' *Canadian Weekly*, 27 Jun 1964
Kallmann, Helmut. 'The acceptance of O Canada,' *CanComp*, 8, Apr 1966
Lortie, Jeanne d'Arc. 'Ô Canada,' *Dictionnaire des oeuvres littéraires du Québec* vol 1, ed Maurice Lemire (Montreal 1978)
Fraser, John. 'O Canada given official status,' Toronto *Globe and Mail*, 28 Jun 1980
Potvin, Gilles. 'Comment fut composé l'O Canada en 1880,' Montreal *Le Devoir*, 30 Jun 1980
Routhier, Adolphe. 'Quelques notes historiques sur l'O Canada,' Ottawa *Le Droit*, 22 Jul 1980 GP (HK)

'Ô Canada! mon pays! mes amours!' Patriotic song, with words by the Canadian statesman Sir George-Étienne Cartier (1814–73). It may have been sung first by Cartier to the tune of an old French song, 'Je suis Français, mon pays avant tout,' in Montreal 24 Jun 1834 at a banquet marking the official foundation of the *St-Jean-Baptiste Assn or Society. Cartier was a law student at the time and secretary of the society. The historian Louis-P. Turcotte, however, has written that the song probably was not sung by Cartier until the following year, 24 Jun 1835, at a second banquet at the Rasco Hotel in Montreal (*Journal de Québec*, 23 Jun 1874). In any event, the song was an immediate success. That the words were published first in *La Minerve* of 29 Jun 1835 argues in favour of Turcotte's view. There were six verses originally but only four were published to a 'new air' in *Le Chansonnier des collèges* (Quebec 1850). According to John Boyd, in about 1860 Cartier sent a revised version of the text to Ernest *Gagnon who chose (or perhaps composed) a tune and provided it with a 'musical accompaniment' which is said to have been published shortly thereafter. Many years later (1912), to an unattributed tune with 'accompaniment by Ernest Gagnon,' the song was published in Quebec City. It was reproduced in *Le Passe-Temps* of 21 Jun 1913. In this version the sixth verse was omitted, and it was specified that the fifth also might be excluded.

However, it is J.-B. *Labelle's setting – more ballad than patriotic song – which has survived and which in fact may be the 'new air' published in 1850. What is certain is that Labelle's setting was sung in Montreal, in the presence of 4000 people including Cartier, by then minister of the militia, at the premiere of Labelle's *Cantate: La Confédération* 7 Jan 1868 at the City Hall. Gustave *Comte is therefore in error when he writes that Labelle composed his setting in 1874 (*Le Passe-Temps*, 1 Oct 1898). It was composed prior to 1868 and was published in Montreal in the late 19th century by *Yon, Bélair, and Boucher and, with English words by J.M. *Gibbon and a harmonization by Achille *Fortier, in New York by Leo Feist in 1928.

The song was recorded in 78 rpm by Victor *Occellier, Rodolphe *Plamondon, Joseph *Saucier, and others (see listing in *Roll Back the Years*), and Roger *Doucet included it in his LP *Chants glorieux / Songs of Glory*.

BIBLIOGRAPHY

Boyd, John. *Sir George Etienne Cartier, Bart* (Toronto 1914)
Desparois, Lucille. 'Histoire d'une chanson,' *P-T*, 899, Jun 1946
Mailhot, Laurent. 'Ô Canada! mon pays! mes amours!,' *Dictionnaire des oeuvres littéraires du Québec*, vol 1, ed Maurice Lemire (Montreal 1978)
Carrier, Maurice, and Vachon, Monique. 'Ô Canada! mon pays! mes amours!' *Chansons politiques du Québec*, vol 2, (Montreal 1979) (SW)

OCCELLIER, Victor. Baritone, teacher, b Italy, d Quebec City 3 Dec 1916. He studied in France and began his operatic career there. He visited Canada in October 1899 as a member of the Durieu-Nicosias company, to which Salvator *Issaurel also belonged. In Montreal and Quebec he was heard in several roles, including William Tell in Rossini's opera of that name. When the company disbanded in Cuba late in 1899 he went to New York, where he made his *Metropolitan Opera debut 27 Jan 1900 as Valentin in *Faust*. After a single season he returned to Montreal, where he was a popular star 1900–6 at *Sohmer Park, specializing in ballads and operetta. After a farewell performance in 1906 in the title role of *Rigoletto* at the *Monument national he was briefly a member of the Manhattan Opera in New York. He then settled in Quebec City, where he dedicated himself to teaching and to the concert stage. Adrienne *Roy-Villandré (Yohadio) was one of his pupils. The five titles he recorded for *Berliner and the one for *Columbia are listed in *Roll Back the Years*. He wrote some articles for *Le Passe-Temps*.

BIBLIOGRAPHY

'Mort subite de Victor Occellier,' Quebec *Le Soleil*, 4 Dec 1916

GP

Occupational songs, Anglo-Canadian. By far the largest part of that body of folksongs of which the words originated in Canada. The tunes for practically all of them are borrowed from old Irish folksongs. Whereas old-world songs featured tales of the supernatural, domestic tragedy, wars, and romance, most of the songs composed in Canada were inspired by the work of men, particularly those who earned their living on the sea or in the woods. One very popular pattern was 'The Alphabet Song,' in which each letter was related to something familiar in a particular occupation. There is a 'Sailor's Alphabet,' a 'Fisherman's Alphabet,' a 'Shantyboy's Alphabet,' and a 'Miner's Alphabet,' each of which is a vivid reflection of the work of the particular group.

1 The sea
2 Lumbering
3 Farmers, cowboys, and homesteaders
4 Mining

1 THE SEA. Maritime songs naturally predominate along Canada's east coast, particularly in Nova Scotia and Newfoundland. In the 19th century sailors sang many sea shanties, but these died out when sails gave way to steam. However, W. Roy Mackenzie, the first to collect Anglo-Canadian songs, found some old Nova Scotia seamen who remembered the work songs they sang in the great days of sail. In his introduction to *Ballads and Sea Songs from Nova Scotia* he discusses 'the obsolete ritual of shanty-singing,' citing information he gathered from several retired sailors, and he gives the largest number of sea shanties that have been collected in Canada. These include such capstan shanties as 'Santy Anna,' 'We're All Away to Sea,' 'We're Homeward Bound,' 'Rio Grande,' 'Rolling River,' 'Sally Brown,' and 'Lowlands,' and halyard shanties like 'Whisky Johnny,' 'Blow the Man Down, 'Reuben Ranzo,' 'Blow, Boys, Blow,' and 'The Wild Goose.' Much later Helen *Creighton still was able to get some shanties from singers who had sailed from the Nova Scotia ports of Lunenburg and Liverpool, and five of these may be heard on her record *Folk Music from Nova Scotia*. Fewer shanties were noted in Newfoundland: Elisabeth Greenleaf, who made the first major collection, found only four fragments – 'Homeward Bound,' 'Haul on the Bo'line,' 'Jolly Poker,' and 'Sally Brown' – and Kenneth *Peacock's vast *Songs of the Newfoundland Outports* includes only one – 'Blow the Wind Westerly' – which came not from a sailor but from a woman.

The sailors sang shanties only while working, but they sang many other kinds of sea song in their leisure hours. For example, 'Wadham's Song,' composed in 1765, is a detailed guide to the landmarks and hazards around the coast of Newfoundland, and 'The Ryans and the Pittmans,' descended from the old British sea song 'Spanish Ladies,' describes the life and loves of a Newfoundland fisherman. From other songs we get a very clear picture of the experiences of fishermen, sailors, and whalers. Most of these others fall into two groups: those that describe a particular voyage, and those that tell of tragedy at sea. 'The Old *Polina*' tells how the whaling ships raced from Dundee in Scotland to St John's each spring, and 'The Greenland Whale Fisher' describes a whale hunt that ended in tragedy when the thrashing of the whale overturned the small boat containing the harpooners.

'The Ferryland Sealer,' which Kenneth Peacock calls 'one of the best native ballads to come out of Newfoundland,' is a graphic account of a 19th-century expedition when 'some were killing, some were scalping, some were hauling on board,' until in the evening 'they counted nine hundred fine scalps in the hold.' Similarly 'The Sealing Cruise of the *Lone Flier*' gives a detailed description of a 1929 voyage in which the crew got its catch but suffered a number of minor mishaps. Two different ballads describe 'The *Greenland* Disaster' when 48 sealers were frozen to death on the ice in 1898, and another tells how 'The *Southern Cross*,' a famous sealing vessel, disappeared in a storm in 1914 with 170 men on board.

Fishing songs fall into the same patterns. 'A Crowd of Bold Sharemen' describes a trip to the Labrador coast to fish for cod, and 'High Times in Our Ship' is a lively account of a fishing expedition on the French shore. 'The Petty Harbour Bait Skiff' tells of the loss of a small fishing boat in a sudden storm, and 'The Loss of the *Regalus*' tells of another sunk near Cape Race.

One unusual ballad, 'The Ghostly Seamen,' incorporates the superstition that drowned sailors board the ships that pass the site of their disaster. Peakock says this song was composed by Harry L. Marcy in 1874. See also Disaster songs.

Besides the ballads describing particular voyages and disasters there were many more lighthearted songs inspired by the Maritimers' work. 'A Noble Fleet of Sealers,' 'The Sealers' Song,' and 'The Sealers' Ball' all tell of the celebrations when the fleet reached port, and even the dance songs reflect the Maritimers' dependence on the sea, as in 'I'se the B'y That Builds the Boat,' 'The Feller from Fortune,' *'Lukey's Boat,' and 'Harbour Grace.' Some emphasize the sailors' fondness for rum: F.W. Wallace wrote a lively ditty telling how drunken seamen survived a dangerous trip on 'The *Mary L. MacKay*,' and 'In Canso Strait' tells how a crew triumphed over its drunken captain.

A smaller number of songs came from the sailors of the Great Lakes. Like those from the east coast, most describe particular voyages or shipwrecks. The two most popular were 'The *Bigler's* Crew,' a humorous account of a flat-bottomed scow hauling timber from Buffalo to Milwaukee, and 'Red Iron Ore,' telling of the hardships suffered by the crew of the *E.C. Roberts* in hauling ore from Escanaba to Cleveland. Most of the other Great Lakes songs tell dismal tales of ships lost in storms. 'The *Persian's* Crew' is the best-known; others chronicle the loss of the *Asia*, the *Maggie Hunter*, the *Belle Sheridan*, the *Antelope*, and a dozen more. Dr Ivan H. Walton of Ann Arbor, Mich, made the largest collection of Great Lakes songs, and some of the Canadian songs were published in *Fowke's *Folklore of Canada* (Toronto 1976). C.H.J. Snider researched and published a few in his Toronto *Evening Telegram* column 'Schooner Days,' and he and his friend Stanley Bâby sang some of them on the recording *Songs of the Great Lakes*.

2 LUMBERING. Work in the lumberwoods inspired the greatest number of native songs in New Brunswick and Ontario, and some lumbering songs have been sung all across Canada. They fall into three groups. First come those that describe life and work in the woods, often taking the form of an account of a winter spent in a particular camp. One pattern is so common that it sometimes is called simply 'The Lumbercamp Song,' and some version of it was known by nearly every man who worked in the woods. Patterned on an English music-hall ditty about 'Jim the Carter Lad,' it sometimes is called 'A Jolly Shanty Lad'or 'Jack the Shanty Lad,' and describes all the activities in a camp from daybreak until evening. Mrs Greenleaf, who collected it in Newfoundland as 'The Lumbercamp Song,' described the tune as 'the best, most robust, and most finished air in the Dorian mode that I have ever heard.' The same tune was used for two other Newfoundland songs, 'The Sealing Cruise of the *Lone Flier*' and 'The Herring Gibbers,' and one from the Great Lakes, 'The *Bigler's* Crew.' Other songs are more localized, like 'Turner's Camp,' 'Anstruther Camp,' 'The New Limit Line,' 'Hogan's Lake,' 'The Banks of Mullen Stream,' or 'The Winter of '73.' Some are moniker songs, naming all the men in the camp, as in 'Hauling Logs on the Maniwaki,' 'The Squire Boys,' and 'MacDonald's Camp.' In Newfoundland 'Twin Lakes' and 'The Badger Drive' are the best-known local lumbering songs.

While these are fairly straightforward accounts of work in the woods, other songs emphasize the hardships endured by the shantyboys. An early one told of a bitter winter spent in 'Canaday-I-O'; this was later adapted to tell of similar hardships in 'Michigan-I-O,' and gave the pattern for a famous Texas song, 'The Buffalo Skinners.' Another widespread ditty told of a man who worked for a tough boss on 'The Rock Island Line,' and the same pattern was localized in the Maritimes as 'The Fox River Line' and 'The Scantaling Line.'

Almost as numerous are the ballads that describe death in the woods or on the rivers. The most widespread is 'The Jam on Gerry's Rocks,' which tells how 'the foreman young Munroe' was swept away when the jam broke. In the Maritimes the favourite is 'Peter Amberley' (*'Peter Emberley'), about a lad from Prince Edward Island who was crushed when a log rolled on him in the Miramichi woods. Less widely known Miramichi ballads tell of similar accidents that killed 'Guy Reed' and 'John Ladner.' In Ontario they sing of 'Jimmy Whelan,' 'Jimmy Judge, 'The Haggertys and Young Mulvanny,' and 'Johnny Doyle,' all of whom were drowned on river drives, and 'Harry Dunn,' who was killed by a falling limb down in 'the woods of Michigan.'

More unusual are two other ballads about woods tragedies. In 'Lost Jimmy Whelan' the drowned shantyboy rises from his grave to ask his sweetheart to stop mourning for him: a counterpart of the old British ballad 'The Unquiet Grave.' A New Brunswick ballad, 'The Dungarvon Whooper,' tells how the ghost of a camp cook, who had been killed, returned to fill the forest with 'fearful whoops and yells.'

A somewhat smaller group of songs tell of the shantyboys and their girls, and the lively times the boys had when they came out of the woods in the spring with their winter's pay in their pockets. Widely popular was a debate between two girls who loved 'The Farmer's Son and the Shantyboy.' 'Ye Maidens of Ontario' or 'The Maids of Simcoe' also emphasize the contrast between the sober farmers and the adventurous raftsmen, and several other songs stress the girls' preference for 'The Roving Shantyboy.' The sailors' ditty 'Jack Tar Ashore' provided the pattern for 'The Lumberman in Town,' also known as 'When the Shantyboy Comes Down,' and 'Duffy's Hotel' and 'The Grand Hotel' tell of riotous times on the east and west coasts respectively. 'How We Got Up to the Woods Last Year,' also called 'Drunk on the Way,' 'Conroy's Camp,' and 'Holmes Camp,' all emphasize the loggers' fondness for liquor, and 'Save Your Money While You're Young' points the moral: 'You'll need it when you're old.' The main sources for lumbering songs are Louise *Manny's *Songs of Miramichi* and Edith Fowke's *Lumbering Songs from the Northern Woods*, although every major folksong collection contains some. Old-time shantyboys may be heard singing on the recordings *Lumbering Songs from the Ontario Shanties* and *Folksongs of the Miramichi*. Edward D. Ives describes the most famous of the logger songmakers in *Larry Gorman: The Man Who Made the Songs*.

3 FARMERS, COWBOYS, AND HOMESTEADERS. Other occupations have inspired fewer songs. The solitary work of farming did not stimulate singing as fishing and lumbering did, but a few verses circulated. In 'The Scarborough Settler's Lament' a Scot compared 'Canada's fields of pine' unfavourably with 'Auld Scotia's glens'; and 'The Backwoodsman,' a tale of a lively country spree, was sung from Nova Scotia to Saskatchewan. Edward Ives has described *Lawrence Doyle: The Farmer Poet of Prince Edward Island*, who wrote many ditties about local events, including a description of 'When Johnny Went Ploughing for Kearon'; and another Island poet, Dan Somers, wrote of 'The Harvest Excursion.'

In the West both homesteaders and cowboys borrowed songs from the USA. In the 1870s, when the first ranches were established in the region that was to become Alberta, most of the cattle were driven up from Texas, nearly 2000 miles to the south, and the ranchers hired US cowboys who brought with them the songs that were being sung at home in the southwest. Popular Texas songs like 'The Old Chisholm Trail,' 'The Streets of Laredo,' 'Bury Me Not on the Lone Prairie,' and 'The Tenderfoot' were sung on Alberta ranches, but the Canadian cowboys do not seem to have composed many songs of their own. Similarly, when homesteaders began to break the prairie sod, they adopted and adapted US songs: 'The Little Old Sod Shanty' was popular in Saskatchewan, and 'The Greer County Bachelor' was transformed into 'The Alberta Homesteader.' 'Dakota Land' and other US parodies of the old hymn 'Beulah Land' were rewritten in Canada as 'Prairie Land,' 'Alberta Land,' and 'Saskatchewan,' 'where winds are always on the blow.' However, it is probable that *'The Red River Valley,' originally thought to be a US song, was composed about the Red River in Manitoba.

4 MINING. Mining songs also are comparatively rare in Canada. Few songs about the Cariboo or Klondike gold rushes have survived (see Klondike), although northern prospectors like to sing *'When the Iceworms Nest Again,' derived from a Robert W. Service composition of 1910. A 'Cobalt Song' which L.F. Steenman wrote in 1910 became popular with the silver miners of northern Ontario, and they also sang an adaptation of the US railroading ditty 'Drill, Ye Tarriers, Drill.'

George Korson noted a few union songs from Cape Breton in *Coal Dust on the Fiddle*, as well as a Nova Scotia version of an English love song about 'The Jolly Wee Miner Men.' Helen Creighton collected another version of the love song 'The Jolly Miner,' and includes two songs (see Disaster songs) about the 1791 Springhill disaster in *Maritime Folk Songs*. In 1966 a song competition in Cape Breton stimulated some compositions, and the miners' choral group Men of the Deeps was organized to popularize mining songs through concerts. The director of the Men of the Deeps, John C. *O'Donnell, has published songs from their repertoire in *The Men of the Deeps* and they have made a record with the same title.

Until the publication in 1979 of Philip J. *Thomas's *Songs of the Pacific Northwest*, which includes examples of songs of logging, mining, fishing, and ranching, there was no record of the occupational songs indigenous to British Columbia.

See also Trade union songs.

BIBLIOGRAPHY

Murphy, James. *Murphy's Sealer's Song Book* (St John's, Nfld 1911)
– *Songs Their Fathers Sung; For Fisherman* (St John's, Nfld 1923)
– *Songs Sung By Old Time Sealers of Many Years Ago* (St John's, Nfld 1925)
Rickaby, Franz. *Ballads and Songs of the Shanty-boy* (Cambridge, Mass 1926)
Mackenzie, W. Roy. *Ballads and Sea Songs from Nova Scotia* (Boston 1928; repr Hatboro, Pa 1963)
Greenleaf, Elisabeth, and Mansfield, Grace. *Ballads and Sea Songs of Newfoundland* (Cambridge, Mass 1933; repr Hatboro, Pa 1968)
Walton, Isaac H. 'Songs of the Great Lakes sailors,' *J of the International Folk Music Council*, vol 3, 1951
Doerflinger, William. *Shantymen and Shantyboys: Songs of Sailor and Lumberman* (New York 1951); repr as *Songs of the Sailor and Lumberman* (New York 1972)
Ives, Edward D. 'The lumberman in town,' *Northeast Folklore*, vol 2, Winter 1959
Creighton, Helen. *Maritime Folk Songs* (Toronto 1962, 1976)
Fowke, Edith. 'American cowboy and western pioneer songs in Canada,' *Western Folklore*, vol 21, 1962
– '"The Red River Valley" re-examined,' *Western Folklore*, vol 23, Jul 1964; *Alberta Historical R*, vol 13, Winter 1965
Ives, Edward D. *Larry Gorman: The Man Who Made the Songs* (Bloomington, Ind 1964)
Korson, George. *Coal Dust on the Fiddle* (Hatboro, Pa 1965)
Peacock, Kenneth. *Songs of the Newfoundland Outports*, 3 vols (Ottawa 1965)
Manny, Louise, and Wilson, James Reginald. *Songs of Miramichi* (Fredericton 1968)
Fowke, Edith. *Lumbering Songs from the Northern Woods* (Austin, Tex 1970)
Ives, Edward D. *Lawrence Doyle: The Farmer Poet of Prince Edward Island* (Orono, Me 1971)
O'Donnell, John. *Men of the Deeps* (Waterloo, Ont 1975)
Thomas, Philip J. *Songs of the Pacific Northwest* (Vancouver 1979)

DISCOGRAPHY

Folk Music from Nova Scotia. Recorded by H. Creighton. (1956). Folk FM 4006
Folksongs of the Miramichi. 1959 Miramichi Folk Festival. Folk FE 4053
Lumbering Songs from the Ontario Shanties. Recorded by E. Fowke. (1961). Folk FM 4052
The Men of the Deeps. O'Donnell cond. 1975. Wat CSPS 898
Songs of the Great Lakes. Recorded by E. Fowke. (1964). Folk FM 4018 EF

O'CONNOR, Billy (William). Singer, pianist, songwriter, agent, b Kingston, Ont, 9 Jan 1914. His father, Tommy (Thomas John) O'Connor (b Kingston 1871, d Toronto 1947), was a pianist-entertainer who during the late 1880s worked in the USA with Lew Dockstader's Minstrels and was accompanist to the magicians Blackstone and Thurston, and who later performed throughout eastern Ontario as part of the team Crosby and O'Connor. The younger O'Connor was taught piano by his father after the family moved to Toronto in 1919. He served as an entertainment corporal in the Canadian Army during World War II and began working in Toronto nightclubs in 1947. His radio career began in 1948 with CBC broadcasts from the Club Norman and continued on that network into the early 1960s and also on network broadcasts originating from CFRB 1954–9 and from CHUM in 1961. His CBC TV career began with 'Four for the Show,' which led to star billing on 'The Late Show' 1954–6, 'Club O'Connor' in 1957, and 'Saturday Date' 1958–9. His programs were noted for introducing new talent, including *Juliette, Sylvia Murphy, Rhonda Silver and Vanda King, Peter *Appleyard, and the Two Tones (of whom one was Gordon *Lightfoot).

In 1960 O'Connor turned full-time to Billy O'Connor Enterprises, an agency founded in 1954. He booked the *CNE Grandstand in 1969, establishing the policy – which continued into the 1970s – of presenting individual concerts. Also in 1969 he began booking for (and performing at) the CNE Bandshell. For over 30 years he took his show to southern Ontario prisons and hospitals, performing for inmates and patients.

O'Connor's recordings include a 1948 hit with his song *'Saskatchewan' (also recorded in the USA as 'Washington') and the LP *Together Again* (1968, Arc AS 769), a reunion of his 1950s trio – the guitarist Kenny Gill, the accordionist Vic Centro, and the bassist Jack *Richardson – assisted by the drummer Doug MacLeod. An affiliate of PRO Canada, O'Connor has had songs (including 'Saskatchewan') published by BMIC and Broadland Music. MM

Octobre. Instrumental and vocal rock group founded in Montreal in 1971 by Pierre Flynn (composer, keyboard player, b Quebec City 1954), Mario Légaré (bass), Jean Dorais (guitarist), and Pierre Hébert (drums). In 1979 Gérard Leduc (keyboards, saxophones) joined the group, and Richard Pelletier replaced Hébert. The group's first LP, *Octobre* (Trans-World PGP 13001), was made in 1972. Employing a progressive style of music moving increasingly towards jazz, Octobre has sung of revolt, struggle, and conflict, as such titles as 'La Maudite Machine,' 'Violence,' and 'Insurrection' demonstrate. Françoy Roberge described the group in *Le Devoir* (14 Mar 1978): 'Octobre, with its drive [and] its sharply defined contrasts, comes across like the figure of a black angel. It has much of the natural energy of Santana and the sharpness of Chicago, and it knows how to evoke fantasies.' Later he adds: 'Its directness of language and choice of material occasionally call to mind the philosophy expressed in the singing of [Léo] Ferré, the philosophy of the fist, and yet, despite all, of hope.'

The group has performed at the Capitol Theatre in Quebec City (1973), the Outremont Cinema in Montreal (1974, 1976, 1978), L'Évêché in the Nelson Hotel in old Montreal (1975), the Astrolabe in Ottawa (1976), and elsewhere. During these years it made the LPs *Les Nouvelles Terres* (1974, Trans-World ZOX-6015), *Survivance* (1976, Trans-World TI-6023), and *L'Autoroute des rêves* (1977, CBS PFS 90439, for which Richard *Grégoire wrote orchestral arrangements). In 1978 the group toured New Brunswick, Ontario, and Quebec. Its concert at the *St-Denis Theatre that year was recorded and released as *Chants de la nuit* (2-CBS GFC 80.006).

BIBLIOGRAPHY
Germain, Georges-Hébert. 'Octobre sur ses nouvelles terres,' Montreal *La Presse*, 26 Oct 1974
Petrowski, Nathalie. 'Octobre's Pierre Flynn about to explore new areas of music,' *MSc*, 280, Nov–Dec 1974
Germain, Georges-Hébert. 'Octobre et le grand départ vers l'inconnu,' Montreal *Le Devoir*, 26 Nov 1977 ST

O'DONNELL, John (Clark). Teacher, choir director, pianist, b Portland, Me, 8 Jun 1935; BA (St Francis Xavier) 1958, M ED (Gonzaga) 1962, M MUS (London) 1970. He began teaching at *St Francis Xavier U in 1966 and became chairman of the Music Dept in 1970. He has been choirmaster of St Ninian's Cathedral, Antigonish, NS, and has performed as a pianist on CBC radio's 'Music in the Evening.' He became president of the *CFMS in 1977. O'Donnell founded the Men of the Deeps, a folk choir of Cape Breton miners, in 1967 and conducted them until 1969. He resumed that function in 1973. The choir toured Canada and China in 1976, and prior to 1980 produced three records, all under the title *The Men of the Deeps*, one for Apex (1967, AL71647) and two for Waterloo (1975, CSPS 898-W5; 1976, CSPS 1011-WR7), and a songbook of the same name (Waterloo 1975).

BIBLIOGRAPHY
Cameron, Silver Donald. 'Underground in China,' *Weekend Magazine*, 27 Nov 1976 CF

Offenbach. Montreal blues-rock band. It evolved from a succession of rock bands in the late 1960s, one of which, Les Gants blancs, included 'Gerry' (Gérald Boulet, singer-pianist-organist-synthesizist, b St-Jean d'Iberville, Que, 1946) and 'Johnny' (Jean Gravel, guitarist, b Granby, Que, 1948), who were the only remaining original members of Offenbach in 1979. At its formation in 1969 Offenbach was completed by the singer-organist Pierre Harel (who left in 1973), the bass guitarist 'Willie' (Michel Lamothe, son of Willie *Lamothe), and the drummer Denis Boulet (brother of 'Gerry'), replaced in 1972 by 'Wezo' (Roger Belval).

Initially Offenbach performed a mixture of pop songs of the day, blues, and original material. An early work, in English, was the suite *Offenbach Pop Opera*. In 1972 the band made its first LP, *Offenbach Soap Opera* (Barclay 80137), singing in French. Its second, *Saint-Chrone de néant* (Barclay 80153), was a recording of a performance of its *Mass for the Dead* at St Joseph's Oratory, Montreal, 30 Nov 1972. Offenbach created the score for Harel's feature film *Bulldozer*; some of the music is heard on an LP of the same name (1973, Barclay 80182). While the band was based in France 1973–5, it toured there and in Holland, Belgium, and Switzerland, and appeared in the film *Tabarnac*. The music for the film was released on a two-LP set, *Tabarnac* (Deram ADEF-1178). Returning to Montreal, Offenbach became one of the leading rock bands in Quebec, even though its reliance on blues-oriented material left it little in common with Québécois pop music. It appeared in major concert halls and clubs throughout the province and, after the release in 1976 of its first LP entirely in English (*Never Too Tender*, A & M SP 9025), toured across Canada. In 1977 *A & M released a French LP, *Offenbach* (SP 9027). That year 'Willie' and 'Wezo'were replaced by Norman Kerr and Pierre Lavoie, respectively, and guitarist Jean Millaire was added. The personnel continued to vary, and in 1979, for concerts 30 and 31 Mar at the *St-Denis Theatre with Vic *Vogel's big band, it comprised Boulet, Gravel, John McGale (guitar), Breen Leboeuf (bass guitar), and Robert Harrison (drums). The LP *Traversion* (Kébec Disc KD-L963) was released at this time and its popularity in France resulted in radio and TV engagements for the group. This LP was chosen rock album of the year at the Gala de l'Assn du disque et de l'industrie du spectacle québécois (ADISQ) of 1979.

Geoffrey O'Hara

Among Offenbach's most popular songs are 'Pourquoi j't'icitte,' 'Québec rock,' 'Dimanche blues,' 'Câline de blues,' 'Everyday I Get the Blues,' 'Le Blues me guette,' and 'Chu un rocker.' After one of the band's club appearances in Toronto Paul McGrath (*Globe and Mail*, 18 Jan 1978) made special mention of Boulet's voice: 'a voice that for sheer throat-ripping volume has no equal anywhere in the great dominion ... with his full tenor he makes the blues mean something different, and at the same time forms the band's trademark.'

BIBLIOGRAPHY
Dostie, Bruno. 'Quebec's rock and roll bad guys make the push into English Canada,' *CanComp*, 118, Feb 1977
Caron, Claire. 'Affiliates join Offenbach in midst of group's success,' *MSc*, 298, Nov–Dec 1977
Petrowski, Nathalie. 'Offenbach is on the way back once more, *CanComp*, 140, Apr 1979
Viau, Serge. 'Prêt à mordre dans la marché américain,' *Perspectives*, 31 May 1980 MM

O'HARA, Geoffrey. Composer, singer, lecturer, b Chatham, Ont, 2 Feb 1882, d St Petersburg, Fla, 31 Jan 1966; hon D MUS (Huron, S Dak) 1947. He played the piano as a child, and at 12 was a singer and organist in a Chatham Anglican Church. In 1904 he joined Lew Dockstader's Minstrels and went on to sing light opera at Daly's Theater, New York. Later he travelled the Lyceum and Chautauqua vaudeville circuits as a singer, lecturer, and community song leader. Appointed instructor of native Indian music in 1913 by the US Secretary of the Interior, he collected and recorded songs of the Navajo and other tribes. He also taught 1936–7 at Teachers' College, Columbia U, and lectured on songwriting at Huron College. During World War II he visited military camps as a singing instructor and morale builder. He was president in 1925 of the International Lyceum and Chautauqua Association, board member in 1941 of ASCAP, and president in 1945 of the Composers-Authors Guild.

O'Hara's first work, a ragtime composition, *Coloured Fireworks* (Canadian American 1904), was written under the name Geoffrey de Vere. His first hit song, 'Your Eyes Have Told Me' (Ricordi 1913), was recorded by Caruso. He is remembered best for the songs *'Give a Man a Horse He Can Ride' (1917) and *'K-K-K-Katy' (1918), both written while he was visiting in Kingston, Ont; 'There Is No Death' (Chappell 1919) and 'The Living God' (Huntzinger 1930), both with words by Gordon Johnstone; *'Wreck of the Julie Plante' (Ditson 1921) and 'Leetle Bateese' (Ditson 1921), settings of verses by the Canadian poet W.H. Drummond; and the barbershop-quartet favourite 'The Old Songs' (Boston Music 1927). He also composed 12 operettas 1927–48, listed in *Catalogue of Canadian Composers*, and some 500 hymns, patriotic songs, and popular tunes. With J.M. *Gibbon and O. *O'Brien he prepared the songbook *Canadian Folk Songs, Old and New* (London 1927, 1949). Recordings of his songs 1913–27 and of his singing 1914–18, for Victor and HMV, are listed in *Roll Back the Years*. EBM

O'Keefe Centre, Toronto

L'Oiseau-phénix. Ballet based on a Canadian legend collected by Marius *Barbeau. The music, scored for medium orchestra, was composed by Clermont *Pépin, and the choreography was by Ludmilla Chiriaeff. Paired with Stravinsky's *Les Noces*, the ballet was premiered 1 Sep 1956 under Pépin's baton by Les Grands Ballets Canadiens at the *St-Denis Theatre as part of the *Montreal Festivals. Every night a phoenix steals golden apples from the apple tree of a rich peasant. Each of his three sons is summoned in turn to watch the tree closely. The first falls asleep, the second gets drunk, but the third and youngest manages to capture the bird, which immediately turns into a beautiful young maiden before the eyes of the amazed villagers. The youth is given her hand in marriage, and the ballet ends with a wedding and merry-making. The introduction, *Ronde villageoise*, in a transcription for two pianos by the composer, was recorded in 1968 by Victor *Bouchard and Renée *Morisset (CBC SM-61). (DA)

O'Keefe Centre for the Performing Arts. Toronto entertainment venue, home in the 1960s and 1970s of the *COC and the National Ballet of Canada. Located on Front Street between Yonge and Scott streets, it was built in 1960 and owned until 1968 by the O'Keefe Brewing Co. In 1968 ownership was transferred to Metropolitan Toronto. Designed by Earle C. Morgan and Page and Steele of Toronto, with Eggers and Higgins of New York as consultants and V.L. Henderson as acoustician, the theatre seats over 3200 on two levels facing an 18-m-wide proscenium stage. Though intended as a 'multi-purpose entertainment centre,' the theatre's size has fitted it mainly for spectacle. The complex acoustic design includes moveable panels attached to the walls of the auditorium and an acoustic shell (added in 1961) which can be lowered from the stage tower for band and orchestra performances. Amplification is necessary for stage productions, including operas.

O'Keefe Centre opened 1 Oct 1960 with a pre-Broadway production of *Camelot* starring Julie Andrews, Richard Burton, and Robert *Goulet. Seldom dark, it has been host to productions of

Anne of Green Gables, **Johnny Belinda*, and Cliff *Jones' **Kronberg 1582*, leading Broadway shows, and many stage plays, and to performances by the Royal Winnipeg, Bolshoi, Royal, and Kirov ballet companies, the Metropolitan and D'Oyly Carte opera companies, the *TS and the New York Philharmonic, the Duke Ellington and Count Basie orchestras, the rock groups Jefferson Airplane and Steppenwolf (*Sparrow), and entertainers Harry Belafonte, Tom Jones, and Sonny and Cher, among many others. Hugh P. Walker, the centre's first managing director was succeeded in 1976 by Tom Burrows. In 1979 John Kruger was appointed interim general manager.

BIBLIOGRAPHY

Henderson, V.L. 'Acoustic considerations at the O'Keefe Centre,' *CMJ*, vol 6, Summer 1960

Mercer, Ruby. 'O'Keefe Centre: a house for all seasons,' *OpCan*, Fall 1971

AM

ONDERET, Maurice. Violinist, pedagogue, b Mons, Belgium, 13 Jan 1899; premier prix (Brussels Royal Cons) 1920. His father taught him solfège and theory. In 1915 he obtained a diploma in violin from the Mons Cons and in 1918 he enrolled in the classes of Alfred Marchot at the Royal Cons of Brussels. Winner, there, of the Adolphe-Canler virtuosity prize in 1923, he also performed in recital and taught 1923–7 at the Cons de la Louvière. In 1927 he emigrated to Canada to teach at the *McGill Cons, and ca 1930 he was a member of the first *McGill String Quartet. He was concertmaster 1930–41 of the *Montreal Orchestra and appeared as soloist in concertos by Bach, Brahms, Mendelssohn, and Vieuxtemps. He gave the Canadian premiere of the Sibelius *Concerto* with the *Promenade Symphony Concerts in Toronto in 1937 and repeated it in Montreal in 1938. He was concertmaster of the CSM Orchestra 1941–5 and of the *Little Symphony of Montreal 1942–5 and gave several recitals on CBC radio. He taught 1943–6 at the *CMM and was a member of the *Dubois String Quartet, the Montreal Trio, and the Jean-*Lallemand Quartet. Late in 1946 he returned to Belgium, taught at Mons and La Louvière, and performed as a soloist in Belgium and Germany. In 1948 Bosworth published his *Méthode de violon* in five volumes, as well as the treatise *Le Staccato*. Returning to Montreal Onderet taught 1965–71 at the *École normale de musique and the Collège St-Laurent, and in 1967 inaugurated violin classes at the Cons de Chicoutimi. With William *Stevens he recorded the Franck *Sonata* (Select SSC 13.016) in 1969. Among his pupils are Nöel *Brunet, Alexander *Brott, Mildred *Goodman, Roméo *Mastrocola, Lionel Renaud, and Lucien *Sicotte. In 1971 Onderet retired to his native city of Mons. IP-C

Ondes Martenot. Electronic instrument invented by the Frenchman Maurice Martenot in 1928 and introduced to Canada in 1950 by Andrée *Desautels, who invited to Montreal the inventor's sister Ginette Martenot to give a recital and demonstration on CBC radio. The instrument is based on the physical phenomenon of beats occurring between two high-frequency waves. An audible frequency that consists of the difference between the two high-frequency waves is produced. The pitch of the instrument is controlled by means of a keyboard similar to that of a piano, or by a ribbon to which is attached a metal ring worn on the performer's middle finger. Movement of the ribbon to the right or the left produces a sliding upwards or downwards in pitch. The keyboard may be moved laterally as well, producing a vibrato effect. The sound may be barely audible if desired; the volume is controlled by a very sensitive key which also permits many effects, such as staccato.

Ginette Martenot returned to Canada to tour 1958–9 for *JMC. The instrument was used for the first time in the theatre in Montreal when Andrée Desautels performed on it her incidental music for a 1954 production of Molière's *Dom Juan* at the Théâtre de Nouveau-Monde. Jean *Laurendeau, an ondist and clarinetist who graduated from the Paris Cons and the École normale, took part in four JMC tours 1965–9, performing works for ondes with piano and/or percussion. In January 1968 he conducted an ondes Martenot class at the *CMM, the first in North America. In November 1976 Laurendeau formed the Ensemble d'ondes de Montréal with ondists Suzanne Binet-Audet, Marie Bernard, Lucie Filteau, and Johanne Goyette. In 1979 the ensemble gave a concert in Quebec City, sponsored by the Assn de musique actuelle, and another in Montreal at the Musée d'art contemporain at which it premiered José *Evangelista's *Carrousel* and an arrangement for ondes of Claude *Vivier's *Pulau Dewata*.

Canadian composers who have used the ondes Martenot in their works include Claude *Champagne (*Altitude*, 1959), Gilles *Tremblay (*Cantique de durées*, 1960; *Kékoba*, 1965), Clermont *Pépin (*Quasars – Symphonie no. 3*, 1967), André *Prévost (*Sonate* avec piano, 1967), Micheline Coulombe *Saint-Marcoux (*Modulaire*, 1967; *Séquences*, 1968; *Ishuma*, 1973–4), Claude Vivier (*Prolifération*, 1969), François *Dompierre (*Sonate* avec piano, 1974) and Richard-Gaudreault *Boucher (*Angoisse des fuyantes créations*, 1974; *Begonia Rex*, 1975, which calls for four ondes Martenot players). Gabriel *Charpentier, Jean-Marie *Cloutier, and Georges *Savaria also have used the instrument in incidental music for the stage or as an accompaniment for dancing.

BIBLIOGRAPHY

Gingras, Claude. 'Les 50 ans des ondes Martenot,' Montreal *La Presse*, 21 Apr 1979

(PR)

O'NEILL, Charles. Bandmaster, composer, teacher, organist, cornetist, b Duntocher, near Glasgow, of Irish parents, 31 Aug 1882, d Quebec City 9 Sep 1964; diploma RMSM (Kneller Hall) 1909, B MUS (McGill) 1914, D MUS (McGill) 1924. Childhood piano lessons were followed by organ study under Albert Lister Peace in Glasgow and theory instruction under Archibald Evans in London. At 15 O'Neill took a position as organist at Grimsby, Lincolnshire, England, and played cornet in the local band. He moved to Boston in 1901, to New York two years later, and to Kingston, Ont, in 1905 to serve as cornet soloist with the newly formed Royal Canadian Horse Artillery Band.

The Dept of National Defence sent O'Neill to train as a bandmaster at the RMSM (Kneller Hall) in 1908. On his return to Canada in 1910 he succeeded Joseph *Vézina as music director of the Royal Canadian Garrison Artillery Band at Quebec Citadel. He continued his theory and composition studies with Herbert *Sanders of Ottawa and became one of the earliest B MUS graduates of *McGill U. In 1919 he attained the rank of captain, and in 1922 he became music director of the newly created *Royal 22nd Regiment Band at Quebec Citadel, developing the ensemble into one of the finest in Canada. He made a name for himself also as a conductor at the *CNE in Toronto (eg, feature band 1927, Composite Permanent Force Band of Canada 1930), as director of a CBC orchestra in Quebec (ca 1935–7), and as a guest conductor in several Canadian and US cities and in London in 1937 at the coronation of George VI. As a fearless but just adjudicator (eg, at the CNE in 1923 and

Capt Charles O'Neill

many years thereafter) he gained wide respect. At the US State and National Band Contests he judged alongside John Philip Sousa and Edwin Franko Goldman in 1928. He was president of the American Bandmasters' Assn 1933–4 and honorary president of the *CBA 1960–4. He also was vice-president of the *Dominion College of Music of Montreal.

In 1937 O'Neill left his position with the Royal 22nd Regiment and began an association with the U of Wisconsin (as summer school instructor and acting director) and the State Teachers' College at Potsdam, NY (teacher of conducting and composition 1937–47, head of the Music Dept 1942–7). O'Neill returned to Canada and taught theory and composition at the *RCMT 1948–54. He retired to Quebec City but continued to compose.

O'Neill's largest composition is his doctoral exercise, the cantata *The Ancient Mariner* (Coleridge text, scored for chorus and orchestra, ms). His orchestral works include a *Prelude and Fugue in G* (1945–6), an *Irish Fantasy* (1958), an *Irish Rhapsody* (1959), many shorter pieces, and many arrangements. A number of choral works and pieces for small wind ensemble also were published, but his main output was band music. *The Land of the Maple and Beaver* for band was published by Boosey & Hawkes before 1936. He left 10 overtures: *Silver Cord* (ca 1930, G. Schirmer), *Knight Errant* (ca 1935, Rubank and Waterloo), *Builders of Youth* (1937, Fischer; Goldman Band, Camden CAL 240), *Aladdin's Lamp* (1940, Fischer), *Concert* (ca 1940, ms), *Festival* (1943, ms), *Nobility* (1943, Remick), *Majesty* (1945, Remick), *Fidelity* (1947, Remick), and *Sovereignty* (1949, Remick). Shorter compositions for band include *Mon Ami*, a march published by *Waterloo in 1928; marches for the Royal 22nd Regiment (piano arr, Waterloo, recorded on RCA PC/PCS 1003); marches for the Royal Canadian Mounted Police (Harris 1960; RCA PC/PCS-1004); the marches *The Emblem* (Waterloo 1930; RCA PC/PCS-1006) and *Nulli secundus* (Waterloo 1931); and the popular fantasia *Souvenir de Québec* (Fischer 1930, RCA PC/PCS-1003). Other publishers of his music include Boston, Fox, and Mercury. The musical rights of his estate are administered by CAPAC.

WRITINGS

'The military band as a distinct musical medium,' *MCan*, vol 10, Jan 1929

BIBLIOGRAPHY

Thiele, Charles F. 'Capt. Charles O'Neill,' *MCan*, vol 10, Jan 1929

Hamilton, H.C. 'Captain Chas. O'Neill,' *MCan*, vol 11, Aug–Sep 1930

Falardeau, Sgt Victor. *La Musique du Royal 22e régiment 50 ans d'histoire (1922–1972)* (Quebec City 1976)

Catalogue of Canadian Composers

Contemporary Canadian Composers

(HK, HP)

O'NEILL, Thelma (Grace Isabel) (b Johannes). Pianist, b Hamilton, Ont, 28 Jun 1915; ATCM 1932, L MUS (Saskatchewan) 1934. Her teachers included George Palmer and Lyell *Gustin 1926–46 in Saskatoon, Eva Dumesnil, Robert Casadesus, Alfred Cortot, and Jean Ratelle 1946–8 in Paris at the Conservatoire and the École normale, and Helmut *Brauss in the early 1970s at the *U of Alberta. After 1939 she gave many solo recitals on CBC radio, and she was heard also 1940–5 in two-piano programs with Edmund *Assaly. During her studies in Paris she broadcast works by Violet *Archer and Robert *Fleming on French radio. She has played concertos of Bach, Mozart, Schumann, and Grieg with orchestras in Calgary, Regina, and Saskatoon, has appeared as a recitalist in several Canadian cities, and in Saskatoon has accompanied a number of visiting artists, including Marta *Hidy, George *Lambert, Howard *Leyton-Brown, Albert *Pratz, and the European violinist François d'Albert. Her pupils have included Cedric Abday, Beverly Burrows, Margaret Chandler, Cheryl Cooney, Janice Plitt, Diane Rausch, and Angela Taranger. O'Neill has examined for the *WBM, and in 1968 she joined the teaching staff of *Alberta College. She served 1967–8 as president of the *ARMTA. (EK)

One Third Ninth. Piano trio formed in 1970 in Calgary by the violinist Moshe Hammer, the cellist John Kadz (at that time principals of the *Calgary Philharmonic Orchestra), and the pianist Gloria Saarinen. After several CBC broadcasts, a telecast on 'Music to See,' and concerts in various Alberta centres the members resigned their other positions and in 1973 were appointed artists-in-residence for the province and *Mount Royal College. Under Alberta's sponsorship they have toured the province, giving two-to-four-day workshops and concerts in smaller centres. At Mount Royal College they have taught chamber music and have given three of the six concerts in the annual Carillon Series sponsored by the Chamber Music Society of Calgary, founded in 1975 with Kadz as president. They have given about 100 other concerts annually in Canada and the USA and a 12-concert tour of Europe in the spring of 1978.

Hammer (b Budapest 30 Mar 1946) studied with Heifetz and gave recitals in Israel, Europe, and North America before joining the Calgary Philharmonic as concertmaster in 1970.

Kadz (b Norfolk, Va, 26 Oct 1945) studied with Joseph di Tullio in Los Angeles and played with various US orchestras prior to joining the Calgary Philharmonic in 1970.

Saarinen (b Dunedin, New Zealand, 21 Sep 1934) trained 1956–61 in Europe with Cortot and others and was a member of the Dept of Music at the *U of Calgary 1966–74.

Ontario Arts Council (OAC) / **Conseil des Arts de l'Ontario** (CAO) (Province of Ontario Council for the Arts, POCA, 1963–70). Independent body created by the Ontario government to promote the production, study, and enjoyment of works in the arts. It was established 22 Apr 1963 by Bill 162 as the Province of Ontario Council for the Arts, with 12 volunteer appointees, all private citizens, of whom 5 were to constitute an Executive Committee. This council was to be supported by a paid executive director and staff of officers and administrators, each officer being responsible for a separate discipline such as music, theatre, visual arts, or literature. At its inception the council reported to the provincial legislature and received its annual subvention through the Ministry of Education. It was transferred in April 1972 to the Ministry of Colleges and Universities and in April 1975 to the newly created Ministry of Culture and Recreation. Appointments to the Council, for renewable three-year terms, have been made by order-in-council of the lieutenant-governor. Chairmen have been the Hon J. Keiller Mackay 1963–9, Anthony Adamson 1969–75, and Frank F. McEachren 1975–9, succeeded by Arthur Gelber. Executive directors have been Milton Carman 1963–70 and Louis *Applebaum 1970–9, succeeded by Walter Pitman. Music officers have been Walter Ball (as consultant) 1966–7, James *Norcop 1967–8, Robert *Sunter 1968–76, and Zelda *Heller 1976–80, succeeded by Gwenlyn Creech. Voltr Ivonoffski became the first associate music officer in 1977.

The appropriation to the council in the fiscal year 1963–4 was $300,000, which covered the salaries for two staff members and 30 grants totalling almost $250,000 awarded to arts organizations of all types. By the fiscal year 1977–8 the appropriation had grown to $12 million, grants numbered about 3000, and $2.4 million was paid out for music alone in grants and programs. The administration numbered almost 40, divided into 10 grant-program offices, an information unit, and the support staff. Originally the council met three times a year to study applications and decide the level of assistance to each group submitting requests; later, two more meetings were added. Meetings usually have lasted three days, and several hundred applications have been considered at each. The executive committee has met monthly to consider requests of a limited nature such as short-term grants for projects or emergency funding assistance; by 1980 the committee had not considered requests which exceeded $7500 unless delegated by full council to do so. Members have voted on all grants recorded in the annual report and all decisions have been recorded in official minutes.

In its early years the council saw its task to be the improvement of quality among existing non-commercial arts organizations in smaller communities. To that end it made grants only to established organizations (including *OFSO and the *Ontario Choral Federation, for which it had created administrative offices in Toronto in 1963 and 1971 respectively) and only in response to written requests. In later years grants were made also to individuals, money was provided to commission works from Canadain composers (60 in 1977–8), and there was funding of studies, workshops (eg, the *U of Toronto's Student Conductors' Workshop), and conferences and liaison with educators. A large part of the funding has gone to supplement the annual operating expenses of community-based organizations and institutions. It has been the duty of OAC officers to supply council members with information and opinion on funding requests, supplementing their own findings with evaluations from ministry field officers and with the advice of independent volunteer experts. Some grants have been made conditional upon the applicants' raising matching amounts of money from other sources, to demonstrate community support for the project. Some other council programs have included assistance to groups sponsoring touring performances by professional artists; grants to community orchestras for performances in neighbouring communities and to amateur performing groups to secure the services of professional soloists and instrumental musicians; funding to encourage skilled musicians to live and work in small communities; and the systematic provision of a liaison between touring performers and potential hiring organizations, a function carried out through council literature which provides information on fees and availability and through an annual (October) showcase of performing talent (Contact '72, Contact '73, etc) mounted for four days in Toronto and bringing together Canadian performers and prospective Canadian employers in various types of audition.

The council has assumed administration of some endowment funds – donations or bequests from individuals and foundations. It also has administered the Heinz *Unger Award for young conductors. It has assisted Wintario – Ontario's provincial lottery – in an advisory or consultative capacity.

Of the 1977–8 fiscal year's approximately 170 OAC music grants (not including funds for Ontario organizations' commissions to composers or the several hundred grants made through the Ontour program for Canadian performers' fee subsidies) orchestras (members of OFSO) received a large number, but many other kinds of organization also benefited. Among representative major recipients were the *Bach-Elgar Choir of Hamilton, the Blue Mountain School of Music, radio station CJRT-FM, the *Canadian Music Competitions, the *COC, the *Chamber Players of Toronto, Comus Music Theatre, Co-Opera Theatre, *EMC*, the *Festival Singers, the *Guelph Spring Festival, the *Hamilton Philharmonic Orchestra, the Interprovincial Music Camp, the Kelso Music Centre, the *Kingston Symphony Assn, the *Kitchener-Waterloo SO, the *London SO, the *NYO, the New Chamber Orchestra, *NMC, the North York SO, the *ORMTA, *Quartet Canada, the *St Catharines SO, the *Thunder Bay SO, Toronto Arts Productions, the *TS and the *York Winds.

Over the years the OAC has developed a reputation for astute and productive use of its funds and its powers and for direct and unbureaucratic procedures. Clients were assured of direct access to the officers in their particular disciplines, and grants once decided were processed with dispatch. In 1979, when the Floyd S. *Chalmers Foundation delivered over its entire assets of more than $1 million to the OAC for administration, Chalmers said he chose the council 'because we have so much confidence, so much faith, in the judgement and the program of the arts council' (*Toronto Star*, 3 Sep 1979).

BIBLIOGRAPHY
Ontario Arts Council. Annual Reports. Toronto 1964–
– *Arts info*. Quarterly newsletter, Fall 1980– (TCB)

Ontario Choral Federation. A service organization of and for choirs, established in 1971 with an elected voluntary board, a paid executive secretary, and offices in Toronto. In 1969, prior to the federation's formation the *OAC (then POCA), at the initiative of its music officer Robert *Sunter, commissioned Keith *Bissell and Ezra *Schabas to write a report (*Choral Music in Ontario*, Toronto 1970) and organized a choral conference in Sudbury. A second conference (Guelph, May 1970) endorsed as primary objectives the major Sudbury recommendations: the formation of a choral federation and, through a summer camp for young people, an *Ontario Youth Choir; the development of regional choral festivals and workshops; and the promotion in general of choral music.

Chartered in 1971 and funded largely by the OAC, the Ontario Choral Federation has drawn its membership (376 in 1977) from individuals (119 in 1977), choirs (235 in 1977), corporations, boards of education, universities, schools of music, and other choral associations. Presidents have been Charles *Wilson 1970–2, Roman *Toi 1972–3, John Barron 1973–4, Peter Partridge 1974–6, John *Bird 1976–7, and David R. MacLennan 1977–9, succeeded by Robert Henderson. Executive secretaries have been Jan *Matejcek in 1971, John M. *Hodgins in 1972, Dorothy Trieger in 1973, and Maud McLean in 1974, succeeded by Mary Willan Mason.

Choirs in Contact, initiated by the federation in 1971, became an annual three-day festival of concerts and workshops for member choirs, often featuring guest choirs and conductors of international reputation. Workshop clinicians for the first two years were Lloyd *Bradshaw, Derek *Holman, Brian *Law, and François Provencher (1971), John Barron, Melville *Cook, Deral Johnson, and Brian Law (1972). Guest conductors in the ensuing years were Elmer *Iseler in 1973, 1974, 1978, and 1980, Robert Shaw in 1974, David Willcocks 1975 and 1977, Norman Luboff and Eric Ericson jointly in 1976, and Helmuth Rilling in 1979.

As administrator of the OAC's annual Leslie *Bell Scholarship competition for young choir conductors, the Ontario Choral Federation has commissioned test pieces for the competition from several Canadians (Bissell, *Song for Fine Weather*, 1974; *Morawetz, *The Song My Paddle Sings*, 1975; *Ridout, *Spirit Is Flesh*, 1976; and *Beckwith, *Papineau*, 1977). The OCF began issuing a newsletter in 1970.

See also Alliance chorale canadienne; Nova Scotia Choral Federation. MMI

Ontario Federation of Symphony Orchestras (OFSO) / **Fédération des orchestres symphoniques de l'Ontario** (FOSO). Provincial forum of orchestral entities. It was founded to help create a stable environment for orchestras in Ontario through discussion, the pooling of information, and the co-operative solving of shared problems. The year in which it assumed the form it retained in 1980 was 1963, but 11 years of gestation preceded that date. The need for such a forum was articulated first in 1952 at a meeting of representatives of Ontario community orchestras at Rodman Hall, the home of Mrs David Wright of St Catharines, Ont. Discussions were carried forward at London, Ont, in 1954, at St Catharines again in 1955, when an executive committee was formed with Lloyd Goodwin as chairman, and in 1956, when representatives of seven orchestras elected Mrs Wright as honorary president and Arnold Edinborough as president of the Ontario Federation of Symphony Orchestras (referred to in some documents as Federation of Civic Orchestras of Ontario).

Achieved only to languish, the new organization was revived by its members at Glenhyrst, Ont, in 1963. A new board was installed in 1963 with Larry Agranove as president, and it continued in sufficient health to be recognized in 1964 as the voice of Ontario community orchestras by the newly created Province of Ontario Council for the Arts (*OAC). The council at that time encouraged individual orchestras to apply for grants through the medium of their federation. Accordingly, in 1964 Agranove presented briefs from 13 OFSO member orchestras (Brantford, Deep River, East York, Etobicoke, Hamilton, Kingston, Kitchener-Waterloo, Lakehead, London, Richmond Hill, International of Sarnia and Port Huron, St Catharines, and Windsor), and these prompted the council's first grants to community orchestras and set one part of the pattern for OFSO's development.

During the early years OFSO's affairs were managed directly by its board. The flourishing organization it was to become in the 1970s, however, originated in the arts council's decision, in 1966, to employ a music officer who would serve also as the executive director of OFSO. Walter Ball, the first to hold this dual position, was succeeded in 1967 by James *Norcop, and Norcop in 1968 by Robert *Sunter. In 1970 the functions were separated. The council's music officer remained ex officio on the OFSO board, and the council provided OFSO with funds to support a Toronto office and hire an executive director. Jan *Matejcek became OFSO's first independent executive director 1 Jan 1970.

OFSO conferences, occasional before 1966, were annual thereafter, and those of 1971 and 1972 were of more than provincial significance. Matejcek had broached the concept of a national federation designed to serve Canada's orchestras as OFSO served Ontario's. OFSO invited representatives of Canadian orchestras outside Ontario to discuss the concept at its 1971 conference in London, Ont. The conference, at which 40 Canadian orchestras were represented, appointed a nationally representative steering committee under the chairmanship of Robert Sunter. That November at Ottawa the committee and Kenneth *Winters (who had succeeded Matejcek in June 1971 and was to serve also as executive director of the new national organization) prepared the blue-print for the Association of Canadian Orchestras. Ratification took place at the first ACO conference, in Winnipeg in 1972, and Ezra *Schabas was elected the first president.

The provincial and national organizations were interlocked. The OFSO offices in Toronto provided (and in 1980 continued to provide) premises and administration for ACO; OFSO members automatically were members of ACO; the funding for the joint administration was supplied proportionately by the OAC and the *Canada Council; and the separate OFSO and ACO boards contained common members, the executive director and treasurer serving on both boards and the current OFSO president being automatically a member of the ACO board.

The OFSO newsletter, begun in 1969 by Sunter and continued by Matejcek as a mimeographed sheet in English, became in 1972 the bilingual *The Orchestra Letter / Le Bulletin orchestral* edited by Winters and, in October 1973, the OFSO-ACO periodical *Orchestra Canada / Orchestres Canada*, professionally printed and illustrated with photographs, edited 1973–4 by Ann Hutchinson, 1974–5 by William Schabas, and thereafter by Jack Edds. OFSO and ACO also have published jointly the annual *Directory of Canadian Orchestras and Youth Orchestras / Annuaire des orchestres et orchestres des jeunes canadiens*. However, though in 1980 the two organizations continued to share some personnel and functions, they have retained differences reflected in separate conferences, OFSO's annual, ACO's biennial.

OFSO, which in 1980 represented some 40 orchestras, has concerned itself mainly with expanding the Ontario symphonic environment and improving the lot and the product of the enterprising community orchestra, organizing workshops on performance techniques, season-ticket campaigning, education, fund raising, management, women's committee enterprises, advertising, board development, and other practical matters. The executive director's duties have included visiting all the orchestras in the province, often accompanied by one or two OFSO board members particularly equipped to advise the boards of the orchestras visited. On occasion the entire OFSO board has travelled to meet the board and administration of a member orchestra on its home ground, usually also attending a concert by that orchestra.

ACO, though it has attracted to its membership community and chamber orchestras of those provinces which have no counterpart of OFSO, has concentrated on the concerns of major orchestras: federal funding, parameters for the hiring of foreign players, union relationships, pension plans, amusement tax, apprenticeship systems, professional management training, etc. Notable ACO-organized events have included 'Dialogue '76,' a 1976 meeting with the OCSM (see Unions), and 'Training and Employment of Orchestral Musicians in Canada,' a 1979 two-day national symposium of music educators and orchestral musicians. The natural divergence between OFSO and ACO has been developed under Betty Webster, who succeeded Winters in 1975 as executive director of both organizations.

OFSO presidents after Goodwin, Edinborough, and Agranove have been Albert Jarvis 1965–7, Brooke Townsend 1967–9, Michael Davies 1969–71, Terence Wardrop 1971–3, Ian Grant 1973–5, Douglas Rishor 1975–7, and E.R. Barrett 1977–9, succeeded by Elizabeth Kovac.

ACO presidents have been Ezra Schabas 1972–4, Leonard David Stone 1974–6, Jorgen Holgerson 1976–7, and Douglas Rishor 1977–80, succeeded by Rosemary Bell.

OFSO became incorporated, belatedly, 7 Mar 1977, and that year published the pamphlet *Aims and Objectives: By-Law Number One*.

PUBLICATIONS

Orchestra Canada / Orchestres Canada (6 issues a year 1973–9; became monthly in 1980)
Directory of Canadian Orchestras and Youth Orchestras / Annuaire des orchestres et orchestres des jeunes canadiens, annual, begun 1975–6; *Orchestra Contact List* annual 1973–5
Canadian Orchestras Concert Calendar, annual 1973–7
Directory of Conductors in Canada / Annuaire des chefs d'orchestre au Canada (Toronto [1977])
OFSO Orchestral Resources Guide (Toronto 1977)
Directory of Women's and Volunteer Committees (Toronto 1978–)

BIBLIOGRAPHY

'Music,' Province of Ontario Council for the Arts: Annual Report 1963–4
Schabas, Ezra. *Ontario Community Orchestras* (Toronto 1966)
Sunter, Robert. 'Ontario Orchestras,' *OpCan*, Feb 1969
Winters, Kenneth. 'Orchestras supply mandate for a federation,' *Toronto Telegram*, 19 Apr 1971
'Federation of symphony orchestras is formed,' *CanComp*, 61, Jun 1971
Kraglund, John. 'Ontario,' *CMB*, 4, Spring–Summer 1972
Winters, Kenneth. 'A move towards national unity,' *MSc*, 264, Mar–Apr 1972
Conrad, David. 'The orchestra associations get a Canada Council cold shower,' *PfAC*, Summer 1974
'Dialogue '77,' *OCan*, Nov 1977
'ACO Symposium: training and employment of orchestral musicians in Canada,' *OCan*, Dec 1978–Feb 1979
Fear, Barbara. 'The Ontario Federation of Symphony Orchestras: its first twenty-five years,' *OCan*, Apr 1980

KW

Ontario Music Educators' Association (OMEA). Founded as the music section of the Ontario Educational Assn, it held its first meeting in April 1919 at the OEA Conference in Toronto. Its initial membership consisted of 18 public-school music supervisors and instructors from the provincial normal schools. During the 1920s it concerned itself chiefly with the promotion of compulsory vocal music instruction in elementary schools, and participated in the 'note-name' versus 'tonic sol-fa' controversy. In the next decade it began to lobby for music courses in high schools and for instrumental music instruction at all levels. It initiated an annual concert on the Wednesday night of the OEA Easter Conventions 1933–60. This concert featured elementary and high school music groups from across the province, conducted by such educators as Leslie *Bell, G. Roy *Fenwick,

P.G. Marshall, Harvey *Perrin, Leonard Richer, and Robert *Rosevear. The concerts began to be broadcast over the CBC network in 1938, and were expanded into mass concerts at Toronto's Varsity Stadium during World War II.

In 1949 the OEA music section was reorganized and the OMEA was formed; in May 1974 it became independent of the OEA. In its early days the OEA music section used *Musical Canada* (which featured a 'School Music Department' section) and the *Canadian School Board Journal* as its official magazines, providing these with its announcements and news. The OMEA founded its own journal, *The Recorder*, in September 1958, and in 1980 continued to publish it quarterly.

The OMEA has organized several regional workshops a year, and until the dissolution of its ties with the OEA in 1974 it also held a yearly convention. After that time it continued to hold a general meeting each spring. Guest speakers at conventions and annual meetings have included Karl Ernst, Paul Gehrkens, Sir Ernest *MacMillan, Joseph Maddy, and Paul van Bodegraven. In addition, the OMEA has sponsored symposia on the renaissance in 1968 and the baroque in 1970 and has held joint conventions with the *CMEA in 1967 and 1973. Though instrumental in the founding of the CMEA, the OMEA still had not become formally affiliated with that organization by 1980.

Presidents of the OEA music section have included A.T. *Cringan 1919–22, E.W. Quantz 1922–4, H. Whorlow Bull 1924–5, George B. Cummings 1925–6, P.G. Marshall 1926–7, 1935–7, Emily Tedd 1927–9, Harry *Hill 1929–31, Leonard Richer 1931–3, W. Benson Collier 1933–4, G. Roy Fenwick 1934–5, Marion Rannie 1937–8, Arthur Merriman 1938–9, Leslie Bell 1939–41, Harold Jones 1941–2, Earle *Terry 1942–3, Harvey Perrin 1943–4, George *Smale 1944–5, Quirt McKinney 1945–7, Cyril *Hampshire 1947–8, and Brydon Roberts 1948–9.

OMEA presidents have included Robert Rosevear 1949–50, Lansing *MacDowell 1950–1, 1966–7, Garfield *Bender 1951–2, Lloyd Queen 1952–3, Robert McGregor 1953–4, C. Laughton *Bird 1954–5, Lorne Willets 1955–6, Marion Park 1956–7, Keith *Bissell 1957–8, Richard *Johnston 1958–9, Ken *Bray 1959–60, Bruce Snell 1960–1, John Sutherland 1961–2, Dawson Woodburn 1962–3, Mary Stillman 1963–4, Paul *Green 1964–5, Donald McKellar 1965–6, Nan Allin 1967–8, John McDougall 1968–9, Robert Head 1969–70, Bernard Turcotte 1970–1, James Maben 1971–2, Ron Holland 1972–3, James White 1973–4, Bernice Oak 1974–5, John Ford 1975–6, Baird Knechtel 1976–8, and James Coles 1978–80, succeeded by John Harrison.

BIBLIOGRAPHY
Brault, Diana. 'A history of the Ontario Music Educators Association (1919–1974),' unpubl PH D thesis (ESM Rochester 1977)
– Series of articles, variously titled, in successive issues of *The Recorder*, beginning in vol 20, Dec 1977 (DBr)

Ontario Place Forum. Outdoor amphitheatre, part of Ontario Place, the recreational park on three man-made islands off the Toronto waterfront. Opened in 1971, Ontario Place is operated by the provincial government. The Forum is circular in design, sitting in the basin created by four hills. Under a dome roof, seating for 3000 (originally 2000, expanded in 1977) surrounds a performing area 22.5 m in diameter. The overlooking hills accommodate another 8000 comfortably, and some pop stars have drawn audiences of more than 20,000. A revolving stage 20.4 m in diameter was introduced in 1976 to ensure an equal view for all areas of the audience.

From late May to early September, beginning in 1971, the Forum has been the site of annual series by the *TS (18 concerts each year), the *Hamilton Philharmonic (6 concerts) and the National Ballet of Canada (6 appearances). Multiple appearances have been made annually for several years by the *Boss Brass and the Ivan *Romanoff Orchestra and Chorus. Many leading US pop performers have appeared at the Forum, but the majority of the musicians presented have been Canadian. Ontario Place statistics for the 1978 season established total attendance at over 680,000 for 128 concerts. The 1979 season offered, in addition to the aforementioned staples, choirs, youth orchestras, a variety of bands (military, concert, pipe, drum-and-bugle), jazz bands, stage bands, Canadian and foreign folksingers and dancers, pop groups, and concerts for children. Among other musical entertainments at Ontario Place have been dixieland concerts on a small showboat which tours the lagoon, and performances by Canadian pop artists in a bandshell erected for the purpose in 1979. MM

Ontario Registered Music Teachers' Association (ORMTA) – Ontario Music Teachers' Association (OMTA) 1936–46. Organization formed in Toronto in 1936 to promote and maintain high musical and academic qualifications among its members. In 1980 it was the largest such association in Canada. An earlier OMTA (*Canadian Society of Musicians) was founded in 1885.

In 1936 several local teachers' associations, including those of Owen Sound, Stratford, Guelph, and Sarnia, banded together as the OMTA at a meeting 6 October in Toronto. W.B. Rothwell of Stratford was credited with the initiative. In 1942 the OMTA became affiliated with the *CFMTA, and in 1946 it was incorporated as the ORMTA. The original membership of 131 had grown to about 1200 active, associate, and honorary members by 1979.

The association came to be organized in nine zones – Hamilton, Ottawa, Toronto, western, central, southern, eastern, northeastern, and northwestern – and representatives of the zones formed an administrative council. The zones in turn were divided into branches (38 in 1979), each with its own president and executive and each responsible for its program of workshops, awards, and scholarships and for support of the CFMTA Canada Music Week project. The ORMTA has been responsible for the acceptance of music as an accredited subject in Ontario high schools, whether the studies are in school or in private.

It became customary for a three- or four-day spring convention to be held annually in an Ontario city. The ORMTA quarterly *Notes* began ca 1969. Under the auspices of the Toronto branch the Contemporary Music Selection Committee (see Contemporary Showcase) prepared a series of annotated lists of Canadian piano music, first published in *Musicanada* (Jun–Jul, Aug–Sep 1968). A report commissioned in 1976 from Walter *Kemp was presented in 1977 as *To Listen and To Teach*. The Ontario Provincial Archives hold taped interviews, edited for broadcast, with nine longtime members of the ORMTA.

ORMTA (OMTA) presidents have been: Frank *Blachford 1936–7, Harvey Robb 1937–8, George *Lambert 1938–9, W.B. Rothwell 1939–40, Norman *Wilks 1940–2, Cyril *Hampshire 1942–4, Cora B. *Ahrens 1944–6, Reginald G. *Geen 1946–8, 1953–4, Charles *Peaker 1948–9, Elizabeth Wilson Black 1949–50, Henry Rosevear 1950–1, John J. *Weatherseed 1951–2, Wilfred Powell 1952–3, Phyllis Elworthy Smith 1954–5, Victor Dell 1955–7, Reginald *Bedford 1957–9, Gladys Howey 1959–60, George *Smale 1960–1, Flora Matheson *Goulden 1961–2, Gordon *Hallett 1962–3, Warren *Mould 1963–4, Thursa Williamson 1964–5, Thomas C. *Chattoe 1965–6, Josephine Parrott 1966–8, Court Stone 1968–70, Markwell J. Perry 1970–2, Sister Callistus 1972–4, Helen Van Iderstine 1974–6, and William M. Vaisey 1976–8, succeeded by Eleanor Marzetti. (WV)

Ontario Youth Choir. Mixed choir of 45–75 voices, initiated in 1971 by the *Ontario Choral Federation and sponsored by the *OAC. With members aged 16 to 24 selected annually from across the province, the choir has rehearsed each summer for two weeks at Lakefield College School, near Peterborough. An autumn tour has followed, usually in a region of Ontario, but the itinerary included a concert in Brandon, Man, in 1976 and concerts in Montreal in 1977 and 1979. The choir has been conducted by Brian *Law (1971), Gerald Fagan (1972), Deral Johnson (1973, 1977), Albert *Greer (1974), John Barron (1975, 1979), Jon *Washburn (1976), Robert Cooper (1978), and Richard Householder (1980). Norma *Beecroft's *Three Impressions* were commissioned for the choir in 1973 and Berthold Carriere's three songs from *As You Like It* in 1978. The 1975 choir won the CBC / Canada Council National Radio Competition for Amateur Choirs, and its taped performance won the Beardsall Silver Rose Bowl, top award in the 1976 BBC international competition 'Let the Peoples Sing.' The 1975 choir also made for private release an LP of motets by *Willan, Palestrina, Andrea Gabrieli, Rachmaninoff, and *Somers, partsongs by Debussy and Kodály, and several folksong arrangements (Audat C 148).

BIBLIOGRAPHY
Law, Brian. 'The Ontario Youth Choir 1971 inaugural season,' *The Recorder*, vol 14, Mar 1972

Opera Canada (*Opera in Canada* until issue 14, May 1963). An English-language magazine published in Toronto. From a four-page newsletter dated February–March 1960 it has developed rapidly into one of Canada's most lavishly produced periodicals, reflecting the growing popularity of opera in the country. *Opera Canada* was published until 1966 by the Canadian Opera Guild, then by the Canadian Opera Assn. In January 1976 it became independent, and Ruby *Mercer, its founding editor, became its publisher-editor. Until 1974 there were four issues a year, the first devoted to Canadian productions, the second to festivals, the third to *COC productions, and the last to opera abroad. In 1975 six issues were planned but only five appeared. In 1976 quarterly publication was resumed. In addition to articles *Opera Canada* has featured news reports from Canada and abroad, reviews, and a calendar of operatic events. The roster of contributors and the readership are international. HK

Opéra de chambre du Québec. See Opéra du Québec.

Opéra de Montréal. See Opéra du Québec.

Opéra du Québec. A company devoted to the production of operas, mainly in Montreal and Quebec City. It was created by the *MACQ, and was active on a regular basis for four seasons 1971–5.

1 History
2 Repertoire
3 Artists

An Opéra du Québec production of *Suor Angelica*, 1971

1 HISTORY. Broached many times after the beginning of the 20th century, the idea of state-supported opera in Quebec came nearer to realization in the summer of 1967 when Jean-Noël Tremblay, then Quebec minister of cultural affairs, announced the formation of 'a committee headed by Léopold *Simoneau, charged with drawing up a plan for the organization and operation of a state-supported theatre devoted wholly or in part to opera.' Submitted at the end of 1967, the committee's report was never made public. It was not until February 1971 that a new minister at the MACQ, François Cloutier, announced that 'in response to the very marked interest of Quebeckers in opera, the minister had examined several solutions, including that of a state company.' He further announced that he had opted for a company that was 'flexible in structure,' one that would 'utilize the administrative services of the already existing institutions: the PDA and the Grand Théâtre in Quebec City.' Established as a non-profit company, the Opéra du Québec was incorporated under the Companies Act, with a seven-member board of directors including, ex officio, the managing directors of both the *PDA and the *Grand Théâtre. Its founding president, 1971–3, was H. Marcel Caron; he was succeeded by Jacques Vadboncoeur. Léopold Simoneau was appointed artistic director in 1971 but tendered his resignation at the end of that same year, following a disagreement over the hiring of a guest conductor, on which the management was insistent. Instead of appointing a successor to Simoneau the board set up a committee of three artistic advisers: Pierre *Boutet, Edgar Fruitier, and John *Newmark. An executive director, Émilien Morissette, was subsequently replaced by Gérard *Lamarche.

By the musical and visual quality of its productions the Opéra du Québec immediately won the public's favour. Supported by an initial subsidy of $200,000 from the MACQ, it received additional sums from the *Canada Council and donations from Seagram's and the *du Maurier Council for the Performing Arts. However, despite the desire for permanence expressed at the outset, and massive public support the Opéra du Québec soon faced a considerable operating deficit.

Beginning in 1973, three productions were presented instead of four. With the deficit approaching $1 million in the first months of 1975, a new minister, Denis Hardy, announced the cessation of activities, at least temporarily. Coinciding as it did with the memorable performances of *Tristan und Isolde*, this announcement of the company's demise sparked a sharp outcry from the public and led to some harsh exchanges between the minister in charge and the Opéra management. Inactive thereafter the Opéra du Québec nevertheless staged three performances of *The Barber of Seville* in July 1976 at the PDA, thanks to a special subsidy of $200,000. The production was part of the Arts and Culture program of the Olympics.

Early in 1980 the MACQ announced the establishment of two companies to succeed the Opéra du Québec, both under the artistic direction of Jean-Paul *Jeannotte. The first – Opéra de chambre du Québec, basically a touring company – performed Bizet's *Le Docteur miracle* and Wolf-Ferrari's *Le Secret de Suzanne* in 23 Quebec communities in February and March 1980. The second – Opéra de Montréal, whose performances were scheduled for the PDA – planned three productions for the 1980–1 season and four for the following season.

2 REPERTOIRE. In four seasons the Opéra du Québec presented 13 productions at the PDA, 10 of them presented also at Quebec City's Grand Théâtre, and one at the *NAC, Ottawa. There were 114 performances in all, 82 in Montreal, 30 in Quebec City, and 2 in Ottawa. (The figures do not include the three performances in 1976.) The works presented were *Samson et Dalila, Il Trittico, La Fille du régiment*, and *La Traviata* (1971–2); *Rigoletto, Salomé, Cavalleria Rusticana, I Pagliacci*, and *Manon* (1972–3); *Otello, Don Giovanni*, and *Madama Butterfly* (1973–4); and *Falstaff, La Bohème*, and *Tristan und Isolde* (1974–5).

3 ARTISTS. In its very first season the troupe was proud that, of a total of 49 roles, 41 were given to Canadian singers. Subsequently certain productions – such as *Il Trittico* – were entirely Canadian. Among the singers were Colette *Boky, Clarice *Carson, Anna *Chornodolska, Marcelle Couture, Claire *Gagnier, Louise *Lebrun, Maria *Pellegrini, and Heather *Thomson, sopranos; Fernande *Chiocchio and Maureen *Forrester, contraltos; Jean *Bonhomme, Pierre *Duval, and Jon *Vickers, tenors; Napoléon *Bisson, Bruno *Laplante, Louis *Quilico, Robert *Savoie, and Bernard *Turgeon, baritones; and Claude *Corbeil, Yoland *Guérard, and Joseph *Rouleau, basses. Among the guest singers were the sopranos Roberta Knie, Ursula Schroder, Rita Talarico, and Tatiana Troyanos; the contraltos Rita de Carlo, Mignon Dunn, and Regina Sarfaty; the tenors John Alexander, Robert Calvert, Pier-Miranda Ferraro, Ottavio Garaventa, and Robert Nagy; the baritones Peter Glossop and Sigmund Nimsgern; and the basses Giovanni Foiani and Peter Meven. The conductors were Jacques *Beaudry, Alfredo Bonavera, Franz-Paul *Decker, Jean *Deslauriers (who assumed the position of regular assistant conductor in 1972), Pierre *Hétu, Zubin Mehta, and Nicholas Rescigno.

Those responsible for stage direction were Jan Doat, Carlo Maestrini, Nathaniel Merrill, Albert Millaire, Ernst Poettgen, Peter Potter, and Peter *Symcox. The Opéra du Québec called on the designers Robert Darling, Rudolf Heinrich, Roberto Oswald, Robert Prévost, Jean-Claude Rinfret, Mark Negin, and Hugo Wuetrich.

BIBLIOGRAPHY

Gingras, Claude. 'L'opéra du Québec a été vraiment pensé pour notre publie et nos chanteurs,' Montreal *La Presse*, 10 Feb 1971

McLean, Eric. 'On the demise of L'Opéra du Québec,' *Montreal Star*, 15 Feb 1975

– 'On the demise of L'Opéra du Québec,' *OpCan*, Sep 1975

'Un nouveau souffle de vie anime l'Opéra du Québec,' *Musique périodique*, vol 1, Nov 1976

GP

Opéra français. Founded in Montreal in 1893 as the Société d'opéra français, to present regular seasons of operas and plays at the Théâtre français, located at the corner of Ste-Catherine and St-Dominique streets. Among the shareholders of the company, which was capitalized at $10,000, were Jean-M. Fortier, Edmond *Hardy, and the managing director R. Sallard. On 2 Oct 1893 a troupe of singers and actors recruited from France opened the inaugural season with Lecocq's *La Fille de Madame Angot*. Gabriel Dorel conducted the orchestra of 25 and chorus of 24. There were seven performances a week during the ensuing season, and a large number of comedies, dramas, and operettas were presented, including *La Mascotte, Le Petit Duc, Boccace*, and *Les Cloches de Corneville*. The cast was entirely French in origin, and was headed by Mmes Cécile DeGoyon, Blonville, Hélène Giraud, and Merville and Messrs Belisson, Henri Giraud, and Delafontaine. The 1894–5 season allotted a larger role to opera when Edmond Hardy succeeded Sallard as manager. Among the operas presented were *Carmen, Faust, Rigoletto, La Fille du régiment*, and *Si j'étais roi*. The singer Alice Cléry and the baritones Montfort and Portalier joined the troupe.

The 1895–6 season, the most ambitious, ended prematurely in a scandal. A new director, Arthur Durieu, had engaged such prima donnas as Mmes Essiani, Bennati, and Conti-Bessi and the baritone Vandiric, and the season opened with Thomas's *Le Songe d'une nuit d'été*, followed by *Mireille, Martha, Norma, Lucia di Lammermoor, Carmen, Les Huguenots* (with a reduced score for small orchestra by Dorel), and *William Tell*, among others. Early in 1896 there was talk of the venture's financial difficulties. On the evening of 12 February the curtain failed to rise on *The Barber of Seville*, and, after a lengthy pause, a singer came out to explain to the public that a considerable amount of money was owing to the artists. Meanwhile, members of the chorus had occupied the director's office. The indignant spectators gradually left the hall. The press made much of the affair, writing about the distress of the artists who sought to return to France. The St-Jean-Baptiste Society offered the hall of the *Monument national, where the company gave *Le Prophète* and also a benefit performance 22 February. Ernest *Lavigne offered the artists a week of engagements at the *Sohmer Park concerts. A few, including Mme Bennati, settled in Montreal, but the majority eventually returned to France. That autumn Lavigne tried to reorganize the company with other artists but was only moderately successful. The Théâtre français, which had been renovated in 1895 and equipped with electricity, was used for variety shows until it was destroyed by fire in March 1900.

BIBLIOGRAPHY

Pelletier, Frédéric. 'L'Opéra français,' *Entre-nous*, vol 2, Jan 1931

GP

Opera Guild of Montreal, Inc. A non-profit operatic society founded in 1941 by Pauline *Donalda 'to give recitals and concerts, and to present or arrange for the presentation of operas, musical comedies, symphonies or musical works of all kinds and descriptions.' Pauline Donalda was president and artistic director, and Sara Berne honorary secretary-treasurer and administrator 1941–69. During its existence the guild presented 29 different works in 28 seasons in a total of 33 productions and 65 performances.

Its first production, *Cavalleria Rusticana* and scenes from *Carmen* and *The Barber of Seville*, was presented at *His Majesty's Theatre 3 May 1942, with Mary *Henderson in the roles of Santuzza and Carmen, supported by Canadian and US singers. Gabriele Simeoni conducted and Benjamin Altieri directed the staging. Subsequently one or two productions were presented annually (each usually for two performances) at His Majesty's until 1964, and thereafter in the Salle Wilfrid-Pelletier of the *PDA.

Emil Cooper (b Kherson, Russia, 20 Dec 1877, d New York 16 Nov 1960) was the conductor of most of the productions 1944–60. Other conductors were Wilfrid *Pelletier, Jean *Vallerand, Julius Rudel, Otto-Werner *Mueller, Henry Lewis, Mario *Bernardi, and Bryan Balkwill. Marcel *Laurencelle conducted the chorus.

The works presented were *Così fan tutte* (1943, 1945), *Le Coq d'or* (Canadian premiere 1944), *Hansel and Gretel* (1944), *The Magic Flute* (1945), *Fidelio* (Canadian premiere 1946), *Madama Butterfly* (1947, 1965, 1969), *The Abduction from the Seraglio* (1947), *Rigoletto* and *Samson et Dalila* (1948), *Il Trovatore* and *Otello* (1949), *La Bohème* (1950, 1966), *The Consul* (Canadian premiere 1951), *The Love of Three Oranges* (Canadian premiere 1952), *Louise* (1953), *Boris Godunov* (1954), *Un Ballo in Maschera* (1955), *Don Carlo* (Canadian premiere 1956), *Tosca* (1957), *Falstaff* (Canadian premiere 1958), *Macbeth* (1959), *Carmen* (1960), *Roméo et Juliette* (1961), *La Traviata* (1962), *Faust* (1963), *Don Giovanni* (1964), *The Marriage of Figaro* (1967), and *The Barber of Seville* (1968).

Many leading roles and most of the supporting roles were given to Canadian artists, notably Pierrette *Alarie, Clarice *Carson, Fernande *Chiocchio, Maureen *Forrester, Marguerite *Gignac, Marguerite *Lavergne, Marthe *Létourneau, Gwenlynn *Little, Louise *Roy, Mary *Simmons, Micheline *Tessier, Napoléon *Bisson, Maurice *Brown, Gérald *Desmarais, Yoland *Guérard, Jean-Pierre *Hurteau, Jules *Jacob, Joseph-Victor *Ladéroute, Claude *Létourneau, André *Lortie, Cornelis *Opthof, Louis *Quilico, Joseph *Rouleau, Léopold *Simoneau, André *Turp, and Richard *Verreau. The stage directors included Armando Agnini, Victor Andoga, Roberta Beatty, Bill Butler, Irving *Guttman, Herbert Graf, Vladimir Rosing, Leopold Sachse, Lothar Wallerstein, and Dino Yannopoulos. Among the non-Canadian singers were Herta Glaz, Marilyn Horne, Anna Kaskas, David Lloyd, Blanche Thebom, Hugh Thompson, Margaret Tynes, Astrid Varnay, Elizabeth Vaughan, and Frances Yeend.

The company was financed through gifts from individuals and corporations, but during the final years of its operation it also received subsidies from the *MACQ and the Council of Arts of Greater Montreal. Mme Donalda's illness and her death in 1970 brought about the end of the Opera Guild's activities. The company's assets were placed in a reserve fund and the proceeds – about $2000 per annum – have been distributed in bursaries to young singers and instrumentalists, thereby perpetuating the name of the Opera Guild and its founder.

A different Montreal Opera Guild, founded and directed by Victor *Brault, presented *Carmen* and *Roméo et Juliette* in Montreal in 1939.

BIBLIOGRAPHY

Brotman, Ruth C. *Pauline Donalda* (Montreal 1975) GP

Opera houses. See Concert halls and opera houses.

Opéra national du Québec. Founded in 1948 by Édouard *Woolley to permit opera students in Quebec to sing in important centres. It performed in Quebec City, Montreal (*Ermitage), Trois-Rivières, and some 10 other cities, and toured New Brunswick. Woolley was music director, and also directed the staging. An orchestra accompanied the first productions but soon was replaced by a Hammond organ (played by Roland Roy) and two pianos. Leading roles were given to such guests as Aline Dansereau, Paul de Meule, Gérard *Gélinas, Thérèse Lambert-Gosselin, Marie-Germaine Leblanc, Alphonse Ledoux, Fernand *Martel, Joseph *Rouleau, and Pierre Vidor. Some 40 performances were given of six operas: *Faust* (1949), *Lakmé* (1950; the Quebec premiere at the *Palais Montcalm), *Carmen* (1950), *Roméo et Juliette* (1951), *Rigoletto* (1951), and *La Bohème* (1952). Despite its public success and its value as an advanced school for singers the company disbanded in 1952 for financial reasons. HPn

Opera performance. It may appear an unenlightening coincidence that the first major landmark in the history of opera, Monteverdi's *La Favola d'Orfeo* (1607), was written at the very time when the first permanent European settlements were established in Canada. Yet both opera and Canada were products of the same renaissance spirit of exploration and experiment. Every composer of opera (in the western sense of the term) presumably has known the name Canada, yet the contact of the two, opera *in* Canada, was achieved only in the late 18th century. Even then, opera was too exotic an art form to take root in a young and sparsely settled country.

1 Beginnings
2 1830–1918
3 1918–45
4 After 1945

1 BEGINNINGS. Perhaps the earliest performance is that reported in the *Quebec Gazette* of 13 Feb 1783: 'On Monday evening last was presented at the Thespian Theatre, a part of the Tragedy of *Venice Preserv'd*, with the Comic Opera of the *Padlock*, Singing, Music, &c. The performers supported their respective characters with the greatest propriety and gave infinite satisfaction to a most numerous and respectable audience.' The *Gazette* reported another five performances of *The Padlock* and two of *Lethé* (described as an entertainment) during the period from March to June of the same year. *The Padlock*, a light opera written by Charles Dibdin in 1768, is also the first such work reported performed in Montreal; it was presented in 1786. Other Montreal performances followed: of William Shield's *The Poor Soldier* in 1787, and of Egidio-Romualdo Duni's *Les Deux Chasseurs et la laitière* in 1789. Montreal gave a hearing even to locally composed works: *The Enchanters*, a pantomime by John *Bentley, in 1786, and **Colas et Colinette*, a light opera by Joseph *Quesnel, in 1790 at the *Théâtre de Société. According to the custom of the time, an evening's entertainment would begin with a play, continue with a few short offerings – a song, a recitation, or a dance – and end with the 'after-piece,' a ballad opera or other form of light opera. Examples of works given in Halifax include Thomas Linley's *The Duenna* in 1790, Shield's *Rosina* in 1794, Dibdin's *The Waterman* in 1798 and 1799, Arnold's *The Review* in 1806, and others (see Halifax). In Quebec City Shield's *The Choleric Fathers* was given in 1794 and his *The Poor Soldier* the following year. More unusual were performances of Giovanni Paisiello's *Il Barbiere di Siviglia* in Montreal in 1792 and Grétry's *Richard Coeur-de-Lion* in Halifax in 1798. On the basis of an inspection of volumes of Halifax, Montreal, and Quebec newspapers for selected years, Helmut *Kallmann has estimated that by 1810 as many as 100 opera performances may have taken place in Canada. Most of them undoubtedly were given by strolling companies of actors, but a few were by resident amateur performers. The 'orchestra' may have been a group ranging from three or four players to one or two dozen.

The performance of the same repertoire continued during the first three decades of the 19th century. Examples from the 1820s would include Samuel Arnold's pastiche opera *The Maid of the Mill* and Thomas Arne's *Love in a Village* performed in Montreal in 1825 and, in the same year, what may have been the first operas performed in Toronto: John Braham and C.E. Horn's 'grand romantic opera' *The Devil's Bridge*, Coleman's *The Mountaineers*, and Stephen Storace's *No Song, No Supper*. In his *Three Years in Canada* (London 1829) John Mactaggart mentions that 'Fancy balls, amateur operas, &c. amuse the gentry in winter' in Halifax. The residents of St John's, Nfld, heard *The Duenna* in 1820.

2 1830–1918. The 1830s present something of a hiatus in the history of opera performance in Canada. Research into the reasons for this has hardly begun, but the political unrest and the cholera epidemics of the period may explain the apparent decline. When opera made a comeback in the 1840s and 1850s the old repertoire had been discarded (the Quebec performance of J.-J. Rousseau's *Le Devin du village* in 1846 under Napoléon *Aubin by a local society was an exception) and a new and far more challenging repertoire was introduced. The grand operas of Auber, Bellini, Boieldieu, Donizetti, Rossini, and Verdi made far greater demands not only on the singers but also on the accompanying orchestras. The new repertoire became known to Canadians mostly through single excerpts, overtures, and medleys. However, Willy *Amtmann reports in *La Musique au Québec* (p 363) that four operas were performed in Montreal in the summer of 1841: *La Sonnambula*, *Fra Diavolo*, *Cendrillon* (Rossini's *La Cenerentola*), and *L'Elisir d'Amore*. The singers included Arthur Edward Seguin and his wife, Ann Childe, who had come to North America in 1838, and one Manvers of the Royal Opera House, Covent Garden. Two years later a French company, headed by a Mlle Cavé, presented Auber's *Les Diamants de la couronne* and Adam's *Le Chalet*.

As the population grew and, with it, a network of steamship and rail transportation, famous singers began to include Canada in their tours. Between 1841 and 1854 John Braham, Euphrasie Borghese, Jenny Lind, Auguste Nourrit, Teresa Parodi, Henriette Sontag, and the prodigy Adelina Patti all gave recitals in Montreal, Quebec, or Toronto. Such celebrities undoubtedly inspired local amateurs, and soon the first persistent signs of regular performance were evident. Between 1850 and 1900 major Canadian cities enjoyed performances of numerous travelling US companies headed by famous US prima donnas such as Emma Abbott, Minnie Hauk, Emma Juch, and Clara Louise Kellogg.

Montreal was visited in 1853 by a travelling troupe under Luigi Arditi, and as early as 1871 there was a local production of *Der Fliegende Holländer*. All-Offenbach seasons were offered at the *Theatre Royal in 1874, 1876, and 1877 by a Paris company that starred Zulma Bouffard, a friend of the composer. Emma *Albani and her company came in 1890 and 1892 to the *Academy of Music to present *Lucia di Lammermoor*, *La Traviata*, *Les Huguenots*, and *Lohengrin*, all of course starring the Canadian prima donna. A great period of activity in Montreal, which was to last until World War I, began with the resident *Opéra français (1893–6), which presented French and Italian grand opera as well as operettas and legitimate drama at the Théâtre français. In 1899 both the Charley Opera of New Orleans and the Durieu-Nicosias troupe of Paris invaded Montreal, the first playing at *Her Majesty's Theatre, the second at the *Monument national, for spectacular seasons of French exotica, including Halévy's *La Juive*, Reyer's *Sigurd*, Gounod's *Mireille* and *La Reine de Saba*, and Meyerbeer's *Robert le Diable* and *L'Africaine*. The sophistication of the city's audiences is demonstrated by the fact that Montreal was chosen for the premieres of Victor Herbert's operettas *Cyrano de Bergerac* (1899) and *The Singing Girl* (1899), and for Sousa's *The Charlatan* (1898). A small troupe of singers from the *Metropolitan Opera performed in Winnipeg and Regina in 1899, and the main New York company visited Montreal in 1899 and 1901, bringing Emma Calvé's famed Carmen both times, and returning in 1911 with a production of *Tannhäuser* with Fremstad and Slezak, and of *Aida* with Emmy Destinn, the latter conducted by Toscanini. The Mascagni Grand Opera Company presented fully staged productions of *Cavalleria Rusticana*, *Zanetto*, and *Iris* in Montreal in 1902, directed by the composer. In 1904–5 there were three visits by the Savage English Grand Opera Company, which brought rare performances of Verdi's *Otello* and Wagner's *Parsifal*. The young Florence *Easton (later buried in Montreal) was Gilda in *Rigoletto*.

The most important chapter in the pre-World-War-I history of opera performance in Montreal undoubtedly was that concerning the *Montreal Opera Company (1910–13), the three seasons of which embraced not only a wealth of activity at His Majesty's Theatre but also regular tours to Quebec City, Ottawa, Toronto, and even Rochester, NY. Among the many Canadian premieres offered were Puccini's *Manon Lescaut* and *Tosca*, Mascagni's *L'Amico Fritz*, Giordano's *Fedora*, Charpentier's *Louise*, and Massenet's *Le Jongleur de Notre-Dame* and *Cendrillon*. In the wake of this organization came the *National Opera Company of Canada, which presented one quixotic season, 1913–14, in Montreal and on tour, dominated by such international luminaries as Marie Rappold and Leo Slezak. The era came to an end in March 1914 with a three-week visit of the Quinlan English Opera Company at His Majesty's Theatre; Wagner's complete *Der Ring des Nibelungen* was sung in Canada for the first time (and by 1980 still the only time), along with *Tannhäuser*, *Lohengrin*, *The Flying Dutchman*, and *Tristan und Isolde*.

Opera was slow to take root in Quebec City, largely as a result of clerical opposition to theatrical entertainments, whether spoken or sung. As late as 1911 the archbishop of Quebec exhorted the citizens to boycott the visiting Montreal Opera Company, on the grounds that the libretti of the works being offered were 'detrimental to morals.' Some performances took place as scheduled, but *Manon* and *Thaïs* were banned. Among noteworthy performances was one by a visiting company 10 Jun 1864 of Rossini's *Barber of Seville* (presumably its Canadian premiere) and several in 1879 of Boieldieu's *La Dame blanche*, conducted by Calixa *Lavallée (after two weeks in Montreal) with Canadian singers.

Landmarks in the long and varied operatic history of Toronto began in 1825 with the performances mentioned above and were followed in 1843 by two presentations of Sir Henry Bishop's *The Miller and His Men*. A decade later came 'the whole of the first act of *Lucrezia Borgia*' with local performers and piano accompaniment. On 8 Jul 1853 *Norma*, with Rosa Devries in the title role, became the young city's first fully staged grand opera. Five years later the Holman Juvenile Opera Troupe made the first of several visits that were to culminate in George Holman's settling in Toronto and presenting regular seasons, 1867–73, of opera and drama at the Royal Lyceum Theatre with his *Holman English Opera Troupe.

Toronto, like Montreal, rarely had a season without the visit of a travelling troupe, notably the Emma Abbott Grand Opera Co in the 1880s. In 1883 Emma Albani for the first time sang opera on her native soil: *Lucia di Lammermoor* at the Grand Opera House. *Lohengrin*, *Rigoletto*, *Carmen*, and *Les Huguenots* were the grand operas given in the 1890–1 season, a particularly busy one, with a total of 91 opera and operetta performances. A group of singers from the Metropolitan Opera Co visited in 1892, and the main company presented six operas in 1899. The premiere of a Victor Herbert operetta *The Fortune Teller* took place in Toronto 14 Sep 1898 at the Grand Opera House. In 1905 the Savage English Grand Opera Company gave the first performance in Canada of *Parsifal*, and in 1906 Ruggiero Leoncavallo conducted excerpts from his works. The Montreal Opera Co first visited Toronto in 1911, and the Boston Opera made four visits 1915–17, bringing such treats as the young Maggie Teyte in *Faust* and *La Bohème* and Luisa Villani in Montemezzi's *L'Amore dei tre re*.

It must be stressed that among Canadian cities even Montreal and Toronto, at the turn of the century, rarely had full seasons of opera. The hazards of arranging visits of foreign companies resulted in extreme fluctuations from year to year. Local productions, rare though they were, depended usually on the importing of singers for certain roles. By 1980 little research had been conducted on the orchestras that accompanied grand opera: was the instrumentation reduced? did local musicians participate? It may be assumed that in the main visiting troupes brought their own orchestras. The accommodation of the troupes presented few problems in the larger cities since theatre buildings, no matter how inadequate for grand opera, at least were plentiful. However, the name 'grand opera house,' which adorned auditoriums all across Canada (see Concert halls and opera houses), gave no indication of the actual use and suitability of the building. More likely than not, in all but the largest cities these opera houses rarely accommodated or could accommodate anything more ambitious than operetta.

Operetta, however, did flourish, in local productions and visiting ones. There were few English-Canadian towns where Victor Herbert, Reginald de Koven, and especially Gilbert & Sullivan were not cultivated (eg, Calgary's first operetta was *Trial by Jury* in 1890, and Regina's was *The Pirates of Penzance* in 1909). And there were few French-Canadian towns in which Offenbach, Messager, Lecocq, or Planquette were not popular. Planquette's *Les Cloches de Corneville* had a great vogue across the country and in 1904, in its English adaptation (*The Chimes of Normandy*), was the first operetta presented in Edmonton. Charles *Hutton began his Gilbert & Sullivan productions in St John's in 1894. Another favourite was von Flotow's comic opera *Martha*, of which local productions took place in Halifax and Victoria. Winnipeg heard *Iolanthe* as early as 1883, when the Hess Opera from England visited, and Halifax heard *The Mikado* in 1887, only two years after its premiere. (See also *H.M.S. Parliament*.) London, Ont, for some seasons enjoyed the presence of the Holman English Opera Co, which moved there in 1873. In 1899 Kingston was the first to hear **Leo, the Royal Cadet*, composed by the resident Oscar *Telgmann, who also presented it in other Ontario towns. Grand opera made its appearance in Vancouver in 1891, when the CPR's Vancouver Opera House opened with a production of *Lohengrin* by the Emma Juch English Opera, a US company.

If Canada still had not produced a single enduring company in which Canadian talent furnished the majority of singers, by World War I, she nevertheless had made an impressive contribution to the great companies of the USA and Europe. The first singer to soar abroad, Emma Albani, was also the most famous, but others won international recognition: Francis Archambault, Donald Brian, Edmund *Burke, Craig Campbell, Eugene Cowles, Pauline *Donalda, Louise *Edvina, Kathleen *Howard, Edward *Johnson, Béatrice *La Palme, Christie MacDonald, F.-X. *Mercier, Whitney Mockridge, Irene *Pavloska, Albert Quesnel, and Marie *Toulinguet. (See also USA.)

3 1918–45. World War I dealt a blow to opera performance in Canada, and recovery proved slow. The main professional company to appear in the years prior to the middle of the century was the New York-based *San Carlo Opera Company. Almost every year it visited Canadian cities, from Vancouver and Winnipeg to Toronto and Montreal, providing a wide variety of the standard literature and including some Canadians in its casts. In this period once again Montreal showed the greatest initiative. Resident companies were the *Société canadienne d'opérette, which, despite its name, presented several grand operas 1925–36; the Canadian Opera Company of 1931, which mounted a single production, *Roméo et Juliette* at Loew's Theatre with Edward Johnson and Queena Mario, with Wilfrid *Pelletier conducting; the *Variétés lyriques (1936–55); and Pauline Donalda's *Opera Guild of Montreal, founded in 1941 and active until 1969. In 1940 the *Montreal Festivals (1936–65) for the first time programmed an opera: *Pelléas et Mélisande*. This work, as well as the festival's productions of *Ariadne auf Naxos* in 1946 were Canadian premieres. Among the Canadian premieres given by the Opera Guild were *Le Coq d'or* in 1944 and *Fidelio* in 1946.

Toronto was visited by Antonio Scotti's troupe in 1921 and the Russian Grand Opera Company (which also performed in Montreal) in 1922 and 1923, the latter offering *Boris Godunov*, *Eugene Onegin*, and the Rimsky-Korsakov operas *The Snow Maiden* and *The Tsar's Bride*. Local activity included performances by the *Savoyards, established in 1919, and by the Toronto Opera Chorus, founded in 1920 by the voice teacher Giuseppe *Carboni and active until his death in 1934. It presented amateur performances of Adam's *Le Chalet*, Gounod's *Philémon et Baucis*, and other works. Edoardo *Ferrari-Fontana founded (ca 1927) the Music and Arts League, which presented operatic programs. The Toronto Conservatory Opera Company, established by Ernest *MacMillan and Countess Laura de Turczynowicz, produced several operas, beginning in 1928 with *Hansel and Gretel* and including *Dido and Aeneas* and *Hugh the Drover*, but the company ceased its activities in 1930. Between 1935 and 1939 there was a veritable onslaught of Toronto productions by competing local companies of varying calibre, including the Opera Guild of Toronto and the Canadian Grand Opera Assn, both established in 1936 and performing operas by Verdi, Gounod, Wagner, Puccini, and others. Less ambitious, but enduring for a longer period, were the *Rosselino Opera Company, which presented programs of operatic scenes or of entire operas 1944–51 at *Eaton Auditorium, the *Eaton Operatic Society (1931–65), and the *Canada Packers Operatic Society (1942–55), the last two specializing in Gilbert & Sullivan and other light works.

As in many other Canadian cities outside Montreal and Toronto, in Winnipeg the staple diet of music theatre in the decades after World War I was Gilbert & Sullivan, and such popular favourites as *The Chimes of Normandy* or Balfe's *The Bohemian Girl*. In addition to local amateur productions Winnipeg received occasional visits from such companies as the Royal English Opera and the D'Oyly Carte. The mainstay of musical theatre in Vancouver was *Theatre Under the Stars (TUTS), which presented open-air performances of operettas at *Malkin Bowl 1940–63. In Ottawa H. Bramwell Bailey directed a Grand Opera Co 1949–64. The names of numerous other light opera societies of the period will be found in the entries on individual cities.

Another genre, the folk ballad opera, received an important stimulus 1927–31 in the *CPR Festivals, particularly those at Banff, Quebec, Toronto, Vancouver, and Victoria. It cannot be denied, however, that on the whole Canada was a desert in so far as grand opera was concerned. For the opera lover, even in the largest cities, a professional stage performance was a treat not available at all in some seasons and limited to the standard works in others. It may be noted that the opera composer considered by many the greatest of all, Mozart, has not been mentioned once so far in this article. It may be that the Montreal Opera Guild's production of *Così fan tutte* in 1943 and *The Magic Flute* in 1945 were the first of that master's operas heard in Canada.

There was one bright light, however: the broadcasts, weekly during the season, from the Metropolitan Opera in New York which, beginning in 1931 (and continuing in 1980), have brought superbly performed operas to Canadians from coast to coast, not only providing enjoyment, but also building potential audiences for local productions and establishing critical standards.

4 AFTER 1945. The unprecedented growth of opera in Canada after World War II was aided by a number of factors, including the expansion of broadcasting and recording, the influx of European immigrants for whom attendance at the opera had been a habit, and the growing prosperity of the 1950s and 1960s. More fundamental was the recognition by a few far-sighted men at the *RCMT that opera could grow permanent roots only if training and employment opportunities were developed simultaneously, backed by powerful institutions and private support. In practice this meant the establishment of the *Royal Cons Opera School and the formation of the *CBC Opera Company and close co-operation between the two. Under the initial direction of Arnold *Walter and the later guidance of Ettore *Mazzoleni, with Herman *Geiger-Torel, Nicholas *Goldschmidt, and Ernesto *Barbini as its main figures theatrical and musical, the school rapidly attracted young singers from all regions of Canada. The first production, *The Bartered Bride* (1947), was followed by the first Opera Festival (three productions, 1950), which in turn grew into the *Canadian Opera Company, a company presenting a professional season independent of the school. In 1958 the company began extensive touring and subsequently it gave the first operatic performances ever heard (1967) in many parts of Alaska, the Yukon, and the Northwest Territories. By 1980 the COC had become the longest-established and most productive opera company in Canada's history.

Elsewhere opera companies were formed in less accommodating circumstances. The *Opera national du Québec, a school founded by Edouard *Woolley in 1948, presented four seasons in Montreal, Quebec, Trois-Rivières, and parts of New Brunswick. In 1949 a performance of *Don Giovanni* launched the *Nova Scotia Opera Assn, which mounted several productions in Halifax and toured in other Maritime centres. The Light Opera of Edmonton was established by H.G. *Turner in 1950. The *Regina Conservatory Opera (1951–69) produced one or two operas each year, ranging from standard repertoire to commissioned works. The Grand Opera of Montreal, established by J. Ubald Boyer in 1957 with Roland Leduc and others, gave *Don Giovanni* and *The Barber of Seville* before it ceased operations in 1958.

In chronological order, there followed the *Vancouver Opera Assn (founded 1959), the *Hamilton Opera Company (1961–72, its residue absorbed into Mohawk College Opera Workshop), Quebec City's *Théâtre lyrique de Nouvelle-France (1961–70, renamed the Théâtre lyrique du Québec in 1967), the *Edmonton Opera Assn (founded 1963), Quebec City's *Société lyrique d'Aubigny (founded 1968), Winnipeg's Manitoba Opera Assn (founded 1969 but not presenting a production of its own until 1973), the provincially sponsored *Opéra du Québec (1971–5, performing in both Montreal and Quebec), Calgary's *Southern Alberta Opera Assn (formed 1972), and the Opéra de Montréal (founded 1980, a revival of the Opéra du Québec). Most of these companies have mounted from one to four productions a year, using mainly professional Canadian singers and playing for a period of from several weeks to a few months, with additional performances out of town. The four prairie and British Columbia companies mentioned above formed a co-operative organization, *Opera West, to pool their resources and co-ordinate their schedules.

Operas have been regular features of several festivals. The *Vancouver International Festival featured *Don Giovanni* in its first season, 1958, and continued presenting opera in some of its 11 seasons, although never as a main component of the schedule. The *Stratford Festival presented Britten's *The Rape of Lucretia* in 1956, followed by operas in many seasons until 1975, changing the emphasis from Britten to Gilbert & Sullivan to Mozart and finally to Canadian operas. The Montreal Festivals continued to present operas until 1965 and the *MSO has included opera presentations in its 1964–8 programs. *Festival Ottawa (Festival Canada 1971–7) has featured one or several operas during its annual July season; the emphasis has been on Mozart and on rarely heard works, such as Rossini's *Le Comte Ory* and Massenet's *Cendrillon*. The *Guelph Spring Festival has presented one opera a year.

Other efforts of the mid-20th century deserving recognition include the Opera Guild of Montreal which continued production until the retirement of its director, Pauline Donalda, in 1969; the *Minute Opera of Montreal, which presented shorter works 1949–53; the productions of the *Banff Centre SFA after Ernesto *Vinci established a voice department in 1949; the *McGill Opera Studio, founded in 1956 by Edith and Luciano *Della Pergola; the Toronto Opera Repertoire, established in 1967 and directed by Giuseppe *Macina; the *Dalhousie U Opera Workshop (Halifax) which presented its first production in 1971; and the Opera in Concert series of rarely heard works, accompanied on the piano, established by Stuart *Hamilton in 1974 at the *St Lawrence Centre in Toronto.

Of paramount importance have been the opera presentations of the CBC, in the 1940s and 1950s on radio and, beginning 14 May 1953 with *Don Giovanni*, on TV. These high-quality productions not only have brought opera to areas outside the large cities but have made it possible to present works, both from the traditional and the modern repertoires, that lack conventional box office appeal. Furthermore they have provided employment to Canadian singers during the many months between the short seasons of the major companies. The Toronto-based CBC Opera Company (1948–55), the CBC Toronto TV productions of Franz *Kraemer, and the CBC Montreal TV program 'L'*Heure du concert' (1954–66) have been the corporation's main vehicles for opera. Studio productions declined during the 1970s, but towards the end of the decade there were live telecasts of Festival Ottawa productions (eg, *The Magic Flute* 1977, *The Barber of Seville* 1978). There also were productions in collaboration with the BBC and the PBS (the US educational network), eg, Verdi's *Macbeth* (1978), a CBC French-network production of *Madama Butterfly* (1978), and a live telecast of the COC's 1978 performance of *Joan of Arc*.

Amateur productions of musical comedies and the simpler operas continued throughout Canada. Presentations of a professional calibre have been staged by the Variétés lyriques of Montreal (active until 1955), the Theatre Under the Stars of Vancouver (active until 1963), *Melody Fair of Toronto (1951–4), and *Rainbow Stage of Winnipeg (begun 1954, outdoor performances).

With the growth of Canadian activity visits by foreign opera companies have decreased. The Metropolitan Opera paid regular visits to Montreal and Toronto during the 1950s, but the venues of those cities, the *Forum and *Maple Leaf Gardens respectively, while providing room for large audiences, proved unsatisfactory both as auditoriums for sound and as stages for theatre. By 1980 no feast of opera by visiting troupes had been surpassed by that at the World Festival of *Expo 67, when the major companies of Hamburg, Milan, Moscow, Stockholm, and Vienna made their North American debuts at the *PDA in Montreal.

See also CPR Festivals; Folk-music-inspired composition; Librettos; Musical theatre; Operas.

BIBLIOGRAPHY

Charlesworth, Hector. 'Grand opera in Canada,' *Canadian Courier*, vol 12, 12 Oct 1912

'The present state of grand opera in Canada,' *The Year Book of Canadian Art 1913*, compiled by the Arts and Letters Club of Toronto (Toronto 1913)

Lamontagne, C.-O. 'Lettre à Frédéric Pelletier,' *Entre-Nous*, vol 1, May 1930

Walter, Arnold. 'The present state of opera in Canada,' *Cons B*, Feb 1950

Beraud, Jean. *350 Ans de théâtre au Canada français* (Montreal 1958)

Neel, Boyd. 'Opera,' *The Arts in Canada*, ed Murray Ross (Toronto 1958)

Hamelin, Jean. 'Pourquoi nos chanteurs d'opéra doivent-ils s'exiler?' *Châtelaine*, Jan 1962

Kallmann, Helmut. 'From the archives: the Montreal Gazette on music from 1786 to 1797,' *CMJ*, vol 6, Spring 1962

Mercer, Ruby. 'Canadians like opera,' *Music Across Canada*, May 1963

Kallmann, Helmut. 'History of opera in Canada,' *OpCan*, Sep 1964

'Salute to Canada,' special Canadian issue of *Opera News*, vol 31, 13 May 1967

Morey, Carl. 'Pre-confederation opera in Toronto,' *OpCan*, Sep 1969

Mercer, Ruby. 'A 150-year history,' *OpCan*, Fall 1973

Geiger-Torel, Herman. 'Canada, an operatic desert?' *German-Canadian Yearbook*, vol 2, (Toronto 1975)

Eaton, Quaintance. *Opera Caravan: Adventures of the Metropolitan Opera on Tour 1883–1956* (New York 1978)

Rosenthal, Harold, and Warrack, John. *The Concise Oxford Dictionary of Opera*, 2nd ed (London 1979). Includes entries on Canada, Montreal, Toronto, Vancouver

Potvin, Gilles. 'A short history of opera in Canada,' *Mcan*, 44, Fall 1980

Lussier, Charles A. 'L'Opéra a-t-il un avenir?' *OpCan*, Spring 1981

Kallmann *History of Music in Canada*

Amtmann *La Musique au Québec*

Opera Canada

JBM, HK, (GP)

Operas. The early history of operas composed by Canadians may be viewed as a series of episodes rather than a continuous expansion in which one phase leads into another. Joseph *Quesnel, the first Canadian – and with some justification regarded by some as the first North American – opera composer, was a lone figure. His **Colas et Colinette* (premiered in 1790) was staged in Montreal in 1790 and Quebec City in 1805, and has had revivals, the first in 1963. Quesnel's other opera, **Lucas et Cécile*, is not known to have been performed. Both it and *Colas* are in the style of the 18th-century French comédie mêlée d'ariettes of Duni, Grétry, Monsigny, and Philidor, and are Canadian only by virtue of their composer's residence.

By the middle of the 19th century opera had become an accepted art form among the urban residents of Canada, and by the end of the century performances were fairly common. Touring companies presented the standard 19th-century European repertoire, and amateur groups often staged works by Canadian composers. As the resources of such groups were limited, only smaller works could be undertaken. Calixa *Lavallée's three light operas, *Lou-Lou* (1872), **The Widow* (1882), and **TIQ (The Indian Question Settled at Last)* (1883), all were written, and the latter two were premiered, in the USA. *Lou-Lou*'s scheduled New York premiere was cancelled at the last minute. Two scenes of a projected grand opera – *Le Jugement de Salomon* – are thought to have been performed in Boston in 1886. No opera by Clarence *Lucas is known to have been presented in Canada, but Charles A.E. *Harriss' **Torquil* (1896) had concert performances 22 May 1900 at *Massey Hall, Toronto, and 25 May 1900 at the *Montreal Arena. Other late-19th-century operas were Susie Frances *Harrison's three-act *Pipandor* (late 1880s, based on French-Canadian folksongs), Jules *Hone's *The Grandee*, performed (probably in concert) in Montreal in 1899, and Frank Stone's *Sardianapolis*, performed in Sherbrooke around the turn of the century.

The 20th century witnessed a gradual increase in operas composed by Canadians, and after 1940 there was an outburst of activity, owing to the patronage of the burgeoning *CBC and to the establishment of the *COC and various summer music festivals. Alfred *Laliberté's *Soeur Beatrice* was never staged, though excerpts were sung in concert. Émiliano *Renaud's three-act comic opera *Djymko* probably was not performed. J. Ulric Voyer's *L'Intendant Bigot*, a three-act grand opera, was premiered in Montreal in February 1929 by the *Société canadienne d'opérette and was presented also in Quebec City. Ballad operas by Healey *Willan and Oscar *O'Brien were staged at the *CPR Festivals (1927–31), and Willan's **Transit through Fire* (the first Canadian opera conceived for radio) was broadcast by CBC Toronto in March 1942. Eugène *Lapierre's opéra-comique *Le Père des amours* (1942, based on the life of Joseph Quesnel) was staged at Montreal's *Monument national in December 1942, and his *Le Vagabond de la gloire*, based on the life of Calixa Lavallée, was produced at St-Alphonse Auditorium, Montreal, in November 1947. Graham *George's **Evangeline* was staged in Kingston 1 Dec 1948.

During the 1950s and 1960s, too, most of the operas written were short works (usually one-act); most were commissioned by the CBC and some by the *JMC. Maurice *Blackburn's comic opera **Silent Measures* was telecast by CBC Montreal 21 Apr 1956; his chamber opera **Pirouette* had its premiere 21 Apr 1956 and was performed 30 Jul 1960 at the *JMC Orford Art Centre. Both operas toured eastern Canada for the JMC in 1960. Jean *Vallerand's chamber opera **Le Magicien* also was presented first at the *JMC centre, 2 Sep 1961, and toured the country the following year. Healey Willan's full-scale grand opera **Deirdre*, premiered on CBC radio 20 Apr 1946, was revised for a stage premiere at the *U of Toronto in 1965 and was repeated by the COC in 1966. Barbara *Pentland's chamber opera *The Lake* was produced at the CBC Vancouver studios 3 Mar 1954, while John *Beckwith's **Night Blooming Cereus* (1953–8) was premiered on CBC radio in 1959 and staged later at *Hart House Theatre, *McGill U, and the *U of Western Ontario. Arthur *Poynter's two religious operas, *The Triumph of Our Lord* and *The Birth of Our Lord*, were premiered in 1950 and 1969 respectively in Toronto.

Canada's centenary in 1967 prompted several operas on Canadian themes. Although a few earlier works in the genre – Pentland's *The Lake* and Willan's *Transit through Fire* – had been based on Canadian subjects, many had had foreign settings. Harry *Somers' **Louis Riel* was the most significant of the new works which attempted to say something specific and serious about the Canadian heritage. Composed to a Mavor *Moore and Jacques Languirand libretto (in English, French, and Cree) which treated the Métis rebellions of 1869–70 and 1884–5 and their political consequences, the imposing, eclectic score incorporated traditional or pseudo-traditional tunes, dodecaphony, and electronics. It was commissioned by the COC with funds from the Floyd S. *Chalmers Foundation and premiered 23 Sep 1967 at the *O'Keefe Centre in Toronto. Raymond *Pannell's *The Luck of Ginger Coffey* was premiered 15 Sep 1967 at the O'Keefe Centre. Also composed for centennial year were Murray *Adaskin's *Grant, Warden of the Plains*, premiered at the CBC Winnipeg studios 18 Jul 1967; Kelsey *Jones' **Sam Slick*, premiered at the CBC Halifax studios 5 Sep 1967; and Robert *Turner's *The Brideship*, premiered at the CBC Vancouver studios 12 Dec 1967. Douglas Major's *The Loyalists*, yet another centennial opera, was performed in 1967 at Saint John, NB.

The upsurge of opera composition continued throughout the late 1960s and the 1970s, though most of the products were short or medium-length works for small or relatively small forces. Gabriel *Charpentier's *Orphée*, a 70-minute piece for chorus, dancers, and a small instrumental group including the ondes Martenot, had its premiere 10 Jun 1969 at the inauguration of the *NAC. His *A Night at the Opera* (10 comic operas, each no more than 15 minutes long) was incomplete in 1980, but several of the mini-operas within it had been performed. Raymond Pannell's *Exiles* was commissioned and premiered in 1973 by the *Stratford Festival's Third Stage, and his *Souvenirs* (chamber opera for one singer, 1978) and *Refugees* (1979) were staged in Toronto. Charles *Wilson's *The Summoning of Everyman* (commissioned by the Music Dept of *Dalhousie U in 1972 and premiered there in 1973) was repeated at Stratford's Third Stage in 1974. Tibor *Polgar's *The Glove*, a one-act opera written in 1973 for *Prologue to the Performing Arts and produced for touring by the COC, had over 90 performances by 1976, including a 1975 telecast by the CBC. Violet *Archer's one-act comic opera *Sganarelle* had its premiere 5 Feb 1974 at the opera workshop of the *U of Alberta. The one-act operas *Enkidu* by Somers and *Lady in the Night* by *Symonds were produced in Toronto in 1977 by Co-Opera Theatre. Paul *McIntyre's *Death of the Hired Man* had a reading by Comus Theatre, Toronto, in 1979. Among several short operas for children are those based on Oscar Wilde's *The Selfish Giant* by Barry *Cabena (1970) and Charles Wilson (1972) and John *Rea's *The Prisoners Play*, commissioned by the U of Toronto Opera Dept and premiered by it 12 May 1973.

Among TV operas of the 1960s and 1970s were Ben *McPeek's *The Bargain* (1963), telecast from CBC Montreal in 1966 and staged by Comus Theatre at the Toronto Spring Festival in 1978; Godfrey *Ridout's Christmas opera *The Lost Child*, telecast from CBC Toronto in 1976; and Raymond Pannell's **Aberfan*, which won the Salzburg International TV Opera Prize in 1977.

Despite the increasingly daunting economics of opera production, a few large operas continued to appear in the 1970s. Wilson's **Heloise and Abelard*, a full-length grand opera commissioned by the COC, was premiered by the company 8 Sep 1973, and his *Psycho Red*, also a full-length work, though for smaller forces, was commissioned by the *Guelph Spring Festival and premiered there in 1977. Wilson adapted the Anne Hébert novel for his fourth opera, *Kamouraska*, which had a public reading in 1979 in Toronto. Derek *Healey's **Seabird Island*, its libretto based on a west-coast Indian legend, was premiered in May 1977 at the Guelph Spring Festival and toured Canada the following season. John Beckwith's *The Shivaree*, a full-length work with an orchestra of 20, was completed and had a public reading in Toronto in 1979.

Even when they are modestly produced, however, operas, in their requirement for singers, instrumental musicians, directors of music and stage, designers and makers of sets and costumes, and, in some cases, choreographers and dancers, are among the costliest performing arts. The flowering of opera composition in Canada in the 1960s and 1970s, limited though it was, depended to a large degree on special subsidies provided either by two crown corporations – the CBC and the Canada Council – or by institutions (eg, the COC, the Stratford Festival, the Guelph Spring Festival, the JMC, the university opera schools) that themselves depend upon the Canada Council, the provincial arts councils, or other government-related sources of support. The Chalmers subsidy of *Louis Riel* was a singular instance of private subsidy for an important work – an instance, alas, which did not set a trend. At the beginning of the 1980s it was apparent that of all musical genres, opera would be the one whose survival would be most closely linked to the development of the national and provincial economies.

See also Children's concerts; Composition for ensemble teaching; Librettos; Musical theatre; Opera performance. (SW)

Opera West. Association of western Canadian opera companies. The principle was initiated in 1968 by the *Vancouver and *Edmonton Opera Assns, which joined forces to improve opera standards, sharing manpower and production costs for stagings of *La Bohème* (1969) and *Lucrezia Borgia* (1972). With the formation of the *Manitoba Opera Assn in 1971 and *Southern Alberta Opera Assn in 1972 the practicality of such collaboration became increasingly evident. The four companies were incorporated as Opera West in March 1973, producing their first joint effort, *La Traviata*, the same year. Permanent production facilities were established in Vancouver. Opera West was later joined by affiliate members, the Portland and Seattle operas. The association's presidents have been A. Kerr Twaddle (1973), Frederick L. Scott (1973–5), and E.W. Bert Adamson (1975–7).

BIBLIOGRAPHY

'Opera West,' *OpCan*, Winter 1972 (CC)

Operetta. See Librettos; Musical theatre; Opera performance.

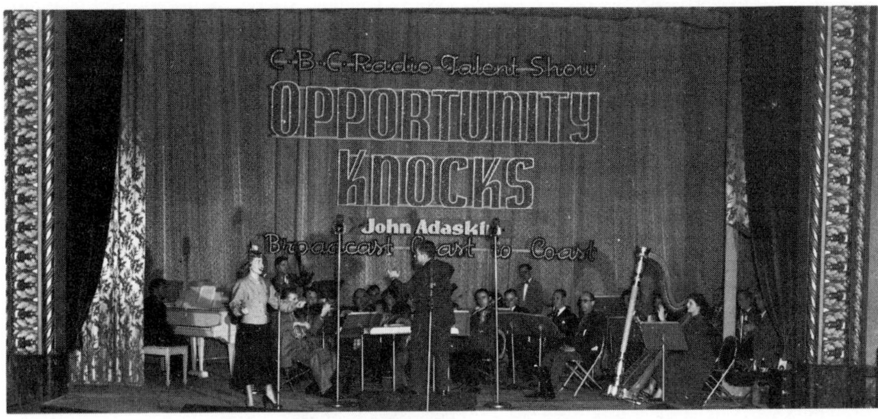

'Opportunity Knocks.' National talent competition sponsored by CBC radio and broadcast from Toronto and Montreal 2 Jul 1947–29 Sep 1957. It was initiated and directed by John *Adaskin, who also conducted the orchestra. There were three series per season, usually of 10 weeks each. Horace *Lapp was the accompanist during the entire life of the show. Adaskin made some auditioning trips across the country but most of the auditions were held in the CBC Toronto studios – out-of-town contestants could submit recordings – and four performers were selected for each broadcast and received professional fees. Weekly winners were chosen at first by studio-audience response and mail-in votes, and later by a panel of judges. Semi-finalists competed again at the end of each series, at which time a Grand Award winner and two or three runners-up were chosen, again by a panel of judges, among whom were Adaskin, Jean-Marie *Beaudet, Helmut *Blume, Herman *Geiger-Torel, Richard *Johnston, and Geoffrey *Waddington. The three Grand Award winners received contracts to appear on the 13-week summer series known as 'Opportunity Winners' and broadcast alternately from Toronto and Montreal. First runners-up each received $100, second and third runners-up each $75. An announcers' competition category was supplanted in 1950 by a composers' category. Composers whose works won first prizes and honourable mentions were Murray *Adaskin (1953), Maurice *Blackburn (1951), Alexander *Brott (1954), Johnny *Burt (1951, 1953), Harry *Freedman (1951), Hector *Gratton (1952), Cal Jackson (1952), Sandy Jones (1954), Walter *Kaufmann (1950, 1951, 1953), Neil McKay (1954), Art *Morrow (1951), Jean *Papineau-Couture (1952), Godfrey *Ridout (1951), John *Weinzweig (1950), and Healey *Willan (1952). 'Opportunity Knocks' was discontinued in 1957.

The Grand Award winners were: Bernard *Johnson, baritone, and Wilfred Reed, tenor (1947); Billy Meek, pop singer, Gratien Landry, tenor, Doreen *Hume (Hulme), soprano, and Les Neal, pop singer (1948); Betty McCaskill and Marthe *Létourneau, sopranos, and Kalle Ruusunen, baritone (1949); Marie-Germaine Leblanc, soprano, Charles Rush, (singer?), and Joseph Rainer, tenor (1950); Fernand *Martel, baritone, Morris Kronick (Maury *Kaye), piano, and William Blaine Williams, baritone (1951); Angela Antonelli, Sylvia *Grant, and Marguerite *Lavergne, sopranos (1952); Roma *Butler, soprano, David Brewster, piano, and Paul Norrback, accordion (1953); Lesia Zubrack (*Romanoff), soprano, Janine Gingras, pop singer, and Anne McCahey, piano (1954); François Auffray, pop singer, Jeannette Franklin, pop singer, and Gordon Fleming, accordion (1955); and Ruth Watson *Henderson, piano (1956).

Among the semi-finalists and runners-up who subsequently made careers in music were: Diane Abran, Herman Apple, Donald *Bell, Napoléon *Bisson, Pierre *Boutet, Norman *Brooks, Fernande *Chiocchio, Corinne Conley, Edith *Della Pergola, Ray *Dudley, Esther *Ghan, Maureen *Forrester, Barbara *Franklin, Donald *Garrard, Robert *Goulet, Sheila *Henig, Irene Loosberg, Margo *MacKinnon, Lois *Marshall, Phyllis *Marshall, Howard *Mawson, Joan *Maxwell, David *Mills, Sylvia Murphy, Arlene *Nimmons, Joseph *Pach, Frank Palmer, Louis *Quilico, Jon Ringham, Joseph *Rouleau, Irene *Salemka, Steven *Staryk, Andrée Thériault, Bernard *Turgeon, and Victor *White.

OPTHOF, Cornelis. Baritone, b Rotterdam 10 Feb 1930. Emigrating to Canada in 1949, he studied voice in Belleville, Ont, in Vancouver with Catharina Hendrikse, and 1957–9 on scholarship at the *RCMT. In 1960 he was a *CBC Talent Festival winner. He sang 1957–64 with the *COC touring company. His roles for the main company of the COC have included Marcello in *La Bohème* (1963), Valentin in *Faust* (1966, 1970), Eisenstein in *Die Fledermaus* (1964, 1969), Amonasro in *Aida* (1972), and Germont in *La Traviata* (1974). In 1967 he created the role of Sir John A. MacDonald in Harry *Somers' **Louis Riel*. He has also sung with many other Canadian (Calgary, Edmonton, Montreal, Ottawa, Vancouver, Winnipeg) and US (Hartford, Miami, New Orleans, the Metropolitan in New York, Philadelphia) opera companies. Performances in 1964 at the *Stratford Festival as the Count in *The Marriage of Figaro* under Richard Bonynge led to an Australian tour in 1965 with Joan Sutherland and many subsequent roles with the soprano, including Germont père in *La Traviata* in Philadelphia in 1975 and a *Metropolitan Opera debut 17 Mar 1976 as Riccardo in *I Puritani*. He was Yeletsky in the Festival Canada (*Festival Ottawa) production of *The Queen of Spades* with Jon *Vickers and Maureen *Forrester.

Opthof's voice, described by *New York Times* critic John Rockwell as 'solid, a little throaty,' has weathered advice, criticism, and praise to be recognized widely for its extreme reliability and useful extension at the top of its range. Opthof may be heard as Filippo on the London recording, with Sutherland, of Bellini's *Beatrice di Tenda* (1966, 3-Lon OSA 1384) and also on a recording of Schoenberg songs with Glenn *Gould (Col M-31312).

BIBLIOGRAPHY

Kirby, Blaik. 'Debut at The Met crowns 23 years of plugging,' Toronto *Globe and Mail*, 3 Oct 1975 (HCs)

Oratorio performance (international repertoire). The history of oratorio performance in Canada may be said to date back to Good Friday, 1646, when a plainsong passion was sung at Quebec, the first known performance of an extended Easter-season program to be given in Canada. It was not until the 18th century, however, that true oratorio was performed. At St Paul's Anglican Church in Halifax the Philharmonic Society, along with officers of the army and navy, is said to have presented an oratorio (unidentified) in April 1769, and in 1789 'several Gentlemen with Musick Bands of the Regiments' sang the final chorus of *Messiah*. While extracts from *Messiah* were given at Quebec in 1793, it was not until 1857 that the work was performed there virtually complete, under Henry *Carter. In December 1857 John *Carter conducted the Sacred Harmonic Choir of Toronto in the first performance of the work in Upper Canada. *Messiah* has remained the most popular of all oratorios, and there have been hundreds of performances in Canada.

350 THE TIMES.

FOR THE BENEFIT OF MRS. ALLEN.
At FERGUSON'S HOTEL, *this evening, Monday, 23d. inſtant, will be performed,*
A CONCERTO SPIRITUALE.

PART 1ſt.

Overture,——Occaſional Oratorio, Handel.
Solo & Chorus——God Save the King.
Recitative——Comfort ye, Comfort ye, &c. } Meſſiah
Air——Every Valley ſhall be exalted. }
Air——Pious Orgies, Pious Airs. Jud. Maccab.
Grand Chorus——Hallelujah, for the Lord.
God omnipotent reigneth. Meſſiah

PART 2d.

Paſtoral Symphony. Meſſiah
Recitative,——And there were ſhepherds, &c. do.
Chorus,——Glory to God, &c. do.
Air,——He ſhall feed his flock. do.
Air,——I know that my Redeemer liveth, &c. do.
Air,——Why do the nations ſo furiouſly rage together, &c. do.
Grand Coronation Anthem.
God Save the King, Long live the King, &c.

Tickets at one Dollar each to be had at the Hotel, of Mrs. ALLEN N°. 13, *rue Ste. Urſule* and at the New Printing-Office.

AU PROFIT DE MADAME ALLEN:
A l'Hotel de FERGUSON, *ce ſoir, Lundi, le 23me du ecurant, ſera exécuté,*
UN CONCERT SPIRITUEL.

1re. PARTIE.

Ouverture,——Occaſional Oratorio, Handel.
Solo et Chorus——God ſave the King,
Récitatif——Comfort ye, Comfort ye, &c. } Meſſie.
Air——Ev'ry valley ſhall be exalted. }
Air——Orgies pieuſes, Airs pieux. Jud. Maccab.
Grand Chorus——Hallelujah for the Lord.
God omnipotent reigneth. Meſſie.

2de. PARTIE.

Simphonie paſtorale. Meſſie.
Récitatif——And there were Shepherds, &c. do.
Chorus——Glory to God do.
Air——He ſhall feed his flock do.
Air——I know that my Redeemer liveth do.
Air——Why do the nations ſo furiouſly rage together, &c. } do.
Grand Coronation Anthem.
God ſave the King, long live the King, &c.

Les billets à 5 Chelins chaque, ſe prendront au dit hôtel, chez Madame Allen, N° 13, rue Ste. Urſule, et à la Nouvelle Imprimerie.

An announcement of a concert of excerpts from Handel's oratorios in *The Times*, Quebec City, 23 Feb 1795

Oratorio enjoyed its greatest popularity in Canada during the 19th century. By the 1840s selections often were performed in concert, and as the number of choral societies increased complete presentations were given more often in concert halls than in churches. In 1842 in Saint John, NB, a choir and 22-piece orchestra performed part of Haydn's *The Creation*, and in October 1845 at two Toronto concerts (conducted by J.P. *Clarke and J.D. *Humphreys) oratorio excerpts, including 'The Horse and His Rider' from Handel's *Israel in Egypt*, were performed. In May 1858 the first complete performance of Haydn's *The Creation* was given by the Hamilton (Ont) Philharmonic Society, and in June of that year what appears to have been the first performance of Handel's *Judas Maccabaeus* was given in Toronto by a 160-voice choir under the direction of Rev G. Onions.

There were several premieres in the last 30 years of the 19th century. Excerpts from Sterndale Bennett's *The Woman of Samaria* were presented in Toronto in 1877. The *Toronto Philharmonic Society under F.H. *Torrington gave Mendelssohn's *Elijah* in 1874 and *St Paul* in 1876 and the Toronto premiere of Gounod's *Redemption* in 1882 and *Mors et vita* in 1886 with Lilli Lehmann as a soloist in the latter. According to Hector *Charlesworth the *Mors et vita* performance preceded the New York premiere by 20 years.

The *Montreal Philharmonic Society (1877–99) gave regular oratorio presentations, many of them local or Canadian premieres. Included were such works as Schumann's *Paradise and the Peri* (1885), Haydn's *The Seasons* (1887), and Beethoven's *Christ on the Mount of Olives* (1893). In London, Ont, the choir of Knox Church gave in 1885 what possibly was the first Canadian performance of Sullivan's *The Prodigal Son*.

Other choirs which gave oratorio performances during the late 19th century included the Berlin (Ont) Philharmonic and Orchestral Society, the Choral Societies of Hamilton and Toronto, the *Mendelssohn Choir of Montreal, the New Westminster (BC) Choral Union, the Ottawa Philharmonic Society, the Sacred Harmonic Society of Hamilton, and the Saint John (NB) Oratorio Society.

While the oratorio declined somewhat in popularity in the 20th century, performances continued to be given regularly, particularly in larger cities. Coleridge-Taylor's *The Atonement* was premiered in Canada in 1904 by the Calgary Philharmonic Society. Torrington conducted a repeat of Gounod's *The Redemption* at *Massey Hall in 1906 with Emma *Albani as a soloist. Elgar's *The Dream of Gerontius* was given its Canadian premiere by the *Montreal Oratorio Society in 1906. The *Association chorale St-Louis-de-France presented Massenet's *Marie-Magdeleine* in 1907 and Pierné's *La Croisade des enfants* in 1909. The first Montreal performance of Franck's *Les Béatitudes* was given by the *Association chorale Brassard in 1921; the first Montreal performance of Honegger's *Le Roi David* by the *Association des chanteurs de Montréal in 1928. The *Toronto Mendelssohn Choir gave the Canadian premieres of Walton's *Belshazzar's Feast* in 1936 and Penderecki's *St Luke Passion* in 1971 and performed Vaughan Williams' *Sancta civitas* in 1932 (first Toronto performance) and Honegger's *Joan of Arc* in 1958, in addition to its innumerable performances of *Messiah* and the Bach *St Matthew Passion*. The *Toronto Jewish Folk Choir sang several oratorios, including Jacob Schaefer's *Biro Bidjan* and *Di Tzvei Brider*, in 1946 and 1960 respectively, and an abridged version of Handel's *Joshua* in 1952. Tippett's *A Child of Our Time* was given its Canadian premiere in 1946 by the *Winnipeg Philharmonic Choir. The choir also gave the North American premiere of Penderecki's *Dies irae (Auschwitz Oratorio)* in 1978 with the *Winnipeg SO. During its existence (1951–66) the *Montreal Bach Choir gave many performances of Bach's *St Matthew Passion*, *St. John Passion*, and *Christmas Oratorio*. The *Vancouver Bach Choir has performed Berlioz' *L'Enfance du Christ*, Honegger's *Le Roi David*, and G. Welton *Marquis' *God and a Child*, the last of which it commissioned and premiered in 1962.

Other 20th-century choirs which have perpetuated oratorio are the *Disciples de Massenet (Montreal), the Edmonton Choral Society, the *Halifax Choral Society, the *Kitchener-Waterloo Philharmonic Choir, the *Winnipeg Oratorio Society, and the *Montreal Elgar Choir.

See also Christmas; Cycle of Musical Festivals of the Dominion of Canada; Easter, Lent, and the Passion; Masses; Oratorio, Canadian (composition and performance); Te Deum laudamus.

(MMl, NM)

Oratorios, Canadian (composition and performance). Large-scale choral-orchestral works, usually on religious, often biblical, texts, but not from the liturgy. In character their librettos may be dramatic-narrative (as in such prototypes from the classics as Bach's *Passions*, Haydn's *The Creation*, and Mendelssohn's *Elijah*) or dramatic-contemplative (as in Handel's *Messiah*). The typical oratorio is laid out in a pattern of choruses and chorales interspersed with recitatives, arias, duets, and trios sung by the solo voices, the whole prefaced by an orchestral overture. Occassionally there are orchestral interludes. Oratorios have been staged, but staging is uncommon; they are done almost invariably in concert style, without action, scenery, or costumes. The particular conditions under which oratorios have been composed and performed in Canada – for and in monasteries, convents, churches, and concert halls – require the admission of organ, piano, and even, latterly, electronic sounds as accompaniment to the voices, as well as the full orchestra of tradition.

The difference between a large cantata and a small oratorio is hard to determine, but normally a cantata uses smaller, more various forces, attempts to fill a smaller dramatic canvas, and admits a much wider latitude in form.

It has been asserted that Alexis *Contant's *Caïn* (1905, and premiered that year) was the first Canadian oratorio. Though it probably was the largest and most imposing work of its kind to have been produced at that time, it in fact was preceded by Frantz *Jehin-Prume's *Oratorio à Léon XIII* (1886; no record of performance), Eva Rose *York's *David and Jonathan* (performed twice in 1887 in Belleville, Ont), and Hugh *Clarke's *Jerusalem* (Presser 1890; composed in Philadelphia). Other early oratorios include Napoléon *Crépault's *La Communion des saints* (performed in Quebec City ca 1880) and Roberta Geddes-Harvey's *Salvator* (C.W. Thompson 1907; premiered in 1912 in Guelph, Ont). *Invoke Her Name with Praise*, a 45-minute oratorio by Cyril C. O'Brien, had its premiere in Halifax, NS, in 1940.

After 1950 some Canadians have produced hybrid works which combine elements of oratorio with elements of other genres, eg, *Ridout in his 'dramatic symphony' *Esther* (1952, premiered that year at the *RCMT under Ettore *Mazzoleni), Paul *McIntyre in his 'melodrama-cantata' *Judith* (1958, premiered in 1959 at the *Vancouver International Festival, with Lois *Marshall in the solo role), Leon *Zuckert in his 'choreographic oratorio' *In the Gleam of the Northern Lights* (1974, commissioned by the Shevchenko Musical Ensemble), and *Anhalt in his 'musical tableau in seven sections on the life of Marie de l'Incarnation,' *La Tourangelle* (1975, premiered that year in Toronto by the sopranos Mary *Morrison and Roxolana *Roslak, the mezzo-soprano Phyllis *Mailing, the tenor Albert *Greer, the baritone Gary *Relyea, and the CBC Festival Orchestra and Choir under Marius Constant).

Among the numerous cantatas, near-oratorios, quasi-oratorios, and oratorio hybrids, the list of clear examples of the genre seems short. The ensuing one, alphabetical by composer, attempts to be representative but cannot claim to be complete (or even authoritative as far as it goes, because of the unavailability of some of the scores for perusal and confirmation). Titles preceded by numbers are discussed in the text following the list.

*Bissell, Keith 1 / *The Passion According to St Luke* 1970
*Boucher, Lydia *L'Oeuvre d'Esther Blondin* 1949
*Chotem, Neil *The Song of Solomon* (radio oratorio) 1951
*Clarke, F.R.C. 2 / *Bel and the Dragon* 1954
Clarke, Hugh 3 / *Jerusalem* 1890
Contant, Alexis 4 / *Caïn* 1905; 5 / *Les Deux Âmes* 1909
*Couture, Guillaume 6 / *Jean le Précurseur* 1912–14
Crépault, Napoléon *La Communion des saints* ca 1880
Geddes-Harvey, Roberta 7 / *Salvator* 1907
Higgin, Clifford *Calvary* ?
*Hooper, Lou 8 / *Ruth* 1920
*Horner, Ralph *St Peter* ?
Jehin-Prume, Frantz *Oratorio à Léon XIII* 1886
*Kunz, Alfred *The Big Land* 1967; 9 / *The Creation* 1972
*Lamoureux, Alfred *La Tragédie d'Esther* ?; *La Samaritaine* ?
Lemieux, J.-L. 10 / *Les Prémices* or *Les Saints Martyrs canadiens* 1947
*Milette, Juliette 11 / *Leur Maison* 1945
O'Brien, C. *Invoke Her Name with Praise* 1940
*Poynter, A. 12 / *The Great Commission* 1963
*Talbot, Robert *Évangéline* ?
*Wilson, Charles 13 / *The Angels of the Earth* 1966
York, E.R. *David and Jonathan* 1887

The works of Crépault, Higgin, Horner, Lamoureux, and York were performed or published (the Higgin published by Breitkopf & Härtel, and performed in London under Sir Henry Wood), but scores have not been located. Those of Lemieux and Milette are known to exist but were not available for study. At least three full-scale orchestrally accompanied oratorios (*Caïn*, *Les Deux Âmes*, and *Jean le Précurseur*) by Quebec composers are of some reputation, and *Caïn* has been performed outside the province (Victoria, BC, in 1980). Other such works may lie in the libraries of churches and religious orders in Quebec, some quite possibly deserving to be brought to light.

Thirteen individual oratorios, twelve of which were available for perusal, are considered in terms of text, forces required, structure, and idiom, followed by evaluation.

1 / Bissell's *The Passion according to St Luke* (Waterloo, 1973). The text is taken from St Luke's gospel, with additions from Wilde, Donne, Bridges, Heber, and the Sussex Mummers' Carol. The scoring is for soprano, alto, two tenor, two baritone, and bass soloists, four-part choir, children's choir, organ, and full orchestra. The seven sections of the work treat the road to Jerusalem, the decision of Judas, the Last Supper, the agony in the garden, the betrayal, Pilate's court, and the Crucifixion and death. Though the work is in a basically tonal 20th-century idiom, it is not so much tonal relations as melodic fragments which unify the structure. The mildly dissonant style proceeds vertically, in harmonic units, rather than by the interaction of contrapuntal lines. As a whole, the work is skilful, singable, and comprehensible. The dissonances – somewhat arbitrary in effect – may derive from Britten, but their relations with one another produce a frequently French-impressionist sound. The work had its premiere at St Paul's Church, Toronto, in 1971 under the direction of the composer.

2 / F.R.C. Clarke's *Bel and the Dragon*. The text comes from the complete apocryphal book of the same name, described in the Apocrypha as 'cut off from the end of [the book of] Daniel.' The scoring is for soprano, tenor, and baritone soloists, double chorus, and full orchestra. Eight leitmotifs, identified in the score, are used in the creation of an overall ternary form, the separate but similar stories 'Bel' and the 'Dragon' constituting the outer sections, a 'triumph' sinfonia providing the middle. The tonal procedures show the influences of Elgar in Daniel's 'nobilmente' triumph music, of Vaughan Williams and Walton in the more harmonically vigorous 'Bel' and 'Dragon' music, and of *Willan in the final Alleluias. Written as a doctoral exercise for the *U of Toronto, the work is generally skilful, showing only occasionally the relative inexperience of the composer at the time of writing.

3 / Hugh Clarke's *Jerusalem* (Presser, 1890). The text is from the scriptures, and the scoring is for soprano, alto, tenor, and bass soloists, vocal sextet, mixed choir, and full orchestra. The form rests on a traditional interlocking key structure, and the idiom is homophonic. This is a strongly made work capable of taking its place in the repertoire, though there is no record of a performance in Canada.

4 / Contant's *Caïn*, in three parts: La Haine, Le Sang, and La Promesse. The text is by Brother Symphorien. The scoring is for soprano, alto, tenor, baritone, and bass soloists, mixed choir, and full orchestra. The traditional interlocking key structure is handled adroitly, and there is some melodic cross-reference though not enough to constitute a major element in the construction. The idiom is of the 19th century, moderately chromatic. The composer's strong melodic, harmonic,

and rhythmic senses are impeded by a text vacillating between poetry and doggerel.

5 / Contant's *Les Deux Âmes*. The work is a setting of a poem by Henri Roullaud and is scored for narrator (a spoken role), tenor and baritone soloists, mixed choir, and full orchestra. The structure's clear definition rises from the close interrelation of keys. The narrative begins with a spoken prologue by an unidentified voice over a continuation of the tonality of the overture. The chorus then represents the Voice of the Groves (B flat), replied to by the Guide (tenor, E flat), and the Traveller (baritone, B flat). A similar alternation – of voices (cities, streams, rocks), Guide, and Traveller – continues until the return of the spoken narrative as an epilogue. The idiom, again, is traditional, moderately chromatic. Both text and music are of high quality, and the work is worthy of retention in the repertoire.

6 / Couture's *Jean le Précurseur*. The libretto is a poem by Albert Lozeau based on a prose text of Antonio LeBel. The scoring is for tenor (l'Historien), baritone (le Précurseur), two soprano, two mezzo-soprano, alto, and two bass soloists, choir, and full orchestra. (The composer states, however, that the five female roles may be reduced to two, the seven male roles to four). The work is laid out in three self-contained sections: The Birth (of Christ as well as of John the Baptist), the Prophecy, and The Martyr. The double-tonality unit (G/E) of the opening reappears strongly in the peroration of part III and ends with the B flat which first appeared toward the end of part I and reappears during part II and at the end of part III. There are other tonal cross-references of smaller orders. The musical idiom is simple, strengthened by references to plainsong and by modal harmonic turns. The music is not infrequently bland to the danger point, but the more massive choral movements show considerable strength, and the elegiac elements contain areas of striking beauty.

7 / Geddes-Harvey's *Salvator* (C.W. Thompson, Boston, 1907). The text is drawn from scripture, with verses by Neale, Havergal, Gerhardt, Milton, Klugh, Heber, and Montgomery. The extant vocal score calls for soprano, contralto, tenor and bass soloists, choir, and organ or piano. It is not known whether an orchestral score exists. The structure has respectable internal symmetries. The musical style is traditional and melodically derivative. In view of the unimaginative quality of the work's melody, harmony, and rhythm, the structure is surprisingly strong. Alas, music cannot live by structure alone.

8 / Hooper's *Ruth*. The text is drawn from Ephesians, the Book of Ruth, Psalm 65, and Psalm 147. The score calls for baritone (Narrator), two soprano, one alto, and one tenor soloists, choir, and small orchestra. Tonally, the work is organized in B flat with conventional oppositions internally, and the musical idiom is traditional. Though he was trained academically, the composer was primarily a jazz musician, and the free flow of the music, melodically, harmonically, and rhythmically, pays tribute to that influence. It has not followed, however, that this combination of merits does justice to the simple beauty of the text, though a conductor (Alan *Reesor) who directed a performance in 1977 stated, 'There are some very exciting moments in it.'

9 / Kunz' *The Creation*. The text is by Laurence Cummings. The scoring is for electronically amplified bass (Narrator), two soprano, and one alto soloists, four-part choir, and full orchestra. The structure depends on the seven-section text (Litany, In principio, Lumen de Lumine, The Elements, Life, God said, In the Image of God, and The Long Sabbath) rather than on either tonality or melodic reference. The largely static harmonies in varying degrees of dissonance combine with vocalises, unvoiced sounds, and aleatoric procedures. The piano is used in experimental ways (eg, wrist-to-elbow sound clusters on the keyboard, and the use of a steel bar and fingernails on the strings).

10 / Lemieux's *Les Prémices*. The libretto is by Arthur Charlebois, a teacher of Lemieux (Brother Barnabé) and himself an oratorio composer. The work is scored for soloists, choir, and two pianos. It is laid out in three sections: Les Sources, Le Temple, and Le Couronnement. The idiom, judging from the small fragments available for study, is remarkable for its directness and expressiveness of innocence. Occasional twists of impressionism perhaps cloud the innocence without increasing the expressiveness. Charlebois has described 'unity and variety' as 'the dominant characteristics' of Lemieux's style.

11 / Milette's *Leur Maison*. The score was not available for study, but the composer (whose religious name is Sister Henri-de-la-Croix) supplied the ensuing information. The work is for choir or double-choir, organ, and piano and is designed in four parts: La Fondation, La Maison menacée, La Maison agrandie, and La Maison vivante. Choral movements alternate with spoken passages supported by accompaniments based on liturgical themes. The title of the work refers to a vision which came, in France, to the founder of the Canadian religious order the Holy Names of Jesus and Mary. In the vision she was encouraged by the Blessed Virgin with the words 'It will be my house and that of my Son.' The oratorio was performed first in 1944, for the centenary of the founding of the Canadian order.

12 / Poynter's *The Great Commission, Part I*. The composer prepared his own text, incorporating quotations from scripture. The score calls for baritone (the Christ), soprano, two mezzo-soprano, contralto, two tenor, and baritone soloists, choir, and full orchestra. The second section is built on E modal minor, in a mirror-like series of tonalities. D modal minor, with which the work begins, reappears briefly during the mirror procedure, and it could be argued that this creates an interlocking structure (D minor/E minor, both modal). The idiom mixes modal, tonal, and whole-tone procedures. An impression of objectives not wholly realized is created.

13 / Wilson's *The Angels of the Earth*. The text is by Wilson MacDonald. The score calls for male and female narrators and soprano and baritone soloists, choir, and a moderate orchestra with, however, a large percussion section. The work is in 16 sections, each named for an angel (The Angel of the Apple Blossom, The Angel with the Dark Hood, The Angel Which Is a Little Child, etc, ending with The Angel of Love). This essentially tonal work in 12-tone idiom – using mildly clashing, reiterated superimpositions of simple intervals – was written for the Canadian centenary, and for performance by the *Bach-Elgar Choir of Hamilton, Ont, under the composer's direction. The premiere took place 19 Jun 1967 at Guelph, Ont, with the soprano Mary Morrison and the baritone James Bechtel as soloists. The text is long-drawn-out and at times platitudinous, and the composer's workmanship, though skilful, is not consistently imaginative enough to sustain a two-and-a-quarter hour contemplative work.

(GGrg, HK, KW)

Orchestral composition. A discussion of the extent and type of orchestral composition in Canada from its beginnings to the 1970s.

1 Before 1900
2 Hints of new influences in the early 20th century
3 Establishment of an orchestral repertoire in the 1940s and 1950s
4 New sounds and techniques with a Canadian flavour
5 The state or orchestral composition and performance

See also Composition competitions; Composition for ensemble teaching; Concertos and concertante music; Film scores; Impressionism; Incidental music; Neoclassicism; Twelve-tone technique.

1 BEFORE 1900. Orchestral compositions by Canadians have been produced mainly in the 20th century and particularly after 1950, but there was orchestral writing as early as Joseph *Quesnel's light opera **Colas et Colinette*, performed in 1790, and Quesnel is said to have written symphonies. In 1863 another French immigrant, Antoine *Dessane, wrote a *Suite* for orchestra which displays the influence of César Franck. Both Léandre-Arthur *Dumouchel and Calixa *Lavallée are credited with symphonies which have not been found. (Eugène *Lapierre in his biography of Lavallée says that a symphony may have been performed in 1874.) A performance of Guillaume *Couture's *Rêverie*, a lyrical mood piece, did take place in Paris in 1875, and this work was published by Girod soon after the performance. It was the only Canadian orchestral work to be published before the turn of the century.

Composers during the 19th century wrote very few symphonic pieces, as efforts to form orchestras of any size in Canada rarely were successful. As a consequence musicians could not acquaint themselves with the standard repertoire, or gain experience in trying and hearing orchestral combinations. Most Canadian orchestral composers created works for foreign orchestras, eg, W.O. *Forsyth in his *Romanza*, played in Leipzig in 1888, and Clarence *Lucas in the overtures and operettas performed in England in the 1890s and later.

2 HINTS OF NEW INFLUENCES IN THE EARLY 20TH CENTURY. Orchestral organizations became more prevalent in Canada in the early years of this century, but works for orchestra of symphonic proportions remained rare. The immigrants Douglas *Clarke, Donald *Heins, Leo *Smith, and Allard de *Ridder wrote descriptive symphonic poems, as did the Canadian-born Alexis *Contant, whose *L'Aurore* (1912) contains some striking dissonant textures, and *Champagne, whose *Hercule et Omphale* (1918) is in the tradition of Saint-Saëns. The *Trois Préludes* (1912–15, for piano) by Rodolphe *Mathieu are remarkable in their orchestral version. The third one, *Une Muse*, foreshadows Webern's Klangfarbenmelodie technique (the changing of instrumental colours within one held note or one strand of melody) and is virtually atonal. Another work that was avant-garde for its time, the *Piano Concerto No. 2* by Colin *McPhee, left its Toronto audience bewildered in 1924.

The beginning of the folksong movement as a basis for Canadian composition was marked by Ernest *MacMillan's *Two Sketches for Strings* (1927), Claude Champagne's *Suite canadienne* (with chorus, 1927), and *Miro's *Symphonie canadienne* (early 1930s). The use of melodies that were modal and often metrically fluctuating forced these composers to depart occasionally from diatonic harmonic progressions and regular metres.

The orchestral output of the 1930s included two symphonies of more import than the many written as doctoral exercises and possibly never performed: Percival *Price's *St Lawrence Symphony* (1932), which in fact was written as a doctoral exercise but also was performed, and Healey *Willan's *Symphony No. 1* (1936). Although the latter is traditional in form and much of its harmonic language is indebted to Wagner, there are traces of contrapuntal modal writing.

3 ESTABLISHMENT OF AN ORCHESTRAL REPERTOIRE IN THE 1940S AND 1950S. With the formation of the *CBC in 1936 and the *NFB in 1939 commissions and performances of orchestral works became more frequent. *Weinzweig began writing film scores and incidental music for radio plays in 1941 and also conducted, thus gaining a broad experience of orchestral practice. *Applebaum and *Rathburn followed this pattern later. *Ridout and *Brott also conducted for the CBC (and if the latter's ease in handling orchestral material probably owed more, in the long run, to his work as conductor of the *McGill Chamber Orchestra, which he founded in 1945, it should be remembered that by then he already had written three large and skilful orchestral works). A certain official timidity in the face of contemporary idioms, not to mention the high cost of copying, led the new commissioning agencies to request more short works than long. Champagne, however, realized the importance of major orchestral works in any significant national repertoire, and in his *Symphonie gaspésienne* he created a tone poem in a wide variety of orchestral timbres coupled with melodies that contain characteristic modules of folksong, without exact quotations. He also encouraged his pupils to write for orchestra.

Another area into which the orchestral repertoire was able to expand in the 1940s was ballet music. Several dance companies, each with directors who also were ambitious and competent choreographers, attained a stage of maturity at about that time, and with it came a desire for original music to dance to. The Winnipeg (later Royal Winnipeg) Ballet commissioned Walter *Kaufman's *Visages* and Robert *Fleming's *Chapter 13* in 1947, the Ballets Ruth Sorel of Montreal Jean *Papineau-Couture's *Papotages / Tittle-Tattle* in 1949, and the Volkoff Canadian Ballet John Weinzweig's *Red Ear of Corn* in 1949; such commissions initiated a repertoire of rhythmic-dramatic, economically scored works which was augmented steadily if not extravagantly in the ensuing three decades. (See Ballets.)

When the *CLComp compiled the *Catalogue of Orchestral Music* in 1957, 233 pieces were included, of which most had been written since 1940 and particularly during the years 1950 to 1953. A wide variety of styles is evident in this music as the influences of Bartók and Stravinsky become ever more evident along with a continuing neo-romanticism. Two prolific composers for orchestra – Violet *Archer and Jean *Coulthard – did, in fact, study with Bartók, though it may be said that both show his influence less overtly than do many who did not. In the works of Papineau-Couture the influence of Stravinsky, although transmuted into his own distinct style firmly based on polyphony and the ideal of a strong structure, can be seen in the evolution from neoclassicism to serial procedures in the *Pièce concertante No. 3* (1959). Weinzweig, who had been using 12-tone series, or parts of series, as sources of motives for over a decade, began to have fellow explorers in the materials and procedures of dodecaphony in his pupils Harry *Somers and Harry *Freedman, while Clermont *Pépin and Serge *Garant (both Champagne pupils) discovered serialism through works of Boulez and Stockhausen during their Parisian sojourns of the early 1950s. Other compositional styles entered Canada with the European immigrants Oskar *Morawetz (homophonic neo-romanticism), S.C. *Eckhardt-Gramatté and Talivaldis *Kenins (polyphonic neo-romanticism), Otto *Joachim (free serial writing), and Istvan *Anhalt (strict serial writing). It was in the mid-1950s that the music of Webern and his followers began to have an impact on Canadian composition. Barbara *Pentland's *Symphony for Ten Parts* (1957) reflects Webernian influence in its soloistic scoring for chamber orchestra, pointillism, and Klangfarbenmelodie. Subsequently this trend – modified, be it said, by a variety of other influences including the teaching of Nadia Boulanger, Olivier Messiaen, and Bernard Wagenaar and the ideas of John Cage and Edgard Varèse – yielded a large repertoire for chamber orchestras and ensembles. Among those who contributed to it were *Adaskin, Applebaum, *Beckwith, *Beecroft, *Buczynski, *Cherney, *Dolin, Fleming, Garant, *Glick, *Hambraeus, *Hétu, Kenins, Papineau-Couture, Rathburn, *Mather, *Schafer, *Schudel, Somers, *Symonds, *Turner, and *Wilson.

4 NEW SOUNDS AND TECHNIQUES WITH A CANADIAN ACCENT. In the 1960s the colour contrasts of the post-Webern school were explored, particularly in new percussion effects with instruments from the East, Latin America, and Africa. Varèse's influence is reflected in the percussion-only section of Roger *Matton's *L'Horoscope* (1958) and in the superimpositions of block sonorities that occur in works of François *Morel, Pépin, occasionally André *Prévost, and others. Novel percussive effects were obtained by tapping the string and wind instruments while other timbres were procured by varied bowing, blowing, and fingering techniques, in works by Schafer and Gilles *Tremblay among others. The expanding world of electronic sounds entered symphonic music when Champagne included the ondes Martenot in *Altitude* (1959), a work inspired by the Rocky Mountains. In Somers' *Five Concepts for Orchestra* (1961) the predominant parameters are timbre, rhythm, and dynamics rather than melody or harmonic progression.

Meanwhile, US composers were exploring chance and indeterminacy, led by Cage and Feldman, whose works were introduced to Montreal by *Mercure and to Toronto by *Kasemets. In her *Symphony No. 4* (1959) Pentland had included a cadenza to be improvised by the percussionist. Improvisation was characteristic of jazz, and that genre's playing styles and rhythms had influenced Matton, Freedman, Morel, Weinzweig, and the Third Stream representative Norman Symonds, among others. Spatial indeterminacy and the dimension of sound is explored in Somers' *Stereophony* (1963) by prescribing the arrangement of the players both on stage and throughout the hall. To procure quasi-electronic sounds from the traditional orchestra Mercure devised some indeterminate notation involving time in *Lignes et points* (1964) but pitch, apart from microtonal inflections, is precisely given. More extensive aleatoric sections with indeterminate notation for durations appear in Joachim's *Contrastes* (1967).

Outstanding orchestral works resulting from centennial commissions again demonstrate the variety of techniques and styles to be found: Freedman's *Tangents*, in which the strings are divided into as many as 59 parts and solo instruments are rhythmically independent; Bruce Mather's *Orchestral Piece 1967*, with cluster chords and intervallic cells as its basic material, but written in a traditional notation; and Weinzweig's *Harp Concerto*, which includes new notational signs and serialization of time durations, pitch, and dynamics.

Two works of 1968 incorporate serial technique and aleatoric sections and call on the players to speak. Garant's *Phrases 2* is, in Xenakis' term, a heteronomous work with the orchestra divided in two, each half with a conductor who determines the order of the sequences. A tone-row is used, but some sequences are improvisational. Schafer's *Son of Heldenleben* uses two series and aleatoric elements but reflects another trend, the strong movement towards pastiche and parody through quotation. This work has an accompanying electronic tape. Previously (1967) Anhalt's *Symphony of Modules* and Peter Clement's *Cloud of Unknowing* have combined live with electroacoustic sounds.

In the 1970s orchestral composition reflected the continuation of the exploration of sounds. Robert *Aitken's *Spiral* (1975), which includes microphoned instruments in a variety of key noises and other effects, is an example. In it, colourful blocks of timbre are contrasted with delicate sounds, often evocative of Eastern music. The influence of the Orient was marked in Canadian music of the 1970s, and Aitken, Somers, Tremblay, Schafer, *Vivier, and *Weisgarber all travelled extensively in the East. Vivier's *Siddhartha* (1976) reflects this, as does Schafer's *East* (1972).

Because Canada is a mosaic of cultures one cannot expect a strong uniformity of style in its orchestral repertoire, but some recurring elements can be suggested as being primarily Canadian. Most serious Canadian composers have adopted an intellectual yet independent attitude to the dominant international trends; they have studied and absorbed, but have not necessarily copied. Canadian music does show some characteristics of the European directional emotive surge but more of the North American fondness for repetitive effects producing a relaxed mental withdrawal similar to that prompted by many Eastern musics. The Canadian tendency to a sparse texture supporting a long, expressive line has been noted frequently. Such characteristics frequently are set off by bold use of silence or by sections which give the effect of immobility. Weinzweig's *Dummiyah* (Silence) (1969) and Pépin's *Quasars* (1967), two works that are otherwise dissimilar, nevertheless both illustrate to some degree these elements. Another characteristic present in Canadian music after Somers' combination of tonality and atonality in the 1950s is the willingness of composers who write in a free 12-tone style to allow tonal centres to occur. As Tremblay has pointed out, the overtones do not support in pitch the 12-tone technique, so he combines elements of serialism with a structure that is centred on the harmonics of a particular note, as exemplified in *Fleuves* (1976).

5 THE STATE OF ORCHESTRAL COMPOSITION AND PERFORMANCE. The continuing output of orchestral works (which in the third quarter of the 20th century has exceeded that of solo and chamber pieces) is an indication of the healthy atmosphere. Nadia Boulanger and Olivier Messiaen have been influential teachers abroad, but composers born after 1925 have been mainly Canadian-trained, most often with either Champagne or Weinzweig. They, along with Mercure, Freedman, Morawetz, Tremblay, and others, are known as excellent orchestrators able to guide students in the analysis and use of orchestral sounds and textures.

The *Canada Council, formed in 1957, has been an important source of commissioning funds, as have the CBC, the (later) arts councils of the provinces, and the orchestras themselves. Along with its support to orchestras the Canada Council recommends a 10 per cent Canadian representation in programming. In the 1978–9 season at least six of the major orchestras achieved this percentage, presenting 31 different compositions of which 12 were premieres. Of these, few would be published but through the CBC a larger proportion gradually would become available through recordings.

Among the most frequently performed Canadian orchestral works have been Archer's *Fanfare and Passacaglia*, Brott's *Spheres in Orbit*, Champagne's *Danse villageoise*, Freedman's *Images* (impressionistic poems on three Canadian paintings), *Gellman's *Symphony No. 2*, Hétu's *Symphony No. 1*, Kelsey *Jones' *Miramichi Ballad* (based on folksongs of New Brunswick), MacMillan's *Two Sketches*, Matton's *Mouvement Symphonique II*, Mercure's *Pantomime*, *Kaleidoscope*, and *Triptyque*, Morawetz' *Carnival Overture* and *Overture to a Fairy Tale*, Morel's *Antiphonie* and *L'Étoile noire (Tombeau de Borduas)*, Papineau-Couture's *Pièce concertante No. 2*, Pentland's *Symphony for Ten Parts*, Pépin's *Guernica*, Prévost's *Évanescence*, Ridout's *Fall Fair*, Schafer's *Son of Heldenleben* and *East*, Somers' *Suite for Harp*, *Fantasia for Orchestra*, and *Picasso Suite*, Turner's *Opening Night (Theatre Overture)*, and Weinzweig's *Divertimento No. 1* and *Symphonic Ode*.

BIBLIOGRAPHY

Canadian League of Composers. *Catalogue of Orchestral Music* (Toronto 1957)

Beckwith, John. 'Recent orchestral works by Champagne, Morel and Anhalt,' *CMJ*, vol 4, Summer 1960

Canadian Annual Review (Toronto 1960–)

Canadian Music Centre. *Catalogue of Orchestral Music at the Canadian Music Centre* (Toronto 1963); rev enl *Catalogue of Canadian Music for Orchestra* (Toronto 1976)

Desautels, Andrée. 'The history of Canadian composition 1610–1967,' *Aspects of Music in Canada*

Beckwith, John. 'What every US musician should know about contemporary Canadian music,' *Mcan*, 29, final issue 1970

Canadian Music Centre. *Catalogue of Canadian Music Suitable for Community Orchestras*, compiled by Jan Matejcek (Toronto 1971)

Hepner, Lee A. 'An analytical study of selected canadian orchestral compositions at the mid-twentieth century,' unpubl PH D thesis, New York U 1972

Gillmor, Alan. 'Contemporary music in Canada,' *Contact*, Summer 1975

Beckwith, John. 'A festival of Canadian music,' *Musicanada: A Presentation of Canadian Contemporary Music* (Ottawa 1977)

Schulman, Michael. 'The Canadian symphonic hit and miss parade,' *Mcan*, 36, Aug 1978

Catalogue of Canadian Composers

Contemporary Canadian Composers / Compositeurs canadiens contemporains (EK)

Orchestras. Next to the opera performance the orchestra concert, especially the symphony-orchestra concert, represents the most complex, most exacting, and, at a professional level, most expensive form of music-making in the non-commercial field – non-commercial because the finest orchestra, playing year-round to full houses at the highest feasible ticket prices, cannot earn as much as it costs. Needless to say, the development of an orchestra which can produce a top-level concert with dependable regularity depends on favourable artistic, social, and economic conditions, having directly to do with the number of people, the per-capita income, the musical tradition, and the educational facilities of that orchestra's home city. Canada, with its relatively few

An unidentified Montreal orchestra, 1867

large cities, the great distances and extreme variation in density of population between those cities, and its climate-dictated tradition of grappling with physical necessities before satisfying aesthetic ones, has been slower to develop fine orchestras in great numbers than has its densely populated, vastly wealthier neighbour to the south. Nevertheless, despite the continuing elusiveness of ideal conditions for its production, and despite Canadian history's numerous demonstrations that artistic excellence cannot be sustained without financial support, much glorious playing has been produced by Canadian orchestras.

By 1980 there was little of the world repertoire of orchestral music that had not been performed with high competence and musical integrity by Canada's best orchestras. To be sure, only a few years earlier such a claim could not have been made. Many veteran concert-goers may be surprised to learn that as late as 1967 (Canada's centenary) a section player in a major Canadian orchestra did not devote most of his professional time to that orchestra or earn the bulk of his living from it. That is the case, however, and it is the reason for the avoidance of the word 'professional' in *EMC*'s descriptions of most orchestras and the preference for the more explicit 'full-time' or 'part-time,' 'major' or 'community.' By 1980 the Canadian orchestras financially able to hire a full complement of players on a 52-week contract, guaranteeing each a living wage in return for the first claim on his time (eg, daytime weekday rehearsals, regular evening weekday concerts) still could be counted on one hand, with possibly a finger to spare (the TS, the MSO, the NACO, the Vancouver SO), after which practical compromise was the rule, even with the seven other major orchestras: eg, an annual players' contract agreement for the full orchestra, but for 27 weeks instead of 52 (Quebec SO), or an annual agreement for a 'nucleus' of 35 players (Ontario's London SO) with the complement necessary for a romantic symphony hired on a 'per-service' basis (an agreed fee per rehearsal and concert) when possible and as needed. The remainder of Canada's more than 100 orchestras (the 1979–80 ACO / OFSO *Directory of Canadian Orchestras and Youth Orchestras / Annuaire des orchestres et orchestres des jeunes canadiens* lists 95 excluding the countless school orchestras, but there are notable omissions, especially among chamber orchestras and long-lived radio orchestras) were part-time to a greater or lesser degree or were avowed community orchestras. A few were on the verge of initiating contractual arrangements with some or all of their players. Some of the community and youth orchestras paid only their conductors. Between the extremes lay a wide variety of arrangements. All were subject to conditions in their communities and to the imperatives and priorities of the Canadian economy and its attendant politics, which had developed an orchestra support system different from that of Europe (outright state support) and the USA (massive private support). All were linked through that support system.

For other articles in *EMC* related to orchestras and orchestra performance see Broadcasting; Concert halls and opera houses; Concerts; Conductors; Youth orchestras.

1 HISTORY. Though in the 20th century Canadian musical life centred around the symphony orchestra, until the late 19th century orchestras in Canada were subordinate to theatres and choral societies. They tended to be put together from whatever players were available, to assist with incidental music for plays, to accompany oratorios or cantatas, or just to contribute an overture, a symphonic movement, or an aria accompaniment to the typical 'Concert of Vocal and Instrumental Music' of the day. Such orchestras relied heavily on military bands for their brass and wind players and sometimes had to send to Boston, Buffalo, or some other US city for an essential player who could not be found or 'tolerated in substitution' by someone on another instrument.

In Quebec City ca 1790–1800 there were subscription concerts at which symphonies or concertos by J.C. Bach, Haydn, Pleyel, and Mozart were played, but one wonders whether the instruments used were those suggested by the composers or whether everything within a certain range was given to clarinets, as seems to have been the case in performances there of **Colas et Colinette* in 1807. In at least one instance, though, a very remarkable orchestra was assembled: 'A Grand Performance of Sacred Music,' 26 Jun 1834 under Stephen *Codman, boasted more than 60 players – 22 violins, four violas, six cellos, one double bass, eight flutes, four clarinets, four bassons, four french horns, four trumpets, one trombone, a serpent, a tuba, and two 'double drums.' But this was not typical and certainly was not sustained. *Torrington's orchestras in Montreal in 1868 and Toronto after 1877, *Couture's Montreal Société des symphonistes (1878), the Victoria Amateur Orchestral Society (1880s), and Winnipeg's Apollo Club (1880s) tried valiantly to assemble and train amateur enthusiasts, but the results inevitably were uneven.

It was not until Ernest *Lavigne returned from Europe (where he had been principal cornet with the Roman Zouaves) and established bands in Quebec City and later in Montreal that disciplined instrumental ensembles emerged. Encouraged by the success of the *Bande de la Cité, which gave its first concerts in the mid-1870s, Lavigne formed an orchestra, tempting a number of musicians from Belgium with the prospect of work in the summer at the new *Sohmer Park (opened 1889) and in the winter at a conservatory which was being planned. Though the conservatory did not materialize and some of the Belgians returned to their homeland, a good number stayed, among them the *Goulet brothers, J.-J. and Jean (J.-J. had been the concertmaster of Lavigne's orchestra). After the demise of a significant but short-lived *Montreal Symphony Orchestra formed by Guillaume Couture in 1894, Goulet established from the remnants a second MSO, which made its debut in the 1897–8 season and flourished thereafter for 20 years.

In 1897 Max *Weil, a Leipzig-trained US musician who had joined the Halifax Cons in 1893, led a *Halifax Symphony Orchestra in works of his own and in Schubert's *Unfinished Symphony*. The orchestra survived several seasons.

In 1903 in Quebec City Joseph *Vézina established the Société symphonique de Québec with players from the remarkable *Septuor Haydn as a nucleus, and this proved to be the most durable of Canada's early orchestras, continuing under Vézina's direction until his death in 1924 and gradually being transformed over the years into the major orchestra still playing as the *Quebec SO in 1980.

A string orchestra formed in Ottawa under Donald *Heins became the first Ottawa SO and survived about 20 years.

In 1906 at the *TCM Frank *Welsman assembled an orchestra which, two years later, became the first *Toronto Symphony Orchestra to perform regularly for as long as 10 years; it lasted until 1918 and gave some 18 concerts each season, many with substantial programs which included complete symphonies. By 1914 it had performed Beethoven's third, fourth, fifth, seventh, and eighth symphonies, Tchaikovsky's fourth, fifth, and sixth, Schubert's '*Unfinished*,' Mendelssohn's '*Scottish*,' and Dvořák's '*New World*.'

Around the turn of the century several western cities established amateur orchestras: a Vancouver Symphony Orchestra in 1897 conducted by Adolf Green; a Winnipeg Orchestral Society under Alexander Scott and a later one in that city under Gustav Stephan; and others, in Regina under Frank *Laubach, in Edmonton under Vernon *Barford, and in Saskatoon and Moose Jaw. Max Weil, who had made such an impression in Halifax, formed an orchestra in Calgary in 1913, importing some professional players from the USA, and the concerts were said to be of fine quality, but the costs were too high for the Calgary of that day, and the orchestra did not last out the war years. World War I, indeed, interrupted the evolution of Canada's orchestras in every city save Ottawa and Quebec. Some – notably the *Montreal Orchestra, the MSO, the TSO, and the *Vancouver SO – became established or re-established after the war; but the largest number of major orchestras and significant community and chamber orchestras came into being between 1940 and the early 1970s. In *EMC*, individual entries for the major orchestras and some of the large community orchestras operative throughout the 1970s, and also for some significant orchestras no longer playing in that era, give details of their antecedents and histories.

For orchestras playing in 1980 and regarded as 'major' at that time see Quebec Symphony Orchestra, Toronto Symphony (founded 1923 as the New SO), Vancouver Symphony Orchestra (founded 1933 under Allard *de Ridder), Montreal Symphony Orchestra (founded 1934 as Concerts symphoniques de Montréal; first regular conductor, Wilfrid *Pelletier), London Symphony Orchestra (founded 1937 as London Civic SO under Martin *Boundy), Winnipeg Symphony Orchestra (founded 1948 under Walter *Kaufmann), Hamilton Philharmonic Orchestra (founded 1949 under Jan Wolanek), Edmonton Symphony Orchestra (founded 1952 under Lee *Hepner), Calgary Philharmonic Orchestra (founded 1955 under Henry Plukker), Atlantic Symphony Orchestra (founded 1967 under Klaro *Mizerit), and National Arts Centre Orchestra (founded 1969 under Mario *Bernardi).

For large community orchestras active throughout the 1970s see Regina Symphony Orchestra (founded 1927), Saskatoon Symphony Orchestra (founded 1931), Victoria Symphony Orchestra (founded 1941), Kitchener-Waterloo Symphony Orchestra (founded 1945), Windsor Symphony Orchestra (founded 1947), St Catharines Symphony Orchestra (founded 1948), Kingston Symphony Association (founded 1954), and Thunder Bay Symphony Orchestra (founded 1960 as the Lakehead SO).

For chamber orchestras which flourished in the 1970s see McGill Chamber Orchestra (founded by Alexander *Brott in 1939 as the *McGill String Quartet), Chamber Players of Toronto (first concerts 1969 under Victor Martin), the Orchestre de chambre Pierre-Morin (founded 1970 by *Morin), Manitoba Chamber Orchestra (founded 1972 under Ruben *Gurevich), and the New Chamber Orchestra of Canada (founded 1973, described in the entry on its founder, Bill Phillips).

For radio orchestras playing in the 1970s see CBC Vancouver Chamber Orchestra (founded 1938 under John *Avison), CBC Winnipeg Orchestra (established 1947 under Eric *Wild), CBC Quebec Chamber Orchestra (founded 1954 under Sylvio *Lacharité), and CJRT Orchestra (founded 1975 under Paul *Robinson).

For significant orchestras which did not reach or did not survive the 1970s, see Calgary Symphony Orchestras (four successive organizations, the first founded 1910), Montreal Orchestra (1930–41 under Douglas *Clarke), Promenade Symphony Concerts (Toronto Philharmonic Orchestra, 1934–56 under Reginald *Stewart), Montreal Women's Symphony Orchestra (1940–late 1960s under Ethel *Stark), Little Symphony of Montreal (1942–52 under Bernard *Naylor and others), Ottawa Philharmonic Orchestra (1944–60, founded by Allard de Ridder), 'The Little Symphonies' (CBC radio-program orchestra fl 1948–65 in Montreal under Roland *Leduc), Halifax Symphony Orchestra (1949–67, founded as an opera orchestra under Alfred *Strombergs), CBC Symphony Orchestra (1952–64 under Geoffrey *Waddington), Heinz Unger (York Concert Society, 1952–6), Hart House Orchestra (1954–71 under Boyd *Neel), and New Brunswick Symphony Orchestra (1962–7 under Janis *Kalnins).

2 SUPPORT SYSTEMS. Despite the obvious differences in budget and station, virtually all Canadian symphony and chamber orchestras, major or community, full-time or part-time, high-budget or low-budget, have depended on the same support systems. The largest major orchestras and the smallest community orchestras have assembled volunteer boards of directors who undertake responsibility for raising the necessary money for their operations, for appointing and supporting their conductors, and for appointing and supporting paid or volunteer administrative staff. In the smaller orchestras, the volunteer boards often are themselves the administrative staff and find themselves directly involved in ticket campaigns, arranging for halls, wrestling with performance rights, preparing applications for grants, organizing publicity, printing programs, and even writing program notes. Behind the scenes of any symphony concert, however modest, exists an elaborate network of exacting tasks undreamed of by the man who merely buys his ticket and listens to the concert. Behind the activities of a major orchestra lie thousands of hours of volunteer and paid time by a bewildering profusion of administrators and committees.

The most intensive and unremitting effort of the orchestra board and its committees is, of necessity, fund raising. Canada by 1980 still had neither condoned full state subsidy of orchestras in the European tradition nor marshalled the enormous private subsidies that created and have sustained the orchestras of the USA. Instead, it evolved a system under which, in the 1970s, the orchestras were expected to take in at the box office about 50 per cent of the money they needed, and to raise from private donations and corporate donations about 25 per cent more. The remaining 25 per cent could be requested from some combination of what usually are described as 'the three levels of government, civic, provincial, and federal,' though in fact at the federal level the source of grants has been not a department of the federal government but an independent crown corporation, the *Canada Council, consisting of a paid staff of administrators and a council of volunteer citizens appointed to decide on grants. Some of Canada's provincial arts-support bodies have existed similarly detached from government itself. Traditionally the Canada Council has provided operating grants to only the major orchestras (excluding the NACO, which is alone among Canadian orchestras in being funded directly by the federal government itself) and to a very few of the largest community orchestras and successful chamber orchestras (in the latter half of the 1970s the Kitchener-Waterloo SO, the Regina SO, the Saskatoon SO, the Thunder Bay SO, the Victoria SO, the McGill Chamber Orchestra, and the Chamber Players of Toronto). The several provincial departments of culture and arts councils have provided subsidies for small community orchestras as well as the major ones in their jurisdictions. City governments generally have been less consistent, some providing regular grants and some providing none. Throughout the 1970s all 'government' grants had in common that they must be applied for and justified annually and were considered only in relation to healthy box-office receipts and vigorous fund raising from the private sector. In addition to standard procedures for fund raising, many orchestras have resorted to unusual and imaginative means, particularly through their volunteer women's committees who, over the years, have raised astonishing amounts through rummage sales, dream auctions, fashion shows, book sales, the operating of second-hand stores, and countless other projects and stratagems. Through conferences, workshops, and publications the orchestral federations *ACO and *OFSO – Canada's equivalent to the USA's American Symphony Orchestra League – have devoted themselves largely to pooling experience and solving problems directly related to orchestra support systems.

3 PLAYERS, PLAYER TRAINING, PLAYER PROTECTION. The number of indigenously trained career orchestral musicians has increased with the number of orchestras able to offer annual contracts or even uncontracted regular paid work, but in at least the area of string playing the number has not increased apace. Report upon report has deplored the apparent impossibility of populating the string sections of the country's best orchestras with Canadian-trained violinists, violists, and cellists of international standard, and the necessity of importing players year after year. Though there have been remarkable individual teachers with remarkable individual pupils, and some with several, there has been no national system for the discovery, segregation, and fine training of orchestral musicians comparable, for instance, to the system epitomized by that in effect at the USA's Curtis Institute (where a gifted child is admitted as young as possible and trained completely, as an absolute educational priority, and free of

charge, to play his instrument with the aim of becoming a professional orchestral musician at a high level), and to such systems in both the east and west of Europe. By 1980, however, a number of positive steps had been taken towards the more serious and systematic professional education of musicians in general and orchestral musicians in particular. Practical orchestrally oriented string training programs were receiving new emphasis across the country – at the *Community Music School of Greater Vancouver, at the *U of Alberta and in the advanced training courses at the *Banff SFA, at *Brandon U, at the *U of Toronto and the *RCMT, at the *Écoles Sacré-Coeur et Mitchell de Sherbrooke, and at *Laval U, where the classes of the *Société musicale Le Mouvement Vivaldi had been organized. At the same time, school, youth, and training orchestras had proliferated, many of them adjuncts of the major orchestras and the large community orchestras, and staffed by instructors who also were leading players in those orchestras. By 1980 also, the *NYO – the noted summer school for the elite of gifted young instrumentalists – had been in existence for 20 years and had done much to refine the thinking of music educators on the subject of instrumental training priorities.

On another front, the musicians' union (American Federation of Musicians of the United States and Canada – see Unions) played a significant role in stabilizing the player's economic environment by establishing fee parameters and professional rules. In 1975, AF of M members of Canadian orchestras formed their own professional association, the Organization of Canadian Symphony Musicians / Organisation des musiciens d'orchestres symphoniques du Canada.

4 CONCERTS AND REPERTOIRE. In the 1979–80 orchestra season the major, community, and chamber orchestras listed in the aforementioned ACO / OFSO directory gave close to 1400 concerts. The busiest major orchestras each gave between 120 and 150. The most modest community orchestras, rehearsing perhaps an evening a week during the fall and winter, prepared from 3 to 6.

By far the largest part of the music heard at orchestral concerts in Canada has been from the standard repertoire – Mozart, Beethoven, and the Romantics – but the major orchestras have programmed at least the showier specimens of 20th-century music – eg, Stravinsky's *Sacre du printemps*, Bartók's *Concerto for Orchestra*, Schoenberg's *Verklärte Nacht*, Berg's *Violin Concerto*, Hindemith's *Mathis der Maler Symphony* – and a careful number of less well established pieces by such composers as Boulez, Copland, Messiaen, Nono, Penderecki, Tippett, and Xenakis. The earlier or less radical established moderns – Britten, Debussy, Delius, Mahler, Nielsen, Prokofiev, Ravel, Sibelius, Strauss, Vaughan Williams – have had somewhat more attention; and during the 1970s, after the Canada Council's imposition of a 10 per cent Canadian program content quota, the 14 orchestras receiving Canada Council assistance began to look more frequently and even more searchingly at the orchestral music of Canadian composers. In a paper titled 'The state of Canadian orchestras' and delivered 10 Dec 1979 to the Canada Council, Franz *Kraemer, head of the council's music section, pointed out that in the 1978–9 season '60 different works (by 47 [Canadian] composers) were given at least one performance by an orchestra,' but added that 'most, if not all, of the works performed are part of the established Canadian repertoire. Too few orchestras commission new pieces.' (Some do, however, as may be seen from their entries in *EMC*, and not only those orchestras subsidized by the council.) In the statistics included in the same report it was interesting to note that of the 47 composers whose works had been performed, four – *Morawetz, *Prévost, *Schafer, and *Somers – each had three works performed by orchestras that season, while *Mercure had six.

5 TOURING. In overnight runouts, short regional circuits, national tours, and extended trips abroad, Canadian orchestras during the 1970s became more mobile than ever before. For community orchestras, concerts in nearby towns were at once outings for the players, a search for wider box office, a means of expanding regional influence, and a justification for increased financial assistance from the province. For the major orchestras touring was a psychological spur – giving the players a healthy change in routine and their regular audiences the opportunity to find they missed them when they were not at hand – and the most effective and practical kind of public relations, turning a name into a reality for potential audiences and purchasers of recordings. Tours by major orchestras also came to be recognized as a stimulus to international goodwill, partly because of the immense glamour and dignity of a well-disciplined body of musicians, and partly because of the symphonic repertoire's power to stride across the barriers of language.

However, touring by Canadian orchestras goes back to 1903, when the Goulet MSO travelled to Moncton and Halifax to play at the *Cycle of Musical Festivals. The MSO under Pelletier visited Quebec City in 1935. The TSO under *MacMillan went to Montreal in the mid-1940s and to Detroit in 1951. The Montreal Women's SO under Ethel Stark played in Carnegie Hall in 1947 (the first Canadian orchestra to do so). The Edmonton SO under Lee Hepner went to Fort Saskatchewan in 1956. The Hart House Orchestra and Glenn *Gould, under Boyd Neel, gave a concert at the World's Fair in Brussels in 1958 (playing Bach, Britten, *Ridout, and Morawetz). The McGill Chamber Orchestra under Alexander Brott gave some concerts in the USA in 1959. Probably orchestral visits about and abroad were made before those. Touring in the broad sense, however, got under way in 1960, when the Hart House Orchestra made a 32-concert five-week tour of western Canada, its program including *Blackburn's *Suite* for string orchestra, which had been commissioned for the tour. In 1962 the MSO under its new conductor, Zubin Mehta, with Jacques *Beaudry as associate conductor, made its first European tour (and the first such tour by any Canadian orchestra), giving concerts in Paris, Vienna, Moscow, and Leningrad. It was to make two more European tours in that decade and the next – one of Belgium, France, and Switzerland under Mehta in 1966, and one of France, Switzerland, England, and Czechoslovakia in 1976 under Rafael Frühbeck de Burgos – as well as a tour of Japan in 1970 under Franz-Paul *Decker. But its leading contemporary, the TSO (TS), though it began more gradually (a Carnegie Hall debut in 1963 under *Susskind, and concerts in Port Arthur and Winnipeg in 1964), became the busier touring orchestra during those same decades, visiting Great Britain (London, Glasgow, Cardiff) in 1965 under Seiji Ozawa; touring Ontario and visiting Expo 67 during the 1966–7 season; touring Japan in 1969 and giving concerts in Ottawa and New York that same year under Ozawa; travelling to England, Holland, Austria, and Germany in 1974 under Kazimierz Kord; and touring the Atlantic provinces in 1976, China and Japan in 1978, and Alberta, Saskatchewan, British Columbia, and California in 1979 under Andrew Davis. Its visits to Carnegie Hall became annual, beginning in 1975.

The McGill Chamber Orchestra under Brott maintained a steady touring record – the USSR in 1966, the USA in 1967, Switzerland and France in 1973, Mexico in 1974, and Poland, Czechoslovakia, and Hungary in 1978. The Hart House Orchestra under Neel did not survive into the 1970s, but it made a notable tour of England, Belgium, and Scandinavia in 1966. The Vancouver SO under Kazuyoshi Akiyama made extended tours of Japan in 1974 and of Canada in 1976. In Alberta the Calgary Philharmonic made regional sorties, but the Edmonton SO was more adventurous, touring the Yukon in 1957–8, accompanying the National Ballet on a western Canadian tour in 1968, giving concerts in Winnipeg, Prince George, and Whitehorse under Lawrence Leonard in 1971, and touring the Yukon and the North West Territories under Pierre *Hétu in 1973. The CBC Vancouver Chamber Orchestra under John *Avison toured Saskatchewan in 1967, and 26 players from the orchestra toured western Canada, the Arctic, Alaska, and Montana as the Vancouver Radio Orchestra in 1969 and ventured as far east as Ottawa. The Victoria SO under Laszlo *Gati toured inland British Columbia in 1977 and has visited cities in Alberta and the Yukon. The Hamilton Philharmonic Orchestra under Boris Brott and the London SO under Clifford *Evens visited many southern Ontario towns in the 1970s, and the philharmonic appeared at the Algoma, Guelph Spring, and Shaw festivals, Ontario Place, and the Olympics in Montreal. The Winnipeg SO, under Piero Gamba, made eastern Canadian tours in 1970 and 1978 and has visited many Manitoba and nearby US communities.

Perhaps the busiest of all Canada's orchestras have been two of the most recently created: the Atlantic SO, which, as a way of life, under Klaro Mizerit and his successor Victor Yampolsky, has toured the cities of the Atlantic provinces as it was created to do in 1968; and the NACO under Mario Bernardi, which, two years after its founding in 1969, began the regular tours that have made it a household word in all parts of Canada (it combed the west in 1971, 1974, and 1977, the east in 1973 and 1975) and a name to be remembered in Europe (France, Great Britain, Italy, Poland, and the USSR in 1973, Germany and Italy, including Sicily, in 1978), the USA (1975), and Mexico (1975).

Among the most interesting major touring projects to be undertaken by a Canadian orchestra was announced in 1980. The Quebec SO under James De Preist was engaged by Noranda Mines to make a series of visits to remote Quebec towns, beginning 23 Sep 1980, with a program of specially composed music by Quebec composer-arrangers. The music was to be derived from Quebec traditional and folk music, and Roger *Matton was engaged as ethnomusicologist for the project. Four communities were to be visited on each tour.

Among Canada's many other orchestras, a surprising number have toured, helping to create a flourishing environment for the development of orchestral concerts in communities other than their own, often in communities which have no other opportunity to hear such concerts live. The foregoing has surveyed only the most visible of the many touring programs that have been undertaken.

6 THE COMMUNITY ORCHESTRA IN THE 1970S. There is more to be said about the community orchestras of Canada than will be evident in *EMC*'s individual entries on the largest of them. Of the 42 listed as members of ACO and OFSO in the 1979–80 *Directory of Canadian Orchestras* 28 were in Ontario, 6 in British Columbia, 2 each in Alberta and Sas-

katchewan, and 1 each in Quebec, Nova Scotia, Prince Edward Island, and Newfoundland. No community orchestras were listed for Manitoba or New Brunswick (though in fact a few existed outside the ACO fraternity). For the 1979–80 concert-giving year 11 of the 42 orchestras planned modest seasons of two-to-four concerts on annual budgets of less than $15,000; 22 of them offered more ambitious seasons on budgets of less than $100,000; 7 provided diversified and sophisticated seasons on budgets of less than $500,000; and 2 – the Kitchener-Waterloo SO and the Victoria SO – had highly developed programs and were on the verge of designation as major orchestras, though their 1979–80 budgets remained under $1 million.

The activity and expenditure of a community orchestra inevitably are linked to the size of population in the community it serves. Put truistically, it is unusual for a small community to be able to afford a high-priced orchestra, or for a major city not to support a large community orchestra. Specific factors of tradition and economy introduce variables, however. For instance, the industrially developed regions of Canada have more community orchestras than the agrarian and maritime regions, but within the industrial region a fast-growing industrial city without a university may not have as well-developed a symphony orchestra or symphony audience as a smaller, older, slower-growing university city. In 1980 the burgeoning industrial city of Oshawa, with a population of 120,000, budgeted less than $100,000 for its orchestra, while the venerable university city of Kingston, with a population of 60,000, budgeted considerably more. The development of a community orchestra often has been inhibited, also, by the nearness of a major orchestra. Many examples come to mind. The Windsor SO, though it plays on in a large industrial city of some 250,000 inhabitants, exists in the shadow of a major US orchestra – the Detroit SO, which plays just across the river. The Ottawa SO remains a community orchestra in a city of 300,000 because Ottawa is also the home of a full-time orchestra, the NACO. The several admirable community orchestras surrounding Toronto (the East York SO, the Etobicoke Philharmonic, the Mississauga SO, the North York SO, the York SO) cannot raise large funds and unlimited audiences from the same metropolitan population which supports and attends the $4.5 million-per-annum TS. Conversely, some orchestras gain an advantage from isolation. The role of the Thunder Bay SO, as the only large community orchestra in the vast and sparsely populated area between the Toronto-Hamilton-London-Kitchener axis and Winnipeg, has been acknowledged by higher-than-average funding from the *OAC.

Many of Canada's community orchestras have been shaped by socio-geographic conditions. The Deep River SO (founded 1952) was developed by the nuclear scientists of that small northeastern Ontario community to provide its inhabitants with 'a musical alternative to the northern service of the CBC' and may be the only amateur orchestra anywhere with a membership made up largely of PH Ds in physics. The International SO of Sarnia and Port Huron has drawn its governing board and its players from both sides of the US-Canadian border and given all of its concerts in both cities. The Ottawa SO has co-existed gracefully with the NACO, playing in the same magnificent auditorium (the Opera of the *NAC) and planning its program to complement the more complex fare of the full-time orchestra. The aforementioned community orchestras of suburban Toronto have provided steady playing opportunities and even modest fees for the many advanced student instrumentalists and serious amateurs in the Toronto area. The Okanagan SO has represented at the community-orchestra level the same principle that the Atlantic SO has represented at the major-orchestra level; that is, it has served not one city but several in its region (the Okanagan Valley), with players and board members from each and audiences in each.

By the 1970s most of the community orchestras of Canada had professional musicians conducting them, or were giving gifted young conductors the nearest thing to those invaluable training podiums, the orchestra pits of the small European opera houses, that Canada could provide. Many community orchestras also employed professional administrators, and some had professional players regularly in the principal chairs and in other key positions. Most offered their audiences guest appearances by leading Canadian soloists.

7 SOME CANADIAN COMMUNITY ORCHESTRAS. By 1980 no net fine enought to capture detailed information on all of Canada's community orchestras had been devised. The ensuing list (arranged chronologically within provinces), provides available data on a number of those without entries of their own in *EMC*, but makes no claim to be comprehensive. Orchestras whose only present existence is in history have been included when sufficient information has been found. Others of the kind have been mentioned in the entries on the cities where they flourished.

British Columbia

Penticton Orchestral Society; 1921–ca 1950s; 25–30 members. Conductors included the founder, H.K. Whimster 1921–late 1930s, W.J. Harris 1942–6, and Mr Mossop and Mr Ireland 1946–early 1950s.

New Westminister Symphony Orchestra; begun in 1944; about 50 members. First called the New Westminster Civic Orchestra. Conductors, in order, have included T. Bevan, Jascha Galperin, Gregori *Garbovitsky, Gideon Grau, Willem Bertsch, Leonard *Camplin, Cardo *Smalley, and Bryan *Gooch.

Nanaimo Symphony Orchestra; begun in 1949; 35–40 members. Conductors have included the founder, M. Kuschner 1949–62, succeeded in turn by J.L. Getgood, Heinz Kilian, Ed Gibney, Bryan Gooch, John Lewis, Thomas Petrowitz, Robert Cooper, Bruce Dunn, and Ian Hampton. The orchestra commissioned and premiered *Adaskin's *Nootka Ritual* in 1974. It presented four concerts in the 1979–80 season.

Okanagan Symphony Orchestra; begun in 1959; 55–60 members. Rehearses and performs in Vernon, Kelowna, Penticton, and Salmon Arm. The founder and first conductor, Willem Bertsch, was followed in 1963 by Douglas Talney and in 1964 by Leonard Camplin. Camplin in 1978 was given the official title of resident conductor. The Okanagan Symphony Choir, established in 1970, was directed by Jocelyn *Pritchard. Imant Raminsh succeeded Pritchard in 1978. The orchestra gave 16 concerts in the 1979–80 season.
BIBLIOGRAPHY

Edds, Jack. 'Have instrument – will travel: the story of the peripatetic musicians of the Okanagan orchestra,' *OCan*, vol 5, Jan 1978

Vancouver Philharmonic Orchestra; begun in 1965; 65 members. Established as the Vancouver Metropolitan Orchestra. Conductors have included Annette Coates, Leonard Camplin, Paul Douglas, and Jerry Dormer. Under the last-named, the orchestra gave five concerts in 1979–80.

New Caledonia Symphony Orchestra, Prince George; begun in 1971 as the New Caledonia Chamber Orchestra, with 23 members under Imant Raminsh. Kerry Stratton, appointed conductor of the enlarged orchestra in 1977, led it in 13 concerts during the 1979–80 season.
BIBLIOGRAPHY

Portman, Jamie. 'Community orchestra shows professional commitment,' *Calgary Herald*, 23 Mar 1979

Kootenay Chamber Orchestra, Kimberly; begun in 1975; 13 members and a resident string quartet. Conductor: Zdenek Kriz

Symphonie Canadiana, North Vancouver; 55–60 members; begun in 1975 as a summer orchestra and conducted by its founder, Yodandi Butt

Kamloops Symphony Orchestra; begun in 1976. James Verity, conductor until 1979, was succeeded by Robert Ryker.

Alberta

Crows Nest Pass Symphony Orchestra, Blairmore; 40 members in 1979. Begun in the early 1920s as a string ensemble and conducted until 1959 by Walter Moser. Other conductors have been Roy Upton 1959–71, Richard Burgman 1971–2, and Frank Edl 1972–6. Upton returned to the position in 1977.
BIBLIOGRAPHY

'Crows Nest Pass Symphony,' *Music in Alberta*, Spring 1974

Medicine Hat Symphony Orchestra; 45 members; begun in 1954 as the Medicine Hat Little Symphony and conducted until 1962 by Robert Thompson. Thompson's successor, Alex Shand, was followed by Larry Krantz in 1975, and the new name was adopted that year. In addition to playing for local musical theatre productions and giving concerts the orchestra has sponsored series of recitals by young performers.
BIBLIOGRAPHY

'Medicine Hat Little Symphony,' *Music in Alberta*, Spring 1974

Lethbridge Symphony Orchestra; begun in 1960; 60 members in 1978. Albert Rodnunsky, the founding conductor, served until 1966. Other conductors have been Kenneth Hicken, Peter Heyblom, Wilfred Woolhouse, Lucien *Needham 1970–6, and John Jackson, succeeded by Stewart Grant (the first full-time music director) in 1978. Norbert Boehm was hired as concertmaster in 1974. Besides giving regular concerts in Lethbridge, the orchestra plays in Fort Macleod, Pincher Creek, Taber, and other Alberta communities. A Symphony Chorus was formed as part of the Lethbridge Symphony Association, which also sponsors concerts and recitals by other performers.

Central Alberta String Orchestra, Red Deer; 45 members; begun in 1964. Conductors have been Antoinette Stuppard 1964–9, George Naylor 1969–77, George Ardois 1977–8, and Conrad Wolfe 1978–9. Naylor resumed the post in 1979. The orchestra customarily has given four concerts a season.

Grande Prairie College Community Orchestra; 12 players; founded in 1968 by Gerald Nelson, who conducted it 1968–72 and 1974–6. John Hancock was the conductor in 1973 and returned in 1978. The orchestra has given three concerts annually in the college auditorium.

Saskatchewan

See Regina SO; Saskatoon SO; see also Youth orchestras.

Manitoba

St James Concert Orchestra, Winnipeg; 20 members; founded in 1920 and conducted until 1974 by Fred Stanford. William Roberts succeeded Stanford as conductor.

La Sinfonietta de Saint-Boniface; 25–45 members; founded in 1928 by its only conductor, Marius *Benoist. It made its debut that year at the Walker Theatre assisting in the Cercle Molière production of Daudet's *L'Arlésienne* with Bizet's music. The orchestra, made up of both amateur and professional players, has given annual concerts. With the Société lyrique Gounod it presented the opera *Mireille* in 1935 and that composer's *Roméo et Juliette* in 1936. Other notable performances have included that of Benoist's *La Rencontre dans l'escalier* in 1952 and Berlioz' *L'Enfance du Christ* in 1955. A special concert 29 Nov 1978 at the Centre culturel Franco-Manitobain marked the orchestra's 50th anniversary.

St James Pops Orchestra, Winnipeg; founded in 1955 by its only conductor, William Lord. In 1979 it numbered 36 amateur and professional players who presented one public concert and several informal concerts each year.
BIBLIOGRAPHY
Lord, William A. 'St. James (Man.),' *CanComp*, 23, Nov 1967

Mennonite Community Orchestra, Winnipeg; 70–90 members; established in 1978. Its membership has been drawn from advanced music students at Winnipeg's two Mennonite colleges and from the community. The music directors of the colleges have alternated as conductors for the orchestra's annual series of six concerts. Bejamin *Horch, president of the Mennonite Community Orchestra Society, also founded and conducted the Mennonite SO 1943–55.

Ontario

Harmony Symphony Orchestra, Toronto; begun after World War I and conducted until 1933 by Arthur *Semple. It became an activity of the Harmony Masonic Lodge in 1922, but masonic sponsorship was dropped when women joined the orchestra, which thereupon became a self-supporting group of amateur players. Membership varied between 50 and 90. The orchestra gave between two and six concerts a season, many with guest soloists. With the development of other community orchestras in the Toronto area in the early 1970s, the Harmony SO disbanded. Conductors after Semple included, in turn, Maurice Dunmall, Leslie *Bell, Brian *McCool, James *Gayfer, Henry Rzepus, Stanley Clark, Francis J. Francis, and Alan Doremus.

Brantford Symphony Orchestra; organized in 1953 as the Brantford String Symphony under Harold Neal. (Frederick C. Thomas had conducted a 35-member Brantford SO that flourished throughout the 1920s.) The enlarged orchestra took the new name in 1954. In the 1970s local players made up about half the membership and professional musicians from other areas the other half. Annual series of from four to six concerts a season were given at the Capitol Theatre. Conductors have included Horace Beard 1956–62, Claude W. Keast 1962–8, and Walter *Babiak 1968–74, succeeded by Stanley *Saunders.

Deep River Symphony Orchestra; established in 1952. This 35-member orchestra was formed to provide musical activity for employees of the nearby Chalk River Nuclear Laboratories and their families. The orchestra has been augmented occasionally by visiting players (eg, members of the Petawawa Armed Forces Base band). Two or three concerts have been presented annually, some with guest soloists. The Deep River Choral Society has assisted at some performances. Conductors have included William J.L. Byers, David Ward, James Wegg, Robert Ryker, and Stephen van Heerden.
BIBLIOGRAPHY
'Deep River Orchestra,' *CanComp*, 25, Jan 1968

East York Symphony Orchestra, Toronto; begun in 1953 as the Bennington Heights Community Orchestra. It became the East York Community Orchestra in 1965 and adopted its third name in 1967. The 65 members have been drawn from among Toronto amateur players and music students. In 1965 the orchestra premiered Srul Irving *Glick's *Elegy for Orchestra* and in 1978 it devoted a complete program to works by Keith *Bissell, Samuel *Dolin, Elliott Feldman, Clifford *Poole, and Godfrey *Ridout. Resident conductors have included Milton *Barnes, Orval Ries, Harvey Sachs, David Gray, and Clifford Poole.

International Symphony of Sarnia and Port Huron, Sarnia, Ont, and Port Huron, Mich; begun in 1956 when the Little Orchestral Society of Sarnia (established in 1951) and the Port Huron String Ensemble joined to form the 55-member orchestra whose players and board represent both cities and whose concert series is performed on both sides of the border. Conductors have included the US musicians Harry Begian, Frederic Johnson, Carl Karapetiak, Arthur Stephen, and John Sweeney and, from the Canadian side, Harman Haakman 1959–60, Donald A. McKellar 1968–74, and David Gray 1974–7, succeeded by Brian Jackson.
BIBLIOGRAPHY
Carson, Judith Ann. 'A musical tale of two cities,' *OCan*, vol 3, Mar 1976

Oshawa Symphony Orchestra; begun in 1957 as a small amateur orchestra at Oshawa's O'Neill Collegiate. By 1968 the 60-member orchestra included local amateur musicians, some visiting professional players, and music students. The orchestra has performed in centres throughout the Durham region as well as giving annual series of concerts in Oshawa. Conductors have included Francis J. Francis 1957–63, Edward Oscapella Sr 1963–7, Jacob *Groob 1967–72, and Roy Cox 1972–9, succeeded by Winston Webber.
BIBLIOGRAPHY
'The Oshawa Symphony Orchestra,' *CanComp*, 27, Mar 1968
Chase, Christy. 'Oshawa Symphony: structured force of 63 people who give their spare time to entertain others,' *Oshawa Times*, 18 Mar 1978

Etobicoke Philharmonic Orchestra, Etobicoke (west of Toronto); begun in 1960 under the sponsorship of the recreation committee of Etobicoke township, the 65–70-member orchestra has drawn its membership from amateurs and music students. In 1978 five professional musicians were engaged for first-chair positions. The orchestra premiered Samuel Dolin's *Symphony No. 3* in 1977. It gave nine concerts in the 1979–80 season. The conductors have included Harman Haakman 1960–2, 1965–7, 1971–2, and 1973–4, Hans Bauer 1962–5, Samuel *Hersenhoren 1967–9, and Barry Gosse 1974–5, succeeded by Eugene *Kash.

Eastern Ontario Concert Orchestra; 55-member ensemble established in Belleville in 1961 by its first conductor, Stephen Choma, with amateur players drawn from seven communities in southeastern Ontario. Rehearsals were held first in Batawa, Ont, and concerts were given in Belleville, Trenton, Brighton, Stirling, Campbellford, Picton, Tweed, and elsewhere. Kerry Stratton, who became the conductor in 1976 following Choma's death, was succeeded by Bruce McGregor in 1978.
BIBLIOGRAPHY
'Eastern Ontario Concert Orchestra,' *CanComp*, 25, Jan 1968

York Symphony Orchestra, regional municipality of York (north of Toronto); established in 1961 as the Richmond Hill SO. It became the York Regional Orchestra and, in 1975, the York SO. It has drawn its 55 members from Aurora, Newmarket, Woodbridge, and King City and has endeavoured to give concerts in all these centres (a total of 8–10 concerts a season). Conductors have included Arthur Burgin, Philip Budd, and Clifford Poole.

Ottawa Symphony Orchestra / Orchestre symphonique d'Ottawa; established in 1965 as the Ottawa Civic SO (name changed in 1976). Its 65–75-player membership has included amateur, professional, and student musicians. The annual concert series was held first in Ottawa high schools, but in the early 1970s it was moved to the NAC. The *Ottawa Choral Society has performed with the orchestra. Conductors have included Clifford *Hunt 1965–6, Nicholas *Goldschmidt 1966–7, and James Coles 1969–75, succeeded by Brian *Law.

Huronia Symphony Orchestra, Barrie and Orillia; 45-member regional orchestra formed in 1966 by Muriel Leeper and Lloyd Tufford. John Montague was the conductor 1966–8. After Montague guest conductors were used until 1973, when Arthur Burgin assumed the directorship. By 1979 the orchestra was giving six concerts a season.

Oakville Symphony Orchestra; begun in 1967 as a 60-member amateur orchestra. By 1976 it was presenting six concerts a season. Conductors have been Kenneth Hollier 1967–73 and David Gray 1973–6, succeeded by Anthony Royse.

Peterborough Symphony Orchestra; 35–50-member amateur orchestra begun in 1967. It developed from a nucleus of string players led by Klemi *Hambourg. Besides its annual series of concerts in the city, the orchestra in the 1970s began giving concerts in Cobourg, Port Hope, and Lindsay. In 1977 the orchestra named professional musicians to the positions of concertmaster and principal cello. Conductors have been Brian Jackson 1968–72, Harvey Sachs 1972–5, and Bruce McGregor 1975–8, succeeded by Winston Webber.
BIBLIOGRAPHY
McGrath, Paul. 'Small city, big sound Messiah,' Toronto *Globe and Mail*, 3 Dec 1977

Sault Symphony Orchestra, Sault Ste Marie; established in 1969 by Lajos Bornyi, who remained its conductor until 1978. Under the auspices of the Sault Ste Marie International Assn, formed in 1974, the orchestra began to include among its 45 members residents of Sault, Mich. In 1978 John Wilkinson of the US city succeeded Bornyi as conductor.

North York Symphony; established in 1970 in the borough of North York (Toronto). The 95-member orchestra by 1980 included five professional players and was giving annual series of five concerts in Minkler Auditorium, Seneca College. Walter *Babiak, the orchestra's first conductor, was succeeded by Voltr Ivonoffski. William *McCauley assumed the position in 1973. Under McCauley an affiliated group of 60 amateur players, the North York Repertory Ensemble, was formed in 1975. The North York Philharmonic, another affiliate group of 40 professional players with Steven *Staryk as concertmaster, gave a series of four children's concerts in 1978 under McCauley's direction.

BIBLIOGRAPHY
McGrath, Paul. '... and some surprises from the amateur orchestra,' Toronto *Globe and Mail*, 5 Feb 1977

Mississauga Symphony Orchestra; 40-member community orchestra established in 1972 with a grant from the city of Mississauga. By 1979 it had 80 players, 5 of them professional, and presented 12 concerts a season. Boyd *Neel, the founding conductor, was succeeded by John Barnum in 1978.

BIBLIOGRAPHY
O'Toole, Lawrence. 'Symphony on a shoestring – playing just for the love of it,' Toronto *Globe and Mail*, 19 Nov 1977

Georgian Bay Community Orchestra, Owen Sound; established in 1972 for amateur musicians in the counties of Grey and Bruce. In addition to annual concert series in Owen Sound, performances have been given in other towns in the area. Conductors have included Hermon C. Dilmore, James White, and Eric Woodward.

Woodstock Strings; established in 1972 by a dozen local musicians. In 1979 the 30 players (mainly amateurs from the London-Kitchener-Woodstock area) presented nine concerts. Conductors have included Raymond Neal 1972–7 and Patrick Burroughs (beginning in 1977).

Fanshawe Community Orchestra, London; established in 1973 under the auspices of Fanshawe College. Orchestra members include teachers and students at the college and local amateur musicians. Bruce Richardson, the founding conductor, retained the position in 1980.

Nepean Symphony Orchestra, Nepean (Ottawa); 35 members; established in 1974 by James Wegg, who continued to conduct it in 1980.

University of Guelph Civic Orchestra, Guelph; established in 1974 by its conductor, Stanley Saunders. The membership of 50 has been drawn from among amateur, student, and professional musicians. Concerts have been given at War Memorial Hall on the university campus.

Sudbury Symphony Orchestra; established in 1975 by Metro Kozak with a nucleus of musicians who had been members of the orchestra of the Sudbury Philharmonic Society conducted 1962–73 by Eric Woodward. (A Sudbury orchestra, founded by Emil First in 1953, had amalgamated with the Philharmonic Society in 1962.) In 1980 the Sudbury SO was made up of amateur and student musicians. Stephen van Heerden succeeded Kozak as conductor in 1979.

BIBLIOGRAPHY
'Sudbury Philharmonic Society,' *CanComp*, 32, Sep 1968

North Bay Symphony Orchestra; established in 1977, with Robert Ryker as conductor. The 35 amateur musicians were drawn from the towns of the surrounding area. Concerts have been given in Sturgeon Falls and South River as well as in North Bay. Stephen van Heerden succeeded Ryker in 1979.

Quebec

Orchestre symphonique de Trois-Rivières; 40 members; founded in 1943. The original orchestra gave two concerts annually until its demise in 1949. Its conductors included Joseph Gélinas, Edwin *Bélanger, and Jean-Yves *Landry. In 1973 Daniel Swift established the Ensemble instrumental de Trois-Rivières, a chamber orchestra. Swift conducted until 1977, when he was succeeded by Gilles Bellemare. In 1978, with an enlarged membership and repertoire, the orchestra was renamed L'Orchestre symphonique de Trois-Rivières.

Symphonie laurentienne, Val-David; formed in 1978 by its conductor, Jean-Louis Lalonde; 25–30 members (amateur, student, and retired professional musicians). The orchestra has accompanied the Chorale de Val-David and the Chorale des Deux-Montagnes. It also participated in the 1979 Laurentian regional Choralies.

New Brunswick

See also New Brunswick Symphony Orchestra.

Edmundston Symphony Orchestra. Organized as a 42-member amateur orchestra in 1946. The conductor in 1955 was Georges Guerrette. The orchestra gave an annual series of concerts in Edmundston and also performed in Maine. No longer active

Nova Scotia

See also Halifax Symphony Orchestra.

Chebucto Orchestra, Halifax-Dartmouth; formed for amateur and professional musicians in 1975 under the auspices of the Nova Scotia Dept of Recreation. Kenneth *Elloway, the founding conductor, was succeeded by Brian March in 1980.

South Shore Concert Orchestra, Bridgewater; formed in 1975 under the auspices of the Nova Scotia Dept of Recreation. Robert Raines was the conductor in 1978.

Prince Edward Island

Prince Edward Island Symphony Orchestra, Charlottetown; founded in 1967. Conductors of the 50-member orchestra have included Thomas Hahn 1967–70, Alan *Reesor 1970–6, and William Bartlett, who was succeeded by Czeslaw Gladyszewski in 1979.

Newfoundland

Newfoundland Symphony Orchestra, St John's; founded in 1970 as the St John's SO with 50 members. Peter Gardner was engaged as concertmaster in 1971 and was conductor 1975–6. The orchestra's annual concert series has been given in the *Arts and Culture Centre. Conductors have included Ian Mennie 1970–5 and David Gray, who assumed the position in 1977.

GENERAL BIBLIOGRAPHY
Fricker, H. Cecil. 'The development of the orchestra in Canada,' *Twentieth Century*, 3 instalments, vol 1, Apr, May, Jun 1933
Adaskin, John. 'Radio production in relation to symphony broadcasting,' *CRMA*, vol 1, Apr 1942
MacMillan, Sir Ernest. 'Orchestral and choral music in Canada,' Music Teachers' National Association *Proceedings* (1946)
Pelletier, Wilfrid. 'Orchestras,' *Music in Canada*
Neel, Boyd. 'Small orchestras: musical need,' *SatN*, 19 Feb 1955
Canada Council. Annual Reports (Ottawa 1958–)
'Orchestras,' *CMJ*, vol 3, Winter 1959
Heinze, Sir Bernard. Private report to the Canada Council, Jun 1960
'Ontario Arts Council sponsors orchestra study,' *CanComp*, 10, Sep 1966
Schabas, Ezra. *Ontario Community Orchestras: A Report for the Province of Ontario Council for the Arts and the Ontario Federation of Symphony Orchestras* (Toronto 1966)
– 'The symphony orchestra: progress or decay?' *CanComp*, 16, Mar 1967
'Canada Council reports growth of music in Canada,' *CanComp*, 22, Oct 1967
Edds, John A. 'The case for the community orchestra,' *CanComp*, 26, Feb 1968
Sunter, Robert. 'Ontario orchestras,' *OpCan*, Feb 1969
Potvin, Gilles. 'Performers,' *Aspects of Music in Canada*
CMCentre. *Catalogue of Canadian Music Suitable for Community Orchestras* compiled by Jan Matejcek (Toronto 1971)
Kraglund, John. 'Ontario's 24 – yes 24 – symphonies on quick march,' Toronto *Globe and Mail*, 12 Feb 1972
ACO / OFSO. *Directory of Canadian Orchestras and Youth Orchestras / Annuaire des orchestres et orchestres des jeunes canadiens*, annual, begun 1975–6 (Toronto)
Winters, Kenneth. 'Canadian orchestras in growth,' *CMB*, 10, Spring–Summer 1975
'Orchestras tour Canada and Europe,' Touring Office *Bulletin*, vol 2, Oct 1976
Littler, William. 'Sunday symphonies: community musicians have high standards,' *Toronto Star*, 22 Jan 1977
Reid, Wendy. 'Community orchestras – a self-made success,' *Fugue*, May 1977
Waller, Adrian. 'From coast to coast; the sound of music,' *Reader's Digest*, Jul 1977
Lauzon, Norman. 'Les Ontariens sont-ils plus musiciens que les Québécois?' *Musique périodique*, vol 1, Mar 1977; transl Leonard Rosemarin, 'Is Ontario more musical than Québec?' *OCan*, vol 4, Sep 1977
Directory of Conductors in Canada / Annuaire des chefs d'orchestre au Canada (Toronto 1977)
Dzeguze, Kaspars. 'Sound of symphonies,' *Maclean's*, 26 Dec 1977
Waller, Adrian. 'Music's new awakening,' Imperial Oil *Review*, no. 6, 1977
'Bush-league Bach,' *The Canadian*, 25 Feb 1978
Schulman, Michael. 'The Canadian symphonic hit and miss parade,' *Mcan*, 36, Aug 1978
Thompson, Leslie. 'Pop! goes the orchestra,' *Music*, Dec 1978
Kraemer, Franz. *The State of Canadian Orchestras* (Ottawa 1980)
'Orchestra news letters,' *OCan*, vol 7, Mar 1980
Read, Merilyn. 'Some sympathy for symphonies,' *Maclean's*, 4 Aug 1980
Orchestra Canada, ACO / OFSO newsletter (Toronto, Oct 1973–) 1–6 / KW, 7 / PW

Orchestre de chambre Pierre-Morin. Ensemble of professional musicians – eight violins, two violas, two cellos, contrabass, and harpsichord – formed in Quebec City in 1970 by its leader, the cellist Pierre *Morin, initially to give a concert in the Anglican Cathedral with the harpsichordist Donald Thomson. The group has not received government subsidies as such, but Quebec's *Grand Théâtre has sponsored it for annual seasons of concerts: five in 1971–2 and four in subsequent years. The ensemble has given the premieres of several Canadian works: in 1973 *Images* by Brent Dutton, *Adagio* by Michel Meynaud (the winning work of a competition organized by the orchestra), and the *Concerto* for harpsichord by Pierick *Houdy (North American premiere); in 1974 *Distique* by Rénald St-Pierre; and in 1975 *Miroir fugace* by José *Evangelista (commissioned by the Grand Théâtre). MB-L

Orchestre symphonique de Montréal. See Montreal Symphony Orchestra.

Orchestre symphonique de Québec. See Quebec Symphony Orchestra.

Order of Canada. Highest civilian honour awarded in Canada. Established in 1967, the award is administered by the governor-general with the assistance of an advisory council and is granted to 'Canadian citizens for outstanding achievement and service to the country or to humanity at large.' Any living Canadian may be nominated for membership by any other Canadian. Initially a member of the Order either was made a Companion (CC, limited to 150 living persons) or was awarded the Medal of Service. (Until 1972 there was also a Medal of Courage, but it was never awarded.) In 1972 holders of the Medal of Service took the newly created rank of Officer (OC), and a third level, Member (CM), was introduced. Of the more than 1531 recipients of the Order of Canada by 1981, 87 represented the field of music (in the list below the date of investiture is given after the name).

COMPANION

Marius Barbeau 1967
Mario Bernardi 1972
Maureen Forrester 1967
Raoul Jobin 1967

Luc Lacourcière 1971
Sir Ernest MacMillan 1970
Lois Marshall 1968
Norman McLaren 1973
Wilfrid Pelletier 1968
Louis Quilico 1975
Harry Somers 1972
Jon Vickers 1969
Healey Willan 1967

OFFICER
Harry Adaskin 1975
Murray Adaskin 1981
Pierrette Alarie 1967
Anaïs Allard-Rousseau 1969
Louis Applebaum 1977
Edith Butler 1975
Norman Campbell 1979
Floyd Chalmers 1967
Jean Coulthard 1979
Lionel Daunais 1978
Pauline Donalda 1967
André Gagnon 1979
Serge Garant 1980
Herman Geiger-Torel 1969
Bobby Gimby 1968
Nicholas Goldschmidt 1978
Elmer Iseler 1975
Jean Lallemand 1968
Félix Leclerc 1971
Gilles Lefebvre 1967
Monique Leyrac 1968
Gordon Lightfoot 1971
Eric McLean 1975
John Mills 1980
Mavor Moore 1973
Anne Murray 1975
Boyd Neel 1973
John Newmark 1974
Jean Papineau-Couture 1969
Vida Peene 1970
Aline Hector Perrier 1968
Oscar Peterson 1973
Joseph Rouleau 1978
Léopold Simoneau 1971
Sam Sniderman 1976
Teresa Stratas 1972 (date of announcement, but not invested)
Arnold Walter 1972
John Weinzweig 1974

MEMBER
Frances Marr Adaskin 1977
John Avison 1979
Hélène Baillargeon-Côté 1973
Pierre Béique 1979
Jeannette Bock 1979
Alexander Brott 1979
Anne Campbell 1977
Jean Carignan 1975
Helen Creighton 1976
Raymond Daveluy 1980
Arthur Delamont 1980
José Delaquerrière 1975
Roger Doucet 1980
Jack Dow 1979
W. Allen Fisher 1974
Edith Fowke 1978
Clyde Gilmour 1975
Gertrude Constant Gendreau 1979
Ida Halpern 1978
Godfrey Hewitt 1976
Juliette 1975
Maryvonne Kendergi 1980
Mart Kenney 1980
Nicholas Koudriavtzeff 1973
Willie Lamothe 1979
Helen Law 1979
Roland Leduc 1980
Alan Mills 1974
Pipe Major Malcolm Nicholson 1978
Marie-Thérèse Paquin 1981
Charles Peaker 1974
Lyman Potts 1978
Ignatius Rumboldt 1975
Ethel Stark 1980
Adine Tremblay 1974
Antonio Tremblay 1974

Most of the recipients of the Order of Canada listed above have individual entries in *EMC*. Those who have not are listed in the index.

Orff-Schulwerk (Music for Children). Approach to music education conceived by the German composer Carl Orff (b 1895). It was developed in the 1920s and 1930s while Orff was music director of the Günther-Schule, a school of dance and music in Munich. The guiding principles were contained in his *Orff-Schulwerk* (Mainz 1930–5), of which revisions came later. The first of many foreign versions was *Music for Children* (Mainz 1956–61), an adaptation in English by Arnold *Walter and Doreen *Hall of the *U of Toronto. Orff's approach, developed for children but latterly used also with adults, is based on his belief that the easiest method of teaching music is to draw out the student's inherent affinities for rhythm and melody and allow these to develop in natural ways, leading the child by his intuition from primitive to more sophisticated expression through stages parallel to western music's evolution. Orff accomplishes this by means of a carefully planned program, beginning with speech patterns, rhythmic movement, and two-note tunes, then moving logically into pentatonic melody. Adult pressure and mechanical drill are discouraged. Improvisation is encouraged. Major and minor melody are introduced as the final stage of the program. Orff designed a special group of instruments, including glockenspiels, xylophones, metallophones, drums, and other percussion instruments to fulfil the requirements of the Schulwerk courses.

The Orff approach was introduced formally to North America by Doreen Hall (after special studies in Europe in 1954) in a demonstration in the summer of 1955 at the *RCMT. A course prepared by Hall was introduced in 1956 at the U of Toronto, and a summer course was begun in 1957 at the RCMT. An International Orff-Schulwerk Conference (in which Orff participated) was held at the U of Toronto in July 1962. The RCMT courses were lengthened in 1966 from two weeks to three and were revised to accommodate three levels of instruction leading to a teacher's certificate. They established the RCMT as the major centre for the dissemination of the Orff-Schulwerk method in North America.

Keith *Bissell pioneered the use of the method in the Scarborough schools in 1958, and by 1962 the other major Metropolitan Toronto school systems had adopted it. In 1963 the CBC broadcast the three-part radio series 'Living Through Music,' featuring children from Scarborough trained by Joan Sumberland. The series won an Ohio State Award for educational broadcasting. By the mid-1960s Orff programs were offered in Montreal by the Hungarian-born pianist-composer Gabor Bartha, who opened a studio in 1964, and by Miriam Samuelson at the *École normale de musique ca 1966. A graduate from the École normale, the harpist Donna Hossack, taught the Orff approach 1966–71 in Montreal and St-Lambert, and introduced it to adult classes in Vancouver when she moved there in 1971. In 1972 Carole Irvine-Kurz began giving Orff summer classes to 4-to-12-year-old children for *CAMMAC. Others involved in the spread of Music for Children in Canada include Trudy Le Caine, wife of Hugh *Le Caine and step-daughter of Arnold Walter, in Ottawa; Lois Berkinshaw, author of *Music for Fun, Music for Learning* (Toronto 1977), in Toronto; Sandra Davies at the *U of British Columbia; Jean Woodrow in Edmonton; Mourna-June Morrow, Edna Knock (see Georges *Little), and Beth *Douglas in Winnipeg; Nancy Vogan at *Mount Allison U; Mario *Duschenes in Montreal; and Doreen Coultas at *Memorial U.

Music for Children / Carl Orff Canada / Musique pour enfants, a national association made up of provincial chapters, was formed in 1974. Doreen Hall was the first president, followed in 1977 by Keith Bissell. A twice-yearly bulletin of the same name has promoted the association's aims, and conferences have been held in Toronto (1975), Winnipeg (1976), Ottawa (1977), and Vancouver (1978).

Though Music for Children is used in an increasing number of Canadian schools, there remain sceptics who criticize the relative neglect of early training in reading and technical skills and the absence of a clearcut teaching methodology. They also criticize the limited consideration of 20th-century idioms. Because of these shortcomings the Orff program's popularity with teachers is limited, and there are those who see its value rather as a supplement than as a basic study course. However, its influence on 20th-century music education is established.

BIBLIOGRAPHY
NL of C. Arnold Walter–Carl Orff correspondence (1953–70)
Walter, Arnold. 'Elementary music education: the European approach,' *CMJ*, vol 2, Spring 1958
Bissell, Keith. 'Carl Orff's Music for Children: a reply to the critics,' *Recorder*, vol 6, Oct 1963
Johnston, Richard. 'The word for the method is *zest*,' *Varsity Graduate*, Christmas 1963
Clark, Eileen. 'A report from the Orff Institute,' *Recorder*, vol 7, May–Jun 1965
Walter, Arnold. 'Orff Schulwerk in American education,' *Recorder*, vol 17, Dec 1974, Mar 1975
Hall, Doreen. 'Music for Children's past, present, future,' *Music for Children / Carl Orff Canada / Musique pour enfants*, 4, Feb 1976
Bissell, Keith. 'Orff, song and tradition,' ibid, 6, Jun 1977

FILM
Music for Children (NFB 1958) (KB)

Orford String Quartet / Quatuor à cordes Orford. Distinguished Canadian ensemble founded at the *JMC Orford Art Centre in 1965, encouraged by Gilles *Lefebvre, and coached by Lorand *Fenyves. The original members are Andrew *Dawes (first violin), Kenneth (John) Perkins (second violin; b Brockville, Ont, 8 Jul 1935, a pupil of Ivan Galamian and Fenyves and a former member of the *MSO), Terence Helmer (viola; b Kirkland Lake, Ont, 18 Jul 1940, a pupil of Geza *de Kresz, Kathleen *Parlow, Joseph Gingold, and Arthur Grumiaux), and Marcel St-Cyr (cello; b Quebec City 20 May 1938, a pupil of Lucien *Plamondon, Walter *Joachim, André Navarra, and Léo Koscielny). St-Cyr was succeeded in 1980 by Denis Brott (see Brott family).

The quartet gave its first concert 11 Aug 1965 at the centre. At the time of this quiet yet momentous debut the *Canadian String Quartet and the *Montreal String Quartet had disbanded and the way was open for a young and dedicated group to maintain the tradition. The Orford Quartet embarked immediately on a busy concert schedule arranged by the *JMC, making about 60 appearances a year in small Canadian towns and in the major music centres in Canada and abroad. Its

The Orford String Quartet with the original cellist

Carnegie Recital Hall debut 23 Nov 1967 drew critical acclaim and marked the beginning of an international career.

In the ensuing years the quartet performed throughout North America, and with the support of the *Canada Council or the Dept of External Affairs toured several times in Europe, visiting England, Scotland, Sweden, Holland, Italy, Rumania, Yugoslavia, France, Poland, Belgium, the USSR, and Tunisia. It has competed abroad – for instance, in the European Broadcasting Union's String Quartet Competition in 1974 in Stockholm, where it shared first prize with the Franz Schubert Quartet of Austria – and it has appeared at many festivals. It performed 15 Nov 1977 at the *Musicanada festival in London. It also played by invitation at *Expo 67, at the Montreal Olympics in 1976, and at the United Nations' Habitat Conference in Vancouver in 1976. It has given several recitals each season in Toronto, which became its home city in 1965. It became the quartet-in-residence at the *U of Toronto in 1968, and to mark the university's sesquicentenary as well as the 150th anniversary of the death of Beethoven it presented that composer's 16 quartets in a series at Walter Hall in 1977. The Beethoven cycle was repeated that summer as part of Festival Canada (*Festival Ottawa) at the *NAC, Ottawa. The quartet has given master classes and concerts in various music camps, especially its alma mater, the Orford Art Centre, and it served 1971–4 as the faculty at the Kelso Music Centre (near Oakville, Ont).

Critical reaction to the ensemble has been consistently enthusiastic. 'The members of the Orford Quartet ... have all the individual virtuosity and ensemble rapport to leave the impression that their only concern is with matters of interpretation' (John *Kraglund, Toronto *Globe and Mail*, 17 Jan 1977). The ensemble was awarded the 1975 *Molson Prize and received the *CMCouncil Awards in 1978 for the best Canadian chamber music recording (for Mendelssohn *Quartets No. 1 and 2*) and the best broadcast by a Canadian chamber music group (*Schafer, *Quartet No. 2 ('Waves')* 1977, on CBC radio).

By the late 1970s the repertoire of the Orford Quartet had become impressively broad, encompassing more than 125 works for quartet alone or quartet with other forces. While most of the repertoire was drawn from the traditional literature, there were also some Canadian works, the choice of which had been both representational and discriminating. At the end of the 1979 spring season the repertoire included quartets by *Adaskin, *Beckwith (recorded), *Cherney (No. 2), *Douglas, *Fleming, *Heard, J. *Hétu, von *Kunits, *Morawetz (No. 2), *Papineau-Couture (No. 2, recorded), *Pépin (No. 2, recorded), Schafer (Nos. 1 and 2, both recorded), *Somers (No. 3), *Weinzweig (No. 2, recorded; No. 3), and *Wilson. It also included pieces by *Dolin (*Portrait for Quartet*), *Freedman (*Graphic II*), *Glick (*Suite Hebraïque; Lamentations for Quartet and Orchestra*), *MacMillan (*Two Sketches for Strings*), Stephen Pedersen (*Novella*), Wilson (*Accordion Quintet*), and *Wuensch (*Accordion Quintet*). Nor have 20th-century foreign composers been neglected. In addition to the Bartók quartets and the usual Debussy and Ravel, Berg and Webern, the Orford's list offers quartets of Britten (No. 1), Carter (No. 2), Lutoslawski (No. 2), Penderecki (No. 2), Prokofiev (No. 2), and Shostakovich (No. 8), and numerous other pieces, eg, Crumb's *Black Angels*, Ives' *Three Pieces*, Kirchner's *Quartet and Tape*, Respighi's *Il Tramonto* (with mezzo-soprano), and Vaughan Williams' *On Wenlock Edge* (with tenor).

DISCOGRAPHY

Beethoven *Elegischer Gesang, Op 118; Quartet, Op 18, no. 4*. E.B. Guy sop, Rideout alto, T. Kelen ten, Turgeon bar. 1970. CBC SM-147
- *Quartet, Op 18, no. 4; Quartet, Op 18, no. 5*. 1976. CBC SM-359
- *Quartet, Op 59, no. 3*. 1977. CBC SM-324
- *Quartet, Op 130*. 1978. CBC SM-321
- *Quartet, Op 95; Quartet, Op 135*. 1978. CBC SM-322
- *Quartet, Op 59, no. 2*. 1978. CBC SM-323
- *Quartet, Op 132*. 1978. CBC SM-356

Beethoven *Quartet, Op 18, no. 5* – Brahms *Quartet, Op 51, no. 2*. 1970. CBC SM-153

Berg *Quartet, Op 3* – Haydn *Quartet, Op 76, no. 2*. 1967. CBC SM-95

Boccherini – Paganini – Scarlatti – Carcassi. Lagoya guit. 1969. RCI 280/RCA Red Seal LSC 3142

Chausson *Concert, Op 21*. Kubálek pf, O. Armin vn, 1974. CBC SM-246

Mendelssohn *Quartet, Op 12; Quartet, Op 13*. 1977. Lon LCS-7079

Mozart *Quartet*, K387. 1968. CBC SM-23

Mozart *Quartet*, K465 – Schafer *Quartet No. 1* – Schubert *Quartettsatz*. 1974. Concert Hall SMS 2902

Ravel *Quartet* – Debussy *Quartet*. 1976. Lon LCS-7047

Ravel *Quartet in F* – Pépin *Quartet No. 2* – Bartók *Quartet No. 3*. 1971. RCI 295

Respighi *Il Tramonto*. Marshall sop. 1971. CBC SM-188

Schafer *Quartet No. 2 ('Waves')* – Beckwith *Quartet*. 1979. Mel SMLP-4038

Schumann *Quintet for Piano and Strings, Op. 44* – Mozart *Quartet*, K465. Kuerti pf. 1971. CBC SM-213
- *Quintet for Piano and Strings, Op 44* – Mendelssohn *Quartet, Op 13*. Turini pf. 1969. RCI 275/RCA Red Seal LSC 3137

Somers *Quartet No. 3* – Haydn *Quartet, Op 54, no. 1*. 1967. CBC SM-45

Weinzweig *Quartet No. 3* – Papineau-Couture *Quartet No. 2*. (1975). RCI 362/(Weinzweig) RCI ACM 1

BIBLIOGRAPHY

'Notes on the Orford Quartet,' *CanComp*, 38, Mar 1969

Grudeff, Lillian. 'Strings that sing,' *PfAC*, vol 10, Summer 1973

Littler, William. 'Orford Quartet's birthday is a celebration of success,' *Toronto Star*, 26 Jul 1975

McLean, Eric. 'Recording the Orford Quartet,' *Montreal Star*, 4 Oct 1975

Fraser, John. 'The Orford's search for excellence,' *SatN*, Mar 1976

'Orford: quatuor célèbre,' *Musique périodique*, vol 1, Nov 1976

(BJE)

Organ building. Closely connected and often even essential to the practice of church music, the organ soon followed the first settlers to 17th-century New France. The early instruments, of modest proportions, were imported from Europe. However, it appears certain that an organ was built in Canada as early as 1723. This article traces the evolution and development of organ building in Canada from its origins to 1980, but is concerned essentially with the pipe organ. The more important builders have their own entries.

An organ built by Gabriel Kney and Co Ltd, St John the Evangelist Anglican Church, Ottawa

1 Origins
2 Early builders
3 The years 1880–1950
4 Revival 1950–80
5 Conclusion

1 ORIGINS. It was in Quebec City, in two different churches, that the first organs in Canada were installed. The Jesuit Chapel had its instrument before 1661. *Le Journal des Jésuites* (Quebec 1871) refers to this organ as early as February 1661, and again in 1664. Concerning the one belonging to the parish church, the date of 1664 that was put foward by Nazaire *LeVasseur in *La Musique* (Mar 1919) would seem suspect since it is based on undiscoverable sources. According to LeVasseur, a document dated 22 May 1657 mentions the existence of an organ in that church. This organ apparently did not last very long, since Mgr François de Laval, according to his biographer Louis Bertrand de la Tour (*Mémoires sur la vie de Mgr de Laval*, Cologne 1761), brought back from France in September 1663 an organ which was inaugurated in 1664 and which is mentioned in *Le Journal des Jésuites* (August 1664) as well as in a report to the Holy See from Mgr de Laval himself. This was probably the instrument Paul *Jourdain dit Labrosse undertook to restore 1721-2. Another instrument which the cathedral contracted from Labrosse was delivered in 1723.

In 1744 Mgr de Pontbriand rebuilt the Quebec cathedral and dismantled the organs, whereupon a new organ was ordered from Paris, similar in design to that of the positive organs of 'Saint-Eustache, Saint-Médéric and les Petits-Pères which are the finest in Paris' (letter from the Canon de la Corne to M. de Lavillangevin, 27 Feb 1753; reproduced in the *Bulletin des recherches historiques*, vol 14, December 1908, p 359). The installation was completed in 1753 to general satisfaction and canon Pierre-Joseph Resche (Quebec 1695–1770), who had played the earlier organ 1733–41, became the organist in charge of the new instrument. This must have been a fine instrument, being praised in Paris by the organist of the King of Poland, who had tried it out. Unfortunately it was destroyed, along with the cathedral, by Wolfe's cannons in 1759. Not until October 1802 would the cathedral have another organ, this one built in London by Thomas Elliott (later W. Hill & Son). At about this time another Elliott organ arrived in Quebec City for use in the Anglican cathedral. It was replaced in 1847 by a Bevington organ, also from London.

The first organ to be installed in Montreal was at Notre-Dame Church between 1698 and 1705. In 1792 the parishioners brought from London a seven-stop organ made by the builder Holland. In 1836 they purchased another London organ which had 23 stops and originally was intended for Nicolet, Que. Christ Church (Anglican) in Montreal received from London in 1816 an Elliott organ, a gift from George III. St Paul's Anglican Church, Halifax, was provided with an organ in 1765. This instrument is said to have been obtained as the result of the boarding of a Spanish vessel bound for the south. In 1802 Trinity Anglican Church in Saint John, NB, acquired an organ made in London. The organ played in St James' Cathedral in Toronto in the 1830s also was imported. In Fredericton, St Anne's Chapel possessed an organ in 1848, as did Christ Church Cathedral ca 1860. As for western Canada, the first mention of an organ relates to a barrel instrument sent from London to Victoria in 1859. A pipe organ by J.W. Walker and Sons of London was installed at St John's Anglican Church in Victoria in 1860 and was moved to St John's Anglican Church in Duncan, BC, 53 years later. Also mentioned is the name of John *Bagnall, an organ and piano manufacturer active in Victoria from 1863 on, but there is no trace of any instrument by him. In 1875 the St Boniface Cathedral in Manitoba acquired an organ by Louis *Mitchell.

2 EARLY BUILDERS. Richard *Coates, the presumed creator of seven instruments, arrived in Canada in 1817. He built mainly barrel organs, but one of his manual instruments (1848) has been preserved at the temple of the *Children of Peace in Sharon, Ont. In 1821 Jean-Baptiste Jacotel, a French emigrant, settled in Montreal. In 1824 he built 'a manual and cylinder organ with four foot-pedals' for the Sault-au-Récollet Church. Though he produced little, he appears to have been the first in Canada to have devoted himself primarily to organ building. At his death (1832), his son Jean-Baptiste and son-in-law Auguste Fay undertook to continue the work. The partnership of Fay and Jacotel was short-lived: Fay carried on alone with some success until 1864, installing several instruments on both sides of the St Lawrence River, especially between Quebec City and Trois-Rivières. As for Jacotel fils, he was associated for a while with Toussaint Cherrier, but there are no records of him after 1845.

Joseph Casavant (b 23 Jan 1807, d 9 Mar 1874) was the first Canadian-born organ builder. His first instrument was delivered in 1840 to the parish council of St-Martin-de-Laval Church in the Montreal region. More important, he transmitted his skill as a builder to his sons Samuel and Claver, who played an influential role in organ building in Canada (see Casavant Frères).

In 1836, with the arrival from New England of Samuel Russell *Warren, Canada was introduced to a professional calibre of organ building. Warren lived in Montreal until 1878, when he moved to Toronto. He produced more than 400 instruments, some of which still were in existence in 1980. Another of his achievements was the training of Louis Mitchell, who opened his own workshop in Montreal in 1861.

Quebec City also had one good builder at this time: Napoléon Déry. He produced little, compared with Mitchell or Warren, but, again, in 1980 several of his instruments survived in their original state. The earliest (1874) could be heard at St-Roch-des-Aulnaies. If the St-Joachim organ (1885) lacks eloquence, that of St-Isidore-de-Dorchester (1889) has preserved enough qualities to win over some of the younger Quebec organists to the tracker action; in the period 1950–60 these organists were to have a considerable influence on the evolution of organ aesthetics in Canada and the USA. The Déry organ of St-Michel-de-Bellechasse (1897) may well have elicited the same reaction. Despite the alterations made by Casavant in 1921, the organ of St-Jean-Baptiste of Quebec City still possessed in 1980 the fundamental pipe work of the fine 38-stop organ that Déry had delivered to the parish in 1885 and on which most of his reputation rests.

In 1866 Eusèbe Brodeur took over from Joseph Casavant and built several instruments, some of which have survived in the province of Quebec: those of Cacouna (Rivière-de-Loup), Ste-Monique (Drummond), and Les Cèdres (Soulanges). In about 1890 he went to work for the Casavant brothers, who had been his pupils.

The work of several other organ builders of the period achieved a certain reputation, but its quality cannot be assessed because almost none of it has survived. Joseph Pépin, for example, made several instruments before joining Casavant Frères. Others, including Ovide Paradis in Yamaska from 1854 to ca 1860, Auguste Desrosiers in Louiseville towards 1875, Pierre Beaudoin in St-Henri de Lévis around the same time, and Antoine Couillard in Montreal were amateurs who achieved a certain brief fame but later lapsed into relative obscurity. To this list should be added the names of Godefroy Martel, Charles Paquin, William Dennis, Raymond Roger Charbonneau, and a Monsieur Jodoin, all of whom were engaged in organ building or repair.

Ontario enjoyed some local building, owing to the sporadic efforts of Richard Coates and of the cabinet-makers (ca 1830) Blythe and Kennedy, the creators of the instrument preserved in Ottawa's Bytown Museum. The arrival in Toronto, ca 1848–50, of Edward Roome Lye, and the founding there in 1864 of his establishment, known later as the *Lye Organ Co, provided Upper Canada with a reliable organ manufacturer, which produced between 300 and 400 instruments. Even some of the earliest survived in 1980, at which time William Lye, grandson of Edward, continued to own and operate an organ repair shop.

Ontario had no large organ building firms before the arrival in Toronto of Warren, though some of the following builders were of relative importance: T.F. Roome, who worked in Toronto (fl in the 1860s), Andrus Bros and the Canada Organ Co in London, and Hager & Vogt and Limbrecht, both fl 1849, in Preston (renamed Cambridge). Mention also should be made of John *Thomas, who began working in Montreal in 1832 and who by 1844 had moved to Toronto.

The Maritime provinces possessed organ makers worthy of mention: Watson Duchemin, a Charlottetown wood merchant who ca 1850 for clients in New Brunswick and Prince Edward Island built some instruments of which at least one, of small dimensions, has survived. James Hepburn of Pictou, NS, built an organ with 400 pipes for the local Assembly Hall in 1881. A local newspaper, the *Eastern Chronicle*, commented, 'Congregations should no longer look afield for organs, when such fine instruments can be manufactured here' (George MacLaren: *Antique Furniture by Nova Scotia Craftsmen*, Toronto 1975).

3 THE YEARS 1880–1950. During this period, organ building in Canada enjoyed unprecedented growth in both quantity and quality. The one great name of this period is Casavant Frères, an enterprise launched under quite modest conditions at the end of 1879 by the brothers Samuel and Claver Casavant, sons of Joseph. The business prospered and at the turn of the century already had to its credit instruments of note in St-Hyacinthe, Montreal, and Ottawa. After completing their training in Europe the two brothers strove to stay abreast of the considerable developments occurring in the art of organ building, including the electrification of the bellows and stops. With the collaboration of Salluste Duval, they brought about certain improvements, such as pedals with adjustable combinations. From the Casavant staff emerged several independent builders. Thus in 1910 the Compagnie d'orgues canadiennes, an association which was to last 20 years, began in St-Hyacinthe. Also around this time, Odilon Jacques and a Monsieur Daudelin built standardized instruments of no great significance.

In Ontario the last 20 years of the 19th century saw few new builders, though the Toronto firm of J. Coleman & Sons (fl 1880s) deserves mention, along with J.H. Phillips in Napanee and the diversified firm of R.S. *Williams, which produced some unusual pipe organs. About the time of the establishment of the Karn-Warren Organ Co (1897, after the firm of S.R. Warren & Son was sold to D.W. Karn of Woodstock), the English organ voicer William Potter arrived in Woodstock, following a sojourn in the USA with Wurlitzer. Potter worked at first with Karn-Warren, but when Karn-Warren appeared to be losing impetus he went to work ca 1901 for a cabinet maker named Hay, who, with the help of a pipe maker from England, J.A.G. Webb, began turning out organs. Hay made few instruments and soon preferred to rent part of his workshops to Frank, Russell, and Mansfield Warren, who in 1907 formed the Warren Church Organ Co. These three were the sons of Charles S. Warren, who had succeeded his father, Samuel Russell, in 1882.

The advent of World War I appears to have dealt organ building in Woodstock a crippling blow. However, a reorganization of skilled craftsmen in 1922 resulted in the Woodstock Pipe Organ Builders. This firm installed instruments throughout Canada before it, too, expired in 1948. The organ voicer Potter and the pipe builder Webb, who worked for all the builders in Woodstock after 1897, were largely responsible for the English style which was the hallmark of all this organ building.

Elsewhere in Ontario, the beginning of the 20th century was marked by the appearance of some new builders. Breckels and Matthews of Toronto (later Matthews Church Organ Co) built instruments, interesting samples of which were extant in 1980. It was early in the century, also, that Léonard Morel, a representative of Casavant Frères, arrived in Toronto. In the 1920s he built under his own name a number of instruments, several of which survived in 1980. During the same decade Richard and James Dawson, originally with the Warren Church Organ Co, made organs for a few years under the name of Dawson Bros but were not active for very long. The Franklin *Legge Organ Co, founded in Toronto in 1915, had a longer existence.

In the Maritime provinces there was little local organ building until the 1880s. In 1881 John Bath Reed opened an organ factory in Bridgetown, NS, and the same year he completed an organ for Provincetown Methodist Church. In Saint John, NB, Landry & Son and the Peter Organ Co made instruments of which little is known, except for the organ of Carleton Church in the Gaspé, built by Landry in 1877. The restoration made by Casavant in 1970 has preserved the façade along with a major part of the original pipe work. Also worthy of mention is W.R. Chute (fl 1908) of Dartmouth, NS.

In 1887 the Presbyterian Church of Birtle, Man, acquired an organ with four stops built in Winnipeg by Bolton and Baldwin. The *Musical Journal* described this instrument in 1888 as the only pipe organ west of Winnipeg. This is incorrect, as Victoria and its region had long before that date acquired instruments that had arrived on ships that had sailed around Cape Horn. One of the first in British Columbia was a Bevington & Sons organ that had arrived in 1861 and was installed in Victoria the following year by William Seeley, the organist at Christ Church. Several old instruments survived in British Columbia in 1980, but it is not known whether they were original installations: eg, the extremely interesting US-built Appleton organ (1869) of the Church of Our Lord in Victoria and the London organ in the United Church of Cumberland.

Besides these, British Columbia in 1980 still had several other interesting and relatively old instruments, such as the Lye organ of St Paul's Lutheran Church in Nanaimo, or those of the English type of St Saviour's Church in Victoria and the church at Sooke, instruments recently restored by Hugo Spilker. In Vancouver, Chandos Dix (ca 1890–1940) applied himself chiefly to maintenance but built and assembled a few instruments, including the one in Shawnigan Lake Boys' School. Other old instruments imported from the USA and installed in Canada fairly recently should also be mentioned: in Edmonton, the Colburn organ (1870) of the German Catholic Church and the Chadwick (1900) of the Westend Christian Reformed Church. With the beginning of the 20th century, the West became well supplied with fine instruments coming occasionally from the USA or England, but more often ordered from Casavant.

4 REVIVAL 1950–80. The early 1950s were marked throughout Canada but particularly in Quebec by a deep dissatisfaction with existing organ building. The European revival of interest in the organ finally reached Canada, especially through the new recordings, which gave forth sounds that were variable but enthralling compared with the insipid sounds characteristic of Canadian instruments. Some organists at that time favoured the neoclassicism of Aeolian-Skinner or of Hill, Norman & Beard. Other younger organists, who had played on classical organs in Europe, embarked on a crusade for a return to the aesthetics that had governed earlier organ builders. Montreal succeeded in acquiring excellent Rudolf von Beckerath instruments at Queen Mary Road United Church, at St Joseph's Oratory, and at the Immaculée-Conception Church. The new classical instruments, which were promoted by the *Ars Organi concerts, soon drew an enthusiastic public, and audiences for the concerts were increased when they were broadcast on CBC radio. Along with tracker-action instruments should be mentioned many electro-pneumatic instruments which, like those of the Cap-de-la-Madeleine Basilica or St-Zéphirin Church at La Tuque, Que, allow the baroque repertoire to be heard in sounds authentic to its period, at least in so far as the quality of timbre is concerned.

The renaissance that occurred with Casavant in the late 1950s put Canada in the forefront in North America and was of sufficient intensity to produce in the region of St-Hyacinthe some independent builders of good-quality organs. Karl *Wilhelm, of German origin, who had received his early training under various European builders, began working with Casavant in 1960. In 1966 he set up shop on his own. By 1979 his workshop, located first in St-Hyacinthe, and later in Mont-St-Hilaire, had turned out 73 organs whose rich and powerful sound gave a healthy indication of their pedigree.

Also to be mentioned are the instruments made by the Swiss-born builder Hellmuth *Wolff, who arrived in Canada in 1963 and founded his own establishment in Laval, Que, in 1966. His productions are the fruit of a great deal of knowledge and an ingenious mind, and their purity of form is combined with an eloquence of timbre. André Guilbault, through his association with Guy Thérien, has revived the style his father had evolved at *Providence Organ Inc, an establishment founded in 1946. The tracker-action instruments made there in the 1970s held much promise.

In 1979 Fernand Létourneau opened the firm Orgues Létourneau Ltée in Ste-Rosalie. He had worked with Casavant for 14 years, 4 of them as chief voicer. His company undertook to specialize in the construction of instruments with tracker action and the restoration of organs with tracker and electro-pneumatic action. The Quebec government commissioned him in 1979 to build a 5-stop organ for the Cons de Hull. In 1980 his company was working on the restoration of a 19th-century instrument in Sydney, Australia.

Before Casavant opened its tracker department, some organs of the type had been built in Ontario by Gabriel *Kney, who for a while was the partner of John Bright. Kney arrived from Germany in 1951, settled in Acton, Ont, in 1955, and moved to London, Ont, in 1967. Another Ontario builder, the *Keates Organ Co of Acton, began work in London, Ont, in 1945. Its first organs were electro-pneumatic but the later ones have been tracker or electric. The Knoch Organ Co was founded in London, Ont, in 1954. Principal Organs in Woodstock and Neutel in Brantford, Ont, also have made pipe organs. *Hallman Organs of Kitchener built pipe instruments ca 1964–76. In Fergus, Brunzema Organs Inc opened its doors in 1979. Founded by Gerhard Brunzema (the former artistic director of Casavant), the company has concentrated on the manufacture of organs with tracker action. A positive organ was installed in Pollock Hall, *McGill U, in 1980.

In the West, Hugo Spilker of Victoria has restored old organs and built new ones.

5 CONCLUSION. After 1960, organ building in Canada attained a level of excellence previously unknown. This rapid improvement would have been impossible without the solid infrastructures laid by the preceding generations of organ builders and without the enthusiasm of a living and productive organ school. The situation may be explained, moreover, only in the light of the staunch affection so many Canadians have retained for the organ.

In 1980 there were some dark clouds on the horizon. There was the apparent disaffection of the Christian church for an instrument that has served it so well. There was as well the inexorable rise in production costs, which had made the acquisition of a fine instrument a serious financial undertaking. Fortunately at the same time there was a growing awareness of the importance of protecting as a precious heritage certain authentic examples of 19th- and early-20th-century workmanship, and a timely movement was underway to remodel instruments of the period between the two world wars, thus providing a link, aided by the aesthetic advances being made in contemporary manufacture, with the great organ building traditions of the past.

See also Canadian Piano and Organ Manufacturers' Assn; Mechanical instruments; Organ music; Organ playing and teaching; Reed organs; Morse Robb; RCCO.

BIBLIOGRAPHY

Bridle, Augustus. 'Beginning with the pipe organ,' *Canadian Courier*, vol 12, 12 Oct 1912

Lapalice, O. 'Les organistes et maîtres de musique à Notre-Dame de Montréal,' *BRH*, vol 25, Aug 1919

Hollins, Alfred. 'Organs and organ building in Canada and the United States,' *The Organ*, vol 6, no. 22, 1926–7

Dufourcq, Norbert. 'Précisions historiques sur l'orgue électrique en France, au Canada et aux États-Unis,' *Revue musicale*, Nov 1929

Chapais, Charles. 'La construction des orgues par des Canadiens français,' *Deuxième congrès de la langue français au Canada*, vol 1 (Quebec 1938)

Mackey, Donald. 'Organ in Christ Church Cathedral, Montreal,' *The Organ*, vol 31, Jan 1952

'British Columbia's first pipe organ,' *CBC Times*, Eastern Canada edition, 27 Jun–3 Jul 1954

White, Herbert D. 'The organ of St. Luke's Church, Winnipeg,' *The Organ*, vol 34, no. 133, 1954–5

Steed, Graham. 'The rebuilding of Christ Church Cathedral organ, Victoria, British Columbia,' *CMJ*, vol 2, Summer 1958

Kennedy, D. Stuart. 'Central United Church, Calgary, Alberta, Canada,' *The Organ*, vol 39, no. 156, 1959–60

Dufourcq, Norbert. 'Quelques instruments canadiens,' *L'Orgue*, 118, Apr–Jun 1966

Matthews, E.N. 'Some organ builders in Victoria before 1900,' *The Organ*, vol 46, Oct 1966

Stobie, Charles I.G. 'The organ in St. Andrew's Presbyterian Church, Saint John's, Newfoundland,' ibid, vol 52, no. 206, 1972

Royal Canadian College of Organists Quarterly (Oct 1973–8)

Stobie, Charles I.G. 'The organ of the Anglican Cathedral of St John the Baptist, St. John's, Newfoundland,' *The Organ*, vol 53, no. 211, 1974; vol 54, no. 212, 1975

Crousset, Donald. 'L'orgue de la basilique de l'Oratoire Saint-Joseph du Mont-Royal,' unpubl L MUS thesis, U of Montreal 1975

Bouchard, Antoine. 'Évolution de la facture d'orgue au Canada, entre 1960 et 1975,' *The Organ Yearbook 1978* (Buren, Netherlands, 1978)

– 'The organ in Canada: the first 300 years,' *Mcan*, 35, Apr 1978

Harris, John. 'Organ builder takes skills around world,' Toronto *Globe and Mail*, 19 Jan 1981

Coup d'oeil

Kallmann, Helmut, and Beckwith, John. 'Musical instruments, Making of,' *Encyclopedia Canadiana*

La Musique au Québec (AB)

Organ music

1 Anglo-Canadian
2 Franco-Canadian

1 ANGLO-CANADIAN. Judging by what has been published, organ music in English Canada has a short history confined to the 20th century. Several important compositions remain in manuscript, while many less worthy have found their way, unabashed, into print. The fact is that Canadian publications have been concerned mainly with music suitable for church use, while concert works have had a slender chance of finding a publisher.

A very few pieces by 19th-century Canadians survive – among them two *Preludes and Fugues* by J.E.P. *Aldous, a *Concert Overture* by J. Humfrey *Anger, a student *Prelude and Fugue* by W.O. *Forsyth, three pieces (G. Schirmer, 1890) by Charles A.E. *Harriss, and a *Grand Choeur* by William *Reed. It may be assumed that some of the fine organists who were raised in Canada or arrived and settled in maturity wrote works, for their own use, that remained unpublished and have been lost. From the slim evidence found, however, it may be said that organ literature in English Canada began with the arrival of Healey *Willan in the 1900s.

Willan brought with him some youthful compositions already in print and in 1916 added the celebrated *Introduction, Passacaglia and Fugue* which earned him an enviable reputation amongst concert organists. Willan's instant pre-eminence among English-Canadian organ composers of the time led eventually to a certain complacency on his part. Here was a situation in which it was fatally easy to produce a great quantity of music based on hymn-tunes, and well-fashioned preludes and fugues for local consumption, which in turn found many imitators much less gifted than Willan himself.

It is a pleasure, however, to come across isolated examples of hymn settings such as Florence Durrell Clark's *Prelude on a 2nd Mode Melody of Tallis* (Novello) or Graham *George's *Prelude on 'The King's Majesty'* (No. 1), in which the composer has caught a breath of inspiration from the original.

For music of originality we need to look beyond the confines of the church to the campus, where the composer wrote for either gifted pupils or professional colleagues. Here mention may be made of Violet *Archer's *Sonatina*, Gerald *Bales' *Petite Suite*, Lorne *Betts' *Improvisations on B-A-C-H*, and William *France's *Suites* and various short pieces. More modest contributions come from Hugh *Bancroft, Frederick *Karam, Kenneth *Meek, and Sir Ernest *MacMillan. Of the composers who have chosen a larger canvas and more advanced composing technique, Keith *Bissell in his *Sonata* (1963) has produced an atonal work of real substance in which three movements grow organically from an initial theme of rising fourths, undergoing rich transformation in the elegiac middle movement and assuming an aerial lightness in the mercurial Vivace. Talivaldis *Kenins is represented by his *Suite in D*, an expert and original composition. Kenins is capable of sustaining rhythmic momentum throughout an extended movement, and his writing is notable for its diversity of texture. Gerhard *Wuensch is another composer able to compose on a large plan. His *Toccata nuptialis* is a virtuoso work both in execution and in the demands made on the performer. His ability to think contrapuntally in his fugal writing is masterly – a gift shared to some extent by Graham George in his many compositions.

Two of the most prolific composers writing for the organ in the 1970s – Barrie *Cabena and Derek *Healey – revealed specialist knowledge of the instrument and sensitive ears for colour and registers. Their interest in the neoclassical instrument is apparent in their detailed registrations, though of the two men Healey is much more the romantic at heart. Cabena is best known for his 10 portraits for organ entitled *Cabena's Homage*, composed in 1967 as a commission by the *RCCO. Each piece bears the name of a noted Canadian organist and aptly and wittily portrays its subject, though the 'in-jokes' can be appreciated only by the cognoscenti. Cabena's fluent technique and grasp of form are seen to advantage in his *Sonata da Chiesa*, in which each movement is based on a chorale. Three other works, *Sonata Festiva, Sonata IX*, and *Sonata for Manuals*, show the composer's predilection for baroque forms.

Derek Healey has a large number of compositions to his credit. He possesses a searching mind and an adventurous spirit, both of which hold exciting possibilities for future work. In a series of six voluntaries, composed from 1956 to 1962, he exhibits an interest in neoclassical writing, though No. 5 of the set (sub-titled 'To Montserrat Torrent: Barcelona') has a strong romantic bias. *Partita '65* reveals a melodic gift and a penchant for caricature. In some of his shorter movements the young composer has been influenced by the visionary paintings of Stanley Spencer, eg, in two of *Three Quiet Pieces*, the remaining piece being based on an Ojibway song. Of his more mature works *Variants, Op 23*, is characterized by witty thought, pungent harmony and pulsating rhythm; *Festus, Op 33*, is a bold experiment in musical mosaic; while *Paraphrase: 'Discendi, Amor Santo,' Op 28B*, shows his most advanced stage of 12-tone writing. Two works, *The Lost Traveller's Dream* and *Summer '73, Op 44*, carry the process of experimentation with organ sound still further – the latter being written for organ and tape.

2 FRANCO-CANADIAN. Organ works written in Quebec at the end of the 19th century and in the first half of the 20th were intended mostly for church use. Representatives are R.-O. *Pelletier's *Dix Petits Morceaux pour l'orgue, Op 3*, and *Six Pièces*, Arthur *Letondal's *Prélude grave, Offertoire*, and *Toccata*, and similar pieces by Gustave *Gagnon, Alphonse *Lavallée-Smith, J.-Arthur *Bernier, Joseph and Zénon Paquin, Omer *Létourneau, Benoît *Poirier, and Léon *Ringuet. The works of these composers spring directly from the French tradition of Guilmant, Franck, Vierne, and Widor. Particularly successful in this genre is Amédée *Tremblay's *Suite de quatre pièces pour grand orgue*, of which the final Toccata has enjoyed an enthusiastic revival.

Also to be noted are Conrad *Bernier's *Esquisse* and *Prière en ut majeur*, Alfred *Tardif's *Triptyque marial*, and Bernard *Piché's *Rhapsodie sur quatre noëls* and *Fugue sur l'Ite Missa est alléluiatique*. Claude *Champagne, Auguste *Descarries, and Georges-Émile *Tanguay have written estimable pieces, and Conrad *Letendre's works also have been admired.

The repertoire of the later 20th century has been enriched substantially by Raymond *Daveluy, whose sonatas and *Fantaisie* for organ and string orchestra demonstrate a profound knowledge of the instrument and of contrapuntal technique. While his style derives unmistakably from the French school, the high discipline of the writing suggests Reger or Hindemith.

Among other notable contemporary pieces are Roger *Matton's *Suite de Pâques*, André *Prévost's *Cinq Variations sur un thème grégorien (Salve Regina)*, François *Morel's *Alleluia* in three parts and *Prière*, Maurice *Dela's *Pastorale* and *Suite*, and Otto *Joachim's *Fantasia*. These works, in their blending of timbres and their unexpected sonorities, are authentically modern in concept, but again they suggest the influence of the French masters, though of a later generation: Marcel Dupré and Olivier Messiaen.

BIBLIOGRAPHY
CMCentre. *Catalogue of Canadian Keyboard Music* (Toronto 1971, suppl 1976)
Bryant, Giles. *Healey Willan Catalogue* (Ottawa 1972)
'Canadian church music composers,' *RCCO Q*, June 1974; suppl, Jun 1976 1 / MCk, 2 / GP

Organ playing and teaching. The sound of the organ has been integral to the musical experience of most Canadians because of the firm place church attendance has held in their lives, at least until the middle of the 20th century. The many immigrant components of Canadian society and the attendant variety of Christian denominations explain the country's multiplicity of churches (relative to population figures) and hence of church organs and organists. Canadians of widely divergent backgrounds – from specialist training in church music or virtuoso skills, to main experience with the piano or string or wind instruments, to what might be described as 'dilettante studies' – have filled those many positions.

1 History
2 Canadian College of Organists
3 The 20th century
4 Perpetuation of tradition: teaching, 1920–80
5 Organ reform
6 Theatre organists
7 Summation

1 HISTORY. The earliest reference to organ playing occurs in the *Jesuit Relations* (vol 46, p 163) for February 1661: 'The organ played while the Blessed Sacrament was being taken down, and during benediction.' It mentions further that Pierre Duquet and Michel Feuillon were the musicians who assisted with the musical aspect of the church services. Louis *Jolliet, the Canadian-born explorer of the Mississippi, is known to have played the organ in Quebec City and to have taught others. The names of the first organists at Montreal's Notre-Dame Church have been traced in *Le Canada musical* (1 Dec 1880), which took them from the *Annuaire de Ville-Marie*, and, in more detail, by Ovide Lapalice. The first were Jean-Baptiste *Poitiers du Buisson and Charles-François *Coron, both in the early 18th century. In Halifax the provincial secretary of Nova Scotia, Richard *Bulkeley, acted as organist at St Paul's Anglican Church, and Viere Warner was another 18th-century incumbent. Among the organists at important churches in the early 19th century were Guillaume *Mechtler, for nearly 40 years at Notre-Dame in Montreal, John *Bentley, at both the Anglican and the Catholic cathedrals in Quebec City, Stephen *Codman at the Anglican Cathedral of the Holy Trinity in Quebec, F.H. *Glackemeyer and T.F. *Molt at the Catholic Cathedral in Quebec, and J.-C. *Brauneis II at Notre-Dame in Montreal. The first organist in Toronto may have been W. (or M.) Warren, ca 1833–5 at St James' Cathedral. A highly qualified organist, Edward Hodges, was brought from England in 1838 to fill the same position but found conditions so unsatisfactory that he left for New York a few months later. J.P. *Clarke, at Christ Church, ca 1844–5, was one of the first organists in Hamilton and served later at St James' in Toronto. Margaret *Gilkison, at St James' during the 1840s, was one of Canada's first women organists; another was Esther Fournier (1805–74) of Rigaud, Que, an aunt of the twin brothers *Dumouchel.

In the second half of the 19th century the work of several outstanding organ builders testified to the growing numbers of instruments required for churches, halls, and educational institutions and the many organists required. Relatively few Canadian musicians were organists first and foremost. The most outstanding of these was Samuel Prowse *Warren, son of the organ builder Samuel Russell *Warren. However, like several other talented musicians, he spent most of his adult years in the USA. L.C. Elson, in his *The History of American Music* (New York 1904), called him 'one of the great concert organists of America ... a man who may stand with the church organists of any country and not be relegated to an inferior position.' In New York alone, Warren gave hundreds of recitals. Only a few of the better known organists active in the second part of the 19th century (and in some cases into the 20th) can be named here: Charles *Hutton in St John's, Nfld; the brothers Charles H. and Samuel *Porter in Halifax; the brothers Ernest and Gustave *Gagnon, Edward Arthur Bishop, Antoine *Dessane, and Calixa *Lavallée in Quebec City; Alcibiade *Béique, George *Carter, Alexis *Contant, Charles A.E. *Harriss, Percival *Illsley, J.-B. *Labelle, R.-O. *Pelletier, and F.H. *Torrington in Montreal; Herbert G.R. Fripp and Gustave *Smith in Ottawa; John *Carter, Edward *Fisher, John W.F. *Harrison, F.H. Torrington, and A.S. *Vogt in Toronto; J.E.P. *Aldous, R.S. *Ambrose, W.E. *Fairclough, C.M.L. *Harris, and D.J. O'Brien in Hamilton; A.S. *Sippi and Charles E. *Wheeler in London, Ont; and P.R. MacLagan in Winnipeg. Some organists were employed in several cities in turn, eg, William *Reed in Sherbrooke, Montreal, Toronto, and Quebec City.

It should be noted that in the late 19th century the organ was regarded largely as a substitute orchestra, and, indeed, much of the recital music consisted of transcriptions. A typical program, given by Torrington 23 Mar 1869 at the Wesleyan Church in Montreal ('Grand Concert of Sacred Music') included three organ solos: Mendelssohn's *Organ Sonata No. 1*, the Andante from Beethoven's *Septet*, and Rossini's *Willian Tell Overture*. It is noteworthy, however, that during the previous year Torrington had played Bach's *'St Anne's' Fugue* to an audience whose enthusiasm bewildered at least one of the concert's reviewers: 'We were not a little surprised to find that the severe compositions in the programme, such as the "Organ Sonata" [Mendelssohn, No. 3] and the "Fugue" by J.S. Bach, received so much applause, when it is considered that it requires a musician to thoroughly understand and appreciate them ... Concerts of this description [should] be given once or twice a week at a cheap rate, so as to enable the poorest to hear the best music' (Montreal *Gazette*, 16 May 1868). The correspondent for the *Musical Times* of London was more at ease with this phenomenon: 'The Fugue by J.S. Bach excit[ed] especial interest, a fact which speaks strongly for the growing musical taste of the public in Montreal' (*MT*, 1 Jul 1868).

In any case, Torrington continued to champion the music of Bach. In French Canada some priests discouraged the music of Bach and that of Mendelssohn, not on musical grounds but because the two composers were regarded as 'Protestant musicians.' Despite this attitude, R.-O. Pelletier, like Torrington, and reassured and inspired by a recital by Alexandre Guilmant at the Montreal Cathedral in 1893, also continued to give recitals which included the works of Bach and Mendelssohn.

2 CANADIAN COLLEGE OF ORGANISTS. Pelletier and Torrington also were among those organists working towards the establishment of a professional organization that would unite organists and help raise standards of performance. The model was the Royal College of Organists, which had been established in England in 1864. The *Musical Journal* (vol 2, 15 Feb 1888) of Toronto reported with approval that Torrington and such colleagues as J.E.P. Aldous, G.H. Fairclough, and A.S. Sippi were about to form a College of Organists. Under the presidency of Torrington the organization was active for a few years but did not survive, probably a victim of rivalries and dissension. Leadership was provided next by the American Guild of Organists (chartered 1896), the letterhead of which proclaimed the 'United States and Canada' as its territory. Canadian organists, however, had need of an organization of their own and thus the Canadian College of Organists (*RCCO) came into being at a meeting in Brantford, Ont, in 1909. Albert *Ham was the first president of this organization, which, under its later name, has continued to expand and flourish.

Although the RCCO has served as an examination body, it has never been a teaching organization. Most of the organ teaching in Canada has been carried on by private individuals, who usually employ the instruments in their own churches for the purpose. Conservatories in the larger cities have had organ teachers on their staffs, however, and some institutions have had good instruments as well. For example, the TCM *Yearbook* of 1892–93 states that 'the Directors of the Conservatory, recognizing the importance of the Organ Department, have greatly increased the facilities for organ teaching and practice by purchasing, at large expense, a grand Concert Organ, and erecting the same in Association Hall ... the organ [by S.R. Warren & Son of Toronto] was completed in December, 1889, and is designed expressly to suit the requirements of the Conservatory for teaching, practice, and also for organ recitals and concerts of the most comprehensive character.'

3 THE 20TH CENTURY. Organ playing has reached a high level of excellence in Canada in the 20th century, owing to the standards set by the RCCO, *Ars Organi, and the *Casavant Societies, the teaching by conservatory and private teachers, and the co-operation of organ builders. Of the Canadian virtuoso performers none has achieved a higher reputation than Lynnwood *Farnam, one of the master organists of the century. After holding church positions in Montreal 1904–13 he moved to the USA, as his predecessor S.P. Warren had done. He achieved worldwide recognition for his flawless technique, infallible memory, and profound musicianship. A pupil of Sir Walter Parratt and Wm Stevenson Hoyte in London, Farnam attracted as pupils some of the finest organists in North America, among them the Canadians H. William Hawke, Harold *Ramsay, Frederick *Silvester, and Ernest *White. Through his pupils and their pupils, his influence continues to be felt in North America. Farnam's playing career reached its climax in 1929, the year before his death, when he played the complete organ works of Bach in a New York recital series. His recital 14 Mar 1929 at the Church of St Andrew and St Paul in Montreal may have been his last in Canada.

It should not be forgotten that Ernest *MacMillan, having returned to Canada after World War I, established his reputation primarily as an organist. Like Farnam, he was noted for the technical perfection of his playing. Though his repertoire was broad, he showed a special affinity for the music of Bach. By many of his colleagues in the 1920s he was considered to be without a peer in the country. Although MacMillan continued to give recitals occasionally in later life, his teaching was concentrated in the 1920s. Pupils such as Muriel *Gidley and Charles *Peaker passed MacMillan's precepts along to their own pupils.

Again like Farnam, MacMillan had studied in Great Britain, especially with the Scottish organist Alfred Hollins. Indeed, many of Canada's finest organists came from England and Scotland. This was only natural, because of the similarity of language and church music traditions on both sides of the Atlantic. The stream of immigrant church musicians, begun with Codman in the early 19th century, gained momentum after the middle of the century with the coming of the Carter brothers, Torrington, Charles *Ambrose, J.P. Clarke, Edward Arthur Bishop, etc, and reached its height in the 25 years before World War I. This group, in addition to those named before, included J. Humfrey *Anger, Vernon *Barford, John W. *Bearder, J. Edgar *Birch, Edward *Broome, George *Coutts, Harry *Dean, Arthur *Egerton, Albert Ham, W.H. *Hewlett, W.A. *Montgomery, George Ross, Herbert *Sanders, and Alfred *Whitehead; these men were active in cities from Alberta to Nova Scotia. The most important musician in this distinguished group was Healey *Willan, an organ pupil of Wm Stevenson Hoyte (who also had taught Farnam) in London. Soon after his arrival in Toronto in 1913 Willan became organist at St Paul's Anglican Church. His recital programs of the period reveal a comprehensive repertoire, including much English music. An excellent improviser, Willan earned a glowing review for the extemporization of a complete sonata at a convention of the National Assn of Organists in Albany, NY, in 1923. Willan was heard in many Canadian cities as guest organist. One of the positions he kept until his old age was that of organist for the *U of Toronto.

Willan, who played at the Church of St Mary Magdalene in Toronto for 47 years, was typical of a select number of organists who, when they have found congenial church positions, show lasting loyalty to them. Harry Dean was 47 years at Fort Massey Church, Halifax. Edward Arthur Bishop was 50 years at the Anglican Cathedral of the Holy Trinity in Quebec City. Henri *Gagnon served 1915–61 in the Basilica in Quebec City, the same position occupied 1864–76 by his uncle, Ernest Gagnon, and 1876–1915 by his father, Gustave Gagnon! Vernon Barford was at All Saints Cathedral, Edmonton, for 56 years. Arthur Mews served at Cochrane Street Methodist Church in St.John's, Nfld, for 62 years, and Charles Hutton at St John the Baptist Cathedral in the same city for 63 years.

Over the years many outstanding foreign organists have visited Canada to fulfil individual recital engagements or to tour. Among them have been Marie-Claire Alain, Feike Asma, Walter Baker, E. Power Biggs, Claire Coci, Charles Courboin, Xavier Darasse, Marcel Dupré, Rolande Falcinelli, Virgil Fox, Fernando Germani, Anton Heiller, Geraint Jones, William Krumbach, Sigfrid Karg-Elert, André Marchal, Marilyn Mason, Alexander McCurdy, Flor Peeters, Lionel Rogg, Alexander Schreiner, Louis Vierne, Clarence Watters, Carl Weinrich, and Charles-Marie Widor.

4 PERPETUATION OF TRADITION: TEACHING, 1920–80. The tradition of organ playing, descending as it does (in the three lines affecting Canada most significantly) through the organist-composers Rameau, Saint-Saëns, Franck, and Messiaen in France, Tallis, Byrd, Purcell, and Handel in England, and Buxtehude, Bach, Mendelssohn, and Reger in Germany, is a serious, even a solemn one, with the disciplines of church, polyphony, choral and congregational responsibility, and the extreme technical challenge of the instrument itself ever present to discourage triflers. It is not surprising, then, that perhaps more than in any of the other disciplines there has been a tendency for Canadian organ scholars to attach themselves to authentic tradition and to go to high-level ancestral sources to ensure the attachment. This is particularly so in French Canada, which has produced the majority of Canadian concert organists, most of whom have studied either with the leading organist-teachers of France or with their Quebec pupils. We chart some of these connections, aware that their importance must have varied according to duration and intensity.

Eugène Gigout (teacher of Victoria *Cartier, Paul *Doyon, J.-D. *Dussault, Henri Gagnon, and Alphonse *Lavallée-Smith), the illustrious Marcel Dupré (teacher of François *Aubut, Jean-Marie *Beaudet, Eugène *Lapierre, Jean *Leduc, D'Alton *McLaughlin, Antoine *Reboulot, J.-Élie *Savaria, and Henri *Vallières), Louis Vierne (teacher of Joseph *Bonnet, Paul Doyon, Omer *Létourneau, Georges *Lindsay, J.-Élie Savaria, and G.-E. *Tanguay), and Charles-Marie Widor (teacher of Henri Gagnon, Alphonse Lavallée-Smith, D'Alton McLaughlin, and J.-Élie Savaria) undoubtedly were among the most influential of the French teachers. However, they were by no means the only ones. Bonnet himself, who moved to Canada in 1943 (and taught, in France or Canada, Conrad *Bernier, Henri Gagnon, Magdeleine and Marcelle *Martin, and D'Alton McLaughlin), André Marchal (teacher of Gaston *Arel, Bernard *Lagacé, Claude *Lavoie, and Antoine Reboulot), and Gaston Litaize (teacher of Antoine *Bouchard, Kenneth *Gilbert, Claude Lavoie, and Lucien *Poirier) also provided touchstones to the French tradition, as did Charles Letestu (for Gaston Arel and Lucienne *L'Heureux-Arel), Xavier Darasse (for Réjean *Poirier, André *Laberge, and Hélène Panneton), and Marie-Claire Alain (for the young Dutch-Canadian organist Jan *Overduin).

The close weave of the Franco-Canadian organ fraternity is evident when we note how many of the French teachers taught the same pupils (for instance, the three giants Dupré, Vierne, and Widor all taught Savaria). It becomes more so when we examine the connections between leading Quebec teachers, their French antecedents, and their established pupils. Henri Gagnon (who taught Jean-Marie Beaudet, Jean-Marie *Bussières, Claude *Lagacé, Paul-Émile *Talbot, and Henri Vallières) and Conrad *Letendre (who taught Gaston Arel, Raymond *Daveluy, Kenneth Gilbert, Bernard and Mireille *Lagacé, and Lucienne L'Heureux-Arel) were among the leading figures to emerge between the world wars, and Romain *Pelletier was of particular significance as the teacher of both, and of Georges-Émile Tanguay. Arthur *Letondal was another teacher of Letendre and also counted Arel and Doyon among his pupils. Romain-Octave Pelletier, the father of Romain, was himself one of the teachers of Alphonse Lavallée-Smith and Omer Létourneau. Other important teachers active between the wars included Eugène Lapierre, whose pupils included Françoise Aubut, Gérard *Caron, and Pierre *Grandmaison, and Raoul Paquet, who taught Gérard Caron and Félix-R. *Bertrand. After World War II Bernard Lagacé came into prominence as the teacher of a new generation, including Christopher Jackson, André Laberge, Mireille Lagacé, Lucien Poirier, Réjean Poirier, and Denis *Regnaud. Georges-Émile Tanguay, who taught organ at the *U of Montreal in the post-war era, counted Félix-R. Bertrand, Magdeleine and Marcelle Martin, and André Mérineau among his pupils. Antoine Reboulot, the French organist who moved to Canada in 1967, has been one of the teachers of Antoine Bouchard and Paul-Émile Talbot. Another notable player-teacher, Raymond Daveluy, a pupil of Letendre, E. Power Biggs, and the US organist Hugh Giles, has taught Pierre-Yves Asselin, Paul *Crawford, Mireille Lagacé, and Lucienne L'Heureux-Arel.

The dynamics of organ playing and teaching in English Canada have been established along lines quite different from those which govern the same disciplines in French Canada. Fundamental to the difference has been English Canada's tendency to prefer importation to the assiduous development of native talent. The number of excellent English organists to have been tempted to settle in Canada, both before and after World War II, is quite large, and the influx has had the effect of taking a good many of the main church jobs effectively out of reach for Canadians, even while it also provided a handy team of first-rate, traditionally trained teachers for whose services students would not have to cross the Atlantic. However, because of the great distances separating Canada's main cities, the influence of the English organists tended to be localized, limited to a degree by the areas in which they worked and taught.

Of those mainly influential in Toronto, Willan (a teacher of Gordon *Jeffery, David *Ouchterlony, Charles Peaker, and Ernest White) has been mentioned, and Frederick *Geoghegan also should be noted. Geoghegan, a pupil in England of Stanley Curtis and Sir William McKie, was also a teacher of Giles *Bryant, Derek *Holman, and Douglas *Haas. In Winnipeg Hugh *Bancroft (a teacher of Douglas *Bodle, Donald *Hadfield, Hugh *McLean, Herbert *Sadler, and Winnifred *Sim) was a great influence, as was Sadler, English-born but a pupil in Winnipeg of Hugh Ross, Douglas *Clarke, and Bancroft, and himself the teacher of more than 20 established Winnipeg church organists. Graham Steed became organist at Christ Church Cathedral in Victoria in the 1950s, moved to All Saints Anglican Church in Windsor, Ont, in 1959 and to Truro, NS, in the 1970s. Steed has held appointments as well in Saskatoon and Montreal. The many other English organists who settled in Canada, to a man energetic, capable, and productive, had similar effects on their local ecologies. To name a few who made their names between the wars: Frederick *Chubb (a pupil of A.W. Wilson), the aforementioned Douglas Clarke (a pupil of Henry Wood), T.J. *Crawford (a pupil of H. Sandiford Turner), Maitland *Farmer (a pupil of G.D. Cunningham, as were two other prominent Canadians, Russell *Green and David Ouchterlony), H.A. *Fricker (a pupil of William Longhurst, Frederick Bridge, and Edwin Henry Lemare), Ronald *Gibson (trained in Canada by Arnold Dann), Godfrey *Hewitt (a pupil of A.C. Tysoe), Filmer *Hubble (a pupil of Hugh Ross), Quentin *Maclean (a pupil of Harold Osmund, F.G. Shuttleworth, and Sir Richard Terry), Kenneth *Meek (a pupil of Herbert Sanders and Herbert Fricker), Charles Peaker (who studied in Canada with Ernest MacMillan, as did Frederick Silvester and Ernest White, and with Willan), Eric *Rollinson, Gerald *Wheeler (a pupil of Edgar T. Cook), and Leonard *Wilson (a pupil of Sydney Nicholson, George Oldroyd, and Dom Anselm Hughes).

English-born organists active in Canada mainly in the period between World War II and 1980 include George *Brough (a pupil of the Australian-English organist George Thalben-Ball), Giles Bryant (Willan's successor at St Mary Magdalene Church, and his cataloguer), Barrie *Cabena (a pupil of Sir John Dykes Bower and one of the teachers of Jan Overduin), Frederick Carter (a pupil in England of Harold Darke, as were the English-born Derek *Healey and John J. *Weatherseed, both of whom have had Canadian careers), Melville *Cook (a pupil of Sir Edward Bairstow and Sir Herbert Brewer), Derek Holman (a pupil of Sir William McKie, Eric Thiman, and York Bowen, as well as of Geoghegan), and Brian *Law (a pupil of Holman and Martindale Sidwell).

Leading Canadian-born organists of English Canada whose activity began between the wars included the aforementioned Ernest MacMillan (a pupil of Alfred Hollins), William Hawke (a pupil of Farnam), Charles E. Wheeler (a pupil of Torrington and W.O. *Forsyth), and Ernest White. Few more distinguished, but certainly a great many more, came to the fore after the war, notably Douglas Bodle (a pupil of Bancroft), Arthur Egerton (a pupil of Farnam, Sir Walter Alcock, Sir Walter Parratt, and Percival Illsley), Donald Hadfield (a pupil of Bancroft and Bodle), Norman *Hurrle (the main teacher of Patrick *Wedd), Gordon Jeffery (a pupil of Willan, Peaker, and White and one of the teachers of Overduin), Hugh McLean (a pupil of Bancroft and Sir William Harris and a teacher of Patrick Wedd), Phillips *Motley (a pupil of Alfred Whitehead), Roma Page Lynde (a pupil of Peaker), Winnifred Sim (a pupil of Bancroft and Gibson), Beal *Thomas (a pupil of William Teague, Robert Anderson, and Alex Wyton, all in the USA), Stewart *Thomson (a pupil of Walter *MacNutt), and Patrick Wedd (a pupil of Hurrle, McLean, and J. Laurence Slater).

So it will be seen that not only the ancestral imperatives but the separate ones of Canada's 'two solitudes' have held sway. The young organists of French Canada have studied in the French tradition, the young organists of English Canada in the English, as if the language barrier were a musical one. The efforts at cross-fertilization have been notable but few: Gagnon's supplementary studies with William Reed, Daveluy's with Giles and Biggs, Claude Lagacé's with Clarence Watters (USA), Lavoie's with Biggs. Both French-Canadian and English-Canadian students have availed themselves more readily of tuition in the Austro-German, Flemish, and Italian traditions than in each other's, though again not lavishly. Bernard and Mireille Lagacé, Douglas Haas, and Denis Regnaud took part of their studies with Anton Heiller; André Laberge had lessons in Holland with Piet Kee and Luigi Tagliavini; Gérard Caron, Douglas Haas, and André Mérineau had tuition from Fernando Germani (though Mérineau's main teacher was Conrad Bernier); Charles E. Wheeler, like two of his English-born colleagues, T.J. Crawford and Harry Dean, studied with Paul Homeyer; and Patrick Wedd had lessons from Flor Peeters. The Casavant Societies of Montreal and Toronto did something towards attempting to blend the traditions, or at least establish detente, but in 1980 the two remained fundamentally independent.

5 ORGAN REFORM. The organ reform movement, aiming to sweep aside the orchestra-substitute syndrome of the romantic era and to restore to the organ its baroque sound, began in Europe shortly after World War I and in the USA a decade later. It had little effect in Canada until 1947, when Ernest White returned from New York to establish in London, Ont, the London School of Church Music, in affiliation with the *U of Western Ontario, bringing with him an organ of his own design which had been built by the Aeolian-Skinner Company of Boston. With its exposed pipework on light wind pressure, including mild foundations, strong mixtures, prominent mutations, and thin reeds, it was a revelation to all who heard it. Ernest White's teaching emphasized the stylistic performance of traditional organ literature (in so far as this was possible on an instrument with electro-pneumatic action), employing historically accurate registrations, rigorously controlled rhythm, and extensive use of non-legato touches. Although the London School of Church Music was a teaching institution for only a few years, in 1980 it remained in existence, under the direction of its co-founder, Gordon Jeffery, as a sponsor of organ, choral, and instrumental concerts.

In 1959 an event of far-reaching significance occurred in Montreal with the installation of a two-manual and pedal mechanical-action organ by Rudolf von Beckerath at Queen Mary Road United Church, where Kenneth Gilbert was organist. This was the first mechanical-action organ of fine quality to be installed in Canada since the advent of electro-pneumatic instruments at the end of the 19th century. In 1960 Gilbert, with Bernard and Mireille Lagacé, Gaston and Lucienne Arel, and Raymond Daveluy, established a group known as Ars Organi, dedicated to the performance of the organ literature on fine tracker instruments. These players all acquired new mechanical-action organs in their churches and studios. In 1961 Canada's largest organ building firm, *Casavant

Frères, established a new department to build modern mechanical-action instruments, one of the first of which went in 1963 to *Acadia U in Wolfville, NS, where the Austrian-born organist Eugen F. *Gmeiner was teaching. By 1965 John McIntosh, at the U of Western Ontario, had ordered a mechanical-action organ from Gabriel *Kney and Company. Only a brief time later Antoine Bouchard acquired new instruments by Paul Ott (of Göttingen) at *Laval U in Quebec, and Hugh McLean had a large Casavant tracker installed at the *U of British Columbia in Vancouver. Other universities and conservatories followed suit, so that by 1975 the majority of teaching institutions throughout the country had first-rate instruments available for the use of their staffs and students.

6 THEATRE ORGANISTS. The phenomenon of the cinema organist, who accompanied silent films and provided intermission entertainment, brought a certain levity into a rather unsmiling profession in the 1920s, 1930s, and 1940s. Splendid glamourized instruments designed for appearance (coloured-glass, back-lighted panels to silhouette the performer at his dais console) and sonic surprise (solo stops that trembled like aspens or warbled like canaries) were installed in movie houses in many Canadian towns and cities and became a strong attraction for audiences who enjoyed pop-music recitals (pop in the broad sense, encompassing the Bach-Gounod and Schubert Ave Marias in handy transcriptions, the intermezzo from *Cavalleria Rusticana*, the Berceuse from *Jocelyn*, and the Toreador Song from *Carmen*, gems from Stephen Foster, Gershwin, and Porter, Christmas tunes in season, and the current favourites) between showings of the film program. Some organists made careers of the specialized and tolerant virtuosities of the movie-house repertoire; others kept their work as church organists central and supplemented their incomes with a little or a lot of theatre work. Some achieved wide reputations as popular entertainers. Among them were Paul Michelin and Hanley Wells in Victoria, BC; Julian Hayward and Sydney Kelland in Vancouver; Harold Ramsay and Cyril Godwin in Calgary; Charles Peaker in Regina; Allan Caron, Agnes Forsythe, and Ted Walker in Winnipeg; Al Bolington, Colin Corbett, Ernest *Dainty, Horace *Lapp, Quentin Maclean, Ronnie Padgett, Kathleen Stokes, and Roland Todd in Toronto; Mack White in Montreal; and Harry *Thomas in Halifax.

7 SUMMATION. In 1980 organ playing continued to thrive in Canada. Several universities have instituted programs leading to the B MUS and M MUS degrees in organ performance. Several societies such as the *Amis de l'orgue in Quebec, Ars Organi, the Casavant Society, the Concerts spirituels, the Concerts d'orgue de Montréal, *Pro Organo in St-Hyacinthe, and the Calgary Cecilian Concerts have dedicated themselves to the sponsoring of recitals, and the Goethe-Institut has introduced numerous fine German organists to Canada. The CBC has supported series or organ broadcasts. Visiting and immigrant organists from Europe, the USA, and elsewhere have continued to enrich the Canadian heritage. Although it cannot be claimed that any one distinctively Canadian 'school' of organ playing had emerged by 1980, it could be demonstrated that Canadian instruments, teachers, players, and students could meet the test of international comparison.

Among internationally distributed recordings by organists resident in Canada are the complete organ works of Buxtehude by Bernard and Mireille Lagacé on the French label Calliope and the organ works of Franck by Graham Steed on the English label L'Oiseau-lyre.

See also Organ building; Organ music.

BIBLIOGRAPHY

Smith, Gustave. *Le Guide de l'organiste practicien* (Montreal 1874)
Lapalice, Ovide. 'Les organistes et maîtres de musique à Notre-Dame de Montréal,' *BRH*, vol 25, Aug 1919
Kallmann, Helmut. 'From the archives: organs and organ players in Canada,' *CMJ*, vol 3, Spring 1959
MacMillan, Sir Ernest. 'The organ was my first love,' ibid
AGO / RCCO *Music*, monthly journal, Oct 1967–
RCCO Quarterly, Oct 1973–8

1 / HK; 2, 3, 5, 7 / JSM; 4, 6 / KW

ORLOFF (Orlov), Vladimir (Vadim). Cellist, teacher, b Odessa, Ukraine, 26 May 1928, naturalized Canadian 1977; first prize (Bucharest Cons) 1947. He took his first lessons with his father, a cello teacher, and then studied in Rumania at the Bucharest Cons, making his debut with the Bucharest Philharmonic shortly thereafter. In 1953 he won first prize in the Bucharest International Competition and was designated a state soloist. He also won major awards in competitions in Warsaw in 1955 and in Geneva in 1957. From 1957 to 1964 he toured widely in Rumania, eastern Europe, and China. He was a member 1964–6 of the Vienna Philharmonic Orchestra, taught 1967–70 at the Vienna Academy, and was a jury member for the 1967 International Cello Competition in Vienna. During his years in Vienna he visited other countries. He was a soloist in 1965 with the Philharmonia of Montreal, in 1968 with the Bournemouth SO under Silvestri and the New Philharmonia of London under Boult, and in 1970 with the ORTF orchestra of Paris under Parisot. He also performed at the English Bach Festival in 1969.

Orloff emigrated to Canada in 1971 with his wife, the pianist Marietta Orloff, to become principal cello teacher at the *U of Toronto. He made his Toronto debut at the *St Lawrence Centre in 1971. He subsequently appeared as soloist with several Canadian orchestras, including the Montreal Philharmonia Orchestra, the *Kitchener-Waterloo SO, the *TS (several times, playing concertos of Shostakovitch, Saint-Saëns, Khatchaturian, etc), the *Chamber Players of Toronto, the *NACO, the *Victoria SO, and the *Atlantic SO, and he has given numerous recitals in Toronto. He has recorded Vieru, Khatchaturian, and Schumann concertos for Electrachord, Haydn concertos for Vox, a recital for Supraphon, and encore pieces for Fidelio. In 1975 his recording of works by Kabalevsky, *Coulthard, and *Morawetz was issued by the CBC on the LP SM-305.

See also Discography for *Fenyves.

BIBLIOGRAPHY

Littler, William. 'A little help from friends keeps cellist "going ahead",' *Toronto Star*, 25 Mar 1978 (LL)

J.L. Orme & Sons. Ottawa music, and later furniture, firm, founded in 1861, and one of the oldest surviving names in the Canadian music trade. James Lawrence Orme (d 1893) arrived from Scotland in 1856 and for a few years was partner in a toymaking enterprise in Belleville, Upper Canada (Ontario). In 1861 he became the first paid organist of St Andrew's Presbyterian Church, Ottawa, and to fill a void opened a music store on Sparks St. The firm was incorporated in 1866 as J.L. Orme & Son. Among the goods sold were imported wind instruments, US pianos (Emerson, Dunham & Sons, etc) and Estey reed organs. For some years branch stores were operated in Kingston and Brockville, Ont. In the 1870s and the following decades Orme published music by such

J.L. Orme & Son, Ottawa, ca 1880

Ottawa residents as A.A. *Clappé, F.W. *Mills, and Amédée *Tremblay. He issued his own *Dufferin Galop* (ca 1872) and *Rose and Thistle* quadrilles (1878, dedicated to the Marquis of Lorne), and his son George Lewis Orme (d 1916) wrote the *Loyal Opposition Galop* (1874). The most substantial Orme publications were Clappé's masque *Canada's Welcome* (1879) and Gustave *Smith's piano method *Le Claviste* (1890).

Matthew Orme (d 1937?), a nephew of the founder, arrived from Scotland in 1868 to join the business, and operated it jointly with George L. Orme after J.L. Orme's death in 1893. The company's name was changed to Orme & Son in 1906.

About 1906 an Orme employee, William Hall McKechnie, took over the sheet music and small goods department and operated it on the Orme premises as the McKechnie Music Co until about 1918, when the business reverted to Orme, although the name McKechnie was used until the late 1940s. McKechnie published some 40 dances, ballads, and patriotic songs. Among the last-named were English-language versions of *'O Canada' by George Gillespie (1909), George Holland (1909), and L.E.O. Payment (1912). Ottawa musicians whose works were published by McKechnie included Donald *Heins, Myrtle de Long, Eugene B. Marier, Herbert *Sanders, and Ernest *Whyte.

An Orme Concert Hall, opened on Wellington St in 1900, proved a business failure, but the Martin-Orme Piano Co, a factory opened in 1902, was active until ca 1924. It made between 300 and 500 upright and player pianos each year and won high respect among local musicians. Owain Martin (d 1923), formerly a *Heintzman superintendent, provided the technical knowledge, the Ormes the business skills.

In 1909 a part of the business was sold to C.W. *Lindsay of Montreal, who operated the Ottawa branch for nearly 30 years. Orme & Son continued however, and the chief executives after World War I included Matthew's son Frank L. Orme and sons-in-law Arthur Crawley and Clement S. Harrington. After World War I radios and Victrola gramophones became major sale items; in 1930 refrigerators; and later in that decade furniture. By the 1940s pianos and records made up only 10–15 per cent of sales revenue. About 1950 part of the business became Orme-Bannon (a furniture company on Albert St) and a new J.L. Orme & Sons was established. It was located on downtown Bank St ca 1960–77, and then moved to Highway 31. Managed by James L. Orme (son of Frank L.) until his death in 1979, the store at that time continued to sell furniture and, in keeping with the family tradition, pianos, mostly built by *Lesage.

HK (FH)

Orpheum Theatre / Théâtre Orpheum. An 1100-seat hall located in Montreal on Ste-Catherine St West. Inaugurated in August 1907 as the Bennett Theatre, for 10 years it housed mainly US vaudeville shows. Its acoustic properties led the impresario J.-Albert Gauvin to present recitals and French plays by touring companies there beginning in 1920. By that time the theatre's name had been changed to Orpheum. Until the end of the 1920s, artists appearing there included Clara Butt, Anna Case, the Flonzaley Quartet, Percy Grainger, Bronislaw Huberman, Clara Haskil, Georgette Leblanc, the London String Quartet, the National Civic Grand Opera, the Opéra de Feo, and the Canadian singers Éva *Gauthier, Ulysse *Paquin, and Rodolphe *Plamondon. The *Montreal Orchestra gave its first concerts, in the fall of 1930, at the Orpheum. Under the management of Consolidated Theatres Ltd, it was subsequently a cinema until 1957, when the Théâtre du Nouveau-Monde leased the hall. *Somers' *The Fool* and *Blackburn's *Silent Measures* were presented at the theatre, as were concerts by the Orchestra da Camera (1959). Productions of Brecht and Weill's *The Threepenny Opera* with Monique *Leyrac and Pauline *Julien were staged there in 1961, followed by Breffort and Monnot's *Irma la douce* with Guylaine *Guy in 1963 and Languirand and *Charpentier's *Klondyke* in 1965. Shortly after, the theatre was torn down to make way for an office building. GP

Orpheum Theatre. Theatre-turned-concert hall, located on Granville Mall, Vancouver. Designed by the architect Marcus Priteca, it was briefly a vaudeville theatre (the site of performances by Charlie Chaplin, the Marx Brothers, Rudy Vallee, and others) after it opened in 1927. Though in the 1930s it became a movie theatre, it was one of two halls used by the *Vancouver SO until 1959. Bought by the city in 1973, it was restored to its original grandeur and reopened 2 Apr 1977 as a civic concert hall and the permanent home of the Vancouver SO. Various adjustments were made to the interior by the acoustician Theodore Schultz (of Bolt, Beranek, and Newman, New York) to accommodate the sound of the orchestra, and a system of microphones and speakers was introduced (creating some controversy) to distribute the sound evenly throughout the hall. The acoustics were praised by Vancouver SO concertmaster Gerald Jarvis for 'a European sound, a warm, generous sound quite different from the clinical sound of many North American concert halls' (*Toronto Star*, 4 Apr 1977). Seating 2788, the Orpheum Theatre at the time of its reopening was one of Canada's largest symphony halls.

The interior of the Orpheum Theatre, Vancouver

BIBLIOGRAPHY

Read, Jeani. 'How the Orpheum was saved from a fate worse than death,' *Maclean's*, 4 Apr 1977

'The Orpheum – regal lady on review,' *VSO*, vol 1, Sep 1977

Orpheus Choir of Toronto. Amateur mixed choir founded and conducted 1964–70 by John *Sidgwick. Its debut in a program of carols 26 Dec 1964 at Convocation Hall, *U of Toronto, was followed by a performance 6 Apr 1965 of Bach's *St Matthew Passion* with the *TSO. Sidgwick was succeeded by James Whicher in 1970, Whicher by Lloyd *Bradshaw in 1975. Initially 100 voices, the choir was reduced in 1975 to about 70. Its concerts, five or six annually, have been presented in Toronto churches and halls and on occasion in other Ontario centres. Performing both unaccompanied and with orchestra, the choir has offered a varied repertoire of sacred and secular music of all periods. It commissioned Anton Gartshore's *Sing Thee Noel* and premiered it 16 Dec 1974. MIM

Orpheus Club of Halifax. The second major choir to emerge in Halifax (see Halifax Harmonic Society). It was formed in 1882, with about 75 trained and amateur male voices. After 1886 women were admitted to the chorus as auxiliaries, and for a performance in 1896 of Flotow's opera *Martha* at the Academy of Music there were 32 sopranos, 23 contraltos, 18 tenors, 20 basses, and 12 orchestral players. Conductors were C.H. *Porter 1882–1906 and Harry *Dean 1907–17. The choir opened its own Orpheus Hall 28 Dec 1886. Renovated and reopened 7 Oct 1890 with a grand concert under the patronage of Prince George of Wales (later King George V), the hall was used for subscription concert series, for Spring Festivals (1905–8, sponsored by the Orpheus Club with visiting soloists), and for concerts by other groups. Although an artistic success, the Spring Festival's financial failure forced the Orpheus Club to sell the hall. However, the club continued to present such light operas as Reginald de Koven's *Robin Hood* and works by Gilbert & Sullivan. Activities were suspended after the 1917 Halifax explosion, and the club was reorganized in 1919 as the Halifax Philharmonic Society by Harry Dean.

BIBLIOGRAPHY

Blakeley, Phyllis R. 'Music in Nova Scotia 1605–1925,' unpubl ms

Public Archives of NS. Orpheus Club, 1890–1919 records. MG 20/317 PRB

Orpheus Club (Regina). Women's organization founded in 1915 as the Eva *Clare Studio Club and known 1917–19 as the Clare Music Study Club. Renamed the Orpheus Club in 1919, it incorporated art and literature into its study program and established a choir. Membership has been limited to 45, and meetings have been held every two weeks during the fall, winter, and spring. In 1940 the Orpheus award, later the Ethel Barr Memorial Scholarship, was established for worthy students. Founded in memory of the club's first president, the scholarship has been given to the soprano June *Kowalchuk, the pianist William Pengelly, the actress Francis Hyland, and others. WLB

Orpheus Operatic Society of Ottawa. (Orpheus Glee Club 1906–ca 1916, Orpheus Amateur Operatic Society ca 1916–49). Founded by James A. Smith in 1906, it gave concerts in the Ottawa area for 10 years, then reorganized to perform operettas under its second name. Its first operatic production was *Iolanthe*, at the *Russell Theatre in 1917, and thereafter it staged an operetta each year. Among the works presented were Edward German's *Tom Jones* and *Merrie England*, Gilbert & Sullivan's *The Gondoliers* and *Yeomen of the Guard*, and Gustav Luders' *The Prince of Pilsen*. After a fire at the Russell Theatre in 1927, the group moved to the Ottawa Little Theatre, where it gave concerts and presented operettas such as *H.M.S. Pinafore* and *The Pirates of Penzance*, Oscar Straus' *The Chocolate Soldier*, and Heinrich Reinhardt's *Spring Maid*. Later locations for the society's productions included the Ottawa Technical High School and, after 1968, the Ottawa High School of Commerce. By 1944 the group had begun to stage two operettas a year. In 1949 it incorporated, changing its name to the Orpheus Operatic Society of Ottawa, Inc. Shortly thereafter, owing to the change in public taste, the society turned its efforts to musicals, presenting its first, Rodgers and Hammerstein's *Oklahoma!*, in 1955. Later productions included *Brigadoon*, *Guys and Dolls*, *Kiss Me Kate*, *My Fair Lady*, *Pajama Game*, *Show Boat*, *South Pacific*, and *West Side Story* and the English musicals *Canterbury Tales*, *Lock Up Your Daughters*, and *Oliver*. It also commissioned and performed Berthold Carriere's musicals *Beauty and the Beast* (1970) and *Glengarry Days* (1973).

In 1968 the society began the practice of hiring professional stage directors and designers on an occasional basis. Musical directors have included Berthold Carriere, Joseph Shaver, and Derek *Stannard. The society has been financed through ticket sales, membership dues, and local patronage, augmented in the 1970s by grants from the *OAC and Theatre Ontario. FH

ORR, Hugh (Morton). Recorder player, teacher, instrument builder, b Toronto 7 Jan 1932. In turn he studied piano, cello (with Isaac *Mamott), and recorder, playing the latter instrument (1955–63) with the *Pack Trio and Quartet. Besides pursuing a radio and TV career as arranger, conductor, and performer, Orr has appeared in recital (solo and ensemble) and has lectured in Canada and the USA. His repertoire includes medieval, baroque, and contemporary music, much of it arranged by himself. Author of the two-volume *Basic Recorder Technique* (Toronto 1960), he taught privately for many years and joined the Faculty of Music of the *U of Toronto in 1972. He had made more than 40 recorders and crumhorns by 1977. MFr

OSBORNE, Stanley (Llewellyn). Clergyman, educator, hymnologist, writer, b Clarke Township (near Bowmanville), Ont, 6 Jan 1907; D MUS (Toronto) 1945, TH D (Victoria U, Toronto) 1954, D LITT S (Victoria U) 1972, hon DD (Queen's) 1974. He studied music in his teens with Rita Dudley and Gwendolyn Williams *Koldofsky, and later at the *U of Toronto with Frederick *Horwood (theory), Viggo *Kihl (piano), Sir Ernest *MacMillan and Charles *Peaker (organ), and Healey *Willan (composition). He also studied theology 1929–32 at Emmanuel College and was ordained a United Church minister in 1932. After serving in several charges he served 1948–68 as principal of the Ontario Ladies' College at Whitby. He is one of the few Canadians who has earned doctorates in both music and theology. It is not surprising, then, that his activities have centred on church music. He was co-editor of *The Canadian Youth Hymnal* (United Church of Canada 1939), editor of *Music for Worship* (F. Harris 1947), and editor 1956–9 of the magazine *Jubilate Deo*. He also wrote *The Strain of Praise* (Toronto 1957), a book on church music. In 1968 he was appointed full-time secretary to the joint committee which prepared *The Hymn Book* (Anglican Church and United Church 1971). The book stands as a monument to his work despite controversy over some of his harmonizations of established hymn tunes. In 1975 he completed *If such holy song ... The Story of the Hymns in the Hymn Book 1971* (Toronto 1976). He has written several articles for *EMC*. In 1974 he was named honorary director of the Summer Institute of Church Music at the Ontario Ladies' College, Whitby, having served as director from 1970.

See also Hymnbooks. FRCC

OS-KE-NON-TON (b Louie Deer). Baritone, actor, b Caughnawaga, Que, ca 1890, d Lily Dale, NY, ca 1950. Educated in Muncey near London, Ont, in Caughnawaga, and at Parkdale Collegiate in Toronto, he first worked as a hunter and guide in the Lake of Bays district of Ontario. There his natural singing talent was discovered by the Toronto teacher-singer Leonora James Kennedy, who taught him the rudiments of music and encouraged his further voice studies in New York. As Os-ke-non-ton (or Running Deer, his name as a Mohawk chief) he first sang in the 1920s at the *CNE and in the Toronto *Star* Fresh Air benefit concerts at Bigwin Inn, Lake of Bays. Subsequently he performed 1924–36 as the Indian Medicine Man in Coleridge-Taylor's *Hiawatha* at Royal Albert Hall, appeared in 1926 in Charles Wakefield Cadman's opera *Shanewis*, and gave recitals in 1928 in Toronto and Ottawa. On 25 Jan 1931 he sang with the *TSO in one of its CNR radio broadcasts. He performed in royal command concerts in Great Britain and sang throughout Europe and the USA. His few recordings for Columbia (1920) and HMV (1925) are listed in *Roll Back the Years*.

EBM

Os-ke-non-ton

Ottawa. Canada's capital city, situated in Ontario on the Ottawa River. Settled in the early 1800s, it was called Bellows' Landing (1810), Richmond Landing (1811), and Bytown (1826) after Col John By, who, 1826–32, supervised the building of the Rideau Canal. By 1846, with a population of approximately 7000 (two-thirds Irish, one-third French), Bytown had become a centre of the lumber trade. Incorporated as the city of Ottawa in 1855, it was chosen by Queen Victoria in 1857 as 'the Capital of the Province of Canada' and officially defined by the British North America Act in 1867 as the capital of the Dominion. By 1979 the population of Ottawa, 18,000 at Confederation, had grown to 500,000 (including the suburbs).

A small pipe organ, built in England by Hutter and Kittridge ca 1812 and brought to Bytown in 1823, is preserved at the Bytown Museum. Another organ at the museum was built ca 1830 from local cedar by Blythe and Kennedy and is, if not the oldest, then one of the earliest extant Canadian-built keyboard organs. Newspapers of the late 1830s reveal that Bytown had private music teachers, that a number of girls' schools offered music lessons, and that St Andrew's Church had a singing school. A military band was stationed there, and a Bytown Amateur Band was active by 1842, a Temperance Society Band by 1847, and an Amateur Glee Club before 1855.

John F. Lehmann (b Germany ca 1795, d Ottawa 1850) was choirmaster at Christ Church after 1839 and may have played its Samuel *Warren organ as well, besides teaching piano, violin, guitar, and voice. Lehmann also was the composer of the first known type-set piece of sheet music in Canada, 'The Merry Bells of England' (Lovell, 1840). In 1850 a 1063-pipe Joseph *Casavant organ was installed in Notre-Dame Basilica. The first important visits by artists from abroad included those in 1853 by the duo Anna Bishop, an English soprano, and Nicholas Bochsa, a French harp virtuoso.

Active in Ottawa by the early 1860s were William *Bohrer, who taught piano, voice, and theory and opened a music store, and Herbert G.R. Fripp, who was organist ca 1861–71 at Christ Church and 1871–ca 1877 at St Alban's. In 1862 the two men were co-directors of the Ottawa Musical Union, a choral-orchestral organization of nearly 100 members. The union probably was superseded in 1865 by the *Ottawa Choral Society (formed by Fripp), which presented a Sacred Music Festival that year. After Bohrer moved to Montreal James Lawrence *Orme in 1861 opened a music store on Sparks Street and became the first paid organist of St Andrew's Presbyterian Church.

With Confederation (1867) Ottawa gained both new status and an increased population as the capital of an enlarged country, the site of Parliament and the civil service, and the home of the governor-general. Musical activity expanded accordingly. In 1866 and 1867 Fripp directed several Grand Promenade Concerts and in 1869 he presented oratorio and operatic selections in the first concert of the Ottawa Philharmonic Society. In the same period Stanislas *Drapeau became choirmaster and Gustave *Smith organist at Notre-Dame Basilica. Both men engaged in journalism (musical and other kinds), and Smith taught voice and piano. About 1872 Frederick W. *Mills succeeded Fripp at Christ Church, and in 1874 he became conductor of the Choral Union. The following year Mills composed the operetta *The Maire of St Brieux* for presentation at the private theatricals of Lady Dufferin at Government House – Rideau Hall. The governor-general, Lord Dufferin, and his wife witnessed the first phonographic demonstration in Canada in 1878 (See Recorded Sound: 2 / The technology).

The next governor-general, the Marquis of Lorne, and his wife, Princess Louise, were greeted in 1879 at the Grand Opera House (built 1874) by *Canada's Welcome*, a masque with music by Arthur A. *Clappé. Clappé was the director of the *Governor General's Foot Guards Band, an ensemble formed in 1872 under John Bonner and still active in 1980. Over the years Rideau Hall has been the site of state concerts and recitals by Canadian artists (eg, Ada T. *Kent, *Canadian Brass) and, in 1978, a performance by the *Orford String Quartet of the first work to win the Jules Léger prize for chamber music, R. Murray *Schafer's *String Quartet No. 2*. (See also Sovereigns, statesmen, and other public figures.)

In 1875 the Choral Society took a new lease on life under Edward *Fisher who was also music director of the Ottawa Ladies' College. Fisher was succeeded at the college 1879–86 by J.W.F. *Harrison, who in 1880 reorganized the Philharmonic Society and subsequently presented several oratorios. Harrison also was organist at Christ Church. In the 1880s the Ottawa String Quartette Club flourished, and its two violinists, François *Boucher and Charles Reichling, were teachers to the household of the governor-general, Lord Lansdowne. The other players were R. Sarginson and Robert Brewer. Annie Lampman *Jenkins, sister of the poet Archibald Lampman, gave concerts after moving to Ottawa in 1885 and joined the quartet as pianist. In 1889 Emma *Albani made the first of several appearances at the Grand Opera House.

The 1890s and early 1900s saw an increase in music teaching activity. Ernest *Whyte and Annie Jenkins taught in the 1890s at the Martin Krause School of Music, named after their teacher in Leipzig. Another school flourishing at this time was the Canadian College of Music, which in the 1880s had become affiliated with the London College of Music, London, England. Prominent not only as a teacher but also as an organist and composer, Amédée *Tremblay, who in 1894 replaced Gustave Smith at Notre-Dame Basilica, remained active in Ottawa until 1920. Like Tremblay, Smith, and other Ottawa musicians of the period, Achille *Fortier, another composer and teacher, made his living principally as a civil servant.

In 1894 Annie Jenkins' husband, F.M.S. Jenkins, founded the Schubert Club (a choir) and the 60-player Amateur Orchestral Society, which gave concerts together. J. Edgar *Birch, organist 1895–1934 at All Saints Anglican Church, took over the Schubert Club in 1895, re-organized it the following year as the Ottawa Choral Society, and conducted it until 1914. Under its new name, and with F.M.S. Jenkins as conductor, this group of 175 amateurs gave its first performance – *Messiah* – 29 Dec 1896 in the Grand Opera House. In response to the growing musical and theatrical life of the city, the *Russell Theatre opened in 1897. It was there that Emma Albani sang her farewell concert in 1906. Pauline *Donalda gave a recital at the Russell in 1915.

The Leipzig-trained musician Harry *Puddicombe established the Canadian Cons of Music (1902–37) on Bay St. Puddicombe's brother-in-law, Donald *Heins, a violist, church organist, and teacher at the school, founded the conservatory's string orchestra in 1903 and introduced string training into the public schools.

In November 1904 the president of the Amateur Orchestral Society, Charles A.E. *Harriss (who had been organist at St Alban the Martyr in 1882, moved to Montreal in 1883, but resided in Ottawa again from 1897 until his death) conducted the society in two of his compositions at a state concert for the departure from Canada of the eighth governor-general, Lord Minto. The latter's successor, Earl Grey, set up a competition in 1907 which was won three times by Donald Heins' orchestra. The Ottawa SO, made up of amateurs and professionals, was formed in 1908 by Albert Tassé. In the orchestra's second season, when the musicians' union would not allow the professional players to continue performing with the amateurs, the orchestra lost its wind section but survived as the Ottawa String Orchestra. Tassé authorized Heins to use the name Ottawa SO for the conservatory ensemble in 1910, prior to forming the Ottawa String Quartet in 1914. Heins' Ottawa SO ceased in 1927, when he moved to Toronto. The long-established Orpheus Glee Club, formed in 1906, changed its name to the Orpheus Glee and Operatic Society when it began to present operettas in 1917 and became the *Orpheus Operatic Society when it added Broadway musicals in 1955. Charles *Marchand organized the Bytown Troubadours in Ottawa in 1927. The *Palestrina Choir, an unaccompanied ensemble, was founded in 1921 by Annie Jenkins. Jenkins

Ottawa Symphony Orchestra under Donald Heins, ca 1915

was president 1920–8 of the *Morning Music Club, a concert organization founded in 1892 by Louise Carling. The club began to give only evening concerts in 1946, became the Pro Musica Society of Ottawa in 1962, and continued 1969–74 as the Concert Society of Ottawa. During its long life the club brought many of the world's most prominent musicians to Ottawa.

Another such organization, the Ottawa Music Club, established in 1930 as the Twilight Music Club, has presented four concerts a year, usually featuring young musicians. A gala concert 4 Nov 1980 held to mark its 50th anniversary featured two outstanding young Ottawa musicians, the pianist Angela *Hewitt and the mezzo-soprano Diane Loeb. Hazel Clark, the president of the club in 1936, was program director for 30 years and remained on the executive committee in 1980.

The *Tremblay Concerts, founded in 1929 by Antonio Tremblay, enriched Ottawa's musical life until 1971. Because the Grand Opera House had been destroyed by fire in 1913 and the Russell Theatre had been demolished in 1928, the Tremblay Concerts went on for 12 years (1929–41) at Glebe Collegiate. They continued 1942–69 at the Capitol Theatre and 1970–1 at the *NAC.

In 1927 a 53-bell carillon was installed in the Peace Tower on Parliament Hill as part of the celebrations marking the 60th anniversary of Confederation. Percival *Price was the first Dominion Carillonneur. Robert *Donnell succeeded Price in 1939, Émilien *Allard followed Donnell in 1975, and Gordon *Slater succeeded Allard in 1977. (See also Carillon.)

Despite the Depression, several amateur orchestras and the Ottawa Women's Choir, directed by Wilfred Coulson, survived the 1930s. In 1939 the Ottawa Choral Union (later Ottawa Choral Society) was formed to present choral-orchestral works. Jules *Martel, director 1939–65 of the school of music, *U of Ottawa, formed a choir for a religious congress in 1946. Renamed the *Palestrina Choir in 1948, it gave concerts under Martel until 1958. Allard de *Ridder founded the *Ottawa Philharmonic Orchestra in 1944. He was followed 1950–7 by Eugene *Kash, who set up a much-praised series of children's concerts, and Kash was succeeded 1957–60 by Thomas Mayer. The orchestra disbanded in 1960. The Ottawa Youth Orchestra was founded that year.

H. Bramwell Bailey founded and ran the Ottawa Grand Opera Co 1949–64. Bailey's accomplishments went back to 1923, when he and Cyril J. Rickwood founded the Temple Choir, a masonic ensemble directed 1923–34 by Rickwood, 1934–9 by Bailey, and until the late 1950s by various others. Bailey's semi-professional Grand Opera Co used local singers and players to form a competent ensemble. Productions of *The Bartered Bride, La Bohème, Carmen, Faust, La Gioconda, Samson et Dalila, La Traviata*, and *Il Trovatore* were presented at the Ottawa Technical High School Auditorium.

In 1965 Brian *Law was appointed organist-choirmaster at St Matthew's Anglican Church, where he developed a men's and boys' choir which also gave concerts. The same year he began conducting the Cantata Singers, formed in 1964 and later the resident choir of the NAC. In 1967 he was named conductor of the Ottawa Choral Society, which, along with the Cantata Singers, began to collaborate with the Ottawa Civic SO in 1971. (This orchestra had been formed in 1965 with Col Clifford *Hunt as conductor.) Subsequent conductors were Nicholas *Goldschmidt 1966–7; Goldschmidt, Dirk *Keetbaas, and Ronald Milne 1968–9; and James Coles 1969–75. Brian Law was appointed conductor in 1975, and the orchestra was renamed the Ottawa SO in 1976 (see Orchestras). In 1974 James Wegg became the conductor of the Nepean SO, a community orchestra established in the Ottawa area that year.

The late 1960s and early 1970s were years of expansion in all of the arts in Ottawa owing to the federal government's decision to develop the capital as a showcase for Canadian achievement. The Centennial Choir, organized by Goldschmidt for the Confederation centenary (1967) continued as the *Canadian Centennial Choir. In 1967 also, the CBC inaugurated a Summer Festival (held annually thereafter until 1978 at Camp Fortune in the Gatineau Hills, north of Ottawa), and *Carleton U opened its music department. The U of Ottawa reorganized its School of Music into a Dept of Music in 1969, a year significant also for the opening of the *NAC and the debut of the *NACO under Mario *Bernardi. The annual summer operatic productions which began at the NAC in 1971 were the beginning of the government-supported *Festival Ottawa (Festival Canada until 1977). A multicultural 'Homelands' festival, organized by the Ottawa Folk Arts Council and held in Lansdowne Park in June 1979, featured the music and dances of 30 of the 60 ethnic groups residents in Ottawa.

Ottawa became the location of the *Canada Council offices, the *CBC's head office, the offices of the *CMCouncil and the *Kodály Institute of Canada, and (in 1979) the administration of the *CCA. The *NFB head office was established and has remained in Ottawa, and its operational headquarters were located there also 1940–60. Several of its regular composers (eg, *Fleming, *Blackburn, and *Rathburn) made Ottawa their home. Ottawa music businesses have included J.L. Orme & Son, an instrument and music dealer, sometime publisher, and, as Martin-Orme 1902–ca 1924, a piano manufacturer, and the McKechnie Music Co, a music dealer and publisher. The RCMP Band and the Canadian Armed Forces Band are stationed in Ottawa. Ottawa has become a centre for music research through the facilities or collections of the *National Museums of Canada, the *NL of C, the Public Archives of Canada, and the National Research Council, and among its resident scholars have been Willy *Amtmann, Marius *Barbeau, Yves Chartier, Helmut *Kallmann, Hugh *Le Caine, Edward *Moogk, and Kenneth *Peacock.

Ottawa has been the home of Cammie *Howard and his Western Five and is the birthplace of Paul *Anka, Hubert *Bédard, Maurice Boivin, Jean *Bonhomme, Bessie *Bonsall, Dan A. *Cameron, Bruce *Cockburn, Morris 'Rusty' *Davis, François *Dompierre, Anne *Eggleston, Brian *Ellard, the pianist Gladys Ewart, Ann *Golden, several of the *Huggett Family, Juliette *Gaultier de la Verendrye, Éva *Gauthier, Angela Hewitt, Guy *Huot, Frederick and Ed *Karam, Hélène *Landry, Jeanne *Landry, Djane *Lavoie-Herz, the *Mathé family, Oscar *O'Brien, Joan *Patenaude, Christina *Petrowska, Bill *Richards, Bramwell *Smith Jr, Art *Snider, George Tremblay, and *Valdy.

Compositions inspired by Ottawa include the folksong 'C'est dans la ville de Bytown,' which appeared in Ernest *Gagnon's *Chansons populaires* (Quebec 1865); topical songs by Emmanuel *Blain de St Aubin such as 'Le Chemin des amoreux / The Lovers' Walk' (1882); and the instrumental pieces *New Edinburgh March* (pre-1860) by Mathias Jung, *The Ottawa Rag* (1913) by George E. Lynn, and *Ottawa Symphony* (1942) by Robert *Farnon.

Facing Ottawa on the north shore of the Ottawa River, in the province of Quebec, is the city of Hull, founded ca 1800 as Wrightstown and renamed Hull in 1875. While relying heavily on Ottawa for musical activities, Hull has had its own choirs, bands, and orchestras and is home to the Cons de musique de Hull and the Théątre lyrique de Hull. Among those born in Hull are Yvon *Barette, Léon *Bernier, Hector *Gratton, Clara Lanctot, and Dave *Snider.

BIBLIOGRAPHY

Hanratty, C.J. 'World record broadcast made,' *Canadian National Railway Magazine*, Aug 1927

Hobday, Kathleen. 'A Survey of the Musical Resources of the Province of Ontario,' unpubl paper (Ontario College of Education 1946)

Applebaum, Louis. 'A Proposal for the Musical Development of the Capital Region,' unpubl report (Ottawa 1965)

Van Vlasselaer, J.J. 'Regional reports: Ottawa,' *Mcan*, 34, Jan 1978

(JSw)

Ottawa Choral Society (Union). Name of several Ottawa choirs.

The first Ottawa Choral Society was formed in 1865 by Herbert G.R. Fripp, organist of Christ Church and St Alban's Church, and co-director of the Ottawa Musical Union. A program from 1866 shows that the group sang operatic excerpts.

The first Ottawa Choral Union was formed in 1874, and Frederick W. *Mills was its conductor.

The second Ottawa Choral Society may have been a continuation or revival of the first. Edward *Fisher was its conductor from 1875 until 1879, when he moved to Toronto.

A third Ottawa Choral Society appears to be distinct from its predecessor(s) and has a definable span: 1897–1914. It grew out of the 75-voice Schubert Choir, formed in 1894 by F.M.S. Jenkins (see Annie Jenkins) and led 1895–7 by J. Edgar *Birch. In order to study and perform large choral works Birch replaced the Schubert Choir with a group twice its size, the new Ottawa Choral Society, in 1897, conducting its first concert 11 Jan 1898. The society's repertoire included standard oratorios as well as Stanford's *The Revenge* and Mendelssohn's *Walpurgisnacht* and *Hymn of Praise*. Birch prepared the society for the 1903 *Cycle of Musical Festivals and remained the conductor until it disbanded in 1914.

The second Ottawa Choral Union, 1940–57, has no discernible link with its predecessors, but did continue after 1957 as the fourth Ottawa Choral Society. It was organized in the fall of 1940 to perform for war charities, and presented its first concert – a program of short pieces – 28 Jan 1941 under its founder, W. Allister Crandall. It gave its first oratorio performance – *Messiah* – with orchestral accompaniment in April 1943. The success of this led to an annual program of three oratorios. Frederick *Karam assumed directorship of the union in 1955 and served in that position for 10 years. After the name was changed in 1957, the choir gave its first broadcast – Handel's *Samson* – over CBC radio in 1959. Karam was succeeded by Robert van Dine in 1965. Brian *Law was appointed conductor in 1967, and to mark the centenary of Canada's confederation led the society in a program of Canadian works – *Ridout's *The Dance*, several of *Fleming's partsongs, and Kenneth *Campbell's *Mass Three Four*. The Campbell work was commissioned for the occasion.

The society began performing in the *NAC in 1970, and its success in this new environment led to an expansion of its season to four programs, usually large choral-orchestral works (*Elijah*, the Verdi *Requiem*, *The Dream of Gerontius*, etc). In May 1977 the society joined forces with the Cantata Singers of Ottawa, the Choristers of St Matthew's Anglican Church, a chamber orchestra from the *NACO, and the Ottawa SO, all under Brian Law, for a performance of Britten's *War Requiem* – a bold but not untypical venture for a choir developed in numbers (140 singers), competence, and strength. The society frequently has been accompanied by the NACO. (MG)

Ottawa Philharmonic Orchestra. Formed in 1944 under Allard de *Ridder, after lengthy preparations, begun in 1932, to provide Ottawa with a symphony orchestra. With about 75 players, including bandsmen from the area, the orchestra made its debut 6 Sep 1944. Its official name (until 1952) was the Ottawa Symphony Orchestra, but it was known as the Ottawa Philharmonic Orchestra even in the early years.

Concerts were given at the Capitol Theatre. Conductors were de Ridder 1944–50, Eugene *Kash 1950–7, and Thomas Mayer 1957–60. (Mayer, b Germany 2 Sep 1907, had conducted in Germany, Czechoslovakia, South America, and the USA before moving to Canada as conductor 1955–7 of the *Halifax SO. He also conducted at Stratford and for the CBC.) Concertmasters were Kash 1944–50, Armand Weisbord 1950–7, Willy *Amtmann 1957–9, and Max Rabinovitsj 1959–60. Under Kash, who, while he was concertmaster, had introduced a highly successful children's concert series, the orchestra began a subscription series of five concerts (increased to six in 1954). Under Mayer the philharmonic expanded its schedule to encompass a 24-week season of 60 concerts annually, including school, out-of-town, and weekly CBC broadcast performances, in addition to the regular series. The orchestra was never full-time in its entirety, but in 1957 it established a nucleus of 36 full-time musicians, which increased to 50 by 1959. Though the 1958–9 season probably was its most successful, capped by sell-out performances 16 and 17 Mar 1959 of Beethoven's *Ninth Symphony*, the orchestra was suspended in 1960 when its board could not meet the salary demands of the local musicians' union. Plans for a revival were dropped when the *NAC announced its intention to establish a resident full-time orchestra. The charter, however, was not relinquished until 1971, at which time the philharmonic's papers were deposited at the *NL of C.

The orchestra's repertoire was conventional, though a smaller orchestra – the professional nucleus – played more modern works. Nevertheless, the philharmonic included in its programs works by *Archer, *Brott, *Freedman, *Mercure, *Morawetz, *Rathburn, and *Somers. In 1955 it sponsored a national competition for Canadian composers. The winning compositions, *Festival Concertino* by Neil McKay of London, Ont, was premiered 5 May 1955. A piano concerto, commissioned in 1959 from Mercure, was not completed.

BIBLIOGRAPHY

Kritzwiser, Kay. 'Ottawa's just wild about its band,' Toronto *Globe Magazine*, 8 Nov 1958 (AEB)

OUCHTERLONY, (Guy) David. Organist, teacher, administrator, b Guelph, Ont, 2 Apr 1914; hon D LITT S (Victoria U, Toronto) 1964. A pupil of *Willan, he also studied with Carl Weinrich in New York and with G.D. Cunningham in London. In Guelph he was organist-choirmaster 1927–30 at St Andrew's Presbyterian Church and 1930–2 at St George's Anglican Church. He was music master at, respectively, Appleby College, Oakville, St Andrew's College, Aurora, and Upper Canada College, Toronto. In Toronto he was organist-choirmaster 1933–7 at Holy Trinity Church and 1937–46 at St Andrew's Presbyterian Church, King St, before succeeding T.J. *Crawford in 1946 at Timothy Eaton Memorial United Church. In 1976 he established a choir school at Timothy Eaton. His honorary doctorate was received for service to Canadian church music.

Ouchterlony began teaching at the TCM (*RCMT) in 1940, and served as supervisor of branches 1947–68 and principal 1968–77. Active as an adjudicator throughout most of his teaching career, he was appointed executive director of the *Kiwanis Music Festival Assn in 1978. He is the inventor of the multiple student keyboard (MSK) which has been used widely in conservatory training (see Inventions and devices).

A highlight of Ouchterlony's performing career was a joint recital 28 Jan 1950 with soprano Jeanne *Pengelly at Carnegie Hall, New York. In the 1950s he founded a male choir, the Songmen, which performed in the Toronto area for about 10 years. He was host 1963–4 for CBC radio's 'The Learning Stage' and in 1974 began to perform the same function once a week for CFRB's nightly 'Starlight Serenade.'

Ouchterlony's compositions are mostly short vocal and instrumental pieces. Notable are the anthem 'Trust in the Lord and Do Good' (Thompson 1959), the organ piece *Trumpet Tune* (Gray 1957), and the collection *Anthems, Introits and Descants* for youth choirs (Harris 1974). A *Carol Cantata* (Harris 1975), in which the carols are conceived in the styles of eight nations, had its premiere 21 Dec 1975 at Timothy Eaton Memorial Church.

BIBLIOGRAPHY

Champagne, Jane. 'David Ouchterlony: jack of all trades in an organist's gown,' *CanComp*, 121, May 1977 (MMI)

OVERDUIN, Jan (Garrit). Organist, b Franeker, Holland, 12 May 1943, naturalized Canadian 1962; ARCT 1961, FRCCO 1963, BA (U Western Ont) 1964, FTCL 1966, Associate American Guild of Organists 1967, MA (Waterloo) 1969, M MUS (U Western Ont) 1979. He emigrated to Canada, settling in St Thomas, Ont, in 1955. His organ teachers included Alan Harrington, Barrie *Cabena, Gordon *Jeffery, and Marie-Claire Alain. In 1970 he received a *Canada Council award to study improvisation and choral conducting with Wilhelm Ehmann and Jean Langlais. He was the first to complete successfully at one sitting the associateship and fellowship examinations of the *RCCO, and he also won the Healey Willan Prize. He has been a prize winner at international organ festivals held in London, Ont (1967), Bruges (1970), and St Albans, England (1973).

Between 1967 and 1973 Overduin developed the music program at Rockway Mennonite School in Kitchener, Ont, conducted the Menno Singers, and served as organist-choirmaster at Waterloo First United Church. He moved to London, Ont, in 1973 as organist-choirmaster at Rowntree Memorial United Church and a secondary-school teacher of vocal music and English. He began to teach at *Wilfrid Laurier U in 1978. Through concerts and radio recitals in Europe and in Canada he has become known as one of Canada's most proficient and sensitive young organists. WHK

Overture Concerts Association. Vancouver-based concert agency, founded in 1955 by George *Zukerman (who remained its executive director in 1980) to present live performances in small or remote Canadian centres. The association began with four concerts in Nelson, BC, on a budget of $1800. By 1977 over 5000 concerts (with a total budget of $4.5 million in artists' fees) had been presented in some 70 communities in western Canada, the Arctic, and as far east as northern Ontario. Almost half the artists involved have been Canadian, and in the 1970s the percentage became higher.

Overture Concerts Association has made a practice of working with community groups, which launch membership drives among their citizens. The success of these drives determines the range of presentations, which can include soloists, chamber and choral groups, orchestras (eg, in the Arctic, the Vancouver Radio Orchestra, a touring version of the *CBC Vancouver Chamber Orchestra, in 1969) and opera (including the *COC touring company in 1976–7.) MW

Oxford University Press. British publishing house which opened a Canadian branch in Toronto in 1904. Though the parent firm published music as early as 1659, it did not set up a music department until 1923. In the Canadian branch a music department was established in 1939 with Wallace Gillman as manager until 1946. Freda Ferguson succeeded Gillman. Healey *Willan was a consultant.

The only publisher in Canada to handle concert music exclusively, the Oxford University Press distributed the parent publisher's catalogue (Rawsthorne, Vaughan Williams, Walton, and others) and published about 100 Canadian works. These included sacred and secular choral music, songs, and works for piano, organ, or small ensemble by Robert *Fleming, Sir Ernest *MacMillan, Clermont *Pépin, Godfrey *Ridout, Arnold *Walter, Healey Willan, and others. At first printing was done in the USA from plates; after the mid-1950s octavo material was printed on the premises by the multilith process, while larger sizes were handled by commercial printers in the Toronto area.

The department also published *Music Bulletin* (12 issues, 29 Jan 1941–15 Dec 1942) and (for the *CFMTA) *A List of Canadian Music* (Toronto 1946). When the music department of the Canadian branch closed in 1973, all copyrights to Canadian works were returned to the composers. Responsibility for rental of the staples in the British catalogue was assumed by *Boosey & Hawkes.

BIBLIOGRAPHY
'Oxford University Press. A history of the Canadian branch of the Oxford University Press,' *Canadian Library Association Bulletin*, vol 9, Jan 1953
Oxford University Press, Canadian Branch, 1904–1954 (Toronto 1954)
'Oxford University Press: busy and ambitious,' *CanComp*, 10, Sep 1966 MWl

OXNER, Diane (m MacDonald). Soprano, b Lunenburg, NS, 10 Nov 1928; B MUS (Curtis) 1954. Her mother, Pearl Young Oxner (1899–1968), was active locally for 50 years as a contralto, a teacher, and the conductor of the Lunenburg Male Choir, which performed at the 1939 New York World's Fair.

Diane Oxner attracted attention at the 1950 Halifax Music Festival and studied 1950–4 at the Curtis Institute in Philadelphia. She received honourable mention in the 1954–5 *'Singing Stars of Tomorrow.' Active in Halifax music in the 1950s, she took leading roles in several operas, sang on CBC radio (eg, 'Invitation,' summer 1955) and TV, and appeared at the 1961 *Nova Scotia Festival of the Arts.

In 1958 Oxner began teaching at the New Brunswick Academy of Music and became a church soloist in Saint John. In the years following she performed extensively on radio and in recital in southern New Brunswick and was a soloist with the *New Brunswick SO. In 1974 she moved to Scotland. Her repertoire included many folksongs. She made the LP *Traditional Folksongs of Nova Scotia* (1973, Rodeo CCLP 2011) and also participated in *Canadian Folk Songs: A Centennial Collection* (9-RCA CS-100). PMr

OZOLINS, Arthur (Marcello). Pianist, b Lübeck, Germany, of Latvian parents, 7 Feb 1946; naturalized Canadian 1964; B SC (Mannes College) 1967. He spent his childhood in Buenos Aires and his early teens in Toronto, where he studied piano at the *RCMT with Alberto *Guerrero, Boris *Roubakine, Raoul da Silva, and Jacques Abram. At 14 he was chosen by Walter *Susskind to perform a concerto with the *NYO, and the following year he appeared twice with the *TSO. He spent the years 1963–4 in Paris as a pupil of Nadia Boulanger and Vlado Perlemuter, and the years 1964–7 in New York at the Mannes College of Music, from which he graduated with the highest academic average in the college's history to that date. He continued study with Nadia Reisenberg. In 1968 he won first prize in the *CBC Talent Festival and also in the *Edmonton SO competition.

In the ensuing years Ozolins performed several times with the TS and other major North American orchestras, including the Cleveland Orchestra, the St Louis SO, the *MSO, and the *NACO. He gave a recital of music by Jean *Papineau-Couture, Clermont *Pépin, and Igor Stravinsky at the *Canadian Cultural Centre in Paris in 1977; during that same season he played Tchaikovsky's *Concerto No. 1* with the TS at *Ontario Place and gave recitals in Sydney and Adelaide under the auspices of the Latvian Federation of Australia. True to his origins, Ozolins has been a champion of Latvian piano music in Canada and abroad and has recorded works by the Latvian composer Janis Medinš and the Latvian-Canadian composer Talivaldis *Kenins.

In 1978, on two weeks' notice, Ozolins was the soloist on an eight-city tour of western USA by the *Vancouver SO. He played in the orchestra's send-off concert 4 April in Vancouver, flew to New York for a recital 5 April at Alice Tully Hall, Lincoln Center, and rejoined the tour for rehearsals

Arthur Ozolins

in Salt Lake City the following day. After the tour concert in Los Angeles, in which Ozolins played Chopin's *Concerto in F Minor*, the critic for the *Los Angeles Times* (20 Apr 1978) noted the pianists' 'articulate virtuosity, a seamless legato, ravishing tone at all dynamic levels, deep poetry and startling musical directness. A Chopinist of individual stamp, Ozolins brought both vigor and grace to this exigent work ...' In the fall of 1978 Ozolins was the soloist in Prokofiev's *Concerto No. 2* with the TS on its US tour, which included concerts in Carnegie Hall and the Kennedy Center, and he also appeared in Sweden with the Stockholm Philharmonic and in England with the Hallé Orchestra. He toured the USSR in January 1979, giving recitals in Leningrad, Moscow, and Riga. In addition to his many public appearances he has performed frequently on CBC radio and TV and has been heard on the national networks of Australia, Norway, Poland, Sweden, and the USSR. He has appeared with the Kroll String Quartet. In 1973, with the violinist Marta *Hidy and the cellist Tsuyoshi *Tsutsumi, he formed the Hidy-Ozolins-Tsutsumi Trio.

DISCOGRAPHY
Bach – Bartók – Chopin. 1971. CBC SM-155
Medinš *24 Preludes for Piano*. 1976. 2-Kaibala 60FO2
Papineau-Couture – Rachmaninoff – Prokofiev. 1968. CBC SM-78
Rachmaninoff *Sonata No. 2; Moment musical* – Kenins *Sonata*. 1974. CBC SM-301
Stravinsky *Petrouchka; Four Etudes Op 7* – Chopin *Ballades No. 1 and 4*. 1980. Aquitaine MS 90588
See also Discography for Marta Hidy.

BIBLIOGRAPHY
Littler, William. 'Pianist joins ranks of musical jet set,' *Toronto Star*, 27 Mar 1978 (WS)

P

Pach, Joseph and Arlene. See Duo Pach.

Pacific Salt. Vancouver jazz co-operative, formed in 1970 by Ian *McDougall. In addition to the trombonist McDougall, the founding members were Don Clark (trumpeter, b Creston, BC, 2 Mar 1938), Tony Clitheroe (bass, bass guitar), Oliver Gannon (guitar, b Dublin 23 Mar 1943), Ron Johnston (piano, b Edmonton 25 Aug 1942), and George Ursan (drums, b Regina 3 Aug 1936) – all among the city's first-call studio musicians. The saxophonist P.J. *Perry joined in 1972.

McDougall moved to Toronto in 1973, and Perry to Edmonton in 1975; Perry was replaced by Jack Stafford (b Phoenix, Ariz, 12 Aug 1946), Clitheroe by Torben Oxbol, and Oxbol in 1979 by Tom Haslett (b Vancouver 29 Mar 1949).

Known popularly as Salt, the group has performed in all of the western provinces, often at CBC-sponsored events, and has been heard frequently on the CBC's 'Jazz Radio-Canada.' It has appeared at many school concerts and it toured in 1970 and 1971 for the *JMC.

Salt's 1980 style was essentially the rock-influenced jazz prevalent in the 1970s. The music on the three LPs it had made by 1979 – *Pacific Salt* (1973, CBC LM 302), *Pacific Salt* (1973, Ramophone G1002), and *Pacific Salt Live* (1975, Little Mountain LMR 105; recorded at the Queen Elizabeth Playhouse) – was chosen from compositions by group members (Gannon, Johnston, McDougall, Perry, and Ursan). In concert, by contrast, the group plays the most popular jazz and pop tunes of the day. Gannon's *Country Detour* and *Somaliland*, Clark's *Canned Tomatoes*, and Johnston's *Dumb Boogie* have been among its most popular pieces. In 1976 McDougall, Gannon, and Johnston were reunited in Toronto to make the LP *Three* (Energy E 464), featuring their own compositions.

The band's composers are affiliates of PRO Canada. (JR)

PACK, Rowland (Sterling). Cellist, organist, choir conductor, b London, Ont, 15 Jul 1927, d Toronto 3 Jan 1964. As a child he studied piano with his aunt, Ruby Pack, organ with Thomas C. *Chattoe, and cello with Goldwin Quantz. At 15 he became organist-choirmaster of Robinson United Church, London. In 1947 Pack entered the *RCMT on a Diamond Jubilee Scholarship for studies with Isaac *Mamott (cello), Kathleen *Parlow (chamber music), and John *Weinzweig (theory). He attended master classes with Gregor Piatigorski at Tanglewood, Mass, in 1948, and that same year joined the *TSO. He succeeded Mamott as principal cello in 1953 but resigned in 1957 to devote more time to chamber music (retaining, however, his position with the *CBC SO, of which he was assistant principal cello 1952–64). After several years of recitals with his wife Carol, he formed (1955) the Pack Trio (Carol Pack, spinet, and Hugh *Orr, recorders and krummhorn) and Quartet (the trio with the addition of Donald Whitton, cello).

While conductor (1958–62) of the *Hart House Glee Club, and organist-choirmaster (1958–63) at Thornhill (Ont) United Church, Pack formed the 14-voice Rowland Pack Chamber Singers from the church choir. Specializing in medieval and renaissance music, the singers gave several series (1960–3) with the Pack Consort (a variable expansion of the Pack Trio) at the Heliconian Hall, Toronto, and performed (1962) for *Ten Centuries Concerts. Though untrained in organ building Pack constructed a portative organ for use in the choir's early-music performances.

Reviewing a concert at Heliconian Hall, Udo *Kasemets called Pack 'a model musician – humble, conscientious, hard-working and highly idealistic. Each of his performances is a revelation, an opening of a new door to the many mysteries of music ... While Mr. Pack's knowledge of music theories of ancient times is obviously very thorough, his performances never smack of dry scholarship. What matters to him is the very essence of music, its pulse, its breath' (*Toronto Daily Star*, 20 Nov 1962).

At the time of Pack's untimely death (of Hodgkin's disease), he and two other versatile instrumentalists, Bert *Niosi and Bill *Richards, were planning a CBC radio program around the ancient tune 'Sumer is icumen in,' of which they would compose and perform variations. As a memorial tribute the CBC invited Niosi, Richards, and 11 other composers (*Agostini, *Applebaum, *Freedman, *MacMillan, *Morawetz, *Nimmons, *Ridout, *Schafer, *Surdin, *Symonds, and *Willan) to expand the original idea, each to provide a variation in a particular style. The composite work, dedicated to Pack and performed by colleagues, was broadcast 21 Jun 1964. Two days later, members of the CBC SO and the TSO, Garnet *Brooks, Victor *Feldbrill, the *Festival Singers, Maureen *Forrester, Lois *Marshall, Mary *Morrison, Jan *Simons, and Heinz *Unger collaborated in another memorial concert at *O'Keefe Centre.

Pack's wife Carol (b Wright, m Pack, m Birtch; b Trail, BC, 13 Dec 1927) was a pupil of Ira *Swartz and Max *Pirani in Vancouver and of Lubka *Kolessa and Boris *Roubakine at the RCMT. Besides playing in Pack's recital groups, she was soprano soloist with the Chamber Singers. After Pack's death she taught piano accompaniment and coached voice 1964–71 at the *U of Toronto and developed a music program (1972–5) at the Montessori School, Toronto. She served 1966–8 as accompanist for the *Toronto Mendelssohn Choir and the Festival Singers. In 1975 she returned to the faculty at the U of Toronto.

PAGLIARO, Michel. Singer, songwriter, guitarist, record producer, b Montreal 9 Nov 1948. He sang and played guitar in a succession of Montreal yé-yé bands before meeting with success with les Chanceliers, whose recording of 'Le P'tit Poppy' was a hit in 1966. He began a solo career the following year, taking his style, unique among Quebec pop performers, from the most basic of US rock and roll. He recorded until 1970 in French only, and his successes in that period included the *RCA singles 'Fou de toi,' 'J'entends frapper' (also the title of a popular LP), 'Comme d'habitude,' and the CBS one 'Dans la peau.' Among his most popular records in English have been the Much singles 'Give Us One More Chance,' 'Rainshowers,' 'Lovin' You Ain't Easy,' and, after 1975 when his affiliation with *CBS Records brought him national exposure, the CBS ones 'What the Hell I Got' and 'Dock of the Bay.' He also has made LPs – several entitled *Pagliaro* – for the Much, Amber, RCA, and CBS (Columbia) labels. A 'greatest hits' LP was issued in 1975 under the MP label.

Pagliaro (or simply 'Pag') has performed at most Quebec rock venues, across Canada in 1977, and in Europe in 1976, 1977, and 1979. A Toronto performance brought this observation from Jymn Parrett: 'Even without the trademark sunglasses, Michel Pagliaro remains inaccessible. Black stud leathers compete with disdainful sneer. Slithering, pounding, almost never smiling, Pagliaro the lizard king du monde onstage delivers state of art rock & roll without nice-guy pretensions.' Pagliaro has produced recording sessions for LPs by Walter *Rossi and others. Pagliaro is an affiliate of PRO Canada.

BIBLIOGRAPHY
Vincent, Pierre. 'Michel Pagliaro,' *MSc*, 253, May–Jun 1970
Parrett, Jymn. 'Pagliaro,' *Cheap Thrills*, Mar 1977 MM

Pakistan. Formed in 1947, an independent state within the Commonwealth. The first immigrants to Canada from Pakistan included students, professionals, and trained workers who arrived in the 1960s. Because English is the official language of Pakistan, many already spoke English in addition to their national language, Urdu. In the late 1970s more than 20,000 Pakistanis were living in Canada, with major communities in Edmonton, Montreal, Toronto, and Vancouver.

Although the scriptures of the Koran are chanted in the mosque, instrumental and other vocal music occur outside the religious framework. Historically, musical forms and instruments have been part of the bond between India and Pakistan; however, after the 1947 partition Pakistan encouraged a national recording and film industry distinct from that of India. Public concerts by well-known Pakistanis have been sponsored by the communities in Canada; Mesdi Hassan, who specializes in the vocal form Ghazal, performed in Edmonton, Calgary, Montreal, Toronto, and Vancouver in June of 1977. Amateurs usually provide music at weddings and especially at the dinners following the two religious Eide Festivals. The seven- or eight-member ensembles include sitar or sarod, tabla, sarangi, and harmonium. Musical events are publicized in radio broadcasts and newspaper announcements, eg, in the *Montreal Jung* and the *Toronto Crescent*, which publish articles in English and Urdu.

BIBLIOGRAPHY
Qureshi, Regula. 'Tarannum: the chanting of Urdu poetry,' *Ethnomusicology*, vol 13, Sep 1969
– 'Ethnomusicological research among Canadian communities of Arab and East Indian origin,' ibid, vol 16, Sep 1972 LRH

Palais Montcalm. A municipal building erected 1931–2 in Quebec City at Place d'Youville, on the site of the former Salle Montcalm, with a $150,000 grant from the Canadian government. The architects Ludger Robitaille and Gabriel Desmeules designed a structure enclosing a 1500-seat hall, offices, and a pool.

The palais was inaugurated 21 Oct 1932 with a special concert by the Société symphonique de Québec (*Quebec SO). This was followed by numerous concerts, recitals, shows, and other musical and dramatic entertainments. The palais's first season featured an evening of operatic excerpts with Raoul *Jobin, and a succession of operettas including Planquette's *Les Cloches de Corneville*, Bizet's *Le Docteur Miracle*, Lecocq's *Le Petit Duc*, and Omer *Létourneau's *Mam'zelle Bébé*.

The palais has housed the activities of the *Institut canadien 1932–44, the Quebec SO 1932–59 and 1962–70, and the *Théâtre lyrique de Nouvelle-France, which presented *The Barber of Seville*, *La Bohème*, and other operas 1961–2. In 1940 the CBC installed its offices in the building and began to use the hall for its music programs. In 1961 the hall was renovated and the orchestra pit was enlarged. Variety shows became the main public attractions at the palais ca 1973. (IB)

The Palestrina Choir / Le Choeur Palestrina. Name of two Ottawa choirs. The first Palestrina Choir was organized in 1921 by Annie Lampman *Jenkins and gave three concerts between 1922 and 1924, including a performance of Verdi's *Requiem* 15 Apr 1924. The second choir, a mixed ensemble of about 50 voices, was founded 8 Sep 1946 by Jules *Martel for the Marian Congress in Ottawa. At first it was called the Chorale du Congrès marial and performed at Landsdowne Park. After these performances its members asked to continue working under Father Martel's direction. About 1948, it became the Palestrina Choir / Choeur Palestrina and, following the example of its namesakes conducted by Charles Bordes in Paris and Mgr Raffaele Casimiri in Rome, devoted itself to making better known the polyphonic liturgical music of the 16th-century masters. Nevertheless, the choir included classical and modern works and Canadian and foreign folksongs in its programs. In October 1948 it sang at the Capitol Theatre in Ottawa for the *U of Ottawa centennial celebrations. In 1954 it performed the *Missa Papae Marcelli* at Notre-Dame Basilica to mark the canonization of Pius X and the centenary of the proclamation of the doctrine of the Immaculate Conception. A 1953 radio program was broadcast in the USA. The choir also sang some 50 times on CBC radio and TV and gave about 40 public performances in Ottawa, Montreal, Rouyn-Noranda, Hawkesbury, Cornwall, and other towns. It disbanded in January 1958 owing to lack of funds.

(L-GA, AHC)

PALMER, Catherine (Mary). Organist, choir conductor, educator, b Patterson, NJ, 22 Jan 1928, naturalized Canadian 1961; FRCO 1956. She graduated from the RAM in 1947. In Toronto she was organist 1953–61 of Holy Trinity Church and 1961–5 of the Church of St Mary-the-Virgin. Her anthem 'Christ, My Beloved' (Waterloo 1963) won the *RCCO anthem competition in 1963. From 1964 to 1970 she directed the Palmer Singers, a small Toronto concert choir which specialized in renaissance and baroque music. In 1970 she was appointed music director at Yorkminster Park Baptist Church, which boasts one of the largest and finest organs in Canada. AHC

PALMER, (Robert Henry) **Charles**. Organist-choirmaster, composer, teacher, b Ringwood, Hampshire, England, 24 Jun 1916; BA music (Oxford) 1937, ARCO 1938, MA music (Oxford) 1945, B MUS (Oxford) 1956. He was brought to Canada as a child but was educated and pursued some of his career in England. He studied at Oxford U with Sir Walford Davies and was organist-choirmaster 1938–9 at the Royal Chapel, Windsor Great Park, England, and master of music 1956–61 at Westminster Abbey Choir School.

During Palmer's first professional period in Canada he was organist-choirmaster 1948–52 at Fairfield United Church and 1953–6 at Metropolitan United Church, Victoria, BC. Returning to Victoria in 1961 he became the organist at the Church of St Mary the Virgin, Oak Bay (Victoria), served 1966–9 as conductor of the *U of Victoria Choir, and in 1967 began teaching piano at the *Victoria Cons. Several of his songs have been sung by John *Goss. His choral work 'Fancies' Knell' (1948) and the chamber-orchestral *Little Piece for the Pops* have been performed on CBC radio; *Music for Strings and Brass* (1962) and *Arabesques for Solo Oboe* (1968) have also been performed. His major work, a *Te Deum* for chorus and orchestra (1939), and his *String Quartet* (1956) remain to be heard. A modest man, Palmer has never pressed the cause of his music, and his considerable abilities as a pianist and accompanist have not been widely recognized. DBW

PANNELL, Raymond. Composer, pianist, b London, Ont, 25 Jan 1935. His father was an oboist in the Royal Canadian Regiment Band. Pannell attended the Juilliard School, studying piano with Eduard Steuermann and composition with Bernard Wagenaar and Vittorio Giannini. He took a teaching appointment at the *RCMT in 1959, made a Carnegie Hall debut 25 Jan 1960 at which he played five of his own études, and was a contestant in the 1962 Tchaikovsky Competition in Moscow. He was director in 1966 of an opera workshop at the *Stratford Festival, was appointed assistant director and resident composer of the Atlanta Municipal Theater in Georgia in 1968, and in 1972 became engaged in elementary music education projects for OISE, Toronto. He helped found Co-Opera Theatre, Toronto, in 1975, has served it as general director, and has composed several works for it, including an electronic ballet, *Circe* (1977).

Pannell's compositions (listed in *Contemporary Canadian Composers*) include a *Concerto for Piano and Orchestra* (1967), scores for several Stratford theatre productions (1967, 1968, 1969, and 1973), and a number of operas, including the one-act *Aria da Capo*, premiered in 1963 by the *Royal Cons Opera; the major *COC commission *The Luck of Ginger Coffey* (1967); and the Stratford Festival commission *Exiles* (1973). *The Luck of Ginger Coffey*, with a libretto by Ronald Hambleton based on the Brian Moore novel, had its premiere 15 Sep 1967 and two more performances by the COC that season at O'Keefe Centre, Toronto, but by 1980 had not been revived. Pannell's TV opera **Aberfan* attracted international attention in 1977 when it won the Salzburg TV Opera Prize.

Aberfan has a libretto by Pannell's wife Beverly, as have *Exiles* and the subsequent operas or stage pieces *Souvenirs* (premiered in 1978 at the Toronto Free Theatre with the baritone Donald *Bell in its sole role), *Refugees* (1979, a Toronto Workshop production), and *Downsview Anniversary Song-Spectacle Celebration Pageant* (premiered 1979 at Downsview Secondary School, Toronto).

Reviewing *Souvenirs*, William *Littler remarked on 'the eclectic manner which has hindered Raymond Pannell's acquisition of an individual voice' (*Toronto Star*, 25 May 1978), but appeared to find that manner suitable in the Downsview pageant of the following year, seeing it as 'a talent for adapting existing musical styles. In this case, [Pannell] paraphrased everything from commercial pop to Kurt Weill, climaxing his score with a super chorus celebrating individualism. It brought the house down' (ibid, 17 May 1979).

Pannell has written chamber music and piano pieces as well as theatre works. He is an associate of the *CMCentre and a member of CAPAC and the *CLComp.

WRITINGS

'Aria da Capo,' *OpCan*, vol 4, Feb 1963

'Building a tradition,' *OpCan*, vol 18, Sep 1977

BIBLIOGRAPHY

Marshall, Brenda. 'Raymond Pannell,' *OpCan*, vol 5, Dec 1964

'*The Luck of Ginger Coffey*,' *OpCan*, vol 8, Sep 1967

Schulman, Michael. 'Opera goes co-op with Raymond Pannell,' *CanComp*, 102, Jun 1975

Godfrey, Stephen. 'The Pannells tackle new frontiers,' Toronto *Globe and Mail*, 24 May 1978

Contemporary Canadian Composers / Compositeurs canadiens contemporains

PANNETON, Charles-Marie. Pianist, teacher, composer, b Montreal 15 or 17 Jun 1845 (or, according to *Musiciens canadiens*, 17 Jun 1848), d there 3 Jan 1890. He studied first at Joliette College and later in Montreal with Paul *Letondal. In 1864 he stayed briefly in Leipzig, and the next year he studied in Paris with Antoine-François Marmontel, Camille Stamaty, and a certain Laurent. He made the acquaintance of Rossini. He returned to Canada in 1874, but precarious health kept him from any strenuous activity. After living 1877–81 in Denver, where he was active as teacher, choirmaster, and organist, he taught in Lachine, Montreal, at the boarding school of the Sisters of Ste-Anne. A member of the Société des auteurs, compositeurs et éditeurs de musique of France (SACEM), he was the composer of a few piano pieces and a patriotic song, 'Rallions-nous' (1874, unpublished, words by B. Sulte), written for the *St-Jean-Baptiste celebrations. Jean-Baptiste *Denys, Antonio *Pratte, and Joseph *Saucier were among his pupils. For *La Revue canadienne*, Panneton wrote 'De la musique religieuse' (Nov 1876 and Jun 1877) and several other articles under the title of 'Le Colorado en 1880, suivi de quelques réflections sur les États-Unis en général' (1881).

BIBLIOGRAPHY

Migneault, P.B. 'Feu Charles-Marie Panneton,' *Le Canada artistique*, vol 1, Feb 1890 GP

Pantonal, Inc. The name adopted in the early 1970s by the Institut de sciences musicales Conrad *Letendre, founded in Montreal in 1970 by some of the latter's pupils and disciples, among whom are Michel *Perrault and Jean *Chatillon. The name denotes the sum total of data and principles established, as well as the Research Institute which succeeded that of Letendre.

Since the 1930s Letendre had been working at the definition and establishment of his own findings on harmony, counterpoint, and fugue, in order to infuse, in the words of Chatillon, 'a new spirit into musical research.' Chatillon also stated that 'the Letendre system proposes a rational study of questions of musical knowledge, being founded on simple and clear data such as, for example, the dominant-tonic linkage.' Chatillon continues: 'It carefully weighs each phenomenon that occurs and seeks to reduce it to absolute essentials. Letendre managed to construct a perfectly coherent system which will serve to evaluate the output of composers and to extract useful examples. Thus it builds a musical language – unique and essential – encompassing all valid idioms encountered in the history of music.'

Lacking subsidies, the institute at first financed its research through revenues from the sale of teaching materials resulting from its research. At its foundation in 1970 it had undertaken research in the field of pure music technology or of technology deriving from the generative grammar of musical language. Even though its work was challenged in certain quarters, Pantonal managed to spread its theories and materials in Quebec, but indifference and even resistance from official circles kept the enterprise from being self-financing. It sought aid from the *MACQ, which granted a subsidy of $90,000 for 1976–7; however, this was not renewed. Thereupon, the institute was obliged to abandon its research work for the time being. In 1978 it published *Pantonal – Présentation I*, the first of a series of manifestos intended to serve as an introduction to the views and findings of the institute.

Pantonal then concentrated solely on disseminating elementary- and secondary-level music instruction based on its work. In 1979, in rented quarters, it offered a music initiation course to children from five to eight, a 'course in musicality' to be obtained through choral singing, so as to 'improve reading, metrics, ear training, phrasing, memory,' as well as class teaching for the guitar, based on the popular, folk, and classical repertoires. Among the teachers in Montreal were Michel Perrault, Gisèle Lecours, and Edward Siegner, Pantonal also offered integrated music courses in solfège, dictation, theory, the structure of musical language, and other subjects.

BIBLIOGRAPHY

Chatillon, Jean. 'Le cas Letendre,' *VM*, 14, Dec 1969 GP

'Papillon, tu es volage.' Folksong in the form of a dialogue. It is of French origin and has been found in Canada in several variants, most often in the minor key. An example appears in Ernest *Gagnon's *Chansons populaires du Canada* (Montreal 1865). A somewhat different example, embellished with ornaments and sung in the major, is presented in Marguerite and Raoul d'Harcourt's *Chansons folkloriques françaises au Canada* (Quebec 1956). Marius *Barbeau in *Alouette* (Montreal 1946) cites 13 versions, which nevertheless are very similar musically. The song tells the story of a fair maiden who dismisses her fickle lover. Later, she appears to regret her act and wishes 'love had wings' so that she might be with her sweetheart once more. The song can be heard on LPs by the *Montreal Bach Choir (Vox STPL 511.860) and Jacques *Labrecque (Pathé AT 1029). HP

PAPINEAU-COUTURE, Jean. Composer, educator, administrator, b Montreal 12 Nov 1916; B MUS (New England Cons) 1941, hon D MUS (Chicago Cons College) 1960, hon LLD (Saskatchewan) 1967. He was a grandson of Guillaume *Couture and Mercédès Papineau. He began piano lessons in 1922 with his mother, Marie-Anne Dostaler, and continued 1926–39 with Françoise D'Amour, who also taught him harmony, sight-reading, and music history. He studied counterpoint 1937–40 with Gabriel *Cusson and piano 1939–40 with Léo-Pol *Morin. In 1940, with the assistance of a Quebec government grant, he attended the New England Cons in Boston to work with Quincy Porter (composition), Francis Findlay (orchestral conducting), and Beveridge Webster (piano). With Nadia Boulanger 1941–3 at the Longy School in Cambridge, Mass, he studied Stravinsky's major works and the composition techniques of such French composers as Fauré, Ravel, and Debussy.

From that time onwards, composition became Papineau-Couture's main preoccupation. His earliest acknowledged work is the *Églogues* (1942), composed in Cambridge. In June 1944, after a year spent teaching mainly piano at the Jean-de-Brébeuf College in Montreal, he received another grant which enabled him to resume studies with Nadia Boulanger in Madison, Wisc, and at Lake Arrowhead, Cal. A US patron, Arthur Sachs, invited Papineau-Couture and his wife to spend the winter at his ranch in Santa Barbara along with a few other privileged visitors, including five of Nadia Boulanger's pupils. There they were joined on occasion by Stravinsky and his wife Vera.

Returning to Montreal in 1945 Papineau-Couture was put in charge of piano studies at Brébeuf College. His teaching, however, was concentrated elsewhere. He taught theory, solfège, and dictation at the *CMM 1946–63 and joined the *U of Montreal Faculty of Music in 1951 to teach harmony, counterpoint, and ear training. He served as dean of the faculty 1968–73, and was a pioneer in the development of a course on musical acoustics based on the physical principles of resonance reapplied to the evolution of musical composition. His pupils in theory and composition have included Marcelle *Deschênes-Harvey, Richard *Grégoire, Jacques *Hétu, François *Morel, André *Prévost, and Gilles *Tremblay.

Papineau-Couture's work as an educator has been extended through his participation in the decision-making processes of many organizations concerned with musical training or betterment: the *AMQ (associate secretary 1947–54, president 1962–3), the *QMTA 1948–52, the *JMC (president, Montreal branch 1956–64), the *CMCouncil (president 1967–8), and the Conseil des arts du Québec (chairman of the sub-committee on music 1962–4).

Other organizations were to afford Papineau-Couture further opportunities to promote Canadian music: the *CMCentre of which he was a founder-member and which he served as president 1973–4, the *CLComp (president 1957–9 and 1963–6) and its Montreal concert-giving offshoot the *Society of Canadian Music (secretary 1959–67), and the *SMCQ (founder-member, president 1966–72). He was vice-president 1976–7 and

Jean Papineau-Couture

president 1977–8 of the Humanities Research Council of Canada. He received the 1962 *Prix de musique Calixa-Lavallée and the *CMCouncil Medal in 1973, and was made an Officer of the *Order of Canada in 1969. He is an affiliate of PRO Canada.

Besides book and record reviews (*CMJ*, Autumn 1958, Summer 1959, Winter 1961), Papineau-Couture has written articles for *Le Livre de l'année* (Montreal 1958) and has given many talks, notably before the Ligue Amérique française (1944), the *International Conference of Composers (Stratford, Ont, 1960), the International Federation of the JM World Congress (*PDA, Montreal, July 1967), and ISME (Tunis, July 1972).

The music of Papineau-Couture has evolved between two poles: one of sensitivities and emotions barely held in check, and the other of sheer cerebralism wherein the need for organization becomes both fundamental and natural. Both tendencies are clearly apparent in two periods in the first ten years of his career: an impressionistic period – that of the *Églogues*, a work which speaks of a completed phase and is a reminder of the years of apprenticeship; and a neoclassical period, which begins in 1942 with the *Suite* for piano, grows stronger with the *Concerto grosso*, the *Sonata in G*, the *Suite* for flute and piano, and the *Suite* for piano and four winds, and ends with the *Concerto* (1951–2) for violin and chamber orchestra. The last-named work may be regarded as a turning point in the search for new organizing principles, comparable to those which arose later in the five *Pièces concertantes* (1957–63). The two poles occasionally unite in a desire to support a freer structure, using nevertheless some fixed principle: system, form, text, or plan. This is borne out by such works as *Viole d'amour* (1966), *Sextet* (1967), *Paysage* (1968), and *Chanson de Rahit* (1972), which borrow their mystical notion of sonority from the *Églogues*, yet are fashioned in a neoclassical style interpreted, as in Stravinsky, not as a return to the past but as intellectual utterance, precise and rigorous.

Thus the composer's path issues from a radical development of early writing habits rooted in impressionism (modality, bi-modality, polymodality, the whole-tone scale, chords with simultaneous major and minor thirds), passes through a flirtation with serialism (*Suite* for solo violin, *Canons*), pauses momentarily for a personal application of the theories of Hindemith (*Concerto* for violin and chamber orchestra), and arrives finally at the adoption of total chromaticism employed first 1950–63 with anchor points and then, after the discoveries of the *Fantaisie* for wind quintet, with split planes, beginning with the *Pièce concertante No. 5*. The forms reveal this fixed approach; with the *Psaume CL* Papineau-Couture already

Part of a manuscript page from the first movement of *Sonata in G* for violin and piano (1944) by Jean Papineau-Couture

was moving towards an increasingly pronounced structuralism (the *Pièces concertantes*) and, in such works as *Dyarchie*, *Complémentarité*, and the *Trio* in four movements (1974), towards a system of complementarities (already apparent in the *Trois Caprices* of 1962) which permits the exploitation of symmetry through split planes as well as by a central pivot. (See also Composition, instrumental solos and duos: 2 / Piano solos; Concertos and concertante music.)

Papineau-Couture's intellectualism often has been severely criticized, while insufficient attention is paid to his constant sensibility, which worries the phrases along with syncopated accents or alternatively yields to an insistent, aggressive hammering (an offshoot of an agogic and motoristic style much in favour at the beginning of the century). The composer's output does, however, offer some almost sensuous sonorities (*Oscillations*, *Obsession*, *Slano*, *Nuit*), some examples of a musical poetry which speaks to the heart (*Quatrains*, *Mort*, *Viole d'amour*, *Chanson de Rahit*, *Paysage*, *Le Débat du coeur et du corps de Villon*), and pages which return to a romantic penchant for virtuosity (*Étude in B-flat Minor*, *Mouvement perpétuel*, *Concerto* for piano and orchestra, *Complémentarité*, and *Versègères*). He invites us to laugh with him in *Suite Lapitsky* or even on occasion to rediscover, as if in bewilderment, in the *Poème*, *Symphony No. 1*, *Quartet No. 1*, or the *Pièce concertante No. 3*, the world of the classical 'three B's,' through a thickness in the harmonies, or, in *Papotages*, *Prélude*, *Pièce concertante No. 5* and the piano *Concerto*, that of Stravinsky and Prokofiev, through the unusual intoxication with orchestral sonorities. Gilles *Manny's recording of the last-named work was awarded the prix du Festival du disque canadien in 1969.

SELECTED COMPOSITIONS

STAGE

Papotages / Tittle-Tattle, ballet. 1949 (Mtl 1950). Full orch. CMCentre

Éclosion, pantomime. 1961 (Mtl 1961). Pf, vn, tape. Ms

Many puppet shows, including *Les Voleurs volés* (1949), *Sous la grande tente* (1950), *Le Rossignol* (1962)

ORCHESTRA

Concerto Grosso. 1943, rev 1955 (Mtl 1947, 1957). Chamb orch. CMCentre. RCI 156 (W. *Pelletier)

Symphony No. 1. 1948, rev 1956 (Mtl 1949, Tor 1957). Full orch. Ber (rental). (1948 version) RCI 3 (J.-M. *Beaudet)

Aria from the *Suite for Piano*. 1949. Orch. Ber (rental)

Marche de Guillaumet (excerpt from *Les Voleurs volés*). 1952 (Tor 1952). Med orch. CMCentre

Poème. 1952 (Mtl 1953). Full orch. Ber (rental)

Prélude. 1953 (Mtl 1953). Full orch. Ber (rental). RCI 90 (R. *Leduc)

Trois Pièces. 1961 (Saskatoon 1962). Orch. CMCentre

Pièce concertante No. 5 'Miroirs.' 1963 (Mtl 1963). Orch. CMCentre. Souvenir recording from the PDA (*MSO)

Suite Lapitsky. 1965 (Mtl 1966). Orch. CMCentre

Oscillations. 1969 (Van 1969). Med orch. CMCentre

Obsession. 1973 (Mtl 1973). Sm orch. CMCentre

SOLOIST AND ORCHESTRA

Ostinato. 1952. Str, hp, pf. CMCentre

Concerto. 1952 (Mtl 1954). Vn, chamb orch. BMIC 1960. RCI 117 (*Brunet)

Psaume CL. 1954 (Mtl 1955). Sop, ten, SATB, org, winds. BMIC 1964. RCI 128 (*Mtl Bach Choir)

Pièce concertante No. 1 'Repliement.' 1957 (Mtl 1957). Pf, str orch. BMIC 1961. Col MS 6285 (*CBC SO)

Pièce concertante No. 2 'Éventails.' 1959. Vc, chamb orch. CMCentre

Pièce concertante No. 3 'Variations.' 1959 (Mtl 1959). Fl, cl, vn, vc, hp, str orch. CMCentre. RCI 293 (*Beaudry)

Pièce concertante No. 4 'Additions.' 1959 (Saskatoon 1959) Ob, str orch. CMCentre

Concerto. 1965 (Tor 1966). Pf, orch. CMCentre. RCI 235/RCA CCS-1029. (*Manny)

Paysage (Saint-Denys-Garneau). 1968 (Zagreb 1969). 8 singers, 8 spkr, sm orch. CMCentre. RCI 299 (*SMCQ)

Contraste (Papineau-Couture). 1970 (Mtl 1970). V, orch. CMCentre

CHAMBER MUSIC

Églogues (P. Baillargeon). 1942. Alto, fl, pf. Amérique française 1943. ARCLP 4 (J. *Dufresne pf)/Hallmark RS6 (*Musica Antica e Nuova)

Sonata in G. 1944 (rev 1953). Vn, pf. CMCentre. RCI 92 (*Brunet)/RCI 438 (*Staryk)

Suite. 1945. Fl, pf. CMCentre

Aria. 1946. Vn. BMIC 1966. CBC Expo 29/RCI 245 (B.-J. *Hagen)/Bar BCS 2851/Everest SDBR 3203 (*Staryk)

Suite. 1947. Fl, cl, bn, hn, pf. CMCentre. CBC Expo 11 (*Tor Woodwind Quin)

Quartet No. 1. 1953. Str quar. CMCentre. RCI 363 (*Classical Quartet of Mtl)

Rondo. 1953. 4 rec. AMP 1957

Suite. 1956. Vn. Peer 1966. RCI 222/RCA CCS-1016 (*Staryk)

Trois Caprices. 1962. Vn, pf. Peer 1971. RCI 243 (*Staryk)

Fantaisie. 1963. Ww quin. BMIC 1968. Ca 1969. JMC C30/Alpha DB 95 (Brussels ww quin)

Canons. 1964. Brass quin. CMCentre

Dialogues. 1967. Vn, pf. Peer 1973

Sextuor. 1967. Ob, cl, bn, str trio. CMCentre

Quartet No. 2. 1967. Str quar. CMCentre. RCI 362 (*Orford Str Quar)

Nocturnes. 1969. Fl, cl, vn, vc, hpd, guit, perc. Ms

Chanson de Rahit (Han Suyin). 1972. V, cl, pf. CMCentre

Départ. 1974. Alto fl. CMCentre

Trio in Four Movements. 1974. Cl, va, pf. CMCentre

Versègères. 1975. Bass fl. CMCentre

J'aime les tierces mineures. 1976. fl. Trans-Atlantique (Paris) 1978

Slano. 1976. Str trio. CMCentre

Le Débat du coeur et du corps de Villon (F. Villon). 1977. Spkr, vc, perc. CMCentre

PIANO

Mouvement perpétuel. 1943. BMIC 1949. RCI 134 (*Newmark)

Suite. 1943. BMIC 1959. RCI 251 (A.-S. *Savoie)/Mel SMLP 4023 (*Kubalek)/('Rondo') IRC-SA-1 (W. *Stevens)

Deux Valses. 1944. FH 1955. 1974. RCI 397 (J. Holtzman)

Étude in B Flat Minor. 1945. Peer 1959. RCI 135 (J. *Dufresne)/CBC SM-78 (*Ozolins)/CBC SM-114 (*Fialkowska)

Rondo. 1945. Pf-4 hands. Peer 1960

Aria. 1960. BMIC 1964. Wat CCM-2 (*Cavalho)

Complémentarité. 1971. CMCentre. RCI 384 (J.-P. *Sévilla)

Nuit. 1978. CMCentre

Also one work for hpd, *Dyarchie*. (1971). CMCentre

See also Composition, instrumental solos and duos.

VOICE OR CHOIR

4 works for v(s) on liturgical texts (1944–58): *Pater noster; Ave Maria; Offertoire 'Père, daignez recevoir'; Te mater*. All ms

Complainte populaire (anon). 1946. Sop, bar, pf. CMCentre

Quatrains (F. Jammes). 1947. Sop, pf. CMCentre. RCI 148/CBC Expo 32 (*Alarie)

Mort (F. Villon). 1956. Alto, pf. CMCentre

À Jésus, mon roi, mon grand ami, mon frère (A. Marie). 1960. 2 soli, children's chor. Ms

Viole d'amour (R. Lasnier). 1966. SATB. CMCentre

WRITINGS

'Que sera la musique canadienne?' *Amérique française*, vol 2, Oct 1942

'Training of composers,' *The Modern Composer and His World* (Toronto 1961)

Analysis of 'Pièce Concertante No. 1 for Piano and String Orchestra' (Repliement) / Notes sur la 'Pièce concertante no. 1,' CMCentre Study Course No. 1 (Toronto 1961); repr in *Musicien éducateur du Québec*, vol 5, no. 1, 1974
'Difficultés d'une carrière musicale au début du siècle,' Montreal *Le Devoir*, 2 Jun 1962
'Le danger de la spirale de l'inflation devant la nouveauté,' *Jmc*, vol 14, Jul 1968
– and Papineau-Couture, Isabelle. 'Souvenirs,' [Igor Stravinsky], *CMB*, 4, Spring–Summer 1972

BIBLIOGRAPHY
Potvin, Gilles. 'La jeune musique canadienne: Jean Papineau-Couture, compositeur,' *P-T*, Nov 1946
Beckwith, John. 'Composers in Toronto and Montreal,' *U of Toronto Q*, Oct 1956
– 'Jean Papineau-Couture,' *CMJ*, vol 3, Winter 1959
Poulain, Roch. 'L'oeuvre vocale de Jean Papineau-Couture,' unpubl MA thesis, U of Montreal 1961
'Un musicien, Jean Papineau-Couture,' *Culture-Information (Ici Radio-Canada)*, vol 1, 20 Aug–20 Sep 1966
'Jean Papineau-Couture, a portrait,' *Mcan*, Jul–Aug 1967
Rivard, Yolande. 'Jean Papineau-Couture's return to tone color,' *MSc*, Jul–Aug 1970
Duguay, Raoul. 'Jean Papineau-Couture,' *Musique du Kébèk* (Montreal 1971)
Denis, Clotilde. 'Cérébralisme et lyrisme dans l'oeuvre de Jean Papineau-Couture,' unpubl L MUS thesis, U of Montreal 1972
CMCentre. *Compositeurs au Québec: Jean Papineau-Couture* (Montreal 1974)
Kieser, Karen. 'Canadian composers you'll be hearing from ...,' *Toronto Symphony News*, Jan–Feb 1977
PRO Canada Ltd. 'Jean Papineau-Couture,' pamphlet (1980)
Bail-Milot, Louise. 'Jean Papineau-Couture,' *Contemporary Canadian Composers / Compositeurs canadiens contemporains*
Dictionary of Contemporary Music
MGG LB-M

PÂQUET, (Jeanne Mathilde) **Marguerite**. Contralto, teacher, b Quebec City 10 Nov 1916; B MUS (Laval) 1939. She began to study voice with Sister Saint-Jean-de-l'Eucharistie at the Collège Jésus-Marie de Sillery and at the same time performed as a soloist at St-Dominique Church. She sang on radio stations CHRC and CKCV and took part in CBC operatic and variety programs ('Les Concerts Molson,' 'Concerts intimes,' 'Les Peintres de la chanson'). She studied later under Pauline *Donalda in Montreal and in 1949 she gave some recitals in Quebec City and sang Inez in *Il Trovatore* for the *Opera Guild. That year also she obtained the LaFlèche trophy awarded by *Radiomonde*.

With scholarships from the Quebec government 1952–4 and the French government 1954–5, Pâquet studied in Paris and began to develop her career as a recitalist and soloist throughout Europe and the USA. She continued voice training with Giuseppe Boralevi and Pierre Bernac and studied stage techniques with Georges Wague. She began appearing regularly on French radio and TV and in 1954 sang Suzuki in *Madama Butterfly* at the Théâtre municipal de St-Brieuc.

She was one of the artists selected by Nadia Boulanger to perform under her direction during the marriage ceremony between Prince Rainier of Monaco and Grace Kelly (19 Apr 1956); Boulanger later came to have an important influence on her career. She became a regular soloist for Boulanger and a member of a vocal quartet at the American Cons at Fontainebleau. For eight years she appeared regularly at the Menuhin Festivals in Bath, England, and Gstaad, Switzerland. She also accompanied Boulanger to the USA in 1958 and for three months in 1962, when she sang Lili Boulanger's *Psaume 130* in Boston, New York, Philadelphia, and Pittsburgh.

Pâquet was praised by the critic Maxime Belliard following a recital 23 Nov 1956 at the Salle Gaveau for her 'keen sense of colour and infinitely convincing diction' (*Jours de Paris*). She took part in the St-Germain-des-Prés concert series and those of the Amis de la musique de chambre and sang Mrs Peachum in the French premiere of Britten's version of *The Beggar's Opera* and Pamela in Ivan Semenoff's opera *Le Corsaire*. She sang at various festivals in the provinces and was a soloist with choirs in Montpellier in Bach's *St Matthew Passion*, in Angers in Charpentier's *Te Deum*, and in Metz in Milhaud's *Pacem in terris*. In 1959 she went to South America with the Ensemble vocal et instrumental Roger Blanchard. Later she sang the role of Don Quixote's housekeeper in *Man of la Mancha*, a Jacques Brel production in which Brel took the leading role. The work was presented in Brussels in its European premiere 4 Oct 1968 and in Paris, and was recorded the same year (Barclay 80381).

Marguerite Pâquet returned to Quebec City briefly in 1958, as soloist in Verdi's *Requiem* conducted by Wilfrid *Pelletier, and again in 1959 when she recorded recitals for the CBC. When she was invited by Raoul *Jobin in 1970 to teach singing at the *CMQ, she once again took up residence in her native city.

With the Roger Blanchard ensemble Pâquet recorded works by Marc-Antoine Charpentier (*Leçons des ténèbres pour le mercredi saint* and *Oratorio de Noël*, 1961?; Les Discophiles français DF-730068) and some medieval songs (*Gai, gai, marions-nous*; 1959?; S.M. 33-86) and made the LP *La Chapelle de Charles Quint* (1960?, Le Club français du disque).

BIBLIOGRAPHY
Bonenfant, Yolande. 'Marguerite Pâquet, artiste lyrique,' *Personnalités féminines* (Chicoutimi 1975) AP

PAQUET, Raoul. Organist, teacher, composer, b Lacolle, near Montreal, 2 Dec 1893, d accidentally off Bonaventure Island, Gaspé, Que, 4 Aug 1946; hon D MUS (Montreal) 1946. While studying in Montreal with Arthur *Letondal (piano) and Rodolphe *Mathieu (harmony), he was organist at St-Pierre-Claver Church. He continued his studies in Europe 1919–21 with Abel-Marie Decaux (organ), Marc Delmas (harmony), and Mme Piltan (piano). On his return to Montreal he gave his first recital at St-Jean-Baptiste Church (where he had been appointed organist), performing works by Bach, Franck, Pierné, and Vierne. *Le Canada musical* commented on the 'restraint and balance of his playing, his fine musicianship, and his skill in registration, in which his sense of proportion is acute,' and continued, 'His technique is highly developed' (4 Feb 1922). He returned to Paris briefly in 1923 to study counterpoint with Jean Gallon. On his return to Montreal he was choirmaster at St-Stanislas Church for a year and then organist at St-Sacrement Church in Lachine. Following this appointment he returned to St-Jean-Baptiste, where he was organist until his death.

Paquet had a marked predilection for the music of Bach and was a highly esteemed improviser. He taught at the Institut musical du Canada in 1922, and was on the original teaching staffs of the École supérieure de musique d'Outremont (*École Vincent-d'Indy) and the *Cons national of Montreal; he received the title of founding professor from the conservatory in 1930. Paquet served also as director of the teaching of solfège for the Montreal Catholic School Commission. Among his pupils were his daughter Madeleine, Félix-R. *Bertrand, Lydia *Boucher, Gérard *Caron, Maurice *Dela, Romain *Gour, Ernest Lavigne (b 1905), Sister *Marie-Stéphane, Juliette *Milette, Sister Paul-du-Crucifix (Andrée Paduci), and Georgette Tremblay (*Prix d'Europe 1935). He was a contributor to *MusiCanada* and president of the French section of the Quebec *Casavant Society. He composed some motets, two masses, a *Toccata* for organ, a *Suite* for piano, and *La Croix douloureuse*, an extended canticle sung by Raoul *Jobin in Montreal in 1945.

BIBLIOGRAPHY
'Mort tragique de M. Raoul Paquet,' Montreal *Le Devoir*, 7 Aug 1946
Musiciens canadiens HP

PAQUIN, Louisa (Sister Marie-Valentine). Lexicographer, teacher, b St-Barthélémi, Que, 23 Jan 1865, d Lachine, near Montreal, 9 Jun 1950; hon D MUS (Montreal) 1937. After attending the local boarding school, where she received some music training, she entered the religious community of the Sisters of St Anne and took her first vows in 1887. In 1915 she obtained a diploma from the Chicago Cons after taking correspondence courses in piano for two years from William Sherwood. She taught piano, harp, violin, and guitar in convents in Montreal and later in British Columbia. She was made responsible for music studies in all of the schools of her community in Canada and the USA and reshaped the curriculum; in 1928 the community received a charter from the federal government authorizing it to grant diplomas. She was the founder, and the director 1937–45, of the École supérieure de musique de Lachine. She compiled and in 1922 published anonymously (under the name of her religious community) a *Dictionnaire biographique de musiciens*; a second edition, entitled *Dictionnaire biographique des musiciens canadiens* (Lachine 1935, reprinted Ann Arbor, Mich, 1972), was devoted exclusively to Canadian musicians and was the first work of its kind to appear in Canada. In the preface Frédéric *Pelletier described it as 'the first memorial to our musicians of the past and a mine of information for those of today.' Paquin also wrote an educational work, *La Musique rendue facile* (Lachine 1933). CH

PAQUIN, Marie-Thérèse. Pianist, coach, teacher, translator, b Montreal 4 Jul 1905. After studies in Montreal with Angéline Normandin-McNamara and Alfred *Laliberté (piano) and Louis Michiels (theory), she went to Brussels in 1926 on a scholarship from the *Ladies' Morning Musical Club. In Brussels she studied with Camille Gurickx (piano), Paul Gilson (theory), and Ernest Closson (aesthetics and history). On her return to Montreal in 1927 she became collaborating pianist to the *Dubois String Quartet and accompanied such singers as Léopold *Simoneau and the visiting Lauritz Melchior. She was orchestral pianist for the CSM 1942–53 and the *MSO 1953–63.

Paquin taught 1950–72 at the *CMM, and her workshop, the MTP Opera Studio (1964–70), was frequented by many young singers. She began teaching at the *Banff SFA in 1971 and has taught at the *École Vincent-d'Indy and the *École normale de musique in Montreal. She has been active in such organizations as the *CFMTA and the Ladies' Morning Musical Club, was president 1945–7 of the *QMTA, and became a member of the administrative board of *PDA in 1971 and of the *JMC Orford Art Centre in 1974.

Paquin has published in Montreal, in single volumes, French/English translations of opera librettos. Each contains, in fact, four translations, one literal and one free in each language, the free ones approximating the phonetic patterns of the original language. The series includes *Don Giovanni* (1974), *La Bohème* and *Otello* (both 1975), *Madama Butterfly* and *Così fan tutte* (1978), and *Tosca* (1980). *Ten Cycles of Lieder* (1977) applies the same principle of translation to major works of German song.

Paquin was made a Member of the *Order of Canada in 1981.

BIBLIOGRAPHY

'Marie-T. Paquin traduit des livrets d'opéra,' *Musique périodique*, vol 1, Jan–Feb 1977
Musiciennes de chez nous PR

PAQUIN, Ulysse. Bass, b Alpena, Mich, 20 Jul 1885, d Montreal 16 Nov 1972. He took his classical studies with the Jesuits, first in Chicago and then in Montreal. He was a bank manager, but left the world of finance in 1913 to embark on a singing career. He studied with Albert *Clerk-Jeannotte and Salvator *Issaurel and was a chorister and soloist at the Gesù Church, Montreal, for six years. In 1916 he became choirmaster of St-Sacrement Church in the Montreal suburb of Lachine. In 1920 he settled in New York, where he was soloist at St Patrick's Cathedral and at St Vincent-Ferrier Church, and where he took lessons with Giovanni Martinelli, occasionally singing with him in concert. He toured in the USA and in Quebec. In 1923 he left New York for Paris, where he studied with Rodolphe *Plamondon, singing with him in Paris and in the provinces. Both returned to Canada in September 1924 to undertake, as a duo, a 50-recital tour of Quebec. In the spring of 1925 the two singers made another joint tour, this time of New England.

Paquin gave numerous recitals as soloist or with Canadian and foreign artists and belonged to such groups as the Quatuor montréalais and the Quatuor Arion. He distinguished himself in opera and operetta, playing such roles as Friar Lawrence in Gounod's *Roméo et Juliette*, Escamillo in *Carmen*, the drum-major in Thomas's *Le Caïd*, and Sganarelle in Poise' *L'Amour Médecin*. Some Canadian works have been dedicated to Paquin: *Mensonges* and *Recueillement* by Frédéric *Pelletier and 'Hiver' and 'Été' (from *Saisons canadiens*) by Rodolphe *Mathieu.

Paquin married Luce Chamberland (b Montreal 8 Oct 1884, d there 22 Jul 1932), pianist, accompanist, and chamber player, sister of the violinist Albert *Chamberland. After her death Paquin sharply curtailed his professional activities. IP-C

PARADIS, Gérard. Tenor, actor, b Montreal 9 Feb 1921. He studied singing with Céline *Marier, Pauline *Donalda, Salvator *Issaurel, and Albert *Cornellier, and piano and solfège with Marie-Thérèse *Paquin. He made his radio debut in 1942 on station CKAC and his stage debut 5 Oct 1944 in Offenbach's *Barbe-bleue* at the *Variétés lyriques, where he sang regularly until 1955. He also worked with the *Théâtre lyrique de Nouvelle-France and took part in productions of operettas by Radio-Mutuel. He was heard on CBC radio in 'Théâtre lyrique Molson' and *'Les Joyeux Troubadours' 1951–77 and appeared on CBC TV in 'Les Soirées de chez-nous' in 1958 and 'Toi et Moi en musique' in 1960. His career centred on operetta; he sang such leading roles as Pomponnet in Lecocq's *La Fille de Madame Angot*, Prince Lothar in Oscar Straus' *Rêve de valse*, Parabella in Offenbach's *La Périchole*, Antonin in Hahn's *Ciboulette*, and Grenicheux in Planquette's *Les Cloches de Corneville*.

Paradis's wife is the soprano and actress Jacqueline (Marguerite) Plouffe (b Montreal 11 Feb 1922), a graduate of Montreal's *Cons national with a diploma in diction and phonetics. She was a pupil of Issaurel and Cornellier and made her debut at 17 at the Variétés lyriques, subsequently appearing in more than 30 roles there. A specialist in late-19th-century French operettas, she has sung in many of these on CBC TV and with companies in Quebec and Montreal and has appeared with her husband in plays. IP-C

PARÉ, (Adélard) Alfred (Étienne). Violinist, baritone, b Quebec City 10 Jan 1829, d there 18 Dec 1916. Paré was a civil servant in the Quebec Dept of Crown Lands. He became known, however, for his numerous musical activities in the latter half of the 19th century. Besides skills on the violin, the viola, and the piano, he had, according to *LeVasseur 'a wide knowledge of all matters of music – its history, its literature and its practitioners.' He played second violin in the *Quebec Harmonic Society, the Septett Club, and the *Septuor Haydn and took up the viola in 1875 when the violinists Louis Sigismond Pfeiffer and Joseph *Vézina were recruited into those ensembles. As a singer he premiered C.W. *Sabatier's *'Le Drapeau de Carillon' 15 May 1858.

However, Paré's name was linked particularly to the Septuor Haydn, of which he was president 1871–2, 1875–6, 1877–81, and 1884–6, a member of a committee convened 1874–5 'to decide matters of great importance,' and librarian 1877–8, 1882–4, and 1886–8. In the last-named position he was assiduous in developing the collection of scores later preserved at the *Seminaire de Québec. A 'catalogue of the septuor's library compiled by Mr. Paré' and ready for the printer is mentioned in minutes of 11 May 1874. He was on committees to welcome visiting musicians such as Sabatier, who arrived from Montreal in 1854, and he helped to organize concerts such as the one on 7 Oct 1872 in honour of Antoine *Dessane.

The author (possibly LeVasseur) of an article in *Le Canada musical* called Paré 'a true lover of Sappho.' In an undated letter to Paré, Frantz *Jehin-Prume refers to work 'done with the assistance of music-lovers in whose efforts I am pleased to detect your influence.' This influence appears to have been effective if one compares the dates of Paré's presidency of the Septuor Haydn with the difficulties experienced and overcome by that society in the first 15 years of its existence.

Paré composed the *Quadrilles Malakoff* for piano (Carey Brothers 1885). He was a member of the *AMQ from 1871 until his death.

BIBLIOGRAPHY

LeVasseur, Nazaire. 'Musique et musiciens à Québec,' *La Musique*, 1919–22
– *Réminiscences d'Antan: Québec il y a 70 ans* (Quebec 1926) LP

PARENT, Nil. Composer, teacher, b Quebec City 6 Oct 1945; premier prix musicology (CMQ) 1968. He took courses at the Institut de technologie de Québec 1966–7 while pursuing his musical studies at the *CMQ. Attracted to contemporary music, he took special summer programs in 1965 at Columbia U, New York, with Vladimir Ussachevsky, in 1966 at the *U of Toronto's electronic music studio with Gustav *Ciamaga and Hugh *Le Caine, and, on a *Canada Council scholarship, in 1967 at the Brussels electronic music studio with Henri Pousseur. On grants from the Canada Council and the government of the Netherlands in 1968–9 he did research at the Sonology Institute in Utrecht with Michael Gottfried Koenig and visited studios in Amsterdam, Cologne, Ghent, Geneva, Milan, and Paris. He composed at this time *Des-accords*, a work for nine brass instruments; half of it (four minutes) is devoted to the note E, which, owing to the distribution of instruments around the hall, produces variations of locale, origin, timbre, volume, and duration.

Parent returned to Canada in 1969 and was appointed to the School of Music at *Laval U, where he founded the electronic music studio SMEUL (Studio de musique électronique de l'Université Laval). During the summer of 1971 he worked under Leland Smith at Stanford U, Stanford, Cal, and the next year he took Iannis Xenakis' course at Indiana U in Bloomington. He participated in the 1973 Festival international de musique électroacoustique de Bourges.

In 1973 Parent founded *GIMEL, a performing ensemble which premiered six of his electronic works: *Extension V*, *Polychrome*, *Toudoutoudoux*, *L'Anneau de Rameau*, *Eolos*, and *Signes-Sing*. He wrote other works, among them *Trapèze* (1971) for four groups of 12 singers, and *Ensemble III* (1972) for a mixed ensemble of eight voices, as well as some compositions in the character of theoretical studies, such as *Sone* (1966), *Déserts 1881* (1967), *Mit-Mat* (1970–2), *Downbeat*, and *Imanomroup* (1972).

In 1974 Parent formed the SMEQ (Société de musique expérimentale de Québec). Besides contributing to several journals, he has lectured at the 1975 CAUSM conference in Edmonton and in 1976 at the Massachusetts Institute of Technology, and has produced background music for films, plays, ballets, TV programs, and exhibitions. Parent is a member of CAPAC.

WRITINGS

'Des-accords,' *VM*, vol 2, Mar 1969
'Musique à l'ordinateur,' *Science Dimension*, vol 1, Jun 1970
'Musique et technologie,' *CMB*, 3, Autumn–Winter 1971
'Musique électro-acoustique,' *Media-Art* (1973)
'Les nouveaux sons,' *Québec-Science*, Jun 1975
Synthétiseur: terminologie néologique, 2 vol (Quebec City 1980)

BIBLIOGRAPHY

Schulman, Michael. 'Nil Parent: getting ahead with electro-acoustic music,' *CanComp*, 116, Dec 1976
(MB-L)

PARK, Ron or **Ronnie** (Ronald John). Tenor saxophonist, flutist, bass guitarist, b Edmonton 27 Oct 1944, d Toronto 20 May 1971. In his teens he was a saxophonist in Edmonton with Tommy *Banks and the rock bands The Fendermen and Wes Dakus and the Rebels. He moved to Toronto in 1964, playing tenor saxophone with Sonny *Greenwich and others and bass guitar 1967–9 with organist Art Ayre at *George's Spaghetti House. He was active briefly in Winnipeg (1966) with Bernie *Senensky and in Montreal (1969) as sideman to the trumpeters Ron Proby and Herb *Spanier and worked 1969–70 in New York with George Coleman and Brother Jack McDuff. Returning to Toronto he performed until his death with Lenny *Breau. A fine though uncelebrated player, influenced by Sonny Rollins and particularly John Coltrane, Park recorded as a saxophonist with Dakus and with the pianist Don *Thompson and as a saxophonist and flutist with McDuff (*Moon Rappin'*, 1970, Bluenote BST 84334). He is the dedicatee of the theme *Ronnie* by Senensky. MM

PARKHURST, Edwin (Rodie). Music and drama critic, b Dulwich, near London, 1848, d Toronto 10 Jun 1924. He studied the violin with George Hart in London and moved to Toronto in 1870. He was a reporter for the *Mail* and the *Globe* until specializing as music and drama critic for the *Mail* 1876–98 and the *Globe* 1898–1924. He was music editor of *Saturday Night* and in 1906 founded the magazine *The Violin*, which became **Musical Canada* in 1907 with Parkhurst as editor and proprietor until 1920. He owned a Joannes Baptista Guadagnini violin and participated in amateur chamber music performances. The *Royal Song Folio* which he compiled in 1886 was devoid of Canadian content. For nearly half a century Parkhurst was a major voice in English-language musical journalism. HK

PARLOW, Kathleen. Violinist, teacher, b Calgary 20 Sep 1890, d Oakville, near Toronto, 19 Aug 1963; hon MA (Mills) 1933. She was taken by her mother to San Francisco in 1894 and there took primary lessons in violin with a cousin, Conrad Coward. She gave her first recital at 6 and continued studies until 14 with an expatriate Englishman, Henry Holmes, a pupil of Spohr. Through Holmes' connections she gave concerts at 15 in England, appearing at Bechstein (which became Wigmore) Hall, at Buckingham Palace in the presence of the royal family, and with the London SO. Wishing to study with Leopold Auer, and assisted financially by Canada's High Commissioner Lord *Strathcona, she travelled in 1906 with her mother to St Petersburg (Leningrad). In October Parlow became the first foreign student to enrol at the St Petersburg Cons. Glazunov was then the director, and her classmates included Zimbalist and Piastro. While still a student she gave nine solo recitals in St Petersburg and learned Glazunov's *Concerto in A Minor*, which became a staple of her repertoire. She made five appearances in Finland with the Helsinki Orchestra under Robert Kajanus and met Sibelius.

After her professional debut, in 1907 in Berlin, Parlow began the strenuous life of the travelling virtuoso, touring in Europe and meeting Auer each summer to prepare the next season's repertoire. She gave some 375 concerts between 1908 and 1915. She was a favourite performer in the Netherlands and Scandinavia and was given her famous violin, the 'Viotti' Guarnerius, by the wealthy Björnson family of Norway. In 1907 she was chosen by Glazunov to play his concerto at the Ostend International Music Festival.

Parlow's first North American tour began in November 1910 and by year's end had included New York, Montreal, Quebec, Ottawa, Kingston, and Philadelphia. Concerts in Regina, Moose Jaw, Saskatoon, Calgary, Edmonton, Vancouver, and Victoria followed in 1911, and a March performance with the New York SO under Walter Damrosch preceded her return to England. During her tour she met the pianist Ernesto Consolo, with whom, in New York in 1912, she gave the first of many recitals in North America and Europe.

Residing 1912–25 at Meldreth, near Cambridge, Kathleen Parlow continued to tour. Despite World War I she was able to perform several times in Holland and Scandinavia and even visited (again) the USA. After a 1920 US tour which included her first radio broadcast (Seattle) and ended in San Francisco she toured Honolulu, Japan, Java (Dutch East Indies), Singapore, China, and the Philippines.

In 1926 Parlow left Europe permanently, residing 1926–36 in San Francisco and 1936–40 in New York. After a nervous collapse in 1927 she turned from touring to teaching and quartet playing, making only an occasional appearance in a concerto with orchestra and a final tour (in Mexico) in 1929. She taught 1929–36 at Mills College, Oakland, and summers 1935–41 at Pittsfield, Mass, where she formed the South Mountain Quartet.

In April 1939 Parlow gave a series of lecture-recitals in Toronto. A second series in January 1940 resulted in an invitation to teach at the *TCM. She joined the faculty in 1941. While based in Toronto she appeared with orchestra in concerto performances, played duos with Sir Ernest *MacMillan, and gave concerts with the Canadian Trio (MacMillan and Zara *Nelsova). She also formed the *Parlow String Quartet and gave duo

Kathleen Parlow

recitals with Leo *Barkin and, later, with Mario *Bernardi.

Although her work was affected by the long illness and death (1954) of her mother, to whom she was devoted and who had been with her on all her travels, Parlow continued her activities. In 1956 she received the U of Alberta National Award in music (see Awards). In 1959 she became head of the string department at the London (Ont) College of Music. After breaking the humerus in her left arm in 1960 she recovered to make a memorable return to performance 23 Jun 1961 in London, Ont.

As a performer Parlow was very great indeed. She had a big, pure tone, a suave legato ('as if she were playing with a nine-foot bow,' as one admirer put it) and effortless technique. Her repertoire was enormous: there was probably no work in the great violin repertoire that she had not played. As a teacher she was most successful with those for whom technique was no longer a problem, finding it difficult to systematize and explain mechanics of playing which to her were instinctive. Her pupils in Canada included Andrew Benac, Charles Dobias, Victor *Feldbrill, Sydney *Humphreys, Gerhard Kander, Morry Kernerman, Jack Montague, Joseph Pach (see Duo Pach), Rowland *Pack, James Pataki, Clara Schranz, and Erica Zentner. Among her US pupils were Marilyn Doty, Marjorie Edwards, and Miriam Solovieff.

When Kathleen Parlow died her estate – including the 1735 Guarnerius del Gesù violin once owned by Viotti – was willed to 'students in the string department of the faculty of music at the *U of Toronto, for whom funds would not be otherwise available.' The estate was liquidated and the funds (in excess of $30,000 after encumbrances were removed) were used to establish the Kathleen Parlow Scholarship. The statement in the Maida Parlow French biography concerning the proceeds from the sale of the violin is incorrect.

WRITINGS

'Student days in Russia,' *CMJ*, vol 6, 1961

DISCOGRAPHY

All recordings listed are 78s unless otherwise specified.

Arensky *Serenade, Op 30* – Bach 'Gavotte' from *Partita No. 3* BWV1006 – Rubinstein *Melody No. 1, Op 3*. Orch (Bach unaccompanied). Col A5588

Bach 'Air' from *Suite No. 3*, BWV1088. Pf. HMV 3-7918

Beethoven *Minuet in G*. Pf, Edison Cylinder 28192/Orch. Col A1199/Col A2162

Brahms *Hungarian Dance No. 8* – Chopin *Nocturne No. 2*. Edison Diamond Disc 52354

Chopin *Nocturne No. 2*. R. Gayler pf. Edison Cylinder 28142/C.A. Prince pf. Col A5992, re-release LP Rococo 2001/Orch. Col A5431

Drigo *Valse bluette*. R. Gayler pf. Edison Cylinder 28192/C.A. Prince pf. Col A2162/Orch. Col A1241

Drigo 'Serenade' from *Les Millions d'Arlequin* – Dvořák-Kreisler 'Larghetto' from the *Sonatina, Op 100*; 'Indian Lament.' C.A. Prince pf. Col A5798

Dvořák *Humoresque, Op 101, no. 7* – Tchaikovsky *Melodie, Op 42*. Orch. Col 5412

Halvorsen *Danse norvégienne; Mosaique No. 4* 'Chant de Veslemøy.' Pf. HMV 07919

Kreisler *Liebesfreud*. Orch. Col A5431

Kreisler *Tambourin chinois* – Svendsen *Romance, Op 26*. C.A. Prince pf. Col A5819

Mascagni 'Intermezzo' from *Cavalleria Rusticana* – Gounod-Wieniawski *Fantasia brillante, Op 20*, 'Garden Scene.' Orch. Col A5908

Massenet 'Meditation' from *Thaïs* – Mendelssohn 'Andante' from *Concerto, Op 64*. C.A. Prince pf (Massenet), orch (Mendelssohn). Col A5483

Moore *The Last Rose of Summer*. Orch. Col A1241/Col A2121

Nevin-Parlow *The Rosary* – Schubert-Kreisler *Ballet Music* from *Rosamunde*. 1928. Edison Diamond Disc 52392

Paganini *Moto Perpetuo*. Pf. HMV 3-7917

Sarasate-Bizet *Carmen Fantasia, Op 25*. C.A. Prince pf. Col A5992; re-release LP Rococo 2001

Schubert *Moment musical, Op 94, no 3*; 'Air russe.' Orch. Col A1199/Col A2121

Tchaikovsky *Melodie, Op 42*. R. Gayler pf. Edison Cylinder 29038/Edison Diamond Disc 80326

See Discography for Parlow String Quartet.

BIBLIOGRAPHY

French, Maida Parlow. *Kathleen Parlow: A Portrait* (Toronto 1967)

Hambleton, Ronald. 'Tea with Kathleen Parlow,' *Fugue*, vol 2, Feb 1978

Discopedia

Roll Back the Years GR

Parlow String Quartet. Founded by Kathleen *Parlow shortly after her return to Canada in August 1941 to take up a teaching post at the *TCM. As early as 19 Jan 1941, in a letter to Sir Ernest *MacMillan, she had expressed her wish to form a quartet. Her brainchild gave its first CBC recital 11 Apr 1943, and its first public concert 1 May 1943 at *Eaton Auditorium. The quartet performed regularly until 1958. The original players were Parlow and (until 1952) Samuel *Hersenhoren, violins; John Dembeck, viola (see Dembeck String Quartet); and Isaac *Mamott, cello. Violas after Dembeck were Robert Warburton in 1945, Michael Barten in 1946, and Stanley *Solomon 1946–58. Cornelius Ysselstyn replaced Mamott 1948–9 and on other individual occasions. In 1957 the complement was Parlow, Andrew Benac, Solomon, and Mamott.

Besides performing often on CBC radio, the quartet gave many concerts in Toronto, toured Ontario frequently and Western Canada in 1945, and played occasionally in Quebec and the Maritimes. Its repertoire, in addition to the standard quartets, included those of Bartók, Bridge, Britten, Dohnányi, Fauré, Glinka, Jongen, Kreisler, Turina, and Wolf. Among Canadian works, the quartet premiered James *Gayfer's *String Quartet* (1944), *Weinzweig's *String Quartet No. 2* (1947), and *Morawetz's *String Quartet No. 2* (1956). It also performed *Pépin's *String Quartet No. 1*.

The famous name of its leader ensured the Parlow String Quartet's status as Canada's best-known ensemble of the kind during its 15 years before the public. With the Dembeck and *McGill quartets it perpetuated quartet-playing with dignity and style in the period between the demise of the *Hart House String Quartet and the advent of the *Orford String Quartet.

After a concert at the RCMT, the Toronto critic John *Kraglund described the quartet: 'Miss Parlow is at her best when given an opportunity for robust expression, and Mr. Mamott is ... the most reliable member under any circumstances. Andrew Benac, second violin, and Stanley Solomon, viola, are quick to follow the lead of the other two' (*Globe and Mail*, 21 Jan 1957).

DISCOGRAPHY

Pépin *Quartet No. 1* – Weinzweig *String Quartet No. 2*, 2nd mvt. 1950. RCI 12

Reger *Quartet in F Sharp*, lst mvt – Freedman *Five Pieces for String Quartet*. 1950. RCI 43 LH

Le Parnasse musical. See Fassio, Angelo.

PARR, Patricia (Ann) (m Grebanier). Pianist, teacher, composer, b Toronto 10 Jun 1937; Artist Diploma (Curtis) 1956. She had her first lessons from her mother and studied piano 1942–51 with Mona *Bates and composition 1949–51 with John *Weinzweig. As Patsy Parr, not yet 10, she made her TSO debut 14 Mar 1947 in Haydn's *Concerto in D* and some of her own solo pieces. She made her Carnegie Hall debut in a pops concert with the New York Philharmonic in 1948 and her New York recital debut (Town Hall) in 1949. Also as a child she won CAPAC scholarships for the piano pieces *Nocturne* and *Song to an Indian*. In 1951 she went to Philadelphia for studies at the Curtis Institute. Her teachers were Isabelle Vengerova 1951–6 and Rudolf Serkin 1956–8 for piano and Gian-Carlo Menotti 1952–6 for composition.

By 1955 Parr had appeared nine times in the *Promenade Symphony Concerts in Toronto, and in 1957 she made her first appearance in a TSO subscription concert, replacing Solomon in Beethoven's *Concerto No. 3*. She performed extensively throughout the USA and Canada and taught 1960–3 at the Cleveland Institute (where she was a member of the Concert Arts Trio) and 1967–74 at Duquesne U, Pittsburgh, before returning to Toronto in 1974 as a member of the Faculty of Music at the *U of Toronto. In Canada she made many appearances with the TSO after 1947, and with the *Edmonton and *Winnipeg SOs in 1957.

Active as a chamber musician in the 1970s, Parr was a founder in 1972 (with the violinist Charmion Gadd and the cellist Fritz Magg) of the US-based Trio Concertante, which toured Australia in 1975 and 1978. In 1974 she became a founding member of the University Faculty Trio with the violinist Lorand *Fenyves and the cellist Vladimir *Orloff. She has given duo recitals in Toronto with Orloff and with the violinist Andrew *Dawes, and she appeared as guest pianist with the Guarneri Quartet in 1974 and 1976 at the St Lawrence Centre. In June 1980 in Toronto with Eugene *Rittich she premiered *Morawetz' *Sonata for Horn and Piano*, a CBC commission. MM, PW

PARSONS, Margaret (Elizabeth) (m Poole). Pianist, teacher, b Hanna, Alta, northeast of Calgary, 26 Oct 1914; LRSM 1927, LAB 1929, ATCM 1931, LTCM 1932. She came to Toronto in 1931 to study at the TCM (*RCMT) on scholarship with Norman *Wilks and, later, with Mona *Bates. During the war years she played with the Bates Ten-Piano Ensemble. Parsons and her husband, Clifford *Poole, formed the Parsons-Poole Duo and gave their first recital in 1952. They toured extensively throughout Canada and the USA 1954–65, performing at *Hart House, U of Toronto (winter 1954), with the *TSO 12 Mar 1954, and for the *Women's Musical Club of Toronto in the autumn of 1955, as well as on CBC radio. In 1964 for Capitol Records they made the LP *Parsons-Poole Piano Duo* (Capitol 6088).

Parsons taught at the TCM / RCMT 1933–48 and at the *U of Western Ontario 1948–58. She returned to Toronto and became a teacher at the RCMT in 1965. A noted pedagogy teacher, she has composed and compiled children's piano music for the conservatory's graded examination books (Harris 1949–62) and with her husband has produced the *Parsons-Poole Festival Series for Piano Solo* (Harris) and the **Parsons-Poole Duo Piano Series* (Harris). Among her pupils have been David Johnston, Leon Major, William *McCauley, and Marjan *Mozetich.

PASQUIER, Joël. Pianist, teacher, b Montmorency, near Paris; 25 Sep 1943, naturalized Canadian 1973; premier prix piano, chamber music (Paris Cons) 1962. Son of the violinist Jean Pasquier of the Trio Pasquier of Paris, Joël Pasquier studied 1953–62 at the Paris Cons with Lucette Descaves, Pierre Pasquier, Annette Dieudonné, Geneviève Joy-Dutilleux, and Joseph Calvet. He did his military service 1962–3 as a drummer in a regimental concert band. He studied piano (concerto class) and orchestra conducting 1963–4 with Louis Fourestier at the Marguerite-Long Academy. He gave concerts 1954–65 in France and in 1964 in Tilburg, Holland. In 1965 in the Cannes periodical *Le Journal* Geneviève Via-Mazel wrote of the 'elegance, charm, and sensitivity' of his playing. That year he became the initial grant-holder in a Franco-US university exchange program and thereby was accepted as a pupil of György Sebök and an assistant in the Dept of Music, Indiana U. He performed in 1965 and 1967 in the USA before joining the teaching staff of *Laval U in 1967. In November 1968 he toured cities in Canada and the USA with his cousin, the violinist Régis Pasquier. In the years following he often performed as soloist with the *CBC Quebec Chamber Orchestra, notably 12 May 1975 in Poulenc's *Concerto* and 24 May 1977 in Jean Françaix's *Concertino*. He also played with the *Orchestre de chambre Pierre-Morin. He gave the premiere 16 Apr 1975 of *Variations* by the young composer André Lamarche at the *Institut canadien in Quebec City. Writing of his performance in Quebec City's *Le Soleil* René Dupéré noted 'assured craftsmanship' and 'a concern for detail.' Pasquier was appointed assistant director of the Music School of Laval U in 1977. (MB-L)

Le Passe-Temps. Montreal periodical devoted to music, literature, theatre, fashion, and sports. Its issues ran from no. 1, 2 Feb 1895, to no. 923, December 1949. (Issues which would have been 859, March 1933, to 863, July 1933, were not published, and there was a 10-year gap between issue 881, Jan 1935, and 882, Jan 1945.) Music was predominant, qualifying *Le Passe-Temps* as the longest-lived Canadian music periodical, a longevity record still unsurpassed in 1980. It was issued twice a month until ca 1926 and monthly thereafter.

The founder and owner-editor was Joseph-Émile Bélair (b St-Paul-de-Joliette, Que, 1866?, d Montreal 26 Apr 1933), a printer, ca 1892, with *Le Monde* of Montreal and an amateur flutist. He also invented a music engraving process that was inexpensive and quick. After Bélair's death, which resulted in the publication gap after issue 858, Eddy Prévost became the owner-editor, publishing under the name Éditions du Passe-Temps, Inc. Prévost later shared his work with his brother Roland.

Designed as a periodical for the whole family, *Le Passe-Temps* concentrated on a range of leisure activities, from fashion reports to puzzles (often musical). In a section variously titled 'Supplément musical' (1899), 'Partie musicale' (1900–7), and 'Album musical' (1908–49), the periodical published vocal and instrumental pieces, most of which also were issued for sale as separate sheet music by Bélair and later by Éditions du Passe-Temps. Many of these were French salon and operatic pieces of the day, but in the early decades

LE PASSE-TEMPS

LITTERATURE

Musique — Théâtre — Mode — Sport

ABONNEMENT Un an $1.50 Six mois .75 Payable d'avance.

MONTREAL, 2 FEVRIER 1895 Vol. I — No 1. LE NUMÉRO, 5 CENTS.

BUREAU No 26 Sainte-Elisabeth MONTREAL

AU PUBLIC

LA QUINZAINE

The cover of the first issue of *Le Passe-Temps*

there was a fair amount (though less than half) of Canadian music, including pieces or songs by Claude *Champagne, Alexis *Contant, J.-J. *Gagnier, Jean-Baptiste *Labelle, Jean-Baptiste Lafrenière, Ernest *Lavigne, Calixa *Lavallée, Arthur *Letondal, Rodolphe *Mathieu, Georges Milo, Henri *Miro, Joseph-I. Pâquet, Frédéric *Pelletier, J.-Amédée Roy, Georges-Émile *Tanguay, Charles *Tanguy, Benoît *Verdickt, and Joseph *Vézina.

Under Prévost's editorship, arrangements of Canadian folksongs by Alfred *Laliberté and Henri Miro were featured, and the composers (in addition to non-Canadians) included Alexander *Brott, Claude Champagne, Maurice *Dela, Andrée *Desautels, Hector *Gratton, J.-J. Gagnier, Eugène *Lapierre, and André *Mathieu. Usually the pieces were short and within the capacities of amateur performers. Altogether there must have been about 4000 pieces, and although many were reprints from foreign plates, this remains an impressive number in Canadian music publishing.

Also featured in the periodical were biographical sketches, lessons in the rudiments of music, brief chronicles of Canadian musical life, concert reviews (under various headings, eg, 'Soirées, concerts, etc.,' 'Théâtres et concerts,' and 'Dans le monde artiste'), but rarely long articles. One of the contributors during the Bélair era was Gustave *Comte (1874–1932) whose column 'L'Art et les artistes' was a regular feature. During the Prévost régime *Le Passe-Temps* had New York and Paris correspondents, and published articles by the noted French musicans Isidor Philipp and Maurice Dumesnil. Between 1947 and 1949 J.-J. Gagnier wrote a series of short memoires entitled 'Pointe sèche et crayon gras.' There was no all-Canadian coverage and *Le Passe-Temps* was never intended to be a scholarly publication. One exceptional issue was the special Lavallée number, no. 864, August 1933.

Despite its attractive format and the cheerful cover drawings on the 1945–9 issues (all but three by Jacques Gagnier), the periodical could not maintain itself in the post-war era. Only six issues appeared in 1948, and three in 1949.

BIBLIOGRAPHY

Prince, Lorenzo. 'Quelques souvenirs sur le fondateur du Passe-Temps,' *P-T*, 864, Aug 1933

PATENAUDE, Joan (m Yarnell). Soprano, b Ottawa 12 Sep 1941. She began her studies in Ottawa and was a winner at the Ottawa Music Festival in 1957. She then studied voice in Montreal with Raoul *Jobin and Bernard *Diamant and coached with Charles *Reiner. She attended the *École Vincent-d'Indy and, 1961–3, the *McGill Opera Studio. She won first prize in the 1963 *CBC Talent Festival and in 1964 was awarded a *Metropolitan Opera scholarship which enabled her to study at the Kathryn Turney Long School in New York. She made her *COC debut in 1964 as Micaela in *Carmen* (with Mignon Dunn and Jon *Vickers) and subsequently sang in many productions for the *Stratford Festival, the *Edmonton Opera Assn, and the *Manitoba Opera Assn, and for CBC radio and TV. She made her US debut in 1968 with the New York City Opera and remained with that company until 1970. Subsequently she appeared with several US and European companies including the San Francisco Opera and Spring Opera. She sang in the premiere, 8 Aug 1974 in Albany, NY, of José Raul Bernardo's *La Niña*, and in the North American premiere, in 1975 at Lincoln Center, New York, of Piccinni's *Didon*, revived for her by Newell Jenkins.

In 1976, for an evening called Great Ladies of Shakespeare (which she had initiated in the USA and Canada in 1975), Patenaude commissioned from Harry *Somers the 18-minute scena *Love in Idleness*, for soprano, piano, and stage props, based on the scene between Titania and Bottom in *A Midsummer Night's Dream*. She premiered the Somers 14 Sep 1976 in London. She appeared with the Warsaw State Opera in 1977 and 1978, and sang the Countess in *The Marriage of Figaro* with the COC touring company in 1978. Sponsored by the US State Dept, Patenaude and her accompanist, the Danish-Canadian pianist Mikael Eliasen, gave recitals in Korea and Hong Kong in 1979.

Patenaude's husband, the US baritone Bruce Yarnell, died in a plane crash in 1973.

DISCOGRAPHY

Eggleston – C. Palmer – Rossini – Marin – Literes – Jose Bassa. Reiner pf. 1967. RCI 247

Mayr *Medea in Corinto*. Patenaude (Creusa), Newell Jenkins cond. 1970. Vanguard VCS 10087-89

Songs of the Great Opera Composers. Vol 1: Bizet – Massenet – Saint-Saëns. M. Eliasen pf. 1977. Vol 2: Berg – Barber. Eliasen pf. 1978. 2-Mus H Soc MHS 3433

BIBLIOGRAPHY

Christie, Norma Vale. 'Young soprano knocks image of opera singer,' *Winnipeg Free Press*, 19 Nov 1974 NT

Pathé Frères. Company, founded in 1894 in Paris by Charles and Émile Pathé, which recorded performances by several Canadian-born musicians. The Pathé brothers, former restaurateurs, used as their trademark 'Le Coq,' a reference to their culinary speciality, and a familiar figure in the newsreels made by their company in later years. Pathé Frères's first recordings were on cylinders, but after 1909 they concentrated on discs. They released the first complete opera – *Carmen* – in 1910. Early in 1914 the company set up distribution centres with J.A. Hurteau and Co Ltd, Montreal, and M.W. Glendon, Toronto. Four years later the Pathé Frères Phonograph Co of Canada Ltd opened a sales office in Toronto. It was listed in city directories until 1921. By 1919 branches existed also in Paris, London, Moscow, Brussels, Milan, and New York. Pathé did not record in Canada but made 78s of performances by such expatriates as Emma *Albani, Henry *Burr (as Harry McClaskey), Craig Campbell, Kathleen *Howard, Frank Oldfield, and Cora Tracey, in studios in New York and London. The *Cherniavskys and Gitz *Rice also recorded for Pathé. Pathé, France, was purchased in 1927 by English Columbia; English Pathé, later, by Decca. The name Pathé has survived in France on labels belonging to IME (EMI) and Pathé-Marconi. (EBM)

Le Patriote. Boîte à chansons opened in November 1964 in east Montreal by Yves Blais and Percival Broomfield. Until 1972 it was the only establishment of its kind in Quebec to present singer-songwriters seven nights a week. Located on the second floor of a decrepit building on Ste-Catherine St, the club was decorated in rustic fashion with fishing nets and could accommodate about 300 people. In May 1965 a room on the top floor was furnished with about 170 seats for an experimental theatre, Le Patriote-en-Haut (known as Le Patriote à Clémence 1969–71).

Blais and Broomfield were ardent supporters of Quebec culture, and their success in presenting both new and established performers lay in providing a friendly environment in which they could express themselves. Auditions were required, and it is estimated that more than 5000 Québécois tried out between 1964 and 1978. It was Yves Blais who discovered, for example, Jacqueline Barrette, Claude *Dubois, Louise *Forestier, Diane *Juster, Alain Lamontagne, and Claude Landré. Every important figure in Quebec pop music and Quebec chanson has appeared at Le Patriote, as have many foreign artists, including Barbara, Gilbert Bécaud, Frida Boccara, Pierre Brasseur, Eddie Constantine, Jacqueline Dulac, Marie Laforêt, Nana Mouskouri, Serge Reggiani, Michel Simon, Marina Vlady, and Roger Whittaker. In the summer of 1969 the owners opened boîtes of the same name in Ste-Agathe and in Hull. Open six months of the year, the boîte in Ste-Agathe was more successful than the one in Hull, which closed after five seasons.

Le Patriote has presented the stars of the day, but it also has introduced new talent regularly. Without the help of subsidies, the founders succeeded in making Le Patriote an important stage where Quebec and European singers could test their popularity before moving on to the *PDA. Despite its success Le Patriote experienced financial difficulties and these, along with a security problem, forced it to close its doors in the 1970s. In the fall of 1980 a new 509-seat theatre, the Comédie nationale, was set up in an unused postal station at the corner of Plessis and Ste-Catherine streets and was inaugurated with a production of the rock opera *Starmania*.

Annually 1965–72 Le Patriote awarded the Renée-Claude trophy to an outstanding performer. Among the recipients were Robert *Charlebois, Georges *Dor, Claude Dubois, Louise Forestier, and Alexandre *Zelkine.

BIBLIOGRAPHY

Germain, Georges-Hébert. 'Le Patriote: ten years of Quebec's pioneering nightclub,' *CanComp*, 99, Mar 1975

Bergeron, Raymonde. 'En attendant une politique québécoise de la chanson Le Patriote reçoit des sous pour son théâtre, mais sa boîte à chanson crie S.O.S.!', *Perspectives*, vol 21, 5 May 1979 (BR)

Patriotic songs. Songs expressing love of a country and usually intended for group singing, in unison or harmony. The texts of some Canadian patriotic songs are related to specific events or crises – eg, Confederation, the Fenian Raids, the two world wars. More often they are non-specific, praising the country and proclaiming devotion to it. Many have been written with the intention of providing Canada with its national anthem. Only *'O Canada' has achieved this goal, although several other patriotic songs (eg, *'The Maple Leaf For Ever' among English-speaking Canadians) have enjoyed popularity. As the entries in *Musical Canadiana, a Subject Index* (Ottawa 1967) show, prior to 1921 some 200 patriotic songs had found their way into print. The following survey provides a cross-section; other songs will be found mentioned in the entries Beaver; Centennial celebrations; Confederation and music; Maple leaf; Political songs; Wars, rebellions, and uprisings.

A patriotic song from 1901

Patriotic songs and national anthems essentially are creatures of the 19th-century struggle for the nation state – a single state for all people sharing a common language or culture in a common area. Only a few countries had national anthems in the 18th century. However, there was a growing awareness that folk and popular songs express the characteristics of a people and should be collected and treasured as part of a national heritage. Though not necessarily or even usually patriotic or nationalistic in content, certain songs – for instance in the repertoire of Irish and Scottish music – came to represent the people as a whole.

In French Canada *'À la claire fontaine,' *'Vive la Canadienne,' and similar songs came to be regarded in the early 19th century as embodiments of the people's spirit and invariably were intoned at patriotic rallies and ceremonial occasions. Dance suites, medleys, and song collections of the mid-19th century frequently included these tunes. Examples of medleys include *Chants canadiens* for piano (Crémazie ca 1856), Antoine *Dessane's *Quadrille canadien* (mid-1850s), Ernest *Gagnon's *Le Carnaval de Québec* (1862), and Joseph *Vézina's *Mosaïque sur des airs populaires canadiens* (1880).

Among the Acadians of New Brunswick and Nova Scotia, 'Un Acadien errant,' an adaptation of the words of *'Un Canadien errant' set to the Gregorian tune 'Ave maris stella,' has become the representative song.

Coincidental with the beginnings of sheet music publishing, the first Canadian patriotic songs appeared in the 1830s and 1840s. The earliest were in French, a fact explained by the high degree of political awareness and the Canadian roots of most French-Canadians of the time. Many Anglo-Saxons were recent arrivals whose ties with the mother country were stronger than those with the colony. J.P. *Clarke's songs to texts taken from *The Maple Leaf* (annual anthology begun in 1847) and his song cycle *Lays of the Maple Leaf* (1853) may be considered early attempts to capture the essential spirit of Canada in song. However, after Confederation (1867) English-speaking songwriters outdid one another in churning out patriotic songs. Production reached a peak of fervour during World War I.

The following chronological lists present a selection of songs that either were widely sung or had well-known composers (a few non-Canadians among them). World War I songs are not included since their texts made them unsuitable for continued use in peace-time.

FRENCH-LANGUAGE

'Canada, terre d'espérance,' chant patriotique (words by F.-R. Angers). Napoléon *Aubin. In *Le Canadien*, 1 Jan 1836

'Noble patron,' chant canadien (F.R. Angers). Charles *Sauvageau (Quebec 1843)

'Dans ce banquet patriotique,' chant national (F.-M. Derome). Charles Sauvageau. In *Le Ménestrel*, vol 1, 27 Jun 1844

*'Le Drapeau de Carillon' (O. *Crémazie). Charles W. *Sabatier (Crémazie 1858)

*'Sol canadien, terre chérie' (I. Bédard 1829). In 1842 sung to a traditional tune. A new tune by T.F. *Molt was printed in 1859.

'Avant tout je suis Canadien' (G.-É. Cartier 1835). Sung at first to a traditional tune ('La Pipe de tabac') and later to a new tune by J.-B. *Labelle (ca 1860) and to 'Le Petit Mousse noir'

'Chant du vieux soldat canadien' (O. Crémazie). Antoine Dessane (Crémazie, nd; *Le Chansonnier des Collèges* 1860)

*'La Huronne' (P.-G. Huot). Célestin *Lavigueur (Brousseau Frères, ca 1861, et al)

'La Mère canadienne' (E. *Blain de Saint-Aubin). Antoine Dessane (Sénécal 1862; Turcotte 1862)

'Canadiens, Ô notre patrie' (O. Dufresne). J.U. Marchand (np, 1862?)

*'Ô Canada! mon pays! mes amours!' (G.-É. Cartier 1834). Sung 1834 to a traditional melody. A new tune was composed by J.-B. Labelle in or before 1867.

'Rallions-nous' (B. Sulte). Charles-M. *Panneton 1874

'Ô mon pays, terre adorée' (L. Fréchette). Guillaume *Couture ca 1875 (ms at *U of Montreal)

'Ô Canada, beau pays, ma patrie.' Words and music by C. Lavigueur 1880 (Bernard & Allaire 1880)

*'Ô Canada, terre de nos aïeux' (A.-B. Routhier). Calixa *Lavallée 1880 (A. Lavigne 1880)

'Le Canada' (O. Crémazie). Alfred *Laliberté in *Le Passe-Temps*, 185, 26 Apr 1902. Also settings by Alexis *Contant 1906 (ms at *NL of C) and by J.-J. *Gagnier (Frères des Écoles chrétiennes 1916)

'Ô Canada, ma patrie' (J.H. Malo). Alexis Contant (Yon 1902)

'Hymne à la patrie' (A. Lozeau). J.-J. Gagnier, in *Le Passe-Temps*, 17 Jun 1905

'Canadien, toujours' (Gaston Leury). Charles *Tanguy, in *Le Passe-Temps*, 15 Jun 1907. Also a setting by Alfred *Lamoureux (Gaudin 1925)

'Lève-toi, Canadien!' Words and music by Rodolphe *Mathieu (Édition exclusive de musique canadienne 1934)

A cross-section of contemporary patriotic songs is provided by the sheet music bound together in the album labelled 'Collection de musique composée par des auteurs canadiens ... Exposition provinciale de 1863,' preserved at the BN du Q in Montreal. Collections which contain patriotic songs are *Le Chansonnier des collèges* (1850; musical notation added in 1860 ed) and *Chants des patriotes* (Yon 1893, 1903). See also St-Jean-Baptiste celebrations.

ENGLISH-LANGUAGE

'The Emblem of Canada,' Canadian national song (words from the annual *The Maple-Leaf*). J.P. Clarke; first setting, *Nordheimer ca 1850; second setting in *Lays of the Maple Leaf* (Nordheimer 1853)

'Let's Sing Success to Canada' (W. Mathews). Martin Lazare (Nordheimer 1859)

*'The Maple Leaf For Ever' (A. Muir). Alexander *Muir 1867 (The Guardian 1867?)

'Our Old Canadian Home' (C.P. Woodlawn). C.P. Woodlawn (Nordheimer 1868)

'Canadian National Hymn' (G.C. Hutchinson). F. Muller (Nordheimer 1872)

'Canada, the Gem in the Crown' (J. Davids). F.H. *Torrington (Suckling 1876)

'God Bless Our Wide Dominion,' Dominion Hymn (Marquis of Lorne). Arthur Sullivan(de Zouche 1880)

'May God Preserve Thee Canada' (R.S. Ambrose?). R.S. *Ambrose (Suckling 1887)

*'My Own Canadian Home' (E.G. Nelson). E. Cadwallader (*Daily Telegraph*, Saint John, NB, 1890). Also a setting by Morley McLaughlin (Maritime Steam Lithography 1890)

'Canada for Ever' (A. Muir). Alexander Muir (Whaley Royce 1894)

'The Men of the North' (H.H. Godfrey). H.H. *Godfrey (Whaley Royce 1897)

'The Land of the Maple' (H.H. Godfrey). H.H. Godfrey (Mason & Risch 1897)

'Canada' (H. Boulton). Edward German (Chappell 1904)

'Canada' (W.A. Fraser). Albert *Ham (Whaley Royce 1906)

'A Song of Canada' (P. Semon). Percy Semon (Chappell 1909)

'Mighty Dominion' (W. Mills). Laura *Lemon (Boosey 1910)

'Hail Canada' (J.H. Anger). J.H. *Anger (Whaley Royce 1911)

'O Canada, Dear Canada!' (M. Pugh). G.V. *Thompson (Thompson 1912)

'Our Canada from Sea to Sea' (A. Stringer). Gena *Branscombe (Thompson 1939)

'We Sing a Song to Canada' (F. *Harris). Healey *Willan (B652; Harris 1939)

An album of *Canadian National and Patriotic Songs* was compiled by Theodore *Martens (Suckling 1890). H.H. Godfrey, like E. Cadwallader (fl 1890–1908) an inveterate writer of patriotic songs, had an album of his *Canadian Patriotic Songs and Melodies* published by Canadian American Music in 1902.

After World War I the vogue for patriotic song-writing was clearly on the wane. The main reason undoubtedly was that 'O Canada' had become accepted so widely that there was no incentive for writing another national anthem. Furthermore, the disillusionment of the 1920s and the Depression years stood in direct contrast to the imagery of traditional patriotic songs (remote from every-day reality) and to the naïvety and downright chauvinism of many of the earlier songs. In Canada World War II produced only a fraction of the number of morale-boosting patriotic songs brought forth by World War I.

The pop idiom of the mid-20th century was irreconcilable with the hymnlike music of earlier patriotic songs, and the genre in consequence became more and more the territory of amateur composers. Patriotism was not dead, but it expressed itself in less conventional garb. Examples of post-1950 songs about Canada, with strong admixtures of either folk music or pop are Gilles *Vigneault's *'Mon pays, c'est l'hiver' (1964) (the composer is careful to describe it as 'not a patriotic song') and *'Gens du pays' (1975); and Bobby *Gimby's *'CA-NA-DA,' the theme song for the 1967 centenary of Confederation.

BIBLIOGRAPHY

Silver, B.C. 'The heritage: patriotic song,' *J of Education*, vol 7, Jun 1958

HK

Patronage. The patronage, support, and encouragement of music in Canada, as in other Western countries, has come from four major sectors: church, state, corporations, and individuals.

The first patron, going back more than 300 years, was the Roman Catholic church, which, as did the Protestant churches later, included music in its services and endowed the parishes with musicians, many of whom assumed musical leadership in the community as a whole, serving as organists, conductors, teachers, and performers. Another early example of patronage was the sponsorship of military bands, first by the British and later by the Canadian government's Dept of National Defence. Established in some numbers across the country in the late 18th century, bands gave concerts and provided orchestras with brass and wind players and the community with teachers. (See Bands; Brass.)

Direct government support of music, so common to nearly all European countries, was almost unknown in Canada until the middle of the 20th century. Apart from the support given to such activities by the government of Quebec, there were no government subventions to orchestras, choral societies, opera companies, or music schools, nor had Canada a resource corresponding to the many private benefactors of the USA who gave lavishly to music. There were certain notable exceptions, eg, in Vancouver the Buckerfield family, the B.T. *Rogers, the *Koerners, W.H. *Malkin, David *Spencer; in Regina Franklin N. Darke, Ambrose C. Froom; in Winnipeg the Richardsons; in Toronto the *Masseys, the Eatons, Col A.E. *Gooderham, F.R. MacKelcan, Floyd S. *Chalmers; in Montreal Lord *Strathcona, Frank *Meighen, Charles S. Campbell, Jean *Lallemand, and J.W. McConnell. In general, however, the Canadian well-to-do were tight-fisted towards the arts. Canadian corporate wealth has been relatively modest; many companies are merely branches of US or British ones, a fact which has inhibited donation policies in Canada. Some companies, however, have supported their own musical organizations, eg, the excellent band of the *Anglo-Canadian Leather Company of Huntsville, Ont, in the first quarter of the 20th century, the *Dofasco Male Chorus of Hamilton, the *Canada Packers Operatic Society, and the *Eaton Operatic Society in Toronto.

By the end of World War II a few of Canada's more altruistic political thinkers were foreseeing the necessity of increased government involvement in the support of the arts. A 1946 statement to Prime Minister Mackenzie King from Herman Voaden, president of the Canadian Arts Council (*CCA), made bold and cogent requests for such involvement. The Commission on National Development in the Arts, Letters and Sciences (*Massey Commission) was created in 1949 and tabled in 1951 a report representing the most massive and thorough cultural investigation undertaken in Canada up to that time. The report reminded the federal government that 'In most modern states there are ministries of "fine arts" or of "cultural affairs" ' and that 'Some measure of official responsibility is now accepted in all civilized countries whatever political philosophy may prevail.' These remarks appear to have had the desired chastening effect on a body whose pragmatism was traditional. As Bernard Ostry points out (*The Cultural Connection*, pp 63–4), 'Almost all its recommendations were eventually implemented in some fashion or other. Before it, everything was tentative, incoherent, a patchwork of band-aid remedies – though a patchwork in which the historical eye could perceive a distinctively Canadian pattern. After the Massey Report, Canadian governments, provincial as well as federal, began to be drawn reluctantly toward the need to develop cultural policy more consciously and to try and avoid the patchwork of the past.'

Gradually patterns evolved for the administration of new forms of aid from national, provincial, and civic levels. Education in music began to receive substantial help in every province through educational funds directed to instruction in public and high schools and in university music faculties and departments. In some provinces, especially Quebec, considerable sums were directed to music schools specifically. Municipal governments have given indirect aid to music through grants to schools, have assisted special projects such as music festivals, youth orchestras, and community music schools and have established parks and concert halls and developed recreation programs for these.

The *Canada Council – established in 1957 as a crown corporation, not a department of government – has been a major national source of subsidy for professional musicians and groups. Generally free of political interference, its 21 members, representing all parts of the country, in 1972–3 (to choose a random year as an instance) authorized musical subsidies of $4,243,000: *MSO, $440,000; *COC, $377,000; *Festival Singers, $112,500; the *CMCentre, $85,000, etc. In addition, the council has given a wide range of grants to individual performing musicians for auditions, tours, advanced study, and special projects. Substantial sums have been given annually to Canadian composers for the completion of commissions, including copying costs.

The *CBC, another, older national crown corporation, since its inception has patronized Canadian music through live broadcasting and through recordings of Canadian musicians and groups. It has aired a great deal of Canadian music. It is doubtful whether some orchestras could function without the revenue gained from performing on the CBC, and a large number of excellent freelance musicians, particularly in Montreal, Toronto, Winnipeg, and Vancouver, have depended on it for much of their livelihood. The Dept of National Defence has contributed to its bands and to the communities in which they are stationed. Indeed, 'for years [it] was alone among federal departments in developing a conscious, consistent and imaginative policy and providing the funds to make it work' (Ostry, *The Cultural Connection*, p 41). Another national body, the *NFB, consistently has used Canadian music and musicians to enhance its films.

By 1980 each Canadian province had a provincial arts council or ministry of culture to subsidize music and the other arts. Unlike the Canada Council, the provincial councils supported amateur as well as professional groups and a wealth of community projects of varying descriptions, from workshops, summer music camps, and festivals, to agencies for promoting engagements of Canadian artists. (See: Alberta Culture; British Columbia Cultural Services Branch; Manitoba Arts Council; Ministère des Affaires culturelles du Québec; New Brunswick Cultural Development Branch; Newfoundland Division of Cultural Affairs; Nova Scotia Department of Culture, Recreation and Fitness; Ontario Arts Council; Prince Edward Island Council of the Arts; Saskatchewan Arts Board; and Yukon Arts Council.) At the civic level, most large cities have set up cultural offices to evaluate and administer local requests for aid (eg, the *Community Arts Council of Vancouver).

Other sources of musical patronage have not grown significantly. There is little indication except in the odd instance that churches have maintained the level they once established. Although Canadian laws are liberal (donations by individuals and corporations to registered nonprofit musical groups, including all the important ones, professional or amateur, are tax-deductible) there was scant hope in 1980 that such donations would increase in proportion to need. Some corporations have supported orchestras and opera groups actively, but these have been in the minority, though by 1980 there was noticeable improvement in this area. Non-profit foundations (see Foundations) have helped music considerably, however. What has been lacking is a consistent policy of private aid on an annual or biennial basis. The Council for Business and the Arts, established in 1974 with Arnold Edinborough as president and chief executive officer, and funded by the business sector through annual subscription fees from member corporations, gave promise of moving toward the establishment of such a policy, but by 1980 much remained to be achieved.

By no means least in any assessment of the patronage of music in Canada must be an acknowledgement of the massive gift of time and effort from volunteers. Volunteers in the cause of music have raised funds, conducted ticket campaigns to fill concert halls, organized concerts, promoted and publicized performances, accepted fiscal responsibility for the orchestras, choirs, or composers' circles they support, founded and financed and perpetuated scholarships, and served music in many other ways. Individual volunteer contributions have ranged from making a pan of cookies for a benefit food sale to setting up and administering a national music support organization or filling a virtually full-time position as the president of a major orchestra. By 1980 the Canadian system of support for music had rested for many decades on a substantial foundation of altruistic volunteer help. Without that help the system would have to be redesigned in fundamental ways. Paid staffs would have to be increased and new means of raising more money would have to be found. Alternatives to disbandment at one extreme and full state support (common in Europe but rare in North America) at the other would be difficult to imagine.

The broad pattern of patronage remained, in 1980, a compromise between the European governmental and US private systems, with an ever-increasing tendency towards the former and no great likelihood of significant change in the near future despite governments' calls for increased involvement of private-sector funds.

BIBLIOGRAPHY

Walter, Arnold, 'Problems of patronage in a democratic society,' *CMJ*, vol 1, Spring 1957

Bladen, Vincent. *The Financing of the Performing Arts in Canada* (Toronto 1971)

Pasquill, Frank T. *Subsidy Patterns for the Performing Arts in Canada* (Ottawa 1973)

'How goes the romance between business and the arts?' *Business Q*, vol 39, Autumn 1974

Alderman, Tom. 'Gimme, gimme never gets,' *The Canadian*, 8 Feb 1975

Ostry, Bernard. *The Cultural Connection* (Toronto 1978)

Council for Business and the Arts. *CBAC News*, 6 issues a year, Toronto 1977–

'The corporate money tree,' *Music*, Sep–Oct 1980

Batten, Jack. 'An aid to excellence: when culture and corporation meet,' Imperial Oil *Review*, vol 64, no. 4, 1980 (ES)

PATTERSON, Pat (Muriel Welsh). Composer, writer, b Victoria, BC, 4 Dec 1921; LRSM 1937. She studied violin, voice, and piano in Victoria but is a self-taught composer. In 1946 she settled in Toronto, where she became in turn a radio continuity and program writer 1946–8, a freelance, and the host for the record programs 'Pat's Music Room' (1948–64) and 'Light and Lyrical' (1950) and for the children's show 'Musical Playroom' (1951).

In the mid-1950s for CBC TV's children's program 'Telestory Time' Patterson wrote and performed several hundred songs. She was host 1962–9 and co-host 1969–71 with Helen Hutcheson for CBC radio's 'Trans-Canada Matinee' and host 1978–9 for CBC radio's 'One to One.' She prepared the CBC series 'Festivals of the World' (1976) and 'Thanks for the Use of the Hall' (1977).

Patterson collaborated with Dodi Robb, the writer for 'Telestory Time,' on several children's works, composing music for the CBC radio fantasy *A Carol for Christmas* (1951) and the popular musicals *The Dandy Lion* (1964), *Mrs Red Riding Hood* (1968), *The Popcorn Man* (1969), *Henry Green and the Mighty Machine* (1970, written for the Toronto Young People's Theatre and published in 1972 by New Press), and *The Cabbagetown Kids* (1978, for the *Guelph Spring Festival).

BIBLIOGRAPHY

LeBlanc, Larry. 'Audience participation important ingredient in children's musicals,' *MSc*, 270, Mar–Apr 1973 (MFr)

PAUK, Alex. Composer, conductor, b Toronto 4 Oct 1945; B MUS (Toronto) 1970, B ED (Toronto) 1971. He was a founding member of *ARRAY in 1971 and attended the *OAC student conductors' workshop 1970–2 under Karel Ančerl, Ernesto *Barbini, Victor *Feldbrill, and Boyd *Neel. He studied conducting further 1972–3 at the Toho Gakuen School of Music in Tokyo, then settled in Vancouver. In 1974 he founded the short-lived Array West and helped to found *Days Months and Years to Come, a similar group of composer-musicians. That same year he began teaching at the Vancouver Community College and conducting the Vancouver Youth Orchestra.

Pauk's compositions – more than a dozen chamber works and *Fragmentations* (1972), the latter thrice performed by the *Vancouver SO in 1976 – are experimental, open-ended, and thick-textured. Commissions have come from the *CBC Vancouver Chamber Orchestra, *Canadian Brass, Mary Lou *Fallis, the *NYO, and the Pacific Wind Ensemble. Pauk has composed and conducted for the Pacific Theatre and the Tamahnous Theatre.

Pauk was named 'Vancouver's Musician of the Year' by the *Sun* in 1975. He returned to Toronto in 1979. He is an associate of the *CMCentre and a member of CAPAC.

WRITINGS

'Notes from composers,' *Music*, Dec 1979

BIBLIOGRAPHY

Champagne, Jane. 'Alex Pauk: music's future?,' *CanComp*, 113, Sep 1976

Kieser, Karen. 'Words about music,' *Musicanada*, 30, Nov 1976

Compositeurs canadiens contemporains CF

PAUL, Damis. Organist, pianist, choirmaster, violinist, b St-Hyacinthe, Que, 9 Mar 1827, d South Bend, Ind, 13 Dec 1913. He studied at the seminary at Ste-Thérèse, Que, with Father Charles-Joseph *Ducharme, at the same time as the organ builders Joseph *Casavant and Louis *Mitchell. L.-Nazaire *LeVasseur relates that he was a violinist 1847–57 with the *Quebec Harmonic Society, but it is known that on 7 Mar 1850 he inaugurated Casavant's fifth organ at Notre-Dame Basilica in Ottawa after helping to build and instal it.

Paul was organist 1842–52 at the Montreal Cathedral and 1852–69 at St-Roch Church, Quebec City. His repertoire leaned heavily on transcriptions and paraphrases of opera. Following the restoration by Mitchell of the Elliott organ in the Quebec Basilica, Paul and his son Léopold took part in the inaugural recital, 9 Feb 1864, along with Ernest *Gagnon, James Pearce, and Antoine *Dessane. Paul became the *AMQ's first secretary 7 May 1868, having participated in its foundation a few days earlier.

In the autumn of 1869 Paul left Canada to settle in the USA, first in New York in the French parish, and then in South Bend, Ind, where he ended his career as organist-choirmaster at the Church of Notre Dame.

Paul left works for piano, organ, and voice, including *Scintillation*, a 'grande étude de salon' dedicated to Prince Louis-Napoléon and published in Quebec, Montreal, and the USA in 1863; *Jubilé*, a grand march for piano; and a *Regina coeli* for solo voice and choir.

BIBLIOGRAPHY

Gagné, Richard. 'Un siècle d'activités musicales à St-Roch de Québec,' unpubl musicology thesis, CMQ 1975

RGg

PAUNOVA, Mariana. Contralto, pianist, b Kapinovo, Bulgaria, 13 Jun 1951, naturalized Canadian 1975; diploma (State Music School, Sofia, Bulgaria) 1967, M MUS piano (Cons Santa Cecilia, Rome) 1970, lauréat (AMQ) 1971. After five years of studies in Sofia, she took courses in piano from Jan Ekier in Poland (summer 1967) and worked in Rome 1967–70 with Guido Agosti and Vincenzo Vitale. In 1970 she won second prize at the Francesco Paolo Neglia International Piano Competition in Enna, Sicily, and moved to Montreal as an accompanist at *McGill U. She studied voice the following year with Dina Maria Narici and participated in a Sarah *Fischer concert in 1972. The same year she won the silver medal at the International Singing Competition in Toulouse. In 1973 she won both the *Canadian Music Competition and the *CBC Talent Festival, and that summer she studied Lieder interpretation with John *Newmark at the *JMC Orford Art Centre. She worked on stage deportment and techniques 1973–6 at the *McGill Opera Studio with Edith and Luciano *Della Pergola. She sang with the *Quebec SO (*Messiah*) and the *Montreal Elgar Choir (Mozart's *Mass in C Minor*, Bach's Mass in *B Minor*) and appeared on many CBC radio and TV programs.

In 1976 Paunova made her professional opera debut, singing Suzuki (*Madama Butterfly*) and operatic excerpts during two tours with the Goldovsky Opera Theatre. Her interpretations of Pauline in Tchaikovsky's *The Queen of Spades* at the Festival of Two Worlds in Charleston, SC (1977), and Dame Quickly in *Falstaff* at the same festival in Spoleto, Italy (1978), drew enthusiastic reviews from the critics. In 1978 she made her debut at Carnegie Hall as Isaura in a concert presentation of Rossini's *Tancredi* by the Opera Orchestra of New York. On that occasion Bill Zakariasen described her as having 'a rich voice of distinctively outstanding quality and emotional fervor' (*Daily News*, 16 Mar 1978). She made her debut at the *Metropolitan Opera in April 1979 as Olga in *Eugene Onegin*, a role she repeated in a concert performance of the opera by the *TS in 1980. Mariana Paunova has been a guest singer with the Mormon Tabernacle Choir, the Handel Society (at the Kennedy Center), and at many festivals; she has given recitals in Europe and the USA.

BIBLIOGRAPHY

Jones, Robert T. 'Mariana Paunova: vocal gold,' Charleston *News and Courier*, 12 Jun 1977

AP

The Paupers. Rock band, formed in 1965 in Toronto as the Spats by the drummer (Ronn) Skip Prokop and the guitarist Bill Misener with the lead guitarist Chuck Beale and the bass guitarist Danny Gerrard. As the Paupers, the group initially appeared in Toronto coffeehouses and high schools and made its first recordings for the Roman label. Misener was replaced by the singer and 12-string guitarist Adam Mitchell in 1966 and the group turned to 'psychedelic' rock that same year.

The Paupers' sound was built around extended improvisations by Beale or Gerrard (the latter's solos met with particular acclaim) to a drum accompaniment by the others. After a successful New York debut at the Cafe A Go Go (week of 27 Feb 1967) they performed widely in the USA and in Canada and recorded the LP *Magic People* (1967, Verve Forecast 3026), In 1967 Gerrard was replaced by Brad Campbell, and an organist was added – Peter Sterbach, followed by John Ord. A second LP, *Ellis Island* (1968, Verve Forecast S 3051) reflected a softening of style.

The Paupers' most successful singles – for which, like the rest of their repertoire, the music and words were by Prokop and Mitchell – were 'If I Call You by Some Name' (1966) and 'Simple Deed' (1967). The Paupers disbanded in mid-1968, though they re-formed briefly in Toronto in late 1968 with Mitchell, Ord, Gerrard, Beale, and the drummer Roz Parks.

Mitchell (b Glasgow 24 Nov 1944) then pursued a solo career before turning in the 1970s to record production and working in Toronto or Los Angeles with the Good Brothers, Gordon *Lightfoot, Linda Ronstadt, Ian *Tyson, and others. The oft-recorded 'French Song' is his best-known composition. Prokop, after playing in the USA with various pop artists and recording with Al Kooper and Mike Bloomfield, became co-founder of *Lighthouse. MM

PAVLOSKA, Irene (b Lévi, m Sherwin, m Mesirow). Mezzo-soprano, b St-Jean, Que, 17 Feb 1889, d Chicago 12 Feb 1962. Raised in Montreal, where her parents settled when she was three, she began piano lessons when she was six. She later studied for 18 months with Clara Folin in Frankfurt while in boarding school there. Under the pseudonym Olga Pawloska she sang several small roles with the *Montreal Opera Company in 1911–12. Study with Edmond Duvernoy in Paris was followed by a season 1914–15 in New York and on tour as Juliska Fekete in Kalman's *Sari*. She re-assumed the name Irene and replaced the 'w' in Pawloska with a 'v' in 1914. On 19 Nov 1915 she made her Chicago Opera debut, singing Musetta to Melba's Mimi, and remained associated with that company until her retirement in 1934, singing some 60 roles in four languages including Princess Clarice in the premiere (1921, in French translation) of Prokofiev's *The Love of Three Oranges* under the composer's baton.

Although a delightful exponent of such 'trouser' roles as Siebel in *Faust*, Stéphano in *Roméo et Juliette*, Hansel in *Hansel and Gretel*, and Orlofsky in *Die Fledermaus*, Pavloska was most closely identified with Musetta, a role for which her beautifully schooled mezzo and sparkling personality were ideally suited. She also sang Suzuki in *Madama Butterfly*, Mallika in *Lakmé*, Charlotte in *Werther*, mezzo roles in *Das Rheingold* and *Die Walküre*, and, many times, the title role in *Carmen*. She also appeared in light opera in Canada and the USA (**Rose Marie, The Chimes of Normandy*, and various works by Gilbert & Sullivan).

Irene Pavloska

Pavloska appeared frequently in recital and with orchestras such as (1921–2 season) the Minneapolis SO. She was on the auditioning committee of the *Metropolitan Opera Company in the 1930s. She recorded six items (including 'Musetta's Waltz') for Brunswick ca 1921. Also a composer in a modest way, she wrote a song, 'In My Dreams' (Forster 1926). A sister, Blanche Lévi, studied violin with Alfred *De Sève. Pavloska was buried in Montreal and left her library to *McGill U.

BIBLIOGRAPHY

Moore, Edward C. *Forty Years of Opera in Chicago* (New York 1930)
Davis, Ronald. *Opera in Chicago* (New York 1966)
Roll Back the Years

JBM (GP)

PAYNE, Marjorie (Agnes). Pianist, organist, conductor, b Halifax 1893, d there 1960. Her father, Thomas J. Payne, was the pianist 1900–27 for the North British Society in Halifax. She graduated from the Halifax Cons (*Maritime Cons) and was organist-choirmaster at Robie St Methodist and St Andrew's United churches in Halifax. She succeeded her father as the pianist (until her death) for the North British Society and was the accompanist for many leading artists during their visits to Halifax. A pioneer of music on Halifax radio, and probably the first woman in Canada to conduct for broadcast, she directed the Little Symphony Orchestra 1929–33 at the Lord Nelson Hotel in programs carried locally on CHNS and nationally on the CNR and CRBC networks. She also was music director for such CBC radio programs as 'From a Rose Garden,' 'Songs at Eventide' (with the mezzo soprano Doris Dunlop and orchestra), and 'Harmony Harbour' (1945–60, with the Acadian Male Quartet). RSm

PAYZANT, Geoffrey (Barss). Teacher, philosopher, writer, organist, b Halifax, NS, 7 Mar 1926; LRSM 1948, BA (Dalhousie) 1948, MA (Toronto) 1950, PH D (Toronto) 1960. In Halifax, he studied piano with Georges *Little and piano, organ, and theory with Harry *Dean. In Toronto he studied harpsichord with Greta *Kraus at the RCMT. He has taught English, music, and philosophy 1952–7 at *Mount Allison U and began teaching philosophy, specializing in aesthetics, in 1957 at the *U of Toronto, where he also was chairman 1970–3 of the Dept of Interdisciplinary Studies. He was organist at various churches in Sackville, NB, and in Toronto. He was editor of the **Canadian Music*

Journal 1956–62. CBC radio presented his five-part series 'Keys in Musical Perception' (1970) and the program 'Symmetry in Musical Motion' (1972).

Payzant's book *Glenn Gould: Music and Mind* is a rarity among treatments of performers in that it concerns itself little with *Gould's personal life and public appearances and much with the nature of his philosophies as they developed and with the quality, depth, scope, and variety of his art as it was affected by those philosophies. The author emerges as Gould's most thoroughgoing apologist, apart, perhaps, from Gould himself. He has written the article on Gould for *EMC*.

In the mid-1970s Payzant became a consultant for the York Pioneer and Historical Society on the restoration of 19th-century organs for the museum at the Temple of the *Children of Peace, Sharon, Ont.

WRITINGS

'The Presbyterian organ,' *Organ Institute Q*, vols 5 and 6, Autumn 1955, Spring 1956

'The actual need,' *CMJ*, vol 1, Spring 1957

'Art invention as discovery and elaboration,' unpubl PH D thesis, Toronto 1960

'The competitive music festivals,' *CMJ*, vol 4, Spring 1960

'Performance and the existence of art,' *Dalhousie R*, vol 44, Summer 1964

'Intention and the achievement of the artist,' *Dialogue*, vol 3, Sep 1964

'The new immortality: "readings" in aesthetics,' *Dialogue*, vol 4, Sep 1966

Glenn Gould: Music and Mind (Toronto 1978)

BIBLIOGRAPHY

Clements, Warren. 'Roll out the barrel – carefully,' Toronto *Globe and Mail*, 5 May 1979 (CF)

PEACOCK, Kenneth (Howard). Ethnomusicologist, composer, pianist, b Toronto 7 Apr 1922; ATCM 1935, B MUS (Toronto) 1943. He studied piano at the TCM (*RCMT) with Alma Cockburn in 1935 and Reginald *Godden 1948–9; he also took private lessons in Toronto with Mona *Bates 1939–40 and in Montreal with Michel *Hirvy in 1950. At the *U of Toronto he studied theory 1941–3 with Healey *Willan and Leo *Smith and composition 1944–6 with John *Weinzweig. He continued his composition studies in 1950 with Francis Judd Cooke at the New England Cons, Boston. During this period he also taught piano and theory privately, 1937–46 in Toronto and 1947–54 in Ottawa, and performed as a pianist in several Canadian cities.

Peacock was on the staff of the *National Museum of Man in Ottawa as a researcher on indigenous music and the music of ethnic minorities 1951–72 and a research fellow 1969–72. His many projects for the museum covered virtually every part of Canada. He concentrated on the folk music of Newfoundland 1951–2 and 1958–61 and of various ethnic groups 1962–74, as well as on the music of the Plains Indians 1953–4. Some of his recordings, illustrating the music of several tribes, were released on the LP *Indian Music of the Canadian Plains* (ca 1955, Folk FE-4464). In 1954 he discussed some of his discoveries in 'Folk Songs from Newfoundland,' a series of six broadcasts on CBC radio.

Peacock was one of the first Canadian folk music collectors with a solid musical training. The originality of his work also resides in the fact that it embraces the full range of Canada's ethnic groups. He has published articles in such journals as *Alphabet*, *Bulletin of the CFMS*, *Ethnomusicology*, and the *Journal of American Folklore*. He has contributed to published folk-music collections edited by Helen *Creighton, Robert *Klymasz, and Alan *Mills. He is also a contributor and subject adviser for *EMC*.

Peacock's compositions include *Bridal Suite* (1947, BMI Canada 1950, recorded by Godden), *Children's Suite* (1950), *Idioms* (1950, a work derived from Indian and folk sources), and *Toccata* (1958), all for piano. He also wrote a *Sonata* (1947) for violin and piano, *Essay* (1949) for clarinet and strings, a *String Quartet* (1949), which won the music competition of the McGill Chamber Music Society, and the cantata *Songs of the Cedar* (1950) for mezzo-soprano, flute, cello, and double-bass (Olympic citation, 1952). His work for choir and orchestra *Rituals of Earth, Fire and Darkness* (1950) was inspired by Iroquois texts, and *Essay on Newfoundland Themes* (1961) for orchestra contains elements of Newfoundland folk music. Peacock performs on the LP *Songs and Ballads of Newfoundland* (ca 1956, Folk FG 3505). He is a member of the *CLComp, an associate of the *CMcentre, and an affiliate of PRO Canada.

WRITINGS

Songs of the Newfoundland Outports, 3 vols, National Museum of Man Bulletin 197 (Ottawa 1965)

A Practical Guide for Folk Music Collectors (Ottawa 1966)

Twenty Ethnic Songs from Western Canada, National Museum of Man Bulletin 211 (Ottawa 1966)

'Folk and aboriginal music' / 'La musique folklorique et aborigène,' *Aspects of Music in Canada / Aspects de la musique au Canada*

Songs of the Doukhobors, National Museum of Man Bulletin 231 (Ottawa 1970)

A Garland of Rue, National Museum of Man Folk Culture series 2 (Ottawa 1971)

See also Bibliography for Folk Music; Folk Music, Anglo-Canadian: 1 / Newfoundland.

BIBLIOGRAPHY

Lawless, Ray M. *Folksingers and Folksongs in America* (New York 1960)

Contemporary Canadian Composers / Compositeurs canadiens contemporains (DM)

PEAKER, Charles. Organist, choirmaster, teacher, writer, b Derby, England, 6 Dec 1899, d Toronto 11 Aug 1978; ATCM 1919, FRCO 1929, B MUS (Toronto) 1925, D MUS (Toronto) 1936, hon FRCCO 1973. At 13 he moved to Saskatoon, and in 1919 on a Heintzman scholarship he studied in Toronto with *Willan, *MacMillan, and Ernest *Seitz. He was a theatre musician in Regina and Saskatoon, but after 1926 was associated continually with churches. He was a church organist-choirmaster 1926–8 at St Paul Street United in St Catharines, Ont, and (after a year of organ studies in England) 1930–6 at Rosedale United in Toronto, briefly at Walmer Road Baptist, 1937–44 at Deer Park United, and 1944–75 at St Paul's Anglican. At St Paul's he began annual Advent and Lenten twilight recitals and Good Friday performances of major passions and requiems. He was the conductor 1934–50 of the *Hart House Glee Club and also 1940–2 of the 2000-voice Coliseum Chorus (see CNE Chorus).

One of Canada's foremost concert organists, Peaker performed in 1935 in the USA and in 1954 in England, where his tour included a recital at Westminster Abbey. He continued to perform outside Canada until the late 1960s and was described as 'a flamboyant, dramatic organist with a brilliant technique, a prodigious memory and a keen sense of humour ... Perhaps the most distinctive characteristic of his organ work is his ingenuity in registration and his ability to exploit fully the tonal resources of any organ' (Testimonial program 6 Oct 1975).

Peaker taught 1930–70 at the TCM (*RCMT) and served 1944–5 as its director. He also lectured on choral technique 1952–65 at the *U of Toronto. In 1964 he became university organist. His pupils have included Fred Graham, John *Hodgins,

Charles Peaker

David Low, Roma Page Lynde, Stanley *Osborne, Godfrey *Ridout, and Charles *Wilson.

Peaker edited *Organ Music of Canada* (two vols, Berandol 1969). He was president of the *CRMTA 1948–9 and president of the *RCCO 1941–3. He became honorary president of the latter in 1974. He was made a Member of the *Order of Canada 6 Dec 1974.

WRITINGS

'Music today,' *CRMA*, vol 3, Oct–Nov 1944

'Choral music in Canada,' *CRMA*, vol 4, Oct–Nov 1945

'Church music II,' *Music in Canada*

'Church music, other than Roman Catholic,' *Encyclopedia Canadiana*, vol 2 (Toronto 1957–8)

'Help wanted, male or female,' *CMJ*, vol 3, Spring 1959

'Plain words about organists,' *Music Across Canada*, vol 1, Feb 1963

'MacMillan as organist,' ibid, Jul–Aug 1963

'Wind merchants,' *Fugue*, May 1978

BIBLIOGRAPHY

'Obituaries,' *Mcan*, 37, Nov 1978 MG

PEDERSEN, Paul (Richard). Administrator, composer, b Camrose, near Edmonton, Alta, 28 Aug 1935; BA (Saskatchewan) 1957, M MUS (Toronto) 1961, PH D musicology (Toronto) 1970. His composition teachers were Murray *Adaskin at the *U of Saskatchewan and John *Weinzweig at the *U of Toronto. He was music director 1962–4 of Camrose Lutheran College. He joined *McGill U in 1966 and served 1970–4 as head of the electronic music studio and chairman of the theory department, and 1974–6 as associate dean. He was made dean in 1976. His doctoral research in acoustic and musical psychology resulted in the article 'The mel scale' (*Journal of Music Theory*, Winter 1965) and the dissertation *The Perception of Musical Pitch Structure* (Toronto 1970). His early compositions, including *Quintet* (1959) and *Sonata* for violin and piano (1960), reveal a free atonal style, but works such as *The Lone Tree* and *For Margaret, Motherhood and Mendelssohn* indicate an interest in electronic and computer music, while *Themes from the Old Testament* and *Fantasie* are multi-media compositions. He is a member of CAPAC and an associate of the *CMCentre.

SELECTED COMPOSITIONS

CHAMBER

Woodwind Trios No. 1 and 2. 1956, 1957. Fl, cl, bn. CMCentre

Chorale Prelude No. 2. 1958. Fl (ob or cl), str quar. CMCentre

Sonata for Violin and Piano. 1960. CMCentre

Serial Compositions. 1965. Vn, hn, bn, hp. CMCentre

An Old Song of the Sun and Moon and the Fear of Loneliness (Eskimo song, transl K. Rasmussen). 1973. Amplified sop, electronic fl, amplified pf. CMCentre. RCI 404 (*Lyric Arts Trio)

Wind Quintet No. 2. 1975. Alto fl, eng hn, b cl, bn, hn. Ms

CHOIR
'Ecclesiastes XII' (Bible). 1958. SATB. CMCentre
Cantata and Narrative for Good Friday (liturgical). 1972. SATB, org, narr, soli. CMCentre
Plus several others
ELECTRONIC
The Lone Tree. 1964. 2-track tape
Themes from the Old Testament. 1966. 2-track tape, slide projector
Fantasie. 1967. 2-track tape, 3 slide projectors
Origins. 1967. 16 mm film
For Margaret, Motherhood and Mendelssohn. 1971. 2-track tape. 1971. RCI 373
Also 2 orchestral works: *Concerto for Orchestra* (1961) and *Lament* (1962). 2 works for pf: *Lament* (1958) and *Fugue* (1959)

BIBLIOGRAPHY
Contemporary Canadian Composers / Compositeurs canadiens contemporains
CF

PEEBLES, Joan (Angusta Brownie) (m Oberg). Contralto, teacher, b New Westminster, BC, 5 Jan 1899. After five years as a shool teacher, she won the Hudson's Bay Company medal in 1923 in the first BC Music Festival and thereafter studied with teachers in Vancouver (Mrs. Walter *Coulthard), New York, and Rochester. In Rochester she made her concert debut in 1924 under Eugene Goossens and her opera debut in 1925 as Nancy in *Martha*. She repeated that role, 8 Jul 1926, in the first opera performance ever given at Chautauqua, NY, returning as principal contralto each season until 1942. She toured the USA and Canada 1927–9 with the American Opera Company, winning particular acclaim as Carmen. In the 1930s she was associated with many organizations including the Banff Scottish Music Festival (*CPR Festivals), the Worcester Festival, and opera companies in Detroit and Philadelphia. Her many radio performances included an abridged *Carmen* with Edward *Johnson on radio station CFRB, Toronto, in 1933. In 1942 Peebles retired to Titusville, Pa, where she taught privately till 1974, when she returned to New Westminster. Her only commercial recordings were of excerpts from *Carmen* with Raoul *Jobin (RCA Camden CAL-221) made in 1940 under the auspices of the National Committee for Music Appreciation, New York. JBM

PEENE, Vida (Hampt). Patron, b Hamilton, Ont, 16 Oct 1898, d Lakeland, Fla, 18 Feb 1978. A prominent Ontario volunteer worker and fundraiser for opera, she was president 1952–4 of the *COC Women's Committee, establishing branches in Hamilton and other cities, and an original member 1957–61 of the *Canada Council, 1963–71 of POCA (*OAC), and 1969–73 of the Toronto Arts Foundation. She founded the Canadian Opera Guild in 1960 and served 1964–70 as a director of the *CMCentre and 1968–75 as a board member of *O'Keefe Centre. She was a director of the Canadian Opera Assn in 1952, president of the Central Ontario Drama League 1955–7, and a director of the National Ballet of Canada 1955–8. She was made an Officer of the *Order of Canada in 1970. AHC

Peer-Southern Organization (Canada) Ltd. Opened in Toronto in 1944, under the management of Allister Grosart, as the Canadian branch of the US company founded in 1928 by Ralph Sylvester Peer primarily to publish hillbilly and Latin American pop songs. Southern Music Publishing Co (Canada) Ltd is a *CAPAC affiliate; Peer International (Canada) Ltd is a *PRO Canada affiliate. With its head office in New York, the Peer-Southern Organization in 1978 had branches in 23 countries. The Canadian office moved in 1950 to Montreal in response to the popularity in Quebec of the Peer-Southern catalogue of Latin American music. J. Newman was the first manager in Montreal.

Matthew Heft, who began his career with the company in 1956, became general manager in 1958. (A graduate of the *McGill Cons, Heft was a pianist-accompanist in Montreal in the 1930s. In London 1938–55 he was the manager of the music publishers Francis, Day and Hunter's. He was president 1968–9 and 1979–80 of the *CMPA.) Heft continued as managing director when Peer-Southern returned in 1972 to Toronto.

In Canada Peer-Southern distributes the publications of the parent firm and represents other foreign catalogues which offer the music of Enesco, Sibelius, Virgil Thomson, and Villa-Lobos. It also handles the Southern Library of Recorded (background) Music. The company published music by the Canadians Wilf *Carter, Terry *Jacks, and Alan *Mills and in the mid-1960s, on the Spark label, issued recordings by Tommy *Common, the Band of the Black Watch, and others. Peer International (New York) has published Canadian concert music, including Violet *Archer's *Two Chorale Preludes* for organ, Jean *Papineau-Couture's *Étude in B Flat Minor* for piano, and Robert *Turner's *Four Fragments* for brass quintet.

BIBLIOGRAPHY
'Southern Music: an international publisher,' *CanComp*, 8, Apr 1966
'Peer Southern: an international legend,' *RPM*, 7 Jun 1975
MWl

PELLEGRINI, (Anna) Maria (m Macko, m Thomas). Soprano, b Pescara, Italy, 15 Jul 1943, naturalized Canadian 1965. Emigrating to Canada in 1958, she studied 1960–4 with Ernesto *Vinci at the RCMT, then in London with Joe Macko. She sang with the *COC first (1963) as the High Priestess in *Aida*, then (1965, her debut in a major role) as Gilda in *Rigoletto*. Further COC roles have included Nedda in *I Pagliacci* (1966), Cio-Cio-San in *Madama Butterfly* (1971 and 1975), and Violetta in *La Traviata* (1974 and 1978). She was a 1967 *Metropolitan Opera auditions winner and made her debuts at Covent Garden (1968) and Sadler's Wells (1969) as Gilda and Cio-Cio-San respectively.

Specializing in the Puccini repertoire, she has appeared with the Edmonton, Manitoba, Quebec, Southern Alberta, and Vancouver operas and has sung in Genoa, Trieste, Parma, and Catania in Italy, in Pittsburgh and New Orleans in the USA, in Santo Domingo, and with the Welsh National Opera. She appeared in the 1977 CBC TV production of *Madama Butterfly* with Pierre *Duval, Bernard *Turgeon, Judith *Forst, and a CBC orchestra conducted by Jean *Deslauriers.

After a *Massey Hall operatic recital with Louis *Quilico 10 Apr 1974 Pellegrini's performance of 'Un bel di' from Puccini's *Madama Butterfly* was described by Toronto *Globe and Mail* critic John *Kraglund as 'an ideal summary of her artistic achievements, in evenness throughout her vocal range, exceptionally beautiful highs, musical phrasing and powerful emotional communication.'

BIBLIOGRAPHY
Mercer, Ruby. 'Maria Pellegrini,' *OpCan*, Fall 1971
'Tragic lady of opera,' ibid, Dec 1977
Jones, Gaynor. 'More than a butterfly: Maria Pellegrini is trying to shake her image as the "Butterfly soprano",' *Music*, Jun 1980
(HCs)

PELLERIN, Hector. Baritone, actor, entertainer, b Montreal 31 Oct 1887 or 1888, d there 18 Apr 1953. He studied piano and organ with Alexis *Contant and J.-Daniel *Dussault and made his debut as a cinema pianist at the Ouimetoscope in Montreal. He continued this activity in Sorel, where he lived 1902–9 and where he began singing. He was an organist 1909–11 in Amesbury, Mass, but returned to Montreal to act in plays and revues and appeared at three theatres, the Canadien 1911–12, the Chanteclerc 1912–14, and the National 1914–16.

On the advice of Henri *Miro and Albert *Roberval, Pellerin turned to singing operetta, and in 1917 he was the partner of Jeanne *Maubourg in Audran's *Gilette de Narbonne*. In cabaret he performed mostly his own songs, accompanying himself on the piano in the manner of the French singer Fragson. He sang one season of operetta in *Sohmer Park. He was one of the first radio performers and continued broadcasting until the 1940s as singer, actor, and entertainer.

In 1934 in Montreal Pellerin opened a cabaret, le Versailles, which featured Lucienne Boyer, Jean Clément, Tino Rossi, Jean Sablon, and other such notables of French song. He worked thereafter as master of ceremonies in a succession of Montreal nightclubs, including the Café de l'Est, until the end of the 1940s.

Pellerin recorded a number of songs on Amberol cylinders and discs for Victor, Starr, Edison, Columbia, and Starr-Gennett. A list is given in *Roll Back the Years*. GP

PELLETIER (Peltier). A Montreal family of musicians and writers on music comprising 1 / Romain-Octave I and his elder brother Orphir; the former's sons 2 / Frédéric and 3 / Romain and Victor; and 4 / Romain-Octave II, Frédéric's son.

1 (Jean) **Romain-Octave** I (Octave). Organist, pianist, composer, educator, writer on music, b Montreal 9 Sep 1843, d there 4 Mar 1927; hon D MUS (Montreal) 1919. While very young he displayed a quick ear, correcting the errors of his two sisters who were studying piano. At 11 he was placed in the Collège de Montréal, where he played the organ without previous musical training. When he one day found he could not read a score that was put before him, he decided to study music. He was mainly self-taught, although he did have some lessons from his elder brother Orphir (b Montreal 7 Sep 1825, d there 1855), organist at St Patrick's Church and composer of an *O salutaris hostia* published in *L'Album littéraire et musical de la Revue canadienne* (Feb 1846). Romain-Octave was organist 1857–67 of St James Cathedral, succeeding J.-C. *Brauneis II at the age of 15. At the same time he studied law and at 21 qualified as a lawyer, though he practised this profession very infrequently. One of the few contracts he did draw up was for the marriage in 1866 of the singer Rosita *del Vecchio and the violinist Frantz *Jehin-Prume. He had met the latter on his arrival in Montreal the previous year and had accompanied him in recitals. Pelletier spent some time ca 1866–7 in Hartford, Conn, where he met the organist Samuel P. *Warren. On his return, he was organist 1867–75 at the Church of St James-the-Less on St-Denis St. He surprised and even shocked the clergy and congregation by performing works by Bach and Mendelssohn, who as 'Protestant' composers were deemed unsuitable and – Bach in particular – too austere. After Pelletier's marriage in 1869 he eked out a meagre living giving piano and organ lessons. During a trip to Europe 1871–2 he took lessons in London with George Cooper, William Thomas Best, and John Baptiste Calkin. In Paris he obtained advice from a certain Lebel, organist at St-Étienne-du-Mont, and at St-Sulpice he played works by Bach in the presence of Widor. He took a few piano lessons

Romain-Octave Pelletier I

with Antoine-François Marmontel and later worked in Brussels with the organist Lemmens. On his return to Montreal he resumed teaching; from 1876 to 1907 he taught solfège at the École normale Jacques-Cartier. In the ensuing years Pelletier was invited to inaugurate many organs installed by *Casavant in Canada and the USA. He resumed organ duties at St James Cathedral in 1887 (at the St-Joseph Chapel until the inauguration of the new cathedral on Dominion Square in 1894) and remained the organist there until 1923. Visiting Europe again in 1900, this time in the company of the Casavant brothers, he met Guilmant and Gigout in Paris. When the *McGill Cons opened in 1904 he was appointed teacher of piano.

R.-O. Pelletier was president of the *AMQ 1884–5, 1894–5, 1902–4, 1909–10, and 1915–16 and taught in numerous institutions, including the Institut pédagogique, the convents of Mont Ste-Anne and of the Sisters of the Holy Names of Jesus and Mary, and the *Institut Nazareth. The list of his pupils is extensive and includes Alcibiade *Béique, Victoria *Cartier, Claude *Champagne, Édouard *Clarke, Alexandre-M. *Clerk, Jean *Dansereau, J.-Daniel *Dussault, Nicholas Eichhorn, Septimus Fraser, J.-J. *Gagnier, Alfred *Laliberté, Alfred *Lamoureux, Alphonse *Lavallée-Smith, Émery and Ernest *Lavigne, Antonio *Létourneau, Clarence *Lucas, Albertine *Morin-Labrecque, Joseph *Piché, William *Reed, Léon *Ringuet, and Amédée *Tremblay.

Pelletier was essentially an improviser and composed relatively little. Two masses and some motets for St James have been lost. Among his chief works may be noted *Dix Petits Morceaux pour l'orgue, Op 3* (G. Schirmer 1870); *Six Pièces d'orgue* (possibly published by G. Schirmer but untraceable); *Accompagnement du nouveau manuel de chants liturgiques de l'abbé [Cléophas] Borduas* for organ (Eusèbe Sénécal 1889, Imprimerie moderne 1903), a work highly praised by Guillaume *Couture; *Quatre Noëls anciens* for choir and organ (1890); *Mécanisme du piano ou Nouvelles études techniques* (Lavigne, after 1876); a *Valse-caprice* 'in memory of Chopin' for piano (Boucher); 'Vert et blanc, Canadiens,' a patriotic song; the march *Prince Arthur* for piano or concert band and another piece for concert band, both of which were played at *Sohmer Park under the direction of Ernest Lavigne; and various songs and pieces for piano and for organ.

During his career as an educator, Pelletier gave many lectures, several of which appeared in published collections, namely *Le Toucher du pianiste* (Montreal 1916), *L'Étude de la littérature du piano* (Montreal 1920), *L'Art pianistique* (Montreal 1922) after Boileau's *L'Art poétique*, and *Guide du professeur de piano* (Montreal 1925). He also wrote many articles, including a series of discussions on organ building and playing, published in *La Revue canadienne* (1881–2).

R.-O. Pelletier enjoyed the esteem and admiration of his contemporaries and must be regarded as one of the most dedicated craftsmen of Canadian music during a difficult period, a man of true initiative who, according to Eugène *Lapierre, 'took it upon himself to be serious at a time when the music in vogue most certainly was not.' The avenue Octave-Pelletier in Montreal was named after him, and a vocal quartet bearing his name, conducted by Guillaume *Dupuis, made recordings ca 1918 for Columbia.

BIBLIOGRAPHY

Lapierre, Eugène. 'Les musiciens du passé, Romain-Octave Pelletier,' *Entre-Nous*, vol 1, Jan 1930

Laurendeau, Arthur. 'Musiciens d'autrefois: Romain-Octave Pelletier,' *Action nationale*, vol 35, Jun 1950

Pelletier, Romain. 'Octave Pelletier, organiste et pédagogue (1843–1927),' *Qui?*, vol 4, Sep 1952; repr in *Courtes Biographies canadiennes*, ed Romain Gour (Montreal 1952)

Catalogue of Canadian Composers

Musical Red Book

Musiciens canadiens

2 **Frédéric** ('Fred'). Choirmaster, critic, teacher, composer, physician, b Montreal 1 May 1870, d there 30 May 1944; MD (Montreal), hon D MUS (Montreal). He studied piano with his father, singing with Guillaume *Couture, and harmony and counterpoint with Achille *Fortier. He qualified as a doctor, but soon gave up his practice in favour of music and journalism. He contributed to several newspapers, including the *Journal des Débats*, *Le Nationaliste*, *Le Canada*, *La Presse*, *La Patrie*, and finally *Le Devoir*, of which he was music editor and critic 1911–44. He was appointed choirmaster at St-Léon Church, Westmount, in 1910 and also was choirmaster at Ste-Brigide Church and later at St James-the-Less. The dates of these appointments are not known. In 1922 he conducted the Saint-Saëns Choral Society in *Samson et Dalila*, with Cédia *Brault and Émile *Gour. He was president 1932–5 of the *AMQ and correspondent 1920–44 for the Assn française d'expansion et d'échanges artistiques, which in 1937 became the Assn française d'action artistique. It was in this capacity that he organized in 1931 the first visit of the Paris children's choir the Petits Chanteurs à la croix de bois, who subsequently added to their repertoire his harmonizations of Canadian folksongs. Pelletier taught music history at the *Cons national of Montreal and at the École supérieure de musique (*École Vincent-d'Indy). He was secretary of the municipal medical services, librarian and publicist for the provincial department of health, secretary of *L'Action médicale*, a captain in the 65th regiment of the Mount Royal Fusiliers, and a graduate of the Military Academy in St-Jean, Que.

Frédéric Pelletier also contributed to numerous publications and periodicals, including 1929–31 *Entre-Nous*, a monthly magazine of which he was editor-in-chief. He published *Initiation à l'orchestre* (Montreal 1948), but his memoirs, 'Montréal, fin de siècle,' which were to have been published at his death, apparently have remained in manuscript. He wrote the preface to *Musiciens canadiens*, a work he described as 'the first monument raised to the memory of our musicians of the past.' Pelletier was the Montreal correspondent 1919–22 for *La Musique* and ca 1924–5 for *Musical America*.

Pelletier was also a composer. He wrote an oratorio, *La Rédemption*, and two other choral-orchestral works: *Triptyque d'oraisons* (*Messager canadien* 1943) and a *Stabat mater*. His *Requiem Mass* for three-part male choir and organ (Schola cantorum 1920) was described by Arthur *Letondal as a work of 'deep religious feeling and of real musical worth' (*Le Devoir*, 3 Nov 1920). Pelletier also composed a *Tantum ergo* (Parnasse musical), several motets, and *Ludus puerilis* for organ or orchestra. He was a Knight of the Order of St Gregory the Great.

BIBLIOGRAPHY

'Le Dr Fred Pelletier est décédé,' Montreal *Le Devoir*, 30 May 1944

Biron, Édouard. 'Frédéric Pelletier, artiste chrétien,' ibid, 1 Jun 1944

Letondal, Arthur. 'Frédéric Pelletier,' ibid, 2 Jun 1944

3 **Romain**. Organist, teacher, composer, b Montreal 22 Aug 1875, d there 24 Nov 1953. After studying with Arthur *Letondal (piano and organ) and Achille *Fortier (singing and harmony), he was organist-choirmaster 1909–51 at St-Léon Church in Westmount, and taught counterpoint and fugue, piano, and organ at the *Institut Nazareth. Fleurette *Beauchamp, Gabriel *Cusson, Guillaume *Dupuis, Conrad *Letendre, and Georges-É. *Tanguay were among his pupils. He was a founder-member of the Société des Artistes-Musiciens de Montréal and composed motets and organ pieces. He wrote an important article about his father which appeared in *Qui?* (Sep 1952) and was reproduced in *Courtes Biographies canadiennes* (Montreal 1952). His brother Victor (cellist, teacher, chartered accountant, b Montreal, ?, d after 1953) was a member, secretary, and music librarian ca 1907 of *Goulet's MSO.

4 **Romain-Octave** II. Producer, critic, violinist, b St-Lambert, near Montreal, 26 Aug 1904, d there 11 Jan 1968; BA (Montreal) 1924, LL B (Montreal) 1927. After studies in law 1924–7 at the U of Montreal he became a lawyer and practised that profession 1928–33. He studied violin with Albert *Chamberland. He began writing articles on music in 1922 for *Le Devoir*, *La Revue moderne*, and other publications. In 1933 for the CRBC radio network he began preparing and delivering the introductions to the broadcasts from the *Metropolitan Opera and the New York Philharmonic. He joined CBC Montreal in 1939 as a producer of programs of recorded music and served 1941–4 as assistant record librarian. He became a producer for the CBC IS in 1944 and for the French network of the CBC in 1951. Working for the latter until 1964 he was responsible for the series 'Festivals du Mercredi,' *'The Little Symphonies,' and other programs. He was admired by his colleagues for his erudition in music and in other fields. GP

PELLETIER, Colombe. Pianist, accompanist, coach, b Montreal 12 May 1923; B MUS (Montreal) 1940, BA (Montreal) 1942, L MUS (École normale, Paris) 1952. A pupil of Antonio *Létourneau (piano) and Eugène *Lapierre (theory) at the *U of Montreal, she received scholarships from the governments of France in 1947 and Quebec 1949–52 and 1955 and studied in Paris at the École normale with Jules Gentil and Alfred Cortot. She toured Canada 1952–3 for the *JMC, giving 35 concerts with Marthe *Létourneau and Jean-Paul *Jeannotte. During the summer of 1956 she studied Lieder interpretation with Ernst Reichart at the Mozarteum in Salzburg.

Pelletier has accompanied many Canadian and foreign artists on JMC recital tours: Ginette Martenot and Eugene *Kash 1958–9; Paul *Brodie 1960–1; Gaston *Germain 1965–6; Guy Fallot 1968–9; the violinist Andrzej Grabiec, the singers Bruno *Laplante and Anna *Chornodolska, the oboist Bernard *Jean, and the violinist Adele *Armin 1972–3. She also played for JMC presentations of *Vallerand's *Le Magicien* and Debussy's *L'Enfant prodigue* in 1961–2, Hazon's *L'Amante Cubista* in 1967–8, and Rossini's *The Barber of Seville* in 1976–7.

Concurrently Pelletier accompanied such Canadian artists as Colette *Boky, Claire *Gagnier, Joseph *Rouleau, Robert *Savoie, André *Turp, and Richard *Verreau in concert, on radio and TV, and on tours abroad. She was the official accompanist 1962–7 for the JMC National Competition and an examiner in 1963 for the École normale in Paris.

Pelletier was a coach 1962–73 at the *JMC Orford Art Centre and has served in that capacity for the CBC, the *Montreal Festivals, the *Opera Guild of Montreal, and the Théâtre du Nouveau-Monde. She has recorded Jeannotte's *Propos intimes* with Turp. (HDn, AP)

PELLETIER, Louis-Philippe (Paul). Pianist, teacher, b Montreal 7 Aug 1945; premier prix piano (CMM) 1968. He studied at the *CMM 1960–8 with Lubka *Kolessa (piano), Gilles *Tremblay (analysis), Otto and Walter *Joachim (chamber music), and Irving *Heller (sight reading) and was a teacher and accompanist there 1971–3. He continued his training in Paris 1973–6 with Claude Helffer (piano) and Maurice Martenot and Christine Saîto (relaxation). He taught piano 1976–9 and analysis 1977–8 at the *U of Montreal. During the summer of 1977 in Aix-en-Provence he studied piano with Aloys Kontarsky and Harald Boje and Stockhausen's *Klavierstücke* with the composer. On his return that fall he began to teach piano at *McGill U.

Pelletier's first concerts were given as the winner in 1962, 1964, and 1966 of the *MSO Matinée auditions. He also performed in recital in 1969 and 1970 in Quebec City and in 1975 and 1976 at the *Canadian Cultural Centre in Paris and toured in 1976 in Tunisia, 1977–8 for the *JMC in Quebec and Ontario, and 1978–9 throughout Canada. He is an enthusiastic promoter of contemporary music, and his appearances with the *SMCQ include a performance as soloist at the Canadian Pavilion during *Expo 67; participation in the North American premiere of André Boucourechliev's *Archipel III*, Montreal 1972; a performance at the 9th International Festival of Contemporary Art in Royan, 1972; and participation in the North American premiere of Luc Ferrari's *Société II*, Montreal 1975. In 1976 his performance for the SMCQ of the complete piano works of Schoenberg, Berg, and Webern from memory was hailed by the critic Claude *Gingras as a 'total success' (Montreal *La Presse*, 12 Nov 1976). In 1979 he received the grand prize at the 4th international piano competition of the Arnold Schoenberg Festival in Rotterdam.

Among the Canadian works Pelletier has premiered are Michel *Vinet's *Métamorphose*, Raynald *Arseneault's *Sonata*, Michel *Gonneville's *Contribution à l'étude de phénomènes musicaux ...* – a work he commissioned with a grant from the *Canada Council – and Gilles Tremblay's *Tracantes*. Pelletier has performed often on CBC radio and TV. He accompanied Bruno *Laplante on a recording of songs by *Daunais, Fauré, *Vallerand, and Alain *Gagnon and arrangements by Victor *Bouchard. In addition, he took part in the recordings of Claude *Vivier's *Prolifération* and William *Douglas' *Improvisation III* (see Discography for the SMCQ, RCI 358) as well as Richard *Grégoire's *Cantata* (see Discography for Garant). In 1977 he recorded Mozart's *Adagio in B Minor* K540, Webern's *Variations, Op 27*, and Garant's *Asymétries No. 1, Pièce No. 1*, and *Pièce No. 2* (*Cage d'oiseau*) (RCI 465 and RCI AMC 2). He became a member of the board of directors of the SMCQ in 1977. The *CMCouncil named him artist of the year (special mention) in 1980. (AP, MP)

PELLETIER, (Louis) Wilfrid (sometimes spelled Wilfred). Conductor, pianist, administrator, b Montreal 20 Jun 1896; hon D MUS (Montreal) 1936, hon D MUS (Laval) 1952, hon D MUS (Alberta) 1953, hon D MUS (New York College of Music) 1959, hon D LITT (Hobart College, NY) 1960, hon doctorate (Ottawa) 1966, hon D MUS (McGill) 1968, hon doctorate (U of Quebec) 1978. His first contact with music was through the concert band conducted by his father, a baker by trade. He studied piano, solfège, and harmony with Mme François Héraly 1904–14. He was just 12 when he began his musical career as a percussionist – his brother Albert had introduced him to percussion – in the St-Pierre-Apôtre parish temperance band and in a movie house. In 1910 he became the pianist for the orchestra of the National Theatre, the best-known establishment of its kind at that time. That same year he made a decision that directly affected his future. Having attended a performance of *Mignon* at *His Majesty's Theatre in Montreal, he decided then and there to concentrate his activities on opera. The following summer Henri *Delcellier, the conductor of the Dominion Park concert band in which Pelletier was percussionist, offered him the job of rehearsal pianist with the *Montreal Opera Company, of which Delcellier was the chorus master. The experience was short-lived, however, since the company's financial difficulties brought about its dissolution in 1913. In his disappointment Pelletier decided to leave Canada for the USA and Europe. The opportunity to do so was provided by the *Prix d'Europe competition for which he prepared by studying harmony and composition with Alexis *Contant and performance with Alfred *Laliberté. He was unsuccessful in the 1914 competition but won the prize in 1915.

Despite the fact that World War I was raging in Europe, he went to Paris in the autumn of 1916 with his young wife, Berthe Jeannotte, the sister of Albert *Clerk-Jeannotte. His teachers there were Isidor Philipp (piano), Marcel Samuel-Rousseau (harmony), Charles-Marie Widor (composition), and Camille Bellaigue (opera repertoire). Because of the war, however, he was forced to leave France at the end of June 1917. In view of the insecurity of the musical field in his own country, he decided to try his luck in the USA. There he met the conductor Pierre Monteux, who introduced him into the musical and operatic circles of New York, where he took up residence. He soon was offered the position of rehearsal pianist for French repertoire at the *Metropolitan Opera, which provided him with the undreamed-of and enriching experience of working with Caruso, Farrar, Rothier, Grace Moore, and many other famous singers. Also during this time he joined the touring company of the famous Italian baritone Antonio Scotti as assistant to the conductors Gennaro Papi and Carlo Peroni. It was on one of these tours, on 21 May 1920 in Memphis, Tenn, that Pelletier first conducted a complete opera: *Il Trovatore*. In 1922 he became assistant conductor at the Metropolitan Opera and was engaged by the Ravinia Opera Company of Chicago for its summer season and by the San Francisco Opera. On 19 Feb 1922 he conducted for the first time one of the Sunday Concerts at the Metropolitan; two years later he became the artistic director for this series. On 28 Feb 1929 he became one of the Metropolitan's regular conductors, a position he held until 1950. In 1936 he conceived the idea for and became the director of the 'Metropolitan Opera Auditions of the Air,' a radio competition which

Wilfrid Pelletier

sought to discover talented young singers. During his early years with the Metropolitan he established a firm friendship with Arturo Toscanini, who later invited him on several occasions to conduct his NBC Symphony Orchestra.

It was during Pelletier's association with the Metropolitan that the *Béique and *David families and Jean *Lallemand decided to try to establish a symphony orchestra in Montreal and attempted to interest him in the project. After some initial reluctance, which his father overcame by appealing to his national pride and feelings of gratitude towards Quebec, Pelletier threw his whole energy into the venture. The project came to fruition in 1934, and soon Pelletier became the first artistic director of the SCSM orchestra (*MSO). The orchestra gave its first concert in January of 1935, and the same year one of Pelletier's most cherished ideas was realized: the Matinées symphoniques pour la jeunesse were inaugurated 16 Nov 1935. (The Young People's concerts for the English-speaking members of the CSM's audience were inaugurated 22 Oct 1947.) He was greatly encouraged by the interest aroused by the MSO and planned another large-scale project, the *Montreal Festivals; he conducted its inaugural program, the *St Matthew Passion*, in June 1936 in the chapel of the Collège St-Laurent. (Years later he also conducted its final program, Haydn's *The Seasons*, in the Grande Salle of the *PDA in August 1965.)

Through his work with the MSO and the Montreal Festivals, Pelletier was painfully aware of the dearth of first-rate native instrumentalists and saw the need for a conservatory – a Quebec version of the European institution – where the finest teachers from all parts of the world would impart their knowledge free of charge. Through the understanding and capable support of Hector Perrier, who was at that time provincial secretary of Quebec, courses were begun at the *CMM on 1 Mar 1943. Pelletier was appointed its director and held the post until 1961.

In June 1951 Pelletier accepted the position of artistic director of the *Quebec SO and maintained his connection with the orchestra for 15 years. In addition to all these activities, he conducted the Canadian premieres of Debussy's *Pelléas et Mélisande* (Montreal Festivals, 1940; CBC TV, 1956), Honegger's *Jeanne d'Arc au bûcher* (Montreal Festivals, 1953), and Ravel's *L'Enfant et les sortilèges* (CBC TV, 1950). His abiding interest in young people led him to conduct the Children's Concerts of the New York Philharmonic as well as the tours and working sessions of the *NYO 1960–1. In 1961 he accepted the post of director of the music service of the *MACQ. On 21 Sep 1963 he shared the podium with Zubin Mehta, conducting the MSO in the inaugural concert of the PDA in Montreal. In 1964 he was appointed board member of the

Régie de la PDA, and in 1966 the largest of the PDA's three halls was named after him. In 1966 he became one of the founding members of the *SMCQ. On 17 Jan 1971 he conducted the inaugural concert of Quebec City's *Grand Théâtre.

Wilfrid Pelletier was made a Knight of the Order of the King of Denmark in 1946, a Companion of St Michael and St George in 1946, and a Chevalier of the Légion d'honneur in 1947. He was awarded the *Canada Council Medal in 1962 and made a Companion of the *Order of Canada in 1968. In 1971 he received the prize of the Concert Society of the Jewish People's Schools and Peretz Schools, awarded each year to an outstanding Canadian in the world of art. He also received the *CMCouncil Medal in 1975.

Pelletier's discography consists mainly of 78-rpm recordings of operatic excerpts; in these he conducts the orchestras accompanying such famous singers as Rose Bampton, Richard Crooks, Beniamino Gigli, Igor Gorin, John Kent, Giovanni Martinelli, James Melton, Grace Moore, Robert Nicholson, Jan Peerce, Dorothy Sarnoff, Bidú Sayão, Gladys Swarthout, Lawrence Tibbett, and Leonard Warren. In the early 1920s he also recorded piano reductions of works by Bizet, Gounod, Massenet, Offenbach, and Wolf-Ferrari on Ampico piano rolls. As part of a two-piano team with Arthur Loesser, under the direction of Arthur Bodanzky, he made a second series of recordings of a similar nature, for the most part consisting of overtures by Mendelssohn, Rossini, Wagner, and Weber. These recordings are listed in *Roll Back the Years*. In the 1940s Wilfrid Pelletier conducted a series of 78-rpm albums devoted to abridged versions of popular operas such as *Aida*, *La Bohème*, *Carmen*, *Faust*, *I Pagliacci*, *Lohengrin*, *Madama Butterfly*, *The Marriage of Figaro*, *Rigoletto*, *Tannhaüser*, *La Traviata*, and *Tristan und Isolde*. These recordings were made by singers from the Metropolitan Opera, including the Canadians Raoul *Jobin and Joan *Peebles, at the request of the National Committee for Music Appreciation in New York. Selections from certain operas were later rereleased on various LP labels, including Parade. One of Pelletier's rare compositions, 'In the Dark, in the Dew,' 'dedicated to Mme Marie [ie, Maria] Jeritza,' was published by Boston Music in 1923.

As an opera conductor Pelletier was highly esteemed for his profound understanding of the French and Italian repertoire; as a symphony conductor he was perhaps more controversial. He was, nevertheless, the dominant figure in the establishment of a structured musical life in Quebec. Through his determination, his powers of persuasion, and his faith in young musicians and in the future of music in Canada, he succeeded in removing obstacles, overcoming prejudices, and co-ordinating the various musical activities of Quebec in such a way that they have been able to survive numerous set-backs and serious crises.

Pelletier's first marriage ended in divorce. In 1925 he married a second time, taking as his wife the US singer Queena Mario, from whom he was later divorced. In 1937 he married the dramatic soprano Rose Bampton. Two sons, Camille and François, were born of his first marriage. In the early 1970s he took up a life of retirement in New York City. In 1972 he published a volume of memoirs, *Une symphonie inachevée* ... He has also written articles in magazines, including *Vie musicale*, of whose board he was the head 1965–7. His personal papers were deposited in the Archives nationales du Québec in 1973. In about 1958 his name was given to a boulevard in Ville d'Anjou (Montreal), where a primary school also bears his name. In addition, the music school of the Sisters of St Anne in Montreal was named after him in 1965.

Despite the fact that he had not conducted for a number of years, Wilfrid Pelletier made an exceptional appearance 30 Aug 1978, when he conducted one number during a concert in his honour held in the Maurice Richard Arena in Montreal. Roger Lemelin described the event in *La Presse* 1 Sep 1978. Pelletier, who was then over 80, was assisted to the podium, where he was to conduct 'Va pensiero' from Verdi's *Nabucco*. 'At first his trembling baton seemed unsure of the beat, but all at once the rhythm of the music seemed to take over. Visibly moved, the great conductor straightened his back, turned to face the audience, and led them in singing the glorious music.'

WRITINGS

'Orchestras,' *Music in Canada*

'La développement de la musique dans le Québec,' CMCouncil Conference report (Ottawa 1966)

Une symphonie inachevée ... (Montreal 1972)

DISCOGRAPHY (as conductor)

The Art of Gladys Swarthout. RCA Victor O. (1970). Vic VIC 1490

Charles K.L. Davis Sings Romantic Arias From Favorite Operas. Stadium Symphony O of New York. (1958). Everest SDBR 3012

Del Riego 'Oh, Dry Those Tears' – Westendorf 'I'll Take You Home Again, Kathleen.' J. Melton ten, Victor Concert O. Ca 1941. HMV 18219-A (78)

French Opera Arias – Gladys Swarthout. Victor Album M-925 (78)

Gounod *Faust*. Kirsten sop, Di Stefano ten, Tajo bass, Metropolitan Opera O and Chorus. 1949. Cetra 'Opera Live' 1/3

A Grace Moore Program. Victor Album M-918 (78)

Great Scenes from Verdi's Otello. Jepson sop, Martinelli ten, Tibbett bar, Metropolitan Opera O and Chorus. 1939. 6-Victor VM-620 (78)/RCA VCC 1365

Papineau-Couture *Concerto grosso*. CBC Mtl chamb orch. (1958). RCI 156

Pons in Operatic Selections and Songs. De Luca bar, Blaisdell fl. Victor Album M-702 (78)

Richard Crooks Arias. (1969). Vic VIC 1464

Romantic Arias from Favorite Operas (Davis). Stadium Symphony O of New York. Everest 6012

Tenor Arias from the Operas – Richard Crooks. Victor Album M-585 (78)

Verdi *Aida*. Milanov sop, Martinelli ten, Castagna alto, Metropolitan Opera O and Chorus. 1943. Cetra LO 26/3

See also Discographies for Disciples de Massenet; Raoul Jobin; MSO; Léopold Simoneau; Richard Verreau.

BIBLIOGRAPHY

Edwards, Frederick. 'Maestro from Montreal,' *Maclean's*, 15 Feb 1934

Marie-Éve. 'Conversation avec Wilfrid Pelletier,' *P-T*, 908, Mar 1947

McCready, Louise G. *Famous Musicians: MacMillan, Johnson, Pelletier, Willan* (Toronto 1957)

Sabin, Robert. 'Educational systems compared by Pelletier,' *Musical America*, 1 Dec 1957

Freeman, John W. 'Pelly,' *Opera News*, vol 31, 13 May 1967

'Dr. Pelletier looks back on an historical musical career,' *CanComp*, 52, Sep 1970

Huot, Cécile. 'Évolution de la vie musicale au Québec sous l'influence de Wilfrid Pelletier,' unpubl doctoral thesis, Toulouse U 1973

MS (DM)

PENGELLY, Jeanne (Isabel) (b Hesson). Soprano, teacher, b Port Arthur (Thunder Bay), Ont, 10 Feb 1908, d Kingston, Ont, 2 Nov 1977. She studied with Wilfred Coulson, conductor of the Port Arthur Women's Choir, and 1925–8 with Giuseppe *Carboni in Toronto, learning 15 operatic roles and more than 250 songs. Pengelly was soprano soloist 1930–74 at Timothy Eaton Memorial Church in Toronto and a leading singer in the CNR's 1930–1 season of opera broadcasts. She also sang in oratorio and she made her *TSO debut 23 Feb 1932. Her operatic debut was with the *San Carlo Opera in 1933 as Gilda in *Rigoletto*. In 1936 she became the first exclusively Canadian-trained artist to sing with the *Metropolitan Opera, appearing 22 May 1936 as Eurydice in *Orpheus and Eurydice*. Appearances followed the same year with the Chicago Civic Opera as Eurydice and with the Cincinnati Opera as Donna Anna in *Don Giovanni*. She returned to Toronto where she sang the lead in the 1937 Canadian Grand Opera Assn production of *Aida* in *Massey Hall. In 1946 she was a soloist in Beethoven's *Missa solemnis* with the *Montreal Festivals and in 1949 she gave a recital at Carnegie Hall.

Pengelly taught ca 1932–6 at the *TCM and 1950–61 at the *RCMT, her students including Billie Bridgeman, Herb Brown, Maurice *Brown, Johanna White, and the actors Jeff Alexander and Murray Davis.

After her performance with the TSO in Beethoven's *Ninth Symphony*, Pengelly was praised for her 'glorious soprano ringing through the hall like the sound of a thrush. Orchestra chorus and ... golden trumpet all combined were subject to her rich, luscious notes' (Toronto *Telegram*, 22 Mar 1933. MH

PENTLAND, Barbara (m Huberman). Composer, pianist, teacher, b Winnipeg 2 Jan 1912; ATCM 1931, composition diploma (Juilliard) 1939, hon LLD (Manitoba) 1976. A heart disorder curtailed her physical and social activities in childhood and forced her to develop a life of the mind. Composition provided a natural exercise for this, but Pentland's first written attempts, shown to the piano teacher with whom, at nine, she had begun lessons at Rupert's Land Girls' School in Winnipeg, only prompted disapproval. Teacher and parents regarded her desire to compose as eccentric and, probably, too 'exciting' for a delicate child. There was nothing delicate about Pentland's determination, however. She continued to compose, though she learned to keep her efforts private. Her teen-age works were conditioned by a study of the French Revolution and by the heroic music of Beethoven.

Pentland's first encouragement to compose came from Frederick H. *Blair who taught her piano and theory 1927–9 while she was in Montreal attending a boarding school. Her first formal studies in composition, at last with parental permission, began in 1929 with the d'Indy pupil Cécile Gauthiez in Paris where she attended a finishing school. Gauthiez, who continued to teach her by correspondence for a year and a half after her return to Winnipeg in 1930, trained her in French academic polyphony and the lush chromaticism of Franck, both of which shaped her work in the ensuing decade, surviving even in the *Piano Quartet* of 1939. In Winnipeg 1930–6 she continued practical studies with Hugh *Bancroft (organ) and Eva *Clare (piano) and was more active as a performer than at any time previously or later. This phase culminated in a formal debut as a concert pianist, 21 Sep 1936 at the Royal Alexandra Hotel.

The requirements of Pentland's nature were not to be appeased by performance, however. Motivated by the need to develop her skills as a composer she tried for and won (1936) a fellowship to the Juilliard Graduate School where, for the next two years, she submitted to a strict course in 16th-century counterpoint under Frederick Jacobi. At the same time, steady encounters with the new music of the day – of which so much more could be heard in New York than in Winnipeg — incited her to fresh rebellion. Leaving Jacobi, she spent her third year at Juilliard searching for freer and more individual means of expression under the encouraging guidance of Bernard Wagenaar. The

Barbara Pentland

works of Hindemith and Stravinsky became a significant influence at this time, combining, as they did, the strong counterpoint which her studies with Gauthiez and Jacobi had taught her to respect and the harmonic resilience and freedom she had come to crave.

Back in Winnipeg 1939–42 Pentland assimilated what she had learned. While teaching privately and examining for the *U of Manitoba she also composed the incidental music for a radio play, *Payload*; a two-piano 'ballet-pantomime,' *Beauty and the Beast*, for the Winnipeg Ballet; the piano pieces, *Studies in Line*; and the *Concerto for Violin and Small Orchestra*. During the summers of 1941 and 1942 she studied at the Berkshire Music Center with Aaron Copland. The textural transparency and rhythmic vitality of Copland's music prompted in Pentland the desire for similar leavening in her own and set her on the road to the neoclassicism (beginning with the Coplandesque *Variations* and the *Concerto*) which pervaded her work until the mid-1950s.

Seeking exposure for her music Pentland moved in 1942 to Toronto where she supported herself teaching composition and theory at the TCM (1943–9; her pupils included George *Crum and Alan *Detweiler) and made a name as a radical, along with such contemporaries as John *Weinzweig and the young Harry *Somers. The 'radical' image was sustained by the premiere (Toronto 1945, by Harry and Frances *Adaskin) of the *Concerto* in a violin-and-piano reduction and the premieres, also in Toronto, of the *Song Cycle on Poems of Anne Marriott* (1947, by Frances *James and the composer), the *Sonata Fantasy* (1948, by the pianist Harry Somers) and the *Octet for Winds* (1949, CBC radio). Pentland premieres were not confined to Toronto during those years. The *Piano Sonata* was introduced in 1947 by Marie Knotkova in Prague, the *Sonata for Violin and Piano* in 1948 by Frank *Thorolfson and Chester *Duncan in Winnipeg, and the *String Quartet No. 1* in 1949 by the Philadelphia Art Alliance.

Though her association with Weinzweig led her closer and closer to a break with tonality, Pentland's first serious consideration of serialism came during her visits (1947, 1948) to the Edward MacDowell Colony in New Hampshire where Dika Newlin, a disciple of Schoenberg, interested her in that master's development and application of strict 12-tone principles. While Pentland could not sympathize with the neurosis from which Schoenberg's theories seemed to stem, she did respond to the disciplines they propounded. The *Octet for Winds*, her first deliberately serial work, was the result. The *Concerto for Organ*, the *Symphony No. 2*, the *Sonata for Solo Violin*, the orchestral piece *Ave atque vale*, the *String Quartet No. 2* (chosen to represent Canada at the 1956 ISCM

A manuscript page from *News* for voice and orchestra (1970) by Barbara Pentland, showing an aleatoric 'zone'

festival in Stockholm), and the other works composed between 1949 (when she moved to Vancouver where she would teach until 1963 at the *U of British Columbia) and 1954 all show the influence of the Schoenberg technique.

But it was a visit (1955) to Darmstadt that brought Pentland into contact with the final major influence on her style: the music of Anton Webern. The delicate sonorities, the concision of the structures, and the pellucid qualities of thought and texture in this music made to the cool, sharp Pentland intelligence an appeal which the Schoenberg ethic – more tortured and more doctrinaire – could not make. The Webern influence was noticeable immediately in the glacial and elegant *Concerto for Piano and String Orchestra* and the cogent, agile *Symphony for Ten Parts* (written in 1957 in Munich where she lived for a time); indeed, it pervades the fastidious clarity of texture in virtually all the post-1955 works.

While Pentland's mature style – exploiting serial possibilities in a free but uncluttered way, and sound combinations in a sensitive but unsensual and, certainly, unsentimental way – became established in all essentials in 1955, she continued to refine and 'season.' She has incorporated pitch shadings (quarter-tones), aleatoric 'zones,' and other relative novelties in the fabric of her scores. Notable instances are to be found in the *String Quartet No. 3* and *Mutations*. Extra-musical distractions such as light effects, projections, theatrics, however, are eschewed.

Though the large catalogue of her works testifies to the independence of her muse (see also Composition, instrumental solos and duos: 2), Pentland has composed on commission for the Forest Hill Community Centre, Toronto (*Colony Music*), the CBC (*Variations on a Boccherini Tune* and *Trio* for violin, cello, and piano), Gordon *Jeffery (*Concerto for Organ and Strings*), the *Winnipeg SO through a *Canada Council grant (*Symphony No. 4*), the Vancouver RCMT Alumni Assn (*Suite Borealis* for piano), the U of British Columbia Chamber Music Ensemble (*Trio con alea*), and the Hugh *McLean Consort (*Septet* for brass, organ, and strings).

After her resignation (1963) from the U of British Columbia, and in response to a need articulated by the Toronto piano teacher Rachel *Cavalho, Pentland began to produce a variety of teaching material for piano, including many short pieces and three graded books (*Music of Now*, Waterloo 1970) which accustom the student to such 20th-century commonplaces as tone clusters, additive and alternating rhythms, retrograde and inverse canons, unharmonic polyphony, and various applications of serial construction.

Aware that her work may seem austere and uningratiating, Pentland neither revises nor repents. She means what she writes, works arduously to write what she means, and leaves the rest to the performer and the audience, remarking (*Northern Review*) that 'all audiences are more intelligent than they are brought up to be by the musicians who are responsible.' Her position on other musical matters is similarly unobsequious. Interviewed by *Musicanada* she described, with irony, a consequence of Canada's 'colonial' complex: 'What comes from outside the country *must* de facto be superior. Prime example: the opening of our multi-million-dollar "National" Arts Centre with an imported French ballet company dancing to a score by a Greek composer conducted by an American born in Germany!' She went on to find the country's central communications medium regressive: 'CBC radio used to do an excellent job of tying [Canada] together, so that cultural isolation was less obvious; even that is no longer the case.'

In the *Northern Review* article cited above, Pentland, in an oft-quoted inflammatory statement, identified hers as 'the first generation of Canadian composers. Before our time music development was largely in the hands of imported English organists who, however sound academically, had no creative contribution to make of any general value.' But she had not many illusions, either, about her own generation, 'slowly bringing forth our own manner of speech.' Her defence was measured: 'At least we've started something, even if it still leaves [us] in the difficult role of pioneer.'

Pentland was awarded the Diplôme d'honneur by the *CCA in 1977. The citation noted that she had been faced 'with ultraconservative attitudes both towards female composers and new means of expression. However,' it added, 'intolerance from the unthinking has never deterred Pentland ... [she] has contributed to all major categories of music and her catalogue of works is impressive.' The citation quoted her remark 'The creative force has to be such that the laws necessary for its expression should be continually challenged. There is an element of daring in all great art' and stated 'Such an element runs through much of the music of Barbara Pentland.'

In 1958 Pentland married John Huberman, son of the violinist Bronislaw Huberman. She is a member of the *CLComp, an affiliate of PRO Canada, and an associate of the *CMCentre.

SELECTED COMPOSITIONS

STAGE, RADIO, AND FILM

Beauty and the Beast, ballet-pantomime. 1940 (Wpg 1941). 2 pf. ms

The Lake, chamb opera (D. Livesay). 1952 (Van 1954). Sop, alto, ten, bs, sm orch. CMCentre

Incidental music for radio plays and the NFB film *The Living Gallery* (1947). Ms

ORCHESTRA

Lament. 1939 (Wpg 1940). Full orch. Ms

Arioso and Rondo. 1941 (London 1945). Full orch. CMCentre

Holiday Suite. 1941 (Van 1948). Chamb orch (str orch arr 1947). Ms

3 *Symphonies*: *No. 1*, 1945–48 (Mtl 1947 'Adagio' only); *No. 2*, 1940 (Tor 1953); *No. 4*, 1959 (Wpg 1960). Full orch. CMCentre

Variations on a Boccherini Tune. 1948 (Tor 1948). Full orch. CMCentre

Ave atque vale. 1951 (Van 1953). Full orch. CMCentre
Ricercar for Strings. 1955 (Van 1958). Str orch. CMCentre
Symphony for Ten Parts 'Symphony No. 3,' 1957 (Van 1961). Sm orch. BMIC 1961. RCI 215/RCA CCS-1009 (Chamb Ens of the *Wpg SO)
Strata. 1964 (Van 1968). Str orch. CMCentre
Ciné-Scene I. 1968. Chamb orch. CMCentre
Five-Plus 'Simple Pieces for Strings.' 1971. Str orch. CMCentre
Res musica. 1975 (Van 1975). Str orch. CMCentre

SOLOIST(S) WITH ORCHESTRA

Concerto for Violin and Small Orchestra. 1942 (arr vn, pf Tor 1945). CMCentre
Colony Music. 1947 (Tor 1948). Pf, str. CMCentre
Concerto for Organ and Strings. 1949 (London, Ont 1951). CMCentre
Concerto for Piano and String Orchestra. 1956 (Tor 1958). Ber (rental). RCI 184 (*Bernardi pf)
News (news media). 1970 (Ott 1971). Virtuoso v, orch. CMCentre
Variations concertantes. 1970 (Mtl 1971). Pf, orch. CMCentre

CHAMBER

Sonata for Cello and Piano. 1943. CMCentre
At Early Dawn (Hsiang Hao). 1945. Ten, fl, vc. Ms
3 *String Quartets* (1945, 1953, 1969). All CMCentre. (*No. 1*) RCI 141 (*Mtl Str Quar)/Col ML-5764 (*Canadian Str Quar)/(*No. 3*) RCI 353 (*Purcell Str Quar)
Vista. 1945. Vn, pf. BMIC 1951
Sonata for Violin and Piano. 1946. CMCentre
Octet for Winds. 1948. Ww, brass ens. CMCentre
Weekend Overture for Resort Combo. 1949. Cl, tpt, pf, perc. Ms
Solo Violin Sonata. 1950. CMCentre
Duo for Viola and Piano. 1960. CMCentre. RCI 223/RCA CCS-1017 (S. *Humphreys va, H. *McLean pf)
Canzona. 1961. Fl, ob, hpd. CMCentre
Cavazzoni for Brass (transcr from 3 org hymns by G. Cavazzoni). 1961. Brass quin. Ms
Trio for Violin, Cello and Piano. 1963. CMCentre. RCI 242 (Pentland pf, A. *Polson vn, J. Hunter vc)
Variations for Viola. 1965. CMCentre
Trio con alea. 1966. Str trio. CMCentre
Septet. 1967. Hn, tpt, trb, org, vn, va, vc. CMCentre
Reflections. 1971. Acc. CMCentre
Interplay. 1972. Acc, str quar. CMCentre. Mel SMLP 4034 (*Macerollo acc)
Mutations. 1972. Vc, pf. CMCentre
Occasions. 1974. Brass quin. CMCentre
Disasters of the Sun (D. Livesay). 1976. Mezzo, 9 instr, tape. Ms
Phases. 1977. Cl solo. CMCentre

PIANO

Rhapsody 1939. 1939. CMCentre
Studies in Line. 1941. BMIC 1949. RCI 134 (*Newmark)/CCM-2 (*Cavalho)/Lon T.5697 (*Godden)
Variations. 1942. CMCentre
Piano Sonata. 1945. CMCentre
Sonata Fantasy. 1947. CMCentre
2 *Sonatinas* (1951). CMCentre
Two-Piano Sonata. 1953. 2 pf. CMCentre
Toccata. 1958. BMIC 1961. RCI 242 (Pentland)/CBC SM-162 (*Buczynski)
Three Duets after Pictures by Paul Klee. 1959. Pf 4-hands. CMCentre. RCI 242 (Pentland, R. *Rogers)
Fantasy. 1962. BMIC 1966. RCI 242 (Pentland)
Echoes 1 and 2. 1964. Wat 1968. CCM-2 (*Cavalho)
Shadows/Ombres. 1964. Wat 1968. RCI 242 (Pentland)
Three Pairs. 1964. BMIC 1966. CCM-2 (*Cavalho)
Hands across the C. 1965. Wat 1968. CCM-2 (*Cavalho)
Suite borealis. 1966. CMCentre. Mel SMLP 4031 (*Kubalek)
Space Studies. 1967. Wat 1968. CCM-2 (*Cavalho)
Music of Now, Books 1, 2, 3. 1970. Wat 1970
Coral Reef. 1974. CMCentre
Tenebrae. 1976. CMCentre
Angelus – Spectra – Whales. 1977. CMCentre
Several other short pieces for pf and 1 work for hpd *Ostinato and Dance* (1962). Ms

CHOIR

'Ballad of Trees and the Master' (S. Lanier). 1937. SATB. Ms
'Dirge for a Violet' (D.C. Scott). 1939. SATB. Ms
Epigrams and Epitaphs, rounds (various). 1952. 2, 3, 4 vs. CMCentre
'Salutation of the Dawn' (Sanskrit). 1954. SATB. CMCentre
'What is Man?' (Ecclesiasticus 18). 1954. SATB. CMCentre
Three Sung Songs (Chinese, transl C.M. Candlin). 1965. SATB. CMCentre

VOICE

Song Cycle (Marriott). 1942–5. Sop, pf. CMCentre. ('Wheat' and 'Mountains') RCI 20 (F. *James)
Approximately 10 other songs (1932–71), all ms

WRITINGS

'An experiment in music,' *CRMA*, vol 2, Aug–Sep 1943
'Canadian music 1950,' *Northern R*, vol 3, Feb–Mar 1950
' "The Lake": one-act chamber opera; libretto by Dorothy Livesay,' *Canadian Forum*, Apr 1954

BIBLIOGRAPHY

'Ideas on a keyboard, *SatN*, 9 Jan 1951
' "The Lake": a Canadian chamber opera,' *CBC Times*, 28 Feb–6 Mar 1954
Turner, Robert. 'Barbara Pentland,' *CMJ*, vol 2, Summer 1958
'Barbara Pentland in dual role,' *CBC Times*, 27 Jul–2 Aug 1963
Harry Somers in Conversation with Barbara Pentland, CBC radio 'Music of Today,' 29 Apr 1966
Huse, Peter. 'Barbara Pentland,' *MSc*, 242, Jul–Aug 1968
'Barbara Pentland,' *Mcan*, 21, Jul–Aug 1969
BMI Canada Ltd / PRO Canada Ltd. 'Barbara Pentland,' pamphlets (1974, 1979)
Eastman, Sheila. 'Barbara Pentland: a biography,' unpubl M MUS thesis, U of British Columbia 1974
Norma Beecroft in conversation with Barbara Pentland, CBC radio 'Two New Hours,' 11 Nov 1979
Eastman, Sheila. 'Barbara Pentland' *Contemporary Canadian Composers / Compositeurs canadiens contemporains*

KW

PÉPIN, (Jean Joseph) **Clermont**. Composer, pianist, teacher, administrator, b St-Georges-de-Beauce, Que, 15 May 1926; Artist Diploma piano, composition (Curtis) 1944, Artist Diploma (RCMT) 1949. He received his first piano and harmony lessons in his native village from Georgette Dionne-Lagacé. At 12 he was introduced by Wilfrid *Pelletier as both composer and conductor at a matinee of the CSM. Pelletier conducted his orchestration of a minuet by Pépin. On 23 Jan 1939, at the *Palais Montcalm in Quebec City, the Société symphonique (*Quebec SO) presented a Pépin symphony directed by J.-Robert *Talbot who had orchestrated the original piano duet. Pépin received a scholarship of $500 from the orchestra's committee.

In 1937 Pépin earned a special prize from the CPRS for his *Invention* for piano and *Ave Maria*. He spent the years 1939–41 in Montreal studying piano with Arthur *Letondal and composition with Claude *Champagne. On a scholarship to the Curtis Institute in Philadelphia he studied 1942–5 with Jeanne Behrend (piano) and Rosario Scalero (composition). Returning to Montreal, he spent 1945–6 at the *CMM with Jean *Dansereau (piano), Claude Champagne (composition), Louis *Bailly (chamber music), and Léon Barzin (conducting). Three prize awards from *CAPAC enabled him to study 1946–9 at the Senior School of the *RCMT with Lubka *Kolessa (piano), Arnold *Walter (composition), and Nicholas *Goldschmidt (conducting). He won the Eaton Graduating Scholarship of $1000.

Pépin's *String Quartet No. 1* was performed at a student composers' symposium in Rochester in 1948. Other important works of this period include the *Concerto No. 1* for piano and orchestra, performed in 1946 by Pépin with the Montreal Youth SO; *Variations symphoniques*, award-winner in the 1948 centenary competition at Ste-Marie College, Montreal; and *Symphony No. 1*, premiered in 1947 on CBC radio under the direction of Jean-Marie *Beaudet. These works are in the post-romantic tradition but display originality in their construction and in their resourceful instrumentation.

Pépin won the 1949 *Prix d'Europe as a pianist and lived 1949–55 in Paris. He studied piano with Yves Nat and Lazare Lévy and composition with

Manuscript opening page from *Séquences pour cinq instruments* by Clermont Pépin

Arthur Honegger and André Jolivet. At the Paris Cons, he took Olivier Messiaen's analysis course; Boulez and Stockhausen as well as Serge *Garant and Sylvio *Lacharité were among his fellow students. He started using serial techniques, and later declared 'I did not like serial music but it intrigued me. I started using this technique only gradually in my works, which were tonal until then.' The works written in Paris marked a new direction in his style which heretofore had been influenced by Honegger. *Guernica*, a symphonic piece after the painting by Picasso, won him first prize in a competition organized by *Laval U for its centenary (1952). In Paris he performed the two-piano version of his ballet *Les Portes de l'enfer* with his first wife, the pianist Raymonde Gagnon, at a 1953 concert of the Pentacorde group, of which he was a member. Another symphonic work, *La Rite du soleil noir*, after a poem by Antonin Artaud, won second prize in a 1955 competition organized by Radio-Luxembourg.

Returning to Montreal, Pépin taught composition at CMM 1955–64 and became director of studies, before serving 1967–72 as director of the school. His many pupils include Micheline Coulombe *Saint-Marcoux, François *Dompierre, André *Gagnon, Jacques *Hétu, and André *Prévost. Despite his teaching and administrative duties, he pursued his creative activities and produced his *String Quartet No. 2* (1957, his first completely serial piece) and his *Symphony No. 2*, commissioned by the CBC for the *'Little Symphonies.'

Other notable steps in Pépin's career were the *String Quartet No. 3* and *String Quartet No. 4*. Of the latter the composer said that 'it is not the end of my research in serial techniques but rather the beginning.' With *Nombres*, for two pianos and orchestra, Pépin went even further in his use of contemporary techniques. Employing the mathematical procedures formulated by Boulez, he divided the instrumental complement into 12 groups, of which two were pianos. Microphones and speakers arranged throughout the auditorium let the audience feel 'completely surrounded by music.'

Attracted to theatre and dance, Pépin wrote two ballets, **L'Oiseau-phénix* and *Le Porte-rêve*, the first premiered under his direction with choreography by Ludmilla Chiriaeff, the second premiered on CBC TV choreographed by Michel Conte. For the first time Pépin introduced an element of jazz to his music. He wrote incidental music 1956–64 for several productions of the Théâtre-club and the Théâtre du Nouveau-Monde. He returned to large orchestra when, on commission for the *MSO, he wrote *Quasars, Symphony No. 3*, a work that revealed his interest in space sciences.

In 1964 Pépin undertook a series of works entitled *Monade*, a word meaning 'a substance that is simple, active and indivisible.' Commissioned by the *Lapitsky Foundation, *Monade I* consists of sequences of notes, sustained without vibrato, which seek to imitate electronic sounds. *Monade II*, also for string orchestra, remained unfinished in 1980. *Monade III*, commissioned for the 1972 *Montreal International Competition, is a bravura piece for violin and orchestra. In these works Pépin's style moved towards a certain starkness, but his manipulation of sound and rhythm remained characteristic and original. *Prismes et cristaux*, for large string orchestra, marked his return to classicism, inspired by the prelude-and-fugue format. In 1975 Pépin completed another monumental piece, *La Messe sur le monde, Symphony No. 4* for narrator, choir, and orchestra, on a text by Teilhard de Chardin. In *Interactions*, commissioned by *SMCQ, the composer revisited his favourite themes of astronomy and space.

Clermont Pépin's creative evolution, which spans more than four decades, is that of a man who passed smoothly from childhood dreams through the formative discoveries of adolescence to arrive at an early maturity. It displays the intellectual development of one who is anxious to live and to understand his century, searching to exploit fully the expressive possibilities of an art freed from traditional frameworks and enriched by new techniques. After the serial adventure, Pépin admitted 'I am probably very sentimental at heart and very romantic. That, I think, is really one of the reasons why I went into serial music in the first place, because to me serial music is not at all intellectual. On the contrary, the more I go into it, the more I find that it opens an entire new world of emotional expression' (*Thirty-Four Biographies*, Montreal 1964).

In 1963 Pépin was a founder of the Centre d'études prospectives du Québec. He collaborated on *Le Bruit*, a publication of the centre (Montreal 1970). After serving 1972–8 as program-consultant at the *MACQ Pépin again taught harmony, counterpoint, and composition at the CMM and CMQ. He is an associate of the *CMCentre, a member of the *CLComp and of CAPAC. He became a member of the administrative council of CAPAC and was vice-president 1966–70. He served 1969–72 as national president of the *JMC.

Pépin received the 1970 *Prix de musique Calixa-Lavallée. His second wife is the violinist Mildred *Goodman.

SELECTED COMPOSITIONS

STAGE

Les Portes de l'enfer, ballet. 1953. Med orch (2 pf). Ms
Athalie, incidental music. 1956. Ww, brass. Ms
Le Malade imaginaire, incidental music. 1956. Xyl, va, vc, perc. Ms
Other works for the stage
See also *L'Oiseau-phénix*.

ORCHESTRA

Variations. 1944. Str orch. Ms
Concerto No. 1. 1946 (Mtl 1946). Pf, orch. Ms
Variations symphoniques. 1947 (Mtl 1948). Full orch. Ms. RCI 1 (J.-M. *Beaudet)
Symphony No. 1. 1948 (Mtl 1949). Full orch. Ms
Concerto No. 2. 1949 (Mtl 1949). Pf, orch. Ms
Guernica, symphonic poem. 1952 (Quebec 1952). Full orch. CMCentre. Audat 477-4001/CBC SM-4 (*TSO)
Le Rite du soleil noir, symphonic poem. 1955 (Luxembourg 1955). Full orch. CMCentre. RCI 155 (J.-M. *Beaudet)
Adagio. 1947–56. Str orch. Ms
Ronde villageoise, excerpt from *L'Oiseau-phénix*. 1956 (Mtl 1957). Str orch. Ms
Nocturne. 1950–7. Pf, str orch. Ms
Fantaisie. 1957. Str orch. Ms
Fantaisie (based on traditional French folksong). 1957 (Mtl 1957). Ten, SATB, orch. Ms
Symphony No. 2. 1957 (Mtl 1957). Med orch. CMCentre. RCI 212/RCA CCS 1007 (R. *Leduc)
Mouvement (based on traditional French folksongs). 1958 (Quebec 1958). SATB, orch. Ms
Hymne au vent du nord, cantata (A. DesRochers). 1960 (Orford 1960). Ten, sm orch. Ms
Monologue. 1961 (Mtl 1961). Med orch. CMCentre
Nombres. 1962 (Mtl 1963). 2 pf, orch. CMCentre
Three Miniatures for Strings. 1963 (Tor 1963). School orch. OUP 1966
Monade I. 1964 (Mtl 1964). Str orch. Ms. RCA LSC-3128/CRI SD-317 (*McGill Chamb O)
Quasars, Symphony No. 3. 1967 (Mtl 1967). Full orch. Leeds 1976. RCI 387/Sel CC-15.101 (*MSO)
Monade III. 1972 (Mtl 1972). Vn, orch. CMCentre
Chroma. 1973 (Guelph 1973). Full orch. CMCentre
Prismes et cristaux. 1974 (Mtl 1974). Str orch. CMCentre
La Messe sur le monde, Symphony No. 4 (Teilhard de Chardin). 1975. Spkr, SATB, orch. CMCentre

CHAMBER MUSIC

Trois Menuets. 1944. Str quar. Ms
String Quartet No. 1. 1948. CMCentre. RCI 12 (*Parlow Str Quar)
Cantique des cantiques (Bible). 1950. SATB, pf. Ms
Quatre Monodies. 1955. Fl. Leeds 1971. Dom S-69006 (*Aitken)
String Quartet No. 2 'Thème et variations.' 1956. Ms. RCI 295 (*Orford Str Quar)
Suite. 1958. Vn, vc, pf. CMCentre
String Quartet No. 4 'Hyberboles.' 1960. CMCentre
Pièces de circonstance. 1967. Children's choir, school inst ens. CMCentre
Séquences pour cinq instruments. 1972. Fl, ob, str trio. CMCentre
Monade IV – Réseaux. 1974. Vn, pf. CMCentre
Monade VI – Réseaux. 1975. Vn. CMCentre
String Quartet No. 5. 1976. CMCentre
Interactions. 1977. 7 perc, 2 pf. Ms
Nuclées. 1977. Perc. CMCentre

PIANO

Andante. 1939. Ms
Petite Étude No. 1. 1940. West 1948. RCI 132 (R. *Pratt)
Thème et variations. 1940. Ms
Pièce pour piano. 1943. Ms
Petite Étude No. 2. 1946. West 1948. RCI 132 (R. *Pratt)
Petite Étude No. 3. 1947. West 1948. RCI 132 (R. *Pratt)
Sonate en un mouvement. 1947. Ms
Thème et variations. 1947. Ms
Toccata No. 1, Op 3. 1947. CMCentre
Étude – Atlantique. 1950. Ms
Petite Étude No. 4. 1950. Ms
Suite. 1951 (rev 1955). Leeds 1973. ('Allegro leggiero' et 'Fantaisie en hommage à Arthur Honegger') RCI 135 (J. *Dufresne)/('Danse frénétique') RCA CCS-1022 (*Troup)
The Nose, Cradle Song, The Gates of Hell. 1953. FH 1953. (*The Gates of Hell*) Dom S-69002 (*Mould)
Deux Préludes and *Étude No. 5*. 1954. CMCentre
Ronde villageoise, excerpt from *L'Oiseau-phénix*. 1961. 2 pf. CMCentre. CBC SM-61 (V. *Bouchard)
Toccata No. 3. 1961. CMCentre
Also *Trois Pièces pour 'La Légende dorée'* (1956, hpd or pf, Leeds 1971); and *Passacaglia* (1950, org, ms)

VOICE

Cycle Éluard (Éluard). 1949. Sop, pf. CMCentre RCI 148 (*Alarie)/RCI 426 (B. *Laplante)
Also others

WRITINGS

'Musique,' *Vie des arts*, 1, 2, Jan–Feb, Mar–Apr 1956
'Montreal: La Semaine internationale de musique actuelle,' *CMJ*, vol 6, Autumn 1961

BIBLIOGRAPHY

'Clermont Pépin fait honneur à la jeune musique canadienne,' interview with Gilles Potvin, *P-T*, 899, Jun 1946
Saucier, Pierre. 'Profils d'artistes,' Montreal *La Patrie*, 8 Nov 1959
Rudel-Tessier, J. 'The many activities of Clermont Pépin,' *CanComp*, 11, Oct 1966
Sauvé, Wilfrid. 'A meeting with Clermont Pépin,' *Jmc*, Nov 1969
Potvin, Gilles. 'Musique: l'année de Clermont Pépin,' Montreal *Le Devoir*, 6 Apr 1974
Martin, Sylvaine. 'A composer talks about music for competitions,' *CanComp*, 156, Dec 1980
Potvin, Gilles. 'Clermont Pépin,' *Contemporary Canadian Composers / Compositeurs canadiens contemporains*
Dictionary of Contemporary Music

GP

Percussion. Instruments from which sound is obtained by shaking or rubbing, or by blows of the hand, fingers, sticks, or mallets upon wood, metal, a stretched skin, or indeed any other material. While the role of the percussion instruments is chiefly rhythmical, they may be used as well to obtain colour and evoke atmosphere. Berlioz was among the first composers to provide the percussion instruments with a distinctive role. In the 20th century percussion has come to the fore, and it is integral to jazz.

Percussion instruments trace their origins back to remotest antiquity and were man's earliest means of extending the effects of hand clapping and foot stamping. The considerable and steadily increasing number of instruments in this family, including the host of exotic instruments from the Orient, Africa, and South America, has made it difficult to classify them. New instruments made from various materials are being introduced constantly, as are new ways of using the traditional instruments.

Berlioz divided the percussion instruments into two groups: those with a definite pitch, which may assume a melodic role, and those with indefinite pitch, used for rhythmical purposes or simply to make a noise. Doubtless more practical for classification is a division into four groups: skins (timpani, drums, etc), metals (cymbals, bells, Chinese gong, other gongs, etc), keyboard instruments (xylophone, marimba, vibraphone, etc), and accessories (triangle, castanets, whip, claves, woodblocks, etc). Besides expanding its role in the orchestra, percussion has attained a measure of independence. After World War II percussion ensembles were formed and a repertoire was created for them.

In Canada percussion instruments were the first encountered by the European settlers, for the Indians possessed many of their own devising. During the 18th century the European drums in use belonged mainly to the settlers' militia. The organized military activities of the 19th century, however, brought regimental bands whose trained players, including the drummers, often assisted in civilian entertainments. The timpani needed for the major symphonic repertoire remained rare, however. In 1877, at its first concert, the *Montreal Philharmonic Society presented *Messiah*, and the timpanist was imported from Boston, 'since this instrument was unknown in Montreal' (*Musical Red Book*). The *Couture *MSO and the later *Goulet MSO did boast timpanists: documents specify a member of the Schepens family in 1894 and R. McKeown and A. Talbot 1905–6. In the early 1900s the young Wilfrid *Pelletier was the drummer in a temperance band.

Louis Decair became the timpanist in the *Montreal Orchestra in 1930 and the CSM orchestra in 1935. He taught at *McGill U and the *CMM, and his pupils included Michel *Perrault and Louis *Charbonneau. The US timpanist Saul Goodman joined the teaching staff at the CMM in the 1940s and taught Charbonneau and Guy *Lachapelle. Charbonneau succeeded Goodman in 1950 and trained a generation of young percussionists, including Pierre *Béluse (founder of the McGill Percussion Ensemble), Ian Bernard (timpanist with the *NACO), and Vincent *Dionne. Lachapelle taught Marie-Josée Simard, the first woman student at the CMM to obtain a premier prix in percussion. She made her debut with the *SMCQ in 1980 performing *Archipel 5E* by Boucourechliev. In Montreal orchestras the names of Thomas Cavanagh, Robert Leroux, Jean-Guy Plante, and Jean-François Roch deserve mention. Leroux has distinguished himself in concerts of the SMCQ, participating in many premieres of contemporary works.

In Quebec City, Roger Juneau, Serge Laflamme, André Morin, and Georges Turgeon were active in 1980. The ensemble Répercussion has given several concerts there. In Toronto C. Riddy taught percussion at the *Toronto College of Music around 1889. Programs from 1923 of the New Symphony Orchestra (see TS) mention Harry Nicholson, timpanist, assisted by E.C. Whitney and T.J. Burry, percussionists.

When Stravinsky conducted the TSO in *The Firebird* and *Petrushka* in *Massey Hall in 1937, Burry was the timpanist, and Ernest Ainley, Archie Cooper, and Harold Slater were the percussionists. John *Wyre, who succeeded Burry as the TSO timpanist in 1966, assumed an important role as percussion teacher at the *U of Toronto, as founder of *Nexus (with Robert Becker, William Cahn, Michael Craden, Robin Engelman, and Russell Hartenberger) and as a regular performer with the *NMC. Wyre remained the TS' timpanist in 1980, and Donald Kuehn was principal percussionist. Allen Beard and David Kent became the percussionist-members of *ARRAY. Muriel *Kilby made a name as one of the rare marimba virtuosos in Canada.

Harold Hunter became a percussion player in Winnipeg in the 1930s and a member of the *Winnipeg SO, first as timpanist beginning in 1949, then as a member of the percussion section until the late 1970s. Others active in Winnipeg have included Al Doe, William Mulhearn, Greg Hodgson (timpani), and Claude Lemieux.

A certain Mr Burns is listed as the 'drummer' in the 1897 *Vancouver SO. Among the percussionists associated with the orchestra in the 1970s have been Don Adams, William Good, Paul Grant, B.C. Manning, and John Rudolph.

Among other percussionists active in the 1970s were Thomas Miller and Tim Rawlings in Calgary, Brian Jones and Barry Nemish in Edmonton, Max Ball and James Faraday in Halifax, Donald Wherry in Newfoundland, Gregory Law, Lanny Levine, and Lisa Simmermon in Ottawa, and Scott Eddlemon and Dale Bassett Price in Victoria.

The popularity of jazz in Canada, particularly after World War II, resulted in the appearance of such highly specialized drummers as Archie Alleyne, Terry *Clarke, Tom Doran, Larry *Dubin, Jerry *Fuller, Billy Graham, Terry Hawkeye, Clayton Johnston, Reg Keln, Guy Nadon, Émile *Normand, Claude *Ranger, Ron Rully, Gregg Simpson, Norm Villeneuve, Jimmy Wightman, and George Ursan.

The role of percussion has grown further with the rise of pop groups of diverse tendencies. Certain names stand out: Jimmy Ayoub (Frank *Marino and Mahogany Rush), Roger Belval (*Offenbach), Kim Berly (The *Stampeders), Jerry Edmonton (*Sparrow), Denis Farmer (*Harmonium), Whitey Glann (*Mandala), Pierre Hébert (*Octobre), Jerry Mercer (*Mashmakhan, *April Wine), Neil Peart (*Rush), Garry Peterson (*Guess Who), Skip Prokop (The *Paupers, *Lighthouse), Raymond Roy (*Morse Code), and Michel Séguin (*Ville Émard Blues Band). Peter *Appleyard and Warren *Chiasson have had international careers as vibraphonists.

Several Canadians have composed concert works for percussion, among them Gilles Bellemare (*Stridulation*), Walter *Boudreau (*Les Sept Jours*), Vincent Dionne (*En mouvement*), Paul Duplessis (*Hip and Straight*), John *Fodi (*Tettares*), Serge *Garant (*Circuits I*), Sydney *Hodkinson (*Imagind Quarter*), Lothar *Klein (*Design for Percussion and Orchestra*), Alfred *Kunz (*Concerto for Percussion and Orchestra*), Alcides *Lanza (*Sensors I*), Bruce *Mather (*Clos de Vougeat*), Roger *Matton (*Concerto* for two pianos and percussion), William *McCauley (*Five Miniatures for Six Percussion*), Pierre *Mercure (*Structures métalliques I* and *II*), François *Morel (*Étude en forme de toccate* and *Rythmologue*), Clermont *Pépin (*Interactions*), Allan *Rae (*Ode to a Pumpkin*), Micheline *Saint-Marcoux (*Trakadie*, with magnetic tape), Thomas *Schudel (*Trio for Percussion*), Morris *Surdin (*Eine Kleine Hammer-Klapper Musik*), Gilles *Tremblay (*... le sifflement des vents porteurs de l'amour ...* with flute), Barry *Truax (*Nautilus*), Claude *Vivier (*Pulau Dewata*), and John *Weinzweig (*Around the Stage in 25 Minutes during which a Variety of Instruments are Struck*). (See also Chamber music.) John Wyre's *Bells* was commissioned for the contemporary music festival held during Expo 70 in Osaka, Japan. His *Utau Kane NoWa* was commissioned in 1973 for the *Festival Singers and Nexus, and his *Connexus* for percussion and orchestra was premiered by the TS and Nexus in 1978. Composers whose use of percussion within the context of large orchestral works has been particularly resourceful include Mather, Pépin, *Schafer, and Tremblay.

In the late 1960s Avedis Zildjian, a firm with an established reputation, began manufacturing cymbals at its factory in Meductic, NB. In Toronto, Milestone Percussion, founded and operated by Michael Clapham, began making percussion instruments in 1973.

See also Bands; Bells; Chimes; Jazz; Rock.

BIBLIOGRAPHY

'Voyage au pays des percussions,' *Musique périodique*, vol 1, Dec 1976

Emmerson, Frank. 'Drums – making it in Canada,' *Music Market Canada*, Nov–Dec 1978

Folster, David. 'The secret of sizzle and splash,' *Maclean's*, 10 Dec 1979 (GP)

***Performing Arts in Canada*.** Illustrated quarterly founded in 1961 and published in Toronto at first by Performing Arts in Canada Publishing Co and after 1964 by Canadian Stage and Arts Publications Ltd. Its first issue appeared in March 1961; by 1979 more than 65,000 issues were circulated each year in Canada, the USA, and Europe.

George Hencz became president in 1969. James C. McIntosh, Rolf Kalman, Stephen Mezei, Arnold Edinborough, Linda Kelley, and Billyann Bayley have served as editors, and Harman Haakman, Carl *Morey, and Michael Schulman have been among the music editors.

In the 1970s the magazine's regular features included 'Calendar,' a selected listing of concerts, theatre, dance, and other events, subdivided by province, and 'What's Going On,' which provided performing arts news in brief. The magazine offered interviews and articles on prominent musicians and stories on festivals and musical ensembles and printed several editorials on the need to promote artistic efforts. Record reviews appeared in almost every issue. Regular contributors, such as Richard Flohil, Max *Wyman, Michael Schulman, and Ann Montagnes, covered the creative and performance aspects of pop, folk, jazz, concert music, and opera.

The magazine was still being published in 1980.

Performing Rights Organization of Canada Limited. See P.R.O. Canada; P.R.O. Canada Awards.

Periodicals. The first Canadian periodicals to pay attention to music were early literary journals such as *The Montreal Museum: or Journal of Literature and Arts* (Montreal 1832–3), *Le Fantasque* (Quebec 1837–45, 1848–9), *Literary Garland* (Montreal 1838–51), *Le Ménestrel* (Quebec 1844–5), *The Anglo-American Magazine* (Toronto 1852–5), and *L'Écho du cabinet de lecture paroissial* (Montreal 1859–75). Many of their volumes included pieces of music and an occasional article or concert review. Music occupied a regular if not dominant position in magazines devoted to a combined coverage of the arts, beginning with *L'Artiste* (1860) and *Les Beaux-Arts* (1863–4), both published in Montreal. Similar partnerships were evident in many later publications, eg, *Arcadia*, *The Arion*, *Canadian Review of Music and Art*, *Curtain Call*, *Le Nigog*, *Le *Passe-Temps*, and *Qui?*, and continued in the 1970s in **Performing Arts in Canada*. The first exclusively musical periodicals were George F. *Graham's *Canadian Musical Review* (Toronto 1856) and Adélard J. *Boucher's *Le *Canada musical* (Montreal 1866–7, 1875–81). Their fate – a short life-span – was shared by many of the more than 300 periodicals listed on the following pages; even in the late 1970s newly launched titles, such as *Adagio*, *Counterpoint*, *Fugue*, and *La Musique périodique*, disappeared quickly. In early days as in recent ones, opening editorial statements conveyed idealism and an urgent sense of purpose, and the reasons for failure also have remained much the same. They were usually economic – the difficulty of competing with well-established foreign magazines, and the small market for subscriptions and advertising sales – but also technical – in particular the problems encountered in gathering news reports in a vast country. However, many of the failures may be blamed on publishers' lack of judgment – launching magazines without securing funds and copy for at least the first year, starting in the face of local competition, championing parochial causes, attempting to make do with spare-time editors, and other such factors. In addition, the indifference of readers and of Canadian writers (many early magazines had to fill their pages with reprinted articles and news items from foreign publications) must share the blame for the short life and meagre subscription lists of so many Canadian music magazines. Even such excellent efforts as *The *Canadian Music Journal* and *The *Canada Music Book* were unable to attract more than a few hundred individual subscribers, apart from library and subsidized subscriptions (eg, those taken by the Dept of External Affairs for distribution to Canadian embassies, and by *CAPAC and BMI Canada for circulation among their composer-members).

Fortunately, a few periodicals have been able to survive for relatively long periods. Among those of general appeal that lasted nine years or longer were *La Lyre*, **Musical Canada*, and *Le Passe-Temps*; among those of some longevity and still being published in 1980 were **Coda*, **Opera Canada*, *The Ragtimer*, and *Sound Canada*. House organs such as *Journal des Jeunesses musicales du Canada*, the various magazines of the TCM and *RCMT, the *TSO News*, and *Western Music News* have had long runs. The same can be said of several magazines addressed to special professional groups, *The Canadian Bandmaster*, *The *Canadian Music Educator*, the **Canadian Music Trades Journal*, *The Recorder*, *La Revue Saint-Grégoire*, and **RPM*, as well as publications of musicians' union locals. Financial and editorial stability is enjoyed also by fully subsidized journals such as *The *Canadian Composer* and *The*

CANADIAN MUSICAL REVIEW.

VOL. I., No. 1. TORONTO, THURSDAY, MAY 1, 1856. SUBSCRIPTION, 7s. 6d. PER ANNUM. SINGLE COPY, 7½d.

PROSPECTUS OF THE Canadian Musical Review.

MUSIC is becoming an almost general branch of Education in this Province, and not without good reason; for its happy effect on the Mind and Heart cannot be overlooked by any one having the real good of his fellow-countrymen at heart. With a view of promoting more general intelligence in musical matters—both theoretical, practical, and social—it has occurred that the periodical publication of a JOURNAL for the Free Discussion of every matter of Musical interest, as well as for the exposition of CANADIAN ART, must prove acceptable to numerous musical devotees throughout the Province. It is therefore proposed to publish on the 1st of May next, and regularly on the First of each succeeding month (provided a sufficient number of subscribe[illegible] previously received,) a Journal to be called [illegible] "Canadian Musical Review," to consist, at f[illegible] of eight pages of Letter-press and fou[illegible] Music—the Letter-press being de[illegible] [illegible] and Selected Articles on the various [illegible] of Music, Correspondence, and Reviews of Music—the latter so arranged that parties purchasing Music may rely upon being able to select it, on reference to the Review, without any hesitation as to its merits or difficulties. The Musical portion will be chiefly devoted to the publication of meritorious Compositions by Canadian authors.

The general co-operation of the Profession is solicited.

Terms of Subscription:—7s. 6d. per annum. Agents or others sending Ten Subscribers will receive one additional copy for their trouble. Subscriptions invariably in advance.

Communications and Subscriptions to be forwarded (pre-paid) to Mr. GEORGE F. GRAHAM, Professor of Music, Toronto, C. W.

Toronto, May, 1856.

MRS. BEVERLEY ROBINSON'S Soiree Musicale, IN AID OF "THE CITY INDUSTRIAL FARM," *Will take place at the St. Lawrence Hall,* ON MONDAY, MAY 5, 1856, AT 8 O'CLOCK.

For Particulars of Concert (Promenade), see Programme.

Dancing will commence after the Concert.

Family Tickets, admitting four,		25s.
" "	three,	20s.
" "	two,	15s.
Single Ticket, each		10s.
Refreshment Tickets,		1s. 3d.

Tickets can be procured at Messrs. A. & S. Nordheimer's, Small & Addison's, Rowsell's, Maclear's Armour's and of the Stewards.

Toronto, May 1st, 1856.

ORGANS.

SAMUEL R. WARREN, *Corner of St. Joseph and St. Henry Streets,* MONTREAL.

HAS now on hand, and is constantly manufacturing, with greatly increased facilities and many important improvements,

CHURCH ORGANS, Church Harmoniums and Parlour Harmoniums.

CHURCH ORGANS, having Registers in number from four to sixty, will be built to order on short notice, at a low price, on liberal terms—and *guaranteed* to equal in mechanism, quality, power, and variety of tone and combinations any that can be manufactured here or elsewhere.

HARMONIUMS from two to twelve Registers, having a rich ORGAN TONE, and being one of the most perfect and substantial Instruments of the present day.

Montreal, May 1, 1856.

SEEBOLD, MANBY & Co. MANUFACTURERS OF PIANO-FORTES, *Nos. 221 and 223 Notre Dame Street,* MONTREAL.

THE Piano-Fortes manufactured by S. M. & Co. are all warranted to prove satisfactory, and each one has the entire Metalic frame, as also the Metalic damper socket and cover. The cases are made of beautifully grained Rosewood, and highly polished. They are in every respect equal to any Pianos imported into Canada, and 20 per cent cheaper in price.

Music and Musical Instruments.

THE Subscribers have on hand and are selling at reduced prices, every description of Wood and Brass Musical Instruments of the best French, English and German manufacture; also, all the latest Foreign and American Sheet Music.

SEEBOLD, BROTHERS, 221 Notre Dame Street, Montreal.

THE VOCAL TUTOR;

BEING a Practical Course of Musical Instruction, wherein the Rudimentary Knowledge required is familiarized and illustrated in a pleasing and thorough manner, and adapted for the use of Singing Classes, Schools, and Private Tuition. By GEORGE F. GRAHAM, Professor of Music, and Organist of St. George's Church, Toronto.

This work will be sent, *post free*, to any part of the Province, on receipt of the price, 5s., by the author, as above, or of Messrs. Small & Addison, Music Sellers, Toronto.

SMALL & ADDISON, BEG TO INFORM THE PUBLIC THAT Piano-Fortes, Melodeons, Saxe-Horns, DRUMS, &c.,

BY the most eminent Makers, are for sale at their establishment,

Corner of King and Yonge Street, Toronto.

Messrs. S. & A. are Sole Agents for the celebrated Piano-Fortes of Bacon & Raven, Boardman & Gray, Keogh, and Ladd, of Boston, whose Piano-Fortes gained the Prize at the Paris Exhibition; also, a variety by other makers, Lighte, Newton & Bradbury, Fischer, and Lennard & Weber. PIANO-FORTES OF ENGLISH MANUFACTURE, both Square and Cottages, by Broadwood, Collard, and Erard, are in preparation and will arrive in a few days.

MELODEONS

by Smith, of Boston, Hughes & Hale, Philadelphia, and Carhart & Needham, New York, (the Inventor of the Instruments,) and those purchasing from us, will, therefore have the benefit of the *latest and best improvements.* Our prices are the most reasonable in the Canadas. We would call particular attention to our supply just received from Geneva, of

MUSICAL BOXES,

With 4, 6, and 8 of the most popular tunes of the day, and contain all the latest improvements. We have a new assortment of *Music Stools* of descriptions, both Horsehair and Plush, at the lowest Rates.

Being in correspondence with the principal houses both in England and America, the facilities for procuring Music are peculiar to this Establishment. We would also call attention to our new and large assortment of Violins, Violincellos, Fifes, Flutes, Flageolets, Clarionets, Cornopeans, Bugles, Accordeons, Flutinas, Concertinas, Violin Bows, Banjos, Guitars, *Eb* and *Bb* Sopranos, Baritones, and Contra Bass Saxe-Horns. Naples Violin Strings of the Finest Quality. Packages of English Music received every mail, including the latest publications by popular Composers both Vocal and Instrumental.

N. B.—Strangers and others are invited to call and inspect our new and large stock, just received.

Piano-Fortes Tuned and Repaired by the most experienced hands. Our Tuner is the best on the Continent of America and is retained expressly for this Establishment. Cards and Catalogues sent Post Free to any part. Orders punctually attended to.

Country purchasers are particularly warned against Six Octave Piano-Fortes, which only contain 43 Notes. Also, Six and a Quarter, which contain 44 Notes, as these are now being pushed extensively throughout the Canadas. The average compass is [illegible] Notes.

The first issue of the first Canadian magazine devoted exclusively to music

Music Scene, backed by CAPAC and *PRO Canada respectively, by **Musicanada*, sponsored by the *CMCentre and later revived by the *CMCouncil, and to a more limited extent by the journals and newsletters of professional societies of teachers, ethnomusicologists, organists, therapists, manufacturers, and other groups. Though it has proved difficult to maintain self-supporting magazines devoted to general coverage and criticism, a few high-level and only partially subsidized magazines of a specialized nature, such as *Opera Canada* and *Coda*, have found international circles of loyal readers.

Canadian music periodicals have adopted many formats, achieved widely different levels of sophistication, and proceeded from a variety of editorial and critical attitudes. Most, however, have sought to promote recognition of Canadian achievement and discussion of vital issues. Many have succeeded in contributing to the development of taste and the spread of knowledge. Even the least have helped document musical history under the immediate impact of events, though reporting in earlier times often was limited in coverage and regional in bias. The historian's work is aided greatly when a certain period is well documented by periodicals and suffers when it is not, as it did, for instance, as recently as 1962–5, between the demise of *The Canadian Music Journal* and the beginning of *The Canadian Composer*. Unfortunately consultation of many periodicals is made difficult by their rareness on library shelves. In 1980 a program of reproducing certain magazines on microfiche or through reprint was one of the most urgent needs of historical research.

With the escalating costs of paper and printing in the 1960s and 1970s, financial assistance became an imperative in the survival techniques of music magazines, and in response the *Canada Council, the *OAC, the *MACQ, and other national and provincial arts-support organizations developed helpful subsidy programs. By 1980 many music magazines were receiving some support from these sources.

The following list of Canadian periodicals is arranged in alphabetical order by title. Indicated are title and significant title changes; parent organization in the case of house organs; place(s) and dates of publication; normal frequency of publication; relationship to preceding, succeeding, and absorbed periodicals. Annotations are added when helpful in clarifying the predominant subject matter and language. Completeness of information has been difficult to achieve because many periodicals cannot be found in any library and because others lack proper identification of place, issue number, or date of publication. Besides music periodicals proper, magazines devoted only partly to music have been included when music is a regular component (ie, the subject of more than an occasional article or a review column). Newsletters and bulletins are included if their content may be of general interest or documentary value. Excluded are concert programs in the form of magazines, annual reports of organizations, academic calendars, and similar publications.

EXPLANATIONS

‡ The majority of issues feature pieces in musical notation, either in the main body of the magazine or in a supplement.

// The magazine has ceased publication.

Monthly often implies double issues for certain periods, eg, 10 issues per year.

'Continues' or 'continued by' indicate that the numbering system of the older magazine is taken over by the newer one. In other cases of succession the terms 'supersedes' and 'superseded by' are used. The open dash after a founding year (eg, 1967–) signifies that publication continued in 1980.

Acaditout. Centre Culturel de Moncton, NB. Monthly. 1976–7 //

ACA Newsletter. See Alberta Composers' Association.

Accents. Music Education Council of the New Brunswick Teachers' Association. Sackville; Moncton, NB. Three times a year. 1975–

L'Action musicale. St-Jérôme, Que. Bi-weekly; weekly. 1932 //

Adagio. St-Hyacinthe, Que. Bi-monthly. 1975–6 // (classical records; French language)

Ad Lib. Toronto. Monthly. 1944–7? // (pop music; English language)

Afterthought. Ottawa. Monthly. 1970 // (two issues only; pop music)

Alberta Composers' Association Newsletter. Edmonton. Quarterly. 1978–9. // Continued by *Composers West*

Alberta Music Educator. Alberta Music Educators' Association. Calgary; Edmonton. Semi-annual. 1965–8 //

Alberta Music Express. See *Music Express* (II).

Album littéraire et musical de la Minerve‡. Montreal. Monthly (weekly 1873–74). 1849–51, 1872–4. Continues *Album littéraire et musical de la Revue canadienne*

Album littéraire et musical de la Revue canadienne‡. Montreal. Monthly. 1846–8.// Continued by *Album littéraire et musical de la Minerve*

L'Album musical‡. Montreal. Monthly. Prospectus Dec 1881; 1882–4? //

À l'Écoute. L'Alliance des Chorales du Québec. Montreal. Approx ten times a year. 1976–

The Alumni Bulletin. See *The Studio Bulletin*.

The Amateur Musician / Le Musicien amateur. CAMMAC. Montreal. Quarterly. 1964–9. // Continues *CAMMAC Journal*, superseded by *Cammuniqué*. In 1980 title given to *CAMMAC National Office Newsletter*

Les Amis de l'orgue de Québec. *Bulletin*. Approx three times a year. 1968–

Les Amis de la Scène lyrique. *Bulletin*. Montreal. Quarterly. 1978. // Continued by *Aria*

Arcadia. Montreal. Semi-monthly. 1892–3 // (music, art, literature; English language)

Aria. Montreal. Quarterly. 1979– . Continues Les Amis de la Scène lyrique. *Bulletin* (French language)

The Arion. Toronto. Monthly. 1880–1 // (music, literature, drama)

ARRAY Newsletter. ARRAY. Toronto. Irregular. 1972–4 // (four issues only)

L'Artiste. Montreal. Weekly. 1860 // (two issues only; music, literature, religion)

L'Art musical. Montreal. Monthly. 1896–9 //

Association de Musicothérapie du Canada. *Le Journal*. See *Canadian Music Therapy Journal*.

AudioScene Canada. Toronto. Monthly. 1974– . Continues *Electron*

Audio Trade Merchandising. Toronto. Monthly. 1978–

Bass Sound Post. International Institute for the String Bass. Halifax. Quarterly. ?–1971. // Continued by *Probas*

B.C. Pipers Newsletter. Vancouver

Les Beaux-Arts‡. Montreal. Monthly. 1863–4 // (music, art, literature, etc)

The Beaver Rock Paper. Ottawa. Monthly. 1972 // (four issues only)

Beetle. Toronto. Monthly. 1970–5? // (pop music)

Bell Magazine. Bell Piano and Organ Co. Guelph, Ont. Fl 1913 // (no copies located)

Boucher & Pratte's Musical Journal. Montreal. Monthly. 1881–2? // Supersedes *Le Canada musical* (I) (includes a section 'Le Journal musical')

La Boulée: Les carnets de la chanson québécoise. Montreal. 1965–6 // (two or three issues only)

Le Bouscueil. Alliance chorale canadienne. Approx three times a year. 1971–8 //

British Columbia Music Educator. British Columbia Music Educators' Association. Vancouver. Quarterly. 1958–

British Columbia Musician. Musicians Union, local 145. Vancouver. Monthly. 1923–8 //

British Columbia Registered Music Teachers' Association. *Quarterly* (originally bi-monthly) *Bulletin*. Vancouver. 1946–67. // Continued by *Provincial Newsletter*. Vancouver. Four times a year 1972– . Also issued *Music Journal* in the 1960s

British Columbia World of Country Music. See *Country Music News*.

Bulletin. See under name of association.

Le Bulletin orchestral. See *The Orchestra Letter*.

Cadenza. Saskatchewan Music Educators' Association. Saskatoon. 1977– . Continues Saskatchewan Music Educators' Association *Newsletter*

Les Cahiers canadiens de musique / The Canada Music Book. Montreal. Semi-annual. 1970–6 //

CAMMAC Journal / Le Journal de CAMMAC. Montreal. Quarterly. 1959–64. // Continued by *The Amateur Musician / Le Musicien amateur*

CAMMAC Montreal Newsletter. Irregular. 1969–

CAMMAC National Office Newsletter. Montreal. Irregular. Ca 1969–80. // Superseded by *The Amateur Musician / Le Musicien amateur*

CAMMAC Notations. Ottawa-Hull. Irregular. 1970–1 //

Cammuniqué. CAMMAC. Montreal. Bi-monthly. 1970–2. // Supersedes *The Amateur Musician / Le Musicien amateur*

Le Canada artistique (I)‡. Montreal. Monthly. Prospectus Dec 1889; 1890. // Continued as *Canada-Revue* (music, theatre, fine arts, literature)

Le Canada artistique (II)‡. Montreal. Monthly. 1895–? // Continuation of *Le Piano-Canada* (music, fine arts)

Canada Folk Bulletin. Vancouver Folk Song Society. Six times a year. 1978–80. // Supersedes *Come All Ye*

Le Canada musical (I)‡. Montreal. Monthly. 1866–7, 1875–81. // Superseded by *Boucher & Pratte's Musical Journal*

Le Canada musical (II). Montreal. Bi-weekly. 1917–24, 1930 //

The Canada Music Book. See *Cahiers canadiens de musique.*

Le Canada qui chante‡. Montreal (temporarily Quebec). Monthly. 1927–30 //

Canada-Revue. Montreal. Monthly, later weekly. 1891–1909. // Continuation of *Le Canada artistique* (music discontinued 1892)

Canadian Accordion Journal. Willowdale; Don Mills, Ont. Irregular. 1961?–9? //

Canadian Amateur Musicians-Musiciens amateurs du Canada. See CAMMAC.

Canadian Association for Music Therapy / Association de Musicothérapie du Canada. *The Journal / Le Journal.* Vancouver; Montreal. Annual. 1976– . Continues *Canadian Music Therapy Journal*

Canadian Association of Music Libraries / Association canadienne des bibliothèques musicales. *Newsletter / Nouvelles.* London, Ont. Quarterly. 1972–

Canadian Association of University Schools of Music / Association canadienne des écoles universitaires de musique. Journal. Vancouver; Ottawa; Calgary. Irregular. 1971–

Canadian Association of Youth Orchestras. *CAYO News and Views.* Banff, Alta. Irregular. 1978–

Canadian Band Directors' Association. *CBDA Journal.* Penhold, Alta. Quarterly. 1976–

Canadian Band Directors Association (Ontario). *Newsletter.* Brantford, Ont. Bi-monthly. 1970–

The Canadian Bandmaster. Canadian Bandmasters' Association. Kilworthy, Ont. Up to six times yearly. 1949–67 //

Canadian Bandmasters' Association. *Newsletter.* 1933–34? //

The Canadian Bandsman. The Canadian Bandmasters' Association. Toronto; Waterloo, Ont. Generally four issues a year. 1942–9 //

The Canadian Bandsman and Musician (later *The Canadian Bandsman and Orchestra Journal*). Toronto. Monthly. 1913–24. // Absorbed by *Musical Canada*

Canadian Bluegrass Review. Waterdown, Ont. Bi-monthly. 1978–

The Canadian College of Organists Bulletin. Toronto. Quarterly. 1925?–28? // Absorbed by *Musical Canada*

The Canadian Composer / Le Compositeur canadien. Toronto. Monthly. 1965–

Canadian Federation of Music Teachers' Associations. *The News Bulletin.* Winnipeg. Four, later three, times a year. 1946–71. // Supersedes *Canadian Music Teacher.* Continued by *CFMTA Newsletter*

Canadian Federation of Music Teachers' Associations. *CFMTA Newsletter.* Winnipeg. Four times a year. 1975– . Continues *Canadian Music Teacher*

Canadian Flute Association Journal. Vancouver. 1980–

Canadian Folk Music Journal. Toronto. Annual. 1973–

Canadian Folk Music Society Newsletter / La Société canadienne de musique folklorique Bulletin. Moncton, NB; Montreal; Antigonish, NS; Vancouver. Irregular. 1965–

Canadian Guild of Organists' Journal. Toronto. Semi-annual. Ca 1912–? //

The Canadian Journal of Music‡. Toronto. Monthly. 1914–19 //

Canadian Music. Toronto. Monthly. 1940–1 //

Canadian Musical Digest. Toronto. Monthly. 1934 //

The Canadian Musical Herald. Toronto. Fl 1890–1. // Supersedes *The Musical Journal*

Canadian Musical News. Canadian Music Sales Corp. Toronto. Monthly. 1939–ca 1940 //

Canadian Musical Review. Toronto. Monthly. 1856–? // (only one issue located)

The Canadian Music and Drama. Kingston, Ont. Monthly. 1895–? //

Canadian Music Centre Newsletter. Toronto. Monthly. 1964–5. // For French edition see Centre musical canadien *Bulletin de nouvelles.*

Canadian Music Centre Newsletter. Vancouver. Monthly. 1978–

The Canadian Music Educator / Le Musicien éducateur au Canada. Canadian Music Educators' Association / Association canadienne des éducateurs de musique. Toronto; Montreal; Victoria. Quarterly. 1959– . For French titles see EMC entry *The Canadian Music Educator.*

Canadian Music Educators' Association / Association canadienne des éducateurs de musique Newsletter. St Catharines, Ont; Toronto. Generally quarterly. 1968–

Canadian Music Folio‡. Toronto. Monthly. Fl 1892–3 //

The Canadian Musician (I). Later *The Musician.* Whaley, Royce & Co. Toronto. Monthly. Ca 1889–after 1906 //

Canadian Musician (II). Toronto. Bi-monthly. 1979–

The Canadian Music Journal. Sackville, NB; Toronto. Quarterly. 1956–62 //

Canadian Music Library Association Newsletter. Irregular. 1957–8, 1967–71 //

Canadian Music Teacher (I). Canadian Federation of Music Teachers' Associations. Vancouver. Irregular. 1937–46. // Superseded by CFMTA *The News Bulletin*

Canadian Music Teacher (II). CFMTA. Winnipeg. Quarterly. 1971–5. // Continued by *Newsletter*

Canadian Music Therapy Journal (originally *Bulletin*). Canadian Music Therapy Association. Kitchener, Ont. 1973–6. Continued by Canadian Association for Music Therapy. *The Journal*

Canadian Music Trade. Toronto. Bi-monthly. 1979–

Canadian Music Trades Journal. Toronto. Monthly (temporarily semi-monthly). 1900–33. // In 1920 absorbed *Phonograph Journal and Radio Trades*

Canadian Opera Guild News. Toronto. Quarterly 1968–

Canadian Recording Industry Association. *CRIA News.* Toronto. Irregular. 1975–8 //

Canadian Review of Music and Art. Toronto. Monthly (irregular). 1942–8 //

Canadian Stereo Guide. See *Stereo Guide.*

Canadian String Teachers Association. *Notes.* London, Ont. Three times a year. 1977–

Canadian World of Country Music (originally *World of Country Music*). Langley, BC; Toronto. Monthly. 1972–3? //

Canawirl. Hamilton, Ont. Semi-monthly. 1965 //

Capital Country News. Ottawa. Monthly. 1980–

Le Carillon‡. Montreal. Irregular. 1926–7. // Absorbed by *La Lyre*

Carnet musical. Ensemble Claude-Gervaise. Chambly, Que. Quarterly. 1971–5 //

CAYO News and Views. See Canadian Association of Youth Orchestras.

CBC Times. Toronto; Vancouver; Winnipeg. Weekly. 1948–70 // (broadcast schedule, commentary, Eastern, Pacific, and Prairie region editions)

CBDA Journal. See Canadian Band Directors' Association *Journal.*

Centre musical canadien. *Bulletin de nouvelles.* Toronto. Monthly. 1964–5. // For English edition see *Canadian Music Centre Newsletter.*

Chansons populaires‡. Ville d'Anjou, Que. Undated [1970–1?] //

Christian Choir Association of Ontario League News. Hamilton, Ont. Monthly. 1956–?

The Church Choir. Toronto. Monthly. Ca 1905–07? // (one issue located)

Coda. Toronto. Monthly. 1958– (jazz)

Combo. Toronto. Monthly. 1966–? // (pop music)

Come All Ye. Vancouver Folk Song Society. 1972–7. // Superseded by *Canada Folk Bulletin*

Communiqué. See Jeunesses musicales du Canada.

Composers West. Alberta Composers' Association. Calgary. Quarterly. 1979– . Continues *ACA Newsletter*

Le Compositeur canadien. See *The Canadian Composer.*

Con Brio. National Arts Centre Orchestra Association. Ottawa. Semi-annual. 1976–

ConNotes. Royal Conservatory of Music of Toronto. Five times a year. 1980–

Conservatoire de musique de Montréal. *Le Bulletin.* Montreal. Quarterly. 1969–70? //

Conservatoire de musique de Montréal. See also *Le Diapason* and *La Tonique.*

The Conservatory Bi-Monthly (from 1912 *The Conservatory Monthly*). Toronto Conservatory of Music. Toronto. 1902–13 //

The Conservatory Quarterly Review (later *The Conservatory Review*). Toronto Conservatory of Music. Toronto. After 1931 twice a year. 1918–35 //

Contact: the West Coast Music Connection. Richmond, BC. Monthly. 1980–

Continuo. Toronto. Monthly. 1978– . Continues *Early Music Directory*

Counterpoint. Toronto. Quarterly. 1979 // (two issues only)

Country Gentleman. Toronto. 1965 //

Country Music Connection. Edmonton. Monthly. 1976–? //

Country Music News (originally *World of Country Music*, then *British Columbia World of Country Music*). Langley, BC. Irregular. 1972–4 //

Crescendo (I). Toronto Musicians' Association. Five to six times a year. 1958?–

Crescendo (II). Étudiants de l'École Vincent-d'Indy. Montreal. 1966–? //

Crescendo (III). Prince Edward Island Music Educators' Association. Charlottetown. Three to four times a year. 1979–

CRIA News. See Canadian Recording Industry Association.

The Curtain Call. Toronto. Bi-weekly, later monthly. 1929–41 // (music, theatre, etc)

Le Diapason. Association des élèves du Conservatoire provincial de musique et d'art dramatique. Montreal. 1944–? //

Le Disco. Montreal. 1977. // Superseded by *Disco Fever* (partly English, partly French language)
Disco Fever. Montreal. Annual. 1978–? Superseded *Le Disco* (partly English, partly French language)
Disco-mag. Montreal. Undated [1969–?] // (French language)
Disque-ton. Cité d'Anjou, Que. Monthly. 1957?–69? //
Dominion Musical Advertiser‡. Montreal. 1874–? //
Dominion Musical Journal. Toronto. Monthly. 1891–? //
Down Home. Orangeville, Ont. Bi-monthly. 1976– (country music)
Early Music Directory (originally *The Toronto Early Music Directory*). Toronto. Monthly. 1977–8. // Continued by *Continuo*
The Echo. R.S. Williams. Toronto. Fl 1920 //
L'Écho musical (I). Montreal. Monthly. Prospectus 1887; 1888–? //
L'Écho musical (II)‡. Montreal. Bi-weekly. 1913–? //
Educator's Profile. Yamaha Canada Music Ltd. National Education Division. Winnipeg. 1978–9. // Supersedes *Yamaha Education News*
Electron. Toronto. Monthly. 1964–74. // Continued by *Audioscene Canada*
Ensemble. University of Western Ontario. Faculty of Music. London, Ont. Semi-annual. 1976–9 //
Entr'acte. Musicians' Guild of Montreal / Guilde des musiciens de Montréal, local 406. Monthly. 1953–
Entre-Nous. Ed Archambault Inc. Montreal. Monthly. 1929–31 //
Fan Fair Country Music Magazine. St Catharines, Ont. Monthly. 1980. // Continued by *Jamboree Country Music*
Federation of Canadian Music Festivals. *Digest Report*. Winnipeg. Annual. 1950–
The FM Guide (originally *Toronto FM Guide*). Toronto. Monthly. 1971–
Fugue. Toronto. Monthly. 1976–80 //
Guild News. See *Canadian Opera Guild News*.
The Guitar Society of Toronto Bulletin. Nine times a year. Fl 1978
Gumbo. Montreal. Monthly. 1970 // (pop music; English language)
Halifax Conservatory of Music Journal. Monthly. 1937–8? //
Histoire du Rock. Montreal. Weekly. Undated. [1975?–7?] //
Hoot. Guild of Canadian Folk Artists. Toronto. Bi-monthly. 1963–7 //
Hot Wacks. Kitchener, Ont. Quarterly. 1979–
Ici Radio-Canada. Montreal. Weekly. 1966– (broadcast schedule, commentary). Supersedes *La Semaine à Radio-Canada*
In Tune. Yamaha Canada Music Ltd, Keyboard Division. Four times a year. 1977–9 //
Jamboree Country Music. St Catharine's, Ont. Monthly. 1980–
Jazz Happenings. Vancouver. Monthly. 1978?–
Jazz Ottawa. Ottawa. Bi-monthly. 1976–
Jazz Panorama. Toronto. Fl ca 1947 //
Jeunesses musicales du Canada
– 1 French-language periodicals in chronological order:
  Journal des Jeunesses musicales du Canada. Montreal. 1951–3
  Le Journal musical canadien. Montreal. Approx six times a year. 1954–61
  Jeunesses musicales. Montreal. Quarterly. 1962 (two issues only)
  Journal des Jeunesses musicales du Canada. Montreal. Four to six times a year. 1962–71
  J.M.C. Bulletin. Montreal. Six times a year. 1974–6
  Communiqué. Montreal. Irregular. 1976–
– 2 English-language periodicals in chronological order:
  Musical Youth Magazine. Montreal. Bi-monthly. 1955–7?
  J.M.C. Musical Chronicle. Montreal. 1958–61
  Jeunesses Musicales Chronicle. Montreal. Quarterly? 1962–71
  J.M.C. Bulletin. Montreal. Six times a year. 1974–6
  Communiqué. Montreal. Irregular. 1976–
  J.M.C. Bulletin. See Jeunesses musicales du Canada.
  J.M.C. Chronicle. See Jeunesses musicales du Canada.
Journal. See under name of association.
Le Journal de CAMMAC. See *CAMMAC Journal*.
Le Journal de musique. Fl 1897
Journal des Jeunesses musicales du Canada. See Jeunesses musicales du Canada.
Le Journal musical. See *Boucher & Pratte's Musical Journal*.
Le Journal musical canadien. See Jeunesses musicales du Canada.
Jubilate Deo. Toronto. Bi-monthly. Fl 1957–? // (church music and worship)
Keynote. Junior Symphony Society and Vancouver Academy of Music. Vancouver. Irregular. 1966?–
Kodaly Institute of Canada. *Notes*. Ottawa. Quarterly. 1976–
Logos. University of Ottawa, Music Dept. Ottawa. Irregular. 1974 // (partly English, partly French language)
Le Lutrin: bulletin d'information de l'Orchestre symphonique de Québec. Five issues a year. 1979–
La Lyre‡. Montreal. Monthly. 1922–31. // Absorbed *Le Carillon*
Magazine Rock. Laval, Que. Undated. [1972] // (French language)
Manitoba Music Educator. Manitoba Music Educators Association. Winnipeg. Three, later four, a year. 1960–
Manitoba Music Educator Newsletter. Manitoba Music Educators Association. Winnipeg. Annual. 1959–74 //
Marche et manoeuvres. Fédération des associations musicales du Québec. Montreal. Monthly. 1975–
Maritime Arts Review. Halifax Symphony Society. Halifax. 1955–6? //
The Mendelssohn Chorister. Toronto Mendelssohn Choir. One to three issues a year. 1948–? //
The Mendelssohnian. Toronto Mendelssohn Choir. Irregular. 1937–9 //
Le Ménestrel‡. Quebec. 1844–5 // (music, literature)
Le Montréal musical. See *Montréal qui chante*.
Montréal qui chante‡. (1912–13 called *Le Montréal musical*). Montreal. Varies from weekly to monthly. 1908–20? //
The Mouthpiece. Canadian National Institute for the Blind. Toronto. Quarterly. 1970–5 //
The Muse. Toronto. Monthly. 1949–50 //
Music across Canada. Canadian Music Centre. Monthly. 1963 //
Musical Canada (until 1907 *The Violin*). Toronto; Waterloo, Ont. Monthly. 1906–33. // Ca 1924 absorbed *The Canadian Bandsman and Orchestra Journal*. In 1928 absorbed *The Canadian College of Organists Bulletin*
Musical Galaxy. Toronto. 1875–? //
The Musical Journal. Toronto. Monthly. 1887–90? // Superseded by *The Canadian Musical Herald*
Musical Journal. See also *Boucher & Pratte's Musical Journal*.
Musical Life. Regina. Monthly. 1933–? //
Musical Life and Arts. Winnipeg. Semi-monthly. 1924–5 //
Musical News. Toronto. Monthly. 1979 // (two issues only)
Musical Review of Canada. Lachute, Que. Monthly. 1933–4 //
The Musical Visitor. Duart, Ont. Fl 1881 //
Musical Youth Magazine. See Jeunesses musicales du Canada.
MusiCanada‡. Montreal. Bi-monthly. 1922–3 // (French language)
Musicanada (I). Canadian Music Centre. Toronto. Approx eight times a year. 1967–70 //
Musicanada (II). Canadian Music Council. Ottawa. Quarterly. 1976– (continues numbering of *Musicanada* (I))
Music Bulletin from the Oxford University Press. Toronto. Irregular. 1941–2 //
Music Canada. Toronto. Monthly. 1970–1 // (pop music)
Music Canada Quarterly. Malton, Ont. Quarterly. 1972–6 // (pop music)
Le Music express (I). Montreal. Weekly. 1972 // (pop music)
Music Express (II) (originally *Alberta Music Express*). Calgary; Vancouver; Willowdale, Ont. Monthly. 1976– (pop music)
Music for Children – Carl Orff Canada – Musique pour enfants. *Bulletin*. Toronto. Irregular. 1975–
Music Hall Éclair (originally *Music Hall Digeste*). Montreal. Monthly. 1964–5 // (French language)
The Musician. See *The Canadian Musician* (I).
Le Musicien amateur. See *The Amateur Musician / Le Musicien amateur*.
Musicien éducateur du Québec. Fédération des Associations des Musiciens éducateurs du Québec. Ste-Foy, Que. 1967–74 //
Le Musicien québécois. Charny, Que. Bi-monthly. 1974–5 //
Music in Alberta. Alberta Music Conference. Calgary. Quarterly. 1972–4 //
Music in London. London, Ont. 1967–? //
Music Journal. See British Columbia Registered Music Teachers' Association.
Musick. Vancouver Society for Early Music. Quarterly. 1979–
Music Magazine. Toronto. Six times a year. 1978–
Music Market Canada. Toronto. Monthly. 1977–
Music McGill. McGill University. Faculty of Music. Semi-annual. 1976–
Music Research News. Canadian Music Research Council. Victoria; London, Ont. Semi-annual. 1976–
The Music Scene. Toronto. BMI Canada, later PRO Canada. Six times a year. 1967– . For French edition see *La Scène musicale*.
Music Thunder Bay. Thunder Bay Symphony Orchestra. 1971?–? //
Musicworks. Toronto. Quarterly. 1978– (new and avant-garde music)
Music World. Toronto. Semi-monthly. 1957–8 //
La Musique. Laval University 1923–4. Quebec. Monthly. 1919–24 //
Musique d'Église. ?–1927 //
Musique et musiciens. Saint-Hyacinthe, Que. Monthly. 1952–4 //
Musique liturgique. Mont Laurier, Que. Irregular. Ca 1965–9? //
La Musique périodique. Beaconsfield, Que. Irregular. 1976–7 // (five issues only)
National Shevchenko Musical Ensemble Guild of Canada. *Bulletin*. Toronto. Two to four times a year. 1972–
The New Brunswick Minstrel‡. Saint John, NB. Monthly. 1864–? //
The New Brunswick Registered Music Teachers' Association Newsletter. Sackville, NB. Irregular. 1965–
The New-Music (I)‡. Toronto. Monthly. Fl 1916 //
The New Music (II). Toronto. Monthly. 1978–9 // (pop music)
News from the Faculty of Music. See University of Toronto.
Newsletter. See under name of organization.

Le Nigog. Montreal. Monthly. 1918 // (music, literature, art)
Notes. Ontario Registered Music Teachers' Association. Quarterly. Ca 1969–
Notes. See also Kodaly Institute of Canada.
Nova Scotia Music Educators' Association Newsletter. Truro, NS. Quarterly. Fl 1975–6
Observer. Toronto. Weekly. 1891–? // (music, drama)
Ontario Choral Federation. *Newsletter*. Toronto. Bi-monthly. 1970–
Ontario Federation of Symphony Orchestras Newsletter. Toronto. Irregular. 1969–72. // Superseded by *The Orchestra Letter / Le Bulletin orchestral*
Ontario Journal of Music and Dramatic and Literary Review. Hamilton, Ont. Monthly. 1889–? // (one issue located)
Ontario Registered Music Teachers' Association. *Notes*. See *Notes*.
Opera Canada (*Opera in Canada* 1960–3). Toronto. Quarterly. 1960–
Opus. University of Western Ontario. Faculty of Music. Irregular. 1964–
Opus XIV. Music Council of the Newfoundland Teachers' Association. Manuels, Nfld. 1979–
Orchestra Canada / Orchestres Canada. Ontario Federation of Symphony Orchestras and Association of Canadian Orchestras. Toronto. Ten times a year. 1973– . Supersedes *The Orchestra Letter / Le Bulletin orchestral*
The Orchestra Letter / Le Bulletin orchestral. Ontario Federation of Symphony Orchestras and Association of Canadian Orchestras. Toronto. Irregular. 1972–3. // Superseded by *Orchestra Canada / Orchestres Canada*
Ottawa Guitar Quarterly. Ottawa Guitar Society. 1970–4? //
Overtures. Canadian Opera Company. Toronto. Three to four times a year. 1975–
Pacific Harbor Light. See *Victoria Home Journal*.
Le Passe-Temps‡. Montreal. Bi-weekly, later monthly. 1895–1935, 1945–9 //
Performing Arts in Canada. Toronto. Quarterly. 1961–
Philharmonic Bulletin. Montreal Philharmonic Society. Fl 1896 //
Phonograph Journal of Canada (later *Phonograph Journal and Radio Trades*). Toronto. 1919–26. // Absorbed by *Canadian Music Trades Journal* (no copies located)
Piano-Canada‡. Montreal. Monthly. 1893–5. // Continued as *Le Canada artistique*
Pop. Toronto. Fl 1972
Pop-Eye. Montreal. 1970–? // (French language)
Pop jeunesse. Laval, Que. Weekly. 1972–? //
Poppin. Vancouver. Monthly. 1969–70 //
Pourquoi chanter? Montreal. 1976–8 //
Prenons notre musique en main! Syndicat de la Musique du Québec. Montreal. Irregular. 1979–
Probas. International Institute for the String Bass. Halifax. 1972–? // Continues *Bass Sound Post*
'Prom' Magazine. Toronto. Monthly. Fl 1946 // (pop music)
Québec Rock. Montreal. Monthly. 1977–
Qui? Montreal. Quarterly. 1949–54. // First issue also in English as *Who?*
La Quinzaine musicale et artistique‡. Conservatoire national de musique et Schola cantorum. Montreal. Bi-weekly. 1930–2? //
The Rackett. Vancouver. Quarterly. 1978– (early music)
The Ragtimer. Weston, Ont. Bi-monthly. 1967–Preceded by *The Ragtime Society Newsletter*. 5 volumes
Rainbow. Toronto. Bi-weekly. 1972–3 // (pop music)
RCCO Newsletter and *RCCO Quarterly*. See Royal Canadian College of Organists.
The Recorder. Ontario Music Educators' Association. Toronto. Quarterly. 1958–
The Record Exchange. Toronto. Monthly. 1948?–? //
Record Month. Toronto. Monthly. 1976–7? //
Record News. Toronto. Monthly. 1956–61? //
Record Week. Mississauga, Ont. Weekly. 1975–7? //
Red Shoes. Burlington, Ont. Monthly. 1980– (pop music)
Le Rêve du pianiste. Montreal. Fl ca 1907 //
La Revue Saint-Grégoire. Société des Musiciens d'église de la province de Québec. Quebec. Irregular. 1949–63 //
Royal Canadian College of Organists. *RCCO Newsletter*. Toronto. Monthly. 1963–73. // Superseded by *RCCO Quarterly*
Royal Canadian College of Organists. *RCCO Quarterly*. Toronto; Kitchener, Ont; Halifax. 1973–8. // Superseded by *Yearbook Digest and Newsletter*, 1980–
Royal Conservatory of Music of Toronto Monthly Bulletin. Toronto. Four to eight issues a year. 1948–64. // Continued by *The Bulletin*. Four to eight issues a year, irregular after 1970. 1964–74 //
Royal Conservatory of Music of Toronto. See also *ConNotes*, Conservatory, and Toronto Conservatory of Music.
RPM. Toronto. Weekly. 1964– (pop music)
Saskatchewan Music Educators' Association Bulletin (later *Journal*). Saskatoon. Semi-annual? Ca 1957–70? //
Saskatchewan Music Educators' Association Newsletter. Regina. Quarterly. Ca 1965–76? // Continued by *Cadenza*
La Scène musicale. Toronto. BMI Canada, later PRO Canada. Six times a year. 1967– . For English edition see *The Music Scene*.
La Semaine à Radio-Canada. Montreal. Weekly. 1950–66. // Superseded by *Ici Radio-Canada* (broadcast schedule, commentary)
Shades. Toronto. Monthly. 1979–? (pop music)
Sharps & Flats. Manitoba Registered Music Teachers' Association. Winnipeg. Quarterly. 1960–?
Singalong. Vancouver. 1957–8 //
Sing and String. Toronto. Quarterly. 1959–65 //
Sir Ernest MacMillan Fine Arts Club Newsletter. Vancouver. Ca 1951–? //
Son Hi-fi Magazine. Montreal. Monthly. 1979–
Sono: Sonorisation au Canada. Montreal. Semi-annual. 1973–8 //
Soul. Toronto. Monthly. 1965–7? // (pop music)
Sound Canada (originally *Sound*). Toronto. Monthly. 1970– (audio and equipment)
The Steede Report to the Music Industry. Montreal. Semi-monthly. 1975–9 //
Stereo Guide (originally *Canadian Stereo Guide*). Toronto. Five times a year. 1972–
Studies in Music from the University of Western Ontario. London, Ont. Annual. 1976–
The Studio Bulletin (originally *The Alumni Bulletin*). Lyell Gustin Piano Studios. Saskatoon. Annual with gaps. 1941–
Symphony News. Edmonton Symphony Society. Four times a year. 1965?–? //
Tam Ti Delam. La Société des Festivals populaires du Québec. Montreal. Monthly. 1976–
Tempo. Toronto. Bi-monthly. 1979– (pop music)
Le Tic-Toc-Choc. Journal du Studio de musique ancienne de Montréal. Bi-monthly. 1979–
La Tonique. Association des élèves du Conservatoire de musique de la province de Québec. Montreal. Fl 1960
Toronto Conservatory of Music Alumni Gazette. Annual? Fl 1916 //
Toronto Conservatory of Music Monthly Bulletin (later *Toronto Conservatory of Music Bulletin*). 1935–47 //
The Toronto Early Music Directory. See *Early Music Directory*.
Toronto FM Guide. See *The FM Guide*.
Toronto Music Guide. Monthly. 1971 //
Toronto Symphony News (originally *T.S.O. News*). Toronto. Irregular. 1945–
Touring Office of the Canada Council / L'Office des tournées du Conseil des Arts du Canada. *Bulletin*. Ottawa. 3 issues a year. 1975–
Tripper. Canada's musical exchange trip magazine. Scarborough, Ont. Semi-annual. 1979–
The / Le Troubadour. Canadian Folk Arts Council / Conseil canadien des arts populaires. Toronto; Montreal. Quarterly. 1965–6, 1971, 1976–
Turlutterie: la musique contemporaine. Alliance des chorales du Québec. Montreal. Quarterly. 1980–
The Underground. Old Time Country Music Club of Canada. Montreal. Irregular. 1967–9, 1971–
University of Toronto, News from the Faculty of Music (originally *Newsletter*). Three times a year. 1970–
Upbeat. Vancouver Musicians' Union, local 145. Monthly. 1959–?
Vancouver Canadian Music Centre Newsletter. See Canadian Music Centre.
Vancouver Opera Association. *VOA News*. Quarterly. 1967–9 //
Vancouver Opera Journal. Vancouver Opera Association. Quarterly. 1977–
Vancouver Symphony Orchestra. Quarterly. 1977–
Variations. Orchestre symphonique de Montréal / Montreal Symphony Orchestra. Seven times a year. 1977–80 //
Vibrations. Montreal. 10 times a year. 1978–9 //
Victoria Home Journal (first two issues called *Pacific Harbor Light*). Victoria. Monthly. 1891–5 // (music, society, drama, etc)
Vie musicale. Ministère des Affaires culturelles du Québec. Quebec. Quarterly. 1965–71 //
The Violin. See *Musical Canada*.
Violin Makers Journal. Violin Makers Association of British Columbia. Vancouver. Irregular. 1957–64 //
Waterloo Convention Review. Canadian Bandmasters' Association. Waterloo, Ont. Annual. 1948–53 //
Waterloo Festival Review. Waterloo Band Festival. Waterloo, Ont. Annual. 1948–55 //
Westcoast Music. Vancouver. 10 times a year. 1980– . First titled *Open Door*
Western Music News. Western Music Co. Vancouver. Monthly, later irregular. 1934–55? //
Who? See under *Qui?*
The Winnipeg Folk Festival Newsletter. Bi-monthly. 1976–7? //
Winnipeg Town Topics. Weekly. 1898–1913 // (music, drama)
World of Country Music. See *Canadian World of Country Music* and *Country Music News*.
Yamaha Education News. Yamaha Canada Music Ltd, National Education Division. Winnipeg. Two to three times a year. 1975–8. // Superseded by *Educator's Profile*
Zounds. Mississauga, Ont. Monthly. 1975 // (pop music)

BIBLIOGRAPHY

Kallmann, Helmut. 'A century of musical periodicals in Canada,' *CMJ*, vol 1, Autumn 1956, Winter 1957
– 'A check-list of Canadian periodicals in the field of music,' ibid, Winter 1957
CMLA. *Union List of Music Periodicals in Canadian Libraries* (Ottawa 1964). *Supplement* (Ottawa 1967). CAML. Rev edn, ed Larry Lewis (London, Ont, 1980)
'Canadian music is making news,' *CanComp*, 31, Jul–Aug 1968
Groetzinger, Deanna, and Stuewe, Paul. 'Small magazines: fugues are music, but Music sure isn't Fugue,' *Quill and Quire*, Aug 1978

Fowke, Edith. 'In the past ... earlier Canadian folk magazines,' *Canada Folk Bulletin*, vol 2, Mar–Apr 1979
'Orchestra news letters,' *OCan*, vol 7, Mar 1980
McMorrow, Kathleen. 'Music periodicals: Canadian music periodicals,' Music Library Assn *Notes*, vol 36, Jun 1980
HK

PERRAULT, Joseph-Julien. Choirmaster, composer, b Montreal 8 or 18 May 1826, d Varennes, near Montreal, 22 Aug 1866. He studied theology 1844–7 at the Grand séminaire de Montréal and 1847–9 at the Séminaire de Saint-Sulpice in Paris. He was ordained a priest in Paris in 1849.

Perrault returned to Canada to serve as a teacher and choirmaster 1850–3 at the Collège de Montréal. He was choirmaster 1859–61 and 1863–6 to the parish of Notre-Dame. A self-taught musician and an outstanding score-reader familiar with orchestral instruments, he presented a Haydn mass on St-Jean-Baptiste day in 1860 and conducted two long-remembered performances (in 1861 at the Cabinet de lecture paroissial) of the symphonic ode *Le Désert* by Félicien David.

Among Perrault's publications are *Recueil de cantiques* (Chapleau 1859, 1869) and *Messe de Noël: 'Deo Infanti'* (1859–60), to which he added a *Credo* and a *Magnificat* in 1865 (Ateliers du Nouveau-Monde 1870, Boucher ca 1882). His four-part harmonizations of two plainsong masses – a *Messe des morts* (with L.-A. *Barbarin) and the *Messe du second ton* by Du Mont – were published by Boucher. Eugène *Lapierre edited a modern version of the *Messe de Noël* (Boucher 1945). Perrault composed a number of motets, psalms, and choruses with accompaniments for organ and orchestra.

BIBLIOGRAPHY

'Feu Messire Joseph-Julien Perreault,' *Canada Musical*, vol 1, 1 Oct 1866
Myrand, Ernest. *Noëls anciens de la Nouvelle-France*, 2nd edn (Quebec 1907)
Kallmann, Helmut. 'Joseph-Julien Perrault,' *DCB*, vol 9
(CMr)

PERRAULT, Michel (Brunet). Composer, conductor, percussionist, teacher, b Montreal 20 Jul 1925. He first studied timpani and theory at the *McGill Cons 1941–3 and later enrolled at the *CMM where he worked 1943–6 with Gabriel *Cusson (harmony), Réal *Gagnier (oboe), and Louis Decair (timpani). He was timpanist 1944–6 with the *MSO and 1945–6 with the CBC *'Little Symphonies' orchestra. In Paris 1946–7 he studied at the École normale de musique with Nadia Boulanger, Arthur Honegger, and Georges Dandelot. On his return to Montreal he studied with Conrad *Letendre. He worked 1949–50 as a composer and conductor for the CBC, obtaining the Radiomonde prize in 1950 for his radio scores. He served 1957–60 as percussionist and assistant conductor of the MSO and 1958–60 as music director of Les Grands Ballets Canadiens. He was a teacher at various institutions and undertook research in musical pedagogy, developing a curriculum and learning materials known by the name of *Pantonal. Practical testing of his methods has continued in Montreal and in various schools throughout Quebec.

As a composer Perrault has distinguished himself by his sense of form, his mastery of the instruments of the orchestra, and his successful utilization of Quebec folk music. Concerning his style, he has said: 'I'm a classicist living in the wrong period. Dodecaphonism, serialism, or any other "ism," are not for me. I like a folk tune and the harmony that goes with it' (*Thirty-four biographies*). He has received commissions from the CBC, Les Grands Ballets Canadiens, and the *Victoria SO. Perrault has not produced any new works after 1970. He is a member of CAPAC and founded his own music publishing firm in Montreal, Les Publications Bonart.

SELECTED COMPOSITIONS

STAGE

Commedia del arte, ballet. 1958. Ms
Sea Gallows, ballet. 1958. Med orch. Bonart. (1963). RCI 185 (CBC Mtl orch, Perrault cond)
Suite canadienne, ballet. 1965. Ms
Also incidental music for several plays, notably *Antigone* (1949), *Caligula* (1950), *La Farce du pendu dépendu* (1950), and *Huon de Bordeaux* (1950)

ORCHESTRA

Monologues. 1954. Str orch. Bonart
Mambo della Destra. 1961. Full orch. Ms
Centennial Homage, overture for BC's second century. 1966. Full orch. Bonart 1966
Works for sm orch, including *Les Fleurettes* (1947), RCI 7 (J.-M. *Beaudet); *Promenade* (1954); *Scherzo* (1954); 8 arr of French-Canadian folksongs published by Bonart, 3 recorded: CBC SM-103 (*Maxwell)
Several works for soloist(s) and orch, including for vc: *Les Trois Cônes* (1949, ms) and *La Belle Rose* (1952, Bonart); for tpt: *Fête et parade* (1952, Bonart), *Pastiche espagnol* (1956, Bonart), and *Pastiche tzigane* (1957, Bonart); for hp: *Margoton* (1954, Bonart) and *Jeux de quartes* (1961, ms); also *Esquisses en plein air* (Saint-Denys-Garneau) for sop and str (1954, Bonart); *Le Saucisson canadien* for 4 sax and str (1955, Bonart); *Bérubée* for pf and orch (1959, Bonart); *Serenade per tre fratelli* for 3 hns and orch (1962, ms); a *Concerto* for double-bass (1962, ms); and a *Concerto* for hn (1967, Bonart)

CHAMBER MUSIC

Triangulaire (Les Trois Cônes). 1945. Cl, hp, str quar. Ms
Les Aquarelles. 1946. Vn, pf. Ms
Sonata. 1946. Vn, pf. Ms
Solitude. 1948. Vn, pf. BMIC 1951
Quartet. 1953. Sax quar. Bonart. RCI 91 (A. *Romano)
Trio. 1954. Vn, vc, pf. Bonart. RCI 125 (*Bress)
Sextet. 1955. Cl, hp, str quar. Bonart. RCI 125 (*Mtl Str Quar)
Also works for jazz ensemble published by Bonart: *Prélude et fugue à l'américaine* (1956); *Half and Half* (1957); *Real Gone* (1957), *Two Three-Part Fugues* (1957); *All Wet* (1959); *Blues Prelude and Fugue* (1959); and the suite *Three Shades* (1959)

CHOIR OR VOICE

Anne de Bretagne. 1953. SSA. Bonart
Plus matin que la lune. 1953. V, hp. Ms
Fontaines noires; douces fontaines. 1956. Ten, 2 hp. Bonart

(JC)

André Perrault Ltée. Record store, opened in 1958 on rue des Cascades in St-Hyacinthe, near Montreal, and at first specializing in popular music. In 1970 the founder-owner André Perrault (b St-Hyacinthe 17 Nov 1935) added to his business a mail-order counter reserved for classical and educational recordings and cassettes. By 1978 orders were arriving from 71 countries as well as Canada and the USA. In 1978 customers numbered more than 100,000 and orders were filled from a stock of some 40,000 titles. A system of perforated cards containing numerous items of information about each customer's preferences allows a rapid delivery of information on the latest issues likely to be of interest to him or her.

André Perrault began publishing a catalogue in 1971. It was comparable in size to others of the same kind (*Bielefelder, Gramophone Classical Catalogue, Schwann Record and Tape Guide*) and by 1978 it covered close to 200 different labels, including some of an esoteric nature, such as Calliope and Edici, Charlin, Harmonia Mundi, Psallite, and the German Wergo. Perrault was the founder-director of the magazine *Adagio* (discontinued in 1976 after five issues appeared at two-month intervals) and launched the 1976 Canadian Grand Prix du disque classique, which was conferred that year only.

In 1978 Perrault opened a US branch of his mail-order counter in Winooski, Vt. That same year, he published his catalogue in English.

BIBLIOGRAPHY

Gingras, Claude. 'André Perrault: le phenomène du disque-par-la-poste,' Montreal *La Presse*, 26 Oct 1974
Inglis, Alexander. 'Success in St-Hyacinthe,' *Fugue*, Nov 1977
Quig, James. 'The better music trap,' *The Canadian*, 4 Feb 1978
Cloutier, Laurier. 'L'Homme du mois,' *Revue Commerce*, Jan 1979
ST

PERREAULT, Geneviève. Mezzo-soprano, b Quebec City 18 Oct 1939; B MUS voice (Laval) 1962, LRCT 1965. After studying voice in Quebec City with Rolande *Dion and three times winning a prize at the Quebec Music Festivals (*Canadian Music Competitions), she received a scholarship to the RCMT and the *Royal Cons Opera School, where she worked 1962–5, mainly with Ernesto *Vinci. She sang Colas 6 Oct 1963 in the *Ten Centuries Concerts revival of *Colas et Colinette*. She attended the *Banff SFA in 1962 and 1964 on scholarships and sang Dame Quickly (*Falstaff*) on tour in Alberta in August 1964. On her return to Toronto that year she made her *COC debut as Mercedes in *Carmen*, a role she sang on tour in 1966 as well as the opera's title role. She sang with the COC in such works as Stravinsky's *Mavra* (1965), *Cavalleria Rusticana* (1966), *The Tales of Hoffmann* (1967), Raymond *Pannell's *The Luck of Ginger Coffey* (1967), and *Salome* (1968). In November 1964 she sang Suzuki in *Madama Butterfly* with the *Théâtre lyrique de Nouvelle-France. She has appeared on CBC radio and TV and performed in recital and concert with the *TSO, the CBC orchestras, and the *Quebec SO. She continued her voice training in New York with Cornelius Reid and in California with Beatrice Rowe, and then left for Europe. In 1969 she won the Netherlands Prize ('s-Hertogenbosch) and then studied in Zurich with Enzo Mascherini. Settling in 1973 in West Germany, she first worked with the Landestheater in Cobourg and then moved in 1976 to the Stadttheater in Giessen; at the same time she continued her studies in Cologne under Joseph Metternich. She was married to the bass Maurice *Brown. AP

PERRIN, Harry Crane. Educator, administrator, composer, organist, b Wellingborough, Northhamptonshire, England, 19 Aug 1865, d Exeter, England, 6 Nov 1953; D MUS (Trinity, Dublin) 1901, FRCO. He was educated at Wellingborough and at Trinity College, Dublin; held church positions in Rathfarnham, Ireland, and Lowestoft, England; and served as organist-choirmaster and director of the musical societies 1892–8 at Coventry Cathedral and 1898–1908 at Canterbury Cathedral. He resigned from the cathedral to accept positions in Canada as director of the *McGill Cons, Montreal, and the first professor of music at McGill U, positions he held until his retirement in 1930. His term was distinguished by three main achievements: the establishment of a university orchestra in 1909, the development of a Canadian system of music examinations, and the founding in 1920 of the McGill U Faculty of Music, which he served as dean until 1930. Perrin was a product of the English cathedral tradition. His gifts as an administrator, so important in the formative years of the faculty, were supplemented by his wide experience in music, not only as a respected organist but also as an able composer.

Perrin wrote songs, choral works, cantatas, and organ and orchestral pieces. His cantata, *Abode of Worship*, and the choral setting, *Pan's Pipes*, were published by Breitkopf, and the *Song of War* by Weekes. Other songs and sacred works were issued by Novello.

It was Perrin's belief that music had a special role to play in Montreal as a bridge between the

English- and French-language groups and he campaigned earnestly for the building of an adequate concert hall. His first impressions of Canada are recorded in his article 'Music in Canada' in *University Magazine* (April 1911) and his many essays, articles, and lectures are deposited in the McGill U Archives.

BIBLIOGRAPHY
McGill Music Month: April 10 to May 8, 1975, 70th Anniversary pamphlet (Montreal 1975) EM

PERRIN, Harvey (Dale). Educator, conductor, violinist, violist, arranger, b Batesville, Ind, 20 Jul 1905, naturalized Canadian 1926; BA (Toronto) 1933, B PAED (Toronto) 1937. Moving to Canada in 1910 he studied at the Kitchener Cons and in 1919 played violin and viola in the Kitchener-Waterloo Orchestra. He studied at the *U of Toronto with Frank *Blachford, H.A. *Fricker, Luigi von *Kunits, George *Lambert, and Ettore *Mazzoleni. He was a member of the *Toronto Mendelssohn Choir in the late 1930s and early 1940s.

Perrin was the conductor 1944–56 of the Harvey Perrin Choir, heard in concert and on CBC and CFRB radio, and 1958–69 of the *Toronto Men Teachers' Choir. He directed the massed choirs 1958–71 at the May Festival Concerts of Toronto school children at *Massey Hall. His choral arrangements were published 1944–66 by G.V. *Thompson.

Perrin was for many years a music teacher in Toronto schools and was associate director 1947–58 and director 1958–71 of music for the Toronto Board of Education. He lectured 1946–66 at the city's summer schools on school music methods and in 1966 visited Hungary on behalf of OISE to study Kodály's principles of music education. He was the editor and one of four authors of the resulting publication *The New Approach to Music*.

Perrin was president of the music section of the Ontario Educational Assn (later *OMEA) and 1969–71 of the *Canadian Music Festival Adjudicators' Assn. He adjudicated at competition festivals for some 35 years in Canada and in the West Indies.

Perrin's daughter, Patricia Krueger (b Toronto 4 Oct 1944), became the keyboard player with the *TS in 1974.

See also School music.

WRITINGS
- and Wright, Don. *Let's Read Music* (Toronto 1952)
The Canadian Singer, vol 7 (Toronto 1955)
- et al. *Songs for Today*, 9 vols (Waterloo 1958–70)
- ed. *The New Approach to Music*, 2 vols (Toronto 1969, 1972)
'Music summer schools I have known,' *Recorder*, vol 15, Mar 1973 (WL)

PERRONE, John or **Juan** (Joseph). Guitarist, composer, b Toronto 17 Jan 1935. He studied guitar with Clark Russel in Toronto in his mid-teens, with Andrés Segovia and Alirio Diaz at the Accademia Musicale Chigiana in Siena in 1963, and with Manuel Lopez Ramos at Estudio de Arte Guitarrístico in Mexico City in 1969. He himself has taught privately and at the *RCMT, which he joined in 1968. Schooled in classical and flamenco styles, Perrone has given recitals in Canada and the USA and has participated in CBC radio and TV programs, including the 1969–70 TV series 'Islands and Princesses.' He has composed music for the 1967 CBC TV production of García Lorca's play *Yerma* (in which he appeared) and for film documentaries. Each of his LPs, *Forbidden Games* (1969, CTLS 0120 / GRT 9217-209), *Alma de Juan* (1970, CTL 477-5132), and *Vaya con Juan* (1972, CTL 477-5163), includes 10 pop song arrangements and 2 of his own works. The latter two LPs are named for Perrone compositions. His *Estudio de Juan* and *Vals de Juan* are published by Beechwood Music (Hollywood). Others are published by Conestoga Music (Toronto). Perrone is a member of PRO Canada. MM

PERRY (originally, Guloien). Family of saxophonists prominent in western Canada: notably 1 / Paul and 2 / P.J., Paul's son.

1 **Paul**. Tenor saxophonist, bandleader, b Wadena, south of Regina, of Norwegian parents, 3 Oct 1916. The second eldest of eight children, he taught himself and his brothers Edward, Howard, and Jim Guloien to play saxophone. He led a dance band, in which his brothers played, 1939–40 in Medicine Hat, Alta, and 1940–4 in other western Canadian cities including Calgary (Penley's Pavilion) and Regina (Trianon Ballroom). In 1945 Perry, with Jim Guloien and the pianist Geoff Hall, bought Varsity Hall at Sylvan Lake (south of Edmonton), and the Paul Perry Orchestra performed there May to September each year until about 1965. The band also toured each spring in central Alberta. Many distinguished jazz musicians played in Perry's bands, among them his son P.J., the trumpeters Chuck Barber, Arnie Chycoski, Don Clark, Bobby *Hales, and Herbie *Spanier, the trombonist Ray Sikora, the pianists Chris *Gage, John Gittens, Ralph *Grierson, and Ron Johnston, and the drummers Jerry *Fuller, Stan Perry (no relation), George Ursan, and Jim Wightman.

Paul's brothers Howard Guloien (b Wadena 8 Feb 1923) and Jim Guloien (b Wadena 6 Aug 1927) also have had careers as dance band musicians.

2 **P.J.** (Paul John). Tenor, alto and soprano saxophonist, flutist, b Calgary 2 Dec 1941. After playing piano and clarinet as a boy, he joined his father's dance band at 14 as a baritone saxophonist. For several years he spent summers playing at Sylvan Lake, and winters at such Vancouver nightclubs as the Cave (with, in turn, Chris Gage, Dave *Robbins, Fraser *MacPherson, and Bobby Hales) and the Cellar. In 1959 he moved to Toronto, where he played in the jazz bands of Ron *Collier, Sonny *Greenwich, and others. In 1962 he went to Montreal and joined the quartet of Maury *Kaye. After living 1963–6 in Europe, playing in London (notably with Annie Ross and Brian Auger), Nice, and Berlin, he returned to Vancouver. There he was a member 1972–5 of *Pacific Salt. In 1975 he moved to Edmonton, working there extensively with Tommy *Banks' jazz group, big band, and studio orchestra, with his own jazz band, and (on call) with the *Edmonton SO (he played the alto saxophone solo in that orchestra's recording of Ibert's suite *Paris*). He performed in Europe during the summer of 1979 as part of an RCI-sponsored 'all star' sextet. Writing of Perry's LP *Sessions*, Mark Miller referred to Perry as one of Canada's finest bebop saxophonists, noting a 'sharp, vibrant style ... In tone and technical facility, especially in the upper registers of his horn, he's reminiscent of Phil Woods' (Toronto *Globe and Mail*, 7 Sep 1978). P.J. Perry was the subject of a 90-minute 'Jazz Radio-Canada' broadcast in 1979. Perry has composed a few jazz themes, including *Torkin' with Torben* recorded with Torben Oxbol for *Sessions*. Perry is an affiliate of PRO Canada.

DISCOGRAPHY
Sessions. Perry alto sax, Tildesley tpt and flhn, McFetridge or Banks pf, Oxbol db, Ranger drums. 1977. Suite 1001
Perry also appears on three Pacific Salt LPs and others with Banks' big band at Montreux, trombonist Curt Watts (CBC LM-425), and blues singer Clarence 'Big' Miller (RCI 474). MM

PERSSE, Thomas (Henry). Tenor, b Limerick, Ireland, 4 Sep 1862, d Venice, Cal, 19 Apr 1920. He was a small child when his parents settled in Toronto. Going to Winnipeg as a youth, he was employed as a surveyor by the CPR and later (1885) saw action in the Riel Rebellion.

Persse's earliest singing appearances were in Gilbert & Sullivan roles 1884–5 with the Winnipeg Operatic Society, of which he was a founding member. After study with Frederick E. Bristol and George Sweet in New York he made his professional debut with the Marie Greenwood English Grand Opera Company at Poughkeepsie, NY, in November 1887. Thereafter he was associated with various US opera companies, notably the Castle Square Opera for which, ca 1895–9 in Boston, Philadelphia, and New York, he sang such roles as Canio in *I Pagliacci*, Faust, Manrico in *Il Trovatore*, Don José in *Carmen*, Turridu in *Cavalleria Rusticana*, and the title role in *Lohengrin*. Of a Toronto appearance with the Kellogg English Opera Company in 1889 the *Globe* wrote: 'Mr. Persse has a clear, bright voice and sings with a great deal of animation.'

In 1910 Persse and his wife, the soprano Edith Mason, settled in California where he acted in motion pictures until his death.

BIBLIOGRAPHY
Clark, Archie L. 'From silver mines to opera,' *Winnipeg Free Press*, 21 Nov 1959 JBM

Perth County Conspiracy (Does Not Exist). Informal association of musicians, in the folk manner, originally members of a community of performers, artists, and crafts people in the Stratford area of Perth County, Ont. It began ca 1968 with a duo, Cedric Smith and Richard Keelan, both of whom sang and played guitar at the Black Swan coffeehouse in Stratford. Other musicians joined on a casual basis, among them the singer-guitarist Terry Jones, the pianist George Toros, and the bass guitarist Michael Butler. Friends and family often participated in performances. A series of concerts 1969–71 included several in Toronto (*Massey Hall, *Mariposa Folk Festival, etc).

After 1971 Perth County Conspiracy appearances became sporadic – some separated by years – as members pursued other interests. Smith, for example, an actor at the *Stratford Festival, participated in productions in Toronto, including the 1974 staging of Barry Broadfoot's *Ten Lost Years*, for which he wrote songs, and the 1977 musical *The Road to Charlottetown*, on which he collaborated with the poet Milton Acorn.

Later performances included tours across Canada by various members of the group; a tour (1975) of eastern Europe by Keelan, Smith, and others; and an appearance (1978) at the Leacock Festival of Humour in Orillia, Ont, all under the Perth County Conspiracy name.

The group made two LPs for Columbia (*Perth County Conspiracy Does Not Exist*, ELS 375; *Perth County Conspiracy Does Not Exist – Alive*, GES 90037) and one for the CBC (LM-85), before establishing its own label, Rumour, in 1972. Rumour released two more of the group's LPs (one of which, *Breakout to Berlin* – 1975, VKC 1015 – was recorded in East Germany) and also issued *Ten Lost Years and Then Some* (Rumour Six).

Writing in *The Canadian Composer* (March 1971), Richard Flohil referred to 'the Conspiracy's mixture of music, amiable anarchy, and guerilla theatre. Words from Dylan Thomas, William Shakespeare, and British poet Christopher Logue are mixed with the Conspiracy's gentle satire.'

BIBLIOGRAPHY
Flohil, Richard. 'Rough notes on a gentle conspiracy,' *CanComp*, 58, Mar 1971
– 'How to make the Conspiracy work,' *CanComp*, 100, Apr 1975
Johnson, Bryan. 'The flowers are gone for PCC,' Toronto *Globe and Mail*, 8 Jan 1977 (LL)

Peterborough. Ontario city on the Otonabee River (part of the Trent-Severn Waterway). It was settled ca 1820 by County Cork Irish, was named Peterborough in 1827, and was incorporated in 1905. It developed into a lumbering and milling town. The population grew from 2000 (1850) to 58,000 (1975) with the industrialization of the city.

A group of well-educated settlers in the area – the Langtons, Stewarts, and Stricklands – wrote of the travails of early backwoods life, and their accounts include mention of music – folksinging in the lumbercamps and informal music-making at the house of singing teacher Thomas Choate (fl 1839–1900) in nearby Warsaw. Organized music began in the churches; a concert of vocal and instrumental music took place in 1844 at a bazaar at St John's Church.

Brass band concerts under a Mr Rackett were heard in 1858 at the Histrionic Club. The city's longest-lived band began in the early 1860s as that of the 57th Regiment. It was re-formed by Rupert Gliddon in 1890 as the 40-member Regimental Concert Band and gained a reputation as one of Canada's finest, appearing at the *CNE in Toronto for some 20 years. After World War I it was directed by Capt W.H. Peryer until 1950 and became, in turn, the Peterborough Citizen's Band and the Peterborough Civic Concert Band.

Instrumental music appeared in the schools in 1872, the emphasis remaining on band instruments though string instruction was to be given periodically. The Peterborough Cons (fl 1905–31) was directed by Rupert Gliddon (b, Cornwall, England, 1867, a cornet player whose parents settled in Bowmanville, Ont, when he was three and who studied under Arthur Hartmann in England and Robert Teichmüller in Leipzig) and his wife Thérèse, a pupil of A.S. *Vogt. The conservatory offered instruction by Toronto and local teachers including Alice Roger Collins, Lina *Drechsler Adamson, Harry *Field, Lora Logan Hooper, Dorothy *Allan Park, and Leo *Smith. The *Hart House Quartet, Herbert Menges, and Arthur Friedheim appeared in its concert hall. Later both *Trent U (established 1963) and Sir Sanford Fleming College (established 1967) included music on their curricula. The Kawartha Lakes Music Camp, begun in 1971 under Canon Jack Clough, has offered 10-day training programs at Lakefield College School in nearby Lakefield.

A Philharmonic Society was giving concerts as early as 1879 in the Old Methodist Church. A Peterborough SO was formed in 1923 by Rupert Gliddon (who also formed a conservatory orchestra and a 60-voice Madrigal Club) and continued until the early 1930s. A new Peterborough SO, begun under Klemi *Hambourg in 1958 as a string orchestra, grew to a 40-piece orchestra by 1967 (see Orchestras).

In 1900 George W. Mulligan directed a specially organized 100-voice Royal Chorus for the visit of the Duke of York (later King George V). Mulligan also conducted the Royal Chorus and the Canadian General Electric Glee Club in a grand concert in 1901. The Peterborough Amateur Opera, organized ca 1908 by Richard Devey (organist-choirmaster at St John's Church), won the Earl Grey Trophy in 1910 for its production of *The Geisha*. (The leading role was sung by Lavina Hallihan of the city, whose later studies were financed by Governor-General Grey, and who enjoyed a concert career in Canada and the USA.) Dorothy Allan Park's Madrigal Singers (fl 1927–42) presented many guest instrumentalists and appeared frequently in Toronto. Martin Chenhall, organist-choirmaster at St Paul's Presbyterian Church, conducted the Peterborough Male Voice Choir in the 1920s in concerts and in Gilbert & Sullivan productions at the Grand Opera House. The choir took second place in the Glee Club Festival of Male Voice Choirs in New York in 1929. Choirs active in the 1970s include the Bonachords, the Coventry Singers, and the Peterborough County Youth Choir.

Three halls have served Peterborough: Hill's Music Hall (1860–80), seating 700 and operated by a Mr. Hill who was an amateur organ builder; The Bradburn (1876–1974), a small auditorium on the third floor of a commercial building; and the Grand Opera House (1906–40), a two-balcony theatre which housed musical comedy performances and offered recitals by Dame Clara Butt, Edward *Johnson, Sir Harry Lauder, and Lillian Nordica. A 350-seat theatre was opened in 1973 at Trent U. The Canadian Concert Assn (founded by J.J. Craig in 1937 and affiliated with *Community Concerts in 1942) has presented series of visiting artists. The Peterborough Arts and Water Festival, an annual 10-day outdoor affair begun in 1971, has presented many Canadian pop and jazz performers. Musicians born or raised in Peterborough include Brian and Lawrence *Cherney, the violinist Julia Grover Choate (granddaughter of Thomas Choate), Agnes Logan Green, Norman *Hurrle, Paul *McIntyre, and Helen Davies *Sherry.

BIBLIOGRAPHY
Poole, T.W. *A Sketch of the Early Settlement and Subsequent Progress of the Town of Peterborough* (Peterborough 1867, 1941)
Collins, Alice Roger. 'The Gliddons,' *Real People*, 9 and 10 (London, Ont [1936])
Choate, Richard F. 'Peterborough's "Golden Age" of music,' *Peterborough Examiner*, 22 Apr 1950
Peterborough: Land of Shining Waters: An Anthology (Toronto 1967)
Cox, Musa I. 'Women in Music,' *Portraits: Peterborough Area Women Past and Present* (Peterborough 1967)
Dixon, Bailey Associates, Ltd. 'Report No. 2 "Cultural Facilities Study, Peterborough Performing Arts" ' (March 1976) (JW)

'Peter Emberley.' The story of a young man from Prince Edward Island who was fatally injured in the Miramichi lumberwoods when a log rolled on him. John Calhoun, a friend of the lad, composed the verses in 1881 and a local singer, Abraham Munn, set them to a traditional Irish tune. The ballad is the favourite lumbering song of New Brunswick; it also was sung along all the east coast of Canada and in Ontario lumbercamps. The tune is the theme of the second movement of Kelsey *Jones' *Miramichi Ballad*. The song is published in Edith *Fowke's *The Penguin Book of Canadian Folk Songs* and was recorded by Tom *Kines for the nine-LP set *Canadian Folk Songs: a Centennial Collection* (RCA Victor CS-100-7). Words to the variant 'Peter Amberlay' were published in W. Roy Mackenzie's *Ballads and Sea Songs from Nova Scotia* (Cambridge, Mass, 1928). A 'Peter Rambelay,' to a different tune, can be found in Helen *Creighton's *Songs and Ballads from Nova Scotia*.

BIBLIOGRAPHY
Manny, Louise. 'The ballad of Peter Amberley,' *Atlantic Advocate*, vol 53, Jul 1963 (EF)

PETERSON, Oscar (Emmanuel). Pianist, singer, composer, b Montreal, of West Indian parents, 15 Aug 1925; hon LLD (Carleton) 1973, hon LLD (Mount Allison) 1978, hon LLD (Concordia) 1979.

Oscar Peterson

His father, a CPR porter, led the family band in concerts in Montreal church and community halls. Peterson was the fourth of five children. He played trumpet at five but switched to piano at eight after a year-long battle with tuberculosis. He was guided first by his sister Daisy (m Sweeney, later a piano teacher in Montreal). At 12 he took piano lessons briefly from Lou *Hooper; later he attended the *CMM, and at 15 he studied with Paul *de Marky. At about that time Peterson won an amateur contest sponsored by the radio personality Ken Soble in Montreal and Toronto and began his own radio show, 'Fifteen Minutes Piano Rambling,' on the Montreal station CKAC. In 1941 he was featured on CBM's 'Rhythm Time,' and by 1945 he had been heard nationally on the CBC's 'Light Up and Listen' and 'The *Happy Gang.' Peterson was a member 1944–7 of Johnny *Holmes' orchestra before playing 1948–9 at the Alberta Lounge with his own trio (Austin 'Ozzie' Roberts, bass, and Clarence Jones, drums, or, briefly, Ben Johnson, guitar). The trio was heard on Montreal radio station CFCF in broadcasts from the lounge.

The first of the 16 78s Peterson made 1945–9 for *RCA Victor reveal the predilection for boogie-woogie which had earned him the nickname 'The Brown Bomber of Boogie-Woogie'; the last of those recordings suggest the influence of bebop. The other sound document of Peterson's Montreal years is the sound-track for Norman *McLaren's NFB film *Begone Dull Care* (1949).

Though Peterson had declined requests from Jimmie Lunceford and Count Basie to move to the USA and join their bands, he accepted an invitation from the US impresario Norman Granz to be 'planted' in the audience at Granz' Jazz at the Philharmonic (JATP) presentation at Carnegie Hall, 18 Sep 1949, and to be brought onstage as a surprise guest. Peterson's appearance that night brought the following report from Michael Levin: 'A Montreal citizen, Oscar Peterson, stopped the Norman Granz Jazz at the Philharmonic concert dead cold in its tracks here last month. Balancing a large and bulky body at the piano much in the fashion of Earl Hines, Peterson displayed a flashy right hand, a load of bop and [George] Shearing ideas, as well as a good sense of harmonic development. And in addition, he scared some of the local modern minions by playing bop ideas in his *left* hand, which is distinctly not the common practise. Further ... Peterson impressed musicians here by not only having good ideas and making them, but giving them a rhythmic punch and drive which has been all too lacking in too many of the younger pianists' (*Down Beat*, 21 Oct 1949).

Under the guidance of Granz, who was to be his manager for over 30 years, Peterson formed a trio (piano, guitar, and bass) in the USA in 1951 and rose during the 1950s to the forefront of jazz musicians through his appearances with JATP shows and his recordings. His version of 'Tenderly' was especially popular. He toured Europe in 1952, 1953, and 1954 with JATP and annually thereafter with his trio, often in the company of the singer Ella Fitzgerald. In 1953 he made the first of many appearances in Japan. The growth of Peterson's popularity is reflected in his first-place standing in the piano category of the *Down Beat* readers' poll as early as 1950 (repeated 1951–5, 1959–63, 1965–7, 1972; he won the magazine's critics' poll in 1953). He has won many other such polls.

In 1958 Peterson changed his trio to piano, bass, and drums; in the early 1970s he performed exclusively as a solo pianist, returning later to a variety of small-group formats. Peterson has played at many European jazz festivals, including that at Montreux, where several of the concerts in which he appeared in 1975 and 1977 (as leader or sideman) were recorded. During the years 1967–71 he recorded in Villingen, West Germany, for Saba (later MPS). LPs also have been issued of concerts in Tokyo, Amsterdam, Paris, London, and Tallinn, USSR. (The recording in Tallinn was made during a tour of the USSR which Peterson undertook in 1974 for the Canadian Dept of External Affairs but cancelled before its completion.)

Throughout his career Peterson has made Canada his home base, living in Montreal until 1958 and in Toronto after that time. In 1960 in Toronto, with Ray Brown and Ed Thigpen (his bassist and drummer of the day) and Phil *Nimmons, he opened the Advanced School of Contemporary Music which, in its three-year existence, drew students of jazz from cities throughout North America. The faculty grew to include Eric Traugott (trumpet), Butch Watanabe (trombone), and Ed *Bickert (guitar). Peterson's own pupils included the Canadian pianists Carol Britto, Brian Browne, and Wray *Downes. Four volumes of his *Jazz Exercises and Pieces for the Young Jazz Pianist* were published in the mid-1960s.

Peterson has performed at the *Montreal, *Stratford, *Shaw, and *Vancouver International festivals – he made an LP at Stratford in 1956 – and has appeared frequently in Canadian nightclubs including the Town Tavern, Toronto, where he recorded *On the Town* in 1958.

Though virtually ignored by the CBC for many years after his early career in radio, Peterson was heard often in the 1970s on CBC radio, in concert presentations (eg, 'Jazz Radio-Canada') and profiles (on 'That Midnight Jazz' in 1973 and 'The Entertainers' in 1975). On CBC TV he was seen in the specials 'Oscar Peterson Inside' (1967) and 'A Very Special Oscar Peterson' (1976) and in a performance with a 37-piece orchestra of an orchestration by Rick *Wilkins of his *Canadiana Suite* (1979) accompanied by appropriate scenic film footage. A CTV series, 'Oscar Peterson Presents,' was filmed in Vancouver in 1974. Peterson also was host in the mid-1970s for BBC TV's 'Piano Party.' In 1980 the CBC telecast a 13-week series, 'Oscar Peterson and Friends,' and the single program 'A Little Special,' devoted to Peterson.

Peterson's sidemen (see Discography) rarely have been Canadians; nevertheless he has employed, at one time or another, the bassists Michel *Donato and David *Young, and the drummers Jerry *Fuller, Stan Perry, and Ron Rully.

Through his studies with Paul de Marky, Peterson follows in the pianistic tradition of Franz Liszt. Impressionist and late-romantic influences also have been detected in his playing; after a concert in Toronto, Hugh Thomson observed: 'His version of "Tenderly" leans heavily on Debussy and Ravel in its harmonies, and his "Little White Lies" had definite echoes of Rachmaninoff' (*Toronto Daily Star*, 11 Oct 1950). In jazz Peterson has acknowledged the influence of Art Tatum, Teddy Wilson, Hank Jones, and Nat King Cole (whom Peterson resembles especially on the rare occasions he chooses to sing).

Gene *Lees, writing in *Maclean's* (July 1975), quoted the Argentinian composer-pianist Lalo Schifrin as saying 'Oscar is a true romantic in the 19th-century sense, with the addition of the 20th-century Afro-American jazz tradition. He is a top-class virtuoso.' Lees added 'This response is common. Peterson has astounding speed. Only Phineas Newborn and the late Art Tatum, one of his idols and mentors, have equalled him. And he has a power of direct swing that Tatum never equalled. His ideas are not always original; on a poor night, he falls back on his own highly identifiable phrases of musical vocabulary and some he got from others, such as a curious spinning chromatic figure of Dizzy Gillespie's. But these alone can be electrifying – the brilliantly clear and perfectly balanced runs, like streams of sparks, the great chords whacked into perfect place in the swing with the left hand that plays tenths effortlessly and could, I suppose, if he wanted, encompass twelfths, the dizzying passages in octaves that utilize a left hand as proficient as the right.' Peterson was afflicted in the 1970s with arthritis in his hands; it did not affect his abilities noticeably and by the end of the decade had subsided.

Peterson's best-known composition is his *Canadiana Suite* (1963, Tomi Music 1964; comprising jazz themes inspired by cities and regions of Canada). The suite received a National Academy of Recording Arts and Sciences 'Grammy' nomination as jazz composition of 1965 and has been recorded by Peterson's trio and by Peterson with Nimmons 'N' Nine Plus Six (in an orchestration by Phil Nimmons). He completed an *African Suite* in 1979. Among his other works for his jazz group are *Hallelujah Time, Blues for Big Scotia, Blues for Smedley, The Smudge, Bossa Beguine*, and *Hymn to Freedom*. He wrote and recorded *Blues for Allan Felix* for Woody Allen's film *Play It Again Sam* (1972) and won a Canadian Film Award in 1978 for his score to the feature film *The Silent Partner*. He has written scores for the documentaries *Big North* and *Fields of Endless Day*, the latter an *NFB / OECA-produced history of blacks in Canada.

Peterson has won Grammy Awards in 1975 for his LP *The Trio*, in 1979 for *Oscar Peterson Jam at Montreux '77*, and in 1980 for *Jousts*. He was made an Officer of the *Order of Canada in 1973 and was inducted into the *Juno Award Hall of Fame and made an honorary member of the *CMCouncil in 1978. He is an affiliate of BMI.

DISCOGRAPHY

1 PETERSON PIANO, OTHER MUSICIANS AS INDICATED

I Got Rhythm. Composite personnel. Armand Samson and Ben Johnson guit, Bert Brown, Albert King, and Austin Roberts db, Frank Gariepy, Roland Verdun, Russ Dufort, Mark Wilkinson, and Clarence Jones drums. 1945–9. (1976). 2-RCA FXMI 7233

Tenderly. Major Holley or Ray Brown db. 1950. Verve MGV 2046

Keyboard. Holley or Brown db. 1950. Verve MGV 2047

Nostalgic Memories. Ellis guit, Holley or Brown db, Bellson drums. 1950, 1954. Verve MGV 2045

Four LP transcription discs for RCI: solos and duets. Roberts db. 1951. RCI 37, 38, 39, 40

2 PETERSON PIANO (AND VOICE WHERE INDICATED), RAY BROWN BASS, OTHERS AS INDICATED

Evening with Oscar Peterson. 1950, 1951. Verve MGV 2048

Pastel Moods. Ashby or Ellis guit. 1952, 1953, 1954. Verve MGV 2004

Recital. Kessel or Ellis guit, Stoller or Bellson drums. 1952, 1953, 1954. Verve MGV 2044

Romance. Peterson v, Kessel guit, Stoller drums. 1952. Verve MGV 2012

Jazz at the Philharmonic. Kessel guit, Stoller drums. 1952. Verve MG, vol 8

Oscar Peterson Sings. Peterson v, Kessel guit. 1953. Clef MGC 145

Jazz at the Philharmonic. Ellis guit. 1953. Verve MG, vol 9

Jazz at the Philharmonic. Ellis guit. 1954. Verve MG, vol 10

Jazz at the Philharmonic. Ellis guit. 1955. Verve MG, vol 11

In a Romantic Mood. Orch, Russ Garcia cond. 1955, 1956. Verve MGV 2002

Oscar Peterson Plays Count Basie. Ellis guit, Rich drums. 1956. Verve MGV 8092

Oscar Peterson at the Stratford Shakespearean Festival. Ellis guit. 1956. Verve MGV 8024

Soft Sands. Orch, Peterson v, Ellis guit, Levey drums. 1957. Verve MGV 2079

Newport Jazz Festival 1957. Eldridge tpt, Stitt alto and ten sax, Ellis guit, J. Jones drums. 1957. Verve MGV 8239

At the Concertgebouw. Ellis guit. 1958. Verve MGV 8268

On the Town. Ellis guit. 1958. Verve MGV 8287

My Fair Lady. Gammage drums. 1958. Verve MGV 62119

3 PETERSON PIANO, RAY BROWN BASS, ED THIGPEN DRUMS, OTHERS AS INDICATED

Jazz Portrait of Sinatra. 1959. Verve MGV 68334

Jazz Soul. 1959. Verve MGV 68351

Fiorello! 1959. Verve MGV 68366

Porgy and Bess. 1959. Verve MGV 68340

Swinging Brass. Orch, Garcia cond. 1959. Verve MGV 68364

Trio. 1961. Verve MGV 68420

Sound of the Trio. 1961. Verve MGV 68480

Very Tall. Jackson vib. 1961. Verve MGV 68429

West Side Story. 1962. Verve MGV 68454

Put on a Happy Face. 1962. Verve MGV 68660

Something Warm. 1962. Verve MGV 68681

Bursting Out. Orch. 1962. Verve MGV 68476

Affinity. 1962. Verve MGV 68516

Night Train. 1962. Verve MGV 68538

Oscar Peterson with Nelson Riddle. Orch, Riddle cond. 1963. Verve MGV 68562

We Get Requests. 1964. Verve MGV 68606

Oscar Peterson Plays. 1964. Verve MGV 68591

Canadiana Suite. 1964. Limelight LM 82010

Oscar Peterson Plus One. Terry tp, flhn, v. 1964. Mer MG 20975

Eloquence. 1965. Limelight LM 86023/Trip 5560

Action. MPS/BASF 21 20668

Peterson also recorded two series of LPs devoted to individual songwriters.

- For Clef he recorded music by Cole Porter (MGC 603), Irving Berlin (MGC 604), George Gershwin (MGC 605), and Duke Ellington (MGC 606) with Kessel and Brown in 1952; by Jerome Kern (MGC 623), Richard Rodgers (MGC 624), and Vincent Youmans (MGC 625) with Ellis and Brown in 1953; and by Harry Warren (MGC 648), Harold Arlen (MGC 649), and Jimmy McHugh (MGC 650) with Ellis and Brown in 1954.
- For Verve he recorded music by Porter (MGV 62052), Berlin (MGV 62053), Gershwin (MGV 62054), Ellington (MGV 62055), Kern (MGV 62056), Rodgers (MGV 62057), Warren and Youmans (MGV 62059), Arlen (MGV 62060), and McHugh (MGV 62061), all with Brown and Thigpen in 1959.

4 PETERSON PIANO, SAM JONES BASS, BOBBY DURHAM DRUMS, OTHERS AS INDICATED

Girl Talk. Or Brown db, Hayes drums. 1967. MPS/ BASF 21 20669

The Way I Really Play. 1968. MPS/BASF 21 20670

My Favourite Instrument. Solo piano. 1968. MPS/ BASF 21 20671

Mellow Mood. 1968. MPS/BASF 21 20962

Travelin' on. 1968. MPS/BASF 21 20963

Motions and Emotions. Orch, Ogerman cond. 1969. MPS/BASF 21 20713

Hello Herbie. Ellis guit. 1969. MPS/BASF 21 20723

Tristeza on Piano. 1970. MPS/BASF 21 20734

5 PETERSON PIANO (OR OTHER INSTRUMENTS AS INDICATED); OTHER MUSICIANS AS INDICATED

NOTE: NHØP is Niels-Henning Ørsted Pedersen.

Walking the Line. Mraz db, Price drums. 1970. MPS/BASF 21 20868

Another Day. Mraz db, Price drums. 1970. MPS/BASF 21 20869

Tracks. Solo piano. 1970. MPS/BASF 21 20879

In Tune. Singers Unlimited, Mraz db, Hayes drums. 1971. MPS/BASF 21 20905

Reunion Blues. Jackson vib, Brown db, Hayes drums. 1971. MPS/BASF 21 20908

Great Connection. NHØP db, Hayes drums. 1971. MPS/BASF 21 21281
History of an Artist. Ashby, Kessel, or Ellis guit, Brown, Jones, or Mraz db, Durham or Hayes drums. 1972, 1973, 1974. 2-Pablo 2625.702
Oscar Peterson Featuring Stephane Grappelli. Grappelli vn, NHØP db, Clarke drums. 1973. America AM 6129 and 6131/2-Prestige 24041
The Trio. Pass guit, NHØP db. 1973. Pablo 2310.701
Canadiana Suite. Nimmons 'N' Nine Plus Six, NHØP db. 1973. CBC LM-303
Oscar Peterson in Russia. NHØP db, Hanna drums. 1974. 2-Pablo 2625.711
Oscar Peterson and Dizzy Gillespie. Gillespie tpt. 1974. Pablo 2310.740
'Satch' & 'Josh.' Basie pf and org, Green guit, Brown db, Bellson drums. 1974. Pablo 2310.722
Oscar Peterson and Harry Edison. Edison tpt. 1974. Pablo 2310.741
Oscar Peterson and Roy Eldridge. Eldridge tpt. 1974. Pablo 2310.742
À la Salle Pleyel. Pass guit. 1975. 2-Pablo 2625.705
Oscar Peterson and Jon Faddis. Faddis tpt. 1975. Pablo 2310.743
Oscar Peterson and Clark Terry. Terry tpt. 1975. Pablo 2310.741
Joust. Gillespie tpt, Edison tpt, Eldridge tpt, Faddis tpt, Terry tpt (individually). 1974–5. Pablo 2310.817
The Oscar Peterson Big 6 at Montreux. Thielemans hmca, Jackson vib, Pass guit, NHØP db, Bellson drums. 1975. Pablo 2310.747
Ella and Oscar. Fitzgerald v, Brown db. 1976. Pablo 2310.759
Porgy and Bess. Peterson clavichord only, Pass guit. 1976. Pablo 2310.779
Oscar Peterson Jam Montreux '77. Gillespie tpt, Terry tpt, Davis ten sax, NHØP db, Durham drums. 1977. Pablo 2308.208
Oscar Peterson and the Bassists. Brown db, NHØP db. 1977. Pablo 2308.213
Satch and Josh Again. Basie pf and org, Heard db, Bellson drums. 1978. Pablo 2310.802
The London Concert. Heard db, Bellson drums. 1978. Pablo 2620.111
The Paris Concert. Pass guit, NHØP db. 1978. Pablo 2620.112
The Silent Partner. Terry tpt, Carter alto sax, Sims ten sax, Jackson vib, Heard db, Tate drums. 1979. Pablo 2312.103
Night Child. Pass guit, NHØP db, Bellson drums. 1979. Pablo 2312.108
The Personal Touch. Peterson pf and v, Terry tpt, Bickert or Leitch guit, Young db, Fuller drums. 1980. Pablo 2312.113

Peterson also appears on many LPs as a member of JATP or Pablo concert parties or jam sessions and has recorded as an accompanist or guest soloist with Lester Young (Verve 8144), Buddy DeFranco (Verve 8210), Stan Getz (Verve 8251), the Modern Jazz Quartet (Verve 8269), Louis Armstrong (Verve 8322), Armstrong and Ella Fitzgerald (2-Verve 8811), Coleman Hawkins (Verve 8346), and Gerry Mulligan (Verve 8559), among many others.

BIBLIOGRAPHY

Dingman, Harold. 'Oscar Peterson,' *Liberty*, Jan 1946
Whiston, Henry F. ' "Watch Peterson," say Canadians,' *Down Beat*, 10 Mar 1950
Simon, George. 'Oscar!' *Metronome*, 14 Oct 1954
Freeman, D. 'Can piano be mastered? No, says Oscar Peterson,' *Down Beat*, 25 Jan 1956
Lees, Gene. 'The trouble with jazz piano; the viewpoint of Oscar Peterson,' *Down Beat*, 29 Oct 1959
Kritzwiser, Kay. 'Oscar Peterson: muscular giant of the jazz piano,' Toronto *Globe Magazine*, 4 Feb 1961
DeMicheal, Don. 'Oscar Peterson: on the teaching of jazz,' *Down Beat*, 27 Sep 1962
Wallace, Clarke. 'Jazz school with an Oscar,' *Weekend Magazine*, 26 Jan 1963
Ramonet, M.C. 'Délicat Oscar,' *Jazz Hot*, May 1966
Cressant, P. 'Oscar Peterson,' *Jazz Hot*, Sep 1969
Lees, Gene. 'The face behind the performer,' *Hi Fidelity and Musical America*, Aug 1970
Postif, F. 'Oscar Peterson,' *Jazz Hot*, Apr 1973
Lyons, Len. 'Oscar Peterson,' *Contemporary Keyboard*, vol 4, Mar 1978
Boulton, Marsha. 'The piano man,' *Maclean's*, 4 Jun 1979
de Sackville-Hunt, Marguerite. 'The elusive Oscar,' *PfAC*, vol 16, Fall 1979 MM

La Petite Maîtrise de Montréal. Children's choir school founded in 1938 by Alfred *Bernier, who was its sole director. He undertook to assemble a choir of boys of from 8 to 15, first approaching the Garnier school in the parish of the Immaculée-Conception. After a general audition he selected the first 43 members from among the 500 children in the school. Later members were drawn from a dozen Montreal schools. Father Bernier intended in this way to found a maîtrise, or choir school, organized along the lines of the famous Vienna Boys' Choir, to provide boys from working-class districts with a complete subsidized education. Along with academic studies there were classes in solfège, diction, and choral literature, sacred and secular. In the spring of 1939 the group began to appear in concert. Critics were extremely encouraging, commenting on the blend and purity of the voices, the subtleties of the shading, and the clear diction. Over a period of five years the Petite Maîtrise gave numerous concerts and took part in operas and radio broadcasts. However, despite the generosity of the Jesuits, Jean *Lallemand, and a few other benefactors, the plan for a school was realized only partially. Without government subsidy, the ensemble was forced to cease its activities in 1944. IP-C

Le Petit Ensemble vocal. Vocal quartet founded in 1956 and directed by George *Little with members of his *Montreal Bach Choir to present vocal chamber music from the Middle Ages to our time. The original quartet – the soprano Claire *Grenon-Masella, the alto Marcelle Dumontet, the tenor Paul-Émile Smith, and the bass Claude *Létourneau – was increased later to a sextet, the sopranos Margo *MacKinnon and Renée Beaumier, the tenor René *Lacourse, the bass Roland *Gosselin, and others joining the ensemble as additions or replacements. The group offered CBC series built around various nations and subjects and performed throughout Canada in public concerts and festivals. Several programs were presented jointly with the Montreal Consort of Ancient Instruments and with the Montreal Bach Choir. During *Expo 67 the ensemble performed polyphonic music by early composers and part-songs by Canadians including François *Brassard, Robert *Fleming, Kelsey *Jones, and Barbara *Pentland. Its last public concert took place 19 Jun 1971 during the CBC Toronto Festival.

DISCOGRAPHY

Azzaiolo *Villote del fiore* – Gesualdo madrigals. 1962. Vox STDL 500.900
Concert. Mtl Consort of Ancient Instruments, Joachim cond. 1969. CBC SM-112/A of D SDD 2159
Dufay motets. Consort of Viols, Lyman org, Joachim cond. Ca 1963. Vox STDL 500.990
Monteverdi *Lagrime d'amante al sepolcro dell'amata*; arie; canzonette. 1962. Vox STDL 500.910 NT

'Petit rocher de la haute montagne.' Canadian song from the early 18th century, which exists in several versions. The text was published first in Quebec City in 1863 by Bishop Joseph-Charles Taché (in *Forestiers et Voyageurs*, a volume of the journal *Soirées canadiennes*) and F.-A.-H. LaRue (*Le Foyer canadien*, vol 1). In his *Chansons populaires du Canada* (Quebec City 1865) Ernest *Gagnon reproduced the text in 11 verses along with Taché's description of the story. Gagnon also presented two versions of the melody, one in the minor mode and one in the major – the first seems more in keeping with the character of the piece. *Canada's Story in Song* by Edith *Fowke et al (Toronto 1965) gives seven verses and the melody in the minor.

The first song to describe a Canadian event, 'Petit rocher' describes the last moments of the person whom legend casts as the author, a coureur de bois named Jean Cadieux (baptized in Boucherville, near Montreal, 12 Mar 1671). He died in May 1709 after defending his family against the Iroquois at the Sept-Chutes portage on the Ottawa River. Cadieux diverted the Indians' attention while his family, protected by the Virgin Mary, managed to navigate the rapids in a canoe. Prior to dying of exhaustion, he dug his own grave and lay in it. Before doing so he wrote 'Cadieux's Lament' on a piece of birch-bark which his companions later discovered on his breast or, according to another legend, fastened to a tree. Voyageurs from a post nearby are said to have set the lament to music.

The song is found on LPs by Alan *Mills (Folk 2-FW 3000, Folk FW 6929) and the *Montreal Bach Choir (Vox STPL 511.860).

BIBLIOGRAPHY

Kohl, J.G. *Kitchi-Gami* (London 1860)
Fréchette, Louis. 'Cadieux,' *La Légende d'un peuple* (Paris 1887)
Montigny, Louvigny de. 'Cadieux et sa complainte,' *Proceedings and Transactions of the Royal Society of Canada* (Jun 1933)
Barbeau, Marius. 'La complainte de Cadieux, coureur de bois (ca. 1709),' *JAF*, 264, Apr–Jun 1954
Laforte, Conrad. 'La complainte de Cadieux,' *Dictionnaire des oeuvres littéraires du Québec*, vol 1, Maurice Lemire ed (Montreal 1978) (HP)

Les Petits Chanteurs à la Croix de Bois. A 100-voice choir of men and boys founded 22 Nov 1933 by Henri Vermandere (Brother Séverin; b Courtrai, Belgium, 17 May 1904) with the assistance of his brother Joseph *Vermandere. The choir at first was called the Petits Chanteurs de la Nativité d'Hochelaga, since its rehearsals were held 1933–43 in Hochelaga in Montreal's east end. At the request of Frédéric *Pelletier, who wrote to Mgr Fernand Maillet, director of the Petits Chanteurs à la Croix de Bois in Paris, the Montreal choir became affiliated with the latter in 1935 and took the same name as the Paris choir. The first concert took place in *Plateau Hall in 1936; at this time the ensemble contained 150 voices. The choir's repertoire of 200 pieces included Gregorian chant, religious works of the 16th century in particular, and secular works. The choir gave more than 300 concerts, appearing in Montreal, Quebec City, Lévis, Valleyfield, Nicolet, and other cities. At Wilfrid *Pelletier's invitation it participated in Roger-Ducasse's *Sarabande* with the *CSM in 1937 and was the angels' choir in the 1938 *Montreal Festivals production of *Parsifal*. After a brief interruption in 1943 the choir resumed activities in Ville St-Laurent when Brother Séverin was appointed to the École supérieure Beaudet. He was there 1944–56. Subsequently he continued his work in St-Césaire, Que, with young singers who also took the name Petits Chanteurs à la Croix de Bois. This choir ceased to exist in 1961. ST

Les Petits Chanteurs de Granby. A training choir of about 100 children's and men's voices. It was founded in 1931 in Granby (60 km east of Montreal) by Brother Julien Hamelin of the Frères du Sacré-Coeur. The ensemble enjoyed the official patronage of the city. It began touring in the early years of its existence, giving concerts throughout Quebec, in the Maritimes, and in western Canada. It also performed in New England and made a European tour in 1969. Its conductors were Brother Hamelin 1931–44, Brother Emmanuel Quintal 1944–57, Brother Auguste Châtelain 1957–9, Brother Cyrille Viens 1959–72, Jules Leblanc 1972–8, and Richard Ducas 1978–9, succeeded by Gérard Lehoux. Its repertoire includes religious works, folksongs, and contemporary music. The choir has participated in liturgical services and other church functions and has performed regularly on radio and TV, accompanied occasionally by an instrumental ensemble. It made tours in the Abitibi (1974 and 1978) and Lac St-Jean (1975) regions and Louisiana (1975) and took part in the Canadian film *Parlez-nous d'amour* by Jean-Claude Lord (1976). In March 1979 it performed with the *Sherbrooke SO in Roger *Matton's *L'Escaouette*.

DISCOGRAPHY

Chants de Noël. RCA LCP-3000
La Chasse aux papillons. RCA PCS-1206
Concert religieux et profane. RCA LCP-1022
Minuit, chrétiens. RCA LCP-1002/ CGP-278
Noëls religieux et populaires. RCA LCPS-1063
Also three 78s of Christmas carols for RCA GP, ST

Les Petits chanteurs du Mont-Royal. Choir and choir school founded in 1956 by Father Léandre Brault of the Congregation of the Holy Cross (b Montreal 22 Jan 1920, d there 12 Nov 1971), who patterned it on the European choir schools. His successor, Charles Dupuis, was the director 1969–78 and Gilbert Patenaude took over in 1978. In addition to professional music training, the young singers receive a complete academic education. The ensemble exists primarily to serve the needs of St Joseph's Oratory on Mount Royal, Montreal; for religious ceremonies at the oratory men's voices are added. The choir made numerous *JMC tours throughout Canada between 1965 and 1970 and performed in New York and in Paris where it took part in a 1967 concert combining choirs from five continents. In 1969 it recorded Harry *Freedman's cantata *The Flame Within* (CBC SM 142 / Decca DL 75244) for Paul Almond's film *Act of the Heart*. It sang in 1975 in Springfield, Mass, in 1976 in Utica, NY, and in 1978 at *Massey Hall in Toronto. It took part in a CBC TV Christmas program with the tenor Luciano Pavarotti in 1978. Its repertoire, although consisting mainly of renaissance pieces and Gregorian chant, also contains a selection of French and Quebec folksongs.

DISCOGRAPHY

Hymnes eucharistiques. Brault cond. Radio-Marie RM 36618
Jeux de la XXIe Olympiade – Montréal 1976, Musique des ceremonies officielles / Games of the XXI Olympiad – Montreal 1976, Music of the Official Ceremonies (arr Vogel). Disciples de Massenet, Orpheus Choir, Vogel cond. 1976. Poly 2424-124
Joie de Noël. Daveluy org, Brault cond. RCA 10 PPKM 1 339
Nous avons vu le Seigneur. 1972. Office catéchistique du Québec 41973
Panorama: Renaissance songs. Sel M 298-104
Les Petits chanteurs du Mont-Royal: mass *O Magnum Mysterium* – motets – renaissance songs. Brault cond. RCA Victor LM 2501
Les Petits chanteurs du Mont-Royal. 1975. PCMR 008
Les Petits chanteurs du Mont-Royal: Bach *Cantata No. 147* ('Jesu bleibet meine Freude') – carols. Daveluy org, Dupuis cond. 1978. Telson AE 1517
Renaissance / Musical Renaissance: Hassler – Lassus – Palestrina – et al. 1968. RCI 237/Madrigal MAS 417/Oryx EXP 36
Viens vers le Père. U. Parr org, Brault cond. Radio-Marie RM 36418

BIBLIOGRAPHY

Perreault, Jean-Guy. 'Une maîtrise: les Petits chanteurs du Mont-Royal,' unpubl L MUS thesis, U of Montreal 1971 (PR)

Les Petits violons. School founded in Montreal in 1965 by Jean *Cousineau to make violin studies more accessible to young children. In the summer of 1965, knowing that there were no institutions specializing in teaching this instrument, Cousineau worked out a method of instruction and submitted it to Sinichi Suzuki, the Japanese teacher. That fall Cousineau started importing from Japan instruments suited to his pupils' size and set up a class at the Institut Cardinal-Léger. The following year he established one at the *École Vincent-d'Indy. In 1968 he began to teach annually some 75 students aged 3 to 20 at his own studio. According to his *Méthode de violon* (in five notebooks, the first of which was published in 1968 by Les Petits violons) the mastery of a piece rests on a study of finger positions and on memory work rather than reading the score. Cousineau saw music as an art of communication, and for him the concert – presented by an orchestra in which each member sometimes is a soloist – is a logical outgrowth of individual instruction and the ideal setting in which to evaluate the technique and communicative skills of each young player.

In this spirit, the Ensemble des petits violons, a selected group of 15 adolescents trained at the school, was formed in January 1974. The members of the school and ensemble have performed in the *Salle Claude-Champagne of the *PDA, Montreal, at the *Institut canadien and the *Grand Théâtre in Quebec City, and elsewhere. After a concert by the ensemble at the *NAC, J.-J. Van Vlasselaer remarked on 'the precision in the attack, the well-chosen tempos, the interpretation bursting with vitality' (Ottawa *Le Droit*, 23 Jul 1977). Les Petits violons have appeared often on CBC and CFTM-TV. They played in the JMC Pavilion at *Expo 67, performed for ISME at the 1968 congress in Dijon, France, and the 1978 congress in London, Ont, and appeared in the 11th annual Quebec City Summer Festival in 1978. The ensemble began receiving grants annually from the *MACQ in 1976.

DISCOGRAPHY

Jean Cousineau dirige les Petits violons: Telemann – Mozart – Beethoven – Britten – Kreisler. 1977. Lon LUL 509
Les Petits violons: Bartók – Fauré – Corelli – Paganini – Mozart. 1976. Lon LUL 501
Les Petits violons: Cousineau *La Légende du feu; Suite québécoise; Mistassini; Reel à bouche* (folklore). A. Millaire narr. 1976. Lon LUL 505

BIBLIOGRAPHY

Pontaut, Alain. 'Il était une fois quinze petits violons,' *L'Actualité*, Dec 1976
Van Vlasselaer, Jean-Jacques. 'Les rêves et les réalisations de Jean Cousineau,' Ottawa *Le Droit*, 23 Jul 1977 AP

PETROWSKA, Christina (m Brégent). Pianist, poet, graphic artist, b Ottawa 30 Dec 1948; B MUS (Juilliard) 1968, M SC (Juilliard) 1969. She studied at the *RCMT 1956–62 with Boris *Berlin and made her debut at 15 at Town Hall, New York, with the Municipal Arts Orchestra. She continued her piano studies at the Juilliard School 1962–9 with Irwin Freundlich, Rosina Lhévinne, and Jeaneane Dowis. She also attended the New York City College and the Chamber Music School of Blue Hill, Me, in 1966, the Aspen Music School in Colorado in 1969, the Internationale Ferienkurse in Darmstadt, Germany, in 1970, and the Paris American Academy (where she was artist-in-residence) in 1968 and 1970. In addition she worked in Berlin with György Ligeti. She received eight grants from the *Canada Council between 1964 and 1975, and one from the French government in 1975. Arthur Balsam and Ventsislav Yankoff were also among her teachers.

Petrowska has given recitals in Canada, the USA, and Europe. In 1971, at the Ukrainian Institute of America in New York, she played works of Gilles *Tremblay, Stockhausen, and others. Two years later, at the *Canadian Cultural Centre in Paris, she performed Serge *Garant's *Pièce No. 2 (Cage d'oiseau)*, Michel *Vinet's *Métamorphose*, and *Geste* by her husband, Michel-Georges *Brégent. She has given several performances of Olivier Messiaen's *Vingt regards sur l'enfant Jésus*.

Although the classics and romantics have a place in her repertoire, Petrowska has been described as 'an extraordinary specialist in unplayable modern music for piano' (Claude *Gingras, Montreal *La Presse*, 10 Nov 1972). She has premiered several works, including Luis de Pablo's *Affettuoso*, Michel Vinet's *Aleph*, Marian Kouzan's *Constructor*, Micheline Coulombe *Saint-Marcoux's *Assemblages*, and Paul Huebner's *Ocotillo*, a work dedicated to her.

Petrowska performed on the ORTF in 1968, at the Kiev Cons in 1971, with the *SMCQ in 1972 and 1976, at the *NAC in 1975, in Carnegie Recital Hall and on various New York radio stations in 1977, as well as on the CBC. In 1978 she won a prize at the first international piano competition of the J.F. Kennedy-Rockefeller Foundation at the Kennedy Center in Washington.

By 1980 Petrowska had made two recordings, one of works by Saint-Marcoux, Vinet, Boulez, Huebner, and Mario Davidovsky (1973, RCI 396), the other containing Brégent's *Geste* (RCI 409, released in 1976). Several exhibitions of her graphic art, including her 'musicographical' poems on Boulez' *Sonate No. 3* (which were approved by the composer), have been held in Canada, the USA, and France. Her poems have been published in several journals and newspapers. Some were collected in *Go Away Sisyphus* (New York 1971). In 1978 she was a New York correspondent for **Musicanada*.

WRITINGS

'Musical chairs and the new revolution,' *CMB*, 7, Autumn–Winter 1973
'The concept of *Geste*,' *CMB*, 9, Autumn–Winter 1974 HP

The Philharmonic Music Club. Vancouver concert organization formed in 1922 on the initiative of Mrs W.E. Green who became its first president. It was established, with the support of music teachers, to promote the work of local performers, especially those just starting professional careers. It presented concerts by musicians new to the city, supported philanthropic performances (eg, at the Veterans' Hospital), and offered scholarships to young performers.

Normally the club sponsored six concerts each year. The first was held in Glencoe Lodge; later ones were presented in other halls including the playhouse adjoining the *Queen Elizabeth Theatre and the Vancouver Art Gallery. Among the artists presented were Milla *Andrew, Marion *Barnum, Donald *Bell, Clifford *Evens, Audrey *Farnell, Audrey *Johannesen, Joseph *Pach, Betty *Phillips, Arthur *Polson, Patricia and Thomas *Rolston, and Malcolm *Tait. The club presented also the Vancouver Junior Symphony, the Salieri Ensemble, and other groups.

When the club disbanded in 1966, its papers were deposited in the Vancouver City Archives.

BNSG

Philippines. In December 1978 some 65,000 Filipinos were living in Canada. Of these, 77 per cent had arrived during the 1970s. Many chose to reside in the Toronto area; smaller groups settled in Calgary, Montreal, Ottawa, Vancouver, and Winnipeg, and others in Newfoundland and New Brunswick, and in Kingston and London, Ont. Most are Visayans (Ilongos and Cebuanos from the Central Philippine Islands), while the rest are Ilocanos and Tagalogs from Luzon. Almost all are Roman Catholics, and the majority speak English.

The Filipino Assn of Canada, with branches in many cities, has sponsored events at which traditional songs and dances have been presented. Occasionally amateur community dance groups have expanded their repertoires to present semi-professional stage performances emulating those of the internationally renowned Bayanihan Dance Troupe of Manila, a group which has helped to codify a pan-Filipino cultural identity both in the Philippines and abroad.

Perhaps the greatest single contribution to Philippine music and dance in Canada has been that of George Aguinaldo of Toronto, who has co-ordinated community activities and who in 1966 founded the Fiesta Filipina Dance Troupe which has achieved a high level of performance and has travelled extensively. Its dances are accompanied by gangsa (gong), nose flute, and bamboo jew's harp for Hill Tribe dances; kulintangan (gong row), gabbang (xylophone), and agung (pair of gongs) for Moslem dances; and a traditional rondalla or small string ensemble for Hispanic dances. The troupe was one of three selected by the Canadian Folk Arts Council to perform at the Montreal Olympics in 1976. In recognition of his efforts, Aguinaldo received a medal from the United Council of Filipino Associations in Canada.

Other performing groups active in Canada in 1980 were the Folklorico Filipino of Canada (Toronto), led by Peter Palomera, and the Alberta-based Kariligan Dance Troupe of the Philippines.

In June 1978 the Filipino Assn of Canada sponsored a Philippine Cultural Week in Toronto, which featured arts, crafts, folkdances, and concerts at *O'Keefe Centre. Pagkakaisa '79, the first Philippine National Day picnic, in Toronto's High Park in June 1979, celebrated the Filipino contribution to Canada and featured an amateur singing contest.

In July 1979 a 50-member company from the Philippines toured North America and appeared in Toronto in a presentation of *Walang Sugat*, a Filipino zarzuela (or operetta) by Severino Reyes y Rivera. The Philippine composer José Macéda visited Montreal in 1973. Among Philippine-born artists who have resided in Canada are the soprano Eleanor *Calbes and the Vancouver violinist Gilopez Cabayo.

When Gilles *Tremblay visited Quezon City to lecture at the U of the Philippines in 1972, three of his compositions – ... *Le Sifflement des vents porteurs de l'amour*, *Champs I*, and *Réseaux* – were performed at the Cultural Centre in Manila. SO

PHILLIPS, Avis (Ruth). Soprano, teacher, b Winnipeg 16 Nov 1900; ATCM 1918, ARCM voice 1925, ARCM piano 1925. After piano studies in Mount Forest, Ont, with Alice Roger Collins, she attended the RCM 1921–5 under Aubyn Raymar (piano) and Edith Grepe (voice). Subsequently she sang in Napier Miles' opera productions under Adrian Boult in Bristol, England, and studied 1927–30 with Edgar Schofield and Alfred Boyce in New York, also singing as a paid soloist in churches there. In 1928 she gave recitals in Montreal and Quebec. She continued to study (eg, in 1934 with Reinhold von Warlich in Salzburg). In 1934 she sang with the *Montreal Orchestra and gave recitals in Winnipeg; Calgary; Kelowna, BC; and Victoria, BC. She was the first Vancouver singer to perform in concert and on radio with the *Vancouver SO and sang on CNRV radio and was a soloist in two *Malkin Bowl concerts. She continued to perform until the 1940s.

Phillips began teaching in 1930 in Vancouver. During several years as a drama and speech instructor at the Vancouver Community College (Langara campus) and more than 30 years as a private teacher of voice and accompaniment, she has taught Milla *Andrew, Norah Halliday, Phylis *Inglis, Betty *Phillips, Scott Robertson, Jacqueline Smith, and Ann Watt. BNSG

PHILLIPS, Betty (Muriel) (m Richardson, m Haworth). Mezzo-soprano, actress, b Vancouver 17 May 1923; BA (British Columbia) 1976. In her mid-teens she sang in school choirs and in the early 1940s she studied voice with in turn Mignon Duke Gidy, Avis *Phillips, and Phylis *Inglis and piano with Phyllis *Schuldt. She appeared at *TUTS for the first time in a 1945 production of *Robin Hood*. She took the second lead in *The Student Prince* (1948) and the leads in *Roberta* and *Countess Maritza* (both 1949) and in *The King and I* (1958 and 1959).

Phillips' radio career began in 1948 with a CBC Vancouver pop-music series and has included regular appearances 1953–65 on the CBC's 'Leicester Square to Broadway'; variety work in 1955 on the BBC; solo, recital, and folksong performances on the CBC; and many British Columbia school broadcasts 1970–2. On CBC TV she sang Rosalinda in *Die Fledermaus* in 1954, co-starred 1956–7 with Ernie Prentice on 'Lolly-too-dum,' and was hostess 1965–7 for 'Bazaar.'

Phillips has performed at the *Vancouver International Festival and with the *Vancouver SO and has appeared in *Vancouver Opera productions (Flora in *La Traviata*, 1961; Nicklausse in *Tales of Hoffmann*, 1961; Zulma in *The Italian Girl in Algiers*, 1965; and the Witch in *Hansel and Gretel*, 1966) and in Vancouver Playhouse productions (*The Boy Friend*, 1963; *Threepenny Opera*, 1966; *Walking Happy*, 1968; and *The Show-Off*, 1969). She has performed in musical comedy throughout Canada – on tour (1967) with *One Hundred Years of Musical Comedy*, at the 1968 *Charlottetown Festival in **Anne of Green Gables* and **Johnny Belinda*, and at Winnipeg's *Rainbow Stage in *Fiddler on the Roof* (1971). She sang locally on CBC radio and in Theatre-in-the-Park productions of *The Sound of Music* (1974) and *Fiddler on the Roof* (1975), while studying drama 1972–7 at the U of British Columbia.

In 1962 Phillips married the actor, writer, and librettist Peter Haworth, who has collaborated with Leonard *Wilson, Healey *Willan, and the English composer Robert Simpson (see Librettos). BNSG

PHILLIPS, Bill or William. Trumpeter, conductor, composer, b Guelph, Ont, 19 Sep 1937; ARCT 1958, BA (Toronto) 1958. His teachers were Joseph Umbrico in Toronto and Maurice André in 1970 at the Paris Cons. He served as principal trumpet 1961–2 with the *Hamilton Philharmonic Orchestra and the National Festival Orchestra, Stratford, 1963–4 with the *Winnipeg SO and the *CBC Winnipeg Orchestra, and 1965–6 with the BBC SO and the English Chamber Orchestra. He was assistant conductor 1964–5 of the Lausanne Chamber Orchestra. In Great Britain 1966–70 Phillips studied composition with Edmund Rubbra and John White and conducting with Alexander Gibson and Neville Marriner, taught at the RCM, and was music director of the London Gabrieli Brass Ensemble, with which he made nine LPs. He was the trumpet soloist on the Beatles' 1967 hit single 'Penny Lane.' He returned to Canada, served 1970–2 as principal trumpet of the Hamilton Philharmonic Orchestra, and became a founding member of *Canadian Brass. In 1972 he founded the Classical Brass and was its music director and first trumpet until 1974. He became the conductor of the *Toronto Jewish Folk Choir in 1978.

Phillips founded the New Chamber Orchestra of Canada in 1973 and continued to serve as its artistic director in 1980. The orchestra has given annual concert series in Toronto with leading Canadian soloists and with guest conductors such as John *Avison, Alexander *Brott, Neville Marriner, and Klaro *Mizerit. Milton *Barnes was named the orchestra's composer-in-residence, and his *Shebetim* (1974) and *Concerto for Violin* (1976, commissioned by the orchestra through a Canada Council grant) have been premiered by the orchestra, as have Phillips' *Changes* (1976) and *City of Youth* (1977).

Among Phillips' other compositions are *Brass Trio* (1969), *Brass Quintet* (1973), and *Peace* (1975) for string orchestra.

PHILLIPS, Stu (Stuart). Balladeer (baritone), songwriter, b St-Eustache, near Montreal, 1933. Known as 'The Travelling Balladeer,' Phillips sang as a youth on amateur radio shows in Montreal (CJAD and CFCF) and Verdun (CKVL) and at 16 worked his way west, appearing at rodeos and carnivals. He wrote and later recorded (for *Rodeo) many ballads based on Canadian history, including 'The Champlain and St Lawrence Line' and 'Dollard des Ormeaux.' During the 1950s he was a radio announcer-singer in Edmonton; Vernon, BC; and Calgary. In 1953 he starred in *Finian's Rainbow* with the Edmonton Light Opera. He began his TV career in the mid-1950s on CHCT-TV, Calgary, and appeared 1960–1 on CBC TV's 'The Outrider.' While host 1961–5 for CBC Winnipeg TV's 'Red River Jamboree,' Phillips performed in the USA and recorded for Columbia.

Moving to Nashville and adopting a more urbane style Phillips made hit recordings of the country songs 'Bracero' (1966), 'The Great El Tigre' (1966), 'Vin Rosé' (1967), and 'Juanita Jones' (1967) and several LPs, all for RCA. Radio, TV, and personal appearances continued throughout the USA and (on occasion, into the mid-1970s) in Canada.

An affiliate of PRO Canada, Phillips had a folio of 13 songs published by BMI Canada in 1963. MM (RGn)

Piano building. In Canada piano building can be traced back to the second decade of the 19th century. It grew into a major industry during the period from 1890 to 1925, employing about 5000 to manufacture products valued annually at several million dollars.

In the early 19th century, as the demand for musical instruments increased with the growing population, it became apparent that the importing of so unwieldy an instrument as the piano in any numbers from Europe was not feasible in terms of cost and the risk of damage during long transport in damp cargo holds. Moreover, imported pianos, made primarily in Germany and Great Britain, were found to react unfavourably to the Canadian climate.

The first builders in Canada – skilled British or German craftsmen – worked in small workshops with few assistants, producing probably no more than one or two pianos per month. Most of their time must have been spent tuning and repairing. One of the earliest builders was Frederick Hund, active in Quebec City in 1816 and later in partnership with Gottlieb Seebold. The firm of G.W. Mead (Mead, Mott & Co) was active in Montreal from about 1827 to 1853. John Morgan Thomas was established in Montreal by 1832 and moved to Toronto in 1839 but it is not known when he began to build pianos.

Among builders and early companies known to have existed by the 1840s were in Montreal, William Dennis (fl 1834–53), Isaac Reinhardt (b 1808, d 1846), Thomas D. *Hood (fl 1848–77), and John Stephenson (fl 1848); in Quebec City, Milligan (fl 1844), Richard Owen (fl ca 1840), and J.M. Pfeiffer

A combination piano-radio-gramophone made by the Craig Piano Co, Montreal, 1929

(fl 1849); in Saint John, NB, A. Laurilliard (ca 1850); in Halifax, B. Slade (fl 1832), and H. & J. Philips (fl 1845–59); in Toronto, John and James Mead (fl 1840), the O'Neill Brothers (fl 1844), Thomas & Smith (1840), and Reynolds & Duffett (opened 1849). (Dates are taken from the documentation for surviving instruments – eg, a Laurilliard piano in the New Brunswick Museum, Saint John; one from Mead, Mott & Co in the Château de Ramezay, Montreal; and a Richard Owen piano in the Royal Ontario Museum, Toronto – or from contemporary advertisements or city directories.)

The 1851 census lists 4 individual piano builders or companies in Upper Canada (all in Toronto) and 13 in Lower Canada (10 in Montreal, 3 in Quebec City). By the year of Confederation (1867) larger piano manufacturing firms were being established. The company of John C. Fox (formerly of New York, and located 1862–8 in Kingston) produced about 500 pianos a year (see Weber Piano Co). In Montreal Mead Bros & Co had evolved from Mead, Mott & Co, and the Craig Piano Co was established in 1856. Theodore *Heintzman, trained in Berlin and New York, began building pianos in Toronto in 1860 and formed a company in 1866. Though not active as manufacturers until ca 1890, A. & S. *Nordheimer in 1842 began a business as agents for pianos and dealers in musical merchandise in Kingston, and in 1844 moved to Toronto.

In the favourable conditions following Confederation the new industry prospered. The population of eastern Canada was growing rapidly in size and wealth, and the completion of the Canadian Pacific Railroad in 1885 made possible the shipment of pianos to the newly settled western provinces. With a few exceptions (*Bagnall, later Goodwin, in Victoria; Amherst Piano Co in Amherst, NS; Fraser & Sons in Halifax; Edmund E. Kennay in Saint John, NB), the piano manufacturers centred in southern Ontario and the Montreal region. The most important names at the turn of the century were, in Toronto, Heintzman, Gerhard *Heintzman, *Mason & Risch, *Mendelssohn, *Newcombe, Nordheimer, and *Gourlay, Winter & Leaming; in Guelph, *Bell; in Bowmanville, *Dominion; in London, Ont, *Evans; in Woodstock, *Karn; in Listowel, Morris, Feild, Rogers; in Oshawa and Toronto, R.S. *Williams; in Kingston, Wormwith; in Ottawa, Martin-*Orme; in Montreal, Craig, Foisy, and *Pratte; in Ste-Thérèse, *Willis, *Lesage, and Sénécal et Quidoz. Retail branches or warehouses were sufficient for the young cities of Winnipeg, Regina, Saskatoon, Calgary, Edmonton, and Vancouver – none of which appear to have established piano manufacturing.

As a further incentive for Canadian manufacturers, the protective tariff of 1879 discouraged competition from US manufacturers; however, even stiffer tariffs in the USA (45 per cent in 1903) stifled Canadian exports to that country. Export to other continents also developed slowly. In 1893 only 135 pianos left Canada – mostly for Great Britain, Australia, and the USA, whereas Canada imported nearly four times that number from the USA alone. By 1903, however, the balance had swung, with 509 exports and only 367 imports, and during the early years of the 20th century trade experts observed that the quality of most Canadian pianos was so high that Canadians tended to import the pianos of only the most renowned makers such as Steinway in New York, and the cost of these imports limited the demand.

The industry thrived throughout the early 20th century (with a decrease during World War I), and advertising was designed to stir interest in the piano among all the members of the average family. Whereas in the 19th century the piano in Canada had been associated largely with genteel young ladies, in the 20th, slogans like 'a piano for every parlor,' and the 'Music in the Home' campaign of the *Canadian Bureau for the Advancement of Music gradually made a piano seem an integral part of life. The growing number of amateur musicians and the increasing appeal of pop music provided a fertile ground for the introduction of the *player piano.

Over 100 piano manufacturing companies, individual builders, and makers of accessory parts flourished at some point during the peak era of the industry, ca 1890 to 1925. Many of these (Bell, Dominion, Karn) also built organs. During the first 12 years of the 20th century the number of pianos manufactured in Canada more than doubled, increasing from about 12,000 in 1900 to about 30,000 by 1912. In 1900 most accessory parts (hammers, actions, strings, keys, etc) were imported, but eventually these, too, came to be made by Canadian manufacturers. Among the best known were Otto *Higel Co, Ltd (1896–1944, manufacturers of piano actions and piano rolls), A.A. Barthelmes (1889–1911, piano actions), D.M. Best & Co (founded 1900, piano hammers and strings), W. Bohne & Co (hammers and strings), J.M. Loose & Co (keys and keyboards), and Wagner, Zeidler & Co (keyboards), all of Toronto, and Sterling Action & Keys Co, Brantford. Best survived to become a subsidiary of Heintzman in 1973. In 1899 piano manufacturers united to form the *Canadian Piano and Organ Manufacturers' Assn, which existed until 1975, when it became the keyboard committee of the Music Industries Assn of Canada (MIAC). The unofficial magazine of the trade was the **Canadian Music Trades Journal* (1900–33).

World War I caused a setback for the piano manufacturing industry. Woods, metals, and fuel were withheld from 'luxury industries,' and experienced craftsmen joined the armed forces. Faced with a shortage of experienced men, many piano firms had to hire women trainees (the *Sherlock-Manning company of London, Ont, later of Clinton, Ont, may have been the first in Canada to pay its female employees the same wages as male.) With the closing of the German export trade to customers in Great Britain and the British Empire (representing 60,000 German pianos a year), a potentially large market was opened for the Canadian piano. Most Canadian manufacturers, however, did not take full advantage of the situation, partly because of prohibitive freight rates, and partly because an entirely new system was needed to construct an instrument practical for export; the manufacturers were unwilling to undertake a two-standard system.

In the 1920s several factors conspired to cause a gradual decline of the piano industry. The player piano craze began to wane. Radio and sound films appeared. Fewer new houses had the space for a piano. Economic conditions were unstable, and family savings were spent on work-saving appliances – refrigerators, washing machines, vacuum cleaners, and automobiles – rather than on luxuries like the piano. An unofficial study undertaken in the late 1920s found that four in five Canadian homes had a phonograph and/or radio, but only one in five had a piano. As a result of the declining demand several companies amalgamated or were taken over by others (eg, Gerhard Heintzman in 1927 and Nordheimer in 1928 by Heintzman; Craig in 1930 by Lesage; and *Doherty in 1920 and Gourlay, Winter & Leeming in 1924 by Sherlock-Manning). Others just went out of business (eg, *Morris in 1923, Evans Bros ca 1933). Some piano companies introduced new smaller models, even vying with one another to produce the smallest, in an effort to appeal to apartment dwellers and owners of small homes. (The Weber Co in 1921 created a five-octave, three-foot grand piano, custom-designed for a Winnipeg family.)

Only the strongest companies survived the Depression. Among those which ceased to exist were Bell, Craig, Dominion, Weber, and Williams. In 1940 only Lesage, Quidoz, and Willis & Co were still active in Quebec. (Lesage remained so in 1980; Willis went bankrupt in 1979.) In Ontario the 1940 survivors were Sherlock-Manning Pianos Ltd, and Heintzman Co Ltd (which merged under the Heintzman name in 1978), and Mason & Risch (still operating in Canada, but taken over by a US firm in 1948). In New Westminster, BC, a firm known as the Edmund Piano Co was active until the 1950s.

Statistics after 1935 have indicated a small but steady overall increase in the demand for and production of pianos. The figures (relative to population growth) are small compared with those of the earlier, peak years of the industry, however. Radio, the phonograph, and, subsequently, TV and more sophisticated home sound systems have displaced the piano as the focus of home entertainment. Other musical instruments, notably the guitar and the 'multi-gadgeted' electronic organ have become more popular with people whose interest in playing is purely recreational. Whereas the piano was, at one time, the foundation of nearly every child's musical education, trends in music education which began around the 1940s have caused students to choose a wider variety of instruments, especially the accordion, band instruments, and, more recently, string instruments. Even so, it has been estimated that in the late 1970s nearly half of all music students played the piano.

By the 1940s and 1950s foreign manufacturers began moving into the Canadian market; Mason & Risch was bought by a large US corporation. By the 1960s the Japanese pianos – notably Yamaha – were being strongly merchandised. Generally lower-priced and widely available, they competed so briskly with pianos of Canadian manufacture that in many instances they were being ordered in quantity by schools and conservatories which formerly had used Canadian instruments.

In 1980 pianos were manufactured by two Canadian-owned companies: Heintzman Ltd (Hanover, Ont), which in addition to its own pianos produced the Sherlock-Manning line, and Lesage Pianos Ltd. The ownership of each had been retained by the original family since its founding. However in January 1981 ownership of

Heintzman Ltd passed from the Heintzman family to Sklar Manufacturing Co.

In so far as their status can be determined, distributors and retailers have been omitted from the ensuing list of piano builders and assembly plants. Many of the pre-1860 names represent individual craftsmen rather than manufacturers. Minor name changes (eg, from 'piano and organ co' to 'organ and piano co') have not been indicated. A date generally refers to the years during which pianos were built, not to a company's entire lifespan.

Amherst Pianos, Amherst, NS; fl 1908–23. Later became Cumberland Piano Co
George Anderson, Saint John, NB; fl 1855–71
John *Bagnall, Victoria, BC; ca 1871–85. Taken over by Charles Goodwin & Co
Beethoven. See R.S. Williams. See also Georges Ducharme.
*Bell Piano and Organ Co, Guelph, Ont. Pianos built 1888–1934. Absorbed Mendelssohn Piano Co in 1919. Taken over by Lesage Pianos in 1934 and continued as a brand name
Belmont. See Lesage.
Berlin Piano & Organ Co, Berlin (Kitchener), Ont; fl 1905
Bernhardt's Furniture, Windsor, Ont; fl 1957. Produced Miessner electronic pianos
Robert Blouin, Sherbrooke, Que; fl 1966
Blundall Piano Co, Toronto; 1900–after 1912
Bowles, Quebec City; mid-19th century
Thomas Boyd, Uxbridge, Ont
Brantford Piano Co. See Morris Pianos.
Brockley and Misener, Halifax; 1857–63. T. & A.W. Brockley 1863–97
Brown, Montreal; fl 1874
George Brown, John Munro and Co. Moved from Boston to Montreal ca 1860
Canada Organ and Piano Co. See R.S. Williams.
Canadian Organ and Piano Co; fl 1874–5
Canadian Piano Co. See Thomas F.G. Foisy.
Cecilian Piano Co, Toronto; before 1915–22. Player pianos only. Absorbed by Stanley
Louis Charbonneau, Montreal; fl 1889
V.W. Claude & Co, Montreal; fl 1898
F.C. Cline, Kingston, Ont; 1868
Clinton. See Doherty Pianos.
Colonial Piano Co, Ste-Thérèse, Que; before 1915–27. Made Saint-Saens piano
Craig Piano Co, Montreal; 1856–1930. Preceded by Labelle & Craig. Absorbed by Lesage in 1930
E. Cross & Co, Toronto; fl 1898
Crossin (& Martens) Piano Mfr Co, Toronto; 1883–after 1908
Cumberland Piano Co, Amherst, NS, and Toronto. Formerly Amherst Pianos
David & Michaud, Montreal; 1917–23. See also Michaud.
William Dennis, Montreal; fl 1834–53
*Doherty Pianos, Clinton, Ont; 1907–20. Absorbed by Sherlock-Manning in 1920 and continued as a brand name to early 1930s. Introduced brand name Clinton in 1913
Dominion. See Rainer & Co.
*Dominion Organ and Piano Co, Bowmanville, Ont. Pianos built 1879–ca 1935
Georges Ducharme, Montreal; fl 1891–8. Made Beethoven Pianos
Noah Durant, Vankleek Hill, Ont; fl 1908
Edmund Piano Co, New Westminster, BC; ca 1924–after 1952
Ennis (& Ennis) Co, Hamilton, Ont; 1863–1911. Later a brand name of R.S. Williams
*Evans Bros Piano & Manufacturing Co; Ingersoll, Ont, ca 1871–90, then at London, Ont, until ca 1933
Everson. See R.S. Williams.
Featherston Piano Co, Montreal; 1893–9
Thomas F.G. Foisy (Canadian Piano Co), Ste-Thérèse-de-Blainville, Que, 1888–91, Montreal 1891–1914. Absorbed by C.W. Lindsay 1914
Foster-Armstrong Co; Toronto head office fl 1910; Kitchener, Ont, before 1915–24. Absorbed by Sherlock-Manning. Made Haines Bros pianos
J.C. Fox, Kingston, Ont; 1862–8. (See *EMC* entry for Weber Piano Co.)
W. Fraser and Sons, Halifax; ca 1856–ca 1890. Absorbed H. & J. Philips
Charles Goodwin & Co, Victoria, BC; 1885–ca 1891. Continuation of John Bagnall
*Gourlay, Winter & Leeming, Toronto. Pianos built 1904–24. Took over R. McMullen. Absorbed by Sherlock-Manning in 1924
Grinnell Bros, Windsor, Ont; fl 1928
Haines Bros. See Foster-Armstrong Co.
Haydn Piano Manufacturing Co, Montreal; fl 1898
*Heintzman, Toronto. Began in 1860 as private builder; continued 1866–1977 as a company in Toronto and then at a plant built in 1962 at Hanover, Ont. Absorbed Gerhard Heintzman and Nordheimer
Gerhard *Heintzman, Toronto; 1877–1927. Absorbed by Heintzman
Henry Herbert. See Mason & Risch.
J.W. *Herbert & Co, Montreal; fl 1837
Henry & Francis Hoerr, Toronto; fl 1890
Thomas D. *Hood, Montreal; fl 1848–77
Frederick Hund, Quebec City; fl 1816
Hund & Seebold, Quebec City; until 1824. See also Seebold, Manby & Co.
Henry G. Hunt, New Brunswick; fl 1850s
Joseph T. Hunt, Saint John, NB; fl 1845–55
Imperial Piano Co, Toronto; fl 1901
International Piano Co, Toronto; fl 1928
Jackson & Co, Peterborough, Ont; fl 1889
*Karn Piano Co, Woodstock, Ont. Piano building began in the late 1880s. Karn Morris Piano & Organ Co ca 1909–20. Absorbed by Sherlock-Manning. Continued as a brand name until 1957
Kennay & Scribner, Saint John, NB; fl 1851; later continued as Edmund E. Kennay (fl 1871)
Kilgour Piano & Organ Co, Hamilton, Ont; fl 1888–99
Knott & Sons, Hamilton, Ont; 1871–ca 1914
Kreisler. See Mason & Risch.
Krydner. See R.S. Williams.
Labelle & Craig, Montreal; 1854–6. Continued as Craig
J.-Donat Langelier (became Langelier-Valiquette in 1963). Began ca 1915 at Pointe-aux-Trembles, Que. Continued ca 1930 in Montreal. Not a manufacturer. See Pratte.
Lansdowne Piano Co, Toronto; ca 1885–90. (See *EMC* entries for Gerhard Heintzman; Nordheimer.)
A. Laurilliard, Saint John, NB; fl ca 1850
Layton Bros, Montreal. (See *EMC* entry for Blind.)
*Lesage Pianos / Les Pianos Lesage, Ste-Thérèse-de-Blainville, Que; founded 1891. Absorbed Craig Piano Co, Bell Piano and Organ Co, and Weber Piano Co. Brand names include Belmont and Schumann
P.W. Leverman & Co; Halifax 1889–97
C.W. *Lindsay & Co, Montreal; ca 1880–ca 1950. Dealer only, but for some years sold Craig, Lesage, and other pianos under the Lindsay name
Liszt Piano Co; fl 1908
Lonsdale Piano Co, Toronto; before 1915–22
R. McMullen & Co, Kingston, Ont. Absorbed by Gourlay, Winter & Leeming
W.H. Manby, Montreal; fl 1857–61. Preceded by Seebold & Manby
Martin-Orme Co, Ottawa; 1902–ca 1924. (See *EMC* entry for Orme & Sons.)
*Mason & Risch, Toronto. Began building pianos in 1877. Until 1878 Mason, Risch & Newcombe. Brand names included Kreisler and Henry Herbert
*Mead, Montreal; 1827–ca 1853. (Mead, Mott & Co, Mead Brothers & Co)
J. & J. *Mead, Toronto; 1840–ca 1844
*Mendelssohn Piano Co, Toronto; ca 1886–1919. Absorbed by Bell Piano and Organ Co. Continued as a brand name by Bell and 1934–72 by Lesage Pianos
Oswald *Michaud, Montreal. Private workshop, 1937–early 1950s. See also David & Michaud.
Milligan, Francis, Quebec City; fl 1854–64
Milligan, George, Quebec City; fl 1844
Moir, George and William, Halifax; fl 1852
*Morris Pianos, Listowel, Ont; established 1892 as Morris, Feild, Rogers Co, successors to Brantford Piano Co. Continued as Karn Morris Piano Co ca 1909–20, and as Morris Pianos 1920–ca 1924
Mozart Piano Co, Toronto; before 1912–20. Absorbed by National Piano Co ca 1918, but built pianos to 1920
National Piano Co, Toronto; before 1915–29. Absorbed Mozart ca 1918
*Newcombe Piano Co, Toronto; 1878–1926. Continued as brand name by Willis ca 1934–79
A. & S. *Nordheimer Piano & Music Co, Toronto. Pianos built ca 1890–1927. Absorbed by Heintzman and continued as a brand name until late 1960s
O'Neill Brothers, Toronto; fl 1844
Ontario Piano Co, Toronto; fl 1928
J.L. *Orme & Sons, Ottawa. See Martin-Orme.
Oshawa Piano & Cabinet Co, Oshawa, Ont
Richard S. Owen & Son, Quebec City; fl ca 1840
Palmer Piano Co, Uxbridge, Ont; fl 1908
Percival Piano Co, Ottawa; fl 1918
J.M. Pfeiffer, Quebec City; fl 1849
H. & J. Philips. Halifax; 1845–59. Taken over by W. Fraser and Sons
Plaola, Oshawa. Player pianos only
*Pratte Piano Co (La Compagnie de pianos Pratte), Montreal; fl 1889–1926, then linked to J.-Donat Langelier
Prince Piano Co, Toronto; fl 1895–1914
*Quidoz Piano. See Sénécal et Quidoz
Rainer & Co, fl 1866, Whitby, Ont; fl 1872, Guelph, Ont; used Dominion as a brand name
Rappe, Weber & Co, Kingston, Ont; fl 1868–9
Isaac Reinhardt, Montreal; discontinued in 1846
J. Reyner, Kingston, Ont; fl 1870
Reynolds & Duffett, Toronto; fl 1849
Saint-Saens. See Colonial Piano Co.
Schubert. See R.S. Williams.
Schumann. See Lesage.
Schumann Piano Co, Toronto
Seebold, Manby & Co, Montreal; fl 1856. See also Hund & Seebold.
Sénécal et Quidoz, Ste-Thérèse-de-Blainville, Que; ca 1897–1938. Continued as Quidoz Piano 1938–66
*Sherlock-Manning Pianos. Pianos built at London, Ont, 1910–30; at Clinton, Ont, 1930–78. Merged with Heintzman in 1978. Absorbed Doherty Pianos, Foster-Armstrong Co, Gourlay, Winter & Leeming, and Karn Piano Co. Doherty was used as a brand name until early 1930s.
Slade, B., Halifax; fl 1832
Small & McArthur, Uxbridge, Ont; fl 1898
Smith. See John Morgan Thomas.
William Snyder, Berlin (Kitchener), Ont
Standard Piano Co, Toronto; fl 1898
Stanley Piano Co, Toronto; 1896–1924. Absorbed Cecilian in 1922
John Stephenson, Montreal; fl 1848
Stevenson & Co, Kingston, Ont; ca 1887–91. See also Weber and Wormwith.

Sumner & Brebner, Ingersoll, Ont; fl 1906–11
C.L. *Thomas & Co, Hamilton, Ont (Western Pianoforte Manufactory of Canada); ca 1856–ca 1893
John Morgan *Thomas (Thomas & Smith), Toronto; fl 1840
*Uxbridge Piano Co, Uxbridge, Ont, ca 1899; also a second company of the same name fl 1914–15
S.R. *Warren, Montreal; built pianos ca 1845
*Weber Piano Co, Kingston, Ont; 1871–ca 1887. Continued as Stevenson & Co until 1891, as Wormwith until 1918, and as Weber Piano Co 1919–39. Absorbed by Lesage Pianos in 1939
G.M. Weber, Kingston, Ont; ca 1881–95
Werlich Brothers, Preston (Cambridge), Ont; fl 1908. Player pianos only
Western Pianoforte Manufactory of Canada. See C.L. Thomas & Co.
R.S. *Williams, Toronto; factory built in Oshawa in 1889 (Canada Organ and Piano Co 1873–1902). Pianos built from 1873 until early 1930s. Brand names included Beethoven, Canada, Ennis, Everson, Krydner, Schubert.
Williams & Leverman, Halifax; 1871–89
*Willis & Co, Montreal; factory Ste-Thérèse-de-Blainville; ca 1900–79
Wormwith, Kingston, Ont; 1891–1918. Continuation of Weber Piano Co and Stevenson & Co, using Weber as a brand name. Renamed Weber Piano Co in 1919
Wright Piano Co, Strathroy, Ont; 1908–24 (1908 is the date of the company's charter)

BIBLIOGRAPHY

'The piano and organ industry,' *Industrial Canada*, Feb 1904
Nixon, D.C. 'Making Canadian pianos,' *Canadian Courier*, 12 Oct 1912
Blyth, G. Gerald. 'Pianos in the making,' *Canadian Forestry Magazine*, vol 16, Oct 1920
Massicotte, E.-Z. 'Quelques anciens pianos,' *BRH*, vol 37, Oct 1931
Whitmore, Joseph A. 'The Canadian piano industry,' *Canadian Music Teacher*, vol 4, Aug 1940
McCook, James. 'Pioneers preferred pianos,' *The Beaver*, Winter 1954
MacLaren, George. 'Pianoforte companies in Nova Scotia,' *Antique Furniture by Nova Scotia Craftsmen* (Toronto 1961, 1975)
Allen, Robert Thomas. 'A piano is polite,' *The Canadian Magazine*, 14 Oct 1972
Kallmann, Helmut, and Beckwith, John. 'Musical instruments, making of,' *Encyclopedia Canadiana*
Canadian Music Trades Journal, monthly (Toronto 1900–33)
Music Market Canada, six issues a year (Toronto 1977–)

FH (HK)

Piano playing and teaching

1 Instruments in early Canada
2 Teaching
3 Public performance
4 Place occupied by the piano in the 1970s
5 The traditional perspective
6 Teaching publications

See also Canadian Bureau for the Advancement of Music; Jazz; Piano teams; Prodigies; Ragtime.

1 INSTRUMENTS IN EARLY CANADA. In Canada, as in Europe, there was a period when both harpsichords and pianos were played. According to Frédéric *Glackemeyer, there was only one piano in Quebec City in 1783. He and a competitor, Francis *Vogeler, did much to change this situation. In 1784 Glackemeyer advertised 'FOR SALE / FIVE elegant PIANOFORTES! arrived in the latest ships ... for a very reasonable price.' He also advertised piano and harpsichord strings and the tuning and repair of these instruments. In 1791, the year of Mozart's death, the expenses of a local musical society included '£3 10s 6d for the use of a Piano Forte.' (Indeed, a Mozart piano concerto

A square grand piano in a home on the prairies, ca 1889

was performed 6 Dec 1792 at a concert in Quebec City.) Advertisements in newspapers indicate that the instrument was well established by the mid-19th century in all the larger centres.

Difficulties encountered in taking pianos to the Prairies were considerable but not insurmountable, at least for a privileged minority. In 1830 Governor Sir George Simpson, taking his bride to Fort Garry (Winnipeg), arranged for the forwarding of her piano. Pianos could be sent by sea to the west coast. When William John Macdonald landed at Victoria for the Hudson's Bay Company in 1850, he was invited to the Langford residence, where he found the eldest daughter 'an excellent pianist.'

Until the third decade of the 19th century all pianos were imported. However, when Canadian firms entered the field the growth of the industry was rapid. (See Piano building.)

2 TEACHING. Most of the early teaching was done privately, though some of the teachers advertised their studios as 'academies of music.' Inevitably the first teachers were Europeans who had emigrated; later their numbers included Canadians who had gone abroad for advanced studies. Most were active in various other branches of the profession in addition to teaching. The German-born T.F. *Molt (1795–1856) began to teach in Quebec City in 1823, then returned to Europe for further study. While there he met Czerny and Moscheles, as well as Beethoven. Molt wrote the first piano-instruction book published in Canada (*Elementary Treatise on Music / Traité élémentaire de musique*, Quebec 1828) and several published in the USA. In *L'Album musical* (1882) Gustave *Smith recalls some of the music teachers active in the province of Quebec in 1856. Jean-Chrysostome *Brauneis II, the first of a long line of Canadian musicians who completed their studies abroad, introduced the sonatinas of Clementi and the studies of Cramer and Czerny. Paul *Letondal, a blind musician, as a youth was a pupil of Kalkbrenner (or possibly of one of his disciples; Letondal was born in 1831, and Kalkbrenner died in 1849). Charles Wugk *Sabatier emigrated from France and was the first virtuoso pianist to live in Quebec City and Montreal. In Toronto the Scottish organist and pianist James Paton *Clarke was an advocate of the Johann Bernhard Logier system which entailed the use of a hand-strengthening device called the Chiroplast and advocated group instruction. The work of these teachers and their contemporaries reflected their particular backgrounds.

After the middle of the century the piano became the accepted household instrument in middle-class families, and no young lady was spared the lessons necessary to acquiring a basic skill in the rendition of dance and parlour pieces and song accompaniments. Lady Dufferin's account of facilities in one Canadian convent in the 1870s reads like a foretaste of music-school conditions in the age of the 'practice module' a century or so later: 'In one hall there are 12 glass boxes, each containing a piano so that pupils can practise simultaneously; whilst in another glass house sits the mistress, overlooking, but, happily for her, not overhearing' (*My Canadian Journal 1872–1878*, Toronto 1969, p 24). Piano teaching remained largely the domain of the private teacher, except in Toronto and the province of Quebec, although after World War II many teachers joined the staffs of conservatories and universities in all parts of the country.

Noted teachers across Canada have included Frank Harrison in Fredericton; Harry *Dean in Halifax, NS; Jean *Dansereau, Paul *de Marky, Auguste *Descarries, Stanley *Gardner, Yvonne *Hubert, Lubka *Kolessa, Alfred *Laliberté, Arthur *Letondal, Paul *Loyonnet, Germaine *Malépart, Dorothy *Morton, Léo-Pol *Morin, and Émiliano *Renaud in Montreal; Guy *Bourassa, Constantin Klimoff, Hélène *Landry, and Berthe *Roy in Quebec City; Ethel Barnes, Annie *Jenkins, Harry *Puddicombe, and Ernest *Whyte in Ottawa; J.E.P. *Aldous in Hamilton, Ont; G.D. *Atkinson, Mona *Bates, Boris *Berlin, Margaret Miller *Brown, Hayunga *Carman, Rachel *Cavalho, H.M. *Field, Edward *Fisher, W.O. *Forsyth, Reginald *Godden, Alberto *Guerrero, Lubka Kolessa, Vigo *Kihl, Waugh *Lauder, Ernest *Seitz, Pierre *Souvairan, Richard *Tattersall, and Frank *Welsman in Toronto; Jean *Broadfoot, Alma *Brock-Smith, Eva *Clare, Gwendda Owen *Davies, S.C. *Eckhardt-Gramatté, Leonard *Heaton, Phyllis *Holtby, Leonard *Isaacs, Roline Mackidd, John *Melnyk, and Grace Rich in Winnipeg; Peggy Sharpe and Lorne *Watson in Brandon, Man; Lyell *Gustin in Saskatoon; Jenny *Lerouge Le Saunier, Alexandra (Sandra) *Munn, and Edward *Lincoln in Edmonton; Jessie Ackland, John Duval, Leonard *Leacock, Gladys *Egbert (b McElvie, the first Canadian to go to London on an RSM scholarship), and Boris *Roubakine in Calgary; Gertrude *Huntley Green, Stanley Shale, Winifred Scott Wood, and Robin *Wood in Victoria, BC; and Barbara *Custance, Mrs Walter *Coulthard, Kum-Sing Lee, Glenn Nelson, Robert *Silverman, Ira *Swartz, and J.D.A. *Tripp in Vancouver. This is to name only a few of the many who have given of themselves, to their pupils and to the musical life of their communities, in a way which never will be surpassed, perhaps never equalled. During World War II, Montreal was fortunate in having Isidor Philipp as a teacher at the *CMM, and other important European teachers (eg, Arthur Friedheim, E. Robert Schmitz) visited Canada at other times.

3 PUBLIC PERFORMANCE. Only in the second half of the 19th century were pianists heard in solo recital (see Concerts: 2 / 1800 to 1899), and the prior tradition of varied programs (songs, operatic arias, instrumental solos, etc) lingered long. Pianists were involved in these as soloists, in chamber music, and as accompanists, and often were required to play versions of the accompaniments of concertos. In centres without orchestras the piano's function as a surrogate orchestra, not only in rehearsal situations but also in public performances, was a commonplace of 19th-century music-making. In Toronto in 1853 the first act of *Lucrezia Borgia* was given with piano accompaniment. In 1895 in Montreal Saint-Saëns' *Danse macabre* was performed in an arrangement for two pianos, eight hands. Wherever an orchestra was stipulat-

From a Nordheimer advertisement, 1904

ed, pianos could appear instead, and continued to do so well into the 20th century.

Although only a few students could go abroad to study, many in or near the larger cities could hear visiting pianists. In the 19th century von Bülow, Thalberg, and Gottschalk were among the visitors. Later d'Albert, Friedheim, Gabrilovitch, Godowsky, Hofmann, Paderewski, de Pachmann, Pugno, Rosenthal, Rubinstein, and Sauer were among the many virtuosi who came. Composer-pianists such as Dohnányi, Grainger, MacDowell, Medtner, Prokofiev, Rachmaninoff, and Ravel were heard playing their own works. In 1913 Harold Craxton, England's finest accompanist and later the teacher of many Canadians in London, toured with Clara Butt. (In London he was also an accompanist of *Albani.) At a time when many Canadian cities still were isolated these visits made teachers and students aware of international standards. Most of these pianists and many others are represented in the remarkable collection of piano recordings owned by Ralph *Gustafson, the Canadian poet.

In the late 19th century and in the 20th, Canada was to produce a number of distinguished players of its own, many of course 'finished' abroad. Victoria *Cartier, Alfred Laliberté, Calixa *Lavallée, Salomon *Mazurette, Émiliano Renaud, and Moïse *Saucier were among the outstanding players in the late years of the 19th century, and the first prodigies – Berthe *Roy and Ellen *Ballon – were not far in the future. In 1924 in Toronto A.S. *Vogt was able to write (*Musical Life and Arts*, 1 Dec 1924): 'We have attracted to this country teachers of piano and violin playing who compare favorably with the foremost instructors of the most populous centres of the older parts of the world. In my opinion the actual standard of piano playing in some parts of Canada is much higher than that of England, and it is a significant thing that in recent years the piano and violin have almost completely monopolized the attention of young Canadian students.' (He did appear to take for granted, however, that the teachers all had come from abroad; an assumption impressively but not completely borne out by the record, as the *EMC* biographies of such early Canadian-born teachers as Harry Marshall Field, W.O. Forsyth, Stanley Gardner, Waugh Lauder, Arthur Letondal, Angelo *Read, J.D.A. Tripp, and, indeed, A.S. Vogt himself demonstrate.)

In the second half of the 20th century Glenn *Gould and Oscar *Peterson (a pupil of Paul de Marky) attained the highest levels of world fame as virtuosi and as musicians of striking individuality. Numerous others, however, at various times in the late-19th and 20th centuries, also achieved celebrity. Among them, the following have entries in *EMC*: William Aide, Henri Brassard, Agnes Butcher, Jane Coop, Barbara Custance, Jean Dansereau, Raymond Dudley, Janina Fialkowska, Harry M. Field, Monica Gaylord, Reginald Godden, Paul Helmer, Sheila Henig, Gertrude Huntley Green, Margaret Ann Ireland, Diedre Irons, Marek Jablonski, Muriel Kerr, Ida Krehm, Antonín Kubálek, Anton Kuerti, André Laplante, Waugh Lauder, Djane Lavoie-Herz, Louis Lortie, André Mathieu, Mari-Elizabeth Morgen, Arthur Ozolins, Patricia Parr, Louis-Philippe Pelletier, Christina Petrowska, Ross Pratt, Claude Savard, Ernest Seitz, Jean-Paul Sevilla, Robert Silverman, Elyakim Taussig, Freda Trepel, Malcolm Troup, and Ronald Turini. (See also Piano teams; Prodigies.)

Also notable in some instances as concert pianists but particularly active as chamber musicians, sonata or Lieder partners, or coach-accompanists have been Frances Marr *Adaskin, John *Avison, Leo *Barkin, Dale *Bartlett, Mario *Bernardi (prior to his rise as a conductor), Carol Birtch, Victor *Bouchard, Guy Bourassa, Ada *Bronstein, George *Brough, John *Coveart, Chester *Duncan, Bryan *Gooch, Alberto Guerrero, Stuart *Hamilton, Paul Helmer, Anna *Moncrieff Hovey, Weldon *Kilburn, Gwendolyn Williams *Koldofsky, Greta *Kraus, Gordon *Kushner, Janine Lachance, Émery Lavigne, Roline Mackidd, Diane Mauger, Renée *Morisset, John *Newmark, Arlene Nimmons (see *Duo Pach), Marie-Thérèse *Paquin, Marjorie A. *Payne, Colombe *Pelletier, Charles *Reiner, Jacqueline *Richard, Gloria Saarinen, Claude Savard, Dorothy *Swetnam Hare, Linda Lee *Thomas, Edmond *Trudel, Bruce Ubukata, and a number of others.

4 PLACE OCCUPIED BY THE PIANO IN THE 1970S. In Canada, as elsewhere in the world, by the 1970s the piano recital no longer dominated the musical scene. After World War II other instruments – violin, cello, flute, clarinet, guitar – and instrumental groups such as the traditional chamber music combinations and early-music consorts took an increasing share of public attention. The opportunities for solo performance, never numerous for the pianist resident in Canada, became proportionally fewer. Much greater encouragement in the way of grants and scholarships was given than formerly, but the problem of how the young pianist would earn a living had become an acute one, not peculiar to Canada.

The teaching of advanced students took place principally in the universities. Those studying piano did so with one or more of a variety of motives. Some saw their studies as part of a broad education. Others wished to become general practitioners in music, for which competence at the piano was useful. Some expected to teach and hoped to play professionally as much as possible. A few continued to aspire to careers as solo performers. In Quebec the conservatoires strongly emphasized performance.

Some Canadian institutions (*RCMT, *WBM, *Western Ontario Cons) and one English one (*Trinity College) continued to conduct local examinations throughout the country, a legacy from Britain. At its worst, the examination system has reinforced the North American enthusiasm for diplomas and has tended to limit learning to the playing of the few pieces required for an examination, thus narrowing the musical perspective. However, both inside the examination framework and outside it, some encouraging developments have taken place. Good editions of the classics have come to be used more and more. Teachers have realized that the counterpart of Schumann's *Album for the Young* is to be found in the works of Bartók, Prokofiev, and others. Publishers have encouraged Canadian composers to write for students.

Perhaps the most urgent need is for a general recognition that nearly all young people who learn to play the piano will become amateurs, either in the old sense of being lovers of music or in the contemporary sense of playing without being paid (or in both senses). If this is so, their need is for training which will enable them to become perceptive listeners, to be at home at the keyboard, to sight-read with ease, and to find pleasure in playing.

5 THE TRADITIONAL PERSPECTIVE. The enduring traditions of piano playing and teaching have descended from remarkably few source figures – most of them performer-teachers and some of them composers as well – who lived in Austria, Germany, France, Russia, or England in the 19th century, who enjoyed fame as teachers, and who attracted pupils from far and wide, Canadians among them. In constructing the appended genealogical tables, working backwards from a mass of individual teacher-pupil connections, it was instructive to see how swiftly the lines converged upon a handful of these legendary eminences: Kalkbrenner, the German virtuoso, whose life spanned those of Schubert and Chopin; Moscheles, the Czech-German teacher of Mendelssohn; Reinecke, the German composer-pianist, an associate of Mendelssohn and Schumann; Busoni, the idiosyncratic Italo-German composer and a titan among the virtuosi of his day; the Vienna-trained Hungarian Liszt, a renowned composer, the most famous of all pianists, and a pupil of Czerny (who studied with Beethoven, Clementi, and Hummel); the Vienna-trained Austrian-Pole Leschetizky, like Liszt a pupil of Czerny, and possibly the most influential of all piano teachers; France's Marmontel, the arbiter of the French school of piano playing, the teacher of Bizet, d'Indy, Debussy, and Paladilhe; Saint-Saëns, the illustrious French composer-pianist; Anton Rubinstein, the great Russian virtuoso, composer, and elder contemporary of Tchaikovsky; Nicolas Rubinstein, the famous teacher, brother of Anton; and Tobias Matthay, the English-trained arbiter of the English school of piano playing. From these descended others of near-comparable fame: Thalberg, often described as Liszt's only rival; Mathias and his noted French pupil Philipp; Dannreuther and his distinguished English pupil Samuel; Vogrich and his famous US pupil Hutcheson; Krause, a teacher of Arrau and Fischer; Diémer, a teacher of Casadesus, Cortot, and Schmitz. The list is long, and a glance down the 'generations' on the charts will give an idea of the numina contained therein.

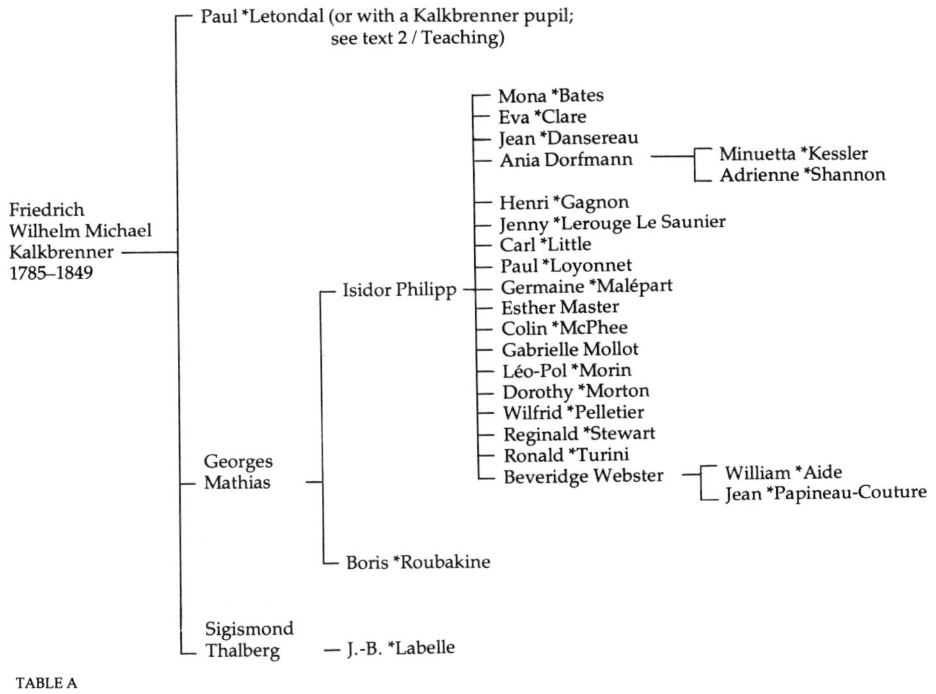

TABLE A

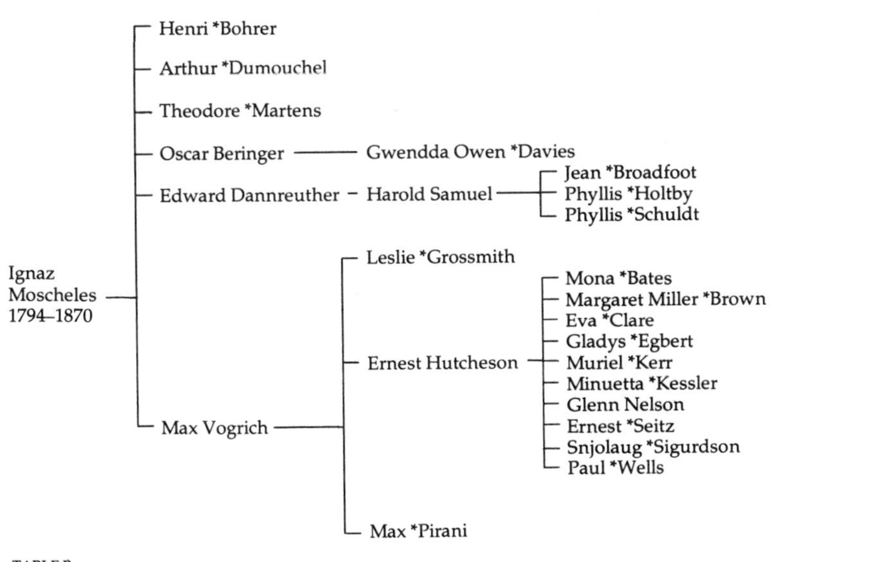

TABLE B

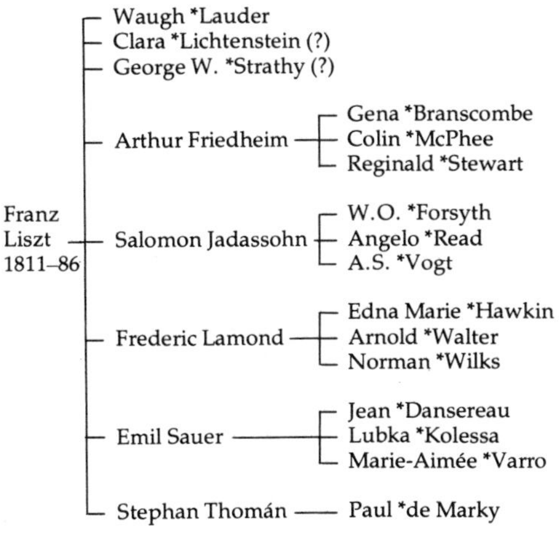

TABLE C

The tables follow each line of descent from a foundational figure to its points of contact with Canada. Each of those points of contact – a Canadian performer or teacher – has under his name in *EMC* a biography which will delineate his or her contribution to music and will name some of his pupils, when pertinent.

Inevitably such tables are limited in the information they can provide and should be regarded only as what they are: an outline of the routes by which certain high traditions of piano playing and teaching may have been transferred from the ancestral countries to Canada. What they do not reveal is anything beyond the point of contact and possible transfer. Moreover, they can imply nothing of the success of such transfer, or of the duration of the attempt to effect it. The Canadians in question may have had several years or only a few master classes with the teachers they have claimed; it is possible, too, that one may have absorbed more in a single lesson than another absorbed in hundreds. Learning cannot be bought, injected, or applied like paint, and its fruits are not easily measured. It is true, nevertheless, that many of the outstanding teachers and performers of Canada appear in these tables, and it is interesting to know that the pedagogical skills which enabled them to achieve as much as they undoubtedly did were not developed in a vacuum of nationalist isolation; these pianists were conscious of tradition and made an attempt to become a part of it.

The tables cannot be at all helpful with the figure whose 'pianistic pedigree' cannot be assembled readily. Perhaps the most striking instance of their failure may be demonstrated by the instance of the late Chilean-Canadian Alberto Guerrero, whose playing was much admired and whose extraordinary teaching abilities may be judged by the list of his pupils, which included William Aide, John *Beckwith, Raymond Dudley, Robert Finch, Gordon *Fleming, Glenn *Gould, Stuart Hamilton, Paul Helmer, Horace *Lapp, Pierrette *LePage, Bruce *Mather, Gordon *McLean, Gerald Moore, Arthur Ozolins, and Malcolm Troup. As nearly as it has been possible to ascertain, Guerrero studied only in his native Chile. That is not to say, however, that he or his teachers may not have trained in Europe. It is possible, though, that he was a genuine progenitorial figure, beholden to no one for the enlightenment he transmitted.

It remains to be pointed out that the tables cannot and do not claim exhaustive coverage of the Canadian connection with the European piano tradition; they were assembled from information in hand, and since in 1980 much information remained to be collected and analysed their content must be regarded as partial, as indicative rather than definitive. Their order is chronological by (and within) culture rather than by individual. Tables A to F (Kalkbrenner to Busoni) represent the Austro-German tradition, G and H (Marmontel and Saint-Saëns) the French, I and J (the Rubinsteins) the Russian, and K (Matthay) the English.

6 TEACHING PUBLICATIONS. The following is a list of musical albums published by Canadians for use in piano instruction in the early stages:

1854

Molt, T.F. *The Pupil's Guide and Young Teacher's Manual* (Jameson)

1890

Jeffers, Thomas Charles. *The Art of Pianoforte Teaching* (Toronto)

Smith, Gustave. *Le Claviste* (J.L. Orme & Son)

1900

Vogt, A.S. *Modern Pianoforte Technique*, 2 parts (Whaley Royce)

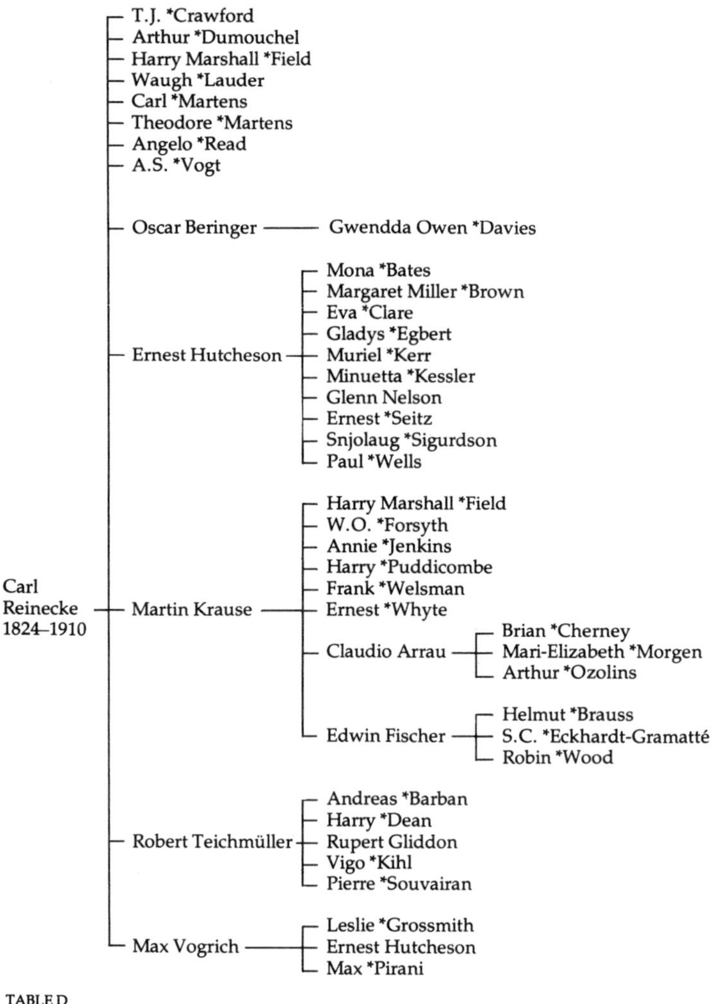

TABLE D

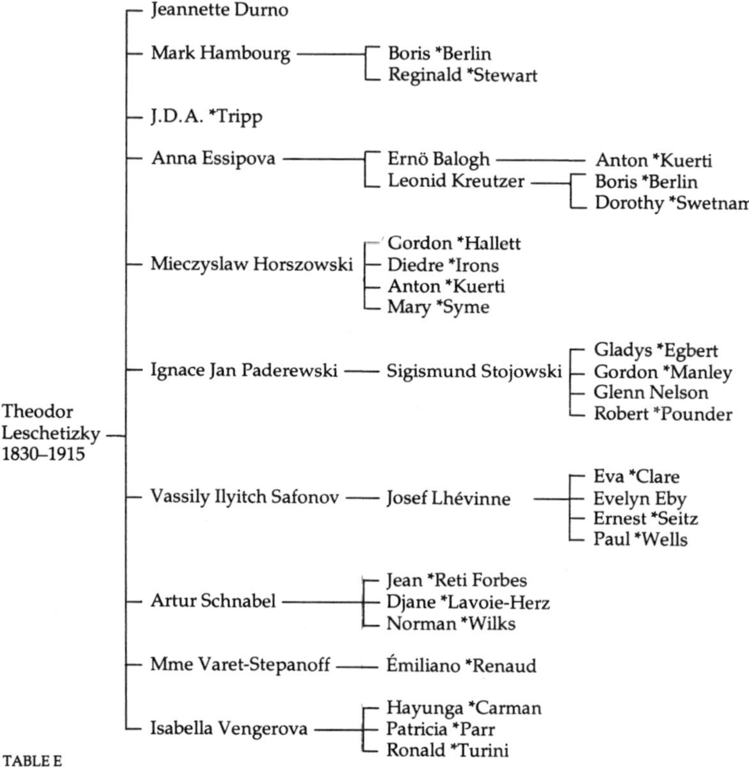

TABLE E

1918
Renaud, Émiliano. *Renaud-Phone Piano Method*. Included recordings
1920
Morin-Labrecque, Albertine. *Méthode de piano*, 2 vols (Montreal)
1922
Morin-Labrecque, Albertine. *L'Art d'étudier le piano* (Montreal)
1929
Kammerer, Hope. *The First Period at the Piano* (Waterloo)
1930
Berlin, Boris, and MacMillan, Ernest. *The Modern Piano Student* (F. Harris)
1932
Berlin, Boris, and MacMillan, Ernest. *Our Piano Class* (F. Harris)
1934
Kammerer, Hope. *The Second Period at the Piano* (Waterloo)
1936
Kelly Kirby Kindergarten Method. *Kelly Kirby Sightreading* (F. Harris)
– *Kelly Kirby Workbooks* (F. Harris)
1937
Ahrens, Cora B. *Daily Sight Playing Exercises for Piano*, 4 vols (Waterloo)
1939
Berlin, Boris, and Magee, Edward. *Four Star Sight Reading*, 8 vols (London, Oakville, Ont)
1940
Berlin, Boris, Boyle, Muriel, and Wilks, Norman. *The Boris Berlin Musical Kindergarten Piano Method* (Heintzman)
1946
Berlin, Boris. *The ABC of Piano Playing*, 2 vols (F. Harris)
Ca 1950
Rose, Myrtle, and Guerrero, Albert. *The New Approach to the Piano*, 2 vols (F. Harris)
1951
Williams, Edith. *Playtime Piano Method* (Waterloo)
1965–6
Peterson, Oscar. *Jazz Exercises and Pieces for the Young* (Ray Brown Publications)
1968
Bubniuk, Irene. *Preliminary Piano Work for the Student of Music* (Bubniuk Music Ltd)

In almost all cases the above are works based on systematic approaches, prepared by teachers rather than composers. After 1950 in Canada more and more works have appeared that are written by composers working in the tradition of creative piano pieces of modest demands (the tradition of Bach's *Little Preludes*, Schumann's *Album for the Young*, and Bartók's *Mikrokosmos 1–4*). Examples are:

*Beckwith *Six Mobiles*
*Cherney *Intervals, Patterns and Shapes; Six Miniatures*
*Fiala *Ten Postludes*
*Joachim *Twelve Twelve-Tone Pieces*
*Kasemets *1 + 1: Twenty Piano Studies for Beginners*
*Kenins *Twelve Diversities*
*Pentland *Music of Now* (books I, II, III); *Space Studies; Three Pairs*
*Wuensch *Mini-Suite; Six Little Etudes; Twelve Glimpses*

Instructional albums with music by several different composers include *Fourteen Piano Pieces by Canadian Composers* (F. Harris), *Music of Our Time* (Waterloo), and *Horizons*, books I and II (Waterloo).

The compiler of the post-1950 list above, the Toronto piano teacher Rachel Cavalho, has been influential in persuading composers to write pieces for the early stages of instruction. In her

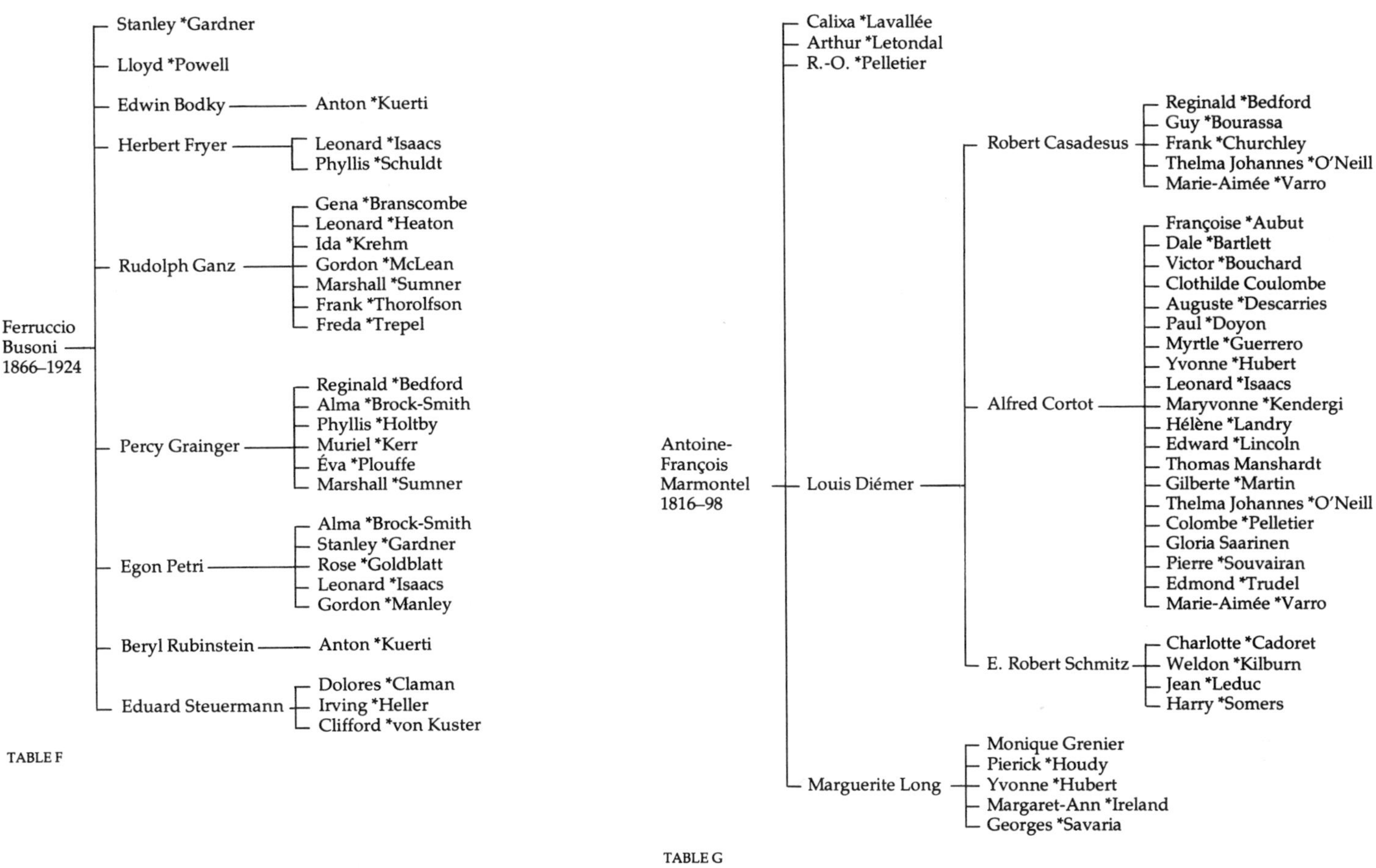

TABLE F

TABLE G

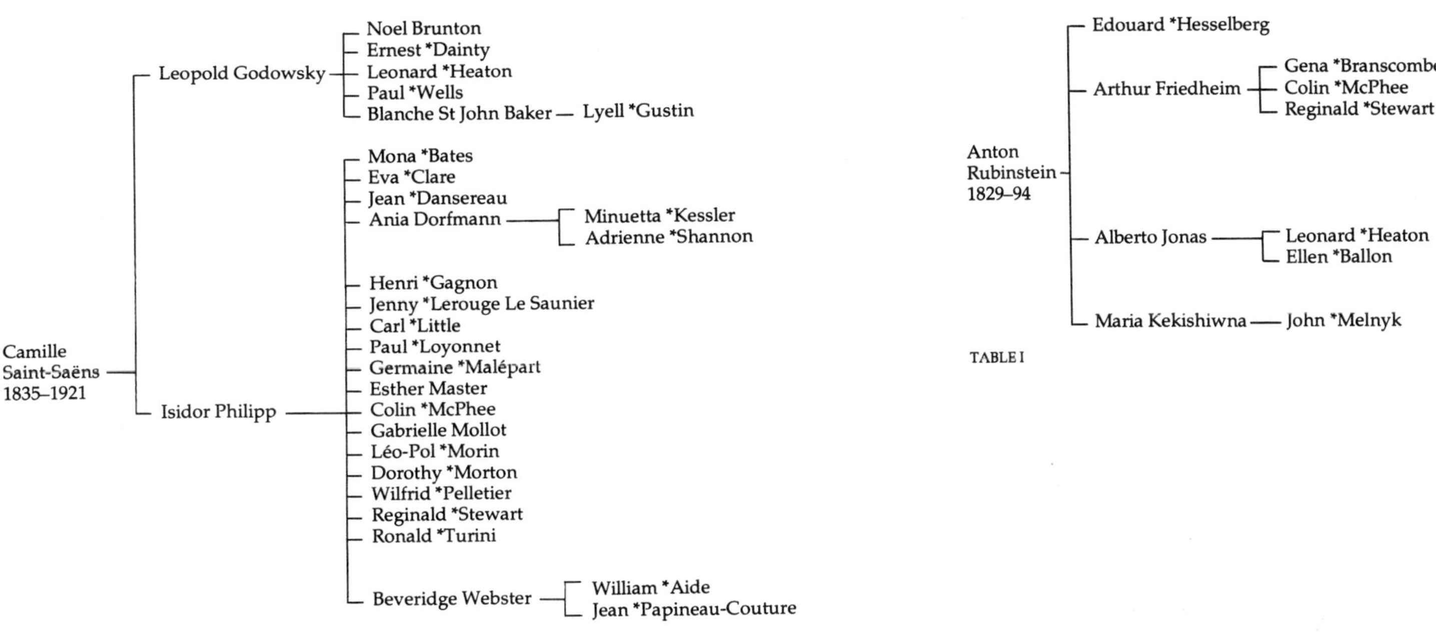

TABLE I

TABLE H

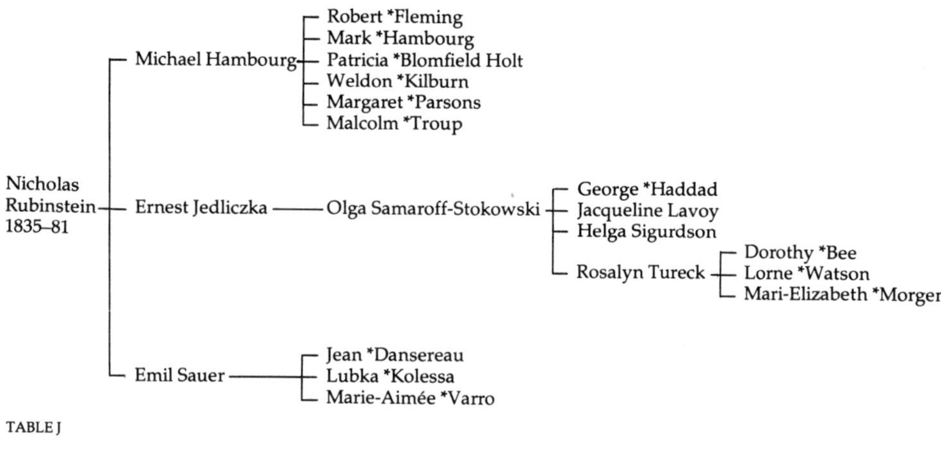

TABLE J

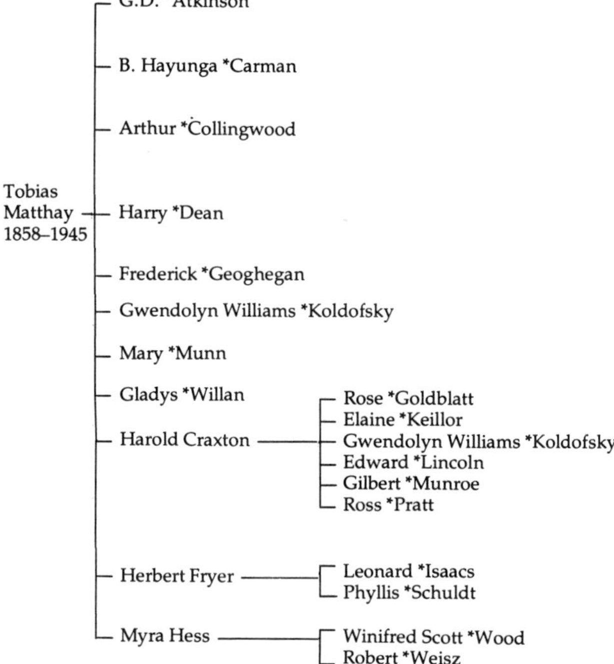

TABLE K

view many of the earlier methods 'do not use original material ... anchor hands, mind and ears on middle C, and completely ignore the 20th century.'

BIBLIOGRAPHY

Musicus. 'Musical hints, No. IV: music and pianoforte teaching,' *Literary Garland*, vol 3, Jul 1845

Pelletier, R.-O. *Le Toucher du pianiste* (Montreal 1916)

– *Étude de la littérature du piano* (Montreal 1920)

– *L'Art pianistique* (Montreal 1922)

– *Guide du professeur de piano* (Montreal 1925)

Sainte-Cécile des Anges, Sister. 'Le piano et sa technique,' unpubl D MUS thesis, Montreal 1947

McCook, James. 'Pioneers preferred pianos,' *Beaver*, outfit 285, Winter 1954–5

Ahrens, Cora, and Atkinson, G.D. *For All Piano Teachers* (Oakville, Ont, 1955)

Churchley, Franklin E. 'The piano in Canadian music education,' unpubl D ED thesis, Columbia 1958

McCook, James. 'Some notes on musical instruments among the pioneers of the Canadian west,' *CMJ*, vol 2, Winter 1958

Cavalho, Rachel, and Elsaessar, Ralph. 'Canadian piano music for teaching,' *Mcan*, 2 articles, 12, 13, Jun–Jul, Aug–Sep 1968

Beaulieu, Mary L. 'A survey of keyboard music of Canadian composers since 1900,' unpubl MA thesis, Indiana 1970

CMCentre. *Canadian Keyboard Music / Musique canadienne à clavier* (Toronto 1971)

Chapman, Norman B. 'Piano music by Canadian composers after 1940,' unpubl PH D thesis, Case Western Reserve U 1973

Reti Forbes, Jean. *Notes on Playing the Piano* (priv publ 1974)

Grant, Margaret. *Your Child and the Piano* (Toronto 1976)

1–4 / RP, 5 / KW

Piano teams. Performers on 'one piano, four hands' (piano duettists); on two pianos (duo-pianists); or on more (eg, the Five Piano Ensemble, the Ten-Piano Ensemble). Most duo-pianists play also as piano duettists, but the larger repertoire has grown around the former for several reasons. The duo-pianist has a keyboard and a bench to himself; compositions designed for two pianos distribute responsibility and opportunity for display more evenly between the players because neither is limited to the upper or the lower half of the keyboard; and two grand pianos, with the pianists facing one another across them, are more effective visually.

One of the earliest Canadian piano teams was that of Reginald *Godden and Scott Malcolm, formed ca 1929 and heard in North America and England during the 1930s; their many transcriptions for duo added considerably to the repertoire. Etta Coles and Naomi Yanova (Mrs John *Adaskin), who formed a team in 1929, made their New York debut in 1934 and continued to perform until 1938 with orchestras such as the *Montreal Orchestra, the *TSO, the Buffalo SO, the *Promenade Symphony Concerts, and the Rochester Civic SO. In Winnipeg during the 1930s Gwendda Owen *Davies performed duos with Mary Scarlett Wood, Cécile Henderson, and Marjorie Dillabough. Possibly the longest-lived of Canadian two-piano teams have been the husband and wife Reginald *Bedford and Evelyn Eby, who appeared together first in 1938 in Chicago and later in London, New York, and Toronto. They remained active in 1979. Other teams formed during the 1930s were Gordon *Hallett and Clifford *Poole, who gave concerts 1936–42 in Toronto and Montreal and were heard over CBC radio; Stanley *Gardner and Rose *Goldblatt who performed in recital 1936–45 on CBC Montreal; Alma *Brock-Smith and Virginia Johnson, who performed widely and were heard often on radio in the Vancouver, Seattle, and San Francisco areas; Georgina Russell and Olga Guilaroff, who played in

Montreal in the 1930s and 1940s; and Madeline Bone and Elsie Bennett, Mona *Bates pupils who joined forces ca 1937 and made their New York debut in 1950. Thelma Johannes *O'Neill performed 1940–5 and again during the early 1950s in the Saskatoon area with Edmund *Assaly, frequently playing his *Suite* for two pianos. In British Columbia Phyllis *Schuldt and Mary *Munn formed a team which flourished 1940–52. Schuldt played 1955–68 with Boris *Roubakine, giving the premieres (both ca 1965) of Jack *Behrens' *Four Pieces for Three Hands* and *Three Pieces for Four Hands*. The composer Kelsey *Jones and his wife Rosabelle began to play piano duos during the early 1940s and harpsichord duos in the mid-1960s. They still were performing in 1980 and in their repertoire was Jones' *Theme and Variations* (1961) for piano four-hands.

Several teams emerged during the 1950s. Jeanne *Landry performed with Jean-Marie *Beaudet and also with Josephte *Dufresne, with whom she recorded *Matton's *Concerto pour deux pianos et percussion* (RCI 145). The duettists Pierre *Beaudet and Guy *Bourassa began to give public and radio recitals ca 1950 and recorded works by *Archer and *Beckwith (RCI 113). Dorothy *Morton and Esther Master of Montreal (still active in 1980) began their partnership in 1955. They have been heard live and in radio broadcasts and have recorded works of Chopin, Infante, and Schumann (CBC SM-207) and of Saint-Saëns (CBC SM-242). Harry Heap and his sister Margaret Heap Sangster became known as duo-pianists about this time, appearing with the TSO and other orchestras and playing on the CBC and the BBC.

Husband and wife teams originating in the 1950s or 1960s include Robin *Wood and Winifred Scott, who played on radio and TV in Canada and England and whose repertoire included Wood's two-piano work *Pieces*, and Margaret *Parsons and Clifford Poole, who performed together 1954–65, made a recording (Cap 6088), and edited the *Parsons-Poole Duo Piano Series* (published by Harris). The internationally renowned duo-pianists Victor *Bouchard and Renée *Morisset made their debut as a team in 1952 and have appeared in Europe, Canada, and the USA. Bouchard and Morisset have recorded together and in 1964 won a joint *Prix de musique Calixa-Lavallée. *Hétu's *Sonata, Op 6* (1962) and *Fiala's *Sonata* (1970) are dedicated to them, and they have premiered works for orchestra and two pianos by Matton and by *Pépin.

Jocelyn *Pritchard and Patricia Elliott (b Saskatoon 20 Nov 1919, d Toronto Aug 1977) performed together 1960–8, mostly in western Canada. Their repertoire included Archer's *Three Sketches for Piano* (1957), *Kenins' *Folk Dance, Variations and Fugue* (1968), an arrangement of *Morel's *Ronde Enfantine*, and their own *Fantasy on Earth Tunes*. (Garth) *Beckett and (Boyd) *McDonald, pupils of Lyell *Gustin and Alma Brock-Smith, established their partnership in 1966 and have appeared in concert in Canada, the USA, and Europe. They premiered *Mather's *Sonata* for two pianos in 1970 (and recorded it on RCI 354) and *Turner's *Concerto* for two pianos and orchestra in 1972.

In the late 1970s several other Canadian two-piano teams were active. Vancouver-based Joyce Rawlings and Don Stagg formed a team in 1973. Both are pianists and harpsichordists, and they have arranged and transcribed many works as duos, have appeared in Canada and the USA, and have been heard over CBC radio; in 1975 they took part in the New York Harpsichord Festival. In Quebec Lorraine *Vaillancourt and her brother Jean-Eudes *Vaillancourt have performed live and on radio and TV; they began as a team in 1965. Also based in Montreal in the 1970s were the brother and sister team Ireneus and Luba Zuk. The composer Bruce Mather and his wife Pierrette *LePage have specialized in new music and have recorded several works. Leslie Kinton and the US-born James Anagnoson (both teachers at the *RCMT in 1980) have given concerts in North America and Europe and have played on CBC radio and TV. Another husband and wife team, the *Camerata members Kathryn Root and Elyakim *Taussig, have appeared as duo-pianists with the TS and made a Wigmore Hall debut in London in 1973. The Toronto pianists Jane *Coop and Adrienne *Shannon were awarded the 1976 Floyd S. *Chalmers Foundation prize for their duo recital at the *St Lawrence Centre, Toronto.

A number of Canadian pianists have formed teams with non-Canadians. Bradford Tracey (b 1956, Sydney, NS) and Rolf Junghanns formed a keyboard partnership at the Schola Cantorum Basiliensis in 1973. Performing on historic instruments from the Fritz Neumeyer Collection, they have toured in North America (1977, 1979) and have recorded duos on the Toccata label (FSM 53625 and FSN 52622). The Canadian pianist Ralph Markham (b 1949, Vancouver) and the US pianist Kenneth Broadway, both pupils of Vronsky and Babin, have toured in Europe and North America. Also noteworthy are the long-established and internationally known duo-pianists Arthur Gold, who is Canadian-born, and Robert Fizdale.

In *A History of Music in Canada* *Kallmann refers to an 1850s Toronto concert at which the overtures to Mendelssohn's *A Midsummer Night's Dream* and Rossini's *La Gazza ladra* were performed by eight hands and twelve hands respectively. The Five Piano Ensemble – Alberto *Guerrero, Viggo *Kihl, Ernest *Seitz, Norah de *Kresz, and Reginald *Stewart – flourished in Toronto ca 1926. The Ten-Piano Ensemble was founded by Mona Bates in Toronto in 1931 to raise funds for the needy. Its changing personnel comprised the leading Bates pupils of the moment; it survived for a number of years and gave many performances during World War II to raise money for the war effort. Evelyn Eby, Millicent Lusk, Alma Sheasgreen (Brock-Smith), and Reginald Bedford were presented by the Lyell Gustin Piano Studios in Saskatoon, 9 May 1928, in a four-piano recital of works by Bach, Chopin, Saint-Saëns, and Tchaikovsky.

Farnaby, Bach, Clementi, Mozart, Beethoven, Schubert, Mendelssohn, Chopin, Schumann, and Brahms all wrote duos or concertos for two (or more) keyboards and orchestra or made duo arrangements of other works. The genre remained popular and was employed by Saint-Saëns, Parry, Debussy, Rachmaninoff, Reger, Stravinsky, Bax, Milhaud, and others. Piano duet arrangements of major symphonies were popular with enthusiasts in the late 19th and early 20th century, not so much for public performance as for exploration and study before the days of the gramophone. Published solo-piano concertos usually have had their orchestral parts arranged for a second piano, and though the prime purpose of this is to permit a teacher or coach to rehearse with a soloist preparing for a performance with orchestra, the two-piano versions often are played in public as well.

Among Canadians (besides those previously mentioned) who have written keyboard duos are *Betts, *Bottenberg, *Fleming, *Huse, *Kasemets, *Kolinski, *MacMillan, and *Papineau-Couture. In 1954 Gilles *Tremblay premiered his *'Mouvement'* for two pianos with Serge *Garant, and in 1959 Barbara *Pentland premiered her *Three Duets after Pictures by Paul Klee* (piano four-hands) with Robert *Rogers. (NM)

PICHÉ. A Montreal family of musicians comprising 1 / Joseph and his sons 2 / Eudore and 3 / Bernard.

1 **Joseph**. Organist, teacher, b Montreal 1877, d there January 1939. He was a pupil of Alexis *Contant (piano), Romain-Octave *Pelletier (organ and piano), and Achille *Fortier (harmony). After serving as organist in the churches of Notre-Dame-du-St-Rosaire in 1898, St-Denis in 1900, and Sacré-Coeur 1908–26, he became the regular organist at St-Victor Church in 1930. He also taught 1905–37 at the Collège Ste-Marie and after that at Jean-de-Brébeuf. His wife, Yvonne Corbin (b Montreal 1877, d there 1951), also studied piano with Alexis Contant and Romain-Octave Pelletier. She gave her first recital in Montreal at 14. After their marriage she began conducting choirs and became deputy organist at the Immaculée-Conception, St-Sacrement, and St Patrick's churches.

2 **Eudore**. Organist, producer, b Montreal 1906, d there 1967. He was a member of the Society of Jesus for several years. He published a collection of folksong arrangements, *Chansons du vieux Québec* (Beauchemin 1939). After an administrative position with the *Encyclopédie Grolier*, he became a radio producer for the CBC. He was also organist ca 1950–65 at Ste-Madeleine Church in Outremont and 1965–7 at St-Joseph Church in the Town of Mount Royal.

3 (Paul) **Bernard**. Organist, composer, b Montreal 10 Apr 1908; lauréat organ (AMQ) 1929. His early musical studies were with Hervé Cloutier. He became organist in 1926 at St-Nicolas Church in Ahuntsic and then moved to Notre-Dame-de-la-Défense. He was awarded a grant by the Delphic Study Club of Montreal in 1929 and won the *Prix d'Europe in 1932. He entered the Brussels Cons, where he studied with Paul de Maleingreau (piano, organ, fugue, counterpoint), and then went to Paris to work with Charles Tournemire. He was the regular organist 1931–45 at the Trois-Rivières Cathedral and gave a daily recital there for six weeks in 1934, devoting half of each day's program to Bach; he thus performed three-quarters of the composer's work during the town's tricentenary celebrations that year. In 1945 in the Quebec City Basilica he performed the music for the NFB film on the *Casavant company, *The Singing Pipes / Le Vent qui chante*. In 1945, under the impresario Bernard *Laberge, he undertook the first of several tours in the USA and Canada. He gave recitals in Toronto, Kitchener, and Hamilton. He was the organist 1945–66 at St Peter and St Paul Church in Lewiston, Me, and also taught there and gave recitals in about 20 states. In 1966 he joined the staff of the Cons de Trois-Rivières, where he taught until his retirement in 1973. He has written some pieces for organ, including a *Rhapsodie sur quatre noëls* (Gray 1947), another rhapsody published by Fischer, and two masses for equal voices. His *Fugue sur l'Ite Missa est alleluiatique* was recorded by André *Mérineau.

BIBLIOGRAPHY
Dion-Lévesque, Rosaire. *Silhouettes franco-américaines* (Manchester, NH, 1957) (ST, SW)

PIERCE, Glen (Wallace). Educator, conductor, b Winnipeg 3 May 1911; BA (Manitoba) 1932, LRSM 1933. He studied piano in Winnipeg with Leonard *Heaton and in London with Harold Craxton and choral conducting at the Juilliard School with Fritz Mahler and Peter Wilhousky. He taught piano privately 1934–8 and later joined the Winnipeg school system where music eventually became his principal subject. While teaching 1947–66 at Daniel McIntyre High School he achieved extraordinary results with his choirs. He conducted the *U of Manitoba Choral and Orchestral Society 1949–51 and, after serving as assistant conductor 1946–53, succeeded Filmer *Hubble as conductor 1953–5 of the Manitoba Schools Orchestra. In 1966 he became supervisor of school music in Winnipeg, retiring in 1976 to private teaching. RG

PIERCEY, Sheila (Kathleen). Soprano, b Halifax, NS, 18 Nov 1933; ARCT voice 1957. She was a pupil of Leonard *Mayoh, became a church soloist, and sang on occasion with the *Halifax SO. Moving to Toronto in 1956, she continued her voice studies with Ernesto *Vinci, appeared with the *Royal Cons Opera 1957–9 and the *CBC Opera 1957–8, and made her *COC debut 1957 as the Dew Fairy in *Hansel and Gretel*. Other COC roles 1957–71 included Marie in *The Bartered Bride* (1961), Zerlina in *Don Giovanni* (1963), Adele in *Die Fledermaus* (1964), Parasha in *Mavra* (1965), Rose and a 'Voice in the Pit' in the premiere (1967) of *The Luck of Ginger Coffey*, Musetta in *La Bohème* (1968), and Olga in *The Merry Widow* (1971). She sang 1958–71 in many of the COC's touring and *Prologue productions. The 'First Girl' in the stage premiere (1960) of John *Beckwith's **Night Blooming Cereus*, she has sung also in operas or musicals at the *Banff Centre SFA in 1957, 1960, 1961, 1962, 1966, and 1967, the *Stratford Festival in 1959, *Rainbow Stage in 1964, and the *Charlottetown Festival in 1965. A natural vivacity made her outstanding in comedy and soubrette roles. In the 1970s she began teaching voice at *Dalhousie U and assisting in the opera department there. (JBl)

Pierre Bourque Saxophone Quartet / Quatuor de saxophones Pierre-Bourque. Founded in Quebec City in 1963 by the soprano saxophonist Pierre *Bourque and three of his pupils at the *CMQ – Claude Brisson, alto; Rémi Ménard, tenor (replaced by Jacques Larocque in 1971); and Jean Bouchard, baritone. The quartet made its debut in 1964 in Quebec City and subsequently played in other Canadian towns, giving 54 concerts 1965–72 for the *JMC. It has performed abroad through exchange programs, touring 1970–1 in France, in 1972 in Sweden, and in 1973 in the USA, and it was the Quebec delegate to the fifth Biennale of Bordeaux (1972), where it won a silver medal. Despite touring, the players continued to teach in Quebec conservatories. The ensemble took part (1973) in a Canadian evening at the ORTF along with the duo pianists *Bouchard and *Morisset and the soprano Louise *Lebrun under the auspices of the Communauté radiophonique des programmes de langue française. It has enjoyed a particular success in France, where its members were described as 'four virtuosi ... playing in the purest spirit of chamber music' (*Carrefour*, 31 Mar 1971).

The quartet's repertoire ranges from transcriptions of classical and romantic works to original contemporary pieces, and it has given the premieres of several works by Quebec composers, notably *Tempo I* (1967) by Marc *Fortier, *Saxologie* (1972) and *Phonie M.A.* (1976) by Pierre Genest, and *Saxi-Phonie-Saties* (1972) by Alexander *Brott. In 1969 it recorded works by Absil, Dubois, *Fiala, and Françaix on *Jeunesses musicales 20 Canada* (RCI 279 / RCA LSC-3141). MB-L

PIGGOTT, Audrey (Margaret). Cellist, teacher, composer, b London 21 Mar 1906, naturalized Canadian 1952. She studied cello and piano 1924–9 at the RCM, London, and received an ARCM in both. She continued 1929–30 with the cellist Diran Alexanian at the École normale in Paris. She taught 1931–9 in England and 1947–50 at the BC Institute of Music and Drama, and in 1971 she began teaching at the *Community Music School of Greater Vancouver. She has given recitals and performed with orchestras in Great Britain, Holland, and British Columbia; on the CBC; and as a member of the *de Rimanoczy Quartet, the Kessler and Camosun trios, and other chamber groups. she has composed *Elizabethan Songs for Female Voice* (Western ca 1957) and *Two 2-part Songs* (Western ca 1957). CF

PILTCH, Bernie (Bernard David). Saxophonist, clarinetist, flutist, b Montreal 12 Aug 1927. He took clarinet lessons from Herbert Pye at the TCM in the 1940s and was a composition pupil of Gordon *Delamont in the 1950s. Piltch began playing in the Toronto dance band of Jack Evans in 1943. He later joined the bands of Bobby *Gimby, Benny Louis, Bert *Niosi, and Art *Hallman. Playing in the bebop style, he was a soloist in the 1950s in the jazz groups of Rob *McConnell and Norman *Symonds and worked until the mid-1960s with Ron *Collier's bands. He had become a leading Toronto studio musician by the late 1950s and played regularly in CBC radio and TV orchestras. He was the saxophonist 1968–75 with the *TS and in 1970 he was the soloist in the orchestra's performance of Symonds' *The Nameless Hour* and (with David *Young) its premiere of Harry *Freedman's *Scenario*. John *Wyre's *Bernie*, for bass clarinet solo, choir, and percussion group, is dedicated to Piltch, who premiered it 13 Nov 1976 with *Nexus and the *Festival Singers. His jazz recordings, as an alto saxophonist, include LPs with Collier and Paul *Hoffert.

In 1976 Piltch began to perform occasionally in Toronto jazz clubs with his sons Rob, a guitarist (a pupil of Eli *Kassner), and David, a bassist. Both sons have played and recorded with Kathryn *Moses and Ted *Moses and have worked with David *Clayton-Thomas (Blood, Sweat & Tears), Hagood *Hardy, Bernie *Senensky, and others. Individually they have played as sidemen to leading US musicians at Toronto jazz clubs.

BIBLIOGRAPHY
Waxman, Ken. 'Like father, like sons,' *Maclean's*, 6 Feb 1978 MM

Pipe bands. See Bands: 7 / Pipe bands, Highland.

PIRANI, Max (Gabriel). Pianist, teacher, b Melbourne 4 Aug 1898, d London 5 Aug 1975. His studies at the Melbourne Cons and later with Max Vogrich in New York preceded the formation (1923) of the Pirani Trio with the violinist Leila Doubleday (later Pirani) and the cellist Charles Hambourg. The trio toured widely in Europe, the Commonwealth, and the USA until 1940. In 1926 Pirani joined the faculty of the RAM. After several visits to Canada in the late 1930s, he served 1941–7 as director of the piano department of the *Banff SFA. He was a lecturer and recitalist 1942–4 at the *Western Ontario Cons in London, Ont, and the founding director 1945–7 of the Music Teachers' College at the *U of Western Ontario. His Canadian pupils included Dorothy *Bee, Gordon K. *Greene, Audrey *Johannesen, Warren *Mould, and John *Searchfield. In 1948 he returned to England, thereafter publicizing and developing the technique of Emanuel Moor and completing the definitive biography *Emanuel Moor* (London 1959). In Pirani's obituary in *The Times* (12 Aug 1975) Sir Thomas Armstrong wrote: '[Pirani's] methods derived from the main-stream of European pianism ... and they were always at the service of an exceptionally broad and discriminating musicianship.' GKG

Pirouette. One-act opera by Marthe Morisset-Blackburn (libretto) and Maurice *Blackburn (music). It was a *JMC commission (1960) and was premiered 30 Jul 1960 at the *JMC Orford Art Centre with Cécile *Vallée as Béatrice, Pierre *Boutet as Jean, and Gilles *Lamontagne as Michael, with Charles *Reiner at the piano. The story of *Pirouette* turns upon the chance meeting in Rome of three Canadian music students, Béatrice, her brother Jean, and Michael, and the friendships that develop despite various comic misadventures. Paired with Blackburn's *Une Mesure de silence* (**Silent Measures*) it received about 100 performances across Canada during a 1960–1 JMC tour. Three excerpts from *Pirouette*, by the original cast with Jacqueline *Richard at the piano, were recorded for release on a 45-rpm disc by JMC (CD-JMC 7). GP

Place des Arts (PDA). Performing arts complex located in the heart of Montreal. It comprises a large hall and two theatres, rehearsal rooms, workshops, offices, several boutiques, and an 800-car garage, all linked by underground passages to the Place-des-Arts subway station to the north and the huge commercial Desjardins complex to the south. It was on the initiative of Jean Drapeau, mayor of Montreal, that some citizens conferred in 1955 to plan an organization bearing the name Centre Sir George-Étienne-Cartier. That organization eventually gave birth to the PDA. The designs of Montreal architects Affleck, Desbarats, Dimakopoulos, Lebensold, Michaud, and Sise were unveiled in 1959. Appeals were made to the public and to governments to finance the project. A round-the-clock 'grande nuit' at the *Forum, televised free by the CBC, brought in considerable amounts of money, including subsidies of nearly $5 million from the province of Quebec and the city of Montreal. Work began 11 Feb 1961. The Grande Salle (renamed Salle Wilfrid-Pelletier 13 June 1966) was inaugurated 21 Sep 1963 with an *MSO concert conducted jointly by Wilfrid *Pelletier and Zubin Mehta. In 1964, after a union dispute, and when installation costs had reached $25 million, the Centre Sir George-Étienne-Cartier corporation was dissolved and replaced by the Régie de la PDA, a public administrative body with a board of directors comprising a president and eight members. Louis A. Lapointe had been president of the original corporation 1957–64. François Mercier succeeded him in 1964 as president of the Régie. Mercier was followed by Marcel Piché in 1968, Raymond Crépault in 1973, and Jean-Claude Delorme in 1974. Directors-general have been Claude Robillard 1957–61 and Maurice Germain 1961–4, succeeded by Gérard *Lamarche.

The Salle Wilfrid-Pelletier is made of reinforced concrete, except the roof which is of steel. There are 2963 seats, or 2885 when the orchestra pit is in use. The proscenium measures 23 x 11 m; the stage floor 51 x 18 m. The hall has five foyers, including the large central Piano nobile, dominated by a giant triptych by Louis Archambault, *Les Anges radieux*.

The coming of *Expo 67, with its attendant World Festival, hastened the construction of a second building, begun 3 May 1966. The Édifice des théâtres comprises two halls, built one over the other: the Théâtre Maisonneuve and Théâtre Port-Royal. It was designed by the Montreal architects David, Barott, Boulva, and Dufresne and was inaugurated without ceremony 30 Apr 1967. It is located to the southeast of the Salle Wilfrid-Pelletier and has a large glass facade affording a view of the city. The Théâtre Maisonneuve, which

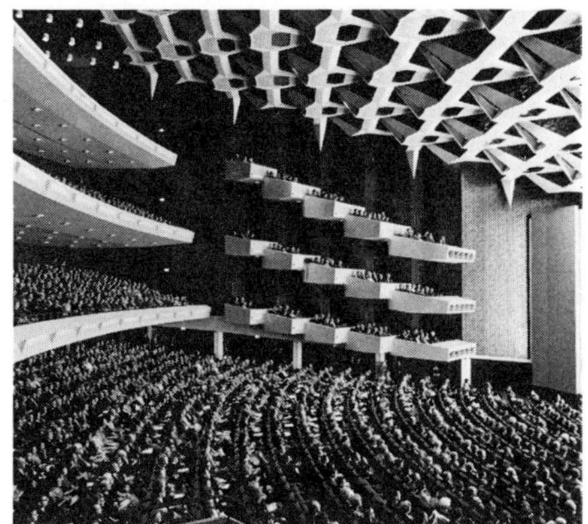

Salle Wilfrid-Pelletier, Place des Arts, Montreal

occupies the upper part of the building, is a modern version of a theatre in the Italian style. It can accommodate 1290 spectators. The proscenium measures 18.5 x 9 m, the stage floor 25.4 x 15 m. The pit can hold 57 musicians and the shell is collapsible. The Théâtre Port-Royal has 823 seats in a tiered seating arrangement looking squarely into a wide and fully-opened stage, without flies. The proscenium opening can be extended to 29.2 m.

Top Canadian and international names in entertainment, music, dance, theatre, and song have appeared at the PDA, including Harry Belafonte, Maria Callas, Yvon Deschamps, Maynard *Ferguson, Dietrich Fischer-Dieskau, Ida *Haendel, Vladimir Horowitz, André *Laplante, Jean Lapointe, Michel *Louvain, Anne *Murray, David Oistrakh, and Ginette *Reno. The MSO established offices there and began giving most of its concerts in the Salle Wilfrid-Pelletier. The *Opera Guild, the *Opéra du Québec, and Les Grands Ballets Canadiens have performed there, and the *McGill Chamber Orchestra, the *Ladies' Morning Musical Club and the *Pro Musica Society began giving concerts in the Théâtre Maisonneuve. The Régie itself established a cultural animation program in the Piano nobile: Sons et brioches, presented in collaboration with the *JMC beginning in 1972; Concerts midi, with members of the MSO, beginning in 1974; the Midis de la PDA 1975–7; and Les Heures de la Place 1977–8. An information periodical *Placedart* was published 1968–75 (37 issues). During the 1975–6 season the PDA welcomed 1,322,756 spectators.

BIBLIOGRAPHY

'La Place des Arts de Montréal,' *Alcan News*, Sep 1963

'La Grande Salle, Place des Arts,' *Royal Architectural Institute of Canada J*, Nov 1963

'La Place des Arts du Québec a un an,' *L'Actualité*, Oct 1964

Cahier spécial sur l'Édifice des théâtres. Montreal *Le Devoir*, 29 Mar 1967

Duval, Laurent. 'Derrière le béton,' *Culture vivante*, 17, May 1970

Institut québécois. Public opinion poll (1975)

PDA Annual Reports (1975, 1976)

Gingras, Claude. 'En 15 ans, la Place des Arts est devenue la place de tout le monde,' Montreal *La Presse*, 30 Sep 1978

(LD)

Plainsong or plainchant. The sung monophony of religious rites (most often Christian, but also Hebrew, Moslem, and Buddhist) prior to the ascendancy of polyphony in the 13th century. Known at that time by several names including 'cantus ecclesiasticus,' its single (or fifth-or-octave-doubled) unmeasured line was redefined by the Roman church as 'cantus planus,' or plainsong, to distinguish it from the plural lines of the new polyphony and the stabilizing harmonies and metred time divisions that ensued. Plainsong was perpetuated in the Christian church in varieties both eastern (Armenian, Byzantine, Syrian, etc) and western (Ambrosian, Gallican, Gregorian, Mozarabic, etc). It was predominantly the Gregorian which reached Canada – first through the French Roman Catholic Church and later through the Church of England; but other varieties were introduced by late-19th- and early-20th-century immigrants from Armenia, Syria, Ukraine, and elsewhere. In the 1970s no comprehensive study of the extent, diversity, and authenticity of plainsong practice in Canada had been published. This article will examine only the Roman Catholic and Anglican traditions.

See also Anglican church music; Missionaries; Religions and music; Roman Catholic church music.

Plainsong was sung first in Canada when Jacques Cartier landed at Labrador 14 Jun 1534. Later the Jesuit missionaries, in their efforts to convert the natives to Christianity, taught them the Te Deum, the Magnificat, the Ave Maria, and hymns translated into their tongue and adapted to traditional plainchants. It is probable that most of the church music sung in New France was plainsong. The oldest preserved composition written for use in Canada is the 'Prose de la Ste-Famille' (ca 1700), attributed to Father Charles-Amador *Martin and published first in the 1801 edition of *Le Processional* [sic] *romain*. The melodic element of the 'Prose de la Ste-Famille' is a good example of 'plein chant musical français'; this work and the development of religious music in 17th-century Quebec are discussed at length in Willy *Amtmann's *Music in Canada 1600–1800*. An 18th-century publication, *Le Rituel du diocèse de Québec* (Paris 1703), contained a number of pieces in plainsong notation suitable for specific occasions such as burials and benedictions. The **Graduel romain, Processional* [sic] *romain* and *Vespéral romain* were printed for the diocese of Quebec in 1800, 1801, and 1802 respectively. These contained the first music printed in Canada and appeared with the traditional square notation on a four-line staff.

During the 19th century plainsong was used extensively, but there was an increasing tendency to provide accompaniment for it, perhaps because few church choirs had sufficient training to maintain the pitch of an unaccompanied line without assistance. Included among several publications of accompaniments were J.-B. *Labelle's *Le Répertoire de l'organiste* (the first edition of which was published in 1851) and Pierre-Minier *Lagacé's *Les Chants d'Église, harmonisés pour l'orgue suivant les principes de la tonalité grégorienne* (Paris 1860). Following the publication of Lagacé's book a disagreement over the matter of plainsong accompaniment arose between Ernest *Gagnon (who sided with Lagacé) and Antoine *Dessane, who resigned his position as organist at Notre-Dame because of this dispute. Romain-Octave *Pelletier's accompaniments to the *Manuel de chants liturgiques* by Father Cléophas Borduas (Montreal 1890) and Ernest Gagnon's *Accompagnement d'orgue des chants liturgiques* (1903, 1912, Boucher 1917–18) are other noteworthy examples of plainsong accompaniment.

The 19th century had witnessed the development of a number of theories on authentic plainsong, ie, that which was in keeping with lost medieval tradition. Pope Pius X's *Moto proprio* of 1903, which outlined the functions of liturgical music, declared Gregorian chant as the proper and only music of the Roman Catholic Church. It also helped to resolve disagreements and had wide influence in French Canada, where it inspired a strong tradition based on the edition issued by Solesmes, the abbey in France long recognized as a guardian of Gregorian tradition. The *Schola cantorum, founded in Montreal in 1915, included Gregorian chant in its first curriculum and introduced a diploma course in plainsong accompaniment. It has organized choir competitions for Gregorian singing and has published works which it considers faithful to Gregorian principles and to the precepts of the *Moto proprio*. With the creation of the Faculty of Music at the *U of Montreal in 1950 a long-standing affiliation between the university and the Gregorian Institute of Toledo, was reconstituted as a direct affiliation between the institute and the faculty. This arrangement remained in effect until 1967 when the university discontinued all affiliations.

A notable centre for the practice of plainsong, and specifically Gregorian chant, is the Benedictine monastery founded in 1912 at St-Benoit-du-Lac, Que. Recordings of plainsong have been made there, and Dom Georges Mercure, the monastery's foremost authority on the subject (Dom Oscar *O'Brien was a later authority) published the book *Rythmique grégorienne* (St-Benoit-du-Lac 1937). Another centre, Toronto's St Michael's Cathedral Choir School, was established in 1937 by Mgr *Ronan, who had studied Gregorian chant at Solesmes and who taught 1923–56 at St Augustine's Seminary, Scarborough, Ont. Among other teachers of plainsong were Louis *Bouhier, one of Montreal's leading specialists in Gregorian chant and the author of *Quatre-vingt Motets en chant grégorien et en musique moderne pour les saluts du Saint-Sacrement* (Montreal 1907); Ethelbert *Thibault; and Eugène *Lapierre, the author of *Traité sommaire d'accompagnement grégorien* (Montreal 1949) and *Gregorian Chant Accompaniment* (Toledo 1949).

Vatican II, the second international policy council of leaders of the Roman Catholic Church, which met in 1962, 1963, and 1964, decided to move away from Latin to a greater use of the vernacular accompanied by more modern types of music. As a result plainsong was reduced or abandoned altogether in many Roman Catholic churches, although during the 1970s there appeared to be a trend towards restoring at least some of the Gregorian propers with Latin words, a practice neither forbidden nor discouraged by Vatican II.

Among Quebec musicians who have contributed significantly to the perpetuation of plainsong are Placide Gagnon, Germain *Lalande, Conrad *Latour, Jules *Martel, and Clément *Morin, all teachers and conductors who have trained choirs in the tradition. The writings of Charles-Hugues *Lefebvre, particularly the series on 'Musique d'église – instruction de S.S. Pie X sur la musique sacrée,' in *La Musique* in 1919, were an important influence.

During the 19th century the English tractarian movement had worked for a restoration of Catholic worship and liturgical music within the Church of England. The effects of this movement were felt somewhat later in Canada. Early in the 20th century Arthur Dorey, choirmaster at Christ Church Cathedral, Ottawa, tried to introduce plainsong into the service. His attempts lost impetus under his successor. In 1921 Healey *Willan became precentor of the Church of St Mary Magdalene in Toronto and began to adapt Gregorian chant to the texts of the propers of *The English Hymnal*. These propers and also antiphons and responsories have continued in regular use in Anglican churches. Dalton *Baker, who taught plainsong 1924–32 to his 40-voice boys' choir at St Peter's Church in Toronto, helped to establish the tradition in central Canada. In British Columbia Leonard *Wilson led the campaign.

Willan's accompaniments to plainsong hymns may be found in the Presbyterian *Book of Praise* (1918, 1972), the United Church *Hymnary* (1930), the Anglican *Book of Common Praise* (revised 1938), and the joint United and Anglican churches' *Hymn Book* (1971), the last of which contains harmonizations by Margaret *Drynan and Robert Hunter Bell as well. Willan was editor of *The Canadian Psalter*, Plainsong edition (1963). He based the pointing of the psalms (ie, the allocation and phrasing of the words of the psalm in relation to the notes of the chant) entirely on the Briggs and Frere psalter – *A Manual of Plainsong for Divine Service* by Henry Bremridge Briggs and Walter Howard Frere (London 1902) – a new edition of the Helmore psalter of 1850. In 1950 Willan co-founded the Gregorian Assn of Toronto (later the Gregorian Assn of Canada). The association was established to promote a wider use of plainsong but it declined after Willan's retirement as its music director in 1963; by 1968 it had become virtually inactive.

Canadian medievalists with a wide knowledge of plainsong include Gaston *Allaire, Terence *Bailey, Andrew *Hughes, and Neil K. Moran.

BIBLIOGRAPHY

Pelletier, J.R. 'L'Évolution de la musique religieuse au Canada français,' unpubl D MUS thesis, Laval 1932

Pierre-Alphonse, Brother. 'Chant et musique sacrés dans la Nouvelle-France,' unpubl MA thesis, U of Ottawa 1948

La Revue Saint-Grégoire. Official publication of the Quebec Société des Musiciens d'Église (Mar 1949–63)

Martel, Jules. 'Church music I'; Peaker, Charles. 'Church music II,' *Music in Canada*

Marie-Pauline de l'Assomption. 'Évolution de la situation de la musique liturgique à Montréal,' unpubl L MUS thesis, U of Montreal 1964 (RB)

PLAMONDON. Montreal family of musicians: 1 / Rodolphe, 2 / Arthur (Rodolphe's brother), 3 / Ernest-Gill (Rodolphe's nephew), and 4 / Lucien (Rodolphe's son). Also active in music, to a lesser degree, have been Antoine, Petrus, Geneviève, Guy, René, Luc, Gérard, and Jean-Paul.

1 (Joseph Marcel) **Rodolphe**. Tenor, teacher, cellist, b Montreal 18 Jan 1876, d there 28 Jan 1940. In his youth he studied cello with Louis *Charbonneau and solfège with Frédéric *Pelletier. On the suggestion of C.-O. *Lamontagne, who had married his sister Rose-Annette, Plamondon also took voice lessons from Guillaume *Couture. He occasionally sang solos at St James Cathedral and at the Gesù Church. He left for France in October 1895 and studied cello with Monteschi at the Rennes Cons, obtaining a medal seven months later. That summer he was engaged at the casino in Paramé, a suburb of St-Malo. His friends urged him to concentrate on singing and Plamondon went to Paris in November 1896. While working as a cellist at the Folies-parisiennes, he continued his instrumental training with Ferdinand Ronchini and studied voice with an elderly choirmaster named Castex. After consulting different teachers he finally chose to study with the tenor Pierre-Émile Engel. He sang in churches and salons where he met among others Massenet and Reynaldo Hahn.

In June 1897 Plamondon was in London and appeared with Melba at Windsor Hall and in various fashionable salons. In Paris he took more lessons from Engel and made his official debut 31 Dec 1897 at a concert at the Dominicans' Church in the Faubourg St-Honoré in which the baritone Jean-Baptiste Faure and the organist Charles-Marie Widor participated. Returning to London he sang at the Albert Hall 21 June 1898 with Melba, Clara Butt, and Pol Plançon. It was suggested that Plamondon accompany Melba to the USA, but he

Rodolphe Plamondon

chose instead to sing supporting roles for the opera season in Vichy in 1899 and Cairo in 1900.

On his return to Paris Plamondon worked again as a cellist at the Casino de Paris and was hired as the tenor soloist at St-Roch Church. In 1903 he married Marie Dufriche, a pianist who frequently played his accompaniments. They appeared together in recital at the Salle Pleyel 2 Feb 1904, and a favourable critical reception helped to further Plamondon's singing career. In Monte Carlo shortly afterwards he sang the leading roles in Gounod's *Faust*, Berlioz' *La Damnation de Faust*, and Boito's *Mefistofele*. In the summer of 1905 he achieved great success as Iopas in Berlioz' *Les Troyens à Carthage* before 12,000 people at the Théâtre antique in Orange. After singing in Rubinstein's *The Demon* in Monte Carlo (1906), Plamondon made his debut at the Paris Opera 6 May 1906 in the title role in *La Damnation de Faust*. There he later sang Hippolyte in Rameau's *Hippolyte et Aricie* (1908) and Castor in the same composer's *Castor et Pollux*. Except for the title role in the tenor version of Gluck's *Orphée*, which he later sang in Angers, and the role of Admète in *Alceste*, which he sang in Geneva, his operatic career seems to have ended before World War I.

Plamondon built an enviable reputation as a concert and oratorio soloist, eventually appearing with virtually every distinguished musical body in France and elsewhere in Europe. A list compiled by Gustave *Comte (*La Musique*, 1920) revealed that he must have sung in *La Damnation de Faust* (in both its staged and its original concert form) 250 times, Franck's *Les Béatitudes* 70 times, Berlioz' *L'Enfance du Christ* 150 times, Bach's two major *Passions* 50 times each, Beethoven's *Missa solemnis* 30 times, Bach's *Mass in B Minor* 30 times, and the Verdi *Requiem* 20 times. He also sang in such rarely performed works as Weber's *Euryanthe* (the role of Adolar in a concert performance under the direction of Vincent d'Indy; Plamondon was one of d'Indy's favourite singers), Elgar's *The Dream of Gerontius* (premiered in France at the Trocadéro de Paris 1906), and Edgar Tinel's *Franciscus* (sung in Tournai, Belgium, in 1908 and at the Montreal *Forum in 1926).

World War I obliged Plamondon to cancel numerous engagements in Germany and Austria. He took part in many patriotic demonstrations and in 1917 he toured the south of France with Saint-Saëns, singing the premiere of the song cycle *La Cendre rouge, Op 146* with the composer at the piano. In Poitiers he sang in *Le Déluge* under the direction of Saint-Saëns, who held the Canadian singer in high esteem and in fact dedicated to him his last work, the song 'À Saint-Blaise' (Durand 1921). Plamondon sang it in Montreal 19 Oct 1924.

Plamondon first returned to Canada in the summer of 1906 and gave a concert that fall at the *Monument national in Montreal and another at the *Auditorium de Québec. He did not visit Canada again until 1920, when he appeared at the Monument national with the pianist Jean *Dansereau in a recital of songs by Beethoven, Berlioz, Debussy, Fauré, Franck, and Méhul. Frédéric Pelletier wrote of Plamondon on that occasion: 'His artistry does not make itself obvious; it exists, and the least knowledgeable listener comes under its influence without realizing it, attributing to the voice alone the emotions he feels, not suspecting that sung by other more beautiful voices these pieces would bore him' (*Le Devoir*, 21 Apr 1920). A banquet was given in the singer's honour a few days later (24 April) at the Viger Hotel.

In 1923 Plamondon returned to Paris, where he met the bass Ulysse *Paquin; together they gave several recitals in Europe and in 1924 in Canada and New England. Another concert, in which Marie-Thérèse *Paquin, Jean-Baptiste *Dubois, and the *Assn Chorale Brassard took part, drew a full house to the Monument national in 1926, and Plamondon received a resounding tribute from his countrymen, who awarded him $2000, raised by popular subscription. Drawn by a vague plan for a conservatory, he returned to Montreal for good in 1928. He sang in the premiere of Healey *Willan's *L'Ordre du Bon Temps*, B20, at the 1928 *CPR Festival in Quebec City; he had taken part in the first festival the preceding year. In 1930 he and his son Lucien (a cellist) made a trans-Canada tour sponsored by the CPR. Plamondon established his own teaching studio in Montreal and also taught 1935–6 and 1939–40 at the École supérieure de musique (*École Vincent-d'Indy). Among his pupils were Louise *André, Germaine *Bruyère, Reine *Décarie, the tenors Richard Manning and Georges Toupin, and the CBC producer Claude Garneau.

Plamondon often sang music by Alfred *Laliberté, Rodolphe *Mathieu, and other Canadian composers. He premiered Mathieu's *Harmonie du soir* under the direction of Paul Paray in 1924 at the Concerts Lamoureux in Paris.

Plamondon's singing was described again by Pelletier after the 1926 recital at the Monument national: 'Here is artistry free of the ostentation so common among tenors concerned primarily with showing off their voices, using music only as a means to that end. With [Plamondon] it is exactly the opposite; the voice, warm and enveloping, is merely an instrument obedient to the spirit of the music, which he interprets with a devotion that is by turns serene and moving. Hearing him one has the impression that he is the priest of that cult of intangible beauty that is music' (*Le Devoir*, 19 Jan 1926).

In 1925 and 1926, near the end of his performing career, Plamondon made about a dozen records for Starr. Most of them featured French art songs (see *Roll Back the Years*). Plamondon's name was given to a street in Chicoutimi and in 1911 to an avenue in Montreal.

BIBLIOGRAPHY

Comte, Gustave. 'Rodolphe Plamondon,' *La Musique*, vol 2, Aug–Oct 1920

Gour, Romain. 'Rodolphe Plamondon, ténor classique,' *Qui?*, vol 5, Jun 1954

2 (Joseph) **Arthur**. Tenor, teacher, b Montreal 9 Jun 1881, d near Paris between 1939 and 1945; lauréat (AMQ). He studied piano with Émery *Lavigne and then voice with Guillaume *Couture, and became a soloist at the Montreal cathedral. He subsequently studied and gave concerts

in Paris. He married the soprano Alice Michot, who returned to Montreal with him in 1908 and was later a member of the *Montreal Opera Company. They founded the École de chant Plamondon-Michot, but returned to Paris in 1920. During this period Plamondon appeared in recital, singing songs by Louis Aubert with the composer at the piano. The Plamondons moved to New York in 1927, but returned to Paris two years later. Alice Raymond, who taught Raoul *Jobin, was a pupil of Alice Michot, and Albertine *Morin-Labrecque and Henri *Prieur were pupils of Plamondon. Plamondon died in the St-Denis concentration camp during World War II.

3 (Jean Paul) **Ernest-Gill**. Violinist, conductor, b Montreal 7 Jan 1896. He moved with his family to Seattle, Wash, ca 1900, and was introduced to the violin at six by his father, Gonzalve-Alphonse, a bassist, and later took lessons from a German musician named Schmidt and from Moritz Rosen. At 12 he was the soloist in a Paganini concerto and appeared frequently in concert and recital. When World War I forced him to abandon a period of study in Paris with Jacques Thibaud, he spent some time in New York and then went to Montreal, where he gave some recitals with the pianist Mme Damien Masson and met Wilfrid *Pelletier. He toured with Pelletier and the tenor Arthur Dufresne in eastern Canada and the USA. Later the success of a concert with Paul *Dufault at *His Majesty's Theatre, Montreal, earned him engagements across Quebec. Returning to Seattle, he became assistant concertmaster of the Clemmer Theatre orchestra; several successive periods in Montreal and Seattle ensued. Around 1920 he joined J.-J. *Goulet's orchestra at the Imperial Theatre, Montreal, and became its concertmaster and assistant conductor. He next worked in the orchestras of Jeremiah *Shea (at the Capitol Theatre until 1922) and Dave Levine (Palace Theatre). Returning to Seattle in 1925, he was the concertmaster of Sam Wineland's orchestra until the advent (ca 1927) of talking pictures, which brought about the orchestra's dissolution.

Plamondon then began an important radio career: he later estimated that he had participated in several thousand broadcasts. He also directed his own radio orchestra 1927–30 in Seattle and served 1929–30 as concertmaster of the Seattle SO under Karl Krueger. He then went to San Francisco, where he was concertmaster in an NBC orchestra directed by Mahlon Merrick, and he served 1933–6 as assistant music director to Meredith Willson and 1936–42 as regular conductor of ABC and NBC orchestral programs such as '45 Minutes from Broadway,' 'From Out of the West,' 'Stringtime,' and 'Waltz Time.' He directed the orchestra of the two networks 26 Jan 1940 in *The City of St. Francis*, a historical pageant presented before 12,000 persons for the *San Francisco Chronicle*'s 75th anniversary. He moved to Los Angeles in 1942 to head the department of music of ABC's western division. In 1945 he left his musical career to enter the business world.

4 **Lucien**. Cellist, teacher, b Paris ca 1907. He studied the cello with Francis Touche at the Paris Cons and appeared as soloist at the Touche concerts and with the Paris SO. He was the original principal cello of the CSM orchestra (*MSO) and he played the Schumann *Concerto* with the orchestra 29 Nov 1935. Marcel *Valois wrote at that time: 'His playing shows the greatest authority. He is an honest and sincere artist' (*La Presse*, 30 Nov 1935). In 1936 he performed the Elgar *Concerto* with the *Montreal Orchestra. A member of the Société de musique de chambre Euterpe and 1928–30 of the Durieux String Quartet, he also gave numerous concerts on the CRBC (later CBC). In 1930 he made a Canadian tour with his father, and at the Windsor Hotel, Montreal, he premiered Rodolphe *Mathieu's *Sonata* with the composer at the piano. In 1940 he was a cellist in Erno Rapee's orchestra at Radio City Music Hall, New York. Later, he was a member of the *Quebec SO, and ca 1953 he began teaching at the *CMQ. It is not known whether he pursued his musical career further. Pierre *Morin, Marcel St-Cyr, and Cécile Lanneville (*Prix d'Europe 1963), to whom he gave his Maggini cello, were among his pupils.

Other members of the Plamondon family, distant relatives of the preceding, have been active in music.

The painter Antoine Plamondon – b Ancienne-Lorette, near Quebec City, 29 Feb 1804, d Neuville, near Quebec City, 4 Sep 1895 – organized musical evenings at Neuville and performed at these as a pianist and violinist. He was also an organist and choirmaster in Neuville.

Petrus Plamondon – merchant, clerk, b Quebec City 30 Jun 1844, d there 7 Mar 1900 – was a member of small vocal ensembles and president 1870–2 of the *Union musicale de Québec.

In the same city Geneviève Plamondon – soprano, b Quebec City 25 May 1933; L MUS voice (Laval) – participated in a number of religious concerts, often as soloist with the *Chanteurs St-Coeur-de-Marie.

Three of the Plamondons from St-Raymond-de-Portneuf, near Quebec City, have distinguished themselves in music. Guy Plamondon (tenor, b 6 Jan 1921) studied with Émile *Larochelle, Raoul Jobin, and Jean-Paul *Jeannotte. He sang on the CBC and participated in productions of the *Théâtre lyrique de Nouvelle-France and in concerts.

Guy Plamondon's nephew René (tenor, b 14 Jan 1931) studied under Olga Kondakowa in Shawinigan and Édouard *Woolley in Montreal. He sang in the choirs of the *Opéra national du Québec and the *Opera Guild.

Luc Plamondon (lyricist, b 2 Mar 1942) has written for several Quebec singers, among them Renée *Claude, Nicole Croisille, Diane *Dufresne, Emmanuelle, Donald *Lautrec, Monique *Leyrac, and Ginette *Reno. He also wrote the lyrics for Michel Berger's rock-opera *Starmania* (1979).

Gérard (Gerry) Plamondon (b St-Hyacinthe, Que, 26 Jan 1933) acted as impresario for the pop singers Bruce and Eric, the Aristocrats, and the Sultans. He has worked also as a record producer.

Jean-Paul (Gene) Plamondon – country singer, guitarist, b Plamondon, north of Edmonton, 13 Aug 1938 – has appeared at the Grand Ole Opry in Nashville, Tenn. He has made several tours in western Canada. His birthplace was founded in 1908 by Joseph Plamondon, a keen amateur musician. JBM, GP, (AP)

Plateau Hall / Auditorium le Plateau. Montreal concert auditorium built in the early 1930s by the Montreal Catholic School Commission. Adjoining the school of the same name, it is situated on Calixa-Lavallée St, in the centre of Lafontaine Park. It seats 1307 – 807 on the main floor, 500 in the balcony.

The CSM (*MSO) gave about 1500 concerts there between 1935 and 1963, when the orchestra moved to the *PDA. The *Montreal Women's SO and the Montreal Youth SO also played there. Among renowned performers who appeared at Plateau Hall were Anderson, Flagstad, Gieseking, Horowitz, *Jobin, Wilhelm Kempff (Beethoven's 32 *Sonatas* in 1961), Rostropovich, Erna Sack (12 recitals in one season), and Solomon. Igor Stravinsky and the violinist Samuel Dushkin gave a joint recital there in 1937.

After 1963 the hall came to be used for the presentation of variety shows, pop or folk-music concerts, and occasional concerts of serious music. GP

Plate numbers. See Publishing.

Player pianos and nickelodeons
1 Player pianos
2 Nickelodeons

1 PLAYER PIANOS. The player piano was the most common automatic musical instrument in use in the first three decades of the 20th century and could be found in thousands of private homes. It was operated pneumatically, by means of perforated paper rolls which activated the hammer mechanisms. The most highly developed example of this type was the reproducing piano, usually a grand, the rolls of which could repeat a pianist's performance 'photographically,' reproducing nuances of dynamics and variations of tempo exactly. Noted examples of the reproducing piano were the 'Welte-Mignon,' the 'Ampico' (American Piano Co), and the 'Duo-Art' (Aeolian Co). In the late 1970s the capabilities of the reproducing piano still had not been duplicated even by the most sophisticated electronic high-fidelity equipment.

Only a few Canadian manufacturers made their own player pianos. Many simply converted their regular models by inserting player mechanisms purchased from other companies. The major manufacturer of mechanisms was the Otto *Higel Co, which began making player actions in 1906. Among Canadian companies which produced player pianos were the *Bell Piano and Organ Co, *Heintzman, Martin-*Orme, *Mason & Risch, and R.S. *Williams. *Doherty Pianos manufactured the Doherty Attachable Piano which converted any standard piano into a player, and the *Legge Organ Co built a self-player organ which operated on hand-recorded rolls. Higel established a roll-perforating operation in Toronto and produced a variety of rolls, many of which have survived in good condition.

Canadian pianists whose performances were reproduced on player rolls included Ellen *Ballon, Mona *Bates, Jeannette Durno, Willie *Eckstein, Gertrude *Huntley Green, Vera *Guilaroff, Wilfrid *Pelletier, Reginald *Stewart, Harry *Thomas, and Louis *Waizman.

Most player piano mechanisms wore out during the 1940s and 1950s. Rather than being repaired, the majority (approximately 80 per cent) were converted into conventional pianos. By the early 1960s a few enthusiasts had developed acceptable methods of restoration. As the complete process is a lengthy and sometimes expensive one, many owners do their own restoration. In 1978 Doyle Lane moved his collection of player pianos from Vancouver to Hillsborough, NC.

See also Piano building.

2 NICKELODEONS. The coin-operated nickelodeon, a variant of the player piano, was popular in Canada. Standard nickelodeons were installed in restaurants, cafés, ice cream parlours, drugstores, pool halls, and saloons from coast to coast. The term 'nickelodeon' began with 5-cent silent films, but quickly became associated with any form of entertainment that could be purchased for a nickel. The fully automatic electric nickelodeon was the forerunner of the jukebox. It was characterized by colourful art glass windows above the keyboard. Wurlitzer and Seeburg were the prime

A 1927 Heintzman player piano, from the Smythe Collection, Winnipeg

manufacturers. Interesting variations on the standard nickelodeon were the Violano Virtuoso, which contained a mechanically played violin with its own piano accompaniment; the Seeburg KT, an orchestrion which simulated piano, tambourine, mandolin, castanets, and xylophone; and the piano-nickelodeon, which could be played both manually and mechanically. Few of these variations were seen in Canada. The Violano in the Smythe collection was recovered from the Olympia Café in Brandon, Man. The Camrose Café in Camrose, Alta, was known to have an orchestrion which occupied the entire rear wall. Harry Hurtig of Thunder Bay, Ont, operated 35 nickelodeons in that area, including six Violanos – none remains today.

In the late 1970s the only known noteworthy examples of nickelodeons (fewer than 15) in Canada were in the Smythe collection (Winnipeg) and the Vinen collection (St Thomas, Ont). In 1980 isolated instruments were known to exist in Provost, Alta, Edmonton, Montreal, Toronto, and Vancouver.

See also Barrel organs; Instrument collections; Music boxes.

BIBLIOGRAPHY
Bowers, David G. *Put Another Nickel in* (New York 1968)
Givens, Larry. *Re-enacting the Artist* (New York 1970)
Ord-Hume, Arthur W.J.G. *Player Piano* (London 1970)
Carson, Susan. 'Play it again, Sam, Terry, Piero, Alice,' Toronto *Globe and Mail*, 18 Dec 1976
Roehl, Harvey N. *Player Piano Treasury* (New York 1976)
Lower, Thelma Reid. 'Mechanical memories,' *Music Market Canada*, vol 1, Dec 1977
Issues of the *Canadian Music Trades Journal*, Toronto (1900–33)

(TS)

PLOUFFE (Plouf), **Éva** (Marie) (m Stopes, m Lassère). Pianist, b Sorel, near Montreal, 7 Mar 1877, d ?. She studied piano with the Sisters of the Congregation of Notre-Dame in Sorel and, beginning in 1893, in Montreal with Victoria *Cartier, Arthur *Letondal, and Romain-Octave *Pelletier. During those years she composed a few pieces, one of which, *Théo*, a waltz, was published and enjoyed some success. She continued her studies in 1900 with Edwin Klahre at the New England Cons in Boston. Returning to Montreal in 1901, she gave a recital in Karn Hall 4 April. As a soloist in two concerts in 1902 with the *Goulet MSO, she played Mendelssohn's *Serenade and Allegro giojoso* and the Grieg *Concerto*. She organized the *Mendelssohn Trio and was its pianist 1904–6, leaving it to study in London with Percy Grainger. Few details of her life and career after 1906 are known. Her name appears 1906–7 in the list of members of the *Ladies' Morning Musical Club, and Mme Cécile Léger apparently asked her in 1916 to replace a soloist at the last minute. From time to time Plouffe shared concerts with the *Dubois String Quartet, playing, among other works, the César Franck *Sonata* with Albert *Chamberland. *Le Canada musical* made reference in 1920 to the return from England of Mme Plouffe-Stopes, and two years later she attended a banquet 14 June in honour of Salvator *Issaurel.

Nothing is known of Plouffe's activities for the next ten years, but on 4 Dec 1932 she played the Grieg *Concerto* with the *Montreal Orchestra at *His Majesty's Theatre. Thomas *Archer, in *The Gazette* (5 Dec 1932), said: 'it is a music that is easy to listen to, has a sweep to it and is unfolded with much charm and grace of manner. Mme Lassère caught the two last-named qualities to a nicety. She never overstressed the point and was content to let the music sing for itself.' Apparently Plouffe ended her career soon after her second marriage, to Édouard Lassère of Louisiana, and she remained subsequently in the USA.

BIBLIOGRAPHY
'Silhouettes musicales,' *P-T*, 67, 16 Oct 1897
'Mme Plouffe-Stopes,' *Canada musical*, Sep 1920
Musical Red Book
Musiciens canadiens

(AP)

Monsieur Pointu (b Paul Cormier). Violoneux, b Les Escoumins, Que, on the north shore of the St Lawrence River, of Acadian parents, 10 May 1922. He was one of a family of musicians who travelled throughout the province. At nine he began to learn the violin on an instrument made for him by his father and at 12 he was playing for dances in north shore communities. After military service during World War II, Cormier performed on CBJ radio in Chicoutimi and later settled in Montreal, playing in hotels, in nightclubs, and for dances. In 1950 he won a contest for violoneux in the Lac St-Jean/Chicoutimi/Saguenay/Charlevoix region. He worked 1954–60 as a mechanic, but maintained his musical skills and returned to his career, playing for several years in the Montreal area.

In 1970 Cormier was auditioned and accepted by Gilbert Bécaud to improvise a jig as accompaniment to the French pop singer's rendition of the song 'La Vente aux enchères' during a concert tour of Quebec. Taking the stage name 'Monsieur Pointu' from the expression 'La vie est triste, mais le bonheur est pointu,' he continued to perform with Bécaud for three years, the engagement entailing four tours in Europe (with three month-long engagements at the Olympia in Paris) and concerts in the Middle East and Africa. He toured again with Bécaud in the late 1970s, and his own popularity grew through his association with the singer. He has performed in Canada and the USA and has opened shows for the singers Julie Arel and Ginette *Reno. His performances include songs – some his own – monologues, mime, dance, and some novelty fiddling, eg, the use of a violin bow attached to a sewing machine.

The film *Monsieur Pointu* (NFB 1974), which combined both actual and animated-cartoon film footage of a Cormier performance, received an Academy Award nomination and won several other awards. Cormier's recordings include the LPs *Monsieur Pointu* (Franco TCM-973), *Monsieur Pointu* (Able ABB 7052), and *S'il vous plaît ...* (Pax TO-9218). Cormier is a member of CAPAC. He is also an amateur painter.

BIBLIOGRAPHY
Kroll, Stephen. 'Country is just as important in Quebec, too,' *CanComp*, 85, Nov 1973

MM

POIRIER, Benoît (Fidèle) (b Benjamin Perry). Organist, composer, b Tignish, PEI, 17 Oct 1882, d Chomedey, near Montreal, 7 Oct 1965; BA (St-Joseph) 1902, hon MA (St-Joseph) 1928. He was only 13 when he first played the organ at St-Joseph U in Memramcook, NB, and in 1897 he played at St Thomas Church. In 1903 he began teaching at the Collège de Montréal and accompanied the Trappist Father Guillaume on a tour of the city's seminaries and important churches to promote the methods of plainsong performance of the Benedictines of Solesmes, France. Poirier was for a time the organist at the Séminaire de philosophie and successively at the churches of Ste-Hélène in 1906, St-Patrice in 1908, St-Vincent-de-Paul in 1909, and St-Jacques in 1914. He also served 1921–54 as organist at Notre-Dame Church, succeeding J. Daniel *Dussault. He gave organ recitals at all of these churches and taught 1921–5 for the Dames du Sacré-Coeur at Sault-au-Récollet, Que.

Poirier was elected a member of the board of the *Schola cantorum in 1919 and was its president 1923–5; he was a member of the board of examiners of the *Cons national, and was director and principal teacher 1953–9 at the Cons Royal de Montréal. He left some compositions for organ and for piano, eg, his *Rhapsodie d'airs canadiens* for piano (Archambault 1922), of which a version for brass band by Joseph *Vézina was performed the same year by Sousa's band in Montreal, Toronto, and Philadelphia. He also wrote numerous motets, patriotic songs, an 'Ecce fidelis' (Archambault 1922), and harmonizations of the *25 Cantiques d'après le style grégorien* (Schola cantorum 1923).

CG (DM)

POIRIER, Lucien. Organist, musicologist, teacher, b St-Alphonse-Rodriguez, near Joliette, Que, 29 Nov 1943; BA (Séminaire de Joliette) 1965, premier prix organ (CMM) 1969, L LITT (Strasbourg) 1971, M MUS (Strasbourg) 1972. He began his music studies in 1958 at the Séminaire de Joliette (piano and organ) and continued at the *CMM with Bernard *Lagacé (organ) and Kenneth *Gilbert (harpsichord). He was awarded a grant by the Quebec Ministry of Education and continued his training 1969–72 in Europe with Eduard Müller in Basel (harpsichord) and Gaston Litaize in Paris (organ). He was the regular organist 1965–9 at the cathedral in St-Jean, Que. In 1966 he began teaching organ and harpsichord. He continued teaching these at *Laval U, beginning in 1972, and the *U of Montreal in 1974, along with musicology which became a specialty. He also has given courses at other universities. He is an active recitalist and has been heard in organ and chamber music broadcasts on CBC radio.

As both musicologist and performer Poirier has been interested primarily in medieval and renaissance music and in the works of J.S. Bach and his immediate predecessors. However he also has championed the contemporary French composer Georges Migot and, under the aegis of the Assn des amis de l'oeuvre et de la pensée de Georges Migot (founded 1976; Poirier is an active member), he has made an LP of Migot's organ music (1978, GM 30002). He edited the *Second Livre d'orgue* of Migot (A. Leduc 1979), and his edition of the third book of Migot's organ music was in preparation in 1980. Poirier is a contributor to *EMC*.

Poirier is the brother of Réjean *Poirier. His wife, the flutist Louise LeComte, was winner of a *Prix d'Europe in 1969.

WRITINGS
'Georges Migot et la musique d'orgue,' unpubl M MUS thesis, Strasbourg 1972

'Pachelbel, sa vie, son oeuvre,' record jacket notes for *Pachelbel* (Arion ARN 38273) recorded by B. Lagacé (May 1974)
'À propos des oeuvres pour flûte douce de Georges Migot,' *Carnet Musical*, vol 12, Jul 1975
– and Poirier, Réjean. 'Musique pour orgue,' *Dictionnaire de la musique: Science de la musique II*, ed Marc Honegger (Paris 1976)
Notes accompanying recordings of Bach's complete works for harpsichord, by Mireille Lagacé, on the Calliope label (CAL 1651, 1652, and 1653, released 1979)
HPn

POIRIER, Réjean. Organist, harpsichordist, teacher, composer, b St-Alphonse-Rodriguez, near Joliette, Que, 22 Apr 1950; premier prix organ (CMM) 1971, certificat d'études supérieures harpsichord (CMM) 1971. He studied piano and organ 1960–5 with his brother Lucien, organ 1965–6 with Antoine *Bouchard at *Laval U, and organ under Bernard *Lagacé and harpsichord with Kenneth *Gilbert 1967–71 at the *CMM. He continued his studies 1971–3 with Xavier Darasse at the Toulouse Cons and won several international awards including a first prize at the 1973 J.S. Bach International Organ Competition in Bruges.

On his return to Montreal (1973) Poirier divided his time between the teaching of organ, harpsichord, and keyboard harmony (at the *U of Montreal, Laval U, *Concordia U, the St-Laurent Cegep, Vanier College, and the *JMC Orford Art Centre) and concerts and broadcasts, mainly for CBC radio. He began researching the use of graphic symbols in composition as a substitute for traditional notation. He participated in the founding of the *Pro organo in 1969, the Concerts d'orgue de Montréal in 1974, and the *Studio de musique ancienne de Montréal in 1974, co-directing the latter with Christopher *Jackson. He has given many recitals in Canada, the USA, and Europe.

Poirier has written *Hallucinations I* for trumpet, organ, and percussion (premiered in Toulouse in January 1973), *Trope* for two percussion and piano (1973, commissioned by the Toulouse Cons for its chamber music class), and *Arcane* for organ, of which he gave the premiere in Montreal in May 1977.

WRITINGS
See Lucien Poirier. HPn

POITIERS DU BUISSON (Dubuisson), **Jean-Baptiste**. Organist, merchant, b diocese of Amiens, France, ca 1645, d Montreal 27 Mar 1727. He lived 1670–98 in New England before settling in Montreal, where he was active mainly in commerce. According to the records he appears to have been the first regular organist of Notre-Dame Church, from 1705 to at least 1718. In the beginning he received no salary and that undoubtedly is why in 1705 and 1707 the churchwarden-treasurer remitted the amount for his pew (10 francs). In 1713 'M. Dubuisson, organist, was given a stipend of 100 francs per annum.' He received occasional gratuities: 100 francs in 1715 and the same sum again in 1718 'for having played the organ for several years.' His successor ca 1721–34, Charles-François *Coron, is not mentioned until 1722 or 1723 at which time 'Sr Coron, organist, was paid for 20 months of playing the organ ... 83 francs 15 sols in silver or 50 francs in merchandise.'

BIBLIOGRAPHY
'Souvenirs artistiques de Notre-Dame de Montreal,' *Canada musical*, 1 Dec 1880
Lapalice, Ovide-M. 'Les organistes et maîtres de musique à Notre-Dame de Montreal,' *BRH*, vol 25, Aug 1919
GP

Poland. The first Polish settlement in Canada was established by Kazubian peasants in 1860 at Wilno, in Renfrew County, south of Pembroke, Ont. The immigration of Poles was steady and sizeable by 1900 and reached its peak in the 1950s; the 1971 census registered 316,425 Polish-Canadians – the fifth largest group among Canada's minorities. (Almost half were living in the cities of southern Ontario, the rest in Alberta, Manitoba, British Columbia, and Quebec). Though some Polish-Canadians are Jewish, most belong to the Roman Catholic church, which has played a central role in the preservation of Polish cultural traditions in Canada.
1 Traditions
2 Musicians of Polish origin or descent
3 Polish visitors
4 Canadian visitors to Poland

1 TRADITIONS. The rich Polish folk music tradition is demonstrated by some 40 flourishing dance, choral, and instrumental ensembles. With few exceptions (including one group which participated in the Winnipeg *CPR Festival of 1928), these ensembles were founded in the 1950s and 1960s. Performances occur at national celebrations, social gatherings, and multicultural events. The preferred dances are Krakowiak, Polonaise, Kujawiak, Mazurka, Oberek, and Góral. Usually a performance offers a suite of dances from a particular region. Accompaniment may be supplied by accordion, violin, drums, and, occasionally, mandolin and clarinet. Among the best-known Canadian ensembles are the Polish 'Sokol' Choir (Winnipeg; founded in 1914 and awarded first prize in the 1976 World Festival of Polish Choirs in Koszalin, Poland) and Podhale (Montreal; founded in 1965). Choral ensembles often are drawn from the elders because the mother tongue is better preserved by them. Besides folksongs, the repertoire includes examples of the Polish 'learned' tradition. The Archives of the Canadian Centre for Folk Culture Studies of the *National Museum of Man in Ottawa held, in 1975, 450 folksongs, 51 instrumental pieces, and 5 folk instruments collected in Renfrew County by John Glofcheskie. (In 1973–4 Glofcheskie prepared for the centre a study entitled 'The musical folklore of Canada's oldest Polish community.')

2 MUSICIANS OF POLISH ORIGIN OR DESCENT. Canadians Walter *Buczynski, Victor *Feldbrill, Janina *Fialkowska, Anna-Marie *Globenski, Eugene *Kash, and John *Weinzweig have Polish antecedents. Native Poles prominent in Canadian musical life include the pianists Leo *Barkin, Marek *Jablonski, Czeslaw Kaczynski (erstwhile director of the Trois-Rivières Cons and in the 1970s a piano teacher at the *CMM), and Frédéric Bertozisky (head of the Académie internationale de piano in Montreal); the violinists Ida *Haendel, Henryk Szeryng (who spent a year in Montreal during the 1940s), and Henri Czaplinski (who taught Harry *Adaskin and Ernest *Farmer); the soprano Adelina Czapska who taught 1940–50 in Montreal (Napoléon *Bisson, Marie-José Forgues, and Alphonse Ledoux were among her pupils); the cellist Martin Hoherman, who lived briefly in Toronto and Winnipeg during the 1950s; the US pianist Emanuel Ax, who arrived in Canada from Poland as a child with his parents in 1959 and studied in Winnipeg with Jean *Broadfoot; Czeslaw Gladyszewski, appointed conductor of the *Sherbrooke SO in 1973; the choir director Alexsander Charuba; the composers Harry *Freedman, Mieczyslaw *Kolinski, Peter Paul *Koprowski, Herbert *Ruff, and Boleslaw Szczeniowski (also an engineer in Montreal); the musicologist Ramón Pelinski of the universities of Ottawa and Montreal; and the Chopin scholar Mateusz Glinski (b Warsaw 1892, d Welland, Ont, 1976), who was visiting professor 1959–65 at Assumption College, Windsor, Ont.

There have been two Chopin societies in Canada. The first, La Société Frédéric Chopin au Canada (Quebec City, 1926–ca 1974) was founded by Léo *Roy and was essentially a single-handed crusade. The Frederic Chopin Society of Canada, founded in 1974 in Toronto, presents music of the romantic period in authentic style and promotes young Canadian pianists in recital.

3 POLISH VISITORS. In the 19th century several Polish musicians performed in Canada. Among these were the soprano Marcella Sembrich (1880s), the violinist Henryk Wieniawski (1872), the pianist Ignace Jan Paderewski (1892), the tenor Wladyslaw Mierzwinski (1880s), and the bass Edouard de Reszke (1890s). Twentieth-century visitors have included the composers Lucjan Kamienski, Felix Labunski, Witold Lutoslawski, and Krzysztof Penderecki; the harpsichordist Wanda Landowska; the pianists Alexander Brailowsky, Halina Czerny-Stefanska, Tadeusz Kerner, Witold Malcuzynski, Artur Rubinstein, Halina Siedzieniewska, and the Polish-American Ruth Slenczynska; the violinists Bronislaw Huberman (father-in-law of Barbara *Pentland) and Wanda Wilkomirska; and the cellist Roman Jablonski.

Polish groups which have appeared in Canada include the folk ensembles Mazowsze and Slask, the Warsaw Philharmonic (under Witold Rowicki), the Poznan Children's Choir, and the Szczecin Choir, which toured (1978) in an exchange with the *Vancouver Bach Choir which had performed in Poland in 1977. Paul Kletzki, Kazimierz Kord, and Stanislaw Skrowaczewski have conducted in Canada, and in 1974 Kord led the *TS on a European tour. Under the sponsorship of the *JMC several young Polish musicians have performed in Canada.

4 CANADIANS VISITORS TO POLAND. Similarly, many Canadian musicians have appeared in Poland. Bertha *Crawford sang annually in Warsaw 1919–34. Jean-Pierre *Ferland in 1963, Pauline *Julien in 1964, Monique *Leyrac in 1965, and Donald *Lautrec in 1967 have been winners of the International Song [competition] Festival at Sopot. In 1975 the pianist John *Hendrickson won third prize and a special music critics' prize at the Frederic Chopin International Piano Competition in Warsaw. Other Canadians who have appeared in Poland include Marek Jablonski in 1964, Suzanne *Shulman with Claude *Savard in 1971, Hugh *McLean in 1973 and 1975, Maureen *Forrester in 1973 and 1976, the *NACO in 1973, Mario *Bernardi in 1975, the *McGill Chamber Orchestra in 1977, the *CCMC in 1978, and the *Lyric Arts Trio in 1978, performing compositions by Robert *Aitken, Bruce *Mather, and Paul *Pedersen at the Warsaw Autumn International Festival of contemporary music. Joan *Patenaude performed Nedda in *I Pagliacci* with the State Opera in Warsaw in 1977 and returned to sing the leading roles in *Madama Butterfly* and *La Traviata* in 1978. (RPl)

POLGAR, Tibor. Conductor, composer, b Budapest 1907, naturalized Canadian 1969. He was a conductor of the Hungarian Radio SO 1925–50, the Philharmonia Hungarica in Germany 1962–4, and the U of Toronto SO 1965–6. He was an instructor in the *U of Toronto Opera Dept 1966–75 and a coach for the *COC. He often employs Hungarian idioms in his compositions. His short opera *The*

Glove, commissioned in 1973 by *Prologue to the Performing Arts for performance by the COC, has a libretto by George Jonas based on a poem of Schiller. With its original Prologue cast – Riki *Turofsky, Michael Burgess, and Avo Kittask – it was telecast 5 Nov 1975 by the CBC. By May 1976 it had been given more than 90 performances. In 1978 Polgar composed the score for the Canadian film *In Praise of Older Women* and appeared briefly in it as a pianist. Polgar is a member of CAPAC and an associate of the *CMCentre.

SELECTED COMPOSITIONS

Kérök 'The Suitors,' opera. 1954 (Budapest 1954). Ms

A European Lover 'Musical satire disguised as an opera' (George Jonas). 1965 (ca 1966). CMCentre

The Last Words of Louis Riel, cantata (J. Robert Colombo). 1966–7. CMCentre

The Troublemaker (Jonas). 1968. CMCentre

Variations on a Hungarian Folk Song. 1969. Hp, str, tim. CMCentre

The Glove, comic opera (Schiller-Jonas). 1973 (CBC 1974). CMCentre

Three Poems in Music. 1977. Orch. CMCentre

Also other orch, chamb works at CMCentre, v and choir works, many arr of German and Hungarian folksongs

BIBLIOGRAPHY

Schulman, Michael. 'Tibor Polgar: seeing his music appreciated by the public,' *CanComp*, May 1976

– 'Two films, two music scores, two less-than-happy composers,' ibid, Feb 1979 CF

Political songs. In contrast to *patriotic songs, which are broad in appeal and generally avoid controversy, political songs usually display intense partisanship and relate to specific events or situations, such as elections, strikes, unemployment, or discrimination. They vent grievances and scorn, often through satire, and are meant to boost morale and rouse support.

No study of political song in Canada as a whole has come to the attention of *EMC*'s editors. *Chansons politiques du Québec* (Montreal 1977 and 1979) does treat the subject, but only in relation to the one province, covering the period 1765–1858. It appears that among the folk songs collected and sheet music printed in Canada political songs have a small place. Political parties, election campaigns, and the trade union movement have inspired little original music, although new words or adaptations of existing verses to new situations have been fairly common.

In the 18th century satirical songs of a political nature were common. An early instance is mentioned in the *DCB* entry on Rigaud de Vaudreuil (vol 2, p 570, of English edition): '[Raudot] had been greatly offended in the spring of 1708 when satirical songs written about him by persons of Vaudreuil's entourage began to circulate in the streets of Quebec.' A 'Chanson sur les Élections' printed in the Quebec *Gazette* for 24 May 1792 and to be sung to the tune of 'air du haut en bas' is a typical example from an 18th-century newspaper. Such songs frequently were printed separately on broadsides. The BN du Q preserves several examples. The music is to be sung to a familiar tune, identified in each case.

Political crises, such as the unrests of the 1830s, the Fenian Raids, the Northwest Rebellion, the South African War, and the two world wars all produced songs (see Wars, rebellions, and uprisings), and so did *Confederation (eg, 'The *Anti-Confederation Song'). Most of this music is patriotic rather than political, but 'Un *Canadien errant,' 'La Mère canadienne,' and 'Le *Drapeau de Carillon' combine both elements. Another such song, 'La Prise de Toronto,' presumably sung in 1837 and expressing support for William Lyon Mackenzie in his fight against the 'Family Compact' of Toronto, was published in *New Frontiers*, vol 3 (Summer 1954). The manuscript is preserved at the National Museum of Man in Ottawa.

In his *Candid Chronicles* (Toronto 1925) Hector *Charlesworth mentions an election song 'Ontario, Ontario' which had an unfortunate effect on the Liberals' chances at the polls in the general election of 1882. But very little election music has been published or printed as a give-away; one example is the *Civic Reform March* [no words] by Cecil Birkett, issued in Ottawa in 1900 [no publisher], distributed free 'with the compliments of Alderman W.D. Morris, candidate for Mayor for 1901. Platform – Honest Civic Government.' Other examples are 'La Mairie' and 'La Mairie à Longueuil,' adapted to the tunes of 'La Fille de Mme Angot' and 'Partant pour la Syrie' respectively and written for the 1904 municipal election at Longueuil, Que.

On the whole, 20th-century songwriters in Canada have remained of the persuasion that music and politics inhabit separate spheres of life. Moreover, their audience, the Canadian public, in particular the English-speaking majority, has not been prone to strong political sentiment – protest marches and political rallies have been rare. It is a pity, from a musical and historical point of view, that such significant political episodes as the Depression and the many industrial strikes have reverberated so faintly in song.

'Protest songs of English Canada' (1978), a research essay by a Carleton U student, Mary-Jane Lipkin, identifies and examines 32 songs, from the songbooks of *Creighton, *Fowke, *Peacock, and John *O'Donnell, and from other sources. Most are miners' and loggers' songs protesting economic exploitation. Characteristic titles are 'The Irish Labourer,' *'Hard, Hard Times,' 'Drill Ye Tarriers,' 'The Estevan Strike Song,' 'The Loggers' Plight,' and 'Bowser Boys of Seventy Twa.'

The 'quiet revolution' in Quebec, the Acadian movement in the Maritime provinces, and the many protest and 'liberation' movements of the 1960s and 1970s brought about change. The songs of some of the urban folksingers, and of the chansonniers of Quebec (Georges *Dor, Jean-Pierre *Ferland, Claude *Gauthier, Félix *Leclerc, Sylvain Lelièvre, Claude *Léveillée, Raymond *Lévesque, Jacques *Michel, Gilles *Vigneault) and Acadia (Edith *Butler and Calixte Duguay) had a political component (see *Chansonniers), as had the content of the cabarets and revues of those decades. Often the 'politics' depended on the emphasis of the performance and the mood of the audience, however, rather than on bold statements or overt satire. Indeed, the persistent broad-brush mockery and caustic wit of the songs of Nancy White for CBC radio's AM network news-commentary program 'Sunday Morning' in the late 1970s were exceptional in the genre.

See also *H.M.S. Parliament*; Musical theatre; *My Fur Lady*; Octobre; *Spring Thaw*.

LITERATURE

1879 Père Louison [Rémi Tremblay]. *Chansonnier politique du 'Canard'* (Montreal: Presses à vapeur du 'Canard'). A collection of 10 satirical songs covering 18 months of a particularly eventful period of Quebec political life between March 1878, when the elected government was dissolved by the lieutenant-governor, and October 1879, when the Conservatives took over from the Liberals. Some songs attack politicians directly. Rémi Tremblay (1847–1926) was a soldier and journalist who settled in Ottawa in 1896 as a translator. He died on Guadeloupe Island.

1893 *Chants des Patriotes*, 'recueil noté de chansons patriotiques canadiennes et françaises' (Montreal: Yon). The second edition (1903) has 54 songs, some 20 more than the first, including *'Ô Canada,' 'Le Drapeau de carillon,' and *'Ô Canada! mon pays! mes amours!,' as well as folk songs and French patriotic songs such as 'La Marseillaise' and 'La Chant du départ.' The book carries the tunes but no accompaniments.

1967 Dick MacDonald, compiler, ed. *Singing Headlines* (Montreal: self-publ). 16 songs, not all political. 'News highlights from Canada's past as interpreted in song'

1970 *Raoul Duguay. *Manifeste de l'Infonie* (Montreal: Les Éditions du Jour). Political poetry and music

1971 R. Duguay. *Lapokalipsô* (ibid). Political poetry and music

1973 Yvon Deschamps. *Monologues* (Montreal). Poems of a political and satirical nature; no music

1975 John C. O'Donnell, ed. *The Men of the Deeps* (Waterloo, Ont). The volume includes miners' and union songs.

1976 N. Brian Davis, ed. *The Poetry of the Canadian People 1720–1920* (Toronto). No music

1977, 1979 Maurice Carrier and Monique *Vachon. *Chansons politiques du Québec*, 2 vols (Montreal). Chronological compilation of some 230 political songs in French, all with melody, tune-reference, and pertinent publishing and background information. By 1980 this remained the most significant study of the political song of any region of Canada.

1979 Philip J. *Thomas. *Songs of the Pacific Northwest* (Vancouver). The book includes political songs and some songs of striking miners.

DISCOGRAPHY

Come Hell or High Water / Songs of the Buchans Miner. 1975–6. Breakwater 1001

The Men of the Deeps. O'Donnell cond. 1967. Apex AL7-1647

The Men of the Deeps. 1975. Wat CSPS 898

The Men of the Deeps 'II.' 1976. Wat CSPS 1011

BIBLIOGRAPHY

Vanasse, Jean-Paul. 'Tout cela est bien plus que chansons,' *Liberté*, vol 10, Jan–Feb 1968

Fowke, Edith. 'Labour and industrial protest songs in Canada,' *JAF*, vol 82, Jan–Mar 1969

Dictionnaire des oeuvres littéraires du Québec, vols 1 and 2 (Montreal 1978, 1980)

Maurice Pollack Foundation. Established in 1955 by Maurice Pollack (merchant, philanthropist, b Kanele, Kiev, 28 Jan 1885, d Quebec City 16 Dec 1968). After arriving in Canada in 1902, Pollack settled in Quebec City, where he opened a department store and became prosperous. He set up a foundation to aid Canadian organizations. The foundation has allocated most of its funds to institutions in Quebec, notably to *Laval U, *McGill U, the *Quebec SO, and the *MSO. In 1966 it earmarked a fund for the eventual construction of a concert hall at McGill U. It was not until 1973 that the decision was made to transform and enlarge the former Assembly Hall of the Royal Victoria College, renamed the Strathcona Music Building in 1971, into a modern concert hall, to be named Maurice Pollack Hall in accordance with the terms of the contract drawn up between the foundation and McGill. Inaugurated in 1975, it became McGill's first modern concert facility (specifically designed as such).

The Pollack Foundation is made up chiefly of members of the family. Maurice Pollack was its president until 1968. At his death he was succeeded by his son Charles C. Pollack.

POLSON, Arthur (Ludwig). Violinist, composer, conductor, b Vancouver 2 Mar 1934. His father wrote pop songs, including 'The Hope Mountain

Waltz' recorded by US bandleader Bob Crosby. Polson began violin lessons with his father at four and studied subsequently with Joy Calvert and Gregori *Garbovitsky in Vancouver and Louis Persinger in California. He was a member 1954–62 of the *Vancouver SO, concertmaster 1962–4 of the *Victoria SO, and briefly (1965) deputy concertmaster of the Vancouver SO. He played for 12 years in the *Cassenti Players. He became concertmaster of the *Winnipeg SO and the *CBC Winnipeg Orchestra in 1966 and has conducted the latter frequently, introducing new works by Alan Hovhaness and others. In 1967 he formed the Festival Quartet of Canada and in 1970 he organized the Festival Players of Canada. He has performed as a soloist and chamber musician in Canada and the USA, appearing for example at *Expo 67 and in 1966 and 1968 at the *Stratford Festival. He taught 1970–1 at the *U of Manitoba and was conductor of the Greater Winnipeg Schools Orchestra.

Polson is a prolific composer. His works include a *Concertino* (1957) for violin and strings, *Tension No. 2* (1958) for violin (or flute) and orchestra, *Introduction and Scherzo* (1959) for cello and orchestra, *Concerto* (1965) for bassoon and strings (written for George *Zukerman), a *Concerto* (1974) for flute, strings, and percussion commissioned by the *Manitoba Chamber Orchestra, and a *Concerto* for trumpet and orchestra commissioned by the Winnipeg SO and premiered 24 Feb 1978 by the orchestra and Ramon Parcells. Other works include a *Quartet* (1964) for violin, oboe, clarinet, and bassoon, an *Organ Concerto* (1969), two *String Quartets*, and various other chamber pieces and songs. His *Duo No. 5* for horn and piano has been recorded by Gloria Johnson and William *Aide. Polson is a member of CAPAC and an associate of the *CMCentre.

Polson's wife Nora (b Borrowman), an actress and singer, was born in Vancouver. She spent five years as a child actress in Hollywood and later was associated with productions of the Greater Vancouver Operatic Society and the *Vancouver Opera Assn.

DISCOGRAPHY

Brahms – Leclair – Polson *Dracula Fantasy*. Aide pf. 1968. CBC SM-64

Kreisler. Isaacs pf. 1971. CBC SM-91

Pentland *Trio* for violin, cello, and piano. J. Hunter vc, Pentland pf. 1967. RCI 242

Polson *Improvisation* for violin and orchestra. CBC Wpg O, Wild cond. 1968. CBC SM-68 (LI)

Polydor Ltd / Ltée (Polydor Records of Canada Ltd, 1966–73). Canadian recording branch of the international entertainment conglomerate PolyGram Inc. Polydor Records of Canada Ltd was established in 1966 with head offices in Montreal. Presidents have been Fred Exon 1966–70 and Evert Garretsen 1970–5, succeeded by Timothy Harrold in 1975. In 1979 branch offices existed in Toronto, Winnipeg, Calgary, and Vancouver. Polydor Ltd (later PolyGram Distribution Inc) is devoted largely to the distribution and marketing in Canada of recordings on labels owned by PolyGram, among them Deutsche Grammophon and Philips, as well as Barclay, Mercury, MGM, and Polydor.

Several Canadians have recorded for the Polydor label in Canada, the USA, Britain, or France. They include the guitarists Randy Bachman and Pat Travers; the singers Garfield French, Joey Gregorash, Félix *Leclerc, Claude *Léveillée, Monique *Leyrac, Jacques *Michel, and Diane Tell; and the pop (or rock bands) the Bells, Goddo, *Maneige, and Moxy.

When *London Records of Canada (1967) Ltd was taken over by PolyGram Inc in 1980, PolyGram Distribution Inc began to distribute the London labels in Canada. CGa, MM

POMER, Anne or **Ann** (b Pomerenski, m Toffan, m James, m Lazzari). Violinist, conductor, teacher, b Gimli (north of Winnipeg) 1 Mar 1913, d Rome 2 Jan 1971; LRSM. Her teacher in Winnipeg was John *Waterhouse. She attended chamber music classes given by the Budapest String Quartet in Minneapolis and took lessons with Boris Kroyt while there. She was a member 1938–42 of Frank *Thorolfson's Winnipeg Chamber Orchestra and played 1939–43 in Waterhouse's studio concerts and, after 1943, in his Winnipeg Chamber Music Society presentations. During the 1940s she led a studio string orchestra (at first made up of her pupils, but later including other Winnipeg players). In 1958 she became the founding conductor of the Winnipeg Chamber Ensemble, a 16-piece string orchestra which gave 13 concerts in its four-year history. She also played for many years in the *Winnipeg SO and in CBC orchestras.

Pomer's pupils in Winnipeg included John Graham (later a viola recitalist in England), Victoria Jakimovitch (Winnipeg SO, *MSO), Mary Kryschuk (m *Stanick), Patricia Pats, Elsie Paziuk (Winnipeg SO), and Gwen *Thompson. Pomer later moved to Rome where she formed a string ensemble, Complesso Classico a Plettro, the first orchestra in Italy conducted by a woman.

Pomer's brother Victor Pomer (b Winnipeg 9 Jun 1930, and also a pupil) was concertmaster of the Winnipeg Chamber Ensemble and played with the Winnipeg SO from the late 1940s until 1969, when he joined the *NACO. Her second husband, Edmund James, was a violist and a teacher at the *Bornoff and *Konrad conservatories. (FH)

PONTBRIAND, Henri. Tenor, teacher, b Sorel Que, 18 Jan 1894, d Rawdon, near Joliette, Que, 12 Jun 1969. After training as a naval draughtsman he moved to Montreal ca 1916 and took lessons from Albert *Clerk-Jeannotte (voice) and Victoria *Cartier (piano). He appeared in concerts with Émile *Taranto and Léo-Pol *Morin before going to Paris to study 1921–2 with Louis Delaquerrière. He lived 1922–8 in New York and continued his studies with Enrico Rosati and Caruso's coach, Salvatore Fucito. He gave concerts at the Waldorf-Astoria and Vanderbilt hotels, among others, alternating with Richard Crooks and Jan Peerce. In San Francisco he performed with an orchestra conducted by Albert Coates. On his return to Montreal in 1929 he opened a teaching studio and sang on the CNR radio station and on CKAC, in particular on 'L'Heure provinciale.' His repertoire included opera and art songs. His studio, which he closed in 1932, was frequented by many pupils, including Jeanne *Desjardins, Mary *Henderson, and Jacques *Labrecque. In 1933 he moved to Rawdon, Que; there he devoted himself to town planning and tourist accommodation. He was president of the *JMC centre in Joliette in 1961. GP

POOLE, Clifford. Pianist, teacher, b Reddish, near Manchester, 25 May 1916. He was taken to Canada as a child and settled in Toronto where he studied piano with Mona *Bates. With another Bates pupil, Gordon *Hallett, Poole formed the Poole-Hallett Duo, which gave concerts 1936–42 in Toronto and Montreal and on CBC radio. In 1938 Poole made his solo debut at *Eaton Auditorium, Toronto. He served in the RCAF during World War II and occasionally, while on leave, performed with the Bates Ten-Piano Ensemble. With his wife, Margaret *Parsons, he formed the Parsons-Poole Piano Duo and toured Canada and the USA extensively 1954–65. (See Parsons for discography and publications.)

Poole taught 1938–41 and 1943–8 at the TCM / *RCMT. In 1948 he joined the staffs of the *Western Ontario Cons and the Music Teachers' College, both in London, Ont. In 1956 the conservatory and college became constituent parts of the *U of Western Ontario, and Poole served 1957–60 as principal of both. In 1963 he rejoined the piano dept of the RCMT and began teaching piano at the Faculty of Music, *U of Toronto. Beverley *Cavanagh, Chia-Yue Chou, Zenovia Kushpeta, Clifford *von Kuster, Marjan *Mozetich, Howard Munn, Halyna Mychalczuk, and Raymond *Pannell have been among Poole's many pupils. Between 1949 and 1962 Poole and Margaret Parsons composed, compiled, and edited much piano music for young players.

In 1968 Poole was appointed music director at St Anne's Anglican Church in Toronto. He directs the St Anne's Music and Drama Society, which specializes in productions of Gilbert & Sullivan operettas. Poole became conductor of the York Regional SO (York SO) in 1973 and of the East York SO in 1978, maintaining both positions simultaneously.

PORTER, Charles Henry. Organist- choirmaster, teacher, composer, b Naugatuck, Conn, 1 Feb 1856, d New Haven, Conn, 26 Sep 1929. Porter is known to have been in Halifax as early as 1877, when he conducted the Halifax Philharmonic Union in the inaugural concert of the Academy of Music. Except for the mid-1880s, when he studied in Leipzig, Porter was organist-choirmaster 1881–1906 at St Matthew's Presbyterian Church and a founder (1882) and the conductor, until 1906, of the *Orpheus Club in Halifax. He was a member ca 1890 of the Leipzig Trio, with Heinrich *Klingenfeld (violin), and Ernst Doering (cello).

For his work as the first director (1887–1900) of the Halifax Cons (*Maritime Cons of Music) Porter was described as 'one of the Fathers of Music in Halifax, for it is through his patient and capable teaching that Halifax can boast of so many home-reared artists in the piano and organ branches' (Halifax *Herald*, 15 May 1907). After his resignation from the conservatory Porter pursued a career as an executive with the Equitable Life Assurance Co, but maintained his other musical affiliations in Halifax until 1906, when he moved to New Haven. In 1903 he was Sir Alexander Mackenzie's associate conductor for the Halifax presentations of the *Cycle of Musical Festivals.

Porter's compositions include *Violin Sonata, Op 1* (Kistner 1886), 'Serenade' (G. Schirmer 1887, words by C.G.D. Roberts), and a *Te Deum in C* (G. Schirmer 1891). His Christmas anthem 'Sing unto the Lord' was performed often at St Matthew's.

Porter's brother Samuel (d Halifax before 1895) was organist-choirmaster 1876–87 at St Paul's Cathedral, Halifax, and the violist and leader of the Haydn Quintette in the early 1880s.

BIBLIOGRAPHY

Talbot, Hugo ed. *Musical Halifax 1903–4* (Halifax 1904)

Halifax Evening Mail, 30 Sep 1929

Minutes of St Matthew's Church, Halifax, NS

Blakeley, Phyllis R. 'History of music teaching in Nova Scotia,' unpubl ms, 1966 (SAB)

PORTMAN, Jamie (James Bickle). Journalist, critic, b North Battleford, Sack, 6 Oct 1935; BA (St John's, Manitoba) 1957. During his youth he studied piano and organ. He was a reporter 1954–6 for the *Winnipeg Free Press* and moved to the *Calgary Herald* in 1957. He was editorial writer and music and theatre critic with the *Herald* from 1962 to 1971, when he became entertainment editor. In 1975 he was appointed fine arts correspondent for Southam News Services.

WRITINGS

'Alberta's gutsy theatre in a pioneer setting,' PfAC, vol 13, Summer 1976 RDM

Portugal. Although some Newfoundland placenames bear witness to early visits and Spanish-Portuguese traditions have survived in a Montreal synagogue, the Portuguese community in Canada did not begin to grow until 1953 when immigrants, largely from Madeira, were sponsored by the Canadian government as agricultural workers in Ontario. Immigration followed from the Azores and the Portuguese mainland. The 1971 census lists more than 96,000 Portuguese in Canada. By 1978, however, more than 100,000 lived in Ontario (Toronto, Hamilton, Cambridge, and London) and 50,000 in Quebec, the majority in Montreal. Communities existed also in Manitoba.

The Portuguese have tended to maintain their cultural traditions and the first generation has not been assimilated readily in Canada. Musical traditions include regional folkdances, often accompanied by an ensemble of piccolo, castanets, bass drum, triangle, accordion, and clay jug (bica); brass bands; and the urban songs known as fado, usually accompanied by the mandolin and the Portuguese 12-string guitar. In Canada the brass bands often have been affiliated with local Portuguese Catholic churches, their rehearsals and weekly dances held in the church halls. The larger communities have supported clubs which offer language training, folkdancing, and entertainment by local and Portuguese performers. The Toronto and Montreal communities have supported several clubs and folkdance groups, Portuguese TV programs, and daily radio broadcasts.

Among Portuguese musicians who have taken up residence in Canada are Armando *Santiago, director of the *CMQ, and Germano Rocha, the singer and guitarist, who settled in Montreal. Michael *Miller was born in Portugal. Portuguese musicians who have performed in Canada include the guitarist Jose Duarte Costa, who toured 1966–7 for the *JMC; the popular fado singer Amalia Rodriguez, who has appeared in several Canadian cities; the singers Rui Mascareñas, Antonio Rios, Faly Molina, Anita Guerreira, and Lino Teixeira; and the accordionist Joao Benevides.

The Gulbenkian Foundation of Lisbon assisted with the cost of Kenneth *Gilbert's research for his edition of the Scarlatti sonatas.

BIBLIOGRAPHY

Anderson, Grace M., and Higgs, David. *A Future to Inherit: The Portuguese Communities in Canada* (Toronto 1976)

(LRH)

POTVIN, (Joseph Edmond) Gilles. Critic, producer, music consultant, administrator, impresario, translator, b Montreal 23 Oct 1923. With Helmut *Kallmann and Kenneth *Winters he is an editor of *EMC* and specifically in charge of the French-language edition. From 1940 to 1948 he studied privately in Montreal with Armand Renaud (theory, solfège), Agostino Salvetti, Jules Dubois, and Jean *Belland (cello), Oscar *O'Brien (harmony), and Rodolphe *Mathieu (analysis), while working as a bank employee and later as a journalist with the daily *Le Canada* (1946–8). At this time he was a cellist in the Montreal Youth Orchestra and a member of the *Montreal Elgar Choir and the Berlioz Choir. He worked 1947–8 as a publicity agent for the *Casavant Society and the Geo.-A. Robert concert agency. He then joined the CBC, where he held various positions: record librarian 1948–50; public relations officer and editor of *La Semaine à Radio-Canada* 1950–3; producer, notably of the radio programs 'Sérénade pour cordes' and 'Premières' 1954–7 and 'Concerts pour la jeunesse' on TV 1957–8; and director 1962–5 of the auditions and casting department. He joined the staff of the *Canada Council as head of the music section briefly at the beginning of 1966, but in June he was appointed head of music production with CBC IS (renamed RCI in 1972), where he became special consultant for recorded music programs in 1971 in addition to working as a producer 1975–7. He initiated numerous RCI projects in the recording field: the LPs *Colas et Colinette* and *The MSO* (1967), the series *Jeunesses musicales 20 Canada* (1969), and the complete works of François Couperin performed by Kenneth *Gilbert (1970–1). His LPs *Chantal Juillet* (RCI 439) and *Harry Somers: piano music* (3-RCI 450-452) earned Grands prix du disque-Canada awards from the *CMCouncil in 1978 and 1979 respectively. From 1966 to 1972 he was the CBC delegate to the annual sessions of the International Rostrum of Composers at the Unesco centre in Paris.

Potvin was one of the founders of *Minute Opera and its administrator 1949–53. He spent the 1953–4 season in Europe having received a scholarship in administration from the Quebec government. He spent some time working in various theatres and festivals including that in Aix-en-Provence, where he was assistant to the stage director. During this period he was also correspondent for *The Gazette*, the Montreal daily to which he had been contributing as a freelancer since 1949. On his return he was appointed instructor for the *McGill Opera Studio, where he staged Purcell's *Dido and Aeneas* in 1957.

Active also as an impresario, Potvin presented in partnership with Jacques Dupire a 1944–5 Quebec tour by André *Mathieu. He was associated 1951–3 with the Musical Arts Series and presented recitals by Walter Gieseking in Canada and New York 1952–5 and, together with Françoys *Bernier, recitals by Wilhelm Kempff 1961–4. He also presented the pianists Solomon and Ross *Pratt, the organist Fernando Germani, and the *Montreal String Quartet.

In 1946 he had begun writing reviews of concerts and other articles in Montreal newspapers and periodicals such as *Le Quartier latin, Notre Temps, Le Passe-Temps, L'Autorité*, and occasionally *Le Canada*. He subsequently became the Montreal correspondent for *Musical America*, *Opera Canada*, and *Opera* (London). He also contributed to *Châtelaine*, the *Journal musical canadien* of the *JMC, and other publications. At different periods he has provided the program notes for the *MSO, the *Pro Musica Society, and the *Opéra du Québec. After working for a short time in 1961 as critic for the daily *Le Nouveau Journal*, he was regular critic for the dailies *Le Devoir* 1961–6 and *La Presse* 1966–70, and in 1973 returned to *Le Devoir*.

Potvin was managing editor 1970–6 of the **Canada Music Book* and contributed to *Thirty-four Biographies* and *Contemporary Canadian Composers* as well as to *Sohlmans Musik-lexikon* and *The New Grove*. At the request of the Canada Council he acted as consultant to the firm of Urwick, Currie & Partners for the study and report entitled *An Assessment of the Impact of Selected Large Performing Companies upon the Canadian Economy* (Ottawa 1974). That same year he was a member of the task force, appointed by the *MACQ and headed by Jean-Paul *Jeannotte, on the state of symphonic music, opera, and dance in Quebec, and he contributed to its report. Since 1970 Potvin has conducted research into the life and career of Emma *Albani, publishing an annotated translation of her autobiography *Forty Years of Song* under the title *Mémoires d'Emma Albani* (Montreal 1972). He has written several articles and given lectures on the subject. He was an instructor in Canadian music 1970–1 at the *École normale de musique in Montreal.

Potvin was a member of the board of the CMCouncil 1968–77 and national president of the JMC 1976–80. In 1960 he married Micheline *Tessier. Hubert *Bédard is his first cousin.

WRITINGS

'Clermont Pépin fait honneur à la jeune musique canadienne,' interview, *P-T*, Jun 1946

'La jeune musique canadienne: Jean Papineau-Couture, compositeur,' *P-T*, Nov 1946

'Alexander Brott compositeur,' *P-T*, May 1947

'La musique dans un paradis,' Montreal *Le Canada*, 11, 12 Sep 1947

– and Kendergi, Maryvonne, eds. *Aspects de la musique au Canada* (Montreal 1970)

'Emma Albani,' *Opera*, Apr 1972

'Albani,' *Perspectives*, 15 Apr 1972

'Albani – ma vie,' *Maclean*, Dec 1972

'Éva Gauthier: il y a 50 ans, elle fit découvrir Gershwin aux Américains,' *Perspectives*, 27 Oct 1973

'Symphony orchestras and opera in Canada,' 'Jeunesses musicales du Canada,' *Arts and Culture* (Montreal 1976)

BIBLIOGRAPHY

Laurence, Monique and Clément, Josephte. 'Entrevue avec M. Gilles Potvin,' *Coups d'archet*, Nov 1961

La Poudrière. Built in 1822 on St Helen's Island, near Montreal, this building originally was used to store gunpowder and house an army supply depot.

The building was converted 1957–8 by Jeanine C. Beaubien for use as the playhouse of the Montreal International Theatre, of which she became the artistic director at the time of its foundation in 1957. The transformation into an intimate theatre, with 180 seats and a revolving stage, was entrusted to the architect Jean Fournier de Belleval. The renovation has preserved the original appearance of the building, with its two arches, its three-metre-thick walls, its open-air courtyard surrounded by a stone wall, and its two lodges in the Norman style.

The theatre has been used for chamber music concerts and numerous recitals by singers and instrumentalists. In 1973 the management began programming the *du Maurier 'mini-opera' productions which have included Mozart's *Bastien et Bastienne*, Wolf-Ferrari's *Le Secret de Suzanne*, Menotti's *The Medium*, *Vallerand's *Le Magicien*, Bizet's *Docteur Miracle*, a stage version of Debussy's *L'Enfant prodigue*, and Donizetti's *Rita ou le mari battu*. ST

POUNDER, Robert (Martin). Pianist, organist, teacher, b Moose Jaw, Sask, 28 Nov 1913; ATCM 1934, LRSM 1935. He studied with Esme Rose, Minnie Ruttan Armstrong, Sigismund Stojowski, and Boris *Roubakine. Pounder was the organist 1926–78 at Knox-Metropolitan United Church and taught piano 1954–78 at *Alberta College, Edmonton, where he specialized in work with younger students. John *Hendrickson, David Hoyt, and Neil Hughes were among his pupils. He began examining for the *WBM in 1945 and adjudicating at competition festivals in 1950. He has accompanied singers and instrumentalists, appeared in chamber recitals, and given piano workshops for both teachers and students.

Pounder was president 1947–9 of the *SRMTA, 1957–9 of the *ARMTA, and 1957–9 and 1963–7 of the *CFMTA. In 1972 the province awarded him an Alberta Achievement Award for his service to the arts.

BIBLIOGRAPHY

Lee, Clayton. 'He finally gets a Sunday off,' *Edmonton Journal*, 23 Jun 1978; repr in CFMTA *Newsletter*, Winter 1979

RDM

POWELL, Lloyd (Ioan). Pianist, teacher, b Bridgenorth, Shropshire, of Welsh parents, 22 Aug 1888, d Vancouver 25 Mar 1975. At 10 he entered the RCM and later he studied in Berlin and (with Busoni) in Basel. In 1919 he began teaching at the RCM, and later he became an examiner for the *AB of the RSM, travelling in that capacity to Asia, Australia, and South Africa and often performing and lecturing before audiences rarely exposed to classical music. Having adjudicated annually in Canada since the 1930s, Powell moved to Toronto in 1951 and settled in Vancouver in 1954. There he taught privately, broadcast for the CBC, adjudicated, performed, and lectured. At the *U of British Columbia he gave recital series which included Beethoven's 32 piano sonatas and the complete piano works of Charles Ives. Powell was the subject of a CBC documentary (23 Feb 1976).

WRITINGS

'Composers I have met and known,' series in BCRMTA *Music J*, vol 4, Aug 1969, Nov 1969, Feb 1970 WLB

Powwow singers. Those who provide the songs at the traditional ceremonial meetings, or powwows, of North American Indian tribes. Corrigan describes three types of powwow: 1 / the winter powwow, held privately on reserves or in towns near reserves by and for individual Indian bands in a band hall or school, and employing local singers and dancers; 2 / the public powwow, organized in response to outside sponsorship and designed to demonstrate Indian singing and dancing to the non-Indian (such powwows in fact are shows, put on for fees, as entertainments at festivals, or to celebrate the opening of a new highway, or for any other such reason); and 3 / the annual summer powwow, a large public affair usually held on reserve land during July and August, attracting up to 8000 visitors from a radius of 400 miles and involving costumed dancers, solo singers, and singing groups.

Music obviously plays a large role in all three types. The religious and magical overtones of the powwow, once central to it, have diminished with the changing times, and in the 1970s powwow circuits, winding back and forth across the US-Canadian border and covering the whole territory of the Indians, were regarded by many as circuits of weekend dance festivals at which widely separated members of particular Indian 'nations' could seek out relatives and friends. In fact, however, the social significance of the powwow has remained strong – for the elders a perpetuation of tradition, for the young a means of finding and confirming personal and ethnic identity. There has been virtually no 'white' influence on the powwow music, though it has grown more overtly dramatic than the traditional music. The texts are in dialect, but some of the most popular have been translated into English.

Some young singers and drummers have established reputations and are paid to perform on the circuits. A circuit serves the Indians of one 'nation,' and the various circuits overlap. There are many recordings, both commercial and field, of Powwow singers, including most of the groups mentioned in the ensuing statement written for *EMC* by the noted singer Winston Wuttunee:

> In Indian tradition every day began with songs. One or two spiritual songs would be sung for guidance and then others such as grass dance songs, round dance songs or sun dance songs would be sung as a way of offering thanks for a new day. The spiritual songs sung were special dream songs or other religious songs that have been passed down from generation to generation. Sweetgrass would burn simultaneously and in this way the songs were purified and carried up to the Great Spirit. The burning of sweetgrass for ceremonial purposes is centuries old. An Indian likes to carry sweetgrass on him in his pocket or in his hat band. Sweetgrass was the only grass on the prairies the buffalo would not eat. Favourite hand drums had the skin of a big dog on them because when a dog howled it was heard from far away, consequently those dogskin drums carried far away. In the old days an Indian would strive to obtain his own special songs through dreams or through periods of fasting and praying. The songs thus obtained were used as guidance songs for that person's spiritual and physical well-being. Some of these songs have survived on Indian reserves and can be sung only by certain people who have inherited the right or won favour in some way. Herbs were and are used to make singers sound better and they work today as they have been working for centuries. What the ingredients of the herbs are, are not for everyone to know. The only people who do know are those who have been directly informed through a dream or who have been given the knowledge as a gift.
>
> Powwow singers today respect each others' traditions and culture. Singers of today are quite different from those old singers, so much has changed and so much is gone, like the buffalo. When old men sing, who still retain that old Indian-ness in their voice and style of drum playing, everyone is quiet and all remember stories of days gone by. Today there are certain groups from the prairie provinces who have gained national recognition by their fine singing. They are as follows:
>
> ALBERTA
> Old Agency singers – Bloods and Blackfeet, Cardston area
> Bullhead and Sarcee singers – Sarcee
> Smallboy singers – Smallboy Camp
> SASKATCHEWAN
> Thunderchild Juniors
> Mosquito Juniors
> Battleford Friendship Centre Drummers
> Littlepine Singers
> Poorman Drummers
> MANITOBA
> Sioux Valley Travellers
>
> The powwow circuit begins in May and lasts until December. Those singers mentioned above and others will follow the major powwows across Canada and into the States. Good powwow singers (groups) can pick up $5,000.00 easily as prize money during the powwow duration. Certain groups' singing does make dancers dance with more enthusiasm and zest, therefore, these groups (above) are in much demand.
>
> There are organized groups of non-Indians who sing well. They are welcomed everywhere. They lack the quality that the Indian singer has and are readily picked out as non-Indians. Today much has changed, but Indian singers still sing in memory of a once beautiful and useful culture. We sing to try to capture that which is almost lost, like the almost extinct Whooping Crane and the buffalo. Through our music we remain Indians. Our music is us.

See also Bridge music; Indians.

BIBLIOGRAPHY

Corrigan, Samuel W. 'The plains Indian powwow: cultural integration in Manitoba and Saskatchewan,' *Anthropologica*, n.s., vol 12, no. 2, 1970

POYNTER, Arthur (Robert). Composer, choir conductor, b Hamilton, Ont, 16 Nov 1913, d Toronto 30 Jun 1981; BA (McMaster) 1943, B DIV (McMaster) 1946. Following ordination as a Baptist minister, he served 1948–58 in Toronto churches; studied composition 1950–4 at the *U of Toronto with John *Beckwith, Godfrey *Ridout, S. Drummond Wolff, and John *Weinzweig; and lectured 1955–63 at McMaster Divinity College. He organized, and directed 1946–58, the Toronto Baptist Choral Society (which in 1950 premiered his first opera, *The Triumph of Our Lord*) and directed 1958–64 the Oratorio Society. In 1962, with the sponsorship of the Audrey S. Hellyer Foundation, he established the Christian Performing Arts to present the Christian message through music, drama, and dance. His compositions include anthems, song-cycles, and oratorios, (See Oratorios, Canadian) and a second opera, *The Birth of Our Lord*, part of which was performed in 1969 at Yorkminster Park Baptist Church, Toronto. Two more operas, along with other works, were in preparation when he was stricken with illness in 1972. His publishers include *Harris and *Jarman. He is an associate of the *CMCentre. FMB

PRATT, Paul. Clarinetist, pianist, conductor, teacher, composer, public administrator, b Longueuil, near Montreal, 25 Nov 1894, d there 8 May 1967; lauréat clarinet (Cons national) 1912. He studied piano with the Sisters of the Holy Names of Jesus and Mary in Longueuil and later with Orpha-F. *Deveaux and Arthur *Letondal in Montreal. He also studied clarinet with François *Héraly. In 1913 he taught piano and clarinet at the Collège de Longueuil, where he conducted the orchestra and band until 1920. He was bandmaster and conductor of the orchestra of the Longueuil Concert Society, as well as a solfège teacher for the Société St-Jean-Baptiste. A member 1916–17 of the Symphonie Dubois and 1919–39 of the *Canadian Grenadier Guards Band of Montreal, he played bass clarinet 1931–41 in the *Montreal Orchestra and contrabass clarinet 1935–46 in the *CSM orchestra. He played also with the *Little Symphony of Montreal and with the Van der Meerschen band in St-Lambert.

As mayor of Longueuil 1935–66 Pratt was decorated by George V in 1935 and George VI in 1939 for his activities as mayor and as War Campaign president. While visiting Cuba in 1946 he was invited to conduct an orchestra in Havana. He was president 1956–7 of the Quebec and Ontario Divisions of the *CBA. He was music director of the Longueuil South Shore Band, the Gais Longueuillois Quartet, and, 1950–67, the Metropolitan Concert Band of Montreal. Among his compositions are marches, waltzes, a *Fantaisie-Impromptu* for band, and some piano pieces.

BIBLIOGRAPHY

'His Worship Mayor Paul Pratt of Longueuil, Que., is President Ontario-Quebec Chapter C.B.A.,' *CanB*, Jun–Jul 1956 (MH-D)

PRATT, Ross (Drury). Pianist, teacher, b Winnipeg 20 Apr 1916; hon ARAM ca 1950, hon FRAM 1959. He studied as a child with Esther Dyson and in his teens with Leonard *Heaton, winning the Aikins Memorial Trophy at the 1931 *Manitoba Music Competition Festival. Awarded a scholarship to the RAM, London, he studied 1934–9 with Harold Craxton and in 1939 made his London recital debut at Wigmore Hall and was soloist with the BBC SO under Sir Henry Wood. On his return to Canada Pratt settled in Montreal, gave recitals, and appeared with orchestras throughout North America. His New York debut 1 Nov 1941 at Town Hall 'established [him] as one of the most gifted of the younger generation of keyboard artists' (Noel Strauss, *New York Times*) and was the prelude to an extended tour of Canada, the USA, and Mexico. He also played for CBC and NBC broadcasts and gave sonata recitals with the violinists Noël *Brunet and Arthur *LeBlanc. His Winnipeg appearances included a joint recital (1944) with the Canadian mezzo-soprano Jean Watson. He also performed with the *TSO (the John Ireland *Piano Concerto*) and the *Little Symphony of Montreal (Mozart's *Concerto in G*, K453).

At the end of World War II Pratt played for the British armed forces in the Far East and then toured Australia. In 1949 he returned to London, teaching 1949–53 and 1960–6 at the RAM and ap-

Ross Pratt

pearing as a concerto soloist, recitalist, and chamber musician in Britain, continental Europe, Mexico, and Iceland. He was the pianist 1957–64 in the Robert Masters Quartet of London, toured as accompanist to the cellist Florence Hooton, gave recitals with Frederick *Grinke, Arthur *Davison, David *Martin, Zara *Nelsova, and William Primrose, and performed with the Royal Philharmonic Orchestra, the Liverpool Philharmonic, and many other orchestras.

Pratt continued to make frequent appearances in Canada (eg, as soloist in Rachmaninoff's *Concerto No. 3* in 1949 and Brahms' *Concerto No. 2* with the *Winnipeg SO in 1955 and in the Canadian premiere of Benjamin Lees' *Concerto* in 1957 with the *CBC SO) and, while on leave 1965–6 from the RAM, was a visiting teacher at the *U of Alberta. Subsequently he taught 1967–73 at the *CMQ, became director of chamber music at *CAMMAC in 1969, began lecturing on keyboard literature at *Carleton U in 1970, and gave lecture-recitals on Mozart, Liszt, Debussy, and 20th-century composers in several Canadian cities. He was a member 1968–71 of the Trio de Québec with Liliane Garnier-Lesage (violin) and Traugott Schmöhe (cello).

Pratt's repertoire has included Arnell's *Concerto No. 1* (of which he gave the British premiere), Rachmaninoff's *Rhapsody on a Theme of Paganini* (Canadian premiere with the *Montreal Orchestra 18 Feb 1940), Milhaud's *Second Piano Concerto*, 10 of the Mozart concertos, both Ravel concertos, and many others. His programs have included solo pieces by Violet *Archer, Jean *Coulthard, Robert *Fleming, Oskar *Morawetz, Jean *Papineau-Couture, Barbara *Pentland, and John *Weinzweig, in addition to a wide range of music drawn from the 18th- and 19th-century piano literature.

WRITINGS

'Opportunities for musicians in Canada,' *MT*, vol 97, Nov 1956

'Chopin in Britain,' *CMJ*, vol 5, Autumn 1960

DISCOGRAPHY

Beethoven *Sonata, Op 81a* – Coulthard 2 *Studies; Quiet Song* – Somers *Strangeness of Heart*. 1953. RCI 93

Piano music of Medtner. (1967). Bar BC 12871

Ravel – Medtner – Carbonelli – Boyce – Purcell – Barclay. 1951. RCI 47

Schumann – Pépin – Somers – Gratton – Archer. (1958). RCI 132

See also Discographies for Hyman Bress; Noël Brunet; and Arthur Davison (SRM)

Pratte. A trade name of pianos which began to be manufactured in Montreal in 1889. Arriving in Montreal around 1875, Louis-Étienne-Napoléon Pratte (b Princeville, Que) opened a music store and began to deal in pianos. In 1882 he was joined for a short time by his young brother Antonio (b Princeville 1865, d Saint-Célestin de Nicolet 9 Jan 1943). After taking music lessons from Dominique *Ducharme and Charles-Marie *Panneton Antonio studied piano manufacturing as an apprentice 1882–9 with the *Dominion Organ and Piano Co, in Bowmanville, Ont. Another brother, Évariste (ca 1867–1913), accompanied him and studied tuning. Both then went to New York for further training before returning to Canada. In 1889 Antonio Pratte began turning out pianos to which he gave the name L.-É.-N. Pratte; Évariste handled sales and L.-É.-N. promotion and advertising. The Pratte Piano Company / La Compagnie de pianos Pratte was formed officially in 1895 and immediately acquired the Cornwall reed organ factory in Huntingdon, Que; it brought in skilled workmen from the USA and Europe. Between 1894 and 1909 Antonio Pratte obtained patents from the Canadian, US, and even European governments covering improvements he made to the upright piano.

An 1896 advertisement for Pianos Pratte

In 1896 the firm proudly listed names belonging to 'the elite of Canadian musicians and teachers who have chosen and purchased the Pratte piano in preference to all the US ones,' adding that its pianos 'possess artistic qualities not found in any other US or European pianos. Their system guarantees in addition to the rarest musical qualities, maximum solidity and durability in extreme climates' (*L'Art musical*, Nov 1896). In 1898 Victoria *Cartier introduced the Pratte piano to Europeans at a concert in the Institut national des jeunes aveugles in Paris. The Pratte firm won a grand prize at the Paris International Exposition in 1900 and in the same year offered its patrons the first Canadian-made player piano.

L.-É.-N. Pratte was founder and owner-publisher of the monthly magazine *L'Art musical* (issued from Oct 1896 to Jan 1899).

In 1911, when L.-É.-N. Pratte died, Antonio Pratte became head of the company. In 1912 Antonio's first grand piano, the design of which he had been developing since 1896, was introduced to the public at a concert at the Ritz-Carlton Hotel in Montreal by Victoria Cartier. Also at this time Pratte produced a new kind of harmonium 'with a transposing keyboard' for use in churches and chapels. The Pratte Piano Company began manufacturing phonographs in 1918 under the name of the Prattephone Co.

In 1926 the company merged with the firm of J.-Donat Langelier Ltée, which in 1963 merged with N.G. Valiquette to become Langelier-Valiquette Ltée.

BIBLIOGRAPHY

'Le palais de musique de L.E.N. Pratte,' *Le Commerce de Montréal et de Québec et leurs industries en 1889* (Montreal 1889)

Pelletier, Frédéric. 'Le piano Pratte,' *La Musique*, vol 4, Jan 1922

Biographies canadiennes-françaises (Montreal 1923)

Roll Back the Years

Kallmann *History of Music in Canada*

Musiciens canadiens DM (ST)

PRATZ, Albert. Violinist, conductor, teacher, b Toronto 13 May 1914. He studied in Toronto with Broadus Farmer and Luigi von *Kunits, in the USA in 1933 with Michel Piastro and summers during the early 1930s with Mischa Mischakoff, and in Europe 1936–7 with William Primrose. He began his career in 1929 in a CFRB radio orchestra under Alexander *Chuhaldin and made his solo debut in 1937 in the Tchaikovsky *Concerto* at the *Promenade Symphony Concerts under Reginald *Stewart. He played 1933–41 in the *TSO and various CRBC and CBC orchestras and was orchestra conductor 1940–3 for CBC Winnipeg.

After moving to New York and serving 1943–6 in the US army Pratz was a member 1946–53 of the NBC SO under Toscanini and of various New York studio and pit orchestras, the associate conductor for the production of *One Touch of Venus*, and the violin soloist in the original production of *Oklahoma!*. He returned to Canada in 1953 and played that year with the cellist Isaac *Mamott and the pianist Glenn *Gould in the Festival Trio at the first *Stratford Festival. He served 1953–61 as concertmaster of the *CBC SO and taught 1953–62 at the *RCMT. With the CBC SO he conducted several broadcasts and was soloist in concertos by Brahms (1953), Vieuxtemps (1954), *Weinzweig (premiere, 1955), Tchaikovsky (1956), Viotti (1957), and Lalo (1960). Pratz also conducted the orchestra for the CBC radio series 'Let's Make Music' and 'The Music Box' and was heard in many CBC recitals, often accompanied by Leo *Barkin. He was concertmaster 1955–60 and a soloist on several occasions with the *Hart House Orchestra.

After playing first violin in the short-lived (1961–3) but significant *Canadian String Quartet, Pratz taught 1964–6 at *Brandon U, where he organized the Wawanesa String Ensemble for on-campus concerts. Appointed concertmaster of the Buffalo Philharmonic in 1965, he also conducted that orchestra occasionally. He returned to the TS in 1969, was appointed acting concertmaster in 1970, and served as concertmaster 1971–9. With the TS his solo work included performances of the Weinzweig *Concerto* (for CBC TV 1971), Bruch's *Concerto No. 1* (1972), Brahms' *Double Concerto* (with the cellist Peter Schenkman, 1972), Bach's *Brandenburg Concertos No. 4 and 5* (1973 and 1976 respectively), Mozart's *Sinfonia concertante* (with the violist Stanley *Solomon, 1975), and Bruch's *Violin Concerto No. 3* (1977). Of the last-named performance John *Kraglund wrote (Toronto *Globe and Mail*, 30 Mar 1977): 'Pratz contributed warmly singing tone [and] technical precision ... If he could be faulted, it was only in what seemed like excessive restraint – compared to the orchestral part – in the finale. Hometown or not, it was an interpretation that warranted a wealth of bravos.' With the CBC Festival Orchestra he participated in the Canadian premiere (4 Mar 1973) of Berio's *Concertino 1951*.

Pratz also has played in many Toronto studio orchestras for recordings, film scores (eg, Louis *Applebaum's score, largely for solo violin, for Harry Rasky's *Homage to Chagall*), and jingles. Pratz taught at the *U of Toronto while a member of the Canadian Quartet and continued to teach privately thereafter. His pupils have included

Albert Pratz

Dean Franke, Raymond Gniewek, Myron Moskalyk, Bill *Richards, Steven *Staryk, Campbell *Trowsdale, and David *Zafer. Pratz has composed instrumental pieces, including *Melanie Waltz* and *A Tango*, arranged by Fred Rous and published by *Canadian Music Sales in 1956 and 1957 respectively, and others recorded by his CBC orchestra.

DISCOGRAPHY

AS VIOLINIST

Berg – Shostakovich – Tanaieff – Prokofiev – Gould pf. 1953. Hallmark RS-3

Bruch *Violin Concerto, Op 58*. CBC Festival O, Feldbrill cond. 1976. CBC SM-329

Concert Miniatures for Violin and Piano: Bloch – Falla – Albeniz – et al. Taussig pf. 1970. CBC SM-159

Korngold – Willan – Szymanowski – Chaminade. Kushner pf. 1950. RCI 42

Morawetz *Duo* – Willan *Sonata in E Minor*. Barkin pf. Ca 1956. RCI 124

Morawetz *Sonata No. 1* – Turner *Sonata*. Barkin pf. (1963). RCI 194

The Voice of the Stradivarius: Chopin – Lully – Moszkowski – et al. Orch, Hyslop cond. London SDD-2118 B

Weinzweig *Violin Concerto*. CBC SO, Waddington cond. 1962. RCI 183

AS CONDUCTOR

Albert Pratz and His Orchestra (title of four LPs): songs and instrumental selections by L. Agostini – Burt – Pratz – Rous – Symonds – R. Toth – et al. Solos by Fiore fl, Lewis bsn, Niosi sax; vocals by Dale and Koster. 1960. RCI 171–174

Rous *Totem Pole Suite*. CBC Light O. 1962. RCI 186

BIBLIOGRAPHY

Moorsom, Val. 'Albert Pratz: year of '79,' *Toronto Symphony News*, issue 6, 1979 (MMI)

PRÉVOST, (Joseph Gaston Charles) **André**. Composer, teacher, b Hawkesbury, Ont, 30 Jul 1934; premier prix harmony, composition (CMM) 1960. Although Ontario-born, he belongs to a Quebec family of venerable lineage; he is a great-grandson of Gustave *Smith. He first studied in St-Jérôme, then pursued his classical studies at the Séminaire de St-Thérèse and the Collège de St-Laurent. In 1951 he enrolled at the *CMM where he studied harmony and counterpoint with Isabelle *Delorme and Jean *Papineau-Couture and composition with Clermont *Pépin. He won the Sarah *Fischer Concerts composition prize in 1959. Bassoonist in a reed trio, he obtained a Chamber Music Award from the *Amis de l'art foundation that same year. Assisted by grants from the *Canada Council and the Quebec government, he studied analysis with Olivier Messiaen at the Paris Cons and in 1961 worked with Henri Dutilleux at the École normale.

André Prévost

Returning to Canada in April 1962, Prévost began teaching at the Séminaire de Joliette and at the Collège des Eudistes in Rosemont. In June 1963 he obtained the *Prix d'Europe for composition and in November of that year his symphonic work *Fantasmes* won a prize from the Amis de l'art foundation. (It won another from the *MSO in 1964). After its US premiere, 17 Mar 1977 by the *TS in Carnegie Hall, Harold Schonberg noted in the *New York Times* that 'it does convey a real urgency and is an impressive work.' During the summer of 1964 he studied electronic music with Michel Phillipot at the ORTF, Paris. In the fall of 1964 Prévost joined the Faculty of Music, *U of Montreal. In the spring of 1964 he conceived a plan for a large musical work on 'Man and His World,' the theme of *Expo 67. Shortly thereafter the work was commissioned officially by the *MACQ. During the summer of 1964 he went to the Berkshire Music Center in Tangelwood where he worked and consulted with Gunther Schuller, Donald Martino, Aaron Copland, and Zoltán Kodály. In the fall of 1965 the Jacques Verdon and Gilles *Manny recording of his *Sonata* for violin and piano received a prize at the Festival du disque in Montreal. In January of 1966 *Ten Centuries Concerts of Toronto, in collaboration with the *CMCentre and the Canadian Confederation Centennial Commission, commissioned his *Suite for String Quartet*. The work was premiered in 1968 in Toronto by the *Orford String Quartet. On 29 Apr 1967 *Terre des Hommes*, for large orchestra, three choirs, and two narrators, to a poem by Michèle Lalonde, was premiered under the direction of Pierre *Hétu at the Salle Wilfrid-Pelletier (*PDA) at the inauguration of the Expo 67 World Festival.

By the late 1970s Prévost had received and completed more than 20 commissions from orchestras and other organizations. Among the resulting works was *Paraphrase* for string quartet and orchestra, commissioned by the TS and premiered in 1980 by the orchestra and the Orford String Quartet. Prévost became a member of the Board of Directors of the CMCentre in 1971 and president of the Groupe Nouvelle-Aire in 1973. In 1977 he received the *CMCouncil Medal. In St-Jérôme an auditorium is named after him.

Prévost's concept of a musical aesthetic resembles that of Xenakis, in that it involves a 'world of sonority in movement.' However, his modes of expression and writing are independent of all schools and determinism. He uses contemporary techniques and writing procedures freely. The notion of 'structure,' of extreme importance to some composers, remains for him a complementary factor, an outcome, dependent upon the work itself and upon its 'life breath.' Up to the late 1970s the whole of his output illustrated this concept. He is a member of the *CLComp, an affiliate of PRO Canada, and an associate of the CMCentre.

SELECTED COMPOSITIONS

ORCHESTRA

Poème de l'infini. 1960. Orch. CMCentre

Scherzo. 1960. Str orch. CMCentre

Fantasmes. 1963. Orch. Ber 1970. RCI 230 / RCA LSC 2980 / Vic VICS-1040 (*MSO)

Célébration. 1966. Med orch. CMCentre

Pyknon. 1966. Vn, orch. Okra (rental)

Terre des hommes (M. Lalonde). 1967. Orch, 3 choirs, 2 narr. CMCentre. CBC Expo-1 (*MSO)

Diallèle. 1968. Orch. CMCentre

Évanescence. 1970. Med orch. Ric 1971. RCI 332/RCA VCCS-1640 (*NACO)

Hommages. 1971. Str orch. CMCentre

Chorégraphie I. 1973. Orch. CMCentre

Cello Concerto. 1973–6. Vc, orch. CMCentre

Chorégraphie II ($E = MC^2$). 1976. Orch. CMCentre

Chorégraphie III. 1977. Orch. CMCentre

Chorégraphie IV. 1978. Orch. CMCentre

Le Conte de l'oiseau (P. Delorme). 1979. Orch, 2 narr. CMCentre

CHAMBER

Pastorale. 1955. 2 hp. Ms

Fantaisie. 1956. Vc, pf. Ms

Quartet No. 1. 1958. Str quar. CMCentre

Électre, incidental music. 1959. Ob, perc. Ms

Mobiles. 1960. Fl, str trio. CMCentre

Sonata. 1961. Vn, pf. BMIC 1968. CBC SM-172 (*Staryk)/Bar JAS-19002 (G. *Manny pf)

Trois pièces irlandaises. 1961. Guit, fl, ob, vn, vc, pf. Ms

Sonata. 1962. Vc, pf. Ric 1974. 1971. RCI 356/VDE 3035 (Fallot vc, Lamasse pf)

Triptyque. 1962. Fl, ob, pf. CMCentre. RCI 297 (*Ens instr du Qué)

Movement for Brass Quintet. 1963. Ms

Ode au Saint-Laurent (G. Lapointe). 1965. Narr, str quar. CMCentre

Suite for String Quartet. 1968. CMCentre

Quartet No. 2 'Ad Pacem.' 1972. Str quar. CMCentre. RCI 394 (*Purcell Str Quar)

Also *Improvisation I* for vn, *Improvisation II* for vc, *Improvisation III* for va, *Improvisation IV* for pf, and *Improvisation V* for v and pf. All 1976. All CMCentre

KEYBOARD

Cinq Variations sur un thème grégorien (Salve regina). 1956. Org. CMCentre

Four Preludes. 1961. 2 pf. Ms

VOICE AND CHOIR

Soleils couchants (Verlaine). 1953. SSATBB. CMCentre

Musiques peintes (G. Lapointe). 1955. High v, pf. CMCentre. RCI 426 (B. *Laplante)

Geôles (M. Lalonde). 1963. Mezzo, pf. CMCentre. Allied ARCLP 4 (J. *Dufresne pf)

Psaume 148. 1971. SATB, 4 tpt, 4 trb, org. CMCentre

Missa de profundis. 1973. SATB, org. CMCentre

WRITINGS

'Propos sur la création,' *VM*, 7 Oct 1967

'Formulation et conséquences d'une hypothèse,' *CMB*, 1, Spring–Summer 1970; repr in *Musiques du Kébèk* ed Raoul Duguay (Montreal 1971)

BIBLIOGRAPHY

Heller, Zelda. 'André Prévost,' *MSc*, 244, Nov–Dec 1968

Lalonde, Michèle. 'Le poème en tant que composante musicale,' *Musiques du Kébèk* (Montreal 1971)

Lefebvre, Marie-Claire. 'André Prévost,' *Cahier des Musialogues* (Montreal 1972)

Loranger, Pierre. 'André Prévost: *Évanescence*,' *CMB*, 4, Spring–Summer 1972

CMCentre. *Compositeurs au Québec: André Prévost* (Montreal 1975)

PRO Canada Ltd. 'André Prévost,' pamphlets (1975, 1979)

Gingras, Claude. 'André Prévost: 35 oeuvres en 25 ans de musique,' Montreal *La Presse*, 5 Mar 1977

Kieser, Karen. 'Canadian composers you'll be hearing: André Prévost,' *TS News*, Mar–Apr 1977

Richer-Lortie, Lyse. 'André Prévost: L'orchestre est un instrument admirable,' Montreal *Le Devoir*, 4 Feb 1978

Robert, Véronique. 'Prévost portrays fate of mankind,' *MSc*, 308, Jul–Aug 1979

Richer-Lortie, Lyse. 'André Prévost,' *Contemporary Canadian Composers / Compositeurs canadiens contemporains*

PR

Percival Price

PRICE, (Frank) **Percival**. Carillonneur, campanologist, composer, teacher, b Toronto 7 Oct 1901; B MUS (Toronto) 1928, carillonneur diploma (Beiaardschool te Mechelen) 1927. His teachers in Toronto included his mother and, later, E. Lois Wilson (theory), Frank Burt and William Hawke (organ), Hayunga *Carmen (piano), and H.A. *Fricker (orchestration).

Price's interest in carillons arose during a trip to the Low Countries in 1921, and his appointment that year as carillonneur at Metropolitan Church in Toronto was the first such appointment outside Europe. Moreover, the carillon on which he was to perform, donated by Chester Massey in memory of his wife, was the first carillon installed in North America. Price was appointed carillonneur at Park Ave Baptist Church, New York in 1925, but he did not assume the position and take charge of the church's new Laura Spelman Memorial Carillon until early in 1926. He continued his studies at the famous training centre for carillonneurs, the Beiaardschool in Mechelen (Malines), Belgium, where his main teachers were Jef Denyn and Jef van Hoof. Price was the first non-European to graduate. In 1932-3 he studied in Vienna with Arthur Willner (composition) and worked on *The St. Lawrence*, his major work, a 'romantic symphony' in four movements (Islands, Rapids, Flatlands, Mountains). He submitted this to the *U of Toronto as a doctoral exercise, and, although it was rejected, it did receive performances, one (the premiere) under Reginald *Stewart at the *Promenade Symphony Concerts in 1934 and another by the *TSO under the composer 30 Oct 1934. The work earned Price in that same year a travelling scholarship awarded by the Pulitzer Prize Committee to 'the student of music in America that may be deemed the most talented and deserving, in order that he may continue his studies with the advantage of European instruction.' In 1935 he went to Basel – his tenth trip overseas – where he studied conducting with Felix Weingartner at the Musikschule.

Meanwhile Price had been consultant in the design of the carillon at the Peace Tower (Parliament Buildings) in Ottawa and he inaugurated the bells on 1 Jul 1927. That year he was appointed Dominion Carillonneur, in charge of the Peace Tower carillon. He retained the position until 1939. He was a driving force in the formation (Ottawa 1936) of The *Guild of Carillonneurs in North America and served as president 1947-9 and later as archivist.

In 1939 Price joined the staff at the U of Michigan, Ann Arbor, to teach composition and campanology and to serve as University Carillonneur at the Burton Memorial Tower. He retired from these positions in 1972 as professor emeritus, remaining active as recitalist, consultant, and lecturer.

As a recitalist Price has performed on more than 100 carillons in many countries. On his travels he has accumulated the wealth of documentation – verbal, pictorial, and sound-recorded – that has made him a world authority on campanology. An early research trip took him to the USSR and the Balkan countries in 1930, and in 1933 he wrote *The Carillon*, one of the first books in English on the subject. His treatise 'Carillons of North America,' written the same year, was unpublished in 1980. During the 1970s he worked on another book, *Bells and Man*, based on his realization that the bell is man's most universal musical instrument and an artefact of great social, religious, and iconographic significance.

Price's practical experience and theoretical grasp have enabled him to work as a consultant and to effect reforms and innovations. During and after World War II he served as consultant to the Inter-Allied Commission on the Wartime Preservation of Artistic and Historic Monuments in War Areas and to the Vatican Commission for the Restoration of Bells. Under the auspices of the Canadian Army's Enemy Science and Technology Investigation section he undertook a survey of the sequestration and destruction of bells for war purposes. He aided Austrian, Belgian, Dutch, West German, and Italian government commissions in locating their removed bells. After the war Price continued his research in Mexico, the Near East, China, East Germany, and other countries.

It is as a musician, however, that Price has felt his strongest attraction to bells. He has added the semantron (or semanterion), the struck wooden percussion board which preceded the church bell, to the carillon as a rhythm instrument. He has placed a choir of 100 voices in a bell chamber and has used a team of ten ringers to produce Russian-style bell ringing on the carillon. His ideas have influenced the design of the modern carillon.

Price has written several hundred compositions and more than 500 arrangements for carillon. His *Kellosavel Variations* were selected at the 1952 Olympic Games in Helsinki as an outstanding Canadian work. Like many of his other pieces, the *Canadian Suite* (early 1930s) was written for performance on the Peace Tower carillon. Among the published carillon works is *Air for Carillon* (OUP and Fischer). In addition to carillon solos and duets, he has written for carillon and choir, and carillon and various instruments. Among the last is a three-movement *Concerto* for carillon, brass, and percussion. His works not using the carillon include the *Yamachiche Suite* for piano trio or strings and *The St Lawrence*. Among the performances of the latter are two by the Warsaw Philharmonic Orchestra under Jerzy Bojanowski in 1973. Price has written 4 compositions and 20 arrangements for handbells.

In 1975 Price was elected honorary president of the World Federation of Guilds of Carillonneurs.

WRITINGS

The Carillon (London 1933)

Campanology Europe 1945-47 (Ann Arbor 1948)

'Mr. Handel and his carillon,' Guild of Carillonneurs in North America *Bulletin*, vol 20, May 1969

Other articles in the *Galpin Society Journal* and *EMC*

BIBLIOGRAPHY

Macbeth, Madge. 'Canada's first carillonneur,' *Maclean's*, 15 Oct 1927

Hamilton, H.C. 'Percival Price, Dominion Carillonneur,' *MCan*, vol 11, Dec 1930

Catalogue of Canadian Composers

(FMB)

PRIEUR, Henri. Tenor, b Montreal 17 Apr 1893, d there 22 Aug 1970. Revealing a rich voice as a youth, Prieur was encouraged to study music and trained 1911-20, with Arthur *Plamondon, Jean *Riddez, and Albert *Roberval. He made his debut in 1911 in Montreal as Mylio in *Le Roi d'Ys* and later sang in *Mireille* and *La Damnation de Faust* (1918), *Les Béatitudes* (1921), Verdi's *Requiem* (1922), and Coleridge-Taylor's *Hiawatha* (1923). He appeared 6 Feb 1923 as the Narrator in the premiere of Guillaume *Couture's **Jean le Précurseur*. Also noted as a Lieder singer, Prieur performed in concerts in Montreal, Quebec, Ottawa, and various major US centres. He was a soloist in 1918 at the Gesù Church in Montreal and in 1926 at St-Viateur in Outremont. He married the pianist Esther *Wayland. Beginning in 1918 he recorded six songs for HMV (listed in *Roll Back the Years*).

GB

La Prima Ballerina. Neoromantic ballet in two acts by Heino Heiden. The music, by Godfrey *Ridout, is scored for large orchestra and was written on commission from the National Ballet of Canada. The ballet had its premiere 26 Oct 1967 in the Salle Wilfrid-Pelletier of the *PDA, Montreal, as part of the World Festival of *Expo 67. The production was designed by Lawrence Schafer, and the *MSO was conducted by George *Crum. Leading dancers were Lois Smith, Hazaros Surmejan, Daniel Seillier, and Yves Cousineau. The story is based on an incident in the life of Maria Taglioni. The great dancer's coach is captured by bandits. The bandit chief recognizes her and, finally, releases her so she can perform; the circumstance leads to a ballet within a ballet.

Nathan Cohen wrote that Ridout's score 'features a theatrical sensibility rare among Canadian composers ... a pastiche ... of 19th century opera and drama and suffused with a disarming instrumentation' (*Toronto Star*, 27 Oct 1967). The choreography was weak and conventional, however, and after the first Toronto stage performances – 29 and 30 Apr and 1 May 1968 – the ballet was dropped from the repertoire. The score stands, nevertheless, as one of the very few expert large-scale (70-minute) ballet scores by Canadian composers, and the 5-minute *Overture*, a *Suite No. 1*, and a *Suite No. 2* are listed in the *CMCentre orchestral catalogue. *Suite No. 1* was premiered 1 Aug 1971 by the *TS under Victor Feldbrill at the *Ontario Place Forum.

KW (PW)

PRINCE, Henry. Music dealer, bandmaster, composer, b ?, d Montreal 1888? In 1854 he acquired the instrument retailing and sheet music business of Mead, Brother and Co, continuing its operation under his own name. The bulk of his stock was imported from the USA and Europe. However, from 18 Jul to 16 Sep 1857 in the *Montreal Daily Transcript and Commercial Advertiser* he advertised 'NEW CANADIAN MUSIC ... National melodies of Canada and the Compositions of various popular Canadian composers.' Though Prince did not advertise publications of his own, he issued sheet music from 1854 to 1878, most of it printed and copyrighted in the USA. Most of the compositions were by Canadians, including Prince himself, William Powell, and I. *Suckling.

Prince was a prolific composer of quadrilles, polkas, and other dance music. His works include the patriotic songs 'Form! Riflemen Form!' (1859) and 'Shoulder to Shoulder on to the Border,' as well as *Mermaid Polka* (dedicated to the ladies of Canada) and *Irresistible Polka* (for the ladies of Montreal). Some of Prince's most 'Canadian' compositions, including the *Jubilee or Celebration Polka* (1855), dedicated to executives of the Canadian

The Montreal Galop, published by Henry Prince, Montreal, late 1850s

Grand Trunk Railway, were published in the USA with Prince listed on the cover as an agent.

Prince remained in business until 1888. A bandmaster of note, he led the Volunteer Militia Rifle Band and played a cornet solo at a Grand Military Concert (17 Sep 1857) in Montreal. Gustave *Smith called Prince 'a true gentleman' and remarked on his 'fine talent on a cornet à piston' (*L'Album musical*, Feb 1882). MC

Prince Edward Island Council of the Arts. Formed in 1974; an autonomous body of representatives of the arts community, with headquarters in Charlottetown. In 1980 Edward Rice was the executive director. After an initial study of Prince Edward Island cultural resources the council set about helping in the co-ordination, planning, and development of the province's arts activities. Its 12-member board, representing arts organizations, has served as an adviser to the provincial minister responsible for cultural affairs.

BIBLIOGRAPHY

Hodge, Sandra. 'PEI Arts Council report,' CCA *Arts Bulletin*, Sep–Oct 1977

Prince Edward Island Music Educators' Association. Formed 6 Jun 1962 at a meeting at Prince of Wales College, Charlottetown.

The PEIMEA has concerned itself with setting higher standards for teachers, ensuring musical instruction in schools, identifying deficiencies and suggesting changes in the provincial music curriculum, and sponsoring musical events.

The PEIMEA has not held its own annual convention but has provided representatives for the committee of the *NSMEA autumn convention, and many of its members have attended that convention. It has become the custom of the PEIMEA to arrange workshops for school music teachers each spring. In 1971 the PEIMEA was host, in Charlottetown, to the *CMEA convention, and in 1973 it became an affiliate of the national body. As a supplement to the publications of the CMEA, the PEIMEA in 1970 began issuing to its members the newsletter *Crescendo*, published four times annually.

Christopher *Gledhill was the first president, followed by Gabriel Chiasson 1964–6 and 1970–2, Sister Mary Winnifred 1966–8, Royston Mugford 1968–70, Cornelius Zaat 1972–4, Allan Graham 1974–6, and Gerard Rutten 1976–8. Joan Davies succeeded Rutten in 1978.

The association made Sister Mary Winnifred an honorary life member in 1975 and conferred the same honour on Royston Mugford in 1979. (AGra)

The Princess Patricia's Canadian Light Infantry Band. Recruited in Toronto in 1919 under the direction of Capt Thomas William James and stationed in Winnipeg 1920–39. It achieved prominence in 1924 at the British Empire Exhibition in Wembley, London, and gave a series of concerts at principal London theatres. It also broadcast a concert from the Savoy Hill radio studios. On returning to Winnipeg the band was honoured by a visit from Serge Rachmaninoff, who conducted it in a transcription of his *Prelude in C-sharp Minor*. When James retired in 1936 interim conductors were used until Lieut Al Streeter assumed direction in 1939, but the band was dispersed by the call to arms of World War II.

In 1950 the band was revived in Calgary (many members were recruited in England and Holland) under the direction of Capt A. Brown, and in 1953 it served in Korea and Japan. That year Capt F.M. *McLeod became music director and in 1954 the band appeared at the Empire Games in Vancouver. While on a tour of duty in Germany 1957–9 with the Canadian Brigade the band, under Capt Herbert A. *Jeffrey (director 1957–64), appeared in the Netherlands in 1958 on the occasion of Queen Elizabeth of England's state visit to that country. In 1959 it visited the Gaza strip, performing for troops stationed there, and became the first Canadian band to participate in the Royal Tournament in England. Returning from Europe, the band was stationed 1959–68 in Edmonton and then relocated in Calgary, where it amalgamated with the Lord Strathcona Horse Band.

In 1967 the band performed in the Grand National Tattoo in Victoria and Vancouver and at *Expo 67 and made an extensive tour of Alberta. It toured Europe again in 1969, 1970, and 1973. The band has appeared regularly in the Stampede Parade in Calgary and was selected in 1976 along with the *Royal 22nd Regiment Band to represent Canada in the Tournament of Roses parade in Pasadena, Cal. In 1978 it played at the opening of the Commonwealth Games. The band was under the direction of Capt G.C. Naylor 1964–8, Capt P.A. Medcalf 1968–9, Capt J. Dowell 1969–72, and Capt Leonard *Camplin 1972–8, succeeded by Maj Jean F. Pierret.

DISCOGRAPHY

Princess' Patricia's Canadian Light Infantry Band Salutes the 60th Diamond Jubilee of the Regiment. 1979. Westmount WSTM 7321-5

BIBLIOGRAPHY

'Regimental Band,' *The Patrician*, vol 20, 1967
'Regimental Band: a brief history,' ibid, vol 26, 1973
(HK, JK)

PRITCHARD, Jocelyn (May) (b Rogers). Pianist, choir conductor, b Yarmouth, NS, 24 Jul 1928; L MUS (Dalhousie) 1947, AMA 1948, BA (Alberta) 1951. She studied piano 1935–45 with her mother, Margaret Sinclair Rogers; 1945–7 at the Maritime Academy of Music with Harry *Dean; and 1948–51 in Edmonton with Vernon *Barford and at the *U of Alberta with Richard S. *Eaton.

Pritchard began teaching university extension courses in 1951 and has taught piano and theory privately in various centres for more than 25 years. With Patricia Elliott she formed a two-piano team which performed 1960–8 in western Canada. She also founded (Edmonton, 1961) the 15-voice Da Camera Singers.

In 1963 Pritchard moved to Vernon, BC, and became a central figure in the development of music in the Okanagan Valley. She was organist-choirmaster at Trinity United Church, pianist with the Okanagan Symphony Trio, founder (1969) and conductor of the Okanagan Symphony Choir, conductor of the Festival Players (a chamber group), an examiner for the *WBN, and co-ordinator, in Vernon, of a Festival of Canadian Music in 1971 and a Festival of Contemporary Music in 1973. In 1974 she received a *Canada Council grant to act as a music resource person in the Okanagan Valley. In 1975 Pritchard moved to Vancouver. (DD)

Prix Archambault. Created in 1940 by Edmond Archambault, president of Ed *Archambault Inc, and awarded annually to encourage advanced students in the pursuit of their musical studies. The competition was supervised by the *MSO's Matinées symphoniques committee until 1943 when its administration was entrusted to Maurice Crépault of the Archambault firm. Crépault remained in charge until 1962, when the competition was terminated.

The competition was limited to piano in the early years but in 1943 a string category was added and in 1944 voice. The winner in each category received an award of $100 and a performance with orchestra in the Matinées symphoniques series. In addition, the prize winners took part in a concert organized by the Archambault company. The competition was open to all Canadian pianists under the age of 22, string players under 24, and singers under 25. A compulsory piece and sight reading tests were added to the performance fare of each category.

Among Prix Archambault winners, Paule-A. Bailly (1940), Jacqueline Lavoy (1942), Lise DesRosiers (1943), Jeanne *Landry (1945), and Monique Munger (1955) were laureates of the *Prix d'Europe as well. The Prix Archambault may be credited with having discovered other young artists who went on to make distinguished careers for themselves, among them Fernande *Chiocchio, Marguerite *Lavergne, Joseph *Rouleau, Sylvia *Saurette, Léopold *Simoneau, and Ronald *Turini. CH

Prix de musique Calixa-Lavallée. An annual prize established in 1959 and awarded by a jury of the St-Jean-Baptiste Society of Montreal to a resident of Quebec whose 'accomplishment and distinction in the field of music have served or are serving the higher interests of the people of Quebec both in Quebec and abroad.' The amount of the prize was raised in 1976 from $500 to $1000. It is accompanied by a medal 'Bene merenti de patria.' The winners listed below all have entries in *EMC*.

1959 Léopold Simoneau and Pierrette Alarie
1960 Jacques Beaudry
1961 Françoise Aubut
1962 Jean Papineau-Couture
1963 Gilles Lefebvre
1964 Victor Bouchard and Renée Morisset
1965 Louis Quilico
1966 Gilles Vigneault
1967 Joseph Rouleau
1968 Gilles Tremblay
1969 Roger Matton
1970 Clermont Pépin
1971 Colette Boky
1972 Claire Gagnier
1973 Gaston Germain
1974 Pauline Julien

1975 Félix Leclerc
1976 Jean Carignan
1977 Lionel Daunais
1978 Monique Leyrac
1979 Serge Garant GP

Prix d'Europe. Study grant created by the Quebec government in 1911 through the initiative of J.-Arthur Paquet, businessman, organist, and the treasurer of the *AMQ. With the approval of the academy's secretary, J.-Arthur *Bernier, and the members of the board, the project was presented to the Quebec premier, Sir Lomer Gouin, who supported it. A law to promote the development of musical art was passed by the Legislative Assembly 24 Mar 1911. The Prix d'Europe, offered annually, was set originally at $3000, raised to $5000 in 1959, and to $8000 in 1973. In 1961 its funding was assumed by the *MACQ and its administration by the AMQ. Initially participants competed in their respective categories for one main prize. In 1960 two categories were created: keyboard instruments and voice, alternating with orchestral instruments and composition. In 1974 the original formula of having only one prize winner was reinstated. Prix d'Europe winners have been:

1911 Clotilde Coulombe piano
1912 Léo-Pol *Morin piano
1913 Omer *Létourneau organ
1914 Hector (Jean) *Dansereau piano
1915 Wilfrid *Pelletier piano
1916 Graziella *Dumaine voice
1917 Germaine *Malépart piano
1918 Jean Kaster cello
1919 Lucille Dompierre piano
1920 Ruth Pryce violin
1921 Auguste *Descarries piano
1922 Anna-Marie Messénie piano
1923 Conrad *Bernier organ
1924 Gabriel *Cusson cello
1925 Paul *Doyon piano
1926 Lionel *Daunais voice
1927 Rita Savard piano; Henri Mercure composition
1928 Brahm Sand cello
1929 Jean-Marie *Beaudet organ/piano
1930 Gilberte *Martin piano
1931 Lucien *Martin violin
1932 Bernard *Piché organ
1933 Edwin *Bélanger violin
1934 Georges *Lindsay organ
1935 Georgette Tremblay organ
1936 Noël *Brunet violin
1937 Georges *Savaria piano
1938 Marcel Hébert piano
1939 Paule-Aimée Bailly piano
1940 Suzette Forgues cello
1941 Marcelle *Martin organ
1942 Claude *Lavoie organ
1943 Berthe Dorval piano
1944 Jacqueline Lavoy piano
1945 Claude *Létourneau violin
1946 Jeanne *Landry piano
1947 Lise DesRosiers piano
1948 Raymond *Daveluy organ
1949 Clermont *Pépin piano
1950 Josephte *Dufresne piano
1951 Anna-Marie *Globenski piano
1952 Janine *Lachance piano
1953 Kenneth *Gilbert organ
1954 Monik *Grenier piano
1955 Léon *Bernier piano
1956 Monique Munger piano
1957 Jean *Leduc organ
1958 Lise *Boucher piano
1959 Rachel *Martel piano
1960 Jacqueline *Martel voice; Gisèle Daoust piano
1961 Jacques *Hétu composition; Pierre Ménard violin
1962 Colette *Boky voice; John *McKay piano
1963 Cécile Lanneville cello; André *Prévost composition
1964 Claude Ouellet voice; Claude *Savard piano
1965 Alain *Gagnon composition
1966 Monique Gendron organ; Bruno *Laplante voice
1967 Micheline Columbe *Saint-Marcoux composition; Jacques Larocque saxophone
1968 Roland Richard voice; Lucie Madden organ
1969 Louise LeComte recorder
1970 John Whitelaw harpsichord
1971 not awarded
1972 Marie *Laferrière voice; Karen Quinton piano
1973 Raynald *Arseneault composition; Marcel St-Jacques flute
1974 Jacinthe *Couture piano
1975 Denis *Bédard harpsichord
1976 Robert Langevin flute
1977 Michel Franck piano
1978 Gilles Carpentier clarinet
1979 Chantal Juillet violin
1980 Marie-Danielle Parent voice

Special grants were awarded to Norman Herschorn (violin, 1924) and Alice Ste-Marie (piano, 1926). In 1938 Marcel Hébert drowned shortly after winning the competition and the grant was given to Noël Brunet. In 1971 the prize was withheld, since no candidate performed at a sufficiently high level.

BIBLIOGRAPHY

Morin, Léo-Pol. 'Le Prix d'Europe,' Montreal *La Patrie*, 5 instalments, 5, 12, 19, and 26 Jun, 26 Jul 1926 CH

P.R.O. Canada (Performing Rights Organization of Canada Limited) / S.D.E. Canada (Société de Droits d'Exécution du Canada Limitée); known 1940–77 as BMI Canada Limited. Established in 1940 and operated for the first seven years as a Canadian presence of the US organization Broadcast Music Inc, to license in Canada the parent company's repertoire. Some Canadian composers were affiliates of the US organization and their works were a part of that repertoire.

In 1947, however, BMI Canada assumed a more active role on behalf of Canadian affiliate composers, writers, and publishers, attracting new affiliates and protecting their performing rights and administering their royalties, under the directorship of Wm Harold Moon (b Toronto 10 Jul 1908, a pioneer in Canadian radio and TV, the recipient in 1974 of the first Canadian Music Hall of Fame Award and the man for whom BMI Canada established the Wm Harold Moon Award, in honour of his dedication to Canadian music). By 1980 the organization had grown to represent 9477 Canadian writers and composers and 1750 publishers.

On 1 Jul 1976 BMI Canada changed its status from that of a subsidiary of Broadcast Music Inc to an organization owned and operated by Music Promotion Foundation, a Canadian non-profit corporation. On 15 Jul 1977 it changed its name to Performing Rights Organization of Canada Ltd. The head office remained in Don Mills (Toronto) Ont. In 1948 a Montreal office was opened, the first locally based performing-rights office in Canada. A Vancouver office was opened in 1968, the first performing-rights office in western Canada.

Managing directors have been Wm Harold Moon 1947–73 and S. Campbell Ritchie 1973–80, the latter succeeded by Jan *Matejcek. Gordon F. Henderson, QC, became PRO Canada's first president in 1977. Jean L. Howson joined BMI Canada in 1947 as director of art-music publications and was succeeded in 1956 by Ronald R. *Napier, who was head of the publishing division 1959–69 and became manager of concert music administration in 1963.

While PRO Canada's primary function has continued to be the collection of licence fees and distribution of performance royalties to affiliates, it has assisted affiliates and the music community at large in other ways as well. In the early years broadcasters were provided with programming information and workshops. In 1947 BMI Canada established a publishing division. Claude *Champagne served 1949–65 as editor-in-chief of the contemporary music dept.

During the 1950s BMI Canada was the agent for Associated Music Publishers of New York and carried a large stock of the publications of Breitkopf, Schott, Universal, and other publishers. By 1969, when it was sold to *Berandol, the publishing division held the largest number of copyrights of Canadian popular and serious music in Canada.

Promotion of Canadian music outside the country has been a long-standing mandate of the organization. In 1950 BMI Canada co-operated with the Oklahoma SO in devoting one in a series of 13 broadcasts of 20th-century music to works by Canadians. In 1953 BMI Canada co-operated with Broadcast Music Inc in presenting at Carnegie Hall, New York, a concert of Canadian music conducted by Leopold Stokowski. Liaison with and assistance to music organizations has continued through financial and/or volunteer assistance to the *CMCouncil, the *CMCentre, the Healey Willan Centennial Committee, the Academy of Country Music Entertainment, Melbourne Records, CBC recordings, the *NYO, and Canada Music Week.

The organization's head office has made its biographical files of Canadian writers and composers available without charge for research purposes. Profiles of affiliated composers of serious music have been published in brochures in French and English. These were preceded in the late 1940s by mimeographed sheets. Profiles include lists of compositions and works recorded.

In 1951 BMI Canada began to provide Canadian broadcasters with listings of all recorded Canadian music registered with the organization. The lists were titled 'Yes, There *is* Canadian Music / Oui, Notre Musique *existe*!' They were discontinued in March 1977.

The organization's six-times-yearly magazine **The Music Scene* and its French-language counterpart *La Scène musicale* made their appearance in 1967 and continued under the same names after the organization's 1974 change of status and name.

In 1972, under the leadership of Lehman Engel, the organization began monthly musical theatre workshops in Toronto for aspiring composers. These workshops led, in 1974, to the first annual Showcase of Songs from Musical Shows, produced in Toronto to expose the workshop's products to producers and directors. In 1970 and 1971 PRO Canada sponsored a series of five workshops for film composers. In 1980 it introduced a second series and expanded the audiences to include film producers and directors, along with composers. In addition, PRO Canada has sent its personnel and guest panelists to speak to groups of affiliates or music industry arts students across the country.

In 1980 *PRO Canada awards included annual student composers' awards, biennial orchestra awards, and an annual award to a student lawyer for a paper on copyright. (see also Copyright.) An annual awards dinner (the first one held in 1969) honoured affiliated songwriters and publishers.

Subsequent to the establishment of its autonomy in 1976 PRO Canada made direct contact with the major foreign performing right societies and publishing companies through a new International Dept headed by Jan Matejcek. Royalties have been collected in Canada for many foreign copyrights and the foreign societies have reciprocated by administering the performance rights in Canadian copyright works performed abroad.

Foreign publishers with catalogues administered in Canada by PRO Canada have included Ricordi, Breitkopf, Universal and Peters.

BIBLIOGRAPHY

Cruickshank, Ralph. 'BMI Canada, a tribute,' *CME*, Spring 1970

'The BMI Canada story,' *Record Week*, 2 May 1977

P.R.O. Canada Awards. Awards and scholarships granted by *PRO Canada (formerly BMI Canada) in five categories: annual student composers' awards, annual songwriters' awards, 'special' awards, awards to orchestras, and an annual copyright award.

Young Canadians engaged in formal music studies became eligible to compete for the US-based BMI Awards to Student Composers at their inception in 1951. Canadian winners of these awards include Steven *Gellman and Peter *Huse (1963), Hugh *Hartwell and John *Mills-Cockell (1966), John *Hawkins and John *Rea (1968), Denis *Lorrain (1969, 1972), Donald Steven (1969), and Michel *Longtin (1972).

In 1967 BMI Canada established Centennial Scholarships in composition at the *RCMT and *Simon Fraser U and from 1975 to 1978 the organization offered $50 cash prizes to composition students at all Canadian universities and community colleges. In 1979 these programs were replaced by a major composition competition (P.R.O. Canada Student Composer Awards), offering up to $5000 to young Canadians studying in Canada and abroad.

P.R.O. Canada's Annual Songwriters' Awards (formerly BMI Canada Awards) were first presented in 1969 at an awards dinner for affiliate writers and publishers of popular music. Winners receive Certificates of Honour. Others honoured at the annual dinners have included those individuals or organizations which have made outstanding contributions to the development and growth of Canadian music. Special plaques were presented to the CBC, the CRTC, and the Canadian Assn of Broadcasters in 1972 and to George Hamilton IV and posthumously to Healey *Willan in 1973.

In 1974 the Wm Harold Moon Award was established to honour those BMI affiliates who had done most to promote Canadian music internationally during the preceding year. Winners include R. Murray *Schafer (1974), Randy Bachman (1975), Harry *Somers (1976), Hagood *Hardy (1977), Serge *Garant (1978), the *Irish Rovers (1979), and Frank *Mills (1980). A winner of this award received a plaque and $500 until 1978, when a piece of Canadian art supplanted the cash prize.

P.R.O. Canada Orchestra Awards, begun in 1978, have offered biennially $10,000 in cash prizes to Canadian orchestras for imaginative programming of contemporary music. The first winners of these (1978) were the *Quebec SO, the Lethbridge SO, the *Regina Symphony, and the *New Brunswick Youth Orchestra. A special citation was made to the *NACO.

The P.R.O. Canada Copyright Award (established in 1978, first awarded in 1979) has offered an annual prize of $2500 to a Canadian law student, or lawyer in his/her first year of articling, for an essay on the subject of copyright as it relates to music. The 1979 winner was Bruce M. Green; the 1980, Gordon J. Zimmerman.

BIBLIOGRAPHY

MSc, annual May–Jun issues (1969–), lists Certificates of Honour winners.

PROCTOR, George (Alfred). Musicologist, teacher, administrator, violinist, b Toronto 13 May 1931, ARCT 1950, BA (McMaster) 1952, M MUS (ESM Rochester) 1956, PH D (ESM Rochester) 1960. He was a pupil of John A. Montague and Kathleen *Parlow at the *RCMT.

While a student at the ESM Proctor played 1953–4 with the Rochester Philharmonic. On his return to Canada he taught 1954–7 at *McMaster U. He worked 1959–61 as a musicologist at the *National Museum of Canada, researching old-time fiddle music, and played 1959–60 in the *Ottawa Philharmonic. He taught 1961–4 at the *U of British Columbia, 1964–5 at the *U of Western Ontario, and 1965–7 at the ESM, where he was a member in 1966 of the Eastman Chamber Orchestra. He held the Pickard-Bell Chair 1967–74 at *Mount Allison U as head of the Dept of Music. He served 1974–8 as assistant dean (graduate studies) of the Faculty of Music at the U of Western Ontario and in 1980 continued to teach as a member of the faculty.

A scholar in many areas of Canadian music, Proctor prepared the 1971 CTV University of the Air series 'Canadian Music of the 20th Century,' shortly thereafter receiving a *Canada Council grant to present the topic in book form. The book was published by the U of Toronto Press in 1980.

Proctor has written articles for *EMC* and *The New Grove*.

WRITINGS

'The Works of Nicola Matteis, Sr.,' PH D thesis, U of Rochester 1960

'Musical styles of Gaspé songs,' *Contributions to Anthropology*, vol 2, National Museums of Canada (Ottawa 1963)

'Old-time fiddling in Ontario,' ibid

'The Bachelor of Music degree in Canada and the United States,' *CME*, vol 7, Jan–Feb 1966

'Music education – an historical view,' *Recorder*, vol 10, Jun–Jul 1968

'Music at Mount Allison,' *MSc*, 259, May–Jun 1971

Sources in Canadian Music: A Bibliography of Bibliographies / Les Sources de la musique canadienne: Une bibliographie des bibliographies (Sackville, NB 1975, 1979)

'Neoclassicism and Neoromanticism in Canadian music,' *Studies in Music from the University of Western Ontario* (London 1976)

Canadian Music of the Twentieth Century (Toronto 1980)

(NV)

Procure Générale de musique Ltée. A music firm established in Quebec City by Omer *Létourneau. After acting as an unofficial adviser to the firm of Gauvin & Courchesne (founded in 1914 by the impresario J.-A. Gauvin and the cellist Hermann Courchesne), Létourneau purchased it in 1934 and renamed it Procure générale de musique. The offices and retail store were located at Place d'Youville above the Lindsay department store. Working with his son Paul, Omer Létourneau offered a selection of sheet music as well as string and wind instruments. He also established the Éditions de la Procure générale de musique Enr'g, which published many of his own works and pieces by J.-Arthur *Bernier, François *Brassard, Léon *Destroismaisons, and Joseph *Vézina. Scores and educational texts continued to be published until the mid-1940s, but the retail business was always the firm's main activity. In 1945 the firm moved to new premises on D'Aiguillon St, and in 1966 Edwin *Bélanger, Létourneau's son-in-law, became the proprietor. At this time the company began to sell popular music. When in 1977 its premises were destroyed by fire the business moved to the Côte d'Abraham. MB-L

Prodigies. Children endowed with phenomenal intellectual and technical abilities which enable them to function, in art or science, as adults. A child may be bright or appealing – or cleverly exploited – without being a prodigy. Among Canadian musicians there are many who gave recitals at six or seven, but often, on the evidence extant, it is difficult to be certain whether these offered ordinary beginners' programs performed neatly or advanced music performed with mature authority.

Possibly the first Canadian to be considered a prodigy was Tom Haliburton (b probably at Annapolis Royal, NS, 18 Jan 1821, d Massachusetts 3 Nov 1847), son and namesake of the author of the famous Sam Slick novels. Haliburton studied music in Germany and was known among his friends as 'the American Mozart.' Other prodigious Canadian children have included Clermont *Pépin, who at eight began to compose a symphony for piano four-hands; and André *Mathieu, who gave his first piano recital at six and had his earliest piano compositions published shortly thereafter.

Among Canadian pianists, Willy *Eckstein was known at 12 as 'The Boy Paderewski,' and Ellen *Ballon at six passed the AB of the RSM and RAM exams. Other piano prodigies include Gilles Breton of Quebec City; Winnipeg-born Valdine Conde, who made her debut (1938) at nine with the New York Civic Orchestra playing Saint-Saëns' *Concerto in G Minor*; Toronto-born Muriel Albert, who was composing at three and whose appearance at 12 (ca 1944) as a pianist with the Buffalo Philharmonic won 10 curtain calls; Glenn *Gould, who read music at three, composed at five, and completed an ATCM at 12; Marian *Grudeff; Vancouver-born (ca 1946) Andrea Kalanj, who played Beethoven's *Concerto No. 3* with the *Vancouver SO at nine; Angela *Hewitt; Diedre *Irons; Elaine *Keillor, who gave her first public performance before she was three and completed her ARCT at 11; Muriel *Kerr; Minuetta *Kessler; Mari-Elizabeth *Morgen; Patricia *Parr; and Berthe *Roy. The jazz pianists Chris *Gage, Oscar *Peterson, and Doug *Riley, all of whom showed phenomenal abilities while very young, might also be considered prodigies. Ernest *MacMillan began organ study at eight and made his debut shortly thereafter.

Emma *Albani made her debut as a singer, pianist, and harpist at eight, and an international career was predicted for her when she was 14. The boy soprano Bobby Breen (b Jackie Boreen, Toronto 1927, d England 1972) sang in Jack *Arthur's Toronto revues, appeared at nine on Eddie Cantor's CBS radio show, and performed until 1942 in Hollywood films – he recorded for Decca, Bluebird, and other labels and spent his later career working in US nightclubs. Another boy soprano, Gérard Barbeau (1936–ca 1959), sang at 12 on Montreal radio and in his mid-teens gave recitals of arias and art songs which brought comparisons to Erna Sack and Lily Pons. (Soon afterwards, he entered the priesthood.) The soprano Marie Gauley, at three, won five firsts at the Kiwanis Festival. Other singers, including Deanna Durbin, Jackie *Rae, and René *Simard, have enjoyed highly successful childhood careers.

Two of Canada's 19th-century violin prodigies were Flavien *Sauvageau (son of Charles) and

George *Fox, who at six drew astonished praise from Eduard Reményi. In the 20th century Arthur *LeBlanc and Noël *Brunet made early debuts, as did Donna *Grescoe and Betty-Jean *Hagen. Kayla Mitzel (b Winnipeg 1915) was a pupil of Geza *de Kresz and Louis Persinger and greatly successful as a child in concerts in Europe and the USA. Betty-Ann Fischer (b Kitchener, Ont, 1925, d Wiarton, Ont 1979) overcame finger deformation to give her first violin recital at six and play the Mendelssohn *Concerto* with the TSO at 11. Later, as Betty Fischer-Byfield, she was a member of the TS. Victor Schultz (b Winnipeg 1959) won the top instrumental award at the *Manitoba Music Competition Festival at 11, after less than four years' study. He later studied in New York with Ivan Galamian and Dorothy De Lay and was a soloist with the TS. The cellist Lorne *Munroe, whose teacher Dezsö *Mahalek was a prodigy in Europe, won the senior cello class of the Manitoba Music Competition Festival at 10. Foreign-born Canadian musicians who were prodigies include Rex *Battle, S.C. *Eckhardt-Gramatté, Piero Gamba (conductor of the Winnipeg SO), Anton *Kuerti, and Leo *Smith.

BIBLIOGRAPHY
'The unusual lives of child prodigies,' *Fugue*, Nov 1977
Brown, Dick. 'Prodigious! But what do you do when you grow up?' *Today*, 21 Jun 1980

Profession of music. Music as a full-time occupation. To earn a livelihood as a musician – particularly in a single discipline such as composing or singing or playing an instrument – has not been possible in Canada for any considerable number of people until relatively recently. More so than in Europe, the musician in Canada has had to depend on a combination of activities, some of them non-musical, to support himself.

The earliest paid musicians were the tambours and pipers in the French regiments in 17th-century Canada and the organists in the cathedrals of Quebec and Montreal, but their engagements were only part-time. The full-time musician, who appeared late in the 18th century, was nearly always from Europe, since the colony lacked the training facilities to produce its own. To survive he had to be a jack-of-all-trades, and indeed the careers of such men as Frederick H. *Glackemeyer and J.-C. *Brauneis, père, are fascinating in the mixture of activities as bandmasters, church organists, music-storekeepers, piano tuners, occasional composers, teachers, and leaders of musical societies.

The church, the regimental band, and the private teaching studio remained the backbone of the profession throughout the 19th century, and although the music trade and the building of keyboard instruments provided more and more jobs, many of the publisher-dealers (eg, A.J. *Boucher, Peter Grossman, Edmond *Hardy, Ernest *Lavigne, and Henry *Prince) were practising musicians as well.

Among the earliest Canadian-born professionals were Charles *Sauvageau (1804?–49) and J.-C. *Brauneis fils (1814–71), the latter perhaps the first to receive a European education, though such foreign training became almost the rule, among gifted musicians who could afford it, from the late 19th century onwards (see Education, professional).

In Europe the 'compleat musician' of the 18th century (Haydn, Mozart, and most of their contemporaries were composer-virtuoso-conductor-teachers as a matter of course) gave way to the mainly-composer, the conductor-only, or the performer-sometime-teacher of the 20th century. Similarly, Canadian musicians in the late 19th and the 20th centuries tended more and more towards specialization, especially in the larger cities, where many teachers (but very few organist-choirmasters) could make a living.

New (for Canada) specializations arose, such as music journalism and school teaching and, in the 20th century, orchestra conducting, orchestra playing, opera singing, university teaching, scholarship, librarianship, concert management, arranging, jingle writing, and music administration. New technologies have produced further professional specializations, eg, the broadcast producer, the program director, the commentator, the recording technician, and the electronic music laboratory technician.

Much of the credit for progress towards the establishment of music as a profession must be given to the *unions – first established in 1887 and responsible especially for the improvement of the instrumental ensemble player's lot (orchestra, band, pop band). But credit must go also to the professional organizations for teachers, organists, composers, and others. Conditions, even by 1980, could not be described as ideal, however; for example, until the late 1960s no Canadian orchestra could offer full-time year-round (52-week contract) employment.

In the early 20th century the theatre and movie orchestra formed the orchestra players' main support; in the 1930s this role passed to the *CBC, which became the main support, or at least provided a decisive supplementary income, not only for the players but also for singers, arrangers, solo performers, and composers. (It should be added, however, that unlike European broadcasting systems, eg, the BBC or Radio France, the CBC has not established full-time employment for orchestral musicians or choral singers.) To some extent the recording studios and the universities (as employers of teachers and as sponsors of performing ensembles) had taken over as guarantors of professional musical life by 1980, though in the 1970s in at least Halifax, Quebec, Montreal, Ottawa, Toronto, Hamilton, London, Winnipeg, Calgary, Edmonton, and Vancouver the major symphony orchestras were the most significant employers of practising instrumental musicians.

Most musicians, fortunately, have preferred to combine a variety of activities not only because of economic necessity but also because of inclination. The designation of musicians' major areas of activity in *EMC* biographies gives evidence of an amazing versatility even today. There have been only a few Canadian musicians whose exclusive (or nearly so) activity is composition (*Somers, *Freedman), or choral conducting (*Bradshaw, *Iseler, *Lacourse). Opera singers, orchestra players, school teachers, and several successful orchestra conductors provide more numerous instances of single-activity concentration.

The economic aspect is one side of professionalism; training and qualification are the other. (There are hundreds of amateurs earning 'professional' wages because as, for instance, part-time drummers or trumpeters in bands they belong to unions.) One reason for the slow growth of professionalism has been the small size of the market; for many years the only avenue for real success was the one which led abroad (see Emigration). Another reason was the lack of facilities for post-conservatory training until after World War II. Those who could not afford to go abroad for advanced study were at a great disadvantage although there are examples of fine musicians trained almost exclusively in Canada – *Contant, J.-J. *Gagnier, *Morel, *Ridout, Amédée *Tremblay, and such stars of the performer's art as Maureen *Forrester, Don *Garrard, Glenn *Gould, Lois *Marshall, Teresa *Stratas, and Jon *Vickers. Nevertheless, immigrants maintained an advantage over Canadians in claiming key positions (and in 1980 continued to do so in the fields of conducting, master teaching, and musicology). This has made it difficult to establish Canadian traditions in the various branches of music. By 1980, however, high professional standards were prevalent in all areas of music in Canada.

BIBLIOGRAPHY
Walter, Arnold. 'Music in a technological age,' *CMJ*, vol 1, Spring 1957
Payzant, Geoffrey B. 'The actual need,' ibid
'The status of the professional musician in Saskatchewan: memorandum on a music conference,' unpubl report, Saskatchewan Arts Board, Regina 1969
Vachon, Marie. 'Survey on the socio-economic status of Canadian composers of serious music,' unpubl MA thesis, Carlton U 1975
Swan, Susan, and White, Nancy. 'The woman as music-maker: classical music: popular music,' *Communiqué*, May 1975
Van Daele, Christa. 'From pedestal to podium: women in serious music,' *Miss Chatelaine*, Fall 1977
Whittaker, Herbert. 'Ten years later – a history of Contact,' Canada Council Touring Office *Bulletin*, Jan 1980

(HK)

Prologue to the Performing Arts. Volunteer organization founded in 1966 in Toronto to serve as a liaison between boards of education and the *COC, the National Ballet of Canada, and Young People's Theatre and to present in intermediate schools live productions planned jointly by the performing companies, the prologue organization, and the education authorities.

The first program was a package series consisting of an opera, a ballet, and a play, each work an hour long, tailored for students in grades 7, 8, and 9, and available to a client-school at an all-in-one fee of $1000. In its first season Prologue for the Performing Arts presented 37 such series (111 performances by the three companies), and by 1970 it was giving 101 series in Toronto alone and 52 in Windsor, Ottawa, and other Ontario centres, a total of 387 individual performances that year. The number of performing companies supplying productions increased from 3 in 1967 to 12 in 1976, and the audience was broadened from exclusively intermediate-level students to primary, junior, and secondary level.

When performing groups from outside Ontario were invited to appear (eg, Les Grands Ballets Canadiens, 1973–4), the provincial endeavour assumed a national complexion, though prologue productions did not tour outside Ontario. The broader program was made possible by the co-operation of other provincial governments and increased financial support from the *OAC.

Prologue to the Performing Arts is governed by a board and operated from a Toronto office under the supervision of a professional administrator (Mary Carr 1969–76, succeeded by Joan McCordic). There is no regular musical director in the organization's employ. The presentations are prepared and manned entirely by the companies which provide them. Prologue's involvement is in the initial planning and the organization of the market.

Prologue has commissioned (among other works) two operas: *The Spirit of Fundy* (1972) by Norman *Symonds and *The Glove* (1975) by Tibor *Polgar and George Jonas, both works given special productions for students by the COC. *The Glove* was telecast on CBC in 1975. The COC also provided productions of Pergolesi's *La Serva Padrona* (1967), Menotti's *The Old Maid and the Thief* (1968 and 1973), Wolf-Ferrari's *The Secret of Suzanne* (1969), Argento's *The Boor* (1969), and

Donizetti's *Rita* (1970). Opera performances are accompanied by piano.

Choral works have been composed for the organization by Keith *Bissell and Brad Warnaar. (JP)

Promenade Symphony Concerts. Toronto summer series (1934–56) given by an orchestra of 75–90 players formed and conducted by Reginald *Stewart. Established with the assistance of the Toronto Musical Protective Assn to provide summer employment for musicians, the orchestra was known first as the Promenade SO and after 1940 as the Toronto Philharmonic Orchestra.

The weekly concerts (May through October) were presented at the 5600-seat Varsity Arena on the *U of Toronto campus and were broadcast by the CBC and heard in the USA during the late 1930s. Admission prices were low, even for the day, ranging downwards from one dollar each for the best reserved seats to 25 cents each for the first 1000 unreserved seats.

Concertmasters were Harold *Sumberg 1934–40, Eugene *Kash 1941–2, Albert *Steinberg 1943–4, John *Dembeck in 1945, and Hyman *Goodman 1946–56.

After Stewart's resignation in 1941 such guests as Maurice Abravanel, Sir Adrian Boult, Alexander *Brott, Hans Kindler, Victor Kolar, André Kostelanetz, Sir Ernest *MacMillan, Ettore *Mazzoleni, and Heinz *Unger were engaged. Soloists included Jessica Dragonette, Percy Grainger, James Melton, Jan Peerce, Gregor Piatigorsky, William Primrose, Efrem Zimbalist, and the Canadians Barbara *Custance, Ray *Dudley, George *Haddad, Betty-Jean *Hagen, Lois *Marshall, Zara *Nelsova, Patricia *Parr, Albert *Pratz, and Harold Sumberg.

Premieres included Percival *Price's *St Lawrence Symphony* (1934) and *Willan's *Symphony in D Minor* (1936), *Coronation Te Deum* (1937), and *Marche solennelle* (1937). North American premieres included Vaughan Williams' *Suite for Viola and Orchestra* (1937) and Walton's *Crown Imperial* (1940). Tchaikovsky was the most frequently performed composer, followed by Wagner. RWJ

Pro Musica Society / Société Pro Musica. Founded in 1948 in Montreal by Mrs Constant Gendreau, with financial assistance from her husband, to present chamber music from all periods. The first concert, 17 Oct 1948, was given by the Stuyvesant String Quartet and the clarinetist Clark Brody at the Ritz-Carlton Hotel. Mrs Gendreau was the president 1948–79 and was succeeded by Gabriel *Charpentier, who became the artistic director. In 1980 Clément *Morin was the only remaining member of the original board.

The society has received financial assistance from individuals and corporations. Each level of government has given annual grants – the province beginning in 1949, the city of Montreal 1952–3, and the *Canada Council in 1972. Until 1964 tickets were available only by subscription. Thereafter the use of larger halls (eg, the Maisonneuve Theatre in the *PDA in 1979) made single-ticket sales possible.

The society's programs have earned respect over the years for the care with which they have been chosen, and its many sources of revenue have enabled it to maintain high standards, to offer young people's matinee concerts 1961–71, and to present special series under the name Montreal Concerts. Many concerts in the latter series were devoted to complete sets of works of Beethoven: the quartets performed in 1955 by the Vegh Quartet; the piano trios in 1960, 1966, and 1977 by the Beaux Arts Trio; the piano sonatas in 1961 by Wilhelm Kempff; and the sonatas and variations for cello and piano in 1965 by André Navarra and Jacqueline Dussol. In 1959 six Beethoven quartets and the complete Bartók quartets were performed by the Hungarian Quartet and the Juilliard Quartet. In the regular concerts Jean-Pierre Rampal and the Pasquier Trio performed Mozart's quartets for flute and strings.

Works given their first Montreal performances under Pro Musica auspices include Schoenberg's *Quartet No. 1*, *Suite* for piano, and *Woodwind Quintet* and Berg's *Lyric Suite*. Canadian works premiered by the society include *Freedman's *Three French Songs*, *Hétu's *Sonate* (1962), and *Pépin's *Séquences*. The revised version of Claude *Champagne's *Quartet* was given its first performance in its final version. In 1974 Pro Musica began offering one concert of Canadian works each season.

Among Canadian performers presented by Pro Musica have been the duo-pianists *Bouchard and Morisset, Maureen *Forrester, Glenn *Gould, the *Montreal and *Orford string quartets and Ronald *Turini. IP-C

Pro Organo. A non-profit-making society founded in St-Hyacinthe, Que, in 1970 to increase awareness in Quebec of the organ and its repertoire through recitals by organists of repute and by serious young performers beginning their careers. The society has been subsidized chiefly by the *MACQ. Pro Organo has established centres in various towns. Each centre is autonomous with respect to both its constitution and its activities, but ties of mutual assistance are maintained.

In 1970 at the instigation of the organist Jean Morissette, a central committee was constituted that included Morissette, the organists Jacques Desroches, Réjean *Poirier, and Paul Vigeant, and the organ builder Guy Thérien. The centres in St-Hyacinthe, St-Jean, and Joliette all were inaugurated during the first year, followed in 1971 by those of Trois-Rivières and Varennes. In 1980, only the centres of Trois-Rivières (Pro-Organo Mauricie Inc), Joliette (Pro-Organo Lanaudière Inc), and St-Hyacinthe (Société culturelle Pro-Organo St-Hyacinthe Inc) were active, and each offered an average of four recitals a season. The central committee was dissolved in 1973.

Incorporated in 1973, Pro-Organo Mauricie was set up principally by Jean Girouard, president 1971–3. Subsequent presidents have been Fernand Beaudet 1973–4, Jean Thiffault 1974–6, and Louis-Georges Pérusse 1976–8, followed by Camille Langis. Pro-Organo Lanaudière was incorporated in 1975. Its first president, Jacques Desroches 1970–2, was followed by Éliette Martineau 1972–7 and Yvette Roy. The concerts of this centre are distinguished by the presence, in addition to the organists, of various soloists and instrumental groups. In 1978 the regional centre of St-Hyacinthe was incorporated. Its presidents have been Paul Vigeant 1970–1, and Jean Morissette.

Among the numerous Quebec organists who have taken part in Pro Organo recitals are Gaston *Arel, Denis *Bédard, Raymond *Daveluy, Jacques Desroches, Sylvain Doyon, Noëlla Genest, Lucienne *L'Heureux-Arel, Bernard and Mireille *Lagacé, Jean Morissette, Bernard *Piché, Réjean Poirier, Denis *Regnaud, and Paul Vigeant. Foreign organists who have been invited to perform include Gillian Weir, who played at the Notre-Dame-du-Cap Basilica in January 1979. HP

PROPHET, Orval (William). Singer, guitarist, songwriter, b Edwards, near Ottawa, 31 Aug 1922. After singing 1944–9 with Bill Sheppard's country band on CFRA's 'Fiddler's Fling' (a travelling radio show which appeared throughout the Ottawa Valley), Prophet toured Canada in 1949 with Wilf *Carter and was recorded by Decca on Carter's recommendation.

As Orval (Rex) Prophet, 'The Canadian Playboy,' he was the second Canadian (after Hank *Snow) to record in Nashville. His 'Going Back to Birmingham,' 'Judgement Day Express,' and 'Molly Darling' were hits in the USA and Canada in the early 1950s. In the late 1950s, as Johnnie Six, he recorded (again for Decca) the hit 'Mademoiselle,' had his own radio show on WWBA (Nashville), and toured with Johnny Cash. Further recordings (as Orval Prophet) appeared on the Harmony, Caledon, and Broadland labels and included (by 1978) six LPs and the singles 'Lois and Me' (1962), 'Run Run Run' (1962), 'Mile After Mile' (1971), 'Leroy Can't Go Home' (1977), and 'Ol' Amos' (1978), all minor hits.

Prophet has continued to live in Edwards, except for a few months in 1958 in Nashville, but has toured widely in North America and has appeared on CBC TV and CTV. An affiliate of PRO Canada, he has written songs with Ken MacRae (including 'Judgement Day Express'), Dallas Harms, and others. He received the 1978 Big Country Award for outstanding performance by a male country singer and in 1979 was inducted into the *RPM* Canadian Music Industry Hall of Fame. The singer Ronnie *Prophet is a cousin.

BIBLIOGRAPHY

Foster, Don. 'Interviewing Orval Prophet,' *World of Country Music*, Dec 1972

Grealis, Walt. 'Orval Prophet – inducted into hall of fame,' *RPM*, 14 Jul 1979 MM

PROPHET, Ronnie (Ronald). Singer, guitarist, comedian, b Hawkesbury, near Ottawa, 26 Dec 1937. A second cousin of Orval *Prophet, he made his debut at 15 in Ottawa on CFRA's country music show 'The Happy Wanderers.' At 17 he moved to Montreal, where he sang at various nightclubs until 1961. He then pursued his career in the USA, settling in Nashville in 1969. Though by 1980 he had continued to live there (operating Ronnie Prophet's Carousel club in the 1970s), he toured widely in Canada in the mid-1970s and starred on CBC TV's 'Country Roads' (summer 1973) and 'The Ronnie Prophet Show' (summer 1974) and on CTV's 'Grand Old Country,' which began in 1975 and which won the Big Country Award in 1976 and 1977 as the TV series of the year. Prophet himself won a Big Country Award for outstanding performance by a male country singer in 1975 and a Juno Award as male country vocalist in 1977. Prophet's one-man touring show has combined song, comedy, and a skilful use of the guitar. After making several LPs privately he began recording for *RCA in 1975 and by 1977 had made two LPs for that company. (RGn)

PROTERO, Dodi (Dorothy Ann) (b MacGregor, adopted McIlraith, m Crofoot). Soprano, b Toronto 13 Mar 1933. While a pupil 1949–59 of James Rosselino she sang during the early 1950s in the *Rosselino Opera's production of *La Traviata*. She also studied in Venice 1955–7 with Toti Dal Monte, in Vienna in 1957 with Ferdinand Grossmann, in Munich in 1963 with Lorenz Fehenberger, and in New York 1967–70 with Rosa Bok and 1975–6 with Oren Brown. She made her European debut in 1955 as Papagena in *The Magic Flute* with the San Carlo Opera in Naples and appeared at the Cologne Opera, at the 1959 Salzburg Festival as Clarice in Haydn's *Il Mondo della luna*, and at the 1960 Glyndebourne Festival as Papagena. She made her *COC debut in 1960 as Ciboletta in *A Night in Venice*. Further COC roles included Gretel in *Hansel and Gretel* (1962, 1963), Musetta in *La Bohème* (1965), Parasha in *Mavra* (1965), Oona in the premiere (1967) of *The Luck of Ginger Coffey*, and Marcellina in *Fidelio* (1970). She appeared in 1962 at Sadler's Wells, London, toured Europe in 1963 with the Mozart Opera of Salzburg, sang at the *Stratford and *Vancouver International festivals, and performed with the *Vancouver, Southern Alberta, and several US operas. She sang Mrs Bedwin in *Oliver!* on Broadway in 1966. She has sung on the CBC, the BBC, and several European networks, and appeared with the *TSO, the Mozarteum Orchestra, and other orchestras. She taught at the *Banff SFA in 1969, 1970, 1976, and 1977, and at the U of Illinois 1976–8. In 1974 she began teaching privately in New York.

DISCOGRAPHY

D'Albert *Tiefland*. Vienna SO, Moralt cond, Protero (Nuri). 1957. 2-Epic SC-6025

Mozart *La Finta Giardiniera*. Camerata Academia des Salzburger Mozarteums, Paumgartner cond, Protero (Sandrina). 1957. Epic LC 3543 (excerpts)

Pergolesi *La Serva padrona*. Camerata Academia des Salzburger Mozarteums, Hager cond, Protero (Serpina). 1958. Philips A 00494L (excerpts)

Protestant church music (Baptist, Congregational, Methodist, Presbyterian, and United, for the purposes of this article). The first protestant church music to be heard in Canada was sung by French Huguenots who during the 17th century brought with them to Acadia the French Psalter of 1562. They resisted the prohibitions (1627) of reformed worship in New France and, it is said, roared their psalmody with such vigour from their ships that they astonished the Indians on shore.

After the Huguenots' return to France ca 1630, reformed church song was not heard again until the early 18th century, when Anglican worship was initiated in Nova Scotia (see Anglican church music; Hymnbooks, protestant; Hymnology; Hymn singing). Canadian Presbyterians, mostly from Scotland, brought with them to the Maritimes the metrical psalms ca 1750. Congregationalists and Baptists from New England brought the hymns of Isaac Watts.

Methodists reached Newfoundland in 1765 and Nova Scotia in the 1770s, though the greatest number arrived ca 1790 as part of the Loyalist migration to the upper St Lawrence River and the Bay of Quinte. To the Methodists, singing was as important as preaching, and their meeting houses resounded with the hymns of John and Charles Wesley. Their singing was unaccompanied, and leadership rested upon those who remembered a few tunes from former days. What they may have lacked in finesse they made up in verve, vigour, and volume.

The 19th century heralded enormous church expansion. Congregations multiplied until by the 1850s they were to be found as far west as the Pacific coast, and Canadian hymnbooks made their appearance.

Although a few Roman Catholic and Anglican churches had had organs installed during the 17th and 18th centuries (eg, the Jesuit chapel, Quebec City, before 1661 – probably the earliest – and St Paul's Anglican Church, Halifax, in 1756), Protestant congregations did not follow suit until the 19th century.

At the beginning of the century all singing was unaccompanied. In the Presbyterian church neither organs nor hymns were allowed; only metrical psalms were permitted. The psalter came without music and the congregation depended upon a precentor for the lead. How much he knew depended upon his own initiative and ability. Congregations which did not have a copy of the psalter waited upon the precentor to 'line out the stanzas.' Permission was given later for the use of a bass viol ('the Lord's fiddle') or a flute to support the singing. An early-19th-century Presbyterian service in St Catharines, Ont, prompted this remark: 'At the conclusion of the service, the clergyman gave out a hymn, which was sung by a party of young men who sat in the church gallery. The sound of a miserably played flute and a cracked flageolet, united with the harshness of the voices, produced a concert both disagreeable and ludicrous' (John Howison, *Sketches of Upper Canada*, Edinburgh 1821, pp 134–5).

In the 1850s 'a carnal instrument' (ie, an organ) was installed in a Presbyterian church in Brockville, Ont; another was installed in London, Ont, and a third in Toronto. A furor erupted in the courts of the church. John Robertson, a parishioner of St Andrew's Church, Toronto, stated that he felt compelled to leave that congregation as he could not 'conscientiously continue to attend upon the public worship of God in a church where a musical instrument is used in praising God' (appendix, *A Memorial to the Presbytery of Toronto*, Toronto 1859).

Generally speaking, while the Presbyterian clergy remained opposed to the introduction of organs, the laity was sympathetic to such innovations. The issue was not resolved until 1872, when the General Assembly of the Presbyterian church decided not to enforce any uniformity of usage but to extend liberty in the matter to each congregation. Even so, some Presbyterian churches did not secure organs until after 1900.

Baptist, Congregational, and Methodist congregations did not suffer such pains. For them, as for Anglicans and Roman Catholics, the organ was considered an adornment to Christian praise. Organs began to appear early in the 19th century, and by 1850 the rush was on. Every urban church that could afford it wanted a pipe organ; rural churches settled for melodeons.

Psalmody was losing its appeal by the mid-19th century. Precentors, on the whole, were poorly trained; their place was usurped gradually by choirs under the direction of the organists. Soon choirs dominated the singing. Later, finding psalms and hymns too confining, they sought works in which the congregation could not join, and so the demand for anthems grew. Thus the choir, originally created to assist the congregation in its worship, became a performing body. The quality of performance, however, was generally low. Edward Hodges, an outstanding English musician and composer who came to Toronto in 1838, so deplored the music in the church and city that he left almost immediately for another position in New York. The situation was lamented in the *Musical Journal* of 15 Jan 1888: 'We are looking hopefully for the day when we shall have in our midst some reliable institution for the training of choirmasters and organists for the service of the Church ... How lamentably ill-judged are the majority of the "voluntaries" we hear in our churches!'

By the end of the 19th century, however, the situation in music had improved greatly. Internationally known artists performed in Canada with some regularity, and standards of composition and performance were being established at newly founded conservatories. Well-trained church musicians had begun to arrive in some numbers from Great Britain; among them were Vernon *Barford, Edgar *Birch, Edward *Broome, Albert *Ham, Charles A.E. *Harriss, William *Hewlett, Percival *Illsley, Frederic *Lord, Horace *Reyner, and Frederick H. *Torrington. The study and pursuit of church music as a career gained credibility as training at the hands of competent teachers began to make itself felt.

By the 1920s an entire generation of church musicians was being trained in Canada, notably under Hugh *Bancroft in Winnipeg (and later Vancouver), Frederick *Chubb in Vancouver, Healey *Willan and Ernest *MacMillan in Toronto, and Alfred *Whitehead in Montreal. The Canadian College of Organists (*RCCO) instituted examination procedures for its members, leading to associateship and fellowship diplomas.

A revised *Methodist Hymn and Tune Book* was published in 1917 and the *Presbyterian Book of Praise* followed in 1918. In 1925 the United Church of Canada was formed through an amalgamation of Methodists, Presbyterians, and Congregationalists, and in 1930 *The Hymnary* of the United Church of Canada appeared, providing a richer pattern of congregational song than had been found in prior Canadian hymnals. With minor revisions *The Hymnary* was adopted by the Baptists in 1936. *The Hymn Book*, a joint production by the Anglican and United Churches, was published in 1971, followed by the Presbyterian *Book of Praise* in 1972 (a more conservative collection), and the Baptist *Hymnal* (a mixture of light and serious music) in 1973.

The style and practice of music in Canadian protestant churches has varied. At one extreme has been the light music associated with Moody and Sankey before the turn of the century, the pop music of the 1920s, the evangelical songs of the Billy Graham crusades in the 1950s, 1960s and 1970s, and the rock and gospel-singing of the 1960s and 1970s. At the other extreme has been the noblest music of the church in Christendom, extending from the 16th century to the late 20th, and including works by Canadians such as W.H. *Anderson, Violet *Archer, Gerald *Bales, F.R.C. *Clarke, Robert *Fleming, Graham *George, Derek *Holman, Walter *MacNutt, Bernard *Naylor, Arthur *Poynter, Healey Willan, and Alfred Whitehead.

Some congregations have gravitated towards songs such as 'What a wonderful change in my life has been wrought' (music by C.H. Gabriel, words by R.H. McDaniel). Some have desired a liberal supply of the hymns of Isaac Watts and the Wesleys. Others have responded best to contemporary writers such as Walter Farquharson, F. Pratt Green, Fred Kaan, and Brian Wren.

In the 1970s most churches had adult choirs, and some had junior choirs as well. Occasionally a church would support a comprehensive music program with as many as three or four choirs. In the more numerous rural congregations the resources have been fewer. Not infrequently there is neither choir nor organ and the congregation must depend upon a pianist and/or song leader.

After 1940 many churches that had been accustomed to melodeons or pianos installed electronic organs, sometimes to the dismay of tradition-minded organists concerned with the limitations such instruments impose. The electronic gadgetry of rock groups captivated a few congregations. Brass ensembles (once a rarity except in *Salvation Army services) began to be heard more frequently.

Nonconformist churches of the reformed tradition have leaned toward freedom in the order of worship. But with such freedom, certain misunderstandings concerning the nature of Christian worship have been construed as norms, and church music at times has become entertainment rather than worship, especially in those churches where liturgical fitness is secondary to performance.

Two working axioms have emerged for church musicians in the 20th century. Firstly, the noblest church music has arisen out of the matrix of sound liturgical practice; and secondly, the music of any church reflects the capabilities and competence of the organist-choirmaster. Consequently, if one were to hazard a guess about future developments in church music in Canada, one might cite the growth and expansion of training courses for organist-choirmasters. Signs have pointed in that direction: a Summer Institute of Church Music was inaugurated at Whitby in 1970, church music has been added to the courses in the faculty of music at *Wilfrid Laurier U in Waterloo, and similar initiatives have been taken in other parts of Canada.

See also Religions and music for a directory of other *EMC* articles related to protestant church music.

BIBLIOGRAPHY

Christie, Rev George. *The Use of Instrumental Music in the Public Worship of God* (Halifax 1867)

Middleton, J.E. 'Music and the theatre in Canada,' *Canada and Its Provinces*, vol 12 (Toronto 1914)

MacMillan, Rev Alexander. *Hymns of the Church* (Toronto 1935)

Reed, T.A. 'Church music in Canada,' ms, Metropolitan Toronto Library nd

Clark, S.D. *Church and Sect in Canada* (Toronto 1948)

Peaker, Charles. 'Church music II,' *Music in Canada*

'Church music,' *Encyclopedia Canadiana* (Ottawa 1957–)

Osborne, S.L. *The Strain of Praise* (Toronto 1957)

A History of the Christian Church in Canada, 3 vols (Toronto 1966–72)

Rennie, F.H. 'Spiritual worship with a carnal instrument,' unpubl M TH thesis, U of Toronto 1969 (SLO)

Providence Organ Inc / Orgue Providence Inc. Organ manufacturing company founded in 1946 by Maurice Guilbault (1903–69) and named for its location in a suburb of St-Hyacinthe, Que. Guilbault had worked for *Casavant, and initially his instruments had nothing unusual about them. In 1968 he handed over control of the business to his son André (b St-Hyacinthe 28 Nov 1937), who teamed up with a voicer from Casavant, Guy Thérien (b St-Jean-d'Iberville, Que, 29 Nov 1947). The young partners changed the firm's policy and began to manufacture tracker organs. Their instruments – especially those in Ste-Anne-de-la-Pocatière Cathedral (1974), the Cons de Rimouski (1975), the Benedictine retreat in Joliette (1976), and the *U of Western Ontario, London (1977) – testify to the spirit that returned to Canadian organ manufacture after 1960. The company has shown an enlightened interest in historic Canadian organs; its 1972 restoration of the Warren-Casavant organ in St Patrick's Church, Montreal, was particularly successful. In 1979 the firm adopted the name Guilbault-Thérien Inc.

BIBLIOGRAPHY

Bulletin des Amis de l'orgue de Québec, 11, 12, 26, Apr, Nov 1970, Mar 1975 AB

PRYSTAWSKI, Walter. Violinist, teacher, b Toronto 12 Feb 1933; Artist Diploma (Toronto) 1953. After studies 1944–53 with Elie *Spivak at the TCM he was a member 1953–8 of the *TSO and 1956–9 of the *CBC SO. He studied further with Wolfgang Schneiderhan in Switzerland, where Prystawski was concertmaster 1960–9 and soloist with the Lucerne Festival Strings, recording with them (DG 138947) the Vivaldi *Concerto* for 2 violins. He was concertmaster 1967–9 of the Basler Orchestergesellschaft and a member 1966–9 of the Lucerne Trio. He taught at the Lucerne Cons prior to his return to Canada in 1969 to serve as concertmaster of the *NACO, a position he retained in 1980. He has continued to perform as a solo artist, in recital and on radio, and has taught at the *U of Ottawa. (FF)

Psychology of music. The scientific investigation of the relationship of music to the human mind. The first courses in the psychology of music in Canada were set up in 1935 by C.C. (Cyril Cornelius) O'Brien at the Maritime Academy of Music in Halifax. As head of the academy's dept of psychology until 1947, O'Brien – b Halifax 22 Mar 1906; D MUS (Montreal), D PAED (Montreal), PH D psychology (Ottawa) – taught courses in the psychology of music, administered tests of musical talent, and wrote articles on music aptitude tests (1935), tonal memory (1943, 1953, 1958), and tone colour discrimination (1945). (See Bibliography for information on all articles, books and theses cited.) In Montreal Rodolphe *Mathieu had begun music aptitude tests in 1930 at his *Canadian Institute of Music and continued until 1956.

Despite these early beginnings, only a few Canadian universities offered courses specifically in the psychology of music in the late 1970s: the *U of Saskatchewan, the *U of Western Ontario, and *Wilfrid Laurier U.

In the late 1960s and the 1970s, while most Canadian research related to the psychology of music was being done in the psychology departments of universities, there was a modest amount done in the wider field of music education. At the *U of Victoria, research has been carried out on the musical creativity of school children (Vaughan and Myers 1971); and at the U of Western Ontario there have been studies on the judging of instrumental performances of secondary school students (Fiske 1975). In addition, occasional masters' theses in education have dealt with topics related to the psychology of music (eg, Walley 1970, Cooper 1972).

A major part of the research done in Canada in the psychology of music has been in the area of psychophysics. Several studies on right-hemisphere dominance of the brain in the perception of musical stimuli have been carried out at *McGill U (Doehring 1972, Bartholomeus et al 1973 and 1974, Kallman and Corballis 1975). Also at McGill, studies have been done which relate to questions of order perception in music (Bregman and Campbell 1971) as well as on the discrimination or simultaneous and successive musical tones (Doehring 1968, Doehring and Ling 1971). At the *U of Toronto in the laboratory directed by C.D. Creelman, doctoral theses have been produced that deal with the learning of 'absolute pitch' (Cuddy 1965) and the perception of pitch structure in music (Pedersen 1970). L.L. Cuddy has continued her work on 'absolute pitch' and the absolute judgment of pitch (1968, 1970, 1971) at *Queen's U. Theses done under Cuddy's direction include studies in musical interval recognition (Thonigs 1973), tonal memory (Dewar 1974), perception of auditory temporal patterns (Miller 1974), and the perception of tone sequences (Cohen 1975). Work on 'absolute pitch' also has been carried out at the U of Western Ontario (Siegel 1974).

Another major area of Canadian research is the field of experimental aesthetics. Under the direction of D.E. Berlyne of the U of Toronto several studies have been undertaken dealing with arousal theory and information theory as related to the arts. Berlyne in 1960 and 1974 has presented a general exposition of his theories on the psychological function of the 'arousal mechanism' in responses to the arts as well as specific studies on the psychosomatic effects of pitch complexity and duration (Berlyne et al 1966, 1967). His colleagues have investigated multidimensional scaling of responses to music (Hare 1975) and the effects of varying uncertainty level on responses to musical stimuli (Crozier 1974). An experimental study of symbolism in music (Nelson and Herczeg 1972) done at the *U of Alberta also could be included in the broader category of experimental aesthetics.

A related area of experimentation is the application of psychophysical research to music composition. The suggestion of the possible use of the mel scale in composition is one example (Pedersen 1965). Another is the use of biofeedback in electronic music; work has been done in this area by David *Rosenboom (1974). The evolution of *Muzak is yet another.

In summary, during the 1960s and 1970s Canadian work in the psychology of music concentrated largely on psychophysics and experimental aesthetics.

See also Acoustics research in Canada; Music therapy; World Soundscape Project.

BIBLIOGRAPHY

O'Brien, C.C. 'The measurement of music talent,' *NS J of Education*, series 4, vol 6, Mar 1935

– 'Part and whole methods in the memorization of music,' *J of Educational Psychology*, vol 34, Dec 1943

– 'Tone colour discrimination of grade seven boys,' *J of Genetic Psychology*, 67, Sep 1945

– 'Atypical tonal memory,' *J of Psychology*, 35, pp 267–70, 1953

– 'Facets of exploration in tonal memory,' *Acoustical Soc of America J*, 30, Apr 1958

Berlyne, D.E. *Conflict, Arousal and Curiosity* (New York 1960)

Pedersen, P.R. 'The mel scale,' *J of Music Theory*, vol 9, Spring 1965

Berlyne, D.E., and Nicki, R.M. 'Effects of the pitch and duration of tones on EEG desynchronization,' *Psychonomic Science*, vol 4, pp 101–2, 1966

Berlyne, D.E., et al. 'Effects of auditory pitch and complexity on EEG desynchronization and on verbally expressed judgments,' *Canadian J of Psychology*, 21, Aug 1967

Cuddy, L.L. 'Practice effects in the absolute judgment of pitch,' *Acoustical Soc of America J*, 43, May 1968

Doehring, D.G. 'Discrimination of simultaneous and successive tones,' *Perception and Psychophysics*, 3, no. 4B, 1968

Cuddy, L.L. 'Training the absolute identification of pitch,' *Perception and Psychophysics*, 8, no. 5A, 1970

Bregman, A.S., and Campbell, J. 'Primary auditory stream segregation and perception of order in rapid sequences of tones,' *J of Experimental Psychology*, 89, Aug 1971

Cuddy, L.L. 'The absolute judgment of musically-related pure tones,' *Canadian J of Psychology*, 25, Feb 1971

Doehring, D.G. 'Discrimination of simultaneous and successive pure tones by musical and non musical subjects,' *Psychonomic Science*, vol 22, no. 4, 1971

Doehring, D.G., and Ling, D. 'Matching to sample of three-tone simultaneous and successive sounds by musical and nonmusical subjects,' *Psychonomic Science*, vol 25, no. 2, 1971

Vaughan M., and Myers, R.E. 'An examination of musical process as related to creative thinking,' *J of Research in Music Education*, vol 19, Fall 1971

Doehring, D.G. 'Ear asymmetry in the discrimination of monaural tonal sequences,' *Canadian J of Psychology*, vol 26, Mar 1972

Nelson, T.M., and Herczeg, A. 'Symbolic content in Wagner's music,' *J of Symbology*, vol 3, no. 2, 1972

Bartholomeus, B. et al. 'Absence of stimulus effects in dichotic singing,' *Bulletin of the Psychonomic Soc*, vol 1, no. 3, 1973

Bartholomeus, B. 'Dichotic singer and speaker recognition,' *Bulletin of the Psychonomic Soc*, vol 2, no. 4B, 1974

– 'Effects of task requirements on ear superiority for sung speech,' *Cortex*, vol 10, Sep 1974

Berlyne, D.E., ed. *Studies in the New Experimental Aesthetics* (Washington, DC 1974)

Crozier, J.B. 'Verbal and exploratory responses to sound sequences varying in uncertainty level,' *Studies in the New Experimental Aesthetics* (Washington, DC, 1974)

Rosenboom, David. *Biofeedback and the Arts: Results of Early Experiments* (Vancouver 1974)

Siegel, J.A. 'Sensory and verbal coding strategies in subjects with absolute pitch,' *J of Experimental Psychology*, 103, Jul 1974

Fiske, H.E., Jr. 'Judge-group differences in the rating of secondary school trumpet performances,' *J of Research in Music Education*, 23, Fall 1975
Kallman, H.J., and Corballis, M.C. 'Ear asymmetry in reaction to musical sounds,' *Perception and Psychophysics*, 17, Apr 1975
THESES
Buddy, L.L. 'Practice effects in pitch perception,' PH D thesis, U of Toronto 1965
Pedersen, P.R. 'The perception of musical pitch structure,' PH D thesis, U of Toronto 1970
Walley, C.S. 'A study of one aspect of psychophysiological research as it relates to the evaluation of school music programs,' M ED thesis, U of Manitoba 1970
Cooper, G.A. 'Children's perception of musical pitch,' MA thesis, McGill U 1972
Thonigs, A.N.M. 'Musical interval recognition,' MA thesis, Queen's U 1973
Dewar, Kathryn M. 'Context effects in recognition memory for tones,' PH D thesis, Queen's U 1974
Miller, J. 'Perception and mis-perception of brief auditory temporal patterns,' MA thesis, Queen's U 1974
Cohen, A.J. 'Perception of tone sequences from the Western-European chromatic scale: tonality transposition and the pitch set,' PH D thesis, Queen's U 1975
Hare, F.G. 'The identification of dimensions underlying responses to music through multi-dimensional scaling,' PH D thesis, U of Toronto 1975
JOURNALS
Journal of Experimental Aesthetics. Journal of the Aesthetic Research Centre of Canada (Vancouver 1974–)
Scientific Aesthetics – Sciences de l'Art. Quarterly journal (New York 1976–)

PP

Publishing. From 1800, when the first music is known to have been printed in Canada, until the late 20th century music publications have appeared in three distinct formats: in volumes, such as collections of church music, of songs, or of instructive material, often issued by book publishers rather than music publishers; in newspapers and magazines, usually in special supplements (see Periodicals, in which entry such magazines are identified); and as separate pieces of sheet music or albums devoted to single compositions or composers. The earliest known dates in each category are 1800 (see *Le Graduel romain*), 19 Sep 1831 (the song 'La Parisienne' in the Montreal newspaper *La Minerve*), and 1840 ('Le Dépit amoureux' by Napoléon *Aubin and *Deux Valses* by Charles *Sauvageau, lithographed by Aubin of Quebec City, and 'The Merry Bells of England' by J.F. Lehmann, typeset by John *Lovell of Montreal). With respect to sheet music publishing it should be noted, however, that John *Neilson had begun to prepare the vocal score of *Quesnel's *Colas et Colinette* for print in 1809 but abandoned the project after the composer's death. An advertisement in the Quebec *Gazette* in 1818 offers for sale the bandmaster Alexander Kyle's *March* dedicated to the Duke of Richmond, and a year later J.-C. *Brauneis II advertised an overture and a piano piece. No copies of the music have been found and it is possible that these composers sold handwritten copies on demand. In any case, the dependence of Canadian musicians on US publishers, evident from such examples as Alexander Duff's *Montreal Bazaar Waltz* (New York, ca 1830) or 'O for a Thousand Tongues to Sing,' 'as sung by the Indians of the Upper Canada Mission' (Baltimore, ca 1831), demonstrates the lack of local publishing facilities before 1840.

By the 1850s sheet music publishing flourished on a modest scale, and by 1867, the year of Confederation, some 600 works by Canadian and foreign composers had been published. Among the publishers were E.G. Fuller of Halifax, NS, J. & A. McMillan of Saint John, NB, J. & O. *Crémazie (principally booksellers) and Robert *Morgan of Quebec City, Adélard J. *Boucher, J.W. *Herbert, John Lovell (best known as a directory publisher), and Henry *Prince of Montreal, A. & S. *Nordheimer of Toronto, and Peter Grossman of Hamilton, Ont. Only Boucher and Nordheimer were to survive into the 20th century as music publishers. But although the names of publishers have changed, certain aspects of the business have remained remarkably stable. First, the quantity of titles issued annually has remained between 100 and 300, with the largest production in the decades 1890–1920, when *Whaley Royce of Toronto and J.-E. Bélair (*Le *Passe-Temps*) of Montreal boasted the largest catalogues. Secondly, in the majority of cases publishing has been a side activity, economically speaking, to the importing and retailing of foreign music and of instruments. Thirdly, the choice of music for publication always has emphasized local needs, supplementing rather than duplicating the great classics of popular and concert music which form the basis of European and US publishing. (A large proportion of the outputs of most publishers has consisted of Canadian editions of fashionable foreign compositions.) Another aspect which has not changed in more than a hundred years is the primacy of the Toronto region in publishing, established by Nordheimer's early lead in the field.

Within this relatively constant framework, however, there have been profound changes. Thus the 19th-century output of sheet music consisted mostly of songs and salon pieces for use at the parlour piano and for dancing, with smaller amounts destined for performance in churches or by bands. Local colour was supplied by the titles (see Composition, topical), and patriotic songs were in great vogue. While most music was well within the amateur performer's reach, special beginners' 'teaching pieces' rarely were published. On the other hand, 19th-century publishers produced a relatively large number of multi-page volumes of substantial works, eg, *Telgmann's **Leo, the Royal Cadet*, C.A.E. *Harriss' **Torquil*, and the Count of Premio-Real's *Seize Mélodies*, to name but a few.

By contrast, mid-20th-century production was destined primarily for the classroom or the teaching studio, with a small but significant amount for the concert hall.

Competition festivals, conservatory examinations, choirs, and school bands and orchestras provided the bulk of the publisher's market. Folksong anthologies and pop music folios also formed an important part of some publishers' catalogues. Only a small part of the concert music written in Canada was published, however, owing to the discrepancy between high printing costs and the small domestic demand and to the difficulty Canadian firms without foreign connections experienced when they attempted to break into the international market. However, several mid-20th-century music houses did have foreign ties, eg, the Canadian branches or sister companies of *Boosey & Hawkes, *Leeds, *Oxford University Press, and G. *Ricordi. Of the purely Canadian firms, BMI Canada (see PRO Canada) took the lead in publishing Canadian concert music from 1947 to 1969.

Two developments, in concert and popular music respectively, marked music publishing after 1960.

The realization that the publishing of extended concert works, in particular those for orchestra, chamber ensemble, and the operatic stage, was beyond the possibilities of commercial firms, led to the establishment of the *CMCentre for the free circulation of scores and the rental of performance parts, reproduced from clear manuscript through photocopying. Commercial publishers continued nevertheless to produce the full scores and instrumental parts of concert works, sometimes with *Canada Council financial support, but in view of the great amount of music turned out after 1940, only an operation like that of the CMCentre has been able to provide access to the full range of the literature. Some composers have experimented with self-publishing, but the disadvantages of this are obvious.

The change in the field of popular music was on an international scale. It was brought about by the ascendancy of the sound recording as the prime means of disseminating such music. Whereas until the 1950s many popular songs were recorded only after the 'song plugger' had stimulated the sale of sheet music and distributed free copies to radio stations, now the reverse became true, and songs were printed only if and when the sale of recordings had established them as hits. Accordingly the very definition of the term 'music publisher' has changed. In addition to the conventional music firm that produces printed sheet music and albums for sale, there is now a music publisher who does little or nothing of this sort, but derives income from the legal control of the copyrights.

EMC provides individual entries for the publishing firms listed below. In many of the entries reference will be found to the use or non-use of plate numbers, the numbers (often preceded by initials) found at the bottom of each page of music. While serving the publisher as a purely internal housekeeping device, these numbers are invaluable to the researcher and collector in establishing the volume and chronology of a company's production and in identifying relationships to foreign publishers.

Alliance chorale canadienne
Anglo-Canadian Music Company
Ed Archambault Inc
Edwin Ashdown Ltd
Berandol Music Ltd
W.H. Billing
La Bonne Chanson
Boosey & Hawkes (Canada) Ltd
A.J. Boucher
William Briggs
Canadian Music Sales Corporation
Chappell & Co Ltd
Chatillon, Jean
Conservatoire national de musique
A. Cox & Co
J. & O. Crémazie
C.C. De Zouche
W.R. Draper Co Ltd
École Vincent-d'Indy
Édition Belgo-Canadienne
Empire Music Publishers Ltd
Fassio, Angelo
Galipeau Musique Inc
Hardy, Edmond
Frederick Harris Music Co Ltd
Heintzman & Co Ltd
J.W. Herbert & Co.
Imrie & Graham
Irving's Series of Five Cent Music
Jarman Publications Ltd
Jaymar Music Ltd
E.C. Kerby Ltd
Laurent, Laforce & Boudreau
Lavigne, Arthur
Leeds Music (Canada)
Leslie Music Supply
L'Herbier, Robert
Robert Morgan
Musgrave
Neilson, John
Neufeld, Kornelius
A. & S. Nordheimer
Oxford University Press

Le Passe-Temps
Peer-Southern Organization (Canada) Ltd
Henry Prince
Procure générale de musique Ltée
G. Ricordi & Co (Canada) Ltd
H.H. Sparks Music Co
Strange & Co
I. Suckling & Sons
Gordon V. Thompson Ltd
Waterloo Music Co Ltd
Western Music Co Ltd
Whaley, Royce & Co Ltd

See also Canadian Music Publishers Association; CAPAC; Copyright; Hymnbooks; Manuscript books; PRO Canada; School songbooks; Theory textbooks.

BIBLIOGRAPHY

LISTS OF PUBLICATIONS

Complete List of Canadian Copyright Musical Compositions (entered from 1868 to January 19th, 1889), compiled from the Official Register at Ottawa (np 1889)

NL of C. *Canadiana* (Ottawa 1950– ; monthly national bibliography; scores listed 1953–)

CMLA. *Musical Canadiana: A Subject Index* (Ottawa 1967)

BN du Q. *Bibliographie du Québec* (Quebec 1968– ; monthly bibliography)

Jarman, Lynne, ed. *Canadian Music: A Selected Checklist 1950–73* (Toronto and Buffalo 1976)

Creelman, Gwendolyn et al. *Canadian Music Scores and Recordings: A Classified Catalogue of the Holdings of Mount Allison University Libraries* (Sackville, NB, 1976)

Arcand, François. *L'Industrie de la musique*, 3 vols (Quebec 1980)

The most comprehensive record of Canadian music publications is the *NL of C's unpublished Union List of Canadian Music Publications, pre-1951. Each of some 10,000 publications is entered by composer, title, date of publication, and name of publisher. The list also includes music by Canadian composers published in other countries; a glance at *EMC*'s list of compositions for *Lavallée, *Whitehead, *Willan, and others will explain the importance of this procedure. It may be of interest also to note that the first orchestral scores of Canadian music known to have been published were those of *Couture's *Rêverie* (1875 by Girod in Paris), and of *Lucas' *As You Like It Overture* (1899 by Chappell in London). The first full score published in Canada probably was that of Willan's orchestral accompaniment to *'O Canada' (B54), issued by F. *Harris in 1941. The first miniature score was that of Murray *Adaskin's *Serenade Concertante*, published by G. Ricordi (Canada) in 1956. The first vocal score of a stage work to be published in Canada must have been Jean-Baptiste *Labelle's *La Conversion d'un pêcheur de la Nouvelle-Écosse* (A.J. Boucher, ca 1869).

STUDIES AND ARTICLES

'Music publishing in Canada: a discussion,' *ConsB* (Nov 1948). Features comments by Sir Ernest MacMillan, G. Ridout, B. Pentland.

[Darch, Robert]. *Music and Paper* (Toronto 1962)

Series of articles on individual publishers, issued intermittently, *CanComp*, 1–18, May 1965–May 1967

Kallmann, Helmut. 'Music Library Association digs up our musical past,' ibid, 11, Oct 1966

Chatillon, Jean. 'À la recherche de l'ancienne musique Québécoise,' *VM*, 9, Oct 1968

Hare, John. 'The beginnings of music printing in Lower Canada,' *Canadian Notes and Queries*, 5, May 1970

Kallmann, Helmut. 'Canadian music publishing,' *Papers of the Bibliographical Society of Canada / Cahiers de la Société bibliographique du Canada*, vol 13, 1974

Potvin, Gilles. 'L'édition musicale est morte,' Montreal *Le Devoir*, 29 Mar 1975

Dostie, Bruno. 'The changing scene: sheet music publishing in Quebec,' *CanComp*, 127, Jan 1978

Farrell, David. 'Industry lacking aggressive publishers,' *MSc*, 308, Jul–Aug 1979

Calderisi, Maria. 'Sheet music publishing in the Canadas,' *The Bibliographical Society of Canada, Colloquium III 1978 / La Société bibliographique du Canada, IIIe Colloque, 1978* (Toronto 1979)

Frank, Alan, and Oliver, Michael. 'The publisher's role,' *MSc*, 312, Mar–Apr 1980

Thériault, Yves. 'Quebec music publishers view future with optimism,' *MSc*, 314, Jul–Aug 1980

Calderisi, Maria. *Music Publishing in the Canadas, 1800–1867 / L'Édition musicale au Canada 1800–1867* (Ottawa 1981)

PERIODICALS AND DIRECTORIES

Canadian Music Trades Journal (Toronto 1900–33)

Music Market Canada (Toronto 1977–)

CMPA. *Directory*, various editions (Toronto)

Guide du spectacle et du disque (Quebec 1978)

RPM. *Canadian Music Industry Directory*, annual (1965–80)

– *Canadian Music Industry Who's Who* (Toronto 1976, 1977)

HK

PUDDICOMBE, Harry (b Henry). Teacher, b London, Ont, 14 Jun 1870?, d Ottawa 7 Jun 1953. Son of a cabinet maker, he sought a career in music instead of learning his father's trade. At 21 he went to Leipzig to study with Martin Krause in the hope of becoming a concert pianist. Nervousness in performance prevented him from fulfilling that ambition, but after five years in Leipzig he began his long career as a piano teacher in Ottawa. In 1902 he established the Canadian Cons of Music on Bay Street, Ottawa. Teachers at the conservatory included his brother-in-law Donald *Heins and Herbert *Sanders. Puddicombe was director until 1937, when the building was acquired by the municipality for school purposes. He continued to teach until shortly before his death. Able and dedicated, he is remembered not only for his high standards but for the warmth and humour with which he pursued his profession. Among his pupils were Yvon *Barette, Gladys Ewart, Hélène *Landry, Olive Munro, Ethel Thompson, and Elise Tye. JSw

PUKARA, Karl. Accordionist, arranger, teacher, b Sudbury, Ont, 31 May 1931. A largely self-taught accordionist who plays both stradella and free-bass instruments, he has performed on Toronto radio stations and in 1960 on CBC TV's 'Talent Caravan.' With his former pupil Iona Reed (winner of the 1962 Prague World Accordion Championship), he has performed in many Canadian and US cities.

Pukara began teaching privately in Sudbury in 1957 and founded the Karl Pukara Music Studio there in 1964. The studio was incorporated in 1969 as Karaccordion Ltd. The name Regional Cons of Music (by which it is known unofficially) came into use in the early years of Pukara's activity, but the studio did not prepare students for university entrance until 1964. Pukara is also a festival adjudicator and examiner.

The Karl Pukara Accordion Orchestra, formed in 1957, has won many competitions including the Canadian Open Band Accordion Competition (six times to 1978) and many in the USA. For the orchestra, and for soloists and duos, Pukara has transcribed works by Bach, Beethoven, Chopin, Dvořák, Gershwin, Grieg, Haydn, Mahler, Mancini, Tchaikovsky, and others. (DBr)

Purcell String Quartet. Founded in 1968 by four principals of the *Vancouver SO: Norman Nelson and Raymond Ovens, violins; Simon Streatfeild, viola; and Ian Hampton, cello. Of the original membership only Hampton remained by the end of 1979.

Nelson had been succeeded in the summer of 1979 by Sydney Humphreys, and by that time the second violin chair had had five occupants. Ovens was succeeded in 1970 by Frederick Nelson, Nelson in 1976 by Robert Growcott, Growcott in 1977 by Joseph Peleg, and Peleg in 1979 by Bryan King.

The viola chair had had two incumbents. Streatfeild was succeeded in 1969 by Philippe Etter.

Norman Nelson, Streatfeild, and Humphreys have entries in *EMC*. Brief biographies of the other Purcell personnel follow here.

Ovens (b Bristol 14 Oct 1932) had been a member of the London SO, the Boyd Neel Orchestra, the BBC SO, and the Royal Philharmonic Orchestra, and served 1968–70 as assistant concertmaster of the Vancouver SO. Frederick Nelson (b Beloit, Kan, 3 Oct 1946) had joined the *Quebec SO in the spring of 1968, the *MSO in the fall of 1968, and the Vancouver SO in 1970. After leaving the Purcell Quartet he was concertmaster 1976–8 of the *Regina SO and the *Saskatoon SO. Growcott (b Shropshire, England) had been a member of the Royal Liverpool Philharmonic, the London Philharmonic, and the Bournemouth SO. Peleg (b Debrecen, Hungary, 22 Sep 1946) had played 1966–9 in the Royal Philharmonic Orchestra. Bryan King (b Norwich, England, 17 Mar 1948) was a pupil of Margaret Major and Gwen *Thompson, a member 1973–5 of the *Victoria SO, and assistant concertmaster of the *Vancouver Opera Assn orchestra. Etter (b London 12 Sep 1935) had been principal viola 1962–5 at Sadler's Wells and 1966–9 of the Royal Philharmonic Orchestra, and was principal viola 1969–73 of the Vancouver SO. Hampton (b London 13 Mar 1935) had been a member of the Academy of St Martin-in-the-Fields, the London SO, and the Edinburgh String Quartet, and was principal cello 1966–73 of the Vancouver SO. He joined the *CBC Vancouver Chamber Orchestra in 1967 and was a founder-member of the *Baroque Strings of Vancouver.

The Purcell Quartet gave its first public concert in 1969 for the CBC. Subsequently it has broadcast extensively in Canada and England. It has presented several series at the Vancouver Art Gallery, has toured Vancouver Island for the CBC, and has performed throughout British Columbia, in eastern Canada, and in San Francisco, New York, and London. In 1972 it became the quartet-in-residence at *Simon Fraser U.

The Purcell String Quartet has premiered numerous works by Canadians including, in 1970, *Schafer's *Quartet No. 1*; in 1972, *Freedman's *Graphic II*; in 1973, Bruce *Davis' *Quartet No. 1* and *Quartet No. 2*, Anton *Kuerti's *Quartet No. 2* and *Prévost's *Quartet No. 2*; in 1974, *Coulthard's *Octet* and *Pentland's *Quartet No. 3* and *Interplay*; in 1976, John *Fodi's *Concerto a quattro*, Schafer's *Quartet No. 2*, *Turner's *Quartet No. 3*, and Eugene Wilson's *Five Pieces*; and in 1977, Elliot *Weisgarber's *Quartet*. Of those, the Coulthard, Freedman, Prévost, Schafer, Turner, and Weisgarber were written for the quartet. The group also gave the North American premiere of Mamangakis' *Tetzaktys* in 1977, the Canadian premieres of Lavista's *Diacronia* in 1973 and Britten's *Quartet No. 1* in 1977, and the US premiere of Exton's *Quartet No. 6* in 1976. Besides the Canadian works mentioned above, pieces by *Beckwith, *Eckhardt-Gramatté, *Pépin, and *Somers are included in its repertoire.

DISCOGRAPHY

Brahms *String Quintets, Op 88; Op 111*. Streatfeild va. 1976. CBC SM-318

Freedman *Graphic II* – Prévost *Quartet No. 2*. (1975). RCI 394

Haydn *Quartets, Op 70, no. 4; Op 71, no. 2*. 1970. CBC SM-138

Mendelssohn *Octet, Op 20* – Shostakovich *Octet, Op 11*. Brunswick Str Quar. 1976. CBC SM-304

Mozart *Clarinet Quintet* K581; *Quintet* K407. de Kant cl, Creech hn. 1971. CBC SM-152

– *String Quintets*. Streatfeild va. 1971–2. CBC SM-175-8

Pentland *String Quartet No. 3* – Schafer *String Quartet No. 1*. RCI 353/Mel SMLP 4026 (Schafer only)

Ravel – Chausson – Hindemith. Mailing mezzo. 1973. CBC SM-228

Turner *String Quartet No. 3* – Schafer *String Quartet No. 2.* 1978. RCI 476

BIBLIOGRAPHY

Quigley, Michael. 'Hinterland and metropolis are arenas for Purcell String Quartet,' *MSc*, 278, Jul–Aug 1974
Gothe, Jurgen. 'Presenting the Purcell String Quartet in the hallway, in the library, in the logging camp …' *PfAC*, Winter 1979 (NM, MW)

PUTLAND, Arthur (Kingsley). Organist-choirmaster, teacher, b Hawkhurst, Kent, England, 1898, d Lethbridge, Alta, 6 Apr 1975; LTCL 1913, B MUS (Toronto) 1918, BA (Alberta) 1924, FCCO 1926, MA (Alberta) 1927, FTCL 1927, B PAED (Toronto) 1944. He began organ study at nine with Fraled Hallett and gave his first recital at 13. He moved to Canada in 1915 and, after study at the *U of Toronto, settled in Edmonton in 1918. He attended the *U of Alberta, taught at *Alberta College, and was organist-choirmaster 1918–24 at McDougall Methodist Church. Moving to Fort William (Thunder Bay) he established the first school music program there and was organist-choirmaster 1924–43 at Wesley United Church. In 1934 his choir represented Canada at the Century of Progress Exposition in Chicago. He was organist-choirmaster 1943–64 at Southminster United Church, Lethbridge, and lectured 1957–64 at the Lethbridge Junior College and 1967–73 at the *U of Lethbridge. Besides introits and anthems for church use he wrote *Ode to Canadian Federation* (1937) and organized a musical pageant for the 25th anniversary of the Rotary International in Chicago (1938).

BIBLIOGRAPHY

Stewath, Chris. 'Southern Alberta's "Mr. Music"!' Lethbridge *Herald*, 30 Nov 1974 (CF)

Q

Quality Records Ltd. Independent Canadian-owned record and tape manufacturing company established in 1950 in Toronto, with George Keane as vice-president and general manager. It pressed and distributed various US lines in Canada, entering into a partnership (terminated in 1973) with the US company MGM and handling Buddah, Groove Merchant, Kama Sutra, and Mercury, among other labels. The company was the first in Canada to manufacture cassette and eight-track tapes. It also has distributed such Canadian labels as its own Quality, Birchmount, and Celebration and the independent Broadland, Kanata, and MWC (Music World Creations), and it controls the publishing rights firms Quality Music (a *PRO Canada affiliate and a major song promoter) and Shediac Music (*CAPAC). George Struth became president in 1975. Struth had joined the company in 1959 and was responsible for the promotion of such international hits as The Beaumarks' 'Clap Your Hands' (1960), Ronn Metcalfe's 'Twisting at the Woodchopper's Ball' (1961), and The *Guess Who's 'Shakin' All Over' (1965). In 1975 Quality Records Ltd opened a New York office and introduced the Quality label to the USA. Other Canadian artists to record for Quality include the Young Canada Singers (who made the hit version of *'CA-NA-DA'), *Harmonium, the Haunted, the King Beezz, Jury, Skip Prokop, and Sweet Blindness, all in the pop field. EBM, MM

'Quand les hommes vivront d'amour.' A classic of 1950s chanson québécoise (see Chanson in Quebec). Its simple melody and its humane and generous lyrics (both by Raymond *Lévesque, 1956) made it a great success and ensured its survival despite changing pop styles. A testament to the unending quest for justice and brotherhood, it nevertheless faces the realities of life in which, if there are winners, inevitably there must be losers. The song has been performed or recorded in France by such stars as Bourvil, Eddie Constantine, Jean Sablon, and Cora Vaucaire and recorded in Quebec by its composer (on *Raymond Lévesque*, on *Chansons et monologues de Raymond Lévesque*, on *Raymond Lévesque chante les travailleurs*, and on *5 Chansonniers: le disque d'or*) and by Raymond Berthiaume, the *Disciples de Massenet, the Famille Brassard, the Jérolas, Pauline *Julien, Michel *Louvain, and Simone *Quesnel. Félix *Leclerc, Gilles *Vigneault, and Robert *Charlebois revived the song at the Superfrancofête in Quebec City in 1974, and their performance was recorded (Productions du 13 août, VLC 13). The song was published by Éditions Eddie Barclay (Neuilly-sur-Seine, France, 1956) and later by the Société d'éditions musicales internationales. The song's title is shared by a collection of Lévesque's songs, poems, and monologues (Quebec City, 1968) although the text of the song itself is not included there in its entirety. (BR)

Quartet Canada. Piano quartet formed in 1975 by Steven *Staryk (violin), Gerald *Stanick (viola), Tsuyoshi *Tsutsumi (cello), and Ronald *Turini (piano). It made its debut on CBC TV's 'Music to See' in May 1976 and gave its first public recital that summer at the Courtenay Youth Music Camp. During the 1976–7 season it toured Canada, performing in Vancouver, Victoria, Winnipeg, and several Ontario cities. After its Toronto debut, 31 Mar 1977, John *Kraglund (describing the performance of the Fauré *Piano Quartet, Op 15*) wrote 'there was the nearly flawless give and take that is an essential characteristic of chamber music ensembles' (*Globe and Mail*, 1 Apr 1977). It made its Montreal debut 2 Oct 1977. The group was appointed quartet-in-residence at the *U of Western Ontario in 1977, toured Canada again 1977–8, and visited the Far East in May and June of 1978, performing in Japan, Korea, and Hawaii. In 1980 Yuri Mazurkevich replaced Staryk.

DISCOGRAPHY

Beethoven *Piano Quartet, Op 16* – Kenins *Piano Quartet.* 1977. RCI 471
Brahms *Piano Quartet, Op 25.* 1976. CBC SM-341 PW

Quatuor de jazz libre du Québec (familiarly, Jazz libre). Montreal-based ensemble active ca 1963–74 in the avant-garde style of jazz known as 'free music' and also, in the late 1960s, in pop music situations. It numbered among its original members Jean Préfontaine (tenor saxophone), Yves Charbonneau (trumpet), Maurice C. Richard (bass), and Guy Thouin (percussion). Richard was replaced briefly (ca 1973) by Yves Bouliane. Thouin was replaced by Jean-Guy Poirier, and Poirier by Mathieu Léger. The pianist Pierre Nadeau joined the quartet for an LP made in 1965 for RCI (271) and issued commercially later by *London (NAS 13515). Jazz libre worked in Montreal with Robert *Charlebois, Yvon Deschamps, and Mouffe in the revues *Peuple à genoux* (1968), *L'Osstidcho* (1968), and *L'Osstidchomeurt* (1969) and toured with Charlebois and Louise *Forestier in 1969 in France. Though part of the first *Infonie (1969), Jazz libre maintained its own identity as a performing ensemble. In 1973 the quartet moved into Amorce, a nightclub in Old Montreal, and continued to perform there until the club's destruction by fire in June 1974. It also performed in 1973 at the Autunno musicale di Como, a music festival in Italy. The quartet was not active after 1974, but the tradition of free improvisation it established in Montreal was sustained in turn by the Atelier de musique expérimentale and the Ensemble de musique improvisée de Montréal.
DM, MM

Quartet Canada

Quatuor de saxophones Pierre-Bourque. See Pierre Bourque Saxophone Quartet.

Quebec City. Capital of the province of Quebec. It was founded 3 Jul 1608 by the French navigator Samuel de Champlain on the site of the Indian village of Stadaconé at the mouth of the St Charles River. Situated on a cliff surmounting the St Lawrence River, Quebec City (Kébec: an Algonquin word meaning 'narrows') remained a fur-trading post until the arrival in 1615 of the first missionaries, the Recollets, followed in 1617 by the farmer Louis Hébert, in 1625 by the Jesuits, and in 1639 by the Ursulines and Hospitalières. Quebec City became the seat of the government of New France in 1663, achieved village status in 1792, and became a city in 1833.

Compared with the English colonies in North America, Quebec's progress was slow. However, it remained for a long time the most populous of New France's settlements, with 1600 inhabitants in 1663, when Montreal had 500 and Trois-Rivières 400. By 1980 the city's population had reached 200,000. In the early 1970s Quebec City and 22 surrounding municipalities were reconstituted as the Quebec City Urban Community, with a total population of close to 500,000. As the capital of its province, Quebec City is the seat of the *MACQ and thereby has a marked influence on music throughout the province.

Early Quebec society consisted of the missionary and teaching clergy, the ruling class composed of the governor and intendant surrounded by their 'little Versailles,' seignorial landowners, merchants, and settlers. Religious musical activity was of the most general sort; social entertainments, theatrical performances, and full-dress social dancing were reserved for the well-to-do. Coming from France, the early settlers transmitted their old-country life-styles to their offspring, along with the crafts and the oral and sung folk traditions they had brought with them.

Instruction in music probably was given as early as 1620 at the 'seminary' built that year by the Recollets, but there is no information about its nature. Later on, music became a relatively thriving activity at the *Seminaire de Québec. In 1632 Father Paul Le Jeune, the Jesuit superior, began a school at which, in 1635, Indian and European children learned to read and to sing Gregorian chant. He originated the custom of translating the liturgy into the native language. Numerous hymns were translated by the priests posted in

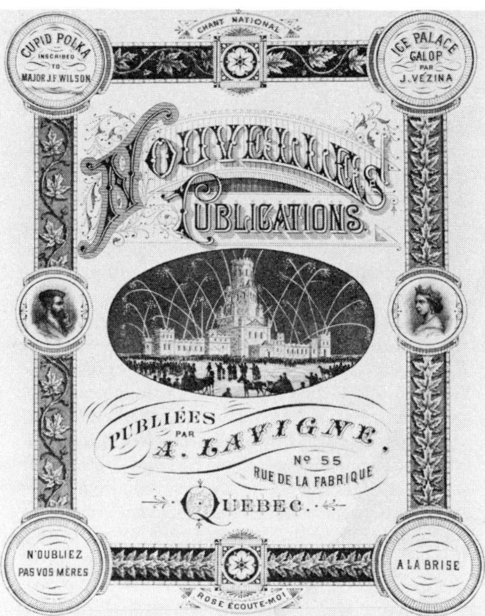

An advertisement for new publications by Arthur Lavigne, Quebec 1884

Quebec City and by the missionaries and Ursulines.

Instruments were played. In 1636 Father Le Jeune noted that the Indians requested that 'some of our young people dance to the sound of a hurdy-gurdy' played by a young Frenchman (*Jesuit Relations*, vol 9, p 269). In a letter dated 3 Sep 1640 Marie de l'Incarnation reported that 'Agnès Chablikuchich was given to us ... She has made great progress while with us, both in the knowledge of the mysteries of the faith and in propriety ... in reading and playing the viol' (*Correspondance*, published by Dom Guy Oury, Solesmes 1971). The presence of violins and flutes at marriages and midnight masses was recorded first in 1645.

In the church, the organ was the instrument most in use, and its presence was reported as early as 1644 on the occasion of the building of the first rectory, although this date, advanced by *LeVasseur, remains doubtful (see Organ building). There is no doubt that the organs in Quebec were the first in North America. The manufacture of organs began very early, according to information in the *Bulletin des recherches historiques* (Feb 1897). Some time after 1664 an ecclesiastic is believed to have copied 'the French model,' an organ that Mgr de Laval, first bishop of Quebec, is said to have had sent from France in 1663. Military music, the sole preserve of the bands of the Carignan-Salières Regiment, which had arrived in 1665 to subdue the Iroquois, was played for the most part by fifes and drums (see Bands 1 / Exordium).

Singing, the principal medium for the communication of the liturgy, remained also the most common form of musical expression on ceremonial occasions; anniversaries, commemorative services, and distinguished visits doubtless were enhanced by the performance of motets and cantatas by Henry Du Mont, Jean-Baptiste Morin, André Campra, Élisabeth Jacquet de la Guerre, Nicolas Bernier, and Louis Marchand, which were in vogue at the time in Paris. Certainly various editions of these works, dating from 1703 to 1750, were in existence in Quebec City at the time, though their mere presence cannot be taken to signify, particularly in the absence of substantiating evidence, that the works were performed. Historians and musicologists, eg, Andrée *Desautels and Willy *Amtmann, hold different opinions on this matter.

The serpent, a bass bugle in vogue in France at the time, probably was used in Quebec City to accompany church singing; a copy has been discovered of Campra's *1er Livre de motets à 1, 2 ou 3 voix avec basse continue* (1710) signed 'Jean-Baptiste Savard, serpent player of the cathedral in Quebec.' As late as 1836 another serpent player, Étienne Montminy, was a member of the militia band the *Musique canadienne, whose conductor was Charles *Sauvageau.

Louis *Jolliet and Charles-Amador *Martin are among the few known musicians active in Quebec City during the 17th century. The clergy, led by the Jesuits, constantly warned the population against the dangers of gatherings at which there was dancing until the late hours. Despite this, social events such as the Mardi Gras ceremonial ball were held. According to documents found, printed, or recopied, the minuet, gavotte, and tambourin, probably played on court instruments, were the most popular dances (see Dancing, pre-Confederation).

Several treatises have been discovered, including *Principes de la flûte traversière ou flûte d'Allemagne, de la à bec ou flûte douce* (Paris 1741), suggesting that these instruments were taught. The Ursulines taught viol, guitar, and harp, as well as dancing. The Augustines of the Hôpital général taught viol, guitar, and subsequently accordion at the boarding school they ran from 1725 until 1868. Later on, the two orders taught violin, piano, and harmonium.

In the 19th century, in the vaults of the Hôpital général, some dozen viols and bass viols made in Paris by the firm of Nicolas Bertrand were discovered. It is possible that these instruments were concealed during the siege of Quebec City in the mid-18th century and then forgotten. Colonists, soldiers, and missionaries had brought their songs from France; the tunes have survived in many musical variants, whereas the words have been transmitted more faithfully. Locally composed songs were few in number. According to the ethnomusicologist Marius *Barbeau, '19 out of 20 of our songs are of European descent' (*Chansons populaires de vieux Québec*, Ottawa 1935). Few instruments were used in the performance of folk music. The violin, which was easy to carry, played reels that may have been Scottish or French in origin. Native music left no mark on the folk music of the colonists, though some Christian hymns appear to have influenced native songs, particularly those of the Hurons of Lorette, near Quebec City.

The conquest of New France by England in 1760 left the population economically drained and ill-equipped to develop cultural pursuits. It relied on the clergy, who, however, were not always appreciative of the importance of secular culture. Until the Act of Union of 1841, which favoured the development of Montreal, the musical life of Quebec City, while depending largely on newcomers, was more active than it had ever been before. In February 1770 *La Gazette de Québec* advertised subscription concerts 'for gentlemen,' and in 1789 the Quebec Assembly began to present winter-season concerts. Musical activity was initiated mainly by musicians of German origin who had arrived in 1776 with the corps of mercenaries to bolster the British positions. Former soldiers settled in Quebec City, where they taught, imported music and instruments, and arranged concerts. They were joined later by other immigrants. Among the names that stand out are F.-H. *Glackemeyer, T.F. *Molt, Francis *Vogeler, and J.-C. *Brauneis.

After the conquest and during most of the 19th century the military band, usually British, stood at the centre of musical activity; it played transcriptions of the classical repertoire, adding strings, church choirs, and solo voices for concerts. On occasion comic operas in English were presented by itinerant theatre companies from the USA (see Opera performance).

Open-air concerts were given on the Esplanade early in the 19th century and at the Terrasse later. Others took place in the halls of Le Manège, the Sewell Theatre, and the Union Hotel, and at the Salle des Glacis. The programs were extremely varied, alternating orchestral selections with songs and chamber pieces. The *Quebec Harmonic Society and the *Société musicale Saint-Cécile performed excerpts from the standard works of the day, as was the custom in Europe. Quartered in the citadel, the regimental band paraded every Sunday on its way to services at the Cathedral of the Holy Trinity, built in 1804. John *Bentley and Stephen *Codman were organists there, as was Edward Arthur Bishop from 1874 to 1924.

Chamber music also held a place of honour at the close of the 18th century and throughout the 19th. Numerous amateur ensembles were active, the main ones being the Sewell Quartet and, 50 years later, the *Septuor Haydn. Jonathan *Sewell, chief justice of Lower Canada, provided his ensemble with recently written works; scores of the last three Mozart quartets bearing the inscription 'Sewell 1793' have survived. The Septuor Haydn continued the Sewell tradition but adopted a repertoire of a more symphonic nature. Formed as the result of a conflict within Antoine *Dessane's Septett Club, the Septuor may be considered the forerunner of the *Quebec SO.

Several instrument makers, among them the *Lyonnais family, who began making string instruments ca 1825, attained prominence. Advertisements of the period promoted the wares of three piano manufacturers, Owen, Milligan, and Pfeiffer.

The first volumes of music printed in Canada were the **Graduel romain* (1800), the *Processional* [sic] *romain* (1801), and the *Vespéral romain* (1802), published by John *Neilson in Quebec City. Neilson also published the libretto of **Colas et Colinette* (1808) and intended to print the music; however, the death of Joseph *Quesnel appears to have halted the project. In 1819 Jean-Denis *Daulé, a priest who had fled the French Revolution, published the *Nouveau Recueil de cantiques à l'usage du diocèse de Québec* in two parts, one containing the text and the other the music.

During the second half of the 19th century, musical life was stimulated by musicians of professional calibre, eg, the organist-composer Antoine Dessane, the pianist-composer Charles W. *Sabatier, the violinist, publisher, and impresario Arthur *Lavigne, the pianist-composer Calixa *Lavallée, and the conductor Joseph *Vézina. To these may be added the names of such distinguished musical families as *Gagnon, *Roy, *Bernier, Vézina, and, later, *Létourneau. A position as church organist was poorly paid but secure, and such a position in a leading church often was handed down from father to son.

After taking place for a long time in the halls of hotels, most concerts came to be given at the *Academy of Music, a magnificent hall inaugurated in 1853, at *Tara Hall, and, later, at the *Auditorium, which opened in 1903.

In 1868 a group of musicians and teachers founded the *AMQ in a first attempt to regulate the teaching of music. The creation of the Société symphonique de Québec (1902), which in 1942 became the Quebec SO, and of the École de musique at *Laval U (1922) were decisive advances. After a somewhat sluggish start the two institutions, both initiated by Quebec City musicians, began to prosper. The foundation of the Société symphonique, one of the first orchestras in the country and the oldest still active in 1980, was prompted less by popular demand than by the desire of musicians to perform serious music. Playing without remuneration, they in fact contributed to the operating costs from their own pockets. Such enthusiasm eventually aroused the interest of the general public. After playing in the Auditorium and later at the *Palais Montcalm, the Quebec SO presented its concerts at the *Grand Théâtre. Several small ensembles have been drawn from orchestra personnel over the years, eg, the Ensemble Gilbert-Darisse during the 1930s, that of Sylvio *Lacharité at the *Concerts Couperin, the *Orchestre de chambre Pierre-Morin, and the *Ensemble instrumental de Québec.

In 1921, following the US pattern, Laval U created its École de musique, the first music school at a French-Canadian university. Dedicated at first to liturgical music, it nonetheless produced from the outset young musicians destined for international careers, among them the violinist Arthur *LeBlanc, the pianist and conductor Jean-Marie *Beaudet, and the tenors Raoul *Jobin and Léopold *Simoneau. With the *CMQ, founded in 1944, the school has shared responsibilities for general, vocal, and instrumental teaching in the Quebec City area. The *Institut canadien has staged several musical events for its subscribers while the CMQ became noted for its Lundis du conservatoire. The *Club musical de Québec, founded in 1891, continued in 1980 to arrange for appearances by internationally known performers. In the field of opera, one of the first companies to achieve a certain stability was the *Théâtre lyrique de Nouvelle-France (Théâtre lyrique du Québec). The *Société lyrique d'Aubigny, begun in 1968, also has staged some operas and operettas.

In the realm of military music the *Royal 22nd Regiment Band has continued to make its mark and has performed both in Canada and abroad, particularly under the direction of Charles *O'Neill and Edwin *Bélanger. Ernest *MacMillan conducted an ensemble drawn from the band in performances at the second of the three *CPR Festivals held 1927, 1928, and 1930 in Quebec City.

It was only in the mid-20th century that composition became a regular activity. Prior to 1950 pioneers such as Joseph Vézina, Robert *Talbot, Léo *Roy, and Omer *Létourneau composed discreetly, almost timidly, with little hope of having their works performed in the near future. More numerous and confident after 1950, the city's composers have not adhered to any particular school; their personalities have developed along individual lines, though without any radical break with the past. In 1980 the most active were Marcelle *Deschênes-Harvey, whose work lies in the field of electro-acoustic music, Alain *Gagnon, Jacques *Hétu, Roger *Matton, and Nil *Parent, founder of the group *GIMEL. Long neglected, contemporary music has been taken up in the city by the Assn de musique actuelle de Québec (AMAQ), founded in 1978 and counting the composers Bernard Bonnier, Pierre Genest, and Gisèle Ricard among its members.

The *Archives de folklore at Laval U have been regarded as among the most important in this field on the North American continent. Luc *Lacourcière, Conrad *Laforte, and Roger Matton were closely associated with their development.

Throughout the 20th century in Quebec City a choral tradition has been maintained by such ensembles as the *Maîtrise du Chapitre, the Choeur symphonique de Québec, the *Choeur V'la l'bon vent, les *Rhapsodes, the *Ensemble vocal Chantal-Masson, and the *Chanteurs Saint-Coeur-de-Marie.

Among the musicians born in Quebec City or environs, and who either have individual entries in *EMC* or are listed in the index, are Denyse Angé; Denis Bédard; Joseph-Arthur, Maurice, Conrad, Gabrielle, Françoys, Madeleine, and Pierre Bernier; Edwin, Marc, and Guy Bélanger; Édouard Biron; Maurice Blackburn; Antoine Bouchard; Victor Bouchard; Guy Bourassa; Pierre Boutet; Henri Brassard; Jean-Chrysostome Brauneis II; Jules Bruyère; Jean-Marie Bussières; Jean Carignan; Octave Hardy dit Chatillon; Jean-Marie Cloutier; Camille Couture; Léonce Crépault; Raymond Dessaints; Léon Dessane; Léon Destroismaisons; Pierre Flynn (of the group Octobre); France Dion; Rolande Dion; Télesphore-Octave Dionne; Danièle Dorice; Stanislas Drapeau; Joseph-Daniel Dussault; Joseph Gagnier; Henri Gagnon; Serge Garant; J.-Albert Gauvin; Gaston Germain; J.-Alexandre Gilbert; Rolland-G. Gingras; Roland Gosselin; Louis Gravel; Adolphe Hamel; Lucien Hétu; Raoul and André Jobin; Louis Jolliet; Bernard R. Laberge; Janine Lachance; Marthe Lapointe; Émile Larochelle; Célestin Lavigueur; Antonio and Marthe Létourneau; Omer, Paul, Jean, and Claude Létourneau; Nazaire LeVasseur; Robert L'Herbier; Pierre-Olivier, Joseph, Roch, Léon, and Cyrille-Roch Lyonnais; Joseph-Désiré Marcoux; Fernand Martel; Jacqueline Martel; Charles-Amador Martin; Rodolphe Mathieu; Anna-Marie Messénie; Léo-Pol Morin; Renée Morisset; Ernest Myrand; Paul-G. Ouimet; Marguerite Pâquet; Alfred Paré; Nil Parent; Geneviève Perreault; Alys Robi; Pierre Rolland; Maurice Rousseau; Philéas, Léo, and Berthe Roy; Adrienne Roy-Villandré; Marc Samson; Charles and Flavien Sauvageau; Jacques Simard; Léopold Simoneau; Paul-Émile Talbot; Robert Talbot; Georges-Émile Tanguay; Edmond Trudel; Monique Vachon; Séraphin Vachon; Richard Verreau; and François and Joseph Vézina.

BIBLIOGRAPHY

Smith, Gustave. 'Du mouvement musical en Canada,' *Album musical*, 12 articles, Dec 1881–Dec 1882

Gagnon, Ernest. 'Physionomie de Québec en 1674,' *Louis Jolliet* (Quebec 1902 and other editions)

– 'La Musique à Québec au temps de Monseigneur de Laval,' *Pages choisies* (Quebec 1917)

LeVasseur, Nazaire. 'Musique et musiciens à Québec,' *La Musique* (1919–24)

Roy, Pierre-Georges. *La Ville de Québec sous le régime français* (Quebec 1930)

Pouliot, Léon. *Le Père Paul LeJeune, s.j.* (Montreal 1957)

Lacoursière, J., Provencher, J., and Vaugeois, D. *Canada-Québec, synthèse historique* (Montreal 1970)

Malouin-Gélinas, France. 'La Vie musicale à Québec 1840–45,' *CMB*, 7, Autumn–Winter 1973

– 'La Vie musicale à Québec de 1840 à 1845, telle que décrite par les journaux et revues de l'époque,' unpubl M MUS thesis, U of Montreal 1975

Aspects de la musique au Canada

History of Music in Canada

Music in Canada

La Musique au Québec (JB-T)

Quebec Harmonic Society / Société harmonique de Québec

Quebec Harmonic Society / Société harmonique de Québec. According to Nazaire *LeVasseur, it was through Frédéric *Glackemeyer that the first of several musical societies using this name was founded in Quebec City in January 1820; Glackemeyer was its president and director. Its aim was 'not only to contribute to the progress of an agreeable art and to the pleasures of the privileged class of citizens, but also to assist public charity.' Its existence was intermittent: 1820–1 (nine concerts), 1847–57, 1861 (one concert), 1870, and 1878. Among its later directors and conductors were Antoine *Dessane and a certain Ziegler (1855), Damis *Paul and a Mr Roschi (1857), Antoine Dessane and Frederick W. *Mills (1870), and Célestin *Lavigueur (1878).

In 1847 the players were recruited from among the best amateurs in Quebec City and from English regimental bands in the garrison there, and the orchestra resembled the classic Viennese type. Rehearsals and concerts were held in 1820 at the Union Hotel, in 1847 in the assembly room of the former parliament, in 1857 in the Salle de Musique, in 1861 in the National School, and in 1878 in the Victoria Hall.

The orchestra's repertoire is known partly from the contents of the orchestra folders preserved in the library of the Petit séminaire de Québec and through a few programs. From the names of the principal composers which appear (Abel, Beethoven, Gossec, Haydn, Handel, Hérold, Kalliwoda, Mendelssohn, Mozart, Pleyel, Ries, Rossini, Vanhal, and Weber) one can form a fair idea of the musicians' competence and also observe the remarkable taste of the society's organizers. In 1855 Antoine Dessane presented the first act of Boieldieu's *La Dame blanche* and two other concerts which were welcomed enthusiastically. At about that time vocal selections, for which a choir director was responsible, were added to the programs.

Financial difficulties brought about the demise of the society in 1857, and attempts to revive it – in 1861, 1870, and 1878 – were unsuccessful. Nevertheless, it was known for the quality of its musicians and its repertoire and for a considerable time it was patronized by 'the smartest society in Quebec.' It was superseded by the Septett Club, a new association headed by Dessane.

BIBLIOGRAPHY

Quebec City *Le Canadien*, 19 Jan 1820

Quebec City *L'Événement*, 3 Apr 1878

LeVasseur, Nazaire. 'Musique et musicians à Québec,' *La Musique* (1919–20)

Michaud, Irma. 'Antonin Dessane, 1826–1873,' *BRH*, Feb 1933

Kallmann, Helmut. 'Beethoven and Canada: a miscellany,' *CMB*, 2, Spring–Summer 1971 LPr

Quebec Music Educators' Association

Quebec Music Educators' Association (QMEA). An association of English-speaking music educators of Quebec formed in 1968. Its origins date back to 1939 when Irvin *Cooper, music supervisor with the Montreal Protestant School Board, gathered together a group of English-speaking music educators then working for the board. The following year an informal association was formed with Cooper as president. Membership broadened and English- and French-speaking music teachers from the Montreal Catholic School Commission joined the organization.

In 1963 the group adopted the name Quebec Music Educators / Éducateurs de musique du Québec (QMEEMQ). Its objectives were to raise the level of music teaching in Quebec, promote the professional development of its members, provide a platform for the discussion of mutual problems, and, finally, to act as spokesman for musicians in all things pertaining to music education. Also in 1963, on the initiative of Horace White, a music consultant with the Montreal Catholic School Commission, the Assn of Catholic Music Educators (ACME) was founded in order to pursue essentially the same objectives among English-speaking Catholic music educators.

In 1966 the French-speaking members of QMEEMQ began joining the newly formed *FAMEQ; in 1968 the two anglophone organizations merged to form the Quebec Music Educators' Assn (QMEA). A revised constitution confirmed the association's objectives: to stimulate an active, intelligent, and universal interest in music education and to collaborate with all who pursue the same goals, to acquire all possible knowledge relating to music education, to disseminate such knowledge in order continually to improve the quality of music education in the province, to promote the professional growth of its members, to establish standards and a code of ethics for the profession, and to encourage the discussion of problems in music education. Since 1968, it has issued the bulletin *QMEA Newsletter* approximately five times a year. It became affiliated with the *CMEA in 1975.

The presidents of QMEA have been Horace White 1968–9, Beth Newell 1969–70, Sister Mary O'Neill 1970–1, Edward J. Duplantis 1971–2, Elaine McDonald 1972–3, Archie Etienne 1973–4, Stan Waters 1974–6, Lorraine Thibeault 1976–8, and Roger Cook 1978–80. LT

Quebec Music Festivals. See Canadian Music Competitions.

Quebec Music Teachers' Association (QMTA) / **Association des professeurs de musique du Québec** (APMQ). Founded in Montreal in 1942 at a meeting organized by Mary Covert, piano teacher, music critic, and correspondent for the *Musical Courier*. The QMTA obtained a charter from the Quebec government during its first year and became affiliated with the *CFMTA in 1945. It held its first provincial convention in Montreal in 1964. It has awarded prizes to students at its J.S. Bach competition festivals in 1976, 1977, and 1978, at a Bartók competition festival in 1979, at its annual recital, and at the one given during Canada Music Week. Among the activities arranged for its members are conferences, concerts with guest musicians, and participation in a chamber music club. Its records were kept at first by Edna Marie *Hawkin, later by Pauline Bentham. In 1978–9 the QMTA had 195 official members and 22 associate or student members. Presidents have been Edna Marie Hawkin 1942–5, Marie-Thérèse *Paquin 1945–7, Ruth Blanchard 1947–9, Roger *Filiatrault 1949–51, Frances Goltman 1951–3, Félix-R. *Bertrand 1953–7, Leon Kofman 1957–60, Françoise D'Amour 1960–2, Anthony Zaplaski 1962–3, Madeleine Provost 1963–5, Daphne Sandercock 1965–7, Maurice Valentyne 1967–9, Muriel Shoobridge 1969–71, Juliette McLaren 1971–4, Viola Benson 1974–7, and Georges *Lindsay 1977–9, succeeded by Susan Giday. An information bulletin is published twice a year. HP

Quebec Symphony Orchestra† / **Orchestre symphonique de Québec**. The earliest founded (1902) of the 11 major orchestras flourishing in Canada in 1980. It was established by a group of young instrumentalists in Quebec City after a highly successful presentation 24 and 25 Jun 1902, under Joseph *Vézina, of Théodore Dubois's oratorio *Le Paradis perdu* for *Laval U's golden jubilee. Vézina agreed to conduct the orchestra, and as the Quebec SO it gave its first concert 28 November at *Tara Hall with J.-Alexandre *Gilbert as soloist.

The public's favourable reception encouraged the musicians to ask the more experienced instrumentalists of the *Septuor Haydn to join them, and on 3 Feb 1903 a constitution was adopted and the name Société symphonique de Québec (SSQ) chosen. The orchestra consisted of about 40 players and included Nazaire *LeVasseur and Arthur *Lavigne, a member of the Septuor Haydn who was the SSQ's first president. The SSQ received its charter in 1906 and adopted the motto 'Arte alitur fulgetque' ('Art nourishes and enlightens').

Staunchly supported by Laval U, the *Séminaire de Québec, the City of Quebec, and

The Quebec Symphony Orchestra under James De Preist, 1978

the provincial government, the SSQ inaugurated 31 Aug and 1 Sep 1903 both its first season and the *Auditorium de Québec with a concert in which Rosario *Bourdon, Paul *Dufault, Émiliano *Renaud, and Joseph *Saucier took part. In 1907 the orchestra won the Earl Grey Trophy in Ottawa and performed at the *Monument national in Montreal. From then on, it presented at least two concerts a year – generally 1928–35 under the auspices of the Société du bon parler français and the *Club musical de Québec. It also played every year on radio station CHRC (in the series 'L'Heure provinciale,' rebroadcast in Montreal by station CKAC). After Vézina's death in 1924, Robert *Talbot became the conductor. A special concert 21 Oct 1932 marked the inauguration of the *Palais Montcalm.

In the fall of 1935 the SSQ entered a difficult period. A group of young dissident musicians, who wanted to increase the quantity and quality of the concerts and in particular to perform the works of the great composers, got together under the direction of Edwin *Bélanger to form the Cercle philharmonique de Québec (CPQ). The CPQ was incorporated 25 Feb 1936 after a first concert 10 Dec 1935 at the Palais Montcalm. The initial season consisted of four public concerts and, as an important innovation, three free educational concerts for school children. In the next seven years the CPQ presented a total of 45 regular and educational concerts compared to a total of 31 by the SSQ. Nevertheless, immediately after Arthur *LeBlanc's homecoming concert 27 Oct 1938 the SSQ attempted a reorganization. A new charter committed the orchestra to 'symphonic and educational concerts with the co-operation of about sixty professional and semi-professional musicians.'

During the 1941–2 season the SSQ presented no concerts. The CPQ also experienced financial and recruiting problems. It was obvious that a merger was essential for survival. The amalgamation took place 25 Jun 1942; the name Orchestre symphonique de Québec was adopted, and Edwin Bélanger became the conductor of the 65 musicians. Wilfrid *Pelletier, who since 1942 frequently had been a guest conductor, succeeded Bélanger in 1951, bringing to the Quebec SO the prestige of his reputation and instilling a new vigour.

The appointment in 1960 of Françoys *Bernier as director general led to a radical structural change. The 54 musicians (60 per cent were Canadians) signed a contract for a 30-week season consisting of 60 to 70 concerts. In addition the orchestra became a much-valued proponent of decentralization: numerous centres, among them Chicoutimi, Sept-Îles, Thetford Mines, and Trois-Rivières, and others in the Abitibi and Gaspé regions, were able for the first time to hear a professional symphony orchestra.

Besides the international repertoire – in which French music held a special position – Bernier made it a point of honour to promote Canadian composers' works. He established a tradition, still continued in 1980, of commissioning and giving premieres of new works. By 1978 the orchestra had premiered *Matton's *Mouvement symphonique No. 1* (1960), *Garant's *Ouranos* (1963), Matton's *Te Deum* (1967), Alain *Gagnon's *Prélude* (1969), Jacques *Hétu's *Concerto* for piano and orchestra (1970), Vic Angelillo's *Tangente I* (1971), *Vigneault, *Léveillée, and *Chotem's *Le Dict de l'aigle et du castor* (1972), Matton's *Mouvement symphonique No. 3* (1974), and *Prévost's *Chorégraphie II* (1976).

Until the 1950s, guest soloists were usually Canadians – eg, Jean-Marie *Beaudet, Victor *Bouchard and Renée *Morisset, Paul *Doyon, Jacques *Gérard, Lubka *Kolessa, Georges *Lindsay, Calvin *Sieb, and Richard *Verreau. A few foreign artists, eg, the soprano Marcella Denya and the harpist Marcel Grandjany, appeared. Pelletier and after him Bernier engaged soloists of international reputation, and the orchestra's audiences heard Wilhelm Kempff in the complete cycle of Beethoven's piano concertos, David Oistrakh in Mendelssohn's *Violin Concerto*, Régine Crespin, Alicia de Larrocha, Arturo Benedetto Michelangeli, Henryk Szeryng, Jon *Vickers, and others. The conductors Sergiu Celibidache, Franz-Paul *Decker, Vladimir Golschmann, Pierre Monteux, Michel Plasson, and several others appeared as guests.

Bernier, who followed Pelletier in 1966 as artistic director, was succeeded in turn by Pierre Dervaux in 1968. Dervaux (b Juvisy-sur-Orge, near Paris, 1917) studied piano and composition at the Paris Cons and played in the Pasdeloup orchestra as timpanist; he then conducted at the Opéra-Comique, the Paris Opera, the Concerts Colonne, and the Orchestre philharmonique de la Loire. While pursuing an international career, he was artistic director of the Quebec SO until 1975. Though prevented by financial constraints from enlarging the 65-musician ensemble, Dervaux nonetheless conducted some remarkable performances, including Messiaen's *Chronochromie* (1970) in the presence of the composer, who declared he was very pleased with the orchestra.

From among the several guests who conducted the orchestra during the 1975–6 season, James De Preist (b Philadelphia 21 Nov 1936, a nephew of the illustrious US contralto Marian Anderson) was selected as artistic director in 1976. De Preist studied at the U of Pennsylvania with Vincent Persichetti (composition) and won a prize in the 1964 Dimitri Mitropoulos International Competition.

He was assistant conductor of the New York Philharmonic 1965–6, principal guest conductor of the Symphony of the New World in New York 1967–9, and assistant conductor of the National SO in Washington, DC, 1972–5. Under De Preist the Quebec SO celebrated its 75th anniversary with performances of *The Rite of Spring* to great acclaim in Quebec and 21 Oct 1977 in Washington. De Preist became the artistic director of the Oregon SO in 1980 but retained his position with the Quebec SO as well.

During the 1977–8 season the orchestra initiated an annual competition for young Quebec musicians. At the first competition – for strings only – the cellist Johanne Perron won the $500 prize and an invitation to perform as soloist with the orchestra. The following year's competition was for flutists.

The orchestra's concertmasters have been J.-Alexandre Gilbert 1903–31, Alphonse St-Hilaire 1931–3, Gilbert *Darisse 1933–60, Stuart Fastofky 1960–3, Jean-Louis Rousseau temporarily 1963, and Hidetaro *Suzuki 1963–76, succeeded by Malcolm Lowe.

An important figure in the development of the Quebec SO is (Jean Charles) François Magnan – b St-Casimir-de-Portneuf, Que, 11 May 1929; B LITT (Laval) 1949 – who, in addition to having been a violinist in the orchestra 1948–67, was its personnel director 1960–6, secretary general 1966–72, and then director general. He studied violin with Calvin Sieb 1946–53 at the *CMQ and with the aid of various scholarships worked under Antonio Brosa in London 1955–6 and Yvonne Astruc in Paris 1963–5. He taught sight-reading 1956–61 at the CMQ and 1956–67 at Laval U and gave the introductory course in the history of music 1964–5 at the Petit séminaire de Québec. He was artistic director of Quebec City's summer festival in 1969, 1970, and 1971. He was a violinist in the CBC's 'Les Petits concerts' orchestra 1956–70 and has given recitals in Paris and Quebec. He married the pianist Madeleine *Bernier.

Presidents of the Quebec SO have been Judge Thomas Tremblay 1942–8, Raymond Cossette 1948–51, Donat Demers 1951–3, René Blanchet 1953–8, Charles Laflamme 1958–9, Pierre Côté 1959–61, Isidore-C. Pollack 1961–3, Wilbrod Bhérer 1963–7, Aimé Déry 1967–70, Jean-Marie Poitras 1970, Charles Martin 1970–1, Paul-A. Chaput 1971–2, Jean Grenier 1972–3, Paul A. Côté 1973–6, Jacques Dionne 1976–7, and Gilles Moisan 1977–9, who was succeeded by Henri Grondin.

After presenting its early programs in the Auditorium, the Military Manège, and Laval U's convocation hall, the Quebec SO played regularly 1932–71 at the Palais Montcalm, occasionally revisiting the Auditorium (renamed the Capitol Théâtre). It moved to the Salle Louis-Fréchette of Quebec City's *Grand Théâtre in 1971. In 1978 its season included a 'Grande musique' series and an 'Invitation' series, both covering a wide repertoire. The important place given to contemporary music in its 1977–8 schedule earned for the orchestra a certificate of honour and a $2000 prize from *PRO Canada. The Quebec SO youth concerts, initiated in 1936, came under the leadership of Mario *Duschenes at the beginning of the 1969–70 season.

In addition to assisting the productions of the Théâtre lyrique du Québec and the *Opéra du Québec, the Quebec SO has presented large-scale choral works with the Choeur symphonique de Québec. This 120-voice mixed choir, a cultural and social organization of about 100 amateur choristers augmented by a group of some 20 paid singers for the public performances, was formed by Françoys Bernier in August 1964. Conductors after Bernier have been Jocelyne Desjardins 1964–5, André Martin 1965–6, Pierre Loranger 1966–8, Marcel *Laurencelle 1967 and 1969, and Élise Paré-Tousignant briefly in 1969, followed that year by Chantel *Masson. Masson began alternating with Charles Dumas in 1977. Claude Duguay served 1964–76 as president of the choir and Jean-Noël Legault succeeded him.

The Quebec SO has allocated part of its annual budget to the choir, and the repertoire has been selected by mutual agreement. The choir has participated annually in two of the orchestra's concerts and has accompanied it on tour in the province. In 1967 it presented Matton's *Te Deum*. Among other works it has performed are *Champagne's *Altitude*, Orff's *Carmina burana*, Haydn's *The Creation*, Mozart's *Mass in C Minor* and *Requiem*, Bach's *Mass in B Minor* and *St John Passion*, Handel's *Messiah*, Beethoven's *Ninth Symphony*, Verdi's *Requiem*, Honegger's *Le Roi David*, and Mahler's *Symphony No. 2* ('Resurrection').

The Quebec SO published the bulletins *Sur une note de musique et d'information* (1974) and *Sur une note d'information* (1974–7). In 1977 it began reporting its activities in the magazine *Le mois à Québec* and between September 1979 and June 1980 five issues of an orchestra news bulletin, *Le Lutrin*, had appeared. The 1978 budget of the Quebec SO was $1,300,000, based on subsidies from the *Canada Council, the *MACQ, and Quebec City and donations from private citizens.

DISCOGRAPHY

Matton *Mouvement symphonique No. 1* – Lekeu *Adagio pour quatuor d'orchestre, Op 3* – Milhaud *Suite provençale*. De Preist cond. 1977. RCI 454

BIBLIOGRAPHY

'Les noces d'argent de la Société symphonique de Québec,' Quebec City *L'Événement*, 28 Apr 1928

Tanguay, A.-P. 'L'Orchestre symphonique de Québec,' *Musique et musiciens*, vol 2, Apr 1954

Poirier-Blanchard, Céline. 'L'organisation de la musique symphonique à Québec de 1935 à 1942 – dissension et fusion,' unpubl B MUS thesis, Laval U 1976

Edds, Jack. 'Art nourishes and enlightens: the mission of the Quebec Symphony Orchestra,' *OCan*, vol 3, Mar 1976

'L'Orchestre symphonique de Québec a eu de bon chefs,' *Musique périodique*, vol 1, Oct 1977

Bernier, Maurice. 'Les 75 ans de l'OSQ,' *Mois à Québec*, 8 instalments in vol 1 and 2, Oct 1977 to May–Jun 1978

Novak, Barbara. 'James De Preist awakens Quebec City,' *Music*, vol 2, Jan–Feb 1979

Beaulieu, Nicole. 'À la conquête de tous les publics,' *Perspectives*, 5 Apr 1980

'Quebec Symphony captivates the north,' *Music*, Feb 1981

MS (AP,GP)

Quebec Woodwind Quintet† / Quintette à vent du Québec. Ensemble formed in Montreal in the autumn of 1971, and composed of Jean C. *Morin, flute; Bernard *Jean, oboe; Jean *Laurendeau, clarinet; Jean-Louis Gagnon, french horn; and René Bernard, bassoon. It gave its first concert in Trois-Rivières on 20 Apr 1972, followed by another in Alma which was given a delayed broadcast by CBC radio in its 'Grands concerts' series. *Canada Council grants enabled it to act as the quintet-in-residence at the music camp in Métabetchouan, Que, in 1974 and at the *JMC Orford Art Centre 1975–7. The quintet also went on *JMC tours 1974–6 in Quebec, Ontario, and Saskatchewan. In 1977 it appeared in Tunisia and made debuts in London (9 November at St John's Church, Smith Square) and in Paris (10 November at the Salle Gaveau) as part of *Musicanada, performing works by *Hétu, *Jones, *Mather, *Papineau-Couture, and *Saint-Marcoux (her *Genesis*, a work it had commissioned and had premiered at the Orford centre in August 1975). In the London *Sunday Times* on 10 Nov 1977, Felix Aphrahamian wrote that the Hétu work had been 'superbly played by the Quebec Wind Quintet.' The group recorded Hindemith's *Kleine Kammermusik*, Ibert's *Trois Pièces brèves*, Mather's *Eine Kleine Bläsermusik*, and *Genesis* (1977, Société nouvelle d'enregistrement SNE-501).

See also Discography for Jean-François Sénart.

GP

Queen Elizabeth Theatre. Home of the *Vancouver Opera Assn and (1960–77) the *Vancouver SO. Principally an opera and ballet hall, seating 2820, it was designed by the Montreal firm Affleck, Dimakopoulos, Lebensold, Desbarats, Michaud and Sise and was opened officially 15 Jul 1959 by Queen Elizabeth II, who on that occasion gave her name to the theatre. The gala orchestral concert was conducted by Sir Ernest *MacMillan and Nicholas *Goldschmidt, and Betty-Jean *Hagen and Lois *Marshall were the soloists. The first actual use of the hall – 11 July – was for a *Vancouver International Festival concert by the Vancouver SO conducted by Herbert von Karajan. The stage is 18.3 m deep and 35.7 m wide, and the proscenium is 10.5 m high and 20.4 m wide. An adjoining 647-seat playhouse opened 1 Feb 1961. For financial reasons the concert hall's ceiling was built 3 m lower than designed, with a consequent reduction of acoustic vitality. The orchestra pit holds 72 musicians. As a venue for a wide variety of presentations – concerts, recitals, opera, ballet, musical comedy, etc – the QE, as it is known popularly, was Vancouver's main centre for the performing arts until 1977, when the remodelled *Orpheum Theatre began to share this function. Among the famous artists and groups who appeared at the QE in the first season were the Obernkirchen Children's Choir, the Moiseyev Dance Company, George *London, Sammy Davis Jr, and the actor Vincent Price. Subsequent seasons saw performances by the New York City Ballet in its Canadian debut (1961), the *Stratford Festival's Gilbert & Sullivan Company (1962), *The Best of *Spring Thaw* (1963), the Royal Ballet with Margot Fonteyn and Rudolf Nureyev (1965), and the Bolshoi Ballet (1966). Among those who conducted orchestral concerts are Charles Munch, Igor Stravinsky, and Bruno Walter. BNSG

Queen's Hall. First hall in Montreal built expressly for concert use. A 1200-seat auditorium with organ, it was built in 1880 on the northwest corner of Ste-Catherine and Victoria streets. It served as the home of the *Montreal Philharmonic Society (1880–9) and the *Mendelssohn Choir of Montreal (1881–90) and was the scene of Emma *Albani's three recitals on her return to Canada in March 1883. Queen's Hall was converted to a theatre in 1891 and destroyed by fire in 1899.

Queen's Own Rifles of Canada Band. One of Canada's oldest and most famous volunteer militia bands, formed in Toronto in 1862 under the direction of Adam *Maul. Its early directors included William Carey 1875–9 and John *Bayley 1879–1901. Under Bayley's leadership the band quickly gained international recognition. The young Herbert L. *Clarke was a cornet soloist 1886–ca 1891. The 'Rifles' toured Canada from east to west and, as Alfred *Zealley remarked, 'charmed their way through most of the United States' (*Famous Bands of the British Empire*, London 1926). In 1910 the band made a triumphal tour of England under the direction of G.L. Timpson. Captain Richard B. *Hayward served as its director 1921–8. In 1922 and 1923 the band won the First Class 'A' band contest at the *CNE in Toronto.

A souvenir publication, 1912

During that time it also assisted the 2300-voice *Canadian National Exhibition Chorus in performances at the Coliseum. In 1928 Hayward was succeeded by Capt James Buckle; during World War II Buckle maintained a highly efficient band which performed for numerous parades and in concert. After the war Capt William T. *Atkins was appointed director. Serving 1947–68, he organized the band into a first-class musical ensemble which performed often at the Royal Winter Fair and for hockey nights at *Maple Leaf Gardens, appeared at many other fairs, and gave park concerts. Directors who followed Atkins were Capt Jack Long 1968–71 and Capt John O'Brien 1971–7, the latter succeeded by Capt George Gresham.

DISCOGRAPHY

The Band and Bugles of the Queen's Own Rifles of Canada. O'Brien cond. Nd. Private recording (JK)

Queen's University. Founded in Kingston, Ont, by the Presbyterian Church in 1841 and a non-denominational university after 1912. It is noted for its law, medical, and sciences faculties, for graduate programs in many disciplines, and for the collections of Canadiana (including concert programs and early Canadian sheet music) in the Douglas Library.

Although the need for a department of music was debated at the turn of the century, the first music instruction was offered in the summer of 1932, when a course of vocal music was given by Eduardo Petri of the *Metropolitan Opera. Petri returned to Queen's to train a choir in 1933 and possibly in 1934.

In 1935 Frank Llewellyn Harrison (b Dublin 29 Sep 1905) accepted an invitation to create a music program, became resident musician, and began teaching music appreciation courses. His program included the development of a record collection and the establishment of university choral and orchestral societies. A full-credit course in music was introduced in 1938, and Harrison was taken on staff in 1942. He left for the USA in 1946, later taught at universities in England (Oxford) and the Netherlands, and had a distinguished career as an editor, ethnomusicologist, and music historian. He revisited Queen's as a guest lecturer in 1980.

Graham *George joined Queen's U as both teacher and resident musician in 1946 and served as acting head of the Music Dept from its inception in 1968 until 1971. In the late 1940s the university initiated a BA with a music concentration and in 1969 it introduced a four-year B MUS program designed to prepare students for teaching careers. Other staff members who made significant contributions to the development of the department and its programs during the 1960s and 1970s include F.R.C. *Clarke and David Smith.

In 1971 Istvan *Anhalt became head of the department, and a period of expansion was begun. From approximately 30 students in 1970 enrolment grew to 170 in 1978, with a faculty of 42 (15 full-time and 27 part-time). Degrees offered in 1979–80 were B MUS (music education, theory and composition, history and literature), BA (minor), and BA (medial). In 1973 the department moved into its own building, Harrison-Le Caine Hall, which boasts, among other facilities, an electronic music studio (directed by David Keane) and a library.

Queen's has conferred honorary doctorates on Marian Anderson, Allen *Fisher, Frank L. Harrison, Sir Ernest *MacMillan, Stanley *Osborne, Godfrey *Ridout, Alfred *Whitehead, and Healey *Willan. The in-residence *Vaghy String Quartet was brought to Kingston in 1968 by the university and the *Kingston SO under the *OAC program for enriching the cultural life of Ontario communities. It has taught at the university and occupied the first string chairs in the Kingston SO. Other performing ensembles have included the Queen's Choral Ensemble, Chamber Orchestra, Chamber Singers, Collegium Musicum, Contemporary Ensemble, Glee Club (active late 1930s–60s), Improvization Group, Jazz Ensemble, Musical Theatre, and Wind Ensemble.

See also Archives; College songs; Music education research.

BIBLIOGRAPHY

Smith, David C.M. 'A degree program in music begins at Queen's,' *MSc*, 254, Jul–Aug 1970 (JPG)

QUESNEL, (Louis) **Joseph** (Marie). Merchant, composer, violinist, playwright, poet, actor, b St-Malo, France, 15 Nov 1746 or 1749, d Montreal 4 Jul 1809. (Research by John Hare of the U of Ottawa has revealed that Quesnel's birthdate probably was 1746, not 1749 as has been assumed.) Following a family tradition young Quesnel became a sailor, visiting Pondicherry, Madagascar, Guinea, and Senegal on a three-year voyage 1768–71 and French Guyana, the Antilles, and Brazil in 1772. In 1779 he commanded the corsaire *L'Espoir* and was sailing from Bordeaux to New York with munitions and provisions for the American rebels when the ship was captured by the British off Nova Scotia, and Quesnel was taken to Halifax. Approaching Sir Frederick Haldimand, governor of Quebec, who happened also to be a family acquaintance, Quesnel was allowed to go free and settle in Canada. Early the following year he married a Canadian, Marie-Josephte Deslandes in Montreal. The certificate calls him a 'négociant,' a wholesale merchant or trader. It appears that Quesnel was more than the village merchant described in Jules Fournier's *Anthologie des poètes canadiennes* (1920); in fact he was a successful trader who exported furs to France and imported wine. (A journey, probably in 1787, to the region around Michilimackinac and the source of the Mississippi and another, 1788–9, to England and France provide the evidence for this.) As far as is known Quesnel remained henceforth in Canada (residing in Boucherville near Montreal but returning to Montreal before his death). Of his 13 children, 2 became widely known: Frédéric-

Joseph Quesnel

Auguste as a member of the legislative assembly of Lower Canada and Jules-Maurice as an explorer after whom the British Columbia city Quesnel is named.

By family background and schooling Quesnel had acquired a knowledge of French literature and music. The plays of Molière, the writings of Boileau, and a violin are said to have been his steady companions. Stimulated by the lack of sophisticated entertainment in the new world, he set about applying his talents to performing and writing for the amusement of himself and his friends, and limned the situation in a poem:

I made my way to Canada, and here
Was welcomed with all manner of good cheer:
I'd no complaint. But – music? Oh, the pity!
At table, naught but some old drinking ditty;
In church, two or three worn-out old motets
Sung to a gasping organ out of breath.
Oh, hideous all. So for my heart's release,
See me composing music! First, a piece
For some religious business – grave or gay?
Was it or was it not, for Christmas Day?
I can't remember; but I mixed up wholly:
Gaiety, pathos, sweet, sour, melancholy,
Through every flat, sharp, natural ran the gamut:
Never before was I so brilliant, d— it!
And what was the result? Why, in a rage,
They said my airs were fitter for the stage.
One swore the service almost made him dance,
Another urged I be sent back to France;
Everyone fell upon me in a rout;
The Sex joined in (especially the devout):
'Good God,' said one, 'this irreligious din
Would lead the Saints in Paradise to sin.'
'O Christ,' another said, 'when the notes swell
'Tis like the imps at loggerheads in hell!'
'Twas then, apprised of Novelty's reward,
I saw my hopes all going by the board.
– Well, to the ear (if at all delicate)
My music, *entre nous*, is rather flat:
But did they want a Handel, a Grétry?
By God, then, they must find him oversea;
And my own little public work, I thought,
Deserved a better public than it got.
(Épître à M Labadie,' *Joseph Quesnel 1749–1809*, ed Michael Gnarowski, Montreal 1970, transl John Glassco)

According to Huston, Quesnel's compositions included songs, duos, motets, quartets, and symphonies, but none of these have survived. Extant, in addition to many literary works, are the vocal parts of two operas, **Colas et Colinette* and **Lucas et Cécile*, along with the second violin part and the libretto for the former. Quesnel wrote *Colas et Colinette* after his European visit, during which, in Bordeaux, he probably heard some of the latest French operas. Quesnel's charming works are among the first operas written in North America; based on French models they reveal melodic inventiveness and technical competence. *Colas* was staged first in Montreal, 14 Jan 1790 (12 days before Mozart's *Così fan tutte* was premiered in Vienna) by the *Théâtre de Société, an enterprise of

Quesnel, Louis *Dulongpré, and others, that was begun in 1789.

Quesnel remained active as a writer of poems (of which at least 34 survive), including 'Lecture to young actors' ('Adresse au jeunes acteurs du Théâtre de Société à Québec,' 1804). His plays include *Les Républicains français (ou, La Soirée du cabaret)*, a one-act prose comedy in which he expressed his preference for the British monarchy, and the one-act verse comedy *L'Anglomanie (ou, Le dîner à l'anglaise*, 1802) in which he ridiculed the aping of foreign manners. Although *Les Républicains français* includes sung passages, the tunes are those of existing French songs.

The revival of *Colas et Colinette* in Quebec in 1805 and 1807 and Quesnel's letters to the publisher John *Neilson regarding the printing of the music of the opera attest to the reputation he had achieved. For some years the memory of 'Le père des amours,' as he was called affectionately by the French poet Joseph Mermet, was kept alive. William Notman, the photographer, reported in 1868 that Quesnel 'has been described as a gentleman of cheerful temperament and nice tastes, who was happy in promoting the happiness of other people.' Indeed, Quesnel attempted not to scale the heights of Parnassus but to supply a need for wholesome diversion and to encourage the appetite for music and drama among his 10,000 contemporaries in Montreal.

The concluding lines of the 'Épître à M Labadie,'

> This vision of the future I can see
> And prophesy such fame for you and me
> As shall make us renowned through Canada,
> And hailed from Vaudreuil to Kamouraska,

indeed have become true for Quesnel, if not for Labadie (a local schoolteacher). Eugène *Lapierre based his opéra-comique *Le Père des amours* (1942) on Quesnel's life. *Colas et Colinette* received several performances subsequent to its revival in 1963 in Godfrey *Ridout's restoration and has been recorded and published. A complete edition of Quesnel's surviving works is being undertaken by John Hare of Ottawa. The *CMCentre has granted Quesnel the associate status reserved for deceased composers whose works the centre holds.

BIBLIOGRAPHY

Huston, James, ed. *Le Répertoire national* (Montreal 1848–50, rev 1893)

Notman, William. *Portraits of British Americans*, vol 3 (Montreal 1868)

Laperrière, Lucienne. 'Bio-bibliographie de Joseph Quesnel,' ms, U of Montreal 1943

Kallmann, Helmut. 'Joseph Quesnel, pioneer Canadian composer,' *CanComp*, 3, Oct 1965

Gnarowski, Michael, ed. *Joseph Quesnel, Selected Poems and Songs / Quelques Poèmes et chansons* (Montreal 1970)

Séminaire de Québec. Archives. FO Verreau 45

PAC. John Neilson papers, MG 24/B1. Frederick Haldimand papers, MG 21/273

Lande private collection

ILLUSTRATION

Portrait in the Château de Ramezay, Montreal HK

QUESNEL, Simone (m Poulin). Contralto, teacher, b Pointe-au-Chêne, Que, or Ottawa?, 19 Mar ca 1915. She studied voice with Céline *Marier for about 10 years and in 1931 gave a recital at the Delphic Study Club, which gave her a grant. Thus she was able to take courses in harmony and counterpoint with Claude *Champagne and Georges-Émile *Tanguay. Devoting herself at first to opera as a soprano, she performed with several troupes: she toured for four years with the Compagnie d'opéra franco-italienne, directed by H. Maurice Jacquet, and sang Micaela and Frasquita in *Carmen* with the *San Carlo Opera Company and Fanchon in Firmin Bernicat's *François-les-Bas-Bleus* and Serpolette in *Les Cloches de Corneville* with the *Société canadienne d'opérette.

Around 1942 Quesnel turned to popular ballads and embarked on a successful career in radio as an entertainer, singing mostly on the two CBC networks ('Musicale,' 'Serenade for Strings,' 'Star Time,' 'Stringtime,' 'Sunday Night Show'), as well as on CKAC (the title role of *Mireille* in 'L'Heure provinciale') and CKVL ('Chansonniers canadiens,' 'The Songs of Simone'). Shortly after the advent of TV she performed on the CBC program 'Connaissez-vous la musique?' and later she sang on 'Music Hall' and 'Tour de chant.'

Quesnel founded and was the director ca 1949-after 1956 of the Choeur des midinettes, composed of garment workers. Around 1956 she opened a private studio in Montreal. Her pupils include Diane *Dufresne and Pierre *Lalonde.

Quesnel recorded art songs with Albert *Viau on the Bluebird label in 1942 and the song *'Quand les hommes vivront d'amour' (Vedette 1001). She was often accompanied by Maurice Meerte's orchestra, with which she apparently made some LPs on the Music-Hall label. She was described by Odette Oligny as a 'consummate musician' who sings with 'infinite sensitivity' (Montreal *Le Samedi*, 17 Aug 1957).

BIBLIOGRAPHY

Hughette. 'Cette chanteuse qui a nom Simone Quesnel!' *Radiomonde et Télémonde*, vol 19, 27 Apr 1957 AP

Quidoz Piano Ltée. Firm of piano builders founded as Sénécal et Quidoz ca 1897 in Ste-Thérèse-de-Blainville (renamed Ste-Thérèse), Que. Its founders were Joseph Sénécal (b Montreal 1872, d Ste-Thérèse 1935) and Georges Quidoz (b Veminez, Haute-Savoie, France, 7 Jan 1870, d Ste-Thérèse 29 Jun 1932). The son of a shoemaker, Joseph Sénécal arrived in Ste-Thérèse at about 13 and learned his craft from the technicians at Thomas F.G. Foisy. In 1891, when this company moved to Montreal, Sénécal joined Lesage & Piché where he was manager for a few years. Around 1897 he went into partnership with Georges Quidoz, who had come to Ste-Thérèse at about 17 and who supplied the capital. In 1901 a fire destroyed the factory but it was soon rebuilt and the company prospered. Before the Depression the company was able to offer nine different models and produced 1700 to 1800 instruments annually, chiefly upright pianos but also some baby grands and player pianos.

When Georges Quidoz died his sons Julien and Gérard and Sénécal's son Philippe took over the management of the business. In 1938 Philippe sold his interests to the Quidoz brothers and the company became Quidoz Piano Ltée. A showroom was opened in Montreal about two years later. In the 1960s production was reduced to some 1200 pianos a year, a drop attributed to increasing imports of Japanese pianos, obsolete equipment, and the Quidoz' lack of interest in developing the business. In 1966 the company liquidated its stock and closed shop. (FH, LO, GP)

QUILICO(T). Family of musicians of Italian origin: 1 / Louis, 2 / Lina, his wife, and 3 / Gino, their son.

BIBLIOGRAPHY

Roewade, Svend. 'Opera is the Quilico family business,' *Music*, Oct 1979

1 **Louis.** Baritone, teacher, b Montreal 14 Jan 1925 of an Italian father and a French-Canadian mother. He was a solo chorister in the choir of St-Jacques Church in Montreal, studied singing with Frank H. *Rowe, and in 1947 won a prize in a competition organized by the St-Jean-Baptiste Society. At the urging of the pianist and vocal coach Lina Pizzolongo (who was to become his wife in 1949) he continued his studies 1947–8 at the Cons Santa Cecilia in Rome with Teresa Pediconi and the famous baritone Riccardo Stracciari. On his return to Montreal he worked 1948–52 with Pizzolongo and Martial Singher at the *CMM and sang supporting roles at the *Variétés lyriques in the *The Barber of Seville* (the role of Pedrillo, 1949) and *La Traviata* (1951). With the aid of a scholarship from Mannes College, New York, he studied there 1952–5 with Singher, with Ralph Herbert and Désiré Defrère (staging), and with Emil Cooper (repertoire). He obtained first prize in the radio competitions *'Nos Futures Étoiles' and *'Singing Stars of Tomorrow' in 1953, and went on a 1953–4 *JMC tour with the mezzo-soprano Rolande *Garnier. He also participated in the CBC TV programs 'Music Hall,' 'Serenade for Strings,' and 'Silhouette.'

Louis Quilico as Falstaff with Clarice Carson in an Opéra du Québec production

In 1954 Quilico made his professional stage debut in the role of Rangoni in *Boris Godunov* with the *Opera Guild of Montreal. Though he won the 'Metropolitan Opera Auditions of the Air' in 1955, he nonetheless made his New York debut with the New York City Opera, singing Germont in *La Traviata* 10 Oct 1955. In 1957 he sang the title role in excerpts from *Wozzeck* in the CBC TV program 'L'*Heure du concert' and was Masetto in *Don Giovanni* for the *Montreal Festivals. The following year he sang in the North American premiere of Nicolas Nabokov's *Symboli Chrestiani* with the *MSO. At the 1959 Spoleto Festival in Italy he sang the title role in Donizetti's *Il Duca d'Alba*, his 'very fine voice somewhat reminiscent of Gobbi's in its richness of colouring' (Andrew Porter, in *Opera*, September 1959). Quilico received a grant from the Canada Council in 1960. He made his Covent Garden debut that year opposite Joan Sutherland as Germont in *La Traviata* and was a member of that company 1960–3. He sang Rigoletto in his debut at the Bolshoi Theatre, Moscow, in 1962. In 1963 Quilico made his Paris Opera debut as Rodrigo in *Don Carlos* and, at the inauguration of the ORTF auditorium, participated in the premiere of Milhaud's oratorio *Pacem in terris* under Charles Munch. He was a member of the cast for the premiere (Geneva 1966) of the opera *La Mère coupable* by the same composer. He appeared twice at the *Stratford Festival – in a solo recital in 1967 and in arias and duets with Lois *Marshall in 1970. He gave several recitals at *Expo 67 and was Iago opposite Jon *Vickers and Teresa *Stratas in *Otello* in the lavish World Festival stage performances with the MSO at *PDA. Also in 1967 he sang Creon opposite Ernst Haefliger and Marilyn Horne in a *Massey Hall performance of *Oedipus Rex* with the *TS 17 May under the supervision of Stravinsky and conducted by Robert Craft, appeared as Rigoletto with the *Vancouver Opera, and sang in *Messiah* with the *Toronto Mendelssohn Choir. In January 1968 he participated in a concert performance of Verdi's *Alzira* with the American Opera Society at Carnegie Hall.

Besides appearing regularly, beginning in the 1960s, with the Vienna Opera, the Teatro Colón of Buenos Aires, the Teatro Massimo of Palermo, the Rome Opera, and the Paris Opera, Quilico performed frequently with the *COC (Iago in *Otello* 1960, the title role in *Rigoletto* 1962, 1969, 1973, and 1978, Germont in *La Traviata* 1966 and 1970, the title role in *Macbeth* 1966 and 1971, Amonasro in *Aida* 1968, Scarpia in *Tosca* 1968 and 1972, Enrico Ashton in *Lucia di Lammermoor* 1971, Michele in *Il Tabarro* 1975, and the title role in *Simon Boccanegra* 1979) and with the *Opéra du Québec (the High Priest in *Samson et Dalila* 1971, Germont 1972, Tonio in *I Pagliacci* 1973, and the title role in *Falstaff* 1974). In 1969 he sang Scarpia at the Bolshoi Theatre and in Leningrad, Bucharest, and Budapest. In February 1972 for the *Metropolitan Opera he replaced at short notice the regular Golaud (Thomas Stewart) in *Pelléas et Mélisande*, and on 1 Jan 1973 he made his official debut there as Germont, performing subsequently in *Rigoletto*, as Choroebus in *The Trojans*, and as Amonasro in *Aida*. He also sang Macbeth on CBC TV in 1973. During the 1974-5 season, he performed in various centres, including Covent Garden (*La Traviata*), San Francisco (*Luisa Miller*), Hartford (*La Forza del Destino*), New Orleans (*Il Tabarro* and *I Pagliacci*), and Baltimore (*Tosca*). For *Festival Ottawa at the *NAC he has sung Germont (1978) and Pandolphe in Massenet's *Cendrillon* (1979). In 1979 he was the star of the CBC TV program 'Portrait de Louis Quilico.'

In 1970 Quilico began teaching at the Faculty of Music, *U of Toronto, where his pupils have included Peter *Barcza, John *Dodington, Avo Kittask, Roelof Oostwoud, Janis Orenstein, Gino Quilico, and Gary *Relyea. Following a concert at the Montreal *Forum with the MSO, Gilles *Potvin wrote: 'Completely relaxed and in remarkable form, Quilico dominated the concert, giving stirring performances of two excerpts from Verdi, the great scene of Rodrigo's death from *Don Carlo* ... and the sombre "Eri tu" from *Un ballo in maschera* ... Quilico's voice, through its power, extremely smooth timbre and evenness of register, is a continual source of wonder and delight ... Here is an artist at the height of his career, an artist whose name for a long time now has been written large in the history of singing in Quebec' (Montreal *Le Devoir*, 22 Jan 1976). Quilico was awarded the 1965 *Prix de musique Calixa-Lavallée and named a Companion of the *Order of Canada in 1975.

DISCOGRAPHY

Bellini *I Puritani*. London SO, Rudel cond. 1973. Audio Treasury 3-ABC ATS 20016

Darwin – Song for a City: Verdi *Rigoletto* 'Cortigiani.' Royal Phil O, Bonynge cond. 1975. Decca SXL.6719

Donizetti *Gemma di Vergy*. New York Opera O, Schola Cantorum, Queler cond. (1977). 3-Col QAL 34409-344011

Donizetti *Maria Stuarda*. London SO, John Alldis Choir, Ceccato cond. 1971. Audio Treasury ABC ATS 20010-13 A-F

Handel *Hercules*. Vienna Radio O, Vienna Academy Chorus, Priestman cond. 1967. RCA Victor Red Seal LSC 6181

Highlights from Gluck: Iphigénie en Tauride. Paris Cons O, Prêtre cond. 1963. Angel 35632

Massenet *Esclarmonde*. National Phil O, John Alldis Choir, Bonynge cond. (1976). Decca SET 612

Massenet *Thérèse*. New Phil O, Linden Singers, Bonynge cond. 1974. Lon AOSA 1165

Milhaud *Pacem in terris*. Utah Symphony, University Choir, Abravanel cond. (1965). Vanguard (7) 1134

Monteverdi – Smith – Morawetz – Vaughan Williams – Cadoret – et al. Newmark pf. 1967. CBC Expo 22

Opera Gala: Campra *Tancrède* 'Quittez vos fers, goûtez un sort plus glorieux.' Provincial Instr Ens. 1973. DG 2538 244

Puccini *Tosca*. Lorange sop, Aragall ten, Bisson bar, New Philharmonia O, Guadagno cond. 1977. 2-Zafiro SA Dorado ZOR-1011

Verdi *Aida* (extracts). Royal Opera House O, Pritchard cond. 1963. Decca SXL.6068/Lon 25798

Verdi *Il Trovatore*. Lamoureux O, Saint-Paul Chorus, Fournet cond. 1966. Philips 837.469

BIBLIOGRAPHY

'Something to hear,' *Time*, 23 Oct 1964

Stevenson, Florence. 'Return of the native,' *Opera News*, vol 31, 13 May 1967

Ashley, Audrey. 'Except for his income tax life is sweet for the singer,' Montreal *Gazette*, 22 Jul 1978

Roewade, Svend. 'Louis Quilico ... a man of many parts,' *Performance*, Sep–Oct 1978

Moisan, Daniel. 'Louis Quilico après 183 opéras,' *Aria*, vol 2, Summer 1979

Creative Canada, vol 2

2 **Lina** (b Pizzolongo). Pianist, coach, teacher of singing, b Montreal 20 Jan 1930; lauréat (AMQ) 1946, premiere prix piano (CMM) 1948. She studied 1943-6 at the *AMQ, 1947-8 at the *CMM with Yvonne *Hubert, and in 1949 at the École normale de musique de Paris with Alfred Cortot. She performed as soloist with the *CSM (1945), the CBC Montreal orchestra (1949, 1950, 1951, 1952), and on CBC TV (1953). She was a teacher at the CMM. In 1970 she joined the Faculty of Music, *U of Toronto. As coach and accompanist she has remained a central force in the careers of her husband and her son.

3 **Gino**. Baritone, b New York 29 Apr 1955. He studied 1976-8 with his father and mother and with James *Craig and Constance *Fisher in the Opera Dept, U of Toronto. He made his debut 8 Jun 1977 as Mr Gobineau in a production of Menotti's *The Medium* by Comus Music Theatre, Toronto. The following year he played Papageno in *The Magic Flute* in Milwaukee. In 1979 he made his COC debut as Escamillo in *Carmen* and sang Paolo in that company's production of *Simon Boccanegra*, with his father in the title role. He played Ford in a scene from *Falstaff*, again with his father in the title role, on the 1979 CBC TV program 'Portrait de Louis Quilico.' He continued his training 1979-80 at the École d'art lyrique of the Paris Opera.

BIBLIOGRAPHY

King, Paul. 'A chip off the old,' *Toronto Star*, 15 Sep 1979

ST

Quintette à vent du Quebec. See Quebec Woodwind Quintet.

QURESHI, (Anna) **Regula** (b Burckhardt). Ethnomusicologist, cellist, b Basel 13 Jul 1939, naturalized Canadian 1968; MA Germanics (Pennsylvania) 1962, M MUS (Alberta) 1973. She studied cello 1958-60 at the Curtis Institute and music history and ethnomusicology at the *U of Alberta after 1963. A scholar 1963-9 of Urdu and Hindi language and literature and of the art music of India and Pakistan, she has given numerous lecture-recitals on sarangi, Indian music, and Muslim chant in Alberta, the USA, Pakistan, and Switzerland and has contributed articles to *The New Grove Dictionary*. For the Provincial Museum and Archives of Alberta she collected and recorded, 1970-4, examples of the province's ethnic folk music. She is a contributor to *EMC*. She was a cellist 1964-7 with the *Edmonton SO and performed 1965-72 with various *U of Alberta chamber orchestras.

WRITINGS

'Tarannum: the chanting of Urdu poetry,' *Ethnomusicology*, vol 13, Sep 1969

'Ethnomusicological research among Canadian communities of Arab and East Indian origin,' *Ethnomusicology*, vol 16, Sep 1972

RDM

R

RACICOT, Caroline. Pianist, teacher, administrator, b Montreal 3 Feb 1862 or 1864, d there 17 Dec 1950. She received her early musical training 1877-85 from the Sisters of the Congregation of Notre-Dame in Pointe-aux-Trembles, Montreal Island, and continued her studies with Marguerite Sym and Arthur *Letondal. She took singing lessons from Guillaume *Couture and organ from Romain-Octave *Pelletier. William *Bohrer later taught her piano and harmony at the *Dominion College of Music. She began her career in 1894 as a piano teacher at the convent in Pointe-aux-Trembles and at the Collège de Boucherville.

Racicot founded the Racicot Cons in Montreal in 1910 and was its director until 1918, when she temporarily gave up this position for health reasons. The institution had become affiliated in 1917 to the Institut Lanctôt, also known as the Hirondelles. In 1926-7 Racicot was still the school's director, and her name appears as a teacher of piano and theory, along with those of J.-J. *Goulet (violin, solfège), Alfred *Lamoureux (singing, harmony, solfège), and Oscar Arnold (woodwind, brass). Ernest Langlois, Alexis *Contant, Alfred Masino, and Rose McMillan also taught there, and Antonio *Létourneau was a student.

With Rose McMillan (artistic director and singing teacher), Gustave *Labelle (cello), and J.-J. Gagnier (violin), Caroline Racicot founded in 1921 a second school, the École de musique de Montréal, under the patronage of the Countess of Minto and Francis Casadesus, director and founder of the Fontainebleau Cons, France. In 1922 it was announced that Émile *Taranto would join the staff. J.-J. Gagnier led the orchestra class, which gave its first concert 24 Apr 1923 at the Mount Royal Hotel. Paul *Dufault taught there and Gabriel *Cusson was among the students. The École de musique de Montréal became the Collège de musique de Montréal in 1923. HP

Radio Canada International. See Broadcasting: 7; CBC; CBC recording.

RAE, Allan. Composer, b Blairmore, near Lethbridge, Alta, 3 Jul 1942. After three years in Calgary as a trumpeter in the Canadian Army Band he studied composition and arranging at the Berklee College of Music, Boston. He was a composer and conductor 1966-70 for CBC Calgary TV and radio. He studied electronic composition 1970-3 with Samuel *Dolin at the *RCMT and taught it there for a year (1973-4) before returning to Calgary.

Rae's compositions include *String Quartet No. 1* (second prize in the nationwide Second-Century Week Composition Competition in 1967 at the *U of Calgary); the jazz works *Suite of Modes* (1966) and *Sleeping Giant* (1967), which won awards in the Czech International Composers Competition; *A Prayer* (1969, for choir, orchestra, and jazz group, commissioned by the *Calgary Philharmonic); *A Day in the Life of a Toad* (1970, for brass quintet); *String Quartet No. 2* (1971); and several other chamber works. Later concert music includes three symphonies (1972, 1978, and 1978); concertos for harp, string bass, and piano (1976, 1977, and 1978 respectively); *Four Brass Quartets* (1975); *Improvisations* for string quartet and for woodwind quartet (both 1977); and *Whispering of the Nagual* for chamber ensemble (1978).

Rae has written scores for several musicals, including *You Two Stay Here and the Rest Come with Me* (1968–9), *Trip* (1969–70), *Where Are You Now That We Need You Simon Fraser?* (1971; book by Christopher Newton), *Beware the Quickly Who* (1971; book by Eric Bentley), and *Charles Manson AKA Jesus Christ* (1972; book by Fabian Jennings). Works for mixed media include *Celebration* (1974) and *Scarecrow* (1975). He contributed scores to productions at the *NAC of *The Tempest* (1973), *The Killdeer* (1975), and *Can You See Me Yet?* (1976).

Rae is a member of the *ACA, a member of the *CLComp, an associate of the *CMCentre, and an affiliate of PRO Canada.

BIBLIOGRAPHY

Schulman, Michael. 'Allan Rae develops craft from copying scores,' *MSc*, 278, Jul–Aug 1974

RAE, Jackie (John Arthur). Singer, songwriter, producer, b Winnipeg 1922 or 1924. At three he began performing with his sister Grace and brother Saul as the Three Raes of Sunshine on the Famous Players vaudeville circuit. As a child he participated also in Jack *Arthur's productions at Shea's theatres in Toronto and appeared in the USA. For service in World War II as a Spitfire pilot he received the Distinguished Flying Cross in 1943.

After the war Rae became a CBC variety producer, responsible for radio shows starring the comedians Wayne and Shuster, the singer Gisèle (*MacKenzie), Jack Arthur, and others. He was head of CBC radio and TV variety 1952–6 and was the singing host of his own CBC TV show 1956–7. In 1958 he moved to London, where he appeared on the Granada and BBC TV networks; his shows included 'Jackie Rae Presents,' 'Chelsea at Nine,' and 'Saturday Night at the Paladium.' He produced for TV and radio and performed in English clubs and cabarets. In 1976 he returned to Toronto and in 1978 he became executive producer of the *CTL.

Rae began composing songs in the 1940s with Lou *Snider, with whom he shared a CJBC radio program in 1948. It was not until the late 1960s, however, that he met with substantial success as a songwriter. His 'Please Don't Go,' recorded first by Donald Peers in England, was an international hit as recorded by Eddie Arnold and received an ASCAP award in 1969 as country song of the year. 'Happy Heart,' co-written with James Last, sold a million copies in 1970 as recorded by Andy Williams and was recorded also by Petula Clark, Ed Ames, and others. Rae's other hits include 'When There's No You' and 'I've Got My Eyes on You,' both written with Les Reed.

Some of Rae's songs have been published by EMI Music or by Jar Music, which he established on his return to Canada. He is a member of CAPAC.

BIBLIOGRAPHY

Brydon, Arthur. 'Jackie Rae: his future isn't in Canada,' *The Globe Magazine*, 7 Jun 1958

Waxman, Ken. 'This songwriter's life began at 40 – and he's going strong,' *CanComp*, 130, Apr 1978 MM

'The Raftsmen' / 'Les Raftsmen.' Canadian song originating in the Ottawa Valley in the second half of the 19th century. It is attributed to a raftsman or logger; according to the song, 'Across Bytown [Ottawa] they went today. They've packed their grub, they cannot stay.' E.-Z. *Massicotte was the first to record this song, which exists in both French and English and is sometimes called 'Bing on the Ring,' after the refrain. 'The Raftsmen' preserves the memory of a period when the hard life of the backwoods was mixed with a certain joie de vivre. The NFB has made filmstrips based on this song. It was recorded in the mid-1920s as 'Les Raft-Man' by Charles *Marchand (Starr 15245 and Col 4047F) and later was included on two LPs by Jacques *Labrecque (Lon MLP 10014; RCI / RCA CS 100-7) and others by Alan *Mills (Folk FP 29) and the *Chorale de l'U St-Joseph (Col FL 234). The song has been published in *Canada's Story in Song*, edited by *Fowke, Mills, and *Blume (Toronto 1965). An arrangement by Ruth *Watson Henderson for baritone, choir, and piano was published by *Thompson in 1975. HP

Ragtime. Musical genre of Afro-American origin, dating from the 1890s, popular until the late 1910s, and revived in the mid-20th century. In its strictest form, ragtime adheres to a composed score of four themes, each of 16 bars, syncopated in rhythm, and ordered AABBACCDD. It takes its inspiration and unique character from the melodic and rhythmic vivacity of Afro-American folksongs and dances.

Ragtime was preceded immediately by the 'cakewalk' dance craze in both black and white societies, and by such racist (but popular) 'coonsongs' as 'The Bully,' sung on US stages by May Irwin (1862–1938, a native of Whitby, Ont) and recorded on her Victor 78s of 1907. Elements of both fads, especially their characteristic syncopation, prepared the North American public for ragtime.

Ragtime is dated generally from the first published piece called a 'rag' – William H. Krell's *Mississippi Rag* (1897), which in fact was a cakewalk. The genre proliferated in sheet-music form, the easiest pieces (or adaptations of more difficult works) receiving wide performance in North American and European parlours. Ragtime's leading figure is the composer-pianist Scott Joplin (1868–1917), and its most popular composition is his *Maple Leaf Rag* (1899). (The work was named after the Maple Leaf Club in Sedalia, Mo, where Joplin was working. The proprietors were Will and Walker Williams, said to have come from London, Ont, and to have named the club after the popular symbol of their homeland.)

In the years following, ragtime was played by such bands as John Philip Sousa's (often under the direction of Herbert L. *Clarke), commercialized by Tin Pan Alley, and exaggerated into exhibitionistic and technically extravagant novelty pieces by Mike Bernard, Zez Confrey, and others, including, in Canada, Willie *Eckstein and his protégés Vera *Guilaroff and Harry *Thomas.

Despite its black origins ragtime has had many white exponents, of whom Joseph (Francis) Lamb (b Montclair, NJ, 1887, d Brooklyn, NY, 1960) is considered the greatest and, with Joplin and James Scott, completes the triumvirate of the genre's main composers. Lamb lived after 1901 in Berlin (Kitchener), Ont, while studying at St Jerome's College. There he wrote several songs and waltzes, published by H.H. *Sparks, as well as his earliest rags (listed in *They All Played Ragtime*), including *Walper House Rag* (1903) and *Rapid Rapids Rag* (1905). By 1907 Lamb had moved to New York, working in the Brooklyn fabric industry and composing his finest pieces only as a hobby.

Many Canadian composers in this idiom also were white, with the exception of Shelton Brooks (whose *'Some of These Days' and *'Darktown Strutters' Ball' have been called ragtime songs), Nathaniel *Dett (who wrote *After The Cakewalk – March Cakewalk* in 1900 while still in Canada), and Lou *Hooper. The earliest, of whom little is known, were Toronto publisher W.H. *Hodgins, who wrote *A Rag Time Spasm* (1899), and G.A. Adams, composer of *The Cake Winner* (Amey & Hodgins 1899).

Later Canadian or Canadian-born composers and/or pianists who worked, if only briefly, in the ragtime style included Tom Brown of the *Six Brown Brothers, Eckstein, J.B. (Jean Baptiste) Lafrenière, Geoffrey *O'Hara (under the surname 'de Vere'), and Charles Wellinger.

J.B. Lafrenière (b Maskinongé, near Trois-Rivières, Que, ca 1875, d Montreal ca 1911) was a trained pianist. He worked in Montreal in the El Dorado Orchestra (1890s) and at the Ouimetoscope, Français, and National theatres (1900s). Lafrenière wrote waltzes and marches (some published in *Le *Passe-Temps*) as well as *Balloon Rag*, *Taxi Rag*, and (his best-known piece) *Raggity Rag* (Delmar 1907), which was reprinted in *The Ragtimer* (vol 6, no. 2, 1967).

Charles Wellinger (b Ottawa ca 1888, d England ca 1943), apparently also a trained pianist, worked in Hamilton, Ont, with I.W. Lomas at the opera house and probably with Lomas' Royal Connaught Winter Garden Dance Orchestra. He wrote and published several songs, waltzes, and rags. His *Intermission Rag* (Roger Graham 1919) was arranged for orchestra, and his most popular work, *That Captivating Rag* (Wellinger 1914), has been reprinted by *The Ragtimer* (vol 6, no. 1, 1967) and recorded by John *Arpin.

The publication in 1950 of the history *They All Played Ragtime* marked the renewal of interest in the music, an interest which had faltered with the rise of jazz prior to the 1920s (though in Canada ragtime still was being recorded in the 1920s by Eckstein, Thomas, and Guilaroff). During its revival ragtime found a champion in Canada in the US-born pianist 'Ragtime' Bob Darch who appeared in various Toronto nightclubs, including, 1959–62, Club 76 (where he also presented, among others, Joseph Lamb – then in his 70s and only recently rediscovered). The Ragtime Society, founded in Toronto in 1962 by John Fisher and others, has focused international attention on ragtime with its publication (*The Ragtimer*), its recordings (for the Scroll label), and its annual 'Ragtime Bash' which draws performers and fans from many parts of North America.

The leading pianist in Canada during the revival era has been John Arpin, a Darch protégé. A less formal approach to ragtime, heard in nightclubs rather than concert halls, was exemplified in the playing of (Douglas) Alexander 'Ragtime' Read (b Niagara Falls, Ont, 1923, d Mississauga, Ont, 1980), who performed on CBC radio and TV and who made five LPs 1962–7 for CTL. Ragtime enjoyed a few years of mass popularity in North America in the mid-1970s as a result of the success of the US film *The Sting* (1974), whose score employs several Joplin rags. Various Canadian pianists of the 1970s, concert and pop, have made ragtime a part of their repertoires. These include Scott Cushnie, Ron Davis, Dave Flowitt, Monica *Gaylord, and Gordon Sheard of Toronto; Mitch Parks of Winnipeg; Charles Foreman of Calgary; and Buck Evans of Edmonton.

David Lee (b Hamilton, Ont, 1934), a Dundas, Ont, lawyer, began composing rags in 1974 and by 1977, through his own Dun-Val Music, had published and recorded 11 works. Austin Kitchen of Mississauga, Ont, and Rodney J. Anderson and Helena Bowkun of Toronto have composed and performed their own rags. Guitarists Colin Linden and David Wilcox have included rags in their performances.

In the 1970s ragtime compositions were played by groups as diverse as *Canadian Brass (whose LP *Rag-ma-tazz* includes rags by Ben *McPeek and Eldon *Rathburn), *Nexus, *One Third Ninth, the Stratford Ensemble (see Raffi *Armenian), and many traditional or dixieland jazz bands.

BIBLIOGRAPHY
Blesh, Rudi, and Janis, Harriett. *They All Played Ragtime* (New York 1950)
The Ragtimer, Toronto 1967– MM

Rainbow Stage. Canada's longest-surviving outdoor theatre, located in the natural setting of Kildonan Park in north *Winnipeg. It opened 7 Jul 1954 with the aim of presenting operettas and musicals using local performers. In 1956 the Winnipeg Summer Theatre Assn was founded to administer the theatre, and in 1966 the non-profit organization Rainbow Stage Inc was chartered, with Jack Shapira (a popular Winnipeg band leader in the 1950s) as executive producer.

After several seasons of poor weather a triodetic dome was constructed over the theatre in 1970. Further renovations in 1975, prolonged by a labour dispute which forced a temporary move to the *Manitoba Centennial Concert Hall, provided 2342 seats (a reduction of 600 from the original) and modernized facilities.

The first full-length musical to be presented was *Brigadoon*, in the fall of 1955. The number of productions each season has fluctuated, and during the first few years musical variety shows were presented. Most of the productions have been of Broadway musicals: *Annie Get Your Gun* (1956), *Kiss Me Kate* (1956), *The King and I* (1958, 1963, 1969, 1979), *Guys and Dolls* (1959), *Damn Yankees* (1960), *The Boy Friend* (1961, 1975), *Pal Joey* (1962), *The Music Man* (1962, 1968), *My Fair Lady* (1966), and *The Sound of Music* (1967).

Stars for some productions have been imported, but leading local directors and performers have been employed when possible, and several have become perennial favourites of Rainbow audiences, or have made names for themselves elsewhere. These include the directors John Hirsch and Peggy Jarman Green; the conductors Filmer *Hubble and Eric *Wild; the singing actors Evelyne *Anderson, Len Cariou, Ed Evanko, Cliff Gardiner, Morley *Meredith, and Bill Walker; the chorus director James Duncan; and the dance director Arnold Spohr. Other Canadian performers at Rainbow Stage have included Jan *Rubeš, Roma Hearn, Catherine *McKinnon, and Wally *Koster.

BIBLIOGRAPHY
Shapira, Machelle. *Over the Rainbow: Celebrating Our 25th Anniversary: Rainbow Stage Theatre* (Winnipeg 1979)
Keys, Janice. 'Rainbow's pot of gold is music,' *Winnipeg Free Press*, 7 Jul 1979 (GHr)

RAMSEY, Harold (Arthur). Organist, choirmaster, composer, teacher, b Yarmouth, England, Aug 1901, d Salmon Arm, near Kamloops, BC, 29 Jan 1976; L MUS (McGill) 1919, hon FTCL 1952. He moved to Calgary at 10, studying music at *Mount Royal College and becoming organist of Hillhurst United Church at 13 and of Knox United Church at 15. After training with Lynnwood *Farnam in New York in the early 1920s he was a vocal coach for Paramount Studios in New York and Hollywood and organist at Broadway's Rivoli Theater. He moved in 1932 to England, where he became a leading theatre organist, performing on some 1000 BBC broadcasts, appearing weekly at London's Granada Theatre, and touring with his Rhythm SO, Eight-Piano SO, and the revue *Radio Rodeo*. His signature tune was the theme from Gershwin's *Rhapsody in Blue*. In 1950 he returned to Calgary, where he was organist-choirmaster 1950–71 at Wesley United Church, founder (1952) of the Calgary Choral Society, and director (1951–62) and teacher of voice and organ at Mount Royal College Cons. He retired to Salmon Arm, BC, in 1971, but continued to teach and compose. His songs were published by *Chappell, *Boosey & Hawkes, and others. His 'Britain, Remember!' (Ascherberg 1941) became a Royal Air Force theme during World War II, and *Rodeo March* (Boosey & Hawkes) was adopted as the theme song of the Calgary Stampede.

DISCOGRAPHY
Beaumont *Twentieth-Century Folk Mass*. Calgary Choral Soc, Mount Royal College O, Ramsey arr and cond. 1963. Lon SLP 20042
Many 78s for Decca in England (LFP)

RANDLE, Doug (Harry Douglas). Composer, lyricist, arranger, pianist, b Calgary 26 Jan 1928. He studied piano as a boy with Grace Webber in Calgary and played 1945–50 in western Canadian cities with the dance bands of Sonny Fry and Bobby Roberts. Living 1948–57 in Vancouver, Randle was an arranger for Pat Doyle's dance band, for the Ray Norris jazz quintet, and for various CBC radio and TV shows. He studied composition 1955–7 with Allard de *Ridder.

After working 1957–61 in England for the BBC and in the recording and film industries with Wally Stott, Norrie Paramor, and others, Randle settled in Toronto as a freelance composer-arranger and scriptwriter, his work including projects for the CBC and *NFB. He has composed two children's musicals, *The Emperor's New Clothes* and *The Magic Planet* (book and lyrics by Eli Rill), the CBC-commissioned radio musical *Lady Emma* (1968, recorded on CBC LM-50), the pieces heard on the LP *Songs for the New Industrial State* (1970, Kan 5), and the stage musical *Of Moon and June and Honeymoon and Countless Plastic Things* (1973, produced at Old Angelo's in Toronto and at the opening festivities of *Hamilton Place).

In reviewing *Of Moon and June* ... Blaik Kirby had praise for 'songs as literate as Cole Porter's but usually a lot more sober' (Toronto *Globe and Mail*, 15 Feb 1973).

Randle is an affiliate of PRO Canada.

BIBLIOGRAPHY
'Profiles: Doug Randle,' *MSc*, 237, Sep–Oct 1967 (CF, MM)

RANGER, Claude. Drummer, composer, teacher, b Montreal 3 Feb 1941. He began playing in a Montreal cabaret in his late teens and later worked in showbands led by André Lacombe (Rainbow Room), Robert Lavoie (Le Mocambo), and Marcel Doré (Casa Loma). By the mid-1960s a leading figure among Montreal jazz musicians, Ranger was sideman to Lee *Gagnon, Pierre *Leduc, and others and led his own octet, which was heard frequently in the late 1960s on the CBC's 'Jazz en liberté.' He was a member 1969–71 of Brian *Barley's Aquarius Rising.

In 1972 Ranger moved to Toronto, where he played in clubs and in concerts with Lenny *Breau, Sonny *Greenwich, Doug *Riley, and the pianist Don *Thompson and such leading US jazzmen as George Coleman, James Moody, Sonny Rollins, and Phil Woods. Though he was a member 1976–8 of the trio of the pianist George McFetridge, accompanying the pop singer Vic Franklyn, he continued to play jazz occasionally. He played, for example, in Thompson's quartet at the 1977 International Jazz Festival in Larens, Holland. In 1978 he joined Moe *Koffman's quintet.

Ranger has recorded with Barley, Gagnon, Koffman, the guitarist (Michael) Munoz, P.J. *Perry, Riley, Herb *Spanier, and Thompson.

One of the most volatile performers in Canada, an aggressive sideman, and an adventurous (if only occasional) leader, Ranger has been hailed by Barry Tepperman (*Coda*, Jan 1975) as 'indisputably the finest drummer on the Canadian scene, a fiery dancer of stick and skin.' His playing reflects the influence of the US drummers Elvin Jones, Max Roach, and Tony Williams. He has taught drums privately in Montreal and Toronto and has written a book (unpublished) of advanced rhythm studies. Greg Pilo is among his pupils.

Ranger, who studied arranging for three years with Frank Mella in Montreal, had composed more than 80 works for jazz group by 1976 (most of them dating from the 1960s), including *Le Pingouin*, recorded by Barley, and *Tickle*, recorded by Riley's Dr Music. Ranger is a member of CAPAC.

BIBLIOGRAPHY
Gallagher, Greg. 'Claude Ranger: the career of a jazz drummer turned composer,' *CanComp*, 112, Jun 1976
Miller, Mark. 'Claude Ranger,' *Down Beat*, 5 Oct 1978
MM

Rapport de la Commission royale d'enquête sur l'enseignement des arts dans la province de Québec, commonly called the Rioux Report. It was submitted to the lieutenant-governor in August 1968 by the commission's president, Marcel Rioux, on behalf of the vice-president, Jean Ouimet, and commissioners Jean *Deslauriers, Réal Gauthier, Fernand Ouellette, and Andrée Paradis, and was published in 1969 by the Éditeur officiel du Québec in three volumes divided into three tomes. The report touches all the arts but attaches a particular importance to music because 'man was born of sound (the word) and his essence abides in sound.'

In volume 1 the report traces the history of music teaching in Quebec from the early beginnings of the colony and outlines, down through the last 100 years, the respective roles of the religious orders, the *AMQ, and the conservatories, university music faculties, and schools, stressing throughout the growth of musical life.

Volume 2 describes in detail music education at the pre-school, elementary, secondary, collegiate, and higher levels, as well as professional, preprofessional, and paraprofessional training, and makes recommendations in these areas. The report next discusses the training of teachers. Though music is not included in the section dealing with 'art education and disturbed children,' subsequent chapters are concerned with the organization of adult education and the role of music in this context. The report touches on music in the chapters entitled 'The responsibilities of a ministry of cultural development' and 'Suggestions for a cultural policy' (cultural democracy).

Volume 3 contains appendices such as 'Musical education in Hungary and the physical and intellectual development of the child' by Jacquotte Ribière-Raverlat. The report introduces the idea of 'open pedagogy' as well as the concepts of preprofessional and paraprofessional levels, the preprofessional leading to a concentration on music to produce professional musicians and the paraprofessional providing all students with the possibility of pursuing their musical education in complementary courses throughout their studies.

Finally the report makes three recommendations: 1 / that music (as well as the other arts) be present at all levels of education, especially at the pre-school level (at least half the time to be devoted to the arts), at the elementary level (30 minutes a day), and at cycle I of the secondary level, becoming optional with cycle II and at the collegiate and higher levels; 2 / that special consideration be given to instrumental music, particularly that for strings (violin), for the playing of which very intensive training is required during a student's early years; 3 / that all the institutions currently teaching music be grouped together under the administrative tutelage of the Ministry of Education, that some of their resources be pooled, and that musical education be given, wherever possible, in the schools, colleges, and universities rather than in separate institutions.

RATHBURN, Eldon (Davis). Composer, b Queenstown, NB, 21 Apr 1916; L MUS (McGill) 1937. After early piano studies with Eric *Rollinson in Saint John, NB, where he also played in Don *Messer's band, Rathburn won a CPRS scholarship for his compositions *Silhouette* (1936) and *To a Wandering Cloud* (1938). At the *TCM 1938–9 he studied composition with Healey *Willan, organ with Charles *Peaker, and piano with Reginald *Godden. For his *Symphonette* (1943) he received first prize in the Los Angeles Young Artists' Competition (1944). He was a danceband pianist, church organist, and radio arranger 1939–47 in Saint John before joining the *NFB, Ottawa, where he was a staff composer 1947–76. He taught film-music composition 1972–6 at the *U of Ottawa. In common with other NFB composers, Rathburn developed a light-textured and economical style readily adaptable to the mood of a film.

By 1976, in addition to many concert works, Rathburn had composed 185 film scores (mostly shorts for the NFB) including *To the Ladies* (1947), *Family Circle* (1949), *Children's Concert* (1951), *The Romance of Transportation* (1952), *Who Will Teach Your Child?* (1952), *City of Gold* (1957; the basis for a symphonic suite of the same name), *Universe* (1960), *Drylanders* (1963; his first feature-length score), *Pillar of Wisdom* (1968), *Labyrinth* (1967, shown at the NFB pavilion at *Expo 67 and recorded on Dominion, LAB 650S), *The World of Paul Kane* (1973), *The Road to Green Gables* (1975; for CBC TV), and *Who Has Seen the Wind* (1977; feature film). The NFB scores (1947–64) are listed in *Musique et cinéma*. Rathburn is a member of the *CLComp, a member of CAPAC, and an associate of the *CMCentre. See also Film scores.

SELECTED COMPOSITIONS

ORCHESTRA

Silhouette (arr). 1940. Orch. Ms
Symphonette. 1943 (rev 1946). Orch. Ms
Cartoon No. 1. 1944. Med orch. Ms
Cartoon No. 2. 1946. Med orch. CMCentre. RCI-41 (*TSO)
Suite (Family Circle). 1949. Orch. Ms
Images of Childhood. 1950. Orch. Ber (rental). RCI 19 (*TSO)/CBC SM-119 (*CBC Wpg orch)
Suite (Children's Concert). 1951. Orch. Ms
Overture to a Hoss Opera. 1952. Sm orch. CMCentre
Nocturne. 1953. Sm orch. CMCentre
Overture Burlesca. 1953. Orch. Ms
Variations and Fugue on Alouette. 1953. Sm orch. Ms
Milk Maid Polka. 1956. Med orch. CMCentre
Gray City. 1960. Med orch. CMCentre
City of Gold. 1967. Orch. CMCentre
Aspects of Railroads. 1969. Orch. CMCentre
Steelhenge. 1974. Steel band and orch. Ms
Three Ironies. 1975. Brass quin and orch. CMCentre

CHAMBER

Miniature. 1949. Ww quar, brass quar. CMCentre
Parade. 1949. Picc, ww quar, brass trio, perc. CMCentre
Pastorella. 1949. Ob, str trio, db. CMCentre
Waltz for Winds. 1949 (rev 1956). Ww quar. CMCentre
Second Waltz for Winds. 1949. Ww quar. CMCentre
Conversation. 1956. 2 cl. Jay 1971. Dom S-69004 (*Galper cl)
Bout. 1971. Guit, db. CMCentre

Eldon Rathburn

The Metamorphic Ten. 1971. Accor, mand, banjo, guit, db, hp, pf, cel, 3 perc. Ber (rental). 1974. Crystal Records S504 (instr ens, Rathburn cond)
Two Interplays. 1972. Sax quar. CMCentre
The Canadian Brass Rag. 1974. Brass quin. Ms. Boot BMC-3004 (*Canadian Brass)
The Nomadic Five. 1974. Brass quin. CMCentre
Turbo. 1978. Brass quin. CMCentre
Five works for pf; five works for v; two multi-media works: *Of Many People* (1970) and *It All Depends* (1974)

WRITINGS

'My most successful work: Labyrinth' *CanComp*, 30, Jun 1968

BIBLIOGRAPHY

'Music from the films,' *CBC Times*, 28 Apr–4 May 1962
'Music can often communicate better than dialogue: a profile of NFB's Eldon Rathburn,' *CanComp*, 35, Dec 1968
Contemporary Canadian Composers
Creative Canada, vol 1
Musique et cinéma (CF)

RAVEL, (Marie Thérèse) **Ginette** (b Gravel, m Marcotte). Singer, lyricist, b Joliette, Que, 6 Oct 1940. She studied elocution with Mme Jean-Louis Audet and began her singing career in 1959 at the cabaret La Cave in Montreal. Subsequently she recorded two singles, 'Le Secret de l'amour' and 'Par ce cri,' for *RCA Victor. She sang in Paris 1963–4 and was hostess in Montreal for CKAC radio's 1964 'Grand Prix du disque' and for CFTM-TV's 1966 variety show 'À La Catalogne.' In 1967 she sang in Port-au-Prince, Haiti, and in 1968 she represented Canada at the International Song Festival in Sopot, Poland, where she won second prize with Jean-Pierre *Ferland's 'Je reviens chez nous.' While living 1971–3 in France she sang in cabarets, at the *Canadian Cultural Centre and the Théâtre Récamier in Paris, and at the 1972 Festival de la chanson in Reims. Returning to Canada she lived 1973–5 in retirement in the Laurentians, successfully overcoming a lung disease and a problem with alcoholism and later recording two of her own songs (music by Marc *Fortier), 'Je suis fragile' and 'Du sable dans ma voix.'

Ravel returned to the stage in 1976 with a recital at the Boîte à chansons in Montreal's Hôtel Meridien, after which Claire Caron wrote ' "With time I acquired softness, with time I became a flower ..." It is undoubtedly with these words taken from the first song [of the evening] that Ginette has best described her state of mind [and] best allayed the anxiety of an audience which wondered what she had become. All softness, tenderness, sensuousness, she has discovered a repertoire of songs to her taste' (*Le Journal de Montréal*, 6 Aug 1976). Ravel appeared there again in 1977 with a recital of Ferland songs and in 1978 with some of her own compositions. In 1979 she gave a program of her own songs, 'Encore une historie d'amour,' at *PDA.

Ravel made several LPs for RCA, among them recordings of concerts in Montreal at the Comédie-Canadienne (1966, PCS-6000) and the PDA's Théâtre Maisonneuve (1968, PCS 1186). RCA has collected and reissued her most popular recordings on the LP *Mes Grands Succès* (PCS-1025) and on two others, both with the title *Succès souvenirs* (CGPS 309, CGPS 346). In the 1970s Ravel began recording for *Kébec-Disc. She is a member of CAPAC.

WRITINGS

Je vis mon alcoolisme (Montreal 1978) ST (MM)

Brother RAYMONDIEN (b Auguste Schuller). Organist, composer, educator, essayist, b Brunstadt, a suburb of Mulhouse, Alsace, 6 Oct 1882, d Croix, northern France, 24 Aug 1947. He studied with the Christian Brothers of Belfort and entered their community in 1895. At about 17 he studied organ, violin, double-bass, and harmony at the Paris Cons. He emigrated to Canada in 1904. In 1908 he began spending his free time composing religious and secular works. He was an accomplished master of Gregorian music, and in 1914 the Christian Brothers published his *Solfège-Manuel du chant grégorien*.

Brother Raymondien's compositions, however, became increasingly individualistic. Their number has been estimated at close to 300 and includes some 20 masses. For organ he wrote variations on well-known hymns, as well as an arrangement of Canadian tunes for the *Saint-Jean-Baptiste celebrations. Offertories, motets, faux-bourdons, hymns, organ accompaniments, and orchestrations of carols complete this abundant output of religious inspiration. Among his 80 pieces of secular music are five operettas for use in the colleges of his order including *L'Ange du Canada*, the orchestration of an unpublished song by the tenor F.-X. *Mercier entitled 'France et Canada,' and an extended concert piece for band, *Voix patriotiques*, based on three Canadian airs treated in cyclical form. In 1934 the last-named work was adapted for organ.

Brother Raymondien taught literature 1921–8 at the Académie commerciale de Québec and was director of music. He founded the 82-piece La Salle Concert Band in 1926 and composed more than 20 pieces for it. After sojourning 1928–9 in Belgium he returned to Quebec, spending 1929–31 in Yamachiche and 1931–8 at his order's provincial house in Ste-Foy. An essayist and educator, he wrote numerous articles and gave courses to promote religious music, and founded a study group, le Fratello, devoted to the study of art and artists. In 1935 the bishop of Rimouski, Que, appointed him his adviser on religious music. He was being considered in 1938 to head a project to reform teaching in Quebec, but he left Canada that year to settle in Dijon, where the German occupation did not interfere with his musical activity. In 1950 his friends and relatives in Canada erected a monument to his memory in the cemetery at Croix.

WRITINGS

'Conférence grégorienne,' *La Musique*, vol 3, Jan–Sep 1921; also other articles in this periodical 1920–4
'Les grands orgues de Sainte-Anne de Beaupré,' Montreal *Le Devoir*, 8, 15, 22 Feb 1936

BIBLIOGRAPHY

Archives of the Christian Brothers (Ste-Foy, Que) GB

RCAF Blackouts. Entertainment troupe organized during World War II by air force personnel; also, the name of one of its shows.

The troupe was organized early in 1943 to perform at air bases in Canada and overseas. The cast of about 35 singers, instrumental musicians, dancers, and comedians gathered at Rockliffe Air Force Station, Ottawa. Flight Lieut Robert Coote, an English singer-actor (previously successful in Hollywood and later Col Pickering in the original Broadway production of *My Fair Lady*), was in charge of production.

The shows exploited the versatility of the cast. Members of the 12-piece pit orchestra also appeared as actors and soloists, and performers were responsible for erecting and striking sets, maintaining costumes, and loading and unloading equipment. Original music and lyrics were written by cast members: Henry Singer, Sam Levine, John Gallant, Bryant Fryer, Wishart *Campbell, and Fran Dowie. The songs 'Why Am I Always Joe?' (Singer) and 'You've Been Darn Swell' (Levine) were published in an RCAF songbook. The orchestra, which included Levine (string bass), Gallant (piano), D'Arcy *Shea, and Stanley *Solomon, was conducted by George *Calangis.

In May 1943 the troupe began a tour of western Canada, starting in Yorkton, Sask, and continuing across the prairies to the west coast and as far north as Annette Island, Alaska. In December it performed for service personnel in the British Isles and at the end of the war it entertained troops in Belgium, Holland, France, and Germany. The final performances were given in September 1945 in the south of England. Ten songs, from the second RCAF show, by Kenneth *Bray, Maurie Hyman, Lloyd Edwards, and Sir Walford Davies, were published in the collection *All Clear* (np, nd). SL

RCA Limited / Limitée. Record company which began as the Victor Talking Machine Co in Camden, NJ, in 1901. Its records were pressed and distributed in Canada by the *Berliner Gramophone Co of Montreal. In 1924 Victor purchased Berliner and formed the Victor Talking Machine Co of Canada. Edgar Berliner remained president until 1930. Victor in turn was purchased by the Radio Corporation of America (RCA) in 1929 and RCA Victor was created. (Artists recorded by Victor before 1929 are discussed in the Berliner entry.)

RCA Victor was one of the two record companies in Canada to survive the Depression. RCA retained the North American rights to the Berliner mascot, 'Nipper,' associated with the HMV (His Master's Voice) series and maintained him (and the Victor name) until the early 1970s. Victor first issued long-playing records (33⅓ rpm) in 1931 and followed these with 45-rpm discs in 1949 and improved long-playing discs (again 33⅓ rpm) in 1950. Stereophonic sound refinement was brought out in 1958.

Under the direction of A. Hugh *Joseph and others, RCA Victor recorded many Canadian performers for its Victor or Bluebird labels, among them the country and folk artists Joseph *Allard, Joe *Bouchard, Paul *Brunelle, Wilf *Carter, Omer *Dumas, Willie *Lamothe, Hank *Snow, Isidore *Soucy, and George *Wade. Other performers in the Bluebird line included Mart *Kenney and His Western Gentlemen, and various other performers in the series La *Bonne Chanson.

A major RCA Victor recording employing Canadians took place in Canada in 1941, when crew and equipment were sent to St-Laurent, near Montreal, to record, in the historic chapel there, the *Montreal Festivals performance of Fauré's *Requiem*, Mozart's 'Ave Verum' K618, and the Agnus Dei from the latter's *Mass in C Minor* K427, with Les *Disciples de Massenet, the Montreal Festivals Orchestra under Wilfrid *Pelletier, the soprano Marcelle Denya, and the baritone Mack Harrell.

Performers in the LP era (after 1950) have included Carroll *Baker, Tommy *Hunter, Ronnie *Prophet, and many other country artists; the *MSO, the *NACO, and the *TS among orchestras; the *Festival Singers and the *Toronto Mendelssohn Choir among choral groups; the tenors Raoul *Jobin and Richard *Verreau among classical singers; and the pop singers and groups the *Guess Who, Raymond *Lévesque, Michel *Pagliaro, and Sloche.

RCA Victor collaborated with the *CBC's RCI to issue commercially the series *Music and Musicians of Canada* (17 records) and *Canadian Folk Songs: A Centennial Collection* (9 records), as well as several individual LPs. In 1969, with the CBC's RCI, RCA released 10 records in the JMC 20 series which commemorated the *JMC's 20th anniversary.

Edward Preston (b Hamilton, Ont, 1931), who joined RCA in 1967, was appointed vice-president and general manager of RCA Records (Canada) in 1975 and played a considerable role in promoting Canadian performers. For some years the company had a pressing plant in Smith Falls, Ont, and modern recording studios on de Maisonneuve Blvd in Montreal and on Mutual St in Toronto; all three were discontinued in the late 1970s.

BIBLIOGRAPHY

'RCA Victor records releases seventeen centennial albums,' *CanComp*, 12, Nov 1966
'RCA-CBC music anthology an important step forward,' ibid, 2 instalments, 18 and 19, May and Jun 1967
'Jack Feeney and country music,' *CanComp*, 126, Dec 1977
Roll Back the Years (EBM)

RCI. See Broadcasting: 7; CBC; CBC recording.

REA, John. Composer, teacher, b Toronto 14 Jan 1944; B MUS (Wayne State) 1967, M MUS (Toronto) 1969, PH D (Princeton) 1978. His teachers included *Weinzweig, Babbitt, and Sessions. In 1973 he joined the staff of *McGill U as a lecturer in composition and theory. He won a BMI Award for Student Composers (1968), third prize in the fourth International Competition for Ballet Music (Switzerland 1969) for *The Days / Les Jours*, and the John Adaskin Memorial Award for *Anaphora* (1970). His opera *The Prisoners Play* was commissioned in 1972 by the *U of Toronto Opera Dept, which gave the premiere 12 May 1973 at the MacMillan Theatre. The *York Winds commissioned *Reception and Offering Music* and premiered it 22 Mar 1976; and *Jeux de Scène* was composed for the Vancouver group *Days Months and Years to Come. Rea is a member of the *CLComp and an affiliate of PRO Canada.

SELECTED COMPOSITIONS

STAGE

The Days / Les Jours, ballet. 1969. CMCentre
The Prisoners Play, opera (Paul Woodruff). 1973. CMCentre

CHAMBER

Sonatina. 1965. Fl, pf. CMCentre
Prologue, Scene and Movement (classical Latin palindrome). 1968. Sop, va, 2 pf. CMCentre
Sestina. 1968. Chamb ens. CMCentre
Fantaisies and/et Allusions. 1969. Sax quar, snare drum. CMCentre
Anaphora. 1970. Chamb ens. CMCentre
Anaphora III. 1974–7. Str quar. Ms
Reception and Offering Music 'Anaphora IV.' 1975. Ww quin, perc. CMCentre
Jeux de Scène 'fantaisie-hommage à Richard Wagner.' 1977. Hn, ob, vc, picc, fl, pf, mar, 3 gl, blacksmith's anvil. CMCentre

PIANO

What You Will. 1969. 2 or 4 hands. Jay 1971
Anaphora II. 1971 (rev 1972). CMCentre
FOR-M-A. 1977. Ms
Also *Piece for Chamberorchestra* (1967, rev 1971), and *The Four Corners of the Year* for v (1968), both ms; 2 works for tape, *S.P.I. 51* and *STER 1.3* (both 1969), recorded on Marathon MS 2211

WRITINGS

'Richard Wagner and R. Murray Schafer: two revolutionary and religious poets,' *CMB*, 8, Spring–Summer 1974
'Conversation between Brian Cherney and John Rea,' *Array Newsletter*, vol 2, Fall 1974
'Franz Liszt: "New paths of composition: the Sonata in B Minor as paradigm",' unpubl PH D thesis, Princeton 1978

BIBLIOGRAPHY

MacMillan, Rick. 'Musical quotations enhance new John Rea works,' *MSc*, 296, Jul–Aug 1977
PRO Canada Ltd. 'John Rea,' pamphlet (1979) CF

READ, Angelo (McCallum). Teacher, composer, organist, b near St Catharines, Canada West (Ontario), 22 May 1854, d Port Maitland, Ont, 15 Jul 1926. His early musical training took place in St Catharines and in the USA. In the early 1880s he spent several years in Leipzig, where his teachers included Robert Papperitz, Carl Reinecke, Alfred Richter, and Salomon Jadassohn. He then spent a year in Vienna studying Leschetizky's piano methods.

By 1889 Read had become organist at St Thomas Church and music teacher at Ridley College, St Catharines, but in 1894 he settled in Buffalo. For many years he divided his teaching activities between Ridley College and d'Youville College of Buffalo, also making a name for himself as a conductor of choirs in both cities. He was music director of the Buffalo Cons in the early 1920s.

Read was one of the earliest Anglo-Canadian composers. Among his major works are the Christmas cantata *A Song of the Nativity, Op 12* (G. Schirmer 1899); the dramatic cantata *David's Lament, Op 15* (ibid 1902); the Lenten cantata *It Is Finished, Op 17*; a *Mass* in B flat; and several concert overtures. The publishers of his shorter works for piano, voice, church choir, etc, include *Anglo-Canadian, Ditson, Presser, G. Schirmer, *Suckling, and *Whaley Royce. He also composed a 'Canadian Flag Song' (Anglo-Canadian 1914). In 1886 he read an essay on 'The encouragement of Canadian composition' before the *Canadian Society of Musicians. He wrote on 'The North American Indian and music' for *Musical America* (vol 6, no. 9, 1907). HK

Rebecca Cohn Auditorium. Part of the *Dalhousie (University) Arts Centre complex, and the major concert hall in Halifax.

The auditorium opened officially 19 Nov 1971 with a concert by the *Festival Singers, the Dalhousie Singers, members of the *Atlantic SO, and musicians from Dalhousie U. For the preceding 10 months, however, the auditorium had been used for musical events, including a recital by Isaac Stern and a performance of *Così fan tutte* by the university's music department.

The auditorium's construction, at a cost of about $5 million, was made possible, in part, through a bequest from the estate of Rebecca Cohn, a Halifax patron of the arts. The multipurpose hall was designed by architects Fowler, Bould & Mitchell Ltd. The proscenium opening is 18.6 m wide and 7.8 m high, and the stage is 9.6 m deep. In 1974 the stage floor was replaced by one suitable for ballet. The auditorium, which seats 1041, has been praised for its acoustics.

Though owned by the university, the auditorium has been managed by Dalhousie Cultural Activities, and its program organized and supervised by a board of directors comprising community leaders and university members, with subcommittees for music, theatre, film, and dance. The first administrator, John Cripton, was succeeded in 1973 by Erik Perth.

The auditorium is a venue for symphony, chamber, jazz, and pop concerts, opera, musical theatre, drama, dance, and film. Among the many performers and groups who have appeared there are Vladimir Ashkenazy, Harry Belafonte, Carlo Bergonzi, *Canadian Brass, the *COC, the Duke Ellington Orchestra, the Entre-Six Dance Company, Maynard *Ferguson, the Guarneri String Quartet, Moe *Koffman, the *NACO, the National Ballet of Canada, John Ogdon, Elisabeth Schwarzkopf, the Toronto Dance Theatre, the *TS, and Pinchas Zukerman. Resident ensembles include the Atlantic SO, the Dalart Trio, the Scotia Chamber Players, and *NOVA MUSIC. The Atlantic Opera Society and the *Kiwanis Music Festival also use the auditorium. JBk

---

REBOULOT, Antoine. Organist, pianist, teacher, composer, b Decize, Nièvre, France, 17 Dec 1914, naturalized Canadian 1978; premier prix organ (Cons national de Paris) 1936, premier prix composition (Cons national de Paris) 1947. In Paris he studied at the Institut national pour les Jeunes Aveugles and later with Marcel Dupré (organ) and Henri Busser (composition) at the Cons national.

Reboulot taught piano and pedagogy and was organist successively in Perpignan, in Versailles, and at St-Germain-des-Prés in Paris (where he succeeded his teacher André Marchal in 1945). He performed as pianist and organist in Europe and North America.

In 1967 Reboulot settled in Quebec, where he taught piano 1967–70 at the *Cons de Trois-Rivières and 1970–2 at the *CMQ. He also taught improvization, piano, organ, and keyboard harmony 1970–8 at *Laval U and in 1972 began teaching at the *U of Montreal. His pupils include Antoine *Bouchard, Victor *Bouchard, Gilles *Manny, and Renée *Morisset.

Reboulot has given many organ recitals in Ontario and Quebec and has participated in the *Ars Organi series and in the summer concerts at St Joseph's Oratory in Montreal. For Ducretet-Thomson Reboulot has recorded music by Franck (1954, 320C022), Mozart, Schumann, and Liszt (1955, 320C106), and Bach (1957, 300C056). A second recording of Bach was issued on the Euterpe label (1964, EU 3002). He performs his *Variations sur le nom d'Henri Gagnon* on the recording *Hommage à Henri Gagnon* (1974, Alpec A-75008).

Of Reboulot's compositions, which include piano and chamber music pieces, some 10 works for organ have been published by the Schola Cantorum of Paris.

Reboulot married the pianist Lise *Boucher, who studied with him in Paris. IP-C

Record collector clubs. Formal and informal groups devoted to study of the history of recorded sound through the collection and preservation of recordings and sound-reproducing equipment, the research of performers' careers, and often the compilation of discographies. Their work supplements that done formally by libraries and archives. The best-known collector clubs in Canada are the Montreal Vintage Music Society and the West Mississauga Jazz Muddies.

The Montreal society was formed in 1966 by Jim Kidd, Dick Bourcier, Hank Fleischman, and Jack Litchfield. Prominent members have included the discographers Litchfield and the late Edward B. *Moogk, the broadcasters Kidd and Henry Whiston, and the writers Len Dobbin and Ron Sweetman. Membership in 1979 reached 22.

The Mississauga club was formed in 1971 in the Toronto area by Eugene Miller (who at the time had been secretary of the International Assn of Jazz Record Collectors since 1966). The Mississauga group established informal affiliation with the international association. In 1979 notable members were Keith Miller, a piano-roll and sheet-music collector; Joe Showler, a jazz-film collector; and Ross Wilby, owner of the label Jazz Studies.

The Montreal and Mississauga clubs began meeting annually in 1972, as the Canadian Congress of Collectors, to exchange information and recordings, to hear guest speakers and performers, and to honour Canadian musicians (eg, Les *Allen and Trump *Davidson in 1975, Lou *Hooper in 1976).

Other prominent clubs include 78s Revisited, developed in 1968 from a CBC Vancouver radio show 'The Record Collector' and numbering approximately 40 members (some from Bellingham, Wash) who meet informally on a monthly basis; and the Antique Phonograph Society, founded in 1969 by John Stephen of Oshawa, Ont, and centred in Toronto with a membership of more than 50. Similar groups are active throughout the country, meeting regularly in libraries or private homes to listen to and discuss recordings of mutual interest.

See also Discography. MM

Recorded sound

1 Introduction
2 The technology
3 The industry
4 Recording studios
5 The records
6 Collections

See also Discography; Record collector clubs.

1 INTRODUCTION. The invention of sound recording and reproduction in the late 19th century and the continuing improvements and refinements in the techniques and technologies of this invention have had a profound effect on music as an art, a recreation, and a business. The ability to store a unique performance for rehearing at any time in the future and to make an unlimited number of copies of that performance was perceived at once as a blessing and a threat. On the one hand sound recording has 'democratized' music by overcoming the conventional limitations of time and place (an achievement which is especially important in sparsely populated Canada, where tours by performers are hard to arrange in outlying regions), by providing higher standards of performance (where formerly the local church soloist's performance had been accepted as the criterion for excellence), and by making available, all for the same price, the oldest and the newest, the homegrown and the most exotic music.

On the other hand, the availability of so much music at the flick of a finger has helped to undermine the role of music as self-expression through singing and instrumental playing and has turned it into a spectator entertainment (although movements discussed in *EMC* entries such as JMC and CAMMAC have helped to restore the balance between active and passive forms of enjoying music; see also School music, Choral singing). Sound recording has catered to all levels of musical taste,

Recording an Indian band in British Columbia, ca 1910

and since it operates on the principles of business, the relationship between artistic merit and sales promotion (especially in the case of contemporary concert music) has been distorted: a composer who has established a reputation in a heavily populated country with a strong recording industry will have far more opportunities to have his work recorded and widely distributed than will a composer of equal distinction living in a country that represents a small market. Since even in the late 1970s the Canadian recording industry remained essentially a branch plant controlled by headquarters in New York, London, and other foreign cities, the Canadian composer in 1980 still could not be described as well served by recording. Nevertheless, as countless *EMC* entries for Canadian composers and performers in both the popular and the concert fields reveal, the overall number of recordings is high. (The *NL of C's collection of commercial recordings of Canadian interest exceeds 30,000 items, and a complete collection might contain between 40,000 and 50,000.) Many of the recordings of Canadian music have been made by the CBC (see CBC recordings), without which this music might be almost unknown beyond Canada's borders; many other recordings are the result of connections Canadian musicians have established in other countries. Some recordings by Canadians – eg, those of Pierrette *Alarie, Maureen *Forrester, Kenneth *Gilbert, Glenn *Gould, Oscar *Peterson, Léopold *Simoneau, and Jon *Vickers – have achieved world recognition, and many discs by pop artists have been international hits. Although sound recording has not destroyed live musicmaking (indeed, to some extent it has enhanced it), it is clear that the dissemination and appreciation of the work of Canadian composers and performers depend as much on recordings as on concert and broadcast performances, and that the future of Canadian music hinges on a strong recording industry. (The *CMCouncil planned its 1981 conference around that very theme.)

2 THE TECHNOLOGY. The history of sound recording begins with the 'phonautograph' of the French inventor Léon Scott de Martinville, who in 1857 was able to record sound waves on a cylinder covered with soot. Twenty years later another Frenchman, Charles Cros, conceived in theory the principle of reversibility, ie, not only recording but also reproducing the voice. In the same year, 1877, the US inventor (the scion of a Canadian family) Thomas Alva Edison accomplished the practical demonstration of a 'talking machine.' Edison covered his cylinder with tinfoil as opposed to the soot used by de Martinville, enabling it to retain the indentations made by sound waves and to play back what had been recorded. In 1878

Edison's invention was exhibited all over the world, including Canada, when a machine was lent to the governor-general, Lord Dufferin, at Rideau Hall in Ottawa. On 17 May 1878 Lady Dufferin wrote in her diary (*My Canadian Journal 1872–1878*, Toronto 1969, p 292): 'This morning we had an exhibition of the phonograph. Two men brought this wonderful invention for us to see. It is quite a small thing, a cylinder which you turn with a handle, and which you place on a common table. We were so amazed when we first heard this bit of iron speak that it was hard to believe there was no trick! But we all tried it. Fred sang "Old Obadiah," D. made it talk Greek, the Colonel sang a French song, and all our vocal efforts were repeated. As long as the same piece of tinfoil is kept on the instrument you can hear all you have said over and over again ... The last performance was for D. to say something which should be repeated by the machine to a public exhibition in Ottawa in the evening.'

For some years Edison put his talking machine on the shelf and turned to other research work. It was the Scot Alexander Graham Bell, who in 1870 had settled in Brantford, Ont, and who became famous for his invention of the telephone, who in company with his cousin Chichester Bell and the British-born scientist Charles Sumner Tainter discarded Eidson's tinfoil record, using instead wax-covered cardboard cylinders and thus contributing to a greatly improved sound reproduction. This improvement led to the formation in 1886 of the American Graphophone Co, succeeded two years later by the Columbia Phonograph Co (see CBS Records Canada Ltd). Becoming aware of others' interest in the talking machine, Edison brought out a 'perfected' phonograph for commercial production in 1888. Both the Edison and the Bell-Tainter machines used wax-cylinder recordings and both applied the 'hill and dale' method of engraving sound waves in a vertical manner. It was Emile Berliner (see Berliner Gramophone Co) who decided upon the use of a disc record in place of the cylinder and introduced the lateral cut method of recording by causing the engraving tool to move from side to side in the groove. Berliner also invented a 'master' record, which made possible the pressing of any required number of any given record. In the earliest days of the cylinder machines, if 100 copies were needed, the performer had to repeat his efforts at least 25 times. Berliner's gramophone was first issued commercially in 1889, and the first discs, made of hard rubber, were 12½ cm (5 inches) wide. Berliner took out a Canadian patent in 1897 and that year in Montreal set up a company which early in 1900 issued the first Canadian-made disc recordings. These were 18-cm (7-inch) discs, followed in 1901 by 25½-cm (10-inch) and in 1903 by Deluxe 30-cm (12-inch). Double-sided discs were issued in 1908.

Early recordings lack the high and low extremes of sound, and despite refinements in record materials the record of early 1925 essentially was identical to that of 1889. The performer or performers would record into horns of varying sizes, and the sound vibrations were recorded directly on a wax disc by means of a diaphragm to which the engraving tool was attached. But by 1919 two former Royal Air Force officers, Lionel Guest, a former aide to a Canadian governor-general, and Horace Owen Merriman (b Hamilton, Ont, 1888, d Ottawa 1972), had begun to experiment with electrical recording by microphone. The first commercial recording of this type made anywhere was the one Guest and Merriman made during the ceremony of the burial of the Unknown Warrior in Westminster Abbey on 11 Nov 1920. The new technique revealed bass and treble sounds hitherto unknown on recordings. However, largely because of their huge inventories of acoustically recorded discs, the major record companies showed little interest. Finally, in 1925, they were forced into recording electrically to compete with the radio's better sound quality. From then on, also, recording was not confined to a small studio but was done on location or from broadcasts. The proceedings on Parliament Hill in Ottawa during Canada's Diamond Jubilee 1 Jul 1927 were recorded, and so, during the following summer, was the 2200-voice *Canadian National Exhibition Chorus in Toronto.

A limitation of the early disc was its playing time of three to four minutes per side. Most of the record firms experimented with a longer-playing record. In the early 1930s Victor (see RCA Ltd) brought out a 33⅓-rpm (revolutions per minute) record, but a combination of technical and economic problems forced the company to abandon the effort, except in its practical application for broadcast transcription discs, generally 40-cm (16-inch). Neither this experiment nor the many improvements in recording technology after World War II had a Canadian ingredient. The major steps, listed here for orientation, included the 'ffrr' (full-frequency range recording) technique introduced by English Decca in 1944, the 33⅓-rpm long-playing record (LP for short; earlier recordings had been standardized at 78 rpm) first issued by Columbia in 1948, the small 45-rpm record first released by Victor in 1949, the stereophonic recording (requiring two microphones or sets of microphones and two playback speakers) patented in 1932 but not pressed commercially in Canada until 1958 (by *Sparton), the quadraphonic record introduced ca 1970, the direct-to-disc recording technique revived in Canada by RCA in 1976, and the laser beam and digital experiments of the late 1970s. Along with the development of disc recordings, there has been a growing refinement of tape-recording techniques. The principle of magnetic recording was discovered as early as 1900, but it was applied widely only after World War II. Offshoots of the reel-to-reel tape recording are the cartridge and cassette tape recordings, which gained great popularity in the 1960s.

While still not a perfect substitute for natural sound, the recorded sound resulting from the vast post-1950 advances in refinement of technique and sophistication of equipment in certain ways has surpassed it. The new technology's unlimited powers in the manipulation of speed, pitch, reverberation, colour, etc, to say nothing of the splicings, combination of independently recorded sounds and other 'plastic surgeries' which became the stock-in-trade of the revision of the sound object, profoundly affected composition (see Electronic music). They also created a new type of listener, the 'hi-fi buff,' an enthusiast absorbed by the search for the ultimate in sound reproduction. He is served by annual audio shows in which manufacturers and distributors exhibit their latest gadgetry and by a number of magazines that review, with varying emphasis, audio equipment and new recordings.

3 THE INDUSTRY. The following chronological list includes a selection of Canadian record companies and labels and provides brief notes on the dates and scope of activity where known. No attempt has been made to indicate all name changes and take-overs.

E. Berliner, Montreal, established 1899 (*Berliner Gramophone 1904–24; taken over by Victor 1924). Made equipment, pressed discs, and produced the Berliner Gram-O-phone label. Music in a variety of genres. Began to distribute Victor (His Master's Voice) records in 1901

Edison label cylinders and, from 1913 on, also discs, distributed by R.S. *Williams, Toronto, ca 1900–26. Music in a variety of genres. Apparently no Canadian production

Columbia (see CBS; Canadian branch 1904–23 under various names, 1924–Depression and 1954–76 as Columbia Records, then as CBS). Canadian pressing began 1912. In early 1930s distributed by *Canadian Music Sales, 1939–54 by Sparton. Variety of musical genres

*Canadian Vitaphone Co, Toronto, 1913–16. Discs pressed from Columbia masters

*Pathé Frères (Paris). Distribution centre established in Montreal 1915; Pathé Frères Phonograph Co of Canada 1918–ca 1921. Apparently no Canadian production

*Brunswick-Balke-Collender of Canada, Toronto. Subsidiary of US firm. Active in Canada in recording business 1917–34, later made only billiards. Made equipment 1917–34, records 1920–34. Pressing and distribution taken over by Compo, 1932. Canadian artists were recorded by US parent company; repertoire mainly classical.

Phonola Co of Canada (Pollock Manufacturing Co), Kitchener, Ont. Records 1918–mid-1920s. By 1914 made Phonola equipment and distributed Fonotipia, Odeon, Jumbo labels; from 1918 on also Otto Heineman records

*Starr Co of Canada (at first Canadian Phonograph Supply Co), London, Ont, 1918–30. Distributed Starr-Gennett (USA) label. Records pressed by Compo; label taken over by Compo 1930 and continued until early 1950s. Various genres of music. Featured Canadian performers

*Compo, Lachine, Que, 1918–64. Acquired by MCA 1964. Pressing plant for Phonola, Starr-Gennett, Decca, etc. Produced Apex label 1921–71, and again beginning in 1979, and also Domino, Melotone, Microphone, Sterling, Lucky Strike, Compo and other labels. Various genres of music

*RCA, Toronto. Canadian activity began 1924 under the name Victor Talking Machine of Canada, Montreal, acquiring its previous Canadian distributor, E. Berliner. Name changed to RCA Victor 1929, RCA early 1970s. Classical music series and labels have included Bluebird and, especially, Red Seal.

(NB: Compo and RCA Victor were the only record companies in Canada to survive from the 1920s to the post-Depression era.)

*Sparton of Canada, London, Ont. Begun 1930. Pressed and distributed for Columbia 1939–54, then became independent. Popular music

Celtic, Antigonish, NS, 1933. Label of Scottish music; taken over by Rodeo. Scottish and Irish fiddle music; Gaelic and Cape Breton songs

CBC Recordings, begun 1945, RCI Transcription Service established 1947. Domestic series 1966–80. All genres of music

*Capitol Records of Canada, London, Ont, ca 1946. Set up by Musicana Records (USA) as distributor of Capitol (USA) records and pressing plant of Musicana Records. Taken over by Capitol 1947, distributed by Regal Records 1947–54, made subsidiary of Capitol (USA) 1954, became Capitol Records EMI of Canada in 1955. Has produced records of popular music and distributed Angel and Seraphim classical records

Regal Records, London, Ont. Pressed Capitol Records 1947–54

Tip Top, Newmarket, Ont, 1948–80. Founded and operated by Max Boag (pseudonym Harry Glenn). Commercial and (especially after 1962) custom recordings

*Rodeo Records. Montreal 1949–56, Halifax 1956–69, Peterborough, Ont, 1969. Ceased new production in mid-1970s. Also produced Banff label (established 1953), Celtic label (taken over 1960), Caprice label (for French-Canadian market), and Melbourne label (for classical music; established 1973 and taken over by *Waterloo Music 1977)
*Beaver Records, Toronto, 1950–6. Produced classical music recordings (*Toronto Mendelssohn Choir) pressed by RCA Victor
Dominion, Toronto, 1950–early 1970s. Label of pop music records issued by Canadian Music Sales
*Quality Records, Toronto, begun 1950. Producer of Quality, Birchmount, and Celebration labels; distributor of Broadland, Kanata, and Music World Creations; also presser and distributor of US discs and tapes
Allied Record Corp, Montreal, 1950s–early 1960s (see Sam Gesser). Over 100 LPs by Canadian performers
Alouette, Montreal, begun 1952. Label of Ed *Archambault Inc
*Hallmark Recordings, Toronto, 1952–9 as a label, 1958–ca 1968 as a recording studio. Produced recordings of classical music; on Spiral label, pop music; on Songs of My People label, music of ethnic minorities
Gavotte, Toronto, 1952–5. Label of G.V. *Thompson, Ltd. Produced and distributed a variety of musical genres
Banff. Label established 1953 by Rodeo (above)
CBS Records Canada Ltd, Toronto, 1954. See notes under Columbia, 1904, of which this is a Canadian revival. Distributor of True North, Aquitaine, and Attic
Orfeo, Montreal, 1954
Alvina, fl 1954. Label for pop music records
Aragon, Vancouver, fl 1955. Label for pop music records
*Rococo, Toronto, begun in 1955. Label of Ross, Court & Co. Reissues of historical recordings including Canadian singers. In 1966 began to distribute also Cantilena label
Club de disque JMC, Montreal, begun in 1956. See JMC.
*Arc Records, Toronto, begun in 1958. Pop and rock performers
Select, Montreal, 1959. Label of Ed Archambault Inc. Classical, church, and pop music
*Canadian Talent Library, Toronto, begun 1962. Issued primarily through a variety of commercial record companies. All genres of music
*Waterloo Music Co. Began producing records in 1971. In 1977 took over Melbourne label from Rodeo
*Canada Baroque Records, Montreal, 1962–ca 1973. Taken over by Everest (USA) in the late 1960s. Produced classical music. Associated labels were Janus and Pirouette.
CAPAC-CAB recording project, Toronto, begun 1963. Distributed through various commercial record companies. Features light and serious Canadian music. See CAPAC.
*Gamma Records Ltd, Montreal, begun in 1965. Devoted mainly to recordings of Quebec performers and chansonniers
Cantilena, Toronto, 1966 (see John Stratton). Reissues of historical recordings, distributed by Rococo
*Polydor Records of Canada, Montreal, 1966–73; became Polydor Ltd in 1973, PolyGram in 1978. Labels include Festivo, Resonance; also distributor of Casablanca, Capricorn, Barclay, Mercury, Philips, DGG, and London after 1980
*London Records of Canada, Montreal, begun in 1967 (London Gramophone Corp of Canada, Montreal 1948–67). Subsidiary of Decca of London. Also produces Ace of Clubs, Ace of Diamonds, and Airdale labels. Has distributed independent Canadian labels such as Aquarius, Attic, Axe, Boot, Gamma, Goldfish, Rodeo, Banff, Caprice, Celtic, Melbourne, and Select at one time or another, and also various European labels. Own production includes various genres of music. After the 1980 takeover of Decca by PolyGram the latter distributed the London label.
Aquarius, Montreal, begun 1968. Pop music recordings distributed by London Records and later by Capitol
Sackville, Toronto, begun 1968. Jazz label (see *Coda*). Distributes Onari label
*GRT of Canada Ltd, London, Ont (later Toronto), 1969–79. Subsidiary of General Recorded Tape, USA. Distributor of foreign tape recordings and later also discs. Distributor of Canadian labels AXE and Daffodil, both comprising pop music
*A & M Records of Canada, Toronto, begun 1970. Canadian outlet for US company whose catalogue of pop music features several Canadian performers
*True North Records, Toronto, begun 1970. Pop and folk music label distributed by CBS
Fundy Records, Sackville, NB, begun 1971
Kanata Records, Toronto, begun 1971. Pop music label
*Boot Records, Toronto, begun 1971. Produces pop music records and, beginning 1973, Boot Master Concert series of classical recordings
ASTRA Records, Montreal, begun 1972. Formed by Canadian Assn of Broadcasters
Goldfish, Richmond, BC, begun 1973. Pop music label distributed by London Records
Melbourne, Peterborough, Ont, begun 1973. Classical music label of Rodeo; taken over by Waterloo Music in 1977
Onari, Toronto, begun 1973. Jazz label (see Bill Smith) distributed by Sackville
Attic Records, Toronto, begun 1974. Pop music label distributed by London Records until 1978, then by CBS
*Kébec-Disc Inc, Montreal, begun 1974. Chansonnier and light music label, also handling the Gatsby, Le Nordet, Solution, and other labels. Distributed in Quebec by Trans-Canada Musique Service, in Europe by RCA
Masters of the Bow, Toronto, begun 1974. Reissues of historical discs (see James Creighton). Also produces Baton label for similar series devoted to conductors
Aquitaine, Toronto, begun 1975 (see Eleanor Sniderman). Classical music label. International distribution by CBS
*Berandol Records, Toronto, begun 1975. In 1978 established Bear 'n' Doll label for children's recordings
Music Gallery Editions, Toronto, begun 1976. Devoted to new, experimental, and native music. See CCMC.
Umbrella, Toronto, begun 1976. The direct-to-disc label introduced by *Nimbus 9 Productions. Classics, jazz. Acquired in 1979 by Sine Qua Non, Toronto. Records reissued on Ultra-Fi label
Tapestry Records, Ottawa, begun 1978. Recordings of carillon, *Canadian Brass, distributed by RCA
Magnum, Toronto, begun 1979. See GRT of Canada, 1969.

The total production of disc recordings in 1979 amounted to nearly 88 million, of pre-recorded tapes to nearly 21.5 million. The value of sales at the distributor's net selling price in that year was about $215 million for discs and about $63 million for pre-recorded tapes. In 1980 the main organizations serving the recording industry were the *Canadian Recording Industry Assn (CRIA) / L'Association de l'industrie canadienne de l'enregistrement, established in 1963 as the Canadian Record Manufacturers' Assn, and the Canadian Independent Record Producers Assn (CIRPA) / Assn canadienne des producteurs de disques indépendants, formed in 1974 with headquarters in Toronto. CIRPA's aims included the building of both domestic and international markets for Canadian records. It has organized symposia on the record industry and record production. Another organization, the *Canadian Academy of Recording Arts and Sciences (CARAS) was formed in 1975 in Toronto, where it shares offices with CRIA. CARAS in 1976 became the sole governing body of the *Juno Awards.

In Montreal an industry organization, the Assn du disque et de l'industrie du spectacle québécois (ADISQ), was founded in 1978 and at a gala at the *PDA in 1979 made the first awards – the Félix Trophy – honouring contributions to the Quebec recording industry.

4 RECORDING STUDIOS. With the growth of highly sophisticated recording and editing equipment after the middle of the 20th century, recording studio facilities became complex and costly sound laboratories staffed by highly skilled technicians. Until about 1970 such studios were few in Canada, and most recording stars had to travel to New York or to European centres. For a number of reasons, among them the *CRTC's broadcast quotas for Canadian music content established in 1970, the situation then changed. For example, while Toronto in 1970 had only three studios of international calibre (RCA Victor, Eastern Sound, and Toronto Sound), two years later there were five 16-track studios in that city, and Montreal even had a 32-track studio. Many Canadian studios were equipped with the latest and most complex equipment, and certain tax advantages helped to attract foreign recording groups, especially in the pop field. In addition to commercial records, studios (rented out at hourly rates) are used to produce jingles, demonstration records, interviews, and other recordings. By 1977 Toronto had become the third-largest jingle producer in North America (see Jingles).

Among studios active in the 1970s were: in Halifax, Audio Atlantic; in Dartmouth, Solar Audio and Recording; in Montreal, Bobinason, Son Montréal, Son Québec, Studio A, Les Studios Marko, and Studio Tempo; in Longueuil, Que, Studio Saint-Charles; in Quebec City, P.S.M. Studio; in Morin Heights, Que, Le Studio; in Ottawa, Marc Studios; in Toronto, Comfort Sound, Inception Sound, Kensington Sound, Kinck Sound, Manta, Sound Canada, Sound Kitchen, Sounds Interchange, Sound Stage (see Nimbus 9 Productions), Thunder Sound, Zanza Sound Productions; in Elmira, Ont, *Mercey Brothers; in Hamilton, Ont, Grant Ave Studio; in St Jacobs, Ont, the Waxworks; in Winnipeg, Century 21, Kolossal Studio, Roade Recording, Wayne Finucan; in Saskatoon, Studio West; in Edmonton, Century 2, Damon Sound, Machine Shop; and in Vancouver, Little Mountain Studio, Mushroom, Ocean Sound, PBS Studios, Pinewood Productions.

5 THE RECORDS. The first recordings made in Canada were those made 17 May 1878 by the governor-general, Lord Dufferin, and his guests at Rideau Hall in Ottawa. Unlike Dufferin's, a recording made 10 years later, 11 Sep 1888, by another governor-general, Baron Stanley of Preston, has survived, if only in a copy made in 1935. One of the world's earliest extant recordings, for many years it was misattributed to Sir Henry Stanley,

the explorer of Africa. In fact, it was made at the Toronto Industrial Exhibition (*CNE) as a message of greeting to the US president and people. During the 1890s the new invention was put to use in the service of the study of native Indian music. Again Canada was one of the first countries in which this was done. Franz Boas and James A. Teit recorded in British Columbia in the early 1890s and Alexander T. *Cringan in Ontario 1897–1902. The recordings of the former were owned by the American Museum of Natural History in New York and transferred to the Archives of Traditional Music, Indiana U, Bloomington, Ind, and those of the latter were preserved at the National Museum of Man (see National Museums) in Ottawa.

The first Canadian commercial recordings, by the E. Berliner company in Montreal, were released in 1900. From the list of these 18-cm (7-inch) discs given in *Roll Back the Years* it is difficult to judge which were recorded in Montreal and which merely pressed there; it appears that the baritone Joseph *Saucier was the first Canadian to record for a Canadian label. (His biography, however, indicates that he spent the years 1897–1902 in Paris.) Other Canadians who made recordings in the first decades of the new century included Emma *Albani 1904–5, Henry *Burr 1903–ca 1930, Pauline *Donalda 1906–8, and Harry *Macdonough 1898–1919. Herbert L. *Clarke, US-born but raised in Canada, recorded as both a bandleader and a cornet soloist. The first Canadian ensemble to have recorded (1902) was the Belleville (Ont) Kilties Band (see Bands: 6 / Civilian bands) under William F. Robinson.

The tenors Burr and Macdonough, who embarked on careers as professional recording artists in the USA, were among the world's most prolific, each making several thousand discs for a variety of companies. Another Canadian who made recording his main career early in the century was Rosario *Bourdon, who began recording for Victor as a cellist in 1909 and two years later became co-director of music for Victor in the USA. By and large, those Canadians who made records did so outside their home country. Canada itself was mainly an importer of recordings, although there was a ready market for homegrown products in French Canada, which had musical traditions of its own. Before 1930 and in the early 1930s this market was supplied by recordings of the fiddling of Joseph *Allard, the singing of La *Bolduc, the folksinging of Conrad *Gauthier, the harmonica playing of Henri Lacroix, the singing of Charles *Marchand alone or with his Bytown Troubadours, and many others. Unfortunately Canadian pianists, violinists, and other concert virtuosos have left lamentably few recorded performances: there are a few discs by Kathleen *Parlow, Rosario Bourdon, and Boris *Hambourg, but the performances of Alfred *De Sève, Harry M. *Field, or Émiliano *Renaud are only some of those that do not appear to have been preserved. Renaud's teaching recordings, the Renaud-Phone Piano Method, Inc (1918), feature his demonstrations of the method but are not typical of his playing in a wider, artistic sense. The number of singers who recorded in the first three decades of the century is considerable, but usually even the opera stars, such as Pauline Donalda, Louise *Edvina, Sarah *Fischer, Jeanne *Gordon, Edward *Johnson, Irene *Pavloska, and Rodolphe *Plamondon, had to content themselves with singing popular parlour ballads rather than operatic arias, though Donalda, Edvina, Gordon, and Johnson did record a few of the latter. Other Canadian singers, among them the tenors Craig Campbell, Charles Dalberty, José *Delaquerrière, Paul *Dufault, Émile *Gour, Harold *Jarvis, Édouard *LeBel, and Geoffrey *O'Hara, and the baritones Arthur *Blight, Louis *Chartier, C.-É. Brodeur, J. Hervey Germain, Placide Morency, Frank Oldfield, Hector *Pellerin, and Joseph Saucier, specialized in the light concert repertoire. As the list shows, the field was a male preserve.

The same restriction to light-weight music applied to performances by symphony orchestras and to choirs. A few dance bands and other ensembles devoted to light music made records in the first third of the century. *Roll Back the Years* documents the discs made by the *Six Brown Brothers, Dave Caplan's Toronto Band, Jack Denny and his Mount Royal Hotel Orchestra, Henri *Miro's Orchestra (and Band), the Windsor Hotel Orchestra of Harold Leonard, and Guy *Lombardo and His Royal Canadians.

Canadians who made recordings during the 1930s include Les *Allen, Wilf *Carter, Omer *Dumas, Percy *Faith, Henri Lacroix, Lombardo, Will Osborne, Hank *Snow, and Isidore Soucy. However the Depression years and World War II dealt recording a blow. Discs featuring major Canadian concert ensembles such as the *Hart House String Quartet, the *TSO, the *Toronto Mendelssohn Choir, or the CSM (*MSO) were few, and were restricted to short items usually from the light repertoire. The 1941 recording of the Fauré *Requiem* by the *Disciples de Massenet and the *Montreal Festivals Orchestra under Wilfrid *Pelletier (see RCA Ltd) was a notable exception. However, the discs of La Bolduc, the *Alouette Vocal Quartet, and Father *Gadbois's La *Bonne Chanson had a devoted audience.

A new era for concert music was ushered in by the CBC's 1945 issue of an album featuring *Willan's *Piano Concerto* and *Champagne's *Suite canadienne*. The CBC continued its recording series, but most of the over 1300 releases were not intended for sale to the public. However, after World War II recording opportunities for Canadian performers, both at home and abroad, increased enormously, and in 1980 there were few of professional calibre whose performances had not been recorded. It is true, however, that the opportunities were greatest for those performing pop music (about 90 per cent of the records sold in Canada) and those having established contacts with US or European recording companies.

Nevertheless, several companies have endeavoured to bring out discs of concert music by Canadian performers. Beaver and Hallmark in 1952 were among the first, the former recording the Toronto Mendelssohn Choir, the latter helping to make known young performers of the day, including Forrester, Gould, *Marshall, and the *Festival Singers. Canada Baroque Records, Melbourne, Boot, and Aquitaine came into existence later. Concert-music releases by such enterprises, to be economically feasible, have had to be subsidized or alternated with releases of pop music (as in the case of Boot Records, the Canadian Talent Library, or the CAPAC-CAB recordings).

In Quebec in the early 1950s the chansonniers and other pop artists singing in French started to develop a market of their own. Robert *Charlebois, Pauline *Julien, Félix *Leclerc, Ginette *Reno, René *Simard, and Gilles *Vigneault, to name only a few, have made highly successful recordings bearing both Canadian and French labels (see also Chansonniers).

Recordings of country music in Canada began to appear in 1932, when Canadian Victor included Wilf Carter in its list of performers. For a discussion of Canadian recordings and record companies involved in the genre, see Country music: 1 / Early history and 3 / Media.

Formal recognition of achievement in the recording industry in Canada began in the mid-1960s, when the annual Juno Awards were established. Others (listed in *Awards: 1 / Honours bestowed) include the Big Country Award, the CMCouncil citation for the Canadian record of the year (offered in solo, chamber music, orchestral, choral, educational, folk, jazz, and composition categories, and for Canadians' recordings made in foreign countries), the Festival du disque, the ADISQ Recording and Showbusiness Awards, and the Moffat Awards. Commercial success in Canada brings a performer or group rewards in the form of 'gold records' (for 50,000 albums or 75,000 singles sold), 'platinum' (for 100,000 albums, 150,000 singles sold), double platinum (200,000 albums), triple platinum (300,000), etc. A special award, not won by a Canadian by July 1980, is awarded for the sale of one million units. Burton Cummings' *Dream of a Child* is the only Canadian recording to reach the triple platinum level by 1980. Double platinum awards went to Dan *Hill in 1978, Angèle *Arsenault and Hagood *Hardy in 1979, and Anne *Murray and Ginette Reno in 1980. *BTO, *Beau Dommage, *April Wine, André *Gagnon, *Rush, Trooper, *Chilliwack, *Harmonium, Prism, Carroll *Baker, Frank *Mills, Anne Murray, Triumph, and Heart each have earned more than two platinum awards. By July 1980 more than 45 Canadian performers or groups had earned gold records (some for several albums). The *Irish Rovers, and Claudja Barry were platinum winners for singles; over 20 other Canadian performers or groups won gold singles.

The dearth of recordings of Canadian compositions, apart from those made by the CBC, has been the subject of many discussions. In 1964, when the *CMCentre was compiling information on Canadian recordings (*Newsletters* no. 2 and 3, October and November 1964), only seven recordings of Canadian compositions were found to be available for retail purchase. The situation improved somewhat during the next 15 years, but, as a glance through the lists of works in *EMC* entries on Canadian composers will show, by 1980 only a small fraction of concert compositions was available on recordings which could be purchased. Those experts who had studied the production and distribution aspects concluded that only a subsidized program for the recording and dissemination of Canadian compositions would solve the problem. (A *Canada Council program of subsidies for recordings of Canadian music was suspended in 1979 but resumed in 1980.)

The recording of Canadian folk and native music sung by traditional or professional singers was in somewhat better shape than that of Canadian composers. A good deal was done in this field in the LP era by the US company Folkways Records, which had issued some 35 Canadian LPs by 1980, and by the CBC in the set of nine LPs *Canadian Folk Songs / Chansons folkloriques du Canada* issued with RCA in 1967 (RCI/RCA CS-100).

There have been occasional releases by other companies, and a vast amount of field-recorded folk music has become available to the student through the holdings at the National Museum of Man, the *Archives de folklore at *Laval U, and other archives. Some ethnic minorities have issued private printings of their folk music, often in harmonized arrangements for choir or instrumental ensemble. In 1980 there remained, however, a deplorable shortage of commercially distributed recordings of Indian and Inuit music.

Another area that awaited action in 1980 was the reissuing of out-of-print recordings of Canadian interest. One step in this direction was the release of *The Original Dumbells* (Aquitaine ELS 385), made in 1977 from discs in the collection of

Edward B. *Moogk. Another was the reissue of songs of La Bolduc on the Apex LPs ALF 1505 and ALF 1515. In this context, several Canadian reissue projects not specifically concerned with Canadian content deserve mention: the Rococo series, initiated by Ross, Court & Co, and the Cantilena series (begun 1966) compiled by John Stratton, both of which include Canadian singers; and the Masters of the Bow label of James Creighton's Historic Recording Society, started in the early 1970s.

Another important category of Canadian recordings is that devoted to educational aims. As early as 1918 Émiliano Renaud made a set of discs to accompany his course of piano study by correspondence. More recently Rachel *Cavalho's *Music for Young Pianists* was recorded by Hallmark, and Waterloo issued her 2-volume *Contemporary Canadian Music for Young Pianists*. The *New for Now / Dans le vent* series on the Dominion label devotes volume 1 to Canadian piano pieces played by Warren *Mould, with commentary by David *Ouchterlony; volume 2 to music for clarinet played by Avrahm *Galper and others; and volume 3 to music for the flute, played by Robert *Aitken.

6 COLLECTIONS. By 1980 a complete collection of commercially released recordings representing Canadian performers and/or compositions would contain about 50,000 items, not counting cartridge and cassette duplications of disc releases. The discography in *Roll Back the Years* lists 5500 such items prior to 1930 alone.

The largest collection of Canadian recordings in 1980 was that of the NL of C, which contained over 30,000. Of these, 19,593 were obtained (Sep 1969 to Jun 1980) on 'legal deposit,' ie, through a 1969 law requiring record companies to send the library a copy of each new release of Canadian interest. A collection of earlier recordings, dating back to 1900, was initiated as a Centennial project by Edward B. Moogk and deposited at the NL of C; historical records have been added from time to time through purchases, donations, and bequests, and there is a supplementary collection of private recordings.

Other large collections with substantial Canadian components are those of the CBC in Montreal and Toronto and of the *U of Toronto. The CMCentre's various regional libraries and the CBC program archives contain many non-commercial tapes of concert and broadcast performances, as do various folklore archives of field recordings of folk music. The Sound Archives of the PAC have specialized in collecting documentary recordings of political and historical rather than artistic interest.

See also Archives; Libraries; RPM MAPL Logo.

GENERAL BIBLIOGRAPHY

Beckwith, John. 'Recordings,' *Music in Canada*

Gould, Glenn. 'The prospects of recording,' *High Fidelity*, vol 16, Apr 1966

Stone, Kurt. 'Review of records,' *MQ*, vol 53, Jul 1967

Roberts, John. 'Communications media,' *Aspects of Music in Canada*

'How the CAPAC-CAB committee helps finance composers,' *CanComp*, 67, Feb 1972

LaClare, Leo. 'Lord Stanley and the demonstration of the Edison perfected phonograph in Canada, 1888,' *Recorded Sound*, 50–1, Apr–Jun 1973

Beaulieu, Michel. 'Sa richesse: 1500 vieux disques de folklore,' *Perspectives*, 3 Aug 1974

Littler, William. 'A history of Canadian music on thirteen records,' *CanComp*, 98, Feb 1975

MacMillan, Rick. 'Melbourne aims to keep recordings in catalogue,' *MSc*, 287, Jan–Feb 1976

Oram, Robert. 'Tax relief called keynote to sound investment,' 'Independent record trade not breaking any records,' Toronto *Globe and Mail*, 11 Sep 1976

Gingras, Claude. 'The Canadian presence in world production,' *Mcan*, 30, Nov 1976

Waxman, Ken. 'Be your own A & R man, producer, artist, distributor ... and flak,' *AudioScene Canada*, Jan 1977

Collins, Winston. 'The quiet boom in rock recording,' *Weekend Magazine*, 6 Aug 1977

Novak, Barbara. 'Heavenly sounds in the Music Church,' *Fugue*, Oct 1977

Labbé, Gabriel. *Les Pionniers du disque folklorique québécois 1920–1950* (Montreal 1977)

A Chartology of Canadian Popular Music January 1965–December 1976, compiled by Brendan J. Lyttle [Toronto 1977]

Welling, Ernie. 'New recording techniques,' *OpCan*, Summer 1978

Feihl, John, and Murphy, Brian. *List of Controversial and Obscure CanCon Material* (Ottawa 1978)

Guide du spectacle et du disque (Quebec 1978)

'Young Edmonton record industry thriving,' Saskatoon *Star Phoenix*, 7 Feb 1979

Guay, Caroline. 'Quoi de neuf pour les enfants,' *Mcan*, 39, Jun 1979

Hogan, Dorothy. 'What makes good children's records,' ibid

Moogk, Edward. 'Early recordings,' *Mcan*, 40, Sep 1979

'The vinyl solution,' *Maclean's*, 19 Nov 1979

Roberts, John P.L. 'A national shame,' *Mcan*, 41, Winter 1979–80

Whitney, Kathy. 'Canada recording studio guide: a comprehensive listing of recording studios across Canada,' *Canadian Musician*, vol 1, Sep–Oct 1979

Miller, Mark. 'Canada's do-it-yourself track to recording all that jazz,' *PfAC*, Spring 1980

Arcand, François. *L'Industrie de la musique*, 3 vols (Quebec 1980)

Roll Back the Years

Statistics Canada. *Production and Sales of Phonograph Records and Pre-Recorded Tapes in Canada / Production et ventes de disques de phonographe et rubans pré-enregistrés au Canada*, monthly reports (Ottawa 1973–)

PERIODICALS

Canadian Music and Trades Journal 1900–33

Phonograph Journal of Canada, fl 1923. Later *Phonograph Journal and Radio Trades* (no copies located)

RPM 1964–80

Sound 1970–6; *Sound Canada* 1976–

Sono: Sonorisation au Canada 1973–

AudioScene Canada 1974–

Record Week 1975–

Record Month 1976–

Music Market Canada 1977–

HK, EBM

REDDEN-BOWER, Finvola (Mhairi) (b Redden, m Bower). Folksinger, songwriter, b Timmins, Ont, 28 Nov 1940. She was named for an Irish folksong, 'Finvola the Gem of the Roe.' She was raised in Nova Scotia and learned many folksongs from her father, Fred, and studied voice, theory, and composition 1958–9 on a *Nova Scotia Talent Trust grant with Bernard *Diamant and others at the *McGill Cons.

The Redden Family (Finvola, her brother Angus, and their father) sang for presentations by Helen *Creighton. Finvola sang at the first two *Mariposa Folk Festivals (1961, 1962) and on concert-lecture tours with Creighton at various Canadian and US universities. She gave seven concerts at *Expo 67.

Among the few songs she wrote in the folk idiom are 'Boat Song' (arr Richard *Johnston) and 'My Cottage-O' (arr Kenneth *Peacock), both published by *Waterloo. An orchestration of the latter song was used in the *NFB production *Songs of Nova Scotia* (1958). MM

Red Ear of Corn. Ballet in two acts by Boris Volkoff. The music, composed in 1949 by John *Weinzweig, was commissioned by the Volkoff Canadian Ballet; it is scored for medium-sized orchestra. The ballet was premiered as part of the second Canadian Ballet Festival 2 Mar 1949 at the *Royal Alexandra Theatre, Toronto. Samuel *Hersenhoren conducted the orchestra.

The title refers to red ears of corn occasionally found by huskers in early Quebec. A red ear's finder was rewarded with the bride of his choice. In composing the music Weinzweig drew on elements of Indian and French-Canadian dance-song while maintaining his own sparse, incisive style.

Scenes from the ballet were filmed in 1950 by the *NFB, and the 'Barn Dance' was repeated that year by the Volkoff company at the third Canadian Ballet Festival. The three-movement suite extracted from the score and premiered in 1951 was performed by the *CBC SO in 1956 and 1959, the *NACO in 1969, the *CBC Winnipeg Orchestra in 1971, the *Atlantic SO in 1972, the *Edmonton SO in 1975, and the *TS in 1977. The 'Barn Dance' has been played alone many times. For recordings of the suite see Weinzweig Compositions. (CM)

'The Red River Valley.' One of the best known folksongs in the prairie provinces. It is also widely known in the USA, where it was thought to be a Texas adaptation of an 1896 popular song, 'In the Bright Mohawk Valley.' Later research by Edith *Fowke indicates that it was known in some five Canadian provinces before 1896 and that it was probably composed at the time of the Red River Rebellion of 1870.

The best-known form is short and generalized (a man is asked to 'Remember the Red River Valley and the girl who has loved you so true'), but earlier versions told of an Indian or half-breed girl lamenting the departure of her white lover, a soldier who came west.

Marius *Barbeau included the song (as 'Remember the Red River') in *Come A Singing!* (Ottawa 1947). A recording by Joyce *Sullivan is included in *Canadian Folk Songs: A Centennial Collection* (9-RCA Victor CS-100).

BIBLIOGRAPHY

Fowke, Edith. ' "The Red River Valley" re-examined,' *Western Folklore*, vol 23, Jul 1964

EF

REED, William. Organist, choirmaster, composer, b Montreal 9 Sep 1859, d Quebec City 2 Nov 1945. An organ pupil of R.-O. *Pelletier and Dominique *Ducharme, he won a scholarship at 19 to study at Keble College, Oxford. He is said to have been chosen organist of the college from among 30 contestants. Reed was organist-choirmaster 1884–8 at St Peter's Anglican Church in Sherbrooke, Que, 1888–9 at American Presbyterian and St John the Baptist churches in Montreal, 1899–1900 at St Andrew's Presbyterian Church in Toronto, and 1900–13 at Chalmers Presbyterian and St Andrew's Presbyterian churches in Quebec City. In 1901 he was guest organist, along with his pupil Henri *Gagnon, at the Buffalo Pan-American Exposition. Reed was afflicted by deafness early in his career and after 1913 had to confine himself to composing and writing for *The Etude* and other magazines.

Reed's major works include the Christmas cantata *The Message of the Angels* (Ditson 1910), the cantata *The Burden of the Cross* (Ditson or Presser 1912), the Easter cantata *The Resurrection and the Life* (Ditson 1911), and the *Grand Choeur in D* for organ (Vincent 1901), which Henri Gagnon considered 'one of the very best Canadian compositions' (letter to Helmut *Kallmann, 20 Jan 1954). His approximately 50 printed works also include shorter sacred and secular choral and organ pieces published by Curwen, J. Fischer, H.W. Gray, *Harris, *Nordheimer, Presser (or Ditson), G. Schirmer, A.P. Schmidt, Vincent, and *Whaley Royce.

Reed should not be confused with the English

violinist and composer William (Henry) Reed (1876–1942), the friend of Elgar. HK

Reed organs. Keyboard instruments which produce sounds by means of vibrating metal tongues ('reeds'), one for each note. The vibration is caused by air forced into or out of a set of two bellows. Related instruments are accordions, bagpipes, concertinas, and mouth organs. All have a common ancestor in the ancient Chinese sheng or cheng, a mouth organ with bamboo pipes and freely vibrating reeds.

Although the 15th-to-17th-century regal was a type of reed organ, the modern instrument originated in France as the *orgue expressif* (1810). The first reed organs used the air compression principle, but the suction method, developed in France about 1835, was refined in the USA some 20 years later, and the 'American organ' became the dominant type in North America.

The small reed organs built in Canada about the middle of the 19th century were called melodeons or cottage organs; the larger models, introduced after 1860, were known as harmoniums, cabinet organs, parlour organs, and, popularly, pump organs.

Among the first melodeon builders in Canada were William Townsend (Toronto, late 1840s), R.S. *Williams (Toronto, early 1850s), and probably Abner Brown (Montreal, fl 1848–74). The Montreal pipe-organ builder S.R. *Warren and the Guelph, Ont, brothers William and Robert *Bell were other pioneer reed organ makers. Their instruments commonly had keyboards of four or five octaves, two small horizontal bellows, and modest foot treadles to pump the bellows. Many came with detachable legs and thus were portable (early versions of the 'missionary' organ); others were larger and heavier, similar in style to the so-called square piano.

The American organ was built in Canada as early as 1865 by R.S. Williams and soon afterwards by W. Bell, D.W. *Karn, and many other companies. It had enlarged, vertical bellows and was encased in a solid desk-style cabinet, with drawstops over the keyboard. Until the 1870s it remained fairly simple in design and was less than four feet in height.

By the late 1870s, however, demand had grown and competition among manufacturers was increasingly keen; in Ontario, companies such as *Dominion (Bowmanville), *Doherty (Clinton), and *Thomas (Woodstock) entered into the production and assembling of reed organs. As a result, factories grew in size and number, though many were merely parts and assembly shops. While most were located in Ontario and in southern Quebec, a few could be found in New Brunswick and Nova Scotia and in Victoria, BC.

Equipment became more sophisticated and later instruments were built with more complex actions and elaborate case designs. Gradually the methods of voicing the reeds became less individual. Many such instruments resembled High Victorian furniture rather than organ consoles.

Cheaper, lighter, and requiring less maintenance than pianos, reed organs were at their most popular ca 1870–1910, and public demand was increased by highly exaggerated newspaper advertisements. Most models were intended for home use, though some were found in auditoriums. As early as the 1870s larger companies manufactured some two-manual models for church and orchestra use. In most instances these lacked foot pedals and required two operators – a player and someone to pump the handle located on one side of the instrument. Like single-manual reed organs,

An Uxbridge cabinet organ, late 19th century

these had less individuality of sound than pianos or pipe organs.

During the height of their popularity, thousands of reed organs were produced each year. Several manufacturers also built pianos and in this period reed organs and pianos often looked much alike. Some of the larger companies established factories and agencies in England and Australia. The advent of other forms of music-making and entertainment (the player piano after 1901 and, later, the gramophone and radio) led to a decline in popularity, and by the 1930s even the larger builders had sold their businesses or switched to dealing exclusively in pianos and/or gramophones. Only *Sherlock-Manning continued to build Doherty reed organs until the 1950s.

Fortunately, many individual instruments have survived and may be found in private homes and in museums such as Black Creek Pioneer Village, Toronto; the Brome County Historical Society, Knowlton, Que; the Bruce County Historical Museum, Southampton, Ont; the Fort Malden National Historic Park Museum, Amherstburg, Ont; the Ontario Pioneer Community Foundation, Kitchener, Ont; the Trent River Museum, Trent River, Ont; the Western Development museums in Yorkton and Saskatoon, Sask; and the Glenbow-Alberta Institute, Calgary.

Among experts on reed organs in Canada in the 1970s were William L. Keizer of Ottawa, Tim Classey of Toronto, and Jan van der Leest of Truro, NS.

LIST OF MANUFACTURERS

Acadia Organ Co, Bridgetown, NS, fl 1878–82
C.W. & F.M. Andrus (Andrews?), Picton, Ont, fl 1857
Andrus Brothers, London, Ont, ca 1859–74
Annapolis Organs, Annapolis, NS, fl 1880
John *Bagnall & Co, Victoria, BC, 1863–85 (harmoniums by 1882)
*Bell Organ and Piano Co (name changes), Guelph, Ont, 1864–1928
Daniel Bell Organ Co, Toronto, 1881–6
Berlin Organ Co, Berlin (Kitchener), Ont, fl 1880
G. Blatchford Organ Co, Galt, Ont, fl 1895; Elora, Ont, fl 1896
Abner Brown, Montreal, fl 1848–74
Canada Organ Co, London, Ont, ca 1865–?
Canada Organ Co, Toronto, 1875
Chute, Hall & Co, Yarmouth, NS, 1883–94
Compensating Pipe Organ Co, Toronto, fl 1900–10
Cornwall, Huntingdon, Que, before 1889–95 (see Pratte)
Cowley (or Conley) Church Organ Co, Madoc, Ont, fl 1890
Dales & Dalton, Newmarket, Ont, fl 1870
R.H. Dalton, Toronto, 1869–82?
Darley and Robinson (see Dominion Organ and Piano Co)
W. *Doherty & Co, Clinton, Ont, 1875–1920 (later owned by *Sherlock-Manning Co)
*Dominion Organ and Piano Co, Bowmanville, Ont, 1873–ca 1935
Eben-Ezer Organ Co, Clifford, Ont, 1935
Gates Organ and Piano Co, ca 1872–82 Malvern Square, NS; 1882–after 1885 Truro, NS
Goderich Organ Co, Goderich, Ont, fl 1890–1910
A.S. Hardy & Co, Guelph, Ont, fl 1874
John Jackson and Co, Guelph, Ont, fl 1872–3, 1880–3?
D.W. *Karn Co, Woodstock, Ont, ca 1867–1924
J. & R. Kilgour, Hamilton, Ont, ca 1872–88 as dealers, 1888–99 as piano and organ company
McLeod, Wood & Co, Guelph, Ont, fl 1869–72; later R. McLeod & Co, London, Ont, fl 1874–5
Malhoit & Co, Simcoe, Ont, fl 1875
Charles Mee, Kingston, Ont, fl 1870
John M. Miller (later Miller & Karn and D.W. Karn), Woodstock, Ont, fl 1867
Mudge & Yarwood Manufacturing Co, Whitby, Ont, 1873–?
New Dominion Organ Co, Saint John, NB, fl 1875
William Norris, North York, Ont, fl 1867
Ontario Organ Co, Toronto, 1884
Oshawa Organ and Melodeon Manufacturing Co, 1871–3 (see Dominion Organ and Piano Co)
*Pratte, Montreal, 1889–1926 (harmoniums built ca 1912)
Rappe & Co, Kingston, Ont, ca 1871–ca 1887
J. Reyner, Kingston, Ont, ca 1871–ca 1885
Sherlock-Manning Organ Co, London, Ont, later Clinton, Ont, 1902–78 (reed organs built 1902–1950s)
J. Slown, Owen Sound, Ont, fl 1871–89
David W. & Cornelius D. Smith, Brome, Que, 1875–?
Smith & Scribner, Chatham, Ont, fl 1864–5
Frank Stevenson, North York, Ont, fl 1867
Edward G. *Thomas Organ Co, Woodstock, Ont, 1875–?
James Thornton & Co, Hamilton, Ont, fl 1871–89
Toronto Organ Co, Toronto, 1880
William Townsend, Toronto, fl late 1840s
*Uxbridge Organ Co, Uxbridge, Ont, fl 1872–1909
S.R. *Warren and Son, Toronto, fl 1878–ca 1910
Elijah West, West Farnham, Que, fl 1860–75
Thomas W. White & Co, Hamilton, Ont, 1863–after 1869
R.S. *Williams & Sons, Toronto, 1854–ca 1952 (reed organs built in 19th century only)
Wilson & Co, Sherbrooke, Que
Wood, Powell & Co, Guelph, Ont, fl 1883–4
Woodstock Organ Factory, Woodstock, Ont, fl 1876 (see D.W. Karn) (TC, HK)

REESOR, (Frederick) **Alan** (Edwin). Teacher, organist, conductor, composer, b Markham (near Toronto) 14 Jun 1936; B MUS (Toronto) 1957, M MUS (ESM, Rochester) 1965. He studied piano with Gertrude Jackson and organ with Wilfred Powell and John McIntosh. After several years as a high-school music teacher and conductor in Oshawa, Ont, he settled in Charlottetown and served 1970–6 as chairman of the Dept of Music, *U of Prince Edward Island. Conductor of the university's choirs till 1973, he also conducted the Prince Edward Island SO 1970–6 and became the organist-choirmaster of St Peter's Anglican Cathedral in 1971. His compositions include *Variations on an Original Theme* for string orchestra (1963), two *Hymn Preludes* (Thompson 1967), and music for the Ukrainian-Canadian film *The Cruel Dawn* (1967). CF

Regina. Capital city of Saskatchewan. Originally called 'Pile of Bones,' from the Cree word Wascana, it became the capital of the Northwest Territories in 1882 with the coming of the railway and was renamed Regina after Queen Victoria. It was incorporated as a town in 1883 and as a city in 1903, when its population was almost 6000. It was designated the provincial capital in 1905. Its population had risen to 35,000 by 1923 and ca 150,000 by 1980.

During its first 10 years, Regina could claim a Musical Club, a Musical and Literary Society, a Glee Club, a Minstrel Club, a North West Mounted Police Band, and several church choirs. The community also supported a brass band, which in 1886 had 14 instruments. A Choral Society, formed in 1889, held weekly rehearsals and attempted to provide 'free instruction in vocal music and to assist at charitable entertainments.' Ten years later the Musical and Dramatic Society staged *The Pirates of Penzance* but ran into difficulties over the non-payment of performing rights. In 1899, also, a small troupe from the *Metropolitan Opera brought *The Chimes of Normandy* to Regina. Emma *Albani included Regina in her farewell tour of 1906.

Frank L. *Laubach, a professional musician who arrived from Scotland in 1904, was the undisputed leader in the city's musical affairs until his retirement in 1922. He founded the Regina Philharmonic Society in 1905 and the Regina Orchestral Society, which first performed in 1908 and was succeeded by the Regina Choral and Orchestral Society, in 1919 (first concert 1920). In 1908, with F.W. Chisholm of Indian Head and other musicians, he founded the *Saskatchewan Music Festival, the second such competition to be established in Canada. The first year (1909) it attracted 25 entries and more than 200 participants. Also in 1909, Laubach directed the Regina Operatic Society in performances to inaugurate the Regina Theatre. In 1913 Laubach and Charles Shrimpton wrote and produced a three-act musical comedy, *The Mystic Light*.

The Regina Male Chorus Club, formed under A.L. Wheatley in 1911, gave its first concert in 1912. Another choir, the Queen City Classics, was organized in 1920 by John Henry. The *Regina Musical Club, founded in 1907 as the Regina Women's Morning Musical Club, and the *Orpheus Club, founded in 1915 as the Eva *Clare Studio Club, promoted the study as well as the performance of music. Throughout the first half of the 20th century the needs of Regina's musicians were catered for by William George Franklin Scythes (b Thornton, Ont, 1876, d Regina 12 Dec 1961), who in 1907 established the W.G.F. Scythes Co music store.

When Laubach retired, in 1922, the Regina Choral and Orchestral Society split into three groups: the *Regina SO under W. Knight *Wilson, the Regina Choral Society under George *Coutts, and the *Regina Male Voice Choir (formerly Male Chorus Club) under Dan A. *Cameron. In 1924 these groups merged again as the Regina Philharmonic Assn. In 1926 the Regina SO separated again from the Philharmonic Assn. Wilson, its conductor 1923–41 and 1945–55, also conducted the orchestra which accompanied films at the Capitol Theatre, taught violin at the Regina Cons (*Cons of Music, U of Regina), and formed a junior orchestra at the conservatory. In 1927 Wilson formed the Regina Orchestral Society and instituted its subscription concert series. *Darke Hall was the orchestra's home 1929–70. In 1970 it moved into the newly opened *Saskatchewan Centre of the Arts.

Cameron conducted the Regina Male Voice Choir 1923–46 and was head of the voice department at the Regina Cons 1923–39. In addition, he conducted the Bach Ladies' Choir and Regina Ladies' Choir. Lionel Allen succeeded him 1946–59 as conductor of the Male Voice Choir.

During the 1920s and 1930s the CPR sponsored music programs in the Hotel Saskatchewan. The Great West Canadian Folksong-Folkdance and Handicraft Festival of 1929 also was sponsored by the CPR. (See CPR Festivals.) In these years and later, the Celebrity Concert Series (see Fred M. Gee) sponsored by the Rotary Club brought to Regina Marian Anderson, Clara Butt, Richard Crooks, Jascha Heifetz, Jeanette MacDonald, Tertius Noble, Jan Peerce, Lily Pons, Leontyne Price, Risë Stevens, Lawrence Tibbett, and others. The Kinsmen Club, the Regina Registered Teachers' Assn (founded 1925; see SRMTA), and the University Women's Club also supported musical activities. The Rotary Club began sponsorship of a Regina Festival of Christmas Carols ca 1940 at Knox-Metropolitan United Church.

The Regina Queen City Band, founded in 1943 by Mrs A.B. Mossing, was taken over by the Lions Club in 1946 and renamed the Regina Lions' Junior Band. By 1976 it encompassed six bands with some 500 participants. The Mossing family continued its support and also subsidized other bands. D'Arcy Mossing, the founding music director of the Regina Separate School Band (formed in 1950), also was director 1955–7 of the Lions Band. Another Mossing – Robert L. – became director of the latter in 1970.

Regina's most important music school has been the Cons of Music, U of Regina (Regina Cons), founded in 1911 as part of Regina College (later University). Staff members such as W. Knight Wilson and Dan A. Cameron made important contributions to every aspect of the city's musical life. Richard Watson, director in the early 1950s, also founded the *Regina Conservatory Opera in 1951. Howard *Leyton-Brown, appointed director of the conservatory in 1955, had begun conducting the Conservatory Chamber Orchestra (later the *U of Regina Chamber Orchestra) in 1953 and also conducted the Regina SO 1960–71. Barbara *Cass-Beggs, who taught 1955–64 at the conservatory, formed the *Saskatchewan Junior Concert Society (originally named the Regina Junior Concert Society), which toured with a series of concerts for children. In 1962 an Inter-collegiate Chorus and an Inter-collegiate Orchestra were formed under Lloyd Blackman. The 1965 *CFMTA Conference, organized by Dorothy *Bee, was held in Regina. The Regina SO Chamber Music Series at the Globe Theatre and the Masterpiece Series sponsored by the Mendel Art Gallery provided another dimension of concert life in the 1970s.

The multicultural Mosaic Festival and a German Oktoberfest were established as annual festivals – the former in 1964, the latter in 1975. The Regina Folk Arts Festival began in 1969; the Saskatchewan Highland Festival, a piping and dancing competition, in 1970 at Fort Qu'Appelle.

Among Regina-area natives active in music have been Gordie *Brandt, the composer Peter Clements, Helen *Dahlstrom, Nina *Dempsey, the bass-baritone Norman Farrow, Edith *Fowke, Barbara *Franklin, Gaelyne *Gabora, Audrey *Johannesen, Muriel *Kerr, Ethel Codd *Luening, the pianist Gary Kosloski, and June *Kowalchuk.

BIBLIOGRAPHY

'Banner of music rides high in fortunes fair or foul,' Regina *Leader-Post*, 31 Aug 1940

Cameron, Dan A. 'Twenty-one years of music,' Regina *Leader-Post*, 25 Nov 1950

– 'Music and drama in Regina,' *50 Years of Progress 1903–1953* [Regina 1953]

(WLB)

Regina Conservatory. See Conservatory of Music, University of Regina.

Regina Conservatory Opera. Founded in 1951 by Richard Watson, director of the Regina Cons (*Cons of Music, U of Regina) and a former member of the D'Oyly Carte Opera. Howard *Leyton-Brown became conductor in 1952 and producer in 1955. The productions were accompanied by the Regina Cons String Orchestra, augmented as necessary, and the company presented one or two operas each season, including *Faust, Così fan tutte, Don Giovanni, Carmen, Amahl and the Night Visitors, Dido and Aeneas*, and two commissioned works, Frank *Thorolfson's *The Qu'Appelle River Legend* in 1956 and Jack *Behrens' *The Lay of Thrym* in 1968. The final full production staged by the company was *Hansel and Gretel*, given in *Darke Hall in January 1969. WLB

Regina Male Voice Choir. Successor to the Regina Male Chorus Club founded in 1911 by A.L. Wheatley. At the time of its first concert, 1 Apr 1912, that choir numbered 29. When in 1914 many of its members joined the armed forces, it was forced to disband. The attempt to revive the club produced instead, in 1920, the mixed chorus known as the Regina Choral Union. The male section of the choir, led by George *Coutts in 1922 and Dan *Cameron in 1923, competed in the provincial music festivals and became the Regina Male Voice Choir in 1923. It gave its first annual spring concert in 1924. This choir, the Regina Ladies' Choir, and the Bach Ladies' Choir sang together 1932–8 as the Regina Philharmonic Society, though the three groups continued to perform independently as well.

Cameron was the conductor of the Regina Male Voice Choir until 1945. Subsequent conductors included Lionel Allen 1946–60, Ernest A. Moore 1960–3, David Graham 1963–5, Allen Wortman 1965–6, William Otis 1966–70, R.A. Wetzstein 1970–2, Tudor Davies and Raymond Hoffman 1972–3, Peter Pasklar 1973–5, David Escott 1975–8, Larry Kloponshak in 1978, and Ken Danylczuk 1978–9, succeeded by Charles Willett.

In 1946 the choir began to present a Saskatchewan musician as soloist at each annual concert. Among those chosen have been William *Morton (1946), Erica Zentner (*Davidson) (1947), Patricia Grant Lewis (*Elliot) (1948), Barbara *Franklin (1950), Irene *Salemka (1952 and 1959), Jon *Vickers (1953), Marilyn Duffus (1955), Lesia Zubrack (1956), Helen Hájnik (1960), Audrey *Johannesen (1961), Nancy Greenwood (1964), Catherine Vickers (1970), and Patricia Knox (1979).

Over the years the choir has performed at memorial services, conventions, and festivals and has given concerts in Regina and throughout southern Saskatchewan.

BIBLIOGRAPHY

'Male Voice Choir has proud record,' Regina *Leader-Post*, 6 Sep 1969

(WLB, VH)

The Regina Musical Club. Founded in 1907 by Mrs Forget and its first president, Mrs R. Rimmer, as the Regina Women's Morning Musical Club to promote music and foster the careers of young artists in the community. As the constitution and policies changed, the name became the Regina Women's Musical Club in the early 1950s and, later, the Regina Musical Club, open to all. Membership has ranged from 100 (1913) to 1000 (1945).

The club's concerts, held initially at the YMCA and latterly at *Darke Hall, have varied from solo and chamber recitals to choral performances and opera. Lois *Marshall, Kathleen *Parlow, John

Charles Thomas, Jon *Vickers, Portia *White, and others have performed for the club and the *COC touring company has been presented under its sponsorship. In 1970 it became the host for *JMC concerts in Regina. With the *CFMTA it has co-sponsored a young artists' series. The Regina Musical Club has provided scholarships for the Regina Music Festival and for the *U of Regina. WLB

The Regina Symphony Orchestra. Community orchestra founded as the Regina Orchestral Society by Frank *Laubach. Its inaugural concert was given 3 Dec 1908. Becoming the Regina Choral and Orchestral Society in 1919 and merging briefly with the *Regina Male Voice Choir as the Regina Philharmonic Assn in 1924, it returned to independent status as the Regina Symphony in 1926, presenting its first regular season 1927–8 under W. Knight *Wilson.

For many years an orchestra of 50 players, it grew to 70 in the 1960s. Its home was *Darke Hall 1929–70 and became the *Saskatchewan Centre of the Arts in 1970. It has appeared occasionally in schools and on tour in southern Saskatchewan.

Preferring the traditional repertoire to the contemporary, the orchestra nevertheless has performed works by Murray *Adaskin, Robert *Fleming, Pierre *Mercure, Godfrey *Ridout, and John *Weinzweig, and it gave the premiere 24 Aug 1970 of Adaskin's *Fanfare*.

Regina Symphony conductors have been Laubach 1908–22, Wilson 1923–41 and 1945–55, Arthur *Collingwood 1941, John Thornicroft 1955–8, Paul *McIntyre 1959–60, Howard *Leyton-Brown 1960–71, Boris *Brott 1971–3, Ted Kardash 1973–4, Timothy Vernon 1975–6, and guest conductors 1976–8; Gregory *Millar took over the post in 1978.

In 1976 65 players were engaged for 14 concerts over a 30-week season and at that time most were teachers and students for whom the orchestra was a part-time occupation. Five woodwinds were full-time employees, however, and their duties included many in-school and chamber concerts. In May 1979 the Regina SO joined the *U of Regina in a production of *Madama Butterfly* with Maria *Pellegrini in the title role and Millar as music director. It was presented in Regina and Saskatoon.

BIBLIOGRAPHY

Leyton-Brown, H. 'Regina Symphony Orchestra,' *CanComp*, 28, Apr 1968

'Great expectations await the Regina Symphony,' *OCan*, vol 6, Dec–Feb 1979 (WLB)

REGNAUD, Denis. Organist, harpsichordist, teacher, b St-Hyacinthe, Que, 6 Jan 1945; B MUS (Montreal) 1966, M MUS harpsichord (Vienna Academy) 1971, M MUS organ (Vienna Academy) 1972. He took lessons in violin and then organ and harmony at the *Institut Nazareth, Montreal, and continued his studies 1963–6 at the *U of Montreal, chiefly with Bernard *Lagacé. He was awarded a scholarship in 1967 by the Montreal Austrian Society and worked until 1972 at the Vienna Academy with Isolde Ahlgrimm (harpsichord) and Anton Heiller (organ). He returned to Montreal briefly in 1970 to participate in the *Ars Organi festival. He played in May 1971 in a series of recitals on Bruckner's organ in St-Florian, Austria, appeared that October at the International Festival of Young Organists in Biel, Switzerland, and gave four organ recitals for schools in the French département of Jura. In December 1972 he performed on the 18th-century organ of San Jacopo Church in Florence. That year he began to teach at the U of Montreal, where he was put in charge of the baroque music workshop; he also taught 1972–3 at the St-Laurent Cegep (Montreal) and the *U of Ottawa. In 1976 he was appointed organist at St Patrick's Church, Montreal. He has given organ and harpsichord recitals on CBC radio and in several towns in Quebec and Ontario. IP-C

REID, Robert. Tenor, choir conductor, business executive, b Toronto 30 Jun 1928. He studied 1947–50 with Arthur Bartlett and 1950–60 with Dorothy *Allan Park. He won the Senior Silver Tray at the Toronto *Kiwanis Festival in 1952. He was a soloist with the *Toronto Mendelssohn Choir in performances of *Messiah* and the *St Matthew Passion* in 1954 and at Carnegie Hall with the New York Oratorio Society in *Messiah* in 1955. That same year he sang in *Acis and Galatea* at the *Stratford Festival.

During the 1950s Reid made guest appearances with the *Bach-Elgar Choir of Hamilton, the Bach Society of Toronto (under Sir Ernest *MacMillan), the *Halifax SO and Choral Society, the *Hamilton and Toronto Philharmonic orchestras, the *Kitchener-Waterloo SO and *Philharmonic Choir, the *Ottawa Choral Society, and the Sudbury SO and Choral Society. He sang also with the *Eaton Operatic Society under Godfrey *Ridout. Reid was heard frequently on radio in recital and in oratorios and operettas, including CBC presentations of *The Pirates of Penzance* and *The Mikado*. He also conducted Gilbert & Sullivan productions in Toronto.

In 1961 Reid moved to Belleville, Ont, where he was director 1961–78 of the Bridge Street United Church Choir. During the 1960s and 1970s there, he conducted the *St Matthew Passion, Messiah, The Creation, Elijah*, the Brahms and Fauré *Requiems*, Elgar's *Choral Ode*, and other large works, with choirs of up to 120 voices, soloists from Toronto, and instrumentalists from Kingston. He has continued singing and has appeared in performances of the *St Matthew Passion* in London, Ont, and at St George's Cathedral, Kingston. NM, DS

REILLY, Tommy (Thomas Rundle). Harmonica player, composer, teacher, b Guelph, Ont, 21 Aug 1919. His father, Captain James Reilly (1886–1956), a trumpeter and violinist, led (in Guelph, 1920–5) one of the first jazz bands in Canada. The younger Reilly studied violin at 8 and began playing harmonica at 11 as a member of his father's Elmdale Harmonica Band. The band won several *CNE competitions and Reilly won medals for solo playing in southern Ontario festivals. In 1935 the family moved to London. Though Reilly had played in England 1935–7 and continental Europe 1937–9, it was not until his arrest (while studying at the Leipzig Cons) and subsequent internment 1939–45 in prisoner-of-war camps that he developed his virtuosity on the harmonica. Returning to London in 1945 Reilly began parallel careers as a concert soloist, a popular BBC radio and TV performer, and a studio musician-composer.

One of the leading exponents of the harmonica as a concert instrument, Reilly has performed with many European symphony orchestras and in recital. In the absence of a concert repertoire for the instrument he has transcribed works by Bach, Chopin, Mozart, Smetana, Sarasate, and others. Various composers have written works for Reilly, including Michael Spivakovsky (*Concerto*, 1951), Robert *Farnon (*Prelude and Dance for Harmonica and Orchestra*), James Moody (several works with orchestra and others with string quartet or strings and woodwinds), Matyas Seiber (*Old Scottish Air for Harmonica, Strings and Harp*), and Richard Rodney Bennett (*Suite* for harmonica and piano).

Reilly himself has composed short harmonica pieces, incidental music for the stock-music libraries of Chappell and other companies, and theme music for BBC TV and radio. He also has recorded music for the sound-tracks of many US and European films and for several US TV series. In addition to writing textbooks for harmonica, Reilly gave master classes 1966–8 at the Städtische Musikschule in Trossingen, Germany, and taught 1967–71 at the Tommy Reilly International Club in Surrey, attracting pupils from around the world. In 1967 he designed a concert harmonica, later manufactured by Hohner as the Silver Concerto Chromonica.

WRITINGS

Play Like the Stars (London 1952)
Progressive Exercises (London 1954)
Studies for the Chromatic Harmonica (London 1954)
Tommy Reilly Harmonica Course (London 1969, Oslo 1971)

DISCOGRAPHY

The Life of Reilly. J. Moody and His Players. (1965). World Sound T 541
Chromonica Rallye mit Tommy Reilly. (1967). Concorde ORL-ST 5002
Colours of My Life. (1968). Poly 184 107
Melody Fair. Kai Warner Singers and Orchestra. (1969). Poly 222 002
Latin Harmonica. Kai Warner and His Orchestra. (1970). Poly 184 367
The Harmonica of Tommy Reilly: Scarlatti – Bach – Rachmaninoff – Farnon – et al. Ørnung pf, str quar. (1971). Poly 2382 002
The Music of Robert Farnon: Farnon *Prelude and Dance for Harmonica and Orchestra*. R. Farnon Orchestra. (1971). Poly 2382 008
Wand'rin' Star. (1971). Poly 2384 029
Tommy Reilly Plays Fried Walter. Berlin Studio Players, Walter cond. (1971). Apollo Sound AS 1008
Harmonica Parisien. T. Reilly and His Orchestra. (1972). Poly 2382 016
Warm Latin Sounds. T. Reilly and His Orchestra. (1975). Philips 6382 081
The Silver Sound of the Harmonica: Jacob *Quintet for Harmonica and String Quartet* – Moody *Quintet for Harmonica and String Quartet*. Hindar Quar. (1975). Argo ZDA 206
Music for Two Harmonicas: Moody – Jacob – Tausky – Reilly – et al. S. Groven hmca, Armon Str Quar, others. (1976). Poly 2922 008
Tommy Reilly, Harmonica: Moody – Jacob – Tausky – Vaughan Williams. Academy of St Martin-in-the-Fields, Marriner dir. (1977). Argo ZRG 856
Also many singles (78s and 45s), beginning in 1951, for Parlophone, Metronome, Oriole, Fontana, Philips, and other labels, as soloist with various popular orchestras, and two instruction LPs for Hohner MM

REIMER, William. Bass-baritone, b Chilliwack, near Vancouver, 8 Apr 1931. He grew up in Yarrow, BC, and studied voice at the *Mennonite Brethren Bible College in Winnipeg. At the 1960 *Vancouver International Festival he sang Noye in Britten's *Noye's Fludde*. He enrolled at the Music Academy in Detmold, Germany, in 1961 and graduated in 1964. In 1966 he began teaching at the State School of Music in Hanover.

Reimer's voice is particularly suited to Lieder and oratorio. He has performed with the Vancouver and Winnipeg CBC orchestras and with the *Toronto Mendelssohn Choir. He is soloist in the Philips European recordings of Bach's *Missae breves* (LY 839 799) and *Cantatas* BWV 74 and 147 (Phi 6500386) and Telemann's *Frühlingskantate* (Phi 6500079), *Trauerkantate* (Phi 6500078), and *Mutzenbecherkantate* (Phi 6500074). HR

REINER, Charles. Pianist, accompanist, teacher, b Budapest 7 Apr 1924, naturalized Canadian 1956. In 1947 he received a concert diploma from the Franz Liszt Academy after studies with Arpad Hanak, Arnold Szekely, and Bela Böszörmenyi-Nagy. He won the 1948 International Competition for Musical Performers in Geneva and in 1949 was awarded first prize for virtuosity by the Geneva Cons, where he had studied with Dinu Lipatti and Louis Hiltbrandt. After performing in various European centres he won first prize (1950) in a United-Nations-sponsored competition of the International Refugees Organization. He moved to Montreal in 1951 and made his recital debut 27 Nov 1952 at the Ritz-Carlton Hotel. In an impressive career as accompanist he has performed with Colette *Boky, Hyman *Bress, Maureen *Forrester, Antonio Janigro, Arthur *LeBlanc, Igor Oistrakh, Joan *Patenaude, Louis *Quilico, Jean-Pierre Rampal, Ruggiero Ricci, Joseph *Rouleau, Henryk Szeryng, Richard *Verreau, and others. Reiner has also given recitals in North America, Europe, and Africa, and has appeared innumerable times on radio and TV. He was a founding member of the Canadian Piano Quartet (1963–6) – with Morry Kernerman (violin), Robert Verebes (viola), and Dorothy Bégin (cello) – and of the *Musica Camerata Montreal in 1971. He began teaching at *McGill U in 1955 and taught 1965–7 at the Cons de Trois-Rivières. He has taught at the *École normale de musique in Montreal as well. His pupils have included André-Sébastien *Savoie and Mikael Eliasen.

DISCOGRAPHY

Mann *Sonata, Op 17* – Glinka *Sonata in D Minor* for viola and piano. Verebes va. (1978). RCI 459

Szeryng Plays the Music of Fritz Kreisler. Mer SR 90348/Philips 6833 164

Tartini *The Devil's Trill*. Szeryng vn. (1963). RCA 1037

Treasures for the Violin: Bartók – Debussy – Brahms – Rimsky-Korsakov – Gluck – et al. Szeryng vn. (1964). Mer SR 90367/Philips 6833 193

Vitali – Tartini-Kreisler – Gluck-Kreisler – Schumann-Heifetz – Wieniawski – et al. Szeryng vn. (1960). RCA LM 2421

See also D. Brott; J. Bruyère; A. Fine; and A. Garami; and also the Discographies for Bress; LeBlanc; Patenaude; and Rouleau. GP

Religions and music. The many religions of Canada are touched upon in numerous articles in *EMC*. The Christian churches have been centres of activity for amateur musicians and providers of employment for professional ones throughout much of Canada's history; and though the large amateur choirs which have played so important a role in Canadian concert life ostensibly are unconnected to churches, the ranks of most of them have been filled by church-trained choristers, and the leaders in many cases have been career church musicians. Compositions to religious texts, whether for use in places of worship or for performance in concert, form easily the largest part of Canadian choral music. Relevant genres, forms, rituals and practices, and historic publications, are treated in the following *EMC* entries:

Anthems, motets, and psalms
Cantata
Choral music
Choral singing
Christmas
Easter, Lent, and the Passion
Graduel romain
Grand chantre
Hymnbooks, protestant
Hymnology
Hymn singing
Masses
Oratorio performance
Oratorios, Canadian (composition and performance)
Organ music
Plainsong
Te Deum laudamus
Union Harmony

For specific compositions on religious texts see:
An Apostrophe to the Heavenly Hosts (Willan)
Brébeuf (Willan)
Caïn (Contant)
Jean le Précurseur (Couture)

The religious music of denominations, sects, and national groups is discussed in the following entries:

Amish
Anglican church music
Arabic music
Children of Peace
Doukhobors
Greek Orthodox church music
Hutterites
Jewish cantors
Jewish religious music
Lutherans
Mennonites
Moravian missions in Labrador
Protestant church music
Roman Catholic church music
Salvation Army
(See also articles on individual countries.)

Religious music education is discussed in the following entries:

Choir schools
Maîtrise du Chapitre de Québec
Missionaries in the 17th century
Schola cantorum
Singing schools
Ward Method
(See also Royal Canadian College of Organists.)

RELYEA, Gary (Weston). Baritone, b Highland Park, Mich, 9 Apr 1942, naturalized Canadian 1972. He studied piano at the U of Michigan and voice 1967–71 with Howell *Glynne and Louis *Quilico at the *U of Toronto.

After his professional debut in 1970 as Pilate in *The St Matthew Passion* with the *NACO, Relyea continued to sing at the *NAC in Festival Canada (*Festival Ottawa) productions, including Strauss' *Ariadne auf Naxos* (1977; Harlequin) and Britten's *A Midsummer Night's Dream* (1978; Demetrius). With the *COC he made his debut (1972) as Charles La Tour in *Symonds' *The Spirit of Fundy*, and he has sung Monterone in *Rigoletto* (1973), Germont in *La Traviata* (1978), and other roles.

Relyea first sang at the *Guelph Spring Festival in 1971 and subsequently appeared there in such roles as Lockitt in *The Beggar's Opera* (1976) and Dr Shadow in the premiere of Charles *Wilson's *Psycho Red* (1978). At the *Stratford Festival he appeared as The Man in the premiere (1973) of Raymond *Pannell's *The Exiles* and Harlequin in *Ariadne auf Naxos* and sang the title role in Jean *Vallerand's *Le *Magicien* (1975).

Relyea has sung with the *Atlantic SO (1973), the *Hamilton Philharmonic (1973, 1976), the *TS (Stravinsky's *Pulcinella* 1976, Bach's *Magnificat* and Stravinsky's *Les Noces* 1977), the NACO (Britten's *War Requiem* 1976), and the *MSO and *Winnipeg SO (Brahms' *A German Requiem* 1976–7 season). He has been a soloist with the *Ottawa Choral Society (the title role in *Elijah* and Christus in the *St Matthew Passion*), the *Festival Singers, and the *Toronto Mendelssohn Choir.

With *New Music Concerts in Toronto Relyea sang in Ligeti's *Nouvelles Aventures* in 1972 and premiered Serge *Garant's *Rivages* 15 May 1976, also touring Europe with the group that year to sing the Garant work. In Toronto in 1975 Relyea was a soloist in the premiere of *Anhalt's *La Tourangelle*. He sang in Montreal for the first time 8 Feb 1973 in an *SMCQ performance of *Nouvelles Aventures*. In 1977 he created the role of the father in the TV opera **Aberfan*. MM

RENAUD, Émiliano. Pianist, composer, organist, teacher, b St-Jean-de-Matha, near Montreal, 26 Jun 1875, d Montreal 3 Oct 1932. He studied piano with his mother, later with Paul *Letondal, and still later with Dominique *Ducharme. He was organist at 12 at the Collège de Montréal and held the same post at Ste-Marie College, where he continued his academic studies. Engaged in 1892 as a teacher and choirmaster in Church Point, NS, he returned to Montreal the following year. He was appointed organist at St Mary's Church in Oswego, NY, in October 1896, but returned to Montreal the following May. In September 1897 he left again, this time to work in Vienna and then in Berlin with Mme Varet-Stepanoff, a pupil of Leschetizky.

Renaud returned in 1899 to Montreal and was the soloist 20 Apr 1900 with the *Goulet *MSO in *Windsor Hall, playing his own *Concertstück* for piano and orchestra; a further performance was given by the same ensemble in January 1903. Reviewing the premiere, the critic in the *Montreal Daily Star* of 21 Apr 1900 wrote: 'He plays with virility and great bravura. In his composition he has fulfilled the requirements of modern musical thought in that he has had something of value to express and has expressed it cleanly and lucidly. This young artist is full of promise and possesses an interesting personality.'

Renaud became an outstanding virtuoso, specializing in the romantic repertoire. He gave recitals in Canada, the USA, and England. After three appearances in Windsor Hall in March 1904 he was hailed as the Canadian Paderewski. He began teaching at the *McGill Cons in 1904, the year of its opening. Among his pupils were J.D. Archambault, Alfred *Laliberté, and Maurice *Rousseau. He taught ca 1908 at the Indianapolis Cons and made a North American tour with the singer Emma Calvé. He resided for a time in Boston, and in 1915 began a career in New York as a performer and teacher. In 1918 he launched a method of teaching piano with the aid of records, the Renaud-Phone Piano Method, Inc, endorsed by Paderewski and the US critic James Gibbons Huneker.

Renaud returned to Montreal in 1921 and there devoted himself to teaching and composition until his death. In the fall of 1924 he gave three recitals at Wigmore Hall, London, performing Schumann's *Études symphoniques* and *Fantasia Op. 17*, Mendelssohn's *Variations sérieuses*, Brahms' *Variations on a Theme by Handel*, and his own transcriptions of songs by Schubert, Schumann, Wolf, and Tchaikovsky. In 1925 he presented an elementary 30-lesson piano course on the *La Presse* radio station CKAC. For this he also published a book of lessons and exercises (Montreal 1925). He gave a recital of his own works 17 Feb 1930 at the Ritz-Carlton Hotel in Montreal, with the tenor Rodolphe *Plamondon and the violinist Émile *Taranto. Among the works heard were *Prelude, Fugue and Chorale; Sept variations sur un thème original; Concerto without orchestra* and other piano pieces; a *Romance* and a *Sonata* in one movement for violin and piano; and some songs.

In addition to a great number of piano pieces, songs, and chamber music, Renaud's output includes *Djymko*, a 'musical farce' in two acts (prologue and two tableaux) for which he also wrote the libretto. Several works were published by Ditson, White Smith, and New Music in the USA, by *Archambault in Canada, and in 1922 in the magazine *MusiCanada*, of which he was director and president. His compositions were recorded by Brunswick and *Starr (see *Roll Back the Years*); *Prelude, Fugue and Chorale* has been recorded by

Émiliano Renaud

Josephte *Dufresne. Articles on Émiliano Renaud appeared in several journals, including *L'Art musical* (Oct 1898), *Le *Passe-Temps* (17 Mar 1900), and *Le *Canada musical* (17 May 1919).

BIBLIOGRAPHY

Comte, Gustave. 'Comment l'un des nôtres qui dût jadis s'expatrier est sur point de faire fortune avec son art,' *P-T*, 613, 21 Sep 1918

'Émiliano Renaud fatally stricken,' Montreal *Gazette*, 4 Oct 1932

GP

RENO, Ginette (b Raynault). Pop singer, b Montreal 28 Apr 1946. At 14 she began participating in amateur contests, including 'Les Découvertes de Jean Simon' at the Café de l'Est in Montreal, where she was ranked first. She performed 1960–4 in nightclubs and radio and TV studios throughout Quebec and took singing lessons with Roger Larivière. In 1961 her first single 'Non papa' and 'J'aime Guy' for Apex, followed soon after by 'Roger,' gained her immediate popular acclaim. Singing with equal ease in English and French, she patterned her career on the US show-business tradition. She was called a 'discovery' in the 1964 Gala des artistes of the weekly *Radiomonde* and scored a tremendous hit that year with 'Tu vivras toujours dans mon coeur.' Her repertoire subsequently consisted mainly of sentimental ballads.

Reno made the first of many appearances at the *PDA in 1965 and at the *NAC in 1969 and performed at the Comédie-Canadienne in 1963 and 1969 and at the *Grand Théâtre de Québec in 1974 and 1976. At the Olympia in Paris she took part along with other Quebec artists in the revues 'Vive le Québec' (1967) and 'Musicorama' (1968). The Quebec public voted her Miss Radio-Television in 1968, and she was awarded a trophy at the MIDEM festival in Cannes that same year. She also performed at the Garden of Stars at Man and His World and won three trophies at the Montreal Festival du disque (most popular singer, strongest commercial value, and best LP). She performed in concerts with the *MSO at the PDA and the NAC in 1969.

In 1969 Reno signed a contract with Decca and gave two shows on BBC TV. She returned to London in January 1970 to sing at the Savoy Theatre, and in 1971 to host a series of programs with the singer Roger Whittaker. In 1972 she won first prize for performance at the Tokyo International Song Festival with Les Reed's 'I Can't Let You Walk out of My Life.' While pursuing her career in Quebec, she lived in Los Angeles 1974–6, studying at Lee Strasburg's studio of dramatic art.

At the 1975 *St-Jean-Baptiste celebrations, the crowd assembled on Mount Royal gave Reno a lengthy ovation following her rendition of the Jean-Pierre *Ferland song 'Un peu plus haut, un peu plus loin.' With Ferland the previous year she had recorded the song 'T'es mon amour, t'es ma maîtresse,' another hit. On CBC TV she participated in a number of special programs, including 'Bonjour Canada' (1970), 'Spécial Ginette Reno' (1972), 'Gershwin 76,' 'Vingt-cinq ans ensemble' (1977), and 'Superstar' (1978 and 1979). She made tours in various parts of Canada in 1968 and 1970 and in Quebec in 1969, 1970, and 1976 and also sang in the USA, where she was invited to appear on the Johnny Carson, Merv Griffin, and Dinah Shore TV shows in 1978.

After Reno's 1977 recital at the PDA Pierre Beaulieu wrote: 'What a Colossus of the stage, what a magnificent performer, what a voice, what soul, what warmth she radiates ... Ginette Reno is music pure and simple, music with no nationality, no boundaries, ageless, beyond time. Ginette Reno is the soul of music, a succession of notes that she rethinks, reworks, to which she gives new life and finally delivers to us through her own view of things, her warmth, her voice and her incredible talent' (Montreal *La Presse*, 1 Jun 1977).

Reno has received *Juno Awards in 1969, 1971, and 1972. 'Les Yeux fermés,' 'Aimez-le si fort,' 'La Dernière Valse,' 'Reste auprès de moi,' and 'Le Sable et la mer' may rank among her greatest hits, along with 'À ma manière' and 'Je ne suis qu'une chanson,' composed for her by Diane *Juster.

DISCOGRAPHY

Les Grands Succès d'une vedette, Ginette Reno. (1968). Apex ALF-71802
Ginette Reno à la Comédie-Canadienne 69. 1969. Grand Prix GPS-3304
Ginette Reno. Ca 1969. Grand Prix GPS-3301
Ginette Reno. Ca 1969. Parrot PAS.71032
Ginette Reno. (1970). Grand Prix GPS-3307
Aimez-le si fort. Ca 1970. Grand Prix GPS-3310
Ginette Reno collection No. 1. Ca 1970. Lero LS-773
Ginette Reno collection No. 2. Ca 1970. Lero LS-774
Beautiful Second Hand Man. (1971). Parrot PAS.71045
Ginette Reno à la Comédie-Canadienne. À guichet fermé. Ca 1971. Grand Prix GPS-1399
Ginette Reno album souvenir. (1971). Grand Prix GPS-100
Ginette Reno en spectacle au Casa Loma. Ca 1971. Apex ALF-1595
Quelqu'un à aimer. Ca 1971. Apex ALF-71597
Touching Me, Touching You. (1972). Parrot PAS.71058
Aimons-nous. Ca 1974. Trans-World TWK-6507
En direct de la Place des arts. Ca 1974. Trans-World International TWI-8000
Ginette Reno. Ca 1974. Trans-World TWF-9532
Mes Plus Belles Chansons. Ca 1974. Trans-World TWK-6506
Ombre et soleil. Ca 1974. Grand Prix GPS-3314
The Best of Ginette Reno. (1975). Parrot PAS.71074
Ginette Reno Toute ma carrière 21 disques d'or. (1977). Les Archives du disque québécois AQ 21013
Ce que j'ai de plus beau. 1978. Melon-Miel MM 501
Trying to Find a Way. 1979. Honey-Dew HD 1000
Je ne suis qu'une chanson. 1979. Melon-Miel MM 502

BIBLIOGRAPHY

Rudel-Tessier, J. 'Ginette Reno: l'escalier de la gloire, ça se monte lentement,' Montreal *La Presse*, 23 Apr 1970

Juster, Robert. 'Rencontre avec Ginette Reno,' *Madame*, vol 1, Jun 1974

David, Thérèse. 'Une femme qui prend l'amour par la main,' *Le mois à Québec*, vol 1, Nov 1977

Beaulieu, Pierre. 'Ginette Reno: "Cette année vous allez avoir droit à un show!",' Montreal *La Presse*, 7 Oct 1978

Grigsby, Wayne. 'If you haven't seen me, you simply don't know,' *Maclean's*, 30 Oct 1978

(BLH)

RENSHAW, Rosette (Rose Madelaine). Composer, pianist, teacher, translator, b Montreal 4 May 1920; BA (McGill) 1942, B MUS (Toronto) 1944, D MUS (Toronto) 1949. She attended the *École Vincent-d'Indy 1936–8 and studied piano, theory, and composition with Alfred *Whitehead and Claude *Champagne in Montreal. She was a pupil of Nicolas Nabokov at the Peabody Cons in Baltimore, and, in 1951, of Nadia Boulanger at the Paris Cons. In France, she studied also at the American Cons in Fontainebleau. She worked as early as 1942 as a translator in the House of Commons in Ottawa and performed the same function later in the Secretary of State's office. She conducted research in French-Canadian folk music and, after 1946, commented for the CBC on the music scene in Ottawa. In England she lectured at the Bath Festival, Yehudi Menuhin's school, and the RCM. Also during this period she spent some time in India studying the music of that country with the aid of a grant from Unesco. On CBC TV she provided commentary for a 1957 concert of Indian music given by Ravi Shankar in the program series 'L'*Heure du concert,' and presented two programs on the same subject in 1960. She taught 1956–7 at the École Vincent-d'Indy and in the 1960s at *McGill U, and began teaching at the State U College in New Paltz, NY, at the beginning of the 1970s. She has composed a few folksongs, a *Symphony in G* as a requirement for her D MUS degree, and *Madrigal for Strings* (1949). (DM)

Requiems for the Party Girl. Cycle of arias composed in 1966 by R. Murray *Schafer. The text, also by Schafer, is based on writings of Kafka and Camus. The work was commissioned for Canada's centenary by the CBC and was premiered 21 Nov 1967 on radio by the mezzo-soprano Phyllis *Mailing and the Vancouver SO Chamber Players. It won the Fromm Foundation Prize in 1968. Later performances were given by the New York Philharmonic under Bruno Maderna (21 Jan 1972) and by the BBC SO under Pierre Boulez. *Requiems* and *From the Tibetan Book of the Dead* (the latter premiered in 1968 on the CBC by Mailing and the *U of British Columbia Chamber Singers under Cortland *Hultberg and also performed at the 1971 ISCM congress in London) were combined with new material as *Patria II*. The new work, completed in 1972 as the second part of a mixed-media stage trilogy, was premiered 23 Aug 1972 at the *Stratford Festival under the direction of Serge *Garant, again with Phyllis Mailing in the solo role. In *Patria II* the Party Girl whose collapse and suicide are documented in *Requiems* is more fully explored in the composite figure of Ariadne, who is in turn a schizophrenic mental patient, a six-year-old child, and a dead spirit.

DISCOGRAPHY

Neva Pilgrim sop, Chicago U Contemporary Chamber Players, Shapey cond. (1969). CRI SD 245
Mailing sop, Ensemble de la SMCQ, Garant cond. 1970. RCI 299
Mailing sop, Schafer cond. 1975. Mel SMLP 4026

BIBLIOGRAPHY

Mather, Bruce. 'Notes sur "Requiems for the Party-Girl" de Schafer,' *CMB*, 1, Spring–Summer 1970

(MCv)

RETI FORBES, Jean (b Sahlmark, m Reti, m Forbes). Pianist, teacher, musicologist, editor, b Saltcoats (near Yorkton), Sask, 19 May 1911, naturalized US 1965, d Athens, Ga, 7 May 1972; ATCM 1930, LRAM 1933. She received her early training at the *Regina Cons and studied 1932–3 in London at the RAM with Harry Isaacs (piano) and Adam Carse (composition). She taught 1934–9 at the Regina Cons and played an important role (1938) in the drafting and adoption of the first provincial bill in Canada to regulate the certification of music teachers. She studied in 1939 with Schnabel and Sessions in New York and subsequently toured the USA.

In 1943 she married Rudolf Reti (1885–1957), Viennese composer, critic, and scholar, and contributed to the writing of his *The Thematic Process in*

Music (London 1951, 1961). After his death she edited and supervised the publication of his *Tonality, Atonality, Pantonality* (London 1958) and *Thematic Patterns in Sonatas of Beethoven* (London 1967).

Following a successful European tour in the early 1960s Reti Forbes joined the Dept of Music at the U of Georgia, where she compiled and annotated an 800-page catalogue of the Olin Downes papers. Her last work, *Notes on Playing the Piano,* was published privately in 1974.

BIBLIOGRAPHY

Forbes, W. Stanton. 'Jean Reti Forbes: 1911–1972, concert pianist and scholar,' Dr D.A. Ledet papers, U of Georgia

Laidlaw, Max. 'News and views in music,' Regina *Leader-Post*, 20 May 1972 WLB

REUBART, (Glen) **Dale, Jr.** Pianist, teacher, b Kansas City 19 Jan 1926, naturalized Canadian 1971; BA (Missouri) 1952, M MUS (Southern California) 1956, DMA (Southern California) 1965. His teachers included Harold Bauer, Carl Friedberg, Conrad Bos, and Ingolf Dahl. He taught piano 1956–60 at the U of Southern California and 1960–3 at Western Washington State College, and in 1963 began teaching at the *U of British Columbia.

Specializing in 19th- and 20th-century piano music, Reubart has performed as soloist, chamber player, accompanist, and lecture-recitalist in several North American centres and has written articles on performance practices. He received research grants from the U of British Columbia in 1969 and the *Canada Council in 1970 to study performance practices in the music of Chopin and Liszt. He considers himself 'a teacher who performs rather than a performer who teaches' (Calgary *Herald*, 19 Jan 1972).

WRITINGS

'Performance in the academic community: opportunity and dilemma,' *CAUSM J*, vol 1, Fall 1971

'Toward a history of musical performance: tapes of the Gustafson Collection,' *CAUSM J*, vol 3, Fall 1973 SLH

REYNER, Horace (Waters). Organist, choir conductor, b England 23 Oct 1866, d Montreal 31 Aug 1912. He studied with Alfred Broughton, whom he succeeded (1883) as organist of St Mark's Parish Church, Leeds. Arriving in Canada in 1887 he held church positions, first in Kingston, Ont, and then in Montreal. He taught 1896–9 at the *Dominion College of Music and 1904–5 at the *McGill Cons. He was the founder-conductor 1897–1901 of the 50-voice Motet Choir and 1902–8 of the *Montreal Oratorio Society. He served 1895–7 as conductor of the Montreal Orchestral Assn and 1896–7 as conductor of the Handel and Haydn Society. Reyner conducted the Canadian premieres of several works, notably Elgar's *The Dream of Gerontius* (1906). In 1906 he became organist-choirmaster of the Chief Methodist Episcopal Church in Duluth, Minn, and in 1911 he was invited to conduct the St Paul SO in festivals.

BIBLIOGRAPHY

Musical Red Book NT

Les Rhapsodes. An amateur mixed choir founded under the name L'Écho in 1962 in Quebec City by Pierre Fréchette. The name Les Rhapsodes was adopted in 1964, and the group received its provincial charter in 1970. It began with 15 singers, but after 1965 the number remained steady at about 30. The first concert was given in August 1963 in the Quebec City Arena. Subsequently the choir has offered between 5 and 15 concerts each year in city churches (St-Jean-Baptiste, St-Thomas-d'Aquin, Sts-Martyrs-Canadiens), at the *Institut canadien, and at the Bonaventure Hotel in Montreal. Though specializing in unaccompanied works, it has sung occasionally with ensembles such as the *Orchestre de chambre Pierre-Morin.

At first the group sang mainly popular, folk, and religious songs, but its repertoire expanded 1971–8 under the energetic direction of Louis Lavigueur, who added works ranging from renaissance to contemporary and conducted premieres of Canadian works including Gilles Ouellet's *Invocation* (1975) and André Picard's *Fanaison* (1976). Lavigueur followed two previous directors, Fréchette 1962–70 and Michel Keable 1970–1, and himself was succeeded by Fred Mooney in 1978. Mooney was followed that same year by Gisèle Pettigrew.

The choir became a member of the *Alliance chorale canadienne in 1963 and went on to participate in such activities as the Choralies internationales canadiennes. In addition, it sang at *Expo 67 and toured Quebec that year. It won first prize 1970–5 in the *Canadian Music Competitions and participated in the 1976 *Ontario Choral Federation's Choirs in Contact in Hamilton. In 1964 it began to be heard annually on the CBC radio series 'A cappella.' Its LP *Chantons tous Noël* was made with the assistance of the organist Claude *Lavoie (1977, RHP 1501).

Les Rhapsodes have received subsidies from the *Canada Council, the *MACQ, and the office of the Quebec high commissioner for youth, sports, and recreation.

Presidents of Les Rhapsodes have included Corinne Poulin 1963–4, Robert Rousseau 1964–5, Claude Larochelle 1965–7, François Painchaud 1967–8, 1969–70, Jean Crête 1970–1, France Duval 1971–2, Lorraine Ouellet 1972–4, Josée Lalonde 1974–6, Richard Noël 1976, Andrée Nicole 1977, Jean-Pierre Pellegrin 1977–8, Claude Jacques 1978–9, and Jean Giroux in 1979, succeeded by Marc-André Bluteau in 1980. (MB-L)

Rhythm and blues. See Blues.

The Rhythm Pals. Country music trio formed in 1946 in New Westminster, BC, by the accordionist and baritone Marc Wald (b Bismarck, ND, 1922), the string bassist and tenor Mike Ferbey (b Saskatoon 1926), and the guitarist and tenor Jack Jensen (b Prince Rupert, BC, 1925). Wald and Ferbey had toured western Canada in the late 1930s with Sleepy (Leslie Frost) and Swede (Nels Nelson) and the Tumbleweeds from Saskatoon.

The Rhythm Pals made their debut on CKNW radio's 'Bill Rae's Roundup.' Regular appearances followed on CBC Vancouver radio's 'Burns Chuckwagon' and other shows. In 1948 the Rhythm Pals performed on US TV, one of the first Canadian groups to do so. They toured with Wilf *Carter in 1950, worked briefly in Hollywood, and in 1958 moved to Toronto. While starring in 1959 on their own CBC show 'Swing Easy,' they joined 'The Tommy *Hunter Show' on CBC radio. Subsequently they were regular performers on most of Hunter's radio and TV shows until 1977. They had their own 'Chuckwagon Show' 1963–6 on CBC radio. Besides touring widely in Canada they have performed, as part of CBC concert parties, in many other countries.

The Rhythm Pals made some 78s in 1953 with *Juliette for Aragon and subsequently made LPs for *Arc, *Decca, Banff, and Arpeggio and four for *CTL. In 1978 they recorded *The Best of the Rhythm Pals* (2-Ross Sound RS 1040), which included such songs as 'Blue Shadows' (their theme on radio and TV) and *'Bluebird on Your Windowsill' (which they had introduced on CKNW in the late 1940s). Among other songs associated with the Rhythm Pals are 'Big Lazy River,' 'Broken Hearts and Faded Dreams,' 'Never Ending Song of Love,' and the hymn 'Lead Me Gently Home.'

The Rhythm Pals won *Juno Awards as best country group of 1965, 1967, and 1968. They remained active in 1980, thus qualifying as one of the longest continuing groups in Canadian pop music.

BIBLIOGRAPHY

Ruddy, Jon. 'Rhythm Pals: 25 profitable years making it small,' *Toronto Star*, 19 Feb 1972

Rasky, Frank. 'A pop group that doesn't keep splitting but goes on and on,' *Canadian Panorama*, 3 Feb 1973 MM (MD)

RICCIO, Pat (Patrick Joseph). Alto and baritone saxophonist, flutist, arranger, composer, b Port Arthur (Thunder Bay), Ont, 3 Dec 1918. He was raised in Toronto and began his career in 1939.

Riccio joined the RCAF in 1941, serving as music director of the RCAF Streamliners, a 15-piece dance band which performed in England for the BBC and, alternating with Glenn Miller's (US) Army Air Force Band, at the Queensbury Club in London. Although the Streamliners made no recordings, they are said to have been the equal of the dance bands of the US (Miller) and British (Squadronaires) services.

Returning to Toronto after World War II, Riccio played in, or wrote arrangements for, the local dance bands of Bert *Niosi, Mart *Kenney, Art *Hallman, and others. He won polls (conducted by the CBC's 'Jazz Unlimited') as best alto saxophonist (1947) and best baritone saxophonist (1949). He later led big bands and small jazz groups in nightclubs, ballrooms, and concert halls in the Toronto area. He has performed with CBC concert parties in Europe and the Middle East.

Riccio's big band was recorded in 1961 (*Arc AS 3001) at the Jubilee Pavilion in Oshawa, its home for several years. His small groups have made LPs for Arc, *Quality, and *CTL; the personnel for the CTL recording (CTLS 071, made in 1965) included the distinguished US jazz musicians Teddy Wilson (piano) and Ed Thigpen (drums).

A pupil of John *Weinzweig and Gordon *Delamont, Riccio has arranged music for several pop singers (Wally *Koster, Patti Lewis, Norma Locke, Billy *O'Connor, and others) and for use on numerous CBC programs and has written songs, jazz themes, and the musical *Pauline*.

Riccio's son Pat (John) Riccio Jr played piano in his teens with Bobby Kris and the Imperials, worked during the 1960s in CBC Halifax pop music shows, and became music director ca 1975 for Anne *Murray.

BIBLIOGRAPHY

Norris, John. 'Pat Riccio,' *MSc*, 241, May–Jun 1968 MM (HM)

RICE, Gitz (Ingraham). Songwriter, entertainer, pianist, b New Glasgow, NS, 5 Mar 1891, d New York 16 Oct 1947. He studied at the *McGill Cons before joining the first division of the Canadian Expeditionary Force at the outbreak of World War I. He fought in many major campaigns and played piano on occasion for the Princess Pat's Comedy Co (see Dumbells). Though he was invalided at Vimy Ridge in 1917 he stayed in the service as officer-in-charge (lieutenant) of musical entertainments for the army in Canada, supervising diversion for some 70,000 soldiers each week. He subsequently worked in vaudeville, staging his own revues, and again entertained the troops in World War II.

Rice's songs included 'Keep Your Head Down, Fritzie Boy' and 'We Stopped Them at the Marne' (Leo Feist 1918), 'On the Road that Leads Back Home' (Ricordi 1918), and 'Some Day I'll Come Back to You' and 'Burmah Moon' (Henry Burr 1919). *'Dear Old Pal of Mine' was his greatest hit. His purported role in the authorship of 'Mademoiselle from Armentieres' is unsubstantiated. Other Rice songs were published by Delmar in Montreal and Chappell and Ditson in the USA.

Rice's recordings of his 'Life in a Trench in Belgium' for Columbia and 'Fun in Flanders' for Victor, both with Henry *Burr, were popular. He also recorded as a singer for Victor and *Pathé and in the late 1920s made piano rolls for Ampico. *Roll Back the Years* lists his recordings as well as many of the artists who recorded his songs. EBM

RICHARD. A Sherbrooke family of musicians: 1 / Ti-Blanc and 2 / Michèle, his daughter.

1 **Ti-Blanc** (b Adalbert). Violoneux, radio and TV host, b Martinville, near Sherbrooke, Que, 13 Aug 1920, d Sherbrooke 22 Feb 1981. Initially an accordionist, he began playing the violin at 15 and in the following year joined the Log Cabin Boys in Sherbrooke. In 1940 he formed his own group, Les Copains de l'Est. He began performing on CHLT radio, Sherbrooke, in 1937, and had broadcast more than 3000 times for that station by 1956. He was host 1956–65 for 'Ti-Blanc Richard et ses gais lurons' on CHLT-TV, Sherbrooke, and performed regularly on CFCM-TV, Quebec City ('Signé Ti-Blanc Richard'), CFTM-TV Montreal ('À la Canadienne'), and other stations across the province. Ti-Blanc Richard performed widely in concert, clubs, and festivals in Quebec and the rest of Canada, and the northeastern USA. He also contributed to the sound-tracks of several Quebec films including *L'Apparition* and *Quelques Arpents de neige*.

Richard's repertoire, which combined traditional Quebec folk music with country music, included many of his own compositions and arrangements. One of Canada's leading novelty fiddlers, at times he employed a baseball bat, a hockey stick, a broom, or an axe handle for a bow. He also played with a violin bow attached to a pedal-operated sewing machine.

Richard made 28 78s for *RCA Victor, several 45s for Meteor, and, beginning in the late 1960s, a dozen LPs for *London, including two volumes of *Le Disque d'or de Ti-Blanc Richard* (1970, Lon SDS 5086; 1973, SDS 5133). In addition, he made several LPs for RCA, excerpts of which were reissued in 1974 on the LP *20 Succès souvenirs de Ti-Blanc Richard et Ses Joyeux Copains* (RCA Gala KTL 2-71915-1-4). The musical rights of his estate are administered by CAPAC.

BIBLIOGRAPHY
Sylvain, Jean-Paul. *Ti-Blanc Richard super violoneux* (Montreal 1974)
'Genuine Canadian country music,' *CanComp*, 112, Jun 1976

2 **Michèle** (Michelle). Singer, entertainer, actress, b Sherbrooke 17 Apr 1946. She first sang professionally at 10 on her father's CHLT-TV program and two years later made the single 'Main dans la main.' In 1963 she received the Meritas trophy as discovery of the year at the Gala des artistes (organized in Montreal by the weekly *Radiomonde et Télémonde*), in recognition of her success with the hit singles 'Quand le film est triste' and 'J'entends siffler le train.' That year she was host on 'Chansons intimes avec Michelle Richard' on CHLT-TV and co-host on 'Chez Isidore.' She also appeared on 'Dans le bon temps' on CFTM-TV, Montreal. During the summers of 1965 and 1966, she was co-host on CFTM-TV's 'Jeunesse d'aujourd'hui.' Also at this time she recorded 'La Plus Belle pour aller danser,' 'Ca va, je t'aime,' and 'Les Boîtes à gogo,' all popular hits.

In 1967 Richard made a six-week world tour of Canadian armed forces bases with Daniel *Dorice and Les *Cailloux. That year she won the MIDEM trophy at Cannes, was named Miss Radio-TV '67 at the Gala des artistes organized by Publications Péladeau, and participated in CJMS radio station's Musicorama tour in Quebec and New Brunswick. She took part in a similar tour in 1970. She performed that year for the film *L'Explosion* in Sicily. After the 1970 release of the single 'Mon Coeur d'enfant' she was co-host with Michel *Louvain of CBC TV's 'Zoom en liberté' and later enjoyed a tremendous success with her appearance at the International Pavilion at Man and His World. The following year she recorded 'Les Hommes, non, non, non,' and in 1974 she was the star of the Musicorama western-music tour covering 42 towns in Quebec, Ontario, and New Brunswick.

Richard acted 1974–5 in the CBC TV serial 'Mont-Joye' and appeared in a musical comedy, *Madame mon père*, staged in 1975 at the Théâtre des Variétés by Gilles Latulippe. She performed on the CBC TV program 'Vedettes en direct' in 1976 and was host 1977–8 for 'Le Réveil de Michèle' on the Verdun radio station CKVL. In 1978 she was the star of the revue at the Caf' Conc' in Montreal. In 1974 she began to spend several months each year in Miami, where she has performed in nightclubs. She has recorded some 60 singles and 20 LPs, most of which, including *Le Disque d'or de Michèle Richard* (1974, TC 49001), were produced and distributed by Trans-Canada.

BIBLIOGRAPHY
Matti, Jacques. *Michèle Richard raconte Michèle Richard* (Montreal 1969)
Levesque, Denis. 'Le monde du spectacle ne serait pas ce qu'il est sans Michèle Richard,' *TV-Hebdo*, 17 May 1975 DM, MM, AP

RICHARD, Gloria. Soprano, teacher, teaching consultant, b Ste-Anne, NB, 21 Apr 1934; B MUS (Montreal) 1963, M MUS (Montreal) 1965, B ED (New Brunswick) 1970. After two years of musical studies at Notre-Dame-d'Acadie College, Moncton, she obtained her professional teaching diploma (piano and singing) in 1953. She then turned to teaching and producing radio programs on CBAF, Moncton. She resumed her voice studies at the *École Vincent-d'Indy 1960–3 and at the *U of Montreal 1963–5 with Pierrette *Alarie, Louise *André, Bernard *Diamant, and Roy *Royal. She won first prizes in the 'CBC Trans-Canada Talent Caravan' (1959 TV competition) and at competition festivals in New Brunswick in 1957, 1958, and 1960, in Quebec City in 1961, and in Toronto. She was the winner of the 1963 *JMC National Competition. In 1963 and 1964 she received grants from the *Canada Council and in 1964–5 she undertook a JMC tour. She was one of the winners of the 1967 *Montreal International Competition. Between 1960 and 1970 she performed in recital as well as on CBC radio and TV in Halifax, Moncton, Montreal, and Toronto and she has sung with the symphony orchestras of Edmonton, Halifax, Montreal, Quebec, and Toronto. She taught singing 1976–9 at the *U of Ottawa. She became a teaching consultant for musical education in New Brunswick, employed by the province's Ministry of Education. In 1963, with the pianist Claude *Savard, she recorded Lully's 'Chant de Vénus,' the 'Nocturne' and 'Rondeau' from Campra's *Fêtes vénitiennes*, Duparc's *La Vie antérieure*, and three songs by Brahms (Club du disque CD-JMC-3). (SPI)

RICHARD, Jacqueline. Pianist, coach, choir and orchestra conductor, b Montreal 8 Mar 1928; B MUS (Montreal) 1953. She studied piano with Marie-Thérèse *Paquin who taught her the skills of opera accompaniment. She was awarded the Quebec Lieutenant-Governor's medal in 1953. Her first *JMC tour, with the violinist Gilles *Lefebvre, was followed by several others, notably with Louise *Roy 1950–1, Don *Garrard 1954–5, Fernande *Chiocchio 1956–7, and Napoléon *Bisson 1958–9. She was rehearsal pianist 1950–65 for the classes of Rachele Maragliano-Mori and Martial Singher at the CMM and was involved in the opera productions of the *Montreal Festivals, the *Opera Guild, and the CBC. In 1963 she founded the *Boutique d'opéra where, in a period of two years, with the co-operation of young singers, she presented 75 performances of operatic works such as *L'Oca del Cairo* by Mozart and *The Medium* by Menotti. On a 1964 *Canada Council grant she studied conducting with Hans Swarowsky in Nice. After coaching 1965–7 for the *Royal Cons Opera School, she sojourned in Vienna prior to her engagement by the Deutsche Oper-am-Rhein in Düsseldorf. She then worked with Rolf Liebermann, first at the Hamburg Opera and later (1973) at the Paris Opera. She prepared the singers for *Parsifal* at the 1975 Bayreuth Festival. She was coach and conductor in 1976 for the Courtenay Youth Music Centre and in 1977 became director of the Centre Opera Studio at *Wilfrid Laurier U, Waterloo, Ont. In 1978 she directed *The Barber of Seville* for the *Vancouver Opera.

BIBLIOGRAPHY
MacNiven, Elina. 'Artists in profile: Jacqueline Richard,' *OpCan*, Feb 1966
Villeneuve, Pâquerette. 'Jacqueline Richard,' *Perspectives*, 7, 16 Feb 1974 (TC-C)

The Richard Eaton Singers (formerly University Singers). Choir formed by Richard *Eaton in 1951 at the *U of Alberta in Edmonton and conducted by Eaton until 1967. He was succeeded by Sandra *Munn in 1967, and Munn by Larry Cook in 1973. The name Richard Eaton Singers was adopted in 1968 in memory of the founder. This 110-voice choir has specialized in the performance of the standard large choral-orchestral works from Bach to Orff. In 1970 the choir toured Great Britain and competed at the Tees-Side International Eisteddfod and the Bournemouth Festival, receiving first prize at the latter. BH

RICHARDS, Bill (William Francis Caven). Violinist, composer, arranger, editor, b Ottawa 28 Mar 1923. In Ottawa he studied piano with Herbert *Sanders and violin with David Shuttleworth and Jack Cavill; in Toronto he studied violin with Broadus Farmer in 1939, Elie *Spivak in 1946, and Albert *Pratz in 1953. Richards began his radio career at eight playing violin solos on Ottawa and Hull stations. He joined the RCN in 1942 and was a featured performer and orchestra member 1943–5 in *Meet the Navy*. He has been a leading studio musician, contractor, and concertmaster of many radio, TV, and recording orchestras. He was host and arranger 1954–9 for CBC radio's 'Guest Time,' conductor-arranger 1958–9 for 'Trans-Canada Talent Show,' and music director in 1959 for 'Swing Easy.'

Richards' compositions include scores for the CBC's productions of *Sleeping Beauty* (1957), *I Knock on the Door* (1968), and *So Great a Sweetness* (1969); a *Flute Quartet* (1964); the tune *Hi Diddle Fiddle*

(1953) recorded by the Albert Pratz Orchestra; and some fiddle tunes – two recorded by the composer for Spiral in 1957 and one heard in the film *The Pyx*. Richards made two LPs in 1962 for *CTL (5016 and 5035) with a quartet featuring the organist Lou *Snider.

Elected to the executive of the Toronto Musicians Assn (AF of M, local 149) in 1958, Richards became assistant secretary in 1960 and served 1965–77 as editor of the union's publication *Crescendo*.

Richards' first wife, the actress Billy Mae (Dinsmore) Richards, performed in *Meet the Navy*. Their daughter Judi (b Toronto 12 Aug 1949) has sung in Montreal with vocal groups which accompany leading Quebec pop artists in concerts and on records. As a member of the bilingual vocal trio Toulouse she made the 1977 hit single 'It Always Happens This Way' / 'C'est toujours à recommencer.' Her songs have been recorded by Toulouse, Renée *Claude, Patsy Gallant, and others. She married the monologist Yvon Deschamps.

Richards' second wife, Victoria Polley, a violinist, studied with John *Konrad in Winnipeg and was concertmaster of the National Ballet orchestra before joining the *TSO in 1967.

BIBLIOGRAPHY
Kroll, Stephen. 'Judi Richards: behind Quebec's biggest stars,' *CanComp*, 100, Apr 1975

RICHARDS, Dal (Dallas Murray). Clarinetist, saxophonist, arranger, conductor, b Vancouver 5 Jan 1918. He was a member of the *Kitsilano Boys' Band in his youth and began his professional career in the late 1930s as a clarinetist and saxophonist in the Vancouver dance bands of Sandy DeSantis and Stan Patton. In 1940 he succeeded Mart *Kenney as music director and bandleader at the Hotel Vancouver's Panorama Roof. He remained there for 25 years, and during that time his orchestra was heard on the CBC radio network. The 11-piece orchestra featured, in turn, the singers *Juliette, Beryl Boden, and Richards' wife, Lorraine McAllister, and over the years included the trumpeters Chuck Barber and Gordon *Delamont and the saxophonists Stan Patton and Lance *Harrison. The orchestra appeared elsewhere on the west coast and made the LP *Dance Date with Dal* (1964, Lon EB 12). Although Richards left the Hotel Vancouver in 1965, he has continued to appear in the Vancouver area with his orchestra and has been music director of CBC and CTV shows, Variety Club telethons, and half-time shows at the British Columbia Lions' football games. He made the LP *Canadian Football Songs* (1968, CTLS 5104 / RCA CTLS 1104) (see also Sports).

Lorraine McAllister (b Saskatoon 12 Apr 1924) sang with the dance bands of Ken Peaker (Saskatoon), Johnny *Holmes (Montreal), and Art *Hallman (Toronto), before joining Richards in the late 1940s. They were married in 1951. Besides singing with Richards, she starred on many CBC radio and TV shows from Vancouver and on CBC TV's 'Holiday Ranch' from Toronto. She has appeared at *TUTS. MM, JR

RICHARDSON, Jack (Arnold). Record producer, bassist, b Toronto 23 Jul 1929. He studied bass privately 1945–8 and theory at the *RCMT in 1946. He worked 1947–8 with Benny Louis, was the bassist in 1956 in Norman *Symonds' jazz octet, and played throughout the 1950s with leading Canadian dance bands and in CBC Toronto radio and TV orchestras.

As a producer 1960–8 with the advertising firm McCann-Erickson, Richardson won many Canadian Broadcast Executives Society awards for his innovative use of popular Canadian performers in Coca-Cola radio jingles. He produced albums 1965–6 by Bobby *Curtola, Michel *Louvain, the *Guess Who, the Staccatos, and many others as sales premiums for Coca-Cola. Richardson became president and head of production of *Nimbus 9 Productions in 1968 and subsequently supervised recording sessions in Canada and the USA by the Guess Who, Mitch Ryder, Alice Cooper, Poco, and the Brecker Brothers. In 1969 he received *Billboard* magazine's 'Trendsetter' award for his work in opening US markets to Canadian artists.

BIBLIOGRAPHY
'The giant's awakening,' *Axes, Chops & Hot Licks* MM

RICHARDSON, (John) **Leland**. Businessman, carillonneur, b Toronto 4 Feb 1906, d Montreal 13 Sep 1969. A boyhood interest in bells led to studies 1927–9 at the Beiaardschool te Mechelen (Royal Flemish Carillon School) in Belgium with Jef Denyn. He returned to Toronto and served 1929–31 as carillonneur at Metropolitan United Church. He gave his first concert at Soldiers' Tower, *U of Toronto, 6 Apr 1930, and until his death continued to play the carillon there in weekly recitals and for New Year's Eve, Remembrance Day, and convocation ceremonies. He played twice-daily recitals during the summers 1960–9 at Rainbow Tower, Niagara Falls, and gave guest recitals on carillons throughout North America. Though employed as an insurance salesman, Richardson won fame for his avocation as a carillonneur. He developed a repertoire of more than 500 melodies – folksongs, hymns, pop songs, and classical pieces – played from memory and often in part improvised. See also Carillon. (MH, MM)

RICHER-LORTIE, Lyse (b Richer, m Lortie). Teacher, administrator, b Montreal 11 Sep 1939; BA (Montreal) 1958, B MUS (Montreal) 1960, M MUS piano (École Vincent-d'Indy) 1961, L MUS (Montreal) 1969. She studied 1951–61 at the *École Vincent-d'Indy with Yvonne *Hubert (piano) and Claude *Champagne (composition) and 1965–70 at the *U of Montreal with Serge *Garant (composition) and Maryvonne *Kendergi (musicology). She received a scholarship from the *Ladies' Morning Musical Club and was a prize winner of the *MSO's Matinées symphoniques in 1958 and of the Ottawa Music Festival in 1959.

Richer-Lortie taught piano 1956–63 at the École Vincent-d'Indy and solfège and Canadian music history 1966–75 at the U of Montreal where 1970–4 she was in charge of the workshop on research into the history of music in Canada. She received bursaries from the Quebec government in 1968 and 1971 and from the *Canada Council 1974–5.

In 1971 Richer-Lortie prepared the inventory of the Wilfrid *Pelletier collection for a prospective acquisition by the BN du Q. That same year she became the administrative director of MUSCADØC – the computerized processing of data on music in Canada – a project which she discussed in *CMB* (Spring–Summer 1974) but which was put in abeyance in 1975.

Richer-Lortie has given lectures and papers at conferences and is the author of articles on Canadian composers in the *Dictionary of Contemporary Music, Le Musicien éducateur* (nos. 2, 3, 1974), *Contemporary Canadian Composers / Compositeurs canadiens contemporains, The New Grove*, and *EMC*. She became vice-president of the Montreal *CMCentre in 1977. She took part in the 1978 CBC radio programs 'Au fil des arts' and 'Aux vingt heures' and has contributed to CBC TV's 'L'Observateur.' ST

G. Ricordi & Co (Canada) Ltd. Canadian branch of the Italian firm which was established in Milan in 1808 and became the publisher of Rossini, Donizetti, Bellini, Verdi, and Puccini. Gordon *Wry acted as Ricordi's Canadian agent early in the 1950s. Bruno Apollonio, who had been a music publisher in Trieste, took on the agency in 1953 and established G. Ricordi & Co (Canada) Ltd in Toronto in 1954. Apollonio served as managing director and his wife, Wally, took charge of promotion.

Besides distributing and promoting in Canada the catalogue of the parent firm, Ricordi (Canada) has published orchestral works by *Adaskin, *Aitken, *Freedman, *Gellman, *Joachim, *Mercure, *Morawetz, *Morel, *Prévost, and *Somers. Printing is done by the W.R. *Draper Co of Weston, Ont. Plate numbers are not used. *Leeds Music (Canada) took over the sales of Ricordi's printed music (including the Canadian publications) in 1963 and began negotiating the grand rights of Ricordi operas and supplying rental orchestral parts in 1975; *Boosey & Hawkes assumed these functions in 1980. Ricordi is a *PRO Canada affiliate; a subsidiary company, Summit Music Ltd, is a *CAPAC affiliate.

BIBLIOGRAPHY
Kraglund, John. Column, Toronto *Globe and Mail*, 25 Aug 1955
Morgan, Kit. 'Ricordi & Co.,' *MSc*, 274, May–Jun 1969
MWl

RIDDELL, Wayne (Kerr). Organist, choir conductor, teacher, b Lachute, Que, 10 Sep 1936; B MUS (McGill) 1960. He studied with Juliette Rodrigue and Kenneth *Gilbert and served as organist-choirmaster at several Montreal churches, including Westmount Park United 1958–65 and Erskine and American United 1965–72, before assuming that function at the Church of St Andrew and St Paul in 1972. Riddell has taught at Marianopolis College and 1961–4 in the protestant schools. In 1969 he was made director of choirs and vice-chairman of the department of school music at *McGill U. He founded the *Tudor Singers of Montreal in 1962 and continued to conduct them in 1980. NT

RIDDER, Allard de. Conductor, violist, composer, b Dordrecht, Holland, 3 May 1887, d Vancouver, 13 May 1966; B MUS (Toronto) 1943, D MUS (Toronto) 1946. He studied violin and conducting in Holland and at the Cologne Cons. His teachers included Johan Wagenaar, Fritz Steinbach, and Willem Mengelberg. He was a guest conductor at Arnhem, The Hague, and Amsterdam and in other European cities. For two seasons he conducted the National Opera in Amsterdam. In 1919 he emigrated to the USA and, after brief seasons with the Boston and Richmond (Va) orchestras, became assistant conductor and violist of the Los Angeles Philharmonic. Many of his orchestral works received their premieres at this time.

In 1930, on the invitation of Mrs B.T. *Rogers, de Ridder conducted a concert by the *Vancouver SO (re-formed for the occasion). This led to further concerts, four a year until 1933 when he moved to Canada as regular conductor of the orchestra. He retained that position until 1941. Shortly after moving to Vancouver he formed the Allard de Ridder Chamber Music Quartette. In 1934 he organized Stanley Park summer concerts, sponsored by BC Electric and persuaded W.H. Malkin to finance the construction of the *Malkin Bowl. He was a guest lecturer 1936–7 at the *U of British Columbia.

Moving in 1941 to Toronto, de Ridder joined the *Hart House String Quartet, taught at the

*TCM, and appeared as guest conductor of the *Promenade Symphony Concerts in 1942 and the *TSO in 1943. In 1943 he was a guest-conductor of the National SO, Washington. He founded and was the conductor 1944–50 of the *Ottawa Philharmonic Orchestra and continued to guest-conduct in Vancouver before returning permanently to that city in 1952. He became conductor of the Holland Choir there and in 1957 appeared with the Vancouver SO in a performance of his *Variations on a Swabian Folk Song.*

In his later Vancouver years de Ridder taught conducting, viola, and composition. His pupils in Canada included John *Avison, Bryan *Gooch, Hans Gruber, Klemi *Hambourg, Ricky *Hyslop, Arnold McLeod, and Doug *Randle. De Ridder was revered by his students for his knowledge, his insistence on discipline in performance and writing, and his special insights into the music of Beethoven, Mendelssohn, and Reger.

De Ridder's orchestral compositions include a violin concerto; four symphonic poems (*Titania, On the Ocean, Song of Lamia,* and *In the Woods*); a *Sketch* for flute, violin, and orchestra; an *Overture in D*; an *Intermezzo*; a string quartet; a scherzo for unaccompanied choir (*Beware of Love*); and several songs.

BIBLIOGRAPHY

Mason, Lawrence. 'Classified summary of principal works by Allard de Ridder and W.O. Forsyth,' Toronto *Globe*, 18 Jul 1936

BNSG

RIDDEZ, Jean (Arthur). Baritone, teacher, b Lille, France, 10 Mar 1875, d Montreal 2 Sep 1939, naturalized Canadian ca 1928; premier prix voice, declamation, opéra-comique (Lille Cons) 1897, premier prix voice, opéra-comique, opera (Paris Cons) 1900. A member, 1900–10, of the Paris Opera, he made his debut in the title role of *Rigoletto* and thereafter undertook numerous roles, notably in Ernest Reyer's *Sigurd* and *Salammbô*, Saint-Saëns' *Henry VIII* and *Samson et Dalila*, Xavier Leroux's *Le Chemineau*, and Massenet's *Thaïs*. From 1908 to 1910 he sang the title roles in *Lohengrin* and *Faust* and the leading tenor roles in other operas. He participated in several cantatas composed by candidates for the Prix de Rome, including those by Caplet and Ravel.

Reverting to the baritone register Riddez participated with great success 1912–13 in the productions of the *Montreal Opera Company, making his debut 12 Nov 1912 in Massenet's *Hérodiade*. With the same company he sang in *Rigoletto* (the title role), *Roméo et Juliette, Le Jongleur de Notre-Dame* (Massenet), *Tosca, Carmen, Tales of Hoffmann, Thaïs,* and *Noël* (Erlanger).

With the Boston Opera Riddez sang Golaud in *Pelléas et Mélisande* and other roles of the French repertoire. With the large orchestras of Paris he performed works by Charpentier (*La Vie du poète*), Dubois (*Le Baptême de Clovis*), and other French composers. He sang five seasons in Lyons and taught at the conservatory there.

Invited to sing *Thaïs* in 1920, Riddez moved to Montreal where he devoted himself mainly to teaching, privately and in such institutions as the *École normale de musique. Among his pupils were Albert *Cornellier, Geneviève Davis-Lebel, Conrad *Latour, Charles *Marchand, and Henri *Prieur.

Riddez was made an officer of the French Instruction publique in 1907. He was a member of the Assn des maîtres du chant français and deputy teacher and jury member of the Paris Cons and the American Cons at Fontainebleau. He wrote articles 1927–8 for *La Lyre* and recorded six songs (listed in *Roll Back the Years*) for HMV and Columbia.

Riddez' daughter Juanita (dramatic soprano, b Vichy 15 Apr 1915) studied with her father and 1936–9 at the Paris Cons where she obtained a deuxième prix in opera. She made her debut 24 Jun 1947 at the Opéra-Comique as Poussette in *Manon* but gave up singing shortly afterwards. Riddez' other daughters, Sita, Mia, and Lygie, are known in the world of theatre and dance in Montreal.

WRITINGS

'La grande pitié du chant,' *Canada musical*, 8 instalments, Jan–Jun 1921

BIBLIOGRAPHY

'Jean Riddez,' *Entre-Nous*, vol 1, Apr 1930
Musiciens canadiens

HPn

RIDEOUT, Patricia (Irene) (m Dissmann). Contralto, b Saint John, NB, 16 Mar 1931. She studied piano 1941–3 with Beatrice Price and voice 1946–8 with Agnes Forbes in Saint John. She went to Toronto on an RCMT scholarship in 1949 and attended the *Royal Conservatory Opera School 1952–5. In Toronto her only teacher – whom she continued to consult until 1970 – was Ernesto *Vinci. She had performed in theatricals in Saint John and continued to do so in 1950 as a singer and dancer with the Red Barn Theatre in Muskoka, Ont. She taught singing in 1954 at University Settlement, Toronto, and was a soloist in opera productions in 1954 and 1955 at the *Banff SFA. Her first important operatic role was Madame Flora in a 1955 Royal Conservatory Opera School production of Menotti's *The Medium* at Hart House. In the *Globe and Mail*, 16 Apr 1955, John *Kraglund wrote 'That this performance achieved such stark realism was due largely to Patricia Rideout's sharply etched characterization.'

Rideout's career began in earnest in 1955 with the role of Annina in an Opera Festival Assn (*COC) production of *La Traviata*. This was followed in 1956 by her recital debut at the Toronto Art Gallery (Art Gallery of Ontario) and her appearance as Bianca in the Canadian premiere (*Stratford Festival) of Britten's *The Rape of Lucretia*, with Regina Resnik (Lucretia), Jennie Tourel, and Jon *Vickers. (Eighteen years later, at the 1974 *Guelph Spring Festival, Rideout sang the title role in that same opera, again in a cast that included Vickers.) She was an original member 1956–68 of the *Festival Singers. For the Opera School (Opera Festival, COC) she sang Mercedes in *Carmen* (1956), the Sandman in *Hansel and Gretel* (1957), and Maurya in the Canadian premiere (1958) of Vaughan Williams' *Riders to the Sea* (with Teresa *Stratas).

In opera, Rideout's most recurrent major role was perhaps Suzuki in *Madama Butterfly*, which she sang at the 1960 *Vancouver International Festival (with Stratas, *Verreau, and *Quilico) and in 1962 and 1971 for the COC. But she sang many other roles for the COC, for the Stratford and Guelph Spring festivals, and, especially, for the CBC, on both TV (*Il matrimonio segreto* 1958, *Peter Grimes* 1959, *Riders to the Sea* 1962, *Rigoletto* 1964, *The Barber of Seville* 1965, *Eugene Onegin* 1966) and radio (*Madama Butterfly* and *The Marriage of Figaro* 1960, *Dido and Aeneas* 1963, *The Fool* in 1968, and others, including the premieres or broadcast premieres – see list – of several Canadian operas).

For CBC TV, besides opera, Rideout's work has ranged from a Brahms recital in 1960 to Schoenberg's *Pierrot Lunaire* and Walton's *Façade* with Glenn *Gould in 1975 and Krenek's *Wanderlied im Herbst* with the same artist in 1977. For CBC radio she has sung in *Pierrot Lunaire* (1962), Mahler's *Kindertotenlieder* and Elgar's *Sea Pictures* with the

Patricia Rideout as Lucretia at the 1974 Guelph Spring Festival

*TSO in 1965, and *Somers' *Five Songs for Dark Voice* with the TSO in 1966 and has given 'Distinguished Artists' recitals in 1968, 1969, 1970, and 1974, offering songs of Barber, *Beckwith, Berg, Debussy, Hindemith, Mozart, Ravel, Schoenberg, and Webern.

Rideout has been in demand constantly as a soloist with Canada's major choral and orchestral societies, singing *Messiah* in Winnipeg (1960), Toronto (1961, 1966, 1974, 1975), and Hamilton (1977); Beethoven's *Ninth Symphony* with the *Calgary Philharmonic (1964), the TSO (1966), and the *MSO (1974); Bach's *Magnificat* at the Stratford Festival (1964) and Beethoven's *Mass in C* at the Guelph Spring Festival (1970) with the Festival Singers; Vaughan Williams' *Serenade to Music* with the same choir in Toronto and Boston in 1965; and numerous other works in Toronto with the *Toronto Mendelssohn Choir and / or the Festival Singers, notably Britten's *Spring Symphony* (1966) and *Cantata academica* (1967), Copland's *In the Beginning* (1966), Haydn's *Nelson Mass* (1967), Bach's *Mass in B Minor* (1975, 1978) and *Christmas Oratorio* (1977), and Mendelssohn's *Elijah* (1976).

Rideout's most significant achievement, however, has been her sustained and vital participation in the performance of contemporary music. In the tradition of Frances *James, and on a level with her colleagues Mary *Morrison and Phyllis *Mailing, Rideout has lent an adaptable soft-edged dark mezzo, a fine intelligence, and sound musicianship to many exacting assignments from *Ten Centuries Concerts and *NMC in Toronto and the *SMCQ in Montreal. For example, in 1976, for NMC, she sang in George Crumb's *Night of the Four Moons* in Toronto, Stockholm, Bergen, Saarbrücken, Geneva, Bourges, Nantes, and Brussels. For the same group in 1977 she sang John Cage's *Five Songs for Contralto* and *The Wonderful Widow of Eighteen Springs* at a special birthday concert for the composer in Toronto. And she has made a specialty of Bruce *Mather's *Madrigals* I, II, and III. No. III was written for her and was given its European premiere (Royan, France, 1972) and its US premiere (Boston, 1976) by her. She also gave the European premiere of Somers' *Evocations* (Royen, 1972). Below are premieres in which Rideout participated between 1956 and 1977:

Beckwith *Night Blooming Cereus*, CBC Radio 1959; *Jonah*, CBC Radio 1964; *Canada Dash – Canada Dot*, Toronto 1967
*Beecroft *Rasas II*, Toronto 1973
Börtz *Nightflies*, ISCM, Boston 1976
*Freedman *Fragments of Alice*, Sweden 1976
Gould *So You Want to Write a Fugue*, CBC TV 1963
*Jones *Sam Slick*, CBC Radio 1967
*Kenins *Gloria*, Guelph Spring Festival 1970
Lanza *Kron'Kelz '75*, Toronto 1976

Mather *Madrigal I*, Toronto 1967; *Madrigal III*, CBC Toronto Festival 1971
Pannell *Push*, Toronto 1976
*Schafer *Lustro*, CBC Toronto Festival 1973
Sigurbjørnsson *Solstice*, Iceland 1976
Somers *Evocations*, CBC Radio 1966; *Louis Riel*, Toronto 1967; *Improvisation*, CBC Montreal Festival 1968
*Turner *The Brideship*, CBC 1967
*Wilson *Heloise and Abelard*, Toronto 1973

Rideout has had important assignments as well in the first performances in Canada of works of Berio (*El mar la mar* 1972), de Banfield (*Lord Byron's Love Letter*, CBC TV 1957), Davies (*Leopardi Fragments* 1971), Ligeti (*Nouvelles Aventures* 1972), London (*Portrait of Three Ladies*), Schoenberg (*Pierrot Lunaire* 1962), Stravinsky (*Mavra*, CBC radio 1964; *Requiem Canticles* 1968), Xenakis (*N'Shima* 1976), and others.

DISCOGRAPHY

Mather *Madrigal II* (Morrison sop, SMCQ, Garant cond); *Madrigal III* (Beluse marimba, Morris hp, Mather pf). Ca 1973. RCI 369
Somers *The Fool*. Roslak sop, Astor ten, Brown bass. 1968. RCI 272/RCA LSC 3049/Mel SMLP 4029
Somers – Schoenberg – Hindemith – Barber. Somers, Helmer both pf. 1970. CBC SM-108
Stravinsky *Mavra*. Belink sop, Simmons sop, Kolk ten, CBC SO, Stravinsky cond. 1964. Col MS 6991
See also Discography for Festival Singers.

BIBLIOGRAPHY

Creative Canada, vol 2

KW

RIDOUT, Godfrey. Composer, teacher, writer, conductor, b Toronto 6 May 1918; hon LLD (Queen's) 1967, hon FRCCO 1975. At the *TCM he studied with Charles *Peaker (organ and counterpoint), Ettore *Mazzoleni (conducting), Weldon *Kilburn (piano), and, on a scholarship received for *Ballade for Viola and Strings* (1938), with Healey *Willan. *Ballade* brought Ridout his earliest recognition and was performed in Canada, the USA, and Great Britain. Another ambitious early work was the full-length dramatic symphony *Esther*, premiered (1952) at *Massey Hall with Lois *Marshall and James *Milligan as soloists under the direction of Mazzoleni. Between *Ballade* and *Esther*, the bulk of Ridout's professional work – with the exception of the oft-performed *Two Etudes* for strings (1946) – comprised many radio-drama scores and symphonic arrangements of popular music for the *CBC, and some film scores for the *NFB.

Ridout began teaching at the TCM in 1940 and at the *U of Toronto in 1948; in 40 years of teaching his pupils have included Walter *Babiak, Walter *Buczynski, Hugh *Davidson, Alan *Detweiler, Ben *McPeek, Welford *Russell, Alfred *Strombergs, and Charles *Wilson. Assistant editor of *Canadian Music* 1940–1 and the *Canadian Review of Music and Art* 1942–3, Ridout has contributed to other Canadian music publications and began writing program notes for the *TS in 1973. He has served 1949–58 as music director of the *Eaton Operatic Society, Toronto, and honorary vice-president of the Gilbert & Sullivan Society, Toronto branch.

Ridout's articles on Sullivan, Elgar, and Willan, and on church music, betray his particular enthusiasms as a music historian of Victorian and Edwardian Great Britain and suggest the formative influences on him as a composer. He himself has noted the lasting impact of his first hearing of Holst's *The Planets*. While these leanings could be foreseen easily, given his English-trained teachers, there is much more to Ridout than is suggested by the epithet 'bloated Edwardian' tacked onto him by one of his colleagues.

Godfrey Ridout

His early assignments for the CBC and the NFB gave Ridout an intoxicating exposure to jazz and a respect for popular music and resulted in extraordinary versatility and fluency of musical craft and a keen appreciation of just how much chaos in music a paying public will endure. Wide knowledge of the historical repertoire also informs his works. He can write occasionally in the serial manner without 'sounding serial.' He can hold on to rhythmic patterns with almost baroque tenacity. He can (and did in several contributions to *Spring Thaw*) produce stylistic parodies of unerring accuracy and telling wit; and this gift he put to good use in his idiomatic reconstruction (1964, from a second violin part) of the orchestral score of *Quesnel's opera **Colas et Colinette* of 1790.

Essentially an eclectic, Ridout yet does not lack for individuality. His music, though intensely felt, is prevailingly sunny and affirmative; it eschews the 'doom and gloom' manner and self-conscious profundity of much 20th-century concert fare. Ridout likes fun in music and cannot easily resist concluding a work with a 'good tune.' He sees no need to strive for ever-new styles, or for a progress through styles, or for the role of musical inventor; style for him is a means of communication, not the 'message' itself. In this aloofness from contemporary conformity, Ridout in the end may be perceived to be more original than many innovators and one of the determined communicators of our day.

Two works separated by more than two decades reveal much of the stylistic consistency and growing refinement of Ridout as a composer. *Two Etudes* (1946, revised 1951) and *Concerto Grosso* (1974) are works for string orchestra (though the concerto has also a solo part for piano in the fast outer movements). Both works are held together mainly by short motives (more often of rhythmic than of melodic identity) that recur, sometimes in persistent repetition or sequence, sometimes greatly transformed. (The slow movement of *Concerto Grosso* even has a serial theme that occurs in all of the Schoenbergian permutations, though against the disjunct angularity of the tone row Ridout has set a cohering bass that moves almost entirely by step, with the result that it sounds like Ridout, not Schoenberg.) The dramatic excitement, however, comes not from the integrating power of motives, but from discontinuities, sudden surges, which both works have in abundance. Similarly, the closing movements of both works achieve cumulation by fast tempo, driving rhythms, and brevity and by final terse cadences that leave the listener astonished but pleased. If both works proceed from the same stylistic premises, they are yet individual: the *Two Etudes* are a young man's effort – bold, impulsive and dramatic; the *Concerto Grosso* is more polished, sophisticated, knowing – it testifies to the composer's understanding of the concerto grosso principle, which he reinterprets in a manner that is fresh.

The *Cantiones mysticae*, three works for solo voice and orchestra, perhaps are the most deeply felt of all of Ridout's creations. It is no accident that their texts are sacred or that the composer himself chose them; for the music he writes to these words would convince any sensitive listener that the composer has strong spiritual convictions. Then too, the combination of redolent poetry and the expressive potential of the richly accompanied solo voice seems to trigger Ridout's highest creative powers. The melodies are fluid and finely arched, having none of the rhythmic rigidity that crops up here and there in his purely instrumental compositions; and they fit the texts like a glove.

The first of the *Cantiones mysticae*, performed in Carnegie Hall under Stokowski (1953), sets three of Donne's *Holy Sonnets* (nos. 15, 1, and 7). The two outer pieces are in the composer's best rhapsodic manner; the gentle centre piece 'Thou Hast Made Me' would seem a perfect baroque aria were it not for the ominous music that suddenly occurs at the words 'despair, death, terror,' and the occasional eccentric modulation. *The Ascension, Cantiones mysticae No. 2* (1962) is written to liturgical texts for Ascension Day and is in two continuous sections: the first, joyous, interpreting quite literally the words 'God is gone up with a merry sound ... the sound of the trumpet ... Alleluia'; the second, elegiac, at the words 'Lo the fair beauty of Earth' and boasting one of Ridout's most glowing melodies. In the third and most ambitious of the cantiones, *The Dream of the Rood* (1972), the animistic Cross narrates and comments on the poetically told story of the Crucifixion. The orchestral forces (winds, brass, and organ) are handled with exceptional brilliance and Ridout adds a large chorus in the introduction and at the close; it replaces the baritone soloist at especially poignant moments of the text.

By way of sad contrast, note must be taken of the three-act CBC TV opera *The Lost Child* (1975), a charming tale of the disappearance of the Christ Child from a church crèche on Christmas Day. While there are splendid musical ideas, Ridout cannot overcome the handicap of a fundamentally flawed libretto that in a one-hour work has far too many characters, far too many plot digressions, far too many bits of dialogue, simply far, far too many words for the music ever to take flight.

The public will know Ridout best from his many occasional works for orchestra. They are widely performed, addressed to the widest possible audience, and intended to please. Yet they are highly professional works. *Music for a Young Prince* was commissioned to celebrate the opening of the St Lawrence Seaway (1959) and with the young Prince Charles in mind. The two outer movements, 'Dreams' and 'Pageantry,' are everything they claim to be, the latter in the best Elgarian tradition. The inside movements are superb genre pieces. The third, 'The Cowboy and the Injun,' evokes memories of Ferde Grofé; but Ridout is much better. The second, a train ride 'From the Caboose,' is a veritable tour de force of orchestral realism (Ridout is a train nut). Ridout's instructions to the trombonists, telling them how to produce the final sounds of this movement (the release of air-brake pressure at the end of the ride) illustrate the exactitude by which he achieved this remarkable movement: 'The desired effect is gained by removing the mouth piece, reversing it, holding the cup against the tube opening at a slight angle and blowing through the shank.'

A CBC commission for a United Nations concert in New York produced the orchestral frolic *Fall Fair* (1961), a shorter, less striking, but characteristic and popular work. The most recent of Ridout's occasional works, *George III, His Lament*, was commissioned by the *NACO for the Ottawa celebration of the 1976 bicentenary of US independence. The subtitle describes it as 'variations on a familiar theme' but what Ridout does not say is that the identity of the theme becomes clear only towards the end. To identify it here would only spoil the fun.

Ridout is a member of CAPAC, which he served 1966–73 as a director, and of the *CLComp. He also is an associate of the *CMCentre.

SELECTED COMPOSITIONS

STAGE

The Lost Child, TV opera (John Reid). 1975. CMCentre

See also *La Prima Ballerina*.

ORCHESTRA

Festal Overture. 1939. Full orch. CMCentre. RCI 41 (*CBC SO)

Two Etudes. 1946 (rev 1951). Str orch. Chap 1960

Music for a Young Prince. 1959. Full orch. CMCentre

Fall Fair. 1961. Full orch. GVT 1966. Audat 477 4001 (*TSO)

Overture to Colas et Colinette (Quesnel). 1964. Med orch. GVT 1971. Sel SSC-24.160 (CBC Mtl O, P. *Hétu cond)

Frivolités canadiennes (from melodies by Vézina). 1973. Full orch. CMCentre. 1974. CBC SM-226 (*CBC Van Chamb O)

Jubilee. 1973. Full orch. CMCentre

George III, His Lament. 1975. Med orch. CMCentre

Kids' Stuff. 1978. Orch. CMCentre

SOLOIST(S) AND/OR CHOIR WITH ORCHESTRA

Esther, dramatic symphony (H. Voaden). 1952. Sop, bar, SATB, orch. Ms

Cantiones mysticae (Donne). 1953. Sop, orch (pf). FH 1956

The Dance (Carmina burana CXXXVII, transl J.A. Symonds). 1960. SATB, orch. Novello 1964

Pange lingua (Aquinas). 1960. SATB, orch. Wat 1960.

The Ascension, Cantiones mysticae No. 2 (Propers for Ascension and the Ascension Day Hymn by Bishop Venantius Fortunatus). 1962. Sop, tpt, str. FH 1971

Four Sonnets (J.E. Ward). 1964. SATB, orch. GVT, Novello 1964

In Memoriam Anne Frank 'A Song of Strength' (text arr B. Attridge). 1965. Sop, full orch. Ms

Folk Songs of Eastern Canada (traditional). 1967. Sop, full orch. GVT 1970

Cantiones mysticae No. 3, Dream of the Rood (anon). 1972. Bar (ten), SATB, orch, org. Ms

Concerto grosso. 1974. Pf, str orch. CMCentre. 1975. CBC SM-289 (*Chamber Players of Toronto)

CHAMBER AND KEYBOARD

Prelude in F. 1958. Pf. GVT 1958

Three Preludes on Scottish Tunes. 1959. Org. Novello, GVT 1960

Introduction and Allegro. 1968. Ww quin, vn, vc. CMCentre

Prelude for Organ (arr by F.R.C. Clarke from 'Four Sonnets'). 1968. GVT 1968

March (arr from 'Partita academica'). 1969. Org. CMCentre

Two Dances for Guitar. 1976. Solo guit. Ms

Tafelmusik. 1976. Ww ens. CMCentre

CHOIR

'Ave Maria' (liturgical). 1954. SSA. GVT 1972. Poly 2917 009 (*Festival Singers)

The Domage of the Wise (R. Hambleton). 1969. SATB. 1969. CBC SM-86 (*Tudor Singers of Mtl)

2 arrangements for SATB: 'Sainte Marguerite' and 'J'entends le moulin.' Both Wat 1960. Recorded CBC SM-19 (Festival Singers) and CBC SM-219 (Kelvin High School Choir of Wpg) respectively

Plus other works for choir, and a few for v

WRITINGS

'Fricker farewell,' *CRMA*, vol 1, Dec 1942

'Two west coast composers,' *CRMA*, vol 3, Dec–Jan 1944–5

'Canadian composing,' *Here and Now*, vol 1, Dec 1947

'Elgar the angular Saxon,' *CMJ*, vol 1, Summer 1957

'Healey Willan,' *CMJ*, vol 3, Spring 1959

'Sir Ernest MacMillan: an appraisal,' *Music Across Canada* Jul–Aug 1963 / *CME*, vol 6, 1964–5

'Aspects of Arnold Walter,' *CanComp*, 38, Mar 1969

'Orpheus in Ecclesia or the River Lute,' *Canadian J of Theology*, vol 15, nos. 3–4, 1969

'Sir Ernest MacMillan: a considered appraisal,' *CanComp*, 82, Jul 1973

'Healey Willan,' *Mcan*, 42, Spring 1980

'Fifty years of music in Canada? Good Lord, I was there for all of them!' *U of Toronto Q*, vol 50, Fall 1980; and *The Arts in Canada* (Toronto 1980)

BIBLIOGRAPHY

Kidd, George. 'Godfrey Ridout,' *CanComp*, 6, Feb 1966

'Godfrey Ridout,' *Mcan*, 12, Jun–Jul 1968

'Interview: a musical conservative,' *CanComp*, 93, Sep 1974

CAPAC. 'Godfrey Ridout,' pamphlet and recording (1975)

Gilbert, Amy. 'Godfrey Ridout,' *TS News*, Jan–Feb 1975

MacMillan, Keith. 'Canadian composers you'll be hearing,' ibid, Apr–May 1977

Tennyson, Jean. 'Godfrey Ridout,' *The Varsity*, 5 Apr 1978

Gilpin, Wayne. 'Godfrey Ridout, choral music with orchestra,' unpubl M MUS thesis, U of Alberta 1978

Winters, Kenneth. 'Godfrey Ridout,' *Contemporary Canadian Composers / Compositeurs canadiens contemporains*

HO

RIGNOLD, Hugo (Henry). Conductor, violinist, b Kingston-on-Thames, England, 15 May 1905, d London 30 May 1976; hon ARAM.

Rignold's father, Hugo Charles Rignold (also conductor, violinist, b Swansea, Wales, 19 May 1873, d Winnipeg 12 Jan 1949), took the family to Winnipeg in 1910. There he conducted in vaudeville, was choirmaster 1923–33 at St Ignatius Church, and formed and directed a 60-piece orchestra.

The younger Rignold studied violin with his father in Winnipeg and in 1921 returned to England on a scholarship to the RAM where he studied with Hans Wessely (violin), Leon Goossens (oboe), and Lionel Tertis. After 13 years as a freelance violinist he conducted orchestras 1945–7 in Cairo and Palestine. Appointments followed with the Sadler's Wells Ballet in 1947, the Liverpool Philharmonic 1948–54, the Royal Ballet 1955–60, and the Birmingham SO 1960–8. In the years following he was a guest conductor of orchestras in various countries.

Rignold's sisters Catherine and Patricia were active in music: the former as a cellist in Winnipeg chamber groups in the late 1920s and early 1930s, and the latter as a singer in England on the BBC.

MM

RILEY, Doug (Douglas Brian). Composer, arranger, producer, pianist, organist, b Toronto 24 Apr 1945; B MUS (Toronto) 1967. His teachers were Lawrence Goodwill (RCMT 1950–6), Paul *de Marky (Montreal 1956–60), and Patricia *Blomfield Holt (RCMT 1961–4) for piano and John *Weinzweig and Mieczyslaw *Kolinski (U of Toronto) for composition and ethnomusicology respectively. Under Kolinski, he did postgraduate work in the music of the Iroquois.

In his teens Riley played rhythm and blues with the Silhouettes at the Toronto nightclub the Blue Note. In 1968 he was the arranger and second keyboard player for Ray Charles' LP *Doing His Thing* (ABC S-695). He has been the arranger and pianst for 'The Ray Stevens Show' (CTV 1969–70) and 'Rolling on the River' (CTV 1970–2) and music director for 'Music Machine' (CBC 1973–4), for Tommy *Ambrose's 'Celebration' (CBC 1975–6), for 'The Wolfman Jack Show' (CBC 1976–7), and for specials starring Anne *Murray, Lou Rawls, and others.

The 16-member band Dr Music (a name Riley has used as a personal pseudonym, the 'Dr' taken from his initials) was formed by Riley to sing and play for 'The Ray Stevens Show' and has continued intermittently (latterly with a reduced personnel) to perform in clubs and concerts. It toured western Canada in 1971 and made three LPs 1972–4: *Doctor Music* (GRT 9233-1003), *Doctor Music II* (GRT 9233-1004), and *Bedtime Story* (GRT 9233-1005), the last largely of jazz compositions by Riley and band members Claude *Ranger and Don W. *Thompson. Dr Music's most popular singles were 'One More Mountain to Climb' (1971), 'Sun Goes By' (1972), and 'Long Time Comin' Home' (1972).

Riley has led jazz groups in Toronto clubs – one, completed by Thompson, Ranger, and the saxophonist Michael Stuart, made the LP *Dreams* (1975, PMR-007) at *George's Spaghetti House. In a review of *Dreams*, Chuck Berg (*Down Beat*, 20 Apr 1978) observed: 'Riley's playing reflects the varied influences of Waller, Tatum, Powell, Evans, Hancock and Corea. His improvisations are emotionally moving, structurally complex and technically sophisticated.' Riley played piano for Sonny *Greenwich 1974–5 and has been an occasional sideman to Moe *Koffman and a member of the *Boss Brass.

Riley's compositions include scores for the ballets *Lies, Wishes and Dreams* and *Sessions for Six* (in the National Ballet of Canada repertoire) and *Jeux en blanc et noir* (premiered at the 1975 *Shaw Festival); scores for the feature films *Foxy Lady, Cannibal Girls, The Naked Peacock*, and *Dreams of America*; a musical version of *Mandragola* (libretto by Alan Gordon), premiered 13 Oct 1977 on CBC radio and later issued on an LP (CBC LM-448); and various student works, among them a *String Quartet* (1966) played by the Armin Electric Strings. Riley began writing jingles in 1964, and has written several hundred in collaboration with, among others, Mort Ross (with whom he established the Revolver label, ca 1969) and Tommy Ambrose (through Trudel Productions).

Riley has arranged music for, played piano or organ on, or produced LPs by the Canadians Tommy Ambrose, David Bradstreet, Dianne Brooks, David *Clayton-Thomas, Dan *Hill, Klaatu, Moe Koffman, Gordon *Lightfoot, Bob McBride, Kathryn *Moses, Anne Murray, Walter *Rossi, and Sylvia *Tyson, and the US performers the Brecker Brothers and Bob Seger.

Riley is a member of CAPAC. He is married to the violinist Adele *Armin.

BIBLIOGRAPHY

Flohil, Richard. 'From ballet to rock, Doug Riley's a hard man to keep pace with,' *CanComp*, 68, Mar 1972

Waxman, Ken. 'Doug Riley: renaissance musician,' *Audio Scene Canada*, Apr 1977

MM

RINGUET, Léon (b Ringuette). Bandmaster, composer, organist, pianist, teacher, b Louiseville, near Trois-Rivières, Que, 3 Jan 1858, d St-Hyacinthe, Que, 20 Sep 1932. His early musical training took place at the Collège de St-Césaire, near Montreal, and at St-Joseph U in Memramcook, NB. He later studied in Montreal with Paul *Letondal (piano) and Romain-Octave *Pelletier (organ). He moved to St-Hyacinthe in 1880 and was for more than 50 years organist-choirmaster of the cathedral and conductor of the Philharmonic Society Concert Band; he also served 1885–1928 as conductor of the 84th Battalion Infantry Band and in 1930 he became conductor of the Drummondville Concert Band. He wrote over 100 pieces (Op 107 was published in 1919), including numerous parlour pieces, marches for concert band, and pieces for organ, piano, and violin; they were published in the USA by Coleman and Presser and in Canada by *Archambault and *Whaley Royce. He contributed to several music journals, including *The Etude*. In 1941 the town of St-Hyacinthe built a bandshell and dedicated a plaque in his memory. Léon-Ringuet Ave, Montreal, was named after him in 1972, and the Salle

Léon-Ringuet on the St-Hyacinthe campus of the Bourgchemin regional Cegep was inaugurated in 1976.

BIBLIOGRAPHY

Gosselin, J.-E. 'Léon Ringuet,' *P-T*, 909, Apr 1947 GP

RINGUETTE, Wellie or **Willy**. Violoneux, composer, b Franklin, NH, 6 Feb 1898, d Trois-Rivières, Que, 10 Sep 1969. At eight he began playing a violin made by his father. After the family moved to the Trois-Rivières area in 1915 Ringuette worked as a lumberjack but continued to play, his popularity growing with his appearances at dances and fiddling contests throughout the province and, after 1927, with his recordings for *Starr and *Columbia (the latter made in New York). The extent of his discography is not clear; *Pionniers du disque folklorique* lists 12 78s made in the late 1920s, but Phil Hresko, in his liner notes to *Jean Carignan* (Philo FO 2001), suggests there may be about 100. Considered by *Carignan, who has perpetuated the Ringuette repertoire, to be with Joseph *Allard the finest violoneux of the day, Ringuette was known especially for his interpretation of waltzes. He composed those classics of French-Canadian fiddling *Valse joyeuse*, *Les Pionniers* (Marche Lancier), *Yvon Valse*, and *Ronfleuse Gobeil*. Little is known of Ringuette's later life. MM

Rioux Report. See *Rapport de la Commission royale d'enquête sur l'enseignement des arts dans la province de Québec*.

RITTICH, Eugene (Danny). French hornist, teacher, b Calgary, of Hungarian parents, 15 Aug 1928; Artist Diploma (Curtis) 1951. After studies in Kelowna, BC, and with Douglas Kent in Victoria, he continued his training 1945–51 at the Curtis Institute where his teacher was Mason Jones.

Rittich became principal horn of the *TSO in 1952 and co-principal (with Frederick Rizner) in 1973. He was principal horn 1952–64 of the *CBC SO and a founding member of the Toronto Winds and the *Toronto Woodwind Quintet.

Rittich became a horn teacher at the *U of Toronto in 1956 and the brass coach for the *NYO in 1960 and subsequently has prepared many pupils for careers in orchestras and chamber groups. Notable among these have been Evan Philpotts of the *NACO; John MacDonald, who was a principal of the Hessischer Rundfunk orchestra in Frankfurt and winner of the horn classes in the 1978 Munich International Music Festival; Carla Goldberg, principal of the Bodensee SO, Germany; James MacDonald of the *York Winds, Toronto; Jean Gaudreault of the *MSO; Kirk Laughton of the *Atlantic SO; Daryl Caswell of the *Calgary Philharmonic; and others in the *Edmonton SO and the *London (Ont) SO. Rittich commissioned *Weinzweig's *Divertimento No. 7* and *Morawetz' *Sonata for Horn and Piano* and premiered both works on CBC radio in 1980, the divertimento with the *CBC Vancouver Chamber Orchestra and the sonata with Patricia *Parr. SC

The Riverboat. Coffeehouse in Toronto's Yorkville district. Seating about 100 in a narrow basement room, with a small stage occupying part of a side wall, it was opened in October 1964 by Burnie Fiedler (its owner and manager until it was leased in 1977 to Ron Carlyle) and became the best-known coffeehouse in Canada. By the mid-1970s the sole remaining coffeehouse in Yorkville, it closed 25 Jun 1978 after four concerts each by Dan *Hill and Murray *McLauchlan; reopened, under different management, 3 Aug 1978, as the Ship of Fools; and closed again in mid-1979.

The Riverboat was the showcase in the late 1960s for numerous emerging Canadian folk-inspired performers, including Bruce *Cockburn, Gordon *Lightfoot, Murray McLauchlan, and Joni *Mitchell, many of whom Fiedler presented later at *Massey Hall. Most major US folk performers also appeared at The Riverboat. Several songs that became popular, including 'Changes' (Phil Ochs) and 'Clouds' (Mitchell), were composed in the club's upstairs backroom.

Fiedler (b Berlin 8 Dec 1938) arrived in Canada as an infant. He opened the Mousehole, also a coffeehouse, in Yorkville in 1963 and was involved in other similar ventures. In 1973 he became a partner of Bernie Finkelstein in Finkelstein-Fiedler Co Ltd, an artist-management and concert-promotion agency which has directed the careers of Ronney Abramson, Cockburn, Hill, and McLauchlan.

BIBLIOGRAPHY

Goddard, Peter. 'The Riverboat changes hands and ends a golden age,' *Toronto Star*, 19 Nov 1977 MM

Rivers. Rivers were of paramount importance in the early development of Canada. Unlike the rivers of Europe, girded by castles and woven into legend, Canadian rivers have served more practical purposes: at first, with the Great Lakes, as the country's transportation network – to be supplanted by the railway – and later as an integral part of the logging industry and a source of hydro-electric energy. Like the rivers in Europe, those in Canada have been admired for their natural beauty, and to this may be attributed the many descriptive titles to be found in Canadian music. The first Canadian songs inspired by rivers were those of the voyageurs, including *'Youpe! Youpe! Sur La Rivière!'. Thomas Moore, who travelled with the voyageurs on the St Lawrence River in 1804, was inspired to write a *'Canadian Boat Song.'

Several individual rivers have enjoyed prominence in titles of music, but none more than the St Lawrence, beginning in the late 1850s with C.W. *Sabatier's mazurka *Promenade sur le fleuve Saint-Laurent*. Other examples are A.J. *Boucher's quadrille *Les Canotiers du St-Laurent* (ca 1860–6), the popular *Sunrise on the St Lawrence* (1910) by Maxine Heller (pseudonym for Frederick *Harris), Gena *Branscombe's song 'By St Lawrence Water' (1925), Percival *Price's romantic symphony *The St Lawrence* (1932–3), André *Prévost's *Ode au Saint-Laurent* (1965) for narrator and string quartet, and André *Gagnon's suite *Le Saint-Laurent* (1977) available on an LP of the same title.

Next in popularity would seem to be the Red River in Manitoba, given lasting fame in the folksong *'Red River Valley.' Other similarly titled pieces include *Gigue de la Rivière Rouge* by the violoneux Arthur-Joseph Boulay, 'Red River' from Violet *Archer's choral suite *Landscapes* (1950), Graham *George's *Red River of the North* (1970), Eric *Wild's *Red River Jig* (1973), and at least three dance tunes by fiddler Andy *Dejarlis. (Dejarlis honoured northern Ontario's Rainy River with a waltz, as did Burton *Kurth with the song 'Road to Rainy River.')

The Saguenay River in Quebec inspired 'Capes Trinity and Eternity' (one of F.T. *Egener's eight *Canadian Scenes*), *La Traverse du Saguenay* by the violoneux Louis 'Pitou' *Boudreault, a *Reel du Saguenay* recorded by the harmonicist Henri Lacroix, *Paul Jones du Saguenay* recorded by the accordionist Tommy Duchesne, and the song 'By the Deep, Blue Saguenay' (1944) by Carlotta Fisher. André *Mathieu's symphonic poem *Mistassini*

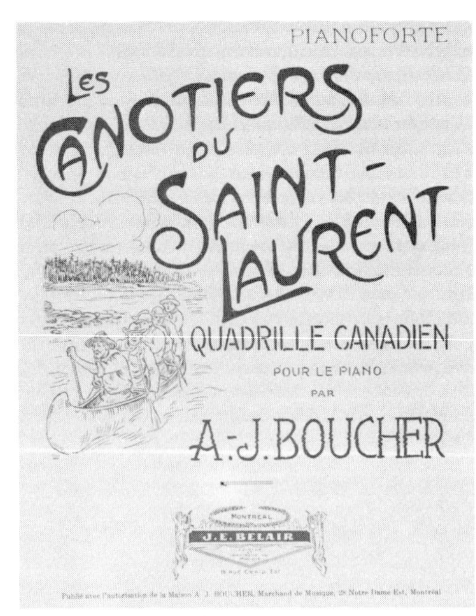

was named for a river and lake in the Saguenay region.

From New Brunswick's Miramichi River come the folk songs 'The Miramichi Fire' and 'The Miramichi' and Kelsey *Jones' orchestral suite *Miramichi Ballad*. The Ottawa River is celebrated in songs by Oskar *Morawetz ('To the Ottawa River,' 1949, words by Archibald Lampman) and Ann *Eggleston ('Night on the Ottawa River,' 1967), the Saskatchewan in 'By the Saskatchewan' from Ivan Caryll's and C.M.S. McLellan's 1910 US musical *The Pink Lady* and in Marguerite *Spencer's piano suite *By the River Saskatchewan*. British Columbia's Fraser River inspired at least two songs: 'My Home by the Fraser,' a hit record in the late 1940s for country singer-songwriter Keray Regan (who also composed a 'Peace River Waltz'), and 'Fraser River' by Gladys Davenport Goertz.

Other pieces with references to rivers in their titles include Mrs G.A. Gilbert's 'Come to the Vale of the Beautiful Don' (ca 1870), J.F. *Johnstone's 'The Humber Fairy' (1886), and Eugene Clair's 'Where the Dreamy Humber Flows,' all about the rivers which flow through Toronto; Joseph Lamb's *Muskoka Falls – Indian Idyll* (1902); A.A. Penn's 'To the Coaticook River of My Boyhood' (1909); W. Spence's *Moonlight on the Rideau* (1937); and various country and Quebec folkdances. Ian *McDougall's *British Columbia Centennial Suite* (1971) comprises six movements, each named for one of the province's rivers.

Films about Canadian rivers have had scores by Lucio *Agostini, Maurice *Blackburn, Robert *Fleming, Harry *Somers, John *Weinzweig, and others. The CBC TV program 'Canadian Express,' 13 Sep 1978, presented 'Songs of the Valleys,' which included folksongs ('Banks of the Miramichi,' 'Where the Ottawa River Flows,' etc) sung by Marie *Hare, Tom *Kines, and others.

See also Lakes; Occupational songs.

ROBB, (Frank) Morse. Inventor, designer, b Belleville, Ont, 28 Jan 1902. After studies 1921–4 at *McGill U he returned to Belleville and in 1926 began research on an electronic organ. His chief goal was to produce an instrument for church use which would save space and require little maintenance. Robb was one of the first anywhere to succeed in developing an electronic organ. The sound-producing mechanism of the Robb Wave Organ involved a system of 12 shafts, each representing one note of the scale in all its octaves. On each shaft were mounted sets of tone discs. Each disc was edged in the shape of sound-waves photographed from a cathode ray oscillograph and corresponded to an organ stop. The shafts and discs were made to rotate before tiny coils and magnets which in turn translated the wave design into electric currents to be fed through a vacuum-tube amplifier into two loudspeakers. Different speeds of rotation produced different pitches. The organ's console had all the usual couplers of traditional pipe organs.

In November 1927 a small trial instrument was demonstrated in Belleville and at the *Toronto Daily Star*'s CFCA radio studio. Boris *Hambourg put Robb in touch with the General Electric Co at Schenectady, NY, but no commercial exploitation of the invention resulted. Robb had filed the first patent application for a Sound Reproducing Instrument 29 Sep 1927 and obtained the patents for Canada 23 Oct 1928 and for the USA 23 Dec 1930. Additional patents for wave organ inventions (eg, experiments with a touch-sensitive keyboard) were obtained during the 1930s. In 1931 Robb resumed experimentation and signed an agreement to work with the organ builders *Casavant Frères for their mutual benefit; however the Depression caused the company to back out of the agreement the following spring.

Robb produced a five-octave one-manual instrument in 1932 and demonstrated a two-manual, 32-pedal note-wave organ in Belleville in April 1934. Soon afterwards Lady Eaton, Edward *Johnson, Alexander and Ernest *MacMillan, and Frederick *Silvester visited Robb to hear the organ. In November the Robb Wave Organ Co was formed. Altogether between 16 and 20 instruments were built. Silvester played on one at a Toronto *Promenade Symphony Concert 30 Jul 1936. Wave organs were installed at Eaton's Montreal and Toronto stores; Robb and the Montreal organist Warner Norman provided demonstrations. Critical response, while recognizing the need for further improvements, was warm, but unfortunately Robb was unable to obtain private or government funding for further production, and in 1938 he abandoned the project. HK

ROBBIN, Catherine (m Dodington). Mezzo-soprano, b Toronto 28 Sep 1950; BA (Toronto) 1977. She studied with Dorothy *Allan Park at the *RCMT, with Jacob Hamm and Phyllis *Mailing in Vancouver, and with Audrey Langford in London and took master classes and private lessons with Ré Koster in Canada, the USA, and France and with Sir Peter Pears in England. After a professional debut in 1972 in *Messiah* with the *St Catharines SO she performed in recital and in oratorios and concerts with the Buffalo Philharmonic, the *Hamilton Philharmonic, the *CJRT Orchestra, and the *Thunder Bay SO. Among choirs with which she has appeared are the *Bach-Elgar Choir of Hamilton, the *Festival Singers of Canada, and the *Vancouver Bach Choir. In 1978, with the violist Rivka Golani-Erdész and the pianist Jane *Coop, she performed Michael *Colgrass' set of songs *New People* at a CBC public concert taped for later broadcast. She has performed in England and the USA, and in 1979 she toured in France for JM and appeared at the Bordeaux Festival (in Beethoven's *Symphony No. 9*) and the Saint-Lizier-en-Ariège Festival. She has been heard over CBC radio and Radio France. Her operatic roles have included Frédéric in *Mignon* (1976, for Stuart *Hamilton's Opera in Concert series, Toronto) and Lucretia in *The Rape of Lucretia* (1979, Aldeburgh, England). She won the Caplet Award at the 1978 Concours international de chante de Paris, a silver medal at the 1978 Geneva Concours international, and the Gold Award at the 1979 Benson & Hedges International Competition for Concert Singers. She is the wife of the bass John *Dodington. NM

ROBBINS, Dave (David). Trombonist, teacher, composer, arranger, b Greenburg, Ind, 14 Aug 1923, naturalized Canadian 1965; B SC music education (Sam Houston State Teachers' College) 1943, M SC (Southern California) 1951. After his university studies he moved in 1951 to Vancouver where he taught, in turn, at a city high school, at Vancouver Community College, and at the *U of British Columbia (trombone 1959–66, theory 1966–9). In 1978 he established a jazz and commercial music department at Vancouver Community College and began teaching at the Courtenay Youth Music Camp. With Gary Guthman and Fraser *MacPherson he coached the New Westminster Secondary Schools Jazz Ensemble (conducted by Bob Schaeffer) that won a first prize at the 1978 Reno International Jazz Festival.

Robbins was a trombonist 1948–54 with the US trumpeter Harry James' big band, and again 1971–2 and 1973–4 on its European tours. He was principal trombone 1960–74 with the *Vancouver SO, played for 10 years with the *CBC Vancouver Chamber Orchestra, and worked in various Vancouver studio and pit orchestras.

Robbins' own big band, pre-eminent in Vancouver during the 1950s and 1960s, was heard nationally 1960–6 on 'CBC Jazz Workshop' (alternating weekly with Phil *Nimmons) and other CBC programs and appeared at the 1962 Seattle World's Fair. For the band, the CBC commissioned works by the Canadians Al Macmillan, Ian *McDougall, Doug Parker, Ray Sikora, Robert *Turner (*Robbins' Round*), and others and from US composers Dick Grove and Lalo Schifrin. The Vienna-born composer and bassist Paul Ruhland, who lived ca 1952–64 in Vancouver, was commissioned to write for the band *Contrasts*, *Passacaglia*, *Brass Fantasia for Large Jazz Orchestra*, and *Twelve Tone Suite for Twelve Piece Jazz Orchestra*. Robbins, Parker, and Dave Pepper were among the band's arrangers. With the Vancouver SO the band gave the North American premiere (ca 1965) of Richard Rodney Bennett's *Piece for Jazz Band and Orchestra* and the Canadian premiere (25 Feb 1966) of John Dankworth and Matyas Seiber's *Improvisations for Jazz Band and Symphony Orchestra* and performed Rolf Liebermann's *Concerto for Jazz Band and Symphony Orchestra*.

Robbins' own compositions include film and radio scores and, inspired by his experiences on one of several trips for the CBC to United Nations peacekeeping installations, the four-movement *Jazz Impressions of the Middle East* (1967). He has arranged music for such CBC programs as 'Parade' (TV), 'Sound of the Sixties' (TV), 'Music-Canada' (radio and TV), and 'Variety Showcase' (radio). His recordings include *The Dave Robbins Band* (1970, CBC LM-89) and the privately released *Everywhere* (1973) by US tenor saxophonist Corky Corcoran, a fellow Harry James alumnus for whom Robbins composed and conducted the big-band accompaniment. Robbins is an affiliate of PRO Canada.

BIBLIOGRAPHY
'David Robbins' Jazz,' *CBC Times*, 10–16 Mar 1962
Smith, Bob. 'Dave Robbins,' *MSc*, 243, Sep–Oct 1968 MM

ROBERT, Lucien. Violist, b Montreal 12 Feb 1899. He studied violin with Eugène *Chartier and began his career as a teacher. He played in short-lived groups such as the Assn philharmonique de Montréal (1920). In Trois-Rivières he played 1924–9 in cinemas. In Montreal he was a member in 1930 of the *La Presse* SO at radio station CKAC and 1930–1 of the *Durieux String Quartet. He played 1930–41 in the *Montreal Orchestra, becoming its principal violist, and was principal viola 1935–63 and associate principal 1963–9 with the CSM orchestra and principal 1942–52 with the *Little Symphony of Montreal. With the latter he was the soloist in Weber's *Andante e Rondo ungarese* and Hindemith's *Trauermusik*. A sought-after chamber player, he belonged 1933–4 to the Société de musique de chambre Euterpe, 1934–9 to the *Montreal String Quartet, 1939–40 to the Jean *Lallemand Quartet, and 1944–5 to the Quartet of the CMM under the guidance of Louis *Bailly with whom he took advanced studies 1943–8. Robert was a member 1944–50 of the *McGill String Quartet and the principal viola, for a few seasons, of the *McGill Chamber Orchestra. He has played in many CBC chamber music broadcasts. (IP-C)

ROBERTS, John (Peter Lee). Administrator, b Sydney 21 Oct 1930, naturalized Canadian 1961. After studying piano in Sydney and voice in London he settled in Canada in 1955 and joined the *CBC. He was a music producer 1955–7 at CBC Winnipeg, program organizer 1957–65 and supervisor of radio music 1965–71 at CBC Toronto, head of radio music and variety 1971–5 for the English Services Division, and special adviser in music and arts development 1976–7.

At the CBC Roberts developed competitions for young composers, amateur choirs, and solo performers and increased the commissioning of music by Canadian composers. He initiated the annual CBC Festivals across Canada and worked to establish the conditions under which a large number of CBC broadcast recordings could be made available for purchase by the public. Through his initiative, Igor Stravinsky, Michael Tippett, Joan Sutherland, Pierre Boulez, Hermann Scherchen, and others visited Toronto for engagements with the CBC.

As a CBC musical official Roberts sat on the jury of the International Beethoven Piano Competition (Brussels 1970) and was a delegate to the International Rostrum of Composers (Paris 1969, 1971).

Roberts served 1968–71 and 1975–7 as president of the *CMCouncil. During his presidency the *Canada Music Book* (1970–6) began publication and *Musicanada* was revived (1976). He was president of the *CMCentre 1971–3 and was appointed executive director of the centre in 1977.

Roberts was the first chairman 1969–70 of the Radio and Commercial Recording Group of the International Music Centre, Vienna. In 1973 he became the first Canadian to be elected to the executive of the International Music Council, which he served 1975–6 as vice-president and 1978–9 as president. When Canada was host in 1975 to the 16th IMC general assembly, Roberts was the chief planner of the concurrent first *World Music Week. He was the organizer 1975–7 of International Music Day, vice-president 1975–6 of the *CCA, chairman of The Arts in Human Settlement (Habitat, 1976, Vancouver), and vice-president in 1976 of the International Institute of Audio-Visual Communication and Cultural Development, Vienna.

In 1972 the CLComp honoured Roberts with a special award for service to Canadian music.

WRITINGS
'Communications media,' *Aspects of Music in Canada* / 'Les moyens de diffusion,' *Aspects de la musique au Canada*
'Stravinsky and the CBC,' *CMB*, 4, Spring–Summer 1972

'Music on radio and the youth of tomorrow,' *50 Years of Music on Radio* (Vienna 1973) / *CMB*, 8, Spring – Summer 1974
'First World Music Week in Canada / Première Semaine mondiale de la musique au Canada,' *CMB*, 10, Spring – Summer 1975

BIBLIOGRAPHY
Champagne, Jane. 'The CBC's resident promoter of music,' *CanComp*, 70, May 1972
Winters, Kenneth. 'Awarding commissions "fascinating and harrowing," ' *MSc*, 266, Jul-Aug 1972 (LL)

ROBERVAL, Albert. Conductor, stage director, tenor, teacher, actor, b Florence 23 Oct 1869, naturalized Canadian 1923, d Montreal 4 Oct 1941. He received all his training in Paris where he studied harmony with Massenet, counterpoint and fugue with Charles René, and voice with Paul Lhérie, and also took lessons in piano and organ. He made his debut as a singer but soon turned to conducting at the suggestion of Massenet, three of whose operas he conducted at the Grand Théâtre in Bordeaux. After performances in Buenos-Aires, Madagascar, and Algeria he arrived in Montreal in 1905 to act at the Théâtre français. At the Bijou Theatre he sang in operettas including Planquette's *Les Cloches de Corneville* and Messager's *Les P'tites Michu*. He worked 1907–9 for the Manhattan Opera Company, New York, as chorusmaster and assistant to Cleofonte Campanini. He then travelled as director of an operetta company to the Orient, and the tour included a trip to Batavia (Djakarta). He lived 1909–13 in Marseilles, where he directed the Théâtre du Gymnase and conducted the then-new Viennese operettas by Lehar.

After military service, ending in 1916, Roberval settled in Montreal where he remained active as conductor, stage director, and teacher until his death. In various theatres and for several companies he conducted and staged many operas and operettas including *Carmen, Mireille, Thaïs, Martha, Véronique,* and *La Mascotte*. With his wife Jeanne *Maubourg he directed a school at which Pierrette *Alarie, Fleurette *Beauchamp, Léonide Letourneux, Henri *Prieur, Honoré *Vaillancourt, and others studied opera performance. Roberval served 1923–4 as artistic director of the *Société canadienne d'opérette and conducted many of its productions both in the theatre and on radio station CKAC; he appeared also as an actor on this station. In 1938 he conducted and staged Leroux's opera *Évangéline*.

BIBLIOGRAPHY
'Montréal perd un artiste de grande valeur,' Montreal *La Presse*, 6 Oct 1941 GP

ROBI, Alys (Alice) (b Robitaille, m Ciamarra). Singer, b Quebec City 4 Feb 1923. At seven she made debuts in Quebec City both at the Capitol Theatre in the revue *Ten Nights in a Bar Room* and on radio stations CHRC and CKCV. She won several amateur contests including the Catelli Talent Competition and studied singing, dancing, and acting, her teachers including Jean *Riddez in Montreal.

Robi had gone to Montreal at 12 to act and dance with the comedienne La Poune at the Théâtre National where her contract was extended for 75 weeks. In 1937 she sang on radio station CKAC in the program 'La Veillée du samedi soir' along with such stars as Amanada Alarie and Gratien Gélinas. She sang in cabarets and, while at the Esquire Club in 1942, attracted the attention of CBC radio producer Morris *Davis who introduced her to the conductors Lucio *Agostini and Allan *McIver. These contacts led to appearances on CBC, and Robi's popularity began to grow.

Robi turned to the Latin American repertoire, for which she had a particular affinity and in which she gained world recognition. Popular with the Canadian Armed Forces, she was proclaimed 'torch singer' of the year in 1943 by the Montreal weekly *Radiomonde*. She sang on CBC English network programs, especially on 'Latin American Serenade' (1944–8). She received two LaFlèche trophies (French and English) for the best pop singer of the year in 1944 and won a Beaver trophy in 1945. Soon afterwards, she was working in such chic New York cabarets as The Blue Angel and on leading US radio programs of the day such as 'The Contented Hour.' In 1947 she went to Europe where she took part in the first regular BBC TV programs and sang in major nightclubs.

Robi's career was curtailed drastically by injuries suffered in a car accident in Hollywood in 1948. (Though widely reported in the French-language press and in many interviews with Robi, the accident is not mentioned in the article about her by Ken Johnstone, who attributed her disappearance from the public eye to a mental breakdown.) She attempted several comebacks (1952, 1954, 1965, 1971) but was unable to re-establish her former status. In 1974 she sang at La Seine, a nightclub in the east end of Montreal.

In the 1940s Robi made many 78s for RCA Victor. Some of these were extremely popular and a selection ('Tico-Tico,' 'Amor, amor,' 'Besame mucho,' 'Jalousie,' etc) was reissued in 1954 on the LP *Les Succès d'Alys Robi* (RCA Gala CGP-101). Robi's autobiography, *Ma Carriere, ma vie*, was published in Montreal in 1980.

BIBLIOGRAPHY
Johnstone, Ken. 'The courageous comeback of Alys Robi,' *Maclean's*, 11 Jun 1955
Sylvain, Jean-Paul. 'Une émouvante soirée: Alys Robi,' *Nouvelles illustrées*, 13 Apr 1963
Poronovich, Walter. 'Alys Robi mirrors 1940s era of musical magic,' *Montreal Star*, 5 Mar 1974 (DA, MM, GP)

ROBINSON, Augusta (Louise) **Beverley** (m Houston). Mezzo-soprano, b Toronto 12 Feb 1859, d there 9 Sep 1935. Her grandfather, Sir John Beverley Robinson, was chief justice of Upper Canada. After study with Emilio Agramonte in New York, Rosine Laborde in Paris, and Alberto Randegger and George Henschel in London, she began her career in England ca 1890 and quickly established herself as an admired exponent of the sentimental ballads (especially those by her friend Maude Valérie White) then so much in vogue. She toured Canada 1896–7 as a member of Emma *Albani's concert party and thereafter confined her appearances to Canada, retiring in 1898, soon after her marriage. She possessed a light, well-schooled voice.

Robinson's husband, Stewart Field Houston of Niagara Falls, Ont, served 1900–10 as manager of *Massey Hall, Toronto, and managed the Canadian tours of many leading artists of the day.

BIBLIOGRAPHY
'Mrs. Stewart Houston,' *Canadian Who's Who* (Toronto 1910) JBM

ROBINSON, Paul (Evans). Administrator, conductor, broadcaster-writer, double-bassist, b Toronto 21 Mar 1940; BA philosophy (Toronto) 1962, MA philosophy (Toronto) 1965. At the *RCMT 1955–7 he studied theory with *Weinzweig, double bass with Charles Rose and Gurney Titmarsh, and piano with *Dolin. He studied double-bass 1957–60 with Frederick Zimmermann in New York, philosophy 1958–65 at the U of Toronto, and conducting in 1969 with Herbert von Karajan and Bruno Maderna at the Mozarteum in Salzburg, obtaining a conducting diploma from the latter. He taught 1966–9 at the U of Hong Kong and 1970–2 at the State U of New York at Fredonia.

Robinson had conducted the Society of the Friends of New Music 1960–1 at the *U of Toronto. He resumed conducting in Hong Kong as music director 1967–9 of the Victoria Chamber Symphony. Appointed music director of radio station CJRT-FM in 1972, he began to conduct the *CJRT Orchestra in 1975. With that orchestra he presented the premieres of *Buczynski's *Lyric* for piano and orchestra in 1977 and *Schafer's *Hymn to Night* in 1978 and the Canadian premiere of Britten's *Suite on English Folk Tunes* in 1979. His books *Karajan* (Toronto 1975), *Stokowski* (Toronto 1977), and *Solti* (Toronto 1979) are drawn from the CJRT-FM radio series 'The Art of the Conductor' and have been published also in Great Britain, the USA, and Japan.

Robinson succeeded Franz *Kraemer as director of music programming 1979-80 for Toronto Arts Productions (Town Hall, *St Lawrence Centre).

JBk

ROBSON, (Charles William) **Sherwood**. Educator, choir conductor, b Vancouver 27 May 1913; B ED (British Columbia) 1962. His teachers included John *Goss (voice) and Frederic Staton (voice, choir training) in the early 1940s and Burton *Kurth (voice, organ, piano) in the 1950s. After teaching music and conducting choirs 1935–61 in Vancouver schools, he served 1963–74 as supervisor of elementary school music in North Vancouver. In 1957 he served as first president of the *BCMEA. In 1938 Robson was narrator and soloist in the first British Columbia Dept of Education broadcasts on CBC radio, and later he served on the department's music advisory committee. With Paul J. Bourret of Edmonton, and others, he adapted for Canada the 8-vol US schoolbook series *This Is Music* (Toronto 1966–71).

Robson was choirmaster 1938–9 at Central Presbyterian Church and organist-choirmaster 1942–52 at West Point Grey United Church. He was conductor 1948–50 of the *Vancouver Bach Choir and 1948–54 of the Sherwood Robson Chorale, the latter formed at the request of the CBC and heard on radio nationally and regionally. BNSG

Rock. Urban pop music of the mid-20th century. The term 'rock' was used first in the late 1940s in the titles of US rhythm and blues songs and, as in 'rock 'n' roll,' came into general use by 1954 to describe a specific pop style drawn as much from country and western as from rhythm and blues.

Variations – rock *and* roll and, simply, rock, among others – had distinct applications at the time (see Charlie Gillett's *The Sound of the City*, New York 1970). These applications were blurred by the continual evolution of the music and are of little direct relevance to its development in Canada. Variations in style have been many over the years, giving rise to a host of descriptions reflecting rock's assimilation of aspects of other music styles (eg, the folk-rock of the mid-1960s, the jazz-rock of the mid-1970s) or reflecting in an abstract sense the cultural milieu from which certain styles have developed (eg, acid or psychedelic rock of the late 1960s, heavy-metal rock of the mid-1970s, and punk rock of the late 1970s). All of these styles originated in the USA or England and have been adopted by Canadian musicians.

In its earliest and most basic form, rock is characterized by a three-chord harmonic structure and an emphasized 4/4 rhythm. Though these elements remained the basis of much of rock music 25 years later, the music has moved into areas more complex rhythmically, harmonically, and melodically as its proponents' musicianship has grown and as the breadth of influences on which they drew has increased. It differs from other popular music in its tendency to extremes: in its volume (and its willingness to embrace the developing technology of sound production and reproduction), in its reliance on rhythm, in the frequent aggressiveness of its performance, and in the control which that performance holds over its audience – predominately white and in the teens or twenties.

Rock was heard first in Canada on US radio and recordings, and Canada has remained a major market for US (and later, British) performers, live and recorded. Many US musicians toured Canada in the late 1950s, usually on a nightclub circuit. Ronnie *Hawkins made Toronto his base ca 1960 and exerted a significant influence, personally and through his band the Hawks (later The *Band), on the development of rock music in that city.

In the USA the popularity of rock gave rise to many recording companies devoted to the genre; in Canada it did not, and very few records, relatively speaking, were made in the 1950s and early 1960s. Those Canadians with successful recording careers usually had moved to the USA. In the 1950s they included the *Crew-Cuts, the *Diamonds, and the Rover Boys (the last originally from Toronto and best known for the single, 'Graduation Day,' 1956). The first Canadian-made record to achieve international popularity was 'Clap Your Hands' (1960, *Quality), by the Montreal quartet the Beaumarks.

The popularity of US rock in Canada encouraged Canadian youths to form rock bands and led existing groups, especially those devoted to country music, to change styles or to incorporate some rock hits in their repertoires. (Some of these artists, such as Bob Regan and Lucille *Starr, the Albertans Dick Damron and Ray *Griff, the Manitoban Ray St Germain, and the Ontarians Jack Bailey, Dallas Harms, and Terry Roberts, eventually returned to country music as rock moved away from its country roots.)

Also popular were instrumentals by such bands as the Classics (see Chilliwack) and the Vancouver Playboys on the west coast, Wes Dakus and the Rebels from Edmonton, the Esquires (or S'Quires) and the Masquerades from Calgary, the Squires from Winnipeg, the Hi-Tones and the Esquires from Ottawa, and the Corvairs from Quebec. Their styles were patterned after those of US and British bands (the Ventures, the Shadows, Johnny and the Hurricanes, etc). Instrumentals, by eliminating the barrier of language, vastly increased the potential audience for Quebec groups.

With the rise of the Beatles about 1964 and the subsequent popularity of many other British bands, Canadian youths began to form rock bands in quantity. By 1966 there were an estimated 1400 bands, amateur and professional, in Toronto alone. Many Canadian bands were influenced directly by English bands; three, for example, openly imitated the Rolling Stones before finding styles of their own: the Du-Cats, the Haunted, and the Ugly Ducklings. Other British bands served as models for the British Modbeats, Jack London and the Sparrows (later *Sparrow), and especially Liverpool (later Aerial, whose repertoire in the late 1970s still consisted largely of Beatles songs).

The Beatles' influence was felt in Quebec in the style known as yé-yé (a translation of 'yeah, yeah,' part of the chorus of the Beatles' 'She Loves You') which co-existed with the chansonnier movement in the 1960s. The most popular of the yé-yé performers were the Classels, a Montreal quintet formed in 1962, who performed in white wigs and stage costumes and were best-known for their recording of 'Avant de te dire adieu' (Trans-Canada). Other popular performers included the Baronets, the Bel-Air, the Bel Canto, César et ses Romains, the Chanceliers (of whom Michel *Pagliaro was a member), Tony Roman (later an influential record producer), the Sinners, the Sultans, and the Têtes blanches. Their repertoires were in large part translations of British and US hits, but some bands – eg, the Classels, the Baronets, and the Chanceliers – performed original material, often slower in tempo, with a less distinctive beat, and closer to the more romantic music of the chansonnier.

The post-Beatles era in Canada was divided into two periods by the introduction in 1970 of the *CRTC's Canadian content broadcast regulations. Only a few Canadian companies (most of them independent and controlled by managers or promoters) recorded rock bands in quantity before 1970. A contract with a US company was much more desirable and ensured greater chances of access to Canadian radio stations which generally were unsympathetic to Canadian rock except for those specimens already popular in the USA. Thus, only a few singles remain as evidence of the many leading Canadian bands and performers of the 1960s.

In Toronto these 1960s musicians included David *Clayton-Thomas and the Shays (and later the Bossmen); Bobby *Curtola; Tommy Graham and the Big Town Boys ('It Was I,' 1965 *Capitol); the Jon-Lee Group or Jon (Finley) and Lee (Jackson) and the Checkmates ('Bring It Down Front,' 1967 *Sparton); *Kensington Market; Ritchie Knight and the Mid-Knights ('Charlena,' 1963, 'That's Alright,' 1966 *RCA); Bobby Kris and the Imperials ('Walk on By,' 1966 Columbia); Luke (Gibson) and the Apostles; Robbie Lane and the Disciples – stars of CTV's 'It's Happening' ('What Am I Gonna Do?', 1966 Capitol); the Last Words ('I Symbolize You,' 1966 *Columbia); Little Caesar and the Consuls ('My Girl Sloopy' which also was a US hit, 'You Really Got a Hold on Me,' and 'You Laugh Too Much,' 1965–6 Red Leaf); Jack London and the Sparrows; the Lords of London ('Cornflakes and Ice Cream,' 1967 Apex); *Mandala; Motherlode ('When I Die,' 1969 Revolver); the *Paupers; Stitch in Tyme ('Got to Get You into My Life,' 1967 Yorkville); and the Ugly Ducklings ('Gas Light,' 1967 Yorkville). Much of Toronto rock of the 1960s showed a marked influence of rhythm and blues.

Edmonton was the home of the singer Barry Allen ('Lovedrops,' 1966 Capitol); Wes Dakus and the Rebels – the group with which Allen often sang ('Hobo' and 'The Hoochi Coochi Coo,' 1967 Capitol); and the King Beezz ('I Can't Explain,' 1966 Quality), all of whom toured widely. The *Stampeders from Calgary were popular, as was Winnipeg's *Guess Who. In Ottawa the leading groups were the Esquires ('Love's Made a Fool of You,' 1965 Capitol) and the Staccatos (*Five Man Electrical Band). In Vancouver the Collectors (Chilliwack), Mother Tucker's Yellow Duck ('One Ring Jane,' 1968 Duck), and Tom *Northcott and the Poppy Family (see Terry Jacks) were popular; as were the Haunted ('1-2-5,' 1966 Quality), Influence (see Walter Rossi), J.B. and the Playboys or the Jaybees ('Don't Ask Me to Be True,' 1965 RCA), and the Rabble among English-speaking bands in Montreal.

For these and other performers, recordings served largely as promotion; rock musicians of the 1960s were sustained by work at dances in teen clubs and high schools, appearances in *coffeehouses (generally the domain of the most original performers and located in the late 1960s in such areas as Toronto's Yorkville and Vancouver's Gastown), and occasional performances in concert (usually opening for US bands). Of these performers, only Curtola, the Guess Who, Kensington Market, Little Caesar and the Consuls, Motherlode, Northcott, Five Man Electrical Band, Sparrow (as Steppenwolf), and the Stampeders had any impact in the USA.

With the introduction of the CRTC's broadcast regulations the Canadian recording industry made rock a major focus of its activity. Increased production (with a corresponding rise in quality) and the ground-breaking international popularity of the Guess Who opened markets outside Canada to the country's musicians. Success abroad usually ensured success in Canada. Many performers came to the fore: in 1970 the Bells (from Montreal) with 'Stay Awhile' (Polydor), Chilliwack, *Edward Bear, and *Mashmakhan; in 1971 the Five Man Electrical Band, Ocean (Toronto) with 'Put Your Hand in the Hand' (Yorkville), *Lighthouse, and the Stampeders; in 1972 *April Wine, and Keith Hampshire (Toronto) with 'Daytime, Night-Time' (*A & M); in 1973 Bachman-Turner Overdrive (*BTO), Terry Jacks, Painter (Calgary / Vancouver) with "West Coast Woman" (Elektra), Skylark (Vancouver) with 'Wildflower' (Capitol), Ian *Thomas, and Wednesday (Oshawa, Ont) with 'Last Kiss' (Ampex); in 1974 Bill Amesbury (Toronto) with 'Virginia' (Yorkville), Frank *Marino and Mahogany Rush, and Gino *Vannelli; in 1975 Heart (US musicians based in Vancouver and often acknowledged as a Canadian band) with 'Magic Man' (Mushroom); and in 1976 Burton Cummings (see Guess Who) and Sweeney Todd (Vancouver) with 'Roxy Roller' (London).

With the introduction of rock music on FM radio stations, where it was common to hear lengthy pieces of music programmed, it was no longer necessary for rock musicians to strive for the hit single of three minutes' duration as required by AM radio; the longer pieces of music accommodated by an LP now could receive wide exposure, and thus the LP became an item as saleable as, and independent of, the single.

The popularity of several Canadian bands of the late 1970s grew through a combination of LP radio exposure (and consequent sales) and concert appearances: Toronto's FM (*Black Noise*, Passport), Max Webster (*Mutiny up My Sleeve* and *High Class in Borrowed Shoes*, Anthem), *Rush, and Triumph (*Rock and Roll Machine*, Attic) and Vancouver's Prism (*Prism* and *See Forever Eyes*, GRT) and Trooper (*Two for the Show* and *Knock 'em Dead Kid*, MCA). Klaatu, formed ca 1974 in Toronto, achieved international notoriety in 1977 with the LP *Klaatu* (Capitol) largely because the similarity of its music to that of the Beatles gave rise to speculation that Klaatu was in fact a re-formed Beatles, a rumour enhanced by the musicians' refusal to perform publicly or to reveal their identities.

In Quebec Robert *Charlebois introduced elements of rock into the music of the chansonniers in the late 1960s by playing an electric guitar and employing a back-up band. Thereafter, rock became a major influence on many Quebec pop performers of the 1970s, among them Aut'Chose, Contraction, *Harmonium, *Maneige, *Morse Code, *Octobre, *Offenbach, Pagliaro, Sloche, *Ville Émard, and Gilles *Valiquette. (See also Chanson in Quebec.)

Many Canadians did not align themselves to one specific international style or trend. Some, however, could be described as folk-rock (the Knack and the Stormy Clovers of Toronto and *Three's A Crowd), acid-rock (the Paupers – and Chilliwack, though only briefly), jazz-rock (the Bossmen and Chimo, both involving the pianist Tony Collacott; Aquarelle; Maneige; Ted *Moses' small groups; *Pacific Salt), heavy-metal-rock (Goddo, Moxy, Rush, and Triumph of Toronto; April Wine and Mahogany Rush of Montreal; BTO in Vancouver; Painter / Hammersmith of Calgary, or punk (Battered Wives, the Diodes, and the Viletones in Toronto; the Action in Montreal; and DOA and Pointed Sticks in Vancouver). A few transcended these categories and stand as the most original of Canadian rock bands: The Band, Influence, and Kensington Market.

Traditionally, however, originality in Canadian bands has not been a quality appreciated by Canadian audiences, whose standards have been developed by constant exposure to US and British groups. Canadian musicians following US or British models have stood a greater chance of success in Canada than those forging their own identities. The popularity of Chilliwack, for example, rose dramatically after the band turned from the experimental nature of its first LPs (as the Collectors) to a mélange of US pop styles; The Band's unique qualities were recognized first in the USA, and its national (as opposed to local) popularity grew in Canada as it grew internationally; and though critically acclaimed in Canada and in New York, neither Influence nor Kensington Market met with substantial popular success and both were relatively short-lived as a result.

Many Canadian-born musicians have had careers in rock as leaders of, or sidemen in, internationally successful US bands. Among them are David Clayton-Thomas with Blood, Sweat & Tears; Gene Cornish (b Ottawa 14 May 1945, guitarist 1964–71 with the Rascals, New York); and Corky Laing (b Montreal 26 Jan 1948, drummer 1969–74 with Mountain, New York). Dewey Martin (drummer, b Chesterville, Ont, 30 Sep 1942), Bruce Palmer (bass guitarist), and Neil *Young were members 1966–8 of Buffalo Springfield in Los Angeles; Alexander 'Skip' Spence (b Windsor) was drummer 1965–6 with Jefferson Airplane and guitarist later with Moby Grape in San Francisco; Floyd Sneed (b Calgary 22 Nov 194?) was drummer of Three Dog Night, a group formed in 1968; and Zal Yanovsky (b Toronto 19 Dec 1944) was guitarist 1965–7 of the Lovin' Spoonful, New York.

Ricky Bell (piano), Brad Campbell (bass guitar), Ken Pearson (organ), and John Till (guitar) were members of Janis Joplin's Full Tilt Boogie Band and continued briefly on their own after her death in 1970. Jon Finley (singer), Michael Fonfara (organist), Peter Hodgson (bass guitar), and others, formerly of Jon and Lee and the Checkmates, were members at various times 1968–ca 1970 of the band Rhinoceros in New York. Graham Lear (drummer, b Toronto?) joined (Carlos) Santana about 1976; Prakash John (bass guitarist) and Whitey Glann (drummer), formerly of Mandala, have toured and recorded with Alice Cooper and Lou Reed; Scott Cushnie (pianist) was an informal member of Aerosmith in the late 1970s; and David Wilcox (guitarist, b Montreal 26 Apr 1957) played for the singers Maria Muldaur and Charlie Rich before forming his own band in Toronto in 1975.

Among singers, Jack Scott (b Windsor 24 Jan 1936) left Canada in the 1940s and made the hits 'My True Love' in 1958 and 'Burning Bridges' in 1960. Terry Black of Vancouver worked in the mid-1960s in Los Angeles; his most successful record was 'Unless You Care' (1964). After moving to New York ca 1965, Andy Kim (b Andrew Youakim, Montreal ca 1947) made a series of hit records beginning in 1968, for (in turn) Steed, Uni, and Ice, including 'How'd We Ever Get This Way?,' 'Baby I Love You,' 'Be My Baby,' and 'Rock Me Gently,' and co-wrote 'Sugar Sugar' and other songs for the Archies. The DeFranco Family, originally of Port Colborne, Ont, made a series of hit records 1973–4, the biggest of which was 'Heartbeat, Its a Lovebeat,' after it moved to Los Angeles.

Similarly, several Canadians became a part of the British rock scene, among them Stacey Heydon (b Windsor 3 Jul 1954, became lead guitarist for David Bowie in 1976), Philip Rambow (singer-songwriter, b Toronto, a member 1974–5 of the Winkies and leader 1977–8 of his own band), and guitarist singer Pat Travers (b Toronto 12 Apr 1954, enjoyed substantial popularity with his own hard rock band, which began in 1976 and toured North America in 1978). The Toronto band Mainline spent the winter of 1970 in England, and many other Canadian groups have toured there for shorter periods.

From its inception, rock, as part of the 'Top 40' pop-music radio format, has been the domain of private radio. In 1978 more than half of the 450 Canadian radio stations surveyed in *RPM's *Canadian Music Industry Directory* (Toronto) programmed some percentage of rock; 16 presented it exclusively. Programming, however, has tended to be controlled by US consulting firms and, when not so controlled, has reflected closely the popularity trends documented by the US trade publications *Billboard, Cashbox,* and *Record Week.* The Canadian publications *RPM, The Steede Report* (begun in Montreal in 1975, edited by Derek H. Steede), and *Record Week* (Toronto 1975–7) have served similar functions in the formation of playlists for Canadian radio.

Programs devoted to rock became a part of the CBC radio schedule in the 1970s with 'The Great Canadian Gold Rush' (Vancouver) and '90 Minutes with a Bullet' (Winnipeg). The Canadian TV networks have presented rock shows, the most important, with respect to Canadian musicians, begin the CBC's 'Let's Go,' seen weeknights 1964–5 and 1967–8, each day from a different city – Halifax, Montreal, Toronto, Winnipeg, and Vancouver.

Until the mid-1960s little attention was paid to rock by daily newspapers except as news or novelty. With the 1970s' introduction of the 'rock critic' (whose responsibility in fact extends to all types of pop music) coverage began to rival that of any other music. The turnover among rock journalists has been high – the leading writers in Canada have included Peter Goddard (Toronto *Telegram* 1968–71, *Toronto Star* beginning in 1972), Jeani Read (Vancouver *Province* 1970–9), and Juan Rodriguez (*Montreal Star* and, after 1975, Montreal *Gazette*). Others include Pierre Beaulieu, David Farrell, Larry LeBlanc, Martin Melhuish, Wilder Penfield III, and Nathalie Petrowski.

The first survey of rock music in Canada was Ritchie Yorke's *Axes, Chops & Hot Licks* (Edmonton 1971), a subjective and sometimes inaccurate account of the subject, with only an incidental historical perspective. Yorke is also the author of *A History of Rock and Roll* (Toronto 1976) and other pop music books and has contributed to Toronto newspapers and international journals.

Several Canadian magazines or newspapers have been devoted to rock, usually dividing their editorial coverage between international and Canadian musicians. These publications have included *CanaWirl* (Hamilton 1965); *Gumbo* (Montreal 1970); *Afterthought* (Ottawa 1970); *Music Canada* (Toronto 1970–1), succeeded by *Music Canada Quarterly* (Toronto 1972–6) and *Record Month* (Toronto 1976–7?); *Beetle* (Toronto 1970–5?); *Cheap Thrills,* later *Stagelife* (Toronto late 1970s); *Zounds* (Mississauga, Ont, 1975); *Quebec Rock* (Montreal 1977–); *Public Enemy* (Vancouver 1978–); *The New Music* (Toronto 1978–9); and *Canadian Musician* (Toronto 1979–).

BIBLIOGRAPHY

Roy, François. *Dix Ans de Rock* (Montreal 1977)
Flohil, Richard and Harry, Isobel. 'Coming to terms with the new wave,' *CanComp*, 149, Mar 1980
'Different voices on the new music,' ibid

MM

Rococo Records. Label for LP reissue of rare 78s and cylinders. It was introduced in the mid-1950s by Ross, Court & Co, a firm established in 1951 in Toronto by André Ross and Leonard and Peter Court as a retail outlet for historic and European recordings. In 1972 Court moved to England, opening a store – The Old Record – in Twickenham, and Ross assumed sole direction of the Rococo label, moving to Coral Gables, Fla, but maintaining a stockpile in Canada and continuing to market Rococo records from Toronto.

The first Rococo record (R-1, a 10-inch LP released in April 1955) featured singers Sir Charles Santley, Francesco Marconi, Selma Kurz, Emilie Herzog, Felia Litvinne, and Feodor Chaliapin (a rare 1901 recording). By 1977 some 400 LPs of vocal and instrumental music had been released. Among Canadian artists represented are Emma *Albani, Thérèse *Deniset, Pauline *Donalda, Louise *Edvina, Jeanne *Gordon, and Edward *Johnson. Rococo distributes Cantilena Records, a label established in 1966 on similar principles by John *Stratton, and has released under its own label a few LPs of vaudeville and music hall performances.

BIBLIOGRAPHY

Vinci, Ernesto. 'Rococo Records,' *CMJ*, vol 2, Summer 1958

EBM

Rodeo Records Ltd. Parent company to several labels in the country and folk fields and to one in the classical field. It was founded in 1949 in Montreal by Don Johnson and George Taylor. The latter, a retired British army officer, took control in 1952 when Johnson moved to the USA. The company moved to Halifax in 1956 (where a recording studio was opened that year) and, in 1969, to Peterborough, Ont.

The Rodeo label has carried country music exclusively and was supplemented by the formation in 1953 of the Banff label and the acquisition in 1960 of the Celtic label (whose catalogue of Scottish music started in 1933). Other Rodeo country labels are Caprice (designed for the French-Canadian market) and Rodeo International. Rodeo has been distributed by *London Records.

Among the performers recorded for the Rodeo labels are Mac *Beattie, Omar *Blondahl, Winston 'Scotty' *Fitzgerald, Marie, Johnny Mooring, Vic *Mullen, Les Petits Chanteurs de la Vierge, Stu *Phillips, Lucille *Starr, and Graham *Townsend.

In 1973 Rodeo established the serious-music label, Melbourne, with the assistance of BMI (PRO) Canada. The label was taken over by *Waterloo in 1977 and continued as its serious-music label. Melbourne had issued more than a dozen LPs by 1980, among them recordings of *Somers' **The Fool*, *Schafer's *Threnody* and *String Quartet No. 2 ('Waves')*, and *Beckwith's *Quartet* and two albums of electronic music, by such performers as Robert *Bauer, Davis *Joachim, Antonin *Kubálek, William *Kuinka, the *Orford String Quartet, the *Toronto Mendelssohn Choir, Christopher *Weait, and David *Zafer.

Rodeo controls four music publishing companies: Banff Music (PRO Canada), Jaspar Music (PRO Canada), Melbourne Music (CAPAC), and Rodeo Music (PRO Canada).

BIBLIOGRAPHY

'Country music – Canadian style,' *CanComp*, 37, Feb 1969

(EBM)

RODERMAN, (Leon) **Ted** or **Teddy**. Trombonist, b Toronto 21 Mar 1924, d Hollywood, Fla, 18 Sep 1980. He studied privately in Toronto 1937–41 with Harry Hawe and played overseas with *The *Army Show*. Returning to Toronto he became one of the leading trombonists in that city, playing in the dance bands of Frank Bogart, Bert *Niosi, and others; with the *CBC SO (principal 1954–64) and the *TSO (principal 1957–8); with the big bands of *Nimmons 'N' Nine Plus Six 1965–74, and others; and with CBC studio orchestras. Roderman led studio groups for one LP of pop songs arrangements for the CBC and for three for the CTL – *Teddy Roderman's Six Trombones* (1967, RCA CTLS 1094 / Camden CAS 2359), *The New World Trombones of Teddy Roderman* (1970, CTL 477-5126), and *Making It with You* (1971, CTL 477-5144).

ROFF, Joseph (b Roffinella). Composer, priest, b Turin, Italy, 26 Dec 1910, naturalized Canadian 1945, naturalized US 1964; BA music (Toronto) 1944, FTCL 1945, B MUS (Toronto) 1945, MA languages (Toronto) 1946, D MUS (Toronto) 1948. Raised in England, where he studied piano and organ in Oxford and Manchester, he moved to Toronto in 1942 and continued his studies at the *U of Toronto with Leo *Smith and Healey *Willan. Roff resided in Toronto until 1956, serving as a parish priest, and then moved to New York where, in 1968, he became composer-in-residence at St Joseph's College for Women in Brooklyn. He has composed orchestral, organ, piano, and, especially, choral music. His compositions (those to 1950 are listed in the *Catalogue of Canadian Composers*) include *Reverie* (1948), premiered 6 Apr 1951 by the *TSO and performed also by the Detroit SO; *Three Fragments* (1952), played by the *CBC SO; and *Niagara* (1953), a suite inspired by Niagara Falls and premiered 19 Aug 1953 at the *Promenade Symphony Concerts, performed 15 Feb 1959 by the TSO, and recorded in 1965 by the Rome SO (Major 3003). He wrote the music for *Lady of Mexico*, a musical produced in 1962 in New York off-Broadway. More than 700 of Roff's choral pieces have been issued (largely in the USA) by over 40 publishers, including BMI Canada, Belwin, the Gregorian Institute of America (of which he was a staff composer), C. Fischer, J. Fischer, H.W. Gray, E.C. *Kerby, Parnasse musical, T. Presser, *Waterloo ('God Bless Canada,' 1953), Warner Brothers, and World Library.

Leo Smith (Toronto *Globe and Mail*, 7 Apr 1951) thus described *Reverie*: 'Built on a melody which floated on the surface of a harmony tinged with chromaticism, it is far from commonplace.'

In 1971 Roff received the New England Liturgical Award for original contribution to the arts of America. (DS)

ROGERS, Mrs B.T. (b Angus). Patron, b Manchester 12 Mar 1869, d Vancouver 14 Oct 1965. Mary Isabella Angus acquired her love of music from her mother's family (Fairweather) and as a girl learned to play the violin. With her parents she moved as a child to Toronto and at about 16 to Victoria where she later taught school. She settled permanently in Vancouver after her marriage to Benjamin Tingley Rogers, who became the founder of the BC Sugar Refinery.

Mrs Rogers was deeply committed to the encouragement of musical life in Vancouver. From the 1930s to the 1950s, with the support of her husband, she gave very considerable financial and moral support to the *Vancouver SO, thus ensuring its survival and development. She was an initiator of the *Vancouver Woman's Musical Club and backed Lily Laverock and other impresarios in their efforts to present artists of international stature to Vancouver audiences. She adamantly shunned publicity, but was awarded the MBE (Member, Civil Division, Order of the British Empire) in 1946, in recognition of her dedication to music in Vancouver.

Her daughter Elspeth married Jan *Cherniavsky. BNSG (ML)

ROGERS, Robert (Garland). Pianist, teacher, b Carberry, near Brandon, Man, 15 Sep 1936; BA (British Columbia) 1957, MA (Washington) 1960. A pupil of Lorne *Watson in Brandon and of Leonard *Heaton in Winnipeg, Rogers moved in 1954 to Vancouver where his teachers were Frances *Adaskin and Ira *Swartz. He studied as well 1958–60 with Berthe Poncy Jacobson and Randolph Hokanson at the U of Washington. On his return to Vancouver in 1960 he taught privately for several years and in 1966 joined the faculty of music at the *U of British Columbia. He taught 1971–6 at the Courtenay Youth Music Centre. He has been a soloist on occasion with the *CBC Vancouver Chamber Orchestra and the *Vancouver SO and orchestral pianist with both groups.

Rogers has participated in the premieres of Jean *Coulthard's *Sonata Rhapsody* (1 Mar 1963) and *Lyric Sonatina* (13 Jan 1972), Barbara *Pentland's *Mutation* (13 Feb 1973) and *Disasters of the Sun* (23 Jan 1977), Eugene Wilson's *Cello Sonata, Piano Trio* (22 Jan 1976, with the composer) and *Viola Sonata* (5 Feb 1976), and Elliot *Weisgarber's *Fantasia à Ire* (7 Mar 1975). For the CBC he has performed works by Beethoven, Elliott Carter, and Pentland and has recorded Pentland's *Three Duets after Pictures by Paul Klee* with the composer and Coulthard's *Five Part-Songs for Voices and Piano* under Hugh *McLean. BNSG

ROGERS, William Keith. Composer, b Charlottetown 16 Mar 1921; M MUS (Juilliard) 1948. Early success in competitions encouraged Rogers to enter the Juilliard School in 1939 where he studied piano with Arthur Newstead and composition with Vittorio Giannini, Bernard Wagenaar, and Frederick Jacobi. He taught piano and theory 1948–50 at the Hamilton Cons of Music (*RHCM) and then became musical director of CFCY radio, Charlottetown, continuing his studies with Nadia Boulanger in Paris in 1952 and 1954–5 and with Ernst Toch at Tanglewood in 1954. Rogers moved to Montreal in 1960 and later retired from music. Though his musical output is not large, it varies in style and form. His *Coronation Tribute* (commissioned by the CBC) is a well-made piece in the tradition of Elgar and Walton, the *Sonatina* for viola and piano is infused with neo-romantic warmth, and the dodecaphonic *Six Short Preludes on a Tone Row* for piano combine lyricism and stern craft. Rogers is an affiliate of PRO Canada.

SELECTED COMPOSITIONS

Sonata. 1943. Vn, pf. Ms

Three Songs from Emily Dickinson. 1947. SATB. BMIC 1948. CBC SM-19 (*Festival Singers)

String Quartet No. 1 in D Minor. 1948. CMCentre

Sonatina. 1952. Va, pf. BMIC 1954. RCI 223/RCA CCS-1017 (*Humphreys va). 1968. CBC SM-78 (O. Green va, Barkin pf)

Two Christmas Carols. 1952. SSAA. BMIC 1952

A Coronation Tribute. 1953. Full orch. CMCentre. RCI 90 (R. *Leduc cond)

Six Short Preludes on a Tone Row. 1963. Pf. BMIC 1963. CBC SM-43/(*Turini)/(No. 1, 3, 4, 5, 6) CCM-1 (*Cavalho) BJE

Rolland, Pierre. Oboist, english horn player, broadcaster, teacher, b Quebec City 13 Oct 1931; B MUS (New England Cons) 1957. He studied at the *CMM 1947-54 with Fernand Gillet (oboe), Jeanne *Landry (harmony), Gilberte *Martin (theory, solfège), and Jean *Papineau-Couture (dictation). In 1954 he became oboist with the *Halifax SO. He worked 1955-7 with Gillet at the New England Cons and spent two summers at Pierre Monteux's school in Hancock, Me. He played in the *Ottawa Philharmonic 1957-60 and during this period was an announcer on radio station CKCH in Hull. He completed his training at the Paris Cons 1960-1 with Étienne Baudo (oboe), Maurice Franck (theory), and Eugène Bigot and Louis Fourestier (conducting). He became the english horn player with the *MSO in 1961 and was president of the committee of the Musicians' Assn for a number of years. On CBC radio he has been host of 'Music de chez-nous,' 'Invitation à la musique,' and 'Faisons de la musique' and an interviewer on 'Les Musiciens par eux-mêmes.' He began to teach oboe in 1970 at the St-Laurent Cegep and in 1973 at the *U of Montreal; he also taught 1974–5 at the *École normale de musique and for several years at the *École Vincent-d'Indy. In 1978 he took charge of the instrumental ensemble of the *UQAM.

Rolland founded the Pierre-Rolland Quintet, which shortly afterwards became the Ensemble Pierre-Rolland. The group made its debut 30 Nov 1970 at the *Salle Claude-Champagne. On that occasion it comprised Rolland (oboe and english horn), Jeanne Baxtresser (flute), Eugène *Husaruk (violin), Leslie Malowany (viola), and Jack Mendelsohn (cello). Husaruk was replaced by Otto *Armin. Clermont *Pépin composed *Séquences* expressly for the group. Depending on the repertoire, the ensemble has added other musicians, as it did for a retrospective program of Canadian music presented 15 Feb 1976 for the *Pro Musica Society.

Rolland also played with the CBC *'Little Symphonies,' the CBC Montreal orchestra, and the *SMCQ Ensemble and has conducted the *CBC Quebec Chamber Orchestra. A member of the founding council of the Quebec Youth Orchestra in 1977, he later became coach for the wind and percussion sections. He began to review records for the *Journal des JMC* in 1965 and for the Montreal daily *Le Devoir* in 1975. (HP, PR)

ROLLINSON, Eric (Thomas). Educator, organist, b London 16 Jan 1911, d Toronto 17 Apr 1963; FRCO 1931, B MUS (Toronto) 1942. He moved to Canada in 1932 and spent the next 10 years as an organist-choirmaster in Saint John, NB, and Hamilton, Ont. In 1942 he joined the faculty of the *TCM. Adjudicator, lecturer, recitalist, and author of books on theory, he became a leading teacher of theory and organ in Toronto. The Rollinson Prize for *RCCO examinations was established in recognition of his work in that college as president 1943–5, editor, and examiner.

WRITINGS

Elementary Harmony and Counterpoint (Oakville 1953)

Free and Double Counterpoint (Oakville 1959)

Musical Notation (Oakville 1960) FRCC

ROLSTON, Thomas (Edmund). Violinist, violist, teacher, b Vancouver 31 Oct 1931; LRSM 1949, ARAM 1961. After violin study in Vancouver with Douglas Stewart, he attended the Mannes College of Music in New York, training 1949–50 under Roman Totenberg. He studied 1950–3 with David

*Martin at the RAM and was a member 1951–8 of the Philharmonia Orchestra of London. He attended the Brussels Cons 1956–7 and returned to Canada in 1958 to take up a position (retained until 1964) as concertmaster and associate conductor of the *Edmonton SO and to teach at the *U of Alberta where he remained until 1979. He premiered Jean *Coulthard's *Concerto* with the *Vancouver SO in 1959 and helped found the *U of Alberta String Quartet in 1969. Rolston introduced the *Suzuki method of violin instruction to Canada, founding in 1964 the Society for Talent Education which by 1974 had instructed some 600 pupils. He began teaching also at the *Banff SFA, serving as head of the string department 1965–71, music co-ordinator 1971–7, and music director 1977–9. In 1979 he became the first director of the school's new year-round program for advanced studies. In 1974 he received an Alberta Achievement Award in recognition of his work as an educator.

Rolston's wife, Isobel Moore (b Glasgow 27 Mar 1931), studied at the Royal Scottish Academy, with Max *Pirani at the RAM, and in Vienna at the Akademie für Musik. She was harpist 1960–70 with the Edmonton SO, taught at the U of Alberta 1962–79, and joined the piano department of the Banff SFA in 1967. In 1979 she became a member of the permanent staff of the school's program for advanced studies.

Rolston and Moore have performed as a duo, winning second prize at the 1956 Munich International Competition and appearing in 1961 at Wigmore Hall, London. Their association with Coulthard has inspired several works, including *Fantasy* (1961, premiered in 1963). The Rolston Trio, formed in 1965 with Claude *Kenneson, has given many recitals and broadcasts. The Rolstons' daughter, Shauna (b 31 Jan 1967), also has performed as the trio's cellist.

DISCOGRAPHY

Brahms *Quintets; Sextets*. Hungarian Quartet, Rolston viola. 1971. Pathé Marconi (unreleased)

Bartók *Two Rhapsodies*. Székely vn, I. Moore pf. 1974. Hungaroton SLPX 11357 (BH)

Roman Catholic church music. The arrival of the first settlers and missionaries in New France marked the beginning of the significant role Roman Catholic church music was to play in Canada. The church became the principal centre of elaborate musical activities involving a considerable number of musicians – singers, choirmasters, organists, and composers – many of them of high repute. This article presents a broad survey of the church's origins in Canada and of its chronological development as exemplified in the province of Quebec.

See also Choir schools; Hymn singing: 3 / Denominations; Organ building; Plainsong; Religions and music.

1 Under the French regime
2 Explorers and missionaries
3 The Indians
4 Religious orders
5 After the conquest of 1760
6 Early Canadian compositions
7 Liturgical song handbooks and collections
8 Choirs and repertoire
9 Vatican Council II

1 UNDER THE FRENCH REGIME. Historical documents report that two Récollet priests sang the mass in Quebec City 25 Jun 1615. According to Samuel de Champlain, who had founded the city in 1608, this was the first instance of sung mass. Another documented early church-music performance was the singing of the *Te Deum* in 1615. The *Te Deum* is known to have been sung again by French settlers on their return to Quebec in 1633 after the four-year occupation of the town by the British, led by the Kirke brothers. Two years later, the Roman Catholic liturgy had been resumed in regular services, and High Mass and Vespers were sung every Sunday and feast day at the small Notre-Dame de Recouvrance Church.

Other events were celebrated with the *Te Deum*, in particular the birth in 1638 of the future Louis XIV, the arrival of the Ursuline nuns in 1639, and the arrival of Mgr de Laval, Quebec's first bishop, in 1659 (when there was singing not only in Latin and French, but also by the Algonquins and the Hurons in their own languages). In 1665, upon the arrival of the lieutenant-general, the marquis de Tracy, with the Carignan-Salières regiment, the *Te Deum* was sung to the accompaniment of an organ (probably the one brought from France by Mgr de Laval) and the regiment's fifes and drums. The same music was used to celebrate the end of a compaign into Iroquois country. It is reported that on the occasion of the death of the Queen Mother of France, Anne of Austria, 'Monsieur Tallon ... signalized ... his respect for that great Princess's memory, by causing a Service to be chanted with music in the principal Church of Quebec, on the 3rd of August of the year 1666. This Service would have seemed magnificent anywhere, but its effect in a country where nothing like it had ever been seen exceeded all description' (*Jesuit Relations*, vol 50, p 107). In 1690 the victory over the British forces led by Sir William Phips (who later became governor of Massachusetts) was hailed with a *Te Deum* in Quebec City's Cathedral; undoubtedly under the direction of the *Grand Chantre (Mgr de Laval had created the post in 1684). The peace treaty of 1701 with the Indians and the treaty of Utrecht (1713) were celebrated in similar fashion.

2 EXPLORERS AND MISSIONARIES. All expeditionary departures and returns were marked by the singing of hymns, as during the encampment of the Sulpicians François Dollier de Casson and René de Galinée on the shore of Lake Erie, when it was reported that 'Sundays and feast days were highlighted by the singing of High Mass' (Faillon, vol 3 p 299). On 4 Jun 1671 a cross was erected at Ste-Marie-du-Sault. The French people present sang the *Vexilla regis* and then the *Te Deum*. Examples of this type of story are plentiful in the reports on daily life in New France at the time.

See also Missionaries in the 17th century.

3 THE INDIANS. Montreal's first chapel was built in 1680 at the Fort de la Montagne (two towers on the Grand Séminaire's land were still standing in 1980). François Vachon de Belmont, a Sulpician priest who had come to Canada that same year, wished the Iroquois to 'sing High Mass and Vespers on feast days in their own language.' He had ordered an organ from France and in the meantime accompanied with a lute the young Indians to whom he taught plainsong. In a letter sent to him 6 Jun 1682, the superior general of the order of St-Sulpice, Monsieur Tronson, makes an allusion to those who wish to hear 'the Gloria, the Credo, the Sanctus, the Agnus Dei and the Vespers in the Indian language ... and who would do well not to fail to inquire whether you have the Pope's permission' (copy of letter at the Archives du Séminaire de Saint-Sulpice, Montreal).

The Jesuits had initiated a similar practice around the same period; during Mgr de Laval's visit to their Laprairie mission, 20 May 1681, the *Veni creator* was sung in Iroquois. The following day, mass was sung by the Iroquois in their own language, a custom still observed in 1980 at the Indian reserve of Kahnawaké (formerly Caughnawaga) near Montreal. To this end a 20-voice mixed choir was formed under Father Conrad Hauser in 1927 at the reserve's St-François-Xavier mission. The choir was heard on CBC radio in 1940 and gave a public concert in Montreal in 1942. It performed once more on CBC radio in 1948 under its new director, Alfred *Bernier.

In several libraries there are published collections of anthems in the Indian language, among them *Aiamieu Kushkushkutu Mishinaigan* (Quebec City 1847, 1856).

4 RELIGIOUS ORDERS. The year after her arrival in Canada (1639) Marie de l'Incarnation wrote: 'We sing better than they do in France' (4 Sep 1640). Twenty-one years later, shortly after Mgr de Laval's arrival, she reported the bishop's concern 'that we may have become vain in our singing ... He fell short of eliminating our singing. He lets us keep only our Vespers and Tenebrae ... As for High Mass, he wants it sung with a straight voice, having not the slightest consideration for what is done either in Paris or in Tours' (13 Sep 1661). In Montreal the church of the Hôpital functioned as a parish church for a long time. Liturgical singing was provided by the nuns as well as by two choirs, one made up of the choristers and priests of the seminary and the other formed by the nuns. The two choirs sang together only for special celebrations such as the High Mass of 11 Apr 1665.

5 AFTER THE CONQUEST OF 1760. On the occasion of the coronation and wedding of George III, as prescribed by an episcopal order issued 4 Feb 1762, the *Te Deum* was sung in every parish. The order was reissued on 17 May 1763 to mark the surrender of the colony to England. After Admiral Nelson's victory over the French troops in the battle of the Nile, at Aboukir in 1798, the bishop of Quebec gave this order: 'A solemn mass of thanksgiving shall be celebrated in every church in the diocese, at the end of which the Te Deum, the Domine salvum fac regem and the prayer for the King shall be sung' (episcopal prescription of 22 Dec 1798). When Queen Victoria ascended the throne, 20 Jun 1837, the ecclesiastical authorities ordered the singing of the *Te Deum*, a decision opposed by several parishioners, who showed their displeasure by leaving the church.

6 EARLY CANADIAN COMPOSITIONS. The oldest extant composition attributed to a Canadian is the Prose 'Sacrae familiae,' believed to be by Charles-Amador *Martin. The first Canadian hymn (more accurately a Christmas carol), *'Jesous Ahatonhia,' was written ca 1642 in the Huron language and attributed to Father Jean de Brébeuf, but the music – the first few bars at least – was that of a 16th-century French song. It appears that the first French-language sacred song was composed in 1694 by a Sulpician priest, Joseph de la Colombière. One of the first choral masses, dating from the mid-19th century and based upon Christmas carols, was the *Messe de Noël: 'Deo infanti'* which Joseph-Julien *Perrault wrote for Notre-Dame Church, Montreal, and which was published by the Ateliers du Nouveau-Monde in 1870. It was reissued by *Boucher ca 1882 along with Perrault's four-voice harmonizations of the plainsong masses of Henry Du Mont (*Messe royale* and masses on the second and fourth modes) and his *Messe des morts*. These settings of the mass long remained a part of the church's choral repertoire in Quebec and in other French-speaking centres of Canada. In June 1880 the same *Messe royale* by Du Mont,

this time in an arrangement by Gustave *Gagnon, was sung in Quebec City on the Plains of Abraham during the *St-Jean-Baptiste celebrations. (See also Masses.)

7 LITURGICAL SONG HANDBOOKS AND COLLECTIONS. Nearly all of the earliest notated prayer-books brought from France were destroyed by fire, in particular the blaze which ruined the Ursulines' monastery in 1650 and three other fires which devastated the Montreal Hôtel-Dieu in the space of less than 50 years. Most of the few copies that survived the fires were lost or worn out in use. A few copies of the *Rituel du diocèse de Québec* (Paris 1703) were extant in 1980. Copies of works with musical notation published in Quebec City – eg, **Le Graduel romain* (1800), *Le Processional* [sic] *romain* (1801), and *Le Vespéral romain* (1802) – have become extremely rare. Several handbooks contained only the words; notable among these were Jean-Baptiste Boucher-Belleville's *Recueil de cantiques des missions, des retraites et des catéchismes* (Quebec City 1795) and Jean-Denis *Daulé's *Nouveau Recueil de cantiques à l'usage du diocèse de Québec* (Quebec City 1819). The tunes (about 200) for the latter were published separately. *Le Paroissien noté*, first issued in Quebec City in 1873 by P.G.Delisle, was republished many times; Langlais et Fils issued the 21st edition in 1911. At the beginning of the Kyriale, it features Du Mont's *Messe royale* and *Messe du second ton*. Besides the Kyriale and the Vespers, *Excerpta e cantibus liturgicis* (Montreal 1872) contains numerous psalms in fauxbourdon. T.F. *Molt's *La Lyre sainte* (Quebec City 1844 and 1845), a collection of short choral pieces, was the first of many such important collections compiled by musician priests – Louis *Bouhier, Léon *Destroismaisons, Charles-Émile *Gadbois, Roméo *Larivière, Conrad *Latour, Charles-Hugues *Lefebvre, Jules *Martel, R.(Roméo?) Vandandaigue, and others. After the modifications brought about in 1963 by Vatican II the Canadian episcopate updated a *Livret des fidèles* (Montreal 1966), the handbook most commonly used. Its musical contents include the tunes of the canticles, 86 psalm refrains, 24 alleluias, simple psalmodic formulae, a Latin kyriale, and a full-scale French kyriale.

Plainsong found in Canadian handbooks prior to Vatican II is related to the Gregorian tradition and is based on the 'Medicean' version which came into use at the beginning of the 17th century. Its two main characteristics are abridged vocalizations and accents prolonged by borrowing notes from the neighbouring neumes. With the restoration of Gregorian chant at the Abbey of Solesmes in France during the 19th century new publications appeared whose authenticity later was sanctioned by the name Vatican Edition. Formerly such publications were described as being in the style of Solesmes. Canadian seminarians who had been trained in the style popularized it in their own dioceses. To facilitate the performance of liturgical chant, Canadian musicians prepared numerous books of organ accompaniment, and these in turn gave rise to occasional heated polemics. Among the musicians who produced plainsong accompaniments were Jean-Baptiste *Labelle (1851), Pierre-Minier *Lagacé (1860), R.-O. *Pelletier (1890), Ernest *Gagnon (1903), and Eugène *Lapierre (1949). (See also Organ music.)

8 CHOIRS AND REPERTOIRE. Several months after assuming the leadership of the Catholic church Pius X, the first pope to have a deep interest in and knowledge of music, revealed his thoughts on sacred music in the *Motu proprio* (22 Nov 1903), which became law for musical performance within the church. Basic changes were made. Mixed choirs had to replace female members with boys from choir schools; the polyphonic repertoire was to be cleared of whatever material had been transcribed from opera or secular music; accompanied masses which were fashionable in the major churches of Montreal and Quebec, especially for special occasions, were strictly forbidden; only organ accompaniment was allowed.

The event stimulated a golden age of church choirs, and each parish was proud to make known its choir's size and the singers' names. The *Vade-mecum du chanteur, paroissial* began publication in Montreal in 1933. At Easter or Christmas time the largest newspapers would publish the musical programs of the main churches. Special instruction became available to choirmasters who wished to increase their knowledge. Religious music, mostly Gregorian, was introduced into the curricula of the universities in Montreal, Quebec City, and Ottawa, and specialized institutions such as the *Schola cantorum were formed. Several dioceses established sacred-music councils.

In the province of Quebec the Abbey of St-Benoit-du-Lac, located near Sherbrooke, became a North American centre of Gregorian musical culture, largely because of the research and leadership provided by Dom Georges Mercure. In 1936 under his guidance the monks of St-Benoit made a series of 12 78s entitled *Rythmique grégorienne*. These and numerous other records issued subsequently have exerted considerable influence.

A sacred-music code was published in 1952 for the ecclesiastical regions of Quebec City, Montreal, Ottawa, Rimouski, and Sherbrooke. Its text was accompanied by a list of works recommended for worship. A similar initiative was taken in Toronto by Mgr *Ronan of St Michael's Cathedral.

The performance of Gregorian chant has made continuous progress. In Montreal a choir composed of choirmasters was formed in the spring of 1964 with a view to demonstrating by means of recordings the decrees of Vatican II, which still were in force (see below).

9 VATICAN COUNCIL II. In its first constitution, 2 Dec 1963, the council stated: 'The Church recognizes Gregorian chant as the proper chant of the Roman liturgy. In liturgical actions it is therefore this chant, other things being equal, which must be in the *first place*' (*Sacrosanctum concilium*, article 116). In spite of this edict, approved by 2147 cardinals and bishops, three French priests who were church music composers – Fathers Gélineau, Deiss, and Julien – came to Canada to predict the end of Gregorian chant by January 1965. They undoubtedly had advance knowledge of the second ordinance of the Canadian episcopate, the prescription of 26 Sep 1964, which decreed that beginning on 22 Dec 1965 during a mass celebrated in the presence of the congregation all texts save the Canon '*may* be read or sung in the vernacular' (*La Réforme luturgique*, p 111). This text clearly indicated an alternative, a possible choice between Latin and the vernacular. But novelty prevailed, and as early as January 1965, in Canada as in France and elsewhere, the Latin, Gregorian, and sacred polyphony were sacrificed as being counter to 'the spirit of Vatican II.'

A new kind of music replaced these, or at any rate a restoration of what had been prohibited until then by the 1903 *Motu proprio*. A liturgical creativity emerged, particularly in televised masses. Less than five years after these changes, Guy de Fatto, a French jazz musician-turned-priest, proposed his own music. Following his example young guitarists, lyricists, and writers of a music called 'rhythmic' imposed it on the faithful. In the face of this innovation, some organists resigned. Although expressly prescribed by Vatican II, sacred music teaching has come to be ignored almost everywhere, and in Quebec the specialist journal *La Revue Saint-Grégoire* ceased publication.

In 1980 there was hope, however, that the centuries-old art of plainsong might be preserved. In September 1975 the Strasbourg Gregorian Convention considered the findings of a survey of church music experts and groups. The survey had been initiated by La Psallette de Strasbourg, and its findings were published in a general report, *Congrès Grégorien international* (Strasbourg 1975). During the convention, at which 13 countries, including Canada, were represented, laymen, well-informed musicians, musicologists, and university teachers decided to take the necessary steps to preserve the Gregorian melodies, 'the musical treasure of western civilization.'

BIBLIOGRAPHY

Vachon de Belmont, François. *Histoire du Canada* (Quebec 1840)

Faillon, Étienne-Michel. *Histoire de la colonie française en Canada*, 3 vols (Ville-Marie 1865, 1866)

Lagacé, Pierre-Minier. 'De la musique,' *Le Foyer canadien*, vol 4 (Quebec 1866)

Myrand, Ernest. *Noëls anciens de la Nouvelle-France* (Quebec 1899)

Laurendeau, Arthur. 'Chamber and church music in Montreal,' *The Year Book of Canadian Art*, compiled by the Arts and Letters Club of Toronto (Toronto, London 1913)

Gagnon, Ernest. 'La musique à Québec au temps de Monseigneur de Laval,' *Pages choisies* (Quebec 1917)

Maurault, Olivier. *Marges d'histoire*, 3 vols (Montreal 1929, 1930)

Lapierre, Eugène. *La Musique au sanctuaire* (Montreal 1932)

Pelletier, Joseph-Romuald. 'L'Évolution de la musique religieuse au Canada français,' unpubl D MUS thesis, Laval 1932

Lefebvre, Charles-Hughes, ed. *Documents officiels sur la musique sacrée parus depuis cinquante ans* (Montreal 1934)

Martimort, A.-G. and Picard, F. *Liturgie et musique* (Paris 1958)

La Réforme liturgique, Documents du Saint-siège et de l'Episcopat canadien (Montreal 1963–4)

Oury, Dom Guy, ed. *Correspondence de Marie de l'Incarnation* (Solesmes 1971)

'La musique ne va plus à la messe,' *Musique périodique*, vol 1, Nov 1976

Amtmann *Musique au Québec*

Jesuit Relations

Martel, Jules. 'Church music I,' *Music in Canada* (CMr)

ROMANDINI, (Giuseppe Alexander Antonio) **Tony**. Guitarist, composer, arranger, teacher, b Montreal 27 Jul 1928. He studied guitar 1937–40 with a teacher named Calabrese in New York and at 15 played with Maynard *Ferguson in Montreal. He worked 1952–8 in Montreal nightclubs, including the Casa Loma, with the accordionist Gordie Fleming and the singer Yolanda Lisi. During these years he took part in the CBC radio program 'Jazz Workshop.' He also played clarinet and saxophone in various clubs and his talents as a jazz guitarist gained recognition. He became a freelance studio musician with the CBC in 1948 and with CFTM-TV when it opened in 1961. Romandini also gave concerts of classical music in France and Germany during the 1960s and appeared with the *MSO, notably in 1970 in Manuel de Falla's *La Vida breve*. He composed the score for Jean-Claude Labrecque's documentary *60 Cycles* and wrote for the CBC and the NFB. He has written several jingles and many instrumental pieces. He performed in concert with Buddy De Franco, Arthur Fiedler, Dizzy Gillespie, Michel Legrand, Jo Moutet, and Oscar *Peterson and recorded with Maynard Ferguson (RCI 265) and Yvan *Landry (CBC LM-22), among others. He was the arranger and conductor for recordings of Monique Doss and Daniel Lachance and served as an accompanist on recordings by Edith *Butler, Jean *Carignan, Lucien *Hétu, Tex *Lecor, and Raoul *Roy. He taught 1974–7 at *Concordia U and 1977–8 at the Cons de Hull, before joining the faculty of *McGill U in 1979.

DISCOGRAPHY

Tony Romandini. 1962. Evans Music Corp EMC LP 33-0644
Bella Musica Tony Romandini. 1964. RCA Gala CGPS-141
Guitare de danse / Dance to the Guitar. 1965. RCA Gala CGPS-197/RCA Camden CAS 936
Tony Romandini guitarist, banjo player, composer and six sensational sidemen. A. Lacombe guit, G. Fleming acc and pf, H. Mackem vib, R. Simard perc. T. Dixon db, N. Ayoub cl, eng hn, and sax. 1965. CTL M-1063
The Tony Romandini Quintet. 1967. CBC LM-19
TR guitar. 1975. CBC LM-407
See also Peter McCutcheon; Discography for Serge Garant. ST (MM)

ROMANELLI, Luigi. Orchestra leader, violinist, b Belleville, Ont, 29 Nov 1885, d Murray Bay, (La Malbaie) Que, 29 Jul 1942. He was the son of the Italian-born harpist Joseph Romanelli 1859–1944, a concert and theatre musician in Toronto) and a nephew of Rocco Romanelli (d 1941), a violinist known as 'Romanelli the Great,' who toured briefly with Enrico Caruso in the USA and accompanied Nellie Melba.

In his youth Luigi Romanelli played the violin on Toronto street corners for a young dancer, George Weitz (later of *George White Scandals* fame). Romanelli made his stage debut at 12 as an actor with Mary Pickford (then known as Gladys Smith). In 1904 he joined a vaudeville troupe from Christie Lake, Ont, the Marks Brothers Touring Co, as a violinist. He performed as well with the Cummings Stock Co before touring Canada 1906–12 as a violin soloist. He studied in Toronto around this time with Jan *Hambourg. Thereafter an orchestra musician in various Toronto theatres, and briefly orchestra director at the Strand, Romanelli became music director of the Allen Theatres chain after a period of study (1918) in Europe. His was one of the first theatre orchestras to accompany silent films with descriptive music. The Romanelli orchestra at Shea's Theatre was the first in Canada to broadcast on radio (1922, over CFCA).

Romanelli became music director for United Hotels in Canada in 1923. One of Canada's most popular orchestra leaders, at his death he had performed at the King Edward Hotel, Toronto, for more than 20 years, and at Manoir Richelieu, Murray Bay, Que, for four summers. Romanelli's 11-piece radio orchestra the Monarchs of Melody, was heard on CRBC and CBC and, occasionally, on NBC's 'Blue' network in the USA. Over the years its personnel included Johnny *Burt, the saxophonist Nat Cassels, Trump *Davidson, the trombonist-arranger Red Ginzler, Alfie *Noakes, and the bassist Gurney Titmarsh. The Luigi Romanelli Orchestra made some 78s for HMV, Edison, and Bluebird. Romanelli also led a concert ensemble which included his father, Joseph, Leo *Barkin, Charles *Mathé, and Titmarsh. His brother-in-law, violinist Enrico Del Greco, was concertmaster.

Two of Romanelli's brothers were violinists and orchestra leaders in Toronto. Don (1891–1960) played in his teens with the dance band of Charles Bodley, organized bands as early as 1918 for the Lake Ontario cruise ships *Cayuga* and *Chippewa*, and led the orchestra at the Royal York Hotel in the early 1930s. Leo (1902–61) joined the Monarchs of Melody at 17 and later became assistant director, assuming the leadership on his brother's death. He returned to the King Edward Hotel in 1952. (HM)

ROMANO. A Montreal family of instrumentalists, comprising 1 / Giulio, 2 / Pietro, Giulio's half-brother, and 3 / Arthur, Giulio's son.

1 **Giulio**. Clarinetist, b Naples 8 Mar ca 1882, naturalized Canadian, d Afragola, near Naples, 19 Jul 1962. He studied music in Italy and arrived in Canada at 14. His teachers in Montreal included Joseph Moretti. Later he was active as an instrumentalist and conductor in theatres. In 1930 at his initiative a group of musicians met to form what came to be known as the *Montreal Orchestra. During this period he also taught at the *McGill Cons. In addition, he was founder and director of the Giulio Romano Orchestra, which was composed entirely of women. He performed on CBC radio. His second wife was Jeanne Girard, pianist and teacher.

2 **Pietro**. French-hornist, b Naples 30 May 1907, naturalized Canadian 1932, d Montreal 13 Nov 1966. He started to play the french horn at five. Arriving in Canada at 13, he began playing at the Imperial Theatre in an orchestra led by his half-brother. He played french horn 1931–41 in the *Montreal Orchestra and later until ca 1963 in the *MSO. He also belonged 1941–52 to the *Little Symphony of Montreal and played in the Henri *Miro Orchestra and the Capitol and Palace theatre orchestras.

3 **Arthur**. Saxophonist, clarinetist, oboist, english-hornist, teacher, b Naples 23 Mar 1914, naturalized Canadian, d Montreal 16 Jan 1964. He studied with his father, with Alfred Gallodoro in New York, and with Marcel Mule in France, and at first played in cabarets. He was a Canadian pioneer in the classical music repertoire for saxophone. With the CSM (*MSO) in 1949 he performed Jacques Ibert's *Concertino da camera*. He played english horn, oboe, and saxophone in the MSO ca 1952–62 and frequently appeared as saxophonist with the *Quebec SO. He also taught the saxophone 1949–62 at the *CMM and 1955–64 at *McGill U and founded the Romano School of Music. In the early 1950s with his pupils Nick *Ayoub, Gerald Danovitch, and Frederick Nichols (later replaced by Gilles Moisan) he formed the Romano Saxophone Quartet, which performed chiefly on CBC radio. Several Canadian works were composed for the quartet, including George *Fiala's first *Saxophone Quartet* and Alexander *Brott's *Three Acts for Four Sinners*. In 1953 the quartet recorded Michel *Perrault's *Quatuor* and works by Jean Françaix and Gabriel Pierné (RCI 91). Lee *Gagnon and Alvinn Pall are also among Romano's pupils. Romano was founder and president of Seward Ltd, which sells and repairs instruments, sells scores, and has studios for teachers. In 1979 the company was managed by his daughter. In 1978 the first Arthur Romano Competition for composition was organized at the UQATR, in collaboration with the Assn of Saxophonists of North America, to encourage the composition of original works for saxophone. HP

ROMANOFF, Ivan (b Pezhuk). Conductor, violinist, arranger, composer, b Toronto, of Ukrainian parents, 8 Mar 1914. He played in a mandolin orchestra as a boy and studied violin at the TCM with Alexander *Chuhaldin, Chris Dafeff, Broadus Farmer, and Kathleen *Parlow. In the early 1930s he was a violinist in Chuhaldin's radio orchestras and in Stanley *St John's dance band. He played also in the *Promenade Symphony Concerts and in CBC orchestras before serving in the RCN as director 1943–6 of the 'Scena Russki' segment of *Meet the Navy*. He studied 1947–9 at the Academy of Musical Arts in Prague with Jindřich Feld (violin), Václav Talich (conducting), and Milo Dolenžil (composition). In 1947 he conducted the Czech Philharmonic Orchestra in a concert of works by *Pentland, *Somers, and *Weinzweig at the Prague Spring Festival. Returning to Canada in 1949, he led a string ensemble on CBC radio's 'Continental Moods' in 1950, played viola briefly with the *Solway String Quartet in 1951, and directed CBC productions of Hulak-Artemowsky's *The Cossack beyond the Danube* (21 Nov 1951; Canadian premiere) and Rimsky-Korsakov's *May Night* (21 May 1952).

Ivan Romanoff

Romanoff formed the Ivan Romanoff Orchestra and (male) Chorus in 1953 for the debut of his CBC radio show 'Songs of My People.' The program continued weekly until 1963 and was followed by 'Continental Holiday' (1964 and again 1970–2), 'Continental Rhapsody' (1965–70), 'The Music of Ivan Romanoff' (1972–3), and 'Music of Our People' (1973–6). 'Rhapsody,' a CBC series in 1958 and 1959, was the first multilingual folksong-and-dance TV presentation seen nationally. TV specials followed. Romanoff's ensemble, performing songs from 40 countries, has appeared in New York, Winnipeg, and several Ontario cities and an average of seven times each season at *Ontario Place. Its recordings include three 78s made for the *Hallmark affiliate label Songs of My People in 1954 (with soloists Leopoldine Pichler and Jan *Rubeš) and the LPs *Rhapsody with Romanoff* (1958, Col FS 501), *Ballads of the Cossack* (1960, CBS GL 10048), *Continental Rhapsody* (1968, CBC LM-55 / Cap SN 6281), *Ukrainian Rhapsody* (1969, Cap ST 6299), two for RCI (258 and 343), *Ukrainian Christmas* (1969, CBC LM 67 / Cap ST 6333), and *To Life, To Love To Music* (1977, Boot BOS 7183).

Ukrainian Christmas features Romanoff's second wife, the soprano Lesia Zubrack (b Saskatoon, of Ukrainian descent, 22 Apr 1931), a pupil of George *Lambert at the RCMT and the winner of *'Opportunity Knocks' in 1954, *'Singing Stars of Tomorrow' 1954–5, and *'Nos Futures Étoiles' in 1955. She sang minor roles 1954–7 for the *COC and became a featured performer on – and scriptwriter and songwriter for – Romanoff's programs.

Romanoff himself has composed songs in several national styles, as well as jingles and incidental music for CBC TV movies. He has been described as 'a mixture of Mantovani, Werner Müller and Sampson Galperine of Moiseyev fame rolled into one versatile, talented, but temperamental violinist, composer, arranger and bandleader' (Walter Kanitz, *Toronto Daily Star*, 24 Sep 1960). Romanoff and his wife are members of CAPAC.

BIBLIOGRAPHY
'Our singing citizens,' *CBC Times*, 20–26 Dec 1953
Levitch, Gerald. 'Ivan Romanoff, everyone's favorite continental,' *CanComp*, 96, Dec 1974 MM

RONAN, John (Edward). Administrator, teacher, choirmaster, composer, b Colgan, near Brantford, Ont, 28 Oct 1894, d Toronto 15 Oct 1962; MCG, LCSC (Rome, Pontifical School of Sacred Music) 1936. He attended Hamilton Teachers College at 16, taught locally, and later went to St Michael's College in Toronto and studied composition privately with Healey *Willan. He entered St Augustine's Seminary, Scarborough, Ont, in 1916 and, after ordination in 1922, studied Gregorian chant in New York with Dom Mocquereau at the Pius X School and later in France at Solesmes Abbey. On his return to Canada Ronan taught Gregorian chant 1923–56 at St Augustine's Seminary, organized and taught music classes briefly in Toronto separate schools, became the city's archdiocesan director of church music in 1923, and established the Boys Sanctuary Choir at St Michael's Cathedral in 1926. While attending the Pontifical School of Sacred Music in Rome 1932–5 he visited Paris for lessons with Nadia Boulanger and Louis Vierne. On his return to Toronto he took charge of music at St Michael's Cathedral and in 1937 founded the St Michael's Cathedral Choir School, which he directed until his death. In 1947 he was made a Domestic Prelate in recognition of his achievements and in 1962 he became Protonotary Apostolic.

Monsignor Ronan was an influential teacher and many of his pupils, including John *Arab, Bernard *Turgeon, and members of the *Four Lads and the *Crew-Cuts, have had successful careers. A prolific composer, he often wrote at the request of choirs and churches in Canada and the USA. Although most of his works are short liturgical pieces such as anthems, introits, graduals, offertories, communions, and *Tenebrae* settings, he also arranged some Irish folksongs. RPn

ROSÉ, Alfred (Eduard Emmerich). Conductor, composer, pianist, music therapist, b Vienna 11 Dec 1902, naturalized Canadian 1955, d London, Ont, 7 May 1975. His mother was Gustav Mahler's sister. He studied piano principally with Richard Robert and theory with Franz Schmidt, Arnold Schoenberg, and Karl Weigl. He became an assistant conductor and coach 1922–7 of the Vienna State Opera. At this time he toured Europe as a pianist with the Rosé String Quartet, founded by his father, the violinist Arnold Rosé. He was music director of the Calderon Festivals of the Vienna Burgtheater 1923–4 and of the Max Reinhardt Theatre in Vienna. After three years in Berlin he returned to Vienna where he conducted the Volksoper and taught 1932–8 at the Volkskonservatorium. Moving to Cincinnati in 1938, he taught piano and theory, coached, and lectured there until 1948.

In 1946 Rosé directed a summer workshop in opera at the *Western Cons of Music, London, Ont, and in 1948 he moved to that city to teach at the *U of Western Ontario. In 1973 he retired with the rank of professor emeritus. In 1950 he became organist-choirmaster at St Martin's Church. He was a pioneer in music therapy and set up programs at Westminster Hospital in 1952 and the London (Ont) Psychiatric Hospital in 1956.

As a composer Rosé's most productive years were the 1920s and 1930s. Of his many songs 10 were published (1927–8, Doblinger, Krämer) in Austria. His *Adagio* for cello and orchestra (1941) was premiered in 1974 in London, Ont. Other works in larger forms are *Sonata in A* (1936) for piano and *Tryptichon* (1937) for large orchestra.

Rosé's connection with Mahler and his extensive collection of scores and letters (the latter now at the U of Western Ontario) made him a valued source of information for researchers.

See also Music therapy.

WRITINGS
'From Gustav Mahler's storm and stress period,' *CMJ*, vol 1, Winter 1957
– et al. 'Music therapy at Westminster Hospital,' *Mental Hygiene*, vol 43, Jan 1959 (CF)

Rose Latulippe. Three-act ballet by Brian Macdonald to music (1966) by Harry *Freedman, commissioned for the Royal Winnipeg Ballet by the Canadian Centennial Commission. The story takes place in a community on the St Lawrence River in 1740 and concerns a pious young girl apparently bewitched by the devil but saved by the love and devotion of her family and fiancé. Freedman's music is serial in technique and evokes much regional colour through characteristic dance rhythms and melodic figures. *Rose Latulippe* was premiered 16 Aug 1966 by the Royal Winnipeg Ballet at the *Stratford Festival in a production also presented 12 Apr 1967 on CBC TV's 'Music Canada' and repeated 8–19 Aug 1967 at the *Charlottetown Festival and 25–26 Aug 1967 at the *Royal Alexandra Theatre in Toronto.

Rose Latulippe was also the subject of an earlier ballet of that name, produced in Montreal and presented in 1953 on CBC TV to mark the inauguration of the network between Montreal and Toronto. The score was by Maurice *Blackburn, the choreography by Françoise Sullivan.

The French-Canadian legend was the subject of a third ballet with the same title, premiered in May 1979 by the Compagnie de Danse Eddy Toussaint. The 55-minute score was by Michael McLean. Choreography was by Toussaint.

BIBLIOGRAPHY
'Standing ovation for first full-length Canadian ballet,' *CanComp*, 11, Oct 1966
'*Rose Latulippe* a Canadian legend and ballet: working notes from the diary of its choreographer, Brian Macdonald,' *Dance Magazine*, Dec 1966 (CM)

Rose Marie. Popular US operetta (and later, movie), partly responsible for the widely held image of Canada as a land solely of Mounties, mountains, and snow. Book and lyrics are by Otto Harbach and Oscar Hammerstein II, and the score is by Rudolph Friml and Herbert Stothart. *Rose Marie* opened 2 Sep 1924 at the Imperial Theater in New York and ran for 16 months (557 performances). A touring company, which included Irene *Pavloska, gave the Canadian premiere 12 Jan 1925 at Toronto's *Royal Alexandra Theatre. Later productions in Canada included those by the *Variétés lyriques (1937, 1945, in French), *TUTS (1940s), *Melody Fair (1951), the *Eaton Operatic Society (1959), and many amateur groups.

Rose Marie is perhaps best known around the world as a movie. Four versions were made: the first two in 1928 as silent pictures (one was not released); the third and most popular in 1936, with Nelson Eddy and Jeanette MacDonald; and a fourth in 1954.

Set in the Rocky Mountains, on the plains of Saskatchewan, and in the ballroom of the Château Frontenac hotel in Quebec City, the operetta was intended to appeal to US audiences' taste for the exotic. Rose Marie La Flamme is in love with Jim Kenyon of the Northwest Mounted Police. Kenyon has been accused of murder and Rose Marie stands ready to save her lover's life by giving herself to another. But Kenyon is vindicated, the Mounties get their man, and the lovers are reunited. (The plot underwent extensive changes in each of the movies.)

Among the show's most popular songs were 'Rose Marie,' 'Indian Love Call' (a duet for Rose Marie and Jim), and 'Totem Tom-Tom.' Excerpts were recorded in 1925 by the Victor Light Opera Co (Vic 35756), and the complete operetta in 1958 (RCA Victor LSO 1001) by a cast starring Julie Andrews and Giorgio Tozzi.

BIBLIOGRAPHY
Mason, Lawrence. ' "Rose Marie" a winner: brilliant musical play delights full house at Royal Alexandra,' Toronto *Globe*, 13 Jan 1925
Berton, Pierre. *Hollywood's Canada: The Americanization of the National Image* (Toronto 1975) (DC)

ROSENBERG, Neil V. (Vandraegen). Folklorist, teacher, b Seattle, Wash, 21 Mar 1939; BA history (Oberlin College) 1961, MA folklore (Indiana) 1964, PH D folklore and history (Indiana) 1970. Before and during his years at university he played banjo, mandolin, and other fretted instruments in folk or bluegrass groups in California (Redwood Canyon Ramblers 1958–60, 1963), Bloomington, Ind (Pigeon Hill Boys 1962–7), and Bean Blossom, Ind (Bill Monroe's Brown County Jamboree 1963–8), and organized festivals in Roanoke, Va, in 1966, and Bean Blossom in 1967 and 1968.

Rosenberg moved to Canada in 1968 to join the department of folklore at *Memorial U, St John's, Nfld. He served 1978–9 as acting head of that department, 1968–76 as archivist, and thereafter as director of the university's Folklore and Language Archive. In St John's, Rosenberg played banjo, guitar, and mandolin 1970–2 with Sneed Hearn and the Smiling Liberators and in 1972 joined another group, the Crooked Stovepipe. He also performed 1967–76 with Peter Aceves (Nardaez) and in the Atlantic provinces with George Hector, John Lacey and Gordon Quinton, Vic *Mullen, the Phillips Brothers, and Shelly Posen.

Rosenberg has researched both the traditional folk music and the pop music of North America; his particular interest has been the relationship between the two. He has become known as an authority on the country music called bluegrass. He has written three books and many articles and reviews (published in *Ethnomusicology*, *Bluegrass Unlimited*, the *Journal of American Folklore*, and the *JEMF Quarterly*, among others) and has contributed to the *New Grove Dictionary* and to *EMC*. By 1978 he had edited and annotated nine LPs of bluegrass for RCA, Folkways, Rounder, and other labels. He served 1979–80 as president of the Folklore Studies Assn of Canada.

WRITINGS
– and Casey, George J., and Wareham, Wilfrid W. 'Repertoire categorization and performer-audience relationships: some Newfoundland examples,' *Ethnomusicology*, vol 16, Sep 1972
Bill Monroe and His Blue Grass Boys: All Illustrated Discography (Nashville 1974)
Country Music in the Maritimes: Two Studies, Memorial U reprint series (St John's 1976)
'Studying country music and contemporary folk music traditions in the Maritimes: theory, techniques and the archivist,' *Phonographic Bulletin*, 14, May 1976
Folklore and Oral History (St John's 1978)
'Goodtime Charlie and the Bricklin: a satirical song in context,' *J of the Canadian Oral History Assn*, vol 3, no. 1, 1978
'A preliminary biblioqraphy of Canadian old time instrumental music books,' *CFMJ*, vol 8, 1980 FH

ROSENBOOM, David (Charles). Composer, keyboardist, teacher, b Fairfield, Iowa, 9 Sep 1947. His teachers included Salvatore Martirano and Gordon Binkerd (composition) and Lejaren Hiller (electronic and computer music) 1965–7 at the U of Illinois and Soulima Stravinsky for piano, and others for violin and viola, percussion, trumpet, and conducting. After serving 1967–8 as composer-in-residence at the State U of New York, Buffalo, and 1968–70 as lecturer at New York U, he joined the faculty at *York U, Toronto, where he taught composition, electronic music, and experimental aesthetics until 1979.

Rosenboom was a founder and director of the Aesthetic Research Centre of Canada, established in 1971 on Vancouver Island. He set up its Laboratory of Experimental Aesthetics at York U, co-edited with John Grayson its *Journal of Experimental Aesthetics* in 1974, and became director of the records division of its affiliated A.R.C. Publications and Recordings in 1975. He has researched the relationship of neurophysical functions and musical perception and is the author of many articles and the editor of the book *Biofeedback and the Arts* (Vancouver 1974).

These interests are reflected in the compositions/performances on Rosenboom's LPs *Brainwave Music* and *On Being Invisible*. His *The Seduction of Sapientia* was commissioned by Peggie *Sampson, and his songs with J. Jasmine are heard to his accompaniment on the LP *J. Jasmine ... My New Music*. He has composed film and TV scores. Characteristic of Rosenboom's idiom in the early 1970s was a hypnotic harmonic simplicity underlying complex rhythmic patterns passing through slow phase shifts (*How Much Better If Plymouth Rock Had Landed on the Pilgrims*). In declaring 'We try to start from nothing each time we begin,' he sums up his continuing attentiveness to the deep sources of the artistic impulse and his determination to channel them afresh.

Rosenboom has appeared as composer and performer on CBC TV, CTV, and TV Ontario, and in the USA on CBS and NET. He also has directed ensembles at York U, 1970–5, and the improvisatory group Light. He is an affiliate of PRO Canada.

COMPOSITIONS

And Come up Dripping. 1968. Ob, analog computer. Composer Performer Edn 1969. Pressed by Triton Records for inclusion in the book / record series *Growing with Music* (Englewood Cliffs, NJ 1971)

How Much Better If Plymouth Rock Had Landed on the Pilgrims. 1969–72. Various instr ens, computer-assisted elec instr, birds, outdoor environments, included in *Pieces, An Anthology*, ed M. Byron (Vancouver 1975). Also *And Out Came the Night Ears*. 1978. Pf interfaced to an elec system. Ms. Both recorded on *Rosenboom and Buchla, Collaboration in Performance*. (1978). 1750 Arch Records (perfs include Rosenboom)

Piano Étude I. 1971, 1 or 2 pf, optional brain signal controlled elec processing. *Portable Gold and Philosopher's Stones*. 1972. 4 brainwave perfs, computer-aided electronics. *Chilean Drought* (with J. Humbert). 1974. Speaking and chanting vs, pf, brainwave perf, electronics, optional perc. All publ in *Biofeedback and the Arts*. All recorded on *Brainwave Music of David Rosenboom*. (1976). A.R.C. ST 1002

Patterns for London. 1972, keyboards, various ens, jazz players, publ in *Pieces, An Anthology* (see above). *Is Art Is*. 1974. Various ens. A.R.C. 1975. *191V75* (with J.B. Floyd). 1975. 2 pf, Ms. All recorded on *Suitable for Framing*. (1975). A.R.C. ST 1000 (perfs include Rosenboom and Trichy Sankaran)

The Seduction of Sapientia. 1975. Va da gamba, voltage controlled resonators. In *Pieces, An Anthology* (see above). (1975). Music Gallery Edn MGE 7 (*Sampson)

Keyboard Encounter (with C. McDermed and D. Buchla). 1976. 2 pf, Ms. (1976). Ocean Records, Composers Cassettes, vol 1 (Buchla and McDermed)

J. Jasmine ... My New Music (with J. Jasmine). 1976–8. Pf, v, instr. Chéz Hum-Boom Publishing 1978. (1978). A.R.C. DR 001

On Being Invisible. 1977. Hybrid computer wave analysis and synthesis system, brain signals, touch sensors, small acoustic sources. Ms. (1977). Music Gallery Edn MGE 4 (AL)

ROSEVEAR, Robert (Allan). Teacher, conductor, french hornist, adjudicator, b East Orange, NJ, 9 Jul 1915; BA (Cornell) 1937, B MUS (ESM, Rochester) 1939, M MUS (ESM, Rochester) 1943, hon D MUS (Western Ont) 1979. He joined the Faculty of Music, *U of Toronto, in 1946. There he developed an undergraduate program to train school music teachers and served 1968–72 as the first chairman of the Music Education Dept. He taught 1947–58 at the Ontario Dept of Education summer school and at various music camps. He has lectured and written on music education, was president 1949–50 of the *OMEA, has adjudicated festivals, and has been an *RCMT examiner. He was the founding conductor 1946–50 of the RCMT Symphonic Band and 1962–74 of the U of Toronto Concert Band and the conductor 1953–9 of the U of Toronto SO. In 1978 he was made a professor emeritus of the U of Toronto.

WRITINGS

'Music education in the United States,' *Harvard Dictionary of Music* (Cambridge, Mass 1969)

'Concert band as an instrument and as a market for composers,' *CanComp*, 39, Apr 1969

The French Horn: A Compilation of Information for the Music Educator, self-publ (Toronto 1974) PS

ROSLAK, Roxolana. soprano, b Chortkiv, Ukraine, 11 Feb 1940, naturalized Canadian 1953; Artist Diploma (Toronto) 1964, B MUS (Toronto) 1964. She studied voice as a child in Edmonton with Mrs. J.B. Carmichael and later at the *U of Toronto and the *RCMT with Howell *Glynne, Irene *Jessner, and Ernesto *Vinci. She made her *COC debut in 1963 as the Milliner in *Der Rosenkavalier*. After a season 1965–6 at Covent Garden she returned to Toronto in 1967 to create the role of Marguerite in *Somers' **Louis Riel*. Other roles with the COC have included Musetta in *La Bohème* (1968), Donna Elvira in *Don Giovanni* (1970), and Micaela in *Carmen* (1970).

Roslak was the featured soloist on the *Toronto Mendelssohn Choir's 1972 European tour, and has appeared in recital, in oratorio, and in Royal Ballet (Covent Garden) and *TS presentations of Stravinsky's *Les Noces*. She sang the Indian Princess in the premiere (1977) of **Seabird Island* and on the Canadian tour (1978) of that opera. She made her New York debut 19 Dec 1978 at Alice Tully Hall, Lincoln Center, accompanied by Stuart *Hamilton in songs of Debussy, Hindemith, and Webern and the Kuyas from Somers' *Louis Riel* and by Patricia *Parr (piano), Lorand *Fenyves (violin), and Daniel Domb (cello) in Shostakovich's *Romanzen-Suite*.

Roslak is heard on the recording of Somers' **The Fool*; and with pianist Glenn *Gould she recorded Hindemith's *Das Marienleben* (1976, Col M2-34597). (HCs)

Rosselino Opera Company. Founded in 1941 in Toronto by James Rosselino. Rosselino (tenor, b Jacob Roessler in Regina ca 1890, d Toronto 1960) went in 1924 to Italy where he sang as Giacomo R. Rosselino and taught music and English. Active in New York during the 1930s, he moved in 1939 to Toronto where he gave recitals in 1942 and 1945 and taught privately and at the Central Technical High School opera workshop.

Rosselino's small company provided valuable experience for his pupils among whom were William *Morton and Dodi *Protero. Monthly concerts or opera performances were offered at Rosselino's studio, and more ambitious programs, either of opera excerpts or of full productions, were staged 1944–51 at *Eaton Auditorium. The company presented *La Traviata* 1946, 1947, 1949, and 1950; Flotow's *Martha* in 1948 with Pina Guido of New York in the title role; and *Lucia di Lammermoor* in 1951. Performances were given in Hamilton, London, and Guelph. Company members included the sopranos Dedena Morello and Lilli Washimoto, the mezzo-soprano Merle Stewart Denny, and the baritone Bruno Pasquale. Weldon *Kilburn served as accompanist or, when a small orchestra was used, as conductor. The company's demise coincided with the rise of the Opera Festival Company of Toronto (later *COC).

Rosselino continued to direct the Central Technical opera classes and productions during the 1950s. (DS)

ROSSI, Walter (Carmen) (b Rossignuoli). Guitarist, singer, composer, b Naples 29 May 1947. One of the leading quitarists in Canadian rock, Rossi began his career as a sideman to several successful US and Canadian pop musicians in Montreal in 1965 as a member of the Soul Mates and then toured with the US rhythm and blues singer Wilson Pickett and appeared on the LP *Wicked Pickett* (Atlantic S8108). He was a member 1967–8 of the Montreal band Influence, a quintet which played in Toronto and New York and made the LP *Influence* (ABC S-630), an eclectic collection of pop music. After working in turn with the Buddy Miles Express in the USA (recording *Them Changes*, Mer 61280) and 1970–1 with Luke (Gibson) and the Apostles in Toronto, Rossi formed his own short-lived band, Charlee, which made an LP of the same name (1972, RCA LPS 4809). As a studio quitarist, in Montreal intermittently for many years, he has appeared on LPs by Boule Noire (George Thurston), Patsy Gallant, Michel *Pagliaro, Tony Roman, and Nanette Workman.

In 1976 Rossi began a solo career with the LP *Walter Rossi* (Aquarius AQR 514). Concerts and nightclub appearances followed in eastern Canada, along with the LPs *Six Strings, Nine Lives* (1978, Aquarius AQR 519) and *Diamonds for the Kid* (1979, Aquarius AQR 526). The most popular songs from the LPs include 'Chasin' Rainbows' and 'Mediterranean Romance.' Rossi won a *Juno Award as most promising male vocalist of 1979. His music is copyrighted by his own company Hit Man Music – an incorporated name in keeping with his rather menacing stage image. He is a member of CAPAC.

BIBLIOGRAPHY

Petrowski, Nathalie. 'An ironic honour for one of popular music's hard workers,' *CanComp*, 152, Jun 1980 MM

'Le Rossignol y chante.' According to Marius *Barbeau, the proper title of a song also known by its refrain, 'Gai lon la, gai le rosier.' There are several songs which employ the image of the nightingale bearing a message of love, among them *'J'ai cueilli la belle rose,' 'Rossignol du vert bocage,' 'Rossignolet des bois,' and 'Au bois du rossignolet.'

Ernest *Gagnon in *Chansons populaires du Canada* (Quebec 1865) maintains that 'Le Rossignol y chante' comes from the French provinces of Saintonge and Bas-Poitou which provided Canada with many settlers between 1640 and 1680. The song was collected ca 1830 by Edward Ermatinger, a fur trader employed by the Hudson's Bay Company in western Canada. His version, which he obtained from Canadian voyageurs in Oregon, differs from the one published by Gagnon in 1865. Another variant, with the title 'Par derrièr' chez mon père,' is given by Marguerite and Raoul d'Harcourt in *Chansons folkloriques françaises au Canada* (Quebec 1956). It is interesting that in the text the French line 'Je donnerais Versailles, Paris et St-Denis' became in Canada 'Je donnerais

Québec, Sorel et St-Denis' and even returned to France in this form.

Joseph *Saucier, the first Canadian to record the song, made a 78 of it in 1904 (Col E 2364). The *Alouette Vocal Quartet also recorded it (Bluebird B 1256-B) as did the *Chorale de l'U St-Joseph. Claude *Champagne made two four-part arrangements of the song, both performable by either mens' or womens' voices. *Le Rossignol y chante* is also the title of a collection of folksongs by Marius Barbeau (Ottawa 1962).

BIBLIOGRAPHY

JAF, 264, Apr–Jun 1954 HP

ROUBAKINE, Boris. Pianist, teacher, b of Russian parents, Clarens, Switzerland, 9 May 1908, d Calgary, 30 Apr 1974. He studied piano with his mother 1916–20 and Mathilde de Ribaupierre in Lausanne. He studied theory and composition with Aloys Fornerod 1926–8 in Switzerland and piano with Paul *Loyonnet, composition with Dukas, and piano literature with Nadia Boulanger 1928–30 at the École normale de musique, Paris.

Roubakine performed often in Switzerland and taught 1930–40 at the Institut de Ribaupierre. As the piano partner of the violinist Bronislaw Huberman 1939–46 he toured in many parts of the world, including the USA and Canada.

Roubakine lived for a few years in New York before moving in 1949 to Canada, where he taught at the Senior School of the *RCMT and later at the *U of Toronto. After settling in Canada he performed throughout the country and in Holland and Switzerland with the violinist Betty-Jean *Hagen and came to be known nationally as a teacher, examiner, and adjudicator. After 1957 he headed the piano department of the *Banff SFA. He gave lecture-recitals and pedagogy workshops at the *U of Alberta 1955–60 and taught piano at the *U of British Columbia 1961–7 and at the *U of Calgary from 1967 until his death. Among his pupils were William *Aide, Gwen Beamish MacMillan, Howard Fuller *Brown, Ann *Burrows, Diana *McIntosh, Arlene Nimmons Pach (*Duo Pach), Arthur *Ozolins, Willard Schultz, Tony Strong, and the Swiss pianist Nicole Wickihalder.

An accomplished landscape photographer, Roubakine exhibited in Europe and the USA and gave lectures on photography, donating the proceeds to a piano scholarship fund. After his death the fund was continued in his memory to maintain the scholarships and publish the photos.

In a tribute to Roubakine the *Gazette de Lausanne* stated, 'He combined a very personal feeling for romantic lyricism with lucid intelligence and his playing had deep expressive life. He was ... a teacher of great authority and vast culture.'

Roubakine Auditorium in the Donald Cameron Hall at the Banff Centre commemorates his work there and a portrait by Holly Middleton hangs in the hall. The U of Calgary named a recital hall in his honour. CF

ROULEAU, Joseph (Alfred Pierre). Bass, b Matane, near Rimouski, Que, 28 Feb 1929. He studied with Édouard J. *Woolley and Albert *Cornellier privately in Montreal and 1949–52 with Martial Singher at the CMM. He won the 1949 *Prix Archambault in Montreal and was a semifinalist in the CBC's 1950–1 *'Singing Stars of Tomorrow.' A *JMC concert tour of eastern Canada followed in 1951. On a Quebec government bursary he studied 1952–4 in Milan under Mario Basiola and Antonio Narducci. By 1950 he had sung small roles with the *Opéra national du Québec and the *Minute Opera in Montreal. He sang Colline to Irene *Salemka's Mimi in the New Orleans

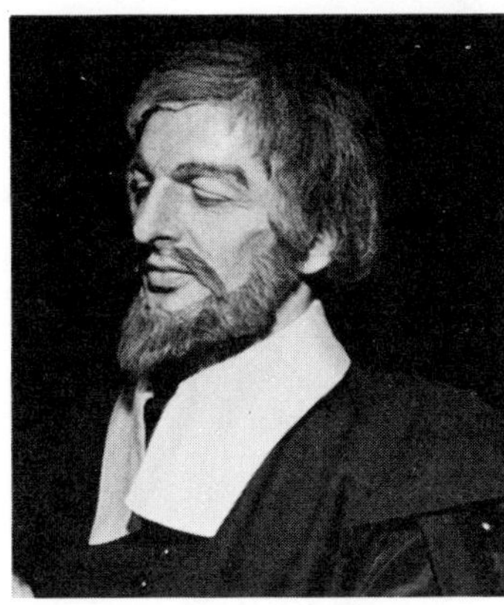

Joseph Rouleau in *Lucia di Lammermoor*

Opera's *La Bohème* in 1955 and made his *Opera Guild of Montreal debut as Philip II in *Don Carlos* in 1956, appearing also in concert and on radio and TV.

Engaged by Covent Garden, Rouleau sang with the company in Cardiff, Manchester, and Southampton prior to his London debut as Colline 23 Apr 1957. Leading roles followed in over 40 productions there during the next 20 years. His Count Rodolfo in Bellini's *La Sonnambula*, in 1960 with Joan Sutherland, led to an association with the soprano which included his debut at the Paris Opera that year as Normanno in *Lucia di Lammermoor* and a 1965–6 Australian tour during which he won high praise particularly for his Assur in Rossini's *Semiramide*. In Sydney, *The Sun* observed: 'Joseph Rouleau, as Assur, grew into magnificent stature, sang his fourth aria with outstanding artistic expression and intelligence.' He has sung in South America, South Africa, and Israel, and his tours of the USSR (1965–6, 1966–7, 1969–70), singing *Faust*, *Don Carlos*, and *Boris Godunov*, brought particular acclaim.

In Canada, he has appeared often with the *MSO, the *TS, the *Quebec SO, and other orchestras. For the *COC in 1967 he sang Basilio in *The Barber of Seville* and created the role of Bishop Taché in *Somers' **Louis Riel*. He sang Ramfis in the COC's *Aida* in 1968 and made his New York City Opera debut as Méphistophélès in *Faust* the same year. Between 1974 and 1976 he gave 55 performances at the Paris Opera including the title role in Massenet's *Don Quichotte*. In Paris he was praised for his singing of the title roles in concert performances at the Théâtre des Champs Elysées of Rossini's *Mosè* and Boito's *Mefistofele*.

Rouleau has appeared with several European and US orchestras, among them the Philharmonia in London, the Amsterdam Concertgebouw, the New York Philharmonic, the Israel Philharmonic, and the Orchestre de la Suisse romande. His Judas in Massenet's *Marie-Magdeleine*, with Régine Crespin in the title role, was admired in New York in 1976. His repertoire has encompassed more than 70 roles.

Rouleau made Montreal his home again in the late 1970s. In 1977 he was elected president of the Mouvement d'action pour l'art lyrique de Québec, a pressure group of singers whose efforts resulted in the establishment in 1980 of the Opéra de Montréal. Rouleau was awarded the 1967 *Prix de musique Calixa-Lavallée and was made an Officer of the *Order of Canada in 1977.

DISCOGRAPHY

Beethoven 'Ode to Joy' from *Symphony No. 9*. Choirs of Rutgers U, MSO, Pelletier cond. 1967. CBC EXPO 1

Berlioz *L'Enfance du Christ*. St Anthony Singers, Goldsbrough O, C. Davis cond, Rouleau (Herod and the Householder). 1961. Oiseau-Lyre SOL 60032, 60033

– *L'Enfance du Christ*. John Alldis Choir, London SO, C. Davis cond, Rouleau (Householder). 1976. Philips 6700-106

Donizetti scene from *Anna Bolena*. Maria Callas, Philharmonia O, Rescigno cond. 1959. Angel 35764

Gounod *Roméo et Juliette*, highlights. Paris Opera O, Lombard cond. 1965. Angel S 36287

Grand Opera Festival: 'Coronation Scene' from *Boris Godunov*. Lanigan ten, Covent Garden O and Chor, Downes cond. 1968. Decca SET 392-393

Great French Opera Arias. Ambrosian Singers, Royal Opera House O, Covent Garden, Matheson cond. 1974. Lon OS 26379

Haydn *Harmoniemesse*. Choir of St John's College (Cambridge), Academy of St Martin-in-the-Fields, G. Guest cond, Runnet org. 1966. Lon Argo Z515

Massenet *Marie-Magdeleine*. Choir and orch, A. Morss cond, D. Roth org. 1976. BJR BJRS 1381-1382

Mathieu – Sauguet – et al. Savard pf. 1972. RCI 365

Mozart – Ravel – Mussorgsky. Reiner pf. 1967. RCI 250/CBC EXPO 3

Rossini *Semiramide*. Ambrosian Opera Chor, London SO, Bonynge cond, Rouleau (Assur). 1966. 3 Lon 1383/(excerpts) Lon OS 26086/(excerpts) Lon 26168

Stravinsky *Renard*. O de la Suisse romande, Ansermet cond. 1965. Lon 25929

Sullivan *Ruddigore*. Glyndebourne Festival Chor, Pro Arte O, Sargent cond, Rouleau (Sir Roderic). 1963. 2 HMV ASD 563, 564

BIBLIOGRAPHY

'Joseph Rouleau,' *OpCan*, vol 3, Sep 1962

McLean, Eric. 'From Matane to Covent Garden,' *Montreal Star*, 29 Jun 1974 (GBr, FH)

ROUSSEAU, (Joseph Édouard) **Maurice.** Civil servant, composer, pianist, b Quebec City 11 Nov 1904. A pupil of Berthe *Roy for piano and Émiliano *Renaud for composition, he wrote chiefly for piano: four *Préludes*, two *Études*, two *Fairy Tales*, and a *Choral varié et berceuse*. Bela Böszörmenyi-Nagy, Paul *Doyon, and John *Newmark have played his works in recital. His *Poème* for violin and piano was performed in Quebec City by Geza *de Kresz and Ruggiero Ricci. His song *Neige printanière* was in the repertoire of the tenor Fernand Francell. He is a member of CAPAC. GP

ROUSSEL, Paul (Joseph Wilfrid Paul-André). Critic, writer, radio producer; b Montreal 5 Nov 1924, d 12 Sep 1977. After teaching himself piano, he studied theory at the *CMM 1943–5 with Jean *Vallerand. He was Vallerand's successor as critic 1945–54 on the Montreal daily *Le Canada*. He also contributed to the weeklies *Notre temps* and *L'Autorité* and published some poems in reviews such as *Gants du ciel*. A member of the CBC staff 1955–77 he worked first as editor of *La Semaine à Radio-Canada* and then as a producer of recorded music programs, including the series 'Vienne la nuit,' devoted to the life and work of the great composers. He published *Mozart raconte en 50 chefs-d'oeuvre / Mozart Seen through 50 Masterpieces* (Montreal and Toronto 1973). He also wrote *Votre Discothèque* (Montreal 1973) and was program annotator 1951–62 for the *MSO. Roussel published the collection of short stories *La Dame en coup de vent* (Montreal 1971) and a translation of Eric *McLean's *The Living Past of Montreal* under the title *Le Passé vivant de Montréal* (Montreal 1964). An amateur painter, he exhibited his work in several Montreal art galleries. GP

ROWE, Frank H. (Francis Henry). Baritone, teacher, b Blackman, England, ca 1880, d ?. He was a soloist at St John's Church in his native town and sang with the Moody-Manners opera troupe for three years. He later studied with Vittorio Maria Vanzo in Milan. On his return to England he sang for a time with the Carl Rosa troupe, and in 1910 he took part in Sir Thomas Beecham's operatic season at Covent Garden. Two years later he moved to Montreal and taught 1913–ca 1923 at the Columbian Cons (later *Canadian Academy of Music). He also taught at *McGill U and gave many private lessons. His pupils included Thomas *Archer, Pierre *Duval, Maureen *Forrester, Louis *Quilico, and André *Turp. He gave recitals in Montreal, Toronto, Ottawa, and Quebec City with his friend the organist and pianist Frederick H. *Blair. They were returning from England on the *Athenia* when it was torpedoed in September 1939. Blair lost his life but Rowe was saved. Following a recital for the *Club musical de Québec, Louis *Gravel wrote: 'The voice is rich enough in timbre, though somewhat lacking in warmth and resonance ... the high notes are effortless; when sung with constraint they have a pleasing sound' (*La Musique*, vol 2, Dec 1920). GP

ROY. Quebec City family of musicians: 1 / Philéas; 2 / Léo, son of Philéas, and 3 / Berthe, daughter of Philéas.

1 **Philéas** (Alphonse). Organist, pianist, band conductor, choirmaster, writer, astronomer, b Quebec City 9 Nov 1857, d there 23 Nov 1939. He studied with Damis *Paul (organ and piano), Célestin *Lavigueur (violin), and Calixa *Lavallée (harmony). He succeeded Nazaire *LeVasseur to serve 1881–99 as organist at St-Roch Church and was a teacher at the *Séminaire de Québec and at the Collège de Lévis. Besides his two children he taught J.-Arthur *Bernier and Alphonse *Tardif. He conducted the *Union musicale, the 9th Infantry Regiment Band, and the Union Lambillotte.

In 1899 he settled in New York with his family. He taught piano at the New York College of Music and played the organ in several churches in New York and in Woonsocket, RI. He was interested in astronomy and built an observatory near his residence. In 1887, during a stay in France, he worked with Camille Flammarion to found the Société astronomique de France. At an international competition in 1892 he won a prize from that society. He wrote articles for several publications.

2 **Léo**. Composer, writer on music, pianist, organist, teacher, b Quebec City 27 Nov 1887, d there 4 Sep 1974. As a child he studied harmonica, xylophone, piano, organ, trumpet, trombone, horn, and double-bass with his father. In New York in 1899 he studied harmony and composition with Homer N. Bartlett. He composed his Op 1, *Berceuse* for piano, in 1903. Eleven years later he had reached Op 47. He took a position as choirmaster at Trois-Rivières in 1912, but returned to New York before finally settling in 1920 in Quebec City, where he pursued a career as a writer and teacher.

In 1926 Roy founded the Société Frédéric Chopin au Canada and became co-editor of the periodical *La Lyre* of Montreal. He was music critic 1926–32 for the Quebec City daily *Le Soleil* and commentator 1928–31 for the radio concerts of the *TSO. Luigi von *Kunits, director of the orchestra at that time, presented several of his works in the 1930–1 season. His overture *Hail to the Exhibition* was performed in Toronto in 1930.

A somewhat eccentric and controversial figure, Roy curtailed his activities after 1930, although he continued to write and compose. His friends attributed his voluntary retirement to the opposition he aroused in music circles. A fervent admirer of Chopin, in 1949 he was named representative and correspondent of the review *L'Anné Chopin* by the Chopin Institute of Warsaw.

Léo Roy (*Le Canada musical*, Sep 1917)

Berthe Roy

He contributed to *Grove's Dictionary* (5th edn) and in 1955 became a corresponding member of the Frédéric Chopin Society of Warsaw. During his travels Roy made the acquaintance of Fauré, Medtner, Paderewski, Rachmaninoff, and Saint-Saëns.

Between 1903 and 1958 Roy appears to have composed about 350 original works and made 800 harmonizations and 400 free-style transcriptions of folksongs, including 160 Bohemian, Czech, and Slovak and 47 Iroquois. He also set to music 62 poems by Émile Nelligan. By far the majority of these works remained in manuscript form. Among his compositions for piano are *Hommage à Chopin*, 'Polonaise héroïque' (1908), *Sérénade, Op 42* (1912), two highly unusual works: *Prélude No. 20* (1919), with the notes G, A, and B to be played as flats and indicated thus as a 'key-signature,' and *Prélude No. 25* 'on two notes' (1930), and two satirical pieces dating from 1914.

In addition to numerous artices on music, in which he advanced his own ideas, Roy produced more than 2000 pieces on subjects as varied as anthropology, ethnology, zoology, philosophy, and aesthetics.

Dr Guy Marcoux, one of Roy's small circle of friends and disciples, established the Léo Roy Foundation for the purpose of conserving his documents and manuscripts and of making his works known. In a speech 20 Sep 1979 at a service commemorating the fifth anniversary of Léo Roy's death, Marcoux stressed that Roy 'was not a man of compromise; he never abandoned his convictions in order to obtain success. In the first fifty years of his life I believe he attempted, unsuccessfully, to communicate with his fellow citizens.' It will be for posterity to establish the real or relative value of Léo Roy's vast output if and when more of them are published and performed.

WRITINGS

'Quebec composers,' *MCan*, Nov 1930

'La vérité sur Sabatier,' *Action nationale*, vol 57, Apr 1968

BIBLIOGRAPHY

LeVasseur, Nazaire. 'Le pic et la plume. Travailleurs. L'un d'eux,' *P-T*, 2 Apr 1921

Asselin, P.-A. 'Léo Roy: une figure de proue,' *L'Information médicale et paramédicale*, vol 32, 7 Oct 1980

3 **Berthe**. Pianist, teacher, b Quebec City 8 Feb 1889, d there 9 Nov 1951; hon D MUS (Laval) 1943. At three she showed surprising talents, including an exceptional memory. After studying piano with her father, she made her debut at eight at the Château Frontenac hotel. In New York, among some 700 contestants, she was chosen to receive a scholarship from the National Cons of Music, where she studied with Rafael Joseffy. She worked also with Gaston Dethier (piano) and Romualdo Sapio (singing). During a three-year stay in Paris she took courses at the Conservatoire with Antoine-Émile Marmontel (piano) and Anna Arnaud (singing). She could play from memory all of the fugues of Bach's *Well-tempered Clavier* and transpose them into all keys. She allegedly accomplished this feat in the presence of guests of the organist-composer Alexandre Guilmant at his house in Meudon. Guilmant is said by Madeleine Gleason-Huguenin to have declared: 'I do not believe there is anyone present who could do as much.'

Numerous concerts in the USA and Europe earned Berthe Roy the highest priase, in particular during a North American tour 1907–8 with the violinist Jan Kubelík. The tour included a concert 25 Mar 1908 at *Massey Hall in Toronto. She settled in 1914 in Quebec City, where she gave private lessons and taught at *Laval U. Several of her pupils won the *Prix d'Europe: Lucille Dompierre (1919), Anna-Marie Messénie (1922), Conrad *Bernier (1923), and Henri Mercure (1927). Her booklet *Amateur et artiste* was published in Montreal in 1944. She died in poverty after being paralysed for 10 years.

BIBLIOGRAPHY

[Gleason-Huguenin], Madeleine. 'Mme Berthe Roy,' Montreal *La Patrie*, 22 Jul 1933

1 / GP, 2 / (SW), 3 / GP

ROY, Louise (m Morin). Soprano, b St Boniface (now Winnipeg), 25 May 1924; ARCT 1946, Artist Diploma (Toronto) 1951. Her studies with J. Roberto Wood in Winnipeg and Ernesto *Vinci at the *RCMT led to first awards (1949) in the CBC's *'Singing Stars of Tomorrow' and *'Nos Futures Étoiles' and scholarships to the Kathryn Turney Long Summer School of the *Metropolitan Opera and the Rollins Summer School of Theatre in Lennox, Mass.

An early member of the *COC Roy sang Donna Anna in *Don Giovanni* (1950), the Countess in *The Marriage of Figaro* (1951), Ludmila in *The Bartered Bride* (1952), and the Foreign Woman in *The Consul* (1953). She performed with the *CBC Opera Company and 'Théâtre lyrique Molson,' in concert with many Canadian orchestras and choirs, and on tour for the *JMC. She was one of Canada's leading dramatic sopranos at the time of her retirement in the mid-1950s.

Roy returned to performance with a recital 10 May 1974 at Town Hall in Toronto, after which the critic John *Kraglund wrote, 'Miss Roy is still blessed with the strong, beautiful voice which won her earlier acclaim' (Toronto *Globe and Mail*, 13 May 1974). MB

ROY, Raoul. Folklorist, collector, singer, b St-Fabien-sur-mer, near Rimouski, Que, 6 Jan 1936. He attended the École de Marine in Rimouski 1954–6, after which he studied the oral tradition of folk literature at *Laval U. In 1958 he decided to concentrate on research into folklore and the collection and recording of folksongs. He studied and performed 1959–61 in England and in 1961 founded the Centre d'art du Pirate in St-Fabien-sur-mer. As a folksinger he took part in *Chansons folkloriques du Canada*, a set of nine LPs produced by CBC IS for RCA Victor and RCI (1967, CS-100); he was one of those who conceived the idea and he wrote the French liner-notes. In addition he recorded four albums of folksongs for Select: CM-298.068, M-298.095, SSP-24.152, SSP-24.177, and a fifth, which was a co-production of Select (SSP-24.177) and RCI (RCI 273). His wife, the singer Louise Poulin, took part in some of the recordings. The 700 to 800 songs or variants which he collected on tape in many parts of Quebec are deposited in the *Archives de folklore of Laval U. He published a collection of 50 Canadian folksongs, *Le Chant de l'alouette* (Quebec City and Montreal 1969).

BIBLIOGRAPHY

Béliveau, André. 'Raoul Roy: les retrouvailles de notre folklore et de sa poésie,' Montreal *Magazine de la Presse*, 23 Sep 1967 / *CanComp*, 23, Nov 1967
Rudel-Tessier, J. 'Le folkloriste Raoul Roy: chez nous, à Saint-Fabien, le quotidien était folklorique,' Montreal *Photo-Journal*, 4–11 Oct 1967 HPn

ROYAL, Roy. Baritone, teacher, producer, administrator, critic; b Edmonton 6 Mar 895, d Montreal 5 Mar 1968. He studied in Edmonton with Eva Gagné-Saint-Germain, a pupil of Guillaume *Couture and Romain Bussine, and 1919–21 at the Paris Cons with A.L. Hettich. From 1921 to 1924 he studied in Vienna, Milan, and Rome. In 1924 he entered the Paris Schola Cantorum as resident baritone, thus ensuring an opportunity to study and perform the classical repertoire.

In 1926 Royal began teaching in Paris, concurrently performing widely in France, Belgium, and England and occasionally in Canada. During World War II he was interned 1940–4 at St-Denis. Though his health had been undermined, he returned to his career. In 1945 he resumed teaching and began writing music criticism in Paris for the weekly *La Bataille* and the daily *L'Époque*.

Claude *Champagne urged Royal to return to Canada, but it was not until 1951 that he settled in Montreal to teach voice and elocution at the *CMM and the *École Vincent-d'Indy. Colette *Boky, Sylvia *Saurette, Bruno *Laplante, and Claude *Corbeil were among his pupils. He wrote criticism 1951–4 for the weekly *Le Petit Journal* prior to joining the CBC International Service as director of its recording program (RCI). He was head of music 1959–64 for the CBC French network.

BIBLIOGRAPHY

Potvin, Gilles. 'En Roy Royal, la musique canadienne perd un ami,' Montreal *La Presse*, 9 Mar 1968 GP

Royal Alexandra Theatre. Toronto landmark and cultural centre, located on downtown King St West near Simcoe St, on grounds formerly occupied by Upper Canada College. Named after Queen Alexandra, it was built in 1907 at a cost of $750,000 by a Toronto syndicate headed by Cawthra Mulock and including the stockbroker R.A. Smith, the manufacturer Stephen Haas, and the entrepreneur Lawrence Solman.

The 'Royal Alex,' as it is known affectionately, was designed by Peter Lyle who, using New York's New Amsterdam Theater as a model, incorporated novel features such as air conditioning which required tons of ice and .9 m-thick concrete floors which made it Canada's first fireproof theatre. He employed gently curving lines to achieve excellent acoustics, thus creating a feeling of intimacy between performer and audience. Cantilevered balcony construction made the Royal Alexandra the first Canadian theatre to offer an unobstructed view of its proscenium arch from all vantage points. The auditorium (comprising orchestra level, balcony, gallery, and four private boxes) seated 1525. Its stage was 22.5 m wide and 10.95 m deep, while the proscenium was 11.4 m in height (*Construction*, November 1907).

The theatre opened 26 Aug 1907 with the musical revue *Top of the World* by Mark Swann and soon was established as one of the leading playhouses in North America. Fred and Adele Astaire, Fanny Brice, Eddie Cantor, Maurice Chevalier, Marie Dressler, Margot Fonteyn, George Formby, Al Jolson, Sir Harry Lauder, Beatrice *Lillie, Alicia Markova, Edith Piaf, and Ethel Waters have performed on its stage, as have the Boston Grand Opera, the *Dumbells, Anna Pavlova's Ballet Russe, the D'Oyly Carte, and the Royal Winnipeg Ballet. Scores of local companies and performers have appeared there.

A Canadian work, Joseph Nevin *Doyle's comic opera *The Golden Age*, was performed in 1915, and some of the operetta productions of the *Savoyards were given in the Royal Alex. In March 1930 the TCM's opera company appeared in *Hansel and Gretel* and Vaughan Williams' *Hugh the Drover*, and in 1936 the Opera Guild of Toronto presented *Tosca*, *Cavalleria Rusticana*, and *I Pagliacci*. In 1941 and 1943 the *San Carlo Opera gave performances of several popular operas.

In 1948 the *Royal Cons Opera presented *Rosalinda*, the Broadway version of Strauss' *Die Fledermaus*. The company presented an annual season in the early 1950s and under the name Opera Festival 1954–9. (The company became the *Canadian Opera Company in 1960 and moved to the *O'Keefe Centre, but returned to the Royal Alex 18 years later to present its 1978 spring season.)

John *Weinzweig's ballet **Red Ear of Corn* had its premiere at the Royal Alex in 1950, in a production by the Volkoff Canadian Ballet, and the Canadian revues **My Fur Lady* and (the annual) **Spring Thaw* appeared there, along with many US touring musicals (*As Thousands Cheer*, *Bittersweet*, *Bloomer Girl*, *Carmen Jones*, *Chu Chin Chow*, etc).

In 1962 the trustees of the Cawthra Mulock Estate decided to sell the theatre. It was purchased in February 1963 by the Toronto entrepreneur Edwin Mirvish who commissioned the designer Herbert E.D. Irvine to restore it to its original Edwardian splendour. Under Mirvish's ownership it has flourished again, although in direct competition with the O'Keefe Centre.

The first production to be staged in the newly restored theatre was the Broadway show *Never Too Late* (1963). Successful shows presented thereafter included *The Best of Spring Thaw*, *By George*, *Don't Bother Me, I Can't Cope*, *Godspell*, *Grease*, *Oh Kay!*, *The Wiz*, and the popular **Hair*, which had a run of 53 weeks and grossed $3.25 million.

The theatre's managers have been Lawrence Solman 1907–33, William Breen 1933–9, Ernest Rawley 1939–56 and 1958–63, and Edwin De Rocher 1957 and 1963–9. Yale Simpson succeeded De Rocher in 1969.

BIBLIOGRAPHY

Young, Roly. 'Cavalcade of musicals; recalling bygone hits; show prices are down,' Toronto *Globe and Mail*, 19 Jun 1948
– 'Oldtime amateur shows kept press scribes busy; summer theatre notes,' ibid, 14 Aug 1948
'Royal Alexandra Theatre,' *Centre Stage*, Oct 1976
Metropolitan Toronto Library. Royal Alexandra Theatre records, clippings, etc (JBk)

The Royal Canadian College of Organists / Le Collège royal canadien des organistes. A national association of organists and church musicians founded 1909 as The Canadian Guild of Organists, renamed The Canadian College of Organists in 1920, and granted the prefix 'Royal' in 1959. Headquarters are in Toronto, and in 1976 there were 1200 members.

1 Organization
2 History
3 Publications
4 Presidents

1 ORGANIZATION. RCCO membership is open to organists, choirmasters, and all those who support its aims:

a. To promote a high standard or organ playing, choral directing, church music and composition.
b. To hold examinations in organ playing, choir directing, theory and general knowledge of music; to grant diplomas to members of the College who pass such examinations.
c. To encourage organ recitals and other musical events; to afford opportunities among members for discussion of topics of musical interest and for meeting socially.

The college is governed by an elected national council with a president and executive committee.

Since 1969 local centres (each with its own elected executive) have been grouped into regions, each also with an executive. In 1976 the regions and local centres were: British Columbia (Vancouver, Vancouver Island), Alberta (Calgary, Edmonton), Prairie (Regina, Saskatoon, Winnipeg), Western Ontario (Chatham, London, St Thomas, Sarnia, Stratford), Central Ontario (Brantford, Hamilton, Kitchener, Niagara Peninsula), Toronto, Georgian Bay (Owen Sound, Huronia), East Central Ontario (Oshawa, Peterborough), Laurentian (Bay of Quinte, Kingston, Ottawa, Pembroke), Montreal, and Atlantic (Fredericton, Halifax, Moncton, Pictou County, Saint John). National and regional conventions are held in alternate years.

Although not a teaching institution, the RCCO, as an examining body, maintains graded standards and offers examinations for Fellowship (FRCCO, in organ or choir training; before 1959 FCCO), Associateship (ARCCO, in organ or choir training; before 1959 ACCO). It offers as well a Pre-Associateship Examination and Preliminary Examination in Service Playing. The Diploma of Fellowship (honoris causa) is also granted. Scholarships in memory of Healey *Willan and Eric *Rollinson are awarded annually, and for members and students there are educational resources, workshops, recitals, and tours of organ installations.

The RCCO thus combines various functions served in other countries by separate organizations (as in Great Britain by the Royal College of Organists, the Royal School of Church Music, and the Organ Club). It fosters the interests of young musicians through student groups and competitions in performance and composition. The college's national placement service aids development of the parish music program. The college archives are on deposit in the library of *Wilfrid Laurier U, Waterloo, Ont. The RCCO is a member of the *CMCouncil.

2 HISTORY. Though organists had attempted to form a professional organization in the 19th cen-

A meeting of the Canadian College of Organists in the early 1920s. Included are (top row, 1st and 2nd from left) Ernest MacMillan and William Hewlett, (top row, right) Alfred Whitehead, (middle row, 2nd from left) Herbert A. Fricker, (4th) Percival Illsley, (6th) Albert Ham, (9th) Healey Willan, (11th) George M. Brewer, (front row, 6th from left) Nellie Ham.

tury, the first concrete step toward founding the RCCO was taken 27 Oct 1909 by eight musicians who met at the Cons of Music in Brantford, Ont, and passed a resolution recognizing 'the importance of establishing a college of organists, similar to that of England, in Canada' (Brantford *Daily Expositor*, 28 Oct 1909). Their desire was realized in December 1909 when the Canadian Guild of Organists was founded, with Albert *Ham as president. Frederick C. Thomas of Brantford was secretary and designed the guild's crest which has continued in use. By the first convention, held in Toronto in 1911, members had enrolled from all nine provinces except New Brunswick and Prince Edward Island, and a scheme of examinations had evolved similar to that of the RCO of Great Britain. The first fellow of the guild, by examination, was Alfred *Whitehead.

In 1920, with the change of name to the Canadian College of Organists, the college absorbed Canadian members of the American Guild of Organists. Although in 1939 there were only 245 members in eight centres, the period following saw steady expansion. By the college's 50th anniversary in 1959 membership had reached 1300 in 32 centres.

One of the college's most significant achievements was its British Organ Restoration Fund (1943–52), under the chairmanship of Healey Willan, which raised more than $30,000 for the installation of a new organ at Coventry Cathedral. An 'RCCO Headquarters Building Fund' was established in 1954.

The RCCO since 1959 has sought solutions to problems peculiar to the practice of church music in Canada. Convention sites have been diversified (eg, Vancouver 1969, Halifax 1973), and presidents have travelled to centres across the country. The examination system has been revised in accordance with the Canadian church music situation. A plan for regional government proposed in 1969 by Barrie *Cabena has been adopted, a nation-wide study was conducted (1974–6) of the professional life of church musicians, and special project grants were awarded as incentives for local centre development. Steps were taken to inaugurate a program and examination in French to meet the special needs of the Quebec Roman Catholic parish, a field which previously had not been a concern of an association built upon British and American models.

The college has fostered international relations and in 1967 was host to the International Congress of Organists.

3 PUBLICATIONS. The *NL of C holds a copy (vol 5, Dec 1916) of *The Canadian Guild of Organists' Journal*, which was published twice a year. Since ca 1923 the college has issued intermittent bulletins and newsletters. A yearbook containing the membership roll, examination regulations, and sample exam papers was introduced in 1939 and later replaced by the *RCCO Quarterly* (1973–8) and then the *Yearbook Digest and Newsletter* (1980–). The college has published separate reports on church acoustics and console standardization. News of the college's activities have been published in *Musical Canada* (1921–33), the US monthly *The Diapason* (1933–68), and in the American Guild of Organists' official magazine, *Music* (1967–).

4 PRESIDENTS. Following Albert Ham, who was first president in 1909–21, presidents have been Percival J. *Illsley (1921–2), Healey Willan (1922–3), Charles E. *Wheeler (1923–5), Herbert A. *Fricker (1925–6), John W. *Bearder (1926–7), Ernest C. *MacMillan (1927–8), William Henry *Hewlett (1928–9), Thomas J. *Crawford (1929–30), Alfred Whitehead (1930–1), Richard *Tattersall (1931–2), Herbert *Sanders (1932–3), Healey Willan (1933–5), Alfred Whitehead (1935–7), George D. *Atkinson (1937–9), Paul *Ambrose (1939–41), Charles *Peaker (1941–3), Eric T. Rollinson (1943–5), Frederick C. *Silvester (1945–7), Eric Dowling (1947–9), John J. *Weatherseed (1949–51), Reginald *Geen (1951–3), D'Alton *McLaughlin (1953–5), Gordon D. *Jeffery (1955–7), Muriel Stafford *Gidley (1957–9), James Hopkirk (1959–61), Henry Rosevear (1961–3), George T. Veary (1963–5), Clifford C. McAree (1965–7), H. Barrie Cabena (1967–9), James Chalmers (1969–71), Robert H. Bell (1971–2), Graham *George (1972–4), Walter H. *Kemp (1974–6), Gordon Atkinson (1976–8), and Markwell J. Perry (1978–80). WHK

Royal Canadian Mounted Police. See Bands: 5 / Police bands; Mounties.

Royal Canadians. See Guy Lombardo.

Royal Commission on National Development in the Arts, Letters and Sciences. See Massey Commission.

Royal Conservatory of Music of Toronto (Toronto Conservatory of Music until 1947). Incorporated in 1886 and opened the following year with an enrolment of 200 students and a staff of some 50 teachers. Edward *Fisher, who had been influential in its organization, became the first music director, and Marion Ferguson registered the students. The conservatory quickly became the most prominent conservatory in Canada and one of the important music-training institutions of the British Empire, establishing its pre-eminence through professional training, a nation-wide examining system, and a faculty which provided much of the leadership for the growth and development of music in Canada. Although in the 1960s and 1970s its programs accommodated major changes in the development of music in higher education, the conservatory has continued to play an important role in the musical life of Canada.

In 1887 instruction was offered in practical and theoretical music as well as elocution, foreign languages, public school music, acoustics, piano tuning, and vocal anatomy and hygiene. Teachers were available for saxophone (1888) and for guitar and zither (1893). At this time Toronto's musical life enjoyed a vigorous rivalry among several music schools and the aspiring figures associated with them. The TCM became affiliated with the *U of Trinity College in 1888 and with the *U of Toronto in 1896 for the purpose of preparing candidates for university degree examinations. The conservatories provided the instruction and the universities conducted the examinations.

From its inception, the conservatory was a large-scale enterprise and by 1892 its activities were organized under two departments – the Academic Dept, for young students and amateurs, and the Collegiate Dept, which offered programs in professional training for performers and teachers. Examinations at the Junior, Intermediate, and Final levels led to the Associate diploma (ATCM). The Fellowship (FTCM, begun in 1890 and offered until 1914 when it was replaced by the Licentiate, LTCM; see also Diplomas) was awarded to students who completed two advanced courses of study. The exacting standards of advanced work at the conservatory were recognized by the U of Toronto; recipients of conservatory diplomas were exempted from the first and second year B MUS examinations. The first graduate in pianoforte was J.D.A. *Tripp in 1893; in that year 265 certificates were issued and 30 students received diplomas. The remarkable growth in these early years was associated with the appointment of many distinguished musicians to the teaching faculty. A three-manuel organ was installed by *Warren and Sons in 1889, to the considerable benefit of the work of the organ teachers, A.S. *Vogt and J.W.F. *Harrison. J. Humfrey *Anger, appointed in 1892, developed an outstanding theory program.

When it opened, the conservatory occupied two upper floors over a music store at the corner of Yonge St and Wilton Ave (later Dundas Square) but in 1897 a new building with more extensive facilities was erected at the corner of College St and University Ave. This structure included a reception hall, offices, 33 classrooms, a lecture hall, and a concert hall in which the Warren organ was housed. In 1899 25 studios and classrooms were

This cover design was familiar to thousands of Canadian children and teenagers.

added, as well as a two-manual organ built by Edward *Lye and Sons. To accommodate out-of-town students, in 1902 two adjacent houses (to the south) were remodelled as a ladies' residence, and another house (to the west) provided 15 additional teaching studios. This expansion of physical facilities was required to cope with the tremendous growth in all departments during Edward Fisher's regime, 1886–1913.

Shortly after moving to College Street, the conservatory introduced the *Fletcher Music Method for young children and operated a special Normal Session in the summer of 1898, and in that same year established local examination centres in several Ontario towns. The conservatory extended its teaching with the establishment of branches in residential areas of Toronto. Bertha *Drechsler Adamson formed the Conservatory String Quartet (1901–4) and later developed a string orchestra. In 1906 Frank *Welsman founded and directed the Toronto Conservatory Orchestra which, two years later, became the *TSO. Some of the graduates of this early period were Frank *Blachford (violin 1897), Mona *Bates (piano 1907), and Cora *Ahrens (piano 1911).

In 1911 the board of directors reorganized the conservatory into a private trust to ensure that all profits would remain for artistic development. By 1912 there were 2000 students registered and among the staff were outstanding musicians such as A.T. *Cringan (school music), Albert *Ham (singing and organ), Frank Blachford (violin), Edward *Broome (organ), and Leo *Smith (cello and theory). By the time of Fisher's death (1913) the institution was exerting a significant influence on music education in Canada.

Augustus Vogt, widely known as the conductor of the *Toronto Mendelssohn Choir, became principal of the conservatory in 1913. He worked closely with Sir Edmund Walker, president of the conservatory, in developing closer ties with the university in order to provide continuity and financial stability for the conservatory; at that time, Walker was chairman of the university's board of governors. By an act of the Ontario Legislature (1919), the property and assets of the conservatory were vested in the university, and in 1921 the conservatory's operation came under the control of the university through a board of trustees, members appointed annually by the university. The fusion of the two institutions was reinforced further in 1918 by the appointment of Vogt as dean of the Faculty of Music which opened in 1919. This dual appointment, together with the physical presence of both institutions in the same building (until 1962) did much to cement the relationship.

In 1924 the conservatory purchased the *Canadian Academy of Music, and its president, Col Albert *Gooderham, was appointed chairman of the board of trustees of the TCM. By the late 1920s the large number of conservatories in Toronto had dwindled to two – the other being the *Hambourg Conservatory. These developments enabled Vogt to consolidate the position of the TCM; it had been the largest in the city probably from the beginning of the century and was soon virtually without a rival in Toronto. Vogt gave vigorous leadership to the institution in several ways. One of the most significant developments was the resident program in performance (1914–52) leading to the Licentiate. During Vogt's term Healey *Willan, who had succeeded Anger as head of the theory department, was appointed vice-principal (he served 1920–36) and Luigi von *Kunits in 1924 became conductor of the Conservatory Orchestra. Vogt increased the number of local centres of examination, and near the end of his regime (1913–26) the number of students had grown to almost 7500 and the number of examination candidates exceeded 16,000.

Ernest *MacMillan was named principal in 1926, and in the following year assumed as well the deanship of the Faculty of Music. The early years of his term were characterized by a diversity of artistic activities and developments. Efforts were made to improve the library. Courses in *Dalcroze eurythmics were introduced in 1927. MacMillan conducted the Conservatory Choir, which gave annual presentations of the *St Matthew Passion* and performed other large choral works, giving concerts in co-operation with the TSO. The *Conservatory String Quartet (1929–46, re-established by Elie *Spivak; its predecessor flourished 1901–4) created much interest in chamber music. In 1930 Donald *Heins succeeded von Kunits as conductor of the Conservatory SO. An opera company was formed which staged several productions during its existence 1928–30.

A number of significant curriculum changes occurred in the 1930s, such as a major revision of the piano syllabus in 1934, improvements in sight-reading and ear tests, and more rigorous theory requirements for the Associate diploma. In 1935 the examination system based on grades I to X was introduced, and by an agreement with the Ontario Dept of Education credit could be claimed for conservatory grades in secondary schools and as entrance requirements for university admission. Frederick *Silvester's career – as registrar of examinations 1929–46 and registrar of the conservatory 1946–66 – was associated with many of these developments.

At the request of the university president and conservatory board, and with the support of the Carnegie Foundation of the USA, Ernest Hutcheson (then president of the Juilliard School) undertook a feasibility study concerning the expansion of music education in Canada. He found the conservatory to be less of a school than a clearing house for private teachers – the conservatory furnished studio facilities and administrative services for which the teachers returned a percentage of their fees. Hutcheson suggested that teachers who were not salaried would be interested primarily in maintaining gifted students for their own classes and would be concerned somewhat less with providing a well-rounded education in all aspects of music, including theoretical subjects. He therefore advocated a smaller faculty, to be hired on a salary basis, with a greater commitment to comprehensive programs for senior students of professional calibre. He recommended also a preparatory division and summer courses.

Although the Hutcheson Report (1937) was not implemented at the time (partly because of World War II), its recommendations led in 1946 to the establishment of a senior division within the conservatory. The Depression and the war also help explain a drop in registration. In the 1940–1 season there were 4654 students registered for tuition and 12,495 for examinations. In 1942 the burden of other duties prompted Sir Ernest MacMillan's resignation as principal. His successor, Norman *Wilks, died in 1944 after a short term as principal, and Charles *Peaker served as director until 1945.

The long association between TCM and the Frederick *Harris Music Co dates back to the first publication of the conservatory's introductory piano books in 1916 and vocal studies in 1924. Other firms which published conservatory examination books were *Anglo-Canadian, *Heintzman, *Nordheimer, Gordon V. *Thompson, and *Whaley Royce, but by 1944 Frederick Harris had become the TCM's exclusive publisher. In that year Harris turned over his shares in the firm to the university, stipulating that the profits be used for scholarships and bursaries and in effect vesting control of the company in the U of Toronto.

In recognition of the conservatory's wide influence, and with the consent of King George VI, its name was changed 1 Aug 1947 to Royal Conservatory of Music, Toronto, and the names of the diplomas were changed to conform. The ATCM became the ARCT (Associate, Royal Cons of Toronto) and the LTCM became the LRCT.

During Ettore *Mazzoleni's term as principal – 1945–68 – the school grew at an unprecendented rate, owing in part to the return of World War II veterans whose studies were supported by DVA allowances. Mazzoleni had been director of the Conservatory Orchestra since 1934. Two other prominent figures who contributed to the achievements of this period were Edward *Johnson, who served 1947–59 as chairman of the board, and Arnold *Walter, who was appointed director of the new Senior School in 1946. The senior school offered a two-year program with professional performance training combined with related courses in theory and history. The initial success of the project gave rise to other curriculum revisions including, in 1948, a three-year program leading to an Artist Diploma. Walter also headed the conservatory's Opera School (begun in 1946), which provided training in all aspects of opera production. Nicholas *Goldschmidt (music director), Felix Brentano and later Herman *Geiger-Torel (stage director), and Mrs Floyd S. *Chalmers (Women's opera and concert committee) assisted Walter in the exciting developments that led to the Opera Festival and the eventual formation of the *COC in 1959. (See Royal Conservatory Opera School.)

The artistic excellence achieved in these new ventures was accompanied by the sense of excitement brought by the war veterans and other students to the many challenging opportunities which arose after the difficult years of World War II. Some of the most gifted young Canadians converged on the RCMT and the U of Toronto in the late 1940s and early 1950s to take full advantage of the new programs. Among those who went on to develop distinguished musical careers were John *Beckwith, Mario *Bernardi, George *Crum, Ray *Dudley, Victor *Feldbrill, Gisèle *MacKenzie, Glenn *Gould, Elizabeth Benson *Guy, Betty-Jean *Hagen, Gordon *Kushner, Andrew *MacMillan,

Lois *Marshall, James *Milligan, Mary *Morrison, Phil *Nimmons, Clermont *Pépin, Patricia *Ridout, and Jon *Vickers. Others such as Lorne *Betts, Harry *Freedman, Harry *Somers, and Andrew *Twa studied composition on an individual basis with John *Weinzweig. Together with students enrolled in the new Faculty of Music degree program, performers and composers thrived in a climate of artistic accomplishment and optimistic enthusiasm for the future.

The activities of the Senior School were integrated during the overall reorganization of 1952 when the university created two main operational divisions under the omnibus designation Royal Conservatory of Music: the School of Music with Mazzoleni as principal continued the traditional conservatory programs in preparatory teaching and examining, continued to offer the Associate diploma (ARCT), and retained responsibility for the Opera School; the Faculty of Music with Arnold Walter as director offered programs leading to degrees and to the Licentiate (taken over from the School of Music) and Artist diplomas of the U of Toronto; and Boyd *Neel became chief administrative officer in 1953 when he was appointed dean of the Conservatory. In 1952 the Licentiate in its new setting became a teacher's diploma; the Artist Diploma had superseded it as the credential of the advanced program in performance. In 1954 the original letters patent of the TCM were revoked and all assets were assigned to the U of Toronto.

The continued expansion of both institutions in the 1950s created serious space problems, necessitating once again an expansion and improvement of physical facilities. In 1963 the School of Music moved to the old McMaster Building on Bloor St (where it continued to function in 1980). The renovated quarters included a 265-seat Concert Hall, a recital hall, three organs, and two small electronic music studios. In 1962 the Faculty of Music moved to the new Edward Johnson Building of the U of Toronto. The Artist Diploma continued in coexistence with the Faculty's degree program in performance, introduced in 1965. An electronic music studio was established in 1966 by Samuel *Dolin.

David *Ouchterlony, supervisor of branches 1947–68, became principal of the School of Music in 1968, at a time when further administrative changes were about to take place. In 1969 responsibility for the Opera School was transferred to the university. In 1970, with a reorganization of its music departments, the university restored to the School of Music the more historically accurate name 'Royal Conservatory of Music' and the dean of the Faculty of Music became the chief executive of music with the right to wield authority over both the faculty and the conservatory. Although such an arrangement existed during John Beckwith's term as dean (1970–7), the conservatory functioned in fact as a separate unit along the same lines that had prevailed until 1952. Under Ouchterlony 1968–77 it was responsive to a growing interest in the study of music as a humanizing, avocational activity in contemporary life. Gordon Kushner served as acting principal in 1978, prior to the appointment of Ezra *Schabas as principal later that year.

The conservatory's summer activities began in 1938, with courses in ear training and piano pedagogy by Charles Peaker, Alberto *Guerrero, and Boris *Berlin. The principal of the conservatory was automatically director of the summer school, until 1950 when the position was made separate. Frederick Silvester was the first incumbent, followed by Berlin in 1952 or 1953, and Mazzoleni in 1956. In Mazzoleni's last term (summer 1962) a special *Orff course was introduced, the classes being given in the new Edward Johnson Building. Under Richard *Johnston (director 1963–7) and Gordon Kushner (appointed director in 1968) the summer school has become an increasingly important part of the conservatory's program.

Over the years the conservatory has had a faculty of teachers of whom many have achieved national recognition, and some international. Among them have been Boris Berlin, Madeline Bone, Hayunga *Carman, Reginald *Godden, Alberto Guerrero, Gordon *Hallett, May *Kelly Kirby, Earl *Moss, and Ernest *Seitz (piano); Greta *Kraus (harpsichord); Irene *Jessner, Emmy *Heim, Weldon *Kilburn, George *Lambert, Dorothy *Allan Park, and Ernesto *Vinci (voice); Isidor Desser, Eugene *Kash, Geza *de Kresz, Kathleen *Parlow, and Elie Spivak (violin); Marcus *Adeney and Leo Smith (cello); Frederick J. *Horwood, Eric *Rollinson, and Molly *Sclater (theory); Samuel Dolin (composition); Wes Wraggett (in charge of the electronic music studio after 1978); and Madeleine Lasserre (eurythmics). Warren *Mould (registrar 1966–76) recorded eight graded albums of the conservatory's books of piano music in 1971 (RCP-GI to RCP-GVIII).

In 1980 the RCMT offered instruction in keyboard, voice, and orchestral and other instruments and a complete range of theoretical studies, speech arts, and drama. At that time, in addition to the main Bloor St building, there were numerous branches in metropolitan Toronto. In 1978 the conservatory conducted 58,300 graded examinations in 275 centres throughout Canada, leading to grade certificates and Associate diplomas in performer, teacher, and composer categories. Among other continuing features of its operation were the summer school, special workshops, correspondence courses in theory, and junior and intermediate orchestras.

The Wednesday Noon Hour Recital Series, the Thursday Twilight Concerts, and the annual recitals at the *CNE have become familiar recurring events, and the tradition of free student recitals is long established.

PUBLICATIONS

The Conservatory Bi-Monthly (Jan 1902–1912)
The Conservatory Monthly (1912–Oct 1913)
The Conservatory Quarterly Review (1918–35)
The Toronto Conservatory of Music Bulletin (1935–47)
Royal Conservatory of Music of Toronto Monthly Bulletin (1948–64)
The Bulletin (1964–74)
ConNotes (May 1980–)
Toronto Conservatory of Music Alumni Gazette (1914?–16?)

BIBLIOGRAPHY

Horwood, F.J. *The Toronto Conservatory of Music, A Retrospect (1886–1936)* (Toronto 1936)
Hutcheson, Ernest. 'Report on a Short Survey of the Toronto Conservatory of Music,' unpubl report, U of Toronto 1937
Sinclair, Lister. 'A scholarship school of music,' *CRMA*, vol 5, Aug–Sep 1946
Batten, Jack. 'Those musty muted halls of music,' Toronto *Globe and Mail Magazine*, 30 Jan 1971
Donskov, Lesa, and Graves, Donald. 'A History of the Royal Conservatory of Music and the Faculty of Music, University of Toronto 1886–1962,' unpubl paper, Centre for Higher Education, OISE [1972]
Cornell, Pamela. 'The Conservatory comes alive,' U of Toronto *Bulletin*, 20 Nov 1978
Dicknoether, Robert. 'A giant music machine with 57,000 students,' *Music*, Dec 1978 (JPG)

Royal Conservatory Opera School, Toronto 1946–69 (Opera Dept, Faculty of Music, *U of Toronto 1969–78; Opera division, beginning in 1978). The first opera classes at the *TCM were those initiated by Ernest *MacMillan in 1926 when he became principal there. They were directed by

A scene from *Gianni Schicchi*, a production of the Opera Division, University of Toronto, 1979

Countess Laura de Turczynowicz (b Laura Blackwell, St Catharines, Ont, ca 1877, d California ca 1953), whose European operatic career had centred in Munich and Bayreuth before World War I. The Coservatory Opera Company performed *Hansel and Gretel* and *The Sorcerer* (week of 16 Apr 1928 at the Regent Theatre); Purcell's *Dido and Aeneas* and von Suppé's *Boccaccio*, with Bach's *Peasant Cantata* as a curtain-raiser (week of 1 Apr 1929 at *Hart House); and, in November, as part of the *CPR Festival, Vaughan Williams' *Hugh the Drover*. The latter opera and *Hansel and Gretel*, the final productions of this company, were given in March 1930 at the *Royal Alexandra Theatre.

The hiatus in operatic training at the TCM, caused by the Depression and World War II, lasted until 1946 when Arnold *Walter, director of the Senior School of the TCM (*RCMT 1947), established the Opera School as a division of that school to provide a two-year comprehensive training program for young singers and a production unit for the display of Canadian operatic talent. The prefix 'Royal,' granted August 1947, began to be used four months after the school was opened.

Nicholas *Goldschmidt was music director and conductor of the Royal Cons Opera School 1946–57 and Felix Brentano was stage director 1946–8, succeeded by Herman *Geiger-Torel (who continued to direct individual productions for the school until his death in 1976, alternating with a number of others including Werner Graf, Giuseppe *Macina, Andrew *MacMillan, and Leon Major). With the reorganization of the RCMT in 1952, Walter became director of the Faculty of Music (U of Toronto) and Ettore Mazzoleni was named principal of the School of Music (RCMT) and (general) director of the opera school, retaining that position until 1966. He also conducted and coached. Peter Ebert was director and stage director in 1967–8, followed by Anthony Besch 1968–9 and Georg Philipp in 1969. Ernesto *Barbini joined the music staff in 1953, assumed Goldschmidt's duties in 1957, and was music director from 1961 until his retirement in 1975, when he was succeeded by James W. *Craig, who had been a coach and conductor 1958–64 and had resumed those duties in 1971. The school's conducting and coaching staff has included, at different times, Mario *Bernardi, George *Brough, George *Crum, Tibor *Polgar, and Alfred *Strombergs.

In 1969 the school became a department of the Faculty of Music, with Ezra *Schabas as chairman 1969–78, followed in 1978 by Constance *Fisher (who had joined the staff in 1972 as a stage director and instructor). Fisher was designated divisional co-ordinator of the opera division. The department thenceforth offered a two-year post-graduate diploma in operatic performance. Until 1969 no diploma or degree was given to those who attended the opera school program of training.

The first opera school presentation of operatic excerpts was at Hart House Theatre 16 Dec 1946. A full production of Smetana's *The Bartered Bride* followed in April 1947 at *Eaton Auditorium. Mrs Floyd *Chalmers founded the Opera and Concert Committee of the RCMT to assist in the presentation and promotion of complete opera performances by the school – six by 1950. In November 1950 the Toronto citizens who had assisted the Royal Conservatory Opera Company with the first Opera Festival (*Rigoletto, Don Giovanni,* and *La Bohème,* in February at the Royal Alexandra Theatre) formed the Opera Festival Assn which, in assuming all budgetary and administrative responsibilities for the annual festival, assured the opera school of a continuing showcase for its talent and a focus for its activities. After 1954, however, the Opera Festival (later the *COC) employed professional singers, and the participation of Opera School students was limited to the chorus and minor roles. (The change in 1957 to a fall season precluded further student participation.)

In 1963 the opera school was relocated in the U of Toronto's Edward Johnson Building, the MacMillan Theatre of which had been designed specifically for its stage use. The building's inaugural ceremonies, 2 Mar 1964, heralded a week of events which included a performance 4 March of Britten's *Albert Herring*. The new facilities permitted a more adventurous and professionally oriented approach to training and performance, and in line with this a course in the technology of theatrical production was established in the fall of 1964.

For serious students of opera on both sides of the footlights, Opera School / Dept productions – a minimum of two a year – have constituted what possibly is Canada's most rewarding continuous operatic program, at least as regards repertoire. The established opera companies of Canada are bound, because they depend for survival on box-office popularity, to the few operas they can be sure will draw crowds. The Opera School, with its different mandate, lower production costs, and sure subsidy, is relatively independent of the box office and may study and present works chosen for particular interest or challenge from the whole range of opera. It thus has been in a position to present the premiere of Raymond *Pannell's *Aria da capo* in 1963, the English-language premiere of the English composer Humphrey Searle's *Hamlet* in 1969 (following the world premiere, that same season, in German, in Hamburg), the stage premiere of *Willan's *Deirdre* in 1965, and the Canadian premieres of Paisiello's *Il Mondo della Luna* in 1962, Orff's *Die Kluge*, Cherubini's *The Portuguese Inn*, and Holst's *The Wandering Scholar* in 1966, Rossini's *The Turk in Italy* in 1968, Robert Ward's *The Crucible* and Richard Rodney Bennett's *The Mines of Sulphur* in 1976, and Janáček's *Katya Kabanova* and Paisiello's *The Barber of Seville* in 1977. It gave the first Toronto performances of Ibert's *Angélique* in 1953 (the first production of this work by a Canadian company), Vaughan Williams' *Riders to the Sea* in 1958, Douglas Moore's *Gallantry* and Rossini's *The Marriage Contract* in 1960, Stanley Hollingsworth's *The Mother* and Respighi's *Maria Egiziaca* in 1961, and Nino Rota's *Silent Night* in 1963. In addition the school has presented Poulenc's *Dialogues des Carmélites* in 1967, Debussy's *Pelléas et Mélisande* in 1968, Strauss' *Ariadne auf Naxos*, and Ravel's *L'Enfant et les sortilèges* in 1969 and similarly unhackneyed operas by Monteverdi, Gluck, Mozart, Weber, Stravinsky, Hindemith, Weill, Martinu, and Berkeley.

After 1969 the U of Toronto SO accompanied opera productions. Previously the RCMT orchestra, or a chamber orchestra of professional musicians, or pianos had been used.

Many of the school's former students have established professional careers. Among them are Milla *Andrew, Leonard *Bilodeau, Jean *Bonhomme, Victor *Braun, Don *Garrard, Marguerite *Gignac, Robert *Goulet, Alexander *Gray, Elizabeth Benson *Guy, Nicole *Lorange, Phyllis *Mailing, Ermanno *Mauro, Lois *McDonall, James *Milligan, Mary *Morrison, Cornelis *Opthof, Maria *Pellegrini, Patricia *Rideout, Teresa *Stratas, Lillian *Sukis, Heather *Thomson, Bernard *Turgeon, Jon *Vickers, and Jeannette *Zarou.

BIBLIOGRAPHY

'Canada's first school of opera,' *CRMA*, vol 5, Oct–Nov 1946

Mazzoleni, E. 'How the Royal Conservatory created a Canadian operatic tradition,' *OpCan*, 4, Nov–Dec 1960

– 'Cultural boom,' ibid, Feb 1964

Ebert, Peter. 'Royal Conservatory Opera School,' *OpCan*, Feb 1968

Besch, Anthony. 'Opera School workshop,' *OpCan*, Dec 1968

Peglar, Kenneth W. *Opera and the University of Toronto 1946–1971* (Toronto [1971])

FILMOGRAPHY

The Opera Class (NFB 1951) PW

Royal Hamilton College of Music 1965–80 (Hamilton Conservatory of Music 1897–1965). Founded in 1897 in Hamilton, Ont, by C.L.M. *Harris, its director until 1907. Situated at first in the former home of Robert Steele, it was moved in 1899 to the Main and Charles streets building previously occupied by the Hamilton College of Music (founded by D.J. O'Brien in 1888 as the Hamilton Musical Institute, renamed in 1889, and open until 1898). The conservatory was moved again in 1904 to its subsequent location on James St South, where its facilities included a recital hall on the second floor, studios on the first, and a meeting room in the basement.

Under Harris' directorship the conservatory was incorporated in 1904 by the province of Ontario and became affiliated in 1906 with the *U of Toronto. The syllabus was expanded to include art, physical culture, dance, musical kindergarten, and elocution, as well as lessons in piano, strings, winds, organ, and guitar. The conservatory offered three examination systems: its own and those of the U of Toronto and the *U of Trinity College, Toronto. Because of its affiliation it was possible for its students to prepare for the U of Toronto B MUS degree and proceed directly to the final examination. Harris also formed the Orchestral Club (which continued until 1914), the Art Culture Club, and a choral group.

A triumvirate of staff members – J.E.P. *Aldous (director 1889–1908 of the Hamilton School of Music), W.H. *Hewlett, and Bruce *Carey – were known as administrative officers and succeeded Harris, who had resigned in 1907. This administration presented internationally known artists in the recital hall and occasionally, after 1912, in the newly opened Royal Connaught Hotel. The U of Toronto proposed and carried out 'disaffiliation' in 1918, when the HCM set up a competing system of examinations.

In the same year Carey resigned, and Hewlett became the conservatory's first principal, remaining in the position until 1939. During his term of office branches were opened in the east end of Hamilton and in suburban Westdale. Subsequent principals have been Cyril *Hampshire 1939–44, Reginald *Bedford 1944–8, Reginald *Godden 1948–53, Lorne *Betts 1953–9, the church organist Harold Jerome (a staff member, 1920–57, and a former pupil of Hewlett) 1959–67, Gladys *Whitehead 1967–74, and Jonathan Watts 1974–80.

The conservatory awarded an associate diploma (AHCM) in piano, violin, voice, speech arts, and drama. When the conservatory received a royal charter 15 May 1965 and was renamed the Royal Hamilton College of Music, it began offering, in addition to the renamed associate's diploma (ARHCM), a licentiate diploma (LRHCM) and an honorary fellow's degree (FRHCM), the last-named awarded that year for the first time to Sir Ernest *MacMillan, Charles *Peaker, and Healey *Willan. Other recipients have been Mario *Bernardi, Charles *Camilleri, Victor *Feldbrill, G. Roy *Fenwick, Nicholas *Goldschmidt, Marta *Hidy, Harold Jerome, Anton *Kuerti, Phyllis *Mailing, Bertha *Carey Morrow, Frank *Thorolfson, Lorne *Watson, and Gladys Whitehead.

By 1978 the teaching staff of the RHCM had grown to 118, including Community Service teachers and 73 full-time staff giving private instruction. Students numbered between 2500 and 3000. Through the in-school instruction program given by the Community Service teachers, an additional 3800 students received specialized attention. Later inclusions in the main syllabus were courses in the *Suzuki string method, jazz, theatre, and visual arts. Besides the main faculty on James St and five branches in the Hamilton area, the RHCM maintained several branches in the Windsor area and one each in Leamington and Oakville, Ont.

The early records of the RHCM are not extant. According to Jonathan Watts, the Board of Governors in 1960 authorized their destruction. Because of financial problems the college closed its doors in 1980.

BIBLIOGRAPHY

Hamilton Conservatory of Music, a Brief History (1961)

Gee, Ken. 'Deathrites of a school,' *Mcan*, 43, Summer 1980

Royal Hamilton College of Music (Hamilton Conservatory of Music). Annual *Calendars* (HL)

Royal Hamilton Light Infantry Band. Formed in 1866 by Peter Grossman as the 13th Battalion Band, at the request of the commander of the 13th Battalion Voluntary Militia, and known under a succession of names as the name of the battalion changed. It was called the band of the 13th Regiment 1900–10, of the 13th Royal Regiment 1910–20, of the Royal Hamilton Regiment 1920–7, and of the Royal Hamilton Light Infantry 1927–57 and 1962–8.

Grossman, who had been the bandmaster of Hamilton's first military band (founded in 1856, attached to the Independent Artillery Company of the militia), led the 13th Battalion Band until 1869. He was succeeded for one year by George R. Robinson who, in turn, was succeeded for one year by W. Blachard. Robinson, a graduate of the RSMS (Kneller Hall), London, and an outstanding trainer, returned in 1871 and remained bandmaster until 1916. In keeping with the latest developments in US bands, Robinson added clarinets, saxophones, french horns, flute, oboe, and bassoon to the usual complement of cornets, trombones, euphoniums, and tuba.

During its first 10 years of existence the disciplined 40-piece band competed successfully throughout eastern Canada and the northeastern USA. It was the principal band at the 'Peace Jubilee' at Berlin (*Kitchener) in 1871 and played for the governor-general and his wife during their visit to Hamilton in 1879. In 1900 the band was invited to give a concert for the Maple Leaf Club of Denver, Col, and in 1901 it was chosen to play at a state dinner in Toronto in honour of the Duke and Duchess of Cornwall and York (later King George V and Queen Mary).

Every winter for many years, under the auspices of the 13th Battalion, the band gave weekly public concerts in the Drill Shed. In the summer it often filled as many as five or six engagements a week, including garden parties, park concerts, and moonlight excursions aboard paddle-wheel steamers on Lake Ontario. By 1912 five of its former members had become bandmasters with other Canadian militia bands.

Robinson was the first in the militia to receive the honorary commission of bandmaster with the rank of lieutenant. He remained senior to all other bandmasters in the service until his retirement in 1917. Walter, one of Robinson's three sons, all of whom were band members, succeeded his father in 1916 and served as bandmaster until 1924. Under his direction the band won first prize at the 1921 *CNE competition. He was succeeded by David Anderson, who served for 10 years. Robinson returned to lead the band 1936–9.

Bandmasters subsequent to Walter Robinson were W. Sharman 1939–42, H.J. Holder 1942–50, H.G. Patterson 1950–7, L. Sharman 1961–6, and A.T. Dharmaratnam 1966–8. The band was disbanded in 1957, reconstituted in 1962 for the regimental centennial, and disbanded again in 1968.

BIBLIOGRAPHY

Semper Paratus, ed Bereton Greenhous (Hamilton 1977)

(JBk)

Royal Regiment of Canada Band. Toronto-based volunteer militia band attached to the Royal Regiment of Canada (founded in 1862 as the 10th Battalion Volunteer Militia). The band received its first set of drums and instruments in 1863. It is one of the oldest permanently organized bands in Canada and, reflecting the changes in the name of the regiment, has been known as the band of the 10th Battalion Royal Grenadiers 1881–1900, of the 10th Regiment Royal Grenadiers 1900–20, of the Royal Grenadiers 1920–36, and of the Royal Regiment of Toronto Grenadiers in 1936. It assumed in 1939 the name by which it continued to be known in 1980.

On 1 Jul 1867 the band presented a formal concert in Queen's Park, Toronto, in celebration of Confederation. Of the early bandmasters, Capt John Waldron, appointed director of music in Fenruary 1888, made a great contribution to the band's development; by 1904 it boasted 'complete double and single reed choirs, saxhorn and brass cylindrical sections, flutes, percussion instruments and string basses.'

From the early part of the 20th century until 1926, the director was Warrant-Officer Harold Bromley. Bromley was succeeded by Lieut Walter M. *Murdoch, who remained until 1958. Under Murdoch the band's membership was increased to 60, and it won the Dominion Championship for Class 'A' bands at the *CNE repeatedly 1927–31. The band played at *Massey Hall in the 1930s, at the opening of *Maple Leaf Gardens in 1933, for the 100th anniversary of Toronto's incorporation in 1934, and at the reception of King George VI by Toronto in 1939. It has played, in fact, for every reigning monarch from Victoria to Elizabeth II and for many world statesmen.

The band has been heard often at civic functions in Toronto and at that city's St James' Cathedral in Remembrance Day services. In 1967 as the official band for the Ontario centenary it played at celebrations in Queen's Park, toured Ontario, and commissioned *The Royal Regiment Ceremonial* by John Cook. The band performed in Cyprus in 1971 and at liberation anniversary celebrations in Louvigny, France, in 1974. In 1976 it appeared in Philadelphia in the RCMP's Musical Ride, as part of the US Bicentennial festivities.

The band's later directors have been Capt Stanley H. Clark 1958–68 and Capt E.J. Robbins 1968–72, succeeded by Capt Gino A. Falconi. Recordings made by the band prior to 1980 were *Cyprus 71* (Stereo Vintage Record SCV 120) and *In Concert and on Parade* (1975, Periwinkle PER 7328).

BIBLIOGRAPHY

Goodspeed, Maj D.J. *Battle Royal* (Toronto 1962)

(HK, JK, NM)

Royal 22nd Regiment Band. The regimental band of the 'Van Doos'. It was formed in Quebec City in 1922 from the 20 members of the former Royal Canadian Garrison Artillery Band and employed the same director, Capt Charles *O'Neill. The new ensemble acquired the instruments and music library of the earlier band. In 1923 the Royal 22nd band began performing on Dufferin Terrace, Quebec City, at the *Orpheum Theatre, and on radio station CKAC in Montreal. The ensemble also played in 1927 and 1930 at the *CNE, Toronto, in 1931 on the CPR radio station's 'L'Heure musicale,' and later on the CRBC via the Quebec City station CHRC. In 1937 O'Neill resigned and was succeeded by Capt Edwin *Bélanger.

During World War II the ensemble gave concerts primarily to encourage recruiting; it resumed its usual activities when the war ended. It played in 1952 in Japan and Korea and received medals from South Korea and the United Nations. The next year it went to Great Britain for the coronation of Elizabeth II and to Germany for the visit of the Duke of Edinburgh and performed on the BBC. (Twelve of the bandsmen had played in England in 1937 at the coronation of George VI.) Accompanied by such artists as the vocal quartet of Collégiens troubadours, Pierre *Boutet, and Claire, Eve, and Gérald *Gagnier, it made 'artistic military gala' tours in Quebec 1954, 1955, and 1956. Another tour, entitled 'The Army on Parade,' was undertaken 1955 and 1956 in Quebec and New Brunswick.

The band was heard 1959–65 on the weekly program 'Je me souviens' on radio station CHRC. Concerts under the stars at the Citadel, Quebec City, began in 1961 and became a tradition. The band participated in the launching ceremonies of the Telstar and Early Bird satellites in 1962 and 1965 respectively. It gave its first concert in the Salle Wilfrid-Pelletier of the *PDA in 1963, and it has returned there annually. It performed in 1964 at the formation of the Quebec chapter of the *CBDA.

After a series of concerts in Quebec and Ontario schools in 1966 the Royal Van Doos made its contribution to the 1967 centennial celebrations: five concerts in New York during Canada Week, followed by others at the National Trade Fair in Vancouver and Victoria, at the Capitol Theatre in Quebec City, and at *Expo 67. In addition, ten of its members participated in the military tattoo presented across Canada. The band gave concerts in France and Germany in 1969 and performed in the opening festival of the *Grand Théâtre in Quebec City in 1971. Its 50th anniversary was celebrated in 1972 with tours in Germany and Cyprus; it returned to Cyprus the following year. A 1975 European tour of Germany, Belgium, and Holland included the International Festival of Military Bands in Limoges, France. The band played at the 1976 Rose Bowl in Pasadena, Cal, and at the convention of the France-Canada Assn on the Côte d'Azur in 1977.

In addition to military marches, the repertoire of the Royal 22nd Regiment Band includes selections based on folk tunes, arrangements of classical works, film music, musical comedy, jazz, and light music, as well as works by such Canadian composers as Howard *Cable, Robert *Farnon, James *Gayfer, Gérald Gagnier, Armand *Ferland, and Charles O'Neill.

The band's conductors have been O'Neill 1922–37, Bélanger 1937–61, Capt Armand Ferland 1961–5, and Maj Jean-François Pierret (premier prix percussion, Brussels Royal Cons) 1965–78, succeeded by Maj Charles-August Villeneuve. From 1960 to 1972 Robert Vocelle and Onil Leblanc conducted a stage band, a small light-music ensemble featuring soloists. In 1978 the full band consisted of 35 instrumentalists: winds, brass, two double basses, percussion, and piano.

The official march of the Royal 22nd Regiment, *Sambre et Meuse*, was replaced in 1935 by *Le Royal 22e régiment*, written by O'Neill, and *Le Royal 22e régiment* was replaced ca 1939 by the song *'Vive la Canadienne,' also in an O'Neill arrangement. Théodore Botrel, the poet from Brittany, wrote 'Gloire au 22e!', a marching song publised in *La Musique* (February 1922) in an arrangement for two voices and piano by Omer *Létourneau. Charles-Émile *Gadbois wrote the *Marche lente du Royal 22e régiment*.

DISCOGRAPHY

La Citadelle. 1974. Franco FR 49002

Concert sous les étoiles. 1978. Franco FR-799 (private recording)

Je me souviens / The Van Doos – Band of the Royal 22nd Regiment. 1964. RCA PCS 1006 / 1007

BIBLIOGRAPHY

Falardeau, Sergent Victor. *La Musique du Royal 22e régiment: 50 ans d'histoire (1922–1972)* (Quebec 1976)

HP

ROY-VILANDRÉ, Adrienne ('Yohadio') (b Roy, m Vilandré, m Ruzé d'Effiat). Soprano, folklorist, b Lévis, Que, 13 Feb 1893, d Montreal 23 Oct 1978. After taking voice lessons in Quebec City with Isa Jeynevald-Mercier, Victor *Occelier, and Berthe *Roy she made her debut at the *Club musical de Québec. She went to Paris in 1922 and studied with Jane Bathori for two years. She returned in 1926 and was one of the first singers to perform the works of Honegger, Milhaud, and Poulenc in Canada. Drawn to folk music, she became interested in Indian songs after meeting Marius *Barbeau, who taught her the dialects of various tribes. Delving into the traditional songs of the Gitksans, Hurons, Kootenays, Nisrae, Omakas, Sioux, Tuscaroras, and many other tribes, she became a pioneer in gathering and preserving this musical heritage. She performed the songs in traditional costume while accompanying herself on such instruments as the tom-tom and the chichigwan. She gave hundreds of recitals across Canada (eg, for the Alliance française and at the Canadian Institute of Music and *Expo 67), in the USA (notably in New York for the local French-Canadian community and in the studios of the French composer Charles Lagourgue), and in France (Cannes and Paris). She also performed on the CBC, the Montreal radio station CKAC, and the Ottawa TV station CBOFT. She contributed to the Montreal periodicals *Le Miroir*, *L'Autorité*, and *Le Jour*. In 1934 the Iroquois of Caughnawaga, Que, made her an honorary member of the tribe and gave her the name 'Yohadio' ('clear voice of the woods') in recognition of her interest in Iroquois songs and traditions. She received a medal from the city of Paris (1957), was made a Chevalier du Bon Parler français (Montreal), and was invested with the

Order of St John of Jerusalem (a Yugoslav honour, 1973). In 1963 her first LP, *Chants indiens*, won a prize for the best recording of Canadian folklore. Her second marriage was to the ninth marquis de Ruzé d'Effiat.

DISCOGRAPHY

Chants indiens / Indian Songs. 1963. Lon MLP 10030
Chansons populaires du Canada français / Popular Songs of French Canada. F. Beauchamp pf. 1964?. Lon MLP 10057
Chants amérindiens / Indian Songs of North America. 1966. Poly 542-506
Canada 100 / Indian Folk Songs of Canada. (1967). Poly CP 5002
A Chorale of Caughnawaga. (1967). Poly (number unknown)
Chants amérindiens. M. Vilandré sop, N. Gagnon ten, R.A. Le Clerc bass. (1972). YDO 8001
Reflets de traditions québécoises, vol 2. 1975. OP 249
Yohadio (voix claire). (1976?). Self-publ
Also some folk recordings made ca 1935

BIBLIOGRAPHY

Duval, Monique. 'Mme Roy-Vilandré: 25 années consacrées à la chanson indienne,' Quebec *Le Soleil*, 19 Nov 1970
Lotbinière-Harwood, Suzanne de. 'The story of clear voice of the woods,' *Montreal Star*, 27 Dec 1975
Fitzgerald, John. 'Marquise's heart beats to the tom-tom,' Montreal *Gazette*, 11 Aug 1977 AP

RPM. Variously titled (*RPM Weekly, RPM Music Weekly, RPM Magazine*, etc) weekly trade magazine of 'the radio and recording industries and the allied arts,' with emphasis on news, feature articles, and radio programming surveys. Generally geared to the English-Canadian market it began publication in Toronto 24 Feb 1964 and was reaching a small but world-wide circulation of 5000 by 1976. It suspended publication briefly at the end of 1980 but resumed operations at the end of January 1981.

Under the direction of its founder-publisher-editor Walt *Grealis *RPM* has offered steady and vocal support for Canadian talent, lobbying successfully for the *CRTC Canadian Content Broadcast Regulations and in 1971 introducing the *RPM MAPL Logo and initiating 'Communication,' an annual dialogue between the recording and broadcast industries.

To focus attention on Canadian artists *RPM* in 1964 inaugurated the RPM Gold Leaf Awards (later known also as the *Juno Awards) and in 1974 established the Canadian Music Hall of Fame Awards and the Big Country Awards along with the latter's governing body, the Canadian Academy for Country Music Advancement (known after 1976 as the Academy of Country Music Entertainment). In 1976 RPM initiated the Canadian Music Industry Awards. RPM publications included the annual *Canadian Music Industry Directory* (begun in 1965), the *Canadian Music Industry Who's Who* (1976, 1977), and a *Directory of Canadian Recording Studios* (1979).

BIBLIOGRAPHY

Klees, Stan. 'The story of RPM Magazine,' *RPM*, 4 Mar 1978
Gallo, Nancy. 'RPM – 15 years of communication,' ibid, 24 Feb 1979
Linden, J.J. 'RPM's Walt Grealis looks back and ahead,' ibid MM

RPM MAPL Logo. A symbol designed by Stan Klees and introduced in 1971 by **RPM* to indicate the extent of an individual recording's compliance with *CRTC Canadian Content Broadcast Regulations regarding music, artist, production, and lyrics (MAPL). Adopted by *CRIA, the symbol, a quartered circle, contains a letter (M, A, P, or L) in each quarter. A blacked-in quarter indicates positive Canadian content: for example the letters M and P on a black background indicate that the music was composed by a Canadian and that the production was wholly recorded in Canada. The symbol appears on record labels and jackets, and in *RPM* programming lists, adjacent to the title of each composition recorded.

RUBEŠ, Jan (Ladislav). Bass, actor, director; b Volyně, southern Bohemia, Czechoslovakia, 6 Jun 1920. He studied with Hilbert Vavra in Prague (graduating from the Prague Cons in 1945), Hermann Gurtler in Geneva, and Herbert Janssen in New York. He made his opera debut in 1940 in Prague, as Basilio in *The Barber of Seville*, and became a leading singer in the Prague Opera. He represented Czechoslovakia at the International Music Festival at Geneva in 1948 and was a first-prize winner.

In 1949 Rubeš emigrated to Canada and gave his first Canadian performance as Betto in *Gianni Schicchi* with the *Royal Cons Opera. He was a soloist 1949–58 with the *CBC Opera and an original member (1950) of the Opera Festival Company of Toronto (later the *COC). By 1977 he had appeared in more than 50 COC productions of about 30 operas and had participated in some 20 national tours. He served 1974–6 as the COC's touring director. Rubeš has been guest soloist with the Frankfurt, Central America, and New York City operas.

Rubeš's repertoire comprises about 90 roles in six languages, including Mephisto in *Faust*, Bluebeard in *Bluebeard's Castle*, Boris in *Boris Godunov*, Daland in *The Flying Dutchman*, the King and Ramfis in *Aida*, Figaro and Bartolo in *The Marriage of Figaro*, Collatinus in *The Rape of Lucretia*, Kecal in *The Bartered Bride*, and Il Maestro in Cimarosa's comic intermezzo *Il Maestro di Cappella*. He commissioned Tibor *Polgar's chamber opera *A European Lover* (1965), which he subsequently performed throughout Canada. He also has sung widely in oratorio and has taken leading roles in such musicals as *South Pacific* and *The King and I*. He has appeared at the *Montreal, *Stratford, and *Vancouver International festivals and with the *MSO, the *TSO, and other symphony orchestras in Canada, the USA, and Mexico.

Rubeš has been heard on radio (notably as singer and host 1953–63 for the CBC's 'Songs of My People'), has appeared on TV ('Parade,' 'L'*Heure du concert,' and 'Guess What?'), and has acted on stage and in films. He has directed productions for the COC (*La Bohème*, on tour 1974–5, 1975–6), the Stratford Festival (*The Fool, Ariadne auf Naxos*, 1975), and the *Vancouver Opera (*La Bohème*, 1976; *Die Fledermaus*, 1977).

In 1954 Rubeš made two 78s with Ivan *Romanoff's orchestra for the Songs of My People label (SP1-2109, SP2-2109) and in 1974 he made the LP *Jan Rubes Sings 'Guess What'* (RCA KCLI-5006), a program of folk and children's songs.

After Rubeš's performance as the Leporello to George *London's Don Giovanni in the Gunther Rennert production at the 1958 Vancouver International Festival, John *Beckwith wrote in the Autumn issue of the *Canadian Music Journal* 'in the second act where they are required to impersonate each other, Mr. Rubes even managed to adopt a bit of Mr. London's sneery vocal tone ... [Rubes's] mounting cheekiness through "Madamina il catalogo" until, towards the end of this aria, he footled Donna Elvira's hem with mock roguishness, bred respect both for his comic stature and for Mr. Rennert's imaginativeness as a director.'

In a review (*Opera Canada*, Winter 1980) of the COC's Canadian premiere of Alban Berg's *Lulu* in the completed three-act version, William *Littler praised Rubeš's 'wonderfully seedy Schigolch, a character study which marked the veteran basso's triumphant return to a company he had served for a quarter of a century.'

Jan Rubeš

Rubeš has performed often at Toronto's Young People's Theatre, founded and directed by his wife, the actress Susan Douglas.

WRITINGS

'To translate or not to translate?' *OpCan*, 14, May 1963
'An actor is on his own,' ibid, 39, Sep 1969

BIBLIOGRAPHY

Kirby, Blaik. 'Jan Rubes: 821 and counting,' Toronto *Globe and Mail*, 20 Mar 1973
Schulman, Michael. 'Jan Rubes in 2,000 beds!' *PfAC*, vol 10, Fall 1973
Mercer, Ruby. 'Guess what next,' *OpCan*, vol 16, Apr–May 1975
Schulman, Michael. 'Interview: Jan Rubes,' *CanComp*, 141, May 1979
Creative Canada, vol 1 (HCs)

RUBIN, Ruth (b Rosenblatt, Rivkah). Folksinger, ethnomusicologist, collector, b Montreal 1 Sep 1906. Born to Jewish parents who had immigrated to Canada from Russia, she sang during her youth but only began to study seriously when she was living in New York in the 1920s. Her interest in Jewish folk music grew until, in 1944, she decided to specialize in the field. She began to give lecture recitals in New York; their success brought her engagements elsewhere in the USA and in Canada. At the same time she continued her research and collected songs. Having established her authority in the field, she began to publish articles. Her first book, *A Treasury of Jewish Folk Song* (New York 1950), was received with enthusiasm and was followed by *Voices of a People* (New York 1963) and *Jewish Folk Songs* (Oak 1965). Her study 'Yiddish folk songs current in French Canada' appeared in the *Journal of the IFMC* (vol 12, January 1960).

Beginning in 1945, Rubin made many 78s for Oriole. Her first LP, *Jewish Children's Songs and Games* (1954, with banjo accompaniment by Pete Seeger), also appeared on Oriole. For Folkways she made the LPs *Jewish Folk Songs* (FW 8740) and *Jewish Life* (FG 3801); for other labels, she made *Yiddish Love Songs* (Riverside RLP 12-647) and *Ruth Rubin Sings Yiddish Folksongs* (Prestige International INT 13019). She has appeared several times in Canada, notably at the Pavilion of Judaism of *Expo 67.

Rubin's work has earned her praise from folklore specialists such as Marius *Barbeau and Edith *Fowke. Following one of her concerts at Carnegie Recital Hall, Robert Shelton called her 'one of the last major authorities on Yiddish Folk Song' and noted: 'It was a fine performance by a scholar who knows how to breathe the passion of human experience into song' (*New York Times*, 22 Apr 1968).

In 1967 Rubin opened an archives bearing her name in Haifa, Israel. She has deposited research files and 2200 songs at the *National Museum of Man in Ottawa.

BIBLIOGRAPHY
Encyclopedia of Folk, Country and Western Music (New York 1969) GP

RUBINSTEIN, Eli. Composer, arranger, conductor, b Bucharest 23 Apr 1929, naturalized Canadian 1972; B MUS conducting, composition (Bucharest) 1954, M MUS (Bucharest) 1955. His string trio, an atonal work, obtained second prize at the Moscow Youth Festival in 1956. In Rumania he composed a *Sinfonietta* for full orchestra, five ballets, several songs on Rumanian texts, chamber music, music for films, and works for the synagogue.

Rubinstein emigrated in 1963 to Israel where he served 1964–5 as conductor of the light music orchestra of the Israel State Radio (KOL). He wrote the music for several films including *Sabina and Her Men* and *Allo 999* (both ca 1966). He wrote music for commercials and the song 'For You Jerusalem,' which was popular in 1967.

Rubinstein moved to Canada in 1968 and settled in Montreal. In 1973 he became musician-in-residence at that city's Saydie Bronfman Centre and there founded the Big Band, composed of some 25 players aged 16–25. The Big Band has given several concerts in public and over the CBC, its repertoire comprising show tunes, folksongs, disco, and rock. Rubinstein is the founder and conductor of the Laval Community Centre Choir, which specializes in Hebrew folksongs and which has appeared with the Big Band. He founded the 45-member Workmen's Circle Choir which sings mostly his compositions and his arrangements of Hebrew and Yiddish music. The choir has appeared in synagogues and has given concerts 1975, 1976, and 1977 at the *Salle Claude-Champagne. Rubinstein has written incidental music to several English-language and Yiddish or Hebrew plays performed in Canada and the USA. He also teaches piano and composition.

In 1971 Rubinstein received the J.A. Segal prize 'for the most important contribution to Jewish music for the theatre in Canada.' His music is influenced by eastern European and oriental music, French impressionism, jazz, and Hebrew and Yiddish folk music. To mark *Jewish Music Month in October 1979, the music committee of the Canadian Jewish Congress, Quebec Region, commissioned him to write *Erev Shabbat* for violin and piano, premiered 25 Oct 1979 at Samuel Bronfman House by Luis and Berta Grinhauz. Rubinstein is a member of CAPAC. (AR)

RUFF, Herbert (Alexandre). Pianist, accompanist, conductor, composer, b Idaweiche, near Breslau, Germany (which became Wroctaw, Poland), 16 Sep 1918, naturalized Canadian 1958. He took piano lessons 1924–8 in Vienna from Lotte Kleine and studied for two years at the Stern Cons in Berlin with Walter Gieseking (piano) and Paul Graener (composition). At 13 he left the conservatory to devote himself more fully to jazz and light music, without however abandoning serious music. With the help of the composer Theo Mackeben, he began ca 1933 a career as film composer, working at first in Germany and then in Switzerland and Czechoslovakia. In the orient 1939–52 he worked for Radio Hong Kong, taught at the Nanking Cons (piano and composition 1947–52), and promoted contemporary music on behalf of the Alliance française and the Arts Council of Great Britain. The latter in 1951 commissioned his *Sonata in D* for piano and violin (Attar 1966), which was well received by European and US critics.

Ruff arrived in Montreal in 1952 and was hired shortly afterwards as pianist and composer by the CBC. His assignments were chiefly in children's TV series (including 'Bobino,' 'Le Pirate Maboule,' 'Maigrichon et Gras Double,' 'La Ribouldingue,' 'Es-tu d'accord?'). Other children's series on which he collaborated – 'Sol et Gobelet,' 'Grujot et Délicat,' 'Nic et Pic,' and 'Picotine' – enjoyed international acclaim. In 1968 he was awarded the BMI trophy for best composer of children's music, in recognition of both the quality and the quantity of his output (more than 1000 programs), and a BMI certificate of honour for the best TV signature tunes ('Le Sel de la semaine' and 'La Boîte à Surprise,' among others).

Ruff has written some 30 concert works, including *Variations on a Scottish Theme*, *Rhapsody* for piano and orchestra, and *Trio* for clarinet, viola, and piano, as well as dance music, especially for the Ballets Chiriaeff, precursor of Les Grands Ballets Canadiens. He has composed the music for the film *Saint François d'Assise*, which in 1962 was awarded a first prize by Catholic TV in Monte Carlo, and music for film documentaries for various provincial government departments and for Quebec Hydro. He has written the music of more than 2000 songs (including 'C'est dans le temps du Carnaval,' which has lyrics by Gilles *Vigneault) and was involved in the renaissance of the Quebec chanson, serving as composer, arranger, or conductor for recordings by Pauline *Julien and Jacques *Labrecque.

In 1974 Ruff recorded the music of *Tante Paule reconte à Pascale* (TRR-4001); in 1975 he made five LPs on the Fantel label: *Picotine* (FA-39401), *Nic et Pic* vol 1 (FA-39402), *Fanfreluche* (FA-39404), *Piccolo* (FA-39405), and, with Mario *Duschesnes (recorder), *Thèmes musicaux avec l'Oncle Herbert* (FA-39411). He is an affiliate of PRO Canada.

BIBLIOGRAPHY
Morgan, Kit. 'Herbert Ruff,' *MSc*, 247, May–Jun 1969
Pedneault, Hélène. 'Herbert creates music for French network's children's shows,' *MSc*, 289, May–Jun 1976
(CG, DM)

Rumania. Immigration to Canada began in 1898 with an influx of Rumanian Jews, followed by three distinct waves, 1900–13, 1920–9, and post-1945. Immigrants during the first two periods settled on the prairies, in Montreal, and in several Ontario centres. Nearly 100 Rumanian singers and dancers took part in the Great West Folk Festival (*CPR Festivals) in 1929 in Regina. In 1961 there were more than 43,000 Rumanian-Canadians. Cultural organizations have been maintained in Montreal, Windsor, and Hamilton, Ont, and in communities in Saskatchewan, usually with the church (Orthodox or Greek-Catholic) as the centre.

Rumanians brought to Canada a rich, ancient, original, and orally maintained musical culture which, in the new social context, has been modified in content and form, function, degree of vitality, and manner of circulation and interpretation. The church music belongs to the Romanized Byzantine tradition, the priests having the liberty to modify it. The folk music is characterized by strophic forms and by strong and varied rhythmic structures analysed first by Béla Bartók ca 1920 in terms of parlando rubato (rhythmic leeways based on the rhythms of speech).

Though epic song is perpetuated only by the elders, lyric song has survived, its original themes now mixed with others invented in Canada. Of the repertoire which, in the old country, accompanied the 'rites de passage,' some wedding songs have survived but funeral songs have not. A repertoire of dances has been maintained in reduced form, but the accompanying calls, lyrical or satirical, have been lost. Traditional instruments (pipe, bagpipe, Jew's harp, ocarina, drum) have been supplanted to some extent by clarinet (taragot), accordion, and piano. A study of Rumanian-Canadian music in Toronto and Montreal was undertaken in 1974 by the ethnomusicologist Emilia Comisel with sponsorship from the *National Museum of Man.

Rumaniam musicians visiting Canada have included the violinist, conductor, and composer Georges Enesco (the teacher of Ida *Haendel in London and of Sydney *Humphreys and Arthur *LeBlanc in Paris), the soprano Marina Krilovici (*COC 1968, 1969), and the violinists Silvia Marcovici and Stefan Ruha. Rumanian-born musicians resident in Canada include the guitarist and composer Robert Feuerstein and his wife, the pianist Sarah Feuerstein, Laszlo *Gati, Eugene *Gmeiner, Luciano and Edith *Della Pergola, Eli *Rubinstein, Aura (Rully), and Rémus *Tzincoca. The Canadian bass Joseph *Rouleau sang the leading roles in 1968 productions in Bucharest of *Boris Godunov* and *Don Carlos*. Charles *Reiner and Robert *Weisz studied in Geneva with the Rumanian pianist Dinu Lipatti. (EC)

RUMBOLDT, Ignatius (Aloysius). Choir director, organist, educator, b Curling (renamed Corner Brook), Nfld, 30 Nov 1916. He studied violin with Catherine Ryan and voice, piano, and organ with Charles *Hutton. He was music director 1936–52 at St Bonaventure's College, Holy Cross School, St Patrick's Hall School, and Mount Cashel Orphanage (all in St John's) and, during the same years, organist-choirmaster at St John the Baptist Cathedral in St John's. A visiting lecturer 1952–60 at the Faculty of Education, *Memorial U, he became full-time music specialist at the university in 1960 and consultant to the Extension Service for which, ca 1961, he organized the St John's Extension Choir and Orchestra (later the St John's SO) and co-ordinated choral and orchestral activities throughout the province. In 1962 he helped found the *Music Council of the Newfoundland Teachers' Assn. He was music director 1953–60 for CJON radio and TV in St John's and conducted the CJON Glee Club for two LPs of Newfoundland folksongs (Rodeo RLP 83 and 84) and the St John's Extension Choir for another (RCA CC-1024). He has broadcast frequently on CBC radio. He was music director 1975–7 at New Regional College in Corner Brook and returned in 1977 to Memorial U's Extension Service as director of Glee Clubs. Rumboldt was a member of the *Canada Council 1965–8 and was made a Member of the *Order of Canada in 1975.

BIBLIOGRAPHY
Morgan, Bernice. 'Ignatius Rumboldt – Mr. Music,' *M.U.N. Gazette*, 28 Aug 1975

Rush. Rock trio formed in 1968 in Toronto by the guitarist Alex Lifeson (b Surnie, BC, 27 Aug 1953), the singer and bass guitarist Geddy Lee (b Gary Lee Weinrib in Toronto 29 Jul 1953), and the drummer John Rutsey. The trio's first LP was *Rush* (1973, Moon MN 100 / Mer SMR-1-1011). Rutsey was replaced in 1974 by the drummer-lyricist Neil Peart (b Hamilton, Ont, 12 Sep 1952). The first of several tours in the USA followed during which Rush opened concerts for other bands. However, the band had toured as a headliner in Canada by 1976 and in the USA and England by 1977, playing as many as 200 concerts a year.

The leading Canadian practitioner of the high-volume, high-energy 'heavy metal' style popular in the mid-1970s, Rush nevertheless met with mixed critical response. Aftet the British debut, 2 Jun 1977 in Manchester, *Melody Maker* (11 Jun 1977) referred to the concert as 'a tour de force of their best known numbers like "Anthem," "Lake Side Park," "2112" and "Something for Nothing," all carefully executed with lights, tape effects, smoke bombs and massive searchlights ... Individually Rush are more than competent, and exciting if you enjoy thundering drum rolls, lengthy guitar solos and pounding bass lines. Their quasi-political lyrics [influenced by the writings of Ayn Rand] are an unusual feature, but it was difficult to hear them with Geddy Lee's high-pitched shriek.'

Rush's other LPs include *Fly by Night* (1974, Mer SRM-1-1023); *Caress of Steel* (1975, Mer SRM-1-1046); *2112* (1976, Mer SRM-1-1079), one of the group's several extended compositions; *All the World's a Stage* (1976, 2-Mer 7508), recorded in concert at *Massey Hall; *A Farewell to Kings* (1977, Anthem ANR-1-1010); and *Hemispheres* (1978, Anthem SANR-1-1015). *Permanent Waves* (1979, Anthem ANR-1-1021) was its most successful release to that date. Rush's music is published by Core Music; its members belong to CAPAC.

In 1977, with its managers Ray Danniels and Vic Wilson, Rush established the record label Anthem, affiliated to the US company Mercury. The Anthem roster includes the Toronto bands A Foot In Cold Water and Max Webster, the latter group having toured extensively in North America with Rush.

Rush won *Juno Awards as most promising new group of 1974 and group of the year for 1977 and has received gold record sales awards in Canada and the USA for several of its LPs. Rush should not be confused with the Montreal rock trio Frank *Marino and Mahogany Rush.

BIBLIOGRAPHY

Flohil, Richard. 'Living the rock'n'roll lifestyle,' *CanComp*, 97, Jan 1975
Weiner, Andrew. 'Rush!' Toronto *The City*, 15 Jan 1978
Snowdon, Annette. 'Rush rock,' *The Canadian*, 21 Jan 1978
MacGregor, Roy. 'To hell with Bob Dylan,' *Maclean's*, 23 Jan 1978
Gallo, Nancy. 'SRO / Anthem: five years and still growing,' *RPM*, vol 29, 1 Apr 1978 MM

RUSSELL, Anna (Ann Claudia) (b Russell-Brown, m Denison, m Goldhammer). Comedienne, contralto, pianist, b London 12 Dec 1911, naturalized Canadian 1943, naturalized US 1955; ARCM 1939. Her mother was Canadian. Anna moved to Canada in 1939 after studies at the RCM 1934–9 with Arthur *Benjamin and (composition) Vaughan Williams and a brief career as a folk-singer on the BBC. After her Canadian radio debut in 1940 on the CFRB English music-hall series 'Round the Marble Arch' she was heard on CBC's 'Jolly Miller Time' and was co-host with Syd Brown on CJBC's 'Syd and Anna.' In the 1940s she was an understudy for, but also actually appeared in, the title role in scenes from *Carmen* with the *Rosselino Opera. She married the Canadian artist Charles Goldhammer.

Russell's first one-woman show as a parodist and 'musical cartoonist' (Clyde *Gilmour) was sponsored by the Toronto IODE and was presented 11 Feb 1942 at *Eaton Auditorium. She performed with the *TSO and Sir Ernest *MacMillan (who had encouraged her unusual talent) at their annual Christmas Box concert in 1944 and again in 1945 and 1949. She made her US debut at New York's Carnegie Recital Hall 2 Oct 1947 and performed in Town Hall 10 Feb 1948. Her satirical parodies of concert music and opera gained her international popularity and she appeared subsequently with leading US orchestras, in recital, and in *Anna Russell's Little Show* (1955) and *All by Myself* (1960) on Broadway. She played the Witch in *Hansel and Gretel* with the New York City and San Francisco operas and was the voice of the witch in the 1954 puppet film of the opera.

Russell's recitals, until 1953 usually accompanied by John *Coveart, continued into the 1970s in North America, England, and Australia. She has performed in every major Canadian city and appeared in the 1953 **Spring Thaw*, the 1959 *Vancouver International Festival, and the 1977 *Stratford Festival. She also was featured on a CBC TV special and portrayed the Duchess of Crakentorp in the *COC production of *Daughter of the Regiment* in 1977. That same year she referred to herself as 'the Rip Van Winkle of Toronto – a bit decrepit but not yet passed away. I still have one of the great voices of the decayed – a roar rather than screech, in a comfy basso nonprofundo' (*Toronto Star*, 29 Mar 1977).

WRITINGS

The Power of Being a Positive Stinker (New York 1955)
The Anna Russell Song Book (London 1960)
The Writings of Anna Russell and Cora C. Russell (New York 1965)

DISCOGRAPHY

The Anna Russell Album. 2-Col MG 31199. Re-issue of *Anna Russell Sings?* H. Dworkin pf; 1951; Col ML-4594; and *Anna Russell Sings ? Again!* Coveart pf; 1952; Col ML-4733
Anna Russell in Darkest Africa. E. Rankin pf. 1954. Col ML-5195
Anna Russell Live at the Sydney Opera House. 1973. EMI
Guide to Concert Audiences. E. Rankin pf. 1953. Col ML-4928
Humperdinck *Hansel and Gretel*. 1954. Franz Allers cond. RCA XLXA 1013
The Practical Banana Promotion. E. Rankin pf. 1956. Col ML-5295
Square Talk on Popular Music. Jiggs Carol's orch. 1955. Col ML-5036

BIBLIOGRAPHY

Gilmour, Clyde. 'Anna *had* to be a clown,' *Maclean's*, 15 Jun 1953
Mallet, Gina. 'Anna in a mere cameo? Not likely,' *Toronto Star*, 8 Oct 1977 (JBl)

RUSSELL, Welford (Hamilton). Surgeon, composer, b Neepawa, Man, ca 1901, d Toronto 23 Apr 1975; MD (Toronto) 1925. The son of missionaries, he studied organ in Ireland with Henry Bishop. He was a physician by profession, first as a missionary doctor 1925–41 in India and later as chief surgeon 1945–69 at the Lockwood Clinic in Toronto.

Russell was also a successful composer of vocal and church music. In Toronto he studied composition with Richard *Tattersall and Godfrey *Ridout, cello with Joyce *Sands, and voice with Weldon *Kilburn. He composed eight choral works (Waterloo 1962–6), *Eleven Introits for All Seasons* (Leeds 1974), and more than 50 songs, many published by BMI Canada and Waterloo. His style was conservative, lyrical, and rhythmically flexible. His part-song 'Who Is at My Window, Who?' was recorded by the *Festival Singers (Sera S 60085), and three other songs, 'Come Hither, You that Love,' 'My Lute, Awake!,' and 'O Waly, Waly up the Bank,' were recorded by Lois *Marshall (SDD-2155). LCk

Russell Theatre. Located at the corner of Queen and Elgin streets in Ottawa; it opened 15 Oct 1897. The building was designed by J.-B. Elfatrick and Sons in an Italian renaissance style and contained 1500 seats in a parterre, two semi-circular balconies, and 10 boxes. An immense curtain separated the hall from the stage, which had more than 50 adjustable scenic panels and a lighting system permitting various colour effects considered daring for the time. Used for operas, recitals, orchestra concerts, plays, and other shows, the theatre was frequented by the capital's élite. Destroyed by fire 7 Apr 1901, it was rebuilt to the original plans by the architect J.M. Wood of Detroit. Under the management of Ambrose J. Small, the New Russell Opera House was inaugurated 5 Oct 1901. Operas were presented, there was vaudeville by touring companies, and US symphony orchestras gave concerts. The Ottawa SO under Donald *Heins, the *Ottawa Choral Society, and Annie *Jenkins' Palestrina Choir performed there regularly, and the *Toronto Mendelssohn Choir was a visiting attraction. Among the singers and instrumentalists who appeared were Emma *Albani, Geraldine Farrar, Amelita Galli-Curci, Nellie Melba, Edward *Johnson, Fritz Kreisler, and Sergei Rachmaninoff. The National Capital Commission expropriated the land to make room for Confederation Square, and the Russell Theatre closed its doors 14 Apr 1928.

L-GA

Russia. See Union of Soviet Socialist Republics.

RUZICKA, Bob (Robert Lloyd). Dentist, singer-songwriter, b Thorsby, near Edmonton, 6 Nov 1943; DDS (Alberta) 1967, M SC (Alberta) 1971. Ruzicka began playing guitar at 12 and wrote his first songs while studying dentistry at the U of Alberta. In 1967 he began a career in dentistry, practising for a year in Inuvik, NWT (where he also performed extensively), and thereafter in Edmonton (until 1977) and Nanaimo, BC.

Ruzicka sang several of his songs about the North in the CBC TV documentary 'Songs for a Vanishing Friend' (1970), and other Ruzicka songs have been heard in various CBC specials. Ruzicka has appeared on many CBC and CTV variety shows and starred on the former's 'Homemade Jam' in 1975 and 'Ruzicka' 1976–7. By 1977 he had recorded five LPs – for Signpost, MCA, and *RCA.

Ruzicka's songs have been recorded by Jimmy Arthur Ordge ('Mail Order Bride' and 'Muk Tuk Annie'), George Hamilton IV ('Dirty Old Man'), Judy Collins ('Down and Losing' or 'The Dealer'), and others. His 'Yes I Can (Anyway You Want It)', as recorded by *Valdy, was a hit in 1976. Ruzicka's songs are published by Lions Gate Music, New York. He is an affiliate of PRO Canada.

BIBLIOGRAPHY

Brown, Dick. 'I love my music but I hate the business,' *Weekend Magazine*, 21 Jun 1975 RGn, MM

S

S. Sabathil & Son Ltd. Vancouver harpsichord makers. The company was established in 1960 by Simon (b ca 1896) and Sigurd (b 1939) Sabathil, who had immigrated to Canada from Marianské Lázně, Czechoslovakia. By the 1970s the company was producing three clavichord models and nine harpsichord models, including three with double keyboards and one with pedal. Other instruments have been custom-made, including a double-ended one. Sabathil & Son have employed aluminum frames in their instruments to achieve stable tuning and audibility in modern halls. The keyboards and some basic materials are imported. Sabathil instruments have been purchased by colleges, conservatories, and individuals in North

America and Europe. About 30 per cent of the instruments (produced in the 1970s at a rate of about 100 annually) have been sold in Canada. Two demonstration records have been issued.
FCR

SABATIER, Charles (-Désiré-Joseph) **Wugk** (not Waugh). Pianist, composer, teacher, b Tourcoing, France, 1 Dec 1819, d Montreal 22 Aug 1862. His father was an immigrant from Saxony named Wugk, and under this name he was registered 1838–40 as a student at the Paris Cons; the name Sabatier must have been added early in his professional career. The claim in the Toronto *Globe*, 25 Sep 1856, that he had conducted opera in Brussels is very doubtful; that he was pianist to the Duchess of Montpensier is probably true.

Sabatier is believed to have arrived in Canada in 1848, living first in Montreal and moving in 1854 to Quebec, where he taught, played the piano at private gatherings and in public, and performed on church organs. In 1856 he was a guest at Toronto's *St Lawrence Hall, playing his own works. From Quebec he moved to St-Jean-Chrysostome-de-Lévis, thence to St-Gervais and to Chambly (as music teacher in a convent) before settling in Montreal. There Calixa *Lavallée and Dominique *Ducharme were among his pupils. In May 1860 he founded the journal *L'Artiste* with Paul Stevens and Édouard Sempé, but only two issues appeared. For the visit of the Prince of Wales he wrote a *Cantata* (with words by Sempé) performed under his baton 24 Aug 1860 by the 250 singers of the Montreal Musical Union, an orchestra, and soloists, including the young Adelina Patti and Emma *Albani. (In June 1861 at the Convent of the Sacré-Coeur, Gustave *Smith and Albani performed a *Grand Duo* for two pianos that Albani had composed on the themes of the cantata.)

To his Canadian contemporaries Sabatier must have seemed the very embodiment of the romantic artist. As a truly gifted virtuoso he won the respect of his colleagues; as a temperamental and restless but handsome man, inclined to an immoderate and bohemian life style, he was a fascinating subject for gossip among the public.

The *Cantata in Honour of the Prince of Wales* has an overture and nine vocal numbers. Sempé's libretto, with an English translation by Mme J.L. Leprohon, appeared in print; the music was published only in part. Sabatier's piano music includes *La Prière des anges*, *La Solitude*, *Mes Derniers Quadrilles*, and many operatic fantasies. Since the *Marche aux flambeaux* (dedicated to Moscheles) is Op 153 and the *Mazurka caprice* Op 190, we may assume he wrote far more than the 30 titles of which we have record. Among Sabatier's published songs are 'Sancta Maria,' 'L'Alouette' (not the famous song), 'La Montréalaise,' and the song that has kept his name alive, *'Le Drapeau de Carillon.' The *NL of C holds the original manuscripts of *Le Bouton de rose* (polka), *Fleur de mai*, and *Mazurka caprice*. A.J. *Boucher wrote and published *Souvenir de Sabatier*, a waltz suite of tunes from the *Cantata*. A street was named in Sabatier's honour in Montreal in 1955.

BIBLIOGRAPHY
La Minerve, 6 Aug 1860
Journal de l'Instruction publique, 18 Sep 1862
LeVasseur, Nazaire. 'Musique et musiciens à Québec,' *Musique*, Oct, Nov, Dec 1920
Letondal, Arthur. 'Un musicien oublié,' *L'Action nationale*, vol 2, Oct 1933
Roy, Léo. 'La verité sur Sabatier,' ibid, vol 57, Apr 1968
Champagne, Guy. 'Cantate en l'honneur de son altesse royale le Prince de Galles,' *Dictionnaire des oeuvres littéraires du Québec*, vol 1, ed Maurice Lemire (Montreal 1978)
Kallmann, Helmut. 'Charles-Désiré-Joseph Wugk,' *DCB*, vol 9
HK

Charles Wugk Sabatier

Sacred music. See Religions and music.

SADLER, Herbert J. Organist, choir conductor, teacher, b Bristol 6 Sep 1894, d Winnipeg 21 Apr 1955. Sadler and his parents arrived in Canada in 1911 and settled in Winnipeg. He had been trained as an organist and he served four years in that capacity at St Peter's Anglican Church. His appointment in 1919 as organist-choirmaster at Westminster United Church (a position he was to hold until his death) made him aware of the necessity to complete his organ training. Studies in the early and mid-1920s with Hugh Ross and in the late 1920s with Douglas *Clarke and Hugh *Bancroft led to his ACCO and FTCL diplomas.

With Filmer *Hubble, Sadler shared the directorship of the *Winnipeg Philharmonic Choir during World War II, and with an augmented Metropolitan Church Choir he prepared a number of public performances, including one of Sullivan's cantata *The Golden Legend*. He composed a number of pieces for use by his church choir and set the first section of Longfellow's *Hiawatha* for a performance by the larger choir along with the two sections set by Coleridge-Taylor. He gave numerous organ recitals, and the *Casavant instrument at Westminster Church, for which he drew up the specifications, was regarded for many years as Winnipeg's finest concert organ.

It was, however, as a teacher that Sadler made his most lasting mark. Among the many practising Winnipeg church musicians who studied with him were Barry Anderson, Eila Buchanan Alford, Allan Borbridge, Minnie Boyd, Beth Cooil, Evelyn Gregory, Frans *Niermeier, Edith Patterson, Maurine Pottruff, Mary Scarlett Wood, B. Franklin *Shinn, and Helen M. Young.
RG

St Catharines. Ontario city located on Lake Ontario west of Niagara Falls and incorporated in 1876. Known informally as 'the Garden City,' it was centred on the earlier Welland Canal. The present-day canal runs along the city's eastern limits. The population grew from 3500 in 1845 to over 115,000 by 1975.

The earliest documented musical events in St Catharines took place in the second-floor room of the town hall (the County Building), built in 1848. Fowler's Hall (1864), seating 500, also was widely used, as was Runchey's Hall in nearby Port Dalhousie (later a part of St Catharines). The Grand Opera House opened in 1877 and two years later boasted an orchestra formed by J.H. Hyde. The house presented vaudeville (eg, the Marks Brothers Co) and plays until 1925.

The Rodman Hall Arts Centre, opened in 1960 in the Merritt estate in west St Catharines, includes a recital hall for chamber music. *Brock U, where a music department was established in 1970 under Ronald Tremain, has two theatres and offers a concert series annually. The city's public library is another site of concerts. The Lincoln County Music Assn, which in 1933 established the Lincoln County Music Festival (later the Garden City Kiwanis Music Festival), was founded in 1922, and the St Catharines *Community Concerts Assn in 1930. The earliest band in the area, the Thorold Reed Band (1851), has survived into the 1970s. A St Catharines Philharmonic was formed in 1857, the St Catharines Brass Band in 1860, and a choral group in 1864. The Lincoln and Welland Regimental Band (1863) gave regular summer concerts at Montebello Park for over 80 years. Later organizations include the *St Catharines SO, the Clan MacFarlane Pipe Band (1953, a consistent winner in band competitions in Canada and the USA), and the St Catharines Madrigal Singers (1973, formed and conducted by Leonard Atherton and in 1977 renamed the Niagara Madrigal Singers).

James Sugden, the organist for many years (after 1860) at St George's Anglican Church, was among those who promoted interest in music in St Catharines. Another was the organist Angelo M. *Read, a native of the city and a teacher at Bishop Ridley College (later Ridley College). Subsequent music directors at the college were W.T. Thompson, A.C. Gore-Sellon and, 1923–64, Sydney George Bett – b Grimsby, England, 1896, d St Catharines 1964; D MUS (Toronto) 1933. Bett was followed by Peter Partridge 1964–9, Peter Orme 1969–71, John Butler 1971–2, and Michael Tansley, appointed in 1972. The composer Eric Dowling was organist-choirmaster 1928–42 at St Paul United Church (following Charles *Peaker) and after 1942 at St George's Anglican. He was president 1947–9 of the *RCCO.

Notable musicians born or raised in St Catharines include the pianist Anahid Alexanian, the organist-teacher Robert Hunter Bell, the opera singer Laura Blackwell de Turczynowicz (b St. Catharines ca 1877, d California ca 1953; an opera singer in Europe and the USA; an opera director in San Diego, Cal, and Victoria, BC, in the 1920s; and head of the new Conservatory Opera Company established at the *TCM in 1928), Billy *Bissett, Clayton *Hare, the cellist David Hetherington, Gene *Lees, the soprano Kathryn Newman (COC 1960–71), and the trumpeters Joe Umbrico and Kenny *Wheeler. St Catharines was the site in 1954 of the founding meeting of *OFSO and became the location of the *CMEA Resource Centre directed by Wallace Laughton. (EL)

St Catharines Symphony Orchestra. Founded in St Catharines, Ont, by Jan Wolanek in 1948 as the St Catharines Civic Orchestra. This community orchestra's governing body assumed the name St Catharines Symphony Assn in 1963 and changed it again in 1978 to Niagara Symphony Assn to reflect increased regional responsibilities.

The first concert, 30 May 1948, was followed by a three-concert series in the 1948–9 season. The orchestra at first comprised some 40 local musicians supplemented by members of the Buffalo Philharmonic Orchestra. Wolanek was succeeded by F.R.C. *Clarke 1957–8, Clarke by Leonard (Alexander) Pearlman (b Winnipeg 12 Jan 1928, a pupil of Hans Swarowsky and, after conducting the St Catharines orchestra 1958–64, a teacher at the Peabody Institute in Baltimore), and Pearlman by Milton *Barnes 1964–72. Under the direction 1972–80 of Leonard Atherton (b Harrow, England, 25 Oct 1941, a 1963 Oxford graduate, conductor 1964–6 of the National SO of Bolivia, a teacher 1968–72 in Philadelphia and conductor 1978–9 of the Toronto Youth SO) the 60-member St Catharines orchestra has presented up to four pairs of subscription concerts annually, a three-part choral series (with the orchestra's Symphony Chorus, Cantata choir, and Madrigal Singers), a pop series, and young people's concerts, all at *Brock U's Thistle Theatre. On Atherton's resignation the orchestra instituted a search for a successor and engaged guest conductors for the 1980–1 season.

Considered a model community orchestra, the St Catharines SO developed several programs designed to enhance the musical life of the city. It established a junior string ensemble which in 1965 became the St Catharines Junior Symphony under the violinist Paul van Dongen; in 1973 on the Brock U campus it opened Symphony House, which has served as the orchestra's administrative headquarters and a teaching centre for the city's youth; and for several years it has sponsored chamber and in-school recitals by ensembles drawn from its ranks. On grants from the *Canada Council the orchestra has commissioned Milton Barnes' *Psalms of David* (1973) and Ronald Tremain's *Seven Medieval Lyrics* (1974). In 1976 *OFSO commissioned Norman *Symonds' *Forest and Sky* for the St Catharines SO in memory of Albert Jarvis, whose concept of the small-city orchestra as a versatile community resource affected the musical development not only of St Catharines but of similar cities throughout Ontario.

BIBLIOGRAPHY

Edds, John A. 'The case for the community orchestra,' *CanComp*, Feb 1968

Lampard, E.H. 'On a winter's day just 25 years ago the city's symphony orchestra was born,' *St Catharines Standard*, 17 Feb 1973

Carson, Judith Ann. 'The St. Catharines Symphony Orchestra,' *OCan*, vol 3, May 1976

White, Peter. 'A tiny orchestra takes some giant steps,' Toronto *Globe and Mail*, 4 Dec 1976 (JE)

St David's Welsh Male Voice Choir. Latest in a linked succession of choirs in Edmonton. The first, the Orpheus Male Voice Choir, was organized in 1908 by a group of men who had emigrated from Europe. They approached Jackson Hanby to act as conductor and prepare them to compete in the *Alberta Music Festival. This choir was directed 1909–14 in turn by Claude Hughes and Herbert Wild. Its ranks depleted by World War I, the choir suspended activities until 1917, when its surviving members approached William John Hendra, a local voice and string teacher, to develop a permanent organization. This became the Edmonton Male Chorus. Between 1917 and 1947 its membership fluctuated between 40 and (in its peak year, 1932) 65 singers. Hendra guided this group to many achievements, including trophies in the Alberta Music Festival, before retiring in 1947. That year a general reorganization and amalgamation of this and two other choirs (the Edmonton Welsh Male Chorus and the smaller St David's Welsh Male Chorus) resulted in a new Edmonton Welsh Male Chorus. This organization sang for several years under various conductors, of whom the most nearly permanent (1954–7) was Douglas *Millson. In 1957 the choir was reorganized again, this time as the 20-voice St David's Welsh Male Voice Choir, which continued to sing in 1980, conducted by Berwyn Griffiths. RDM

St.-Denis Theatre / Théâtre St-Denis. Built in 1915 on St-Denis St north of Ste-Catherine St in Montreal and inaugurated 4 Mar 1916.

This 2380-seat theatre was intended for use as a French-language cinema and a stage for popular plays and operettas. In 1920 it began to present such famous performers as the tenor Hipolito Lazaro and the violinist Jascha Heifetz, and in 1921 it offered appearances by the orchestra of Milan's La Scala under Toscanini, the Boston Orchestra under Monteux with Vincent d'Indy as soloist, and the troupe of Antonio Scotti. In 1922 the *San Carlo Opera Company presented among other works Strauss' *Salomé*, and for a month the Russian Grand Opera presented a repertoire that included *Boris Godunov* and Rubinstein's *The Demon*. Besides such celebrities as Emma Calvé, Alfred Cortot, Mischa Elman, Tita Ruffo, Jacques Thibaud, and Théodore Botrel, the bard from Brittany, the theatre welcomed in 1923 the *Toronto Mendelssohn Choir and was the locale for the premiere of *Couture's **Jean Le Précurseur*. Casals appeared there in 1925, and a grand benefit concert for Emma *Albani was staged the same year. Maurice Ravel performed his own works there in 1928.

After several changes of ownership, the St-Denis Theatre was purchased in 1925 by Joseph Cardinal, who leased it in 1933 to the France-Film Company directed by Alexandre De Sève. At that time the hall was devoted almost entirely to the French cinema. World War II interrupted film-making in France, and France-Film joined with the *Montreal Festivals to present a brief opera season in 1941 with artists from the *Metropolitan. The company continued this annual presentation alone until 1945. In 1943 France-Film worked with *Canadian Concerts & Artists to organize the St-Denis Vendredis artistiques. To the operas were added recitals and symphony concerts with the Montreal Philharmonic Orchestra (conducted by Fitelberg, Horenstein, Kostelanetz, Kurtz, Maazel, Monteux, *Pelletier, and Stravinsky, with the soloists Dorfman, Elman, Francescatti, Heifetz, Malcuzynski, and Stern) and guest orchestras including those of Detroit, Minneapolis, Pittsburgh, and Toronto.

Dance and music-hall entertainments were another feature of the fare at the St-Denis, and among those appearing in the latter were Gilbert Bécaud, Maurice Chevalier, Fernandel, Luis Mariano, Yves Montand, and Tino Rossi. In 1960 the first artists from the Soviet Union to come to Canada performed there, as did other Soviet artists in the following years (Ashkenazy, Gilels, Kogan, the Oistrakhs father and son, Richter, and Vishnevskaya), and the state orchestras of Moscow and Leningrad. The Montreal Festivals used the theatre 1955–7 for the summer seasons, presenting *The Marriage of Figaro* and *Don Giovanni* among other works.

The St-Denis once more became a theatre devoted to French films after the opening of the *PDA in 1963. In 1972 two small adjoining halls, the Chevalier and the Pierrot, were built; they are now known as St-Denis 1 and 2. In 1977–8 the theatre was modernized (reducing the seating capacity to 2300), and equipped to stage big variety shows and recitals. The Kébecspec agency has presented the following performers: Cano, Chick Corea, Claude *Dubois, Diane *Dufresne, Raoul *Duguay, Jean Lapointe, Paul Piché, and Jean-Luc Ponty. GP

SAINTE-MARIE, Buffy (Beverly) (m Bugbee, m Wolfchild). Singer-songwriter, guitarist, mouth-bow player, b Piapot Reserve, Craven, near Regina, of Cree parents. Her exact birthdate has never been confirmed, though 20 Feb 1941 or 1942 have been published in press biographies and reference works. Orphaned when a few months old, she was adopted by a part-Micmac family and raised in Wakefield, Mass. She later was adopted according to tribal customs on the Piapot Reserve by a Cree family related to her natural parents. At 17 she took up the guitar, and by her early twenties she had become an important figure in Greenwich Village (New York) folk music circles. She has been noted for her commitment to social causes, especially those of the native peoples of North America.

Sainte-Marie attained international success during the 1960s and 1970s, and she appeared frequently as well in most major Canadian cities. Her earliest Canadian performances included an appearance at the 1964 *Mariposa Folk Festival. She also performed at *Expo 67 and in 1977 at the Winnipeg Folk Festival and before Queen Elizabeth II at the Silver Jubilee celebrations in Ottawa. She starred on CBC TV's 'Superspecial' (taped in 1975 at *Ontario Place and telecast 20 Mar 1978) and has appeared on several other CBC radio and TV shows. She also has been seen in Canada as a regular performer, beginning in 1975, on the (US) NET network's children's show, 'Sesame Street.' The songs she has written range from the ballad 'Until It's Time for You to Go' (a hit for Elvis Presley and also recorded by Claude *Gauthier, Catherine *McKinnon, Odetta, and others) to such protest songs as 'The Universal Soldier' (which she wrote at Toronto's Purple Onion coffee house and which became a hit as recorded by Donovan). Her songs about the native peoples include 'Native North American,' 'Now That the Buffalo's Gone,' 'Soldier Blue,' and 'My Country 'Tis of Thy People You're Dying.' Many are included in *The Buffy Sainte-Marie Song Book* (Belwin Mills / Grosset & Dunlap 1971). Her recordings include over a dozen LPs for Vanguard, MCA, and ABC of her own songs and others by various folk-influenced songwriters, including Leonard *Cohen and Joni *Mitchell. She has set to music 'God Is Alive, Magic Is Afoot,' a passage from Cohen's novel *Beautiful Losers*.

BIBLIOGRAPHY

Hale, Barrie. 'The rebirth of Buffy Sainte-Marie,' *The Canadian*, 14 Jan 1978 MM

St Francis Xavier University. Roman Catholic institution founded at Arichat, NS, in 1853 as St Francis Xavier College. In 1855 it was moved to Antigonish, NS. It gained university status in 1866 and awarded its first degrees in 1868. Its ladies' college, Mount St Bernard College, was founded ca 1883. In 1894 students at that college became eligible for degrees from St Francis, a move which established the latter as the first co-educational Catholic university in North America. In 1980 the ladies' college existed as a residence only, and St Francis offered degrees at the undergraduate and graduate (master's) levels.

A music department was founded at Mount St Bernard in 1883, and particular attention was given to the study and performance of Gregorian chant. St Francis established a music major program in 1945, a degree program (BA in music) in 1975, and two-and-a-half-year courses in liturgical music and jazz studies in 1979. Sister St Michel of the Eucharist (Mary Byrne) served 1945–70 as chairman of the university's Music Dept. John C. *O'Donnell, who became chairman in 1970, has established a strong presence in the community at large.

In 1979–80 the department offered a BA MUS (honours and major), BA (major and minor in music), and diplomas in liturgical music and jazz studies. In that school year seven teachers (five full-time and two part-time) and 40 students met at classes in the department's own building.

In addition to its own holdings and those of the music library, the department has access to the

Dept of Celtic Studies' recording archives, augmented by materials from that department's Gaelic Language and Folklore Project (initiated in 1977). Within the first two years of the project's existence more than 350 field recordings of Scots-Gaelic songs, collected by John Shaw, had been classified and catalogued, and some texts had been transcribed. A small number of fiddle recordings had been made.

The university has sponsored recitals on the department's two *Casavant pipe organs and a Performing Arts Series. Resident performing groups have included the University Wind Ensemble under James Hargreaves, the University Singers under Sister Agnes MacAdam, the Stage Band under Donald Hughes, and the Renaissance Singers.

BIBLIOGRAPHY
'Interview: John Shaw,' *Canada Folk Bulletin*, vol 3, May–Jun 1980 (JCm)

St-Hyacinthe. A Quebec city on the Yamaska River, some 50 km east of Montreal. Founded in 1748, a municipality in 1849, and a town in 1857, it was named after the patron saint of Jacques-Hyacinthe-Simon Delorme, the local seigneur. In 1979 it was an industrial centre with a metropolitan population of 40,000.

The Séminaire de Saint-Hyacinthe was founded in 1811 and soon began to give courses in music; a certain Cléophas Larue is said to have taught the young Calixa *Lavallée when he attended that institution. Lavallée's father, Augustin, had settled in the town around 1848, working as a string-instrument maker and as a manufacturer of organ pipes in Joseph Casavant's modest factory, in addition to conducting an amateur band. At 10 Calixa was the regular organist of Notre-Dame-du-Rosaire Church. Télesphore Urbain was a later incumbent, followed by Conrad *Letendre and Ferrier Chartier, among others.

Music was taught at the convent of the Sisters of the Sacred Heart, founded in 1842, as well as at the convents of the Sisters of the Presentation of Mary (founded 1858) and the Sisters of St Joseph. St-Hyacinthe became known around the world for *Casavant Frères, the organ manufacturers founded in 1879 by Joseph's sons, Samuel and Claver Casavant, both born there.

One of the leading figures of the town was Léon *Ringuet, who arrived in 1880 to conduct the Société philharmonique, a concert band founded the preceding year. Ringuet was the organist-choirmaster at the cathedral and a teacher. One of his pupils, L.-J. Oscar *Fontaine, was assistant organist at the cathedral before moving to the USA in 1904. In 1979 the concert band celebrated its centenary, under the direction of Gilles Saint-Amant.

Conrad *Letendre and Charles-Émile *Gadbois were two prominent residents born early in the 20th century. In addition to being organist at Notre-Dame-du-Rosaire, Letendre taught at the seminary and the academy. Bernard *Lagacé, born in St-Hyacinthe, was his pupil, as was Gaston *Arel, the organist at the cathedral in 1945. Letendre also collaborated with Gadbois in his publishing enterprise *La Bonne Chanson, founded there in 1937.

It was in St-Hyacinthe that the *JMC originated in 1949, and the St-Hyacinthe centre remains one of the most active in the movement. The town had several concert bands such as the Patro, founded in 1906, and choirs such as the Ménestreles and Gloria Laus, as well as the Variétés canadiennes, founded in 1945. For a long time concerts were held in the hall of the seminary and at the Corona cinema. The Bourgchemin Cegep has a modern 800-seat hall, the Salle Léon-Ringuet.

St-Hyacinthe is the birthplace of Willie *Lamothe, Louis-Philippe *Laurendeau, Damis *Paul, the violinist and composer Georges Paul, the record distributor André *Perrault, the organists Paul Vigeant and Denis *Regnaud, the pianist and teacher Miville Bois, and the pianist-arranger-composer Gérald Locas. The town has spawned a number of pop music groups, including the Hou-Lops, the Sultans, and the Aristos. The firm *Providence Organ Inc was founded in 1946 in the suburb of Providence. GP

St-Jean-Baptiste celebrations. Popular annual celebrations in French Canada on the days before or after 24 June, the feast day of St-Jean-Baptiste. Following a tradition the origin of which is lost in antiquity, many people, among them the Gauls, lit fires to celebrate the summer solstice. According to the *Jesuit Relations* and the *Journal des Jésuites*, this tradition was revived on the banks of the St Lawrence in 1636. In 1646 the *Journal* reported that 'on 23 June the fire for St-Jean was lit at half-past eight in the evening ... One heard five cannon shots and two or three discharges from muskets.'

It is not known why St-Jean-Baptiste came to be considered the patron saint of French Canada. One legend has it that a great many French-Canadians bearing that given name persuaded the journalist and patriot Ludger Duvernay to adopt it as the name of the national society of French-Canadians which he founded in 1834. In any case that was the name he chose, and the St-Jean-Baptiste Society of Montreal took the maple leaf and the beaver as its emblems. The founding was celebrated 24 Jun 1834 by a banquet to which 60 guests were invited – Irish, US, and Canadian. Many among them sang their interpretations of patriotic songs, including George-Étienne Cartier who sang *'Ô Canada! mon pays! mes amours!' The celebration became annual, and gradually more elaborate, and spread to other localities in Quebec, in Acadia (1880), and in the francophone regions of Ontario, the Canadian west, and even the USA. The celebrations were suspended 1838–42 because of political troubles.

Quebec City had its first official celebration in 1842. The procession to the cathedral was led by a civic band, the *Musique Canadienne, which also played patriotic songs during the ensuing banquet. T.-F. *Molt, the regular organist 1840–9 at the Quebec Basilica, was the first church musician to participate in the St-Jean-Baptiste celebrations and ca 1845 he organized a choir for the occasion. The Montreal St-Jean-Baptiste Society was reorganized in 1843 with a parade to mark the festivities. The Temperance Band, the first to participate, made its appearance in 1846. Soon, other bands joined: those of the Collège de Montréal in 1847 and the Collège de Ste-Marie in 1850, Joseph *Maffré's band in 1851, the Chasseurs canadiens and the Christian Brothers' band in 1868, the *Bande de la Cité and the St-Henri and Ogdensburg, NY, bands in 1877, and those of Longueuil, Maisonneuve, and St-Vincent-de-Paul, and the Shamrocks, in 1879. Several musicians dedicated compositions to St-Jean-Baptiste societies in Quebec, Montreal, and Ottawa: for example, Charles *Sauvageau's 'Chant canadien' (1843) and 'Chant national' (*Le Ménestrel* 1844), both for voice and piano, J.-C. *Brauneis II's *Marche de la Saint-Jean-Baptiste* (Lovell and Gibson 1848), and Célestin *Lavigueur's 'Á notre saint patron' (1877) for voice and piano.

A solemn mass was usual in most parishes in Montreal and Quebec. Thus, at Notre-Dame in Montreal 'the worthy M. Barbarin conducted 200 voices which, with the orchestra, offered up Haydn's *Second Mass* with masterly hands and throats' (*La Minerve*, 25 Jun 1868). Other masses were sung in other years: Haydn's in 1869 and 1879, Rossini's in 1870 and 1871, and one by Father Cléophas Borduas in 1893, the 250th anniversary of the founding of Montreal. In 1935, at the church of St-Jean-Baptiste in Montreal, a *Mass* by *Contant and an *Ave Maria* by *Lamoureux were performed; in 1936, the *Descarries *Mass*.

Twice the celebrations achieved exceptional dimensions. In 1874 60,000 visitors, half of them Franco-Americans, invaded Montreal to celebrate in grand style the 40th anniversary of the founding of the St-Jean-Baptiste Society and to join in a huge national convention of French-Canadians. A hymn, 'Rallions-nous,' was composed by Charles-Marie *Panneton to words by Benjamin Sulte. The minutes of the society mention for the first time floats, numbering 15 on that occasion, and also 31 bands in the procession. The choir of the Collège de Montréal sang the eucharist in Notre-Dame Church. A banquet in the hall of Bonsecours Market and a musical jubilee on St Helen's Island were among the memorable events. J.-B. *Labelle wrote and conducted a cantata for the occasion.

The celebration in Quebec City in 1880 coincided with another national convention of French-Canadians. Band concerts in the public squares on the evening of 23 June drew enormous crowds. The next day a choir of more than 500 voices performed Gustave *Gagnon's arrangement of Du Mont's *Messe royale* accompanied by the bands of the 9th Battalion and the *Union musicale. Calixa *Lavallée's national song *'O Canada,' composed for the occasion, was performed that day. Some 20 floats took part in a parade of 112 associations and numerous bands from Canada and the USA.

Parades became more and more elaborate over the years. A particular theme was chosen each year. For example, in 1928 34 floats each took for a theme a folksong, and the song was sung by a choir following the float. That same year, on 28 June, Guillaume *Couture's oratorio **Jean le Précurseur* was presented at the Delorimier Stadium in Montreal; it was revived 22 Jun 1964 in a performance at the *PDA. The 1931 theme 'Women in Canadian history' included a float representing Emma *Albani singing for Queen Victoria.

In 1939, at Lafontaine Park in Montreal, under the general theme 'Canada has remained faithful,' a float illustrated two songs: 'Isabeau ou l'anneau fatal' and *'J'ai cueilli la belle rose.' Folk music was honoured again in 1950 and 1952. Quebec chanson in the world context was featured in the framework of 'The International Personality of Quebec,' the theme of the 1967 celebrations. The following year Gilles *Vigneault opened the parade singing *'Mon Pays.' In 1970 a need for change in the format, and considerable political unrest, forced the authorities to put an end to the traditional parade.

Many musical activities have accompanied the week-long celebrations. Notable among these have been the promenade concerts, the first of which took place in the hall at Bonsecours Market in 1869. On 25 June *La Minerve* reported that 'the Orphéonistes sang some jolly tunes by Octave Labelle and Zotique Pagé (comic songs full of wit and fun).' Such lively dances as the lancers (a variant on the quadrille), cotillions, and quadrilles were danced. The pattern was repeated in later years with much success; at the *Monument national in 1893 such artists as Victoria *Cartier, Blanche Labelle, Rosario *Bourdon, and J.-J. *Goulet took part. A military sketch, *Devant l'ennemi*, was presented 24 Jun 1879 at a grand dramatic and musical evening at the *Theatre

Royal; a literary and musical session, during which Oscar *Martel played his own *Fantaisie coquette*, took place 24 June 1880. There were gala evenings in 1898, 1901, and 1903 and evenings of folk music in 1919, at the Monument national. In 1929 a competition for poets and musicians was organized with a view to creating new Canadian songs; the best were presented to the public 22 Jun 1929 at the Delorimier Stadium. Henri *Miro's cantata *Vox populi* was performed on 24 June. Concerts of instrumental and vocal music were presented 1903–48 in parks and public squares, especially in Lafontaine Park.

The celebrations continued more or less in the traditional manner until the early 1960s. In 1964 the Commission des Fêtes du Canada Français was created, and that year 43 chansonniers performed at five bandstands on St Helen's Island, Montreal. Week-long celebrations took place in 1965 and 1968, with international dances, band festivals, and popular concerts.

After 1970 celebrations were held in the streets of Old Montreal, and in 1975 and 1976 on Mount Royal. In 1977, 275 municipalities in 19 regions of Quebec took part in the national holiday. In Montreal, on the night of St-Jean-Baptiste, the team of artists gathered at the Olympic stadium included Colette *Boky, Pierre *Duval, the *Disciples de Massente, Félix *Leclerc, Claude *Léveillée, and Robert *Savoie. In 1978 regions, towns, and villages organized their own activities, engaging noted singers and instrumental musicians as well as local ones. The holiday was celebrated in more than 1000 places in 1979.

In 1959 the St-Jean-Baptiste Society of Montreal initiated its annual acknowledgement of the merits of a composer or performer, the *Prix de musique Calixa-Lavallée.

BIBLIOGRAPHY

Chouinard, H.-J.-B. *Fête nationale des Canadiens-français célébrée à Québec en 1880* (Quebec 1881)
Annales de la Société Saint-Jean-Baptiste de Québec, vol 4: 1902 (Quebec 1903)
Rudel-Tessier, Danièle. 'Montréal 1874: 150,000 habitants, 60,000 visiteurs. Ah, mes aïeux, quelle belle Saint-Jean ce fut!' *Perspectives*, vol 17, 21 Jun 1975
Vaugeois, Denis. 'La Saint-Jean, fête de la fierté,' *Forces*, vol 43, no. 2, 1978

ST

ST JOHN, Stanley. Bandleader, pianist, conductor, b Sunderland, northeast of Toronto, 19 Feb 1904. Raised in Sunderland and in nearby Uxbridge, St John commuted to Toronto for studies at the *TCM. His teachers included Viggo *Kihl, Ernest *Seitz, and Paul *Wells for piano and Reginald *Stewart for conducting. While studying mathematics and physics at the U of Toronto he led a dance band at the university and in resort areas around Toronto. Leading bands – often from the piano – for private social functions in the city, he gradually became the leading society orchestra leader in Toronto and was in residence for several years at the Royal York Hotel and, after 1952, at the King Edward Hotel, sustaining several orchestras under his name at the same time. In 1946, Trent Frayne wrote: 'In and around Toronto for more than 10 years now people in the upper bracket have operated on the conviction that no party is complete without the St. John beat. It's sort of like having forks on the table.' St John's orchestra also performed 1935–41 at the *CNE and was heard in the 1940s on CFRB and CBC radio. He continued to lead orchestras in Toronto until the mid-1970s.

BIBLIOGRAPHY

Frayne, Trent. 'Melody merchant,' *Maclean's*, 1 Oct 1946

MM

A dance at Saint John (*Canadian Illustrated News*, 26 Dec 1874)

Saint John. New Brunswick city at the mouth of the Saint John River on the Bay of Fundy. Developing on the site of a series of French and English forts dating back to 1631, Saint John became, in 1785, the first Canadian city to be incorporated. By 1824 it had a population of 8000, including many descendants of the Loyalists – opponents of the American Revolution – who had arrived in 1783. Saint John became a centre of fishing and shipbuilding and in 1975 had a population of 100,000.

In early Saint John music was the special enthusiasm of the educated Loyalists and the British officers. New Brunswick's solicitor-general 1784–1808, Ward Chipman Sr, was noted for the soirées at his home, in which he entertained his guests with the latest songs from London.

A notable Loyalist musician, Stephen *Humbert, moved in 1783 from New Jersey to Saint John, where, in 1796, he opened a Sacred Vocal Music School (see Singing schools). An ardent Wesleyan Methodist, in 1801 (a time when many churches damned music as irreligious) Humbert compiled **Union Harmony*, the first Canadian music book with English text.

Some church deacons, who objected to 'dance music in the House of God' were prevailed upon, only after considerable resistance, to permit the singing of a 'copper tune' during the collection. Even as late as 1867 no organ was permitted at St Andrew's Presbyterian Kirk, and after that only a feeble one. Some churches were not averse to music, however. In 1802 Trinity (Anglican) Church, with the help of a £200 donation from a wealthy merchant, imported an organ from London.

Colin Campbell, in 1801, advertised violins, military and common fifes, and an Aeolian harp, as well as the most fashionable music from Scotland, Italy, and elsewhere. Educational institutions, such as the Music Academy set up by the Irishman Arthur Corry in 1822, improved musical standards and gave students the opportunity to perform.

Of many choral societies, the first was the Phil-Harmonic Society, established in 1824. Another was the Catch and Glee Club, formed in 1833 by an Irish immigrant. In 1837 a member of St Andrew's Kirk who opposed the minister's suppression of music organized a sacred Music Society which for at least eight years thereafter, under a former regimental bandmaster named Weisbecker, performed selections from the works of Handel, Haydn, and Mozart. Another Sacred Music Society, founded by Stephen Humbert, made its first public appearance in 1840 at the Baptist Church.

A Mechanics' Institute was built in 1840 and henceforth provided a needed platform for comic opera and concerts. In 1832 the Hermann troupe from Munich had brought performances of music by Mozart, Beethoven, Rossini, and Weber to the city. The St Luke family, in an extended stay in the early 1840s, gave concerts and trained a local choir. During Christmas week 1841, the St Lukes gave three concerts. In March 1842, with the help of his children and a 22-piece orchestra, St Luke presented a concert which included eight excerpts from Haydn's *The Creation* and a violin concerto by de Bériot. After a farewell concert in 1843 the St Lukes moved on to Halifax. In 1853 Saint John was visited by the Norwegian violinist Ole Bull.

Among several briefly successful musical organizations was the Harmonic society of 23 singers, formed in 1854 under the conductor and organist Theodoric Wichtendahl. The society performed secular and sacred music including excerpts from opera and oratorio (eg, *Messiah*) and drew capacity audiences to the seven-or-so concerts it presented 1855–6. Early in 1857 Wichtendahl resigned his $75-a-year post after a dispute with the society's executive over his failure to develop an orchestra. Wichtendahl's successor, Signor de Angelis, gave two concerts, but the society seems to have disbanded in 1857.

Later enterprises were the Saint John Oratorio Society, organized by Thomas Morley in 1882; the Euterpian Club under James Ford (Ford prepared the 150-voice Festival Chorus for its participation in the *Cycle of Musical Festivals held in April 1903); and the Saint John Choral Society, directed by Ernest S. Peacock, which performed, among other works, *Messiah* (1911, 1912, and 1913), *The Creation* (1912), and Cowen's *The Rose Maiden* (1913).

Saint John has had a succession of music halls – and destructive fires. The Mechanics' Institute (1840–1914) survived longer than most. The Academy of Music, built on Germain St in 1872, was destroyed in the great fire of 1877. The Opera House, built in 1891 – used for comic operas and operettas in its early days, for burlesque later, and for movies ultimately – burned down in 1959. When the Imperial Hall, constructed in 1920, ceased being a theatre, Saint John was left without a large concert hall, and subsequent concerts have taken place in the Saint John High School auditorium.

Vocal music in Saint John owed much to David *Thomson, who had arrived from Scotland in 1914. After World War I he formed the Brunswick Singers, a male quartet which also performed with Don *Messer as the Lumberjacks Quartet. In 1937 Thomson began to lead the popular Capitol Theatre singsongs and founded the mixed-voice Carriden Choir which performed throughout New Brunswick and on the CBC national network until 1967. As provincial music supervisor 1949–65, Thomson effected major changes in school music throughout New Brunswick.

In the 1890s the Rev James Anderson, an advocate of Tonic Sol-Fa, gave instruction to Saint John teachers. In 1898 Morton Harrison organized and conducted a high school orchestra; Harrison's orchestra, later conducted by William C. Bowden, survived until after World War II. Catherine Robinson, in the early 1900s, was Saint John's first full-time school music teacher.

James Brown, an organist from England, was supervisor of music for Saint John schools from 1923 until shortly after World War II. He was interested especially in boys' choirs and organized several non-competition festivals in the schools. After World War II Douglas Major (composer, b England 1902, d Saint John 1969), who was associate conductor of the Carriden Choir, organist-choirmaster at St Paul's Anglican Church, and a public school music teacher, wrote an opera, *The Loyalists* (libretto by Patricia Collins), which was performed in Saint John in 1967.

In the 1950s orchestral activity increased dramatically in Saint John owing to the development of such groups as the Saint John SO, founded 1950 by Kelsey *Jones; the *New Brunswick SO; the *New Brunswick Youth Orchestra; and the regularly visiting *Atlantic SO.

Eldon *Rathburn, who spent the early years of his career in the city, composed the concerto *Steelhenge* premiered by Saint John's Lancaster Kiwanis Steel Band and the Atlantic SO in 1974. The band, formed in 1972 of high school students and directed by Walter Ball, has toured the Maritimes, performed at the 1976 Montreal Olympics, and made two records for RCA.

In 1967 the city adopted as its official song *'My Own Canadian Home,' which had been published in Saint John in 1887.

Musicians born in Saint John include Berkley *Chadwick, Stompin' Tom *Connors, Jane *Coop, Bruce *Holder, Frances *James, the songwriter Michael F. Kelly, Ned *Landry, the composer and teacher Edward Betts Manning, Catherine *McKinnon, Patricia *Rideout, and Gordon *Wry.

See also Instrument collections: New Brunswick.

BIBLIOGRAPHY

Harper, J. Russell. 'The theatre in Saint John, 1789–1817,' *Dalhousie R*, Autumn 1954

– 'Spring tide: an enquiry into the lives, labours, loves and manners of early New Brunswickers,' unpubl ms, National Gallery of Canada (Ottawa)

Elliott, Carleton. 'Music in New Brunswick,' *The Arts in New Brunswick* (Fredericton, NB, 1967) (EMD, PMW)

St John's. Newfoundland's capital city, situated on the east edge of the Avalon peninsula. John Cabot is said to have entered St John's Harbour in 1497. The first permanent residence at St John's (establishing its claim as the first community in the new world to be settled by Europeans) was built in 1528. With its protected harbour and proximity to Europe, St John's became an important fishing, trading, and strategic centre. It was incorporated as a city in 1888. The first trans-Atlantic wireless message, 12 Dec 1901, was received there on Signal Hill. The city's population – more than 3000 by 1800, 20,000 by 1835, and 135,000 by 1975 – has remained a consistent one-quarter of Newfoundland's total population.

The predominantly Irish and Welsh immigrants have perpetuated their strong vocal and instrumental folk traditions and the hymn-singing of their ancestral faiths. It is known that in the 18th century the fiddle and the flute were popular instruments. An entry in the 1810 subscription list of *The Gazette* shows that one of the subscribers paid his bill in barter, with the music of his fiddle: 'Augustin Macnamara, commenced Nov. 1, 1810, to be paid for in fiddling.' Irish nuns from Dublin and Cork arrived in St John's in the 1840s to teach, and music was among the subjects they offered. The bishop of Newfoundland wrote to the London journal the *Parish Choir* (23 Dec 1848) reporting the activities of his church's Parochial Choral Society. Mr Henry Earle accompanied congregational singing at St Thomas' Church on a seraphine (reed organ) in the mid-19th century.

The amateur theatricals which were the mainstay of the St John's stage during the 19th century usually included music. Thomas Linley's *The Duenna*, the first opera given in the town, played for almost a fortnight at the end of May 1820. Proceeds went to victims of the great fire of 1817, which had ruined businessmen and destroyed many homes. Theatricals were presented first at the Amateur Theatre or at the Globe Tavern and after 1822 at the New Amateur Theatre, the foremost stage in St John's prior to the fire of 1846. There, performances were presented by talented local inhabitants and by officers of the garrison at Fort Townsend. In 1852 the Hearn family arrived and gave vocal and dramatic performances in the old Court House. Around 1860 professional touring companies began to visit St John's. During the 1860s and 1870s performances took place in the Mechanics' Hall or the Fishermen's Hall; in the 1890s concerts and lectures were given at the Athenaeum.

A Choral Society presented *Messiah* in 1884 and Gade's *Crusaders* in 1885 with piano and harmonium accompaniment. It was also during the 1880s that Charles *Hutton began his rich and varied contribution to the musical life of St John's. One of his pupils, Ignatius *Rumboldt, succeeded him 1936–52 as organist-choirmaster at St John the Baptist Catholic Cathedral.

In the first 20 years after World War II the St John's population more than doubled as Newfoundlanders left the 'bays' for urban centres. The musical life of St John's benefited from this population shift but also from many related changes: the overall improvement of economic conditions, the expansion in radio and TV services, the growth of *Memorial U, the development of the public education system, and the employment of specialist music teachers. Prior to 1949 musical training was provided by private teachers or was available at the city's denominational colleges or larger schools. The *TCL courses of study were introduced in St John's as early as 1900, and the TCL examiners' annual visits, begun at that time, continued in 1980. (In 1978 there were five TCL centres in the province.)

Andreas *Barban, an immigrant who settled in St John's in 1947, became an important piano teacher and broadcaster. Eric *Abbott, who began teaching music in the St John's schools in 1948, also performed on radio and gave hundreds of piano, organ, and cornet recitals.

The number of visiting performers increased after World War II. *Community Concerts presented Vivian Della Chiesa, Eugene Istomin, George *London, Dorothy Maynor, Lois *Marshall, and William Primrose, among others. During the 1950s and 1960s *Canada Council assistance enabled distinguished Canadian symphonic, operatic, and ballet ensembles to visit the city and other parts of the province.

In these years competition festivals and new ensembles multiplied. In 1951 the Kiwanis sponsored the foundation of the Music Festival Assn of Newfoundland. Barban was active in preparing syllabi, adjudicating, and accompanying. Competitors in the annual St John's festival increased from 1400 in 1952 to more than 12,000 in 1974.

Ignatius Rumboldt, visiting lecturer 1952–60 at the Faculty of Education, Memorial U, and music director 1953–60 for CJON radio and TV, formed the St John's Extension Choir and Orchestra and two new university glee clubs in the early 1960s. The Extension Orchestra, conducted 1963–6 by Barban, went on to become the basis of the St John's SO, established in 1970 and conducted by Ian Mennie 1970–5, and Peter Gardner 1975–7, succeeded by David Gray. The orchestra became the Newfoundland SO in 1978.

An event of signal importance for music was the opening, 22 May 1967, of the *Arts and Culture Centre, which has provided a focus for the cultural life of the city. Its 1017-seat auditorium, regarded as one of the finest in Canada, has provided a permanent home for the Newfoundland SO and a platform for visiting groups and individual artists.

In 1968, the same year that he became director of the Booth Memorial Brass Band, Eric Abbott was appointed director of the Avalon Consolidated School Board. Sister Mary Catharine Burke directed the *school music broadcast series 'Music in the Classroom' 1968–73. In 1970 Sister Paschal Carroll of the Presentation Order was appointed music consultant to the Dept of Education. The school music program which she helped devise was introduced in the autumn of 1972. The expansion of music education, although especially impressive in St John's, has occurred throughout the province. In 1973, for example, Newfoundland had 16 school bands and orchestras and about 250 glee clubs and choirs. One of these, the Glee Club of Our Lady of Mercy College, performed at *Expo 67 and won the *FCMF's George S. Mathieson Trophy. The formation of a music department at Memorial U in 1975 was a logical extension of the rapid post-war development in music education.

The folk music of Newfoundland has been maintained in a vital tradition extending from 1497 to the present. Gerald *Doyle's important folk compilation *Old-Time Songs and Poetry of Newfoundland* (St John's 1927, 1940, 1955, 1966, 1978) helped give it particular impetus in the 20th century. The Commodore's Quartet in the late 1940s, and many others subsequently, have helped keep traditions alive. Newfoundland folksongs have formed a large part of the repertoire of groups such as the Anchor-Killick Chorus, a mixed choir founded in 1974 and directed by Frances Dawson, and the popular women's choir the Canterbury Singers, directed by Eileen Stanbury.

Among noted musicians born in St John's have been Eric Abbott, the baritone Donald Brian, Roma *Butler, the soprano Lynn Channing, the pop singer Mary Lou Collins, the harpist Carla Emerson (who returned to St John's in 1962 after playing in the Royal Philharmonic in London, and who began teaching at Memorial U in 1976), the pop singer Mary Lou Farrell, the organist Charles Hutton, and the pianist Karen Quinton. Newfoundland-born Arthur *Scammell retired to St John's, and the folksinger Omar *Blondahl settled there in 1955.

See also Folk music, Anglo-Canadian: 1 / Newfoundland.

BIBLIOGRAPHY

O'Neill, T.H., and Young, R.A. 'Old-time theatricals in St. John's,' *The Book of Newfoundland*, vol 2, ed J.R. Smallwood (St John's 1937)

Walker, Ralph. ' "Pop" bands in Newfoundland,' ibid, vol 4 (St John's 1967)

Withers, J.W. 'Dirty, diseased and dangerous – and always exciting. St. John's in 1807,' ibid, vol 5 (St John's 1975)

Rowe, Frederick W. *Education and Culture in Newfoundland* (Toronto 1976)

St Lawrence Centre. A theatre complex in Toronto, located east of *O'Keefe Centre on Front St and built as the city's centennial project. It was designed by Gordon S. Adamson and Associates and opened in February 1970 after eight years of planning. The completed single building houses the 483-seat Town Hall and 831-seat Theatre. A second building, planned for classrooms and rehearsal space, was never built. The hall is used mainly for chamber concerts, public debates, and film presentations, while the theatre, adaptable for thrust-stage, proscenium, and caliper formations, is in use year round for dramatic presentations. The complex is owned by the city and operated by Toronto Arts Productions (formerly

Toronto Arts Foundations). General directors have been Mavor *Moore 1966–70 and Leon Major 1970–80. Major's successor, Edward Gilbert, assumed the position with the title of artistic director.

Louis *Applebaum was music consultant 1968–71. Franz *Kraemer was music director 1971–9, succeeded by a team: Costa Pilavachi, music administrator, and Paul *Robinson, director of music programming. Robinson resigned in 1980 and Pilavachi continued in sole charge of music. Music presentations have included several series each year under a variety of titles, some carried forward from year to year. In the 1980–81 season the Music Canada Series featured both young and established Canadian performers, the Connoisseur Series offered rarely performed music, the Festival Series was devoted to chamber groups of international standing, the Grand Pianists Series presented noted Canadian and foreign virtuosi, and the Schubert Series concentrated on that composer's songs. In previous years there were Brahms and Schumann festivals, series of recitals by leading violin virtuosi, etc. Among ensembles that have appeared at the centre are the Concentus musicus of Vienna, the Amadeus, Guarneri, Juilliard, Lindsay, and *Orford string quartets, and the Beaux Arts Trio. Among instrumentalists have been the violinists Ida *Haendel, Nathan Milstein, Ruggiero Ricci, and Steven *Staryk, and the pianists Emanuel Ax, Anton *Kuerti, Louis *Lortie, and William *Tritt. Among singers have been the sopranos Elly Ameling, Gundula Janowitz, Jessye Norman, and Margaret Price, the mezzo-sopranos Tatiana Troyanos, Lois *Marshall, and Frederica von Stade, and the contralto Maureen *Forrester. Canadian Sound, a festival of music by Canadian composers and performers was presented in 1976.

BIBLIOGRAPHY

Littler, William. 'Toronto's St. Lawrence Centre now finished,' *CanComp*, 46, Jan 1970

Moore, Mavor. 'St. Lawrence Centre,' *OpCan*, vol 11, Feb 1970

Doherty, Tom. 'Building the magic box,' *PfAC*, vol 10, Fall 1973

Littler, William. 'Two men of note follow in Kraemer's footsteps,' *Toronto Star*, 16 Jun 1979

CF

St Lawrence Hall. Toronto civic building which served in the mid-19th century as the centre of the city's musical life. It was designed in a neoclassical style by the Toronto architect William Thomas and opened in 1850. Located on the southwest corner of King and Jarvis streets, it was attached by a market annex to the city hall at Front and Jarvis. The four-storey St Lawrence Hall included ground-level stores and upper-level offices. A third-floor auditorium, 30 m by 12 m, seated 1000 for concerts and speeches. A raked balcony at the north end served as a speaker's platform, and a thrust stage was located at the south end. Musical activity in the hall included recitals by Jenny Lind (1851), Ole Bull (1853), Adelina Patti (1853, 1860), and Sigismund Thalberg (1857), presentations by the Toronto Vocal Music Society and *Toronto Philharmonic Society, minstrel shows, and, later, Gilbert & Sullivan productions by Upper Canada College students. In the late 19th century, however, new halls more conveniently located brought about a decline in the use of St Lawrence Hall.

In 1967, as a Toronto centennial project, the building was restored, and the auditorium came into use again for social functions and chamber music concerts. The building also houses the administrative offices and rehearsal rooms of the National Ballet of Canada.

BIBLIOGRAPHY

Arthur, Eric. *Toronto: No Mean City* (Toronto 1964)

Ontario Association of Architects. *St. Lawrence Hall* (Toronto 1967)

'Toronto's pre-confederation music societies'

MH, MM

SAINT-MARCOUX, Micheline Coulombe (b Coulombe, Micheline). Composer, teacher, b Notre-Dame-de-la-Doré, near Roberval, Que, 9 Aug 1938; B MUS (Montreal) 1962, premiere prix composition (CMM) 1967. She studied piano and harmony 1956–8 with François *Brassard in Jonquière, Que, and worked 1960–3 with Yvonne *Hubert (piano) and Claude *Champagne (composition) at the *École Vincent-d'Indy. She then became a pupil of Gilles *Tremblay and Clermont *Pépin at the *CMM. Awarded the *Prix d'Europe for composition in 1967, she lived 1968–70 in Paris, studying electronic music with the Groupe de recherches musicales of the ORTF and taking courses with Pierre Schaeffer at the Paris Cons. The Groupe de recherches musicales commissioned her to write a work, *Arksalalartôq*, which was premiered 26 Feb 1971 in Paris. While she was in Paris she studied privately with Gilbert Amy and Jean-Pierre Guézec. In 1969, with five young composers from different countries, she founded the Groupe international de musique électroacoustique de Paris (GIMEP). She took part until 1973 in its concerts in Europe, South America, and Canada. Two of her works, *Bernavir* and *Trakadie*, were premiered in 1970 by GIMEP. *Makazoti*, commissioned in 1971 by the CBC IS, originally was conceived for the Swingle Singers and was the first of a set of three vocal works influenced by the composer's obvious desire to return to her roots.

Coulombe Saint-Marcoux returned to Quebec in 1971 and formed the Ensemble Polycousmie with the Montreal percussionists Guy *Lachapelle, Pierre *Béluse, and Robert Leroux in an attempt to integrate electronic techniques with percussion and dance. From this association came *Épisodes*. With her three associates, for the series 'Sons et images,' she recorded a program telecast by the CBC in November 1972; she recorded another, utilizing *ondes Martenot, in April 1973 with Jean *Laurendeau. In April 1972, with Jacques Thériault, she organized three evenings of electronic music in a gallery in Montreal's Old City; the dance companies Groupe de la Place royale and Groupe Nouvelle Aire participated. In 1977 she was a guest on several programs in the CBC TV series 'Femme d'aujourd'hui'; one dealt with the treatment of the voice in contemporary music.

Coulombe Saint-Marcoux has received commissions from the *MSO for *Hétéromorphie*, from the CBC Montreal orchestra for *Alchera*, and from the *SMCQ for *Ishuma*, which was presented 14 Nov 1976 on CBC TV as part of a program on three Canadian composers. In addition to her frequent lectures and appearances at professional gatherings, she has been a jury member for several competitions, such as the *CBC National Radio Competition for Young Composers in February 1976. She began teaching at the CMM in 1971. Her works of the late 1970s employed texts by young Quebec composers. By then she had abandoned the serialism of some of her earlier works and was seeking a more original organization of her sound world, often selecting one interval, or several, to serve as basic modules for elaboration within several parameters. Saint-Marcoux was appointed to the boards of *CAPAC and the *CMCentre in 1974. She also is an associate of the centre.

Micheline Coulombe Saint-Marcoux

SELECTED COMPOSITIONS

ORCHESTRA

Modulaire. 1967 (Mtl 1968). Full orch, ondes M. CMCentre

Hétéromorphie. 1970 (Mtl 1970). Full orch. CMCentre

Luminance. 1978 (Thunder Bay 1978). Full orch. CMCentre

CHAMBER

Chanson d'automne (Verlaine). 1963 (rev 1966). Sop (ten), fl, vn, pf or sop (ten), pf. CMCentre

Evocations doranes. 1964. Picc, 3 fl, ob, cl. Ms

Sonata. 1964. Fl, pf. CMCentre

String Quartet. 1966. CMCentre. RCI 363 (*Classical Quar of Mtl)

Équation I. 1967. 2 guit. CMCentre

Séquences. 1968 (rev 1973). 2 ondes M, perc. CMCentre

Trakadie. 1970. Tape, perc. CMCentre. RCI/CAPAC RM-222 vol 13 (*Lachapelle)

Makazoti (N. Audet, G. Marsolais). 1971. 8 vs, fl, cl, tpt, trb, vn, db, perc. CMCentre

Épisode II. 1972. 3 perc. CMCentre

Alchera (N. Brossard). 1973. Mezzo, fl, cl, trb, vn, vc, 2 perc, hpd (Hammond org), tape, lights. CMCentre

Ishuma (Inuit texts, P. Chamberland). 1974. Sop, trb, vn, db, 3 perc, ondes M, Hammond org. CMCentre. RCI 422 (*SMCQ)

Genesis. 1975. Wind quin. Arch 1978. Soc nouvelle d'enregistrement SNE-501 (*Que WW Quin)

Miroirs. 1976. Hpd, tape. CMCentre

Moments. 1977. Sop, fl, va, vc. CMCentre

PIANO

Doréanes. 1961. GVT 1969. ('Brouillard épais') Dom S-69002 (*Mould)

Variations. 1963. Ms

Kaleidoscope. 1964. CMCentre

Assemblages. 1969. CMCentre. RCI 396 (*Petrowska)

TAPE

Bernavir (N. Audet). 1970

Arksalalartôq; Contrastances; and *Moustières*. All 1971

Zones. 1972. RCI 373

Also music for the film *Tel qu'en Lemieux* (1973) and 1 work for choir and 6 perfs, *Wing Tra La* (1964)

WRITINGS

'Reflections of a young composer,' *CanComp*, 33, Oct 1968

'L'influence de la machine sur la musique du XXe siècle,' Montreal *Le Devoir*, 27 Jun 1970

'À la recherche d'une nouvelle "écoute",' ibid, 5 Apr 1972

BIBLIOGRAPHY

Thériault, Jacques. 'On devrait faire plus confiance à l'auditeur,' Montreal *Le Devoir*, 13 Apr 1970

'Coulombe-Saint-Marcoux ... a young composer of great talent,' *CanComp*, 51, Jun 1970

'An avant-garde composer's insights into her career,' ibid, 89, Mar 1974

Pilon, Denise. 'Musique du Canada à l'Espace Cardin,' *CMB*, 8, Spring–Summer 1974

CMCentre. *Compositeurs au Québec: Micheline Coulombe Saint-Marcoux* (Montreal 1975)

Lord, Catherine. 'Pourquoi la création est-elle si difficile pour les femmes?' *Châtelaine*, Jun 1975

Potvin, Gilles. 'Micheline Coulombe Saint-Marcoux,' *Contemporary Canadian Composers / Compositeurs canadiens contemporains*

(JT)

The St Mary Magdalene Singers. Choir of 25, organized in 1939 by Healey *Willan at the Church of St Mary Magdalene, Toronto, to sing the unaccompanied choral literature. The church's two choirs, Ritual and Gallery, had given recitals together throughout Ontario since Willan's appointment as precentor in 1921. To the singers of the Gallery choir he now added the remaining members of his Tudor Singers (formed in 1933 with 22 voices to perform madrigals and balletts of England's Tudor period – Byrd, Gibbons, Weelkes, Dowland, etc – and reduced to 10 voices in 1938, to sing a repertoire broadened to include di Lasso, Vittoria, and Palestrina). Besides performing in church the St Mary Magdalene Singers continued the Tudor Singers' tradition of *Hart House Christmas concerts and gave secular concerts as well. In September 1945 they won great praise for two recitals at Town Hall, New York. After Willan's death in 1968 the singers continued under the direction of Giles *Bryant, who augmented their established repertoire of 16th- and 17th-century music and works by Willan with music of the 20th century. As the Choirs of St Mary Magdalene Church, they also give recitals of plainsong and liturgical music. In 1975 Robert Bell succeeded Bryant.

DISCOGRAPHY

Faire Is the Heaven: Vaughan Williams – et al. Bryant cond. (1975). SMM 7504

Healey Willan at St. Mary Magdalene's. Bryant cond, Gartshore org. (1973). SMM 0002

Hodie: Motets and Carols for the Advent of the Christ Child. Bryant cond. (1972). Church of St Mary Magdalene QC 982

Music for Holy Week: Willan – Weelkes – Victoria – Tallis – Palestrina. Bryant cond. (1974). SMM 7403

Music for Mass and Evensong: Willan – Byrd – Farrant. Bryant cond, Gartshore org. 1971. Choirs of the Church of St Mary Magdalene J 10122B

Rorate coeli: Plainsong for Advent and Christmas. Bryant cond, Gartshore org. 1975. SMM 7506

Willan *Brebeuf and His Brethren*. Gallery Choirs of St Mary Magdalene and Timothy Eaton Memorial, Ouchterlony org, Cavall narr. 1967. TBC Recording Ltd

Willan *Missa brevis No. 1*: 'Ave verum corpus'; 'Faire in Face'; 'Hail Gladdening Light'; 'In Youth Is Pleasure'; 'Rise Up My Love'; 'I Beheld Her ... ' Willan cond. RCI 11 (MDr)

SAKOS, Kenneth (b Tsakos, Kyriabos). Tenor, b Neapolis, Laconia, Greece ca 1903, d Kitchener, Ont, 26 Feb 1960. He arrived in Renfrew, Ont, as a young man and settled in Kitchener in 1925. He studied there with J.G. Galloway and in Toronto with Giuseppe *Carboni. He studied further in Italy and sang 1929–34 in Italian and Greek opera houses. After his Toronto debut in 1935, Lawrence *Mason hailed him as the best Canadian tenor since Edward *Johnson. Sakos toured in 1936 with the *San Carlo Opera Company, sang 1937–8 with the Chicago Civic Opera Co, and appeared in concerts, but in 1939 he retired to assist his brother in running a restaurant in Kitchener. His voice has been described as lyrical, easy, sweet, and brilliant. His opera scores and books were donated to the Kitchener Public Library in 1972. HK

SALEMKA, Irene (m McGillivray). Soprano, b Steinbach, near Winnipeg, 3 Oct 1931; hon LL D (Saskatchewan) 1972. Her voice studies with Marjorie Cathcart in Weyburn, near Regina, Sask, Lloyd *Slind and Mme A. *Birkett in Regina, and Fred J. Smith in Montreal led to awards on CBC radio's *'Opportunity Knocks' (1951) and *'Singing Stars of Tomorrow' (1953). She made a *COC debut in 1953 as Cio-Cio-San in *Madama Butterfly* and a *Montreal Festival debut in 1952 as Juliette in Gounod's *Roméo et Juliette* opposite Raoul *Jobin. She completed her training under Hans Löwlein in Germany and has returned occasionally to Canada, singing with the COC as Susanna in *The Marriage of Figaro* (1960) and Anna Glawari in *The Merry Widow* (1973), performing on CBC radio and TV, and appearing as Olympia, Giulietta, Antonia, and Stella in the *Vancouver Opera Assn's *The Tales of Hoffman* (1961) and as Donna Elvira in the *Stratford Festival's *Don Giovanni* (1966).

Salemka was a soloist itinerantly with the opera companies of New Orleans (1955), Washington (1956), Basel (1956), Sadler's Wells (1956–7), Covent Garden (1963), Rome (1963), Vienna (1963), and Hamburg (1963), with the Bolshoi Theatre in Moscow (1963), and at various European festivals including the Edinburgh (1961) and was also a leading soprano (1956–64) with the Frankfurt State Opera. There she appeared in such roles as Cio-Cio-San, Mélisande, Lauretta in *Gianni Schicchi*, Anne in *The Rake's Progress*, Cleopatra in *Julius Caesar*, Sophie in *Der Rosenkavalier*, Pamina in *The Magic Flute*, and Concepción in *L'Heure espagnole* during her tenure, and returned as Micaela in *Carmen* (1966). She also sang with the Frankfurt SO under Solti and Hindemith and appeared in the German films *Madame Dubarry* (1965) and *The Merry Widow* (1965). Salemka's lyric soprano was described in *The Times* of London as 'a voice of rare quality, haunting yet resolute, mellow yet ringing and always perfectly controlled.'

DISCOGRAPHY

Aus dem Essener Musikleben: Rameau arias. Essen Opera House O, König cond. 1964. GEMA 062019

Mozart *Don Giovanni*: excerpts. Watson, Streich, Salemka [Donna Elvira], Haeflinger, Fischer-Dieskau, Berry, RSO Berlin, Löwlein cond. 1964. DG 136415

Musical Soirée with John van Kesteren. Concertgebouw O. 1967. Philips 844046

Timber!!: excerpts. CBC orch, Chotem cond. 1954. RCI 119 (WLB)

Salle Claude-Champagne. Auditorium of the *École Vincent-d'Indy, located in Outremont, Montreal. Dedicated to Claude *Champagne, it was inaugurated 22 Nov 1964. With the participation of the pianist Guy *Bourassa, an orchestra made up of teachers from Quebec conservatories, and the school's own choir, this first concert was devoted to five works by Champagne: *Hercule et Omphale*, the *Concerto* for piano and orchestra, and *Symphonie gaspésienne* conducted by Roland *Leduc, and *Suite canadienne* and *Altitude* conducted by Rémus *Tzincoca. In the intermission a bust of Sister *Marie-Stéphane, the founder of the École, by the Canadian sculptor Sylvia Daoust was unveiled.

The plan for the hall was prepared by Geza Häffner. The main floor seats 990, with an additional 317 in the balcony and 50 in the two boxes. Electrically controlled sliding curtains make it possible to divide the hall in two. The hall has a large Ruffatti organ with 60 stops, a radio control booth, a recording room, an audio control centre, etc. The sound may be varied and controlled as desired by means of movable wooden panels. The ceiling above the stage has three acoustic baffles to improve the sound of the organ. Designed for use by the school's advanced students, the hall also is leased to organizations such as the CBC and the *Montreal International Competition.

In 1980 the building of the École Vincent-d'Indy, and with it the Salle Claude-Champagne, was purchased by the U of Montreal. CV

Salvation Army / Armée du Salut. Religious and charitable organization founded in London by William Booth in 1865. The Salvation Army commenced its evangelical work in Canada in 1882, and as early as 1883 it used bands of wind instruments, drums, tambourines, fifes, fiddles, and concertinas in any combination for open-air meetings, indoor services, park concerts, and parades. Over the years the bands have been standardized along the lines of the British brass band: cornets, flugelhorn, tenor and baritone saxhorns, euphoniums, trombones, and bombardons. The early Salvationists also sang vigorously for their open-air ministry and often accompanied their songs on English concertinas. Hamilton, Kingston, and Toronto were important centres of the army's musical activity in the early days. The first Canadian Staff Band was formed in Toronto in 1889. By 1914 it had become known for the high standard of its playing. Tragically, most of its members were lost in the *Empress of Ireland* disaster of that year. It was not until 1969 that the Canadian Staff Band was reconstituted, with full-time officers from national headquarters and laymen from central Ontario corps bands.

The Salvation Army band movement in Canada probably reached its peak during the 1930s, when well-trained ensembles could be found attached to most corps (congregations), even in small towns. These bands often included English immigrants. Many brass players in Canada have been products of the movement; during World Wars I and II Salvationist musicians were prominent in the bands of the Canadian armed forces, and a number of Salvation Army bands also functioned as militia units.

Outstanding conductors who were encouraged and developed within the movement include Norman Audoire at Toronto's Earlscourt Corps ca 1927–30 and at the Montreal Citadel ca 1930–60, Alfred Pearce with Toronto's Dovercourt Corps 1917–31 and the Metropolitan Silver Band 1931–49, and Henry Merritt at the Winnipeg Citadel 1930–45. Eric *Abbott also conducted Salvation Army bands in St John's, Nfld. Canadian composers represented in the band music journals include Norman Audoire, Morley *Calvert, James Merritt, Percy Merritt, and Kenneth Rawlins. During his term as Territorial Music Secretary (see below), Rawlins produced the first *Canadian Band Journal* (Toronto 1954, 1963, 1965).

The development of choirs, or 'songster brigades,' dates back to 1892. While they have not received the widespread recognition accorded the bands, songster brigades represent an important branch of the army's music. Notable leaders have been Ben Smith at the Peterborough Temple 1926–72, Ed Judge at the London Citadel 1940–70, and Eric Sharp in Toronto with the Danforth Corps 1940–77 and at Agincourt thereafter.

In the late 19th century the Salvationists' practice of setting 'heavenly words to secular tunes' gave their music a popular appeal which drew large crowds and attracted many converts. A leading exponent of this practice was Jack Addie, who left England and settled in Ontario in the late 19th century. One of the army's most colourful pioneers, he reportedly wrote more than 100 such songs. Many amateur songwriters published their works in the magazine *Canadian War Cry* (Toronto 1884–), which functioned partly as a weekly song sheet. Early contributors included Tom Mitchell, Aggie Cowan, William Stacie, and Annie Fry. Another Canadian publication was *The Salvation Soldiers' Songbook* (Toronto nd), a book of words without music. Music by Salvationist composers from many countries has been published at the army's international headquarters in London. Among the first Canadian choral compositions to be published in *The Musical Salvationist* (London 1866–) were works by Sarah Graham of Lindsay in 1886, Gustavius Grozinsky of Edmonton in 1895, and William Hawley of Calgary in 1895. A few songs by Canadians appeared in the international collection *The Song Book of the Salvation Army*, published first in London in 1930. A Canadian supplement, *Songs of Faith* (Toronto 1971), includes many compositions by Sidney Cox (1887–1975), at one time a Salvation Army officer in western Canada. Another notable Canadian contributor to Salvation Army choral music was John Wells (1903–78) of Vancouver.

The Salvation Army provides music instruction through its junior bands and junior choirs, the latter known as 'singing companies.' In addition, summer music camps (pioneered by Alfred Keith in 1940) have become an important aspect of the army's musical training. In 1977 nearly 1300 students attended the music camps established in almost every province (eg, the National Music Camp at Jackson's Point, Ont). Although youth activities in the 1960s incorporated popular music, using small combos for accompaniment, the older hymns and marching tunes have continued to dominate programs and services.

Less visible on street corners in the 1970s, army musicians nevertheless have continued to provide music for hospitals, prisons, and other institutions. After World War II the army took an increasing interest in festivals, musicals, and other sorts of entertainment, and this sophisticated the repertoire. In 1955 the position of Territorial Music Secretary was created to ensure the coordination of all musical activities including tours, recordings, festivals, broadcasts, and curricula for the music camps. Incumbents have been Kenneth Rawlins 1955–68 and Norman Bearcroft 1968–76, succeeded by Robert Redhead in 1976. Bands and songsters frequently participate in exchanges, and the Agincourt Songsters, the Earlscourt Band, the Canadian Staff Band, the Danforth Songsters, and the London Citadel Band all have toured in Britain. In addition, the last three have made private recordings. In 1978, in Canada and Bermuda (the available official figures were combined), there were 115 senior bands with a total membership of 2257, 79 youth bands comprising 891 members, 2580 songsters, and 1734 singing company members.

BIBLIOGRAPHY

Avery, Gordon. *Companion to the Song Book of the Salvation Army* (London 1961)

Boon, Brindley. *Play the Music, Play!* (London 1966)

Royan, Don. 'Salvation Army Band,' *Bands By the Bow*, compiled by Norman Draper (Calgary 1975)

MacGuire, Bee. 'Sound the trumpet! Tell the message!' *Montreal Scene*, 13 Dec 1975

Moyles, R.G. *The Blood and Fire in Canada* (Toronto 1977)

JPG

SAMPSON, Peggie (b Margaret). Viola da gambist, cellist, teacher, b Edinburgh 16 Feb 1912, naturalized Canadian 1973; B MUS (Edinburgh) 1932, Licence de Concert (École normale, Paris) 1932, D MUS (Edinburgh) 1961. She began cello lessons at eight with Ruth Waddell in Edinburgh and continued with Guilhermina Suggia in London and Portugal. She was a pupil 1929–32 and teaching assistant 1937–44 of Donald Francis Tovey at the U of Edinburgh and studied summers 1930–4 in Paris with Diran Alexanian (cello) at the École normale and with Nadia Boulanger (theory) privately. During the 1930s she gave recitals in England and Holland, performed the Elgar *Concerto* under Tovey, and played in the Glyndebourne Festival orchestra under Fritz Busch. She also studied intermittently 1935–7 with Emanuel Feuermann and ca 1946 with Pablo Casals in Prades. She was a freelance cellist 1944–51 in London, giving recitals and playing in the Carter Trio.

Peggie Sampson

Sampson emigrated to Canada in 1951 to teach theory, history, and cello at the *U of Manitoba and remained in that post for 20 years. She also taught cello privately in Winnipeg and in 1962 received a special grant from the U of Manitoba to set up an experimental class for unusually gifted children. (Several participants in this class – Stephen Cira, Laurie Duncan, Mayda Narvey, Dace Stauvers – subsequently entered the profession.) Her cello pupils in Winnipeg included Gisela *Depkat, John Derksen, Kenneth *Murphy, Paul Pulford, and Lynn Rudiak.

Sampson was extremely active as a cellist in Winnipeg during the 1950s and 1960s, appearing as solo recitalist, as a member of the Corydon Trio (with Lea *Foli and Gerald *Stanick), and in various ensembles for the University Chamber Music Group. After one such concert, describing a performance by Sampson and the pianist Mario *Bernardi of Brahms' *Sonata in F*, Kenneth *Winters praised the cellist's 'great range, subtlety and command' (*Winnipeg Free Press*, 15 Jan 1963).

Around 1960 Sampson began to develop an interest in the viola da gamba and collaborated with Christine *Mather in founding the *Manitoba University Consort (1963–70). By the end of the 1960s the gamba had supplanted the cello as her main instrument. In 1970 she joined the staff at *York U, Toronto, to teach theory and develop a program for viols. Probably the foremost viola da gambist in Canada, she has been sought increasingly for recitals and for performance of the obbligatos in the Bach *Passions*, playing the latter with several Ontario choirs and in 1973 in a TV performance in Madrid. Invited three times to the Aldeburgh Festival, she gave a recital there with Peter Williams in 1972, participated in a Handel program with George Malcolm and his singers in 1974, and gave a recital in the Maltings, with Malcolm at the harpsichord and her pupil Christel Thielmann playing second gamba, in 1976. She also appeared in the Connoisseur Series (1975) at *St Lawrence Centre, Toronto, in a concert billed as 'Peggie Sampson and Friends.' The friends included her Hart House Consort of Viols (Christel Thielmann, Rosamund Morley, Alison Mackay, and others, a professional group which grew out of her York U classes) and the New York harpsichordist Kenneth Cooper. With the consort she gave a series of recitals 1976–7 at *Hart House, U of Toronto, and during the 1977–8 season she appeared as a soloist at York U, Wilfrid Laurier U, Guelph U, and the U of British Columbia and in the Toronto Spring Festival. She taught 1973, 1974, and 1975 at the U of Victoria Summer School and, after retiring in 1977 from York U, taught part-time at *Wilfrid Laurier U. She also played and taught at the 1977 Conclave of the Viola da Gamba Society of America in Baltimore.

Sampson has premiered works of S.C. *Eckhardt-Gramatté (*Duo concertante* for cello and piano, 1959), Bernard *Naylor (*On Hearing Mrs. Arabella Hunt Singing*, 1970), Murray *Adaskin (*Two pieces*, 1972), David *Rosenboom (*The Seduction of Sapientia*, 1975) and Rudolf *Komorous (*At Your Memory the Transparent Tears Fall like Molten Lead*, 1976). All save the Eckhardt-Gramatté were commissioned by Sampson – the Naylor privately, the others with *Canada Council grants – to pioneer a modern repertoire for the viola da gamba. In 1976 she formed Quatre en Concert – Christine *Harvey (soprano), Michael Purves-Smith (oboe), Deryck Aird (violin) – to perform music of the 17th and 18th centuries. They toured Ontario in 1976, from Montreal to Saskatoon in 1977, and Holland in 1978.

WRITINGS

'Creative music for children,' *Sharps and Flats*, vol 3, Jan, Mar, Jun 1963

DISCOGRAPHY

Eckhardt-Gramatté *Duo concertante; Suite No. 6* – Tovey *Elegiac Variations*. Irons pf. (Ca 1966). RCI 224/RCA CCS-1018

Handel – Bach – Locke. Redekop-Penner hpd. 1969. CBC SM-110

Ortiz – de Chambonnières – Schenk – Cabezon – Couperin – anon. Redekop-Fink hpd. 1974. CBC SM-229

Ortiz – Schenk – Buxtehude – Marais – Bach – Bloch. Redekop-Penner hpd. 1968. CBC SM-69

Rosenboom *The Seduction of Sapientia* – M. Adaskin *Two Pieces for Solo Viola da Gamba* – Sampson *Improvisation on a Theme from Tobias Hume*. 1976–7. Music Gallery Editions MGE7

Works for Viola da Gamba and Harpsichord: Marin Marais and Tobias Hume. S. Shapiro hpd. (Ca 1977). Orion ORS 74162

BIBLIOGRAPHY

Winters, Kenneth. 'Whither the music student,' *Winnipeg Free Press*, 30 Jun 1962

'Dr. Peggie Sampson,' *Sharps and Flats*, vol 5, Apr 1965

FILMOGRAPHY

Playing the Viol (York U 1972) KW (BN)

Sam Slick. A comic chamber opera in three scenes, for eight voices and medium orchestra. It was composed in 1967 by Kelsey *Jones to Rosabelle Jones' libretto based on Thomas Chandler Haliburton's *The Clockmaker, or the Sayings and Doings of Samuel Slick of Slickville* (Halifax 1836), the first English-language Canadian book successful abroad. Haliburton's fictitious Yankee, the unscrupulous Sam Slick, first appeared in a Halifax newspaper in 1836 and was a device for poking fun at Nova Scotia. The opera relates the comic adventures of Slick (tenor) and his companion and casual employer The Squire (bass) as they roam the province. Three other performers sing multiple roles. A CBC centennial commission, *Sam Slick* was premiered from Halifax 5 Sep 1967 in a broadcast performance conducted by Ettore *Mazzoleni, with Robert Peters (Slick) and Maurice *Brown (The Squire).

BIBLIOGRAPHY

'Samuel Slick of Slickville hero of new comic opera,' *CanComp*, 22, Oct 1967

CF

SAMSON, (Joseph Jean) Marc. Critic, b Lauzon, near Quebec City, 14 Oct 1929. After taking piano lessons at the Collège de Lévis from Father Alphonse *Tardif he studied at the *CMQ ca 1948–50 with Hélène *Landry and Henri *Vallières (piano), Séverin *Moisse (solfège), and Father Tardif (harmony). He joined the Quebec City newspaper *Le Soleil* in 1964 as reporter and music critic. His writings may be found in *La Vie musicale au Canada français* (1964), *Esquisses du Canada français* (1966), *The New Grove Dictionary, Sohlmans Musiklexikon*, and *EMC*, and have appeared in the periodicals **Canada Music Book, *Musicanada, Variations*, and *Actualité*. He has taken part in several CBC radio and TV programs. He is a member of the Music Critics' Assn. He married the pianist Louise *Forand. AP

SANBORN, Eddie (Edmund William). Conductor, violinist, b Farnham Centre, southeast of Montreal, 27 Jan 1896. Raised in Barre, Vt, where he took up the violin at 8 and led a band in high school, he joined the orchestra of Oscar Goodfriend at the *Auditorium in Quebec City at 17 and succeeded Goodfriend as conductor at 18. After serving 1919–21 as concertmaster at the Princess Theatre in Montreal, he was the orchestra leader 1921–38 at Loew's Theatre, Montreal, and conducted for many leading entertainers of the day. Also in the 1920s he began a 30-year radio career, conducting orchestras on CKAC (including the one heard on 'Étoiles de France') and on CFCF. Under the pseudonym Philias Malouin he played country and folk music on French-language radio. Sanborn also led a string quartet at Montreal's Ritz-Carlton Hotel in the late 1930s, conducted an orchestra on the *SS Tadoussac*, and contracted orchestras for summer resorts. After service as music director of **The Army Show* during World War II, he resumed his radio career and conducted orchestras in the Montreal nightclubs Café de l'Est and Quartier Latin.

BIBLIOGRAPHY
Wardwell, William. 'Fame was a fiddle ...' *Montreal Star*, 6 Jan 1978 MM

The San Carlo Opera Company. Touring organization founded in New York in 1913 by the Italian-American impresario Fortune Gallo (1878–1970). Until its disbandment in the early 1950s, the company – 100 strong, including 30 instrumentalists – toured annually in the USA and Canada, visiting cities and towns poorly served by other companies. For some years it was the only professional opera heard in many Canadian cities. Although it has not been possible to trace the San Carlo's first appearance in Canada, the company visited Toronto frequently after 1914 and Vancouver annually after 1919, and appeared also in Montreal, Winnipeg, Hamilton, Ont, and elsewhere. A typical bill for a week at Montreal's *St-Denis Theatre (23–8 Oct 1922) offered *Salomé, Lohengrin, Faust, Tosca, Aida*, and *Madama Butterfly*. Among the Canadian artists who appeared with the company – some over extended periods of time, some for one or two guest performances – were Elizabeth Campbell (under the pseudonym Maddalena Carreno), Pauline *Donalda, Margaret George, Mary *Henderson, Raoul *Jobin, Jeanne *Pengelly, Simone *Quesnel, and Joseph Royer (sometimes under the pseudonym Giuseppe Battistini). Another Gallo venture, the Fortune Gallo English Opera Co, established to perform light opera in English – mainly Gilbert & Sullivan – lasted only two seasons, 1920–2, but finished one tour which included performances in Montreal and Winnipeg.

BIBLIOGRAPHY
Gallo, Fortune T. *Lucky Rooster* (New York 1967) JBM

SANDERS, Herbert. Organist, choir conductor, composer, teacher, writer, pianist, b Wolverhampton, England, 20 Sep 1878, d Montreal 18 May 1938; ARCM 1896, FRCO 1900, D MUS (McGill) 1912. A pupil of Charles Swinnerton Heap and Charles W. Perkins (organ) and of Charles H. Kitson (theory), he held organ posts in England at Camphill Presbyterian Church, Birmingham, and St Mary's Methodist Church, Truro, Cornwall. He was an orchestral violinist as well. He moved to Canada in 1907 and was organist for a year at Chalmers' Presbyterian Church, Guelph, Ont, and 1908–29 at Dominion Methodist Church, Ottawa. He gave organ recitals across Canada and was regarded as an excellent accompanist. He also directed the Ottawa Oratorio Society and served as president of the Ottawa Arts and Letters Club and as music critic for the *Ottawa Journal*. He taught at the Canadian Cons and privately. His pupils included Kenneth *Meek, Charles *O'Neill, and Bill *Richards.

In 1929 Sanders accepted a unique position as music director of the new *Tudor Hall in the J.A. Ogilvy Department Store in Montreal. There, until his death, he gave regular noon-time organ recitals and arranged for appearances by other artists. He was organist in the 1930s at Westmount Park Melville United Church (later Westmount Park United).

Sanders composed many sacred songs, anthems, and organ pieces. Twice he was awarded the Clemson Gold Medal for composition by the American Guild of Organists. His patriotic song 'We Are Coming, Mother Britain' was published by McKechnie in 1916. His other publishers included *Anglo-Canadian, Boston Music, Ditson, Weekes, and Josef Williams. He was associate music editor of *The Methodist Hymn and Tune Book* (Toronto 1917) and contributed several tunes to that publication. He wrote articles for many musical journals (*Etude, Musical Quarterly, The American Organist*) and was editor of the CCO (*RCCO) bulletin, which appeared 1928–ca 1933 in *Musical Canada*. He was president of the CCO 1932–3. The *NL of C has a collection of his manuscripts.

BIBLIOGRAPHY
Palmer, T.J. 'Dr. Herbert Sanders taking over new, important organist post in Montreal,' *MCan*, vol 10, Jul 1929
Hamilton, H.C. 'Dr. Herbert Sanders,' *MCan*, vol 12, May 1931 FH

SANDS, Joyce (b Feldtmann, m Hornyansky). Cellist, teacher, b Clairmont, Western Autralia, 6 Mar 1902; naturalized Canadian 1935; LRAM 1919. Raised in England she studied cello there with Hélène Dolmetsch and 1920–4 in Belgium at the Royal Flemish Cons, Antwerp, with Arnold Godene. She also studied theory and composition privately in Brussels with Joseph Jongen. As a member of the Buyssc String Quartet she toured Belgium. She also gave some recitals in Europe before moving in 1929 to Canada to join the newly formed Harisay String Quartet – Vino Harisay and Murray *Adaskin (violins), Tom Brennand (viola) – in Toronto.

Sands gave her first solo recital 10 Jan 1930 at *Hart House and was soloist in Saint-Saëns' *Concerto in A Minor* 2 Dec 1930 with the *TSO. Besides teaching at the *TCM she played 1931–6 in the TSO, organized the Fireside Music Club for chamber concerts in private homes, and founded and played in the Arcorda Trio. She lived 1936–8 in Capetown, South Africa, and briefly in England, where she appeared in recital at Wigmore Hall before returning to Toronto in 1939. She was a member again 1940–5 of the TSO and a teacher at the TCM and played in the early 1940s with the *Conservatory String Quartet. In 1952 she moved to Ottawa, where she was the cellist 1953–4 with the Carleton String Quartet, principal 1957–9 of the *Ottawa Philharmonic, and a member 1958–9 of the New Chamber Music Ensemble. She established another Fireside Music Club and added a concert series for young people in 1965. The club continued until the early 1970s. Her Somerset Chamber Music Club (1975–6) was planned along similar lines. FH

Sängerfeste (singers' festivals). Occasions organized to perpetuate German singing and social traditions. In Canada the gatherings have been centred mainly in communities of southern and western Ontario. The German cultural heritage of Waterloo County, Ont, was firmly established by immigration patterns of the 19th century (see Germany). Not content to exercise their love of singing only in the home, church, or school, settlers in these smaller urban communities had founded male and/or mixed choirs by the 1860s. Athletic clubs (Turnvereine), modelled on those in Germany, organized festivals of gymnastics, theatre, choral music, and dance. Emphasis on song soon lessened the importance of the other events.

Berlin (renamed Kitchener, 1916), Ont, was the site of the first major Sängerfest in Canada, 6–9 Aug 1862. Towns and cities represented were Berlin and Waterloo, the neighbouring communities of New Hamburg, Phillipsburg, Wellesley, and Bridgeport, and Toronto, Buffalo, and Detroit. In addition to performances by the 200 singers, athletic and dramatic events, band concerts, a picnic, and a gala ball were held. The success prompted another festival in Waterloo the following year. On this occasion Berlin and Waterloo formed a choir of 200 voices, which joined with other guests and four bands to entertain 2000 people. The German Club of Hamilton mounted a festival in 1866 on the plains of Burlington. Choirs from Toronto, Buffalo, Erie, Pa, and elsewhere sang for the 5000 visitors.

The first German-Canadian Choir Federation (Deutsch-kanadischer Sängerbund) was founded at a meeting 12 Nov 1873 in Hamilton. Thereafter, the larger Sängerfeste were to be organized by the federation rather than by individual clubs. A new Canadian Choir Federation, formed 24 May 1893 in Berlin, consisted of three choral groups during the years 1904–14: Concordia (Berlin), Liederkranz (Toronto), and the Male Choir (Elmira). German-Canadian choirs were active also in the Peninsula Choir Federation, a US organization (founded in Michigan in 1887) which changed its name to the Lake Erie Choir Federation to allow participation by Ontario and New York choirs. This federation held festivals in Ontario at Waterloo (1890, 1902), Hamilton (1891), and Berlin (1898). The principal song and music festivals held in Canada were at Waterloo (1874, 1885, 1902), Berlin (1875–77, 1879, 1886, 1897, 1898, 1906), Berlin and Hamilton (1890), Berlin and Waterloo (1912), Toronto (1895, 1900, 1907), Bowmanville (1884), Guelph (1887), Port Elgin (1888), Sarnia (1894), Erie, Pa, (1889), Bridgeport (1904), and Elmira (1905).

The Concordia Club of Berlin (founded in 1873) was a focus for the life of German song in North America. It was host for three of the most spectacular of the Sängerfeste. In 1875 the largest festival of its kind to that time lasted three days and attracted 15 choirs – from Montreal, Toronto, London, Detroit, Chicago, Rochester, Buffalo, and elsewhere – and 10,000 visitors to the city. At the 1879 festival, 500 choristers entertained 12,000 people; English-Canadian choirs also appeared. The 1886 festival was deemed to be one of the most impressive ever held in North America. In three days five full concerts were given, among them a performance of *The Creation*.

The coming of World War I and the rise of anti-

The Sängerfest in Berlin (now Kitchener), Ont, 1875

German sentiments caused a suspension of the activities of the local institutions which had sustained the song festivals. Although individual clubs revived after World War II the enthusiasm for German-Canadian choral traditions – eg, festivals in Kitchener in 1955 (the city's centenary) and 1959 – the success of initial attempts to re-establish the former popularity and scope of the Sängerfest have been hindered by social change and the reorientation of leisure in the postwar period.

See also Kitchener-Waterloo; Theodore Zoellner.

BIBLIOGRAPHY

Breithaupt, W.H. 'The Saengerfest of 1875,' *22nd Annual Report of the Waterloo Historical Society* (Kitchener 1935)

Staebler, H.L. 'Random notes on music of nineteenth-century Berlin, Ontario,' *37th Annual Report of the Waterloo Historical Society* (Kitchener 1949)

Leibbrandt, D. Gottlieb. 'One hundred years of Concordia,' *Waterloo County Historical Society*, vol 61, 1973

'100 Jahre Concordia,' *Nachrichten* (Kitchener 1973) (WHK)

SANTIAGO, Armando. Composer, conductor, teacher, administrator, b Lisbon 18 Jun 1932, naturalized Canadian 1972; premier prix music history (Lisbon Cons) 1954, premier prix composition (Lisbon Cons) 1960. After lessons in singing and piano he studied conducting with Hans Münch in Lisbon and Franco Ferrara in Siena. In 1960 he went to Paris to study the techniques of musique concrète with Pierre Schaeffer in the research service of the ORTF. On grants from the governments of Portugal and Italy he worked 1962–4 in Rome with Boris Porena privately and with Goffredo Petrassi at the Accademia Santa Cecilia, obtaining a diploma for advanced studies in composition. Later, he taught theory and composition and conducted the orchestra classes in Lisbon.

Arriving in Quebec in 1968, Santiago became a teacher at the Cons de Trois-Rivières and served 1974–8 as director. During the 1977–8 season he conducted the *CBC Quebec Chamber Orchestra in a concert of his own works. He has composed a *Suite* for bassoon and piano (1960), *Soneto de Camões* for baritone and string orchestra (1966), a *Sinfonia* (1966, written for the JM) *Sonata 1968* (commissioned by the U of Lisbon), *Simetrias* (1970), *Prismes* (1970), *Heterogenia-Movimento per 32 solisti* (1971, commissioned by the Gulbenkian Foundation of Lisbon), *Undecassônia* (1975), and other works, for orchestra and for solo instruments. In 1962 he wrote the score for Ernesto de Sousa's film *Dom Roberto*. Santiago became director of the *CMQ in 1978. He is a member of CAPAC. ST

Sarah Fischer concerts, Sarah Fischer scholarships. See Fischer, Sarah.

SARGENT, Margaret (m McTaggart). Ethnomusicologist, b Fort William (Thunder Bay), Ont, 6 May 1921; B MUS (Toronto) 1942. She studied with Healey *Willan and Leo *Smith at the *U of Toronto and transcribed Huron and Iroquois music (1948) under Marius *Barbeau at the *National Museum, Ottawa. In 1950 she collected English and Irish folklore in Newfoundland and in 1951 she studied American Indian music with George Herzog at Indiana U on a Unesco fellowship and examined folk music collections in Edinburgh, Dublin, and London. She worked during the 1960s with Ida *Halpern on the music of the Kwakiutl.

WRITINGS

'Seven songs from Lorette,' *JAF*, vol 63, 1950

'Folk and primitive music in Canada,' National Museum *Bulletin* 123 (Ottawa 1951)

'Folk and primitive music in Canada,' *J of the International Folk Music Council*, 4, 1952

'A preliminary survey of folk music in BC,' CFMS *Newsletter*, vol 2, Jul 1967 (DD)

Sarnia. Ontario city settled in 1807. It was known first as Fort Rapids, later as Port Sarnia, and in 1856 it was incorporated as the town of Sarnia. It became a city in 1914. Its population was 55,576 in 1979. Sarnia is located on the St Clair River just south of Lake Huron and opposite Port Huron, Mich. Immediately to the south lies 'Chemical Valley,' Canada's greatest concentration of petrochemical industries.

Church and band music preoccupied Sarnia's first musicians. At St Andrew's Presbyterian Church, which had a choir soon after it opened in 1841, Francis Laird led congregational singing classes 1861–77. After years of argument about the propriety of instrumental music in the church, St Andrew's installed an organ in 1883. Its first organist, A.A. *Clappé, had become conductor of the Sarnia Citizens' Band in 1879. He was also a teacher, the conductor of the Mozart Choral Union, and bandmaster of the 27th Battalion Band. About 1884 he left for the USA.

In 1910 the 130-voice combined choirs of St Andrew's Presbyterian and St George's Anglican churches, with soloists from Toronto, performed *Messiah* under Charles Patchett, organist at St George's 1904–41. Other pioneers were the organist and bandmaster William Philp and his successor (1910) as leader of the Citizens' Band, W.E. Brush. Brush also conducted several other local military, church, and school bands.

Before World War I most of Sarnia's secular musical ensembles were bands. The Sarnia Garrison Band (later the Lambton Regimental Band), formed in 1875, was followed by the Citizens' and 149th bands. The Sons of Scotland Highland Pipe Band, formed in 1910, enlisted *en masse* in the 70th Battalion in 1915 and re-formed after the war as the Imperial Pipe Band.

Among organizations performing between the two world wars were a Sarnia SO (formed in 1915), a Sarnia Male Chorus (formed in 1919; its accompanist, Mrs A.W. Mills, was also an organist at Central Baptist Church), an Imperial Theatre Orchestra (formed 1919), a Philharmonic Choral Society (formed 1920 to perform Gilbert & Sullivan), and a Sarnia Orchestra (formed in 1938).

The Polymer (later Polysar) Glee Club, established in 1948, presented Broadway musicals, Gilbert & Sullivan operettas, and variety concerts. In 1951 under Adrian Strybos the three churches of the Dutch community formed the 85-member Solo Deo Choir, which in 1980 continued to perform weekly in the churches and to give two major public concerts annually. It has been conducted 1952–61 by George Hale, 1961–5 and again after 1970 by J.D. Murray, and 1965–70 by Ronald Klinck. Among other choral groups have been the David Stone Singers, 1961–7, which became the Tudor Singers in 1967, and the Art Christmas Aggregation, formed in 1975.

A significant post-war development was the Sarnia Little Symphony Society, organized in 1950 under Walter Stern and amalgamated in 1956 with the Port Huron (Mich) String Ensemble. Renamed the International SO of Sarnia and Port Huron it made its debut in 1957 and in 1980 continued to perform in the USA and Canada. Until 1974 (see Sault Ste Marie) it was the only adult community orchestra in North America with players and board members from both sides of the border (see Orchestras).

Organizations which have brought visiting artists to Sarnia include the Musical Literary Society (1895–8), the Women's Tuesday Musical (fl 1907–16, 1919–28), the Sarnia Music Club (formed in 1935 and later renamed the Sarnia Music and Drama Assn), and the Sarnia *Community Concerts Assn. In the years between 1944 and 1978, Community Concerts presented more than 120 Canadian and non-Canadian soloists and ensembles of stature, including Pierrette *Alarie and Leopold *Simoneau, Rose Bampton, Victor *Bouchard and Renée *Morisset, the *COC, Clifford Curzon, Eileen Farrell, Maureen *Forrester, William Kapell, Lois *Marshall, Erica Morini, Leontyne Price, Louis *Quilico, Bidú Sayão, Cesare Siepi, Teresa *Stratas, the Stuttgart Chamber Orchestra, Ronald *Turini, and Portia *White.

The Canadian Concert Series, organized in 1962, has presented such musicians as Robert *Aitken, Lorand *Fenyves, Marek *Jablonski, the *London SO Sinfonia, Yuri and Dana Mazurkevich, and the *Orford String Quartet at the Sarnia Public Library.

In the early years of the 20th century young musicians received their training from private teachers and from the Sisters of St Joseph Music School, which opened in 1905. In 1928 Sarnia music teachers organized the Lambton chapter of the OMTA, which in 1946 became the Sarnia branch of the *ORMTA. This organization promoted music instruction in the schools, set up the Lambton County Music Festival (in 1930), and sponsored recitals, workshops, and lectures. A Sarnia chapter of the *RCCO was established in 1953. Irene Harrington Young, a piano teacher who has composed for children and contributed musical articles to children's magazines, has lived near Sarnia for many years.

Brian *Barley and R. Murray *Schafer was born in Sarnia. Gwen Beamish (*MacMillan) settled in Sarnia in 1952 and has been an important teacher, performer, and organizer there. The rock band Max Webster, which came to prominence in 1976, was formed in Sarnia.

BIBLIOGRAPHY

Mason, Lawrence. 'Ontario's vistas: journeyings in the rich field of provincial music and drama: Sarnia,' Toronto *Globe*, 11 Jul 1925

'Music has its place of importance in the life of Sarnia.' *Sarnia Canadian-Observer*, 18 Jul 1925

'The Sarnia Citizens' Band 100 years old and active,' Sarnia *Gazette*, 26 Jan 1977 (GBm)

'Saskatchewan.' Song composed by the Swift Current businessman William W. Smith during the 1930s, when the prairie farmers were suffering not only from the Depression which destroyed the markets for their grain but also from the prolonged drought and dust storms which caused the period to be known as 'the dirty thirties.' Smith used the pattern of the gospel hymn 'Beulah Land,' which already had been used for several other sets of words in the American and Canadian west. His graphic chorus ran:

We sit and gaze across the plains
And wonder why it never rains,
And Gabriel blows his trumpet sound:
He says 'The rain, she's gone around.'

It was published by Gage in *Fowke, *Mills, and *Blume's *Canada's Story in Song* (1960) and included on a record of the same title (Folkways 3000). Smith's song should not be confused with the 1948 pop song of the same title by Billy *O'Connor. EF

Saskatchewan Arts Board. Autonomous provincial arts-subsidy board established 3 Feb 1948, the first agency of its kind in Canada (and, it is claimed, in North America) to have an annual allocation of funds received from government sources but disposable independent of government control.

From its inception the board has worked to encourage greater participation in the arts throughout the province, and in particular to support and encourage professional activities. The 15-member board, appointed annually by order-in-council, reports to the Saskatchewan Dept of Culture and Youth established 1 Apr 1972 and directed in 1980 by deputy minister Elizabeth Dowdeswell. The board chairman in 1980 was R.J. Marcotte; the executive director was Joy Cohnstaedt.

Board meetings, at least two a year, have been held to refine arts policies and evaluate grant applications, sometimes with the advisory assistance of panels of arts professionals. The board's annual provincial allocation of monies has been supplemented by earned revenues and donations. In 1948 the budget was $4400; in 1980 it exceeded $1 million, about half of it disbursed in grants.

The board established a Young Artists and Concert Series in 1950, following a successful tour of the province by the pianist Thelma Johannes *O'Neill. Gordon *Hancock, appointed 1958, was director of the series for some time. All the cultural projects for the province's 1955 golden jubilee celebrations – including a composition competition and the presentation of Neil *Harris' musical *Saskatchewan Ho!* – were planned by the board. In 1965 it assumed responsibility for the *Saskatchewan Music Festival Assn. It has sponsored the Saskatchewan Summer School of the Arts (founded 1962), held annually at the Echo Valley Centre near Fort Qu'Appelle.

To groups and individuals the board has provided assistance in the form of operating grants, project grants, and travel grants. Among groups which have received such assistance are the Greystone Singers, the *Regina and *Saskatoon SOs, the Saskatoon Chamber Music Society, the Saskatoon Chamber Singers, the Saskatchewan Choral Federation, the *Saskatchewan Junior Concert Society, and the Moose Jaw International Band Festival. The Organization of Saskatchewan Arts Councils (founded 1974) also has received support. In September 1969 at Fort San the board organized a panel discussion which resulted in the report (unpublished in 1980) 'The status of the professional musician in Saskatchewan.' In 1977 the board began publication of the newsletter *Saskatchewan Arts*. In 1978 in co-operation with the *Canada Council's Touring Office, it sponsored Contact Saskatchewan, a showcase for the province's performers. That same year it published *Contact Saskatchewan: A Directory for the Performing Arts*.

The work of the board has been complemented by that of the Cultural Activities Division of the Dept of Culture and Youth. The division was established in November 1972; its executive director in 1980 was Louis Julé. It has emphasized the support of community and pre-professional activities through a program of grants and has sponsored the Saskatchewan Talent Program, a series of regional and provincial contests for performers. The Dept of Culture and Youth and the SAB cosponsored a 1975 Study of the Arts in Saskatchewan, a series of small conferences which culminated in a major provincial one at Saskatoon in October 1975.

BIBLIOGRAPHY

George, Graham. 'Music where the wind blows free,' *CMJ*, vol 6, Spring 1962

Riddell, W.A. *Cornerstone for Culture: A History of the Saskatchewan Arts Board from 1948 to 1978* (Regina 1979)

(MSr)

The Saskatchewan Centre of the Arts. A theatre complex at the Wascana Centre in *Regina in commemoration of Canada's centenary. It opened 24 Aug 1970 to serve southern Saskatchewan as a centre for performing arts and exhibitions. Designed by Izumi, Arnott, and Sucijama, the Estevan brick and Manitoba Tyndall stone structure houses Centennial Theatre (seating 2029), Hanbidge Hall (seating 1600), Jubilee Hall, and various conference rooms and lobby display areas. The theatre, with three balconies, has a large stage whose front lowers hydraulically to form an orchestra pit for 100 musicians. Owned by the province, the centre is the home of the *Regina SO and has been host to the Bolshoi Ballet, the Vienna Boys' Choir, the *Stratford Festival production of *The Comedy of Errors*, Gary *Karr, Anton *Kuerti, Gordon *Lightfoot, Guy *Lombardo, Teresa *Stratas, the *TS, and many others. IMM

The Saskatchewan Junior Concert Society. Founded by Barbara *Cass-Beggs in 1956 as the Regina Junior Concert Society to sponsor musical presentations for children with an eye to developing future audiences. It was incorporated under the new name in 1959. In the first year staff members of the Regina Cons gave three concerts. Subsequent years have seen spring and fall tours of about 30 Saskatchewan communities, presenting up to 50 concerts to as many as 30,000 children. The folksinger Alan *Mills and the puppeteer Daniel Llords each have toured three times. Other artists have included Howard *Leyton-Brown, Malcolm Lowe, Lloyd Blackman, Juliette Alvin, Eugene *Kash, Tom *Kines, the *Baroque Trio of Montreal and the *Huggett Family. WLB

The Saskatchewan Music Council. An organization founded in Saskatoon and Regina in 1967 by Lloyd Blackman, David *Kaplan (chairman), and Rj *Staples. Active 1967–72, the council's function was to act as a central forum for provincial musical organizations. Its meetings were held in Regina and Saskatoon on an irregular basis (1967, 1970, 1972), with representatives from universities, schools, the communications media, the *SRMTA, music businesses, and the provincial government. Speakers such as Arnold *Walter in 1967 and Richard *Johnston in 1970 were a feature of these meetings, as were university student performers. The council advocated improved school music curricula and better teacher training and encouraged the provincial Dept of Education to sponsor a greater number of seminars, classes, and workshops. It also stimulated an increased awareness among broadcasters of the need for a balance between popular and 'classical' programming and petitioned for a CBC FM station in Saskatchewan. (DK)

Saskatchewan Music Educators' Association. Founded 24 Apr 1957 at a meeting organized by Rj *Staples at the Teachers' College in Saskatoon and chaired by Lloyd Blackman. Membership began at 73 and neared 300 in 1978 apart from associate and student members. The SMEA became affiliated with the Saskatchewan Teachers' Federation, as a special subject council, and also with the *CMEA. Its original aims included improving practices in music education and advising the Saskatchewan Teachers' Federation. The SMEA comprises an executive and representatives from eight regions, from various special interest groups, and from the universities of Regina and Saskatchewan. An official magazine has been published intermittently beginning in 1957 under the titles *Bulletin*, *Journal*, *Newsletter*, and *Cadenza*. SMEA presidents have been Reginald McFarland 1957–8, Blackman 1958–9, 1963–5, Don *Cowan 1959–61, Mikel Kalmakoff 1961–3, David *Kaplan 1965–7, William Otis 1967–9, Tom Magnuson 1969–70, Blaine McClary 1970–2, Al Browne 1972–4, Phil Johnston 1974–6, Brian Hartsool 1976–7, and Dennis Humenick 1977–9, who was succeeded by Joan Hunker. Honorary presidents have been Staples 1957–72, and Herbert *Jeffrey 1972–8, succeeded by Don Cowan. On Staples' death in 1972 a fund was established in his name to provide scholarships for two music education students each year, one at the *U of Regina, the other at the *U of Saskatchewan. Choral and band clinics, a feature of the first annual meeting, were supplanted in 1974 by performances by the Provincial Honour Band, Orchestra, and Choir. IMM

Saskatchewan Music Festival Association. Co-ordinating body founded in 1909 to promote the appreciation, performance, and study of music through competition festivals and concerts. During its first year it held, at Regina, a one-day festival which drew 25 entries. The next festival was held in Saskatoon, the third in Prince Albert, and the fourth in Moose Jaw. The fifth, in Regina, drew 236 entries. In 1979 the 46 affiliated community festival branches organized 58 spring festivals, attracting musicians from 350 Saskatchewan communities.

Based in Regina, the association's affairs have been governed by a volunteer board of directors and administered by a salaried staff. (Gordon *Hancock, executive director 1958–76, was succeeded by Kathleen Keple.) The association became a member of the *FCMF and affiliated with the British Federation of Music Competition Festivals.

Responsible for the co-ordination of all festival activities (including the provincial semi-finals and finals), the association has undertaken to publish an annual syllabus, to select adjudicators (who have included Sir Hugh Roberton, Dorothy *Bee, Helmut *Brauss, and Gordon *McLean), to administer community assistance and promotion programs and a Provincial Awards Program (including prizes for the winners of the Saskatchewan finals leading to the *National Competitive Festival of Music), and to sponsor concerts by outstanding winners. The associaton has viewed its role as one of supporting and supplementing the existing music education network in Saskatchewan.

In 1955 the association offered eight awards and scholarships; in 1980 it offered 45, many established to honour Saskatchewan musicians. (Individual festivals also have offered hundreds of awards.) Test pieces, chosen each year for the fall syllabus, have included pieces by Saskatchewan composers. In 1979 the syllabus featured 749 classes, for school and community choirs, orchestras and bands, for solo voices, and for instruments.

The association's plans for 1980 included a greater emphasis on the performance of Saskatchewan music, to be achieved through a promotional project, 'The Festival Celebrates Saskatchewan.' In 1980, in addition to the use of compositions by Saskatchewan composers as test pieces in some regular classes, the syllabus offered three special classes – not competitions – in which music by Saskatchewan composers would be performed 'on a recital basis.' In one of these the performer could choose from a short list of set pieces; in another, he could play a Saskatchewan composition of his own choice; in the third, the composer or arranger of a work could perform or conduct it himself.

Also in 1980 a concerto competition was scheduled in honour of the 71st anniversaries of the festival association, the *Regina SO, and the Regina Cartage and Storage Co; first prize was a $1000 scholarship offered by the last-named sponsor and an opportunity to perform with the Regina SO.

In 1980, apart from a wartime suspension of activities 1915–19, the association's record of activity was unbroken.

BIBLIOGRAPHY

'Proud record of 50 years' service,' Regina *Leader-Post*, 8 May 1963

Rodwell, Lloyd. 'The Saskatchewan association of music festivals,' *Saskatchewan History*, vol 16, Winter 1963

Hancock, Gordon. 'Music festivals play key role in training young,' Regina *Leader-Post*, 25 Aug 1973 NM

Saskatchewan Registered Music Teachers' Association (SRMTA). The Regina Music Teachers' Assn, formed in 1925, became the Saskatchewan Provincial Music Teachers' Assn in 1930. The provincial association, in turn, affiliated with the *CFMTA in 1935 and obtained a provincial charter under its present name in 1938, becoming the first in Canada to do so. Among the founders were Lyell *Gustin, Edith Mash, George Palmer, and Henry J. Record. In 1978 membership stood at 220, with branches in Prince Albert, Regina, Moose Jaw, Saskatoon, and Weyburn. The *SRMTA Newsletter* began in 1954 and has been published thrice annually. The SRMTA archives are held at the *U of Saskatchewan in Saskatoon. The organization has co-operated with other RMTAs in support of the CFMTA Young Artist Series, originated by Lyell Gustin in 1942, through which outstanding students, selected at public auditions, have been sent on tours of the western provinces. SRMTA presidents have been Alma W. Ward 1930, Marion B. Kinne 1931, Henry J. Record 1933, 1935–6, George C. Palmer 1934–5, Helen Davies *Sherry 1936–7, Grace E. Knowlden 1937–8, Lyell Gustin 1938–40, Maude McGuire 1940–2, Dan A. *Cameron 1942–4, Lucille Murphy 1944–5, Mrs A.B. McKenzie 1945–7, Robert *Pounder 1947–9, Marjorie Wilson 1949–51, Gordon *Hancock 1951–3, Gertrude Greaves 1953–5, Dorothy *Bee 1955–7, Mrs L.E. Collard 1957–9, Jean McCulloch 1959–61, Betty Godley 1961–3, May Woodley Benson 1963–5, Joyce Johnson 1965–7, Walter Thiessen 1967–9, Ethel Weare 1969–71, Louise McPherson 1971–3, Margaret Muirhead 1973–5, Margaret Kippen 1975–7, and Joan Faron 1977–9, succeeded by Bernice Ringler. (GGrv)

Saskatoon. Saskatchewan city settled in 1883 as a temperance colony by pioneers from Ontario. It was incorporated as a town, with a population of 544, in 1903, and as a city, with five times that number, in 1906. Its population had grown to 25,000 by 1925 and to 142,000 by 1976, and it was well-established as an agricultural, industrial, and medical centre and a university city.

Saskatoon's first concert, 1 Dec 1884 by the Pioneer Society, featured solos, duets, choruses, readings, and recitations. The erection ca 1900 of the Saskatoon Music Hall and the Dulmage Hall indicates a quickening of musical activity. Cairns' Hall, opened 29 Sep 1903, was built by J.F. Cairns, who previously had owned a theatre in Chatham, Ont, and had managed the Grand Opera House in London, Ont. In 1903 the church organist and piano tuner F.W. Musselwhite formed the Saskatoon Choral Society. Musselwhite also conducted the first concert of the Saskatoon Orchestra, with John Jackson as concertmaster, at Cairns' Hall 16 Mar 1905. The same year, Saskatoon was visited by a concert and operatic ensemble conducted by Frank *Laubach.

In the early 1900s the main musical activities were solo recitals, band concerts, minstrel shows, vaudeville, and Gilbert & Sullivan operettas by local and visiting groups.

In 1908 Blanche St John-Baker, a pupil of Leopold Godowsky and Olga Varet-Stepanoff, opened a piano studio. She taught in Saskatoon until 1920 and developed many talented pianists – including Lyell *Gustin – but later settled in Los Angeles.

1908 was also the year of the founding of the 78-member Saskatoon Philharmonic Society, the city's first important musical organization. Organized and conducted by William Preston, the society gave its first concert in the Lyric Theatre in January 1909. In May 1909 it won a prize in Regina for its performance of *H.M.S. Pinafore* at the first *Saskatchewan Music Festival. (Saskatoon was the location in 1910 of the second provincial festival and continued to be the biennial location of the festival.)

In 1910 members of the Philharmonic Society, performing as the Grand Vaudeville Co in a repeat production of *H.M.S. Pinafore*, inaugurated the Empire Theatre, which provided a home to music and drama for more than 20 years. During these decades, the Philharmonic (later Orpheus) Society continued to present musicals.

In 1912 Saskatoon had four bands and two orchestras. Another indication of the expanding musical scene was the founding that year of the *Women's Musical Club and the opening, by Mr and Mrs Robert Bell, of the Bell Cons in the Odd Fellows' Hall on 3rd Ave. The Bells and their teachers – including the aforementioned John Jackson – offered lessons in piano, strings, theory, and voice and produced such noted musicians as Thelma Johannes *O'Neill and Mabel Sanda. George C. Palmer (1879–1968), a native of Bristol who settled in Saskatoon in 1915, opened the Palmer School of Music and taught piano. Five years later Lyell Gustin opened his piano studios, from which many leading Canadian pianists and teachers were to emerge.

After 1900 numerous solo artists and performing companies visited Saskatoon. The tenor Harold *Jarvis sang there in 1905 and the San Francisco Opera performed in 1908. In 1910, at $5 a ticket, Nellie Melba gave a joint recital with the violinist Jan Kubelík. Two years later Ernestine Schumann-Heink appeared at the Empire Theatre, and the Sheehan English Opera presented *Il Trovatore*. The tenor John McCormack sang at the Empire Theatre in 1913. Other attractions 1910–20 were Kathleen *Parlow (1911) who gave a recital during her first Canadian tour, the *Cherniavsky Trio (1914), Clara Butt (1914), the *Chautauqua, the Gilbert & Sullivan Festival Opera, the De Koven Opera, the *San Carlo Grand Opera, the Shuberts, the Gallo English Opera, the Royal English Opera, and the Boston Opera. Individual artists who appeared in Saskatoon prior to 1930 included Harold Craxton, Marcel Dupré, Arthur Friedheim, Percy Grainger, Boris *Hambourg, and Edward *Johnson. The *Hart House String Quartet also played there.

The Saskatoon Oratorio Society under William Preston, with Fred M. *Gee as organist, gave the Saskatoon premiere of the complete *Messiah* 3 and 4 Dec 1913. Irene Moore, a music critic for Saskatoon newspapers until 1920, provided comprehensive reporting, interviews, and vignettes on local musicians. By 1920 Lyell Gustin had become a major figure on the music scene, his piano studios a centre for the musical milieu. In 1924 he founded the *Musical Art Club, which continued to sponsor monthly performances and lectures for more than 50 years.

The Depression and the drought of the 1930s and the attendant decline in population slowed musical growth, but development continued, especially in music education. In 1931 a chair of music was established at the *U of Saskatchewan, and Arthur *Collingwood, who founded the *Saskatoon SO in 1931 or 1932, was appointed dean. In 1931 Lyell Gustin organized a series of musical appreciation programs for grades 7 and 8 in four city schools. These programs continued until 1938, the final one, in the Third Avenue Church, with the participation of 3000 children. Also in 1931 the Saskatoon Music Teachers' Assn was formed; George C. Palmer, who taught 1935–50 at the U of Saskatchewan, was the first president. In 1939 the *CFMTA held its biennial convention in Saskatoon.

The slow recovery of the musical community from the Depression, the drought, and World War II began in the mid-1940s. The Saskatoon Kinsmen Club in 1944 began a Celebrity Concert Series that was to present internationally known musicians to Saskatoon audiences for the next 26 years (eg, Mischa Elman, Zara *Nelsova, Lily Pons, Artur Rubinstein). The U of Saskatchewan – which established a Dept of Music in 1952 – presented an operetta or musical annually 1951–5 in the Capitol Theatre. Productions included *Naughty Marietta*, *The Desert Song*, *Countess Maritza*, *Brigadoon*, and *Finian's Rainbow*. The Dept of Music also established a Sunday evening recital series which presented distinguished performers.

In 1952 a Saskatoon Oratorio Society (Saskatoon Choral Society after 1959) was organized with Victor Kviesis as conductor. Its first performance, 3 and 4 Feb 1953, in the Third Avenue United Church, was of Mendelssohn's *St Paul*. Over the years, with a membership that has remained between 60 and 80, the society has presented Bach's *St Matthew Passion*, Handel's *Messiah*, *Judas Maccabaeus*, and *Solomon*, Haydn's *The Creation*, Mozart's *Requiem*, Beethoven's *Christ on the Mount of Olives* and *Missa solemnis*, Mendelssohn's *Elijah*, Brahms' *A German Requiem*, and Britten's *War Requiem*. The presentations have been financed entirely by ticket sales.

The Saskatoon Lyric Theatre Society survived five years and produced Smetana's *The Bartered Bride* in 1955. Robert Solem in 1963 became the conductor of the Greystone Singers, a mixed choir founded in 1959 to celebrate the 50th anniversary of the U of Saskatchewan. The singers have performed in Saskatchewan, Alberta, and North Dakota, have given annual workshops in Saskatchewan centres, and have appeared with the Saskatoon SO.

Also in 1959 Murray *Adaskin, who had become head of the Dept of Music at the U of Saskatchewan in 1952 and was conductor of the Saskatoon SO 1957–60, organized the first Summer Festival of Music. In 1962 Saskatoon was host to the convention of the *Federation of Canadian Music Festivals.

The Saskatoon Boys' Choir was formed under Don Forbes in 1960. *Humphrey and the Dumptrucks were formed in 1967. In 1968 Murray Adaskin founded the *Amati String Quartet. Probably the decade's most significant event was the 1967 opening of the *Saskatoon Centennial Auditorium, which provided a permanent home for the Saskatoon SO and a fulcrum for the city's musical life. In 1976 Ruben *Gurevich became the first full-time conductor of the Saskatoon SO.

Saskatoon is the birthplace of Walter *Babiak, the bassist Kim Brandt, the pianist-teacher Irena Bubniuk, Neil *Chotem, Mike Ferbey of the *Rhythm Pals, the singer Lorraine McAllister Richards, the pop singer Susan Pesklevits *Jacks, the pianist David Swan, and Lesia Zubrack *Romanoff.

BIBLIOGRAPHY

'A musical city,' *The Capital*, anniversary number 1909

Kasemets, Udo. 'The Saskatoon summer music festival, 1959,' *CMJ*, vol 4, Autumn 1959

Gustin, Lyell. 'Music in the early days of Saskatoon,' paper ed by Mrs T.C. Vanterpool, repr *Alumni Bulletin*, no. 13, 1966

History of Theatre in Saskatoon 1897–1955, 2 vols, index prepared by U of Saskatchewan drama students (Saskatoon 1974) (WLB, IMM)

Saskatoon Centennial Auditorium. Home of the *Saskatoon SO. Acoustically excellent and seating 2003 in the orchestra and three balconies, the auditorium was designed by Kerr Cullingworth Riches Associates and, following construction funded by municipal, provincial, and federal governments, opened 1 Apr 1968 with a performance by the Saskatoon SO of Orff's *Carmina burana*. The Saskatoon Centennial Auditorium Foundation Board was formed to govern its operation and maintenance. Maureen *Forrester, Harry Belafonte, the *NACO, the Royal Winnipeg Ballet, the *TS, and other solo artists and ensembles have appeared there. JSn

Saskatoon Symphony Orchestra . Community orchestra of some 40 members, founded in 1927. It adopted its present name in 1931 or 1932. Previous Saskatoon orchestras had been formed in 1909, 1913, and 1924, conducted by William Preston, John Jackson, and Allan Clifton respectively. Under Arthur *Collingwood 1931(2?)–47 the orchestra performed only short pieces, overtures, and movements from symphonies. After 1950 it began to present complete works including concertos, and for many years it closed its season with an oratorio.

Neil *Chotem, Maureen *Forrester, Robin *Harrison, Gary *Karr, Zara *Nelsova, Igor Oistrakh, Thomas *Rolston, Steven *Staryk, Jon *Vickers, and George *Zukerman and the conductor Fiora Contino have performed as guests of the orchestra, which has presented series of concerts annually save during 1956–7, when activities were suspended for one season. The orchestra commissioned a Canadian composition for the first time in 1957 while under the leadership of Murray *Adaskin; subsequently it has attempted to commission a Canadian work each year. Those who have received commissions include Adaskin, *Archer, *Cable, Chotem, *Fleming, *Freedman, *Kasemets, *Kenins, *Papineau-Couture, *Rathburn, *Weinzweig, and Luigi Zaninelli. In February 1959 the orchestra gave the North American premiere of Milhaud's *Suite provençale*. In 1962 it initiated a development program which included, in sequence, a summer workshop, junior strings, junior SO, and junior chamber orchestra. The *Suzuki method of instruction also was introduced.

The orchestra's conductors after Collingwood have included J.D. Macrae 1947–50, Victor Kveisis 1950–6, Adaskin 1957–60, Alex Reisman 1960–3, David *Kaplan 1963–9, 1970–1, Franz Zeidler 1969–70, and Dwaine Nelson 1971–6. In 1976 Ruben *Gurevich, founder and conductor of the *Manitoba Chamber Orchestra, became the orchestra's first full-time music director and conductor. Except for the years 1950–6 (when it appeared at the Capitol Theatre), the orchestra rehearsed and performed at the *U of Saskatchewan from its inception until 1967. At that time the *Saskatoon Centennial Auditorium became its permanent home.

During the 1977–8 season the orchestra presented 44 in-school concerts and clinics, 10 concerts on tour, and three special presentations, in addition to its 10 pairs of subscription concerts. In January 1978 it gave the premiere of S.C. *Eckhardt-Gramatté's *L'Île* 'La Mer Sargasso,' the pencilled ms of which had been found by Gurevich among the composer's papers.

BIBLIOGRAPHY

'Saskatoon Symphony Orchestra,' *CanComp*, 27, Mar 1968

Adaskin, Murray. 'Saskatchewan,' *CMB*, 3, Autumn–Winter 1971

Barris, Ted. 'Love is a rock symphony,' *CanComp*, 89, May 1973 (FVE)

SAUCIER. Family of Montreal musicians: 1 / Moïse, 2 / Joseph, son of Moïse, and 3 / Marcel, grandnephew of Moïse.

1 **Moïse**. Pianist, organist, teacher, b Montreal October? 1840, d there 24 Aug 1912. He took piano lessons from Paul *Letondal and went ca 1865 to Paris to study with Camille Stamaty (piano) and Laurent (harmony). In its first issue, 1 Sep 1866, *Le Canada musical* mentioned his return. The next issue (1 October) reported 'We are strongly convinced that Montreal has a real Canadian artist at last ... Just back from Paris, Mr Saucier exhibits aplomb, an attack remarkable for its precision and security, a technique that is tidy, brilliant, and vigorous, and a touch that is perfectly even.' According to the same review Saucier's repertoire consisted of 'Thalberg's grandiose fantasies, Weber's lighthearted rondos, Chopin's imaginative scherzos, Beethoven's classical sonatas, Gottschalk's enchanting inspirations, Stamaty's pleasant transcriptions; no school, no genre is excluded; the artist is familiar with them all.' Saucier ca 1871–2 was one of the first members of the *AMQ. He was the organist at various Montreal churches, including St-Joseph where he served for 25 years. Marie-Thérèse Brazeau and Euphémie Codère were among his pupils.

2 **Joseph**. Baritone, choirmaster, teacher, pianist, b Montreal 24 Feb 1869, d there 10 Apr 1941. He studied piano with his father and later with Charles-Marie *Panneton and Dominique *Ducharme, and first played in public at 10. At 18 he decided in favour of singing and took lessons from Paul Wiallard and Achille *Fortier. After serving as a soloist at the Gesù Church and St James Cathedral, he was organist- choirmaster in 1897 at St-Louis du Mile-End. At the end of that year he left for Paris where, as a non-diploma student at the Paris Cons, he studied voice with Auguste-Jean; he also performed successfully in Paris and London. Returning to Canada in June 1902 he sang the role of Satan in Théodore Dubois's *Le Paradis perdu* during the 50th anniversary celebrations of *Laval U. Saucier had prepared the role with the composer himself. He went to Paris again but returned to Montreal in 1903, becoming choirmaster at Immaculée-Conception Church. He served 1907–8 and 1911–12 as president of the *AMQ. He took part 16 Nov 1913 in the premiere of Alexis *Contant's oratorio *Les Deux Âmes*. He became a soloist at St-Louis-de-France Church in 1914 and served there as choirmaster 1927–36.

Joseph Saucier

Joseph Saucier was one of the most admired Canadian singers of his time. In concert and as a soloist in oratorio he brought a sense of style to singing that was disciplined and warm in sound. Although he seldom sang opera he enjoyed a success as the High Priest in *Samson et Dalila* in Worcester, Mass (1923). He frequently was soloist with the *Goulet *MSO and is thought to be the first (ca 1900) French-Canadian musician to record on cylinder or disc in Canada. A list of his recordings is given in *Roll Back the Years*.

Saucier's wife, Octavie Turcotte, a niece and pupil of Dominique Ducharme, accompanied him on the piano in many of these recordings, as well as in recital. Their son Jean, a neurologist, was a violinist, and Jean's son Pierre was a critic 1956–60 with the Montreal daily *La Patrie*.

BIBLIOGRAPHY

Valois, Marcel. 'Le chanteur Joseph Saucier,' Montreal *La Presse*, 12 Apr 1941

3 **Marcel**. Violinist, teacher, b Montreal 6 Nov 1912; lauréat (Montreal) 1935, teaching certificate (Montreal) 1950, B MUS (Montreal) 1951. On his mother's side he was a cousin of Father Alphonse *Tardif. He studied violin 1919–25 with Albert Devault, 1925–8 with Alfred *De Sève, 1929–30 with Raphael Kellert, 1930–2 with Jeanne Labrecque, 1932–6 with Camille *Couture, and 1936–7 with Maurice *Onderet. He also took piano, harmony, and composition from Antonio *Létourneau and organ from Eugène *Lapierre. Between 1931 and 1935 he often performed in concert in Canada and the USA and on radio station CKAC. He taught at St-Guillaume College in l'Épiphanie, Que, at St-Louis College in Terrebonne, Que, and at St-Viateur High School in Montreal, but after 1935 confined himself exclusively to teaching in his Montreal studio. Among his pupils were Jean *Cousineau, Roméo Galipeau, Jacques Perron, and Henriette Tardif. A number of the songs he wrote were performed by well-known artists such as Jean *Lalonde. He published 'Valsons, valsons mon amour' (Montreal 1940, at his own expense) and a *Gavotte* for violin and piano (St-Viateur Library 1936). Fernand Robidoux made a 78 of his song 'Miarka, ma jolie' (London FC-134). GP

Sault Ste Marie. Ontario city across the St Mary's River from Sault Ste Marie, Mich. As early as 1668 there was a small settlement of fur traders on the site. The permanent settlement was established in 1792. Sault Ste Marie was incorporated as a town in 1887 and as a city in 1912. Steel became the major industry. Succession duties from the estate of Sir James Dunn, chairman and president of Algoma Steel, were allocated by the federal government as foundation money for the *Canada Council. In the mid-1970s Sault Ste Marie's population was more than 80,000 including large numbers of Croatians, Italians, and Ukrainians.

Bands have been an important part of the city's musical life. The Band of the 227th Regiment, formed ca 1915 and conducted for several decades by Harry R. Pearse, marched to war in 1916 to the strains of Pearse's privately published *Men O' the North*, the 227th's band march. A bandshell was named in Pearse's honour in 1971. In 1975 the Kiwanis Concert Band was formed.

The violin teacher Edward Hanelt founded a community orchestra in 1939, and in the 1930s and 1940s John Blackburn taught voice; Doreen *Hume was the latter's most noted pupil.

The Northmen Male Chorus was established in 1937 and in 1942 formed the nucleus of the Northernaire's Choral Society. In 1949 Gordon Christie, supervisor of music for the Board of Education, formed the 45-member Ladies' Choral Society, which was renamed the Gordon Christie Singers in 1965 and was conducted by Christie until 1972. Subsequent conductors have been Anton Gartshore 1972–3, Patty Gartshore 1973–4, John F.M. Wood 1974–7, and Albert E. Furtney 1977–8, succeeded by Rodger J. Beatty. The choir has sung sacred music, folk music, and show tunes and usually has given one concert at Christmas and one in the spring.

In the 1940s Croatian and Ukrainian orchestras were active. The Sault Chamber Orchestra of the 1960s developed in 1969 into the Sault SO under the direction 1969–78 of Lajos Bornyi. John Wilkinson became conductor in 1978. Some of the orchestra's members have come from Sault Ste Marie, Mich; indeed, the orchestra and the Sault Chamber Players have been sponsored by the Sault Ste Marie International Assn, established in 1974. Local instrumental standards have been raised by the Sault Music Festival, initiated in 1937 by the Algoma Music Teachers' Assn (affiliated with the *ORMTA in 1946) and the Kiwanis Club. In the 1970s the event became the second largest competition festival in Ontario.

Artists of international calibre have appeared in Sault Ste Marie as part of the *Algoma Fall Festival, which began in 1973. Nicholas *Goldschmidt, engaged as festival consultant in 1975, conducted productions and organized the Algoma Festival Chorus. Other performing groups in the Sault in 1980 included the Sault Opera Society, directed by Arno Ambel; the Musical Guild, conducted by Frank Elliott; the Sir James Dunn Choir, directed by James Whicher; and the St Luke's Cathedral Choir of Men and Boys, led by John Wood.

During the 1920s music teachers were assigned to the public schools, and by 1946 three music specialists were working in the school system. Music training establishments flourishing in Sault Ste Marie in 1980 included the Algoma Cons and the Algoma Music Camp, the latter directed by Ed Gartshore, a leading violin teacher in the city for many years and director also of the Gartshore Music Centre.

Gary *Buck, Ned Ciaschini (arranger and member of Percy *Faith's orchestra), Claire *Grenon-Masella, Doreen Hume, the singer Debbie Lori Kaye, Joseph *Laderoute, Gino *Silvi, and Eric *Wild were born in or near Sault Ste Marie. (CEG)

SAUNDERS, Stanley. Administrator, teacher, conductor, clarinetist, b Newport, Gwent (then Monmouthshire), Wales, 3 May 1927; B MUS (Wales) 1951, M MUS (Oregon) 1968, DMA (Oregon) 1970. He toured Europe 1948–51 as a clarinet soloist, was a founding member of the National Youth Orchestra of Wales, and performed on BBC TV, British Independent TV, and, later, on the CBC and US networks. He was a music specialist 1951–8 for the Glamorgan Education Authority in Wales prior to emigrating to Canada in 1958. He taught 1958–74 at *Mount Allison U, establishing the summer Instrumental Music Camps and conducting the University Symphonic Band and (1965–74) the *New Brunswick Youth Orchestra. He moved to the *U of Guelph in 1974 as music director and conductor of the U of Guelph Civic Orchestra and the Brantford SO. He served 1974–6 on the board of the *CCA and was appointed to that of *OFSO in 1974, that of the Canadian Assn of Youth Orchestras in 1975, and that of the *NYO in 1976. He became president of the NYO in 1979.

WRITINGS

'A study to adapt selected instrumental and vocal compositions of the renaissance as a practical guide for secondary school use,' unpubl DMA thesis, Oregon 1970

'A concept of music education for the Canadian community: the needs and aspirations of the Maritime provinces,' *CME*, vol 15, Winter 1974

'The role of the music director: on and off the podium,' *OCan*, vol 4, Jul 1977 (RAK)

SAURETTE, Sylvia (m Hübert). Soprano, b Letellier, south of Winnipeg, 27 Sep 1935; diploma (École Vincent-d'Indy) 1961. She studied in Winnipeg with Cora Doig James and Doris Mills *Lewis, then in Montreal at the *École Vincent-d'Indy with Pierrette *Alarie, Louise *André, Bernard *Diamant, and Roy *Royal. A top award winner at the *CNE in 1959, at the *Kiwanis Music Festival, Toronto, in 1960, and at the *Montreal Festivals and the *Amis de l'Art competition in 1960, she also won the *Prix Archambault that year and was a finalist in the CBC and *JMC national competitions in 1963. With the Montreal Brass Quintet she premiered Alexander *Brott's *World Sophisticate* in 1962. She has given many radio and TV recitals and has appeared as soloist with several symphony orchestras, including those in Montreal, Toronto, Quebec, Winnipeg, and London, Ont, and also with the *McGill Chamber Orchestra. She sang Donna Anna in *Don Giovanni* at the 1966 *Stratford Festival, and in 1968 she joined the Hambourg State Opera, where she sang supporting roles, notably in *Parsifal* and *The Magic Flute*. For personal reasons she declined a four-year contract there and returned in 1969 to pursue her career in Canada. With the *Opéra du Québec she sang in the 1971 production of Puccini's three one-act operas, *Il Trittico*, appearing as Lauretta in *Gianni Schicchi* and Suor Genovieffa in *Suor Angelica*. Saurette, accompanied by Claude *Savard, has recorded music of Roussel and Poulenc (1963, CD-JMC 3). (SPI)

SAUVAGEAU, (Louis) Charles. Conductor, composer, teacher, b Quebec City 9 May 1804 (?), d there 16 Jun 1849. The circumstances of his birth have remained mysterious, and different dates have been advanced. It is probable that he received his early training from Jean-Chrysostome *Brauneis I. With his brother Benjamin he played 1831–2 under Brauneis in a band organized by Joseph-François-Xavier Perrault, colonel of the Quebec militia. Sauvageau formed the Orchestre Quadrille in 1833 and led it until his death, when Benjamin replaced him. He also organized a band of 12 players, the *Musique Canadienne in 1836, and for a time (1841–4) conducted the band of the Petit Séminaire, where he taught 1841–9. He also organized concerts with his best private pupils. His son Flavien (b 1831, a child prodigy of the violin) died in the tragic fire at the St-Louis theatre 12 Jun 1846. Sauvageau was probably the first Quebec native to devote his life to music. *Le Ménestrel* (15 Aug 1844) described him as 'notre musicien national.' However, his few compositions are but pale imitations of the popular music of his day.

COMPOSITIONS

2 *Valses*. Pf. Aubin 1840

Le Dépit amoureux (Aubin). Pf. Aubin 1840

2 *Valses* (arr W.H. Warren). *Literary Garland*, vol 3, Sep 1841

'Chant canadien: Noble patron' (F.R. Angers). V, pf. Québec 1843 (sung at banquet of St-Jean-Baptiste Society Jun 1843). Also v, pf. Sénécal, Daniel & Cie 1859/*J de L'Instruction publique*, Jun 1859. Also v. *Chansonnier des Collèges*, 3rd ed 1860

Le Ménestrel printed a number of Sauvageau's compositions in 1844: *Valse du Ménestrel; Gallopade; Solo de Violin sur D'Auld Robin Grey*; 'Chant national' (F.M. Derome), sung at the banquet of the St-Jean-Baptiste Society.

WRITINGS

– ed. *Notions élémentaires de musique, tirées des meilleurs auteurs et mises en ordre par Charles Sauvageau* (Quebec 1844)

BIBLIOGRAPHY

Roy, P.-G. 'Le jeune prodige Flavien Sauvageau,' *BRH*, vol 43, Jun 1937

– 'A propos de musique,' ibid, Dec 1937

Malouin-Gélinas, France. 'La vie musicale à Québec 1840–1845,' *CMB*, 7, Autumn–Winter 1973 JH

SAVARD, Claude. Pianist, teacher, b Montreal 16 Oct 1941; premier prix piano (CMM) 1963. He studied in Montreal with Marie-Louise Boisvert and 1959–63 at the *CMM with Germaine *Malépart. On a *Canada Council grant he worked 1963–9 in Paris with Vlado Perlemuter and Suzanne Roche. He was a recipient of the *Prix d'Europe in 1964, won international competitions in Vercelli in 1964, Geneva in 1965, and Lisbon in 1966, and was awarded first prize unanimously at the competition in Munich in 1966. In February 1967 at the Maison canadienne in Paris he premiered Alain *Gagnon's *Sonata No. 3*, which had been composed for him the previous year.

Savard was official accompanist (voice and violin) in 1966, 1967, 1969, and 1970 at the *Montreal International Competition and a jury member in 1969 for the Montevideo International Competition. In 1970 he gave recitals at Carnegie Recital Hall in New York and at Festival Canada in Marburg, Germany. In 1971 he made his *MSO debut in February in Mendelssohn's *Concerto No. 1* and gave a recital at Wigmore Hall, London. In 1972, sponsored by the Department of External Affairs, he gave 17 recitals in Latin America. He studied 1972–6 with Irving *Heller. In the summer of 1973 he performed Jean *Papineau-Couture's *Pièce concertante No. 1* 'Repliement' with a CBC Toronto orchestra. As a soloist with different orchestras he played on many radio and TV stations in Europe, South America, and Canada. For the CBC program 'Concerto' he performed, among other works, Bach's *Concerto* for three keyboards and orchestra in June 1974 with Victor *Bouchard and Renée *Morisset and Poulenc's *Concerto* for piano in September 1974. He played Ravel's *Concerto for the Left Hand* with the *TS in August 1976 and Ravel's *Concerto in G* in the CBC series 'Concert populaire' in July 1977.

Savard has accompanied a number of singers and instrumentalists, including Pierrette *Alarie, Josephte Clément (Fauré, Duparc; 1963; CD–

Claude Savard

JMC-3), Andrew *Dawes, Bruno *Laplante, Nicole *Lorange, Jean-Pierre Rampal, Joseph *Rouleau, Marcel Saint-Jacques, Sylvia *Saurette; Suzanne *Shulman, and Léopold *Simoneau. For the JM he toured several European countries in 1966 and Canada in 1967–8, 1969–70, 1971–2, and 1972–3.

In the *New York Times* Allen Hughes described Savard's recital 27 Mar 1975 at Carnegie Recital Hall: 'Hearing him play a stimulating program ... one regretted that the demand for pianists of his intelligence, sensitivity and skill is not greater than it is.' Savard began teaching piano in 1975 at the *U of Montreal and in 1977 at the Cons de Trois-Rivières. He performed 9 Mar 1978 in Town Hall, New York.

WRITINGS

'Les concours internationaux: pour ou contre?' *VM*, 8, May 1968

DISCOGRAPHY

Beethoven *Sonata No. 26* 'Les Adieux' – Alain Gagnon *Sonata No. 3*. 1968. CBC SM-52

Debussy *Images* – Alain Gagnon *Sonata No. 3*. 1969. RCI 274/Sel CC.15007

Morawetz *Fantasy, Elegy and Toccata* – Morel *Deux Études de sonorité*. 1971. CBC SM-182

See also Gloria Richard; Sylvia Saurette; Suzanne Shulman; and Discography for Joseph Rouleau.

BIBLIOGRAPHY

Samson, Marc. 'L'évolution de Claude Savard,' Quebec City *Le Soleil*, 24 Feb 1968

McLean, Eric. 'Savard has taste, technique,' *Montreal Star*, 3 Feb 1971 HP

SAVARIA. Montreal family of musicians, probably of Corsican descent: 1 / Joseph-Élie, 2 / Georges, son of Joseph-Élie, and 3 / Marie, daughter of Georges.

1 **Joseph-Élie.** Organist, teacher, b Lachine, near Montreal, 16 Dec 1886, d Montreal 4 Oct 1973; lauréat (AMQ) 1903. While singing as a boy soprano in various churches he studied piano, solfège, and harmony with Jean-Noël *Charbonneau. He began studying organ ca 1903 with Alphonse *Lavallée-Smith and was organist 1905?–ca 1920 at St-Charles Church and ca 1920–ca 1927 at Notre-Dame-du-Très-Saint-Sacrement Church, Montreal. He taught ca 1911–ca 1918 at the Collège de St-Jérôme, and during 1912–13 undertook further training in Paris with Marcel Dupré, Louis Vierne, and Charles-Marie Widor. He taught organ at the *Schola cantorum, organ and piano 1926–9 at the Séminaire de Joliette, and organ and piano at the *Cons national in Montreal, where he also was a director. He was regular organist 1927–66 at the Ascension of Our Lord Church in Westmount. In 1957 he received a medal from the diocesan commission for sacred music. Pierre *Brabant and Antonio *Thompson were his pupils.

2 **Georges.** Pianist, ondist, teacher, administrator, composer, b Montreal 27 Mar 1916. He took piano and organ lessons from his father and private theory lessons from Claude *Champagne. In 1937 he received the *Prix d'Europe for piano. He went to Paris to study harmony and theoretical subjects with Louis Aubert, piano with Lazare Lévy, Marguerite Long, and Pierre Lucas, and, at the Schola cantorum, counterpoint with Daniel Lesur and organ with Olivier Messiaen. The war interrupted his studies; he was interned in a camp near Paris but he escaped and returned to Canada in 1943. His book, *Hors de portée* (Mandeville, Que, 1980) describes these experiences.

As a pianist Savaria gave recitals 1943–56 in Quebec and performed on radio and TV; he played the Schumann *Concerto* in 1944 and 1947 with the *Quebec SO and in 1948 at the *MSO Matinées. He was a music consultant and producer 1953–64 with the CBC and wrote the incidental music for many TV dramas (including Lorca's *Yerma* and *House of Bernarda Alba*). He also contributed to productions by the Nouvelle Compagnie théâtrale, the Théâtre de l'Égregoire, Les Grands Ballets Canadiens (*Médée* 1960), and documentaries by the ORTF in 1963 and Radio Québec in 1970.

Having studied the *ondes Martenot 1959–60 with the instrument's inventor through correspondence courses, Savaria was the ondist in some background scores for Shakespeare productions at the 1959 *Stratford Festival and in the premiere in 1960 of Claude Champagne's *Altitude* by the *CBC SO.

As early as 1952 Savaria taught piano at the *CMM and in 1965 he received a permanent appointment there. Céline Boucher and Albert *Grenier are among his pupils. He taught piano 1976–8 at the Cons de Trois-Rivières and was its director 1978–80. During these years he developed an interest in school music and worked to promote music and the plastic arts in the district of Mauricie, especially in St-Léon-de-Maskinongé.

Savaria composed a piano concerto in 1951 and songs and piano pieces, some of which were published in *Le Passe-Temps* (*Pavane de Michel* in 1946) and by the Éditions laurentiennes (*Variations canadiennes*).

Savaria's daughter Marie (b Montreal 29 Sep 1956; premier prix flute and chamber music, Versailles Cons, 1976) was a pupil 1970–1 of Wolfgang Kander in Montreal, 1971–4 of Jean-Paul *Major at the CMM, and 1974–6 of Roger Bourdin at the Versailles Cons. She taught flute and theory at the École Ste-Croix in Montreal and in 1977 began teaching flute at the Cegep in Trois-Rivières.

BIBLIOGRAPHY

Prévost, Roland. 'La jeune musique canadienne – Georges Savaria,' *P-T*, 905, Dec 1946 (DA)

SAVOIE, André-Sébastien. Pianist, accompanist, teacher, b Montreal 25 Jul 1935. He studied piano 1952–8 with Charles *Reiner at the McGill Cons. He won various competitions and was awarded scholarships from the Quebec government and the *Canada Council which allowed him to study 1958–61 with Carlos Vidusso in Italy and 1962–4 with Joseph Dichler at the Vienna Academy. After his return to Montreal Savoie gave many recitals in eastern Canada and on radio and TV. In 1977 he was the soloist in a performance of André *Mathieu's *Concerto No. 3* ('Concerto de Québec') with the Tunis Orchestra under Raymond *Dessaints at the Municipal Theatre in Tunis and repeated the work with the CMM summer concerts SO, conducted by Dessaints at the Maurice Richard Arena in Montreal. Savoie taught 1966–9 at *Laval U and joined the faculty at the *CMM in 1969. He is a brother of the baritone Robert *Savoie.

DISCOGRAPHY

Berlioz *Les Nuits d'été*. Peters ten. 1967. Madrigal MAS-412

J. Hétu – Morel – Papineau-Couture – Somers. 1965. RCI 251

Pianofiesta: Villa-Lobos – Albeniz – Mignone – Ponce – Mompou. 1975. RCI 418

Le Piano romantique: Alain Gagnon *Sonata No. 4*. 1968. Madrigal MAS-416

Somers *Sonata No. 3*. 1976. RCI 451

See also Discography for Jean Morin. NT

SAVOIE, Robert. Baritone, b Montreal 21 Apr 1927. He studied for five years with Pauline *Donalda and made his debut in 1948 with the *Opera Guild as the Second Philistine in *Samson et Dalila*. For the next four years he sang secondary roles with this company as well as taking part in various contests, notably *'Singing Stars of Tomorrow' in Toronto in 1950–1 and *'Nos Futures Étoiles' in Montreal. He then worked on repertoire with Antonio Narducci in Milan. He made his Milan debut as Scarpia in *Tosca* at the Teatro Nuovo and sang an important role in Di Viroli's *La Madre* under the name Roberto Savoia.

After returning to Canada in 1954, Savoie pursued a career in radio and TV as well as on stage. With the Opera Guild he sang Rodrigo in *Don Carlo* (1956), the title role in *Falstaff* (1958), Leporello in *Don Giovanni* (1964), Sharpless in *Madama Butterfly* (1965 and 1969), Marcello in *La Bohème* (1966), and Figaro in *The Marriage of Figaro* (1967) and in *The Barber of Seville* (1968). He also took part in many Canadian productions at the *Montreal Festivals, including *The Marriage of Figaro* (1956), *Don Giovanni* (1957), *L'Heure espagnole* (1961), and *Così fan tutte* (1962), and in 1958 he helped found the Grand Opéra de Montréal, for which he again sang the title role in *The Barber of Seville*.

In 1961 Savoie signed a five-year contract with Covent Garden, making his debut as Schaunard in *La Bohème* and then singing the title role in *Rigoletto*. In 1966 he also sang with Sadler's Wells, London, and the Scottish Opera, Glasgow. In France he has performed in many theatres, and in 1966 he sang the role of Dourakin in the French premiere of Prokofiev's opera *The Gambler* in Toulouse. The critic Claude Rostand praised him and the production: 'A work of the first order; a beautiful voice, healthy, well managed: a distinguished artist' (*Figaro littéraire*, 31 Mar 1966).

Savoie next appeared in Johannesburg, singing in *Falstaff* and Britten's *War Requiem*, and at *Expo 67 (Valentin in *Faust*). In 1967 he sang Lescaut in *Manon* with the Théâtre lyrique du Québec and the next year he participated in the *Stratford Festival, singing Dandini in *Cenerentola*. He was soloist in *Matton's *Te Deum* in 1969 when it was premiered in France with the orchestra and choirs of the ORTF. In 1970 in southern France he sang Sancho in a touring production of Massenet's *Don Quichotte*, with Joseph *Rouleau in the title role. He sang *Falstaff* in Washington at the inauguration 9 Sep 1971 of the John F. Kennedy Center. In 1972 he again sang Rodrigo in *Don Carlos*, this time in the original French version for the BBC, with other Canadian singers – Édith *Tremblay, André *Turp, Émile *Belcourt, and Joseph Rouleau.

In 1973 Savoie was artistic director of a series of mini-operas presented in Montreal and Quebec City by the Théâtre de la *Poudrière. He has sung

Robert Savoie

at Carnegie Hall (*The Damnation of Faust*, 1972) and for the *Opéra du Québec (Lescaut and Leporello in 1973, Ford in *Falstaff*, and Sharpless in 1974). He participated in the performances *Festival Ottawa in 1977. In that year he was named vice-president of the Mouvement d'action pour l'art lyrique du Québec and in this capacity he has worked to establish a permanent opera company in Quebec. Robert Savoie's repertoire includes 95 roles in six languages. He is a brother of the pianist André-Sébastien *Savoie.

DISCOGRAPHY

La Bonne Chanson présente nos plus belles chansons, vol 4. La Bonne Chanson choir, Grassi dir. RCA Victor LCP-1035

Matton *Te Deum*. ORTF Chorus and Phil O, Bernier cond. 1969. RCI 290/Sel SSC-24.188

BIBLIOGRAPHY

Who's Who in Opera (New York 1976)

Bergeron, Raymonde. 'C'est ici que nous voulons chanter!' *Perspectives*, 19, 12 Feb 1977 (CH)

Savoyards. Operetta company founded in Toronto in 1919 by George *Stewart and his son Reginald. Its financial support came from the Canadian Operatic Society, founded in 1920 for the express purpose of providing such assistance. The Savoyards made their debut in Gilbert & Sullivan's *The Gondoliers* at the Princess Theatre during the week of 3 May 1920. George Stewart staged the production and Reginald conducted the orchestra. Ruth Cross starred as Tessa, Kenneth Angus played Giuseppe, Elwood Genoa was the Duke of Plaza-Toro, and A.J. Rostance was Don Alhambra. Cross also had a leading role in *The Pirates of Penzance*, the Savoyards' second production.

In addition to Gilbert & Sullivan, the company occasionally performed the light operas of Edward German and Robert Planquette. It staged two productions a year, some of them at the *Royal Alexandra Theatre. Owing to Reginald Stewart's increasing commitments as a concert pianist and conductor, the Savoyards dissolved after approximately eight seasons. (DS)

SCAMMELL, Arthur. Schoolteacher, songwriter, singer, b Change Islands, Nfld, 12 Feb 1913; BA (McGill) 1942, hon LL D (Memorial) 1977. His mother was a church organist in the Change Islands. At 15 he wrote the song *'Squid-jiggin' Ground,' adapting his own lyrics to an Irish fiddle tune, 'Larry O'Gaff,' as a high-school project. Scammell taught school in the early 1930s in the Newfoundland outports and after 1942 in the Montreal suburb Mount Royal. He continued to write songs, however, and gave private recitals and school concerts in Newfoundland. He also wrote articles on local folksong for the *Atlantic Guardian*, and his songs, verses, and sketches of outport life were published in *My Newfoundland* (Montreal 1966). The discographer Michael Taft has called Scammell the first person to record specifically for the Newfoundland market – in 1943 he made five 78s (nine tunes, including 'Squid-jiggin' Ground') and distributed them privately. After his retirement to St John's he made the LP *My Newfoundland* (1974, Audat 477-9043). Scammell is an affiliate of PRO Canada. (RGn)

SCHABAS, Ezra. Administrator, teacher, clarinetist, writer, b New York 24 Apr 1924, naturalized Canadian 1967; Artist Diploma (Juilliard) 1943, B SC (Juilliard) 1947, MA (Columbia) 1948. He studied at the Juilliard School with Arthur Christmann (clarinet), Hans Letz (chamber music), and Rose Marie Grentzer (music education) and, while serving with the US forces in France during World War II, attended the conservatory in Nancy. He returned to France in 1949 to the American Cons at Fontainebleau. He also studied at Columbia U 1946–8 and 1951, at the ESM in 1950, and privately in New York with David Weber and in Paris with Gaston Hamelin. In 1952, after academic appointments in New York, Massachusetts, and Ohio, he joined the Faculty of Music at the *U of Toronto, where he taught clarinet until 1978 and served 1952–60 as director of the RCMT Concert and Placement Bureau. Among his pupils have been Brian *Barley, Paul Grice, Howard Knopf, Timothy Maloney, Peter Smith, and Patricia Waite. He became chairman of the university's performance and opera departments in 1968. That same year, in collaboration with POCA (*OAC), he established the U of Toronto Student Conductors' Workshop. He was organizer and chairman of Canada's first 'Teaching Opera Conference,' sponsored in 1976 by the university opera department. He was appointed principal of the *RCMT in 1978.

Schabas was a freelance clarinetist until 1960 with CBC orchestras, performed with the Paganini and *Parlow string quartets, was a member 1956–60 of the *Toronto Woodwind Quintet, and served 1958–61 as music manager of the *Stratford Festival. He was a conductor of CBC and student ensembles; an instructor 1960–2, auditioner 1960–2 and 1965, and academic administrator 1960–2, 1964, and 1965 for the *NYO; and a woodwind instructor in 1975 for the JM World Orchestra.

Schabas' practical knowledge of music education and administration and his experience as an organizer have made him a valued consultant and board member, and his informed and outspoken views have made him an authoritative guest lecturer and contributor to panel-discussions and periodicals. He served 1972–4 as the first president of the *ACO. He has lectured in Canada, the USA, South America, and Europe, was editor 1962–3 of the *Canadian Music Educator* and Canadian editor 1954–62 of the *Musical Courier*, and has contributed to *Opera Canada, The Recorder, Performing Arts in Canada*, the *Globe and Mail*, and *Canadian Composer*, among other periodicals. He has written articles for *The New Grove Dictionary* and *EMC*. His reports *Ontario Community Orchestras* (Toronto 1966) and *Choral Music in Ontario* (Toronto 1970, in collaboration with Keith *Bissell) were commissioned by the OAC. A third report, *Toronto's New Orchestra* (Toronto 1976), was commissioned jointly by the *COC, the National Ballet of Canada, the OAC, the *TS, and the CBC. (MMI)

SCHAFER, R. (Raymond) **Murray**. Composer, writer, educator, b Sarnia, Ont, 18 Jul 1933; LRSM 1952, hon LL D (Carleton U) 1980. Suppressing a

R. Murray Schafer

youthful urge to become a painter, he entered the *RCMT and the *U of Toronto in 1952 to study with Alberto *Guerrero (piano), Greta *Kraus (harpsichord), John *Weinzweig (composition), and Arnold *Walter (musicology). In view of Schafer's later proclivities, however, his casual contact with Marshall McLuhan at the university might be singled out as the strongest and most lasting influence on his intellectual development. Disillusioned by what he came to view as the confining atmosphere of the university, Schafer terminated his formal studies in 1955 and embarked upon an intensive autodidactic routine with an emphasis on languages, literature, and philosophy. The LRSM remains his only formal diploma.

When in 1956 Schafer left Canada his plan was to study music at the Vienna Academy. Once there, however, his main attention was absorbed by medieval German – an early manifestation of his strong interest in unusual and exotic languages. After nearly two years in Vienna he went to England, where he studied briefly and informally with the composer Peter Racine Fricker. During his lengthy stay in Britain Schafer supported himself largely by journalism (the major result of which was a book, *British Composers in Interview*) and by the preparation of a performing edition of the poet Ezra Pound's little-known opera *Le Testament* (1920–1) broadcast by the BBC in 1961. It was also in England, 1 Jul 1960, that he married his first wife, the Canadian mezzo-soprano Phyllis *Mailing.

Back in Toronto Schafer organized in 1961 and for a time directed the *Ten Centuries Concerts. He then began 12 years of teaching, first (1963–5) as artist-in-residence at *Memorial U, and then (1965–75) at *Simon Fraser U. It was at Simon Fraser, with the aid of grants from Unesco and the Donner Canadian Foundation, that he set up the *World Soundscape Project dedicated to the study of man's relationship to his acoustic environment. Schafer moved in 1975 to a farm near Bancroft, Ont, but has remained affiliated with the project. In September 1975 he married Jean Elliott. During 1976 and 1977 he brought to completion a labour of love begun 16 years earlier – the preparation of a complete edition of the musical writings and musical works (including the two operas) of Ezra Pound.

Schafer's earliest extant works – the *Concerto for Harpsichord and Eight Wind Instruments*, the *Sonatina for Flute and Harpsichord (or Piano)*, and the *Partita for String Orchestra* may be singled out – reveal a debt to his teacher Weinzweig in particular and to the currents of post-war serialism in general. Their very titles recall the kind of neoclassical dodecaphonism fashionable in the 1950s. However the *Minnelieder*, a setting of 13 love songs from medieval Germany, though neoclassi-

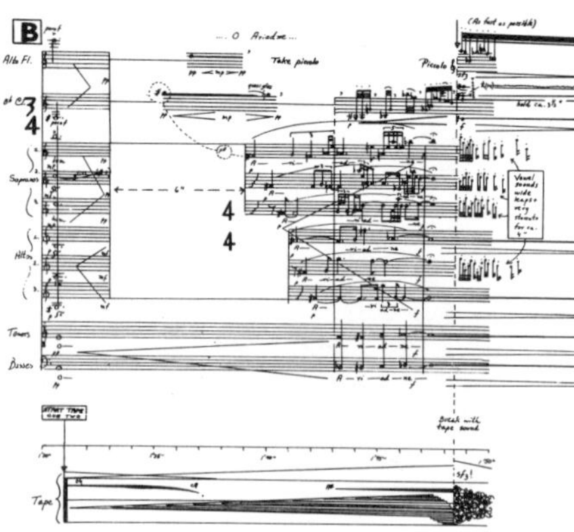

A manuscript page from *From the Tibetan Book of the Dead* by R. Murray Schafer

cal in flavour, generate an atmosphere which the composer acknowledges to be Mahlerian. Significantly, Schafer has singled out this expressive work as his first important achievement.

In the early 1960s Schafer began to draw on diverse mid-20th-century compositional techniques and on the language, literature, and philosophy of ancient and recent cultures, and to explore the mythology and symbolism of modern life. The result was a succession of chillingly effective multimedia studies on 20th-century urban themes of alienation and psychoneurosis. *Protest and Incarceration, Canzoni for Prisoners*, the bilingual TV opera *Loving*, and *Requiems for the Party Girl* (winner of the Fromm Foundation Prize, 1968) reflect a searching, wide-ranging social consciousness which motivates and informs all of Schafer's activities.

Canzoni for Prisoners, five interconnected movements for orchestra, is a sombre, pointillistic, and somewhat Webernesque work of great textural delicacy which may be viewed as an anti-fascist statement dedicated to that committed species of non-violent conscientious objector which became a force in Western society in the mid-1960s. *Requiems for the Party Girl*, the central episode in a planned triptych called *Patria*, documents the mental collapse and suicide of a young woman who becomes a poignant symbol of acute loneliness and alienation in the dehumanized labyrinth of contemporary urban society. Characteristically, in this and many later works, Schafer utilizes the full resources of the multimedia theatre in a hybrid form the composer has referred to as a 'Theatre of Confluence' (a kind of neo-Gesamtkunstwerk which reflects Schafer's urge to explore the relationships between the arts).

An important aspect of Schafer's multi-faceted career has been his deep involvement in music education. His unique and imaginative booklets – *The Composer in the Classroom, Ear Cleaning, The New Soundscape, When Words Sing*, and *Rhinoceros in the Classroom* – illustrate the composer's experiences with students and are among the first attempts to introduce Cageian concepts of creative hearing and sensory awareness into the Canadian classroom. As an adjunct to his teaching Schafer has composed several works for youth orchestra and choir. *Statement in Blue, Threnody* (a moving and bitter commentary on the bombing of Nagasaki based on comments by survivors), and *Epitaph for Moonlight* introduce young musicians to an unusual range of sounds while involving them in the creative process through a minimal use of aleatoric techniques.

As the self-styled 'father of acoustic ecology' Schafer has been concerned about the damaging effects of technological sounds on humans, especially those living in the 'sonic sewers' of urban environments. His booklets *The Book of Noise* and *The Music of the Environment* are reasoned but impassioned pleas for anti-noise legislation and improvement of the urban soundscape through the elimination or reduction of potentially destructive sounds. Coincidental with his critical exploration of the new soundscape has been a search for alternative life-styles which has led Schafer to a growing preoccupation with eastern thought and religion. His mature music reveals an ever-widening stylistic and linguistic boundary along with a tendency towards mysticism and a kind of oriental quietism. The sources are of a rich and unorthodox diversity, ranging from 13th-century Persian love poems in *Divan i Shams i Tabriz* (part 1 of *Lustro* and the product of a 1969 *Canada Council-sponsored visit to Persia and Turkey) to fragments of a Bruckner symphony in *Music for the Morning of the World* (part 2 of *Lustro*), the verse of Rabindranath Tagore in *Beyond the Great Gate of Light* (part 3 of *Lustro*), the sounds of the sea and the poetry of Hesiod, Homer, Melville, and Pound in *Okeanos*, and Middle Egyptian hieroglyphs in *Arcana*. The first complete performance of *Lustro* was given in 1973 by the CBC and the second in 1975 as a special event of the General Assembly of the International Music Council (held that year in Canada) that preceded *World Music Week.

Although Schafer's outlook is largely internationalist, there have been signs in the mid-1970s that he is retreating into a more parochial culture to avoid contact with the garish and unhealthy aspects of the sonic landscape. His search for spiritual unity has led to a synthesis of 20th-century avant-garde techniques with the spirit of 19th-century romanticism. The highly original result has secured him a special status among Canadian musicians of his generation. He received the *CMCouncil's first Composer of the Year Award in 1977 and the first Jules Léger Prize for New Chamber Music (for his *String Quartet No. 2*) in 1978. In 1980 he was awarded the Prix international Arthur-Honegger for *Quartet No. 1*. He is an affiliate of PRO Canada and an associate of the *CMCentre.

SELECTED COMPOSITIONS

STAGE

Patria II (Schafer). 1972 (Stratford 1972). Ber 1978. See also *Requiems for the Party Girl* (under 'Chamber') and *From the Tibetan Book of the Dead* (under 'Choir').

Patria I 'The Characteristics of Man' (Schafer). 1974. Mezzo, mime, actors, 32-v chorus, chamb ens. Ber 1979

See also *Loving*.

ORCHESTRA

In Memoriam: Alberto Guerrero. 1959 (Van 1962). Str orch. CMCentre

Partita for String Orchestra. 1961 (Van 1963). CMCentre. CBC SM-15 (*CBC Van Chamb O)

Canzoni for Prisoners. 1962 (Mtl 1963). Full orch. Ber 1977

Untitled Composition for Orchestra. 1963 (Tor 1966). Sm orch. Ms

Statement in Blue. 1964 (Tor 1965). Youth orch. BMIC 1966, UE 1971. 1970. Mel SMLP 4017 (Lawrence Park Collegiate O, J. McDougall cond)

Son of Heldenleben. 1968 (Mtl 1968). Full orch, tape. UE 1976. RCI 387/Sel CC-15.101 (*MSO)

No Longer than Ten Minutes. 1970. Rev 1972 (Tor 1971). Full orch. Ber 1977

East (meditations on a text from *Ishna Upanishad*). 1972 (Bath, England, 1973). Sm orch. UE 1977. RCI 434 (*NACO)

Train. 1976 (Tor 1976). Youth orch. Ber 1978

Cortège. 1977. Ms

SOLOISTS AND/OR CHOIR WITH ORCHESTRA

Concerto for Harpsichord and Eight Wind Instruments. 1954 (Mtl 1959). CMCentre. RCI 193 (K. *Jones hpd)

Protest and Incarceration (Rumanian poets). 1960 (Tor 1967). Mezzo, orch. CMCentre

Brébeuf, cantata (Brébeuf, transl Schafer). 1961 (Tor 1966). Bar, orch. CMCentre

Threnody (Japanese children). 1966, rev 1967 (Van 1967). Choir, orch, tape. Ber 1970. 1970. Mel SMLP 4017 (Lawrence Park Collegiate O and Choir, J. Barron cond)

Lustro. 1970–2 (CBC Tor 1973). Comprising:
- Part 1: *Divan i Shams i Tabriz* (Jalal al din Rumi). 1969, rev 1970. 6 solo vs, orch, tape. UE 1977
- Part 2: *Music for the Morning of the World* (various). 1970. V, 4-track tape. UE 1973
- Part 3: *Beyond the Great Gate of Light* (Tagore). 1972. 6 solo vs, orch, tape. UE 1977

Arcana (Middle Egyptian hieroglyphs, transl D.B. Redford). 1972 (Mtl 1973 orch version). V, orch (v, chamb ens). Ms. UE 1975 (chamb version). RCI 434 (*Morrison)

North / White. 1973 (Van 1973). Hp, pf, snowmobile, str. UE 1975

Adieu Robert Schumann (Clara Schumann, adapt Schafer). 1976. Alto, orch. CMCentre

CHAMBER

Minnelieder (medieval German). 1956. Mezzo, ww quin. Ber 1970. RCI 218/RCA CCS-1012 (Mailing mezzo, *Tor WW Quin)

Sonatina for Flute and Harpsichord (or Piano). 1958. Ber 1976

Five Studies on Texts by Prudentius. 1962. Sop, 4 fl. BMIC 1965

4 pieces from *Loving: The Geography of Eros* (1963), and *Air Ishtar, Modesty, Vanity* (all 1965). V, chamb ens. CMCentre

Requiems for the Party Girl (Schafer) from *Patria II*. 1966. Mezzo, chamb ens. BMIC 1967. RCI 299 (*Mailing mezzo, SMCQ)/Mel SMLP 4026 (Mailing, instr ens, Schafer cond)/CRI SD 245 (Pilgrim sop, Chicago U Contemporary Chamb Players, Shapey cond)

Minimusic. 1967. Any comb of instr or v. UE 1971

Sappho (Sappho). 1970. Mezzo, hp, pf, guit, perc. Ms

String Quartet No. 1. 1970. UE 1973. RCI 353/Mel SMLP 4026 (*Purcell Str Quar)/Concert Hall SMS 2902 (*Orford Str Quar)

The Enchantress (Sappho). 1971. V, exotic fl, 8 vc. Ber 1978

Hymn to Night (Novalis, Friedrich von Hardenberg). 1976. Sop, chamb ens, tape. Ms

String Quartet No. 2 ('Waves'). 1976. Ber 1977. Mel SMLP-4038 (*Orford Str Quar)

The Crown of Ariadne. Ca 1979. Hp, perc. Ms. Aquitaine MS 90570 (*Loman)

Music for Wilderness Lake (soundscape). 1979. 12 trb, O'-Grady Lake. Ms

CHOIR

Four Songs on Texts of Tagore. 1958. Sop, mezzo, alto, SA. CMCentre

Gita (Bhagavad Gita). 1967. SATB, brass, tape. UE 1977

Epitaph for Moonlight (Schafer). 1968. SATB, bells (optional). BMIC 1969, UE 1971. CBC SM-274 (*Festival Singers) /Mel SMLP 4017 (Lawrence Park Collegiate Choir, J. Barron cond)

From the Tibetan Book of the Dead (Bardo Thödol) from *Patria II*. 1968. Sop, SATB, alto fl, cl, tape. UE 1973

Yeow and Pax – retitled *Two Anthems* (Bible). 1969. SATB, org, tape. Ms

In Search of Zoroaster (sacred books of the East). 1971. Male v, SATB, perc, org. Ber 1976

Miniwanka or the Moments of Water (North American Indian dialects). 1971. SA (SATB). UE 1973. RCI 434 (*Van Bach Choir)

Tehillah – retitled *Psalm* (Psalm 148). 1972, rev 1976. Mixed chorus, perc. Ber 1976. RCI 434 (*Van Bach Choir)

Apocalypsis (Revelations, bp nichol, Schafer). 1977 (London, Ont 1980). Ms. Comprising:
- Part 1: *John's Vision*. 12 choirs, brass instr, perc, home-made instrs
- Part 2: *Credo*. 12 choirs, tape

VOICE

Three Contemporaries (Schafer?). 1954–6. Mezzo, pf. Ber 1974

Kinderlieder (traditional, Brecht). 1958. Mezzo, pf. Ber 1975. CBC SM-141 (*Mailing mezzo)

Dream Passage (Schafer). 1969, preliminary study for *Patria II*. Mezzo, tape. Ms

La Testa d'Adriane (Schafer). 1977. V, acc. Ms. Mel SMLP-4034 (*Morrison sop)

ELECTRONIC

Kaleidoscope. 1967. Multi-track tape

Okeanos (Hesiod, Homer, Melville, Pound). 1971. 4-track tape

Also a work for pf solo, *Polytonality* (1954). Ber 1974

Several works in all categories, now withdrawn by the composer. These include *The Judgement of Jael* (1961), *Dithyramb for String Orchestra* (1961), *Opus One for Mixed*

Chorus (1962), *Divisions for Baroque Trio* (1962–3), *Invertible Material for Orchestra No. 1* (1963), *Festival Music for Small Orchestra* (1966), *Sonorities for Brass Sextet* (1966).

WRITINGS

Review of record of Harry Partch: *U.S. Highball – A Musical Account of a Transcontinental Hobo Trip*, *CMJ*, vol 3, Winter 1959

'International Folk Music Council: twelfth annual conference,' *CMJ*, vol 4, Autumn 1959

'Review of works by Alwyn, Vaughan Williams, Rubbra, Walton,' *Notes*, vol 17, Dec 1959

'Two musicians in fiction,' *CMJ*, vol 4, Spring 1960

'Review of I. Stravinsky and Robert Craft: *Conversations with Igor Stravinsky*; M. Tippett, *Moving into Aquarius*, *CMJ*, vol 4, Summer 1960

'Music and the Iron Curtain,' *Queen's Q*, vol 67, Autumn 1960

'The limits of nationalism in Canada,' *Tamarack R*, 18, Winter 1961

'Ezra Pound and music,' *CMJ*, vol 5, Summer 1961; partial reprint in *Ezra Pound: A Collection of Critical Essays* ed Walter Sutton (Englewood Cliffs, NJ, 1963)

'The Canadian String Quartet,' *CMJ*, vol 6, Spring 1962

'Music ... 1961/62 in Toronto,' *Canadian Art*, vol 19, Jul–Aug 1962

'A perspective for musical appreciation,' *Recorder*, vol 5, Dec 1962

British Composers in Interview (London 1963)

'Short history of music in Canada,' *Catalogue of Orchestral Music at the Canadian Music Centre* (Toronto 1963)

'Opera and reform,' *OpCan*, vol 5, Feb 1964

'What is this article about?' *Canadian Forum*, vol 44, Dec 1964

The Composer in the Classroom (Scarborough, Ont, 1965) / *Schoepferisches Musizieren* (Vienna 1971)

– writer, narrator. 'In search of Charles Ives,' CBC radio 'Tuesday Night,' 13 Sep 1966

'The philosophy of stereophony,' *West Coast R*, vol 1, Winter 1967

Ear Cleaning (Scarborough, Ont, 1967) / *L'Oreille pense* (Scarborough 1972) / *Schule des Hörens* (Vienna 1972)

'The future of music in Canada,' *Proceedings and Transactions of the Royal Society of Canada*, vol 5, Jun 1967

'Music and education,' *MSc*, 239, 240, Jan–Feb, Mar–Apr 1968

'Cleaning the lenses of perception,' *Arts Canada*, vol 25, Oct–Nov 1968

The New Soundscape (Scarborough, Ont, 1969) / *Der Schallwelt in der wir leben* (Vienna 1971)

'A basic course,' *Source: Music of the Avant Garde*, vol 3, Jan 1969

'The city as a sonic sewer,' Vancouver *Sun*, 11 Mar 1969

The Book of Noise (Wellington, New Zealand, 1970)

When Words Sing (Scarborough, Ont, 1970) / *Wenn Worte klingen* (Vienna 1972)

'A Middle-East sound diary,' *Focus on Musicecology*, vol 1, 1970

'Threnody: a religious piece for our time,' *AGO / RCCO Music*, vol 4, May 1970

'Discovering the word's soul,' *Music Educators J*, vol 57, Sep 1970

Review of Pierre Demers, ed *Le Bruit: 4e pollution du monde moderne*, *CMB*, 2, Spring–Summer 1971

'Lärmflut – eine Montage,' *Musik and Bildung*, vol 3, Jul 1971

'Thoughts on music education,' *CMB*, 3, Autumn–Winter 1971; repr in *Australian Music Educator's J*, Spring 1972

A Survey of Community Noise By-laws in Canada, Soundscape Document no. 4 (Vancouver 1972)

The Public of the Music Theatre: Louis Riel – A Case Study (Vienna 1972)

The Music of the Environment (Vienna 1973); repr in *Cultures*, vol 1, 1973

'Where does it all lead?' *Australian J of Music Education*, 12, Apr 1973

The Vancouver Soundscape, Soundscape Document no. 5 (Vancouver 1974)

'Notes for the stage work "Loving" (1965),' *CMB*, 8, Spring–Summer 1974

'The theatre of confluences (notes in advance of action),' *CMB*, 9, Autumn–Winter 1974

Rhinoceros in the Classroom (London 1975)

'The graphics of musical thought,' *Sound Sculpture*, ed John Grayson (Vancouver 1975); repr in *Festschrift Kurt Blaukopf*, ed I. Bontinck and O. Brusatli (Vienna 1975)

E.T.A. Hoffmann and Music (Toronto 1975)

Creative Music Education (New York 1976)

Smoke: A Novel (Vancouver 1976)

'Exploring the new soundscape,' *Unesco Courier*, vol 29, Nov 1976

The Tuning of the World (Toronto 1977)

'Music in the cold,' *Vanguard*, Apr 1977. Repr *Music in the Cold* (Toronto 1977)

– ed, commentator. *Ezra Pound and Music: The Complete Criticism* (New York 1977)

– ed. *European Sound Diary*, Music of the Environment Series no. 3 (Vancouver 1977)

– ed. *Five Village Soundscapes*, ibid no. 4 (Vancouver 1977)

A Chaldean Inscription, priv publ (Toronto 1978)

'Ten Centuries Concerts: a recollection,' *Only Paper Today*, vol 5, Toronto 1978

'The real reason for a poor mail service,' Toronto *Globe and Mail*, 16 Sep 1978

Open Letter, double issue devoted to Schafer's writings on music, 4th series, Fall 1979

BIBLIOGRAPHY

'Murray Schafer – a portrait,' *Mcan*, 14, Oct 1968

Ball, Suzanne. 'Murray Schafer: composer, teacher and author,' *MSc*, 253, May–Jun 1970

Mather, Bruce. 'Notes sur "Requiems for the Party Girl" de Schafer,' *CMB*, 1, Spring–Summer 1970

Bissell, Keith. Review of *The Composer in the Classroom, Ear Cleaning, The New Soundscape, When Words Sing*, *CMB*, 2, Spring–Summer 1971

Such, Peter. 'Murray Schafer,' *Soundprints* (Toronto 1971)

Kasemets, Udo. Review of *Threnody*, *CMB*, 5, Autumn–Winter 1972

Rea, John. 'Richard Wagner and R. Murray Schafer: two revolutionary and religious poets,' *CMB*, 8, Spring–Summer 1974

BMI Canada/PRO Canada Ltd. 'Murray Schafer,' pamphlet (1975, 1979)

Potter, Keith, and Shepherd, John. 'Interview with Murray Schafer,' *Contact: Today's Music*, 13, spring 1976

Skelton, Robert. 'Weinzweig, Gould, Schafer: three Canadian string quartets,' unpubl PH D thesis, U of Indiana 1976

MacMillan, Rick, ed. 'Schafer sees music reflecting country's characteristics,' *MSc*, 293, Jan–Feb 1977

– 'Grand apocalypse from an Ontario farm house,' *Fugue*, Oct 1977

Adams, Stephen. 'A bibliography of R. Murray Schafer,' *Open Letter*, 4th series, Fall 1979

Kasemets, Udo. 'Murray Schafer,' *Contemporary Canadian Composers/Compositeurs canadiens contemporains*

FILM

Bing, Bang, Boom (NFB 1975)

Music for Wilderness Lake (Fichman-Sweete Productions 1980)

AMG

SCHALLEHN, Henry. German musician active in Toronto in the middle of the 19th century: violinist, clarinetist, bandmaster, and teacher. Schallehn may be the Henry Schallehn (1815–27 Jun 1891) described in H.G. Farmer's *The Rise and Development of Military Music* (London 1912) as bandmaster of the 17th Lancers Band 1845–57, director of the Crystal Palace Band in 1854, and music director of the RMSM (Kneller Hall) 1857–9, all in England. David Sale's thesis, 'Toronto's preconfederation music societies,' dates Schallehn's Toronto activites 1847–51. In 1849 Schallehn advertised in the Toronto *Globe* as a teacher of piano, guitar, and voice. He also participated 1849–50 in the *Toronto Philharmonic Society's concerts and performed as conductor, concertmaster, piano accompanist, and violin and clarinet soloist, besides appearing with other musical societies in Toronto and Hamilton. In 1850 he was the singing master 'pro tem' at Upper Canada College, and in 1851 the city directory listed him as a 'professor of music.' In 'Music in Toronto' (*The Mail*, 21 Dec 1878) he is remembered as 'a versatile musician ... a clever clarinet player and ... bandmaster of the 71st Regiment.' He was the composer of the *Cathcart Polkas* (Nordheimer 1848), *Scotch Fusilier's Guards Polka* (Nordheimer 1848), *Ontario Quickstep March* (Nordheimer 1848), *Assembly Galop* (Mead, Brothers ca 1848), and other dances.

A brother, Ferdinand, was a violinist, and another, Theodore, a pianist whose published music includes *The Lilla Polka* and *The Amy Polka* (Nordheimer 1850) and *Niagara Polka* (Sage [Buffalo] 1853). HK

SCHERMAN, Paul (Isidor). Conductor, violinist, b Toronto 12 Sep 1907. Raised (1912–20) in London (where he was a scholarship pupil of Leon Bergman and Hans Wessely at the RAM), Paris, and Berlin, Scherman returned to Toronto and studied violin with Luigi von *Kunits at the TCM and theory with Louis *Waizman privately. Later studies were taken with Albert Maieff in New York 1927–30, William Primrose in Toronto and London 1937–9, Dimitri Dounis in New York 1946–7, and Nadia Boulanger in Paris 1955–7. As a violin soloist Scherman toured 1923–6 in Ontario and made his radio debut in 1925 on CFCA, Toronto. He played in various Toronto theatre and radio orchestras and was a member of the New SO under von Kunits for two concerts in the 1925–6 season and for the entire 1926–7 season.

While a violinist 1932–52 with the *TSO Scherman appeared occasionally as soloist with the orchestra – for instance, in Wieniawski's *Concerto No. 2* 22 Mar 1946. Until 1944 he performed as Isidor Scherman. He was assistant conductor 1947–55 of the TSO and made his conducting debut 7 Feb 1947 in a pop concert. In the 1940s he also conducted orchestras for several CBC radio programs, including 'The Northern Electric Hour' and, under the name Don Miguel, 'Latin American Serenade.' As a violinist he participated 1950, 1951, and 1953 at the Casals Festival in Prades. Scherman was one of the *CBC SO conductors 1952–7 and conducted its 1955 *Stratford Festival presentation of Stravinsky's *A Soldier's Tale*. Scherman's appearance 24 Oct 1955 as conductor with the Orchestre national in Paris was followed by engagements with the BBC Scottish Orchestra in 1955, the Vienna Radio Orchestra in 1955, the Vienna SO in 1956, and the London Philharmonic Orchestra in 1959. Settling in London he was a member 1958–60 of the Royal Philharmonic Orchestra and then became a freelance violinist, playing in studio orchestras in the 1970s. MM

SCHILDER, Marie (b Rodker). Contralto of Finnish and Polish extraction, b London, 26 Apr 1903. She studied voice with Anton Tausche 1926–8 in Vienna and 1929–33 at the Vienna Academy and the Mozarteum in Salzburg. She won first place in the International Competition for Voice and Violin in Vienna in 1932. She became a specialist in Lieder, oratorio, and the vocal parts in chamber music. She appeared as soloist with the Royal Choral Society, London, in 1933, in recital in Brussels in 1934, as soloist with the Edinburgh and Newcastle Bach societies in 1938, and in recital on the BBC. She settled in Canada in 1939. She sang on CBC radio and appeared frequently 1946–56 with the *Friends of Chamber Music and 1956–64 with the *Vancouver SO. In 1960 she began to teach at the *U of British Columbia. Her pupils included Lloyd *Burritt and Ian *Docherty. Her warm contralto voice reflects a strong personality and a dramatic flair, recalling the grand style of another era. CF

SCHIØTZ, Aksel. Tenor, teacher, b Roskilde, Denmark, 1 Sep 1906, d Copenhagen 19 Apr 1975. The famed Danish singer, knighted for his service in the Resistance during the Nazi occupation in World War II, was forced to pursue a teaching career when a surgical operation partially paralyzed his face and severely impaired his voice. He gradually resumed his singing career, but as a baritone. He taught for 13 years, 1955–68, in North

America, first working at the *RCMT in the summer of 1955 while appearing at the *Stratford Festival. After teaching at the *U of British Columbia Summer School, giving recitals, and broadcasting 1956–8 for CBC Vancouver he taught again 1958–61 at the RCMT and performed throughout southern Ontario. He also gave recitals in 1961 at the *Vancouver International Festival before taking an appointment at the U of Colorado. He returned to Denmark in 1968 and completed his book, *The Singer and His Art* (New York 1970). His Canadian pupils included Alan *Crofoot, Evaleen Dunlop, Albert *Greer, Mona Kelly, Phyllis *Mailing, Randall Marsh, James *Stark, John *Stratton, and James Whicher.

Schola cantorum. Founded in Montreal 19 Mar 1915 by Jean-Noël *Charbonneau. It was inaugurated 15 September as the Diocesan School of Sacred Music by Archbishop Georges Gauthier of Montreal. Its first individual and group lessons were attended by 84 students. The program included theory, solfège, voice, liturgical Latin, Gregorian chant, liturgy, choral ensemble, elementary keyboard, organ, Gregorian-chant accompaniment, music history, harmony, and composition. The teachers were Salvator *Issaurel, Arthur *Laurendeau, Arthur *Letondal, Benoît *Poirier, and Ethelbert *Thibault. The institution was affiliated 1917–19 with *Laval U and 1919–38 with the *U of Montreal. Among the graduates were Camille Duquette of *Archambault, Charles *Goulet, and Clément *Morin. Duquette worked for the Schola cantorum's publishing program, which was designed to promote Canadian sacred music. It published Frédéric *Pelletier's *Messe de requiem*, Alphonse *Lavallée-Smith's *Messe des morts*, Roméo *Larivière's *Cantique pour une première messe*, and several anthologies. The 1927 reorganization of the *Cons national of Montreal by Eugène *Lapierre led to a gradual decline in the school's enrolment, and in 1938 it was integrated in the Institut musical du Canada organized by Charbonneau in 1922.

School music

1 INTRODUCTION. Musical activities and music instruction began to appear in some form or other in many Canadian schools with the appearance of a formal system of education in the mid-19th century. Their importance in the Canadian curriculum was slight, however, until the 1930s, and the main advances were made in the period following World War II.

The importance attached to music in education, as in life, has varied widely, usually, but not always, increasing in proportion to the degree of sophistication and urbanization in the community and fluctuating according to the socio-economic level and the cultural heritage of its citizens.

The fact that the British North America Act has made education a provincial concern has had a profound influence on the progress of music education. The various provincial and municipal authorities have solved their educational problems in a variety of ways, selecting the solutions which they deemed wisest and best according to existing circumstances. This apportioning of responsibility to the provinces has all the advantages provided by geographical proximity, but on a national scale it has resulted in a lamentable lack of uniformity in the educational procedure, especially as it pertains to music.

Over the years each province has evolved its own bureaucracy, which often bears little resemblance to that of its neighbours and which pays varying and sometimes scant attention to music and the other arts. Across Canada wide variations continued to exist in 1980, particularly in budgeting, curricula, scheduling, and training and certification of teachers, not to mention the kinds of musical activities and the calibre of experience available to the children. The requirements and activities in a given year of mathematics study show considerable similarity from one province to the next. This is not the case in music. Discrepancies have abounded even between one school and another, not only in a single province but also within the same area. Trends toward decentralization of authority within a province in the 1970s made it increasingly difficult for those making the decisions concerning music education to collaborate formally with their counterparts in other provinces.

Given the principle of provincial jurisdiction, much of this variation has been unavoidable and perhaps even of little long-range significance. However, decentralization has had a detrimental effect on the development of music in the schools and has made it difficult to assess progress or to compare achievement between provinces. Other problems in music education in Canada stem from the teachers themselves. Despite much concern, there is, on the whole, little consensus on the part of Canadian teachers as to the objectives or the philosophy of school music except in the most general, fundamental terms. Efforts of national organizations such as the *CAUSM and the *CMEA have been productive in the setting of standards.

Yet serious unanswered questions continued to exist in the collective mind of the Canadian school music profession. Differences of opinion and uncertainty exist, not only as to curricular problems in music, such as choral versus instrumental instruction or what constitutes 'good' or 'bad' music, but also in professional problems: the length and the kind of training required of music teachers-in-training, the function and relative importance of the classroom and the specialist music teacher, the 'professional musician' who is becoming a teacher and the professional teacher who is learning about music, the relationship between mere entertainment and the acquisition of performing skills in music, the integration of performance and non-performance activities, the competition festival, and, more recently, the importance of creative work in the developing of musicianship in children and the ideal ratio of creative and re-creative activities in the classroom. Any evaluation of music instruction is thus made increasingly difficult because of vague and shifting criteria.

By far the most important and pressing need of the profession as a whole at the threshold of the 1980s was a sound philosophical foundation for the teaching of music as an essential ingredient of the school curriculum, a justification which is unique to music but valid in today's educational system and which is acceptable to the general public and to the educational authorities alike. Spurious justifications (contributions to physical health, social skills, citizenship training, etc) offered in the past have tended to cause confusion in the minds of teachers because of their lack of educational significance or uniqueness to music. Even in the 1970s the distinctive role of music in aesthetic education – one of encouraging perception, reaction, and general sensitivity – seemed to be understood by few music educators and even fewer administrators and parents.

The importation of systems of music instruction developed in Europe and Asia and highly successful in the countries of origin has found many converts in Canada. For example, the system evolved by Zoltán Kodály and his disciples has been found particularly relevant to Canada, perhaps because of its firm pedagogical foundations and the prior existence and wide acceptance in Canada of one of its basic techniques, the 'moveable doh' or Tonic Sol-fa system. Inevitably, however, these imported techniques need considerable clarification and some adaptation for effective incorporation into Canadian schools. Such adaptation presupposes a thorough grasp of the system to be adapted as well as a mature understanding of the Canadian need itself – no small accomplishment. (See Teaching methods.)

Strangely enough, some of these problems seem to have been solved in a given area of the country only to arise a decade or so later there, or in some other area, as innovative teachers seek to incorporate so-called 'new' ideas. Moreover, there is at least as much resistance to change in the teaching profession as there is in other professions.

Increasing importance is being attached to research in music education, and many more studies than ever before are being carried out. The results of this work promise to shed new light on pedagogical procedures and other problems. (See Canadian Music Research Council; Music education research.)

A poor teacher can do more harm than good, especially in music, and a supply of adequately trained music teachers has been a perennial problem because training in music is long, and acceptable short cuts are few. After the middle of the 20th century university music schools across Canada began to produce increasing numbers of talented graduates whose musical expertise and teaching potential brightened the educational future of Canadian youth and the developing maturity of the Canadian music teaching profession. It is ironical, however, that this promising supply of young teachers has appeared in the face of severe economic difficulties in the field of education.

A long view of the situation reveals, however, that the problems and uncertainties outlined above have brought about only partial impairment of the progress of music education in the schools. Experience across Canada has shown that when a dedicated musician-teacher works industriously and enthusiastically to introduce or improve music instruction in the schools of his or her area, the results are almost incredible. The enthusiasm generated among the participating students by this gifted master teacher spreads first to the parents and then to the school administrators and the general public. Neighbouring schools often are spurred to develop a similar or supplementary program in music. Many communities in Canada can testify to the experience of being 'put on the map' culturally by such means. What must be acknowledged in the face of such evidence is that, with a few notable exceptions, the impetus for expanding and improving instruction in Canadian schools has come from uniquely talented pioneer teachers rather than from the established educational hierarchy.

Nearly every province seems to have had at hand imaginative, visionary men and women who, at appropriate times and grasping all available opportunities, have taken the lead in developing music in their schools. On occasions, successors to these pioneers in music have suffered reverses, thus demonstrating that music programs can deteriorate in much less time than it takes to create them. Nevertheless, these unselfish individuals and their supporters, many quite unknown beyond their own provinces or their immediate areas of action, have contributed much more than they were aware of, and Canada is deeply in their debt.

See also Children and music; Choir schools; Competition festivals; Composition for ensemble teaching; John Adaskin Project; School music broadcasts; School songbooks; Solmization; Summer camps and schools; Teaching methods; Theory textbooks; Universities.

2 EARLY PATTERNS OF MUSIC INSTRUCTION. The resources of pioneer communities were devoted to stressing the fundamentals of education to the exclusion of music. The idea that music was not part of the core curriculum, which was understandable enough in a pioneer society, has persisted. For example, in Ontario, one of the provinces which began first and has progressed furthest in school music, a senior education official during the 1950s, fortunately atypical, used the word 'frill' in connection with music study in the school curriculum. This image has been difficult to dispel and has been extremely detrimental to the advancement of school music in Canada, although, as we have seen, school authorities readily make room for music activity when good teachers are present.

Initial development in the older parts of Canada invariably reflected the musical heritage of the settlers. It was French music that was taught to Quebec children by Mother *Marie de St-Joseph after 1639 and by Martin *Boutet after 1651. (These two were the first known to have taught music in Canadian schools.) It was German music that was taught at the Clinton Township school in the Niagara Peninsula during the opening decades of the 19th century, as witness the music notebooks preserved at the Jordan, Ont, Museum of the Twenty (see Manuscript books).

In the main, a child's exposure to music lessons in the late 18th and early 19th centuries was at *singing schools – which had more in common with Sunday schools than with public schools – or, if the parents could afford it, through private lessons. Throughout the 19th century, school music remained tied to the wealth of a family; it was offered, usually for an additional fee, at the many private young ladies' academies, at the convent schools and seminaries of Quebec, and at Toronto's Upper Canada College. (See Classical colleges and seminaries; Ladies' colleges and convent schools.)

When vocal music did appear in urban elementary schools it often was taught by people outside the school system – local private music teachers and church choir directors – with assistance from the classroom teacher. The time allotted was usually less than one hour a week, but this was increased later, particularly in the senior grades. The activity usually consisted of rote-singing and instruction in the rudiments of music. Development in rural schools followed later in a pattern similar to that of the urban centres, but standards were rarely as high. The experiences of one Ontario rural school teacher are recounted in Alistair P. Haig's 'Henry Frost: pioneer (1816–1851)' in the *Canadian Music Journal* (Winter 1958).

Initially elementary school teachers were expected to teach music, yet few were at all capable, and those only because they happened to possess some love for and training in music. In the course of the 19th century, however, the training of teachers was expanded to include some music and some form of licensing or certification in the subject, and the provinces began to set down and approve courses of study in music. By the 1930s some provinces had appointed provincial directors of music to supervise and co-ordinate musical efforts.

While vocal music eventually became an obligatory part of elementary school education, the first appearance of music activities in the high schools invariably was extra-curricular, some time later appearing as an elective curriculum offering. It was at this level that the first formal instruction in instrumental music was begun, usually in wind instruments and often sponsored by local service clubs. In many urban centres string instruments were introduced, sometimes at pre-secondary levels, and many orchestras, and many more bands, were formed. The earliest school ensemble recorded in history was at the *Séminaire de Québec.

It is interesting to note that the instrumental teaching was almost always done in class though at times it was supplemented by individual teaching sessions or by private lessons outside the school. In most cases, in elementary and particularly in secondary schools, extra-curricular activities, both vocal and instrumental, were undertaken to supplement the often insufficient time scheduled during school hours.

3 THE ATLANTIC PROVINCES. Vocal instruction in the schools began in Nova Scotia after the Normal College (later the Nova Scotia Teachers' College) opened in Truro in 1855. So great was the musical interest of the first principal, Dr Forrester, that he paid from personal funds a portion of the salary of his part-time music instructor. A singing program and Tonic Sol-fa instruction similar to those implemented in Nova Scotia were introduced in New Brunswick in 1872. This program became an official part of the elementary school curriculum in 1887 and was accepted much more widely in the early 1900s. The province's first full-time music instructor was Mary McCarthy, appointed in Moncton in 1905. She was succeeded by Frank Harrison, appointed to teach in Fredericton, in 1907. In-service training and special summer schools in music were held to alleviate the shortage of qualified music teachers in both of the larger Maritime provinces. Later in Nova Scotia summer programs for teachers were expanded greatly, especially in the 1950s under the direction of Catherine *Allison, who also, 1957–66, headed the newly formed music department of the Nova Scotia Teachers' College in Truro.

Competition festivals played a very large part in the development of school music programs in Nova Scotia and New Brunswick. By contrast, in Prince Edward Island and Newfoundland music training was more heavily indebted to the Roman Catholic school system. A festival initiated in Saint John, NB, just after 1900 was emulated in other centres in the province. Between 1930 and 1960 in Nova Scotia, the competition festival movement was responsible in large measure for the continuing interest in and the improved quality of, choral music.

Better-trained teachers, the enhanced stature of music in the school curriculum, and expanding music programs in the schools resulted in a great new interest in instrumental music instruction, especially in the high schools. Bands increased in number, and their calibre improved. The instrumental movement culminated in the *New Brunswick Youth Orchestra (1965) and the Halifax Schools Symphony Orchestra, both formed in the 1960s. New Brunswick's first provincial supervisor of music, David *Thomson, was appointed in 1949, and his salary was paid by the Kiwanis Club. In 1980 there were two: Gloria *Richard, consultant for the French-language division, and Douglas Hodkins, consultant for the English-language division, of the Dept of Education. Paul *Murray was appointed music consultant for the Nova Scotia Dept of Education in 1967. In Prince Edward Island Christopher *Gledhill, appointed in 1961, was succeeded by William Bartlett in 1978. All have engaged in formulating province-wide curricula and co-ordinating music education throughout their respective provinces.

All four provinces have vigorous associations of music educators, founded in the 1960s, and three of these – the *NSMEA (Halifax) in 1963, the *PEIMEA (Charlottetown) in 1971, and the *Music Council of the Newfoundland Teachers' Assn (St John's) in 1977 – have been hosts to national conferences of the CMEA.

By 1980 degree courses in music and music education were being offered by the music departments of *Acadia, *Dalhousie, *Mount St Vincent, and *St Francis Xavier universities in Nova Scotia; by *Mount Allison U and the *U of Moncton in New Brunswick; by the *U of Prince Edward Island; and by *Memorial U of Newfoundland.

See also Charlottetown; Halifax; Moncton; Saint John; St John's.

4 QUEBEC. Attempts to systematize music teaching in Quebec public schools began when the Protestant School Board of Montreal in 1931 appointed G.A. Stanton superintendent of music for protestant schools, and the Catholic School Commission of Montreal in 1934 appointed Claude *Champagne director of music education for catholic schools. The need for a music program was recognized in some schools, but obstacles to the enforcement of a coherent and effective system were so numerous that music teaching usually was left to the initiative of the classroom teacher who had some competence in the subject and could obtain authorization to devote some time to it. In establishments directed by religious orders, especially convent schools for girls (see Ladies' colleges and convent schools), music was given greater consideration; piano, violin, and singing were taught and, above all, choral singing because of its function in the rituals of the church. When the Manécanterie des Petits Chanteurs à la Croix de Bois of Paris visited the province in 1931, numerous choir schools of the same sort sprang up across Quebec. In so far as the public schools were concerned, however, a lack of sufficiently qualified music teachers remained the major problem.

A report of 1853, which deplored the lack of general training among teachers (of 2000 only 400-odd were suitably qualified), led to the establishing of teachers' training colleges in the province. In Montreal the École normale Jacques-Cartier served this function, and in 1871 it appointed R.-O. *Pelletier teacher of solfège and Gregorian chant. In his 35 years in the position Pelletier strove to provide school teachers with a basic musical training which they in turn could impart to the children in their charge in the cities and towns of Quebec. During his tenure music became a part of the qualification for a teaching diploma. Champagne took the teaching of music in the primary grades to heart. He wrote solfège exercises expressly for individual teachers and students. His successor 1942–6 was Raoul *Paquet; Paquet's, 1947–57, was Alfred *Mignault.

A royal commission of enquiry on teaching (Parent Report, 1966) made important recommendations, eg, 'Besides a general music education which is the right of everyone, more advanced training for those children who want it must be offered in the regular school curriculum.' A subsequent enquiry into the teaching of the arts in Quebec (*Rioux Report, 1969) was to lead to a greater preoccupation with the teaching of the arts in general, and music in particular. George *Little was put in charge of this area at the Ministry of Education, with Lorraine Boutin as music consultant. The music teachers formed the professional association *FAMEQ.

Several Quebec Catholic school boards appointed music consultants or co-ordinators. In Montreal Monique Leduc, Caroline Guay, and Michèle Clerk have held these positions. In the protestant system eminent educators have worked in this area, particularly Frank *Hanson, Irvin *Cooper, W.J. Hislop, and W.P. Percival, but in 1980 there was no specialist in charge of music.

In spite of the resolutions made by the commissions of enquiry, new program structures, and a co-ordination of effort, the future of music teaching at the elementary level in Quebec has remained problematic. In 1976–7 only 350 teachers, or 12 per cent of the teacher force, were specialists in music. Caroline Guay revealed that in Montreal, whereas 40 per cent of secondary schools had some sort of school band at the end of the 1960s, this percentage had fallen to 30 in 1979. Choral music also appeared on the decline; in 1979 only 2 of 59 secondary schools in the Catholic School Commission had choirs.

Throughout Quebec organizations such as the *JMC and *Educanima have contributed a great deal to the spread of a taste for music. The teaching of string instruments has flourished, largely because of groups such as the *Petits Violons and the *Société musicale Le Mouvement Vivaldi. The methods of Orff, Corneloup, and Kodály, the préconservatoires, and the music departments in the *Cegeps have contributed toward the accessibility of music training. In 1980 it remained for the efforts to be unified and the initiatives to be coordinated in such a way as to achieve even more decisive results.

See also Conservatoire de musique du Québec; Écoles Sacré-Coeur and Mitchell of Sherbrooke.

5 ONTARIO. The first official recognition of music as a part of public education came in 1848 when J.H. Robertson and, a month later, J.P. *Clarke were appointed to the Toronto Normal School at the instigation of Egerton Ryerson, who had been chief superintendent of education for Upper Canada since 1844. H.F. *Sefton occupied the position at the normal school 1858–82. In his report of 1850, Ryerson listed more than 5700 Canada West students in some sort of vocal music classes out of a total elementary school population of over 150,000 (approximately 4 per cent). By 1935 43 per cent of the students in the public and separate schools in Ontario had regular music instruction, and by 1950, 86 per cent.

The first summer courses for music teachers were given by the *U of Toronto in 1887 but these did not continue on a regular basis. In 1918 they were taken over by the Dept of Education. Duncan McKenzie (b Glencarse, Scotland, 1885) directed the summer school in the 1920s and was director of music for the Toronto schools. The summer schools expanded to such an extent that in the late 1930s they were being held in two centres: Toronto under P. George Marshall and London, Ont, under G. Roy *Fenwick.

Vocal music prospered but mainly in the urban centres as each city appointed a music director for its schools. As early as 1853 Hamilton appointed a vocal-music teacher, and in 1856 London followed. Music became a school subject in Toronto and Hamilton in the 1870s and in Ottawa and London in 1906 and was offered continuously in those cities thereafter. Some of the pioneer teachers were particularly durable, serving for many years in one location. For example, Alexander T. *Cringan, Canada's foremost exponent of Tonic Sol-fa, laboured in Toronto in various capacities for some 44 years beginning in 1886. By 1920 nine normal schools, each with its own music instructor, were training teachers for elementary schools, and the Ontario College of Education, also with a music department, was preparing secondary school teachers.

The first provincial music supervisor, G. Roy Fenwick, was appointed in 1935. He actively promoted the cause of music through his several books, many radio broadcasts, inspectoral visits throughout the province, and adjudication at competition festivals. During his tenure the Dept of Education sponsored in outlying areas community concert series featuring young Canadian artists. These highly successful series, in addition to ever-increasing instrumental music instruction, were administered by Brian S. *McCool, who later succeeded Fenwick as provincial music supervisor.

Inter-school competitions provided a challenge to teachers and students alike and stimulated interest in music. Competition festivals also greatly influenced the course of music in the schools of Ontario. At first sponsored by local boards of education (eg, Toronto, in 1920), these later were administered by community groups or service clubs and remained very popular. The Toronto *Kiwanis Music Festival, begun in 1943, became the largest in Canada. In 1945 there were 47 competition festivals and 71 non-competition (ie, without comparative marks and stressing the festive and 'workshop' approaches), with a total of some 40,000 participants. One of the oldest annual school-music concert festivals, the Toronto May Festival (or Spring Festival Concert) had its 94th recurrence in 1980 at its accustomed site: *Massey Hall.

It was after World War II that instrumental music came to the fore, especially in the secondary schools of larger centres; 70 orchestras and 55 bands were reported in 1950. The impetus for this flowering, which continued into the 1960s, was attributable mainly to the return of service men and women who had experiences at first hand the importance of music in the war effort and the impact of a developing system of instrumental instruction in classes which diminished, in part at least, the need for the private studio lesson. At this time, several smaller urban centres had developed performing groups which became known nationally and internationally. Two examples are the Listowel District Secondary School Choir (conductor, Lorne Willets) and the *Barrie Central Collegiate Band (conductor, W. Allen *Fisher). The groups from these several centres were glowing models which provided lasting inspiration to many in the profession.

In 1960 80 per cent of Ontario elementary schools had some form of music supervision. In Toronto in that year 72 of 90 schools had string programs, the first of which had been initiated in 1949.

Another factor in the expansion of instrumental music, especially at the secondary school level, was the appearance of Canada's first university degree program designed especially for training potential school music teachers. This course, initiated at the U of Toronto in 1946, has had a strong, continuing influence. By 1980 undergraduate music education programs were bring offered by large music departments at the *U of Western Ontario and *Queen's U and by smaller departments at *McMaster U, the *U of Windsor, *Wilfrid Laurier U, and the *U of Ottawa. Graduate work in music education was being offered at the U of Toronto and the U of Western Ontario.

The largest and oldest of the provincial music educator associations, the *OMEA, was founded in 1919. It has encouraged the professional development of school musicians through regular workshops and conferences and was host to CMEA conferences in London, Ont, in 1967 and in Ottawa in 1973.

6 THE WESTERN PROVINCES. The development of school music for the most part followed the pattern established in the older settled regions except that in the newer parts of Canada (British Columbia, Alberta, Saskatchewan, and Manitoba) the beginnings were considerably later. Vocal music was reported in the elementary schools of Manitoba in 1893 and emerged in Alberta and British Columbia mostly in the 1930s, although in Calgary the first supervisor of school music, Dr Frederic Rogers, was appointed in 1916, and Miss Koney taught Tonic Sol-fa at the Vancouver Normal School in the early 1920s. Vancouver's first music supervisor, Fred Waddington, was appointed in the mid-1930s.

Instrumental music instruction seems to have had a somewhat earlier beginning in Saskatchewan than in the other western provinces, perhaps because of the sterling efforts of a pioneer teacher, Rj *Staples. Staples began teaching in the 1920s, went to Manitoba for some years, and returned to serve 1949–69 as Saskatchewan's supervisor of school music. By 1938 the Manitoba Schools' Orchestra of 400 (established in 1929 as the Winnipeg Junior SO with more than 200 violins and 75 mandolins, drawing heavily on players reared in Polish and Ukrainian traditions) was flourishing under P.G. Padwick. It was in the mid-1950s that bands made the greatest impact in this section of Canada. Extra-curricular instruction in strings was given in Calgary at this time. Rapid expansion followed in the 1960s, when instrumental music became an established part of the curriculum in most urban centres.

Competition and non-competition festivals have proved beneficial in this region as well, with 43 reported in Manitoba alone. Both competition and non-competition festivals were held in Calgary for more than 50 years (beginning in the 1920s), strongly supported by the local public and separate school systems. Experiments in school broadcasts in Vancouver were conducted in the early 1930s by Mildred McManus, Burton *Kurth, and Sherwood *Robson, the latter becoming the first president of the *BCMEA in 1957.

Notables in Manitoba school music include Ethel *Kinley, supervisor of music for Winnipeg schools 1937–47, Beth *Douglas, teacher at the Manitoba Teachers' College 1943–56, and Lola *MacQuarrie, music director for Winnipeg schools 1955–65 and president of the CMEA 1963–5.

In 1980 accredited degree music-education and teacher-training programs were offered at the universities of *Manitoba and *Brandon in Manitoba, at the universities of *Saskatchewan and *Regina in Saskatchewan, at the universities of *Alberta, *Calgary, and *Lethbridge in Alberta, and at the universities of *British Columbia and *Victoria in British Columbia.

Music educators' associations became established in all four provinces, although the association in Alberta was dissolved in 1969 and some of its members became associated with the Alberta Teachers' Assn Fine Arts Council. All of these associations have been host to CMEA national conventions: the *MMEA (Winnipeg) in 1960, the *SMEA (Regina) in 1969, the *AMEA (Calgary) in 1965 and (Edmonton) in 1975, and the BCMEA (Vancouver) in 1962 and 1979.

7 CONCLUSION. Though Canada as a whole has been slow in assuring music a firm place in the basic curricula of its schools, by 1980 the emerging philosophy of Canadian music education appeared sound, based as it was on an increasing concern for the individual student and yet not geared merely to the requirements of an elite. The approach reflected a belief in the need for educating Canadian youth to their full potential, according to their personal needs and capabilities, aesthetic as well as vocational.

The following have been most helpful in supplying basic information to the author for their respective regions: Catherine Allison (Nova Scotia), Nancy Vogan (New Brunswick), Dawson Woodburn, Brian McCool, and Paul *Green (Ontario), Alan Janzen (Manitoba), Cyril *Mossop (Alberta), and Donald Gibbard and Sandra Davies (British Columbia). The section on Quebec was prepared by Gilles *Potvin.

BIBLIOGRAPHY

BIBLIOGRAPHY

Bradley, Ian L. 'Education,' *A Selected Bibliography of Musical Canadiana* (Victoria 1976)

BOOKS

Hodgins, John George. *Documentary History of Education in Upper Canada*, 28 vols (Toronto 1894–1910)

The Toronto Normal School, Jubilee Celebration 1847–1897 (Toronto 1898)

Marcoux, J.C. *L'Enseignement de la musique dans la province de Québec*, brochure (Quebec 1924)

Montreal Music Year Book, 1931, 1932

Hill, Harry. *School Music, Its Practice in the Classroom* (Waterloo, Ont, 1934)

Marshall, P. George. *The Pedagogy of School Music* (Toronto 1937)

Centennial Story (Toronto 1950)

Fenwick, G. Roy. *The Function of Music in Education* (Toronto 1951)

Kallmann, Helmut. *Audio-Visual Aids to Music Education in Canada*, ISME series Technical Media in Music Education, mimeographed (np 1957)

Conference on Music in the Schools of the Atlantic Provinces, mimeographed report (Sackville, NB, 1960)

Russell, Vera E. *Teaching Music in Canadian Schools* (Toronto 1967)

Music Education and the Canadians of Tomorrow, report of the CMCouncil annual meeting and conference [Toronto 1968]

Churchley, Frank. *Music Curriculum and Instruction* (Toronto 1969)

ARTICLES

Blain, Emmanuel. 'De l'enseignement de la musique,' *Journal de l'instruction publique*, vol 4, Feb, Mar, Apr 1860

Legendre, Napoléon, 'Le chant dans les écoles,' *L'Écho*, vol 2, Quebec 1877

Hesselberg, Edouard. 'A review of music in Canada,' *Modern Music and Musicians* (New York, Toronto [1913])

Cooper, Irvin. 'School music in Quebec,' *The School*, Secondary edn, vol 30, Dec 1941

Atkinson, Roy. 'We need music supervisors,' *B.C. Teacher*, vol 27, p 94, 1947

Beck, Stan N. 'Cinderellas of the school-room,' *Vancouver Sun Magazine Supplement*, 30 Apr 1949

Fenwick, G. Roy. 'Music in the schools,' *Music in Canada*

St-Robert-Marie, M. 'Pourquoi un cours d'initiation à la musique dans nos collèges,' *L'Enseignement secondaire*, vol 38, no. 3, 1959

Gaboury, P. 'Notre enseignement de la musique est-il culturel?' ibid, vol 40, no. 1, 1960

St John, J. Bascom. 'Always a place for music,' Toronto *Globe and Mail*, 13 May 1960

'Music education in Manitoba,' *CanComp*, 14, Jan 1967

'Calgary school board emphasizes music enjoyment,' ibid, 16, Mar 1967

Richard, G. 'Music education in New Brunswick schools,' *Profile*, vol 2, Apr 1967

Bissell, Keith. 'School music today and tomorrow,' *MSc*, 238, Nov–Dec 1967

Schafer, R. Murray. 'Music and education,' ibid, 2 instalments, 239, 240, Jan–Feb, Mar–Apr 1968

Journal of Education, issue devoted to music education, vol 14, Apr 1968

Little, George. 'Music education in Quebec,' *MSc*, 2 instalments, 241, 242, May–Jun, Jul–Aug 1968

Bird, C. Laughton. 'Composer in the school,' *Mcan*, 19, May 1969

Walter, Arnold. 'The growth of music education,' *Aspects of Music in Canada*

Trowsdale, G.C. 'Vocal music in the common schools of Upper Canada: 1846–76,' *J of Research in Music Education*, vol 18, Winter 1970

Morey, Carl. 'Misalliance: the state of music education,' *PfAC*, Summer 1971

Schafer, R. Murray. 'Thoughts on music education,' *CMB*, 3, Autumn–Winter 1971

Fulton, William E. 'Music in the Halifax schools,' *MSc*, 274, Nov–Dec 1973

Creech, Robert. 'Remarks on music education,' *CMB*, 10, Spring–Summer 1975

Dumesnil, Thérèse. 'L'école a des trous de musique!' *Châtelaine* (May 1979)

Price, Bonnie. 'Music education: why it's declining,' Montreal *Gazette*, 1 Dec 1979

Proctor, George. 'Education in music: Canada,' *The New Grove*, vol 6

THESES

Marie-Stéphane, Sister. 'La musique au point de vue éducatif,' U of Montreal 1936

Fraser, Arthur M. 'Music in Canadian public schools: survey and recommendations,' Columbia U 1951

Smith, Alan Arthur. 'A study of instrumental music in Ontario secondary schools during 1954–55,' U of Toronto 1956

Brown, Aldred Malcolm. 'A study of teacher education and certification for the teaching of music in Canadian public schools,' Florida State U 1960

Trowsdale, G.C. 'A history of public school music in Ontario,' U of Toronto 1962

Coultas, Helen D. 'A study of organization for music education in the elementary schools of Alberta,' U of Alberta 1965

Lefrançois, Guy Ronald. 'Developing creativity in high school students,' U of Saskatchewan 1965

Takoski, Leonard Tony. 'A history of the Manitoba Schools Orchestra 1923 to 1964,' U of Manitoba 1965

Feld, Judith. 'Performance repertoire of Ontario secondary school bands and orchestras,' U of Toronto 1968

Hayward, Dorothy V.M. 'Qualifications of school music teachers in the province of New Brunswick in 1967–1968,' Acadia U 1968

Smith, D.C.M. 'A proposal for a high school of music for Metropolitan Toronto,' U of Toronto 1968

Pilote, Gilles. 'L'enseignement du solfège dans les écoles élémentaires de la CECM: Claude Champagne et ses contributions,' McGill 1970

Mills, Isabelle M. 'Canadian music: a listening program for intermediate grades with teaching guide,' Columbia U 1971

Bates, Duane. 'The status of music education in 1969–70 in the cities of southern Ontario having a population in excess of 100,000,' U of Illinois 1972

Patterson, Lawrence W.A. 'Undergraduate programs for music teacher preparation in Canadian colleges and universities,' U of Illinois 1972

Mauger, Louise. 'L'évaluation du système d'enseignement musical à l'élémentaire dans une région de Montréal pour l'année 1972–73,' U of Montreal 1973

Pilote, Gilles. 'L'enseignement de la musique au Québec, Claude Champagne et la Commission des Écoles catholiques de Montréal,' Strasbourg 1973

Bouvry, Nicole Lefebvre. 'Analyse du système actuel de l'enseignement musical au secondaire,' U of Montreal 1974

Challice, Elizabeth G. 'A study of the qualifications and some of the problems of those teaching music in the Calgary public elementary school system,' U of Calgary 1974

Rankin, Bob. 'A primary general music curriculum for North Vancouver Schools,' U of British Columbia 1976

Vogan, Nancy. 'A history of public school music in the province of New Brunswick 1872–1939,' ESM Rochester 1979

PERIODICALS

Accent (Music Education Council of the NB Teachers' Assn)

Alberta Music Educator

British Columbia Music Educator

Bulletin (SMEA)

Canadian Music Educator

Child Study

Crescendo (PEIMEA)

École

École ontarienne

Journal (SMEA)

Journal of Education

Manitoba Music Educator

Le Musicien éducateur (FAMEQ)

Newsletter (Music Council of the Newfoundland Teachers' Assn)

Newsletter (NSMEA)

Profile

QMEA Newsletter

Recorder (OMEA)

KBr

School music broadcasts. Radio and TV programs designed to supplement school classes. Before the advent of the CBC in 1936, private Canadian radio stations experimented with school broadcasting as early as 1927, when the Vancouver station CNRV provided for school children a weekly evening hour that included a music segment directed by Miss A. Roberts, the assistant music supervisor for Vancouver schools. (BBC radio, the pioneer in the field, had begun school broadcasts only a few months earlier.) On 19 Mar 1928 the Halifax station CHNS produced an experimental two-hour program that included the Harmonica Band of St Patrick's (Boys') School directed by Cyril O'Brien.

Because education in Canada is a matter of provincial jurisdiction, school broadcasts were initiated and developed largely in the individual provinces prior to the formation of co-operative programming among the four western provinces in 1941 and the creation of the Maritime school broadcast network in 1943. Provincial and regional school programs developed as joint presentations of the provincial departments of education and the CBC, with the latter supplying the technical facilities and resources. A National Advisory Council on School Broadcasting was established in 1943 to set up between the federal agency of the CBC and the provincial departments of education the liaisons necessary for the production of national school broadcasts.

1 Provincial school broadcasts
2 National school broadcasts

1 PROVINCIAL SCHOOL BROADCASTS

The Maritimes and Newfoundland. The first regular school broadcast series in Canada began in the fall of 1928 on CHNS Halifax. The two-hour weekly program for the junior and senior high schools of mainland Nova Scotia included vocal music, instrumental music performed by school bands and by the Wolfville School orchestra conducted by Basil C. Silver, and some music instruction. A series for Cape Breton schools was begun in 1930 on CJCB in Sydney. On the initiative of the CBC the departments of education of New Brunswick and Prince Edward Island in 1943 joined Nova Scotia to form the Maritime school broadcasts network, and in 1944 Douglas B. Lusty was appointed network organizer by the CBC. The music portion – 'Junior School Music' – was prepared by Irene McQuillan, director of music for Halifax schools. This 15-minute weekly series, which emphasized singing for grades 1 to 3, ran for 20 years (1942–62) and in 1943 won an Ohio State Award. John *Arab was an original participant. Other series on music appreciation were broadcast for junior high school students, notably by Harold *Hamer of *Mount Allison U. When the French station CBAF in Moncton inaugurated a school series in 1954, it included 'Chantons ensemble' for grades 1 to 3, directed by Sister Marie-Lucienne. Newfoundland joined the Maritimes network (Atlantic network after 1954) in 1949 and began contributing to the school broadcasts in 1952. Its first music program was a concert of Christmas carols in December 1953 on the National School Broadcasts network. However, Newfoundland did not originate music programs until 1967, when a series for grades 1 to 4 was presented. After that, 'Music in the Classroom,' directed 1968–73 by Sister Mary Catherine Burke, was part of the Atlantic school broadcasts. Although Atlantic school broadcasts terminated in June 1975, local programs, including 'Let's Sing a Song' (1974–5), 'Something to Sing About' (1976–7), and 'Old Times and New' (1978–9), continued to be heard in Newfoundland. Paul O'Neill, who in 1955 became the CBC producer of many of these series in St John's, continued in that position in 1980.

Quebec. In 1925 on Montreal station CKAC Émiliano *Renaud gave a series of piano lessons designed for a general audience, but school broadcasts as such were still some distance in the future. The Quebec Dept of Education was created in 1964 and immediately began supporting broadcasts for elementary schools under its jurisdiction. However, in 1941 'Radio-Collège,' intended as a high-school supplement but designed also to interest adult listeners, had been organized by the CBC and broadcast on eight French network stations. Claude *Champagne was in charge of music, prepared the weekly series 'Invitation à la musique,' and acted as host until 1945, when he was succeeded by Jean *Vallerand, who remained in the position until the conclusion of the series in 1956. At the request of the Quebec (Protestant) Dept of Education, Ontario school broadcasts, including 'Music for Young Folk,' were made available to English- language stations in Quebec beginning in 1945. With the demise of 'Radio-Collège' French-language school broadcasts were relegated to the limbo of reassessment until a change in government took place in 1960. The first two French-language school series – broadcast 1963–4 and 1964–5 under the name 'Place à la musique' – were designed for secondary students. 'Faisons de la musique,' begun in 1965 and aimed at elementary school students, emphasized singing, using French and English folksong, and employed elements of the *Kodály method, *Orff-Schulwerk, and the *Martenot method. The English series 'Making Music,' for grades 1 to 4, was initiated in 1973. Notable contributors to these series have included Marie Bolduc, Micheline Gerber, Monique Leduc, Pierre Perron, and Margaret Tsé. The Office de Radio-Télédiffusion du Québec, the provincial educational broadcasting system, was established in 1968. Its introductory music programs were broadcast through the CBC and some private stations. Beginning in 1972 its programs were broadcast from Radio-Québec's own studios in Montreal.

Ontario. In 1940–1 CBC Ontario stations carried the CBS 'School of the Air' programs, which included a 26-week music series. The success of these focused attention on the need to develop school programs relevant to Ontario curricula and culture. Organized and informed pressure was applied by the Ontario Education Association, the Ontario Federation of Home and School, the CBC, and other interested groups on the hitherto indifferent and unresponsive Ontario Dept of Education. The province's first school broadcasts were presented in 1942–3, as an experimental series of 10 45-minute music appreciation programs with various soloists and with Sir Ernest *MacMillan conducting the *TSO. G. Roy *Fenwick, provincial music supervisor, was content director. George Drew, elected premier of Ontario in August 1943, also undertook the education portfolio. He and his wife (Edward *Johnson's daughter) were interested in the potential benefits of radio to education, and Drew ensured the necessary funds for regular school broadcasts to be planned and presented by the Dept of Education in co-operation with the CBC. Leslie *Bell prepared the scripts and Fenwick was commentator 1944–60 for the series 'Music for Young Folk,' designed originally for grades 7 and 8 and later for all levels – primary, junior, and senior. Paul *Scherman conducted the orchestra for the early series. 'Music for Young Folk' was presented in various formats until 1964. 'Junior School Music' for grades 3 and 4 was a series that stressed vocal music, with Fenwick as host and Leo *Barkin as accompanist for the soloists. As with all school broadcasts, supplementary notes were distributed prior to the series to assist classroom teachers. The CBC produced all the Ontario series and broadcast them on a network of stations – 15 in 1944, increased to 27 by the 1960s. After 1964 programs of a more experimental nature, designed for kindergarten to grade 9, were produced. 'Hear Out' (1969–70, an exploration of sound in all its manifestations), 'The Kodály Approach' (1970), and 'Use Your Voice' (1971–2) received Ohio State Awards. Some of the many performers, writers, and composers who contributed to more than 30 years of broadcasts were C. Laughton *Bird, Lloyd *Bradshaw, the *Hamilton Philharmonic Orchestra, the *Hart House Orchestra, Betty Kovacs, Digby Peers, Hugh *Orr, R. Murray *Schafer, Harry *Somers, Mary *Syme, Lloyd Thomson, the TSO, and Rudi *van Dijk. With the increased use of TV, film, and tape recorders and the advent of tape and cassette service provided by the provincial educational resource centres, live broadcasts became impractical. In the early 1970s few new series were developed, and by 1976 production of Ontario school broadcasts had ceased.

Manitoba. Experiments in school broadcasts began as early as 1925 in Manitoba, but music was not included until 1927, when the unique series of Saturday morning instructional orchestra rehearsal broadcasts began on the Winnipeg station CKY. An orchestra of young musicians of 8 to 18 years under P.G. Padwick was joined by music students in their homes throughout the province in rehearsal sessions conducted via radio. Each Easter all the students would gather in Winnipeg for a massed concert, which was broadcast. The series ran continuously 1927–38 and intermittently thereafter until it ceased in 1949. (See also Youth orchestras, Manitoba). CKY also carried a school music segment as part of the province's school broadcasts in 1938–9. However, regular series did not begin until 1941, when the four western provinces agreed to co-operate in shared school-broadcast programming, with Manitoba providing the primary music series 'Music and Movement' prepared by Beth *Douglas and Elizabeth Harris. School choirs and approaches to choral singing were an integral part of the province's music broadcasts from the outset. Beginning in 1944, leading music educators such as Winnipeg's successive school music supervisors – Ethel *Kinley, Marjorie Horner, and Lola *MacQuarrie – supervised the graded programs carried by the CBC and co-ordinated by Gertrude McCance, the director of Manitoba school broadcasts. For the graded programs themselves (play songs for primary children, narrative and dramatic for elementary, and socially connotative for upper-elementary and junior high) the successive planners were, for primary Frances Christie, Lola MacQuarrie, Beth Douglas, and Roberta Stone; for elementary Douglas, Gertrude Lowry, and Shirley Gibb; and for junior high Muriel James, Margaret Thomson, James Duncan, and Glen *Harrison. Betty Friesen gave instruction in rhythm instruments 1970–5. The *Winnipeg SO performed on the broadcasts 1950–65. TV series were fewer, because of cost, but still significant. Frances Martin designed a sight-singing series in 1969, and Edna Knock prepared another in 1972. A three-part series, 'Orchestrally Speaking,' was produced in 1975 for secondary schools with the help of the Greater Winnipeg Youth Orchestra. Manitoba's school music broadcasts won Ohio State Awards in 1952 for 'Let's Sing Together' (a series that continued in 1980) and in 1961 for the series 'Music for Juniors.'

Saskatchewan. Saskatchewan's regular school broadcasts began in 1941, although some experimental series had been tried in the 1930s and the CBC had carried the British Columbia school broadcasts in 1940–1. Because the province had agreed to become part of the western provinces' co-operative program, in which locally prepared series were to be supplemented by series from the other participating provinces, the first music series heard in Saskatchewan's public schools – 'Music and Movement' – originated in Winnipeg. In 1945 Rj *Staples, newly appointed provincial music supervisor, initiated the series 'Making Music Together,' which reflected his distinctive ideas on music education. The broadcasts presented 'a simple graduated approach to music reading for voices and classroom instruments' that combined movement, singing, and performance on instruments, the latter often made by the children themselves (Lambert *School Broadcasting in Canada*, p 68). Gertrude Murray, who worked closely with Staples, prepared the primary-grades series 'Rhythmic Patterns,' heard in the early 1950s. Saskatchewan continued to contribute series such as 'Sounds and Songs' to the western programs, and Staples was involved in their creation, 1948–66 as scriptwriter, arranger, and/or commentator, and 1966–70 as a consultant. In 1980 the music appreciation broadcasts 'Listening to Music' (for grades 5 to 8) continued to be heard throughout the western region. The television series 'Jeremiah's Music Lesson,' for primary grades, was begun in 1968 and was shared by other western provinces in the 1970s.

Alberta. Music became a part of Alberta school broadcasts in 1937–8, when an experimental series on station CJOC, Lethbridge, included singsong sessions conducted by Agnes Davidson. The following year three series, one for elementary grades by Janet McIlvena and two for intermediate levels by Glyndwr Jones and T. Jenkins respectively, were broadcast for the first time on the provincial educational network. In addition to these, Alberta in 1941 broadcast the results of its co-operative programming with the other three western provinces and added music series from Winnipeg. Janet McIlvena continued her influential elementary school programs 'Sing and Play,' which were heard on the provincial network until 1958. Hazel Robinson developed programs for primary grades – 'Music Makers' – that ran 1950–4. All series employed direct teaching at all grade levels and included a mixture of folk-singing and general music appreciation. Crystal Fleuty and Anne Wheeler were among those who developed the programs. TV series, begun in the 1960s, have included 'Making Music' and 'Tune-Up Time,' the latter initiated in 1977 and still telecast in 1980. Responsibility for school broadcasts, which are regarded as an essential part of Alberta's educational program, was assumed in 1980 by the Alberta Educational Communications Corporation, working in consultation with the provincial department of education.

British Columbia. Six programs on music appreciation by Cyril *Mossop and F.T. Marrige, broadcast in 1936 over the privately owned station CKOV in Kelowna, marked the beginning of serious school music broadcasts in the westernmost province. Because of the interest aroused, the provincial department of education authorized a 10-week experimental series, 'Musical Pathways,' prepared by Mildred McManus and narrated by Sherwood *Robson, and heard on Vancouver's CBR and four private stations in 1938. The official 'British Columbia Radio School' was launched in the fall of 1938 and for grades 1 to 12 included three series of music programs which became a regular part of school broadcasts. Magdalene Barton's 'Listening is Fun,' organized and narrated 1945–61 by Philip J. Kitley, won an Ohio State Award in 1956. Robert *Chesterman's program 'Masters of the Keyboard' also won an award in 1961. Ann *Mortifee and the singer-guitarist Lloyd Arntzen have performed on the British Columbia programs. Only one TV music series has been produced: 'Music and Man,' with John *Avison. In 1980 BC school broadcasts continued to include programs for primary grades and, as a participant in the western regional program, to use series prepared in Manitoba ('Let's Sing Together') and Saskatchewan ('Listening to Music').

2 NATIONAL SCHOOL BROADCASTS. By 1941 the CBC had established effective network coverage of most of Canada, had created school programs as part of its participation in and contribution to the CBS 'School of the Air' broadcasts (including a series on Canadian and British folk music), and had made clear its interest in the field of education. The CBS programs heard in Canada in their turn had provoked a strong reaction in favour of Canadian productions relevant to Canadian conditions and culture. Most of the provinces had developed local school programs, many using CBC facilities and some using CBC resources and expertise. Partly as a result of a national conference in 1942 and one experimental series of national school broadcasts, the National Advisory Council on School Broadcasting was established in 1943 to provide the means of co-operation between the federal agency and the provincial educational authorities. That same year the CBC named R.S. Lambert national supervisor of the school broadcasts department.

All national broadcasts were co-ordinated and packaged in Toronto and were carried on the CBC network of stations or affiliate stations. The music series, designed mainly for grades 3 to 9, emphasized music appreciation and included concerts by orchestras (eg, the TSO, the Winnipeg SO, and the *Vancouver SO), opera performances (Gluck's *Orpheus* in 1949, Britten's *Let's Make an Opera* in 1951 and 1961, and Gilbert & Sullivan's *The Pirates of Penzance* in 1953 and *H.M.S. Pinafore* in 1956), dramatizations of composers' lives, and series employing Canadian singers, instrumentalists, and composers. Several of the national series received Ohio State Awards – 'Music in the Making' in 1960, '*Let's Make an Opera*' in 1962, and 'The Folk Element in Music' (with Edith *Fowke) and the Orff series 'Living through Music' in 1964. However, because of wide differences in levels of music teaching in Canadian schools, these relatively sophisticated broadcasts were not widely used, and regular programs ceased in 1966, although special series, such as the 1978 'Harry Somers' History of Music in Canada' appeared sporadically thereafter.

Experiments in national school telecasts began in 1954 and were produced in Toronto. Two of these early programs – Eugene *Kash's 'Magic of Music' and the series 'Music to See' – won Ohio State Awards in 1956 and 1958 respectively. Regular TV series started in 1960 and included 'Rhythm and Melody' for grades 2 and 3. The 1961–2 telecasts included music programs for high-school students. 'Music – From Bach to Rock,' a five-part series of music appreciation programs produced by Rena Elmer with Boris *Brott as host, was telecast first in 1969 and has been repeated many times across Canada. It won an Ohio State Award in 1970.

By 1980 the only regular national school broadcast to continue uninterrupted was the annual Christmas broadcast begun in 1949. As in the past it offered a concert of carols by a school choir selected from 1 of the 10 provinces.

BIBLIOGRAPHY

Rose, Mary J. 'A history of school broadcasting in Canada,' unpubl thesis, Northwestern U 1951

Kallmann, Helmut. 'Audio-visual aids to music education in Canada,' ISME series, *Technical Media in Music Education*, mimeographed (np 1957)

Lambert, Richard S. *School Broadcasting in Canada* (Toronto 1963)

Peers, Digby. 'Radio school broadcasts,' *CME*, vol 12, Winter 1970

Lyseng, Mary. 'The history of educational radio in Alberta,' unpubl M ED thesis, U of Alberta 1976

Lambert, Richard S. 'Music in school broadcasting,' *Music in Canada*

Walter, Arnold. 'Music education,' *Aspects of Music in Canada* DPr, KW, PW

School songbooks. Collections of songs for classroom use, generally arranged according to pedagogical principles in progressive order of their application in teaching and accompanied by explanatory sections and glossaries, and sometimes incorporating instruction in rudiments or chapters on music appreciation. Books recommended or authorized for use in Canadian schools are included in this survey, and others of interest are discussed. See also Solmization.

The earliest authorized music textbook in Canada was Henry Francis *Sefton's *Three Part Songs* (James Campbell & Son, 1869), which contained a large number of British tunes and some from Canada and other countries. Like other educational material of the time, 19th-century songbooks aimed at rousing a student's interest in music, acquainting him with standard works, and encouraging socially approved behaviour.

This belief in the refining influence of music was evident in S.H. Preston's adaptations of *The Public School Music Reader* (Canada Publishing Co 1885) and *The High School Music Reader* (Canada Publishing Co 1885) by John Tufts and H.E. Holt, two US music educators. According to Preston, any teacher could learn a carefully graded series of exercises and songs for classroom presentation. Hand signs, syllables, numbers, and time-names were used to develop proficiency in tonal awareness and music reading.

In Alexander *Cringan's *The Canadian Music Course* (Canada Publishing Co 1888) and *The Educational Music Course* (4 vols, Canada Publishing Co 1898–1907), syllables of the Tonic Sol-fa system ('doh' as the tonic of the prevailing key rather than 'doh' as C) replaced the actual notation. Cringan later wrote *The New Canadian Song Series* (Canada Publishing Co 1931–4).

Nineteenth-century Quebec songbooks included *Le Chansonnier des collèges* (bureau de 'l'Abeille' 1850, 1854, 1860; only the 1860 edition included the music), *Chansonnier de tous les âges* or *Nouvelle Lyre canadienne* (Chapleau 1858), and *Le Chansonnier des écoles* (A.J. Boucher 1876; the fourth edition, 1887, was authorized by the Roman Catholic School Commission of Montreal).

Among songbooks of the early 20th century were *The King Edward Music Reader* (Morang Educational Co 1903; compiled by H.J. Minchin and W.A. McIntyre and used in British Columbia, Saskatchewan, and Manitoba) and Charles E. Whiting's *The New Public School Music Course* (Educational Book Co 1912). Whiting's course was published in four readers, the first of which was used in New Brunswick; it assumed that the child was acquainted with the Tonic Sol-fa system and that the appreciation of excellence in music was possible only through familiarity with folksongs.

Popular in Quebec was *Chansons de Botrel pour l'école et le foyer* (Beauchemin 1903, 1931, 1942, 1953), which contained several songs on Canadian subjects by Théodore Botrel (poet, singer, composer, b Dinan, France, 14 Sep 1868, d Pont-Aven, France, 1925), who toured Quebec several times prior to 1922. Louis *Bouhier sponsored his appearances in Montreal.

Tufts and Holt's *New Normal Music Course* (Educational Book Co 1914; used in Saskatchewan and Manitoba) comprised graded exercises and songs grouped into sections, each illustrating a specific musical idea or fact (eg, 'Devotional and patriotic songs,' 'Divided beat in 3 / 8 and 6 / 8 time,' 'Easy chromatic progressions. Further study of after-beat note'). The prototype for this publication was S.H. Preston's *The Normal Music Course* (Canada Publishing Co 1883).

Another noteworthy publication was *The Progressive Music Series* (Gage 1921; by Horatio Parker and others), which reflected contemporary musical and pedagogical aims and grouped its songs in chapters according to the particular musical problems or sophistications they contained (eg, 'Syncopation,' 'Modulation to remote keys'). Suitable for supplementary use at this time were the *School and Community Song Book*, edited by A.S. *Vogt and Healey *Willan (Gage 1922, 1929, 1931, 1951); the *High School Song Book*, edited by James Walker (Renouf 1920; entirely religious in content); and *Le Chansonnier canadien pour l'école et le foyer* (Beauchemin 1931), by Uldéric S. Allaire.

In summary, these early songbooks demonstrated a belief in song, in particular folksong, as an efficacious means not only of broadening and conditioning musical tastes but also of imparting social mores. They also propounded systematic approaches to musical learning, most notably the Tonic Sol-fa system.

Concern with extending a student's musical reach was uppermost in later publications such as E.M. Coney and F.T.C. Wickett's *The New Canadian Community Song Book* (Gage 1936; used in British Columbia and Nova Scotia), R.T. Bevan's *Songs for Young Canadians* (Thomas Nelson nd probably 1930s), Ernest *MacMillan's *A Canadian Song Book* (Dent 1937), Ethel A. *Kinley's *The Manitoba School Song Book* and *A Song Book for Ontario Schools* (both Clarke Irwin 1940, collections which included classical songs, Lieder, and conservative contemporary pieces), Joseph *Beaulieu's *Mon école chante* (Laprairie 1956–64; part of the La *Bonne Chanson collection and widely used in Ontario and Quebec), Marjorie Horner's *The Classroom Chorister* (Clarke Irwin, 1959), and Thomas *Legrady's *Lisons la musique* (Fides, 1970; based on Kodály methods). An earlier collection, Harry *Hill's eight-volume *The Singing Period* (Waterloo 1933–8), included pictorial reproductions of famous pieces of art and attempted to correlate music and other classroom themes such as ethics, courtesy, nature study, and safety habits.

The imparting of music-reading skills, however, remained a prime objective. Roy *Fenwick, one of the authors of *The High Road of Song* series (3 vols, Gage 1943) and editor of *The New High Road Music Series* (8 vols, Gage 1954–60), felt that the power to read music was the key factor in keeping singers and players musically active after they left school. Leslie *Bell, in *The Chorister* (2 vols, Gage 1947, 1950), reflected a similar belief. Through carefully graded song material which avoided emphasis on mechanical drill, Bell hoped to develop an appreciation for music and an understanding of its theory. He took into account the limitations of the adolescent voice, thus encouraging greater participation. Similar respect for young voices is evident in Don *Wright's *The Collegiate Choir* (2 vols, Waterloo 1938, 1939) and *Youthful Voices* (3 vols, Thompson 1945, 1949, 1954).

Concern for the tastes of young people was taken into consideration in the textbooks of the 1950s and 1960s. Beautifully illustrated, easy-to-read materials taught them about the structure and theory of music by encouraging exploration, creativity, and problem-solving. This approach is evident in Lola *MacQuarrie and Beth *Douglas' *Treasure Tunes* (Clarke Irwin 1961); in *Slind and *Churchley's *Basic Goals in Music* (8 vols, McGraw Hill 1964–72), which uses folk materials from many lands; and in *Songtime* (8 vols, Holt, Rinehart and Winston 1963–7; by Vera Russell and others) and *Songs for Today!* (Waterloo 1970; by Richard *Johnston and others). Other titles of interest are Charles-Émile *Gadbois's *La Bonne Chanson à l'école* (La Bonne Chanson 1938–51), Ken *Bray and others' *For Young Musicians* (Waterloo 1961, 1967, 1972, 1974) and *Music for Young Canada* (3 vols, Gage 1967–9), Keith *Bissell's *Let's Sing and Play* (2 vols, Waterloo 1973, 1975), Monique Leduc's *Je chante avec mes amis* (Commission des écoles catholiques de Montréal 1975), and Joachim Sandvoss' *A First Book of Songs for the French Classroom* (Empire Music 1975).

Choral arrangements of Canadian folksongs, typified in *Fowke and Johnston's *Folk Songs of Canada, Chansons de Québec,* and *More Folk Songs of Canada* (Waterloo 1954, 1957, 1967) and in Johnston's *Chansons canadiennes-françaises* (Waterloo 1964), are used often in schools.

School music books of the later 20th century continued to reflect many of the aims of earlier texts: the desire to develop musical sensitivity, love of music, reading and aural skills, and knowledge of rudiments, forms, and procedures. Greater variety in presentation and implementation, however, is evident in those approaches which call on the student to analyse, listen, and perform.

BIBLIOGRAPHY

Weir, Don. 'Elementary school choral repertoire,' *Recorder*, vol 9, Nov 1966–Jan 1967 (NK)

SCHOTT, Adam (Joseph). Bandmaster, b Mainz 1794, d Poona, India, 4 Aug 1864. This son of the founder of the German publishing house B. Schott's Söhne became a bandmaster in the British army. He is said to have served 1825–36 with the 79th Cameron Highlanders and 1841–7 with the 14th regiment in Canada. These regiments were stationed in Quebec City 1825–8, 1833, and 1845–7. Schott is said to have instructed Pierre-Olivier *Lyonnais in the art of string-instrument building and to have played cello in the *Quebec Harmonic Society. In 1830 he played his clarinet and basset horn at a concert in Montreal with his father-in-law and brother-in-law, the bandmasters James Ziegler Sr (d Toronto 1833) and Jr. He lived briefly 1830–1 in New York but returned to Canada, where he founded the Société Ste-Cécile at the Petit *Séminaire de Québec in 1833 and served as its director until 1836. In 1838 he helped to establish the London branch of B. Schott's Söhne. He was bandmaster 1844–56 of the Grenadier Guards and served partly in India during those years, but not in Canada. He is reported to have been an excellent musician and published a *Journal pour musique militaire* in three series and a collection of 16 *Tänze und Märsche* for band (both Schott). HK

Schubert Choir. Mixed ensemble of from 100 to 150 voices, formed in Brantford, Ont, as an enlargement of the Brantford Male Choir and active 1906–41. Its conductor was Henri K. *Jordan, except during his war service, 1914–20, when he was replaced by Clifford Higgin. The choir specialized in short works, unaccompanied and accompanied, of the 19th and early 20th centuries. It rapidly gained public favour, giving one or two concerts a year, sometimes with a visiting orchestra (Pittsburgh 1909, *Welsman's TSO 1910, *TSO 1926, 1928, Boston Festival Orchestral Club 1912, the Little Symphony of New York 1922, 1936) or a guest artist (Richard Crooks 1923, Percy Grainger 1933, 1937).

After a late-April concert in 1928 the Toronto *Globe*'s critic Lawrence *Mason judged the Schubert Choir the best mixed ensemble in Canada next to the *Toronto Mendelssohn Choir. The same critic, after a concert 30 Apr 1930, praised the 'finished ensemble work and assured responsiveness to Mr. Jordan's magnetic leading.' As the result of a triumphant *Massey Hall performance in November 1928 in Toronto, the choir was invited to sing in July 1929 at the National Eisteddfod of America in Scranton, Pa, where it won the first prize for large choirs in competition with three US groups. In 1939 Olin Downes, on behalf of the New York World's Fair, invited the choir to sing 25 July at the fair. The previous night, the choir appeared at St Thomas Church, New York City. Howard Taubman of the *New York Times* was lavish in his praise of its 'fine-grained pianissimo' and many other features, ranking it with 'our well-known ensembles.' The aging Jordan conducted the choir's last public concert 23 Apr 1941 in Brantford and a private concert 18 Nov 1941. On his retirement the Schubert Choir was dissolved.

BIBLIOGRAPHY

NL of C. Jordan scrapbooks HK

SCHUCH, Edward (Washington). Choirmaster, teacher, critic, bass, b Manchester 20 Feb 1848, d Toronto 3 Mar 1940. He was educated in Toronto at Upper Canada College and served as choirmaster at several of Toronto's Anglican churches, including St James' Cathedral 1892–6. While choirmaster 1886–92 and 1898–1904 at the Church of the Redeemer he conducted a series of popular monthly 'services of praise.' He participated in concerts and was bass soloist in a performance (1883) of Haydn's *The Creation* in Berlin (Kitchener), Ont. He conducted several amateur choral societies, including the Toronto Harmony Club ca 1892 and the Toronto Vocal Society 1892–3, and taught voice at a number of schools. Among his pupils were Mabel *Beddoe and Bertha *Crawford. He was music critic for the *Globe* and *Saturday Night* and editor 1888–90? of the *Musical Journal*. (WLk)

SCHUDEL, Thomas. Composer, administrator, bassoonist, teacher, b Defiance, O, 8 Sep 1937; B SC music education (Ohio) 1959, MA music theory (Ohio) 1961, DMA (Michigan) 1971. He began teaching at the *U of Regina in 1964, rising to head of the music department in 1974, and was principal bassoonist with the *Regina SO 1964–7 and 1968–70. He won first prize in the International Competition for Symphonic Composition at Trieste, Italy, for his *Symphony No. 1* (1972). Dependent on instrumental colour, his compositions are atonal and develop structurally from small motivic cells. He has written other orchestral pieces (eg, *Variations for Orchestra*, 1976), chamber works (including a *String Quartet*, 1967, and a *Trio* for percussion, 1977), and choral pieces (*Psalm 23*, ca 1968). He is an affiliate of PRO Canada and an associate of the *CMCentre. CF

SCHULDT, Phyllis (Mairi) (b Ward). Pianist, teacher, b Aldershot, England, 10 Apr 1911; ARCM 1933, GRSM 1934. The daughter of musicians, descended from five generations of oboe players on her father's side, she was taken to live in Vancouver while a child. In 1929, acting on advice from Ernest *MacMillan, she studied (on scholarship) at the RCM under Herbert Fryer, Arthur *Benjamin, and Harold Samuel and accompanied the soprano Marjorie Avis, the baritone Keith Faulkner, and the bass-baritone William Parsons on tours of England. Returning to Vancouver in 1934, Schuldt became a leading performer and private teacher there. For some 20 years she was the piano partner of Jean *de Rimanoczy in public appearances and on radio and accompanied John *Goss (in his recitals and with his Singers, 1943–8), Donald *Bell (on tour, 1967, during which they premiered Oskar *Morawetz' *Four Songs* on poems of Bliss Carman), and others. She was a duo-pianist 1940–52 with Mary *Munn and 1958–66 with Boris *Roubakine, giving the first Canadian performance of two Handel *Preludes and Fugues* in 1963 and the premieres of Jack *Behrens' *Four Pieces for Three Hands* and *Three Pieces for Four Hands* (ca 1965). She became an adjudicator for the *CFMTA in 1935, joined the faculty at the *U of British Columbia in 1959, and began examining across Canada for the *RCMT in 1964. Her pupils include Harold *Brown, Don *Garrard, Errol Gay, Steven Henrikson, Sharon Krause, Hugh *McLean, and Betty *Phillips. (MW)

SCHULLER, Auguste. See Brother Raymondien.

SCLATER, Molly (Mary Lindsay). Teacher, author, organist-choirmaster, b Edinburgh 28 Dec 1912; ATCM 1938, ACCO ca 1938, B MUS (Toronto) 1939. Her family settled in Toronto in 1923. She studied at the TCM with Marion Copp (voice) and Muriel *Gidley (organ) and took classes 1935–9 at the U of Toronto. She began to teach theory and organ at the TCM (*RCMT) in 1938 and continued to do so in 1980. She was organist-choirmaster 1947–58 at Kimbourne Park United Church and 1963–73 at St Cuthbert's Anglican Church.

WRITINGS

- and Sinclair, Kathryn, and Berlin, Boris. *Keys to Music Rudiments* (Toronto 1968, 1969)
- and Sinclair, Kathryn, and Andrews, William G. *Keys to Music Analysis and Melody Writing*, 4 vols (Toronto 1972–6, later revisions)
- and Andrews, William G. *Introduction to Materials of Western Music* (Toronto 1977) MMl

Scotland. The history of Scottish music in Canada has to be seen against a background of emigration, especially from the Highlands, which effectively started after the failure of the 1745 rebellion, intensified during the Victorian era, and has continued unabated. The Scottish contribution to Canadian life and culture thus has been profound, and is by no means limited to Nova Scotia. All the other provinces, particularly Ontario and British Columbia, show the effects of Scottish settlement and enterprise. This phenomenon has received some attention from social and economic historians, but its musical aspects have been neglected. The present article is no more than a preliminary survey; part of its purpose is to refer readers to other entries in *EMC*, where individual topics are treated in more detail.

The contributions of Scotland to music in Canada may be considered under two main headings:

1 Classical music, jazz, and popular music (in the western European and North American traditions)
2 Traditional Scottish music.

1 CLASSICAL MUSIC, JAZZ, AND POPULAR MUSIC (IN THE WESTERN EUROPEAN AND NORTH AMERICAN TRADITIONS). Many outstanding Canadian composers, performers, and teachers either emigrated from Scotland and settled in Canada or were born to Scottish or Scottish-emigrant parents or their near descendants. Among those born in Scotland are Dorothy *Allan Park, the pipe-major Farquhar Beaton, Keith and Jim *Blackley, Noel Brunton (a director of music at *Mount Allison U), Dan A. *Cameron, James Paton *Clarke, Frank *Connell, George *Coutts, Thomas J. *Crawford, Alexander *Cringan, the pipe-major Archie Dinan, Bertha *Drechsler Adamson, Jeanne *Dusseau, the pipe-major James Fraser, the country singer Johnny Forrest, Margaret *Gilkison, Stanley *Hoban, George *Kindness, Frank *Laubach, May *Lawson, Alexander *MacMillan, the composer Neil McKay, Norman *McLaren, Christine *Mather, George S. *Mathieson, the music educator Duncan McKenzie, John *Moncrieff, Elizabeth *Morrison, Alexander *Muir, Charles *O'Neill (of Irish parents), the pianist Isobel Rolston, the organist George Ross, Peggie *Sampson (of English parents), Molly *Sclater, David Dick *Slater, Donald Alexander Smith (Lord *Strathcona), Reginald *Stewart, George William *Strathy, Richard *Tattersall, W. Davidson *Thomson, the pipe-major John Wilson, and W. Knight *Wilson.

An extraordinary number of Canadian jazz musicians have been Scots, eg, the trombonist Jim Abercrombie, the clarinetist Ian Arnott, the pianist Ian Bargh, the trumpeter Charlie (Dr McJazz) Gall, Jim *Galloway, the trumpeter-guitarist Malcolm Higgins, the clarinetist Alistair Lawrie, Jim *McHarg, and Murray *McLauchlan.

Musicians of Scottish descent (often mixed with English, French, or Irish) are legion. A few names will give an idea of the pervasiveness of Scots ancestry in Canadian music: W.H. *Anderson, Beth *Douglas, William *Douglas, Maureen *Forrester, Glenn *Gould, Sir Ernest *MacMillan (partially trained in Scotland, and once invited to be Sir Donald Francis Tovey's successor at the U of Edinburgh), Lola *MacQuarrie, Lois *Marshall (who has recorded several of Marjory Kennedy-Fraser's arrangements of Scottish and Hebridean songs), Mary *Morrison, and Quentin *Maclean.

Calixa *Lavallée's mother, born in Canada, was of Scottish descent. Emma *Albani (whose maternal grandmother was of Scottish origin) was 'discovered' as a young girl by a Scottish balladeer named Crawford, who invited her to perform at his concerts and taught her many Scottish songs. Albani, Pauline *Donalda, and Sarah *Fischer sang frequently in Scotland, in concerts, recitals, and opera, as, later, did Milla *Andrew, Clarice *Carson, and Joseph *Rouleau. Clara *Lichtenstein, born in Budapest, took her musical training in Scotland.

Scots who performed in Canada during the 19th century included the singers David Kennedy (b Perth 1825, d Stratford, Ont, 1886, the father of Marjory Kennedy-Fraser), who travelled widely in Canada 1866–86, performing with his singing family, and in fact died in Canada shortly after an appearance in Sarnia, Ont, and John Wilson (b Edinburgh 1800, d Quebec City 1849). Scottish-born Sir Alexander Campbell Mackenzie, principal of the RAM, was conductor for the *Cycle of Musical Festivals in 1903. The soprano Mary Garden sang in Montreal in 1912, and the pianist James Friskin played there in 1926 and 1946. Marjory Kennedy-Fraser, accompanied by her sister Margaret Kennedy, sang 20 Sep 1929 at the Royal York Hotel, Toronto, in a recital which was part of a series of six concerts of British and Canadian music organized by the CPR. Harry Lauder toured Canada 1930–1 with Jerry *Shea. Sir Hugh Roberton toured Canada with his Glasgow Orpheus Choir and was a favourite adjudicator at Canadian competition festivals. Roberton's nephew David *Thomson modelled his Carriden Choir on that of his uncle.

The *Montreal Bach Choir sang at the Edinburgh Festival in 1958, the *MSO played there under Rafael Frühbeck de Burgos in 1976, and *Canadian Brass and the *Toronto Mendelssohn Choir performed there in 1980. Canada was represented at the International Festival of Youth Orchestras (Aberdeen, 1977) by the George Brown College Orchestra, conducted by Leonard Atherton, and by Hélène *Gagné, who was a guest instructor. In 1979 a series of exchange tours was initiated by the Scottish Philharmonic Trust and the Scottish Canadian Philharmonic Foundation (Toronto), with the aim of strengthening ties between the two countries, particularly in the area of classical music. A visit to Toronto by the Scottish Chamber Orchestra of Edinburgh was the first of the exchanges. As part of the exchange series the *Orford String Quartet, the *Purcell String Quartet, the Galliard Ensemble, the Guelph University Choir, and the Stratford Ensemble performed in Scotland in 1980. The foundation also undertook a campaign to raise $100,000 toward the restoration of Queen's Concert Hall in Edinburgh.

The White Heather Concerts, conceived in Toronto in the late 1940s by the Scots-born performer Neil Kirk (b Willie Robertson), became annual events in many Canadian and US cities. In them a touring concert party of Scottish and Scottish-Canadian performers presented a variety of musical entertainments and skits. Among the featured performers in certain years was the noted Scottish tenor Kenneth McKellar.

2 TRADITIONAL SCOTTISH MUSIC. This section examines vocal music (songs in English, Scots, and Gaelic and psalms and hymns), instrumental music (solo and ensemble performance on Highland bagpipes and drums, fiddle, and accordion and composition in Scottish idiom for these instruments), and dance. See also Folk music, Anglo-Canadian: 2 / Nova Scotia and New Brunswick, 4 / Ontario and the Prairies.

Vocal music. Because emigration from Scotland has been uninterrupted, it is difficult to know the age of songs found in Canada. According to Calum I.N. MacLeod, the oldest of a variety of song types within the Scottish-Gaelic tradition in Canada is the heroic ballad, its texts from Celtic cycles whose roots lie in pre-Christian Ireland. One of these, *Bàrdachd Ghàidhlig á Albainn Nuaidh*, was recorded in Nova Scotia in 1952. Like Newfoundland, Nova Scotia has been relatively isolated from outside influences, and thus this and other Gaelic songs collected there represent the earliest Scottish vocal traditions in Canada. MacLeod has found that several types of Gaelic song have survived, among them epics, laments, and work songs. The last, usually strophic and rhythmical, include songs for rowing, churning, milking, weaving, spinning, quern-grinding, and waulking (ie, fulling cloth). Gaelic psalms have continued to be sung in Nova Scotia and in a few other places in Canada (such as Toronto), where church services are held in Gaelic. (For a brief description of the Gaelic Language and Folklore Project, see St Francis Xavier U.)

Scottish songs in English and Scots form a distinctive but less distinguishable category of vocal music, since their history is intertwined with that of English folksong, and they are part of the common heritage of English speakers in Canada. One also must include in this class Scottish music-hall songs (such as those of Harry Lauder and Andy Stewart). Many old songs of Scottish origin, however, have been recorded, especially in Nova Scotia, Prince Edward Island, and Ontario, by the National Museum of Man and by individual collectors. The commercial success of the folksong revival, too, has made popular many Scottish songs, both old and new; John Alan *Cameron, for example, includes Scottish material in his repertoire. Lastly, one must mention the musical influence of the Presbyterian church in Canada, whose hymnary to some extent differs from that of other English-speaking churches (see Hymnbooks, protestant).

Instrumental music. Separate articles in *EMC* are devoted to Bagpipes, great Highland; and to pipe bands (see Bands: 7). This subsection considers briefly Scottish fiddle and accordion music. Scottish fiddle playing had developed a distinctive style of bowing and ornamentation by the 18th century, and there are many compositions in the Scottish style for violin, mainly slow airs, marches, strathspeys, reels, and jigs. Fiddlers often play bagpipe tunes too. Some of the Gaelic airs are of great antiquity, and many of the dance tunes go back to the 18th century. We may be sure that fiddlers accompanied the early Scottish settlers to Nova Scotia and Upper Canada, but precise information is not available.

In 1980 Nova Scotia remained the heartland of Scottish fiddling, such players as Angus Chisholm and Winston 'Scotty' *Fitzgerald being widely known. Other centres of Scottish fiddling have been the Ottawa Valley, Glengarry County in Ontario, and the Red River settlement in Manitoba. In Montreal the Scottish Caledonian Society in 1867 sponsored a fiddling competition in which reels, strathspeys, and Scottish airs were heard. Indeed, a hundred years later the most famous living player of Scottish fiddle music was a French-Canadian from Montreal, Jean *Carignan, who was influenced directly by the famous Scottish fiddler James Scott Skinner, and several old Scottish pipe and fiddle tunes have survived in Quebec, under French names. Canadian country fiddlers such as Ned *Landry (New Brunswick) and Johnny Mooring (Nova Scotia) have played many Scottish dance tunes. In Nova Scotia in 1980 the old Scottish custom of ensemble fiddling continued in practice: at the gatherings of strathspey and reel societies up to 200 fiddlers have played together in quasi-unison. See also Fiddling.

Individual fiddlers have played often with Scottish dance bands, but the usual melody instrument in these ensembles has been a three-row button or piano accordion. The best such band in Canada has been that of Stan Hamilton (lead accordion, Robert Frew), whose recordings have been admired both by dancers and by connoisseurs of music. This band dissolved in the late 1970s; but another excellent band in the Toronto area was led by Angus MacKinnon (fiddle), and others have continued to be active. Such groups are in great demand for balls organized by Scottish societies and Scottish country dance groups in Canada and the USA. An annual event of the kind has been the St Andrew's Ball, at Toronto's Royal York Hotel, which in three ballrooms uses a Scottish dance band, a regular dance band, and a Highland pipe band (the *48th Highlanders, to play for Highland dancing exclusively).

Dance. Scottish dance is of two kinds: country and Highland. The revival and worldwide popularity of the former naturally has included Canada, where countless societies are dedicated to it, and where it has appealed to people of all nationalities and from all walks of life. George Emmerson, long resident in Ontario and a leading authority on the history of Scottish dancing, has noted in Cape Breton and elsewhere interesting local variants of steps and of dances, and Canadians such as Bob Campbell (Oakville, Ont) have composed and published new dances.

Highland dancing, originally a form of ritual dance for men, has become an almost balletic display, and by the mid-20th century most of the dancers were women. Highland dancing is seen above all at the Highland Games. In the years between 1960 and 1980 Canadians have attained international standards in this exacting art; a climax was reached in 1967, when the first three places in the World Adult Championship (at Gourock, Scotland) went to dancers from Canada: in order, Angus Clay-Mackenzie (Edmonton), Scott Porter (Verdun, Que), and Beth Buchanan (Vancouver).

DISCOGRAPHY

See also Discographies for Jean Carignan; Folk music, Anglo-Canadian: 2 / Nova Scotia and New Brunswick.

SONG

Gaelic Mouth-Music. Recorded by C.I.N. MacLeod. 1952. 2-Rodeo RO-128, RO-152 (78s)

FIDDLE MUSIC

Chez Isidore: Isidore Soucy et son ensemble. RCA Victor CGP 128

Les Danses de nos campagnes: Tommy Duchesne et ses chevaliers. Disques C-473

Rodeo Records Salute to Sydney, Cape Breton Island. Banff RBS 1051

Winston 'Scotty' Fitzgerald. Celtic CX 40

SCOTTISH DANCE BANDS

Angus MacKinnon and the Scots Canadians: Scottish Dance Music. Scotscan AJM-001

On with the Dance, with Ed Brydie's Scottish Dance Band. Col ELS 304

Scottish Dance Time: Stan Hamilton and the Clansmen. Notes by George S. Emmerson. 2 records: Clansmen SP 214, Sparton 216

Scottish Dance Time: Stan Hamilton and His Flying Scotsmen. Notes by George S. Emmerson. Clansmen SMT 70-2

Stan Hamilton and the Flying Scotsmen: Scottish Dance Music. RCA Victor PCS-1041

Stan Hamilton: Scottish Dance Time. Notes by George S. Emmerson. 2-RCA Victor PCS-1136, PCS-1137

BIBLIOGRAPHY

Fraser, Alexander. 'The Gaelic folk-songs of Canada,' *Proceedings and Transactions of the Royal Society of Canada*, vol 9, 1903

Creighton, Helen, and MacLeod, Calum. *Gaelic Songs in Nova Scotia*, National Museum of Man Bulletin no. 198 (Ottawa 1964)

'Canada takes top awards,' *The Piper and Dancer Bulletin*, Sep 1969

MacLeod, Calum I.N. *Bàrdachd Ghàidhlig á Albainn Nuaidh: Scottish Gaelic Poetry from Nova Scotia* (Glasgow 1970)

Emmerson, George S. *Rantin' Pipe and Tremblin' String: A History of Scottish Dance Music* (Montreal 1971)

– *A Social History of Scottish Dance: Ane Celestial Recreation* (Montreal 1972)

Macdonald, John H., et al. *Highlanders '72* (Toronto 1972)

Scott, Gail. 'Jean Carignan: the fiddler the rest call the best,' Toronto *Globe and Mail*, 23 Feb 1974

Fergusson, Donald A. ed. *Fad Air Falbh As Innse Gall: Beyond the Hebrides: Including the Cape Breton Collection* (Halifax 1977)

Kimber, Stephen. 'Highland fling on new sod,' *Maclean's*, 20 Aug 1979

JOURNALS

B.C. Pipers' Newsletter (Vancouver)

The North American Scotsman (St Catharines, Ont, 1969–)

The Piper and Dancer Bulletin (Hamilton, Ont 1945–)

FILMOGRAPHY

Celtic Spirits (NFB 1978)

The Fiddlers of James Bay (NFB 1980) (DW)

Seabird Island. Opera by Derek *Healey on a libretto by the Vancouver playwright Norman Newton. The story is based on a legend of the Tsimshian (west-coast Indian) tribe. Commissioned by the *Guelph Spring Festival, the *Canada Council, and the Floyd S. *Chalmers Foundation, *Seabird Island* was premiered 7 May 1977 at the festival by the singers Donald *Bell (the Prince), Garnet *Brooks (the Shaman), Barbara Ianni (the maid), Ingemar *Korjus (the King), Phyllis *Mailing (the Queen), and Roxolana *Roslak (the Princess) and the Stratford Festival Ensemble conducted by Nicholas *Goldschmidt. William *Littler found the opera 'reminiscent of the ritual of Noh or Kabuki' and described its 'interesting variety of techniques within a generally tonal framework. Pentatonic scales, ecclesiastical modes, percussion textures full of atmospheric rattles and metallic tinkling, and a tape of electronically distorted sea sounds are all brought into play' (*Toronto Star*, 9 May 1977). *Seabird Island* was broadcast 27 Jun 1977 on 'CBC Monday Night.' In 1978 a production featuring the same cast (with the exception of Bell, who was replaced by Korjus and of Janos Tessenyi, who sang the role of the King) toured to Toronto, Montreal, Ottawa, Banff, and Vancouver.

BIBLIOGRAPHY

Healey, Derek. '*Seabird Island*,' *OpCan*, Mar 1977 MM

SEARCHFIELD, John (Welbank). Organist, choirmaster, teacher, critic, conductor, writer, b Chester, England, 3 Mar 1930; BA (Oxford) 1951, ARCM 1952, LRAM 1953, MA (Oxford) 1966. His teachers included Douglas Hawkridge and C.H. Trevor (organ), Max *Pirani (piano), and Maurice Miles and Sir Adrian Boult (conducting). After emigrating to Canada in 1955 Searchfield worked as an organist-choirmaster in Brantford, Ont, until 1958, when he took a similar position in Calgary. There he began to conduct the Calgary Festival Chorus in 1959 and the CBC Calgary String Orchestra in 1968. In addition to his other activities he was a producer at CBC Calgary 1964–7, began teaching organ, theory, and harpsichord at the U of Calgary in 1967, and became the harpsichordist with the Calgary Baroque Ensemble in 1968. He became organist- choirmaster at Christ Church in 1969. He has written on music for the Calgary *Albertan*, and he contributed reports on Alberta 1970–4 to the *CMB*.

BIBLIOGRAPHY

Dawson, Eric. 'No party hats but Calgary's Festival Chorus is celebrating,' Calgary *Herald*, 10 Mar 1979 RDM

Sea shanties. See Occupational songs, Anglo-Canadian: 1 / The sea.

SEFTON, Henry Francis. Teacher, choirmaster, b Ireland 18?, d Toronto Dec 1882? He was engaged by Egerton Ryerson (who established the educational system in Ontario) and in 1858 moved to Canada from Ireland to teach music in Toronto's Normal and Model schools. Remaining there as music master until 1882, he also taught in public schools and at the Mechanics' Institute, applying the fixed-doh sight-singing systems of the Paris pedagogue Guillaume-Louis-Bocquillon Wilhem

Marie-Claire and Richard Séguin

and of John Hullah. He compiled the earliest music books in Ontario intended specifically for school use: *Three-part Songs* (Toronto 1869, 1879), which included 18 of his own songs, and *A Manual of Vocal Music* (Toronto 1871). *Nordheimer in 1860 published his song 'Welcome to Canada' with lyrics by Rev E. Denroche and a dedication to HRH the Prince of Wales. His successor, Alexander T. *Cringan, considered Sefton a 'fine theoretical musician.'

See also School music. HK

Les Séguin. Richard and Marie-Claire Séguin; twin brother and sister singer-songwriters, b Pointe-aux-Trembles, Montreal, 27 Mar 1952. As Les Nochers they first sang in 1966 in cafés and boîtes à chansons. In 1967–8 they sang as the duo Marie et Richard and were named 'Découverte 1968' at Le *Patriote in Montreal. Their distinctively personal singing style has been developed from characteristics of both folksinging and contemporary popular music. With other musicians, they founded La Nouvelle frontière (1969–71), a group with which they made two LPs for Gamma: *La Nouvelle frontière* (GS 137) and *L'Hymne aux quenouilles* (GS 143). After 1971 Les Séguin performed as a duo until 1977 when they began to include additional musicians. At the same time each began to pursue a separate career. Between 1973 and 1976 they made one LP a year: *Séguin* (Warner WSC 9013), *En attendant* (Warner WSC 9015), *Récolte de rêve* (Kot'ai KOT 3307), and *Festin d'amour* (CBS PFS 90385). In *The Canadian Composer* Bruno Dostie described the Séguins' particular sound: 'It's a product of acoustic instruments, soft percussion (no drums) and vocal harmonies that manages to synthesize medieval laments, baroque figured passages, Celtic rhythms, and the blues.'

In 1978 Richard Séguin collaborated with Serge Fiori of the group *Harmonium on the LP *Deux cents nuits à l'heure* (CBS PFS 90456) which won three of the 1979 ADISQ recording and showbusiness awards in Montreal. In 1979 he produced his first solo record (CBS PFC 80018), which reflected a style inspired by US folk-rock. Marie-Claire continued to display her sense of poetry and her vocal intensity on LPs made in 1978 and 1979 (CBS PFS 90452 and CBS PFC 80019).

Richard and Marie-Claire Séguin have worked with several lyricists. Their most popular songs include 'Sam Seguin,' 'Nous voyagerons,' and their version of Félix *Leclerc's 'P'tit train du Nord.' They are members of CAPAC.

BIBLIOGRAPHY

Kroll, Stephen. 'Twin talent,' *CanComp*, 80, May 1973

L'Heureux, Christine, and Pedneault, Hélène. *Les Séguin* (Montreal 1977)

Dostie, Bruno. 'A woman writer discovers her strength and begins to explore,' *CanComp*, 129, Mar 1978 (BLH)

SEITZ, Ernest (Joseph). Pianist, teacher, songwriter, b Hamilton, Ont, 29 Feb 1892, d Toronto 10 Sep 1978; Fellow, Royal Society of Arts, London 1954. For seven years a pupil of A.S. *Vogt in Toronto, Seitz studied 1910–14 with Josef Lhévinne in Berlin. His plans for a concert career in Europe were frustrated by the outbreak of World War I. He returned to Toronto and later studied in New York with Ernest Hutcheson. Seitz appeared at *Massey Hall some 18 times with the *TSO before 1946, in works of Bortkiewicz, Chopin, Rubinstein, Tchaikovsky, and others, and in the North American premiere, 11 Feb 1930, of Constant Lambert's *Rio Grande*. He was heard also in recital there, elsewhere in Ontario, in western Canada (1926), and on CKNC, CFRB, CRBC, and CBC radio.

At his most active as a pianist in the 1920s and 1930s, Seitz also accompanied Arthur *Blight, Ferdinand Fillion, and Luigi von *Kunits and was a member of the Five Piano Ensemble. He made his New York recital debut 4 Dec 1922, having performed there in April of that year as a soloist with the *Toronto Mendelssohn Choir. Other US engagements included those with the New York Philharmonic, the Boston SO, and the Philadelphia Orchestra. He also performed twice (1922, 1924) in Toronto with the New York SO. After a Seitz recital, Hector *Charlesworth wrote (*Globe and Mail*, 6 Nov 1942): 'Mr. Seitz in technical equipment and musical inspiration ranks among the foremost contemporary pianists ... As an interpreter [he] has dignity and authority that arouse the confidence and expectation of listeners ... His touch combines both tenderness and nobility, and is unique in its variety of emotional colour ... Especially in Liszt numbers, he revealed a superb quality with the left hand that sets him apart from most pianists, but he unites with this asset a beautiful balance of style.'

Seitz taught 1916–46 at the *TCM, where his pupils included Naomi *Adaskin, André *Asselin, Ewart *Bartley, Muriel *Gidley, Reginald *Godden, Scott Malcolm, Adelmo *Melecci, Earle *Moss, Harold Packer, Charles *Peaker, and Lorne *Watson. Despite his prominence as a concert pianist and his success as a teacher, Seitz was known best as the composer of the melody of the 1918 ballad *'The World Is Waiting for the Sunrise' (words by Gene Lockhart). Other Seitz songs included 'Laddie Boy' (1932), 'When Moonbeams Softly Fall' (1935; words by Donald *Heins), and 'The Sky's the Limit' (1943; words by G.L. Creed). Seitz retired from performance in 1945 and became president of the family business, an automobile dealership in Toronto.

WRITINGS

'Technique and other essentials for a pianist,' *CQR*, vol 1, Nov 1918

'Some observations on examinations,' *CQR*, vol 11, Summer 1929

BIBLIOGRAPHY

'Ernest Seitz,' *Musical Canada*, vol 6, Jan 1925

Hunter, Carl. 'Conservatory portrait gallery no. 2 – Mr. Ernest Seitz,' *CQR*, vol 10, Winter 1928

MH, MM, PW

Séminaire de Québec. Teaching establishment founded in Quebec City by François de Laval, the first bishop of New France. The Grand Séminaire was created in 1663 to provide for the training of an indigenous clergy. The Petit Séminaire, begun in 1668, offered a classical education leading to the liberal professions. As early as 1666 Bishop Laval is believed to have introduced a course in church music into the seminary's program.

The Société Sainte-Cécile, which was to serve as the hub of musical activities at the seminary – and indeed, to play an important role in the artistic life of Quebec – was not formally established until 200 years later. It came into being as a student instrumental group in 1833, but was not given permanent status or named until 1869. (It is not to be confused with the Société Sainte-Cécile founded in Montreal by A.J. *Boucher in 1860 or the *Société musicale Sainte-Cécile.) Much later, in 1927, its regulations defined it as follows: 'The Société Sainte-Cécile, Brass Band or Concert Band, is a musical society made up of pupils boarding in the adult division of the Petit séminaire de Québec'; its purpose was to 'initiate the students into the art of instrumental music, to develop their appreciation of it, to make them proficient in playing an instrument and also to enhance public gatherings.'

In the spring of 1833 in the Petit Séminaire Adam *Schott organized an orchestra which performed during the end-of-year examination period. The first official concert was given 15 Aug 1834 at the time of the public examinations. Schott was replaced by James Ziegler Jr, commander of the 66th Regiment, who transformed the orchestra into a military band 1836–8. The program of a concert given 6 Apr 1837 contained Boieldieu's overture to *The Caliph of Bagdad*. The leadership of the society changed hands fairly often. Its musical directors were Vincent Mazzocchi 1838–41 and Charles *Sauvageau 1841–4; Ziegler returned 1844–8 and was followed by James Ross 1848–58, a certain Sprake during the summer of 1858, Father Sébastien Morel 1858–9, Sprake again 1859–61, Célestin *Lavigueur 1861–5, Charles J. Millar 1865–7, Lavigueur again 1867–8, E. Rochette 1868–73, Father Georges Frazer 1873–5, Henry McKernan ca 1875–82, and Father Thomas Marcoux 1882–4. Among those who taught at the seminary during this period were Sauvageau 1841–9, Antoine *Dessane 1849–50, Louis Sigismond Pfeiffer 1851–2, and Lavigueur for 30 years. Morel had come from Europe to be organist-choirmaster at the cathedral. Ross, Sprake, and McKernan were regimental band directors; McKernan also taught English and bookkeeping at the seminary.

Joseph *Vézina took over as music director 1884–1924. Vézina made some radical changes. He excluded wind instruments so that the band could play at religious ceremonies, but in 1900 he readmitted the woodwinds. Even after 1914, when the ensemble had become little more than a military band, Vézina slowly directed the repertoire towards classical non-religious works (such as excerpts from Weber's *Der Freischütz* and medleys of Verdi and Donizetti operas). A report of a meeting of the society 1 Jun 1897 described the repertoire played until then as follows: 'quick steps, galops, some waltzes, that was in reality the sum total of the program of almost all its music sessions.'

Father Pierre-Chrysologue Desrochers, a music teacher at the seminary, euphonium player in the society, and its deputy conductor, gradually took over the position of director, which he held until his death in 1947. Robert *Talbot replaced him briefly. Around this time the Société Sainte-Cécile began to decline. Father Marc Letarte was director 1947–50 and 1951–60, and Edwin *Bélanger, teacher at the seminary for 22 years, served as interim director in 1950–1, but between 1960 and 1962 the ensemble was left to its own devices. Its last director was the violinist Claude *Létourneau 1962–ca 1967. With him ended the activities of this society, the oldest of its kind in Canada. The more relaxed attitude towards the students' use of leisure time and the boarders' freedom to come and go from the school had made mandatory rehearsals virtually impossible.

A. Bégin, Ernest *Gagnon (piano, organ), J.-A. *Gilbert, T.F. *Molt, G. Raineri, and M. Range are some of the others who taught at the seminary at different periods. Edwin Bélanger, Émile *Larochelle, and Joseph Vézina are among the best-known students.

BIBLIOGRAPHY

Vézina, Raymond. 'La Société Sainte-Cécile,' *Aspects de l'enseignement du petit séminaire de Québec 1765–1945* (Quebec 1968)

HP

SEMPLE, Arthur (Emil). Flutist, conductor, civil servant, b Toronto 9 Mar 1876, d there 9 Feb 1963; Fellow Toronto College of Music, LRAM, LAB, before 1912; B MUS (Toronto) 1915. He was the principal flute in the *Welsman *TSO in its early years and with other Toronto orchestras and bands and gave recitals and concerto performances. He also served as organist-choirmaster in St Luke's Anglican and Zion Congregational churches, taught 1912–13 at the *Toronto College of Music, and joined the staff of the *Hambourg Cons in 1913. He wrote flute solos, church music, and a cantata, *Blest Pair of Sirens*. He is remembered as the founder around the end of World War I of the Harmony SO, which he conducted until the mid-1930s. He was the founder and first president (1944) of the Toronto Flute Club. Semple served 1899–1939 as private secretary to Ontario's premier George W. Ross and to six successive provincial secretaries. HK

SÉNART, Jean-François. Choir conductor, b Anglet, France, 27 Apr 1943; BA (Montreal) 1962. He came to Canada in 1952 and later studied literature at the U of Montreal. In 1965 he enrolled at the *CMM, where he studied orchestration with Jean-Louis Martinet and orchestra conducting with Raymond *Dessaints and Pierre Dervaux. He took advanced courses in 1973 with Dervaux in Nice and in 1977 with Piero Bellugi in Siena on a grant from the *Canada Council. He founded the *Choeur Kattialine in 1962. A member of the college of instructors of the *Alliance chorale canadienne, for which he was the animateur in 1969 and 1970, he became recognized as an 'international instructor' by the choral movement À Coeur Joie. He conducted workshops on 16th-century choral music at the 1971 and 1974 Choralies internationales in Vaison-la-Romaine, France. In 1973 he began the extended series of choral programs 'A Cappella' on CBC radio. Made up primarily of young professional singers, the A Cappella ensemble has broadcast more than 70 programs in about 15 languages. Sénart founded the Ensemble vocal de Montréal in 1976 and was in charge of the orchestral department at the *École Vincent-d'Indy in 1974. He was a teacher and conductor of the orchestra and choir at the St-Laurent Cegep 1969–77 and became director of choral activities at the *U of Montreal in 1973 and assistant conductor of the Orchestre des jeunes du Québec in 1979.

DISCOGRAPHY

La Fleur des musiciens de Pierre de Ronsard. A Cappella choir. 1974. RCI 408

Folklore du Canada: Quebec and neo-Canadian songs. CBC vocal ens. 1975. RCI 429

Noël de la paix. Ens vocal de Mtl, Quebec WW Quin. 1976. RCI 435 (ST)

Sénécal. Montreal publishers under a succession of names – Sénécal & Daniel 1854–6, Sénécal,

Daniel et Cie 1857?–9, Eusèbe Sénécal 1860–80, Eusèbe Sénécal & Fils 1882–96, and Eusèbe Sénécal et Cie 1897–1902 – whose output included music. Sénécal & Daniel published such newspapers and periodicals as *La Patrie* (1855–7) and *Journal de l'instruction publique / Journal of Education for Lower Canada* (1857–9). The latter contained only brief notices of music teachers' activities until in 1859 two issues appeared with important music inserts: T.F. *Molt's *'Sol canadien' (February) and Charles *Sauvageau's 'Chant canadien' (June). Eusèbe Sénécal published the *Journal* on his own after 1860, but music seems not to have been included. However, one or two pages of music, besides musical announcements, chronicles, and reviews, appeared monthly in the *Écho du cabinet de lecture paroissial* (1859–75) after Sénécal took it over in 1862. This official publication of a literary circle formed in 1857 aimed to cover national and international news and opinion from the moral viewpoint of the group. The publication of music was discontinued after 1863 because of the cost of typesetting. Several sheet music publications of Sénécal, Daniel et Cie (including 'Sol canadien' and 'Chant canadien') and of Eusèbe Sénécal have survived. All are typeset and dated, in keeping with the practice of periodical publishers, and cover the years from 1859 to 1863. Among the composers are Antoine *Dessane, Mathias Jung, and Charles Wugk *Sabatier. In later years Eusèbe Sénécal & Fils published Father Cléophas Borduas's *Nouveau Manuel de chants liturgiques* (1888), R.-O. *Pelletier's *Accompagnement du nouveau manuel de chants liturgiques* (1889), and P.L. Paré's *Recueil d'introïts et de motets* (1891).

BIBLIOGRAPHY

Beaulieu, André, and Hamelin, Jean. *La Presse québécoise, des origines à nos jours*, 2 vols (Québec 1973, 1975)
Calderisi, Maria. 'Music publishing in Canada: 1800–1867,' unpubl MA thesis, McGill 1976 MC

SENENSKY, Bernie (Bernard Melvyn). Pianist, composer, photographer, b Winnipeg 31 Dec 1944. He began piano studies at 9 with Clara Pearlman and was guided in jazz at 17 by Bob Erlendson. After playing 1962–6 in Winnipeg and Edmonton nightclubs and crossing Canada in a series of hotel engagements, he settled in 1968 in Toronto, where he became one of the city's leading accompanists. In Toronto clubs he has played for such US jazzmen as George Coleman, Art Farmer, Art Pepper, Zoot Sims, and Phil Woods and has been music director or accompanist to the singers Salome *Bey, Ginette *Reno, Joe Williams, and others. In December 1976 he worked with Elvin Jones in Montreal. He became a member of Moe *Koffman's quintet in 1979. Senensky has recorded as sideman to Bey, Koffman, the saxophonist Eugene Amaro, the trombonist Russ *Little, the guitarist (Michael) Munoz, Herbie *Spanier, Fred *Stone, and others. He formed his own trio in the early 1970s; on *New Life* (1975, RCI 416/PMR-006), an LP of his compositions, the trio is completed by the bassist Michel *Donato and the drummer Marty Morell. Jack Batten described Senensky as a 'remarkably secure player, hitting all the notes in the sort of hard and true manner that gives the listener a sense of comfort' and praised a 'whizzingly impressive technique' (Toronto *Globe and Mail*, 12 Aug 1976). Senensky is affiliated with PRO Canada, and his compositions, which have been recorded by Red Rodney, Don (W.) *Thompson, and others, are copyrighted by his own company, Beloved Gift Music. His photographs of musicians have appeared on record covers and in *Coda, Down Beat*, and *The Encyclopedia of Jazz in the 70s*.

BIBLIOGRAPHY

Miller, Mark. 'Bernie Senensky,' *Down Beat*, vol 42, 18 Dec 1975
Waxman, Ken. 'Bernie Senensky maintains high profile on jazz scene,' *MSc*, 292, Nov–Dec 1976 MM

Septuor Haydn. Founded in Quebec City in 1871 by Arthur *Lavigne (first violin), L.-Nazaire *LeVasseur (second violin), Alfred *Paré (viola), Narcisse Hamel (cello), Édouard Gauvreau (contrabass), Octave Chavigny de Lachevrotière or Cyrille Duquet (flute), and J.-A. Defoy (piano). Through at least one of its members the group was connected to the recently dissolved Septett Club founded in 1857 by Alfred Paré and some musicians from the *Quebec Harmonic Society. An 'unfortunate misunderstanding' between the Septett Club members William Campbell (cello) and Paré appears to have led Paré to found the Septuor instrumental Haydn. At the first meeting, 21 Aug 1871, Ernest *Gagnon and Édouard *Glackemeyer were elected music director and honorary president respectively. The septuor made its official debut 25 Aug 1871 in Haydn's *Symphony No. 73*, 'The Hunt' (it is not specified whether the work was played in its entirety), and the overture to Rossini's *Cenerentola*. The occasion was the conferring of the *AMQ diplomas in the hall of the École nationale, on the rue d'Auteuil. The group performed some 10 overtures and various other pieces during its first year.

Alone or with the participation of the *Union musicale, the *Société musicale Sainte-Cécile, and the Quatuor vocal de Québec, the group took an active part in Quebec City's musical life. LeVasseur, in his *Réminiscences d'antan*, wrote: 'In the hall adjoining the gas inspection offices, the Septuor Hayden [sic] annually for many years gave series of brilliant soirées with an orchestra and singing. The governors-general, when in town, the lieutenant-governors and their retinues, and the cream of the city's society were invited and were eager to attend.' Six of the septuor's members took part in the World's Peace Jubilee in Boston in 1872, and in addition the group presented 17 concerts that year. In 1873 it gave 16 concerts and went on a two-month tour with the violinist Frantz *Jehin-Prume.

In 1874 the ensemble leased a hall in the Masonic Building in order to present monthly concerts there and organized a performance of Félicien David's symphonic ode *Christophe Colomb* on the occasion of the bicentenary of the archdiocese of Quebec City. In December 1888 the augmented ensemble gave some concerts in the Basilica, including one for the Feast of the Immaculate Conception (the players on that occasion being Defoy, Gauvreau, LeVasseur, and Paré, along with 'Messrs. Courchênes, Dorval, Dufresne, Leclerc and Prince'). The ensemble was invited by Gustave *Gagnon to participate in a rehearsal of a Gounod mass for the coming Christmas celebrations. The *Morning Chronicle* made special mention of the septuor's presence at a concert of 22 Apr 1889 at the *Académie de musique.

The date of the Septuor Haydn's demise cannot be determined. In all likelihood it did not die but merged with the Société symphonique de Québec (*Quebec SO), formed in February 1903. In the orchestra's ranks appear the names of J.-A. *Gilbert, LeVasseur, and Lavigne – all sometime members of the Septuor Haydn. The septuor's library, one of the largest of the time, contained 25 quintets by Félicien David, several series of orchestral and chamber works donated to the ensemble by Édouard Glackemeyer, and many other works. The material has been deposited at *Laval U.

BIBLIOGRAPHY

Un amateur. 'Le Septuor Haydn de Québec,' *Canada musical*, 1 Jul 1875
LeVasseur, L.-Nazaire. *Réminiscences d'antan* (Quebec City 1926) (CH)

Serbia. Immigration to Canada by the peoples of this eastern portion of modern *Yugoslavia began in significant numbers after World War II, and by the mid-1970s some 50,000 Serbian-Canadians lived and worked in the industrial areas of southern Ontario. Others lived in Ottawa, Montreal, and Vancouver. Industry, mining, real estate, and hostelry have been favoured occupations.

In the mid-1970s among Serbian-Canadians music was used mainly for weddings and for dances and picnics sponsored by churches, youth groups, and political organizations. Bands of one or two accordions, electric guitar, and drums played a variety of popular circle dances (kolo), especially šest, žikino, čačak, and malo, as well as popular songs in Serbian and English. Some 10 of these bands have flourished in Canada; and 2 or 3 others, which use only acoustic instruments, including the tamburica (long-necked plucked lute), have catered to the pre-World-War-II generation of immigrants. In the 1970s about 10 folkdance groups (with accordions, electric guitar, and drums) and four choirs served the young people in the Serbian community and exchanged visits with similar groups in the USA. One of the groups, Hajduk Veljko of Toronto, was named the outstanding Serbian group in North America in 1975 by the Serbian Radio Hour broadcast from Detroit, Mich, and by CHIN radio in Toronto.

In 1980 numerous traditional songs, such as bečarac and svatovac, continued to be sung at weddings, and immigrants from Montenegro occasionally performed song dances at weddings. In 1975 the archives of the *National Museum of Man held 10 Serbian folksongs collected in Canada. A frula (flute) or gaide (bagpipe) player occasionally has been heard, and in 1979 two gusle (one-stringed, bowed lute) players – Todor Jevrić and Mitar Crnogorac, both from Montenegro – were living in Toronto. TR

Serialism. See Twelve-tone technique.

SÉVILLA, Jean-Paul. Pianist, b Oran, Algeria, 26 Mar 1934; premier prix piano (Paris Cons) 1952, premier prix chamber music (Paris Cons) 1953. He studied 1948–52 at the Paris Cons, primarily with Blanche Bascourret de Gueraldi and Marcel Ciampi. In 1952 he received the prix d'honneur and undertook his first European tours. In 1954 he obtained first prize at the JM Competition in France and in 1959 he was awarded first prize by unanimous decision at the Geneva International Competition for Musical Performers.

For the *JMC Sévilla toured Canada in 1961–2 as a member of a trio and in 1962–3 as a solo recitalist. He gave courses in performance in 1962 at the *JMC Orford Art Centre. He made his US debut in 1961, his Mexican debut in 1964, and his South American debut in 1967. In Montreal he gave the first Canadian performances of sonatas by Henri Dutilleux and Alberto Ginastera.

In 1971 at the *U of Ottawa Sévilla presented a series of concerts of French music which included Canadian premieres of works by Tisné, Dukas, Delvincourt, and Constant. In January 1972 at a public recital taped for broadcast by CBC Toronto he premiered *Complémentarité*, a work dedicated to him by its composer Jean *Papineau-Couture. In March 1975 Sévilla performed Ravel's piano repertoire at the *NAC to mark the 100th anniversary of the composer's birth. Prior to that time he had played Ravel's complete piano works in recitals in France, Belgium, Spain, and Argentina.

Sévilla began to teach at the U of Ottawa in 1970, and under the university's aegis he has given summer courses in France, particularly in Aix-en-Provence and Perpignan. Angela *Hewitt, Heather Huber, Charlotte Sheng, and Andrew Tunis are among his pupils. A sabbatical 1978–9 in Paris was spent working on a performing edition of the piano works of Fauré and giving lecture-recitals on them at several French conservatories.

Sévilla possesses a secure technique and a wide musical culture. His repertoire extends from Bach to 20th-century composers, some of whom (eg, Castérède, Dutilleux, and Jolivet) have dedicated works to him. His programs, however, have shown a preference for music of the romantic and impressionist periods.

DISCOGRAPHY

Delvincourt *Sonate* for violin and piano. L. Garnier vn. (1953). Club National du Disque (JM de France)

Papineau-Couture *Complémentarité* – Schumann *Études symphoniques, Op 13*. 1972. RCI 384

Schubert *Sonatas, Op 147 and 164*. (1968?). Harmonia Mundi HMO ORTF 30.903

See also Discography for Louise Lebrun. YC (ST)

SEWELL, Jonathan. Lawyer, violinist, b Cambridge, Mass, 6 Jun 1766, d Quebec City 12 Nov 1839. The son of a United Empire Loyalist, Sewell was educated in Bristol, England, before moving to New Brunswick in 1785. Called to the bar in Lower Canada in 1789 he enjoyed a distinguished career in law, rising from solicitor-general in 1793 to chief justice of Lower Canada 1808–38 and also becoming a member in 1796 and speaker in 1804 of the legislature. An amateur actor and poet and a violinist of some proficiency, he was chosen to lead a small orchestra organized by the Duke of Kent, who was in residence in Quebec 1791–4 as commander of British forces. However, chamber music was his abiding passion, and he led ensembles made up of amateur musicians, some from the legal profession. One such quartet comprised Sewell, the notaries Archibald Campbell (violin) and Édouard *Glackemeyer (flute), and the shipbuilder J. Harvicker (cello). These ensembles established a tradition perpetuated by the Quintette Club, the Septett Club, and the *Septuor Haydn. Copies of works of Haydn and Mozart with Sewell's signature survive, indicating that they probably were performed in Canada as early as three years after they were written. This music is now held in the *Laval U library.

BIBLIOGRAPHY

Notman, W. *Portraits of British Americans* vol 2, (Montreal 1867) MHl, HK

Shadow on the Prairie. Ballet in one scene by Gweneth Lloyd (choreography) and Robert Fleming (music). The score was commissioned by the Royal Winnipeg Ballet and composed in 1951. The ballet was premiered 30 Oct 1952 in Winnipeg. The production toured extensively in 1954 in Canada and the USA. The story concerns a Scottish couple on the prairies and depicts the wife's growing fear and loneliness during a long winter. Excerpts from the ballet were filmed in 1953 by the NFB. Fleming's music, neoclassical and containing some folk elements, was arranged in 1953 into a concert suite which in 1954 was rescored for larger orchestra and premiered 9 Feb 1955 by the *TSO under Sir Ernest *MacMillan. A study score of the ballet suite was published by the *CMCentre, and a recording (1955, RCI 129) of the orchestral version was made by MacMillan and the TSO. SW

Shaftesbury Hall. The auditorium in Toronto's first YMCA, built at Queen and James streets in 1872 to designs by the architects Smith and Gemmel. The hall was on the ground floor with a direct entrance from the street, a double gallery, and a seating capacity of about 1500. The *Toronto Philharmonic Society performed there until 1879, and occasional tenants included the Theodore Thomas Orchestra (1873), the Mendelssohn Quartette Club (1877), the *Queen's Own Rifles Band (1878), and the *Toronto String Quartette (1886–7) along with educational and temperance groups. The building was sold to the Sons of England in 1886, and later the name was changed to Bijou Hall. It was demolished in 1901. RPn

SHANNON, Adrienne. Pianist, b Hamilton, Ont, 24 Jul 1950; ARCT 1968, M MUS (Juilliard) 1973. A pupil of Boris *Berlin at the *RCMT and Ania Dorfmann at the Juilliard School, she has performed with the *TS, the *MSO, the *Hamilton Philharmonic, and the *St Catharines and *Windsor SOs and has appeared in recital across Canada, in New York, and in Sion, Switzerland. She has performed on CBC radio and TV, RAE radio in Italy, and RIAS radio in Berlin. She placed fourth in the 1973 Munich International Competition, first in the 1975 *MSO Concours, and fourth in the 1976 Busoni International Piano Competition and was a semi-finalist in the 1978 Leeds International Piano Competition. In 1974 she joined the faculty of the RCMT. Shannon and Jane *Coop made their Toronto debut as a two-piano team in 1976 at the *St Lawrence Centre and their performance earned them the Floyd S. *Chalmers Foundation Award. They also have appeared as duo-pianists with the *NACO and the TS and have given recitals on CBC radio.

Shaw Festival. Established at *Niagara-on-the-Lake, Ont, as a platform for the plays of Bernard Shaw. It began with an eight-performance 'Salute to Shaw' at the town's court house in 1962. A professional company established in 1963 flourished under the direction of Andrew Allan 1963–5, Paxton Whitehead 1966–77, Richard Kirschner 1977–8, and Leslie Yeo 1978–80, succeeded by Christopher Newton, and its summer season increased in duration from three weeks in 1963 to 22 weeks in 1976. The 830-seat Festival Theatre was opened in 1973. Though music was introduced to the festival in 1966 with a concert by the *Hart House Orchestra, it was only in 1970 that another music presentation was attempted – a new-music series directed by Robert *Aitken at St Mark's Church with the *Lyric Arts Trio and the *Orford Quartet. The same groups returned for 'Music Today '71' and, with the addition of *Nexus, for 'Music Today '72.' In 1973 the *NACO, *Canadian Brass, the *Festival Singers with Lois *Marshall, and the Orford Quartet gave concerts, and in 1974 *Camerata began the first of three seasons of concerts on various historical and stylistic themes with such guests as Maureen *Forrester and Moe *Koffman. Members of the Camerata also gave master classes at the festival in 1974 and 1975. After a season's hiatus, music returned to the festival in 1978 with the *Huggett Family, the *York Winds with Judy *Loman, the entertainers Dinah *Christie and Tom Kneebone, and the musical melodrama *Lady Audley's Secret*. The International Concert Series, an impressive winter season, began in 1973–4 with 12 attractions, including Renée *Claude, the Contemporary Music Orchestra of Paris, and the *COC. This winter series continued with 19 events of similar calibre in 1974–5, 15 in 1975–6, 7 in 1976–7, and 10 in 1977–8.

BIBLIOGRAPHY

Shaw Festival: History 1977 (Niagara-on-the-Lake 1977)

Shawnigan Summer School of the Arts. Training centre founded in 1971 and directed by J.J. *Johannesen and located at the Shawnigan Lake School for boys (north of Victoria, BC) until 1974, when it moved to St Michael's School in Victoria. Courses, private tutoring, and master classes have been offered in strings, winds, keyboard instruments, and composition for advanced students (over 16), teachers, and professionals. Courses have also been introduced in flute (1974), chamber music (1975), and electronic music (1978). An opera centre was opened in 1979. Jean *Coulthard and Rudolf *Komorous have taught composition and Phyllis *Mailing voice. Instrumental instructors have included Robert *Aitken, Gary *Karr, Tsuyoshi *Tsutsumi, and the *Orford String Quartet, as well as several from abroad. The Shawnigan International Festival (which became the Victoria International Festival in 1979), presents students and staff in concert during the school term, on Vancouver Island and in Vancouver city. The school is assisted financially by the BC government, the *Canada Council, and corporate donors.

SHEA, George Beverly. Bass-baritone, b Winchester, near Ottawa, 1 Feb 1909; hon DFA (Houghton College) 1956, hon D Sacred MUS (Trinity, Deerfield, Ill) 1969. He was taught to play the violin by his father, a Methodist minister, and the piano and organ by his mother. Shea lived 1917–21 in Houghton, NY, and 1921–8 in Ottawa and began singing at religious meetings in the Ottawa Valley. He returned to the USA and studied singing 1928–9 with Herman Baker at Houghton College, NY. While a medical secretary 1929–38 in New York, he studied privately with Emerson Williams and Manley Price Boone and sang on radio stations WMCA and WHN. In Chicago he was a singer and announcer 1938–44 on WBMI and sang humns 1943–52 on WCFL's 'Songs of the Night' and 'Club Time.' He became a soloist with Billy Graham's evangelical crusade in 1947 and retained the position for over 30 years, performing at rallies and on radio and TV. With the crusade he has visited Canada many times.

Considered among the foremost exponents of popular sacred song, Shea made 46 LPs 1950–77 for RCA Victor, including *Southland Favourites* (1965, RCA LSP 3440), which won a Grammy Award for best gospel or other religious recording in 1965. Shea has composed songs published by Chancel Music, including the highly successful 'I'd Rather Have Jesus' (1939), 'Blue Galilee' (1947), and 'I Will Praise Him' (1971). He also compiled song collections, notably *George Beverly Shea Favourites* (1957), *The Crusade Soloist* (1963), and *Songs That Lift the Heart* (F.H. Revell 1972, a collaboration with Fred Bauer). His autobiography, *Then Sings My Soul*, written with Fred Bauer, was published in 1968 by F.H. Revell (Old Tappan, NJ). FH

SHEA, Jerry (Jeremiah James). Violinist, conductor, b Montreal 5 Feb 1884, d there 18 Oct 1960. After studies in Montreal with Jean *Goulet and in New York he toured US theatres with a string quartet at 16. Though he was successful in the USA as music director 1904–6 for the Klaw and Erlinger (New York) company's touring production of the opera *Ben Hur* and conductor of the Chicago Concert Orchestra, Shea chose to return to Montreal in 1906 and spent the rest of his professional life there except for a tour 1930–1 with Harry Lauder. In Montreal he conducted orchestras for silent films, vaudeville, and opera at the major theatres and for broadcasts on CKAC, CFCF, and CBC radio. He conducted the premieres 16 Nov 1913 of Alexis *Contant's *Les Deux Âmes* and *L'Aurore*. At the Imperial Theatre 1914–15 he initiated and conducted Sunday concerts of classical music by a 50-piece orchestra (a forerunner of the *MSO). He was also music director of Adanac Films, an early Canadian company, and organized entertainment for the St Lawrence cruises of the Canada Steamship Lines. In 1930, when talking pictures had caused widespread unemployment among theatre orchestra musicians, Shea founded the Canadian Musicians Benevolent and Educational Assn and was its first president. He conducted *The Mikado* in 1952 and *The Gondoliers* in 1953 for the *Montreal Festivals.

Shea's son (John) D'Arcy Shea – b Montreal 4 Feb 1921; A MUS (McGill) 1942, L MUS (McGill) 1948 – was a pupil of Rachel Gilbert at the McGill Cons 1938–42 and in Paris 1959–60 and of Herbert Menges in London 1959–60. He was second violin of the *McGill String Quartet from 1949 to the early 1950s and a member of the MSO 1947–59, 1961–8 and the TS 1972–7, prior to becoming principal second violin with the *Vancouver SO in 1977. (JDS)

SHEAN, Ranald. Violinist, teacher, conductor, b Edmonton 6 May 1914. Violin lessons in Edmonton with Percy Humphrey were followed by study in Vancouver in the 1930s with Gregori *Garbovitsky. Shean was one of the founders and a conductor 1941–2 of the Edmonton Philharmonic (*Edmonton SO) and was its concertmaster 1945–52. He was an organizer and the second conductor, 1953–60, of the Edmonton Junior Symphony (renamed Edmonton Youth Orchestra). Shean taught privately in Edmonton prior to establishing in 1966, and serving as director of, the Edmonton Cons of Music. In 1973 he became a teacher and assistant director at *Alberta College. Considered an outstanding string teacher, particularly of young children, he has counted among his pupils Susan Cottrell, Tamara Fahlman, Ernie Kassian, Robert Klose, John Lowry, Mark Lupin, Nick Pulos, David Rhein, Yvonne Vercohnin, and Marlin Wolfe. Many of his pupils have been accepted as members of the *NYO. In 1977 he was presented with an Alberta Achievement Award for his service to music in the province. PW

SHEPPARD, W. (William) **Spurgeon** ('Spurge'). Bandmaster, cornetist, composer, arranger, b Saint John, NB, 2 Nov 1869, d Waterloo, Ont, 26 Jul 1955. He played cornet as a young man with the *Waterloo Musical Society Band and was for many years bandmaster of the Galt Kiltie Band and the Cornwall Band and assistant director of the Kitchener Musical Society Band. Later he became bandmaster of the New Hamburg Citizens' Band and assistant director of the Waterloo Musical Society Band. Sheppard was president 1949–50 of the CBA (*CBDA), and was made a life member in 1954. Several of his marches (*Pro patria, Silver Trumpets, Down the Line, Military Spirit*, etc, and an arrangement of melodies from Sullivan's *H.M.S. Pinafore*) are published by *Waterloo Music. Several others, and a transcription for band of Mozart's *Symphony No. 39*, are in manuscript. EBM

Sherbrooke. City in southern Quebec, located about as far south of Quebec City as it is east of Montreal. With its suburbs it has a population of more than 100,000 (1978); it has been called 'Queen of the Eastern Townships' or of 'L'Estrie,' the more recent name for the area.

The Loyalists who arrived from the USA after 1776 to populate these tracts of land brought with them their reels and folksongs. The first hamlet was formed around a mill established in 1796 by Gilbert Hyatt and in 1818 this little settlement was named Sherbrooke after the governor in chief of Canada, Sir John Coape Sherbrooke. The places of worship were the location of most of the musical activity 1820–70 and such activity intensified after 1870. The diversity of religious affiliations resulted in numerous churches. Singers such as George Armitage and Fred H. Bradley were attached to Trinity (Methodist) Church, built in 1856; other local performers gave concerts there as well, under A.F. Waterhouse, with well-known guest soloists, including the organist Lynnwood *Farnam, and the soprano Marie Hollinshead. Such works as Mendelssohn's *Hymn of Praise*, Gounod's *Gallia*, and Rossini's *Stabat mater* were presented.

In the early years of the 20th century, the organists William *Reed, Mme Holland, Alfred *Whitehead, and later Graham *George were connected with St Peter's Anglican Church (which dates from 1844). The singers Cecil Bowen and Arthur Dorey were members of the choir of St Peter's and the latter organized festivals – the gathering of several choral groups to perform oratorios. At Plymouth Church the organist Frank Stone presented his opera *Sardianopolis* with local artists. Frequent concerts including an annual 'Musical May' were held at the church and it became known as a centre for the performance of music of good quality. Well-known singers were invited for the Burns Concerts at St Andrew's Presbyterian Church. Bertha, Evelyn, and Clifford Price of the Adventist Church played an important role in the organization of musical groups. Bertha, a mezzo-soprano and pianist, also taught young people and ca 1914–18 led a youth orchestra that was very popular; Evelyn, a violinist, and Clifford, a cellist, played in various ensembles, including the first Sherbrooke SO 1923–7.

St Michael's Cathedral was the centre of vigorous Roman Catholic musical activity. A two-keyboard Couillard organ, installed in 1874, was inaugurated by Rosa d'Erina, who was also a singer. H.-O. Doré, a teacher at the Collège de Sherbrooke, conducted a mixed choir there. Liturgical singing was provided by the students from the Séminaire St-Charles under the direction 1875–1910 of a Father Roy. When the seminary organized its own services in 1910, the lawyer Ernest Sylvestre founded the Sherbrooke Cathedral Choir. Besides music for the church service, operas, oratorios, and cantatas were presented. In 1918 the cathedral acquired a three-keyboard *Casavant. One of its long-time resident organists was Louis-Édouard Codère, head of a musical family which was influential in the community. His wife, b Joséphine Doherty, a pianist and composer, was decorated in 1929 by the ministry of education of France for her work as a musical organizer. Oscar Cartier, pianist, organist, and composer, succeeded Sylvestre as director of the choir and adapted masses by Gounod, Dubois, and Palestrina (*Missa Papae Marcelli*) for his 50-voice male choir.

The Gregorian revival at the end of the 1930s and the foundation of the Gregorian Institute by Bishop Maurice O'Bready (the hall of the Centre culturel of the university was named after him) with the assistance of the Benedictines of St-Benoit-du-Lac brought about the departure of most of the choristers. Thus it was that the choirs of St-Jean-Baptiste, St Patrick, and Ste Thérèse-d'Avila acquired singers who continued in the style used 1910–40 by the cathedral choir. This choir followed the Gregorian reform of the Benedictine abbey at Solesmes, France, with Paul-Émile Letendre as organist and director. From 1950 to 1967 J.-B. Marcoux conducted a choir school which he had founded. In the early 1960s the Choeur Pie X assumed the cathedral choir's earlier function of musical stimulus to the region.

The St-Jean-Baptiste Choir founded by Eugène Caron, organist and composer, was taken over by the lawyer Georges Sylvestre in 1925 and for more than 25 years remained the centre of musical life in the eastern sector of the city. Groups devoted to light music were formed, and Allan *McIver and Germaine Janelle became known as the accompanists of the Minstrel Shows. Les Chanteclers, an unaccompanied choir, were founded in 1935 by H. St-Pierre. In 1971 Héritage, a 60-voice choir conducted by Marc Bernier, was set up to propagate the Quebec chanson.

Towards the end of the 19th century Mrs Henry Odell organized about 100 women to form the Ladies' Musical Club, which sponsored concerts by such artists as Emma *Albani and J.-B. *Dubois. The *Union musicale de Sherbrooke, a cultural association active 1892–6, was reorganized in 1921. The Schubert Music Club (1926–ca 1950), which consisted of some 30 local musicians, presented the baritone Gordon T. Brand, the violinist Audrey Cook, the tenor Alfred O'Shea, the pianist Paul *de Marky, and the Metropolitan Opera tenor Richard Crooks, among many solo artists of note. Two associations, Le Jeudi musical (1936) and l'Art intime (1943) helped stimulate musical activity until ca 1960 through public performances which their members were expected to give and through financial aid to young musicians such as the cellist Émile Préfontaine and the composer Serge *Garant.

Between 1938 and 1974 the Sherbrooke Concerts Society, affiliated to *Community Concerts, presented artists of world reputation such as Mischa Elman, Bidú Sayão, and Rudolf Serkin at the Granada Theatre (which became the Festival Cinema). It was in Sherbrooke, 19 Jan 1950, that Noël *Brunet and Suzette Pratte gave the first *JMC concert. The annual summer Festival des Cantons began in Sherbrooke in 1974; traditional music has been a principal component of its numerous concerts, amateur competitions, and other entertainments.

The Sherbrooke Concert Band (or the Harmonie de Sherbrooke) was founded in 1882 as a municipal band. It was directed successively by François *Héraly, J.-J. *Goulet, Charles Delvenne, Georges Sylvestre, Sylvio *Lacharité, and Marcel Marcotte. Instrumental groups from the polytechnical schools partially took over from the Sherbrooke Band when it ceased its activities in 1968. The Victoria Band (1876) was connected with the 53rd Regiment and directed by two musicians from England, J. Whiteley and J. Eave. The brass band of Uldéric Brien, founded after World War I, bore the colours of the 54th Regiment.

In 1923 Irwin Sawdon, a licentiate of the RCM, founded the Sherbrooke SO with 50 local musicians. Alfred-Sévère Bourgeault was its concertmaster. The group disbanded in 1927 when Sawdon returned to England. In 1932 the violinist Paul-E. Fortier founded a group of instrumentalists who played for their own pleasure. The *Sherbrooke SO was reorganized by Sylvio Lacharité in 1939. The Ensemble classique optimiste de Sherbrooke, founded in 1974, had a membership of 65 young instrumentalists by 1980 (see Youth Orchestras), with Chantal Juillet as concertmaster and Czeslaw Gladyszewski and Jacques Clément as conductors.

Mme Holland, who had taken her studies at the Paris Cons, taught organ, piano, and voice at the end of the 19th century. Wilfrid *Pelletier's first teacher, Ida Campbell (Mme François Héraly), was her pupil. Eugénie Caron (Mme Charles O'Shea) began teaching organ and piano in 1900. Subsequently the violinists A.-S. Bourgeault, Horace Boux, and Laurent Champigny taught strings while Paul-Marcel Robidoux and Réjane Marcotte, a pupil of Léo-Pol *Morin, were among the numerous piano teachers. Pianists were trained mainly at the Mont Notre-Dame and Jésus-Marie convents. The Séminaire St-Charles had its own concert band and orchestra. In 1958 the Filles de la Charité du Sacré-Coeur established a music course which developed into a music school; it was affiliated 1964–70 to the *U of Montreal so that its students might attain the B MUS degree.

The *Écoles Sacré-Coeur and Mitchell were the first public schools in Canada to offer music as the main subject concentration, and several of Sherbrooke's polytechnical schools have shown a particular concern for the teaching of music. The Sherbrooke Cegep initiated its own music department in 1970. The U of Sherbrooke, to which the *École Vincent-d'Indy was affiliated 1970–8, announced in 1979 that its own School of Music would open for registration in 1981, with Brian *Ellard as director. *Bishop's U in Lennoxville, near Sherbrooke, opened its music department in 1967 and established the practice of presenting concerts in its Centennial Theatre. The concerts at the nearby *JMC Orford Art Centre in Magog also have enriched the concert-going opportunities of the people of Sherbrooke.

Among the musicians born in or near Sherbrooke are Eugène Caron, Gabriel *Charpentier, Clémence *Desrochers, Claude *Gingras, Ralph *Gustafson, Sylvio Lacharité, Denis *Langelier, Robert Langevin, Édouard *LeBel, Marcel Marcotte, Allan *McIver, Claude Paradis, Émile Préfontaine, Ti-Blanc and Michèle *Richard, Rénald Saint-Pierre, and William-Arthur *Wayland.

BIBLIOGRAPHY

'The story of music in Sherbrooke: outstanding pioneer contribution to the art reviewed for centenary,' *Sherbrooke Daily Record*, 31 Jul 1937 (CP)

Sherbrooke Symphony Orchestra / Orchestre symphonique de Sherbrooke. A community orchestra of about 45 players, founded in 1939 in Sherbrooke, Que, by Silvio *Lacharité, its first director, Horace Boux, a violin teacher, and some interested citizens. It began modestly, performing in parish halls or in the hall of the St Charles seminary. The repertoire comprised such works as Schubert's *Unfinished Symphony*, Grieg's *Peer Gynt* suite, overtures, Strauss waltzes, and Brahms' Hungarian dances. The decision to use the Granada cinema, with its excellent acoustics, as a concert hall allowed the orchestra to become more ambitious. The first concert there took place 13 Feb 1945.

The practice of augmenting the orchestra with musicians from the *MSO or the *Quebec SO began at this time and has provided a stimulus for local players, among whom in the 1940s was Serge *Garant, at that time a clarinetist. The concerts (three to six each year) were enhanced by noted soloists such as the pianists Leon Fleisher, Glenn *Gould, Paul *Loyonnet, and Witold Malcuzynski, the violinists Albert Brusilow, Henryk Szeryng, and Joseph Szigeti, and the contralto Maureen *Forrester.

The orchestra played 1960–4 in the auditorium of the St Charles seminary and in the cathedral, presenting such works as Beethoven's *Ninth Symphony*, Honegger's *Le Roi David*, and Handel's *Messiah*; it moved in 1964 to the large hall of the U of Sherbrooke's Centre culturel. For its 25th anniversary (1964), the orchestra commissioned Serge Garant to write *Ennéade* and premiered it 18 February under Lacharité. After the latter's departure in 1969 Claude Paradis – founder of the Choeur Pie X of Sherbrooke, choirmaster at the cathedral, and music teacher at the Collège de Sherbrooke – took over the duties temporarily. He conducted Berlioz' *L'Enfance du Christ* and Bach's *St. John Passion* and *Magnificat* and organized Beethoven and Mozart festivals and numerous concerts of baroque music.

Czeslaw Gladyszewski, a graduate (MA) of the École supérieure de musique of Poznan, Poland, was invited to the *JMC Orford Art Centre in June 1972 and agreed to direct the orchestra as regular guest conductor 1972–6. Guy Robitaille, Raymond *Dessaints, and Pierre *Rolland shared conducting duties in 1976–7, and Roland *Leduc took over the position in 1977. During the 1977–8 season the orchestra welcomed among others the pianist Lise *Boucher (in Mendelssohn's *Concerto in G Minor*), the baritone Robert *Savoie (in Mozart arias), and the french horn player Paul Marcotte and the flutist Robert Langevin (in Mozart concertos). It also made a tour of the Eastern Townships under the aegis of the regional touring organization, the Tournestrie, visiting the towns of Cookshire, Disraeli, La Guadeloupe, Magog, Plessisville, Richmond, St-Hyacinthe, and Stanstead.

The orchestra received $6000 in 1977–8 from the *Canada Council to engage three instrumental coaches and to recruit a permanent artistic director, and it received $8300 in 1978–9 from the *MACQ. The presidents have been Horace Boux 1939–40, Paul-Émile Fortier 1940–2, 1943–4, 1945–6, Marcel Fortier 1942–3, Gérard Gingras 1944–5, Jacques Olivier 1946–50, 1952–7, Charles-Émile Bélanger 1950–2, Philippe Dionne 1957–8, Jacques Lagassé 1958–9, Georges Sylvestre 1959–60, André D'Etchevery 1960–1, Gaétan Côté 1961–5, Julien Giroux 1965–6, Charles Goulet 1966–9, Gérard Larochelle 1969–70, Gérard Lasalle 1970–2, Gilbert Decouvreur 1972–4, Roger Desbiens 1974–6, Antoni Trias 1976–7, and René Dorais 1977–8. Antoni Trias again became president in 1978.

BIBLIOGRAPHY

Paradis, Claude. 'L'Orchestre symphonique de Sherbrooke (OSS),' *L'Estrie*, vol 2, Nov 1979 (CP)

Sherlock-Manning Pianos Ltd (Sherlock-Manning Organ Co 1902–10; Sherlock-Manning Piano and Organ Co 1910–30). Manufacturer located 1902–30 in London, Ont, and 1930–78 in Clinton, Ont. The company was established in 1902 as the Sherlock-Manning Organ Co by J. (John) Frank Sherlock (b ca 1851, d 31 Dec 1931) and Wilbur Manning, both lately of the W. Doherty Co (*Doherty Pianos Ltd). According to *Industrial Canada* (February 1904), about 100 reed organs were produced each month by 50–60 employees. By 1914 Sherlock-Manning was seeking to establish regular export trade in Australia, New Zealand, and South America, having had some success with organ sales to these countries. During World War I the firm is reputed to have been the first piano company in Canada to train and employ women in its production plant. By 1920 Sherlock-Manning had the capacity to produce 1500 pianos per month; that number increased greatly as the firm purchased financially embarrassed or bankrupt piano companies including Doherty Piano and Organ; Foster-Armstrong Co, Kitchener; the *Karn Piano Co; and, from the trustee, *Gourlay, Winter & Leeming, Ltd. The last-named three companies became divisions within the Sherlock-Manning organization, and their pianos were produced in the firm's London factories. In 1930 Sherlock retired, selling his interests to Manning. The company was incorporated that year as Sherlock-Manning Pianos Ltd, (although it continued to produce reed organs until the 1950s) and completed its relocation in Clinton, Ont. The firm continued production – in the mid-1960s it was the smallest of five existing manufacturers in Canada – until it merged in 1978 with *Heintzman & Co, continuing as Heintzman, Ltd, with a factory in Hanover, Ont. FH

SHERRY, Helen (b Davies). Soprano, teacher, adjudicator, b Levenshulme, near Manchester, England, 15 Sep 1884, d Saskatoon 27 Feb 1964. Her father was organist at St John's Church, Peterborough, Ont, and she was a part-time music supervisor in Peterborough public schools and music teacher at the Normal School. She studied with Albert *Ham in Toronto and then with Bicetti at the RAM. After marrying in 1911 she lived in Deloraine and Neepawa, Man, and frequently sang oratorio in Winnipeg. She made her *Massey Hall debut in 1917 and sang on CNR radio's symphonic hour from Toronto in the late 1920s. Moving to Saskatoon she taught 1917–44 at the Saskatoon Normal School and was choirmaster 1917–47 at Knox United Church and 1947–53 at St John's Anglican Cathedral. She was president 1941–3 of the *Musical Art Club of Saskatoon. She also examined for the *WBM in Alberta and Saskatchewan. As a teacher, lecturer, clinician, and adviser to rural schools she was a pioneer in the development of music in Saskatchewan. Her pupils included Émile *Belcourt, Mary-Jean MacArthur Jamieson, Lloyd Jamieson, and Mae Strasser Daly. WLB

'She's Like the Swallow.' Distinctive Newfoundland variant of a large family of songs about unhappy love. Both Maud Karpeles (1930) and Kenneth *Peacock (1960) collected it, and its beautiful tune has made it popular with many singers. It has been arranged for choral and other use by several composers, including Keith *Bissell, James *Campbell, Ben *McPeek, and Harry *Somers. The swallow simile seems to be found only in Newfoundland, but the other verses turn up in various British love laments such as 'Died for Love' and 'Must I Go Bound.' Karpeles included it in *Folk Songs from Newfoundland* (London 1971). It may be heard on the LP *Songs, Fiddle Tunes and a Folktale from Canada* (Folk FG 3532) and, as 'She's Like a Swallow,' is the title song of an LP by Bonnie *Dobson. EF

SHIELDS, Jimmie (James). Tenor, b Vineland, near St Catharines, Ont, 19 Aug 1912. Raised in Hamilton, Ont, he made his radio debut on CHML at 18 and performed in Toronto in 1932 on CKNC as 'The Golden Masked Tenor' and 1933–6 on the independently syndicated 'Neilson Show' and various CBC programs, specializing in Irish, Scottish, and English ballads. One of the most popular 'Irish tenors' in Canada of the day, he rose to further fame 1937–41 in New York and Hollywood, singing with the orchestras of Morton Gould and Eddie Duchin and on the radio shows of Jack Benny, Fred Allen, and Fibber McGee and Molly and starring (1939) on his own weekly NBC program, 'Enna-Jettick Melodies.' After appearing 1942–6 as the 'Singing Sergeant-Major' in *The *Army Show* and studying voice 1946–7 in New York with Alfredo Martino, Shields was a leading tenor 1948–54 with the *CBC Opera, where his robust lyric tenor served the Italian repertoire handsomely. He appeared at *Massey Hall during the 1940s and 1950s, sang with the *Royal Cons Opera (Rodolfo in *La Bohème* 1951, 1954; Pinkerton in *Madama Butterfly* 1951, 1953, 1956), and continued to perform for CBC radio and TV, notably 1948–64 on 'Bod's Scrapbook,' and again on CHML. Declining personal appearances after 1956, he retired in 1964.

BIBLIOGRAPHY
'The story of Jimmie Shields,' *CBC Times*, 16–22 Mar 1952
Brydon, Arthur. 'For St. Patrick, he'll bare his Irish charms on TV,' *Globe Magazine*, 14 Mar 1959 VW

The Shining People of Leonard Cohen. Pas de deux choreographed by Brian Macdonald to a taped montage by Harry *Freedman. Excerpts of nine erotic poems from Leonard *Cohen's *The Spice-Box of Earth* are spoken and become a part of Freedman's mixture of various natural sounds (including the singing voice of Mary *Morrison) altered electronically. Although commissioned by the Royal Winnipeg Ballet for a performance before Queen Elizabeth II during her visit in July 1970 to Manitoba's centennial celebrations, it was premiered 18 Jun 1970 by request of the Paris Festival at the Théâtre de la Ville, and its Canadian premiere took place in July in Ottawa. It has been performed in Canada by the Royal Winnipeg Ballet and Les Grands Ballets Canadiens.

BIBLIOGRAPHY
Campbell, Francean. '*The Shining People of Leonard Cohen*,' *CMB*, 1, Spring–Summer 1970
Cohen, Susan H. '*The Shining People of Leonard Cohen*,' *Ballet-hoo*, 5, Oct 1970 MCv

Shinn Conservatory of Music. Winnipeg school opened in 1922 by William H. (Henry) Shinn and closed in 1967 by his son B. (Bonar) Franklyn Shinn. The elder Shinn (b Ledbury, Herefordshire, England, 23 Nov 1873, d Winnipeg 29 Apr 1954) moved to Winnipeg in 1912 and taught privately until 1922. He opened a conservatory in the Alfred Building and moved in 1947 to the new building on Furby St which housed 14 studios and a 250-seat recital hall. Besides the Shinns, who taught piano, organ, voice, and theory, instructors included A.A. Zimmerman and Carl Horoschuk (violin), Albert Whiteman (voice), and James Thomson (winds). W.H. Shinn retired in 1951 and, on his death, was succeeded as president by his son. The younger Shinn (b Barry Dock, South Wales, 7 Jul 1911), who studied with his father and Herbert J. *Sadler, and 1933–6 at the RAM, began teaching at the Shinn Conservatory in 1926. He also conducted 1936–9 the Winnipeg Metropolitan Choir and was organist-choirmaster 1939–67 in various United churches. His few compositions to 1950 are listed in the *Catalogue of Canadian Composers*. After 1967 B.F. Shinn, a highly skilled lens grinder, devoted himself to a career in astronomy. The conservatory building was taken over by George *Kent. (CC)

SHULMAN, Suzanne (m Rosenbaum). Flutist, b Toronto 30 Nov 1946; Artist Diploma (Toronto) 1967. Her teachers were Nicholas *Fiore and Robert *Aitken at the *U of Toronto and (in 1967) Christian Lardé, Michel Debost, Marcel Moyse, and Jean-Pierre Rampal in Paris. She has toured for the *JMC in Canada (1968, 1969) and in the USA (1970), for JMFrance (1970, 1973), for JMBelgique (1971), and for the JMC and the Canadian External Affairs Dept in Poland (1971) and South America (1972). She was a soloist with the *NYO on a 1970 tour and has performed with the *TS (1971), the *McGill Chamber Orchestra (1974), the BBC Scottish and Welsh orchestras, and others in Canada, Poland, and Spain. She gave two recitals in 1971 at Wigmore Hall, London, one with the pianist Claude *Savard and one with the French harpist Catherine Michel. With Savard she has recorded music by Martinu, Roussel, and Leon *Zuckert (1975, RCI 425). As a member of the Pro Arte Trio (with Jane *Coop, piano, and Belva Spiel, soprano) she made the LP *Folk songs in Concert Form* (Folk FTS 31314) in 1978. She is a founding member of *Camerata. WS

SHUTTLEWORTH, Barbara. Soprano, b Toronto 18 Apr ca 1944; B MUS (Juilliard) 1970. She made her debut at five on the CBC radio program 'Small Types Club' and was heard regularly in that series for the next eight years. She studied piano with John *Coveart and Helen Wilson at the *RCMT and voice with Judith Litante in California. At Juilliard 1965–70 she studied with Suzanne Bloch (theory and harmony) and Jennie Tourel and Beverly Johnson (voice). While a member of the Juilliard Opera Theater she sang in productions of Harold Farberman's *The Losers*, Richard Rodney Bennett's *The Mines of Sulphur*, and Poulenc's *La Voix humaine*. She has been a member of the New York Chamber Soloists, and she joined the New York City Opera in 1971. Among her roles with that company have been Kristina in Janáček's *The Makropoulos Affair*, Clorinda in Rossini's *La Cenerentola*, and Miss Jessel in Britten's *The Turn of the Screw*. (She repeated the last-named role with the *NACO in concert performances in Ottawa and Toronto in 1975.) With the Santa Fe Opera she sang Nellie in Lee Hoiby's *Summer and Smoke* and the soprano lead in the premiere of Luciano Berio's *Opera*. She also has appeared with the Baltimore Opera, the *Vancouver and *Edmonton Operas, and the Welsh National Opera, and she made her *COC debut in 1976 as Musetta in *La Bohème*. Other COC roles include Wanda in *The Grand Duchess of Gerolstein* and Susanna in *The Marriage of Figaro*. She has sung at the Newport (Rhode Island) Music Festival and at the Wexford Festival in Ireland. In 1972 she was Lisette in a CBC TV production of Puccini's *La Rondine*. She made her New York Philharmonic debut in March 1973 in a performance of Haydn's *L'Incontro Improviso* conducted by Pierre Boulez.

Barbara Shuttleworth's father is the dance-band leader Bob Shuttleworth. Her mother, the soprano Frosia Gregory (b Toronto 11 May 1922, a pupil, at the Juilliard School, of Anna E. Schoen-René), sang on various CBC radio shows during the 1940s and 1950s and was host for the children's show 'Frosia Tells a Story' (1950) and the TV program 'A Date with Frosia' (1954). She also appeared in **Spring Thaw*. She was known especially for her folksong performances, in which she sang and played the autoharp. SW (NM)

SICOTTE, Lucien. Violinist, teacher, b Montreal 22 Sep 1902, d there 23 Sep 1943. He studied violin in turn with Émile *Taranto, Alfred *De Sève, and Maurice *Onderet and theory with Oscar *O'Brien and Claude *Champagne. With the founding in 1934 of the CSM (*MSO), he became assistant to the concertmaster Albert *Chamberland. Together in 1935 they played Bach's *Concerto in D Minor* for two violins and orchestra and Sicotte was soloist 17 Nov 1938 in the Beethoven *Concerto* under Sir Ernest *MacMillan. He was second violin 1929–36 in the *Dubois String Quartet and, ca 1930, in the first *McGill String Quartet and also appeared in public recital and was heard on radio. His repertoire included sonatas by Franck, Beethoven, and others. In 1934 he founded the *Montreal String Quartet in which he played first violin. He commuted to New York in 1936 for lessons with Louis Persinger and in 1937 spent six months in Brussels with Alfred Dubois, returning then to the CSM, the quartet, solo work, and teaching. In 1939 he attended Georges Enesco's interpretation classes in Paris, but his return to Canada was hastened by the onset of World War II. With the dissolution of the quartet (1939?) he continued to perform in concert and on radio and to teach. His pupils included Gilles *Baillargeon and Jean *Vallerand. Jean Papineau-Couture's *Sonata in G* (1944) is dedicated to Sicotte's memory. IP-C

SIDGWICK, John (Robert Lindsay). Organist, choir conductor, teacher, adjudicator, b Limpsfield, Surrey, England, 29 Jan 1923, d Toronto 26 Nov 1973; ARCM 1946, ARCO 1946, B MUS (Cambridge) 1948, FRCO 1953, MA (Cambridge) 1954. He was a boy chorister at St George's Chapel, Windsor, a music scholar at Felsted School, Essex, and an organ scholar at Clare College, Cambridge U. He first visited Canada during RAF service 1942–6 and returned to Toronto to serve 1949–51 as music master of Upper Canada College. He then held positions 1952–60 at Metropolitan United Church and 1960–73 at St Clement's Anglican Church in Toronto. Concurrently he was organist-choirmaster 1951–73 at the *U of Trinity College. He founded and directed the Madrigal Singers of Toronto in the early 1950s. He conducted 1955–60 the *Bach-Elgar Choir of Hamilton and was chorusmaster 1960–4 of the *Toronto Mendelssohn Choir and founding director 1964–70 of the *Orpheus Choir of Toronto. He taught at the U of Toronto and the *RCMT and was a commissioner for the RSCM. He adjudicated at competition festivals across Canada. Sidgwick accompanied and conducted the choir engaged for the private recording *62 Hymns for Broadcast*, produced by the Anglican Church of Canada for its use. His death ended a career of quiet significance to choral music in Canada. An annual award provided by a memorial fund established in his name in 1974 and administered by the *RCCO was offered first in 1977. MMl

SIEB, Calvin. Violinist, teacher, b Newark, NJ, 30 May 1925, naturalized Canadian 1970. He began studying violin at six in Newark with Mandel Svet and continued 1938–43 with Hans Letz at the New York College of Music, 1945–8 at the Juilliard School, and 1949–50 at Chatham Square School. He took classes in composition and musical aesthetics in the spring of 1950 with Nadia Boulanger at the American Cons at Fontainebleau and studied violin 1950–1 with Jacques Thibaud in Paris. A winner of the 1951 Marguerite Long-Jacques Thibaud International Competition, he returned to New York, where Wilfrid *Pelletier offered him a teaching post at the *CMQ and a position as assistant conductor of the *Quebec SO – which position he retained until 1954. Later he taught at both the CMQ and the *CMM. He has been concertmaster 1954–8 of the CBC *'Little Symphonies' orchestra and 1959–79 of the *MSO (with 1977–8 a sabbatical year). He gave up his duties at the CMQ after settling in 1960 in Montreal, where he continued to teach at the CMM. Sieb has performed often on CBC radio and TV. He was soloist in 1959 at the *Stratford Festival and 1964–7 at the Pablo Casals Festival in Puerto Rico. He was rehearsal leader 1969–70 for the MSO's Matinées symphoniques and coached the strings of the JM World Orchestra in 1972 in Germany, in 1975 in Belgium, and in 1978 in England. He was a member of the jury at the 1970 Enesco International Competition in Bucharest and in 1966 became a member of the music advisory committee of the *Montreal International Competition. During his 1977–8 sabbatical he was one of the concertmasters in the Toulouse

(France) Orchestre du Capitole, and in 1979 he settled in that city as concertmaster.

BIBLIOGRAPHY
Peterson, Maureen. 'MSO concertmaster Sieb takes a bow after 20 years,' Montreal *Gazette*, 28 Apr 1979 CLE

SIGURDSON, Snjolaug (Anna). Pianist, teacher, b Arborg, north of Winnipeg, 5 Nov 1914, d Winnipeg 22 Aug 1979; ATCM 1932, LRSM 1933, LMM 1936. She studied with Eva *Clare in Winnipeg, and then with Ernest Hutcheson and Muriel *Kerr in New York. She made her New York debut in 1950 at Times Hall, and later performed frequently at Town Hall and the Carnegie Recital Hall. She taught in New York and in 1958 began teaching in Winnipeg. Her pupils included Helen Choi, Thora Asgeirson Dubois, Carla Lother, and Nancy Smith. She was a recitalist for the CBC and performed the Schumann *Concerto* and the Fauré *Ballade* with the *CBC Winnipeg Orchestra. In 1968 she played the Franck *Symphonic Variations* with the Icelandic SO in Reykjavik. Her first cousin, (Agnes) Helga Sigurdson (b Riverton, near Arborg, Man, 6 Apr 1917), also a pianist, pursued her career in the USA after 1948. RG

Silent Measures / Une Mesure de silence. Comic opera in one act by Marthe Morisset-Blackburn (libretto) and Maurice *Blackburn (music). Composed 1954–5 in Paris, the work was premiered 21 Apr 1956 on CBC TV ('Concerts pour la jeunesse') with Claire *Gagnier as Martine, Jean-Paul *Jeannotte as Bobino, and Yoland *Guérard as Antonin, and Charles *Reiner at the piano. The work was staged by Jean Gascon and produced by Françoys *Bernier. The following 17 November it was presented in *Eaton Auditorium, Toronto, in a double bill with Harry *Somers' **The Fool*. On 15 Mar 1959 it was given at the *Orpheum Theatre in Montreal. The following summer several performances were given at the *Poudrière, followed by 100 performances during the *JMC 1960–1 tour on a double bill with the same composer's **Pirouette*. In August 1962 *Silent Measures* was produced with orchestra, under Jean-Marie *Beaudet, as part of the *Montreal Festivals.

The setting of the opera is Montreal in the period 1908–13. Martine discovers her husband's stinginess when he refuses her request for money to buy a new dress, and she pretends to be deaf and dumb to convince him to change his mind. She succeeds, with the complicity of their neighbour, Bobino. The libretto was translated into English by Guy Glover. Three excerpts, sung by Marthe *Létourneau, Jean-Paul Jeannotte, and Jules *Bruyère and accompanied by Charles Reiner, were recorded by the JMC (CD-JMC 1). GP

SILVER, Annon Lee (m Lumsden). Lyric soprano, b Glace Bay, NS, 18 Nov 1938, d London 28 Jul 1971; BA (Mount Allison) 1957, B MUS (Mount Allison) 1958. After graduation from *Mount Allison and ca 1963 from the RCM she continued voice study in London with Maggie Teyte, in Switzerland with Frederick Husler, and in Italy with Giorgio Favaretto. She received many awards, including the first Dame Maggie Teyte Prize and a top vocal award in the *JMC Centennial Competition in 1967 resulting in a CBC recording. Her operatic debut in 1963 was with the Glyndebourne Festival Opera as Amor in Monteverdi's *L'Incoronazione di Poppea*, a production later recorded. More study in 1964 in Switzerland was followed by another Glyndebourne engagement and several in Europe and Canada. She appeared with the *MSO at *Expo 67. In 1969 she was Sophie in Michael Redgrave's production of *Werther* at Glyndebourne, and in 1970 she created the role of Miss Atalanta Lillywhite in Nicholas Maw's *The Rising of the Moon* and sang Pamina in the touring company's *The Magic Flute*. Other important operatic roles included Blondchen in *The Abduction from the Seraglio* at the Bath Festival, Norina in *Don Pasquale* with the Phoenix Opera, Gilda in *Rigoletto* with the Welsh National Opera, Marzelline in *Fidelio* at the Grand Théâtre, Geneva, and several (Zerlina in *Don Giovanni*, Sophie in *Der Rosenkavalier*, Gretel in *Hansel and Gretel*) during two years with the Frankfurt Opera. For BBC TV she gave master classes with Carl Ebert and Gerald Moore and sang Mozart arias with the Amadeus String Quartet. She gave many recitals with her pianist-husband Ronald Lumsden. Critics praised her 'excellence in all styles and techniques of singing' and her 'sure sense of character.' On her tragic death at 32 a tribute in *The Times* (2 Aug 1971) remembered 'her voice of unmistakable, individual quality and ... her particular vivacious charm and endearing personality.'

DISCOGRAPHY
Handel *Messiah: Excerpts*. Payne alto, W. Evans ten, Opie bass-bar, London Little Symphony O and Chorus, Davison cond. (1968). Music for Pleasure SMFP 2108
Monteverdi *L'Incoronazione di Poppea*. Glyndebourne Festival Chorus, Royal Philharmonic O, Pritchard cond, Silver sop (Amor). (1964). 2 Angel S36165-36166
Rossini *La Regata Veneziana* – Britten *On This Island* – Ives *Three Songs*. Lumsden pf. Ca 1968. CBC SM-38 RSm

SILVERMAN, Robert. Pianist, teacher, b Montreal 25 May 1938; BA (Sir George Williams) 1960, B MUS performance (McGill) 1964, M MUS performance, literature (ESM, Rochester) 1965, Artist Diploma (ESM, Rochester) 1968, DMA performance (ESM, Rochester) 1970. He began piano study at 4 and appeared in recital at 5 and with the *MSO at 14. After his professional debut in 1961 in Montreal and a first prize in the Quebec Music Festivals in 1961 he studied 1961–3 on a *Canada Council grant at the Vienna Academy of Music with Richard Hansen. His other teachers have been Dorothy *Morton at *McGill U, Cecile Genhart at the ESM, Jeaneane Dowis in New York, and Leonard Shure, Paul Badura-Skoda, and Lili Kraus in various master classes. In 1967 he won first prize at the *JMC Concours national and performed twice at *Expo 67.

Silverman was pianist-in-residence 1967–9 at Nazareth College, Rochester, and has taught at the U of California 1969–70 and the U of Wisconsin-Milwaukee 1970–3. He began teaching at the *U of British Columbia in 1973. His Vancouver pupils have included Sharon Krause and the first winner of the S.C. *Eckhardt-Gramatté prize, David Swan. Silverman has performed with the MSO, the *TS, the *NACO, the *Vancouver SO, the Rochester Philharmonic, and the Milwaukee SO, has toured (1971) with the American Wind Symphony, and has given recitals in Chicago, Toronto, Montreal, Washington, and London (Wigmore Hall, 1968). After Silverman's Chicago recital the critic R.C. Marsh noted 'a sensitivity to the artistic value of contrasts, not only between successive works, but internally in the works themselves' and commended his grasp of various idioms (*Sun-Times*, 3 Jan 1972). He has performed with the Curtis, Fine Arts, and *Purcell string quartets. He premiered Jacques *Hétu's *Concerto* in 1970 with the *Quebec SO and both performed and recorded it with the BBC SO during *Musicanada in 1977. With the TS he gave the first concert performances of *Somers' *Second Piano Concerto* (5, 6 Dec 1978). He made a successful New York recital debut 7 May 1978, toured the USSR that same year, and toured Australia in 1979. Silverman's Liszt recording was awarded the 1977 Grand Prix du disque by the Budapest Liszt Society.

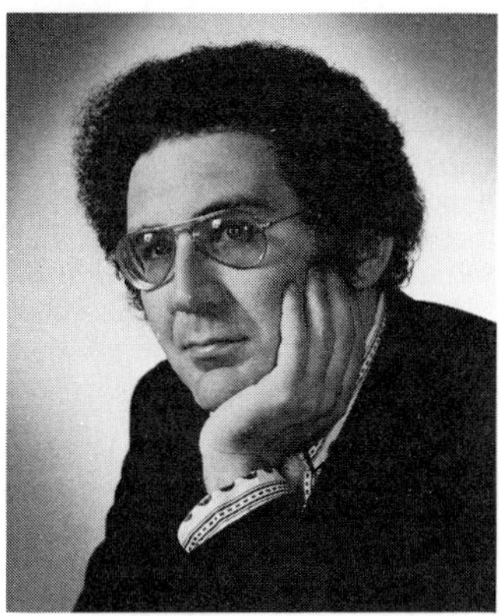
Robert Silverman

DISCOGRAPHY
Bartók *Dance Suite*; 14 *Bagatelles*. 1974. Orion ORS 74152
Beethoven *Sonata, Op 111* – Hindemith *Sonata No. 3*. 1969. CBC SM-90
Chopin *Sonata in B Flat Minor* – Liszt *Sonata*. Ca 1967. JMC 8
Copland *Piano Sonata; Passacaglia; Four Piano Blues; The Cat and The Mouse*. 1972. Orion ORS 7280
Hétu *Concerto*. BBC SO, Bernardi cond. 1977. RCI 477
Liszt *Variations* on Bach's Weinen, Klagen, Sorgen, Zagen; 2 *Transcendental Études; Scherzo and March*. 1975. Orion ORS 76226
Martin 8 *Preludes* – Prokofiev *Sonata No. 6*. 1978. Orion ORS 79328
Schumann *Sonata in F Minor; Bunte Blätter*. 1971. Orion ORS 7146

BIBLIOGRAPHY
Grescoe, Paul. 'When Silverman came home, his career took off,' *SatN*, Jul–Aug 1976
Hancock, Geoff. 'Music, made in Canada, for the world to hear,' *UBC Alumni Chronicle*, Spring 1978 (CF)

SILVESTER, Frederick (Caton). Organist, choir conductor, administrator, composer, b Darwen, near Manchester, England, 21 Jan 1901, d Toronto 24 Jun 1966; FRCO 1931; FRCCO 1943. He studied organ with C. Spencer Heap in England and, after moving in 1921 to Canada, with Lynnwood *Farnam in Saskatoon. During his eight years there, he was organist at the First Baptist Church and Knox United Church. He moved to Toronto in 1929, studied at the *TCM with *MacMillan (organ) and *Willan (theory and composition), and was organist 1931–8 at the Church of the Messiah and 1938–66 at Bloor Street United Church, where he led the choir in many large works. At the TCM he served at first, 1929–46, as registrar of examinations, and then, 1946–66, as registrar. He gave organ recitals in many parts of Canada and on the CBC and was president 1945–7 of the *CCO. He was also assistant conductor and coach 1942–57, and conductor 1957–60, of the *Toronto Mendelssohn Choir. Of his work with the choir, George *Kidd wrote, 'The overall effect is one of good discipline, a clear understanding, and a sincerity that spreads itself over all sections' (Toronto *Telegram*, 15 Dec 1957). Silvester wrote a number of short choral works (published by Harris) and songs.

BIBLIOGRAPHY
A Responsive Chord: The story of the Toronto Mendelssohn Choir 1894–1969 (Toronto 1969) RPn

SILVI, Gino. Arranger, choir conductor, singer, saxophonist, clarinetist, b Sault Ste Marie, Ont, of Italian parents, 23 May 1914. After playing saxophone and clarinet in the dance bands of Morgan Thomas, Len Allen, and Bill Andrews in Hamilton, Ont, and 1941–6 in a Canadian army band in Toronto, he was a member of Art *Hallman's orchestra (and the vocal quartet of that orchestra) in the late 1940s, of the Howard *Cable Concert Band into the early 1950s, and of CBC orchestras under Lucio *Agostini and Samuel *Hersenhoren. In 1949 he joined the Bill Brady Sextet (a vocal group heard on radio station CKEY, Toronto) and soon succeeded Brady as the leader. Silvi's subsequent ensembles sang on such CBC radio shows as 'Trans-Canada Hit Parade,' 'Gino and *Juliette' (summer 1954), and, with Norma Locke, 'Dream Street' (summers 1955–9). For 'Dream Street' he also was the arranger and conductor. In 1958, for 'Juliette,' he formed an octet, the Gino Silvi Singers (a name also used by some of his earlier groups). On camera the men – Alex Ticknovich, Rick Stainsby, Vern Kennedy, and John Garden – appeared as the Romeos; the women – Angela Antonelli, Fran Groat, Sylvia Wilson, and Carol Hill – as the Four Mice. Augmented at times to as many as 30, the singers also performed 1960–2 on 'Sing, Sing, Sing,' an occasional program in the CBC TV series 'Parade.' They received All-Canada awards from *Liberty* magazine 1959–60, 1960–1, and 1961–2. Among the other singers to perform for Silvi were Babs Babineau, Laurie *Bower, Bernard *Johnson, Gordon *Lightfoot, Margo *MacKinnon, and Margaret Stilwell. Under his direction the Romeos made the LP *Rendezvous with the Romeos* (Col FL 291), and in 1963 a group known as the Silvi Girls recorded for CTL (SO23). After leaving radio work in 1965, Silvi taught instrumental music first for the North York (Toronto) board of education and then, beginning in 1968, for the Metropolitan (Toronto) Separate School Board.

MM

SIM, (Margaret) **Winnifred** (b Johnston). Pianist, organist, teacher, b Winnipeg 28 Jun 1930; AMM piano 1949, AMM organ 1954, ARCCO 1965, ARCT 1966, FTCL 1973. She studied piano with her aunt, Winnifred Hubble Frayne (sister of Filmer *Hubble), and Gwendda Owen *Davies and organ with Hugh *Bancroft, John Clarke, and Ronald *Gibson. She was organist-choirmaster 1947–65 at Sparling United Church and 1965–75 at Westworth United Church, Winnipeg, and in 1977 assumed that position at Elim Chapel. She has given recitals in public (debut 1952) and on CBC radio. She became the organist for CBC TV's 'Hymn Sing in 1965 and succeeded Eric *Wild as the program's music director in 1977. Also one of Winnipeg's busiest accompanists, she has been the recital partner of the violinist Lea *Foli, the singers Peter *van Ginkel and Nona Mari, and many others. She became an official accompanist at the *Manitoba Music Competition Festival ca 1950 and has recorded as accompanist to the Hymn Sing Chorus and van Ginkel.

Sim began teaching organ, repertoire, and service playing for the *Canadian Mennonite Bible College in 1970 and joined the staff of the college in 1977. She has conducted workshops in accompanying and in the training of church choirs. Her son Bryan William (b 4 Jan 1954) is a jazz musician. Her daughter Margot Elinor (b 24 Jan 1957) is a soprano and the winner of a 1977 *Women's Musical Club of Winnipeg scholarship.

SIMARD, Jacques. Oboist, teacher, b Quebec City 23 Feb 1941; premier prix oboe (CMQ) 1958, premiers prix, oboe and chamber music (Paris Cons) 1962. At nine he began studying oboe at the *CMQ with Réal *Gagnier. He studied 1958–61 at the Paris Cons with Étienne Baudo (oboe), Norbert Dufourcq (history), and Fernand Oubradous (chamber music). Under the aegis of the JM, he played Jacques *Hétu's *Quatre pièces* in 1961 at Carnegie Hall. He toured for the *JMC in 1962 with the harpsichordist Donald Thompson and in 1962–3 as a member of the Trio canadien with Gail Grimstead (flute) and Pierre *Hétu (piano); the trio gave the premiere of André *Prévost's *Triptyque*. In 1963 Simard made his debut with the *MSO (simultaneously with Pierre Hétu's debut as a conductor). In 1966 he was appointed principal oboe with the *Quebec SO and in 1970 he founded the *Ensemble instrumental du Québec. In 1968 with the pianist Jeanne *Landry he recorded sonatas by Hindemith, Dutilleux, and Poulenc (RCI 337 / CBC SM-60). He and the pianist Louise *Forand performed together 1970–3; they gave duo-recitals on the CBC, in 1971 in Stratford, Ont, and in 1972 at the *JMC Orford Art Centre. He began teaching at the CMQ in 1966.

In 1973 Simard married Barbara Todd – flutist, teacher, b Birmingham, Ala, 2 Apr 1946; B MUS (Oberlin) 1968. She began flute lessons at 11, and her teachers 1963–8 were William Kincaid, Robert Willoughby, Julius Baker, Murray Sharp, and Marcel Moyse. She toured 1967–8 in the USA before joining the Quebec SO in 1968 as principal flute and becoming a teacher at *Laval U. She and the guitarist Paul Gerrits formed a duo 1969–73 and made tours of Quebec. She joined the Ensemble instrumental du Québec in 1970 and became a member of the Quebec SO Woodwind Quintet in 1975.

GP (MB-L)

SIMARD, René. Singer, b Chicoutimi, Que, 28 Feb 1961. His father was a choirmaster on the Île d'Orléans where he spent his childhood. At nine René was the prize winner on the program 'Les Découvertes de Jen Roger' (CFTM-TV, Montreal). This brought him to the attention of the impresario Guy Cloutier, who quickly made the boy soprano an international pop music star. With his first show at the *PDA in 1971, the 'p'tit Simard' captured the hearts of Quebec audiences, as did his first hit recordings: 'Ave Maria' (1971), 'L'Oiseau' (1971), and 'Un enfant comme les autres' (1972), all for the Nobel label owned by Cloutier. In 1974 he was chosen to represent Canada at the International Festival of Song in Tokyo. There he won first prize for performance and the Frank Sinatra trophy, which was presented by Sinatra himself. Acclaimed in Japan and also in Paris, where he made his debut at the Olympia in 1975, Simard embarked on a career in the English-speaking world. He appeared frequently on the US TV networks, with artists such as Bing Crosby, Bob Hope, Liza Minnelli, and Andy Williams, and with Liberace both in Las Vegas and in 1977 on a tour of the USA. That year he returned to Quebec to sing in 25 towns. He was host 1977–9 of 'The René Simard Show,' a CBC English-language TV variety series produced in Vancouver. In these programs he showed a preference for a US style of performance – becoming an adept dancer in the process – and by that very fact seemed to have moved away from the prevailing Quebec ideas of entertainment.

René Simard passed smoothly through the voice-change period, and his popularity, the result of a well-focused voice and a carefully selected repertoire, continued to grow. His repertoire consists of sentimental ballads such as 'Ma mère est un ange' (written by his brother Régis) and disco songs, which easily reach a wide audience of all ages. Among his other major hits for Nobel are 'Les dimanches après-midi' (1974), 'Maman, laisse-moi sortir ce soir' (1975), 'Bébé bleu' (1975), 'Fernando' (1976), 'Bienvenue à Montréal' (theme song of the 1976 Montreal Olympics), 'Never Know the Reason Why' (1977), and 'You're My Everything' (1978). He also had made about 20 LPs for Nobel by 1978, including two with Les *Disciples de Massenet. He has appeared in the documentary films *Un Enfant comme les autres* (1972) and *René Simard au Japon* (1974) and he took part in the Quebec feature film *J'ai mon voyage* (1974) and CFTM-TV's teleplay 'Les Berger.'

Undoubtedly it is Simard's pleasant personality and easy-going manner – apparent even in his childhood – which more than anything else have won him international stardom. Assessing Simard's popularity as a boy soprano, Patrick Conlon wrote: 'Simard's impish onstage exuberance appeals particularly to young girls (who want to marry him) and older women (who want to mother him). His repertoire ranges from filial tributes such as 'Ma mère est une [sic] ange' to eye-dampening hymns such as 'Ave Maria'. He works the audience to the limit, strutting and grinning across the stage like a pint-sized vaudevillian' (*Maclean's*, 3 Nov 1975). After his second engagement at the PDA Linda Nantel wrote in *Photo-Journal* (19 Dec 1977) that 'his superior talent and great facility of expression have made him "great" in every sense that word encompasses of professionalism.' Simard's younger sister Nathalie began appearing with him when she was nine, but soon began her own career as a singer. By 1980 (at age 11) she had made three LPs: *Nathalie chante pour ses amis*, *Joyeux Noël ... Nathalie*, and *Nathalie Simard*.

BIBLIOGRAPHY

Vincent, Pierre. 'Petit René Simard deviendra-t-il grand?,' Montreal *La Presse*, 9 Mar 1972
– 'Two brothers win in Quebec,' *CanComp*, 84, Oct 1973
Kearns, Hilda. 'Going up Canada's biggest star is 13,' *Montreal Star*, 18 Jun 1974
Berthiaume, Christiane. 'Le p'tit Simard: une "entreprise" compliquée,' Montreal *La Presse*, 11 Jul 1974
Taschereau, Yves. 'Mais qu' est-ce-qui fait donc grimper le p'tit Simard,' Montreal *Le Devoir*, 31 Aug 1974
Nicaise, Jean-Pierre. 'René Simard, un enfant pas "abîmé" malgré tout,' *Perspectives*, vol 16, 12 Oct 1974
Kirby, Blaik. 'René Simard: Quebec's kid superstar goes after bigger game,' Toronto *Globe and Mail*, 8 Nov 1975
Dostie, Bruno. 'Les journées studieuses de René Simard,' Montreal *La Presse*, 5 Aug 1978
Beaulieu, Pierre. 'I love you, René, même si tu chantes comme aux USA,' Montreal *La Presse*, 21 Aug 1978
Vézina, Marie-Odile. 'Petit Simard devenu grand,' *Perspectives*, 12–19 May 1979

(BLH, DM, MM)

SIMMONS, Mary (m Bernstein). Soprano, b Philadelphia 29 Jul 1928. She studied violin in Philadelphia with Louis Angeloty for 10 years and voice in New York with Therese Schnabel, receiving the Marian Anderson Scholarship in 1945 and 1946. She first sang in Canada in 1946 with the *TSO and returned in 1947 to appear with the *Toronto Jewish Folk Choir and the TSO under Emil Gartner. Recitals for the CBC and its international service followed, and in 1953 she was engaged for the title role in the *CBC Opera Company production of *Turandot*. In 1954 she made her concert debut in New York and her stage debut (as Magda in *The Consul*) in Cleveland. Visiting Canada again for a performance in 1955 with the TSO, she met the Toronto businessman Jack Bernstein and subsequently married him and took up residence in Toronto.

Highly regarded as a Lieder singer, particularly for her integral presentations (1968, 1977) of Schubert's *Die Winterreise*, Simmons has appeared mainly in recital, as a soloist with orchestra, and on CBC radio ('Distinguished Artists,' etc). Her relatively few opera roles in Canada have included her 1953 Turandot and her 1957 Cressida (in Walton's *Troilus and Cressida*) with the CBC Opera, Santuzza (1961) in *Cavalleria Rusticana* and Sieglinde (1962) in *Die Walküre* with the *COC, and Donna Elvira (1964) with the *Opera Guild of

Montreal. She sang with the TSO in the Canadian premiere (1957) of excerpts from Berg's *Wozzeck*, with the *CBC SO in the premiere (24 Mar 1958) of *Weinzweig's *Wine of Peace*, with the TSO and *Toronto Mendelssohn Choir under Heinz *Unger in the Toronto premiere (York Concert Society, 1964) of Mahler's *Symphony No. 3*, and with the TSO in the first Canadian performance (1966) of one movement from Bernstein's *Jeremiah Symphony*. She may be heard on the recordings of Stravinsky's *Pulcinella* with the Cleveland Orchestra conducted by the composer (1953, Col ML 4830), in *Wine of Peace* (RCI 182), and in Stravinsky's *Mavra* and *Le Faune et la bergère* with the CBC SO (Col MS 6991). Of her 1977 performance of *Die Winterreise*, John *Kraglund wrote that there were numerous highlights, including 'an intensely moving performance of "Der Lindenbaum," sung with folklike simplicity and without sentimentality,' adding that ' "Irrlicht," with its leisurely pace and careful shaping of phrases, was another example, not only of Miss Simmons' artistry, but of the art of Lieder singing' (Toronto *Globe and Mail*, 4 Aug 1977). (JBl)

SIMONEAU, Léopold. Tenor, teacher, administrator; b St-Flavien, near Quebec City, 3 May 1918; BA (Laval) 1941, hon D MUS (Ottawa) 1969, hon D MUS (Brock) 1971, hon D MUS (Laval) 1973. In 1939 he began voice study with Émile *Larochelle. He continued 1941–4 with Salvator *Issaurel in Montreal. At Issaurel's studio he met the soprano Pierrette *Alarie, who became his wife in 1946. His stage debut was with the *Variétés lyriques as Hadji in *Lakmé* (1941). His first major roles were with the variétés, in *Mignon*, *The Daughter of the Regiment*, *Mireille*, *La Traviata*, and *The Barber of Seville*, usually opposite Alarie. His first recitals were broadcast by the CBC, and in 1943 he attempted his first Mozartean role, Basilio in the *Montreal Festivals' production of *The Marriage of Figaro* under Beecham. In 1944 he won the *Prix Archambault, the award leading to his debut with the *CSM orchestra under Wilfrid *Pelletier. He continued his studies 1945–7 in New York with Paul Althouse. In May 1945 he was acclaimed in Montreal as Ferrando in *Così fan tutte* and Tamino in *The Magic Flute* (Canadian premiere of the latter opera, staged by the *Opera Guild) and in the Berlioz *Te Deum*. Simoneau's first US opera appearances were in Central City, Col, and New Orleans.

Simoneau's career took on an international dimension in 1948 when he made his Paris debut at the Opéra-Comique in Gounod's *Mireille*. He coached in Paris with Berl Lilienfeld and in Vienna with Erik Werba, continuing to perform at the Opéra-Comique and the Paris Opera until 1954, appearing in the standard roles and, in June 1953, as Tom in the French premiere of Stravinsky's *The Rake's Progress* (*Le Libertin*). The critics compared him with Edmond Clément. His reputation as a Mozart specialist grew steadily after 1950, when, at the Aix-en-Provence and Glyndebourne festivals and elsewhere, he sang all the main tenor roles: Ottavio, Ferrando, Tamino, Belmonte, and Idamante in *Idomeneo*. He also was heard in Gluck operas (Pylade in *Iphigenia in Tauris* and Orpheus in the tenor version of *Orpheus and Eurydice*) and as Paolino in Cimarosa's *Il Matrimonio segreto*. During the 1952 Festival du XXe siècle in Paris, he appeared in a historic production of Stravinsky's *Oedipus Rex* with the composer as conductor and Jean Cocteau as narrator. In 1953 he sang in *Don Giovanni* at La Scala in Milan under von Karajan, and in 1954 he was with the Vienna State Opera in London for its Royal Festival Hall appearances. He was heard shortly afterwards at the Teatro Colón in Buenos

Léopold Simoneau

Aires and at the Salzburg and Edinburgh festivals.

In the USA and Canada Simoneau appeared with major symphony orchestras and made numerous concert tours, often with his wife or as a member of the Bel Canto Trio with the baritone Theodor Uppman. He made several appearances at the Lyric Opera in Chicago, including one as Alfredo in *La Traviata* opposite Maria Callas. In Toronto he sang in *Don Giovanni* with the *COC in 1956 and in *The Abduction from the Seraglio* in 1957. For the Montreal Festivals he sang in 10 performances of *Don Giovanni* in 1957 and in 8 of *The Abduction from the Seraglio* in 1960. In 1958 he repeated Ottavio in the *Vancouver International Festival's *Don Giovanni* with George *London as the Don and Joan Sutherland in her North American debut as Donna Anna. He appeared at the *Stratford Festival in recital in 1962 and in a concert version of *The Abduction from the Seraglio* in 1969. His performance 18 Oct 1963 as Ottavio at the *Metropolitan Opera (his only role with that company) won him a public ovation; according to Theodore Strongin, he sang 'with intelligence as well as beauty of sound' (*New York Times*, 19 Oct 1963). He repeated that role for the last time in April 1964 at the *PDA for the Opera Guild, in two performances that marked his farewell to the operatic stage. He had sung the role 183 times. He continued to appear in concert and oratorio, however, and a *Messiah* (1967) and a Berlioz *Requiem* (1969) with the *Toronto Mendelssohn Choir were memorable. His final public appearance, 24 Nov 1970, was with the *MSO in *Messiah*.

Appointed to the faculty of the *CMM in 1963, Simoneau left in 1967 to join the *MACQ as deputy head of the music division. At the ministry's request he prepared a report on the situation of opera in Quebec that led to the creation in 1971 of the *Opéra du Québec. Appointed to the company as artistic director, he resigned at the end of the same year after a policy disagreement. He joined the faculty of the San Francisco Cons in September 1972 and taught 1973–6 at the *Banff SFA.

Simoneau is numbered among the most distinguished Canadian singers of the century. His international reputation as a Mozart singer is attested by his presence at major festivals and events dedicated to this composer, as well as by his recordings. He is honoured also as an interpreter of French music both on stage and in the concert hall. An extensive legacy of recordings preserves this patrician singer's art. One of these – *Concert Arias and Duets* of Mozart, with Pierrette Alarie – was awarded the 1961 Grand Prix du disque by the Académie Charles Cros, Paris. Simoneau and Alarie were awarded the 1959 *Prix de musique Calixa-Lavallée, thus becoming the first recipients of this important honour. In 1971 Simoneau was made an Officer of the *Order of Canada. He was a member 1968–71 of the Régie de la PDA, and a judge at the *Montreal International Competition in 1977. In *Le Devoir*, Montreal (1 and 8 Dec 1962) Simoneau published a two-part article entitled 'De la futilité des traductions des oeuvres lyriques.'

DISCOGRAPHY

I / RECORDINGS BY SIMONEAU

Beecham in Rehearsal: The Abduction from the Seraglio. Beecham Choral Soc, Royal Phil O, Beecham cond. 1956. HMV SLS 846

Berlioz *L'Enfance du Christ*. Choral Art Soc, Little Orchestra Soc, T. Scherman cond. 1953. 2 Col ML 4874-4875

– *Requiem*. New England Cons Chor, Boston SO, Munch cond. 1959. RCA Victor LDS 6077/RCA Victrola VICS 6043

Duparc *Songs*. A. Rogers pf. 1958. West XWN 18788

Gluck *Iphigénie en Tauride*. Paris Cons O, Giulini cond. 1952. Vox PL 7822/Vox OPX 212/3-Pathé-Marconi DTX 130-132

Handel *Messiah: Excerpts*. London Handel Soc O and Chor, Goehr cond. 1958. Perfect 15006

Méhul – Thomas – Massenet – Donizetti – Verdi – Flotow. Berlin RIAS SO, P. Strauss cond. 1957. DGG LPEM 19101/Decca DL 9968

Mozart *The Abduction from the Seraglio*. Royal Phil O, Beecham Choral Soc, Beecham cond, Simoneau (Belmonte). 1957. 2-Angel S-3555 BL/2-Pathé-Marconi FCX 700-701

– *Arias*. O du Théâtre des Champs-Élysées, Jouve cond. 1955. Ducretet-Thomson 270-C-088

– *Così fan tutte*. Philharmonia O and Chor, von Karajan cond. 1954. 3-Angel 3522 CL/3-Pathé-Marconi FCX 484-486/(excerpts) Electrola 80574

– *Don Giovanni*. Vienna SO and Chamb Choir, Moralt cond. 1955. 3-Epic LC 3191-3193/3-Philips PHC 9057-9059

– *Famous Opera Arias*. Hollweg sop, Vienna SO, Paumgartner cond. 1954. Epic LC 3262

– *Idomeneo*. Glyndebourne Festival O and Chor, Pritchard cond, Simoneau (Idamante). 1958. 3-Angel 3574 C/L

– *The Magic Flute*. Vienna State Opera Chor, Vienna Phil O, Böhm cond, Simoneau (Tamino). 1955. 3-Lon A-4319/ (excerpts) Lon OS 25046

– *Requiem*. Westminster Choir, New York Phil SO, Walter cond. 1956. Col ML 5012

Offenbach *Les Contes d'Hoffmann*. Paris Concerts O and Chor, LeConte cond, Simoneau (Hoffmann). 1957. Epic SC 6028

Schubert – Mozart – Dela. Lachance pf. 1965. CBC Expo 33

Schumann *Spanische Liebeslieder*. Marshall sop, Sarfaty mezzo, Warfield bar, Gold and Fizdale pfs. 1961. Col MS 6461

Verdi *La Traviata: Highlights*. Morales sop, Lamoureux O, Dervaux cond. 1953. Philips NOO 639R

II / RECORDINGS WITH PIERETTE *ALARIE, SOPRANO

Bach *Mass in B Minor*. Amsterdam Phil Soc Chor and O, Goehr cond. 1959. 2-Van 216-217

– *Mass in B Minor*. Vienna Academy Chor, Vienna State Opera O, Scherchen cond. 1959. 3-West WST 304/Mus Guild MS 6301

Beethoven 'Ode to Joy' *Symphony No. 9*. Choirs of Rutgers U, MSO, Pelletier cond. 1967. CBC Expo 1

Bizet *Carmen*. Paris Concerts O and Chor, LeConte cond, Alarie (Micaela), Simoneau (Don José). 1959. 3-Epic BC 1056-1058

– *Les Pêcheurs de perles*. Chorale Elisabeth Brasseur, Lamoureux O, Fournet cond, Alarie (Leila). 1953. 2-Epic LC-3087-3088/Philips PHC-2-016/(excerpts) Philips GBL 5574

Cimarosa – Donizetti – Verdi – Puccini – Gounod – Halévy – Massenet. Berlin RIAS SO, Schaenen cond. 1959. DG SLPM 138056

Couperin *Motet de Sainte Suzanne*. Ens Vocal de Paris, O de Chamb Gérard Cartigny, Bour cond. 1954. Ducretet-Thomson London DTL 93077

Delibes *Lakmé: Highlights*. Lamoureux O, Jouve cond, Dervaux cond. 1952. Philips NOO 638R

Famous Duets from the French Opera: Bizet – Massenet – Gounod. O du Théâtre des Champs-Élysées, Ingelbrecht cond, Dervaux cond. 1953. Ducretet-Thomson 93018/Sel M 298.004

Gluck *Orphée et Eurydice*. Blanchard Vocal Ens, Lamoureux O, Rosbaud cond, Alarie (Amor). 1956 2-Epic SC 6019/(excerpts) Fontana 700 476 WGY

Gounod *Faust*. Vienna State Opera Chor, Vienna Festival O, Rivoli cond, Alarie (Marguerite). 1962. Guilde Inter-

nationale du Disque (catalogue no. unknown)/(excerpts) Concert Hall SMS-2374
Handel *Messiah*. Vienna Academy Chor, Vienna State Opera O, Scherchen cond. 1959. 3-West WST 306/3-Mus Guild MS 6302/(excerpts) West 14095
Haydn *Airs*. NACO, Bernardi cond. 1970. RCI 332/RCA VCCS 1650
Love Duets: Gounod – Massenet – Cilèa. Berlin Radio SO, Schaenen cond. 1959. DG LPM 18593
Monteverdi – Haydn – Schubert – Cornelius – Schumann. Lachance pf. 1968. CBC SM-50
Mozart *Arias and Duets*. CBC Mtl orch, J.-M. Beaudet cond. Ca 1955. RCI 147
– *Concert Arias and Duets*. Amsterdam Phil O, Goehr cond. 1959. Guilde Internationale du Disque MMS 2183
– *Lieder*. Newmark pf. 1955. RCI 146
– *Opera Arias*. O du Théâtre des Champs-Élysées, Jouve cond. 1955. Ducretet 93089/Sel SC 12.017
Quesnel *Colas et Colinette*. CBC Mtl orch, P. Hétu cond. 1968. RCI 234/Sel CC-15.001/Sel SSC-24.160
Schumann *Duets*. Newmark pf. (1962). RCI 198

BIBLIOGRAPHY (for Alarie and Simoneau)
'Pierrette Alarie et Léopold Simoneau,' *Musique et Musiciens*, vol 1, Dec 1952
'The Simoneaus: "Their lives blend as happily as their voices",' *OpCan*, vol 2, Feb–Mar 1961
Blackburn, Marthe. 'Elegance is the hallmark in the home of Pierrette Alarie and Léopold Simoneau,' *Jmc*, Jan 1966
Kutsch, K.J., and Riemens, L. *A Concise Biographical Dictionary of Singers* (Philadelphia 1969)
Samson, Marc. 'La (curieuse) rançon de la gloire au Québec,' Quebec *Le Soleil*, 26 Aug 1972
Gingras, Claude. 'Les Simoneau: dernier acte,' Montreal *La Presse*, 2 Sep 1972
Rivard, Yolande Piette. 'La nouvelle vie des Simoneau,' ibid, 8 Sep 1973
Lee, M. Owen. 'Simoneau: a Mozart prince,' *Mcan*, 33, Oct 1977
Creative Canada, vol 1 GP (NM)

Simon Fraser University. Non-denominational university founded in Burnaby, BC, in 1963, with undergraduate and graduate programs operating on a year-round tri-semester schedule. It was named after Simon Fraser (explorer, fur trader, 1776–1862) who gave his name to the Fraser River.

Musical activities have developed slowly and have been structured loosely. From its inception in 1965 the Centre for Communications and the Arts (within the Faculty of Education) offered non-credit workshops in dance, film, music, theatre, and visual arts, conducted by resident and visiting artists. The aim was to awaken a sensitivity to the arts rather than to turn out professional artists.

The resident musicians 1965–72 have included the composers Jack *Behrens, Bruce *Davis, Peter *Huse, R. Murray *Schafer, and Phillip Werren and the mezzo-soprano Phyllis *Mailing. Short-term residents have been Cornelius Cardew, Udo *Kasemets, Olivier Messiaen, and Christian Wolff. In the early 1970s the emphasis shifted from single musicians to in-residence ensembles and from composers to performers. These have included Mailing 1965–7 and 1970–5, the *Lyric Arts Trio 1971–2, the *Purcell String Quartet appointed in 1972 (and still resident in 1980), the early music specialist David *Skulski 1973–6, and the conductor Jon *Washburn in 1974.

In addition to performing and conducting workshops, the ensembles have made frequent tours of British Columbia. Mailing served 1966–8 as conductor of the 32-voice Simon Fraser University Choir and its subsection, the Simon Fraser University Chamber Singers. David Keane took over 1968–70 during Mailing's absence. In 1970, on her return, Mailing reorganized the choirs as the *Madrigal Singers. The funding of the in-residence ensembles has been supported by the *Canada Council and the *Koerner Foundation.

The heads of the Centre for Communications and the Arts were Bruce Attridge 1965–6, Tom Mallinson 1966–8, Patrick Lyndon 1968–70, and Nini Baird 1970–2. In 1972 the department was divided into the Dept of Communication Studies and the Centre for Communications and the Arts, the latter directed by Nini Baird until 1976. Another reorganization in that year transformed the Centre for Communications and the Arts into the Centre for the Arts within the Faculty of Interdisciplinary Studies. Evan W. Alderson was appointed the reorganized centre's head.

The Centre for the Arts has developed credit courses in dance, film, music, theatre, and the visual arts. Courses have been offered in music history and the basics of music; a minor credit degree program in music was scheduled for implementation 1980–2. Ingrid Buch and the composer David McIntyre have taught music, and Barry *Truax was appointed jointly by the centre and the Dept of Communication Studies. The latter, chaired by William H. Melody, includes in its syllabus courses, towards a degree in communication, on such topics as the theory and uses of tape recordings. It has provided the base for the Sonic Research Studio developed by Schafer after 1965 and for the *World Soundscape Project initiated by Schafer in 1971.

The music specialist in the Faculty of Education was Joachim Sandvoss (d 1979). Sandvoss' successor, Robert Walker, was appointed in 1980.

Besides attracting outstanding practising musicians to its ranks, the university has been visited by close to 200 ensembles and soloists whose programs have given much emphasis to contemporary Canadian music.

BIBLIOGRAPHY
Baird, Nini. 'Centre for Communications and the Arts,' *Communications 70*, Apr 1970
– 'Music an unstructured experience at Simon Fraser,' *MSc*, 267, Sep–Oct 1972

SIMONS, Jan. Baritone, teacher, b Düsseldorf, Germany, 11 Nov 1925, naturalized Canadian 1944. He studied voice with Emilio de Gogorza in New York 1950–3, with Emmy *Heim and Ernesto *Vinci at the *RCMT 1953–8, and with Yvonne Rodd-Marling in London in 1970. He has given numerous public recitals, specializing in Lieder, and has sung in radio and TV oratorio performances in Canada, Europe, and Japan. He was a soloist at the *Stratford Festival's first concert (1955) and sang the vocal part in the Canadian premiere (1956) of the ballet *Dark Elegies* (to Mahler's *Kindertotenlieder*) by the National Ballet of Canada. He recorded a duet recital with Elizabeth Benson *Guy for the CBC (RCI 199) and in 1964 was a soloist with the *Montreal Bach Choir in the NFB film *Selections from the Christmas Oratorio*. He was a founding member of the *Festival Singers and became director general of *CAMMAC in 1969. He joined the *McGill U Faculty of Music in 1961 and has also taught at Marianapolis College 1963–7, CAMMAC in 1957, and Vanier College in 1973. NT

Singing and voice teaching. An examination of the development of the art of singing in Canada from its earliest documented incidences to its flourishing state in the late 20th century. The emphasis is on the exceptional contribution of those singers who, perhaps more than artists in any other field, have contributed in a major way to Canada's reputation abroad after 1850.

1 The early years
2 Singers
3 Voice teaching
4 Awards and competitions

1 THE EARLY YEARS. Singing, by individuals or groups, was the first musical activity to occur in New France, and subsequently the most widely practised. In the earliest days after their arrival in 1534 Jacques Cartier and his companions must have heard those traditional Indian songs which have so interested historians and ethnologists. The French, who sang the mass and hymns in thanksgiving upon landing, were the first to perform European music on North American soil. They also brought along folksongs from several regions of France. Great numbers of these songs have been collected in the ensuing years – the first ones by Ernest *Gagnon in the middle of the 19th century – and bear witness to the importance of singing in the life of the country's earliest settlers (see Folk music, Franco-Canadian). Singing not only held a place of honour in the services and rituals of the church but also flourished as a part of daily life, at social gatherings and benefit concerts, on journeys or during work in the fields, at political meetings and on patriotic feast days, in prize-giving ceremonies at the end of the school year, and in many other social settings. As singing did not require special training or accompaniment by instruments, it lay within everyone's capacity, and any person could practise it according to his ability, even without a knowledge of the rudiments of music.

It was only towards the end of the 18th century that singing came to be regarded in Canada as a means of artistic expression, requiring special study and the development of a technique which included tone projection, placement of the voice, breath control, and interpretation. It was at this time that the first visits of theatrical companies with singers trained in Europe made Canadians aware that the voice in its natural state left much to be desired and could be improved through study, contrary to the prejudice which held that a fine natural voice could be destroyed if entrusted to a teacher. Nevertheless, it was not until the middle of the 19th century that Canada welcomed its first specialized voice teachers. Until then the study of singing was not distinct from that of music in general, as witness T.F. *Molt's *Traité élémentaire de musique vocale* (Quebec 1845) which, despite its title, is no more than a work of music theory and ear training, never dealing with the voice itself.

2 SINGERS. It is astonishing that in spite of this situation Canada in the mid-19th century was able to produce one singer destined quickly to attain the highest pinnacle of international fame. Emma *Albani had studied only with her father when she gave her first public performance in 1856, but the excellence of her training was manifest even then; just two more years of study in France and in Italy prepared her for the stardom she was to enjoy from 1870 onward.

During the next hundred years numerous singers born or raised in Canada and trained at least partly (and often entirely) in Canada have attained national or international fame in opera, oratorio, concert, and recital, establishing Canada as a country known for its exceptional singers. Among these are Pierrette *Alarie, Milla *Andrew, Émile *Belcourt, Donald *Bell, Colette *Boky, Jean *Bonhomme, John *Boyden, Cedia *Brault, Victor *Braun, Edmund *Burke, Clarice *Carson, Pierre Charbonneau, Fernande *Chiocchio, Claude *Corbeil, Alan *Crofoot, Odette *de Foras, Rosita *del Vecchio, Pauline *Donalda, Paul *Dufault, Graziella *Dumaine, Céline *Dussault, Jeanne *Dusseau, Pierre *Duval, Florence *Easton, Louise *Edvina, Sarah *Fischer, Maureen *Forrester, Judith *Forst, Don *Garrard, Éva *Gauthier, Jacques *Gérard, Gaston *Germain, Jeanne *Gordon, Alexander *Gray, Elizabeth Benson *Guy, Denis *Harbour, Mary *Henderson, Kathleen *Howard, Doreen *Hume, Jean-Pierre *Hurteau, Frances *James, Raoul *Jobin, Edward *Johnson, Gladys *Kriese-Caporale, Béatrice *La Palme, Gabrielle *Lavigne, Louise *Lebrun, Nicole *Lorange, Germaine Manny, Lois *Marshall, Nicholas *Massue, Ermanno *Mauro, Joan *Maxwell, François-Xavier *Mercier, Morley *Meredith, James *Milligan, Norman *Mittelmann, Allan *Monk, Cornelis *Opthof, Mona Paulee, Mariana *Paunova, Irene *Pavloska, Rodolphe *Plamondon, Albert Quesnel, Louis *Quilico, Joseph *Rouleau, Irene *Salemka, Sylvia *Saurette, Robert *Savoie, Léopold *Simoneau, Teresa *Stratas, Lilian *Sukis, Micheline *Tessier, Heather *Thomson, Marie *Toulinguet, Huguette *Tourangeau, Édith *Tremblay, Bernard *Turgeon, André *Turp, Richard *Verreau, Lyn *Vernon, Jon *Vickers, Peter *van Ginkel, and Jeannette *Zarou. Several of these artists became known also as teachers, many while still at the height of busy performing careers.

In addition to performing the traditional repertoire, some singers have specialized in contemporary works (in particular those by Canadians). Notable among these specialists have been Billie Bridgeman, Josèphe *Colle, Jocelyne Coutu-Fleury, Rosemarie *Landry, Margo *MacKinnon, Phyllis *Mailing, Mary *Morrison, Gary *Relyea, Roland Richard, Patricia *Rideout, Roxolana *Roslak, and Pauline *Vaillancourt.

In 1980 several young singers showed exceptional promise, among them Marie *Laferrière, Marie-Danielle Parent (*Prix d'Europe 1980), and Catherine *Robbin (Gold Award, Benson and Hedges International Competition for Concert Singers 1979).

3 VOICE TEACHING. In the early 19th century singing began to be taught as a minor subject in convents, colleges, and seminaries, often by teachers of dubious competence. One of Montreal's first distinguished voice teachers was Mme Petipas, who, along with her husband, M d'Anglars, gave private instruction and taught in several institutions from 1868 until 1880, when the couple returned to France. 'These distinguished artists have introduced to this city the serious and logical teaching of voice and French declamation,' wrote *Le Canada musical* (1 Aug 1880).

At about the same time, priests such as L.-A. *Barbarin and J.-J. *Perrault taught singing in their own way, from a liturgical point of view. It was this milieu which produced Guillaume *Couture, who pursued his studies 1873-87 in Paris with Romain Bussine, a pupil of Manuel Garcia. Couture did not take up a singing career, but he had several voice pupils, among them Achille *Fortier, Édouard *LeBel, Ada Moylan, and Rodolphe Plamondon. Later, Fortier, Marie Contant, Charles *Labelle, and Céline *Marier (all of whom became teachers) also studied in Paris with Bussine.

In subsequent years, voice teaching in Canada acquired a more solid foundation with the arrival of eminent foreign masters as well as Canadian teachers who had received their apprenticeship in the great schools of France, Italy, England, and Germany. This gave rise to several generations of singers who, while possessing remarkable voices, did not identify themselves with particular schools or traditions. The Canadian singer became known for the ability to sing in several languages and various styles.

Among teachers prominent in Montreal in the 20th century have been Louise *André, Albert *Clerk-Jeannotte, Albert *Cornellier, Adelina Czapska, Reine *Décarie, José *Delaquerrière, Edith and Luciano *Della Pergola, Bernard *Diamant (also in Toronto), Roger *Filiatrault, Sarah Fischer, Ruzena *Herlinger, Salvator *Issaurel, Roger Larivière, Arthur *Laurendeau, Ria *Lenssens, Jeanne *Maubourg, Dina Maria Narici, Alice Raymond, Frank H. *Rowe, Albert *Roberval, Jan *Simons, and Mrs A.C. Wieland. In Quebec City, the most eminent have been Rolande *Dion, Adine Fafard-Drolet, Louis *Gravel, Émile *Larochelle, Guy Lepage, F.-X. Mercier, and Isa Jeynevald-Mercier.

In Toronto and other Ontario cities the main teachers have been Dorothy *Allan Park, Dalton *Baker (also in Vancouver), Giuseppe *Carboni, Bertha *Carey Morrow, Gina Cigna, Francesco *D'Auria, Eduardo *Ferrari-Fontana, Nina *Gale, Howell *Glynne, Albert *Ham, Elliott *Haslam, Emmy *Heim, Irene *Jessner, Weldon *Kilburn, George *Lambert, Campbell *McInnes, Otto *Morando, Aksel *Schiøtz, Helen Simmie, Rechab Tandy, Adine Tremblay, Ernesto *Vinci (also in Halifax and Banff), and Albert Whitehead.

Among teachers active in Winnipeg have been W.H. *Anderson, Nina *Dempsey, Thérèse *Deniset, Simone Estelle (the last two in St Boniface), John *Goss (also in Vancouver), Stanley *Hoban, George *Kent, May *Lawson, Doris *Lewis, Victor *Martens (also in Kitchener-Waterloo), Frederick *Newnham (also in Nova Scotia), Gladys *Whitehead (also in Hamilton), and the J. Roberto Wood (also in Victoria). In Alberta, Odette de Foras, Glyndwr Jones (also in Vancouver), Jean *Létourneau, and Lucien *Needham have trained singers, as have Alicia *Birkett and Helen Davies *Sherry in Saskatchewan. In British Columbia, Nancy Paisley *Benn, Donald Brown, Isabelle *Burnada, Caterina Hendrikse, Gideon *Hicks, Phylis *Inglis, Frances James, Phyllis Mailing, Avis *Phillips, and William *Morton have been among the leading teachers. Teodor Brilts, Audrey *Farnell, Gloria *Richard, and Mariss Vetra (also in Toronto) have been prominent in the Maritimes, and Eleanor Jerrett in Newfoundland.

4 AWARDS AND COMPETITIONS. In the late 19th century Béatrice La Palme and Ada Moylan were awarded *Strathcona scholarships, and in 1916 for the first time the Prix d'Europe was given to a singer, Graziella Dumaine. Lionel *Daunais won it in 1926. In the 1950s the radio competitions *'Singing Stars of Tomorrow,' *'Nos Futures Étoiles,' and *'Opportunity Knocks' stimulated the discovery of many young singers, among them several who have pursued international careers. The *Montreal International Competition was devoted to singing in 1967, 1970, 1973, 1977, and 1981. During the 1977 competition, a 'Colloque sur le chant' featured such eminent personalities of the singers' world as Rose Bampton, Clarice Carson, Maureen Forrester, Don Garrard, and Bidú Sayão, the accompanist Gerald Moore, and the opera directors Lotfi Mansouri and Terry McEwen.

See also Art song; Choir schools; Choral singing; Hymn singing; McGill Opera Studio; Opera performance; Oratorio performance (international repertoire); Oratorios, Canadian (composition and performance); Regina Cons Opera; Royal Cons Opera School; Singing schools.

BIBLIOGRAPHY

Molt, T.F. *Traité élémentaire de musique vocale* (Quebec 1845)
Graham, George F. *The Vocal Tutor* (Montreal 1854)
Legendre, Napoléon. 'Le chant dans les écoles,' *Canada artistique*, Apr 1890
Slater, David. *Vocal Physiology and the Teaching of Singing* (London 1911)
Mercier, François-Xavier. 'Classement et pose de la voix,' *La Musique*, 3 articles, vol 1, Oct, Nov, Dec 1919
Riddez, Jean. 'La grande pitié du chant,' *Canada musical*, 8 articles, Jan to Jun 1921
Mercier, François-Xavier. *Technique de musique vocale* (Quebec 1928)
Gour, Romain. *La Palme-Issaurel* (Montreal 1948)
Lawson, James Terry. *Full Throated Ease: A Concise Guide to Easy Singing* (Vancouver 1955)
André, Louise. 'L'éducation de l'artiste chanteur,' unpubl D MUS thesis, U of Montreal 1957
Nielsen, Gerda. *A New Guide to Good Singing* (Willowdale 1975)
Delaquerrière, José. *Savoir chanter* (Montreal 1976) GP

Singing schools. A New-World echo of an English movement to renovate psalm-singing. The schools appeared first in New England in the early 18th century. They were organized by itinerant musicians, who for a period of months or years would teach the rudiments of musical notation and choral singing in meeting houses or rented halls. The new reading skills greatly increased the repertoire of psalm tunes. From New England the movement spread to the English-speaking areas of Canada.

An early instance in Canada is that of Amasa Braman, a Connecticut singing master who taught psalm-singing in Liverpool, NS, ca 1776-8. Reuben McFarlen offered to teach the rules of psalmody in his singing school in Halifax in 1788, and Stephen *Humbert, from New Jersey, opened a Sacred Vocal Music School in Saint John, NB, in 1796. While the singing school movement had produced several hundred tunebooks in the USA, Humbert's *Union Harmony* (1801 and later editions) was the first and for many years the only Canadian compilation of its kind. In Toronto (then York) Joseph B. Abbot proposed to open a 'School in the principles of Church Music' in 1810, but as late as 1837 Mrs Anna Jameson noted with regret the lack of a singing school. The *Children of Peace organized singing classes in Sharon, Ont, about 1819. At that time the movement began to fade in the USA as a simpler, more homophonic type of church music came into fashion. In rural and frontier areas, however, singing schools lived on until the late 19th century. In Merivale, near Ottawa, George Stiles developed a choir of 100 young people who rehearsed twice a week and sang at social events and concerts in the 1880s, and in Regina a visiting musician, R.B. George, held a 'convention' of 30 pupils, to teach them to read and sing and prepare a concert in a mere five-day period. As these examples show, singing schools should not be considered forerunners of the modern conservatories.

See also Literature with musical content: 1 / Anglo-Canadian.

BIBLIOGRAPHY

Trowsdale, G.C. 'Vocal music in the common schools of Upper Canada: 1846-1876,' *J of Research in Music Education*, vol 18, Winter 1970
McMillan, Barclay. 'Tune-book imprints in Canada to 1867: a descriptive bibliography,' *Papers of the Bibliographical Society of Canada*, vol 16, 1977 HK

'Singing Stars of Tomorrow.' National voice competition initiated, organized, and broadcast 1943-56 by the CBC, and sponsored by York Knitting Mills and, later, by Canadian Industries, Ltd. Each season some 46 young singers, chosen at regional auditions, were heard with an orchestra conducted by Rex *Battle in national broadcasts on Sunday afternoons over a 23-week period. On the basis of their radio performances of art songs and operatic or oratorio arias, semi-finalists and finalists were heard again in three additional broadcasts, during the last of which the winners were named.

Because the contest began during World War II, only female singers participated during the first years, and awards were limited to single prizes of $1000, $500, and $250 respectively. In 1947 male singers began to compete and a grand award of $1000 went to the contestant with the highest marks, $750 went to the contestant of the other sex nearest in marks to the winner, and second awards of $500 each went to the male and female runners-up. In the case of ties for second awards between two men or two women, additional second awards were made. By 1953 the grand award had been increased to $2000, and the top award to a singer of the opposite sex had grown to $1000. The two second awards remained at $500 each, but four honourable mentions of $100 each had been added.

Among the judges over the years were A.A. Alldrick (*A.A.A.), Thomas *Archer, Rex Battle, Hector *Charlesworth, Jean Dufresne (Marcel *Valois), Rhynd Jamieson, Bernard *Naylor, and Healey *Willan. John *Adaskin was the producer of the broadcasts.

The following list gives the names of prize winners and those who received honourable mentions:

1943–4
1 Claire *Gagnier, Trois-Rivières, Que; 2 Evelyn *Gould, Toronto; 3 Jane Harkness, Toronto
Honourable mentions: Margaret Royle, Vancouver; Pierrette *Alarie, Montreal; Nancy Douglas, Toronto; Lillian Smith, Toronto

1944–5
1 Evelyn Gould, Toronto; 2 Jane Harkness, Toronto; 3 Simone Flibotte, Montreal, and Gwendolyn Smart, Ottawa
Honourable mentions: Joan Ryan, Montreal; Muriel Niven, Calgary; Kaye Connor, Vancouver; Alexandra Belugin, Newmarket, Ont

1945–6
1 Simone Flibotte, Montreal; 2 Audrey *Farnell, Amherst, NS; 3 Marie-José Forgues, Montreal
Honourable mentions: Elizabeth McCaskill, Edmonton; Marie-Germaine Leblanc, Moncton; Victoria Douglas, Toronto

1946–7
1 Marie-José Forgues, Montreal; 2 Victoria Douglas, Toronto, and Louise *Roy, St Boniface, Man; 3 Elizabeth McCaskill, Edmonton
Honourable mentions: Beth Corrigan, Toronto; Simone Rainville, Quebec City

1947–8
1 Gilles *Lamontagne, Quebec City; 2 Elizabeth Benson *Guy, Bridgewater, NS; 3 Ernest *Adams, Vancouver; 4 Yolande Lagrenade, Montreal
Honourable mentions: Louise Roy, St Boniface, Man; Simone Rainville, Quebec City; Marie Germaine Leblanc, Moncton; Glenn Gardiner, Merlin, Ont; Morley Margolis (*Meredith), Winnipeg

1948–9
1 Louise Roy, St Boniface, Man; 2 Morley Margolis (Meredith), Winnipeg; 3 Ernest Adams, Vancouver; 4 Lois *Marshall, Toronto
Honourable mentions: Doreen Hulme (*Hume), Sault Ste Marie, Ont; Glenn Gardiner, Merlin, Ont; Esther *Ghan, Toronto; Roger *Doucet, Montreal

1949–50
1 Lois Marshall, Toronto; 2 Abramo Carfagnini, Montreal; 3 Doreen Hulme (Hume), Sault Ste Marie, Ont, and Andrée Lescot, Montreal; 4 Pierre *Boutet, Quebec City
Honourable mentions: Marie-Germaine Leblanc, Moncton, NB; Claire Duchesneau, St-Lambert, Que; Robert *Savoie, Montreal; Wilfred Read, Hamilton

1950–1
1 June *Kowalchuk, Regina; 2 Pierre Boutet, Quebec City; 3 Marguerite *Gignac, Windsor, Ont; 4 Robert Savoie, Montreal
Honourable mentions: Doreen Hulme (Hume), Sault Ste Marie, Ont; Mary *Morrison, Winnipeg; Donald *Garrard, Vancouver; Joseph *Rouleau, Montreal

1951–2
1 Marguerite Gignac, Windsor, Ont; 2 Robert Savoie, Montreal; 3 Joan *Hall, Winnipeg; 4 John Dunbar, Victoria
Honourable mentions: Patricia Snell, Toronto; Barbara *Franklin, Regina; Jon *Vickers, Prince Albert, Sask; James Lamond, Calgary

1952–3
1 Don Garrard, Vancouver; 2 Joan Hall, Winnipeg; 3 Irene *Salemka, Weyburn, Sask; 4 James *Milligan, Huntsville, Ont
Honourable mentions: Roma *Butler, St John's, Nfld; Donald *Bell, Vancouver; William Goertzen, Winnipeg; Yolande DiPaolo, Winnipeg

1953–4
1 James Milligan, Huntsville, Ont; 2 Gladys *Kriese, Winnipeg; 3 Norman *Mittelmann, Winnipeg; 4 Roma Butler, St John's, Nfld
Honourable mentions: Thomas Hender, Cobourg, Ont; Liliane Durand, Montreal; Floriane Cotnoir, Noranda, Que; Stanley Martin, Victoria, BC

1954–5
1 Lesia Zubrack, Prince Albert, Sask; 2 Bernard *Turgeon, Edmonton; 3 Emily Cundari, Windsor, Ont; 4 Gaston Harnois, Shawinigan Falls, Que
Honourable mentions: Norman Mittelmann, Winnipeg; Marguerite *Lavergne, Montreal; Diane *Oxner, Lunenburg, NS; Pieter (Peter) *van Ginkel, Winnipeg

1955–6
1 Marguerite Lavergne, Montreal; 2 James Whicher, Wiarton, Ont; 3 Joan *Maxwell, Winnipeg; 4 Pieter (Peter) van Ginkel, Winnipeg
Honourable mentions: Roma Butler, St John's, Nfld; Victor *Braun, Windsor, Ont; Norman Mittelmann, Winnipeg; Ilona Kombrink, Toronto

SIPPI, Charles A. (Augustus). Educator, organist-choirmaster, physician, b Hyderabad, India (Pakistan), 25 Jul 1844, d London, Ont, 15 May 1906; D MED (Dublin), hon MA (Kenyon College, Ohio). Though of Italian descent Sippi was third-generation Irish. He attended the Royal College of Surgeons, Dublin, and the U of Dublin while studying organ with an uncle, John A. Sippi, and voice with Alexander Roche (or Roache). After emigrating to Canada in 1865 he practised medicine in Port Stanley, on Lake Erie, but moved to London, Canada West (Ontario), where he taught English, classics, and physiology 1864–74 at Hellmuth College (*U of Western Ontario). Eventually music occupied most of his time. He was manager of A. & S. *Nordheimer's London, Ont, music store 1874–87 and served as organist-choirmaster of Cronyn Memorial Church. As a cofounder, and the first president 1885–7, of the Ontario Music Teachers' Assn (*Canadian Society of Musicians) he campaigned for the certification of music teachers and increased music teaching in public schools. George B. *Sippi was his brother. Their father, a retired British bandmaster, also lived in London, Ont.

BIBLIOGRAPHY
Rose, G.M. *A Cyclopedia of Canadian Biography* (Toronto 1886–8)
Goggio, Emilio. 'The Italian contribution to the development of music in Ontario,' *CRMA*, Oct–Nov 1945, Dec–Jan 1946 HK

SIPPI, George B. (Buckley). Organist, choirmaster, teacher, b Bombay 10 Mar 1847, d London, Ont, 18 Sep 1915. His family returned in 1854 to Ireland from India, where his Italian grandfather had settled. He attended Queen's College in Cork and studied piano and organ with his uncle, John A. Sippi, but also played the violin well enough to appear in local concerts. After studying medicine briefly he followed his elder brother Charles A. *Sippi to London, Ont, in 1870. He taught music 1870–6 at Hellmuth College (*U of Western Ontario) and, after a short period in Montreal as organist-choirmaster at St Martin's Church, served for 37 years as organist-choirmaster at St Paul's Cathedral, London, Ont. An able performer and choirleader he also was an avid student of church music and music history. He assembled at the cathedral a collection of about 350 volumes of choral music, which, with his private library of musical literature, was donated to the U of Western Ontario after his death. In 1907 the Bishop of Huron, recognizing the unusual 'precision, solemnity and power' of Sippi's choir, appointed him director of diocesan music. Sippi's published compositions include *The Oddfellows Galop* (Nordheimer 1875) and a setting of W.H. Drummond's 'Canadian Forever' (Whaley Royce 1915).

BIBLIOGRAPHY
See C.A. Sippi. HK

Sir Ernest MacMillan Fine Arts Club. Founded in 1936 by Marjorie Agnew and other teachers at Templeton Junior High School in Vancouver to foster fine-arts activities among the students. Sir Ernest *MacMillan approved the use of his name and maintained an interest in the club's progress as it spread from school to school in Vancouver and other cities, including Whitehorse in the Yukon. On occasion he was a visitor at club functions. Besides literary, visual-art, and dance activities, the club presented concerts and gave music scholarships. It opened the summer season at the *Malkin Bowl for many years and presented a total of 30 annual concerts for the Canadian National Institute for the Blind. Student members were recruited as ushers at Denman Auditorium and the *Orpheum Theatre and thus were enabled to hear many notable performers. Marjorie Agnew was the club's driving force throughout its 40-year existence, and it was with her failing health that the club fell dormant in the mid-1970s. Donald *Bell, Betty-Jean *Hagen, Gregory *Millar, and Heather *Thomson are alumni. BNSG

SIRULNIKOFF, Jack. Composer, teacher, clarinetist, b Winnipeg 11 Dec 1931; A MUS performance (McGill) 1956, B MUS composition (McGill) 1956, MA composition (Bennington) 1960, M MUS (Toronto) 1971. His composition teachers include István *Anhalt, Henry Brant, Lionel Nowack, and John *Weinzweig. He was a teaching fellow 1958–60 at Bennington College, Vt, and there wrote incidental music for Ionesco's *Victims of Duty* and had his opera, *This Evening* (1960), and his *Green Mountain Overture* (for band) performed. The opera was produced again at Piermont, NY, by the Rockland Lyric Theater. Sirulnikoff was in charge of music for theatre and dance 1960–1 at Smith College and there wrote incidental music for Molière's *Le Médecin malgré lui*. In Canada, he taught 1962–6 in Ontario secondary schools, in 1966 at the Nova Scotia Teachers' College in Truro, and later in Metropolitan Toronto public schools. Sirulnikoff has provided stock music for the *NFB and has arranged for the CBC. His compositions may be divided into three categories: light music (*Foreign Affairs*, *Polka Dots*), music for amateur performers (*Little Suite* for brass trio, *Ceremonial Piece II* for two trumpets and piano), and works utilizing serial methods and dodecaphony (*Movement for Orchestra*). He has experimented with electronic music and jazz. Sirulnikoff is an associate of the *CMCentre and a member of CAPAC. PK

SISKIND, Jacob (Kohos). Critic, broadcaster, b Montreal 9 Jun 1928. His first piano teachers included Rose *Goldblatt and, 1939–44, Alfred *Laliberté. At McGill U 1944–9 he studied mathematics, physics, and music. Among his teachers were Helmut *Blume, Maitland *Farmer, and Kenneth *Meek (organ and piano) and Rachel Gilbert (violin). Other teachers included Yvonne *Hubert at the *CMM and Bernard Simons privately. He took some private lessons with Benno Moiseiwitsch in 1953.

Siskind began writing music criticism for the *McGill Daily* in 1945 and was a reviewer for the Montreal *Standard* from 1949 until that weekly's demise in 1951. He taught piano privately 1950–65 and also, during those years and later, coached many young performers in preparation for competitions. He returned to McGill U for courses 1953–6 in psychology and English, freelancing meanwhile for the *Montreal Star* and writing fiction under pseudonyms for US pulp magazines. In 1956 he joined the *Montreal Star* as theatre editor, and in 1965 he became entertainment editor of the Montreal *Gazette*. In 1966 he was co-host with Uriel Luft of CTV's weekly show 'Arts Calendar and Review.' In 1971 he was appointed critic of music, drama, and ballet for the *Gazette*, and after 1974 he wrote exclusively on music and ballet. He was briefly (1977–8) arts editor and music critic for the new daily *Ottawa Today*, and in 1978 he began freelancing for the Toronto *Globe and Mail*. He was music, dance and drama critic 1978–80 for the *Ottawa Journal* and in 1980 joined the *Ottawa Citizen*.

Siskind has been heard often as a commentator on the CBC programs 'Sights and Sounds' (local, Montreal) and the national network's 'New Records' and 'Arts National.' Between 1973 and 1980 he was both writer and commentator for several CBC recorded-music series, including 'Great Keyboard Performances of the 20th Century,' 'Musically Speaking,' and 'The Art of the Interpreter.'

A candid writer and engaging speaker on performances of traditional music, Siskind expresses views that are at once informed and subjective and have aroused lively discussion. He writes and talks with unbounded enthusiasm of performers whose work he enjoys, pianists in particular. He has shown no great affection for contemporary music. Although he is generally sympathetic to its performers for their efforts on its behalf, his appraisal of the music itself tends towards impatience and scepticism. His contributions to the field of musical comment thus veer between persuasive supportiveness and outright polemic.

WRITINGS

'Music in Montreal,' *Canadian Annual Review*, ed John Saywell (Toronto 1960)

Reviews, *CMB*, 1 and 2, Spring–Summer 1970, Spring–Summer 1971

'The role of recordings,' *CMB*, 11/12, (Autumn–Winter 1975, Spring–Summer 1976 (FCR)

Six Brown Brothers. Vaudeville act which helped to introduce the saxophone into popular music. Formed in 1910 as the Brown Brothers Saxophone Quintette (or Five Brown Brothers) by five brothers from Lindsay, Ont, and led by alto saxophonist Tom Brown, the group first recorded for Columbia in 1911. By 1914 it had become a sextet, the members playing soprano, alto, C-melody, tenor, baritone, and bass saxophones. Sources differ as to the group's personnel in later years. Brian Rust, in *The Dance Bands* (New Rochelle 1972) and *The American Dance Band Discography 1917–1942* (New Rochelle 1975), states that Alex, Fred, Verne, and William Brown all had been replaced by 1915, while *Moogk, in *Roll Back the Years*, suggests that the brothers performed together with a sixth unrelated member for the length of the group's career. The Six Brown Brothers appeared in the Broadway shows *Chin-Chin* (1914), *Jack 'O Lantern* (1918), *Tip Top* (1920), and *The Bunch and Judy* (1922) and performed until 1925 on US vaudeville circuits. Further recordings of expertly arranged and exuberantly played ragtime, novelty pieces, popular songs, and selections from *Chin-Chin* and *Tip Top* were made for Victor and (as the Saxo Sextette) Columbia; they included the Tom Brown compositions 'Chicken Walk,' 'That Moaning Saxophone Rag,' and 'Bull Frog Blues' from the 1910s and a very early version (9 May 1917) of *'Darktown Strutters' Ball.' An extensive discography is included in the later Rust book and in *Roll Back the Years*. MM

SKULSKI, (Murray) David. Oboist, early music specialist, b Moose Jaw, Sask, 29 Nov 1942. After early training in New Westminster and Burnaby, BC, and experience with the Vancouver Junior SO, Skulski studied at San Fernando Valley State College, Cal, and at the *U of British Columbia. He became a freelance oboist in 1963, performing for the CBC and with a number of Vancouver chamber ensembles. He played 1966–8 in the Orquesta Sinfónica de Xalapa, Mexico. Returning to Vancouver he founded the Hortulani Musicae in 1968 and was a performing member until 1976. He founded the *Vancouver Society for Early Music in 1970 and managed it until 1975. He became the founder-manager of the Towne Waytes in 1974, and he has helped to establish other early-music ensembles. He was music resident at *Simon Fraser U from the fall of 1973 to the spring of 1976 and taught summer courses in renaissance music in Breiteneich, Austria, in 1972. MW

SLATER, David (Dick). Organist, teacher, composer, choir director, b Glasgow 1869, d Toronto 31 Mar 1942. He studied music in Glasgow and in London where he obtained an ARCM. He came to Canada in 1911 to teach voice at the *TCM, and he also taught at the Ontario Ladies' College, Whitby. For some years he was an organist-choirmaster in Toronto, first at Parkdale Presbyterian Church and then at Westminster Church. He wrote articles on vocal training for the *Conservatory Quarterly Review* and a book, *Vocal Physiology and the Teaching of Singing* (London 1911). Approximately 150 of his compositions were published, mainly by *Harris, Larway, and Presser (often in *The Etude*). These included songs, anthems, piano pieces for pedagogical use, and orchestral transcriptions of some of his piano pieces. In those compositions he published before coming to Canada he often used pseudonyms. For instance, piano pieces were attributed to 'Paul Ambroise,' a number of the earlier songs to 'Kenneth Rae,' and his songs for children to 'Erland Hunt.' A fourth pseudonym was 'Leon Aubry.' Some of the works published in Great Britain and most, if not all, of the North American publications appeared under Slater's own name. Two sets of 12 piano pieces for young players – *Pictures from Holidayland* (ca 1916) and *Pictures from Storyland* (ca 1919) – were published by Harris, and a similar set – *Pictures from Fairyland* – was published by Presser in 1917. *Graded Course of Vocal Studies* (3 vols) was published by Harris in 1924.

BIBLIOGRAPHY

'Musical bibliographies of Canadian composers: no. 3,' Toronto *Globe*, 10 Jul 1936 EK

SLATER, Gordon (Frederick). Carillonneur, b Toronto 22 Aug 1950. He studied piano 1954–64 with Carmel Archambault at the *RCMT and bassoon 1968–71 with Nicholas *Kilburn at the *U of Toronto. His first carillon teacher 1959–68 was his father, James B. Slater (carillonneur at Metropolitan United Church, Toronto). Later, 1973–4, he worked with Robert *Donnell in Ottawa. While organist-choirmaster 1969–72 at Riverdale Presbyterian Church, Toronto, and a pipe organ builder, tuner, and repairman 1970–7 at the *Legge Organ Co in Islington (Toronto), Slater was carillonneur at Soldiers' Tower, U of Toronto, 1969–77, at Rainbow Tower, Niagara Falls, Ont, 1972–5, and the Carlsberg Carillon, *CNE, 1975–6. On 1 Apr 1977 he became the Dominion Carillonneur at the Peace Tower in Ottawa.

DISCOGRAPHY

Bells and Brass. Canadian Brass. 1978. Tapestry GD 7371

The Bells at Niagara Falls Volume I. 1974. Vantage CABR-1044

Peace Tower Christmas. 1979. Tapestry GD 7373

BIBLIOGRAPHY

'Bells and brass combine to make unique recording,' *CanComp*, 139, Mar 1979

Moffatt, Janet. 'Carilloneur [sic] as superstar,' Ottawa *Sunday Post*, 16 Dec 1979 FH

SLATTER, John. Bandmaster, composer, arranger, b London 21 Feb 1864, d Toronto 7 Dec 1954. After studies at the British Army Training School of Music, he became a euphonium soloist with the First Life Guards Band in London in 1882. In 1884 he joined the Victor Herbert Orchestra in New York. He played trombone and euphonium 1885–96 with leading US bands and orchestras, including the Detroit SO and the band of John Philip Sousa. In 1896 he became bandmaster of the recently formed *48th Highlanders Regimental Band in Toronto, a position he held with the rank of captain until 1944. Under his direction, the band visited world fairs in the USA, toured Canada several times, and performed for the royal visits of 1919 and 1939. During World War I Slatter supervised all army bands at Camp Borden, north of Toronto, training some 63 bands and over 1000 buglers. He also organized the Toronto cadet band, one of the first school bands in Canada. Many Canadian bandmasters and soloists came under his tutelage.

Slatter was the editor of the band-and-orchestra section of *Musical Canada* and contributed a series of articles on 'Phrasing and expression in music' (May, June, August 1907) as well as arrangements for brass quintet of such favourites as 'The Blue Bells of Scotland.' From 1931 to 1933 he was the first president of the *CBA, the founding of which he had advocated since 1918, and he did much to give leadership to the Canadian band movement. He compiled and arranged several band collections, including *Regimental Marches of Famous Scottish Regiments* (Canadian American Music 1901), *National Airs and Regimental Marches* including *'O Canada' and 'The *Maple Leaf For Ever' (R.S. Williams 1911), *Canadian Patriotic Band Book* (R.S. Williams ca 1919), and three sets of Scottish bagpipe books for band. Slatter also compiled *The New Excel Edition for Piston Trumpet Band* (Whaley Royce 1951) and arranged a Scottish medley for band,

The Bonnie Brier Bush (Waterloo). Several of his marches and arrangements for band are published by *Waterloo. His recordings on Edison cylinders, as conductor of the 48th Highlanders Band and also as conductor of the *Starr-Gennett Military Band, are listed in *Roll Back the Years*. He was awarded the OBE.

Slatter's brother Henry Arthur (clarinetist, bandmaster, b London 1866, d ?) was a member of the Band of the Grenadier Guards 1884–1905 and moved to Vancouver in 1911, where he directed the band of the 72nd Seaforth Highlanders 1911–14 and 1919–25. Another brother, Albert, was bandmaster of the 7th London Fusiliers.

BIBLIOGRAPHY

'Henry Arthur Slatter,' *British Columbia Musician*, 1 May 1928 (JK)

SLIND, Lloyd (Hilmer). Educator, b Dahlton, near Saskatoon, 21 Jun 1910; B SC (Saskatchewan) 1933, B MUS (Montreal) 1947, LRSM 1948, D ED (Florida State) 1955. He was a pupil of Arthur *Collingwood at the *U of Saskatchewan and of Dan *Cameron at the Regina Cons, then taught 1935–9 in Saskatchewan schools. After service in the RCNVR and studies at the *U of Montreal, he was music director 1947–9 at William Dawson High School, Montreal, supervisor of music 1949–51 in Regina public schools, and a voice teacher at the *Regina Cons. He taught 1951–5 at Florida State U and studied composition and conducting there with Kodály. After teaching 1953, 1954, and 1955 at the Victoria Summer School of Education and 1955–6 at the Vancouver Normal School, he taught 1956–75 in the Faculty of Education at the *U of British Columbia. He conducted workshops 1954–66 in Canada and the USA and wrote extensively on music education. Slind was a founding member in 1957 and president 1958–9 of the *BCMEA and a founding member of the *CMEA (1960) and the ISME (Canadian delegate 1961–4).

WRITINGS

Melody, Rhythm and Harmony for the Elementary Grades (New York 1953)

More Melody, Rhythm and Harmony (New York 1956)

Play and Sing Book (Boston 1956)

- and Davis, D. Evan. *Bringing Music to Children: Music Methods for the Elementary School Teacher* (New York 1964)
- and Churchley, F., eds. Basic Goals in Music series, 8 vols, 6 LPs (Toronto 1964–72). Slind was also co-author of the following vols in the series:
- and Churchley. *Basic Goals in Music 4* (1964), 2nd edn with Churchley and Terry, issued as *Whales and Nightingales* (1972)
- and Churchley. *Basic Goals in Music 5* (1964)
- and Churchley. *Basic Goals in Music 6* (1965)
- Churchley and Cowan. *Basic Goals in Music* (1966)

BNSG

SLOAN, T.R. (Thomas Reginald). Lawyer, composer, b Hamilton, Ont, 21 May 1889, d there 3 Nov 1950. He studied law at Osgoode Hall, Toronto, and music at the Hamilton Cons (*RHCM). Although Sloan was a successful and prolific composer of songs and of short works for band, orchestra, or choir, music remained an avocation. (A practitioner of civil and criminal law, he became a King's Counsel in 1946.) Beginning to compose in the 1930s, he produced over 40 pieces including 'All Pals Together' which was popular with US and British military bands and became the signature tune of the English band leader George Scott-Wood, who recorded it for Regal Zonophone; 'God Bless the Shores of England,' recorded by the *Coliseum Chorus for Victor; 'Victory Cavalcade,' introduced by Al Jolson; and 'That Indefinable Feeling,' sung by Rudy Vallee and recorded by the King Cole Swingsters. Sloan's publishers included Mills Music, Shapiro & Bernstein, Campbell-Connelly, G.V. *Thompson, and the Hamilton firm Primogram. Sloan joined the CPRS in 1939 and was later a member of its advisory committee. The musical rights of his estate are administered by CAPAC. Sloan was chairman 1945–50 of the Band Concert Committee of the Hamilton Parks Board and initiated weekly band concerts in the city's parks.

Slovenia. The first substantial Canadian immigration from Slovenia (the northwestern region of the Kingdom of Serbs, Croats, and Slovenes, which was renamed *Yugoslavia in 1929) occurred 1918–29. Peasants and labourers moved to Ontario, many becoming farmers on the Niagara peninsula. An influx of professionals and tradesmen to Toronto began after World War II. In 1976 there were an estimated 50,000 Slovenian-Canadians. In large Slovenian settlements, the first musical organization to be formed usually has been a choir, sponsored by a church (Roman Catholic is the major denomination) or cultural association. In the mid-1970s a dozen Slovenian choirs flourished in major cities from Montreal to Vancouver. Folk dance groups were associated with less than half of these groups. There also were several bands, each consisting of a singer, an accordionist, a clarinetist, a trumpeter, and, occasionally, a guitarist, which played polkas and waltzes at weddings and at parties sponsored by cultural associations. The most famous Slovenian-Canadian musician is the accordionist Walter Ostanek of St Catharines, Ont. One of Canada's Mr Polkas (Gaby *Haas is another), Ostanek has made many recordings for the Arc, Axe, and Marathon labels and is known throughout North America. TR

SMALE, George (Albert). Organist-choirmaster, educator, b Delaware Township, near London, Ont, 12 May 1905; ATCM organ 1934, ATCM voice 1934. After studies with George Lethbridge in London, Smale moved in 1927 to Brantford, Ont, where he served as organist-choirmaster at a succession of churches including Zion United 1939–70. He became music director for Brantford Schools in 1937, served 1945–70 as music director of the Ontario School for the Blind (renamed the W. Ross Macdonald School), and was principal 1970–4 of the *Western Ontario Cons, London, Ont. He also taught 1937–57 at the Ontario Dept of Education summer school in Toronto. He founded and was the conductor 1937–45 of the Varié Singers, a female choir which performed throughout Ontario, and was the conductor 1946–53 of the Cockshutt Male Choir, which under his direction achieved a high performance standard and was invited to perform on the CBC several times. Smale has been president of the music section of the Ontario Educational Assn (*OMEA) 1944–5, of the *ORMTA 1960–1, and of the *Canadian Music Festival Adjudicators' Assn 1973–5. He set up in the Brantford Music Festival a scholarship for performance of Canadian compositions and was host 1975–6 on a voluntary basis for a CKWR-FM, Kitchener, radio show devoted exclusively to Canadian music.

Smale's wife Marnie (Margaret), a staunch supporter of music in Brantford for over 40 years, served 1950–4 as president of the Brantford Music Club and 1960–2 as president of the Brantford SO Assn. She resumed the latter position in 1977. (GKG)

SMALLEY, Cardo (Brooks). Violinist, violist, conductor, b London 13 Mar 1910, d Victoria, BC, 7 Sep 1977. He studied in Port Arthur (Thunder Bay), Ont, with his father, B. Gunton Smalley (1887–1942), a graduate of the RAM who moved to Canada in 1910, organized and conducted the Thunder Bay Philharmonic 1910–29, and was organist-choirmaster at the First Baptist Church.

In 1930 the younger Smalley performed as a solo violinist on CJOR radio, Vancouver. He continued his studies in Vancouver with Jean *de Rimanoczy and William Primrose and, on scholarship, with Szymon Goldberg at the *U of British Columbia. In 1932 he joined the *Vancouver SO, becoming assistant concertmaster in 1937 and associate concertmaster in 1965. In 1933 he became concertmaster of the CNRV Concert Orchestra, a forerunner of the *CBC Vancouver Chamber Orchestra of which he was concertmaster until 1956 and a member until 1970. He was also concertmaster ca 1935–56 for concerts sponsored by BC Electric at the *Malkin Bowl. Smalley was a leading Vancouver studio and radio musician, concertmaster 1944–5 of the CBR Symphony, and music director of the Gipsy Strings, a CBC radio orchestra which intermittently ca 1944–59 broadcast programs of Hungarian, Rumanian, and Russian gypsy music. Retiring from the Vancouver SO in 1967, Smalley was music director 1967–73 of the New Westminster SO and a teacher 1970–3 at Douglas College (New Westminster). In 1973 he joined the *Victoria SO and began teaching at the *Victoria Cons. The Vancouver jazz guitarist Felix Smalley was his brother. (BNSG)

SMITH, Bill (William Ernest). Saxophonist, clarinetist, composer, editor, photographer, record producer, b Bristol, England, 12 May 1938. He studied aeronautical design at the North Staffordshire Technical Institute in Alsager, England, before moving in 1963 to Toronto. There he collaborated with John *Norris in the production of *Coda*, 1963–76 as art director, after 1967 as co-publisher (with Norris), and after 1976 as co-editor (with David Lee). He was a founder in 1968 (and has been co-producer with Norris) of Sackville Records. He has written extensively for *Coda* and also has contributed to other music publications. His photographs have appeared in books (eg, *For What Time I Am In This World*, Toronto 1977), in jazz magazines published in North America and Europe, and in a series of exhibitions entitled *Imagine the Sound*, begun in 1979.

Having played drums and trumpet in England before 1963, he took up the soprano saxophone during a sojourn there 1966–7, studying with Ronnie Beer and, after his return to Toronto, with Paul *Brodie, Brian *Barley, and James Warburton. He began performing publicly in 1973 with Stuart *Broomer. Becoming the leading soprano saxophonist and clarinetist of the avant garde of Canadian jazz, he has been a founder and member of a succession of performing groups, including the All-Time Sound Effects Orchestra, the *CCMC 1974–7, and the Avant Garde Jazz Revival Band 1975–6. He also was a founding member of Air Raid in 1978 and the New Art Music Ensemble (NAME) in 1979. He has composed several pieces for these groups, among them *Goat's Hill Road* – recorded by Smith and Broomer (for the LP *Conversation Pieces*, 1976, Onari 002) and by the Toronto saxophonist Maury Coles – and *Somewhat Surprised* (published in *Music Works*, Winter 1978). Smith is a member of CAPAC. The Onari label, under which Coles, the guitarist Lloyd Garber, and NAME (completed by David Lee, cello and bass, and David Prentice, violin) also have recorded, is an outgrowth of Onari Productions, established by Smith and his wife Clomin Onari in 1973 to promote concerts in Toronto by US and Canadian jazz musicians.

BIBLIOGRAPHY
Miller, Mark. 'The free spirits of N.A.M.E.,' Toronto *Globe and Mail*, 6 Oct 1979
– 'A new kind of jazz moves in,' *CanComp*, 144, Oct 1979
MM

SMITH, Gustave. Teacher, organist, composer, writer, painter, draftsman, b London 14 Feb 1826, d in or near Ottawa 6 Dec (Feb?) 1896. His grandfather, a well-to-do English manufacturer of metal goods, traded with Napoleon and eventually settled in France; his father, educated at Oxford U, and his Swiss mother, a fine amateur musician, lived in Paris, but Gustave was born on a visit to England. At eight he became a pupil of his mother's teacher, P.J.G. Zimmermann, at the Paris Cons. He continued his studies until 1844, though presumably not as a regular student but as an 'observer.' Health problems necessitated a sojourn in Marseilles, and in the next dozen years he also studied painting, fought as a corporal in the 1848 revolution (on the republican side), travelled in Germany and India, and in 1856 obtained from Auber, the director of the conservatory, a testimonial letter stating that he had completed the courses in harmony and 'haute composition.' For an act of bravery (rescuing a wounded comrade in 1848) he was appointed a Chevalier of the Legion of Honour in 1860.

Smith came to Canada in March 1856 and worked at first for a German painter, Ruther. He married Hermine Leprohon, daughter of the wood sculptor Louis-Xavier Leprohon, in 1857, became a convert to Roman Catholicism, and served ca 1860 as organist-choirmaster at St Patrick's Church, Montreal. He taught at the Dames du Sacré-Coeur convent at Sault-au-Recollet – where Emma Lajeunesse (*Albani) was among his pupils – and wrote an *Abécédaire musical* which remained in print for some 60 years. He contributed a series of articles on music teaching to *Le Pays* in 1858 and wrote eight articles on 'Musique et musiciens' (under the name Diérix) and a column, 'Chronique musicale' (signed Caecilius), for *L'Écho du cabinet de lecture paroissial* in 1862. With his father-(or brother-)in-law, Leprohon, he established a small printshop in 1863. They took over the young magazine *Les Beaux-Arts* at the beginning of 1864, turning it into 'une revue des sciences, des lettres, de l'industrie.' The magazine had few subscribers and ceased publication in May.

After a year in New York and two in New Orleans (ca 1866–8) as music teacher and organist at St Patrick's Church there, Smith returned to Canada and settled in Ottawa. For the departments of Agriculture, Railways, and Public Works in turn, he worked as a draftsman and cartographer. For many years he also was organist at Notre-Dame Basilica. He taught music at the Grey Nuns' convent and the Collège d'Ottawa and established a music school at the corner of Rideau and King Edward streets. In 1868 he served for 10 months as co-editor of *Le Courrier d'Ottawa* and in 1869 he delivered a lecture on 'Les Beaux-arts' before the Institut canadien-français. The Montreal periodical *L'Album musical* printed Smith's series 'Du mouvement musical en Canada,' covering 25 years of music, the first critical survey to be written. He also wrote for other periodicals and newspapers – eg, *L'Ordre* in Montreal and *Le Foyer domestique* in Ottawa (later *Album des familles*) – and painted in water-colour. He became deaf towards the end of his life and suffered a stroke in 1894.

Although his life story is insufficiently known, Smith appears to be one of the most versatile and interesting pioneers of the second half of the 19th century. He was a product of both the British and the French civilizations, and his activities encompassed music, the visual arts, and journalism. Most of his compositions were occasional pieces, but his musical instruction books won a great measure of popularity. The *NL of C preserves some of his papers and scores in manuscript.

Smith was the great-grandfather of the composer André *Prévost. See also Charles Écuyer.

SELECTED COMPOSITIONS
PIANO
L'Aragonaise. *Les Beaux-Arts*, vol 1, Sep 1863
La Comète. S.T. Pearce nd
Dolly's Quadrilles. S.T. Pearce ca 1858
Doux Souvenirs. 1886. Ms
En Avant !!! Pre-1864. Ms?
Souvenirs de la Savoie. F. Boucher 1884
Valse. *Le Foyer domestique*, vol 3, 1 Dec 1878
CHOIR
'Ave Maria.' A. Lavigne 1874
Cantate à l'occasion du 50ème anniversaire de la fondation du Petit Séminaire de Sainte-Thérèse (A. B. Routhier). 1875. Ms?
'O salutaris.' *L'Écho du cabinet de lecture paroissial*, vol 4, 1 Mar 1862
'Le Pape-Roy ou l'Univers catholique' (G. Smith). L.J. Pregen 1860
'Prosternez-vous' (?). *Le Foyer domestique* 1877
Several masses. All ms

WRITINGS
Le Parfait Musicien ou Grammaire musicale (Montreal 1859)
Abécédaire musical (Montreal 1861); 38th edn (Montreal 1901); 78th edn (Montreal 1920)
Compte-rendu de la réception de l'orgue de la chapelle Wesleyenne, le 5 février 1861 (Montreal 1861)
'Du mouvement musical en Canada,' *Album musical*, 12 instalments, Dec 1881-Dec 1882
Le Guide de l'organiste, 2nd edn (Montreal 1874), 3rd edn (Montreal 1879)
Le Gamma musical (Ottawa 1887)
Le Claviste (Ottawa 1890)
'Souvenirs et relations de voyages (1844–1856),' unpubl ms (1895–6). Copy at NL of C
Articles for newspapers, periodicals

BIBLIOGRAPHY
Boutet, Edgar. 'Organiste et journaliste,' Ottawa *Le Droit*, 8 Nov 1958
HK

SMITH, Leo (Joseph Leopold). Composer, cellist, writer, teacher, b Birmingham, England, 26 Nov 1881, d Toronto 18 Apr 1952; B MUS (Manchester) 1902, hon FRMCM (Manchester College) 1925. Smith's mother was an accomplished pianist, his father a teacher. One of seven children, Smith was a child prodigy on the cello, studying with W.H. Priestley in Birmingham and Carl Fuchs in Manchester. He gave a full solo recital at eight during the Harrison concert series at Birmingham Town Hall. Studies followed at the Royal Manchester College of Music, where he was later a junior instructor, and with Henry Hiles at Manchester U. A cellist in the Hallé Orchestra, he also played in chamber groups and (on a freelance basis) on tours to various centres in northern England. Compositions from his years as a student and young professional include a *Symphonic Movement in E Minor* (now lost) and many songs, among them some to texts by his brother Arnold, a poet. He was for five years a member of the orchestra of the Royal Opera House, Covent Garden. From this period he recalled playing under such conductors as Richter and such composers as Delius, Elgar, Debussy, and the young Bartók.

Smith emigrated to Canada in 1910, almost immediately joining the *Welsman TSO and becoming principal cellist for that orchestra during its last season (1917–18). His appointment to the teaching staff of the *TCM was announced in the fall of 1911. There he taught theory, composition, history, and cello and played in the Cons Trio and later (1929–41) in the *Cons String Quartet. He was also a member of the *Toronto String Quartette and the *Academy String Quartet. Revealing gifts as a literary stylist, he became a contributing editor 1918–35 to the *Conservatory Quarterly Review*, often writing more of the contents of each issue than his title would suggest. Early in his Toronto years Smith married the violinist Lena Hayes (188?–1956).

Leo Smith

Smith's professional career broadened considerably in the 1930s and 1940s. He was principal cellist 1932–40 in the TSO and held a similar position with the Toronto Philharmonic Orchestra (*Promenade Symphony Concerts) from 1938 to the mid-1940s. He also wrote the program notes for the latter. Smith played an active, though characteristically little-publicized, role as executive committee member 1946–51 of the AF of M Toronto local 149. Acquiring skill on the viola da gamba, he encouraged other musicians to cultivate the viol family, using the historic chest of viols belonging to *Hart House. He later gave concerts on these instruments and introduced them into some of his works.

Composition, writing, and teaching continued to absorb Smith. His three textbooks, *Musical Rudiments* (Boston 1920), *Music of the 17th and 18th Centuries* (Toronto 1931), and *Elementary Part-Writing* (Oakville, Ont, 1939), all achieved wide use and went into several editions. Appointed lecturer in the Faculty of Music, *U of Toronto in 1927, he became a professor on the inauguration of the honour music program in 1938, a post he held until his retirement in 1950. Remembered as a gentle, soft-spoken (at times even dreamy) Englishman, an erudite scholar, and a sensitive performer, Smith influenced a large number of young professionals through several generations that saw crucial changes in higher education in music. His pupils included Marcus *Adeney, Louis *Applebaum, John *Beckwith, Keith *Bissell, Howard Fuller *Brown, Kenneth *Peacock, Margaret *Sargent, and Bertha *Tamblyn. On his retirement, Smith was persuaded by friends to take up a position as critic with the *Globe and Mail*, where he provided a model of thoughtful, elegantly expressed comment until his death in 1952.

Smith said of his own music that he wished 'to pipe Canadian tunes' but feared they would always be 'sung to an English ground bass.' Though showing liberal acceptance of modern trends, he preferred in his own music to continue in the vein of impressionism, tinged with modality and Celtic lilt, which marked the music of composers in his youth such as Bax, Delius, or Edward MacDowell. He applied this approach with success to settings based on Canadian folk sources or texts by leading Canadian poets. He incorporated Quebec fiddle tunes in *Tambourin* for violin and piano, arranged West-Coast Indian songs for concert use, and set well-loved verses such as Duncan Campbell Scott's 'When Twilight Walks in the West' with the same sensitiveness found in his leisurely, finely felt settings of Shakespeare, Blake, Swinburne, and other poets of the English tradition. Though at its best in understated and perhaps elegiac harmonies, as seen in the Scott song or the Delius-like *A Summer Idyll*, and leaning frequently on 6/8 folk-dance rhythms, Smith's music can also achieve dramatic impact, as in his version of the Tsimshian song 'Nalkina,' taken from Marius *Barbeau's collection and translated by Scott as 'Whose Brother Am I?' His later output contains several works for voices with a few instruments, the major cycles of these being the *Four Trios* for high voice, cello, and piano, on Elizabethan English lyrics, and *London Street Cries* (also titled *Old London Street Cries* in some copies) for one or two solo voices, cello, and piano – the latter an interesting revival of a genre cultivated by Weelkes, Gibbons, and their contemporaries. His *String Quartet in D* was performed in Canada and also in Britain as part of a BBC program in 1935 devoted to music in Canada. His *Cello Sonata in E Minor* won a CPRS prize in 1943. Smith's manuscripts and writings are held in the *NL of C.

COMPOSITIONS
ORCHESTRA
An Ancient Song (Henry VIII). Ms
Divertissement in Waltz Time. Orch (pf). Ms
Elegy for Small Orchestra. Ms
Little Pretty Nightingale. Ms
Occasion for Strings. Ms
A Summer Idyll. 1945. Cl, str. Ms. RCI 233/Cap ST 6261 (*CBC Wpg O)
CHAMBER
Celtic Trio. Pf trio. Ms
Four Pieces from *The Book of Irish Country Songs*. Vc, pf. Priv publ
Four Pieces on an Old English Style. Vc, pf. Schmidt 1946
A Horse Race Ballad. Vn, vc, hp. Ms
Old London Street Cries. 2 singers, vc, pf. Ms
Quartet in D. 1932. Str quar. Ms
Shakespearean Music (arr). 2 treb viol, gamb (viol, gamb, hpd). Ms
Sonata in E Minor. 1943. Vc, pf. Ms
Three Ravens. Pf trio. Ms
Trio (Pavane). Treb viol, gamb, hpd. Ms
2 arr of French Canadian folk tunes for vn, pf: *Tambourin* and *Trochaios* (both 1930). Both FH 1960
4 trios for v, vc, pf: *The Passionate Shepherd, Her Reply, Spring's Welcome, Little Peggy Ramsay*
Several other works for vc, pf, including *Father O'Flynn* and *Indian Romance* (1935). Both ms
Many other arr publ by FH and G. Schirmer
PIANO
Suite for Piano. Ms
Three Pieces for Piano. FH 1937
Many arr for pf publ by GVT and others
CHOIR
'Beloved and Blest' (Swinburne). Male vs. G. Schirmer 1914
'Christmas Bells,' part song (Longfellow). G. Schirmer 1916
'Fresh from the Dewy Hill' (Blake). Female vs. Alexander & Cable 1929
'Night' (Swinburne). Male vs. G. Schirmer 1914
'On Dante's Track' (Swinburne). Male vs. G. Schirmer 1914
'We Are the Music Makers' (O'Shaughnessy). Female vs. Alexander & Cable 1930
VOICE
Five Songs (Blake, Browning, Swinburne). Ca 1912. V, pf. WR 1912
Four Songs (Leigh Hunt, Poe, Swinburne). V, pf. G. Schirmer 1914
'To One in Paradise' (Poe). Ca 1924. V, pf. Ms
Songs of Experience (Blake). 1941(?). V, pf. Ms
Three Songs (D.C. Scott). V, pf. FH 1930
Also 23 other works for v and pf, 3 works for v and instr, and arr for v and instr
Many other arr, including 5 of French-Canadian folk-songs, 6 of Elizabethan songs and ballads, and several arr of Old English songs using Elizabethan instr

WRITINGS
'The development of string music,' *Canadian Courier*, vol 12, 12 Oct 1912
'On having photisms,' 'Coloured music,' *CanJM*, vol 2, Sep 1915
'A survey of music in Canada,' *British Association for the Advancement of Science Handbook of Canada* (Toronto 1924)
'Music in our universities,' *Canadian Forum*, vol 5, Aug 1925
'Music,' *Encyclopedia of Canada* vol 4 (Toronto 1936)
'William Byrd: instrumental music,' *CRMA*, vol 2, Aug–Sep 1943
'Competition reveals outstanding talent,' *CRMA* series, vol 2, Oct–Nov 1943, Dec 1943–Jan 1944; vol 3, Feb–Mar, Apr–May 1944

BIBLIOGRAPHY
McCarthy, Pearl. *Leo Smith: A Biographical Sketch* (Toronto 1956) JB

SMITH, Nellie (m Loukides). Contralto, b Skipton, near Bradford, Yorkshire, 1906, d Toronto 12 Jun 1958; LRAM. She began her career in England, singing in concert and on radio before moving to Canada in 1930. In November 1933 she made her North American debut with the *Toronto Mendelssohn Choir in Mendelssohn's *Elijah*. She also was a soloist with the choir 1944–50 in its annual performances of Handel's *Messiah*. She made her *TSO debut 15 Apr 1947 as a soloist in Beethoven's *Symphony No. 9*. In 1948 she sang in *Messiah* and Bach's *St Matthew Passion* for the CBC, and in 1949 she made her *CBC Opera Company debut as Widow Sedley in Britten's *Peter Grimes*. She sang in the company's 1951 performance of Britten's *Albert Herring*, and in 1952 repeated her role in *Peter Grimes*. Smith also was a member of the CBC Light Opera Company and sang leading roles in all of its Gilbert & Sullivan productions. These included Ruth in *The Pirates of Penzance*, 1948, 1949, and 1950 and the Duchess of Plaza-Toro in *The Gondoliers* in 1952. She made her last major appearances as the Mother in Menotti's *The Consul* in 1953 and 1954 for the Opera Festival of Toronto (*COC). Smith taught 1944–58 at the TCM (*RCMT), where her pupils included Margaret Abbott and Gordon *Wry.

SMITH, W. (William) **Bramwell Jr.** Bandmaster, administrator, trumpeter, b Ottawa 3 Mar 1929. While studying trumpet 1945–9 with Ellis McLintock Sr at the *RCMT he appeared with various dance bands. He moved to Washington, DC, as trumpet soloist (1949–57) with the US Marine Band. While in Washington he was chairman 1962–7 of the brass and winds department of American U and founder in 1959 of a ceremonial group, the Herald Trumpets, and of the Repertory Brass Ensemble. He also composed and arranged music for official functions, including the presidential inauguration of John F. Kennedy in 1960, and was a music consultant for the White House. As head clinician for Leblanc-Holton musical instruments he toured North America for a short time, conducting orchestras and bands and playing at university seminars. On his return to Canada he served 1967–75 as music director of the RCMP Band and directed the RCMP Centennial Review in 1973 (See Bands: 5 / Police bands). In 1975 he was appointed educational consultant for Yamaha of Canada. He has recorded as a soloist (*Bram Smith and His Trumpet*, 1957, Golden Crest 4012) and as music director of the RCMP Band (*Dynamic Sound*, 1972, Polydor 2917 068). His pupils have included his son, W. Bramwell Smith III (b Silver Springs, Md, 26 Dec 1952), who later studied in Toronto with Arnie Chycoski and Don Johnson and in 1974 became the lead trumpeter of *Nimmons 'N' Nine Plus Six. (JK)

SNELL, 'Peggy' (Margaret) (b Young). Arts patron, b Toronto 18 Jun 1904; BA (Toronto) 1928. Her interest in music developed through organizing concerts for children. She joined the TSO Women's Committee in 1940 and remained a member in 1980, was president 1961–3 and for 20 years (1950–70) a member of the executive of the *Women's Musical Club of Toronto, and was a founding member (1960) of the *NYO, secretary 1965–7, and vice-president 1971–3, and remained on its board until 1978. She worked 1971–6 on the national committee of the *Canadian Music Competitions, served 1969–72 on the board of governors of the *Stratford Festival, and was made a senator of the festival in 1972. She was a founding member and the president 1970–2 of the *Chamber Players of Toronto.

SNIDER (Sniderman). Family of musicians in Toronto: 1 / Jack Sniderman and 2 / Lou Snider and 3 / Art and Dave Snider, sons of Jack.

1 **Jack**. Teacher, composer, drummer, b Russia 1897, d Delray Beach, Fla, 10 Oct 1977. Moving to England and then to Canada, he played drums in pit bands in Toronto and, during the 1920s, at the B.F. Keith Theatre in Ottawa. In Ottawa he formed and conducted the Young Judea Orchestra. He took his family in 1930 to Toronto, began playing saxophone and violin, and joined Charlie Hannigan's Mountaineers, a country band which broadcast on CKCL and performed regularly at Playter's Hall. He taught until 1975 in Toronto, privately and at the United Music School opened by his son Art. He taught all his sons. His compositions include *Judea* (for the Young Judea Orchestra), *Melody for Heavy Bells* (late 1920s, for Percival *Price, and a part of the Dominion Carillonneurs' repertoire for over 50 years), and such songs as 'Sweet Caroline' (1923, recorded by Tommy *Ambrose in 1960) and 'Oriole' (1976, recorded by Lee Sanford).

2 **Lou** (Louis). Organist, pianist, composer, b Toronto 13 Jun 1918. At 10 he began playing piano at the B.F. Keith Theatre in Ottawa. In Toronto he made his radio debut in 1931 on CKCL and also played with the Mountaineers. He served intermittently 1937–66 as music director for Ken Soble's amateur show on CKCL, then on CHML, and finally on CHCH-TV. During a long association with CBC radio, he was the organist for the children's show 'Just Mary' (late 1930s to mid-1960s, except for a period of RCAF service in World War II) and for the *Happy Gang 1948–51, co-star of shows with Jackie Rae and with the Australian singer Peggy Brooks, and music director (summer 1951) for 'Time for a Song' starring Brooks and Howard Manning. His own shows were heard on CBC (eg, 'Lou Snider and Rhythm' with the bassist Murray Lauder and the drummer Reef McGarvey in 1953) and on CHUM (1958). He later played in cocktail lounges in the Toronto area and produced industrial shows. He played piano 1978–9 for Suzanne Stevens on the Global TV show 'For Lovers Only.' He has made the LPs *Holiday in Canada* (1957, Decca 8666), *Popular Songs by Lou Snider* (1960, RCI 175, with Peggy Brooks), *Lou Snider and Lloyd Edwards* (1963, CTL 019), and *Lou Snider Plays Snider* (1970, Scope 477-5701). The last-named presents 10 of his own piano pieces (many reflecting the influence of Chopin), 2 by Art Sni-

der, and 1, *Judea*, by their father. Lou Snider also appears as organist on two LPs by Bill *Richards. Several of Snider's songs were published by BMIC. He is an affiliate of PRO Canada.

3 **Art** (Arthur). Pianist, arranger, record producer, b Ottawa 24 Aug 1926. He studied arranging with Benny Louis and harmony with Phillip Podoliak. In his teens he played piano in Toronto dance bands and in 1946 he began coaching pop performers. He managed many singers in the years following, among them, briefly, Gordon *Lightfoot. In 1948 he established the United Music School which he sold in 1956 to his brother Dave (trumpeter, b Hull, Que, 16 Aug 1920, who later converted the school to the Dave Snider Music Centre, which retailed sheet music). Art Snider worked in the 1940s as a conductor's copyist and directed the chorus 1956-65 for CBC TV's 'Country Hoedown' and 1965–70 for 'The Tommy *Hunter Show.' He established Chateau Records (1956–61), which released some 30 LPs and 60 singles by the Allen Sisters, Tommy *Ambrose, Trump *Davidson, the Hames Sisters, Pat Hervey, Gordon Lightfoot, and others. In 1967 he established Sound Canada, a studio which has produced recordings for various labels including his own, Periwinkle, begun in 1973 with a roster which included Mickey Andrews, Dave Broadfoot, Ina Harris, the Peaches, Tammi Rafferty, and Lee Sanford. MM

SNIDERMAN, Eleanor (b Koldofsky). Record producer, patron, b Toronto 9 Sep 1920. The sister of the violinist Adolph *Koldofsky and the wife of Sam *Sniderman, she helped establish the sound-recording archive of the *U of Toronto Faculty of Music in 1963 and continued to assist in its later development. She has worked as a volunteer with the *Women's Musical Club of Toronto and the *Canadian Music Competitions and professionally with *Boot Records and, later, her own company. For Boot's Master Concert Series label she produced best-selling recordings by *Canadian Brass and the guitarist Liona *Boyd. In 1975 she founded Proclaim Publications, incorporated with the broad aim both of publishing and of recording and launched that year with Anton *Kuerti's integral recording of the Beethoven piano sonatas on the company's Aquitaine label. The Kuerti album was followed in 1976 by three more Aquitaine releases presenting the violinist Victor Schultz, the tenor Alan Woodrow, and the cellist Gisela *Depkat with the pianist Raffi *Armenian. A recording taken from a 1951 recital given by Lotte Lehmann and Gwendolyn *Koldofsky was released in 1977. The *Canadian Children's Opera Chorus recorded Menotti's *Chip and His Dog* in 1979. By 1980 Aquitaine had released some 40 recordings, of which two had won *Juno Awards: in 1976 Anton Kuerti's Beethoven set and in 1979 Judy *Loman's performance of R. Murray *Schafer's *The Crown of Ariadne*. The Kuerti recordings were the first of classical music to receive a Juno. Eleanor Sniderman has said that her purpose is to produce high-standard indigenous recordings of outstanding Canadian performers, to supervise personally all aspects of their production, and to provide maximum promotion. In 1976 she signed a contract with *CBS Records for international distribution of Aquitaine recordings.

BIBLIOGRAPHY

Littler, William. 'Canadian classics take off,' *Toronto Star*, 28 Aug 1976

Cuthbert, Art. 'Eleanor of Aquitaine,' *Audio Scene*, Sep 1976

Fetherling, Doug. 'Classical hustle,' *The Canadian*, 31 Dec 1976

Dzeguze, Kaspars. 'Eleanor, for the record,' *Maclean's*, 8 Oct 1979

(AHC)

SNIDERMAN, Sam (Samuel). Record retailer, patron, b Toronto 15 Jun 1920. The family business, Sniderman Radio Sales and Service, was established in Toronto on College St in 1929 by his brother Sidney. Sam Sniderman introduced the sale of records in 1937, and eventually this became the backbone of the business. In 1959 a second outlet was opened in a Yonge St furniture store. In 1961 the two outlets were consolidated as Sam the Record Man on downtown Yonge St. With extensive and wide-ranging holdings, the store claims the largest selection of retail records in the world. In 1969 a national Sam the Record Man franchise chain was established, with a wholly owned subsidiary, Roblan Distributors Ltd (of which Sniderman became president, his son Robert vice-president, and Sidney Sniderman secretary-treasurer), set up as its supplier. By 1979 71 stores were in operation. A second franchise system of mini-dealerships began in 1978; 39 were in operation in 1979. Sniderman's sales in 1978 accounted for over 10 per cent of the national retail record business, his major competition coming from chains owned by large record companies.

A colourful personality, Sniderman has given substantial support to the Canadian music industry by his enthusiasm and by the exposure his stores have afforded records by Canadians. With his wife, Eleanor *Sniderman, he made possible the recordings archive at the Edward Johnson Building, *U of Toronto, in 1963, donating many recordings and arranging the donation or acquisition of many others. He also has assisted the *Mariposa Folk Festival financially. In 1977 he became a member of the three-man *CNE Grandstand Attractions Committee. Sniderman was made a Member of the *Order of Canada in 1976 and has received many other awards and tributes for his contribution to Canadian music.

BIBLIOGRAPHY

Franklyn, Stephen. 'Yes this is Sam the Record Man,' *Weekend Magazine*, 14 Dec 1965

Rasky, Frank. 'The long-playing war,' *Canadian Magazine*, 20 May 1967

Adilman, Sid. 'The unknown side of Sam the Record Man,' *Toronto Life*, Jul 1969

Waxman, Ken. 'Yes, this is Sam the Record Man,' *Financial Post Magazine*, Sep 1968

Levitch, Gerald. 'Self-made Sam,' (*Toronto Star*) *The City*, 6 May 1979

MM

SNOW, Hank (Clarence Eugene). Singer-songwriter, guitarist, b Liverpool, NS, 9 May 1914, naturalized US 1958. He began playing guitar as a child. Leaving home at 12, he worked on fishing boats and trans-Atlantic ships and in the fish-processing plants of Nova Scotia. Inspired by his life-long hero, the US country singer-yodeller Jimmie Rodgers, whom he heard first in 1930, Snow began to perform shortly afterwards and made his radio debut ca 1933 on CHNS, Halifax, with the show 'Clarence Snow and His Guitar.' In 1936 he made his first recording for Victor: 'Lonesome Blue Yodel' (in the Rodgers style) and 'The Prisoned Cowboy,' both his own songs. In the next 10 years he was popular in Canada, touring widely and playing for national broadcasts on the CBC and for local programs in the Maritimes. Albums of Snow's songs were published by *Thompson (*Cowboy Songs by Hank the Yodelling Ranger* 1942) and *Canadian Music Sales. Snow was accompanied by the Rainbow Ranch Boys, and for some of his dozen or more 78s 1936–42 for Victor was joined by the singer Anita Carter. In 1946 Snow

Hank Snow

went to the USA, adopting a cowboy image and developing some popularity in Texas. He returned to Canada briefly in 1947 and 1949 and then settled permanently in the USA.

In 1950, with the assistance of fellow Rodgers disciple Ernest Tubb, Snow became a regular performer at the Grand Ole Opry on WSM in Nashville. He made that city his home and in 1979 still appeared with the Opry. His recording for RCA Victor of his *'I'm Movin' On' (1950) was one of the most successful singles of the first 50 years of recorded country music. It was followed by such hits as 'Golden Rocket' (1950), 'Rhumba Boogie' (1951), 'Bluebird Island' (1951), 'The Gold Rush Is Over' (1952), 'I Don't Hurt Anymore' (1954), and 'I've Been Everywhere' (1962). Snow has made over 45 LPs for the RCA Victor or Camden labels, including *Rodgers Songs* (LSP-2043) and *Hank Snow Sings in Memory of Jimmie Rodgers* (LSP-4306), and others of Christmas songs, railroad songs, and sacred songs. Several collections of his hits have been issued, among them *The Best of Hank Snow* (vol 1, LSP-3478; vol 2, LSP-4708) and *The Hits of Hank Snow* (vol 1, KEL1-8093; vol 2, KEL1-8098). Some of Snow's early 78s were reissued on the LP *The Old and the Great Songs* (Cam CAS 836). Sales of Snow's records reached some 60 million by the late 1970s.

Snow returned frequently to Canada in later years for concert and TV appearances and has been acknowledged, along with Wilf *Carter, as one of the fathers of country music in Canada. He was inducted into the Country Music Hall of Fame, Nashville, in 1976 and into the *Juno (Awards) Hall of Fame in 1979.

BIBLIOGRAPHY

The Hank Snow 25th Anniversary Album (Nashville 1961)

MacLeod, Stewart. 'My Gawd, you've got to be the greatest, Hank,' *Weekend Magazine*, 9 Sep 1967

O'Malley, Martin. 'In silver heels and silver toes in dazzling rhinestoned reds in cabin cruiser, in Lincoln Continental – it don't hurt anymore,' Toronto *Globe Magazine*, 10 Jul 1971

Durden-Smith, Jo. 'Nashville gothic,' *Maclean's*, May 1972

Brown, Dick. 'Hank Snow's lament,' *Canadian Magazine*, 1 Mar 1975

(MD)

SNOW, Michael (James Aleck). Pianist, trumpeter, composer, film maker, sculptor, painter, b Toronto 10 Dec 1929. Although more immediately recognized as the creator of the *Walking Woman* sculpture-graphics series (1961–7) and of such films as *Wavelength* (1967) and *La Région centrale* (1970–1), Snow has also been involved for many years in improvised music. A self-taught musician, encouraged during visits to Chicago in the late 1940s by the pianist Jimmy Yancey, Snow played in Toronto traditional-jazz groups while a student 1948–52 at the Ontario College of Art. He took up the trumpet in the early 1950s and after a period in Europe (1953–4) playing in hotel orchestras he worked in Toronto as a pianist with the trumpeter Mike White 1958–61 and with his own bebop groups 1958–62. In the early 1960s he was drawn to free jazz through his association with the *Artists' Jazz Band in Toronto and with the movement's leaders in New York. He continued to perform with the Artists' Jazz Band and was a member 1966–7 of the Toronto New Music Ensemble and a founder in 1974 of the *CCMC. His own music, exemplified by the Chatham Square solo albums, extends into the medium of sound the intensive exploration of ideas and techniques characteristic of his work in the visual arts. In his films, beginning with *New York Eye and Ear Control* (1964), he has often drawn musical and visual elements together to create an 'image-sound composition.' He received a *Molson Prize in 1979.

DISCOGRAPHY

Music for Piano, Whistling, Microphone and Tape Recorder. 1970–2. 2-Chatham Square 1009/10

WITH OTHERS

Mike White *Mike White's Imperial Jazz Band.* 1958. Hallmark CS-6

Carla Bley (Jazz Composer's Orchestra) *Escalator Over the Hill.* (1974). 3-LP-EOTH

See also Discography for the Artists' Jazz Band; CCMC.

BIBLIOGRAPHY

Reid, Dennis. *A Concise History of Canadian Painting* (Toronto 1973)

Hale, Barrie. 'The inventions of Michael Snow,' *The Canadian*, 31 Dec 1976

Creative Canada, vol 1 MM

'Snowbird.' Pop song by Gene *MacLellan. Only his second composition, it was written in the late 1960s, apparently with Anne *Murray's voice in mind. The snowbird is a metaphor for freedom. A single by Murray (Cap 72623) introduced her, and the song, to pop and country music audiences internationally in 1970, selling over one million copies in that year alone. As a result, MacLellan received a special *Juno Award for 1970 as composer of the year. 'Snowbird' has appeared on LPs by many singers, including Burl Ives, Loretta Lynn, Al Martino, Elvis Presley, and Andy Williams, and instrumental versions have been recorded by the duo pianists Ferrante and Teicher and the bandleaders Bert Kaempfert and Lawrence Welk. It is the title tune of the LP by the guitarist Chet Atkins which won the 1971 Grammy Award for best country instrumental performance. It is included also on the composer's LP, *Gene MacLellan*. 'Snowbird' was published in 1970 by Beechwood Music of Canada and appears in Edith *Fowke's *Canadian Vibrations* (Toronto 1972). MM

Société canadienne d'opérette Inc. One of the first opera companies in Quebec, founded in Montreal by Honoré *Vaillancourt and chartered 14 Jul 1921. Its aim was 'to develop the artistic abilities of the members and to instil in the public a liking for good wholesome music' and also 'to work for the establishment of a lyric theatre for and by Canadians.' The troupe was financed chiefly by its president, Rodolphe Monty, and by shareholders, who numbered about 200 by the end of the 1925–6 season.

As its inaugural presentation the society gave Offenbach's *Les Brigands* 16 Oct 1923 at the *Monument national under the musical direction of Albert *Roberval. There were nine productions in 1923–4, including Carl Zeller's *L'Oiseleur* , Offenbach's *La Chanson de Fortunio*, Donizetti's *La Fille du Régiment*, and Strauss' *The Gypsy Baron*.

For 10 consecutive seasons (1923–33) the society offered the public a wide choice of operettas, comic operas, and operas, including *Les Cloches de Corneville, La Fille de Madame Angot, Monsieur Beaucaire, Waltz Dream, Martha, Le Pré aux clercs*, and *The Barber of Seville*, at the Monument national and *His Majesty's Theatre in Montreal or at the *Auditorium in Quebec City. In 1929 *L'Intendant Bigot*, a Canadian opera with music by J.-Ulric Voyer, was presented in Montreal and Quebec.

At the end of the 1930–1 season, the society had given more than 300 performances and could look with pride on its company of 60 performers, 46 choristers, 26 musicians, and 23 administrators and technicians, a total of 155 persons divided into an opera section and a drama section.

Besides engaging some established singers, Vaillancourt also provided opportunities for a host of young performers, including Amanda Alarie, Fournier de Belleval, Camille *Bernard, Louis *Bourdon, Charles-Émile Brodeur, Lionel *Daunais, Geneviève Davis-Lebel, Fabiola Hade, Émile Lamarre, Caro *Lamoureux, Léonide Letourneux, Roméo Mousseau, Paul *Trépanier, and Irène Trudeau. Other artists appearing in the casts were Fleurette *Beauchamp, Louis *Chartier, Marie-Rose Descarries, Élisa Garneau, Armand Gauthier, Conrad *Gauthier, Blanche Gonthier, Charles *Goulet, Arthur Lapierre, Hercule Lavoie, Ernest Loiselle, Fabiola Poirier, Gaston Saint-Jacques, Lucille Turner, and Paul Valade. The company engaged as well such stars as José *Delaquerrière, Jean Grimaldi, Jeanne *Maubourg, and Albert Roberval. Roberval and Vaillancourt shared the artistic directorship, and J.-J. and Jean *Goulet and Sylva Alarie were among the conductors.

Shortly after its foundation, the society launched a popular subscription campaign, selling for a dollar the privilege of contributing a brick towards a proposed four-storey building at 3774 St-Denis St to house its administration and rehearsals. This building, still standing in 1980, was opened with a concert 3 Aug 1925. In 1931 a second subscription campaign was begun for the construction of a national theatre. The sudden death of Vaillancourt early in 1933 put an end to the project, and the company itself only survived another few months under the triumvirate of J.-A.-E. Cartier, Daunais, and Roberval. But the way had been paved for the *Variétés lyriques, established three years later.

Many of the society's vocal scores, orchestra parts, chorus parts, original librettos, translations, and programs are preserved in the Albert Duquesne Collection at the Montreal City Library.

BIBLIOGRAPHY

Album-souvenir de la Société canadienne d'opérette, 28 May 1925

Montreal Music Year Book 1931 and *1932* (Montreal 1931, 1932)

Gour, Romain. *La Palme-Issaurel* (Montreal 1948) PL

Société de musique contemporaine du Québec (SMCQ). Founded in Montreal in 1966 through the efforts of Wilfrid *Pelletier (then director of the music section of the *MACQ), by Jean *Papineau-Couture (president 1966–72), Maryvonne *Kendergi (who became president in 1972), Serge *Garant, and Hugh *Davidson. Jean *Vallerand and Pierre *Mercure also were associated with the initiation of the project. As defined in its statutes, the objective of the SMCQ was to 'disseminate and promote contemporary music, international and Canadian.' The first concert, 15 Dec 1966 at the *Salle Claude-Champagne, Montreal, included works by Boulez, *Schafer, *Mather, and Garant. At first exclusively subsidized by the MACQ, the society later received support from the *Canada Council and the Council of Arts of Greater Montreal. Each season the society has organized a series of six to eight concerts, given in Montreal by the SMCQ Ensemble or by guest groups and soloists. Directed by Serge Garant, the SMCQ Ensemble has varied in size, on occasion numbering as many as 30 musicians, depending on the requirements of the individual program.

Board members of the Société de musique contemporaine du Québec (1969–71): (seated left to right) Serge Garant, Maryvonne Kendergi, Jean Papineau-Couture; (standing left to right) Jean Laurendeau, Bruce Mather, Gilles Tremblay, Jean-Paul Jeannotte, Guy Lachapelle

The SMCQ's guests have included several prominent composers and their best-known interpreters, notably Luciano Berio and the soprano Cathy Berberian in 1968, Olivier Messiaen and the pianist Yvonne Loriod in 1970 and 1978, Karlheinz Stockhausen and his group in 1971, Mauricio Kagel and the Kölner Ensemble für neues Musiktheater in 1974, and Earle Brown in 1976. Among other noted visiting performers have been the duo-pianists Alfons and Aloys Kontarsky in 1972 and 1979, the Percussions de Strasbourg in 1973, and the organists Xavier Darasse in 1975 and Werner Jacob in 1977. The SMCQ Ensemble has appeared in Canadian cities, including Toronto and Vancouver, and at the 9th Festival of International Art at Royan in 1972, the 5th biennial festival 'Reconnaissance des musiques modernes' in Brussels in 1973, the US bicentennial festival in Washington in 1975, and the ISCM World Music Days in Boston in 1976, the last-named followed by a Canadian tour in collaboration with *NMC. The ensemble gave concerts in England, France, Germany, and Belgium in the autumn of 1977 as part of the *Musicanada and *CAPAC-sponsored Rendezvous with Canada series. Pollack Hall, *McGill U, became its Montreal home in 1975.

The SMCQ premiered, presented, or repeated, between 1966 and 1980, more than 500 works of 20th-century composers, including such classics of the era as Schoenberg's *Pierrot Lunaire* in 1968 and complete works for the piano in 1976, and Varèse' *Déserts, Intégrales, Ecuatorial, Ionisation*, and *Octandre* at a concert in 1975 marking the 10th anniversary of the composer's death. About 20 works by Canadian composers were commissioned and introduced by the SMCQ Ensemble during this period, notably *Tremblay's *Souffles (Champs II)* (1968), *Beecroft's *Rasas I* (1968), Jacques *Hétu's *Cycle, Op 16* (1970), Schafer's *Music for the Morning of the World* (1971), *Hawkins' *Waves* (1971), Garant's *Circuits II* (1972), *Morel's *IIKKII (Froidure)* (1972), Papineau-Couture's *Obsession* (1973), Mather's *Madrigal V* (1973), *Saint-Marcoux's *Ishuma* (1974), Alcides *Lanza's *Plectros IV* (1975), *Cherney's *Concerto de Chambre* (1975), Marcelle *Deschênes-Harvey's *Moll, opéralilliput pour six roches molles* (1976), Donald Steven's *Images (Refractions of Time and Space)* (1977),

Otto *Joachim's *Uraufführung* (1977), and *Pépin's *Interactions* (1977). In the years prior to 1980 the SMCQ also gave the Canadian premieres of Gilbert Amy's *Sonata pian' e forte* (1974) and Iannis Xénakis' *épéï (puisque, depuis, since)* (1976) and the first Montreal performance of Elliott Carter's *A Mirror on which to Dwell* (1978). Among the soloists who participated in SMCQ concerts 1966–80 were the *Tudor Singers, John Hawkins, Bruno *Laplante, Phyllis *Mailing, Gilles *Manny, Bruce Mather and Pierrette *LePage, Mary *Morrison, Gary *Relyea, Patricia *Rideout, and Lorraine and Pauline *Vaillancourt.

In the numbers of its concerts and in the interest it has stimulated, the SMCQ has demonstrated its success in accomplishing its primary objectives. On the occasion of its 10th anniversary concert Eric *McLean wrote (*Montreal Star*, 10 Dec 1976): 'The Society deserves the warmest congratulations on such an important birthday ... today, [it] can not only rely on a considerable number of expert interpreters, but a new generation has also entered the field ... Just as important as the development of the ensemble, a faithful audience has been created for this repertoire and it is growing'.

DISCOGRAPHY

Garant *Offrande I* (Morrison sop, SMCQ Ens, Garant dir); *Circuits II; Offrande III* (SMCQ Ens, Garant dir). 1970–3. RCI 368/RCI AMC 2

Mather *Madrigal II*. Morrison sop, Rideout contralto, SMCQ Ens, Garant dir. 1972. RCI 369

Morel *Départs; IIKKII (Froidure)* (SMCQ Ens, Garant dir); *Radiance* (Husaruk vn, Kudlak va, J.-L. Morin vc, SMCQ Ens, Garant dir). 1970–2. RCI 367

Music of Today / Musique d'aujourd'hui, vol 2: Schafer *Requiems for the Party Girl* (Mailing mezzo, SMCQ Ens, Garant dir) – Papineau-Couture *Paysage* (Tudor Singers, SMCQ Ens, Garant dir). 1969–70. RCI 299

Music of Today / Musique d'aujourd'hui, vol 3: Garant *Jeu à quatre* – Hawkins *Remembrances*. SMCQ members, Garant dir. 1968–9. RCI 300/(*Jeu à quatre*) RCI AMC 2

Music of Today / Musique d'aujourd'hui, vol 4: Beecroft *Rasas I* (SMCQ Ens, Garant dir) – J. Hétu *Cycle, Op 16* (J. Hawkins pf, SMCQ Ens, Garant dir). 1970. RCI 301

Saint-Marcoux *Ishuma* (M. Forget sop, SMCQ Ens, Garant dir) – Garant ... *chant d'amours* (P. Vaillancourt sop, J. Fleury-Coutu mezzo, R. Richard bar, J.-L. Morin vc, SMCQ Ens, Garant dir). 1976–8. RCI 422/(... *chant d'amours*) RCI AMC 2

SMCQ: Vivier *Prolifération* (J. Laurendeau ondes M, L.-P. Pelletier pf, Laflamme perc) – W. Douglas *Improvisation III* (J. Laurendeau cl, L.-P. Pelletier pf) – Heard *Voices* (MacKinnon sop, J.-P. Major fl, S. Mustard vc, Hawkins pf, Lachapelle perc, Garant dir). 1969–70. RCI 358

Gilles Tremblay *Souffles (Champs II); Vers (Champs III)*. SMCQ Ens, Garant dir. 1970. RCI 370

Vivier *Lettura di Dante* (P. Vaillancourt sop, SMCQ Ens, Garant dir) – Aitken *Shadows II: Lalita* (Aitken fl, SMCQ Ens, Garant dir). 1973–4. RCI 411

BIBLIOGRAPHY

Gingras, Claude. 'Fondation d'une société de musique contemporaine,' Montreal *La Presse*, 19 Nov 1966

Mather, Bruce. 'La Société de musique contemporaine du Québec,' *Mcan*, 25, Dec 1969

Thériault, Jacques. 'The SMCQ is ahead of the game, because the MSO cannot change with the changing times,' *CanComp*, 46, Jan 1970

Kendergi, Maryvonne. 'SMCQ's audience, program expand,' *MSc*, 256, Nov–Dec 1970

McLean, Eric. 'Composers outstanding with new music,' *Montreal Star*, 13 Apr 1973

Aprahamian, Felix. 'A splash from Canada,' London *Sunday Times*, 9 Nov 1977

Fleuret, Maurice. 'Des Canadiens à Paris,' *Nouvel Observateur*, 680, 21–7 Nov 1977

Schulman, Michael. 'Contemporary music groups thriving across Canada,' *MSc*, 303, Sep–Oct 1978

HPn (ST, CV)

Société des Concerts symphoniques de Montréal. See Montreal Symphony Orchestra.

Société lyrique d'Aubigny. Non-profit organization founded in Quebec City in 1968 to perform opera and oratorio and financed by various governmental and professional bodies. Léandre Lapierre was president 1968–70 and Jean-Pierre Audet succeeded him in 1970. The society has maintained a volunteer choir, which grew from an initial 35 members to about 60 in 1977, and an orchestra, which increased from 24 in 1968 to 45 in 1977, at which time the growth appeared to stabilize; the singers have provided their own costumes. For its soloists the society has called upon young Quebec singers such as Jacqueline *Martel and Marie-Cécile Nadeau. The approximately 20 concerts and performances each year have been conducted by Guy *Bélanger or his father, Edwin. The program has offered operas and religious works. Among the operas have been complete stage performances of Gounod's *Faust* (1969, 1978), Bizet's *Les Pêcheurs de perles* (1970, 1974), Gounod's *Mireille* (1971), and Delibes's *Lakmé* (1971). Performances were given at the *Palais Montcalm until 1972, when the society moved to the *Grand Théâtre and also began to appear around the province of Quebec for various associations. The society has presented, among other notable performances, the Canadian premiere of Puccini's *Messa di Gloria*. MB-L

Société musicale Le Mouvement Vivaldi. Decentralized organization established in 1973 to promote the teaching of string instruments by the method developed by Claude *Létourneau. It continued the work begun by Létourneau in Quebec City under the name Les Jeunes Violonistes, bringing together teachers, parents, students, and benefactors in Quebec, Ontario, New Brunswick, and even France.

The Létourneau method is a Canadian adaptation of the principles of Shinichi Suzuki and Zoltán Kodály and concentrates on the total development of the child (beginning at age three) through the playing of string instruments (Létourneau began his teachings in 1965 with violin; he extended the principles to cello in 1967 and viola in 1970). The child acquires a working knowledge of theory in direct relation to the instrument and is exposed to original music based mainly on the folk music of the region.

In 1965 Létourneau applied his method to about 50 violin students aged 6 to 17, at the same time undertaking to train teachers who wanted to use it. In 1968 a group of Létourneau's pupils took part in the ISME congress in Dijon. The following year some teachers he had trained formed the École Les Jeunes Violonistes to develop new methods and study programs and to increase and diversify the group's activities. One result was the Vivaldi music camp, begun in 1970 and held each summer at a different location in the Quebec City region; its purpose was to provide both teachers and students with intensive study sessions based on the Létourneau method. Beginning in 1971, voluntary groups of parents joined forces to help manage the movement's resources.

In April 1973 the Société musicale Le Mouvement Vivaldi replaced the École Les Jeunes Violonistes and adopted new structures that reflected this evolution. Thus two co-ordinated organizations were founded, offering programs with regular examinations and certificates: the Académie Vivaldi with four levels for students and the Institut Vivaldi for teachers. The courses for teachers have been co-ordinated with the school of music program of *Laval U; more than 150 took them between 1965 and 1980. The name Vivaldi was adopted in homage to the great 18th-century composer whose works were mostly for strings and who devoted his life to teaching the young. Létourneau has served the organization as president and director general, with Wilfrid *Pelletier as honorary president. Books and records on the Létourneau method have been published by the Éditions Les Jeunes Violonistes and, beginning in 1974, by the Éditions de la Volute. (DM)

Société musicale Ste-Cécile. A 50-voice amateur mixed choir founded 15 Dec 1869 in Quebec City by Antoine *Dessane. Dessane, the organist at St-Roch Church at the time, served as the society's president and director until his death in 1873. The society then was reorganized by Célestin *Lavigueur, who gave it a constitution and the motto 'Te Deum laudamus!' However, as early as 1872 Nazaire *LeVasseur had almost complete responsibility for directing it, and he remained its director until 1885. In 1881, at the invitation of the organist Adolphe *Hamel, the society left St-Roch for St-Patrice Church. The same year it published the *Historique de la Société musicale Sainte-Cécile de Québec*, which recorded its activities in detail. It is not known what became of the society after 1885.

The repertoire consisted mainly of masses by Gounod, Haydn, Mozart, Rossini, and Weber, as well as those by Gustave *Gagnon, J.-B. *Labelle, and J.-J. *Perrault. These works were performed at Easter and as part of such special celebrations as the Feast St Cecilia and the pilgrimage to Ste-Anne-de- Beaupré. In 1874 the society began presenting some of the works with instrumental accompaniment, presumably with the assistance of the *Septuor Haydn and the *Union musicale de Québec, which took part regularly in the society's events. (An orchestra of the Société Sainte-Cécile was established ca 1870 but lasted only two years; it was under the successive direction of Célestin Lavigueur, Frédéric Geay, and Calixa *Lavallée.)

One of the many masses premiered in Quebec by the society was Rossini's *Petite Masse solennelle*. It was warmly received despite the fact that the scores, ordered from Belgium in December 1879, arrived only three weeks before Easter. 'The choir was large and the music powerful,' wrote *Le Provincial* (20 Mar 1880). Participating were Frantz *Jehin-Prume, Calixa Lavallée, and Arthur *Lavigne (conducting the orchestra), J.-A. Defoy (piano), and Alexandre Defoy (harmonium). On 20 Nov 1881 Gounod's *St Cecilia Mass*, the first work in the society's repertoire, was revived at St-Sauveur Church.

The Société Sainte-Cécile occasionally sang in the parishes around Quebec City (Ange-Gardien, Deschambault, St-Michel-de-Bellechasse, Ste-Marie-de-Beauce). It also organized moonlight musical excursions on the St Lawrence on the *Union* and the *Saguenay*. It gave about five concerts a year, presenting excerpts from operas and operettas (*Le Trouvère*, Hervé's *Le Petit Faust*) and vocal works by Halévy, Mendelssohn, Thomas, and others. Félicien David's *La Perle du Brésil* was performed 12 Mar 1878 with 'ensemble playing of the highest order,' according to the anonymous author of the *Historique*.

The society should not be confused with the Société Ste-Cécile of the *Séminaire de Québec, which originated in 1833. Another Société Sainte-Cécile was founded and directed by A.J. *Boucher in Montreal in 1860–1; it presented four concerts, singing in particular Rossini's *Stabat Mater*. (AP)

Société symphonique de Québec. See Quebec Symphony Orchestra.

The Society of Canadian Music / La Société de musique canadienne. Founded December 1953 in Montreal at the behest of the *CLComp to ensure the performance of Canadian compositions, draw the attention of the press to them, and encourage established concert organizations to include them more regularly on their programs. Until its incorporation by the Quebec government in 1957, the society was known as the CLComp's Concert Committee. Its first concert, by a CBC orchestra under Geoffrey *Waddington, took place 3 Feb 1954 at *Plateau Hall. Members from the CLComp selected the programs and performers, and members from the business community administered the finances. Jean *Lallemand was president, and the composer Jean *Papineau-Couture was secretary.

In its 15 years (1954–69) the Society of Canadian Music organized 15 concerts, ranging from solo recitals to choral-orchestral presentations. At the *Orpheum Theatre it presented (15 Mar 1959) the chamber operas *Une Mesure de silence* / **Silent Measures* (by Maurice *Blackburn) and *The *Fool* (by Harry *Somers). Almost all the programmed works were by CLComp members, but occasionally composers of the past were represented to afford a wider panorama of Canadian music. Owing largely to the society's efforts, the *SMCQ, when it began giving concerts in 1966, found an audience receptive to Canadian music. This accomplished, the society began re-evaluating its role. In 1969 it decided that its assets, augmented by generous gifts, would be turned over to Les *Amis de l'art to establish a fund for an annual scholarship to be given to a composition student. This prize has been given alternately to students at *McGill U and the *U of Montreal, thus perpetuating the objectives of the society. IP-C

Sohmer Park. A Montreal amusement park established in 1889 by Ernest *Lavigne, who wanted to revive the happy experience of the Viger Garden concerts of 1885. With his partner, Louis-Joseph Lajoie, Lavigne rented the historic property located between the St Lawrence shoreline and Salaberry, Notre-Dame, and Panet streets on the site of the Jardin Guilbault. The park was named after the make of pianos of which Lavigne & Lajoie were the distributors. It was inaugurated in May 1889 with a concert by the *Bande de la Cité. This brass band was supplanted in 1890 by a symphony orchestra, made up mainly of Belgian conservatory graduates recruited by Lavigne during his travels, and of the best Montreal musicians. Several of them were to form in 1894 the nucleus of *Couture's *MSO.

Sohmer Park had many attractions: while sampling refreshments, adults could enjoy overtures, Viennese waltzes, and military marches and could applaud such singers as Louis Vérande or Victor *Occelier in performances of ballads or operettas. Meanwhile the children could play to their hearts' content on the rides and other attractions. For a modest price Montrealers had access to all kinds of exhibitions, variety shows, and circus acts, even to contests featuring the great champions of wrestling and boxing.

Soon Sohmer Park became so popular that a pavilion with a capacity of 7000 was built in 1893 to house winter events. Around this time, Lavigne tried unsuccessfully to establish a permanent troupe of European artists able to perform a different opera or operetta every evening for four months. Even so, the park presented itinerant troupes in such operettas as *La Fille de Madame Angot*, *La Mascotte*, *La Périchole*, or *Les Cloches de Corneville* and various instrumental ensembles including the Theodore Thomas Orchestra. In 1909, on the death of Lavigne, Xavier Larose took over the direction of the orchestra. Larose was followed by J.-J. *Goulet 1912–14, (Peter?) Van der Meerschen 1914–16, and J.-J. *Gagnier 1916–19. On 24 Mar 1919 the pavilion was destroyed by fire. The land was acquired by the C.S. Campbell estate and what had been for more than 30 years the most popular amusement park in Montreal became a simple playground.

BIBLIOGRAPHY
'Les musiciens du Parc Sohmer,' *P-T*, 31, 2 May 1896
Massicotte, Édouard-Z. 'Brève histoire du Parc Sohmer,' *Cahiers des dix*, 11, 1946
– 'Leur dernier succès,' *BRH*, 52, Jan 1946
Gagnier, J.-J. 'Pointe sèche et crayon gras,' *P-T*, series, 908–20, Mar 1947–Dec 1948
Chevrotière, A. de la. 'Le Parc Sohmer fut le symbole d'une ère insouciante et gaie,' *Voix nationale*, Jul 1954
De Vaux, Agathe. 'L'histoire de l'OSM,' *Variations*, vol 1, Oct–Nov 1977 (CH)

'Sol canadien, terre chérie.' One of the earliest Canadian patriotic songs. Isidore Bédard intended the words as a national song. Two stanzas were published anonymously in 1827 and all four in the *Gazette de Québec* 1 Jan 1829. At first they were sung to the tune of 'Ah! quel tourment,' while *Le Chansonnier des collèges* (2nd edn 1854) refers to the tune of 'Ah! quelle, quelle inquiétude.' The poem was sung as well to an original tune by T.F. *Molt, published as an insert in the February 1859 issue of *Le Journal de l'instruction publique* and in the *Recueil de chansons canadiennes et françaises* (1859). When Molt wrote the music remains unknown. The *Recueil* (p 341) states that the song 'sums up admirably the feelings of French Canadians at the time of its composition. They were submissive to British rule, despite the daily strain placed on their loyalty by its oligarchic nature, because they abhorred the thought of annexation by the USA.'

BIBLIOGRAPHY
Lortie, Jeanne d'Arc. 'Sol canadien,' *Dictionnaire des oeuvres littéraires du Québec*, vol 1, ed Maurice Lemire (Montreal 1978) HK

Solmization. General term indicating the use of syllables instead of letter-names, numbers, or other designations for the seven tones of the diatonic scale. Two systems of solmization have dominated: that employing the 'fixed do' and that employing the 'movable doh.' The seven syllables in use in the two systems differ in spelling but have almost identical pronunciations. They are do (doh), re (ray), mi (me), fa (fah), sol (soh), la (lah), and si or ti (te). The syllable forms in parentheses are those used in the Tonic Sol-fa system. In the 'fixed do' system, usually referred to as solfège or solfeggio, 'do' always represents the pitch with the letter-name C, re is D, mi is E, etc. This principle applies regardless of tonality. While following the letter-name system the 'fixed do' plan utilizes vocal sounds which are highly suitable for singing.

In the 'movable doh' system (commonly known as Tonic Sol-fa), doh is assigned to the tonic centre of the phrase. Doh is the first degree or tonic of the scale, ray is the second or supertonic, me is the third or mediant, etc. The shifting pitch and staff position of doh emphasize the principle of tonality and provide greater flexibility of application, particularly in music of a tonal nature.

The modern systems of solmization are derived from the 11th-century work of Guido d'Arezzo, who used the initial syllables of the first six lines of a hymn to St John, attributed to Paulus Diaconus of the eighth century.

Ut queant laxis,
Re-sonare fibris
Mi-ra gestorum,
Fa-muli tuorum
Sol-ve polluti,
La-bii reatum, Sancte Ioannes.

Each phrase of this hymn begins successively one note higher than the preceding one with the sounds of the hexachord, the syllables being Ut, Re, Mi, Fa, Sol, and La, and the original sounds being the hexachord C D E F G A. These syllables also were used for the hexachords on F (F G A B flat, C D) and G (G A B C D E). By the mid-17th century, the seventh tone, si (possibly taken from the last line of the hymn), completed the octave. Do replaced ut in most European countries when the Guidonian syllables began to assume a fixed position and ut became C.

SOLFÈGE. Solfège, derived from the Italian solfeggio, is the comprehensive French term for the teaching of the elements of music, notation, and ear training. It embraces the 'fixed do' principle and is used mainly in the schools of France, Belgium, and Italy, in training systems derived from them, and at certain US professional training institutions. The solfège system would appear to be advantageous and more significant in the training of highly motivated professional musicians, especially instrumentalists, emphasizing as it does the fixed position of do and encouraging the achievement of an absolute pitch sense.

TONIC SOL-FA. Tonic Sol-fa is a highly comprehensive and carefully graded system which was perfected by the Englishman John Curwen in the mid-19th century to assist in the development of singers' aural senses through the use of 'the modulator,' and of their ability to read notation first through 'the elementary notation' and finally 'the established notation,' ie, staff notation. Utilizing the movable doh, it is used most widely in England and the English-speaking countries, in Germany, where it is known as Tonika-Do, and in Hungary.

The central idea of Tonic Sol-fa instruction is that through an aural examination of each of the scale tones (first in context and then in isolation) and of their function in the formation of chords, the relationship of sounds within a given key may be established mentally and ready for instant recall. Later this feature is extended to include the interrelationship of one key to another, and modulation thus is clarified.

The 'elementary notation' makes use of the first letter of each of the syllables (doh, ray, me, fah, soh, lah, te) with chromatic alterations written out in full as follows, the sharpened syllable names ending in 'e' and the flattened endings in 'a.'

Flattened chromatic		Sharpened chromatic
	t	
ta		le
	l	
la		se
	s	
		fe
	f	
	m	
ma		re
	r	
ra		de
	d	

Exact indications are given for notes of higher or lower octaves by means of super- or subscripts; d' is an octave higher than d; t, is a half-tone below d. Curwen changed the seventh tone name, si, to te, so that each syllable would begin with a different letter. Another important tonal relationship was recognized when the tonic of a relative minor scale was set as lah, following the course of its historical evolution and maintaining the same doh for relative major and minor modes, ie, major and minor scales with the same key signature. To assist the learner visually, Curwen evolved an ingenious system of hand-signs so that a different position of the hand represented each of the scale tones. These have proved particularly useful with children.

Canadian children have been educated in both solfège and Tonic Sol-fa, depending on the prevailing philosophy. Henry Francis *Sefton taught the fixed-do system after his arrival from Ireland in 1858. Alexander T. *Cringan, a graduate of the Tonic Sol-fa College in London, used the Tonic Sol-fa system with marked success after 1886.

The movable-doh system has been used widely in Canadian schools, particularly in those which perpetuate the English choral tradition, although its use in the teaching of instrumental music has met with limited success – instrumentalists in most cases preferring to call notes by their letter names, particularly keyboard players who have chords as well as melodic lines to read. However, the noted Hungarian educator Zoltán Kodály has indicated his preference for the Tonic Sol-fa for the teaching of sight-singing, and the widespread interest shown during the 1970s in adapting the *Kodály principles for Canadian schools has stimulated new activity in Tonic Sol-fa training.

Some solmization textbooks published in Canada are:

Labelle, Charles. *Petit Traité de Solfège* (Montreal 1892)

Champagne, Claude. *Initiation pratique au solfège* (Montreal 1938)

Solfège pratique (Montreal 1939)

Solfège scolaire (Montreal 1940)

Solfège et chant, cinquième année (Outremont 1943)

Solfège pédagogique (Montreal 1948)

Le Solfège à l'École (Ottawa 1951, Montreal 1960)

Solfège élémentaire, 4ème et 5ème année (Quebec City 1955)

Solfège manuscrit à changements de clefs, 44 leçons pour voix moyennes (Montreal 1958)

Marie-Jocelyne, Sister. *Solfège*, 2 vols (Rosemont Que, 1960) KBr

SOLOMON, Stanley. Violist, artists' manager, b Toronto 3 Apr 1917. After violin studies 1927–39 at the *TCM with Luigi von *Kunits, Vino Harisay, and Elie *Spivak, he attended the Curtis Institute on scholarship, training (1939–42) as a violist with Max Aronoff, Louis *Bailly, and Oscar Shumsky. During RCAF service 1942–4 he toured Canada and Europe as concertmaster and assistant conductor of the **RCAF Blackouts* review. He was briefly with the Baltimore, Columbia Music Festival, Columbia, and Toronto Philharmonic orchestras before joining the *TSO in 1946. He became principal viola in 1949 (and retained that position in 1980). He has been a member of the *Parlow String Quartet 1946–58 and of the *Hart House Orchestra 1954–68, becoming manager of the latter in 1966. His Stanley Solomon Concert Artists Management (1963–9) represented such Canadian artists as Howell *Glynne, Hyman and Erica *Goodman, Sheila *Henig, Mary *Simmons, Steven *Staryk, and David *Zafer.

Solomon's two children have followed careers in pop music. Maribeth (b Toronto 23 Jun 1950) was a pianist with Tony Kosenic and Jerry Jeff Walker and in 1975 began working with Micky Erbe as an arranger, composer, and producer for Mickymar Productions. Lenny (violinist, b Toronto 28 Sep 1952) formed the Lenny Solomon Band after working for seven years with Myles Cohen as Myles and Lenny, a successful *GRT and Columbia recording team and the winners of a 1975 *Juno Award. MH

SOLWAY, Maurice. Violinist, teacher, b Toronto 10 Mar 1908. He began violin studies at 4 and entered the *U of Toronto Faculty of Music at 15. He played 1923–6 in the New SO (later *TSO) and 1933–49 in the TSO. He studied violin 1926–8 with Ysaÿe in Brussels and made his concert debut there in 1928. In 1947 he founded the Solway String Quartet, with Jacob *Groob (and successively Charles Dobias and Berul *Sugarman) as second violin, Robert Warburton (and in turn Ivan *Romanoff and Eugene Hudson) as viola, and Marcus *Adeney as cello. The quartet gave public and CBC concerts until the early 1970s and toured small Ontario towns for the Dept of Education. Its programs mixed standard repertoire with arrangements of familiar tunes, quartets by *Coulthard, *Gayfer, *MacMillan and *Weinzweig, and other works by *Applebaum, Leo *Smith, and *Willan. With Andrés Segovia the Solway String Quartet gave the Canadian premiere (1951) of the Castelnuovo-Tedesco Guitar Quintet. Solway began to compose in 1956 and has produced some 40 works for solo violin or piano. Several have been published by BMI Canada and Boosey & Hawkes. He has appeared in two films: *The Violin* (1973), for which he composed the music and which won numerous honours, including an Academy Award nomination; and *Divertimento* (1974) to music of Mozart. Robert Thomas Allen's book version of *The Violin*, illustrated with stills from the film, is published (Toronto 1976), and the music may be heard on the LP *Music from the Film The Violin and Folk Songs and Dances from around the World* (1973, RCA KXL1-0029).

WRITINGS

'Ysaÿe – gentle giant of the violin,' *Music*, Jun 1980 (SLH)

'Some of These Days.' Song by Shelton Brooks, the composer of *'Darktown Strutters' Ball.' It was introduced by Sophie Tucker in 1910 at Chicago's White City Park and published that year by Will Rossiter, Chicago. It became Sophie Tucker's theme song, and she recorded it six times – the first ca 1911 on an Edison cylinder – and sang it in two movies: *Broadway Melody of 1938* (1937) and *Follow the Boys* (1944). The song has been recorded by many others, including Louis Armstrong (1929), Bing Crosby (1932), and Coleman Hawkins (1935). MM

SOMERS, Harry (Stewart). Composer, b Toronto 11 Sep 1925; hon D MUS (Ottawa) 1975, hon LL D (Toronto) 1976, hon D LITT (York) 1977. He began piano study in the fall of 1939 after meeting a doctor and his wife – both accomplished pianists – who exposed him to classical works. Somers later recalled, 'A spark ignited and I became obsessed with music.' During the 1940s he studied piano and composition, intending to pursue both as a career. His piano teachers were Dorothy Hornfelt 1939–41, Reginald *Godden 1942–3, Weldon *Kilburn 1945–8, and E. Robert Schmitz in the summer of 1948. Somers was a gifted pianist and gave several recitals in the late 1940s, including one of Barbara *Pentland's music and one of his own in March 1948 at the *RCMT. He had begun composing without guidance in 1939, but in 1941 he joined the class of *Weinzweig. Except for a period of service 1943–5 with the RCAF he was with Weinzweig until 1949, when a $2000 Canadian Amateur Hockey Assn scholarship afforded him a year in Paris with Milhaud. Milhaud's influence on Somers' music was minimal, however.

Harry Somers

Though in 1948 Somers gave up his plans for a career as a pianist to devote himself to composing, he nevertheless mastered the guitar during the 1950s. He continued to compose prolifically, avoiding those kinds of employment which would sap his creative energies. (He drove a taxicab until he found he could make a living as a music copyist. The latter activity refined the meticulous hand which always marks a Somers manuscript.)

In 1960, on a *Canada Council fellowship, Somers returned to Paris to observe trends and to compose. He also studied Gregorian chant at Solesmes. Back in Toronto he found for the first time that he could live on commissions. Many of these came from the CBC. He also became concerned with the teaching and performance of Canadian music in schools. He participated in the first phase of the *John Adaskin Project in 1963 and was special consultant for school music in North York (Toronto) 1968–9. He was host on a CBC series of televised youth concerts in 1963 and on the CBC radio series 'Music of Today' 1965–9.

An $18,000 grant from the Canadian Cultural Institute in Rome allowed Somers to live 1969–71 in Rome, where he completed *Voiceplay* and *Kyrie*, fruits of a growing interest in new vocal techniques. Late in 1971 he returned to Canada via the Far East, where he experienced various aspects of Eastern music and philosophy.

Somers' first wife, Catherine Mackie, died in 1963. In 1967 he married the Canadian actress Barbara Chilcott.

Somers is one of Canada's most important composers and one of the few to receive international recognition; his music has been performed in the USA, Central and South America, Europe, and the Soviet Union. Unusually versatile, he has produced major scores for stage, concert hall, film, radio and TV and has employed voices, instruments, and synthetic sounds in a wide variety of forms, traditional and new. His commissions indicate the level at which his work has been appreciated. The *Stratford Festival commissioned his *Five Songs for Dark Voice* for Maureen *Forrester; the *Vancouver International Festival his *String Quartet No. 3* for the Hungarian Quartet; the CBC numerous works including *Evocations*, *Movement for Orchestra*, *The Crucifixion*, and (for Cathy Berberian) *Voiceplay*. *Kuyas* was commissioned for the 1967 *Montreal International Competition; **Louis Riel* by the Floyd S. *Chalmers Foundation for the *COC; *Lyric* by the Koussevitzky Foundation; *Stereophony* by the *TSO; **The Fisherman and His Soul*, *Ballad*, and *House of Atreus* by the National Ballet of Canada; and *Music for Solo Violin* by a triumvirate of the Canada Council, the *Guelph Spring Festival, and the violinist Yehudi Menuhin, who also gave its premiere.

Manuscript opening page from *Kuyas* by Harry Somers

Although in the course of his career Somers has absorbed many influences (eg, Weinzweig, Bartók, baroque counterpoint, 12-tone procedures, and Gregorian chant) his music has retained certain trademarks, independent of trends such as the serialism of the 1950s. Many of these can be found in his student works. The piano pieces of 1939–41, written before his studies with Weinzweig, are mood essays with descriptive titles and a marked interest in non-functional harmonic colour. A favourite device is the parallel movement of fourths, fifths, triads, and chords of the seventh and ninth. This persists in the works of the 1940s (eg, the introduction to the first movement of *North Country*).

The *String Quartet No. 1*, the first large work written under Weinzweig's guidance, contains a number of elements carried forward into, and refined during, the late 1940s and 1950s: the extended melodic line (probably a result of exercises designed by Weinzweig to exploit a single line); ostinatos, often with a strong rhythmic drive; points of tonal repose in non-tonal contexts; the accumulation and release of tension (often through textural density) over an extended arc; and finally the use of rhetorical, declamatory gestures at climactic moments.

By the time of *North Country* these elements had evolved into a distinctive style in which the communication of intense feeling was balanced by effective scoring and driving rhythms were contained within compact ternary structures. The first movement of *North Country* evokes a bleak, rugged landscape through the slow unfolding of spare melody in the violins' high tessitura against a quasi-ostinato of short rhythmic figures.

Over the years Somers' 'long line' has functioned as a vehicle for intensity as well as a provider of continuity. Two main types of line are used. One unfolds slowly within a small range of pitch and often is accompanied thinly by nervous rhythmic interjections. Characteristic of this line are a falling minor second in a long-short rhythm, sharp dynamic fluctuations in otherwise sustained elements or short melodic segments, silences of varying lengths interrupting the line, and a built-in accelerando at the point of climax (often associated with the falling second). Examples can be seen in the final page of the *Rhapsody* (1948), the opening of *Stereophony* (1963), and *Music for Solo Violin* (1973). The second type of line may include one or more of these traits but is more active rhythmically, with wider intervals and greater range, and usually is accompanied by one or more continuous voices. Examples are the violin's theme in the Prologue of the *Symphony No. 1*, the opening of *Lyric*, and several of the long vocal solos in *Louis Riel*.

Another Somers device, dating from the 1940s and recurrent, has been the deliberate use of tension in manipulating the listener's emotions. In the 1950s he generated such tensions with neobaroque counterpoint and with a juxtaposition of contrasting styles – for instance, the superimposition of tonal on non-tonal material. The effectiveness of Somers' counterpoint can be seen in the *Passacaglia and Fugue*, in which each section grows to a climax through the accumulation of imitative voices. Of 14 large works written between 1951 and 1959, 10 involve some fugal writing. Style juxtaposition, which first appeared in the second movement of the *Suite for Harp and Chamber Orchestra* (1949), was less successful in works of the 1950s (**The Fool* and *Piano Concerto No. 2*) than in *Louis Riel* (1967), where folksong, tonal writing, taped material, and Somers' own atonal fabrics work together to achieve a high dramatic impact.

Tension is produced also by sharp fluctuations in volume (Somers calls them 'dynamic unrest') which may be applied to single notes, to segments of a melodic line, or (especially in orchestral works) to sustained vertical aggregates. In fact, the growth pattern of many of Somers' works is an extension of a crescendo-decrescendo dynamic shape. A striking example is the fifth of *Five Concepts for Orchestra* (1961). The broad structure of many of the post–1940 works is ternary – eg, *Symphony No. 1, Five Concepts, Twelve Miniatures* – and this probably is a result of the tendency to plan works around the build-up, achievement, and release of tension.

The orchestral works of the 1960s grew, in part, from Somers' music, 1959–60, for the film *Saguenay*, in which he worked with non-thematic colours and textures. At first this affected only abstract works (*Lyric, Five Concepts*) but later it led to experiments with other dimensions: visual (*Movement*), spatial (*Stereophony*), and theatrical (*The House of Atreus*). In these works tonal or modal elements (common in pre–1959 works) are present no longer. The basis of pitch organization is a 12-tone series. Although Somers used a series in the mid–1940s, he did not employ it throughout a work until 1951 (*Symphony No. 1, 12 x 12*). His subsequent use of series (in all major works including *Louis Riel*) has been flexible and intuitive, tailored to complement other dimensions of a given work, not growing out of theoretical speculation.

In 1963 Somers began showing particular interest in the voice, using phonetic sounds, timbral inflections, and minute ornamentation. In *Twelve Miniatures, Evocations*, and *Louis Riel* these colour a traditional treatment of words. However, in two large works of the 1970s the fabric consists mainly of non-semantic sounds and colour inflections. *Voiceplay* is a wordless lecture demonstration of new vocal techniques for singer/actor, and *Kyrie* is a 25-minute work for vocal quartet, choir, and instruments. In *Kyrie* the text is derived exclusively from the phonetic sounds of the words 'Kyrie eleison, Christe eleison.' The sounds, Somers believes, contain the real meaning of the words.

The earmarks of Somers' style are reflected in his works for solo instruments (in particular the piano and the violin), and small combinations of instruments. For discussion of some of these see Composition, instrumental solos and duos: 2 / Piano solos.

Somers has worked extensively in the Electronic Music Studio, U of Toronto, but has used taped materials only in *Louis Riel*. He has experimented with graph notation (*And*) and improvisation (*Improvisation*), but by 1976 he had not persisted along these lines.

Somers has been honoured variously – by the Critics' Award (1965) of the Cava dei Tirreni Summer Festival, Italy; by the Italian Government Award; by his investiture as a Companion of the *Order of Canada (1972); by the Wm Harold Moon Award (1976), and by doctorates from several universities. On the occasion of the awarding of his honorary degree from the U of Toronto John *Beckwith said: '[Somers'] music has been created ... out of a mastery of the technical processes of his time, out of a wide intellectual curiosity, out of a sense of his relation to tradition; at a more essential level it has been created out of pain and isolation and (like all good music) out of love – in other words altogether out of an extraordinary feeling for the human condition ... Through it all runs a remarkable elemental quality which ... identifies the Somers style like a thumbprint. "Simplicity" is a dangerous word to describe such a quality of style because, though it is direct and elemental in the way it "grabs the ear," its layers of reference often lie deep and it can be profitably experienced afresh many times ... The music has spoken to us – and *for* us to the rest of the world – with an eloquence and force that few segments of our musical repertoire have matched.'

Somers is an affiliate of PRO Canada, an associate of the *CMCentre, and a member of the *CLComp.

COMPOSITIONS

STAGE, FILM, TELEVISION

The Homeless Ones, TV operetta (M. Fram). 1955 (CBC-TV Tor 1956). Narr, vs, orch. Ms

Faces of Canada, incidental music. 1956 (CBC-TV Tor 1956). Full orch. Ms

Ballad, ballet. 1958 (Ott 1958). Full orch. Ms

Saguenay, film score. 1956. Chamb orch. Ms

Movement (formerly *Abstract for Television*). 1961 (CBC-TV Tor 1962). Full orch. Ric 1964

The House of Atreus, ballet. 1963 (Tor 1964). Full orch (chamb orch). Ms

The Gift, incidental music. 1965 (CBC-TV Tor 1965). Ms

And, dance. 1969 (CBC-TV Tor 1969). Sop, mezzo, ten, bar, dancers, chamb ens. Ms

Images of Canada, incidental music for TV. 1972–5 (Tor 1973, 1976). Various ens. Ms

Death of Enkidu: Part I, chamb opera (M. Kinch). 1977. 5 vs, actor, female dancer, fl, cl, 2 hns, hp, pf, 3 perc. CMCentre

The Merman of Orford, mime. 1978. Fl, hn, vc, perc. Ms

See also *The Fisherman and His Soul; The Fool; Louis Riel.*

ORCHESTRA

Sketches for Orchestra. 1946 (Tor 1947, Rochester 1948). Ms. RCI 88 (R. *Leduc)

Slow Movement for Strings (mvt 2 of *String Quartet No. 1*). 1946. (Tor 1946). Str orch. Ms

Scherzo for Strings. 1947 (Tor 1947). Str orch. AMP 1948. RCI 41 (*TSO)/RCI 238 (*Hart House O)

North Country. 1948 (Tor 1948). Str orch. BMIC 1960. RCI 154 (*CBC SO)

Symphony No. 1. 1951 (Tor 1953). Ber (rental)

Prelude and Fugue for Orchestra. 1952 (Tor 1952). Ms

Passacaglia and Fugue. 1954 (Tor 1954). BMIC 1958. RCI 180 (*CBC SO)/Louisville LS 661 (Louisville O, Whitney cond)

Little Suite for String Orchestra on Canadian Folk Songs. 1955 (Tor 1956). BMIC 1956

Fantasia for Orchestra. 1958 (Mtl 1958). BMIC 1962. RCI 230/RCA LSC 2980/Vic VICS 1040 (*MSO)

Lyric for Orchestra. 1960 (Washington 1961). BMIC 1963

Symphony for Woodwinds, Brass and Percussion. 1961 (Pittsburgh 1961). Peters (rental). CBC SM-134 (*Feldbrill)

Five Concepts for Orchestra. 1961 (Tor 1962). BMIC 1964

Stereophony. 1963 (Tor 1963). Kerby 1972

Picasso Suite. 1964 (Saskatoon 1965). Sm orch. Ric 1969. CBC SM-241 (*Atlantic SO)

Those Silent, Awe-Filled Spaces. 1977 (Ott 1978). Orch. Ms

Variations. 1979. Str orch. CMCentre

SOLOIST(S) WITH ORCHESTRA
Piano Concerto No. 1. 1947 (Tor 1949). Ms
Suite for Harp and Chamber Orchestra. 1949 (Tor 1952). BMIC 1959
Piano Concerto No. 2. 1956 (Tor 1956). Ber (rental)
Five Songs for Dark Voice (Fram). 1956 (Stratford 1956). Alto, chamb orch. Ber 1972 (v, pf). CBC SM-73 (*Mailing, *CBC Van Chamb O)/RCI 286/RCA LSC 3172 (*Forrester, *NACO)
CHAMBER
Duo. 1943. 2 vn. Ms
String Quartets No. 1 and 2 (1943, 1950). Both CMCentre. (No. 2) CBC SM-263 (*Vaghy Str Quar)
Suite for Percussion. 1947. Pf, 4 drums. Ms
Mime. 1947. Vn, pf. Ms
Rhapsody. 1948. Vn, pf. CMCentre. RCI 244 (*Duo Pach)
Woodwind Quintet. 1948. Ms
Trio. 1950. Fl, vn, vc. CMCentre
Sonata No. 1. 1953. Vn, pf. BMIC 1968. RCI 221/RCA CCS 1015 (*Hidy, *Duncan)
Sonata No. 2. 1955. Vn, pf. BMIC 1968. RCI 222/RCA CCS 1016 (*Staryk, L. *Boucher)
Movement for Woodwind Quintet. 1957. Ms
String Quartet No. 3. 1959. Ber (rental). CBC SM-45 (*Orford Str Quar)
Sonata for Guitar. 1959. Solo guit. Kerby 1972. RCI 409 (*Strutt)
Twelve Miniatures (Haiku, transl H.G. Henderson). 1964. Sop, rec (fl), va da gamba (vc), spinet (pf). BMIC 1965. RCI 217/RCA CCS 1011 (*Morrison, *Fiore, *Buczynski, D. Whitton vc)
Theme for Variations. 1964. Any comb of instr. Ber (rental)
Etching – The Vollard Suite (from *Picasso Suite*). 1964. Fl. Ric 1969. CBC SM-114 (Michalska fl, *Armenian)
Kuyas (Cree). 1967. Sop, fl, perc. Ber (rental)
Improvisation. 1968. Narr, singers, ww, str, 2 perc, pf. CMCentre
Music for Solo Violin. 1973. Ber 1975. RCI 413 (Menuhin vn, Somers commentator)
Zen, Yeats and Emily Dickinson (Zen poetry, Yeats, Dickinson). 1975. 2 actors, sop, fl, pf, tape. CMCentre
PIANO
Strangeness of Heart. 1942. BMIC 1947. RCI 93/RCI 132 (R. *Pratt)/1976. RCI 450 (K. Quinton)
In ms: *Étude* (1943); *Flights of Fancy* (1944); *Dark and Light* (1944)
5 Piano Sonatas. 1945–57. CMCentre. (No. 1) RCI 450 (*Godden)/(No. 2) RCI 450 (*Helmer)/(No. 3) RCI 251 and RCI 451 (*Savoie)/(No. 4) RCI 451 (J. *McKay)/(No. 5 'Lento') CBC SM-102 (*Buczynski)/(No. 5) RCI 452 and Mel SMLP 4023 (*Kubálek)
Three Sonnets. 1946, orch version 1952 (No. 2 and 3 only). BMIC 1948 (pf). 1976. RCI 450 (K. Quinton)
In ms: *Solitudes* (1947); *Four Primitives* (1949)
12 x 12: Fugues for Piano. 1951. FH 1955 (No. 1), BMIC 1959 (complete). RCI 452 (J. *Couture)
CHOIR
'Where Do We Stand, O Lord?' (Fram). 1955. SATB, BMIC 1955. RCI 130 (*Waddington)
Two Songs for the Coming of Spring (Fram). 1955. SATB. BMIC 1957. RCI 206 (*Mtl Bach Choir)
'God, the Master of This Scene' (J. Taylor). 1962. OUP 1964, GVT 1973. Cap ST 6258/Ser S-60085 (*Festival Singers)
Gloria (liturgical). 1962. SATB, 2 tpt, org. OUP 1964, GVT 1973. CBC SM-53 (*Tudor Singers of Mtl)/RCA LSC 3043 (*Tor Mendelssohn Choir)
'The Wonder Song' (Somers). 1963. SATB. BMIC 1964. CBC SM-19 (*Festival Singers)
Crucifixion (Passion Psalm). 1966. SATB, eng hn, 2 tpt, hp, perc. Ms
Five Songs of the Newfoundland Outports (traditional, coll Peacock). 1968. SATB, pf. GVT 1969. RCI 339/CBC SM-105/RCA LSC 3154 (*Festival Singers)
Kyrie (liturgical). 1972. SATB, soli, instr ens. publ *Exile*, vol 1, no. 3, 1973
Three Limericks (anon, W.H. Auden). 1980 (Guelph 1980). SATB, mezzo, instr ens. CMCentre
VOICE
'Stillness' (Somers). 1942. Sop, pf. Ms
Three Songs (Whitman). 1946. V, pf. CMCentre. RCI 20 (F. *James)
'A Bunch of Rowan' (D. Skala). 1947. Med v, pf. BMIC 1948
'A Song of Joys' (Whitman). 1947. Med v, pf. Ms
Three Simple Songs (Fram). 1953. Mezzo. CMCentre
'Conversation Piece' (Fram). 1955. High v, pf. BMIC 1957
Evocations (Somers). 1966. Mezzo, pf. BMIC 1968. CBC SM-13/CBC SM-108 (*Rideout, Somers pf)
Voiceplay (Somers). 1971. Singer/actor. CMCentre
Love-In-Idleness, operatic scene (Shakespeare, *Midsummer Night's Dream*). 1976. Sop, pf. CMCentre

WRITINGS
'The agony of Maurice Lowe: a reply,' *Canadian Forum*, vol 35, Sep 1955
Analysis of Suite for Harp and Chamber Orchestra, CMCentre Study Course no. 1 (Toronto 1961)
'Stereophony for Orchestra,' *Music Across Canada*, vol 1, Mar 1963
'Composer in the school: a composer's view,' *Mcan*, 19, May 1969
'A letter from Rome,' *CMB*, 1, Spring–Summer 1970
'Harry Somers' letter to Lee Hepner,' *CMB*, 3, Autumn–Winter 1971
'How "Music for Solo Violin" was born,' *CMB*, 10, Spring–Summer 1975
'Dr. Somers replies,' *News* from the Faculty of Music, U of Toronto, vol 6, Summer 1976

BIBLIOGRAPHY
Lowe, J.M. 'Agony of modern music,' *Canadian Forum*, vol 35, Sep 1955
Beckwith, John. 'Composers in Toronto and Montreal,' *U of Toronto Q*, vol 26, Oct 1956
Olnick, Harvey. 'Harry Somers,' *CMJ*, vol 3, Summer 1959
'Harry Somers: a portrait,' *Mcan*, 4, Sep 1967
Winters, Kenneth. 'Somers: in the spring of his career,' Toronto *Telegram*, 5 Jul 1969
Loranger, Pierre. 'Harry Somers: *The Picasso Suite*,' *CMB*, 1, Spring–Summer 1970
Hepner, Lee. 'An analytical study of selected Canadian orchestral compositions at the mid-twentieth century,' unpubl PH D dissertation, New York U 1971
Harry Somers CBC radio documentary tape (1972)
Such, Peter. 'Harry Somers,' *Soundprints* (Toronto 1972)
Duke, David. 'Neo-classical composition procedures in selected works of Harry Somers, 1949–59,' unpubl MA thesis, U of North Carolina 1973
Smith, Frances Jean. 'An analysis of selected works by Harry Somers,' unpubl M MUS thesis, U of Western Ontario 1973
Butler, Edward Gregory. 'The five piano sonatas of Harry Somers,' unpubl DMA thesis, U of Rochester 1974
Beckwith, John. 'Harry Somers,' *Dictionary of Contemporary Music*
Cherney, Brian. 'Harry Somers,' *Contemporary Canadian Composers*
– *Harry Somers* (Toronto 1975)
Schulman, Michael. 'Harry Somers: in the midst of journey into himself,' *MSc*, 284, Jul–Aug 1975
Callwood, June. 'The informal Harry Somers,' Toronto *Globe and Mail*, 1 Dec 1975
Fraser, John. 'The music of Somers: witty, thoughtful and dead-right,' *SatN*, vol 91, Jan–Feb 1977
Littler, William. 'Early Somers concerto spends time well,' *Toronto Star*, 14 Mar 1977
PRO Canada Ltd. 'Harry Somers,' pamphlet (1979) BC

Songs. In addition to *EMC* articles on individual chansons, folksongs, and pop songs entered under their titles, see the following:
Art song
Ballads
Chanson in Québec
Children's songs, traditional
College songs
Country music
Disaster songs
Flag songs
Folk music
Folk music, Anglo-Canadian
Folk music, Franco-Canadian
Lullabies
National and royal anthems
Occupational songs
Patriotic songs
Political songs
Trade union songs
See also:
La Bonne Chanson
'Concours de la chanson canadienne'
Composition competitions
Composition, topical
Granby Song Festival
Indians
Inuit
School songbooks
Gordon V. Thompson Ltd

Many of *EMC*'s entries on individual countries mention characteristic songs (folksongs, etc) perpetuated in Canada.

Sorel. City situated 60 km east of Montreal at the junction of the St Lawrence and Richelieu rivers on the former site of Fort Richelieu, built in 1642, and the seigneury given in 1672 to Pierre de Saurel, a captain in the Carignan-Salières regiment. Loyalists arrived in the area around 1781, and the settlement was called William-Henry and later Sorel; it was incorporated as a city in 1889. Located on an important waterway, the town experienced a period of rapid industrial growth in the 19th century through the establishment of shipyards, steelworks, and foundries. In the 1970s it had a population of about 20,000.

Although there was some musical activity early in the English régime, it did not develop until schools began to be established in the mid-19th century. In 1783 Frédéric *Glackemeyer taught piano to the daughters of Baron von Riedesel, the commanding officer of the regiment of Brunswick mercenaries stationed in Sorel (these lessons may have taken place in Quebec City).

The arrival of the Sisters of the Congregation of Notre-Dame in 1858 marked the beginning of some exceptionally fine music teaching (especially of piano); among their pupils were Charlotte *Cadoret, Victoria *Cartier, Anna Charbonneau, Estelle Giroux, Juliette Paradis, Cordile Paul, and Éva *Plouffe. A musical evening in 1913 devoted to works of Cécile Chaminade prompted the composer to send compliments to Juliette Paradis who had organized the event. The Brothers of the Christian Schools and later the Fathers of the Sacred Heart and the Brothers of Charity established choirs and brass bands. Henry Emery was director of the Cercle Ste-Cécile orchestra in the late 19th century.

In the early 20th century several Belgian musicians settled in Sorel, including Bosman, Clement, De Kestellier, and especially Auguste *Liessens, one of those who, in the period 1913–54, provided leadership for the musical life in the town. Georges Codling, a pupil of Camille *Couture, Eugène *LaPierre, and Liessens, was a teacher at the Académie du Sacré-Coeur, assumed the directorship of the Calixa-Lavallée Concert Band in 1940 and of the Carignan School Band, and was the composer of two masses. The town's radio station, CJSO, presented many programs featuring local artists.

Choirmasters and organists made a large contribution to the town's musical life. Christ Church, erected in 1778 and said to be the first Anglican parish church in Canada, had Charles Coxhead as leader of the singing, towards the end of the 18th century; some of the parish's organists or choirmasters were Alexander Wright ca 1860–80, Lily Theodosia Wright 1880–ca 1920, and Theodosia Wright-Riopel 1936–61. In the Catholic churches the following deserve mention: Eugénie Smith-Champagne 1887–1945 and Éliane Champagne-Carpentier, organists at St-Joseph; Albéric Latraverse, choirmaster 1904–66 at Ste-Anne; Henri DeGrandpré, choirmaster, and Richard Bernard, organist, at St-Pierre, the town's first Catholic parish. The choir of St-Pierre began the regular practice of Gregorian chant in 1932, at first under the direction of Émile Mineau and later under his brother Adrien.

Sorel over the years has welcomed Emma *Albani, La *Bolduc, Rose Bampton, Marcel Grandjany, Marcel and Yvonne *Hubert, Raoul *Jobin, Arthur *LeBlanc, Léopold *Simoneau and Pierrette *Alarie, Henryk Szeryng, the *Disciples de Massenet, the *MSO, and the foremost names in French and Quebec popular song. The town played host to the *Community Concerts 1941–ca 1954 and to the 1973 festival of the *Fédération des harmonies du Québec. A *JMC centre, established in Sorel in 1958 through the initiative of Frans Liessens (son of Auguste) and others, has presented young artists in recital. Musical events have been held also in the town's churches and in the Georges-Codling Auditorium and the Fernand-Lefebvre Secondary School Auditorium.

The proximity of Montreal and Trois-Rivières has always encouraged students, such as Henri *Pontbriand, Walter *Boudreau, and Pierre-M. Plante, to attend the music schools, conservatories, and universities of those cities. Frans Liessens' son Frederick became a member of the McGill Percussion Ensemble. For young students the École Huguette-Aussant gives instruction at the local level. The conductor Jacques *Beaudry, the pianist Anna-Marie *Globenski, and the organist Claude *Lagacé are among the musicians born in Sorel or the area.

BIBLIOGRAPHY

Valois-Liessens, Louise. 'Sorel et musique,' *Voix métropolitaine*, vols 12 and 13, 28 Nov 1972–3 Jan 1973

LV-L

SOSA, Raoul (Raùl). Pianist, teacher, b Buenos Aires 27 Jul 1939, naturalized Canadian 1973; diploma (Buenos Aires Cons) 1957. After studying 1951–7 at the Buenos Aires Cons with Rafael Gonzalez (piano) and Lita Spena (piano and theory) he made his debut in 1959 at the Teatro Colón and took part in numerous chamber music concerts. He was a finalist in the 1962 International Van Cliburn Competition. He continued his training 1963–7 with Magda Tagliafero in Paris and Salzburg on a French government scholarship and later worked with Stanislav Neuhaus in Italy. He played in 1965 at the Salle Chopin-Pleyel in Paris and made his London debut in 1967 at Wigmore Hall. He won first prize in the 1964 Jean-Hubert Biermans International Competition and was among the prize winners of the 1966 Magda Tagliafero International Competition, the 1966 Maria-Canals Competition, and the 1967 Santiago de Compostela Competition. He was a finalist in the 1968 *Montreal International Competition for piano and won second prize in the 1970 Olivier Messiaen Competition in Royan.

Sosa began to teach at the *CMM in 1967, and he made a recital tour the same year for the JM of Belgium. He played for the *Ladies' Morning Musical Club in 1971 and toured western Canada and Quebec for the *JMC 1973–4. His recital 18 Mar 1977 at the *Salle Claude-Champagne was greeted enthusiastically by the critics: Claude *Gingras described the pianist as an 'altogether exceptional musician' (*La Presse*) and Gilles *Potvin thought him 'a first-rate artist' (*Le Devoir*). He appeared in another recital at the *PDA in February 1978.

Sosa has played on occasion with the *SMCQ Ensemble (Berg's *Chamber Concerto* 1972), and has performed as soloist with the *Quebec SO, the *MSO, the *TS, and the Orchestre Lamoureux in Paris, in concertos by Brahms, Prokofiev, and Tchaikovsky. He has appeared on the CBC TV series 'Les Grands Concerts' and 'Les Beaux Dimanches,' and a 1978 broadcast for the CBC radio series 'Récital' earned him the *CMCouncil award for the year's best radio program by a Canadian soloist.

Sosa taught 1970–3 at the *JMC Orford Art Centre, was an adjudicator for the 1977 *CBC Talent Festival, and has served accredited music-training institutions as an examiner. His recording of piano music of Schubert for the Select label (1977, CC 15.127) contains the *Wanderer Fantasy, Op 15*; the *Sonata in A Minor, Op 143*; the *Impromptu in A Flat, Op 90 no. 4*; and four Ländler.

Sosa's wife, Claudette (pianist, teacher, b Quebec City 29 Jul 1940), studied 1953–63 at the *CMQ with Guy *Bourassa (piano), Gilles *Tremblay (analysis), Françoise *Aubut (counterpoint and fugue), and Georges-Émile *Tanguay (harmony). She studied further 1963–7 with Magda Tagliafero on a grant from the French government. She has given recitals and has appeared as soloist with the Quebec SO. She was a teacher and accompanist 1973–7 at the CMM and has taught in institutions in Val d'Or and Sorel and at the JMC Orford Art Centre.

BIBLIOGRAPHY

McLean, Eric. 'Raoul Sosa,' *Montreal Star*, 4 Feb 1978

(AP, NT)

SOUCY, Isidore. Violoneux, composer, b Ste-Blandine, near Rimouski, Que, 7 Sep 1899, d Montreal 7 Dec 1963. In his teens the best violoneux in his hometown, Soucy went to Montreal in 1924. He worked for the city until 1926, when he began recording for *Starr. Soucy was heard on CKAC radio, Montreal, in the 1920s and also performed in Conrad *Gauthier's Veillées du bon vieux temps at the *Monument national. In the 1930s Soucy began playing on radio shows and was the leader or a member of several popular groups, among them les Vive-la-Joie, the Trio Soucy, and the Famille Soucy.

The first, whose name translates as the revellers, was completed by Donat Lafleur (an accordionist with whom Soucy formed a duo which, over a period of some 15 years, made 9 78s for Starr and 10 for Bluebird) and Jimmy Dabate and performed on radio station CHLP. The Trio Soucy – Isidore, his son Fernando (singer, violoneux, b Montreal 1927, d 1975), and the accordionist René Alain – was formed in 1951; it performed in Montreal nightclubs and made many records. The most popular of these were 'Prendre un verre de bière mon minou,' 'Un Festin de campagne,' and 'Les Fraises et les framboises,' the last selling over 100,000 copies, an exceptional figure for the day. Isidore and Fernando formed the Famille Soucy with other family members: Eugène, Thérèse, Marie-Ange, and Fernande. The family made its radio debut in 1956 with a nightly program on CKVL, Verdun. It made its TV debut on NBC while touring in the USA and performed 1960–2 on CFTM TV, Montreal. Its 'Chez Isidore' was the most popular TV variety show of its day. The Famille Soucy also performed in the Montreal nightclubs El Mocambo and Casa Loma.

After Soucy's death, Fernando continued to sing and play the violin. He made two LPs entitled *Les Veillées du bon vieux temps* for Dominion (LPS 48001, LPS 48002), both of music by his father. Under Fernando, the Famille Soucy performed at *Expo 67. Isidore Soucy himself is said to have made some 1200 recordings, among them 78s for Columbia, Starr, and Bluebird and such LPs for Dominion as *Chez Isidore* (LPS 48004), *Noel Chez Isidore* (LPS 48006), and *Garden Party* (LPS 48007). Collections of his most popular 78s have been reissued on LP, including *20 Grands Succès d'hier: Isidore Soucy* (MCA Coral CB 37004). The musical estates of Isidore and Fernando Soucy are administered by CAPAC.

BIBLIOGRAPHY

Laframboise, Phil. 'Avec un violon payé $125 en 1924 il est devenu millionnaire du disque en 1962,' *Telé-Radiomonde*, 20 Oct 1962
Pionniers du disque folklorique québécois

MM

Soundscape ecology. See World Soundscape Project.

SOUTHAM, Ann. Composer, teacher, b Winnipeg 4 Feb 1937; Licentiate Diploma (Toronto) 1963. After studies with Samuel *Dolin (composition) at the *RCMT and with Pierre *Souvairan (piano) and Gustav *Ciamaga (electronic music) 1960–3 at the *U of Toronto she began teaching at the RCMT in 1966. Her association with the New Dance Group of Canada (later Toronto Dance Theatre) began in 1967, and she became composer-in-residence in 1968. By 1977 she had composed over 20 electronic scores for the company. Southam's earlier works, especially for piano, are lyrical atonal pieces, and lyricism remains an important element of the later electronic scores and of such works as *Counterparts* for orchestra and tape and *CounterPlay*, a CBC commission for string quartet and tape. Of *Waves* (based on electronic wave forms), commissioned and premiered (1 Apr 1976) by Milton *Barnes' Toronto Repertory Orchestra, John *Kraglund wrote: 'Its cycles of sounds were effectively achieved by the location of sections of the orchestra in a semi-circle ... While there was an element of chance music in the style, the effect was pretty controlled ... alternating long lyrical lines with angular, staccato phrases – interrupted by silences.' Southam is a member of the *CLComp and of PRO Canada and an associate of the *CMCentre.

See also Ballets.

SELECTED COMPOSITIONS

CHAMBER

Rhapsodic Interlude for Violin Alone. 1963. Ms. Mel SMLP-4121 (*Zafer)
Momentum. 1967. Pf pre-recorded on tape, va, vc, hpd, 2 perc. Ms
Configurations. 1973. Pf, tape. Ms
CounterPlay. 1973. Str quar, tape. Ms
Integruities (G. Arbour, M. Thompson). 1975. Pf, narr, tape. Ms
Interviews (Arbour, Thompson). 1976. Pf, narr, tape. Ms
Towards Green. 1976. Fl, cl, vn, va. ms
Waves. 1976. Str orch. Ms
Networks. 1978. Fl, va, trb, pf, vc, perc. Ms

PIANO

Suite for Piano. 1960. Ms
Four Bagatelles. 1961. Ber 1974. Mel SMLP-4031 (*Kubálek)
Three in Blue. 1965. Ber 1966. CCM-2 (*Cavalho)
Quodlibet. 1966. Ber 1967. CCM-2 (Cavalho)
Five Pieces in a Jazz Manner. 1970. Ms
Others, including *Sea Flea* (1962). BMIC 1963

ELECTRONIC

A Thread of Sand. 1969. Tape
Boat, River, Moon. 1972. Tape. Mel SMLP 4024
Sky-Sails (O'Huigan). 1973. Tape. Ber CSPS 645
L'Assassin Menace. 1974. Tape
Mythic Journey. 1974. Tape
The Reprieve. 1975. Tape
Nighthawks. 1976. Tape
Rude Awakening. 1976. Tape
Several other electronic works, mostly for dance; also scores for Toronto Arts Productions

BIBLIOGRAPHY

Mitchell, C.J. 'Warmth a characteristic of Ann Southam's electronic music,' *MSc*, 269, Jan–Feb 1973
BMI Canada Ltd. 'Ann Southam,' pamphlet (1977)
Colgrass, Ulla. 'Electronic sound: Ann Southam on sound and space,' *Fugue*, vol 2, Sep 1977
Edwards, Barry. 'Some first recordings: composer of the month: Ann Southam,' ibid

South and Central America, Mexico, the West Indies. Although Canada and the Latin American countries are part of the western hemisphere, their musical relations have been limited, for the most part, to many visits back and forth between performers and composers. The native cultures of Mexico and South and Central America have little in common with those of North America, and the Spanish and Portuguese settlements in the southern countries of the hemisphere were established 200 years earlier than were the French and British settlements in the northern countries. The developments have been along lines these differences would suggest, intermigration has been slight, and post-World-War-II commercial activities linking Canada and individual South American countries have had minimal cultural impact. The two cultures are drawn to each other's music by fascination with the exotic, but have remained distinct.

Nevertheless, a few Latin American musicians have settled in Canada. Among the first was the Chilean pianist and teacher Alberto *Guerrero, who arrived in Toronto, via New York, in 1919. The vibraphonist Jimmy *Namaro was born in Mexico but was brought to Canada as a child, as was the danceband pianist Billy Munro, born in the British West Indies. The tenor Édouard *Woolley, born in Haiti, settled in Montreal in 1938. During the early 1940s the Inca Taky Trio, a folk group from Peru, moved to Montreal and broadcast to South America for the CBC's International Service. A member of the group, the famous many-voiced singer Yma Sumac, soon departed for the USA where she pursued an exceptionally successful solo career.

The Cuban-born pianist Zeyda *Suzuki moved to Quebec City in 1963. The conductor and violinist Ruben *Gurevich immigrated to Canada from Uruguay during the late 1960s. His father also moved to Canada and became a violinist with the *Winnipeg SO. The Argentinian pianist Raoul *Sosa, a teacher at the *CMM, settled in Montreal ca 1967. Other immigrants from Argentina in the late 1960s and early 1970s were Alcides *Lanza, director of *McGill U's Electronic Music Studio, and the MSO violinist and teacher Luis Grinhauz and his wife, the pianist Berta Rosenhol-Grinhauz. The Mexican violinist and conductor Manuel Suarez led the *Thunder Bay SO 1972-4.

Although few South Americans have chosen to live in Canada, many have visited. The famous Venezuelan pianist Teresa Carreño played in Montreal as early as 1883, when she appeared as assisting artist at Emma *Albani's comeback concerts. She was heard later in Toronto as well. The Chilean pianist Rosita Renard performed in Montreal in 1918.

In 1944 representatives from Canada and Brazil exchanged notes which constituted 'an agreement for the promotion of cultural relations.' As a result the *Alouette Vocal Quartet travelled to Brazil, as did the composers Claude *Champagne and Sir Ernest *MacMillan, both of whom conducted programs of Canadian works. Champagne wrote a piece entitled *Quadrilha brasileira*, which was premiered by the Brazilian pianist Arnaldo Estrella. In return the Brazilian composer Heitor Villa-Lobos visited Canada in 1952 and conducted the CSM Orchestra at *Plateau Hall in Montreal in a concert which included two of his own works and compositions by Ernesto Drangosch of Argentina and Humberto Allende of Chile. He returned in 1958 to conduct the *CBC SO and the *TSO.

In 1946 the CBC International Service began regular short-wave music broadcasts to South America, and these encouraged further visits by South American artists. Some of those who travelled to Montreal to perform for these broadcasts were the pianist Guiomar Novaes of Brazil, the tenor Ramón Vinay of Chile, the aforementioned Arnaldo Estrella, and the Brazilian composer José Siqueira, who conducted a program of his own works. In 1948 a special concert of Brazilian and Canadian music was broadcast in honour of Brazil's Independence Day.

Among other South American visitors to Canada have been the Brazilian soprano Bidú Sayão, who has performed in concert and opera and who served as a judge in the 1977 *Montreal International Competition; the pianists Martha Argerich of Argentina, Claudio Arrau of Chile, Jorge Bolet and Horacio Gutiérrez of Cuba, Nelson Freire of Brazil, and Antonio Bujardo Octavio of Venezuela; the violinist Jaime Laredo of Bolivia; the Cuban guitarist Leo Brouwer, who has performed with the flutist Robert *Aitken; and the Mexican conductor Eduardo Mata. In 1965 the Brazilian composer Francesco Mignone visited Canada as a jury member for the Montreal International Competition – that year in piano. Mignone's *Tres preludios sobra temas canadenses*, based on French-Canadian folksongs, have been recorded by the pianist André-Sebastien *Savoie (RCI 418).

Orchestras heard in Canada include the Orquesta Sinfónica Nacional de México, which, under Luis Herrera de la Fuente, presented a program of works by José Pablo Moncayo, Silvestre Revueltas, and Carlos Chávez (Montreal 1958); and the Brazilian National Symphony, which performed with the conductor Eleazar de Carvalho at the *NAC in November 1977. The National Children's Choir of Argentina has appeared in Canada, as has the politically oriented Chilean group Quilapayun. In 1967 the Consejo Interamerica de Musica (CIDEM) held its fifth general assembly in Toronto. Arnold *Walter was a founding member and president 1969-72.

Numerous Canadian musicians have paid visits to South America. Probably the first to do so were J.-B. *Labelle and Calixa *Lavallée, both of whom toured there in 1857. The violinist Frantz *Jehin-Prume spent some time in Mexico, Brazil, and Cuba in the mid-1860s before settling in Montreal. In 1890 Emma Albani performed in Verdi's *Otello* opposite Francesco Tamagno in Mexico City. Edward *Johnson sang at Buenos Aires' Teatro Colón in 1916.

The pianist Jean *Dansereau gave several recitals and broadcasts 1942-3 in Rio de Janeiro; Ellen *Ballon, the dedicatee of Villa-Lobos's *First Piano Concerto*, premiered it in Rio in 1946; and Raoul *Jobin sang in *Werther* and Gluck's *Armide* at the Teatro Colón in 1948. Other noted Canadians who have appeared at that famous opera house include Maureen *Forrester, George *London, Joseph *Rouleau, Léopold *Simoneau, and Jon *Vickers. The sopranos Anna *Chornodolska and Louise *Lebrun have sung in Mexico City, the tenor Pierre *Duval in Chile, and the tenor André *Turp at the Municipal Opera in Rio de Janeiro. The contralto Portia *White toured in Central and South America in 1946.

Herman *Geiger-Torel spent many years as a stage director at opera houses such as the Teatro Colón in Buenos Aires, the SODRE National Theatre in Montevideo, and the Municipal Theatre in Rio de Janeiro prior to settling in Canada.

In 1957 in Mexico City Alexander *Brott received first prize at the Pan-American conducting competition. The same competition was won the following year by Boris *Brott, with second prize to Otto-Werner *Mueller. Others who have conducted in Latin America are Laszlo *Gati, Gregory *Millar, who was director of the National Opera of Mexico 1973-5, Paul *Pratt, Heinz *Unger, and Reginald *Stewart.

Maureen Forrester and Calvin *Sieb have participated in the Casals Festival in Puerto Rico, and Gerard *Kantarjian was a member of the festival orchestra 1960-7. The pianists André *Asselin, Arthur *Ozolins, and Claude *Savard, the flutist Suzanne *Shulman, and the chamber group *Camerata have performed in South America. The chanteuse Pauline *Julien and the tenor Raoul Jobin have sung in Havana. The group *Stringband gave a series of concerts in Mexico in 1977.

A 1977 production of *The Barber of Seville* by the Southern Alberta Opera Association

Colin *McPhee composed *Tabuh-Tabuhan* (1936) at the request of Carlos Chávez for the National Orchestra of Mexico. John *Weinzweig spent part of a sabbatical in Mexico in 1968 and composed *Dummiyah* there. In 1968 Talivaldis *Kenins' *Suite in D* for organ (1967) was premiered by Christian Grundman at Caracas, Venezuela. In 1977 John *Rea's *D'après Vasarely* was heard for the first time in a performance at the U of Santa Fe, Argentina. In 1979 the Montreal composer Micheline Coulombe *Saint-Marcoux was a guest at the 'Curso Latino Americano de musica contemporanea' in São João de Rei, Brazil.

Light music from South America, Mexico, and the Caribbean has enjoyed lasting success in Canada, mainly through radio broadcasts (eg, the popular CBC radio series of the 1940s, 'Latin American Serenade') and telecasts. The Argentine tango and the Brazilian conga, bossa nova, and rumba have been heard in countless programs featuring performers such as Claudette Jarry, Henri *Miro, Alys *Robi, and Chicho *Valle. The guitarist Art DeVilliers, who studied in Brazil, has specialized in bossa nova. Gene *Lees has collaborated with the Brazilian composers Antonio Carlos Joabim and Armando Manzaneiro. Billing themselves as 'Sukay,' the Montreal musicians Quinton and Edmond Badoux played Sukay – the folk music of the Andes – at the 1977 *Mariposa Folk Festival. Other proponents of Latin American music in Canada in 1980 were Memo, Marty Morell, and Dick Syncona Smith. (GP)

The Southern Alberta Opera Association. Established 12 Apr 1972 by the baritone Alexander *Gray and several Calgary citizens to present performances of professional quality. The first production (30, 31 Mar 1973) was *La Bohème* directed by Herman *Geiger-Torel and conducted by Stefan Minde, with Maria *Pellegrini, Ermanno *Mauro, Alexander Gray, Peter Milne, and Claude *Corbeil. Other productions, at first two, then – beginning in 1977 – three a year in Calgary's *Alberta Jubilee Auditorium, have included *Rigoletto* (1973), *Carmen* (1974), *Madama Butterfly* (1974), *Faust* (1975), *Die Fledermaus* (1976), *Lucia di Lammermoor* (1978), and *The Merry Widow* (1979). The orchestra has been drawn largely from the *Calgary Philharmonic Orchestra and the *Edmonton SO, and the conductors 1973-9 were Franz-Paul *Decker, Walter Ducloux, Anton Guadagno, Harman Haakman, Alfredo Silipigni, Samual Krachmalnik, Boyd *Neel, Ernesto *Barbini, and Howard *Cable. Stage directors included Irving *Guttman, John Leberg, Jean *Létourneau, Douglas Campbell, and Peter *Symcox. Singers for the first seven seasons included Peter *Barcza, Napoléon *Bisson, Colette *Boky, Jean *Bonhomme, Pierre *Duval, Judith *Forst, Jerome Hines, Ann Howard, Allan *Monk, Cornelis *Opthof, Gail Robinson, and Heather *Thomson. Alexander Gray was succeeded as artistic director in 1975 by Brian M. Hanson, who also became business administrator. Financial support for the association has been provided by the Calgary Regional Arts Foundation, the Province of Alberta, private and corporate donors, and the box office.

BIBLIOGRAPHY

'Southern Alberta Opera Association,' *OpCan*, vol 17, Feb 1976 (RDM)

SOUTHWORTH, Jean. Journalist, critic, b Omemee, near Lindsay, Ont, 9 Jan 1923; BA History (Toronto) 1944. She studied organ with Godfrey *Hewitt. She joined the news staff of *The Ottawa Journal* in 1948, served 1953–75 as music and drama editor, and later was a staff writer and reporter. She was chairman 1972–4 of the Ottawa Centre of *RCCO.

SOUVAIRAN, Pierre (Julien Arnold). Pianist, teacher, b Montreux, Switzerland, of French parents and nationality, 30 Jul 1911, naturalized Swiss 1931, naturalized Canadian 1959; Diplôme de Virtuosité (Ribaupierre) 1930. After studies with André de Ribaupierre at the Institut Ribaupierre in Lausanne he continued 1931–3 with Robert Teichmüller at the Leipzig Cons and briefly in 1933 with Alfred Cortot in Paris and Rudolf Serkin in Bern. He taught 1938–53 at the Bern Cons, gave recitals, and premiered many Swiss compositions in concert and on radio. In 1953 he joined the faculty of the *U of Toronto, where his students have included Mary Nan Dutka, Anne *Eggleston, Ralph Elsaesser, Mari-Elizabeth *Morgen, and Ann *Southam. Continuing to perform annually in Europe, Souvairan has appeared also in Canada, in recital, with chamber ensembles, and with such orchestras as the *CBC SO. He played Beethoven's *Triple Concerto* 29 and 30 Oct 1963 with Albert *Pratz, Theo Salzman, and the *TSO. Of a Souvairan recital in Toronto of works by Beethoven, Fauré, Ravel, and Schumann, Michael Schulman wrote in the *Globe and Mail*: 'There was nothing of pretense or self-consciousness in either Souvairan's manner or his music-making. He began each piece practically in the same motion with which he returned to the bench – no inward-searching pregnant pauses here. And the music, too, was unencumbered by arbitrary interpretive touches imposed from without' (6 Feb 1976).

DISCOGRAPHY

Bartók *Piano Concerto No. 3* – Chopin *Ballades No. 3, 4* – Schumann *Fantasiestücke, Op 12*. 1956. Hallmark 6012

Beethoven *Bagatelles, Op 126* – Schumann *Fantasiestücke, Op 12*. 1969. CBC SM-94/Sel CC 15.037

Beethoven *Sonata No. 32* – Schumann *Humoreske, Op 20*. 1973. Boot BIC 9000

Fauré *Nocturne, Op 63* – Honegger *Toccata and Variations* – Bartók (various). 1976. Gallo 30-132

Honegger *Petite Suite* – Regamey *String Quartet No. 1* – Moeschinger *Sonata*. 1950. Decca LXT 2849

See also Discography for Lorand Fenyves; Albert Pratz.

(WS)

Sovereigns, statesmen, and other public figures. Certain dignitaries, explorers, and political and religious leaders have contributed to Canada's

musical history through their own musical talents, as patrons of the arts, or passively as dedicatees of Canadian compositions. Information on compositions which treat Canadian dignitaries in retrospect will be found under History of Canada in music. See also Coronations.

In his 17th-century work *Histoire du Montréal* (transl R. Flenley as *A History of Montreal 1640–1672*, Toronto 1928), François Dollier de Casson described Maisonneuve (1612–76), the founder (1642) and first governor of Montreal, as a practitioner of music: '[the divine hand] maintained in him such a lively fear of the Day of Judgement, that in order not to be driven to seek the company of the wicked for recreation, he had learnt to play the lute, to be able to pass his time alone when he had no other companions' (Flenley pp 70–1). According to Eric *McLean, this lute has been preserved by the Sulpicians.

Claude-Thomas Dupuy, the Intendant of New France 1726–8, is known to have had a strong interest in music. In his biography *Claude-Thomas Dupuy* (Montreal 1969) Jean-Claude Dubé states that the intendant had imported instruments into Canada, that he was a performer, and that his tastes in music were cultivated. Dupuy made a list of his music library, which included many Lully operas, Campra motets, and Clérambault cantatas. Another music-loving (and equally corrupt) politician was Dupuy's successor, François Bigot (1703–ca 1777), the last intendant (1748–60) of New France. Bigot is known to have given balls, masquerades, and other entertainments which were the talk of Quebec. This was much to the regret of at least one local curé who is said to have commented 'Observe all these lascivious manners, which can lead only to sin' ('La Correspondance de Madame Bégon, 1748–1753,' *Rapport de l'Archiviste de la Province de Québec pour 1934–35*). In the *Journal du Marquis de Montcalm durant ses campagnes en Canada de 1765 à 1769* (ed H.-R. Casgrain, Quebec 1895), one reads that 'The Intendant [Bigot] assembled many guests to hear a concert given by his officers and their wives' but that this laudable effort was followed by a gambling party (entry of 18 Dec 1757).

One of the earliest of Canadian-born explorers was Louis *Jolliet (1645–1700), the discoverer of the source of the Mississippi River, and one of the first organists in Canada. Explorers of the Canadian north in the 19th century included Ferdinand Wentzel, a Norwegian in the service of the North West Company, who mastered both the flute and the fiddle and compiled a collection of voyageur songs which survived until at least 1890. Due to the inclusion of several obscene songs, the collection was never published. Edward Ermatinger, a Swiss-born explorer who worked for the Hudson's Bay Company, also wrote down voyageur songs which, unlike Wentzel's, have survived.

Inuit music was notated by (Sir) William Edward Parry during his exploration of the Northwest Passage in several expeditions 1819–27. To help pass the time he carried several flutes and even a *barrel organ on his ships the *Fury* and the *Hecla*. Parry was co-author of an 'opera,' *The North West Passage, or Voyage Unfinished*, performed aboard his ship in 24 degrees below zero centigrade. The performance undoubtedly set a precedent in operatic history for geographical location, and a record for temperature.

The future Duke of Kent and father of Queen Victoria, Prince Edward (1767–1820), spent the 1790s in Quebec and Halifax as commander of the Royal Fusiliers' regiment, and probably was the first royal visitor to Canada to exhibit a strong interest in music. His regimental band, which cost him £800 a year, was said to have been excellent. It participated in subscription concerts, played at dances, and gave outdoor performances. In Halifax Prince Edward erected a bandstand (still intact in 1980), and while stationed in Quebec he took a personal interest in the activities of Frédéric Henri *Glackemeyer.

The prince's grandson (later King Edward VII), who visited Canada in 1860 as the Prince of Wales, was the dedicatee of the first major Canadian composition written for a dignitary, C.W. *Sabatier's *Cantata in Honour of the Prince of Wales* (ca 1860). The visit also inspired Antoine *Dessane's *Marche – Cantate pour la visite du Prince de Galles* and shorter pieces such as Henry *Prince's *The Prince of Wales Galop* and Henry Francis *Sefton's 'Welcome to Canada.'

During the following 80 years the fashion of dedicating songs, dances, and marches to sovereigns and statesmen blossomed. When Prince Arthur, younger son of Queen Victoria, visited Canada in 1869–70, a march by F.J. Hatton, a galop by Hunter Gowan, and a mazurka by William *Bohrer were named for him. To honour the same visit G. Raineri wrote *Dominion State Ball Galop*, and J.C. *Brauneis II, the *Royal Welcome Waltzes*. The golden jubilee (1887) of Queen Victoria inspired F.H. *Torrington's 'Queen's Jubilee,' and *Vézina's *Le Jubilé de la Reine*, while her diamond jubilee (1897) resulted in over 15 published Canadian compositions. Following the visit of the Prince of Wales (later Edward VIII), Lillian Casselman wrote the song 'His Smile,' arranged by Jules *Brazil and published in Toronto in 1921. Among the songs composed to mark royal events are Oscar *O'Brien's 'King's Jubilee' (English words by Charles F. Larkin, French by Hector Beauregard) published in *La Presse*, Montreal, on 13 May 1939 during the royal tour of King George VI and Queen Elizabeth. Godfrey *Ridout's *Music for a Young Prince* (written in honour of Prince Charles) was commissioned by the CBC for the opening of the St Lawrence Seaway and the attendant royal tour in 1959.

There have been numerous 'welcome' and 'farewell' pieces written for the monarch's representatives in Canada, the governors-general. The oldest in print is probably Vincenzo Mazzocchi's *Welcome to Canada* (1839), dedicated to Baron Sydenham. Judging by the number of pieces written for them, the most popular of crown representatives were Lord and Lady Dufferin (in office 1872–8) and the Marquis of Lorne and Princess

Louise (who followed 1878–83). *Canada's Welcome* (1879), a masque written by A.A. *Clappé, director of the *Governor General's Foot Guards Band, and dedicated to the latter couple was the largest of these compositions. Lady Dufferin organized theatrical and musical performances at Government House (see Frederick W. Mills) and was the author of poems which were set to music and published in Canada. G. Raineri wrote the *Dufferin Galop* for the Dufferins' visit to Halifax in 1873. Princess Louise, a daughter of Queen Victoria, herself has been credited with a number of compositions.

The Marquis of Lorne wrote the words for the 'Dominion Hymn' (1880), and Arthur Sullivan set them to music, but the work failed to gain acceptance as a national anthem. Lorne and his wife were the dedicatees of *Lavallée's *Cantate en l'honneur du Marquis de Lorne et de la Princesse Louise*, performed for them at Quebec 11 Jun 1879 by more than 300 singers and instrumentalists. Célestin *Lavigueur's *Soyez la bienvenue* was written especially for Princess Louise herself.

According to the *Encyclopedia Canadiana* Sir William Robinson, lieutenant-governor of Prince Edward Island 1870–3, was 'a musical composer of some note and author of a number of well-known songs.'

In the 20th century governors-general who have taken an interest in music include Earl Grey, who held office 1904–11. He organized contests for amateur orchestras, choirs, and solo instrumentalists and singers. Winners included the Société symphonique de Québec (*Quebec SO) and the Ottawa SO. For the diamond jubilee of Canadian confederation, Lord Willingdon (governor-general 1926–31) composed a suite which was performed in Ottawa 1 Jul 1927 by the Chateau Laurier Orchestra and broadcast nationwide over the CNR network. He also founded the Willingdon Arts Competition for Excellence in Music, Literature, Painting and Sculpture, and under a nom de plume wrote several songs. Prior to his appointment in 1952 Vincent Massey, the first Canadian-born governor-general, had demonstrated his devotion to the arts – as a patron of the *Hart House String Quartet, and as chairman of the Royal Commission on National Development in the Arts, Letters and Sciences, known as the *Massey Commission. He was the dedicatee of *The Vincent Massey March* by the Montreal violinist and composer Maurice *Zbriger. In 1978 Jules Léger (governor-general 1974–9) established the Jules Léger Chamber Music Prize (see Composition competitions).

Other distinguished patrons of music in Canada included Lord Strathcona (1820–1914), a benefactor of several music institutions and musicians, and creator of the Montreal Scholarship (later the *Strathcona Scholarship) for studies at the RCM; and Lord Beaverbrook, who commissioned Louise *Manny to collect and record songs of the Miramichi (New Brunswick) lumbermen. Among Canadian prime ministers none has been known for an interest in music but three are noteworthy for the number of musical dedications they have received. These are Sir John A. Macdonald, Alexander Mackenzie, and Sir Wilfrid Laurier, the last-named a patron of Eva *Gauthier and a friend of Emma *Albani. Examples of works written for these prime ministers are the *Loyal Opposition Galop* by George *Orme, the *Sir John A. Macdonald Waltz* by Annie Douglas, *The Premier's NP* [National Policy] *Galop* by Arthur Koerber, the *Ministerial Galop* (dedicated to the Liberal party and featuring Mackenzie's picture on its printed cover) by A. Overell, *Vive Laurier* by Alexis *Contant, and 'Our Chieftain' by 'an Ottawa lady.' Sir George-Étienne Cartier and Macdonald, joint leaders 1857–62 of the governing ministry of the Province of Canada, both had funeral marches written for them: the *Grand Requiem March* (1873) by A. Koch, and the *Sir John A. Macdonald Funeral March* (1891) by Charles *Bohner. Cartier himself was the author of the words of two songs (see Patriotic songs). Macdonald was a friend of Albani, and 18 Feb 1889 in a letter to Dr James Williamson he wrote 'She sang for me on my birthday. Was it not kind of Her? I was charmed with her voice' (*The Letters of Sir John A. Macdonald and His Family*, ed J.K. Johnson, Toronto 1969).

Among later 20th-century tributes to Canadian prime ministers is 'Dief Will Be the Chief Again' (1975), a salute to John Diefenbaker by Bob Bossin of *Stringband. An LP, *Graham Townsend Salutes Canada's Prime Ministers 1867–1967* (London SBS 5275) comprises fiddle tunes named for each Canadian prime minister up to and including Lester Pearson.

Federal cabinet ministers of the 1970s with an interest in music have included Mitchell Sharp, an accomplished pianist, and Paul Hellyer, tenor. On a municipal level Paul *Pratt (b 1894), mayor 1935–66 of Longueuil, Que, was a composer, conductor, and clarinetist.

Among the few Canadian compositions honouring religious dignitaries are Emma Albani's 'Hymne à Pie IX' (ca 1864), Lavallée's *Marche funèbre 'Hommage à Pie IX'* (ca 1878), Gustave *Gagnon's *Marche pontificale* (1886), written for Quebec's Cardinal Taschereau, and *Jehin-Prume's *Oratorio à Léon XIII*.

Soviet Union. See Union of Soviet Socialist Republics.

Spain. Immigration to Canada by Spanish peoples was slow until 1950, by comparison with that from most other European nations. Nevertheless, by the 1970s there were some 30,000 Spanish-Canadians, concentrated in cities in Quebec, Ontario, and British Columbia.

The great music of the early Spanish church has had little currency in Canada (though the *Montreal Bach Choir has performed and recorded music of the renaissance and a mass by Victoria) and 18th-century opera and orchestral music have had virtually none. From the 19th century an occasional piece by Arriaga may be heard (the *Orford String Quartet plays his *Quartet No. 3* and the *CJRT Orchestra has performed his *Symphony in D*) but nothing of Eslava or Pedrell. Most performed are the nationalist composers – Albéniz, Falla, and Granados and, to a lesser extent, Turina – who straddled the 19th and 20th centuries; and even they are represented on Canadian programs by relatively few works, notably Falla's *El Amor Brujo* on symphony programs and his *Seven Popular Songs* at recitals and Granados' *Goyescas* and Albéniz's *Iberia* in the repertoires of several pianists. Pieces by later Spanish composers (Mompou, Nin) are heard from time to time, but those by Halffter, for instance, and Esplá remain all but unknown. By contrast the music played by both classical and Flamenco guitarists has proved widely appealing to Canadians.

Spanish folk music and dance have been sustained in Canada by several amateur ensembles such as that of the Club Hispano in Toronto, which performs both folk and classical music. Flamenco, the dance music of the Spanish gypsies, is played in Canada by Spanish-Canadians (eg, Juan Garcia, owner of the Toronto restaurant Embrujo Flamenco) and by other guitarists including Lenny *Breau, John *Perrone, David Phillips (accompanist to the Paula Moreno Spanish Dance Co of Toronto), Juan (John) Thomas, and the duo Harry and David Owen. Many Canadian classical guitarists also include Flamenco in their repertoires. The Canadians Harry and David Owen, Ian Ayre McConkey, and Juan Thomas have studied guitar in Spain; Eli *Kassner, John Perrone, Thomas, and others offer instruction in Spanish guitar music (see also Guitar). The outstanding Flamenco and classical guitarists of Spain, including Carlos Montoya, Andrés Segovia, and Narciso Yepes, have appeared in Canadian cities, giving concerts and master classes.

It is known that Emma *Albani sang at the Gran Teatro del Liceo in Barcelona during the 1884–5 season. Other Canadians who have performed in the opera house include André *Turp in 1961–2 (awarded the Medalla de Oro in 1963 for his performance in *Werther*), France *Dion in 1964, Joseph *Rouleau in 1963–4, Louis *Quilico 1966–7, and Nicole *Lorange in 1976. Lorange also recorded arias and duets with the tenor Jaime Aragall. Irving *Guttman was a guest director in 1969, 1971, and 1973. Heinz *Unger was a popular guest conductor of Spanish orchestras. The pianist Sheila *Henig, the Orford Quartet, and Gaston *Germain have toured in Spain.

Among Spanish musicians resident in Canada have been the conductor Henri *Miro; the pianist José Iturbi (conductor 1968–9 of the *Calgary Philharmonic Orchestra); the violinist Victor Martin (born of Spanish parents in France), conductor 1968–77 of the *Chamber Players of Toronto; the composer José *Evangelista; the composer Luis de Pablo (b Bilbao 28 Jan 1930), who began teaching at the *U of Ottawa in 1974; and Rafael Frühbeck de Burgos, conductor 1975–6 of the *MSO.

The cellist Pablo Casals appeared many times in Canada. He was an assisting artist 1 and 2 Feb 1915 with the *Toronto Mendelssohn Choir at *Massey Hall. His pupil Gaspar Cassado played for the *Ladies' Morning Musical Club of Montreal in 1937. Victoria de los Angeles sang in Toronto in 1953, 1958, and 1972, and Teresa Berganza in 1964. The pianist Alicia De Larrocca appeared with the *TS in Toronto, New York, and Washington in 1977 and has performed on many other occasions in Canada. For the JMC the guitarist Alberto Ponce toured Canada in 1963–4, the guitarist Renata Tarrago in 1966–7 and 1967–8, the soprano Monserrat Alavedra in 1968–9, the soprano Maria Muro in 1973–4, and the Quartet Tarrago in 1975–6 and 1976–7.

The immigration in the 1960s of Sephardic Jews from the Near East introduced into Canada a repertoire of old Spanish romances and songs sung in Ladino. (GP, RPl, KW)

SPANIER, Herb or **Herbie** (Herbert Anthony Charles). Trumpeter, flugelhornist, pianist, composer, b Cupar, near Regina, 25 Dec 1928. He played guitar and harmonica at five, bugle in Regina cadet bands, and trumpet in high school. One of the first bebop jazzmen in Canada, he played with Paul *Perry 1947–8 and his own Boptet 1948–9 in Regina and worked in Chicago 1949–50 and Toronto 1950–4 before joining Paul *Bley in New York 1954–5 (and later in Los Angeles, 1958–9) and touring in 1955 with Claude Thornhill in the USA. An influential jazz musician in Montreal 1956–8 and 1960–71 and in Toronto after 1971 he taught briefly in 1957 at Sir George Williams U, performed in various dance orchestras, joined *Nimmons 'N' Nine Plus Six in 1970, and began playing occasionally with David Amram in 1975. His own groups have been heard in clubs and concerts and frequently, during the 1960s, on CBC radio's 'Jazz en liberté.' Characterized by Barry Tepperman as 'an emotionally brilliant and immediately accessible player ... with one of the most ingeniously expressive vibratos of the post-bop era' (*Coda* Aug 1975) Spanier has been featured on recordings by Nimmons and Amram (*Summer Nights, Winter Rain*, 1975–6, RCA KPL1-0169) and, with the saxophonist Alvin Pall, the pianist Bernie *Senensky, the bassist Michel *Donato, and the drummer Claude *Ranger, on an album of his own compositions, *Forensic Perturbations* (1972, RCI 376). He is an affiliate of PRO Canada. MM

H.H. Sparks Music Co. Toronto music and publishing house run ca 1900–10 by Harry H. Sparks. It issued over 200 pieces of music, beginning with Canadian songs for the South African War and continuing with dance, ragtime and march music, and songs, often reflecting local colour or patriotic spirit. Many are designated Star Edition; perhaps half have a copyright notice. The composers, all writing in a popular idiom, include Fenton S. Fansher, Arthur Wellesley *Hughes, Joseph F. Lamb, J. Cecil Rolls, Charles E. Wellinger, William Westbrook, and one Harry Herbert, possibly a pseudonym for Harry H. Sparks. HK

Sparrow (Steppenwolf). Toronto blues band which became a popular US hard-rock group after its re-formation (1967) as Steppenwolf in Los Angeles. Formed as the Sparrow in 1964 by the singer Jack London, with the guitarist Dennis Edmonton, the bass guitarist Bruce Palmer (replaced by Nick St Nicholas), and the drummer Jerry Edmonton, it was joined in June 1965 by the singer-harmonica player-guitarist John Kay (who would replace London) and the pianist-organist Goldy McJohn. One of many Toronto groups influenced by the Hawks (see The *Band), it appeared 1965–6 in Yorkville coffee houses and recorded on the Capitol label, then worked in 1966 in New York, briefly in Los Angeles, and in San Francisco. Other recordings from this period were compiled on *John Kay and the Sparrow* (Col CS 9758). After the dissolution in 1967 of the Sparrow in San Francisco, Dennis Edmonton began a solo career under the name 'Mars Bonfire,' his recordings including the LP *Faster Than the Speed of Life* (1969, Col CS 9834). Kay, with Jerry Edmonton and McJohn, formed Steppenwolf, taking the name from the popular Hermann Hesse novel and initially drawing on the Sparrow's repertoire. A succession of lead and bass guitarists, including St Nicholas 1969–70, occupied the other positions in the quintet. Steppenwolf performed extensively in major North American halls and also in Europe, and by 1972 it had released 10 LPs with ABC/Dunhill (8 receiving gold record sales-awards) and three million-selling singles, Mars Bonfire's 'Born to Be Wild' (1968) and Kay's 'Magic Carpet Ride' (1969) and 'The Monster' (1970). Dominated by Kay's gruff voice, Steppenwolf's musical product was a tough, sometimes menacing, high-volume rock which lost its popularity as it became increasingly formulized. Steppenwolf first disbanded in 1972. Thereafter Kay (b Germany 12 Apr 1944) made the solo LPs *Unsung Songs and Little Known Heroes* (1972, Dunhill D5X 50120) and *My Sporting Life* (1973, Dunhill D5X 50147) and a hit version of 'I'm Movin' On' (1972). He re-formed Steppenwolf with Edmonton in 1974, but the new group's three albums for Columbia Records failed to recapture past success. Several bands formed by former members were active under the name Steppenwolf in the late 1970s, and the question of ownership of the name was taken eventually into the US courts. In 1980, a band under Kay's leadership toured as John Kay and Steppenwolf. Steppenwolf was listed in 1975 by *Billboard* magazine as the 199th of the 200 most-popular recording acts of the previous 30 years.

BIBLIOGRAPHY

Yorke, Ritchie. 'The ones who wouldn't wait,' *Axes, Chops & Hot Licks* (Edmonton 1971) MM

Sparton of Canada, Ltd. Record manufacturing company established in 1930 in London, Ont, by a US company, Sparks-Worthington. Sparton of Canada manufactured radios, phonographs, and household appliances and became the Canadian presser and distributor 1939–54 for Columbia records and thereafter, until 1969, for ABC-Paramount, Disneyland, Hifirecord, and its own Sparton label. It was the first company in Canada to press stereo records. Besides many records from the Sparton (USA) catalogue, the company issued 78s, singles (45s), or LPs by Ward *Allen, Paul *Anka, Joyce *Hahn, Cliff *McKay, Jimmy *Namaro, the fiddler Bob Scott, Don and Priscilla *Wright, and other Canadians. (EBM)

SPENCER, David. Patron, b Toronto 27 Oct 1915; BA (British Columbia) 1938. A lawyer by profession, Spencer became a member of the music section of the *Community Arts Council of Vancouver after World War II and served as its chairman for two years. As donor and adviser he has assisted in the establishment and development of the *Vancouver Opera Assn, the Courtenay Youth Music Centre, the *Edmonton Opera Assn, and the *Community Music School of Greater Vancouver. He believes that a proportion of an organization's maintenance monies should always be reserved for capital investment and is an advocate of the development of endowment funds and investment policies.

SPENCER, Herbert. Conductor, violinist, composer, b Liverpool 28 Feb 1875, d Montreal 24 Dec 1945; Associate, Dominion College of Music. As a child he studied violin with Henry Lawson, piano with Helen Beer, and theory with W.J. Doran. Emigrating to Canada in 1891 he continued his studies in Montreal with Horace *Reyner and Charles *O'Neill. In a long career as a theatre and hotel orchestra director he conducted at the Lyceum, *His Majesty's, and Loew's theatres in Montreal and at the Château Frontenac hotel in Quebec. For some 20 years he was music director for the theatrical producers Sparrow and Jacobs. Spencer is said to have improved the quality of music in the movie houses by using a symphonic orchestra and programming 'music of the masters.' In the 1920s, with the Mount Royal Concert Orchestra of Montreal, he pioneered in orchestral radio broadcasts.

Spencer founded and was the violin in a trio in Montreal (1899–1904, with Louis *Charbonneau, cello, and a Mrs Turner, piano). He played first violin in the *CSM in its early years and became an arranger for the CBC ca 1938. His unpublished compositions include the operetta *The Cavaliers* (W.A. Tremayne), which was produced by the Lyric Operatic Society of Montreal. His song *'The Wreck of the Julie Plante' (W.H. Drummond) was sung by Pauline *Donalda at the *Russell Theatre in Ottawa in 1915. Several of his short pieces and folksong arrangements for orchestra or band were heard on CBC radio. The CBC has preserved some of Spencer's manuscripts in its Montreal music library. (FH)

SPENCER, Marguerita (b MacQuarrie). Composer, pianist, organist, teacher, b Glace Bay, NS, 28 Dec 1892; L MUS (McGill) 1934. She studied with Harry *Dean at the Halifax Cons, with Mary Mitchener, Helen Davies *Sherry, and Lyell *Gustin in Saskatoon (where she settled in 1922), with Clara *Lichtenstein at the *McGill Conservatorium, and with Boris *Roubakine and Bela Böszörmenyi-Nagy at the *Banff SFA. She was organist at Westminster and First Baptist churches in Saskatoon and was the organ partner in a 1954 series of duo-recitals on the CBC with the pianists John Whelan and Norman Dahl. She has published some songs ('June Magic,' Thompson 1956, 'Two Shakespeare Songs,' Thompson 1961) and two *Prairie Suites* (Harris 1953, 1959). In manuscript are many works for piano, string quartet, voice, and instrumental combinations. Her *24 Preludes in All Keys* for piano were completed in 1971. She was president of the *Musical Art Club 1943–5. She was the pianist in a recital of her songs and piano pieces for the *Women's Musical Club of Saskatoon 4 Apr 1978. GGrv

Elie Spivak

SPIVAK, Elie. Violinist, b Uman, Ukraine, 2 Feb 1902, d Toronto, 23 Jul 1960. He studied at the Paris Cons 1910–15 with Bertholier and at the Royal College of Manchester 1916–21 with Adolf Brodsky. He founded (in Manchester, 1923) the Elie Spivak String Quartet, the first ensemble to give chamber music concerts over the new BBC network. After a year (1925) in New York he moved to Toronto, where he taught and played. He was first violin 1929–42 of the *Conservatory String Quartet and concertmaster 1931–48 of the *TSO. In 1945 he gave the North American premiere of the Khachaturian *Violin Concerto* with the Boston Pops Orchestra. He was the first Canadian musician invited to Israel, touring the country for five months in 1950 as guest of the Jerusalem String Quartet. He led the Spivak String Quartet 1951–6 and with this group, with orchestra, and as soloist was heard frequently over CBC radio. He examined for the *RCMT and adjudicated for *Kiwanis Festivals and the *CNE. He taught violin at the RCMT from 1929 until his death. He also taught in the University Settlement music school. Many of his pupils – including Doreen *Hall, Julian Kolkowski, John Montague, Pearl Palmason, Walter *Prystawski, Steven *Staryk, and David *Zafer – have occupied important teaching and playing posts across Canada and in the USA. His playing was known for warmth of tone and depth of feeling. Colleagues recall his sensitivity and gentleness as an artist and as a man.

BIBLIOGRAPHY

Sumberg, Harold. 'Elie Spivak 1902–1960,' *CMJ*, vol 5, Autumn 1960 WS

Sports. Canadians have adopted nearly every known athletic activity or sport, and some have been inspired by a favourite one to compose a popular song or a short band or piano piece. Such pieces were common during the late 19th and early 20th centuries, when boating, cycling, golf, and hockey became popular and social-athletic clubs proliferated, many with their own songs.

One of Canada's earliest sports, lacrosse was invented by the Indians. Pieces composed in its honour include the song 'La Crosse, Our National Game,' arranged by H.F. *Sefton (mid-1870s) and the piano piece *Lacrosse Jersey* (1892), written by Nellie Smith and dedicated to the Toronto Lacrosse Club. Archery as a sport was introduced to Canada ca 1850, and in 1859 Henry *Prince dedicated a piano piece entitled *The Arrow Flight Galop* to the ladies of the Montreal Archery Club. Rowing became a competitive sport in Canada in 1848, and while canoeing had begun as a means of transportation, by the mid-19th century it, too, was popular as a recreation. Canoeing and boating pieces include 'Les Canotiers du Saint-Laurent,' signed by a lady, 'D.D.' (*Écho du Cabinet*, 1863), a quadrille of the same name by A.J. *Boucher, 'Yachting Song' by Herbert L. *Clarke and John Imrie (Imrie & Graham 1890), and *Midland Regatta Schottische* by Campbell Shaw (1894). Among works dedicated to specific clubs were Emma Blackstock's 'A Starry Night' (nd) and Matthew de S. Wedd's song 'You and Canoe' (1896), both for Toronto's Royal Canadian Yacht Club; William Spence's *Royal St. Lawrence Yacht Club* (nd) and Mrs Converse's *The St. Lawrence Yacht Club Waltz* (1893), both for the Royal St Lawrence Yacht Club in Montreal; Miss C. Geddes Armstrong's *Splash and Dash Polka* (1892), for the Ottawa Rowing Club; and Lotte Marks' *Argonaut Waltzes* (1899), for the Argonaut Rowing Club of Toronto. Several pieces were dedicated to the Canadian rowing champions Ned Hanlan (see Edwin Gledhill) and Lewis Scholes.

Bicycling took Canada by storm in 1876; clubs soon were established and races organized. Many pieces appeared in tribute to the new fad: *The Bicycle Belle March* (1895) by G.A. Watts, 'A Corker Bicycle Song' (1895) by J.F. *Davis, *Wheeling by Moonlight* (1896) by T. Echel, 'Queen of the Wheel' (1897) by G. Deane, and 'On Wings of Steel' (1907) by Herbert H. *Godfrey. R.S. Peniston dedicated 'Wheeling' (1891) to the Wanderers' (Bicycle) Club of Toronto. A more recent song was Paul (Tex) *Lecor's 'Ti-Bicycle.'

Cricket probably was played first in Nova Scotia during the 18th century. Although it never became widely popular in Canada and appears to have been almost ignored by composers, Mrs H.S. Scadding did write *The Cricketers' Waltzes* (ca 1875) for the Toronto Cricket Club. Curling, a sport closely identified with Canada, is thought to have been introduced by General Wolfe's soldiers at Quebec ca 1760. Sometime before 1871 a Mr Stevenson wrote *The Curling Club Polka* for piano. Golf, first played at Montreal in 1873, was eulogized in Edward Atherton's song 'Far and Sure' (1903). In 1929 R.C. *Larivière wrote *Valse des petits gymnastes* in honour of the sport of Greece. *The Lawn Tennis Dance* (1889) by J.F. Davis and 'Tennis' (1915) by Wilson MacDonald both praised that sport. Football, popular in Canada in the 20th century, inspired Ambeault's song 'Argonaut Two-step' and William *Eckstein's 'Alouettes, Alouettes, Alouettes' (self-publ 1955). The *Canadian Talent Library lists a recording, *Canadian Football Songs* (CTL S-5104), which includes 'The Day of the Grey Cup,' 'Go Argos Go,' and 'Tigercat Marching Song.' Another recording, RCA 75-1013, features the official Grey Cup song for 1969.

Ice hockey – claimed by some to have originated in Halifax, NS, in 1828 – is the game identified most often as Canada's national sport. Songs dealing with the game and its players include Eugene Platzman's 'Hockey' (1929), William *McCauley's 'Clear the Track, Here Comes Shack' and 'Warming the Bench' (both 1966), Anna *McGarrigle's 'Hommage à Henri Richard' (ca 1974), Bob King's 'Ballad of Gordie Howe,' Alec Somerville's 'Hockey Night in Canada' (recorded on Arc 257), and Oscar Thiffault's 'Le Rocket Richard' (recorded on Carnival C-500). Pierre *Mercure composed *Jeu de hockey* (1961) for electroacoustic tape. Pierre Létourneau's song 'Maurice Richard' is recorded (La Compagnie 124), as is Hervé Brousseau's 'Mon Patin' (Select SP 12.078).

Horse racing has been especially popular in Ontario and British Columbia, and its most important centre has been the Woodbine Race Track in Toronto, home of the Queen's Plate (established in 1836, the oldest stakes race in North America). The *2.10½ Galop* by 'B.C.' was dedicated in 1881 to O.B. Sheppard, secretary of the Woodbine Park Assn. Albert *Nordheimer wrote his 'Hunting Song' (1908) for the Toronto Hunt Club. Winter sports – sleighing, skating, skiing, snow-shoeing, tobogganing – inspired Henry Russell's 'The Canadian Sleigh Song' (ca 1840), J. Smythe's *The Sleigh Polka* (1849, dedicated to the Montreal Sleigh Club), W. Braybrooke Bayley's 'Belle of the Rink' (Suckling 1877), J. *Vézina's 'Chant de l'Union des raquetteurs' (1886), W. Delaney's 'The Joyous Skaters' (1886), E. Buron and P. de Sale's 'En nouant sa raquette' (ca 1896), and A. Tessier's 'Vive la raquette' (1916). Others were Harold F. Palmer's 'The Snow Shoe Tramp, a Song of the North West' (pre–1859), written for the Snow Shoe Clubs of Canada; C.E. St Clair's 'Snow Shoe Galop' (nd), written for the Montreal Snow Shoe Club; and H.A.G. Austin's *Valses Asketyn* (1886), dedicated to Ottawa's Taché Hill Sliding Club.

Miscellaneous sports songs of more recent years have included 'Marilyn' (Canadian Music Sales 1954), by Leslie *Bell, written in honour of Marilyn Bell's 1954 marathon swim across Lake Ontario. Some of the songs composed for the Olympics are included on the recording *10 Chansons finalistes du concours de la chanson d'adieu* (Solo SO-21101). Marc *Gélinas and Marcel Lefebvre's song 'Les Expos sont là,' theme song of the Montreal baseball team, has been recorded in its French version (Marco DM 777) as a single, and also in an English version by Pat McDougall, 'The Expos Song' (Marco DM 778). J. Larin's 'La Chanson des sports' is included in a two-record set (2-RCA Gala KTL-2-7018) and also on RCA Gala CGP-181.

BIBLIOGRAPHY
Musical Canadiana (FH)

Spring Thaw. Toronto revue recurrent annually from 1948 to 1971, by 1980 still a record of longevity in Canadian musical theatre. The first production, devised by the New Play Society under Dora Mavor Moore and directed by her son Mavor *Moore, was a last-minute replacement for an uncompleted play. It opened 1 Apr 1948 and had three performances at the Museum Theatre. The revue's stylistic origins have been attributed to the *Arts and Letters Club spring revues and to Gratien Gélinas's **Fridolinons* in Montreal. A combination of topical and satirical songs, dances, and skits, mostly on Canadian subjects, *Spring Thaw* was staged in a succession of Toronto theatres – Museum, Avenue, Radio City, Odeon Fairlawn, Crest, *Royal Alexandra, Playhouse, and Global Village. At the height of its success, runs extended into mid-summer and in 1962, 1964, and 1967 it toured Canada.

Spring Thaw was produced by Dora Mavor Moore until 1961, when Mavor Moore bought the production rights. He, in turn, leased them 1966–9 to Robert Johnson, in 1970 to Howard Bateman and John Uren, and in 1971 to Andrew Alexander. The revues directors included Moore, Brian Macdonald and James de B. Domville, Leon Major, Paxton Whitehead, Don Harron, Moni Yakim, and Robert Swerdlow. Harron (1967) and Swerdlow (1971) wrote their own productions. Songs and skits for the revues were contributed by various composers and writers, including Lucio *Agostini, Pierre Berton, Morris *Davis, John *Fenwick, Harron, Ray Jessel and Marian *Grudeff, Keith *MacMillan and Ronald Bryden, Ben *McPeek, Raymond *Pannell, Swerdlow, Frank Tumpane and Godfrey *Ridout, and (Johnny) Wayne and (Frank) Shuster. Among the performers were Salome *Bey, Dinah *Christie, Jack Duffy, Don *Francks, Barbara *Franklin, Robert *Goulet, Frosia Gregory, Barbara Hamilton, Judy Lander, Rich Little, Catherine *McKinnon, Margo *MacKinnon, Andrew *MacMillan, and Dean Regan. In the *Canadian Theatre Review*, Ross Stuart wrote: 'After the *Dumbells, *Spring Thaw* was the most significant phenomenon in the development of musical theatre in Canada. Although it followed in the tradition of earlier revues, it far excelled them all.' Attempts in 1976 by Robert Johnson and Tedde Moore (Mavor's daughter) to revive *Spring Thaw* were not successful, but in 1977 students at *York U recreated 30 sketches and songs from *Spring Thaw* under the title *The Review of Revues*.

BIBLIOGRAPHY
Frayne, Trent. 'They kid Canada for fun and profit,' Toronto *Star Weekly*, 14 Apr 1962
' "Spring Thaw" calling Canadian composers,' *CanComp*, 2, Aug 1965
Batten, Jack. 'Spring Thaw grows up,' *Canadian Magazine*, 11 Feb 1967
Franklin, Stephen. 'Don Harron's Spring Thaw,' *Weekend*, 25 Mar 1967
Stuart, Ross. 'Song in a minor key: Canada's musical theatre,' *Canadian Theatre R*, 15, Summer 1977
Harron, Don. 'Remembering Spring Thaw,' *Toronto Life*, Apr 1979
Ross, Val. 'One more flight of the Canada goose,' *Maclean's*, 24 Mar 1980 MH, MM

'Squid-jiggin' Ground.' One of Newfoundland's best-known songs. Its words, an account of high jinks on the squid-fishing grounds, were written by the 15-year-old Arthur *Scammell in 1928 as a high-school project and adapted to an Irish fiddle tune, 'Larry O'Gaff.' Published in Gerald Doyle's *Old-time Songs and Poetry of Newfoundland* (second edition, 1940) it was copyrighted by Scammell in 1944, issued as sheet music by BMI Canada, and appeared later in other folksong collections. It has been recorded by Scammell, Omar *Blondahl, George Hamilton IV, Harry *Hibbs, Ed *McCurdy, Alan *Mills, Dick *Nolan, Hank *Snow, and others. The tune was played on the Peace Tower carillon in Ottawa to mark the entry of Newfoundland into the confederation of Canada in 1949.

The Stampeders. Rock band formed in Calgary in 1964. Originally a sextet known as the Rebounds, they played in Calgary and Toronto and made two minor hit records (singles), 'Morning Magic' in 1967 for MWC (Music World Creations, founded by the band's manager, Mel Shaw, and distributed by *Quality) and 'Be A Woman' in 1968 for MGM. The band was re-organized in Toronto as a trio in 1968 by the founding members, Rich Dodson (guitarist, b Sudbury, Ont, 1 Jul 1947), Ronnie King (bass guitarist, b Rotterdam 1 Aug 1947), and Kim Berly (drummer, b Dawson Creek, BC, 24 Jul 1948). Each sang and contributed songs to the repertoire. The trio's recording of Dodson's 'Carry On' was a major Canadian hit in 1971 and was followed the same year by his 'Sweet City Woman,' an international hit. As a result they received the 1971 *Juno Award as vocal and instrumental group of the year. Though the success of 'Sweet City Woman' typecast the band in a rather frivolous pop vein, its true style was exuberant hard rock. The single 'Wild Eyes' (1972) was the first to reflect this accurately. Other hits included 'Devil You' (1971) and 'Hit the Road Jack' (1975), both successful in the USA, and 'Minstrel Gypsy' (1973) and 'New Orleans' (1975). The group's first two LPs and *The Best of the Stampeders* received gold record sales awards.

The Stampeders were one of the top touring bands in Canada for most of the 1970s and appeared in TV specials on the CBC and Global networks. They also toured widely in the USA (where, in 1974, they were the only Canadians to perform at the American Song Festival, held at Saratoga, Cal, and seen on ABC TV) and performed in Brazil (1972) and in European countries (1972, 1973). They were especially popular in the Netherlands, where they won an Edison Award in 1973 for their first European LP (a combination of their first two Canadian LPs). In 1976 a second drummer and a three-man brass and reed section were added. In December of that year, however, Dodson left to pursue a solo career. He was followed in 1978 by Berly. King switched to guitar and was joined by his brother Roy (bass guitar) and two other musicians; the band resumed in 1979 as the Stampeders Featuring Ronnie King.

DISCOGRAPHY

Against the Grain. 1970. MWCS 701
Carryin' On. 1971. MWCS 702
Rubes, Dudes and Rowdies. 1972. MWCS 704
From the Fire. 1973. MWCS 705
New Day. 1974. MWCS 706
Backstage Pass. 1974. MWCS 707
Steamin'. 1975. MWCS 708
Hit the Road. 1976. MWCS 709
Platinum. 1977. MWCS 710
Best of the Stampeders. (1977). Tee Vee International TA 1072

BIBLIOGRAPHY

LeBlanc, Larry. 'Confidence comes after that first hit,' *MSc*, 266, Jul–Aug 1972
Goldman, Mark David. 'Sweet city woman and her friends,' *Weekend Magazine*, 21 Apr 1973
'The Stampeders: taking rock and roll happiness across the land,' *CanComp*, 108, Feb 1976 MM

STANDING, Russell (Elmer). Teacher, pianist, composer, b Belmont, Man, 10 Apr 1893, d Toronto 21 Jun 1977; ATCM 1919. He studied piano with Leonard *Heaton and singing with James Isherwood. Although confined to a wheelchair from the age of seven (because of the effects of polio) he established his own piano studio and also, for 50 years, was one of Winnipeg's best-known theory teachers. He sang ca 1916–25 in the choir of St Paul's Church and later in that of the Home Street United Church, and was a member of the Winnipeg Choral Society. An active member of the *MRMTA, he was president 1935–6 and 1948–50 and later was made a life member. He was a member of the *CFMTA and the editor of its news bulletin 1951–67. Standing served as an examiner for the *WBM and on the music selection committee of the *Manitoba Music Competition Festival. After retiring and moving to Toronto he continued, on a limited basis, to teach theory by correspondence and was made a life member of the *ORMTA. Hugh *McLean was a pupil. Standing composed a number of pieces for piano, several songs, and sacred choral works, none published. JBk

STANGELAND, Robert (Alan). Teacher, administrator, pianist, b Chicago 18 Nov 1930, naturalized Canadian 1969; B MUS (Miami) 1952, M MUS (ESM, Rochester) 1953, DMA (ESM) 1963. Beginning lessons at 10, he continued his training at Miami U, Oxford, O, and the ESM with Cecile Genhart and others. At university he won five scholarships. He has taught piano 1955–9 at the U of Wyoming, 1959–65 at the *U of Alberta in Edmonton, and 1965–6 at Louisiana State U. He returned to the U of Alberta in Edmonton in 1966 and became chairman of the Dept of Music in 1969. In the ensuing years he has strengthened the work of the department particularly in the field of piano performance studies. He has given many recitals, has appeared as soloist with North American orchestras, and has performed on radio and TV. He has lectured on piano literature and technique in public and on radio. He was vice-president of the Alberta Music Conference 1971–4.

WRITINGS

'A pedagogical study of the Chopin etudes,' unpubl DMA thesis, Eastman 1963
'Forerunners of the keyboard étude,' *CAUSM J*, vol 1, Jan 1972
– and Sasonkin, M. 'Music education, another view,' *Music in Alberta*, vol 3, Spring 1974
'The art of piano teaching: do we practice it?' *Piano Q*, 86, Fall 1974 RDM

STANICK, Gerald. Violist, teacher, administrator, b Winnipeg 9 Nov 1933. He studied in Winnipeg with John *Konrad and Richard Seaborn and at the U of Indiana with David Dawson. He was principal viola 1958–63 of the *Winnipeg SO and the *CBC Winnipeg Orchestra and was a founding member, with Lea *Foli and Claude *Kenneson, of the Corydon Trio (fl 1959–62). He taught in Winnipeg (where his pupils included Rennie Regehr) and 1963–8 at the U of Wisconsin at Madison (where James Creitz was his pupil). As a member of the Fine Arts Quartet, resident at the Madison campus, Stanick toured in many countries and recorded for the Concert Disc label. He was music director 1968–74 of the Wisconsin College-Cons in Milwaukee and head of the string department 1974–7 at the *U of Victoria (BC), prior to joining the music faculty of the *U of Western Ontario, where he teaches viola and chamber music and where *Quartet Canada, of which he was a founding member, became quartet-in-residence in 1977. Besides performing regularly and widely as a chamber musician Stanick has appeared as soloist with many Canadian and US orchestras. (KMr)

STANNARD, Derek. Bandmaster, trumpeter, arranger, b Southport, Lancashire, England, 24 Sep 1929, naturalized Canadian 1958; ARCT (1957), ARCM (1961), LRAM (1962). He played trumpet at 17 in the Hallé Orchestra and spent his national service period in the Band of the Irish Guards. Moving to Canada in 1953 he joined the RCAF Tactical Air Command Band in Edmonton and transferred, in 1958, to the Lord Strathcona Horse Band (Royal Canadians) in Calgary. He studied in England 1960–3 at the RMSM (Kneller Hall), graduating with the medal of the Worshipful Company of Musicians. He was music director 1963–9 of the Royal Canadian Regiment, London, Ont, and associate director 1969–72 of the NORAD (North American Air Defense) Command Band. In 1967 he was assistant conductor of the *London SO and directed the London Youth Symphony Orchestra. In 1972 he became Commanding Offier and music director of the Central Band of the Canadian Forces, Ottawa. In 1961 he wrote *Miniature Suite Canadienne* for concert band.

See also Bands: 3 / Regular armed forces. WHK

STAPLES, Rj. Administrator, conductor, trumpeter, b Grenfell, near Regina, 1904, d Richmond, BC, 9 Nov 1972; BA (Manitoba) 1931. In his home town he played in the dance and theatre orchestras and directed the band. In the late 1920s he was a trumpeter in theatre, hotel, and symphony orchestras in Regina. He took his professional training at the U of Manitoba, the Winnipeg Teachers' College, the U of Saskatchewan, Columbia U, and Florida State U, continuing to supplement his studies until 1954. His teachers included Ernst von Dohnányi, Robert Shaw, Irvin *Cooper, Harvey Brooks, and Marion Atkinson. He taught music or was principal 1924–33 in various Saskatchewan and Manitoba schools. He was music director 1933–45 at Central Collegiate, Regina, and also served 1935–40 as adviser to the Saskatchewan Dept of Education and 1940–5 as chairman of the provincial committee on school music courses. He moved to Moose Jaw as music director of the Teachers' College, then became supervisor of music (1949–69) for Saskatchewan schools. He lectured on school music methods 1948–66 at the *U of Saskatchewan and frequently at other schools and summer schools. Staples was conductor 1949–54 of the Regina Civil Service Choir. As a scriptwriter, arranger, and commentator 1948–66 and consultant and arranger 1966–70 for the CBC, Staples has been credited as the guiding force behind the development of *school music broadcasts in Saskatchewan. He was president 1938–44 of the Regina MEA, honorary president 1955–69 of the *SMEA, and charter member and vice-president 1960 of the *CMEA. Besides writing many school-music textbooks and guides for the classroom teacher and developing some music-education devices, Staples composed or arranged numerous choral pieces. He was a member of CAPAC.

See also Inventions and devices; School music; School music broadcasts.

WRITINGS

Music Manual for the Classroom Teacher (Regina 1947, rev 1961)
Let's Play the Classroom Instruments (Brooklyn 1958)
– ed. *Saskatchewan Sings*, 2 vols (Toronto 1964)
Music Activities for the Primary Grades (Toronto 1969)
Other teaching manuals and series of instrumental and choral textbooks.

BIBLIOGRAPHY

Weweler, Johanna Peebles. 'Rj Staples: innovative Saskatchewan music educator,' unpubl MA thesis, U of Saskatchewan 1973
Cowan, Don. 'Rj Staples, pioneer music educator,' *CME*, vol 17, Summer 1976 BNSG

STARK, Ethel (Gertrude). Violinist, conductor, teacher, b Montreal 25 Aug 1916; lauréat (AMQ) 1927, diploma (Curtis) 1934, fellow (Royal Society of Arts) 1980, hon LL D (Concordia) 1980. She took her first violin lessons from Alfred *De Sève and then worked with Saul *Brant at the *McGill Cons as a winner of the MacDonald scholarship. At the Curtis Institute in Philadelphia she studied 1928–34 with Lea Luboshutz (violin), Louis *Bailly (chamber music), and Artur Rodzinski and Fritz Reiner (conducting). She also studied violin with Carl Flesch.

In 1934 Stark became the first Canadian woman to perform as soloist in a program broadcast across the USA, playing the Tchaikovsky *Concerto* with the Curtis Symphony Orchestra under Fritz Reiner. She also participated in the Canadian premiere of Ernest Bloch's *Sonata No. 1* with Charles *Reiner on CBC radio and those of Samuel Barber's *Concerto, Op 14* and Ralph Vaughan Williams' *Concerto Accademico* with the CBC *'Little Symphonies' Orchestra. She performed with the CSM Or-

Ethel Stark

chestra (Tchaikovsky *Concerto*, 1936), the *TSO, the CBC Montreal orchestra (Mendelssohn *Concerto*), and other orchestras. She was also one of the first in Canada to perform Richard Strauss' *Sonata, Op 18* and Respighi's *Sonata in B Minor*. She premiered two works on CBC radio in 1946: Violet *Archer's *Sonata for Violin and Pianoforte* (which is dedicated to Stark) with the composer at the piano; and Hugh Poynter *Bell's *Sonata* with John *Newmark at the piano.

In 1940 Ethel Stark founded the *Montreal Women's Symphony Orchestra, the first Canadian symphony orchestra composed exclusively of women; she conducted it until the late 1960s. She was also the founding director of the New York Women's Chamber Orchestra in 1938, the Ethel Stark Symphonietta in 1954, and the Montreal Women's Symphony Strings 1954–68. She was a guest conductor with the TSO in 1946, the *Quebec SO in 1950, the Miami SO in 1957, 1958, and 1962, the Kol-Israel of Jerusalem in 1952 and 1962, and the Tokyo Asahi and Nippon Hoso Kyokai in 1960, as well as the CBC Montreal orchestra on several occasions. On a *Canada Council grant she went to Europe in 1962 to research violin methodology. As violinist or conductor she has taken part in an estimated 300 or more radio programs in Canada, the USA, and Europe.

Stark taught in 1951 at the Catholic U of Washington, 1952–63 at the *CMM, and 1974–5 at *Concordia U. Among her pupils are Tadek Horn and Edna Wolteger, winners of Congress of Strings scholarships in the USA, and Antoinette Groulx and Gratiel Robitaille, both members of the *MSO. In 1976 she received the award given each year by the Concert Society of the Jewish People's Schools and Peretz Schools to an outstanding Canadian artistic personality. She was made a Member of the *Order of Canada in 1980.

BIBLIOGRAPHY

Fitzgerald, John. 'Plaudits abroad don't help the conductor at home,' Montreal *Gazette*, 28 Apr 1976 (CH)

STARK, James (Arthur). Musicologist, tenor, b Minneapolis, 11 Jun 1938, naturalized Canadian 1971; BA (Minnesota) 1960, M MUS (Toronto) 1963, PH D (Toronto) 1973. He studied with Aksel *Schiøtz in Toronto. He received a PH D for his thesis on vocal performance practices of the early baroque period. Pursuing a career in performance and musicology, he taught voice and music history 1963–4 at the U of Colorado and 1966–74 at the *U of Western Ontario, where he specialized in oratorio and Lieder and gave regular recitals with the pianist Clifford *von Kuster. He became chairman of the Dept of Music at *Mount Allison U in 1974.

WRITINGS

'Giulio Caccini and the "Noble Manner of Singing",' *CAUSM J*, vol 1, Fall 1971

'Vocal gymnastics,' *CAUSM J*, vol 5, Fall 1975 GKG

STARK, Phil (Philip). Tenor, actor, b Darmstadt, Germany, 1919, naturalized Canadian 1963. He trained as a violinist before studying voice at the Hochschule in Frankfurt. After engagements in various central European houses and with the Staatstheater in Wiesbaden and the Grand Théâtre municipal in Bordeaux he moved to British Columbia in 1958 and to Toronto in 1960. He has sung with the *COC 1960–5 and regularly after 1967 and has appeared with the *Vancouver Opera, at the *Stratford Festival, and on CBC radio and TV. He has specialized in character roles, and in these has sung with such sopranos as Birgit Nilsson (Pang to her *Turandot*, Herod to her *Salome* in Hartford, Conn). He made his *Metropolitan Opera debut 27 Oct 1973 as Herod opposite Grace Bumbry's *Salome* and subsequently sang Mime in *Siegfried* (1974) and Aegisthus in *Elektra* (1975). GK

STARR, Lucille (Raymonde Marie) (b Savoie, m Regan, m Cunningham). Singer, b St Boniface, Man, 13 May 1938. She began her career as Lucille Starr in Vancouver in 1954, and two years later with the singer-comedian-guitarist-fiddler Bob Regan (b Dawson Creek, BC, 1932) she formed the country duo the Canadian Sweethearts, moving to Los Angeles shortly thereafter. She was known sometimes as Fern Regan during this period. The duo appeared on many US and Canadian TV shows, including ABC's 'Country America,' and toured in Europe, Asia, and South Africa. The duo recorded for *A & M, and several of its singles were hits, including 'Freight Train' and 'Blue Canadian Rockies' (mid-1960s). A versatile singer in many pop-music styles, Starr also recorded alone for A & M; her biggest hit was 'The French Song' ('Quand le soleil dit bonjour aux montagnes'), sung in French and English and popular during 1965 in Canada, the USA, Europe, Australia, Asia, and south Africa. Her other hits for A & M, Epic, and Dot included 'Yours,' 'Crazy Arms,' 'Missing You,' 'Jolie Jacqueline,' and 'Bonjour Tristesse.' Among her LPs for A & M is the two-record *Lucille Starr* (SP 9015), a re-issue of her earlier *Say You Love Me* (LP 100) and *Canadian Sweethearts* (LP 106). Starr was heard on the popular US TV comedy 'The Beverly Hillbillies,' yodelling for the character Cousin Pearl.

The Canadian Sweethearts continued to perform together until 1977. Starr then pursued a solo career, living in Sarnia, Ont, but maintaining a Los Angeles residence, while Regan began to appear with the singer Patricia Lane. MD, MM

Starr. Name of a record company; later also of a label in the *Compo line. The Starr Piano Co of Richmond, Ind, founded in 1872, began issuing vertical-cut recordings in 1915 and established studios in Richmond and in New York. Early in 1917 the newly formed Canadian Phonograph Supply Co (Starr Co of Canada, 1918–30) of London, Ont, began to distribute Starr-Gennett records and phonographs in Canada. In 1918 Starr-Gennett began making lateral-cut discs which were pressed at the newly formed Compo Co of Lachine, Que. Guy *Lombardo and His Royal Canadians made their first recordings (in the USA, 1924) for Starr-Gennett, and the label's US jazz and blues issues are legendary. In the late 1920s Starr began recording French-Canadian performers, the list growing over the years to include the tenor Rodolphe *Plamondon and the baritones Alex J. Bédard, J. Hervey Germain, and Hector *Pellerin, as well as many folk performers: the harmonica players Louis Blanchette and Henri Lacroix; the accordionists Tommy Duchesne and Arthur Pigeon; the fiddlers J.O. *LaMadeleine and Isidore *Soucy; La *Bolduc and the singers Eugène *Daignault, Ovila *Légaré, Charles *Marchand, and Marcel *Martel, among others. In 1930, when the Starr Piano Co discontinued its recording activity, the Starr name was taken over by Compo and continued in use until 1953. The discographers Alex Robertson and George Humble have published the *Canadian Gennett and Starr-Gennett 9000 Numerical* (Montreal 1972), and *Roll Back the Years* includes lists of five other numerical series. (EBM)

STARYK, Steven. Violinist, teacher, of Ukrainian descent, b Toronto 28 Apr 1932; hon D LITT (York U) 1980. At six he began violin studies with John Moskalyk, continuing 1949–50 with Elie *Spivak, Christopher Daffef, John *Dembeck, and Albert *Pratz and 1950–1 in New York with Misha Mischakoff, Oscar Shumsky, and Alexander Schneider. Staryk was a member 1950–2 of the *TSO and 1952–6 of the *CBC SO and also played with several chamber orchestras. In 1956 he won second prizes in the International Competition for Musical Performers in Geneva, and the Carl Flesch International Competition in London and became the youngest (to that date) concertmaster of the Royal Philharmonic Orchestra under Sir Thomas Beecham. In 1960 he became concertmaster of the Concertgebouw Orchestra and the Amsterdam Chamber Orchestra and began three years of teaching at the Amsterdam Cons. He gave master classes in Osaka in the summer of 1962.

On the recommendation of George Szell, Staryk became concertmaster of the Chicago SO in 1963 – the first Canadian to hold the position – and on several occasions he appeared with that orchestra as soloist. He retained the position until 1967. While in Chicago he taught at Northwestern U and at the American Cons. He also made his Montreal debut during this period, playing two concertos, the Haydn in C and the Mozart in G, 26 Apr 1964 with the Montreal Chamber Orchestra. He returned to Montreal in 1965 for the *Society of Canadian Music, his program comprising *Papineau-Couture's *Suite* for solo violin, *Adaskin's *Divertimento No. 1* (with Ida Elizabeth Busch and Lise *Boucher), and *Somers' *Sonata No. 2* (with Boucher). After performing 1967–8 in Europe, as soloist with various orchestras and in recital, Staryk taught 1968–72 at the Oberlin College Cons in Ohio.

In 1969 with a fellow faculty member, the US pianist John Perry, he formed the Staryk-Perry Duo, which in the ensuing 10 years gave recitals in many of the major cities of the USA and Canada and in 1979 toured Texas. The duo premiered Harry *Freedman's *Encounter* 8 Aug 1975 at the Courtenay Youth Music Centre (where Staryk gave summer classes 1972–6, having returned to Canada to serve as head, 1972–5, of the string department at the *Community Music School of Greater Vancouver; Staryk also gave classes in 1972 at the *Shawnigan Summer School of the Arts). The duo also recorded Papineau-Couture's *Sonata in G*.

Staryk was visiting professor 1973–4 at the *U of Victoria. In 1975 he became visiting professor at the *U of Ottawa and in 1976 he began teaching at the *U of Western Ontario, where *Quartet Canada, of which he was the founding violin, had been appointed quartet-in-residence. He also began teaching at the *RCMT in 1975 and taught at the *U of Toronto during the 1978 term. His pupils hold

Steven Staryk

positions in major orchestras in Canada, the USA, England, and Holland. Canadians among them are Jan Böbak (concertmaster of the *Atlantic SO), Julian Kolkowski of the TS, and Winston Webber, Angela Cavadas, Gwen Hoebig, Ralph Manson, Myron Moskalyk, and Daniel Ohrbach. In 1978 Staryk was an adjudicator for the the Tchaikovsky Competition in Moscow.

Sometimes called a violinist's violinist and usually regarded as the leading Canadian-born violinist of his generation, Staryk has won the respect of his peers and of the critics for his virtuosity, but there is occasional mild dissent over his communicative powers. After his performance of the Walton *Concerto* with the TS in 1977, John *Kraglund wrote: 'There is nothing in the violin repertoire which is beyond his technical ability, even a concerto which was composed for Jascha Heifetz ... The Walton concerto calls for warmly romantic expression alternating with ... passages brittle in mood as well as sound. Staryk coped superbly with both ... even at its harshest the music was neither strained nor ugly' (*Globe and Mail*, 5 Jan 1977). William *Littler took a somewhat different view of the performance: 'For all its technical assurance and interpretive intelligence, it has about it a coolness and almost Olympian detachment that have the effect of telling an audience it isn't needed, that everything is under control, that the outcome has been predetermined. However true this may be, it tends to lessen the quantity of electricity in the air' (*Toronto Star* 5 Jan 1977).

Staryk retains high favour with Canadian composers. The violin concertos of George *Fiala (1973, premiered 11 Oct 1974 with the *Winnipeg SO), Talivaldis *Kenins (1974, premiered 31 Aug 1974 with the *CBC Vancouver Chamber Orchestra), Srul Irving *Glick (1976, premiered 24 Oct 1976 with the *Victoria SO), and Paul *Hoffert (1976, premiered July 1976 at Blue Mountain School, near Collingwood, Ont, where Staryk spent the summers of 1976 and 1977 as artist-in-residence) are dedicated to Staryk, as are the aforementioned *Encounter* by Freedman and Lothar *Klein's *Paganini Collage* (1967, premiered 13 Apr 1971 by the TS). Concertos from the international repertoire played by Staryk with Canadian orchestras include the Bach in E (TS 1971), the Kurt Weill (*NACO 1972), the Mendelssohn in E minor (TS 1974, NACO European tour 1978), the Wieniawski No. 2 (Staryk's *MSO debut 1976), the Walton (TS 1977), the Prokofiev No. 1 (NACO 1978), and the Stravinsky (NACO European tour 1978). During the 1970s Staryk played two Guarneri violins, an unnamed one dating from 1740 and the one known as the 'Baltic', made by Giuseppe Bartolomeo Guarneri (called del Gesù, the most famous member of the illustrious Cremona family of violin makers). In 1979 the Baltic was exchanged for the numinous Stradivarius 'ex-Barrere' of 1727.

DISCOGRAPHY

Bach *Concerto in E* BWV1042. Tor Chamb O, Neel cond. 1977. Umbrella UMB-DD9
– 4 *Sonatas* BWV1020–1023. Gilbert hpd. 1965. Bar BCS 2858
– *Sonata in G; Sonata in F*. Gilbert hpd. Orion ORS 74148
Bartók *Two Portraits, Op 5*. Royal Phil O, Kubelik cond. 1958. Cap SG 7186
– *Sonata No. 1* – Beethoven *Sonata No. 8, Op 30, no. 3*. Perry pf. Masters of the Bow MBS 2006
Bartók – Satie – Hindemith – Prévost. Schwarz pf. 1971. CBC SM-172
Bonporti *Concerto, Op 11, no. 8*. Leonhardt hpd, Amsterdam Chamb O, Rieu cond. 1961. Telefunken SAWT 9415
Brahms – Coward – Dinicu – Hubay – Kálmán – Monti – Sarasate. Royal Tziganes, Staryk cond and vn. Philips 870034BFY
Every Violinist's Guide: Dancla – Dont – et al. 1963. HMV HQS 1124
Farnon *Rhapsody*. London Festival O, Farnon cond. 1963. Poly 2382 008
Fiocco *Allegro* – Brahms *Sonata in D Minor*. Bernardi pf. Ca 1969. CBC SM-39
Fiocco – Handel – Mozart – et al. Niwa pf. 1967. Orion ORS 7027
Freedman *Encounter* – Walton *Sonata*. H. Bowkun pf. Ca 1976. CBC SM-342
Haydn – Leclair – R. Mathieu – Papineau-Couture – Willan. Boucher pf. 1966. RCI 243
Haydn – Leclair – Sarasate – Saint-Saëns. Boucher pf, London Festival O, Gamley cond. 1963, 1966. Sel CC 15069
Hoffert *Concerto for Contemporary Violin*. Orch, Hoffert cond. 1978. Ultrafi ULDD 12
Italian Baroque Concerti: Corelli – Marcello – Torelli – Vivaldi. Baroque Chamb O, Staryk vn and cond. 1959. Bar BC 2880
Italian Baroque Sonatas: Corelli – Locatelli – Nardini – Veracini. Gilbert hpd. 1966. Bar BCS 2874
Kenins *Concerto*. CBC Van Chamb O, Avison cond. 1975. CBC SM-293
Mozart *Concerto No. 3* K216. NACO, Bernardi cond. 1971. CBC SM-174
– *Concerto No. 5* K219. NACO, Bernardi cond. 1972. RCI 382/RCA KRLI 0007
Paganini *Caprices, Op 1, no. 1, 2, 5, 9, 13, 14, 16, 17, 19, 20, 21, 24*. 1969. Mus H Soc MHS 1122/Sel CC 15076
– *Concerto No. 1*. Norddeutscher Rundfunk SO, Michael cond. Masters of the Bow MBS 2003
Papineau-Couture *Sonata in G* – Prokofiev – et al. Perry pf. 1975. RCI 438
Prokofiev *Sonatas, Op 80, no. 1; Op 90, no. 2*. Bernardi pf. 1968. AofD SDD 2152/Mus H Soc MHS 1135
– *Violin Concerto No. 1*. Van SO, Akiyama cond. 1973. CBC SM-235
Solo Sonatas: Geminiani – Pisendel – Stamitz – Hindemith – Papineau-Couture (*Aria* for solo violin) – Prokofiev. 1964. Bar BCS 2851
Somers *Sonata No. 2* – Papineau-Couture *Suite* for solo violin – Beethoven *Sonata in A Major, Op 12, no. 2*. Boucher pf. 1965. RCI 222/RCA CCS 1016
Staryk Plays Kreisler. Corwin pf. 1976. CBC SM-299/Masters of the Bow MBS 2005
Tchaikovsky *Chanson triste, Op 40, no. 2*; 'Andante Cantabile' from *Op 11*; *Melodie, Op 42, no. 3*. Members of the Concertgebouw O of Amsterdam, Staryk vn and cond. 1961. Imperial IPE 5084
Vladigerov *Vardar, Op 16*. Royal Tziganes, Staryk vn and cond. Imperial ILPT 117/World Record Club T P339
Wieniawski *Selections*. Kotowska pf. 1960. HMV HQM 1139/Mus H Soc MHS 1131
Several of the above recordings have been included in the Everest set SDBR 3203 and the Orion set ORS 7027.
Staryk has also recorded as concertmaster with the Amsterdam Chamb O, the Royal Phil O, the Capitol SO, the Chicago SO, the Concertgebouw of Amsterdam, and others. See *Discopaedia*.

BIBLIOGRAPHY

Widerman, Jane. 'Why Canada's foremost violinist isn't famous,' *Fugue*, vol 1, Mar 1977

Kellogg, Pat. 'Steven Staryk: no profit in his own country,' *PfAC*, Winter 1978 (JBk)

STEINBERG, Albert. Violinist, conductor, b Toronto 11 May 1910. His teachers in Toronto included Broadus Farmer, Luigi von *Kunits, and Kathleen *Parlow (violin) and Ettore *Mazzoleni and Reginald *Stewart (conducting). He also studied violin privately 1935–7 in New York with Mishel Piastro and conducting in Maine with Pierre Monteux. After a debut at 14 on radio station CFCA, Toronto, he performed throughout Ontario and toured the USA 1927–8 on the Chautauqua vaudeville circuit and western Canada in 1929. He was a member 1936–46 of the *TSO and conducted orchestras on the CBC radio programs 'Music Time' and 'Summer Concert' (1943), 'Thursday Concert' (1944), 'String Orchestra' (1945), and 'Variety Time' (1946). He was concertmaster 1943–4 for the *Promenade Symphony Concerts orchestra and assistant conductor and concertmaster 1946–51 of the *Vancouver SO. He was also music director 1946–51 of the Vancouver Junior SO, founder in 1947 of the Vancouver SO students' and children's concerts, and a founding member of the Vancouver Chamber Sinfonietta 1947–51, the Steinberg String Quartet 1947–51, and the *Friends of Chamber Music in 1948. He left Canada to play 1952–6 in the Los Angeles Philharmonic Orchestra. After 1956 he played in various studio orchestras, including that of Percy *Faith. He conducted for 'The Red Skelton Show' on CBS TV (1970) and NBC TV (1971). In 1973 he became music director of the Young Artists' Symphony of Los Angeles. BNSG

STEINBERG, Ben. Teacher, organist, choirmaster, composer, b Winnipeg 22 Jan 1930; B MUS (Toronto) 1961. A soloist at 8 in the synagogue choir conducted by his father, Cantor Alexander Steinberg, he began conducting choirs himself at 12 and soon participated in services as a composer and organist. At the *RCMT 1948–51 and 1957–60 he studied composition with *Dolin and *Weinzweig and piano with Weldon *Kilburn. After teaching 1953–8 in public schools in the Toronto area and studying music education at the *U of Toronto he served 1961–4 as head of the music department at Winston Churchill Collegiate and thereafter in the same capacity at Forest Hill Collegiate, Toronto. He was director of school music 1950–60 and music director 1960–9 at Holy Blossom Temple, and in 1970 he became music director at Temple Sinai. His method for youth choirs, *Together Do They Sing* (New York 1961), was commissioned and published by the Union of American Hebrew Congregations.

Steinberg's music includes three services (two published – 1963 and 1969 – by Transcontinental Music and one – 1969 – by New Horizon Music); works for choir and/or soloist and organ (some published by Transcontinental Music and Israeli Music Publications); *The Vision of Isaiah* (1970) for tenor, choir, and organ or instrumental ensemble; *Yerushalayim* (1973) for soprano, choir, and orchestra; *Echoes of Children* (1979), a cantata for soloist, narrator, chorus, and orchestra; and instrumental works including a suite for flute and string trio based on Israeli folksongs. Of Steinberg's music Michael Isaacson wrote, 'While conservative, pragmatic and always well-mannered, it is also gratefully mindful of its tradition in a deeply lyrical way' (*Journal of Synagogue Music*, June 1973). Steinberg has presented Jewish music on the CBC and has given many lecture-recitals on it in Canada and the USA. He is a contributor to *EMC*, a member of the *CLComp, an associate of the *CMCentre, and a member of CAPAC.

See also the Jews. CF

STEVENS, William (Jervis). Pianist, teacher, b Montreal 6 Jan 1921, of US parents; B MUS (McGill) 1943. He studied piano with Germaine *Malépart 1941–7 and Yvonne *Hubert (after 1948), graduating from the *CMM in 1949. Following World War II (when he toured with **Meet the Navy*) he studied composition with *Champagne. He made his Montreal debut in 1950 at the Ritz-Carlton Hotel and his New York debut in 1954 at Town Hall. He was the soloist in 1958 in the premiere of Violet *Archer's *Piano Concerto* on radio with the *CBC SO. In 1960 he received the Harriet Cohen Commonwealth Medal. After many appearances in the USA and Canada he made a Carnegie Hall debut, 28 Jan 1962. He has appeared regularly on Canadian radio and TV, giving many concerts for children as host on the CBC TV series 'Let's Talk Music' (1961–74). He was soloist with the *TS in 1977 and the same year appeared with Anna *Russell for one of the CBC TV 'Musicamera' series. He became a teacher at the *École normale de musique in 1961 and at the *École Vincent-d'Indy in 1967. He has adjudicated at many competition festivals.

DISCOGRAPHY

Exploring Music I and II, educational series of 26 recordings. 1968–9. Quebec Dept of Education and Radio-Québec RQA-1

Impressions: Ravel – Schubert – Brahms – Debussy – Morel. 1967. Laurentien CTM 6036

Liszt – Fauré – Papineau-Couture – Debussy – Dohányi. 1959. IRC SA-1 (International Records SA-1)

Mozart – Scriabin – Stevens – et al. 1970. CTL 477-65138

William Stevens Plays the Romantics: Rachmaninoff – Chopin – Debussy – Scriabin – Brahms – Liszt. 1961. Laurentien CL 4001

NT

STEVENSON, Scotty (John) (b Stephenson). Singer-songwriter, guitarist, b Onoway, near Edmonton, 25 Jul 1932. He began playing guitar at 12 and appeared later with Gaby *Haas and on Edmonton radio with Omar *Blondahl. His recording career began in 1952 with the RCA single 'Edmonton Waltz.' He completed 4 LPs for RCA and 10 for London before he began recording for Maple Haze in 1978. His other singles include his first hit, 'Alberta, the Province of Riches Galore' (1953), and the subsequent minor hits 'Twelve-Foot Davis,' 'Big Treaty,' 'Dandelion Wine,' and 'Take Me Back to Old New Brunswick' – all of his own composition and all issued on the LP *Travelling Through the Years* (Lon EBX 4196).

While living 1955–70 in Montreal, Stevenson appeared in nightclubs throughout eastern Canada and northeastern USA, leading the Canadian Nighthawks 1957–66. One of the top Canadian country bands of the day, the Nighthawks comprised the guitarist Bernie MacLean, the bass guitarist Ruthie MacLean, the steel guitarist Buddy Ackers, and the fiddler Johnny Brown.

In 1970 Stevenson returned to Edmonton, where he continued to perform, alone or with his daughter Debbie, in nightclubs and on TV. Writing in the *Montreal Star* (5 Sep 1970), Dick MacDonald commented, 'Perhaps it is the simply stated, uncomplicated pride and longing in Scotty's own compositions which contribute to his popularity.' Stevenson is an affiliate of PRO Canada.

RGn

STEWART. Scottish-born family of musicians, 1 / George and 2 / Reginald, son of George.

1 **George** (Watson). Conductor, teacher, organist, french hornist, b Glasgow 1870, d near Woodbridge, Ont, 24 Nov 1961. He studied with George Bloine in Berlin, taught singing at the Academy in Edinburgh, and toured for two seasons with the Berlin Meister Orchestra. In 1912 he emigrated with his family to Canada and settled first in Medicine Hat, Alta, where he conducted a band, an orchestra, and an operatic society. He moved to Toronto in 1917, began teaching at the *Hambourg Cons in 1918, and later was principal of that conservatory's Deer Park Branch. He was organist at St Columba's United Church and played the french horn with local orchestras. He produced operettas for the *Eaton Operatic Society and for the *Savoyards, which he formed with his son Reginald in 1919. During the 1930s he was a producer for Canadian Industries Ltd's 'Opera House of the Air,' which originated in the Toronto studios of the broadcasting system which existed in Canada prior to the establishment of the CRBC (*CBC).

2 **Reginald** (Drysdale). Conductor, pianist, teacher, administrator, b Edinburgh 20 Apr 1900; hon D MUS (Western Ont) 1949. He studied with H.T. Collinson (choirmaster of St Mary's Anglican Cathedral in Edinburgh), with Arthur Friedheim and Mark *Hambourg in Toronto, and with Nadia Boulanger and Isidor Philipp in Paris. During the 1920s he was music director of the Savoyards, taught 1921–4 at the *Canadian Academy of Music, played in 1921 with the *Hambourg Trio, toured western Canada as a pianist in 1925 and conducted *The Yeomen of the Guard* that same year for CNRT radio, and made many other appearances in Ontario, including several 1926–8 with the Five Piano Ensemble in Toronto. Stewart also made some piano rolls for Duo-Art at this time. While conductor of a large radio orchestra heard nationwide 1929–31 on a network sponsored by Imperial Oil, he spent some time in England, where he was guest conductor and soloist 6 Apr 1930 with the London SO.

When Ernest *MacMillan was named conductor of the *TSO in 1931, the rivalry-by-definition that existed between him and Stewart (both Bach-lovers, both superior performers, skilled administrators, talented conductors, and charismatic figures) became a matter for partisanship. Stewart's supporters felt he should conduct the TSO. MacMillan, once firmly in charge, proposed a TSO summer series to counter the *Promenade Symphony Concerts (which Stewart founded and conducted 1934–41). In the *Globe and Mail* Augustus *Bridle predicted 'a scrimmage, with our two chief conductors in the spotlight, each beating time to outspot the other' and suggested (idealistically and unfeasibly) an amalgamation of the Proms and the TSO, with Stewart and MacMillan in joint command. Helmut *Kallmann has commented on the conflict between the two conductors, 'I suspect that the rivalry, as in the case of Wagner and Brahms, was between the followers rather than the masters.' If so, the partisanship was durable. A *Mayfair* article (February 1953) stated, 'The 22 years that have passed since MacMillan won the board of directors' nod as permanent conductor [of the TSO] have not dimmed the conviction of some music lovers that it was the younger Stewart who showed the greater promise.'

Stewart was music director in the 1930s for Canadian Industries Ltd's 'Opera House of the Air' and founder and conductor 1933–41 of the *Toronto Bach Choir, which presented annual performances of the *St John Passion*. During this period he also conducted (1935) on NBC radio from New York and led orchestras in New York, Washington, and Detroit. In May 1936 he conducted the orchestra of the Opera Guild of Toronto in performances of *Tosca, Cavalleria Rusticana*, and *I Pagliacci*. He made his New York Town Hall debut 6 Mar 1937, toured Canada and the USA as a concert pianist, and was a soloist with the Chicago SO and the New York Philharmonic. He was conductor 1942–52 of the Baltimore SO and director 1941–58 of the Peabody Cons in Baltimore; he left the conservatory to undertake a major recital and conducting tour, 1958–60, of Europe and South America. On visits to Canada during these years he conducted the premiere of *Somers' *Five Songs for Dark Voice* with Maureen *Forrester 11 Aug 1956 at the *Stratford Festival and was a guest conductor of the *CBC SO twice in the 1955–6 season and once in each of the 1959–60 and 1960–1 seasons. He also operated a summer school in Oakville, Ont, in 1961. He became artist-in-residence at the Music Academy of the West in Santa Barbara, Cal, in 1962 and later was appointed head of the piano department there. His pupils have included Glen *Morley, Stanley *St John, Albert *Steinberg, and John *Weinzweig.

WRITINGS

'Impressions and comparisons: recent musical developments in Britain compared with conditions in Canada,' Toronto *Globe*, 15 Jul 1933

'Good music made popular,' Empire Club of Canada *Addresses* (1934–35)

'The business of conducting,' *Etude*, Mar 1946

DISCOGRAPHY

AS CONDUCTOR

Boccherini – Vivaldi: *Cello Concertos*. Baltimore Cons O, Parisot vc. Ca 1954. Counterpoint 555

Ives *Symphony No. 3* – Donovan *Oboe Suite*. Baltimore Little Symphony, Genovese ob. Ca 1954. Vanguard 468

AS PIANIST

Bach Program: *Jesu, Joy of Man's Desiring*; *Partita No. 1*; et al. Ca 1964. Educo 3018

Beethoven *Sonatas No. 8 and 14*; *Bagatelles, Op 126, no. 1 and 2*; *Rondo, Op 51, no. 1*. Ca 1964. Educo 3019

Debussy – Ravel. Ca 1964. Educo 3024

Favorite Pieces by Chopin. Ca 1964. Educo 3051

Masterpieces of the 17th and 18th Centuries. Ca 1964. Educo 3053

More Favorite Pieces by Chopin. Ca 1964. Educo 3052

Schumann *Carnaval*; *Toccata, Op 7*; et al. Ca 1964. Educo 3023

Recordings of Chabrier, Godowsky, Rubinstein, and Schumann made for Victor in 1938

BIBLIOGRAPHY

Hamilton, H.C. 'Reginald Stewart,' *MCan*, vol 10, Dec 1929

Mullens, Raymond. 'A Stewart conquers London,' *Maclean's*, 15 Aug 1930

Brusque, M. 'Conductio ad absurdum; Reginald Stewart's resignation as conductor of the Promenade Concerts,' *Canadian Forum*, vol 21, Sep 1941

(MDr)

STIRLING, Georgina. See Toulinguet, Marie.

STONE, Fred or **Freddie**. Flugelhornist, trumpeter, composer, writer, teacher, b Toronto 9 Sep 1935; B MUS (Metropolitan College, London) 1964. The son of Archie Stone (b London 1905, the orchestra leader 1936–60 for Toronto's Casino Theatre), he studied trumpet 1950–5 with Donald Reinhardt during summers in Philadelphia and composition 1955–60 with Gordon *Delamont and 1960–2 with John *Weinzweig. He worked with Benny Louis at 16 and played 1955–67 in various CBC Toronto orchestras. He has appeared in both symphonic and jazz contexts, performing with the Toronto, Winnipeg, Detroit, Cleveland, Buffalo, Ottawa, and San Diego SOs and with Ron *Collier 1960–73, Phil *Nimmons 1965–70, the *Boss Brass 1968–70, and *Lighthouse 1969–70. He participated in the premieres of Norman *Symonds' *The Nameless Hour* and *Democratic Concerto*. He toured North American and Europe 1970–1 with the Duke Ellington Orchestra and thereafter worked extensively in Toronto with his own bands (usually comprising his pupils) and sometimes used an amplified flugelhorn and a computer-synthesizer. Besides teaching privately in Toronto he was artist-in-residence 1972-3 at Centennial College and taught 1973-5 at Humber College and in 1976 at George Brown College and its affiliated Blue Mountain School of Music. He has given workshops and lectures on improvisation and has written articles published 1971-3 in the European Jazz Federation's *Jazz Forum* and an unpublished 'Treatise on Improvisation.'

Stone has composed scores for the *NFB, two suites for electric flugelhorn and symphony orchestra (1969), and over 200 works for his small group and big band. His works for jazz orchestra, many of them CBC commissions, include *Leah* (1965), *Maiera* (1965, recorded by Ellington), *Reflections on a Theme* (1969), *Sunshine and Pretty Things* (1969), *Rice Lake Suite* (1970), *For Igor* (1972), *Tribute to Igor Stravinsky* (1972), *Idea for Orchestra* (1974), *Uranus* (1974, recorded by Moe *Koffman with Stone as soloist), *Stone Poem* (1974), *Alphera* (1974), and *Young Peoples' Guide to the Jazz Orchestra* (1976).

According to Barry Tepperman '[Stone's] writing, like his playing, is pungent, moodily brassy rather than brazen, and exploits perfectly the colours and range of his massed throngs, building over a small ensemble ... within the larger organism' (*Coda*, October 1972). Stone has been described by Mark Miller as 'an original stylist' who 'generally takes things fast and loose, scattering quick bursts of notes in all directions and maintaining just the slightest connections to the tunes' harmonic structures' (Toronto *Globe and Mail*, 11 Jul 1978).

DISCOGRAPHY

Symonds *The Nameless Hour*. TS, Feldbrill cond. 1969. CBC SM-104

The Music of Fred Stone. K. Moses fl, Senensky pf, Boyd db, Craden perc, Magadini drums. 1972. RCI 377

With Ellington: *New Orleans Suite*. 1970. Atlantic S-1580 – *Afro-Eurasian Suite*. 1971. Fantasy 9498

Others as soloist with Bruce Cockburn, Collier, Koffman, Lighthouse, and Nimmons

BIBLIOGRAPHY

Flohil, Richard. 'My life with the Duke,' *CanComp*, 53, Oct 1970

MM

Strange & Co. Established in Toronto ca 1881 as Strange & Billing, wholesale and retail dealers in cheap editions of printed music. By 1883 the partnership had dissolved, and Frederic Strange remained independent until the firm's end, ca 1900. He was one of the few Canadian publishers who were also typographers, and his publications bore an S & Co plate number (those of the Strange & Billing period often a cryptic H.S.). About half of his numerous publications – some 560 vocal and instrumental pieces – appeared in a series, the Canadian Musical Library, about which the most noteworthy fact is the lack of Canadian content. Some specimens lack an imprint. However, Strange did publish some Canadian compositions, eg, Annie Douglas' *Sir John A. Macdonald Waltz* (1882) and pieces by Edwin *Gledhill, Carl *Martens, and G.W. *Strathy. HK

STRATAS, Teresa (b Anastasia Stratakis). Soprano, b Toronto 26 May 1938; Artist Diploma (Toronto) 1959. The youngest of three children of Greek immigrant restaurateurs in Toronto and later in Oshawa, she began voice lessons at 12 and made her radio debut singing Greek pop songs at 13. After high school she became a secretary while harbouring ambitions to become a nightclub singer. She studied 1954-8 at the RCMT with Irene *Jessner, the final three years on scholarship, and received the 1959 Eaton Graduating Scholarship. She was cast by Herman *Geiger-Torel as Nora in a 1958 production of Vaughan Williams' *Riders to the Sea* at Hart House and made her debut in professional opera 13 Oct 1958 to great acclaim as Mimi in *La Bohème* with the Toronto Opera Festival (*COC). Co-winner of the 1959 *Metropolitan Opera Auditions, she made her debut with the Metropolitan in October 1959 as Poussette in *Manon*. She also appeared with the *TSO in 1959. At the 1960 *Vancouver International Festival she sang Cio-Cio-San in *Madama Butterfly*, a performance broadcast 22 Jul 1960 by the CBC. She created the title role in Peggy Glanville-Hicks' *Nausicaa* at the Herod Atticus Theatre in Athens in 1961 and made her Covent Garden debut as Mimi that same year.

Teresa Stratas

At the Metropolitan Stratas moved quickly into major roles, first as a replacement for Lucine Amara as Liù in *Turandot*, then as Micaela in *Carmen*. In 1962 she sang Cio-Cio-San with the COC, toured the USSR in recital, and created Queen Isabella in the premiere (posthumous) of Manuel de Falla's *Atlantida*, which also was her debut at La Scala, Milan. While continuing to perform with the Metropolitan she sang with the Bolshoi, Vienna State, Berlin, Bavarian State (Munich), and San Francisco operas. Her Metropolitan repertoire has included Mimi, Zerlina in *Don Giovanni*, Liù, Micaela, Nedda in *I Pagliacci*, Cherubino in *The Marriage of Figaro*, Marguerite in *Faust*, *La Périchole*, Gretel in *Hansel and Gretel*, Lisa in *The Queen of Spades*, Sardulla in the US premiere of Menotti's *The Last Savage*, Mélisande in *Pelléas et Mélisande*, Marenka in *The Bartered Bride*, and Jenny in *Mahagonny*. She also sang Violetta in *La Traviata* at Munich, Susanna in *The Marriage of Figaro* and Despina in *Così fan tutte* at the Salzburg Festival and the Paris Opera, and Desdemona in *Otello* at *Expo 67. She took the leading roles in Norman *Campbell's 1972 CBC TV production of Puccini's *La Rondine* and in the 1974 film of Strauss' *Salome* with the Vienna Philharmonic under Karl Böhm. She was chosen by the conductor Pierre Boulez to sing the title role in the first performance – Paris Opera, 28 May 1979 – of the completed version (the unfinished portion of the third act scored by the Austrian composer Friedrich Cerha) of Alban Berg's *Lulu*.

Stratas possesses a lyric soprano, smooth and rich throughout its range. Her singing is allied to a strong stage personality and an instinctive and communicative dramatic sense. She is endowed with a delicate sense of comedy, but she yields most completely to those roles demanding direct emotional expression. Reviewing the Metropolitan Opera telecast of *Mahagonny*, Andrew Porter wrote: 'Close up, the intelligence, subtlety and precision that distinguish Teresa Stratas's Jenny were even more apparent. She is an arresting artist. One began to regret every moment the cameras left her – when, for example, she moved into the refrain of "Benares" and her eyes and mouth caught to perfection the "Wouldn't it be wonderful *if* ... and yet I know it can't be" expression of Weill's music. The opera took life from her' (*New Yorker*, 24 Dec 1979).

Stratas became an Officer of the *Order of Canada in 1972, and the *CMCouncil named her artist of the year in 1980.

WRITINGS

'Thoughts on the day of a performance,' *Fugue*, Mar 1979

DISCOGRAPHY

Berg *Lulu*. Paris Opera O, Boulez cond. 1979. 4-DG 2711 024

Glanville-Hicks *Nausicaa*. Athens SO and Chorus, Surinach cond. (1964). CRI 175

Lehar *The Merry Widow*. Berlin Phil O, Karajan cond, Chorus of the 'Deutsche Oper Berlin,' Hagen-Kroll cond, Stratas (Valencienne). (1973). DG 2707 070

Mozart *Così fan tutte*. Strasbourg Phil, Lombard cond, Stratas (Despina). (1978). 3-RCA FRL 3-2629

Opera Gala: Verdi 'Willow Song' and 'Ave Maria' from *Otello*. Bavarian State Opera O, Gerdes cond. (1968). DG 2538 244

Smetana *Die Verkaufte Braut*. Müncher Rundfunkorchester, Krombholc cond, Chor des Bayerischen Rundfunks, H. Franz cond. (1975). Eurodisc Quadrophonie 89 036 XGR

Verdi *Otello*. Bayerisches Staatsorchester, Gerdes cond, Chor der Bayerischen Staatsoper, Baumgart cond. DG 2537 017

BIBLIOGRAPHY

'Three stars return home in triumph,' *OpCan*, vol 3, Sep 1962

Coleman, Emily. 'So one day the star got sick,' *New York Times*, 22 Jan 1967

Gravina, Peter. 'Pistol packin' soprano,' *OpCan*, vol 12, Spring 1971

Winters, Kenneth. 'Teresa Stratas – a swallow returns,' Toronto *Telegram*, 19 Jun 1971

Maheu, Renée. 'Stratas – Lulu,' *Mcan*, 40, Sep 1979

Colgrass, Ulla. 'A will of iron a voice of gold,' *Music*, Mar-Apr 1980

O'Toole, Lawrence. 'Voice at the top,' *Maclean's*, 23 Jun 1980

Sargeant, Winthrop. 'Profiles: presence,' *New Yorker*, 26 Jan 1981

(HCs)

Stratford. Ontario mill town (Little Thames until 1831) located on the Avon River 75 km west of Hamilton, in Perth County, and incorporated as a city in 1885. It was the site of railway shops ca 1880-1952, and became the home of the *Stratford Festival in 1953. The extraordinary and, in 1980, continuing success of the festival won for the city an international prestige enjoyed by few if any Canadian towns of comparable size (population 25,500 in 1979) and provided it with a new economic focus.

Stratford's first band is believed to have been formed about 1850 when the population was less than 1000. A Stratford band was bold enough to travel 700 km in 1878 to compete in a festival in Montreal. By 1900 there was a short-lived orchestra of 50 directed by a blind conductor, Roger W. Roberts, who also owned the town's music store. Other bands in the area included the Brodhagen Brass Band (1904), the New Hamburg City Band (1908), the Grand Trunk Railway (CNR) Concert Band (whose conductors included Charles A. *Bird), and the Stratford Boys' Band directed by James Malone.

Among performance venues were the Town Hall (400-500 seats, built in 1857) and the Theatre Albert (1100 seats, 1901, also known as the Opera House or the Brandenburger Theatre). The Theatre Albert in its first 25 years housed locally produced musicals, by the GTR Minstrels and other groups, sponsored by such organizations as the Imperial Order of Daughters of the Empire and the Knights of Pythias. It also provided a stage for touring productions by the *Dumbells and the San Francisco Opera. (Later a movie house, it was rented 1956–63, then purchased, by the Stratford Festival, and was renovated and renamed the Avon Theatre.) Stratford was also on the *Chautaugua Ontario summer circuit.

Until World War II, music was largely the domain of church organists, who, in addition to their appointed duties, taught, supervised public and normal school music programs, administered festivals, and conducted choirs, orchestras, and massed groups in performances of oratorios and operettas. In 1887 a choir of 1000 children and 1000 adults performed under the baton of W.J. Freeland (Stratford's first school music director) at a public school concert in the Skating Rink. Freeland also formed the Stratford Juvenile Select Choir, which presented 'a cantata' at the Town Hall in 1889.

James Bottomley, Freeland's successor, continued the annual school concerts and organized the Stratford Public Schools Music Contest 1901–12. He also initiated annual Good Friday performances of Stainer's *The Crucifixion*, Rossini's *Stabat Mater*, and other works. These concerts, which combined all of the city's church choirs, continued until 1946 under the direction of L.R. Bridgeman, Talman J. Gotby, and others. Bottomley's Men's Choral Union and Masonic Temple Choir both were formed in 1918. The latter, under the direction of Frank Creasy and Peter Wilson, presented operettas of Gilbert & Sullivan.

W.B. Rothwell was director of music 1923–50 at the Normal School, succeeding Bottomley. Rothwell supported the 1926 founding of the Perth County Music Teachers' Federation (later Stratford Music Teachers' Assn) and was president 1927–30 and 1940–6 of its first project, the Perth County Music (competition) Festival (later the Stratford Music Festival and finally the Kiwanis Music Festival). In 1942 Rothwell was national president for *Kiwanis Music Festivals. He also founded, and directed 1935–45, the 40-voice Stratford Ladies' Choir. The organist John Blackburn succeeded Rothwell as music supervisor at the Normal School.

J.T. Priest, a school music director 1930–68, organized and led, with violinist Henry Clark, the Civic Orchestra, an amateur ensemble made up of school music students and interested community members. Several of the churches used small instrumental groups for regular services as well as special events. Priest and Norman O'Leary composed the annual musicals given at the Stratford Collegiate.

Stratford choirs prior to 1940 included Irene Jocelyn *Bird's 45-voice Orpheus Girls' Choir, Helene Smith's 50-voice Corona Girls' Choir, and F.P. (Paddy) Polley's Alpha Juvenile Choristers. Among later musical organizations were the Aeolian Trio (1936–66; founding members were Bailey *Bird, violin; Charles Tretheway, cello; and Anne Tretheway, piano); Gordon Scott's *Elizabethan Singers (1953–9) and Stratford Boychoir, the latter formed in 1972; the various Stratford Festival orchestras; the Stratford Festival City Rhythm Band, begun in 1957 and comprising senior citizens; the *Perth County Conspiracy (based at the Black Swan coffee-house); and the CNR Band, which in 1980 still was giving weekly outdoor concerts.

Musicians born or raised in Stratford and its environs include Cora B. *Ahrens, Bailey and John *Bird, Martin *Boundy, John *Boyden, Barbara *Collier, Richard Manual (see The *Band), the pianist Kathryn Root, Campbell *Trowsdale, Ward *Allen, the teacher W. Caven Barron, Lloyd *Bradshaw, and Nora *Clench – the last three in St Mary's.

Stratford Ensemble, with its conductor Raffi Armenian (extreme right)

BIBLIOGRAPHY
Karr, Jack. 'The Avon; an old theatre is re-born,' *OpCan*, May 1964 (GJ)

Stratford Festival (the Stratford Shakespearean Festival Foundation of Canada). Annual performing-arts festival established at Stratford (Ont) in 1953 'to promote interest in, and the study of, the arts generally and literature, drama and music in particular.' Fresh productions of the plays of Shakespeare have dominated the festival from its inception, as they were intended to. However, though music from the beginning has been cast in supporting roles (as background to the dramas or alternative fare for theatre tourists), the festival's music directors, composers, and performers often have contrived to transmute what has been described as a poor-relation's portion of the festival budget into memorable musical events.

1 Performance
2 Composition

1 PERFORMANCE. Music at Stratford began in 1953, under the direction of Louis *Applebaum, with 16 poorly attended afternoon concerts in the 1147-seat Tent Theatre. Only one concert, by the *Elizabethan Singers of Stratford, was presented in 1954. However, with the move to the 950-seat Concert Hall (in fact a converted badminton hall) in 1955, Stravinsky's *The Soldier's Tale* and concerts by the *Hart House Orchestra and Festival Chorus (later the *Festival Singers) were offered in what was called 'The Inaugural Season of Music.' The 1956 season boasted a production of Britten's *The Rape of Lucretia* featuring Jon *Vickers, concerts by the Festival Orchestra, Festival Chorus, and various soloists, and the first of three years of jazz programs, which included a concert recording (1956) by Oscar *Peterson and a performance by Duke Ellington of his Shakespearean suite *Such Sweet Thunder* (1957). After the English Opera Group's presentation in 1957 of Britten's *The Turn of the Screw* and a concert by the *CBC SO, music moved to the Avon Theatre. Two seasons there saw productions of *The Beggar's Opera* (1958) and *Orpheus in the Underworld* (1959) and, significantly, the creation in 1959 of the Orchestra Workshop under the direction of leading chamber musicians, to attract and hold players who would form the National Festival Orchestra. Master classes, in later years independent of the Orchestra Workshop, continued until 1969 and were revived in 1971. In 1960 concerts were presented in the Festival Theatre for the first time, while stage productions, including the Gilbert & Sullivan operas *H.M.S. Pinafore* (1960), *The Pirates of Penzance* (1961), *The Gondoliers* (1962), *The Mikado* (1963), and *The Yeomen of the Guard* (1964) continued at the Avon Theatre. Saturday morning chamber concerts, introduced in 1960, increased from three to eight per season. An *International Conference of Composers and the International String Congress also were held in 1960.

In 1961 two distinguished US musicians who were instructors in the Orchestra Workshop, the cellist Leonard Rose and the violinist Oscar Shumsky, were named in a directorial triumvirate with Glenn *Gould (who had been a regular performer at Stratford since 1953) to succeed Applebaum. The Rose-Shumsky-Gould seasons, 1961–4, and the following three, 1965–7, under Shumsky alone, were highlighted by the three players' joint and solo performances, by the continuing expansion of the Festival Concert series, and by the Festival Choral Workshop 1963–5 under Elmer *Iseler. Opera productions, including *The Marriage of Figaro* (1964, 1965), *Don Giovanni* (1966), and *Così fan tutte* (1967), Weill's *Mahagonny* (1965), Britten's *Albert Herring* (1967), Rossini's *Cinderella* (1968), and Gabriel *Charpentier's **An English Lesson* (1968), continued until they were deemed prohibitively costly. By 1969, the second of Victor *Di Bello's two years as musical director, casual concerts proliferated, and full-scale opera had ceased. After 1969, under the direction of Andrée Gingras 1970–3 and Raffi *Armenian 1973–6, concerts decreased in number but expanded in range to include jazz performers and leading Canadian folk musicians as well as chamber and recital programs. The Stratford Festival Ensemble, founded and conducted by Raffi Armenian, performed regularly 1974–6. (It served also during those years as the professional nucleus of the *Kitchener-Waterloo SO, and after 1976 it continued in that function and performed also as an independent itinerant chamber unit called the Stratford Ensemble. In 1980 it was renamed the Canadian Chamber Ensemble.)

Special concert programs met a mixed reception. The 'Music at Midnight' series (which presented unscheduled appearances by the festival's guest musicians and chamber concerts by members of the resident festival orchestra) flourished 1969–76 at the Rothman Art Gallery, but 'Music For A Summer Day,' a notable day-long mini-festival (1972) was repeated only in 1973, then dropped. Although major productions of opera were not resumed, in 1971 the Third Stage (the badminton court again, in disguise) became the home for chamber opera and experimental productions, eg, R. Murray *Schafer's *Patria II: *Requiems for the Party Girl* (1972), Gabriel Charpentier's *Orpheus* (1972), Raymond and Beverly *Pannell's *Exiles* (1973, a Stratford commission), Charles *Wilson's *The Summoning of Everyman* (1974), Gian-Carlo Menotti's *The Medium* (1974), Harry *Somers' **The Fool* (1975), Jean *Vallerand's

Le Magicien (1975), and Richard Strauss' *Ariadne auf Naxos* (1975).

No productions were mounted in 1976 or the following year under the new music director Berthold Carriere, appointed in the fall of 1976. In fact the 1977 music program was limited to six concerts of pop music. The 1978 season was somewhat expanded: an opening gala featuring the *COC and the National Ballet of Canada; a Third Stage production of Bernstein's *Candide* with Caralyn Tomlin, Ed Evanko, and Andrea Martin; concerts by Liona *Boyd, Oscar Peterson, and Louis and Gino *Quilico; and appearances by Bruce *Cockburn and Dan *Hill. The 1979 season offered the musical play *Happy New Year* (music of Cole Porter, adapted by Burt Shevelove); jazz concerts by the Gary Burton Quartet, Dizzy Gillespie, the Preservation Jazz Band, and Sarah Vaughan; and concerts by *Valdy and Kate and Anna *McGarrigle.

2 COMPOSITION. Incidental music for Stratford's theatre productions has been commissioned from various composers and performed by the Stratford Festival Theatre Orchestra as required. Louis Applebaum scored over 30 productions between 1953 and 1977, and John Cook and Gabriel Charpentier more than 10 each. Others who have provided incidental music are Cedric Thorpe Davie (1954–5), Harry Somers (1960), Duke Ellington (1963), Godfrey *Ridout (1964), Raymond Pannell (1967–9, 1973), Stanley Silverman (1967–70), Alan Laing (1967, 1972–5), Harry *Freedman (1971, 1975), Pierre Philippe (1971), and Berthold Carriere (1974, 1975). Concert works have been commissioned from Serge *Garant, Bruce *Mather, Gabriel Charpentier, and Steven *Gellman (all premiered at the Saturday morning chamber music concerts in 1968) and from John *Hawkins, Brian *Cherney, and Gilles *Tremblay (premiered in 1969).

BIBLIOGRAPHY

Articles in *CMJ*, vols 1–6, Autumn 1956–61; vol 1, Summer 1957
Stratford Shakespearean Festival Foundation of Canada. *Fanfare*, quarterly publication 1966–
Thompson, David. 'Opera at the Stratford Festival 1953/1967,' *OpCan*, vol 8, Sep 1967
Applebaum, Louis. 'Stratford's music festival,' *The Stratford Scene*, ed Peter Raby (Toronto 1968)
Stratford Festival Story. Annual brochures (Stratford)
Shaw, Grace Lydiatt. *Stratford Under Cover* (Toronto 1977)
Littler, William. 'Where has all the summer festival music gone?' Toronto *Star*, 20 Aug 1977
Timmerman, Nicola. 'Stratford's Berthold Carriere: a musical director with panache,' *CanComp*, Oct 1978 (LCf)

Strathcona Scholarship. Established in Montreal in 1895 by Donald Alexander Smith, statesman, financier, and philanthropist (b Forres, Moray, Scotland, 6 Aug 1820, d London 21 or 29 Jan 1914), who became Baron of Strathcona and Mount Royal in 1897. A prominent figure in Canadian history, Lord Strathcona contributed considerable sums of money to musicians, societies, and teaching establishments during his career in Canada.

With his cousin Lord Mount Stephen, Lord Strathcona created in 1885 the Montreal Scholarship of the RCM. This award, granted first to Ella Walker ca 1886–91, then to a Miss Russell ca 1891–4, became in 1895 the Strathcona Scholarship with Lord Strathcona as sole donor. It allowed the winners free tuition at the RCM for three years (with a possible two-year extension) as well as an annual living allowance of 50 guineas. Béatrice *La Palme (1895), the singer Ada Moylan (1898), Lynnwood *Farnam (1900). Pauline *Donalda (1902), Arthur *Egerton (1911), Sarah *Fischer (1917), Rose *Goldblatt (1930), and Alexander *Brott (1939) were among the recipients, as were also Christina Barrie-Dickson and Jules Lamontagne.

Lord Strathcona was honorary president and a member of numerous music societies and was associated with *McGill U as governor, chancellor, and special benefactor over a considerable period of time. Between 1896 and 1913 he continued to help young Canadian artists, including Éva *Gauthier and Kathleen *Parlow, while holding the post of Canadian High Commissioner in London. The Strathcona Music Building of McGill U was named in his honour in 1971.

BIBLIOGRAPHY

Gould, Joseph. 'Music,' *Arcadia*, vol 1, 15 Dec 1892
McGill U Archives. RG 39
Musical Red Book NT

STRATHY, George (William). Teacher, pianist, conductor, composer, b Scotland 19 Aug 1818, d Toronto 4 Dec 1890; B MUS (Trinity College, Toronto) 1853, D MUS (ibid) 1858. He probably came to Canada in 1835. He studied music in Germany with Friedrich Schneider (Kapellmeister in Dessau) and, according to an ad in the *Globe* (6 Oct 1849), with Mendelssohn. No confirmation of this has come to light, nor has it for another claim that he studied with Liszt. By late 1847 he had settled in Toronto as a piano, organ, and theory teacher. He was accompanist for the *Toronto Philharmonic Society and briefly (1849–50) its conductor. The B MUS he received from the *U of Trinity College was only the second granted in Canada, and Strathy was appointed that same year (1853) to teach at the college; he was the first person in Canada to hold the academic title 'Professor of Music.' He was also the first person in Canada known to have received a D MUS.

Strathy continued to teach piano and theory privately and, ca 1862–9, at the Toronto Musical Institute (which may simply have been his own studio). Of his many concert appearances in Toronto, one, 11 Sep 1862, offered Beethoven's 'Grand' (probably the 'Archduke') *Trio* and the other, 25 Sep 1862, presented vocal and instrumental music under the patronage of the governor of the Province of Canada, Lord Monck. In 1867 Strathy attempted to form an orchestra, and in 1879 he founded the Pianoforte Players Classical Club, which presented, among other music, piano transcriptions of symphonies and paraphrases of other major works. He continued to hold his university position, but a student paper, *Rouge et Noir* (vol 2, no. 2) reported in 1881 that the music program had a professor, 'but we have seen nothing of him – no graduates – no lecture – no examinations – it is time for a change.' (Strathy, in a letter to the editor of *Arion*, retorted that the lectures had been cancelled because of an insufficient enrolment.) In 1852, *Nordheimer published Strathy's *Recreation Polka* and *Magic Bell Polka* and later the *Musical Journal* (1887–90), I. *Suckling & Sons, and *Claxton printed some 10 piano pieces and songs. Strathy was also one of three editors of *A Selection of Chants and Tunes* (Toronto 1861). (EK)

STRATTON, John (Reginald). Record historian and producer, baritone, b Toronto 1 Aug 1931; BA (Trinity College, Toronto) 1954, MA (Toronto) 1958, PH D philosophy (Toronto) 1969. A specialist in the history and recordings of dramatic singing, Stratton has contributed articles to the *Record Collector* on Florence *Easton and Dmitri Smirnoff, and part of his doctoral research appeared (April–July 1966) in the *Journal of the British Institute of Recorded Sound* as 'Operatic singing style and the gramophone.' For these journals he has written several pieces on the Mapleson Cylinders (the earliest recordings taken during live performances in the theatre). In 1968 he gave the opening lectures ('Crisis in the art of singing') at the new quarters of the British Institute of Recorded Sound. He is also a contributor to *EMC*. Through his own record label, Cantilena, founded in 1966 in Toronto and distributed by *Rococo Records, Stratton had released by 1977 over 35 LPs of rare 78s by singers of the past, including Florence Easton and Edward *Johnson. Stratton himself studied voice in the 1950s: in Toronto with Gina Cigna and Aksel *Schiøtz, and in New York with Easton and Herbert Janssen. He has recorded for Cantilena three recital LPs (1967–74) of songs, opera excerpts, and sacred works. By profession a teacher of philosophy, Stratton joined the faculty at Ryerson Polytechnical Institute (Toronto) in 1971.

STREATFEILD, Simon (Nicholas). Conductor, violist, b Windsor, England, 5 Oct 1929; ARCM 1949. After viola studies 1946–50 with Frederick Riddle at the RCM he played in the London Philharmonic, was principal viola of the Sadler's Wells Orchestra and the London SO, and was a founder of the chamber orchestra the Academy of St Martin-in-the-Fields. After moving to Canada he served 1965–9 as principal viola, 1967–71 as assistant conductor, 1971–2 as acting music director, and 1972–7 as associate conductor of the *Vancouver SO. Dividing his time between Canada and Great Britain, Streatfeild has been guest conductor of the City of Birmingham SO, the Scottish National and various BBC orchestras, and the Royal Choral Society. In Canada he was a founding member 1966–8 of the *Baroque Strings of Vancouver and the founding director 1967–9 of the Courtenay Youth Music Camp. In 1968 he became conductor and director of the *Vancouver Bach Choir. A founding member 1968–9 of the *Purcell String Quartet, he later rejoined the quartet as second viola for its series of recordings of the Mozart and Brahms string quintets. In 1977 Streatfeild became a visiting professor at the *U of Western Ontario. (MW)

Stringband. Group of folk singers and instrumentalists formed in 1971 at the *U of Toronto by Marie-Lynn Hammond and Bob Bossin. Stringband first worked in Ontario coffeehouses and universities, and by 1977 had made tours in western Canada, the Maritimes, the Northwest Territories, and the Yukon. The group has performed on CBC radio and TV, and on CTV. In 1977, sponsored by Canada's Dept of External Affairs, it gave 15 concerts in Mexico. Both Hammond – whose voice has been described by Jack Batten as 'a deep, rich, entrancingly lovely vehicle' (*Chatelaine*, November 1976) – and Bossin are bilingual singers, and each plays a variety of instruments (acoustic guitar, banjo, autoharp). Stringband's varied repertoire includes the members' own songs (including Bossin's 'Dief Will Be the Chief Again,' a minor record hit in 1975), traditional songs, fiddle tunes, and novelty pieces. The fiddlers Jerry Lewycky, Ben Mink, and Terry King, in turn, have toured with Stringband, and each is heard on one of its first three LPs – *Canadian Sunset, National Melodies*, and *Thanks to the Following*. King performed for the fourth – *Maple Leaf Dog* (1979) – and then was succeeded by Zeke Mazurek. The LPs were issued under the group's own label, Nick. Other musicians have participated in Stringband's recordings and, on occasion, its performances.

After a 1977 New Year's Eve concert in Toronto Hammond left Stringband to pursue a solo career and released the LP *Marie-Lynn Hammond* (Black Tie Records BTR 1001) late in 1978. She was succeeded by the singer-songwriter Nancy Ahern, and the group was known briefly as the Whilom Stringband, eventually reverting to its original name.

Writing in *Saturday Night*, Doug Fetherling called Stringband 'one of the most distinctive and independent groups in Canadian music at the moment and also, perhaps, one of the most culturally significant.' He continued, 'Theirs is the music that goes with pine furniture and Greg Curnoe paintings on the wall.'

BIBLIOGRAPHY
'Stringband's music is home-made and friendly,' *CanComp*, 89, Mar 1974
Fetherling, Doug. 'Stringband's search for a Canadian style,' *SatN*, Jun 1976
Ross, Val. 'Between the notes,' *Weekend Magazine*, 29 Jan 1977 MM

String instrument building. Traditionally, the French word 'lutherie,' used in both French and English, denotes the art of building string instruments that are bowed – violins, violas, cellos, and bass viols or double-basses – and of making the bows themselves. By extension, it includes the building of other instruments of the viol family and of plucked-string instruments such as the guitar, lute, and mandolin. 'Luthier' is the name given to a person who devotes himself to building, maintaining, and repairing these instruments. This entry deals only with instruments of the violin family. The *EMC* entries Guitar; Instruments: medieval, renaissance, and baroque; and Lute provide information on the principal builders of other string instruments in Canada.

String instrument building is both an art and a science, and its principles and laws have been defined over the centuries, culminating in a 'golden age' in 18th-century Italy, chiefly in Cremona, with three famous names: Amati, Guarneri, and Stradivari. The three represent a pinnacle of achievement which in 1980 remained unsurpassed. In addition to Cremona, other cities – Naples, Venice, and Milan in Italy, Paris and Mirecourt in France, and Mittenwald in Germany – subsequently acquired reputations as centres for string instrument building. Besides the professional makers who learned their skills through apprenticeship with masters or, more recently, in schools for instrument building, self-taught amateurs occasionally have acquired astonishing mastery of the art.

In Canada numerous luthiers have belonged in the amateur category but have remained little known, in part because adequate records have not been kept. As early as 1930 the Toronto firm R.S. *Williams & Sons contemplated compiling a dictionary of Canadian string instrument builders and for this purpose had gathered information on several hundred amateur luthiers, some of whose dates went back as far as 1750 (see 'R.S. Williams & Sons' in *Universal Dictionary of Violin and Bow Makers*).

The presence of a violin in Quebec City as early as 1645 is documented. Someone, probably Martin *Boutet, played it at a wedding. There is no indication, however, that this instrument or any others were built locally at this time, even though the types of wood required for their construction – fir, spruce, and maple – were found in abundance in Canada. It may be supposed that amateurs managed to build many of the instruments used for accompanying social dancing and other entertainments. In 1788 in Quebec City F.-H. *Glackemeyer advertised that he repaired guitars

The Bayeur violin, once belonging to Claude Champagne, won 6th prize in the 1921 Le Monde musical competition in Paris

and sold strings and bridges. Around 1820 Pierre-Olivier *Lyonnais learned from the bandmaster Adam *Schott how to make violins and was the first of a line of string instrument builders of this name, the last of whom died in 1921.

History has preserved few names of luthiers from this period. At L'Assomption, near Montreal, Pierre Martel, the grandfather of Oscar *Martel, built violins, two of which were said to have been displayed in Paris in 1877, earning him considerable praise (*Coup d'oeil*). Oscar's father also was a string instrument builder. Augustin *Lavallée and his son Charles are believed to have built some 150 violins in the second half of the 19th century. In 1879 Lavallée père successfully restored a valuable Guarnerius, belonging to Frantz *Jehin-Prume, after it had been severely damaged in an accident. Trefflé R. Gervais, born in Quebec in 1863, went to Boston in 1877 as an employee of Gould & Sons and subsequently produced many highly prized instruments. Gould also trained T.-O. *Dionne, who in 1890 opened a workshop in Montreal where he in turn trained his successor, Rosario *Forget.

However, it was the *Bayeur brothers, Rosario and Albert, who first attracted international attention to Canadian string instrument building when a violin of theirs belonging to Claude *Champagne placed sixth in a competition assessing tone quality in Paris in 1921. Camille *Couture also won bronze medals at Wembley, England, in 1924 and 1925. The following were active in Montreal in the late 19th and early 20th centuries: Adolphe Blanchette (known particularly for his bows), D.-H. Dansereau, J.-H. Davignon, Ovide Richer, and Hormisdas Saint-Cyr. After 1930 the names of Pierre Dalphin, Claude Fougerolle, Jean Gobeil, Ivo Loerakker, Cyrice Martin (father of the violinist Lucien *Martin), Napoléon Rhéaume, Antoine Robichaud, Jules Saint-Michel (b Szentmihaly), and Anton *Wilfer deserve mention.

In Quebec City Charles-Lévis Laterreur (b St-Isidore, Dorchester, near Quebec City, 23 May 1904) built some 70 violins and 200 guitars. In 1968 a bursary from the *MACQ enabled him to perfect his skills in Europe with master builders. Italian-born Sylvio de Lellis came to Canada in 1964 and settled in Quebec City in 1971. In 1979 the MACQ granted him a subsidy to open a school for string instrument building, the first in Canada. Léonard Otis of Chicoutimi received a bursary from the MACQ in the late 1970s. In Moncton ca 1920 Joseph LeBlanc built for his son Arthur *LeBlanc two violins which are preserved in the museum of the *U of Moncton. Joseph Kun, originally from Czechoslovakia, was active in Ottawa after World War II.

In Toronto the firm of R.S. Williams hired George *Heinl in 1912. He worked 1920–6 in Ottawa and later opened his own establishment in Toronto, where he was succeeded by his son and two grandsons. The Parisian August(e) Delivet made several instruments for R.S. Williams (1920–7). Another Williams employee, George *Kindness, opened his own shop in Toronto in 1921. William Knaggs allegedly won a prize at an exhibition in Paris in 1900, but no substantiating evidence has been found. Other distinguished luthiers include James *Dyer, who worked for Heinl for a year, and Piet *Molenaar, who opened a workshop in 1951. Otto Erdész, who established a shop in Toronto in 1975, has won special renown for his violas.

In Winnipeg James *Croft began making violins in 1915. He was succeeded by his son Henry James Croft. Another Manitoba string instrument maker, Sid *Engen, set up shop in Dauphin in 1919. His copies of instruments by Stradivari and Guarneri won prizes at exhibitions in the USA. Born in Owen Sound, Ont, in 1879, Peter Murray Bell settled in Calgary at the beginning of the 20th century, and his instruments enjoyed a considerable reputation. Leif Karlsson, of Swedish descent but trained in the school at Mittenwald, also became active in Calgary. In Vancouver 'Doc' (Warren Fulton) Porter began building instruments ca 1920. By 1980 he had made more than 100 violins.

Despite respectable results, the art of string instrument building in Canada has not attracted significant world attention. This relative neglect notwithstanding, numerous fine Canadian craftsmen have found and have continued to find in the practice of this art a pastime both useful and rewarding, and their work commands admiration. At the professional level the necessity for luthiers to devote themselves primarily to repair work and restoration, and the difficulty of recruiting apprentices interested in exercising a skill that does not conform to the norms of the industrial age, have slowed down the production of new instruments, despite a steadily increasing demand.

BIBLIOGRAPHY
Bachmann, Alberto. *An Encyclopedia of the Violin* (New York and London 1925; New York 1966)
Massicotte, É.-Z. 'Violons et luthiers,' *BRH*, vol 41, Apr 1935
Royer, Henri. 'Lutherie à Québec,' *R Saint-Grégoire* (Mar 1951)
Henley, William ed. *Universal Dictionary of Violin and Bow Makers* (Brighton, England, 1959–60)
Vannes, René. *Dictionnaire universal des luthiers* (Brussels 1972)
Bardsley, Alice. 'Violin making an art,' *Atlantic Advocate* (Oct 1973)
Colgrass, Ulla. 'Violinmaker scoffs at "Stradivarius sauce",' *Music*, Mar–Apr 1979 GP

String instrument playing and teaching. See the following entries:
Cello
Double-bass
Guitar
Harp
Instruments: medieval, renaissance, and baroque: 1 / Playing and teaching
Lute
Violin and viola playing and teaching

STROMBERGS, Alfred. Conductor, opera coach, pianist, teacher, b Liepaja, Latvia, 19 Feb 1922, naturalized Canadian 1954; ARCT 1958, ARCCO 1960. He studied piano, conducting, and composition 1940–3 at the Latvian State Cons, Riga, and was a ballet conductor and opera coach (1943) and conductor (1944), in Latvia. After four years in Germany he moved to Canada in 1948.

He taught piano at the Halifax Cons (*Maritime Cons of Music), founded and was the conductor 1949–55 of the Halifax Symphonette (later *Halifax SO), was the conductor and music director of the *Nova Scotia Opera, and conducted the orchestra for the Halifax Ballet Guild. After studies in conducting with Leonard Bernstein and Lukas Foss at Tanglewood in 1953 he studied composition with Godfrey *Ridout at the *RCMT. He served 1957–68 as conductor of the *Stratford Festival Theatre Orchestra, 1957–71 as a coach with the *COC, and 1960–71 as head coach of the *Royal Cons Opera School. He was appointed vocal coach and opera conductor at the *U of Alberta in 1971 and head of the voice and opera department there in 1972. He was music director 1972–3 of the opera division at the *Banff SFA and chorusmaster 1973–4 for the *Edmonton Opera.

BIBLIOGRAPHY
MacNiven, Elinor. 'Profile: Alfred Strombergs,' *OpCan*, Dec 1966 RDM

STRONG ROURKE, Alice (b Strong, m Rourke). Soprano, b Chatham, Ont, 6 Jun 1906; BA (Toronto) 1929. She studied voice in Toronto with Nina *Gale, Jeanne *Dusseau, Eduardo *Ferrari-Fontana, Ernesto *Vinci, and others. Though she made her stage debut as Solveig in the 1930 *Hart House Theatre production of *Peer Gynt* and sang Nedda in the 1936 Opera Guild of Toronto production of *I Pagliacci*, it was in productions of Gilbert & Sullivan that she enjoyed particular popularity in the Toronto area for over 20 years. She also gave recitals throughout Ontario and on radio and was soloist in turn at Deer Park United and Lawrence Park Community churches before moving in 1953 to the USA. SLO

STRUTT, Michael. Guitarist, lutenist, teacher, b Prestbury, Cheshire, England, 14 Apr 1945. Raised in the Manchester area, Strutt began piano lessons in 1956, studied guitar 1963–5 with Terrence Usher, and took up the lute. He continued his studies 1965–6 with Julian Bream and in 1974 with José Tomas and José Luis Rodrigo in Alicante, Spain. A recitalist and chamber musician on BBC TV Strutt, playing the lute, won that network's 1968 'New Faces' competition. He moved to Canada in 1969 and performed in Regina, Victoria, Vancouver, and Seattle and with the Okanagan SO. He played on CBC radio and TV and taught 1971–2 at the *U of Victoria before moving in 1973 to Montreal. He began teaching at *McGill U in 1974, at the *U of Ottawa in 1976 (establishing a lute-major program there), and at Vanier College, Montreal, in 1977. At the 1974 Concurso Internacional de Guitarra he won a full scholarship to the Santiago de Compostela Master Class and a series of concerts in Alicante province in 1975. Continuing his performing career in Canada and the USA he has specialized in the 16th-century repertoire for lute and in contemporary music for guitar. He is heard on a recording of Harry *Somers' *Sonata for Guitar* (RCI 409). He is a contributor to *EMC*. BNSG

STUBBS, Janet (Helena). Mezzo soprano, b Toronto; LLB (Toronto) 1969, Artist Diploma opera (Toronto) 1975. She studied with Helen Simmie at the *RCMT and, after a brief career in law, with Bernard *Diamant at the *U of Toronto. She joined the *COC in 1974 and has appeared as Schwertleite in *Die Walküre* (1976), Margret in *Wozzeck* (1977), Cherubino in *The Marriage of Figaro*, Maddalena in *Rigoletto*, and Annina in *Der Rosenkavalier* (all 1978) and in the title roles of *Cinderella* and *Carmen* in 1979. She has sung with the *Edmonton Opera Assn (1977, 1979) and has performed in concert and oratorio with the *Calgary Philharmonic and many Ontario orchestras, including the *London, *Kitchener-Waterloo, and *Thunder Bay SOs. In 1976 she made her *TS debut in Stravinsky's *Pulcinella*. She has appeared with *Camerata, the Cantata Soloists, the Voirin Ensemble, and *NMC, has sung several times at the *Guelph Spring Festival, and has appeared in Festival Canada (*Festival Ottawa) productions of *La Traviata* (1975), *The Magic Flute* (1975, 1977), and *Ariadne auf Naxos* (1977). In 1977 she was a soloist with Sir Peter Pears in a performance of the Bach *Magnificat* by the *Ottawa Choral Society, and Sir Peter subsequently selected her for his 1978 Master Class at Aldeburgh. She has performed often for CBC radio and TV. In January 1979, with the *CJRT Orchestra, she gave the Toronto premiere of Britten's *Phaedra*.

BIBLIOGRAPHY
Fraser, John. 'Janet Stubbs: a rare voice "drifts" to greatness,' Toronto *Globe and Mail*, 2 Mar 1976 NM

Studio de musique ancienne de Montréal. Ensemble of professional and student singers and instrumentalists dedicated to the performance of pre-1750 German, English, French, and Italian music 'in an informed and authentic spirit.' The ensemble was founded by Hélène Dugal and its music directors Christopher *Jackson and Réjean *Poirier in September 1974 and was incorporated in 1976. Performances involving from 20 to 70 musicians have provided Montreal audiences with hearings of published or manuscript works in the playing or singing styles of their individual periods, adhering in particular to traditional pitch standards. Supported by donations from private citizens and subsidies from the *Canada Council, the *MACQ, and the Council of Arts of Greater Montreal, the group has worked gradually to replace modern instruments with replicas of historical ones.

The studio has given an average of three concerts a season in Montreal in places selected for their acoustics and ambiance, such as the chapel of the Grand Séminaire, St-Pierre-Apôtre Church, and Redpath Hall (*McGill U). Tickets are sold individually or by subscription.

The first concert, devoted to Monteverdi and Carissimi, took place in December 1974. The next season Claude *Gingras drew attention to the 'high musical and musicological quality' of the ensemble's performance (*La Presse*, 1 Dec 1975). In 1975 the group performed at the Abbey at St-Benoit-du-Lac and organized a colloquium in Montreal on 17th-century Italian music. The ensemble toured Quebec in 1977, performing works by Bach, and the same year broadcast 13 programs for the CBC radio series 'Les Goûts réunis.' During the summer of 1980 it gave 22 concerts on a tour of France and Spain. (BL)

I. Suckling & Sons. Music publishers and retailers in Toronto ca 1875–ca 1894. Isaac Suckling was a retired English bandmaster and music teacher; his son George H. (b England ca 1856, d Vancouver ca 1930) had worked for *Nordheimer and eventually returned to that firm as general representative and superintendant of agencies; his son Henry also worked for the family firm and later was a treasurer for the CPR; and another son, Isaac Edward (1862–1938) became an impresario and the first manager 1894–1900 of *Massey Music Hall in Toronto. The Suckling store was located at 107 Yonge St. It was an agency for Chickering pianos. The firm's earliest publication was copyrighted in 1876. Plate numbers were used from 1881 onwards and reached nearly 500. Suckling's remarkable catalogue included music by the majority of Anglo-Canada's trained composers, including J.E.P. *Aldous, R.S. *Ambrose, Francesco *D'Auria, A.E. *Fisher, W.O. *Forsyth, J.A. *Fowler, Edwin *Gledhill, C.A.E. *Harriss, J.D. *Kerrison, Clarence *Lucas, Angelo *Read, and F.H. *Torrington. The firm also issued the first edition of the *University of Toronto Songbook* (1887) and *Canadian National and Patriotic Songs* (1890). Its series included *Choice Compositions for the Pianoforte* and *Collection of Standard Glees and Part Songs*. A coup was the acquisition of the rights for a Canadian edition (1890) of Paderewski's famous *Menuet*, first published in 1887. Paderewski himself appeared in Toronto under Suckling's management, as did such other noted performers as Chaliapin, Galli-Curci, Hofmann, Kreisler, Melba, Nordica, and Ysaÿe. HK

Sudbury. Mining community in northern Ontario. Settled in 1883 and incorporated as a city in 1930, Sudbury by the mid-1970s had a population of 100,000 from a variety of national origins including Ukrainian, Italian, Finnish, and Croatian.

According to a city directory, in 1911 Sudbury had 2 music teachers and 2 music stores. The 1930 directory listed 11 teachers and 5 stores. One of the earliest musical organizations was the Sacred Heart College Band, founded in 1916. The Sacred Heart College Choir later sang on local radio broadcasts.

Other Sudbury choirs have included the Sudbury Chamber Singers directed by Douglas Webb, the Bel Canto Chorus directed by Donald Weir, the Sudbury Ladies' Choir directed by Louise Innes, and the Marian Singers directed by Chrissie Nemis. Nemis, who also directed the choir at Christ the King Church and taught in the separate school system, was named citizen of the year in 1977. Among ethnic ensembles have been the Dnipro Choir (Ukrainian), the Caruso Club Choir (Italian), the Finnish Male Chorus, and the Croatian Tamburitza Ensemble. The 1978 Choirs in Contact of the *Ontario Choral Federation was held in Sudbury.

Eric Woodward (organist, conductor, b England 1902), settled in Sudbury in 1956 and founded the Sudbury Philharmonic Society in 1957. This choral-orchestral ensemble performed Mendelssohn's *Elijah* and *Hymn of Praise*, Elgar's *In the Bavarian Highlands*, and other works. In 1962 it merged with the Sudbury SO, founded in 1953 and conducted by Emile First, to give three concerts a year for six or seven years, but then the two organizations separated again. Metro Kozak, director of music at Cambrian College, became the conductor of a reconstituted Sudbury SO in 1975 and shifted the programming more definitely towards the symphonic repertoire. The 65-member orchestra has given four or more concerts annually in the Great Hall of Laurentian U.

Other musical groups have included the Sudbury Band, founded in 1943, and the Karl *Pukara Accordion Orchestra, organized in 1957. The Sudbury-born Pukara established the Regional Cons of Music (also known as the Karl Pukara Music Studio) in 1964. Two other Sudbury schools have offered music programs: Cambrian (community) College, which offers a three-year diploma course in music, and Marymount College. A branch of the *ORMTA was formed in Sudbury in 1943 and has co-sponsored the annual Kiwanis Music Festival. Founded in 1960, Laurentian U, with Woodward as director of cultural affairs, has sponsored concerts and recitals. Performances by local and visiting artists have been organized by the *JMC, Cambrian College, St Andrew's Place, the Dante-Alighieri Society, and Spectrum – the Sudbury Arts Festival.

In 1959 Germain *Lemieux, who collected many folksongs and legends in the Sudbury area, was made director of the U of Sudbury's Institut de folklore (Centre franco-ontarien de folklore after 1975).

Musicians born in Sudbury include Trump *Davidson (who formed there ca 1925 what possibly was the first jazz-style group in Canada) and the guitarist Rich Dodson (of the *Stampeders). The 11-member co-operative group Cano was formed in Sudbury and gave its first concerts in 1975. It has toured in Quebec and recorded for *A & M Records.

BIBLIOGRAPHY
Dostie, Bruno. 'Cano: a new group from Sudbury – with something different to say,' *CanComp*, 117, Jan 1977

(MKz)

SUGARMAN, (Abram) **Berul**. Violinist, teacher, b Toronto 28 May 1908. He studied violin with Broadus Farmer 1918–20 (see Ernest Farmer), with Luigi von *Kunits 1920–31, and with Arthur Hartmann, Mischa Mischakoff, and others in the 1930s. He was a member of the *TSO 1925–38 and of the Indianapolis SO 1938–40 and rejoined the TSO in 1942. He played in Toronto symphony, silent-movie, hotel, and radio orchestras, including those of Alexander *Chuhaldin and Reginald *Stewart, the *CBC SO, the York Concert Society, the *Hart House Orchestra, and many Toronto chamber groups, including the *Solway String Quartet and his own Galant Chamber Music Players 1956–67. He was chamber music instructor 1967–72 for North York (Toronto) schools. For chamber ensembles he has arranged French-Canadian folksongs, edited neglected works of Pergolesi, Schobert, and Schubert, and in 1962 reconstructed a lost minuet from Mozart's *Eine kleine Nachtmusik* (all unpublished). (SLH)

Sugar Shoppe. Pop group formed in Toronto in 1967 by the singer-pianist Peter Mann with the singers Laurie Hood, Lee Harris, and Victor Garber. All but Garber were conservatory-trained; Mann previously had worked in theatre and TV. Accompanied by a small band, Sugar Shoppe sang what Mann described as 'jazz oriented folk-rock' (Toronto *Telegram*, 19 Sep 1969). Its first single, a version of *'CA-NA-DA' for the Yorkville label, was its most successful; three others were released by late 1968. Sugar Shoppe performed widely in the USA and Canada in nightclubs (eg, in Las Vegas) and on TV (eg, 'The Ed Sullivan Show' in 1969). It also made two LPs before disbanding in April of 1970. The members continued in music and theatre, Garber meeting with the most success in the 1970s, starring as Jesus Christ in the movie of the musical *Godspell* (soundtrack: Arista 4005) and as Anthony Hope in the Broadway production of *Sweeney Todd* (cast recording: RCA CBL2-3379). Garber also appeared with Hood in Mann's rock-musical *Jack – A Flash Fantasy*, telecast 28 Feb 1974 by the CBC.

BIBLIOGRAPHY
Kirby, Blaik. 'How sweet it is for the Sugar Shoppe,' Toronto *Globe and Mail*, 3 May 1969

MM

SUKIS, Lilian. Soprano, b Kaunas, Lithuania, 29 Jun 1939; ARCT voice 1961, ARCT piano 1962, BA (McMaster) 1962, Artist Diploma (Toronto) 1965. Her family moved to Germany during World War II and emigrated in 1950 to Canada, settling in Hamilton, Ont. In 1962 she moved to Toronto, where she studied with Irene *Jessner, Greta *Kraus, and Arnold *Walter at the *Royal Cons Opera School. In 1964 she won the Rosebowl in the *Kiwanis Festival. That same year she appeared as Lady Billows in *Albert Herring* during the opening of the MacMillan Theatre (*U of Toronto) and as Alice Ford in Verdi's *Falstaff* at the *Banff SFA. She also made her *COC debut in 1964, as Kate Pinkerton in *Madama Butterfly*. In 1965 she won the Eaton Graduating Scholarship and sang the title role in the stage premiere of *Willan's **Deirdre* at the opera school and the Countess in *The Marriage of Figaro* at the *Stratford Festival. She studied at the *Metropolitan Opera Studio and School during the mid-1960s and made her Metropolitan debut 17 Mar 1967 as Helen Niles in the premiere of Martin David Levy's *Mourning Becomes Electra*. She made her New York Town Hall debut in 1969 and in the same year joined the Munich State Opera. At the Munich Olympic Festival (1972) she sang the title role (which had been written for her) in the premiere of the Korean composer Isang Yun's opera *Sim Tjong*.

During the 1970s Sukis sang with opera houses in Bayreuth, Frankfurt, Graz, Hamburg, Munich, Salzburg, and Vienna. Her roles have included the Countess in Strauss' *Capriccio*, Fiordiligi in *Così fan tutte*, Leïla in *Les Pêcheurs de perles*, Mélisande in *Pelléas et Mélisande*, Micaela in *Carmen*, Mimi in *La Bohème*, Pamina in *The Magic Flute*, Servilia in *La Clemenza di Tito*, Violetta in *La Traviata*, Woglinde in *Das Rheingold*, and the title role in Strauss' *Daphne*. She has appeared in Mozart's *Ascanio in Alba* and his religious play-with-music *Die Schuldigkeit des ersten Gebotes*. In 1977 she was Frau Fluth in a film version of Nicolai's *Merry Wives of Windsor* and also recorded the role for London (3.Lon 13127). In 1979 she sang Lisa in *The Queen of Spades* at *Festival Ottawa.

BIBLIOGRAPHY
McBride, Ken. 'Canadian artists in profile: Lilian Sukis,' *OpCan*, May 1965
Wults, Phillip. 'A singer's struggle,' *Music*, Jun 1978
Mercer, Ruby. 'Lilian Sukis,' *OpCan*, Winter 1978

SW

SULLIVAN, Joyce (Anna) (b Solomon, m Scott). Singer, b Toronto 4 Jul 1924. A pupil of Emmy *Heim at the RCMT, she was a member 1947–54 of the *Leslie Bell Singers and a mezzo-soprano soloist with them in various concerts and broadcasts, including a 1951 radio performance of Pergolesi's *Stabat mater*. In the early 1950s she was heard in her own light-music shows on CBC and on Jack *Arthur's 'Mr. Showbusiness.' After appearing occasionally 1952–4 and 1956–7 on CBC TV's 'Showcase,' she co-starred on the same show 1957–9 with Robert *Goulet. In 1960 she was the host for CBC radio's 'Talk of the Town.' During the 1960s she was a soloist with the Carl *Tapscott Singers, appearing on the LP *Great Hymns of All Time*. She also recorded *Folk Songs of Canada* (1956, Hallmark CS-3) with Charles *Jordan and *The Songs of Joyce Sullivan* (1965, CTL 069) and participated in the nine-record *Canadian Folk Songs: A Centennial Collection* (RCA CS-100). She continued to perform, less frequently, until 1970.

BIBLIOGRAPHY
Rasky, Frank. 'Don't call me sweet,' *SatN*, 1 Mar 1958

MM (PG)

SUMBERG, Harold. Violinist, conductor, teacher, b Rochester, NY, 25 Aug 1905, naturalized Canadian 1920s. After studies at the Dovercourt Music School in Toronto and violin lessons (1922–7) with Willy Hess at the Hochschule für Musik in Berlin, Sumberg taught 1927–56 at the *TCM. He was a member 1929–45 of the *Cons String Quartet and directed the Sumberg Studio String Orchestra, made up of his violin and viola pupils Nathan Green, Phyllis Gummer, Stephen *Kondaks, Eveline Maguire, Samuel Margolian, Victor Zuchter, and others. Joining the *TSO in 1927 he served as principal second violin from 1932 to 1957. He was also concertmaster 1934–40 for the *Promenade Symphony Concerts and was a member (1930s) of the New World Chamber Orchestra under Samuel *Hersenhoren. Sumberg appeared in concert throughout the 1930s with Alberto *Guerrero and was a member in the late 1940s of the Sumberg-Ysselstyn-Guerrero Trio (later Sumberg Trio, with Cornelius Ysselstyn and Leo *Barkin). He played often on radio and in 1945 became music director of CBC radio's 'Intermezzo.' He also initiated the CBC series 'Symphony for Strings' (1946–8), on which he premiered Godfrey *Ridout's *Two Etudes* (dedicated to him) and Harry *Somers' *Scherzo*. He organized in 1948 the 20-member Toronto Women's Orchestra, conducted 1948–56 the Canadian Little Symphony, which performed throughout Ontario, and was principal second violin 1952–65 of Heinz *Unger's York Concert Society. In 1961 Sumberg returned to the TSO (retiring in 1975) and in 1973 he became director and violin-viola instructor at the YMHA Music School in Toronto. RTr

Summer camps and schools. Each summer musicians of all ages and abilities meet at music camps and schools across Canada to participate in programs of specialized instruction, supervised music-making, and, often, social and recreational activities. At many of these, music is one facet of a larger arts program. Such programs may be sponsored by universities, community colleges, school boards, musical organizations (including performing groups), or private concerns, and some have received support from federal and/or provincial arts councils and agencies, through direct grants or through monies for scholarships for students.

The teachers may be established performing musicians or teachers from schools, conservatories, or universities. Many summer music programs feature noted artist-performers who give master classes and conduct workshops. Levels of instruction and opportunities for performance vary. Some programs offer instruction in solo-instrumental and chamber music performance, others workshops in orchestra, opera or musical comedy, still others vocal and choral tuition. Most schools have entrance requirements. Some hold auditions. Though some camps call themselves schools, certain differences in essential nature identify them.

Music camps usually are located in rural, woodland settings, often near natural swimming facilities, and offer one to eight weeks in residence, attracting students at all levels and both professional and amateur adult performers. The *CAMMAC centres in the Laurentians of Quebec and the Muskoka district of Ontario encourage family participation. A few camps were founded during the 1940s and early 1950s: several by the *Salvation Army, the first ca 1940; C.F. *Thiele's short-lived Bandberg, a band camp for boys in Waterloo, Ont, in 1946; the *JMC Orford Art Cen-

A practice hut at the JMC summer camp

The Pacific Jazz Workshop at Courtenay Youth Music Centre, 1979

tre near Magog, Que, in 1951; the aforementioned CAMMAC centres in 1952 and 1978; and the Camp musical St-Jean, Île d'Orléans, Que, in 1952. Interest in and support for such camps increased in the late 1950s and 1960s, and by the 1970s music camps could be found in every province. Not all were residential. The Kelso Music Centre's Children's Music Workshop at Oakville, Ont, for instance, was a day camp.

Music summer schools, whether urban or rural, often are operated by accredited educational institutions, and many offer intensive studies which lead to scholastic credits. One of the first to program such high-level courses was the *Banff SFA, established in 1933. The *RCMT Summer School, begun in Toronto in 1938, traditionally has been attended from all parts of Canada by music teachers seeking refresher courses and master classes. An organization which operates independently (ie, not linked to a parent institution) but is sufficiently important and unusual to be singled out in this context is the *NYO, which, despite the name 'orchestra,' is in fact a summer school for the intensive conditioning of talented instrumentalists in the techniques and traditions of ensemble playing.

The ensuing list – which makes no claim to be comprehensive – describes some camps and schools in chronological order of foundation within each province. Those with entries elsewhere in *EMC* may be named but are not described here.

BRITISH COLUMBIA

Camps

Okanagan Summer School of the Arts, Penticton; established in 1960 for students of all ages and levels of proficiency, from beginner to professional. Music courses include string workshops (*Purcell String Quartet in-residence in 1979), wind ensemble, piano, guitar, voice, and songwriting.

BIBLIOGRAPHY
'Holiday with a purpose,' *Beautiful British Columbia*, Summer 1977

Victoria Summer School of Music, at St Michael's University School in Victoria; established in 1964 for young music students. String instruction, string ensemble performance, and piano classes have been offered. The founding directors, who continued to teach in 1979, were Clayton *Hare and Dorothy *Swetnam.

Courtenay Youth Music Centre, Courtney; established in 1967 as the Courtney Youth Music Camp and directed first by Simon *Streatfeild, then by Robert *Creech. In 1979 among the many programs and activities offered were a two-week workshop for the BC Summer Youth Choir, an opera workshop which prepared the premiere of *Freedman's *Abracadabra*, full instrumental programs, a Kodály teachers' workshop, and a jazz workshop. Public concerts, recitals, and other opera productions have been presented by faculty and students.

BIBLIOGRAPHY
Rivers, Clair. 'Summer music from Courtney,' *Beautiful British Columbia*, Summer 1975
Docherty, Ian. 'Youth music camp the Courtenay way,' *OpCan*, May 1976
Mertens, Susan. 'Courtenay Youth Music Centre,' ibid, Dec 1977

*Shawnigan Summer School of the Arts; established 1971

Summer schools

*University of British Columbia summer school, Vancouver; established in the mid-1950s. It offered high school band and orchestra workshops, opera workshops, master piano classes, and chamber music classes.

BIBLIOGRAPHY
Marquis, Weldon. 'The summer school program at U.B.C.,' *CME*, vol 3, no. 4, 1962

Credit and non-credit summer courses, including master classes, are given yearly at the U of British Columbia, *Simon Fraser U, and the *Victoria Cons.

ALBERTA

Camps

Alberta Music Camp, Sylvan Lake; founded in 1960, originally at Morley, by Arthur Dee, offering band instruction for children and adults

Alberta Summer Music Workshops; established in 1960 and sponsored by *Alberta Culture. They were held in various locations throughout the province until 1967, when they settled permanently at Camrose. Band, orchestral, instrumental, and choral programs have been offered for students aged 10 to 22 and for teachers.

BIBLIOGRAPHY
'Provincial summer music workshop,' *Music in Alberta*, Spring 1973

Schools

Courses are offered at the *Banff SFA, *Alberta College, the *U of Alberta, and the *U of Calgary.

SASKATCHEWAN

Camps

School of the Arts, Echo Valley Centre, Fort Qu'-Appelle; sponsored by the *Saskatchewan Arts Board. In 1963 the arts board, the Saskatchewan chapter of the *CBA, and the *Canadian Bureau for the Advancement of Music organized the first annual music workshop. By 1967 the music program was integrated with the other summer arts programs and centred at Echo Valley. By 1979 students of 10 to 18 years could enrol for band and orchestra programs, instrumental instruction, a jazz clinic, and courses in Highland piping and drumming. Directors have included Frank *Connell, Vernon Bell, and Jim Ellemers.

BIBLIOGRAPHY
Mitchell, John O. 'Music instruction courses at Saskatchewan Summer School,' *CanComp*, 30, Jun 1968

Schools

Summer courses are offered at the *U of Regina and the *U of Saskatchewan.

MANITOBA

Camps

International Music Camp, located at the Peace Garden on the US-Canadian border near Boissevain, Man, and Bottineau, N Dak. It was established in 1956 by Merton Utgaard, who remained the director in 1979. The camp's students (junior high-school to adult) and faculty are drawn from both countries. A broad program (band, jazz, instrumental ensemble, orchestra, piano, guitar, choir, theory, piping, and drumming) is supplemented by credit courses for music teachers.

BIBLIOGRAPHY
Lawrence, Marguerite. 'International Music Camp,' *Sharps & Flats*, vol 4, Oct 1965
Wright, A.G., and Newcomb, S. 'International Music Camp band,' *Bands of the World* (Evanston, Ill, 1970)

Schools

Summer courses are offered at *Brandon U, the *U of Manitoba, and the Manitoba Teachers' College.

ONTARIO

Camps

Inverness Music Camp, on Lake Rosseau; established in 1957 and directed 1957–61 by Marcus *Adeney. String, wind, and keyboard programs were offered for students, amateurs, and professionals on holiday.

Inter-Provincial Music Camp; established in 1962. By 1969 the senior division (14 to 19 years) was located at Manitou-Wabing Sports and Arts Centre in Parry Sound, and the junior division (grades 5 to 9) at Camp Wahanowin near Orillia. A wide range of practical choral and instrumental activity has been offered, including participation in stage, rock, and jazz bands, symphony orchestras, and chamber ensembles.

The Junior School of Arts of Northern Ontario (JSANO), Kirkland Lake; established in co-operation with Northern College in 1963. The varied summer arts program for children and adults in 1979 included instruction in piano, guitar, woodwinds, and brass.

Ontario Youth Music Camp, Beaverton, on Lake Simcoe; established in 1963 and sponsored by the Ontario chapter of the CBDA for high-school-age students. Directors have included Frank Banks, Wilfred Manning, Harry Hamilton, and Allan J. Ford.

BIBLIOGRAPHY
'Ontario Youth Music Camp prepares for biggest year,' *CanComp*, 17, Apr 1967

Elliot Lake Centre Summer School of the Arts / Centre d'Elliot Lake Programmes d'été – Arts; begun in 1966. In the 1970s the varied arts programs for students over 16 included voice and opera workshops, study of Lieder and oratorio, and instruction in guitar.

Algoma Music Camp, at Camp Pauwating, north of Sault Ste Marie; established in 1966 by Ed Gartshore, who remained camp director in 1980. It admits both resident and day campers. While the camp at first emphasized string instruction, in the 1970s it added wind, brass, voice, piano, guitar, band, and orchestra training. The Algoma Music Camp Orchestra, active year-round, attended the 1976 Canadian Festival of Youth Orchestras at Banff. John Montague conducted. (See also Youth orchestras.)

BIBLIOGRAPHY

'Music camp schedules concert,' *Sault Star*, 18 Aug 1977

Kawartha Lakes Music Camp, Lakefield; established in 1970 at Lakefield College School and sponsored by the Kawartha Lakes Music and Arts Foundation. Courses have been offered in strings, brass, woodwinds, keyboards, percussion, voice, and theory.

Kelso Music Centre, Oakville; established in 1971. The centre has supported two summer programs, the first, a quartet camp, for advanced string quartet players coached 1971–4 by the *Orford String Quartet and thereafter by the *Vaghy String Quartet; the second a day camp for children of 12 and under.

*Ontario Youth Choir; begun 1971

Blue Mountain School of Music, near Collingwood; established in 1974 for students of all ages, and offering orchestral programs, participation in concert and stage bands, and a contemporary music program. It had ceased operations by 1979.

BIBLIOGRAPHY

White, Peter. 'Young music school struggles to be heard,' Toronto *Globe and Mail*, 24 Jul 1976

Toronto Summer School of Music; begun in 1977. Essentially a day school, but with a few residents. It has specialized in string training (solo and ensemble) and has offered courses in conducting techniques.

Artsperience, North Bay; begun in 1978. This summer arts program, sponsored by Canadore College for children of 6 to 15 years and for adults, has offered choral and choral conductors' workshops, and organ, guitar, piano, string, woodwind, and brass courses. Recitals by faculty members have been a feature.

*CAMMAC on Lake Rosseau; begun in 1978

Schools

*Royal Conservatory of Music of Toronto Summer School; begun in 1938. In 1980 it offered master classes in various disciplines, special courses for teachers, courses leading to examinations, courses in teaching methods (eg, *Orff, *Kodály), choral workshops, theory programs, and special events such as the *CAPAC-MacMillan lectures and faculty and student recitals.

Piano Teachers' Workshop, Geneva Park, on Lake Couchiching; begun in 1969 under the direction of Myrtle Rose *Guerrero. Teaching methods, theory, study of repertoire, and contemporary music

Summer Institute of Church Music, Ontario Ladies' College, Whitby; begun in 1970 for church musicians. Programs have included organ and service playing, choral techniques and repertoire, and harmony.

George Brown College Summer School of the Performing Arts, Toronto; established in 1977 as an orchestral training course for young musicians. The Youth Orchestra performed that year at the International Festival of Youth Orchestras in Scotland. In 1979, under the name Symphony Canada, the orchestra of amateur and professional players aged 12 to 31 toured in the Hawaiian Islands. Conductors have included Leonard Atherton, Robert Raines, and Victor *Feldbrill.

BIBLIOGRAPHY

Atherton, Leonard. 'Young Canadian musicians a success at the International Festival of Youth Orchestras,' *OCan*, vol 4, Nov 1977

Summer courses have been provided also by the Ontario Department of Education, by the *ORMTA, and by several universities, including Carleton, McMaster, Queen's, Waterloo-Lutheran, Toronto, and Western Ontario.

Some community orchestras have offered summer programs for student musicians, eg, the Summer Strings of the International Symphony Orchestra of Sarnia and Port Huron, the Oshawa Symphony Assn Summer School of Music at Durham College, and the *St Catharines Symphony Summer School for all orchestral instruments.

QUEBEC

Camps

*JMC Orford Art Centre; begun 1951

*CAMMAC; begun 1952

Camp musical St-Jean; begun in 1952 for the boys of the *Maîtrise du Chapitre de Québec and held in various locations on the Île d'Orléans. In 1974 the camp settled at St-Jean on the island, and was so named. Until 1976 it was restricted to members of the choir school. However, for the two final years of its existence (1977 and 1978) it was opened to the general public.

Camp musical d'Asbestos; established in 1960 under the name Camp musical de l'Harmonie d'Asbestos and restricted to members of that band until 1966, when registration was opened to all young band musicians of 14 years and over

Villa Musica, at St-Jean-des-Piles (near Trois-Rivières); operated 1961–70 by its founding director, Czeslaw Kaczynski

Camp musical du Lac St-Jean, Metabetchouan; begun in 1963. Courses in solfège, theory, and history; a broad range of instrumental instruction (including organ, piano, and guitar), singing, and chamber music

Camp musical Accord Parfait, Lac Simon (Portneuf County); begun in 1964 for music students aged 9 to 17 years. Piano, strings, woodwinds, brass, percussion, and guitar

Camp musical de Lanaudière, St-Côme; begun in 1967 for students aged 9 to 17 years. Instrumental instruction, piano, and singing; also string orchestra and chamber music instruction

Vivaldi Music Camp, begun 1970. See Société musicale Le Mouvement Vivaldi.

Camp musical St-Alexandre, Inc, Kamouraska; begun in 1971 for music students aged 10 to 17 years. Courses for beginners and advanced students in theory, singing, and various instruments

Camp musical du Nord-Ouest québécois, Barraute; begun in 1973; directed in 1979 by Hélène Poirier

Camp musical du Domaine Forget, St-Irénée; begun in 1978 by Françoys *Bernier, its co-director with Marie Tremblay. Sessions devoted to orchestral and band instruments, renaissance music, and various other subjects, including traditional art and music

Schools

Summer music courses have been given at *Laval U beginning in 1937, at UQAM beginning in 1969, at the *U of Montreal 1958–72, at the *École normale de musique in Montreal 1954–76, and at the *École Vincent-d'Indy. The *McGill Conservatorium offered music workshops for children in 1978 and 1979.

NEW BRUNSWICK

Instrumental Music Camps, *Mount Allison U, Sackville; established in 1959 by Stanley *Saunders, who was succeeded as director in 1974 by Rodney McLeod. The camps offer instruction in individual instruments and participation in orchestra, band, and choral programs, and in chamber music.

New Brunswick Summer Music Camp, Rothesay; begun in 1969 to offer instrumental training (including piano and organ). Clayton Hare, the director 1969–77, was followed by Robert Skelton and Peter Ellis.

NOVA SCOTIA

Summer Music Camp, Acadia U, Wolfville; begun in 1967 by Janis *Kalejs. Subsequent directors were M.W. Harvey and Peter H. Riddle.

Nova Scotia Summer Music Camp, Truro; begun ca 1975 and directed 1975–9 by Ronald *MacKay

PRINCE EDWARD ISLAND

Youth Music Camps, *U of Prince Edward Island, Charlottetown; begun in 1975 and directed by Hubert Tersteeg. Choral, orchestral, instrumental, and band courses for students aged 9 to 17

NEWFOUNDLAND

Summer Instrumental Music Camp, first in Stephenville, then in Burin; established in 1972 by the Extension Service of *Memorial U, for music students aged 9 to 19. The founding director, D.F. Cook, continued in the position in 1979. Private and ensemble instruction in all band and orchestral instruments

GENERAL BIBLIOGRAPHY

Johnston, Richard. 'Summer schools in transition,' *CanComp*, 2, Aug 1965

CMCentre. *Summer Music Camps / Camps d'été en musique* (Toronto 1972)

Freedman, Harry. 'The composer at camp,' *Mcan*, 43, Summer 1980

'Summer music camps in Canada,' ibid

Van Vlasselaer, J.J. 'Musical islands in the summer landscape,' ibid

Brosseau, Cécile. 'Le Domaine Forget, un sanctuaire des arts,' Montreal *La Presse*, 29 Aug 1980

(NM, LO, DSm, PW)

SUMNER, Marshall. Pianist, teacher, b Melbourne 22 Sep 1907, naturalized Canadian 1956; B MUS (Chicago Musical College) 1933. He studied 1923–7 at the U of Melbourne and 1927–33 with Percy Grainger, Rudolph Ganz, and Alexander Raab at the Chicago Musical College. Following his debut in 1933 with the Los Angeles Philharmonic playing Rachmaninoff's *Third Piano Concerto*, he performed with the Minneapolis SO and the Chicago SO and toured Australia with visiting artists for the Australian Broadcasting Corporation. In 1950 he moved to Vancouver, where he taught piano 1959–72 at the *U of British Columbia (Lyn *Vernon and Andrea Kalanj were among his pupils) and performed frequently over CBC radio, as recitalist and as soloist with the *CBC Vancouver Chamber Orchestra. During his term 1964–6 as president of the *Philharmonic Music

Club of Vancouver he commissioned works from Jean *Coulthard, Elliot *Weisgarber, and others. After retirement he remained active as an adjudicator and teacher. DD

SUNTER, Robert (Henry Anthony). Administrator, critic, b Liverpool 20 Nov 1931, naturalized Canadian 1975. As a child he studied piano and sang in the choir of St Francis Xavier's College. After coming to Canada in the early 1950s he worked for several Ontario newspapers, including the *Peterborough Examiner* under Robertson Davies, gaining experience as a reporter, editor, and manager. With the *Vancouver Times* 1963–4 he was editorial-page and news editor. Sunter joined the *Vancouver Sun* in 1964, and in 1966 he became music editor and critic. He moved to Toronto in 1968 to become the music officer of the *OAC and served in that position until 1976. These were years of expansion and progress at the arts council, and Sunter's resourcefulness, fairness, and diplomatic skill played no small part in that progress. At first (until 1972) his duties included serving as executive director, then advisory director, of *OFSO, and he remained closely associated with that organization during his full term with the OAC. In those years, too, he was one of the architects of *ACO and served as adviser and ex-officio board member of the *Ontario Choral Federation and *Prologue to the Performing Arts. In May 1976 Sunter was appointed head of radio music for the English Services Division of the *CBC. He married the soprano Riki *Turofsky. KW

SURDIN, Morris. Composer, arranger, conductor, b Toronto 8 May 1914, d there 19 Aug 1979. At six he began violin lessons with Louis Gesensway in Toronto, and soon the lessons were expanded to include counterpoint and harmony. Gesensway moved to the USA to play in the Philadelphia Orchestra, and in 1937 Surdin joined him for a further year of study. He also studied conducting in 1945 with César Borré in Toronto and composition in 1950 with Henry Brant in New York. A conductor and a composer of incidental music for the *CBC (on staff 1939–41 and freelance after 1947), Surdin also worked in the USA as an arranger for the Philadelphia Pops and as a composer and conductor 1949–54 for the CBS network. With the playwright Ray Darby he collaborated on several CBC radio productions, including the musical comedy *The Gallant Greenhorn* (1949) and the series 'Once upon a Time' (1949, directed by Esse Ljungh, later also produced for CBS as 'Once upon a Tune'). Surdin wrote the music for almost all of W.O. Mitchell's radio plays, including the series 'Jake and the Kid' (1950–72), a light-hearted situation comedy set in a Saskatchewan farming community. He composed incidental music for 'CBC Playhouse,' 'CBC Stage' (continuing his association with Ljungh), 'Adventure Theatre,' 'Festival,' and 'Hatch's Mill' and the film score for the Hollywood feature *Hospital* (1971). Several of his works were commissioned: *The Remarkable Rocket* (1961, for the National Ballet of Canada), two accordion concertos (1966 and 1976, both for Joseph *Macerollo), *Wild Rose* (1967, with W.O. Mitchell for the Mac 14 Theatre Society of Calgary), *Suite Canadienne* and *A Feast of Thunder* (1970 and 1972, for the Shevchenko Musical Ensemble of Toronto, with whom he toured Ukraine in 1970), *Eine Kleine Hammer-Klapper Musik* (1976, for the *TS), and a Viola *Concerto* (1978, for Rivka Golani-Erdész).

Surdin displayed great competence and facility as a composer, particularly of music to accompany theatrical situations. He had a keen sense of the relationship between 'dialogue time' and 'musical time' and was adept at underlining humour and suspense with supportive sound. Avoiding 'modern' or 12-tone music, he wrote in a traditional style, often drawing on folk tunes for inspiration. He was the author of *A Sense of Priority* (Toronto 1973), a study of musical resources in Metropolitan Toronto's Borough of York. In 1978 the *U of Calgary acquired all of Surdin's manuscripts, a collection said to contain more than 2000 incidental scores for radio dramas, films, and stage pieces. Surdin was a member of the *CLComp and CAPAC and an associate of the *CMCentre.

SELECTED COMPOSITIONS

STAGE, FILM, RADIO, AND TV

The Remarkable Rocket, ballet. 1961. CMCentre. (Excerpts) Col MS 6763 (Tor Philharmonia O, Susskind cond)
Wild Rose, musical (W.O. Mitchell). 1967. Ms. 'The Arithmetic of Love' Dom LP 1368 (Al *Baculis Singers)
Over 2000 scores for radio, TV, and NFB films

ORCHESTRA

Credo. 1950. Ms
Two Symphonic Hoedowns from *The Gallant Greenhorn*. Ca 1950. Ms
Eine Kleine Hammer-Klapper Musik. 1976. CMCentre
Several works for str orch, including *Four X Strings* (1947), *Time* (1966), *Alteration* (1970), *Five for Four* (1977), *A Group of Six* (1977), *Who's on Bass?* (1977), all ms; 3 works for band

SOLOISTS WITH ORCHESTRA

Softly as the Flute Blows. 1947. Fl, str. Ms
A Spanish Tragedy (Surdin). 1955. Orch (sop, orch). CMCentre
Five Shades of Brass. 1961. Tpt, orch. CMCentre
Concerto for mandolin and orchestra. 1961–6. CMCentre
2 *Concertos* for accordion and string orchestra. 1966, 1976. Ms. (No. 1) RCI 238 (*Macerollo)
Two Solitudes. 1967. Hn (eng hn), str. CMCentre
Berceuse. 1977. Hn, orch. CMCentre
Concerto for Viola and Orchestra. 1978. Ms
3 works for TTBB and orch, *Suite Canadienne* (1970), *Billy Carney-O* (1971), and *Sea Song* (1971). Ms

CHAMBER

Carol Fantasia for Brass. 1955. Ms
Mandolin and Guitar. 1961. Ms
Elements. 1965. 2 vn, cbn, hpd. Ms
Matin. 1965. Ww quar. Ms
Quartet in G Minor. 1966. Str quar. Ms
Canadian Folk Songs. 1968. Acc. B & H 1970
Piece for Woodwind Quintet. 1969. CMCentre
Serious I–VIII. 1969. Acc. B & H 1970. (*No. I, II, V*) RCI 385 (*Macerollo)
Serious IX–XVI. 1973. Acc. Self-publ 1976
Trinitas in morte. 1973. 3 ob, bn, 3 hn, tim, 8 vc, 2 cbn. Ms
An Odd Couple. 1975. Cl, db. Ms
Heritage Suites I–IV. 1975–7. Brass quar. CMCentre
Sly-d Trombones. 1975. Trb(s), bass trb(s). CMCentre
Landscapes. 1978. Solo hp. CMCentre
Deux Fabliaux pour violoncelle seul. 1979. Ms

VOICE

Prairie Boy (W.O. Mitchell). 1964. V, pf. B & H 1965. Cap ST 6087 (*Agostini cond)
4 works for v, vc, hp. *A Thought*, *Music Fair*, *Quartet for Trio*, *Three Plus 1 for 3*. (All 1976). Ms
Several works for pf, and for v, pf. Also 3 choral works, 'A Big Bear,' *Peg-Leg's Fiddle*, 'Wonnerful Bad Luck Song.' (All 1977). CMCentre

WRITINGS

'Agostini & Surdin,' *CanComp*, 38, Mar 1969

BIBLIOGRAPHY

Bennett, Ray. 'Surdin: the music machine,' Toronto *Telegram*, 11 Nov 1967
'Morris Surdin says: " ... the main difficulty in collaborating with a writer is trying to get inside his mind",' *CanComp*, 48, Mar 1970
'Canada's music ambassadors to the Ukraine,' *CanComp*, 54, Nov 1970
Flohil, Richard. 'The musical resources of a community,' *CanComp*, 77, Feb 1973
Graham, June. 'Composer both loose, disciplined,' *Saskatoon Star Phoenix*, 15 Aug 1975
Schulman, Michael. 'At last, recognition for Morris Surdin's music,' *CanComp*, 129, Mar 1978
Contemporary Canadian Composers / Compositeurs canadiens contemporains NM

Walter Susskind

SUSSKIND (Süsskind), **Walter**. Conductor, pianist, b Prague 1 May 1913, d Berkeley, Cal, 25 Mar 1980. After studies at the Prague Cons (piano with Josef Hoffmeister, composition with Josef Suk and Alois Hába, and conducting with George Szell) he made his debut in 1934 as assistant conductor at Prague's German Opera House and remained at the historic house until it closed in 1938 under the Nazi occupation. Thereafter he conducted the Carl Rosa Opera 1942–5, Sadler's Wells on a 1945 German tour, the Scottish Orchestra 1946–52, the Victoria SO of Melbourne, and the Philharmonia Orchestra of London, before succeeding Sir Ernest *MacMillan as conductor and music director of the *TSO in 1956. An orchestral workshop which Susskind initiated in 1960 at Stratford, Ont, led directly to the founding of the *NYO, which Susskind served as music director 1960–4 and conducted during the 1961 and 1963 sessions and on the 1966 European tour. He also conducted the *Toronto Mendelssohn Choir 1960–4, the *CBC SO as a frequent guest, the *COC productions of *Carmen* (1961), *Die Walküre* (1962), *Der Rosenkavalier* (1963), and *Don Giovanni* (1963), and many Canadian premieres, including (CBC SO, 1958) *Weinzweig's *Wine of Peace*, (*Vancouver SO, 1959) Pierre *Mercure's *Triptyque*, and (TSO, 1960) *Morawetz' *Symphony No. 2*. He appeared as a pianist with the TSO, usually performing Mozart concertos, and in 1958 accompanied Teresa *Stratas in recital. He conducted the TSO for the CBC TV productions of Strauss' *Elektra* (1961) and Mozart's *The Magic Flute* (1965). Leaving the TSO in 1965, he freelanced in Europe and the USA, then was conductor and music director 1968–75 of the St Louis SO and taught at the U of Southern Illinois, returning occasionally to conduct the TSO. Susskind conducted performances recorded by the TSO, the Toronto Mendelssohn Choir, the CBC SO (see Discographies of aforementioned), the Toronto Philharmonia, the St Louis SO, and several leading London orchestras.

BIBLIOGRAPHY

Kraglund, John. 'Walter Susskind conducting ... ' *Mayfair*, Dec 1955 (MCv)

'Suzanne.' Love poem and song by Leonard *Cohen. The poem, written in 1966 in Montreal and later published in *Selected Poems 1956–1968* (Toronto 1968), became one of Cohen's earliest songs. It was recorded first for the LP *In My Life* by the US singer Judy Collins, who learned it from Cohen over the telephone, then by Chad Mitchell, Spanky and Our Gang, Leon Bibb, Tom *Northcott, Roberta Flack, and others. Cohen himself recorded 'Suzanne' in 1967. That same year a recording by Noel Harrison was a minor hit on North American charts. The song was published by Project Seven Music (New York) and appeared in the folio *Songs of Leonard Cohen* (New York 1969). MM

SUZUKI, Hidetaro. Violinist, conductor, b Tokyo 30 Jun 1939. After some early studies in Tokyo he worked 1956–63 with Efrem Zimbalist at the Curtis Institute. He was a finalist in the 1962 International Tchaikovsky Competition in Moscow and a finalist in the 1963 and 1967 Queen Elisabeth Competitions in Brussels, and won second prize in the 1966 *Montreal International Competition. While he was concertmaster 1963–77 of the *Quebec SO he also performed with the orchestra as soloist and guest conductor. In addition he taught at the *CMQ, where Pierre Mongrain was one of his pupils. Suzuki has toured in the USA, Japan, the USSR, France, Belgium, Cuba, and Canada, both as a soloist with orchestra and in recital, accompanied by his wife, the pianist Zeyda *Suzuki. At *Ontario Place in Toronto he played the Tchaikovsky *Concerto* 26 Jul 1976 with the *TS conducted by Victor *Feldbrill. His large repertoire, extending from the classics to contemporary works, is served by a strong technique and a keen musicality. In 1978 he became concertmaster of the Indianapolis SO.

DISCOGRAPHY

Beethoven *Sonata in F, Op 24; Sonata in A, Op 47*. Z. Suzuki pf. Japan 1977. Toshiba SRS-527

– *Variations in E Flat, Op 44*. Serkin pf, Léonard vc. 1968. Marlboro Recording Soc MRS 4B

Franck *Sonata* – Ravel *Sonata; Tzigane*. Z. Suzuki pf. 1976. Sel CC 15-119

Hidetaro Suzuki Violin Encore Album: Dvořák – Tchaikovsky – et al. Z. Suzuki pf. Japan 1977. Toshiba LRS-528

Music of the World: Dvořák – Tchaikovsky – Kreisler – Wieniawski. Z. Suzuki pf. Japan 1964. Gakken Co Ltd SG-118 JASRAC 8429 (MS)

SUZUKI, Zeyda (b Ruga). Pianist, teacher, b Havana, Cuba, 29 May 1943. She gave her first concert at 5 for the JM in Cuba and then performed on radio and TV. She studied at the Havana Cons. At 12 she took lessons from Nola Sahig, and in 1959 she enrolled at the Curtis Institute for studies with Rudolf Serkin which led to her diploma in 1963. That year she settled in Quebec City with her husband, the violinist Hidetaro *Suzuki. In 1961 they began playing as a team, notably in Quebec City, Montreal, Ottawa, and Stratford, Ont, and recording together. She took part in the Bay Chamber Festival in Camden, Me, in 1962, 1966, and 1972 and toured Japan in 1964, 1966, 1973, and 1976, Cuba in 1965, and France in 1973 and 1976. She was a member 1970–4 of the *Ensemble instrumental du Québec, with which she made an LP (RCI 297). In 1974 she played Rodolphe *Mathieu's *Sonata* for piano and participated in a performance of his *Quintette* at the *Pro Musica Society concerts and at the *Institut canadien in Quebec City. She taught 1970–8 at *Laval U, then moved to Indianapolis. MB-L

Suzuki method. Music-teaching system developed by the Japanese violinist and educator Shinichi Suzuki (b 1898) and widely disseminated after World War II under the name Talent Education (Saino-Kyoiku). At first a violin method, it subsequently was adapted for the teaching of the other string instruments and of flute and piano.

The Suzuki method became widely used in Canada, particularly by string teachers, after its introduction by Thomas *Rolston in Edmonton in 1964, by Jean *Cousineau in Montreal in 1965, and by Claude *Létourneau (see Société musicale Le Mouvement Vivaldi) in Quebec City in 1965. Suzuki himself visited Montreal in 1966 with a class of his pupils and made similar visits to London, Ont, and Winnipeg in 1972 and to Edmonton and Montreal in 1977. In 1967 the Women's Committee of the *Hamilton Philharmonic Orchestra established the Philharmonic Children's School as a Canada Centennial project. The school, under the direction of Marta *Hidy, offered training in violin and cello by the Suzuki method.

Suzuki was not the first to advocate class instruction and imitative methods for very young string players. John *Konrad, who began teaching at the *Bornoff School in Winnipeg in 1937 and directed the school under his own name after 1949, was famous for the phenomenal results he achieved working along these lines, and it would be interesting to know in detail the extent to which his methods resembled those developed independently across the Pacific by the Japanese educator.

The most significant difference may well reside in the fact that Suzuki is not only an extraordinary teacher, as Konrad was, but also a pragmatic evangelist who has made it a specific concern to disseminate his ideas internationally and who has not lacked gifted and enthusiastic disciples.

By 1974, 10 years after engaging the Manchuria-born violinist and Suzuki pupil Yoko Wong to found Suzuki classes in Edmonton, Rolston and his assistant had taught some 600 young players according to the system. Cousineau, who had developed a method along Suzuki lines but adapted to Canadian conditions, submitted his ideas to Suzuki in Japan in 1965, published a teaching manual, *Canadian Music* (Tokyo 1965) in English and Japanese, and, on his return to Montreal, founded the École des petits violons.

Alfred *Garson, a Suzuki pupil, has sat on the board of the Suzuki Assn of the Americas and has published *The Suzuki Teaching Method* (London 1971), and his articles on the method have appeared in the *Canadian Music Educator*, the *Music Educators Journal*, and *Music in Education*.

Garson, in a description of the method submitted to *EMC* in 1977, wrote: 'Canadian teachers have not hesitated to develop and adapt the method to suit their needs. As a result there are now some astonishing public performances by children's orchestras, chamber groups, solo performers, conductors and even composers ... Canadian teachers emphasize reading more than do the Japanese. They introduce it at an earlier stage without, however, sacrificing Suzuki's stress on memorization. This exemplifies a spirit of independence, initiative and enterprise, virtues lauded by Suzuki himself.' Typical of such adaptations is that of Létourneau, whose Société musicale Le Mouvement Vivaldi combines principles of Suzuki and Kodály.

The essentials of the Suzuki method appear to be an early beginning, imitation, group learning, and parent involvement. Children as young as two-and-a-half or three are accepted and introduced to music one simple step at a time. They learn to play as they learn to speak, by hearing a sound and then reproducing it. They imitate not only their teachers but also their peers and find confidence in the common enterprise. Parents are essential to the success of the training and are involved directly as home teachers.

By 1980 in Canada the method, or adaptations of it, had been introduced at the *U of Regina by Howard *Leyton-Brown, at the Cons de musique de Hull, at the McGill Preparatory School of Music in Montreal, in the school string programs of the elementary schools in Lethbridge, Alta, in the youth string program of the *Saskatoon SO, at the *Community Music School of Greater Vancouver, and in numerous other string-training centres. In 1978 the Suzuki representative Haruto Kataoka gave master classes to teachers at the Northwest Community College in Terrace, BC, on piano teaching by the Suzuki method.

BIBLIOGRAPHY

Knechtel, Baird. 'Music man from Matsumoto,' *Recorder*, vol 9, Sep–Oct 1966

Garson, Alfred. 'The Suzuki teaching method,' *BC Music Educator*, vol 15, Oct 1971

Gaffe, Janis. 'Suzuki philosophy of learning,' *Recorder*, 2 instalments, vol 16, Dec 1973, Mar 1974 (AG)

SVEEN, Olaf. Accordionist, composer, b Surndal, Norway, 18 Apr 1919, naturalized Canadian 1954. Taught to play the accordion by his father and grandfather and by noted Norwegian players, Sveen moved to Canada in 1949. He settled on a Saskatchewan farm, then began touring the province's dance halls with, in turn, Eddie Mehler's Southern Playboys (who were heard also on CKRM radio, Regina), the Western Five Orchestra and, 1955–62, his own group, Olle and His Playmates (heard often on CHAB radio, Moose Jaw). Sveen moved in 1962 to Edmonton, where he performed for social gatherings and in local nightclubs and taught 1962–7 at the Roberts-Tait Music Schools and later privately. He has been heard in Edmonton on his own Scandinavian-music programs 1965–71 on radio station CKUA and, beginning in 1976, on QCFM. In 1977 he won the third annual Old Time Accordion Championships at Kimberley, BC. After his first LP, for Aragon in 1954, Sveen made over 25 others (by 1977) for Point (now MCA Coral) and *London. His publications include the folios of his waltzes, polkas, and other dance tunes – *Olaf Sveen's Old Time Instrumental Music* (Empire 1961), *Scandinavian Dance Tunes* (Berandol 1971), and *Music for Accordion Souvenirs* (Waterloo 1973) – and the book *Nordmann i Canada* (Trondheim, Norway, 1977).

BIBLIOGRAPHY

Ferguson, Ted. 'Olaf the king,' *The Canadian*, 18 Feb 1978 (RGn)

SWARTZ, Ira. Pianist, teacher, b Walla Walla, Wash, 23 Jul 1902. He was a pupil during the 1920s of J.D.A. *Tripp and Gertrude *Huntley Green in Vancouver, Paul Pierre McNeely and Boyd Wells in Seattle, and Maxim Schapiro in San Francisco and in the 1940s of Arthur *Benjamin in Vancouver. One of the first soloists with the *CBC Vancouver Chamber Orchestra (playing Bach's *D-Minor Concerto*), Swartz also performed under Allard de *Ridder at the *Malkin Bowl concerts and at the Promenade Concerts in the (now demolished) Denman Auditorium. Until the mid-1950s he was particularly known as a recitalist and chamber musician. Debussy and Ravel were a specialty, and his CBC recitals often featured works of those composers. With Jean *de Rimanoczy he performed all of the violin-and-piano sonatas of Mozart and Beethoven. He also toured (ca 1951) in British Columbia with the Russian violinist Robert Kitain. Swartz has taught piano privately in Vancouver for over 50 years. His pupils include Bryan *Gooch, Kari-Jo Miller, and Robert *Rogers. BNSG

Sweden. Natives of this kingdom in the eastern part of the Scandinavian peninsula settled in Canada as early as 1812, as members of the Red River Colony (Winnipeg). It was not until 1890, however, that significant numbers arrived in the prairies from the USA. In 1971 there were 101,870 people of Swedish origin in Canada.

Musicians of Swedish birth or origin who have lived in Canada include the baritones Peter *Barcza (born in Stockholm to Hungarian parents)

and Ingemar *Korjus (born in Stockholm to Estonian parents); the pianist and teacher Clarence Dahlgren and the violin builder Sid *Engen, both of Dauphin, Man; the composers Bengt *Hambraeus and Richard *Johnston; the country singer Nels Nelson, of Sleepy and Swede and the Tumbleweeds; and the Winnipeg violinist Alma Wahlberg.

Swedish visitors to Canada have included Jenny Lind, who created a sensation in Montreal and Toronto in 1851, and Kristina Nilsson, who toured North America in the 1870s and appeared in Montreal with the Theodore Thomas orchestra in 1884. The 'Prince of tenors,' Jussi Björling, sang several times in Canada, and the Wagnerian tenor Set Svanholm also made appearances. The composer Karl-Birger Blomdahl visited Canada in 1954 to investigate contemporary composition, and again in 1960 as the Swedish representative to the *International Conference of Composers at Stratford, Ont. The mezzo-soprano Kerstin Meyer sang at the 1959 *Vancouver International Festival, and the soprano Elisabeth Söderström appeared with the *TS in 1980 and the *COC in 1981.

The illustrious dramatic soprano Birgit Nilsson, who has sung in Canada as a member of the *Metropolitan Opera and often in concert (notably with Jon *Vickers, William Wilderman, and the TS conducted by Zubin Mehta), performed at the Montreal World Festival during *Expo 67 with both the Hamburg Opera (as Elektra) and the Royal Swedish Opera (as Isolde). Sixten Ehrling conducted the latter company and also led the *MSO in a Scandinavian gala. Ehrling also has been a guest of the TS and the *Vancouver SO.

Other visiting performers from Sweden have included the Fresk Quartet, which toured for the *JMC in 1970–1, 1972–3, and 1974–5; the Kyndel String Quartet; and the pop group ABBA which in 1979 was seen with the Swedish pop singer Ted Gardestad in 'Listen to the Music / Lyssna Till Musiken,' a joint production of CBC TV and Swedish Television TV-2.

Emma *Albani performed in Stockholm in 1888. Canadians who have visited Sweden in the 20th century include the *Hart House String Quartet, the *Hart House Orchestra, Gertrude *Newton, Ida *Krehm, the *Orford String Quartet (co-winner of first prize in the 1974 European Broadcasting Union's String Quartet Competition in Stockholm), Arthur *Ozolins, and Patricia *Rideout with other members of Toronto's *NMC group. Both Armas *Maiste and Glen Mossop have studied in Sweden, the latter with the assistance of a Canadian-Scandinavian Foundation award. Robert *Aitken has given master classes in Ingesund and at the Swedish Radio Music School in Stockholm. He and the flutist Per Øien recorded a three-record set of the complete flute music by the brothers Doppler for the Swedish company Bis in 1978–9. In 1980 the *Toronto Consort performed in Göteborg.

Swedish folk music relies mainly on two instruments – the accordion and the violin. In Canada 'Swedish violins' are produced by a few luthiers including Leif Karlsson of Calgary. Swedish folk music has been performed by the singing Bellman Quartet (named for C.W. Bellman, 'the Robert Burns of Sweden') which appeared at the *CPR's New Canadian Folksong and Handicraft Festival in Winnipeg in 1928, and by Selma Johanson de Coster who sang at the Great-West Canadian Folksong-Folkdance and Handicraft Festival in Regina in 1929.

Scandinavian-Canadian composers of old-time dance music include Olaf *Sveen, Agnar Tollefsen, Quintan Spitzer, and Edwin Erickson, all of whom have used Swedish themes and forms in their compositions. In addition to Sveen, Tollefsen, and Erickson (all accordionists), outstanding performers of Swedish old-time dance music include the violinists Graham *Townsend, Frankie Rodgers, and Andy *DeJarlis, the clarinetist Veikko Saarista, and the groups the Emeralds, the Cottonpickers, Quinton and the Polka Dots, and the Calgary CBCN Oldtimers.

Traditional Swedish music is heard in Canadian cities in the annual celebrations of the Swedish festival of Santa Lucia, held 13 December.

SWETNAM, Dorothy (m Hare). Pianist, teacher, accompanist, examiner, adjudicator, b Glace Bay, NS, 27 Mar 1911; B MUS (Mount Allison) 1933. She studied with Noel Brunton, a pupil of Godowsky', at *Mount Allison U. In 1934 she went to Japan to head the piano department at the Canadian Academy in Kobe and also studied in Tokyo with Leonid Kreutzer. She returned to Canada in 1941. She has taught at Mount Allison U, *Mount Royal College in Calgary, the *Banff SFA, and the Victoria Summer School of Music, which she co-founded with her husband, Clayton *Hare, in 1963. She lived 1955–70 in the USA (her husband taught 1955–65 at the U of Portland, Ore), and during those years she accompanied a number of singers, including Betty Allen, Elisabeth Söderström, and Ernst Haefliger. She returned to Canada in 1970 and settled in Calgary, where she continued to teach and perform. Swetnam has been an examiner for the National Guild of Piano Teachers (USA), the Washington State Music Teachers' Assn, and the *U of Alberta and has adjudicated at festivals in Nova Scotia, New Brunswick, and the four western provinces. She has toured in Canada, the USA, the orient, and Bermuda and has performed in concert and on CBC broadcasts with her husband.

BIBLIOGRAPHY
Dawson, Eric. 'Early musical years tough but rewarding for city pianist,' *Calgary Herald*, 24 Feb 1979 WLB

Swinging Shepherd Blues. Tune by Moe *Koffman, written as *Blues a la Canadiana* and renamed *Swinging Shepherd Blues* in 1957 when it was recorded, with the composer playing the flute, for inclusion on the LP *Hot and Cool Sax*. Released on a single (Jubilee 5311), it was a hit internationally (reaching number 36 on *Billboard* magazine's Top 100 in 1958) and also was a success as copied (ie, played virtually in its original form) by the US flutist Johnny Pate (Federal 12312). By 1979 it had been recorded over 300 times. Versions were made by Count Basie, Herbie Mann, Mantovani, David Rose, and others; a vocal version, with lyrics by Rhoda Roberts and Kenny Jacobson, was made by Ella Fitzgerald. A second set of lyrics was written to the tune in the mid-1970s by members of the Bug Alley Band of Montreal. *Swinging Shepherd Blues*, whose copyright has been held in turn by Benell Music Co (the original publisher), Kahl Music Inc, and Nom Music, has remained Koffman's signature tune for over 20 years. He has recorded it several times, and his 1973 single (GRT 1230-51) was a minor hit in Canada. Evidence of the width of the tune's popularity was its inclusion as an encore (played on a bamboo flute) in a program given by the Shanghai Ballet on its Canadian tour of 1977. MM

Switzerland. Emigration from Switzerland to Canada began in the late 18th century. By 1871 some 3000 people of Swiss descent were living in Canada; by 1977 their numbers had reached 20,000. While festivities organized by Swiss-Canadian societies for Switzerland's National Day (1 August) have included dancers, singers, and yodellers chosen to help preserve Swiss popular traditions in Canada, the greatest Swiss contribution to Canadian music has been made by a few individuals.

Among Swiss-born musicians who have lived in Canada are Napoléon *Aubin (who settled in Canada in 1835), Ettore *Mazzoleni (1929), the cellist and former *Calgary Philharmonic manager Kurt Trachsel (1936), Edward *Laufer (1939), Boris *Roubakine (1949), Pierre *Souvairan (1953), Jean-Pierre *Vetter (1955), Regula *Qureshi (1960s), Hellmuth *Wolff (1963), the baritone Pierre *Mollet (who began to teach at the *CMM in 1969), the *MSO conductor Charles Dutoit (1976), and the Montreal-based violin maker Pierre Dalphin (1977). Willi Germann, the promoter of Vancouver Planetarium jazz concerts in the mid-1970s, was born in Switzerland. Gustave *Smith and A.S. *Vogt had Swiss-born mothers. Edward Ermatinger, who according to Marius *Barbeau was the first (1830) to notate French folksongs in the New World, was of Swiss-Italian descent but born on the isle of Elba and never a Swiss resident. The organist Victor Togni (1935–65), born of Swiss parents in Tanganyika, studied 1951–7 in Geneva, Rome, Paris, and London, then served at St Columkille's Cathedral in Pembroke, Ont, and at St Basil's Church and St Michael's Cathedral, Toronto, before his death in an automobile accident near Gananoque, Ont.

Musicians who lived in Switzerland before settling in Canada are Mario *Duschenes and Lorand *Fenyves. Swiss artists who have appeared in Canada include Ernest Ansermet, who was a guest conductor with the *MSO and conducted the Orchestre de la Suisse romande at *Expo 67, the pianists Karl Engel and Bela Siki (both of whom toured for the *JMC during the 1950s), and the Geneva Quartet. Canadians who have been resident performers in Switzerland include Kenneth Asch (*Ascher Duo), Donald *Bell, Garnet *Brooks, the tenor Paul Frey, James *Milligan, Walter *Prystawski, and Irene *Salemka. Canadian visitors to Switzerland include the MSO, which performed there under Zubin Mehta in 1966. In 1969 the Toronto Youth Orchestra under Jacob *Groob placed first in the International Symphony Festival at St Moritz, and John *Rea's ballet *The Days* placed third in the International Competition for Opera and Ballet Composition. Several Canadians have won prizes or medals in the International Competition for Musical Performers in Geneva, including Rafael *Masella (1949), Steven *Staryk (1956), James Milligan and Micheline *Tessier (1957), Gabrielle *Lavigne (1969), the mezzo-soprano Marie *Laferrière (1975), the pianists Ick Choo Moon and Philip Thomson (1977), and the bassist Joel Quarrington who won a silver medal and tied for second prize (1978; no first prize was awarded that year.) Among those who have appeared at the International Jazz Festival at Montreux are *Dionysos and Yvan *Landry (1971), Oscar *Peterson (who recorded there in 1975, 1977, and 1979), several groups – the Tommy *Banks Band with the vocalist 'Big' Miller, the U of Regina Jazz Band, the York U Sextet, and the jazz-rock group Aquarelle – in 1978; and Salome *Bey, Ed *Bickert, and Fraser *MacPherson, whose 1979 performances were recorded along with Peterson's (RCI 503).

Major Swiss compositions which have been performed in Canada include a number of Honegger symphonies, as well as his *Jeanne d'Arc au bûcher* (1953, *Montreal Festivals, with *Pelletier conducting, and numerous other performances elsewhere) and *Pacific 231*. Frank Martin's *Petite Symphonie concertante* and *Jedermann Monologues* have been performed, as have his oratorio *Golgotha* and his 'profane oratorio' *Le Vin herbé*, both on CBC radio. In 1975 Rolf Liebermann's *Concerto* for jazz band and orchestra was heard in a concert at Pollack Hall in Montreal.

SYMCOX, Peter (John Fortune). Director, producer, set designer, critic, b Chelmsford, England, 7 Jun 1925, naturalized Canadian 1964; MA English literature (Oxford) 1947. He studied piano 1932–47 along with French and English literature and fine arts. Next he took courses in staging at the Old Vic Theatre School, where he staged his first productions. He also worked at Covent Garden. Shortly after his arrival in Montreal in 1953 he was hired as a set designer for CBC TV, and in 1968 he began to produce music programs, directing Britten's *The Burning Fiery Furnace*, Verdi's *Macbeth* (1973), and Puccini's *Madama Butterfly* (1976) and special programs (eg, 'Les Beaux Dimanches') featuring Vladimir Ashkenazy, Grace Melzia Bumbry, Maureen *Forrester, Jerome Hines, Marek *Jablonski, André *Laplante, Roberta Peters, Shirley Verrett, and others. In 1969 he presented a one-hour version of **Colas et Colinette* on the program 'One of a Kind.'

Symcox directed for several companies, including the Mountain Playhouse in Montreal (Sandy Wilson's *The Boy Friend* in 1961, for which he also designed the sets), the Pittsburgh Opera (*Roméo et Juliette* and *Rigoletto* in 1972, *Don Giovanni* in 1973), the *COC (*Rigoletto*, 1973), the Hartford, Conn, Civic Opera (*Otello*, 1973), the *Opéra du Quebec (*Madama Butterfly*, 1974), the Milwaukee Florentine Opera (*The Tales of Hoffmann*, 1975, *La Bohème*, 1976, *Macbeth*, 1979), and the Teatro nacional of the Dominican Republic (*Madama Butterfly*, 1975). Symcox has been an adjudicator for drama festivals and has contributed articles to periodicals and newspapers, including the *Montreal Star*. GP

SYME, Mary (Yvonne). Pianist, composer, broadcaster, b London, Ont, ca 1918; ATCM 1933, LTCM 1935, BA (McMaster) 1938. She taught at the Hamilton Cons (*RHCM) 1942–6 and studied piano with Hayunga *Carman in Toronto, making her orchestral debut 6 Nov 1945 with the *TSO. She continued her studies in New York under Horszowski and made her recital debut in 1949 in Town Hall. She has performed throughout Canada and she toured Europe in 1950. She later appeared with the Chicago SO. She has given numerous recitals on CBC radio since 1944. In 1963 she became hostess of the CBC children's program 'Playroom.' She has adapted the *Kodály approach to music education for a series of Ontario school broadcasts. The CBC received an Ohio State Award in 1970 for 'Rhythm Patterns,' the fourth program of the series.

See also School music broadcasts.

WRITINGS

'Music for children offers opportunities for composers,' *CanComp*, 4, Dec 1965 EK

SYMONDS, Nelson. Guitarist, b Halifax 24 Sep 1933. He began playing on the banjo at 9 and took up the guitar at 11, first performing for dances in Halifax with his cousins Ivan and Leo Symonds (both guitarists), then 1951–5 in Sudbury, Ont, and on tour 1955–8 with carnivals in Canada and the USA. Settling in Montreal in 1958 and beginning to play jazz, he was a member until 1962 of Alfred Wade's Stablemates, then performed in various Montreal clubs (eg, the Black Bottom intermittently 1963–8, Café La Bohème 1968–71) and (in a duo with his longtime bassist Charles Biddle) 1971–7 in several Laurentian resort communities. He has accompanied such US jazzmen as Art Farmer, Benny Golson, and Jimmy Heath during club or concert appearances in Montreal. Symonds has been heard on the CBC's 'Jazz en liberté' and 'Jazz Radio-Canada.' One of the most original of Canadian jazzmen, he plays in an essentially linear style in the tradition of Charlie Christian, but employs an aggressive attack and angular, headlong phrasing. His use of chords, which is sparing, reflects the influence of Django Reinhardt.

His cousin Ivan Symonds (b Halifax 17 May 1933), whose style is more chordal than Nelson's, moved to Montreal in 1960 and worked until 1977 at Rockhead's Paradise, the last six years as leader of his own trio. He opened his own club, Le Jazzbar C + J, in 1978. MM

SYMONDS, Norman. Composer, clarinetist, saxophonist, b near Nelson, BC, 23 Dec 1920. Raised in Victoria, BC, Symonds began playing clarinet in his teens. While serving 1938–45 with the RCN he played in Halifax with a dixieland band led by the saxophonist Charles 'Bucky' Adams. He studied clarinet, piano, theory, and harmony at the *RCMT 1945–8, then composition privately with Gordon *Delamont. Working as clarinetist, alto and baritone saxophonist, and arranger in the Toronto dance bands of Leo Romanelli, Bobby *Gimby, and, 1949–66, Benny Louis, he also led a jazz octet 1953–7. The group included at various times Ed *Bickert, Ron *Collier, Ross Culley, Bernie *Piltch, Jack *Richardson, and Jerry *Toth and performed in Toronto and at the 1956 *Stratford Festival.

As perhaps the leading figure in the third-stream movement growing in Canada at that time, Symonds wrote some jazz works employing classical forms (eg, *Fugue for Reeds and Brass*, *Fugue for Shearing*, and two *Concertos* for jazz octet), and others for jazz group or soloist and string or symphony orchestra. His *Concerto Grosso* was premiered and recorded in 1957 by Ron Collier's quintet with the *CBC SO under Victor *Feldbrill and played in 1957 by the Collier group with the Tri-City Symphony in Davenport, Ia, and in 1966 with the *TSO. After the TSO performance, John *Kraglund (Toronto *Globe and Mail*, 9 Nov 1966) called the work 'more successful than most scores in this hybrid idiom' and noted that 'while Symonds ... employs a classical form ... he does not try to bridge any gap, real or imaginary. The impression is that he has used the orchestra to provide a sort of pseudo-jazz background for the jazz quintet. There are occasional exceptions, as when the brass answers the quintet – in concerto grosso style – or in the dialogue between the timpani and the jazz drums, and in the brief fugue which is begun by the jazz musicians and builds up in the full orchestra.' Symonds' other third-stream orchestral works include *Autumn Nocturne*, premiered in 1960 by a CBC string orchestra with the tenor saxophonist Rick *Wilkins as soloist; *The Nameless Hour* (dedicated to Albert Camus), premiered in 1966 by the TSO under Victor Feldbrill and the flugelhorn player Fred *Stone and later (after it was revised for other solo instruments) recorded by an orchestra under Collier with the pianist Duke Ellington as soloist; *The Democratic Concerto*, commissioned by the *Winnipeg SO, which gave its premiere in 1967 with Stone's quartet; and *Impulse*, commissioned by R.W. Finlayson for the TS (and also performed by the *NYO), a work which integrates elements of jazz in the music but does not use jazz musicians in its performance. Several of Symonds' other works also have drawn on jazz: *Opera for Six Voices*, presented in 1961 on CBC radio; the mixed-media incidental score for *Man, Inc.* (with Jacques Languirand), produced at the *St Lawrence Centre, Toronto, in 1970; *Black Hallelujah*, a collaboration with Russ *Little, seen on CBC TV in 1971; and *Lady in the Night*, produced in Toronto in 1977 by the Co-Opera Theatre with Julie Amato in the lead and the composer as conductor.

Some of Symonds' work in the 1970s has been in evocation of the vastness and wonder of nature. His travels 1968–9 across Canada under a Canada Council senior fellowship resulted in a 13-part radio series, 'Travelling Big Lonely' (with scripts written and music chosen by Symonds), heard in 1971 on the CBC and later issued by RCI on a 13-LP set of broadcast transcriptions. He completed the orchestral work *Big Lonely* (commissioned, premiered, and recorded by the NYO) in 1975 and has composed such pieces as *The Story of a Wind* and *The Land* (for CBC TV), *Four Images of Nature* (for the Guelph Meistersingers), and *Forest and Sky* (commissioned by *OFSO for the *St Catharines SO). Symonds' nature pieces depart in some essentials from his third-stream works. They are expressionist in their sombre but strong colour and their concern with conveying feelings directly, in 'sound-images' rather than in 'sound-arguments,' in rhetoric rather than logic. Like his jazz works, they make effective use of ostinatos and other patterns, and the instrumental timbres are carefully judged, but the purpose is different. The result is usually a large-boned, moody but essentially simple statement distinct from the relaxed colloquy of his third-stream pieces.

In addition to those organizations mentioned above, a number of others have commissioned works from Symonds, notably *Canadian Brass (*Diversions*), the *Canadian Electronic Ensemble (*Quintet* for clarinet and four synthesizers), the *COC (*'Charnisay Versus LaTour,'* an opera written for student audiences and produced by the COC for *Prologue to the Performing Arts, which presented it on tour in Ontario in 1972), the *Festival Singers (*At the Shore*), and Imperial Oil (*The Gift of Thanksgiving*, premiered 9 Sep 1980 by the TS under Andrew Davis).

A special area of Symonds' interest has been theatre music for young people, and with the creative participation of public-school classes he developed two plays with music, *Laura and the Lieutenant* in 1974 and *Sam* in 1976, both of them performed by the students upon completion. In a series of CBC radio broadcasts in 1979 Symonds described and discussed these creative workshops. Symonds was scriptwriter and host 1975–6 for several programs on the CBC series 'Music of Today' and co-host in 1976 (with Norma *Beecroft) of its summer series 'Ad Lib.' He is an associate of the *CMCentre, a member of the *CLComp (for whose 25th anniversary in December 1976 he prepared a CBC radio documentary), and a member of CAPAC.

SELECTED COMPOSITIONS

STAGE, RADIO, AND TV

Age of Anxiety, radio play (Auden). 1959. Jazz tentet. Ms

Opera for Six Voices, radio opera (J. Reeves). 1962. 6 vs, jazz band, str orch. Ms

Tensions, ballet. 1966. Jazz quin, orch. CMCentre

The Story of a Wind (Concerto for TV). 1970. V, narr, jazz ens. Ms

Man, Inc., mixed-media stage work (J. Languirand). 1970. Jazz orch, 3 vs, perc, dancers, actors. Ms

'Charnisay Versus LaTour' (or *The Spirit of Fundy*), opera (Symonds). 1972. CMCentre

The Land (Concerto for TV). 1973. Narr, v, jazz ens. Ms

Lady of the Night, opera (H. Alianak). 1977. Ms

ORCHESTRA

Concerto Grosso. 1957. Jazz quin, orch. CMCentre. RCI 181 (Ron *Collier Quin)

Autumn Nocturne. 1960. Sax, str orch. CMCentre

Pastel Blue. 1963. Str orch. Kerby 1973. CTL S-5030 (*Hart House O)

The Nameless Hour. 1966. Improvised instrumental solo, str orch. Leeds 1969. CBC SM-34/CBC SM-104 (F. *Stone

flhn)/Decca DL 75069/MPS BASF 21704 (Ron *Collier Orch)
Democratic Concerto. 1967. Jazz quar, orch. CMCentre
Impulse. 1969. CMCentre. RCI 477 (B. *Brott cond)
Big Lonely. 1975. Kerby 1975. RCI 431 (*NYO)
Forest and Sky. 1977. CMCentre
The Gift of Thanksgiving. 1980. Orch. CMCentre
CHAMBER
Fugue for Reeds and Brass. 1952. Ms
Fugue for Shearing. 1957. Pf, jazz ens. Ms
A Six Movement Suite for Ten Jazz Musicians plus Four Songs and Incidental Music (Auden). 1959. V, jazz tentet. Ms
Fair Wind. 1965. Jazz ens. Ms. Decca DL 75069 (Ron *Collier Tentet)
Diversions. 1973. Brass quin. Kerby 1975. CBC SM-320 (*Canadian Brass)
Bluebeard Lives. 1975. Str quin, tape. Ms
The Canterville Ghost (Wilde). 1975. Narr, chamb ens. Ms
Quintet for Clarinet and Synthesizers. Ca 1976. Ms. RCI 484 (J. *Campbell)
Also two concertos for jazz octet (1955, 1956), *Hambourg Suite* (1956) and other works for jazz group
CHOIR
At the Shore (Bible). 1976. SATB, perc. CMCentre
Four Images of Nature (Symonds). 1976. SATB. Ms

WRITINGS
'clJasAsiZcaZl = third stream music,' *CanComp*, 37, Feb 1969
'The Spirit of Fundy,' *OpCan*, Winter 1971
'Solving a problem: how to find a good libretto,' *CanComp*, 68, Mar 1972

BIBLIOGRAPHY
McNamara, Helen. 'The skill of the skull: Canada's greatest jazz composer,' *Music World*, vol 1, 22 Jun 1957
'CBC will preview a new jazz opera,' *OpCan*, Sep–Oct 1961
'Third stream jazz composition,' *CanComp*, 24, Dec 1967
'Man, Inc., multi-media co-authorship,' *CanComp*, 47, Feb 1970
McNamara, Helen. 'Norman Symonds,' *International Musician*, Jul 1970
'Big Lonely: work in progress,' *CanComp*, 57, Feb 1971
West, Linda. 'Norman Symonds: a denizen of the deep,' *That's Showbusiness*, 19 May 1976
Schulman, Michael. 'Norman Symonds: a third stream composer finally comes of age,' *CanComp*, 151, May 1980
Contemporary Canadian Composers / Compositeurs canadiens contemporains MM (CF)

Syria. Immigration to Canada from Syria began in 1882. The first wave consisted mainly of small merchants; the second wave, beginning in 1946 (including Palestinians), was mainly of blue-collar workers; the third wave, beginning in 1962 (including Palestinians) brought white- and blue-collar workers in about equal numbers.

Immigrants of Syrian origin have tended to retain their heritage more completely than have those of other Arabic nationalities. In the 1970s, while there was a trend towards acculturation among second-generation Syrian-Canadians, the third generation was divided between those who were assimilated almost completely to Canadian culture and those who adhered very strongly to the culture of Syria. Syrian-Canadians have been noteworthy for their preservation of the authentic classical Arabic music tradition, a tendency found also among Syrians in their homeland. While the composition of the performing group at a Syrian-Canadian concert is similar to that at other structured performances in the Arab-Canadian community (see Arabic music), such performances by Syrians feature classical music and only occasionally include commercialized Arabic music. Members of the audience at these concerts frequently dance the 'Dabkah' and the belly dance. Authentic folk singing, with or without instrumental accompaniment, tends to be reserved for private gatherings of Syrians from particular localities, although classical music also may be performed on such occasions. Among Canadian musicians of Syrian parentage are Paul *Anka, Edmund *Assaly, King *Ganam, and George *Haddad.

GDS

T

TAIT, Malcolm (James) (b Miller-Tait). Cellist, teacher, b Vancouver 21 Jan 1931. He studied cello in Vancouver with Mildred Johnston 1936–44 and Dezsö *Mahalek 1944–8 and began playing professionally at 17. After further study in 1953 with Pierre Fournier and André Navarra in Paris, he returned to Canada and served 1954–7 as principal cello of the *Vancouver SO and 1955–6 as a member of the *de Rimanoczy Quartet. He was principal cello 1957–67 of the *TSO and 1960–9 of the *Stratford Festival orchestra and taught 1960–6 at the *RCMT. Artist-in-residence in 1967 at the *U of New Brunswick, Tait joined the faculty at *Brandon U in 1968 and subsequently performed with the *Brandon U Trio, as a solo recitalist, and as a member of the *Cassenti Players for that group's 1974–5 national tour. Among his pupils are the cellists Van Burden, Lyndamae Harris, Janet Horvath, and Ingrid Seidl-Frohmuller and the bassists Cameron Lowe and David Murray.

KN

TALBOT, Paul-Émile. Organist, teacher, b Quebec City 1 Sep 1934; lauréat piano (Laval) 1951, BA (Laval) 1955, Diplôme d'études supérieures in Gregorian chant (Laval) 1958, premier prix organ (CMQ) 1960. He studied Gregorian chant 1954–8 at *Laval U and with the Benedictines at St-Benoît-du-Lac, then enrolled at the *CMQ, where his teachers were Henri *Gagnon (organ), Andrée Gauthier-Germain (solfège), Magdeleine *Martin (history, analysis), and Françoise *Aubut (theory). On a Quebec government scholarship he continued his training 1960–3 with Donald Willing at the New England Cons, Boston, and in the summer of 1965 he took private lessons from Antoine *Reboulot in Paris. Concurrently with these activities he taught solfège 1959–69 at the CMQ and held successively the positions of president of the Assn des professeurs of the CMQ, vice-president of the Syndicat des professeurs de l'État du Québec, and president of the conservatories section of the last-named. He was assistant director of the CMQ 1969–71 and its director 1971–8. While organist 1961–73 at St-Charles-Garnier Church, he took part in concerts by various Quebec ensembles and was soloist at the 1971 concert marking the fifth anniversary of Les *Amis de l'orgue de Québec, of which he was a founding member. (CH)

TALBOT, (Jean) **Robert**. Violinist, violist, educator, administrator, composer, b Montmagny, near Quebec City, 2 Dec 1893, d Quebec City 24 Aug 1954; diplôme supérieur (AMQ) 1917, lauréat (AMQ) 1918, D MUS and hon D MUS (Laval) 1933. After taking law at Laval U, he began music studies with J.-A. *Gilbert (violin), Berthe *Roy, and Joseph *Vézina. He obtained a teaching certificate from the *AMQ in 1919, probably the first violinist ever to do so. That September he went to New York to study at the Institute of Musical Art under Franz Kneisel, Albert Stoessel, and Louis Svenčenski. Returning to Canada in 1922, he gave a series of concerts in western Canada. Talbot served 1922–35 as secretary and 1932–54 as director (the positions concurrent 1932–5) of the School of Music at *Laval U. He also taught harmony and violin at Laval; his pupils included Maurice *Blackburn, François *Brassard, Gilbert *Darisse, Marthe *Lapointe, and Henri Mercure (*Prix d'Europe for composition, 1927). He founded the

Robert Talbot

Schubert String Quartet in 1921 and the Talbot String Quartet ca 1924 and was the conductor 1924–41 of Quebec City's Société symphonique (*Quebec SO).

The author of articles for various periodicals and of books on music theory, Talbot was a member of the Société française de musicologie (Paris), the International Musicological Society (Basel), the Musical Assn of London, and the Diocesan Commission on sacred music in Quebec. His compositions, none of which were published, include the oratorio *Évangéline*; the opera *Celle qui voit*; a symphony, a *Poème* for violin and orchestra; a string quartet; orchestral pieces; organ pieces; and several songs.

WRITINGS
'M. J.-A. Gilbert,' *La Musique*, vol 1, Aug 1919
Cycle des Quintes: Des propriétés de l'intervalle de quinte dans la science, dans l'histoire, dans la pédagogie de la musique (Quebec 1940)
Phonétique, vol 1 of series *Grammaire de la musique* (Quebec ca 1941)
'Avons-nous une culture musicale nationale?,' *Culture*, vol 3, Sep 1942
'Beethoven, le moderne,' *Les Carnets viatoriens*, Apr 1945

BIBLIOGRAPHY
'J.-Robert Talbot,' *La Lyre*, vol 2, Jan 1924
'M. J.-Robert Talbot,' Quebec *L'Événement*, 14 Apr 1928

DM

TAMBLYN, Bertha (Louise). Composer, singer, lecturer, b Oshawa, Ont, 1877, d Toronto 19 Dec 1954. She studied music at the Ontario Ladies' College in Whitby, and later at the TCM with A.S. *Vogt, J.H. *Anger, D.D. *Slater, Leo *Smith, and T.J. *Crawford. In the 1920s, with the pianist Lenore Stevens, she gave recitals throughout southern Ontario, often performing her own songs. Publication of these began in 1922, and by 1950 over 40 songs, anthems, and piano pieces had been issued by *Canadian Music Sales, Frederick *Harris, G.V. *Thompson, *Waterloo Music, Lorenz (Dayton, O), and Hall and McCreary. Bertha Tamblyn was adept at writing distinctive songs for children. Collections of the latter – *Holly Time Songs* (1938) and *We Are Seven* (1939) – are published by Thompson.

BIBLIOGRAPHY
Hamilton, H.C. 'Bertha Louise Tamblyn,' *MCan*, vol 10, May 1929
Catalogue of Canadian Composers EK

TANGUAY, Georges-Émile. Composer, organist, teacher, pianist, b Quebec City 5 Jun 1893, d there 24 Nov 1964; lauréat (AMQ). In Quebec City his teachers were Léon Dessane and J.-Arthur *Bernier, and in Montreal Arthur *Letondal and Romain *Pelletier. He spent the years 1912–14 in

Paris studying organ with Louis Vierne and harmony with Félix Fourdrain. In 1920 he returned there to work with Édouard Mignan (organ), Georges Caussade (harmony and counterpoint), and Simone Plé-Caussade (piano) and to attend Vincent d'Indy's classes at the Schola cantorum. He studied organ with Pietro Yon and Gaston Dethier in New York. Upon his return to Montreal in 1925, he became organist at Immaculée-Conception Church, a position he held for 20 years.

Tanguay taught at the *Cons national and in 1943, when the *CMM was founded, he was appointed to teach harmony there. He also taught this subject and later organ as well at the *U of Montreal. Among his pupils were Marcel Beaulieu, Jeannine Bégin, Léon *Bernier, Maurice *Blackburn, Marcel *Laurencelle, the sisters Gilberte, Marcelle, and Magdeleine *Martin, Lucien *Martin, P.-E. *McCaughan, André *Mérineau, Renée *Morisset, and Micheline *Tessier.

Tanguay composed relatively little, and most of his works were written during the early years of his career. Léo-Pol *Morin described his *Lied* for organ as 'a serious work, more elaborate than those preceding it, displaying the same refined lyricism that has come to characterize this musician' (*Papiers de musique*, Montreal 1930). The *CMCentre has granted him the associate status reserved for deceased composers whose works it holds.

COMPOSITIONS

ORCHESTRA

Romance. 1915. Vn, hp, orch. Ms
Danseuses devant Aphrodite (arr). Ca 1920. Roudanez
Pavane (arr). 1925. Med orch. RCI Canadian Album No. 2 (J.-M. *Beaudet)
Lied (arr). 1947. Str orch. RCI Canadian Album No. 3 (J.-M *Beaudet)

CHAMBER MUSIC

Souvenir. Ca 1912. Vc, pf. Durand 1914
Apaisement (arr). Ca 1920. 2 ww quin, hp. Roudanez
Hommage à Couperin (arr). Ca 1920. Cl, bn, str quin. Roudanez
Lied (arr). Ca 1930. Str quar. Ms

PIANO

Air de ballet. Ca 1912. Durand 1913
Menuet. Ca 1912. Durand 1914
Scherzo-Valse. Ca 1912. Durand 1914
Sarabande. Ca 1912. Archambault 1916
Causerie. Ca 1912. *P-T*, 3 Nov 1917
Gavotte et Musette. Ca 1912. *P-T*,?
Pavane. 1914. Ditson 1921
Trois pièces brèves. Ca 1920. Roudanez 1921

CHORAL

'Cor Jesu.' 1912. SATB. *P-T*,?
'O Salutaris.' 1912. SATB, bar. Bélair 1916
Graduel et Trait (excerpt from *Messe de Requiem*). 3 men's vs. *P-T*, 1 Dec 1917
'Cor Jesu.' SATB. *L'Action catholique*
Also 2 pieces in ms for org, *Prière* (1915) and *Lied* (1924)

GP

TANGUY, Charles. French hornist, teacher, composer, b France ca 1845, d ?; premier prix french horn (Académie de Valenciennes and Paris Cons). At first a member of the Pasdeloup and Théâtre lyrique orchestras in Paris, he became sergeant-bugler and then bandmaster of a regiment during the Franco-Prussian War. He later played in orchestras in England, Scotland, Ireland, and Switzerland as well as at the Théâtre-Italien in Paris. He taught brass instruments at the Cons de Valenciennes and was director of the Société chorale de St-Quentin, France, prior to his appointment to teach at the Bordeaux Cons. He was a conductor of choral and instrumental societies in France and continued to work as an instrumentalist, visiting New Orleans as principal french horn with the Opéra français. He was made an officer of the Académie by the French government in 1907, the year he settled in Montreal as a teacher of brass instruments, voice, violin, and piano. J.-J. *Gagnier and Guillaume *Gagnier were among his pupils.

Tanguy composed numerous sentimental ballads, piano pieces, and patriotic songs which were published in *Le *Passe-Temps*. One of these songs, 'Canadien toujours,' with lyrics by Gaston Leury (*Le Passe-Temps* nos. 316 in 1907, and 909 in 1947) enjoyed a certain popularity, as did 'Patrie,' to a poem by Albert Ferland (Yon 1909).

BIBLIOGRAPHY

'M. Charles Tanguy,' *P-T*, 316, 4 May 1907

GP

TAPSCOTT, Carl (Harry). Choir conductor, tenor, arranger, organist, b Toronto 14 May 1910; ARCT 1948. A pupil of Albert Whitehead (voice), Tapscott began his career in the late 1920s as a tenor soloist on the Toronto radio stations CFCA, CKGW, and CKNC and sang for 22 years on CFRB. An organ pupil of Stanley Drummond Wolff, he has been organist-choirmaster in various Toronto churches. During World War II he was choral director for the RCN's *Meet the Navy* and conducted the 'Sea Shanty Choir,' from which the Commodores (or Commodores Quartette) were formed (1943). As part of *Meet the Navy* the group – Harvard Reddick (lead tenor), Tapscott (second tenor and arranger), John Ringham (baritone), and Donald Parrish (bass) – gave a royal command performance in England and toured in Europe. After the war the Commodores performed throughout Canada, on CBC radio, and at the *CNE. They recorded a few folksongs, spirituals, and sea-shanties for Gavotte. In 1954, with the Four Gentlemen (see William Morton), the Commodores formed the nucleus of the Carl Tapscott Singers, a 12-man Toronto choir which gave popular CBC broadcasts until 1967 and made eight LPs and several singles for *Hallmark, *Columbia (eg, 'Great Hymns of All Time'), *RCA, *Capitol (eg, 'Songs for a Family Christmas'), Epic, and *CTL. With the addition of eight female voices they became the Carl Tapscott Choir and performed in 1968 on CBC radio's 'Songs of Faith.' Some of Tapscott's many arrangements for his choirs have been published by *BMI Canada, *Berandol, G.V. *Thompson, *Waterloo, and Frederick *Harris.

(CF)

Tara Hall. Auditorium located at 119–123 Ste-Anne St, Quebec City. The building housed a Wesleyan chapel 1816?–49?, the Lecture Hall – a public hall for cultural pursuits – 1849?–74, a theatre known as Victoria Hall 1874–6, and finally Tara Hall, after the acquisition of the building in 1876 by the St Patrick's Literary Institute. Partially destroyed by fire in 1887, it was rebuilt the following year. It began to be used regularly for musical events at the turn of the century; before then virtually the only such occasion was a concert by the violinist Camilla Urso 3 Dec 1864. Among the early 20th-century activities were a symphonic concert 5 Dec 1902 conducted by Joseph *Vézina, the first concert of the 1904–5 season of the *Quebec SO 28 Nov 1904, a 'Concert, comedy and operetta given by the Zouaves of Quebec City...under the direction of M. Léon Dessane' 25 May 1905, and a gala evening 7 Mar 1907 with the violinist Arthur Hartmann and the pianist Adolphe Borschke. Gradually surpassed by other halls, Tara Hall in retrospect appears a cultural centre of limited importance, used during the 19th century mainly by Irish immigrants. After it was destroyed again about 1917, most likely by fire, it was not rebuilt.

BIBLIOGRAPHY

Hawkins' Picture of Quebec with Historical Recollections (Quebec City 1834)
Le Moine, J.M. *Historical Notes on Quebec and Its Environs* (Quebec City 1890)
Gale, George. *Historic Tales of Old Quebec* (Quebec City 1923)

LP

TARANTO, Émile. Violinist, teacher, b Montreal, of Italian parents, 1878, d there 27 Aug 1936. At six he began studying violin with Frantz *Jehin-Prume, and by 1894 he was a member of *Couture's *MSO. He also gave many recitals at that time. In June 1903 he went to Brussels to study with Eugene Ysaÿe, who recorded his impressions of his pupil in October of the same year: 'I am completely satisfied with the progress of M. Taranto, and I believe that by prolonging his stay for a year we may hope to obtain a very artistic result. I am both interested in him and fond of him.' Taranto returned to Montreal, played Bruch's *Concerto No. 1* 8 Apr 1904 with the *Goulet MSO, and served 1904–7 as that orchestra's concertmaster. Also in 1904 he founded the *Mendelssohn Trio. He participated in concerts by the Beethoven Trio and in 1907 and 1914 toured Europe. In February 1930 at *Windsor Hall he performed *Sonate en un mouvement* and *Romance on the G String* by Émiliano *Renaud, with the composer at the piano. Concurrent with his career as a concert artist, he spent much time teaching, notably at Villa-Marie, Mont-Ste-Marie, in convents in Lachine, at the St-Louis-de-Gonzague Church, and at the Académie Marie-Rose. His pupils included Jean *Deslauriers, Marthe *Lapointe, Annette *Lasalle-Leduc, and Lucien *Sicotte. Taranto wrote a few pieces for violin including *Danse caprice* (*Musi-Canada*, February 1923) and *Mouche à feu*.

CG

TARDIF, (Georges) Alfred (Father Hilaire-Marie, Order of the Friars Minor). Organist, pianist, composer, b Laconia, NH, 7 Feb 1903, d Montreal 16 Mar 1978; lauréat piano (Montreal) 1929, lauréat organ (AMQ) 1934, D MUS (St Louis) 1959. In 1924, after completing his general education in Trois-Rivières, he entered the order of the Franciscan Fathers; in 1930 he was ordained priest. He took piano lessons in Trois-Rivières with J.-Antonio *Thompson (1919), and studied harmony in Montreal with Benoît *Poirier and organ there with Eugène *Lapierre and Raoul *Paquet and in Quebec City with J.-Arthur *Bernier. He studied voice with Rodolphe *Plamondon and took summer courses at the Juilliard School, New York, with Luisa Stojowski (piano) and Robert Ward (composition). In 1931 he obtained a diploma from the Bryant School of Piano Tuning and Repairing in Washington. In addition to his activities as chaplain, general teacher, preacher, and missionary in Europe (1941–5), the USA (Biddeford, Me, 1939–41, 1958–60; Pittsfield, NH, 1945–7, 1953–5), and Canada (Andover, NB, and St Charles, Man, 1947–53; Niagara Falls, Ont, 1955–8), he occasionally taught organ, piano, harmony, and singing. He gave many recitals and became known as an authoritative interpreter of the works of Bach, Franck, Widor, and others. In addition to two masses for mixed voices, he wrote several works for organ, including *Triptyque marial* (Fassio 1947), performed by Jean Langlais at Ste-Clotilde Church in Paris and on the radio there, as well as *Liturgical Harmonies* (Gray 1951). He left the priesthood in 1967.

WRITINGS

Ornements musicaux des maître anciens (Montreal 1959)
Orgues et organistes: problèmes d'aujourd'hui (Montreal 1965)

BIBLIOGRAPHY
Dion-Levesque, Rosaire. 'Le Père Hilaire-Marie Tardif, O.F.M. de Pittsfield, N.H.,' *Silhouettes franco-américaines* (Manchester, NH 1957) ST

TARDIF, Alphonse. Organist, pianist, teacher, b Plessisville, south of Quebec City, 11 Mar 1885, d Lévis, near Quebec City, 8 Mar 1951. In 1898 he entered the Collège de Lévis, where he studied with Philéas *Roy (piano) and Wilfrid Roy (organ). He was the college's organist 1905–7 and again from 1909 until he was ordained a priest in 1912. He subsequently had organ and piano lessons for eight years from Henri *Gagnon and on a Quebec government grant continued his studies 1922–5 in Paris with Abel-Marie Decaux and Joseph *Bonnet (organ), Sylva Hérard (piano), and Georges Caussade (harmony and counterpoint). On his return to Canada he resumed his organ duties at the Collège de Lévis and taught there and at *Laval U. Among his many pupils were Jean-Marie *Beaudet, Victor *Bouchard, Claude *Lavoie, and Georges *Lindsay. Shortly after Tardif's death, Eugène *Lapierre wrote, 'There are many music teachers in our province, but we had very few of his ability and calibre' (*Le Devoir*, 17 Mar 1951) GP

TATTERSALL, Richard. Organist, pianist, teacher, b Thornliebank, near Glasgow, 23 Mar 1879, d Toronto 26 Feb 1950. He studied in Glasgow with Herbert Walton and Philip Halstead, and later in Germany. After 1893 he was organist in various Glasgow churches and led choirs in Dunoon and Thornliebank. He emigrated to Canada, settled in Toronto in 1908, and was organist at several churches: St Thomas' Anglican 1908–15, Old St Andrew's United 1915–33, and St Paul's United 1935–47. He taught piano and organ 1918–20 and 1929–41 at the *TCM and was music director 1925–44 at Upper Canada College. He was the pianist 1909–12 of the Brahms Trio with George Bruce, Lina *Dreschler Adamson, and later Nora Hayes, and he also played in the *Hambourg Trio in its early years. He helped Ernest *MacMillan prepare many performances of the *St Matthew Passion*, beginning in 1923. He was president 1931–2 of the CCO. Welford *Russell was one of his pupils.

BIBLIOGRAPHY
'Richard Tattersall,' *MCan*, vol 4, Dec 1909
'Biographical: Richard Tattersall,' *Canadian Journal of Music*, vol 1, Feb 1915
'Portrait gallery no. 18 – Richard Tattersall,' *CQR*, vol 14, Winter 1932 RPn

TAUSSIG, Elyakim (Peter). Pianist, teacher, b Bratislava, Czechoslovakia, 27 Feb 1944, naturalized Israeli 1949, naturalized Canadian 1976; BA Islamic studies (Jerusalem) 1965, Artist Diploma (Toronto) 1969, M MUS (Toronto) 1970. He studied piano with Edith Kraus in Israel 1951–65 and with Anton *Kuerti in Toronto 1968–70 and received the first M MUS in performance granted by the *U of Toronto. He was an award winner at the 1970 Busoni Competition in Italy. He has performed in Europe and Israel, and in Canada with the *TS, the *Vancouver SO, and other orchestras. He has played as a duo-pianist with his wife, Kathryn Root, as a soloist and chamber musician (and the music director) with *Camerata, which he helped found in 1972, and in recorded recitals with Adele *Armin (CBC SM-145), Albert *Pratz (CBC SM-159), Peter Schenkman (CBC SM-160), and Marta *Hidy (CBC SM-161). *Morawetz' *Fantasy* was commissioned for him in 1973 and is included on Taussig's recording of solo piano works by Bartók, Liszt, and others (1975; CBC SM-279). In the early 1970s Taussig became known as a player of fluent technique and bold style. The critic John *Kraglund (Toronto *Globe and Mail*, 27 Nov 1972) found his Beethoven and Schubert 'at times hard and scintillating, at others meltingly lyrical [though] often for the sake of contrast rather than for musical reasons.' He noted, however, that Bartók invoked Taussig's 'sensitivity to tone colour and his ability to communicate on a more thoughtful level.' Taussig taught 1972–3 at the U of Toronto and 1973–6 at the *U of Western Ontario. (WS)

Teaching aids. See Inventions and devices.

Teaching methods. See the following entries:
Dalcroze Eurythmics
Fletcher Music Method
Kelly Kirby Kindergarten Method
Kodály
Martenot method
Orff-Schulwerk
Pantonal Inc
Suzuki method
Ward method
Theory textbooks

Te Deum laudamus / We Praise Thee O God. Greatest non-biblical hymn of the Christian church. It has been translated from the Latin into many languages and has been sung in worship since the fifth century in innumerable settings, including several by Canadians. In 17th-century Canada the Te Deum was sung on ceremonial and festive occasions, such as the baptism of the Micmac chief Membertou and his tribe by the Jesuit Jesse Fléché in 1610, and during Bishop Laval's welcome to the lieutenant-general of the forces, Marquis de Tracy, 30 Jun 1665 (*Jesuit Relations*).

Two Te Deums by James P. *Clarke were published in his *Canadian Church Psalmody* (Toronto 1845). Before 1867 *Nordheimer published a *Te Deum and Jubilate* by the Toronto organist Henry Martin, and in 1888 the same firm issued a *Te Deum* by the Winnipeg organist Frederick Jaffery.

Of four choir-and-organ settings by Healey *Willan the earliest, in B flat (B252, 1906, H.W. Gray 1909; F. Harris 1937), requires a baritone soloist; an E-flat one (B254, 1912) was not published; a second Te Deum laudamus in B flat (B53), completed in 1937 for the coronation of George VI and published in 1938 by Harris, specifies 'double choir with antiphons' (a later version with organ accompaniment was published by Peters in 1963 as *Festival Te Deum*, B259); and the last one, in F (B260, 1953, rev 1955), was published by Concordia in 1956.

Sir Ernest *MacMillan's setting with orchestra (1936), written for the TCM's 50th anniversary and premiered on that occasion in 1937, has been sung 1948, 1956, 1968, and 1976 by the *Toronto Mendelssohn Choir, on the last-named date with the *MSO at the opening ceremonies of the Olympic Games.

Other 20th-century settings by Canadians include Placide *Vermandere's, commissioned by the CBC, premiered 13 May 1945 to mark the end of World War II, and repeated in 1947 and 1957; Arthur *Egerton's (Western 1950); Gerald *Bales', with trumpets and timpani (Waterloo 1962), written for the Cathedral Church of St Mark, Minneapolis; Rogert *Matton's, with baritone and orchestra (1967), dedicated to the *Quebec SO on its 65th anniversary and premiered 27 Nov 1967; Barrie *Cabena's, for unison voices, choice of keyboards, and optional trumpet (Jaymar 1967), written for the choirs and congregations of the Episcopal Diocese of Michigan; and F.R.C. *Clarke's *Festival Te Deum* premiered 11 Mar 1973 in Kingston.

A *Te Deum* (1950) by Violet *Archer makes non-specific use of the title to convey the general intention of her three-movement setting of verses from Psalm 104, Psalms 13 and 30, and the Apocrypha.

See also Roman Catholic church music.
(MMI, KW)

TELGMANN, Oscar (Ferdinand). Conductor, educator, composer, violinist, b Mengeringhausen, Germany, ca 1855, d Toronto 30 Mar 1946. He began to study music when his parents emigrated to Canada and settled in Kingston, Upper Canada (now Ontario). His mother was trained as a concert pianist. On his father's death in 1882 Telgmann, the eldest son, supported his brothers and sisters – all trained musically – by forming a family ensemble, the Telgmann Concert Party, which toured for several years. In 1892 he established the Kingston Cons of Music and School of Elocution, which he and his wife, Alida Jackson, operated for over 25 years. It was from his pupils and his family that the first Kingston SO was formed in 1912. Telgmann, the founder-conductor, continued to direct the orchestra and to teach till he retired in 1938. His most important composition was the 'Canadian military opera,' **Leo, The Royal Cadet*. He also wrote the operettas *The Miller and the Maid* and *King of Siam* as well as songs, marches, and other pieces. The *British Whig March* (1900) and *The Mascot* (dedicated to the Queen's U rugby team) were among his published works. In 1895 he established the monthly *The Canadian Music and Drama* and became its editor. Only the first two issues have been located. Telgmann played a key role in the musical development of *Kingston for over 50 years, and several of his children became professional musicians. PB

Ten Centuries Concerts. A Toronto organization which produced concerts 1962–7 of unfamiliar but important works. It developed from discussions among Gordon *Delamont, Harry *Freedman, R. Murray *Schafer, Harry *Somers, and Norman *Symonds, and its name reflected the time span from which repertoire would be drawn. Calling on the resources of many different and usually unrelated musical groups in Toronto, Ten Centuries Concerts presented an extraordinary variety of programs, including, in the first season, Joseph *Quesnel's **Colas et Colinette*, Falla's *El Retablo de Maese Pedro*, and the 10th-century liturgical drama *Quem quaeritis*, which shared a concert with Stravinsky's *L'Histoire du soldat*. Events, often broadcast later on the CBC, were held in the concert hall (Walter Hall) of the Edward Johnson Building, *U of Toronto, and the initial response was sufficient to sell out the first season of seven concerts by subscription. Essay-length program notes were mailed to subscribers before each concert. In 1967 Ten Centuries Concerts gave four concerts at *Expo 67 and also commissioned works from Norma *Beecroft, Ron *Collier, Bruce *Mather, André *Prévost, and Norman Symonds. However, audience interest by then had declined, and the directors found the burden of voluntary work overwhelming. After the spring presentations of 1967 the series was discontinued. Three programs were presented in the spring of 1970 at the *St Lawrence Centre, but no further attempt was made to revive the concerts. Though subsequent organizations have assumed parts of Ten Centuries Concerts' responsibility (particularly, in regard to 20th-century music, *Kasemets' Isaacs Gallery Concerts and *NMC), no other (by 1980)

The Telgmann family ensemble of Kingston, Ont

had offered a repertoire comparable in the length of its historical perspective, the rarity of its material, and the high quality that pervaded its extraordinary variety.

DISCOGRAPHY

A chamber ensemble of Ten Centuries Concerts is listed as the performing group, conducted by Howard Cable with the soloist Mary *Morrison, in a recording of Serge *Garant's *Anerca*.

BIBLIOGRAPHY

'Ten Centuries Concerts: a recollection,' Toronto *Only Paper Today*, vol 5, Jun 1978 (CM)

ten HOOPE, Karel (Joseph). Organist, conductor, critic, composer, b Amsterdam 28 May 1917, naturalized Canadian 1958. He studied at the Amsterdam Cons and in Utrecht at the School voor Katholieke Kerkmuziek. He emigrated to Canada in 1951 and studied composition with Robert *Turner in Vancouver. Settling in New Westminster, BC, ten Hoope formed two choirs – the Karellers (1955–63) and the *Handel Society of Music in 1966. He was music critic 1954–74 for *The Columbian*. In Vancouver he conducted the *Vancouver Bach Choir 1961–5 and became music director at Holy Rosary Cathedral in 1969. Most of his compositions were written for use in the cathedral; they include four masses, four wedding songs, and several motets. A *Proper of the Mass, Mass I for the People*, and *Mass II for the People* are published (Empire 1966). TRL

TERRY, (William) **Earle**. Educator, choir conductor, b Toronto, 9 Jul 1912; BA (Toronto) 1938, B PAED (Toronto) 1940, M MUS (Montreal) 1950. He was supervisor of music 1935–43 and 1945–6 in New Toronto and became music director for the London, Ont, Board of Education in 1947. He has been a guest professor at *McGill U, the *U of British Columbia, and the *U of Victoria and a choral instructor at the *U of Western Ontario 1954–74. In London, Ont, he founded the Earle Terry Singers (1948–63), a female choir which broadcast regularly on CBC radio and in 1953 represented Canada in Brussels at the first ISME conference. Terry was the founder and conductor of the Conservatory Choir, which sang with the Cleveland Orchestra during its visits to London in the late 1950s and 1960s. He was president 1942–3 of the music section of the Ontario Educational Assn (later *OMEA) and has written music-education texts for elementary schools.

WRITINGS

– Churchley, Frank, and Slind, Lloyd. *Whales and Nightingales*, Basic Goals in Music Series, vol 4 (Toronto 1972)

BIBLIOGRAPHY

Foy, Jane. 'Earle's girls,' *London Free Press*, 22 May 1978

GKG

TESSIER, (Hélène) **Micheline** (m Potvin). Soprano, teacher, administrator, b Paris 21 Jul 1932 of Canadian parents; lauréat voice (AMQ) 1950, BES (Quebec Ministry of Education) 1970. She studied voice with Roger *Filiatrault 1945–9 at the *École normale de musique in Westmount and 1949–53 privately. She took theory with G.-É. *Tanguay and Gilberte and Raymonde *Martin. With a Sarah *Fischer Concerts Scholarship (1951), and grants from the *Amis de l'art (1952) and the Quebec government (1955, 1957), she continued her training 1953–7 in New York, mainly at Mannes College with Martial Singher (voice), Paul Ulanowsky (repertoire), and Otto Guth and Rudolph Fellner (repertoire and opera). She was a member of the Juilliard Opera Theatre.

During the summers of 1955 and 1956 with the Marlboro Festival in Vermont Tessier performed cantatas by Rameau and Bach and the soprano part in Schoenberg's *Quartet No. 2*, and sang Lieder of Adolf Busch with Rudolf Serkin at the piano. She was a finalist in the 'Metropolitan Opera Auditions of the air,' and also, by unanimous consent of the jury, received the first-prize medal at the 1957 Geneva International Competition for Musical Performers. That summer she sang Elvira in 10 performances of *Don Giovanni* for the *Montreal Festivals, and in 1958 she appeared as Nanetta in *Falstaff* for the *Opera Guild.

While under contract 1959–60 to the Detmold Landestheater in Germany, Tessier's roles included Violetta in *La Traviata*, Dorotha in Weinberger's *Schwanda*, and Karolka in Janáček's *Jenufa*. She sang in other German cities, especially Hanover where she was acclaimed for her performance in *La Traviata*: 'Micheline Tessier captivated the audience...She breathed life into the role of Violetta...the evening's success was due to her convincing artistry' (*Hannoversche Presse*, 11 Feb 1960).

On her return to Montreal Tessier worked with Bernard *Diamant, made her debut at the *COC (Micaela in *Carmen*, 1961), gave recitals 1962–3 for Community Concerts, and performed on CBC radio and TV. With the tenor Jean-Louis Pellerin and the bass Gaston *Germain she formed the Trio canadien Bel Canto which toured eastern Canada 1963–5 for the *JMC. Tessier sang leading roles in TV productions of Stravinsky's *Pulcinella*, Menotti's *The Telephone*, and Bernstein's *Trouble in Tahiti*.

Soloist with the *MSO in 1958 and 1963, the *Quebec SO, the *McGill Chamber Orchestra, and the *NACO, Tessier also sang in 1965 with the Bordeaux SO. At the *Théâtre lyrique de Nouvelle-France she appeared with great success as Musetta in *La Bohème* (1962), Tosca (1963), Cio-Cio-San in *Madama Butterfly* (1964), and Fiordiligi in *Così fan tutte* (1970). She sang Eudoxie in a 1964 Carnegie Hall concert performance of Halévy's *La Juive* organized by the Friends of French Opera. In December 1968 she went to the USSR, sang Tosca and Cio-Cio-San in the opera houses of Odessa, Tbilisi, and Yerevan, and gave a recital of French songs on Moscow TV. In 1971 she sang a supporting role in Puccini's *Suor Angelica* at the *Opéra du Québec.

By 1971 Tessier was concentrating primarily on teaching voice and stage techniques. She taught 1967–9 at the École normale and 1969–74 at *UQAM, where she staged chamber operas by Schubert, Chabrier, Roussel, and Delibes, and 1974–6 at the Lionel-Groulx Cegep. She became head of the music department of the Marguerite-Bourgeoys College in 1976. She was elected to the board of directors of the *CMCouncil in 1977. In 1960 she married Gilles *Potvin.

DISCOGRAPHY

Bach – Vivaldi – Handel. Arts Quebec Instr Ens: J. Morin fl, Verdon vn, Salvetti vn, Onofreyo va, Carpenter vc, M. Lagacé org and hpd. 1965. Pirouette JAS 19003

Soirée chez Bach: Le Petit Livre d'Anna Magdalena. Quatuor double of Mtl, B. Lagacé org and hpd, Courville cond. 1966. Madrigal MAS 404-U

WRITINGS

'A warm welcome in the snow,' *OpCan*, vol 10, May 1969

'Atelier lyrique du Rhin,' ibid, vol 18, Mar 1977

BIBLIOGRAPHY

'La Charmante Micheline,' *Soviet Union Today* Feb 1969

GP

Tétrachromie. Ballet by Ludmilla Chiriaeff (choreography) and Pierre *Mercure (music), commissioned by Les Grands Ballets Canadiens for the inauguration of the *PDA, Montreal, in 1963. The form of the ballet was suggested to Chiriaeff by the rhythm and nature of life's seasons, and the movements were associated with the colours green, yellow, red, and white. Decor and costumes were by Jean-Paul Mousseau. The work was rehearsed but never presented because the festival at which it was to be performed was cancelled. The scoring of the music is for clarinet, bass clarinet, alto saxophone, percussion, and magnetic tape. In December 1964 the work was recorded for Columbia (MS 6763) by members of the Toronto Philharmonia Orchestra. The original tape of the recording has been lost. DA

Théâtre de Société. Enterprise devoted to drama and opera; it was established in Montreal in 1789 and located in the residence of Louis *Dulongpré. Dulongpré was a painter and teacher of music and dance who emigrated from France in 1778. A detailed contract, signed 11 Nov 1789 by Dulongpré and six citizens, including Joseph *Quesnel, specified 'that the said Mr. Dulompré [sic] will supply three complete sets, painted on canvas, to the Théâtre de Société, which will be set up in his house...[He] will supply either candles or lanterns necessary for lighting the said theatre; the three abovementioned sets will represent a room, a forest, and a street...[He] will pay for the music, the wig-maker, the tickets, cost of programs, theatre attendants...The said Mr. Dulompré is also required to have the theatre ready several days before a performance, as well as providing the lighting and musicians required for rehearsals.' The theatre opened 24 Nov 1789 with *Le Retour imprévu*, a comedy by Regnard, which was followed by Florian's *Deux Billets*, 'a one-act prose comedy with ariettas.' *Les Deux Chasseurs et la laitière* was performed there 29 Dec 1789. The first productions of Quesnel's *Colas et Colinette* were given in the theatre on 14 Jan 1790, and of Didbin's *The Padlock* and Shield's *The Poor Soldier* on 22 Apr 1790. The Théâtre de Société helped to create a climate for the arts in Montreal. At the end of 1790, however, a citizen publicly denounced the management for trying to make social distinctions in its seating arrangements and 'to limit admittance to the parterre to a small number of persons of good birth or of the nobility.' It is not known when the theatre's activities ceased; however at the beginning of 1805 *Les Deux Chasseurs et la laitière* was performed there again.

BIBLIOGRAPHY
'Théâtre de Société à Montréal,'' *Quebec Gazette*, 31 Jan 1805
Massicotte, É.-Z. 'Un théâtre à Montréal en 1789,' *BRH*, vol 23, Jun 1917
Hare, John E. 'Le Théâtre de Société à Montréal, 1789–1791,' *Bulletin du Centre de recherche en civilisation canadienne-française*, vol 16, Apr 1978
La musique au Québec GP

Théâtre lyrique de Nouvelle-France (Théâtre lyrique du Québec 1966–70). Founded in Quebec City in 1961 by the bass Roger *Gosselin and the soprano Nelly Mathot, this company offered a regular season for 10 consecutive years. Its initial production – *The Barber of Seville* with Colette *Boky, Roger *Doucet, Fernand *Martel, Roger Gosselin, and Napoléon *Bisson in the leading roles and Edwin *Bélanger conducting – was given in Chicoutimi in May 1961. The first offering in Quebec City itself was Delibes's *Lakmé*, with Boky in the title role, in April 1962 at the *Palais Montcalm. With the support of the *MACQ the company became more efficiently organized, with Roger Gosselin as sole artistic director until the 1966–7 season. The baritone Gilles *Lamontagne, Gosselin's successor, served until 1970, when the company was dissolved.

Although only one work was presented during its first two seasons, three and often four productions were offered subsequently, first at the Palais Montcalm and later (1964) in the hall of Quebec City's Académie commerciale. The repertoire was along the lines of that of the Opéra-Comique in Paris. In addition to traditional French works such as *Lakmé* (1962, 1965), *Werther* (1963, 1968), *Les Pêcheurs de perles* (1964, 1969), *Mignon* (1966), *Mireille* (1965), and *Manon* (1967), it included the operettas *Le Pays du sourire* (1965), *The Merry Widow* (1966), *La Périchole* (1967), *Monsieur Beaucaire* (1968, 1969), and *Ciboulette* (1970) and operas by Rossini (*The Barber of Seville*, 1961, 1963, 1967), Verdi (*La Traviata*, 1965), Puccini (*La Bohème*, 1962, 1967; *Madama Butterfly*, 1964; *Tosca*, 1963, 1968, 1969) and Mozart (*Così fan tutte*, 1964, 1970). At first all works were sung in French, but increasingly often they came to be given in the original language.

Though semi-professional in character at the beginning, the productions – employing almost exclusively Canadian casts and technical crews – reached an estimable level. Among the artists who sang leading roles were the sopranos Pierrette *Alarie, Clarice *Carson, Marcelle Couture, Marguerite *Gignac, Jeanne Guihard (Mrs Roger Gosselin), Suzanne Lapointe, Thérèse *Laporte, Micheline *Tessier, and Cécile *Vallée; the contraltos Réjane *Cardinal and Geneviève *Perreault; the tenors Léonard *Bilodeau, Pierre *Boutet, Pierre *Duval, Jean-Louis Pellerin, Guy Plamondon, Paul *Trépanier, André *Turp, and Richard *Verreau; the baritones Dominic Cossa, Jacques Jansen, Gilles Lamontagne, and Robert *Savoie; and the basses Claude *Corbeil and Yoland *Guérard. Sylvio *Lacharité was music director 1962–5, followed 1967–70 by Jean *Deslauriers. Guest conductors were Wilfrid *Pelletier, Pierre *Hétu, Louis Fourestier, Ernesto *Barbini, and Charles Dumas. Among the producers were Roland Laroche, Herman *Geiger-Torel, Jacques Létourneau, and Roger Gosselin. Besides performing in its home city the company took productions of *The Merry Widow* and *Manon* to Montreal, appearing at the Salle Wilfrid-Pelletier (*PDA), and made several tours of Quebec. By 1970 the annual budget had reached a half-million dollars, and a considerable deficit caused the troupe to cease activities.

BIBLIOGRAPHY
Boeckh, Sherry. 'Théâtre Lyrique de Nouvelle-France,' *OpCan*, Dec 1965
Gosselin, Roger. 'L'Opéra au Québec...six pieds sous terre?' *Musicien québécois*, Aug – Sep, Oct – Nov 1974, Dec – Jan 1974–5 MS (GP)

Théâtre lyrique du Québec. See Théâtre lyrique de Nouvelle-France.

The Theatre of Neptune (Le Théâtre de Neptune). Masque written by Marc Lescarbot in 1606. Lescarbot (lawyer, traveller, writer, b Vervius, France, ca 1570, d Presles, France, 1642) visited Port Royal during the winter of 1606–7. *The Theatre of Neptune*, the earliest known entertainment conceived and performed in New France by Europeans, was presented 14 Nov 1606 by Frenchmen and Indians under the author's direction in barges and canoes on the waters before Port Royal (the first successful French settlement in North America and known since 1710 as Annapolis Royal, NS). Written to welcome the port's founders, Samuel de Champlain and Jean de Biencourt de Poutrincourt, on their return from coastal explorations, the masque includes two musical cues – a trumpet call and the singing 'in four parts' ('en Musique à quatre parties') of the song 'Vray Neptune.' The text was published in Lescarbot's *Les Muses de la Nouvelle-France* (Paris 1609) and later translated by H.T. Richardson as *The Theatre of Neptune in New France* (Boston 1927). However, the music has not survived, and its authorship is in doubt. Marius *Barbeau has conjectured that Lescarbot may have borrowed the melody of the French folk song 'La Petite Galiotte de France,' while Willy *Amtmann in *Music in Canada* has suggested that Lescarbot himself may have composed the melody. A version of *The Theatre of Neptune*, translated by R. Keith Hicks and with incidental music by Healey *Willan, was performed 6 May 1954 at the *Arts and Letters Club in Toronto.

BIBLIOGRAPHY
Girard, Gilles. 'Le Théâtre de Neptune en la Nouvelle-France,' *Dictionnaire des oeuvres littéraires du Québec*, vol 1, ed Maurice Lemire (Montreal 1978)

Theatre Royal. The first Montreal theatre bearing this name was located on St-Paul Street and inaugurated in December 1825. Built at the initiative of John Molson and a group of citizens, it was Canada's first house designed specifically for entertainments that required a proper stage. An orchestra conducted by Messrs Duff and Honey was featured, but most of the presentations were plays. In August 1843 a French comic opera troupe put on Auber's *Les Diamants de la couronne* and Adam's *Le Chalet* under the direction of a Mlle Cavé. The theatre was demolished 1844–5 to make way for the Bonsecours market.

A second Theatre Royal, seating 1500 and located on Côté Street, was inaugurated in 1852 by the Irish soprano Catherine Hayes. A German orchestra, the Germania Music Society, played there that same year, performing nine times in two weeks with great success and featuring the Austrian pianist Alfred Jaell. Soon after his arrival in Montreal, the young Calixa *Lavallée frequented the theatre with his patron Léon Derome and performed there in 1855. The soprano Adelina Patti, the violinist Ole Bull, and other stars were heard there around the same time. With the passing years and the construction of new halls uptown the Theatre Royal lost its prestige, and when it closed in 1913 its sole fare was burlesque comedy and vaudeville.

BIBLIOGRAPHY
Géraud, Jean. *350 ans de théâtre au Canada français* (Montreal 1958)
Johnson, Sydney. 'Montreal's theatres of the past,' PDA inaugural program, Sep – Oct 1963
Collard, Edgar Andrew. 'Theatre Royal: its rise and fall,' Montreal *Gazette*, 30 Oct 1971
Amtmann *Musique au Québec* GP

Theatre Under the Stars (TUTS). Vancouver company which produced operettas and musicals 1940–63 at the *Malkin Bowl. TUTS was founded under the auspices of the Vancouver Park Board by the board superintendent A.S. Wootten, the conductor Basil Horsfall, and the actor E.V. Young, with advice from Gordon *Hilker, to provide entertainment in Stanley Park. In the 1930s attempts had been made by Young and Stanley *Bligh to establish outdoor theatre at Brockton Oval, and these ventures set the precedent for TUTS. After TUTS' first season (which opened 6 Aug 1940 and presented *The Geisha*, the plays *A Midsummer Night's Dream* and *As You Like It*, and selections from grand opera) its program was devoted mainly to operettas (*The Firefly*, **Rose Marie*, *The Red Mill*, *Naughty Marietta*, and others). In 1944 the Park Board established the BC Institute of Music and Drama under the direction of Glyndwr Jones to train young performers during the winter months. The institute, whose staff included Basil Horsfall (voice), Barbara *Custance and Phyllis *Schuldt (piano), and Nicholas *Fiore (flute), closed in 1950 shortly after it was renamed the Cons of Music, British Columbia.

In 1949, when the Civic Theatre Society was established to take over control from the Park Board, TUTS began producing six-to-eight-week summer seasons of such musicals as *Finian's Rainbow*, *Brigadoon*, *Oklahoma!*, *Annie Get Your Gun*, *South Pacific*, *The King and I*, *Kismet*, *Guys and Dolls*, and *Carousel*. In 1952 TUTS premiered **Timber!!*. In 24 seasons TUTS presented 104 productions, many, after 1944, also touring in British Columbia. Though established foreign artists often were engaged for leading roles, TUTS employed as well such Canadians as Ernest *Adams, Milla *Andrew, Donald *Bell, Harold *Brown, Eleanor *Collins, Don *Francks, Don *Garrard, Robert *Goulet, *Juliette, Don *McManus, Karl Norman, Barney Potts, and Betty *Phillips. Conductors included Bligh, Horsfall, Lucio *Agostini, Beverley *Fyfe, and Harry Pryce. TUTS' operations were supervised 1940–9 by Hilker, 1949–54 by Hubert S. Banner, and 1955–60 by Bill Buckingham. Plagued by bad weather and facing competition from the *Vancouver International Festival, TUTS made the 1963 season its last. In its 24 summers TUTS contributed greatly to the Vancouver scene and assisted significantly in the development of many performers' careers. It was the prototype for *Melody Fair in Toronto, *Rainbow Stage in Winnipeg, and the Forum at *Ontario Place in Toronto. (BNSG)

A page from Theodore F. Molt's bilingual *Elementary Treatise on Music / Traité élementaire de musique*, 1828

Theory textbooks. This entry provides a list of some of the theory books written by Canadians. 'Theory,' in this context, is a broad term encompassing the standardized rudiments of notation and terminology and the analytical and practical study of norms and principles of harmony, counterpoint, orchestration, arranging, and the forms of composition. Voice technique instruction books and sight-singing manuals are mentioned in the entries on Singing and Solmization; treatises on instrumental performance techniques are cited in the entries on the playing and teaching of individual instruments or families of instruments. See also School songbooks.

Canadian contributions to the literature of music theory have been designed most often for the elementary student at the school or conservatory and only rarely for the advanced student who has the choice of many well-established foreign textbooks and who provides only a very small market for the Canadian author. A critical study of the Canadian theory literature had not appeared by 1980.

The need for Canadian theory manuals arose in the early 19th century, when each choirmaster and bandmaster had to teach the fundamentals of melodic and rhythmic notation as he rehearsed his group. Hence the early compilations of church music nearly always had an introductory chapter devoted to theory. For example, *Humbert's *Union Harmony* of 1816 included an 'Introduction to the Grounds of Musick'; *Daulé's *Nouveau Recueil de cantiques* of 1819, a 'courte méthode pour apprendre à les mettre en plain chant'; Mark Burnham's *Colonial Harmonist* of 1832, a chapter 'Rudiments to the Art of Singing'; Alexander Davidson's *Sacred Harmony* of 1838 (and again the *Canadian Church Harmonist* of 1864), an 'Introduction to the Science of Music'; *The Harmonicon* of 1841, an 'Introduction to Vocal Music'; and J.P. *Clarke's *Canadian Church Psalmody* of 1845, a set of 'Introductory Lessons and Exercises.'

Along with many forgotten books the appended list contains several that were used by generations of students, eg, certain works by J. Humfrey *Anger, Frederick *Horwood, Gustave *Smith, and Leo *Smith and a few others embodying original approaches, ie, those by Orpha-F. *Deveaux and Gordon *Delamont. Graham *George's *Tonality and Musical Structure* (London 1970), which propounds an original theory of the relation of form to key change, does not fall into the textbook category.

Stevenson, A. *The Vocal Preceptor or Key to Sacred Music From Celebrated Authors* (Montreal 1811)
Molt, T.F. *Elementary Treatise on Music / Traité élémentaire de musique* (Quebec 1828)
Sauvageau, Charles, ed. *Notions élémentaires de musique* (Montreal 1844)
Molt, T.F. *Traité élémentaire de musique vocale* (Quebec 1845)
Smith, Gustave. *Le Parfait Musicien ou Grammaire musicale* (Montreal 1859)
– *Abécédaire musical* (Montreal 1861). Subsequent editions appeared under such titles as *Nouvel Abécédaire, Abécédiare musical, Le Célèbre Abécédaire*. The 78th printing appeared in 1920.
– *Le Gamma musical* (Ottawa 1887)
Héroux, G.P.O. *Méthode d'harmonie*, a set of 12 cards, each numbered as one lesson (np, registered 30 Jan 1892)
Anger, J.H. *Form in Music* (Toronto 1898, rev edn Boston 1900)
– *Elements of Harmony* (Toronto 1902)
– *A Treatise on Harmony*, 3 vols (Toronto 1905, Boston 1906–12); edn rev by H. Clough-Leighter from posthumous annotations of the author (Boston 1919)
– *The Modern Enharmonic Scale* (Boston 1907)
– *A Key to the Exercises in Part I & II of A Treatise on Harmony*, 2 vols (Boston 1909, 1913)
Ham, Albert. *The Rudiments of Music and Elementary Harmony with Test Papers* (London 1910, 1919)
Marie de St Mathieu, Sister. *Précis de la théorie musicale* (Montreal 1911, 11th edn 1954). The author also wrote *Théorie musicale, Recueils d'exercices sur la théorie, Recueils d'exercices sur le précis, Corrigé des exercices sur la théorie*, and *Corrigé des exercices sur le précis*. All appeared in English: *Abridgement of the Musical Theory, Musical Theory, Exercises Based on the Musical Theory, Exercises Based on the Abridgement, Key to the Exercises Based on the Musical Theory*, and *Key to the Exercises Based on the Abridgement*.
Ham, Albert. *Musical Ornaments and Graces and Their Interpretation*, Novello's Canadian Music Text-Books, vol 1 (London 1914)
Deveaux, Orpha-F. *Les Principes de la musique* (Montreal 1918)
– *Les Principes de l'harmonie* (Montreal 1919)
Smith, Leo. *Musical Rudiments* (Boston 1920)
Morin-Labrecque, Albertine. *Recueil de modèles et de dictées musicales* (Montreal nd)
Ham, Albert. *Outlines of Musical Form*, Novello's Canadian Music Text-Books, vol 3 (London [1924])
Stoupanse, Al. *Traité simple et pratique d'harmonie consonante à l'usage du Conservatoire National de Musique* (Montreal [1924])
Marie-Stéphane, Sister. *Manuel d'harmonie* (Outremont, Que, 1926, 3rd edn 1958)
Grey Nuns of the Cross. *Petite Théorie musicale suivie d'un supplement* (Ottawa 1925). English transl *The New Manual on the Elementary Theory of Music* (Ottawa 1927)
Sisters of the Holy Names of Jesus and Mary [Sister Marie-Stéphane]. *Théorie de la Musique* (Montreal 1929). English transl *Musical Theory* (Montreal 1946)
Cooper, Irvin. *Circle of Fifths* (Toronto 1933)
Smith, Leo. *Elementary Part-Writing* (Oakville, Ont, 1939)
Burke, William E. *Theory of Music*, vol 1 (Waterloo, Ont, 1941), vol 2 (Waterloo, Ont, 1931, rev 1943)
Ahrens, Cora B. *Rudiments of Music*, 9 vols (Toronto 1943–6)
Létourneau, Omer. *Théorie musicale* (Quebec 1943)
– *Questionnaire de la théorie musicale* (Quebec [1943?])
– *École de la dictée musicale* (Quebec 1943?)
Horwood, Frederick J. *The Basis of Music* (Toronto 1944)
Soeurs de la Charité de Québec. *Questionnaire de la Grammaire musicale* (Quebec 1945)
Horwood, Frederick J. *The Basis of Harmony* (Toronto 1948)
Rollinson, Eric. *Elementary Harmony and Counterpoint* (Oakville, Ont, 1954)
Burke, William E. *Condensed Harmony of Music* (Waterloo, Ont, 1956)
Horwood, Frederick J. *Elementary Counterpoint* (Toronto 1958)
Lagacé, Claude. *Sixteenth Century Counterpoint* (Toledo, O, 1958)
Soeurs de la Charité de Québec. *Questionnaire de la théorie musicale* (Quebec 1959)
Dubois, Jules. *Théorie élémentaire de musique* (Montreal 1961)
Bray, Kenneth, Snell, D. Bruce, and Peters, Ralph M. *For Young Musicians*, 2 vols, workbooks (Waterloo, Ont, 1961–74)
Lyons, Jean. *Harmony Course*, 3 parts (Vancouver 1961–73)
Marquis, Welton. *Twentieth Century Music Idioms* (Englewood Cliffs, NJ, 1964)
Delamont, Gordon. *Modern Harmonic Techniques*, 2 vols (New York 1965)
Chatillon, Jean. *Le Procès des clefs* (Trois-Rivières 1969)
Delamont, Gordon. *Modern Contrapuntal Techniques* (New York 1969)
Wharram, Barbara. *Elementary Rudiments of Music* (Oakville, Ont, 1969)
Chatillon, Jean. *Initiation aux structures de la musique pantonale*, 3 vols (Trois-Rivières 1969, 1970, 1975)
– *L'Emploi des accords ascendants par les grands compositeurs* (Trois-Rivières 1971)
Lawless, James, and Podoliak, Tela. *Writing music*, 3 vols (Waterloo, Ont, 1972, 1973, 1974)
Baron, Michael. *Précis pratique d'harmonie* (Montreal 1973)
Delamont, Gordon. *Modern Twelve-tone Techniques* (New York 1973)
Hepner, Lee. *Dimensions of Music* (Toronto 1973)
Wharram, Barbara. *Theory for Young Beginners* (Oakville, Ont, 1974)
Lawless, James. *The New Theory Book*, 3 vols (Waterloo, Ont, 1975, 1976)
McEachern, Jim. *Contemporary Music Theory* (Winnipeg 1975)
Delamont, Gordon. *Modern Melodic Techniques* (New York 1976)
Lawless, James. *Complete Answers Book* (Waterloo, Ont, 1978) HK, DM, (GP, PW)

THIBAULT, Éthelbert. Gregorianist, b Manchester, NH, 26 Mar 1898, d Montreal 20 Aug 1953; PH D (Angelicum, Rome) 1923, L SC (Institut catholique of Paris and Sorbonne) 1926, teaching diploma (Institut grégorien, Paris) 1927. He studied theology 1918–22 at the Grand Séminaire de Montréal and was ordained priest 23 Dec 1922 at St-Sulpice Church in Paris. He then undertook studies in philosophy, science, and Gregorian chant in Rome and in Paris. Back in Montreal, he studied organ and accompaniment with Eugène *Lapierre and was appointed to teach sciences at the Séminaire de philosophie. He also taught Gregorian chant there as well as at the Grand Séminaire 1927–35 and at the *Schola cantorum. He was music director 1931–7 for the CKAC radio program 'L'Heure catholique,' and in 1936 he founded the *Choeur Pie X, which he directed. He gave summer courses 1942–53 at the Gregorian Institute of America in Toledo, O. He was appointed to the Faculty of Music at the *U of Montreal in 1951 and was briefly its dean in 1953.

In collaboration with Lapierre, Thibault published a *Messe des saints martyrs canadiens* (Archambault 1937), wrote plainsong accompaniments, and prepared a set of six Gregorian recordings (Archambault 1935). Thibault wrote the accompaniment to a plainsong *Messe votive solennelle pour la victoire* performed 9 Feb 1941 at Notre-Dame Church, Montreal. In addition, he published *The Kyriale* (Gregorian Institute of America, 1951), a selection, in modern notation, of plainsong chants for the mass and the creed (with indications for rhythmic interpretation) and for a complete requiem mass. (CMr)

THIELE, Charles (Frederick). Publisher, bandmaster, cornetist, composer, arranger, b New York 1884, d Waterloo, Ont, 3 Feb 1954. He was a solo cornetist and the director of several New York bands before organizing and directing the Thiele Concert Party, which included his wife, also a cornetist, and their daughter Carolyn (Mrs Wilfred Bender), a saxophonist. The party performed at band festivals and toured extensively on the Lyceum and Chautauqua vaudeville circuits. Moving to Waterloo in 1919 as director of the *Waterloo Musical Society Band, Thiele founded the *Waterloo Music Co and the Waterloo Metal Stamping Co for the manufacture of music stands, drums, and non-musical hardware. He was the editor 1928–33 of **Musical Canada*. He was an organizer and the first president, 1924–48, of the Ontario Amateur Bands Assn, which administered the *CNE band contests, and a founding member in 1931 and president 1934–5 of the *CBA. He was named an honorary life-member of the American Bandmasters' Assn. In 1932, on the Waterloo Musical Society's 50th anniversary, he organized the *Waterloo Band Festival, for many years (1932–40, 1946–58) Canada's foremost annual band competition. In 1946 he established the Waterloo Music Camp for Boys, naming it Bandberg (a play on the name Bamberg, Ont, a nearby community). Thiele's subsequent illness curtailed the camp's development. Noted for his unconventional programming, Thiele composed marches, notably *Chatham Kilties*, and made band arrangements of such works as Beethoven's *Fifth Symphony*. His publishers were Belwin in the USA and Waterloo in Canada. He also compiled and arranged *The Pocket Dictionary of Musical Terms* published by Waterloo Music (nd). It includes a short section on the rudiments of music. (EBM)

THISTLE, Lauretta (b Finlayson). Writer, critic, b New Glasgow, NS, 23 Jun 1917; BA English (Mount Allison) 1936. She studied piano privately and voice 1933–6 at the Mount Allison Cons and also privately with Charles Underwood. She began reviewing music, dance and theatre for the *Ottawa Citizen* in 1945 and continued to do so in 1980. She has contributed articles to the *Canadian Composer*, the *Music Scene*, the *Canada Music Book*, and other periodicals and prepared the entries 'Dance in Canada' for the *Dance Encyclopedia* (New York 1967) and 'Ballet' for the *Encyclopedia Canadiana*. CF

THOMAS. Family of organ and piano builders; also the trade name of a line of organs. John Morgan Thomas (fl 1832–75) began building organs in Montreal in 1832 and established a partnership in Toronto with Alexander Smith in 1839. In 1840 the partners obtained a patent for a metallic frame around the tuning pegs of a piano, designed to take pressure off the case. In 1844 the headquarters were located on King St West, and it was here that Thomas built the first organs to be placed in St Michael's Cathedral and Holy Trinity Church. By 1856 the company was known as John Thomas & Son. In fact, Thomas had five sons active in the trade.

Charles L. Thomas, in partnership with a Mr Drew, established the Western Pianoforte Manufactory of Canada, active ca 1856–ca 1893 in *Hamilton, Ont, and known at times as C.L. Thomas & Co. In 1870 Western Pianoforte was producing some 70 pianos a year. A C.L. Thomas square piano may be seen at the Wellington County Museum, Elora, Ont.

John J. Thomas served his brother Charles' firm as manager ca 1878–84 and was supervisor of the piano department at *Bell Piano and Organ in the 1920s.

Edward G. Thomas founded the Thomas Organ Co in 1875 in Woodstock, Ont. The company was managed later, however, by James Dunlop, who acquired a part interest in 1891 (on Thomas' death) and full interest in 1895 (when the firm became the Thomas Organ and Piano Co; incorporation followed in 1919). A prosperous export trade with Britain was begun in 1893, and orders for organs came later from Australia, New Zealand, Holland, and Germany. At the turn of the century the firm produced an estimated 150 *reed organs and 1000 piano stools and benches a month. In 1916 it began to manufacture record cabinets. In the 1920s it introduced the Thomas Orchestral and Symphony models of reed organ. Late in the decade the firm enjoyed a slight surge in the sales of its portable organs. By the mid-1940s, however, when James Dunlop's son, John G., was president, it had turned to furniture building, and later it became a subsidiary of the Whirlpool Company of the USA and relinquished the Thomas name.

Of John Morgan Thomas' other sons, Thomas L. Thomas worked for R.S. *Williams & Co and Frank J. Thomas was a piano builder. FH

THOMAS, (Roy) **Beal**. Organist, choirmaster, teacher, b Longview, near Dallas, Tex, 14 Mar 1940; B MUS (Southern Methodist) 1962, M Sacred MUS (Union Theological Seminary) 1964. His organ teachers in the USA were William Teague, Robert Anderson, and Alex Wyton. He was organist-choirmaster 1965–70 at Christ Church Cathedral, Vancouver, and in 1971 became music director at Christ Church Cathedral, Victoria. Under his direction the choir of the Vancouver Cathedral travelled to England in 1968, visiting Chester, Norwich, and Lincoln and singing evensong daily for a week in the cathedral of each city. Thomas taught 1966–8 at the Anglican Theological College, Vancouver, began teaching at the *Victoria Cons in 1970, was head of the music department at St Michael's School, Victoria 1972–4, and became head of music at the Norfolk House School for Girls, Victoria, in 1975. His compositions include two settings of the mass, a congregational mass, and a 'Tantum ergo.' PFB

THOMAS, Harry (Reginald Thomas Broughton). Pianist, b Bristol, 24 Mar 1890, d Montreal 11 Jul 1941. A self-taught musician, he moved to Canada in 1909 and performed in Montreal 1909–22 and for a few years in Halifax NS, as an accompanist to silent films. With the advent of 'talkies' he turned to work in Montreal nightclubs. He recorded his popular *Delirious Rag* (written with Willie *Eckstein) for Victor in 1916 and made piano rolls for Rythmodik and Duo-Art 1919–20. The Harry Thomas Trio (1920–2), with the saxophonist Alex Lajoie and the xylophonist Howard Wyness, performed at the Regent Theatre, Montreal, and recorded for HMV, Compo, and Victor. Thomas' recordings are listed in *Roll Back The Years*. EBM

THOMAS, Ian. Singer-songwriter, guitarist, producer, b Hamilton, Ont, 23 Jul 1950. He began his career as a member 1969–71 of the rock band Tranquility Base (the pop group-in-residence 1970–1 with the *Hamilton Philharmonic), which recorded for RCA. As a CBC producer 1972–4 in Toronto, Thomas was responsible for the program 'National Rock Works' and for CBC LM recordings by more than 20 performers, including Bearfoot, Bim, and Cal Dodd. He has produced commercially released recordings by James Leroy, D'Arcy Wickham, and others and has written, produced, and performed many jingles. His own first LP, *Ian Thomas* (1973; GRT 9230-1037), included 'Painted Ladies,' a hit single in Canada and the USA. He had made five more LPs for GRT by 1979 and had appeared on TV and performed in clubs and concert halls in several Canadian centres. His recordings of his songs 'Long Long Way,' 'Liars,' 'Coming Home,' and 'Time Is the Keeper' have been popular in Canada, and his 'Everyday' was a hit in Germany as recorded by the German group Lineman. In a review of the LP *Still Here* (GRT 9230-1067), Peter Goddard called Thomas 'perhaps the most underrated musician in Canadian pop music' and stated that the LP 'shows Thomas at his best – writing and singing strong, commercial songs, but ones which haven't lost any of the basic feel of rock 'n' roll' (*Toronto Star*, 5 May 1978). Thomas received a *Juno Award in 1974 as 'most promising new male vocalist.' An affiliate of BMI Canada until 1974, he was a member of CAPAC thereafter.

BIBLIOGRAPHY

Taylor, Peter. 'Writing songs "just plain hard work" for Ian Thomas,' *MSc*, 277, May – Jun 1974

Flohil, Richard. 'Ian Thomas,' *CanComp*, 104, Oct 1975

Niester, Alan. 'Ian Thomas in retreat? No, he's just biding his time,' Toronto *Globe and Mail*, 30 Jun 1979 (MM)

THOMAS, Linda Lee (m Washburn). Pianist, teacher, b Lethbridge, Alta, 5 Feb 1947; ARCT piano 1963, ARCT voice 1965, B MUS (Montana) 1968, M MUS (Montana) 1969. Raised in Cardston, she studied piano locally with Thelma Smith, in nearby Lethbridge with Beatrice Foster, and in Calgary with Gladys *Egbert. She also studied 1965–9 at the U of Montana and in 1976 with Menahem Pressler. After touring 1969–72 as principal solo pianist with the Royal Winnipeg Ballet she was the pianist 1972–4 for the *Vancouver Opera Assn. In 1973 she began giving CBC recitals and became the orchestral pianist for the *Vancouver SO. The following year she joined the staff of the Vancouver Community College. In 1975 she became the co-ordinator of the Masterpiece Chamber Music Series at the Vancouver East Cultural Centre. The piano trio she formed in connection with the series – with the violinist Gwen *Thompson and the cellist Ian Hampton – continued to perform in 1981 as the Masterpiece Trio. She has appeared in recital, in chamber concerts (eg, with the *Purcell String Quartet), and in concertos with the *NACO, the *Winnipeg SO, and the Seattle SO. Her repertoire includes works of Mozart, the German Romantics, and 20th-century French composers. With the Vancouver SO she premiered (1976) Michael *Baker's *Struggle for Dominion*. Her playing of five piano pieces by Calixa *Lavallée may be heard on the LP *Early Music from Quebec* (1972, CBC SM-204). In 1975 she recorded Colin *McPhee's *Concerto* for piano and wind octet with members of the *CBC Vancouver Chamber Orchestra (CBC SM-308). She married the choir conductor Jon *Washburn. BNSG

THOMAS, Philip J. (James). Collector, composer, singer, teacher, b Victoria, BC, 26 Mar 1921; BA

English and history (British Columbia) 1948. By profession a children's (visual) art teacher, he began working in the Vancouver school system in 1952 and also has given courses at the U of British Columbia Summer School and at the Vancouver Art Gallery. Thomas has collected (on tape) many folksongs relating to British Columbia and, in researching documentary materials relating to the province's history, has uncovered other songs in diaries, archival papers, newspapers, and books. He has adapted or composed tunes for those songs for which the original music was not given or had been lost. His own songs include 'Far from Home' and 'Way Up in the Monashee Range.' In 1975 the 500 songs in his collection were deposited with the provincial archives. Some have been published in periodicals and books, including *British Columbia Library Quarterly* (July 1962; 10 songs and an accompanying article), *More Folk Songs of Canada* (Waterloo 1967; two songs), and *Canadian Folk Songs for the Young* (Vancouver 1975, three songs). His own book, *Songs of the Pacific Northwest* (Saanichton, BC, 1979), includes 49 songs.

Self-accompanied on the guitar or banjo, Thomas has sung in concert and on CBC radio. Tapes of his performances have been included in the instruction kits *The Cariboo Wagon Road 1858–1868* (Vancouver 1964) and *Solo Flight* (Vancouver 1970). Thomas was a co-founder (1959, with his wife, Hilda, Rolf Ingelsrud, and Al Cox) of the Vancouver Folk Song Circle, which, as the Vancouver Folk Song Society, published the periodical *Come All Ye* 1972–7 and the *Canada Folk Bulletin* 1978–80. It also began producing 'Folk Circle' for radio station CFRO-FM in 1975 and opened the Green Cove coffeehouse in 1977. Thomas was a director 1974–9 of the *CFMS. He is a contributor to *EMC*.

BIBLIOGRAPHY

Bartlett, Jon. 'The P.J. Thomas collection of British Columbia folk songs,' *CFMJ*, vol 4, 1976 (FEC)

THOMPSON, Alan (Dales). Radio producer, composer, b Middlesbrough, England, 7 Apr 1901, d ?; LLCM ca 1925. After living 1912–16 in Toronto, he returned to England, where he studied 1921–5 with Cuthbert Harris (organ) and with Sir Henry Wood and Percy Pitt (conducting, orchestration, and theory). He performed in England as a concert organist, then moved to Canada in 1926 and settled in Vancouver. An organist for silent films 1927–30 at the New Orpheum Theatre in Vancouver, he also gave recitals in California and throughout the Pacific northwest and was a freelance radio organist, conductor, and announcer. Following World War II he became staff announcer and later music producer for CBR (CBC) radio in Vancouver. Programs with which he was associated included 'Classics for Today,' 'Music in Nature,' and the series 'Distinguished Artists' as well as broadcasts of the CBC Bach Festival and the *Vancouver SO. He was organist-choirmaster at a succession of Vancouver churches: Ryerson United, St Paul's Anglican, and Shaughnessy Heights United. In 1950 he was named production director for WEW, a radio station owned and operated by St Louis (Mo).

Among Thompson's compositions are an incomplete cantata, *Moses* (1951); two shorter choral-orchestral pieces, *Dunkirk* and *Per ardua ad astra* (both 1942); *Three Preludes for Organ* (1934); *Toccata on the Hymn Tune 'Leoni'* (1938); and several published songs, including 'O Father, like a Child Asleep' and 'Reverie of a Soldier' (both BMIC 1946), 'Prayer for Easter Day' and 'This Human Way' (both BMIC 1947), 'Where He Sleeps' (BMIC 1948), and 'The Oxen' (BMIC 1949). Some of his songs were performed in a recital tour by Jean Browning Madeira ca 1950. He was an affiliate of BMI Canada (PRO Canada). FH

THOMPSON, (William) **Don** or **'D.T.'**. Saxophonist, composer, arranger, b Drumheller, near Calgary, 19 Sep 1932. He played saxophone and clarinet at 12, first performed publicly at 15, and began promoting his own jazz concerts, 'Jammin' the Blues,' in Edmonton at 17. He moved in 1952 to Toronto and toured 1954–8 with Anne Marie *Moss in Canada and the USA. A bebop-inspired tenor saxophonist, Thompson organized and composed for various small groups and led one of Toronto's leading big bands, appearing regularly 1959–65 at the First Floor Club before joining Lionel Hampton's orchestra 1965–6 in the USA. He performed during the 1960s on many CBC TV shows, including 'Club Six' and 'Music Hop,' and has worked extensively in Toronto studios. In 1971 he began to tour and record with Anne *Murray, writing arrangements for some of her albums and for others by Gordon *Lightfoot and John Allan *Cameron. On his return to jazz performance in 1976 he drew praise from Jack Batten in the Toronto *Globe and Mail* for an 'alert, nicely-swinging full-toned style' (23 Sep 1976). His brother Lloyd (b Drumheller 4 Nov 1933) worked during the late 1950s in Europe as a bassist with such US bebop musicians as Dizzy Reece and Don Byas.

BIBLIOGRAPHY

Norris, John. 'Profile: Don Thompson,' *Coda*, vol 4, May 1962 MM

THOMPSON, Don (Donald Winston). Pianist, bassist, vibraphonist, drummer, composer, arranger, recording engineer, b Powell River, north of Vancouver, 18 Jan 1940. After childhood piano lessons he took up the string bass and the vibraphone in his teens. He is essentially self-taught on all instruments. In Vancouver 1960–5 he was sideman to Chris *Gage (playing bass or vibraphone) and Dave *Robbins (bass) and accompanied the visiting US jazzmen Barney Kessel, John Handy, and others in local nightclubs. With the drummer Terry *Clarke he joined Handy's quintet in the USA in 1965, touring widely and making two LPs, of which *Live at Monterey* was among the most popular jazz recordings of the 1960s.

Thompson returned to Vancouver in 1967 (after working briefly in Montreal with Lee *Gagnon that year) and moved to Toronto in 1969. He quickly became that city's first-call studio bassist, a standing he maintained until the mid-1970s, when he curtailed this aspect of his career. In 1969 he became a member of the *Boss Brass and also began playing in the jazz group led by Sonny *Greenwich (for whom he has been pianist and, informally, music director). He was a member of Moe *Koffman's group (as bassist 1970–4 and as pianist 1975–8) and joined Ed *Bickert's in 1974. He has worked on occasion with Lenny *Breau (as both bassist and drummer), Jimmy *Dale, Doug *Riley, and others and has accompanied such US musicians as Paul Desmond, Jim Hall, Frank Rosolino, Milt Jackson, and James Moody. His work with Desmond and Hall, on LPs recorded in 1975 at the Toronto jazz club Bourbon Street, brought Thompson international recognition. (In addition to playing bass, he was the recording engineer on both occasions.) In 1976 he toured with Hall in Japan (Clarke completing the trio) and appeared with Desmond, Bickert, and the drummer Jerry *Fuller at the Monterey Jazz Festival. He has appeared in US clubs and concerts with Desmond and Hall. In 1977, leading his own band from the piano, he performed at the EBU-sponsored International Jazz Festival in Larens, Holland.

Despite his proficiency and the wide appreciation of his bass playing, Thompson has claimed the piano to be his main interest. As described by Jack Batten (Toronto *Globe and Mail*, 7 Dec 1976), 'Thompson's piano influences come from a great tumble of players – Cecil Taylor, Keith Jarrett, Bill Evans, maybe a dash of McCoy Tyner and a lick of Red Garland – but his own style is utterly distinctive. There's a sense of peace in his touch – even when he falls into swirling passages – that is instantly identifiable.' Thompson's compositions include pieces arranged for, and recorded by, Koffman (*Bilbo*, *Days Gone By*, *Wildlife*, and others), Riley (*Gandalf* and *Dreams*), and his own groups. Perhaps his best-known composition is *Country Place*, a ballad reflecting the influence of Keith Jarrett. Thompson's LP with Ed Bickert received the *Juno Award as the best jazz recording of 1979. He is an affiliate of PRO Canada.

DISCOGRAPHY

Love Song for a Virgo Lady. Thompson pf, Park ten sax, Greenwich guit, Donato db, Fuller drums. 1969. RCI 303/Sack 2003

Secret Love. Thompson vib, Bickert guit, Binstead db, Clarke drums. 1970. RCI 350

Country Place. Thompson pf and vib, Perla db and b guit, LaBarbera drums. 1976. PM PMR-008

Don Thompson Quartet Live. Thompson pf. Stuart ten and sop sax, Homme db, Ranger drums. 1977. RCI 480

Ed Bickert / Don Thompson. Bickert guit, Thompson db. 1978. Sack 4005

WITH OTHERS

Handy: *Live at Monterey*. Thompson db, Clarke drums, and others. 1966. Col CS-9262

– *Second Album*. Thompson, Clarke, and others. 1966. Col CS-9367

– *Spirituals to Swing*. Thompson, Greenwich guit, Clarke and others. 1967. 2-Col CG-30776

Jay McShann: *Man from Muskogee*. McShann pf, Thompson db, and others. 1972. Sack 3005

Hall: *Live!* Hall guit, Thompson db, Clarke drums. 1975. Horizon 705

– *Commitment*. Thompson pf, Clarke drums, and others. 1976. Horizon 715

– *Live in Tokyo*. 1976. King

– *Jazz Impressions of Japan*. 1976. King

Pat LaBarbera: *Pass It On!* LaBarbera ten and sop sax, Thompson pf, and others. 1976. PM PMR-009

Others as sideman to Guido *Basso, Bickert, Desmond (see Bickert Discography), Jim *Galloway, Greenwich, Koffman, Riley, as a member of the Boss Brass, and as a studio accompanist

BIBLIOGRAPHY

Gallagher, Greg, and Barnes, Lilly. 'Love of jazz dispels contrasts between musicians-composers,' *MSc*, 263, May–Jun 1975

Miller, Mark. 'Don Thompson,' *Down Beat*, 13 Jan 1977

– 'Don Thompson: sideman in the spotlight,' *Jazz Forum*, 58; issue 2, 1979 MM

THOMPSON, Gordon V. (Vincent). Songwriter, music publisher, b Humberstone (now part of Port Colborne, Ont, on Lake Erie) 9 Aug 1888, d Toronto 12 May 1965. Several factors contributed to Thompson's gravitation towards songwriting in his teens: the singing at the missionary meetings of which his mother was an ardent supporter; a song publisher's advertisement soliciting compositions; and the convenience of a printshop owned by his brother. His 10 *Life Songs* (Revival Publishing Bureau 1909) were sold door-to-door by Thompson and his U of Toronto classmates as a means to finance their studies. Since the songs appealed strongly to the religious sentiments of Ontarians, some eventually sold over 100,000 copies. Cover photos show that singers like Arthur *Blight, Harold *Jarvis, H. Ruthven McDonald, and John W. *Whyte featured them in their

Gordon V. Thompson

recitals. Five *Heart Songs* ('Sacred solos with bright piano settings') followed in 1911, introducing the Thompson Publishing Co of Toronto.

With his *March National* and *Song National* ('O Canada, Dear Canada!' with words by Martha Pugh), both issued in 1912, Thompson turned from religion to patriotism. This proved to be another financially rewarding field when, during the first years of World War I, the Canadian demand for wartime songs could be filled without US competition. In 1914 Thompson acquired the rights of 'For King and Country' by the Australian Robert Harkness, and sold about 100,000 copies. He later acknowledged Harkness as an inspiration for his own war songs. Their very titles reflect the progress of the war: 'Where Is My Boy Tonight?' (1915), 'Red Cross Nell and Khaki Jim' (1916), 'Three Cheers for the Lads of the Navy' and 'When We Wind Up the Watch on the Rhine' (1917), 'For the Glory of the Grand Old Flag' and 'Back to the Farm with a Farmerette' (1918), and 'You Are Welcome Back at Home, Sweet Home' (1919). With the series of eight *Songs of the Homeland* (1915–16) Thompson added such songwriters as Jules *Brazil and Lewis Owen to his catalogue.

In 1918 Thompson founded the Authors and Composers Association of Canada to protect the rights of songwriters and to lobby for changes in *copyright legislation. This campaign was taken over later and broadened by the Canadian Authors Assn founded in 1921 by J.M. *Gibbon, B.K. Sandwell, and others. Thompson's work 1919–32 as manager of the Canadian branch of Leo Feist, a US music publisher, and as president of Gordon V. *Thompson Ltd (founded in 1932) curtailed his songwriting. His last success, the 'Quintuplets' Lullaby' of 1935, was followed by only a few songs, including 'In an Eastern Canadian Port' (1944) and 'Jesus is Lord' (1956), ending his production where it had begun, on a religious theme.

Altogether Thompson wrote and published about 60 songs, usually supplying both the words and the music. They were written for the day and owed their success to their unabashed 'corniness' and guaranteed promotion. A list of those recorded up to 1930 may be found in *Roll Back the Years*. Thompson may be regarded as Canada's prime example of the songwriter-publisher.

WRITINGS

'Recollections,' *CME*, vol 5, Mar – Apr 1964 HK

Gordon V. Thompson Ltd. Toronto music publishing, distributing, and retailing firm established in 1932. It was preceded by Gordon V. *Thompson's Revival Publishing Bureau (1909) and the Thompson Publishing Company (1911), which in 1919 was taken over by the US firm Leo Feist Ltd (remaining, however, under Thompson's management). Feist in turn was taken over by the NBC-owned Radio Music Co, and this name was adopted in Canada in 1930. When NBC found it advantageous to dissolve the company, Thompson purchased the Canadian branch in 1932, though the CPR and Associated Screen News held shares for some years. The company did business in the *Heintzman building on Yonge St 1919–47, then occupied a midtown location on Yonge St, and eventually moved to Birch Ave.

After 1932 Thompson continued to distribute Feist's catalogue of popular songs and became distributor for the large US firm Carl Fischer Inc. He was one of the few music dealers in Canada to build an expanding enterprise during the Depression years. This was due in large part to his shrewd instinct for 'spotting a winner' and for recognizing trends in taste. Furthermore he cultivated community contacts, co-founding the Toronto *Kiwanis Music Festival and taking a great interest in the *Canadian Bureau for the Advancement of Music. Thompson's promotion was significant in the careers of such country stars as Wilf *Carter, Hank *Snow, and Don *Messer. Thompson put his own 'Quintuplets' Lullaby' on the market when the Dionne sisters were making front page news and acquired the copyright of Weir's English words for *'O Canada,' which turned out to be the ones most widely accepted. (Thompson was generous in allowing other publishers to use Weir's text in songbooks and eventually offered its copyright to the government of Canada for $1. See also National and royal anthems.)

Thompson's success as a publisher of patriotic songs (in that period of World War I when Canada had joined the conflict but the USA had not, and US publishers had not begun to cash in on the war-song craze) was repeated in World War II. He acquired the North American rights to 'There'll Always Be an England' (selling 130,000 copies) and issued two Canadian songs that became widely sung among the Allies: Ernest *Dainty's *'Carry On' (written in 1928 but not a hit until the war) and Freddie *Grant's *'You'll Get Used to It.' Successful peacetime acquisitions were the copyright for *'The Blue and White' and *Gimby's *'CA-NA-DA' of 1967.

In the 1930s the firm had begun to publish educational materials, from instruction books to vocal, choral, band, and orchestral music. For school and community use Thompson supplied Canadian adaptations of US community songbooks (*Canada Sings*, 1935; *Merrily We Sing*, 1935; *Sociability Songs*, 1937) in addition to J.M. *Gibbon's *Northland Songs* (1936, 1938), *Canada in Song* (with Leslie *Bell, 1941), and *Pioneer Songs of Canada* (with Irvin *Cooper, 1941). The *Dominion Piano Class Books* first printed in 1935) by Margery M. and Peter C. Kennedy, Don *Wright's textbook series *Youthful Voices* (1940, 1964), the theory books by Frederick J. *Horwood, and the series *Let's Explore Music* edited by G. Roy *Fenwick and Richard *Johnston are educational publications which have had wide use. Thompson began publishing Gena *Branscombe in 1930, Carmen *Lombardo in 1932, Ernest *MacMillan in 1934, Percy *Faith in 1939, Leslie Bell in 1941, Ernest *Seitz in 1942, and Wishart *Campbell in 1943.

About 1950 the company embarked on the publishing of larger-scale concert music, by *Archer, *Bissell, *Champagne, Robert *Fleming, *Freedman, *Morawetz, *Ridout, *Somers, *Walter, *Willan, and others. The extensive choral catalogue includes the *Festival Singers of Canada Choral Series. Among other publications are *The Catholic Book of Worship* (1972) and Ridout's reconstruction (1963, published 1974) of *Quesnel's **Colas et Colinette*. Thompson's printing has been done by the W.R. *Draper Co of Weston, Ont; plate numbers have not been used.

During the early 1950s the firm issued sound recordings on the Gavotte label (see Edward B. Moogk), but printed music remained its chief interest. It has served as the Canadian distributor for such companies as Big Three Music Corp, Bourne Inc, and the rental catalogue of G. Schirmer, all of New York, and Montgomery Music of Buffalo.

After Thompson's death in 1965 John C. *Bird became president of the firm, a CAPAC affiliate, and of its subsidiaries, Chanteclair Music, a PRO Canada affiliate, and G.V. Thompson, Inc, of Niagara Falls, NY.

BIBLIOGRAPHY

'Silhouette: Gordon V. Thompson,' *Music World*, vol 1, 22 Jun 1957

Thompson, Gordon V. 'My first 50 years of music publishing in Canada,' *CanComp*, 1, May 1965

'Gordon V Thompson Limited has stake in Canadian music,' *CanComp*, 16, Mar 1967 HK, MWI

THOMPSON, Gwen (Gwendoline Linda Louise), (m Robinow). Violinist, teacher, b Winnipeg 30 Mar 1947; B MUS performance (Indiana) 1969. A pupil of Anne *Pomer James, John *Waterhouse, and S.C. *Eckhardt-Gramatté in Winnipeg and of Josef Gingold, Ivan Galamian, and Jascha Heifetz in the USA, she was a member 1961–6 of the *NYO and concertmaster for its 1966 European tour. She played 1963–4 in the *Winnipeg SO and the *CBC Winnipeg Orchestra, toured the west 1966–7 with the pianist Diedre *Irons for the *JMC, and in 1967 was associate concertmaster of the Orchestra of the International Federation of the Jeunesses musicales at Mount Orford. After completing her studies she moved to London, Ont, where she served 1971–5 as concertmaster of the *London SO and was a teacher at the *U of Western Ontario. She has taught at the *Banff SFA (summer 1972) and the Interprovincial Music Camp, Manitouwabing, Ont, (1972, 1973, 1974). In 1975 she became head of the string department of the *Community Music School of Greater Vancouver and began teaching at the *U of British Columbia. In Vancouver she has appeared frequently as soloist, chamber musician, and CBC recitalist. She served 1975 and 1977 on the teaching faculty of the NYO, and in 1977 was appointed concertmaster and leader of the *Baroque Strings of Vancouver. In the mid-1970s with the pianist Linda Lee *Thomas and the cellist Ian Hampton she formed the Masterpiece Trio. (PS)

THOMPSON, Joseph-Antonio (Antoine). Organist, composer, choir conductor, bandmaster, teacher, b Montreal 22 Nov 1896, d Trois-Rivières, Que, 8 Mar 1974; lauréat organ (Laval) 1923, D MUS (Montreal) 1950. He received his musical education in Montreal with Jean-Noël *Charbonneau and Élie *Savaria (piano), and in Quebec City with J.-Arthur *Bernier (organ). He occasionally replaced Bernier on the organ at St-Jean-Baptiste Church. In 1916, at the age of 20, he was appointed organist of Notre-Dame-des-Sept-Allégresses Church in Trois-Rivières, and from then until his death he played a leading role in that city's musical development. In 1920 he directed the music for the Compagnons de Notre-Dame, a theatre company he helped found. He taught piano and organ at the seminary, the Académie de la Salle, and the Collège séraphique. In 1930 he succeeded Giuseppe *Agostini as conductor of the Philharmonie de La Salle, and in

1941 he founded the Choeur mixte (later Choeur Thompson), which he directed until 1955. Under his direction the choir presented in 1953 Handel's *Samson* and in 1954 two Bach cantatas. He was the first artistic director 1937–9 of radio station CHLN and produced and announced many musical programs. During the same period he founded the vocal quartet Chevaliers du guet, for whom he arranged numerous folksongs. He also gave private lessons and taught solfège and harmony in the public music courses offered 1930–70 by the Quebec government.

Thompson composed some 60 works, all still unpublished in 1980. Among them are *Les Sept Paroles du Christ* (1933) for four-part unaccompanied choir, premiered in 1937 on the CKAC radio program 'L'Heure provinciale'; five masses, including a *Messe de Noël* (1935) and a *Messe de Pâques* (1941) on Gregorian themes; and works for concert band, numerous motets, organ and piano pieces, hymns, and songs. He also wrote the symphonic poem *Mon Pays* (1936).

Two of Thompson's sons, who were his pupils, became active musicians: Marcel is an organist and Claude began to conduct the Petits Chanteurs de Trois-Rivières in 1956. Émilien *Allard, Gabriel *Charpentier, Jean-Yves *Landry, Marcel Roux, and Alfred *Tardif also studied with him. Appointed in 1949 a member of the Interdiocesan Commission on sacred music, Thompson received the Pro Pontifice et Ecclesia medal from Pius XII for his contribution to musical liturgy. He is the author of *50 Ans de vie musicale à Trois-Rivières* (Trois-Rivières 1970). When the Capitol Theatre in Trois-Rivières was renovated in 1979 it was renamed the Salle J.-Antonio-Thompson.

BIBLIOGRAPHY
'Le témoinage de Marcel Roux sur J.-Antonio Thompson,' Trois-Rivières *Le Nouvelliste*, 19 Mar 1974
Lord, René. 'Un concert en hommage à J.-A. Thompson,' ibid, 15 Mar 1975 GP

THOMSON. Winnipeg musical family, 1 / W. Davidson Thomson and 2 / Stewart, his son.

1 **W.** (William) **Davidson**. Baritone, choir conductor, teacher, b Perth, Scotland, 22 Jan 1886, d Winnipeg 3 Jun 1961. Emigrating to Canada in 1903 he worked on a ranch in Northern Ontario, where he was remembered for his lusty open-air renditions of Scottish songs. He moved to Winnipeg in 1906, studying voice with Rhys Thomas and beginning a 38-year association with Knox United Church, first as a soloist, then as choirmaster. He was also choirmaster 1944–58 at Augustine United Church and was in demand as an oratorio soloist. He impressed as a 'natural' singer, but in fact had been coached by Reinald Werrenrath and Louis Graveure in New York and Albert Visetti in London. Thomson conducted the Great-West Life, United Scottish Society, and St Andrew's Society Male choirs in Winnipeg in the 1920s. In the summer of 1931 he directed the Winnipeg *Tribune*'s 'Nights of Community Song,' six concerts in city parks, heard by over 100,000 people and featuring massed choirs and bands and such leading Winnipeg soloists as the soprano Gertrude *Newton, the contralto May *Lawson, and the pianist Joe Lyon. Thomson taught singing, and Jon *Vickers was briefly among his pupils. Later (1955–7) he reviewed vocal and choral performances for the *Winnipeg Free Press*.

BIBLIOGRAPHY
Horner, M. 'For auld lang syne,' *Winnipeg Free Press*, 26 Aug 1961

2 **Stewart** (MacMillan). Architect, pianist, organist, choir conductor, b Winnipeg 14 Apr 1930; B ARCH (Manitoba) 1952. His teachers were his father and Glen *Pierce (voice), Leonard *Heaton (piano), and Walter *MacNutt (organ). Though an architect by profession, Thomson has pursued a parallel career as one of Winnipeg's busiest and most reliable accompanists and chamber musicians. In 1955 he married the soprano Phyllis *Cooke and has been her partner in many recitals in Winnipeg and other Manitoba centres and on CBC radio. The Thomsons commissioned and premiered 18 Oct 1976 Bernard *Naylor's *Three Feminine Things*. Thompson was organist-choirmaster at St James Anglican Church ca 1951–3, took the same position at St George's Anglican Church in 1956, and served 1967–75 as chorusmaster of the *Winnipeg Philharmonic Choir. RG, SRM

THOMSON, David. Educator, choir conductor, b Portree, Isle of Skye, 27 Sep 1895, d Saint John, NB, 23 Feb 1979. His family settled in Saint John, NB, in 1914. After army service in World War I, Thomson, a self-taught musician, formed the Brunswick Singers, a male quartet – Bernard C. Bean and Lester Rowley, then Alfred E. Stafford (tenors), Thomson (baritone), and Graham Allwood, then Omar Thomson (bass) – which was heard on national radio, sang at the 1938 British Empire Exhibition Music Festival in Glasgow, and performed as the Lumberjacks Quartet with Don *Messer. Thomson was choir director at Central Baptist Church in Saint John and also led the popular Capitol Theatre singsong broadcasts begun in 1937 on CHSJ. That same year he founded and was the only director of the 40-voice Carriden Choir, which sang throughout New Brunswick and on the CBC national network until 1967. Modelled on the Glasgow Orpheus Choir of Thomson's uncle Sir Hugh Roberton, the Carriden Choir specialized in unaccompanied part-songs, madrigals, and ballads. Its extensive library was presented in 1967 to the U of New Brunswick in Saint John.

For the Canadian Legion Thomson was district supervisor in charge of recreation for servicemen 1942–6, and for the Kiwanis Club he directed the project 'Let New Brunswick Sing,' 1946–9, which undertook to persuade the provincial government of the need for a school music program. When in 1949 such a program was begun, Thomson was appointed provincial supervisor, and thereafter until 1963 he organized school music teaching in New Brunswick, established and adjudicated school music festivals, ran summer schools 1950–67 at the U of New Brunswick in Fredericton, and conducted workshops in rural areas. Active on the founding committee of the *CMEA, he also assisted in the formation of the *Music Education Council of the New Brunswick Teachers Assn.

See also School music.

BIBLIOGRAPHY
Sweet, Jean. 'He started the whole province singing,' Saint John *Times-Globe*, 12 Jul 1963
McCullagh, Harold. *The Man Who Made New Brunswick Sing* (St Stephen, NB, 1978) PW

THOMSON, Heather (m Price). Soprano, b Vancouver 7 Dec 1940. A pupil 1954–6 of Phylis Dilworth *Inglis in Vancouver, in 1961 she was a *CBC Talent Festival winner and a finalist in the *Metropolitan Opera regional auditions. She then studied with Irene *Jessner at the *RCMT and made her *COC debut in 1962 as the Dew Fairy in *Hansel and Gretel*, followed in 1963 by Mimi in *La Bohème*. While a member 1964–6 of Sadler's Wells, where she sang Mimi, Anne Trulove in *The Rake's Progress*, and Marguerite in *Faust*, she also appeared with the COC as Rosalinda in *Die Fledermaus* (1964) and as Marguerite (1966). Other COC roles have included Giulietta/Antonia in *The Tales of Hoffmann* (1967), Liù in *Turandot* (1969), Donna Elvira in *Don Giovanni* (1970), Tatiana in *Eugene Onegin* (1972), Marguerite again (1974), and the title role in *Manon Lescaut* (1975). In 1973 she created the role of Heloise in the COC's premiere of Charles *Wilson's **Heloise and Abelard*. She was the Countess in *The Marriage of Figaro* for Festival Canada (*Festival Ottawa) in 1971, Nedda in *I Pagliacci* for the *Opéra du Québec in 1973, and Hanna in the *Quebec SO performance of *The Merry Widow* at the Montreal Olympics in 1976. She has appeared with the Edmonton, Manitoba, Southern Alberta, Vancouver, Boston, New Orleans, Pittsburgh, and San Diego operas. In 1969 she made her New York City Opera debut as Marguerite and in 1974 her European debut as Violetta in *La Traviata* at the Augsburg opera house, where her husband, the US tenor Perry Price, was a leading tenor.

Heather Thomson as Marguerite in *Faust*

BIBLIOGRAPHY
Cansino, Barbara. 'Heather Thomson's three busy lives,' *PfAC*, Winter 1977 (HCs)

THOROLFSON, Frank. Educator, pianist, organist, conductor, composer, b Winnipeg, 5 Feb 1914, of Icelandic parents, d Hamilton, Ont, 26 Mar 1977; ATCM 1932, LAB 1933, M MUS (Chicago Musical College) 1952, hon FRHCM 1972. His father, Halldor Thorolfson, was a singer and the conductor of the Winnipeg Icelandic Choral Society and of church choirs. Frank studied piano with Eva *Clare and R.H. Ragnar in Winnipeg and orchestral conducting on scholarship at *McGill U. He served 1944–6 in the Canadian army and subsequently (1947–52) attended the Chicago Musical College, where his teachers were Rudolph Ganz (piano), Hans Rosenwald, and Paul Nettl. During this period he was Ditson Scholar in musicology in 1947 and 1948 and held administrative and teaching positions 1949–51 at the Chicago Metropolitan School of Music and the Chicago Musical College. Returning to Canada he taught 1955–8 at the *Regina Cons of Music, serving also in Regina as organist at Knox-Metropolitan United Church. He was appointed music director at *McMaster U in 1959 and served 1965–70 as the first chairman of that university's music department, teaching history and aesthetics. He was chancellor 1972–7 of the *RHCM.

Thorolfson founded (and directed 1938–42) the Winnipeg Chamber Orchestra and conducted several other performing groups, including the Chicago Bach Chorus 1947–52, the *U of Manitoba SO 1942–4 and 1946, the Regina Ladies' Choir 1953–8, and the *Bach Elgar Choir of Hamilton 1960–1. Thorolfson's opera *The Qu'Appelle River Legend* (1955) was commissioned for Saskatchewan's Golden Jubilee (1956). His *Saskatchewan Scenes* for piano were composed in 1957. Thorolfson's first wife was the Winnipeg violist Irene Diehl.

BIBLIOGRAPHY

Goodridge, Ingibjorg S. 'Frank Thorolfson, A.T.C.M., L.A.B., MUS.M., F.R.H.C.M.,' *Icelandic Canadian*, Summer 1977 (FAH)

Three's A Crowd. One of the first Canadian folk-rock bands. It was formed in 1964 in Vancouver by the singer Donna Warner, the singer-guitarist Trevor Veitch, and the singer-guitarist Brent Titcomb and was known as the Bill Schwartz Quartet (with apologies given nightly for Schwartz's absence). The trio appeared in coffeehouses in western Canada then moved in 1965 to Toronto. Its first single, 'Bound to Fly' (Epic), was a hit in 1966. By 1967 the group had added the singer-guitarist David *Wiffen, the bass guitarist Ken Koblun, and the drummer Richard Patterson. Its most notable accomplishments that year were performances at *Expo 67 and the *Mariposa Folk Festival and the LP *Christopher's Movie Matinee* (RCA Victor DS 50030). In 1968 two singles, 'Bird without Wings' and 'Let's Get Together,' were minor hits in Canada, and Three's A Crowd made its first appearances in the USA. Further personnel changes left the group in 1969 with Wiffen, Patterson, Colleen Peterson (previously an occasional singer with the group), the guitarist Bruce *Cockburn, and the bass guitarist Dennis Pendrith. Based in Ottawa, the newly constituted group appeared in Ontario coffeehouses (eg, Le Hibou and the *Riverboat) and starred in 1969 in the CBC TV series 'One More Time.' It disbanded in 1969.

Three's A Crowd won *Juno Awards in 1966 and 1967 as folk group of the year. In the 1970s, Titcomb enjoyed a successful career as a coffeehouse and concert performer and as the composer of such songs as 'Sing High, Sing Low' and 'I Wish the Very Best for You' for Anne *Murray; Peterson received the Juno Awards of 1967 and 1977 as best new female singer and has performed to critical acclaim in the pop and country fields. Veitch served as lead guitarist for Tom Rush in the early 1970s, and Pendrith has played for Cockburn and Murray *McLauchlan. MM

Thunder Bay. Ontario city formed through an amalgamation of the twin cities Fort William (which, as Fort Camenestigouia or Kaministiquia dates back to 1679) and Port Arthur (established in 1870), both incorporated in 1907. They became Thunder Bay in 1970, named for the bay they share on the west brow of Lake Superior. The population (about 110,000 in 1976) is a mixture of European cultures with a large Finnish component.

One of the twin cities' first musical organizations was a Philharmonic Society founded in 1888. A successor was the Thunder Bay Philharmonic, a choral society and orchestra founded (soon after his arrival in 1910) by B. Gunton Smalley (1887–1942, a graduate of the RAM, organist-choirmaster at the First Baptist Church and father of Cardo *Smalley). That same year the society gave the first local performance of *Messiah*. In subsequent years it also performed Mendelssohn's *Elijah*, Samuel Coleridge-Taylor's *Hiawatha*, and Smalley's *The Legend of Nanna Bijou* (about the sleeping giant who guards the harbour). The Philharmonic Society made the first musical broadcast from the twin cities in 1929, the year Smalley retired. The first music competition was held in 1927. The orchestra continued to function and had renewed success in the late 1930s under the direction of Ralph Colosimo. However, with the onset of World War II it was dissolved. A new ensemble, the *Thunder Bay SO, was formed in 1960 and became the city's most significant musical organiztion.

Thunder Bay choirs have included the Port Arthur Ladies' Choir, formed in 1924 under Wilfred Coulson, who also taught singing. It specialized in 14th to 16th-century music and the work of early 20th-century English composers such as Elgar and Holst, and performed at the CPR English Music Festival (see CPR Festivals) held at Toronto's Royal York Hotel in 1929. The Fort William Male Choir, established in 1927, was conducted 1945–78 by Norman John Kleven (1915–78). The choir won the Canadian Centenary Choir Competition in Saint John, NB, in 1967, toured in Europe several times, and represented Canada in the BBC's 'Let the Peoples Sing' competition in 1970. Ethnic choral groups of the area include the Finnish Otava Male Choir. A choral group formed in 1957 gave concerts and performed *Die Fledermaus* in 1976. A notable earlier production was Rita Ubriaco's of *Amahl and the Night Visitors* in 1953.

Thunder Bay has had a vareity of city, industrial, military, and school bands. There have been several pipe bands, the earliest of which, the MacGillivray Pipe Band, was formed in 1917. The Lake Superior Regimental Band was founded ca 1907 and continued to perform during World War II.

Jean McMichael (1898–1955) conducted her own orchestra and participated in the radio program 'School of the Air.'

Thunder Bay is the site of *Lakehead U and is the birthplace of Kenneth *Campbell, Bobby *Curtola, Mona Kelly *Bernardi, Hugh *Le Caine, Doris Mills *Lewis, Myrna *Lorrie (born in nearby Cloud Bay), Jeanne *Pengelly, Pat *Riccio, and the folk music scholar Margaret *Sargent.

The bay (as distinct from the city) is commemorated in B. Gunton Smalley's song 'Lovely Thunder Bay' (Armand-Greig 1925). (JCr, PMW)

Thunder Bay SO. Community orchestra founded in 1960 as the Lakehead SO. Its players were drawn from the Fort William-Port Arthur area. When those cities amalgamated in 1970 as Thunder Bay, the orchestra changed its name accordingly. Prior to 1967 its conductors were René Charrier, Douglas Dahlgren (the orchestra's founders), and, 1964–7, C.H. Bateman.

Under Boris *Brott, 1967–72, the orchestra began to import players on a per-concert basis from the *Hamilton Philharmonic, the *Winnipeg SO, and the orchestras of Duluth, Minneapolis, and St Paul, Minn. This practice undoubtedly raised the calibre of performance but proved to be costly and was thought eventually to be inhibiting the development of Thunder Bay's own resources. Under Brott's regime, however, the orchestra began a musicians-in-residence program, engaging the Princeton String Quartet to live in Thunder Bay and teach in the city's first Symphony School of Music. The orchestra's next conductor, Manuel Suarez (violinist, b Mexico City 4 Feb 1943, a pupil of Galamian at the Curtis Institute and Boris Belinsky at the Moscow Cons) put greater emphasis on the employment of local players and continued to develop the instrumental teaching programs. Some players still were brought in for concerts, however.

Suarez was succeeded in 1974 by Dwight Bennett (b Campbellford, Ont, 28 Dec 1945, a pupil of Karel Ančerl, Ernesto *Barbini, Victor *Feldbrill, Elmer *Iseler, and the Metropolitan Opera's Tibor Kozma in Toronto, and of Franco Ferrara and Bernard Haitink in Europe; and a winner of the Heinz Unger Award). Under Bennett's leadership a symphony chorus was formed for the presentation of choral-orchestral works such as the Verdi *Requiem*, Mendelssohn's *Elijah*, and Beethoven's *Symphony No. 9*, and the orchestra consolidated its position as one of the foremost community orchestras in Ontario, with a resident professional musician in every principal chair. In 1978 the orchestra had 53 members, of whom 22 were full-time. Groups from the orchestra – quartets, quintets, and a chamber orchestra – and the full orchestra have travelled frequently to northwestern Ontario towns to give concerts. Several operas (*The Marriage of Figaro, Hansel and Gretel, Carmen, Madama Butterfly*) have been staged, using the orchestra and chorus and imported soloists. During the 1978–9 season some 20 orchestral, choral-orchestral, and children's programs were presented.

Guest soloists have included Anna *Chornodolska, Maureen *Forrester, Lorand *Fenyves, Ingemar *Korjus, Anton *Kuerti, André *Laplante, Lois *Marshall, Yuri Mazurkevich, Arthur *Ozolins, Robert *Silverman, Steven *Staryk, and Ronald *Turini. Among the guest conductors have been Victor Feldbrill, Laszlo *Gati, and Harman Haakman. Works commissioned by the orchestra include *Saint-Marcoux's *Luminance*, which it premiered in April 1978. The orchestra has received financial assistance from the *Canada Council, the *OAC, the City of Thunder Bay, and corporate and individual donors.

BIBLIOGRAPHY

'Thunder Bay Symphony touring orchestra,' *OCan*, vol 7, Jan 1980 NM

Timber!! Musical comedy by Dolores *Claman with orchestration by Neil *Chotem and lyrics by Douglas Nixon and David Savage. It was premiered 23 Jul 1952 at *TUTS, Vancouver, and broadcast on CBC radio in an abridged form 1 Aug 1952. Set in British Columbia, it concerns the love of a logger for the daughter of a lumber magnate. The original cast included Thora Anders, Don *Garrard, Len Hayman, Lorraine McAllister, Barney Potts, Jacqueline Smith, and Frank Wade. A vocal score was published in 1952 by BMI Canada.

DISCOGRAPHY

Timber!! (excerpts). Juliette, Salemka, B. Johnson, H. Ramer, Chotem cond. 1954. RCI 119 BNSG

TIQ (The Indian Question Settled at Last). 'A melodramatic musical satire' in two acts. The libretto by Will F. Sage incorporates poems by Phillips Hawley and the music was written by Calixa *Lavallée. The work probably was written in 1865–6, and there is no proof of its performance. The action takes place among the US-west-coast Sioux and depicts the clashes that occur between Indians and whites, until 'the Indian question is settled at last.' The vocal score, comprising an overture and 26 musical numbers, was published by Russell Brothers, Boston, in 1883. An excerpt – *Marche indienne* – was arranged for band by J.-J. *Gagnier and conducted by him in Montreal in 1933. GP

TODD, Dick (Richard James). Singer (baritone), b near Calgary, 4 Aug 1914, d New York 1975. As a teenager in Montreal he sang and played trumpet with George Sims' dance band, then worked with his own band on Caribbean ship cruises. Performing first on Montreal radio at 19, Todd later sang with the CBC orchestras of Lucio *Agostini and Allan *McIver, his programs also heard 1937–8 in the USA. He went to New York in 1938, singing briefly with Larry Clinton's orchestra, then achieved great popularity on the NBC radio shows 'Magic Keys of RCA' (1938), 'Melody and Madness' (1938–9), 'Avalon Time Show' (1940), and 'Showcase' (1940). He also appeared in film shorts for Paramount. Following World War II service he resumed his career on NBC's 'Your Hit Parade' (1945). A husky crooner, Todd was often called the Canadian Crosby and was the subject of the Tommy Dorsey-Bing Crosby 'I wonder where Dick Todd is tonight?' radio comedy-routine. Todd recorded for Victor in Montreal in 1936 and New York in 1938. Some of his many 78s for Bluebird (1938–42, listed in *The Complete Entertainment Discography*, New Rochelle 1973) were reissued on *Blue Orchids* (2-Bluebird AMX2-5509). Further recordings, some as late as 1968, appeared under Decca and other labels. MM

TOI, Roman. Composer, choir conductor, organist, b Estonia, 18 Jun 1916, naturalized Canadian 1957; ARCT composition 1973, PH D (Union Graduate School, Ohio) 1977. Toi studied 1942–3 at the Mozarteum, Salzburg, under Clemens Krauss, and at the Institute of Advanced Studies in Montreux, Switzerland. After radio, theatre, and choral work in Europe, Toi moved in 1949 to Montreal and in 1951 to Toronto. There he began conducting the Estonian Male Choir in 1952 and was organist-choirmaster 1952–68 at Centennial United Church and conductor 1957–72 of the Estonia Mixed Choir. He also has conducted at choral festivals in Canada, the USA, Europe, and Australia and was president 1973–4 of the *Ontario Choral Federation. He began teaching at the *RCMT in 1974, after studies there with Samuel *Dolin. Composing within a tonal framework and acknowledging the influence of Vaughan Williams, Toi has written three symphonies (1969, 1972, 1974), nine cantatas (1953–77), and over 80 choral works, of which some are standard repertoire among Estonian choirs and are among the most frequently performed works by an Estonian-born composer living outside Estonia. Toi is an affiliate of PRO Canada. RM

Toronto. Ontario's capital city, founded as York on the north shore of Lake Ontario by Lieutenant-Governor John Graves Simcoe in 1793, the site near that of previous Indian settlements and the French Fort Rouillé. It was the capital of the province of Upper Canada 1796–1841 and of United Canada 1849–51 and 1855–9, and was designated the capital of Ontario in 1867, the year of Canada's Confederation.

The settlement's population, less than 200 in 1799, consisted originally of civil service and garrison personnel. In 1834, when it had reached 9252, York was incorporated as the city of Toronto. Before World War I most Torontonians were of English, Irish, and Scottish extraction, but successive waves of immigration from many parts of the world, beginning early in the 20th century, significantly altered the city's ethnic balance. In 1953 13 area municipalities amalgamated to form the Municipality of Metropolitan Toronto, which by 1979 had a population of more than 2.5 million.

Because of Toronto's early designation as the capital of Ontario it became a major centre of administration, commerce, education, and industry; and because of its magnetism as the most populous city in English Canada it became the national headquarters for many cultural organizations, supported the largest number of book and music publishers and the richest libraries in Canada, and rivalled Montreal as a broadcast production centre and employer of professional artists.

1 1793–1918
2 1918–1945
3 1945–1980
4 Toronto-born musicians

1 1793–1918. The progress of music in the Toronto of the 19th and early 20th centuries was linked intimately with the city's burgeoning population and prosperity. From a few hundred souls, population grew to more than 300,000. In the 1830s and 1840s performing groups were established, auditoriums were erected, and later in the century education, publishing, and piano building began to thrive, and many touring artists and ensembles of world fame visited Toronto to perform.

On 30 Jul 1793, when the schooner *Mississauga* took Simcoe to Toronto for the first time, the Queen's Rangers band was on board ship. But the first extant reference to a musical event in Toronto is an itemized account including '7 Dollars Paid musick by Order' for a ball and supper, 4 Jun 1798, to celebrate the king's birthday. In 1810 Joseph B. Abbot proposed to open 'a School in the principles of Church Music.' In the same year the performance of a company of actors from Montreal featured a group of songs between a play and a farce. In 1811 a 'double Key'd Harpsichord and Piano Forte inlaid with Sattinwood and of beautiful Mechanism' were sold at an auction. The largest single expense in a statement for the 'Subscription Assemblies 1814' was £22 15s Od for 'Music for the season.'

By the 1820s there were occasional public concerts, but when a company from Rochester, NY, presented Coleman's opera *The Mountaineers* 22 Dec 1825 at Mr Frank's Assembly Room, it was the first time that William Lyon Mackenzie, editor of the *Colonial Advocate*, had been to a theatre in North America since his arrival five years earlier. The first theatre building, a converted Methodist chapel, opened only in 1834.

Visiting artists of international fame appeared from the 1840s onward; among the first were John Braham (1841), Ole Bull (1844, 1857), the Germanians (an orchestra; 1850, 1852), Jenny Lind (1851), Adelina Patti (1853, 1860), Henriette Sontag (1854), Sigismund Thalberg (1858), Henri Vieuxtemps (1858), Louis Moreau Gottschalk (1864), Frantz *Jehin-Prume (1865), Anton Rubinstein (1872), Henri Wieniawski (1872), and Hans von Bülow (1876). Many of these artists performed at *St Lawrence Hall, opened in 1850. The Royal Lyceum Theatre, opened in 1848, accommodated larger-scale musical and non-musical shows in Toronto, although programs of operatic excerpts and truncated versions of popular operas given by four or five performers were more frequent than were complete performances.

Norma, given 8 Jul 1853 at the Royal Lyceum by the visiting Artists' Italian Opera, was the first grand opera, complete with orchestra and chorus, to be presented. Rosa Devries sang the title role and Luigi Arditi conducted. Thereafter, touring companies visited the city regularly, and by the beginning of the 20th century most of the popular Italian and French repertoire had been heard.

In 1883 Emma *Albani made her first Canadian appearance in a complete opera (*Lucia di Lammermoor*), as a member of Her Majesty's Italian Opera. The company's second production was *Il Trovatore*. In the 1890–1 season 91 performances of 24 works were given in Toronto, though only 4 were grand operas: *Lohengrin*, *Rigoletto*, *Carmen*, and *Les Huguenots*. A group of singers from New York's *Metropolitan Opera supported Adelina Patti in a short version of Rossini's *Semiramide* in 1892, and the main company performed six operas in 1899 at the Grand Opera House, a theatre opened in 1874 after the Royal Lyceum had burned down. After 1910 Toronto was on the circuits of the *Montreal Opera Co and the *San Carlo Opera.

Local operatic production was unsuccessful. A few operas were presented in concert form, eg, *Il Trovatore* and *La Sonnambula* in 1866 by the *Musical Union under John *Carter, but the only company to produce opera on a regular basis was the *Holman English Opera Troupe, resident 1867–73 at the Royal Lyceum.

The first church organ was probably the one at St James's Anglican Cathedral; it was imported from England in the late 1830s. The first music published in Toronto (though actually printed in New York) was William Warren's *A Selection of Psalms and Hymns* (1835). Both 'firsts' are evidence of the close relationship between music and religion that characterized 19th-century Toronto. The predilection for choral singing and the taste for oratorio were the results. Until the mid-20th century nearly all the leaders in musical life were also the leading figures in church music.

Despite the number and importance of visiting artists, most concerts were produced by local musicians. Among the leading mid-19th-century figures were the conductor and composer J.P. *Clarke, the singer J.D. *Humphreys, the university's president John *McCaul, the violinist and music dealer Abraham *Nordheimer, the three *Schallehn brothers, and the pianist and teacher G.W. *Strathy. Local groups date back at least to 1822, when the West York Militia Band played at the Orange celebrations of 12 July 1822. A group of amateurs organized the Toronto Musical Society in 1835, and a Harmonic Society gave concerts in 1840.

The first substantial choral-orchestral organization, however, was the *Toronto Philharmonic Society of 1845–7. The initiator and guiding spirit of this group and of several of its successors was McCaul, the musical leader, Clarke. The fortunes of the Philharmonic were uneven, as were those of the Toronto Vocal Music Society (1851–3), the Metropolitan Choral Society, founded in 1857 by Martin Lazare, the Musical Union, formed in 1861 by John Carter, and other groups. However, these groups introduced to Toronto audiences many of the classical overtures, symphonies, and oratorios, even though the larger works rarely were presented in their entirety. An early exception was Handel's *Messiah*, performed 17 Dec 1857 by the Sacred Harmonic Choir under Carter; another, his *Judas Maccabaeus* presented under the Rev G. Onions in 1858.

Apart from a volunteer militia band – the *Queen's Own Rifles, organized 1862 under the direction of Adam *Maul and continuing to flouish in 1980 – the only stable ensembles were those founded after Confederation. The Philharmonic Society was revived in 1872 with J.P. Clarke as conductor and achieved great distinction 1873–94 under his successor, F.H. *Torrington. Nearly as important was Edward *Fisher's Toronto Choral Society (1879–91). Many other societies were formed, dissolved, and re-formed in the last quarter of the century. Some of them used the same names as their predecessors, and their activities ranged from serious musical performance to popular quasi-educational meetings for those interested in learning to read music and to sing.

Among the choir directors were Humfrey *Anger, Arthur E. *Fisher, John W.E. *Harrison, Elliott *Haslam, J.D.A. *Tripp, and A.S. *Vogt. Their societies presented Toronto with a widely varied vocal repertoire, from solo songs and glees to the choral masterpieces of Gounod, Handel, Haydn, Mendelssohn, and Schumann. Cantatas and oratorios won a much warmer reception in the city than did operas. Since orchestras had to be assembled for oratorio and other major presentations, programs also would include overtures or even symphonies and concertos.

All attempts at forming regular orchestras failed, however. Strathy had tried it in 1867, Torrington in 1877. The latter was able to assemble 100 instrumentalists for the festival of 1886, the largest enterprise of the Toronto Philharmonic Society. But although he established an Orchestral School at his *Toronto College of Music, Torrington had to rely once again on an ad hoc ensemble for the festival of 1894 which marked the opening of Massey Music Hall (later known as *Massey Hall, and Canada's most famous concert auditorium). A Toronto SO formed by Francesco *D'Auria in 1891 was short-lived, as was the Toronto Permanent Orchestra, optimisitically inaugurated by Torrington in 1900.

Toronto had to wait several more years for its first enduring orchestra, the *Toronto SO, formed by Frank *Welsman in 1908 on the basis of the Toronto Conservatory Orchestra he had established two years earlier. Welsman's orchestra introduced to Torontonians the classical symphonies and works by Debussy, Sibelius, Tchaikovsky, Richard Strauss, and Wagner and accompanied Elman, Carreño, Kreisler, Rachmaninoff, Schumann-Heink, and other celebrities. Personnel shortages forced its eclipse before the end of World War I.

At the beginning of the 20th century Toronto justifiably was known as 'the choral capital of North America.' This fame was based on several new concert choirs and a multitude of fine church choirs. Albert *Ham led the *National Chorus (1903–28), Edward *Broome the *Toronto Oratorio Society (1910–12 and 1914–25) and Herbert M. Fletcher two 'graded' choirs formed in 1904, the People's Choral Union for beginners and the Toronto Choral Union (later renamed Schubert Choir) for advanced choristers, which were active until the war. There was even a Young Socialist Choir (1914–17). But the most important and long-lived group proved to be the *Toronto Mendelssohn Choir. Established in 1894 by A.S. Vogt to perform unaccompanied works, the choir was disbanded in 1897 and reorganized in 1900 on a larger scale. After 1904 the choir made frequent visits to the USA, while US orchestras joined it (and some of the other large choirs) in concerts and oratorio presentations.

Possibly the first string quartet in Toronto was one formed by the violinist Ferdinand *Griebel ca 1853. It is reported that all the Mozart and Beethoven piano trios and quartets were played in the early 1870s, but the performances may have been private. An increase in chamber music concerts during the 1880s resulted directly from the expansion of musical education in this decade. The musicians who came together as teachers at the newly established conservatories formed such ensembles as the *Toronto String Quartet(te) (1884), the Conservatory String Quartette (1901), the Brahms Trio (ca 1909), the *Hambourg Trio (1912), the *Academy String Quartet (ca 1912), the Schumann Trio, and the Toronto Ladies' Trio. Prominent chamber music players included John *Bayley, Frank *Blachford, Bertha *Drechsler Adamson, A.E. Fisher, the *Hambourg brothers, Heinrich *Klingenfeld, Luigi von *Kunits, Carl *Martens, Leo *Smith, Richard *Tattersall, and Frank Welsman. Many chamber music recitals took place under the auspices of the *Women's Musical Club, founded in 1897.

During the greater part of the 19th century specialized music teaching was exclusively in the hands of individual musicians. In addition to their private teaching many also held part-time posts in private schools. After 1844, when Egerton Ryerson became chief superintendent of education in Upper Canada, vocal music gained an important place in the public elementary school curriculum. The Toronto Normal School, opened in 1847, appointed a music instructor the following year. The leading school music educators during the following decades were H.F. *Sefton and A.T. *Cringan.

THE EXHIBITION SONG CRAZE
TAKE ME TO TORONTO FAIR
BY
GORDON V. THOMPSON.

An early 20th-century publication

The rise of a prosperous middle class made possible the establishment of conservatories. The Canadian Cons (fl 1876) may have been the first; an equally short-lived music school under the direction of J. Davenport *Kerrison followed at the end of the 1870s. The Toronto Cons of Music, founded in 1886 by Edward Fisher, continued to flourish in 1980 as the *Royal Cons of Music of Toronto. Others schools included the *Toronto College of Music, founded in 1888 by F.H. Torrington; W.O. *Forsyth's Metropolitan School of Music, founded in 1893 and absorbed in 1912 by the *Canadian Academy of Music (founded in 1911 and financed by Albert *Gooderham); and the *Hambourg Cons of Music, founded in 1911.

Although both the *U of Toronto (King's College until 1850) and the *U of Trinity College conferred B MUS degrees early in their histories (respectively on J.P. Clarke 1846 and G.W. Strathy 1853), they set up examination systems only in the 1880s (Trinity) and 1890s (Toronto), without, however, offering regular instruction. Instead, the preparation of candidates was left to certain affiliated conservatories.

The foundations laid in the 1840s by such pioneer piano builders as J. and J. *Mead, O'Neill Brothers, and J.M. *Thomas, and by the music dealer-publishers A.&S. *Nordheimer, paved the way for Toronto's national supremacy in instrument building and music publishing. Probably the first keyboard instrument manufactured in York was the 'fine-toned and handsomely ornamented Chamber Organ' offered for sale in 1825 by Richard *Coates. In the second half of the 19th century *Gourlay, Winter & Leeming; *Heintzman; Gerhard *Heintzman; *Mason & Risch; *Newcombe; and Nordheimer were among prominent piano builders. Edward H. *Lye, S.R. *Warren & Son, and R.S. *Williams were major pipe and reed organ makers. In 1913 the *Canadian Courier* claimed that 'Toronto alone produces more pianos than New York, Chicago or Philadelphia.' Of the many retail music dealers who imported and published music, *Anglo-Canadian Music Co, Nordheimer, *Suckling & Sons, and *Whaley Royce were by far the most productive.

Among the journalists and critics who contributed to the discussion of music were Augustus *Bridle, Hector *Charlesworth, Edwin *Parkhurst, and Edward *Schuch. The first Canadian music periodicals in English were published in Toronto, among them George F. *Graham's *Canadian Musical Review* (1856), *Musical Galaxy* (fl 1875), and the *Musical Journal* (1887–90?). Much longer runs were achieved by the *Canadian Music Trades Journal* (1900–33) and **Musical Canada*, begun in 1906 as *The Violin* and continuing until 1933.

2 1918–45. In the next period of Toronto's history the rise in popularity of the gramophone and radio, the hardships of the Depression, and the increased ethnic diversity of the population changed the emphases of musical culture. On the one hand music became a more passive amusement, and, on the other hand, new standards of professional accomplishment were introduced. Unfortunately, World War II interrupted or terminated many worthwhile activities.

During the 1920s the accompaniment of silent films, of vaudeville, and of other theatrical entertainment provided a measure of employment for orchestral musicians. Examples were the extravaganzas produced by Jack *Arthur at Shea's Theatre after 1918. In the 1930s talking movies made the movie house orchestras obsolete, but Toronto became the centre of English-language radio broadcasting, supplying musicians with new opportunities. As early as 1922 the *Romanelli Orchestra had participated in a broadcast, the first by an orchestra in Canada. Luigi von Kunits, who founded the New SO in 1923 (the *TSO after 1927), recognized the potential of broadcasting. In 1929 he and members of the TSO inaugurated North America's first transcontinental radio series. Von Kunits' successor, Ernest *MacMillan, expanded the length and number of annual concerts and, during his 1931–56 tenure, developed the orchestra into a first-rate ensemble. Other orchestras in the inter-war years included the Toronto Conservatory SO under Donald *Heins and later Ettore *Mazzoleni, the U of Toronto SO founded by John *Weinzweig, and the *Promenade Symphony Concerts under Reginald *Stewart.

In both symphonic and choral music, Stewart and MacMillan were rivals during the 1930s. In addition to leading the TSO, MacMillan gave annual performances of Bach's *St Matthew Passion* with the TCM Choir. Stewart and his *Toronto Bach Choir presented the *St John Passion* annually 1933–41. Although no longer so predominantly devoted to choral music, Toronto still produced many new choral groups. These included the Orpheus Society, founded in 1920 by Dalton *Baker; the Coliseum Chorus (later the *Canadian National Exhibition Chorus), under H.A. *Fricker 1922–34; the *Hart House Songsters and Canadian Singers founded 1924 by Campbell *McInnes; the *Hart House Glee Club (1933–72); the *Bishop Strachan School Chapel Choir (founded 1925); the Freiheit Gezangs Farein, founded in 1925 and succeeded in 1934 by the *Toronto Jewish Folk Choir; Healey *Willan's Tudor Singers (1933–40) and *St Mary Magdalene Singers (founded 1939); the *Toronto Men Teachers' Choir (1941–76); and the Harvey Perrin Choir (1944–56). The Toronto Mendelssohn Choir, under H.A. Fricker 1917–42, continued to be the centre of musical life.

Between the two world wars, visits to Toronto by the San Carlo Opera Co and the Metropolitan Opera touring company were frequent. Efforts to found a permanent local opera company were persistent, but futile. Several amateur groups specializing in Gilbert & Sullivan did achieve a measure of continuity, however. Among these were the *Savoyards, founded in 1919 by George and Reginald Stewart; the *Eaton Operatic Society (1931–65); the *Canada Packers Operatic Society (1942–55); and the Toronto Light Opera Society, founded in 1943 by Howard and Frederick *Mawson. The TCM's Conservatory Opera Company, begun by MacMillan during the late 1920s, failed during the Depression. Beginning in 1936, Harrison Gilmour's Opera Guild of Toronto and Braheen Urbane's Canadian Grand Opera Assn competed for audiences and funds. These companies brought to the stages of the *Royal Alexandra, Massey Hall, and *Maple Leaf Gardens several operas, including *Aida, Faust, Cavalleria Rusticana, I Pagliacci, Tosca, Rigoletto, Tannhäuser,* and *Lohengrin*. Although Urbane's company was short-lived, Gilmour's continued to produce operas sporadically even after the outbreak of World War II. During the 1940s the *Rosselino Opera Co sought to provide young performers with experience.

Less hindered by financial vicissitudes than opera and better able to capitalize on the opportunities provided by broadcasting, chamber music was relatively active. The *Hart House String Quartet (1923–45) became Canada's most famous chamber ensemble of the day and one of the few to tour abroad then. Other chamber groups included the Five Piano Ensemble, formed in 1926 by Norah *de Kresz, Alberto *Guerrero, Viggo *Kihl, Ernest *Seitz, and Reginald Stewart; the Conservatory Trio (1926); the revived *Conservatory String Quartet (1929); the Ten-Piano Ensemble, organized in 1931 by Mona *Bates; the Toronto Chamber Music Society, founded in 1931 by A.D. *Jordan; the New World Chamber Orchestra, founded and conducted 1932–40 by Samuel *Hersenhoren; the Canadian Trio, formed in 1941 by Kathleen *Parlow, Zara *Nelsova, and Sir Ernest MacMillan; and the *Parlow String Quartet (1941–58).

Many of the musicians just named were among the foremost teachers of the period. For the institutions at which they taught, the 1920s and 1930s were years of consolidation and retrenchment after the earlier growth spurt. The Canadian Academy of Music and the Toronto College of Music, amalgamated in 1918, were absorbed in 1924 into the TCM, which in 1921 had been placed under the jurisdiction of the board of governors of the U of Toronto. A Faculty of Music, set up in the university in 1918 as an entity separate from the TCM, in fact maintained intimate links with it, so that from 1918 to 1942 the dean of the faculty and the principal of the TCM were the same person, first A.S. Vogt and later Ernest MacMillan. The latter, through the combination of these and other positions, occupied a position of influence and prestige in his city unique in the musical history of Canada.

School music owed much to the efforts of A.T. Cringan, Eldon Brethour, P. George Marshall, Duncan McKenzie, and other supervisors and teachers.

Toronto music critics and journalists of the period 1918–45 included Augustus Bridle at the *Toronto Daily Star*, Lawrence *Mason at the *Globe*, and Hector Charlesworth at *Saturday Night*. Bridle had been instrumental as well, in 1908, in creating the *Arts and Letters Club, which counted among its members many of Toronto's prominent musicians. A variety of other organizations came into being in this period. The *Canadian Bureau for the Advancement of Music, founded in 1917, and the Canadian Performing Rights Society (1925–45; *CAPAC thereafter) were national in scope; the *Ontario Music Educators' Assn, founded in 1919, and the *Ontario Registered Music Teachers' Assn, founded in 1936, were of provincial significance; while the *Vogt Society, founded in 1936, was of local importance.

New music publishing firms established in Toronto included *Canadian Music Sales and Gordon V. *Thompson. *Boosey & Hawkes of London opened a Toronto branch, and the Toronto office of *Oxford University Press created a music department.

The number of piano manufacturers declined, but in 1919 Franklin *Legge opened a new organ factory, and Toronto became a centre of the recording industry. Recording companies which had offices or Canadian headquarters in Toronto included *Columbia Records and *Brunswick. Among violin makers and repairers in Toronto, the most prominent have been George *Kindness 1911–60s and George *Heinl, who opened in 1912 an establishement that continued to do business in 1980.

At the *Canadian National Exhibition (opened as the Industrial Exhibition in 1879 and renamed CNE in 1904) military bands had long been a main attraction. A.L. Robertson helped to organize a band competition in 1921 and continued to administer it for nearly 40 years. Toronto bands of this period included those of the Queen's Own Rifles, the Toronto Regiment (conducted 1926–58 by the musicians' union official Walter *Murdoch), and the *Royal Regiment of Canada. Richard *Hayward founded the Toronto Police Band in 1926 and led the Toronto Concert Band 1925–39. L.F. *Addison formed the *Toronto Symphony Band in 1935 and John *Slatter led the *48th Highlanders Band 1896–1946. Bands made up a large proportion of the ensembles competing in the *Kiwanis Music Festival, the first of which was held in 1944 at *Eaton Auditorium.

3 1945–80. The post-war period saw an enrichment of musical life in Toronto commensurate with the notable growth of the city's population and wealth. Toronto benefited greatly from the increased post-war government financing of the arts, education, and broadcasting. It became as well a centre for rock and jazz, with excellent broadcasting and recording facilities. Groups such as the *Boss Brass, the *Crew-Cuts, the *Diamonds, the *Downchild Blues Band, *Kensington Market, and *Sugar Shoppe have been established in Toronto (see also Rock; Jazz). In addition, the significant wave of new immigration added a great variety of professional skills and popular traditions to the fabric.

After World War II the city's most distinguished performing groups, the Toronto Mendelssohn Choir and the TSO, continued to appear at Massey Hall, *Ontario Place Forum (opened 1971), and elsewhere. In 1956, after his 25th season as conductor of the TSO, Sir Ernest MacMillan resigned. Subsequent conductors of the TSO (TS after 1967) were Walter *Susskind 1956–65, Seiji Ozawa 1965–9, Karel Ančerl 1969–73, Victor *Feldbrill as resident during two seasons of guest conductors 1973–5, and Andrew Davis, who succeeded Ančerl in 1975. The other two major symphonic organizations were the *CBC SO (1952–64), a full-scale broadcasting orchestra which specialized in contemporary music, and Heinz *Unger's York Concert Society (1952–65), which pioneered in the Canadian performance of Mahler.

Among smaller post-war orchestral groups have been the Toronto Women's Orchestra founded in 1948 by Harold *Sumberg, the *Hart House Orchestra (1954–71) founded by Boyd *Neel, and the *CJRT Orchestra, founded in 1975 and conducted by Paul *Robinson. Community orchestras such as the Harmony SO (founded by Arthur *Semple ca 1919), the East York and North York SOs, the Etobicoke Philharmonic, and the Mississauga SO also have added to Toronto-area concert life. (See Orchestras.)

Toronto has sustained its excellent reputation as a choral centre. Elmer *Iseler and the *Festival Singers (1954–79) set a new standard for choral singing in Toronto and Canada. Under Iseler's direction both that choir and the Toronto Mendelssohn Choir enjoyed international recognition. Other choral groups have included the *Leslie Bell Singers, the *Don Wright Chorus (1957–62), Roman *Toi's Estonian Mixed Choir (1957–72), and the *Orpheus Choir, founded in 1964 by John *Sidgwick. Ethnic, school, and church choirs too numerous to name have carried on Toronto's amateur choral tradition.

Chamber music received a boost after the war when the Women's Musical Club resumed its concert series (1946) and Walter *Homburger, through his International Artists Concert Agency, began to present recitalists of world renown. Many new chamber ensembles were formed, among them the Sumberg-Ysselstyn-Guerrero Trio (late 1940s), the *Solway String Quartet (1947–early 1970s), the Marcus *Adeney String Quartet (fl 1950s), the *Dembeck String Quartet (1950–61), the *Spivak String Quartet (1951–6), the *Pack Trio (formed 1955), the Galant Chamber Music Players (founded 1956 by Berul *Sugarman), the Jack *Groob Trio (formed 1956), the *Toronto Woodwind Quintet (founded 1959), the *Canadian String Quartet (1961–3), William *Kuinka's Mandolin Chamber Ensemble (1964–9), the *Orford String Quartet (formed 1965, and by 1980 regarded as the country's foremost quartet), the *Chamber Players of Toronto (founded 1968), the *Brodie Saxophone Quartet (founded 1972), the *York Winds (founded 1972), *Camerata (founded 1972 by Elyakim *Taussig), the Ararat Trio (1973–6; Gerard *Kantarjian, Gisela *Depkat, and Raffi *Armenian), Peggie *Sampson's Quatre en Concert (formed 1978), the U of Toronto Faculty Trio (formed 1974 by Lorand *Fenyves, Vladimir *Orloff, and Patricia *Parr), the Gadar Trio (formed 1976 by Kantarjian, Rivka Golani-Erdész, viola, and David Miller, cello), and *Canadian Brass (which moved in 1976 from Hamilton to Toronto).

Of pianists who lived in Toronto during the period 1950–80, Glenn *Gould, Anton *Kuerti, and Oscar *Peterson achieved the greatest recognition nationally and internationally. Of singers who lived there during the same period, Maureen *Forrester, Lois *Marshall, and Louis *Quilico enjoyed world fame. Other noted residents included the pianist Antonin *Kubálek, the clarinetist James *Campbell, the singers Mary *Morrison and Patricia *Rideout, the harpsichordist Greta *Kraus, the teacher Boris *Berlin, the pianist-accompanists Leo *Barkin and George *Brough, and the pop singers Gordon *Lightfoot and Anne *Murray.

Among post-war endeavours in musical theatre have been the *CBC Opera Co (1948–55), **Spring Thaw* (1948–71 and 1980), *Melody Fair (1951–4), Giuseppe *Macina's Toronto Opera Repertoire (founded 1968), Opera in Concert (founded 1974 by Stuart *Hamilton), Co-Opera Theatre (formed 1975 by Raymond *Pannell), and Comus Music Theatre (formed 1975 with Michael Bawtree, Maureen Forrester, Gabriel *Charpentier, and Douglas Annett as directors).

The expanding concert life of the city was served by several new halls, including MacMillan Theatre and Walter Hall at the Edward Johnson Building, U of Toronto, and Town Hall at the *St

Toronto's new concert hall under construction, 1980

Lawrence Centre. A new Massey Hall was scheduled to open in 1982.

In the late 1940s Herman *Geiger-Torel, Nicholas *Goldschmidt, Ettore Mazzoleni, and Arnold *Walter began to work to establish the permanent opera company which had eluded all previous pioneers. Like the TSO, the *Canadian Opera Company had its roots in the RCMT. The *Royal Cons Opera School, established in 1946, has produced singers who have helped ensure the permanence not only of the COC but of other Toronto groups and companies all over Canada. The *Canadian Children's Opera Chorus, founded in 1968, has participated in many COC and Toronto area productions.

Education in all fields of music was reorganized and improved after World War II. New programs in school music, which significantly increased the numbers of teachers, students, and aspiring performing artists, were created by C. Laughton *Bird, Keith *Bissell, Jack *Dow, and Harvey *Perrin at the elementary and secondary levels and by Robert *Rosevear at the post-secondary level. To satisfy the growing interest in the accordion, guitar, saxophone, and recorder, Eric *Mundinger, Eli *Kassner, Paul Brodie, and Hugh *Orr established private schools or studios, and Joseph *Macerollo pioneered free-bass accordion classes at the the RCMT.

The RCMT and U of Toronto Faculty of Music moved to larger quarters, and in 1968 a new music department was organized at *York U. Those responsible for these schools have included Ettore Mazzoleni, Arnold Walter, Boyd Neel, John *Beckwith, Gustav *Ciamaga, David *Ouchterlony, Ezra *Schabas, and, at York, Sterling *Beckwith and Alan Lessem. Community colleges such as George Brown, Humber, and Seneca also have offered study programs and special events. The librarians Jean Lavender, Kathleen McMorrow, Ogreta *McNeil, and Isabel Rose and the sound archivist and discographer James *Creighton built up for Toronto the foremost musical research and listening facilities in Canada.

For school choirs and instrumental ensembles, and for student singers and instrumentalists of all grades, the Kiwanis Festival continued in 1980 to provide opportunities to evaluate their achievements through competition, as did the annual competitions held during the CNE. The *National Competitive Festival of Music, established in 1972 at the CNE, gave top winners from Kiwanis and other competition festivals across Canada a chance to compete for higher honours.

Sophisticated audiences have supported a number of performing groups devoted to music of the avant-garde – among them, *ARRAY, the *Artists' Jazz Band, the *Lyric Arts Trio, and *Nexus – and the series *Ten Centuries Concerts, the Isaacs Gallery Concerts (and others of Udo *Kasemets), and *New Music Concerts. The city has enjoyed numerous concert festivals devoted to the works of individual composers (eg, Bach, Beethoven, Brahms, Mendelssohn, Messiaen, Mozart, and Schubert), although by 1980 a continuing annual concert festival had not been established, despite numerous attmpts. However, long-lasting performance festivals in other areas have included the May (or Spring) Festival Concerts at Massey Hall, established in 1886 for choirs and performing groups from the city's public schools; the festivals of ethnic groups such as the Latvians, the Chinese, and the West Indians (Caribana); the annual multi-national celebrations of *Caravan, established in 1969; and the *Mariposa Folk Festival.

At the hub of musical activity in all genres – classical, avant-garde, church, pop, jazz, commercial, etc – in English-speaking Canada, Toronto has become a headquarters for many arts organizations, sometimes to the chagrin of other cities and regions of the country which have resented and criticized what they feel is an excessive concentration. In 1980 Toronto was the location of the national offices of *ACO, CAPAC, the *CLComp and *CMCentre, the *CMPA, the *Canadian Academy of Recording Arts and Sciences, the Canadian Bureau for the Advancement of Music, the *NYO, and *PRO Canada and for years was the seat of the *CMCouncil and the *CCA. It became the headquarters for several provincial organizations as well, including the *OAC, *OFSO, the *Ontario Choral Federation, and *Prologue to the Performing Arts.

Composers resident in Toronto after World War II have included Lucio *Agostini, Robert *Aitken, Louis *Applebaum, John Beckwith, Norma *Beecroft, Keith Bissell, Walter *Buczynski, Gustav Ciamaga, Michael *Colgrass, Gordon *Delamont, Samuel *Dolin, John *Fodi, Harry *Freedman, Srul I. *Glick, John *Hawkins, Udo Kasemets, Talivaldis *Kenins, Lothar *Klein, Edward *Laufer, William *McCauley, Ben *McPeek, John *Mills-Cockell, Oskar *Morawetz, Phil *Nimmons, Raymond Pannell, Tibor *Polgar, Godfrey *Ridout, Harry *Somers, Ann *Southam, Morris *Surdin, Norman Symonds, John Weinzweig, and Healey Willan. Among them, Applebaum, Bissell, Buczynski, Glick, Mills-Cockell, Ridout, Somers, Surdin, and Weinzweig were born in Toronto.

The many facets of the city's musical life have been assessed by such critics as Jack Batten, John Beckwith, Leslie *Bell, Udo Kasemets, John *Kraglund, William *Littler, and Kenneth *Winters.

In music publishing Toronto flourished, although most of the activity was in the distribution of foreign imports. But the newly established branches of such foreign firms as *Chappell & Co, *Leeds Music, and G. *Ricordi & Co did their share of Canadian publishing. New publishers were *Berandol Music, *Jarman Publications, and E.C. *Kerby. Berandol was preceded by BMI Canada (PRO Canada), which, though primarily a performing rights organization, in the years 1947–65 built the largest catalogue of Canadian serious music in print.

Many phonograph and recording companies which flourished during the 20th century had offices in Toronto. In addition to the aforementioned Columbia and Brunswick, these companies have included *Quality Records (1950), *Beaver (1950), *Hallmark (1952), *Capitol (1954), *Rococo (mid-1950s), Cantilena (1966), *Nimbus 9 (1968), *GRT (1969), *True North (1970), *Boot (1971), and Aquitaine (1975, see Eleanor Sniderman). By the 1970s Toronto had become a recording studio centre of international importance.

4 TORONTO-BORN MUSICIANS. In addition to a number mentioned above, musicians born in Toronto, many of whom have individual entries in *EMC* or are listed in the index, include John and Murray Adaskin, Christopher Allworth, Tommy Ambrose, Terence Bailey, Gerald Bales, Brian Barley, Milton Barnes, Ewart Bartley, Stuart Broomer, Edmund Burke, Allan Burt, Howard Cable, Elizabeth Campbell, Tommy Common, John Coveart, Bertha Crawford, Paul Crawford, Alan Crofoot, George Crum, Bruce Davis, Gordon Day, Alan Detweiler, Victor Di Bello, John Dodington, Robert Donnell, Wray Downes, Margaret Drynan, Gil Evans, Percy Faith, Robert and Dennis Farnon, Victor Feldbrill, Clifford Ford, James Gayfer, Steven Gellman, Hyman and Erica Goodman, Evelyn Gould, Teresa Gray, Marian Grudeff, Susie Frances Harrison, Samuel Hersenhorne, Dan Hill, Eugene Hill, John Hodgins, Margaret Huston, Daryl Irvine, Harold Jarvis, Cliff Jones, Eugene Kash, Mart Kenney, Nicholas Kilburn, Michael Kilburn, Paul Kilburn, Warren Kirkendale, Moe Koffman, Ida Krehm, Beatrice Lillie, Ruth Lowe, Russ Little, Murray McEachern, Ellis McLintock, Rika Maniates, David Martin, Bruce Mather, Howard and Elizabeth Mawson, Ed Moogk, Mavor Moore, Carl Morey, Anne Marie Moss, Earl Moss, Warren Mould, Alfie Noakes, Albert and Gerald Nordheimer, Hugh Orr, Joseph Pach, Patricia Parr, Alex Pauk, Kenneth Peacock, John Perrone, Albert Pratz, Percival Price, George Proctor, Dodie Protero, John Rea, Robert Reid, Jack Richardson, Leland Richardson, Doug Riley, Catherine Robbin, Jamie Robbie Robertson, Teddy Roderman, Ivan Romanoff, Dorothy Sandler Glick, Paul Scherman, Suzanne Shulman, Barbara Shuttleworth, Gordon Slater, Lou Snider, Michael Snow, Stanley Solomon, Douglas Stanbury, Steven Staryk, Albert Steinberg, Fred Stone, Teresa Stratas, Joyce Sullivan, Carl Tapscott, Earle Terry, Graham Townsend, Malcolm Troup, Riki Turofsky, Denny Vaughan, Ruth Watson Henderson, Kenny Wheeler, and Charles Wilson.

GENERAL BIBLIOGRAPHY

'Music in Toronto: reminiscences of the last half century,' Toronto *Mail*, 21 Dec 1878

'The Toronto music festival,' *MT*, 1 Aug 1886

Taylor, Conyngham Crawford. *Toronto 'Called Back' from 1877 to 1886* (Toronto 1886)

Harrison, Susie Frances. 'Choirs and choir singing in Toronto,' *Dominion Illustrated Monthly*, vol 1, pp 748–52, 1888

Adam, G. Mercer. *Toronto, Old and New* (Toronto 1891)

Dixon, F.E. 'Music in Toronto, as it was in the days that are gone forever,' Toronto *Daily Mail and Empire*, 7 Nov 1896

Godfrey, H.H., ed. *A Souvenir of Musical Toronto* (Toronto 1897)

Tasker, William Frederick. 'Music in Toronto,' *The Westminster*, vol 14, Jan 1909

MacMillan, Ernest. 'The musical season in Toronto,' *Canadian Forum*, vol 8, May 1928

Hobday, Kathleen M. 'A survey of the musical resources of the province of Ontario,' unpubl paper, Toronto College of Education 1946

Beckwith, John. 'Composers in Toronto and Montreal,' *U of Toronto Q*, vol 26, Oct 1956

Firth, Edith G. *The Town of York*, vol 1, 1793–1815 (Toronto 1962); vol 2, 1815–34 (Toronto 1966)

Schafer, R. Murray. 'Music...the four seasons 1961–62 in Toronto,' *Canadian Art*, vol 19, Jul – Aug 1962

Morey, Carl. 'Pre-Confederation opera in Toronto,' *OpCan*, Sep 1969

– 'Canada's first operatic ensemble,' ibid, Sep 1970

Locke, William R. 'Ontario church choirs and choral societies, 1819–1918,' unpubl DMA thesis, U of Southern California 1972

Kallmann *History of Music in Canada*

'Toronto's Pre-Confederation Music Societies 1845–1867'

HK, CM, (NM, PW, PMW)

Toronto Bach Choir. Formed in 1933; the performing ensemble of the Bach Society of Toronto. Reginald *Stewart was its sole conductor (1933–41). In the program for the first concert, 27 Apr 1933 at Yorkminster Park Baptist Church, the president of the organization, Victor Ross, apparently overlooking the contributions of Ernest *MacMillan and H.A. *Fricker, wrote: 'The need has long been felt by many music lovers of Toronto for an organization which would devote itself to the popularization of the inspiring music of Johann Sebastian Bach...The objects of the society will be to memorialize and popularize the works...by means of lectures and performances of his choral and instrumental compositions, including the performance annually by the Bach Choir of at least one major choral work.' It was proposed to present a program of cantatas each December and the *St John Passion* every spring. Performances were given at Yorkminster Church, Convocation Hall (*U of Toronto), or *Eaton Auditorium. The choir numbered about 150 voices and was assisted by a 45-member orchestra, of which Elie *Spivak was concertmaster. Among the accompanists were Helen Cherrie, D'Alton *McLaughlin, Frederick *Silvester, and Healey *Willan. Soloists included Norman Cherrie, Hubert Eisdell, Irving Levine, Eileen *Law, Frank Oldfield, and Jeanne *Pengelly. Lawrence *Mason described a presentation of the *St John Passion* as a 'splendid addition to the city's major annual fixtures' and added that 'Reginald Stewart is adding more dramatic touches to the straightforward simplicity of his readings in recent years' (Toronto *Globe and Mail*, 17 Apr 1939). With the *Promenade Symphony, the choir gave the premiere 3 Jun 1937 of Willan's *Te Deum laudamus in B Flat* B53.

DS

Toronto College of Music. One of three music schools to open in the city during the 1880s – the others being the TCM (*RCMT) and the *Metropolitan School of Music. The college was founded in 1888 by F.H. *Torrington and by 1890 had 400 students and a faculty of about 50. That same year it became affiliated with the *U of Toronto. It granted certificates, medals, diplomas, and, in conjunction with the university, B MUS and D MUS degrees. In addition to courses it provided practical experience in orchestral playing and organ, and the Pembroke Street building housed a concert hall with a three-manual pipe organ. Among the faculty members, of whom some also taught at other Toronto schools, were Bertha *Drechsler Adamson, G.D. *Atkinson, Herbert L. *Clarke, A.T. *Cringan, W.E. *Fairclough, H.M. *Field, W.O. *Forsyth, W. Elliott *Haslam, T.C. Jeffers, Leonora Kennedy, Heinrich *Klingenfeld, Clarence *Lucas, Arthur E. *Semple, and A.S. *Vogt. Among musicians who attended the school were Bessie *Bonsall, Florence *Brimson, Ernest *Dainty, A.D. *Jordan, and Fannie Sullivan. After Torrington's death the college amalgamated (1918) with the *Canadian Academy of Music, which was absorbed in turn (1924) by the TCM. An earlier Toronto College of Music, founded in 1879 by J. Davenport *Kerrison, lasted about four years. (CF)

Toronto Conservatory of Music. See Royal Conservatory of Music, Toronto.

Toronto Consort. Formed in Toronto in 1972 to perform early vocal and instrumental music. Its original members were the tenor Frank Nakashima, the counter-tenor Garry Crighton, the tenor David Walker, the baritone David Klausner, and the bass Timothy McGee, who was its director un-

Toronto College of Music

til 1978. Nakashima was replaced in 1974 by Katharine Pimenoff, and Pimenoff by Penelope Tibbles, who appeared with the group 1976–7. Alison Mackay replaced Walker 1975–6 and joined the group in 1978. The sopranos Jean Edwards and Emily van Evera joined in 1977. The tenor David Fallis replaced Walker in 1978. In 1980 the membership consisted of Crighton, Edwards, Klausner, Mackay, and Fallis.

The group's repertoire covers the medieval and renaissance periods and ranges from liturgical works to bawdy popular songs. Frequently the music performed has been transcribed by consort members directly from manuscript material. Programs have been planned around the works of individual composers or groups ('The Music of Guillaume Dufay,' 'Music by Orlando Lasso and his Contemporaries'); places and periods ('France and Italy in the 14th Century,' 'A Century of German Song'), rulers ('Long Live Fair Oriana!,' 'Music for Lorenzo the Magnificent'), and other themes.

Many of the consort's working collection of more than 100 accurate replicas of historical instruments were made by members of the group. Among these are bagpipes, bandora, cittern, cornetto, crwth, dulcian, flute, gemshorn, harpsichord, lute, organetto, orphorium, psaltery, rackett, rauschpfeife, rebec, recorder, regal, shawm, vielle, and viol. It has become customary for the members to explain texts, music, and instruments prior to the performances.

The consort has performed throughout Ontario, at St Paul's Church in New York City, and at the Folger Library in Washington, DC. In 1977 it toured Nova Scotia, and in 1978 it was invited to perform for the visiting archbishop of Canterbury on Baffin Island, NWT. In 1980 it performed in Regina, Calgary, and Vancouver and toured in Austria, Sweden, England, and West Germany (giving there, in Hanover, the European premiere of Lothar *Klein's *Musica Antiqua*, which it had premiered with the *TS in 1976). In Toronto the consort has performed mainly at the U of Toronto's Walter Hall and at St Andrew's Presbyterian Church. It has performed also on CBC radio and TV.

In 1974 its members became the nucleus of the annual summer Early Music Workshop at the U of Toronto's Scarborough College. *Buczynski's *Consortium* for four players (1975), Klein's *Musica Antiqua*, and Ben *McPeek's *My Lute and I* (1978) were written for the consort.

DISCOGRAPHY

Music for Early Instruments. 1974. CBC SM-229

To Syngen and to Pleye. 1976. Ber 9020 (ML, NM)

Toronto Jewish Folk Choir. Organized in 1934, a successor to the Freiheit Gezangs Farein (Freedom Singing Society). The earlier choir, founded in 1925 by a group of immigrant factory workers, began annual spring concerts in 1926 under Hyman Riegelhaupt. (The Young Socialist Choir, fl 1914–17, may be regarded as the precursor of both organizations.) Riegelhaupt conducted the new choir for two years and was succeeded by Henry Dobkowski. The composer Jacob Schaefer was a guest conductor in 1928, 1935, and 1936. Emil Gartner (b Vienna 1913, d Toronto 1960) succeeded Dobkowski in 1939. At that time the choir's repertoire consisted mainly of Yiddish and Hebrew folk songs and operettas which reflected the struggles and aspirations of the Jewish community in general and the working class in particular. As the choir under Gartner became more accomplished and increased in size (130 voices by the late 1940s) its repertoire expanded to include Canadian folk songs; large 18th- or 19th-century works by Handel (1942, *Judas Maccabaeus*; 1952, *Joshua*), Mendelssohn (1945, *Elijah* excerpts), and Schubert (1948, *Song of Miriam*); and 20th-century works by Jacob Schaefer (1945, *Tzvei Brider*; 1946, *Biro Bidjan*), Benjamin Britten (1949, *Ballad of Heroes*), Max Helfman (1949, *Di Naye Haggadah: The Glory of the Warsaw Ghetto*), and the Soviet composers Yuri Shaporin (1944, *Birth of Russia*) and Dmitri Shostakovich (1951, 1953, *Song of the Forests*).

The choir also commissioned works from Bernard Rogers (*A Letter from Pete*, premiered 7 Apr 1948) and John *Weinzweig (*To the Lands Over Yonder*, premiered 28 Jan 1950). During Gartner's tenure the choir presented such guest performers as Igor Gorin, Charles *Jordan, Alexander Kipnis, Lois *Marshall, Jan Peerce, Regina Resnik, Paul Robeson, and Jennie Tourel. Fagel Freeman Gartner, the director's wife, was the choir's accompanist. The *TSO often assisted the choir, and on one occasion the two organizations, with Daniel Duno and Mary *Simmons as soloists, gave a joint concert, after which the critic for the *Globe and Mail* (26 Mar 1947) described the choir as 'well balanced and artistically responsive...with an excellently blended choral tone.' Even then, at the height of its fame, the choir retained its working-class character and most of its members still learned their parts by ear.

After Gartner's death in an automobile accident the Toronto Jewish Folk Choir continued on a more modest scale, under Douglas Webb and Esther Cronenberg in the 1960s, Searle Freedman 1971–5, and Melvyn Isen 1975–8, succeeded by Bill *Phillips. JBk

The Toronto Mendelssohn Choir. Canada's famous and oldest-surviving mixed-voice amateur choir, begun 1894 by Augustus Stephen *Vogt as the Mendelssohn choir of Toronto, a group of 75 voices founded on Vogt's Jarvis St Baptist Church choir. Succeeding the *Toronto Philharmonic Society, which had ceased operations in 1894, the new choir, already grown during the first months of rehearsal to 167 voices, gave its first concert 15 Jan 1895 in the new Massey Music Hall (*Massey Hall). The repertoire, for the three years under its original name, was largely unaccompanied (for reasons, probably, of both choral discipline and fiscal prudence) and, apart from single short pieces by di Lassus, Gounod, and Chaminade, contained no music by any internationally known composer except the choir's namesake, Mendelssohn, five of whose pieces were performed.

Despite the choir's success with critics and public Vogt disbanded it in 1897, only to revive it 19 Sep 1900, after three years of canny long-term planning, under a constitution requiring the an-

The Toronto Mendelssohn Choir under Walter Susskind in a concert performance of *Aida* at Massey Hall, 1961

nual re-audition of members. The reconstituted Toronto Mendelssohn Choir made its debut 16 Feb 1901, again at Massey Music Hall. Vogt's wishes to venture beyond the repertoire for unaccompanied choir led to associations 1902–7 with the Pittsburgh SO conducted by Victor Herbert and 1908–12 with the Theodore Thomas (Chicago) SO under Frederick Stock. The choir's only performance, 6 Feb 1917, with the *Welsman TSO (1908–18) was directed jointly by Vogt and the orchestra's conductor, Frank Welsman.

Having re-established the choir on principles which would continue to serve it for years to come, Vogt gave up the leadership in 1917 because of his increasing responsibilities as principal of the *TCM. Subsequently the Welsman TSO disbanded and, as a result, Vogt's chosen successor, Herbert Austin *Fricker, again looked south for an orchestra.

Having known Leopold Stokowski in England, Fricker made the Philadelphia Orchestra his first choice. That association, which lasted 1918–25, was followed by a collaboration 1926–31 with the Cincinnati SO under Fritz Reiner. The choir continued its frequent performances in the USA, begun in 1905 by Vogt with the first of nine appearances in Buffalo. Other US cities visited between 1905 and 1954 included New York (five times); Baltimore, Boston, Cincinnati, Cleveland, Detroit, and Philadelphia (twice each); and Chicago. Presentations in Toronto with the Detroit SO (1932), the *Hart House String Quartet (1933), and the New World Chamber Orchestra (1934) preceded a long and continuing relationship with the TSO. The outbreak of World War II, which depleted the choir's male sections, forced suspension of the 1939–40 season. However, a reorganized choir was able to give about two concerts each year for the war's duration. Another setback was Fricker's retirement, marked by a performance 23 Feb 1942 of his favourite work, Bach's *Mass in B Minor*.

Under Fricker the choir had given its first performances of Vaughan Williams' *A Sea Symphony* (1921), Boito's *Mephistopheles* in a concert version (1923), Elgar's *The Dream of Gerontius* (1925), Beethoven's *Missa solemnis* (1927), Bach's *Mass in B Minor* (1929), Handel's *Messiah* (1932), and Mendelssohn's *Elijah* (1933) and the Canadian premieres of Walton's *Belshazzar's Feast* (1936) and Berlioz' *Requiem* (1938). Vogt's repertoire had been relatively modest, containing many small-scale pieces. However, he did introduce a few such larger works as Mendelssohn's *Die erste Walpurgisnacht* (1906), Elgar's *Caractacus* (1909), Pierné's *Children's Crusade* (1910), Verdi's *Requiem* (1911), and most of Brahms' choral music, including *A German Requiem* (1908). Comparing the choir's first two conductors, one critic insisted that both were great, but added that under Vogt the choir had developed a diamond-like purity of tone, whereas under Fricker the sound was softer and darker-hued. The Toronto Mendelssohn Choir's third conductor was Sir Ernest *MacMillan. Like Fricker, MacMillan took over in wartime; like Vogt, he brought to the choir a choir of his own. Vogt's had been his church choir; MacMillan's was the TCM choir developed in the previous two decades and heard annually since 1923 in Bach's *St Matthew Passion*. The merger, though a difficult one involving both choristers and administrations, was accomplished surprisingly smoothly. The choir's first performance under MacMillan, 29 Dec 1942, was in Handel's *Messiah*, which thereafter became an annual Christmas presentation. MacMillan also introduced the *St Matthew Passion*, which then became an Easter annual. The two works were recorded in 1952 and 1953 respectively for *Beaver Records and were performed with the same soloists in 1954 at Carnegie Hall. Although the choir came to be identified with these two works, it varied its repertoire, offering, for instance, Verdi's *Requiem* during its 1942–3 season and a three-day Bach Festival in 1950 to commemorate the bicentenary of the composer's death. MacMillan resigned as conductor in 1957 but resumed his association with the choir as honorary president 1962–73. The choir honoured him in 1968, on his 75th birthday, with a performance of some of his favourite pieces, and the concert was telecast on the CBC.

Frederick *Silvester, who had been the choir's assistant conductor since 1946, succeeded MacMillan, assuming the duties of chorusmaster and conductor but working with various orchestra conductors. In his three seasons Silvester introduced the choir to the new choral idiom represented by Honegger's *Joan of Arc* (performed in 1958) and often prepared the choir for performances conducted by Walter *Susskind with the TSO. On his retirement in 1960 Silvester was succeeded as chorusmaster by John *Sidgwick (who had been the leader 1952–4 of a small chamber choir drawn from the Toronto Mendelssohn Choir) and as conductor by Susskind. This four-year partnership, which gave Toronto performances of Orff's *Carmina burana*, Berlioz' *The Damnation of Faust*, Bloch's *Sacred Service*, and Mahler's *Third Symphony*, terminated in 1964 with Susskind's departure from the TSO and Sidgwick's resignation to form his own *Orpheus Choir.

In 1964 Elmer *Iseler, a choir member since 1950 and occasionally assistant rehearsal conductor, became the Toronto Mendelssohn Choir's sixth conductor. He began his tenure by preparing the choir for the Canadian premiere (1964) of Britten's *War Requiem*, conducted by Susskind, and for a performance under Ernesto *Barbini of *Messiah*. Iseler himself first conducted the choir in public, augmented by his own *Festival Singers and two other choirs trained by Lloyd *Bradshaw, in the spring of 1965 at the Festival of Choral Music. That same year at the sesquicentenary of the Handel and Haydn Society of Boston the choir presented a program which included Godfrey *Ridout's *The Dance*, MacMillan's arrangement of 'Blanche comme la neige,' and Stravinszky's *Symphony of Psalms*. Performing in the company of the world's great choirs the Toronto choir nevertheless made a strong impression. 'There is something fresh, stimulating, vital, about the Iseler-Mendelssohn combination, and the result vocally and musically is remarkable. Diction is superb. Chords and polyphonic textures are always in perfect balance' (*Boston Globe*, 31 Oct 1965). The choir travelled to Montreal for centennial celebrations 1 Jul 1967 at the *PDA and a concert at *Expo 67. Also in 1967 it commissioned and premiered John *Beckwith's *Place of Meeting*.

Like Vogt and MacMillan before him, Iseler brought to the Toronto Mendelssohn Choir a choir of his own. The Festival Singers became the professional nucleus of the larger choir in 1968. Two others, the *Bach-Elgar Choir of Hamilton and John Sidgwick's Orpheus Choir, were enlisted for a special performance of Berlioz' *Requiem* on the 100th anniversary (1969) of the composer's death. The Mendelssohn Choir's own 75th anniversary season, 1969–70, was marked by its first presentation of Handel's *Israel in Egypt* and was followed in 1971 by the Canadian premiere of Penderecki's *St Luke Passion* (the latter was so successful that the work was repeated in 1972).

A tour of Europe, first planned for 1915 and postponed because of the outbreak of World War I, was finally managed in August 1972. With *Canadian Brass, the soprano Roxolana *Roslak, and the organist Ruth *Watson Henderson, the choir performed in England, Paris, and Lucerne and was lauded for 'the well-trained voices united to form a firm organic unit in which the clever structuring never detracted from the life and fervour of the singing' (*Der Bund*, 20 Aug 1972) and for 'a firm, clean ensemble with remarkably strong male parts and light flexible articulation' (*Financial Times*, 24 Aug 1972). That same year, the annual *Messiah* performances in Toronto included one 'sing-along' performance. The audience participation proved popular, and the sing-along was repeated annually 1972–6.

In 1973 the Mendelssohn 100 Voice Choir, a 'choir within a choir' incorporating the Festival Singers, was formed to facilitate CBC broadcasts and performances at such smaller Ontario cities as Barrie and Orillia and at the *Shaw Festival at Niagara-on-the-Lake. The full choir, numbering about 190, performed during the 1974–5 season with the *NACO and the *Hamilton Philharmonic and appeared 25 Oct 1975 with Canadian Brass at Kennedy Center in Washington, DC. For the 1976 Olympics it participated with the *MSO at PDA in the Solemn Opening Session 13 July under Rafael Frübeck de Burgos and in a special arts and culture program 15 July under Iseler. In the tradition established by Vogt the Toronto Mendelssohn Choir in the 1970s continued to audition its members annually and to draw its programs from the major works with orchestra at one end of that range and hymns of the Christian church or short unaccompanied works as disparate as *Willan's **An Apostrophe to the Heavenly Hosts* and R. Murray *Schafer's *Epitaph for Moonlight* at the other, maintaining the while its reputation as one of the world's great choirs. It made its debut at the Edinburgh Festival in 1980.

A Toronto Mendelssohn Youth Choir – a 60-voice mixed group aged 14 to 19 – was founded by the senior organization in 1977. Under the leadership of Gerald Fagan it quickly established a pattern of annual concerts in May and at Christmas. In 1979 its Christmas concert was given jointly with the Toronto Symphony Youth Orchestra.

DISCOGRAPHY

Bach *St Matthew Passion*. Full orch, MacMillan cond, Milligan (Jesus), Johnson (Evangelist), Marshall sop, Morrison sop, Newton sop, Stilwell alto, Lamond ten, Brown bar, Tredwell bar. 1953. 3-Beaver LPS 002

Bell-Lloyd *Rosy Dawn* – Graves *Men of Heaven*. Fricker cond. 1926. Brunswick 10261 (78)

Great Hymns. Iseler cond. 1975. CBC SM-302

Gloria: Gabrieli – Rachmaninoff – Stewart – Stanford – Willan – Vaughan Williams – Somers. Iseler cond. 1968. RCA LSC 3054/Mel SMLP 4030

Handel *Messiah*. Full orch, MacMillan cond, Marshall sop, Palmateer alto, Vickers ten, Milligan bar. 1952. 3-Beaver LPS 001/3-RCA Victor LM 6134/(excerpts) 1-Beaver LPS 1003/RCA Victor LM-2088

Lavallée *O Canada*. Iseler cond. 1965. RCA 57-3386 (45)

MacMillan – Vaughan Williams – Ives. Iseler cond. 1969. CBC SM-105/RCA LSC 3154

Make We Merry: Vaughan Williams – Willan – Britten – et al. Iseler cond. 1970. CBC SM-80/RCA LSC 3174

Palestrina *Adoramus te; Exultate Deo*. Fricker cond. 1926. Brunswick 10260 (78)

Pierné *The Children's Crusade*. TSO, Susskind cond, Bishop Strachan School Chapel Choir, Elliott sop, Guloien sop, Morrison sop, McCollum ten, Young bar. 1960. 2-Beaver LPS 003

Star Spangled Banner – *Scots wha hae*. Fricker cond. 1926. Brunswick 10262 (78)

Tribute to Her Majesty Elizabeth II: Handel anthems. CBC Orch, MacMillan cond, Vickers ten. 1953. Beaver LPS 1002

We Magnify Thee: Rachmaninoff *Songs of the Church, from 'All Night Vigil.'* Iseler cond. 1970. CBC SM-179

BIBLIOGRAPHY

Smith, Ocean G. compiler. *The Toronto Mendelssohn Choir: A History 1894–1948* (Toronto 1948)

[McLean, Maud]. *A Responsive Chord: The Story of the Toronto Mendelssohn Choir 1894–1969* (Toronto 1969)

McLean, Maud. 'Contemporary works contribute to Mendelssohn Choir's fame,' *MSc*, 273, Sep – Oct 1973

Jones, Donald. 'Choirmaster's dream led to musical fame for Toronto,' *Toronto Star*, 31 Dec 1976

Kraglund, John. 'Mendelssohn Choir forms youth branch,' Toronto *Globe and Mail*, 20 Dec 1977

Metropolitan Toronto Music Library. Vertical files. Bound programs 1895–1952 (OM)

The Toronto Men Teachers' Choir. An amateur group founded in 1941 by Murray Dobson and Alec Turner with about 10 members; it later had as many as 70. It gave its first public concert 27 Apr 1942 at *Eaton Auditorium. Under the direction of Eldon Brethour 1941–58, Harvey *Perrin 1958–69, James Maben 1969–74, and Bev Stainton 1974–6, the choir gave annual concerts until 1976, usually at *Massey Hall or Eaton Auditorium. It also performed in the USA, throughout southern Ontario, and at *Expo 67. On 26 and 27 Oct 1965 it participated in a performance of Brahms' *Alto Rhapsody* with Maureen *Forrester and the *TSO. Renamed the Toronto Men's Choir in 1975, it disbanded the following year. Recordings of the annual concerts (1950–69) were released privately by the choir.

BIBLIOGRAPHY

McIver, Murdoch. *A Musical History: The Story of the Toronto Men Teachers' Choir*, priv publ (Toronto nd)

The Toronto Oratorio Society. One of several large choirs in early 20th-century Toronto. It was founded in 1910 and survived 15 years despite a period of inactivity 1912–14. It was an outgrowth of the choir at the Jarvis St Baptist Church, where its conductor, Edward *Broome, was organist. The 200-voice choir presented annual festivals of two or three concerts at *Massey Hall, engaging such orchestras as the New York Philharmonic, the Cleveland Orchestra, the Cincinnati SO, and the Detroit SO. The orchestras also presented their own concerts. In 1924 the New SO (later *TSO) appeared with the society. At first the repertoire was drawn from the standard oratorios, including *Messiah, Elijah*, and *St Paul*, but shorter choral pieces and more contemporary works were added later. A children's chorus under the aegis of the society also performed under Broome's direction at Massey Hall. The organization disbanded in 1925 when Broome moved to Calgary.

An earlier choral group of the same name was founded first (1903) as the Sherlock Vocal Society by the conductor J.M. Sherlock and renamed the Toronto Oratorio Society in 1906. It gave annual concerts from 1904 until about 1909. RPn

Toronto Philharmonic Society. Name of a succession of concert societies (1845–7, 1848–50, 1853–5, 1872–94), connected by a certain continuity of leadership: John *McCaul, the U of Toronto president, and James P. *Clarke worked together in most of the early societies as president and conductor, and F.H. *Torrington led the group during its final 22 years.

The first Toronto Philharmonic Society was organized after two concerts in October 1845, initiated by McCaul and conducted by Clarke and J.D. *Humphreys respectively, had demonstrated the existence in Toronto of musical talent and of audiences for classical music. The new society made its debut 26 Dec 1845 at the New City Hall, and during that season it gave five more concerts under Clarke, with a French violinist, Bley, as concertmaster, and strong support from the 81st Regimental Band under T.C. Crozier. The programs mixed choral, orchestral, solo instrumental, and solo vocal selections. Movements of Mozart and Beethoven symphonies were programmed in 1847, but financial problems led to the organization's collapse that year.

A new Toronto Philharmonic Society appeared in 1848, with F.W. Barron, principal of Upper Canada College, as president, and Humphreys, Henry *Schallehn, and George W. *Strathy as its leading musicians. Concerts were given at City Hall, the Royal Lyceum Theatre, *St Lawrence Hall, and Temperance Hall. Short vocal and instrumental pieces were popular, as were operatic overtures. Among the overtures were those to *La Cenerentola, Der Freischütz, Anacreon*, and *Semiramide*. The society faltered after two seasons and was followed by another McCaul-Clarke collaboration, the Toronto Vocal Music Society (1851–3), which placed more emphasis on choral music. Its repertoire included excerpts from Handel's *Acis and Galatea, Dettingen Te Deum*, and *Messiah*, Haydn's *The Creation*, and Beethoven's *The Mount of Olives*. When a Mr Paige was appointed conductor in April 1853, Clarke's supporters left the society, and its eclipse resulted.

The Toronto Philharmonic Society was revived by the same leaders and gave its first concert 25 Apr 1854. The programs, performed at University College and St Lawrence Hall, continued along the old lines – oratorio choruses, operatic excerpts, and vocal and instrumental solos – but the concertmaster, Ferdinand *Griebel, played a *Violin Concerto* by de Bériot, and the orchestra took up the challenge of the Funeral March in the *Eroica* symphony. Financial problems brought about the end of the organization in the spring of 1855.

On 1 Oct 1872 the Toronto Philharmonic Society was revived yet again. This time it outlasted the combined ages of all its predecessors. McCaul

A concert of the Toronto Philharmonic Society from a sketch by W. Cruickshank (*Canadian Illustrated News* 22 Dec 1877)

and Clarke resumed their prior functions, and Robert Marshall was concertmaster. Rehearsals of *Messiah* began in October and culminated in a performance 28 Feb 1873 before an overflow audience at *Shaftesbury Hall. The orchestra comprised 30 musicians, the chorus about 160. The event marked the ageing Clark's farewell performance. Marshall assumed the conductor's duties for a short time, but a vigorous younger musician, F.H. Torrington, after a debut concert with the society 17 Nov 1873, led it to its greatest heights, making it the leading and most stable ensemble in late 19th-century Toronto. The stability, however, belonged to the chorus only; a permanent orchestra proved elusive despite attempts to establish one. The society presented the Canadian premieres of Mendelssohn's *Elijah* (1874) and *St Paul* (1876) and Gounod's *Redemption* (1882, the year of its composition). By 1890 *Messiah* had been given six times, *Elijah* five, and *The Creation* three. There also were performances of Mendelssohn's *Walpurgisnacht*, Handel's *Judas Maccabaeus* and *Samson*, Sullivan's *The Golden Legend*, and other large choral-orchestral works typical of the European repertoire of the period. Symphonies still were represented in most instances by single movements, but Haydn's *Surprise Symphony* and Mendelssohn's *Symphony No. 2, 'Hymn of Praise'* were performed in their entirety. A Miss Boyd and the German Franz Rummel were heard in Beethoven piano concertos (one of them the *Emperor*) and in 1893 François *Boucher, a member of the orchestra, played a Bruch violin concerto (probably the *G-Minor*). Unlike its sister organization in Montreal the society did not venture into the realm of complete opera performance.

In the Festival of 1886 the Toronto Philharmonic Society was joined by other forces to form an adult choir of 1000, a children's choir of 1200, and an orchestra of 100. Lilli Lehmann and Max Heinrich were the guest singers, and the main works offered were Handel's *Israel in Egypt* and Gounod's *Mors et vita*. The success of Torrington's endeavours was a factor in Hart Massey's decision to build a music hall in Toronto (see Massey Hall). Concerts were given until 1879 at Shaftesbury Hall, and later at the Grand Opera House and the Pavilion Music Hall. The concertmasters over the years included R.L. Cowan, John *Bayley, and Bertha *Drechsler Adamson. Torrington resigned as conductor in 1894, and the society dispersed. Its members joined other choristers, however, to sing in the Festival Chorus under Torrington's direction until 1912.

A separate organization by the same name was led 1896–8 by J. Humphrey *Anger. Its performances included *Messiah* in 1897.

BIBLIOGRAPHY
'The Philharmonic Society: first public concert: The Messiah,' Toronto *Mail*, 1 Mar 1873
Lehmann, Lilli. *My Path Through Life* (New York, London 1914)
'Toronto's Pre-Confederation Music Societies'
Metropolitan Toronto Library. Torrington scrapbooks

(HK,RPn)

Toronto String Quartette (Toronto String Quartet). Three independent ensembles of the same name active respectively 1884–7, in 1894, and from 1906 to the mid-1920s.

1 1884–7. The Toronto Quartette Club, formed to enlarge public interest in chamber music, sponsored a series of five concerts (winter 1884) by a Toronto String Quartette, with Henri Jacobsen and John *Bayley as the regular violins, a Mr *Martens (either Carl or Theodore) as viola, and a Mr Kuhn as cello, and assisted on one occasion by a Mr Whitaker, double-bass. The following season the same players, augmented by F.H. *Torrington, A.E. *Fisher, a Mr Haslam, and a Mr Daniels, presented Mendelssohn's *Octet for Strings* among other works. The 1885–6 season offered a series of 12 Monday Popular Concerts and a change in personnel: A.E. Fisher, viola, and Ludwig Corell, cello. The program contained works by Schumann, Beethoven, and Haydn, as well as the Mozart *Clarinet Quintet*, with a Herr Kegel of New York as the clarinet, and piano trios of Hummel and Reissiger with Carl Martens as pianist. Teresa Carreño and Emma Juch were among the other guest performers at these concerts. In 1886, to ensure the continuation of the quartet, A.&S. *Nordheimer and some Toronto citizens organized the Chamber Music Assn, which sponsored the 1886–7 series of six concerts at *Shaftesbury Hall. However, in spite of popular acceptance, the quartet was forced to disband in September 1887 when Corell and Jacobsen moved to the USA.

2 Fl 1894. A second Toronto String Quartette, with Messrs Bayley, Anderson, Napolitano, and Dinelli, is reported in the *Musical Courier* (31 Dec 1894) as performing for a small but appreciative audience.

3 1906 to mid-1920s, possibly interrupted for a few years about 1918–20. The third Toronto String Quartette presented its first concert 23 Jan 1907. Frank *Blachford was the first violin throughout its existence. The other original members, Roland Roberts, Frank Converse Smith, and Frederic Nicolai, were replaced by Benedick Clarke (ca 1914) and Erland Misener (ca 1923), second violins; Alfred Bruce and Albert Aylward, violas; and Leo *Smith (ca 1914), cello. In addition to its regular concerts the group performed for the *Women's Musical Club of Toronto (1909) and in many Ontario towns, and presented musicales in private homes in Toronto, Buffalo, and other cities. Its repertoire ranged from Haydn to Hugo Wolf and Debussy. Guest pianists included Paul *Wells (1915 in Lekeu's *Piano Quartet*) and Healey *Willan (1916 in his *Trio*, B98). HK, PW

Toronto Symphony. In 1980 and for many years prior to that time English-speaking Canada's principal large symphony orchestra, founded in 1906 as the Toronto Conservatory Symphony Orchestra, becoming the Toronto Symphony Orchestra in 1908, re-started (after a five-year hiatus, and with mostly different personnel) as the New Symphony Orchestra in 1923, renamed the Toronto Symphony Orchestra (TSO) in 1927 and that name amended to the Toronto Symphony (TS) in 1967.

1 Predecessor organizations
2 1906–18
3 1922–31
4 1931–65
5 1965–80

1 PREDECESSOR ORGANIZATIONS. In the 1870s the *Toronto Philharmonic Society under F.H. *Torrington organized the city's first regular full orchestra, which performed standard symphonies and concertos, in full or (more often) in part, as a component of the society's concerts, in *Shaftesbury Hall and the Horticultural Pavilion. By the 1880s membership had become more professional, drawing players from theatre-pit orchestras such as that of the Grand Opera House. However, the group was essentially a dependent one, since the society's main emphasis was on choral music. The *Toronto Mendelssohn Choir, formed under A.S. *Vogt's direction in the 1890s, started in 1902 to bring guest orchestras from the USA to play its accompaniments and occasionally to present orchestral concerts as well. Thus the city, which had welcomed the touring Theodore Thomas Orchestra in 1873, had opportunities by the early 1900s to hear the orchestras of Chicago, Minneapolis, Philadelphia, and elsewhere.

Meanwhile there were several attempts to organize a permanent local ensemble, independent of choral affiliation. One such group, calling itself the Toronto Symphony Orchestra, appeared in 1890–1 with Francesco *D'Auria as conductor. A Toronto Permanent Orchestra started by the indefatigable Torrington in 1900 evidently did not live up to its name. In 1901 yet another TSO, conducted by James Dickinson, gave a single concert, intended as the first in a continuing series – for which, however, support did not materialize.

2 1906–18. Then in 1906 Frank *Welsman formed a Toronto Conservatory Symphony Orchestra with Bertha *Drechsler Adamson as concertmistress and with a personnel made up of staff and students of the TCM. After two successful seasons, it became more firmly established under a directorial board led by a prominent businessman, H.C. Cox, dropped the direct connection with the conservatory and the 'Conservatory' part of its name, and presented a flourishing annual concert series in *Massey Hall. Toronto finally had its own regular symphonic orchestra.

The early Welsman years show a predominance of standard late-18th- and 19th-century European music – Schubert's *Unfinished*, Dvořák's *New World*, and symphonies by Haydn, Mozart, and Beethoven. The third and fourth symphonies of Mendelssohn and the last three of Tchaikovsky were played, but, surprisingly perhaps, none by Brahms. An all-Wagner program was given in 1911. Novelties for the time included symphonies by Goldmark and Kalinnikov and Strauss' *Death and Transfiguration*. Ballots for a request concert (1913) show that among symphonies the *Pathétique* was the most popular, among overtures the *Midsummer Night's Dream*, and among other pieces the *Second Hungarian Rhapsody*.

Guest artists included many world-renowned musical figures: the violinists Fritz Kreisler, Eugène Ysaÿe, Carl Flesch, and the 17-year-old Mischa Elman; the pianists Wilhelm Backhaus, Vladimir de Pachmann, and Sergei Rachmaninoff, the latter playing his own *Second Concerto*; the singers Clara Butt, Johanna Gadski, Alma Gluck, Louise Homer, Leo Slezak, and Ernestine Schumann-Heink. Elgar conducted the touring Sheffield Choir in his oratorio *The Dream of Gerontius* with the TSO in April 1911, but otherwise neither guest conductors nor works by English composers were much in evidence.

In keeping with the social temper of the era, the concerts may have had a certain class appeal: 'Music [had been] an important part of the social and cultural life of well-to-do Toronto in the latter half of the nineteenth century' (Davies, *Over the Years*). However, pop concerts were added to the schedule at the end of the first TSO season (April 1909), with a uniform admission price of 25 cents. The orchestra travelled to nearby Ontario centres for a few concerts each season. Frank *Blachford was the 'concertmeister' (as spelled in the program) beginning in that 'expansion' season of 1908–9. Leo *Smith joined the cello section shortly after his arrival in 1910 and later became principal, as well as program annotator. Other noted members included, in the later seasons, Jack *Arthur, Luigi *Romanelli, and the young Harry *Adaskin.

The TSO weathered the World-War-I years, but with increasing difficulty (scattered players, curtailment of travel affecting guest artists, waning audience support), and in 1918 it was obliged to discontinue. This first regularly based phase of 11 years (13 counting the two preliminary years under TCM auspices) had provided a professional standard worthy of international-calibre guest artists and a broad, though conservative, repertoire.

3 1922–31. Five years went by before another such musical ensemble and supporting organization could emerge. In the interim the local musical scene had changed significantly. Movie-theatre orchestras (eg, Shea's Hippodrome, the Uptown) were the new employers of professional instrumentalists. Eager for the challenge of more serious fare, in 1922 a groups of players persuaded Luigi von *Kunits to conduct them in an orchestra. Louis Gesensway, a section violinist (later a violinist with the Philadelphia Orchestra and a composer), and Abe Fenboque, the first flutist, were the chief organizers. Several of the string players were von Kunits' pupils. Moses Garten was the concertmaster. Rehearsals were held that winter in von Kunits' home. On 23 Apr 1923 the New Symphony Orchestra gave its first public concert in Massey Hall. It was announced that 'the concert will commence sharp at Five o'clock in the evening, this hour being selected because of the engagements of the Musicians in theatres etc., which prevents any other choice. However this will give everyone an opportunity to hear an hour or so of the best music and leave the Massey Hall in time to reach home before evening dinner.'

Two more concerts followed shortly, and a board of directors led 1923–31 by Albert *Gooderham, was formed to ensure financial support for future seasons. Twenty twilight concerts were given in 1923–4, but, though artistically impressive, they met with indifferent attendance, and the number was reduced to 10 or 12 a season for the succeeding few years, while the board and an especially active women's committee worked gradually to increase the size of audiences.

On 7 May 1924 a particularly striking program – and one of the rare examples to feature originally composed music – brought together the past, current, and future conductors: Welsman conducted von Kunits' *E Minor Violin Concerto* with the composer as soloist, and Ernest *MacMillan conducted the orchestra, of which he later was to become the regular director, in the premiere of his own *Concert Overture in A*.

In 1923 each player received a fee of $3.95 for each concert, including rehearsals. By the 1925–6 season this honorarium had increased to $14. There were 58 players listed in the program for the reorganized orchestra of 1923, and only 4 or 5 had been members of Welsman's TSO; by 1929–30 membership had increased to 64. Tickets cost 75 cents, 50 cents, and 25 cents in 1923; in 1924 the top price was raised to $1; in 1926 seats were 50 cents for the top gallery and $1 for the rest of the auditorium, with season tickets available for dollar seats only.

The orchestra gave its first children's concert at 5 pm 31 Jan 1925. Four such concerts were presented during 1925–6, but none were attempted again until 1930. Once resumed, however, they became a fixture of each season.

In conjunction with the orchestra's concerts in 1923 an announcement states that 'Miss E. Lois Wilson will give a series of lectures on Symphonies and their Meaning on Monday evenings preceding the concert, at 8:15 p.m. in the Women's Art Association. These lectures will fully interpret and explain the program to be given by the orchestra at its next concert. Themes are illustrated at the piano' (quoted by Davies, p 41). This is an early example of a supplemental activity later to become familiar in the orchestra's work.

In 1927, by a decision of the board, the name New Symphony Orchestra was changed to Toronto Symphony Orchestra. Notably, the players listed now included more veterans (11) of the Welsman years. Grant Milligan had succeeded Garten as concertmaster in 1926 and in turn was succeeded by Donald *Heins in 1927.

In 1929–30 a new departure brought change, sudden development, and wider recognition. The CNR sponsored a series of 28 weekly one-hour radio broadcasts by the orchestra. Performed live from the Arcadian Court of the Robert Simpson Co department store (C.L. Burton, president of Simpson's, was a member of the TSO board of directors), these were Canada's first national broadcasts of serious music, and they proved highly successful. Von Kunits had revitalized the orchestra, and it became established on a more secure and more elaborate organizational base than in the 1908–18 period – with loyal subscribers, committed guarantors, an orchestra association, and a women's committee. The choice of music in the 1920s seldom ventured outside conservative tradition (Brahms' *Third Symphony*, Schumann's *Second*, Beethoven's *Eroica*, the Schubert *C Major*, all presented in the first year or two, were, however, an indication of serious high aims); local soloists were more usual than the stellar international artists of the pre-war years.

4 1931–65. At von Kunits' sudden death in the summer of 1931, Ernest MacMillan was selected to be the new conductor. He was anxious to shift the concert time from 5 pm to an evening hour and did so on a few occasions during his first season. As it happened, by 1933 the talking motion picture had transformed entertainment life; many of the former theatre musicians moved into other areas of work – particularly radio broadcasting – and now were free to play evening concerts on a regular basis. Longer programs and more ambitious repertoire eventually resulted. An assistant conductor was appointed for the first time: Donald Heins, concertmaster 1927–31, held this new position 1931–42. Ettore *Mazzoleni was named to the higher-level position of associate conductor in 1942 and retained it until 1948. Heins' actual successor as assistant conductor, however, after a hiatus of five years, was Paul *Scherman, who occupied the position 1947–55. In a move that was unusually bold for a depression period, the board increased ticket prices in MacMillan's first season to a range from 50 cents to $2.50.

MacMillan introduced the orchestra and its audience in the 1930s to the Sibelius symphonies (including the *Seventh*, then quite new) and to a substantial quota of English contemporary music (Elgar, Delius, Bax, Walton). Holst's *The Planets* became the most often repeated piece in his régime, and the TSO eventually recorded it. MacMillan's correspondence of the time reveals how diplomatically he had to deal with guarantors and especially women's committee stalwarts who objected to unfamiliar works – even though few were modern in any advanced or progressive sense. Finances were precarious, and in several seasons towards the end of the decade MacMillan turned back his own fee to help offset the deficit.

Sir Ernest MacMillan rehearsing the Toronto Symphony Orchestra, 1930s

In 1935 the TSO presented its first 'Christmas Box' concert. This became an annual event recurrent until 1957. Alongside a selection of Christmas music and carol arrangements in which audience members could join, the players gave original burlesque performances and skits. Stunt acts included the 'Sumvak Sisters' (the violinists Elie *Spivak and Harold *Sumberg dressed in a Siamese-twin gown) performing on a single instrument, one fingering and one bowing. The blind pianist-entertainer Alec Templeton was a frequent guest, and the recently knighted conductor entered into the spirit, appearing dressed as Santa Claus, as a young boy in knee-pants auditioning for a place in the violin section, or as a professor giving a musicological analysis of a current song hit, or conducting (during World War II) Mossolov's *The Iron Foundry* in overalls, with a monkey-wrench for a baton. (The eventual disappearance of this tradition may be attributable to the retirement of MacMillan, since his personality had marked it; but other factors, especially the growth and the changing social patterns and tastes of Toronto in the 1950s and 1960s no doubt were responsible as well.)

World War II was a difficult period for the orchestra, but it survived as its predecessor had not survived World War I. Suspension of its concerts was considered seriously in 1940, but the importance of music to wartime morale was stressed by a number of its leading supporters, and it took on a new spirit of cultural vitality. In 1943 a campaign of many years succeeded when the Toronto City Council approved its first grant to the orchestra (in the sum of $1500).

In 1944 the idea of pop concerts was revived (Welsman had given them regularly, and there had been some in the early years of von Kunits' tenure). Paul Scherman conducted eight such concerts that season. The series was expanded, and the Robert Simpson Co assumed sponsorship to broadcast them. MacMillan and other conductors participated, but Scherman remained the principal conductor of these. After 1951 a new sponsor, Canada Packers Ltd, took over, and in 1955 the pop series was moved from Friday evenings to Sunday afternoons. From then until revision of the provincial Lord's Day Act in 1960 admission was free, voluntary donations being solicited at the door. Pop concert audiences continued large and loyal through the change of time but declined with the reimposition of a ticket charge in 1960, and this, added to other complications, led to the series' discontinuance in 1961.

The immediate post-war years – 1945–50 – were the most successful the TSO had known. Performance improved in artistic calibre. The string section, whose fine quality was a legacy from von Kunits, was admired particularly. Audiences increased until, in 1946, each subscription concert had to be given twice. To the subscription series and pop concerts (all broadcast on radio at least in part), the occasional recordings, and the children's concerts were added students' concerts. These, a series begun in 1940–1, were designed for secondary-school students. School music teachers, various members of the TSO including the conductor, and a city-wide student committee (Victor *Feldbrill, then a teenager at Harbord Collegiate Institute, was its first president) all contributed educational preparation and lectures which preceded the concerts.

Works by the Canadians Robert *Farnon, Robert *Fleming, Allard *de Ridder, Arnold *Walter, and Healey *Willan were presented during the 1940s, and in 1947, with the sponsorship of *CAPAC, MacMillan led the orchestra in its first live concert of Canadian music. (One of von Kunits' radio broadcasts with the orchestra in 1930 had had an all-Canadian program.) Repertoire innovations continued to be made only with caution, however. Symphonies by Harris and Copland were heard, but US contemporary music in a broad sense, surprisingly, was neglected. Canadian soloists regularly shared guest billing with such international luminaries as Heifetz, Myra Hess, Schwarzkopf, Arrau, or Rubinstein. Although Stravinsky had appeared as guest conductor of his own *Firebird* and *Petrushka* as early as 1937, other guest conductors were not numerous: Enesco, Kindler, Monteux, Munch, Sevitzky, and Stokowski are a few from the 1940s.

In 1951, at the height of the orchestra's popularity, it was engaged to give its first US concert, in Detroit. The Joe McCarthy 'witch hunts' then were having their terrorizing effects on immigration to the USA, and six TSO players were refused entry. They were replaced for the concert, and the engagement went ahead. For the following season, further US concerts had been booked (New York, Boston, Philadelphia), and in order to fulfil them the management decided not to renew the contracts of the six players. This led to a general outcry in the community against this response to an unjustified smear. The incident of the 'Symphony Six' (Ruth Ross, Dirk *Keetbaas, William *Kuinka, Abe Mannheim, John Moskalyk, and Steven *Staryk) became a controversial and divisive one, causing several board resignations. MacMillan's stature (he had taken a 'no-comment' position) and the prestige of the orchestra both suffered.

At length, MacMillan announced he would resign as conductor at the end of his 25th season, 1955–6. His successor, Walter *Susskind, chose a Canadian, Glenn *Gould, as soloist for his inaugural concert and was acclaimed later in the same season for an outstanding performance of Berlioz' *Damnation of Faust* with James *Milligan as Mephistopheles. Although (as MacMillan had since 1942) Susskind combined the conductorship of the TSO with that of the Toronto Mendelssohn Choir, his true flair was operatic, and concert performances of operas were added to the schedules.

He also appeared as soloist-conductor in piano concertos by Mozart and Ravel. Though Czech-born and -trained, Susskind had spent a large part of his early career in Great Britain, and British music was more prominent than Czech in his repertoire. Among newer works, he conducted Toronto's first live *Sacre du printemps*, and introduced pieces by Webern, Schoenberg, and Berio. During his years as musical director, many leading guest conductors appeared – among them Barbirolli, Beecham, Krips, Leinsdorf, Sargent, and Steinberg.

It was also during the Susskind years that the orchestra came through one of its most severe crises. The character of the local audience was changing as new immigrant groups began to alter the Toronto cultural scene and the concert fare which for so long had satisfied the middle-class anglophile failed to satisfy the new audience. Moreover, the wealthy guarantors – the *Massey family, Cox, Gooderham, Lady Kemp, Mrs Edmund Boyd – who in former days could be counted on to help out with deficits, were dying away, and no replacements were to be found. The Women's Committee's giant rummage sale – an annual civic event in Toronto since 1954 – helped fund-raising, but needs and costs were mounting alarmingly. The public granting agencies were just beginning their at first tentative and uncertain patterns of aid. Players' morale was low because of discouraging wage-negotiation results and a continuing feeling of being regarded as on a lower social rung. Because of a dispute between the players' committee and their union executive, a particularly acrimonious union election took place in 1960. A year later the TSO had to delay the start of its subscription season, cancelling the first two concerts, because of the lack of an agreement over players' contracts. J.W. Elton, the orchestra's manager since 1934 (having taken over from his father, H.J. Elton, manager since 1924), resigned in 1961, and his place was taken by Walter *Homburger, already at that period one of the country's most experienced arts administrators.

The orchestra's first appearance in Carnegie Hall, New York, 3 Dec 1963 under Susskind, with Lois *Marshall as soloist, was a marked success and gave a timely boost to morale. The early 1960s nevertheless were an uneasy period for the orchestra's members. By 1965–6 the season had increased only from the 26 weeks in MacMillan's best post-war years to 30 weeks. The *CBC SO – all but 20 of whose members also played in the TSO – disbanded in 1964, causing further anxiety. Although some members were engaged by Heinz *Unger's spring York Concert Society series, the *Promenade Symphony Concerts which provided supplementary employment from the 1930s to the 1950s were a thing of the past. Orchestral performance was a precarious career in Toronto, and the goal of year-round contracts was still some seasons away.

5 1965–80. When in 1965 Susskind resigned after a 10-year association with the orchestra, fortunes already were starting to turn. A new co-operative agreement with the *COC meant late-summer and early-fall employment – an arrangement which was to last until 1976. Subscriptions surged dramatically with the appointment of Seiji Ozawa (b Manchuria of Japanese parents 1 Sep 1935) as conductor.

Ozawa's tenure lent a fresh flavour to orchestra music in Toronto. Dynamic in style, sometimes daring in taste, he introduced music by such composers as Ives (*Symphony No. 4*, in the difficult single-conductor version) and Messiaen (*Turangalîla*, later recorded). Early in his conductorship the civic nature of the institution was symbolized by its performance at the opening ceremonies of Toronto's new City Hall. A tour in 1966 to Great Britain (Commonwealth Festival) and France was followed in 1969 by a more extensive one to Ozawa's own country, Japan. From this, and from the conductor's emphasis on contemporary Japanese works, especially those of Takemitsu, may be traced a marked influence on Toronto's musical tastes, notably in percussion performance and in composition. In Canada's centennial year, 1967, the TSO became the TS. The name-change went hand-in-hand with the design of a new logo by the typographer Allan Fleming. In honour of the centenary the orchestra introduced specially commissioned pieces by Otto *Joachim and Luigi Nono. Ozawa's Toronto sojourn, though brief, had a tonic effect on orchestra and public. At his departure he was named 'musical director emeritus.'

Seiji Ozawa, conductor of the Toronto Symphony 1965–9

Karel Ančerl, conductor of the Toronto Symphony 1969–73

Whereas Ozawa had led the TS at an early, even still formative, point of his brilliant career, his successor was a distinguished European conductor of exceptionally broad experience. Karel Ančerl (b Tucapy, Czechoslovakia, 11 Apr 1908, d Toronto 3 Jul 1973) assumed the Toronto post in 1969. The Soviet invasion of Czechoslovakia had occurred the previous year while he was in North America, and this circumstance prevented him from continuing his regular engagement in Prague, as he had planned.

Ančerl's impact on the orchestra represented a serious challenge to its standards, and one which it met with distinction. A strong technician with a sharp ear, he had an almost scholarly rehearsal manner and an individual rapport which soon won players' respect. In repertoire his concerts were in the conservative mainstream (though by now this included Stravinsky and Bartók), with a new emphasis on Czech works (Janáček, Martinu, Suk) previously seldom heard in Toronto. A 1970 Beethoven-bicentenary festival of six concerts at *O'Keefe Centre (slightly larger in seating capacity than Massey Hall) proved one of the organization's all-time successes, both artistically and financially. A Brahms festival the following year fared similarly.

It was during Ančerl's regime, in the summer of 1971, that the orchestra began to give summer concerts at the lakefront outdoor *Ontario Place Forum. At one of the early events Ozawa, returning as guest conductor, drew an audience of over 12,000. Ančerl's own programs were uncompromising in quality, drew large crowds, and were credited with creating new friends for the orchestra among Torontonians who had never attended the Massey Hall concerts.

The following year – 13 Jan 1972 – a return to the pop concerts series was initiated by Victor Feldbrill, who remained associated with this phase of the orchestra's schedule throughout the 1970s. Feldbrill's connection with the TS is in fact a unique one. Beginning as a teenage fan and student-committee president, he was a section violinist in the 1950s, assistant conductor 1956–7, and conductor of the youth concerts starting in 1969, assuming responsibility also for many of the 'Family Pops' from 1972 on. In 1973 he suddenly was thrust into further responsibility. Ančerl, known to be seriously ailing at the time of his appointment, died shortly after celebrating his 65th birthday in Toronto, July 1973. During the following two seasons Feldbrill, as resident conductor, assisted with program planning and the choice of a succession of guest conductors, also himself conducting many concerts. One immediate crisis was the already contracted European tour of 1974 which Ančerl was to have directed. Kazimierz Kord was engaged as guest conductor, and the tour went ahead, with visits to centres in England, Belgium, West Germany, and Austria.

A new artistic director and principal conductor took up duties in the fall of 1975. Andrew Davis (b Ashridge, Hertfordshire, England, 2 Feb 1944) was approximately the same age Seiji Ozawa had been at the time of his appointment. Equally vibrant in personality, he had a more versatile repertoire and a cooler and perhaps tidier approach to performance. His concerts in the first few seasons broadened Toronto's exposure to orchestral music by presenting Schoenberg and Berg works previously unplayed in Toronto, the entire cycle of Stravinsky ballets, a Borodin cycle (later recorded), and the cycle of the Mahler symphonies. Also included was a strong emphasis on English composers – Elgar in particular, but also Britten and Tippett. The Canadian premiere of Tippett's *Fourth Symphony* (1979) was a highlight. Davis' several appearances as soloist-conductor (piano, harpsichord) also enhanced the programs.

In 1974 the TS organized the Toronto Symphony Youth Orchestra, with Feldbrill as its first conductor and leading TS players as section coaches. It has appeared on several occasions in joint concerts with the parent organization. (See Youth orchestras.)

Under Davis' direction the TS resumed recording in a more comprehensive way than ever before, the contract with a major international label (Columbia) ensuring wide distribution. Concerts were given in New York and at Washington's Kennedy Center in 1977. A memorable event was the three-week tour of China and Japan early in 1978, with two Canadian soloists, Maureen *Forrester and Louis *Lortie. Sponsored by the Canadian Dept of External Affairs, this was one of the most elaborate cultural exportations the coun-

Andrew Davis, conductor of the Toronto Symphony 1975–

try had ever undertaken. A film documentary was made by the CBC. During the visit of the Peking Opera to Toronto on its 1980 tour, many of the orchestra members were able to renew musical contacts they had made while in China. Other notable TS tours were those to Quebec and the four Atlantic provinces in 1976 and to the three westernmost provinces and California in 1979.

Three conductors held the intermittent post of assistant conductor during the 1960s: Boris *Brott 1963–4, Nicklaus Wyss 1966–7, and Kazuyoshi Akiyama 1968–9. Concertmasters from the MacMillan years through 1980 were Elie Spivak 1931–48, Hyman *Goodman 1948–67, Gerard *Kantarjian 1967–70, Albert *Pratz 1970–9, and Moshe Murvitz. TS program annotators have been Ettore Mazzoleni 1932–48, Marcus *Adeney 1948–66, John *Beckwith 1966–70, Kenneth *Winters 1970–2, and Godfrey *Ridout.

Harry *Freedman was associated with the orchestra for 25 years, 24 of them as oboe and english horn and the 25th (1970–1) as composer-in-residence. His *Graphic I* was premiered by the TS under Ančerl in October 1971. Although criticized for performing fewer Canadian-composed works than other Canadian orchestras, the TS between 1960 and 1980 commissioned and performed works by *Hawkins, Joachim, *Klein, *Morawetz, *Schafer, *Somers, and others, and performed pieces by many other Canadian composers.

By degrees, beginning in the mid-1960s, the board of directors was enlarged and made more representative of facets of the community such as business, education, religion, communications media, and the arts. Presidents of the board after Gooderham have been Vincent Massey 1931–4, J.E. Hahn 1934–6, A.E. Bishop 1936–9, W.G. Watson 1939–53, Trevor Moore 1953–6, 1961–2, T.S. Johnston 1956–61, R.W. Finlayson 1962–4, E.A. Pickering 1964–7, Robert Chisholm 1967–9, Frank McEachren 1969–73, James Westaway 1973–5, and Terence Wardrop 1975–8, succeeded by Alan Marchment. The continuing vital activities of the Women's Committee and a Junior Women's Committee (founded in 1955) led in the 1970s not only to a reliable additional source of fund-raising each year but also to an impressive program of educational support for the TS. A brochure of 1975–6 lists Symphony Seminars, addressed to junior-high-school and high-school students, and Symphony Preludes, geared to those of elementary-school age, both offered by TS personnel in the schools themselves, as well as 'Symphony Street,' a children's series given in other community settings such as public libraries. In that season more than 200 events, were organized by the women's groups, in addition to the more formal children's and students' series in Massey Hall by the full orchestra.

In 1979–80, 21 of the 98 orchestra members were women. A photo from von Kunits' fifth season (1926–7), however, shows only one woman, the harpist Heloise Macklem. In a 1909 program conducted by Welsman, 11 out of 61 players were women.

In the late 1970s the TS' 98-member aggregation was contracted for 48 weeks of each year, with an annual budget ($4.5 million) which ranked it as the only Canadian orchestra in the 'top ten' of North American orchestras. Its 1979–80 subscription concert individual tickets cost from $3.35 to $15. Its policy of a variety of subscription series of differing appeals and its sound conservatism of programming placed it on a firm foundation as it faced the challenge of moving to new quarters – the new Massey Hall, designed by Arthur Erickson in a newly developing area of west-downtown Toronto and scheduled to open in 1982.

DISCOGRAPHY

MAC MILLAN AS CONDUCTOR

Adaskin *Serenade concertante* – Morel *Esquisse* – Fleming *Shadow on the Prairie*. 1956. RCI 129

Coulthard *Ballade (A Winter's Tale)* – MacMillan *Two Sketches* – Weinzweig *Interlude in an Artist's Life*. (1946). CBC IS Canadian Album No. 2 (4 78s)

Elgar *Imperial March, Op 32* – Holst *The Planets*. ?. 4-RCA Victor 11-8412-8415 (78s)

Elgar *Pomp and Circumstance Marches, Op 39, no. 1–4*. ?. 2-RCA Victor 8226, 8227 (78s)

Jacob *A William Byrd Suite* – Haydn *Serenade* (Andante cantabile from *Quartet, Op 3, no. 5*). ?. 2-RCA Victor 8725-8726

McMullin *Rocky Mountain Suite* (Sketch No. 2) – Rathburn *Images of Childhood* – Freedman *Symphonic Suite*. 1950. RCI 19

Milhaud *Suite française* – Britten *Kermesse canadienne* – Benjamin *Red River Jig*. 1950. RCI 18

Rachmaninoff *Concerto No. 3*. William Kapell pf. Mid 1940s?. International Piano Archives IPA 507

Ridout – Morawetz – Somers – Rathburn – Weinzweig – Vallerand. 1951. RCI 41

Tchaikovsky *Symphony No. 5*. ?. Beaver LP 1001/Victor Bluebird LBC 1093

See also Discographies for Lois Marshall; Toronto Mendelssohn Choir.

GEOFFREY WADDINGTON AS CONDUCTOR

Adaskin *Ballet Symphony* – Brott *Violin Concerto* – Dolin *Scherzo* – Freedman *Nocturne*. Dembeck vn. 1952. RCI 71

SUSSKIND AS CONDUCTOR

Matton *Concerto pour deux pianos* – Morawetz *Piano Concerto No. 1*. Bouchard and Morisset pfs, Kuerti pf. 1965. Cap SW 6123. Matton *Concerto* also released on CRI SD 317

Pierné *The Children's Crusade*. 1960. 2-Beaver LPS 003

See also Discography for Toronto Mendelssohn Choir.

OZAWA AS CONDUCTOR

Berlioz *Symphonie fantastique* – MacMillan *Two Sketches for Strings* – Freedman *Images* – Mercure *Triptyque* – Morel *L'Étoile noire*. 1966. 2-Col M2S-756. MacMillan, Freedman, Mercure, and Morel issued on Col MS 6962 and on Odyssey Y 31993. Berlioz issued on Odyssey Y 31923

Messiaen *Turangalîla* – Takemitsu *November Steps*. 1967. RCA LSC-7051

Takemitsu *Asterism; Requiem; Green (November Steps II); The Dorian Horizon*. 1968. RCA LSC-3099

JEAN DESLAURIERS AS CONDUCTOR

Morawetz *Symphony No. 2* – Turner *Three Episodes* – Pépin *Guernica*. 1965. CBC SM-4. Morawetz also issued on CBC SM-104

FELDBRILL AS CONDUCTOR

Beecroft *Improvvisazioni concertanti No. 1* – Freedman *Tangents* – Ridout *Fall Fair*. Fiore fl. 1972. Audat 477-4001

Weinzweig *Concerto for Piano and Orchestra* – Symonds *The Nameless Hour*. P. Helmer pf, F. Stone flhn. 1969. CBC SM-34/CBC SM-104

ANČERL AS CONDUCTOR

Beethoven *Symphony No. 6*. 1972. CBC SM-150

Martinu *Symphony No. 5*. 1971. CBC SM-218

Pépin *Guernica*. 1972. Audat 477-4001

Willan *Symphony No. 2*. 1970. CBC SM-133

KAZUYOSHI AKIYAMA AS CONDUCTOR

Respighi *The Fountains of Rome*. 1972. CBC SM-218

Stravinsky *The Firebird*. 1980. CBC SM-5004

DAVIS AS CONDUCTOR

Borodin The Three Symphonies; Overture and Polovtsian Dances from *Prince Igor*. Tor Mendelssohn Choir. 1976. 2-Col M2 34587

Brahms *Symphony No. 4*. 1976. CBC SM-327

– *Symphony No. 2*. 1977. CBC SM-336

– *Symphony No. 1*. 1978. CBC SM-353

Janáček Suite from *The Cunning Little Vixen; Taras Bulba*. 1977. Col M 35117

Respighi *La Boutique fantasque*. 1979. Col IM 35842

Strauss *Rosenkavalier Suite* – Bizet *Carmen Suite* – Massenet *Scènes pittoresques*. 1980. CBC SM-5003

Tchaikovsky *The Nutcracker*. Tor Children's Chorus. 1978. 2-Col M2 35196

BIBLIOGRAPHY

Saunders, Henry S. 'Toronto's orchestras: works played 1908 to April 1st 1937,' typescript copy at NL of C

Wood, Christopher. 'History and career of the Toronto Symphony Orchestra,' *Curtain Call*, vol 2, Nov 1939

Honderich, Ruth. 'The Toronto Symphony,' *CRMA*, vol 5, Oct – Nov 1946

Beckwith, John. 'Time TSO came to grips with contemporary music,' *Toronto Daily Star*, 27 Feb 1960

Davies, Doris L. *Over the Years* (Toronto 1961)

'Toronto Symphony Orchestra performs Canadian compositions,' *CanComp*, 14, Jan 1967

Winters, Kenneth. 'Ancerl family in Germany, now Toronto will be home,' Toronto *Telegram*, 13 Sep 1968

– 'Ozawa,' Toronto *Telegram*, 26 Apr 1969

Morey, Carl. 'Toronto Symphony Orchestra,' *PfAC*, Winter 1971

The Welsman Memoranda (Toronto 1971)

Edinborough, Arnold. *A Personal History of the Toronto Symphony* (Toronto 1972)

Weait, Christopher. *The New Symphony Orchestra: The Toronto Symphony Orchestra: The Toronto Symphony: A Master List of Personnel 1922–1972* (Toronto 1972)

Kraglund, John. 'Ancerl aimed TS at greatness' and 'Death critical loss for TS,' Toronto *Globe and Mail*, 4 Jul 1973

MacMillan, Keith. 'Jack Elton: an appreciation 1902–1975,' *TS News*, May 1975

Hathaway, Tom. 'Chronicles of music: on Andrew Davis,' *Canadian Forum*, vol 56, Sep 1976

Schulman, Michael. 'Toronto: good music is for everybody,' *PfAC*, Spring 1977

Deacon, Tom. 'Andrew Davis both challenges and reassures Toronto Symphony audiences,' *Fugue*, Feb 1978

Potvin, Gilles. 'L'OST en Chine,' Montreal *Le Devoir*, 18 Feb 1978

Craven, George. 'The tour of the Toronto Symphony to the People's Republic of China,' *Fugue*, May 1978

Rusk, J. 'Knowledge of business keeps symphony in key,' Toronto *Globe and Mail*, 24 Feb 1979

Pearce, John. 'Performing arts: reaching for the top: excellence at the TSO,' *Toronto Life*, Sep 1980

Toronto Symphony. Archives

FILMOGRAPHY

The Toronto Symphony Orchestra, 2 films with MacMillan as conductor (NFB 1945)

Music East, Music West (CBC 1978)

JB

Toronto Symphony Band. Formed in 1915 by Harry Jose and R.L. Jose (the latter a french hornist) to promote summer employment for the musicians of the *Welsman *TSO and Toronto's theatre orchestras. Under the direction of Luigi von *Kunits the band played for many summers at the *CNE, Hanlan's Point Park, and Scarborough Beach Park and each spring at the Toronto Skating Club carnivals. It also gave radio braodcasts. When the TSO became a full-time orchestra, many of the musicians had to leave the band. In 1935 it was reorganized under L.F. 'Puff' *Addison, continued to perform in the Toronto area, and during the early years of World War II made over 100 broadcasts for the CBC. In 1950 Maurice M. Dunmall became the band's director. Dunmall conducted many concerts in Toronto, including those sponsored by the *Toronto Daily Star* and given at the Queen's Park band stand. Dunmall resigned in 1958 and was succeeded by George Anderson. In 1959 the band's president and co-founder, R.L. Jose, died, and the group's activities ceased. NM

Toronto Woodwind Quintet (Toronto Winds 1972–8). Founded in 1956 by Gordon *Day (flute), Perry *Bauman (oboe), Ezra *Schabas (clarinet), Eugene *Rittich (horn), and Nicholas *Kilburn (bassoon) – all but Schabas principals in the *CBC SO and/or the *TSO. Schabas was succeeded by Stanley *McCartney in 1960, Day by Nicholas *Fiore in 1962, Kilburn by Christopher *Weait in 1970, and Bauman by Melvin *Berman in 1971. For the first few years of its existence the quintet performed only on CBC radio. In 1958, however, it began to appear publicly, mostly within Ontario. It was at its most active during the 1960s, performing with the pianists Jacques Abram, Mario *Bernardi, and Anton *Kuerti and with the *Festival Singers, Judy *Loman, Phyllis *Mailing, and the Montreal Brass Quintet. In 1965 it became one of the first groups to participate in the TSO-sponsored Prelude Concerts for school children. In 1966 it played at the *U of New Brunswick. It appeared in several *Ten Centuries Concerts. In 1967 it was the resident woodwind quintet on the teaching staff of the *NYO, performed in Toronto at the International Congress of Organists and in Montreal for one week at the Canadian government Pavilion at *Expo 67, and appeared in a festival at *Memorial U in St John's, Nfld.

The group featured Canadian works in most of its programs and premiered Lucio *Agostini's *Suite in a Popular Style* (ca 1960), Harry *Freedman's *Quintet* for winds (1962; written for the group), *Eckhardt-Gramatté's *Woodwind Quintet* (1963), and *Weinzweig's *Woodwind Quintet* (1965). In 1964 it participated with the Festival Singers in the first performance and the recording of Freedman's *The Tokaido*.

The group changed its name to the Toronto Winds in 1972. Under its new name it continued to perform locally, appearing at the *Stratford Festival in 1973 and 1975. In 1974 it gave concerts in Great Britain. The group ceased activities in 1978.

DISCOGRAPHY

Bartos *Suite from 'Le Bourgeois Gentilhomme'* – Freedman *Quintet* for winds. (1965). RCI 208

Beethoven *Quintet*, Op 4. Ca 1969. CBC SM-36/CBC SM-193

Dela *Petite Suite maritime* (extracts) – Papineau-Couture *Suite* – Mozart *Quintet* K452. Newmark pf. 1967. CBC Expo 11

Hindemith – Souris – Reicha. 1973. CBC SM-238. (Recorded under the name the Toronto Winds)

Pijper *Woodwind Quintet* – Addison *Serenade* for wind quintet and harp. Loman hp. Ca 1969. CBC SM-35/CBC SM-186

Schafer *Minnelieder* – Kasemets *Quintet* for wind instruments – Weinzweig *Woodwind Quintet*. Mailing mezzo. (1967). RCI ACM-1 (Weinzweig only)/RCI 218/RCA CCS-1012

Telemann *Suite in B Minor* – Fiala *Chamber Music for Five Woodwind Instruments*. Ca 1965. CBC SM-22/CBC SM-186 (Fiala only)/CBC SM-193 (Telemann only)

See also Discography for the Festival Singers. NM

***Torquil: A Scandinavian Dramatic Legend*.** Opera by Charles A.E. *Harriss on a text by Edward Oxenford. This two-and-a-half-hour work (which, the composer stipulates on the score, 'may be sung by Choral Societies but must be given without Costume or Action') was published in 1896 by *Whaley Royce. It was premiered, in an orchestration by the Boston flutist Paul Fox, at *Massey Hall, Toronto, 22 May 1900, by the Boston Festival Orchestra, *Torrington's Festival Chorus, and soloists – Flora Provan (soprano), Isabella Boulton (contralto), Leon Moore (tenor), and Gwilym Miles (bass) – under the composer's baton. The work was repeated with the same orchestra and soloists in Ottawa at the *Russell Theatre the following day and at the *Montreal Arena 25 May, assisted in each city by a large local choir. All three performances were for the benefit of families of soldiers fighting in South Africa, and, at least in Ottawa, the performers were draped patriotically in red, white, and blue. Despite its subtitle, *Torquil* betrays no attempt by the composer to capture a Scandinavian musical idiom. Influences range from Mendelssohn to Wagner. Only the vocal score is extant, and an excerpt ('Alas for Me') is reproduced in *A History of Music in Canada*. An excerpt from the second-act finale, orchestrated by Godfrey *Ridout, was performed in 1965 on CBC radio. NT

TORRINGTON, F.H. (Frederick Herbert). Conductor, organist, violinist, teacher, administrator, b Dudley, near Birmingham, 20 Oct 1837, d Toronto 20 Nov 1917; hon D MUS (Toronto) 1902. After early local training Torrington studied piano, organ, theory, and choral music for four years in Kidderminster with James Fitzgerald. He became organist at 16 at St Ann's Church in Bewdley.

In 1856 Torrington emigrated to Canada, settling in Montreal, where he worked first as a piano tuner and then as organist-choirmaster at St James St Methodist Church. He also taught privately and at several schools, was conductor of instrumental and choral groups including the Montreal Amateur Musical Union, and for three years was bandmaster of the 25th Regiment, Queen's Own Borderers. He played in an orchestra and performed frequently as an organist and solo violinist. In 1869 he organized the Canadian section of an orchestra directed by Patrick S. Gilmore for a performance at the First Peace Jubilee in Boston. Torrington moved to Boston that year and was organist at King's Chapel, a teacher of piano and organ at the New England Cons, a conductor of various choral groups in the area, and a member of the first violins in the Harvard (later Boston) SO. He also gave organ recitals in Boston, New York, and other eastern US cities.

In 1873 he returned to Canada as organist-choirmaster at the Metropolitan Methodist (later United) Church in Toronto and conductor 1873–94 of the re-formed *Toronto Philharmonic Society. Rapidly becoming a central figure in musical life in Toronto, he conducted the Canadian premieres of Mendelssohn's *Elijah* (1874) and *St Paul* (1876) and later organized the first Toronto Music Festival (1886) at the Horticultural Pavilion of Allan Gardens with a 1000-voice choir, orchestra, a children's choir, and Lilli Lehmann and Max Heinrich as soloists. In 1894 he organized a second festival to open *Massey Music Hall, for which event the Festival Chorus was formed. Made up mainly of singers from the disbanding Toronto Philharmonic Society, the new choir gave annual performances of *Messiah* and other oratorios until 1912. At his farewell performances on 12 and 13 March Torrington conducted the Festival Chorus with the *Welsman TSO.

Torrington's influence extended beyond Toronto, as he was music director ca 1874–82 at the Ontario Ladies' College in Whitby and conductor of the Hamilton Philharmonic Society in the 1880s. In 1888 he founded the *Toronto College of Music, which in 1890 became the first musical affiliate of the *U of Toronto. He remained the director until his death. He was president of the *Canadian Society of Musicians in 1892. He also conducted a succession of amateur or semi-professional orchestras in Toronto which, taken together, were the city's closest approximation to symphonic

F.H. Torrington, a painting by J.W.L. Forster

groups before Frank Welsman formed his Toronto Symphony Orchestra in 1906. Typical of these were an amateur orchestra of 50–70 students, organized in 1877, which gave several concerts each year, and another group (1900–1) called the Toronto Permanent Orchestra. Also, under the auspices of the Toronto College of Music he founded the Orchestral School to provide playing experience for 100-or-so members. Leaving his post at Metropolitan Church in 1907, he moved to High Park Methodist Church, where he remained until 1914. The composer of the patriotic songs 'Canada, The Gem in the Crown' (I. Suckling 1876) and 'Welcome Home, Brave Volunteers' (Imrie & Graham 1885), he also wrote 'Our Country and King' (1901) for chorus and some organ music.

Torrington's major achievement was the development of a strong choral tradition in Toronto, but he also had a personal influence on many musicians in Montreal and Toronto, through his orchestras and teaching. His pupils included G.D. *Atkinson, Mary Kerr Austin, Ernest *Dainty, H.K. *Jordan, Whitney Mockridge, and Charles *Wheeler. A full-length portrait of Torrington by J.W.L. Forster, commissioned by friends and former students and completed in 1899, was hung, many years later, in the U of Toronto's Edward Johnson Building.

BIBLIOGRAPHY

'Dr. F.H. Torrington,' *Commemorative Biographical Record of the County of York* (Toronto 1907)

Blewett, Jean. 'Mr. Torrington and his work,' *Canadian Magazine*, vol 35, May 1910

Seranus [S.F. Harrison]. 'Dr. F.H. Torrington,' *MCan*, vol 6, Mar 1912

Bridle, Augustus. 'Two pères de musique,' *Sons of Canada* (Toronto 1916)

Charlesworth, Hector. 'Dr. Torrington's memory honoured,' *SatN*, 27 Sep 1924

Metropolitan Toronto Library. Scrapbooks, vertical files

RPn

Toth. Czechoslovakian-Canadian family of musicians: 1 / Carl, and 2 / Rudy, 3 / Jerry, and 4 / Tony, sons of Carl.

1 **Carl** (b Karol). Violinist, cimbalom builder, b near Stare Karasnow, Czechoslovakia, 1905, d Toronto 1958. He moved to Canada in 1925 and made his home in Toronto in 1933, working as a gypsy fiddler and a master cabinet maker. The Carl Toth Gypsy Orchestra was heard in Hungarian clubs in Toronto, and Toth himself performed occasionally on CBC radio. He made about 10 cimbaloms (Hungarian dulcimers), modifying the traditional type, and also a few violins.

2 **Rudy**. Composer, arranger, conductor, pianist, cimbalom player, b Stare Karasnow, Czechoslovakia. As a child he played cymbalom for his father.

During the 1940s he attended the *TCM where his teachers were Boris *Berlin (piano), John *Weinzweig (harmony), and Ettore *Mazzoleni (conducting); concurrently he worked in the Toronto dance bands of Stan Patton, Ellis *McLintock, Bert *Niosi, and others. He studied piano in Paris with Gaby Casadesus in 1950 and completed his conducting studies with Leonard Bernstein at Tanglewood and Walter *Susskind in Toronto. Toth began his CBC career in the late 1940s as pianist for Howard *Cable, had his own radio show in 1951, and worked until ca 1965 as music director for CBC TV shows starring Joan *Fairfax, Wally *Koster, Denny*Vaughan, and others.

In the mid-1960s Toth turned increasingly to the writing of jingles, 1965–70 in partnership with Jerry Toth, Dolores *Claman, and Richard Morris as Quartet Productions, and thereafter with Jerry as Seven-O Productions. (Seven-O Inc was established in the USA in 1980 to facilitate the Toths' work in that country.)

Toth's later work in TV has included the orchestration (with Jerry) and conducting of the CBS production of *Once Upon the Brothers Grimm* (an Emmy Award nominee), and of several CBC specials. Recordings of his music include *Toronto*, inspired by the city and commissioned and distributed by the *Toronto Star*; and two LPs of children's music designed for use in public schools. Toth has continued to perform on the cimbalom, in works by Bartók, Kodály, and Stravinsky, with the *TSO, the *Ottawa Philharmonic, the Buffalo SO, and the Ivan *Romanoff Orchestra. He is a member of CAPAC.

Rudy Toth's wife, Josephine Chuchman (violinist, b Edmonton, and a pupil of Elie *Spivak at the RCMT), played at 14 in the *Promenade Symphony Concerts orchestra and 1952–8 in the TSO. She later played in ballet, opera, and studio orchestras in Toronto. She has collaborated as a lyricist on several of her husband's projects.

3 **Jerry** (b Jaroslav). Alto saxophonist, clarinetist, flutist, arranger, composer, audio consultant, producer, b Windsor, Ont, 15 Nov 1928. His teachers in Toronto were Frank Hiron (saxophone) and Herbert Pye (clarinet, at the TCM). During 1953 he studied woodwinds in Los Angeles with Dale Eisenhuth. He played 1945–53 in the dance bands of Stan Patton, Bobby *Gimby, Trump *Davidson, and others and was co-leader 1952–7 with the trombonist Ross Culley and the saxophonist Roy Smith of a 17-piece jazz band. He was a member of Phil *Nimmons' jazz bands until 1974 and also studied orchestration with Nimmons. Toth began playing in CBC orchestras in 1954 under Jack *Kane and became a leading Toronto studio musician. He was chief arranger or music director for the CBC's 'Parade' ca 1957–60. In the mid-1960s he began writing and producing jingles with his brother Rudy and others. He has produced recordings by several singers and has served as audio consultant for many TV productions. He has composed and arranged music for CTL LPs by Bobby Edwards' Fat City Guitars (which recorded his *Fat City Suite in E Major*, CTL 477-5162) and Ted *Roderman and for the LPs *The Music of Jerry* (1969, CTL 477-5116) and *The Twelve Sides of Jerry Toth* (1973, CTL 477-5171), by Toth's orchestra, and *Moment of Love* (1972, Warner WSC 9008), by Toth's singers, both essentially studio groups. Written by Rudy Toth, and recorded with the composer as piano soloist, 'Moment of Love' was a hit in Canada. Toth also has recorded as a soloist with Phil Nimmons and with the *Boss Brass and has continued to lead small jazz groups in Toronto clubs. He is a member of CAPAC.

4 **Tony**. Oboist, english hornist, saxophonist, clarinetist, copyist, b Windsor. Among his teachers were Herbert Pye (clarinet, TCM), Maurice Morel (oboe, english horn, and clarinet, Paris 1960), and Virginia Markson (flute). He began his professional career in London, Ont, while studying commerce 1950–5 at the U of Western Ontario. Returning in 1955 to Toronto he has divided his time between work as a copyist and performance as an oboist, clarinetist, and english hornist in radio, TV, and recording orchestras. In the 1970s he was the baritone saxophonist and copyist for *Nimmons 'N' Nine Plus Six. (MM)

TOULINGUET, Marie (b Stirling, Georgina). Soprano, b Twillingate, Nfld, 3 Apr 1867, d there 21 Apr 1935. She studied with Mathilde Marchesi in Paris, made her debut there in 1893, and for about 10 years enjoyed a successful concert and opera career, particularly in Italy where she sang at La Scala before the Italian royal family. She returned to Newfoundland in 1893 to perform in recital at the Methodist College Hall, St John's. On that occasion she sang arias by Meyerbeer, Handel, and Verdi and the songs 'Harbour Bay' (F.L. Moir), 'The Holy City' (S. Adams), and 'Venetian Boating Song' (Tosti). In 1896 Toulinguet sang again in St John's, this time in the Roman Catholic Cathedral. The following year, at the Brooklyn Academy of Music, she sang arias from Giordano's *Andrea Chenier* and Handel's *Serse*. Also in 1897, she toured with Mapleson's New Imperial Opera singing in Weber's *Der Freischütz* and other works. While with that company she performed in Montreal. In the same year she performed with the Boston Harmony Orchestral Society.

After many years abroad Toulinguet returned to Twillingate, where, 29 years after her death, a citizens' committee raised a monument over her previously unmarked grave. Her professional name was derived from the old Breton name for Twillingate; in Newfoundland she was known also as Twillingate Stirling. Her only recording (Milan ca 1904), surviving in a private collection, reveals a high soprano of great brilliance and agility.

BIBLIOGRAPHY

NL of C. Music Division vertical files JBM

TOURANGEAU, (Marie Jeannine) **Huguette** (m Thompson). Mezzo-soprano, b Montreal 12 Aug 1940; deuxieme prix (CMM) 1964. She graduated in pedagogy and piano from the Collège Marguerite-Bourgeoys and in 1958 enrolled at the CMM for voice study with Ruzena *Herlinger, repertoire with Otto-Werner *Mueller, and declamation with Roy *Royal. In 1962 she was soloist in Monteverdi's *Vespro della Beata Virgine* for the *Montreal Festivals. In 1964 she made her debut as Mercedes in *Carmen* under Zubin Mehta, who encouraged her to take part in the *Metropolitan Opera regional auditions. A finalist among the 5000 candidates, she won a $2000 prize from the Fisher Foundation and was engaged to sing 1964–5 with the Metropolitan National (touring) Company.

In the summer of 1964 Tourangeau sang Cherubino in *The Marriage of Figaro* under Richard Bonynge's direction at the *Stratford Festival, and during the 1965–6 season she appeared in the title role of *Carmen* in 56 North American cities with the Metropolitan National Company and repeated the role with the New York City Opera. During *Expo 67 she appeared as Siebel in *Faust*. Around that time she began to appear and record with Joan Sutherland and Bonynge. She was heard in Seattle (Mallika in *Lakmé*), London (Urbain in *Les Huguenots*), and San Francisco (Elisabetta in *Maria Stuarda*, Adalgisa in *Norma*, and Orlofsky in *Die Fledermaus*). At the Hamburg State Opera, in the title role (originally alto castrato) of Handel's *Julius Caesar* and then in *Carmen*, she was a marked success. In the fall of 1972 she appeared in Vancouver and Edmonton performances of *Lucrezia Borgia*.

Huguette Tourangeau

On 28 Nov 1973 Tourangeau made her Metropolitan Opera debut as Nicklausse in *The Tales of Hoffmann* (the *New York Times* described her as 'splendid'). The same year, she sang Bertarido in Handel's *Rodelinda* at the Holland Festival. Tourangeau excels also in light opera, and in 1972, and again in 1973, with the Santa Fe Opera, she sang the title role of *The Grand Duchess of Gerolstein*. In June 1974 she joined Joan Sutherland in Australia for the inaugural season of the Sydney Opera House. Other important roles Tourangeau has sung in the 1970s include Dorabella in the Metropolitan Opera's *Così fan tutte* (1975), Arsace in *Semiramide* for the *Vancouver Opera (1975), Rosina in the *Edmonton Opera's *The Barber of Seville* (1976), the title role in *Carmen* (16 performances) for the Sydney Opera (1977), and Elisabetta in *Maria Stuarda* at Covent Garden (1977, her debut there). In 1978 she sang Zerlina in *Don Giovanni* at the Metropolitan, in 1979 Orpheo in *Orpheo ed Euridice* at the Holland Festival, and Carmen with the *Société lyrique d'Aubigny at the *Grand Théâtre in Quebec City.

In 1977 Tourangeau became the first recipient of the *CMCouncil's Artist of the Year award. Her voice is a light and flexible mezzo-soprano adaptable to the wide range of the mezzo repertoire, from Rossinian coloratura to the robust sound required by the trouser roles of German opera or the lyric mezzo of the French heroines. Her husband, Barry Thompson, was manager of the Vancouver Opera 1975–8.

DISCOGRAPHY

Arias from Forgotten Operas: Balfe – Bizet – Donizetti – Auber – Massenet – Verdi. O de la Suisse romande, Bonynge cond. (1971). Lon OS 26199

Donizetti *Lucia di Lammermoor*. Chor and O of the Royal Opera House, Covent Garden, Bonynge cond, Tourangeau (Alisa). (1972). Lon OSA 13103

– *Maria Stuarda*. Chor and O of the Bologna Teatro Comunale, Bonynge cond, Tourangeau (Elisabetta). (1976). 3-Lon OSA 13117

Handel *Messiah*. Ambrosian Singers, English Chamber O, Bonynge cond. (1970). Lon OSA 1396/(Excerpts) Lon OS 26254

Leoni *L'Oracolo*. John Alldis Choir, Finchley Children's Music Group, National Phil O, Bonynge cond. 1975. 2-Lon 12107

Massenet *Esclarmonde*. Alldis Choir, National Phil O, Bonynge cond, Tourangeau (Parseis). (1976). Lon OSA 13118

– *Songs*. Bonynge pf, R. Kilbey vc. 1975. Decca SXL 6765

– *Thérèse*. Linden Singers, New Philharmonia O, Bonynge cond. Tourangeau (Thérèse). (1974). Lon AOSA 1165
Meyerbeer *Les Huguenots*. New Ambrosian Opera Chor, New Philharmonia O, Bonynge cond, Tourangeau (Urbain). (1972). Lon OSA 1437/(Excerpts) Lon OS 26239
Offenbach *The Tales of Hoffmann*. Suisse romande Chor, O de la Suisse romande, Bonynge cond, Tourangeau (The Muse and Niklausse). (1972). Lon OSA 13106
Thomas *Mignon*. Vancouver Opera Chor and O, Bonynge cond. 1977. 3-BJRS 1441-1443
Verdi *Rigoletto*. Ambrosian Opera Chor, London SO, Bonynge cond, Tourangeau (Maddalena). (1973). Lon OSA 13105/(Excerpts) Lon OS 26401

BIBLIOGRAPHY
Chalip, Alice Grace. 'Fame, elsewhere,' *Montreal Star*, 6 Jan 1973
Zakariasen, William. 'Tourangeau, French Canadian,' *Opera News* (Oct 1973)
Coleman, Francis. 'Huguette Tourangeau at Covent Garden: impressive,' *Mcan*, 35, Apr 1978

FILMOGRAPHY
The Dream and the Destiny / Le Rêve et la destinée (Hambourg 1972) GP

TOWNSEND, Graham (Craig). Fiddler, mandolinist, composer, b Toronto 16 Jun 1942. His father, Fred Townsend (b Reading, Berkshire, England, 24 Apr 1900), was Don *Messer's square dance caller for many years. The younger Townsend was raised in the Ottawa Valley, where he was influenced by Irish traditional fiddlers. At 9 he won the '30 and Under' fiddling competition at the *CNE, Toronto, and at 13 he made his first recordings for *Rodeo. Townsend has performed in the USA and Europe and widely in Canada. He was a frequent guest on the CBC's 'Don Messer's Jubilee' throughout that program's history. He won the open class of the *Canadian Open Old Time Fiddlers' Contest in 1963, 1968, 1969, and 1970 before retiring from competition. He has made over 25 LPs for the Banff, London, Audat, Rounder, and Point labels. Recordings for Point were reissued as *Best of Graham Townsend* (MCA Coral CB 34010). He also has made an LP as a mandolinist.

Among the most impressive fiddlers in Canada, Townsend is fluent in the many regional and ethnic styles and has assisted the folklorists Dorothy and Homer Hogan of Guelph in the documentation of the Canadian fiddle tradition. His descriptions of fiddle styles are included in their notes to *The Great Canadian Fiddle* (1977, Springwater S6; recorded by Townsend with his father, his wife, Eleanor, the banjoist Maurice *Bolyer, and others) and in part 2 ('Canadian Fiddle Culture') of *Canadian Folk Culture* (Scarborough, Ont, 1977). He also has served as a consultant for, or co-producer of, CBC radio programs about Canadian country music by David Pritchard and Alan Guettel.

Townsend's wife, Eleanor (fiddler, b Reed in Dungannon, northwest of Stratford, Ont, 8 Jan 1944), won the women's class at the Canadian Open Old Time Fiddlers' Contest in 1967, 1969, 1970, and 1974 and placed second in the traditionally male-dominated open class in 1975. She has won open competitions at the CNE. In 1977 she began teaching old time fiddling at Seneca College, Toronto. Her LPs include *Mrs. Country Fiddle* (Marathon MMS 76048). Graham and Eleanor Townsend are key members of Maple Sugar, a performing group initiated by Dorothy Hogan of Guelph, Ont, in the early 1970s and dedicated to the preservation of Canada's folk heritage. Other members of the troupe include the singer-guitarist James Gordon, the step dancers Donny and Gina Gilchrist, and Les Danseurs québécois. Active especially in the late 1970s, Maple Sugar has appeared in various forms at folk festivals in Canada and the USA and made the LP *Songs of Early Canada* (Springwater S1/S2). MM (MD)

Trade union songs. Although rich in occupational songs, Canada has not been particularly productive of trade union songs. A sealers' strike in St John's in 1902 inspired two ballads that were printed in Newfoundland booklets, and a strike by Canadian Northern Railway workers along the Fraser River in 1912 led Joe Hill, the songwriter associated with International Workers of the World, to write 'Where the Fraser River Flows' to the tune of 'Where the River Shannon Flows.' Several songs came out of strikes 1912–13 in the Nanaimo coalfields, the best known being 'Bowser's Seventy-Twa,' a satirical description of the militia sent in by Attorney-General Bowser. In Cape Breton during a strike in 1910 the Glace Bay miners sang 'Arise Ye Nova Scotia Slaves' and attacked 'The Yahie Miners,' whom they accused of taking their jobs.

The Winnipeg General Strike of 1919 was not celebrated in song, though it is the basis of the musical *The Conquest of Winnipeg* by Stuart *Broomer, but a lesser-known strike, in 1931, of miners in the Bienfait-Estevan coalcamps of southeastern Saskatchewan inspired Cecil Boone to write 'The Estevan Massacre' to the tune of 'Kevin Barry.' In the On-to-Ottawa Trek of 1935 the unemployed marchers' theme song was 'Hold the Fort,' and many picket lines have resounded to 'Solidarity Forever' and 'We Shall Not Be Moved.'

In Ontario M.T. Montgomery wrote 'United Steelworkers Are We' to the melody used in *'Squid-jiggin' Ground,' and in Buchans, Nfld, steelworkers composed half a dozen songs to familiar tunes during strikes in 1971 and 1973. Similar songs undoubtedly have been composed during other industrial disputes, but these usually have not survived beyond the struggle that inspired them.

Texts of various trade union songs appear in 'Labor and Industrial Protest Songs in Canada' in the *Journal of American Folklore* (vol 82, Jan–Mar 1969), and the *Travelers sing a few on the LP *A Century of Song*. EF

Transit through Fire: An Odyssey of 1942. First opera commissioned by CBC radio. The music by Healey *Willan, to a prologue and four scenes by John Coulter, was orchestrated by Lucio *Agostini. Norman Cherrie, Frances *James, Charles *Jordan, J. Campbell *McInnes, William *Morton, and Howard Scott sang in the premiere, 8 Mar 1942, with chorus and orchestra under Sir Ernest *MacMillan. A recording of the hour-long work is in the CBC Program Archives. Ettore *Mazzoleni led the Conservatory SO, chorus, and soloists in a concert performance 18 Feb 1943 at Convocation Hall, *U of Toronto. The libretto, which has been published (Toronto 1942), concerns a young man's reaction to war.

Transportation. Of the various means of travel by land, sea, and air, only the railways, with the rhythmic clickety-clack of the wheels and the scream of the locomotive whistle, have provided an obvious subject for imitation in music. Perhaps the best known international example is Arthur Honegger's orchestral work *Pacific 231*, inspired by a US locomotive. Canadian composers fascinated by railroad sound have included André *Mathieu, who at four composed a piano piece, *Les Gros Chars* (*The Big Train*), subsequently published by Southern; Eldon *Rathburn, in his

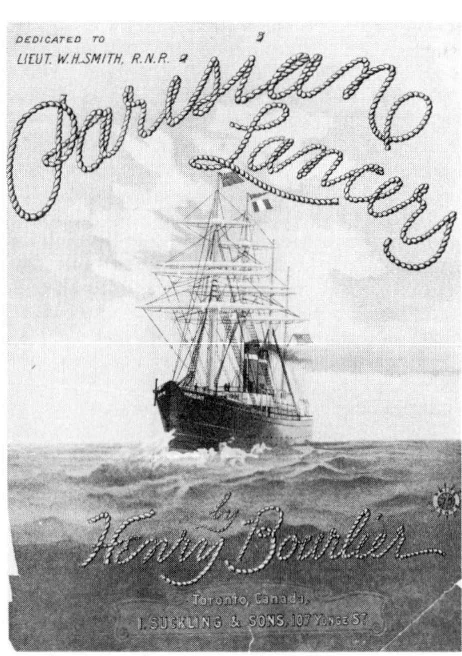

The *Parisian*, an Allan lines steamship, 1888

Aspects of Railroads for orchestra (1969); and Godfrey *Ridout, in the second movement ('From the Caboose') of his *Music for a Young Prince* for orchestra (1959). Louis *Applebaum set railway timetables in his chamber work *Algoma Central* for soprano, harp, and flute (1976). Rathburn's *Turbo*, composed in 1978 for *Canadian Brass, celebrates the modern fast train. Oskar *Morawetz' symphonic poem *The Railway Station* (1980, commissioned by the *NYO) was inspired by Archibald Lampman's poem of that name. In a three-part narrative song, 'Canadian Railroad Trilogy,' Gordon *Lightfoot recounts the story of the building of the CPR.

Most other Canadian pieces ostensibly inspired by the railway are 19th-century dances which, typically for their time, bore any label which, by referring to a current matter, might promote sales. Railway building was a topic of great importance in 19th-century Canada, and the purveyors of dance took notice. Examples are *The Canadian Grand Trunk Railway Gallop* by 'W.H.' (1853); *The Grand Trunk Waltzes* by Charles d'Albert (featuring a picture of the newly opened Victoria Bridge in Montreal, ca 1859); the *C.P.R. Lancers* by N.S. Smith (1880s); *Chemin de fer du Pacifique*, a quadrille by Jules *Hone (nd); and *Q.M.O. & O. Galop* (Quebec, Montreal, Ottawa and Occidental) by Roch *Lyonnais. *Ottawa & Gatineau Ry.* is the title of a march by Alice Allen-Heeney, published in 1898. Descriptive pieces include *A Trip to Niagara* (1905) by Clifford V. Baker and *A Trip from Montreal to Lachine on the G.T.R.*, reported by the Toronto *Musical Journal* (15 Jul 1887) to have been performed by the Victoria Rifles band on Dominion Square in Montreal to the accompaniment of 'bells, whistles, steam, etc.'

Sea travel by steamship on the Great Lakes, on the St Lawrence and its tributaries, or on the waters of Manitoba and the Atlantic and Pacific coasts was not only a necessity but a popular recreation. The names of many steamships have been celebrated in music. Examples include *Success to the Steam Ship 'Secret'* (ca 1871) by E. George Straker, dedicated to the mayor of Quebec, Pierre Garneau; the *Parisian Lancers* (1888) by Henry Bourlier, named after an Allan lines steamship; and the *Peerless Rockaway* (nd) composed by C.J. Arthur Marier of Ottawa and played on Ottawa river moonlight excursions. The *Chicora Waltz* (1881) dedicated by Edwin *Gledhill to the captain and the officers of the palace steamer *Chicora*, the *Cayuga Two Step* (1906) by W.H. *Hodgins, and the *S.S. Noronic March* (1921) by W.D. Martin recall famous Great Lakes ships. (See also Disaster songs.)

The airplane and the automobile developed in an age when sheet music titles related less often to everyday objects. Songs written about aviation in 1918 include Morris Manley's 'Up in the Air'; Florence Benjamin's 'Come with Me in My Aeroplane,' dedicated to the boys of the Royal Air Force; and Will J. White's 'Flying.' World War II produced Wishart *Campbell's 'We're Flying to a New Horizon' (1943), Walter Ewin's 'The Eagle of the Sky!' (1941), R. Beaudry's 'Votre avion va-t-il au paradis?,' and Mario Dépangher's *La Marche des aviateurs* (1946). Canadian automobile songs include D.F. Harrison's 'My Ragtime Automobile,' written in the early 20th century, and Nelson H. Bell's 'Mister Buick: "The Hero of the Road" ' (copyright by the McLaughlin Motor Car Co of Oshawa, Ont) and ' "Pontiac": That's the Car for Me' (copyright by General Motors of Oshawa), both dating from 1927. The third movement of George *Fiala's orchestral suite *Montreal* – 'Métro: allegro giusto' – is descriptive of the city's subway.

See also Sports for music related to bicycles, canoes, sleighs, and yachts. (FH, HK)

The Travellers. Folk group formed in Toronto during the summer of 1953 by Sid Dolgay (mando-cello), Jerry Gray (banjo and lead singer), and Helen Gray, Jerry Goodis, and Oscar Ross (singers). Sam Goldberg was music director until 1961. Helen Gray and Ross were replaced, respectively, by Simone Cook (m Johnston) in 1954 and Marty Meslin in 1955. Meslin left in 1957. The Travellers made their TV debut in 1954 on the CBC's 'Haunted Studio' and were finalists in 1956 on 'Pick the Stars.' In 1958 they recorded the first of many LPs, assisted by the bassist Jack Lander, who continued to record with the group until 1963. In 1961 the Travellers appeared at the first *Mariposa Folk Festival and toured Canada with Jacques *Labrecque. In the same year Goodis and Goldberg left, and the guitarist Ray Woodley joined the group.

The following year, with Eugene Dolny as music director, the group performed in the USSR, presenting 'A Musical Tour of Canada' in 19 concerts. An LP was released to commemorate the tour; though spoken introductions and audience reaction were recorded in the USSR, the performances in fact were recorded in Canada. A tour of Canada in 1963 was followed in 1964 by a royal command performance in Charlottetown and a tour of Britain. Dolgay and Johnston left the group in 1965 and 1969 respectively and were replaced by the string bassist and bass guitarist Joe Lawrence and the singer Pam Fernie. Dolny also left in 1965, and until 1970 there was no official music director. In addition to making a centennial album, and an LP for the Canadian Labour Congress, the Travellers toured Canada again in 1967, giving some 100 concerts, including several in the Northwest Territories and the Peace River district of Alberta. In the late 1960s they began giving annual children's concerts in Toronto, most of them at Minkler Auditorium, Seneca College. With a new guitarist and music director, Ted Roberts, they performed at the opening of the Canadian Pavilion at Expo 70, Osaka, before an audience which included the Japanese royal family. In 1971 the Travellers entertained Canadian troops stationed in Germany and Cyprus. They returned to Cyprus the following year with another new member, the drummer Don Vickery, and in 1974 Aileen Aherne replaced Fernie.

In the late 1970s the group reduced its itinerary, continuing its children's concerts and performing for conventions. Over the years, it has made many commercials. In 1979 the Travellers were Aherne, Gray (the only remaining original member), Lawrence, Roberts, and Vickery. The Travellers' repertoire has reflected the diverse ethnic make-up of Canada and has included songs of the native peoples. It also has offered comic and satirical routines. An adaptation for Canadian audiences of Woody Guthrie's 'This Land Is Your Land' has enjoyed wide popularity, and all royalties have been assigned to the Woody Guthrie Foundation.

DISCOGRAPHY

Across Canada with the Travellers. 1958. Hallmark CS-7
The Travellers Sing Songs of North America. 1959. Hallmark CS-9
The Travellers' Quilting Bee. 1960. Col FS 512
Introducing the Travellers. 1961. Col BN 26013
The Travellers on Tour. 1962. Col FS 545
Something to Sing About. 1963. Col FS 610
We're on Our Way Again, the Travellers. 1964–5. Col EL 103
A Century of Song. 1967. Arc AS 261
This Land, the Travellers Centennial Album. 1967. Arc AS 250
Sea to Sea, the Iron Miracle. 1968. CNE 68
The Travellers Applaud Canada. 1968. Arc AS 268
The Travellers Sing for Kids. 1970. RCI 352/CBC LM-82/Kanata 3/Caedmon ML-7001
The Travellers Still Travelling. Harmony HES 6003

BIBLIOGRAPHY

Rasky, Frank. 'Singers in search of the sound of Canada,' *Canadian Weekly*, 27 Sep 1965
Adilman, Sid. 'The Travellers about as Canadian as you can get eh?' *Star Week*, 6 Jan 1973 (JBk, MM)

TREDWELL, Eric (Alfred Stanley). Baritone, b Bristol, England, 2 Aug 1906; BA (Toronto) 1945. Raised in Canada, he studied voice in Victoria, BC, with Gideon *Hicks and 1929–30 in Munich with Julius Schweitzer. Returning to Canada he made his radio debut in 1931 on CNRT, Toronto, and studied 1931–40 at the TCM with Dalton *Baker, Hubert Eisdell, Ernesto *Vinci, and Albert Whitehead. A leading soloist in choral and orchestral concerts in Toronto from the 1930s to the early 1950s, Tredwell was heard on the CRBC and CBC, and in 1933 he sang for the first time with the *Toronto Mendelssohn Choir (with which he recorded the *St Matthew Passion* in 1952). He was soloist 1938–51 at Bloor St United Church. In 1940 he made his debut with the *TSO, and in the mid-1940s he appeared with the *Ottawa Choral Union in *Messiah* and Verdi's *Requiem*. In the 1940s also he was a member of the CBC Madrigal Singers and sang leading roles in Gilbert & Sullivan operas with the CBC Light Opera and others with the *CBC Opera Company. For many years also a public school teacher, Tredwell retired from performance in 1957, after two years with the *Festival Singers, to become vice-principal of a Toronto school. MM, PW

TREMBLAY, (Pierre-Joseph) **Amédée**. Organist, composer, teacher, b Montreal 14 Apr 1876, d Los Angeles 1949. He began study at 12 with Father Sauvé, the organist at St-Joseph Church, Montreal, continuing with Alcibiade *Béique (piano and organ) and Father Cléophas Borduas (Gregorian chant). Though he competed successfully for the post of organist at the Dominican Church, St-Hyacinthe, he accepted instead a post at St-Joseph Church in Montreal, which he held 1892–4. In 1894 he founded a choral society, the Orphéon de St-Joseph, which became the Orphéon Goulet when J.-J. *Goulet succeeded Tremblay as director in 1895. Tremblay was organist 1894–1920 at Notre-Dame Basilica in Ottawa and

Amédée Tremblay

was a prominent figure in the musical life of the capital as an organist, composer, and teacher. His pupils included Wilfrid Charette, Oscar *O'Brien, and his own son, the composer George (Amédée) Tremblay. He moved to Salt Lake City, Utah, in 1920 as organist at the Cathedral of the Madeleine, then settled in 1923 in Los Angeles as organist at St Vincent's Roman Catholic church, remaining there until his death.

Like Alexis *Contant, Tremblay was one of the few major musicians of his time whose training was exclusively Canadian. Though to some degree self-taught, he wrote works which attracted the attention of Guillaume *Couture and Vincent d'Indy. His best-known work, *Suite de quatre pièces pour grand orgue* (J. Fischer 1924), dedicated to Joseph *Bonnet, is noted for its finale, a brilliant toccata. Tremblay also wrote two masses, some motets, and a few patriotic songs. His operetta *L'Intransigeant* was produced in Ottawa in 1906. With Achille *Fortier and Alfred *Laliberté, Tremblay was among the first to make concert arrangements of French-Canadian folksongs. His collection, *Dix-huit Chansons populaires du Canada* was published in 1902 in Ottawa by Orme. Other works were published in *Le *Passe-Temps* and by *Archambault.

His son George (b Ottawa 14 Jan 1911) was a pupil of Arnold Schoenberg in Los Angeles, where he took up residence in 1923, and there founded in 1965 the School for the Discovery and Advancement of New Serial Techniques. George Tremblay's works, which reflect a wide range of influences, are listed in Vinton's *Dictionary of Contemporary Music* and include three quartets, three sonatas, and three symphonies. GP

TREMBLAY, (Marie) **Édith** (Louise Ginette) (m Gallienne). Soprano, b Arvida (renamed Jonquière), Que, 11 Apr 1947; deuxième prix voice (CMQ) 1971. She studied voice 1964–71 with Guy Lepage and René Bianco at the CMQ and during the same period took part in a 1967 matinée of the *Quebec SO and in such programs as 'Quebec sait chanter' on CFTM-TV and 'Recital de Quebec' on CBC radio. She won second prize in the 1971 *CBC Talent Festival and went to Paris where she studied voice and solfège 1971–2 with Janine Micheau at the Cons national. She obtained third prize in the 1971 Concours international de chant in Toulouse and first prize in both opera and French art song at the 1972 Concours international de chant in Paris.

Under contract 1972–4 to the Opéra de Wallonie, a company of the Royal Theatre of Liege, Belgium, Tremblay performed the roles of Musetta (Puccini's *La Bohème*), Charlotte (Massenet's *Werther*), Fata Morgana (Prokofiev's *The Love of Three Oranges*), Minnie (Puccini's *The Girl of the*

Golden West), Fatme (Grétry's *Zémire et Azor*), Giulietta (Offenbach's *Les Contes d'Hoffmann*), Lisa (Tchaikovsky's *The Queen of Spades*), and Desdemona (Verdi's *Otello*). With that company and orchestra conducted by Marcel Desiron she recorded Leonora's aria 'Pace, pace, mio Dio' from *La Forza del Destino* (1973, Alpha SP 6014). She was hailed as 'a singer with great style and an impeccable evenness of tone' for her performance as Cio-Cio-San in *Madama Butterfly* with the same troupe in Namur, Belgium (*Le Progrès*, 26 Oct 1973).

In a Radio France broadcast Tremblay took the part of Mimi in Leoncavallo's *La Bohème* and participated in a recording of Menotti's *The Old Maid and the Thief*. For the BBC she sang the role of Élisabeth in the original French version of Verdi's *Don Carlos*, in a cast which included André *Turp, Robert *Savoie, Émile *Belcourt, and Joseph *Rouleau; she repeated the role in her US debut in 1973 with the Boston Opera Company directed by Sarah Caldwell. In 1975 she was the soprano soloist in Verdi's *Requiem* at the Royal Albert Hall in London, and the next year she sang the role of the Second Prioress (Poulenc's *Dialogue des Carmélites*) in Tourcoing, France.

In March 1976 Édith Tremblay returned to live in Quebec City. AP

TREMBLAY, Gilles (Léonce). Composer, teacher, pianist, ondist, b Arvida (Jonquière), Que, 6 Sep 1932; premier prix piano (CMM) 1953, premier prix analysis (Paris Cons) 1957, L MUS counterpoint (École normale, Paris) 1958. After private lessons with Jocelyne *Binet (counterpoint), Isabelle *Delorme (solfège), Jean *Papineau-Couture (acoustics), and Edmond *Trudel (piano), he entered the *CMM, where he studied 1949–54 under Claude *Champagne (composition, theory) and Germaine *Malépart (piano). He attended summer courses 1950, 1951, and 1953 at the Marlboro School of Music in Vermont and studied music history 1952–3 with Jean *Vallerand at the *U of Montreal. A meeting with Varèse in 1952 made a deep impression on him. After presenting his *Mouvement pour deux pianos* with Serge *Garant at the CMM in 1954, he went to Paris to continue his training 1954–61.

He enrolled at the Paris Cons, working 1954–7 with Yvonne Loriod (theory, piano) and Olivier Messiaen (analysis). It was at this time that he met Pierre Boulez. He also studied the ondes Martenot 1956–8 with Maurice Martenot, obtaining a première médaille for his performance on that instrument. He became interested in electroacoustical techniques while attending the summer courses given in Darmstadt by Stockhausen. He took advanced studies in counterpoint 1957–8 with Andrée Vaurabourg-Honegger. On *Canada Council grants 1958–61 he was able to attend sessions 1959–61 with the Groupe de recherches musicales headed by Pierre Schaeffer at the ORTF. There he met several composers, including Boucourechliev, Ferrari, and Xenakis. During the summer of 1959 he taught analysis at the *JMC Orford Art Centre. In 1960 a grant from the Kranichsteiner Musikinstitut allowed him to return to Darmstadt to attend the summer classes given by Pierre Boulez and Henri Pousseur. Also in that year he composed his first important work for orchestra, *Cantiques de durées*, which was to be premiered in Paris in 1963 by the Domaine musical under Ernest Bour.

Upon his return to Montreal in 1961 he taught again during the summer at the JMC Orford Art Centre. He taught analysis 1961–6 at the CMQ and in 1962 began to teach analysis and composition at the CMM; he also collaborated 1962–3 on the scripts or music for the CBC radio series 'Paroles

Gilles Tremblay

de poètes' and 'L'Homme américain' with Fernand Ouellette and for 'Festivals,' of which he was the host for 39 weeks. His production 1966–7 of the sound-tracks for the Quebec Pavilion at *Expo 67 earned him the 1968 *Prix de musique Calixa-Lavallée. Tremblay took part in the conference on Canada, in 1968 at Cerisy-La-Salle, France, and in the 24th (1970) Avignon Festival, where, with the Trio vocal de Montréal, he presented his work *Kékoba* at a concert in homage to Varèse. He was a member of the jury for the International Composition Competition at the 1971 Paris Biennial and for the 1972 International Flute Competition at the 9th Festival d'art contemporain in Royan. Also in 1972 he embarked on a tour of the Far East (Japan, Korea, the Philippines, China, Java, Bali, and India) as the recipient of a bursary from the Canada Council. After his return he served again on juries in 1973 and 1976 and was invited to give lectures at the U of Montreal, at the JMC Orford Art Centre, in Los Angeles, and elsewhere.

Along with his numerous duties Tremblay continued to compose on commission for festivals or for organizations such as the *SMCQ, the *CBC, and the *NACO. The *MSO commissioned one of his major works, *Fleuves*, and premiered it in 1977 under Serge Garant. The CBC has presented some of his compositions at the International Rostrum of Composers: *Deux Pièces pour piano* in 1964, *Kékoba* in 1966, *Souffles (Champs II)* in 1970, and *Solstices* in 1972.

Tremblay joined the board of the SMCQ in 1968 and served 1975–7 on the advisory board of the Canada Council. He received the *CMCouncil Medal in 1973, and the *CMCouncil named him Composer of the Year for 1977. He is an associate of the *CMCentre, a member of the *CLComp, and an affiliate of PRO Canada. His brother Dominique, a violinist, studied at the CMQ and played in the *Quebec SO before turning to Quebec traditional music in 1968.

The aesthetic of Gilles Tremblay is concerned above all with sonority. Yet we should hesitate to reduce so rich an output to one word. It therefore seems necessary to dismantle the word 'sonority' and reassemble it in a more subtle form in which the notion of timbre is both encompassed and extended. Far from referring solely to original combinations of timbres, the word should invite us to consider sound as a complex network of events, both material and immaterial, real and potential – in other words to examine sonority according to a number of dual perspectives, all necessary for a precise and full understanding of the inner meaning of Tremblay's work.

The quest for more supple timbres has led the composer to explore the instrument's alter ego, its

Part of a manuscript page from *Oralléluiants* by Gilles Tremblay

otherness, its reverse side, its shadow: to draw from it an ultimate sonority. In *Souffles (Champs II)*, for example, the musicians must blow into their wind instruments without causing the column of air to vibrate. The ensuing sound, lightly coloured by the various pitches, exists, as it were, apart from the instrument. Again, at the very beginning of *Oralléluiants*, the contrabass players are required to explore their highest harmonics. In the same work, a chord played fortissimo in the low register by three bass players must cause an 'invisible' (according to the indication in the score) high B flat to emerge. This note is not produced directly by any one of the instruments but rather by the convergence of the harmonics of all three. It thus exists outside the instruments, freed from the material entities of instruments.

In these fringe areas the uniform and rigorous structuring of (equal) tempering of pitches holds no sway. Instead, it yields to an infinite number of non-tempered approximations and divisions which the composer purposely exploits, as when he specifies, for example, that a performer should play the fifth or seventh harmonic of a given fundamental. In his work the composer attempts to discover in each instrument an area of proximity that corresponds as accurately as possible with that of other instruments. In *Oralléluiants*, the percussionists have to imitate the high pitches and penetrating sounds of an aluminum sheet being crumpled slowly in front of a microphone. In *Solstices*, one section of the work intervenes in another to influence the latter, to render it 'akin.' At the outset this piece is divided into four regions which correspond to the four seasons. The 'winter' region, marked by long cross-fades, can intervene in the 'summer' region, for example, in an attempt to make it 'akin' on the level of its rhythms and contrasting elements.

Certain sections of Tremblay's works are designated 'en mobile.' In these instances, the notes are blockframed in the score. The performer may choose the order in which he will play them, but he must respect the pitches indicated. If the notes are enclosed in a triangle, the instrumentalist must give priority to the elements inscribed at the base of the triangle, whether notes, dynamics, or timbres. Frequently several instruments are playing 'en mobile' simultaneously. In such cases, all the proximities are possible within the defined networks. From the perspective of the work, this presupposes a virtual identity, or at least a strong relationship between the different sounds of a network, so that one aggregate of sounds may come into contact with any other aggregate without incurring a lack of affinities, all the while remaining within the limits set by the composer. The original equilibrium of the network or area remains unchanged despite the many possible displacements within it, following a concept wherein the field of proximities is virtually unlimited and where one note gets closer and closer (as it were) to being 'like' another, in spite of the pitch differences the composer has assigned to both inside the blocked frames. The actual diversity in timbres, which Tremblay obtains through optimum extension, leads ultimately to a sonority or, rather, to a vast incorporeal sound coextensive to itself. Thus from a real and maximum diversity we arrive at an omnipresent and unequivocal virtuality. The non-tempered field is more than simply latent; it is an actual and constant presence in every note – to the extent, one might add, of obliterating the individual notes, dematerializing them in favour of the omnipresent, but never fully articulated, non-tempered field. The real note gives way to the virtual without the latter losing its non-present or incorporeal quality. Thus one is made to feel a non-presence *as* a non-presence.

If the preceding outline has shown the composer's fundamental aesthetic to be a logical extension of 'sonic elements,' we now must take a look at his use of rhythmic pulse which may be qualified as indefinite, yet occupies an important place in Tremblay's work. The 'duration-breath' describes a time lapse from the attack until the extinction of the breath of the singer or wind instrumentalist. Often this length of time limits the 'en mobile' activities of other instrumentalists, whose playing must evolve according to the choice of the dynamics of attack, a choice which in many cases is made at the moment of playing. In the 'duration-resonances' the time lapse is a function of the natural resonance of the instrument until all vibration ceases. In the 'duration-arcos' the length of the bow's stroke becomes the controlling element. This undefined rhythmic element is in actual fact a duration derived from the sonic reality of the instrument.

Finally there are the 'reflexes,' the one major element that does not come down to a consideration of sonority. The reflexes designate ways of playing in which a choice made spontaneously by one instrumentalist sets off a precise reaction among several possibilities available to another instrumentalist. These reflex actions may assume the character of a duel in performance, with one player provoking another or several others, even trying to frustrate him or them by a rapid and unexpected choice. Thus the reflexes have a tendency to create a 'rhythmic pulse based on tension,' wherein the tempo is broken up by reactions and counter-reactions. This rhythmic pulse is nonetheless closely tied to the durations of indefinite type. At one moment an instrument may exhibit a continuous time lapse until its natural extinction; at another, two or several musicians diffract the tempo, giving it a tension that often is very strong. This tension-induced rhythm is the reverse counterpart of those indefinite rhythms. Strict time (as a common element, integral to all situations in motion) is both the focus and the point of reversal, so that the first rhythmic element is essentially the 'other' of the second, and vice versa. Thus, a preoccupation with sound elements is the primary unifying force of Tremblay's work. An infinitely pointillistic sound indicates each sound always differently, obliterating the sound (as, it is said, the name indicates and kills the object it names), and in the single real sound one hears the continual coming-into-being of the non-tempered field.

COMPOSITIONS

ORCHESTRA

Cantique de durées. 1960. 7 gps of instr (50 perfs). CMCentre

Jeux de solstices. 1974. CMCentre. RCI 477. See Discography.

Fleuves. 1976. Full orch, pf, perc. Sala 1976

Vers le soleil. 1978. CMCentre

CHAMBER

Mobile. 1962. Vn, pf. CMCentre

Champs I. 1965 (rev 1969). Pf, 2 perc. Sala 1974. RCI 370. See Discography.

Kékoba (Tremblay). 1965 (rev 1967). Sop, mezzo, ten, perc, ondes M. BMIC 1968. RCI 240. See Discography.

Souffles (Champs II). 1968. 2 fl, ob, cl, hn, 2 tpt, 2 trb, 2 perc, db, pf. Sala 1975. RCI 370 (*SMCQ)

Vers (Champs III). 1969. 2 fl, cl, tpt, hn, 3 vn, db, 3 perc. Sala 1974. RCI 370 (*SMCQ)

'... *le sifflement des vents porteurs de l'amour* ...' 1971. Fl, perc, microphones. CMCentre

Solstices (ou Les jours et les saisons tournent). 1971. 1, 2, 3, or 4 gps of 6 soli: fl, cl, hn, db, 2 perc. CMCentre. RCI 298. See Discography.

Oralléluiants. 1975. Sop, fl, b cl, hn, 3 db, 2 perc, microphones. CMCentre

Compostelle I. 1978. 18 inst. Sala 1978

PIANO

Deux pièces pour piano: 'Phases,' 'Réseaux.' 1956–8. Ber 1974. RCI 228/RCA CCS-1022 (*Troup)/('Phases') CBC SM-162 (*Buczynski)

Traçantes. 1976. Sala 1976

ELECTRONIC

Exercise I (1959); *Exercise II* (1960)

Sonorisation du Pavillion du Québec. 1967. 24-channel sterophony

Also music for the NFB film *Dimension Soleils* (1970)

WRITINGS

'Thèse analytique sur La Messe de Guillaume de Machaut,' unpubl thesis, Paris Cons 1956.

– et al. 'Hommage à Messiaen,' *Melos*, 25, Dec 1958

'Les sons en mouvement,' *Liberté* 59, Sep–Oct 1959

'Vers une nouvelle écoute' and other articles in *Musiques du Kébèk*, ed Raoul Duguay (Montreal 1971)

'Notice (1967) pour "Phases" (1956) et "Réseaux" (1958),' *VM*, 7, 1967

'Note pour *Cantique de durées*,' *Revue d'esthétique* (Paris 1968)

'Le bruit, prospective négative et prospective positive,' *Le Bruit, 4e pollution du monde moderne* (Montreal 1970)

'Oiseau-nature, Messiaen, musique,' *CMB*, 1, Spring–Summer 1970

'R. Murray Schafer: *The Book of Noise*,' *CMB*, 2, Spring–Summer 1971

'Le point de vue d'un compositeur,' *Vie spirituelle*, vol 56, Mar–Apr 1974

'Olivier Messiaen,' *Dictionary of Contemporary Music*

DISCOGRAPHY

Canadian Music in London, Paris and Bonn / Musique canadienne à Londres, Paris et Bonn: Tremblay *Jeux de solstices*. Nouvel O phil de Radio France, Tremblay cond. 1977. RCI 477

Music of Today / Musique d'aujourd'hui, vol 1: Tremblay *Solstices (ou Les jours et les saisons tournent)*. J. Morin fl, J. Laurendeau cl, G. Masella hn, R. Desjardins db, Lachapelle and Béluse perc, Tremblay cond. 1970? RCI 298

Tremblay *Champs I*. Tremblay pf, Lachapelle and Béluse perc. 1970. RCI 370

Tremblay *Kékoba*. Colle sop, Chiocchio mezzo, G. Morgan ten, Tremblay ondes M, Lachapelle perc. (1969). RCI 240

BIBLIOGRAPHY

Martin-Dubost, Paul. 'Le *Cantique de durées* de Gilles Tremblay,' *Vie des arts*, 31, Summer 1963

'Gilles Tremblay – a portrait,' *Mcan*, 24, Nov 1969

Thériault, Jacques. 'Gilles Tremblay,' *MSc*, 252, Mar–Apr 1970

'Gilles Tremblay,' *Musiques du Kébèk*, ed R. Duguay (Montreal 1971)

CMCentre. *Compositeurs au Québec: Gilles Tremblay* (Montreal 1974)

BMI Canada / PRO Canada Ltd. 'Gilles Tremblay,' pamphlets (1975, 1980)

Richard, Robert. 'Gilles Tremblay,' *Vie des arts*, 86, Spring 1977

Contemporary Canadian Composers / Compositeurs canadiens contemporains

Creative Canada, vol 1

Dictionary of Contemporary Music

'Review of Records' RR

Tremblay Concerts / Les Concerts Tremblay. Organized in Ottawa by Antonio Tremblay. The first subscription series (1929) presented Edward *Johnson, the English Singers, Jacques Thibaud, Rachmaninoff, and Kathryn Meisle. The concerts continued with assistance from Tremblay's wife, Adine, and daughter Suzanne, until 1961, when Earl Crowe assumed control, retaining the Tremblay name. At Glebe Collegiate 1929–41, the Capitol Theatre 1942–69, and the *NAC 1970–1 Tremblay Concerts presented solo recitalists, orchestras and chamber groups, popular performers of the day, Broadway musicals, operas, and ballets. Artists ranged from Nellie Melba, Artur Rubinstein, and Fritz Kreisler to Victor Borge, Harry Belafonte, and Petula Clark. Crowe also presented two concerts each year by Canadians. Tremblay (b 1887?, d 1 Dec 1974), a translator for the federal government, had presented his first concert – by Galli-Curci at the Capitol Theatre – in 1921 as the agent for the Montreal impresario. His wife, Adine Tremblay (b Gagnon, Quebec City) studied piano with her great uncle Gustave *Gagnon and voice with Alice Dion-Parent, Berthe *Roy, and (in Montreal) Jean *Riddez. She appeared frequently in recital. Constance *Lambert was among her pupils.

Shortly before Tremblay's death he and his wife were made Members of the *Order of Canada, the first couple to be so honoured. (AEB)

Trent University. Non-denominational, predominantly undergraduate institution in Peterborough, Ont, with some graduate programs at the master's level. It was opened officially in 1964 by the governor-general, Georges Vanier. Emphasis has been on small-group teaching in the liberal arts.

By 1980 Trent still did not have a music department and had offered no credit courses in music. The extension department, however, had presented guest lectures by conductors of the Peterboro SO (see Orchestras) and by local organists. Honorary degrees have been conferred on Edith *Fowke (1975), whose folksong collecting has included shanty songs from Peterborough County; on Gilles *Vigneault (1975); and on Gordon *Lightfoot (1979). In 1969 Joseph Wearing, a teacher at the university, instituted the Town and Gown Concerts, a joint university-community series presenting local and touring Canadian artists.

In 1973 the *Chamber Players of Toronto inaugurated the university's 350-seat theatre. Extracurricular music has included Gilbert & Sullivan productions, a music society begun by Peter MacKinnon, a jazz club, and an Otonabee College residency by the Hamilton Philharmonic Institute (a group comprising young musicians studying and performing with the *Hamilton Philharmonic Orchestra). Champlain College created an in-residence appointment for the conductor of the Peterborough SO in 1975.

BIBLIOGRAPHY

Symons, T.H.B. 'Trent Unviersity,' *Peterborough: Land of Shining Waters* (Toronto 1967) (JW)

TRÉPANIER, (Joseph Horace) **Paul**. Tenor, b Noranda, Que, 6 Aug 1939. After studying privately 1961–4 with Albert *Cornellier and taking courses at the *École Vincent-d'Indy, he attended the *CMM 1964–7. There he studied voice with Léopold *Simoneau and repertoire with Janine

*Lachance. He attended the *Royal Cons Opera School on scholarship in 1967 and achieved notable successes in the school's productions of *The Magic Flute* (singing Tamino) and *Pelléas et Mélisande* (singing Pelléas) under the direction of Ernesto *Barbini (music) and Peter Ebert (staging). At the school Trépanier studied operatic acting and stage techniques with Ebert. After participating in the 1968 Glyndebourne Festival, he sang the role of Sir George-Étienne Cartier that fall in the *COC production of *Somers' *Louis Riel* and the following year in the CBC TV production of that work. In 1969 he appeared in COC productions of *Rigoletto* and *Elektra* in Toronto before resuming his studies with Simoneau and Lachance.

In 1970 Trépanier sang Ferrando in *Così fan tutte* with the Théâtre lyrique du Québec and Wilhelm in *Mignon* with the CBC and was a soloist in Beethoven's *Ninth Symphony* with the *Atlantic SO. On a *Canada Council grant he went to Munich in 1970–1 and London in 1971–2 to improve his knowledge of the German and English languages and repertoire. In 1973 he sang Tamino at the *Banff SFA, in 1974, Hubert in *Chanson gitane* at the *PDA and Gonzalve (*L'Heure espagnole*) on CBC TV. Also in 1974 he sang with the *NACO in the Canadian premiere of Rossini's *Le Comte Ory* and was the Narrator in that orchestra's presentation of Berlioz' *L'Enfance du Christ*, first in Ottawa then at Carnegie Hall. He was a founding member in 1974 of the *Ensemble cantabile de Montréal.

Trépanier sang the title role in Bizet's *Docteur Miracle* at La *Poudrière, Montreal (summer 1975), and repeated the role of Cartier with the COC in Toronto, Ottawa, and at the John F. Kennedy Center in Washington that year. Shortly afterwards he toured Canada in *JMC productions of *The Magic Flute* and *The Barber of Seville* (Count Almaviva; French-language version 1975–6, English-language version 1976–7). As a concert and oratorio soloist he sang in 1976 with the *Edmonton SO in *The Creation* and in 1978 with the *MSO in its summer concert series and in *Messiah*. Also that year he performed at the Festival de Namur, Belgium. In 1980 he repeated his interpretation of the Narrator in the *Guelph Spring Festival production of *L'Enfance du Christ*. Trépanier is the possessor of a lyric tenor of pleasing timbre. He has recorded songs by Stojowski, Jean-Paul *Jeannotte, Vellones, and Maurice *Dela with the pianist Janine Lachance (1977, RCI 470). (DA)

TREPEL, Freda (m Kaufmann). Pianist, teacher, b Winnipeg 1 Mar 1919, naturalized US ca 1960; LRSM 1933, ATCM 1934, B MUS (Chicago) 1940. She began piano study at five and was soon winning classes at the *Manitoba Music Competition Festival, alone and in chamber ensembles with her sisters Anne (who played the violin) and *Shirley. She won the Aikins Memorial Trophy, that festival's highest instrumental award, in 1932. She studied 1936–41 on scholarship with Rudolph Ganz at the Chicago Musical College and made her Chicago debut in 1941. A New York debut followed in 1944 and also recitals in Rome, Stockholm, Paris, London, and many Canadian cities. She married Walter *Kaufmann in 1950 and that year was soloist in the premiere of his *Concerto* with the *Winnipeg SO. Moving in 1957 with her husband to Indiana, she began teaching privately. In 1960 she joined the teaching staff at Indiana U. SRM

TREPEL, Shirley. Cellist, b Winnipeg 1 Mar 1924. Sister of Freda *Trepel and Anne. She studied with Daniel Saidenberg (Chicago) and later with Emanuel Feuermann and Gregor Piatigorsky. She made her New York debut at Carnegie Hall in 1949 and enjoyed some success as a recitalist and concerto soloist. She married (and later divorced) the violinist Berl Senofsky and occasionally performed with him in duo. She became principal cello of the Houston SO in 1963. The conductor-composer André Previn wrote a concerto for her in 1968. She began teaching at Rice U, Houston, in 1975. SRM

Trinity College of Music, London. Established in 1872 to provide a comprehensive music education and, through its external examinations department, to examine and award certificates and diplomas (ATCL, LTCL, FTCL). The TCL pioneered in establishing systems for local examinations in performance and theory in England and her colonies. The first centres were set up in South Africa, India, Ceylon, and Australia in 1881. Theory exams were offered in Canada in 1887, and practical examiners began their annual visits in 1908 to conduct 'impartial, thorough and efficient' appraisals of Canadian students prepared by local teachers. A TCL local centre was established in Winnipeg in 1926.

By 1978 there were 20 centres in eight provinces: 5 in Newfoundland, 4 each in British Columbia and Ontario, 3 in Saskatchewan, and 1 each in Alberta, Manitoba, New Brunswick, and Nova Scotia. During World War II resident Canadians, including Arthur *Collingwood, H.A. *Fricker, Henry Rosevear, and *Willan, examined for the TCL. Visiting examiners after 1908 have included Ronald Chamberlain, Albert Mallinson, Adolph Mann, David Robinson, Harold Rutland, and Mary Tweedie. Among the Canadians to whom the TCL has awarded honorary fellowships are Collingwood, Fricker, Lyell *Gustin, Gordon *Jeffery, Nellie Mould, Rosevear, and Leonard *Wilson.

BIBLIOGRAPHY

Rutland, Harold. *Trinity College of Music: The First Hundred Years* (London 1972) PW

Trio de guitares Laval. See Laval Guitar Trio.

Trio lyrique. A vocal trio founded in Montreal in 1932 by the baritone Lionel *Daunais, who enlisted the contralto Anna *Malenfant, the tenor Ludovic Huot, and the pianist-arranger Allan *McIver. The voices it brought together, and more particularly its repertoire, comprising folksongs and original songs by Daunais, sung in French or English, made the Trio lyrique a unique ensemble. All the arrangements were by McIver. The ensemble was heard first on private radio and was engaged in 1933 by the CRBC for its network series 'One Hour with You.' The program – for which Giuseppe *Agostini conducted the orchestra – was extended for 87 weeks. For six months in 1936 the trio performed for the CBS network in New York. Later it was active mainly on CBC radio, for which it took part in countless programs, but it also gave public concerts. Jules *Jacob replaced Huot in the early 1940s. The ensemble ceased its activities in the mid-1960s but was revived temporarily in the autumn of 1971 (with Guy Piché as tenor) for a CBC retrospective of Daunais's work. In 1954 the trio made the LP *Chansons de Lionel Daunais* (RCI 106). GP

Trio Victoria. Formed in 1965 as trio-in-residence of the Victoria School of Music (later *Victoria Cons of Music). The original members were Robin *Wood (piano), Jean Angers (violin), and Hans Siegrist (cello). Angers was succeeded by Jack *Kessler in 1967, Kessler by Sydney *Humphreys in 1970, Humphreys by Derek Collier in 1972, Collier by Harry Cawood in 1973, and Cawood by Humphreys in 1975. Siegrist was succeeded by James Hunter in 1967. Wood and Humphreys had been associates 1954–65 in England as members of the St Cecilia Trio. Trio Victoria gave six concerts during its first season, tripling that number by 1970. In 1972 it travelled to Hawaii. It has also toured British Columbia and the northwestern USA, and has performed on CBC radio and TV. It performs the standard repertoire for piano trio with the addition of contemporary European and Canadian works. PFB

TRIPP, J.D.A. (John David Alvin or Alexander). Pianist, teacher, b Dunbarton, east of Toronto, 10 Jan 1867, d Vancouver 26 Nov 1945; ATCM 1889. The first graduate of the *TCM, where his teachers included Francesco *D'Auria and Edward *Fisher, Tripp also studied 1891–2 in Berlin with Moritz Moszkowski and 1896–8 in Vienna with Theodor Leschetizky. Moszkowski was impressed with his pupil's work. He wrote: 'Mr. Tripp's playing is marked by a full, rich, penetrating tone, pearly passage playing, and surety in all technical difficulties' (letter in *Canadian Music Trades Journal*, Nov 1900). Tripp performed in Europe and the USA and gave several cross-Canada tours. On 11 Apr 1907 he was the soloist in Liszt's *Hungarian Fantasy* at *Massey Hall in the first concert given by the TCM Orchestra. Founder and conductor 1893–1908 of the Toronto Male Chorus, he also taught ca 1890–1910 at the TCM and was the conservatory's first examiner to visit the Pacific coast. In 1910 he moved to Vancouver, where he conducted the Tripp Choir 1910–12 and became the city's leading piano teacher. His pupils included John *Avison, Harold *Brown, Hayunga *Carman, H.C. *Hamilton, Kenneth Ross, and Ira *Swartz. Tripp continued to perform and was heard on CBR radio broadcasts with the Seattle SO. In 1942 he presented a recital (Bach, Beethoven, Brahms, Schumann, Scarlatti, Chopin, Moszkowski, and Rubinstein) at the Hotel Vancouver to mark his 75th birthday. A group of Tripp's piano pieces, composed during his Toronto years, were published by *Whaley Royce, and a song, 'The Salt Sea Foam,' was published in 1894 by *Anglo-Canadian. He wrote 'Music in British Columbia' for the *Yearbook of Canadian Art* (London, Toronto, 1913).

BIBLIOGRAPHY

'J.D.A. Tripp,' *MCour*, vol 37, 2 Nov 1898 (BNSG)

TRITT, William. Pianist, b Point-Claire (Montreal) 27 Dec 1951; B MUS (Montreal) 1969, M MUS (Montreal) 1969. He studied 1962–9 in Montreal at the *École Vincent-d'Indy with Sister Lucille Brassard, Yvonne *Hubert, and Gilles *Manny prior to advanced studies in 1971 with Yvonne Lefébure at St-Germain-en-Laye, France, and 1972–4 with György Sebok at the U of Indiana. He was artist-in-residence 1974–5 at *Dalhousie U. A semi-finalist at the 1969 Munich Festival, he also won the 1970 *MSO Concours, the 1971 *CBC Talent Festival, and the 1971 Internatioanl Stepping Stones of the Quebec Music Competitions (*Canadian Music Competitions) and was third-place winner in the 1971 *Montreal International Competition. In 1976 he founded the Dalart Trio with the violinist Philippe Djokic and the cellist William Valleau. Tritt has been a soloist with the MSO, the TS, the Vancouver SO, and other Canadian orchestras and has performed often on CBC radio and TV. While pursuing his career mainly in Canada and the USA, he made his first LP in Europe in 1974 for the Guilde Internationale du Disque. Released in 1975 (Concert Hall SMS 2937) it contained works by Haydn, Brahms, Bach-Busoni, and Jacques *Hétu. Reviewing it, the May 1975 issue of

William Tritt

Harmonie magazine noted 'a flawless technique ... a very solid architecture, a communicative spirit ... and a beautiful vigour.'

BIBLIOGRAPHY
'William Tritt,' *Adagio*, vol 1, Feb 1976 (PR)

TROCHU, Pierre. Composer, percussionist, b Montreal 8 Jan 1953; B MUS (Montreal) 1974, M MUS (Montreal) 1977. He studied 1970–7 with Serge *Garant (composition) and Robert Leroux and Guy *Lachapelle (percussion) at the *U of Montreal. He also took courses in mathematics and computer science 1970–4 at the university and enrolled at the electronic music studio at *McGill U, where he worked 1973–5 with Alcides *Lanza and Bengt *Hambraeus. His first work, *Pluton*, was composed in 1971; the following year he wrote the music for an educational film, *La Percussion*, commissioned by the Quebec Ministry of Education. In 1974 he won the first *CBC National Radio Competition for Young Composers for *Orange* (for mezzo-soprano, flute, piano, and two percussionists) premiered in April 1972 at the U of Montreal. He also composed the instrumental works *Modulo 5 ou la Naissance du rythme*, premiered in May 1974 at Cowansville, Que, (*FAMEQ congress), and *Miracrose*, premiered in April 1977 by the *SMCQ Ensemble. In the second CBC National Radio Competition for Young Composers he took first prize for *Eros*, a work for magnetic tape performed in January 1976 at the U of Montreal. He was awarded grants in 1975 and 1976 from the *Canada Council and composed the sound track for the CBC radio program 'Portrait de Jean-Jules Richard' (1975) and incidental music for a dramatic work, Jacques Godbout's *Le Bébé d'artifice* (Prix Gilson 1975). In July 1976 his *Solstices de liberté* was presented by Médiateq as part of the activities surrounding the Montreal Olympic Games. Trochu is an associate of the *CMCentre and an affiliate of PRO Canada.

BIBLIOGRAPHY
Proulx, Michelle. 'Pierre Trochu – music, politics and the word,' *MSc*, 294, Mar–Apr 1977 (IPn)

TROIANO, Dom or **'Tricky'** (Domenic Michaele Antonio). Guitarist, singer, songwriter, b Mondugno, Italy, 17 Jan 1946, naturalized Canadian 1955. Raised in Toronto, Troiano began playing guitar at 15. After working with Ronnie *Hawkins' Hawks and with Robbie Lane and the Disciples he was a member of the related groups the Rogues (Toronto 1964–6), *Mandala (Toronto/USA 1966–9), and Bush (Arizona 1970–1). He recorded *Domenic Troiano* (1971, Mer SRM 1-639) then played lead guitar 1972–3 with the US band the James Gang for two LPs (*Straight Shooter*, 1972, ABC/Dunhill ABCX-741; and *Passin' Thru*, 1972, ABC/Dunhill ABCX-760) and on some tours. While with the James Gang he also recorded his own LP, *Tricky* (1972–3 Mer SRM 1-670). He joined the *Guess Who in 1974 for its last LPs (*Flavours* and *Power in the Music*) and final concerts.

In 1976 he formed the Domenic Troiano Band in Toronto, appearing in nightclubs and local concerts and recording *Burnin' at the Stake* (1977, Cap ST-11665), *The Joke's On Me* (1978, Cap SW-11772) and *Fret Fever* (1978, Cap ST-11932). In the front rank of rock guitarists Troiano is a fluent blues player whose style began, in the 1970s, to incorporate elements of jazz. Co-written with Roy Kenner, Burton Cummings, and others, his songs have been recorded by the bands mentioned above and by Three Dog Night and others. Among the best known are 'Writing on the Wall' and 'I Can Hear You Calling.' For Shawne Jackson, who has sung on his LPs, Troiano produced the internationally successful single 'Just as Bad as You' (1973) and the LP *Shawne Jackson* (1975, RCA APL1-1320). He is an affiliate of PRO Canada.

BIBLIOGRAPHY
LeBlanc, Larry. 'Troiano and Kenner make it as James Gang writers, members,' *MSc*, 269, Jan–Feb 1973
Lamont, John. 'The outer limits of a guitarist extraordinaire,' *Stagelife*, Sep 1977
LeBlanc, Larry. 'Domenic Troiano: Canadian guitarist with Bush, Guess Who, Mandala and James Gang goes solo,' *Guitar Player*, vol 12, Jan 1978 (PG)

'Trois Beaux Canards.' See 'V'la l'bon vent.'

Trois-Rivières. Founded on the north shore of the St Lawrence River in 1634 by Sieur de Laviolette as a trading post between Quebec City and Montreal. The town derived its name from the three mouths of the St Maurice River, on which it is located. It became a city in 1857 and had a total population of some 100,000 by 1980. Renowned at first for its forges, the city is an industrial centre known for its paper and textile mills.

Musical life does not appear to have been very vigorous at the beginning of the 19th century, if one is to judge by the comments of John Lambert, a visiting traveller: 'The amusements of Three Rivers consist of the before-mentioned parties [tea parties, *conversazioni*, and *petits soupers*] and a few dances in the winter. Sometimes assemblies are held at one of the taverns, in which there is a subscription ball once a fortnight during the winter season ... Concerts and plays are unknown in Three Rivers, unless sometimes a few strollers arrive from the States and pass through the town on their way to Quebec City' (*Travels through Canada and the United States of America in the Years 1806, 1807 and 1808*, vol 1, London 1816, p 496).

However, the historian Benjamin Sulte, in his *Mélanges historiques* (vol 19, Montreal 1932), refers to the presence of five 'master-singers,' including a Monsieur Leclerc and a Dr Charles Alavoine, both ca 1730, as well as Jean-Baptiste Badeaux, a 'good singer' ca 1754, and his son Joseph 'possessing a powerful voice.' The latter's son, Dr Georges-Édouard Badeaux, was active ca 1830–70. Sulte also mentions a clarinetist named Hippolyte Godin.

At the Ursuline Convent (founded in 1697) and the seminary (opened in 1860) music presumably was taught. Beginning in 1872 a local orchestra performed at the town hall, accompanying a choir in works by Mozart and Rossini. A pianist from Trois-Rivières, Bernadette Dufresne (1873–1923, a pupil of Calixa *Lavallée in Boston), gave a recital in 1899 with the violinist J.-J. *Goulet. In 1901 the Cathedral's grand organ (a *Casavant) was inaugurated. Its first regular organist was Mme Ph. Aubry. Among those who followed her in the position were Nazaire Marchand, J.-François Paradis, and Bernard *Piché.

At the Notre-Dame-des-Sept-Allégresses Church, J.-Antonio *Thompson was organist from 1916 until his death in 1974. For 58 years Thompson was an exceptional force as teacher, band conductor, and choir director. In 1930 he succeeded Giuseppe *Agostini as conductor of the Philharmonie de La Salle and he began giving free lessons in solfège. He founded the Choeur Thompson (1941) and the vocal quartet Les Chevaliers du guet and was music director of radio station CHLN 1937–9. In 1956 his son Claude became the director of the Petits Chanteurs, a choir school whose performing group has been heard on CBC radio and in numerous public concerts.

The Union musicale was founded in 1878 and, as early as 1909, an ensemble of some 20 musicians bearing the name of the Trois-Rivières SO presented two concerts and *Le Désert* by Félicien David. The violinist Joseph Gélinas (who had founded a string quartet in 1937) reorganized the orchestra in 1943 and acted as conductor. His successors were Edwin *Belanger 1946–7 and Jean-Yves *Landry 1947–9. In 1978 a young composer, Gilles Bellemare (b Shawinigan, Que, 1952), revived it under the name Orchestre régional de Trois-Rivières and assumed conducting duties. A municipal band was directed 1889–1914 by Henri Weber and later by Émile Quiquemberg.

Another guiding spirit was Father Jean-Gers Turcotte (b Trois-Rivières, 1887, d ?), choirmaster at the cathedral and the seminary, teacher, pianist, composer, and graduate of the Schola cantorum of Rome. In 1910 he presented Gounod's *Jeanne d'Arc* at the seminary and later, in 1913, *Joseph* by Méhul.

Arthur *Plamondon opened a voice studio in 1915, and in 1919 the Assn lyrique was founded 'to develop local talents, display them on home ground and give the public an opportunity to enjoy them.' In addition to concerts, the association presented *Les Cloches de Corneville* by Planquette and, later, *Si j'étais roi*, by Adam.

The tricentennial festivities in 1934 were an occasion for celebration in which music played an important role. Father Turcotte organized a 700-voice choir which took part in concerts and shows of a historical character. Concerts were held at that time in the La Salle auditorium and later at the Capitol Theatre, which opened in 1928 with a season of French operetta. Roger *Filiatrault opened a voice studio in 1936; among his pupils was Irène Allard-Moquin, who sang Debussy's *La Demoiselle élue* with the CSM orchestra.

The Concert Society, affiliated with *Community Concerts, was organized in 1939 but met with competition from the Club musical, which presented Canadian artists exclusively. In 1942 Anaïs Allard-Rousseau combined these endeavours to form Les Rendez-vous artistiques, which presented internationally known artists such as Raoul *Jobin and Malcuzynski. The same year she founded the André-Mathieu Club for young people, which in 1950 became the local branch of the *JMC, a movement of which she was the national president 1954–6.

At the beginning of the century, Trois-Rivières began to be visited by the leading Canadian and foreign artists, eg, Théodore Botrel, Albert *Chamberland, Edmond Clément, Alfred Cortot, Béatrice *La Palme, Albert Larrieu, F.-X. *Mercier, Léo-Pol *Morin, Rodolphe *Plamondon, the *Dubois String Quartet, Jean *Riddez, Émile *Taranto and Eugène Ysaÿe.

Opened in April 1964 as a preparatory school, the *Conservatoire de musique du Québec à and directed successively by Czeslaw Kaczynski, Raymond *Daveluy, Armando *Santiago, and Georges *Savaria. The Music Module of the *UQATR, which began in 1969, was directed by Jean *Chatillon, succeeded by Lorraine Casaubon in 1974. A Cultural Centre, complete with a modern hall, houses most of the musical events. The Capitol Theatre in 1979 was renovated by means of a public subscription and was renamed the Salle J.-Antonio-Thompson.

Among musicians born in Trois-Rivières or in the region are Gaston *Arel, Nick *Ayoub, Paule-Aimée Bailly, A.J. *Boucher, Gilles Carpentier, Maurice *De Celles, Josephte *Dufresne, Graziella *Dumaine, Ernest and Gustave *Gagnon, Noëlla Genest, Jacques *Hétu, Jules *Jacob, Pauline *Julien, Marie *Laferrière, Jean-Yves Landry, Alphonse *Lavallée-Smith, Gilles *Manny, Sister *Marie-Stéphane, Alphonse *Martin, François-Xavier Mercier, Guy Piché, Léon *Ringuet, Myke Roy, Claude Thompson, and Pierre Vidor.

BIBLIOGRAPHY

Thompson, J.-Antonio. *Cinquante Ans de vie musicale à Trois-Rivières* (Trois-Rivières 1970) GP

TROUP, Malcolm. Pianist, teacher, b Toronto 22 Feb 1930; PH D musicology (York, England) 1968. He studied under Norman *Wilks and Alberto *Guerrero at the *RCMT and made his debut at 17 with a CBC Toronto orchestra playing Rubinstein's *Concerto in D.* He continued his studies 1950–2 with Sidney Harrison at the GSM and 1954–6 with Walter Gieseking in Germany and was awarded the Harriet Cohen Commonwealth Medal in 1955. He has performed widely in Canada, Europe, and South America, in concert and at festivals. He has played with the London SO, the Hallé Orchestra, the Berlin SO, the Bucharest Philharmonic Orchestra, and the BBC SO. In Canada he has appeared with the *CBC SO and the Toronto, Winnipeg, Halifax, and Victoria SOs. In the 1960s he lived in South America. He was music director 1970–5 of the GSM and became head of music and pianist-in-residence at City U, London, in 1975. Troup has been a member of the *Canada Council International Jury and was a judge for the first S.C. Eckhardt-Grammatté competition (1976) and for the *CBC Talent Festival (1978). His thesis topic was 'Messiaen and the modern mind.'

DISCOGRAPHY

Debussy *Images* – Villa-Lobos *Rudepoêma*. CBC SM-25

Liszt – Mather *Fantasy* – Schumann – selections. 1967. CBC SM-48

Music and Musicians of Canada, vol 16: Tremblay – Pépin – Beckwith – Messiaen. 1967. RCI 228/RCA CCS-1022 (WS)

TROWSDALE, (George) Campbell. Educator, violinist, b Stratford, Ont, 17 Oct 1933; ARCT 1953, B MUS (Toronto) 1954, B ED (Toronto) 1957, M ED (Toronto) 1959, ED D (Toronto) 1962. His teachers included Cora B. *Ahrens (piano and theory) in Stratford and Elie *Spivak, Albert *Pratz, and John Moskalyk (violin) in Toronto. In the late 1950s Trowsdale became a member of the *Hart House Orchestra and played occasionally in the *TSO. Appointed in 1961 to the faculty of education at the *U of British Columbia he also joined the *CBC Vancouver Chamber Orchestra in 1964 and became concertmaster in 1968. He has performed alone and as a chamber musician in Vancouver and on CBC radio, his repertoire reflecting his interest in contemporary music. Trowsdale's teaching employs elements of the methods of *Orff, *Kodály, *Schafer, and others. He has worked – especially at the elementary level – to develop a fully integrated musical curriculum in the belief that music education should produce listeners as well as performers.

WRITING

'A history of public school music in Ontario,' unpubl ED D thesis, Toronto 1962

'Vocal music in the Common schools of Upper Canada: 1846–1876,' *J of Research in Music Education*, vol 18, Winter 1970

'Public institutions and music education: a profile of the Polish music schools,' *CAUSM J*, vol 2, Jul 1972

'History of music education as a field of study: a consideration of status, research and needs,' *CAUSM J*, vol 3, Spring 1974 BNSG

TRUAX, Barry (Douglas). Composer, researcher, b Chatham, Ont, 10 May 1947; B SC (Queen's) 1969, M MUS (British Columbia) 1971. After training in mathematics and physics at *Queen's U and in composition with Courtland *Hultberg at the *U of British Columbia, Truax studied 1971–3 at the Institute of Sonology, Utrecht U, with G.M. Koenig and Otto Laske. On his return to Canada in 1973 he began teaching in the Dept of Communication, *Simon Fraser U, and became a research assistant (later research director) with the *World Soundscape Project there. Though his early works (1969–71) were for piano solo, piano and cello, and voice ensemble, Truax later concentrated on electronic and computer composition. At Utrecht U and Simon Fraser U he has programmed computers as 'interactive compositional systems' for use by other composers. His own compositions include four *Sonic Landscapes* (1970, 1971, 1975, 1977); *She, A Solo* (1973) for mezzo-soprano and tape, premiered 10 Apr 1974 by Phyllis *Mailing and sung 17 Feb 1975 in Utrecht by Ileana Melita; four *Soundscapes* (1974) for tape, broadcast on the CBC; *Trigon* (1974–5) for flute, piano, voice, and tape, premiered 9 Dec 1975 by Mailing and others for the *Vancouver New Music Society; and *Nautilus* (1976) for solo percussion and four-channel tape. *Sonic Landscape No. 3, She, A Solo, Trigon,* and *Nautilus* were recorded with Mailing, the flutist Kathryn Cernauskas, the percussionist Russell Hartenberger, and the pianist Arlie Thompson and released on the LP *Sonic Landscapes* (1977, Mel SMLP 4033).

Sonic Landscape No. 1 was recorded by the french hornist James MacDonald for Music Gallery Editions (MGE 21).

See also Electronic music.

WRITINGS

'The computer composition – sound synthesis programs POD4, POD5 and POD6,' *Sonological Reports*, no. 2 (Utrecht 1973)

'Some programs for real-time computer synthesis and composition,' *Interface*, vol 2, 1973

'General techniques of computer composition programing,' *Numus West*, 4, Fall 1973

'Computer music in Canada (1975),' *Numus West*, 8, Spring 1975

'A communicational approach to computer sound programs,' *J of Music Theory*, vol 20, Fall 1976

See also Bibliography For World Soundscape Project.

(CF, MM)

TRUDEL, (Joseph Jean) Edmond. Pianist, conductor, teacher, composer, b St-Roch (Quebec City) 10 Apr 1892, d Quebec City 13 Sep 1977. He studied 1912–15 at the Paris Cons with Félix Fourdrain (composition, harmony), Alfredo Casella, Joaquin Nin, and Lazare Lévy (piano). He also took courses with Alfred Cortot. On his return to Canada in 1915 he was appointed choirmaster at St-Sauveur Church in Quebec City. He also organized chamber music concerts with Omer *Létourneau, P. Ernest Lavigne, and Robert *Talbot. In 1921 he went to Paris to study orchestral conducting with André Caplet and later with Paul Paray, and a grant from the Quebec government in 1924 enabled him to stay until 1928. He then settled in Montreal where 1928–9 he conducted operettas presented by a French troupe at the *St-Denis Theatre.

Trudel was music director 1929–30 at radio station CKAC and later conducted concerts 1931–7 on CNRM (the CNR radio station) and in the CKAC series 'L'Heure provinciale' and 'Syrup Symphonies,' the latter series broadcast from *Tudor Hall. With Alexander *Brott and Jean *Belland he founded the Montreal Trio in the early 1930s. At the CRBC and later the CBC he frequently served as a conductor or piano accompanist.

Trudel conducted the CSM (*MSO) 1935–8 during its first three seasons. After one of his concerts, a critic for *La Presse* wrote: 'His very French way of understanding and viewing a score, the concern for detail which never allows him to lose sight of the unity of a work, his highly developed sense of colour and contrast were all noted and strongly applauded' (5 Feb 1935).

Trudel taught 1943–56 at the *CMM and served 1944–7 and 1950–2 as president of the *AMQ. Among his pupils were Monique Fournier, François *Morel, Gilles *Tremblay, and Ronald *Turini. He composed some religious works. ST

True North Records. Major independent company founded in 1970 in Toronto by Bernie Finkelstein. Beginning with the album *Bruce Cockburn*, it had released some 30 LPs by 1978, including 9 by *Cockburn and 7 by Murray *McLauchlan. Others recorded include Ronney Abramson, Luke Gibson, the US guitarist and folksinger David Rea, John *Mills-Cockell, and Mills-Cockell's band Syrinx. Many of the recordings were produced by Gene Martynec, formerly of *Kensington Market. True North releases are distributed in Canada by *CBS Records and in the USA and Europe by Island Records.

Finkelstein (b Toronto 12 Aug 1944), a leading figure in the Canadian music industry, was manager 1966–7 of the *Paupers and 1967–9 of Kensington Market. His partnership with Burnie Fiedler (the Finkelstein Fiedler Co, Ltd, formed in 1973) has managed the careers of Abramson, Cockburn, McLauchlan, and Dan *Hill.

BIBLIOGRAPHY

Farrell, David. 'Bernie Finkelstein True North chief,' *Record Week*, 25 Oct, 1 Nov 1976

Waxman, Ken. 'Bernie Finkelstein helps turn Canadian folk singers into folk heroes,' (*Toronto Star*) *The City*, 25 Jun 1978 MM

TSUTSUMI, Tsuyoshi. Cellist, teacher, b Tokyo 28 Jul 1942. Early studies with his father and with Hideo Saito led to his debut at 12 with the Tokyo Philharmonic and a youthful career as a soloist and recitalist in Asia and Europe. He continued his studies in 1961 with Janos Starker at Indiana U and soon became Starker's assistant. He won first prizes at the 12th International Music Competition in Munich and the International Casals Competition in Budapest (1963). Later awards included the Arts Festival Prize (1970) from the Cultural Ministry of Japan, the Torii Music Prize (1971) for outstanding achievement by a Japanese musician, and the Ysaÿe Medal (1973). His interest in contemporary works for cello has drawn particular recognition, and several composers have written works for him. Lukas Foss chose him to give the premiere (1969) of his *Cello Concerto* with the Berlin Radio Orchestra. Tsutsumi began teaching at the *U of Western Ontario in 1968 and at the *Banff SFA in 1970, drawing students from North America and Europe. While continuing to tour internationally, he has performed regularly at the *Stratford Festival and appeared as soloist with the *TS and other leading

Canadian orchestras. He began performing with the *Hidy-Ozolins-Tsutsumi Trio in 1973 and with the violinst Steven *Staryk, the violist Gerald *Stanick, and the pianist Ronald *Turini formed *Quartet Canada in 1976.

DISCOGRAPHY

Bach *Unaccompanied Cello Suites*, complete. 1968–9. 4-CBS (Sony) SONS-30082

– *Unaccompanied Cello Suites No. 3 and 6*. 1969. Col MS90325

Bach *Unaccompanied Suite for Cello No. 1* – Kodály *Unaccompanied Sonata for Cello, Op 8*. 1968. CBS (Sony) SONC 16003

Beethoven *Cello Sonata No. 3* – Brahms *Cello Sonata No. 1*. Kobayashi pf. 1971. CBS (Sony) SONC 16024J

Brahms *Cello Sonata No. 2*. 1963. Comensoli pf. Qualiton

Brahms *Concerto in A Minor* for violin and cello – Dvořák *Concerto in B Minor*. Japan Phil SO, Akiyama cond, Unno vn. 1969. CBS (Sony) SONW 20065-66J

Brahms *Cello Sonata in D Major* – Chopin *Cello Sonata in G Minor*. Nakamura pf. 1975. CBS (Sony) 23 AC8

Japanese Contemporary Works for Unaccompanied Cello: Mayuzumi – Irino – Shimoyama – Mamiya. 1969–71. CBS (Sony) SONC 16022J

Mamiya *Japanese Folk Songs; Uta* – de Falla *Suite populaire espagnole; Danse rituelle du feu*. Mamiya pf. 1972. CBS (Sony) SOCN-12XJ

Reger *Suite No. 2* – Hindemith *Sonata, Op 25, No. 3* – Ysaÿe *Sonata, Op. 28*. 1971. CBS (Sony) SOCL-112-XJ

Schubert – Beethoven – Cassado – Davidoff – Saint-Saëns. Penneys pf. 1970. CBS (Sony) SONC 16018-J

Tchaikovsky *Trio in A Minor*. Nakamura pf, Unno vn. 1974. CBS (Sony) SOCM 59

Yashiro *Concerto*. (1960). NHK SO, Iwaki cond. 1964. Japan Col OS 10025-J

See also Discography for Marta Hidy. GKG

Tudor Hall / Salle Tudor. A 300-seat hall built in 1929 by Ogilvy's on the fifth floor of its department store on Ste-Catherine St, Montreal. It contained a pipe organ with three manuals. Its excellent acoustics were attributed to its oak-panelled walls. For a long time free noon-hour recitals were given daily by the organist Herbert *Sanders. Many artists and ensembles performed there, including the *Hart House String Quartet with Sir Ernest *MacMillan, the Fisk Jubilee Singers, one of whose members was Martin Luther King, the Vienna Boys' Choir, and the Royal Chapel choir of London. The hall was used by the radio stations CFCF and CKAC for their musical programs. In 1931 the first Canadian TV programs, telecast by the experimental station VE9AF, originated in this hall. The hall was administered by Ogilvy's as a public service until 1957, when its use was discontinued owing to the expansion of the store. GP

The Tudor Singers of Montreal / L'Ensemble Vocal Tudor de Montréal. Mixed choir founded in 1962 by Wayne *Riddell to perform unaccompanied music of the 16th and 17th centuries. They gave their first concert 19 Apr 1963 at Redpath Hall and have continued to perform regularly in the Montreal area and for the CBC. In 1964 they won the first Leslie *Bell Memorial Choral Competition for adult amateur choirs. With the addition in 1966 of singers from the defunct *Montreal Bach Choir, the Tudor Singers added to their repertoire works of the baroque and the 20th-century, also presenting Canadian works at *SMCQ concerts. Prior to 1975 membership ranged from 17 to 35 augmented for larger presentations. Under Riddell's continuing direction the choir premiered Bruce *Mather's *La Lune mince* (SMCQ, 2 Apr 1970) and Kelsey *Jones' commissioned *The Hymn to Bacchus* (16 May 1972) and, under Serge *Garant, gave the first North American performance of Jean *Papineau-Couture's *Paysage* (SMCQ, 2 Apr 1970). Also presenting one large-scale traditional work annually, the Tudor Singers have per-

The Tudor Singers of Montreal with their conductor, Wayne Riddell (top row)

formed Handel's *Judas Maccabaeus* (1968) and *Messiah* (1969) and Bach's *Christmas Oratorio* (1971), *St John Passion* (1972), *Magnificat in D* (1973), *Mass in B Minor* (1974), and *St Matthew Passion* (1975). Soloists have included Maureen *Forrester, Claude *Corbeil, Joan *Patenaude, Lois *Marshall, John *Martens, Gaston *Germain, Ann *Golden, and Christina Jones. Initially an amateur choir, the Tudor Singers were re-organized in 1975 by Riddell as a professional ensemble of 19 voices.

DISCOGRAPHY

Anhalt *Cento*. Anhalt cond. RCI 357

K. Jones *The Prophesy of Micah*. Riddell cond. 1971. RCI 355

Mozart – Bach – Somers – Britten – Byrd – Phillips: motets, hymns. Riddell cond. 1968. CBC SM-53

Music of Today, vol 2: Mather *La Lune mince* (Riddell cond) – Papineau-Couture *Paysage* (SMCQ Ens, Garant cond). 1970. RCI 299

Palestrina – Poulenc – Ridout – Morley: selections. Riddell cond. 1969. CBC SM-86 NT

'Tumbling Tumbleweeds.' Cowboy song identified with the country-music group Sons of the Pioneers, of which the New Brunswick-born composer Bob Nolan was a member. It was written ca 1933 as 'Tumbling Leaves' in Los Angeles and revised in 1934 as 'Tumbling Tumbleweeds,' an evocation of the prairie west. Introduced in 1935 in the movie of the same name by Gene Autry (who sang it again in 1945 in *Don't Fence Me In*), it was performed also by Roy Rogers in *Silver Spurs* (1943) and by the Sons of the Pioneers in *Hollywood Canteen* (1944). Recordings were made by Autry, the Sons of the Pioneers, and other country artists and by such pop singers as Jo Stafford and Patti Page. As recorded by Bing Crosby (Decca 3024) it was a hit in 1940. The song was published by Williamson Music and Sam Fox and has remained popular with small male-voice ensembles.

Nolan (b Robert Clarence Nobles, 1 Apr 1908, d Los Angeles, 16 Jun 1980) was raised in New Brunswick and Boston, moved at 14 to Arizona, and settled later in California. With Dick Weston (also known as Leonard Slye or Roy Rogers) and Tim Spencer he founded (Los Angeles 1933) the Sons of the Pioneers, with whom he toured until 1949 and recorded until 1957. Nolan wrote over 1200 songs, among them the group's other major hit, 'Cool Water.' MM

TUPPER, Reginald de Havilland. Bassoonist, administrator, b Wimbledon, Surrey, England, 1883, d Montreal 1 Sep 1967. He studied at the Cathedral Choir School in Worcester with Hugh Blair and at the RCM for four years. Before emigrating to Canada he played for two years in the Llandudno SO, North Wales, and, later, in the London New SO and the Covent Garden Opera Orchestra. Active in Montreal after 1912, he became bassoon instructor in 1921 at the *McGill Cons and later (1927) secretary of the conservatorium and of the Faculty of Music and Musical Examining Board, McGill U. He became vice-director of the conservatorium in 1939. Retiring from administration in 1948, he lectured on music until 1955. He played bassoon and wrote the program notes 1930–41 for the *Montreal Orchestra and conducted the McGill Cons Orchestra for 13 years. One of his string quartets was performed in 1912 by the King Cole Club, London, and his *Suite of Old English Pieces* was played 14 Jan 1934 by the Montreal Orchestra.

WRITINGS

'McGill Conservatory [sic] of Music,' 'Musical criticism,' *Montreal Music Year Book 1931* (Montreal nd) NT

TURGEON, Bernard (Joseph Roméo Vianney). Baritone, administrator, b Edmonton 20 Oct 1932. He began his musical training in Edmonton with his mother and continued with Jean *Létourneau. He studied 1951–5 at the *RCMT with George *Lambert and Ernesto *Vinci, 1959–60 in Vienna with Ferdinand Grossmann, Heinrich Schmidt, and Helmut Froschauer, and 1960–3 in London with Walter Jensch. He appeared in several *Royal Cons Opera School productions 1951–5 in Toronto and in 1955 won the top men's award in CBC's *'Singing Stars of Tomorrow.'

Turgeon began singing with the *COC in 1952, appeared 1960–3 with Sadler's Wells, and also, during the 1960s, performed with the *Edmonton, Pittsburgh, and San Diego Opera Companies. He sang with the Welsh National Opera in 1962, the *Vancouver Opera in 1964, 1965, and 1979, and the *Opéra du Québec in 1973. In the course of these engagements he developed a repertoire of operatic roles which has included Amonasro in *Aida*, Bartolo in *The Barber of Seville*, Conochar in *Deirdre*, the Father in *Hansel and Gretel*, Malatesta in *Don Pasquale*, Masetto in *Don Giovanni*, Maurizio in *The School for Fathers*, Papageno in *The Magic Flute*, Marcello and Schaunard in *La Bohème*, and Tonio in *I Pagliacci*. He has sung at festivals in Stratford, Ont, in 1956 and 1965, Vancouver in 1958, 1962, and 1964, Edinburgh and Glyndebourne in 1960, and Colorado in 1967. He has performed in recital and concert throughout Canada, and he toured the USSR in 1971, 1972, and 1976. As a concert soloist he has appeared with the London Philharmonic Orchestra, the *MSO, the *TSO, the *Vancouver SO, and other orchestras.

Perhaps Turgeon's most distinctive achievement has been the creation of the title role in the COC production of *Somers' *Louis Riel*. So close was his identification with the role that he was re-engaged for the revivals of the opera in 1968 and 1975 and for the CBC's TV production in 1969. Following the premiere John *Kraglund wrote: 'Both words and music were impressively served by Bernard Turgeon in the title role, for he appeared to be completely bilingual. In his dramatic interpretation he brought out the contradictory aspects of Riel's character, a curious blend of mysticism, realism, warm simplicity, patriotism and madness. And in musical terms he ranged from impassioned declamation in political arguments to ecstatic lyricism in his vision of himself as the reincarnation of David and his exchange with his mother and sister' (Toronto *Globe and Mail*, 25 Sep 1967).

Turgeon was head of the voice and opera departments at the *U of Alberta 1967–75 and the

Bernard Turgeon as Louis Riel

*Banff SFA 1970–8 and began to teach at the *U of Victoria in 1978.

DISCOGRAPHY

Beethoven *Elegischer Gesang*. Orford Str Quar. 1970. CBC SM-147

Gilbert & Sullivan *Trial by Jury*. Glyndebourne Festival Chor, Pro Arte Orch, Sargent cond. Ca 1960. Angel S-35966

Hutchinson – Mussorgsky – Tchaikovsky – Robinson – Ireland – Saint-Saëns. Brough pf. 1967. CBC Expo 27

Mussorgsky – Franck – Duparc – Ravel: songs. Helmer pf. 1970. CBC SM-121

BIBLIOGRAPHY

'Canadians in profile: Bernard Turgeon,' *OpCan*, Summer 1973

Mercer, Ruby. 'An interview with Bernard Turgeon,' *OpCan*, Oct 1975 (RDM)

TURINI, Ronald. Pianist, teacher, b Montreal 30 Sep 1934; premier prix (CMM) 1950. Born of a US-Italian father and a Canadian mother of Danish origin, he had piano lessons as a very young child from his mother and from Frank *Hanson at the *McGill Cons. He enrolled at the *CMM at nine and studied there with Yvonne *Hubert, Germaine *Malépart, and Isidor Philipp until 1950. Prior to his graduation he made his debut at the *MSO's Matinées symphoniques under Wilfrid *Pelletier. He won the *Prix Archambault in 1950. He entered Mannes College, New York, in 1953, and had lessons there with Isabelle Vengerova and later with Olga Stroumillo, who introduced him to Vladimir Horowitz. Horowitz taught the young pianist for five years and became the major influence on his playing.

Turini toured 1956–7, 1957–8, and 1958–9 for the *JMC and in 1958 won second prizes at the Concorso Pianistico Internazionale Ferruccio Busoni in Bolzano, Italy, and the International Competition for Musical performers in Geneva. The following year he gave a series of recitals in Switzerland. After winning second prize at the 1960 Queen Elisabeth International Music Competition in Brussels he toured Canada under the auspices of the *Canada Council. Harold C. Schonberg described his Carnegie Hall debut in the *New York Times* of 24 Jan 1961: 'He was resplendent. For in addition to technical expertness, there was a quality of aristocracy to the performance.' Turini returned there in 1964 and 1967.

Turini continued to receive highly favourable reviews and soon acquired an international reputation. He toured in the USSR and South America in 1963, 1965, and 1968. As a concerto soloist he performed in the USA with the National SO of Washington, DC, in 1968 and with the San Antonio SO in 1970 and also with the Melbourne SO on its North American tour in 1971. In 1965 he played in the Concertgebouw in Amsterdam and in several recital halls in London including Wigmore Hall. In 1967 he performed at the *Institut canadien in Quebec City and at the Canadian Pavilion at *Expo 67, was a soloist with the London Philharmonic Orchestra under Sir Adrian Boult, and gave recitals in France and Ireland. The following year he played Rachmaninoff's *Concerto No. 3* with the *TS. He performed with the *Orford String Quartet on a 1969–70 JMC tour and in a 1976 chamber music recital at *PDA.

Ronald Turini

Turini was a soloist with the MSO, both in Montreal in 1953, 1957, 1958, 1969, 1974, and 1979 and on tours of Europe in 1962 and 1976 and appeared in recital at the PDA in 1966, 1972, and 1975. After a Turini recital Claude *Gingras remarked that his performance of Schubert's *Impromptu, Op 142 no. 3*: 'displayed a deep lyricism, a sound of refined quality, and admirable control of keyboard and pedal, at the same time investing these pages with the improvisational qualities which suit them' (Montreal *La Presse*, 21 Apr 1972). In 1974 he gave a recital on BBC radio and appeared with the Royal Philharmonic Orchestra and the Bournemouth SO.

In 1975 Turini became a founding member of *Quartet Canada and began teaching at the *U of Western Ontario, where the members of the quartet were appointed artists-in-residence. He continued his solo career, however. In 1977 he played the Schumann *Concerto* with the *Quebec SO. He gave a *St Lawrence Centre solo recital in Toronto in 1979 and appeared with Ida *Haendel in a series of duo-sonata recitals for Montreal's *Pro Musica Society in 1980. Eric *McLean praised him for a 'splendid performance' of the Grieg *Concerto* at the PDA and noted that 'the piano part was played with admirable restraint, without subtracting anything from the technical display with which Grieg endowed the piece' (*Montreal Star*, 11 Apr 1979).

DISCOGRAPHY

Beethoven – Scriabin – Liszt – Ravel. (1965). RCI 211

Hindemith *Sonata* for viola and piano; *Sonata, Op 11, no. 4*. W. Trampler va. 1967. RCA LSC-3012

Schubert – Ginastera – Rachmaninoff. 1969. RCI 283/RCA LSC-3145

Schumann – Liszt – Hindemith – Scriabin. 1961. RCA LSC-2779

See also Discographies for Orford String Quartet; Quartet Canada. (PR)

Turkey. Turkish immigrants, largely from Ankara and Istanbul, began to settle in Canada in the 1960s. The 1971 census lists 6400 Turks living mainly in large urban centres. Social gatherings sponsored by organizations in the larger Turkish communities in Burlington, Ont, Toronto, and Montreal are the main occasion for traditional music and folk dance. Traditional Turkish folk music uses the saz, a long-necked plucked instrument, the zurna, an oboe-like instrument, and the davul, a type of drum. Turkish popular music uses classical and folk as well as modern instruments. However, differences between the Turkish musical system and that in use elsewhere create difficulties in the practice of traditional forms outside of Turkey, and especially in the handing on of these forms to the younger generation. Transcriptions of some Turkish music are held at the National Museum of Man. There was a Turkish Pavilion at the 1978 Toronto *Caravan sponsored by the Turkish Folklore and Cultural Assn and the Turkish-Canadian Friendship Assn. Toronto's CHIN radio station has broadcast a regular program that includes both folk and popular Turkish music.

The *JMC sponsored the Turkish violinist Ayla Erduran on Canadian tours in 1960–1 and 1961–2. Visits to Canada by other Turkish musicians include those by the Whirling Dervishes of Turkey (a folk group which performed in Montreal in 1973), by another folk dance group in 1976, by the singer Mustafa Sagyasar in 1978, by the pianist Idil Biret – a Nadia Boulanger pupil who gave recitals in Canada as a child prodigy, appeared with orchestra during the 1960 *Montreal Festivals, and performed at *Hart House in 1979 – and by the violinist Suna Kan, who was soloist with the *CBC Winnipeg Orchestra in 1979.

The ethnomusicologist and anthropologist Asen Balikci (b Turkey 30 Dec 1929) made extensive recordings of Inuit songs, games, and legends while working at the National Museum of Man.

BIBILIOGRAPHY

Basgöz, Ilhan. 'Turks in the Canadian social mosaic,' unpubl report, National Museum of Man (Ottawa 1973–4) (IMG)

TURNER, Edward (Rainey). Harpsichord maker and historian, b Noranda, Que, 23 May 1940. He studied at the school of art and design at the Montreal Museum of Fine Arts before moving in 1962 to Vancouver. During the 1960s, prompted by an interest in folk music, he began making banjos, and in 1971 he turned to instrument building full-time, sharing a workshop with Ray *Nurse, Michael Dunn, and Tim Hobrough. As his interest turned to renaissance instruments, he decorated (in 17th-century style) three harpsichords built by Dunn for the *Vancouver Society for Early Music. Thereafter he concentrated on harpsichord building. On grants from the Bronfman and *Koerner foundations, in 1975 and 1977 respectively, he studied early keyboard instruments in the U of Edinburgh's Russell Collection (for which he became a consultant draughtsman, preparing full-sized plans and researching the instrument's histories for other builders). By 1977 Turner himself had completed 12 harpsichords in 16th-, 17th-, and 18th-century styles.

BIBLIOGRAPHY

McAlpine, Mary. 'True to the harpsichord,' Vancouver *Sun*, 9 Apr 1976 BNSG

TURNER, Herbert G. Teacher, b Oxford, England, 26 Feb 1883, d Edmonton 4 Jul 1963. After voice and trumpet studies in England and a brief period of military service Turner moved to Edmonton in 1907. There he and his wife, Eileen McEcheran Turner, opened a voice studio in 1913. He was also a founder of AF of M local 390 and secretary-treasurer 1936–62 of the *Alberta Music Festival Assn. The Turners founded the Light Opera of Edmonton (1950–67), which produced over 25 shows. After Turner's death, it continued for four years under his wife's direction. His pupils included Robert *Goulet; hers included Lois *McDonall. RDM

TURNER, Robert (Comrie). Composer, radio producer, teacher, b Montreal 6 Jun 1920; B MUS (McGill) 1943, M MUS (Peabody College) 1950, D MUS (McGill) 1953. His teachers included Douglas *Clarke and Claude *Champagne at *McGill U, Herbert Howells and Gordon Jacob at the RCM 1947–8, Roy Harris at the George Peabody College of Teachers in Nashville, Tenn, 1947–50, and Olivier Messiaen at Tanglewood 1949. His responsibilities as a CBC Vancouver music producer 1952–68 included the broadcasts of the *CBC Vancouver Chamber Orchestra. He taught at the *U of British Columbia 1955–7 and at *Acadia U 1968–9 before joining the faculty at the *U of Manitoba in 1969. A confessed eclectic, Turner in his music has responded to a variety of influences, includng jazz and modal and quartal harmony. Even in dissonance or when using a 12-note theme as source material, he usually has maintained a tonal centre. Most of his compositions have been written on commission or for particular occasions and reflect his belief that music should be 'precisely notated, emotional in content and listener-oriented' (*Musicanada*, May 1970). His lyric drama *The Brideship*, for which George Woodcock provided the libretto, was a CBC commission for Canada's centenary and was premiered on radio 12 Dec 1967 under the direction of Hugh *McLean, with a cast which included Audrey *Farnell, Phyllis *Mailing, Patricia *Rideout, and Garnet *Brooks. Turner is a member of the Composers' Guild of Great Britain and the *CLComp, an associate of the *CMCentre, and an affiliate of PRO Canada. He married the percussionist Sara Nan Scott in 1949.

COMPOSITIONS

STAGE, RADIO, AND TV

The Brideship, lyric drama (Woodcock). 1967. 8 solo vs, orch. Peer (rental)

A few works for radio and TV, plays and documentaries

ORCHESTRA

Opening Night, theatre overture. 1955. Full orch. BMIC 1960. CBC SM-163 (*CBC Wpg O)/RCI 179 (*CBC SO)

Lyric Interlude. 1956. Full orch. CMCentre

Nocturne. 1956. Med orch. Ber 1972. CBC SM-63/RCI-334/A of D SDD-2121 (*CBC Van Chamb o)

A Children's Overture. 1958. Med orch. CMCentre. CBC SM-63/RCI-334/A of D SDD-2121 (*CBC Van Chamb O)

The Pemberton Valley. 1958. Med orch. ms

Symphony for Strings. 1960. Str orch. CMCentre. RCI-214/RCA CCS-1008 (*CBC Van Chamb O)

Three Episodes. 1963. Full orch. CMCentre. CBC SM-4 (*TSO)

Eidolons '12 Images for Chamber Orchestra.' 1972. Wat 1977. CBC SM-265 (*CBC Van Chamb O)

Variations on 'The Prairie Settler's Song.' 1974. CMCentre. CBC SM-331 (*CBC Van Chamb O)

SOLOIST(S) WITH ORCHESTRA

Four Songs (Wilfred Watson). 1959. Sop (ten), orch (pf). CMCentre

The Third Day, cantata (medieval and renaissance sources, adapt Peter Haworth). 1962. Soli, SATB, med orch. CMCentre

Concerto for Two Pianos and Orchestra. 1971. CMCentre

Johann's Gift to Christmas (Jack Richards). 1972. Narr, full orch. CMCentre

Chamber Concerto for Bassoon and Seventeen Instruments. 1973. Wat 1977

Capriccio Concertante. 1975. Vc, pf, full orch. CMcentre

CHAMBER

Lament. 1951. Fl, ob, cl, bn, pf. CMCentre

Sonata. 1956. Vn, pf. CMCentre. RCI-194 (A. *Pratz vn)

Robbins' Round. 1959. Jazz band. CMCentre

Variations and Toccata. 1959. Ww quin, str quin. Ber (rental). RCI-215/RCA CCS-1009 (Chamb Ens of Wpg, *Feldbrill cond)

Mobile (Elder Olson). 1960. SATB, 7 perc. CMCentre

Serenade for Woodwind Quintet. 1960. CMCentre. CBC SM-139 (*Van WW Quin)

Four Fragments. 1961. Brass quin. Peer 1972

Robert Turner

Fantasia. 1962. Org, brass quin, tim. CMCentre

The Phoenix and the Turtle (Shakespeare). 1964. Mezzo, fl, b cl, cl, str trio, cel, hp. CMCentre

Suite in Homage to Melville (Melville). 1966. Sop, alto, va, pf. CMCentre

Diversities. 1967. Vn, bn, pf. CMCentre. RCI-239 (*Cassenti Players)

Trio for Violin, Cello and Piano. 1969. CMCentre

Fantasy and Festivity. 1970. Hp. CMCentre. CBC SM-188 (J. *Loman)

Nostalgia. 1972. Sop sax, pf. CMCentre

Others, including 3 string quartets (1949, 1954, 1975)

PIANO AND ORGAN

Sonata Lyrica. 1955 (rev 1963). Pf. CMCentre

Six Voluntaries. 1959. Org. BMIC 1968. RCI-226/RCA CCS-1020 (H. *McLean)

And others

CHOIR AND VOICE

Two Choral Pieces (Wallace Stevens, e.e. cummings). 1952. SATB. RCI-70/('Anyone Lives in a Little How Town') RCI-206 (*Mtl Bach Choir)

A few other works for choir and v(s), including several arr of Canadian folk songs

WRITINGS

'Barbara Pentland,' *CMJ*, vol 2, Summer 1958

BIBLIOGRAPHY

'*The Brideship*,' *CBC Times*, 9–15 Dec 1967

Garvie, Peter. 'Robert Turner,' *MSc*, 245, Jan–Feb 1969

'Robert Turner,' *Mcan*, 29, final issue 1970

BMI Canada Ltd / PRO Canada Ltd. 'Robert Turner,' pamphlets (1975, 1979)

Creative Canada, vol 1

Contemporary Canadian Composers / Compositeurs canadiens contemporains JHn

TUROFSKY, Riki (Rita Nan Ricky) (m Sunter). Soprano, b Toronto, 20 Feb 1944. She began studies with the British Columbia Opera Ensemble, making her debut in 1967 in its touring production of *Hansel and Gretel*. She was awarded a place in the San Francisco Opera's Merola program in 1967 and studied at the Music Academy of the West with Martial Singher and Lotte Lehmann and 1968–70 at the *U of Toronto with Irene *Jessner, graduating in opera performance. After singing Oscar in the 1970 *Vancouver Opera Assn production of *Un Ballo in Maschera* she appeared that same year as Zerlina in *Don Giovanni* with the *COC.

Turofsky made her New York City Opera debut 27 Oct 1972 as Frasquita in *Carmen* and has performed with the Chattanooga Opera (1972), the Houston Grand Opera (1973, alternating with Beverly Sills in *The Daughter of the Regiment*), the Kansas City Lyric Opera (1975), and (in her European operatic debut, 10 Jun 1976) the Netherlands Opera as Curley's Wife in Carlisle Floyd's *Of Mice and Men*. She sang Titania in the 1978 *Festival Ottawa production of Britten's *A Midsummer Night's Dream*.

Turofsky toured Europe in 1971 as soloist with the *Festival Singers and has sung with the *TS and the *Toronto Mendelssohn Choir, the *Hamilton Philharmonic, the *Bach-Elgar Choir, and the *McGill Chamber Orchestra. R. Murray *Schafer's *Hymn to Night* was commissioned for her, and she gave the premiere with the *CJRT Orchestra in 1978. She sang the Princess in the TV premiere (CBC, 1975) of Tibor *Polgar's *The Glove*. In 1980 for the Aquitaine label she recorded a song recital, *Jade Eyes* (AQD 9064), with the guitarist Michael Laucke.

Turofsky married the OAC music officer, later CBC radio music official, Robert *Sunter.

WRITINGS

'The young performing musician,' *CMB*, 10, Spring–Summer 1975

BIBLIOGRAPHY

Batten, Jack. 'Bye-bye Brunhild,' *Maclean's*, Oct 1974

Adilman, Sid. 'Riki's singing a new tune,' *Toronto Star*, 2 Apr 1978 MW

TURP, André. Tenor, b Montreal 21 Dec 1925. He took voice lessons from Édouard *Woolley and Frank H. *Rowe and then worked at the *CMM with Ruzena *Herlinger. He was awarded a Quebec government grant in 1949 and went to Italy to study with Hélène Vita. He made his stage debut in 1950 in operettas with the *Variétés lyriques and took part in several CBC programs. In 1956 he sang Cavaradossi in *Tosca*, Rodolfo in *La Bohème*, and Roméo in *Roméo et Juliette* in New Orleans. With the *Opera Guild of Montreal he sang Cavaradossi (1957), Fenton (*Falstaff*, 1958), and Macduff (*Macbeth*, 1959). With the *MSO in 1959 he sang Jason in Cherubini's *Medea*. Shortly thereafter he made his New York debut with the American Opera Society as Fritz in a concert performance of Offenbach's *The Grand Duchess of Gerolstein*, an operetta he had sung in 1958 on CBC TV.

Turp made his debut with the Royal Opera, Covent Garden, 5 Feb 1960 as Edgardo in *Lucia di Lammermoor* opposite Joan Sutherland. He was with that company for several seasons and appeared in numerous roles including Turridu (*Cavalleria Rusticana*), des Grieux (*Manon*), Rodolfo, Pinkerton (*Madama Butterfly*), Cavaradossi, Alfredo (*La Traviata*), and Rinuccio (*Gianni Schicchi*). He also sang the leading tenor roles in Gluck's *Iphigénie en Tauride*, Walton's *Troilus and Cressida*, and Tippett's *The Midsummer Marriage*.

In 1961 Turp was invited to Glyndebourne, where he sang in Henze's *Elegy for Young Lovers*, among other works. He participated in numerous performances at the Opera and the Opéra-Comique in Paris, augmenting his usual repertoire with the leading roles in *Louise* and *Werther*. He has performed in theatres in Switzerland, Portugal, and Spain. In 1963 the Teatro del Liceo, Barcelona, conferred on him a gold medal for his performance of Werther, a role he sang with great success more than 500 times in Europe and America.

In Montreal Turp sang Ferrando in *Così fan tutte* (1962) and Angelo in Gilbert Bécaud's *Opéra d'Aran* (1965). He sang Hoffmann in *The Tales of Hoffmann* with the *COC in Toronto and Montreal in 1967 and repeated the role with the New York City Opera in 1973.

Turp has sung opposite Montserrat Caballé, Régine Crespin, Rita Gorr, Victoria de los Angeles, Beverly Sills, and other operatic luminaries. In 1973 for the BBC he sang the title role in Verdi's *Don Carlos*, revived in French for the first time in 100 years, in company with the Canadians Édith *Tremblay, Émile *Belcourt, Robert *Savoie, and Joseph *Rouleau. 'Critics have acknowledged his noble and passionate voice, with its glorious tim-

André Turp

bre, evenly balanced in all registers' (Renée Maheu in *Le Devoir*, 12 Apr 1976).

In 1976 Turp was a founding member of the Mouvement d'action pour l'art lyrique du Québec. A resident of England, Turp in 1980 continued to sing at Covent Garden and tour in Europe and South Africa. He reminisced about his career on the CBC TV program 'Propos et confidences' (28 Feb and 7 and 14 Mar 1978).

DISCOGRAPHY

Berlioz *Roméo et Juliette*. London SO, Monteux cond, Resnik mezzo, Ward bass. 2-Mus Guild S-6206/2-West 8127-2

Cherubini *Medea* (selections). Columbia SO, Gamson cond, Farrell sop. Odyssey Y-32356/Col 6032/Philips 30.1.399

Dubois *Les Sept Paroles du Christ*. Choeurs de Montréal, Renaud dir. 1960. Apex ALF 71700

Music at the Canadian Pavilion: Jeannotte *Propos intimes*. C. Pelletier pf. 1967. CBC Expo-26

BIBLIOGRAPHY

Nadeau, Monic. 'André Turp se vide le coeur au sujet de la piètre situation des chanteurs d'opéra du Québec,' *Télé-Radiomonde*, 9 Oct 1965

Bergeron, Raymonde. 'La merveilleuse histoire d'André Turp, chanteur d'opéra,' *Perspectives*, vol 21, 6 Jan 1979

GP

Turvey. Musical play by Donald Harron (book) and Norman *Campbell (music). Based on Earle Birney's novel *Turvey* (winner of the 1949 Leacock Award for humour), it concerns the misadventures of a hapless soldier, Private Thomas Leadbetter Turvey, during World War II. *Turvey* was first dramatized (without music) by Harron and produced in 1957 at the Avenue Theatre in Toronto by the New Play Society under Mavor *Moore. The musical version was premiered 25 Jul 1966 at the *Charlottetown Festival with Jack Duffy as Turvey and Kate Reid, Jean Cavall, Eric House, and Harron in supporting roles. John *Fenwick, conductor of the first production, scored a dance sequence, and Campbell contributed 16 songs, which were, according to Nathan Cohen, 'varied and pleasant, recalling the military and popular melodies of World War II.' Cohen commented that '[Campbell's] ballads were particularly agreeable' (*Toronto Daily Star*, 3 Aug 1966). Revised by Harron and Campbell as *Private Turvey's War*, it was staged again at the 1970 Charlottetown Festival with Alan Lofft as Turvey and Catherine *McKinnon and Douglas Chamberlain in supporting roles. This production was presented at the *NAC in 1970.

TWA, Andrew. Composer, violist, accountant, b Ellisboro, near Regina, 13 Dec 1919. He studied viola with Richard Ainsworth in Brandon, Man. In 1945 he moved to Toronto, where he studied violin and viola with Elie *Spivak and composition with John *Weinzweig. In 1949 he won the McGill Chamber Music Society Award for his *String Quartet* (1948). He taught viola 1949–52 at the *RCMT and was a violist 1950–1 with the *TSO. He was a founding member, and treasurer 1952–8, of the *CLComp. He played 1963–4 in the Harmony SO (Toronto) and was conductor in 1962 of the Scarborough Choral Society and music director 1965–8 of the Scarborough Music Guild. He was assistant conductor 1972–3 and conductor 1973–4 of the York Regional SO. His compositions include the orchestral works *Prairies* (BMIC 1950), *Serenade for Clarinet and Strings* (1948, recorded by Avrahm *Galper, RCI 86), *Serenade for Bassoon and Strings* (1951, Ber 1970), *Symphony* (1953, premiered by the TSO in 1954), and *Oxford Sinfonia* (1978). Works for smaller forces include the above-mentioned string quartet, a sonata for solo violin (1948), a sonata for violin and piano and one for viola and piano (both 1951), *Tonomoda* for horn and string bass (1974), and *Monody and Multiplex* for solo horn (1978, performed by Fergus McWilliam for Norwegian radio in 1978). Twa was the founder and general manager 1970–1 of *Berandol Music. He is a member of PRO Canada and an associate of the *CMCentre. NM

Twelve-tone technique (dodecaphony; 12-note technique). Method of composing which dissociates from tonality the 12 pitches of the well-tempered chromatic scale, subjecting them to rules of a kind of abstract polyphony in which conventional harmony plays no part. The early (pre-1924) atonal pieces of Schoenberg, Berg, and Webern attempted to eliminate all tonal implication, but until Josef Matthias Hauer devised (1912–21) and Schoenberg refined the 12-tone technique there was no system for ensuring the at least theoretical equality of the pitches.

The 12-tone technique begins with the ordering of the 12 notes of the scale into a set or row or series. Three corollary sets or rows are obtained from the inversion, retrograde, and retrograde-inversion of the set (see figure). By transposing the set and its three corollaries through the full chromatic span, retaining the integrity of the intervallic relationships, the composer produces 48 distinct but related forms which constitute the material for a strict 12-tone composition. It should be mentioned that serialism need not be 12-tone serialism and that many composers work with series using fewer than 12 pitches or series which use one or more of the 12 pitches more than once. Stravinsky's *In Memoriam Dylan Thomas* and Britten's *The Turn of the Screw* exemplify the use of shorter rows. Pierre Boulez, notably in *Structures I*, and Milton Babbitt in *3 Compositions for Piano* have extended serialist principles into areas other than pitch, into duration, dynamics, and articulation, and several other composers have followed their lead.

In Canada, John *Weinzweig pioneered dodecaphony in a way that was selective and individualistic from the outset, employing the row as the source of various motives (*Piano Suite No. 1*, 1939) rather than exploiting it systematically. Weinzweig's contemporary, Barbara *Pentland, was introduced to the serial method by Dika Newlin, a pupil of Schoenberg, but was not inspired to use it until she heard the music of Webern in 1955. Once persuaded, however, she used the method with great freedom. A kind of '12-tone school' developed at the *U of Toronto from Weinzweig's use of the technique as a training for young composers. Notable among the products of this 'school' are certain works of Harry *Somers,

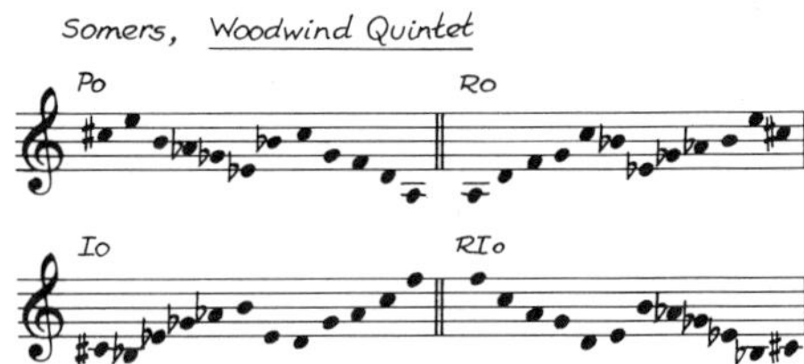

The row, retrograde, inversion, and retrograde inversion upon which Harry Somers' *Woodwind Quintet* is based

whose piano fugues *12 X 12* (1951) reflect Bach and Schoenberg and whose *Woodwind Quintet* (1948) explores the Weinzweigian principle of motivic selection from the 12-tone row. Works of Norma *Beecroft, Bruce *Mather, and several others also carry forward the open-minded approach to serialism advocated by Weinzweig.

The severely exploitive, highly mathematical applications of serialism pioneered in France by Boulez found a strong response in French Canada – particularly in Serge *Garant's *Asymétries No. 1* (1958), *Offrande I-III* (1969–71), and *Circuits 1* (1972) and *III* (1973) – but also in English Canada in Udo *Kasemets' works of the 1950s.

Otto *Joachim's serialism, of which a forthright example is the *Twelve 12-tone Pieces for Children* (1961), derives more directly from the Viennese prototypes and from Krenek, and John *Beckwith's – (in *A Chaucer Suite* (1961), and the 'Children's Song' from *The Trumpets of Summer* (1964) – belongs with the non-chromatic approach of Stravinsky and Britten, though full chromatic series are used, 1963–7, in the *Concertino, Circle with Tangents*, the other movements of *The Trumpets of Summer*, and other works of that period.

To summarize – or, rather, to risk summarizing – it may be said that dodecaphony's strictest (as distinct from strict) adherents in Canada have been *Anhalt (from 1950 to 1965), Garant (occasionally with modifications), and Kasemets (in the works 1950–60). Those who have written some strict works are Beckwith, *Ford (from 1969 to 1972), *Hartwell, *Hawkins, Joachim (until the late 1960s), *Laufer, *Papineau-Couture, and Pentland (after 1955). Those who incorporate a modified dodecaphony in most of their works are Beckwith (between 1960 and 1973), *Buczynski, *Cherney (1960s), *Dolin (1940s–1960s), *Fodi (1965–7), Ford (late 1960s to early 1970s), *Freedman (1940s–1960s), Joachim (until about 1969), *Prévost (after 1959), Somers, and Weinzweig. Composers some of whose works employ a modified series include Beecroft, Lorne *Betts, Alexander *Brott, Dolin (1960s and 1970s), Garant (though most are strict), Hawkins, *Henninger, *Hodkinson, *Klein, Laufer, Mather, *Mercure (the late works), *Morel, Pentland (after 1955, along with some strict works), Gilles *Tremblay, *Vallerand, and *Wilson. Composers whose works demonstrate traces of dodecaphonic influence include Murray *Adaskin, *Applebaum, *Douglas, *Eckhardt-Gramatté, *Pedersen, *Schafer, and Robert *Turner. The jazz composers Gordon *Delamont (the author of the textbook *Modern Twelve-Tone Techniques*), Doug *Riley, and Don *Thompson (1970s) have employed dodecaphony in some of their compositions.

Although 50 years after the 12-tone technique had been introduced its major products remained incomprehensible to a large part of the concert-going public, its influence on composers, including many of the foremost Canadians, was at once pervasive and catalytic.

BIBLIOGRAPHY

Leibowitz, René. *Introduction à la musique de 12 sons* (Paris 1949)

Gould, Glenn. 'The dodecacophonist's [sic] dilemma,' *CMJ*, vol 1, Autumn 1956
Marquis, Welton. *Twentieth Century Music Idioms* (Englewood Cliffs, NJ, 1964)
Perle, George. *Serial Composition and Atonality* (Berkeley-Los Angeles 1971)
Proctor, George A. *Canadian Music of the Twentieth Century* (Toronto 1980)
See also Bibliography for Somers; Weinzweig.

CF, KW (JB)

Two Gentlemen of Verona. Stage musical by Galt *MacDermot (music) and John Guare and Mel Shapiro (book, after Shakespeare). It was premiered 27 Jul 1971 at the New York Shakespearean Festival in Central Park under Shapiro's direction, and the production was transferred to the St James Theater, opening 1 Dec 1971. It won a Tony Award for best musical of the 1971–2 Broadway season and subsequently toured North America, beginning a three-week Toronto run at *O'Keefe Centre 22 Jan 1973. It encompassed a variety of popular idioms and was described by Herbert Whittaker in the Toronto *Globe and Mail* as the 'least reverent, most completely engaging Shakespeare in history ... It is glorious musical Shakespeare' (7 Feb 1972). A recording (1971, ABC Dunhill BCSY 1001) starred the original cast, including Clifton Davis, Jonelle Allen, Larry Kent, and Edith Diaz.

MCv

(Tyson) Ian and Sylvia. Folksingers who attained international prominence in the 1960s. Ian (Dawson) Tyson (b Victoria, BC, 25 Sep 1933) began his career in 1956 at the Heidelberg Cafe in Vancouver while studying at the Vancouver School of Art. He also played guitar with a rock band, the Sensational Stripes, in lower British Columbia before moving in 1959 to Toronto. There, at the First Floor Club, he sang blues with Don *Francks, then folk music with Sylvia Fricker (b Chatham, Ont, 19 Sep 1940), who also played guitar and autoharp and had performed in other Toronto coffee houses.

Ian and Sylvia became a professional team in 1961 and married in 1964. In 1961 they appeared at the *Mariposa Folk Festival and gave their first US performances at folk clubs in New York and Chicago. Caught up in the folk revival in North America, they rose quickly to the forefront of the movement with their first LPs and the popularity of Ian's song *'Four Strong Winds.' With a repertoire of traditional songs, blues, pop tunes, their own songs, and other contemporary folk-styled material (they were among the first to sing Gordon *Lightfoot songs), they performed throughout North America, making the transition from clubs to colleges and festivals. Part of their concert at the 1963 Newport Folk Festival was released on the LP *The Evening Concerts* (Vanguard 78148). Ian and Sylvia appeared in 1966 in England on BBC TV and performed 30 Apr 1967 in New York at Carnegie Hall. A recording by the US group We Five of Sylvia's song 'You Were on My Mind' was a major hit internationally in 1965, and another by Ian and Sylvia themselves ('Lovin' Sound,' written by Ian) was a minor hit in Canada in 1967.

By 1968, when they had formed the Great Speckled Bird as their back-up band (previously they had been accompanied by a third guitarist, eg, David Rea or Red Shea, and a bassist), Ian and Sylvia had moved away from traditional music to a synthesis of country music and rock. The Great Speckled Bird lasted about eight years, surviving as many reorganizations of personnel, and at one time or another included such notable musicians as the guitarists Amos Garrett and David Wilcox. Initially Ian and Sylvia met with mixed if not hostile reaction from their old fans, but they were successful in reaching a new and wider audience

Ian and Sylvia Tyson

– they appeared, for example, in rock events, including the Atlanta Pop Festival and the Festival Express which crossed Canada in 1970. Country music alone became the dominant influence on their work, together and individually, in the 1970s. Their weekly CTV series 'Nashville North,' begun in 1970, became 'The Ian Tyson Show' (with Sylvia only an occasional guest) in 1971 and continued until 1975. In 1974 Sylvia (later joined by Doug Lennox and Bill Garrett) became host for the weekly CBC radio folk-music show 'Touch the Earth.'

Ian and Sylvia made their last appearances together in 1975, thereafter recording and touring separately. With the breakup of the Great Speckled Bird in 1976 Ian briefly and unsuccessfully attempted to establish himself in Nashville, then settled on a ranch near Calgary, dividing his time between music and the breeding of cutting horses. He formed a new band, the North-West Rebellion, in 1977, and toured Canada in 1978. On his own, Tyson adopted an aggressive and blunt performing manner in the so-called 'outlaw' style of certain Texan country singers of the day. Writing in *The Canadian*, Roy MacGregor noted, 'Tyson's voice works ... like a pull of good whisky; rich and carrying, it edges close to the nasal passage before retreating safely, riding that fine country line that so very few voices find.'

Sylvia toured Canada in 1977 and 1978. In 1978 she formed Salt Records, which released her LP *Satin on Stone* and announced plans to issue others by singers heard on 'Touch the Earth.' Two of her songs from this period, 'River Road' and 'Cool Wind from the North,' were recorded by other performers. Writing in the Toronto *Globe and Mail* (29 Nov 1976), Paul McGrath referred to Sylvia's 'distinctive voice that some loved and others found affected.' He continued: 'She has a touch of a warble in her singing reminiscent of Loretta Lynn ... her songs, while written in faithful down-home style, have a sophistication that I would like to think comes from her Canadian roots ... They aren't hung up on the blues or on defining right-of-middle-of-the-road; they usually have simple stories to tell ... topics usually left unsung in the country vein.'

Ian and Sylvia's songs during their years as a team were published by Witmark Music; songbooks were issued by that company in conjunction with several of their LPs and usually bore the same titles. Sylvia's songs thereafter were published by her own company, and Ian's by Newtonville Music. Ian and Sylvia are members of ASCAP.

DISCOGRAPHY

Ian & Sylvia. 1961. Vanguard VSD 2113
Four Strong Winds. 1962. Vanguard VSD 2149
Northern Journey. 1963. Vanguard VSD 79154
Early Morning Rain. 1964. Vanguard VSD 79175
Play One More. 1964. Vanguard VSD 79215
So Much for Dreaming. 1965. Vanguard VSD 79241
Nashville. 1966. Vanguard VSD 79284
Lovin' Sound. 1967. MGM SE 4388
Great Speckled Bird. 1970. Ampex A 10103
Ian & Sylvia's Greatest Hits, vol 1. (1969). 2-Vanguard VSD 5/6
Ian & Sylvia's Greatest Hits, Vol 2. (1970). 2-Vanguard VSD 23/4
Ian and Sylvia. 1971. Col C 30736
You Were on My Mind. 1973. Col KC 31337

IAN TYSON

Ol Eon. 1974. A&M SP 9017
One Jump Ahead of the Devil. (1978). Boot BOS 7189

SYLVIA TYSON

Woman's World. (1975). Cap SKAO 6430
Cool Wind from the North. 1976. Cap ST 6441
Satin on Stone. 1978. Salt SR 101
Sugar for Sugar, Salt for Salt. 1979. Salt SR 102

BIBLIOGRAPHY

Batten, Jack. 'Sweet song of success,' *Maclean's*, 21 Aug 1965
Hale, Barrie. 'Sylvia solo,' *Canadian Magazine*, 2 Aug 1975
MacGregor, Roy. 'Ian Tyson's lament,' *The Canadian*, 11 Dec 1976
Snider, Norman. 'The public and private lives of Sylvia Tyson,' *Toronto Life*, Nov 1978

FH (MM)

TZINCOCA, Rémus (Pétru). Orchestra and choir conductor, composer, teacher, administrator, b Jassy, Rumania, 15 Sep 1915, naturalized Canadian 1965; diploma in orchestral conducting, theory, and pedagogy (Jassy Cons) 1938, premier prix conducting (Paris Cons) 1948. At the Jassy Cons 1933–8 his teachers were Antonin Ciolan (conducting) and Alexandre Zirra and Constantin Georgesco (theory). He taught 1937–40 and 1943–4 in Jassy and 1940–2 in Bucharest. He was secretary of music studies at the Bucharest Opera and music director 1940–2 at the patriarchal cathedral of that city and became conductor of the Jassy Opera in 1943. He continued his studies in conducting at the Paris Cons with Louis Fourestier and Eugène Bigot. He also took private lessons 1947–50 with Georges Enesco and 1945–50 with the brothers Jean and Noël Gallon while serving 1946–50 as director of the Société philharmonique de Laval, France. In 1950 he arrived in the USA, and in 1952 he appeared as guest conductor at the Ipswich Festival, Ipswich, Mass. He founded the Newport Music Festival, Newport RI, and directed it 1953–5. In New York City he founded the Orchestra da Camera (1954–6).

At the invitation of Wilfrid *Pelletier, Tzincoca moved to Montreal and taught 1959–77 at the *CMM. He directed the orchestra classes there and was in charge of orchestra and ensemble conducting. He founded a second Orchestra da Camera (1959), this time with principal players from the *MSO. During its only season it gave three concerts at the *Orpheum Theatre, two featuring works by Bach, and the third Canadian music, and it premiered Jacques *Hétu's *Symphony for Strings*. Between 1960 and 1965 Tzincoca also directed a choir and taught choral conducting at the *École Vincent-d'Indy. The choir won first prize at the 1962 Quebec Music Festivals, participated in the 1964 inauguration ceremonies of the *Salle Claude-Champagne, and the same year performed Tzincoca's oratorio *Sur la montagne*.

In 1964 in France Tzincoca premiered *La Chèvre de M. Séguin*, a musical tale by Henri Tomasi, with the chamber orchestra and youth choir of the ORTF. At the Palais de Chaillot in Paris, he conducted the Pasdeloup Orchestra in the European premiere of Claude *Champagne's *Altitude*. The same year he conducted Jean *Vallerand's *Cordes* *en mouvement* on the ORTF. He has returned to Rumania several times since 1973 and conducted *Die Walküre* at the Bucharest Opera in 1979. He has appeared as guest conductor with several orchestras, including the Orchestre Lamoureux de Paris, the London Philharmonic Orchestra, the Tonhalle Orchestra in Zurich, the Cleveland Orchestra, and the Bordeaux SO. He was a jury member in 1962, 1964, and 1971 at the annual examinations of the Paris Cons. He has performed on CBC radio and conducted the *CBC Quebec Chamber Orchestra in his *Ballade No. 2* (1977). In 1977 he became a consultant to the board of the *Cons de musique du Québec.

Among Tzincoca's compositions are 15 songs composed 1955–70 to texts by Musset, Pillat, and Valéry; *Béatitudes* (1969, a revision for soloists, choir, and orchestra of the 1963 oratorio *Sur la montagne* which used Byzantine thematic material); two *Ballades*, one (1952) for choir and orchestra, the other (1954) for orchestra; a *Liturgie Byzantine* (1957) for unaccompanied mixed choir; and a *Symphonie* (1978). Jean Vallerand described *sur la montagne* as a piece that is 'extremely well written for voices and has a deep inner lyricism' (*La Presse*, 15 May 1964). Tzincoca is a member of CAPAC.

WRITINGS

'L'école française de direction d'orchestre,' Montreal *La Presse*, 13 Apr 1963 HP

U

Ukraine. Towards the end of the 19th century large numbers of Ukrainians began to arrive in Canada; the majority settled in the Prairie provinces. By the late 1970s there were over 500,000 Ukrainian Canadians, the largest concentrations in Edmonton, Winnipeg, Toronto, and Montreal. Their cultural heritage has been perpetuated in Canada by the Ukrainian-Canadian Arts Council, the Ukrainian Cultural and Educational Centre (Winnipeg), the Ukrainian Youth Federation, and the Ukrainian Youth Assn (SUM), and by many choirs, instrumental ensembles, and dance groups. Musical traditions have been maintained in five genres: authentic folk, liturgical, classical, country, and pop. Folk music is the strongest and most popular of these, and has retained in Canada archaic features and forms such as the ritual folksong cycle and the epico-balladic song. Field studies conducted during the 1950s and 1960s by Tetjana Koshetz, Jaroslav Rudnyckyj, Kenneth *Peacock, Robert *Klymasz, and others indicated that almost the entire Ukrainian folk music tradition had been re-established in Canada. In the 1970s this tradition continued to serve as a source of inspiration for other forms of music-making.

Alongside the cultivation of folk music there existed a growing interest in operetta and choral music. After World War II this diversification was intensified by the impact of radio and sound recording, contact with the mainstream of Canadian musical life, the arrival of a Ukrainian cultural elite in the form of political refugees from the homeland, and the emergence during the 1960s and 1970s of a new generation of Ukrainian-Canadians with wider musical tastes. Choral singing, a traditional predilection of Ukrainians, developed along religious, artistic, and recreational lines. Key figures have included Nestor Horodovenko (1885–1965) in Montreal and Oleksander Koshetz (1875–1944) in Winnipeg. The latter made a further significant contribution through his choral settings of Ukrainian folksongs, a complete edition of which was published 1949–56 by Winnipeg's Ukrainian Cultural and Educational Centre, which also preserved Koshetz' manuscripts and papers. Another guardian of the Ukrainian choral tradition is Paul Macenko, a Winnipeg musicologist, composer, and music critic who in the 1950s began to promote educational workshops for the training of church cantors (*djaky*) and choral conductors, and who in 1980 still was at work. Noteworthy Ukrainian-Canadian choral groups have included the Oleksander Koshetz Memorial Choir of Winnipeg, the leadership of which was assumed by Walter Klymkiw in 1952. This choir, which has toured in Canada and performed over CBC radio and TV, remained the country's leading Ukrainian choral group in 1980. Other noted choirs at that time were the Voloshky Singers of Vancouver, the Centennial Ukrainian Choir of Calgary, the Ukrainian National Youth Federation Mixed Choir of Winnipeg, and the Prometheus and Dibrova Choirs (male and female respectively) of Toronto.

Generally speaking, Ukrainians are members of the Greek Catholic or Greek Orthodox churches (Eastern Rite). (See Greek Orthodox church music).

For both accompaniment and solo performances, Ukrainian-Canadian folkdance ensembles and choirs have continued to use traditional string instruments – the dulcimer-like cymbaly, the many-stringed bandura, the lyre-like kobza, the hurdy-gurdy known as a lira – in addition to the mandolin, and the violin. In 1980 among the best-known folk groups were the Dnipro Ensemble of Edmonton, the Hoosli Ukrainian Folk Ensemble of Winnipeg and the Shevchenko Musical Ensemble of Toronto. The Dnipro Ensemble was organized as the Dnipro Male Chorus in 1953 in Edmonton by Roman Soltykewych (1909–76). With the addition of women's voices in 1971 it became the Dnipro Chorus. An orchestra, led by John A. Achtymichuk, and dancers were added in 1974. Maria Dytyniak became the director in 1976. The ensemble has performed throughout Alberta, in the USA in 1974, and in Ottawa in 1976. It has appeared on radio and TV, and in 1979 it toured the South Pacific and Australia.

Founded in 1951 as a male chorus, the 120-member Shevchenko Musical Ensemble of Toronto (chorus, orchestra, dance group), added its orchestra when Eugene Dolny became director in 1952. It has performed throughout Canada, and in 1970 it visited eight Ukrainian cities. For that tour the ensemble commissioned Morris *Surdin's *Suite Canadienne*. It also commissioned *A Feast of Thunder* from Surdin and works from Leon *Zuckert in 1974 and Ben *McPeek in 1977.

Some Ukrainian communities have organized ensembles out of which professional musicians, in particular orchestral players, have emerged. Saskatoon's Yevshan Ukrainian Orchestra was founded in 1974, by its first conductor Bohdan Wowk, to perform Ukrainian-Canadian symphonic music. Instrumental compositions by Ukrainian-Canadians have attained a high standard, and major Canadian symphony orchestras have performed works by George *Fiala and Edmonton's Serhij Yaremenko. Fiala's *Capriccio* for piano and orchestra (1962) was performed during the late 1960s by the pianist Tatiana Nikolayeva and the USSR Radio and Television SO. Fiala's *Symphony No. 4*, subtitled 'Ukrainian,' was dedicated to the 100th anniversary of the City of Winnipeg and to Winnipeg's Ukrainian community. That anniversary also was honoured by Leon Zuckert's *Fantasia on Ukrainian Themes* (1973).

Ukrainian country and pop music came to the fore during the 1960s and 1970s, particularly in Winnipeg, where country music was pioneered by the husband-and-wife team *Mickey and Bunny (Sklepowich) and Ukrainian pop found protagonists in the D-Drifters-5. The Montreal male voice and instrumental quartet Rushnychok also made a distinctive contribution to the trend. A considerable amount of Ukrainian pop music has been recorded on the V label by Mike Domish and the folksinger and choir conductor Mae Chwaluk (b Seech, Man, 8 Aug 1917).

While their native traditional and national music has been preserved proudly by Ukrainian-Canadians, the broader musical life of their adopted country also has claimed their attention. Musicians who have contributed to musical life in Canada include the accordionist Ted *Komar; the CBC TV (Winnipeg) producer Ernie Zuk; the conductors Ivan *Romanoff and Ted Kardash; the composers Larysa Kuzmenko, Zenoby Lawryshyn, and J.B. Weselowsky; the fiddler Al *Cherny; the mezzo-sopranos Renata Babak and Hanna Kolesnyk (former members of the Bolshoi and Kiev Operas respectively); the pianists and teachers Richard *Gresko, Lubka *Kolessa, John *Melnyk, John Melnyk Jr, and Ireneus and Luba Zuk; the singers Ed Evanko, *Juliette (Sysak), Debbie Lori Kaye, and Wally *Koster; the bass Cecil Semchyshyn; the sopranos Anna *Chornodolska, June *Kowalchuk, Roxolana *Roslak, and Lesia Zubrack; the string bassist and mandolinist William *Kuinka; the violinists Walter *Babiak, Michael Barten (the *Metropolitan Opera Orchestra in 1966), Philip Bassa, George *Bornoff, Mikhail Brat, Donna *Grescoe, Basil Gresko, Frederick *Grinke, Halyna Holynska (1902–76), Michael Humenick (b 1909), Eugene *Husaruk, John Moskalyk, Anne *Pomer, Walter *Prystawski, and Steven *Staryk; the violist Gerald *Stanick; and the cellist Olga Kwasniak. Jury Krytiuk, the co-founder of *Boot Records, and John Cripton, the director of the Canada Council's Touring Office until 1980, are both of Ukrainian descent.

The bass Yosyp Hoshuliak (b Ukraine, 7 Oct 1922) settled in Canada in 1950. Living in Toronto, he has appeared in recital, performed with the *COC, the *Manitoba Opera Assn, and Stuart *Hamilton's Opera in Concert, and (with the Canadian SO under Ernesto *Barbini) has recorded *Bass Arias and Monologues* (1975, Boot BMC 3005).

Several Ukrainian artists have visited Canada. In 1961 Yuri Lutsiv, the director of the Lvov Philharmonic, conducted the *Calgary Philharmonic while its leader, Henry Plukker, conducted orchestras in Lvov and Kiev. The soprano Tamara Didyk, the mezzo-soprano Valentina Reka, the tenor Anatoli Solovianenko, and the bass Andrei Kikot all appeared at *Expo 67 in Montreal, as did the bandurists Yulia Gamova, Eleonora Mironiuk, and Valentina Parkhomenko. In 1978 the conductor Anatoly Avdievsky, the baritone Dimitri Gnatiuk, the coloratura soprano Evgenia Miroshnitchenko, members of the Shevchenko State Opera and Ballet Theatre, and the pianist Alla Tolstych performed in 16 Canadian centres in an exchange arranged by the governments of Canada and the USSR.

Victor *Feldbrill conducted several orchestras in Ukraine during a tour in 1963, and the Oleksander Koshetz Memorial Choir performed there in 1978.

Special Ukrainian events in Canada have included the annual National Ukrainian Festival held each summer at Dauphin, Man. Toronto's Canadian-Ukrainian Opera Assn has offered Ukrainian operatic works. In 1975 it presented Semen Hulak-Artemovsky's *The Cossacks Beyond the Danube* (1863), and in 1979 in Toronto it gave the

North American premiere of Anatole Vachnianyn's *Kupalo*, a work which had received only one previous performance, in Ukraine in 1929. Also in 1979, the Vesnivka Girls' Choir of Toronto presented the children's operetta *Koza Dereza* by Mykola Lysenko.

Canadian musicians who, in addition to several mentioned above, were born in Ukraine include Sara and Jacob *Barkin, Boris *Berlin, Jan *Cherniavsky, Jacob *Groob, John *Konrad, Peter *Koslowsky, Nicholas *Koudriavtzeff, Isaac *Mamott, Vladimir *Orloff, Elie *Spivak, and Maurice *Zbriger.

DISCOGRAPHY

Album of Songs. Anthony Derbish and Alexander Ticknovitch singers, Ivan Romanoff Chorus and O. Arka T-32956

'The Bandura player.' Adam Timoon, I. Romanoff Quartet. Col C-10520

'I Gaze at the Skies.' Adam Timoon, I. Romanoff Quartet. Col C-10521

Mae Chwaluk Does 'More Ukrainian Country Style' Songs. V Records VLP 3049

Mae Chwaluk's Ukrainian Country Farm Party, vols 1 and 2. V Records VLP 3067–68

St Nicholas Choir Sings. Vladimir Sloboda dir. (1977). V Records SULP-3119

Ukrainian Classics. Yosyp Hoshuliak bass, Barkin pf. 1967. RCA T 55819

Ukrainian Christmas Songs. Recorded by Laura Boulton. Folk FW 6828

Ukrainian Songs. Surma Male Choir. London MLP-10007

Yevshan Ukrainian Orchestra. 1976. Wowk Enterprises Ltd

Also a recording by soprano Stefa Fedchuk, with Coveart pf. (Ca 1966). RCA Victor CC-1005

Several recordings by the Prometheus and Dibrova Choirs and the Baturyn Band, the Shevchenko Musical Ensemble, all of Toronto; and by the Dnipro Ensemble of Edmonton

BIBLIOGRAPHY

Simpson, G.W. *Alexander Koshetz in Ukrainian Music* (Winnipeg 1946)

Bassa, Philip. 'Ukrainian musical culture in Canada,' unpubl MA thesis, U of Montreal 1951

Wytwycky, W. 'Ukrainian music in Canada,' *Ukraine: A Concise Encyclopedia*, vol 2 (Toronto 1971)

Klymasz, Robert B. 'Social and cultural motifs in Canadian Ukrainian lullabies,' *Slavic and East European J*, vol 12, 1968

Macenko, Paul. *Narysy fo istoriji ukrajins'koji cerkovnoji muzyky* (Winnipeg 1968)

Klymasz, Robert B. *A Bibliography of Ukrainian Folklore in Canada, 1902–64*, National Museum Anthropology Paper 21 (Ottawa 1969)

– *An Introduction to the Ukrainian Canadian Immigrant Folksong Cycle*, National Museum Bulletin 234 (Ottawa 1970)

– *The Ukrainian Winter Folksong Cycle in Canada*, National Museum Bulletin 236 (Ottawa 1970)

Marunchak, M.H. *Ukrainian Canadians: A History* (Ottawa, Winnipeg 1970)

'Canada's music ambassadors to the Ukraine,' *CanComp*, 54, Nov 1970

Klymasz, Robert B. 'Ukrainian folklore in Canada: an immigrant complex in transition,' unpubl PH D thesis, Indiana U 1971

– ' "Sounds you never before heard": Ukrainian country music in western Canada,' *Ethnomusicology*, vol 16, 1972

Henderson, Alan, and Proracki, Anthony. 'Ukrainian-Canadian folk music of the Waterford area,' *CFMJ*, vol 2, 1974

Pelinski, Ramón. 'The music of Canada's ethnic minorities,' *CMB*, 10, Spring–Summer 1975

Ukrainian Cultural and Educational Centre Archives. Winnipeg

FILMOGRAPHY

Poltava (West Wind Film Group 1974) (RK)

UNGER, Heinz (Heinrich). Conductor, b Berlin 14 Dec 1895, d Toronto 25 Feb 1965; D JURIS (Greifswald) 1917, State Music Teacher's Diploma of Prussia. His music teachers in Berlin included

Heinz Unger

Wilhelm Klatte and Theodor Schoenberger (theory) and Eduard Moerike and Fritz Stiedry (a few conducting lessons). While a law student he heard Bruno Walter conduct Mahler's *The Song of the Earth* in Munich in 1915 and decided on the spot to become a conductor and a champion of Mahler. Soon afterwards he had his first conducting experience with the Berliner Symphonie Verein, an amateur orchestra, in part of Beethoven's *Symphony No. 5*. In 1919–20 he made his professional debut, conducting the Berlin Philharmonic Orchestra in several Mahler concerts, including the *Symphony No. 1* and *The Song of the Earth*. He conducted some of the Konzerte des Anbruch series 1920–2, led the Berlin SO and Berlin Philharmonic combined in Mahler's *Symphony No. 8* in a 1923 performance that had to be repeated three times, and for nine seasons, 1924–33, directed the concerts (usually six per season) of the Gesellschaft der Musikfreunde, engaging the Berlin Philharmonic. In 1921 he became the founder and conductor of the Caecilienchor of Berlin. He appeared as guest conductor in other German cities, in Vienna, and in Oslo, and at the suggestion of Artur Schnabel in 1924 he undertook the first of 13 trips to the Soviet Union. On these visits he led concert and radio orchestras in Moscow, Leningrad, Kharkov, Kiev, Odessa, Tiflis, and other cities, and in the mid-1930s he was under contract with the Leningrad Radio Orchestra for annual six-month seasons. Unger's enthusiasm for the musicianship of Russian and Ukrainian orchestras and the responsiveness of their audiences was dampened eventually by his experiences with Soviet bureaucracy, and he wrote a book of memoirs (*Hammer, Sickle and Baton*, London 1939) describing enticement and disenchantment.

In 1933 Unger settled in London. He conducted the Northern Philharmonia 1933–47 and was a guest with the major British orchestras including the London Philharmonic, with which he made over 100 wartime appearances throughout Great Britain. In the 1930s he conducted in other countries, notably Spain, made his North American debut with the *TSO 9 Nov 1937, and was invited to repeat the engagement in 1938, which he did. Having enjoyed his visits to Toronto, Unger determined to settle there after leaving the Northern Philharmonic in 1947. He moved to Toronto in 1948. During the next few years he often was a guest conductor with the *Promenade Symphony Concerts and built up an amateur orchestra. He filled a total of 24 engagements 1952–64 with the *CBC SO and, as a guest, conducted CBC orchestras in Vancouver, Winnipeg, and Montreal ('L'*Heure du concert' on TV, etc), building a high reputation with audiences and critics alike. To provide a concert outlet for his talents, his supporters formed the York Concert Society, which organized annual series of four spring concerts, using a classical-size orchestra of top players from the TSO and the CBC SO. Most concerts were held at *Eaton Auditorium, but works demanding a larger orchestra were performed at *Massey Hall. The York Concert Society made its debut in a Beethoven concert 23 Apr 1953 and maintained a high standard in the ensuing 12 years of its existence. It provided above all a welcome complement to the TSO series, from which its program differed substantially. Its guest artists included Betty-Jean *Hagen, Lubka *Kolessa, Anton *Kuerti, Moura Lympany, Lois *Marshall, James *Milligan, Mary *Simmons, and others. Because of financial difficulties there was no 1961 season, and in 1963, when Unger was ill, the first guest conductor, the expatriate Canadian Harry Newstone, was engaged for one concert. After Unger's death Hans Bauer led the remaining concerts of the society's final season, the last on 29 Apr 1965.

After World War II Unger had renewed his travels as a conductor, appearing particularly in Spain, but also in Latin America, Switzerland, and Germany and filling engagements in Great Britain as a guest on the BBC. An invitation by Furtwängler before the latter's death in 1954 led to two concerts with the Berlin Philharmonic in 1956, Unger's first return to his native city since 1933.

Primarily a guest conductor, Unger programmed only works of whose merit he was convinced. His repertoire, though focused on the Austro-German masters from Bach to Richard Strauss and the young Schoenberg, was large. Among contemporary composers he favoured conservative works. He gave the Canadian premiere of Nielsen's *Symphony No. 4* and featured Canadian scores by *Brott, *Freedman, *Karam, *Mercure, *Morawetz, *Somers, and *Willan, introducing some to foreign audiences. Besides the Viennese classics and Bruckner his great love was the music of Gustav Mahler, which he championed with the fervour of an apostle. He introduced some of Mahler's works to the USSR, Spain, and Latin America and gave the London premiere of the *Symphony No. 5*. In Canada he introduced three of the symphonies – *No. 2* in 1958, *No. 5* in 1959, and *No. 9* in 1963 – as well as other works.

In Unger's preparation of a score for performance, no detail was left to chance. At this stage he shunned other conductors' recordings. A characteristic of his rehearsal technique was his exploitation of the potential of each phrase for articulation and dynamic shading. His tendency to explain the music to his orchestra, resented by some players anxious to try the notes, possibly was connected with the deafness which threatened his later years. In concert he tended at times to overconduct, but he always succeeded in bringing the music to life and conveying its emotions to the audience.

In 1958 Unger was named an honorary director of the Gustav Mahler Society of America, in 1959 he was awarded the Mahler medal of the Bruckner Society of the USA, and in 1961 he was elected an honorary member of the Vienna Gustav-Mahler-Gesellschaft. In 1965, his 50th anniversary as a conductor, the West German government presented him with the Commander's Cross of the Order of Merit of the Federal Republic of Germany. A few weeks later, upon arriving home after recording the first three movements of Mahler's *Symphony No. 6* for its Canadian premiere on CBC radio, he died of a heart attack. A Heinz Unger scholarship, administered by the *OAC, was set up to assist promising young conductors (see Awards). Unger's widow donated his extensive score library to the *NL of C.

WRITINGS

'Music,' *Playtime in Russia*, ed Hubert Griffith (London 1935)

Hammer, Sickle and Baton (London 1939)

'Has the Canada Council hit a wrong note?' *Globe Magazine*, 22 Jul 1961

DISCOGRAPHY (78s)

Mendelssohn *Athalia Overture*. National SO. Decca DK 1298

– *Fingal's Cave Overture*. National SO. Decca DK 1120/Lon T5271

– *Ruy Blas Overture*. National SO. Decca DK 1326/Decca GAG 1326

– *Italian Symphony*. National SO. 4-Decca DK 1370-1373/EDA Set 1/4-Decca Z 882-885

Schubert *Overture in the Italian Style*. National SO. Decca DK 1327

BIBLIOGRAPHY

'All about Heinz Unger,' *MCour*, 13 Aug 1925

Lee, Betty. 'Heinz Unger, a portrait of a maestro,' *Globe Magazine*, 13 Jul 1957

Stoddard, Hope. 'Heinz Unger: The conductor is the explorer,' *International Musician*, 16 Mar 1959

HK

Union Harmony: or British America's Sacred Vocal Musick. Compiled and published in Saint John, NB, by Stephen *Humbert in 1801 and printed, probably in New England, by C. Norris and Co. It was Canada's first English-language book of music (appearing one year after *Le *Graduel romain*, the first Canadian book of music). Later editions appeared in 1816 ('much enlarged and improved'), 1831?, and 1840. Copies of the 1801 edition sold for $1 each, but none are known to have survived. In format the 1816 edition (also printed by Norris) follows New England models. It has a preface, a section explaining the rudiments of notation and sight singing, a glossary, the collection of pieces (of 'the most approved English and American composers'), and an index of the tunes. Its direct inspiration probably was *Holden's Union Harmony or Universal Collection of Sacred Music* (1793, 1796, 1801), which is similarly large; both have over 300 pages, double the size of contemporary standard books of the kind. Both compilers also defend the propriety of fuguing tunes which, according to Humbert, 'when judiciously performed, will produce the most happy effect, without the least disorder of jargon, especially when it is considered we do not sing to please men but the Lord.' 'If those who are hearers,' he continued, 'were as assiduous to learn Sacred Musick, as they too generally are the giddy amusements of the day, we should have less hearers and more performers of this animating part of divine worship.' The first two thirds of the collection – tunes of Belknap, Holden, Holyoke, Kimball, Read, and Swan – are probably survivors of the 1801 edition as they can be traced to prior sources. The last third offers pieces by Cole, Edson, Ingalls, Jenks, Maxim, Sanger, and Wood, all to be found in publications of 1801–16. Notably absent are pieces by Gram, Lyon, and Morgan and pieces from the shape-note books of Law or Wyeth, or from the Baptist collections. The bulk of pieces by English composers such as Dixon, Leach, and Williams are traceable to American publications, but those from Beaumont's *The New Harmonic Magazine*, published in Britain, are an exception. Humbert himself wrote 14 of the pieces and possibly 3 unsigned ones if titles such as 'Canada' and 'Halifax' are an indication. The Humbert compositions range from simple hymns and fuguing tunes to complex anthems and multiple-movement odes with internal contrasts of meter and texture. His *Elegy on Sophronia* (the wife of a friend) is secular, as are several other odes in the collection.

UNION HARMONY:

OR

BRITISH AMERICA'S SACRED VOCAL MUSICK.

FROM THE MOST APPROVED ENGLISH AND AMERICAN COMPOSERS, WITH SOME ORIGINAL MUSICK ON SPECIAL OCCASIONS.

TO WHICH IS PREFIXED A CONCISE INTRODUCTION.

While I live, will I praise the Lord:
I will sing praises unto my God, while I have any being.
146 PSALM, 2d VERSE.

SECOND EDITION, MUCH IMPROVED AND ENLARGED.

SAINT JOHN (*New-Brunswick*:)

Published by STEPHEN HUMBERT, and sold at his Store, Market Wharf.—Sold also by MARTIN G. BLACK, *Halifax*; BENJAMIN & GEORGE DEWOLF, *Windsor*; and by the principal Booksellers in the BRITISH PROVINCES.

1816.

C. NORRIS & CO. PRINTERS.

BIBLIOGRAPHY

McMillan, Barclay. 'Tune-book imprints in Canada to 1867: a descriptive bibliography,' *Papers of the Bibliographical Society of Canada*, vol 16, 1977

(DJR)

Union musicale de Québec. Choral society founded 20 Sep 1866 in Quebec City and active until at least the 1920s. Ephrem Dugal (b St-Michel-de-Bellechasse, Que, 23 Dec 1835, d there 29 Jun 1905), a founding member, was its president for nearly 40 years, as well as being choirmaster at St-Jean-Baptiste Church from 1871 until his death.

The inaugural concert 22 Nov 1866 presented the *12th Mass*, falsely attributed to Mozart. The choir and the soloists, Elzéar Déry and Napoléon *Legendre, were accompanied by a small orchestra made up of Arthur *Lavigne, Célestin *Lavigueur, Nazaire *LeVasseur, Joseph *Vézina, and other city musicians. A concert band was established in 1870 when eight brass players became members. The band's numbers slowly increased, largely through the assistance of regimental musicians. The conductors were Vézina, Ernest *Lavigne, and, from 1876 until after 1922, Georges Landry. The original library of the Union musicale was destroyed by fire in 1881.

For several decades the Union musicale was the only choir in Quebec City presenting the great choral masses (eg, Beethoven's *Mass in C*, Cherubini's *Coronation Mass for Charles X*, Haydn's *Imperial Mass*, Schubert's *Mass in E Flat*, and Weber's *Mass in G*), and the operettas and oratorios of French composers such as Félicien David (*La Perle du Brésil* in 1878), Dubois, Franck, and Gounod. The Union musicale's repertoire also contained Joseph-Julien *Perrault's *Messe de Noël* and excerpts from Guillaume *Couture's **Jean le Précurseur*. These large-scale works generally were offered with orchestral accompaniment.

Calixa *Lavallée's *Cantata* in honour of the Marquis of Lorne and Princess Louise was presented 20 Apr 1879, and Lavallée conducted Gounod's *Messe solennelle de Sainte-Cécile* 22 Nov 1879. A mass by Ambroise Thomas was given 22 Nov 1891 on the choir's 25th anniversary. Its 50th anniversary, 22 Nov 1916, was marked by the Canadian premiere of Franck's oratorio *Les Béatitudes*, repeated 13 December. After the premiere of Massenet's *La Vierge* 14 Apr 1919, Octave Bourdon remarked on the quality of the performance given by the 'imposing array of choristers and instrumentalists' (*La Musique*, April 1919).

The position of conductor-organist was held by Gustave *Gagnon 1866–76, Joseph Otten 1876–8, and Georges Hébert 1878–1917; J.-Arthur *Bernier was appointed organist in 1917. Petrus *Plamondon was president 1870–2 and Ernest *Gagnon honorary director 1866–76.

The Union musicale sang the services (including that for St Cecilia's Day) at St-Jean-Baptiste Church 1867–79 and from 1882 until after 1922. Between 1879 and 1882 it performed in the churches of St-Patrice, St-Roch, and Bon Pasteur, among others. In addition it presented several concerts with the *Société musicale Saint-Cécile between 1869 and some time after 1885.

BIBLIOGRAPHY

LeVasseur, Nazaire. 'Musique et musiciens à Québec,' *La Musique*, vol 4, Sep–Oct 1922

AP

Union musicale de Sherbrooke. Cultural society active 1892–6 and reconstituted in December 1921. It contributed to the musical life of the Eastern Townships, where it introduced public teaching of solfège, encouraged choral singing, and organized local performances of operas and operettas in concert form. Its principal conductors were Oscar Cartier (Gounod's *Faust* 1922 and Lalo's *Le Roi d'Ys* 1924), Léonidas Bachand (Gounod's *Mireille* 1926 and *Roméo et Juliette* 1927, Thomas's *Mignon* 1928, and Oscar Straus' *The Last Waltz* 1930), and Charles Delvenne, the cellist and the director of the Sherbrooke Concert Band (Lehar's *The Count of Luxembourg* 1929, Offenbach's *Le Mariage aux lanternes* and Bizet's *Carmen* 1931, Hahn's *Ciboulette* 1932, and Thomas's *Le Caïd* 1933). Andrien Leblanc conducted Massenet's oratorio *Marie-Magdeleine* in 1946 for the society's 25th anniversary.

After 1932 the Union musicale's musical activities merged with those of the newly formed *Sherbrooke SO. It continued its literary evenings in affiliation with the Alliance française and other cultural groups, and occasionally presented solo artists in recital.

The pianist Mme Euphémie Codère, who studied in Montreal with Dominique *Ducharme, Paul *Letondal, and Moïse *Saucier, was active in the society as early as 1892, and was its president

1924–54. She was succeeded by Mrs Fred H. Bradley, who helped found the Sherbrooke Symphony Concerts in 1946 and who remained president of the union in the 1970s.

Among those who gave recitals for the society and became honorary members were Théodore Botrel and Jean *Riddez in 1922, Edmond Clément and the tenor Rodolphe *Plamondon in 1924 (the last three from the Paris Opera, the bass Ulysse *Paquin in 1924, Eugène *Lapierre and Salvator *Issaurel in 1932, and Sylvio *Lacharité in 1946.

BIBLIOGRAPHY
'L'Union musicale de Sherbrooke,' *P-T*, Jan–Feb 1949
Union musicale de Sherbrooke: 40e anniversaire (Sherbrooke 1961) (CP)

Union of Soviet Socialist Republics. The USSR is made up of 15 Union Republics comprising many language- and cultural groups. Some of the groups are well-represented in Canada, and some, because of their distinct individuality or because their homelands did not form part of the Soviet Union at the time of emigration, are treated separately in *EMC*, in the entries for Armenia, Estonia, Latvia, Lithuania, and Ukraine. Three religious groups, many of whose followers have come from either Tsarist Russia or the Soviet Union – the Doukhobors, the Jews, and the Mennonites – also have separate entries. The present article will deal essentially with the Russian component in the Canadian mosaic and also with cultural relations and exchanges between Canada and the Soviet Union as a whole.

1 Immigration
2 Musicians of Russian origin in Canada
3 Russian visitors
4 Canadians in the USSR

1 IMMIGRATION. Large-scale immigration from Tsarist Russia to Canada began in the mid-1870s, when the Mennonites settled in southeast Manitoba. In 1899 7000 Doukhobors followed, and the period from 1880 to the beginning of World War I witnessed the mass immigration of Jews from Russia, Ukraine, and Tsarist-ruled Poland, and of Ukrainians. Immigration declined in the period between the two world wars and became slow again after a wave about 1950, though in the 1970s a number of Jews arrived via Israel or directly from the Soviet Union, and many of the musicians among these found employment in Canadian symphony orchestras. In the 1971 Canadian census figures, 160,000 Canadians cited the USSR as their birthplace; however, the 'division by mother tongue' indicated that 31,740 spoke Russian, 309,860 Ukrainian, and 49,890 Yiddish. Few have settled in the Atlantic provinces, and the largest concentrations may be found in Edmonton, Montreal, Toronto, and Vancouver. Russian cultural organizations in the larger Canadian centres have sponsored social gatherings, plays, bazaars, choirs, balalaika orchestras, and folk dance groups. Two Russian pavilions, Novgorod and Volga, were in operation during the 1978 Toronto *Caravan. The Russian Orthodox church has preserved liturgical musical traditions (see Greek Orthodox church music), and some congregations have offered Russian language and history classes.

2 MUSICIANS OF RUSSIAN ORIGIN IN CANADA. Among Russian-born musicians in Canada have been Alexander *Chuhaldin; S.C. *Eckhardt-Gramatté; Gregori *Garbovitsky; the *Hambourg family; Constantin Klimoff (d 1974, a piano teacher in Quebec City); Vladimir Lancman (Landsman), a violinist and teacher in Montreal; the *TS violinist Jascha Milkis; Kornelius *Neufeld; the Toronto oboist Simon Trubashnik; the Toronto baritone Alexander Tumanov; the cellist and *CMM teacher Yuli Turovsky, a former member of the Borodin Trio, and his wife, Eleanor, a violinist and violist with the *MSO; and the conductor Victor Yampolsky, who became music director of the *Atlantic SO in 1977. Canadian musicians of Russian ancestry include the *Adaskin family, Milla *Andrew, Ida *Krehm, Zara *Nelsova, Boris *Roubakine, and the pianist Zadel Skolovsky.

3 RUSSIAN VISITORS. Perhaps the first musician from Russia to visit Canada was the cellist Henri Billet, billed as the 'premier violoncelle de la musique privée de l'Empereur de Russie' in announcements of an appearance 24 Aug 1841 at the Théâtre royal in Quebec City. The Baron Rudolph de Fleur, 'late pianist and inspector general of military music to His Majesty the Emperor of Russia' (Toronto *Patriot*, 16 Jul 1844), gave performances described as 'exquisite and decidedly the most scientific ever witnessed in Toronto' (ibid, 23 Jul 1844). He also visited Charlottetown in 1847. Basil Schütz was sent to North America by his family and is known to have played the piano in a Montreal theatre ca 1845. He returned to Russia with a Canadian wife of Scottish descent, and their daughter Françoise-Jeanne, born in 1861, became the famous soprano Félia Litvinne. Other visiting Russian musicians have included Anton Rubinstein (Toronto 1872); Ossip Gabrilowitsch, who played in Montreal in 1902; Sergei Rachmaninoff, who gave the first of many Canadian concerts in Toronto in 1909; the violinist Mischa Elman (1913); Prokofiev, who stayed in Montreal for a few months, ca 1920–1, presumably completing there the orchestration for *Love of Three Oranges*; the Russian Grand Opera, a company of exiles under Leo Feodoroff, which appeared twice in Montreal, twice in Toronto, and once in Hamilton during the 1922–3 season with productions of French, Italian, and Russian operas, including *Boris Godunov, The Queen of Spades*, and *Eugene Onegin*; Feodor Chaliapin, who sang in Montreal and Toronto in the mid-1920s; Vladimir Horowitz, Nikolai Orloff, and Gregor Piatigorsky, all of whom performed in Canada in the early 1930s; and Igor Stravinsky, who made his first visit in 1937 and in the 1960s recorded several of his works with the *Festival Singers and *CBC SO.

In the mid-1950s an active exchange of artists, initiated by Nicholas *Koudriavtzeff, began between Canada and the USSR. Though exchanges were not always on an 'official' basis, a cultural agreement was signed by the two countries in 1960. It may be said without exaggeration that Canadians abroad have had their most enthusiastic audiences in Moscow and Leningrad and that their Soviet tours have brought them great prestige at home. Conversely, Soviet artists have enjoyed notable success in Canada. Among Soviet and expatriate Soviet artists to perform in Canada in the mid-20th century have been Mstislav Rostropovich, Vladimir Ashkenazy, Emil Gilels, Leonid Kogan, David and Igor Oistrakh, Sviastoslav Richter, Lazar Berman, the Moscow State SO, the Moscow Chamber Orchestra, the Moscow Philharmonic Orchestra, the Borodin Trio, the Borodin String Quartet, the Red Army Chorus, and the Leningrad Philharmonic Orchestra. *Expo 67 introduced the Bolshoi Opera to Canada (indeed to North America). An exchange tour of Canada was arranged for the Moscow Chamber Choir in 1978 following a tour of the USSR made by the Festival Singers in 1977.

4 CANADIANS IN THE USSR. Among Canadian musicians who visited (pre-Soviet) Russia were Emma *Albani, who sang opera there in 1873 and 1878; the soprano Bertha *Crawford, who sang in Petrograd in 1915 and Moscow in 1916; and Kathleen *Parlow, who studied 1906–7 at the St Petersburg Cons with Leopold Auer. The MSO played in Moscow and Leningrad in 1962. The violinist Betty-Jean *Hagen, the pianist Elaine *Keillor, the cellist Michael *Kilburn, and the pianist Raymond *Pannell were contestants in the 1962 International Tchaikovsky Competition in Moscow. The pianist Barbara *Custance studied Russian teaching methods in Moscow in 1968, and the pianist Karen Quinton (*Prix d'Europe 1972) studied 1973–5 with Tatiana Nikolayeva at the Moscow Cons. André *Laplante shared second prize at the 1978 Tchaikovsky International Piano Competition in Moscow. Canadian musicians who have performed in the USSR include Jacques *Beaudry (1957, the first North American conductor to appear in the Soviet Union after World War II), Donald *Bell (1962), John *Boyden (1968), Henri *Brassard (1978), Alexander *Brott (1962), Renée *Claude (1971), the *Elgar Choir of British Columbia (1961), Victor *Feldbrill (1963, 1966–7), Maureen *Forrester (1961), Glenn *Gould (1957, 1959), Margaret-Ann *Ireland (1960, 1962), Jean-Paul *Jeannotte (1961), Pauline *Julien (1967), the *Kitsilano Boys' Band (1962), Claude *Léveillée (1968, 1972), Monique *Leyrac (1968), Joseph *Macerollo (1978), Fraser *MacPherson (1978), Phyllis *Mailing with William *Aide (1971), Lois *Marshall (1958, the first of seven tours by 1978), Oscar *Peterson (1974), Louis *Quilico (1962–3), Robert *Silverman (1978), Teresa *Stratas (1962, 1963), Micheline *Tessier (1968), the *Travellers (1962), Bernard *Turgeon (1971, 1972, 1976), Ronald *Turini (1962, 1963), and George *Zukerman (1978).

Music of Russian romantic composers – notably Tchaikovsky, Mussorgsky, Rachmaninoff and, to a lesser degree, Glinka, Borodin, Rimsky-Korsakov, Scriabin, and Glazunov – has been extremely popular with Canadian audiences in the 20th century. The expatriate Stravinsky has been the dominant figure of Russian music after 1900, but several Soviet composers – notably Prokofiev, Shostakovich, Khachaturian, and, less often, Kabalevsky – have been represented steadily on Canadian programs. Kabalevsky visited Canada in 1978 (and several times previously), but by that year neither early nor recent works of Canadian composers had been adopted into the Soviet repertoire, though Canadian artists occasionally had performed such works on visits to the USSR. Overtures have been made. In the fall of 1977 the composer Harry *Somers and the *CMCentre's John Peter Lee *Roberts spent two weeks in the USSR meeting members of the Union of Soviet Composers, performers, and critics, and playing for them recordings of Canadian works. In 1978, in exchange, the Soviet composer and the pianist Andrei Eshpai visited the CMCentre.

BIBLIOGRAPHY
Parthun, Mary Lassance. 'A rich harvest of Russian emigrés,' *Music*, vol 2, Dec 1979

Unions. Fraternal organizations formed to protect part-time or full-time performing musicians through the establishment and maintenance of standards for working hours and conditions, wages, and other economic benefits. The need for such unions first arose in Canada during the latter half of the 19th century as the demand for musical and theatrical entertainments rapidly increased in growing towns and cities. Instrumental musicians were needed to provide the accompaniments for opera and musical theatre and to perform in concerts, yet they were at a disadvantage when negotiating fees for their work.

One of the earliest musicians' organizations in Canada was the Toronto Orchestral Assn. Founded in 1887, the association held its meetings in quarters located above Thomas *Claxton's Music Store on Yonge Street. In December 1888, with the summer Opera Season on Toronto Island, it negotiated its first agreement, guaranteeing its members a weekly payment of $12 for nine performances. It later changed its name to the Toronto Musical Protective Assn, with Claxton as president, and in 1897 it decided to admit bandsmen as well as orchestral players. In 1901 the name was changed to the Toronto Musicians' Assn. Among other early Canadian organizations was the Assn protectrice des musiciens de Montréal (Musicians' Protective Union of Montreal), formed in 1898 with Edmond *Hardy as president. It was later known as the Féderation des musiciens de Montréal and in 1946 became the Guilde des musiciens de Montréal (Musicians' Guild of Montreal).

In 1897 the newly formed (1896) American Federation of Musicians invited the Toronto Musical Protective Assn to become a member local, and in 1901 both the Toronto association and its Vancouver counterpart joined the US organization. Associations in Hamilton, London, and St Catharines affiliated in 1903, in Montreal and Berlin (Kitchener) in 1905, in Brantford and Edmonton in 1907, in Saskatoon in 1910, in Windsor in 1911, in Quebec in 1917, and in Halifax in 1938.

In 1901 the AF of M expanded its name to the American Federation of Musicians of the US and Canada. In 1979 it had a total Canadian membership of approximately 33,000, served by 38 Canadian locals, the majority (25) in Ontario, the largest (local 149, with approximately 8000 members in 1979) in Toronto. The Musicians' Guild of Montreal (local 406) was next with a membership of 2664, followed by Ottawa, Vancouver, and Winnipeg (approximately 1200 members each), Calgary (about 1100), and Edmonton and Quebec City (approximately 800 members each).

It has been the custom for the Canadian locals to send delegates to the AF of M annual conventions and for one of these delegates to be elected, by the entire convention, as vice-president from Canada, a position created in 1967. Prior to that time (1909–66) national officers for Canada sat as members of the executive committee of the International Executive Board. Walter *Murdoch (president, Toronto Musicians' Assn, local 149, 1931–58) held this position 1935–64. J. Alan Wood (president, Toronto Musicians' Assn, local 149, 1960–79 succeeded Murdoch in 1965.

Within Canada, locals have held two national conferences annually, primarily to deal with provincial and federal legislation affecting the Canadian music industry. The national AF of M executive assumed responsibility for the negotiation of union agreements with the CBC, CTV, the NFB, and the recording industry, and with companies producing commercials in which music is used. In 1979 the AF of M in Canada established a national office in Toronto, with Wood as president.

No provincial bodies or union officers have been created, each local being autonomous, setting its own wage scale, and holding jurisdiction over its assigned territory. Most locals have elected a number of officers, including a president, two vice-presidents, and a secretary-treasurer, all of whom usually have served as trustees for the local. Individual locals have issued monthly bulletins, eg, local 149's *Crescendo*, local 406's *Entr'acte*, and local 145's *British Columbia Musician*. In addition, the *International Musician*, the official monthly journal of the AF of M of the US and Canada, has been sent to the members of all Canadian locals. Membership in the AF of M has not been mandatory in Canada, and many private teachers and composers have become members of other professional organizations. However, most instrumentalists, particularly those who earn their livelihoods from performing in public, have joined the union.

In order to join an AF of M local in 1980 a musician was required first to apply and to pay an admission fee. Upon acceptance by the local membership he or she was expected to pay annual dues and to adhere to the prescribed rules of the local. Members transferring from one local to another, either within Canada or from the USA to Canada, were subject to the requirements of the new local regarding waiting periods or performance restrictions. (Some locals have imposed certain restrictions on immigrant orchestral musicians, requiring them to perform exclusively with the orchestra by which they are employed and forbidding freelance work until a set time has elapsed. This has been done to protect the rest of the local members from loss of employment.) Within Canada an internal agreement between lcoals has enabled union members to move and work (at prevailing rates of pay) within the jurisdictions of different locals. The same agreement has established a portable pension plan, to which all members have contributed, irrespective of locale. Individual locals have negotiated agreements with symphony orchestras, concert halls and theatres, convention sites, radio stations, and other organizations employing musicians within the locals' jurisdictions and in most cases have obtained exclusive contracts for the employment of union musicians. However, the union never has represented itself as an employment agency for its members. Instead it has been concerned with the protection of its members against exploitation and with the maintenance of goodwill between those members and their employers.

In addition to protecting its members' rights, the union has established rules of professional conduct applicable to all AF of M members. Under those rules, members have been required to refrain from any activities that might be prejudicial to the union or to any of its members. For example, a union member is liable to a fine for lateness at a playing engagement or rehearsal, and, if unable to fulfil a contract, is expected to provide and pay for an approved substitute. Fines can be imposed as well for unprofessional conduct during a playing engagement or for improper attitudes towards fellow musicians during rehearsal or performance. A union member can be fined for accepting less than union fees.

For many years the AF of M has worked to counteract in the music industry and in the media developments that it deems detrimental to the livelihood of its members. During the 1940s an agreement reached with the recording industry resulted in the establishment of the Music Performance Trust Fund, an attempt to offset the lack of royalties paid to recording musicians and the decreasing opportunities for employment resulting from the growth of commercial and domestic use of recorded music. In 1948, through financial contributions from the recording industry to the Trust Fund, 'make-work' programs, including free public concerts in parks, hospitals, homes for the aged, and elsewhere, were made possible. Such performances, to encourage 'live music,' continued, co-sponsored by the Trust Fund and a municipal agency and/or a private industry. At the discretion of its trustee, the Trust Fund has been used also to pay for the services of union members who form the nucleus of a civic or community orchestra, for concerts given by that orchestra, provided no admission is charged. Non-union players in such orchestras have received, on occasion, union-scale wages paid from the Trust Fund, but only with the understanding that they must contribute all or most of their pay to the orchestra to assist in its maintenance.

In March 1978 the Syndicat de la musique du Québec (Music Union of Quebec) was formed, as a result of disputes between the Musicians' Guild of Montreal and some of its members. *Le Devoir* (Montreal, 7 Nov 1980) reported that by the end of 1980 the group claimed a membership of approximately 700 but had not yet signed a collective agreement with any major employer.

The Organization of Canadian Symphony Musicians (OCSM / l'Organisation des Musiciens d'Orchestres Symphoniques du Canada (OMOSC) was formed in 1974 and had its inaugural meeting in Toronto in August 1975. An organization within the AF of M, OCSM functions as a lobby to improve the working conditions and enrich the life style of musicians in symphony orchestras. In 1980 all 11 major symphony orchestras were members, representing approximately 1000 Canadian musicians. OCSM has concerned itself with issues such as instrument insurance and the charges made by airlines for instrument transport, income tax deductions, immigration regulations, auditioning procedures for orchestral appointments, mandatory retirement for symphony musicians, study grants, and the disparity across the nation of 'fees per service,' which in many cases govern the salaries of symphony musicians.

Singers who are not also instrumentalists are not eligible for membership in the AF of M, but instead can be members of the Canadian Actors' Equity Association for live stage performances such as operas and musicals and either the Union des artistes (UDA) or the Assn of Canadian Television and Radio Artists (ACTRA) for performance on TV and radio and in commercials.

Canadian Actors' Equity originally was a part of the US organization Actors' Equity. In 1955 Canadian branches of Actors' Equity were formed, initially to protect artists engaged for the newly established *Stratford Festival, but later for all English-speaking stage performers. On 1 Apr 1976 the Canadian branches gained autonomy; the Canadian Actors' Equity Assn was formed to protect Canadian artists involved in stage, ballet, and opera productions.

UDA and ACTRA originally were one organization, founded in Montreal in November 1937 under the name Union des artistes lyriques et dramatiques, to represent performers who worked on the stage, in films, or on radio (and later TV). It was affiliated with the American Federation of Radio Artists (AFRA, later American Federation of Television and Radio Artists, AFTRA). The union became formally a part of the Canadian Council of Authors and Artists (CCAA) in 1952 and affiliated with the Fédération internationale des acteurs (FIA) in 1953. In 1956 CCAA was granted a national charter from the Canadian Congress of Crafts and Labour (later Canadian Labour Congress). A 1959–60 strike by Quebec members of CCAA against the CBC was not supported by the rest of the union, and in consequence the French-speaking branches refused to forward their fees to CCAA. In 1960 a permanent split in CCAA took place, with UDA re-establishing its independence and taking jurisdiction over all French-speaking performers who retained membership and CCAA continuing to represent the English-speaking members. In 1980 UDA represented all non-instrumental musicians who wished for union affiliation. Meanwhile, in 1960, the time of the division in the CCAA between French-speaking and English-speaking performers, the CCAA had become a loose federation of autonomous branches. A new, more tightly structured organization emerged in 1962 to include, particularly, radio and TV artists. On 1 Jan 1963 ACTRA began operations, to serve an English-speaking membership from all parts of Canada.

In 1980 UDA maintained jurisdiction over French-language (and some other non-English-language) stage, radio, and TV productions, recordings, cassettes and commercials; ACTRA protected members' rights and fees in English-language radio, TV, and the recorded media; while Equity concerned itself with live stage performances. However, the three organizations had developed harmonious reciprocal agreements which allowed members of one organization to perform in the jurisdiction of one of the others, provided the membership and permit requirements were fulfilled properly. When instruments were involved, similar reciprocity existed between the three organizations and the AF of M. All four organizations, however, had adopted nationalistic positions emphasizing the protection of Canadian artists against the incursion of imported performers, while domestically undertaking the protection of musicians from unfair exploitation and encouraging the profession of music as a viable and respected occupation.

See also Trade union songs. ML (JBk, AP, HP)

United States of America. The similarities between Canada and its southern neighbour are many. Both are New World pioneer societies settled largely by adventurers, fortune seekers, missionaries, colonizers, idealists, and refugees from repressive old-world societies; both share an emphasis on technology and materialism mixed with religious puritanism; both know extremes of climate, large geographical distances, and mixed settlements of people of many ethnic and linguistic origins. The obvious differences lie in the strong French component in the Canadian population, the Canadian allegiance to the British crown, from which the USA broke away two hundred years ago, and, perhaps most significant in the musical context, the two populations' different rates of growth. For example, not only did the US population in 1980 exceed that of Canada by a ratio of ten to one, but comparisons of numbers of orchestras, music publishers, recording companies, library holdings, artist managements, professional schools, and so on, also reveal wide disparities. As an example, by the time the first sheet music was printed in Canada, ca 1840, US publishers already had issued more such music than Canada has issued in its entire history (to 1980).

For these reasons it is easy to forget that, if age be dated from the first settlement, Canada is the older of the two countries, and that despite the faster growth of the USA, Canada may claim the first organ (Quebec ca 1657), the first opera (*Quesnel's **Colas et Colinette*, 1790), and the first earned B MUS (Toronto 1846).

1 17th and 18th centuries
2 19th century
3 20th century
4 Individuals with US careers

1 17TH AND 18TH CENTURIES. It should be borne in mind that for the larger part of these two centuries political boundaries bore no resemblance to those of modern times; certainly there was no US/Canadian border, real or dreamed of, until the second Treaty of Paris in 1783. Thus, Louisiana was settled by the French, and even in the 20th century remained a stronghold of survivals of French culture (Acadian, or 'Cajun'), boasting a wealth of transplanted French song which has had an enduring fascination for scholars, as has its counterpart in Acadian New Brunswick.

It is well to remember, too, that from the first Treaty of Paris (1763) to the second – that is, between formal recognition of the British conquest of New France and British Recognition of American independence – Canada and New England, as colonies of Great Britain, were essentially one country. As the English-speaking protestant population increased after 1760, Canada provided a field for the singing-school movement (see Singing schools) that had arisen in the USA and, with it, for the numerous hymn-and-rudimentary-instruction books published in New England. Perhaps this explains the dearth of Canadian English-language church music publications until ca 1850.

From the USA also came strolling companies of actors, singers, and instrumentalists, many of European origin, whose performances entertained audiences from Halifax to Montreal. John *Bentley is one of those who arrived in Canada in this way. Among the Loyalists who moved to Canada after the Revolution were some musicians, eg, Stephen *Humbert, Jonathan *Sewell, and David Willson (see Children of Peace).

2 19TH CENTURY. Because the USA grew so rapidly, it provided an abundance of employment for its own talented musicians, and few emigrated to Canada, where the need was supplied, instead, largely by immigrants from Belgium, France, Germany, and Great Britain. Many of those who did move to Canada from the USA were the children of French-Canadian expatriates, eg, Jean-Baptiste *Labelle (a native of Plattsburgh, NY, 1828), Charles Labelle (from Champlain, NY, 1849) (see Labelle family), Orpha-F. *Deveaux (b Hartford, Conn), and Chambord Giguère (b Woonsocket, RI). There were, of course, some Anglo-Saxons among the US arrivals: the Holman family in 1858 (see Holman English Opera Troup), Edward *Fisher in 1875, Samuel Porter ca 1876, followed by his brother Charles H. *Porter ca 1877, Arthur Bird (1856–1923; organist, pianist, conductor, and composer) in 1877, and Herbert L. *Clarke, the cornet virtuoso, in 1880.

Even early in the century the USA had developed a significant music trade. Publishers such as Firth & Pond, Lee & Walker, O. Ditson, and later in the century G. Schirmer exported large quantities of printed music to Canada, while instrument companies supplied pianos and reed organs. Canadian music education and musical taste were shaped by US instruction books, hymn collections, and song albums, which in quantity far outweighed those from Europe.

European celebrities – Ole Bull, Jenny Lind, Henri Vieuxtemps, and others – would hardly have visited Canada had it not been on the way from New York to Detroit or from Boston to Chicago. US artists (eg, Louis M. Gottschalk) also performed in Canada, and whole orchestras visited (the Germanians – an orchestra of Berliners which settled in Boston ca 1850 – in the middle of the century and the Theodore Thomas Orchestra first in 1873). The National Opera performed in Canada in 1888, the Charley Opera of New Orleans, in 1899. In 1896 the Kneisel String Quartet of Boston made the first of several appearances in Montreal.

In the reverse direction there began, about the middle of the century, a slow but steady flow of Canadian musicians to the USA, where employment opportunities were easier and audiences more sophisticated (see also Emigration). Many of these Canadians not only managed to make decent livings but also made outstanding contributions to the musical development of their adopted country. This was true especially in music education. Calixa *Lavallée, who served as choirmaster at the Boston Catholic Cathedral, became president of the Music Teachers' National Assn and was a pioneer in the holding of 'all-American' concerts; Philip C. Hayden was the founding father of the Music Educators' National Conference; and Hugh A. Clarke became one of the first two university professors of music (both appointed in 1875) and the author of many textbooks.

In the area of performance, Samuel P. Warren distinguished himself as a concert organist (see Warren family); Alfred *De Sève, who succeeded Lavallée at the Boston Cathedral in 1891, was a member of and occasional soloist with the Boston SO; the violinist François Boucher settled in Kansas City (see Boucher family); and the pianists Salomon *Mazurette and Waugh *Lauder found appreciative audiences in Detroit and Chicago respectively.

Other Canadians who have lived in the USA will be listed below.

3 20TH CENTURY. While a strong British orientation prevailed in Anglo-Canadian universities and churches during the first half of the century, and while immigration came mostly from Europe, a US influence of overwhelming strength began to assert itself in several other areas of musical life. This resulted from the development of such mass-distribution media as sheet music, phonograph records, radio, movies, and finally television, as well as from the growth of important US music schools – the Eastman School, the Curtis Institute, the Juilliard School, and the New England Cons, which had outstanding teachers and were much closer than Leipzig, London, and Paris. Furthermore, a powerful, near-monopolistic concert industry made strong inroads into Canada (see Community Concert Associations).

From 1930 to about 1955 Canadians listened to more broadcasts of US orchestras and opera productions than of Canadian groups; they avidly read the *Etude*, *Musical America*, and the *Musical Courier*, but could not support a music magazine of their own for any length of time; they obtained more advanced music degrees from US than from Canadian universities (see Education, professional); they heard, in their concert halls, many minor US performers, in addition to the famous ones, to the disadvantage of Canadian artists of similar or higher calibre; the Canadian hit parade was the Broadway (and Paris) hit parade; the musicians' unions were directed largely from the USA; border cities such as Windsor and Detroit shared music-teaching facilities and symphony musicians; and the *Haskell Opera House, straddling the Quebec-Vermont border, has served citizens of both countries.

In short, Canada enjoyed easy access to the best the USA had to offer, but at the same time was swamped by some of the worst and all but lost its musical initiative. After World War II, however, the process was slowed by a conscious effort to develop Canadian resources, from graduate music schools and schoolbooks to concert bureaus and a home-based recording industry. The establishment of the *CLComp, the *CMCentre, the *CRTC, the *ACO, and other national organizations, has gone far towards making musical relations between the two countries more balanced.

US immigration to Canada began to increase during the middle of the 20th century. Many US teachers came to Canadian universities. Richard *Johnston, Robert *Rosevear, and Ezra *Schabas were among the first. The introduction of musicology into the Canadian university curriculum in the mid-1950s brought a wave of scholars, eg, Andrew *Hughes, Weldon *Marquis, Donald McCorkle, and Harvey Olnick.

Another influx of US musicians, in the late 1960s, was due partly to political developments and partly to the appeal of a country in which artistic challenge and potential were high.

Among immigrants in the 1960s and 1970s have been the conductor and writer (*Toscanini*, London, New York, 1978) Harvey Sachs, the composer Michael *Colgrass, three members of *Canadian Brass, several in the new music groups *Nexus and *NOVA MUSIC, and numerous orchestral players. The US conductor James De Preist became artistic director of the *Quebec SO in 1976.

Prominent European-born musicians who have lived in the USA and resettled in Canada include Ernesto *Barbini, Ernst *Friedlander, Nicholas *Goldschmidt, Anton *Kuerti, and Boris *Roubakine.

Canadian concert artists and performing groups have visited the USA for many years. The *Toronto Mendelssohn Choir made its first US appearance in Buffalo in 1905 and for many years was accompanied both in Toronto and on tour in the USA by the Pittsburgh Orchestra or the Chicago SO. With Percy Grainger as soloist the *Winnipeg Male Voice Choir made its first US tour in 1922. In 1947 the *Montreal Women's SO became the first Canadian orchestra to play in Carnegie Hall, New York. The TSO performed in Detroit in 1951 and began annual visits to Carnegie Hall in 1973. The *MSO made its US debut in 1976. Many Canadian soloists have had significant careers in the USA (eg, Colette *Boky, Judith *Forst, Glenn *Gould, and Louis *Quilico). Lois *Marshall and Maureen *Forrester, besides making many solo appearances in the USA, became members of the New York Bach Aria Group in the mid-1960s. As Canada's contribution to the US bicentennial celebrations, *Somers' **Louis Riel* was performed by the *COC at Washington's Kennedy Center. In 1979 the Birmingham (Alabama) Festival of Arts devoted its 10-day program to Canadian artists.

4 INDIVIDUALS WITH US CAREERS. The following list provides brief notes on some Canadian-born or Canadian-trained musicians whose careers have been pursued mostly in the USA. Those who have entries of their own in *EMC* are named but not annotated. The selection of individuals has much to do with the number of years they spent in Canada, the ties they kept with Canada after emigration, and the importance of their contribution to Canada. The list is in chronological order by date of birth. (In addition to these, many others, some with *EMC* entries, others without, have had important connections with music in the USA. See also Blues; Country music; Dance bands; Guitar 2 / Jazz; Jazz; Metropolitan Opera; Rock.)

Composers

Hugh Archibald Clarke, b 1839 (See Clarke family.)

Calixa *Lavallée, b 1842

George *Grant-Schafer, b 1872

Edward (Betts) Manning, b Saint John, NB, 1874, d New York 1948. He studied composition with Edward MacDowell in New York, with Humperdinck in Berlin, and with Vidal in Paris and violin with Henry Schradieck in New York. He taught privately in New York and, later, at Oberlin Cons in Ohio and Teachers' College, Columbia U. His largest work, the three-act opera *Rip Van Winkle* (to his own libretto), was premiered by the Charlotte Lund Opera Co at Town Hall, New York, in 1932.

L.J. Oscar *Fontaine, b 1878

Cedric (Wilmot) Lemont, b Fredericton, NB, 1879, d New York 1954. He studied at the *U of New Brunswick, at the Faelten Piano School and the New England Cons in Boston, and at Capitol College, Columbus, O, completing an M MUS. In 1906 he began teaching at the Walter Spry Music School (later Chicago Institute of Music). He acted as organist-choirmaster at churches in Fredericton and Chicago and taught privately in Fredericton and Brooklyn, NY. He was a contributor to various music journals and collaborated on three volumes of the *American History and Encyclopedia of Music*. Several hundred of his compositions, mostly anthems and pedagogical pieces, were published by Ditson, C. Fischer, and Presser; his set of studies *Facile Fingers* was a best-seller. Lemont's materials for junior- and intermediate-level piano students employed variegations of harmony and rhythm uncommon in the Teaching music of the period.

Gena *Branscombe, b 1881

Nathaniel *Dett, b 1882

Lorraine (Noel) Finley (m Fitch), b Montreal 1899, d Greenwich, Conn, 1972. Her teachers included J.-J. *Goulet (violin) and Ada Richardson (piano) in Montreal, Louise Héritte-Viardot and Frank La Forge (voice) in Germany and New York, respectively, and Percy Goetschius and Rubin Goldmark (composition). In addition to her numerous published compositions, which include a *Symphony in D*, she translated into English, from 20 different languages, the words of more than 600 works ranging from the short pieces in *National Anthems of United Nations and Associated Powers* and Mozart concert arias to Milhaud's opera (her version, 1937) *Le Pauvre Matelot*.

Colin *McPhee, b 1901

Gerald Strang, b Claresholm, Alta, 1908. He studied at Stanford U (BA 1928), at the U of California at Berkeley, and at the U of Southern California. His composition teachers included Charles Koechlin, Arnold Schoenberg, and Ernest Toch. Strang was Schoenberg's teaching assistant 1936–8 and editorial assistant 1936–50. He taught after 1938 at various California colleges and lectured on electronic music 1969–70 at the U of California at Los Angeles. He initiated the New Music Workshops in 1933, became director of the New Music Society of California in 1936, and edited the *New Music Edition* 1935–40. He was a consultant on building design and acoustics after 1950 for several US college and music departments and worked on computer and electronic music 1964–9 at the Bell Telephone laboratories in New Jersey and after 1964 at the U of California at Los Angeles.

Charles Jones, b Tamworth, Ont, 1910. He studied violin at New York's Institute of Musical Art and composition under Bernard Wagenaar. He taught 1939–44 at Mills College, Oakland, Cal, and later at the Music Academy of the West in Santa Barbara, at the Bryanston School in England, and at the Seminar of American Studies in Salzburg. In addition he began teaching composition in 1951 at the Aspen Music School in Colorado and has taught in New York at the Juilliard School and the Mannes College of Music, where he was head of composition 1972–7. Jones' own compositions include four symphonies, six string quartets, two piano sonatas, and *Allegory* for divided orchestra (1970). His *Sonatina* for violin and piano (1942) and *String Quartet No. 6* (1970) were recorded by CRI in 1972.

George Tremblay, b 1911. (See Amédée Tremblay.)

Reuel (or Ruel) Lahmer, b Maple, Ont, 1912. He was taken to the USA as a child and there studied at Columbia U and Cornell U, developing his abilities as composer, organist, choir director, and folksinger. He taught in the 1940s at Cornell and at Carroll College, Waukeska, Wisc, and served as head of the theory department at Colorado College. He was organist 1951–62 at the Church of the Ascension, Pittsburgh. He has composed choral, chamber, and orchestral works.

Henry Dreyfus Brant, b 1913. (See Saul Brant.)

Minuetta *Kessler, b 1914

Dorothy Cadzow, b Edmonton 1916. After receiving a BA in music from the U of Washington she studied composition at the Juilliard School with Frederick Jacobi and Bernard Wagenaar. In addition to freelance arranging and teaching, she began teaching theory, orchestration, and composition at the U of Washington in 1959. Her compositions include works for orchestra, piano, and voice.

Robert Lenard *Barclay (b Basham), b 1918

Galt *MacDermot, b 1929

Sydney *Hodkinson, b 1934

Songwriters

Cowles, b 1860. (See Musical theatre below.)

James Gardiner MacDermid, b Utica, Ont, 1875, d 1960. His teachers included B. Sanders in London, Ont, G. Tyler and F.E. Woodward in Minnesota, and A. Williams and G. Hamlin in Chicago. In addition to performing in recital and concert, he toured as accompanist to his wife, the singer Sybil Sammis MacDermid. His compositions include secular and sacred songs, many published by Forster Music Publishers Inc and by Horace J. Carver.

Geoffrey *O'Hara, b 1882

Organists

Édouard and Arthur *Dumouchel, twins, b 1841

Samuel P. Warren, b 1841. (See Warren family.)

Paul Ambrose, b 1865. (See Ambrose family.)

George H. Fairclough, b 1869. (See William E. Fairclough.)

J.-Ernest Philie, b St-Dominique de Magog, Que, 1874, d Montreal 1955. He studied organ and singing and taught in the Eastern Townships before taking a position ca 1900 as organist in Manchester, NH. After nine years there he moved to Woonsocket, RI, later to Fall River, Mass, and around 1920 to Springfield, Mass. He retired to Montreal in the 1950s. He wrote several masses, a cantata for choir and orchestra (*Le Pays*), and patriotic songs. His publishers were Theodore Presser and White, Smith.

BIBLIOGRAPHY

Dion-Lévesque, Rosaire. Silhouettes franco-américaines (Manchester, NH, 1957)

Lynwood *Farnam, b 1885

Ernest *White, b 1901

Bernard *Piché, b 1908

Gérard *Caron, b 1916

Pianists

Calixa *Lavallée, b 1842

Salomon *Mazurette, b 1847

Waugh *Lauder, b 1858

Jeannette Durno (m Collins), b Walkerton, Ont, 1876, d Los Angeles 1964. She studied at the conservatory of the Ladies' College in Rockford, Ill, and with J.J. Hattstaedt at the American Cons in Chicago. She gave her first recital at seven and later made her professional debut in Vienna, where she also studied witb Leschetizky. She taught in Chicago and appeared as soloist with many US and European orchestras. Her Canadian pupils included Evelyn Eby *Bedford, Neil *Chotem, and Lyell *Gustin.

Gwendolyn Williams *Koldofsky, b 1906

Arthur Gold, b Toronto 1917. His teachers included Josef and Rosina Lhévinne at the Juilliard School. With the US pianist Robert Fizdale he formed a two-piano team which has toured the USA, Canada, and Europe. Gold and Fizdale have premiered material for prepared piano by John Cage and have had works composed for them by Auric, Barber, Milhaud, Poulenc, and Virgil Thomson.

Zadel Skolovsky, pianist, b Vancouver 1921. With his Russian-born parents he moved to the USA in 1923. His piano teachers were Isabelle Vengerova at the Curtis Institute and Leopold Godowsky. A Naumburg Award winner (1939), he has performed with the major orchestras of Canada and the USA and has toured Europe. He premiered Milhaud's *Concerto No. 4* (dedicated to him) in 1950 with the Boston SO under Charles Munch. He has recorded for Philips and Columbia. In 1975 he began teaching at the U of Indiana.

Marion *Barnum, b 1926

Raymond *Dudley, b 1931

Mari-Elizabeth *Morgen, b 1944

Strings (violin unless otherwise stated)

Oscar *Martel, b 1848

François Boucher, b 1860. (See Boucher family.)

Alfred *De Sève, b 1860

Chambord (Joseph Emile) Giguère, b Woonsocket, RI, 1877, d after 1957. The son of French-Canadian musicians who moved to the USA ca 1874, he studied in Montreal with Émile Daudelin, Frantz *Jehin-Prume, and Oscar Martel and in Brussels with César Thomson and Eugène Ysaÿe. In addition to teaching briefly in England and playing in Belgian orchestras during the early years of the 20th century, he taught in New England for more than 50 years and appeared in concerts in New England and Canada.

BIBLIOGRAPHY

Dion-Lévesque, Rosaire. *Silhouettes franco-américaines* (Manchester, NH, 1957)

Kathleen *Parlow, b 1890 (in the USA 1926–40)

Ernest Gill Plamondon, b 1896. (See Plamondon family.)

Louis Gesensway, b Dvinsk, Latvia, 1906, d Philadelphia 1976. He arrived in Canada as a child, studied violin with Luigi von *Kunits in Toronto, and toured Canada 1916–18 as a prodigy. He studied later at the Curtis Institute and in Budapest with Kodály. He played 1923–6 in the New SO (*TSO) and 1926–71 in the Philadelphia Orchestra. He composed chamber and orchestral works and devised a scheme of 'colour harmony.'

Albert *Pratz, b 1914 (in the USA 1943–53)

William Waterhouse, b 1917. (See John Waterhouse.)

Suzette Forgues, cellist, b Montreal ca 1920. She studied in Montreal with Gustave *Labelle and J.-B. *Dubois and appeared as soloist with the CSM in 1937. She won the *Prix d'Europe in 1940 and studied in New York with Emmanuel Feuermann. She became principal cello of the New York City Center in 1947.

Lorne Munroe, b 1923 (cello). (See Munroe family.)

Klemi Hambourg, b 1928. (See Hambourg family.)

Lea *Foli, b 1933

Pierre Ménard, b Quebec City ca 1940. He studied with Calvin *Sieb at the *CMQ. He won the Prix d'Europe in 1961 and later moved to the USA, where he became second violin of the Vermeer Quartet, which has toured in the USA and Canada.

Martin Foster, b Rochdale, England, ca 1950. He emigrated to Canada in 1956 and later studied at *McGill U and the *CMM, completing his premier prix in violin at the latter in 1970. His teachers have included Taras *Gabora in Montreal and Dorothy Delay at the Juilliard School. He has played in the JM World Orchestra and the Aspen Chamber Symphony and was a founding member of the Gagliano String Quartet in 1971 and the American String Quartet in 1974.

Other instruments

E.N. L'Africain (trumpet 1887–1902 with the Boston SO)

Alexandre *Laurendeau, b 1870 (oboe; in the USA 1900–20)

Percival *Price, b 1901 (carillon)

Gloria Agostini, b 1923 (harp). (See Agostini family.)

Claude Hill, b 1934 (a harpist with the Metropolitan Opera Orchestra from 1962)

Conductors

Bruce Carey, b 1877. (See Carey family.)

Rosario *Bourdon, b 1885

Wilfrid *Pelletier, b 1896

Reginald *Stewart, b 1900

Daniel Saidenberg, conductor, cellist, b Winnipeg 1906. His family moved to the USA when he was an infant. He studied cello 1919–21 with André Hekking at the Paris Cons and 1925–30 at the Juilliard School. A member of the Philadelphia Orchestra 1926–30 and principal cello with the Chicago SO 1930–7, he was head of the cello department 1933–7 at the Chicago Musical College. He began guest conducting orchestras in the eastern USA in 1933, and in 1941 he formed the Saidenberg Little Symphony. He began conducting the Connecticut SO in 1946.

Albert *Steinberg, b 1910

Brock McElheran, b Winnipeg 1918. He studied at the *U of Toronto (BA 1939, B MUS 1947) and at the *TCM; among his teachers were Nicholas *Goldschmidt and Ettore *Mazzoleni in Toronto and Stanley Chapple at Tanglewood, Mass. In 1947 he began to teach at the State U College at Potsdam, NY. He has been choral director for the Saratoga and Tanglewood Festivals and he served 1972–9 as conductor of the *Montreal Elgar Choir.

Gregory *Millar, b 1929

School music

Joseph (Bennett) Sharland, b Halifax, NS, ca 1837, d Boston 1909. Early in life he moved to Boston, and later he became the accompanist or conductor for a number of choral societies and for more than 25 years served as a teacher and supervisor of school music. He edited several school songbooks.

Philip (Cady) Hayden, b Brantford, Ont, 1854, d Keokuk, Ia, 1925. He studied at Oberlin Cons in Ohio, then served as school music supervisor 1888–1900 in Quincy, Ill, and 1892–? in Keokuk, Ia. In 1907 he helped organize the founding meeting of the Music Supervisors' (later Educators') National Conference (MENC). He conducted various choirs and wrote lyrics and music for children's songs. He founded the magazine *School Music* and edited it 1900–25.

Edwin (Ninyon Chaloner) Barnes, b Oromocto, near Fredericton, NB, 1877, d Landover Hills, Md, 1952. He studied in Canada, the USA, and England, earning a D MUS ED in 1924. He was named director of school music for Massachusetts in 1906 and for Rhode Island in 1914 and served 1922–47 as head of the music department of the District of Columbia Public Schools. He was executive director of the Stephen Foster Memorial Foundation and wrote books and brochures about US music.

Private or conservatory teaching

Kate Sara Chittenden, b Hamilton, Canada West (Ontario), 1856, d New York 1949. She was a teacher 1873–6 at Hellmuth College, London, Ont, and served 1879–ca 1906 as organist at Calvary Baptist Church in New York. She was head of the piano departments 1890–1914 at the Catharine Aitken School in Stamford, Conn, and 1899–1930 at Vassar College in Poughkeepsie, NY, and dean 1892–1933 of New York's Metropolitan College of Music (reorganized in 1900 as part of the American Institute of Applied Music). In 1887 she founded the Synthetic Piano School, later part of the institute. Her pupils numbered more than 3000.

Katherine Burrowes, b Kingston, Ont, ca 1869, d ? 1939. She studied with J.C. Batchelder in Detroit and Karl Klindworth in Berlin and taught 1895–1903 at the Detroit Cons. In 1903 she founded the Burrowes Piano School in Detroit. A specialist in teaching methods for children, she composed studies and simple pieces and devised *The Burrowes Course of Music Study for Beginners* (1895) and *The New Success Music-Method* (1917).

Evelyn Ashton Fletcher, b 1872. (See Fletcher Music Method.)

Jeannette Durno, b 1876. (See Pianists above.)

Léopold *Simoneau, b 1918

Pierrette *Alarie, b 1921

University (musicology unless otherwise stated)

Hugh Clarke, b 1839 (all-round, theory). (See Clarke family.)

George *Bornoff, b 1907 (string pedagogy)

Wilfred Conwell Bain, b Shawville, Que, 1908. At 10 he moved to the USA, where he studied at Houghton College (BA 1929), Westminster Choir College (B MUS 1931), and New York U (MA 1936, D ED 1938). The recipient of several honorary degrees, he was dean of music 1938–47 at North Texas State U and 1947–73 at Indiana U, where he established an opera department.

BIBLIOGRAPHY

Thorpe, Day. 'Wilfred Bain,' *Musical America*, Apr 1964

Michael Winesanker, b Toronto 1913. A pupil of George Boyce (piano) and Healey *Willan (theory), he later studied musicology with Otto Kinkeldey at Cornell U. He received a B MUS (Toronto) in 1933, an MA (Michigan) in 1941, and a PH D (Cornell) in 1944. He taught piano and theory 1940–2 at the *Hambourg Cons, 1945–6 at the U of Texas, and 1946–76 at Texas Christian U, where he was named chairman of the music department in 1976.

Jaroslav Mráček, b Montreal 1928. He studied piano with Alberto *Guerrero at the RCMT and completed his B MUS (Toronto) in 1951. He studied further in the USA completing an MA (Indiana) in 1962 and a PH D in musicology (Indiana) in 1965. He began teaching at San Diego State U in 1965. His special fields of scholarship have been 17th-century instrumental music and Czech renaissance music. He is the editor of *Seventeenth Century Instrumental Dance Music* (Sweden 1978) and the author of articles for *EMC* and the *New Grove*.

H. Colin Slim, b Vancouver 1929. He studied with Harry and Frances *Adaskin, Ida *Halpern, and Irwin Hoffman at the U of British Columbia (BA 1951) and with Otto Gombosi, Arthur Merritt, Walter Piston, and John Milton Ward at Harvard (MA 1955, PH D 1959). A specialist in renaissance music, he taught 1958–65 at the U of Chicago and 1965–72 at the U of California at Irvine. He returned to the latter in 1974 as chairman of the Historical Musicology department. He is the author of *Musica nova: Monuments of Renaissance Music* (Chicago and London 1964) and the two-volume *A Gift of Madrigals and Motets* (Chicago and London 1972).

(John) Warren Kirkendale, b Toronto 1932. He attended university in Canada (BA, Toronto 1955), Germany, and Austria (PH D, Vienna 1961), worked in 1963 as a reference librarian at the Library of Congress, Washington, and taught 1963–7 at the U of Southern California and subsequently at Duke U, North Carolina. A lecturer in Europe and North America, he has contributed articles to *Acta Musicologica*, the *Journal of the American Musicological Society*, and other publications.

Singers (opera and concert)

Emma *Albani, soprano, b 1847 (lived in the USA 1852–6 and 1864–8)

Charles Hedmont, tenor, b Portland, Maine, 1857, d London 1940. He studied as a youth in Montreal and later in London and Leipzig. He made his debut in 1881 in Berlin as Tamino, and sang for seven seasons at the Leipzig Stadttheater. He appeared in Gewandhaus concerts under Nikisch. He toured North America several times and sang the title role in *Lohengrin* with the Emma Juch company in Toronto in 1890 and Vancouver in 1891. In 1914 he sang Wagner roles in Montreal with the Quinlan Opera.

(William Thomas) Whitney Mockridge, tenor, b Port Stanley, Canada West (Ont), 1861, d Capetown 1956. He studied with F.H. *Torrington and made his debut with the *Toronto Philharmonic Society in 1879. He was soloist with various US organizations and a member of the Carl Rosa Opera Company 1882–4 and the American Opera Company in 1886. He settled in England in 1893, but returned occasionally to the USA to teach.

Albert P. Quesnel, tenor, b Montreal ? ca 1870. He sang in St Paul, Minn, in Chicago, and in St Louis and settled in New York, where he made his Metropolitan Opera debut, 20 Feb 1901, as Zorn in *Die Meistersinger*. He sang there again during the 1905–6, 1907–8, 1913–14, and 1915–16 seasons. While he appeared in many US cities, he seldom was heard in Canada. He recorded six Edison Blue Amberol Cylinders (see *Roll Back the Years*).

Edward *Johnson, b 1878

Francis Archambault, bass, b L'Assomption, Que, 1879, d Montreal 1914. He studied with Frank Dossert in New York and with Jacques Bouhy in Paris. In 1904 he toured North America as Amfortas in a concert version of *Parsifal* presented by Walter Damrosch and the New York SO. He sang in concerts in Paris and London ca 1906 and was a member 1909–10 of Henry Russell's Boston Opera. He made test records 1909–10 for American Columbia.

BIBLIOGRAPHY

Gour, Romain. 'Francis Archambault,' *Qui?*, vol 4, Fall 1953

Kathleen *Howard, b 1880

Forrest Lamont, tenor, b Athlone, Adjala Township, Ont, 1881, d Chicago 1937. He grew up in Massachusetts, studied in Italy, and made his debut in Rome in 1914. A principal tenor 1917–30 with the Chicago Opera, he taught, and in 1919–20 made 10 recordings for Okeh.

Elizabeth Campbell (b Findlay), mezzo-soprano, b Toronto 1883, d Toronto 1969. After church and concert appearances in Toronto she sang with the Century Opera (New York) 1914–15, Max Rabinoff's Boston Opera 1915–16, the *San Carlo Opera 1916–17 (as Maddalena Carreno), the Aborn English Grand Opera 1917–18, and the Society of American Singers 1918–19. She lived and taught in Paris from 1920 until the late 1950s.

Joseph Royer, baritone, b Quebec City 1884, d Phoenix, Ariz, 1965. He moved to New Hampshire as a child. After 1916 he often sang with the San Carlo Opera Company. He toured with light opera companies in South America and South Africa during the 1920s and made his Metropolitan Opera debut 16 May 1936 as Escamillo in *Carmen*. He sang with companies in Chicago, Cincinnati, Philadelphia, and St Louis.

Éva *Gauthier, b 1885

Irene *Pavloska, b 1889

Jeanne *Gordon, b 1893

Mary *Bothwell, b 1900

James Eby, bass, b Saskatoon 1911. He was heard first over CRBC radio in 1933. In 1946 he left Canada to study in New York. He has toured with opera companies in Canada and the USA and has recorded with the Early Music Foundation of New York. He made his home in Wallkillm, NY.

Jack Barkin, b 1914. (See Barkin family.)

Mary *Henderson, b 1914

Jean Dickenson, soprano, b Montreal 1914, to US parents. She was raised in India, South Africa, and the USA. She was a pupil of Florence Hinman in Denver. She became a regular performer 1937–50 on NBC radio programs and was a favourite of radio audiences in Canada. She appeared with the Denver and Milwaukee SOs, the *Promenade Symphony Concerts, and the *Little Symphony of Montreal, performed in productions of the Denver and San Carlo opera companies, and made her Metropolitan Opera debut 26 Jan 1940 as Philine in *Mignon*.

Norman Farrow, bass-baritone, b Regina 1916. After vocal studies 1938–40 at the Juilliard School, he made his debut in New York in 1940, and in 1946 helped to organize the New York-based Bach Aria Group. He has sung with the group on many North American tours and on recordings. He has appeared as soloist with both US and Canadian orchestras. He began teaching at the U of North Carolina in 1969.

Mona Paulee, mezzo-soprano, b Edmonton 1916. Raised in Portland, Ore, she won the 'Metropolitan Opera Auditions of the Air' in March 1941. She appeared with that company 1941–6, toured Central America and Europe during the early 1950s, and appeared on Broadway in *The Most Happy Fella* in 1956. She later taught in California.

Emilia Cundari (m Vezzetti), soprano, b Detroit 1930. Raised in Windsor, Ont, she studied at Marygrove College in Detroit (B MUS, BA 1953) and with Edith Piper at the Juilliard School. During the mid-1950s she sang with the Detroit, Toronto, and Windsor SOs and appeared 1953–5 with the New York City Opera. She was an apprentice 1956–9 with the Metropolitan Opera. In 1959 she moved to Italy, where she participated in 1959, 1960, and 1961 in the Sacred Music Festival in Perugia and sang with the Rome Opera and the Teatro Sociale in Como. She also sang on European radio and appeared at various festivals. She returned to North America in the 1960s and in the 1970s was a voice teacher at Marygrove College. She has recorded for Columbia, Harmonia-Mundi, Victor, and Music Guild.

Salli Terri (b Stella Tirri, m Biggs), singer and folklorist, b London, Ont, ca 1935. she moved to Detroit as a child and studied music at Wayne State U. She also studied at the U of Southern California and the U of California at Los Angeles. An arranger and soloist for many years with the Los Angeles-based Roger Wagner Chorale, she has made several recordings for Capitol (reissued by Angel) and has toured with the John Biggs Consort, an ensemble directed by her husband. In 1976 she began to teach at Fullerton Community College, Fullerton, Cal.

Teresa *Stratas, b 1938

Musical theatre

George H. Primrose, minstrel, b London, Canada West (Ontario), ca 1853, d San Diego, Cal, 1919. He began his career in the early 1860s, toured with the Haverly troupe and the Barlow, Wilson, Primrose and West Company, and worked with Lew Dockstader. He is said to have originated soft-shoe dancing.

Eugene (Chase) Cowles, bass, b Stanstead, Canada East (Quebec), 1860, d Boston 1948. He grew up in Vermont. A specialist in comic opera, he sang the role of Will Scarlett in the premiere (1890) of Reginald de Koven's *Robin Hood*. With the Alice Nielsen Opera Company he took leading roles in the premieres of Victor Herbert's *The Fortune Teller* (Toronto 1898) and *The Singing Girl* (Montreal 1899). He later appeared in vaudeville and in Broadway productions of several Gilbert & Sullivan operettas. He composed approximately 40 songs, recorded for Victor in 1906, and made an Edison Diamond Disc of his song 'Forgotten' (Ditson 1894) in 1921.

May Irwin (b Campbell), singer, b Whitby, Canada West (Ontario), 1862, d New York 1938. With her sister Flo she appeared 1877–83 at Tony Pastor's Theater in New York. She went to London and appeared with Augustin Daly's stock company. In 1895, in *The Widow Jones*, she had her first leading role. Later known as 'the peeress of stage widows,' she recorded a few ragtime songs for Victor in 1907.

BIBLIOGRAPHY

Bell, Margaret. 'May Irwin – peeress of stage widows,' *Maclean's*, 1 Jul 1914

Marie Dressler (b Koerber), singer, actress, b Coburg, Ont, 1868, d Santa Barbara, Cal, 1934. Her first success was in *The Lady Slavey*, in 1896. Following vaudeville appearances in Great Britain and the USA she had a second stage success, in *Tillie's Nightmare* (1910). Besides recording ragtime songs for Edison in 1910 she appeared in silent films under the Canadian director Mack Sennett and made 24 talking films 1930–4, winning the Academy Award for best actress of 1930.

BIBLIOGRAPHY

Dugan, James. 'Marie Dressler, queen of the movie queens,' *Maclean's*, 15 Mar 1952

Harry *Macdonough, b 1871

Christie MacDonald, soprano, b Pictou, NS, 1875, d Greenwich, Conn, 1962. She grew up in Boston. Her first starring role (1910) was that of Princess Bozena in Reinhardt's operetta *The Spring Maid*. In 1913 Victor Herbert wrote his operetta *Sweethearts* for her. She recorded songs from these two works for Victor in 1911 and 1913. Her last stage appearance was in a 1920 revival of *Floradora*.

BIBLIOGRAPHY

Bell, Margaret. 'The little princess of the stage,' *Maclean's*, May 1914

Eva Tanguay as Salomé

Donald Brian, singer, actor, b St John's, Nfld, 1875, d Great Neck, Long Island, NY, 1948. At six he moved to Boston. He made his first New York appearance in 1899 and became a matinee idol. His greatest success was as Prince Danilo in the original US production of Lehar's *The Merry Widow* (New Amsterdam Theater, New York, 1907).

BIBLIOGRAPHY

Blum, Daniel. *Great Stars of the American Stage* (New York 1952)

George MacFarlane, baritone, actor, b Kingston, Ont, 1877, d Hollywood 1932. In 1909 on Broadway he sang a lead in de Koven's *The Beauty Spot*. Roles followed in other musicals and in operettas such as Jerome Kern's *Miss Caprice* (1913), *The Midnight Girl* (1914), and *Trilby* (1915). He recorded for Victor and Columbia.

Eva Tanguay, singer, dancer, actress, b Marbleton, Que, 1878, d Hollywood 1947. She acted in variety shows and musicals throughout the USA and reached 'star' status in 1902 with *The Chaperones*, which featured her first song hit, 'My Sambo.' By 1912 she was said to be the highest-paid actress in North America. In 1916 she starred in the motion picture *Wild Girl*. She gained great success with her version of the song 'I Don't Care,' recorded for Nordskog in 1922.

BIBLIOGRAPHY

Dion-Lévesque, Rosaire. *Silhouettes franco-américaines* (Manchester, NH, 1957)

(Robert) Craig Campbell, tenor, b London, Ont, 1878, d New York 1965. In New York he was a pupil of Isidore Luckstone and a soloist for six years at the Church of the Transfiguration. He made his stage debut in 1909 as Alfred Blake in Edmund Eysler's *The Love Cure* at the New Amsterdam Theater. In 1912 he sang Jack Travers in the premiere of Friml's *The Firefly*. He appeared for several years on Broadway and in vaudeville. He was a member 1917–20 of the Society of American Singers and a soloist 1942–54 at St John's Episcopal Church in Jersey City, NJ. He recorded for Columbia, Davega, Pathé, and Perfect.

BIBLIOGRAPHY

Manning, E.B. (pseud). 'Tenor Craig Campbell, one of London's "forgotten" celebrities,' London *Free Press*, 8 Dec 1962

Walter Huston, singer, actor, b Toronto 1884, d 1950; brother of Margaret *Huston. A vaudeville performer for 20 years before becoming a celebrated stage and film actor, he is remembered for his performance of 'September Song' in Kurt Weill's *Knickerbocker Holiday*.

Henry *Burr, b 1885

Estelle Carey, b 1890. (See Carey family.)

Walter Pidgeon, baritone, actor, b East Saint John, NB, 1898. He sang with the E.E. Clive Repertory Company in England and appeared on Broadway in *Puzzles of 1925* before moving to Hollywood and becoming known primarily as a film actor. He recorded for HMV in England ca 1924.

Douglas Stanbury, baritone, b Toronto 1899, d Huntington NY, 6 Dec 1980. As a youth he toured in Canada and New York State with Arthur Pryor's Band and studied 1915–20 with Otto *Morando in Toronto. In 1922 he became principal baritone soloist at the Capitol Theater in New York. During the 1920s he sang with the Chicago Civic and San Carlo operas and continued to appear on Broadway. In the early 1930s he was heard regularly on radio and in 1934 he sang in several opera broadcasts sponsored by Chase and Sanborn and conducted by Wilfrid Pelletier. A transcription of one of these (*Aida*) was released in 1976 by the Unique Opera Record Corp. Stanbury appeared 1926–34 in five Vitaphone film shorts and recorded for Edison, Victor, Cameo, Silvertone, and Oriole.

Ruby Keeler, dancer, singer, b Halifax, NS, ca 1911. She moved with her family to New York, where she eventually joined the Ziegfeld Follies. In the 1930s she went to Hollywood and starred in a number of Busby Berkeley musical films, including *42nd Street*. She retired from show business in 1941 and made a brief comeback in a Broadway revival of *No, No, Nanette* in 1970.

Kaye Connor, lyric soprano, b Vancouver ca 1925. At five she was heard on radio as 'Vancouver's Baby Kaye.' She played children's parts in Hollywood films during the 1930s and later appeared on stage in productions of Victor Herbert's *Romany Love* in Hollywood, New York, and London.

Dorothy Collins (b Marjorie ? Chandler), b Windsor, Ont, 1926. She sang on WJKB radio in Detroit and was discovered in 1942 by the bandleader Raymond Scott. She was heard 1950–7 on NBC TV's 'Your Hit Parade' and appeared in musicals and straw hat productions on Broadway and elsewhere. Her recording included the 1957 hit 'Four Walls.'

BIBLIOGRAPHY

Lee, Betty. 'That virginal Hit Parade girl finds Broadway,' Toronto *Globe and Mail*, 10 Jul 1971

Gisele *MacKenzie, b 1927

Milton Jiricka, tenor, b Saskatoon 1930. He studied at the RCMT and in Italy. After singing in the early 1950s for CBC radio programs, he moved to New York, where he appeared in musicals at Radio City Music Hall and on Broadway. He was seen on the US TV shows of Lawrence Welk and Tennessee Ernie Ford.

Gale Sherwood, soprano, actress, b Hamilton, Ont, 1930. She began singing on Toronto radio stations at three, went to Hollywood ca 1938, and appeared in her first movie in 1939. Following several movie musicals, made during the 1940s, she began to appear in stage operettas and on TV specials. She achieved her greatest recognition performing in nightclubs in Canada and the USA with the baritone Nelson Eddy. She retired in the late 1960s.

Robert *Goulet, b 1933

Len (Leonard) Cariou, actor, director, singer, b St Boniface, Man, 1939. He sang in the chorus at *Rainbow Stage, acted at the *Stratford Festival, and starred in the Broadway musical *Applause* (1970) and in the stage and film productions of Sondheim's *A Little Night Music*. He appeared in the title role of another Sondheim musical, the successful *Sweeney Todd*. For the three musicals he received best actor nominations for Broadway's 'Tony' Awards, winning for *Sweeney Todd*.

Judy Lander, singer, b Winnipeg ca 1948. She began singing in 1964 and studied in the late 1960s with Portia *White and Rosemary Burns. She appeared 1968–9 in a Toronto production of *Jacques Brel Is Alive and Well and Living in Paris* and in 1969 in **Spring Thaw*. In 1973 she performed in the Broadway production of *From Berlin to Broadway with Kurt Weill* and toured the USA in the Jacques Brel show.

Singing evangelists

Aimee Semple McPherson (b Kennedy), b Ingersoll, Ont, 1890, d Oakland, Cal, 1944. After missionary work in India and China she moved to the USA and settled in Los Angeles. Her Angelus Temple Church of the Foursquare Gospel included a radio station for on-air preaching. She recorded songs and sermonettes for Columbia in 1926 and 1931.

George Beverly *Shea, b 1909

Hollywood singers

Deanna (b Edna Mae) Durbin, b Winnipeg 1922. She moved to California at the age of one. In the 1930s and 1940s she appeared in several films, the first of which was *Three Smart Girls*. She was heard regularly on Eddie Cantor's CBS radio show.

Bobby Breen (b Jackie Boreen), b Toronto 1927, d England 1972. He sang in Jack *Arthur's Toronto revues and at nine was heard on Eddie Cantor's radio show. He appeared in several Hollywood films before 1942. During the 1940s and 1950s he toured and performed in nightclubs. He recorded for Bluebird, Decca, and other labels.

See also Dressler, Sherwood, and Tanguay under 'Musical theatre' above.

Others in pop music

Rosario *Bourdon, b 1885

John Murray Anderson, lyricist and director, b St John's, Nfld, 1886, d New York 1954. He was lyricist and director 1919–24 of the Greenwich Village Follies, which rivalled the Ziegfeld Follies. He directed the movie *King of Jazz* (1930) and was the music director 1938–50 for Billy Rose's Diamond Horseshoe and 1942–51 for the Ringling Bros Circus.

Percy *Faith, b 1908

Lucille *Starr, b 1938

Concert management and administration

Bernard R. *Laberge, b 1891

Terry McEwen, b Thunder Bay, Ont, 1929. He worked at the *International Music Store in Montreal, joined Decca records in London in 1950, and in 1959 moved to New York where he was artistic director of the classical section of London Records and a regular intermission panelist for the Metropolitan Opera radio broadcasts. In 1979 he was appointed successor to Kurt Adler (effective 1982) as general director of the San Francisco Opera.

BIBLIOGRAPHY

McLean, Eric. 'McEwen – for the love of opera,' *Montreal Star*, 16 Jun 1979.

Pop songwriters

Shelton Brooks, b 1886. (See 'Darktown Strutters' Ball.')

Carmen *Lombardo, b 1903

Will Osborne (b Oliphant), singer and songwriter, b Toronto 1906. He left Canada ca 1925. Among his songs were 'Beside an Open Fireplace,' 'The Hills of Old Virginia,' 'Mumble Jumble,' and 'Pompton Turnpike.'

Robert Nolan, b 1908. (See 'Tumbling Tumbleweeds.')

Lyrics

George V. Hobard, b Port Hawkesbury NS, 1867, d Cumberland, Md, 1926. He left Canada at the age of 17 and enjoyed success 1900–22 as lyricist and librettist of more than 40 Broadway musicals, including many *Ziegfeld Follies* 1911–20.

James O'Dea, b Hamilton, Ont, 1871, d Long Island, NY, 1914. He grew up in London, Ont, and moved to New York, where he began to write songs. As a lyricist he collaborated with his wife, Anna Caldwell, on 'The Ghost of the Banjo Coon' (ca 1902), 'The Sweetest Girl in Dixie' (1904), and Ivan Caryll's fantasy *Chin-Chin;* with Neil Moret on 'Hiawatha' (Whitney-Warner 1903); with Jerome Kern on 'The Subway Express' for *Fascinating Flora* (1907); and with Victor Herbert on *Lady of the Slipper*.

J. M. Anderson, b 1886. (See 'Others in pop music' above.)

George White (b George Weitz), b Toronto 1890, d Hollywood 1968. A dancer in his youth, working with Luigi *Romanelli in Toronto and later in a team with Bernie Ryan in vaudeville and on Broadway, he wrote and produced the *George White Scandals* (1919–32, 1936, and 1939), Broadway revues which rivalled the Ziegfeld Follies.

Jazz

See Jazz: 8 / Canadians in the USA and Europe.

Country

Wilf *Carter, b 1904
Hank *Snow, b 1914
See also Country music: 4 / Canadian characteristics; Guitar.

Pop and dance, general (includes rock, dance bands)

Guy *Lombardo, b 1902
Paul *Anka, b 1941
David *Clayton-Thomas, b 1941
Joni *Mitchell, b 1943
Neil *Young, b 1945
Gino *Vannelli, b 1952
The *Diamonds, fl 1952–64
The *Crew-Cuts, fl 1954–70s

In the latter half of the 20th century, with the expansion of the recording industry and constant improvements in transportation and communications, it became possible for many Canadian-born pop performers (eg, Anne *Murray, Joni Mitchell, Gino Vannelli, Neil Young) to live in either Canada or the USA while enjoying successful careers in both countries.

BIBLIOGRAPHY

Nixon, D.C. 'Canadian colony in New York,' *CMTJ*, vol 2, Feb 1901
MacMillan, Ernest. 'Musical relations between Canada and the U.S.A.,' *Proceedings of the Music Teachers' National Association* (1931)
MacMillan, Mazzoleni, Walter, J.-M. Beaudet, Peaker. *Proceedings of the Music Teachers' National Association* (1946)
Yocum, John. 'Tin pan alley to Canada, popular music's one way street,' *SatN*, 31 May 1952
Sinclair, Lister. 'Big time,' *SatN*, 14 Nov 1953
BMI Canada Ltd. *Canadian Music at Carnegie Hall: a Report* (Toronto 1954)
Kaplan, M. 'Reflections on music education in the United States and Canada,' *CME*, vol 5, no. 1, 1963
Proctor, George. 'The bachelor of music degree in Canada and the United states,' *CME*, vol 7, Jan–Feb 1966
Thomas, Tony. 'Some Canadians in Hollywood,' *CanComp*, 43, Oct 1969
Beckwith, John. 'What every U.S. musician should know about contemporary Canadian music,' *Mcan*, 29, final issue 1970 (HK)

Université de Moncton. See University of Moncton.

Université de Montréal. See University of Montreal.

Université du Québec à Montréal. See University of Quebec.

Université du Québec à Trois-Rivières. See University of Quebec.

Université Laval. See Laval University.

Universities. Most of Canada's universities provide academic and extracurricular programs in music and therefore have entries in *EMC*. There are entries as well for subjects and subject areas related to higher education in music. See listing below.

It will be noted that most universities are non-denominational, though many of the older ones began under the wing of religious groups and some have continued thus. Education is a provincial rather than a federal jurisdiction in Canada, and most universities have been supported and controlled by their provincial governments. This explains in part the great variety and frequent duplication of teaching programs and degrees.

While some universities offered examinations in music in the 19th century (U of Trinity College, Toronto; Bishop's U, Lennoxville; U of Toronto), they rarely provided instruction, and the history of formally constituted teaching departments dates back only to 1918 when the U of Toronto created its Faculty of Music, followed in 1920 by that of McGill U and in 1922 by the École de musique at Laval U. It should be added that many universities have grown out of colleges (ie, undergraduate schools) which operated their own conservatories, eg, Acadia, Dalhousie, Mount Allison, and Regina.

The music-teaching divisions of universities usually have been called faculties, schools, or departments. In traditional parlance in Canada, a university faculty is a body which administers its own degree (for example, a faculty of music administers the degree B MUS), whereas a department is a faculty subdivision which offers a specialized program leading to the 'parent' faculty's degree (for example, a department of music, within a faculty of arts or of fine arts, offers an honours-music program leading to the degrees BA or BFA). The term 'school of music' typically applies to a music division found in a large state university in the USA; it has been adopted by a few Canadian institutions, and merely characterizes a diversified music division, whether offering a degree in music or not. The head of a faculty is called a dean; the head of a department is called a chairman or head; the head of a school may be called dean, head, or a similar name. In practice, however, one notes a few exceptions in Canadian universities, especially where the term 'department' continues to be applied where 'faculty' might be more appropriate (for example, in the universities of Saskatchewan, Alberta, British Columbia, and Victoria).

In 1980 faculties of music existed at McGill U, the U of Montreal, the U of Toronto, the U of Western Ontario, and Wilfrid Laurier U. Schools of music existed at Acadia U, Brandon U, Laval U, the U of Manitoba, the U of Sherbrooke and the U of Windsor. Departments existed at all the others.

The following universities have entries in *EMC:*
Acadia University
Bishop's University
Brandon University
Brock University
Carleton University
Concordia University
Dalhousie University
Lakehead University
Laval University
McGill University
McMaster University
Memorial University
Mount Allison University
Mount St Vincent University
Queen's University
St Francis Xavier University
Simon Fraser University
Trent University
University of Alberta
University of British Columbia
University of Calgary
University of Guelph
University of Lethbridge
University of Manitoba
University of Moncton
University of Montreal
University of New Brunswick
University of Ottawa
University of Prince Edward Island
University of Quebec
University of Regina
University of Saskatchewan
University of Toronto
University of Trinity College
University of Victoria
University of Waterloo
University of Western Ontario
University of Windsor
Wilfrid Laurier University
York University

See also the following entries:
Archives
Canadian Association of University Schools of Music
Canadian Mennonite Bible College
Cegeps
Classical colleges and seminaries in Quebec
College songs
Community colleges
Degrees
Diplomas
Education, professional
Electronic music
Ethnomusicology
Hart House
Instrument collections
Ladies' colleges and convent schools
Libraries
Mennonite Brethren Bible College and College of Arts
Music education research
Musicology
Rapport de la Commission royale d'enquête sur l'enseignement des arts dans la province de Québec
Royal Conservatory of Music of Toronto
Séminaire de Québec

BIBLIOGRAPHY

Smith, Leo. 'Music in our universities,' *Canadian Forum*, vol 5, Aug 1925
MacMillan, Ernest. 'The place of music in a university curriculum,' *Proceedings of the National Conference of Canadian Universities* (1927)
Collingwood, Arthur. 'Music in education,' *Queen's Q*, vol 44, Winter 1937
Walter, Arnold. 'Music in Canadian higher education,' *The Humanities in Canada*, W. Kirkconnell and A.S.P. Woodhouse eds (Ottawa 1947)
– 'Education in music,' *Music in Canada*
Adaskin, Harry. 'Music and the university,' paper given at the 1955 National Conference of Canadian Universities; report *Royal Architectural Institute of Canada J*, Sep 1955 and *CMJ*, vol 1, Autumn 1956
MacMillan, Sir Ernest. 'Music in Canadian universities,' *CMJ*, vol 2, Spring 1958

'Music education,' University of British Columbia *J of Education*, special issue devoted to music education, Apr 1968
Walter, Arnold. 'The growth of music education,' *Aspects of Music in Canada*
Bédard, Yves. *Oeuvres commentées à l'usage des professeurs d'éducation musicale* (Montreal 1968)
Patterson, Lawrence W.A. 'Undergraduate programs for music teacher preparation in Canadian colleges and universities,' unpubl D ED thesis, U of Illinois 1972
Roman, Zoltan. 'Higher music education in Canada,' *New Patterns of Musical Behaviour* (Vienna 1972)
Green, J. Paul. 'A proposed doctoral program for Canadian universities with specific recommendations for specialization in music education,' unpubl D ED thesis, U of Rochester 1974
Blume, Helmut. *A National Music School for Canada* (Ottawa 1978)

PERIODICALS
CAUSM Journal Ottawa 1971–
Music Research News, newsletter of the Canadian Music Research Council

University of Alberta. Non-denominational university with undergraduate and graduate programs. Founded in Edmonton in 1906, it began to offer instruction in 1908 and awarded its first degrees in 1912. The U of Alberta first offered programs of study at Calgary in 1945 and continued until 1966 when the *U of Calgary was established as an autonomous institution. During the 1930s the U of Alberta's extension department helped to found the *Banff SFA; stewardship for that school was held 1966–78 by the U of Calgary.

The U of Alberta joined the *U of Manitoba and *U of Saskatchewan in 1934 to form the *Western Board of Music, and the board's Alberta examinations were conducted on the university campus. In the years prior to World War II organ recitals were given frequently on the University Memorial Organ in Convocation Hall. After the war John Reymes *King, head of music 1945–7, and Richard *Eaton, head 1947–67, laid the foundations of the first music program in the midwestern provinces to offer professional degrees. The U of Alberta National Awards for distinguished contribution to 'Letters, Music and Painting and the Related Arts' were begun in 1951 (see Awards: 1 / Honours bestowed).

In 1958 a Dept of Fine Arts was established with three constituent divisions, one of which was Music. The umbrella department ceased to exist in 1965, when individual departments of Art, Drama, and Music were constituted. Eaton continued as head of the Music Dept. Thomas *Rolston was acting chairman 1967–9, Robert *Stangeland chairman 1969–78, and Brian Harris acting chairman 1978–9. Stangeland was appointed chairman for a five-year term in 1979.

Music degrees offered in 1978–9 were the D MUS (performance, initiated in 1977), M MUS (applied music, musicology, theory, and composition, initiated in 1968), M ED (music) B MUS (applied music, history and literature, theory, and composition), BA (honours), and B ED (elementary and secondary major). Degrees in music education were offered under the auspices of the Faculty of Education's music program. The first B MUS graduates were Wolfgang *Bottenberg (1961), Lynn Newcombe, and Eileen Turner. Honorary degrees have been awarded to Gladys *Egbert (1965) and Jenny *Lerouge LeSaunier (1966). In 1978–9 the department was composed of 312 students (270 undergraduate and 42 graduate) and 48 teachers (25 full-time and 23 part-time). Among members of the teaching staff in 1978–9 were Violet *Archer (appointed 1962), Helmut *Brauss, Alfred *Fisher, Malcolm *Forsyth, Claude *Kenneson, Edward *Lincoln (also director of the WBM), Alexandra *Munn, and Manus Sasonkin.

After Alfred *Strombergs joined the department in 1971, its voice/opera section presented, each February, operatic productions, either in workshops or fully staged and accompanied by a student orchestra. The first were Vaughan Williams' *Riders to the Sea* and Seymour Barab's *A Game of Chance* in 1972. These were followed by Monteverdi's *The Coronation of Poppea* (1973, the Canadian premiere), Violet Archer's *Sganarelle* (1974, premiere), *Cosi fan tutte* (1975), *Gianni Schicchi* (1976), Bernstein's *Trouble in Tahiti* (1976), *The Magic Flute* (1977), Britten's *A Midsummer Night's Dream* (1978), and Menotti's *The Medium* (1979).

The Fine Arts Centre, shared by the Art, Drama, and Music departments, opened in 1973, providing rehearsal halls, classrooms, teaching studios, practice rooms, an electronic studio, and the Music Resources Centre, which holds collected editions, study scores, music for performance, basic reference material, audio equipment, and recordings. In 1980 the Cameron and Rutherford libraries contained the music reference collection, microforms, the major periodicals, and books on music.

Students, staff, and visitors have presented annually some 200 public performances, some of them on the 40-rank, three-manual *Casavant tracker organ which replaced the Memorial Organ in Convocation Hall in 1978. In addition to the *U of Alberta String Quartet (in-residence ensemble appointed in 1969) performing ensembles have included the university's Symphony Orchestra, St Cecilia Chamber Orchestra, Symphonic Wind Ensemble, Concert Band, Concert Choir, Madrigal Singers, and Brass Quintet, a Collegium Musicum founded and directed by Arthur *Crighton, and two stage bands. The U of Alberta was host to the 1979 *Alberta Composers' Assn's Alberta Composers' Festival.

See also College songs; Music education research.

BIBLIOGRAPHY
Stangeland, R.A. 'Performances mirror department courses,' *MSc*, 253, May–Jun 1970 (AC,PMW)

The University of Alberta String Quartet. Founded in 1969 as quartet-in-residence at the *U of Alberta in Edmonton, with Thomas *Rolston and Lawrence Fisher (violins), Michael Bowie (viola), and Claude *Kenneson (cello). Norman *Nelson succeeded Rolston as first violin in 1979. The quartet has made a specialty of contemporary works. It played Elizabeth Maconchy's *Quartet No. 10* (premiere) and Jean *Coulthard's *Quartet No. 2* at the 1972 Cheltenham Festival. Both works had been written for it. In Great Britain it also played at the Purbeck Festival in Dorset, at the Menuhin School, and in the Channel Islands. Also in 1972 it joined the *Purcell String Quartet for the premiere of Coulthard's *Octet* at the CBC Vancouver Festival. It gave integral performances of the six Bartók *Quartets* in 1974 in Edmonton and at the *Banff SFA. In 1973 it recorded the Coulthard and Maconchy quartets (RCI 386) and quartets of Schubert and Debussy (CBC SM-254). BH

University of British Columbia. Non-denominational undergraduate and graduate teaching and research institution incorporated 1908 in Vancouver, absorbing the *McGill-affiliated McGill University College of Vancouver in 1915 and awarding its first degrees in 1916. Noted in particular for its programs in forestry, geology, and oceanography, it offers a wide range of studies in the arts, sciences, and professions.

While Ida *Halpern introduced courses in music appreciation in 1940, music was not established as an academic discipline at the U of British Columbia until 1946, when the Vancouver brewer Robert Fiddes endowed the appointment of Harry *Adaskin. Frances Marr *Adaskin and Jean *Coulthard were among the department's first teachers. Barbara *Pentland joined in 1949.

Until 1958 the department offered courses for general arts students and presented weekly (or more frequent) concerts featuring the Adaskins and other faculty members and guests. These concerts greatly enriched Vancouver's musical life and prepared the ground for the appreciation of contemporary music.

After 1958 increasing government support enabled the department to expand. Adaskin did not wish to undertake the heavy administrative duties of an expanded department, but remained as a teacher until 1973. His successor 1958–71 was G. Weldon *Marquis. Subsequent heads have been Donald McCorkle (b Cleveland, O, 1929, d Vancouver 1978; one-time director of the Moravian Music Foundation in Winston Salem, NC, and a teacher at the U of British Columbia until 1978 and head of the music department 1972–5), Robert Morris (acting head, 1975–6), and Eugene Wilson (executive secretary, 1976–7). Wallace Berry became head of the department in 1978.

During Marquis' headship, the department underwent rapid expansion. The B MUS program, which began in 1959 with 27 students and 8 faculty members, had 170 students and 41 teachers by 1964. By 1970 the department had 311 students (280 undergraduate, 31 graduate) and 55 faculty members. The figures for 1978–9 were 318 (300, 18) and 64 (27 full-time, and 37 part-time). Degrees then offered were B MUS (general music; performance; composition; music history and literature; opera), MM (majors in historical musicology; ethnomusicology; composition and/or theory; performance; opera; general music), DMA (performance; composition), and PH D (musicology). Later the Faculty of Education offered a B ED, an M ED, and a D ED with majors in music education. (In 1980 Allen E. Clingman and Campbell *Trowsdale of that faculty lectured in the Music Dept.)

The first B MUS graduates, May 1962, included Errol Gay and Zoltan Roman. The first PH D in musicology was granted to Joanne Dorenfeld in 1976.

Throughout the 1960s the department emphasized performance. Many student ensembles – orchestras, a concert band, choirs, chamber groups, and a Collegium Musicum – gave regular free public performances. An opera workshop, begun in 1962, developed further after the US opera director French Tickner (b 1930) joined the faculty in 1964. In that year the university was the first in Canada to offer the B MUS and M MUS as a major in opera. Graduate and undergraduate students were encouraged to study at least one 'historical' instrument, eg, the viola da gamba or the viola d'amore. The department's ethnomusicology program included instruction in such exotic instruments as the Japanese koto, shakuhachi, and shamisen.

After the rapid expansion of the 1960s an increasing emphasis was placed on academic research. Significant work has been done by, among others, Donald and Margit McCorkle (Brahms), Dimitri Conomos (Byzantine music), Ming-Yueh Liang (ethnomusicology), Evan Kreider (Pierre de la Rue), Gregory Butler (rhetoric), John Sawyer (English viol music), and Elliot *Weisgarber (Japanese music). Researchers active in the areas of performance and education have included Allen Clingman, Ronald *de Kant, Cortland *Hultberg, Hans-Karl Piltz, Marie *Schilder, and Robert *Silverman. Undergraduate and graduate students in composition have been encouraged to use the electronic music studios and to take the courses in computer programming.

The department's four-storey building, with 35 practice rooms, 38 teaching studios, one of the largest academic music libraries in Canada (see Libraries), and a 300-seat recital hall, was completed in 1967 and opened in 1968. A tracker-action *Casavant organ was installed in 1970 at a cost of $100,000. The department also acquired one practice and one portative organ; a violin (Saluzzo, 1690) by Goffredo Cappa, a pupil of Amati; a violin by Richard Duke (London, 1764); an early grand piano by Aloys Biber (Vienna, ca 1835); modern replicas of many renaissance and baroque harpsichords and string and wind instruments; and Chinese, Japanese, Korean, and Indo-Pakistani instruments.

The department has presented numerous free public solo and ensemble student and faculty concerts as well as a series by guest performers. The university was host to the Centennial Workshop on Ethnomusicology (initiated by Ida Halpern) in June 1967 and the Northwestern Regional Workshop of the National Assn of Teachers of Singing in June 1978. Sir Ernest *MacMillan received an hon LLD from the university in 1936.

See also College songs; University of British Columbia Chamber Singers.

BIBLIOGRAPHY
'Perspectives: the University of British Columbia,' *CMJ*, vol 3, Summer 1959
Marquis, G. Welton. 'Canadian music at the University of British Columbia,' *CanComp*, 2, Aug 1965
– 'View from the West Coast,' ibid, 26, Feb 1968
– 'Modern, ancient music techniques taught at U.B.C.,' *MSc*, 257, Jan–Feb 1971 TB (PMW)

The University of British Columbia Chamber Singers. Twelve music students assembled in 1962 by Cortland *Hultberg to perform music of the 15th, 16th, and 20th centuries. Their contemporary repertoire includes many works employing electronic tape and other synthetic sounds. The group tours regularly in British Columbia and has appeared in eastern Canada and at universities on the west coast of the USA. It performed at the *CMCouncil conference in 1972 and at the 1978 ISME conference in London, Ont. It gave the premieres of Istvan *Anhalt's *Cento* in 1967, Murray *Schafer's *From the Tibetan Book of the Dead* in 1968, Luis de Pablo's *Portrait imaginé* in 1975, and the Canadian premiere of John Tavener's *The Whale* in 1968. TRL

University of Calgary. Non-denominational institution founded in 1945 as the Calgary branch of the *U of Alberta and granted autonomy as the U of Calgary in 1966. It has developed a wide range of undergraduate and graduate programs.

A Dept of Fine Arts was created within the university in 1959, with Frank *Churchley as chairman; Churchley was succeeded in 1964 by A. Malcolm Brown, and Brown by Zoltan Roman, acting chairman 1967–8 during a period of reorganization. The department was redefined as a Faculty of Fine Arts in 1968, with Richard *Johnston as dean.

Music courses, which had existed at the university since its founding, were consolidated into a Dept of Music within the Faculty of Fine Arts, with Ward Cole as head. In 1973 Johnston was succeeded as faculty dean by J. Marchbank Salmon, and Cole was succeeded as department head by Stanley G. Finn. Alan Robertson succeeded Salmon in 1980.

In 1978–9 the Music Dept offered a B ED and a B MUS (school music, elementary or secondary; performance; theory and composition; history and literature). In 1979 a graduate department was inaugurated, offering an MA (musicology) and an M MUS (composition, school music). In 1978–9 the department was composed of 150 students and 40 teachers (31 full-time and 9 part-time).

Prominent faculty members have included, also, Lois Choksy, Eugene Cramer, Lise Elson, Marilyn *Engle, Charles Foreman, Alexander *Gray, T. Herman Keahey, and John *Searchfield.

In 1980 facilities included two concert halls, a library, a music resource centre and listening laboratory (of which a component was the record collection of the broadcaster Allan Sangster), an electronic music studio, and a computer music studio. The university library tower became the home of the *CMCentre (Prairie region), opened in 1980. Concerts and recitals at the university have been presented in student series, faculty series, and the annual University Concert Series. Visiting performers and teachers have appeared frequently. Performing groups under department sponsorship have included the University SO, Chamber Players, Concert Choirs, Singers, Concert Band, and Jazz Lab. There have been numerous opera productions.

The *Banff SFA was affiliated 1966–77 with the U of Calgary, the university acting as steward for the school during those years.

See also Archives; Libraries.

BIBLIOGRAPHY
Faculty of Fine Arts, U of Calgary. *Repertoire*, annual, 1980– AC (PMW)

University of Guelph. Founded at Guelph, Ont, in 1964 as a non-denominational graduate and undergraduate institution incorporating the Ontario Veterinary College (founded 1862), the Ontario Agricultural College (1874), and the Macdonald Institute (1903). It is noted for its agricultural and veterinary programs. In 1947 Ralph A. Kidd became director of musical activities for the three colleges. Upon the establishment of the U of Guelph, a music division was created within the Faculty of Arts. Nicholas *Goldschmidt was appointed director of music in 1967, and Stanley *Saunders succeeded Goldschmidt in 1974. Among Kidd's responsibilities was the direction of choral activities within the founding colleges on an extracurricular basis. Under Gerald Neufeld, who assumed its direction in 1979, the 50-voice U of Guelph mixed choir presented 15 concerts in Great Britain in August 1979 during its fourth trip overseas. The U of Guelph Civic Orchestra, drawn from both the university and the city of Guelph, has been conducted by the director of music.

Music is offered in the form of electives within the Faculty of Arts, and the BA may be taken with honours in music, the B SC with minor honours in music. In 1978–9 there were 20 teachers in the music division, 4 full-time and 16 part-time.

Begun in January 1968 under the management of Edith Kidd, the university's Thursday noon-hour concerts, sponsored by the Faculty of Arts and by 1970 numbering 10 in the fall and 10 in the winter semesters, became a highlight of campus musical life, presenting solo performers and ensembles from all parts of Canada. The university also has been the site of many of the events of the *Guelph Spring Festival. JPG

University of Lethbridge. Non-denominational university established in 1967 at Lethbridge, Alta. It awarded its first undergraduate degrees in the liberal arts in 1968.

The Music Dept began in 1967 with 38 students (35 in 1977–8). The B MUS program, initiated in September 1972, produced its first graduate, Marcia Swanston, in May 1975. Other degrees offered in 1978–9 were the BA (music major), B ED (music major), and B MUS/B ED (five-year combined degree). Murray *Adaskin received an honorary degree in 1970. Chairmen of the department have been Kenneth L. Kicken in 1967, Lucien A. *Needham 1967–71, Dean G. Blair 1971–6, and John P. Jackson, acting chairman 1976–7. Blair returned as chairman in 1978.

The department has emphasized applied musical studies, including instruction in piano, strings, woodwind and brass instruments, harpsichord, voice, and a selection of historical instruments. In 1978–9 there were seven full-time and seven part-time faculty members.

The Music Dept received a collection of books and music as the bequest of the former department member Arthur *Putland. It has acquired a substantial collection of replicas of early instruments (viols, recorders, harpsichord, and dulciana, among others) and has installed an electronic studio.

The department has established the custom of recital and concert series by faculty members and advanced students. Performing groups have included the U of Lethbridge Choir (founded 1967), Madrigal Singers, Collegium Musicum, Wind Ensemble, and Faculty Trio. The department also established a non-credit conservatory program in applied music and theoretical subjects.

BIBLIOGRAPHY
Needham, Lucien. 'Music at Lethbridge – where quality counts,' *MSc*, 255, Sep–Oct 1970 (AC, PMW)

University of Manitoba. Non-denominational university founded in Winnipeg in 1877. Its first degrees were granted in 1880. Originally located downtown, on Broadway, it moved to its Fort Garry site in 1929 but maintained the Broadway facilities as well for many years. Unlike its various faculties (eg, Arts, Education, Medicine) its School of Music has offered no advanced degrees.

Music has been a focus of much extracurricular activity at the U of Manitoba. At least as far back as the early 1930s the Glee Club presented a Gilbert & Sullivan operetta annually. Starting in 1940, the 80-player University SO, conducted successively by Ronald W. *Gibson, Frank *Thorolfson, and Filmer *Hubble, performed Beethoven and Mozart symphonies and accompanied soloists (eg, Gordon *Kushner, pianist, 1942 and 1945) at the *Winnipeg Auditorium and the Walker Theatre. In the 1940s the university band, chamber music groups (string trios, quartets), and Choral Society flourished, and the Glee Club expanded its repertoire. Most of these groups broadcast over the western network of the CBC.

In 1934 the university joined the *U of Saskatchewan, the *U of Alberta, and the departments of education of the three provinces, to form the *Western Board of Music whose purpose was to devise and administer a diploma program. The program was initiated in 1935. In 1944–5 the university's newly created Dept of Music began providing arts and science students with elective courses in theory and history at the Broadway buildings. The department became the School of Music in 1963. The position of director of music antedated both the school and the department. Incumbents have been: Robert Fletcher (chairman, Advisory Board) 1936, Eva *Clare 1937–49, Ronald W. Gibson 1949–63, Leonard *Isaacs 1963–74, Carl F. Haenselman 1974–8, succeeded by Paul W. Paterson.

University of Manitoba, School of Music, Fort Garry Campus

The school's degree studies began in 1964 with six students enrolled in either the three-year Bachelor or the four-year Honours Bachelor program. The first degrees were awarded in 1967. In 1974 the four-year B MUS program (general, performance, composition, history, music education) was initiated. The university conferred honorary LLDs on John *Waterhouse in 1965 and Filmer Hubble in 1967.

In 1978–9 there were 100 students and 32 teachers (12 full-time and 20 part-time). Most of the part-time instructors have been members of the *Winnipeg SO. The teaching staff has included Peggie *Sampson 1950–70, Christine *Mather 1964–70, Robert Irwin 1964–72, William *Aide 1965–74, Alma *Brock-Smith 1965–79, and Douglas *Bodle 1966–8. Among those teaching there in 1980 were Klara Belkin, Robert *Turner (joined 1969), Marek *Jablonski (joined 1979), Conrad Grimes, and Richard Seaborn.

The school's own building was opened in 1965, its facilities including the 240-seat Eva Clare recital hall, two classrooms, 12 teaching studios, 18 practice rooms, and a library. Free weekly concert series have been presented Wednesdays and Sundays.

The school has developed a collection of replicas of historical instruments and acquired a square piano (Adam Berger, London, 1784) and a Dolmetsch clavichord. The *Men's Music Club of Winnipeg donated a two-manual *Casavant Baroque Organ. The school also acquired a Beckerath tracker practice organ. A synthesizer was installed for use in summer courses in electronic music.

The university has co-operated in an opera workshop with the *Manitoba Opera Assn and participated in a Renaissance Week with the Winnipeg Art Gallery. The *Manitoba University Consort (1963–70) helped advance the cause of early music through public performances on original instruments. Other performing groups have been the U of Manitoba SO, Concert Band and Stage Band, the University Singers, Collegium Musicum, Percussion Ensemble, and Prairie Consort of Recorders.

John Greer, Music Gold Medalist 1976, has written the *U of M March, 1877–1977* for orchestra and chorus. The school for many years has administered the Richardson Foundation Scholarships and several smaller awards.

see also College songs; Music therapy.

BIBLIOGRAPHY
U of Manitoba. *Brown and Gold*, year books (1940–50)
Friesen, Olga. 'The Leonard Isaacs and the University School of Music,' *Sharps & Flats*, vol 5, Feb 1965
'University of Manitoba Music Diploma Association,' ibid, vol 7, Oct 1966
Isaacs, Leonard. 'Music department plays community role,' *MSc*, 252, Mar–Apr 1970 (LW, PMW)

University of Moncton† / Université de Moncton. Founded in 1864, the U St-Joseph of Memramcook, NB, became the U of Moncton nearly a hundred years later, in 1963, when it moved to that city. Neil Michaud – b Edmundston, NB, 14 Oct 1927; BA (U St-Joseph) 1949, MA (Columbia Teachers College) 1964 – was given the task of establishing a music department, which he directed 1964–70. He was succeeded by Brian *Ellard 1970–8, and Ellard by Donald Desroches in 1978. In 1980 the department continued to offer a general B MUS and a B MUS with majors in music education, performance, and pedagogy, as well as in history, harmony, and counterpoint. Teaching is exclusively in French. In 1977–8 there were eight full-time teachers (one of whom was Gaston *Allaire), three assistants, and some 63 students. In 1972 the Notre-Dame-d'Acadie School became affiliated with the U of Moncton as a preparatory music school. Concerts and recitals by students and faculty have been given regularly, and courses in elementary keyboard harmony have been made available to the public. The mixed choir of the U of Moncton (*Chorale de l'U St-Joseph) has played an important role in the community. Established in 1970, by 1980 the folklore section of the Centre for Acadian Studies, of which Father Anselme Chiasson was a director, had accumulated more than 1500 tapes of songs, stories, legends, and oral history. The song collection included 5000 songs and variants, classified according to Conrad *Laforte's *Catalogue de la chanson folklorique française*. More than 1700 pieces of instrumental music were preserved in sound recordings, and there was also a collection of records of traditional and contemporary folksong. Charlotte Cormier, supervisor of the folklore section for six years, published in 1978 *Écoutez tous, petits et grands*, transcriptions of folksongs from southeastern New Brunswick.

BIBILOGRAPHY
Gleason, Marie. 'Folklorist helps Acadians know past,' Toronto *Globe and Mail*, 8 Jul 1975 (GA)

University of Montreal† / Université de Montréal. Canada's largest French-language university, founded in 1919 by a rescript of Pope Benedict XV which made the branch established by *Laval U in Montreal in 1876 an autonomous Roman Catholic institution. A third provincial charter (1967; the others were in 1920 and 1950) defined the U of Montreal as a public institution, dedicated to higher learning and research, in the administration of which students and teachers would have the right to participate. The university was housed 1876–95 in the Grand Séminaire de Montréal and 1895–1942 in a building on St-Denis St; from there it moved to the Mount Royal location it still occupied in 1980. In 1978–9 the university consisted of 12 undergraduate faculties leading to the baccalauréat; the faculty of graduate studies leading to master's and doctoral degrees; two affiliated schools (Hautes Études commerciales and Polytechnique); and a continuing studies program (night classes for adults). Nearly 2500 teachers and as many assistant teachers provided tuition for more than 33,000 students.

On an order from Paul-Émile Cardinal Léger the Faculty of Music was founded 18 Oct 1950 during the rectorship of Mgr Olivier Maurault, whose efforts to establish such a faculty dated from 1939 and became linked with those of the Diocesan Commission on Sacred Music in 1947. Besides organizing and administering its own study and research programs, the new faculty became responsible for co-ordinating the programs of study and academic standards in those schools of music that until then had been affiliated directly with the U of Montreal, the charter of 1950 having decreed that the affiliated schools 'are [now] affiliated by means of annexation to a Faculty' (ie, now express their affiliation by relating to a faculty rather than, as before, to the university as a whole). Thus the *Cons national de musique, the *École normale de musique, the *École Vincent-d'Indy, the Institut des Soeurs de Sainte-Anne in Lachine, the Présentation de Marie school in St-Hyacinthe, the Soeurs de l'Assomption school in Nicolet, the Ursulines school in Trois-Rivières, the Gregorian Institute in Toledo, O, the *Institut Nazareth, and the *Schola cantorum of Montreal all were annexed to the faculty. These affiliations were followed by those of the École de Sherbrooke, the École supérieur de musique in Hull, and the Collège de musique Ste-Croix in St-Laurent.

Courses began 1 Feb 1951. The teaching program was divided into two sections, sacred music and secular music, and covered a comprehensive group of academic subjects. The only instruments taught were the piano and the organ. The faculty was directed until 1953 by Dean Alfred *Bernier, who helped put it on a firm footing. A particular problem at that time was the intractability of the affiliated schools, which saw their autonomy curtailed by the existence of the faculty. Éthelbert *Thibault succeeded Bernier for a short term (1953), after which Jean *Papineau-Couture, secretary of the faculty, undertook its administration on an interim basis until 1955.

Clément *Morin assumed the deanship in 1955 and immediately initiated a program for church musicians. In 1958 he inaugurated summer courses which attracted distinguished guest teachers to the faculty, and in 1961 he established courses in music pedagogy. During his 13 years as dean he devoted himself in particular to stabilization and to standardizing curricula at the affiliated schools.

In 1966 a revolution in the faculty's offerings brought about important changes in orientation and a complete reorganization of the undergraduate programs. Thenceforth the latter led to a B MUS (general, performance; composition theory; history and analysis). Courses in music pedagogy were integrated in 1967 into the university program for the secondary school teaching certificate (licence), a program later (1972) replaced by a BA with a major in music and a minor in education offered in collaboration with the Faculty of Education. It was also in 1967 that the affiliation of the music schools with the faculty was discontinued according to the terms of the new university charter.

Jean Papineau-Couture, dean 1968–73, gave new direction to the faculty by obtaining larger premises, increasing the number of full-time staff members from 6 to 18, introducing more flexibility into the programs, and developing several activities designed to make the faculty's work better known. The Nocturnales, begun in 1968, allowed members of the faculty to present evening concerts of traditional or contemporary works, some of them premieres, in a setting where listening often was enriched by visual elements. The Musialogues, organized by Maryvonne *Kendergi, and begun in 1969 consisted of informal encounters with personalities from the arts world, from both Canada and abroad. The workshops in early music (Gerrit Tetenburg and Jean-Pierre Pinson), baroque music (Réjean *Poirier), contemporary music (Lorraine *Vaillancourt), acting and stage movement (Louise *André and Marthe *Forget), and jazz (Sayyd *Abdul Al-Khabyyr) were offered as much to the faculty as to the community at large.

The U of Montreal Orchestra, conducted 1977–8 by Jean-Eudes *Vaillancourt and thereafter by Serge *Garant, has given many concerts, some in the Nocturnales series. It has joined the 100-voice Chorale de la faculté on occasion to perform large choral-orchestral works, eg, Handel's *Messiah*. The choir was founded by Morin, who turned it over to Jean-François *Sénart in 1973. It should not be confused with the Choeur bleu et or, a U of Montreal choir independent of the faculty, founded in 1949 by Robert Villeneuve, a medical student, directed by Fernand *Graton after 1950, renamed the Choeur des étudiants in 1962, and discontinued in 1965.

A reorganization of faculty academic and administrative structures under the 1973–9 deanship of Gilles *Manny was marked by procedures calling for collegial participation in management. The staff increased to 25, and enrolment grew rapidly to more than 400 students in 1978–9. A special emphasis was placed on the development of graduate studies (M MUS and D MUS in performance or composition, MA and PH D in musicology) and the establishment of research programs. These programs were concerned with music at the elementary level and the application of international techniques of creativity to musical training (initiated in 1972 by Jean-Marie *Cloutier and Sister Alix de Vaulchier), with music data processing (begun 1973, under the direction of Papineau-Couture), with musical paleography (begun 1973, under Clément Morin), with ethnomusicology (begun 1974, under Charles Boilès and Ramón Pelinski), and with musical semiology (begun 1974, under Jean-Jacques Nattiez). Certain of these projects have benefited from special Canada Council or Quebec Ministry of Education grants. Henri Favre succeeded Manny as dean in June 1979, supported by two vice-deans, Robert Léonard and Louise Hirbour-Paquette, and an assistant, Denise Tessier-Vachon.

The Faculty of Music's pioneering course in sacred music, at one time the only one offered in a Canadian French-language university, broadened over the years into an early music study program under Clément Morin, Dujka Smoje, Gerrit Tetenburg, and Jean-Pierre Pinson. More recently, contemporary music has moved to the fore through the teaching of such leading figures as Garant, Maryvonne Kendergi, Papineau-Couture, and André *Prévost. In 1966 the faculty became the first French-speaking university to offer a course on Canadian music. In the area of performance Louise André (organizer of the voice program), Françoise *Aubut (organ), Marcel *Baillargeon (flute), Gisela *Depkat (cello), Réjean Poirier (harpsichord and organ), Antoine *Reboulot (organ and piano), Denis *Regnaud (harpsichord and organ), Claude *Savard (piano), Jacques Verdon (violin), and others have ensured a high calibre of instruction. Massimo Rossi became director of the classes in organology, harmony, orchestration, and instrumentation in 1964. As artists-in-residence, Manny (piano, 1967–73) and Vladimir Landsman (violin, 1975–9) also gave courses.

Studies are facilitated by a record collection, a library, an auditorium, and elaborate audio-visual equipment, including an electronic studio under the direction of Louise Gariépy. The faculty also owns three mechanical-action organs (one *positif* and two two-manual instruments) and a wide variety of percussion instruments.

Before the disaffiliation of the music schools in 1967 the U of Montreal granted diplomas and external-examination certificates (including lauréats, baccalauréats, licences for theory, masters for performance, and doctorates) to the students at its affiliated schools. This system, established before the founding of the university's own Faculty of Music in 1950, continued afterwards. Under it Armand Pellerin, a student at the Institut Nazareth, in 1921 received the first B MUS, and Eugène *Lapierre in 1930 received the first D MUS. Musicians who followed Lapierre's example included Charles *Goulet in 1937, Leslie *Bell in 1946, Félix-R. *Bertrand in 1948, and G. Roy *Fenwick in 1950. One of the first B MUS graduates after the founding of the faculty was Jean-Marie Cloutier in 1953. Among subsequent graduates were Luce Beaudet-Léonard, José *Evangelista, Marthe Forget, Albert *Grenier, Marcelle Guertin, Louise *Laplante, Michel *Longtin, Denis *Lorrain, Lyse *Richer-Lortie, Pierre *Trochu, and Pauline *Vaillancourt. Among D MUS and PH D graduates in the new era have been Louise André, Joseph Berljawsky, Georgette Canuel-Letarte, Alfred *Garson, Louise Hirbour-Paquette, Hortense Morissette, Gaston Ouellet, and William Tortolano. Honorary degrees (D MUS) have been awarded to Wilfrid *Pelletier (1936), Louisa *Paquin (1937), Rosario *Bourdon (1944), Claude *Champagne (1946), and Paul *Doyon (1957).

Several members of the U of Montreal Faculty of Music were closely involved in the founding of the *SMCQ and *CAUSM. The faculty became affiliated to the latter and to the Student Composer's Symposium. It has been represented frequently at international conferences, notably at the meetings of ISME.

The publications of U of Montreal Press (founded 1962) include Marie-Thérèse *Paquin's translation of Italian opera librettos and some Lieder texts, as well as *Essai de stylistique comparée: les variations de William Byrd et John Tomkins* (2 vols, 1979), by Élisabeth Morin. The need to expand facilities led in 1980 to the faculty's acquisition of the École Vincent-d'Indy and the *Salle Claude-Champagne.

See also Archives.

BIBLIOGRAPHY

Léonard, Luce and Robert. 'La faculté de musique de l'université de Montréal à l'heure de la contestation,' *VM*, 12, Jun 1969

Richer-Lortie, Lyse. 'Muscadet ou le traitement électronique de la documentation concernant la musique au Canada,' *CMB*, 8, Spring–Summer 1974

Manny, Gilles, 'Esquisse d'un portrait de la faculté de musique de l'université de Montréal,' *L'Interdit*, 260, Nov–Dec 1977

Nattiez, Jean-Jacques. 'Le groupe de recherches en sémiologie musicale de la faculté de musique,' ibid

ADV (AP)

University of New Brunswick. Founded in 1785 in Fredericton as the Academy of Arts and Science. It became the College of New Brunswick in 1800 (enrolment restricted to Anglicans) and King's College in 1828, the same year that it granted its first degrees. In 1854 King's College offered the first engineering course taught at a Canadian university. King's College became the non-denominational U of New Brunswick in 1859. A second campus was established in 1964 in Saint John. Graduate studies have been offered in several disciplines, but not in music.

Although music is mainly an extracurricular activity at the U of New Brunswick, Arthur Trythall was appointed music director in 1953, to organize amateur choral and instrumental groups. Douglas Start succeeded Trythall in 1961. With Start's retirement in 1978 the post was terminated. In 1962, however, the university established a musician-in-residence program. Paul *Helmer was pianist-in-residence 1962–4. In 1964 the *Duo Pach (Joseph Pach, violin, and his wife, Arlene Nimmons Pach, piano) was appointed resident musicians. The Pachs were joined in 1970 by Andrew Benac (violin), James Pataki (viola), and Ifan *Williams (cello), who formed (with Pach) the *Brunswick String Quartet. In 1973 Paul Campbell replaced Benac and Richard Naill replaced Williams. Both the duo and the quartet have given regular recitals on campus, and Arlene Nimmons Pach, assisted by the other musicians, established a non-credit course in music appreciation.

Concert series by visiting performers have been presented by the university's Creative Arts Committee. A feature of each concert has been an open lecture about the music to be performed. In 1966 the Duo Pach established the annual summer *University of New Brunswick Chamber Music and Jazz Festival. In 1976 the extensive library of David *Thomson's Carriden Choir was presented to the Saint John campus library.

See also College songs. (JCm, PMW)

University of New Brunswick Chamber Music and Jazz Festival. Annual festival of concerts and workshops, organized in 1966 by Arlene Nimmons Pach. The first festival lasted 3 days in July and the tenth lasted 10 days in June, at Memorial Hall (on campus), the Fredericton Playhouse and Christ Church Cathedral. At the first four festivals R. Murray *Schafer served as host, and the *Toronto Woodwind Quintet (in 1966), the Aeolian String Quartet (in 1967), and the mezzo-soprano Phyllis *Mailing (in 1968) were among the featured performers. Jazz was introduced in 1969 by Phil *Nimmons and has remained an integral part of the festival; among others who have taken part are Ed *Bickert, Moe *Koffman, Kathryn *Moses, Nimmons himself (annually), and Oscar *Peterson (who premiered the orchestral version of his *Canadiana Suite* there with Nimmons' band in 1970). Chamber musicians have included Nicholas *Fiore, Erica *Goodman, the English classical guitarist John Mills, and the violinist Mischa Mischakoff (remembered as Toscanini's concertmaster). The *Lyric Arts Trio performed in 1977, and the U of New Brunswick resident groups the *Duo Pach and the *Brunswick String Quartet have been mainstays.

BIBLIOGRAPHY

Hamilton, Andrew, and Creech, Gwenlyn. 'Where nothing happened they made music thrive,' *Music Magazine*, Mar–Apr 1978

MM, PW

University of Ottawa / Université d'Ottawa. Bilingual institution founded in 1848 as the Roman Catholic College of Bytown by the Oblate Fathers of Mary Immaculate. It was renamed the College of Ottawa in 1861 and the U of Ottawa in 1866. Restructured and made non-denominational in 1965, it was divided into 14 faculties offering a wide range of undergraduate and graduate degrees.

A School of Music and Elocution was established in 1931 by Father Conrad *Latour. Latour was succeeded by Father Jules *Martel, who directed the school 1939–65 and conducted the university's Schola cantorum 1939–43. Teachers at that time included Roger *Filiatrault and Hélène *Landry. During the 1930s, 1940s, and 1950s instruction was offered in piano, organ, and strings, but most notably in church music.

In 1959 music became the responsibility of the Faculty of Arts, and in 1969, within the faculty, a formal Music Dept was established under François *Bernier. Luther Dittmer succeeded Bernier as chairman in 1976, and Keith *MacMillan succeeded Dittmer in 1977. Among the teaching staff have been Gerald *Bales, Yves Chartier, Steven

*Gellman, Frederick *Karam, and Jean-Paul *Sévilla. Many *NACO players have provided instrumental instruction. During the 1970s the department underwent considerable expansion, necessitating a move to new quarters – the Pavillon Calixa-Lavallée – in 1974. Student enrolment, 90 in 1970, had increased to 200 by 1978. In 1979–80 there were 16 full-time and 54 part-time teachers, and degrees offered were a B MUS in composition, education, musicology, theory or performance and a BA with specialization (four years) or concentration (three years) in music. Auditoriums included the university chapel and the Odeon Theatre.

The department has sponsored a noon-time recital series, special events – a 'Festival Olivier Messiaen' (including a lecture by Messiaen) in 1970 and a 'Panorame de la musique française' in 1972 – and numerous seminars on contemporary music, etc. Performing groups in 1979–80 included the University Choir / Chorale universitaire (large) and the Chorale Calixa-Lavallée (chamber), both under Richard Ducas; a woodwind ensemble and a brass choir under Robert Oades; and training and string orchestras.

The U of Ottawa has awarded honorary degrees to Sir Ernest *MacMillan (LLD 1959), Wilfrid *Pelletier (D MUS 1966), Lèopold *Simoneau (D MUS 1969), John *Weinzweig (D MUS 1969), Mario *Bernardi (D MUS 1974), and Jules Martel (D MUS 1974). During World Music Week in 1975 it conferred the honorary D MUS on four musicians – Harry *Somers, Jean *Vallerand, Yehudi Menuhin, and Trân Van Khê. *Portrait imaginé*, which the university commissioned from the Spanish composer Luis de Pablo, at the time a guest teacher there, was premiered during the week, under the direction of Françoys Bernier.

BIBLIOGRAPHY

Meredith, Joan. 'University program studies contemporary composers' work,' *CanComp*, 61, Jun 1971 JPG

University of Prince Edward Island, Charlottetown. Non-denominational university established in 1969 by the amalgamation of Prince of Wales College, founded in 1834, and St Dunstan's U, founded in 1855. Bachelor degrees were offered in arts, science, business administration, education, and music. There was no graduate department (and in 1980 that remained the case). Music had been taught in both merging colleges. Thomas Hahn, the first chairman of the new university's Dept of Music, also served 1969–70 as conductor of the PEI SO. Hahn was succeeded in both positions by Alan *Reesor in 1970. Peter Ellis (concertmaster of the PEI SO 1968–77 and a member of the Faculty Trio with the cellist Hubert Tersteeg and the pianist Frances Gray) succeeded Reesor as chairman in 1976. Reesor returned as acting chairman 1978–80. In the 1979–80 academic year there were six full-time and three part-time faculty members. One of the former, Carl B. Mathis, who became the conductor of the University Chorus and the Chamber Chorus in 1972, was chairman of the *Prince Edward Island Council for the Arts in 1974. Hilary Apelstadt began conducting the University Chorus in 1977. William A. Bartlett (succeeded by Marc Apelstadt) was responsible for the university band.

Degrees offered in 1980 were a B MUS in music education (initiated in 1973) and a BA with a major in music. The department's first graduates (1972) were Allan MacLean, Faye Rogerson, Gerard Rutten, and Frederick Shepherd. In the 1978–9 academic year, 26 students were working towards the B MUS degree. The university has a concert hall equipped with modern recording facilities. The department has sponsored an annual series of recitals and concerts by students, faculty members, and guests, and the university's performing ensembles have appeared with the Prince Edward Island SO. The Chamber Chorus has received grants from the *Canada Council to commission works by Keith *Bissell and Harry *Freedman. Through its concerts and its traditional connection with the Prince Edward Island SO, the Dept of Music has established a close relationship with the musical public of Charlottetown. (WB)

University of Quebec† / Université du Québec. Network of higher education and research establishments, created by an act of the Quebec National Assembly 18 Dec 1968. It includes four constituent universities: Montreal, Trois-Rivières (each with a Module de musique), Chicoutimi, and Rimouski. The U du Québec is a self-governing public body administered by a board of directors, as are its component members. The traditional faculties have been replaced by a two-tier structure: departments that include the teachers and the various courses, and modules designed for the students. Under the authority of a dean, the modules are grouped according to field of study, discipline, or objective. Programs are offered at the levels of bachelor, master, and doctor in all the major fields of study except medicine and in some quite new areas. More than half the students are adults taking advanced, evening, or retraining courses.

1 Université du Québec à Montréal
2 Université du Québec à Trois-Rivières

1 UNIVERSITÉ DU QUÉBEC À MONTRÉAL (UQAM). University which serves metropolitan Montreal and defines itself as 'public, urban and "québécoise".' Its originality lies chiefly in its programs in ecology, communications, jurisprudence, urban studies, and sexology. It opened in 1969 in buildings that had housed the Collège Ste-Marie and the École normale Jacques-Cartier. A new campus in the heart of the city was inaugurated in 1979. In 1979–80 UQAM had about 17,500 full- or part-time students and some 1400 teachers in its 16 buildings.

UQAM had a service contract 1969–76 with the *École normale de musique; in 1976 the latter was integrated as the Module de musique and moved into a part of the third floor of the Palais du Commerce on Berri St. In 1978–9 144 students were enrolled. Sister Marcelle *Corneille set up the module and directed it until 1978, introducing many up-to-date teaching methods. Hélène Paul succeeded her as head of the Module de musique in 1978. In 1979 Corneille became director of the regroupement musique (music planning). Those preceding her in the latter post were Louis Cyr 1976–8 and Jean-Marc Tousignant 1978–9.

A baccalauréat with specialization in music education was granted, along with an official teaching certificate, 1969–78. The title of the degree was changed to baccalauréat with specialization in music (B SP MUS) in 1978, though the program remained the same. The B MUS, initiated in 1969, offered four options: performance, musical education, theory, and musicology; a fifth, music therapy for schools, was introduced in 1975. Among the teachers have been France *Dion (voice), Jacques *Hétu (composition), Lucienne *L'Heureux-Arel (organ), Lorraine Prieur-Deschamps (piano), and Pierre *Rolland (oboe, ensemble music).

A laboratory of 10 electric pianos was installed for a group keyboard introductory course under Yolande Leduc. Pierre *Leduc was engaged to teach keyboard harmony. The library in 1980 contained about 4000 books and scores, the record library close to 3000 discs. The Concerts Musiquam have provided public performance opportunities for the Module de musique students.

The Petit Ensemble vocal of the UQAM Module de musique, a 30-to-40-voice mixed choir recruited from among the students, succeeded the Ensemble vocal of the École normale de musique. Formed and directed by Miklos Takacs, it made its debut in 1973 and has performed regularly on the CBC program 'A cappella.' In 1974 the ensemble gave eight concerts in Poland on a cultural exchange with the U of Lublin Folk Dance Ensemble. In June 1975 it placed first in the national finals of the *Canadian Music Competitions and made the LP *Suavi Cantu* (MS-11403-11404). In 1976 it performed in the BBC radio competition 'Let the Peoples Sing'. In 1977 Takacs established a second choral group, the UQAM Choir, made up of about 40 voices and open to the entire university.

A preparatory music school was sanctioned 26 Jun 1978 by UQAM's board of directors. It originated in 1976, under the direction of Sister Marcelle Corneille, with the conservatory operations of the École normale de musique and was designed to offer a graded pre-college, pre-university program of theoretical and practical courses, with examinations and diplomas. Certificates of equivalence were initiated for successfully completed refresher courses at college level. Classes at the preparatory school were designed to accommodate both young and adult students, and teachers and trainees alike were intended to evaluate the effectuality of the program through sustained observation. Among the teaching methods encouraged by the school and advocated by the Module de musique are Corneloup, *Dalcroze, *Kodály, *Martenot, Médau, and *Orff. For the 1978–9 school year the UQAM preparatory music school had an enrolment of 278 students.

2 UNIVERSITÉ DU QUÉBEC À TROIS-RIVIÈRES (UQATR). Founded in 1969 in the heart of the Bois-Francs and the Mauricie region, and deeply rooted in the community, this university's enrolment had reached some 9000 by the 1978–9 academic year. In addition to its 15 departments, UQATR set up a leisure study centre offering a program in recreational science unique in Quebec universities. It also initiated a summer course in French for Canadian and US English-speaking students.

The music section was opened in 1969 as part of the department of plastic arts and modern languages. Jean *Chatillon served 1969–74 as its first head and was succeeded by Lorraine Casaubon. Jacques Larocque was appointed director of the Module de musique in 1971. The module was located 1971–4 in the Antonio-Thompson building and later moved to the Grand Séminaire (Michel-Sarrazin building), where a concert hall was set up in 1979–80. The available music degrees are B MUS (instrumental performance; composition; popular music) and B ENS MUS (baccalaureat in music teaching).

A co-operative arrangement has been made with the Institute de recherche Pantonal of Montreal for the teaching of harmony, counterpoint, and rhythm. Some 100 students attended the Module de musique in the 1979–80 school year, under Lorraine Casaubon (solfège, ear training), Jean Chatillon (theory), Marie *Daveluy (voice), Michel *Dussault (piano), Lise Gauthier (harmony), Jacques Larocque (saxophone), and Marcel Thompson (teaching methods).

The UQATR has published some of its music teachers' instructional material, including theory texts and about 200 instrumental and vocal compositions by Chatillon; books on the *Pantonal system by Lise Gauthier (in collaboration with Michel *Perrault); and *Initiation à la musique pour ensembles de flûte à bec et petites percussions*, by Marcel Thompson. Through the initiative of Jean Chatillon UQATR produced a series of 12 records entitled *Musique québécoise 'nos compositeurs'* (1973–4). Two of these LPs were released on the L'Oiseau-Coeur label in 1979 (see Marie Daveluy and Michel Dussault).

In the 1971–2 season, Marie Daveluy initiated Musique vivante, a concert series by students and student groups, eg, the Jazz Ensemble, led 1971–9 by René Béchard (succeeded by Gaston Rochon); the Ensemble de musique ancienne, founded in 1975 and conducted by Gilles Plante; a 20-voice choir conducted 1971–9 by Thérèse Lupien (succeeded by Lise Gauthier); two saxophone quartets begun in 1971 by Jacques Larocque; a guitar quartet established in 1977 by Marcel Benoît; and a 40-piece concert band, drawn from music students at UQATR, the Cons de Trois-Rivières, the Trois-Rivières Cegep, and the city and area of Trois-Rivières. The band was conducted 1977–9 by Marcel Thompson. Daniel Swift succeeded him. ST

University of Regina. Non-denominational university growing out of Regina College, which was founded in 1911 along with the Regina Cons of Music (later the *Cons of Music, U of Regina). A constituent college of the *U of Saskatchewan in 1934, it was renamed the U of Saskatchewan, Regina Campus, in 1961. In 1974 it gained autonomy as the U of Regina. In 1980 it offered a variety of undergraduate and graduate programs in the arts and sciences.

Regina College operated 1934–61 as a junior college, with the conservatory as its music school. A B MUS program, begun in 1964, antedated the 1968 inception of the Music Dept. Howard *Leyton-Brown served 1964–8 as head of the B MUS program. H. Bruce Lobaugh (musicologist, composer, b Toledo, O, 19 Feb 1930) joined the music staff in 1966 and served 1968–74 as chairman. Thomas *Schudel succeeded Lobaugh in 1974, and J.R. Raum succeeded Schudel in 1978. In 1978–9 degrees offered were B MUS (performance; music history; composition), B MUS ED, BA (major, honours in music history) and M MUS (performance; composition; conducting), and the department had 21 teachers (13 full-time and 8 part-time) and 97 students (80 undergraduate and 17 graduate).

Thomas Schudel has given classes at the department's electronic music studio. Jan van der Gucht, head of the voice department 1961–73, directed the Conservatory Choir and was in wide demand as an adjudicator. Philip May joined the voice department in 1976. For students of opera, workshop classes have been available. Two full operas have been presented annually in conjunction with the *Regina SO (see also Regina Cons Opera). Also in conjunction with the orchestra, the department has presented an annual series of seven chamber concerts in which staff members and noted guests have performed. The university's ensembles – a concert choir, concert band, jazz ensemble, chamber orchestra, chamber singers, collegium musicum, and opera ensemble – have performed regularly in the 500-seat Convocation Hall and the 285-seat Quance Theatre. (AC, PMW)

University of Saskatchewan. Non-denominational graduate and undergraduate institution founded in Saskatoon in 1907. It awarded its first degrees in 1912. Its Regina campus became the autonomous *U of Regina in 1974. Founded in 1931, the Music Dept (the first in western Canada) became the College of Music in 1936. Reconstituted as the Dept of Music in 1952, it enrolled its first graduate student (for the M ED in music) in 1962. Revised B MUS and B MUS ED programs were inaugurated in 1969. In 1975 the department occupied new quarters.

The music program has been directed by Arthur *Collingwood, dean 1931–47; J.D. Macrae, chairman 1947–51; Murray *Adaskin, head 1952–66; and David L. *Kaplan, appointed head in 1966. Adaskin was composer-in-residence 1966–72.

Marjorie Wilson (B MUS 1934) was the department's first graduate; others in the 1930s were Margaret Pippin and Reginald McFarland, who became a member of the faculty. The university, through Collingwood, was involved in the formation of the *WBM, and Lavinia Elsley Collard received the first AMS diploma. Other graduates have included Norman Burgess, dean of the *Mount Royal College Cons, Calgary, Paul *Pedersen, and Glenn Thamer, consultant in fine arts, province of Alberta. Jean *Papineau-Couture received an hon LLD in 1967, as did Lyell *Gustin in 1969.

In 1978–9 there were 155 students (150 undergraduate and 5 graduate) and 27 teachers (12 full-time and 15 part-time). That year the degrees offered were B MUS (theory; composition; history; performance; music education), BA (honours), B ED (elementary; secondary), M ED (music education: general, choral, conducting, applied), and MA (theory; composition; history).

Among the faculty members in 1978–9 were Edward *Bisha and Robert Klose (who had been members of the *Amati String Quartet and, with the pianist Robin *Harrison, had formed the *Canadian Arts Trio), the music educator Isabelle *Mills (also conductor of the university's Quance Chorus), the orchestra conductor Dwaine Nelson, the choir conductor Robert Solem (director of the Greystone Singers), and the teacher of electronic music courses Richard Wedgewood.

In addition to summer sessions, begun in 1960, the department has offered instrumental extension courses and has published an Extension Bulletin in music.

In 1959, to mark the 50th anniversary of the province's decision to locate the U of Saskatchewan at Saskatoon, Adaskin organized a festival offering performances of 80 works, from solo compositions to pieces for large orchestra, half of them composed during the 20th century, 28 of them directly contemporary and being heard in their world, North American, or Canadian premieres, and 10 of them commissioned for the festival. He engaged 21 US and Canadian musicians to perform and teach and set up a related six-week course for 80 young instrumental players. The large budget was met through support from Saskatoon musical and service organizations, private donations, and other outside sources, including the *Canada Council. While the festival was too costly to repeat annually in the university context, it probably was the first event of its kind and scope to be held at a Canadian university, and its influence was inestimable.

The department has been the recipient of the Carnegie (in the 1950s) and Andrusyshen collections of recordings and of the Saskatoon Collection of Early Manuscripts. Its quartet of Amati string instruments was purchased from Stephen Kolbinson in 1959 (see Instrument collections).

The following concert series have been presented: Sunday Evening Recital Series (9 yearly), Faculty Series (12 yearly), Guest Series (two to four guest lecturers), Wednesday Noon Student Series (26 recitals), and Choral/Instrumental Groups Series (6 yearly). At one time the Sunday Evening Recitals were popular with the community, but the audience has been composed increasingly of university members. Among its intramural performing groups have been the University Chorus, the Concert Band, and various brass, woodwind, string, and recorder ensembles. See also Music education research.

BIBLIOGRAPHY

Kasemets, Udo. 'The Saskatoon summer festival of music, 1959,' *CMJ*, vol 4, Autumn 1959

'U of Saskatchewan names Adaskin to new post,' *CanComp*, 13, Dec 1966

Adaskin, Murray. 'University of Saskatchewan to sponsor exhibition-concerts,' ibid (AC, PMW)

University of Toronto. Founded by royal charter at York (Toronto), Upper Canada, in 1827 as the Church of England (Anglican) King's College. It granted its first degree in 1844 and was secularized and renamed the U of Toronto in 1850. Three denominational Toronto universities – Victoria (originally at Cobourg, Ont), St Michael's, and Trinity – entered into federation with it at the turn of the century. In 1980 the U of Toronto offered a complete range of undergraduate and graduate studies, had the largest library in Canada, and was the country's leading centre of graduate education and research.

King's College opened for instruction in 1843. During the following year the university enacted statutes by which a professorship in music and the B MUS and D MUS degrees were established. In 1846 the B MUS degree, the first to be granted in Canada, was earned by James Paton *Clarke. The claim in various reference books that Clarke was made music instructor is not confirmed by the university's archives. The professorship was not implemented. It may be assumed, however, that Clarke, a portégé of John *McCaul, the music-loving first president of King's College, was recommended as a private instructor to interested students. It appears also that the university intended to bestow an honorary D MUS on Clarke in 1856 but that this was cancelled at a late moment.

It was not until the early 1890s that the university, following similar action taken by the *U of Trinity College during the previous decade, established syllabi and administered examinations leading to the B MUS and D MUS degrees. The holder of the bachelor degree was permitted, after an interval of three years, to submit an extensive composition and pass further examinations in order to obtain a D MUS. Among the first graduates were Clarence *Lucas (B MUS 1893) and C.L.M. *Harris (D MUS 1898).

The university did not provide instruction apart from occasional lectures. Instead, examination candidates could take lessons at one of the recently established conservatories. The procedure was recognized formally in a number of affiliations with the university: the *Toronto College of Music in 1890, the *TCM in 1896, and the Hamilton Cons (*RHCM) in 1906. The university's examiners for music degrees in the 1890s were F(rederick?) Archer, W.E. *Fairclough, A.E. *Fisher, and S.P. *Warren. Those who served in the early 1900s were J. Humfrey *Anger, Albert *Ham, C.L.M. Harris, and H.A. Wheeldon; Healey *Willan was appointed as a lecturer and examiner in 1914.

In 1901 the U of Toronto began sending representatives to communities in Ontario and the western provinces to administer practical and theoretical examinations leading to the licentiate diploma. More candidates presented themselves for the diplomas than for degrees – 471 students were examined in 1904–5, and of those, 390 obtained diplomas; but in the five school years 1900–5 only seven degrees were awarded – and a university commission in 1906 blamed the conservatories for making little effort to train students for degrees while exploiting their affiliation for advertising

A student ensemble performing in Walter Hall, Edward Johnson Building, University of Toronto

purposes. The report expressed the hope that the university eventually would set up its own school of music.

This hope was realized when the Faculty of Music was created in 1918. A.S. *Vogt, the principal of the TCM, served 1918–26 as the faculty's first dean; Herbert A. *Fricker, Albert Ham, Ferdinand Albert Mouré (b London 1870, d Toronto 1945), and Healey Willan were lecturers. (Mouré was the university's bursar 1904–38 and organist 1918–30.) In its early years the faculty offered a series of 18 lectures annually in association with its B MUS degree. By 1921 the university had assumed complete responsibility for the TCM (which took over the issuing of diplomas), and in 1924 it sanctioned the purchase of the *Canadian Academy of Music, thus strengthening the TCM's teaching staff and incorporating the province's leading music schools. The Faculty of Music staff remained small however; Healey Willan and Leo *Smith were the only professors in the late 1930s and early 1940s.

Ernest *MacMillan, principal of the TCM 1926–42, was also dean of the Faculty of Music 1927–52. As head of both institutions he promoted closer ties and co-ordinated their lecture series.

The BA (honours music) was established in 1936 as a degree for musicians desiring advanced musical skills in combination with a liberal arts education, or for prospective teachers. In order to provide a more extensive and specialized training for teachers, a three-year B MUS in School Music was introduced in 1946 and the previous B MUS program became known as 'general music.' Arnold *Walter, at the time implementing several recommendations of the 1937 Hutcheson Report (RCMT), was involved also, with Robert *Rosevear, Leslie *Bell, and Richard *Johnston, in the development of the new degree in school music (renamed music education in 1953). The first 19 school music graduates were awarded degrees in 1949. Rosevear and Johnston were faculty members prominent in this program, which has had a far-reaching influence on the development of music in the public (elementary and secondary) schools and ultimately on the expansion of music education courses (the training of school music teachers) in other Canadian universities.

In the years immediately following World War II there was a sense of excitement associated with these departures in professional training, stimulated to a great extent by the return of the war veterans who came in considerable numbers and who, having had to postpone their studies, brought a useful maturity to them. The growth and complexity of such developments within the Faculty of Music and the RCMT's senior division necessitated a major reorganization in 1952. At that time music was restructured into two operational units under the overall title *RCMT: the Faculty of Music, which offered courses leading to degrees and assumed responsibility for preparing students for the diplomas formerly given by the Senior School of the RCMT, and the School of Music, which continued the conservatory programs in performance, teaching, and examining and retained the administration of the *Royal Cons Opera School. Arnold Walter became director of the faculty and Ettore *Mazzoleni principal of the School of Music. Boyd *Neel was appointed dean of the 'umbrella' RCMT in 1953 and retained that position until 1970.

Arnold Walter, in the years (1952–68) of his directorship of the Faculty of Music, presided over an unprecedented expansion involving a number of academic changes. The General Music program was phased out as an extramural degree 1951–5. In its place, composition and the history and literature of music were introduced in the 1953–4 school year as specialized areas of study in the B MUS program. In 1954 M MUS programs in composition, musicology, and music education were initiated. By 1963 all B MUS programs had been extended to four years, and in 1965 a PH D program in musicology and a four-year degree program in performance were introduced. The appointment in 1954 of Harvey Olnick (MA Columbia) to establish the first musicology program in a Canadian university led to an increasing importance of this field of study and to the subsequent development of the U of Toronto music library. Jean Lavender, head librarian for the faculty 1947–73, was succeeded by Kathleen McMorrow.

The space and facilities in the College Street complex could not accommodate the expansion of programs in the 1950s (see RCMT), and new premises were erected to house the faculty; the Edward *Johnson Building, named for the famous Canadian tenor, administrator, and chairman of the board of the RCMT in the 1950s, was occupied in 1962.

In 1968 the faculty was organized into four departments, under Gustav *Ciamaga (composition), Harvey Olnick (history and literature), Robert Rosevear (music education), and Ezra *Schabas (performance). The Royal Cons Opera school became a department of the faculty in 1969 and in the following year offered a two-year postgraduate diploma in operatic performance.

After Walter's retirement in 1968, Boyd Neel continued until 1970 as dean of the RCMT (as that name had been re-applied in the 1952 restructuring) and assumed the duties of director of the Faculty of Music. With Neel's retirement in 1970 (in fact 1971, but he was on leave during his final year, and John *Beckwith was acting dean), nomenclature changed again to accommodate the first major restructuring of the faculty-school-conservatory relationship since 1952.

The concept of an RCMT administrative umbrella shading an academic faculty and a practical school (conservatory) seemed outworn in view of the phenomenal independent developments of that faculty and that school. Therefore the name Royal Conservatory of Music, Toronto was restored to the erstwhile School of Music – to which it belonged historically. The title dean replaced the title director in connoting the head of the Faculty of Music. The new dean of the faculty (John Beckwith, who was to serve 1970–7) undertook duties as the chief executive responsible for academic policies in music throughout the university. And faculty and conservatory thenceforth pursued related but separate courses within the university.

During the 1970s there were a marked increase in graduate enrolment and an emerging interest in contemporary music, ethnomusicology, and the performance practices of early music. Gustav Ciamaga succeeded Beckwith as acting dean in 1977 and became dean in 1978.

The number of B MUS graduates to 1945 was 107. The number of B MUS graduates for the period 1946–68 was 445, of which 324 were in music education. There were 95 BA (honour music) graduates for the period 1941–68. The following list itemizes the number of degrees according to field of specialization for the period 1969–78: music education 326, performance 199, music history and literature 47, and composition 46. In 1956 John *Fenwick was the first recipient of a master's degree.

In 1978–9 the faculty offered the following: Diploma in Operatic Performance, Licentiate Diploma, Artist Diploma, B MUS (music education; composition; history; performance), MA (musicology) M MUS (composition; music education; performance and literature), PH D (musicology), and D MUS (composition). In the same academic year the Faculty of Music consisted of 120 teachers (44 full-time and 76 part-time) and 450 students (400 undergraduate and 50 graduate).

Among members of the faculty in 1978–9 were John Beckwith, Melvin *Berman, Ronald Chandler, Robert Falck, Lorand *Fenyves, Andrew *Hughes, Talivaldis *Kenins, Lothar *Klein, Mieczyslaw *Kolinski, Rika *Maniates, Oskar *Morawetz, Carl *Morey, Harvey Olnick, Vladimir *Orloff, Godfrey *Ridout, Robert Rosevear (emeritus), Ezra Schabas, and John *Weinzweig.

Recipients of honorary degrees have included J. Humfrey Anger (D MUS 1902), F.H. *Torrington (D MUS 1902), Sir Alexander Mackenzie (D MUS 1903), Albert Ham (D MUS 1906), A.S. Vogt (D MUS 1906), John MacKenzie Rogan (D MUS 1907), Sir Frederick Bridge (D MUS 1908), Healey Willan (D MUS 1920), Ferdinand Albert Mouré (D MUS 1922), H.A. Fricker (D MUS 1923), Luigi von *Kunits (D MUS 1926), Edward Johnson (D MUS 1934), W.H. *Hewlett (D MUS 1936), H.K. *Jordan (D MUS 1938), Alexander *MacMillan (D MUS 1943), Sir Thomas Beecham (D MUS 1956), Glenn *Gould (LLD 1964), Lois *Marshall (LLD 1965), Zoltán Kodály (D MUS 1966), Helmut *Kallmann (LLD 1971), Hugh *Le Caine (LLD 1973), Harry *Somers (LLD 1976), and Maureen *Forrester (D MUS 1977).

When it opened in 1962 the Edward Johnson Building, with its 12 classrooms, 40 practice studios, recital and rehearsal facilities, and well-stocked library and listening room, was one of the best such facilities in North America. Its library – the Edward Johnson Library – had grown by 1980 to the largest in Canada (in 1971: 50,000 books and scores, 39,000 LPs; in 1978: 95,000 books and scores, 50,000 LPs). Many of the books and scores came from such donors as Edward Johnson, Arnold Walter, and Herman *Geiger-Torel. The building's electronic studios, developed in the 1960s by Myron Schaeffer, were the second such to be installed in a North American music school. The 500-seat Walter Hall was designed for chamber and solo recitals as well as lectures and came to be recognized as one of Toronto's finest small auditoriums. A two-manual tracker-action *Casavant organ was installed there in the mid-1970s. The 850-seat MacMillan Theatre, inaugurated in 1964 with a performance of Britten's *Albert Herring*, was designed, also with considerable success, for the presentation of operas, guest productions, concerts, and recitals.

The numerous concert series, which have undergone frequent name changes, have included many in conjunction with the CBC as well as continuing guest series and others featuring faculty members, including artists-in-residence such as the *Canadian String Quartet, Anton *Kuerti, and the *Orford String Quartet. In addition to the many student solo recitals, Faculty of Music performing groups have included the U of Toronto SO, known until 1968 as the Royal Cons SO and conducted by Mazzoleni, later by Boyd Neel, and after the change of name by Victor *Feldbrill; the Concert Band under Robert Rosevear (later the Symphonic Wind Ensemble under Melvin Berman); the Concert Choir, under Charles Heffernan; the Opera Chorus; the University Singers; the Repertory Orchestra; and the Jazz Ensemble.

A number of musical activities at the university have taken place outside the Faculty of Music, presented by groups such as the Hart House Chorus (formerly *Hart House Glee Club), the U of Toronto Chorus, and the earlier U of Toronto SO (not to be confused with the faculty orchestra mentioned above) established by John Weinzweig in 1934, open to all U of Toronto students and staff, and independent of the TCM and the faculty. Its conductors included Hans Gruber, Lee *Hepner, Feldbrill, Elmer *Iseler, Keith Girard, Rosevear, and Tibor *Polgar. Many of the university's constituent colleges, schools, and faculties have produced musical entertainments, particularly annual revues or musicals, often with original scores.

In the 1960s, as the musical life of the university became increasingly centred around the Faculty of Music, the campus ensembles have been less prominent. Following Mouré in the university organist's post have been Healey Willan 1932–64, Charles *Peaker 1964–78, and Peaker's successor, John Tuttle. The rich tradition of music activities at *Hart House includes recitals of the Soldier's Tower carillon (in 1980 one of the 11 carillons in Canada). Other university concert locations in addition to those at Hart House and the Edward Johnson Building include Varsity Arena, Varsity Stadium, Convocation Hall, and smaller facilities in several colleges.

A music alumni association became active in 1950. It has provided scholarships, and in its early years it commissioned works by Harry Somers, John Beckwith, Healey Willan, Howard *Cable, and William *McCauley.

University of Toronto Press has published a number of books on Canadian music, including *Music in Canada* (1955), edited by Sir Ernest MacMillan; the **Canadian Music Journal* (1956–62); *A History of Music in Canada 1534–1914* by Helmut Kallmann (1960); *Aspects of Music in Canada* (1969), edited by Arnold Walter; *Discopaedia of the Violin* (1974), edited by James *Creighton; *Harry Somers* (1975), by Brian *Cherney; *Canadian Music: A Selected Checklist 1950–73 / La Musique canadienne: une liste selective 1950–73* (1976), compiled by Lynne Jarman; *Canadian Music of the Twentieth Century* (1980), by George *Proctor; and this *Encyclopedia of Music in Canada*.

For many years the U of Toronto Faculty of Music has been one of the leading schools of its kind in Canada. The musicians and scholars on its faculty are known for their compositions and publications, appearances on national radio and TV networks, and other professional activities. Many entries in *EMC* deal with the careers of its graduates, several of whom have received international recognition as performers and composers, or have become major figures in other areas of Canadian musical life, including universities and cultural organizations.

See also Archives; Carillon; College songs; Degrees; Electronic music; Ethnomusicology; Libraries; Music education research; Musicology.

BIBLIOGRAPHY

The University of Toronto and Its Colleges 1827–1906 (Toronto 1906)
University of Toronto. *Higher Education in Music*, Bulletin no. 2 for 1920–1 (Toronto)
Wallace, W. Stuart. *A History of the University of Toronto* (Toronto 1927)
Reed, T.A. ed. *A History of the University of Trinity College, Toronto, 1852–1952* (Toronto 1952)
Sissons, C.B. *A History of Victoria University* (Toronto 1952)
Payzant, Geoffrey. 'The Faculty of Music in the University of Toronto,' *Recorder*, vol 5, Jun 1963
'March is music month at Varsity,' *Varsity News*, vol 5, Feb 1964
'... and how is Sir Ernest?', 'The toast to the faculty,' *Varsity Graduate*, Summer 1964
U of Toronto Music Alumni Assn. *Directory of Degree Graduates* (Toronto 1964)
Beckwith, John. 'University of Toronto a pioneer in music education,' *MSc*, 258, Mar–Apr 1971
Pegler, Kenneth W. *Opera and the University of Toronto 1946–1971* (Toronto 1971)
Donskov, Lesa and Graves, Donald. 'A history of the Royal Conservatory of Music and the Faculty of Music, University of Toronto 1886–1962,' unpubl paper, Centre for Higher Education, OISE [1972]
Davey, Earle. 'The development of undergraduate music curricula at the University of Toronto, 1918–68,' unpubl MA thesis, U of Toronto 1977
U of Toronto Faculty of Music *Newsletter*, Nov 1970–Summer 1974
News from the Faculty of Music, U of Toronto, 3–4 issues annually (Autumn 1974–) (JPG)

University of Trinity College. Church of England university founded in Toronto in 1851 by the first bishop of Toronto, John Strachan, after King's College, precursor of the *U of Toronto, became secular in 1850. In 1904 'Trinity' was federated with the U of Toronto. While maintaining Anglican ties, Trinity does not restrict enrolment or employment to Anglicans.

On 28 Apr 1853 Trinity appointed George William *Strathy Professor of Music. On 1 Jun 1853 it awarded him the second B MUS granted in Canada (see U of Toronto). In 1858 it awarded him a D MUS. Although Strathy was listed in the university's calendars, in fact his contributions seem to have been limited to occasional lectures. By 1878–9 he had formed a class in theory.

In 1881 *Rouge et Noir*, the student magazine, complained about the neglect of music at Trinity. Later that year, after a candidate (apparently Davenport *Kerrison) applied to be examined, Trinity formally created a Faculty of Music to administer examinations but still offered no course of studies. B MUS candidates had to provide evidence of five years of musical study, to compose 'a song or anthem in four parts, and perform the same publicly,' and to pass an examination in theory. The doctorate required evidence of eight years of study along with the composition and performance of a partsong or anthem in six or eight parts with orchestral accompaniment. Upon refusing to examine the first candidate, Strathy was replaced as examiner in 1882 by the Rev R.F. Dale. In 1883 Frédéric Louis Ritter of Vassar College, New York, was named examiner.

Requirements were changed in 1883 so that B MUS candidates had to pass three examinations at one-year intervals, in harmony, counterpoint, history of music, form in composition, and the use of instruments, and had to compose an exercise in at least four parts with accompaniment. No arts subjects were required. Three years after obtaining a B MUS a student could achieve a D MUS. Women were allowed to take the B MUS examination and received a certificate of passing, but only in 1885 were they offered degrees. Helen Emma Gregory, later a judge, became the first female graduate of Trinity when she received a B MUS in 1886.

In 1885 London's *Musical Standard*, with information gleaned from a US journal, published Trinity's curriculum and examination papers. Practising musicians, deterred from pursuing music degrees in British universities because of their arts prerequisites, requested that Trinity hold music examinations in England. Since Trinity's royal charter of 1852 allowed it 'all such and like privileges as are enjoyed by the Universities of our United Kingdom of Great Britain and Ireland,' it felt entitled legally to decide, in 1885, in favour of simultaneous London and Toronto examinations. In the same year it rejected an application for affiliation from London's Trinity College, a music school. It appointed a former Trinity professor of mathematics, Edward K. Kendall, to serve as acting registrar in England and subsequently named as examiners for England and Canada Edward John Hopkins, William Henry Longhurst, and Edwin Matthew Lott, all prominent English church organists on whom Trinity conferred honorary doctorates in 1886.

In order to meet British standards, Trinity stiffened its matriculation requirements in 1886. Students had to produce certificates of character, 'satisfactory evidence of attainments' in general education, and certificates showing five years of musical study and practice.

The Faculty of Music's affiliation with the *TCM in 1889 exempted conservatory students from some of the faculty's examinations. In 1890 Trinity also held examinations in New York. By the end of the year the faculty had granted five honorary and nine in-course doctorates as well as one honorary and 86 in-course bachelor degrees, the majority to English candidates. Benjamin Agutter received an honorary doctorate in 1889 or 1890 when he replaced John Hopkins as examiner.

The intrusion of a Canadian university into Britain occasioned the publication of increasingly numerous complaints in British music journals. In 1890 35 prominent musicians, including Sir John Stainer of Oxford, submitted to Lord Knutsford, the colonial secretary, 'memorials' condemning Trinity's practice of granting in-absentia degrees in England. Their main argument was that Trinity was lowering standards by not requiring literary tests. It was felt that Trinity had overstepped its powers and could open the door to bogus degrees. Thomas Lea Southgate and Stainer headed a committee which organized criticism, in British journals and newspapers, of Trinity's London 'agency' and graduates. Trinity Provost C.W.E. Body's hurried trip to England failed to counter the criticism, and early in 1891 the university decided to discontinue the examinations in London and New York.

Longhurst and Lott continued as examiners, the latter becoming Professor of Music in 1891, replacing Strathy, with the responsibility of visiting Toronto annually to conduct examinations and give lectures. Other examiners were J. Humfrey *Anger, TCM lecturer (by 1893), and F.J. Karn (1894). In 1898 Edward *Fisher of the TCM was granted a doctorate and Albert *Ham, also of the TCM, was added to the examiner's roster. Trinity established a board of musical studies in 1900 to oversee the affairs of the faculty and to name examiners. In 1901 Ham and C.W. Pearce of Cambridge were examiners, and Ham taught voice culture in the Faculty of Arts. In 1902 Samuel Prowse *Warren replaced Pearce as examiner.

When Trinity became a federated college of the U of Toronto in 1904, thereby surrendering its degree-granting powers in all faculties except Divinity, its Faculty of Music came to an end after having granted 161 B MUS degrees (including one honorary) and 34 D MUS degrees (including six honorary).

After 1904 music at Trinity consisted of a periodically revivified Glee Club, music for church services, and student musicals such as *What, No Crumpets?* and *Saints Alive!* (1948, 1949), both composed by Keith *MacMillan.

BIBLIOGRAPHY
University of Trinity College. Calendars 1853–1903
University of Trinity College, Faculty of Music, Memorials Presented to Lord Knutsford, H.M. Secretary of State for the Colonies, with Appendices, &c (London 1890).
Reed, T.A., ed. *A History of the University of Trinity College, Toronto, 1852–1952* (Toronto 1952)
Watson, Andrew, ed. *Trinity 1852–1952* (Toronto 1952)
Harris, Robin S. *A History of Higher Education in Canada, 1663–1960* (Toronto 1976)
Trinity College Archives. Corporation Minutes 1853–1904; Faculty of Music records (including scrapbooks); Provost Body papers
Kallmann *History of Music in Canada* (HPl)

University of Victoria. Non-denominational university in Victoria, BC. It is the successor of Victoria College, affiliated 1903–62 first with McGill U, then with the U of British Columbia. After gaining its autonomy in 1963 as the U of Victoria it expanded rapidly to offer undergraduate and graduate programs in the arts and sciences.

Although it accepted its first students in 1966, the Dept of Music commenced officially in 1967. Prior to that date some music instruction had been offered by the Faculty of Education. The department moved into its own new building in 1978 and became the School of Music in 1979. The English musicologist Gerald Hendrie 1967–9, Phillip T. Young 1969–77, and Rudolf *Komorous, appointed in 1977, have been its chairmen. (Young, b Milton, Mass, 2 Mar 1926, and educated at Yale U, has played bassoon in the *Victoria SO, taught bassoon, conducted, carried out research in organology, and written articles on the history of woodwind instruments.)

Music degrees offered at the U of Victoria in 1979–80 were B MUS (general, composition and theory, history and literature, performance, education), MA (musicology), M MUS (performance, composition), and PH D (musicology). The first graduates (Spring, 1970) were Sheryl Borris and Merle Naduriak. Maureen *Forrester and Robin *Wood received honorary LLDs in 1978.

In 1978–9 there were 20 full-time and 24 part-time on the teaching staff. These included Frank *Churchley, Sydney *Humphreys, and Gordana *Lazarevich.

Performance, especially of contemporary music, has been emphasized at the U of Victoria. All undergraduate (160 in 1978–9) and most graduate (18 in 1978–9) students have taken individual tuition in an instrument or voice. About one-third of the Victoria SO players have been pupils of members of the department. The Pacific Wind Quintet, in residence 1978–9, consisted of William Benjamin (oboe), Richard Ely (french horn), Lanny Pollet (flute), Jesse Read (bassoon), and Ethan Sloane (clarinet), all members of the department. Performing groups and composers often have been brought in for week-long residences during which they have presented recitals and conducted workshops. Much of the research in the department has been performance-oriented: studies in French baroque performance, in 18th-century Italian comic opera, in organology, and in computer research.

In 1978 the department occupied a new building which provided 48 practice rooms and studios, a recital hall seating 200, and three electronic music studios containing highly sophisticated analog, digital, and hybrid sound-generating equipment including a computer-controlled digital synthesizer with terminal and Decwriter. Advanced mixed and recording facilities (with 2-, 4-, and 8-track tape machines) also were installed. The University Administrative Centre's 1200-seat concert hall, the McPherson Library's collection of scores, books, and recordings (one of the largest in Canada), and a growing collection of medieval, renaissance, and baroque replica instruments (some acquired after 1970 from the *Manitoba University Consort collection), and the organ, built by Georges Mayer of Alsace and donated by Joyce Clearihue, have helped enrich the department's musical life.

Regular public performances have included those in the staff recital series and the student noonhour concerts 'Tuesdaymusic' and 'Fridaymusic.' Student performing groups have included the University Orchestra, Chorus, Chamber Singers, Collegium Musicum, Sonic Lab (a new-music ensemble), and the U of Victoria Little Orchestra. U of Victoria students preparing for their B MUS degrees have been permitted to take solo performance tuition at the *Victoria Cons, which became affiliated with the university in 1968.

BIBLIOGRAPHY
Young, Phillip T. 'Making music is theme of University of Victoria's music training,' *MSc*, 261, Sep–Oct 1971
(TB, PMW)

University of Waterloo. Non-denominational university founded in 1957 at Waterloo, Ont, and incorporated in 1959. It came to be noted in particular for its schools of optometry and engineering.

Musical activities were introduced at first on an extracurricular basis by Paul Berg (b Hartford, Wis, 11 Oct 1907, d Kitchener, Ont, 14 Nov 1975) who, as director of cultural affairs for the university, established and coached choral and instrumental groups and organized art shows, theatrical performances, concerts by visiting performers, and several arts festivals. In 1965 he hired Alfred *Kunz to direct the choirs and ensembles, and these presented annual concerts.

Conrad Grebel College, a church-supported Mennonite residential and academic affiliated college established on the campus, began offering undergraduate courses in music history and theory in 1963, and the university's credit courses in music have been given there. Through cross-registration U of Waterloo students have been able, also, to avail themselves of courses offered by the Faculty of Music at *Wilfrid Laurier U. The new Conrad Grebel College building, opened in 1976, has provided music studios, practice rooms, and a library.

A general BA in music was offered by the Faculty of Arts for the first time in 1974, and an honour BA in music, in 1979. When a Music Dept was established within the faculty in 1977, Wilbur Maust was appointed chairman. The teaching staff comprised four full-time (Maust, Helen *Martens, who had been on staff at Conrad Grebel College since 1965, Leonard Enns, and Kenneth Hull) and five part-time teachers, giving courses in music history, theory, performance, and conducting, as well as a course on computers in music, taught by David Harrison. In addition, members of the Stratford Ensemble were enlisted to provide instrumental instruction.

Along with the facilities provided by the Conrad Grebel College, the university contains the Humanities Theatre (performance home of the *Kitchener-Waterloo SO until September 1980) and the Theatre of the Arts (in the Modern Languages Building). Performing ensembles have included the 35-voice Conrad Grebel College Choir under Leonard Enns; Choral Literature Choir (participation is part of a credit course); 40-piece Orchestra under William H. Janzen Jr; Menno Singers (a community choir sponsored by the university) under Abner Martin, succeeded by Jan *Overduin; 20-voice Chamber Choir under Wilbur Maust; Concert Band conducted by Alfred Kunz, succeeded by George Holmes; and Inter-Mennonite Children's Choir under Helen Martens. A University Choir was begun in 1980. The personnel for these extra-curricular groups has been drawn from both campus and community.
(JCm)

University of Western Ontario. Founded in 1878 as the Western University of London, a denominational school of the Church of England. In the early 1900s the London Cons and the Brantford Cons were affiliates. The university was made non-denominational in 1908 and renamed the U of Western Ontario in 1923. In the 1970s it offered a full range of undergraduate and graduate degree programs, had a well-developed part-time and continuing education faculty including a French-English Summer School at Trois-Pistoles, Que, and maintained affiliation with Huron, Brescia, and King's Colleges. In 1942 the *Western Ontario Cons of Music moved from downtown quarters to the university campus as an affiliated school under the direction of Harvey Robb.

Music at the university previously had consisted of the Sunday Nine O'clock Concerts, summer schools, occasional lectures on music appreciation, and student performing ensembles such as the Orpheus Society Glee Club under Robb, a string orchestra under Zoë Addy-Watson, and a band under Don *Wright. Having received money from the McIntosh estate, however, the university offered music for the first time as a credit subject in 1943. In 1945, with financial assistance from the A.E. Silverwood Foundation, the university established the Music Teachers' College to provide a level of professional training. Max *Pirani was principal 1945–7. As an affiliate of the university, the college offered a two-year diploma course in music pedagogy (MUS G PAED) designed primarily for private music teachers. After Ernest *White's short term, 1947–50, Harvey Robb was the college's principal 1950–7.

In 1956 the college was integrated within the university's Faculty of Arts and Science and offered a BA with music options. Among the teaching staff at this time was Alfred *Rosé, who originally had come to the conservatory to direct summer opera workshops in 1946. Clifford *Poole served 1957–9 as principal of both institutions, which were moved off campus to the A.E. Silverwood Building. In 1960 Clifford *von Kuster became principal of the college, the name of which was changed in 1961 to College of Music.

Major developments took place 1960–73 during Clifford von Kuster's term, and the college developed at an unprecedented rate. School music courses in vocal and instrumental techniques were introduced by Earle *Terry and Donald McKellar respectively; B MUS programs were offered in 1964 and M MUS programs in 1968, the year in which the first B MUS degrees were awarded. The college became the Faculty of Music in 1968 with von Kuster as dean, and the continuing increase in student enrolment required additional full-time faculty, expansion of library resources, and construction of a new Faculty of Music Building which was opened officially in 1972. In 1973, the faculty's departmental chairmen were Paul *Green (Music Education), Gordon *Greene (Music History), John McIntosh (Applied Music), and Gerhard *Wuensch (Theory and Composition), and Hugh *McLean became dean. McLean served in the position until 1980, when he was succeeded by Jack *Behrens.

Degrees offered in 1978–9 were the B MUS (honours: music education, history, performance, theory, and composition), BMA, BA (music), and BA (honours in music); graduate degrees include the M MUS in theory, music education, composition, literature, and performance and the MA in musicology. Honorary degrees have been awarded to Margaret Ferguson (1972), Maureen *Forrester (1974), Edward *Johnson (1929), Paul Henry Lang (1972), Guy *Lombardo (1971), Alfred Rosé (1975 posthumously), Robert *Rosevear (1979), Reginald *Stewart (1949), George Szell (1967), and Jon *Vickers (1972).

In 1978–9 the faculty, with 686 students (609 undergraduate and 77 graduate) and 100 teachers (51 full-time and 49 part-time), was the largest in any Canadian university. Among the teachers in 1978–9 were Ralph Aldrich, Kathryn Bailey, Terence *Bailey, Damiana Bratuz, Kenneth *Bray, Robert *Creech, Philip Downs, Paul Green, Deral Johnson, Clifford von Kuster, Yuri Mazurkevich, John McIntosh, Donald McKellar, George *Proctor, Alvin Reimer, Robert Riseling, Robert Skelton, Gerald *Stanick, and Ronald *Turini. Composers on the faculty included Jack Behrens, Peter Clements, Arsenio Giron, Alan *Heard, Peter *Koprowski, Jerome Summers, and Gerhard Wuensch. The cellist Tsuyoshi *Tsutsumi, for some years an artist-in-residence, became a founding member of *Quartet Canada, which in 1977 was appointed quartet-in-residence.

In 1980 the Faculty of Music's facilities in Talbot College and the adjoining Music Building included a 240-seat recital hall, Talbot Theatre, four organ studios (one, the Organ Recital Studio, with a three-manual *Casavant tracker-action organ), an electronic music studio, and a music library which by 1974 had acquired more than 100,000 items, including 38 letters of Gustav Mahler, obtained from Alfred Rosé, and a special collection, 'Opera 1751–1800,' purchased from Richard MacNutt Ltd. The faculty published a four-volume catalogue of the collection in 1980. Instruments of fine quality in the faculty's string bank were purchased with the assistance of a grant from the Richard and Jean Ivey Fund. Outside the faculty but still within the university precincts, the 2300-seat Alumni Hall and the auditoriums of Althouse and Elborn Colleges have been used for concerts.

Opera workshops were organized 1971–4 by Karin Pendle and after that time by Martin Chambers, and productions have included Menotti's *The Old Maid and the Thief*, John *Beckwith's **Night Blooming Cereus* (1971), Purcell's *Dido and Aeneas* (1972), and Pergolesi's *La Serva Padrona* (1975). Martin Chambers directed *The Magic Flute* in 1978 and Poulenc's *The Dialogues of the Carmelites* in 1979.

Before the founding of the faculty, the most important performing ensemble was the university choir under Alfred Rosé. After 1968, however, the choir was superseded by the faculty's choral ensembles, including the Faculty of Music Singers conducted by Deral Johnson, and instrumental ensembles developed: the symphony orchestra under Clifford *Evens, succeeded by Simon *Streatfeild, the Wind Ensemble under Jerome Summers, and the Symphonic Band under Donald McKellar.

Among special events sponsored by the faculty have been the biannual research symposia organized by the Music Education Dept and an annual New Music Colloquium by the Theory and Composition Dept. The faculty was host to the 13th World Congress of the ISME 12–30 Aug 1978, and has brought to London for lectures and workshops a number of significant musicians and groups, including Pierre Boulez, Karlheinz Stockhausen, John Cage, and Nicolas Slonimsky. The university has continued to serve an important role in enriching London's cultural life through concerts and recitals of the Faculty of Music and the Alumni Great Artist Series, which has featured such artists as Van Cliburn, Elisabeth Schwarzkopf, and the Cleveland Orchestra. In 1976 the music history department began to publish the annual *Studies in Music*, edited by Terence Bailey.

See also Archives; College songs; Libraries; Music education research; Music therapy.

BIBLIOGRAPHY
Talman, J.J. and Talman, R.D. *'Western' – 1878–1953* (London 1953)
Fox, William Sherwood. *Sherwood Fox of Western* (Toronto 1964)
Green, Paul. 'Western announces graduate programs in music,' *Recorder*, vol 11, May 1969
McKellar, Donald. 'Western's music facilities among most progressive in Canada,' *MSc*, 270, Mar–Apr 1973
Kraglund, John. 'London enters the musical go-round,' Toronto *Globe and Mail*, 12 Aug 1978
Gwynne-Timothy, J.R.W. *Western's First Century* (London, Ont, 1978) JPG

University of Windsor. Founded in 1857 at Windsor, Ont, as Assumption College (Roman Catholic). It became a university in 1953 and was granted incorporation as the non-denominational U of Windsor in 1963, affiliating at the same time with Essex College. In 1980 it offered a variety of undergraduate and graduate degree programs and extensive adult education programs.

As early as 1959 music courses and student performing ensembles were organized by Violet Leach and Mateusz Glinski (visiting professor 1959–65). In his first year on the faculty (1964) Carl *Morey developed a minor credit program in music. He established the Music Dept in 1966 and was its head 1967–70. The B MUS program was introduced in 1967 and produced its first graduates in 1971. Paul *McIntyre succeeded Morey in 1970 and introduced an applied-music degree program in 1973. The department became the School of Music in 1977, with McIntyre as its director. McIntyre was succeeded in 1980 by Richard Householder. In 1978–9 the degrees offered were: B MUS (honours: history and theory; school music; applied), BMA, BA (honours, major), Honours BFA in Music Theatre, and Honours BA in Music and Sociology.

The Dept of Asian Studies has offered programs in the performance of eastern music. Canadian music studies have been fostered by a fourth-year seminar on Canadian music, mandatory for all composition students.

The department's facilities include an electronic laboratory. In 1972 the department had approximately 60 degree students and a faculty of 11 (8 full-time and 3 part-time). In 1978–9 the figures were 121 and 27 (12 and 15). Those on staff in 1978–9 included Jens *Hanson (theory and composition), and Edward Kovarik (history). The majority were of US origin or held US degrees.

Performing ensembles have included the University Singers, Orchestra, Concert Band, Chamber Choir, and Community Choir, and the Ensemble X1040Y. In 1978 the U of Windsor Singers commissioned and premiered Derek *Healey's *Brown Season* (text by Thoreau) for flute, percussion, and SATB. Assumption College (University) has sponsored annually a Christian Culture series of lectures and concerts and has presented the Christian Culture Award to 'an outstanding exponent of Christian ideals.' Recipients have included Arnold *Walter (in 1945) and Paul *Doyon (1950).

BIBLIOGRAPHY
'University of Windsor holds Canadian music exhibition,' *CanComp*, 13, Dec 1966
McIntyre, Paul. 'Windsor music students bombarded with ideas first year,' *MSc*, 272 Jul–Aug 1973 (JPG)

Uxbridge Organ Co. Established ca 1872 at Uxbridge, north of Toronto. The company also was known as the Uxbridge Cabinet Organ Co and, after 1898, as the Uxbridge Piano and Organ Co. Advertisements 1878–9 offered reed organs in seven models at prices ranging from $200 to $355 and mentioned installations in central Ontario churches. No trace has been found of the company's activities after 1909. However, the formation of a new, presumably unrelated firm, the Uxbridge Piano Co, with directors in Toronto, was announced in the *Canadian Music Trades Journal* (Feb 1914). This company appears to have been short-lived. FH

V

VACHON, (Marie Reine Aline) **Monique**. Teacher, lecturer, writer, researcher, b St-Frédéric, near Quebec City, 19 Oct 1921; B MUS (Laval) 1958, L MUS (Laval) 1962, D MUS (Laval) 1966, diplôme (École normale supérieure, Laval) 1968, BES (Quebec Dept of Education) 1968. She studied 1955–68 at *Laval U, chiefly with Jocelyne *Binet (counterpoint, formal analysis), Jeanne *Landry (harmony, composition), and Onésime Pouliot (history). She gave courses on music teaching methods 1967–70 at the École normale Laval and 1970–3 at Laval U. In 1973 she was appointed a research officer in the Quebec High Commissioner's Office for Youth, Sports, and Recreation. In collaboration with Maurice Carrier, a teacher of history at UQATR, she has lectured in France, Belgium, Quebec, and New Brunswick and written several articles dealing with political song. She has appeared on CBC radio (eg, 'Au fil des arts') and TV. Monique Vachon is a member of the community of the Soeurs servantes du Saint-Coeur-de-Marie.

WRITINGS
La Fugue dans la musique religieuse de W.A. Mozart (Quebec, Tours 1970)
'Aristote et la musique dans l'education,' unpubl L MUS thesis, Laval 1962
– and Carrier, Maurice. *Chansons politiques du Québec*, 2 vols (Montreal 1977, 1979) HP

VACHON, Séraphin (Dominique). Violinist, conductor, composer, teacher, b Quebec City 15 Dec 1841, d Baltimore, Md, 3 Jan 1875. But for the recollections of Nazaire *LeVasseur, Vachon's life and career might be unknown today. He took violin lessons from Joseph *Lyonnais, soon distinguishing himself through his unusual aptitude; he demonstrated 'marvellous talent,' deep intuition, and a methodical mind. LeVasseur speaks glowingly of Vachon's astonishing virtuosity, his singing tone, 'pure, vibrant and full of vigour,' and his abilities as a sight-reader and improviser. Excessive shyness and perfectionism prevented him from exploiting his gifts. According to LeVasseur 'he was given a hard time in Quebec City.'

When Vachon was about 25 he moved to Montreal. There for a few months he led the LaRue minstrels, with whom he subsequently made several tours in the USA. In 1872 he settled in Baltimore and became the conductor at the Odeon, a variety theatre.

Vachon was known as the Quebec teacher of Roch *Lyonnais and as a composer of skill and wit; most of his compositions remained unpublished, however. The song 'Il ne reviendra pas,' with words by Louis-H. Fréchette, is listed in an undated catalogue published by Arthur *Lavigne.

BIBLIOGRAPHY

LeVasseur, L.-Nazaire. 'Musique et musiciens à Québec,' *La Musique*, vol 2, Aug 1920 LP

The Vághy String Quartet. Formed 1964 at the Juilliard School by the Vághy brothers, Dezsö (first violin) and Tibor (viola) (who had studied in Budapest, Vienna, and Hamburg), Stephen Kecskeméthy (second violin), and Edward Culbreath (cello). The quartet was coached by members of the Juilliard and Amadeus String Quartets and was quartet-in-residence 1966–8 at Bowdoin, Gorham, and Nasson colleges and the U of Maine. Its first appearance in Canada was at *Expo 67 in Montreal. In 1968 it became quartet-in-residence at *Queen's U, Kingston, Ont, and assumed the first chairs of the string section in the *Kingston SO. In 1969 Kecskeméthy and Culbreath were succeeded by David George and Robert Kemble Dodson. Besides the standard repertoire the quartet has played works by John *Fodi, Jacques *Hétu, Otto *Joachim, and Harry *Somers. It premiered Paul *Crawford's *String Quartet: 'La nuit étoilée'* in 1972. It also premiered James Kent's *Cadenza String Quartet* in 1976 and, with the harpist Erica *Goodman, Milton *Barnes' *Divertimento* in 1979. After a recital in Washington, DC, in February 1969, the *Washington Evening Star* critic noted 'playing ... marked by a high degree of individuality ... molded into a unified effort of the highest degree.' A New York debut, 2 Mar 1975, was similarly well received. Peter G. Davis in the *New York Times* (9 Mar 1975) praised a 'large, lush, glamorous ensemble tone ... used ... to excellent effect.' The quartet was the subject of a film, *Vaghy*, produced in 1971 by Quarry Film Production. Its recording of the string quartets of Shostakovich and Szymanowski received the 1977 *CMCouncil award for the best chamber music record.

DISCOGRAPHY

Bartók *String Quartet No. 4* – Crawford *String Quartet: 'La Nuit étoilée.'* 1976. CBC SM-325

Franck *Quintet*. Kubálek pf. 1976. CBC SM-319

Prokofiev *String Quartet No. 1* – Somers *String Quartet No. 2*. 1973. CBC SM-263

Shostakovich *String Quartet No. 8* – Szymanowski *String Quartet No. 2*. 1976. CBC SM-312 (CF)

VAILLANCOURT, Honoré. Baritone, actor, director, administrator, b Montreal 25 Nov 1892, d there 25 Jan 1933. His gifts as a singer and actor were evident at the Collège de St-Jean-Iberville, where he studied solfège. He then studied voice with Arthur *Laurendeau, Salvator *Issaurel, and Albert *Roberval and acting and staging with Jeanne *Maubourg. He made his debut 11 Apr 1917 at the *Monument national as Jean in Massé's *Les Noces de Jeannette*, subsequently appearing in plays and opera in Canada and the USA, singing leading roles in such works as *Carmen, Faust, Lakmé, Thaïs*, and *La Fille du Régiment*, as well as Gounod's *Mireille* and *Philémon et Baucis*, Messager's *Véronique* and *La Basoche*, and Thomas's *Mignon*. He founded the *Société canadienne d'opérette in the summer of 1921 and served it tirelessly, as manager and 1925–33 as artistic director. For 10 seasons, 1923–33, he performed in and directed many productions. His premature death shocked the Quebec theatre world, and the society disbanded a few months later. Vaillancourt recorded three 78s ca 1913–17 for Columbia. The titles of these operetta excerpts are listed in *Roll Back the Years*.

BIBLIOGRAPHY

Cormier, Raphaël. *Biographies canadiennes-françaises* (Montreal 1922)

Gour, Romain. *La Palme-Issaurel* (Montreal 1948) PL

VAILLANCOURT, Jean-Eudes. Pianist, orchestra and choir conductor, teacher, composer, b Port-Alfred, near Chicoutimi, Que, 16 Aug 1940; B MUS (Laval) 1955. He studied piano 1956–9 at the *CMM with Yvonne *Hubert and 1959–61 in New York with Rosina Lhévinne. He taught 1961–6 at the Institut des Arts in Saguenay and founded and directed the Sine Nomine Choir (a mixed choir of 80 voices) and La Chanterelle (a 60-voice children's choir). He took conducting courses 1966–7 with Tullio Serafin in Rome. On a scholarship awarded by the *MACQ for his stage cantata *L'Orphalisiaque* he worked 1967–8 with Louis Fourestier in Paris. In 1969–70 he taught at the École de musique Ste-Croix in Ville St-Laurent, Montreal, and conducted a 16-piece string orchestra at the Vaisseau d'or restaurant, giving two concerts of classical music each evening. In 1970 he began touring as a soloist and as accompanist to the cellist Klaus-Peter Hahn. He has accompanied singers including his sister Pauline *Vaillancourt, Claude *Corbeil, Bruno *Laplante, and Nicole *Lorange.

Vaillancourt's frequent appearances as conductor of the *MSO and the *Quebec SO have been well received by the critics, and he has conducted radio and TV concerts for both the French and the English networks of the CBC. In 1975 he began teaching at the *U of Montreal. In April 1977 he conducted Stravinsky's *Les Noces* there, and the same year he founded the Faculty of Music Orchestra.

Besides the *Chant de la Transfiguration* (a work written for mixed choir, organ, and narrator), Vaillancourt has composed piano pieces, two song cycles, and some film music. ST

VAILLANCOURT, Lorraine. Pianist, conductor, b Kénogami, near Chicoutimi, Que, 20 Sep 1943. She studied 1964–8 at the CMQ with Hélène *Landry and 1968–70 at the École normale in Paris with Jeanne Loriod (ondes Martenot) and Pierre Dervaux (orchestral conducting). She also studied piano with Yvonne Loriod and Anne-Marie de Lavilléon-Verdier. She worked 1971–3 with Serge *Garant and Bruce *Mather (whom she replaced in 1974 as director of the *U of Montreal's contemporary music workshop) and subsequently directed numerous works, notably those of Alain Louvier, Cage, Stockhausen, Crumb, *Somers (**The Fool*), *Vivier, *Tremblay, *Schafer, and Myke Roy. She was music director 1972–5 of the Atelier-laboratoire, a group responsible for the premieres of many works by young Quebec composers. She has participated often as pianist at the Nocturnales (late evening concerts) of the U of Montreal and in *SMCQ concerts. In 1965 she began to appear frequently with her brother Jean-Eudes *Vaillancourt in two-piano recitals on radio and TV and in concerts throughout Quebec. In 1975 Lorraine Vaillancourt began playing duos and trios with the clarinetist Jean *Laurendeau and the percussionist Robert Leroux. The trio devised collectively the incidental music for the 1975 Théâtre du Nouveau-Monde and CBC TV productions of Claudel's *Le Père humilié*. Vaillancourt married the pianist and conductor Léon *Bernier. ST

VAILLANCOURT, Pauline. Soprano, b Arvida, now Jonquière, Que, 2 Feb 1945; M MUS (Montreal) 1976. She studied first with Guy Lepage at the *CMQ, then with Louise *André at the *U of Montreal. Her career as a soloist and recitalist began in 1970. She sang in many important works, notably the Mozart *Requiem* and the Bach *Magnificat* with the orchestra of the Institut des arts au Saguenay, Handel's *Messiah* with the CMQ orchestra (1970), and Brahms' *German Requiem* with the *MSO (May 1977) and the *Kingston and *Kitchener-Waterloo SOs (1978). She specializes, however, in avant-garde repertoire. Frequently engaged by the *SMCQ, the CBC, and the Atelier-laboratoire of the U of Montreal, and a member of Gropus 7 since its inception in 1975, she has premiered several works, including *Orange* by Pierre *Trochu (Toronto, 1973), *Lettura di Dante* and *Liebesgedichte* by Claude *Vivier (SMCQ, 1974–5), ... *chant d'amours* (sic) by Serge *Garant (CBC, March 1975), *Arabesco* by José *Evangelista (Spain, April 1975), and *Three Songs of the Holocaust* by Marvin *Duchow (Montreal, September 1978). She has participated in numerous 'collective creations' of Gropus 7. In April 1975, accompanied by the pianist Jean-Eudes *Vaillancourt (her brother), she made a recital tour in Spain organized by the Caja De Ahorros. Her striking abilities in extemporization are demonstrated on a recording made with *Dionne and Brégent in March of 1976. In November 1976 she became a member of TRIO 3 with the guitarist Michael Laucke and the flutist Sayyd *Abdul Al-Khabyyr. She took part in the SMCQ tour of Germany, England, France, and Belgium in November 1977, performing in *Madrigal IV* by Bruce *Mather and *Ishuma* by Micheline Coulombe *Saint-Marcoux.

DISCOGRAPHY

Evangelista *En guise de fête; Arabesco*. Escrig vc, 15 instr, Franco-Gil cond. 1975. CBS LSP-13224

Garant *Cage d'oiseau*. L.-P. Pelletier pf. 1978. RCI AMC 2

Tchaikovsky – Mussorgsky – R. Strauss – Villa-Lobos. 8 vc, J.-E. Vaillancourt pf and dir. 1974. RCI 417

See also Discography for SMCQ (RCI 411, 422). ST

VALDY (b Valdemar Horsdal). Singer-songwriter, guitarist, b Ottawa, of Danish parents, 1946. After playing guitar for several years im rock and country bands, he adopted a folk-influenced style and gained popularity in 1972 with the release of the LP *Country Man* (Haida HL 5101) and the single 'Rock and Roll Song.' He has toured Canada often, his many appearances making him, according to Jeani Read, 'unquestionably the most public performer in Canada; also – where the insular Lightfoot inspires no more than awe – the most loved.' He has performed in the USA and at the 1976 International Song Festival in Sopot, Poland. His singles have included his own songs 'A Good Song' (1973) and 'Simple Life' (1973), David Bradstreet's 'Renaissance' (1974), and Bob *Ruzicka's 'Yes I Can (Anyway You Want Me)' (1976); his LPs have included *Family Gathering* (1974, Haida HL 5104), *Landscapes* (1973, A & M SP 9013), *Valdy and the Hometown Band* (1976, A & M 4592), and *Hot Rocks* (1978, A & M SP 9034). All but *Hot Rocks* received gold record sales awards by 1978. The last two LPs reflect a broadening of his style to include elements of rock and jazz. His repertoire consists of his own songs, many of them concerned with social issues, and others by such Canadian writers as Bruce *Cockburn, Bruce Miller, and Joe White. He received *Juno Awards in 1972 (outstanding performance) and 1973 (folk singer of the year). He is an affiliate of PRO Canada.

BIBLIOGRAPHY
LeBlanc, Larry. 'Valdy relaxing, enjoying a more simple musical style,' *MSc*, 281, Jan-Feb 1975
Read, Jeani. 'Valdy crack corn, but he don't care / It's money in the bank,' *Maclean's*, 6 Sep 1976
Boulton, Marsha. 'The new Valdy puts his shoes on,' *Maclean's*, 22 Jan 1979 MM

VALIQUETTE, Gilles. Singer, songwriter, guitarist, record producer, b Montreal 7 Apr 1952. Beginning his guitar studies at 12, he continued his musical training 1967–70 at the Collège Lionel-Groulx and then at the St-Laurent Cegep in Montreal. During this time he formed the group Someone, with which he made two singles, one for Visa and one for Canama. At the end of 1971 he joined Marie-Claire and Richard *Séguin, and the following year he became Jacques *Michel's accompanist. At the same time he composed and occasionally performed in student cafés throughout Quebec as well as in boîtes à chansons, including La Butte à Mathieu in Val David and Le *Patriote in Montreal.

In 1972 Valiquette made his first LP, *Chansons pour un café* (Zodiaque ZOX-6008) and was described in *La Presse* (10 Mar 1973) as having 'an easy-going and melodious style, infinitely personal yet never obscure.' He then toured in Quebec and made a second LP, *Deuxième Arrêt* (1973, Zodiaque ZOX-6013), from which the song 'Je suis cool' was popular.

In Montreal Valiquette performed in *St-Jean-Baptiste celebrations in 1973, 1974, and 1975 and appeared for the first time at *PDA 1 Mar 1974 with other young singers. At this time the review *Pop Rock* described him as the best guitarist in Quebec. In 1974 he participated in the Spa Festival, Belgium, and between 1975 and 1977 he made the LPs *Du même nom* (Zodiaque ZOX-6017), *Soirées d'automne* (Trans-World INT TI-6022), and *Valiquette est en ville* (CBS PFS 90386). He toured France, Belgium, Switzerland, and Holland in 1977.

Some of his hits were reissued in 1976 on the LP *Gilles Valiquette 1972–1975* (Trans-World INT TI-6029). Among the best known are 'Quelle belle journée,' 'Fais attention,' 'Samedi soir,' 'Sous un soleil d'été,' 'Un peu de bonheur,' and 'Blanc après noir,' which was included on the LP *Vol de nuit* (1977, CBS PFS 90440). Valiquette toured 1978–9 in Quebec and Ontario as well as in Louisiana and northern Texas.

Valiquette has produced records for the singers Jim and Bertrand, Plume Latraverse, Daniel Lavoie, Robert Paquette, Gilles Rivard, and Richard Séguin. He is an affiliate of PRO Canada.

BIBLIOGRAPHY
Ducharme, André. 'Gilles Valiquette,' *Perspectives*, vol 16, 21 Sep 1974 (HPd)

VALLE, Chicho (Amador). Bandleader, singer, guitarist, b Cienfuegos, Cuba, 2 Jul 1922 or 1924, naturalized Canadian 1961. A pioneer and popularizer of Latin-American music in Canada, Valle began singing in Cuba at nine with the dance orchestra of his brother, Hector. He attended Loyola U in New Orleans and led a trio 1942–6 in that city's nightclubs. Invited to Toronto in 1946 by CBC radio to sing on 'Latin American Serenade,' he made his debut 19 May and, after completing the contracted four weeks, remained in Canada and starred in 1946 on 'Chicho Valle Sings' and 1947–67 on 'Chicho Valle y los Cubanos.' Los Cubanos grew from a trio in 1946 to 10 musicians by 1956 (including the flutist Gordon *Day, the bassist Johnny *Niosi, the pianist Rudy *Toth, and the guitarist Stan Wilson) and later, for special occasions, to a 20-piece concert orchestra of reeds, woodwinds, brass, and rhythm instruments. With a quintet Valle appeared in nightclubs or hotel lounges in Toronto (the Cork Room 1950–63; the Inn on the Park 1966–76), Muskoka, Ont, (Bigwin Inn, summers ca 1950–63), and Montreal (the Skyline Hotel 1965–6). With a trio he appeared in concert with the Buffalo Philharmonic in 1968. Valle was music director 1970–6 for the Four Seasons hotel chain in Canada (of which the Inn on the Park is a part) and thereafter, having retired from performance, maintained a booking agency. He made three LPs: *Chicho Valle y los Cubanos* (1963, CTL 038), *Latin Lustre* (1968, CBC LM-42/Cap SN 6289), and *Este es Chicho Valle* (1970, CBC LM-83). Valle used two theme songs, 'Magic in the Moonlight' and his own 'Buenas Noches Mi Amor.' He is an affiliate of PRO Canada. MM

VALLÉE, Cécile (m Jalbert). Soprano, teacher, b Bonnyville, northeast of Edmonton; B MUS voice (Montreal) 1951, diplôme d'artiste (École Vincent-d'Indy) 1953, premier prix virtuosity (Geneva Cons) 1957. Her voice teacher at the *École Vincent-d'Indy was Reine *Décarie. After winning two competitions, including the 1952 *Prix Archambault, Vallée completed her training 1954–8 with Anna-Maria Guglielmetti in Geneva. In 1957 she sang for Geneva Radio. After her return to Canada, she sang the role of Blanche de la Force in Poulenc's *Dialogue des Carmélites* for CBC TV in 1960. She then participated in several *JMC tours, performing in Blackburn's *Une Mesure de silence* (*Silent Measures) and *Pirouette* (having premiered the role of Béatrice in 1960), *Vallerand's **Le Magicien*, and Debussy's *L'Enfant prodigue*. For the *Théâtre lyrique de Nouvelle-France she sang Mimi in *La Bohème* (1962) and Despina in *Così fan tutte* (1964), repeating the latter role for the Théâtre lyrique du Québec in 1970. She was Gilda in the 1964 production of *Rigoletto* by the Edmonton Professional Opera (*Edmonton Opera Assn) and that same year inaugurated a series of Ravel concerts at the Milan Cons and sang for the JM of Italy in 15 cities. She was a member 1964–5 of the Trio d'opéra JMC with Léonard *Bilodeau and Bruno *Laplante. She toured for the JMC in 1967 with *L'Amante Cubista* by Roberto Hazon and sang Sophie (1968) in the Théâtre lyrique du Québec's *Werther*. Her frequent performances at the *JMC Orford Art Centre and on TV and radio date from 1967. She taught 1970–7 at Marianapolis College and became a soloist at the St James United Church in Montreal in 1975. She began teaching at the *Cons de Val d'Or and the Collège de l'Assomption in Nicolet in 1977. (GB)

VALLERAND, Jean (d'Auray). Composer, critic, administrator, teacher, essayist, conductor, violinist, b Montreal 24 Dec 1915; L LITT (Montreal) 1938, journalism diploma (Montreal) 1941, hon D MUS (Ottawa) 1975. While obtaining his general education and attending university, he studied violin with Lucien *Sicotte 1920–35 and theory and composition with Claude *Champagne 1935–42. In 1941 he succeeded Léo-Pol *Morin as a critic on the daily *Le Canada* and thus began a distinguished career in journalism. He wrote 1941–6 for *Le Canada*, 1948–9 for *Montréal-Matin*, 1952–61 for *Le Devoir*, 1961–2 for *Le Nouveau Journal*, and 1962–6 for *La Presse*.

In 1940 Vallerand won the Schumann trophy at the Festival-concours de musique du Québec for his song 'Les Roses à la mer' (later performed by Jeanne *Desjardins and Mary *Henderson). In 1942 Désiré Defauw and the CSM orchestra (*MSO) gave the premiere of his symphonic poem *Le Diable dans le beffroi*, a work inspired by the writings of Edgar Allan Poe and often performed in the USA and Europe. Between 1940 and 1950 Vallerand composed and conducted incidental music for more than 50 classical and contemporary plays produced on the CBC. His output, if these are included, is relatively large. His *Nocturne* for orchestra received a special mention in 1947 at the Reichold International Competition of the Detroit SO. The *Sonata* for violin and piano was premiered in 1952 by Noël *Brunet and John *Newmark and later transcribed for violin and orchestra. The *String Quartet* was premiered by the *Montreal String Quartet in 1955 and *Quatre Poèmes de Saint-Denys-Garneau* by Marguerite *Lavergne and John Newmark. Two works, *Cordes en mouvement* for string orchestra and *Étude concertante* for violin and orchestra, were commissioned respectively by the *Lapitsky Foundation (1961) and the *Montreal International Competition (1969).

Jean Vallerand

Vallerand's output attests to a solid background and reveals qualities of sensitivity and intellect often found in the music of French composers. In *Le Diable dans le beffroi* he displays a rare mastery in handling orchestral timbres and much imagination in unifying the dramatic elements of program music. Concerning his *Sonata* for violin and piano, which is classical in design, the composer declared: 'In this work, all my efforts are directed towards the identification of form and expression. It is the common denominator of everything I knew about music at the time I wrote it' (*La Semaine à Radio-Canada*, February 1951). Vallerand turned to the serial technique with the 1955 *Quartet*; he subsequently employed it less rigorously in such works as *Cordes en mouvement* and *Étude concertante*. His only opera, **Le Magicien*, for which he also wrote the libretto, is inspired by the commedia dell'arte, and captures the verve and colour of that genre in a score which skilfully underlines the situations and vicissitudes of the action. Between 1969 and 1980 Vallerand has not introduced any new compositions.

In 1944 Vallerand prepared the chorus for the *Opera Guild production of Rimsky-Korsakov's *Coq d'or*. He also conducted the Guild's productions of *Hansel and Gretel* (1944), *Così fan tutte*, and *The Magic Flute* (1945). During this period he frequently appeared as conductor of the CSM orchestra at young people's concerts. He was a regular performer on the CBC's educational series 'Radio-Collège' 1945–56 and frequently conducted ensembles to illustrate his remarks.

Vallerand's musical and academic training made him the logical choice to assist Wilfrid *Pelletier when the *CMM was founded. He was its secretary general 1942–63 and taught orchestration. He taught orchestration and music history at the *U of Montreal 1950–66. After 20 years at the CMM, Vallerand turned to other areas of musical activity. He was head of radio music 1963–6 for CBC Montreal and cultural attaché 1966–70 for the

Quebec government in Paris. In 1971 he was appointed director of music education for the *MACQ; after a reorganization that year he became director of performing arts. He served 1971–5 in that position and 1971–8 as director of the Cons de musique et d'art dramatique du Québec (see Cons de musique du Québec). He helped prepare and draft the report of the task force headed by Jean-Paul *Jeannotte 1974–5. In 1975 he became a teaching consultant at the CMM and in 1976 staff consultant with the MACQ. In 1977 he was appointed secretary general of the Quebec Youth Orchestra.

In the 1940s Jean Vallerand began writing program notes for the *MSO and other musical organizations and appearing as a lecturer. He contributed to numerous periodicals, including *L'Action universitaire*, *Amérique française*, *Culture vivante*, *Gants du ciel*, *Liberté*, *Maclean*, *Musical America*, *Relations*, and *Vie musicale*. He has reviewed cultural events for CBC radio and TV, appearing on such programs as 'La Revue des arts et des lettres,' and often has been a guest on the French-network broadcasts of the *Metropolitan Opera.

Vallerand's versatility has been described accurately by Annette *Lasalle-Leduc: 'In examining the personality of Jean Vallerand, it is difficult to distinguish the composer, the essayist, the educator and the critic. His rather aristocratic spirit, imbued with insatiable curiosity and a rare eclecticism, has been attracted to all aspects of contemporary music and to all forms of thought. The value of his judgments, the quality of his literary language which reveals him to be a humanist, and finally his knowledge of the musician's craft, lend an indisputable authority to his criticism. As for his musical output, since *Le Diable dans le beffroi* (1942), it has espoused in turn the diverse trends of contemporary music. His recent *String Quartet* makes use of serial principles, his *Prélude* for orchestra is a piece of admirable musical and poetic density; moreover, special features of Vallerand's music are its preoccupation with timbre and its richness: ample evidence of his excellence as harmonist and orchestrator' (*La Vie musicale*).

Jean Vallerand is a member of CAPAC and an associate of the *CMCentre.

SELECTED COMPOSITIONS

STAGE, FILM

Marie Stuart, incidental music (Schiller). 1961. Ms
Noces de sang, incidental music (Lorca). 1962. Ms
La Cerisaie, incidental music (Chekhov). 1963. Ms
Payse, ballet based on *Prélude* for orchestra. 1964. Ms
La Fin des étés, film. 1964. NFB
Incidental music for over 50 radio dramas on the CBC
See also *Le Magicien*.

ORCHESTRA

Le Diable dans le beffroi. 1942. Ms. RCI 41 (*TSO)
Cantate (G. Lamarche). 1946. Ten solo, SATB, orch. Ms
Cantate (R. Lasnier). 1946. Ten solo, SATB, orch. Ms
Nocturne. 1946. Ms
Prélude. 1948. Ms. RCI 116 (*Waddington)
Concerto, orchestral version of *Sonata*. 1951. Vn, orch. Ms
Cordes en mouvement. 1961. Str orch. CMCentre. RCI 216/RCA CCS 1010 (*McGill Chamb O)
Réverbérations contractoires. 1961. Ms
Étude concertante. 1969. Vn, orch. CMCentre

CHAMBER MUSIC

Sonata. 1950. Vn, pf. CMCentre. RCI 92 (*Brunet)/Masters of the Bow MBS-2002 (*Bress)
String Quartet. 1955. CMCentre. RCI 141 (*Mtl Str Quar)/ Col MS 6364 (*Canadian Str Quar)

VOICE AND PIANO

'Les Roses à la mer' (Desbordes-Valmore). Ca 1935. Ms
Quatre poèmes de Saint-Denys-Garneau. 1954. CMCentre. RCI 393 (B. *Laplante)/(no. 1 and 3) Allied ARCLP-4 (J. *Dufresne pf).

WRITINGS

'Conquête de la forme: épisode de la vie d'un compositeur,' *Gants du ciel*, Dec 1943
Introduction à la musique (Montreal 1949)
La Musique et les tout-petits (Montreal 1950)
'La musique et la vie intérieure,' *Action universitaire*, vol 16, Jan 1950
'Rencontre avec Varèse,' *Liberté*, vol 69, Sep–Oct 1959
'A look at music in Québec,' *Musical America*, Sep 1963
'Pour que s'arrête le gaspillage de talent,' *VM*, vol 1, 1965
'Le Conservatoire dans la cité,' *Culture vivante*, vol 11, Dec 1968

BIBLIOGRAPHY

Contemporary Canadian Composers / Compositeurs canadiens contemporains GP

VALLIÈRES, Henri (Eugène). Organist, teacher, pianist, b Rivière-du-Loup, Que, 8 May 1901. He entered the *Séminaire de Québec in 1913 and was trained there by Henri *Gagnon, whom he also assisted at the Quebec Basilica. Vallières was the organist at the seminary ca 1920–5. On the death of his father, Eugène, he succeeded him as the organist of St-Patrice Church in Rivière-du-Loup. He went to Paris in 1928 and worked with Marcel Dupré (organ). He also attended the École normale de musique, where his teachers were Paul *Loyonnet (piano) and Henri Potiron (harmony). On his return to Canada, in 1929, he was appointed the organist of Notre-Dame-du-Chemin Church in Quebec City, a post he held until 1972. He taught solfège and piano at *Laval U 1931–70 and piano and organ at the *CMQ 1947–72. His pupils included Lucille Baby, a harpist with the *Quebec SO, and Jeannine Bégin, a teacher at the *CMM. He toured with Arthur *LeBlanc and Raoul *Jobin, and during the 1940s he was music director of 'L'Heure dominicale,' a religious program on CBC radio. He married the pianist Gabrielle Hudson. BM

VALOIS, Marcel (b Dufresne, Joseph Henri Jean). Critic, essayist, b Montreal 17 Mar 1898. After his general education he read law and literature at the U of Montreal and studied piano. He was music critic 1929–54 for the Montreal daily *La Presse* and continued to contribute on a weekly basis until 1971.

Valois was the commentator 1941–2 for a series of recitals – 'Les liedistes français' – in a salon at the Windsor Hotel, in which the soprano Jeanne *Desjardins, and the pianist Marie-Thérèse *Paquin took part. For nine seasons he was a juror for the CBC's *'Singing Stars of Tomorrow.' For CBC radio he prepared and presented the 1973–4 series 'La musique à Montréal 1920–50' and the 1974–5 series 'Théâtre chanté, théâtre dansé.'

In 1957 Valois was named honorary professor of the Faculty of Music at the *U of Montreal and in 1961 he became a fellow of the Royal Society of Canada.

Valois wrote enthusiastic and intelligent articles in a vivid style. They reveal his admiration for genuine artistry and his keen appreciation of the music of French composers, particularly Debussy and Ravel. He was also a perceptive dance critic.

WRITINGS

Figures de danse (Montreal 1943, 1945)
– et al. *Variations sur trois thèmes* (Montreal 1946)
Dance Recaptured, transl Benton Jackson (Montreal 1947)
Le Sortilège de Marcel Proust (Montreal 1964)
Au carrefour des souvenirs (Montreal 1965) GP

Vancouver. British Columbia metropolis: Canada's most important Pacific port and third largest city. Settled in 1862, Vancouver had several early names: Hastings Mills and Gastown (both 1867) and Granville (1870). William Van Horne of the CPR announced in 1884 that the settlement would be the terminus of the transcontinental line and named it after Capt George Vancouver, who in 1792 had visited Burrard Inlet. Only two months after its incorporation as a city, 6 Apr 1886, Vancouver was destroyed by fire. By the end of that year, with reconstruction well under way, the population was 2500. Mostly because of the *Klondike gold rush of 1897–8, Vancouver's population rose quickly from 15,000 in 1892 to 100,000 in 1900. The transcontinental railways (particularly the CPR), the ships, and, later, the airlines brought settlers from both Europe and Asia, grafting a cosmopolitan mixture of races onto the English and Scottish roots of the city and enhancing the variety of its cultural life. Many of the settlers had lived in well-established musical centres in eastern Canada or abroad, and consequently music was an accepted part of the plans and activities of the quickly growing community. The inhabitants of Greater Vancouver numbered 400,000 in 1946 and more than 1,000,000 in 1980.

Dancing on the stump, ca 1910

1 The first half-century
2 1919–45
3 1945–80

1 THE FIRST HALF-CENTURY. A piano dating back to the first settlers and in the possession of the city archives is a relic of pre-1886 musical life in Vancouver. Another relic, at Hastings Sawmill School, is the town's first organ, 'a little groan box' carried to the docks when Lord Dufferin arrived in 1876. Early in 1887 funds were raised by subscription to establish a brass band to welcome the first transcontinental train, which duly arrived 23 May to the strains of 'See the Conquering Hero Comes,' and other musical eulogies.

The first musical leaders in Vancouver were George J. and Fred W. *Dyke, brothers who settled there in 1888. George (violinist, conductor, teacher, impresario, and critic) that same year opened Vancouver's first music supply store (Painton & Dyke) and first music school. He played in trios and quartets, conducted orchestras (eg, that of the CPR Opera House), and brought to Vancouver its first internationally famous performers: *Albani (1897 and 1906), Bauer, Elman, Paderewski, and Rachmaninoff. Fred participated in training the chorus for the 1903 *Cycle of Musical Festivals.

When the city was in its infancy, choral and orchestral societies formed and disbanded frequently, their main purpose being to supply an outlet for the energies of amateur singers and instrumentalists. In 1888, for example, the Vancouver Musical Club invited the participation of anyone who could satisfy the requirement that 'members must have voices of some kind.' In 1890 the 100-voice Vancouver Philharmonic Society combined with the Orchestral Society, which numbered 40 players in 1895, to present a program of overtures, songs, choruses, and other music by Gounod, Bizet, Mendelssohn, Schumann, and others at the Imperial Opera House (which was in operation as early as 1888).

A special operatic event took place in 1891 to inaugurate the CPR's Vancouver Opera House, which opened 9 February. The Emma Juch English Opera, a US touring company which included Mme Juch herself, and other soloists, chorus, and orchestra, was engaged at a cost of $10,000 to perform *Lohengrin* in the new opera house, which itself had cost more than $200,000. Although not usually presented so spectacularly, other artists visited Vancouver at this time, and their concerts usually were sold out. The *Vancouver Woman's Musical Club, formed in 1905 through the efforts of Mrs B.T. *Rogers, Mrs Walter *Coulthard, and others, brought to Vancouver such eminent musicians as Paderewski in 1908 and the New York SO under Walter Damrosch in 1910.

With Vancouver's rapid growth in wealth and population around the turn of the century, moves to found permanent musical organizations became more frequent. A *Vancouver SO gave several concerts beginning in 1897 but soon disbanded. Other orchestras, founded in 1915 and 1919, also failed to last long. In the mean time, some strides were being made in education. The Vancouver school system in 1904 appointed a supervisor of music: George Hicks, who served in the position until 1919. The music programs he established in the schools were not strong enough to produce many proficient musicians, and attempts to establish conservatories – eg, the British Columbia Institute of Music and Drama and George Dyke's Academy of Music – had limited success. Mrs Walter Coulthard, who settled in Vancouver in 1904, and J.D.A. *Tripp, who arrived there in 1910, raised the level of education through their high standards of teaching and performance.

2 1919–45. The major new institution of the period between the wars was the Vancouver SO, revived in 1930 by Mrs B.T. Rogers, who invited Allard de *Ridder to conduct. For instrumentalists, unemployed because of the Depression and the advent of the 'talkies,' which had made the movie house orchestras obsolete, the VSO provided an occupation. De Ridder, who led the VSO 1933–41 at the *Orpheum Theatre (opened 1927) and the Georgia Auditorium, also organized summer concerts in 1934. Sponsored by BC Electric, the concerts took place at the newly built *Malkin Bowl in Stanley Park. Another orchestra created during this time was the Vancouver Junior SO, conducted 1940–6 by Gregori *Garbovitsky. The Australian-English musician Arthur *Benjamin conducted the *Vancouver Sun*'s Promenade Concerts 1941–2.

Radio had a strong influence on orchestral music between the wars. Several radio orchestras had been precursors of the VSO. The Musical *Calangis Family was the staff orchestra 1933–43 on CKCD radio. After 1934 it also performed on CBC. The *CBC Vancouver Chamber Orchestra, founded in 1938 by Ira *Dilworth and conducted by John *Avison, became one of Vancouver's permanent ensembles. There also was a CBR SO, conducted 1941–6 by Arthur Benjamin.

Frederick *Chubb, organist-choirmaster 1912–46 at Christ Church Cathedral, developed his choir into one of the city's outstanding ensembles, leading it in oratorios and cantatas in addition to regular service. Among concert choirs formed after World War I were the *Elgar Choir of British Columbia (1924–75), founded by C.E. *Findlater; the *Vancouver Bach Choir, conducted 1930–4 by its founder, Herbert *Drost, and 1935–40 by Ira Dilworth; the St Cecilia Choristers directed ca 1931–50 by Nancy Paisley *Benn; and the Goss Singers, directed 1943–8 by John *Goss and accompanied by Phyllis *Schuldt. The most important of these, the Vancouver Bach Choir, suspended activities during World War II. In 1930 Drost established the *Western Music Co.

After World War I, recitals continued to be presented by the Woman's Musical Club at various locations and, after 1931, at the Vancouver Art Gallery. Lily Laverock was responsible for bringing artists of international reputation to Vancouver, and in 1937 Gordon *Hilker's Greater Artists Series also began to present renowned recitalists. Many orchestral musicians not only taught but also played in chamber groups. One such musician was the cellist Dezsö *Mahalek, who moved to Vancouver in 1937, developed a large class of pupils, and played in trios and quartets with Allard de Ridder, Adolph *Koldofsky, and Arthur Benjamin.

In 1920, after the previous year's campaign for the introduction of music study into Vancouver schools, the Vancouver Music Teachers' Assn (later *BCRMTA) was formed, with H. Roy Robertson as president. Among the leading private teachers during the years between the world wars were Nancy Paisley Benn, Gideon *Hicks (brother of George Hicks), Avis *Phillips, and Ira *Swartz. During the next two decades, Ira Dilworth worked for the improvement of music study in the schools in Vancouver and throughout British Columbia. Other organizations with educational intent or functions included the *Philharmonic Music Club (1922–66), which gave young musicians opportunities for public performance; the *Sir Ernest MacMillan Fine Arts Club, formed in 1936; the British Columbia Music Festival, begun in 1923; C.E. Findlater's Elgar School of Music (1935–65); and the British Columbia Institute of Music and Drama, established in 1944 by the Park Board in conjunction with *TUTS. The latter presented a series of outdoor musicals and operettas 1940–63 at the Malkin Bowl.

The dance bands of Mart *Kenney and Dal *Richards began in Vancouver in the 1920s, as did the noted *Kitsilano Boys' Band founded in 1928 and conducted by Arthur W. *Delamont.

3 1945–80. After World War II, music in Vancouver developed as rapidly as the population. The VSO, the CBC Vancouver Chamber Orchestra, and the Vancouver Junior SO continued to perform and to improve in quality. Avis Phillips and Phylis *Inglis were teaching a new generation of singers; Barbara *Custance and Ursula *Malkin were noted piano teachers of the day. The *Queen Elizabeth Theatre opened in 1959, and the Vancouver SO performed there 1960–77 successively under Irwin Hoffman, Meredith Davies, Simon *Streatfeild, and Kazuyoshi Akiyama. In 1977 the newly renovated Orpheum Theatre became the orchestra's permanent home. In 1967 the *Vancouver Opera Assn, founded in 1959, with Irving *Guttman as artistic director 1960–74, began using the Vancouver SO as its pit orchestra.

A number of outstanding organists occupied church positions in the post-war era, fulfilling these roles on a high musical level and contributing to the city's concert life as organ recitalists, choir directors, or both. Among these have been Leonard *Wilson 1935–63 at St Michael's Anglican and St James Anglican; a succession of incumbents including Hugh *Bancroft, Thomas Jenkins, Beal *Thomas, and Patrick *Wedd at Christ Church Cathedral; Lawrence *Cluderay after 1947 at St Andrew's Wesley United, St John's Shaughnessy, and St Stephen's Anglican; Hugh *McLean 1957–73 at Ryerson United; and Frederick Carter at St John's Shaughnessy.

The Vancouver Bach Choir continued after World War II as the leading concert choral ensemble. New groups included the Music Makers, a children's choir directed by Nancy Paisley Benn during the 1940s and 1950s; the *Cantata Singers of Vancouver 1958–67, under their founding conductor, Hugh McLean; the Phylis Inglis Singers 1959–67; the Vancouver Welsh Male Voice Choir, formed ca 1962 (see Wales); and the *Vancouver Chamber Choir, formed in 1971 by Jon *Washburn.

Chamber music thrived in Vancouver after 1945. Many new performing groups and concert societies came into existence. Among these were the *de Rimanoczy Quartet, the *Steinberg String Quartet, and the Vancouver Chamber Sinfonietta, all founded in 1947; the *Friends of Chamber Music, formed in 1948 by Ida *Halpern, ethnomusicologist at the *U of British Columbia; the *Cassenti Players, formed in 1954 by George *Zukerman; the Vancouver String Quartet, formed in 1958 by Jack *Kessler and others; the *Baroque Strings of Vancouver, founded in 1966; the *Vancouver Woodwind Quintet and the *Purcell String Quartet, both formed in 1968; and the *Vancouver Cello Club, established in 1969.

The late 1960s were notable for the revival of medieval and renaissance music performed on original instruments or authentic replicas. The Hortulani Musicae, formed in 1968, and the baroque trio the Cecilian Ensemble, formed in 1972, became groups-in-residence of the *Vancouver Society for Early Music, established in 1969. The society also sponsored the orchestra L'Age d'Or 1972–4. The work of these groups and individuals and the growth of a Vancouver community of early-instrument builders (see Ray Nurse, Edward Turner) have led many to consider Vancouver the leading Canadian centre of early music activity. (See also Instruments: medieval, renaissance, and baroque.)

This early-music reawakening was paralleled by a new public interest in contemporary music, the first signs of which were demonstrated in 1950 at the *First Symposium of Canadian Contemporary Music initiated by Jacques Singer. The major continuing contemporary music organizations, both of which perform at the Vancouver East Cultural Centre, have been the *Vancouver New Music Society, founded in 1972 with Phyllis *Mailing as director and president, and *Days Months and Years to Come, formed in 1974.

The *Vancouver International Festival brought noteworthy visiting attractions to the city 1958–68. Vancouver musicians and ensembles have toured under the aegis of George Zukerman's *Overture Concerts, established in Vancouver in 1955, and the *Festival Concert Society, founded there in 1961 by J.J. *Johannesen. A recital series was initiated in 1968 by the Vancouver Art Gallery.

Post-war Vancouver musicians and musical organizations have been fortunate in the patronage of David *Spencer, the *Koerner Foundation, the Vancouver Foundation, and the British Columbia Cultural Fund (established in 1967). Indicative of a new emphasis on education in the broadest sense was the founding in 1946 of the *Community Arts Council of Vancouver, with Ira Dilworth as its first president. Although not an educational body, the council, as a source of well-researched ideas, encouraged the formation in 1959 of a Dept of Music at the U of British Columbia (where Harry *Adaskin had established music courses in 1946) and the opening in 1969 of the *Community Music School of Greater Vancouver. The latter institution, a model for other cities, moved in 1976 to its own premises in Vanier Park and in 1979 adopted the name Vancouver Academy of Music. R. Murray *Schafer was one of the several composers-in-residence at *Simon Fraser U 1966–75 and also directed there the *World Soundscape Project, established with headquarters at the university in 1971. In 1973 the pianist Robert *Silverman moved to Vancouver to teach at the U of British Columbia.

Vancouver pop groups in the 1970s have included *Chilliwack, Heart, *Pacific Salt, Prism, and Trooper. The expansion of the music industry in the late 1960s led BMI Canada (see PRO Canada) to open a Vancouver office in 1968. It persuaded Tom *Northcott to found in 1968 the recording company Stage 3 Productions. The *CMCentre opened a branch in Vancouver in 1977. Two of the finest music libraries in Canada have been developed at the U of British Columbia and the Vancouver Public Library.

Musicians born in or near Vancouver have included Norma *Abernethy, Milla *Andrew, David *Astor, John Avison, Marion *Barnum, Donald *Bell (South Burnaby), Marjorie *Biggar, Lloyd *Burritt, Irenee *Byatt, George Calangis, Dolores *Claman, F.R.C. *Clarke, Jean *Coulthard, James *Creighton, Barbara Custance, Terry *Dale, Clifford *Evens, jazz clarinetist Wally Fawkes, Judith *Forst (Coquitlam), Don *Francks, Don *Garrard, Bryan *Gooch, Ray *Griff, Lance *Harrison, Gordon Hilker, Edmund *Hockridge, Ricky *Hyslop, G. Herald *Keefer, Wallace Laughton, Ursula Malkin, Gordon *Manley, Glen *Morley, Doug Parker, Betty *Phillips, Arthur *Polson, Nora Borrowman *Polson, Dal Richards, Sherwood *Robson, Thomas *Rolston, Malcolm *Tait, Heather *Thomson, and Timothy Vernon.

BIBLIOGRAPHY

'Our new temple of Thespis,' Vancouver *World*, 21 Jan 1891

Tripp, J.D.A. 'Music in British Columbia,' *The Year Book of Canadian Art 1913*, compiled by the Arts and Letters Club of Toronto (Toronto, London 1913)

Forsyth, W.O. 'The winsome, wonderful west,' *CanJM*, Sep 1914

Stoddard, Hope. 'Music in British Columbia,' *International Musician*, Dec 1950

Salisbury, Dorothy. 'Music in Vancouver,' *CLA Bulletin*, Feb 1957

Morgan, Kit. 'Growing is what's happening in Vancouver,' *MSc*, 257, Jan–Feb 1971

Wyman, Max. 'Vancouver's in-house entertainment for Festival Habitat,' *PfAC*, Spring 1976

Docherty, Ian. 'The musical mosaic of Vancouver,' *Mcan*, 32, May 1977

Mertens, Susan. 'Vancouver: land of smiles and tears,' *Mcan*, 35, Apr 1978

Wyman, Max and Mertens, Susan. 'What price glory? An examination of music and the performing arts,' *Vancouver*, vol 12, Jan 1979

Hicks, Graham. 'Musically, Vancouver has come of age,' *MSc*, 307. May–Jun 1979

Colgrass, Ulla. 'Focus on Vancouver,' *Music*, Aug 1980

Miller, Mark. 'Jazz is alive and well and living in Vancouver,' Toronto *Globe and Mail*, 6 Sep 1980 (BNSG)

Vancouver Academy of Music. See Community Music School of Greater Vancouver.

Vancouver Bach Choir. A 150-voice choir founded in 1930 by Herbert Mason *Drost and Harvey P. Wyness. It first appeared publicly in June 1930 at the BC Music Festival and presented Bach's *Christmas Oratorio* 14 Dec 1930 at the *Orpheum Theatre. The choir's conductors have been Drost 1930–4, Ira *Dilworth 1935–40, Hugh *Bancroft 1946–8, Sherwood *Robson 1948–50, Lawrence *Cluderay 1950–9, G. Welton *Marquis 1959–61, Karel *ten Hoope 1961–5, and Meredith Davies with chorusmaster Beverly *Fyfe 1965–8, succeeded by Simon *Streatfeild. Streatfeild continued as conductor in 1981. Jon *Washburn was assistant conductor and chorusmaster 1970–4. Activities were suspended during World War II.

For many years the most significant choir in Vancouver, it has continued its Christmas presentations of such works as *Messiah* (broadcast nationally as early as 1934), Britten's *A Ceremony of Carols*, Berlioz' *L'Enfance du Christ*, and Honegger's *Le Roi David*. Other notable presentations have included Elgar's *The Dream of Gerontius* with Maureen *Forrester and Richard Lewis for 'CBC Wednesday Night' (30 Oct 1957), the premiere of Paul *McIntyre's *Judith* with Lois *Marshall (10 Aug 1958), the first Canadian performance of Bruckner's *Mass No. 3* (1 Aug 1959), 'A Choral Christmas 1960' sung with the Benedictine Monks of Westminster Abbey in Mission, BC, and the premiere of G. Welton Marquis' *God and a Child* (29 May 1962), commissioned by the choir. In 1979 it premiered *Freedman's *Green ... Blue ... White*. The choir has performed with other choirs and the *Vancouver SO. After participating in the opening ceremonies for the *Queen Elizabeth Theatre (15 Jul 1959), the choir made that hall its home.

In June 1971 the Vancouver Bach Choir was the first Canadian choir to perform at the International Koorfestival, Scheveningen, Holland, where its subsidiary Ladies' Bach Choir won a first prize and the full choir a third. The full choir was first in the large choir class of the 1978 BBC 'Let the Peoples Sing' competition. In 1977 the choir toured in Poland, singing in restored castles and cathedrals at Szczecin, Koszalin, Kamien Pomorski, Torum, and Warsaw. While in Europe the choir also sang at the Cathedral of Notre Dame in Paris.

Over the years the Vancouver Bach Choir has changed from a regional ensemble of limited repertoire to a sophisticated organization capable of a wide repertoire in the hands of its recent conductors and such guests as Kazuyoshi Akiyama, Sir Arthur Bliss, Irwin Hoffman, Sir Ernest *MacMillan, Zubin Mehta, William Steinberg, and Bruno Walter. It has recorded music by Bach, Holst, Deems Taylor, Vaughan Williams, and Stanford (ca 1971, Ensemble ES 7002, Hugh *McLean organ) and by R. Murray *Schafer (*Miniwanka, Psalm*, RCI 434). The choir began publishing a quarterly, *Tempo*, in August 1963.

BIBLIOGRAPHY

Lower, Thelma Reid. 'The Vancouver Bach Choir: a retrospect,' *CMB*, 4, Spring–Summer 1972

Mertens, Susan. 'The Bach Choir celebrates,' *Western Living*, May–Jun 1979 TRL

Vancouver Cello Club. Founded in 1969 by Ian Hampton, cello of the *Purcell String Quartet and still the club's president in 1980, to foster interest in cello playing. The organization has promoted interest in the cello repertoire – particularly in works for two or more cellos – and has provided a meeting ground for professional, amateur, and student cellists. Its chief activities have been workshops, master classes, and recitals. Its encouragement of the writing of new music for cello has resulted in works from Jack *Behrens, Robert Buckley, Jean *Coulthard, Alex *Pauk, Audrey *Piggot, and R. Murray *Schafer. The club's extensive library of cello literature is housed in the *Community Music School of Greater Vancouver. JDn

Vancouver Chamber Choir. A 16-voice ensemble formed in 1971 by its conductor, Jon *Washburn. In 1973 it became the first Canadian choir to win a first-place award in 'Let the Peoples Sing,' the international contest sponsored by the BBC and the European Broadcasting Union. In addition to presenting an annual concert series in Vancouver, it has toured in eastern and western Canada and in the USA and has been heard regularly over CBC radio and TV. James Bowman, Lois *Marshall, the *Purcell String Quartet, Nigel Rogers, Colin Tilney, the *Tudor Singers of Montreal, Delia Wallis, and Patrick *Wedd are among the artists who have performed with the choir. The choir itself has been a guest of the *Vancouver SO. In 1977 Washburn established the Vancouver Chorale, an auxiliary ensemble which augments the choir in performances of certain works. The choir's repertoire is wide-ranging, with an emphasis on short and Canadian works and on music which explores new choral techniques. The choir has commissioned and premiered works by several Canadians, including Thomas Baker, David Keeble, Imant Raminsh, R. Murray *Schafer, Jerome Summers, Brian Tate, and Elliot *Weisgarber.

Vancouver Chamber Choir with its conductor, Jon Washburn

DISCOGRAPHY (Washburn conducting)

Christmas Carols from Many Lands. 1977. CBC SM-338

Handel – Debussy – Barber. 1975, 1976. CBC SM-303

Haydn – Britten – Brahms. Baroque Str of Vancouver, Wedd org. 1973. CBC SM-243

The World of Folksongs: Willcocks – Brahms – et al. 1977. CVP 700G

BIBLIOGRAPHY

Cummings, Bob. 'The singers and the sound of the Vancouver Chamber Choir,' *PfAC*, Spring 1978 (MW)

Vancouver International Festival. Initiated in 1949, when Eby Koerner, Mary Roaf, and Elena Arkell Wait, all executives of the *Community Arts Council of Vancouver, discussed with members of Vancouver's academic, artistic, and business circles the possibility of a summer festival. After the success of the Summer School of the Arts at the *U of British Columbia, plans for such a festival were revived in 1954, and in 1955 the Vancouver International Festival was incorporated. Financial support came from the *Canada Council and the *Koerner Foundation, and from corporate and private donors.

The first festival, organized by Nicholas *Goldschmidt, was held in the summer of 1958 in the *Orpheum Theatre, the Georgia Auditorium, and the Hotel Vancouver Ballroom and included orchestral concerts, chamber music recitals, a major choral work (the Verdi *Requiem*), an opera (*Don Giovanni*), a drama (Lister Sinclair's *The World of the Wonderful Dark*, premiere), and an international film festival. Artists included the singers Pierrette *Alarie, Maureen *Forrester, George *London, Lois *Marshall, Aksel *Schiøtz, Léopold *Simoneau, and Joan Sutherland, the pianist Glenn *Gould, the conductors André Previn and

William Steinberg, the mime artist Marcel Marceau, and the Oscar *Peterson Trio. Two $1,000 prizes (one for orchestral music, one for chamber music) were offered to Canadian composers by BMI Canada and CAPAC, the prize-winning works to be given their first public performances at this festival. (Only one winner was named, Paul *McIntyre, for his cantata *Judith*, and the prize was awarded solely by CAPAC.)

The second festival (1959) was even more ambitious. The City of Vancouver and the provincial and federal governments provided monetary support. A new hall (the *Queen Elizabeth Theatre) facilitated a broadened concert schedule. Three works were commissioned: *String Quartet No. 3* by Harry *Somers, for premiere by the Hungarian String Quartet; *Tryptique*, an orchestral work by Pierre *Mercure; and *Four Songs* for high voice and orchestra by Robert *Turner. The festival also presented an array of attractions which included Harry Belafonte, the *Cassenti Players, the *Montreal Bach Choir, Anna *Russell, the Takarazuka Dance Theatre, and the conductors Herbert von Karajan and Bruno Walter, who appeared as guests with the festival orchestra. In an attempt to reduce financial losses the third festival was shorter and the programs were of a more general nature. Stellar attractions were the Peking Opera, symphony concerts conducted by William Steinberg and Carlos Chávez, two performances by the New York Philharmonic (conducted by Leonard Bernstein), the Kingston Trio, Glenn Gould, and Kerstin Meyer.

The fourth season included appearances by Les *Disciples de Massenet, the New York City Ballet, the Red Army Chorus, and the soprano Irmgard Seefried. There was opera again (the North American premiere of Britten's *Midsummer Night's Dream*, with Russell Oberlin and Mary Costa) and a large increase in pop content in the programming generally. Despite this, the festival incurred a considerable deficit and also was harshly treated by the critics. In the *CMJ* (Autumn 1961) Kenneth *Winters called it 'a week of festival in a month of mediocrity' and described the increasing pop-concert bias of the programming as 'a capitulation of patience, foresight and courage in the face of crude economics.'

It was not until early in 1962 that sufficient funds (donated by individuals, the city, and the province and raised partly through the efforts of radio station CHQM) guaranteed a fifth festival. The 1962 program featured the Comédie Française, the *Stratford Festival production of Gilbert & Sullivan's *The Pirates of Penzance*, and the Mormon Tabernacle Choir. In addition, the *Vancouver Opera presented *The Magic Flute*, and audiences heard concerts and recitals by the *CBC Vancouver Chamber Orchestra, the Juilliard Quartet, and the duo-pianists Vronsky and Babin. This was the last season in which an international film festival was included within the festival. Because of the continuing large deficit, a suspension of the 1963 festival was considered, and a new policy was adopted. It was decided that future festivals would be constructed around themes reflecting the life of countries from which Canada had derived its cultural heritage. The provincial government offered more money (on a matching basis), and fund-raising concerts were presented in the winter of 1962–3.

The sixth festival (1963), on a British theme, presented several plays and *The Best of Spring Thaw*. In the winter of 1963, the festival brought the Moscow Circus to Vancouver to raise funds for the 1964 festival. Built on a French theme, the 1964 program included stars of the Paris Opera Ballet, Charles Munch (conducting the *Vancouver SO, which for the first time was playing in the festival under its own name), Zizi Jeanmaire, and Les Ballets de Paris.

In 1965 the Vancouver International Festival changed its name to the Vancouver Festival and dropped the one-country theme. The eighth festival is remembered chiefly for the conducting of Igor Stravinsky and the performance of Margot Fonteyn and Rudolf Nureyev. For the 1966 festival it was decided that the Vancouver Opera Assn, the Playhouse Theatre Co, and the Vancouver SO each would prepare at least one production. The opera presented *Hansel and Gretel*, the festival *Oliver*, and the Playhouse Theatre *Big Soft Nellie* and *The Threepenny Opera*. The orchestra under Meredith Davies performed twice, once to mark the centenary of Busoni's birth. The Bolshoi Ballet and an *NFB presentation were included on the program. The 1967 festival opened with a concert conducted by Sir Arthur Bliss. Puccini's *The Girl of the Golden West* was produced by the Vancouver Opera Assn, and Van Cliburn and George Malcolm gave recitals. The 1968 festival suffered severe losses despite the artistic success of the Robert Joffrey City Centre Ballet and some other events. As a result, the 11th season was the last.

Festival presidents included W.C. Mainwaring 1958–9, General Sir Ouvry Roberts 1960–1, T.N. Beaupre 1962–3, David S. Catton in 1964, Martin A. Linsley in 1965, and R.A.C. Douglas 1966–8. Artistic directors included Nicholas Goldschmidt 1955–62, Dino Yannopoulos 1962–4, and Gordon *Hilker followed by William Crawford in 1964. For three years, 1965–7, in the absence of an artistic director, the festival was supervised by Hugh Pickett, Dora McQuade, and Julia Switzer. Hilker assumed the directorship again for the final year, 1968. (BNSG)

Vancouver New Music Society. Founded in 1972 by a group of musicians, radio producers, and university teachers, including Ian Hampton, George Laverock, Phyllis *Mailing, and Simon *Streatfeild, to initiate performances of contemporary works. After a successful season at the Arts Club Theatre the society made the Vancouver East Cultural Centre its home in 1973. At first, attention was given to early 20th-century works – Webern, Berg, and the young Stravinsky. In 1973 the emphasis shifted to newer music. Of six to eight annual concerts at least one presents a major theatrical work: Harrison Birtwistle's *Down by the Greenwood Side* (1973), Stravinsky's *Renard* (1974), Peter Maxwell Davies' *Eight Songs for a Mad King* (1975, with Donald *Bell) and *Missa super l'homme armé* (1976). The Vancouver New Music Society has commissioned works from Theo *Goldberg (*Daedalus*) and Barbara *Pentland (*Disasters of the Sun*) and has performed works by Robert *Aitken, Micheline Coulombe *Saint-Marcoux, John *Fodi, Serge *Garant, John *Hawkins, Rudolf *Komorous, Bruce *Mather, François *Morel, Alex *Pauk, Gilles *Tremblay, and others.

The society employs Vancouver musicians but regularly imports guest conductors, including Lukas Foss (1974), Udo *Kasemets, Serge Garant, and Peter Maxwell Davies (1976). Such foreign groups as Les Percussions de Strasbourg (1973), the Warsaw Music Workshop, the Kronos String Quartet, and Davies' Fires of London (all in 1976), Stuttgart's Trio Ex Voco (1977) and Tashi (1979) have been presented. The society's presidents have been George Laverock in 1972, Phyllis Mailing 1972–8, and Bruce *Davis.

BIBLIOGRAPHY

Schulman, Michael. 'Contemporary music groups thriving across Canada,' *MSc*, 303, Sep–Oct 1978 MW

The Vancouver Opera Association. Non-profit organization founded in 1959. In the two decades between its first production (*Carmen*, April 1960, with Nan Merriman, Richard Cassilly, and Louis *Quilico) and its 1980 season the Vancouver Opera Assn has given approximately 25 performances of four or five operas each (winter) season at the *Queen Elizabeth Theatre. It also, until 1967, mounted an opera each summer for the *Vancouver International Festival. In 1977 the season was divided between three home productions in September-October and an exchange program with Seattle in the spring. While drawing almost exclusively on the traditional repertoire, the association has attempted a balance between the most popular works (*La Traviata, La Bohème*, etc) and those less often done (Rossini's *L'Italiana in Algeri* in 1966, Massenet's *Le Roi de Lahore* in 1977). It also presented soprano Joan Sutherland's first *Norma* (1963) and first *Lucrezia Borgia* (1972).

Although it has continued to engage important foreign singers for casting, or box-office reasons (eg, Mary Costa, Reri Grist, Marilyn Horne, Dorothy Kirsten, Gloria Lane) the Vancouver Opera Assn, under its artistic directors Irving *Guttman 1960–74 and Richard Bonynge 1974–80, has made regular use of Canadian singers. Milla *Andrew, Donald *Bell, Clarice *Carson, Claude *Corbeil, Gloria Doubleday, Judith *Forst, Ermanno *Mauro, Alan *Monk, Cornelis *Opthof, Maria *Pellegrini, Louis Quilico, Heather *Thomson, Huguette *Tourangeau, Riki *Turofsky, and Lyn *Vernon are among those who have sung in its productions.

Anton Guadagno was named principal conductor in 1980 of the Vancouver Opera Assn orchestra, established in 1977, which replaced the *Vancouver SO. The latter had been the accompanying orchestra 1967–77. Conductors of productions have included Kazuyoshi Akiyama, Mario *Bernardi, Bonynge, James *Craig, George *Crum, Meredith Davies, and Otto-Werner *Mueller; stage directors have been Norman Ayrton, Herman *Geiger-Torel, Bliss Hebert, James Lucas, Lotfi Mansouri, and others. The association has encouraged local singers through two Resident Artist programs (1967–70, 1974–6) and through the Vancouver Opera Guild's 'Opera in the Schools' project. In 1977 a condensed *Il Trovatore* featuring young Canadian singers was performed for a total of some 21,000 elementary school children in British Columbia's lower mainland.

By the 1977–8 season the association's annual budget had reached approximately $1 million, with half of this amount coming from ticket sales (over 6000 subscriptions) and the rest from the *Canada Council, the British Columbia Cultural Fund, the city of Vancouver, and corporate and private donations. The company has been managed 1960–5 by Karl Norman, 1965–7 by James *Norcop, 1967–9 by John Finlay, 1969–75 by Brian Hanson, and 1975–8 by Barry Thompson, succeeded by Hamilton McClymont.

BIBLIOGRAPHY

'The Vancouver Opera Association 1960–4: 5 years of progress,' *OpCan*, Feb 1965

Watmough, David. 'The Vancouver Opera Association,' *OpCan*, Feb 1968

'Vancouver Opera Association,' *OpCan*, Sep 1975

Ewert, Henry. 'Joan Sutherland's 20 year love affair with Vancouver,' *Fugue*, Jun–Jul 1978

Mertens, Susan. 'The dream of international opera fades as Vancouver faces fiscal realities,' *PfAC*, Spring 1979

Forst, Graham. 'Hamilton McClymont: the VOA's high-flying General Director has down to earth plans,' *OpCan*, Fall 1979 BNSG

Vancouver Society for Early Music. Founded in 1969 by David *Skulski, Ray *Nurse, Jon

*Washburn, Hans-Karl Piltz, and Cuyler Page to foster interest in medieval, renaissance, and baroque music. The society has sponsored an annual series of concerts by guests (eg, the harpsichordists Gustav Leonhardt, Alan Curtis, and Colin Tilney, the recorder player Frans Brüggen, the tenor Nigel Rogers, the viola da gambist August Wenzinger, and the trumpeter Edward Tarr) and regular performances by its own two groups-in-residence, Hortulani Musicae and the Cecilian Ensemble. Hortulani Musicae was founded in 1968 by Nurse, Washburn, Skulski, and Doreen Oki to perform renaissance and medieval music on correct instruments. Prominent members have included Ingrid Suderman (soprano), Nurse (lute), Washburn (viola da gamba), John Sawyer (baroque violin, viola da gamba), and Patrick *Wedd (harpsichord, organ). The Cecilian Ensemble, a trio formed in 1972 by Wedd and Carlo Novi (baroque violin) and completed by Susan Napper (viola da gamba, baroque cello) is devoted to baroque music. Another ensemble, L'Age d'Or orchestra, was active 1972–4 under the Vancouver Society for Early Music's sponsorship. Besides performances (eight main series concerts and nine informal recitals in the 1977–8 season) the society has offered public lectures and workshops and has assembled a collection of some 20 accurate replicas of old instruments, built by the present-day Vancouver craftsmen Ross Hill (string instruments), Edward *Turner (harpsichords), Nurse (lutes), Rod Cameron (recorders and flutes), Michael Dunn (guitars and harpsichords), Je Titus (harps), and others. The first issue of the quarterly newsletter *Musick* (Summer 1979) included a history of the society. MW

Vancouver Symphony Orchestra. Until 1930 the history of symphony orchestras in Vancouver was one of discontinuity and uncertainty. The first Vancouver SO, formed in 1897 with 23 players under Adolf Gregory, gave three concerts in Dunn Hall, then disbanded. In 1907 it was revived briefly, with 36 members under Charles Ward. Another group, known as the 'Spare Time Symphony' and conducted by Oscar Ziegler, was playing in 1915 but was disbanded after his death ca 1919. In 1919 Henry Green organized a 60-member orchestra for the Vancouver Symphony Society under the leadership of F.L. Beecher (president) and Mrs B.T. *Rogers (vice-president). This orchestra survived for two seasons, but financial strains and the disappearance of Green (who had been refused an annual salary of $20,000) ended its activities. In 1921 an English musician, William Raven, started the Vancouver Philharmonic, which became officially the Capitol Theatre SO. With the advent of the talking motion picture this orchestra, too, lost its audience.

Very little symphonic music was heard in Vancouver during the 1920s. It was not until 1930 that the Vancouver Symphony Society was revived, largely through the efforts of Mrs B.T. Rogers, by then a notable patron of the arts. The conductor of the re-formed 80-member Vancouver SO was Allard de *Ridder, a pupil of Mengelberg. The first of four concerts in the 1930–1 season took place in the new *Orpheum Theatre on 5 October. In de Ridder's 10 years with the orchestra he increased the annual number of concerts to seven in Vancouver and two in Victoria. The CBC broadcasts of Vancouver SO concerts began during his tenure. De Ridder programmed no Canadian works except four of his own – including his *Violin Concerto*. He did, however, share his podium with several distinguished conductors, including Arthur *Benjamin, Sir Thomas Beecham, Gregori *Garbovitsky, and Sir Ernest *MacMillan. In 1941 de Ridder left Vancouver for Toronto, and the orchestra played for the next six years under a succession of guest conductors, including Barbirolli, *Beaudet, Bernstein, Dorati, Goossens, Klemperer, *Mazzoleni, and Sevitzky.

The Vancouver Symphony Orchestra under Kazuyoshi Akiyama on the Orpheum Theatre stage

Jacques Singer (b Przemysl, Poland, 9 May 1917, d New York, 12 Aug 1980) was engaged as music director in 1947 and greatly expanded the orchestra's activities, inaugurating school and pop concerts, visiting smaller centres, and augmenting the orchestral program with large choral-orchestral works such as Beethoven's *Symphony No. 9*. Though the orchestra was attracting new audiences, it was $40,000 in debt when Singer left Vancouver following the 1949–50 season.

Another period of guest conductors followed before the 1952 appointment of Irwin Hoffman (b New York City 26 Nov 1924), a protégé of Koussevitzky. During his 12 seasons with the orchestra Hoffman maintained a creditable standard of performance and added considerably to the orchestra's repertoire. He was responsible for the premieres of works by 11 Canadian composers, the addition of the popular 'Christmas Box Concerts,' and an increase in the number of school concerts. Also during Hoffman's tenure, the venue of the concerts changed in 1960 from the Orpheum Theatre and Georgia Auditorium to the new *Queen Elizabeth Theatre. Hoffman's wife, the violinist Esther Glazer (b Chicago 5 May 1926, Naumburg Award winner 1950) also made a significant contribution, if not directly to the orchestra, certainly to instrumental performances in Vancouver. She taught 1962–4 at the *U of British Columbia, gave master classes in violin in Victoria, and formed a string orchestra.

When Hoffman left in 1964, Meredith Davies (b Birkenhead, England, 30 Jul 1922) was chosen to succeed him. Davies had made a strong impression when he visited Vancouver in 1961 to conduct the North American premiere of Britten's *A Midsummer Night's Dream* at the *Vancouver International Festival. During his tenure, 1964–70, he rebuilt the orchestra, replacing veteran members with younger players, many from Europe and the USA, and developing the orchestra into an ensemble of high national standing. He also gave the premiere of Ginastera's *Estudios Sinfonicos* and, with the *Vancouver Bach Choir, the Vancouver premieres of several large choral-orchestral works, including Britten's *War Requiem*, Walton's *Belshazzar's Feast*, and Honegger's *King David*, as well as works of Messiaen, Berio, Henze, Penderecki, and contemporary Canadian and US composers, through a commercially sponsored 20th-Century-Music Series unique in Canada. When Davies left Vancouver in the autumn of 1970 the assistant conductor, Simon *Streatfeild (former principal viola with the London SO and the Vancouver SO), served as acting music director until the 1972 appointment of Kazuyoshi Akiyama (b Tokyo 1941). Akiyama, besides conducting the Vancouver orchestra, remained the conductor of the Tokyo SO, principal guest conductor of the Japan Philharmonic Orchestra, music director and conductor of the Osaka Philharmonic Orchestra, and music director of the American SO, succeeding Stokowski. He has guest-conducted the TS, the New York Philharmonic, the Cleveland Orchestra, the Philadelphia Orchestra, the Cincinnati SO, the St Louis SO, and the Hamburg Radio SO.

By 1980 the Vancouver SO under Akiyama had taken its place, with the *MSO, the *NACO, and the *TS, in the topmost echelon of Canadian orchestras, behind only the TS and the MSO in the number of concerts given in the 1979–80 season and boasting the largest subscription list of any orchestra in North America. Along with its usual division of the season into four concert series – a main one of 13 programs, each played three times; a series of 5 'Musically Speaking' programs, each played twice, introduced by guest hosts; and 2 separate pop series – the orchestra has offered special series, eg, in 1977 a Beethoven Festival and in 1978 a Brahms Festival. It also has sponsored solo recitals by famous performers – eg, an appearance by Isaac Stern in 1978.

The orchestra made an extended tour of Japan in 1974 and toured Canada in 1976, performing in Ottawa, Toronto, Hamilton, Montreal, Winnipeg, Saskatoon, and Edmonton. During the Canadian tour the orchestra presented the premiere of *Capriccio Concertante*, written by Robert *Turner for the cellist Zara *Nelsova and her husband, the pianist Grant Johannesen, who toured with the orchestra. Among the many other resident or native Canadian performers who have appeared with the orchestra in the 1970s are Clarice *Carson, Janina *Fialkowska, Maureen *Forrester, Judith *Forst, Don *Garrard, Ida *Haendel, Anton *Kuerti, Gabrielle *Lavigne, John *Melnyk, Arthur *Ozolins, Louis *Quilico, Claude *Savard, Robert *Silverman, Heather *Thomson, William *Tritt, Tsuyoshi *Tsutsumi, and Lyn *Vernon, sharing the spotlight with such distinguished foreign artists as Elly Ameling, Claudio Arrau, Vladimir Ashkenazy, Emanuel Ax, the Beaux Arts Trio, Pierre Fournier, Yo-Yo Ma, Yehudi Menuhin, John Ogdon, Peter Serkin, Isaac Stern, and Henryk Szeryng. Similarly, guest conductors in the 1970s came from both Canada and abroad; among them were Mario *Bernardi, Franz-Paul *Decker, James De Preist, Sixten Ehrling, Arthur Fiedler, André Kostelanetz, Neville Marriner, and John Pritchard.

In April 1977 the orchestra moved to a former but completely renovated home, the Orpheum Theatre.

By 1980 the CBC had released three recordings by the orchestra under Akiyama: Prokofiev's *Violin Concerto No. 1* (SM-235, ca 1973) with Steven *Staryk as soloist; Respighi's *Pines of Rome* and *Roman Festivals* (SM-335) produced in 1978 by the recording engineer Anton Kwiatkowski and acclaimed for its musical and technical qualities; and Holst's *The Planets* (SM-5002, 1979).

The concert masters of the orchestra have been Kathleen Carapata 1919–21, Arthur Gramm 1930–4, Jean *de Rimanoczy 1934–44 and 1951–6, Adolph *Koldofsky 1944–6, Albert *Steinberg 1946–51 (Steinberg also conducted the Vancouver Junior Symphony), Gideon Grau 1956–64, Jack *Kessler 1964–5, and Norman *Nelson 1965–73. Gerald Jarvis succeeded Nelson in 1973. Michael Allerton (b England 5 Mar 1935) was appointed orchestra manager in 1971, succeeding Victor *White.

On 29 Feb 1948 the orchestra presented the premiere of the *Violin Concerto* by the US composer David Diamond. It also has premiered Robert Turner's *Lyric Interlude* (ca 1956), Ernst *Friedlander's *Cello Concerto No. 2* (15 Oct 1961), and Michael *Baker's *A Struggle for Dominion* (26 Sep 1976) and *Symphony No. 1* (1 Oct 1978).

In September 1977 the orchestra began issuing the quarterly magazine – *Vancouver Symphony Orchestra* – which continued to appear regularly in 1980.

BIBLIOGRAPHY

'History and career of the Vancouver Symphony Society,' *Curtain Call*, Mar 1940

'Symphony, often in the red, started Green,' 'Who's who in orchestra's ranks,' Vancouver *Province*, 28 Dec 1963

Lower, Thelma M. 'An orchestra, a chamber group, a string quartet, and a summer music camp,' *CanComp*, 41, Jun 1969

Mitchell, Norah, and Forster, Sheila. *The Symphony Story* (Vancouver 1971)

Rossiter, Sean. 'On the road with the Vancouver Symphony,' *Vancouver*, Sep 1976

Mertens, Susan. 'The good ship VSO,' *Arts Bulletin*, Oct–Nov 1976

Schreiner, John. 'VSO,' *AudioScene Canada*, Apr 1977

Wyman, Max. 'Vancouver: hucksterism in the concert hall,' *PfAC*, Spring 1977

Gothe, Jürgen. 'VSO: very successful orchestra,' *Fugue*, Apr 1978

'Happy birthday to us! The VSO takes a backward glance over 60 years,' *Vancouver Symphony Orchestra*, Sep 1979

Edds, Jack. 'The Vancouver Symphony: a lesson in coordinated management,' *OCan*, Oct 1979

'The Vancouver Symphony travelling show,' *Vancouver Symphony Orchestra*, Mar 1980 (LC)

Vancouver Woman's Musical Club. Founded in 1905 by Mrs B.T. *Rogers, Mrs J.J. Banfield, Mrs C.M. Beecher, (first president 1905–7) and others and incorporated in 1916 under the guidance of Esther Beecher Weld and Mrs Walter *Coulthard. Membership has ranged from 100 to 600; in 1976 it stood at 200. The club's stated objective has been the advancement of music in the cultural, social, and educational life of Vancouver and British Columbia. The club was involved in the campaign in 1919 to introduce music study into Vancouver schools and assisted morally and financially in the formation in 1919 and revival in 1930 of the *Vancouver SO.

In the absence of professional impresarios in Vancouver, the club presented many famous performers in its early years, beginning in 1908 with Paderewski and continuing with such artists as Clara Butt, Mischa Elman, Amelita Galli-Curci, Josef Hofmann, Liza Lehmann, Benno Moiseiwitsch, William Primrose, Sergei Rachmaninoff, Ernestine Schumann-Heink, Luisa Tetrazzini, and Eugène Ysaÿe. In 1910 it sponsored three concerts by the New York SO under Walter Damrosch. From the earliest years, however, the club presented Canadian artists (eg, Kathleen *Parlow, the *Hart House String Quartet), and in 1980 it continued to do so. Barbara *Custance, Judith *Forst, Ross *Pratt, and Robert *Silverman are among the many. As local impresarios emerged, the club concentrated increasingly on the encouragement of young performers.

Over the years concerts have been held at the CPR's Opera House, the Oak Room of the Hotel Vancouver, the Vancouver Art Gallery, and elsewhere. In 1976 the club began holding its concerts at the Koerner Recital Hall of the *Community Music School of Greater Vancouver. (Free concerts have also been provided to hospitals, nursing homes, and other such institutions.) An annual scholarship, established in 1913, helped the careers of Donald *Bell, Jean *Coulthard, Lea *Foli, Arthur *Polson, Robert *Rogers, and Bernard *Turgeon. Besides receiving money awards, winners traditionally are presented in recital by the club. In 1976 a memorial trust fund was established to provide bursaries for Canadian music students. Born in the early years of Vancouver, the Vancouver Woman's Musical Club may claim a special place in the city's musical development. The club's archives, assembled by Mrs G. Inglis (president 1972–4), were presented to the Vancouver City Archives in 1975. (BNSG, JRl)

The Vancouver Woodwind Quintet (after 1976 the Winds of Vancouver). An offshoot of the former Vancouver Symphony Chamber Players. Members were Harriet Crossland (flute), Ronald *de Kant (clarinet), Warren Stannard (oboe), Roland Small (bassoon), and Robert *Creech (horn), succeeded in 1976 by Martin Hackleman. Founded in 1968, it was sponsored until 1970 by the JMC of British Columbia and presented programs jointly with the *Vancouver SO, the Vancouver School Board, and the Musicians' Association's Music Performance Trust Fund. The quintet gave some 40 concerts annually, most often in Vancouver schools but also in public, on provincial tours, and over CBC radio. Drawing on a wide repertoire, including many Canadian works, the quintet recorded music by Carl Nielsen, Ingolf Dahl, and Robert Turner (1970; CBC SM 139). In 1976 it ceased to tour. BNSG

van DIJK, Rudi (Martinus). Composer, b The Hague 27 Mar 1932, naturalized Canadian 1955. After studies 1944–52 at the Royal Cons of The Hague he moved in 1953 to Canada. While a bandsman 1953–6 in the Canadian army he studied composition (summer 1955) with Roy Harris in Toronto. After further studies 1964–5 with Max Deutsch in Paris, van Dijk worked 1965–6 in London for BBC TV. A composer in Ottawa and Toronto for over 15 years, van Dijk also taught 1969–72 at the *RCMT and 1972–5 at Indiana U at Purdue before joining the faculty at the Berklee College of Music, Boston. His compositions include piano and chamber pieces, songs, a *Christmas Cantata* (1967) for children's choir, *Sinfonia Concertante for Piano and Orchestra* (1959), *Four Epigrams* (1962, premiered by the *TSO), and a *Concertante on the B-A-C-H Motif* for flute and string orchestra (1963, premiered by Robert *Aitken with the Toronto Chamber Orchestra). His *The Shadowmaker* (1971–5, to texts from a book of the same title by Gwendolyn MacEwen) was premiered in 1978 by the baritone Victor *Braun and the TS. He is a member of the *CLComp, an associate of the *CMCentre, and an affiliate of PRO Canada.

BIBLIOGRAPHY

PRO Canada. 'Rudi van Dijk,' pamphlet (1979) (CF)

van GINKEL, Peter (Pieter Mathew Joseph). Bass-baritone, b Eindhoven, Holland, 10 Mar 1930. After early training in Holland van Ginkel emigrated to Canada, where his voice teachers were Nina *Dempsey in Winnipeg 1954–6 and Bernard *Diamant in Montreal 1957–60. He was a winner in the 1955–6 *'Singing Stars of Tomorrow.' He sang with the *Vancouver Opera in 1960 and made his *COC debut in Toronto in 1962 as Sparafucile in *Rigoletto*. With the COC Touring Company he sang in *Madama Butterfly* (1962) and *Carmen* (1964). With the *Metropolitan Opera National Company 1965–7 his roles included Figaro in *The Marriage of Figaro*, Marcello in *La Bohème*, and Junius in *The Rape of Lucretia*. In 1967 he created Grant in Murray *Adaskin's *Grant, Warden of the Plains* on the CBC and was affiliate artist at Waterloo Lutheran (*Wilfrid Laurier) U. He has sung 1968–70 with the Chicago Lyric Opera, was a leading bass-baritone with the Braunschweig Staatsoper 1970–2 and the Dortmund Opera 1972–3, and appeared with the San Francisco Opera in 1974. In 1974 he joined the Nürnberg Opera, and in 1976 he was honoured as that company's Star of the Year. In 1978 he returned to the Chicago Lyric Opera to sing the role of Satan in the premiere, 28 November, of Penderecki's *Paradise Lost*.

Reflecting the versatility of his voice, which encompasses both bass and baritone registers, van Ginkel's roles have included *Boris Godunov*, *Wozzeck*, and Deems Taylor's *Peter Ibbetson*, as well as Hans Sachs in *Die Meistersinger*, Wotan in both *Das Rheingold* and *Die Walküre*, Iago in *Otello*, and Jochanaan in *Salome*. Accompanied by Winifred *Sim, he has recorded Vaughan Williams' *Songs of Travel*, Hugo Wolf's *Poems of Michelangelo*, and Beethoven's *An die ferne Geliebte* (1973, CBC SM-257).

BIBLIOGRAPHY

Keys, Janice. 'Singing opera slugging game,' *Winnipeg Free Press*, 14 Oct 1978 (CC)

VANIER, Jeannine. Organist, teacher, composer, b Laval-des-Rapides, near Montreal, 21 Aug 1929; B MUS (Montreal) 1950, L MUS (Montreal) 1952. She studied at the *Institut Nazareth and at the *U of Montreal with Jean *Papineau-Couture and Clermont *Pépin (composition), Jean *Vallerand (history and orchestration), and Conrad *Letendre, Françoise *Aubut, and Georges *Lindsay (organ). She won second prize in the *Casavant Society competition in 1949 and an RCCO prize in 1952. She was the organist 1952–74 at St-Paul-de-la-Croix Church and taught theory and organ 1955–70 at the Institut Nazareth. In 1967 she began teaching ear training and keyboard harmony at the U of Montreal. In 1959 she was awarded a Sarah *Fischer Concerts Scholarship for her composition *Cinq pièces enfantines / Five Pieces for Children* for piano (Waterloo 1960; recorded 1972, with other contemporary Canadian works, by BMI Canada). In 1962 she won the *CAMMAC competition with her *Fantaisie* for three recorders (Berandol 1963), performed in 1965 by Mario *Duschenes's group for a *Canada Baroque recording (BC 1856). Also in 1965 her *Salve regina* was recorded by the *Montreal Bach Choir (RCI 206). NTr

VANNELLI, Gino. Singer, composer, b Montreal 16 Jun 1952. His father, (Joseph) Russ Vannelli, sang with the Montreal dance bands of Bix Belair and Maynard *Ferguson. The younger Vannelli played drums as a youth, studying privately, and with his brother Joe (a keyboard player, b Montreal 28 Dec 1950) formed a rhythm and blues band. He also studied theory at *McGill U. Though Vannelli recorded as early as 1970 (singing under the name Vann Elli for RCA Victor), it was not until 1974 that he made his first US and Canadian hit – 'People Gotta Move' (US A & M). This was followed by such other singles as 'Powerful People' (1975) and 'Love of My Life' (1976), all his own songs. He received the *Juno Award of 1975 as most promising male singer of the year. His recording of 'I Just Wanna Stop,' by his brother Ross (b Montreal 6 Mar 1956), was a million-seller and brought Vannelli a Grammy Award nomination in the USA and a Juno Award as male vocalist of 1978 in Canada.

Vannelli began touring in Canada and the USA in 1975, initially with an unusual band comprising three synthesizists (Joe Vannelli among them) and percussion. He established a home near Los Angeles in 1978 but continued to perform in Canada. His LPs 1973–8 for A & M have met with considerable success: *Crazy Life* (SP 4395), *Powerful People* (SP 3630), *Storm at Sun Up* (SP 4533), *The Gist of the Gemini* (SP 4596), *A Pauper in Paradise* (SP 4664), which includes Vannelli's four-part 'symphony' of the same name, recorded in London with the Royal Philharmonic Orchestra, and *Brother to Brother* (SP 4722). His music is ambitious, intense, and flamboyant, but to the extent that his popularity is built on his physical appearance – he has been described as 'Canada's first export sex symbol since Robert Goulet' (Steven Davey, *Toronto Star*, 25 Nov 1977) – his credibility as a musician has been undermined for many of his critics.

BIBLIOGRAPHY

Jackson, Marni. 'High-flying Gino Vannelli: more than meets the eye,' *Maclean's*, 28 May 1979 CGa, MM

Les Variétés lyriques. Private company founded in Montreal in 1936 by the singers Lionel *Daunais and Charles *Goulet to produce stage works, mainly operettas. During 19 consecutive seasons at the *Monument national – without public or private subsidies of any kind – the company presented a total of 1084 performances: 102 productions of operettas, 15 of operas, and one revue.

The Variétés lyriques succeeded the *Société canadienne d'opérette, which had ceased to exist in 1934 after 10 years of activity. The inaugural show, Lehar's *Land of Smiles* 22 Sep 1936, was followed by six other operettas. There were 426 subscribers the first season. Lopez' *La Belle de Cadix*, given 26 times during the 1930–1 season, held the record for a single production by the company, and the 1951–2 season was the largest, with a total of 97 performances.

When the Variétés lyriques closed its doors 30 Apr 1955 with Offenbach's *La Fille du Tambour-major*, the subscribers numbered 12,487 – not enough, however, to save the operation. The main reasons given for closing were the ever-increasing production costs (at this time no government subsidies were granted to theatre projects) and declining audiences after 1952 caused by the competition from TV.

French operetta was the mainstay of the company. The repertoire included works by some 20 composers, ranging from Hervé and Lecocq to Paul Misraki, Maurice Yvain, and Francis Lopez, and including Audran, Messager, Offenbach, and Planquette. Most of the classics of French operetta were performed at one time or another. Viennese works (by Lehar, Kalman, Fall, and Oscar Straus) were popular, as were US operettas (by Herbert, Romberg, Friml, and Youmans). Romberg's *The Desert Song* was the work most frequently revived by the Variétés.

The company presented its first opera, *Werther*, in its second season and subscribers subsequently heard *Carmen, Manon, The Barber of Seville, Lakmé, Les Contes d'Hoffmann, La Traviata, Mignon, La Fille du régiment, Mireille, Faust, Rigoletto*, and *Madama Butterfly*, at a rate of one opera a season. The entire repertoire was performed in French.

The Variétés lyriques regularly called on outstanding Quebec talents – singers, actors, instrumentalists, and conductors – and many young performers began their careers with the company. Participants included the sopranos Pierrette *Alarie, Rita Bibeau, Yolande *Dulude, Caro *Lamoureux, Marthe *Lapointe, Thérèse *Laporte, Marthe *Létourneau, Jacqueline Plouffe, and Irene *Salemka; the mezzo-soprano Jeanne *Maubourg; the contralto Anna *Malenfant; the tenors Jacques *Gérard, Raoul *Jobin, Jacques *Labrecque, Gérard *Paradis, Léopold *Simoneau, André *Turp, and Richard *Verreau; the baritones Napoléon *Bisson and Louis *Quilico; and the basses Yoland *Guérard, Jean-Pierre *Hurteau, and Joseph *Rouleau. Daunais and Goulet sang numerous roles besides taking responsibility for stage direction and administration.

Actors such as Fred Barry, Paul Berval, Guy Hoffmann, Juliette Huot, Jean-Pierre Masson, Guy Mauffette, and Henri Poitras also appeared. Starting in the second season, stars were brought from Paris. Performers such as Adrien Adrius, Gérard Boireau, Réda Caire, André Dassary, Michel Dens, Rudy Hirigoyen, Jacques Jansen, Armand Mestral, Germaine Roger, and Ugo Ugaro took prominent roles, some for several seasons. Most of the chorus was recruited from Les *Disciples de Massenet.

The orchestra consisted of about 30 musicians, conducted most often by Jean Goulet, but also by Jean-Marie *Beaudet, Lionel Renaud, and, on occasion, Charles Goulet. Maurice Lacasse-Morenoff was in charge of choreography. The sets and costumes were made locally, sometimes from Parisian designs. Daunais and Goulet staged most of the productions, but on occasion invited Henri Montjoye, director of the Gaîté-Lyrique of Paris, to produce a particular work.

Under the resourceful and enthusiastic direction of its two founders, the Variétés lyriques formed an important chapter in Montreal's entertainment history. From 1939 on, the company's avowed objective was 'to make lyric theatre the top artistic attraction of the metropolis, bearing in mind the changing taste of the public.' Its contribution over 20 difficult years, marked by the end of the Depression and by World War II, was remarkable, especially considering that the company received no public or private financial assistance.

BIBLIOGRAPHY

Lefebvre, Marie-Claire. 'Les Variétés lyriques: leur histoire et leur importance,' unpubl M MUS thesis, U of Montreal 1975
Goulet, Charles. *Sur la scène et dans la coulisse* (Quebec 1981) M-CL

VARRO, Marie-Aimée (b Warrot, m Treil). Pianist, b Brunoy, near Paris, 18 Feb 1915, d Neuchâtel, Switzerland, 14 sep 1971, naturalized Canadian 1960. A 1930 graduate of the Paris Cons, she studied with Alfred Cortot and Robert Casadesus and later with Emil von Sauer in Vienna. Her reputation established in Europe, she moved in 1955 to Canada, settling first in Vancouver and later in Halifax. She continued to perform in recital and with major orchestras in Canada, the USA, and Europe, specializing in the romantic repertoire. She premiered Jean *Coulthard's *Concerto* in 1967, and among her recordings of 19th-century music for *Canada Baroque Records (BC 1849, BC 2873) are two Coulthard études (BC 2837). She recorded for Orion (ORS 6912, ORS 7034, ORS 73112) and made three private recordings (1956, 1969, 1971).
BJE

VAUGHAN, Denny (Dennis). Singer, arranger, pianist, b Toronto 20 Dec 1922, d Montreal 2 Oct 1972. He performed in his teens on CFRB radio and with Horace *Lapp and studied at the U of Toronto before touring Europe with *The *Army Show* during World War II. Singing, arranging, and recording 1945–9 with the British dance bands of Carroll Gibbons, George Melachrino, and especially (1947–9) Geraldo, Vaughan became one of England's leading singing idols and was called 'the English Sinatra.' In 1949 he joined Robert *Farnon on the BBC's 'Journey into Melody.' After a year (1951) in New York as an arranger for Eddie Fisher, Ezio Pinza, and Kate Smith, he returned in 1952 to Toronto, starring first on CBC radio and then (1954–7) on CBC TV's 'Denny Vaughan Show.' He moved in 1959 to Montreal, where he led the Queen Elizabeth Hotel Orchestra, which was heard on CBC radio. From 1967 until shortly before his death Vaughan worked in Hollywood as a bandleader and was choral director for such TV programs as the 'Smothers Brothers' Show' and 'Glen Campbell Hour.' Besides recording in England, Vaughan was heard on several LPs of his own arrangements and compositions, including *Denny Vaughan* (ca 1951, Coral 56038) recorded in the USA, *Girls I Knew* (1967, CTL S 5092/RCA CAS 2358), *Denny Vaughan and His Orchestra* (1969, CTL S 5119/RCA CAS 2375) and others for CTL (one, CTLS 5068, accompanying Nick *Ayoub) and RCI. His single of Johnny *Cowell's 'Walk Hand in Hand' (1956, Spiral) was his most successful record. A BMI (PRO) Canada affiliate, Vaughan owned the Clarendon House publishing company. His papers were given to the *NL of C in 1981.

BIBLIOGRAPHY

Willock, David. 'In England he's the voice,' Montreal *Standard*, 14 Jan 1950 MM

VENNAT, Raoul. Music dealer, flutist, b Clairac, France, 14 May 1869, d Montreal 1 Oct 1962. A Montreal resident after 1903, he established a music store which specialized in French music. He initiated 'Les Concerts du lundi,' free concerts of French and Canadian music, heard first ca 1921–3 at the Bouvier Ltée department store, then ca 1923–4 over CKAC radio. Vennat was a founding director (1923) of the *Société canadienne d'opérette. Before his death the business became concerned only with embroidery and fabric. NT

VENNE, Stéphane. Singer-songwriter, arranger, record producer, administrator, b Verdun (Montreal) 2 Jul 1941. He taught himself the rudiments of music and at about 15 began composing songs. Between 1960 and 1966 he wrote and arranged music for several Quebec singers and started to perform on stage and to record. He made three LPs for Select, each one entitled *Stéphane Venne* (1965, SSP 24126; 1966, SSP 24136; 1967, SSP 24150) (see also Discography for Chansonniers). His career was launched when his song 'Un jour, un jour' / 'Hey Friend, Say Friend' was chosen as the theme song for *Expo 67.

As head of production 1967–72 for Barclay Canada Venne produced many hit singles of his own songs, including 'Le Début d'un temps nouveau' for Renée *Claude, 'Attention la vie est courte' for

Pierre *Lalonde, and 'Les Enfants de l'avenir' and 'Le Temps est bon' for Isabelle Pierre. In 1972 he formed Solset Inc to finance his productions. Gilles *Vigneault and Louise *Forestier are among those who have used his services as artistic consultant.

In 1972 Venne arranged and conducted the music for the LP *Stéphane Venne en dix chansons orchestrales* (Barclay 80162), which was made in Paris. The LP *Tranquillement* (Solset SOLT 59603), on which he sings 'C'est pas lundi aujourd'hui,' was released in 1975. For the singer Emmanuelle he wrote, among other songs, 'Le Monde à l'envers,' 'Chanter pour vivre,' and 'C'est pas fini.' He has written as well for Donald *Lautrec, Michel *Louvain, and Melody Stewart. He was conductor and arranger for the LP *Aimons-nous les uns les autres* by Michel Conte and arranger for *Petit Matin* (Le Nordet GVN 1006) by Sylvain Lelièvre. In the 1970s he also produced shows at the *PDA, composed the music for the films *Les Mâles, Où êtes-vous donc?*, and *Heads or Tails*, and wrote jingles.

In 1974 Venne was a principal in the promotion of the Superfrancofête, a French-speaking international festival held in Quebec City. In 1975 he was chairman of the board of directors for Chant'-Août, a festival of Quebec chanson in Quebec City. In 1976 he organized and directed a song competition for the Montreal Olympic Games and opened radio station CIEL-FM in Longueuil, a suburb of Montreal. He was president of *CAPAC 1977-9. He initiated and produced six LPs of programmed background music (*Musique de Québec*) issued in 1979 by *Kébec-Disc (6-KDM 967-972) (see Muzak).

Stéphane Venne is known for his complete professionalism; through his talent and imagination, he has contributed to the enrichment of the Quebec chanson as well as to the success of several performers.

WRITINGS

'It's time now to re-evaluate the composer's role,' *CanComp*, 139, Mar 1979

BIBLIOGRAPHY

Rudel-Tessier, J. 'Stéphane Venne wins Expo song contest,' *CanComp*, 14, Jan 1967

Kroll, Stephen. 'How a composer-producer packages Quebec superstars,' ibid, 91, May 1974

Dostie, Bruno. 'Stéphane Venne, Quebec's man-about-music,' ibid, 130, Apr 1978

(A-MG)

VERDICKT, Benoît. Organist, choirmaster, composer, educator, b Steenhuffel, Belgium, 27 Sep 1884, d Ville St-Laurent, Montreal, 28 Apr 1970. A graduate of the Mechlin Cons, he also studied at the Interdiocesan School of Sacred Music in that city with Edgar Tinel, Aloys Desmet, and Oscar Depuydt. He arrived in Canada in 1906 and was organist 1906-12 in Victoriaville, Que, and 1912-13 in Rochester, NY, and choirmaster 1913-63 at the Sts-Anges Church in Lachine, near Montreal. During his years in Lachine he organized concerts, conducted the local concert band, and taught privately. Gustave Robitaille was among his pupils (piano and theory). Verdickt was director of music education for the Lachine school board and also taught solfège for the Quebec government. He wrote some church music which he published himself, notably *Cantique de mariage* for soloist and two-part choir (1918) and his major work, *Missa pro defunctis* for three-part choir and organ (1941). That his contribution to the community's cultural life was appreciated is evident from an article that appeared at the time of his death: 'There are many among us who owe him their taste and their musical training. For that reason he will always remain a prominent figure in the history of Lachine' (*Messager de Lachine*, 6 May 1970). YL

VERMANDERE (Brother Placide), **Joseph** (Émile). Composer, organist, critic, b Heule, Belgium, 18 Jan 1901, d Montreal 23 Apr 1971; B MUS (Montreal) 1932, L MUS (Montreal) 1935, D MUS (Montreal) 1945. He and his family emigrated to Canada and settled in Montreal in 1908. He entered the Congregation of the Holy Cross in 1912 and took his final vows in 1922. He studied with Benoît-F. *Poirier (organ), Raoul *Paquet (organ and harmony), and Alfred *Laliberté (piano). He was organist and cantor 1919-37 at St Joseph's Oratory, and a teacher and the organist at the Collège Notre-Dame. With his brother Henri (Brother Séverin), who studied organ and composition with him, Vermandere founded in 1938 the boys' choir school of the *Petits Chanteurs à la Croix de Bois. He was attached 1945-56 to Fides, the publishing house run by his community. In addition he served his order as provincial secretary, archivist, and director of publications.

Brother Placide's first published compositions were the motets 'Ecce fideles' (*Annales de St-Joseph* 1921) and 'Quicumque sanus vivere' (ibid 1922; reprinted in *Messager du T.-S. Sacrement*, March 1943). His *Ode à Jacques Cartier* for soloists, chorus, and organ on a text by Louis *Bouhier (Archambault 1935) was performed in 1935 in Notre-Dame Church. Among his incidental music is a 60-minute score for soloists, chorus, and orchestra for Corneille's *Polyeucte*, performed in May 1934, as well as music for Arnoux's *Huon de Bordeaux* (1947) and for Barbier's *Le Roi Cerf* (1948). His *Te Deum* for soloists, chorus, orchestra, and organ was commissioned for CBC radio and broadcast 13 May 1945 under J.-J. *Gagnier to celebrate the Allied victory in World War II. It was revived in 1947 and 1957 at the Collège de St-Laurent. He composed a *Mass in E* for choir and organ (1938), a *De profundis* published in *Chants et motets pour les défunts* (Quebec City 1938), and various folksong harmonizations, motets, and hymns.

Between 1955 and 1960 Brother Placide published numerous poems and articles, as well as music criticism under the initials J.P. in the Montreal weekly *Notre Temps*. The *Catalogue of Canadian Composers* gives a partial list of his compositions. GP

VERNON, Lyn. Mezzo-soprano, b New Westminster, BC, 19 Aug 1944. She studied piano as a child, then 1962-3 and 1964-6 at the *U of British Columbia with Barbara *Custance, Kathryn Bailey, and Marshall *Sumner. Her voice teacher there was Donald Brown. She was a member 1966-8 of the *Vancouver Opera training program, and in 1967 she was a student in the San Francisco Opera's Merola program, winning the Gropper Memorial Award. She furthered her studies at the Zurich Opernstudio then in Geneva, in 1968, with Maria Carpi privately and Herbert Graf and Lotfi Mansouri at the Centre lyrique international. She performed 1968-70 in Zurich, Vancouver (Mrs Noye in *Noye's Fludde*), Geneva (*Carmen*), Berne, and Florence (Waltraute in *Götterdämmerung*), and, after appearing in 1972 with the Australian Opera as Octavian in *Der Rosenkavalier* and Maddelena in *Rigoletto*, she sang 1972-5 as a member of the Zurich Opera. There her roles included Nicklausse in *The Tales of Hoffmann* and Ulrica in *The Masked Ball*. She also, during these years, made guest appearances in Geneva as Annina in *Der Rosenkavalier*, Barbara in Janáček's *Katya Kabanová*, and Flosshilde in *Das Rheingold* and in London with the English National Opera as Octavian. Other European appearances have been with l'Orchestre de la Suisse romande and at the Montreux festival. She made her *COC debut in 1974 as Marina in *Boris Godunov* and Judith in *Bluebeard's Castle*, sang Marie in 1977 in that company's Canadian premiere of Berg's *Wozzeck*, and returned in 1978 to take the title role in Tchaikovsky's *Joan of Arc* and in 1979 to sing *Carmen*. She was the Female Chorus opposite Jon *Vickers in Britten's *The Rape of Lucretia* at the *Guelph Spring Festival (1974). She has sung with the *Edmonton Opera, the *NACO, and the *Vancouver SO. Vernon re-established a home in Canada (at Hudson Hope, BC) in 1975 but has continued to sing abroad, particularly in Switzerland.

Lyn Vernon

BIBLIOGRAPHY

Gothe, Jurgen. 'Down-to-earth diva,' *Fugue*, Oct 1978

BNSG

VERREAU (Verreault), **Richard**. Tenor, b Château-Richer, near Quebec City, 1 Jan 1926. He began singing in his parish church. After winning a *Quebec SO competition for young artists he decided in 1945 to enter *Laval U. He studied there with Émile *Larochelle and took private lessons from Louis *Gravel. In 1949, on a Quebec government scholarship, he went to Paris, where Raoul *Jobin gave him help and advice. In 1951 he signed a six-month contract with the Opéra de Lyon to sing in *Lakmé, Manon, Mireille*, and *Les Pêcheurs de perles*. Returning to Canada in 1952, he met Beniamino Gigli and went to Rome to study 1952-4 with that master of bel canto.

Verreau was a frequent soloist 1953-60 with the *MSO, and in 1956 he made his debut with the New York City Opera, singing Wilhelm Meister in *Mignon*. Immediately thereafter he sang Rodolfo in *La Bohème* and the Duke in *Rigoletto* at Covent Garden. He also appeared there in Berlioz' *The Trojans*. Returning to North America, he sang in *Roméo et Juliette* in San Francisco. His interpretation of the tenor part in Verdi's *Requiem* was greatly admired; he sang it in Montreal in 1957, 1958, and 1962 and at the Hollywood Bowl in the summer of 1958. He was invited in 1960 to the *Vancouver International Festival, and in the same year he became a principal tenor of the New York City Opera, remaining with this company ca 1960-3.

Verreau travelled through Italy, Belgium, France in 1959 and Austria in 1960, and was heard in 1964 in the USSR. He sang in *Tosca* with the MSO in 1963 and on 28 November made his debut at the *Metropolitan Opera in *Faust*. He sang with the *Opera Guild of Montreal (*La Traviata* 1962, *Faust* 1963, *Madama Butterfly* 1965, and *La Bohème* 1966), with the *Théâtre lyrique de Nouvelle-France (*Werther, Tosca* 1963, *Manon* 1967), with the

*Montreal Festivals (*Werther* 1963), and on CBC radio and TV ('L'*Heure du concert,' 'Récital,' 'Music Hall,' 'Sérénade'). In 1965 he repeated his role in *Manon* with the Metropolitan Opera, and in 1967 he repeated the title role in *Faust* with the MSO at *Expo 67.

Verreau's voice has a pleasant sound with a rare velvety quality; however, he is not always at ease in stage roles. In *La Presse* (24 Jul 1968), Gilles *Potvin praised his warm tone 'which keeps its quality throughout the range.' In 1977 Verreau opened an art gallery bearing his name in Quebec City.

DISCOGRAPHY

Bach *Mass in B Minor*. Philadelphia O, Ormandy cond, Temple U Choirs, R.E. Page dir. 1963. Col M3L 280

Berlioz *The Damnation of Faust* (extracts). O Lamoureux, Markevitch cond. 1960. DGG 2538244

Chantons Noël. André Grassi O and Chorus. 1959. RCA LSC-2390

Concert: Adam – Gounod – Bizet – et al. Yvonne Gouverné Chorus, RCA Victor SO, R. Blareau cond. RCA LSC-2645

Handel – Caccini – Stradella – et al. Newmark pf. 1967. RCI 249

Opéra: Quelques Grands Airs. Turin SO. W. Pelletier cond. 1961. RCA LSC-2458

Richard Verreau à l'église. Disciples de Massenet, Goulet dir, J. Martin org. 1958. RCA CCS-1003

Romance: French and Italian romances. André Grassi O. 1961. RCA LSC-2573

Sérénade: Neapolitan airs. André Grassi O. 1960. RCA LSC-2502

CH

VERSCHELDEN, Louis. Baritone, physician, b Ste-Thérèse-de-Blainville (Ste-Thérèse), near Montreal, 11 Jan 1881, d Montreal 18 Mar 1948. He was educated at the Collège de Ste-Thérèse, where he was organist while taking lessons in solfège, piano, and organ. He then studied medicine at Laval U in Montreal (U of Montreal), was a soloist at St James Cathedral, and worked with Guillaume *Couture in 1901 to learn the technique of choral conducting. He was choirmaster 1902–44 at St-Louis du Mile-End (later St-Enfant-Jésus) Church and conducted a 45-voice choir with which Paul-Émile *Corbeil, Émile *Gour, and Joseph *Saucier occasionally sang as soloists.

Verschelden studied voice 1921–4 with Salvator *Issaurel and gave concerts in Montreal at the *Monument national, the *St-Denis Theatre, Salle St-Sulpice, and other halls. He and his daughter Marthe, a soprano and a pupil of Issaurel, often performed together in Montreal, Ottawa, St-Hyacinthe, and elsewhere. He sang the role of Jean in the oratorio *Jean le Précurseur* in 1923, 1924, and 1928 and was a soloist in Massenet's *Hérodiade* and Honegger's *Le Roi David* with the *Assn des Chanteurs de Montréal. In 1931 he was president of the Orphéon de Montréal.

Verschelden's grandniece Paule Verschelden (m Bisaillon, mezzo-soprano, b Montreal 17 Apr 1938) studied with Lina Narducci, made her debut in 1967 in Manuel de Falla's *The Three-Cornered Hat* and in 1969 sang Carmela in his *La Vida Breve*, both with the *MSO. Between 1971 and 1975 she sang with the *Opéra du Québec, notably in *Il Trittico* and *Rigoletto*. She has toured as a member of the *Ensemble Cantabile de Montréal, and in 1976 she sang in Bizet's *Docteur Miracle* at La *Poudrière Theatre in Montreal. Her roles on CBC radio have included Dulcinée in Massenet's *Don Quichotte* and the title role in Thomas's *Mignon*.

BIBLIOGRAPHY

Gaétan. 'Mr Louis Verschelden,' *P-T*, vol 9, Nov 1903

IP-C

VETTER, Jean-Pierre. Pianist, teacher, b Vevey, Switzerland, 18 Nov 1927, naturalized Canadian 1961; diplôme de virtuosité (Lausanne Cons) 1948. After his studies at the Lausanne Cons he took further training 1949–50 in Florence with Rio Nardi and in Siena with Guido Agosti. A scholarship from the French government allowed him to study 1950–5 in Paris with Pierre Kostanoff, whose assistant he became. He gave recitals and played with orchestras in Brussels, Geneva, Lausanne, and Zurich.

Vetter emigrated to Canada in 1955 and subsequently performed with the Calgary and Edmonton SOs. In Edmonton he taught 1955–67 at *Alberta College and played for various organizations, including the *Edmonton Chamber Music Society, the *Edmonton Musical Club, and the Northern Concert Society. He was in charge of the piano class 1967–76 at the *École normale de musique in Montreal; in 1976 he moved to a similar appointment in the music module of *UQAM.

CH

VÉZINA. Quebec musicians: 1 / François and 2 / Joseph, his son.

1 (Xavier) **François**. Master painter, bassoonist, clarinetist, bandmaster, b Quebec City 10 May 1812, d there 12 Feb 1891. He was the original bassoonist in the *Musique Canadienne (founded 1836), as he had been in an ensemble which existed for five or six months in 1831. He was a member also of the Orchestre Sauvageau, which he conducted 1850–60, succeeding the *Sauvageau brothers Charles and Benjamin. His son François (b 1844) was the godson of Charles Sauvageau. Another son, Ulric, became a bassist in the Société symphonique de Québec.

BIBLIOGRAPHY

LeVasseur, Nazaire. 'Musique et musiciens à Québec,' *La Musique*, vol 1, Jul 1919

Roy, Pierre-Georges. 'La première fanfare québécoise,' *BRH*, vol 43, 1937

2 (François) **Joseph**. Bandmaster, organist, choirmaster, teacher, composer, music dealer, publisher, b Quebec City 9 Jun 1849, d there 5 Oct 1924; hon D MUS (Laval) 1922. He was educated at the École St-Jean-Baptiste and the *Séminaire de Québec. Except for instrumental lessons with his father and six months of studies in harmony with Calixa *Lavallée, he was self-taught in music. Owing to a remarkable memory and a capacity for hard work, however, he succeeded in playing and teaching most of the wind instruments and established himself as the leading conductor of musical ensembles in Quebec City and the surrounding area. He enrolled at the Quebec Military College in 1866, began to play the baritone in the band of the 9th Battalion of the Quebec Rifles in 1867, and conducted the band 1869–79. Thereafter until 1912 he directed the band of the 'B' Battery of the Royal Canadian Artillery.

In 1876 Vézina founded the Beauport Concert Band, which made its debut the following December in Quebec City at a concert organized by Célestin *Lavigueur. At a competition for concert bands in 1877 the ensemble received a mention, and the Montmorency Concert Band, which Vézina also conducted, tied for first prize with the band of the 9th battalion. The Beauport band placed first in 1878 in a national competition held in Montreal. Vézina also served 1879–1924 as director of the concert band of the Séminaire de Québec.

For special occasions Vézina added choirs, solo singers, and extra instrumentalists, both Canadian and foreign, to his bands. He conducted 100 band musicians from Quebec City, Beauport, and Fall River, Mass, at the historic performance 24 Jun 1880 of *'O Canada,' which he added as a finale to his *Mosaïque sur des airs popularies canadiens*. Emma *Albani sang under his baton in 1896. When the Duke of York visited Quebec City in 1901, Vézina conducted 250 musicians and 1000 choristers. In 1902, for the 50th anniversary of *Laval U, he conducted a 300-voice choir in two performances of the oratorio *Le Paradis perdu* by Théodore Dubois. His success encouraged J.-Alexandre *Gilbert and Arthur *Lavigne to assemble about 30 of these musicians in 1903 to form the Société symphonique de Québec (*Quebec SO), of which Vézina was the conductor until his death and president 1910–11. The orchestra won the Earl Grey competition in Ottawa in 1907.

Joseph Vézina

In 1908 Vézina organized the musical events for Quebec City's tricentenary celebrations. He served 1911–24 as conductor of the concert band of the cadets of the École St-Jean-Baptiste, and in 1916 he founded the Vézina brass band, which gave summer concerts on the terrace of the Château Frontenac.

For these ensembles, Vézina composed numerous marches and light concert pieces. His earliest known composition is a valse de concert, *The Canadian Rifles*. He also wrote for orchestra, voice, and piano. His three operettas, *Le Lauréat*, *Le Rajah*, and *Le Fétiche*, were premiered by the Société symphonique de Québec with soloists and a choir from Laval U. Several of his tunes have been employed by Godfrey *Ridout in his orchestral suite *Frivolités canadiennes*, recorded by the *CBC Vancouver Chamber Orchestra. Vézina published several of his works through his own publishing firm and ran a music store 1872–9, either alone or in partnership with Alfred Vézina.

Vézina was organist 1896–1912 at St-Patrice Church and choirmaster 1912–24 at the Quebec Basilica. He was president 1914–15 of the *AMQ and in 1922 took part in the establishment of the School of Music of Laval U, where he taught harmony until 1924. He also taught 1879–1924 at the seminary, 1916–24 at the Académie commerciale, and 1917–24 at the Collège Jésus-Marie de Sillery.

A hard-working man of limitless patience and tenacity, Vézina was a leading light in the musical life of Quebec City between 1870 and 1925. A year before his death he conducted 350 choristers and 100 instrumentalists in Gounod's oratorio *La Rédemption*.

Some of Vézina's children have continued the family's musical tradition. Raoul (b Quebec City 1882, d 1954) was the original principal bassoon with the Société symphonique de Québec and served as president 1926–9. He was also a cornetist and taught winds at Laval U and the Séminaire de Québec. His brothers Jules and Arthur were respectively violinist and bassoonist and were members of the Société symphonique.

The Séminaire de Québec has a Joseph Vézina collection, as has the *CMQ, which also holds material pertaining to Raoul and his son Roger.

SELECTED COMPOSITIONS

STAGE

Le Lauréat, opéra comique (F.-G. Marchand). 1906. Ms

Le Rajah, opéra bouffe (B. Michaud). 1910. H. Chassé 1910 (libretto only)

Le Fétiche, opéra comique (A. Plante, A. Langlais). 1912. Quebec *L'Événement* (libretto only)

La Grosse Gerbe, opera comique (incomplete)

ORCHESTRA OR BAND

The Canadian Rifles Waltzes. 1870. band (pf). Morgan 1870? (pf)

Pot-pourri sur des mélodies canadiennes. 1877. Band. Ms. Edison 689,2290 (Edison Concert Band)

La Canadienne. 1878. Band (pf). Ms

Le Voltigeur de Québec. 1879. Band. Ms

Mosaïque sur des airs populaires canadiens. 1880. Orch (band or pf). R. Vézina 1926 or 1927 (pf)

Estrella Valse. 1881. Orch (fl, str or pf). A. Lavigne (pf)

Le Galant artilleur, overture. 1882. Band. Ms

Souffle parfumé. 1882. Orch (band or pf). Lavigne & Lajoie 1887 (pf). RCI 233/Cap ST 6261 (*CBC Wpg O)

Ton sourire. 1882. Orch (band). Ms

Fantaisie caractéristique. 1883. Band. Ms

Grande Valse de concert. 1883. Band, solo cornet. Ms

La Brise 'The Quebec Yacht Club Waltz.' 1886. Orch (band). A. Lavigne nd

Hymne à l'Union commerciale (P. Lemay). 1887. Chorus, band (org). Ms

Le Jubilé de la Reine. 1887. Orch (band or pf). A. Lavigne (pf)

De Calgary à MacLeod. 1889. Band (pf). A. Lavigne (pf)

Le Lys blanc. 1889. Orch (band or pf). Ms

Conversazione. 1891. Orch (band or pf). A. Lavigne (pf)

Vive Champlain. 1898. Harm (pf). Ms

Souvenir d'amour. 1901. Orch. Ms

Friskarina, overture. 1905. Band. Samuels

Several other works and arr for band including *Frontenac* (1879), *B.B. Battery Officers* (1880), *Royal Rifles March* (1890), *Carnaval de Québec* (1894), *17th Regiment March* (1895), *Royal Grand March* (1901), *Chant triomphal* (1923)

Several works for pf including *Les Roses d'or* (A. and J. Vézina 1876) and *Cupid Polka* (Lavigne 1884); a work for fl, *L'Oiseau mouche* (1885); works for voice and choir, including *Je me souviens* (1898) and *En avant* (1914, Bélair 1915, *P-T*, Feb 1915)

BIBLIOGRAPHY

'M. Joseph Vézina,' *La Musique*, vol 1, May 1919

LeVasseur, L.-Nazaire. 'Musique et musiciens à Québec,' ibid, vols 3, 4, 1921, 1922

Du Berger, Jean. 'Le Lauréat,' *Dictionnaire des oeuvres littéraires du Québec* vol 1, ed Maurice Lemire (Montreal 1978) (JB-T)

VIAU, Albert. Baritone, teacher, composer, b Montreal 6 Nov 1910; B MUS (Montreal) 1966, teaching certificate (Quebec Ministry of Education) 1966. He took piano lessons from Arthur Caron, but at about 17 decided to study voice. His teachers were Victor *Brault, Arthur *Laurendeau (voice), Conrad *Letendre (diction), Dom Georges Mercure (Gregorian chant), and Oscar *O'Brien, Michel *Perrault, and Roland Van de Goor (harmony). After studying the classical repertoire he specialized in folk music and traditional songs. He made his debut in 1931 in *Roméo et Juliette* at Loew's Theatre, Montreal, and sang in 1934 in two CRBC series – 'La Petite Histoire' and 'Le Chanteur de lied,' the latter with Léo-Pol *Morin and Jean-Marie *Beaudet as piano accompanists. Paul-Emile *Corbeil engaged him soon afterwards for his quartet the Imperial Grenadiers. He was a soloist on numerous radio programs, singing regularly for 21 years on the CBC's 'Le Réveil rural' and for 20 years on the CBC's (later CKAC's) 'Le Quart d'heure de La Bonne Chanson.' He was a producer 1953–4 for radio station CJMS, continued giving numerous recitals in Canada and the USA, and for 15 years worked with vocal groups as director and arranger. In 1950 he became organist-choirmaster at St-Sixte Church in St-Laurent, Montreal, and in 1965 he began to teach for the Catholic School Commission of Montreal, also giving lessons in voice placement, piano, guitar, and recorder at his studio in St-Laurent. He made some 50 recordings (listed in *Pionniers du disque folklorique*), most of them for La *Bonne Chanson. In addition he recorded 'Le Rêve passe' with the *Canadian Grenadier Guards Band (RCA 216605) and (under the pseudonym Jacques Dupont) recorded 'Partons, la mer est belle,' 'Le Soir sur l'eau,' and 'Le Lac des amours' (Musica CT 12095-96). He wrote over 200 songs, some of which were comic patter songs, as well as hymns and a requiem mass. In 1954 he published *Six Chansonnettes pour bambins et bambines* and in 1958 *Six Chansons enfantines* with the Éditions Albert Viau. PD

VICKERS, Jon (Jonathan Stewart). Tenor, b Prince Albert, Sask, 29 Oct 1926; hon LL D (Saskatchewan) 1963, hon LL D (Laval) 1978. The sixth child in a family of eight, he recalls singing in a Christmas concert at the age of three. His boy's treble had become a robust tenor by the time he had finished high school, and he joined Baptist choirs in Prince Albert and Flin Flon (where he worked in chain stores) and sang leading roles in Gilbert & Sullivan and Victor Herbert operettas. Compulsive about his gift, he sang, in those days, 'for anyone anytime anywhere.'

In 1946 he became assistant manager of a chain store in Winnipeg, but soon the demand for his service as a singer began to encroach on his time, and his employer ordered him to give up singing. Instead he resigned and became a hardware salesman, but continued to sing. Encouraged by Mary *Morrison to study voice formally, he sent a recording of his singing to Ettore *Mazzoleni at the *RCMT. Accepted as a scholarship student in the fall of 1950, he began training with George *Lambert. During his first year in Toronto Vickers sang in 30 oratorio performances for the Board of Education, was soloist in *Messiah* at the *U of Western Ontario, was chosen by Mazzoleni as soloist for the Canadian premiere of Bruckner's *Te Deum* with the massed RCMT choirs, and in the fall of 1951 sang in *Messiah* at Massey Hall with the *Toronto Mendelssohn Choir. In 1952 he won honourable mention in the CBC radio competition *'Singing Stars of Tomorrow' and first prize in Radio Canada's *'Nos Futures Étoiles.' By 1955, despite wide exposure in concert and oratorio and some 28 operatic performances, including *COC appearances as the Duke in *Rigoletto* (1954), Alfredo in *La Traviata* (1955), and Alfred in *Die Fledermaus* (1954), he had received no offers from either the USA or Europe. However, after his performances as the Male Chorus in the *Stratford Festival's production of Britten's *The Rape of Lucretia* and as Don José in a 1956 COC production of *Carmen* with Regina Resnik, he was invited in 1957, on Resnik's recommendation, to sing in concert performances of *Fidelio* and *Medea*, the latter with Eileen Farrell, in New York. Also in 1956 Sir David Webster, general administrator of the Royal Opera House, Covent Garden, visited Canada, heard Vickers, and invited him to London for an audition. A three-year contract with the Royal Opera was the result. After his debut on tour with the Covent Garden company as Riccardo in *The Masked Ball* (January 1957) Vickers received enthusiastic notices, and he subsequently enjoyed great personal success in *Carmen, Don Carlo, Aida*, and *The Trojans*. After his debut at Bayreuth in 1958 as Siegmund in *Die Walküre*, Vickers was acclaimed as the world's leading interpreter of the role. That same year he sang Jason to Maria Callas' *Medea* in Dallas. By the end of the 1959–60 season, having

Jon Vickers

appeared with the Vienna Staatsoper and the Teatro Colòn in Buenos Aires and having sung in *Peter Grimes* and *Fidelio* at the *Metropolitan Opera, he decided to become a freelance artist.

Vickers' roles over the years have represented most of the dramatic and Heldentenor repertoire: Don José, Radames, Don Carlo, Canio, Otello, Tristan, Aeneas (*The Trojans*), Siegmund, Parsifal, Florestan, the Emperor (*Die Frau ohne Schatten*), and, his favourite, Peter Grimes. In the latter role he is noted for the projection of a dramatic dimension rare on the operatic stage. He regards the operas of his repertoire as conveyances for their composers' deepest emotions, intuitions, and beliefs, not as vehicles for voices. Consequently he concerns himself with Nietzschean philosophy in his interpretation of Tristan and conceives Otello as 'the Julius Caesar of the Venetian Empire.' One of Vickers' most significant associations has been with the conductor Herbert von Karajan. He sang in Karajan's first three Salzburg Easter Festivals (1966, 1967, 1968), recorded *Tristan und Isolde, Die Walküre, Otello*, and *Fidelio* and filmed *I Pagliacci* and *Otello* with the conductor, and has sung under his baton in the great opera houses, including La Scala and the Metropolitan.

Though he has given occasional recitals in Canada, notably in Toronto and at the opening of the 1969 *Guelph Spring Festival, Vickers in his maturity has sung little opera in Canada. While this has been blamed on Toronto critics' reactions to his recitals, in the 1960s and 1970s it probably was due to his fees, which by then were justifiably large, and to his time, which was too limited to accommodate the weeks of rehearsal often demanded. Nevertheless, there have been stellar occasions: he sang Otello in four performances in July 1967 at the World Festival (*Expo 67) in Montreal. With the soprano Regine Crespin and the *MSO he sang act 1 of *Die Walküre* at the opening ceremonies of the *NAC, 10 Jun 1969. He was the Male Chorus in the Guelph Spring Festival production (4, 6, and 8 May 1974) of Britten's *The Rape of Lucretia*. With the soprano Birgit Nilsson and the *TS under Zubin Mehta he sang opera excerpts in what was billed as a 'Dream Concert' in Toronto in November 1974. And with the *Opéra du Québec in May 1975 he was Tristan in five Montreal performances of *Tristan und Isolde* and acted as host for the production when it was seen on CBC TV (9 Feb 1977). An eight-city tour of Saskatchewan in 1977 with his accompanist Peter Schaaf culminated in a recital in his home city, Prince Albert, in the church where his father had preached as an elder and where he had sung in the choir as a child. The program included exerpts from *Samson* (Handel), *Die Walküre, Hugh the Drover* (Vaughan Williams), and *Peter Grimes*. He gave his first public performance of Schubert's dramatic song cycle *Winterreise* at the Guelph Spring Festival 9 May 1979. In order to spend more time with his family Vickers limited his performances to 65 a year after 1966. For years at the height of his career he maintained a farm in Ontario, working it himself between engagements to maintain a contact with realities different from those of the operatic world. In 1973, however, he moved to Bermuda.

A *Newsweek* article (15 Mar 1976) on the world's leading tenors described Vickers as 'an austere, reflective Canadian ... goaded by the demands of a protestant work ethic' and continued: '[He] uses his rugged voice with a contemptuous disregard for musical or national boundaries and a compulsion to challenge the brutes of the repertory ... The sound of his muscular, tireless voice is pitted and scarred as if hacked out of a Canadian quarry. But it is clearly made by hand, its imperfections redeemingly human and individual. What he conveys with unrelenting concentration is a profound dramatic sensibility.'

Vickers was made a Companion of Honour of the *Order of Canada in April 1969 and in 1975 won a *Molson Prize presented 21 Jun 1976 at Ottawa.

WRITINGS

'Working with Herbert von Karajan,' *OpCan*, Dec 1969

'On singing Wagner,' *OpCan*, Feb 1970

DISCOGRAPHY

OPERA

Beethoven *Fidelio*. Philharmonia O, Klemperer cond. (1962). 3-Angel S-3625

– *Fidelio*. Berlin Phil, Karajan cond. (1964). 3-Angel SCL-3773

Berlioz *Les Troyens*. Royal Opera O, Covent Garden, C. Davis cond. 1969. 5-Philips 6709002/1-Philips 6500161 (excerpts)/Philips 7300050

Bizet *Carmen*. Paris Opera O, de Burgos cond. (1970). 3-Angel SCL-3767/4X3S-3767/1-Angel S-36829 (excerpts)

Britten *Peter Grimes*. Royal Opera O, C. Davis cond. 1978. 3-Phillips 6769014

Great Tenors of Today. Angel S-36947

Italian Arias. Rome Opera House O, Serafin cond. 1960–1. RCA LSC 2741

Saint-Saëns *Samson et Dalila*. Paris Opera O, Prêtre cond. (1963). 3-Angel S-3639/1-Angel S-36210 (excerpts)

Verdi *Aida*. Rome Opera House O, Solti cond. (1962). 3-Lon 1393/Lon D31164/3-RCA LSC-6158/1-RCA LSC-2616 (excerpts)

– *Otello*. Rome Opera House, O, Serafin cond. (1972). 3-RCA AGL3/RCA LSC-2844 (exerpts)

– *Otello*. Berlin Phil, Karajan cond. (1974). 3-Angel SX-3809

Wagner *Tristan und Isolde*. Berlin Phil, Karajan cond. (1972). 5-Angel SEL-3777

– *Die Walküre*. Berlin Phil, Karajan cond. (1967). 5-DG 2713002/DG 136 435 (exerpts)/DG 2537012 (exerpts)

– *Die Walküre*. London SO, Leinsdorf cond. (1961). 5-RCA LDS 6706/5-Lon OSA 1511/Lon P31249

RECITAL

Glick – Morawetz – Coulthard – Kent. Woitach pf. 1973. CBC SM-180

Scarlatti – Purcell – Dvorak – Beethoven. Barkin pf. 1969. RCI 287/CBC SM-76

WITH ORCHESTRA

Beethoven *Symphony No. 9*. London SO, Monteux cond. (1963). 2-WST 234

Handel *Messiah*. Royal Phil O, Beecham cond. (1959). 4-RCA LDS-6409/RCA LDS-2447 (exerpts)

Opera Gala. Berlin Phil, Karajan cond. (1968). DG 2538 244

Vaughan Williams Serenade to Music. New York Phil, Bernstein cond. (1962). Col MS-7177

Verdi *Requiem*. New Philharmonia O, Barbirolli cond. (1970). 2-Angel S-3757

See also Discography for Toronto Mendelssohn Choir.

BIBLIOGRAPHY

Scholder, Herbert. 'Vickers in American premiere,' *OpCan*, Dec 1964

Kirby, Blaik. 'Vickers: world critics praise him, but Toronto inflicts scars,' Toronto *Globe and Mail*, 6 Mar 1971

McLean, Eric. 'Man on a tightrope,' *Montreal Star*, 31 Jul 1971

Mould, Warren. 'Controversially speaking: here's Jon Vickers,' *Sound*, vol 2, Dec 1971, vol 3, Feb 1972

Littler, William. 'Jon Vickers may study as conductor,' *Toronto Star*, 22 Oct 1973

Kraglund, John. 'Vickers criticizes musical nationalism,' Toronto *Globe and Mail*, 17 Jan 1974

Ardoin, John. 'Jon Vickers,' *The Tenor*, ed Herbert Breslin (New York 1974)

Gingras, Claude. 'Jon Vickers: l'art rongé par l'envie,' Montreal *La Presse*, 6 Jul 1975

Saal, Herbert. 'The puritan and the cavalier,' *Newsweek*, 15 Mar 1976

Blyth, Alan. 'Knight at the opera,' London *Daily Telegraph*, 26 Feb 1977

Johnstone, Bruce. 'Jon Vickers' home-coming,' *Fugue*, Jan 1978

Colgrass, Ulla. 'In pursuit of truth,' *Music*, Aug 1979

FILMOGRAPHY

Jon Vickers – a Man and His Music (CBC TV 1974)

Fidelio; filmed at the 1977 Orange Festival in France (Sunchild Production)

RMr (MM, KW)

Victor. See RCA Victor.

Victoria. Capital city of British Columbia. Established in 1843 on the southern tip of Vancouver Island as a Hudson's Bay Co trading post called Fort Victoria, the town had 148 adult inhabitants by 1855. Within four months of the Fraser River gold discoveries in 1858, Victoria's population had risen to 20,000, and the town was a thriving supply centre and starting point for expeditions to the mainland. Victoria was incorporated as a city in 1862 and designated the capital in 1868. The Klondike gold rush of 1897 further contributed to Victoria's growing population. In 1976 218,250 lived in the capital region. Victoria's geographic isolation from the mainland has had the effect of limiting industrial growth and forcing a degree of self-reliance on its citizens, particularly in the performing arts.

In 1850 the only musical instruments in Fort Victoria are said to have been the flute and fiddle of the chief trader, John Tod. In 1853 the first piano arrived, after a long journey from Europe around Cape Horn. The settlement's first melodeon was heard at the Victoria District Church in 1858; a barrel organ with 30 tunes arrived the following year; and a pipe organ, built by J.W. Walker and Sons of London, was installed at St John the Divine (later St John's) Anglican Church in 1860. The wave of prospectors that descended on Victoria 1858–9 brought enough players on musical instruments for Arthur T. *Bushby and Judge Matthew Baillie Begbie (later Chief Justice of British Columbia) to found the first Victoria Philharmonic Society, first heard in concert 6 May 1859. John *Bayley, inspector of police, conducted, and his son contributed a clarinet solo. This amateur society was short-lived, but others followed soon: the Germania Singverein (probably Canada's first German musical society) in May 1861; Les Enfants de Paris in August 1861; the Victoria Musical Society (an amalgamation of two brass bands) in 1864; and a Glee Club in 1866.

A strong factor in the support of musical societies in Victoria has been the presence of a naval establishment, first British, then Canadian, at nearby Esquimalt. From the earliest days naval officers and band musicians participated in the music making. An officer named Horne in 1860 wrote the *Vancouver Island Waltz*, which apart from Bushby's fragmentary 'Valentine' of 1859 was probably the first music composed locally; it is preserved at the Provincial Archives of British Columbia.

In the last quarter of the 19th century the local Amateur Dramatic and Operatic Society as well as visiting concert companies and Italian and English opera troupes presented performances of operas and other works. For its first production, ca 1880, the society chose Thomas Arne's *Love in a Village*. In subsequent years, directed from the piano by Digby Palmer, it presented much Gilbert & Sullivan and a few Grand operas, eg, Flotow's *Martha* and Verdi's *Il Trovatore*. Visiting opera companies included the Juch Grand English Opera Company (from the USA), which in 1890 presented *Faust*, *Der Freischütz*, *The Bohemian Girl*, and *Carmen*. Herbert Kent, a chronicler of music in Victoria, pointed out that 'the old Theatre Royal on Government St. was very frequently secured for Operatic Companies, and, contrary to the order of things in late years, these organizations found it profitable to give three or four days, and in many cases, a week of grand Opera' ('Musical chronicles of early times,' Victoria *Daily Times*, 14 Dec 1918).

FRENCH SOCIETY

LES ENFANS DE PARIS.

THE

First Concert

OF

THIS SOCIETY

WILL BE GIVEN

In the Victoria Theatre.

FRIDAY EVENING, AUGUST 16th, 1861.

Printed at the British Colonist Office.

PROGRAMME:

PART I.

1. QUADRILLE—*Lurline*.....C. D'Albert
2. CHORUS—*Introduction of the Chalet Opera*.....A. Adam
3. EXIL ET RETOUR—*Chorus*.....Monpou

SOLOS BY A YOUNG LADY HONORARY MEMBER AND MR. FELIX.

4. WALSE—"*Mountain Daisy*".....C. D'Albert
5. SOUVENIRS DE JEUNE AGE—*Pre aux Clers*.....Herold

BY A YOUNG LADY HONORARY MEMBER.

6. LES ENFANS DE PARIS—*Patriotic Chorus*.....A. Adam

PART II.

7. QUADRILLE—*Italian Campaign*.....C. D'Albert
8. SCENE, CHORUS AND SOLOS—*Chalet Opera*.....A. Adam

BY MRS. SANDRIE AND MR. FELIX.

9. OH! MON FERNAND—*Favorite*.....Donizetti

BY A YOUNG LADY HONORARY MEMBER.

10. LA FILLE DE LA NUIT—*Chorus*.....Fourdain
11. LE POSTILLON DE BESANCON—*Chansonnette*.....Berat

BY MR. FELIX.

12. GARIBALDI GALOP.....C. D'Albert

CONDUCTOR, - - - - - - - - - - - M. G. SANDRIE.

The Concert will commence at half-past Eight o'clock, precisely.

An early concert program from Victoria

The Victoria Opera House opened 10 Oct 1885 with a local production of *The Pirates of Penzance* accompanied by an orchestra led by E. Pferdner. Other theatre buildings were erected about the turn of the century. The Victoria Theatre, built in 1892, was the site of Reginald Hincks' Christmas pantomimes; the first was presented in 1910. During World War I Hincks, who for over 40 years produced revues and pantomimes, staged monthly musical entertainments in aid of the Red Cross. Johanna Gadski sang 8 Nov 1912 for the Victoria Ladies' Musical Club, which had been founded in 1906. The Princess Theatre, where the *Dumbells played, opened in 1911 and closed in 1961. Victoria's major auditorium, the 1450-seat Royal Theatre, was inaugurated 29 Dec 1913.

The first Victoria performance of Handel's *Messiah*, on Easter Sunday 1887 with a choir of 200 led by Enrico Sorge, initiated a tradition. In 1892 the Arion Club was organized under William Greig (see Arion Male Voice Choir); in 1980 it was recognized as Canada's oldest extant secular choir. George Taylor and Howard Russell prepared the 250-voice choir that sang in the 1903 *Cycle of Musical Festivals. During her farewell tour Emma *Albani was soloist with the Victoria Musical Society, a chorus led by Gideon *Hicks, in a performance of Cowen's *The Rose Maiden* (May 1906). The Victoria Choral Society under Hicks gave its first concert in 1910.

Among the first instrument builders and technicians in Victoria were John *Bagnall (fl 1863–85), who probably built the first pianos in British Columbia; his successors Charles Goodwin and G.W. Jordan; and William Seeley, who advertised as an 'organ and pianoforte builder, tuner and repairer of all kinds of musical instruments' (*Colonist*, 8 Oct 1871). Systematic research into Victoria's musical life in the 19th century – an extensive computerized investigation of the sources – was begun by Dale McIntosh, *U of Victoria, in the late 1970s.

Victoria has been noted for its English character, and perhaps it is not surprising that all of the leading musical personalities listed here as being active in the first half of the 20th century were English-born. Jesse A. Longfield was organist-choirmaster at St Andrew's Presbyterian Church 1903–39. Stanley Bulley, organist at Christ Church Cathedral, was conductor of the Victoria Choral and Orchestral Union (founded 1934), and with it presented oratorio performances of a high quality. Graham Steed was organist at the cathedral in the 1950s. Jennings *Burnett, organist-choirmaster at St John's Anglican Church, was the most active composer in the city. Leslie *Grossmith, also a composer, was best known as conductor of a theatre orchestra and of operatic productions. Stanley Shale and Gertrude *Huntley Green (the sole native Canadian mentioned in this paragraph) were prominent piano teachers. Victoria's famous Empress Hotel was the location in 1929 and 1930 of *CPR Festivals. William (Billy) Tickle, who was associated with the Victoria local of the AF of M, led the dance bands in the hotel's ballroom, and his trio played during teatime for over 30 years (ca 1927–1960).

Recitals by local and visiting artists were sponsored by the Victoria Ladies' Musical Club (1906–30) and its successor, the *Victoria Musical Art Society. Apart from the Arion Male Voice Choir, however, few ensembles had long lives. One Victoria SO flourished briefly about 1922; another of 42 players made its debut in November 1923 under Drury Pryce. The Victoria Philharmonic Orchestra, a slightly larger group, gave its first concert in December 1931 under Alfred Prescott. However, the *Victoria SO, which continued to play in 1980, was formed only in 1941. The rise of that orchestra was paralleled by that of the naval band stationed at HMCS Naden after World War II. The Naden band played a prominent part in the British Columbia Centennial celebrations in 1958 and has provided music for the Sunset Ceremony at the provincial Legislative Buildings.

The naval establishment at Esquimalt also gave Victoria a unique role in music education after 1954, when the Royal Canadian Navy School of Music (renamed *Canadian Forces School of Music in 1968) was established to train bandsmen, both players and directors. The Victoria School of Music (opened in 1964 and renamed *Victoria Conservatory of Music in 1968) and the Dept of Music at the U of Victoria (opened in 1967) did much to improve educational opportunities. The conservatory became affiliated with the university in 1968. In 1980 the university was one of only seven in Canada that offered doctoral programs in music. These developments, together with the artistic and financial growth of the Victoria SO, have attracted to the city highly qualified professional musicians and thus have encouraged the formation of several chamber ensembles: *Trio Victoria (piano and strings), the duo-pianists Robin *Wood and Winifred Scott, the Pacific Wind Quintet, the conservatory faculty's Baroque Ensemble, and the Ars Nova Ensemble, made up of players from the symphony orchestra. Some of these groups have performed on the Canadian and US mainland and on the CBC.

Choral music is well represented by the Arion Male Voice Choir, the Amity Singers (at one time under Timothy Vernon), the Victoria Choral Society, and several other groups. The Victoria Operatic Society confines its activities to amateur presentations of popular stage musicals and operettas. An opera department has developed at the conservatory under Catherine Young. An extension of this is Opera in Action, an advanced-student and community group which has offered concert versions of full-length operas and mounted several short works, from both the early and the modern repertoires.

By 1980 a flourishing annual competition festival had become a tradition, and an extensive music program existed in the schools.

In the 1970s the principal concert halls were the Royal Theatre (acquired by the municipality in 1973 and thereafter the home of the Victoria SO) and the 835-seat McPherson Playhouse (also municipally owned). On the campus of the U of Victoria a new concert hall and auditorium were opened in 1979. The university, the Victoria Musical Art Society, and other impresario organizations have presented series of recitals and concerts by visiting and local solo artists and ensembles. The city is the location of the *Shawnigan Summer School of the Arts and its attendant Victoria International Festival.

Prominent musicans active in the 1970s included, in addition to those named before, Frances *James Adaskin and Murray *Adaskin, Ian Bradley (educator and bibliographer), Frank *Churchley, Laszlo *Gati, Sydney *Humphreys, Rudolf *Komorous, Christine *Mather, Bernard *Naylor, Charles *Palmer, Margery M. Vaughan (one of the chairmen of the *Canadian Music Research Council), Phillip T. Young (bassoonist and university teacher), and Herman *Bergink, the provincial carillonneur and the regular performer on the Netherlands Centennial Carillon presented to British Columbia by the province's Dutch community in 1967.

Victoria is the birthplace of John *Beckwith, Robert *Creech, the soprano Jeannette Dagger, Richard *Eaton, Phylis *Inglis, Pat *Patterson, the jazz bassist Neil Swainson, Philip *Thomas, Ian *Tyson, Timothy Vernon, and Robin Wood.

BIBLIOGRAPHY

'Victoria Symphony Orchestra,' *MCan*, vol 5, Dec 1924

Learoyd, Eileen, 'At 77, Reginald Hincks still giving Victoria Christmas pantomime treat,' Victoria *Daily Colonist*, 12 Dec 1948

Nesbitt, James K. 'Old homes and families,' ibid, 25 Sep 1949

Salisbury, Dorothy E. 'Music in British Columbia outside Vancouver,' *CMJ*, vol 2, Summer 1958

Smith, Dorothy Blakey. 'Music in the furthest west a hundred years ago,' ibid

Steed, Graham. 'The rebuilding of Christ Church Cathedral organ, Victoria, British Columbia,' ibid

Lee, Phil. 'Royal last stage link with cultural past,' *Victoria Daily Times*, 23 May 1962

Johnson, Audrey St Denys. 'Music on Vancouver Island,' *PfAC*, Winter 1963

Nesbitt, James K. 'Crime and music in Victoria of yesteryear,' *Islander*, 3 Jan 1967

Belford, Margaret S. 'Victoria's singing tower,' ibid, 3 May 1970

MacMillan, Keith. 'Report from Victoria,' *CMB*, 2, Spring–Summer 1971

Garvie, Peter. 'The virtues of limits,' *CanComp*, 65, Dec 1971

Gibbard, Donald. 'Music in the early days in Victoria,' *British Columbia Music Educator*, vol 28, Spring 1975

Gregson, Harry. *A History of Victoria 1842–1970* (Victoria 1977)

Adaskin, Murray. 'Victoria: more beauty than meets the eye,' *Mcan*, 35, Apr 1978 (ASDJ)

Victoria Conservatory of Music. Major British Columbia teaching institution, incorporated in 1964 as the Victoria School of Music. It adopted the name 'conservatory' in September of 1968 and was affiliated with the *U of Victoria in October of that year. In September 1978 the conservatory became affiliated also with Camosun College, offering a two-year performer-teacher course leading to an Associate of Arts in Music diploma. The first director, Otto-Werner *Mueller, was followed by Robin *Wood in 1966, and Wood became principal when Christine *Mather was appointed director of music administration in 1979. Originally located on Pandora St, the conservatory moved to Craigdarroch Castle in 1969 and to the former St Ann's Academy in 1979.

The conservatory offers training (individual and master-class) in many instruments, in voice, in speech arts, and in piano teaching. The program also includes classes in the *Orff, *Kodály, and *Suzuki methods. Three-week summer courses devoted to instrumental training were introduced in 1975. The conservatory also has a two-year teacher-training program.

The student body has grown significantly – from 40 in the school year 1964–5 to 1284 in the school year 1978–9. A number of students from outside British Columbia and, indeed, Canada, have sought admission. By 1979 five conservatory students had been finalists in the *CBC Talent Festival, and in 1977 several won top prizes at the finals of the *National Competitive Festival of Music. The faculty has included Murray *Adaskin, Sydney *Humphreys, James Hunter, Selena James (voice), Jack *Kessler, Arthur *Polson, Winifred Scott (piano), Stanley Shale (piano), Hans Siegrist (cello), Kathleen Solose (piano), and Catherine Young (voice). The group-in-residence is the *Trio Victoria. Some 60 student and 25 faculty recitals were presented in the 1978–9 season.

BIBLIOGRAPHY

Johnson, Audrey St Denys. 'New mecca for music,' *Victoria Daily Times*, 12 Sep 1964 BNSG

Victoria Musical Art Society (until 1930 the Victoria Ladies' Musical Club). Founded 3 Mar 1906 to encourage local performers and to present international artists. Under its aegis Galli-Curci, McCormack, Kreisler, and others performed in Victoria. In 1917 it presented a program of British Columbia composers, including G. Jennings *Burnett, Violet Bridgewater, and Leslie *Grossmith. In 1930 the Victoria Ladies' Musical Club was dissolved by common consent, and the Victoria Musical Art Society was constituted. Mrs J.O. Cameron was its first president. Though the society continued to sponsor visiting musicians, it turned its attention increasingly to the presentation in recital, and to the financial support, of young local musicians – eg, John *Beckwith, Robin *Wood, and Irene *Byatt. By 1977 48 young musicians had been awarded the Victoria Musical Art Society Open Scholarships, established in 1966. MMV

Victoria Symphony Orchestra. British Columbia's largest community orchestra. Several predecessors (see Victoria) had been short-lived, and the new orchestra was founded in 1941 as a 30-piece ensemble by its first conductor, Melvin Knudsen (flutist, b New Westminister, BC, 4 Aug 1908, a conducting pupil in 1935 of Felix Weingartner in Basel). Knudsen was succeeded in 1948 by Hans Gruber (b Vienna 11 Jul 1925, naturalized Canadian 1944, an *RCMT conducting student who took summer courses 1943–7 with Fritz Mahler, Leonard Bernstein, and Pierre Monteux). By 1951 eight concerts were being presented annually, and in 1953 the orchestra made its first tour of Vancouver Island. Gruber was succeeded in 1963 by Otto-Werner *Mueller, Mueller in 1967 by Laszlo *Gati, and Gati in 1979 (after a season of guest conductors 1978–9) by Paul Freeman, former conductor-in-residence of the Detroit SO.

The orchestra experienced its greatest expansion under Gati's direction, increasing its subscription series to 12 pairs of concerts at the Royal Theatre and the McPherson Playhouse. By the mid-1970s it employed from 65 to 80 players, 35 of whom constituted a professional nucleus. An annual six-week summer festival in Victoria parks was begun in 1972, and summer and winter series have been given elsewhere on the island. In 1977 a tour was made in inland British Columbia, the Yukon, and Alberta, and in 1980 a tour of Alaska. The orchestra started a program of concerts and recitals for school children in 1973. Over the years the orchestra has commissioned several works by Canadians including John *Beckwith's *Flower Variations and Wheels* (1962), Michel *Perrault's *Centennial Homage* (1967), Harry *Freedman's *Klee Wyck* (1971), and Srul Irving *Glick's *Concerto* for violin, premiered in 1976 by the orchestra and Steven *Staryk. Among other guests have been the conductors John *Avison, Clifford *Evens, and Arthur Fiedler and the solo performers Paul Badura-Skoda, Anna *Chornodolska, Van Cliburn, Philippe Entremont, Maureen *Forrester, Marek *Jablonski, Giorgio Tozzi, Riki *Turofsky, and Narciso Yepes.

BIBLIOGRAPHY

Salisbury, Dorothy. 'Music in British Columbia outside Vancouver,' *CMJ*, vol 2, Summer 1958

Edds, Jack. 'Orchestra Canada presents ... Victoria Symphony,' *OCan*, vol 4, Mar 1977

Reprise: A Scrapbook, suppl to *Victoria Daily Times*, 28 Jul 1978 (ASDJ)

VIDOR, Pierre (b Trépanier, Russell). Tenor, choir conductor, policeman, b Louiseville, near Trois-Rivières, Que, 3 Sep 1907. He began to study trumpet but turned to singing, which he studied in Montreal with various teachers. He was soloist in CBC radio performances of Honegger's *Le Roi David* in 1941 and Pierné's *The Children's Crusade* the following year. In 1942 also he created the role of Joseph Quesnel in Eugène *Lapierre's comic opera *Le Père des amours*. For the *Opera Guild of Montreal he sang Monostatos in *The Magic Flute* in 1945 and for the *Variétés lyriques he took the title role in *Faust* in 1948 and the Duke in *Rigoletto* in 1949. At the *Montreal Festivals in 1946 he performed Beethoven's *Missa solemnis* and on short notice replaced the tenor Hubert Norville as soloist in the Berlioz *Requiem* under Sir Thomas Beecham. The same year he gave a recital of Schubert's *Die Winterreise* at the Windsor Hotel. In 1950 he repeated Faust for the Montreal Festivals and sang the same role for the *Opéra national du Québec. He sang other leading roles with the Opéra national du Québec and on the CBC, in particular for the program 'Le Théâtre lyrique Molson.'

At the same time Vidor pursued a career in the Montreal police force, which he joined in 1936, becoming a detective-sergeant in 1946, a lieutenant in 1951, and a captain in 1967. He retired that year and was in charge of security for *Expo 67. In 1956 he founded a 40-voice men's choir – the Symphonie vocale des policiers de Montréal, which in 1969 became the Symphonie vocale des policiers de la Communauté urbaine de Montréal – and directed it in many public concerts as well as radio and TV performances. He was succeeded as conductor in 1971 by Jean Ratelle. In 1975 Vidor returned to Louiseville, where he continued to conduct a choir and involve himself in musical and social activities. GP

VIGNEAULT, Gilles. Singer-songwriter, poet, publisher, b Natashquan, North Shore, Que, 27 Oct 1928; BA (Laval) 1950, L LITT (Laval) 1953, hon D LITT (Trent) 1975, hon doctorate (U of Quebec at Rimouski) 1979. While completing his general education in Rimouski and Quebec City he held various jobs such as library assistant, publicist, and archivist. He taught algebra and French 1957–61 at the Institut de technologie in Quebec City and gave summer classes in 1960 and 1961 at Laval U. He also was a writer and host 1960–2 for CBC radio and TV in Quebec City.

Gilles Vigneault

By this time Vigneault was publishing poems and writing songs. In 1959 he founded Les Éditions de l'Arc to distribute his publications; between *Étraves* (1959) and *Silences* (1978) he published nearly 20 collections of poems, stories, and songs. In August 1960, at the request of the audience at the boîte à chansons L'Arlequin in Quebec City, he agreed to sing his earliest song, 'Jos Monferrand' (1957), which had been recorded by Jacques *Labrecque. Vigneault subsequently sang with increasing success in several halls, including the Gesù (1961) and *Plateau Hall (1963) in Montreal. In 1962 he received the Grand prix du disque from the Montreal radio station CKAC. His reputation grew in Quebec and elsewhere with the success of his song *'Mon Pays,' sung first by Monique *Leyrac at the 1965 International Song Festival in Sopot, Poland. He received the 1966 *Prix de musique Calixa-Lavallée from the St-Jean-Baptiste Society, and in June 1966 a float in the annual St-Jean-Baptiste parade in Montreal was dedicated to Vigneault and Monique Leyrac. Also in June 1966 he was given the 1965 Governor-General's Award for his anthology of poems *Quand les bateaux s'en vont*. He wrote the theme for the film *Poussière sur la ville* in 1965 and 'Chanson des enfants' for Gratien Gélinas's play *Hier les enfants dansaient* in 1966.

Besides the concerts he has given in Montreal at the Comédie-Canadienne (annually 1963–8, and in 1970), at the *PDA (1970, 1972), and at the Théâtre du Nouveau-Monde (1973, 1974), and in Quebec City at the *Grand Théâtre (1972), he has sung with the *MSO at the *NAC (1969, 1971) and at the PDA (1969, 1971, 1972). He took part in the *Mariposa Folk Festival in July 1969 and performed at *Massey Hall, Toronto, and in various centres in northern Ontario in 1970. In April 1974 he sang in Ottawa, Toronto, Winnipeg, Edmonton, and elsewhere. Vigneault has made several tours in France – appearing in Paris (1966, 1967, 1969, 1970, 1971, 1974), Strasbourg (1971), Bourges (1974) and elsewhere – and in Switzerland (1969, 1972), Poland, Luxembourg, and Belgium. His LP *Du milieu du pont*, made in France, was awarded the Grand prix du disque de l'Académie Charles-Cros on 2 Mar 1970. In the spring of 1977 he gave 50 recitals at the Théâtre Bobino in Paris; in September he performed at the Théâtre du Nouveau-Monde in Montreal before touring Quebec and New Brunswick. He again toured in France in February 1978 and sang at the Théâtre du Nouveau-Monde in September 1979.

Vigneault is the subject of the films *Ce soir-là* (1968, by Arthur Lamothe), *Miroir de Gilles Vigneault* (1972, made for the CBC by Roger Fournier), and *Why I Sing – The Words and Music of Gilles Vigneault* (made for the *NFB by John Howe during a performance at Le *Patriote, in Ste-Agathe, and telecast 7 Feb 1973 on the CBC TV series 'Adieu Alouette'). Vigneault also appeared in the NFB's *Musicanada* (1975).

After 1960 most of Vigneault's songs were written in collaboration with his music director for concerts and records, Gaston Rochon (b Quebec City 8 Apr 1932). Rochon, who studied cello, clarinet, and composition at the *CMQ, made an LP of Vigneault songs arranged for orchestra, *Dans l'air des mots*, which was released on Vigneault's own label, Le Nordet (1974, GVN-1004). Established in the early 1970s, Le Nordet (Éditions du Vent qui vire) also has recorded Sylvain Lelièvre and Laurence Lepage. Vigneault's song 'Jack Monnoloy,' which won second prize at the 1964 Sopot festival, was the subject of a ballet by Georges Reich at the Comédie-Canadienne in September 1966. Similarly, several of his songs served as the inspiration for the ballet by Brian Macdonald *Tam Ti Delam*, which was staged in November 1974 by Les Grands Ballets Canadiens to an instrumental score by Edmund *Assaly.

Several of Vigneault's texts have been set to music and recorded by other musicians, including Gilbert Bécaud ('Natashquan'), Pierre Calvé ('Quand les bateaux s'en vont'), Robert *Charlebois ('La Marche du président'), and Claude *Léveillée ('L'Hiver,' 'Rendez-vous,' 'Avec nos yeux' and others).

The performers who have recorded, sung, or played Vigneault's songs are numerous. In Quebec they include the *Choeur V'là l'bon vent, Neil *Chotem, Renée *Claude, Françoise *Dompierre, Emmanuelle, the *Ensemble Claude-Gervais, Louise *Forestier, André *Gagnon, Patsy Gallant, Pauline *Julien, Jacques *Labrecque, Monique Leyrac, Isabelle Pierre, Louise Poulin, Ginette *Reno, Marie Savard, Les *Séguin, and Fabienne Thibeault; in France, Frida Boccara, the Compagnons de la chanson, Jacques Douai, Jeanne Moreau, Colette Renard, and Catherine Sauvage.

Like Félix *Leclerc, Gilles Vigneault has created his own style, inspired by the folksongs he heard as a boy in Natashquan. 'Some of my songs recall in their rhythms the old country songs,' he told Marc Gagné (*Propos de Gilles Vigneault*, Montreal 1974), 'because I lived in a world where they still sang drinking songs and where they still liked to square dance.' His rich, vivid lyrics present such likable characters as Ti-Cul Lachance and Caillou Lapierre and approach all subjects in a highly colourful manner: 'L'Air du voyageur,' 'La Danse à St-Dilon,' 'Fer et titane,' *'Gens du pays' (composed for the 1975 *St-Jean-Baptiste celebrations in which he participated in Montreal), *'Les Gens de mon pays,' 'Il me reste un pays,' 'J'ai pour toi un lac,' 'Mademoiselle Émilie,' 'Pendant que,' 'Tire mon coeur,' and 'Le Vent' are but a few of them.

After a recital by Vigneault at the Olympia in Paris, Dominique Bosselet wrote: 'His voice is hard, hoarse, biting, a voice that hurts. And his rustic accent now and then makes some of his songs incomprehensible. Yet after five minutes with this ordinary guy, with his slight build and mobile features, the audience is applauding, and after ten minutes we discover not only that Gilles Vigneault can convey the tragic but that he has a rare humour, and is a poet' (*France-soir*, 21 Apr 1970). A poet deeply rooted in Quebec, Vigneault has become its true ambassador abroad. He belongs to the generation of chansonniers who assured the Quebec chanson of its own identity while giving it at the same time a universal dimension. Vigneault is a member of CAPAC and sat on its board of directors 1970–4. See also Chansonniers.

DISCOGRAPHY

Gilles Vigneault. 1962. Col FS 538
Jack Monnoloy. 1962. Harmonie KHF 90082
Chansons et poèmes. 1963. Harmonie KHF 90211
Gilles Vigneault chante et récite II. 1963. Col FS 544
Tam Ti Delam. (1963). CBS FS 746
Gilles Vigneault. 1965. Col FS 612
Gilles Vigneault à la Comédie-Canadienne. 1965. Col FS 632
Récital à la Comédie-Canadienne. 1965. Harmonie KHF 90233
Bobino 3 octobre 1966. 1966. CBS 223
Gilles Vigneault enregistré à Paris. 1966. Col FL 348
Mon pays. 1966. Col FS 634
Gilles Vigneault. 1967. Col FS 90085
La Manikoutai. Montreal 1967. Col FS 652/(Paris 1968) CBS 63302
Le Nord du Nord. Montreal 1968. Col FS 681/(Paris 1969) CBS 63634
Du milieu du pont. 1969. L'Escargot ESX-70501
Musicorama. 1969. Col FS 710
Les Voyageurs. 1969. Col FS 702
Le Voyageur sédentaire. 1970. L'Escargot ESX-70502
Les Gens de mon pays. 1971. L'Escargot ESC 312
Les Grands succès de Gilles Vigneault. (1971?). Col RS 90001-90002/GFS 90003
Le Temps qu'il fait sur mon pays. 1971. Le Nordet GVN-1000
C'est le temps. (1972). Col FS 90123-90124/GFS 90125
Qui êtes vous Gilles Vigneault? 1972. RCI F-678
Pays du fond de moi. Montreal and Paris 1973. Le Nordet GVN-1002/L'Escargot ESC 318
Gilles Vigneault. 1974. Le Nordet GVN-1003
Gilles Vigneault au Théâtre du Nouveau-Monde. 1974. Le Nordet GVN-1005
Le Québec en chanson. 1974. CBS 80376
Chansons. 1976. Le Nordet 838-1007
J'ai planté un chêne. 1977. Le Nordet GVN-1007
Gilles Vigneault à Bobino. 1977. Le Nordet GVN-1008/1009
Comment vous donner des nouvelles ... 1978. Le Nordet GVN-1010
See also Discography for Chansonniers.

BIBLIOGRAPHY

Robitaille, Aline. *Gilles Vigneault* (Montreal 1968)
Beckett, Barbara. 'The poet of Natashquan,' *CanComp*, 43, Oct 1969
Rioux, Lucien. *Gilles Vigneault* (Paris 1969)
Fournier, Roger. *Gilles Vigneault, mon ami* (Montreal 1972)
Champagne, Jane. 'The roots and reasons for Quebec's music,' *CanComp*, 92, Jun 1974
Gagné, Marc. *Gilles Vigneault* (Quebec City 1977)
'Gilles Vigneault lui-même,' interview with Pierre Nadeau, *L'Actualité*, Sep 1979 (BLH)

Ville Émard Blues Band (familiarly Ville Émard). 'The aggregation of session musicians and hired hands that became the catalyst of Quebec's rock revolution in the mid-1970s' (Juan Rodriguez, Montreal *Gazette*, 11 Aug 1979). It was formed in 1973 by musicians from the bands of Robert *Charlebois, Renée *Claude, Claude *Dubois, and others (including Contraction in its entirety), under the informal leadership of the bass guitarist Bill (Roland) Gagnon (b Verdun, Montreal, ca 1943). Musicians numbered from 18 to 25 and included such prominent performers as the singers Lise Cousineau and Estelle Sainte-Croix, the pianist Pierre Nadeau, the percussionists Denis Farmer, Michel Séguin, and Christian St-Roch, the saxophonists Carlyle Miller and Renald Montemeglio, and the guitarists Rawn Bankley and Robert Stanley. The band made its debut on the CBC TV program 'Décibel,' and the name Ville Émard Blues Band (taken from the name of a Montreal neighbourhood) was invented for the occasion. 'Blues band' is, in fact, a misnomer.

Stephen Kroll, in *Canadian Composer*, described a typical performance: 'The band is loose and the music starts to move all over the stage: a bass player on the left starts jamming with a drummer on the other side; the guitars find somebody to improvise with; some sing. The sound is enormous, a pulsing hybrid of John Coltrane and Santana, as the music weaves a textured tapestry of African-inspired folk songs like *Yamakech* [Yama Nehk], discotheque Latin-rock like *Conkey Donkey* [Kondy Donky] and symphonic compositions like *Ode*.' Nadeau's reworking of 'Ordinaire,' the autobiographical song he wrote with Charlebois and Mouffe, was a highlight of the band's performances.

Though the musicians maintained their associations with other groups and/or performers, they gathered on a co-operative basis for outdoor concerts in Montreal during the summer of 1973 and made their 'grand debut' 27 Oct 1973 at the *U of Montreal. A concert at the *St-Denis Theatre in January 1974 was recorded, resulting in the LPs *Live at Montreal* (2-Funkébec FK 600/1). A 30-concert tour of the province followed, as did another LP, *Ville Émard* (Funkébec FK 602). The band also performed in 1974 at the *Forum in Montreal and on Centre Island, near Toronto.

The band set significant trends for the Quebec pop music that followed, despite the fact that it was very short-lived. It had dispersed by 1975, and the musicians returned to their work as accompanists and studio players or became members of other groups. (Séguin led the percussion-oriented group Toubabou 1974–7, and Farmer and Stanley joined *Harmonium). Bankley gathered some former members under the name Koma for engagements in 1978. Gagnon, however, maintained the Ville Émard co-operative as a management and sound rental company; in 1979 it was based in Pointe St-Charles, a Montreal suburb.

BIBLIOGRAPHY

Rodriguez, Juan. 'Happy blues,' *Montreal Star*, 20 Oct 1973
Kroll, Stephen. 'Ville Émard Blues Band,' *CanComp*, 90, Apr 1974
Rodriguez, Juan. 'Gagnon now wily as well as wild,' Montreal *Gazette*, 11 Aug 1979 MM

VINCI, Ernesto (Ernst Moritz). Teacher, baritone, adjudicator, physician, b Berlin 20 Apr 1898, naturalized Canadian 1944; MD (Berlin) 1924, MD (Milan) 1933. He studied singing, after 1920, at the Hochschule für Musik in Berlin and privately with Ernst Grenzebach and Louis Bachner in Berlin and Milan. Practising medicine in Milan, he sang in recital, in opera, and on radio until 1938, when he moved to New York. There he was referred by Toscanini to Wilfrid *Pelletier, who had been asked to recommend a director for the vocal department of the Halifax Cons (*Maritime Cons of Music). While in Halifax 1938–45 he also lectured at *Dalhousie U and at Pine Hill Divinity Hall, taught singing at the Halifax Ladies' College, and sang in recital and in *The Marriage of Figaro*, *The Abduction from the Seraglio*, and *Dido and Aeneas*. He joined the Faculty of Music at the *U of Toronto in 1945, and there built a reputation as one of Canada's leading voice teachers. He gave summer courses 1945–8 in Winnipeg and 1949–69 at the *Banff SFA, where he was the head of the vocal (later opera) department and touring company. At Banff he sang in Trevor Jones' opera *The Broken Ring* in 1958. He has written articles on voice production and related subjects for *Opera Canada* and the *CBC Times*. His pupils have included John *Arab, Maurice *Brown, Glyn Evans, Marguerite *Gignac, Robert *Goulet, Alexander *Gray, Elizabeth Benson *Guy, Joan *Hall, Avo Kittask, Andrew *MacMillan, Mary *Morrison, Ivanka Myhal, Maria *Pellegrini, Sheila *Piercey, Roxolana *Roslak, Louise *Roy, Alice *Strong Rourke, Bernard *Turgeon, and Portia *White. CF

Ernesto Vinci

VINET, Michel-R. (Raymond). Composer, b Verdun (Montreal) 25 Aug 1950. After completing his general education he studied 1968–9 with Serge *Garant at the *U of Montreal. His first works were played in Canada and abroad and include *Métamorphose* (1970), premiered by the pianist Louis-Philippe *Pelletier in 1971 and recorded (RCI 396) by Christina *Petrowska, and *Acousmie*, for nine instrumentalists, premiered by the *SMCQ Ensemble in 1971. His *Aleph* was commissioned by the CBC for Christina Petrowska, who gave its premiere in December 1973. A second version, *Imp-Aleph*, was completed the same year. Also in 1973 Vinet was awarded scholarships from the *CLComp and the *Canada Council which enabled him to enrol at the Instituut voor Sonologie in Utrecht. After the mid-1970s, ill-health forced Vinet to reduce his musical activities. PR

Viola playing and teaching. See Violin and viola playing and teaching.

Violin and viola playing and teaching. By the late 17th century the popularity of the instruments known as viols had been surpassed by those of the violin family (violin, viola, violoncello). While there is evidence that the fiddle may have originated in ancient central Asia, the modern violin and viola reached the apex of their development during the period 1600–1750, when the master builders of Cremona, Italy – the Amati family, especially Niccolo; the Guarneri family, in particular Giuseppe Antonio, known as del Gesù; the peerless Antonio Stradivari; and a few others – practised their craft. Modern builders, including those in Canada, usually have been content to model their instruments on those of the Cremona masters. (See String instrument building.)

The playing of the violin in Canada dates back to the early days of European settlement in the new land. Instances are reported in volume 27 of the *Jesuit Relations*, which describes a Quebec wedding of 27 Nov 1645 at which two violins were heard. Martin *Boutet, one of the players (Amtmann *Music in Canada 1600–1800*, p 88–9), is said also to have played the violin at a midnight mass at Christmas ca 1645. However, as the viol retained its place of prominence in France (and, by implication, New France) until the early 18th century, it seems likely that in this instance the term 'violin' may have described something other than the modern violin. The Ursuline Mother Superior Marie de St-Joseph (b 1616) brought her viol to the

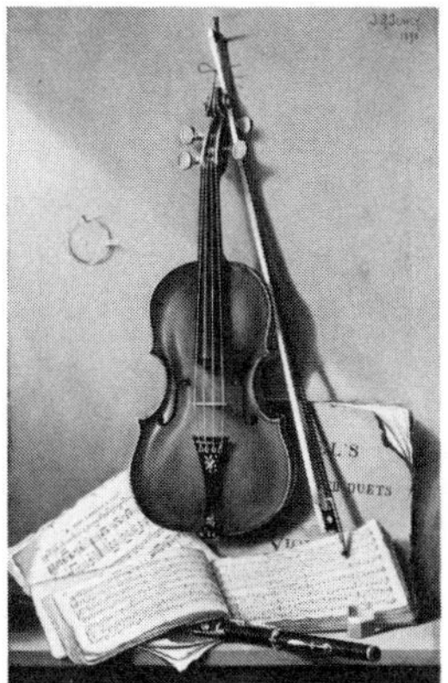

'Music' by Julian Ruggles Seavey, ca 1890

New World, where it was an object of great interest to the Indians (Amtmann, p 74).

In the early 18th century frequent references were made to 'les violons,' a collective term for the bowed string instruments played at the entertainments of the upper echelon of colonial administrators and military officers. Among the French, fiddles (sometimes the dancing master's violons de poche, or pocket fiddles) were used commonly to play dance tunes. Many English-speaking sects, notably the Methodists, considered the instrument sinful owing to this association with 'carnal' activity.

Among the first known violin players in Canada were Joseph *Quesnel in Montreal and F.H. *Glackemeyer (who supposedly had been a child prodigy in his native Hanover) and Jonathan *Sewell, the lawyer and later chief justice, in Quebec City. Other violinist-teachers in Quebec City were the Italian-born Gaetano Franceschini and the Belgian Guillaume *Mechtler (who later lived in Montreal), both active during the 1780s. One of the first musicians in the town of York (later Toronto) was a Mr Maxwell, who played the violin at private and public functions.

There were players enough in Quebec during the 1790s to permit the performance of symphonies, overtures, and concertos. Sellers of violins and violin accessories in the late 18th century included Glackemeyer, James Sinclair, and Francis *Vogeler in Quebec; John Smith in Halifax; Frederick Wyse in Montreal; and Colin Campbell in Saint John, NB.

Famous European violinists who gave concerts in Canada during the 19th century included Ole Bull (1844, 1853, 1857), Eduard Reményi (1880), Camilla Urso (first in 1855, at age 13), Henri Vieuxtemps (1858), Henry Wieniawski (1872), and August Wilhelmj (1880). A few professional musicians resided in Canada at least briefly. A European violinist, Monsieur Bley, appeared in Montreal and Quebec in 1843 and lived in Toronto ca 1845-7. The German Ferdinand *Griebel (1818-58) also lived and performed in Toronto for a few years. The Belgian violinist and teacher Jules *Hone (1833-1913), a pupil of Léonard, arrived in Montreal during the early 1860s; his pupils included François *Boucher, Oscar *Martel, Charles Reichling, and the US-born Jean *Duquette. In 1865 the Belgian virtuoso Frantz *Jehin-Prume (1839-99) made his first visit to Montreal, where he settled a few years later. Jehin-Prume was a pupil of de Bériot, Léonard, Vieuxtemps, and Wieniawski; his own pupils included François Boucher, Béatrice *La Palme (later famous as a singer), Alfred *De Sève, and Émile *Taranto.

The first Canadian-born violinists of distinction were Joseph W. *Baumann of Hamilton, Ont (1847-1905; a pupil of Adolf Brodsky and Joseph Joachim and the teacher of Nora *Clench and George *Fox) and Oscar Martel (1848-1924; a Hone pupil who studied later at Liège and whose pupils included De Sève and Chambord Giguère). Calixa *Lavallée (1842-91), though excelling as a pianist, also appeared in public as a violinist in his younger years.

Two immigrants from Europe must be considered next. Bertha *Drechsler Adamson (1848-1924) studied with Ferdinand David before coming to Canada, where she taught Frank *Blachford, Harry *Adaskin, her daughter Lina, and others. The German-born Charles Reichling (1854-1922) received his training after his arrival in Canada, studying with Jules Hone. He was named violinist to the households of the governors-general Lord Stanley and the Marquis of Lansdowne and was leader of the Ottawa and Montreal String Quartettes.

Two Montreal-born violinists, François Boucher (1860-ca 1936) and Alfred De Sève (1860-1928), had lessons with Jehin-Prume and others (Hone and Martel respectively) before going abroad for advanced studies, Boucher in Liège with Massart, De Sève in Paris with Vieuxtemps. Both men had important careers in the USA, but De Sève had several noteworthy Canadian pupils (eg, Alexander *Brott, Noël *Brunet, Albert *Chamberland, Marcel *Saucier, Lucien *Sicotte, and Ethel *Stark) after he returned to his native city.

Two pupils of J.W. Baumann received acclaim as virtuosos rather than teachers. They were Norah Clench (1867-1938), who went to study in Europe with Brodsky and Ysaÿe, and George Fox (1870-1913). It is possible that Evelyn de Latre Street (b London, Ont, ca 1870) was another Baumann pupil, for her early studies were in Hamilton, Ont. Her main teacher in the 1890s was Hans Sitt, in Germany. She gave recitals in Canada and the USA but little else is known about her career.

Émile Taranto (1878-1936) of Montreal was a pupil of Jehin-Prume and later of Ysaÿe and was the teacher of Jean *Deslauriers, Marthe *Lapointe, Annette *Lasalle-Leduc, and Lucien Sicotte. Frank Blachford (1879-1957) of Toronto began his lessons with Bertha Drechsler Adamson and continued with Hans Sitt, later transmitting his art to many pupils at the TCM (*RCMT). Another important teacher was Camille *Couture. A pupil of Jean Duquette and Ovide Musin (the latter in Liège), Couture taught in Winnipeg and later in Montreal; among those who studied with him were Arthur *Davison, Jean Deslauriers, and Lucien *Martin.

The first conservatories of music in Canada were established during the last years of the 19th century. Teachers at these and at other early institutions included Célestin *Lavigueur (*Séminaire de Québec), Oscar Martel (Collège de Montréal), Alfred De Sève (*McGill), and Frank Blachford and François Boucher (TCM). Among immigrant player-teachers of that era were Heinrich *Klingenfeld, first at the Halifax Cons and later in Toronto, Max *Weil in Halifax and Calgary, and the violist Frank Converse Smith at the *Toronto College of Music.

From the foregoing it is clear that the principal source of artistic violin playing in 19th-century Canada was the Franco-Belgian school, centred at Liège, with a lesser influence from German teachers. In the 20th century violin playing in Canada grew with the population and with the increase in wealth and proliferation of educational facilities which, in turn, gave rise to orchestras and chamber groups. Other contributing factors were the immigration to Canada of Belgians, Britons, eastern European Jews, Italians, and Slavs, all of whom had strong string-playing traditions, and the arrival of a number of outstanding violinists who were excellent teachers. Among these teachers were Donald *Heins (first in Ottawa) and Luigi von *Kunits in Toronto, pupils respectively of Hans Sitt and Otakar Ševčik. Drawing on his own pupils, von Kunits built the string section of the *TSO into one of the finest in North America.

Important teachers in Winnipeg were Phillip Shadwick (d 1932) and John *Waterhouse. Waterhouse taught for more than 50 years; among his pupils were George *Bornoff (who developed his own teaching methods and founded the *Bornoff School of Music in Winnipeg), Frederick *Grinke, Anne *Pomer, and Gwen *Thompson. Shadwick's son Joseph (1898-1956), a violinist and composer, conducted theatre orchestras in Winnipeg and later was concertmaster of the Minneapolis Orchestra in the USA and of the London Philharmonic Orchestra, the Royal Covent Garden Opera Orchestra, and the Sadlers' Wells Orchestra in England.

One of Canada's most significant violinists and teachers during the first half of the 20th century was Kathleen *Parlow (1890-1963), who studied in Russia with Leopold Auer, performed in Europe and North America, led the *Parlow String Quartet 1943-58, and taught many Canadians, including Victor *Feldbrill, Sydney *Humphreys, Joseph Pach (see Duo Pach), and Rowland *Pack.

Other violinists who became noteworthy teachers in the years between the two world wars were Saul *Brant; Albert Chamberland, a pupil of Jean Duquette and De Sève; Alexander *Chuhaldin; Henri Czaplinski, who lived in Canada briefly and taught Harry Adaskin; Broadus *Farmer; Mary Fraser of Truro, NS; Gregori *Garbovitsky, a pupil of Auer; John *Konrad, who took over the Bornoff school and was a pre-Suzuki pioneer in group-teaching methods; Flora Matheson *Goulden, a pupil of Ysaÿe; Geza *de Kresz, who also studied with Ysaÿe and taught Betty-Jean *Hagen, Clayton *Hare and Maurice *Solway; Maurice *Onderet (teacher of Alexander Brott, Noël Brunet, Mildred *Goodman, and Lucien Sicotte); Jean de *Rimanoczy, a pupil of Jenö Hubay and a teacher of George Bornoff and Cardo *Smalley; George Rutherford; Elie *Spivak (teacher of John Montague, Walter *Prystawski, Steven *Staryk, and David *Zafer); Ifan *Williams; and W. Knight *Wilson.

Among those who consolidated their names as teachers after World War II are Claude *Létourneau in Quebec City; Jean *Cousineau, Taras *Gabora, and Arthur *Garami (a pupil of de Kresz) in Montreal; Isidor Desser, Lorand *Fenyves, Carolyn and Joyce Gundy, Eugene *Kash, Jack Montague, and David Zafer in Toronto; Marta *Hidy in Hamilton, Ont; Rosemonde *Laberge in Cornwall, Ont; John Konrad, S.C. *Eckhardt-Gramatté, Anne Pomer, Richard Seaborn, and Arthur *Polson in Winnipeg; Francis *Chaplin in Halifax, and later in Brandon, Man; Thomas *Rolston and Ranald *Shean in Edmonton; Frederick Nelson and Gwen Thompson in Vancouver, to name only a few. It was Rolston, Cousineau, and Létourneau who introduced the *Suzuki method to Canada.

Joseph Berljawsky - b Przemysl, Austria-Hungary (Poland), 1911; a graduate of the Vienna Academy, arrived Canada 1939, founded the Montreal Orchestral Society in 1954 and Ottawa Musica Viva in 1968 - taught in Montreal and Ottawa, for some years commuting between the two cities. See also Canadian String Teachers' Assn; Contemporary Showcase; Les Petits violons; School music; Société musicale Le Mouvement Vivaldi.

Over the years several Canadian violinists have pursued careers abroad – eg, George Bornoff, Arthur Davison, Lea *Foli, Hyman *Goodman, Donna *Grescoe, Frederick Grinke, Betty-Jean Hagen, Adolph *Koldofsky, Albert *Pratz, Steven Staryk, and Albert *Steinberg. In somewhat greater numbers, violinists from abroad have pursued careers in Canada – eg, Hyman *Bress (arrived 1951), John *Dembeck (1941), S.C. Eckhardt-Gramatté (1953), Lorand Fenyves (1965), Arthur Garami (1949), Ida *Haendel (1952), Marta Hidy (1957), Gerard *Kantarjian (1967), Frederick Nelson (1970), Norman *Nelson (1965), Calvin *Sieb (1951), David Zafer (1947), and others. Of the expatriates, Grescoe returned to semi-retirement in Winnipeg; Pratz returned to serve with distinction as soloist, teacher, and TS concertmaster; and Staryk re-established residence in Canada, continuing his career at home and abroad as a soloist and chamber musician.

Among Canadian violinists who developed their careers as soloists, chamber musicians, and orchestral players almost entirely within Canada are Noël Brunet, Arthur *LeBlanc, Lucien Martin, Joseph Pach, Arthur Polson, Thomas Rolston, and Harold *Sumberg. Noteworthy players born after 1940 include Adele and Otto *Armin, Andrew *Dawes, Angèle Dubeau, Chantal Juillet, Kenneth Perkins, Victor Schultz, and Gwen Thompson.

Jean Duquette, Donald Heins, Smythe *Humphreys, Otto *Joachim, Joseph *Mastrocola, and Cardo Smalley have played as both violinists and violists, but numerous others have made careers exclusively on the viola, eg, Paul *Armin, Maurice *Durieux, Philippe Etter, Rivka Golani-Erdész, Osher Green, Terence Helmer of the *Orford String Quartet, Steven *Kondaks, Uri Mayer, Rennie Regehr, Lucien *Robert, Ivan *Romanoff, Stanley *Solomon, Gerald *Stanick, Robert Verebes, and Robert Warburton. Stanick spent several years in the USA as the viola of the Fine Arts Quartet before returning to Canada to teach in Victoria and later in London, Ont, and to serve as the viola of *Quartet Canada. Golani-Erdész and Mayer, both from Israel, have had outstanding Canadian careers, the former as a soloist and chamber musician, the latter as principal viola and assistant conductor of the *MSO.

Canadian composers have made a significant contribution to the violin/viola repertoire. Murray *Adaskin, *Archer, *Barnes, Brott, *Cherney, *Coulthard, Eckhardt-Gramatté, *Fiala, *Freedman, Joachim, *Kasemets, *Kenins, *Klein, *MacLean, *Morawetz, *Papineau-Couture, *Pentland, *Pépin, *Prévost, *Vallerand, and *Weinzweig have written works for solo violin and orchestra, while *Baker, Brott, Cherney, Coulthard, *Fodi, *Ridout, and *Surdin have composed works for viola and orchestra. Surdin's *Viola Concerto* was premiered 20 Feb 1980 by Golani-Erdész and the *CBC Vancouver Chamber Orchestra under Victor Feldbrill. Numerous works have been written for solo violin (eg, Eckhardt-Gramatté's *10 Caprices*, four *Suites*, and *Concerto*; Rodolphe *Mathieu's *Douze Études modernes*; Papineau-Couture's *Suite*; and *Somers' *Music for Solo Violin*) and a few for violin and viola together (eg, Joachim's *Music for Violin and Viola* and *Zuckert's *Sisterly Love*). Jacques *Hétu's *Variations, Op 11* were designed to be playable by violin, viola, or cello.

The violin is heard in country and folk music (see Fiddling; Folk music) and much less often in jazz and rock. Rock violinists of note, however, are Tim Evans of the Original Sloth Band; Ian Guenther, a sideman to Fraser and DeBolt, member of *Lighthouse, and director of the THP Orchestra; Ben Mink of *Stringband and later of Murray *McLauchlan's Silver Tractors and of FM; Nash the Slash (Jeff Plewman) of the Toronto bands Breathless and FM; and Lenny Solomon. Jazz violinists Willy Girard and Sonny Richardson were active during the 1940s in Montreal and Vancouver respectively. Terry King, who replaced Mink in Stringband, has worked in Montreal and Toronto clubs with Jane Fair, Claude *Ranger, and others. Pierre Bournaki has played with the Montreal jazz-rock band Aquarelle.

BIBLIOGRAPHY

Berljawsky, Joseph. 'Violin technique, its evolution and pedagogy: a historical and comparative study,' unpubl doctoral thesis, U of Montreal 1964

Trowsdale, G.C. 'Profile of a beginning string program,' *British Columbia Music Educator*, vol 10, Spring 1967

Kenneson, Claude. 'String renaissance in Alberta,' *CME*, vol 12, Summer 1971

Haydou, Irene. *The Irene Haydou Beginner's Method: Violin*, ed Frank Radcliffe (Berandol 1972)

Adaskin, Harry. *A Fiddler's World* (Vancouver 1977)

Cousineau, Jean. *Méthode de violon: premier cahier* (Outremont, Que, 1979) (FG, HK, NM)

Violoncello playing and teaching. See Cello playing and teaching.

Violoneux. See Fiddling.

'Vive la Canadienne.' National song most frequently sung in Quebec before *'O Canada' became popular. According to Ernest *Gagnon (*Chansons populaires du Canada*, Montreal 1865), this old French tune is a variant of 'Par derrièr' chez mon père.' Marius *Barbeau suggested that it was derived from 'Vole mon coeur vole' which differs slightly from the former. F.-A.-H. LaRue, who examined the words of 'Par derrièr' chez mon père' in the first volume of *Le Foyer canadien* (Quebec 1863), also discussed a variant, 'Les Trois Princesses.' According to Barbeau in *Alouette* (Montreal 1946), the words to 'Vive la Canadienne' probably were written by an oarsman; however he gives no further details. In August 1840 the melody, arranged for piano, appeared in *Literary Garland* as 'The Canadian / a French air.' The melody inspired Charles Grobe's *Variations brillantes sur Vive la Canadienne, mélodie nationale canadienne, Op 113* for piano (Ditson 1859). *La Canadienne*, a fantasy for violin and piano by Jules *Hone (3rd edn, Boucher, nd) is based on the song. Oscar *Martel composed *Variations sur 'Vive la Canadienne'* for violin. The tune also appears in Antoine *Dessane's piano suite *Quadrille sur cinq airs canadiens* (1854, Léger Brousseau, Crémazie 1855). *Vive la Canadienne* is also the title of an operetta in three acts written by Omer *Létourneau in 1924. About 1939 Charles *O'Neill's arrangement of the tune became the official march of the *Royal 22nd Regiment. Éva *Gauthier, Édouard *LeBel, and Joseph *Saucier made 78-rpm recordings of the song, and several choirs, among them the *Chorale de l'U St-Joseph (Col FL 234), included it on LPs.

BIBLIOGRAPHY

Vive la Canadienne!: souvenir du 24 juin 1880, pamphlet (Quebec City 1880) HP

VIVIER, Claude. Composer, b Montreal 14 Apr 1948. He studied 1967–71 at the *CMM with Gilles *Tremblay (composition) and Irving *Heller (piano). Awarded *Canada Council grants 1971–4 he worked with Gottfried Michael Koenig at the Instituut voor Sonologie in Utrecht and with Paul Méfano in Paris. His *Désintégration* was premiered at the Champigny Collectif international under the direction of Méfano and was performed in Cologne and Darmstadt. He continued his training 1972–4 in Cologne with Stockhausen. In some of his works he uses the human voice as a medium through which he succeeds especially well in conveying his spiritual concerns, using texts inspired by ancient and medieval literature. He was director 1975–6 of the contemporary music ensemble of the *U of Ottawa and resident composer with the *NYO in Quebec City in the summer of 1976. He has received commissions from the *SMCQ (*Liebesgedichte*), the secretary of state for cultural affairs of France (*Chants*), the NYO (*Siddhartha*), and the *Festival Singers (*Journal*). At the end of 1976 he undertook a research trip to Asia. Canada Council grants enabled Vivier to compose two major works: *Kopernikus*, an opera in two scenes on his own libretto which was produced at the *Monument national on 8, 9 May 1980 by the *U of Montreal Atelier de jeu scènique and Atelier de musique contemporaine; and *Orion* for orchestra, first performed by the *MSO in October 1980. He is an associate of the *CMCentre and an affiliate of PRO Canada.

A manuscript page from *Kopernikus* by Claude Vivier

SELECTED COMPOSITIONS

CHAMBER MUSIC

Ojikawa (Bible, Vivier). 1968. Sop, cl, perc. Ms

String Quartet. 1968. Ms

Prolifération. 1969 (rev 1975). Ondes M, pf, perc. CMCentre. RCI 358 (*SMCQ)

Hiérophonie (Greek hymn). 1970. Sop, 3 tpt, hn, cl, 2 fl, 1 trb (ten), 1 trb (bass), 2 perc. Ms

Désintégration. 1972. 2 pf, 4 vn, 2 va. Ms

Deva et Asura. 1972. 2 ww quin, brass quin, str quin. Ms

Lettura di Dante (*The Divine Comedy*). 1974. Sop, ob, cl, bn, tpt, trb, va, perc. CMCentre. RCI 411 (*SMCQ)

Liebesgedichte (Virgil, Psalm of David, Vivier). 1975. Vocal quar, cl, ob, hn, bn, 2 tpt, 2 trb. CMCentre

Learning. 1976. 4 vn, perc. CMCentre

Pulau Dewata. 1977. Perc ens or combination of instr. CMCentre

Also works for bn and pf, fl and pf, vn and pf, and vc and pf; for guit; and for vn and cl. All 1975. All ms

CHOIR OR VOICE

Musik für das Ende (Vivier). 1971. 20 vs. Ms

Chants (Vivier). 1973. 2 sop, 3 mezzo, 2 alto. Edns musicales transatlantiques 1975

'Jesus erbarme dich' (Kyrie eleison). 1974. SATB. Chanteclair 1977

'O! Kosmos' (Vivier). 1974. SATB. Chanteclair 1977

'Hymnen an die Nacht' (Novalis). 1975. Sop, pf. Ms

Journal (Vivier, Novalis, L. Carroll). 1977. SATB, 4 soli, perc. CMCentre

Also *Hommage à un vieux corse triste* (tape, 1972), *Pianoforte* (pf, 1975), *Siddhartha* (orch, 1976), *Shiraz* (pf, 1977), *Love Songs* and *Nanti Malam* (both ballets, 1977), *Orion* (orch, 1979), *Kopernikus* (opera, 1980). All ms

BIBLIOGRAPHY

Rochon, Pierre. 'Claude Vivier struggles to portray Canada in music,' *MSc*, 283, May–Jun 1975

BMI Canada Ltd. 'Claude Vivier,' pamphlet (1976)

Moisan, Daniel. 'Kopernicus [sic] ou l'histoire d'une oeuvre lyrique québécoise,' *Aria*, vol 3, Spring 1980 (PR)

'V'là l'bon vent!' Folksong on the theme of the 'trois canards' or three ducks, of which there are some 100 variants. Among the most popular are 'En roulant ma boule' and 'V'là l'bon vent!' 'Lèv' ton pied,' 'C'est le vent frivolant,' 'Suivons le vent,' and 'Descendez à l'ombre' are some of the other titles. The melody and the words of the chorus differ considerably from one version to another, but the story of the king's son who kills one of the three ducks is the same in most; the theme apparently arrived in Canada some time during the 17th century and was well known to the voyageurs. Ernest *Gagnon, in *Chansons populaires du Canada* (Quebec 1865), suggests that the words of the chorus as well as the tune of 'V'là l'bon vent!' are of Canadian origin. The song also appears in two versions in the *Chansons canadiennes* (Montreal 1907) harmonized by P.E. Prévost. Hector *Gratton wrote *Fantasia sur V'là l'bon vent* (1952) for orchestra, and Claude *Champagne made an arrangement for four voices *'V'là l'bon vent'/'Fair Wind'* (Waterloo 1960). The song may be heard on a 78 by Éva *Gauthier (Victor 69 273), and it is included on LPs by Jacques *Labrecque (RCI and RCA CS 100-7), the *Chorale de l'U St-Joseph (Col FL 234), André Bertrand, Les *Cailloux, the Petit Ensemble vocal of the *École normale de musique, and the *Alouette Vocal Quartet. In 1958 Gilles Julien and François Provencher founded the *Choeur V'là l'bon vent in Quebec City.

BIBLIOGRAPHY
Brassard, François. 'Refrains canadiens de chansons de France,' *Archives de folklore*, vol 1 (Montreal 1946)
Barbeau, Marius. 'Trois beaux canards (92 versions canadiennes),' ibid, vol 2 (Montreal 1947)
d'Harcourt, Marguerite. 'Analyse des versions musicales canadiennes des "Trois beaux canards",' ibid, vol 4 (Montreal 1949) HP

VOGEL, Vic (Victor Stéphane). Conductor, composer, arranger, trombonist, pianist, b Montreal, of Hungarian parents, 3 Aug 1935. He taught himself to play piano and violin. Later he studied piano, analysis, and musical theory 1954-5 with Michel *Hirvy in Montreal and took lessons in improvisation 1955-6 with Lennie Tristano in New York. He was an instrumentalist and conductor 1951-65 in Montreal hotels and nightclubs and toured Quebec in 1961 as pianist with the Paris vocal ensemble the Double-Six. He occasionally worked as arranger, pianist, and trombonist in Lee *Gagnon's 10-piece orchestra, notably during the Montreal Jazz Festival in 1962 and 1963, and in 1966 he conducted a group of Quebec jazz musicians on its first CBC-sponsored European tour. As a conductor, arranger, and composer he participated in the CBC radio programs 'Jazz en liberté' 1965-8, 'Jazz Canadiana' 1966-73, and 'Feu vert' 1972-4, and as conductor and accompanist he appeared on the CBC TV programs 'Music-Hall' 1956-66, 'Les Couche-tard' 1961-70, 'Sincèrement Fernand Gignac' 1966-7, and 'Vedettes en direct' 1973-4.

At the opening of the summer festival Man and His World in 1968 Vogel conducted an orchestra of 60 musicians; later in the season he led orchestras for Paul *Anka, Annie Cordy, Mahalia Jackson, Jerry Lewis, and Ann-Margret. He performed there again in 1971, when his band accompanied Gerry Mulligan. On a tour of Cyprus in 1972 he conducted the orchestra of the CBC program 'Les Beaux Dimanches' for the UN Peace Corps. He was the music director of the CBC National Song Competition in 1974.

In 1973 Vogel began to make summer visits to Baden Baden, Berlin, and Rome to conduct their radio orchestras, which have commissioned original scores from him. For the Théâtre des Variétés he has composed some 15 musical comedies, including *La Course au mariage* (1973, Trans Canada TSF 1457). He has written also for Tony Bennett, Eartha Kitt, and Andy Williams. Drawing on the works of André *Mathieu, he made the arrangements and conducted the incidental music for the official ceremonies of the 1976 Olympic Games (see Discography for Les Petits Chanteurs du Mont-Royal). He arranged this music for concert band in 1978. He composed the musical themes used in 1976-7 on both the CBC and CTV news bulletins and also wrote the music for the films *The Capricorn Challenge* (1978) and *Les Maîtres de l'Ungava* (1979, produced by SDA Productions), as well as for several NFB films.

In January 1978 he founded Vic Vogel + 19, a big band which under his direction gave concerts at the El Casino and the Vieux-Montréal Cegep that year. The ensemble performed along with the group *Offenbach at the *St-Denis Theatre in March 1979 and at the Bromont Summer Show the following August. At the *Grand Théâtre in Quebec City Vogel conducted the *Quebec SO 22 Mar 1979 in works by Woody Shaw and Thelonious Monk as part of a gala concert devoted to 'jazz greats.' He has made some LPs as soloist for London and Aris.

BIBLIOGRAPHY
Sherman, David. 'Vic Vogel wants to reach the kids to hustle jazz,' Montreal *Gazette*, 27 Jun 1978 ST

VOGELER, Francis. Music dealer, instrument importer, teacher, b Quebec City, fl 1788-1820. His name suggests that he was of German origin. Vogeler's first advertisement in the *Quebec Gazette*, in June 1788, offers four pianos imported from London as well as sheet music and music books. He was a friend and rival of Frédéric *Glackemeyer, and the two engaged in friendly competition to attract a limited clientele. In 1790-1 both took part in the orchestral subscription concerts of the Quebec Assembly and were remunerated for their services. In 1815 Vogeler was offering for sale 'an elegant bird organ' (Amtmann p 214); at the same time he announced that he taught piano, guitar, the flute, and other wind instruments. In 1819 and 1820 he was having severe business difficulties, as is revealed in his correspondence with his London suppliers.

BIBLIOGRAPHY
Amtmann *Music in Canada 1600-1800* GP

VOGT, A.S. (Augustus Stephen). Choir conductor, administrator, educator, organist, pianist, b Washington, near Kitchener-Waterloo, Ont, of German and Swiss parents, 14 Aug 1861, d Toronto 17 Sep 1926; FRCO, hon D MUS (Toronto) 1906. He received his early education in Elmira, Ont (where his family settled in 1865), and at 12 became the organist at St James Lutheran Church, playing an instrument made by his father, George Vogt, a pipe organ builder who had left Germany after the 1848 revolution. After studies in 1877 in Hamilton, Ont, with L.H. Parker, the younger Vogt in 1878 became organist at the First Methodist Church, St Thomas, Ont. He went to Boston to study 1881-4 at the New England Cons under S.A. Emery and H.M. Dunham and there met Calixa *Lavallée. He continued his studies 1885-8 at the Leipzig Cons with Salomon Jadassohn, Willy Rehberg, Carl Reinecke, Adolf Ruthardt, and others and often heard the famous choir at the Thomaskirche, directed by Gustav Schreck. Settling in Toronto, Vogt served 1888-1906 as organist-choirmaster at Jarvis St Baptist Church, where his choir became known for its unaccompanied singing. He taught piano and organ at the *Toronto College of Music, at several ladies' colleges, and after 1892 at the *TCM. He was Toronto secretary 1889-92 of the first Canadian College of Organists and president 1893-5 of the *Canadian Society of Musicians. He was the only Canadian organist to perform at the 1893 Chicago World's Fair. In the mid-1890s he was the music critic for *Saturday Night*, writing under the pseudonym 'Moderato.'

In 1894 Vogt founded the *Toronto Mendelssohn Choir, initially drawing most of the personnel from his choir at Jarvis St Baptist Church. He suspended the choir's activities 1897-1900, mainly to devise the kind of long-range strategy (including annual auditions for all members) which would ensure its healthy perpetuation. Resuming leadership of the reconstituted choir, Vogt soon developed it into one of the finest in North America. In 1902 he became the first choir director in Toronto to present annual festivals in conjunction with major orchestras. Those he employed most often were the Pittsburgh Orchestra and the Chicago (Theodore Thomas) SO. Katherine Hale (*Canadian Magazine*, February 1909) described him as a magnetic conductor with 'Napoleonic qualities of concentration [and] assimilation, and great determination.' By the time he resigned (in 1917, owing to increasing pressures at the TCM, of which he had become principal in 1913) he had gained an international reputation as a conductor.

A gifted administrator, Vogt devoted the remainder of his life to the TCM, which under his principalship became one of the largest such institutions in the British Empire, establishing examination centres throughout Canada. During a European sojourn (May 1912-April 1913, ostensibly to arrange for the Mendelssohn Choir a tour subsequently made impossible by World War I) Vogt had visited leading European music schools, and undoubtedly his keen assimilative and organizational mind had perceived ways in which their systems could be adapted for use by the TCM. Until 1921 he also made adjudicating trips to western Canada and was very much concerned with providing opportunities for competition. After establishing a closer liaison between the TCM and the U of Toronto, Vogt helped plan the faculty of music at the university and in 1918 was appointed dean.

Vogt's small compositional output shows great understanding of choral craft and effect. Several works were published, including *The Sea* (G. Schirmer 1911) and arrangements of *The Lord's Prayer* (Whaley Royce 1900) and *Crossing the Bar* (Whaley Royce 1906). His composition for women's voices, *An Indian Lullaby* (Whaley Royce 1906), was performed by the Toronto Mendelssohn Choir as early as 1907 and as late as 1945 and also by choirs outside Toronto. His arrangement of *Rule Britannia* (orchestration: Frederick Stock) also was popular. Earlier works included a 'scholarly and very effective' (according to J.D. Logan) *Prelude and Fugue for Organ*, written in Leipzig. Vogt compiled the widely used *Standard Anthem Book* (Whaley Royce vol 1 1894, vol 2 prior to 1909) and, with Healey *Willan, *The School and Community Song Book* (Gage 1922). His *Modern Pianoforte Technique* (Whaley Royce 1900) had been reissued 10 times by 1909. His published articles include 'Choir music in Europe' (*Musical Canada*, Oct 1907) and 'Musical Canada: yesterday and today' (*Musical Life and Arts*, 1 Dec 1924). A teacher for over 30 years, Vogt's pupils included G.D. *Atkinson, Jessie M. Allen, Mona *Bates, Ernest *Farmer, H.C. *Hamilton, William Henry *Hewlett, Ada Twohy *Kent, Ernest *Seitz, Bertha L. *Tamblyn, and George *Ziegler.

Vogt was honoured in various ways after his death. In 1928 a memorial scholarship was set up by former TCM students, and a Vogt Choir (conducted by a pupil, Richard Greene) was established in Guelph. In 1929 the Mendelssohn Choir placed a memorial window in St Paul's Anglican Church, Toronto. In 1936 the *Vogt Society was founded in Toronto.

BIBLIOGRAPHY

Hale, Katherine. 'Dr. Vogt,' *Canadian Magazine*, vol 32, Feb 1909

Logan, J.D. 'Canadian composers / the men and their music, 1, A.S. Vogt, MUS.D.,' *Sunday World*, 14 Mar 1909

Jacques, Edmund. 'Dr. Vogt and his choir,' New York *Evening Post* (11 May 1912)

'Augustus Stephen Vogt,' *MT*, vol 53, Dec 1912

Bridle, Augustus. 'Vogt, a great chorus master,' *The Year Book of Canadian Art 1913* compiled by the Arts and Letters Club of Toronto (London, Toronto 1913)

– 'Dr. A.S. Vogt,' *Sons of Canada* (Toronto 1916)

Atkinson, G.D. 'Dr. Vogt and church music,' *The New Outlook*, Oct 1926

MacMillan, Ernest. 'Augustus Stephen Vogt: an appreciation,' *U of Toronto Monthly*, vol 27, Oct 1926

Uttley, W.V. 'Dr. Augustus Stephen Vogt,' *14th Annual Report of the Waterloo Historical Society* (1926)

Falconer, Sir Robert. 'Address at the funeral service for Dr. Vogt,' ibid

Smith, Leo. 'Editorial comments,' *CQR*, vol 9, Autumn 1926

The Toronto Conservatory of Music, a Retrospective ... (Toronto 1936)

Smith, Ocean G. compiler. *The Toronto Mendelssohn Choir, a History ... 1894–1948* (Toronto 1948)

[McLean, Maud.] *A Responsive Chord: The Story of the Toronto Mendelssohn Choir 1894–1969* (Toronto 1969)

RPn

Vogt Society (later the Society for Contemporary Music). Established in 1936 by the TCM Residence Alumni Assn in honour of A.S. *Vogt to promote the performance and publication of music by Canadian composers. At its first meeting, 11 Feb 1937 at the Art Gallery of Toronto, Elie *Spivak, accompanied by Leo *Barkin, performed works of Leo *Smith and Healey *Willan. A competition for Canadian compositions was established in 1938. Walter *MacNutt's *Suite for Piano*, the first winner, was published by *Harris. Co-winners in 1939 were Florence Biltcliffe (*Piano Prelude*, Harris), and Patricia *Blomfield Holt (*Suite*, violin and piano, Harris). Other composers whose works were performed at Vogt Society concerts included Louis *Applebaum, Oskar *Morawetz, Godfrey *Ridout, and Harry *Somers. After 1941, when the society changed its name to the Society for Contemporary Music, fewer concerts were given, and in 1945 the organization disbanded. The society's presidents were Mrs Geoffrey *Waddington 1936–7, Leo Smith 1937–8, Ewart Walker 1938–41, J. Campbell *McInnes 1941–2, and Arnold *Walter 1942–5. A Junior Vogt Society was established in the late 1930s by Mary Willan (Mason), Francean Campbell (Rich), and Godfrey Ridout. Its concerts were presented in members' homes until 1941.

(MWM)

von KUSTER, Clifford (Austin). Pianist, teacher, administrator, b Turtleford, northwest of Saskatoon, 2 Jun 1921; B MUS (Toronto) 1949. A pupil of Mona *Bates, Margaret Miller *Brown, and Clifford *Poole, he later studied with Carl Friedberg, Eduard Steuermann, Cecile Genhart, and Marcel Ciampi. Appointed in 1952 to the staff of the Music Teachers' College, London, Ont, which was affiliated to the *U of Western Ontario, he became principal of the reorganized college in 1960 and dean when it became the Faculty of Music of the university in 1968. He assembled an efficient team of administrators and teachers, and under his leadership the school became one of the largest in Canada, moving into its own building on the campus in 1973. At this point, von Kuster resigned his deanship to devote himself to teaching. He has served on the boards of the *Western Ontario Cons, the *London SO, and the London Music Scholarship Foundation.

PGD

Vox populi. Suite for orchestra, choir, and soloists by Henri *Miro. The music is based on 14 French-Canadian folk tunes. Completed in September 1928, the work was performed 6 November under the direction of Jean *Goulet at the *Monument national. It was presented again 19 Apr 1929 in Holyoke, Mass, and 24 June at the Stadium in Montreal. The first part, 'Fantaisie,' contains the tunes 'Dans tous les cantons,' *'À la claire fontaine,' 'Gai lon la, gai le rosier,' and *'À St-Malo.' The second is based on *'Isabeau s'y promène' and consists of eight variations preceded by a symphonic introduction. The third part describes a village fête, following the high mass; one hears church bells, a children's choir, and some violoneux, all sustained by the full orchestra. *La Lyre* (vol 4, Sep 1928), reported that the work could be performed with chorus and orchestra or with orchestra alone.

GP

W

WADDINGTON, Geoffrey. Conductor, administrator, violinist, b Leicester, England, 23 Sep 1904, d Toronto 3 Jan 1966; hon LL D (Dalhousie) 1956. His mother, Elizabeth, was a pianist, and his father, Frank, appeared in light opera in England. The family moved to Canada in 1907 and settled in Lethbridge, Alta, where the young Waddington began playing violin at 7. He had his first conducting experience before he was 12, when the conductor of a local theatre orchestra fell ill. In 1921 Waddington won a scholarship to the *TCM. While studying there with Ferdinand Fillion, Luigi von *Kunits, Leo *Smith, and Healey *Willan he toured 1921–5 as a violinist and was a member 1922–6 of the TCM faculty. At the TCM he met his future wife, the concert pianist Mildred Baker. He also played 1925–8 in the *TSO.

Waddington began his radio career in 1922 on CKNC and served 1926–33 as music director of that station and 1933–5 as music director of the CRBC (which took over CKNC's facilities in 1933). On CKNC he conducted orchestras for many sponsored programs, including 'The Neilson Hour' (some 460 broadcasts, 1926–33), which in 1929 became the first variety program to be heard across Canada. He also conducted CKNC's Canadian Eveready Concert Orchestra, which recorded for Victor in 1928. For several years he worked as a freelance conductor, first (1935–6) with an orchestra at the Royal York Hotel in Toronto, then (1939, 1940) with the Winnipeg Summer Symphony for a while (1943) with *The *Army Show*. He was music director 1938–43 at CBC Winnipeg (responsible for 'Geoffrey Waddington Conducts') and at All-Canada Radio Facilities (Alberta) in 1944. In 1945 he began conducting CBC Toronto radio shows – 'The Geoffrey Waddington Show,' 'The Edmund *Hockridge Show' (both 1946–7), and others. In 1947 he was appointed to a casual position (made official in mid-1948) as music adviser and consultant to the CBC English network. He was a co-founder in 1948 of the *CBC Opera Company and won acclaim for broadcasts of *Peter Grimes, Albert Herring, Così fan tutte,* and **Deirdre*. Appointed CBC music director in 1952, he was founder and music director 1952–64 of the *CBC SO and was that distinguished orchestra's most frequent conductor. He led it in some 50 concerts, including its broadcast debut 29 Sep 1952, its public debut 16 May 1955, and its concert 23 Oct 1961 in Washing-

Geoffrey Waddington

ton at the Inter-American Music Festival celebrating the 16th anniversary of the United Nations.

Other highlights of Waddington's conducting career include appearances with the *Promenade Symphony Concerts (1940s) and the TSO (1940s and 1950s), BBC broadcasts of Canadian music from Glasgow and Manchester in 1953, and a concert (29 Jul 1957) and, later, a recording of music for organ (Gordon *Jeffery) and strings presented at Westminster Abbey before the International Congress of Organists. He conducted the first symphonic concerts sponsored by the *CLComp in Toronto (26 Mar 1952) and in Montreal (3 Feb 1954). Waddington also conducted other CBC special broadcasts and series in the 1950s (eg, 'Music for Strings' and a selection of Gilbert & Sullivan operettas). However, he rarely appeared on TV (*The Marriage of Figaro* in 1956, 'Portrait of an Orchestra' in 1962, and several episodes of 'L'*Heure du concert' were exceptions) or in public concert. He was an adjudicator in many of the CBC's contests for performers and composers. In 1959 he received the U of Alberta National Award in Music. With the demise of the CBC SO in 1964 he was appointed music consultant and director of symphonic services, a largely inactive position.

Waddington's experience as one of the first radio conductors in Canada (and probably the most active in his day) shaped his personality on the podium. He was thoroughly professional in his recognition of the practical demands of time slots and studio facilities and in his subordination of personal taste to programming requirements. A shy person, he spoke little at rehearsals. Though he expressed few aesthetic preconceptions about the music at hand, he was able to establish with his players a rapport based on mutual respect and confidence. Despite his conservatory training, his early career was mostly in light music. Nevertheless, he adapted well to the symphonic repertoire. His workmanlike objectivity and trust in his players enabled him to prepare himself to conduct contemporary works in two or three days. From the beginning Waddington's orchestras served as training grounds for musicians who did well on their own later, including Percy *Faith (as an arranger), Robert *Farnon, Samuel *Hersenhoren, Zara *Nelsova, Albert *Pratz, and Paul *Scherman.

In the late 1940s and 1950s, when Canada experienced a cultural expansion which embodied an upsurge of musical talent in performance and composition, Waddington – as the musician with the greatest employment power and programming responsibility in Canada – was able to channel this talent into broadcasting and thus to give it national and international exposure. During this period program series organized by Waddington served as vehicles and outlets for performers and composers alike. Under his direction the CBC's policy of commissioning Canadian composers became a regular practice. He conducted the premieres of many new works, including Murray *Adaskin's *Algonquin Symphony* (1958), *Freedman's *Nocturne* (1952) and *Symphony* (1961), *Matton's *L'*Horoscope* (1958), *Papineau-Couture's *Violin Concerto* (1954), *Somers' *North Country* (1948), *Suite for Harp and Chamber Orchestra* (1949), and *Five Concepts* (1962), *Weinzweig's *Edge of the World* (1946) and *Divertimento No. 3* (first complete performance, 1961), and Willan's *Coronation Suite*, B57 (1953).

WRITINGS

'Music and radio,' *Music in Canada* (Toronto 1955)

'Music will serve you well!' *CBC Times*, 15–21 Jul 1956

DISCOGRAPHY

A. Brott *Songs of Contemplation* – Vallerand *Prelude for Orchestra*. CBC Mtl orch, Marshall sop. 1954. RCI 116

M. McIntyre – Dela – Hamer – Kalnins – Mercure. A CBC Tor orch and choir, Benson Guy sop. 1951. RCI 35

Mercure *Pantomime*. CBC Mtl orch. 1954. RCI 117

Somers – Dolin – Weinzweig – Twa. Iosch hp, Bauman ob, Galper cl, CBC str orch. 1952. RCI 86/(Weinzweig) RCI ACM 1

See also Discographies for N. Brunet; CBC SO; TS. (HK)

George Wade and His Cornhuskers (or Corn Huskers). The most popular Canadian country band of its day. Though much of its history is sketchy, it is known that the band, led by the caller George Wade (b Manitoba ca 1895, d Toronto January 1975?), was based in Toronto and performed for dances in Ontario and Quebec from the mid-1920s probably until the 1940s. The band began broadcasting on CFRB, Toronto, in 1928 and in 1933 became the first group of its type to perform on the CRBC. It was heard regularly until the late 1930s, in turn on the CRBC and the CBC, and toured in the Maritimes in 1933 and in western Canada ca 1935. The band made some 13 78s for Victor's Black Label in 1933, each an arrangement of four or five dance tunes, with calls by Wade. Personnel ranged from 4 to 15; for records, a small group was used – two or three fiddles, banjo, piano, harmonica (or jew's harp), and a singer, 'Pete the Mountain.' Among sometime members of the band were the fiddlers Bill, Francis, and Laury Cormier, Jean *Carignan, Bill Martin, Ted Steven, and Johnny Bentley; the pianist Johnny *Burt (for CFRB broadcasts ca 1931–3 and the Victor 78s); the banjoist 'Doc' Boyd; the guitarist Tony Mont; and the bassist Cecil McEachern. A photograph ca 1930 in *A Pictorial History of Radio in Canada* (Toronto 1975) shows a cellist, a trumpeter, and a drummer among an eight-man group. Carignan has recalled playing saxophone and clarinet with the Cornhuskers for dances. The band appears to have broken up some time after it left regular employment with the CBC. Albums of pieces played by Wade (some composed by Bill Cormier and arranged by Burt) were published by Harry *Jarman ca 1932 and, as part of a six-volume 'Cornhuskers Series of Canadian Square Dance Books,' ca 1947. MD, MM

WAIZMAN (Waizmann), **Louis** (Ludwig). Composer, arranger, librarian, teacher, violist, trombonist, pianist, b Salzburg 6 Nov 1863, d Toronto 24 Aug 1951. Purportedly born in the same house as Mozart, Waizman studied composition privately with Joseph Rheinberger and graduated from the Mozarteum in 1884. He spent 10 years with the Austrian Army Band touring Europe and Africa, then moved in 1893 to Canada. After 10 years in Ottawa he moved to Toronto, where he worked first as a band trombonist and theatre musician (playing viola, cello, and piano) and taught theory and composition. His pupils included Leslie *Bell, Percy *Faith, Robert *Farnon, Samuel *Hersenhoren, Charles *Jordan, Paul *Scherman, and Morris *Surdin. Waizman was a violist 1923–32 and the librarian 1923–46 with the New SO (*TSO) and was also a staff arranger 1933–51 for the CRBC (after 1936, *CBC). On his retirement from the TSO he was made honorary librarian (1946–9), the occasion marked 5 Apr 1946 by the orchestra's third performance of his *Suite de Ballet* dedicated to Luigi von *Kunits. Waizman's other compositions (listed in the *Catalogue of Canadian Composers*) include piano trios, cantatas, orchestral suites, and a piano caprice. Several piano rolls were recorded by the composer after 1910 for Solodant, Solo Art, and Star and Word, and other piano pieces were published in 1927 by *Waterloo and 1928–9 in *Musical Canada*. Several unpublished works are held in the CBC Toronto Music Library. MM

Wales. Immigration of the Welsh to Canada occurred in cycles corresponding to economic depressions in the homeland in the 19th and 20th centuries. Some moved to Canada via the USA and others via the Welsh community established in the Argentine. They settled in coal-mining areas and farming districts of Alberta, Saskatchewan, and Ontario, and some later were drawn to urban centres, mainly Toronto, Winnipeg, Calgary, Montreal, and Vancouver.

An early settlement (ca 1902) was Bangor, east of Regina. Accounts refer to song as an integral part of celebrations in the community. A clergyman in Bangor wrote of a church service: 'The old tradition of the men sitting on one side of the church while the women sat on the other goes back to the days when they sang in four part harmony. At Bangor a Mr. Griffith led the singing. He marched up and down the aisle to make sure everyone kept in tune and kept the tempo properly ... with only 28 people in the congregation, they could carry [various hymns] with a volume comparable to that of a congregation six or seven times their size' (*The Canadian Family Tree*, Ottawa 1967). An eisteddfod (choral competition) was held annually in Bangor during the early 1900s.

Indeed, the Welsh contribution to music in Canada lies mainly in the field of singing. This has been sustained by both the churches (the Welsh protestant service may be held in English or Welsh) and the many St David's societies (named for the patron saint of Wales) across the country. Choral groups include the *St David's Welsh Male Voice Choir in Edmonton, the Welsh Male Choir in Saskatoon (fl 1913 under John Parry), the Welsh Male Voice Choir in Winnipeg (fl 1920s), the Cymric Singers in Vancouver (heard on CBC radio in the 1940s), the Vancouver Welsh Choral Society (1946–54), conducted by Evan Walters), the Vancouver Welsh Male Voice Choir (formed in 1962 and directed in turn by Evan Walters, Lloyd Wade, John Williams, and Enid Lewis), and the Ottawa Welsh Choral Society (directed in 1971 by Roy Morris). The Dewi Sant Welsh United Church in Toronto is the centre of many Ontario activities. The Welsh Club of Ontario began sponsoring annual spring hymn-singing weekends (in Niagara Falls, then in Kingston) called Cymanfa Ganu, which in 1978 attracted 1500 people. By 1977 the International Welsh Assn had held four Cymanfa Ganu in Canada – the fourth in Ottawa. During these festivals, folk singing and dancing and recitations precede the singing of hymns.

The 90-member Rhos Male Voice Choir conducted by Colin Jones toured in Canada in 1967, and in October 1978 the 85-voice Trelawnyd Male Voice Choir of North Wales visited Canada under the sponsorship of the Centennial Choir of Cornwall, Ont. Several Canadian choirs have competed in the eisteddfods in Great Britain: the *Elgar Choir of BC placed first in the girls' choir division of the 1936 National Welsh Eisteddfod, the Anne *Campbell Singers won firsts at the 1968 Tees-Side Eisteddfod (England) and the 1972 Llangollen International Eisteddfod (Wales), the *Leamington Choral Society placed third at the 1970 Llangollen competition, and the *Jeunes Chanteurs d'Acadie won three first prizes there in 1974.

Canadian musicians who have appeared in Wales include Victor *White, principal tenor with the Welsh National Opera ca 1957, Bernard *Turgeon, who sang with that company in 1962, and Joseph *Rouleau and Barbara *Shuttleworth who appeared with it in 1970 and in 1973 respectively; Arthur *Davison, who conducted the National Youth Orchestra of Wales in 1966 and made two recordings with it; and Boris *Brott, who was conductor of the BBC Welsh Orchestra 1974–9. Welsh-born musicians active in Canada include Henry Abley, organist-composer active in Sault Ste Marie, Ont, 1957–9, in Lethbridge, Alta, 1961–7, and in Saskatoon thereafter; Merlin Davies, tenor and voice teacher at *McGill U; Vic Franklyn, a pop singer and recording artist in Toronto in 1972, who began his own nationally syndicated TV show from CHCH, Hamilton, in 1976; Fred M. *Gee; Howell *Glynne; W.J. Hendra (1880–1966), who moved to Canada in 1906 and settled in Edmonton, where he taught voice and strings at *Alberta College 1913–64 and founded, and conducted 1917–47, the Edmonton Male Chorus; Gaynor Jones, who became a music historian at the *U of Toronto in 1971; Glyndwr Jones (1901–75), who moved in 1929 to Calgary, where he taught voice at the *Banff SFA, and in 1944 to Vancouver, where he directed the Canadian Memorial Chapel Choir 1944–70 and was principal of the BC Institute of Music and Drama (see *TUTS); Ernest Morgan (1899–1959), an organist-choirmaster and baritone soloist in Toronto churches and for some years a CBC producer; Robbie Rae, a pop singer who, with his wife, Cherrill (of St Thomas, Ont), recorded the hit single 'Que Sera Sera' for A & M in 1977 and starred on a CBC TV summer series in 1978; Stanley *Saunders; B.F. Shinn (*Shinn Cons of Music); Rhys Thomas, voice teacher and conductor, fl 1903–18 in Winnipeg; Ifan *Williams; and Rhyddid Williams, an organist-choirmaster in Sault Ste Marie and a composer of choral works.

Many Welsh tunes are included in hymn books of the Anglican and United churches in Canada. The theme and setting of Raymond *Pannell's opera **Aberfan* were suggested by the 1966 disaster at that mining village in Wales. (FH, LRH, MM)

WALKER, Alan. Administrator, writer, teacher, radio producer, b Scunthorpe, Lincolnshire, England, 6 Apr 1930; LGSM 1949, ARCM 1950, B MUS (Durham) 1956, D MUS (Durham) 1965. He studied piano with Alfred Nieman at the GSM, London. He lectured 1958–6 at the Guildhall School and was a producer 1961–71 with the BBC. He moved to Canada in 1971 and served until 1980 as head of the music department at *McMaster U and after that time as a teacher there. In 1974 he was made an honorary fellow of the Guildhall School. His wife, the English pianist Valerie Tryon, has continued her career on both sides of the Atlantic.

WRITINGS

A Study in Musical Analysis (London, New York 1962)

An Anatomy of Musical Criticism (London 1966, Philadelphia 1968)

– ed. *Frederic Chopin: Profiles of the Man and the Musician* (New York 1967)
'John Field,' *Listener*, 23 Apr 1970
'Liszt and the Beethoven symphonies,' *Music Review*, vol 31, Aug 1970
– ed. *Franz Liszt: The Man and His Music* (London, New York 1970)
Franz Liszt (New York 1971)
– ed. *Robert Schumann: The Man and His Music* (London 1971, New York 1972)
'Music criticism,' *Encyclopaedia Britannica* (Chicago 1974)
'Schopenhauer and music,' *Times Literary Supplement*, 3 Jan 1975
'Liszt's duo sonata,' *MT*, vol 116, Jul 1975
'The musical imperative,' *Times Educational Supplement*, 11 Jul 1975
Robert Schumann (London, New York 1976) CF

WALTER, Arnold (Maria). Educator, administrator, musicologist, composer, b Hannsdorf, Moravia (now in north-central Czechoslovakia), 30 Aug 1902, d Toronto 6 Oct 1973; DR IURIS (Prague) 1926, hon D MUS (Mount Allison) 1966. The son and grandson of schoolmasters (his grandfather was also the village organist-choirmaster), Walter pursued a classical high-school education in Brno, earning money for private music studies by coaching his fellow students in Latin and Greek. His teachers included Bruno Weigl, a pupil of Bruckner, for harmony and composition. At his father's insistence, he studied jurisprudence at the U of Prague, but on graduating he turned to musicology at the U of Berlin, where his principal teachers were Hermann Abert, Curt Sachs, and Johannes Wolf. At the same time, he studied privately with Rudolf Breithaupt and Frederic Lamond (piano) and Franz Schreker (composition).

After brief medical studies at Masaryk U in Brno, Walter returned to Berlin. However, Berlin in the late 1920s had little to offer to yet another pianist-composer from the provinces. Always resourceful, he developed his talent for writing about music. He contributed to *Melos*, and by the early 1930s he was associated actively with two influential left-wing periodicals: *Die Weltbühne* (as music editor) and *Vörwarts* (as music critic). Because of his political allegiances Walter was forced to leave Berlin in 1933, escaping to Majorca, where he studied folk music, learned three new languages (at one time or another he could converse in four or five languages as well as Latin and Greek), and taught. In 1936, at the outbreak of the Spanish Civil War, he fled to England. There he was engaged in folk music research at Cecil Sharp House and became acquainted with Ralph Vaughan Williams, Imogen Holst, Maud Karpeles, and other eminent folk scholars.

In 1937 Walter accepted a teaching offer from Upper Canada College, Toronto, travelling on a British passport hastily arranged in the absence of any other acceptable document. He taught at Upper Canada College until 1943 and then freelanced before taking a special assignment at the *TCM in 1945 to implement the Ernest Hutcheson Report for the reorganization of higher music education in Toronto. Walter established the Senior School as the TCM's graduate department and initiated the opera school (see *Royal Cons Opera School, *COC). In 1946 he introduced a degree program, the first of its kind in Canada, to prepare music teachers for positions in elementary and secondary schools. After extensive correspondence with the composer-methodologist Carl Orff, Walter introduced courses in Orff's teaching method at the RCMT (1955), the first such courses anywhere in North America. These were supervised by Doreen *Hall, who had studied with Orff in Salzburg in the previous year on a scholarship arranged by Walter and who collaborated 1952–68 with Walter in the preparation of English-

Manuscript opening page of *Sonata for Piano* by Arnold Walter

language versions of Orff's teaching manuals (see Orff-Schulwerk).

With the *U of Toronto's 1952 reorganization of the various music departments under its control Walter became director of the Faculty of Music, with responsibility for all degree programs and for the diploma previously awarded by the Senior School. His tenure 1952–68 as director was a period of extraordinary growth. Academic programs were strengthened, and new programs added at both undergraduate and graduate levels. Under his direction the U of Toronto music library was expanded into the largest of its kind in Canada and one of the finest in North America, and an electronic music studio, the first in Canada, was inaugurated. Both were housed in the new Edward Johnson Building, which he also had helped to plan.

During this time Walter's activities took on national and international dimensions as well. He served as president of the *CMCouncil 1965–6, the *CMCentre 1959 and 1970, and *CAUSM 1965–7 and as chairman of the editorial board of the **Canadian Music Journal* 1956–62. He was president of the International Society for Music Education (ISME) 1953–5 and of the Interamerican Music Council (CIDEM) 1969–72. All of these organizations owed their existence in some degree to his efforts.

Many of Walter's ideas were in advance of their time, and some of his attempts to turn vision into reality met with strong opposition and resentment. An aura of controversy often surrounded his activities. Everything he undertook seemed geared to the unfolding of a master plan for music in Canada, a plan conceived in the first few years after his arrival. At the root of this plan was an awareness that the development of talent, which he found to be abundant, and the development of the market for this talent had to go hand in hand. This required conscious direction, through education of both musicians and audiences, through public and private subsidization, and through group action channelled within strong organizations. He never voluntarily surrendered control of a project until he felt it was secure, and his greatest legacy may well be the institutions he thus helped to create.

Although Walter composed intermittently throughout his life, it could not be said that he was pre-eminently successful in this field. His aesthetic was primarily that of pre-World-War-I Europe, and he seemed not to want to move away from the terrain of Mahler and Strauss, of Debussy and Scriabin and the young Schoenberg. As much of this music was unfashionable and even unknown in Toronto, Walter's compositions struck many listeners as lacking in the dynamism and forward thrust that characterized so many other areas of his life. His works never gained wide acceptance, despite the efforts of friends and colleagues to promote them, and this was a source of great disappointment to him.

In a sense, his best creative energies were invested in teaching and in his many essays, articles, and lectures. His writings, liberally sprinkled with quotations from the world's great authors and thinkers, reflect an enormous erudition. His composition pupils included such diverse musical personalities as Paul *McIntyre, Phil *Nimmons, and Clermont *Pépin. In his teaching and especially in his writing, he sought repeatedly to emphasize the place of music in society and the debt society owes to music. At the time of his death, he was working on a book on music in a technological age.

Of his many honours and awards, he valued particularly the Christian Culture Medal given by Assumption College (Windsor, Ont) in 1945 to 'an outstanding exponent of Christian ideals.' In 1972 he was made an Officer of the *Order of Canada. In 1974 the concert hall of the Edward Johnson Building, U of Toronto, was named Walter Hall in his memory, and the Arnold Walter Memorial Award for performance students was established by the university. The *CMCentre has granted him the associate status reserved for deceased composers whose works the centre holds. The musical rights of his estate are administered by CAPAC.

SELECTED COMPOSITIONS

ORCHESTRA

Symphony in G Minor. 1942. Full orch. CMCentre
For the Fallen (Binyon). 1949. Sop, SATB, orch. Ms
Concerto for Orchestra. 1958. Full orch. CMCentre

CHAMBER

Sonatina for Cello and Piano. 1940. CMCentre
Trio for Violin, Cello and Piano. 1940. CMCentre
Sonata for Violin and Piano. 1940. Ms

PIANO

Suite for Piano. 1945. OUP 1956
Sonata for Pianoforte. 1950. GVT 1951

ELECTRONIC

Summer Idyll (collab Myron Schaeffer, H. Olnick). 1960. Tape. 1967. Folkways FM 3436
Other works in all categories. Also several scores for radio plays

WRITINGS

'What is modern music?' *CRMA*, vol 1, May 1942
'Music a means to unify mankind,' *CRMA*, vol 3, Apr–May, Jun–Jul, Aug–Sep 1944
'Canadian composition,' Music Teachers National Assn *Proceedings* (Pittsburgh 1946)
– et al. 'Music, fine arts and drama in Canadian higher education,' *The Humanities in Canada*, ed Kirkconnell and Woodhouse (Ottawa 1947)
'Toward Canadian opera,' *Here and Now*, vol 1, May 1948
'Music education on the North American continent,' *Food for Thought*, vol 14, Feb 1954
'Education in music,' *Music in Canada*, ed MacMillan (Toronto 1955)
'Carl Orff,' *CMJ*, vol 1, Autumn 1956
– and Hall, Doreen, transls. *Music for Children* by Carl Orff (Mainz 1956–61)
'A Canadian pattern,' 'Problems of patronage in a democratic society,' 'Music in a technological age,' *CMJ*, vol 1, Spring 1957
'The International Society for Music Education,' 'Elementary music education – the European approach,' *CMJ*, vol 2, Spring 1958
'In memoriam: Edward Johnson,' 'Music and electronics,' *CMJ*, vol 3, Summer 1959
'A musical journey to Japan,' *CMJ*, vol 6, Autumn 1961
Music and the Common Understanding, U of Saskatchewan Lecture 9 (Saskatoon 1966)
– ed. *Aspects of Music in Canada* (Toronto 1969)
'The growth of music education,' *Aspects of Music in Canada* / 'Le développement de l'éducation musicale,' *Aspects de la musique au Canada*

'Orff Schulwerk in American education,' *Inter-American Music Bulletin*, May 1970
'A composer's story,' *CanComp*, 77, Feb 1973

BIBLIOGRAPHY
'Dr. Arnold Walter retires as Music Faculty director,' *CanComp*, 26, Feb 1968
Weinzweig, Helen. 'Dr. Arnold Walter honoured by friends, colleagues, alumni,' *CanComp*, 29, May 1968
Ridout, Godfrey. 'Aspects of Arnold Walter,' *CanComp*, 38, Mar 1969
Mercer, Ruby. 'Arnold Walter,' *OpCan*, vol 10, May 1969
Creative Canada, vol 1
Contemporary Canadian Composers / Compositeurs canadiens contemporains PM

Ward method. Initially a liturgical movement as well as a music-training system. It was developed by Justine Ward (USA 1880–1975) to accommodate the directives of Pius X's *Motu proprio* (1903) for the renewal of sacred song. Working mainly with children, the Ward method's aim was to produce singers specialized and experienced in the approved repertoire and tradition. In addition to voice training, the method stresses such special skills as reading in all clefs (beginning with the C clef) and in all keys; figured bass before staff notation; the use of Gregorian modes and polyphony as the melodic materials for solfège; and training in rhythm founded essentially on gesture ('chironomy') and bodily movement. The founder's pedagogy was enriched by the continuous collaboration of Thomas Shields of the U of Washington and Dom Mocquereau of the Benedictine abbey at Solesmes, France.

The Ward method was introduced to central Canada in 1954 by a French Dominican nun, Sister Alix de Vaulchier (b Le Deschaux, France, 19 Mar 1897), who had been sent by the director of the Institut grégorien in Paris. She travelled in all parts of Quebec giving courses to teachers and visiting classrooms in which the method was being taught. At the Congrès international de musique sacrée in Paris in 1957, a map displayed the method's dissemination not only in the Montreal area but also particularly in Baie-Comeau, Jonquière, Amos, and Philipsburg, Que, and Alexandria, Ont. Justine Ward's concept was tellingly demonstrated at the liturgical ceremonies in 1957, 1958, and 1959 which brought together some 500 Quebec children at Cap-de-la-Madeleine. A record of Gregorian chant and hymns, *La Voix des plus petits*, with Vaulchier conducting, was produced in 1958 (Radio-Marie NDC 455 902). Between 1959 and 1965, only *Laval U, a section of which was affiliated with the Ward Institute in Paris, could grant Ward diplomas. Nevertheless, the *U of Montreal continued teaching the method until 1963. After that time Sister Alix de Vaulchier gave her course a new orientation, and while it preserved certain elements of the Ward method, it adopted a new name, 'Pedagogy for class teaching of music,' and was offered solely at the U of Montreal. The reform in liturgy which followed Vatican Council II gave rise to various interpretations, with the result that the Ward method ceased to be applied ca 1966–7.

The Ward method has been expounded in books published 1934–62 in Washington, DC (Catholic Education Press), and in Tournai, Belgium (Desclée). The main Washington publications are the volumes *Music* and *Music Teacher's Guide* (vols 1, 2, 3), *Gregorian Chant* (1949, translated into French and published by Desclée in 1951), and, along with a series of pictures for grade 1, seven volumes for children covering grades 2 to 8, with corresponding teachers' guides. Among the books illustrated by Frances Delehanty and published by Desclée are *Musique pour les classes élémentaires* (1934–41; grades 1 to 4) for use by teachers, *Chants et chansons* (1949–53) for children, and *La Méthode Ward* (Paris 1962, 1967) for use by teachers, illustrated by Denise Donvez and accompanied by a collection of songs for children.

BIBLIOGRAPHY
Monique-d'Ostie, Sister [Mamie Martel]. 'La méthode "Ward",' unpubl L MUS thesis, U of Montreal 1959 (ADV)

WARREN. Family of organ builders and organists: 1 / Samuel Russell and his brothers Thomas and William; 2 / Samuel Prowse, son of Samuel Russell; and 3 / Charles S., son of Samuel Russell, and Frank, Russell, and Mansfield, sons of Charles S.

1 **Samuel Russell**. Organ and piano builder, b Tiverton, RI, 29 Mar 1809, d Montreal 30 Jul 1882. A nephew of the architect Russell Warren and a son of the carpenter Samuel Warren, he was taught wood-working by his father and quickly became interested in organ building. He supplied an organ to Charleston, SC, in 1830 and installed one in Newport in 1834 and another in Providence in 1835. About this time he went to Boston to work with Thomas Appleton. Settling in Montreal in 1836, he built an organ for the church in Rigaud. The following year he entered into partnership with George Mead; the partners built an organ for Sherrington, Que, but dissolved their company shortly after.

While servicing organs in Montreal and the surrounding region, Warren continued to build, installing instruments of his manufacture in St-Ours (1841), St-Isidore de Laprairie (1842), Montreal (St George's Church and a Presbyterian church 1843, St. Thomas' Church 1845), Boucherville (1846), Chambly (1847), and elsewhere. In 1847 he repaired the organs of the Catholic church in Grondines and the Anglican church in Dunham. In Montreal the Hôpital Général acquired a Warren organ in 1848, and the churches of St Patrick and Bon-Secours followed suit in 1850. These are by no means the only Warren organs installed in the Montreal region, and others were acquired after 1853 by clients in Toronto, Hamilton, Ont, Quebec City, and Kamouraska, Que. Though Warren's instruments attracted criticism in 1854 and again in 1863 from such organists as A. J. *Boucher, J.-B. *Labelle, and Paul *Letondal, the success of the firm did not decline. Charles S. took over as head in 1882. In its early years the company was described as 'makers of church, parlour, reed organs, seraphims, melodeons and pianofortes.' As a piano manufacturer Samuel R. had obtained, in 1845, a patent for a 'method of constructing "harmonic" attachments for piano fortes.'

Warren built probably more than 400 organs. Those intact in 1979 – eg, in Chambly, Dunham, and Freligshburg, Que, or in Tignish, PEI – are small instruments but provide eloquent proof of Warren's achievement through the quality of their timbres and the symmetry of their cases. His larger instruments unfortunately have disappeared or been radically altered. In 1861 Gustave *Smith described Warren's development and its debt to European models – eg, the introduction into Canada of the harmonic flutes and free reeds – and his increasing preference for the French organ. Always open to new ideas, he was the first organ builder in the country to adopt the Barker lever (ca 1851) and hydraulic bellows (1860). A fine craftsman, he even built the pipework, occasionally assisted by his brothers Thomas (who was Appleton's partner 1847–50 in Boston and died in the US Civil War) and William (who later settled in Toronto). Until ca 1910 William manufactured mostly small instruments; those extant in 1979 had been considerably altered. Samuel Russell Warren brought a high calibre of professional organ building to Canada and between 1855 and 1860 he transmitted its secrets to Louis *Mitchell and Mitchell's partner Charles Forté.

Samuel Prowse Warren

The Montreal violinist and violist Edwin Sherrard, a founding member of the *McGill String Quartet and later a teacher at the U of Dartmouth, New Haven, Conn, is a great-grandson of S.R. Warren.

It is not known whether W. Warren was related to the family of organ builders. He was the organist at St James' Cathedral, Toronto, in 1834 and at the Anglican cathedral in Montreal from 1838 until his death in 1856. He edited a *Selection of Psalms and Hymns* (Toronto 1834) for use in the diocese of Quebec.

WRITINGS
Compte-rendu de la réception de l'orgue de la Chapelle Wesleyenne (Montreal 1861)
Réponse au sujet de la construction de l'orgue de la Chapelle Wesleyenne et concernant la réception de l'orgue de la Chapelle Wesleyenne (Montreal 1863)

BIBLIOGRAPHY
Classey, T.F. '19th century Canadian organs,' *York Pioneer*, 1966
Owen, Barbara. Letter adressed to Antoine Bouchard, 3 Feb 1975
Coup d'oeil

2 **Samuel Prowse**. Organist, choirmaster, composer, b Montreal 18 Feb 1841, d New York 7 Oct 1915. Initially a piano student, he began taking organ lessons at 11 and gave his first recitals the following year at St Stephen's Chapel in Montreal. After serving eight years as organist at the American Presbyterian Church he continued his training 1861–4 in Berlin with Karl August Haupt (organ), Gustav Schumann (piano), and Paul Wieprecht (theory). He returned to Montreal in 1864, but moved to New York the following year. He gave his first public recital there in January 1866 and was appointed organist of All Souls Unitarian Church in April. He was organist-choirmaster 1868–74 and 1876–94 at Grace Episcopalian Church, where he gave more than 230 recitals, and was organist 1874–6 at Holy Trinity Episcopalian Church and 1895–1915 at the First Presbyterian Church in East Orange, NJ.

Samuel Prowse Warren became widely known as a virtuoso and made several US tours. He served 1880–8 as director of the New York Vocal

Union and in 1896 was a founding member of the American Guild of Organists, becoming honorary president in 1902. He was administrator of the American College of Musicians, a member of the board of the Boston Cons, and an examiner for the *U of Toronto. Several of his songs were published by G. Schirmer. Warren collected manuscripts and rare books, prepared an edition of Mendelssohn's organ works (G. Schirmer 1924), and was the only Canadian to subscribe to the complete edition of Bach's organ works. He transcribed works by Beethoven, Schumann, Wagner, and Weber for organ. His second wife, Jeanne Joséphine Croker-Southward, was a professional singer of French origin.

BIBLIOGRAPHY
Malone, Dumas, ed. *Dictionary of American Biography*, vol 19 (New York) 1936
Baker's

3 **Charles S.** Organ manufacturer. At least two of his instruments are extant: one in St Michael's Cathedral, Toronto (1886) – Samuel Prowse Warren played on it during a visit – and the other in the church at Deschambault, Que (1892). He succeeded his father in 1882 as the head of S.R. Warren and Son and sold the firm ca 1896 to D.W. Karn of Woodstock, Ont. He continued to build organs for the firm Karn-Warren and later retired to Rochester, NY. His sons Frank, Russell, and Mansfield were involved in organ building in Woodstock ca 1900 and formed the Warren Church Organ Co in 1907. (AB)

Wars, rebellions, and uprisings. A survey of songs and other music written in immediate response to armed conflicts in Canada or involving Canadians on foreign soil. Another entry deals with Battle music, and compositions written in retrospect are dealt with under History of Canada in music. The main conflicts reflected in the music of their periods have been:

1 The conquest of New France by Great Britain 1756–60
2 The invasion by US revolutionaries 1775–6
3 The War of 1812
4 The rebellions of 1837–8
5 The Fenian Raids 1866–70
6 The Red River and Second Riel rebellions 1869–70, 1885
7 The South African War 1899–1902
8 World War I 1914–18
9 World War II 1939–45

1 THE CONQUEST OF NEW FRANCE. Of the songs about General James Wolfe, the British commander who died during the battle of Quebec, *'Brave Wolfe' – also known as 'The Death of the Brave General Wolfe' or 'Bold Wolfe' – has achieved the status of a folksong in eastern Canada and New England. Another song that has survived in oral tradition into the 20th century is 'General Wolfe.' Versions of both are among the several war songs printed and commented on in *Fowke's *Canada's Story in Song*. Fowke also provides the words of 'Hot Stuff,' a song – describing the treatment the English soldiers hoped to give the French – written by one of Wolfe's officers and sung to the tune of 'Lilies of France.' The British victory inspired several British composers, among them James Nares, whose 'Not unto Us, O Lord,' a thanksgiving anthem 'for the taking [of] Montreal and making us Masters of all Canada,' is preserved in manuscript at the British Museum. The PAC preserves a printed copy (1760) of John Worgan's 'I Fill not the Glass – A Song on the Taking of Mont-Real [sic] by General Amherst' (the commander-in-chief of the forces in North America and governor-general of Canada 1760–3). Several other songs, for which precise dates of composition and publication are difficult to trace, appeared in the late 18th century. Among these were Charles Thomas Carter's 'The Soldier's Farewell to His Mistress on the Eve of the Battle of Quebec,' Thomas Smart's 'General Wolfe,' and 'On the Death of General Wolfe' (as sung by Mr Sedgwick). Copies of some of these earliest printed examples of musical Canadiana may be found at the Metropolitan Toronto Library, the *NL of C, and the New Brunswick Museum.

2 THE INVASION BY US REVOLUTIONARIES. To celebrate the first anniversary of the Canadian victory over a contingent of US invaders led by General Benedict Arnold in 1775, an *Ode* was performed in Quebec City (see Cantata). A contemporary report by August Ludwig von Schlözer (see Art songs) refers to songs written in honour of Baron von Riedesel, the commander of the German mercenaries sent by the British to fight against the revolutionaries. 'Marching Down to Old Quebec' and the Acadian song 'Le Sergent,' both printed in *Canada's Story in Song*, date from the same period.

3 THE WAR OF 1812 (between Great Britain and the USA 1812–14). This conflict is remembered both in marches and in songs. Victor Pelissier's *March to Canada* (Taws, Philadelphia, ca 1813) cheered the US soldiers, while F.H. *Glackemeyer's *Châteauguay* (performed in 1818 but possibly written earlier) commemorates Lieut-Col de Salaberry, the hero of that battle. 'Come All You Bold Canadians' and 'The *Chesapeake* and the *Shannon*' (sung to the tune of 'A Drop of Brandy O') are given in Fowke's book.

4 THE REBELLIONS OF 1837–8. The most famous song inspired by the unrests of the 1830s is 'Un *Canadien errant,' with words by Antoine Gérin-Lajoie to the old tune of 'Si tu te mets anguille.' Others, also to be found in *Canada's Story in Song*, are 'Farewell to Mackenzie,' written in Markham, Ont, in 1832, and 'The Battle of the Windmill' (to the tune of 'The Girl I Left behind Me'), a song that remained popular for over a hundred years in the St Lawrence River area around Prescott, Ont.

5 THE FENIAN RAIDS. These were assaults on the Canadian-US border by the Fenian Brotherhood, an Irish-US movement organized in Dublin in 1858 and in New York in 1859 and dedicated to the independence of Ireland. The US branch's attempted takeover of Canada, in a series of border raids 1866–70, was rebuffed by some 14,000 volunteers. The raids gave rise to several songs and instrumental pieces. A skirmish in 1866 at Lime Hill, near Fort Erie, Upper Canada (Ontario), in which the Queen's Own Rifles of Toronto were defeated roundly, inspired the Irish-Americans to compose the jeering 'Fenian Song,' later sung on Great Lakes ships. However, when more Canadian troops assembled, the Fenians withdrew across the border, and the Canadian volunteers made up 'An Anti-Fenian Song' to the tune of 'Tramp, Tramp, Tramp, the Boys Are Marching.' These verses, credited to Lachlan McGoun (b Scotland 1837, d Napanee, Ont, 1896, a decorator in Montreal and later in Port Hope, Ont), became fairly widely known and inspired fresh parodies during the Saskatchewan Rebellion, the South African War, and World War I. 'The Chatham Volunteers' was inspired by a threatened raid (which did not occur) on Windsor, Ont, to which the Chatham Volunteer Infantry Companies responded. The song appeared in a local paper and was reprinted in 1963 in a Toronto folk magazine (P. Wyborn, 'The Chatham Volunteers,' *Hoot*, No. 2). W. Roy Mackenzie noted a fragment of a Fenian song in his *Ballads and Sea Songs from Nova Scotia* (1928), and John Murray *Gibbon quoted the 'Song of the Fenian Brotherhood' in *The Canadian Mosaic* (1938).

Among more than a dozen contemporary pieces published with dedications to the volunteers are the songs 'Up Volunteers!' (Nordheimer 1865), 'Shoulder to Shoulder, On to the Border' (with music by its publisher, Henry *Prince), and 'The Canadian Volunteer's Farewell' (Nordheimer 1866), as well as the instrumental compositions *Fort Erie Quadrilles* (R. Morgan, nd) by 'A Lady' and *Canadian Band March* (Nordheimer 1866) by the bandmaster C.P. Woodlawn.

6 THE RED RIVER AND SECOND RIEL REBELLIONS. This episode of Canadian history also produced both vocal and instrumental music. Several songs are about Louis Riel, for example 'Quand je partis ma chère Henriette' (in *Canada's Story in Song*) and 'C'est au champ de bataille' (in *The Penguin Book of Canadian Folk Songs*, compiled by Edith Fowke, Harmondsworth, England, 1973). *The University of Toronto Song Book* (1887) contained 'Pork, Beans, and Hard Tack,' to the tune of 'Solomon Levi,' sung by the volunteers from Winnipeg who were unhappy with their mode of travel and their rations. 'The Toronto Volunteers' on the other hand complained about the cold climate of the prairies. *Imrie & Graham published an album *Toronto's 'Welcome Home' to Her Brave Defenders, from the North-West Rebellion! July 1885*. Other songs of the time may be found in *Canada's Story in Song* and in *Songs of Old Manitoba*. Among instrumental pieces were Dingley Brown's *The Battleford March* (F. Boucher 1885) dedicated to Major General Middleton, Annie Delaney's *Batoche Polka* (Nordheimer 1885), and Joseph *Vézina's march *De Calgary à McLeod, souvenir du Nord-Ouest* (A. Lavigne ca 1886).

7 THE SOUTH AFRICAN WAR. Canadian opinion was divided as to the justness of the cause and the need to send troops to South Africa, but enthusiasm ran high among a large segment of English-speaking Canadians, and over 7000 Canadian soldiers participated in the South African War, most of them in battle action. All of the more than 25 Canadian compositions about the war have English titles. Typical examples are 'Bobs and Victory' by F.H. Burt, 'Tommy Atkins, You're a Dandy' by Arago Easton, 'Young Canada' by Alexander *Muir, and 'The Sons of Canada' by F.H. *Torrington.

8 WORLD WAR I. The fact that World War I involved far larger military forces than Canada had mustered in any previous war accounts for the vast output of music. Over 300 Canadian war and patriotic songs, as well as numerous marches, are known to have been published in the years 1914–18. Most of these were written by those at home, boosting recruitment and morale; not many were born of frontline experience, and Canadian war songs popular in the trenchlines were few.

Other factors contributed to the 'home-front' Canadian boom in war songs. The USA did not join the war until 1917, thus leaving Canadians a North American monopoly in the genre during the first years, and the recent invention of the phonograph had created an additional and most effective means of propagating war music.

It is difficult to single out the most successful among the songs, but certain titles turn up more

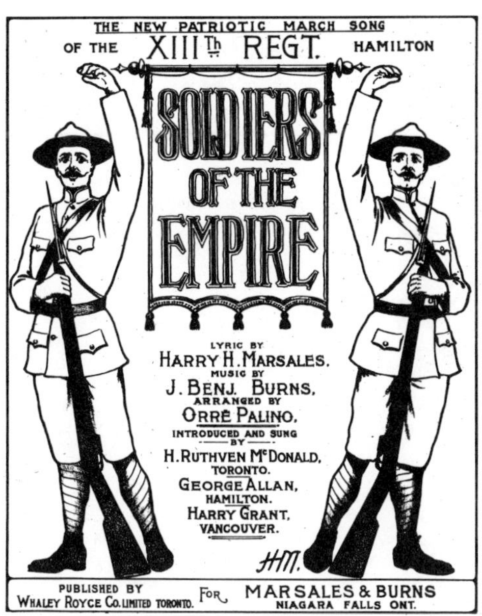

often than others in piles of old sheet music and recordings. Among these are *'We'll Never Let the Old Flag Fall' by M. F. Kelly and Albert Erroll MacNutt (1915), *'Dear Old Pal of Mine' by Gitz *Rice and Harold Athol (written in France in 1918), *'Good Luck to the Boys of the Allies' by Morris Manley (1915), and *'In Flanders Fields' (with words by John McCrae and music by several different composers). A number of songwriters concentrated on war songs, among them Florence M. Benjamin ('Marching Along' and 'Come with Me in My Aeroplane'), Jules *Brazil ('Remember Nurse Cavell' and 'Dreaming of Home'), Morris Manley ('I Love You, Canada' and 'Goodbye Mother Dear'), Geoffrey *O'Hara ('Highlanders! Fix Bayonets!' and *'K-K-K-Katy!' – not a war song but very popular among the overseas troops), Gitz Rice ('Keep Your Head Down, Fritzie Boy' and 'We Stopped Them at the Marne'), Gordon V. *Thompson (*'When Your Boy Comes Back to You,' 'When We Wind Up the Watch on the Rhine,' and 'For the Glory of the Grand Old Flag'), and Will J. White ('Take Me Back to Dear Old Canada' and 'Hip Hip Hooray for the Boys Who Went Away'). Thompson's claim that his 'When We Wind Up the Watch on the Rhine' sold about 100,000 copies in Canada and another 100,000 in the USA is an indication of the wide circulation enjoyed by many of the songs.

French-language war-time songs included Joseph Vézina's 'En avant' (1915; 'chant dédié aux volontaires canadiens-français'). Other songs, recorded or published, included H.W. Ellerton's 'Belgium Put the Kibosh on the Kaiser' (1916), Irene Humble's 'We're from Canada' (1915), E.W. Miller's 'Call of the Motherland' (1914), N. Fraser *Allan's 'The Made in Canada Campaign Song' (1915), and M.F. Kelly's 'By Order of the King' (1915).

More erudite composers also tried their hands at patriotic songs. Gena *Branscombe wrote 'Dear Lad O' Mine' (1915), Donald *Heins 'The Song of the Allies' (1914), and Colin *McPhee 'Arm, Canadians!' (1917).

Marches, in addition to those written for specific regiments, included J.-J. *Gagnier's *Here's to Tommy* (ca 1915), Alexis *Contant's *Les Alliés* (1914), and Arthur W. *Hughes' *March of the Allies* (1915).

See also Dumbells.

9 WORLD WAR II. Canadian songs of World War II were fewer in number than those of its predecessor but had the advantage of being spread by sheet music, records, and radio alike. The aggressive and patriotic tone of World War I songs gave way to an emphasis on humour and nostalgia. Another difference was that the government provided more organized entertainment for the troops – *The *Army Show*, **Meet the Navy*, and the *RCAF Blackouts – and that songs by professional musicians outnumbered those by amateurs.

From the point of view of publishing, an imported English song, 'There'll Always Be an England' (1939), was the greatest hit. Gordon V. *Thompson, who secured the North American copyright early during the war (when it was banned on radio in the still-neutral USA), sold some 130,000 copies in Canada alone. Thompson himself no longer wrote war songs, but he published *'Carry On' and its French-language version, 'En avant' (with music by Ernest *Dainty, composed before the war but the text adapted to the new circumstances), which became the greatest Canadian success of the war. Other popular war songs included 'That's an Order from the Army' and 'H'ya Mom' from *The Army Show*, *'You'll Get Used to It' (Freddy *Grant), 'We're Proud of Canada' (Mart *Kenney), and 'Over Here for Over There' (Jess Jaffrey, Horace Brown, Vida Guthrie). Songs in French included 'Vers la victoire' (Joseph Daniel Plamondon) and 'Dollard t'appelle' (N.M. Peck and Henri Grammont), but the most popular were those by 'Le soldat Lebrun' (Roland *Lebrun), such as 'Je suis loin de toi, mignonne,' 'L'Adieu du soldat,' and 'La Complainte d'une mère.'

War-related concert music included Healey *Willan's radio opera **Transit through Fire* (J. Coulter, B27), and his *The Trumpet Call* (A. Noyes, B55, chorus and orchestra), *Hymn for Those in the Air* (D.C. Scott, B28, incidental music), and *A Marching Tune* (B73, dedicated to the Queen's Own Rifles of Canada); Arnold *Walter's cantata *For the Fallen* (L. Binyon, completed shortly after the war); Alexander *Brott's symphonic poem *War and Peace;* Harry *Somers' piano sonata *Testament of Youth;* and Joseph *Vermandere's *Te Deum* written to celebrate the allied victory and performed on the CBC 13 May 1945. Willan was somewhat out of his element when he wrote a 'popular' war song, 'Speed the Victory' (B758, J.M. *Gibbon), as was Sir Ernest *MacMillan when he wrote 'Canada Calls / Debout Canadiens!' (English D. Hill, French A. Plouffe). Of the many band marches written during the war, *Commando March* by Leslie *Bell and the march-song 'Marche de la victoire' by Joseph *Beaulieu may be mentioned.

Anthony Hopkins' collection *Songs from the Front and Rear – Canadian Servicemen's Songs of the Second World War* (Hurtig 1979) was limited to songs actually sung by soldiers, as distinct from songs intended for but not necessarily popular among them, as exemplified by the early-war-years collections *Le Soldat canadien chante* (Ottawa 1940, compiled by Marius *Barbeau) and *Aux armes canadiens!* (Ottawa 1941).

See also Patriotic songs.

BIBLIOGRAPHY
Musical Canadiana
1–4 / HK, 5 / EF, 6–7 / HK, 8 / (EBM), 9 / (HK, EBM)

WASHBURN, Jon (Spencer). Choir conductor, viola-da-gambist, b Rochelle, Ill, 4 Jul 1942; B SC music education (Illinois) 1965. He studied conducting at the U of Illinois and musicology at Northwestern U and the *U of British Columbia. He moved to Canada in 1965 and became a founding member and gambist of Hortulani Musicae in

John Waterhouse

1969, the *Vancouver Society for Early Music in 1970, and L'Age d'Or baroque orchestra in 1973. His most significant achievement has been his directorship (begun in 1971) of the *Vancouver Chamber Choir; he had been assistant conductor of the *Vancouver Bach Choir (1970–4 and led its Ladies' Bach Choir to first place in the International Koorfest in Scheveningen, Holland, in 1971. He was artist-in-residence at *Simon Fraser U in 1974, became choir director at Vancouver Community College that same year, and was conductor of the Amity Singers of Victoria in 1975. Washburn has shown a keen interest in the works of British Columbia composers, and with the Vancouver Chamber Choir he has premiered Jerome Summers' *Lacrymosa* (1973) and Elliot *Weisgarber's *Night* (1974). He was conductor of the *Ontario Youth Choir for its 1976 session and was a guest conductor of the *Festival Singers in January 1979 in Toronto. Washburn was host for the CBC radio program 'Choral Concert' 1977–80 and in connection with that series compiled the *1979 Canadian Choral Records List* (CBC Vancouver). His wife, the pianist Linda Lee *Thomas, is an active performer and teacher in Vancouver. TRL

WATERHOUSE, John (Fereday Preston). Violinist, teacher, conductor, b Bilston, near Birmingham, England, 28 Oct 1877, d Winnipeg 22 May 1970; FRAM 1947, LL D (Manitoba) 1965. One of Canada's distinguished teachers, he taught violin privately in Winnipeg for over 50 years. He studied violin with Émile Sauret and harmony and counterpoint with Ebenezer Prout and Stewart Macpherson at the RAM, London, and performed as soloist, orchestral player, and conductor in England. He played in the Minneapolis SO before moving in 1914 to Winnipeg, where, with his wife, Cecilia, a pianist who had studied with a pupil of Clara Schumann, he taught and performed, introducing to Winnipeg many English compositions. He conducted the Winnipeg String Orchestra 1934–6. He was also concertmaster 1923–7 of the Winnipeg Orchestral Club (a forerunner of the *Winnipeg SO). He was an honorary life member of the *MRMTA, the Winnipeg *Men's Music Club, and the *MMEA. In 1967 he was one of six recipients of the *CFMTA centennial citation. His pride was in the achievements of his pupils, among whom were Michael Barten, Armand *Ferland, Frederick *Grinke, Ben Loban, Leslie Malowany, Palmi and Pearl Palmason, Anne *Pomer, Hugo *Rignold, Gwen *Thompson, and his son William (James) Waterhouse – violinist, teacher, b Winnipeg 15 Aug 1917, B MUS (Boston) 1950, M MUS (Boston) 1950, LAB (London) 1933, hon RAM 1976.

William studied in England with Rowsby Woof and Michael Head and played there 1935–8 with the Silverman Quartet, 1936–9 with the Boyd *Neel Orchestra and the London String Orchestra, and 1937–9 with the Stornoway Players. He appeared as soloist with the CSM during the 1939–40 season and later, with Martin Hoherman, performed the Brahms *Double Concerto* with the Boston Pops Orchestra and the *CBC Winnipeg Orchestra. He served the major part of his career as a member (1951–75) of the Boston SO. After retiring from that orchestra he returned to his home city and in 1976 joined the Winnipeg SO and began playing duos with the pianist Leonard *Isaacs.

BIBLIOGRAPHY
Sangwine, Jean. 'Dr. John Waterhouse,' *Sharps & Flats*, vol 6, Nov 1965 (PS)

Waterloo. See Kitchener and Waterloo.

The Waterloo Band Festival. An annual band festival and competition held 1932–40 and 1946–58 in Waterloo Park, Waterloo, Ont. Organized by Charles F. *Thiele (bandmaster and the founder of the *Waterloo Music Co) to celebrate the 50th anniversary of the *Waterloo Musical Society, the first festival presented 23 bands (14 in evening parades) and 80 solo contestants. Subsequent festivals, held on the last Saturday in June, drew crowds of up to 25,000 to hear as many as 70 bands from Ontario, Quebec, Wisconsin, Michigan, and (one year) Kamloops, BC, in concerts and parades, and more than 1000 contestants in 100 instrumental competitions. The festival also presented such solo artists as the saxophonist Sigurd Rascher and the Radio City Music Hall cornetist Leona May Smith. In 1937 an evening spectacle, 'The Festival of Empire,' was staged to mark the coronation of George VI. The festivals were discontinued during World War II and abandoned after 1958.

BIBLIOGRAPHY
Waterloo Festival Review Annual (Waterloo 1948–55)
Waterloo Convention Review (Waterloo 1948–53) EHR

Waterloo Musical Society Band. Civic band of 32–45 players, founded in 1882 under the auspices of the Waterloo Musical Society. In its early years it participated in many competitions or tournaments, winning nine prizes in a single year during the 1880s. It accompanied Waterloo singing societies at Sängerfeste in Michigan and New York State, played on pleasure boat excursions on the Great Lakes, and began to perform annually at the *CNE. During the first part of the 20th century, and especially under the leadership of Charles F. *Thiele, it achieved new prominence. (See Waterloo Band Festival.) In the 1970s the band continued to present a concert series each summer in Waterloo, to appear for armed forces veterans' events and civic gatherings, and to participate in Waterloo County Music Festival competitions. Its conductors have included Noah *Zeller 1882–1900, W.H. Walker 1900–1, Arthur Stares 1902–3, Henry Restorff in 1903, W.J. Philip 1903–10, W.A. ('Fritz') Paul 1910–15, J.E. Pillar 1915–16, Enea Trovarelli 1916–18, Thiele 1919–51, Fred Roy 1951–5, and William Gallagher 1955–62. John T. Conrad succeeded Gallagher in 1963. In 1980 the band remained one of the most active amateur organizations in Canada.

BIBLIOGRAPHY
Ronneberg, Ernie. 'Waterloo Concert Band marks 90th anniversary,' *Kitchener-Waterloo Record*, 18 Feb 1972
(EHR)

The Waterloo Musical Society Band in the late 19th century

Waterloo Music Company Ltd. Publishing and instrument retailing firm founded in 1921 by Charles F. *Thiele in Waterloo, Ont. Thiele was sole owner until 1951, when Waterloo Music became a limited company with Thiele as president (1951–4; followed by R.P. Uffelmann 1954–60, Fred Moogk 1960–75, and Howard Underwood). As a local agent for band instruments Thiele set up the company in his home. His first successful business endeavour, the importation and distribution of sheet music suitable for silent film accompaniment, declined with the advent of talking pictures in the late 1920s. In 1927 he turned to educational materials which have proved the mainstay of the company.

Waterloo publishes *Western Ontario Cons and *WBM piano examination books and issues theory, harmony, and history texts for use in elementary and secondary schools. Band music was first published in the 1930s, and the Waterloo band catalogue, offering original works by Canadians and reprints of music by foreign composers, was the largest in Canada by 1960. The choral catalogue, secular and sacred, includes the Waterloo Folk Music Library (begun 1954), edited by Edith *Fowke and Richard *Johnston, and Eric *Wild's Hymn Sing Choral Series (begun 1973). Both series include recordings. Waterloo has published music for piano, accordion, strings, and winds and in the 1970s popular music, including a folio by *April Wine. Canadian composers published by Waterloo include Violet *Archer, John *Beckwith, Keith *Bissell, Kenneth *Bray, Barrie *Cabena, F.R.C. *Clarke, Jean *Coulthard, Samuel *Dolin, George *Fiala, Robert *Fleming, Richard Johnston, Walter *Kemp, Talivaldis *Kenins, James Lawless, Walter *MacNutt, Robert *McMullin, Barbara *Pentland, Godfrey *Ridout, Eric Wild, Healey *Willan, and Gerhard *Wuensch. Performers recorded on the Waterloo label (established in 1971) include J. Chalmers *Doane, John Greenwood, Robert McMullin's Sound 80 Orchestra, and John *O'Donnell's Men of the Deeps. Waterloo acquired Melbourne from *Rodeo Records in 1977 for its classical record issues and established Action Press, its own printing and binding business in 1979. The sale of imported musical instruments accounted for over half of the company's business in the mid-1970s. Waterloo maintains a large instrument repair shop. It opened a retail branch in Ottawa in 1965. Waterloo is a PRO Canada affiliate. Its subsidiary, Peter McKee Music Co Ltd (established in 1966), is a member of CAPAC.

BIBLIOGRAPHY
'Waterloo Music Company: the house that service built,' *Recorder*, vol 7, Nov–Dec 1964
Grayhurst, Denis. 'Waterloo Music,' *MSc*, 240, Mar–Apr 1968
'Educational material, recordings are two aspects of Waterloo Music Company's activities,' *MSc*, 284, Jul–Aug 1975 MWI

WATKIN-MILLS, Robert. Bass-baritone, teacher, b Painswick, Gloucestershire, England, 4 Mar 1849, d Toronto 10 Dec 1930. After study with Samuel Sebastian Wesley in Gloucestershire, Edwin Holland in London, and Federico Blasco in Milan, he made his debut at London's Crystal Palace, 17 May 1884, in a concert with Sims Reeves. Thereafter he sang with great success throughout England, North America (almost annually, after 1894), and Australia 1904–5. In Canada he appeared with the *Montreal Philharmonic Society and other groups. Eschewing opera, he pursued his career exclusively in concert and oratorio, becoming particularly identified with such works as *Messiah* and *Judas Maccabaeus*. Of a London performance of Gounod's *Redemption* in 1893, Bernard Shaw wrote, 'All the gentlemen, especially Mr. Watkin-Mills, were very efficient.' In 1914 Watkin-Mills settled in Winnipeg, where he became choirmaster of Broadway Methodist Church and a founding member and president 1917–19 of the *Men's Music Club. In 1919 he married Elsie Cantell, a singer and organist, and in 1922 the couple moved to Toronto, where they opened a vocal studio and took up positions as choirmaster and organist at Knox Church. The singer made his final public appearance at 77 in *Messiah* at St Paul's Church. At the time of his death the *Musical Times* wrote, 'Though his name does not ring in history and reminiscence as do those of a few of his contemporaries, he was a full member of that band of oratorio singers who were the pride of musical England in the Victorian age.' In England, Watkin-Mills made a few extremely rare records for Pathé (1903) and Odeon (1907–8), the latter listed in *Roll Back the Years*. JBM

WATSON, Gilbert. Dance band leader, pianist, b ca 1898, d Peterborough, Ont, 12 Aug 1959. He studied piano with Michael *Hambourg and Harvey Robb and played at the Allen Theatre in Toronto. He also worked for several music retailers, among them *Mason & Risch (in the Victrola department) and *Whaley Royce (as store manager). In the mid-1920s he formed his own dance band. The Gilbert Watson Orchestra became one of the most popular in Canada and survived until the late 1930s. It played at the Prince George Hotel (where it was heard on the Toronto radio station CFRB) and for several years at the Old Mill. It also appeared in dance pavilions around Toronto. In 1926, in New York, the orchestra made three 78s for Starr and one for Domino. The Domino 78, comprising 'St. Louis Blues' and 'I Just Want to Be Known as Susie's Feller,' with solos by the trumpeter Kurt Little, is possibly the first jazz recording by a Canadian band. Watson retired from music in the late 1930s and subsequently operated a hotel in the Kawartha Lakes region of Ontario.

MM

WATSON, Lorne. Pianist, educator, administrator, b Leamington, near Windsor, Ont, 29 Jul 1919; ATCM 1936, LTCM 1940, BA (Toronto) 1948, MA (New York) 1950, PH D performance (Indiana) 1976, hon FRHCM 1978. His teachers were Ernest *Seitz (piano) and Muriel *Gidley Stafford (organ) at the *TCM and Rosalyn Tureck (piano) 1949–50 in New York. He was a soloist with the TCM SO in 1940. While attending the *U of Toronto 1945–8 he was assistant conductor of the *Hart House Glee Club. He became director of the department of music at Brandon College (*Brandon U) in 1948 and began examining for the *RCMT in the early 1950s. He gave recitals throughout Canada 1949–56. He was co-chairman 1974–6 of the committee which established the S.C. Eckhardt-Gramatté Competition for the Performance of Canadian Music and subsequently was chairman of the competition's national planning committee. Before *Eckhardt-Gramatté's death he worked closely with her to record her particular piano method and, as part of the requirement for his D MUS, completed a paper on it – 'The Eckhardt-Gramatté piano technique' – which is deposited at Indiana U. Watson has been president of the *MRMTA 1952–3 and the *MMEA 1960–1, first secretary 1965–7 and president 1973–5 of CAUSM, and a contributor to *EMC*. In the spring of 1979, during a sabbatical, and on a grant from the *Manitoba Arts Council, he visited 14 European countries to study, compare, and evaluate schools of conservatory type.

SRM

WATSON HENDERSON, Ruth (Louise) (b Watson, m Henderson). Pianist, composer, b Toronto 23 Nov 1932; ARCT 1950, LRCT 1952. After piano studies at the TCM (*RCMT) 1937–45 with Viggo *Kihl and 1945–52 with Alberto *Guerrero, she continued 1952–4 at Mannes College, New York, with Hans Neumann, and summers 1952 and 1953 at Chautauqua, NY, with James Friskin. She also studied composition 1950–1 with Oskar *Morawetz and 1951–2 and 1961–2 with Richard *Johnston. In 1956 she won the grand prize of the CBC's *'Opportunity Knocks.' She taught and was an organist-choirmaster 1957–61 in Winnipeg and 1962–8 in Kitchener, Ont, returning thereafter to Toronto. As a soloist she has performed with the *CBC Winnipeg Orchestra (her assignments including the Canadian premiere of Menotti's *Piano Concerto* in 1958), the *Hamilton Philharmonic, the *Kitchener-Waterloo SO, the *'Little Symphonies' Orchestra, and the *Regina SO. She was accompanist 1968–79 for the *Festival Singers and also has partnered, in individual recitals, Hyman *Goodman, Lois *Marshall, the oboist Harry Sargous (Carnegie Recital Hall 1975), Peter *van Ginkel, and George *Zukerman. Her compositions include four works sung by the Festival Singers and published by Thompson: *Pater noster* (1973), *Two Canadian Folksongs* – 'Mary Ann' and 'Les Raftsmen' – (1975), and an unaccompanied *Missa brevis* (1976). She also has written a *Sonata* for oboe and piano (1976), a *Piano Suite* (1978), three motets (Waterloo 1964, 1968), and other choral works and songs. She is a member of CAPAC.

(MMI)

WAYLAND. Family of musicians: 1 / William-Arthur and 2 / his daughter Esther.

1 **William-Arthur**. Choirmaster, b Sherbrooke, Que, 14 Jun 1868, d Montreal 14 Jun 1946. He studied liturgy, plainsong, Gregorian chant, and organ at the Collège de Montréal and conducted the choir of St-Pierre-Apôtre Church, Montreal, for 17 years and the choir of St-Viateur Church, Outremont, 1918–38. He invited Marcel Dupré to give a recital 25 Jan 1923 on the organ at St-Viateur. Wayland was considered the dean of Montreal choirmasters at the time of his death.

2 **Esther** (m Prieur). Pianist, accompanist, b Montreal 27 Jul 1899. While completing her studies at the convent of the Sisters of the Sacred Heart in Montreal she studied music with Sister *Marie-Stéphane and Victoria *Cartier and at the *McGill Cons. On several occasions she participated in the 'L'Heure provinciale' concerts on radio station CKAC, playing concertos by Schumann, Chopin (E minor), Mozart (D minor), and Beethoven (C minor). With the McGill Cons string orchestra she played in a concert which was repeated 3 Feb 1934 at *Tudor Hall, Montreal. On 11 Jan 1941 she performed Manuel de Falla's symphonic poem *Nights in the Gardens of Spain* at a matinée of the CSM. She taught for 21 years at Trafalgar School, Montreal, where she also gave courses in music appreciation for 13 years. In addition she taught for five years with the Sisters of the Sacred Heart, Sault-au-Récollet, Que. Beginning in 1954 she devoted her energies for many years to the MSO Young People's Concerts, as chairman of the administrative committee. Her husband, the tenor Henri *Prieur, died in 1970.

GB

WEAIT, Christopher (Robert Irving). Bassoonist, teacher, composer, b Surrey, England, 27 Mar 1939; B SC music education (State U of New York) 1961, MA (Columbia) 1966. He studied with Charles Robert Reinhart at State U College and with William Polisi. He became co-principal bassoonist of the *TS in 1968 and performed as concerto soloist with the orchestra in 1976. He has been a member of the Toronto Winds (see Toronto Woodwind Quintet) and Toronto Baroque Trio. Weait taught 1972–4 at *Queen's U and 1973–9 at the *U of Toronto and became woodwind coach of the TS Youth Orchestra in 1974. He has written *Basson Reed-making: A Basic Technique* (New York 1970) and compiled *A Master List of Personnel, 1922–1972* of the TS and its predecessors (Toronto 1972). He has recorded two of his compositions, *Variations for Solo Bassoon* (1972 for Pyramid) and *Lonely Island for Solo Bassoon* (1974 for Melbourne). As vice-president 1975–6 of the International Double-Reed Society, he organized its fifth annual meeting in Toronto in 1976. Weait, his wife Margaret Barstow (cello), and Monica *Gaylord (piano) formed the Canzona Trio, which performed in England and Austria in 1978.

WRITINGS

– and Shea, John. 'Vibrato: an audio-video fluorographic investigation of a bassoonist,' *Applied Radiology*, vol 6, Jan–Feb 1977

DISCOGRAPHY

Four Centuries of Music for Bassoon. Kernerman vn, Barstow vc, Brough hpd. 1973. Pyramid 102/Lyrichord LLST 7277/World Record Club R.03020

Lonely Island: Johnston – Wevers – Coulthard – Weait – Lidov. Gaylord pf. 1976. Mel SMLP 4032

Toronto Baroque Trio: A Baroque Bouquet. Berman ob, Gaylord hpd. 1976. Berandol BER 9009

BIBLIOGRAPHY

MacMillan, Rick. 'Christopher Weait,' *MSc*, 288, Mar–Apr 1976

(PS)

WEATHERSEED, John (Joseph). Organist, choir conductor, teacher, b Hastings, England, 20 Oct 1900, d Toronto 13 May 1965. He received his musical education in England with H.V.W. Batts, R.E. Groves, D. Harold Darke, Oscar Beringer, and Sir Walford Davies. In Canada he was organist 1922–4 at St Luke's Church, Winnipeg, organist-choirmaster 1925–44 at St George's Church, Montreal, conductor 1927–31 of the *Mendelssohn Choir of Montreal, and teacher of organ and piano 1926–43 at the *McGill Cons. In Toronto he taught 1944–63 at the *RCMT and was organist-choirmaster at Deer Park United Church from 1944 until his death. He was president 1949–51 of the *RCCO and 1951–2 of the *ORMTA. For many years he directed the Christmas Choir of the Robert Simpson Co's Toronto department store. Some of his anthems and organ pieces were published by *Harris, *Western Music, and Boston Music (see *Catalogue of Canadian Composers*).

MMI

Weber Piano Company Ltd. Manufacturers of grand, square, and upright pianos, founded as Messrs Weber & Co in Market Square, Kingston, Ont, in 1871. The firm also sold parlour organs and melodeons by other makers. Weber succeeded an earlier piano manufacturer, J.C. Fox, after a transition period of several takeovers and amalgamations by other entrepreneurs. John C. Fox (of J.C. Fox & Co, New York) had established a piano manufacturing firm in Kingston in 1862 and by 1867 was reputed to be the largest piano manufacturer in Canada, turning out about 500 instruments a year. The void left by Fox's demise was filled 1868–71 by J. Reyner; J. Stevenson; Rappe, Weber & Co; F.C. Cline; and John Breden, Jr.

Only Weber & Co survived the transition. By 1873 Weber was building seven or eight square and upright pianos a week. The company won several prizes at provincial exhibitions and in 1876 was awarded a first prize and a silver medal at the Philadelphia World's Fair. John and W.H. Stevenson became the proprietors of Weber & Co in 1881 and later renamed the firm Stevenson & Co. A Kingston piano builder, William Wormwith, assumed control of Stevenson & Co in 1891, continuing as Wormwith & Co at Princess and Ontario streets. This company carried on successfully, producing, in addition to Wormwith pianos, a line of Weber pianos and player-pianos. The factory was destroyed by fire in 1908, but was rebuilt and became incorporated as the Wormwith Piano Co Ltd, with William Wormwith as president. He was succeeded a year or so later by George Y. Chown, and in 1918 he retired from the company. At that time the firm employed about 75 workmen and produced 1800 pianos per year. With Wormwith's retirement, the firm was renamed the Weber Piano Co Ltd in 1919, the controlling interest held by Henry Richardson. In 1920 the firm began exhibiting at the *CNE and exporting some pianos to the West Indies. The staff increased to 100 and production to 2000 units a year. The Weber Piano Co was purchased by *Lesage Pianos in 1939.

Another Kingston piano builder, G.M. Weber, set up business on Wellington St, manufacturing upright instruments ca 1881–95. No connection with the prior Weber firm has been established.

FH

WEDD, Patrick. Organist-choirmaster, harpsichordist, composer, b Simcoe, Ont, 4 Jan 1948; B MUS (Toronto) 1970, M MUS (British Columbia) 1972. At 11 he began organ studies with J. Laurence Slater and at 12 he became organist-choirmaster at St Paul's Church in Port Robinson, Ont. After holding similar positions in St Catharines and Thorold, Ont, he served 1966–9 as sub-organist to Norman *Hurrle at St James' Cathedral, Toronto, and a recitalist in various churches. Wedd studied organ with Hurrle and harpsichord with Greta *Kraus. He was an Albert *Ham Organ Scholar at Trinity College, U of Toronto. In 1969 he won the RCCO's international Young Organists' Competition. He studied 1970–2 on scholarship at the *U of British Columbia and privately with Hugh *McLean. In 1973 he was chosen by the RCCO to attend an organ course in Belgium given by Flor Peeters. Wedd has been organist-choirmaster 1970–5 at St Mary's Anglican Church, then at Christ Church Cathedral, Vancouver. He was co-director 1972–5 of Hortulani Musicae and also has been keyboard player with the *Vancouver Society for Early Music, the Cecilian Ensemble, the *Vancouver New Music Society, and Array West. He was a founding member of *Days Months and Years to Come and founder in 1974 and director of Quorum, an ensemble of six vocalists which gave the first performance by a Canadian group of Stockhausen's *Stimmung* and the premieres of works by Thomas Baker and Alex *Pauk. Wedd's organ recitals have included premieres of works by Baker, Pauk, and Jerome Summers. In 1974 he began a three-year project – the performance of the complete works by Bach for keyboard – and on 17 Aug 1977 he completed it with a recital at the U of British Columbia. Wedd has composed two masses (1975, 1976), several psalm settings (1976, 1977), chants, anthems, psalm tones, hymn arrangements, fanfares, and several settings of Magnificat and Nunc dimittis (1977).

DISCOGRAPHY

An Organ Recital by Patrick Wedd: Bruhns – Byrd – Telemann (arr Walther) – Widor – Vierne. KVP 502

Haydn *Missa brevis*. Vanc Chamb Choir, Washburn cond. 1973. CBC SM-243

Hymns of Herbert O'Driscoll. Christ Church Cathedral Choir, Wedd org and cond. (1976). KVP 601

Music for Christmas: Ahrens – Distler – Mathias – Wedd (arrs) – et al. Christ Church Cathedral Choir, Wedd org and cond. (1976). KVP 603F BNSG

Wednesday Morning Musicale. A Winnipeg concert-giving club. Organized in 1933 by Eva *Clare, who became its first president, it has presented concerts, mostly by local performers, monthly from October to March each year. Its home platforms have been, successively, the Fort Garry Hotel (first seven years), the Music and Arts Building until the late 1940s, and the T. Eaton Company's Assembly Hall. It has offered premieres of works by Lorne *Betts, Chester *Duncan, S.C. *Eckhardt-Gramatté, Leslie *Mann, Bernard *Naylor, and Barbara *Pentland, all natives or one-time residents of Manitoba. Proceeds from performances of such chamber operas as Britten's *Let's Make an Opera* and *Noye's Fludde*, Mozart's *The Impresario*, Pergolesi's *La Serva padrona*, Sullivan's *Cox and Box*, and several by Menotti have supported a scholarship fund for young Manitoba musicians. The Wednesday Morning Musicale maintained its membership at about 200 in 1980. CF

WEIL, Max. Conductor, violinist, teacher, b Philadelphia 1869, d California 1952(?). He studied the violin in Leipzig under Adolf Brodsky and Hans Sitt, then played in Damrosch's SO in New York for two years. He became head of the violin department of the Halifax Cons (*Maritime Cons of Music) ca 1892 but resigned in 1900 to found the Weil School of Music. He took over and enlarged the Haydn Quintette Club and formed the *Halifax SO, which made its debut 24 Apr 1897. He attracted several good teachers to Halifax and helped to develop the public's taste for opera, producing Flotow's *Martha* in 1896 and Gounod's *Faust* and Balfe's *The Bohemian Girl* later. He left Canada in 1908, and it is known that he played principal second violin with the Minneapolis-St Paul SO but returned in 1912 to conduct the second *Calgary SO (debut 27 Jan 1913). With the outbreak of war in August 1914 Weil (who was of German descent) left the country and settled in Los Angeles, where he eventually had a career in real estate. He also composed songs and pieces for string orchestra. He has been described by P.R. Blakeley as a conductor of energy, with a capacity for hard work, a quick eye, and an unerring ear.

BIBLIOGRAPHY

'Mr. Max Weil,' *CMTJ*, vol 2, Feb 1901

Talbot, Hugo, ed. *Musical Halifax 1903–4* (Halifax 1904)

Blakeley, Phyllis R. 'The theatre and music in Halifax,' *Dalhousie R*, 29, Apr 1949 (HK)

WEINZWEIG, John (Jacob). Composer, teacher, administrator, b Toronto 11 Mar 1913; ATCM piano and theory 1934, B MUS (Toronto) 1937, M MUS (ESM, Rochester) 1938, hon D MUS (Ottawa) 1969. The eldest child of Polish-Jewish immigrants, Joseph and Rose (Burstyn) Weinzweig, he first studied music at 14, taking group lessons in mandolin at the Workman's Circle Peretz School in Toronto. That same year, with his brother Morris (1915–74), who later was a saxophonist in Toronto studio orchestras, he began piano lessons with Gertrude Anderson. While attending Harbord Collegiate he played under Brian *McCool in one of the few established school orchestras in Canada at that time. At first Weinzweig played violin parts on the mandolin, but later he took up tuba, tenor saxophone, and bass. He also played in the orchestra of the Central High School of Commerce and later studied piano with George Boyce. Following his own tentative explorations, and with encouragement from both Anderson and McCool, Weinzweig at 19 had resolved to become a composer. He studied 1934–7 at the *U of Toronto with Healey *Willan (counterpoint and fugue), Leo *Smith (harmony), and Sir Ernest *MacMillan (orchestration). While a conducting student of Reginald *Stewart at the *TCM, he founded, and conducted 1934–7, the U of Toronto SO.

In 1937 Weinzweig showed his scores to the composer Howard Hanson, the chairman of the ESM, who was in Toronto for a conducting engagement. Hanson encouraged Weinzweig to enrol at the ESM which, unlike the U of Toronto of that day, offered courses in 20th-century music. There, Weinzweig studied orchestration and composition with Bernard Rogers, conducting with Paul White, and string bass with Nelson Watson and was exposed to much new music not yet accepted in Toronto. Two works in particular, Stravinsky's *The Rite of Spring* and Berg's *Lyric Suite*, caught his attention, the former for its rhythmic potency and the latter for its melodic and motivic use of the 12-tone row.

Weinzweig's fascination with these matters was reflected in the works composed after his return to Toronto in 1938 and before his RCAF service, 1943–5. The second movement of his *Suite for Piano No. 1* (1939), his first (and the first Canadian) music to explore serial technique, used the 12-tone row, whole occasionally but more often as a source of motivic fragments. In other works of those years – the *Symphony* (1940) and the *Sonata* (1941) for violin – the row is used as the basis for long, flowing melodies but is rarely employed in chordal formations. Evident everywhere are the rhythmic vitality and motivic organization which

John Weinzweig

were to function so effectively in Weinzweig's later work. Weinzweig introduced these principles and other concepts of 20th-century composition to his pupils at the TCM (*RCMT), where he taught 1939–43 and 1945–60. His music received some performance, although the works chosen, including *String Quartet No. 1* and *The Enchanted Hill*, represented a style he was fast repudiating.

In 1941 Weinzweig began composing incidental music for the CBC and film scores for the *NFB. His work for such series as *New Homes for Old, White Empire*, and *Whiteoaks of Jalna*, some 100 programs in all, introduced Toronto musicians and Canadian radio audiences to an amount of modern music which would have been resented in concert situations, and which permitted Weinzweig to experiment and to develop the lean, resilient technique which proved so durable an asset. Some of this radio music found a place in the orchestral suites *Our Canada* and *Edge of the World*. Weinzweig gradually lost interest in radio and film, however, and after the last (1945) of his half-dozen scores for the NFB he turned exclusively to concert music, although seldom to full-scale orchestral works. With the exception of the *Violin Concerto, Wine of Peace*, the *Piano Concerto*, and *Dummiyah/Silence*, few of his works require more than a chamber orchestra.

The years immediately following the war were among his most prolific, resulting in *Divertimento No. 1* (which won the silver medal in chamber music at the 1948 Olympics), *Divertimento No. 2*, *String Quartet No. 2*, the *Cello Sonata 'Israel,'* and *Suite for Piano No. 2*. In 1951, with two former pupils, Samuel *Dolin and Harry *Somers, Weinzweig established the *Canadian League of Composers, and the league's first concert, 16 May 1951, was devoted to his works. Weinzweig served 1951–7 as president of the CLComp and was appointed to the Faculty of Music at the U of Toronto in 1952, and because his new duties took much of his time he of necessity reduced his compositional output in the mid-1950s. Nevertheless, the few products of these years, notably the *Violin Concerto* and *Wine of Peace*, are among his most personal and complex scores (see also Concertos and concertante music).

As president of the CLComp he presented a brief to the Fowler Commission on Broadcasting in 1957 and, with John *Beckwith, prepared the *CMCouncil brief to the *Canada Council which resulted in the formation of the *CMCentre. After 1957 he balanced his organizational efforts with his teaching and composing. During a second term as president of the CLComp, 1959–63, he represented Canada at European and Central American conferences. He also served 1973–5 as president of *CAPAC. During this time he com-

A manuscript page from the second movement ('City of brass') of *Wine of Peace* for soprano and orchestra (1957) by John Weinzweig

posed about one piece annually, each the result of a commission, generally from the CBC.

In 1973 the CBC presented publicly a concert of Weinzweig's music performed by a CBC string orchestra (led by the composer) and the *Lyric Arts Trio, the Toronto Winds, the harpist Judy *Loman, and the bassoonist George *Zukerman. Broadcasts followed on 'CBC Tuesday Night' and 'Encore,' 20 and 22 Nov 1973. The previous week (14 and 15 November) the CBC had honoured Weinzweig with a documentary of his life and music, prepared by Lothar *Klein. Another Weinzweig concert, under the composer's direction and featuring the premiere by the soprano Mary Lou *Fallis and the pianist Monica *Gaylord of his song cycle *Private Collection*, was given 7 Jan 1977 at the U of Toronto's Walter Hall and was broadcast on CBC's 'Music of Today,' 15 Mar 1977.

Over the years, Weinzweig's works have been performed frequently abroad. His *Divertimento No. 1* was conducted in Prague in 1947 by Ivan *Romanoff. His *Violin Sonata* was performed that same year in New York by Harry *Adaskin and Frances Marr Adaskin. His *Violin Concerto* was played in 1956 by Frederick *Grinke over the BBC, with Boyd *Neel conducting. His *String Quartet No. 2* was performed in Tel Aviv in 1960 by the Jacob *Groob Quartet, and 'Am Yisrael Chai!' was heard in Israel in a 1964 performance by Les Chanteurs du Québec conducted by Fernand *Graton.

By the late 1960s Weinzweig had come to accept only those projects which interested him, and many of his subsequent compositions resulted from a desire to solve specific problems. *Dummiyah/Silence*, written 1968–9 in Mexico during a sabbatical, explored the possibilities of composing with silence framed by sound. His *Concerto for Harp and Chamber Orchestra*, commissioned by Judy Loman and the Toronto Repertory Ensemble, combined serialized timbres with the harp techniques practised by Carlos Salzedo. *Divertimento No. 4* explored extensions of the clarinet's sound suggested by Bruno Bartolozzi. Weinzweig also synthesized elements of jazz in *Divertimento No. 3* and in the *Piano Concerto*. Later works – *Trialogue, Riffs* for solo flute, and *Impromptus* for piano – offer a seemingly random assembly of many short fragments. In all his works, however varied are the problems engaged or the solutions offered, qualities remain that have characterized Weinzweig's music since 1939: clarity of texture; economy of material; rhythmic energy; tight motivic organization, usually but not slavishly controlled through a personal application of serialism; short melodic outbursts contrasted with long flowing lines; and harmonies which, though often harsh, never lose fully their tonal orientation.

In 1974 Weinzweig began publishing some of his own works, and 'Eskimo Song,' 'To the Lands Over Yonder,' and *Woodwind Quintet* have appeared under his imprint.

John Beckwith has described Weinzweig's music as 'one of the cornerstones of our repertoire ... a distinctive, high-quality body of work by any standards I know of' (*CMB*, Spring–Summer 1973). The difficulties it encountered were the traditional snubs to new music by a conservative society, but they were no easier to rise above on that account. R. Murray *Schafer has written: 'If I were to name [Weinzweig's] principal service to Canada it could be this: that he rode out the first storm of criticism alone, until he could educate enough other composers to offer him the companionship of the Canadian League of Composers. His refusal to admit that music was at a standstill ... gradually won a more benign attitude for the reception of our music' (ibid).

Weinzweig's music, his organizational efforts on behalf of Canadian composers, and certainly also his teaching have had a permanent effect on Canada's musical life. In nearly 40 years of teaching, recognizing the individual needs of his pupils, he has guided composers, scholars, and performers alike, including Murray *Adaskin, Lorne *Betts, Howard *Cable, Samuel Dolin, Harry *Freedman, Jack *Kane, Mavor *Moore, Phil *Nimmons, Kenneth *Peacock, Harry Somers, and Andrew *Twa in the 1940s; Milton *Barnes, Norma *Beecroft, Gustav *Ciamaga, Anne *Eggleston, Srul Irving *Glick, Walter *Kemp, Alfred *Kunz, Edward *Laufer, Bruce *Mather, R. Murray Schafer, Jack *Sirulnikoff, and Kenny *Wheeler in the 1950s; Robert *Aitken, Brian *Cherney, John *Fodi, Clifford *Ford, Richard *Henninger, Paul *Pedersen, Doug *Riley, and Fred *Stone in the 1960s; and Robert *Bauer, Gary J. *Hayes, and David Jaeger in the 1970s. For Schafer, in 1950 when music in Toronto 'was still run by the pommies,' Weinzweig was 'a Parnassus of one, and all the young men who wanted to know about the newer things blustered into his office between 1945 and 1960.' Schafer continues, 'I do not know if he was a good teacher, I only know that he was considerate and that the things he had to offer were not purchasable anywhere else in Canada at that time' (ibid).

Weinzweig was made an Officer of the *Order of Canada in 1974 and was awarded the *CMCouncil Medal in 1978. On his retirement from the U of Toronto in 1978 he was appointed Professor Emeritus. He is an associate of the CMCentre and a member of CAPAC. His wife is the novelist and story-writer Helen Weinzweig.

COMPOSITIONS

STAGE, FILM AND RADIO

The Whirling Dwarf, ballet. 1937 (Tor 1939). Med orch. Ms

4 scores for NFB films: *Mackenzie River; West Wind*: 'Life and Art of Tom Thomson'; *The Great Canadian Shield; Turner Valley*. (1941–5). Ms

Over 100 radio (CBC) drama scores, including *Riel; Whiteoaks of Jalna; White Empire*

See also *Red Ear of Corn*

ORCHESTRA AND BAND

Legend. 1937. Full orch. Ms

The Enchanted Hill. 1938 (Rochester 1938). Full orch. Ms

Suite. 1938 (Rochester 1938). Full orch. Ms

Symphony. 1940. Full orch. Ms

Rhapsody for Orchestra. 1941 (Tor 1957). CMCentre

Interlude in an Artist's Life. 1943 (Tor 1944). Str orch. Leeds 1961. RCI Canadian Album No. 2/RCI Anthology of Canadian Music ACM 1 (*TSO)

Our Canada. 1943 (Tor 1943). Med orch. CMCentre. RCI 41 (*TSO)

Band-Hut Sketches. 1944 (CBC 1944). Band. Ms

Edge of the World. 1946 (Tor 1946). Med orch. Leeds 1967. CBC SM-163 (*CBC Wpg O)

Red Ear of Corn (suite). 1949 (Tor 1951). Med orch. CMCentre. 1967. ('Barn Dance') Dom 1372/Col MS 6763/Citadel CT 6011 (Tor Philharmonia O, *Susskind cond)

Round Dance. 1950 (Tor 1950). Med orch (arr for band by Cable). CMCentre, Leeds 1966 (band). (Band) RCA PCS 1004/Citadel CT 6007 (*Cable Concert Band)

Symphonic Ode. 1958 (Saskatoon 1959). Full orch. Leeds 1962

Dummiyah/Silence. 1969 (Tor 1969). Full orch. CMCentre. RCI 477 (B. *Brott)

SOLOIST(S) WITH ORCHESTRA

Spectre. 1938 (Tor 1939). Tim, str orch. Ms

A Tale of Tuamotu. 1939. Bn, orch. Ms

Divertimento No. 1. 1946 (Van 1946). Fl, str orch. B & H 1950. RCI 182/RCI ACM 1 (*CBC SO, *Day fl)/Dom S 69006 (*Aitken fl, Weinzweig cond)

Divertimento No. 2. 1948 (Tor 1948). Ob, str orch. B & H 1951. RCI 86/RCI ACM 1 (*Bauman ob, *Waddington cond)

Violin Concerto. 1951–4 (Tor 1955). Vn, orch. CMCentre. RCI 183/RCI ACM 1 (*CBC SO)

Wine of Peace (Calderon de la Barca, transl A. Symons, anon). 1957 (Tor 1958). Sop, orch. CMCentre (study score) 1957. RCI 182 (*CBC SO)

Divertimento No. 3. 1960 (Tor 1961). Bn, str orch. Leeds 1963. CBC SM-15 (*CBC Van Chamb O)

Divertimento No. 5. 1961 (Pittsburgh 1961). Tpt, trb, winds. Leeds 1969. RCI 292/RCI ACM 1 (*Deslauriers)

Concerto for Piano and Orchestra. 1966 (Tor 1966). CMCentre. CBC SM-104 (*Helmer)

Concerto for Harp and Chamber Orchestra. 1967 (Tor 1967). Leeds 1969. CBC SM-55/RCI ACM 1 (*Loman hp)

Divertimento No. 4. 1968 (Tor 1968). Cl, str. CMCentre. CBC SM-134 (*Barnes cond)

Divertimento No. 6. 1972 (Tor 1972). Alto sax, str. CMCentre

Divertimento No. 7. 1979 (Van 1980). Hn, str. CMCentre

CHAMBER

String Quartet No. 1. 1937. CMCentre. (Mvt 2) RCI 12 (*Parlow Str Quar)

Sonata. 1941. Vn, pf. OUP 1953. CBC SM-276 (*Hidy)/Masters of the Bow MBS 2002 (*Bress)

Fanfare. 1943. 3 tpt, 3 trb, perc. CMCentre

Intermissions. 1943. Fl, ob. South 1964

String Quartet No. 2. 1946. CMCentre. Col MS 6364 (*Canadian Str Quar)

Cello Sonata 'Israel.' 1949. Vc, pf. CMCentre. RCI 209/RCI ACM 1 (W. *Joachim vc)

String Quartet No. 3. 1962. CMCentre. RCI 362/RCI ACM 1 (*Orford Str Quar)

Woodwind Quintet. 1964. Self-publ 1975. RCI 218/RCI ACM 1/RCA CCS-1012 (*Tor Woodwind Quin)

Clarinet Quartet. 1965. 4 cl. Leeds 1970. Dom S 69004 (*Galper, McCartney, Fetherston, Temoin)

Around the Stage in 25 Minutes During Which a Variety of Instruments Are Struck. 1970. Solo perc. CMCentre

Trialogue (Weinzweig). 1971. Sop, fl, pf. CMCentre

Riffs. 1974. Fl. CMCentre

Contrasts. 1976. Guit. Ms

Pieces of 5. 1976. Brass quin. CMCentre

Refrains. 1977. Db, pf. CMCentre

PIANO AND ORGAN

Suite for Piano No. 1. 1939. CMCentre, FH 1955 (mvt 1)

Improvisations on an Indian Tune. 1942. Org. Ms

Piano Sonata. 1950. CMCentre. CBC SM-162 (*Buczynski)

Suite for Piano No. 2. 1950. OUP 1956 (mvt 2); OUP 1965 (mvt 1 and 3). 1970. (Mvt 2) CBC SM-99 (Angela Florou)

Impromptus. 1973. Pf. CMCentre

CHOIR AND VOICE

'To the Lands Over Yonder' (Inuit). 1945. SATB. FH 1953. Self-publ 1974

'Of Time, Rain and the World' (Weinzweig). 1947. V, pf. CMCentre. RCI 20/RCI ACM 1 (*James)

'Dance of the Masada' (I. Lamdan). 1951. Bar, pf. CMCentre. RCA LSC 3092 (*Fine bass)/Master MA 275 (D. *Mills bass)

'Am Yisrael Chai!'/'Israel Lives!' (Malka Lee, English transl Weinzweig). 1952. SATB, pf. Leeds 1964

Private Collection (Weinzweig). 1975. Sop, pf. CMCentre

WRITINGS

'The new music,' *CRMA*, vol 5, Jun 1942

'A composer looks at the teaching of musical theory,' *ConsB*, Nov 1949

'Notes on a visit to Britain,' *CanComp*, 21, 22, Sep, Oct 1967

'Address' (25 Nov 1967), *Report on the John Adaskin Project Policy Conference*, CMCentre (Toronto 1967)

BIBLIOGRAPHY

Saminsky, L. *Living Music of the Americas* (New York 1949)

'Demonstrating the twelve-tone technique,' *CBC Times*, 13–19 May 1951

Wilson, Milton. 'Music review,' *Canadian Forum*, vol 21, Jul 1951

Beckwith, John. 'Composers in Toronto and Montreal,' *U of T Q*, vol 26, Oct 1956

Kasemets, Udo. 'John Weinzweig,' *CMJ*, vol 4, Summer 1960

'Good reviews for a Canadian composer,' *Maclean's*, Mar 1963

'Professor John Weinzweig: important musical influence,' *CanComp*, 14, Jan 1967

'Weinzweig's "Harp Concerto" wins critical praise,' *CanComp*, 19, Jun 1967

'John Weinzweig, a portrait,' *Mcan*, 9, Mar 1968

Winters, Kenneth. 'Behind the silence lurks more of the same,' Toronto *Telegram*, 17 May 1969

'Weinzweig in Mexico,' *CanComp*, 42, Sep 1969

Seay, Albert. 'Review of Concerto for Harp and Chamber Orchestra,' Music Library Assn *Notes*, vol 26, Mar 1970

Such, Peter. *Soundprints* (Toronto 1972)

Littler, William. 'John Weinzweig: the CBC's birthday concert,' *CanComp*, 78, Mar 1973

Henninger, Richard et al. 'Dossier J.J. Weinzweig,' *CMB*, 6, Spring–Summer 1973

Webb, Douglas J. 'Serial techniques in John Jacob Weinzweig's five divertimentos and three concertos,' unpubl PH D thesis, U of Rochester 1973

Kallmann, Helmut. 'John Weinzweig,' *Dictionary of Contemporary Music*

Henninger, Richard. 'John Weinzweig,' *Contemporary Canadian Composers / Compositeurs canadiens contemporains*

CAPAC. 'Musical Portrait John Weinzweig,' pamphlet and recording (1975)

Champagne, Jane. 'What one man's done to help us understand the composer's role as part of our life,' *CanComp*, 100, Apr 1975

Hines, Malcolm. 'An analysis of Divertimento No. 6 for Alto Saxophone and String Orchestra by John Weinzweig,' unpubl M MUS thesis, Western 1975

Skelton, Robert A. 'Weinzweig, Gould, Schafer: three Canadian string quartets,' unpubl D MUS thesis, Indiana 1976

'Weinzweig works featured by CBC in premiere of Anthology series,' *CanComp*, 139, Mar 1979 (RH)

WEISGARBER, Elliot. Composer, ethnomusicologist, b Pittsfield, Mass, 5 Dec 1919, naturalized Canadian 1973; B MUS (ESM, Rochester) 1942, M MUS (ESM, Rochester) 1943. He studied composition and clarinet at the ESM and composition in Paris 1952–3 with Nadia Boulanger and in Los Angeles 1958–9 with Halsey Stevens. He taught at the Women's College of the U of North Carolina 1944–58 and the U of California 1958–9 and began teaching at the *U of British Columbia in 1960. He has specialized in the teaching of composition and Asian music. His pupils have included Michael *Baker, David Keeble, and Claire *Lawrence. On *Canada Council grants he studied Japanese music in Japan in 1966, 1967, and 1968–9 at the U of Otana and privately, becoming proficient on the shakuhachi, a traditional bamboo flute. In 1974 he toured Canada with the kotoist Miyoko Kobayashi. Weisgarber's compositional style is many-faceted, ranging from traditional works for orchestra and chamber ensemble to pieces which incorporate elements of Japanese folk music, as in *Kyoto Landscapes: Lyrical Evocations for Orchestra*, *Japanese Miscellany* (1970) for piano, and a series of chamber works for Japanese instruments. He is a member of CAPAC and an associate of the *CMCentre.

SELECTED COMPOSITIONS

ORCHESTRA

Sinfonia Pastorale. 1961. Sm orch. Ms

Kyoto Landscapes: Lyrical Evocations for Orchestra. 1970 (rev 1972). CMCentre

Illahee Chanties. 1971. Chamb orch. Ms

Musica serena. 1974. Sm orch. CMCentre

Netori: A Fantasie. 1974. Alto sax, orch. CMCentre

Concerto for Violin and Orchestra. 1974. CMCentre

A Pacific Trilogy. 1974. Orch. CMCentre

Also others

CHAMBER

Sonata for Unaccompanied Violoncello. 1965. Ms

Rokudan Henko-no-shirabe. 1971. 2 koto, 2 shamisen. 1971. Ms

Six Miniatures after Hokusai. 1972. Vn, pf. CMCentre

As We Stood Then, song cycle. 1975. Mezzo (bar), va, pf. CMCentre

Fantasia a Tre. 1975. Vn, hn, pf. CMCentre

String Quartet. 1975. CMCentre

Several more chamber works, including 3 others for Japanese instruments

CHOIR AND VOICE

Num mortuis resurgent?, cantata (Dunstan Massey). 1963 (rev 1973). SATB. CMCentre

Ren-ai to toki ni tsuite 'Of Love and Time' (Shakespeare, Japanese, Tsubouchi Shoyo). 1971. Sop, fl, ob, str trio, hpd. Ms

Illusions of Mortality, song cycle. 1975. V, pf. CMCentre

Other works for choir and v, including 2 for v and Japanese instr

Incidental music for TV and several radio documentaries; a few works for pf

WRITINGS

'Mayonnaise on the sashimi,' *CanComp*, 44, Nov 1969

'A composer explains his "trans-cultural" music,' *CanComp*, 88, Feb 1974

BIBLIOGRAPHY

Contemporary Canadian Composers / Compositeurs canadiens contemporains CF

WEISS PEERY, Irene (Joan) (b Weiss, m Peery). Pianist, teacher, b Cardston, Alta, 11 Apr 1946; B MUS (Juilliard) 1970, M MUS (Juilliard) 1972. At eight she was performing major works in Alberta festivals, winning every class she entered for the next eight years. Gladys *Egbert, with whom she studied 1957–65 in Calgary, was her most significant teacher. Irene Weiss won first prize in the *CBC Talent Festival at 17. Two years later, with the aid of a Ford of Canada scholarship and a *Canada Council award, she went to New York, where she studied 1965–73 with Ilona Kabos and Irwin Freundlich at the Juilliard School. She made a Carnegie Hall debut in 1972. She joined the teaching staff at Utah State U, Logan, to teach senior piano and pre-school music education. She made a 49-concert tour of the North American west coast and Alaska in the 1974–5 season and has been heard on CBC TV ('Centennial Performance') and CBC radio ('Mods Make Music' 1968). GKG

WEISZ, Robert. Pianist, teacher, b Arad, Rumania, 25 Jun 1925, of Hungarian parents, naturalized Swiss 1963 and Canadian 1975; prix de virtuosité (Geneva Cons) 1949. He studied until 1947 at the Franz Liszt Academy in Budapest with Annie Fischer and Bela Böszörmenyi-Nagy and then at the Geneva Cons with Dinu Lipatti. In 1949 he won first prize at the Geneva International Competition for Musical Performers. He then worked with Nadia Boulanger in Paris and Myra Hess in London. He gave recital tours in South America in 1951, Indonesia in 1953, and throughout Europe 1951–67; in Holland the critic of *Het Vaterland* described his technique as the 'perfect servant of an intelligent and sensitive musicianship.' He was artist-in-residence 1967–9 at Indiana U and was appointed to teach piano at *Laval U in 1969. Jacinthe *Couture and Michel Franck, winners of the *Prix d'Europe in 1974 and 1977 respectively, are among his pupils. He has given numerous recitals, performing at the *JMC Orford Art Centre in 1974, in Montreal, and in Quebec City and has appeared on the CBC TV program 'Les Grands Concerts.' With the *CBC Quebec Chamber Orchestra he was guest soloist on the occasion of the 25th anniversary of Lipatti's death. He formed a two-piano team with Jeanne *Landry at Laval U, performing works with orchestra by *Matton in 1971, Bartók in 1972, and Schumann in 1973. The team also gave a recital at the *Salle Claude-Champagne in 1975 and with the *Quebec SO played Martinu's *Concerto* for two pianos in 1976. Between 1950 and 1952 Weisz recorded Schumann's *Faschingsschwank aus Wien, Op 26* and Brahms' *Waltzes, Op 39* (Decca LK 4063), Schumann's *Fantasy, Op 17* (Decca LM 4539), and, with the cellist Paul Tortelier, Schubert's *Sonata in A Minor* ('Arpeggione') and Grieg's *Sonata in A Minor, Op 36* (Pathé-Marconi FALP 570). MB-L

WELDON, Dorothy (Ellen) (m Masella). Harpist, teacher, b Montreal 27 Jul 1929; premier prix harp (CMM) 1951. She studied at the *CMM with Germaine *Malépart (piano) and Marcel Grandjany (harp) and in 1947 made her debut at the Sarah *Fischer Concerts, where she won a scholarship. She toured Quebec for the *JMC, as a soloist in 1952 and as both soloist and accompanist in 1961–2 with the soprano Renée Maheu and in 1968–9 with the soprano Jacqueline *Martel. She participated in the premieres of Michel *Perrault's *Margoton* for harp and strings in 1955 and *Fontaines douces, noires fontaines* for tenor and two harps in 1956 and Kelsey *Jones' *Trio* for flute, viola, and harp in 1955. As a soloist she performed with the *Quebec SO in 1947 and 1951, the CBC *'Little Symphonies' Orchestra in 1951 and 1952, the *MSO in 1958, 1974, and 1978, the *Victoria SO in 1965, and the *McGill Chamber Orchestra in 1971. Her repertoire included Mozart's *Concerto* for flute and harp, Ravel's *Introduction and Allegro*, Debussy's *Danse sacrée et danse profane*, and Pierné's *Concertstück*. She has performed on CBC radio and TV programs, including 'Concerto' in 1975 and 'Les Beaux Dimanches' in 1976, playing among other works Grandjany's *Aria dans le style ancien* and *Weinzweig's *Concerto*. She became a member of the MSO in 1947 and principal harp in 1971. In 1951 she began to teach at the CMM, and Claude Hill, Manon LeComte, and Margot Morris were among her pupils. She and her husband, the clarinetist Rafael *Masella, have appeared together in recital. They premiered Grandjany's *Impromptu* for clarinet and harp in 1955. See also Discography for the Montreal String Quartet. ST

'We'll Never Let the Old Flag Fall.' World War I marching song about the Union Jack. It was written by M. (probably Michael) F. Kelly (music) and Albert Erroll MacNutt (words) and published in 1914, though copyrighted only in 1915, by *Anglo-Canadian Music. In the years following, MacNutt often was identified as the sole author. Originally for voice and piano, the song was arranged also for orchestra, band, and choir. It was performed each evening at the 1915 *CNE (Toronto) by a male quartet with band, as part of a military demonstration, and at the 1916 CNE by massed bands. An advertisement in the *Canadian Music Trades Journal* (May 1916) reported sales of 100,000 throughout the British Empire. Several recordings and piano rolls, including those by the baritones Herbert Stuart of Ontario and Frederick Wheeler, are listed in *Roll Back the Years*. Kelly (b Saint John, NB, ca 1882, d there 1916) and MacNutt (b Truro,

NS, 1891, d 1952) also collaborated on 'By Order of the King' (Anglo-Canadian 1915). FH

'We'll Rant and We'll Roar like True Newfoundlanders.' This lively song recounting a young fisherman's love affairs is a Newfoundland offshoot of the widely known English capstan shanty 'Spanish Ladies,' which described the landmarks sighted during a passage through the English Channel. Pacific whalermen remade the shanty to tell of the 'Talcahuano Girls,' with a chorus: 'We'll rant and we'll roar like true Huasco whalesmen,' and Australian drovers adapted it to voice their farewells to the 'Brisbane Ladies.' The Newfoundland version is credited to Henry W. LeMessurier, deputy minister of customs in St John's. He borrowed some stanzas from the whalers' version and composed the rest ca 1875. James Murphy printed it as 'The Ryans and the Pittmans' in his *Old Songs of Newfoundland* in 1912, and Gerald S. *Doyle included it in his *Old-Time Songs and Poetry of Newfoundland* in 1927. It appears in many later song collections and on various records, including *Folk Songs of Canada* (Waterloo CS3) and *Folk Songs of Newfoundland* (Folkways FW 6931), and several composers have arranged it, including Godfrey *Ridout, whose SATB setting was published by Waterloo in 1958. EF

WELLS, Paul. Pianist, teacher, writer, composer, b Carthage, Mo, 22 Jul 1888, d Jacksonville, Fla, May 1927. He studied with Ernest Hutcheson at the Peabody Cons, Baltimore, and (after performances with the Baltimore and Minneapolis orchestras) continued in Europe with Josef Lhévinne and Leopold Godowsky. His European tours (1912, 1913) included several appearances with the Berlin Philharmonic. Later in 1913 he joined the faculty of the *TCM, where his pupils included Gordon *Hallett, Muriel *Kerr, Scott Malcolm, and Stanley *St John. He made his Toronto debut 15 Oct 1913 and toured western Canada in 1914. He subsequently appeared with the *TSO and performed with the *Toronto String Quartet and the Conservatory Trio. Wells' recitals often included his *Sonata* or other compositions.

WRITINGS

'The psychological side of piano playing,' *CanJM*, Oct 1915
'Combining the teaching of piano technique, touch and tone production,' *CQR*, vol 1, Nov 1918
'The aesthetic aspect of musical study,' *CQR*, vol 1, May 1919
'Psychological phases of piano playing, *CQR*, vol 3, Aug 1921 EK

WELSMAN, Frank (Squire). Conductor, teacher, pianist, b Toronto 20 Dec 1873, d at his summer home, Lake Joseph, Muskoka, Ont, 2 Jul 1952. He studied violin and piano at the *Toronto College of Music and attended the Leipzig Cons 1894–7, working with Martin Krause (piano) and Gustave Schreck and Richard Hofmann (theory). Later, also in Germany, he studied piano with Arnold Mendelssohn. On his return to Toronto he began a career as a pianist, playing in Canadian cities from Quebec to Victoria, and taught at the Toronto College of Music. In 1906 he joined the staff of the *TCM. After 1907 he virtually abandoned his career as a pianist, though he continued to play chamber music. In 1914 he founded the Welsman Studio Club, which for more than 10 years presented bi-weekly piano music programs by students and teachers at the TCM. In 1908 the TCM SO, which he had organized two years previously, became the *Toronto Symphony Orchestra (identified throughout *EMC* as the Welsman TSO to distinguish it from the later TSO) and survived until 1918. He also conducted the *Anglo-Canadian Leather Company Band in Huntsville, Ont, during the summers of 1923 and 1924. In 1918 he left the TCM to teach at the *Canadian Academy of Music, and in 1922 he became the latter's music director. However, in 1924 when the two institutions amalgamated, he returned to the TCM and remained on staff until his retirement in 1951.

Welsman's pupils included Roy Angus, G.D. *Atkinson, Margaret Miller *Brown, Percy *Faith, H.K. *Jordan, and Kate Bryce Marquis Nelson. He was music director 1928–31 of Alma College in St Thomas, Ont, and often crossed Canada as an examiner and a festival adjudicator. He composed several songs and instrumental pieces – eg, a *Minuet* for piano (Whaley Royce 1900) and *Two Songs* (Church 1904). Undoubtedly, however, his main contribution was the establishing of Toronto's first relatively durable symphony orchestra, a group which more than any other prepared the ground for the future TSO.

BIBLIOGRAPHY

'Conservatory portrait gallery, no. 10 – Frank S. Welsman,' *CQR*, vol 12, Winter 1930
Editorial. 'Frank S. Welsman,' Toronto *Globe and Mail*, 5 Jul 1952
The Welsman Memoranda, compiled by Mary E. Jolliffe (Toronto 1971) RPn

Western Board of Music. Examining body established in 1936 by music educators in Alberta, Saskatchewan, and Manitoba. Dissatisfied with the multiplicity of examining bodies in the west and with the lack of uniform examination content and standards, and concerned about the amount of money sent to eastern Canada and England in the form of examination fees, six representatives (one from each of the three prairie universities and the provincial departments of education) met 13 Apr 1934 in Regina. Arthur *Collingwood of the *U of Saskatchewan was the only professional musician among them. Among the results of that meeting were the approval of 'the principle of setting up a uniform standard of music options and music tests for the three prairie universities,' the establishment of a joint board to administer the plan, and the appointment of a syllabus committee.

At a second meeting, 28 Apr 1936 in Saskatoon, it was agreed that 'in addition to a common syllabus, standards of attainment, and fees, there would be prepared, by an inter-provincial committee, common theory papers.' The name 'Western Board of Music' was adopted, and two diplomas, Associate of Music (performance or teaching) and Licentiate of Music (performance) were introduced, the initials AM and LM to be followed by the initial of the province (eg, for Manitoba AMM, LMM; for Saskatchewan AMS, LMS). These were granted by each province's university, though they remained independent of the university's own degree program. Musicians on the WBM in 1936 were Eva *Clare (*U of Manitoba), Collingwood (U of Saskatchewan), and Gladys *Egbert (*U of Alberta).

During the 1940s the common syllabus and sets of theory papers were introduced, music option examinations were accepted for high-school credit by the three provinces, and common books of graded piano pieces were published. In 1954 the WBM was strengthened by representation from the three provinces' RMTAs. By 1977 the WBM syllabus had been revised five times and expanded beyond its original coverage (piano, violin, voice, theory, and sightreading) to include lower strings and most woodwind and brass instruments. Operations were centralized at the U of Alberta in 1973, an executive director (Edward *Lincoln) was appointed in 1974, and all of the prairie universities (seven by this time: Alberta, *Brandon, *Calgary, *Lethbridge, Manitoba, *Regina, and Saskatchewan) and the three RMTAs gained representation on the board.

The WBM has published the three-volume *Explorations* (Leeds 1969, co-edited by Dorothy *Bee and Gordon Wallis) and the two-volume *Horizons* (Waterloo 1973, co-edited by Richard *Johnston, Edward Lincoln, and Gerhard *Wuensch) and has revised, under the editorship of Bee, its eight graded books of piano music (Waterloo 1976).

BIBLIOGRAPHY

'A history of the Western Board of Music,' unpubl paper, Edmonton nd
'Western Board of Music gathers,' *CanComp*, 52, Sep 1970 WLB

Western Five. See Cammie Howard.

Western Gentlemen. See Mart Kenney.

Western Manitoba Centennial Auditorium. Multi-purpose civic hall located on the campus of *Brandon U and connected by a tunnel to the university's school of music. The land on which it is situated was given to the city by the university in exchange for specific guarantees relating to the university's use of the hall. (Though the university pays for such use, it is assured of a venue for its chamber opera productions, chamber orchestra performances, and recitals.) Completed in 1969 at a cost of nearly $2 million, the auditorium is Brandon's main concert hall and features continental seating (crescent arrangement without centre aisles) for 877 people on a raked floor, with a stage 10.5 m deep and a proscenium opening 7.2 m by 14.4 m. The orchestra/forestage lift projects 3.6 m into the house, while the height of the gridiron is 18.3 m, with 21 line positions. A rehearsal hall located beneath the main auditorium is used also for banquets, dancing, and receptions, and the foyer accommodates receptions and exhibits. At stage and trap level are eight dressing rooms, two chorus assembly rooms, and a scene shop. Those who have appeared there include Liona *Boyd, the *Brandon University Trio, *BTO, *Canadian Brass, the *COC, the *Cassenti Players, *Chilliwack, Bruce *Cockburn, Judith *Forst, the Greystone Singers, the *Guess Who, the *Irish Rovers, Anton *Kuerti, André *Laplante, *Lighthouse, Guy *Lombardo, Catherine *McKinnon, the Don *Messer Show, Louis *Quilico, Robert *Silverman, Hank *Snow, the *Tudor Singers, and the *Winnipeg SO. (DRM)

Western Music Company, Ltd. Retailing and publishing firm with headquarters in Vancouver, 1930–70. The company was founded by Herbert *Drost to make available on the west coast a wide selection of printed music, especially for choir. Later, branches were operated in Winnipeg 1938–56, in Toronto 1948–55, and in Victoria 1945–9 and 1954–73. The Vancouver store added records and instruments to its merchandise and in 1937 began to publish music. By 1960 over 450 pieces had been issued, more than half by Canadian composers (W.H. *Anderson, Dalton *Baker, Hugh *Bancroft, Keith *Bissell, Frederick *Chubb, George *Coutts, T.J. *Crawford, Arthur *Egerton, Robert *Fleming, Leonard *Heaton, H.E. *Key, Burton *Kurth, Kenneth *Meek, Adelmo *Melecci, Bernard *Naylor, Clermont *Pépin, Max *Pirani, Alfred *Whitehead, Healey *Willan, and others). Prominent in the catalogue were the Western Series of choral, organ, piano, school-choir, and vocal pieces. Many of the publications were for competition-festival, school, or church use. The firm also published the treatise *Full-throated Ease* by James T. Lawson (1955). The *Western Music News* was issued monthly 1934–40 and once or twice a year thereafter until 1955. Though primarily devoted to advertising the company's merchandise it also provided some documentation of musical life. For some years Western Music was the sole Canadian agent for Novello, J.B. Cramer, Arnold, and other British firms. Its own publications were sold in the USA by the British-American Music Co of Chicago. In 1970 the Western Music copyrights and stock were acquired by *Leslie Music Supply of Oakville, Ont. HK

Western Ontario Conservatory of Music. Teaching and examining body established under the auspices of the *U of Western Ontario in 1934. The conservatory was preceded by two private music schools, the London Cons of Music (1892–1922) and the London Institute of Musical Art (1919–34). The former, founded and directed 1892–ca 1910 by W. Caven Barron (1864–1936) and later directed by F.L. Willgoose, offered instruction in piano, organ, voice, orchestral and band instruments, theory, and the *Fletcher Music Method, leading to three diplomas (associate, teacher's, and fellow's).

Branches were established in residential areas of London and in nearby Woodstock, St Mary's, and Stratford. In 1922 the London Cons was absorbed into the London Institute of Musical Art but continued as an examining board. The institute, which had been established by Albert David *Jordan and was affiliated with the TCM, continued until 1934. In 1930 it introduced a course in the Fletcher Music Method which drew teachers and advanced students from across Ontario. The Western Ontario Cons of Music absorbed the institute in 1934 and discontinued the affiliation with the TCM. Frederick *Newnham, the first director, was succeeded in 1938 by Harvey Robb (b Chesley, Ont, 18 Apr 1888, d London, Ont, 30 May 1957). Examinations in piano, violin, and voice were offered first in 1939. The conservatory became affiliated with the university in 1942 and vacated its downtown premises for an on-campus location. Under Robb's direction the syllabus expanded to include a wide range of practical and theoretical courses and summer workshops in opera, piano pedagogy, and school music, but the conservatory was reduced to an examining body after the formation of the Music Teachers' College in 1945. Robb served 1950–7 as principal of both institutions and was succeeded on his death by Clifford *Poole. Howard Munn became principal of the conservatory in 1960, the same year that a College of Music was established by the university. Under the principalship 1970–4 of George *Smale, the conservatory syllabus was revised and the institution's role as a teaching body was restored. Carl *Duggan became principal in 1974. The Western Ontario Cons has operated in 'academic co-operation' with the university but retains financial independence. The two institutions have shared various buildings on campus, and in many cases the conservatory's examiners are members of the university faculty. In the mid-1970s the conservatory conducted some 5000 examinations annually in Ontario, leading to the associate diploma (A MUS, previously AWCM) and licentiate diploma (L MUS, previously LWCM) in voice, piano, organ, strings, winds, and theory. *Waterloo Music is the publisher of the conservatory's teaching materials. (LCf, JPG)

West Indies. See South and Central America, Mexico, and the West Indies.

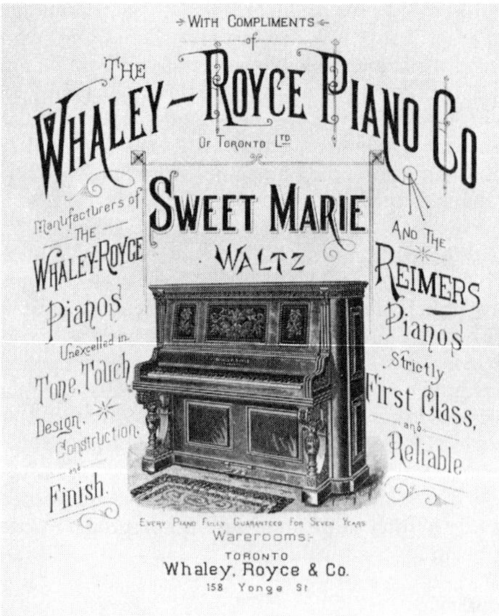

Whaley, Royce & Co Ltd. Toronto instrument dealers and manufacturers and, until 1969, music dealers and publishers. The firm was founded in February 1888 by Eri (sic) Whaley (b Stewarttown, west of Toronto, 6 Feb 1853, d January 1920) and George C. (Cooper) Royce (b Toronto ca 1865, d there 10 Apr 1942). Whaley had been a bandleader in Orangeville, Ont, had composed a *Hanlan Waltz* in 1878, and had worked 1885–7 for Thomas *Claxton. Royce had been employed briefly by a Toronto music dealer; he left Whaley, Royce in 1902 and later was president of the Ferranti Electric Co. After Royce's departure, Whaley was president and general manager. When Whaley died, the firm was bought by W.A. Hunter, H.R. Maddock, and W.H. Myhill. The company occupied in succession several locations on downtown Yonge St until it moved its wholesale division to suburban Scarborough in 1975. It gave up its downtown location in 1976. A branch was maintained 1889–1922 on Main St in Winnipeg.

The advertising slogan used by the company at about the turn of the century – 'Canada's Greatest Music House' – probably was justified. From the beginning Whaley, Royce carried a stock of band instruments, pianos and organs, sheet music, and general musical merchandise; engaged in the manufacture of brass and percussion instruments; and published music. It was one of the few Canadian music houses that had its own engraving, lithographing, and printing facilities (1890–ca 1940) and it did such work for other publishers as well. It also issued a magazine, the *Canadian Musician* (ca 1889–?), which by 1906 had changed its name to *The Musician*, and numerous handsome catalogues, eg, a *Descriptive and Selective Catalogue of Sheet Music and Music Books* (386 pp, ca 1900) and *Catalogue No. 23: Musical Instruments* (200 pp, illustrated, 1923). Whaley, Royce claimed to have built the first cornet in Canada in June 1888 and the first flute, piccolo, and clarinet in 1895. After 1920 only brass instruments and drums were made, however, and the firm has sold mainly imported instruments under the trade name 'Imperial,' its registered name for the best of its own three lines – 'Ideal' and 'Sterling' being the other two. The repair of instruments has been an important and continuing service.

The first Whaley, Royce publications date from 1890. The catalogue grew quickly and during the next 30 years surpassed that of any other Canadian publisher. The output declined later and came to a halt about 1940, after which date only reprints of earlier issues were undertaken, and a very few new items (eg, two pieces by Frank *Haworth, 1958, 1964). Plate numbers appear on many publications; they seem to have begun at number 101, reaching 1000 in 1903 and 1600 in 1923.

Canadian composers published by Whaley, Royce included R.S. *Ambrose, J. Humfrey *Anger, William Caven Barron, Charles *Bohner, Gena *Branscombe, Edward *Broome, Herbert L. *Clarke, Francesco *D'Auria, W.O. *Forsyth, H.A. *Fricker, H.H. *Godfrey, Albert *Ham, C.A.E. *Harriss, Edouard *Hesselberg, A.W. *Hughes, Thomas Charles Jeffers, Clarence *Lucas, Angelo M. *Read, William *Reed, Horace W. *Reyner, Leo *Smith, and A.S. *Vogt. Among the larger publications were Vogt's *Standard Anthem Book* (vol 1, 1894) and *Modern Pianoforte Technique* (1900), Harriss' opera **Torquil*, *New Songs of the University of Toronto* (1899), *Queen's University Songbook* (1903), and *Mount Allison Songs* (1908). Another important publication was the first edition of *'O Canada' with English words (by T.B. Richardson, 1906). Few, if any, other music publishers have published music by so varied a list of Canadians.

Some of these publications belonged to such series as Select Choruses and Part Songs, Octavo Church Music, Band and Orchestra Music, and *TCM examination books, but the series included much non-Canadian music. The main types of music published were educational, sacred, and patriotic, but there was a certain amount of both concert and pop music.

In 1955 the publications division moved to separate Yonge St quarters, and after a fire in 1969 destroyed the stock one of the vice-presidents, Ted (Edward Gordon) Hough (chairman of the *CMPA 1956–7), formed his own music store, Algord Music Ltd, located at yet another downtown Yonge St location. Reprinting of old Whaley, Royce publications continues according to demand.

BIBLIOGRAPHY

'The passing of E. Whaley,' *CMTJ*, vol 20, Feb 1920 HK

WHEELER, Charles E. (Edward). Organist, teacher, composer, b London, Ont, 1870, d there 25 Nov 1949; FRCCO. After early studies with Carl Verrinder, W.J. Birks, George *Sippi, and J.W. Featherston, Wheeler had organ and theory lessons in Toronto with F.H. *Torrington and W.O. *Forsyth respectively. He then studied in Leipzig with Bruno Zwintscher (piano), Paul Homeyer (organ), and Gustav Schreck (theory). On his return to Canada he became organist at First Congregational Church, London, then served for 47 years (1890–1937) at St Andrew's United Church. For many years he also was music director of the London Normal School. He was the first registrar of the Canadian Guild of Organists (*RCCO), vice-president in 1918, and president 1923–5. Wheeler became widely known through his weekly organ broadcasts. Besides teaching piano, organ, and voice he directed various musical societies in London and presented a number of light operas. In later years (1938–45) he was organist at Dundas St Centre United Church. Of his compositions approximately 40 anthems and 10 songs were published (Nordheimer and Anglo-Canadian). He also wrote two cantatas, *Hagar* and *A Song of Praise*.

BIBLIOGRAPHY

Hamilton, H.C. 'Charles E. Wheeler,' *MCan*, vol 10, Sep 1929 EK

WHEELER, (William) **Gerald**. Organist-choirmaster, harpsichordist, teacher, composer, b Richmond, Surrey, England, 26 Mar 1929; ARCM 1951, LRAM 1953, FRCO 1956. A pupil of Edgar T. Cook, the organist of Southwark Cathedral, London, Wheeler was assistant organist 1953–6 at St Paul's Cathedral, then emigrated to Canada where he was organist-choirmaster 1956–65 at St Matthew's Church, Ottawa. He also taught 1960–5 and 1971–3 at *Carleton U. In 1965 he became organist-choirmaster at Christ Church Cathedral in Montreal and began teaching at Marianapolis College. His pupils have included Aubrey Foy, Paul Halley, and Robert Kennedy. He was official organist 1969–73 with the *MSO and became organist and harpsichordist with the *McGill Chamber Orchestra in 1971, relinquishing the harpsichord duties in 1972 but resuming them in 1974. Wheeler has given public recitals and radio and TV broadcasts. In 1975 he was named conductor of the *Canadian Centennial Choir, Ottawa. He has premiered Graham *George's *Five Fugues for Organ* (CBC 1964) and *Sonatinas for Organ* (*Expo 67) and Robert *Fleming's *Fanfares for Brass and Organ* (1969). His recording *Organ Plus* (1977, CBC SM-292) includes works by Monnikendam, Robert Fleming, Mozart, and Piston. Wheeler has composed church and incidental music. NT

WHEELER, Ken or **Kenny** (Kenneth Vincent John). Trumpeter, flugelhornist, composer, arranger, b Toronto 14 Jan 1930. Raised in St Catharines, Ont, where his father, Wilf, played trombone in local bands, Wheeler worked in dance orchestras and later studied trumpet with Ross MacClanathan and harmony with John *Weinzweig at the *RCMT. In 1952 he moved first to Montreal and then to London. Among his teachers in England were Bill Russo (counterpoint) and Richard Rodney Bennett (composition). In 1959 he joined John Dankworth's big band, with which he played until 1965 (at one point alongside the Canadians Art *Ellefson and Ian *McDougall) and for which he later composed the orchestral suite *Windmill Tilter* based on *Don Quixote*.

In the 1960s, by which time he had become a major figure in the British jazz world, Wheeler played bebop with Joe Harriott, Tubby Hayes, Ronnie Scott, and others. Also in the mid-1960s he began playing free jazz with the groups of Tony Oxley and John Stevens, and by the early 1970s he was acknowledged as one of Europe's leading players in this idiom. However, he maintained his interest in more conventional contemporary jazz, performing in the 1970s as soloist with bands led by Ian Carr, Mike Gibbs, John Taylor, the Canadian expatriate John Warren, and others and arranging music for Maynard *Ferguson's English band. In 1971 he began playing in the quartet of the US saxophonist Anthony Braxton, at first occasionally in Europe and 1974–6 as a regular member for tours in Europe and North America. Also in the early 1970s he became a member of the Globe Unity Orchestra (based in Germany) and began leading his own big band in London. He led or co-led several small London groups in the 1970s, including Coe, Wheeler & Co (with Tony Coe), Freedom For a Change, and Azimuth (with Norma Winstone and John Taylor).

Besides playing in Canada with Braxton, Wheeler appeared in concert in Toronto with local groups in 1976 (when he made a recording for RCI at the Mother Necessity Jazz Workshop) and in 1978. He was heard 3 and 4 Nov 1978 on the CBC's 'Jazz Radio-Canada.' In a review of the LP *Gnu High*, Mikal Gilmore commented: 'His rotund, bright tone, smooth rippling flurries, and bluesy, cool stride are reminiscent of mid-60s Miles

Kenny Wheeler

[Davis]. Preferring to play in the uppermost register of his instrument, Wheeler attains a praiseworthy purity of sound, the kind of accuracy that elicits [Dizzy] Gillespie as a comparison' (*Down Beat*, 21 Oct 1976). In *Jazz Now* (ed Roger Cotterell, London 1976), Wheeler is called 'one of the finest trumpeters in jazz, able to express himself musically with directness and poise in almost any context.' Wheeler has composed the themes heard on several of his recordings. His most ambitious compositions, those for big band, are written with specific soloists in mind (including the most adventurous of English free-jazz players) to bring together the jazz avant garde of the 1970s and the more traditional forms of big band orchestration.

DISCOGRAPHY

Song for Someone. Orch with soli. 1973. Incus 10

Gnu High. 1975. ECM 1069

Kenny Wheeler Quintet. Ellefson ten sax, Williamson elec piano, Young db and b guit, Morell drums. 1976. RCI 444

Taylor/Wheeler/Winstone *Azimuth*. 1977. ECM 1099

– *The Touchstone*. 1978. ECM 1-1130

Dean/Gallivan/Wheeler *The Cheque Is in the Mail*. 1977. Ogun OG 610

Deer Wan. 1977. ECM 1102

WITH OTHERS

Dankworth *Bundle from Britain*. 1959. Top Rank RM 314

– *Collaboration*. Also including McDougall trb and Ellefson sax. 1960. Rou SR 52059

– [LP title unknown]. Also McDougall and Ellefson. 1960. Rou SR 52075

– *Jazz from Abroad*. Also Ellefson. 1961. Rou SR 52096

– *What the Dickens!*. Also Ellefson. 1963. Fontana MGF 67525

– *Zodiac Variation*. 1964. Fontana MGF 67543

– *Windmill Tilter*. 1967. Fontana STL 5494

– *Full Circle*. 1972?. Philips 6308 122

Stevens (Spontaneous Music Ensemble) *Karyobin*. 1968. Island ILPS-9079

– *Oliv*. 1969. Poly 2384-009

– *The Source*. 1970. Tangent TGS 107

– *So What Do You Think?*. 1971. Tangent TGS 118

Philly Joe Jones *Trailways Express*. 1968. Black Lion Select 2460 142

Oxley *Baptized Traveller*. 1969. CBS RM 52664

– *Four Compositions*. 1970. CBS S 64071

– *Ichnos*. 1971. RCA Victor SF8215

Gibbs *Mike Gibbs*. 1969. Deram SML 1063

– *Tanglewood '63*. 1970. SML 1087

– *Just Ahead*. 1972

Carr *Solar Plexus* 1970. Vertigo 6360 039

– *Labyrinth*. 1973

Taylor *Pause and Think Again*. 1971. Turtle TUR 302

Braxton *The Complete Braxton*. 1971. 2-Arista Freedom 40112, 40113

– *New York, Fall 1974*. Arista AL 4032

– *Live at the Moers Festival*. 1974. 2-Ring 01010-11

– *Five Pieces 1975*. Arista AL 4064

– *Creative Music Orchestra*. 1976. Arista AL 4080

– Montreux/Berlin Concerts. 1976. 2-Arista 5002

Globe Unity Orchestra *Live at Wuppertal*. 1973. Free Music Productions FMP 0160

– *Evidence*. 1975. FMP 0220

– *Into the Valley*. 1975. FMP 0270

– *Pearls*. 1975. FMP 0380

– *Jahrmarkt/Local Fair*. 1975, 1976. Po Torch PTR/JWD 2

– *Improvisations*. 1977. Japo 60021

Other LPs in England with Bill Bruford, Joe Harriott, Louis Moholo, Alan Skidmore, Norma Winstone, Phil Woods, etc, and in Europe with the Kenny Clarke–Francy Boland Big Band, Friedrich Gulda, and others

BIBLIOGRAPHY

Bavin, Pam. 'Canadians in London 3: Ken Wheeler,' *Coda*, Jun 1962

Miller, Mark. 'Kenny Wheeler,' *Down Beat*, 12 Feb 1976

– 'Jazzman prefers obscurity,' *Globe and Mail*, 12 Aug 1978

Cotterell, Roger. 'Kenny Wheeler: speaking softly but carrying a big horn,' *Jazz Forum*, 57, no. 1, 1979

Miller, Mark. 'Kenny Wheeler's many vehicles,' *Down Beat*, Apr 1980 MM

'When My Baby Smiles at Me.' Song composed in 1919 by the Montreal dance-band pianist Billy Munro. Ted Lewis and Andrew B. Sterling were credited as lyricists, though later their contribution was disputed. Composed in New York while Munro was a member of Lewis' Kentucky Serenaders, the song was inspired by an unsmiling patron who frequented Renton's, the club where the band worked. It was published by Harry von Tilzer, introduced by Lewis in *The Greenwich Village Follies of 1919*, and recorded first by the Serenaders for Columbia. Although it became Lewis' theme song, it was recorded by several other artists (some listed in *Roll Back the Years*) and, as sung by Dan Dailey, was the title song of a Hollywood movie in 1948.

Munro (b British West Indies 1893, d Montreal 16 Oct 1969) studied in London and in 1913 moved to Montreal. There he played at the Jardin de danse in 1917 and with Andy Tipaldi's Melody Kings and recorded some songs, including his hit, for Apex. After his New York years (1919–23?) he returned to Montreal, where he composed a few songs with Willie *Eckstein or Don Davis to lyrics by Sam Howard. In later years his radio show 'Les Talents de Billy Munro' was broadcast on CKVL.

'When the Ice-Worms Nest Again.' The favourite song of prospectors and trappers in the Canadian north and later the theme song for the annual gatherings of silver miners at Cobalt, Ont, and fur trappers at The Pas, Man. Its origin is not clear, but it seems to have been sung first in northern British Columbia and the Yukon and may date from the Klondike gold rush of 1898. Robert W. Service published a piece with this title in his *Twenty Bath-Tub Ballads* in 1938, but the traditional verses differ considerably from his. Wilf *Carter also recorded a slightly different version for RCA-Victor (48-0319). The song is both published (*Fowke and *Johnston's *Folk Songs of Canada*, 1954) and recorded (*Folk Songs of Canada*, CS3) by *Waterloo. EF

'When You and I Were Young, Maggie.' Ballad (1866) by the English-born James A. Butterfield (1837–91) to a poem written in Hamilton, Ont, by G.W. (George Washington) Johnson (b Binbrook, Upper Canada, 1839, d Pasadena, Cal, 1917), a schoolteacher who later taught languages and mathematics at the U of Toronto. The poem was written ca 1864 as a pledge of undying love to Johnson's wife, Maggie Clarke (who was to die in 1865), and published in the collection *Maple Leaves* (Hamilton 1864). It was set to music in Indianapolis, Ind, by Butterfield, who published the song there 19 May 1866. The song became one of the most popular ballads in North America, and it has been recorded by many artists (some listed in *Roll Back the Years*) including Albert Ammons, Henry *Burr, Benny Goodman, Harry *MacDonough, John McCormack, and Frank Munn. The song was heard in the 1976 NDWT (a Toronto theatre company) production of James Reaney's plays, *The Donnelly Trilogy*.

'When Your Boy Comes Back to You.' Patriotic song of World War I. Words and music are by Gordon V. *Thompson. An arrangement for voice and piano by Jules *Brazil was published in 1916 by Thompson's company in Toronto. The song was introduced 6 Jul 1916 by the composer at a sing-song at the Camp Borden (Ontario) army base and was performed by massed bands at the 1916 *CNE. Some 54,000 copies of the sheet music were sold within the first three months. Also arranged for band, orchestra, chorus, and mixed or male quartet, it was recorded by the *Canadian Grenadier Guards Band, by the tenor Charles Harrison with the Broadway Quartet, by the tenor David Irwin, and by the baritone Alan Turner.

FH

WHITE, Ernest. Organist, choirmaster, organ designer, teacher, editor, b London, Ont, 20 Jun 1901, d Fairfield, Conn, 21 Sep 1980; hon FRCCO 1977. He studied violin locally and organ at the *TCM after 1920 with *MacMillan and *Willan and was organist for a short time at Howard Park Methodist Church and Alhambra Ave United Church in Toronto. He moved to New York in 1926 for lessons with Lynnwood *Farnam and was acclaimed for his performance at the St Louis Organists' Convention in 1927. He was organist-choirmaster 1927–35 at St James Episcopal Church, Philadelphia, and 1935–7 at Trinity Church, Lenox, Mass. For 25 years (1937–62) he was associated with the Church of St Mary the Virgin, New York, first as organist, then as music director. While there, it was his custom to give two series of organ recitals each year.

White also became tonal director for the organ builder M.P. Möller, of Hagerstown, Md, designing and supervising installations in the USA and Canada, including those in New York at the Church of St Mary the Virgin, St George's Episcopal Church, and the Interchurch Center Chapel. The St Mary organ was purchased in 1947 by Gordon *Jeffery for Aeolian Hall, London, Ont, and was transferred to the London site under White's supervision. White taught at Bard College (Columbia U) and Pius X School of Liturgical Music in New York 1935–8, at the Music Teachers' College, *U of Western Ontario, 1948–51, at Jordan College (Butler U) and the Christian Theological Seminary in Indianapolis 1963–71, and at the U of Bridgeport, Conn, 1971–3. He became organist-choirmaster at St George's Church, Bridgeport, in 1973. He gave over 1000 organ recitals emphasizing both old and modern repertoire. He was noted also for his trail-blazing editions of early organ music and for his recordings, among which was the first issued of Messiaen's *La Nativité du Seigneur*. Rollin Smith (AGO and RCCO *Music*, August 1977) has said of White, 'That he was able to synthesize the many contingencies of organ playing and organ construction into one pioneering point of view will distinguish his name and stature for many years to come.'

DISCOGRAPHY

Bach *Eight Little Preludes and Fugues*. 1942. Mer MG 15027
Brahms *11 Chorale Preludes*. 1942. Mer MG 10070
Christmas Hymns and Carols. MGM E522
Ernest White Plays Bach: Pastorale; Passacaglia and Fugue in C Minor. 1942. Mer MG 15032
Franck *Three Chorales; Prelude, Fugue and Variation*. 1953. Discuriosities BCL-7280
Messiaen *La Nativité du Seigneur*. 1949. Mer MG 10069
Music for Organ, 2 vols: vol 1 Elmore – Bach – Martini – Arne – Fiocco – Karg-Elert; vol 2 Dandrieu – Karg-Elert – Pachelbel – Schroeder – Bach. Möller Records
Studies in Organ Tone. 1947. Aeolian-Skinner

WRITINGS

'Raymond Nold of St. Mary's,' *American Organist*, vol 24, Jan 1941
– ed. *Ten Christmas Carols from Ancient Sources* (Music Press 1945)
– ed. Masterpieces of Organ Music, folio series (Liturgical Press 1949–53): 61 *Hanff*, 62 *Froberger*, 63 *Tunder*, 64 *Strungk*, 65 *des Près*, 66 *A. Gabrieli*, 67 *Early German Masters*, 68 *Kuhnau*, 69, 70 *Handel*, 71 *Music for Lent*, 72 *Music for Easter*, 73 *Old English Album*
'The use of short-length reeds,' *Organ Institute Q*, vol 7, Autumn 1958
– ed. Choral series no. 61 *Anthems* (Music Press nd)
– and Hawke, H.W., eds. *Ascended Ayres* (Ernest White Editions 1972)

HWH

WHITE, Portia. Contralto, b Truro, NS, 24 Jun 1911, d Toronto, 13 Feb 1968. White was supporting herself as a school teacher when her extraordinary voice, much admired at various amateur functions, won her a scholarship for study with Ernesto *Vinci at the Halifax Cons of Music. She made her formal debut at Toronto's *Eaton Auditorium 19 Nov 1941 and reached the high point of her brief career with a widely acclaimed recital at Town Hall, New York, 13 Mar 1944. Following a tour in 1946 of Central and South America she found herself in vocal difficulties and retired from public singing. In the late 1950s, having renewed her studies, now with Irene *Jessner in Toronto, she resumed her career and sang before Queen Elizabeth at Charlottetown's *Confederation Centre 6 Oct 1964. She recorded a song recital under the title *Think on Me* (White House LP 6901). Dinah *Christie was a pupil of White in the mid-1960s, as were Judy Lander and Anne Marie *Moss. A memorial scholarship in her honour is presented by the *Nova Scotia Talent Trust (established in 1944 to assist White's career).

BIBLIOGRAPHY

Aitken, Margaret. 'Portia White, the new Canadian star of the concert stage,' *SatN*, 8 Apr 1944

JBM

WHITE, Victor. Tenor, administrator, b London 7 Aug 1918. Raised in Prince Albert, Sask, and in the Fraser Valley, BC, he studied during World War II with Ernesto *Vinci in Halifax and Pauline *Donalda in Montreal. Studies continued 1947–52 with Vinci at the *RCMT. White sang in recital and opera for the CBC and appeared with the *Royal Cons Opera as Don Basilio in *The Marriage of Figaro* (1951), Vašek in *The Bartered Bride* (1952), and Yamadori in *Madama Butterfly* (1953). He continued his studies in England with Roy Henderson, sang 1956–8 at the Glyndebourne Festival, became principal tenor (ca 1957–8) of the Welsh National Opera, and appeared as a guest 1957–9 at Sadler's Wells. He also made some recordings (78s) of religious songs. More studies followed in Milan 1958–61, but a throat problem ended his singing career; he returned to Canada in 1961. Turning to a career in administration he served 1963–72 as general manager of the *Vancouver SO. In 1974 he became president of Endeavour, a Vancouver fund-raising organization for the arts, sciences, and health.

BNSG

WHITEHEAD, Alfred (Ernest). Composer, organist, choirmaster, teacher, b Peterborough, England, 10 Jul 1887, d Amherst, NS, 1 Apr 1974; ARCO 1910, FCCO 1913, B MUS (Toronto) 1916, D MUS (McGill) 1922, FRCO (with the Lafontaine Prize) 1924, hon LL D (Mount Allison) 1954, hon

Portia White

LL D (Queen's) 1970, FRCCO 1973. After studies with Haydn Keeton and C.C. Francis, both of Peterborough Cathedral, and later with A. Eaglefield Hull, he emigrated to Canada in 1912 and was the first Fellow by examination (1913) of the Canadian Guild (College) of Organists (*RCCO). He was organist-choirmaster 1912–15 at St Andrew's Presbyterian Church, Truro, NS, and instructor in organ and theory 1913–15 at *Mount Allison U. He moved in 1915 to Sherbrooke, Que, as organist-choirmaster at St Peter's Anglican Church, and then to Montreal, where he served 1922–47 as organist-choirmaster at Christ Church Cathedral. He also taught organ, theory, and composition 1922–30 at the *McGill Cons. Among his pupils were Alexander *Brott, Graham *George, Hector *Gratton, Frances *James, Donald Mackey, Louis Robinson, and Ethel *Stark. During the Montreal years, Whitehead became the acknowledged leader of the city's Protestant church music, and his Cathedral Singers were chosen by Wilfrid *Pelletier to perform major works of Bach with the orchestra of the *CSM in 1936 at the inception of the *Montreal Festivals and also at subsequent festivals. Forced by ill health to withdraw from his arduous duties in Montreal, he became head of the music department at Mount Allison U and served there 1947–53. On his retirement from the university he became organist-choirmaster of Trinity United Church, Amherst, NS, retaining the post until 1971. He was twice (1930–1, 1935–7) president of the CCO and also served as honorary vice-president 1971–3 and honorary president 1973–4 of the RCCO.

Whitehead was a distinguished recitalist, but his finest playing was in the accompaniment of the church service. He was, he said, 'trained to the belief that organ accompaniment ... was the student's chief concern.' As choir director and teacher he combined consummate technique and high standards with unfailing courtesy and good humour. He was a prolific composer of motets and anthems in traditional idiom (in a letter of 1963 he remarks on the 'far too many Whitehead church works'), but the quality of his output was consistently high. His own choice included 'Alleluia, Sing to Jesus' with organ accompaniment based on *Alle Menschen müssen sterben* from Bach's *Orgelbüchlein*; the short motets 'Bread of the World,' 'Grant Us Grace,' and 'Almighty God, Whose Glory'; a 'Benedicite' on the Tonus peregrinus (called by Leo Sowerby the 'best Benedicite' he knew); and three anthems recurrently mentioned in Whitehead's letters: 'Ye Choirs of New Jerusalem,' 'Now God Be with Us,' and 'O Light Beyond Our Utmost Light.' Notable also are the eight-part motet 'Watch Thou, Dear Lord' on words of St Augustine, 'Love Unknown,' many of his short carols for Christmas, and the Brahmsian

Alfred Whitehead

organ *Prelude on Irby* (the tune associated with 'Once in Royal David's City'). The musical rights of his estate are administered by CAPAC.

Whitehead was an internationally recognized authority on some aspects of philately, and just before his death he completed the preparation of a third edition of his book, first published in the 1950s, *The Squared-Circle Cancellations of Canada*. He also was a noted painter, and his works hang in various private collections. A large part of his private library and many of his papers have been deposited at the *NL of C.

SELECTED COMPOSITIONS

CHORAL

'Alleluia, Sing to Jesus' (W.C. Dix). 1932. SATB, org. Schmidt 1934

Eighteen Fauxbourdons and Descants (various). 1932. SATB. Fischer 1933

'Love Unknown' (Crossman). 1932. SATB. Stainer 1932

'Most Glorious Lord of Life' (Spenser). 2 SATB. Gray 1932

'Ye Choirs of New Jerusalem' (St Faulbert of Chartres, transl J.N. Neale). 1932. SATB, org. Schmidt 1933

'Almighty God, Whose Glory' (Liturgy of St James, 2nd century AD). SATB. Schmidt 1933

'Come Sweet Evening Guest' (German). Sop (ten), SATB, org. Boston 1933

Magnificat and Nunc dimittis. 1933. 2 SATB, org. Fischer 1933

'Watchman, from the Height Beholding' (Psalms 22, 27, 118, *Hymns of the Apostolic Church*, transl Rev J. Brownl). 1933. Sop, bar, SATB, org. Boston 1934

'Early One Morning' (Old English folksong). 1934. Women's vs (mixed vs). Schmidt 1940

'Grant Us Grace.' SSATB. Curwen 1934

'O Light Beyond Our Utmost Light.' SATB, org. Boston 1934

'Watch Thou, Dear Lord,' motet (St Augustine). SATB, org (sop, ten duet). Ditson 1934

'The Seven Joys of Mary' (Old English). Sop, SATB. Schmidt 1935

'Benedicite omnia opera.' SATB, org. Gray 1936

'If Ye Then Be Risen with Christ.' Sop, bar, SATB, org. Gray 1937

'Praise Him, Ye That Fear Him' (Revelations 15 and 19). Sop, alto, ten, bass, SATB, org. Gray 1937

'I Beheld a Great Multitude' (Revelations 7). Ten, SATB, org. Curwen 1938

'Now God Be with Us.' SATB. Galaxy 1940

'Through a Long Cloister.' 1940. Male vs. Galaxy 1940

'Bread of the World' (Bishop Reginald Haber). Ca 1946. SATB. Ditson 1948

Over 100 songs, anthems, carols, and other choral works for mixed vs, men's vs and women's vs, publ by Curwen, Ditson, FH, Fischer, GVT, Galaxy, Gray, Novello, OUP, Schmidt, Stainer, and West, 1928–70

Also several arr of English and French- and English-Canadian folksongs, traditional Christmas and Easter carols, and adaptations and arr of early choral pieces for use as anthems

ORGAN

Christmas Slumber Song. Schmidt 1932

Passacaglia. Gray 1932

Prelude on 'Winchester Old,' Christmas pastorale. Ca 1937. Gray 1937

Prelude on a Theme by Orlando Gibbons. Gray 1940

Westminster Suite, arr. OUP 1943

BIBLIOGRAPHY

MacRae, C.F. 'Alfred Whitehead,' *CMJ*, vol 5, Spring 1961

'Alfred Whitehead,' *Atlantic Advocate*, vol 54, July 1964

George, Graham. 'Alfred Whitehead: Doctor of Music,' AGO and RCCO *Music*, vol 4, Nov 1970

'Alfred Whitehead 1887–1974,' ibid, vol 8, Jul 1974

Catalogue of Canadian Composers GGr

WHITEHEAD, (Marion) Gladys (b Manning). Singer, teacher, b Portsmouth, England, 16 Dec 1903; LAB 1923, ARCM 1938, hon FRHCM 1975. Her family settled in Canada when she was a small child. She studied piano 1913–16 with Ethel Maybee and violin with Philip Shadwick in Winnipeg and 1922–3 with Joseph Shadwick in London. Her voice teachers were John Coates and George Dodds in England and W.H. *Anderson, Burton *Kurth, and J. Campbell *McInnes in Canada. She was heard frequently 1933–40 as both a chorister and a soloist on radio station CKY, Winnipeg, and was a member 1937–58 of Anderson's CBC choir, the *Choristers. Whitehead was a soloist in numerous major choral performances, including the Canadian premiere of Tippett's *A Child of Our Time*, and also taught voice privately until 1958 in Winnipeg, though she lived in Kenora after 1949. She lectured on music 1958–66 for the Dept of Education in Kenora and continued teaching privately in that city. In 1967 she was appointed principal of the *Royal Hamilton College of Music, remaining in that position until 1974. She was a teacher of vocal and choral techniques 1967–72 and a voice instructor 1971–7 at *McMaster U. She has examined for the *RCMT, the *WBM, and the *U of Western Ontario and in 1954 began adjudicating at Canadian competition festivals. She was president 1975–6 of the *Canadian Music Festival Adjudicators' Assn. Her pupils have included Evelyne *Anderson, Devina Bailey (*Duggan), James Bechtel, Orville Derraugh, Marilyn Duffus, David Falk, Victor *Godfrey, Peter *Koslowsky, Helen Litz (*Mennonite Children's Choir), Nona Mari, John *Martens, Victor *Martens, Maxine Miller, William *Reimer, Wilmer Neufeld, Phyllis *Cooke Thomson, and George Wiebe.

BIBLIOGRAPHY

'Gladys Whitehead,' *Sharps & Flats*, vol 6, Nov 1965 FAH

WHITNEY, Moxie (Moxam). Bandleader, b Brockville, Ont, 2 Jun 1919. He began his career at 17 as leader and guitarist of the Pacific Swingsters, a Hawaiian music group at a Toronto theatre. He also played guitar for Stanley *St John and other Toronto dance band leaders and was a trumpeter in the RCAF during World War II. In 1946 he formed his own dance band for the Granite Club, Toronto. The band also performed at Lake Louise, Alta (summer 1946), the Banff Springs Hotel, Banff, Alta (summers 1947–60, 1962), and the Royal York Hotel, Toronto (1948–60, 1962–71). In 1961 Whitney was bandleader at the Royal Hawaiian Hotel, Honolulu.

Whitney's Canadian band was heard regularly for many years on the CBC and for shorter periods on US networks. Whitney opened his own booking agency in Toronto in 1962 and was music director until 1971 for the CP hotel chain in Canada. After moving to Grand Cayman Island in the Bahamas as a hotelier in 1971 he returned to Canada in 1975 and became bandleader at the Chateau Laurier, Ottawa, in 1976. He also led a band at the *CNE dance tent (Toronto) in 1977 and 1978. He has made three LPs for Columbia (Harmony label) and one each for CTL and RCA. His band's theme is the Isham Jones and Gus Kahn song 'I'll See You in My Dreams.' (HM)

WHYTE, Ernest. Composer, teacher, b Ottawa 1858, d there 1922. After studies with Martin Krause (piano) and others at the Leipzig Cons ca 1890, Whyte operated the Martin Krause School in Ottawa, teaching piano and voice. Though a man of independent wealth, he was known also to have taught at the Ottawa Cons about 1900. He wrote some 270 songs which reflect a strong German romantic influence. Many were written to poems by Burns, Goethe, Heine, Kipling, Poe, Shakespeare, Tennyson, and Yeats and by the Canadians Wilfred Campbell, Archibald Lampman, and Duncan Campbell Scott. Published are *Twelve Songs* (McKechnie 1907), *Ten Songs* (Orme 1912), and *Twenty-six Songs*, the last in three volumes (Nordheimer 1925–6). Manuscripts of 17 Whyte songs and other papers are held at the *NL of C.

BIBLIOGRAPHY

Saunders, C.E. 'The songs of Ernest Whyte,' *Acta Victoriana*, Christmas 1905 FMB

WHYTE, John M. (Marchant). Evangelist, hymnwriter, singer, b Paris, Canada West (Ontario), 8 Jun 1850, d Toronto 17 Mar 1927. He studied at the U of Toronto and devoted himself to evangelistic and temperance work. Typical of several hundred songs for which he wrote the words or the music, or both, are 'Canada Shall Yet Be Free,' 'Toronto the Good,' and 'Song of Trust.' Many songs appeared in separate editions published by Toronto News Co or Briggs. With his brother D.A. Whyte he edited *Songs of Calvary* (Briggs 1889). *The Great Redemption* (Briggs 1894) and *Nuggets of Gold* (Briggs 1898) contain many of his own melodies. HK

The Widow. Comic opera in three acts by Calixa *Lavallée (music) and Frank H. Nelson (libretto, in English). The vocal score, dedicated to 'His Excellency the Count of Premio-Real, Consul General of Spain for the Dominion of Canada and the British and French possessions in North America,' was published in Boston in 1881 by J.M. Russell and carries the subtitle 'La Veuve.' It consists of an orchestral overture and 30 vocal numbers. The exact date of its first performance is unknown, but an announcement of a production by C.D. Hess' Acme Opera Company at Chatterton's Opera House in Springfield, Ill, 25 Mar 1882, described the work as 'entirely new.' It appears certain that it was presented in Chicago and New Orleans and probable that it had performances in other cities. The action takes place in the south of France and features a dozen or so characters in a succession of amorous intrigues, misunderstandings, real or imagined plottings, and chance encounters, all leading to a happy ending in the best tradition of French comic opera and operetta. An account of the period (*La Nouvelle France*, vol 1, no. 2, 1882) states: 'The music is extremely gay and brilliant. The chorus is melodious and rich in harmony; most of the cavatinas have that seal of elegance and virtuosity that is found only in the good comic operas. The orchestration is the work of a master.'

Excerpts from the work were presented on CBC TV in 'Hommage à Calixa Lavallée,' part of the 1967 series 'Les Beaux Dimanches,' and a stage production was given by the Mohawk College Opera Theatre of Hamilton in 1976. A recording of 11 selections from the work under the direction of Eric *Wild employed an orchestral accompaniment devised from the vocal score by Ovid Avarmaa, the original never having been found. The performers, with the *CBC Winnipeg Orchestra, were Nona Mari (soprano), Joan *Maxwell (mezzo-soprano), Heather Ireland (contralto), Peter *Koslowsky (tenor), Peter *van Ginkel (baritone), Wilmer Neufeld (tenor), and Paul *Fredette (bass) (RCI 231 and RCA LSC-2981). GP

WIFFEN, David. Singer-songwriter, guitarist, b England 11 Mar 1942. He moved to Canada in 1958 and began his career as a blues and folk singer in Yorkville (Toronto) coffeehouses in the early 1960s. After travelling widely in Canada he settled in Ottawa, where he was a member 1967–9 of *Three's A Crowd and co-host 1969–70 with Ann *Mortifee for CJOH-TV's 'Both Sides Now.' His performing career in the early 1970s was hindered by a battle with alcoholism (eloquently expressed in his best-known song, 'More Often Than Not') but had become more stable by 1976 when he resumed regular appearances in coffeehouses and at folk festivals and universities. 'More Often Than Not' has been recorded by Eric Anderson, Ian and Sylvia (*Tyson), and Jerry Jeff Walker. His other songs include 'Driving Wheel,' recorded by Tom Rush; 'Mr. Wiffen Regrets,' recorded by the composer and also by Harry Belafonte; and 'Coast to Coast Fever,' the title song of Wiffen's third and most popular LP (1973, U Artists UALA 172). Roger McGuinn and Anne *Murray also have recorded his songs. Writing of 'Come Down to the River' Barrie Hale observed, 'It is without a doubt a Wiffen song, from that piece of country somewhere between ballad and blues that he staked for his own years ago, with a lovely, easy melody line.' Jack Kapica, in the *Globe and Mail* (Toronto, 7 Apr 1976), praised Wiffen's guitar playing, adding 'but that is secondary to Wiffen's own ... marvellously resonant baritone [which] he works ... much in the manner of the old Fred Neil.' Wiffen is an affiliate of PRO Canada.

BIBLIOGRAPHY

Hale, Barrie. 'Mr. Wiffen regrets,' *The Canadian*, 6 Nov 1976 MM

WILD, Eric (Lees). Conductor, arranger, composer, b Sault Ste Marie, Ont, 11 Feb 1910; ALCM 1925, B MUS (Michigan) 1932. After early training in Sault Ste Marie and studies in conducting and arranging 1928–32 at the U of Michigan, Wild was an arranger 1933–6 for Geoffrey *Waddington and others at the CRBC in Toronto, then went to London with Billy *Bissett's dance band and was principal trumpet and arranger 1936–9 for the BBC TV orchestra. Returning to Toronto he worked 1939–42 as a CBC conductor, then served 1942–5 as musical director of *Meet the Navy*. He rejoined CBC Toronto as conductor for the Wayne and Shuster show, the Alan Young show, and others. In 1947 he was appointed conductor of the newly formed *CBC Winnipeg Orchestra, a post he held until 1974. He was also music director of the Royal Winnipeg Ballet 1955–62 and of CBC TV's 'Hymn Sing' 1965–77. Under his direction the Hymn Sing Chorus, a 16-voice mixed choir, recorded *Eric Wild's Chorus as Featured on Hymn Sing* (Wat CSPS 632), *How Great Thou Art* (Wat CSPS 827), *Come Along and Sing Praises* (Wat CSPS 883), and *Hymn Sing* (RCA PCS-1178). Wild has contributed to many areas of broadcast music, as a conductor, an expert arranger, and a composer of many short works for orchestra, choir, and solo voice. His publishers include *Waterloo, *Berandol, and Harmuse. He conducted premieres of several Canadian works with the CBC Winnipeg Orchestra and the recording of *Lavallée's *The *Widow*. Wild is an affiliate of PRO Canada.

BIBLIOGRAPHY

O'Neill, Dennis H. 'Man of many talents: Winnipeg's Eric Wild,' *CanComp*, 7, Mar 1966
Morriss, Frank. 'Eric Wild,' *MSc*, 248, Jul–Aug 1969 TT

WILFER, Anton. Violin maker, b Luby, Czechoslovakia, 30 Apr 1901, d Montreal 31 Aug 1976. He studied and practised violin making in his home town before travelling in 1946 to Mittenwald, Bavaria, to perfect his work with master craftsmen. In 1951 he moved to Montreal and opened a workshop, Anton Wilfer Co Ltd. He made about 75 violins, 15 violas, 10 cellos, and 3 string basses. Wilfer worked with his sons-in-law, Alois Fogl and Ewald Fuchs, who took over the management of the shop after his death. Fogl (b Mistroveice, Czechoslovakia, 20 May 1925, naturalized Canadian 1955), who also studied in Luby, specialized in the making of bows (about 24 by 1978) and the building and repair of violins. He settled in Montreal in 1949. Fuchs (b Luby 9 Sep 1932, naturalized Canadian 1961) studied for three-and-a-half years in Mittenwald and worked 1950–5 in Switzerland before settling in Montreal in 1956. He had made 50 violins, 4 violas, 1 cello, and 24 guitars by 1978. All three makers' instruments are modelled after those by Stradivarius and Guarnerius.

BIBLIOGRAPHY

Heller, Zelda. 'Tender, loving care at Anton Wilfer's,' *Placedart*, vol 7, Jan–Feb 1972
Provencher, Norman. 'Loving care still lives in violin-makers' shop,' *Montreal Star*, 7 Apr 1976 CH

Wilfrid Laurier University. Non-denominational university at Waterloo, Ont, with origins in the Evangelical Lutheran Seminary (founded 1911) and the Waterloo College of Arts (founded ca 1924 and affiliated 1925–60 with the *U of Western Ontario). It became Waterloo Lutheran U in 1959 and Wilfrid Laurier U in 1973. At that time the Lutheran church relinquished its sponsorship of the university but maintained control of Waterloo Lutheran Seminary, which federated with Wilfrid Laurier U. The university offers undergraduate and graduate degrees.

Ulrich *Leupold taught church music at the seminary and organized choral ensembles at Waterloo College. During the early 1960s Martin Dolbeer and Charles McClain were active in an extension program which included sacred music instruction and annual tours by the university choir. In 1967 a Music Dept was established under Walter *Kemp, who held the university's first full-time appointment in music and was department chairman 1967–75. In 1975 a Faculty of Music was established with Christine *Mather as dean. Mather was succeeded by Gordon *Greene in 1979. An honours B MUS and a BA with a music major were offered in 1979–80; at that time there were more than 140 students and 13 full-time and 24 part-time faculty members, among them Barrie *Cabena, Garth *Beckett and Boyd *McDonald, Victor *Martens, and Jan *Overduin.

Located in MacDonald House, a former men's residence, the faculty's facilities in 1980 included approximately 30 practice rooms, a small library in addition to the music section in the university library (which also houses the *RCCO archives), three organs, instruments for baroque orchestra (used by students of the baroque music program), and an electronic studio.

The faculty has sponsored a Music at Noon concert series, and its opera workshops have presented productions of Ibert's *Angélique*, Monteverdi's *Il Combattimento di Tancredi e Clorinda*, Menotti's *The Consul*, Purcell's *Dido and Aeneas*, Ravel's *L'Enfant et les sortilèges*, Puccini's *Gianni Schicchi* and *Suor Angelica*, Hindemith's *Hin und Zurück*, Mozart's *L'Oca del Cairo*, and Bernstein's *Trouble in Tahiti*. Workshop directors have included Raffi *Armenian, Carol Anne *Curry, Philip May, and Jacqueline *Richard. Workshops have been offered on baroque music, piano, and voice. Performing groups at the university include the Wilfrid Laurier University Choir and Orchestra, the Laurier Singers, and the Chapel Choir. Among graduates of Wilfrid Laurier are Theodore Baerg and Victor Martens. Honorary doctorates have been awarded to Garfield *Bender and Maureen *Forrester.

See also Archives. (JPG)

WILHELM, Karl. Organ manufacturer, b Lichtental, Rumania, 5 Jul 1936, naturalized Canadian 1966. He was of German ancestry and learned his trade in Germany with the firm of Laukhuff and in Switzerland with Metzler. In 1960 he moved to Canada to initiate the production of mechanical-action instruments at *Casavant Frères. There he collaborated in the construction of many organs which since have become widely known. In 1966 he went into business for himself, first in St-Hyacinthe and then at Mont-St-Hilaire, Que. Assisted for a while by Hellmuth *Wolff, then by C. Linde, Wilhelm has produced many organs (73 by 1979), and these have established his reputation throughout North America. Organs he has built can be found in the St-Bonaventure (1967) and St-Mathias (1973) churches in Montreal; in other Quebec centres such as Beaupré (1968), Loretteville (1969), and Amos (1970); and in Toronto, Winnipeg, Dallas, Tex, and Portland, Ore. They are eloquent testimony to the high quality of contemporary organ manufacturing in Canada. Wilhelm restored the historic *Warren and Son organ in Deschambault, Que.

BIBLIOGRAPHY

Bulletin des Amis de l'orgue de Québec, 5, Jan 1969; 8, Nov 1969; 13, Feb 1971; 23, Jan 1974
Bouchard, Antoine. 'Dix ans d'orgue au Québec,' *VM*, 17, Sep 1970 AB

WILKINS, Rick (Herbert Richard). Arranger, tenor saxophonist, composer, b Hamilton, Ont, 1 Feb 1937. His uncle, Doug Hurst, was a jazz pianist in Hamilton in the 1950s. Wilkins took up the saxophone in high school, played and arranged for Jack Ryan's danceband at the nightclub El Morocco, and arranged for Gav Morton's danceband at the Brant Inn. Moving to Toronto in 1957 he played in the dancebands of Benny Louis and others, and in 1960 he began arranging music for the CBC orchestra of Jack *Kane. He studied arranging briefly with Phil *Nimmons at the Advanced School of Contemporary Music in Toronto and thereafter made his living primarily in that field. He has prepared and often conducted music for CBC and CTV pop-music and variety series and specials, with Julie Amato, Tommy *Ambrose, Guido *Basso, *Canadian Brass, Burton Cummings, Anne *Murray, Wayne and Shuster, and others. For CBS TV, Los Angeles, he was music director 1976–7 for a series and several specials starring the US singing group the Jackson Five. He scored Oscar *Peterson's *Canadiana Suite* for a CBC TV presentation in 1979. Wilkins also has written the arrangements for recordings by Peter *Appleyard, Ed *Bickert, Vic Franklyn, Moe *Koffman, Anne Murray (including *'Snowbird' and several LPs), and Ginette *Reno and for his own LPs *My Heart Belongs to Me* (1977, CTLS 5210/New Ventures NV 5003) and *For the Sake of Music* (1978, CTLS 5129). His compositions include scores for CBC TV dramas (eg, 'The Dumbells,' 1976) and documentaries. Wilkins has played in

Toronto studio orchestras and has been a member of the *Boss Brass, Nimmons 'N' Nine Plus Six, and other jazz bands. In 1977 he became co-leader of a jazz quartet with the drummer Pete Magadini. Wilkins is a member of CAPAC. MM

WILKS, Norman. Pianist, teacher, administrator, b Birchington, Kent, England, 9 Jun 1885, d Toronto 20 Nov 1944. As a boy he won a singing scholarship for the Duke of Newcastle Choir. He studied piano in England with Michael *Hambourg and Frederic Lamond and composition with Ebenezer Prout and Joseph Holbrooke, later attended the Brussels Cons, and then studied piano in Germany with Artur Schnabel. He toured North America 1913–14, playing six times with the Boston SO. Interrupting his career to serve in World War I, he earned the Military Cross. After the war he resumed playing and gave recitals in England, Holland, Belgium, Germany, Australia, and the West Indies and appeared with the Queen's Hall, Royal Philharmonic, and continental European orchestras. In Canada 1928–44 his major interest was music education. He lectured and examined for the *TCM, of which he became principal in 1942, succeeding Sir Ernest *MacMillan. He fought what he called 'turning out Beethoven sausages in the examination machine' and emphasized the element of discovery in a student's approach to music. His pupils included Robert *Fleming, Patricia *Blomfield Holt, Weldon *Kilburn, Margaret *Parsons, and Malcolm *Troup. He was president of the OMTA (*ORMTA) 1940–2.

WRITINGS

'Interpretation and examinations,' *CQR*, vol 12, Winter 1929

'On playing Beethoven,' *CQR*, vol 14, Autumn 1931 MHl

WILLAN, Gladys (Ellen) (b Hall). Teacher, pianist, b London 19 Mar 1883, d Toronto 8 Dec 1964; LRAM 1902. At the RAM she studied piano with Francesco Berger and Tobias Matthay and voice with Walter Mackway. She married Healey *Willan in 1905 and followed him to Canada in 1914. In Toronto she coached singers, taught piano privately, and was co-author with Olive Brush of *Let's Play and Sing around the Clock* (Harris 1929) and author of *A Manual of Ear-Training and Sight-Singing* (Harris 1939, 1971). She was music director for Dora Mavor Moore's Shakespeare productions in Toronto high schools. Mavor *Moore was one of her pupils. HK

WILLAN, (James) Healey. Composer, church musician, organist, choir conductor, teacher, b Balham (later a part of London) 12 Oct 1880, d Toronto 16 Feb 1968; ARCO 1897, FRCO 1899, hon D MUS (Toronto) 1920, hon LL D (Queen's) 1952, hon D LITT (Manitoba) 1954, hon D MUS (Cantuar) 1956, hon D LITT (McMaster) 1962, FRSCM 1963, FRHCM 1965. Willan maintained that he was born with the ability to read music, although his forebears – some of them Irish according to an unsubstantiated family legend – were not musicians but doctors, schoolmasters, and clergymen for the most part. His mother had some musical ability and, when he was four-and-a-half, became his first music teacher, a task she shared with his governness, Miss De Bruin, who taught him five-finger exercises. At eight-and-a-half he entered St Saviour's Choir School, Eastbourne, as a probationer and progressed so well in his studies that in six months (a record for the school) he became a regular choir boy. He studied piano and organ, harmony and counterpoint, was successively appointed assistant school librarian, librarian, and assistant librarian at the church itself, then at-

Healey Willan

tained the envied position of 'doctor's boy,' which entailed assisting the church organist by setting out the proper music, dusting the organ keys, and turning on the pneumatic engine. At 11 he began directing choir practices for boys older than himself and played and conducted for the evensong services at St Saviour's, alternating with the adult organist. His voice changed at 14, but he was given an extra year's schooling notwithstanding. When he did take his leave the headmaster and organist-choirmaster Walter Hay Sangster paid him what Willan regarded as a high compliment: 'I shall miss you. You never had a great voice, but you never missed a lead.'

Willan went on to private organ study with William Stevenson Hoyte, organist of All Saints Church in London. Willan credited Sangster and Hoyte with his basic musical education ('unknown men, really, but great teachers') and in later life was fond of quoting remarks of both men, such as Hoyte's 'Any fool can play notes; I want to hear the music!' Willan's natural musical gifts seem to have been congruent with his pleasures: in his mid-teens he would amuse himself by working out double counterpoint, devising a cantus firmus embodying all the possible diatonic intervals, and then doing strict counterpoint of the five species in two, three, four, and five parts above and below the cantus. While studying organ with Hoyte he also studied piano with Evlyn Howard-Jones; he entertained visions of a career as a concert pianist specializing in the music of Brahms, for whose 'dignity, breadth and spaciousness' he felt profound respect; but an injury to his forearm which limited the use of his right hand put an end to that dream.

Willan served as organist-choirmaster at St Saviour's Church, St Alban's, Herts, 1898–1900; Christ Church, Wanstead, 1900–3; and St John the Baptist, Holland Road, Kensington, 1903–13; and gained a reputation as an authority on plainchant in the vernacular (ie, English rather than Latin), an interest which he shared with his friend Francis Burgess, and which was a natural extension of his religious views. Those views had been set in early childhood, when the Church of England was beset by internal conflict between its protestant and Anglo-catholic wings, the latter following the teachings of the Oxford Movement. The Willans were ardent supporters of the Anglo-catholic party, which was bent on re-introducing doctrine and ritual unused in the English church since the reformation. Emotions ran so high that there were riots in the streets, and two members of Willan's family were assaulted physically. This struggle, with its inherent sense of intellectual rigour versus popular sentimentality, informed Willan's attitudes to Christian worship throughout

Manuscript final page of *Introduction, Passacaglia and Fugue* for organ (1916) by Healey Willan

his life. The Anglican church did not allow the use of Latin in its services, but the use of plainsong with English words was acceptable, and Willan spent much time and effort effecting a union between the two. He promoted plainsong in English by example in his churches (except between 1913 and 1921) and by editing, arranging, and publishing it. As an extension of this work he joined the Gregorian Assn in London in 1910.

Besides his church work, Willan made his living 1895–1900 as organist to the St Cecilia Society, 1904–6 as conductor of the Wanstead Choral Society, and in 1906 as conductor of the Thalian Operatic Society. He also read proofs for Novello, taught, and composed a variety of music. In 1904 he was elected an associate of the Philharmonic Society of London, which enabled him to attend orchestra rehearsals including those conducted by Arthur Nikisch, who, Willan maintained, was the greatest conductor he ever heard. In 1905 he married Gladys Ellen Hall (see Gladys Willan), a music student, who was to bear him four children and remain his companion until her death in 1964.

Willan was exposed to his strongest musical influences before the second decade of the 20th century; among continental composers these were Wagner, Brahms, and Tchaikovsky; among British composers Elgar is cited often, but Willan's pupil Godfrey *Ridout is probably correct in his assessment that Parry and Stanford had a greater influence on him, though Willan admired Elgar as a person ('He had a generous, kind mind; a dear chap').

In 1913 Willan received an invitation from A.S. *Vogt, principal of the *TCM, offering him the position of head of the theory department, to succeed Humfrey *Anger. A friend of Vogt's had recommended him after hearing him play in London. Years later Willan said that the numbers 3 and 13 had played an important part in his life and, since the invitation arrived on the third day of the third month in 1913 when Willan was 33, he decided to accept it; however, though Celtic mysticism (inherited or assumed) was an important element in his personality, it is likely that the decision was based more on economic necessity than on numerology. Three weeks after his arrival in Toronto he accepted the post of organist-choirmaster at St Paul's Anglican Church, Bloor St. In 1914 he was appointed a lecturer and examiner for the *U of Toronto. From 1919 to 1925 he served as music director of the university's *Hart House Theatre and in that capacity he wrote and conducted incidental music for 14 plays. In 1920 he became vice-principal of the TCM, a post he held until 1936, when he was dismissed during an economy wave (and amid considerable controversy; see Sir Ernest MacMillan). It has been said that Willan was not very effective as a TCM administrator, his interest tending much more strongly to composition and teaching; but some observers maintain that he resigned in protest against TCM internal politicking. In any case, the incident created a coolness between Willan and MacMillan which lasted for a number of years, though eventually they became reconciled. The controversy died down when Willan was appointed to the U of Toronto Faculty of Music in 1937 (see below).

In 1921 Willan's friend Father Griffin Hiscocks, rector of the small and impecunious mid-town Anglican Church of St Mary Magdalene, solicited his help in finding an organist-choirmaster. Willan nominated himself, resigned from St Paul's on 12 October (he called the act a birthday present from himself), and began an association with St Mary's that was to last till his death. In financial terms the move made no sense whatever, but Father Hiscocks was willing to give him sole charge of all aspects of music, with a free hand to alter the form of service and even the physical structure of the building if necessary. Willan proceeded to institute an Anglo-catholic style of service-music, a style first made evident in the Christmas services of 1921. He never regretted his decision to take the post; in 1963 he said, 'You have a sense of home, absolute completion ... doing the work you want to do and the work you feel you can do.'

Willan was a member of the *Arts and Letters Club of Toronto for more than 50 years, and in 1923 he was elected to a one-year term as the club's president. One of his first tongue-in-cheek acts was to set the constitution to music. The club was a convivial place where he was able to indulge his taste for stimulating intellectual conversation with his peers, enjoy the companionship of fellow artists, and occasionally partake of some of the noble liquid which gave rise to his remark: 'I am English by birth, Irish by extraction, Canadian by adoption, and Scotch by absorption.'

Willan served 1922–3 and 1933–5 as president of the CCO and later was made honorary president and life member of the *RCCO. He was university organist 1932–64 at the U of Toronto, in which post he was required to play at convocations and other ceremonial events and also to give a number of recitals for the students each year. His recital programs were respectable, though he didn't regard himself as a brilliant concert organist and claimed he couldn't play his own major works; generally, organ recitals bored him ('The organ is a dull instrument'), and he facetiously remarked that the only ones he could sit through were those he played himself. In 1933 he served as president of the Authors and Composers Assn of Canada, and in that same year he founded the Tudor Singers, a 10-voice mixed choir that he conducted in concerts of renaissance music until late 1939, when World War II forced its disbandment (see St Mary Magdalene Singers). In 1936 Willan was appointed chairman of the board of examiners in music at *Bishop's U. He taught counterpoint and composition 1937–50 at the U of Toronto and was a guest lecturer in the summers of 1937 and 1938 at the U of Michigan and in the summer of 1949 at the U of California at Los Angeles. In 1943 he was made chairman of the British Organ Restoration Fund, whose aim was to help finance the rebuilding of the organ at Coventry Cathedral. In 1950 he was a co-founder and music director of the Gregorian Assn of Toronto. In 1953 he acceded to the request of the Anglican bishop of Toronto to found and become music director of the Toronto Diocesan Choir School (see Choir schools).

Willan was commissioned to write the homage anthem *O Lord, Our Governour* for the coronation of Elizabeth II in 1953, the first non-resident of Britain to be so honoured. In 1955 he was made an honorary member of the *CLComp, and in 1956 he received the Lambeth Doctorate from the Archbishop of Canterbury, the highest award an Anglican musician can receive from his church and the one Willan prized most highly among all his honours. In 1958 he was made a fellow of the Ancient Monuments Society of England; in 1960 the RCCO established a scholarship in his honour; in 1961 he received the *Canada Council Medal; and in 1967 he was made a Companion of the *Order of Canada and received a diploma from the province of Ontario in recognition of his role in Canadian musical life. The RCCO in 1978 set up a committee to encourage activities marking the centenary of his birth; this evolved into the Healey Willan Centennial Celebration Committee, a group of admirers of Willan, under the chairmanship of Nicholas *Goldschmidt, dedicated to organizing events in his name throughout Canada during 1980. On 4 Jul 1980 the Canadian Post Office issued a commemorative stamp bearing a portrait of Willan. With Emma *Albani, who was commemorated in this way at the same time, he was the first Canadian musician to be honoured thus.

Willan's classroom pupils included Ewart *Bartley, Howard *Brown, Muriel *Gidley, Ida *Krehm, Glenn Kruspe, Horace *Lapp, Scott Malcolm, George *Maybee, Adelmo *Melecci, Stanley *Osborne, David *Ouchterlony, Charles *Peaker, Mgr *Ronan, Margaret *Sargent, Frederick *Silvester, Ernest *White, and Michael Winesanker. Also among his pupils were a few composers whose styles reflect his influence. These include Gerald *Bales, Patricia *Blomfield Holt, F.R.C. *Clarke, Margaret *Drynan, Robert *Fleming, Walter *MacNutt, and Godfrey Ridout. The influence is less apparent in the works of Louis *Applebaum, John *Beckwith, Kelsey *Jones, William *McCauley, Kenneth *Peacock, Eldon *Rathburn, and John *Weinzweig. Willan's daughter, Mary Willan Mason, was a founding member of the Junior *Vogt Society, which flourished from the late 1930s to 1941, and in 1975 became executive director of the *Ontario Choral Federation.

Willan's reputation rests not only on his compositions but also on his work in other fields. As a teacher he instructed by example and encouragement. Godfrey Ridout observed: 'He couldn't teach composition and didn't try to. Rather, he would engage in dialogue about works and suggest improvements.' Though Willan neither understood nor liked mid-20th-century music ('I hear only strange sounds which surprise and disturb me') he was able to maintain good relationships with pupils who did. As Applebaum said: 'He had no truck with some of the newer things that were going on, but that didn't matter ... It never stood in the way of an association between you and him.' As a conductor and choir-trainer he encouraged an appreciation of plainsong and renaissance music, and his ideals of choral tone were widely emulated. In lectures and articles and, above all, in the example he set at St Mary Magdalene, he waged constant war on unworthy church music. Finally, his stature as a public figure served as an encouragement to musicians of succeeding generations.

WILLAN'S MUSIC

Willan often referred to the mass, the central act of worship of his church, as a sacred drama. He also confessed a deep and abiding interest in Wagner. It thus is not surprising that he had a lifelong preoccupation with dramatic music: a 'scena' called *Cleopatra* dates from 1907, and he was working on *The Play of Our Lady* not long before his death. He himself regarded the opera **Deirdre* as his most important work, but this view is not held universally; *Deirdre* has been criticized for a lack of dramatic thrust and insufficient relief in its scoring, and for wearing its post-Wagnerian mantle too heavily. It is said, moreover, if truistically, that he did not write for the future or perhaps even for his own time. Recognizing this himself, he countered by claiming that beauty is timeless, and that his duty as a composer was to add to that beauty using accepted forms and language, rather than to search out the shape and sound of things to come. *Deirdre* remains a masterpiece, flawed perhaps, but full of appealing music. It shared with **Transit through Fire* and **Brébeuf* an origin as a work commissioned by the CBC for radio. *Brébeuf* had two subsequent performances in concert. *Deirdre* was revised quite extensively in 1962 and again in 1964–5 for stage performances. *The Beggar's Opera, The Order of Good Cheer*, and the four ballad-operas all were assembled from folksong sources (including French-Canadian and Indian), an interest that also found expression in numerous arrangements for solo voice and for choir.

The large-scale works for choir and orchestra show strong links with the past. Only occasionally are there hints of the much more personal style that is the mark of the best of his shorter works for unaccompanied choir. Representative of the 'larger' style is the *Te Deum laudamus in B Flat* in which noble elegiac tunes in straightforward harmony combine with bold antiphonal effects in a style reminiscent of Parry and Stanford. The introduction of beautiful lyric lines into this formula (visible perhaps most clearly in 'Come, Thou Beloved of Christ' from the *Coronation Suite* of 1953) recalls Gerald Finzi's approach to this kind of music. These ingredients also are present in many of the larger works for choir and organ, some of which have alternative accompaniments for instruments. There are several patriotic songs in this category as well as choral ballads and anthems.

Willan's orchestral and band works reflect the breadth, dignity, and long melodies he admired in Brahms. The shade of Elgar is there, too, but more in melody and in certain harmonic twists than in orchestration. The most frequent criticism of the two symphonies is directed at what is taken to be a weak sense of orchestral colour. Actually, as Godfrey Ridout has pointed out, the music is its own worst enemy in this matter – it seems to fight against glamour in its orchestration. A parallel with the music of Edmund Rubbra comes to mind. The second symphony, in C minor, definitely is the more popular, but the first does not deserve its comparative neglect. Several marches for band or orchestra tend to be conventional. By contrast, the *Piano Concerto in C Minor* is a surprise. One can find its derivations quite easily, but its vitality, tightness of construction, and flow, coupled with the pyrotechnics of the solo part, make it a work of strong attraction. One cannot claim for it a great depth, but it has immediate appeal and deserves many more hearings. It is significant that a comparison of earlier works in manuscript with later orchestral music shows very few differences in style and approach – indeed, the first movement of the *Symphony No. 1* contains music first sketched about 1910.

Few chamber works are extant. A 1974 performance of parts of a *Trio in B Minor* (1907–15) suggests a very fine work; unfortunately the work is not preserved in its entirety. The *Sonata No. 1 in E Minor* for violin and piano is a popular work in the late-romantic tradition, while the later *Sonata No. 2 in E* is a pastiche of a baroque suite. What exists of a projected string quartet, the *Poem* for string orchestra, makes one wish that more of the work had got past the sketch stage. There are numerous manuscript fragments of works in this genre. The lack of piano music is a disappointment. Only one major work exists: *Variations and Epilogue on an Original Theme* for two pianos. For the rest, Willan's piano output is strictly in the educational category.

With the music for organ one enters a different world. Here Willan was thoroughly at home and made a significant and lasting contribution. One work stands out: the monumental *Introduction, Passacaglia and Fugue* of 1916. Said to have been described by Joseph *Bonnet as the greatest of its genre since Bach (there is stiff competition from Rheinberger, Reger, and Karg-Elert) this is a virtuoso work of great depth, ingenuity, and variety. It is finely spaced and highly colourful. It represents the culmination of Willan's first period of organ composition, which started ca 1906 with a *Fantasia on 'Ad coenam agni.'* The *Preludes and Fugues* in C minor and B minor and the *Epilogue* are the other major works from this period. While not exploring the possibilities of the instrument as searchingly as his masterpiece, they are idiomatic and very typical of their time. They combine an innate Englishness (with a Stanfordian flavour) and a European chromaticism that can be found in Reger and Karg-Elert. (Willan knew and played a few pieces by the latter, but it is doubtful he had heard much Reger at the time he was writing these pieces.) Willan composed a few small pieces for the instrument over the next four decades, but it was not until 1950 that he returned seriously to organ composition. By then his style was considerably pruned and had become more contrapuntal. Chorale preludes were the most frequent expression 1950–60: *Six Chorale Preludes Sets I and II, Five Preludes on Plainchant Melodies*, and *Ten Hymn Preludes Sets I, II, and III* are the major collections. Even in free compositions the economy is evident; typical are *A Fugal Trilogy, Five Pieces for Organ*, and *Andante, Fugue and Chorale*. An exception is the *Passacaglia and Fugue No. 2*, in which he permits himself a more expansive utterance, with a fugue that is arguably his best essay in the form.

The church music takes one into yet another realm. The different religious observances for which he wrote brought forward remarkably different styles. For the Lutheran rite he worked in a simple, straightforward idiom, neither particularly lyrical nor very rich harmonically – a kind of religious Gebrauchsmusik. A *Missa brevis in G* (1954) is a good example, together with various commissioned sets – 7 motets, 10 anthems, and 7 hymn-anthems. For the regular Anglican services his style was closely related to that of the church composers who were the models of his formative years – which, we should remember, were the last two decades of the 19th century. Examples, from the first decade of the 20th, are *The Office of Holy Communion in G*, a *Te Deum in B Flat*, and the *Magnificat and Nunc dimittis in B Flat*. Later Willan threw off some of the chromaticism and the more overt lyricism of this style and wrote in a simpler diatonic vein with a greater reliance on imitation. Such mid-century works as *Magnificat and Nunc dimittis in E Flat*, 'Sing We Triumphant Songs,' and 'O Praise the Lord' show the more recent style at its best. Several hymn-anthems from the early 1960s are in similar vein.

The music composed for the Church of St Mary Magdalene is of a different type, reflecting the needs of the Anglo-catholic liturgy and exploiting its suggestions of a more mystical approach. Willan's deep interest in plainsong and polyphonic music, and his belief in their correctness for this type of service, are clearly evident in this music. Modality, melismatic vocal line, rhythmic freedom based on verbal accentuation, and a strong preoccupation with linear shape rather than vertical congruence combine to form a thoroughly personal idiom. It is this that separates this music from the rest of his output and makes it possibly his most important. The clearest examples are the 14 settings of the *Missa brevis* (1928–63), a set of 11 *Liturgical Motets* (1928–37), of which the three motets to Our Lady (B312–14) are deservedly the most popular, his many plainsong-with-fauxbourdons settings of the Canticles, and an earlier set of *Six Motets* and the *Responsaries for the Offices of Tenebrae* published in 1956. Willan's work as a practising church musician gave rise to a variety of lesser pieces, including hymn-tunes, sacred songs, fauxbourdons, introits, collections of anthems for junior choirs, and many carols and carol arrangements. Finally, three major works for choir must be mentioned. **An Apostrophe to the Heavenly Hosts* is a lengthy piece for unaccompanied double chorus with semi-chorus. Its style is unique in Willan's output, contrasting an almost Russian breadth and sonority with passages of very simple chordal writing in antiphony. 'Gloria Deo per immensa saecula' is more classical in form, consisting of a prelude and fugue. A neglected work, *The Mystery of Bethlehem*, a cantata in six movements, tempts revival.

There are several madrigals and part-songs as well as folksong arrangements for secular choirs, and more than 100 original songs, the vast majority of which are unknown. Willan himself held them in high regard, and they deserve re-examination.

The *NL of C became the custodian of the Willan papers in 1970 and mounted an exhibition – Healey Willan: The Man and His Music – in 1972. Coincident with this, the library published the *Healey Willan Catalogue* compiled by Giles *Bryant, the first such catalogue devoted to the work of a Canadian composer. A supplement was to be issued in 1981. In 1980 F.R.C. Clarke was preparing a study of Willan's life and music. Willan was an associate of the *CMCentre, and the musical rights of his estate are administered by PRO Canada.

See also Anglican church music; Anthems, motets, psalms; Cantata; Coronations; CPR Festivals; Masses; Organ music; Plainsong; Te Deum laudamus.

SELECTED COMPOSITIONS

Numbers given for each category are those assigned in the Bryant *Healey William Catalogue*.

DRAMATIC MUSIC (B1–B42)

The Beggar's Opera B19, ballad opera (Gay). 1927. V, fl, cl, str. FH 1928

The Order of Good Cheer B20, ballad opera (Louvigny de Montigny, transl J. M. Gibbon). 1928. TTBB, fl, ob, vn, vc, hpd. FH 1928

Hymn for Those in the Air B28, incidental music (D.C. Scott). 1942. Narr, sm orch. Ms

See also *Brébeuf* B29; *Deirdre* B30; *Transit through Fire* B27

14 sets of incidental music for Hart House Theatre, 5 other sets of incidental music, 4 other ballad operas (2 lost), other finished and unfinished works and fragments of works

VOCAL MUSIC WITH INSTRUMENTAL ENSEMBLE (B43–B64)

O Lord, Our Governour B56 (various Psalms). Ca 1953. SATB, orch. Ms. HMV ALP 1057 (combined choirs and orch, Boult cond)/1977. Vista VPS 1053 (Exultate Singers, G. O'Brien cond, T. Farrell org)

Coronation Suite B57 (Milton, J.E. Ward, Scriptures). 1952. SSATB, orch. BMIC 1953 (mvts 2, 4, 5). (Mvts 2, 5) RCI 118 (*CBC SO)/(mvt 5) RCA LSC 3043 (*Tor Mendelssohn Choir)

Also 9 large works for choir and orchestra

ORCHESTRA AND BAND (B65–B91a)

Symphony No. 1 B70. 1936. Full orch. Ber (rental)

Symphony No. 2 B74. 1941 (rev 1948). Full orch. Ber (rental). RCI 23 (*CBC SO)/CBC SM-133 (*TS)

Piano Concerto B76. 1944 (rev 1949). Ber (rental). RCI Canadian Album No. 1/RCA DM 1229 (all 78s – Agnes *Butcher pf)/CBC SM-205 (*Henig pf)

Royce Hall Suite for Concert Band B78. 1949. AMP 1952. CUWE-10 (Cornell U Wind Ens)

Overture to an Unwritten Comedy B79. 1951. Med orch. CMCentre. CBC SM-143 (*CBC Van Chamb O)

Three Fanfares B81. 1959. 4 tpt, 3 trb, timp. Ms

3 early works for orch; 12 other works for orch/band, including 5 marches; several unfinished works for orch

CHAMBER (B92–B120)

Trio in B Minor B98. 1907. Vn, vc, pf. Ms

Sonata No. 1 B100. 1916. Vn, pf. BMIC 1955. RCI 124 (*Pratz vn)

Sonata No. 2 B101. Ca 1921. Vn, pf. Bosworth 1923. RCI 42 (*Pratz vn)/RCI 243 (*Staryk vn)

Several unfinished works, including a *String Quartet*, B109, in E minor

PIANO (B121–B142)

ORGAN (B143–B212)

Prelude and Fugue B146. 1908. Novello 1908. Col MD 6798 (Francis Jackson)

Prelude and Fugue B147. 1909. Novello 1909

Introduction, Passacaglia and Fugue B149. 1916. G. Schirmer 1919. Odeon CSD 1550C (Jackson)

Rondino, Elegy and Chaconne B171. 1956. Novello 1957

Fugal Trilogy B176. 1958. OUP 1959, GVT 1973. ('No. 1') Col MS-6798 (Jackson)

Five Pieces for Organ B177. 1958. BMIC 1959. ('Fanfare') St Mark's Cathedral of Minneapolis, Sears SR 101568 (*Bales)

Passacaglia and Fugue No. 2 B178. Ca 1959. Peters 1959. Col MS-6798 (Jackson)/CBC SM-202 (F. *Geoghegan)

Numerous other works for org, including 97 chorale preludes and numerous arrs, some recorded by F. Geoghegan, Francis Jackson, H. *McLean, and Noel Rawsthorn

CHORAL (B212–B664)

The Mystery of Bethlehem B585, cantata (various liturgical sources, transl Athelstan Riley, John Mason Neale). Sop, bass, SATB, org, optional instr. Gray 1923; 1951

Six Motets B303–B308 (various). 1924. SATB. Gray 1924. (No. 1) RCI 11 (*St Mary Magdalene Singers)

'Gloria Deo per immensa saecula' B593 (York Doxology, transl Alan G. McDougall). 1950. SSATB. Western 1952. RCI 207/Cap ST 6248 (*Festival Singers)

The Story of Bethlehem B595 (Bible). 1955. Unison vs, SSAA, org. Concordia 1955

Red Carol Book B429 (various). Willan ed. SATB (unison), pf. FH 1930

Carols for the Seasons B442 (various). Willan arr. Unison (or SS or SA), keybd. Concordia 1959

Canadian Psalter B608, Plainsong Edition (Bible). Willan ed. Unison vs. Anglican Church of Canada 1963

'Hymne à l'occasion du Centenaire de la Confédération canadienne' / 'Anthem for the Centennial of Canadian Confederation' B611 (R. Choquette, Eng adap J. Glassco). 1966. SATB (TTBB or unison vs), pf. BMIC 1966. St Simon's Church T 55562-3 (St Simon's Choir, E. Hanson cond)

See also *An Apostrophe to the Heavenly Hosts* B584.

14 settings of the Missa brevis, 12 settings of the communion service, including Latin masses and Lutheran liturgy

39 fauxbourdons and 15 full settings of the Canticles

11 liturgical motets, over 20 miscellaneous motets

Over 40 anthems, over 30 hymn-anthems, 31 hymn tunes, over 40 fauxbourdons to hymn tunes, numerous plainsong adaptations

Some of the preceding have been recorded by choirs of the Cathedral Church of St Mark (Minneapolis, Minn), the Church of St Mary Magdalene (Toronto), the Church of St Simon-the-Apostle (Toronto), Grace Church on-the-Hill (Toronto), Washington Cathedral (Washington, DC), the *Bishop Strachan School Chapel Choir (Toronto), and the Central College Tudor Singers (Danville, Ky); the choirs of the College of St Nicholas (Chislehurst, England), Concordia College (Moorhead, Minn), and *York U; the Festival Singers; the

Mormon Tabernacle Choir; and the Toronto Mendelssohn Choir.

Among secular choral works: 15 part-songs B614–B664, 14 folksong arrs, other miscellaneous works, and over 100 original songs and numerous folksong arrs for v B665–B766, including *Chansons canadiennes* B743–B744. F. Harris reissued the *Healey Willan Song Albums* B736–B737 and *Songs of the British Isles* B741–B742 in 1980.

WRITINGS

The Bryant *Healey Willan Catalogue* lists 18 articles by Willan, including:

'On hymn playing,' *CQR*, vol 8, Spring 1926

'Church music in Canada,' Royal College of Organists *Calendar* (London 1936–7)

'Organ playing in its proper relation to music in the church,' *Diapason*, vol 29, Oct 1937

'What's wrong with church music in Canada,' *Cap and Gown*, 1959

DISCOGRAPHY

See 'Sound recordings' in the Bryant *Healey Willan Catalogue* for a listing of recordings of Willan's music to 1972; and sections 3 and 4 for listing of recordings and tapes made by and about Willan.

BIBLIOGRAPHY

An extensive bibliography and list of archival collections is included in the Bryant *Healey Willan Catalogue*.

'Mr. Healey Willan: a Canadian appointment,' *MT*, vol 54, no. 846, 1913

Hamilton, Henry C. 'Dr. Healey Willan,' *MCan*, vol 28, Dec 1928

Wood, Christopher. 'Healey Willan: eminent composer,' *CRMA*, vol 4, Oct–Nov 1945

Lehl, Allan P. 'The choral style of Healey Willan,' unpubl MA thesis, ESM, Rochester 1957

McCready, Louise G. *Famous Musicians: MacMillan, Johnson, Pelletier, Willan* (Toronto 1957)

Wagner, Jacob David. 'Healey Willan, his life and organ literature,' unpubl M Sacred MUS thesis, Union Theological Seminary, New York 1957

Ridout, Godfrey. 'Healey Willan,' *CMJ*, vol 3, Spring 1959

Brown, Tom. 'Healey Willan,' *MSc*, 238, Nov–Dec 1967

Coulter, John. 'Lament for Healey Willan,' poem in Arts and Letters Club *Monthly Letter*, Feb 1968

Drynan, George K. and Margaret. 'Healey Willan: his last days,' *Diapason*, vol 59, Apr 1968

MacMillan, Sir Ernest. 'Healey Willan ... 1880–1968,' ibid

Telschow, Frederick H. 'The sacred music of Healey Willan,' unpubl PH D thesis, ESM, Rochester 1969

Marwick, William E. 'The sacred choral music of Healey Willan,' unpubl PH D thesis, Michigan State U 1970

Bryant, Giles. *Healey Willan Catalogue* (Ottawa 1972)

Beckwith, John. 'Healey Willan,' *Canadian Forum*, vol 52, Dec 1972

Johnson, Norman. 'Healey Willan (1880–1968): his life and influences important to his music,' unpubl DMA thesis, Southern Baptist Theological Seminary 1979

Jones, Donald. 'St. Mary Magdalene Church inspired organ masterpieces,' *Toronto Star*, 12 May 1979

Kraglund, John. 'Bumper times ahead for Healey Willan fans,' Toronto *Globe and Mail*, 11 Jan 1980

Bryant, Giles. 'Healey Willan – a personal view,' *MSc*, 311, Jan–Feb 1980

Issue devoted to Willan. *Mcan*, 42, Spring 1980

FILMOGRAPHY

Music In the Wind (NFB 1945)

Man of Music (NFB 1959) TCB, GBr

WILLIAMS. Family: 1 / Ifan, and 2 / Ifan, his son.

1 **Ifan**. Violinist, teacher, conductor, b Carmarthen, Wales, November 1889, naturalized Canadian, d London September 1957; FRAM 1940. He studied at the RAM and was principal violin of its quartet and orchestra. He won numerous prizes and scholarships for violin and chamber music and for several years was a member of the London SO, the Opera Orchestra (presumably Covent Garden), and the Blagrove String Quartette and gave many solo recitals in London and in the provinces. He arrived in Canada in 1920 and was director of the string department, and director 1934–57, of the Halifax Cons (see Maritime Cons). He taught several instruments there and made the conservatory orchestra into a competent ensemble which actively contributed to the local music scene. He founded the Halifax Choral Union (later *Halifax Choral Society) in 1922 and the Ifan Williams String Quartette in 1930. In 1935 he was one of the main organizers of the first Halifax music competition festival. On 13 Jul 1949 he conducted the premiere of Trevor Jones' *Symphony to Halifax* – to a text by Mrs A.G. Baird. The work was composed for the city's bicentenary and dedicated 'to Ifan Williams and the Halifax Choral Union.' During these years, recognizing the need to provide a future supply of musicians for the province, he made pioneering efforts to establish in the Halifax public schools a concert band and an orchestra; these achieved reality only after his time.

2 **Ifan**. Cellist, teacher, b Halifax 10 Jul 1945. He studied cello 1958–64 with Edward *Bisha and was a member 1961–2 of the *NYO. At the Manhattan School of Music, New York, he worked 1964–6 with Bernard Greenhouse (cello) and studied chamber music with Arthur Balsam, Lilian Fuchs, and Benar Heifetz. He then went to England, where he was a member of the Bournemouth SO in 1967, the New Philharmonia of London in 1968, and the London SO in 1969. On his return to Canada in 1970 he joined the *Atlantic SO as principal cello. He was artist-in-residence 1971–3 at the *U of New Brunswick and taught in 1973 at *Mount Allison U. He was a member 1973–6 of the *Classical Quartet of Montreal and of *Musica Camerata Montreal and in 1976 he became principal cello with the Stratford Ensemble and the *Kitchener-Waterloo SO. His performance with that orchestra of the Boccherini *Concerto* exhibited, according to W.J. Pitcher, a 'sunny radiance in the cello tone ... style, technique and musicianship of a high order' (*Kitchener-Waterloo Record*, 31 Jan 1977). In 1977–8, with Irving Ilmer and Raffi *Armenian, Williams presented the complete cycle of Beethoven's piano trios and sonatas in the chapel of Conrad Grebel College (U of Waterloo). 1 / NT, 2 / AP

R.S. Williams & Sons. Instrument building and sales firm established by Richard Sugden Williams (b London 12 Apr 1834, d Toronto 24 Feb 1906). Taken to Hamilton, Upper Canada (Ontario), at four, Williams in the late 1840s was apprenticed to the melodeon maker William Townsend in Toronto. He opened an instrument repairshop in Hamilton (some sources say Kingston) in 1849. He established a business in Toronto in 1854 and began making mandolins, banjos, and, soon afterwards, melodeons. Williams also sold pianos and other instruments and expanded into the manufacturing of pianos and larger reed organs. In 1873 the manufacturing was assumed by the subsidiary Canada Organ and Piano Co (after 1902 Williams Piano Co), and in 1889 the factory was moved to Oshawa, Ont, supervised by Williams' son Robert, who became the company's president after his father's death.

The Toronto business, in 1879 renamed R.S. Williams & Son (later Sons), remained the headquarters for retailing (first on Queen St, later at several successive locations on Yonge St) and also for wholesaling. In the early years there was a sales outlet in London, Ont. By 1905 a branch had been established in Winnipeg and a depot in London (England), and by 1919 there were branches in Montreal and Calgary.

Expansion was rapid. By the end of the century the firm claimed to have the largest instrument factory in Canada. In the 1880s some 150 workers produced about 20 pianos and 6 reed organs each week; in the second decade of the 20th century some 250 men produced about 60 pianos a week. Two Williams pianos were placed in Windsor Castle at the request of Queen Victoria, thus entitling the company to use the crest 'Piano Makers to the Queen.' By the turn of the century grand pianos, uprights, and player pianos were manufactured. Brand names (then or later) included Beethoven, Canada, Ennis, Everson, Krydner, Schubert, and Williams. In 1929 serial numbers had reached 67,000. Williams also built a few pipe organs. One of these (from a church whose identity cannot be ascertained) was reinstalled in 1898 at St Paul's Roman Catholic Church in Toronto and was restored in the 1970s, since it was found still ideally suited for use in the liturgy.

The R.S. Williams & Sons factory in the early 20th century

Mandolins, banjos, and guitars continued to be built, but Williams' successor in the Toronto establishment, his son Richard Sugden Williams Jr (1874–1945), was renowned as an expert in violins. A stock of valuable imported string instruments was maintained, and skilled craftsmen from France, Holland, Italy, and Canada were employed to make violins after Stradivarius and other patterns. One of these was the Paris violin builder August Delivet, who worked for R.S. Williams in Toronto from 1920 until his death in 1927. The firm's illustrated instrument and merchandise catalogues, produced as early as 1860 (no. 31 dates from 1905, no. 36 from 1919), testify to the volume and variety of the business.

By 1900 Williams had become the Canadian distributor for Edison phonographs and records. This association continued until 1926, but when radio for a while replaced recordings in popularity, Williams began to sell Westinghouse, and later Magnavox, radios. A small amount of music publishing was done, but the Williams Musical Library (only 8 numbers known; late 19th century) contained little of significance. Arrangements for band by John *Slatter were advertised in 1919, and also at that time the firm published the *Canadian Bandsman and Orchestra Journal*, a monthly which had begun as the *Canadian Bandsman and Musician* in June 1913 and was absorbed by *Musical Canada* in 1924. Yet another venture of the company was an R.S. Williams School of Music, opened in Toronto in 1929 under the directorship of A.L. Evans.

The Oshawa factory, of which the last president was Frank W. Bull, did not survive the Depression years. The Toronto company, sold to B.A. and F.A. Trestrail in 1928, eventually closed its Yonge St store but continued as a warehouse-type operation until 1951 or 1952, thus making Williams one of the few Canadian music firms to have existed for over 100 years. The last president was Alexander B. Vasey.

The elder Williams was an avid collector of old musical instruments and autographs, exhibiting his collections as early as 1861 at the Toronto Mechanics' Institute. His son Richard S. Jr added to the collection but in 1913 began to present segments to the Royal Ontario Museum. At that time there were 166 instruments, 70 volumes of music, and about 160 letters and manuscript scores of famous musicians. In the late 1970s the R.S. Williams collection remained the largest and most valuable of its kind in Canada. (In 1980 Ladislav Cselenyi was preparing a book on R.S. Williams.)

See also Archives; Instrument collections.

BIBLIOGRAPHY

R.S. Williams musical merchandise catalogues. Representative issues at NL of C and Royal Ontario Museum

'75th anniversary of R.S. Williams & Sons Co., Ltd., an important event this year,' *CMTJ*, vol 25, Sep 1924

'Williams Piano Co., Ltd., Oshawa, celebrates its 75th anniversary,' *CMTJ*, vol 25, Nov 1924

Also information in other issues of *CMTJ*, 1900–32

Henley, William. *Universal Dictionary of Violin and Bow Makers*, vol 5 (Brighton 1960)

Cselenyi, Ladislav, ed. *Musical Instruments in the Royal Ontario Museum* (Toronto 1971)

Windeler, Janet. 'Williams' old junk became museum gem,' *Fugue*, vol 2, Nov 1977 (FH, HK, CM)

Willis & Company Ltd. Montreal piano retailer and manufacturer. At first a retailer of sewing machines, the firm was established at Stellarton, NS, in 1871 and re-established in Montreal in 1875 by A.P. (Alexander Parker) Willis (1845–1934) following his move in 1873 from his native Nova Scotia. In the mid-1880s the piano and organ trade was developed, and by 1888 sewing machines were discontinued. Willis & Co retailed the major Canadian pianos and the Knabe piano from Baltimore. Beginning in 1889 the firm briefly distributed in Quebec the Emerson piano from Boston, and about 1900 it acquired a majority of the shares of the *Lesage & Fils piano factory at Ste-Thérèse-de-Blainville (renamed Ste-Thérèse), near Montreal, to engage in its own manufacturing. The firm sold about 2000 pianos in 1907, including its own and those of the *Dominion, *Newcombe, and Knabe companies. It also represented Dominion Organs, the Cecilian grand piano of Detroit, and the Cable Co of Chicago. Between 1910 and 1925, retail outlets were opened in several Canadian cities, and in March 1914 the main retail centre was established in Montreal at the corner of Drummond St and Ste-Catherine St W. By then the firm also represented Chickering pianos in Canada and the Ampico player piano. The Willis grand piano, first built in 1925 for the company's golden jubilee, did not remain in the Willis line. The company's five-year production fluctuated over the years, ranging from 10,000 (1915–20) down to 850 (1930–5). In 1966 1600 instruments were built. The Willis catalogue of the mid-1970s included eight types of upright piano. The company went bankrupt in 1979. (EK)

WILSON. Winnipeg family of musicians: 1 / J. Kerr Wilson, 2 / Thelma, his wife, 3 / Carlisle and 5 / Eric, their sons, and 4 / Kerrine, their daughter.

1 **J.** (James) **Kerr**. Baritone, choir director, b Winnipeg, of Irish parents, 9 May 1917. He studied voice with Stanley *Hoban and Winona Lightcap in Winnipeg and later with Ernesto *Vinci in Toronto. He was soloist and choir director at Crescent Fort Rouge United Church in the late 1940s and at St James United Church after 1953; he also gave many joint recitals with his wife throughout Manitoba and performed regularly on CBC radio's 'Cross-Canada Matinee' in the 1950s and 'The Happy Land' 1948–53. In 1959 he was invited by the lieutenant-governor of Manitoba to sing at Government House, Winnipeg, for Queen Elizabeth II.

2 **Thelma** (b Guttormson). Pianist, teacher, b Winnipeg, of Icelandic parents, 12 Apr 1919; ATCM 1935, LRSM 1935. She studied in Winnipeg with Louise McDowell and Leonard *Heaton and developed a busy career as a solo performer, accompanist, and teacher. She has given many joint recitals with her husband and with Eric (in Switzerland in 1971 and in Iceland in 1976) and Carlisle and has accompanied many other Winnipeg musicians. She was president of the *Junior Musical Club of Winnipeg 1947–9, the *Wednesday Morning Musicale 1968–9, and the *CFMTA 1975–9.

3 (John) **Carlisle**. Violinist, teacher, adjudicator, b Winnipeg 21 May 1944; AMM 1953, BFA (Wisconsin) 1958, B ED (Manitoba) 1973. His teachers included Egon Grapentin, Anne *Pomer, Victor Pomer, George Rutherford, and John *Waterhouse, all in Winnipeg, and Abe Loft at the U of Wisconsin. In 1977 he was appointed instrumental music consultant for the Winnipeg school system, a post he still held in 1980. He joined the *Winnipeg SO in 1977 and was conductor of the Winnipeg Junior Youth Orchestra 1977–9 and the Winnipeg Youth Orchestra 1979–80.

4 (Thelma) **Kerrine** (m Stewart-Hay). Pianist, teacher, b Winnipeg 21 Jun 1946; AMM 1963, LMM 1968, B MUS (Manitoba) 1969. She studied piano in Winnipeg with Jean *Broadfoot, at the *Banff SFA with Boris *Roubakine in 1962 and Pierre *Souvairan in 1963, and at the U of Manitoba 1966–9 with William *Aide and Leonard *Isaacs. A piano teacher and accompanist, she also has performed as part of a trio with her father and her brother Eric. She served 1973–5 as president of the Junior Musical Club of Winnipeg.

5 **Eric** (James). Cellist, b Winnipeg 23 Sep 1949; B MUS (Juilliard) 1972, M MUS (Juilliard) 1973, D MUS (Juilliard) 1979. He studied in Winnipeg 1955–9 with Kenneth *Murphy, 1959–60 with Peggie *Sampson, and 1960–5 with Claude *Kenneson. Other teachers included Leonard Rose at the Meadowmount School, New York State (summers 1962–4), Guy Fallot and Paul Tortelier at the *JMC Orford Art Centre (summers 1966–8), and Leonard Rose and Harvey Shapiro during his years at the Juilliard School. He won a bronze medal at the 1971 Geneva International Competition and the Morris Loeb Prize in 1972 and also received *Canada Council doctoral fellowships in 1974, 1975, and 1976. Following his 1965 orchestral debut with the Winnipeg SO (Saint-Saëns' *Concerto in A Minor*), he was solo cello 1971–5 of the Juilliard Ensemble and principal cello 1972–4 of the Juilliard Theatre Orchestra. In 1972 he became the cello of the Emerson String Quartet, which has performed in Cleveland, New York, Los Angeles, San Francisco, and Washington, DC, and which won the Naumburg Award in 1978. Wilson has appeared in recital and as a soloist with orchestras in England, Scandinavia, and the USA. In Canada he has given public recitals in Toronto and Winnipeg and has appeared with the CBC Festival Orchestra. He has been heard over the PBS radio network in the USA. In 1970 with the Juilliard Orchestra he gave the New York premiere of the Ligeti *Cello Concerto*, and in 1973 with the Juilliard Chamber Ensemble he gave the North American premiere of Peter Maxwell Davies' *Icons*. He has given master classes at the *U of Alberta and has taught at the San Francisco Cons and the U of Hawaii in Honolulu. In 1979 he joined the Dept of Music at the *U of British Columbia. KW

WILSON, Charles (Mills). Composer, choir conductor, teacher, b Toronto 8 May 1931; B MUS (Toronto) 1952, D MUS (Toronto) 1956. He began piano lessons at six with Wilfred Powell and later studied organ with Charles *Peaker. After writing his first sonata he was encouraged by his high-school music teacher, Harvey *Perrin, to study composition with Godfrey *Ridout at the *RCMT. Although he also attended the Berkshire Music Centre, Tanglewood, studying in 1950 with Lukas Foss and in 1951 with Carlos Chávez, Wilson recognizes Ridout as the strongest influence among his teachers. After a year at the *U of Saskatchewan, Saskatoon, where he taught harmony, conducted the university choir, and completed his doctoral thesis, *Symphony in A* (1956), he was organist-choirmaster 1954–64 at Chalmers United Church, *Guelph. As founder and conductor (1955–74) of the Guelph Light Opera and Oratorio Co (later the Guelph Opera and Concert Singers) he used local singers to present one oratorio and one musical annually. During these years he conducted choirs and bands and taught high school in the Guelph area and was for a time music supervisor of Guelph Township public schools. He conducted 1962–74 the *Bach-Elgar Choir of Hamilton but resigned to devote his time to study and composition.

Although Wilson has composed successful orchestral and chamber works, vocal music claimed his main attention after 1966, as witness his two-hour centenary oratorio *The Angels of the Earth* (premiered Guelph, 1967, by the Guelph Light Opera Company, the Bach-Elgar Choir, and the soloists Mary *Morrison and James Bechtel) and his operas, *The Summoning of Everyman*, *Heloise and Abelard*, and *Kamouraska*. Most of his major works between 1967 and 1980 were commissions, for the *COC, the *Canadian Children's Opera Chorus, the *Festival Singers, *Canadian Brass, and *Dalhousie U.

Psycho Red, the full-length opera commissioned for the 1978 *Guelph Spring Festival – to a libretto by Eugene Benson which treats the triangular role-reversals of a psychiatrist, his wife, and his patient – is resourceful in achieving a neo-Bergian expressionism with a limited orchestra (viola, two flutes, two clarinets, piano, trombone, harp, three percussion, and six-voice choir). The use of the choir as part of the orchestral fabric, and of dances to enact the interior states of the three characters, gives *Psycho Red* its most distinctive sonic and dramatic aspects.

Wilson's style is eclectic – fundamentally diatonic but incorporating serial procedures, electronics, and an occasional mixing of media as ingredients in an expressionist fabric natural to the theatre and invigorating to his concert works. His *Concerto 5 × 4 × 3* and his 'Dona nobis pacem' are recorded. He is an associate of the *CMCentre and a member of CAPAC.

SELECTED COMPOSITIONS

STAGE

The Strolling Clerk from Paradise, chamb opera (Hans Sachs). Ca 1952. Ms

Ballet Score (based on Canadian Indian legend). 1969. Ms

Johnny Fibber, play for children (P.J. Spensley). 1970. Ms

Phrases from Orpheus (D.G. Jones). 1970. SATB, dancers. Ms

The Selfish Giant, children's opera (Oscar Wilde). 1972. CMCentre

The Summoning of Everyman, church opera (Benson, adapted from 15th-century morality play). 1972. CMCentre

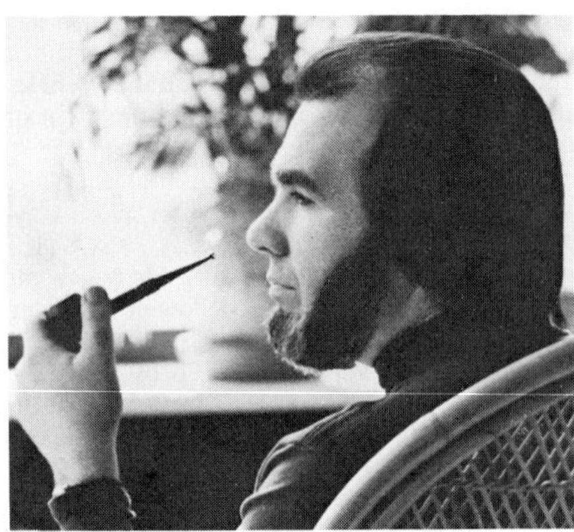

Charles Wilson

Kamouraska, opera (Anne Hébert). 1975. Ms
Psycho Red, 'a dramatic mindscape' (Benson). 1977. CMCentre
See also *Heloise and Abelard*.
ORCHESTRA, SOLOISTS AND/OR CHOIR AND ORCHESTRA
Symphony in A. 1953. Orch. Ms
Sonata da Chiesa for Oboe and Strings. 1960. CMCentre
Cantata 'On the Morning of Christ's Nativity' (Milton, Crashaw, Eliot, Donne). 1963. Sop, ten, bar, SATB, orch. CMCentre
The Angels of the Earth, oratorio (Wilson MacDonald). 1966. Sop, bar, narrs, SATB, orch. CMCentre. See also Oratorios, Canadian: 13.
Theme and Evolutions for Orchestra. 1966. Ms
En Guise d'Orphée. 1968. Bar, str orch. Ms
Sinfonia for Double Orchestra. 1972. CMCentre
Christo paremus canticam (Thomas Traherne, anon). 1973. SATB, orch. CMCentre
Symphonic Perspectives 'Kingsmere.' 1974. Full orch. CMCentre
CHAMBER
3 *String Quartets*. 1950, 1968, 1975. All CMCentre
String Trio. 1963. CMCentre
Concerto 5 × 4 × 3. 1970. Str quin or ww quar or brass trio. CMCentre. 1972. CBC SM-195 (Atlantic Brass Ens)
CHOIR AND VOICE
Three Madrigals on Latin Lyrics (Chaucer, Abelard, anon). 1964. SATB. CMCentre
'And Now Bless the God of All' (Sirach). SATB, org. Wat 1965
'Dona nobis pacem' (liturgical). 1970. SATB, brass (org). GVT 1972. Poly 2917 009 (*Festival Singers)
Image out of Season (various authors). 1973. SATB, brass quin. CMCentre
Missa brevis. 1975. SATB, brass (org). CMCentre
Song for St Cecilia's Day (Auden). 1976. Sop, ten, SATB, orch. CMCentre
Also 6 sets of songs on texts by Stevenson, Blake, D.G. Jones, Spenser, St-Denys-Garneau (transl J. Glassco), and Hébert (1951, 1953, 1962, 1974, 1976, 1977)

BIBLIOGRAPHY

Wolfond, Barbara. 'Two works premiered by Dr. Charles Wilson,' *CanComp*, 30, Jun 1968
Schulman, M. 'Heloise and Abelard – what price Canadian operas?' *PfAC*, vol 10, Winter 1973
Contemporary Canadian Composers / Compositeurs canadiens contemporains (RMr)

WILSON, Leonard. Organist-choirmaster, composer, lecturer, writer, b near Manchester 1911, d Vancouver 22 Apr 1963; LTCL 1929, hon FTCL 1947. Though his family emigrated to Canada when he was 9, Wilson returned to England at 18 for five years of study at the TCL and the RSCM. His teachers included Sydney Nicholson, George Oldroyd, and Dom Anselm Hughes. He was organist 1935–48 at St Michael's Anglican Church, Vancouver, and organist-choirmaster thereafter at the same city's St James Anglican Church, where he developed a standard of high-church musical service similar to that of the renowned choirs of Healey *Willan at the Church of St Mary Magdalene in Toronto. He was appointed local representative of the *TCL in 1942. His compositions included masses, introits, and fauxbourdons. A CBC program about his choir-training methods – 'And Places Where They Sing' – was telecast nationally 24 Mar 1963. Wilson taught liturgical music at the Anglican Theological College, *U of British Columbia, and gave many talks and recitals for the CBC. Some of his lectures were published in *Music of Western Man* (London, Toronto, Vancouver 1958) edited by Peter Garvie from the CBC radio series of that name. Wilson began writing for newspapers in the 1930s and was the regular reviewer 1961–3 for the *Vancouver Sun*. It is said that he was a gentle critic, but his opinions were respected. He was a vice-president of the *RCCO and also, 1957–9, of the *BCRMTA, which established a scholarship in his name after his death. The CBC Vancouver Choir, directed by Hugh *McLean, recorded (RCI 255) his *Lord's Prayer* and his *Missa brevis No. 2*, and for the same disc McLean recorded his organ pieces *Meditation*, *Canzona*, and *Antiphon*.

BIBLIOGRAPHY

'One man's busy week,' *CBC Times*, 23–9 Mar 1963 MDr

WILSON, W. (William) **Knight**. Conductor, teacher, violinist, b Leven, Fifeshire, Scotland, 1887, d Toronto 10 Sep 1961. A pupil of J.M. Cooper and Henri Verbrugghen at the Glasgow Atheneum (the Scottish National Academy of Music), he played in the Scottish SO under Wood, Elgar, and Richter. After his arrival in Canada in 1920 he conducted an Ottawa orchestra until 1922, then was a concertmaster in Toronto. He settled in Regina in 1923 and joined the faculty of the *Regina Cons, where he became director of the string department and organized a junior orchestra. In 1923 he became conductor of a choral-orchestral ensemble which under his direction became the *Regina SO in 1926. He also founded the Knight Wilson String Quartet. During service 1941–5 in the Royal Canadian Ordnance Corps, he organized and directed army bands across the country. Wilson returned to the Regina SO as conductor, remaining until 1955 when he began teaching violin, viola, and orchestration at the *Mount Royal College in Calgary. His pupils included John Thornicroft (who conducted the Regina SO during World War II), Frans Colquhoun, and Jean Fraser.

BIBLIOGRAPHY

Graham, Helen. 'Violinist-conductor vital to city's musical story,' Regina *Leader-Post*, 28 Apr 1979 WLB

WINCHESTER, Jesse (James Ridout). Singer-songwriter, guitarist, pianist, b Shreveport, La, 17 May 1944, naturalized Canadian 1973. Though raised in Memphis, he began his career in Germany in the mid-1960s with a rock band, the Night Sounds. He returned to Memphis but moved in 1967 to Canada to evade the US draft, a fact which lent him a certain notoriety. He worked first in nightclubs throughout Quebec with Les Astronautes, then as a solo performer in coffeehouses in all of eastern Canada. Discovered by Jamie Robbie Robertson (of The *Band), he made his first LP, the widely acclaimed *Jesse Winchester* (1970, Bearsville BR 2012), with Robertson as producer. He toured Canada in 1970 as the opening feature of The Band's concerts and continued to appear in coffeehouses such as the *Riverboat. Despite the popularity of his records in the USA, he was unable to perform there until the amnesty of 1977. He therefore expanded his Canadian activities to include concert hall appearances and toured Europe in 1976. Maintaining his Montreal home, he made his US debut 4 May 1977 at the New York club, the Bottom Line. His most popular songs, including 'Yankee Lady' and 'Brand New Tennessee Waltz,' have been recorded by Joan Baez, the Everly Brothers, Fairport Convention, Wilson Pickett, and others. His own other LPs (to 1979, and all but the last recorded in Canada for the US Bearsville label) were *Third Down, 110 to Go* (BR 2102) – the title an allusion to Canadian football – *Learn to Love It* (BR 6593), *Let the Rough Side Drag* (BR 6964), *Nothing But a Breeze* (BR 6968), and *A Touch on the Rainy Side* (BR 6984). According to Melinda McCracken, 'His songs have an unidentifiable quality, a trace of American romanticism about them, whispers of Vermont, Tennessee, Biloxi, a Yankee Lady, with a very soft feeling to them – there are no edges either in his voice, his electric guitar, which he uses with a round, light tone, or in the words to his songs' (Toronto *Globe and Mail*, 21 Jan 1970).

BIBLIOGRAPHY

MacGregor, Roy. 'Reb without a cause,' *The Canadian*, 9 Aug 1975 MM

Windsor. Southern Ontario city across the Detroit River from Detroit, Mich. First settled in 1834, it was established as the western terminus of the Great Western Railway in 1854 and was incorporated as a town in 1858 and as a city in 1892. It became an automobile manufacturing centre after the Ford Motor Co established a plant in Windsor in 1904. The population of metropolitan Windsor was 196,000 in 1976.

Throughout Windsor's history, choral music has been important. A typical program at All Saints Anglican Church, 12 Mar 1875, offered excerpts from Haydn's *The Creation*, a Mozart mass, Spohr's *Last Judgement*, and Handel's *Messiah*. H. Whorlow Bull (b England 1872, d Windsor 1938) conducted the 100-150-voice Windsor and Walkerville Choral Society 1905–19, during which time it performed *Messiah* (twice), *Elijah* (twice), Mendelssohn's *Hymn of Praise*, Handel's *Judas Maccabaeus*, Gounod's *Faust* (concert performance), Elgar's *For the Fallen*, Stanford's *The Revenge*, Hubert Bath's *The Wedding of Shon Maclean*, and other works. The society usually was accompanied by organ, but sometimes by organ and piano, and occasionally by small orchestra. Oratorios later were performed by the *Border Scottish Choir of Windsor, formed in 1924 and conducted by Bull, the Schubert Choir, formed in 1926, the Windsor Choral Union, formed in 1940, the Windsor Choral Society, established in 1956, and many church choirs.

Before 1920 some 13 Windsor bands performed in light opera, presentations of sacred music, minstrel shows, and military functions. Among the light operas were Richard Stahl's *Said Pascha* in 1900 and Gilbert & Sullivan's *H.M.S. Pinafore* in 1901. Henry Philp was the leader, ca 1925, of the Ford City Brass Band and of the Windsor Battalion Band. Phil Murphy (1902–75) settled in Windsor in 1927 and formed a service club band for boys. After active service as a bandmaster in World War II he returned to the city, and in 1948 he formed the Windsor Federation of Musicians Concert Band (later the 'Music Under the Stars' concert band). In addition Murphy served 1961–74 as conductor of the Detroit Fire Dept Band and was music director of the Windsor Light Opera. Another Windsor bandmaster, prominent in the 1940s and 1950s, was Peter C. Allan, president of the CBA (*CBDA) 1953–4 and a composer of works for band and solo band instruments, many published by *Waterloo.

Attempts to train an amateur orchestra were begun in the early 1920s by the violin teacher Henry

McCaw and continued by H.P.C.S. Stewart, organist at St Andrew's Church. The Border Cities Amateur Orchestral Society, said to have been formed in 1923, may have been McCaw's orchestra or a separate ensemble. The *Windsor SO, founded in 1947 under Matti Holli, became the city's permanent orchestral ensemble and has performed mainly in the Cleary Auditorium. The International Youth SO was founded by Holli in 1966 with board and orchestra personnel from both sides of the US-Canadian border. The Windsor Light Opera Assn began its annual productions of operetta and musical comedies in 1949.

Organizations which, over the years, have sponsored recitals and lectures have included the Windsor Musical Society, founded in 1875, the Derthick Musical and Literary Club, founded ca 1890, the Music, Literature and Art Club, founded in 1903, and the Matinée Musicale, founded in 1926. For chamber and orchestra concerts Windsor residents have benefited from the proximity of Detroit. However, the development and maintenance of Windsor's own ensembles have been inhibited to a degree by that very convenience.

Instruction in music began in 1864 at St Mary's Academy, the first Ontario school of the Sisters of the Holy Names of Jesus and Mary. Salomon *Mazurette taught music there while living in Detroit in the mid-1870s, and his compositions *Recollections of the Past* (Whitney) and a scherzo valse *The Turtle Dove* (Whitney) bore the inscription 'expressly for and dedicated to the pupils of St. Mary's Academy, Windsor, Ont.' In the 1890s and early 1900s private music teaching was supplemented by the Windsor Cons of Music, the Grovenberg Academy, and a Windsor branch of the Detroit Institute of Music. Only the Ursuline School of Music (founded in 1915) and St Mary's Academy continued in the 1970s. Assumption College offered music as part of its curriculum in 1894. H. Whorlow Bull, who in 1909 became supervisor of music in the public schools of Windsor and Walkerville, introduced Tonic Sol-fa and an annual music festival. However, by 1925 Windsor was more dependent on the Detroit Cons, the Detroit Institute of Musical Art, and the Detroit School of Music for musical instruction. The *U of Windsor music courses, introduced in 1959, and its B MUS program, introduced in 1967, were a sign of Windsor's growing independence.

The *Brothers-In-Law, formed in 1963, have been a successful Windsor pop group. Among musicians born in Windsor have been the singer Iris Bala, Victor *Braun, Marguerite *Gignac, the guitarist Stacey Heydon, Margo *MacKinnon, the soprano Jeannine Morand, Émile *Normand, the rock musicians Skip Spence and Jack Scott, and Jerry and Tony *Toth. Musicians born in the surrounding region include Patricia Snell *Crum and Lorne *Watson from Leamington (also the home of the *Leamington Choral Society), Jeanne *Gordon from Wallaceburg, Douglas *Millson from Kingsville, and Sylvia *Tyson from Chatham. The soprano Emilia Cundari received her early training at St Mary's Academy.

BIBLIOGRAPHY
Mason, Lawrence. 'Ontario vistas: II: the border cities,' Toronto *Globe*, 11 Jul 1925
Hall, Frederick A. 'Musical life in Windsor: 1875–1901,' *CMB*, 6, Spring–Summer 1973 (FAH, PMW)

Windsor Hall / Salle Windsor. A hall of 1300 seats adjoining the Montreal hotel of the same name and located on the corner of Peel and Dorchester streets. Built in 1890, it was demolished in 1906 after having served for numerous musical events. The first *MSO gave its concerts there from 1894 until the end of the 1902–3 season. In October

Windsor Hall, the concert hall at the Windsor Hotel, Montreal

1896 the orchestra of the *Metropolitan Opera gave three concerts there under Anton Seidl, and in 1903 Sir Alexander Mackenzie conducted three concerts of English music during the *Cycle of Musical Festivals. Among the many celebrities who performed there were Paderewski, *Albani, Yvette Guilbert, Teresa Carreno, Pol Plançon, Emil Sauer, Moriz Rosenthal, Vladimir de Pachmann, Lillian Nordica, Béatrice *La Palme, Raoul Pugno, Mark *Hambourg, the Kneisel Quartet, Ernestine Schumann-Heink, Josef Hofmann, and Eugène Ysaÿe. In February 1904 the Pittsburgh SO, conducted by Victor Herbert, gave a concert there. The *Montreal Philharmonic Society held its concerts at the hall from 1890 until its disbandment in 1899, and the *Montreal Oratorio Society presented most of its concerts there 1902–6. An advertisement of the time describes Windsor Hall as 'a magnificent hall with incomparable acoustical qualities.' Later, concerts were given in the hotel's ballroom, which also bore the name Windsor Hall.

BIBLIOGRAPHY
De Vaux, Agathe. 'L'histoire de l'OSM,' *Variations*, vol 1, Jan 1978 GP

Windsor Symphony Orchestra. Community orchestra founded in 1947 in Windsor, Ont, by Matti Holli. Its first concert was given 16 Nov 1947 at Patterson Collegiate. Broadcasts on CKLW-FM began in 1948. After performing at Walkerville Collegiate and at the Tivoli Theatre, the orchestra made Cleary Auditorium its permanent home in 1961. Membership has grown from about 45 musicians presenting 10 concerts annually in the 1950s to some 65 players (each of whom received some remuneration) giving 15 concerts annually in the 1970s. In 1977 a concertmaster, principal second violin, viola, and cello were employed on a full-time basis. Soloists have included Otto *Armin, Joseph *Macerollo, Cornelis *Opthof, and the Windsor-born singers Iris Bala, Victor *Braun, and Jeannine Morand. Annual concerts with the *Leamington Choral Society began in 1970.

The orchestra's only regular conductor until his death, Holli – b Tampere, Finland, 12 Dec 1916, d Windsor 11 or 12 Nov 1977; ATCM 1932, M MUS (Detroit Cons) 1948 – studied violin at the TCM and privately 1932–40 with Maurice Warner and theory and composition with Francis L. York at the Detroit Cons. In addition to his duties with the Windsor SO, Holli appeared as guest conductor with Finnish, US, and Mexican orchestras. In 1965 he formed the International Youth SO of student musicians from Windsor, Ont, Detroit, Mich, and nearby communities. On his death, the orchestra named Clifford *Evens interim conductor and artistic adviser pending the appointment of a successor. Lászlo *Gati became that successor in the spring of 1979.

BIBLIOGRAPHY
'Windsor Symphony Society,' *CanComp*, 29, May 1968
(FAH)

Winnipeg. Manitoba's capital city, located at the junction of the Red and Assiniboine rivers on a site once known to the Indians as 'Dirty Water.' Fort Rouge was established there in 1738 by Pierre de La Vérendrye, a fur trader and explorer. The first Selkirk settlers (a group of Highland Scots sent by the Earl of Selkirk and led by Miles Macdonnell) arrived at the Red River Settlement in 1812, and a second fort, Fort Garry, was established in 1821. By the mid-1850s the name Winnipeg was in use. The town's population was 200 in 1870 when Manitoba entered Confederation, but a dozen years later, when the railway had reached Winnipeg, its population had increased to 7000. Thereafter, immigration and other factors increased this number dramatically, to 70,000 in 1904 and 600,000 in the late 1970s. In 1972 12 separate municipal governments, including St Boniface and Fort Garry, were amalgamated to form the metropolitan city of Winnipeg.

As early as 1833 there was a piano in the Red River Settlement, but fiddling was the most popular form of music. 'There was nothing wrong with the fiddling of the early Red River musicians whose lively strains inspired the young gallant of the day to wear out three pairs of moccasins in one night in the swift swirling of the Red River dances' ('Fifty years of music in Winnipeg'). Many of the fiddlers were Métis, and one of them, Pierre *Falcon, achieved a considerable reputation as a songwriter.

In 1870 and 1871 members of the First Ontario Rifles (with Col Wolseley's expedition, sent to restore order after the Red River Rebellion) presented Winnipeg with its first public theatrical and musical performance of record. The Rifles sold some of their instruments when they departed, enabling Winnipeggers in 1871 to form their first band, under Harry Walker. Winnipeg had a reed organ with five stops at Grace Church in 1873, and St Boniface a pipe organ in 1875. A year later Winnipeg boasted a glee club, and on 14 March the City Hall Theatre opened with a concert in aid of the General Hospital. The theatre, which seated 500 and had a gallery across one end, was in use until 1883. That year the Winnipeg Theatre and Opera House (originally called Victoria Hall) was built. It was altered, and was renamed the Walker Theatre, in 1907.

The first Philharmonic Society on the Prairies was founded in Winnipeg in 1880 by Capt W.N. Kennedy, who invited a Professor Hammerschmidt from the USA to be its first conductor. Hammerschmidt was succeeded by Joseph Hecker, a German immigrant who moved to the USA before the society could establish itself with any permanence. Another group performing in the 1880s was the Apollo Club, an orchestra of some 35 amateur musicians. Probably the first virtuoso performer to visit Winnipeg was Frantz *Jehin-Prume ca 1881. In 1883 the Hess Opera from England inaugurated the Princess Opera House with a performance of *Iolanthe*. Until 1899, when it burned down, the theatre was home to the local Operatic Society. The tenor Thomas *Persse, a member of the society 1884–5, appeared in its productions of Gilbert & Sullivan. The founder of the society was P.R. MacLagan, formerly of Montreal, the organist at Holy Trinity Church and a music teacher. Despite these evidences of musical activity, Charles H. Wheeler (a music critic for 25 years) could write in the newly founded Winnipeg *Tribune*: 'Can three musicians be found in the city? Aye, can there be one found? The answer is emphatically NO' (8 Feb 1890).

The *Women's Musical Club began in 1894 as a weekly practice and study group and had expanded by 1899 into an energetic organization for the promotion of all aspects of music and the presentation of concerts. The *Junior Musical Club was founded in 1900, and the Clef Club was incorporated in 1906. Russell E. Chester's article 'Music in Winnipeg 1900–1907' recounts this Winnipeg-born musician's memories of the period.

J.J. *Moncrieff, co-founder of the Winnipeg *Tribune* and vice-president of the Clef Club, was a moving force behind choral music, Winnipeg's chief form of musical expression until the end of World War II. A 250-voice Festival Chorus, prepared by Rhys Thomas, took part in the 1903 *Cycle of Musical Festivals. Moncrieff also was one of the founders of the *Winnipeg Oratorio Society (1908–24) and in 1913 succeeded Ralph J. *Horner as its conductor. With the Board of Trade, the society sponsored an annual spring festival which featured its own members, guest soloists, the Minneapolis SO, and groups such as Burton *Kurth's St Cecilia Ladies' Choir. Together these forces gave impressive performances of the standard oratorios. Other Winnipeg choral groups active before World War I included the Elgar Musical Society, founded ca 1908, the Jewish Folk Choir, founded in 1910, the Choral and Orchestral Society, and the Handel Society.

On 11 Dec 1915 a group of businessmen, meeting in the Hotel Fort Garry to discuss the dearth of male singers in Winnipeg, founded the Men's Musical Club (*Men's Music Club after 1960). The club's objectives were to participate in music making, to encourage young musicians, to sponsor visits by major musicians, and to proclaim 'disapproval, discouragement and condemnation of any scheme, act or organization which in any way had a tendency to debase the standard of music in the Province of Manitoba.' The subsequent history of music in Winnipeg demonstrates that the club acted upon its principles. In 1916 it established the *Winnipeg Male Voice Choir, a 24-voice ensemble which, under its third conductor, Hugh Ross, quickly built an international reputation. In 1918 the club sponsored the formation of another of Winnipeg's most important musical institutions, the *Manitoba Music Competition Festival, which was held first in 1919, with 2500 entries heard in classes scheduled over four days. The competition festival became an important stimulus to music education in the province. In 1951 four sessions daily for two weeks accommodated 19,500 competitors. In 1926 George S. *Mathieson, secretary 1916–44 of the Men's Musical Club (succeeded by Richard W. *Cooke) and co-founder of the competition festival, established the *FCMF, with headquarters in Winnipeg.

Founded in 1922 under Hugh Ross, another choral-orchestral aggregation, the Winnipeg Philharmonic Society, has survived to become the city's most important oratorio choir. It, too, was linked intimately with the Men's Musical Club, which 1929–68 directly administered the ensemble, renamed the *Winnipeg Philharmonic Choir in 1929.

Among other choral groups which flourished between the two world wars were the Winnipeg Choral and Orchestral Society, under Arnold Dann 1922–5 and Ronald *Gibson 1927–9; the Winnipeg Boys' Choir, formed in 1925 by the Men's Musical Club and conducted by Ethel *Kinley 1925–43 and Beth *Douglas 1943–62; the Kelvin High School Chorus, founded in 1932 and conducted by Gladys Anderson Brown 1932–62 and later by Herbert Belyea and John Standing; the Daniel McIntyre High School Chorus conducted by Lola *MacQuarrie and later by Glen *Pierce; the CBC Singers (*Choristers), founded in 1937 by W.H. *Anderson; the Young Women's Musical Club Choir, founded in 1939 by Berythe *Birse, who also established the Winnipeg Ladies' Choir in 1940; the Ukrainian Male Chorus, founded in 1941 (see Ukraine); and the Winnipeg Girls' Choir, founded in 1944 by Beth Cruikshank and Maurine Pottruff.

After World War II choral singing lost some of its former uncontested predominance because of increased interest in instrumental music. Nonetheless, Winnipeg remained one of North America's choral capitals. In 1949 groups under the continuing sponsorship of the Men's Musical Club included the Winnipeg Philharmonic Choir, Male Voice Choir, Boys' Choir, Junior Male Voice Choir, and (Frances Christie's) Juvenile Boys' Choir. Others, post-war, have included the 80-voice choir of the Junior Musical Club, formed in 1949 under Beth Cruikshank; the Oriana Singers under Berythe Birse 1954–66; numerous fine choirs founded in the *Mennonite community under Ernest Enns, Benjamin *Horch, Victor *Martens, and George Wiebe, and particularly the *Mennonite Children's Choir, founded in 1957 by Helen Litz; and, in St Boniface, the Chorale des intrépides, founded in 1960 under Marcien *Ferland. The Kelvin High School Choir, conducted by John Standing, distinguished itself by winning the G.S. Mathieson Trophy in 1975. It also performed on the CBC and BBC and made an LP entitled *Kelvin High School Choir of Winnipeg* (1973, CBC SM-219).

The churches of Winnipeg through their choirs have provided a training ground for young singers and regular employment for a select few in their paid quartets of soloists. Notable in the second and third quarters of the 20th century were the choirs of W.H. Anderson at Crescent Fort Rouge United, Hugh *Bancroft at All Saints' Anglican, Marius *Benoist at the St Boniface Cathedral (Roman Catholic), Ronald Gibson at Holy Trinity Anglican, Conrad Grimes at First Presbyterian, Filmer *Hubble at St Stephen's Broadway United, Herbert *Sadler at Westminster United, and Stewart *Thomson at St George's Anglican, to name only a few. These choirs presented seasonal concerts and oratorios and entered the senior choir classes of the Manitoba Music Competition Festival. Many of the organists and choirleaders also were busy teachers, and Anderson, Bancroft, Hubble, and Sadler in particular had outstanding pupils who, in turn, became leaders in musical life.

City teachers and choirs developed a strong community of oratorio soloists, drawn from the Anglo-Saxon, French, Mennonite, and Ukrainian communities and all well trained in the style. Among the leading sopranos were Nina *Dempsey, Thérèse *Deniset, Devina Bailey *Duggan, Cora Doig James, Olga Irwin, Mary *Morrison, Gertrude *Newton, Sylvia *Saurette, Phyllis *Cooke Thomson, and Gladys *Whitehead. Among the mezzo-sopranos and contraltos were Myfanwy Evans, Gladys *Kriese-Caporale, May *Lawson, Joan *Maxwell, Peggie-Anne Truscott, and Phyllis Worth. One can note among the tenors the *Kent family (notably George), Victor Martens, John *Martens, and Peter *Koslowsky. Among baritones and basses were Orville Derraugh, Ronald Dodds, Roy Firth, Paul *Fredette, Stanley *Hoban, Wallace Lewis, Robert Publow, Cecil Semchyshyn, Alvin Reimer, W. Davidson *Thomson, Albert Whiteman, Kerr *Wilson, and J. Roberto Wood. (Important visiting soloists were not precluded, however, and there were memorable appearances by Maureen *Forrester, Lois *Marshall, James *Milligan, and Patricia *Rideout, among others.)

Any list of Winnipeg accompanists would have to include Audrey *Cooke Belyea, Douglas *Bodle, Jean *Broadfoot, Ada *Bronstein, Chester *Duncan, Cécile Henderson, Anna *Moncrieff Hovey, Gordon *Kushner, Dorothy Lawson, Roline Mackidd, Winnifred *Sim, Thelma *Wilson, and Mary Scarlett (Mrs J. Roberto) Wood. Many among these singers and accompanists also taught effectively, as did Doris Mills *Lewis, herself a chorister more than a soloist but a uniquely gifted teacher of singers.

Winnipeg did not have a permanent symphony orchestra until after World War II (see Winnipeg symphony orchestras), though short-lived groups were formed before that time by John *Waterhouse, Hugh Ross, Marius Benoist (in St Boniface), Bernard *Naylor, Geoffrey *Waddington, Benjamin Horch, and others. The modern Winnipeg SO gave its first concert in 1948 under Walter *Kaufmann. The orchestra's first home was the *Winnipeg Auditorium (opened 1932), its second the *Manitoba Centennial Concert Hall (opened in 1968). Kaufmann was succeeded as conductor by Victor *Feldbrill in 1958, Feldbrill by George Cleve in 1968, and Cleve by Piero Gamba in 1971.

Two other important post-war orchestras have been the *CBC Winnipeg Orchestra, conducted 1947–74 by Eric *Wild and subsequently by Boris *Brott, and the *Manitoba Chamber Orchestra, founded in 1972 by Ruben *Gurevich.

No opera-producing organization was able to establish a firm footing in Winnipeg until the late 1960s. However, musical theatre has always been part of Winnipeg's musical life. In 1911, the year that William *Dichmont's musical play *Miss Pepple (of New York)* was published in Winnipeg, Ralph H. Horner produced his own comic opera, *The Belles of Barcelona*, with an opera company assembled locally. Several touring companies appeared at the Walker Theatre – the *San Carlo Opera in 1919 and 1921; the Gallo English Opera in Gilbert & Sullivan operettas and *The Chimes of Normandy* in 1920; the Royal English Opera in more Gilbert & Sullivan, and in *Chu Chin Chow* and *The Bohemian Girl* in 1920; the D'Oyly Carte in 1928. In the 1940s and 1950s the operetta tradition was carried forward by the vigorous glee clubs and alumni choirs of the major high schools, particularly Kelvin and Daniel McIntyre, which mounted major productions, often with invited soloists. It was in a Kelvin production of *The Mikado* that the guest soprano and former Kelvin graduate Mary Morrison met the young local tenor Jon *Vickers and encouraged him to continue operatic study in Toronto.

In St Boniface the operas of Gounod were performed by the Société lyrique Gounod founded in 1935 by Marius Benoist. The group shortened its name to Société lyrique in 1952 and in subsequent years presented numerous operatic and choral-orchestral works, including Berlioz' *L'Enfance du Christ* and Benoist's *La Légende du vent* and *Onadéga*. The group continued to flourish in 1980.

*Rainbow Stage was founded in 1954, by local theatrical and musical people including James Duncan and Peggy Jarman Green, to present operettas and musicals of professional standard outdoors in the summer in Kildonan Park. After Duncan, Glen *Harrison was its music director 1963–72, and Neil *Harris, Filmer Hubble, and Robert *McMullin have been among its conductors.

The Ukrainian Opera Theatre has presented occasional performances of Ukrainian works, eg, four of *Cossacks in Exile* in 1964. *COC touring productions visited Winnipeg several times prior to 1969, when A. Kerr Twaddle and 13 others founded the *Manitoba Opera Assn; this became Winnipeg's permanent opera-producing organization, presenting works of the standard repertoire such as *Il Trovatore, Madama Butterfly*, and *Tosca*.

Among famed singers who have performed in Winnipeg have been Emma *Albani, twice in 1897, Clara Butt in 1922, Geraldine Farrar in 1922, Dame Nellie Melba in 1923, Elena Gerhardt in 1924, Amelita Galli-Curci in 1927, Ernestine Schumann-Heink in 1928, Tito Schipa in 1929, Edward *Johnson in 1929, Feodor Chaliapin in 1935, Marian Anderson in 1937, Richard Tauber in 1938, Paul Robeson in 1941, and Maggie Teyte in 1947.

The list of visiting instrumentalists, no less impressive than that of the singers, includes Mischa Elman in early 1920s, Josef Lhévinne in 1923, Ignace Jan Paderewski in 1924, Jascha Heifetz in 1924, Sergei Rachmaninoff in 1925, Moriz Rosenthal in 1928, Efrem Zimbalist in 1929, Josef Hofmann in 1933, Yehudi Menuhin in 1938, Artur Rubinstein in 1942, Claudio Arrau in 1942, Isaac Stern in 1943, and Arturo Benedetti Michelangeli in 1949. The Minneapolis SO gave more than 100 performances in more than 30 annual visits to Winnipeg, under three successive conductors: Dimitri Mitropoulos, Antal Dorati, and Stanislaw Skrowaczewski.

The main force drawing these many artists to Winnipeg was Fred M. *Gee, who presented them in his Celebrity Concerts (1927–67). Other concert presenters have included the Women's Musical Club, which gave an annual concert series 1940–65 in the small concert hall of the Winnipeg Auditorium; the Men's Musical Club; the *Wednesday Morning Musicale, founded in 1933 by Eva *Clare; and the *U of Manitoba School of Music. In 1970 the Men's Music Club initiated the Intimacy Concert Series in the Planetarium Auditorium, to provide young musicians with the opportunity of performing in public. The contemporary music series Music Inter Alia, founded by Diana *McIntosh in 1976, has been held at the (new) Winnipeg Art Gallery, which opened in 1972. The annual summer Winnipeg Folk Festival, begun in 1973, has featured Canadian and international folk singers and groups.

Although somewhat in the shadow of choral activity for many years, chamber music received impetus from the increasing number of instrumentalists and the expansion of music education in the 1950s. An early ensemble was the Tudor Quartet, which broadcast over the CBC for several years prior to 1940. Its members were Valberg Leland and Joseph Sera, violins, Eugene Hudson, viola, and Isaac *Mamott, cello. Later ensembles have included the Dirk *Keetbaas Players, a woodwind quintet, 1955–66; the Winnipeg Chamber Music Ensemble, formed in 1958 and conducted by Ann *Pomer; the Corydon Trio, formed in 1959 by Lea *Foli, violin, Gerald *Stanick, viola, and Claude *Kenneson (succeeded by Peggie *Sampson), cello; the *Hidy Trio; the *Manitoba University Consort; and the Festival Quartet of Canada, formed in 1967 by Arthur *Polson. After inauguration in 1965 with a performance by the Amadeus Quartet, the Eva Clare Hall in the U of Manitoba School of Music became the scene of an annual recital series featuring such performers as the Winnipeg-born cellist Zara *Nelsova and the *Orford String Quartet.

Most of the above-mentioned chamber musicians have been prominent teachers. Among others in the instrumental field who have been important as performers or teachers or both are the pianists William *Aide, Jean Broadfoot, Alma *Brock-Smith, Beth Cooil, Leonard *Heaton, Megan Howes, Marek *Jablonski, Roline Mackidd, John *Melnyk, Grace Rich, and Snjolaug *Sigurdson and the violinists George *Bornoff, John *Konrad, George Rutherford, and John Waterhouse. The composer-pianist-violinist S.C. *Eckhardt-Gramatté also was an extraordinary teacher in all three of her disciplines. Among the city's noted theory teachers were Gwendda Owen *Davies (piano also), Frans *Niermeier, and Russell *Standing.

In 1919 the *MRMTA was founded as the Winnipeg Music Teachers' Assn by Eva Clare and others. Its objective – besides maintaining high standards among the private teachers it represented – was to introduce music into schools as an optional credit. In 1935 music became a recognized subject in Winnipeg high schools and Manitoba universities. In 1936 the *Western Board of Music was formed. Ethel Kinley, supervisor of music in Winnipeg schools 1937–47, introduced group instrumental instruction in the last year of her tenure, and the instrumental emphasis was expanded under her successor, Marjorie Horner. P.G. Padwick had established a Manitoba school orchestra program as early as 1923. His work was carried on after 1938 by Ronald Gibson, Filmer Hubble, Glen Pierce, and Frances Port until 1964. Lola MacQuarrie became director of music for the Winnipeg schools in 1955 and was succeeded by Glen Pierce in 1966. The *MMEA was founded in Winnipeg in 1959.

Eva Clare became the first music director at the U of Manitoba in 1937, and the School of Music was set up in 1963 and directed by Leonard *Isaacs. Among notable privately operated schools have been the *Shinn Cons of Music, the *Bornoff School of Music and its successor the Konrad Cons, and the accordion and guitar schools founded by Ted *Komar in 1950 and 1970. The music department of the *Mennonite Brethren Bible College and College of Arts was founded in 1944. The *Canadian Mennonite Bible College, founded in 1947, also has offered music courses.

James *Croft, who arrived in Winnipeg in 1904, and later his son H.J. Croft, made the city a centre of violin rebuilding and repair, and the firm continued to sell instruments and music in 1980. Also prominent in the music business was Tom Tredwell, who was the manager 1938–56 of Western Music (Manitoba) Ltd, and who opened Tredwell's Music Centre in 1956. J.J.H. McLean and Co sold pianos, electric organs, and sheet music.

A Winnipeg Composers' Concert in 1948 featured music by W.H. Anderson, Chester Duncan, Walter *MacNutt, Frans C. Niermeier, and Barbara *Pentland. Other composers who have resided in Winnipeg include S.C. Eckhardt-Gramatté after 1953, Bernard Naylor 1959–68, and Robert *Turner after 1969, as well as Victor *Davies, Neil Harris, Leslie *Mann, and Robert McMullin.

The first Icelanders arrived at Winnipeg in 1875, and in the ensuing years the city's ethnic diversity came to be reflected in musical expression of great variety. The Jewish, Mennonite, Scandinavian, and Slavic communities have produced energetic choral, orchestral, operatic, and folk ensembles. Among Jewish groups have been the Jewish Community Choir and Orchestra and the Jewish Women's Musical Club. The Mennonite community has organized concerts, its choirs have produced oratorios, and its educational institutions have trained many of the city's most active singers, instrumentalists, and church musicians. The large Ukrainian community has been particularly enterprising in folk opera and choral singing. In 1949, at a 75th civic birthday festival, Alec Lubimiw presented ensembles of Estonian, Hungarian, Latvian, Lithuanian, Polish, Ukrainian, and Yugoslavian Canadians. Icelandic, Norwegian, and Swedish male-voice choirs performed in Winnipeg for many years. There also has been a United Scottish Society Male Choir. The Polish 'Sokol' Choir won the Lord Tweedsmuir Trophy in 1964.

In addition to many mentioned above, musicians born in or near Winnipeg, St Boniface, and the other constituent municipalities include Ernest *Adams, Evelyne *Anderson, J.S.P. *Bach, the sopranos Belva Boroditsky and her sister Sara Boroditsky Udow, Lorne M. *Betts, Victor Davies, Beth Douglas, Deanna Durbin, Armand *Ferland, Esther *Ghan, Flora Matheson *Goulden, Donna *Grescoe, Frederick *Grinke, Donald *Hadfield, Joan *Hall, the pianist Jack Henderson, Sheila *Henig, Sydney *Hodkinson, Phyllis *Holtby, Margaret Ann *Ireland, Diedre *Irons, Terry *Jacks, the tenor Robert Jeffrey, *Juliette, Wally *Koster, Gladys Kriese-Caporale, Gordon Kushner, Gisele *MacKenzie, Fraser *MacPherson, David *Martin, Gordon *McLean, Hugh *McLean, Morley *Meredith, Norman *Mittelmann, John *Moncrieff, Mary Morrison, Gilbert, Sheila and Lorne *Munroe, Kenneth *Murphy, George *Murray, Barbara Pentland, Avis *Phillips, Henriette (Platford) Asch (*Ascher Duo), Ross *Pratt, Jackie *Rae, the organist Harold Redekopp, the harpsichordist Joyce Redekop-Fink, the violinist Victoria Polley Richards, Louise *Roy, the mezzo-soprano Elsie Sawchuk, Bernie *Senensky, Winnifred Sim, Ann *Southam, Lucille *Starr, Ben *Steinberg, the violinist Vera Tarnowsky, Frank *Thorolfson, and Ann, Freda, and Shirley *Trepel.

BIBLIOGRAPHY

Begg, Alexander, and Nursey, Walter R. *Ten Years in Winnipeg* (Winnipeg 1890)

Wheeler, Charles H. 'Music in Manitoba,' *The Year Book of Canadian Art 1913*, compiled by the Arts and Letters Club (Toronto, London 1913)

'Fifty years of music in Winnipeg,' *MCan*, vol 16, Aug 1920

Musical Life and Arts, music periodical (Winnipeg 1924–5)

Lamont, Joyce. 'City's musical history began at turn of century,' *Winnipeg Free Press*, 28 May 1949

Maley, S. Roy. 'City's music comes of age,' Winnipeg *Tribune*, 28 May 1949

Hoogstraten, Vinia. 'Winnipeg: where music is king,' *Mayfair*, Apr 1952

Maley, S. Roy. 'The outlook was bleak for culture,' Winnipeg *Tribune*, 6 Apr 1965

'Clubs filled city's musical vacuum,' ibid

'A mellow melody of many tongues,' ibid

Friesen, Olga. 'Historical sketch,' *Sharps & Flats*, vol 6, Nov 1965

Chester, Russell E. 'Music in Winnipeg 1900–1907,' *CMB*, 8, Spring–Summer 1974

FILMOGRAPHY

Listen to the Prairies (NFB 1951). A shorter version is titled *A City Sings.*

WA, KW, PMW

Winnipeg Auditorium. Winnipeg's main concert hall complex from 1932, when it opened, until 1968, when it was supplanted in that function by the *Manitoba Centennial Concert Hall. It was designed jointly by three architectural firms – Northwood & Chivers, Pratt & Ross, and J.N. Semmens – and erected on St Mary's Ave at Memorial Blvd at a cost of $1 million. A Depression unemployment relief project, it was financed by civic, provincial, and federal governments and inaugurated 15 Oct 1932 by the Canadian prime minister, R.B. Bennett. The main auditorium (seating over 4000) and the concert hall (seating 800) shared a single stage – a doubtful economy since it made their simultaneous use impossible. A third auditorium (the assembly hall, seating 400) shared the third floor with the Winnipeg Art Gallery and the Manitoba Museum.

The main auditorium was the home 1947–68 of the *Winnipeg SO, the *Winnipeg Philharmonic Choir, the evening sessions of the *Manitoba Music Competition Festival, and the *Gee Celebrity Concerts. Marian Anderson, Victoria de los Angeles, Glenn *Gould, Jascha Heifetz, Joseph Hofmann, Vladimir Horowitz, Fritz Kreisler, Lois *Marshall, Arturo Benedetto Michelangeli, Gregor Piatigorsky, Ezio Pinza, Sergei Rachmaninoff, Elisabeth Rethberg, Artur Rubinstein, Josef Szigeti, Lawrence Tibbett, Helen Traubel, Leonard Warren, and many others were heard there in recital. The Ballets Russes de Monte Carlo, the Sadler's Wells Ballet, the *San Carlo Opera, and the New York Philharmonic appeared there, and the Minneapolis SO under Mitropoulos and, later, Dorati was for many years an annual visitor. Although it was the largest and one of the finest Canadian buildings of its day, the main auditorium was poor acoustically and was far surpassed in this regard by its successor, the centennial hall. The acoustics were a by-product of its all-purpose design, with unraked floor and removable seats permitting its conversion for social dancing, rollerskating, wrestling, bond rallies, conventions, etc.

The smaller concert hall (described by the English musician William Glock, during an adjudicating tour of Canada in the late 1940s, as one of the country's two best auditoria – the other being the original *Eaton Auditorium, Toronto) was the home 1940–65 of the *Women's Musical Club's annual concert series. It has survived the building's $3-million 1975 remodelling (into the Provincial Archives and Library). (CC)

Winnipeg Male Voice Choir. An enterprise of the *Men's Music Club. Founded in 1916 as a quartet of club members, it had increased by 1918 to 46. On the death in 1920 of its founding conductor, George Price, Cyril Musgrove was brought from England to take over the choir. Musgrove was succeeded in 1921 by Hugh Ross, another Englishman, who served until 1927. Each of these men served also as organist-choirmaster at Holy Trinity Church. Under Ross' direction, the Winnipeg Male Voice Choir became a polished ensemble, which toured the USA in 1922 with Percy Grainger as soloist. A longer tour included a performance, 26 Feb 1923 at Carnegie Hall, which received praise for 'a fine quality of tone, a rich pianissimo, a sonorous forte, and commendable accuracy and finish' (*New York Times*). The choir was placed unequivocally 'in the very front rank' (*New York Post*).

After Ross' departure to assume the conductorship of the Schola Cantorum of New York the choir maintained its arrangement with Holy Trinity Church and imported from England its next three conductors: Douglas *Clarke 1927–9, Peter Temple 1929–31, and Bernard *Naylor 1932–5. Besides presenting many great soloists to Winnipeg (eg, Enesco, Gabrilowitsch, Grainger, Boris *Hambourg, Harold Samuel, Albert Spalding, and Thibaud) the choir often performed with visiting orchestras (eg, 22 May 1926, with the Minneapolis SO in Hermann Goetz' *The Water Lily*). Herbert *Sadler (the conductor 1935–44) and Filmer *Hubble (the conductor 1944–9) saw the choir through the years of World War II, but the ranks had thinned, and the future had become uncertain. However, Walter *Kaufmann became the conductor of a revived choir in 1949, and Kaufmann was followed by Donald Leggat 1953–5, George *Kent 1955–7, and Lucien *Needham 1957–60. The choir never regained its pre-war status, however. In 1960 it broke its tie with the Men's Music Club and continued under a new name, Metro Male Chorus, conducted until 1966 by Barry Anderson and thereafter by Clayton Lee and Herbert Holland 1966–7, James Whan 1967–8, and Archie Stone 1968–77. It assumed the name Winnipeg Male Chorus in 1974.

BIBLIOGRAPHY
Major, G. Sharp. *Crescendo* (Winnipeg 1935) (RG)

Winnipeg Oratorio Society. Founded in 1908 by John J. *Moncrieff and others, to provide Winnipeg with a major choir drawn from the city's many church choirs and capable of undertaking large-scale choral works. It was conducted 1908–9 by Fred Warrington, 1909–12 by Ralph *Horner, and 1913–24 by Moncrieff. Fred M. *Gee was the accompanist during the lifetime of the organization. Concerts were given 1908–18 in Grace United Church and the Walker Theatre and 1918–24 in the Board of Trade Auditorium.

The society's spring festival (Western Canada Musical Festival) was inaugurated in 1908 and recurred annually until the society disbanded after 1924. Each festival (except those of 1915, 1916, and 1917) consisted of six concerts by the Minneapolis SO (under Emil Oberhoffer until 1923), the oratorio society itself, visiting and resident soloists, and public school choirs. Among the works presented were Handel's *Judas Maccabaeus* and *Samson*, Mendelssohn's *Elijah*, *Hymn of Praise*, and *St Paul*, Verdi's *Requiem*, Coleridge-Taylor's *Hiawatha's Wedding Feast* and *The Death of Minnehaha*, Bruch's *Fair Ellen*, Sullivan's *The Golden Legend* and *On Shore, On Sea*, Hamilton Harty's *The Mystic Trumpeter*, and, in concert performances, Gounod's *Faust* and Saint-Saëns' *Samson et Dalila*. The society also performed *Messiah* each December using resident soloists, among them Nina *Dempsey (ca 1922). In 1924 Gertrude *Newton sang in the festival performance of *Elijah*. In addition to its regular season, the society gave concerts during World War I at Tuxedo Hospital, sang in the Armistice Day celebrations, and participated in other special events.

The society also functioned as an impresario, introducing to Winnipeg audiences soloists from elsewhere in Canada and from abroad, among them Paul Althouse, Alfred Cortot, Percy Grainger, Louis Graveure, Boris *Hambourg, Florence Macbeth, Kathleen *Parlow, Louis Persinger, Maggie Teyte, Cornelius van Vliet, and Clarence Whitehill.

BIBLIOGRAPHY
Wheeler, Charles H. 'Music in Manitoba,' *The Year Book of Canadian Art 1913*, compiled by the Arts and Letters Club of Toronto (London, Toronto 1913) JBk

---

The Winnipeg Philharmonic Choir. Winnipeg's principal oratorio choir. It was formed in 1922 as the Winnipeg Philharmonic Society by Hugh Ross – b Langport, Somerset, England, 21 Aug 1898; ARCM, FRCO, BA (Oxford), D MUS (Oxford) – who moved to Winnipeg in 1921 as organist-choirmaster of Holy Trinity Church and conductor of the *Winnipeg Male Voice Choir, and also founded the Winnipeg Orchestral Club in 1923 before moving to New York in 1927 to conduct the famed Schola Cantorum.

A choir of 150 to 200 voices drawn mainly from the city's churches, the philharmonic society made its first public appearance 11 Dec 1922 in a program of part-songs, with the soprano Anna Case as guest soloist. Further performances under Ross included Vaughan Williams' *A Sea Symphony* and Brahms' *A German Requiem*, both with orchestra. Ross was succeeded by Douglas *Clarke during whose term (1927–9) the *St Matthew Passion* was presented. With the appointment of Peter Temple in 1929 the choir, until then an independent organization, became an affiliate of the *Men's Music Club of Winnipeg. The climax of Temple's tenure was a performance of Holst's *The Hymn of Jesus* in 1931.

Bernard *Naylor succeeded Temple, conducting 1932–5. After Naylor and during World War II, Herbert *Sadler and Filmer *Hubble sustained the choir. Dimitri Mitropoulos conducted performances of *Messiah* in 1944 and *Elijah* in 1946, the accompaniment provided by his Minneapolis (later Minnesota) SO. Hubble prepared the choir for these performances.

Naylor returned for one season (1948–9) and was succeeded in 1949 by the new conductor of the revived *Winnipeg SO, Walter *Kaufmann. Subsequent conductors have been Donald Leggat 1953–5, Lucien *Needham 1956–60, Sydney Bryans 1960–6, and Melville *Cook 1966–7. In 1969 control of the choir passed from the Men's Music Club to the Winnipeg SO and Stewart *Thomson served 1967–75 as chorusmaster, succeeded in 1975 by Henry Engbrecht. Performances after 1969 have included Bach's *Mass in B Minor* under George Cleve (1976), Beethoven's *Missa solemnis* under Piero Gamba (1973), and Britten's *War Requiem* (1974) under Brian Priestman.

DISCOGRAPHY
In Concert – The Winnipeg Philharmonic Choir: Schubert *Mass in G* – Handel 3 coronation anthems. S. Richardson sop, J. Martens ten, N. Lohnes bass, B. Anderson org, Engbrecht cond. 1976. WCRC [no number]

BIBLIOGRAPHY
Scarth, Ronald S. 'The Winnipeg Philharmonic Choir: a short historical sketch,' *Sharps & Flats*, vol 5, Jun 1965
(RG)

Winnipeg symphony orchestras. Prior to the formation of the Winnipeg SO in 1946, several orchestras had been established with varying degrees of success.

1 Early orchestras
2 Winnipeg Symphony Orchestra

1 EARLY ORCHESTRAS. In 1880 a philharmonic society was established by Capt W.N. Kennedy, the organist at Grace Church and the mayor of Winnipeg 1875–6. Kennedy asked a Professor Hammerschmidt to conduct, and Hammerschmidt was succeeded by Joseph Hecker, a German immigrant who later moved to the USA. This was the first philharmonic society on the Prairies. During the same period an Apollo Club established a 35-player orchestra. At the turn of the century Alexander Scott conducted a Winnipeg Orchestral Society, and shortly before World War I a permanent orchestra was attempted under Gustav Stephan. In March 1918 John *Waterhouse conducted an orchestra of *Men's Musical Club and *Women's Musical Club members in Beethoven's *Egmont Overture* and *Emperor Concerto* (with the pianist Arnold Dann) and Mozart's *'Jupiter' Symphony*. In 1920 at the annual Festival of Music of the Board of Trade, a Winnipeg SO performed under the baton of Henri Bourgeault. In 1922 Arnold Dann (b England 1891, d USA 1964), who taught music at Wesley College, founded and conducted the Winnipeg Choral and Orchestral Society. That same year Charles Manning conducted a series of orchestra concerts at the Allen Theatre, with Waterhouse as concertmaster. In 1923 Hugh Ross, one of the first conductors brought from England to direct the *Winnipeg Male Voice Choir and the *Winnipeg Philharmonic Choir, formed the Winnipeg Orchestral Club, which gave five concerts

annually until 1927. Peter Temple in 1930 formed a Winnipeg SO which, in its one season, backed by the Men's Musical Club, performed with the Philharmonic Choir and broadcast over the CPR radio network. The orchestra was revived 1934–6 by Bernard *Naylor. A Summer SO under Geoffrey *Waddington, with Albert *Pratz as concertmaster, also survived two seasons (1939, 1940) under the sponsorship of the CBC and the musicians' union. Its activities were curtailed by World War II. Other orchestras, formed by Winnipeg's leading violin teachers – George Rutherford, Philip Shadwick, and John Waterhouse – and composed of their pupils and a few professionals, also were active in the early part of the century. Nevertheless, Winnipeg for many years looked to annual visits by the Minneapolis SO (see Fred M. *Gee) for dependable and recurrent symphonic experience.

Winnipeg Symphony Orchestra under Piero Gamba

2 WINNIPEG SYMPHONY ORCHESTRA. Manitoba's major orchestra. In 1944, with the prospects for a symphony orchestra enhanced by the CBC's plans for a regular broadcasting orchestra, the Winnipeg Civic Music League was organized. The league established a joint stock company, Winnipeg Symphony Orchestra Ltd. Walter *Kaufmann in 1948 became the first conductor, and the 73-piece orchestra's debut concert (16 Dec 1948 at the old *Winnipeg Auditorium) included two of the conductor's compositions. After the initial season of five concerts, 10 performances were presented each year, some with outstanding soloists.

In 1958 Victor *Feldbrill succeeded Kaufmann as conductor and persuaded the board to establish in the orchestra a nucleus of some 45 players on a 26-week-per-year contract. This, together with an increase in size, led during Feldbrill's 10-year tenure to the organization's status as one of Canada's full-time symphony orchestras. During the same period the orchestra became known for the regular inclusion of Canadian works in its programs. Feldbrill conducted or programmed works of *Adaskin, *Archer, *Beckwith, *Betts, *Eckhardt-Gramatté, *Freedman, Greenberg, *Keetbaas, *MacMillan, *Mann, *Matton, *Mercure, *Morawetz, *Morel, Naylor, *Papineau-Couture, *Pentland, *Pépin, *Ridout, Sherman, *Somers, *Symonds, *Turner, *Weinzweig, and *Willan. Among these were several premieres: Pentland's *Symphony No. 4* (1960), Norman Sherman's *Sinfonia Concertante for Bassoon and Strings* (1961), Naylor's *Variations for Small Orchestra* (1961), Eckhardt-Gramatté's *Symphony-Concerto for Piano and Orchestra* (1961), and Lionel Greenberg's *Prelude and Fugue* (1965).

The orchestra moved to the *Manitoba Centennial Concert Hall in 1968, playing its first concert there at the hall's inaugural ceremonies 27 March. George (Wolfgang) Cleve (b Vienna ca 1937, US-trained and previously an assistant to George Szell in Cleveland) succeeded Feldbrill and during his stay, 1968–70, the orchestra assumed control of the Winnipeg Philharmonic Choir and also gave the premiere of Victor *Davies' *Celebrations for Orchestra*. The Italian conductor-pianist and former child prodigy Piero Gamba (b Rome 16 Sep 1936) was appointed music director in 1971, and Ruben *Gurevich became Gamba's assistant in 1973. Gamba, at the time of his appointment, had conducted or guest-conducted in 40 countries, was honorary director of nine orchestras and had recorded with several, and was a winner (1962) of the Arnold Bax Memorial Medal. He was noted for his adroit handling of orchestral accompaniments. A recording of Beethoven's *Emperor Concerto* with Julius Katchen as soloist and Gamba conducting the London Symphony Orchestra received high praise, and Yehudi Menuhin extolled his abilities: 'I should have played with Piero Gamba 30 years ago and every year since' (CBC interview, March 1976). Gamba appeared frequently as his own soloist, conducting a concerto from the keyboard. By the mid-1970s the orchestra of 80 under his direction was giving annually 12 pairs of subscription concerts, 3 or 4 pop concerts, and over 25 children's concerts, and the liaison with the Philharmonic Choir was yielding performances of Bach's *Mass in B Minor*, Beethoven's *Missa solemnis* and *Ninth Symphony*, and Stravinsky's *Symphony of Psalms*. Gamba programmed premieres of Eckhardt-Gramatté's *Symphony No. 2: Manitoba* (1970, with subsequent performances on the orchestra's first eastern-Canadian tour), George *Fiala's *Ukrainian Violin Concerto* (1974), and Arthur *Polson's *Concerto for Trumpet and Orchestra* (1978). Polson became the orchestra's third concertmaster in 1966. The two previous concertmasters were Richard Seaborn 1948–60 and Lea *Foli 1960–6. Short tours have been undertaken frequently, to other Manitoba centres and nearby US cities, and in the spring of 1978 the orchestra visited the Ontario cities of Cornwall, Kingston, Barrie, Ottawa, Niagara Falls, and Waterloo. In March 1979, to mark the 15th anniversary of the Symphonicum Europae organization, of which Gamba was president, the orchestra gave a gala concert in Carnegie Hall, New York, assisted by a number of noted performers including Maureen *Forrester, Gary Graffman, Byron Janis, Yehudi Menuhin, Roberta Peters, Jean-Pierre Rampal, and Peter Ustinov.

Gamba resigned in 1980 after a year during which the orchestra's financial situation – a reported accumulated deficit of $900,000 – drew much public comment. Guest conductors were engaged for the 1980–1 season.

In any comparison of Winnipeg orchestral playing during Ross' time with that of the Winnipeg SO of the 1970s the contrasts are obvious. Because of the mixture of amateur and professional players and the extraordinary instrumental substitutions sometimes required, a performance in the 1920s of Delius' *Brigg Fair* could be called a minor disaster, requiring three tries to get it under way. Yet the last movement of Haydn's *Clock Symphony* was a tour de force, and two of Debussy's *Nocturnes* were quite first rate, enlivened by a kind of pioneer excitement. In the 1960s and 1970s the orchestra achieved a better balance and consistently higher level, and its first chairs were occupied by fine players; but with its maturity came occasional routine performances, the inevitable result of over-exposure and under-rehearsal, the common lot of contemporary orchestras.

Managers of the orchestra have been James Henderson 1949–54, Lawrence Davis 1954–6, Stirling Dorrance 1956–8, Kent Hurley 1958–66, James Emde 1966–7, Leonard David Stone 1967–78, Mark Walker 1978–9, and Tony D'Amato 1979–80, succeeded by Jack Mills.

DISCOGRAPHY

Alfven – Gluck – Chapi – Granados – Puccini – Gimenez. Gamba cond. 1972. CBC SM-233

Beethoven – Liszt – Mercure *Kaleidoscope* – Saint-Saëns. Gamba cond. 1977. CBC SM-334

Davies *The Beginning and the End of the World*. Skitch Henderson cond. 1972. OMNI 1001

Pentland – Turner – Adaskin. Chamb ens of Wpg SO, Feldbrill cond. (1966). RCI 215/RCA CCS-1009

Rossini – Mascagni – Verdi. Gamba cond. 1976. CBC SM-300

BIBLIOGRAPHY

Maley, S. Roy. 'Meet Winnipeg Symphony's 75 talented musician group,' Winnipeg *Tribune*, 7 instalments, 1, 15 Apr, 2, 6, 30 May, 3, 7 Jun 1949

Davis, Lawrence L. 'The story of the Winnipeg Symphony Orchestra,' *Actimist* (sic), Nov 1954

Wpg SO program. 'Farewell concert,' 25 Apr 1968

Cansino, Barbara. 'Winnipeg: a delicate operation,' *PfAC*, vol 14, Spring 1977

Carlyle-Gordge, Peter. 'Variations on a theme of discord,' *Maclean's*, 22 Sep 1980

Kamin, Hope. 'Symphony saved, Miller says,' *Winnipeg Free Press*, 10 Jan 1981 (RG)

Winter. The climatic features peculiar to the winter season in Canada – cold, snow, ice, squalls, and flurries – generally precede and extend beyond the season's three official months by several weeks. In the Canadian north, the land of the *Inuit, winter is very long and lasts almost the whole year. Because of its dominance of the Canadian calendar, this season has always played a determining role in Canadian life, and the country is known abroad largely on account of its winter, from the 'few acres of snow' dear to Voltaire to Gilles *Vigneault's famous song *'Mon Pays' – 'My country is not a country, it's winter.' It is therefore not surprising that winter and all that accompanies it, including the sports practised during this season, have become bound up with characteristic themes developed in various forms of music.

In the 19th century numerous piano pieces referring to winter were published, including *Canadian Winter Galop* (1864 or before) by Charles J. Millar, *The Ice Palace Souvenir March* (1885) by Isabel Howard-O'Keefe, and *Winter Pleasures* (1889) by Charles *Bohner. Mention also should be made of the 20th-century writer-composer-performers Claude *Léveillée ('Soir d'hiver,' 'Bonhomme hiver,' and, to lines by Émile Nelligan, 'Ah comme la neige a neigé') and Gilles Vigneault ('Mon Pays' and 'Ballade de l'hiver'). André *Gagnon wrote the instrumental piece *Neiges* as well as the set of

'The Band of the Mulligan Guards caught in a snow storm on their way to Elmira' (*Canadian Illustrated News*, 13 Mar 1875)

four concertos *Mes Quatre Saisons*, of which the fourth ('Hiver') is based on 'Mon Pays.'

Winter has inspired a number of other composers, for example Rodolphe *Mathieu in *Saisons canadiennes* (before 1927) and Jean *Coulthard in *Ballade (A Winter's Tale)* (1940), 'Soft Fall the February Snows' (1958), and 'A Cold Kingdom,' the first part of her *Choral Symphony* (1967). Claude *Champagne gave the title 'Chanson d'hiver' to the third movement of his *Images du Canada français* (1943). In *Altitude* (1959), 'a sound fresco inspired by the sight of the Rocky Mountains,' Champagne found in snow the inspiration for those passages describing the 'light on the glaciers, the dread of the avalanche, the avalanche itself, the squalls, and the final desolation.' Winter also appears in 'In Winter Cold' (1950) by Leslie *Bell, in 'First Snow,' the fourth piece in *The Seasons* (1952) by Lorne *Betts, in *Les Saisons* (1954) by Maurice *Dela, and in *Boréal* (1959) and *IIKKII (froidure)* (1971) by François *Morel. Serge *Garant used it as a source of inspiration in *L'Homme et les régions polaires*, film music produced for the pavilion of the same name at *Expo 67. The ballet *Pointes sur glace*, to music by Edmund *Assaly on themes of Calixa *Lavallée, was premiered at the *PDA by Les Grands Ballets Canadiens in 1967. R. Murray *Schafer, in *North/White* (1973), uses a snowmobile (a motorized vehicle on skis invented in Quebec by the Bombardier company), as an orchestral sound and also as a realistic symbol of what he calls 'the rape of the North.' Mention must be made of *Pays de neige* (1971) by Michel *Longtin and 'Snow Anthology,' the first movement of *Weatherscapes* (1973) by Derek *Holman.

See also Sports. (HP, PR)

WINTERS, Kenneth (Lyle). Critic, broadcaster, pianist, choirmaster, teacher, b Dauphin, Man, 28 Nov 1929; LRSM piano performer 1951, LRSM piano teacher 1953. With Helmut *Kallmann and Gilles *Potvin he is one of the editors of this encyclopedia, responsible primarily for the text of the English-language edition. He was born into a musical family; his mother, Edythe Kemp Winters, was a pianist, a teacher, and for 50 years the organist at Dauphin United Church. In Dauphin he studied voice 1940–6 with Ursula Koons Dahlgren and piano 1942–3 with Amy Strickland. In 1942 he won the boy soprano classes in the *Manitoba Music Competition Festival and was one of a team of soloists (with Douglas Rain and Ted *Komar) who toured Ontario with the Winnipeg Sea Cadet Band. After the band's concert in *Eaton Auditorium, Toronto, Augustus *Bridle wrote '[Winters] sang Mendelssohn's "O for the Wings of a Dove" as I have never heard it done by a boy since 1890 ... This lad's voice has the grand lustre of a woman's, plus the indescribable etheriality of a boy's' (*Toronto Star*, 18 Jul 1942). In 1946 Ernesto *Vinci awarded him, now a baritone, the highest mark at that year's Manitoba Music Competition Festival, and the Tudor Bowl.

Winters moved to Winnipeg that fall and began several years of study: theory with Gwendda Owen *Davies, voice successively with Mary Wood, Filmer *Hubble, Frederick *Newnham, and George *Kent, and piano 1946–51 with Roline Mackidd and 1951–3 with John *Melnyk, commuting the last two years from Dauphin, where he had set up a piano class. He had begun composing songs, and in 1950 his setting of Blake's 'O Rose, Thou Art Sick' for contralto, flute and string quartet won the first composition award offered by the Winnipeg Jewish Women's Musical Club. During the 1950s and early 1960s he completed a number of songs on verse of Shakespeare, Peele, Pound, Sandburg, and de la Mare and a folksong suite for high voice, flute, viola, and cello.

In 1954 Winters returned to Winnipeg to serve as organist-choirmaster at St Philip's Anglican Church, Norwood, to attend Manitoba Normal School, and to establish a piano class. He also did some vocal coaching, taught school music 1955–6, and in the summer of 1956 sang Buffalo Bill in a *Rainbow Stage production of *Annie Get Your Gun*. He began writing music and dance reviews for the *Winnipeg Free Press* in 1956 and within two years was covering visual arts and movies as well, and writing record and book reviews. This pattern held until 1966, interrupted 1959–60 by a year's study in Paris with Nadia Boulanger (composition) and Annette Dieudonné (solfège). Winters also served in 1962 as music editor for the periodical *Canadian Art*. He composed five incidental pieces – a 'Kitchen Canon,' a 'Pumping Song,' a 'Lullaby,' a 'Winter Aria,' and a 'Games Scene' – and served as music director for John Hirsch's production of James Reaney's children's play *Names and Nicknames* (premiered in Winnipeg, 1 Nov 1963).

Winters moved to Toronto as music and dance critic for the *Telegram* in February 1966 and continued in the position until June 1971, when he was appointed executive director of *OFSO. In the fall of that year he also became the founding executive director of ACO, administering the national organization from the OFSO offices in Toronto. In 1972 he became associated with the planners of *EMC*, and in 1975 he resigned from OFSO / ACO to devote all his time to the encyclopedia.

Winters began broadcasting in 1956 and thereafter was the author of, and commentator for, innumerable CBC radio broadcasts, both reviews ('Critically Speaking,' 'Records in Review,' 'Music Diary,' 'Sound Reviews,' etc) and entire series, notably 'Telemann and Company' (1964), 'The Music of Chopin' (22 programs, 1964–5), 'The Music of Mendelssohn' (21 programs, 1965–6), 'Benjamin Britten' (a 'CBC Tuesday Night' documentary and 8 subsequent programs of the composer's music, 1970), 'Gustav Holst, Planetmaker' (Ohio-Award-winning 'CBC Tuesday Night' documentary and 13 programs, 1974), 'Sir Michael Tippett: A Composer for Our Time' ('CBC Tuesday Night' documentary and 6 programs, 1975), and 'The Way to the Cross' (Good Friday three-hour special, 1978).

WRITINGS

'Music criticism,' *CMJ*, vol 5, Spring 1961

'Ozawa,' Toronto *Telegram*, 26 Apr 1969

'Somers: in the spring of his career,' ibid, 5 Jul 1969

'Teresa Stratas – a swallow's return,' ibid, 19 Jun 1971

'Canada,' *Sohlmans Musiklexikon* (Stockholm 1975)

'RCCO national convention,' AGO / RCCO *Music*, vol 9, Oct 1975

'Violet Archer,' 'Godfrey Ridout,' *Contemporary Canadian Composers*

Also articles for *Canadian Music Journal, Canada Music Book, Canadian Composer, Canadian Art, Music Scene*; program notes for the Toronto Symphony 1971–3

WITMER, Robert (Earl). Ethnomusicologist, bassist, b Kitchener, Ont, 24 Feb 1940; B MUS (British Columbia) 1965, M MUS (Illinois) 1970, PH D (Illinois) 1978. While studying bass with J.P. *Hamilton, the principal bass of the *Vancouver SO, he worked as a player 1962–5 in various Vancouver symphony orchestras and jazz groups. Studies in ethnomusicology followed with Bruno Nettl at the U of Illinois. After teaching there 1969–70 and at the U of the West Indies, Kingston, Jamaica, during a year of field research (1970–1) on Jamaican popular music for a doctoral dissertation, he joined the music department of the Faculty of Fine Arts at *York U, where he has been director 1972–6 and co-director (as of 1976 with John Gittens) of Canada's first program in jazz studies at the university level. He also developed in 1974 York U's ethnomusicology laboratory and archives. One of Canada's first ethnomusicologists to investigate popular-music cultures, Witmer has contributed articles on that subject to *The New Grove Dictionary*. His research materials are held in the U of Illinois and York U archives.

WRITINGS

'The musical culture of the Blood Indians,' unpubl M MUS thesis, Illinois 1970

'Recent change in the musical culture of the Blood Indians,' *Yearbook for Inter-American Musical Research*, vol 9 (1973)

– and Behague, G. 'Brazilian Ketu cult song,' *Folk and Traditional Music of the Western Continents*, ed Bruno Nettl (Englewood Cliffs, NJ, 1973)

'White music among the Blood Indians of Alberta,' *CFMJ*, vol 2, 1974

'African roots: the case of recent Jamaican popular music,' *Proceedings of the 12th Congress of the International Musicological Soc*, vol 1 (1977)

Many other contributions to scholarly journals and papers for learned societies BAC

WOLFF, Hellmuth (Gustav Sylvio). Organ manufacturer, b Zurich 3 Sep 1937, naturalized Canadian 1970. After apprenticing in Switzerland with Metzler and receiving additional training in Holland, Austria, and the USA he worked 1963–5 for *Casavant Frères and helped produce such noted instruments as the one at St-Pascal, near Kamouraska, Que. In 1966 he was associated with Karl *Wilhelm in St-Hyacinthe but he founded his own business later that year in Laval, near Montreal. Between 1966 and 1980 he built about 20 instruments; 2, with 23 and 27 stops, are in New York, 1 in Ithaca, NY, and 1 in Cambridge, Ont. The 19-stop organ he installed in 1973 in the chapel of the Cistercian Abbey in Oka, Que, is ideally suited to the classical repertoire, especially the French. The design and sound of his instruments have earned them an established position in contemporary organ building.

BIBLIOGRAPHY

Bouchard, Antoine. 'Dix ans d'orgue au Québec,' *VM*, 17, Sep 1970

Bulletin des Amis de l'orgue de Québec, 12, Nov 1970; 23, Jan 1974

Bouchard, Antoine. 'The organ in Canada: the first 300 years,' *Mcan*, 35, Apr 1978 AB

Women's Musical Club of Saskatoon. Founded in 1912 by Mrs G.E. McCraney and others, with a membership of 24 (later as many as 40) determined by audition. Monthly meetings, October through April, have been devoted to study papers illustrated by vocal, choral, or instrumental selections. Recital programs by club members (or very occasionally by guest performers) have been given at the December and April meetings and traditionally have been open to the public. Associate membership was introduced for the convenience of interested listeners who are not regular members and the Mrs F.B. (Elizabeth) *Morrison Scholarship was established for the annual recognition of an outstanding winner at the Saskatoon Music Festival. Club members have included Mary Anderson, Evelyn Eby *Bedford, Patricia Kirkpatrick Elliott, Janet Schnell, Alma Sheasgreen (later *Brock-Smith), and Marguerita *Spencer. (JSn)

Women's Musical Club of Toronto. Founded in Toronto ca 1898. It was initiated by Mrs George Dickson, principal of St Margaret's College for Ladies (and the club's first president), Mrs Sanford Evans, a pianist, and Mary Smart, a singer who later organized the club's first choral society. It began its concerts in 1899 and presented over 20 each season during the early years. Performers were drawn from among the club's 'active' members – some 60 women who were teachers and musicians. Such concerts also were open to approximately 300 'associate' members and to out-of-town guests at a 25-cent admission fee. In addition, there were a few open concerts (with a 25-cent charge for non-members) and one or two special evening recitals by out-of-town artists such as the US pianist Olga Samaroff, who appeared in 1908, and Switzerland's Flonzaley String Quartette, which performed in 1911. By the 1920s the number of concerts had decreased to six or eight a year and, apart from the last years of World War II, when activities ceased altogether, has remained at that level to 1980.

Besides choirs, chamber ensembles, and solo performers, the club also has sponsored the occasional program of dance. During the first 30 years, concerts were given in various locations including the concert hall of the TCM, the Masonic Hall, and the Uptown Theatre. Later performances were held 1929–42 at *Hart House Theatre and 1946–77 at *Eaton Auditorium, and in 1977 they began to be located at St Andrew's Presbyterian Church.

The club has maintained a particular interest in young performers; its Junior Organization (fl 1920s) and Rehearsal Club (1931–47) offered them encouragement and opportunities to perform. In addition, a scholarship fund was established in 1930, and in 1951 the first scholarship was awarded to Betty-Jean *Hagen. In 1955 this award was renamed the Mary Osler Boyd Scholarship in memory of a former club president.

Among Canadian performers who have been presented by the club are the *Hart House String Quartet (1925), Paul *de Marky (1926), Eva *Gauthier (1926), Jeanne *Dusseau (1927), Harry *Adaskin (1927, 1933), Ellen *Ballon (1928), Ida *Krehm (1939), the *Little Symphony of Montreal conducted by Bernard *Naylor (1947), Zara *Nelsova (1947, 1951), the *Parlow String Quartet and Sir Ernest *MacMillan (1948), the *St Mary Magdalene Singers (1949), Donna *Grescoe (1950), Glenn *Gould (1953), Betty-Jean Hagen (1953), Maureen *Forrester (1956), Ray *Dudley (1957), Donald *Bell (1958, 1959, 1967), the *McGill Chamber Orchestra (1960), John *Boyden (1961, 1963), Anton *Kuerti (1963, 1965, 1969), the *Festival Singers (1964), *Bouchard and *Morisset (1966), Ronald *Turini (1967), the *Orford String Quartet (1968), Tsuyoshi *Tsutsumi (1971), and Louis *Quilico (1973).

Foreign artists, many making their Toronto debuts, have included Myra Hess (1923), Wanda Landowska (1926), Joseph Szigeti (1926, 1927), Gregor Piatigorsky (1930), Madeleine Grey (1931), Nathan Milstein (1934). Andrés Segovia (1936, 1949), Marian Anderson (1936, 1937), Alexander Kipnis (1937, 1938), Rosalyn Tureck (1948, 1949, 1958, 1960), Francis Poulenc and Pierre Bernac (1950), the Virtuosi di Roma (1952), Dietrich Fischer-Dieskau (1955, 1956), the Hungarian String Quartet (1956, 1969), I Solisti di Zagreb (1957, 1977), Leontyne Price (1957, 1959), the Juilliard String Quartet (1965, 1967, 1972), Jean-Pierre Rampal (1966), the Guarneri String Quartet (1969), Elly Ameling (1970), the Toulouse Chamber Orchestra (1972), the King's Singers (1974), and the Deller Consort (1977).

BIBLIOGRAPHY

Goudge, Helen. *Look Back in Pride: A History of the Women's Musical Club of Toronto* (Toronto 1972) NM

Women's Musical Club of Winnipeg. In 1980 the fourth-oldest existing club of its kind in Canada. It began informally in 1894 when six women – Mrs Gerald F. Brophy, Mrs L.A. Hamilton, Mrs H.A. Higginson, Mrs Angus Kirkland, Mrs F.H. Matthewson, and Mrs Fred Stobart – met weekly in one of their homes. The first general meeting was held in 1897, and a constitution was adopted in 1899. Mrs Kirkland was the first president, 1897–9. Membership, which in the 1930s reached a peak of 850 but later dropped to 350, was opened to men in 1965. The club has encouraged the advancement of music mainly through establishing and maintaining a high standard in its annual recital series.

In earlier years it presented, among others, the singers Clara Butt, Amelita Galli-Curci, Nellie Melba (1910), Lily Pons, Ernestine Schumann-Heink, Eva Tetrazzini, Richard Crooks, John McCormack, and Lauritz Melchior; the pianists Percy Grainger, Ignace Jan Paderewski, and Sergei Rachmaninoff; and the violinist Mischa Elman. In later years the growing prominence of Canadian artists was reflected in the increasing number who appeared in the club's recitals, though not to the exclusion of guests from abroad. A modern cross-section would include the singers Maureen *Forrester, Marguerite *Gignac, Lois *Marshall, Leontyne Price, and Teresa *Stratas; the pianists Claudio Arrau, Glenn *Gould, Diedre *Irons, Arthur *Ozolins, Ross *Pratt, and Freda *Trepel-Kaufmann; the violinist Nathan Milstein; the cellists Zara *Nelsova, Mstislav Rostropovich, Peggie *Sampson, and Eric *Wilson; and the *Orford String Quartet. Such important Winnipeg musicians as Gwendda Owen *Davies, Cécile Henderson, Phyllis *Holtby, Roline Mackidd, and Snjolaug *Sigurdson also have given recitals for the club.

Held formerly in the concert hall of the *Winnipeg Auditorium, the series moved in 1965 to the concert hall of the Winnipeg Art Gallery.

Besides concerts the club has provided scholarships to young Manitoba musicians chosen by audition, the winners being presented in recital. Winona Lightcap, who later became a prominent Winnipeg performer and teacher, was the first recipient of the scholarship, which is awarded as sufficient money becomes available rather than on an annual basis. Other winners have included Deborah Arnason, Laurie Duncan, Flora Matheson *Goulden, Donna *Grescoe, Ruth Campbell Gairdner, Frederick *Grinke, Margo Sim, and Sydney Young McInnis. Many former winners have returned in subsequent years as seasoned recitalists to perform for the club. (SRM)

Women's musical clubs. Associations of music lovers formed with the aim of improving the members' knowledge and appreciation of music, enriching the concert life of the local community, and encouraging young artists. The women's (or ladies') musical clubs in many cases are the oldest surviving musical organizations in their communities. Of the 16 that have entries in *EMC*, only 3 have ceased to exist. In order of founding dates, and listed by their latest names, the 16 are:

1889 The Duet Club, Hamilton
1891 Club musical de Québec (also known as the Quebec Ladies Morning Musical Club)
1892 Ladies' Morning Musical Club, Montreal
1892–1974 Concert Society of Ottawa (Morning Music Club)
1894 Women's Musical Club of Winnipeg
1898 Women's Musical Club of Toronto
1904–64 Calgary Women's Musical Club
1905 Halifax Ladies' Musical Club
1905 Vancouver Woman's Musical Club
1906 Victoria Musical Art Society
1907 The Regina Musical Club
1908–73 Edmonton Musical Club
1912 Women's Musical Club of Saskatoon
1915 Orpheus Club, Regina
1932 Lethbridge Music Club
1933 Wednesday Morning Musicale, Winnipeg

Other clubs are mentioned in some *EMC* entries on individual cities (eg, Brantford; London; Ottawa).

The development of these groups has shown a remarkably consistent pattern. The product of an age when men were supposed to be preoccupied with the harsh realities of business and professional careers and women with the refinements of the arts and with charitable work, the clubs began as series of meetings for discussion and performance in the homes of well-to-do families. Amateur musicians and music teachers took turns in arranging sessions on subjects such as 'The music of Schumann' or 'Ballads and folk songs.' Soon, recitals by professional performers, local or out-of-town, were added to the schedule, and the paying public, male and female, were admitted to such events. In later years some of the clubs admitted men to full membership. Over the years the emphasis on concerts has grown, as has the granting of scholarships, usually funded by bequests from former members.

See also Clubs.

WOOD, Robin (Lawrence). Pianist, teacher, b Victoria, BC, 13 Oct 1924; LRSM 1943, hon LL D (Victoria) 1978. He studied in Victoria with Stanley Shale and continued 1943–6 at Victoria College and the *U of British Columbia. After World War II a scholarship to the RAM (won in 1943 but postponed because of the war) enabled him to study 1946–50 with Vivian Langrish (piano) and Herbert Murrill (composition). He represented Great Britain in the 1949 International Chopin Competition in Warsaw. He made a Wigmore Hall debut in 1951 and won a Boise scholarship, which provided studies with Nadia Boulanger in France and Edwin Fischer in Switzerland. He then settled in England as the pianist, 1954–65, of the St Cecilia Piano Trio and a teacher 1955–65 at the RAM. In 1958 he received a Harriet Cohen Commonwealth Medal.

Wood returned to Canada in 1965 as assistant director of the Victoria School of Music and became director the following year. When the school became the *Victoria Cons of Music (1968, affiliated to the *U of Victoria) Wood continued as principal. In England he has performed with the Royal Philharmonic and the London and Birmingham SOs; in Canada, with the Vancouver and Victoria SOs and the CBC Vancouver and CBC Winnipeg orchestras. He has performed as the pianist in *Trio Victoria and has given radio and TV recitals in Canada and England, alone and in a two-piano team with his wife, the pianist Winifred (Jean) Scott (b Winnipeg 18 May 1924), a pupil of Gwendda Owen *Davies in Winnipeg, of Frank Mannheimer 1944–6 in New York, and of Hilda Dederich, Herbert Murrill and Myra Hess in 1946 at the RAM, London, on an AB scholarship. Scott also studied with Nadia Boulanger in Paris before joining the staff of the RAM in 1948 as a teacher of graduate students. In the ensuing years she played concertos with several British orchestras and gave many BBC recitals. After returning to Canada in 1965 she taught piano 1965–71 at the Victoria School (Cons) of Music, served 1971–3 as registrar of the conservatory, and in 1973 became vice-principal, her duties continuing to include master classes in piano and teacher-training. DBW (KW)

Woodwinds, playing and teaching. The woodwind instruments in wide use in Canada during the 19th and 20th centuries were flute, oboe, clarinet, bassoon, saxophone, and recorder; and, in the orchestra, piccolo, english horn, bass clarinet, and contrabassoon. In 1980, with the exception of flutes made by Jack P. Goosman of Toronto, orchestral woodwinds still were not made in Canada. Flutes were imported from the USA, oboes, clarinets, and saxophones from France (and some clarinets from Japan), and bassoons from Germany, France, Great Britain and, more recently, from the USA.

1 History, in Canada
2 20th century: concert music
3 20th century: jazz and pop
4 Medieval, renaissance, and baroque instrument revival
5 Woodwind music for teaching

1 HISTORY, IN CANADA. The first European woodwind instrument to be played in Canada probably was the 'German [transverse] flute which proved to be out of tune when they came to the Church,' at Quebec on Christmas Day 1645 (*Jesuit Relations*, vol 27, p 113). The fife was used in the regimental music of the French military in Canada after 1650. Other woodwinds were introduced in the 18th century by members of British military bands, some of whom remained in Canada and taught music. The announcement in the Montreal *Gazette* (12 Sep 1796) of a concert performance, by George E. Saliment, of two flute concertos (unidentified) is one of the earliest references to a public solo performance of woodwind music. Among the items offered for sale in the Montreal *Gazette* of 1791 by the Quebec music dealer *Glackemeyer were flutes, apparently the only woodwinds he stocked. Glackemeyer's son Louis-Édouard later became an accomplished amateur flutist.

With the growth of towns during the 19th century, municipal bands were formed, creating thereby a demand for instruments and instruction. The 1836 *Musique Canadienne included clarinet, piccolo, and bassoon. An early teacher of clarinet, flute, and other band instruments in Ottawa in the 1840s was James Balbirnie. Adam J. *Schott and John *Bayley, bandmasters, were fine clarinetists and teachers. In the late 1880s Ernest *Lavigne recruited a number of well-trained Belgian and French musicians for his *Sohmer Park band and newly formed orchestra, and many remained in Montreal as teachers and players. In 1877 the Belleville (Ont) Band imported a quartet of saxophones from France. The *TCM from its inception offered instruction in flute, oboe, clarinet, bassoon, and saxophone. Thus, the standards of woodwind playing in Canada had risen considerably by the turn of the century, when Sousa's band was so widely popular. Canadian woodwind players generally looked to England and France for standards and traditions in those years, but by the 1940s the US influence had become dominant and most of the leading teachers in Canada were trained in the eclectic US style. Some of the players who emerged in the 1960s were entirely products of Canadian instruction, and in the 1970s Canadian orchestras became more inclined than before to audition Canadian-trained players for principal positions.

2 20TH CENTURY: CONCERT MUSIC. Notable woodwind players and teachers before World War II included Hervé *Baillargeon, flute (Montreal); Frank E. Dennis, bassoon (Toronto); Joseph *Gagnier, clarinet, and his sons Armand, clarinet, Lucien, flute, and Réal, oboe, and his grandson Roland, bassoon, all active in Montreal; Alexandre *Laurendeau, clarinet and oboe (Montreal); Montreal's *Masella family, including Frank (clarinet) and his sons Rafael (clarinet), Pietro (oboe), and Rodolfo (bassoon); John McNamee, bassoon (Toronto); Herbert Pye and Robert Rogers, clarinet (Toronto); Arthur *Semple, flute, who founded the Toronto Flute Club in 1944; and Oliver E. Woods, oboe and french horn, who had played in Sousa's band, and his daughter Maxine Woods Shimer, bassoon, the first woman member of the *TSO woodwind section. Both the last-named were members of the Canadian Double Reed Sextet (fl 1933 in Toronto).

It was after the war however, with the growth of full-time orchestras and chamber groups, that Canada could point to a list of resident players, foreign- and Canadian-born, able to contribute significantly as soloists, chamber musicians, orchestra players, and teachers. To name a few active in the period 1945–80: the flutists Robert *Aitken, Jeanne Baxtresser, Kathryn Cernauskas, Robert Cram, Harriet Crossland, Gordon *Day, André-Gilles Duchemin, Mario *Duschenes, Nicholas *Fiore, Kenneth Helm, Albert Horch, Wolfgang Kander, Dirk *Keetbaas, Robert Langevin, Jean C. *Morin, Suzanne *Shulman, and Douglas Stewart; the oboists Perry *Bauman, Melvin *Berman, Harry *Freedman (and english horn), Pierre *Rolland, Harry Sargous, Jacques *Simard, Warren Stannard, and Stan Wood (and english horn); the clarinetists James *Campbell, Avrahm *Galper, Arthur Hart, Emilio Iacurto, Ronald *de Kant, David *Kaplan, Jean *Laurendeau, Leslie *Mann, Stanley *McCartney, James Morton, John Rapson, and Ezra *Schabas; the bassoonists René Bernard, Nicholas *Kilburn, Christine *Mather, James McKay, Norman Tobias, Elver Wahlberg, Christopher *Weait, and George *Zukerman.

Canadian woodwind ensembles have been heard on the CBC and in recital and have made recordings. Among the leading groups have been the *Ayorama Wind Quintet; the Canadian Wind Quintet (*Kingston Symphony members Dale and Donelda Hunter, oboe and flute, Gordon Craig, clarinet, Norman Sherman, bassoon, and Stephen Seiffert, french horn); the Dirk *Keetbaas Players; the Lorien Woodwind Quintet (*Hamilton Philharmonic members Vivian Minden, flute, Sandra Watts, oboe, Wes Foster, clarinet, John Courtney, bassoon, and Robert Hanson, french horn); the Ottawa Saxophone Quartet (Russell Thomas, soprano, Wally Munro, alto, Bruce Tetu, tenor, and Johnny Hinchey, baritone); the Pacific Wind Quintet (*U of Victoria faculty members Lanny Pollet, flute, William Benjamin, oboe, Ethan Sloane, clarinet, Jesse Read, bassoon, and Richard Ely, french horn); the *Quebec SO Woodwind Quintet; the *Quebec Woodwind Quintet; the Sentiri Wind Quintet (Hamilton Philharmonic members Paula Elliott, flute, Jon Peterson, oboe, Wes Foster, clarinet, Thomas Elliott, bassoon, and Gregory Hustis, french horn); the Toronto Chamber Winds (an octet); the *Toronto Woodwind Quintet (Toronto Winds); the *Vancouver Woodwind Quintet; and the *York Winds. (See also Chamber music: 3 / Woodwind quintet.)

The emergence in Canada of the saxophone as a solo concert instrument has been attributed largely to the efforts of Paul *Brodie, founder and director of the Brodie School of Music and Modern Dance and the Brodie Saxophone Quartet and co-founder of the *World Saxophone Congress. Other concert saxophonists include Jean-Guy Brault and Lawrence Sereda (Brodie pupils) and Pierre *Bourque. Brodie and Arthur *Romano (Montreal) have been Canada's leading saxophone teachers; others include Gerald Danovitch (Montreal) and Dave Quarin (Vancouver).

By 1980 instruction in woodwind instruments was offered in many public and high schools, and tuition was available privately and at conservatories throughout Canada. The leading players often taught advanced students at universities which offered performance courses. The woodwind instruments were a popular choice for study, particularly the flute and clarinet, followed in favour by the saxophone. The cost of oboes and bassoons, and the relative difficulty the neophyte has in playing them and learning to overcome the vicissitudes of reed-making, tend to limit the number selecting these instruments. Avrahm Galper and Christopher Weait are among those who have written instruction books.

The *U of Toronto has been the location of two international woodwind meetings: that of the International Double-Reed Society in 1976 and the International Clarinet Congress in 1978.

3 20TH CENTURY: JAZZ AND POP. The saxophone has been used most extensively in popular music and jazz. As early as 1910 the *Six Brown Brothers (originally from Lindsay, Ont) were performing as a saxophone sextet in vaudeville and were among the pioneers of the instrument in popular music. By the late 1920s a saxophone section was an integral component of the dance band; by the 1940s it numbered from four to six players, among them one or more capable of improvised (jazz) solos. Different traditions have developed in jazz according to each of the saxophone's four main registers – soprano, alto, tenor, and baritone. Thus it is necessary to identify which type a jazz musician plays, even though, for the sake of versatility and ensemble work, many saxophonists have become fluent in some or all of the others. By register, the leading jazz saxophonists in Canada in 1980 included: soprano, Jim *Galloway, Bill *Smith, and Michael Stuart; alto, Sayyd *Abdul Al Khabyyr, Moe *Koffman, Alvinn Pall, Leo Perron, P.J. *Perry, Bernie *Piltch, and Jerry *Toth; tenor, Eugene Amaro, Nick *Ayoub, Brian *Barley, Ted Davidson, Art *Ellefson, Lance *Harrison, George Kennedy, Pat LaBarbera, Fraser *MacPherson, Ron *Park, Michael Stuart, John Tank, and Don *Thompson; baritone, Gary Morgan, Freddie Nichols, and Earl Seymour. Such Canadian-born saxophonists as Georgie Auld and Bob Burns have had major careers elsewhere (see Jazz).

The clarinet and the flute usually are secondary instruments for saxophonists; their use in the dance- or big-band context is generally for orchestral effect, and only a few musicians have made reputations as clarinet or flute soloists. The clarinet is heard as a solo instrument most often in swing and dixieland bands. Some of its leading players in Canada have been Howard 'Cokie' Campbell, Henry Cuesta, Lance Harrison, Al Lawrie, Cliff *McKay, Phil *Nimmons, and Bert *Niosi. The Vancouver-born Wally Fawkes has been prominent in British traditional jazz bands. Among jazz flutists, Sayyd Abdul Al Khabyyr, Paul Horn, Moe Koffman, and Kathryn *Moses have enjoyed success.

4 MEDIEVAL, RENAISSANCE, AND BAROQUE INSTRUMENT REVIVAL. The revival of interest in the recorder began in the 1930s and gained momentum after 1950, partly because of the growing popularity of medieval, renaissance, and baroque music. The desire in the 1960s and 1970s for an authentic sound in the performance of such music stimulated the manufacture of replicas of the instruments of those periods, and some began to be made in Canada, including shawms, krumhorns, dulcians, and racketts, all ancestors of the oboe. Because it is relatively easy to play, however, the recorder became the early instrument most widely used by children (*Orff method and others) and by adults for recreational music and as an introduction to music-making. The *CAMMAC Music Centre has utilized recorders in its summer programs. Leading Canadian players and authors of instructional materials for the instrument have been Don *Cowan, Mario *Duschenes, Frank Gamble (Vancouver), Miriam Samuelson (Montreal), and Hugh Orr.

Performers on early wind instruments include Louise Courville, Garry Crighton, Paul Douglas, David Klausner, Alison Mackay, Christine Mather, Timothy McGee, Ray *Nurse, Susan Prior, Michael Purves-Smith, Janet See, David *Skulski, and David Walker.

For a list of early-instrument ensembles see Instruments: medieval, renaissance, baroque: 3 / Ensembles in Canadian universities, 4 / Professional ensembles. See also Instrument collections.

5 WOODWIND MUSIC FOR TEACHING. There is a fairly large body of Canadian music available and useful for instruction purposes by woodwind teachers with pupils at the pre-professional level. This material can be used to expand and supplement traditional woodwind teaching music. Until the 1970s a primary difficulty in this area has been lack of knowledge of such works. However the promotional and informational services of the *CMCentre, the *CMEA, and the *Contemporary Showcase have helped to improve the situation. The primary purpose of such works should be to introduce both the notation and the techniques of innovations in woodwind playing in compositions worthy of public performance without a disproportionate amount of explanation by the teacher. The ideal, for teachers and students, might be a body of graded material, published and printed in a well-edited format with concise instructions for the required new techniques in the printed part, and with separately available recordings by acknowledged performers. The most effective development of instructional material for an instrument tends to occur through the direct involvement of an acknowledged teacher/performer on that instrument. In the accompanying list, for example, there are 30 works for flute, half of them published, seven recorded. Many of these were produced through the exemplary efforts of the flutist Robert *Aitken.

The composer in this genre must be sensitive to the existing capabilities of young players so that he or she may expand and develop technique logically. The composer should seek the advantages of publication, as the great majority of teachers do not have the time to seek unpublished music or the inclination to clarify inconsistencies in manuscripts. Indeed, the publisher of such music has an attractive world-wide market for a product which is in continual demand.

The appended list is a selection of published and unpublished works by Canadian composers for flute, oboe, clarinet, and bassoon with and without accompaniment. The CMCentre chamber music catalogues are a further source of suitable music by Canadian composers for duos, trios, etc. The Contemporary Showcase syllabus and the CMCentre's *Canadian Music: A Selective Guidelist for Teachers* provide timings, and annotations rating the works according to difficulty.

FOR FLUTE

*Applebaum *Essay*. 1971. Fl. Leeds 1971. Dom S-69006
*Baker, Michael *Sonata*. 1963. Fl, pf. Southern 1973
*Barnes *Sonata*. 1965. Fl, pf
*Beecroft *Tre Pezzi Brevi*. 1961. Fl, hp (guit, pf). UE 1962. Dom S-69006
*Bottenberg *Dialogue*. 1972. Rec (fl), hpd (pf)
*Camilleri *Danse lente*. Fl, pf. Wat 1964
– *Meditation*. Ob (fl), pf. Wat 1964
*Coulthard *Lyric Sonatina*. 1971. Fl, pf. Wat 1976
*Cowan *Charm Bracelet*. Fl, pf. B & H 1972
Evans, Robert *Thoronet pour flûte seule*. 1971
*Fleming, R. *Almost Waltz*. 1970. Fl, pf. Jaymar 1971. Dom S-69006
*Fodi *Seven Fantasias*. 1968. Fl
*Freedman *Soliloquy*. 1970. Fl, pf. Leeds 1971. Dom S-69006
*Glick *Petite Suite pour Flûte*. 1960. GVT 1972. Dom S-69006
*Hétu, J. *Quatre Pièces*. 1965. Fl, pf. Éditions Billaudot 1969. Madrigal MAS-402
*Joachim, O. *Expansion*. 1962. Fl, pf. BMIC 1967
*Jones, K. *Rondo*. Fl. 1963. Wat 1972. RCI 219/RCA CC/CCS 1013/Sel CC15.066
*Kenins *Concertante*. 1966. Fl, pf. B & H 1972. Dom S-69006
*McCauley *Five Miniatures*. 1958. Fl, str orch. Leeds 1961. Dom S-69006
*Morel *Nuvattuq*. 1967. Alto fl. RCI 409
*Papineau-Couture *Suite*. 1945. Fl, pf
*Pentland *Sonatina*. 1954. Fl
*Saint-Marcoux *Sonata*. 1964. Fl, pf
*Somers *Etching – The Vollard Suite* from *The Picasso Suite*. 1964. Fl. Ric 1969. CBC SM-114
*Wuensch *Cameos*. 1969. Fl, pf. Leeds 1971. Dom S-69006
– *Three Pieces*. 1971. Fl
*Zuckert *Elegiac Improvisations*. 1970. Fl, hpd (pf). RCI 421
– *The Nightingale at My Window*. 1968. Fl
– *Little Spanish Dance*. 1970. Jaymar 1971. Dom S-69006

FOR OBOE

*Archer *Sonata*. 1973. Ob, pf. Ber 1978
Coulthard *Sonata*. 1948. Ob, pf. RCI 4
Fleming, R. *Three Dialogues*. 1964. Fl (ob), pf (hpd). CBC SM-268
*Klein *À la Rossini*. 1972. Ob (pf optional)
*Turner, R. *Sonatina*. 1951. Ob, pf
*Weinzweig *Divertimento No. 2*. 1948. Ob, orch (pf reduction H. Perry). B & H 1951. RCI 86/RCI ACM 1

FOR CLARINET

*Adaskin, M. *Daydreams*. 1968. Cl, pf
Archer *Sonata*. 1970. Cl, pf. Wat 1973. RCI 412
Camilleri *Three Visions for an Imaginary Dancer and Solo Clarinet*. Fairfield 1968
Coles, Graham *Sonata*. Cl, pf. Ber
*Eckhardt-Gramatté *Ruck-Ruck Sonata*. 1947, rev 1962. Cl, pf
Evans, Robert *Suite Bizarre*. 1967. Cl
*Garant *Asymétries No. 2*. 1959. Cl, pf
Glick *Suite Hébraïque*. 1963. Cl, pf. B & H 1968. Dom S-69004
*Haworth, F. *Shepherd's Purse Suite*. 1958. Cl, pf
Kenins *Divertimento*. 1960. Cl, pf. B & H 1970. Dom S-69004
*Kymlicka *Two Dances*. Cl, pf. Leeds 1970. Dom S-69004
*Mather *Étude pour clarinette seule*. 1962. CBC SM-184
Simeonov, Blago *Monody*. Cl (cl, pf). Wat
– *Poème*. Cl. Wat 1974
Wuensch *In modo antico*. 1971. Cl, pf
– *Variations*. 1971. Cl, pf
Zuckert *Doina: Roumanian Fantasy*. 1970. Cl, pf
– *Sur le lac Baptiste*. 1972. Cl, pf

FOR BASSOON

Coulthard *Lyric Sonatina*. 1969. Bn, pf. Wat 1973. Mel SMLP-4032
*Johnston, R. *Suite*. 1946. Bn, pf (orch). Mel SMLP-4032
*Lidov *Alpha-bits*. 1973. Bn, pf. Mel SMLP-4032
*Weait *Variations*. 1972. Bn. Harmuse 1975. Pyramid 102
Zuckert *Suite*. 1975. Bn

DISCOGRAPHY

New for Now, vol 2: 9 works for cl. Galper, McCartney, Fetherston, Temoin cls, Barkin pf. 1971. Dom S-69004
New for Now, vol 3: 12 works for fl, an illustrated talk by Robert Aitken. Aitken fl, Ross pf, str orch. 1972. 2-Dom S-69006
Four Centuries of Music for Bassoon. Weait bn, Kernerman vn, Barstow vc, Brough hpd. 1973. Pyramid 102
Lonely Island. Weait bn, Gaylord pf. 1976. Mel SMLP 4032

FILMOGRAPHY

The Oboe Reed (U of Toronto Media Centre 1972)

1/ HK, 3/ MM, 5/ CW

WOOLLEY, Édouard (Joseph). Tenor, teacher, actor, composer, b Port-au-Prince, Haiti, 31 Mar 1916, naturalized Canadian 1958; D MUS (Montreal) 1947. In Port-au-Prince he studied voice with Élisabeth de Pesquidoux-Mahy and Henriette Perret-Duplessis, acting with Raoul Nargys, German repertoire with Werner Jaegerhuber, and piano and harmony with Carmen Brouard. He was a choirmaster before moving to Montreal in 1938. He continued his voice studies there with Salvator *Issaurel 1938–44 and opened his own studio in 1942. His pupils included Joseph *Rouleau and André *Turp. At the *Cons national in Montreal he studied organ with Eugène *Lapierre and piano with Edmond *Trudel. His doctoral thesis was entitled 'La phonétique appliquée à l'art du chant.' He made his debut with the *Variétes lyriques in Hahn's operetta *Ciboulette* in 1942 and in his five seasons with that company took a number of roles, notably in Bazin's *Le Voyage en Chine* and Oscar Straus' *Three Waltzes*. He also sang or acted in several CBC programs and took several supporting roles on stage and film as well as TV. Woolley was the founder and artistic director of the *Opéra national du Québec 1948–52. He began to teach art history at the Vieux-Montréal Cegep in 1967 and was director of the Cons national 1971–5. He has written masses for three voices and for four voices, some songs, and a few instrumental works, including *Sous les palmiers* (ca 1958), a suite for violin and piano. *Mazoumbel* (revised 1979), a movement from the suite, was performed in

Montreal in 1979 during a concert of Haitian music. HPn

'The World is Waiting for the Sunrise.' Popular ballad by Gene Lockhart (lyrics) and Ernest *Seitz (music, Toronto 1918), who had conceived the refrain when he was 12. Published in 1919 by *Chappell, the song was recorded over 100 times: initially when its hopeful sentiment appealed to post-war North America, by both singers and instrumentalists, including Morton Downey, Fritz Kreisler, Ted Lewis, John Steel, and others; and later as a popular vehicle for improvisation, by jazz and big band musicians, including the Benny Goodman Quartet and Sextet, Duke Ellington, Bert *Niosi, Mel Powell, Jess Stacy, and Jack Teagarden. A version recorded for Capitol in 1949 by Les Paul and Mary Ford was a million-seller. The song's lyricist, Lockhart (b London, Ont, 1891, d 1957), at the time an actor with the travelling Pierrot Players, began a Broadway career in 1921 and a Hollywood career in 1922. He wrote and directed the Broadway musical revue *Bunk of 1926*. In 1953 he returned to Toronto for a *Melody Fair production.

World Music Week / Semaine mondiale de la musique. Biennial congress begun in 1975 and held under the aegis of the International Music Council. Canada was host to the inaugural congress, 29 Sep to 5 Oct 1975, and for it the schedule of events was organized by the *CMCouncil under the direction of John *Roberts, then president of the council. The purpose of the week was to foster a constructive exchange among musicians of five continents. Nearly 500 delegates from 50 countries attended. The activities took place in turn in Toronto, Ottawa, Montreal, and Quebec City. Prior to the week itself a meeting of the executive committee of the International Music Council was held in Calgary, and the council's 16th general assembly took place in Toronto, as did the International Exhibition of Music for Broadcasting, organized jointly by the *CBC and the International Music Centre, Vienna.

World Music Week's opening event, at the *St Lawrence Centre in Toronto, was highlighted by the premiere of the film *Musicanada*, produced by Malca Gilson and Tony Ianzelo of the *NFB and depicting the musical life of the country, and by a concert of works by the Toronto composers *Aitken, *Beecroft, *Freedman, *Gellman, and *Weinzweig. Discussions on the theme 'Music as a dimension of life' continued for five days in a series of workshops which dealt individually with the roles of the media, the music of young people, the world soundscape, music and tomorrow's public, the role of the composer in a changing world, the role of the performer and the democratization of music, and the preservation and presentation of traditional music and dance. Another important feature was International Music Day (1 October), during which Yehudi Menuhin gave a recital (his program included *Somers' *Music for Solo Violin*) and International Music Council prizes were awarded to Ravi Shankar, to Menuhin, and – posthumously – to Dmitri Shostakovich.

World Music Week played a considerable role in making the public more aware of Canadian music and its performers. Between the 16th general meeting (23 September) and the concluding event (5 October) many recitals and concerts were given by Canadian artists and groups, including Robert Aitken, Émilien *Allard, Edith *Butler, Maureen *Forrester, Félix *Leclerc, Phyllis *Mailing, Hugh *McLean, John *Mills-Cockell, Alexandre *Zelkine, the *Toronto Mendelssohn Choir, the *Festival Singers, the *COC, the *SMCQ Ensemble, the *Lyric Arts Trio, the *Orford String Quartet, the *Quebec Woodwind Quintet, the CBC orchestras of Montreal and Ottawa, the *NACO, the *MSO, and the *TS, and the 'Ksan Dancers in their presentation 'The spirit of our ancestors.' The public had occasion to hear works by *Beckwith, *Fleming, *Forsyth, *Glick, *Healey, *Morel, *Papineau-Couture, *Saint-Marcoux, *Schafer (*Lustro*), Somers (**Louis Riel*), *Tremblay, *Turner, *Vivier, and *Willan in addition to those mentioned above. Among the works commissioned by the CBC for the occasion were ... *chant d'amours* by *Garant, *Icons* by *Hambraeus, and *Ouverture* by *Prévost. Compositions by Baird, de Pablo, Cristóbal Halffter, and Stockhausen also were heard. Among foreign artists who participated were the dancers and musicians of the national theatre of Burma. The concerts, several of which were televised by the CBC and relayed abroad by RCI, took place mostly at the St Lawrence Centre in Toronto, at the *NAC, in *McGill U's Pollack Hall, at the *PDA, and at the *Grand Théâtre in Quebec City. There were several public lectures and exhibitions, and honorary degrees were conferred by the *U of Ottawa on Yehudi Menuhin, Harry Somers, Jean *Vallerand, and Trân Van Khê.

World Music Week was financed primarily through subsidies from Canada's Dept of the Secretary of State and Dept of External Affairs, the CBC, the Alberta, Ontario, and Quebec governments, and the *Canada Council. The council also set aside a special amount for the publication of a full report of the activities in the **Canada Music Book* (double issue 11–12 1975–6).

BIBLIOGRAPHY

Gyokeres, Nancy. 'Representatives from 50 countries listen to Canadian music,' *MSc*, 287, Jan–Feb 1976 AP

The World Saxophone Congress. Founded in 1969 in Chicago by Paul *Brodie and Eugene Rousseau to demonstrate the versatility of the saxophone. The congress has been held in Chicago (1969, 1970), Toronto (1972), Bordeaux (1973), and London (1976). Performers at the third congress, convened in Toronto, included the Canadians Claude Brisson, Gerald Danovitch, I Ching, Moe *Koffman, Rémi Ménard, Alvinn Pall, Jerry *Toth, and the *Pierre Bourque Saxophone Quartet, in addition to distinguished players and groups from abroad. Works were commissioned by the CBC (Violet *Archer: *Sonata*), the *OAC (Rudolf *Komorous: *Dingy Yellow*), and the *Canada Council (John *Weinzweig: *Divertimento No. 6*). The Canadians *Bissell, *Bottenberg, *Dela, *Fiala, *Fleming, *Ford, *George, *Haworth, *Henninger, *McCauley, *Rathburn, *Turner, *Wuensch, and *Zuckert also wrote works for the congress. CF

World Soundscape Project. Established in 1971 with headquarters at *Simon Fraser U. This research enterprise, which has secured Canada a place in the forefront of the study of soundscape ecology, was devised, and in 1980 continued to be directed, by R. Murray *Schafer; among Schafer's associates have been Howard Broomfield, Bruce *Davis, Peter *Huse, Barry *Truax, Hildegard Westerkamp, and Adam Woog. The Donner Canadian Foundation, the *Canada Council, and Unesco have provided financial assistance. Through systematic and critical study the project has endeavoured to contribute to and co-ordinate research on the scientific, aesthetic, philosophic, architectural, and sociological aspects of soundscape ecology, the human community's relationship to its sonic environment. The project's ultimate aim is to make its findings available to planners and designers of future soundscapes.

The sonic environment (or soundscape) – the sum total of all the natural and artificial sounds within any defined area – is an intimate reflection of the social, technological, and natural conditions of that area. Change in these conditions means change in the sonic environment. One of the main tasks of soundscape ecology is to determine whether and how the sonic environment may be controlled and improved.

In studying a specific soundscape it becomes apparent that the image of the soundscape is shaped by the listener's perception of it. The analysis of the image is based on cognitive units such as foreground, background, contour, rhythm, silence, density, space, and volume. From these units have been derived such analytical concepts as keynote, signal, soundmark, sound object, and sound symbol.

Keynote as a musical term refers to the key or tonality of a particular composition. In soundscape studies it refers to a ubiquitous and prevailing sound, usually in the background of the individual's perception, to which all other sounds in the soundscape are related.

Signals, a term borrowed from communication theory, are foreground sounds, listened to consciously, often encoding certain messages or information.

Soundmarks, analogous to landmarks, are unique sound objects, specific to a certain place.

A *sound object*, as defined by Pierre Schaeffer, who coined the term ('l'objet sonore'), is 'an acoustical object for human perception, and not a mathematical or electro-acoustical object for synthesis.' The sound object is the smallest self-contained particle of a soundscape.

Sound symbols, a more general category, are sounds which evoke personal responses based on collective and cultural levels of association.

While the scope of the World Soundscape Project is global, particular emphasis has been placed on the Canadian soundscape. Studies of specific environments have documented salient features, identified differences, and noted trends. Present and future research topics include studies in new sounds; an archive of lost and disappearing sounds; a glossary of sounds in literature; sound association tests; soundscape analyses (eg, events, entertainments, and community soundmarks); the structural analysis of radio programming, car horn sounds and counts, and the sonic environments of schools; the design of acoustic parks; sound typology and morphology; the semantics of sound; and other related topics.

As might have been predicted, it was found that too often the modern soundscape is 'lo-fi' – the signal-to-noise ratio is unfavourable, ie, discrete sounds cannot be heard clearly because of a high ambient noise level. The average citizen, however, considers noise an inevitable by-product of technological progress. This lack of awareness is dangerous not only from the ecological point of view – the data on the harmful effects of sound pollution are overwhelming – but also from the aesthetic.

However, some musicians previously concerned only with the *creation* of sound have become concerned with its *prevention*. Beyond fighting sound pollution, sound ecologists eventually may help to design healthier and more pleasant sonic environments by tapping the resources of such seemingly diverse areas as acoustics, architecture, linguistics, music, psychology, sociology, and urban planning. Creative town planning, legislative action (noise abatement regulations), the design of acoustic parks and playgrounds, and the innovative preservation of worthwhile sounds of past and present may be among the means to achieve such ends. The aim of the World Soundscape Project is 'to provide coherent facts by which decisions can be made not only to control but also to compose the acoustic environment of the future' ('Introduction,' *Music of the Environment Series*).

See also Acoustics research in Canada; Psychology of music.

DISCOGRAPHY

Davis, B. Fawcett, Murray Schafer *Okeanos*. 90-minute quadraphonic tape composition. 1971. Ber rental

Soundscapes of Canada, 10 hour-long radio broadcasts for CBC's 'Ideas' series. 1974. Rental for broadcasts, World Soundscape Project

WRITINGS

Schafer, R. Murray. *The New Soundscape* (Don Mills 1969)

– *The Book of Noise* (Vancouver 1970)

– *A Survey of Community Noise By-Laws in Canada (1972)* (Vancouver 1972)

The Music of the Environment Series, ed R. Murray Schafer (1973–8):

1 *The Music of the Environment* (Vienna 1973)

2 *The Vancouver Soundscape*, with 2 cassettes (Vancouver 1974)

3 *European Sound Diary* (Vancouver 1977)

4 *Five Village Soundscapes*, with 5 cassettes (Vancouver 1977)

5 *A Dictionary of Acoustic Ecology* (Vancouver 1978)

Truax, Barry. 'Soundscape Studies, an introduction to the World Soundscape Project,' *Numus West*, 5, Spring 1974

Sound Heritage, entire issue, vol 3, no. 4, 1974

Davis, Bruce. 'FM radio as observational access to wilderness environments,' *Alternatives*, vol 4, Spring 1975

UNESCO Courier, entire issue, vol 29, Nov 1976

Schafer, R. Murray. *The Tuning of the World* (Toronto 1977); transl *Le Paysage Sonore* (Paris 1979)

(HK, APW)

'The Wreck of the Julie Plante.' A poem by W.H. Drummond, published in *The Habitant and Other Poems* in 1897 and subtitled 'A Legend of Lac St. Pierre.' The roving lumberjacks set it to a tune and carried it to many widely scattered lumbercamps. Franz Rickaby included a fragment (music for one stanza and one other incomplete stanza) in his *Ballads and Songs of the Shanty-Boy* (Cambridge, Mass, 1926), noting that the singer, from eastern Ontario, described it as 'a "Canuck" song, very popular among the French-Canadian shantyboys both at home and abroad.' The US song collector E.C. Beck (*Songs of the Michigan Lumberjacks*, Ann Arbor 1941) heard it from at least nine different lumberjacks in Michigan and Wisconsin, some of whom changed 'Lac St. Pierre' (on the St Lawrence River between Montreal and Quebec) to 'Lak San Clair' (between Lake Erie and Lake Huron). It is included in the *Fowke and *Johnston *Folk Songs of Canada* (Waterloo 1954). It had not been recorded by 1977. The poem has been set to music by H.H. *Godfrey (1899), Herbert *Spencer (Delmar 1907), and Geoffrey *O'Hara (Ditson 1920) in choral and solo-voice versions.

See also Disaster songs. EF

WRIGHT, Don (Donald John Alexander). Choir conductor, arranger, composer, educator, b Strathroy, near London, Ont, 6 Sep 1908; BA classics (Western Ont) 1933. His father was the founder and owner of the Wright Piano Co which was chartered in 1908 and remained active until 1924. He began cello studies at seven and trumpet at ten. With his brothers, Clark, Ernest, and William, he organized the Wright Brothers' Orchestra, which performed 1921–35 in Ontario dance halls. He was a teacher 1934–40 and director of music 1940–6 in London, Ont, schools. He was manager 1946–56 of radio station CFPL, London, and in 1947 he founded the CFPL Chorus, which later became the popular *Don Wright Chorus. In 1955 his arrangement of Warwick Webster's 'Man in a Raincoat,' recorded for the Unique label by his daughter Priscilla (b 14 Aug 1940), was an international hit and resulted in her appearance 1 Jul 1955 on 'The Ed Sullivan Show.'

Wright moved in 1957 to Toronto, where he formed the Don Wright Singers (1957–62) and composed commercials and scores for films and TV. These include CBC TV's 'Trail of '98' (1958) and 'Seaway to the World' (1959). He also composed *Proudly We Praise* (Thompson 1966), a tribute to Canada, which has been performed by school choirs across the country. As an educator he has shown particular interest in the changing voice. His publications, choral and educational, include *The Collegiate Choir* (2 vols, Waterloo 1938, 1939), *Youthful Voices* (3 vols, Thompson 1945, 1949, 1954), *Fun to Read Music* (Thompson 1952), and *Pre-teen Song Settings* (Thompson 1961).

BIBLIOGRAPHY

'Musical salute to Canada a national best-seller,' *CanComp*, 16, Mar 1967 HM

WRIGHT, William Lewis. Teacher, organist, administrator, b Nova Scotia 16 Apr 1878, d Robson, BC, 1970; BA (Acadia) 1903, hon D MUS (Acadia) 1946, hon D MUS (Brandon) 1969. He was the first music graduate of *Acadia U, then studied for four years in Germany with Leopold Godowsky. Returning to Canada he became the first director (1907–47) of the Dept of Music of Brandon College (see Brandon U). He was a founding member of the *MRMTA and president 1936–8. After retirement from the college he was organist at the Community Church in Robson, BC, until his death. PAS

Wright Chorus. See Don Wright Chorus.

WRY, Gordon. Tenor, choir conductor, b Saint John, NB, 7 Oct 1910. His teachers were Agnes Forbes (voice) in Saint John and Albert Whitehead and Nellie *Smith (voice) and Healey *Willan (theory) at the *TCM 1937–40. A church soloist in Saint John at Trinity Anglican and in Toronto at Knox Presbyterian 1937–50 and Grace Church on-the-Hill 1950–77, he also was tenor soloist in several performances of the *St Matthew Passion* under Sir Ernest *MacMillan. As a leading tenor 1949–53 with the *CBC Opera Company he sang Florestan in *Fidelio* (1949), Bob Boles in *Peter Grimes* (1949), and Mr Upford in *Albert Herring* (1950). He was a soloist in the Canadian premiere, 21 Feb 1957, of Britten's *Spring Symphony* and gave the Canadian premiere, 17 Dec 1972, of the same composer's *Fourth Canticle* at Massey College, U of Toronto. Wry was a founding member in 1953 of the *Festival Singers and sang with them until 1974. He also founded the Massey College Singers in 1963 and remained their director until 1979. SWl

WUENSCH, Gerhard (Joseph). Composer, musicologist, pianist, b Vienna 23 Dec 1925; PH D musicology (Vienna) 1950, Artist Diplomas piano and composition (State Academy, Vienna) 1952. While studying at the State Academy he was a freelance accompanist and a staff composer 1951–4 for the Austrian radio network. He studied further 1954–6 at the U of Texas with Paul Pisk and Kent Kennan on a Fulbright Fellowship and has taught at Butler U, Indianapolis, 1956–63, at the *U of Toronto 1964–9, and at the *U of Calgary 1969–73. In 1973 he became chairman of the theory and composition department at the *U of Western Ontario. He completed his PH D thesis on Max Reger and in 1972 received a *Canada Council Research Fellowship for work on a book about the German composer. He also prepared a CBC radio series, 1968–9, on Schoenberg, Berg, and Webern.

While Wuensch was at Butler U his *Mosaic* won first prize at the Syracuse Fine Arts Festival. Written in Canada, his *Music without Pretensions* (premiered at the 1970 *Guelph Spring Festival), *Alberta Set*, and *Prelude, Aria and Fugue* were written for the free-bass accordionist Joe *Macerollo and contribute significantly to the accordion repertoire. Wuensch is a practical eclectic who evades allegiance but whose skills equip him to move easily and with a certain amused detachment through many styles, both as a composer and as a lecturer. More committed than a parodist, more practically involved than a critic, he nevertheless comes across in his compositions as an intentionally commentative artist rather than an originator. He is an associate of the *CMCentre, a member of the *CLComp, and a member of CAPAC.

SELECTED COMPOSITIONS

STAGE

Labyrinth, Op 7, ballet. 1957. Ms

Il Pomo d'Oro, Op 9, comedy-ballet (Allegra Stewart). 1958. Ms

ORCHESTRA AND BAND

Nocturne, Op 6. 1956. Orch. CMCentre

Variations on a Dorian Hexachord, Op 10. 1959. Orch. CMCentre

Symphony No. 1, Op 12. 1959. Ms

Symphony in E Flat, Op 14. 1960. Band. Ms

Symphony, Op 35. 1967. Brass, perc. CMCentre

SOLOIST(S) WITH ORCHESTRA

Piano Concerto, Op 7. 1961. Ms

Ballad, Op 19. 1962. Tpt, orch. CMCentre

Concerto, Op 57. 1971. Pf, chamb orch. CMCentre

Scherzo, Op 58. 1971. Pf, wind ens. CMCentre

Concerto, Op 69. 1976. Bn, chamb orch. Ms

Laus sapientiae, Op 72 (Bible). 1977. Sop, ten, bar, SATB, org, brass choir, orch. CMCentre

CHAMBER

Trio, Op 1. 1948. Cl, bn, pf. CMCentre

Sonatina, Op 15. 1963. Va, pf. CMCentre

Music for Seven Brass Instruments, Op 27. 1966. WIM 1972

Four Mini-Suites, Op 42. 1968. Acc. Wat 1969. (No. 2) AFA-20 863 (A. Abbott)/RCI 385 (*Macerollo)

Cameos, Op 46a. 1969. Fl, pf. Leeds 1971. Dom S-69006 (*Aitken fl)

Music without Pretensions, Op 45. 1969. Acc, str quar. CMCentre

Six Songs, Op 47 (various texts). 1970. V, fl, acc. CMCentre

Suite, Op 40. 1970. Tpt, org. WIM 1972. (1976). Avant AV-1014 (A. Plog tpt, M. Swearingen org)/RCI 406 (A. *Laberge org)

Prelude, Aria and Fugue, Op 54. 1971. Acc, brass quar. CMCentre

Musica Giocosa, Op 70. 1976. Fl, pf. CMCentre

Many other works, including 2 str quar (1955, 1963) and 2 ww quin (1963, 1967), works for hn and pf, cl and pf, fl and pf, and several for solo acc, including *Alberta Set* (1971, B & H 1972)

PIANO

Esquisse, Op 2. 1950 (rev 1970). CMCentre

Mini Suite No. 1. 1969. Leeds 1969. ('Voices from the Past') Dom S-69002 (*Mould)

Twelve Glimpses into 20th Century Idioms, Op 37. 1969. Leeds 1969. ('The Big Leap Forward,' 'Rain Clouds') Dom S-69002 (*Mould)

Valses nostalgiques, Op 61. 1972. Pf 4-hands. CMCentre

Sonata. 1977. Pf 4-hands. CMCentre

Sonatina. 1977. CMCentre

Several other works for pf, org, and hpd (some educational), some published by Avant, Leeds, Wat, WIM

CHOIR AND VOICE

Symphonia sacra, Op 30 (1st Epistle of St John). 1961. Sop, bar, SATB, brass, perc, org. CMCentre

Vexilla regis produent, Op 36 (J. Skelton). 1968. Soli, SATB, org. WIM 1968

Fragments: Beach, Op 63 (M. Atwood). 1972. SAB. Ms

A few works for voice

WRITINGS

'The programme sonatas of J.L. Dusik [Dussek],' _CAUSM J_, vol 1, Fall 1971

'Spielformen in Regers Klaviermusik,' _Mitteilungen des Max-Reger-Instituts, Bonn_, Jul 1971

'Max Reger's choral cantatas,' AGO and RCCO _Music_, vol 6, Feb 1972

BIBLIOGRAPHY

'Stephen Adams talks with Gerhard Wuensch,' _Mcan_, 34, Jan 1978

Schulman, Michael. 'Gerhard Wuensch: interview,' _CanComp_, 131, May 1978 GKG (KW)

WYMAN, Max. Critic, b Wellingborough, England, 14 May 1939. He studied piano and theory as a youth and began his career in journalism with the _Northamptonshire Evening Telegram_ at 14. After studies at Nottingham U and journalistic experience in Wellingborough, Nottingham, and Romford, he worked 1960–7 as an arts critic and feature writer for London newspapers and magazines and 1961–2 as editor of the _South London Advertiser_. He moved to Canada in 1967 and served 1968–76 as music and dance critic for the _Vancouver Sun_, exchanging music for theatre in 1976. He became a contributing editor for *_Performing Arts in Canada_ in 1973 and wrote regular British Columbia columns 1968–76 for *_Opera Canada_ and 1970–5 for the *_Canada Music Book_. He has written for _EMC_, the *_Canadian Composer_, the *_Music Scene_, _Dance in Canada_, and _York Dance Review_ and has prepared reviews and commentaries for CBC radio and TV programs. He is the author of _The Royal Winnipeg Ballet: The First Forty Years_ (Toronto, New York 1978). BNSG

WYRE, John (Harvey). Percussionist, composer, teacher, b Philadelphia, Pa, 17 May 1941, naturalized Canadian 1972; B MUS (ESM, Rochester) 1963. He studied percussion 1956–9 with Fred Hinger of the Philadelphia Orchestra and 1959–64 with William Street at the ESM, Rochester, NY. He played 1964–5 with the Oklahoma City SO and 1965–6 with the Milwaukee SO and served 1966–71 as timpanist with the *TSO, a position he resumed in 1975. He was a founder of I Ching (1969–70) and of *Nexus in 1971 and began to appear as percussionist with *NMC in 1972. He was an instructor 1967–9 with the *NYO and 1971–4 at the *U of Toronto. On 12 Sep 1970 he premiered his composition _Bells_ (commissioned for Expo 70) with the Japan Philharmonic, and in 1972 he repeated the work for his Canadian solo debut with the TS. His _Utau Kane NoWa_ ('singing bell cycle') for voices, bells, cymbals, and gongs was commissioned in 1973 and performed in 1975 by the *Festival Singers and Nexus. His _Bernie_ was premiered by the same forces and the bass clarinetist Bernie *Piltch in 1976. The TS and Nexus gave the premiere 25 Apr 1978 of his _Connexus_.

BIBLIOGRAPHY

Schulman, Michael. 'Bells both realistic and mystical to percussionist,' _MSc_, 272, Jul–Aug 1973 (MM, WS)

YANOVA, Naomi. See Adaskin, John.

Yohadio. See Roy-Vilandré, Adrienne.

YON, J.-G. (Joseph-Georges). Publisher, music dealer, b Montreal 25 Jan 1857, d there 11 May 1945. In 1885 in Montreal he founded the publishing house and music- and instrument-importing firm bearing his name, and managed it until 1921, when his son-in-law, Louis-Joseph Doucet (1874–1950), became the owner. In 1906 Doucet, poet and writer, had married Yon's daughter Yvonne, a pupil of Alexis *Contant.

As a publisher, Yon was active chiefly in the 1890s and 1900s. He published the collection _Chants des patriotes_ (1893, 1903, a collection of songs by Canadian and French composers) which eventually sold 8000 copies. He also published the popular song folios _L'Écrin musical_ (1899), _L'Écrin du chanteur_ (1901), _L'Écrin lyrique_ (1901), _La Gerbe mélodique_ (ca 1901), and _La Rigolade_ (1902), all containing compositions, patriotic and other, by Canadians. He published separately works by Contant, Charles *Tanguy, and Georges Milo. In 1926 the firm opened a phonograph and record department. After the owner's death in 1950, the business was unable to find a purchaser and liquidated its stock before closing its doors in 1952. GP

YORK, Eva Rose (b Fitch, m York, m Wilfred, m Winford). Composer, organist, editor, teacher, b in western Ontario 22 Dec 1858, d after 1935. One of Canada's early women composers, she attended Woodstock College and studied 1881–2 at the New England Cons. She lived ca 1885 in Belleville, Ont, and formed a Philharmonic Society which performed her oratorio, _David and Jonathan_, 11 Jan and 30 May 1887. At the second concert her _Meditation in G_ was performed by the orchestra. In 1887 she left for Iowa. (The Philharmonic Society continued under the direction of W.H. Donley.) By 1890 she had moved to Toronto and was editor of the _Musical Journal_, organist at Grace (Anglican) Church, and a piano, voice, harmony, and English teacher. After the demise of the _Musical Journal_ she continued to teach until ca 1893 and was founder and superintendent ca 1901–13 of Redemption House in Toronto. Little is known of her life after 1913. In 1935 a brief, unrevealing autobiography, _When My Dream Came True_, was published in Toronto. EK

York Concert Society. See Unger, Heinz.

York University. Non-denominational Toronto institution offering part-time and full-time undergraduate and graduate degree programs and non-degree courses. It was founded in 1959 and accepted its first students in 1960. Its first campus – Glendon – opened in 1961. After an initial period of affiliation with the *U of Toronto it became independent in 1965 with the opening of its main campus on the northern outskirts of Toronto. In 1980 undergraduate and graduate degrees could be obtained in arts, sciences, administration, education, fine arts, environmental studies, and law. Degrees obtainable in music were BA (specialized honours), BFA (music), and MFA (musicology).

William *McCauley, the first appointment in music, served 1961–9 as music director, organizing extracurricular musical activities and setting up performing ensembles. One of the latter, the York University Choir, won the 1967 City of Lincoln Trophy awarded by the *FCMF. A Faculty of Fine Arts, created in 1968, offered an interdisciplinary program in drama, music, film, visual arts, and dance. Sterling *Beckwith designed the music program and served 1969–71 as its director. A Music Dept was formed under the chairmanship of Austin *Clarkson in 1973. Alan Lessem succeeded Clarkson in 1975, and the composer David *Lidov was appointed acting chairman in 1979. In 1979–80 the full-time teaching staff numbered 14, including Beckwith, Clarkson, and Lidov and the ethnomusicologists Stephen Blum, Steven Otto, and Robert *Witmer. Edith *Fowke began to teach folklore at York in 1971. The auxiliary staff numbered 12 in 1980.

Aesthetics, electronic and computer music, ethnomusicology, popular traditions and jazz, and performance have developed into specializations. Performance at York has not been structured according to traditional patterns. It has reflected, rather, interests in early, contemporary, and non-western music (supported by collections of eastern and early-European instruments and an electronic laboratory). Performances by staff, students, and visiting artists have been presented regularly in the university's 600-seat Burton Auditorium. See also Archives.

BIBLIOGRAPHY

'York's spirit of adventure found in music courses,' _MSc_, 266, Jul–Aug 1972 (JPG)

York Winds. Wind quintet formed in Toronto in 1972. The founding members were Douglas Stewart, flute (b Winnipeg 6 Dec 1949, a pupil of Robert *Aitken and Marcel Moyse); Lawrence Cherney, oboe (b Peterborough, Ont, 1 May 1946, a pupil of Perry *Bauman, Ray Still, and Robert Bloom); Howard Knopf, clarinet (b Sudbury, Ont, 6 Oct 1947, a pupil of Ezra *Schabas, Robert Marcellus, and Stanley Drucker and one-time member of the Spoleto Festival of Two Worlds Ensemble); James MacDonald, horn (b Portage la Prairie, Man, 31 Jan 1945, a pupil of Leslie *Huggett, Eugene *Rittich, and Barry Tuckwell); and James McKay, bassoon (b Toronto 4 Oct 1944, a pupil of Nicholas *Kilburn, Ferdinand DelNegro, and Leonard Sharrow and one-time member of the Contemporary Chamber Players of Chicago). Knopf was replaced in 1975 by Paul Grice (b Toronto 6 Jun 1943, a pupil of Schabas, Keith Wilson, and Gervase de Peyer; he performed with the London SO, the London Haydn Orchestra, and the Melos Symphonia); MacDonald in 1978 by Harcus Hennigar (b Dartmouth, NS, 27 Oct 1952, a pupil of Eugene Rittich), and McKay in 1978 by Gerald Robinson (b Barrie, Ont, 28 May 1950, a pupil of Nicholas Kilburn, Norman Tobias, Harold Goltzer, and Loren Glickman).

The group has performed throughout Canada and in Europe, where it was heard over radio networks in England, Belgium, and France. It made its London and New York debuts in 1977 and spent three weeks teaching and playing in Israel in 1978. It became ensemble-in-residence at Toronto's *York U in 1975 and served in that capacity at the Blue Mountain School of Music (near Collingwood, Ont) 1975–7. It has appeared in recitals and concerts with William *Aide, Douglas *Bodle, Judy *Loman, the *Orford String Quartet (in Samuel Baron's transcription of Bach's _Art of Fugue_), Gervase de Peyer, William *Tritt, and the Cantata Singers of Ottawa.

Canadian works premiered by the York Winds (with those they commissioned identified by a double dagger) include:

*Cherney ‡_Notturno_ 1974
*Pedersen _Wind Quintet No. 2_ 1975
*Fodi _Variations II_ 1976
*Ford _Alliance for Winds_ 1976
*Mozetich _In the Air_ 1976
Parker, Michael _Cholê_ 1976
*Rea ‡_Reception and Offering Music_ 1976
*Hambraeus ‡_Jeu de cinq_ 1977
*Hawkins ‡_Quintet_ 1977
Jaeger, David ‡_Double Woodwind Quintet_ 1977
*Lanza ‡_acufenos IV_ 1979 NM (ML)

'You'll Get Used to It.' World War II song in quick-march tempo, written in 1940 by Freddie *Grant about life in a camp for German and Austrian nationals (many of whom were refugees) in England

during the hostilities. It appeared first in the November 1941 issue of the newspaper – *Stackeldraht* (sic) – of the camp in Canada to which Grant had been transferred. A version with modified lyrics credited to Gordon Victor (a pseudonym for the song's commercial publisher, Gordon V. *Thompson) was popular as a morale booster during the war, and the title became a catch phrase among the allied forces. This version was sung frequently by the *Happy Gang, recorded by Wilf *Carter (and in the 1960s by the Al *Baculis Singers), and appeared in the folio *Sing With Gracie Fields* (Robbins). In Canada the song was a show stopper as sung by John Pratt to his own lyrics in *Meet the Navy*. Pratt also performed his version in the English movie of the show and on a Victor recording.
FH

YOUNG, David (Anthony). Double-bassist, bass guitarist, composer, b Winnipeg 29 Jan 1940; BA economics (Manitoba) 1964, B COMM (Manitoba) 1966. He was a pupil in 1962 of William Curtis at the Berklee School of Music, Boston, and 1967–9 of Thomas *Monohan at the *RCMT. He played with Moe *Koffman and Hagood *Hardy's Montage in the 1960s and joined the *Edmonton SO in 1970. Prior to a season in 1975 as bassist with Oscar *Peterson he was principal 1972–3 and assistant principal 1973–4 with the *Hamilton Philharmonic Orchestra and principal in 1974 with the *Winnipeg SO. He returned to the Hamilton Philharmonic Orchestra in the fall of 1975. Young has played with Peter *Appleyard and with such US jazzmen as Mose Allison, Red Norvo, Sonny Stitt, and Buddy Tate in Toronto nightclubs. In 1976 he formed the Downes-Young Duo with the pianist Wray *Downes (see Downes for discography). Young also has appeared on LPs by Koffman, Peterson, the US drummer and Toronto resident Pete Magadini (*Polyrhythm*, 1975, Briko BR 1000), Kenny *Wheeler, and others. He has played in recitals and chamber-music concerts (eg, in Schubert's *Trout Quintet* with the *Brunswick String Quartet and others) and has recorded with the *Czech Quartet. Playing bass guitar, he participated in the premiere (with the *TS and Bernie *Piltch) of Harry *Freedman's *Scenario*. Young has composed many songs, some recorded by Appleyard and Magadini. He is a member of CAPAC.

Young's sister, Sydney (Elizabeth) Young McInnis (pianist, b Winnipeg 23 Sep 1934, a pupil of Jean *Broadfoot in Winnipeg, Margaret Miller *Brown 1952–7 at the RCMT, and Rosina Lhévinne at the Juilliard School), has performed widely as an accompanist and soloist in western Canada. She has taught privately and at the *U of Manitoba. In 1978 she was appointed to a three-year term as a member of the *Manitoba Arts Council. MM

YOUNG, Neil (Percival). Singer, songwriter, guitarist, pianist, harmonica player, b Toronto 12 Nov 1945. A son of the Toronto journalist Scott Young, he moved to Winnipeg in his mid-teens and first performed 1962–4 with a rock band, the Squires, in Manitoba and Northern Ontario. He then worked with the Mynah Birds in Toronto's Yorkville coffeehouses and later in Detroit before forming in Los Angeles the celebrated rock group Buffalo Springfield (1966–8) with Stephen Stills, Richie Furay, and the Canadians Bruce Palmer and Dewey Martin. Although Young worked informally 1969–74 in the 'supergroup' Crosby Stills Nash and Young, and briefly again in 1976 with Stills, he concentrated after 1968 on what became one of rock's most successful solo careers of the early 1970s, performing alone and with an accompanying group, Crazy Horse, throughout North America (giving several concerts in large Canadian halls) and in Europe and Japan. In the later

Neil Young

1970s he was active only intermittently as a touring performer but continued to record.

Young is a prolific songwriter, who borrows freely from country and folk music, and an aggressive rock guitarist, but he is above all a haunting singer, his voice in turn strained and forceful or soft, high, and disarmingly childlike. In 1971 he was voted Best Male Singer and Best Composer, and his album *After the Gold Rush* was voted Best Album of 1970 by *Melody Maker* readers. Of his many songs the most popular include 'Expecting to Fly,' 'Broken Arrow,' and 'I Am a Child' written for Buffalo Springfield; 'Country Girl,' 'Helpless,' and 'Ohio' for Crosby Stills Nash and Young; and 'Southern Man,' 'Round and Round,' 'Everyone Knows This is Nowhere,' 'Only Love Can Break Your Heart,' 'Tell Me Why', 'Cinnamon Girl,' 'Old Man' and the million-selling hit (1972), 'Heart of Gold.' His 'Lotta Love' was a hit in 1979 as recorded by Nicolette Larson. Various anthologies of his songs have been published by either Broken Arrow Music or Silver Fiddle Music. With the exception of the soundtrack from his autobiographical film *Journey through the Past* all his albums 1969–74 received gold-record sales awards. Another film, *Rust Never Sleeps*, a documentary of Young in concert, was released in 1979 in conjunction with an LP of the same name.

DISCOGRAPHY

Neil Young. (1968). Reprise 637
Everyone Knows This is Nowhere. (1969). Reprise 6349
After the Gold Rush. (1970). Reprise 6383
Harvest. (1971). Reprise 2032
Journey through the Past. (1972). 2-Reprise 2XS-6480
Time Fades Away. (1973). Reprise 2151
On the Beach. (1974). Reprise 2180
Tonight's the Night. (1975). Reprise 2221
Zuma. (1975). Reprise 2242
American Stars and Bars. (1976). Reprise 2261
Decade. 1966–76 (1976). 3-Reprise 2557 (anthology)
Comes a Time. (1978). Reprise MSK 2266
Rust Never Sleeps. 1978. Warner HS 2295
Live Rust. 1979. 2-Reprise CRS 2296

WITH OTHERS

Buffalo Springfield: *Buffalo Springfield*. 1966. Atco SD 33-200-A
– *Buffalo Springfield Again*. 1967. Atco SD 33-226
– *Last Time Around*. 1968. Atco SD 33-256
– *Retrospective*. (1971). Atco SD 33-283 (anthology)
CSN & Y: *Déjà Vu*. 1969. Atlantic S7200
– *Four-Way Street*. 1970. 2-Atlantic S2- 902
– *So Far*. (1974). Atlantic 18100 (anthology)
Stephen Stills: *Long May You Run*. 1976. Reprise MS 2253-P

BIBLIOGRAPHY

Blinder, Elliot. 'Neil Young: in conversation,' *Rolling Stone*, 30 Apr 1970
Yorke, Ritchie. 'The ones who wouldn't wait,' *Axes, Chops & Hot Licks* (Edmonton 1971)
Stambler, Irwin. *Encyclopedia of Pop, Rock and Soul* (New York 1974)
Dufiechou, Carole. *Neil Young* (New York 1978)
Young, Scott. 'Long may you run: Neil and me: a father's memories of his famous son,' *Toronto Life*, Dec 1980
MM

'Youpe! Youpe! Sur la rivière!' Folksong adapted by Quebec lumberjacks from another song, 'Le P'tit Bois d'l'ail.' The words 'Youpe! Youpe! Sur la rivière,' which form the typically Canadian refrain, are not found in 'Le P'tit Bois d'l'ail,' since it has no refrain. The song tells the story of a man who visits the home of some friends with a companion one evening and tries to court the host's daughter. But she tells him that she doesn't take him seriously and that she knows he loves another. Her father, who has retired for the night, tells his guests and his daughter that they should do likewise. The suitor acquiesces and leaves with his friend. 'Le P'tit Bois d'l'ail' was published with a piano accompaniment by P.E. Prévost in *Chansons canadiennes* (Montreal 1907). The words had been printed previously in *La Lyre canadienne* (Quebec 1886), a work compiled by W.H. Rowan. The *Nouvelle Lyre canadienne* (Montreal 1895) contains an unusual version employing the words of another song, 'Quand j'étais chez mon père,' for the verses and those of 'Youpe! Youpe! Sur la rivière!' for the refrain. 'Youpe! Youpe! Sur la rivière!' can be found in *Folk Songs of Canada* (Waterloo 1954) by Edith *Fowke and Richard *Johnston, with accompaniment for piano and guitar and with both French and English words. Among those who made 78s of the song are Charles *Marchand, singing alone and with the Bytown Troubadours, and Conrad *Gauthier. It appears on LPs by Alan *Mills (Folk FP 29) and by Jules *Bruyère with the choir of *La Bonne Chanson (RCA LPC 1011). HP

Youth orchestras. Canadian youth orchestras fall into three main categories: those attached to public and private schools (including universities, colleges, conservatories, and camps); those connected to and supported by adult community or professional orchestras; and those which represent a city or region and are a young counterpart of the community orchestras.

Among the earliest youth orchestras in Canada were the Manitoba Schools' Orchestra (Greater Winnipeg Schools' Orchestras), founded in 1923, the *Mount Royal College (Calgary) Junior Orchestra (founded as the Baby SO in 1937), the Vancouver Junior SO, begun in 1938, and the Inter-Schools Orchestra of Montreal, organized in 1945. The increase in numbers of adult orchestras in Canada after 1950 created a new demand for home-trained musicians, and many youth orchestras were organized as part of the response to that demand. By the 1960s what could be described as the youth orchestra movement was well under way, and the majority of the new youth orchestras provided not simply recreation for young players but serious professional instruction in instrumental techniques and ensemble playing, the instruction provided in some cases by players in the region's senior orchestras, in others by specialist teachers employed by schools.

Of the youth orchestras formed after 1960 several were subdivided according to age and musical ability. Many accepted members as young as 7 or 8, and some admitted players as old as 30. Some were created to provide the player with a transitional step towards a career in a full-time orchestra. Among these were the Canadian Chamber Orchestra of the *Banff SFA, the Montreal Junior SO, the Orchestre des jeunes du Québec (see list below), the *NYO, and the orchestral training program established at the *RCMT in 1980.

Major Canadian organizations involved in the youth orchestra movement have been the *JMC, which presents concerts throughout the country, the Youth Orchestra Committee of the *OFSO, and the Canadian Assn of Youth Orchestras (CAYO).

The CAYO, which is based in Banff, Alta, was incorporated in January 1977, although its roots go back to the first Canadian Festival of Youth Orchestras, held in Banff in April 1974, and again in 1976. Founding directors of the CAYO (the youth-orchestra counterpart of the *ACO) were Neil M. Armstrong, Rolf Duschenes, Douglas Lauchlan, Gerald Ross, and Frank Simpson. The association's prime concern has been the provision and stimulation of performance and training opportunities for young musicians in Canada. In this connection it has overseen and sponsored the biennial Canadian Festival of Youth Orchestras, initiated at Banff in 1974 to provide a brief but stimulating experience of intensive training for a selected number of youth orchestras (approximately six per festival). Participating instructors have included the violinists Lorand *Fenyves and Eugene *Kash, the violist Stephen *Kondaks, the cellist Claude *Kenneson, the bassist Gary *Karr, the flutist Robert *Aitken, the bassoonist George *Zukerman, members of *Canadian Brass, and the conductors John *Avison, Alexander and Boris *Brott, John Carewe, Oskar Danon, Franz-Paul *Decker, Victor *Feldbrill, and Janos Sandor. The 1978 festival was the subject of a CBC Musicamera TV documentary. An offshoot of the CAYO is the Assn of Canadian Youth Orchestra Conductors, formed in 1976, whose workshops have been held in conjunction with the Canadian Festival of Youth Orchestras.

In 1979, at the time of the CAYO's annual meeting in Montreal, the Quebec Assn of Youth Orchestras / Assn des orchestres de jeunes du Québec was established and the first Festival des orchestres de jeunes du Québec was presented.

The appended list provides brief descriptions of some Canadian youth orchestras. With a few exceptions school orchestras have not been included. (See also Education; Orchestras; Summer camps and schools; Universities.)

British Columbia

Delta Youth Orchestra. Founded in the mid-1970s. Conductors have included Harry Gomez. Member of the CAYO.

Genstar Youth Orchestra of Surrey. Founded in the 1970s as an independent organization with junior and senior divisions. Conductors have included Ian Hampton and Lucille Lewis. Member of the CAYO in 1979

Greater Victoria Schools Senior Symphony Orchestra. Outgrowth of the Greater Victoria School District string program initiated in 1957. For musicians of 14 to 18 years. In 1968 the conductor was Thomas Tucker.

Kamloops Youth Orchestra. Founded in the mid-1970s and affiliated with the Kamloops SO. Conductors have included Victoria Kereluk. A member of the CAYO and of the ACO through the parent orchestra. In the 1930s A. Nelson McMurdo, school music director, established a 100-member schools orchestra. Although activities were suspended during World War II, McMurdo increased participation by the city's pupils until by 1949 Kamloops boasted a 140-member junior symphony orchestra, a 100-member preparatory junior orchestra, and a 60-member string orchestra.

BIBLIOGRAPHY

Beck, Stan N. 'Now come the musical pioneers,' *Vancouver Sun Magazine Supplement*, 23 Apr 1949

Kelowna Music Society Junior Orchestra. Established in the 1970s. A 60-member orchestra of music students of all ages, coached by members of the Okanagan SO

Vancouver Youth Orchestra. Founded in 1938 by the Vancouver Symphony Society as the Vancouver Junior Symphony Orchestra. Original membership numbered about 45. After 1945 the orchestra was under the auspices of the Junior Symphony Society of Vancouver. By the 1960s a three-level system of preparatory, junior, and senior orchestras was in effect. Conductors have included Gaspare Chiarelli, John Chlumecky, George *Coutts, Jean *de Rimanoczy, Gregori *Garbovitsky, Jerold Gerbrecht, Harry Gomez, Adolph *Koldofsky, Frederick Nelson, Alex *Pauk, Simon *Streatfeild, and Garth Williams. Membership open to young players of 7 to 20 years. Member of the CAYO

Alberta

Calgary Junior Philharmonic Orchestra. Founded in 1957 for students in Calgary schools. This orchestra of 75 players of 12 to 18 years was under the auspices of the city's public and separate school boards and the Calgary Philharmonic. Conductors included Jack Mirtle and Frank Simpson.

BIBLIOGRAPHY

Romaine, Edward. 'Calgary youngsters say it with music,' *Weekend*, 11 Mar 1961

Calgary Youth Orchestra. Established in 1968 by its conductor, Frank Simpson, for student musicians under 20. The 80-member orchestra has performed in 1970 in Europe, in 1972 at the International Festival of Youth Orchestras in Switzerland, 1974, 1976, 1978, and 1980 at the Canadian Festival of Youth Orchestras at Banff, Alta. Member of the ACO and the CAYO.

BIBLIOGRAPHY

'Calgary Youth Orchestra: teenagers, tunes and tours,' *OCan*, vol 4, Jan 1977

Edmonton Youth Orchestra. 42-member ensemble founded ca 1952 and conducted until 1955 by Keith *Bissell. By 1965 it had 65 members of 11 to 18 years and was under the auspices of the *Edmonton SO. It participated in the 1972 International Festival of Youth Orchestras in Switzerland and attended the Canadian Festival of Youth Orchestras at Banff in 1976, 1978, and 1980. Conductors have included John Barnum, Ted Kardash, Michael Massey, George Naylor, Ranald *Shean, and Edgar Williams. Member of the CAYO

Mount Royal College Symphony Orchestra, Calgary. Founded in 1937 by Jascha Galperin under the auspices of the *Mount Royal College. For music students of 4 to 12 years, it was known first as the Baby Symphony, then as the Junior Symphony String Orchestra, and after 1944 as the Mount Royal College SO. Conductors have included Galperin, Clayton *Hare, and J.S. Peter *Bach.

Southern Alberta Youth Orchestra, Calgary. Established in the early 1960s as part of Calgary's three-level system of youth orchestras. Open to players of 15 to 20 years. Conductors included John Murray.

South Peace Youth Orchestra, Grande Prairie. Formed in 1973 as a training orchestra within the Grande Prairie Regional College community program. Its members have been drawn from both the city and the surrounding area. Conductors have included John Hancock.

Saskatchewan

Regina Inter-Collegiate Orchestra. Founded in 1962 under the auspices of the Regina Board of Education. Its 80 members have been selected from secondary school students of 12 to 18 years. A 22-member chamber orchestra drawn from its ranks attended the 1974 Canadian Festival of Youth Orchestras in Banff. The founding conductor, Lloyd Blackman, retained that position in 1980. Member of the CAYO

Saskatoon Symphony Society – Orchestral Development Program. Founded by Murray *Adaskin in 1958 as the Saskatoon Junior SO, under the auspices of the *Saskatoon Symphony Society and the Kiwanis Club. It includes junior chamber ensembles, junior strings, and a Junior SO for students from 12 to 20. Conductors have included Alfred Dahl, Michael Bowie, Ruben *Gurevich, Jack Johnson, Dwaine Nelson, and Dorothy Overholt. Member of the CAYO, and also of the ACO through the parent orchestra, the Saskatoon SO

Saskatchewan Youth Orchestra, Regina. Founded in 1967 under the auspices of the Regina Board of Education, the *Saskatchewan Arts Board, the Saskatchewan Dept of Education, and the *SMEA. For students of 12 to 19 years. Conductors have included Lloyd Blackman.

South Saskatchewan Youth Orchestra, Regina. 55-member orchestra founded in 1977, sponsored by the *Regina SO, and conducted by Ernest Kassian. Age range of the players is 13 to 23. Member of the CAYO and the ACO

BIBLIOGRAPHY

Kozma, Andrew. 'Varied program at Sunday concert,' Regina *Leader-Post*, 25 Apr 1979

Manitoba

Greater Winnipeg Schools' Orchestra (known 1939–62 as the Manitoba Schools' Orchestra). It was founded in 1923 by P.G. Padwick for young musicians of 8 to 18 years. Under a succession of names in its early years (eg, Winnipeg Junior SO), it began its unique series of weekly Saturday morning concert-rehearsals on radio station CKY in 1927. These rehearsals were joined 'on air' at home by music students throughout the province. Each Easter the radio members would gather in Winnipeg for a massed concert which also was broadcast. This practice, in effect until Padwick's death in 1938, was resumed in 1940 and continued intermittently until 1949. The name adopted in 1939 reflected the broad membership and objectives of the orchestra. In 1945 provincial tours supplanted the annual massed concerts. In 1949 the orchestra was divided into junior and senior levels, and in 1962 the senior orchestra was renamed the Greater Winnipeg Schools' SO. Following Padwick's death conductors included Ronald *Gibson, Filmer *Hubble, Glen *Pierce, Eric Adams, Frances Port, Arthur *Polson, Richard Seaborn, and Carlisle Wilson (see Wilson family). The orchestra, a member of the CAYO, is also known as the Winnipeg Youth Orchestra.

BIBLIOGRAPHY

Takoski, Leonard T. 'A history of the Manitoba Schools' Orchestra 1923 to 1964,' unpubl M ED thesis, U of Manitoba 1965

Ontario

Bach Youth Ensemble, Toronto. Chamber orchestra established in 1971 by Patrick Burroughs. During the five years of its existence it presented annual series of concerts and toured in western Canada and France.

Brantford Youth Orchestra. Founded in 1967 under the auspices of the Brantford Board of Education and the Brantford SO for players of 10 to 18 years. Conductors have included Claude Chislett, Stanley *Saunders, and Barry Devereux. Member of the OFSO through the Brantford SO

Cambrian Youth Orchestra, Sudbury. Founded in the mid-1970s with a membership of players of 14 to 23 years. It has continued under the auspices of Cambrian College, with Metro Kozak as conductor. It attended the 1980 Canadian Festival of Youth Orchestras at Banff. Member of the OFSO through the Sudbury SO

Georgian Bay Junior Orchestra, Owen Sound. Founded by the Georgian Bay Community Orchestra in 1975 for players of 7 to 14 years. The conductors have included Edouard Bartlett, Malcolm Lacey, and Andrew Shaw. Member of the OFSO through the Georgian Bay Community Orchestra

Guelph Youth Orchestra. Established in the 1970s by a committee of the Guelph Arts Council, which appointed Patrick Burroughs conductor and musical director in 1978

Hamilton Philharmonic Youth Orchestra. Founded in 1965 for players of 12 to 24 years by Glenn Mallory (still the conductor in 1980), under the auspices of the Hamilton Philharmonic Society. It attended the 1980 Canadian Festival of Youth Orchestras in Banff. Member of the CAYO, and of the OFSO through the *Hamilton Philharmonic Orchestra

Huronia Youth and Junior Orchestras, Barrie. Founded in 1973 under the auspices of the Huronia SO and conducted by John Montague. Member of the OFSO through the Huronia SO

International Youth (originally String) Orchestra of Sarnia and Port Huron. Founded in 1976 with members and board drawn from Sarnia, Ont, and Port Huron, Mich, and under the auspices of the International SO of Sarnia and Port Huron. The founding conductor, Richard Lawrence, retained the position in 1980. Member of the OFSO through its parent orchestra

International Youth Symphony, Windsor, Ont, and Detroit, Mich. Founded in 1965 by Matti Holli under the auspices of the International Youth Symphony Executive Committee. Membership open to players under 21. Holli was succeeded as conductor by William Bruce Curry. Member of the OFSO

BIBLIOGRAPHY

'Ontario-Québec orchestra exchanges: International Youth Symphony,' *OCan*, vol 7, Jan 1980

Kingston Youth Orchestra. Founded in 1968 under the auspices of the *Kingston SO. Conductors have included Edouard Bartlett, Clifford Crawley, and James Coles. Member of the OFSO through the Kingston SO

Kitchener-Waterloo Junior Symphony. Founded in 1967 under the auspices of the *Kitchener Waterloo SO Assn. For players 13 and older. The conductors have included Raffi *Armenian, Stuart Knussen, Louis Lavigueur, and Frédéric Pohl. Member of the OFSO through the Kitchener-Waterloo SO

London Youth Symphony Orchestra. Founded in 1961 under the auspices of the Junior Women's Committee of the London SO Assn. For players under 24. The conductors have included Derek *Stannard and James White. Member of the CAYO, and of the OFSO through the *London SO. It performed at the 1976 International Festival of Youth Orchestras at Aberdeen, Scotland, and at the 1974 and 1978 Festivals of Youth Orchestras in Banff.

Niagara Youth Orchestra, St Catharines, Ont. Founded in 1965, with 69 members aged 12 to 16, as the St Catharines Junior Symphony. It was renamed St Catharines Youth Orchestra in 1968 and Niagara Youth Orchestra in 1979. Under the auspices of the *St Catharines SO (Niagara SO) it developed from the School String Ensemble formed in 1961 by Paul van Dongen. Van Dongen was succeeded as conductor by Richard Grymonpre, and Grymonpre by Takng Lai. The orchestra attended the Canadian Festival of Youth Orchestras in 1974 and 1980 in Banff. Member of the OFSO through its parent orchestra

BIBLIOGRAPHY

Philips, Dr J.H.H. 'Paul van Dongen: eleven years of service to the youth of St. Catharine's,' *OCan*, vol 4, Mar 1977

Oakville Youth Orchestra. Founded under the auspices of the Oakville SO. Conductors have included Jean Grieve and Harold Clarkson. Member of the OFSO through the Oakville SO

Ottawa Youth Orchestra. Founded in 1960 by H.E. Morris and M.H. Haycock and run as a night class of the adult division of the Ottawa Board of Education for members of Ottawa and Hull secondary schools and universities. Player age range is 13 to 24. Conductors have included James Coles, Dirk *Keetbaas Sr, and Brian *Law. Member of the CAYO and the OFSO

Peterborough Symphony Youth Orchestra. Founded in 1974 under the auspices of the Peterborough SO. For players of 6 to 25 years. Conductors have included Peter Bartley and George Pyper. Member of the OFSO through the Peterborough SO

Riverdale String Ensemble, Cornwall, Ont. Founded in 1969 by its conductor, Rosemonde *Laberge. Membership open to Cornwall elementary and secondary school students of 8 to 18 years

Thunder Bay Youth Symphony Orchestra. Founded as the Lakehead Youth SO under the auspices of the *Thunder Bay SO. The conductors have included Dwight Bennett, Charles Burke, Roger Gadsen, Tim Maloney, and Kirk Trevor. Member of the OFSO through the Thunder Bay SO

Toronto Symphony Youth Orchestra. Founded in 1974 under the auspices of the *TS. Membership open to players of 13 to 22 years. Conductors have included Leonard Atherton, Victor *Feldbrill, and Ermanno Florio. The orchestra attended the 1980 Canadian Festival of Youth Orchestras. Member of the CAYO and the OFSO

BIBLIOGRAPHY

Scott-Patterson, Helen. 'Youth Orchestra,' *TS News*, vol 40, no. 7, 1979–80

Toronto Youth Orchestra. Founded in 1967 and conducted by Jacob *Groob until its demise in 1972. Its personnel was made up of players of 14 to 21 years. It performed at the 1969 International Festival of Youth Orchestras in St Moritz, Switzerland.

BIBLIOGRAPHY

Mason, Donna. 'Young musicians: how they met a big challenge,' *CanComp*, 31, Jul–Aug 1968

Quebec

Ensemble classique optimiste de Sherbrooke. Ensemble of 55 players of 13 to 20 years, founded in 1974 by the Optimist Club of Sherbrooke. Czeslaw Gladyszewski, the conductor 1974–7, was succeeded by Jacques Clément. The orchestra attended the 1978 Canadian Festival of Youth Orchestras and performed at the 1979 Festival des orchestres de jeunes in Montreal. Member of the CAYO

Montreal Junior Symphony Orchestra. Founded in 1947 by Lewis V. Elvin for players of 11 to 19 years. The orchestra toured in Great Britain in 1954 and in continental Europe in 1961. Elvin was succeeded as conductor by Eugène *Husaruk in 1971. In 1977 Joseph Milo became conductor of the reorganized orchestra of 40 players of 17 to 27 years. Member of the CAYO

Montreal Civic Youth Orchestra / Orchestre civique des jeunes de Montréal. Founded in 1976 by Sandra Wilson with 60 members of 13 to 25 years. The orchestra attended the 1978 and 1980 Canadian Festival of Youth Orchestras and performed at the 1979 Festival des orchestres de jeunes du Québec. Conductors have included Alexander *Brott and Jacques Clément. Member of the CAYO

BIBLIOGRAPHY

'Jacques Clément dirigera malgré Rémus Tzincoca,' *Musique périodique*, vol 1, Jan–Feb 1977

Blanchfield, Cecilia. 'Trip to Banff is a high note for Montreal's Youth orchestra,' Montreal *Gazette*, 27 Jan 1978

Orchestre des jeunes de Chicoutimi. Founded in 1967 by its conductor, Yvon Gaudreault, with 60 players of 10 to 18 years. Member of the CAYO

Orchestre des jeunes du Québec (OJQ). Founded during the summer of 1977 at the *JMC Orford Art Centre and officially established later that year, subsidized entirely by the *MACQ. Members (who must be under 30 years old) are hired for two sessions of 15 weeks each, which include tours within the province. In 1978 each player received a weekly salary of $180. Conductors have included Franz-Paul *Decker, Charles Dutoit, Serge *Garant, and Otto-Werner *Mueller.

BIBLIOGRAPHY

Magnon, François. 'A new orchestra in Quebec,' *OCan*, vol 5, Mar 1978

McLean, Eric. 'For musical pros,' *Montreal Star*, 22 Apr 1978

Petrowski, Nathalie. 'J'ai passé ma période de défoulage électrique, maintenant je veux faire de la musique ...' *L'Actualité*, vol 3, Nov 1978

Orchestre symphonique des jeunes de Joliette. Founded in 1971 by its conductor, Father Rolland Brunelle. Players of 9 to 19 years are drawn from the Joliette region. The MACQ sponsored a tour of the province in 1976, and that same year the orchestra attended the Canadian Festival of Youth Orchestras and the 1979 Festival des orchestres de jeunes in Montreal. Brunelle also formed a junior orchestra of players of 7 to 12 years. Member of the CAYO

Montreal Youth Symphony Orchestra / Orchestre symphonique des jeunes de Montréal. Founded by Fernand *Graton in 1945, the 60-member ensemble of players of 13 to 25 years was active until 1951. The orchestra premiered *Pépin's *Concerto No. 1* (with the composer at the piano), *Perrault's *Petite Suite*, *Morel's *Diptyque*, *Matton's *Danse brésilienne*, *Blackburn's *Charpente*, and *Papineau-Couture's *Symphony No. 1*

New Brunswick

*New Brunswick Youth Orchestra

Nova Scotia

Nova Scotia Youth Orchestra, Halifax. Founded in 1977 under the conductorship of Robert Raines. The orchestra attended the 1980 Canadian Festival of Youth Orchestras in Banff. Member of the CAYO

BIBLIOGRAPHY

MacMillan, Keith. 'Youth orchestras in Canada,' *Mcan*, 11 May 1968

CMCentre. *Youth Orchestras in Canada*, Nov 1971

Lee, Clayton. 'Music and arts,' Calgary *Albertan*, 31 Jan 1976

'Canadian Festival of Youth Orchestras: a summary report,' *OCan*, vol 3, Jul 1976

'Canadian Association of Youth Orchestras,' *OCan*, vol 4, Mar 1977

'The youth orchestra: the indispensable link in the development of Canada's musical community,' *OCan*, vol 4, Jul 1977

Wilson, Sandra. 'Music, mountains, magnificence and magic,' *OCan*, vol 5, Mar 1978
Gingras, Claude. 'Lancement de l'Association des orchestres de jeunes ...,' Montreal *La Presse*, 19 Feb 1979
(NM, SS, ST, PW)

Yugoslavia. Patterns of immigration to Canada from this south-central European country are considered in *EMC* entries for Croatia, Macedonia, Serbia, and Slovenia – four of the republics and cultures which constitute the political and geographic entity of Yugoslavia (so named in 1929 but formed as the Kingdom of the Serbs, Croats, and Slovenes in 1918, and made the Socialist Federal Republic of Yugoslavia in 1945). Other republics in Yugoslavia are Bosnia-Hercegovina and Montenegro; the Montenegrins form the fifth and smallest cultural entity in the country.

Among the musicians of Yugoslavia who have appeared in Canada are I Solisti di Zagreb in 1956, 1957, 1973, and 1978, the soprano Daniza Ilitch (*Eaton Auditorium 1956) and, on tours for the *JMC, the Zagreb String Quartet 1964–5, the Belgrade Trio 1966–7, 1972–3, the piano duo of Lukic and Murai 1968–9, and the Foestrovo Trio 1969–70. The great Yugoslav (Croatian) soprano Zinka Milanov sang in Canada during the visits 1952–5, 1957, 1959, and 1960 of the *Metropolitan Opera.

Folk groups have presented the several cultural heritages of Yugoslavia to Canadian audiences. Among these have been the Yugoslav National Folk Ballet and Kolo (the Yugoslav state company from Belgrade), both in Montreal and Toronto in 1956, and the Lado Folkloric Ensemble of Yugoslavia at *Expo 67. Among Yugoslavian-born musicians active in Canada are the musicologists Dujka Smoje and Gordana *Lazarevich and the folksinger Joso Spralja (of *Malka and Joso). The composer Marjan *Mozetich is of Yugoslavian descent.

Among Canadian musicians who have performed in Yugoslavia are Louise *Forand (piano), Jean *Laurendeau (clarinet, ondes Martenot), and Vincent *Dionne (percussion), who toured as a trio for the JMC, 1968–9. James *Campbell (clarinet) was the winner of the JMC International Competition in Belgrade. Hélène *Gagné toured Yugoslavia as a JM exchange artist.

Yukon Arts Council. Organization founded as an independent society under the Yukon Societies Ordinance in October 1971. Prior to that time, some of its musical responsibilities were carried out by the Whitehorse Concert Assn, active from the late 1950s to 1970. The council has spoken on behalf of a number of cultural groups within the Yukon Territory; in 1979 it began working to enlarge its mandate, striving to become the representative of all cultural, arts, and crafts groups.

The council has planned, scheduled, and promoted annual concert series (featuring classical music and jazz) for the City of Whitehorse and other communities, and has administered the use of a set of risers (for use by choral-orchestral groups) and a grand piano. In an attempt to raise performance and teaching levels, it has co-ordinated, sponsored, and sometimes funded workshops in each of the performing arts. On occasion it has sponsored the attendance of individuals at conferences and workshops outside the territory and has provided assistance to local conferences. It has promoted and publicized the Yukon Music (competition) Festival (held at Whitehorse), and established trophies for the festival's best performer(s). In 1979 it initiated a spring festival of the arts (not a competition).

The council's activities have been supported by grants from civic and territorial governments, proceeds from fund-raising campaigns, receipts from concerts, and fees from workshops it has sponsored. It has received money from private donors for special projects, such as a Grand Piano fund.

Members of the council's board of directors have served as an unpaid executive committee. Presidents have been Maurits van der Veen 1971–3, Michael Heron 1973–5, Wyn Gladman 1975–7, and Esme Myers 1977–8, succeeded by Henry Klassen.

Z

ZAFER, David (Anthony). Teacher, violinist, b London 2 Apr 1934, naturalized Canadian 1973. In England he studied with his father and at the RCM with Antonio Brosa. He moved to Canada in 1947 and continued his studies in Toronto with Elie *Spivak and Albert *Pratz. He was a member 1956–9 of the *TSO, assistant concertmaster 1959–60 of the Baltimore SO, and concertmaster 1960–3 of the orchestra of the National Ballet of Canada and 1970–2 of the *Hart House Orchestra. A teacher at the *U of Toronto beginning in 1966, and with the *NYO, he has numbered among his pupils Joan Barrett, Richard Green, John Lowry, and Rhyll Peel. Zafer gave master classes at the Menuhin School, Surrey, England, in the summer of 1977 and was the string coach for the Toronto Symphony Youth Orchestra 1980–1.

DISCOGRAPHY
Violin Music of the 20th Century: Dohnanyi – Southam – Dolin – Milhaud. Brough pf. 1973. Mel SMLP 4021 WS

ZAROU, Jeannette. Soprano, b Ramallah, Palestine. She emigrated to Canada in 1947, began studies in 1961 with Irene *Jessner at the *U of Toronto, and made her *COC debut in 1964 as the Priestess in *Aida*. She created the title role in the *Royal Cons Opera School's 1966 stage premiere of *Willan's **Deirdre* and repeated the performance for the COC that same year. She was also a winner in 1966 of the *CBC Talent Festival. Other COC roles have included Liù in *Turandot* (1965), Micaela in *Carmen* (1966), Marguerite in *Faust* (1970), Marzelline in *Fidelio* (1973), and Mimi in *La Bohème* (1976). In 1967 she toured with Leonard Bernstein and the New York Philharmonic to sing the soprano part in Mahler's *Fourth Symphony*. A leading lyric soprano 1967–74 with the Deutsche Oper am Rhein in Düsseldorf, she has performed with major European houses in Amsterdam, Berlin, Hamburg, Cologne, Vienna, and Wiesbaden and extensively in concert and recital. Her performance of Ariadne in Strauss' *Ariadne auf Naxos* at the 1975 *Stratford Festival drew praise from John *Kraglund in the Toronto *Globe and Mail* 'not only for the strength and security of vocal performance, but for the emotional impact of both the musical and dramatic interpretation' (1 Aug 1975).

DISCOGRAPHY
Mahler – Morawetz. Coveart pf. 1966. CBC SM-8
Mozart – Handel. Clemens pf. 1972. CBC SM-220

BIBLIOGRAPHY
Mercer, Ruby. 'Zarou: profile,' *OpCan*, vol 9, Dec 1968
Southworth, Jean. 'Heart-rending task for soprano,' Ottawa *Journal*, 22 Oct 1976 HCs

ZBRIGER, Maurice. Violinist, violist, composer, conductor, b Kamenets-Podol'skiy, Ukraine, 10 July 1896, d Montreal 5 Apr 1981. After first studying the violin in his native town he was accepted in the class of Leopold Auer at the St Petersburg Cons, where Jascha Heifetz and Nathan Milstein were among his fellow students. He left Russia in 1920, subsequently playing in cafés in several European cities before arriving in Montreal in 1924. In 1925 he was one of the founders of the Traymore Quartet, which later became the Traymore Salon Orchestra and which made nine 78s for Compo (listed in *Roll Back the Years*). Playing in theatres and restaurants, Zbriger was one of the first musicians in Canada to specialize in gypsy music. As soloist and conductor he took part in many radio programs devoted to this music on CKAC and later the CBC. For a few seasons beginning in 1931 he was violist with the *Montreal Orchestra and in the mid- and late 30s he was a member of the orchestras of the CSM (*MSO) and the *Montreal Festivals.

Zbringer was a prolific composer, who wrote some 250 songs, 42 marches, and 8 overtures. Such singers as Yolande *Dulude and Yoland *Guérard have performed his songs. 'Mother's Lullaby' (1948) was written to mark the birth of Prince Charles of England, and 'Little Bells are Twinkling' (1949) was sung by the noted soprano Erna Sack. His marches include *The Vincent Massey March* (1952) and *Tribute to the Games 76*, which was premiered at the international bandshell of Man and His World in Montreal. In July 1974 *The Campbell 50th Anniversary Overture*, a commission by the Royal Trust Company to commemorate the 50th anniversary of the *Campbell Free Band Concerts, was premiered at the bandshell, and *The Campbell Memorial March* (1956) also was performed on that occasion. Several of Zbriger's works have been published by F. *Harris, *Thompson, Popular Music Publishers Ltd, and *Canadian Music Sales Corporation. He was a member of CAPAC.

BIBLIOGRAPHY
Seligson, Lou. 'Still singing love at 80,' *Montreal Star*, 24 Jan 1974 (DA)

ZEALLEY, Alfred E. (Edward). Bandmaster, french hornist, writer, b Bristol 10 Jun 1878, d Agincourt, near Toronto, 15 May 1961. At 16 he became a bandboy in a military band and in 1898 he attended the RMS Kneller Hall. He lived 1908–14 in Boston, playing in bands and theatre orchestras and leading the Cambridge City Band. During World War I he led the 75th Battalion band of the Canadian Expeditionary Force and became music director of the RCN. After the war he led the Belleville Kilties Band 1918–20 and in 1923 on US tours and lived in Toronto, playing french horn and contributing to *Musical Canada*, the *Etude*, and other periodicals. With J. Ord Hume he wrote *Famous Bands of the British Empire* (London 1926). In 1939 he was asked to form in Halifax the first permanent RCN band, which also was Canada's first active service band of World War II. In 1943 he was appointed Lieut-Commander and music director of the RCN School of Music, Toronto. During the war years he supervised and trained 19 navy bands. He retired in 1945. Autobiographical notes, 'From bandboy to director of the music; memoirs of a musical career,' appeared in the *Canadian Military Journal* (January, February 1948). HK

ZELKINE, Alexandre (Vladimirovitch). Singer-songwriter, b Lyons, France, 14 Feb 1938, naturalized Canadian 1973. Born of a Russian father and a French mother, he made an early debut singing the folk music of these two cultures and accompanying himself on the guitar. In 1956 with two friends in Lyons he founded the group Los Chacos which specialized in Latin American music. He was a member 1957–9 of the opera class of Germaine Piroird at the Lyons Cons. Later he travelled widely and did his military service 1961–2 in North Africa during the Algerian war. In 1963 he worked in Paris as a reporter-photographer and then performed in clubs in Israel. While he was in the USA 1964–6 he sang on some TV programs, including the 'Pete Seeger Show,' and was presented at the 1965 Newport Folk Festival by the US folksinger Theodore Bikel. Zelkine settled in Montreal in January 1966 and performed at the Canadian Pavilion during *Expo 67. In 1968 he gave a series of recitals in Cameroon and at Cornell U in Ithaca, NY, and in 1969 he appeared at Harvard U in Cambridge, Mass. He took part in the *Mariposa Folk Festival in 1970 (returning in 1974) and in 1971 made a tour of the Arctic, also performing in Vancouver and Hawaii. He gave concerts in Senegal in 1972 and sang at the *NAC in 1973. In the 1974 *Juno Awards in Toronto, he obtained the McGowan prize for his LP *Pessimiste* as the 'best contribution to multiculturalism in music.' Zelkine began writing his own songs in 1972. He speaks several languages, and his repertoire includes French, Russian, Israeli, Spanish, South American, Mexican, English, US, Canadian, Rumanian, gypsy, and Yiddish songs. He has mastered several instruments, including the guitar, the balalaika, the charango, and the Andean flute. His audiences respond especially well to the humanity and infectious warmth of his performances.

DISCOGRAPHY

Russian Folk Songs. 1965. Audio Fidelity AFSD 6137
Alexandre Zelkine, vol 1. 1966. Cap T 70002
Alexandre Zelkine, vol 2. 1967. Cap T 70010
Alexandre Zelkine Sings Meadowlands and Other Russian Songs, Old and New. 1968. Monitor MFS 703
Quebec – French Canadian Folk Songs. 1970. Monitor MFS 714
Pessimiste. 1973. U Artists UALA 164F
L'Otage. 1974. U Artists UALA 336G DA

ZELLER, Noah. Bandmaster, teacher, b near Breslau, Canada West (Ontario), ca 1852, d Berlin (Kitchener), Ont, 8 Feb 1914. In 1875 he was the clarinet soloist and from 1878 to 1882 he was the conductor of the 29th Regiment Band of Berlin. In 1882 he became the first conductor of the *Waterloo Musical Society Band. The Waterloo band became a leading musical organization and won many contests – so many that for a time it was barred from competition. In 1900 Zeller resigned to resume his former duties with the 29th Regiment Band. During his years with both bands he also trained the bands at Elmira, New Hamburg, St Jacobs, and Baden, Ont. After a Toronto engagement by the Berlin band *Saturday Night* commented, 'Of all the bands which visit Toronto, except professional bands, it is the best.' Poor health forced Zeller to resign in 1913. EBM

ZIEGLER, George (Henry). Teacher, bandmaster, organist-choirmaster, b Berlin (renamed Kitchener), Ont, 1 Aug 1889; LTCM piano 1909, ATCM organ 1912. He played in the Ziegler Family Orchestra and at 13 became the youngest member of the Berlin Musical Society Band. He studied at the TCM with Humfrey *Anger, G.D. *Atkinson, and A.S. *Vogt, and also in Buffalo and New York. During his student days Ziegler played flute in the *Welsman TSO and served as assistant organist in several Toronto churches. On his return to Berlin (*Kitchener) he founded in 1911 the Ziegler Associated Studios (later the *Kitchener Cons of Music), where he taught piano, organ, band instruments, and theory until his retirement in 1974. His pupils included Harvey Gleiser Jr, J. Ferris *Loth, Kenneth *Sakos, and the Toronto trumpeter Erich Traugott. Ziegler also served on the examining boards of the *RCMT, the Hamilton Cons (*RHCM), the *AB of the RSM and the *Western Ontario Cons of Music, and organized the Kitchener branch of the *ORMTA. He was organist-choirmaster in several Kitchener churches, including (1917–50) Trinity United, where he presented many organ recitals, some of which were broadcast. He also supervised the design and installation of several organs. He directed the Kitchener Musical Society 1924–67; a Ladies' Band (which had 94 members and was said to be the largest of its kind in the world) 1925–32; several junior bands (many of which won honours in *CNE competitions); and the Brass Band of the Scots Fusiliers of Canada. Ziegler composed works for band, organ, and choir, many of which were performed. Most of his manuscripts, however, were destroyed in a fire. JCm

ZOELLNER, (Herman) Theodor. Conductor, teacher, organist-choirmaster, b Dornburg, Saxony (now East Germany), 13 Apr 1854, d West Indies after 1922. The Zoellner family settled in Berlin (Kitchener), Ont, in 1861, and the father, Hans A. Zoellner (d ca 1906), who had been a singer and conductor in Germany, became a leader of local singing societies, directed two *Sängerfeste, and drafted the constitution for the German-Canadian Choir Federation in 1873. The younger Zoellner studied at home with his father and in Cincinnati. In 1880 on his return to Berlin he taught voice and instruments. In 1883 he founded the Berlin Philharmonic Society, dedicated to the performance of such large-scale works as *The Creation* (1883) and *Messiah* (1887). For an 1896 performance of Mendelssohn's *St Paul* there were 160 voices in the choir. The instrumentalists Zoellner engaged to accompany these performances were billed, sometimes, as the Philharmonic Orchestra. He also organized and directed opera, operetta, and other performances, often employing visiting musicians. Zoellner directed two men's choirs, the Sängerbund of Berlin and the Orpheus of Waterloo, and his appointment as conductor of the 1886 International Sängerfest and the 13th Peninsular Sängerfest (1901) attested to his stature as the leading musician of his time in the Berlin-Waterloo area. The first professional musician to teach music in schools in Berlin, Zoellner served as singing master 1897–1922 in the public system and at St Jerome's College. His program was based on the sol-fa system. He involved the entire school population in choral performances in the town rink. He became organist-choirmaster ca 1890 at the Church of the New Jerusalem and held the same position (ca 1898–1908) at St Peter's Lutheran Church. JCm

ZUCKERT, Leon. Composer, violist, b Poltava, Ukraine, 4 May 1904. He studied violin 1916–18 with Boris Bordsky at the Imperial School of Music in Poltava. After living in Poland and Argentina he moved to Canada ca 1929. Between 1929 and 1969 he played in many orchestras in Canada, the USA, and Mexico, including the *Winnipeg SO 1932–4, the *TSO 1951–6 and 1961–3, and the *Halifax SO (*Atlantic SO) 1963–5 (principal viola and assistant conductor) and 1967–9 (violin). He has received commissions from the *CBC Winnipeg Orchestra for *Fantasia on Ukrainian Themes* and from the Toronto Shevchenko Musical Ensemble for *In the Gleam of the Northern Lights*. His symphonic suite *Quetico* was composed for the Christopher Chapman film of the same name. He is married to the poet Ella Bobrow, with whom he has collaborated on several songs. Zuckert is a member of CAPAC and an associate of the *CMCentre.

COMPOSITIONS

ORCHESTRA

My Canadian Travels. 1938. CMCentre
2 *Symphonies*. (1949, 1962). CMCentre
Quetico. 1957. CMCentre
Dnieper (Shevchenko). 1961. SATB chorus, orch. CMCentre
Divertimento Orientale. 1965. Ob, str orch. CMCentre
Impressions of Teneriffe. 1970. CMCentre
Fantasia on Ukrainian Themes. 1973. CMCentre
In the Gleam of the Northern Lights (Bobrow). 1974. TTBB chorus, dancers, orch; or SATB, 2 pf, str, perc. CMCentre
Concerto for bassoon and string orchestra. 1976. CMCentre
Elegia. 1977. CMCentre

CHAMBER

Gypsy Memories. 1938. Vn, pf. CMCentre
Prayer (A. Shum, transl Bobrow). 1960. V, str quar. CMCentre
Prelude en Modo Antiquo. 1964. Brass ens. CMCentre
Song in Brass (P. Zoline). 1964. V, va, brass ens, timp, perc. CMCentre
Psychedelic Suite. 1968. Brass quin. CMCentre. 1972. CBC SM-225 (Atlantic Brass Ens)
Elegiac Improvisations. 1970. Fl, pf. CMCentre. RCI 421 (*Shulman)
Little Spanish Dance. 1970. Fl, pf. Jay 1971. Dom S-69006 (*Aitken)
Sonata Amorfa. 1970. Vn, pf. CMCentre
Suite for Bassoon Solo. 1975. CMCentre

CHOIR

A la Mujer del Poeta (V. Lozano). 1978. TTBB, pf. CMCentre
Longing for Peace (H. Schwartz). 1978. Bar, SATB (TTBB), pf or orch. CMCentre

Also *Piano Pieces*, vols 1–3 (1967–77); several songs including 'Days Come and Go,' 'How Sweet,' 'Spring Thaw,' recorded on Master MA-275 (D. *Mills) and 'Remember,' on Master MA-377 (D. Mills)

WRITINGS

'My most successful work,' *CanComp*, 28, Apr 1968

BIBLIOGRAPHY

Schulman, Michael. 'Leon Zuckert: an old-world composer inspired by travel,' *CanComp*, 128, Feb 1978 NM

ZUKERMAN, George (Benedict). Bassoonist, impresario, b London, of US parents, 22 Feb 1927, naturalized Canadian 1967; MA (Queen's, New York) 1949. The son of a New York newspaper correspondent based in London, Zukerman studied at New York's High School of Music and Art and, before and after World War II service in the US navy, at Queen's College. He also studied privately with Leonard Sharrow, the principal bassoon of the NBC SO. After a tour as a member of the St Louis Sinfonietta in 1949, he joined the *Vancouver SO for a season, returning in 1953 as principal bassoon after two seasons as associate principal of the Israel Philharmonic. He founded the *Cassenti Players in 1954 and became principal bassoon of the *CBC Vancouver Chamber Orchestra and established *Overture Concerts in 1955. He relinquished his position with the Vancouver SO in 1963 in order to concentrate on a solo career, which soon led to his recognition as one of the world's foremost bassoonists and to the bassoon's increased popularity as a solo instrument in Canada. He began annual tours of Europe in 1964 and on each of them searched for unpublished bassoon concertos. He has located about 150 works, including a *Concerto in F Major* misattributed to Mozart, a *Conzertstück* by Franz Berwald, an alternative version of a *Concerto in F* by Hummel, and six quintets by Brunetti (the latter found in the Madrid Palace Library under the eye of Spanish soldiers assigned to guard the treasures as he searched). In 1969, on his first world tour, Zukerman became the first foreign bassoonist to be invited to perform in the USSR. He per-

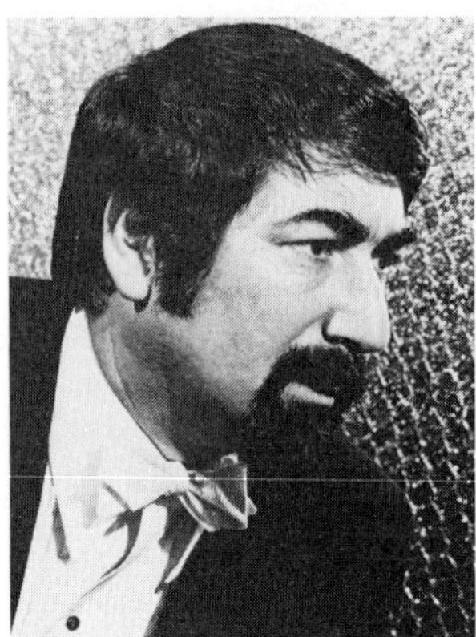

George Zukerman

formed as well in Australia, New Zealand, Pago-Pago, Samoa, and New Caledonia in 1972 and made his second world tour in 1976. He toured the USSR, South Africa and Australia in the spring of 1978. In Canada he has appeared repeatedly in solo recitals and with the Calgary, Edmonton, Halifax, Kingston, Regina, Saskatoon, Victoria, and Winnipeg symphony orchestras and has given lecture-demonstrations for schools, universities, and music clubs. Many Canadian composers have written for him, including Murray *Adaskin, Jean *Coulthard, Theo *Goldberg, Arthur *Polson, Robert *Turner, Elliot *Weisgarber, and John *Weinzweig.

DISCOGRAPHY

Adaskin *Concerto*. CBC Van Chamb O, Avison cond. 1970. CBC SM-143

Adaskin *Divertimento No. 3* (CBC Van Chamb O, Avison cond; 1973) – Danzi *Trio* (B. Tuckwell hn, T. Gabora vn; 1976). RCI 405

Baroque Recital: Galliard – Telemann – Boismortier. 1970. Campi SCG 11.005

Couperin – Corrette – Devienne – Boismortier. Lautenbacher vn, Gode, Wolken, Steinbrecher bns, Württemberg Chamb O, Faerber cond. 1969. TV 34304

Graun – J.C. Bach *Concerti for Bassoon*. Württemberg Chamb O, Faerber cond. 1969. TV 34278

Hummel *Concerto*. Württemberg Chamb O, Faerber cond. 1970. TV 34348/KTVC 34348

Mozart *Concerto* K191 – Weber *Concerto, Op 75*; *Andante and Rondo in Hungarian Style*. Württemberg Chamb O, Faerber cond. 1965. TV 34039

K. Stamitz *Concerto*. Württemberg Chamb O, Faerber cond. 1968. TV 34093

Telemann – Hindemith – Saint-Saëns – Bozza. H. Brown pf, hpd. 1968. CBC SM-72

See also Discography for CBC Vancouver Chamber Orchestra

BIBLIOGRAPHY

Schulman, Michael. 'The business of the bassoon: George Zukerman sounds off,' *PfAC*, Fall 1978 MW

ZVANKIN, Peter (Phinehas Zvi). Composer, b Kherson, Russia, 15 Aug 1879, d Winnipeg 25 Aug 1975. He played clarinet 1903–6 in the Russian Army Orchestra then moved in 1906 to Winnipeg, working in the textile business and pursuing music as an avocation. His compositions, the earliest of which dated from 1934, are all unpublished. They include the orchestral works *Cloudy Skies* (ca 1951) and *Poem* (1950). The latter was played by the *Winnipeg SO in 1951 and again in 1974 in the presence of the 95-year-old composer. He wrote ceremonial pieces for Queen Elizabeth II and President Kennedy, a hymn – 'God Guard Thee Newfoundland' (1949), and songs in English, Hebrew, and Yiddish. The *Catalogue of Canadian Composers* lists his works to 1951. His papers are held in the Provincial Archives of Manitoba.

BIBLIOGRAPHY

'Peter Zvankin,' *Winnipeg Free Press*, 6 Sep 1975 LI

Illustration Credits

Photographers and publishers

Every effort has been made to obtain permission to reproduce the illustrations and musical examples which appear in this volume, although it has not always been possible to identify photographers of unsigned prints obtained from promotion agencies or from the subjects themselves. The editors of the *Encyclopedia of Music in Canada* gratefully acknowledge the courtesy of the following photographers and music publishers in allowing them to use the illustrations which appear on the pages listed below (the letter *a*, *b*, or *c* following each page number identifies the column).

Milton Adamson, Toronto 875c
Arnott, Rogers, Batten, Montreal 860c
Ashley & Crippen, Toronto 7b, 999b
Associated Screen News, Montreal 17a
Fabian Bachrach, New York 400b
S. Bain, Yarmouth, NS 456c
Wayne R. Barrett, St Catherines, PEI 23b, 226a–b
John Bendixsen 415c
Berandol Music Ltd, Toronto 177b, 882a
Blackham 670a
Bruno of Hollywood, New York 108b
Campbell Studios Ltd, Vancouver 738a
Carter (Anthony's of Kerrisdale), Vancouver 717b
Cavouk Portraits, Toronto 43b, 80b, 428a
Colin M. Clark, ARPS, Fergus, Ont 382c, 809c
Robert Courtemanche, Magog, Que 466b
Crombie McNeill, Ottawa 160a
Walter Curtin, RCA, Toronto 22a, 70c, 367b, 377c, 596c, 618c, 628b, 841b, 849c, 894b, 974c, 990c
Studio Desautels 387b
Guy Dubois, Montreal 486b
John Evans Photography Ltd, Ottawa 68a
Henry Fox, Toronto 63a
Gaby, Montreal 387c, 534b, 849a
Hans Geerling, Toronto 464a
Geka, Enr'g 34b
Graetz Bros Ltd, Montreal 74c
Ralph Greenhill, Toronto 188a
Frank Harmantas, Toronto 927a
V. Tony Hauser, Toronto 184b
Horvath Studios, Toronto 435a
Gadi Hoz Photographer, Toronto 721b
Image Maker Photographic Services, Winnipeg 591a–b
Studio Jac-Guy, Montreal 64a, 289b, 537b
Helmut Kallmann, Ottawa 146a–b
Jean-Pierre Karsenty, Montreal 69a, 428c, 486c, 546a
Karsh of Ottawa 143a (portrait only)
R. Kayaert 475b–c
Kitchener-Waterloo Record 131c
Krieber, Quebec City 390b
Lagacé, Montreal 641b
Robert Lansdale Photography, Etobicoke, Ont 547b, 928c, 959a
Vic la Vica Photos Ltd, Calgary 885c
André Le Coz, Montreal 161b, 617b, 694a, 790c
Studio Lipnitzki, Paris 823b
Reginald Litz, Winnipeg 615a
McDermid Studios, Edmonton 52a
Maclean's Magazine, Toronto 406c, 601b–c
Photo C. Marcil, Ottawa 9c
Jack Marshall Ltd, Clarkson, Ont 302c
Bruno Massenet, Montreal 878c
C.A.G. Matthews, Toronto 733c
Francis J. Menten, Montreal 90a
Jean Gainfort Merrill, Toronto 352c
Mia et Klaus, Montreal 724a
Mark Miller, Toronto 100a–b, 503a
Ronald Miller, Master of Photographic Arts, Toronto 261b
Gilbert A. Milne & Co, Ltd, Toronto 119b–c, 165c
Moss Photo, New York 480c
Le Nouvelliste, Trois-Rivières, Que 336b
Andrew Oxenham Photography, Toronto 828c
Panda Associates, Toronto 356b, 605a, 677a–b, 689c, 763a, 920a
Jim Parr, Toronto 381b
Kenneth Peacock, Ottawa 92a–b, 279c, 452b, 468a
Photo / Canada Wide, Toronto 393b
David Portigal & Co, Ltd, Winnipeg 70b
Robert Ragsdale, FRPS, MPA, Toronto 25a, 371b, 619a–b, 648a, 679c, 982c
G. Ricordi & Co (Canada) Ltd, Toronto 617c
François Rivard, Montreal 773b
Everett Roseborough, Toronto 581c
Éditions Salabert, Paris 8b
Wilfrid P. Sauvé, St Lambert, Que 538c
Bernie Senensky, Willowdale, Ont 995b
Paul Smith, Toronto 938a
T. Smythe, Winnipeg 766a
Society Studio, Montreal 557a
Christian Steiner, New York 347c, 402c, 523a
Studio One, Courtenay, BC 900b
G. V. Thompson Ltd, Toronto 984b
Universal Edition (London) Ltd 850a
Luis Vidal, Valencia 943b
Jacques Weiss, Basel 623a
Harold Whyte, Orangeville, Ont 385a
Florence Wyle Estate 171b
Nathan Zassman, Winnipeg 1009b–c

Collections

Some of the institutions listed below have supplied photographic reproductions of paintings, instruments, sheet music, concert programs, and other documents in their collections. Others have provided prints made from photographic negatives. The individuals have lent original prints of historical photographs. Sincere thanks are offered to all.

Archives nationales du Québec 361c
Henri Brunet, Montreal 126b
CBC 347b, 400c, 619a–b, 644c, 938a
Dalhousie University 183c
Glenbow-Alberta Institute 59a–b, 186a–b, 477c, 656b–c, 801b
Mrs Charles Goulet, Montreal 387b
Manitoba Provincial Archives 79b, 293a, 370c, 437b, 654a, 987c
Elizabeth Mullin, Hamilton, Ont 430a
Musée du Québec 267a
National Gallery of Canada 35a–b, 171b, 193a, 979a
National Library of Canada 17c, 41b, 57c, 70a, 77c, 82a, 93a, 94b, 139a, 139c, 141c, 151a, 151b, 156a, 202a, 215a, 217b, 220b, 230a, 272c, 277a, 294c, 334c, 349c, 409b, 419b–c, 447b, 467c, 516c, 517a, 554b, 564a, 574a, 592b–c, 593a, 593b, 600c, 630b–c, 637a, 651c, 680c, 719a–b, 729c, 742a, 743a, 756a–b, 775a, 785a, 789a, 812c, 826a–b, 886b, 911a, 918b, 921b, 930c, 984b, 987a, 994b, 997a, 999c
National Museum of Man 309b
New Brunswick Museum 66b, 944b–c
Notman Photographic Archives, McCord Museum, McGill University 102a, 238c, 262c, 326a, 418a, 473c, 551a, 598c, 633a, 638b, 703b, 796c, 985c, 1005b
Provincial Archives of British Columbia 975c
Provincial Museum of British Columbia 456a
Public Archives of Canada 2b (negative C63001), 58a (PA28920), 78a–b (PA43791), 160b (PA43799), 195b–c (C59500), 252a–b (C252), 404a, (C17797), 451c (C52358), 498b (C110432), 594a (J.A. Castonguay 1965-57), 699a–b (PA112533), 755b (PA118147), 837b (C61578), 843a (C62856), 923c (C66220), 925b (PA52587), 965c (PA11645), 1010a (C62599)
Royal Ontario Museum 455a, 455b, 458c
Séminaire de Québec 105a, 685a
Claudette Taschereau, Montreal 480c
University of Toronto 928c

Index of Illustrations

Index

The index lists those persons, organizations, companies, radio stations, churches, periodicals, schools, etc that do *not* have their own entries in *EMC*. The index concentrates on the Canadian content of the encyclopedia. Non-Canadian performers, teachers, organizations, etc have been indexed only when there is a significant Canadian relationship.

Names beginning with Mac and Mc are treated as though spelled Mac, and put into alphabetical order accordingly. Saint, Sainte, and the corresponding short forms St and Ste are treated as though spelled Saint, and interfiled accordingly.

Subjects are indexed by page and column. The columns are designated by the letters *a*, *b*, or *c* following the page numbers.

This index should be used as a supplement to the encyclopedia itself; it lists only subjects which do *not* have their own entries.

B

This index should be used as a supplement to the encyclopedia itself; it lists only subjects which do *not* have their own entries.

This index should be used as a supplement to the encyclopedia itself; it lists only subjects which do *not* have their own entries.

This index should be used as a supplement to the encyclopedia itself; it lists only subjects which do *not* have their own entries.

C

This index should be used as a supplement to the encyclopedia itself; it lists only subjects which do *not* have their own entries.

This index should be used as a supplement to the encyclopedia itself; it lists only subjects which do *not* have their own entries.

This index should be used as a supplement to the encyclopedia itself; it lists only subjects which do *not* have their own entries.

This index should be used as a supplement to the encyclopedia itself; it lists only subjects which do *not* have their own entries.

D

This index should be used as a supplement to the encyclopedia itself; it lists only subjects which do *not* have their own entries.

This index should be used as a supplement to the encyclopedia itself; it lists only subjects which do *not* have their own entries.

E

This index should be used as a supplement to the encyclopedia itself; it lists only subjects which do *not* have their own entries.

F

This index should be used as a supplement to the encyclopedia itself; it lists only subjects which do *not* have their own entries.

This index should be used as a supplement to the encyclopedia itself; it lists only subjects which do *not* have their own entries.

G

This index should be used as a supplement to the encyclopedia itself; it lists only subjects which do *not* have their own entries.

This index should be used as a supplement to the encyclopedia itself; it lists only subjects which do *not* have their own entries.

H

This index should be used as a supplement to the encyclopedia itself; it lists only subjects which do *not* have their own entries.

I

This index should be used as a supplement to the encyclopedia itself; it lists only subjects which do *not* have their own entries.

J

K

This index should be used as a supplement to the encyclopedia itself; it lists only subjects which do *not* have their own entries.

L

This index should be used as a supplement to the encyclopedia itself; it lists only subjects which do *not* have their own entries.

This index should be used as a supplement to the encyclopedia itself; it lists only subjects which do *not* have their own entries.

This index should be used as a supplement to the encyclopedia itself; it lists only subjects which do *not* have their own entries.

M

This index should be used as a supplement to the encyclopedia itself; it lists only subjects which do *not* have their own entries.

This index should be used as a supplement to the encyclopedia itself; it lists only subjects which do *not* have their own entries.

This index should be used as a supplement to the encyclopedia itself; it lists only subjects which do *not* have their own entries.

This index should be used as a supplement to the encyclopedia itself; it lists only subjects which do *not* have their own entries.

This index should be used as a supplement to the encyclopedia itself; it lists only subjects which do *not* have their own entries.

This index should be used as a supplement to the encyclopedia itself; it lists only subjects which do *not* have their own entries.

This index should be used as a supplement to the encyclopedia itself; it lists only subjects which do *not* have their own entries.

P

This index should be used as a supplement to the encyclopedia itself; it lists only subjects which do *not* have their own entries.

This index should be used as a supplement to the encyclopedia itself; it lists only subjects which do *not* have their own entries.

This index should be used as a supplement to the encyclopedia itself; it lists only subjects which do *not* have their own entries.

R

This index should be used as a supplement to the encyclopedia itself; it lists only subjects which do *not* have their own entries.

This index should be used as a supplement to the encyclopedia itself; it lists only subjects which do *not* have their own entries.

S

This index should be used as a supplement to the encyclopedia itself; it lists only subjects which do *not* have their own entries.

This index should be used as a supplement to the encyclopedia itself; it lists only subjects which do *not* have their own entries.

This index should be used as a supplement to the encyclopedia itself; it lists only subjects which do *not* have their own entries.

This index should be used as a supplement to the encyclopedia itself; it lists only subjects which do *not* have their own entries.

T

This index should be used as a supplement to the encyclopedia itself; it lists only subjects which do *not* have their own entries.

This index should be used as a supplement to the encyclopedia itself; it lists only subjects which do *not* have their own entries.

U

This index should be used as a supplement to the encyclopedia itself; it lists only subjects which do *not* have their own entries.

V

This index should be used as a supplement to the encyclopedia itself; it lists only subjects which do *not* have their own entries.

W

This index should be used as a supplement to the encyclopedia itself; it lists only subjects which do *not* have their own entries.

This index should be used as a supplement to the encyclopedia itself; it lists only subjects which do *not* have their own entries.

X

Y

Z

This index should be used as a supplement to the encyclopedia itself; it lists only subjects which do *not* have their own entries.

This book
was designed by
WILLIAM RUETER
and was printed by
University of
Toronto Press